Huxford's Fine Art Value Guide

VOL II

Huxford's Fine Art Value Guide

VOL II

COLLECTOR BOOKS
A Division of Schroeder Publishing Co., Inc.

The current values in this book should be used only as a guide. They are not intended to set prices, which vary from one section of the country to another. Auction prices as well as dealer prices vary greatly and are affected by condition as well as demand. Neither the Author nor the Publisher assumes responsibility for any losses that might be incurred as a result of consulting this guide.

On the Cover:

TOP LEFT: Dupre, Julien (French, 1851-1910), Harvesters, oil on panel, sgn/dtd 1889, 15x18", C-NY 10/25/89 OE, $35,200

BOTTOM LEFT: Renoir, Pierre Auguste (French, 1841-1919); L'Ombrelle, oil on canvas, sgn, 1878, 24x20", C-NY 5/11/88 OE; $6,600,000

TOP RIGHT: Cottingham, Robert (American, 1935-); Ajax, acrylic on paper, sgn/dtd 1983, 25x40", C-NY 5/4/89 OE, $26,400

MIDDLE RIGHT: Gerome, Jean Leon (French, 1824-1904); Caesar Crossing the Rubicon, Parcel Gilt, dk gr patina base, sgn/mk Siot Fondeur, 30", C-NY 5/24/89 OE, $34,100

BOTTOM RIGHT: Fantin-Latour, Henri (French, 1836-1904); Roses dans un Vase, oil on canvas, sgn/dtd 1892, 16x14", C-NY 5/11/88, $385,000

Additional copies of this book may be ordered from:

Collector Books
P.O. Box 3009
Paducah, KY 42002-3009

@$29.95. Add $2.00 for postage and handling.

Table of Contents

Preface

The second edition of *Huxford's Fine Art Value Guide* has been compiled from auction sales covering a two-year span (1988 through 1989) as reported by twenty-six of the major auction galleries in the United States, Canada, England, and Monaco. It is unique in that the wide, meaningless ranges usually found in art-evaluating guides that are so confusing to the novice have been avoided altogether. Instead, individual items are listed (either by title or description), actual measurements are given, and any and all pertinent information that would affect the assessment of their values is provided for the reader, thereby allowing him much more insight and understanding regarding the realized prices. Abbreviations have been kept to a minimum in order to facilitate comprehension. Every effort has been made to give the most thorough and accurate artist information possible.

Sales are sorted alphabetically by title of work or description rather than by value. (You'll find that often the same item has been sold several times through more than one auction gallery and so will be listed consecutively.) By noting the dates of the sale, a sort of this type makes it obvious which artist's works are appreciating and which are declining in value. Each listing contains the date of the auction through which each item sold, along with a code that identifies the auction house.

Please bear in mind that all values given are auction results; you may find gallery prices much higher due to many factors. For instance, the work of a western artist may bring more in his home territory than it would through an eastern auction house. The gallery owner may have bought an item that was attributed to a particular artist and only after spending much time and effort was then able to assign a positive artist identification. Naturally overhead and operating expenses must also be taken into account.

Acknowledgments

The editors and publisher of *Huxford's Fine Art Value Guide* wish to thank the following auction galleries who have allowed us to use their auction catalogs:

Neal Alford Co., Inc.
Richard A. Bourne Co., Inc.
Butterfield & Butterfield
Christie's
William Doyle Galleries
DuMouchelles
Early Auctions
Fraser Bros. Ltd.
Freeman–Fine Arts of Philadelphia, Inc.
Garth's Auctions, Inc.
Morton M. Goldberg Auction Galleries
C.E. Guarino
Leslie Hindman Auctioneers
Milwaukee Auction Galleries
Phillips
Schrager & Associates, Ltd.
Selkirk's
Robert W. Skinner, Inc.
Sotheby's
Swann Galleries
Waddington's
Weschler's
Wolf's Auction Gallery

Photo Credits

Photos used in this publication have been reprinted through the courtesy and cooperation of the following galleries:Swann Galleries

Butterfield & Butterfield
Christie's
Wm. Doyle (Photographer George Roos)
C.E. Guarino
Phillips
Robert W. Skinner, Inc.
Skinner, Inc.; Auctioneers and Appraisers
Waddington's

Auction Gallery Codes and Pricing Practices

The following codes were used throughout this book to indicate specific auction galleries:

B/B–Butterfield & Butterfield (10% buyer's premium included in post-sale results)

C-E–Christie's East (10% buyer's premium included in post-sale results)

C-L–Christie's London (10% buyer's premium included in post-sale results)

C-M–Christie's Monaco (11% buyer's premium included in post-sale results)

C-NY–Christie's New Port (10% buyer's premium included in post-sale results)

C-SK–Christie's South Kensington (10% buyer's premium included in post-sale results)

CEG–C.E. Guarino (10% buyer's premium included in post-sale results)

DM–Du Mouchelles (10% buyer's premium charged but not included in post-sale results)

FAP–Freeman/Fine Arts of Philadelphia, Inc. (10% buyer's premium included in post-sale results)

FB–Frazier Brothers (10% buyer's premium included in post-sale results)

GAI–Garth's Auctions, Inc. (no buyer's premium charged)

LH–Leslie Hindman (10% buyer's premium charged but not included in post-sale results)

MAG–Milwaukee Auction Galleries (10% buyer's premium charged but not included in post-sale results)

MG–Morten Goldberg (10% buyer's premium charged but not included in post-sale results)

NA–Neal Alford (10% buyer's premium charged but not included in post-sale results)

PHL–Phillips (10% buyer's premium charged but not included in post-sale results)

RAB–Richard A. Bourne (no buyer's premium charged)

RWS–Robert W. Skinner (10% buyer's premium charged but not included in post-sale results)

SA–Schrager & Associates (no buyer's premium charged)

SLK–Selkirk's (10% buyer's premium charged but not included in post-sale results)

SBY–Sotheby's (10% buyer's premium included in post-sale results)

SWN–Swann Galleries (10% buyer's premium included in post-sale results)

WAD–Waddington's (25% buyer's premium charged but not included in post-sale results)

WD–William Doyle (10% buyer's premium charged but not included in post-sale results)

WG–Wolfe's Galleries (10% buyer's premium charged but not included in post-sale results)

WL–Weschler's (10% buyer's premium charged but not included in post-sale results)

Buying Art: Some Questions and Answers

Why do we buy art? For some it is for no other reason than to have something to hang on the living-room wall. For others it is an investment or a way to beat inflation. With the first group, specialized knowledge is of little consequence: as long as you like, buy it. With the second group, reliance on an art-investment guru (often a dealer/broker) is the rule, and again specialized knowledge (other than what guru to use) is of little importance. It is obvious that the above two groups represent extremes. For the majority of fine art buyers, appeal (esthetics) and cost are the factors determining an art purchase. Esthetics are personal and impossible to codify and tabulate in a guide book format. Cost, on the other hand, is the proper domain of a price guide.

Where to buy it? At a dealer's? At auction? Good dealers have wide experience in the art market, are familiar with research methodologies, understand conservation techniques, and stand behind what they sell. Here are some additional characteristics we like to find in a dealer: unpressured selling, pleasant demeanor, and a willingness to help and to answer questions honestly.

The other route to take is that of the auction house. When buying paintings at auction, be aware of the kind of guarantee that is offered. Ask about the provenance and condition of a work. Many auction houses provide this kind of information on the premise that the best customer is an informed customer. In some instances, the buyer must provide the requisite expertise. Here the situation is one of caveat emptor. Keep in mind that though authenticity may be guaranteed, condition rarely is.

How to decide which artist to collect? Both esthetics and cost figure here. Buy the work of an artist that pleases you. The more famous an artist is, the more likely his works are to be esthetically successful (which is precisely why he is famous) and hence more costly. For example: you decide that you like a painting and you think it is right for you. Do some research on the artist. *Who's Who in American Art, Mantle Fielding,* and *Groce and Wallace* (19th-century artists) are standard reference books on American artists. The ten-volume *Benezit* serves for all artists, Europeans and otherwise. These books are available in most libraries and bookstores. In looking at artists biographies, check to see with whom they studied, the prizes they won, and where they exhibited. Have an idea of what kind of work from what period the artist is famous for. Looking at prices may help here. If landscapes by an artist bring consistently higher prices than his portraits, it is obvious that his landscapes are better buys. If the artist whose work you want to purchase is not listed anywhere and does not have an auction record, you might want to think twice before getting involved and buying the painting. Should you buy the painting, realize that it is being bought solely on the basis of its esthetic appeal. (One of the most beautiful watercolors we've ever owned was by an unlisted artist with no price record. It was as if the artist had somehow fallen out of the late 19th century sky to paint this one miraculous work and then disappear. To this date we've never seen another work by this artist. We must report that the watercolor was subsequently sold, and at a profit.)

What other factors determine cost? Bright paintings please. Luminous landscapes and seascapes, ships, genre scenes, beautiful women, children, beach scenes, trompe-l'oeil, still lifes, and garden scenes are all high on the list of desirability. Modern works are sought, based on how successfully they achieve the style (for example, abstract expressionism, cubism, minimalism, constructivism, photorealism, etc.) in which they are painted. Oils are generally worth more than watercolors or pastels by the same artist. However, if an artist is famous for works in pastel, then the price of a pastel by that artist can top the price of an oil.

Size is also a cost factor. Within limits, the bigger a painting is, the more it will be worth. A painting 40" x 50" is considered to be within the upper limits for ideal size. Yet a very large painting by a major artist can be very important, expensive, and destined for a museum. The same size painting by a minor artist presents problems in that no museum is likely to want it, and private homes do not have the wall space necessary to hang it. Of course, some artists specialized in small works, and such should not be overlooked on the basis of size.

The history of a painting can add to its value. Was it exhibited and where? Look for exhibition labels on the back of the painting. Has the painting been reproduced in a catalogue or a book? Is it included in a catalogue raisonne of the artist's works? There is another point to made here: even though they have no current auction records, artists whose biographies show them to have won many prizes and to have been exhibited widely tend to resurface. They were good and highly-esteemed artists in their days, and they may well develop a new following (with resulting auction records). There is some speculation involved here, but there is also a reasonable chance of a pay-off later on.

How important is condition when buying an oil painting? It is most desirable to buy a painting in untouched and pristine original condition. Unfortunately, this is not always feasible. Good restoration requires skill and is expensive. Rips, tears, holes, and areas of paint loss can be acceptable if the damage is minimal. It is also easier to clean a dirty canvas than to repaint one that has been overcleaned. Learn how to use a black (ultraviolet) light to detect areas that have been touched up (impainted) as well as fake signatures. When buying watercolors, pastels, or drawings, be careful about stains and tears. Restoration of works on paper is a very delicate task and can be very costly. Works on paper should be mounted using acid-free mats and boards, if they were not already so mounted at the time of purchase.

How reliable are the prices quoted in an auction price guide? Now let's go to the heart of the matter. Prices stated in a guide represent actual prices paid. It should be remembered, however, that a price guide cannot report on the esthetic value of a painting, its condition, or other factors affecting price (historical backgrounds, exhibition records, etc.) Extremely high or low prices may indicate unusual circumstances at the time of the sale and should be analyzed very carefully, since they may not be representative of the fair market value of a given artist's work. Allowing for the preceding caveats, an auction price guide is invaluable in deciding what to pay for a painting. Prices paid at auction represent a standard criterion by which the value of an artist's work can be assessed in the open market.

A final piece of advice to prospective buyers is to be well informed. Visit museums and galleries; find out what reference books are available at your local library. Purchase as many books on art as your budget will allow, but remember that books on Michelangelo may look very impressive on your coffee table but will not be of much help at your next auction unless you are very rich indeed.

Good luck and happy hunting in your collecting!

Gerard Leduc
Joseph D. Ferrara
FER-DUC Inc.
P.O. Box 1303
Newburgh, NY 12550
(914)565-5990

Listing of Standard Abbreviations

The following is a list of abbreviations that have been used throughout this book in order to provide you with the most detailed descriptions possible in the allocated space.

a .... artist's
a/p .... artist's proof
alb .... albumen
alb/s .... albumenized salt print
ambro .... ambrotype
aqua .... aquatint
arro .... arrowroot print
att .... attributed
bcro .... bichromate, gun bichromate
bl .... blue
blk .... black
brml .... bromoil
brn .... brown
brom .... bromoid print
bstp .... backstamp
C .... Century
ca .... circa, about
calo .... calotype (talbotype)
cbcr .... cibachrome
cbnt .... cabinet photo
cbrn .... carborundum
CDV .... carte de visite
chlr .... chloride
chromo .... chromolithograph
clr .... color, colored
collo .... collotype
cr .... crease
cyan .... cyanotype
dag .... daguerreotype
dk .... dark
drypt .... drypoint
dtd .... dated
dye clr .... dye-transfer color print
ea .... each
ed .... edition
engr .... engraving
etch .... etched, etching
EX .... excellent condition
ferro .... ferrotype
fl .... flourished
fld .... fold, folded
fox .... foxed, foxing
fr .... frame, framed
gr .... green
gstn .... gluestain
gum .... gum print
haft .... halftone
hc .... hand colored
img .... image
imp .... impression
intg .... intaglio
intl .... initialed
inscr .... inscribed
JW .... J Whatman (paper)
L .... from borderline of subject, length
lav .... lavender
lg .... large
litho .... lithograph
ls .... loss
lstn .... light stain
lt .... light, lightly
M .... mint condition
mezzo .... mezzotint
mk .... marked
mrg .... margin
mstn .... matstain
NM .... near mint
nspt .... newsprint
OE .... over estimate (by at least 20%)
oro .... orotone
P .... platemark
p/p .... publisher proof
p/s .... pencil signed
photogr .... photogravure
pk .... pink
pl .... plate
pl/intl .... plate initialed
pl/s .... plate signed
pldm .... palladium
pltn .... platinum
pub .... publisher
remrg .... remargined
repro .... reproduction
rlt .... roulette
rpl .... rippling
rpr .... repaired
rstr .... restored
S .... size of sheet
s/wrp .... shrink-wrapped
scr .... scrape
scrpt .... screenprint
sftgr .... softground
sgn .... signed
sl .... soil
slksc .... silkscreen
sltp .... salt print
slvr .... silver, silver print
sm .... small
srgph .... serigraph
stereo .... stereograph
stn .... stain
stp .... stamp, stamping
stp/s .... stamp signed
stpl .... stipple
tin .... tintype
tp .... tape
tr .... tear, torn
trm .... trimmed
tstn .... timestain
UE .... under estimate (by at least 20%)
unfr .... unframed
VG .... very good condition
w/ .... with
wc .... woodcut
wdb .... woodbury
wht .... white
wm .... watermarked
wstn .... waterstain
yel .... yellow

How to Use this Book

Artists' information lines are in bold. Nationality and birth/death dates are found in parenthesis immediately following the artist's name. If the artist is still living or if the death date is unavailable, the birth date will be given followed by a (-); if the artist is deceased but only the date of death is known, that date will be preceded by a (-). When exact data was not available, the century during which the artist lived/worked is noted. Occasionally the date will signify the years during which the artist flourished, but this is specifically indicated.

Each work of the artist is sorted alphabetically under his/her name, either by title or by the auction catalog's description. If the title does not readily suggest the subject, a descriptive phrase often follows. (Such a phrase when taken directly from the catalog will not be set off by parenthesis; the parenthetical descriptions reflect a layman's view of the work.) Titles in other languages are often translated; these are also in parenthesis.

The auction house from whose catalog the listing was taken will be indicated by a special code at the end of the line. These codes are explained in the section *Auction Gallery Codes and Pricing Practices*, which will also inform you as to which of the galleries do or do not charge a buyers premium and which includes this charge in their post-auction report. The actual sale date is noted immediately following the gallery code, and prices we have listed are just as they appear on any given company's post-auction price sheet.

Because auctions are notorious for extremely high and low hammer prices (which result from a multitude of factors and tend to cloud the issue of market values), whenever an item exceeded its pre-sale estimate by more than 20%, it will be so signified by the letters 'OE' (over estimate) at the end of the listing. Conversely, a hammer price of more than 20% under the pre-sale estimate will be indicated by 'UE' for under estimate. Though admittedly generally inexplicable, such erratic prices may actually be early indicators of oncoming market trends.

When very similar lots sold through the same catalog, the lot numbers are provided so that you may more quickly find the original catalog reference if you so desire.

Some specific explanation may be required in order that you may fully understand each category:

Bronzes, Sculptures, and Assemblages: In this section, each description is for a bronze unless noted otherwise. If two dates are indicated, the first refers to when the work was originally conceived or executed, the second to when the specific bronze in the description line was actually cast. Because of the limitations of our one-line format, in order to differentiate between a work that can be positively linked to a particular studio or foundry and one whose origin can only be attributed, we have placed the name of the studio (or foundry) immediately following the size to indicate attribution – otherwise the manufacturer's name will be given before the date and/or size. When one dimension is given, it is height unless noted otherwise; when both height and length are given, height is first. Bear in mind that size and age have little bearing on the value of a bronze; the artist and the quality of the bronze are the most important worth-accessing factors to consider.

Paintings, Drawings, and Mixed Media: Type of medium used (for instance, watercolor, charcoal, gouache, etc.) will be indicated following the title and/or descriptive phrase at the beginning of each line. Pictures are framed unless stated otherwise. See also Glossary of Terms.

Photographs: Unless a frame or a mat is mentioned, assume that photographs are not framed. Dates given within the line indicate (first) when the negative was produced and (second) when the print was made. A vintage print is one made at the same time the negative was produced (or shortly thereafter), either by the photographer or by someone whose work he approved of or requisitioned. Sizes are actual print measurements (excluding the mat). When a photo is not marked with a studio stamp, attribution will be indicated directly after size.

Prints: Prints are sorted by artist or lithographer. A publisher's mark, when it appears on the print, will be noted directly before the date and/or size. When the publisher is identified after the size, the print is unmarked but is known to be published by that specific company and/or individual. Prints are framed unless noted otherwise. Damage has been listed when that information was given in the auction catalog. (Bear in mind that foxing, tears, and other imperfections in the margins are not as significant as when they extend into the image.) Measurements are usually taken from the platemark as indicated by 'P'. When the dimensions are preceded by an 'S' the size of the sheet is given; 'L' is used when measurements have been taken from the borderline of the subject.

Butterfield & Butterfield, Auctioneers & Appraisers

Founded in 1865, Butterfield & Butterfield celebrates its125th anniversary in 1990. The company conducts auctions in its San Francisco and Los Angeles galleries and extends its scope through a network of regional representatives in London, Tokyo, Arizona, Texas, the Monterey Peninsula, Portland, Reno, Sacramento, San Diego, Santa Barbara, and Seattle.

Butterfield & Butterfield has been responsible for selling property from prominent estates and has been chosen by many notable museums who wish to deaccession property in order to raise funds for new acquisitions. Among these have been the Los Angeles County Museum of Art, San Francisco Museum of Modern Art, Santa Barbara Museum of Art, San Diego Museum of Art, Baltimore Museum of Art, and Phoenix Art Museum.

1989 brought a number of record-setting prices to both galleries: an ebonized cherrywood table set a national record for American Aesthetic furniture, a gold lacquer shodana broke the world record for a single piece of Japanese furniture, and a gentleman's Patek Philippe & Co. wristwatch set a West Coast record for fine timepieces.

The Los Angeles gallery generated excitement with a series of special sales, including the firm's first auction dedicated entirely to Art Deco, Art Nouveau, and Arts & Crafts furniture and decorative arts. A week of sales devoted exclusively to Western American history included an auction of property from the personal collection of Gene Autry and memorabilia from the Custer family. The sale of Thomas Custer's personal revolver set a record for English revolvers, and the sword presented to General Ulysses S. Grant when he took command of the Northern army broke all previous records for American swords.

Other special auctions at Butterfield & Butterfield included a sale of architectural renderings from the 1930s firm of Miller & Pflueger, one of the preeminent proponents of Art Deco and Modern styles. Property from the collection of Whitney Warren, Jr., was sold for the benefit of the Fine Arts Museums of San Francisco.

Butterfield & Butterfield has the largest staff of personal property appraisers on the West Coast. This staff of specialists provides written appraisals for insurance, inheritance tax, estate planning, and family division purposes. Verbal estimates of auction value may be obtained by bringing property to the regular free appraisal clinics in either San Francisco or Los Angeles. Those outside the area may send a photograph and brief description of up to five items for a free auction estimate by mail.

Catalogue subscriptions include post-sale results and a complimentary subscription to the Butterfield & Butterfield monthly bulletin. For a descriptive brochure, write to:

Catalogue Department
Butterfield & Butterfield
220 San Bruno Avenue
San Francisco, CA 94130

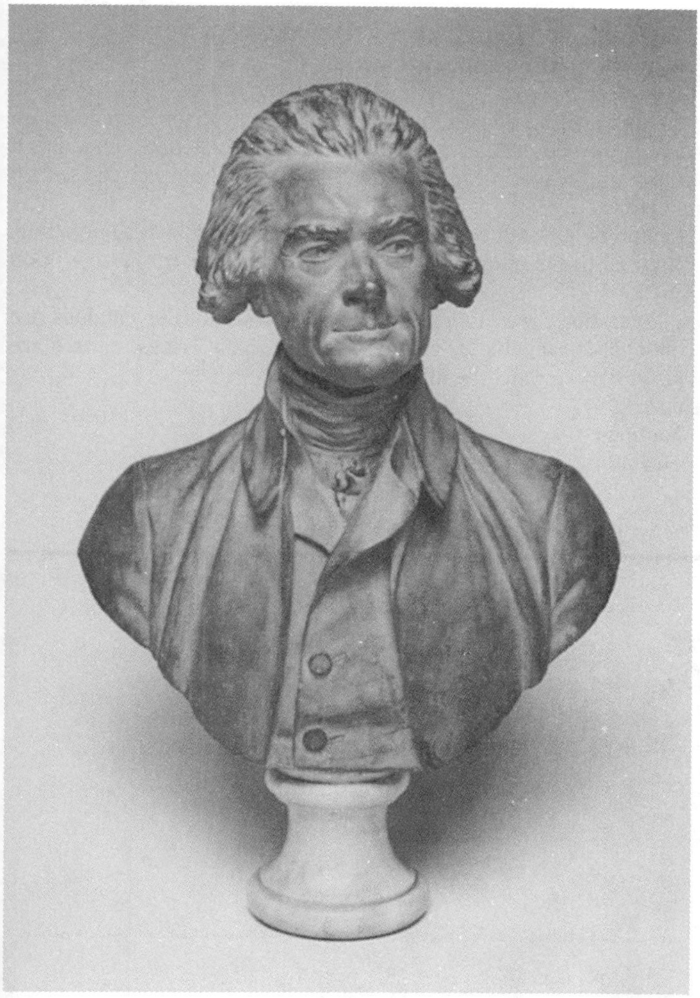

William Doyle Galleries, Inc.

William Doyle Galleries, Inc., has been in business for 15 years; founder William Doyle is Chairman. They conduct bi-weekly sales of fine English and Continental furniture and decorations including paintings and sculpture, silver, porcelain, and rugs. Semi-annual and tri-annual specialty sales feature Old Master's, Modern, European, and American paintings; Americana; Victorian and 19th-century furniture and decorations; books and autographs; prints and drawings; and important estate jewelry.

William Doyle Galleries specializes in estate property and also does appraisals for insurance and estate purposes. They will purchase an entire household, or consign some items and buy the remainder, depending on the client's preference. There is no fee for verbal appraisals done at the gallery on individual items. Fees for written appraisals are based on the number of appraisers involved and the time spent. They can be reached at:

William Doyle Galleries, Inc.
175 East 87th Street
New York, NY 10128
(212)427-2730 (Mon.-Fri. 9 a.m. to 6 p.m.)

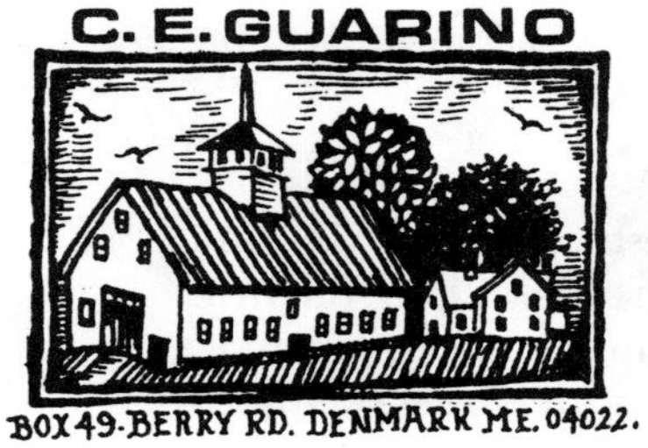

C.E. Guarino – Absentee Auctions

Charles E. Guarino is among the first auction houses to deal exclusively in absentee bidding o lots offered through their Americana Arts Auction catalogs. Established in 1972, Guarino handles variety of graphic arts, rare books, antique maps, paintings, and special sales of American India weavings, beadwork, basketry, and artifacts.

Bidding is by mail or telephone and is handled by the staff on a competitive basis; quotation regarding the amount bid on an item as the auction progresses are given over the phone upo request.

Catalogs containing complete descriptions of the lots and numerous illustrations are available by mail. Individual sales catalogs ar priced at $5.00 – a subscription for twelve months of sales (at least four catalogs) is available by regular mail at $15.00. Prices realized ar sent to bidders and are also included in the catalog for the next consecutive auction. Contact the auctioneer:

C.E. Guarino
Americana Arts Auctions
Berry Rd., P.O. Box 49
Denmark, Maine 04022
(207)452-2123

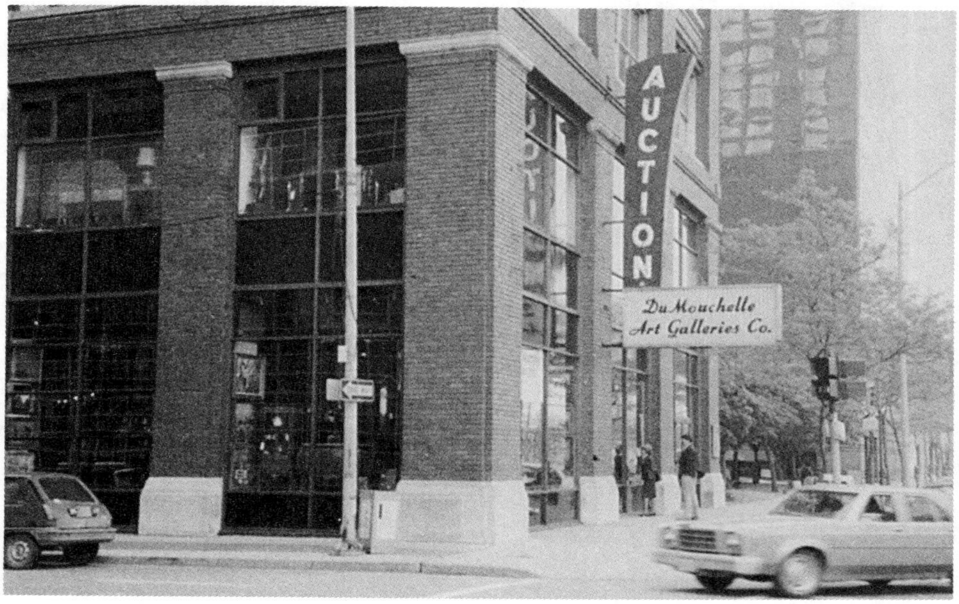

DuMouchelles Art Galleries Company

DuMouchelles is a Detroit area institution that has been known for its auction and appraisal business for more than sixty years Located in downtown Detroit directly across from the Renaissance Center, DuMouchelle's accessibility plays a key role in its success.

Auctions consisting of estate properties and those of individual consignors are held at the gallery one weekend a month, beginning Friday evenings at 7:00 p.m., Saturdays at 11:00 a.m., and Sundays at noon.

Each auction is locally and nationally advertised. Monthly brochures are sent to over 15,000 clients, and fully illustrated catalogues are mailed to subscribers and interested parties all over the world.

DuMouchelle's monthly auctions consist of antiques; fine arts and collectibles such as paintings, graphics, sculpture; Oriental and exotic rugs; fine furniture; jewelry; porcelain; art glass; crystal; antique firearms; fine china; silver; pianos; and vintage cars.

For further information regarding either auctions or appraisal services you may contact them at:

DuMouchelles Art Galleries Company
409 East Jefferson
Detroit, MI 48226
(313)963-6255

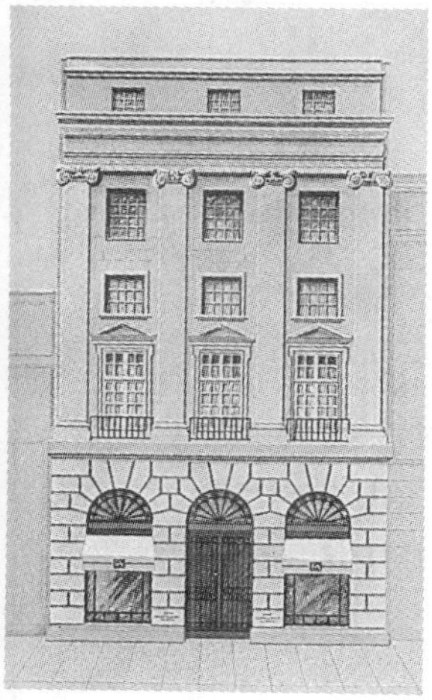

Freeman/Fine Arts of Philadelphia, Inc.

As the oldest auction house in America (having been in continuous operation since 1805), we provide a full-service auction and appraisal firm servicing the legal, banking, and private interests of buyer and seller alike. Our seven-floor gallery in the heart of the Philadelphia business district is easily accessible from every method of local, national, and international transportation.

Ours is a tradition with new ideas offering professional services in personal property and real estate auctions as well as appraisals for estate taxes, insurance, and fair market value. We hold weekly estate auctions and have catalogued sales specializing in period furniture, prints and paintings, decorative arts, fine jewelry, Americana, books and manuscripts, Oriental rugs, and collections.

FREEMAN \ FINE ARTS
OF PHILADELPHIA, INC.
AUCTIONEERS FA APPRAISERS

Freeman/Fine Arts of Philadelphia, Inc.
1808 Chestnut Street
Philadelphia, PA 19103
(215)563-9275
Vice President: James E. Buckley

Serving the Canadian antiques and fine art markets for over 100 years!

We hold two major art and jewellery sales annually
Spring and Fall

CANADIAN & EUROPEAN
ART & FINE JEWELLERY

Our services include insurance evaluations, fair market values, estate evaluations for division and probate.

Regular quality auctions of antiques and fine art are held in our salesrooms every 4-6 weeks.

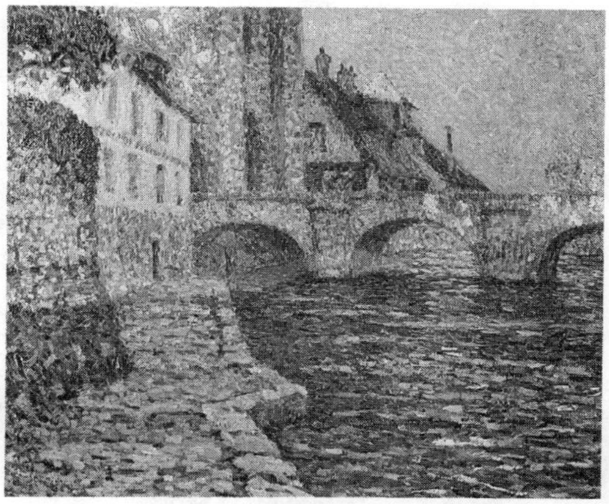

HENRI LE SIDANER
(French School 1862-1939)
'Bridge Near Bruges'
Oil on canvas, 18½ x 22"
Sold for $96,800

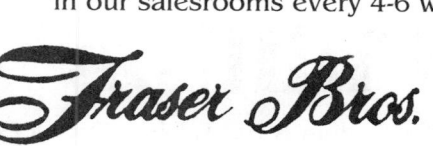

Fraser Bros.

NEW ADDRESS:
8290 Devonshire, Montreal, Quebec H4P 2P7
Telephone: (514) 345-0571
FAX: (514) 737-2423

Auctioneers, Appraisers and Liquidators since 1880
Commissaires-priseurs, evaluaterus et liquidateurs depois 1880

Garth's Auctions, Inc.

Garth's Auctions is one of the most-respected auction houses in the United States. Established in 1956 as an auction firm, Garth's handles 18th and 19th century American, English, and Continental furniture and accessories. Stratford Auction Center, a division of Garth's, sells Victoriana and collectibles of the 19th and 20th centuries.

Garth's has a number of specialty sales including guns, Civil War items, pre-historic and historic Indian artifacts, toys, banks, dolls, blown glass, historical and bitters bottles, art glass, and art pottery.

Catalogs are available by subscription. Gift subscriptions are available at any time. The charge for all catalogs (including post-sale price lists) is $85.00 per year. You may contact the company at:

Garth's Auctions, Inc.
2690 Stratford Road
Box 369
Delaware, OH 43015
(614)362-4771
(614)369-5085

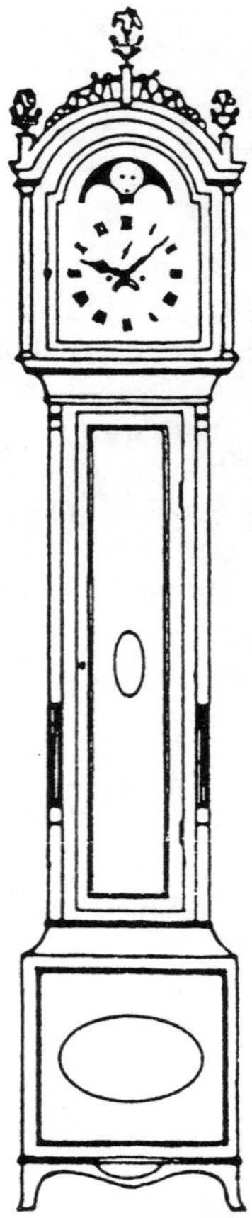

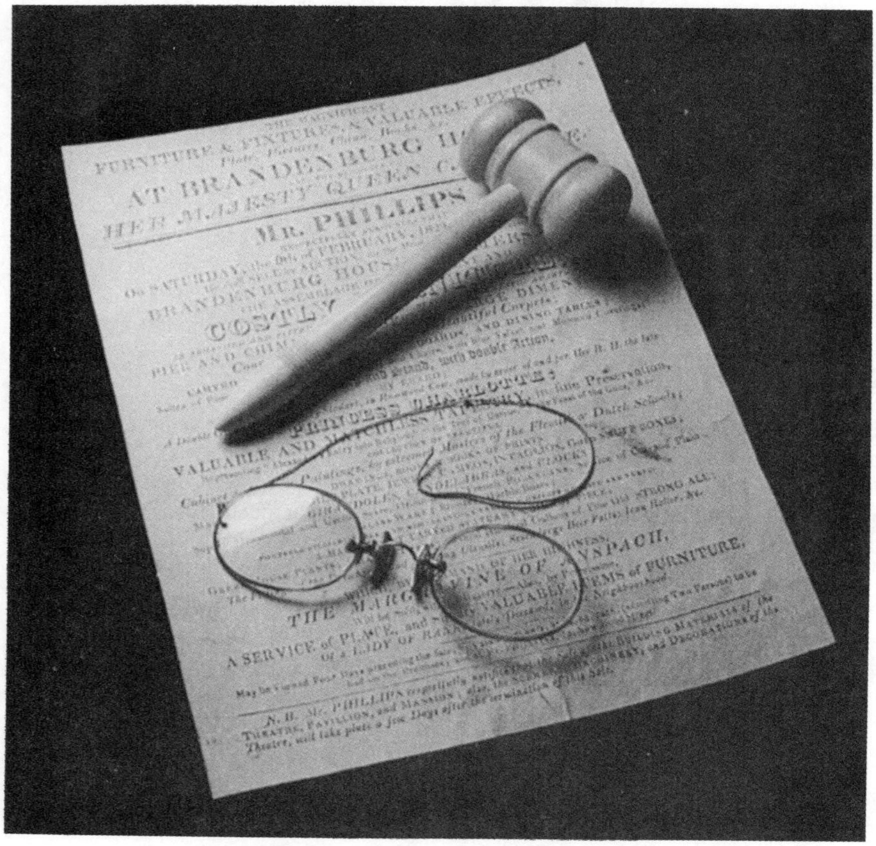
Mr. Phillips

Schrager Auction Galleries, Ltd.

In 1985, Al Schrager bought the sixty three-year old Third Church of Christian Science in Milwaukee, Wisconsin, in which to re-establish his prestigious auction galleries.

The beauty of the building with its two expansive floors of galleries echoes Al Schrager's professional dedication to 'recapturing the beautiful things' in our world. It provides the setting for fine estate auctions which are held regularly. Both buyers and sellers from national and local audiences appreciate his expertise, forthright service, and leadership in the field. He is known not only as the founder of Schrager Auction Galleries but also for his specialization in estate liquidations and appraisal services for insurance and probate purposes for over forty years.

The building, a significant Milwaukee landmark, is a magnificient neoclassic structure with elements of Art Deco. The Auditorium Gallery seats over nine hundred people and is topped with a fifty-nine foot leaded glass ceiling dome which is lit on auction evenings. The gallery is easily accessible from expressways and the airport, as well as any location in the city. For information regarding services, contact:

Schrager Auction Galleries, Ltd.
2915 North Sherman Boulevard
P.O. Box 10390
Milwaukee, WI 53210
(414)873-3738

Selkirk Galleries

Selkirk's, founded in 1830, is an auction house which takes pride in providing the best-possible service to sellers and buyers of all categories of estate property.

We have a full schedule of auction venues which includes four important gallery auctions and nine estate auctions every year. The gallery auctions are widely advertised and draw collectors from around the world. The previews enjoy a regular attendance in excess of 3,000 people. We publish illustrated catalogues with scholarly descriptions of each item in these auctions. These venues are designed for lots ranging in price from $500 to $500,000.

Our monthly estate auctions provide a fast, efficient and effective vehicle for selling lots ranging in price from $10 to $2,500.

Our staff has expertise and experience in selling the following categories of property of all periods: American, European, and Oriental furniture; porcelains; silver; jewelry; American and European painting, sculpture, and bronze; Oriental art; antiquarian books; Oriental rugs; vintage automobiles; designer furs; arms and armor; Art Nouveau; and Art Deco.

Our 28,000 square-foot gallery, salesroom, and warehouse facility is one of the best equipped and most spacious in the world.

We efficiently serve vendors of antiques and fine art throughout the midwestern region.

Selkirk Galleries
4166 Olive Street
St. Louis, MO 63108
(314)533-1700
(314)533-1704 FAX
Bruce B. Selkirk, President
Mark O. Howald, Vice President

Skinner Galleries of Boston and Bolton, MA

Situated in Central Massachusetts in the heart of Nashoba Valley, Bolton is the main headquarters of Skinner, Inc., the nation's fifth largest auction gallery. We have set world auction records, drawing record-breaking bids and attracting international media attention in various categories including American furniture and decorative accessories, textiles, historical bottles, Arts & Crafts-period furniture and accessories, art glass, Oriental rugs, and board games.

The Bolton Gallery is the site of sixty auctions annually and houses fifteen specialty areas consisting of American, English, Continental, and Arts & Crafts period furniture and accessories, fine jewelry, silver, American and European paintings and prints, art glass, antique textiles and needlework, ceramics, books, Oriental art, Oriental rugs and carpets, toys, dolls and games, American Indian art and Ethnographica, tribal art and antiquities, military items, photographs and related hardware, bottles and early glass, musical instruments, and autographs. Special events including lectures, appraisal clinics, and exhibitions are held regularly at the Bolton Gallery.

Centrally located in Boston's historical Back Bay, Skinner's Boston Gallery, part of New England's largest auction and appraisal organization, is the site of special sales of jewelry, musical instruments, and the December Gift Auction. Exhibitions for these sales are held at the Boston Gallery with auctions conducted directly across the street at The Ritz-Carlton. The Boston Gallery provides a backdrop for regularly scheduled lectures, appraisal days, and exhibitions.

For further information regarding Skinner Galleries of Boston and Bolton, telephone: (508)779-6241.

Swann Galleries, Inc.

Swann Galleries is the oldest and largest U.S. auctioneer specializing in Rare Books, Autographs and Manuscripts, Important 19th and 20th Century Photographs and Photographic Literature, Hebraica and Judaica, and Works of Art on Paper. We are known internationally, and we often set record prices.

We conduct some thirty five sales a year during the September–June auction season. At least two major sales are devoted to each of the above special fields. Other auctions include the following subjects: Americana; Art and Architecture; Early Printed Books; Decorative Graphics; Maps and Atlases; Medicine, Natural History, Science, and Technology; Modern Illustrated and Press Books; Modern Literature; Performing Arts and Magic; Sets and Bindings; Sporting Books; and Travel and Exploration.

In addition to these sales, for which detailed catalogues are prepared, we occasionally conduct 'shelf sales,' consisting of good material, principally from institutional or book trade consignors, that was deemed not appropriate for our regular auctions. This material is not catalogued, but shelf lists are available. You bid by shelf and are responsible for packing and removing your purchases.

Our quarterly newsletter, *The Trumpet*, available upon request, gives full information about forthcoming sales and contains a catalogue order form.

For further information, contact Caroline Birenbaum, Director of Communications, at (212)254-4710.

Wolf's is an internationally recognized auction house located in the Historic Warehouse District of Cleveland, Ohio. Wolf's conducts on an annual basis specialized sales which include: American and European Paintings and Sculpture; Prints, Drawings and Books; Americana; Art Glass and Pottery; Jewelry and Wines. Wolf's also conducts bi-monthly auctions that feature a wide range of Furniture and Decorative Arts.

Wolf's welcomes consignments and inquiries. For further information, literature, or catalog subscriptions contact Laura Oviatt. (1-800-526-1991)

Wolf's
Auctioneers and Appraisers
1239 West 6th St.
Cleveland, OH 44113
1-216-575-9653
FAX 1-216-621-8011

Bronzes, Sculptures, and Other Assemblages

AARONS, George (American, 1896-1980)
Testing the Water-A Fountain Sculpture; gr patina, terra cotta base, sgn/dtd 1928, 22", RWS 3/16/89 OE ... **5,000**
ABAKANOWICZ, Magdelena (20th C)
Anonymous Portrait, cotton/resin/sand, 1985, 8x7x5", SBY 10/8/88 OE ... **7,975**
ABDELL, Douglas (20th C)
Aephae-Aekyad (contemporary), sgn/dtd 11-7-77/titled under base, 29", SBY 10/5/88 UE ... **1,100**
ADAMS, Robert (20th C)
Untitled (contemporary), 6/6, brn patina, wood base, sgn/dtd 1978 on base, 5", lot 199, C-E 5/9/89 UE ... **770**
ADNET, Jean & Jacques (French, 20th C)
Female Dancer (stylistic), #6, walnut, sgn/mk Made in France, ca pre-1928, 13", C-NY 6/11/88 OE ... **2,420**
AFRICANO, Nicholas (American, 20th C)
Boy in a Tree (Upright), glass/lead/oil, 1986, 26x25x21", SBY 5/3/88 OE ... **63,250**
Combing His Hair (wall relief), acrylic/metal wire/linoleum tile, intl/titled, SBY 11/11/88 ... **8,800**
High Wire #2 (figure balancing on high wire), oil/wax/acrylic/string/wood, 1979, 10x8x1", lot 300, SBY 10/5/89 ... **6,050**
AGAM, Yaacov (Israeli, 1928-)
Beating Heart, gold-plated brass in 18 graduated parts, sgn, 4x10x7", SBY 10/8/88 ... **6,600**
Beating Heart (Moods), 9 graduated stainless steel hearts, sgn/dtd 1981, 22x24", SBY 5/3/88 ... **11,000**
Beating Hearts (pendant), 19/300, golden patinated metal, 3", lot 183, SBY 2/14/89 ... **495**
Birth of a Flag (multiple sculpture), XXXXIII/L, slksc on acrylic, sgn, 1975, 26x20", Transworld, lot 87, PHL 6/16/88 ... **800**
Orchestration on White (abstract sculpture), oil on aluminum relief, sgn/dtd 1975-6/titled, 69x71x4", SBY 2/19/88 ... **44,000**
AHEARN, John (20th C)
Ricky (bust), painted plaster, 1983, 24x23x9", SBY 2/19/88 ... **5,225**
AITKEN, Robert Ingersoll (American, 1878-)
Metal Tondon Allegorical Relief: Hear No Evil, See No Evil, Speak No Evil; golden patina, sgn, 17" dia, C-E 6/1/88 ... **440**
AIZELIN, Eugene Antonie (French, 1821-1902)
Mignon, rich brn patina, sgn/dtd 1880/mk Barbedienne Paris/Collas Reduction seal, 31", C-NY 5/25/88 ... **4,180**
Mignon (seated lady w/stringed instrument), brn patina, marble plinth, sgn/titled/mk Barbedienne, 26", SLK 11/25/88 ... **3,200**
ALLIOT, Lucien (French, fl 1905-1940)
Untitled, nude kneeling on one knee; brn patina, wood plinth, 15" (w/out plinth), SLK 2/11/89 ... **1,100**
ALONZO, see De Alonzo
AMAGOSTI, A. (Continental, early 20th C)
Lion Attacking a Bird of Prey, veined gr marble base, sgn/dtd 1921, 14", lot 110, C-E 4/19/88 ... **990**
Stag, Doe, & a Fawn; reddish-brn patina w/traces of verdigris, realistic base, sgn/dtd 1929, 18x28", C-E 6/1/88 ... **1,000**
American School (20th C)
Bust of an Indian, 11", lot 380, FAP 4/15/88 ... **220**
ANDRE, Carl (American, 1935-)
2 (9AL), group of 18 aluminum plates, 1980, 1x12x60" overall, lot 233, SBY 10/5/89 OE ... **60,500**
25 Steel Rectangle (contemporary), 25 joined hot-rolled steel squares, 36x41", lot 251, SBY 2/15/89 OE ... **49,500**
ANDREA, see De Andrea
ANGUIER, Michel Andre; after (French, 1612-1686)
Amphitrite (partially draped/standing contraposto), terra cotta, 14", lot 134, C-NY 6/17/89 UE ... **352**
Anonymous (Russian, 19th C)
Balailaika Player, wearing wide-brimmed hat/loose tunic; gilt, rectangular malachite base, 6", C-L 10/6/89 ... **1,485**
Bear & Cub, gilt, rectangular malachite base, 6" long, C-L 10/6/89 OE ... **2,975**
Recumbent Peasant, in traditional dress; gilt, rectangular malachite base, 6" long, C-L 10/8/89 ... **1,022**
Antique, after
Borghese Warrior, red/gr patinae, self base, 25", C-E 6/1/88 ... **1,760**
Antique (Roman, First C A.D.)
Head of a Woman, truncated at neck/wavy parted hair; marble, later stone cube base, 4", lot 139, C-NY 6/17/89 OE ... **770**
Torso of Hercules, truncated neck/standing contraposto/lion skin over left arm; marble, wood base, 18", C-NY 6/17/89 OE ... **20,900**
Antique (Roman, Second C A.D.)
Head of a Youth, truncated neck/shaggy locks of hair; marble, later circular plinth, 5", lot 140, C-NY 6/17/89 OE ... **528**
Antique (Tanagra, style of)
Silenus with a Bacchante, bacchante sitting w/Cupid in her lap & Silenus standing; 10", lt ls/rpr, lot 143, C-NY 6/17/89 ... **660**
Antique (Tanagra)
Bacchante Playing a Flute, laurel-wreathed nude walks/plays flute; terra cotta, 13", ls, lot 142, C-NY 6/17/89 ... **770**
Matron, mature woman in coiled headdress holds hem of skirt w/left hand; terra cotta, 6", lot 144, C-NY 6/17/89 UE ... **110**
APPEL, Karel (Dutch, 1921-)
Clown with Trumpet, 6/8, acrylic on wood, sgn/dtd 77, 48x73x8", SBY 5/3/88 OE ... **24,200**
Dancing Elephant, I/IV, painted wood, sgn/dtd 1978, 46", lot 214A, SBY 2/15/89 ... **22,000**
Flying Bird, glazed ceramic, sgn/dtd, no size given, lot 777, FAP 11/4/88 ... **1,900**
Magician (multiple sculpture), 2/8, hand-painted wood, 1978, 39x34", ABCD Eds, lot 706, SBY 11/5/88 ... **6,600**
ARAKAWA, Shusaku (20th C)
Untitled (abstract assemblage), plaster/radio tube/fiberglass/plexiglas on painted wood, sgn, 82x20x7", SBY 2/19/88 ... **7,700**
ARCHIPENKO, Alexander (Russian, 1887-1964)
Femme Assise, 3/12F, golden-brn patina, sgn/dtd Paris 1912, 1912/1966, 16", lot 57, SBY 2/18/88 ... **41,250**
Femme Assise (surrealistic seated nude), 5/12, brn patina, sgn/dtd/#d, 1912/1966, 16", SBY 5/11/89 ... **99,000**
Madonna, wht marble, sgn, 1936, 25", lot 73, C-NY 10/5/89 OE ... **40,700**

Repose (surrealistic reclining torso), brn patina, sgn, ca 1935(?), 9" long, SBY 2/6/89 41,250
Soldat Qui Marche (highly-styled figure), 5/10, golden-brn patina, sgn/dtd/#d, 1917/later, 46", SBY 5/11/89 154,000
Statuette (Statue on Triangular Base), 2/6, brn patina, sgn/dtd 1914, 1914/ca 1955-57, 30", SBY 5/11/88 OE 121,000

ARMAN (Spanish, 1928-)

Amphetamines (sculpture), accumulation of pills/plastic pill bottles in plexiglas, sgn/dtd 70, 48x48", SBY 5/2/88 OE 41,250
Bad Taste Leads to Crime (contemporary), accordion parts in plexiglas, 1972, 49x49x9", lot 184, SBY 5/3/89 OE 57,750
Casals Marmelade (abstract sculpture), accumulation of cellos/bows in plexiglas, sgn, 1968, 63x53x10", SBY 6/30/88 72,000
En Souvenir de Milton, book fragments embedded in polyester/plexiglas box, sgn, 1972, 40x20x5", lot 68, C-NY 10/4/89 OE 35,200
Long Term Parking (contemporary), plastic toy cars in plaster, 13x8x8", lot 309, C-NY 5/4/89 OE 14,300
Poubelle (sculpture), accumulation of garbage in plexiglas, sgn/dtd 70, 48x36x5", SBY 5/2/88 OE 35,750
Poubelle (sculpture), accumulation of garbage in plexiglas, ca 1970, 40x20x5", SBY 5/2/88 OE 27,500
Statue of Liberty, gr patina, sgn, 30x8x9", lot 100, SBY 2/15/89 16,500
Untitled (Accumulation), sliced violins in polyester & plexiglas, ca 1969, 40x24x4", SBY 10/5/89 OE 71,500

ARMITAGE, Kenneth (British, 1916-)

Bed, painted bronze, intl, 1967, 20x15x10", SBY 10/5/88 1,870
Seasons (contemporary), 1956, 30", SBY 10/5/88 OE 12,100
Sibyl #1 (contemporary), intl, 1961, 44x16x15", SBY 10/5/88 4,125
Sibyl #2 (contemporary), intl, 1961, 40x13x12", SBY 10/5/88 5,500
Sibyl #3 (contemporary), intl, 1961, 40x24x12", SBY 10/5/88 UE 3,300
Sprawling Lady (contemporary), 2/6, brn patina, sgn/dtd 69, 9x26x8", lot 171, C-NY 5/4/89 OE 8,800
Untitled (abstract figure), #2, gr patina, intl, 65", lot 42, SBY 2/15/89 OE 49,500

ARNESON, Robert (American, 20th C)

Self-Portrait: Stomp-`Em; #6, partially-glazed terra cotta, sgn/dtd 1973/titled, 18" dia, SBY 10/8/88 5,500

ARNOLD, Henry (19th/20th C)

Woman in Classical Greek Dress (plays lyre), brn/gr patinae, sgn/mk Colin, ca 1930, 19", lot 71, SBY 11/17/88 2,090

ARNOLDI, Charles (American, 1946-)

Carat (contemporary), acrylic/flashe on wood, sgn/dtd 1981 on verso, 96x94x9", SBY 10/8/88 UE 17,600
Untitled II (square shape/contemporary), painted tree branches, 1981, 77x70x80", lot 295, C-NY 5/4/89 13,200
Untitled: Diptych (slivers of colored wood); acrylic on wood, sgn/dtd 1982, 99x92", SBY 11/11/88 23,100

ARP, Jean Hans (French, 1887-1966)

Applique et Songeur, wht marble, 1960, 22", SBY 5/11/88 90,750

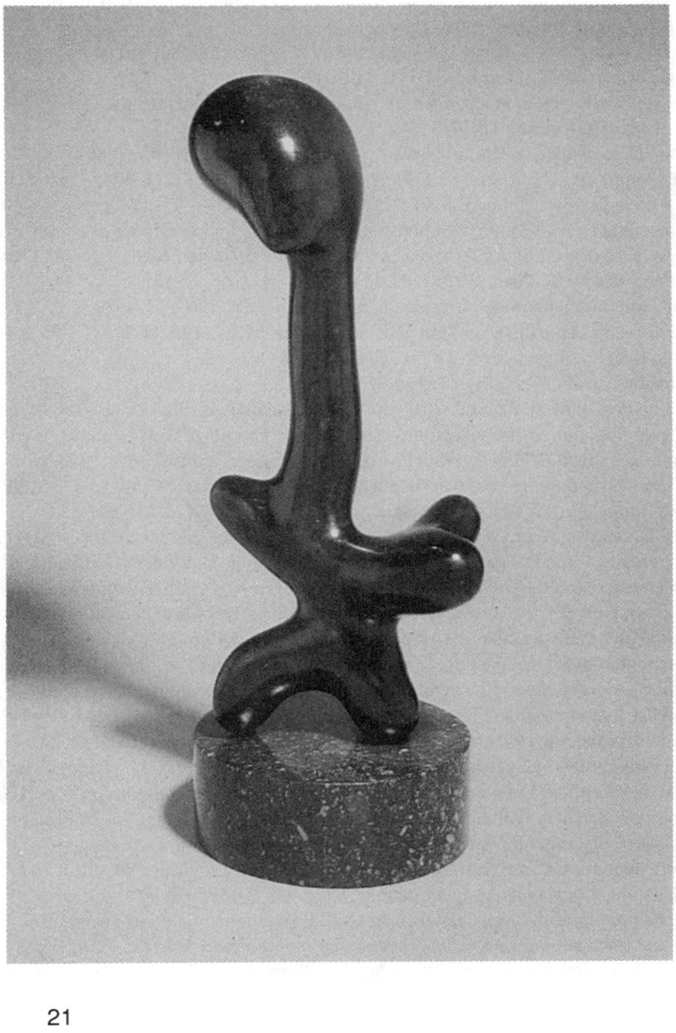

Petite Sphinx, ed of 5, blk patina, 1942, 16", C-NY 5/12/88 OE, $82,500

Assis, limestone, 13", lot 78, WD 11/16/88 UE 62,500
Composition (contemporary wall relief), ed of 5, polished bronze, sgn on verso, 1958, 14x9x2", lot 3, C-NY 5/3/88 OE 30,800
Coupe Chimerique (abstract), 1/3, polished bronze, 1947, 32", SBY 5/11/89 154,000
Feuille sur Cristal (abstract), V/V, golden-brn patina, intl/mk Georges Rudier Fondeur Paris, 1957, 18", C-NY 5/12/88 66,000
Geburstagskonstellation (contemporary relief), ed of 10, painted wood, 1962, 11" dia, lot 139, C-NY 10/5/89 22,000
Grand Batard (abstract), wht marble, rectangular self base, 1960, 21", SBY 5/11/89 OE 203,500
Group of 4: La Famille; #1-4, ed of 3, glass, sgn/dtd, 1966, 18"/22"/28"/36", Fucina Angeli, C-NY 2/16/89 17,600
Homme Vu par un Fleur (contemporary), ed of about 400, polished bronze, ca 1958, 5" long, C-E 5/9/89 OE 4,620
Homme Vu par un Fleur, ed of about 400, 1958, 3", SBY 10/5/88........ 2,750
Metamorphose (Coquille-Cygne-Balance-Toi), ed of 5, polished bronze, 1935, 9", C-NY 5/12/88 30,800
Metamorphose (Coquille-Cygne-Balance-Toi), polished bronze, 1935, 9", lot 135, C-NY 10/5/89 36,300
Pair: Sposi; 1/3, glass, sgn/dtd 1964/mk Constantini FA, 20", C-NY 10/6/88 16,500
Piece d'Echec, 3/5, polished bronze, sgn, 1958, 20", SBY 10/7/88 33,000
Soupir d'Une Fleur (abstract), wht marble, executed 1963, 5x8x8", SBY 5/11/89 OE........ 115,550

ARTSCHWAGER, Richard (American, 1924-)
Perjunta (in 2 parts), blk painted wood w/metal eye hook top, 30x9x1"/20" dia, C-NY 5/4/88 OE 8,250
Relief I (wall relief), clr formica on wood, 29x22", C-NY 11/9/88 OE 46,200

ARYTON, Michael (British, 1921-1975)
Impact (contemporary), 3/12, square base, 1974, 14", lot 210, SBY 10/7/89 4,950

ASHOONA, Ohitoo (Canadian, Inuk artist, Cape Dorset, 20th C)
Polar Bear Carrying Captured Seal, soapstone, 1984, 9x10", RAB 8/1/89 1,300

Austrian School (19th C)
Arab Seated Beneath a Palm, camel lying nearby; cold paint, ca 1900, 14", C-E 9/16/88 550
Box, nude snake charmer/snake on oriental carpet on top; cold paint, 6", C-E 6/16/88 550
India Elephant, in full riding gear w/mahout; #3412, cold paint, mk Geschutet, 9x11", lot 212, RWS 9/24/88........ 2,100
Lamp, Mideastern merchants barter surrounded by wares/carpets; cold paint, blk marble base, 14", RWS 12/10/88 2,000
Pair: Companion Couple (man w/ruffled collar, woman w/wide skirt & key); painted wood, square base, 13", RWS 12/10/88 600
Set of 4: Figural Cardholders (ea a bird: pheasant/grouse/woodcock/partridge); slvr base, mk JC Vickery, 2", RWS 9/24/88........ 1,000

AWRET
Horse & Rider, gr patina, 19", C-E 1/12/88 UE 264

BALLA, Giacomo (Italian, 1871-1958)
Ballerina V (contemporary), 1/9, chrome-plated brass, rectangular plexiglas base, 1922, 21", lot 71, C-NY 10/5/89 UE........ 7,150
Futurist Flower, 37/40 & G/42, lacquered wood, sgn/mk Obelisco Multi-Pli, ca 1925-30, 17x35", C-E 5/13/88 OE........ 3,520

BAREAU, Georges (Flemish, 1616-1686)
Justice, seated half-draped Justice holding scroll/pen; golden reddish-brn patina, sgn, 23", C-E 6/28/88 UE 1,100

BAREAU, Georges; after (Flemish, 1616-1686)
Vox Pacis (man in loincloth w/open arms), square red-mottled marble base w/tag, sgn/dtd 1891, 25", C-E 6/1/88 462

BARLACH, Ernst (German, 1870-)
Der Racher (The Reaper), 8/10, brn patina, sgn, 1914, 24" long, SBY 10/7/88 OE........ 7,700
Lesender Mann, brn patina, sgn/mk H Noack Berlin, 1936/later, 18", C-NY 2/16/89 OE........ 38,500

BARRIAS, Louis Ernest (French, 1841-1905)
Nature Unveiling Herself Before Science, gilt/slvr, gr veined marble base, mk Susse Fres, ca 1900, SBY 2/22/89........ 10,450
Planter (classical draped figure w/lizards on flat ovoid shap/footed base), sgn/mk Barbedienne, 11", C-NY 6/11/88 1,430

BARYE, Alfred (French, 19th/20th C)
Joan of Arc (mounted on horse), brn patina, mk A Barye, 34", C-NY 5/24/89 6,834
Lion & Lioness, gr-brn patina, sgn/mk Thiebaut Freres, 5x7", lot 102, C-E 4/19/88 660
Pointer & a Rabbit, gilt, sgn, 6x8", lot 116, C-E 4/19/88 OE........ 660

BARYE, Antoine Louis (French, 1795-1875)
Bears, adults in playful combat; blk/brn patinae, molded octagonal base, sgn/mk Barbedienne, 9", lot 201, SBY 6/9/89 3,300
Bronze Panel of a Lion, gr patina, sgn/mk Barbedienne Foundry, 23x11", lot 322, WG 4/23/88........ 1,300
Bull (standing w/head held high), rich brn patina, mk Barye, 15x15", C-NY 5/24/89 2,860
Cheval Turc (spirited horse), rubbed blk/brn patinae, veined marble base, sgn, late 19th C, 12", lot 158, SBY 6/9/89........ 15,400
Crouching Bunny, #44, rich brn patina, sgn, 2", C-NY 2/23/89 OE 1,760
Eagle with Outspread Wings & Open Beak, rich brn patina, mk AL Barye, 10x14", C-NY 5/24/89 OE 2,640
Elephant of Senegal (pounding through jungle), gr-blk patina, sgn/mk Barbedienne, late 19th C, 15" long, SBY 6/9/89 3,575
General Bonaparte (on horseback), dk brn patina, mk Barye, 14", C-NY 5/24/89 8,800
Group of Deer, Doe, & Two Fawns, on rocky oval base; rubbed warm brn patina, sgn, late 19th C, 7", lot 152, SBY 6/9/89 2,640
L'Accolade (Arab mare & stallion), brn patina, sgn, 8x14", C-NY 5/24/89 3,300
Lion & Serpent, rich gr/brn patinae, sgn, late 19th C, 10x14", lot 179, SBY 6/9/89........ 2,860
Lion Devouring an Antelope, rich brn/gr patinae, sgn/mk Barbedienne Paris, late 19th C, 5x11" long, lot 182, SBY 6/9/89 1,650
Lion with Boar, standing on prey/on rocky base; rubbed golden-brn patina, sgn, 19x15", lot 202, SBY 6/9/89 6,325
Lion with Dead Alligator, rich gr-brn patina, rectangular base, sgn/mk GM, late 19th C, 13x18", lot 199, SBY 6/9/89 3,300
Lioness of Senegal (standing), golden-brn patina, gr marble base, mk Barye, 8x11", C-NY 5/24/89 1,320
Pair of Plaques: Panther; Leopard (rectangular reliefs); dk brn patina, sgn, 5x3", lot 203, SBY 6/9/89 1,320
Panther of India (crouching/holds prey), gr/blk patinae, oval base, sgn/mk Barbedienne, ca 1825, 8" long, SBY 6/9/89........ 1,650
Panther of Tunisia, crouching on rocky base; rubbed golden patina, sgn, late 19th C, 7" long, lot 194, SBY 6/9/89 770
Percheron (standing stallion), brn/blk patinae, sgn, last half 19th C, 8", lot 191, SBY 6/9/89 2,750
Python Crushing a Crocodile, gr/gray patinae, inscr/mk Barbedienne Fondeur, late 19th C, 7", lot 180, SBY 6/9/89 OE 7,975
Python Crushing a Gazelle, gr-brn patina, sgn/mk Barbedienne Fondeur Paris, late 19th C, 7", lot 183, SBY 6/9/89 3,575
Reclining Doe, rich rubbed brn patina, rectangular molded base, sgn/mk France, late 19th C, 3x6", lot 195, SBY 6/9/89 1,760
Reclining Panther, rich rubbed brn patina, sgn/mk Barbedienne Fondeur Paris, 4x8", lot 192, SBY 6/9/89........ 880

Rhinocerous, rich brn patina, sgn, 4", C-NY 2/23/89 OE 4,510
Seated Basset, gr-brn patina, gr marble base, sgn/mk F Barbedienne Fondeur, 6x11", C-NY 2/23/89 1,650
Seated Cat, on rocky ground; rich verdigris patina, sgn, late 19th C, 4", lot 196, SBY 6/9/89 1,980
Seated Lion, rich rubbed dk brn patina, oval molded base, sgn, ca 1850, 14", lot 155, SBY 6/9/89 OE 8,800
Seated Lion, rubbed dk brn patina, oval molded base, sgn, ca 1850, 14", lot 156, SBY 6/9/89 OE 8,800
Stag Listening, gr-brn patina, mk Barye, 8", C-NY 5/24/89 1,650
Standing Basset, gr-brn patina, gr marble base, 7x9", C-NY 2/23/89 OE 2,860
Standing Elk, sgn/mk Susse Paris, 19x19", lot 2029, DM 2/19/88 4,500
Standing Greyhound: Levrier Espagnol; rubbed blk patina, rectangular base, sgn, ca 1845, 5", lot 153, SBY 6/9/89 1,760
Standing Lion, 10" long, lot 951, FAP 12/8/88 700
Striding Lion, aged male; rubbed golden-brn patina, sgn, late 19th C, 7x12", lot 205, SBY 6/9/89 1,650
Striding Lion, gr-brn patina, mk Barye, 9x17", C-NY 5/24/89 2,860
Striding Tiger, rubbed gr/blk patinae, rectangular molded base, sgn, 20th C, 8x16", lot 204, SBY 11/5/88 2,750
Turkish Horse, gr-blk patina, mk Barye F Barbedienne Fondeur, 7x8", C-NY 5/24/89 5,500
Turkish Horse, head down/rearing back; rich dk brn patina, rouge marble base, sgn, ca 1880, 6", lot 154, SBY 6/8/89 6,600
Turkish Horse, rich dk gr-brn patina, sgn/mk F Barbedienne Fondeur, 7", C-NY 5/24/89 11,000
Two Dogs Pointing Pheasant, rich brn patina, mk Barye 8, 7x11", C-NY 5/24/89 3,300
Virginia Deer Reclining, full-antlered stag leaning to bite flea; #1837, dk brn patina, late 19th C, 10", SBY 6/9/89 5,775
Walking Lion, #16, rich dk gr-brn patina, sgn/mk F Barbedienne Fondeur France, 9x15", C-NY 5/24/89 3,080
Walking Lion, #43, brn patina, mk Barye F Barbedienne Fondeur w/seal, 9x17", C-NY 5/24/89 4,180
Walking Lion, bronze relief, dk brn patina, sgn, 8x16", C-NY 5/24/89 770
Walking Lion, gr-blk patina, rectangular base, sgn, late 19th C, 9x15", lot 206, SBY 11/5/88 2,750
Walking Tiger, #15731 & #6, dk brn patina, mk Barye F Barbedienne Fondeur Paris France, 8x17", C-NY 5/24/89 1,760
Walking Tiger, gr-brn patina, mk Barye Made in France, 8x17", C-NY 5/24/89 1,650

BARYE, Antoine Louis; after (French, 1795-1875)

Stealthy Lion, gr patina, sgn, 39", SLK 9/26/88 1,300

BASALDELLA, see Mirko

BASKIN, Leonard (American, 1922-)

Deadalus, 4/6, brn-blk patina, sgn/dtd 67/mk Bedi-Rassy Art Foundry, 41", lot 269, SBY 4/14/89 8,800
Festina Lente, dk brn patina, intl/dtd 1959/titled, 6", lot 124, C-E 6/1/89 UE 220
Head (contemporary), 6/15, blk patina, sgn/mk Bedi-Rassy Art Foundry, 12", lot 277, SBY 6/28/89 1,760
Head with Bird, 4/8, brn patina, sgn, 10", SBY 1/24/89 OE 1,540
Moan of the Fools of Chelm, dk brn patina, 6", lot 125, C-E 6/1/89 UE 220
Phaedra, 8/12, dk brn patina, sgn, mk Bedi-Makky Foundry Kennedy Gallery, 1969, 31", lot 281, SBY 6/28/89 6,600

BASQUIAT, Jean Michel (European, 20th C)

Double-Sided: All Beef (contemporary); oil/oil stick on canvas w/wood supports, sgn/dtd 1983, 73x35x22", SBY 5/2/88 OE 24,200
Untitled (abstract sculpture), oil/objects/string on wood, 102x48", SBY 2/19/88 23,100

Water-Worshipper, oil & chalk on panel/wooden planks/metal rod/nails/screws, 1984, 83x108x4", C-NY 5/4/88 OE, $35,200

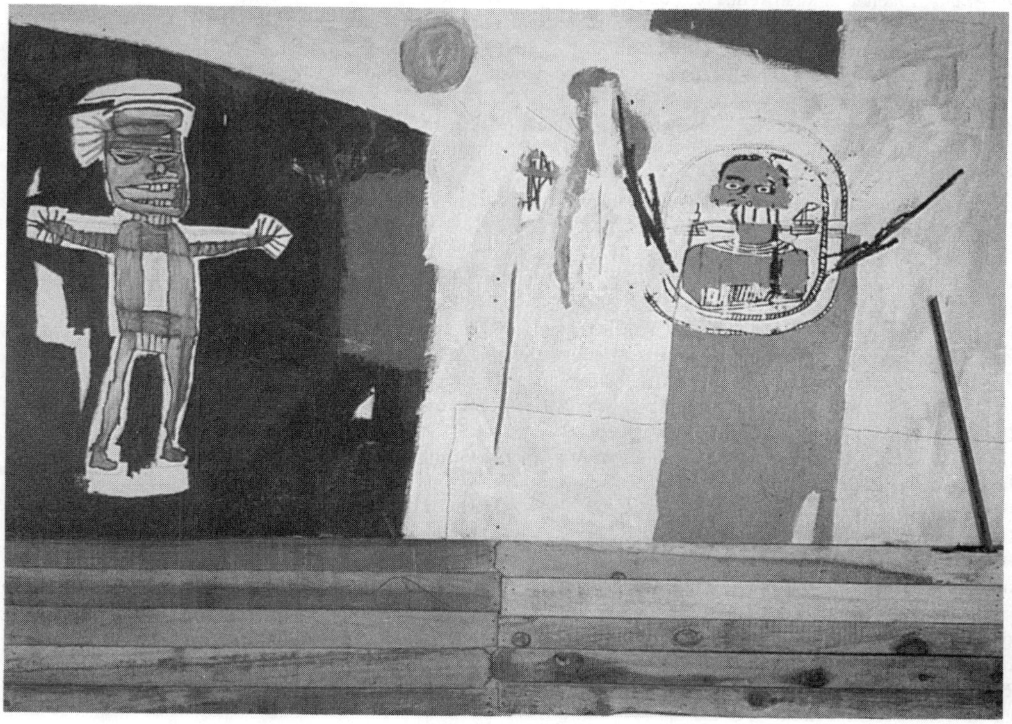

BASTIDE, P.

Napoleon (standing figure), blk patina, sgn, ca late 19th C, 41", SBY 2/22/89 2,750

BATTI, Leon

Napoleon (mounted on horse), rubbed blk patina, verde marble rectangular base, sgn, late 19th C, 21x18", SBY 2/22/89 2,750

BATTIGLIA, E. (Italian, 19th C)
Mona Lisa, After Da Vinci; alabaster, mk La Joconde d'apre Leonarde de Vinci on separate brass tag, 15", RWS 12/10/88 UE 300
BAUERMEISTER, Mary (20th C)
Literatur-e (wall relief in 2 parts), acrylic/plaster straws on panel, 1966, overall 12x21x12", C-E 5/13/88 1,320
Progression 174 to 8 in 19 Rows (wall relief), 8/19, sand/pebbles on particle board, sgn, 1971, 12x12", C-E 5/9/89 OE 5,060
BECKER, Edmond Henri
Joan of Arc (bust-length figural desk seal), slvr/gilt, sgn, 5", lot 462, WAD 6/12/89 300
BECQUEREL, Andre Vincent (French, fl early 20th C)
Two Leaping Deer, mottled gr patina, molded rectangular base, sgn/mk Susse Fes Edts, ca 1925, 29", lot 218, SBY 6/8/88 2,310
Two Lovebirds, perched on branch; slvr, ca 1925, rectangular blk onyx base, mk Susse Freres, 13", lot 452, SBY 12/12/88 550
Untitled, girl in pinafore pulling toy; blk marble plinth, sgn/mk Etling Paris, 9", C-E 12/8/88 1,320
Untitled, girl/fox terrier playing with ring; polychrome bronze/ivory, marble plinth, sgn, 10x9", SLK 5/6/88 950
BEGAS, R. (Continental, 19th C)
Otto Von Bismark (bust), sgn/dtd on base, 1886, lot 386, FAP 4/15/88 1,595
BEHN, Fritz (Austrain, 1878-)
Nude & a Gazelle (leaping), brn patina, sgn/mk Brandstetter, 28" long, lot 72, SBY 11/17/88 3,575
BEIL-HERMANT (American, 19th C)
Pair: Untitled (allegorical wall reliefs), 1 sgn/mk Chicago, 49x63"/48x64", SLK 4/7/89 6,000
BEN TRE, Howard (20th C)
Cast Form Type IV, 1979 (contemporary); sand-cast glass/patinated copper, sgn/dtd 79, 5x7x6", lot 174, C-NY 10/4/89 6,600
Cast Form Type VIII, 1979 (contemporary); sand-cast glass/patinated copper, sgn/mk 1879 P, 7x6x8", C-NY 10/4/89 OE........ 10,450
Dedicant 2, 1986 (contemporary); cast glass/brass/patinated copper/gold leaf/lead, ca 1987, 48x19x8", C-NY 10/4/89........ 22,000
From Andy C, Second Version, 1980 (contemporary); sand-cast glass/copper, 14x13x13", lot 175, C-NY 10/4/89 OE 12,100
BENGLIS, Lynda (American, 20th C)
Bravo (abstract wall relief), bronze & copper painted bronze wire/plaster/gesso, 1973-74, 26x12x14", SBY 5/3/88 7,700
Charles (abstract wall relief), aluminum screen/bunting/plaster/sprayed copper, 1973, 31x18x13", lot 54, C-NY 11/20/88........ 9,900
Gold Luster (wall relief), a/p, ed of 12, painted ceramic, 1982, sgn, 18x27x3", SBY 2/19/88 4,400
Kaudi (abstract wall relief), bronze wire/plaster/gesso/oil base gold leaf, 1980, 37x20x15", SBY 2/19/88 16,500
Knot, a/p, ed of 8, glazed ceramic, sgn, 1980, 18x7x11", lot 289, SBY 10/8/88 5,225
BENNES, J. (19th/20th C)
Jockey on Horseback, rich rubbed golden-brn patina, oval molded base, sgn, late 19th C, 18x19", lot 160, SBY 6/9/89 2,640
BENTON, Fletcher
Stainless: Blue-Blue 2; stainless steel/clr plexiglas/flourescent light (motorized), 1972, 63x36x9", C-E 5/13/88 UE 6,559
BERGE, Edward (American, 1876-1924)
Pair of Bookends: Young Scholar; brn patina, sgn/mk B Zoppo Foundries NY, 9", lot 251, SBY 1/24/89 2,310
BERGMAN, Franz (Austrian, 19th/20th C)
Arab Scribe, sitting cross-legged on low chair; #2746, cold paint, sgn/mk Geschutzt, 4", C-E 9/16/88 UE 66
Two Arabs Crouched in Rush Tent, cold paint, sgn twice/mk Geschutzt, 8", C-E 9/16/88........ 495
Untitled, Arab w/draped harem girl (mechanical); cold paint, mk Namgreb Real Vienna Bronze, 4", C-E 6/16/88 550
BERGMAN, Franz; after (Austrian, 19th/20th C)
Untitled, nude holding rose above head stands on patterned shawl; gr marble base, 12", C-E 10/11/88 330
BERLANT, Tony (20th C)
Page From Her Diary (contemporary), metal collage/nails, ca 1968, 6x6", SBY 10/8/88 990
Self-Portrait in Landscape, metal collage on panel, sgn/titled/dtd 1984 on verso, 54x95", lot 392, C-NY 5/4/89........ 17,600
BERNDORF
Boy & Horse Crossing a River, barefoot child grasps horse's neck; red-brn patina, sgn/mk FR, 14", lot 322, C-E 9/13/88........ 1,320
BERROCAL, Miguel (Spanish, 1933-)
Alice II, 208/500, sgn, 1981-82, 7", lot 330, C-E 11/17/88 660
Alice II (contemporary), 207/500, sgn twice, 1981-82, 7", lot 237, C-E 5/9/89 OE 1,430
Christina, #1194, nickel-plated metal alloy, sgn, 1969-70, 6", C-E 5/13/88 660
Christina, #1911, ed of 9500, nickel-plated metal alloy, sgn, 1969-70, 6x3x2", C-E 5/9/89 OE........ 825
Goliath, #1255, ed of 2000, sgn/mk Orangerie Multiples Cologne Reischauer, 1972, 8x6x4", lot 322, C-E 11/7/88 2,420
Head of Diana (contemporary), ed of 9, blk patina, square self base, 9", C-E 5/9/89 1,430
Mini-David, #1619, nickel-plated aluminum alloy, sgn, 1968, 6", part missing at neck, C-E 5/13/88 330
Mini-David, #2317, nickel-plated aluminum/gold plate, sgn, 1968, 6", lot 354, C-E 11/17/88........ 605
Mini-David, 2179/9500, nickel-plated aluminum alloy w/gold plate, sgn, 1968, 6", SBY 10/8/88........ 880
Mini-Maria, #4114, ed of 9500, chrome, sgn, 1968-89, 2x3x2", C-E 5/9/89 330
Mini-Zoraida, #3121, ed of 9500, nickel-plated metal alloy, sgn, 1969-70, 2x3x1", C-E 5/9/89 385
Multiple Piece Sculpture of Goliath, #1258, polished brass, sgn, 10", lot 3853, B/B 10/9/88 2,475
Portrait de Michele, #2090, nickel-plated steel/copper/enamel/glass, sgn, 4", SBY 10/8/88 880
Portrait de Michele, #03160, brass, sgn, 1969, 4", lot 329, C-E 11/17/88........ 308
Romeo & Juliet, #373, polished brass, sgn, 1966-67, 6", lot 198, SBY 2/19/88 OE 2,860
Romeo & Juliet (contemporary), #1940, ed of 2000, brass, sgn, 6x9x3", lot 235, C-E 5/9/89 3,850
Torrero, 1383/2000, brass, sgn, 1972, 11x9", lot 323, C-E 11/17/88........ 1,870
BERTHOLD, Joachim (European, 1917-)
Seated Woman (contemporary), gr marble, sgn, 15", C-E 5/9/89 OE 1,980
BERTOIA, Harry (American/Italian, 1915-1978)
Bush (contemporary), 19x20x19", lot 33,SBY 10/8/88 OE 13,750
Bush (contemporary), 7x17x15", lot 64, SBY 2/15/89 OE 28,600
Bush (contemporary), 9x23x19", lot 73,SBY 10/8/88 OE 25,300
Dandelion 6, gilded beryllium copper, ca 1965, 39" dia, C-NY 5/4/88 11,000

Sounding Sculpture, beryllium copper, 23x18x4", lot 153, SBY 10/8/88 7,150
Sounding Sculpture, beryllium copper rods/bronze, 26", C-NY 11/10/88 8,250
Sounding Sculpture, beryllium copper rods/bronze, 26", lot 156, C-NY 11/10/88 8,250
Spray, stainless steel rods, bronze base, ca 1965, 26x5x5", lot 87, C-NY 2/14/89 3,850
Spray, stainless steel rods, stainless steel base, ca 1968, 20x8x8", lot 89, C-NY 2/14/89 4,620
Squares (contemporary), copper-painted bronze, ca 1958, 39x7x7", lot 35, C-NY 2/14/89 5,500
Sunburst, gold-plated steel wires on brass stand, 72", lot 445, SBY 10/7/89 19,800
Tree (contemporary), brn patina, 1957, 19", lot 26, WD 5/5/88 4,200
Untitled (abstract, wire attached to 4-legged structure), gilt copper, 45x18x4", lot 15, SBY 2/19/88 5,500
Untitled (contemporary), copper, 9x6x5", lot 233, C-E 5/13/88 1,870
Untitled (contemporary), welded bronze, 1956, 12x21x12", lot 34, SBY 10/8/88 5,225
Untitled (contemporary), 14x23x8", lot 35, SBY 10/8/88 4,950
Untitled (Umbrella), steel, 47", lot 442A, SBY 10/7/89 UE 3,300

BEUYES, Joseph (German, 1921-1986)
Felt Suit (suit on hanger), 81/100, felt/wood hanger, sgn, 1970, 54x27x8", Ed Galerie Rene Block, lot 242, SBY 10/5/89 66,000
Holzpostkarte (contemporary), ed of 120, slksc pinewood, p/s on verso, 1974, 4x6x1", Ed Staeck, lot 236A, SBY 10/5/89 OE 1,925
Sledge (contemporary), sledge/felt blanket/belt/torchlight/fat, 14x36x14", lot 236, SBY 10/5/89 121,000

BEYER, Edith S. (20th C)
Bust of Woman, sgn/mk Roman Bronze Works, 20th C, 27", lot 179, RWS 2/27/88 UE 350

BIEGAS, Boleslas (Polish, 20th C)
Figure with Serpents, blk patina, sgn/dtd 16 November 1917, 34", SBY 10/7/88 13,200

BIELINSKI, W.
Centaur Forward (playing w/football), medium brn patina, sgn, 12", lot 461, WAD 6/12/89 450

BIESBROECK, see Van Biesbroeck

BILL, Max (Swiss, 1908-)
Hexagonal Surface in Space with Complete Circumference, gilded brass, sgn/dtd 1953, 8x12x9", lot 2, C-NY 5/3/88 OE 22,000
Unit of Three Equal Volumes, 2/8, gilt brass, sgn/dtd 1962-68, 13x15x15", lot 33, SBY 2/19/88 13,200
Unity of Three Equal Elements, gilded brass, sgn/dtd 1963, 10x10x9", lot 1, C-NY 5/3/88 OE 19,800

BINQUET, Albert
Clock (Roman numerals/flowers in circle supported by pair of doves), slvr, sgn/dtd 1928, 15" long, lot 66, SBY 3/19/88 1,100

BLAI, Boris (American, 1893-)
Seated Nude, blk patina, sgn, 14", lot 287, SBY 3/17/88 2,200

BLEZER, see De Blezer

BLOCK, Adolph (American, 1906-)
Temptress, bronze relief bolted to wooden plaque, sgn, 25x14", SBY 3/17/88 1,210

BOCK, Richard Walter (American, 1865-)
Indian with Pipe (reclining/mounted on bronze box), blk patina, sgn/dtd 94, 13" long, Winslow Co, SBY 1/24/89 OE 7,150

BOGER
Six Tours, steeplechase jump w/monkey jockeys; 9", lot 952, FAP 12/8/88 800

BOGHOSIAN, Varujan (American, 1926-)
Emperor of Venice (contemporary), mixed media construction, stp/s, titled, 1968, 16x13x11", lot 85, SBY 2/15/89 7,150

BOLOGNA, see De Bologna

BOLOGNE, see De Bologne

BOLOTOWSKY, Ilya (Russian, 1907-)
Marble #10 (wall relief), oil/marble mounted on panel, 1961, 3x4", C-E 5/13/88 OE 1,760

BONEVARDI, Marcelo (Argentinian, 1929-)
Decoy (contemporary), painted burlap/wood construction, sgn/dtd Nov 20 1980/titled, 79x57", SBY 5/16/89 22,000
Entablature III (wall relief), mixed media on fiberboard, sgn twice/dtd 1 Oct 1986 twice/titled, 82x39", C-NY 5/17/89 19,800
Preacher (contemporary), painted burlap/wood construction, sgn/dtd 66/titled, 55x39", SBY 5/16/89 UE 8,800
Two Figures (contemporary), painted canvas/wood construction, sgn/dtd 66/titled, 20x30", SBY 11/21/88 5,500

BONHEUR, Isidore Jules (French, 1827-1901)
Bull, brn patina, gr marble base, mk I Bonheur, 15x25", lot 165, C-NY 5/24/89 OE 10,450
Bull, brn patina, sgn/mk Peyrol, 4x6", lot 172, C-NY 5/24/89 1,430
Bull, golden-brn patina, sgn/mk Peyrol, 16x25", lot 167, C-NY 5/24/89 4,400
Cow, brn patina, sgn/mk Souvenir d'Amite et de Reconnaissance, 8x10", C-NY 2/23/89 OE 3,080
Cow & Bull, brn patina, sgn/mk Peyrol, 12x21", lot 166, C-NY 5/24/89 4,400
Cow & Bull (leaning over gate opposite each other), dk brn patina, sgn/mk Peyrol, late 19th C, 12", lot 161, SBY 6/9/89 3,850
Draft Horse, rubbed brn/blk patinae, molded oval base, sgn/mk Peyrol, ca 1880, 13x17", lot 159, SBY 6/9/89 3,850
Figure of a Bull (standing), dk red-brn patina, oval base, sgn/mk Peyrol, late 19th C, 31x52", lot 187, SBY 6/9/89 OE 29,700
Foxhunt (group of 2 hunters/horse/dog), blk patina, mk D'Estray, 20x23", C-NY 5/24/89 OE 15,400
Horse Drinking, rubbed gr-brn patina, molded rectangular base, sgn, late 19th C, 14", lot 166, SBY 6/9/89 8,250
Huntsman & Three Hounds, gr-brn patina, sgn/mk Peyrol, 15", C-NY 5/24/89 OE 13,200
Jockey on Trotting Horse, dk blk/brn patinae, rectangular molded base, sgn/mk Peyrol, 38", lot 186, SBY 6/9/89 22,000
Jockey on Trotting Horse, warm brn patina, rectangular molded base, sgn/mk Peyrol, late 19th C, 38", lot 162, SBY 6/9/89 38,500
Louis XV Huntsman (figure on horse), rich brn patina, sgn/mk Peyrol, 40", missing sword, C-NY 5/25/88 24,200
Milkmaid & Cow, brn patina, mk Peyrol, 12x21", C-NY 5/24/89 OE 2,200
Mounted Jockey, rubbed orange/blk patinae, rectangular molded base, sgn/mk Estray, ca 1900, 18x23", lot 164, SBY 6/9/89 10,450
Pepin le Bref Dans l'Arene (king slays lion that has attacked bull), gr-blk patina, sgn/mk Peyrol, 20", C-NY 5/25/88 OE 11,000
Stallion, dk brn patina, gr marble base, sgn/mk D'Estray, 14", C-NY 5/24/89 3,300
Standing Stallion, warm brn patina, rectangular base, sgn/mk Peyrol, late 19th C, 27x33", lot 163, SBY 6/9/89 17,600
Steeplechase, brn patina, sgn/mk Boudet 43 Bd Des Capucines Peyrol, 21", C-NY 5/24/89 8,800

Tethered Horse, dk brn patina, sgn, 15", C-NY 5/24/89 ..... **3,520**

BONHEUR, Rosa (French, 1822-1899)

Bull, rubbed dk brn patina, molded oval base, sgn, mid-19th C, 7", lot 184, SBY 6/9/89 ..... **1,980**
Grazing Ewe, rubbed golden patina, molded oval base, sgn, late 19th C, 8", lot 189, SBY 6/9/89 ..... **880**
Reclining Bull, rich dk brn patina, sgn/mk Peyrol, 11" long, C-NY 5/24/89 ..... **2,200**
Reclining Ewe, oval base, 5x9", lot 127, RWS 9/24/88 ..... **925**
Stallion (spirited/high-stepping), rich brn/blk patinae, oval molded base, sgn, late 19th C, 13", lot 185, SBY 6/9/89 ..... **2,750**

BONTECOU, Lee (American, 1931-)

Bird (contemporary), dk brn patina, 1957-58, 7x11", SBY 10/5/88 ..... **1,045**
Untitled (wall relief), canvas/welded metal rods/wire, 1959, 55x45x23", SBY 2/19/88 OE **17,600**

BOREE, after

D'Orythie (allegorical group), dk brn patina, self base, 21", lot 158, C-E 11/1/88 ..... **2,090**

BORGLUM, John Gutson (American, 1867-)

Seated Abrahm Lincoln, rich dk brn patina, sgn/mk Gorham Founders Q501, 21", lot 175, C-NY 5/25/89 ..... **38,500**

BORGLUM, Solon (American, 1868-1922)

Lassoing Wild Horses, rich dk brn patina, sgn/mk Copyright 1900 Roman Bronze Works, 31x33", C-NY 2/2/88 ..... **110,000**

BOTELLO (Austrian, 20th C)

Untitled (contemporary standing figure), #6, 24", RAB 8/21/89 UE **300**
Untitled (head of young girl), #9, 13", lot 367, RAB 8/21/89 UE **300**

BOTERO, Fernando (Colombian, 1932-)

Cabeza de Hombre (a man's head), 2/6, dk brn patina, sgn/dtd, 12", C-NY 5/17/89 ..... **38,500**
El Obispo (figure of a bishop), 1/6, polychromed polyester, 1977, sgn, 47", C-NY 11/21/88 ..... **71,500**
Still Life (plentiful table), 3/6, 1976-77, 50x79x67", SBY 5/16/89 ..... **198,000**
Woman with Serpent, 6/6, sgn, 1983, 44" long, SBY 11/21/88 ..... **66,000**

BOUCHER, Alfred (French, 1815-1934)

Untitled, allegorical winged figure; lt gr-brn patina, sgn/mk Susse Freres, 28", lot 490, SLK 11/25/88 ..... **3,500**

BOURAINE, Marcel (French, 20th C)

Idol (seated w/head tilted back offers covered urn), polychrome, flaring marble base, sgn, ca 1925, 16", SBY 3/19/88 UE **1,210**
Pair of Bookends: Pouter Pigeon (perched); #77 & #78, slvr, sgn, ca 1925, 6", lot 453, SBY 12/12/88 ..... **990**

BOURDELLE, Emile Antoine (French, 1861-1929)

Etude pour l'Heracles, Archer (hunter w/bow); 6/10, gr/brn patinae, sgn/mk Susse Fondeur, 1909/later, 22", SBY 5/11/89 ..... **242,000**
Mask of Hercules, #1, dk brn patina, sgn/mk Valsuani, sgn, ca 1905, 14", lot 34, SBY 10/7/89 ..... **3,850**
Masque: Study for the Sphinx; painted plaster, sgn, 7x6", C-E 11/17/88 ..... **660**

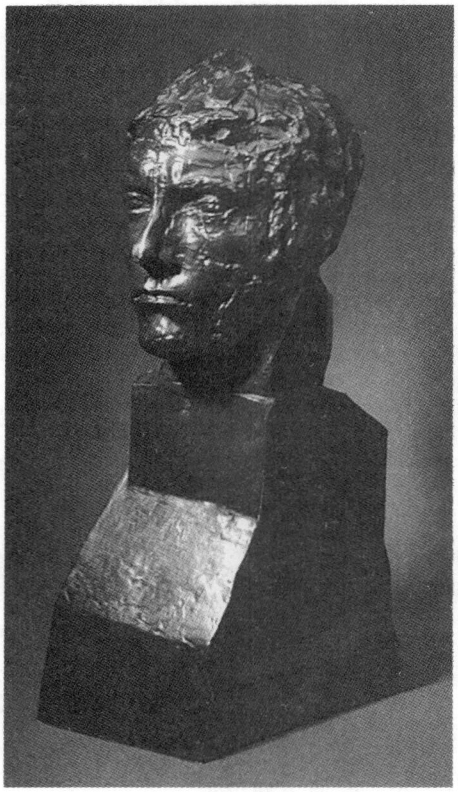

Tete d'Apollo, dk brn patina, sgn/dtd/mk Alexis Rudier Fondeur Paris, 1900/later, 26", C-NY 2/16/89 OE, $71,500

Plaque: L'Ame Pathetique; 6/8, terra cotta, sgn, 15x13", lot 213, C-NY 2/18/88 UE **1,100**
Tete de Bacchante, dk brn patina, sgn/mk Alexis Rudier Fondeur Paris, 8", C-NY 10/6/88 ..... **2,750**
Wind (semi-prone/windblown figure), #d V, gr patina, sgn/mk Valsuani, 1906, 9", lot 33, SBY 10/7/89 ..... **11,000**

BOUVAL, Maurice (French, fl ca 1920)

Figure of a Woman (draped lady in upswept hair); gilt, sgn/mk Joilet, ca 1900, 11", lot 455, SBY 12/12/88 ..... **1,650**
Modestly Posed Nude (full-figured desk seal), gilt, sgn/mk Collin Paris, 5", lot 463, WAD 6/12/89 ..... **320**

BRANDAO, Wilson (20th C)
Resando, wood relief on painted wood, twice sgn/dtd 79, 54x32", C-NY 5/18/88 ... 2,420
BRAQUE, Georges (French, 1882-1963)
Cheval (contemporary horse), ed of 6, dk brn patina, 1939/1944, 8" long, lot 143, SBY 2/18/88 ... 19,800
Ibis (surrealistic bird), ed of 6, blk patina, sgn, 1945/later, 7", SBY 5/11/89 OE ... 36,300
Woman & a Faun (nude w/bow feeds doe), blk patina w/gilt traces, sgn/mk Lastelle, ca 1925, 20", lot 282, SBY 6/8/88 ... 3,300
BRAULT (German)
Javelin Thrower, typical pose; gr patina, rectangular blk marble base, sgn, 20", C-E 6/28/88 UE ... 550
BRAVO, Claudio (Chilian, 1936-)
Bread, ed of 4, painted bronze, sgn w/full signature, dtd MCMLXXIV, 9" dia, SBY 5/16/89 ... 15,400
BRENNER, Victor David (American, 1871-1924)
Portrait Medallion of Ralph Waldo Emerson, brn patina, mk VD Brenner Sc, 7" dia, SBY 6/1/88 ... 275
BRENNER, Victor David; after (American, 1871-1924)
Plaque: Abraham Lincoln; 1907, S Klaber & Co Founders, 10", SLK 9/26/88 ... 250
BROWN, David Lee (American, 20th C)
3-80 (contemporary), polished stainless steel, wooden base, sgn/titled, 19x18x10", C-E 5/13/88 ... 1,760
BROWN, Roger (American, 20th C)
Diner, oil on wood w/metal strips, 1973-74, 8x24x11", SBY 10/8/88 OE ... 8,800
Lewis & Clark Trail (contemporary), oil on canvas/tree trunk sections/fr, 1979, 77x50x16", lot 97, C-NY 10/4/89 ... 20,900
BUCKLEY, Stephen (20th C)
Woven Red Wax (contemporary), wax encaustic on canvas woven on wooden supports, sgn/dtd 1976, 40x48x3", SBY 10/8/88 ... 6,325
BUGGATTI, Rembrandt (French, 1883-1916)
Elephant Blanc, #B4, blk-brn patina, sgn/mk Hebrard, ca 1908, 5x8", lot 284, SBY 6/8/88 ... 20,900
Elephant de l'Inde au Repos, #7, rich blk-brn patina, sgn/mk Hebrard, ca 1910, 18x20", lot 283, SBY 6/8/88 OE ... 66,000
BURTON, Scott (20th C)
Hectapod Table, ed of 6, nickel-plated/polished steel, 1982, 21x24x24", lot 300, SBY 11/11/88 ... 18,700
Hectapod Table (contemporary), polished nickel-plated steel, 21x24x24", lot 311, C-NY 5/4/89 ... 16,500
BUSCH, L.C. (German, 20th C)
Untitled, equestrian figure in half-length suit of armour; gr-brn patina, marble plinth, sgn, 24", SLK 9/26/88 ... 950
BUTLER, Reg (British, 1913-)
Doll, 7/8, golden-brn patina, marble base, intl/mk Susse Fondeur Paris, 1955, 20", lot 76, WD 11/16/88 OE ... 9,000
Girl (standing nude), 1/8, intl/mk Susse Fondeur, 1956-57, 59", SBY 5/11/88 OE ... 115,500
Girl on Her Back (contemporary), 4/8, golden patina, sgn/mk Susse Fondeur, 12" long, lot 212, SBY 10/7/89 OE ... 11,550
Ophelia, 1/8, golden patina, sgn/mk Susse Fondeur Paris, 1955, 22", SBY 10/5/88 OE ... 6,050
BUTLER, Tom (20th C)
EX (contemporary), fiberglass, 1982, 94", lot 280, SBY 2/15/89 ... 6,600
FL (contemporary), fiberglass/resin, 1984, 106", SBY 11/11/88 ... 8,250
HC (contemporary), fiberglass/resin, 1984, 90", lot 271, SBY 2/15/89 ... 7,700
BUTTERFIELD, Deborah (American, 20th C)
Horse (contemporary), mud/sticks, 1978, 31x33x11", lot 60, C-NY 11/20/88 ... 24,200
Horse (contemporary), mud/sticks/wire/steel rods, 1977, 69x109x31", lot 318, C-NY 5/4/89 ... 28,600
Large Horse #4 (3-dimensional figure), wire/wood, 1979, 76x124x30", SBY 5/3/88 ... 27,500
Small Dry Fork Horse (assemblage), sticks/wire, 1978, 29x49x11", SBY 5/3/88 ... 22,000
Untitled (contemporary horse), mud/sticks over wire mesh/steel armature, ca 1976-77, 60x93x41", lot 384, SBY 11/11/88 ... 27,500
CAFFIERI, Jean Jacques; after (French, 1725-1792)
Bust of Benjamin Franklin (sculpture), marble, 20", SBY 3/17/88 ... 6,600
CAIN, Auguste Nicolas (French, 1822-1894)
Pair of Candlesticks (baby birds in nest among stems of 3 flower candle cups), gilt bronze, sgn, 20", C-NY 5/24/89 ... 1,760
Rooster on a Basket, brn patina, gr marble base, sgn, 7", C-NY 2/23/89 ... 1,100
CALDER, Alexander (American, 1898-1976)
Big Bellied Bottle (stabile), painted sheet metal, sgn, 14x27x11", C-NY 11/9/88 ... 60,500
Black Flower in Seventeen (mobile), painted sheet metal/rod, intl/dtd 59, 34x40", lot 10, C-NY 5/3/88 ... 198,000
Black Sails (standing mobile), painted sheet metal/rod, 22x26", C-NY 11/9/88 OE ... 132,000
Black Triangle (contemporary standing mobile), painted metal, intl, 1963-64, 33x28x14", SBY 11/11/88 OE ... 137,500
Black-White Rudder & Ten Reds (hanging mobile), painted sheet metal/rod, intl/dtd 68, 29x124x95", lot 57, C-NY 11/20/88 ... 286,000
Blue Crinkly (standing mobile), painted sheet metal/rod, sgn/dtd 75, 15x23", C-NY 11/9/88 OE ... 121,000
Boomerang (standing mobile), painted sheet metal/rod, sgn, 12x20", C-NY 11/10/88 OE ... 71,500
Boomerang & Polygons (sculpture mobile), painted metal, intl/dtd 72, 37x84", SBY 11/10/88 ... 220,000
Boomerangs & Targets, painted metal mobile, intl/dtd 73, 34x52", SBY 10/5/89 ... 275,000
Could Be Twins (free-standing mobile), painted steel, intl/dtd 71, 7x14", lot 648, SBY 6/30/88 OE ... 68,000
Cow, wire sculpture, ca 1930, 7x19x6", SBY 10/5/89 OE ... 154,000
Double Yellow on Brass (stabile), painted metal/brass, intl, 1964, 6", lot 12, WD 11/16/88 OE ... 23,000
Eleven Polychrome (hanging mobile), painted sheet metal/rod, intl/dtd 61, 41x54", lot 19, C-NY 5/3/88 ... 143,000
Five White & Brass Spiral on Red & Black (standing mobile), painted sheet metal/brass/wire, 1960, 20", C-NY 11/10/88 OE ... 121,000
Hundred Yard Dash (stabile), painted metal, intl/dtd 1969/titled, 26x28x20", SBY 5/3/88 ... 46,750
Maquette for Large Mobile in Black & Silver (contemporary), aluminum/painted steel, intl, 1951, 36x34x18", SBY 5/3/89 ... 231,000
Moon Phases (hanging mobile), painted sheet metal/rod, intl/dtd 65, 45x74", lot 26, C-NY 5/3/88 ... 231,000
Moon Phases (hanging mobile), painted sheet metal/rod, intl/dtd 65, 45", C-NY 5/3/88 ... 231,000
Orange Clef (wall mobile), painted metal, intl/dtd 57, 30x57x23", SBY 2/19/88 OE ... 101,750
Pterosaurus (stabile), painted sheet metal, sgn/dtd 58, 12x19x17", C-NY 11/9/88 ... 66,000

Roxbury Red (hanging mobile), painted metal, intl/dtd 63, 62x104", lot 22A, SBY 5/2/89 OE **682,000**
Snake on a Table, 2/6, dk gr patina, sgn, 46", lot 12, C-NY 2/14/89 ..... **36,300**
Stabile with Two Heads, painted metal, intl, 1955, 17x17x11", lot 112, SBY 5/3/89 OE..... **137,500**
The Constable, wire sculpture w/wooden base, ca 1930, 21x9x9", SBY 10/5/89 OE **165,000**
Toy (standing mobile), painted metal, ca 1955, 17x18x9", SBY 5/3/88 OE..... **57,750**
Two Friends (stabile), red/blk/wht painted metal, sgn/dtd 1971, 6x16x8", lot 69, SBY 2/15/89 ..... **41,250**
Two Holey Blacks (contemporary hanging mobile), painted metal, intl/dtd 61, 29x58", SBY 11/11/88..... **187,000**
Untitled, painted metal hanging mobile, 33x58", SBY 10/5/89 OE **297,000**
Untitled, painted metal mobile, ca 1945, 53x31", SBY 10/5/89 ..... **198,000**
Untitled (abstract stabile), painted sheet metal, sgn/dtd 1945, 6x6x3", lot 129, C-NY 11/10/88 OE **39,600**
Untitled (abstract standing mobile), painted metal, ca 1953, 28x23", lot 129, SBY 5/3/88 ..... **71,500**
Untitled (contemporary hanging mobile), painted metal, intl/dtd 65, 104" wide, lot 125, SBY 11/11/88 OE **451,000**
Untitled (hanging mobile), painted metal, ca 1955, 24x30", lot 80, SBY 10/8/88 OE **36,300**

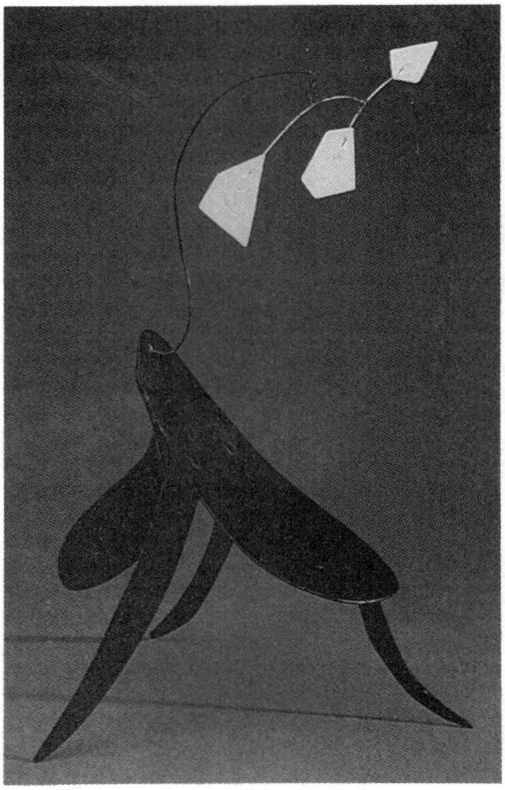

Untitled, mltclr painted sheet metal/rod, sgn, ca 1945, 13", C-NY 5/3/89 OE, $181,500

Untitled (hanging mobile), painted metal, intl/dtd 58, 36x95", lot 18, SBY 11/10/88 OE..... **341,000**
Untitled (Maquette for Chase Manhattan Bank Mobile), painted metal, ca 1967, 14x33", SBY 10/5/89..... **286,000**
Untitled (stabile), red/wht/gray painted metal with brass, intl, ca 1965, 8x9", lot 26, SBY 2/15/89 ..... **37,400**
Untitled (stabile), red/yel/wht painted metal, intl, ca 1968, 17x24x3", lot 19, SBY 2/15/89 ..... **99,000**
Untitled (standing mobile), mltclr painted sheet metal/rod, sgn, ca 1945, 13", lot 4, C-NY 5/3/89 OE..... **181,500**
Untitled (standing mobile), painted metal, ca 1948, 4x5", lot 61, SBY 2/19/88 ..... **20,900**
Untitled (standing mobile), painted metal, ca 1948, 7x14", lot 44, SBY 2/19/88 OE **45,100**
Untitled (standing mobile), painted metal, intl/dtd 62, 20x23x10", lot 157A, SBY 5/3/88 ..... **38,500**
Untitled (standing mobile), red/yel/bl/blk painted sheet metal/rod, 10x43", lot 27, C-NY 5/3/89 OE..... **220,000**
Wheat (standing mobile), painted metal, ca 1958, 32x42x42", SBY 2/19/88 OE **165,000**
14 Black Leaves (contemporary hanging mobile), painted metal, intl/dtd 61, 9x42", SBY 11/11/88 OE **143,000**

CAMARGO, see De Camargo

CAMPBELL (American, 20th C)
Abraham Lincoln (bust), brn patina, sgn/mk Griffoul, 6", lot 100, C-E 4/19/88 ..... **418**

CANOVA, Antonio (Italian, 1757-1822)
Les Trois Graces (The Three Graces), sgn, 65", lot 369, FB 10/17/88 ..... **54,000**

CANOVA, Antonio; after (Italian, 1757-1822)
Bust of Napoleon, Italian wht marble, truncated plinth, ebonized square pedestal, 13", lot 317, C-E 9/13/88 ..... **2,200**
Napoleon (standing figure), rich gr/blk patinae, inscr Canova, ca late 19th C, 28", C-NY 2/22/89..... **2,475**
Pair: Companion Putti (making music/writing); brn/gr patinae, waisted socle, rouge marble plinth, 9", C-E 10/11/88 ..... **495**

CARABIN, Rupert (French, 1862-1921)
Untitled (nude carrying tree stump over shoulder), brn patina, rouge marble base, sgn, ca 1903-04, 24", SBY 11/17/88..... **9,900**

CARDENAS, Augustin (French, 20th C)
Column of Fire (abstract), oak, sgn, 1961, 88", SBY 11/21/88..... **34,100**
Pair: Couple (abstract); #d E/A, sgn/mk Fonderia Tesconi Pietrasanta, 1967, 17"/11", SBY 11/21/88 ..... **16,500**

CARDOSSI, Professor Vittorio (Italian, 19th/20th C)
Dusk (draped figures), marble, sgn, ca 1900, 61", SBY 2/22/88 OE 99,000
CARO, Anthony (20th C)
Floor Piece C 16, rusted/varnished steel, 1975-76, 33x48x36", SBY 10/8/88 25,200
Gray Apron (contemporary), gray painted steel, 1972, 50x58x33", lot 293, C-NY 5/4/89 OE 55,000
Silver Piece XIV, China; welded slvr, 1984, 7x11x10", lot 182, SBY 5/3/89 OE 44,000
Table Piece CCXXXI (sculpture), rusted/varnished steel, 1975, 18x66x24", SBY 5/3/88 OE 20,900
Writing Piece, steel/rusted steel, 1979, 30x35x12", SBY 11/11/88 OE 33,000
CARPEAUX, Jean Baptiste (French, 1827-1875)
Anna Foucard (bust), rich brn patina, sgn/mk Propriete Carpeaux, 20", C-NY 5/25/88 3,850
CARRARA, A. Piazza (Italian, 19th C)
Sultane (bust), alabaster, sgn on verso, 24", lot 384, FAP 4/15/88 605
CARRIER-BELLEUSE, Albert Ernest (French, 1824-1887)
La Liseuse (elaborately dressed woman w/book), parcel slvr/gilt/ivory, sgn/mk Liseuse 24633, 13", lot 21, C-NY 6/10/89 1,265
Liseuse (medieval costumed lady w/book), #3866, gilt/ivory, sgn, late 19th C, 24", lot 361, WAD 11/28/88 OE 2,700
Pair: Royal Guardsmen; #357, rich brn patina, sgn, 22"/18", C-NY 5/25/88 2,200
CARTIER, Thomas Francois (1879-)
Clown (Pierrot w/lute at side & hand at brow), #11, cold paint/ivory, stone base, sgn, ca 1925, 19", lot 285, SBY 6/8/88 3,300
CARVIN, Louis Albert
Seagull Swooping Over Waves, gr/gilt patinae spelter, oval blk/clr mottled marble base, sgn, ca 1930, 35", WAD 11/28/88 1,000
CASTANEDA, Felipe (Mexican, 1938-)
Crouching Woman, wht onyx, sgn/dtd 1977, 15", SBY 11/21/88 OE 11,550
Desnudo Sentado (seated nude), blk onyx, sgn/dtd 1975 on right foot, 13", C-NY 11/21/88 6,600
Seated Female Nude, 1/111, gr patina, sgn/dtd 1970, 10", lot 2854, B/B 10/9/88 3,300
CAUSSE, Julien
Art Nouveau Woman, stands in diaphanous gown on rocky base; gr-brn patina, ca 1900, 15", lot 53, RWS 6/25/88 UE 400
CAVERLEY, Charles (American, 1833-1914)
Portrait Medallion of James Russell Lowell, dk brn patina, copyrighted 1896/mk Calverley SC, 7" dia, C-E 6/1/88 UE 110
CESAR (20th C)
La Poule a Aillettes (abstract), 2/2, welded bronze, sgn/mk Bacquel Fondeur HC, 28", SBY 6/30/88 52,000
CHADWICK, Lynn (British, 1914-)
Figure (contemporary), iron/cement, 11", SBY 10/5/88 OE 11,000
Maquette for Tugon A (contemporary), 1/4, brn patina, sgn/dtd 64, 22x9x8", lot 178, C-NY 5/4/89 OE 14,300
Maquette II: Winged Figures (abstract); #669 & 6/6, blk patina, sgn/dtd 73, 10", SBY 2/6/89 17,600
Maquette IV for Walking Woman, #C6S & 2/9, blk patina, intl, 1984, 18", SBY 10/7/88 18,700
Maquette 7 for Two Watches V (contemporary), 530 3/4, brn patina, sgn/dtd 67, 12", lot 209A, SBY 10/7/89 OE 15,950
Seated Male Figure (contemporary), #68S & 1/6, gray patina/polished bronze, intl, 19", SBY 2/6/89 OE 26,400
Standing Electra (abstract), #581 & 1/9, blk/polished golden patinae, sgn/mk Morris Singer, 1969, 28", SBY 2/6/89 OE 38,500
Taddy Boy (contemporary), 21x11x7", lot 172, C-NY 5/4/89 OE 20,900
Trig III (abstract), 2/4, sgn, 1961, 18", SBY 10/7/88 9,900
Winged Figures, #172 & 4/6, 1955, 22", SBY 10/7/88 OE 34,100
CHAGALL, Marc (Russian/French, 1887-1985)
Platter: Amoureux au Pichet Bleu; glazed ceramic, sgn/mk Chagall Antibes, 12" dia, lot 105, C-NY 2/18/88 OE 60,500
CHALON, Louis (French, 1687-1741)
Inkwell, fan-shaped tray w/bulbous glass inkwell & pansy lid; sgn/mk Colin, 11", C-E 12/8/88 660
CHAMBERLAIN, John (American, 1927-)
Alan's Piece (abstract wall relief), painted/chromium-plated steel, 1975, 30x36x22", lot 33, C-NY 5/3/89 88,000
Arch Brown, painted automobile parts, 37x36", C-NY 11/9/88 OE 143,000
Bent Tynes (abstract sculpture), painted steel, 1983, 70x55x42", SBY 2/19/88 OE 66,000
Blue Flushing (abstract), painted/chromium-plated steel, 1975, 59x63x27", SBY 11/11/88 OE 110,000
Papagayo (abstract), galvanized steel, 1967, 74x48x46", SBY 5/2/88 OE 55,000
Playskool, metal/staples on painted wooden base, sgn on bottom of base, ca 1959-61, 8x6x6", SBY 11/11/88 OE 30,250
Salanangie (abstract), painted steel in 2 parts, 1977, 24x49x30", SBY 5/2/88 OE 46,750
Tonk #1-86 (abstract sculpture), painted metal, sgn, 1986, 13x10x5", SBY 2/19/88 OE 18,700
Tonk #10-83 (contemporary), painted steel, sgn/dtd 1983, 8x7x4", lot 257, SBY 2/15/89 OE 24,200
Tonk #2-83, painted steel, sgn/dtd 83, 6x9x6", SBY 5/3/88 OE 17,600
Untitled (abstract), painted/chromium-plated steel, 1964, 36x30x24", lot 277, SBY 11/11/88 OE 82,500
CHARPENTIER, Alexander (American, 1815-1880)
Untitled, running nude athlete w/3 laurel wreaths; dk brn patina, sgn, ca 1900, 20", lot 117, SBY 6/10/88 OE 1,210
CHATTAWAY, William (1929-)
Standing Woman, 2/6, dk brn patina, sgn/mk Valsuani/dtd 61, 29", lot 391, SBY 10/7/89 OE 3,300
CHAUDET, Antoine Denis; after (French, 1763-1810)
Napoleon (bust), dk brn patina, 22", SBY 2/22/89 7,150
CHAVALLIAUD, Leon Joseph (French, 1858-1921)
George Bernard Shaw, Carrara marble, inscr d'Apres Photos Chavalliaud Reims, 1906, 27", SLK 9/26/88 1,500
CHEMIN, Victor (European, 1825-1901)
Racehorse & Jockey (rider on mount), dk gr-brn patina, Belgian marble base, sgn, 10", C-NY 5/24/89 1,100
CHERET, Joseph
Vase, C-scroll handles, nudes/putti hold theatrical masks; #7, gilt, mk Soleau Paris 1904, 15", lot 70, SBY 3/19/88 2,090
CHEVRE, Paul Romaine
Separating the Cocks (semi-nude boy/cocks on shaped base), rubbed golden-brn patina, sgn, 19", lot 459, WAD 6/12/89 OE 1,200

CHIA, Sandro (20th C)
Boy with Ram (abstract), 3/4, painted bronze, 1983, 60x46x26", SBY 5/2/88 ... 33,000
Figure on Ladder (contemporary), sgn/dtd 83, 18x9x8", SBY 11/11/88... 14,300
Figure with Arrow, ed of 4, brn patina, stp signature/dtd 82/mk Foundra Luigi Tommasi, 17x20", SBY 5/2/88 ... 15,400
Figure with Tear, 1/4, gr patina, stp signature/dtd 82/mk Foundra Luigi Tommasi Pietra Santa, 21", SBY 5/2/88 ... 9,900
Lovers, 6/6, sgn/dtd 86/foundry mk, 27x24x20", SBY 5/3/88 ... 18,700
Lovers (contemporary seated couple kissing), sgn/dtd 86, 27x24x20", lot 317, SBY 10/5/89... 20,900
Reflective Man (contemporary seated figure), bl plaster, sgn, 1984, 70", lot 288, SBY 10/5/89 ... 55,000
Untitled (contemporary figure on knee), 3/6, dk brn patina, sgn, 29", lot 360, SBY 2/15/89... 24,750
Woman with Teddy Bear, AP, ed of 4, sgn/dtd 85, 11x15x8", lot 263, C-NY 5/4/88... 10,450
Woman with Teddy Bear, 1/4, 1985, 38x63x32", lot 73, SBY 5/3/88 ... 41,250

CHIANELLI, Mervine (20th C)
Tenement, bronze/lucite/wood, sgn/dtd 70, 26", lot 187, SBY 2/14/89 OE... 1,760

CHIHULY, Dale (20th C)
Untitled (abstract sculpture), glass, sgn, 13x20x10", lot 136, SBY 2/19/88... 9,900

CHIPARUS, Demetre H. (French, 19th/20th C)
Amazon (draped female figure in semi-repose), slvr/gilt, veined blk marble base, sgn, ca 1925, 37" long, SBY 6/8/88 OE ... 9,350
Antinea (standing exotic female dancer), cold paint/ivory, brn onyx base, sgn/mk Etling, 27", lot 28, C-NY 6/10/89 OE ... 33,000
Ayouta (dancer in flowing full skirt on right foot), polychrome/ivory, stepped onyx base, 1925, 19", lt rpr, SBY 3/19/88... 12,100
Ballet Russes (3 dancers in short tunics w/beaded belts), polychrome/ivory, marble base, ca 1925, 24", SBY 11/17/88 OE... 104,500
Dancer (elaborate dress/arms extended overhead/leg raised), polychrome/ivory, marble base, ca 1925, 22", SBY 11/17/88 OE ... 13,200
Dancer (posed in semi-split w/raised hand), mustard-brn patina, brn onyx base, ca 1925, 29" long, SBY 11/17/88 OE ... 77,000
Dancer of Kapurthala, #69, cold paint/gilt/ivory, variegated marble base, sgn, 22", rpr base, C-NY 6/11/88... 17,600
Dancer with Ring (exotic/on toes), cold paint/ivory, blk veined marble plinth, mk Etling, 18", lot 23, C-NY 6/10/89 OE... 12,100
Egyptian Dancer (crossed legs/arms overhead/cobra headdress), polychrome/gilt/ivory, ca 1925, 12", lot 85, SBY 11/17/88 ... 9,900
First Arrows, standing figure w/bow; parcel slvr/gilt/cold paint/ivory, gr onyx base, sgn, 17", lot 18, C-NY 6/10/89... 3,850
Folie de Printemps, harem dancer; gilt/polychrome, tapered rectangular pedestal, sgn, 13", C-E 3/24/88 ... 2,420
Footsteps, maiden in long skirt w/bare midriff; polychrome/ivorene, stepped gr onyx base, unmk, 17", C-E 9/16/88 ... 330
Grape Harvest, polychrome, marble base, sgn, 13", lot 372, FB 10/17/88 ... 5,400
Hindu Dancer (on toes/arms upheld), polychrome/slvr/ivory, marble base, mk Etling, ca 1925, 24", lot 287, SBY 6/8/88... 20,900
Innocence (demure girl in off-shoulder dress), parcel gilt/ivory, wht onyx base, sgn, 15", lot 17, C-NY 6/10/89 ... 4,950
Kora (dancer on tiptoe/extending hands at either side), parcel gilt/ivory, stepped onyx base, 25", SBY 11/17/88 OE ... 41,250
Les Amis de Toujours, woman & 2 borzois; #10, gilt/cold paint/ivory, onyx base, ca 1925, 26" long, lot 288, SBY 6/8/88 ... 36,300
Les Amis de Toujours, woman & 2 borzois; #40, gilt/ivory, brn onyx base, sgn/mk France, 16", C-E 6/16/88 OE ... 13,200
Les Amis de Toujours, woman & 2 borzois; gilt/cold paint/ivory, onyx base, sgn, 1920s, 26" long, lot 71, SBY 3/19/88 OE ... 26,400
Nymph, reclining harem girl holding grapes overhead; spelter, gr onyx/blk marble base, sgn, 12" long, C-E 3/24/88 OE... 2,640
Reclining Female Nude, #3, gr-brn patina, blk marble base, sgn/mk Etling Paris, 9x29", C-NY 6/11/88 ... 2,640
Russian Dancers, cymbal dancers, slvr/gilt/ivory, variegated marble base, sgn/mk Etling Paris, 23x18", C-NY 6/11/88 ... 28,600
Starfish (exotic dancer), polychrome/ivory, stepped cream onyx/blk marble base, mk Etling, 29", lot 286, SBY 6/8/88 OE... 33,000
Syrian Dancer, on toes w/outstretched arms; gilt, shaped rectangular onyx base, sgn, 14", lot 461, SBY 12/12/88 ... 2,090
Tamara, ballerina tying her shoe; parcel slvr/gilt/ivory, blk marble base, sgn/mk Etling Paris, 15x26", C-NY 6/11/88... 41,800
Untitled (dancer in full gr skirt & skull cap), polychrome/ivory, beige onyx base, 1925, 22", SBY 3/19/88 OE... 15,400
Untitled (dancing nude w/2 seated nude musicians), dk olive-brn patina, marble base, ca 1925, 20" long, SBY 6/8/88 ... 5,500
Vedette, dancer on tiptoe w/extended arms; polychrome, stepped brn onyx base, sgn, 21", C-E 6/16/88 ... 4,180
Vedette (semi-nude dancer), polychrome, tiered brn onyx base, sgn, ca 1930, 32", lot 81, SBY 11/17/88 ... 6,050

CHIPARUS, Demetre H.; after (French, 19th/20th C)
Two Seated Children, polychrome, veined gr marble base, 7x6", lot 2207, DM 5/13/88 ... 650

CHOTKA
Lamp, Arab traders bartering under lantern/tent of oriental rugs; cold paint, sgn, 15", rechromed, C-E 9/16/88... 1,210

CHRISTO (Bulgarian, 1925-)
Double Store Front (wall relief), oil/wood/glass/cardboard/fabric/paper/electric light, 1964, 26x35x3", C-NY 11/9/88 OE ... 154,000
Pair: Double Show Window; 50/65, gr hc plexiglas/aluminum mullions, 1972, 26x24x3", Tanglewood Pr, lot 589, C-NY 11/1/88... 2,420
Wrapped French Post Card Rack (contemporary), mixed media, 1963, 34x10x10", lot 153, C-NY 5/4/89... 77,000

CHRYSSA (Greek, 1933-)
Functioning Electrodes, plastic/neon/glass in plexiglas box, 26x24x13", lot 191, C-E 5/9/89 OE ... 4,620
Study for The Gates No 9, neon tubes in plexiglas box (motorized), 1968, 17x19x13", C-E 5/13/88 OE ... 3,520
Untitled (contemporary), neon in plexiglas/painted wooden box, sgn, 1973-75, 18x18x10", lot 193, C-E 5/9/89 OE... 8,580

CLARA, Juan
Child Teasing, toddler pulling cat's tail; #50 LX, brn patina, self base, sgn/foundry mk, 11", C-E 3/24/88 ... 660

CLARK, James Ippitt (American, 1883-)
Big-Horn Ram, dk brn patina, sgn/dtd 23/mk RBW Inc NY, 8" long, lot 270, SBY 4/14/89... 4,950

CLAUDEL, Camille (French, 1856-ca 1920)
La Valse (nudes embrace as they dance), 7/50, dk brn patina, sgn/stp, 1892/1905, 18", SBY 5/1/89 OE ... 110,000

CLAVE, Antoini (Spanish, 1913-)
Jug: Pipa Fisherman; 1/3, clr glass, sgn/dtd 1964, 13", C-NY 10/6/88... 5,720

CLEMENCIN, Francois Andre
Diana & Hound (running/holding bow aloft, leaping dog), gr-blk patina, marble plinth, ca 1920, 18", lot 222, SBY 4/23/88 ... 6,050

CLESINGER, Jean Baptiste (French, 1814-1883)
Bust of a Lady, wht marble, marble socle, sgn/mk on her left arm Lere Etude, 32", C-NY 5/24/89... 6,050
Grecian Woman, sgn/dtd on base/foundry mk, 28", RAB 8/8/89 UE ... 1,250

CLODION, Claude Michel (French, 1738-1814)
Bacchanal, sgn, 21", lot 373, FB 10/17/88 .... **4,400**
CLODION, Claude Michel; after (French, 1738-1814)
Untitled, Bacchanalian subject of semi-nude revelers/putto; brn patina, 26", SLK 5/6/88 .... **2,300**
COCTEAU, Jean (French, 1889-1963)
Cyclope, 1/3, clr glass, sgn/dtd 1963/mk Opera Che la Fucina Degli Angeli Ed Egidia Constanini, 42", C-NY 10/6/88 .... **2,200**
Face: Dream (contemporary); 1/3, clr glass mounted on metal pole w/14 glass leaves, sgn, 1966, 65", C-NY 10/6/88 .... **7,150**
Face: Dream; 1/3, clr glass mounted on metal pole w/14 glass leaves, sgn/dtd FA 1966, 65", C-E 5/9/89 .... **7,700**
Plate: Faun Playing a Pipe; 8/50, partially glazed gray ceramic, sgn/dtd 1958, 13" dia, lot 591, C-NY 5/10/89 .... **1,320**
COGNEL
Lady in a Feather Hat, gilt, wht alabaster plinth, 11", C-E 10/11/88 .... **330**
COINARD, Roland (20th C)
St Martin of Tours (equestrian group), gr patina, ca 1950, 10", RWS 7/13/89 UE **125**
COLIN, Georges (French, 1876-)
Icarus (standing w/eagle & vulture), gr/brn patinae, shaped wood base, mk Colin, ca 1925, 23" long, SBY 6/8/88 .... **2,310**
Icarus (standing w/eagle & vulture), gr/brn patinae, wood base, mk Colin, ca 1925, 23" long, lot 324, SBY 3/10/89 OE **3,850**
COLOMBIER, Amelie
Carmencita (flamenco dancer w/castinets), gilt, oval marble base (replaced), ca 1915, 22", SBY 6/10/88 .... **1,540**
COLUNGA, Alejandro (Latin American, 20th C)
Nino Agli, 1/9, sgn/dtd 86, 11", lot 202, SBY 5/16/89 .... **1,980**
Twistr's Sistr's Co (surrealistic), painted steel, sgn/dtd 84, 50", SBY 11/21/88 .... **4,675**
COMOLERA, Paul (French, 1818-1897)
Arab Stallion (standing on oval base), golden-brn patina, sgn, 17", lot 455, WAD 6/12/89 .... **1,800**
CONNELLY, Pierce Francis (American, 1841-)
Bust of a Young Woman, wht marble, sgn/mk Fecit Flor, 27", lot 161, SBY 6/28/89 .... **1,760**
CONSAGRA, Pietro (European, -1920)
Agressions (contemporary), #52, sgn, 19", SBY 10/5/88 .... **2,090**
Colloquio (abstract), welded bronze, sgn/dtd 57, 14" long, lot 393, SBY 10/7/89 .... **5,775**
CONSTANT, Maurice
Le Jongleur (minstrel w/mandolin & parrot), gilt/ivory, wht marble base, sgn, 16", C-E 12/8/88 .... **1,430**
Continental School (20th C)
Nubian Archer, cold paint/patinated, 16", lot 390, FAP 4/15/88 .... **880**
Untitled, classical male nude; 11", lot 382, FAP 4/15/88 .... **220**
COOK, Robert
Untitled (contemporary), gr patina, 48x33", lot 259, C-E 5/13/88 OE **2,860**
CORNELL, Joseph (American, 1903-1972)
Astronomer Magician, sculpture constructed of wood/cork/metal/paint/collage, sgn twice, 1962, 7x9x3", SBY 10/5/89 OE **99,000**
Constellation (assemblage), wood/cork/glass/shell/ceramic pipe/metal, ca 1959, 10x16x4", lot 20G, SBY 5/2/89 OE **209,000**
Day (contemporary), box construction of clay pipe/wine glass/metal/collage/cork, sgn, ca 1955, 9x14", SBY 5/3/89 OE **110,000**
France Nuyen (assemblage), mixed media in glass bottle, 1958, 11", lot 99, SBY 5/3/89 .... **28,600**
Lunar Level #2 (assemblage), wood/cork/marble/starfish/metal, 1959, 9x15x4", lot 20J, SBY 5/2/89 OE **132,000**
Trade Winds #2 (assemblage), wood/cork/marbles/glass/pins/sand/metal, ca 1956-58, 11x16x4", lot 20B, SBY 5/2/89 OE **220,000**
Untitled (Blue Sand Tray), wood/tape on glass/wire coil/ball bearing/glass, 1954, 7x8x8", C-NY 5/4/88 .... **13,200**
Untitled (Dovecoat Variant, Medici Princess), stained wood/paper/wooden balls/glass, ca 1952, 15x10x3", C-NY 5/3/89 OE **418,000**
Untitled (Soap Bubble Set Variant), mixed media framed in box, sgn on verso, ca 1960, 9x15x3", lot 6, C-NY 5/3/88 .... **55,000**
Untitled (Window), mixed media box construction, sgn on verso, ca 1953, 17x11x6", lot 52, SBY 10/8/88 .... **41,800**
COUDRAY, Georges Charles (French, 19th C)
Bust of a Young Woman (head turned to side/bow in hair), brn patina, sgn, 21", lot 217, RWS 6/25/88 .... **925**
COULON, Noel
Untitled (damascened medieval equestrian group), brn patina/ivory, blk veined marble vase, sgn, 23", C-NY 6/11/88 OE **12,100**
COUSTOU, Guillaume; after (French, 1716-1777)
Pair: Marly Horses (rearing horses w/attendants), rubbed golden-brn patina, sgn, 12", lot 458, WAD 6/12/89 .... **800**
COYSEVOX, Antoine; after (French, 1640-1720)
Fame, female riding Pegasus; gilt, yel marble base, sgn/mk Jaboeuf & Rouard seal, 19", lot 114, C-E 4/19/88 OE **1,760**
CRAGG, Tony (20th C)
Landscape (Mountain), painted wood wall construction, 1984, 94x124", lot 248, SBY 10/5/89 .... **20,900**
CRAWFORD, Thomas (American, 1813-1857)
Boy with Tambourine, marble, sgn/dtd Fecit Romae MDCCCLIV, 43", SBY 5/24/89 OE **44,000**
CREEFT, see De Creeft
CROZATIER, Charles; after (French, 1795-1855)
Man with Horse, patinated, 22x23", lot 791, FAP 11/4/88 .... **1,650**
CROZIER, William (British, -1931)
Debbie (prone nude), 2/9, sgn/dtd 1979-80/mk Guss H Mayr Munich 1981, 10x50x27", SBY 2/19/88 UE **550**
Debra, 5/9, sgn, 1976-77, 5x17x15", lot 232, SBY 10/8/88 .... **1,650**
Marilyn (nude on back with arms & legs extended), 2/9, sgn/dtd 1975-80, 45x33x38", Hans Mayr Foundry, SBY 2/19/88 OE **7,700**
Nancy (posterior view of sleeping nude), 3/9, sgn, 1970-74/1982, 7x47x22", Hans Mayr Foundry, Munich, SBY 5/3/88 OE **8,800**
CURTS, T.
Arab Water Carrier, turbaned man w/water bag; rocky base, sgn, ca 1900, 18", SBY 6/10/88 .... **1,100**
D'ANGERS, David; after (French, 19th C)
Portrait Plaque of Napoleon, gilt on rectangular antico verde marble, 10x7", lot 3, RWS 6/17/89 .... **325**

D'ILLIERS, Gaston
Horse Jumping (horse over fence), blk patina, sgn, 14", C-NY 5/24/89 .... **2,200**
Jumping Horse (mare clears third fence rail), dk brn-blk patina, rounded rectangular base, 13", lot 214, SBY 6/9/89 OE **2,420**
DAEN, Lindsay
Girl Skipping Rope, IV, 29", RAB 8/21/89 UE **400**
DALI, Salvador (Spanish, 1904-1989)
Hommage a Newton, 5/8, total ed of 12, blk patina, sgn/mk Valsuani Cire Perdue, 1969, 52", C-NY 2/16/89 OE **143,000**
Lilith et la Double Victoire de Samothrace, 6/6, brn patina, sgn, 1966, 7", SBY 10/7/88 .... **13,200**
Persistance de la Memoire (sculpture), 120/150, pate de verre/hanger, sgn/dtd 70/mk Daum, 26", SBY 10/7/88 .... **3,850**
Tete de Dante, III/VI, gr patina w/18-karat gold-plated slvr spoons, mk Maitres Ltd, 1964, 11", C-NY 10/6/88 .... **37,400**
Untitled (melting clock draped over coat hanger), frosty wht glass/gilt hanger, sgn/dtd 70, 30" long, C-E 12/8/88 OE **7,920**
Venus de Milo Hysterique, 201/300, partially painted pate de verre, mk Daum/France, 1983, 14", lot 198, C-E 11/17/88 .... **4,620**
DALLIN, Cyrus Edwin (American, 1861-1944)
The Scout (Indian on horseback), #10, brn patina, intl/dtd copyright 1910/mk Q488 Gorham Co, 23", SBY 5/24/89 .... **11,000**
DALOU, Aime Jules (French, 1838-1902)
Baigneuse se Lavant le Pied, brn patina, sgn/mk Cire Perdue A A Hebrand, 14", lot 1, PHL 11/15/88 OE **23,000**
Bust of a Young Man, brn patina, marble socle, sgn/dtd 1884, 20", lot 169, PHL 6/16/88 .... **750**
Bust of a Young Woman, brn patina, marble socle, sgn/dtd 1876, 19", lot 170, PHL 6/16/88 .... **750**
Paysan Retroussant ses Manches, brn patina, sgn/Susse Freres seal, 12", C-NY 5/25/88 OE **1,650**
DANSON, Duane (American, 20th C)
Young Shopper (sculpture of woman) oil polychromed polyester/fiberglass/accessories, 1973, life-size, SBY 11/10/88 OE **209,000**
DAUMIER, Honore (French, 1808-1879)
Ratapoil (figure), ed of 20, blk patina, mk Alexis Rudier Fondeur Paris, ca 1850/1925, 17", SBY 5/11/88 .... **55,000**
DAVID, Fernand (20th C)
Untitled (nude w/garland of flowers on flower-strewn base), 2/50, golden-brn patina, ca 1930, 21", lot 284A, SBY 6/8/88 .... **1,980**
DAVID, Pierre Jean (French, 19th C)
Johann Gensfleich Gutenberg (standing male figure), golden-brn patina, sgn/dtd 1839/mk Susse Freres, 16", C-NY 5/24/89 .... **1,320**
Johann Gutenberg, holds page of Bible; lt brn patina, sgn/mk Susse Freres, 19th C, 16", lot 76, RWS 9/24/88 .... **400**
DAVIDSON, Jo (American, 1883-1952)
Abraham Lincoln (bust), blk patina, sgn/dtd 1943, 10", lot 260, SBY 4/14/89 .... **1,980**
Bust of a Woman, golden-brn patina, sgn/dtd Paris 1921, 15", lot 163, SBY 6/28/89 .... **2,750**
Bust of Marjorie Merriweather Post (sculpture), painted plaster, sgn/dtd 1940, 17", SBY 3/17/88 .... **1,430**
DAVIS, Debby (American, 20th C)
Pig (full figure), oil on polyadam/fiberglass/hydrocal, 1984, 36x24x10", lot 317, C-NY 5/4/89 .... **4,400**
Pighead No 1, oil on polyadam/fiberglass/hydrocal, 1983, 12x10x8", lot 315, C-NY 5/4/89 .... **1,320**
DE ALONZO, Dominique (French, fl 1910-1930)
Oriental Water Carrier, maiden descending stair; bronze/ivory, sgn, 13", C-E 9/16/88 .... **1,320**
Untitled (medieval lady descending staircase), golden patina/ivory/coral/onyx, 10", SLK 4/7/89 .... **1,500**
Young Girl, bare-breasted w/hands behind back & standing on rocky base; bronze/ivory, sgn, 11", lt ls, C-E 9/16/88 .... **2,860**
DE ANDREA, John (European, 1941-)
Black Woman with Folding Chair (sculpture), oil painted polyvinyl w/metal chair, 1978, life-size, SBY 2/19/88 OE **49,500**
Standing Woman with Gold Ring (nude), polychromed polyester/resin/fiberglass, 67", SBY 11/11/88 .... **49,500**
Untitled (man, nude); polychromed polyester/resin/fiberglass, 1970, 71", SBY 10/5/89 .... **12,100**
DE BLEZER (19th C)
Untitled (nude on tiptoe, swirling drapery overhead), gilt, red marble base, tripod base, 75", C-E 3/24/88 .... **4,950**
DE BOLOGNA, Gian; after (Italian, 1529-1608)
Mercury, w/caduceus, brn patina, marble plinth w/bronze frieze, ca early 20th C, 33", SLK 5/6/88 .... **1,000**
DE BOLOGNE, Jean (Flemish, 1524-1608)
Mercury, 28", left leg/right arm rpr, staff not orig, RAB 4/25/89 .... **300**
DE CAMARGO, Sergio
Opus 175, painted wood construction, sgn/dtd Paris 67/#d, 34x24", SBY 5/16/89 OE **6,600**
DE CREEFT, Jose (American, 1884-)
Head of a Woman, partially polished stone, sgn, 7", SBY 10/5/88 .... **2,750**
Head of a Woman, stone, sgn, 8", lot 276, SBY 6/28/89 .... **3,080**
Mythological Mother with Children (sculpture), stone, 14", SBY 1/24/89 .... **1,650**
Seated Woman, stone, sgn on base, 7", lot 279, SBY 6/28/89 .... **1,320**
DE FOY SUZOR-COTE, see Suzor-Cote
DE KOONING, Willem (American/Dutch, 1904-)
Head III (abstract), 11/12, sgn, 1973, 20", SBY 5/2/88 OE **99,000**
DE LA FUENTE, Manuel
Primavera (reclining nude), Portuguese pk marble, sgn/dtd 1986, 18x14x10", C-NY 5/17/89 OE **17,600**
DE LA MOTHE BORGLUM, John Gutzon (American, 1871-1941)
Two Reclining Nudes, wht marble, sgn, 50" long, SBY 1/24/89 UE **2,200**
DE MARIA, Walter (American, 1935-)
Bronze Shaft/Steel Shaft (contemporary), bronze/steel, titled, 1966, 15x18x3", C-NY 11/9/88 .... **60,500**
Elle (contemporary), carbon steel/stainless steel ball in 2 parts, ca 1966, 3x16x16", C-NY 11/9/88 .... **60,500**
DE MONARD, Louis (French, 1873-)
Rearing Stallion & Groom, rich brn patina, sgn/mk 10 59025, 23", C-NY 5/24/89 .... **3,520**
DE RIVERA, Jose (American, 1904-)
Construction #160, motorized stainless steel, painted wood base, 1971, 9x14x11", SBY 10/8/88 OE **15,400**
Construction #2 (contemporary), stainless steel, 1954, 18x22x20", lot 45, SBY 2/15/89 OE **25,300**

Construction #23 (contemporary), polished, painted square wood base, 8x8x7", lot 187, C-NY 5/4/89 8,800
Construction in Black & Yellow, painted aluminum, 1953, 27x58x28", lot 48, SBY 2/15/89 19,800
Untitled (motorized abstract sculpture), polished bronze, square blk wood base, sgn, 1980, 11", lot 55, C-NY 11/20/88 16,500

DE SAINT-MARCEAUX, Charles Rene (19th/20th C)

Harlequin (standing figure), reddish-brn patina, sgn/dtd 1879/mk Barbedienne/Reduction Mecanique seal, 27", C-NY 5/25/88 2,640

DE SAINT-PHALLE, Niki (American, 1930-)

Drake Eating Man, 3/10, painted ceramic, sgn/dtd 1979, 13" long, lot 121, C-NY 11/20/88 4,620
Lady & the Dragon, 4/7, painted cast polyester resin, sgn, 5x9x10", SBY 10/8/88 OE 13,750
Man Reading Newspaper Sitting on Snake, 3/10, painted ceramic, sgn/dtd 1980, 6x10", lot 120, C-NY 11/20/88 2,200
Oiseau, 3/10, painted ceramic, sgn, 6", lot 122, C-NY 11/20/88 2,200
Personnages a la Tele (double-sided sculpture), painted polyester, sgn, ca 1970, 30x17x10", SBY 2/19/88 OE 27,500

DE SAINT-PHALLE, Niki; & TINGUELY, Jean

Nana, crayon/painted cast polyester resin, sculpted iron base, sgn De Saint-Phalle, ca 1965, 13", SBY 10/8/88 OE 33,000

DEBUT, Marcel (French, 1865-)

Pecheuse de la Ciotat, lady holds lobster/fishing net; red-brn patina, sgn/titled, 26", lot 321, C-E 9/13/88 1,320

DEGAS, Edgar (French, 1834-1917)

Danseuse s'Avancant, les Bras Leves; #19, blk patina, sgn/mk Hebrard Cire Perdue, ca 1882-95/1919-21, 14", SBY 5/11/89 99,000

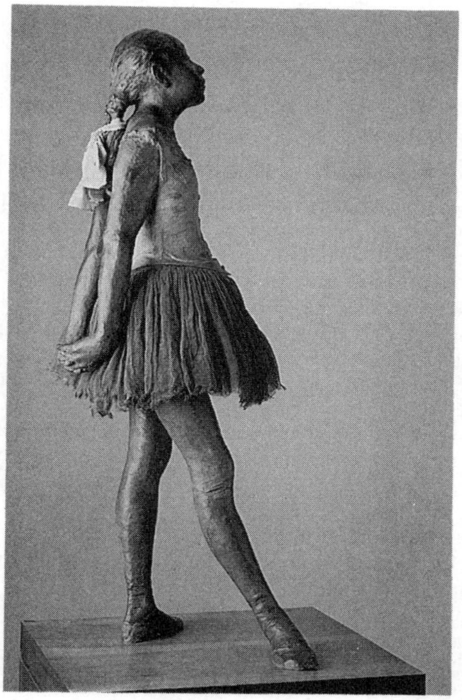

Petite Danseuse de Quatorze Ans, polychrome, sgn/mk B AA Hebrard Cire Perdue, 1879-81/1921, 39", C-NY 11/14/88, $10,175,000

Femme Enceinte (standing nude), 24/B, dk brn patina, sgn/mk AA Hebrard, ca 1896-1911/ca 1919, 17", SBY 5/11/88 49,500
Position de Quatrieme Devant sur la Jambe Cauche, 58/J, brn patina, sgn/mk Hebrard, ca 1890/ca 1919, SBY 5/9/89 286,000

DEJEAN, Louis (French, 1872-)

Elegant Lady (long skirt/flaring cape/wide-brimmed hat), #33, brn patina, sgn, ca 1910, 13", SBY 6/10/88 495

DELABRIERRE, Edouard (French, 1829-1912)

Setter (dog), rich brn patina, gr marble base, sgn, 5x8", C-NY 2/23/89 495
Setter & a Goose, brn patina, gr marble base, sgn, 5x8", lot 272, C-NY 2/23/89 660

DELAGRANGE, Leon Noel (French, 20th C)

Loie Fuller, gilt, sgn/mk Jollet, 17", C-NY 6/11/88 UE 8,250

DELANNOY, P. (Continental, 20th C)

Satyr & Nude, sgn, 17x21", lot 389, FAP 4/15/88 1,045

DELFIN, Victor (20th C)

Horse (head/tail down), steel, intl, 1977, 63", SBY 5/16/89 12,100
Horse (head/tail upraised), steel, intl, 1977, 89", SBY 5/16/89 OE 18,700

DENIS (20th C)

Dancing Lady, nude w/raised knee, open arms, holds globes; medium brn patina, square marble base, 10", RWS 12/10/88 UE 50

DERAIN, Andre (French, 1880-1954)

Les Boules, 6/11, total ed of 15, brn patina, sgn/mk Atelier, 8", lot 36, C-E 2/13/89 OE 6,050
Les Grandes Oreilles, 6/11, total ed of 15, gr/brn patinae, sgn, 7", lot 32, C-E 2/13/89 OE 6,050

DERENNE, after

Nude Disc Dancer, gr patinated metal, blk marble base, sgn, 11", C-E 6/16/88 UE 220

DERUJINSKY, Gleb (Russian, 20th C)

Infant, terra cotta, wood base, ca 1932, 6" wide, lot 121, C-E 6/1/89 990

DESCHAMPS, Leon

En Moisson, woman w/bundle of wheat on rockwork base; golden-brn patina, sgn, 24", C-E 6/1/88 1,100

DESCOMPS, Jean Bernard
Elegant Victorian Lady, brn patina, sgn/dtd 1904/mk Bingin Costenoble Fondeurs Paris, 25", SBY 6/10/88 ... 1,210
DESCOMPS, Joe (20th C)
Lamp, standing elaborately dressed lady holds fan; gr onyx plinth, stepped square base, sgn, 29", lot 463, SBY 12/12/88 ... 4,070
DESCOMPS, Joseph E. (French, 1869-1950)
Untitled (nude w/short curls & back braid swinging garland), slvr, cast circular base, onyx socle, 21", SBY 3/19/88 ... 1,320
DESPIAU, Charles (French, 1874-1946)
Printemps (seated nude), 2/7, blk patina, sgn/mk C Valsuani Cire Perdue, 1923, 14", SBY 2/6/89 ... 9,350
DI SUVERO, Mark (American, 1933-)
Apache (contemporary), welded steel in 2 parts, 1976-77, 54x64x53", lot 221, SBY 10/5/89 ... 165,000
Crochet (Chalon), welded/cut steel in 2 parts, 1974, 26x27x28", lot 77, C-NY 11/20/88 ... 41,800
Herald (abstract), welded steel, 1973, 10x17x10", lot 93, C-NY 10/4/89 ... 38,500
Untitled, welded steel, 1965, 12x10x8", w/sgn photo, lot 162, C-NY 5/4/88 ... 8,250
Untitled (abstract), welded steel in 2 parts, 1980-81, 25x21x11", lot 188, SBY 5/3/89 OE ... 82,500
Untitled (contemporary), steel, 9x13x9", 1969, lot 224, SBY 5/3/88 ... 3,520
Untitled (hanging sculpture), polished brass, ca 1965, 28", lot 195, C-NY 5/4/88 ... 11,000
DINE, Jim (American, 1935-)
Arch (contemporary), 3/3, sgn/dtd 1983, 100x83x35", lot 49, C-NY 11/20/88 OE ... 52,800
Hammer Acts (contemporary wall relief), oil/hammer/wooden plank/steel nails on canvas, sgn/dtd 62, 85x75", C-NY 11/9/88 ... 66,000
Little Reliefs From Los Angeles V (contemporary), painted, 1982-85, 14x15x4", lot 207, SBY 10/5/89 ... 16,500
Metamorphosis of a Plant into a Fan (group of 5 sculptures), aluminum, sgn/dtd 1963-73, 1974, 27x16x12", SBY 2/19/88 ... 16,500
Tennis Shoe, painted tennis shoe/paper collage/painted wood, sgn/titled/dtd 1962, 18x20", lot 11, SBY 5/2/89 OE ... 52,250
DOLIVET, E.
Inkwell, sleeping putti w/mandolin in clouds; golden-brn patina, sgn/mk Thiebaud Freres, 1895, 7" long, C-E 10/11/88 OE ... 715
DOMELA, Cesar (Dutch, 1900-)
Relief No 59A (abstract), copper/brass/iron construction mounted to painted panel, sgn/dtd 1959, 29x46", C-NY 5/12/88 ... 13,200
Relief No 74 (abstract), copper/aluminum/wood construction mounted to painted panel, sgn/dtd 1961, 48x32", C-NY 5/12/88 ... 13,200
DORE, Gustave (French, 1832-1883)
Nude Standing on a Ledge (relief), plaster, mk Original de Gustave Dore, 22", C-NY 11/26/88 ... 12,100
DROUOT, Edouard (French, 1859-1945)
American Indian on Horseback, lt brn patina, rectangular realistic base, 21x24", SLK 9/26/88 ... 2,600
Bust of Diana, wht marble, sgn, 29", C-NY 5/24/89 ... 3,300
Dancing Pan (standing figure), rich brn patina, gr veined marble base, sgn, 20", C-NY 5/25/88 ... 1,320
Farmer & Two Oxen, polychrome, blk veined marble base, sgn, late 19th C, 13", lot 107, C-E 4/19/88 ... 1,760
Indian, semi-prone on bed of plants/rocks; verde antico marble stepped rectangular base, 20x20", C-E 3/22/88 ... 880
Indian, semi-prone warrior on bed of plants/rock; verde antico stepped rectangular base, 10x20", C-E 6/28/88 UE ... 352
Male Youth Fighting a Tiger, gilt, sgn, 22", lot 117, C-E 4/19/88 OE ... 1,430
Running Athlete, brn patina, sgn, 20", C-NY 5/25/88 ... 1,540
DRURY, Edward Alfred (British, 1859-)
Young Girl (bust), gr patina, gr marble base, sgn/dtd 1907, 17", C-NY 5/25/88 ... 1,320
DU PASSAGE, Arthur Marie Gabriel
Horse & Groom (running on realistic base), dk brn patina, molded oval base, late 19th C, 30x44", lot 210, SBY 6/9/89 OE ... 26,400
Mare Harnessed by a Groom, rich brn patina, sgn, 13x29", C-NY 5/24/89 ... 7,700
DUBOIS, Paul (French, 1829-1905)
Florentine Singer, brn patina, sgn/dtd 1865/mk Barbedienne/Reduction Mecanique seal, 15", C-NY 5/25/88 ... 1,650
Pair: Companion Harlequins; brn patina, 33", lot 691, WL 2/26/88 ... 2,000
Saint John the Baptist, brn patina, sgn/dtd 1861/mk Barbedienne/Reduction Mechanique seal, 32", C-NY 5/25/88 ... 1,540
DUBUCAND, Alfred (French, 1828-)
Hunting Group (tethered saddled horse/slain deer/dogs), golden-brn patina, sgn, late 19th C, 9x11", lot 213, SBY 6/9/89 ... 1,430
DUBUFFET, Jean (French, 1901-1985)
Appareil Telephonique (telephone), polyester resin, sgn/dtd 68, 34x33x17", SBY 11/11/88 OE ... 176,000
Chien de Guet II (abstract), epoxy/polyurethane paint, 1969-70, 122x63x43", lot 25, C-NY 5/3/89 ... 528,000
Element Bleu VII (3-dimensional sculpture on base), paint transfer on polyester relief, 1967, 79x54", SBY 6/30/88 ... 16,000
Paysage Contrapontique (abstract), polyurethane w/epoxy paint, 43x50x38", lot 194, C-NY 5/4/89 ... 181,500
DUC, see Le Duc
DUCHAMP, Marcel (French, 1887-1968)
Marcel Duchamp Moule Vif 1967, I/IV, lt brn patina, onyx/blk Belgian marble, sgn, 1966-67/1967, 22x17x9", SBY 5/11/89 OE ... 38,500
DUCHAMP-VILLON, Raymond (French, 1876-1918)
Cheval et Chevalier (1Er Etat), blk patina, sgn/Louis Carre stp/mk Georges Rudier Fondeur, 1914/later, 9", SBY 10/7/88 ... 46,750
Le Cheval Majeur (abstract horse), 6/9, sgn/dtd 1914/mk Louis Carre Editeur Susse Fondeur Paris, 59", SBY 5/9/89 OE ... 1,100,000
DUCHOISELLE (French, 19th C)
Indian Riding in a Canoe, gilt, sgn, 24x36", C-E 6/1/88 ... 4,620
Indian Sitting in a Canoe, golden patina, veined marble base, sgn, 26x42", lot 108, C-E 4/19/88 OE ... 15,400
DUFRENE, M.
Lamp, cylindrical column w/stylized leaf forms & matching final; 3-scroll footed base, sgn, 23", C-E 6/16/88 ... 550
DUMAIGE, Etienne Henri (French, 1830-1888)
Pair: Apres le Combat Grenadier de 1792; Avant le Combat Volontaire de 1972; brn patina, marble base, 28", WL 2/26/88 ... 2,500
DURET, Francisque Joseph (French, 1804-1865)
Tragedy, allegorical draped figure; dk gr-brn patina, sgn, 37", C-NY 5/25/88 ... 1,650
DURHAM, Joseph (1814-1877)
Sunshine, seated nude; wht marble, sgn/mk Sc 1865 Sunshine, 26", C-NY 5/24/89 ... 2,860

DUVERNET
Untitled, young bare-breasted female sitting on her heels holds incense burner; brn onyx base, 19", C-E 12/8/88 OE **1,210**
EBERLE, Abastenia St. Leger (American, 1878-1942)
Bookends: Standing Children; brn patina, sgn/dtd 1911 & 1912/mk Theodore B Starr Inc, 7", lot 78, WD 10/5/88 UE **3,750**
Dancing Figure, sgn/mk Pompeian Bronze Works NY, 1906, 15", lot 212, PHL 6/16/88 .... **2,750**
EISENBERGER, L.
Before the Battle (warrior afixing cloak), gr-brn patina, ca 1920-30, 21", lot 695, WL 2/26/88 .... **700**
ELSNER, Fritz Richter
Untitled (Amazon on horse), rubbed brn/blk patinae, rectangular base, sgn, ca 1925, 23", lot 326, SBY 3/10/89 .... **2,970**
EPSTEIN, Jacob (British, 1880-1959)
Babe with Outstretched Arms, brn patina, 1949, 10", C-E 5/9/89 OE **8,580**
Eighth Portrait of Peggy Jean (head), golden patina, square base, 1921, 10", lot 125, SBY 10/7/89 OE **8,250**
First Portrait of J Ramsay MacDonald, 1/2, dk brn patina, 1926, 19", SBY 10/7/88 .... **7,150**
First Portrait of Kitty (with Curls), golden-brn patina, 18", SBY 10/5/88 OE **11,000**
Isobel Hughes (head), golden patina, sgn, 1950, 12", lot 124, SBY 10/7/89 .... **7,700**
Pola Nerenska (head), golden patina, 1937, 13", lot 126, SBY 10/7/89 OE **7,700**
Ronald Duncan (head), ed of 6, blk/gr patinae, sgn, 1946, SBY 10/7/89 .... **6,050**
Self-Portrait with a Beard, dk brn patina, ca 1918, 15", C-E 5/13/88 OE **3,850**
Sheila (head), brn patina, sgn on back of base, 14", lot 214, C-NY 2/18/88 OE **5,720**
ERIKSEN, Edvard (Danish, 20th C)
Little Mermaid, brn patina, shaped wood base, sgn/inscr Copenhagen & Bartje, 9", C-NY 6/11/88 .... **1,430**
ERNST, Max (American, 1891-1976)
Cheri Bebe, 59/175, brn patina, sgn/mk Valsuani Cire Perdue, 13", C-NY 10/6/88 .... **6,600**
Cheri Bebe (contemporary), 63/175, gr patina, sgn on base, 1973/1975, 13", lot 188, C-NY 10/5/89 .... **6,050**
Chimere (medallion), 4/8, 23-karat gold, sgn/mk Francois Hugo, 1961/1978, 2x3", boxed, lot 136, C-NY 2/18/88 OE **1,870**
Deux et Deux Font Un (abstract), 1956, 14", SBY 5/11/88 .... **41,250**
Deux Tetes (medallion), 23-karat gold, sgn/mk Francois Hugo, 1959/1977, 2x3", boxed, lot 143, C-NY 2/18/88 OE **2,420**
Dream Rose (abstract), II/VI, blk patina, sgn/mk C Valsuani Foundry, 1959, 12", SBY 10/7/88 .... **27,500**
Egyptienne (medallion), 4/8, 23-karat gold, sgn/mk Francois Hugo, 1959/1981, 3x3", boxed, lot 129, C-NY 2/18/88 OE **3,300**
Grand Masque (medallion), 2/8, 23-karat gold, sgn/mk Francois Hugo, 1961/1977, 4x4", boxed, lot 140, C-NY 2/18/88 OE **3,520**
Grand Masque Ovale (medallion), 2/8, 23-karat gold, sgn/mk Francois Hugo, 1959/1977, 11x7", boxed, lot 145, C-NY 2/18/88 OE **17,600**
Grand Masque Strie (medallion), 2/8, 23-karat gold, sgn/mk Francois Hugo, 1959/1977, 10x7", boxed, lot 146, C-NY 2/18/88 .... **9,350**
Grande Tete (medallion), 2/8, 23-karat gold, sgn/mk Francois Hugo, 1959/unknown, 4x4", boxed, lot 127, C-NY 2/18/88 .... **3,520**
Group of 4: Les Quatre Saisons; clr glass, 12" dia, C-NY 10/6/88 .... **17,600**
Homme aux Bras Croses (contemporary), 1/2, slvr, sgn/mk Francois Hugo 2368, 1967/ca 1980, 8x19", lot 208, C-NY 2/18/88 .... **14,300**
Les Deux (medallion), 2/8, 23-karat gold, sgn/mk Francois Hugo, 1959/1976, 6x4", boxed, lot 141, C-NY 2/18/88 OE **6,600**
Madame (contemporary), 2/8, slvr, sgn/mk Exemplaires d'Autre 1858-1558 Francois Hugo, 1960, 7", lot 205, C-NY 2/18/88 .... **14,300**
Madame New Look (abstract), 1/2, slvr, sgn/mk Exemplaires d'Autre 1839-1523, 1961/ca 1980, 11", lot 186, C-NY 2/18/88 .... **14,300**
Masque (medallion), 2/8, 23-karat gold, sgn/mk Francois Hugo, 1959/1976, 3x3", boxed, lot 132, C-NY 2/18/88 OE **3,300**
Masque 1 (medallion), 4/8, 23-karat gold, sgn/mk Francois Hugo, 1959/1979, 2x3", boxed, lot 131, C-NY 2/18/88 OE **3,850**
Masque 2 (medallion), 2/8, 23-karat gold, sgn/mk Francois Hugo, 1961/1981, 3x3", boxed, lot 137, C-NY 2/18/88 OE **3,300**
Monsieur New Look (abstract), 1/2, slvr, sgn/mk Exemplaires d'Autre 1836-1522, 1961/ca 1980, 12", lot 187, C-NY 2/18/88 .... **19,800**
Nez de Cone (medallion), 2/8, 23-karat gold, sgn/mk Francois Hugo, 1961/1977, 3x3", boxed, lot 125, C-NY 2/18/88 OE **3,850**
Petit Masque (medallion), 3/8, 23-karat gold, sgn/mk Francois Hugo, 1960/1977, 2x2", boxed, lot 139, C-NY 2/18/88 OE **1,650**
Petit Ovale (medallion), 3/8, 23-karat gold, sgn/mk Francois Hugo, 1960/1977, 2x1", boxed, lot 133, C-NY 2/18/88 OE **1,870**
Soleil (medallion), 2/8, 23-karat gold, sgn/mk Francois Hugo, 1959/1977, 4x4", boxed, lot 126, C-NY 2/18/88 OE **3,850**
Tete (medallion), 4/8, 23-karat gold, sgn/mk Francois Hugo, 1959/1978, 3x3", boxed, lot 130, C-NY 2/18/88 OE **3,850**
Tete a Cornes (medallion), 5/8, 23-karat gold, sgn/mk Francois Hugo, 1961/1977, 7x5", boxed, lot 128, C-NY 2/18/88 OE **7,150**
Tete Ovale (medallion), 4/8, 23-karat gold, sgn/mk Francois Hugo, 1961/1978, 3x2", boxed, lot 135, C-NY 2/18/88 OE **2,750**
Tete sur Plateau (medallion), 3/8, 23-karat gold, sgn/mk Francois Hugo, 1961, 11" dia, boxed, lot 144, C-NY 2/18/88 OE **22,000**
Tete Triangle (medallion), 2/8, 23-karat gold, sgn/mk Francois Hugo, 1959/1976, 3x3", boxed, lot 138, C-NY 2/18/88 OE **3,080**
Tete 1 (medallion), 5/8, 23-karat gold, sgn/mk Francois Hugo, 1959/1981, 2x2", boxed, lot 134, C-NY 2/18/88 OE **2,200**
Tete 2 (medallion), 2/8, 23-karat gold, sgn/mk Francois Hugo, 1959/1976, 3x3", boxed, lot 142, C-NY 2/18/88 OE **2,420**
Tondo: Oiseau; 2/3, bl glass mounted on wht wood plaque, sgn/dtd 1964, 20x17", lot 206, C-NY 2/18/88 .... **4,950**
ERTE, Romain de Tirtoff (Russian, 1892-1990)
Autumn, 111/250, parcel gilt/brn patina, mk Fine Art Acquisitions, 1980, 15", C-E 3/24/88 UE **2,310**
Diva, standing figure in beaded raiment; 29/50, parcel gilt/gr patina, mk Fine Arts Acquisitions, 1984, 18", C-E 3/24/88 .... **6,820**
Evening in 1921, lady in cowled gown w/full sleeves; 225/250, patinated, mk RKP Int Corp, 1980, 16", C-E 3/24/88 .... **4,620**
Evening in 1922, lady on stepped pedestal w/closed eyes & finger to lips; 140/250, patinated, 1980, 17", C-E 3/24/88 UE **2,860**
Firebird, bird-woman w/winged torso; 126/250, parcel gilt/patinated, mk RKP Int Corp, 1980, 17", C-E 3/24/88 .... **3,740**
Gala, lady in halter dress w/arms held wide; AP, parcel gilt/patinated, mk Fine Art Acquisition, 1980, 15", C-E 3/24/88 .... **2,970**
Globe, lady in windswept dress/upheld slvr orb; parcel gilt/slvr/red patina, mk Fine Art Acquisitions, 1984, C-E 3/24/88 .... **8,250**
Kiss of Fire, couple in theatrical plumage; 282/300, parcel gilt, mk Fine Art Acquisitions, 1984, 21", C-E 3/24/88 .... **4,950**
L'Amour, lady on tiptoe w/ankles & hands chained to red heart on her chest; 161/375, slvr/patina, 21", C-E 3/24/88 .... **2,860**
La Femme et la Panthere, lady clad in exotic animal skin/pet panther; 181/250, mk RKP Int Corp, 1980, 15", C-E 3/24/88 .... **9,020**
La Plume, kneeling lady w/plumed headdress; 34/250, parcel gilt, mk RKP Int Corp, 1980, 15", C-E 3/24/88 .... **5,500**
Le Soleil, lady in arched headpiece w/hanging strands of beadwork; parcel gilt, mk RKP Int Corp, 1980, 18", C-E 3/24/88 .... **8,800**
Victoire, lady holding eagle aloft on her right hand; 210/250, parcel gilt, mk RKP Int Corp, 1980, 19", C-E 3/24/88 .... **16,500**
ESTE, Gaudi (Latin American, 20th C)
Neron (surrealistic dog w/human head), 4/6, dk gr patina, 1988, 35", C-NY 6820 OE **13,200**

ETIENNE-MARTIN
Tete aux Mains, 1/9, gray patina, sgn/mk Artistica Bataglia C Milano, 1951, 23", C-NY 10/6/88 OE ... 17,600

ETROG, Sorel (Canadian/Rumanian, 1933-)
Crusader, wht marble, self base, 1965-67, 45", lot 13, SBY 2/15/89 OE ... 18,700
Crusader (contemporary), ed of 6, plated bronze, sgn, 1965-67, 43", SBY 10/6/88 OE ... 13,200
Entertainer, 1/7, stp sgn, ca 1965, 37", lot 134, SBY 5/3/88 ... 9,900
Odalisque, 2/7, sgn, 11", lot 65, SBY 2/15/89 ... 7,150
Venetian, 1/7, sgn, 23x25x8", lot 154, SBY 10/8/88 ... 10,450

European School (19th C)
Untitled, classical draped figure looking backward over her right shoulder; wht marble, 34", SLK 9/26/88 ... 2,500

FALCONET, Etiene Maurice (French, 1716-1791)
After the Bath (draped standing nude), d'ore patina, sgn, 20", lot 2250, DM 5/13/88 ... 1,700

FALGUIERE, Jean Alexandre Joseph (French, 1831-1900)
Le Vainqueur au Combat de Coq (boy & rooster), brn patina, sgn/mk Thiebaut Foundry, 38", C-NY 5/25/88 ... 3,080
Pegasus Carrying the Poet Towards the Regions of the Dream, rich gr-brn patina, sgn/mk Thiebaut, 29", C-NY 5/24/89 ... 6,050
Phyrne, standing nude; #364, gilt-wash patina, sgn/mk Goupil, no size given, lot 173, C-NY 5/25/88 OE ... 4,180

FARNHAM, Sally James (American, 1876-1943)
Will Rogers on His Pony, rich dk brn patina, sgn, 22", lot 174, C-NY 5/25/89 ... 49,500

FAYRAL
Dancer, bare-breasted/in short skirt/on tiptoe/hands raised in V; gr painted metal, blk marblized base, 17", C-E 9/16/88 ... 330
Espana, bare-breasted figure in split skirt w/pink glass fan; gr patinated metal, blk stepped base, 20", C-E 6/16/88 ... 1,375
Lamp: Two Deco Maidens Kneeling (facing/hands raised to support glass shade); blk marble plinth, 20" long, C-E 9/16/88 ... 1,540
Nymph, Deco nude holding scarf at hips w/tambourine on shoulder; gr marble base, sgn, 23", C-E 3/24/88 ... 1,210

FAYRAL, after
Cymbal Player, girl in tunic w/raised leg; gr patinated metal, sq blk marble base, sgn, 20", C-E 6/16/88 ... 495

FELLOWS, Fred (American, 1935-)
Dancing Back the Past (Indian dancer), 22-50, sgn/titled, 21x17", SLK 4/7/89 ... 2,000

FEUCHERE, Jean Jacques (French, 1807-1852)
Daphnis & Cloe, rich gr-brn patina, sgn/mk Paillard/foundry seal, 21", C-NY 5/25/88 ... 3,850

FEUERMAN, Carole Jeane (20th C)
Brooke with Beach Ball, polyester resin & oil, 21x25x19", SBY 10/5/89 OE ... 23,100

FIOT, Maximillian (French, 1886-)
Pair: Heads of Dogs; brn patina/slvr, sgn/mk Susse Fes Edts Paris Cire Perdu, 8", lot 288, C-NY 2/23/89 OE ... 2,420

FLANAGAN, John (American, 1895-1942)
Portrait Relief of Henry Wadsworth Longfellow, brn patina, mk Grolier Club NY, 8x6", C-E 6/1/88 OE ... 440

FLAVIN, Dan (American, 1933-)
Untitled (contemporary), pink/bl/gr flourescent tubes, 1976, 96", lot 45, C-NY 5/3/88 OE ... 30,800
Untitled (contemporary), 2/3, red/yel/gr flourescent light, 1968-69, 48", lot 237, SBY 2/15/89 OE ... 41,250
Untitled (To Eleanor McGovern), 1/5, flourescent light, 1972, 95", lot 285, SBY 11/11/88 OE ... 55,000

FONSECA, Gonzalo (20th C)
Concinnitas (contemporary), marble, sgn/dtd 1970/titled, 35", SBY 5/16/89 ... 47,300

FONSSAGRIVES-PENN, Lisa (20th C)
Mother & Child (abstract), gr/copper patinae, foundry mk on base, 1982, 18x18x14", lot 418, C-NY 5/4/89 OE ... 81,250

FORAIN, Jeanne (French, 1852-1931)
Concetto Spaziale Natura 1967, 467/500, polished brass, sgn, 1967, 12x9", SBY 2/19/88 OE ... 7,700
Old Woman, #3, blk patina, sgn/mk foundry monogram XX, 20", C-E 5/9/89 ... 1,100

FOURNIER, Paul
Shakespeare, standing/holding open book; square base w/scroll cartouche, sgn, 21", C-E 3/22/88 ... 605

FOYATIER, Denis
Joan of Arc, gr-brn patina, sgn/dtd 1952, 18", C-NY 5/25/88 ... 1,100

FRANK, Mary (20th C)
Leaping Man (abstract sculpture), terra cotta, 1977, 15x21x7", SBY 2/19/88 OE ... 9,900

FRATIN, Christopher (French, 1800-1864)
Arab Stallion (standing), brn patina, sgn/mk MJP Temoignage de Reconnaissance 10 Aout 1888, 16x18", C-NY 5/24/89 ... 2,860
Arab Stallion (standing), brn-gr patina, mk Fratin Daubree, 13", C-NY 5/24/89 OE ... 4,070
Standing Horse (proud stallion), rubbed golden-brn patina, sgn/mk Daubre, ca 1880, 13x16", lot 167, SBY 6/9/89 ... 2,310
Thoroughbred, rectangular marble base, sgn, 24x31", lot 1065, DM 2/19/88 ... 1,300

FREEMAN, William (American, 1927-)
Bronc Rider, shaped realistic base, Bear Paw Bronze, 19", lot 264, WG 4/23/88 ... 1,050

FREMIET, Emmanuel (French, 1824-1910)
Dog Stretching, brn patina, gr marble base, sgn, 4x7", C-NY 2/23/89 ... 935
Goat & Kid (on oval realistic base), golden-brn patina, sgn, 7", lot 457, WAD 6/12/89 ... 600
Joan of Arc (mounted on horse), rich dk brn patina, red marble base, sgn/mk Barbedienne Paris, 31", C-NY 5/24/89 OE ... 4,620
Louis XIII (figure on rearing horse), brn patina, sgn/mk Barbedienne Fondeur VT60, 18", sword missing, C-NY 5/24/89 ... 3,520
Louis XIII (figure on rearing horse), gilt bronze, sgn/mk Barbedienne 46, 18", C-NY 5/24/89 ... 2,860
Racehorse & Jockey (figure mounted on horse), brn patina, sgn, 18" long, C-NY 5/24/89 ... 6,600
Racehorses & Jockeys (group of 2 mounted riders), rich brn patina, sgn, 18x22", C-NY 5/24/89 ... 11,000
Seated Cat, brn patina, sgn, 3", C-NY 2/23/89 OE ... 880
Seated Setter, rich brn patina, sgn, 6", C-NY 2/23/89 ... 715
Stallion (standing), #12, brn patina, sgn/intl/mk Tiffany & Co twice, 11x12", C-NY 5/24/89 ... 2,860
Standing Rooster, rich brn patina, sgn, 3", C-NY 2/23/89 ... 528

Two Seated Dogs, rich brn patina, gr marble base, 6", C-NY 2/23/89	825
FREMIET, Emmanuel; after (French, 1824-1910)	
Two Barge Horses, blk-gr patina on wht metal, sgn, 9", lot 77, C-E 6/1/88	528
French School (18th C)	
Pallas Athena (standing contraposto w/left hand on hip & lion at feet), terra cotta, 22", lot 133, C-NY 6/17/89	2,420
French School (19th C)	
Bull Dog with Collar & Chain, wht marble plinth, 10", lot 338, SLK 2/12/88	275
Bust of Diana, dk brn patina, circular molded antico verde marble socle, 14", rpr socle, lot 392, RWS 12/10/88 UE	425
Cupid & Psyche, seated Psyche on draped lion skin holds Cupid; slate base, 25", lot 333, RWS 6/25/88	1,400
Mercury (figure), blk marble plinth w/bronze relief, 33", SLK 11/25/88	700
Pair: Young Lady (seated on stump w/bird's nest or seashell); dk brn patina, marble base, 17", RWS 12/10/88 UE	200
Putti Lovers, seated on oval rocky plinth gazing into pond; 13" long, C-E 10/11/88	352
Vase (dragonfly lady against tall reeds w/lily pads on base), parcel gilt, Louchet foundry seal, 11", C-NY 6/11/88	1,760
Venus, in long dress standing near column holds quiver of arrows; 20", C-E 10/11/88	770
French School (20th C)	
David, standing above slain Goliath's head; parcel gilt/cold paint, rouge marble base, 9", C-E 10/11/88	264
Stag, brn patina, 13x18", lot 948, FAP 12/8/88	750
FRINK, Elizabeth (British, 1930-)	
Bird (contemporary), brn patina, sgn, 20", lot 211, SBY 10/7/89	12,100
FRISHMUTH, Harriet Whitney (American, 1880-1980)	
Crest of the Wave (nude rising out of wave), ed of 200, gr-brn patina, sgn/mk Gorham Foundry, 21", SBY 3/17/88 OE	14,300
Globe Sundial (seated nude holding up world globe), gr-brn patina, sgn/mk copyright 1921, 43", SBY 5/24/89	19,800
Joy of the Waters, ed of 45, gr patina, sgn/dtd 1920/mk Roman Bronze Works NY, 43", lot 2898, B/B 6/9/88	33,000
Star (nude stretches upward), #195, olive-gr patina, sgn/dtd 1918/mk Gorham 0505, 21", lot 2899, B/B 6/9/88	7,700
Thread of Life (standing nude on naturalistic terrain), brn patina, sgn/mk Gorham Co Founders, 13", SBY 5/24/89	7,700
FUCHS, Emil (American/Austrian, 1866-1929)	
Figure on Point, #1, brn patina, sgn/dtd 1922/mk Roman Bronze Works NY, 23", lot 137, RWS 9/8/89	850
FUENTE, see De La Fuente	
GALLO, Ignacia (20th C)	
Woman & a Hound (running), slvr, rectangular base, sgn, ca 1925, 20", lot 296, SBY 6/8/88	1,320
GARDET, Georges (French, 1863-1939)	
Group of Birds, long-tailed birds seated on branch; gilt, sgn/mk Barbedienne, late 19th C, 10", lot 465, SBY 12/12/88 OE	1,100
Setter (dog), #3333B, golden-brn patina, gr marble base, sgn/mk Societe des Bronzes Seal, 12x22", C-NY 2/23/89	2,860
GASQ, Paul Jean Baptiste	
Victory (winged figure), brn patina, red marble socle, sgn, 36", C-NY 5/25/88	3,080
GAUDENS (19th C)	
Richard Louis Stevenson (tondo relief), dk gr patina, 1887, 18", lot 116, C-E 6/1/89 OE	7,700
GAUDEZ, Adrien Etienne (French, 1845-1902)	
Art Nouveau Woman, windblown gown/stands on zodiac globe; gr/brn patinae, marble base, sgn, 23", lot 56, RWS 6/25/88 UE	600
David (standing figure), rich brn patina, separate swivel base, sgn, 32", C-NY 5/25/88	2,420
Ondine: Winged Nymph (running in tall grasses); #3082, rich brn patina, sgn/titled on separate tag, 12", C-E 9/16/88	220
GAUGUIN, Paul (French, 1848-1903)	
Mask of a Savage, blk patina, 10", lot 31, SBY 10/7/89 OE	25,300
Mask of a Woman, dk brn patina, 16", lot 32, SBY 10/7/89 OE	39,600
GAUSS, Eugen	
Mother & Her Children, veined wht marble, wood base, sgn/dtd 1974, 13", lot 132, C-E 2/1/89	880
Two Children (standing/embracing), wht marble, sgn/dtd 1977, 18", lot 133, C-E 2/1/89 UE	660
GAUTHERIN, Jean	
Mother & Child, in flowing robes holds infant; gilt, sgn/mk Collas Fondeur, ca 1900, 27", lot 466, SBY 12/12/88	1,100
GECHTER, Thomas	
Reclining Spaniel, gr-brn patina, carved wood base, sgn/dtd 1842, 6x10", C-NY 2/23/89	1,100
GEMITO, Vicenzo (Italian, 1852-1929)	
Fisherboy, dk brn-blk patina, sgn/mk Proprieta Artistica, 8", SBY 2/22/89 OE	9,900
GENNARELLI, Amadeo (Italian, 20th C)	
Towards Destiny, nude stretches to push cloud-covered wheel; blk onyx base, sgn, ca 1925, 22" long, SBY 12/12/88 UE	1,430
German School (20th C)	
Roman Stonecutter, wearing toga/apron, w/hammer & chisel; octagonal antico verde marble base, 11", RWS 12/10/88	500
GEROME, Jean Leon (French, 1824-1904)	
Caesar Crossing the Rubicon (man on horse), parcel gilt, dk gr patina base, sgn/mk Siot Fondeur, 30", C-NY 5/24/89 OE	34,100
Washington (figure on horse), gilt bronze, sgn/mk France L354, 16", C-NY 5/24/89	4,400
Washington (mounted on horse), blk marble base, sgn/mk Siot Fondeur Paris, 18", C-NY 5/25/88	6,600
GERZSO, Gunther	
Yaxchilan (word means place of green stones in Mayan, abstract), 3/6, gr patina, sgn/dtd 88, 27x24", SBY 5/16/89	20,900
GIACOMETTI, Alberto (Swiss, 1901-1966)	
Lamp, plaster, 1930-40, 15", lot 356, SBY 5/11/89 OE	33,000
Lampadaire Tete de Femme (floor lamp), blk patina, sgn/intl, 61", lot 110, WD 5/5/88	10,500
Pair: Deux Lampes a l'Etoile (lamps); dk gr patina w/light fittings, sgn twice, 1935-37/later, 16", C-NY 5/12/88	24,200
Petit Buste sur Double Socle, 3/8, brn patina, sgn/mk L Thinot Foundry, cast 1970, 5", SBY 10/7/88	22,000
Petit Buste sur Double Socle (contemporary), 5/8, brn patina, mk L Thinot Fdr Paris, 1940-41/1970, 5", C-NY 10/5/89 OE	38,500
Portrait du Pere de l'Artiste (Plat et Grave), 1/6, gr/brn patinae, mk M Pastori, 1927/early 1960s, 11", SBY 5/11/89 OE	170,500

Tete de Meduse, brn patina, 1935, 10", C-NY 10/6/88 ..... **11,000**

GIACOMETTI, Alberto; & GIACOMETTI, Diego (Swiss, 20th C)

Lamp: Woman's Head; gr/brn patinae, sgn, 1937, 20", SBY 10/5/88 ..... **14,300**

GIACOMETTI, Diego (Swiss, 1902-)

Caryatide, golden painted bronze, ca 1972, 7", lot 204, C-E 11/17/88 ..... **2,750**
Chaise (chair), dk gr patina, 41", lot 180, SBY 2/18/88 ..... **15,400**
Chat Maitre-d'Hotel: Version au Plateau Creux (stylized cat w/bowl); brn patina, ca 1967, sgn, 12", C-NY 5/12/88 ..... **30,800**
Chat Maitre-d'Hotel: Version au Plateau Creux; brn patina, sgn, ca 1967, 12", C-NY 2/16/89 ..... **19,800**
Chat Maitre-d'Hotel: Version au Plateau Creux; lt brn/gr patinae, sgn on base, ca 1967, 12", lot 120, C-NY 10/5/89 ..... **24,200**
Console a Plateaux: Modele aux Grenouilles (2-tier table); dk gr patina w/2 glass tops, ca 1984, 36x49x16", SBY 5/11/89 ..... **44,000**
Deux Caryatides, gr/golden patinae, sgn/intl, 8", lot 190, SBY 2/18/88 ..... **17,600**
Grande Table Basse a Deux Plateaux aux Grenouilles (table), gr/brn patinae, 2 glass tops, 18", lot 182, C-NY 10/5/89 OE **154,000**
Gueridon-Arbre a l'Oiseau Prenant son Envol (table), gr/brn patinae, sgn, ca 1980, 28", lot 121, C-NY 10/5/89 ..... **38,500**
Gueridon-Arbre au Hibou (table), gr patina w/glass top, sgn twice, 1980, 26", C-NY 5/12/88 ..... **38,500**
Gueridon-Arbre au Hibou (table); gr patina w/glass top, sgn/intl, 1980, 26", C-NY 2/16/89 ..... **38,500**
L'Autruche (ostrich w/ostrich egg body), gr patina, ca 1977, sgn/intl, 19", C-NY 5/12/88 ..... **24,200**
La Table-Berceau, Premiere Version (table); gr patina, ca 1963, 55x16x15", SBY 10/7/88 ..... **33,000**
La Table-Berceau, Seconde Version; gr patina, ca 1970, 46x14x15", SBY 10/7/88 ..... **33,000**
Modele de Chaise (chair), dk gr patina/cast iron, ca 1955, 32x20x17", lot 188, SBY 2/18/88 ..... **15,400**
Modele de Chaise (chair), dk gr patina/cast iron, ca 1955, 32x20x17", lot 176, SBY 2/18/88 ..... **14,300**
Pair of Andirons: Chenets Carcasse (contemporary); dk gr patina, sgn/intl, 18x20", lot 158, SBY 2/18/88 ..... **46,750**
Pair: Deux Poigness d'Ameublement: Lionne (lion); gr patina, rectangular base, 1943, 5" long, lot 119, C-NY 10/5/89 ..... **11,000**
Pair: Fauteuil Tete de Lionnes (2nd Version), Pieds Anterieurs en Griffes de Lion (chairs); gr/brn patinae, SBY 5/11/89 ..... **82,500**
Pair: Lampe au Chien et au Faucon (wired for electricity); brn patina, ca 1955, 13", SBY 5/11/89 OE **93,500**
Pair: Les Dompteuses (andirons w/busts & animals), blk patina, ca 1960, 14x20", SBY 5/11/89 ..... **49,500**
Pair: Sellette au Ruban et aux Arbustes (tables); brn patina w/glass top, sgn, ca 1982, 18x24x24", SBY 5/11/89 ..... **71,500**
Petite Table aux Caryatides (table), dk gr patina w/glass top, sgn twice, 18x28x28", C-NY 5/12/88 ..... **41,800**
Table Basse Trapezoidale: Modele aux Cerfs et aux Chiens (table); gr patina w/glass top, ca 1963, 17", C-NY 2/16/89 ..... **49,500**
Table Basse Trapezoidale: Modele aux Cerfs et aux Chiens (table); patina/glass top, sgn, 17", lot 161, C-NY 2/18/89 ..... **44,000**
Table Basse Trapezoidale: Modele aux Cerfs et aux Chiens (table); brn patina/glass top, ca 1963, 17x25x19", C-NY 10/5/89 ..... **35,200**
Table Basse Trapezoidale: Modele aux Cerfs et aux Chiens (table); brn/gr patinae, ca 1963, 17", SBY 5/11/89 OE **71,500**
Table Basse Trapezoidale: Modele aux Harpies (table), brn patina w/glass top, ca 1963, 16", lot 181, C-NY 10/5/89 ..... **34,100**
Table Berceau (table), brn patina w/glass top, ca 1970, 15x44x16", SBY 5/11/89 ..... **35,200**
Table Feuilles: Modele Bas aux Grenouilles (table); gr patina w/glass top, sgn/intl, ca 1980, 20x22x22", C-NY 2/16/89 ..... **49,500**
Table Feuilles: Modele Bas aux Grenouilles (table); gr patina/round glass top, ca 1980, 20", lot 160, C-NY 2/18/88 ..... **60,500**
Table Feuilles: Modele Bas aux Grenouilles (table); gr/brn patinae, w/glass top, ca 1980, sgn, 21x24x23", SBY 5/11/89 OE **99,000**
Tabouret en X, Troisieme Version; gr patina, ca 1965, 17x18x16", lot 187, SBY 2/18/88 ..... **24,200**
Tabouret en X, Troisieme Version; gr patina, 17x18x16", lot 186, SBY 2/18/88 ..... **30,800**

GIAVONNI

Young Minstrel, playing & singing/leans against railing; dk brn patina, shaped base, 19", lot 84, RWS 9/24/88 OE **1,300**

GIBBONS, Arthur

Dey (stabile), lacquered steel, titled on base, 1983, 82x21x46", lot 439, C-NY 5/4/89 ..... **6,050**
Wirra, painted stainless steel, sgn/dtd 84/titled, 42x17x10", SBY 10/8/88 ..... **3,025**

GILBERT, Andre

Two Women Dancing (in short tunics/on toes/holding hands), gilt, circular base on onyx dish, ca 1925, 18", SBY 3/19/88 ..... **3,960**

GILBERT & GEORGE (20th C)

Reclining Drunk (ash tray shaped as a Gordon's Dry Gin bottle), multiple object, sgn, 1973, 9", lot 654, SBY 2/23/89 OE **1,540**

GILHOOLY, David (American, 20th C)

Frog & Vegetable Stand (contemporary), mixed media, sgn/titled/dtd 1972 & 1973, 49x96x24", lot 370, C-NY 5/4/89 UE **6,600**

GILIOLI, Emile (French, 1911-)

Angel, 1/3, polished bronze, sgn, 32", lot 178, SBY 2/14/89 ..... **8,250**
L'Ange (contemporary), #sc06, polished bronze, sgn/mk Susse Fondeur Paris, 1947, 33", SBY 10/5/88 OE **6,050**
La Barque de Pecheur (contemporary), gr-blk patina, 24" long, SBY 10/5/88 ..... **3,575**
La Colombe, 2/6, polished bronze, blk marble base, sgn, 8", SBY 10/5/88 ..... **2,475**
La Petite Histoire Cretoise (contemporary), 1/5, polished bronze, 1950, 17", lot 188, C-NY 2/18/88 OE **5,500**
La Vierge Sage (contemporary), wht stone, sgn/dtd 57 twice on base, 20", SBY 10/5/88 ..... **4,400**
Pair: Babet; La Fleur; ed of 5 & 6, dk brn patina & polished bronze, 13"/15", lot 176, SBY 2/14/89 OE **11,000**
Ravenne (contemporary), marble, sgn on base, 15", SBY 10/5/88 ..... **4,400**
Untitled (contemporary), 1/6, polished bronze, sgn, 10", lot 180, SBY 2/14/89 OE **5,775**

GINNEVER, Charles (American, 1931-)

Maquette for Abacuses, painted welded steel, ca 1966, 12x20x5", C-E 5/9/89 ..... **880**

GLADENBECK, Oscar

Boy Fishing, seated nude on rock w/fish; variated golden/dk brn patinae, rouge marble base, sgn, 7", C-E 10/11/88 ..... **495**
Traveler, in traditional peasant garb w/cane; golden-brn patina, blk marble base, sgn, 11", C-E 10/11/88 ..... **330**

GODCHAUX, Roger (French, 20th C)

Le Ripolin (Arab/child riding elephant), 2/15, dk brn patina, sgn/mk Susse Fres Edts Paris, 23", lot 10, C-NY 6/10/89 ..... **4,950**

GODET, Henri (1863-)

Bust of a Woman (upswept hair w/flowers), cold paint, round blk onyx base, mk Med d'or, ca 1900, 9", SBY 3/10/89 ..... **2,750**

GODWIN, Frances Godwin

Hippo-Campus, plunging sea horse, composition, sgn/dtd/titled, 1936, 22", C-E 6/16/88 ..... **990**

GOLDSCHEIDER (20th C)
Untitled (dancer in fool's costume dances on oval base), EL 4/1759, gr patina, ca 1900, 32", lot 468, SBY 12/12/88 ... 1,870
GONZALES, Julio (Spanish, 1876-1942)
Tete Aigue (abstract head), 4/9, brn patina, sgn/#d/mk C Valsuani Cire Perdue, ca 1934-36, 13", SBY 5/11/89 OE ... 181,500
Tete de Femme Couchee I, 5/9, blk patina, sgn/mk C Valsuani Foundry, ca 1934-36, 9" long, SBY 10/7/88 OE ... 28,600
GORI, A.; after
Bust of a Girl, gilt/wht marble, waisted paneled verde antico socle, square plinth, sgn, 19", C-E 10/11/88 OE ... 1,870
GOULET, Lorrie (American, 20th C)
Shadows, Pyrenees marble, sgn/dtd 1981/copyright mk, 29", SBY 10/5/88 UE ... 660
GRATCHEV, Georgi Ivanovich (Russian)
Equestrian Group of Two Cossacks, brn patina, mottled gr marble base w/molded edge, 19x19", lot 1161, WL 2/26/88 ... 1,600
Sleighs with Horses, brn patina, sgn/foundry mk, 10x20x11", C-E 1/12/88 OE ... 4,180
Troika Scene (figures on horse-drawn sleds), golden patina, sgn/mk Fabr CF Woerffel St Petersbourg, 9", C-NY 5/24/89 ... 7,700
GRAVES, Nancy (American, 20th C)
Byrd (contemporary), polychrome patina, sgn/dtd 7-83 TX/titled, 21x7x9", SBY 11/11/89 ... 27,500
Conjugate (abstract), polychrome patina, sgn/dtd 5-82/titled, 62x50x55", SBY 11/10/88 OE ... 132,000
GRAYRARD, Paul
Reclining Deerhound, rubbed brn patina, sgn/dtd London 1848, 13" long, C-NY 2/23/89 ... 2,420
GREB, Nam (19th/20th C)
Egyptian Mummy, hinged cover opens to reveal nude; polychrome, sgn/mk Bergmann, ca 1900, 9", lot 473, SBY 12/12/88 ... 990
Lamp, maiden/lion cub on oriental rug/lamp above; polychrome, ca 1910, 16", lot 475, SBY 12/12/88 ... 1,100
Lamp, rug merchant unfurls carpet/mosque lamp overhead; polychrome, ca 1900, 20", lot 474, SBY 12/12/88 ... 1,540
GRECO, Emilio (European, 1913-)
Danztarice (surrealistic bust), blk patina, sgn, 25", SBY 5/11/89 ... 71,500
Donna Seduto, brn patina, sgn, 1966, 15", SBY 10/7/88 ... 41,250
Grande Figura Seduto (nude seated on stool), gr patina, ca 1961, 52", SBY 5/11/89 ... 143,000
Tiger Attacking a Peacock, gr patina, sgn/mk F Barbedienne Fondeur X, 7x19", C-NY 5/24/89 ... 3,850
GREENBLATT, Rodney Alan (American, 20th C)
Realm (constructed fantasy castle wall relief), mixed media, intl, 1983, 44x48x10", lot 127, C-NY 11/20/88 ... 5,500
Wishing Well (contemporary), painted & motorized wood construction/lightbulbs/applique, 1982, 86", lot 385, SBY 2/15/89 ... 11,000
GREENE, Saya (American, 20th C)
Isadora Duncan Dancing, scantily clad on rocky base; gr-brn patina, sgn/mk Roman Bronze Works, 1915, 19", RWS 8/20/88 ... 950
GREGORY, after
Apollo & Diana, wolf's head at her feet/his arms around her; dk brn patina, circular moulded base, 20", C-E 10/11/88 ... 1,430
GRETHOFF, after
Troika Sleigh Scene (Russians driving sleigh), 18x11", lot 212, DM 10/14/88 ... 350
GRIMES, Frances (American, 1869-)
Pair: Boy with Duck (fountain groups); rich gr-blk patina, sgn/mk Gorham QHDA, 1914, 30", lot 131, C-E 2/1/89 ... 6,600
GRISARD, L.
Clock, nude/baby satyr winding ball of yarn within marble columns; rectangular clock, sgn/mk France, 18", SBY 6/10/88 ... 1,540
GRIZAR (Russian)
Pair: Recumbent Bears; rectangular malachite base, 8" long, C-L 10/6/89 OE ... 2,975
GROOMS, Red (American, 1937-)
Charlie Chaplin, 61/75, 3-dimension litho/Rives BFK, 1986, bl crayon sgn, 23x18x11", Grooms/Shark's Inc, SBY 5/14/88 OE ... 6,600
Dali Salad, litho/slksc/Arches & Japan/vinyl on paper in dome on stand, 27x28x28", Vermillion/Alexander, SBY 5/13/89 ... 4,950
De Kooning Breaks Through, 22/75, clr litho/BFK Rives, 1987, sgn, plexiglas box, 47x33x9", Shark's Inc, SBY 5/13/89 ... 11,000
De Kooning Breaks Through, 28/75, clr litho/BFK Rives, 1987, sgn in crayon, 47x33x9", Grooms/Shark's Inc, SBY 11/5/88 OE ... 13,200
London Bus, 41/63, clr litho, 1983, p/s, orig plexiglas box, 20x22x14", Shark's Inc, lot 1007, SBY 5/13/89 OE ... 12,650
Pancake Eater, 15/31, 3-dimension litho/slksc/Arches/Mylar/paper shade in plexiglas box, 43x31x3", SBY 5/14/88 ... 3,850
Red's Roxy, 147/200, litho/BFK Rives, 1984, orig plexiglas box w/metal crank handle, 8x6x12", lot 446, C-NY 5/11/88 OE ... 3,080
Red's Roxy, 167/200, clr litho/BFK Rives, 1985, plexiglas box, 8x6x12", Shark's Inc, lot 1008, SBY 5/13/89 OE ... 4,400
Red's Roxy, 28/200, clr litho/BFK Rives, 1985, plexiglas box, 8x6x12", Grooms/Shark's Inc, lot 787, SBY 11/5/88 ... 3,300
Red's Roxy, 73/200, clr litho/BFK Rives, p/s, plexiglas box, 1985, 8x6x12", Grooms/Shark's Inc, lot 656, SBY 2/23/89 ... 3,025
Subway, 37/75, clr litho, 1986, sgn in red crayon, plexiglas box, 15x41x7", Grooms/Shark's Inc, lot 788, SBY 11/5/88 OE ... 13,200
Western Eagle, 4/6, oil painted bronze, steel base, sgn, 33x29x19", C-NY 5/4/88 OE ... 46,200
GROSS, Chaim (American, 1904-)
Acrobat, marble, sgn, 11", lot 295, SBY 6/28/89 OE ... 4,675
Acrobats, 1/6, dk brn patina, marble base on wood block, sgn/dtd 1964, 13", lot 120, WD 4/13/88 ... 3,400
Balancing (2 acrobats on unicycle), wood, sgn twice/dtd 1955 twice/mk & stp twice, 24", lot 227, SBY 5/24/89 ... 13,750
Girl on a Wheel, brn patina, sgn/mk Bedi-R Foundry NYC, 1940, 15", SBY 3/17/88 ... 4,950
Head of a Girl, dk brn patina, sgn/dtd 1947, 7", lot 278, SBY 6/28/89 ... 1,045
Mind of Marc Chagall, 4/6, gr-brn patina, lot 280, SBY 6/28/89 ... 3,300
Mother with Three Daughters (contemporary), #1, brn patina, sgn/mk artist insignia, 30" long, SBY 5/24/89 ... 14,300
Two Acrobats on a Unicycle, lignum vitae, sgn/dtd 1958, 10", lot 293, SBY 6/28/89 ... 4,400
Young Girl, dk brn patina, sgn, 7", lot 299, SBY 6/28/89 ... 880
GROSSMAN, Nancy (American, 1940-)
Head, leather/metal zippers/studs on polyester molds, sgn/dtd 69, 17", lot 99, SBY 2/15/89 OE ... 12,100
Head (contemporary), leather/metal chains/studs/rivets/polyester molds, sgn/dtd 68, 17x8x10", lot 62, C-NY 10/4/89 ... 5,500
GUDEZ, A.
Etoille Dumatin, Hors Concours (allegorical female stands on sphere), 27", lot 12, DM 10/14/88 ... 1,200

GUERBE, see Le Verrier, Max
GUIRAUD-RIVIERE, Maurice (French, 1881-)
Foemina, short-haired nude w/seductive smile; lacquered slvr patina, veined marble base, sgn, ca 1925, 16", SBY 6/10/88 .... **2,200**
Three Men (nude/bending under strain of pulling rope), gr patina, sgn/mk Etling, ca 1925, 36" long, SBY 3/19/88 OE **15,400**
GURDJAN, Akop (20th C)
Untitled (nude w/legs about male peacock), painted terra cotta, sgn, ca 1930, 13" long, SBY 6/10/88 .... **715**
GUTZON, Borglum (1867-1941)
Pearl S Buck (bust), marble, 18", lot 385, FAP 4/15/88 UE **740**
GUYOT, Georges Lucien (French, 1885-1973)
Maternite (monkey/baby seated on branch-strewn base), slvr, sgn, ca 1925, 6", lot 329, SBY 3/10/89 .... **880**
Monkey (turned head/sitting), terra cotta, sgn/mk Sevres, ca 1930, 13", lot 328, SBY 3/10/89 .... **880**
HABBAH (20th C)
Untitled (goat head), copper sculpture, sgn/dtd 62, 16x16", SLK 4/7/89 .... **60**
HACKER, Dieter
Atem, 16x14x17", lot 389, SBY 11/11/88.......... **8,250**
HAFENRICHER, Hans
Untitled (dancer in flowing strapless dress, on left foot), gilt, oval dished gr onyx pl, ca 1920, 10", SBY 3/19/88 .... **1,100**
HAGER, Charles (Belgian, 20th C)
Two Elephants, rich dk brn patina, sgn/dtd 1919/mk Fonderie Natle des Bronzes Bruxelles, 16x40", C-NY 6/11/88 .... **4,180**
HAGUE, Raoul
Swamp Pepperwood (contemporary), carved pepperwood on wooden base, 28x63x19", C-NY 11/9/88 OE **60,500**
Untitled (figure), stone, 16", lot 173, C-E 5/9/89 .... **4,620**
HAJDU, Etienne (French, 1907-)
Couple (contemporary figures), wht marble, sgn twice/dtd 1866, 20", SBY 10/5/88 OE **8,250**
Eos aux Doigts de Rose (contemporary), pk marble, sgn on base, 1959, 21x26", SBY 2/16/89 .... **17,600**
Femme Assise (contemporary), pk marble, sgn/dtd 1955(?), 21", SBY 10/5/88 OE.......... **8,800**
Femme au Chapeau en Profil (contemporary), marble, sgn/dtd 58 on base, 20", SBY 10/5/88 .... **6,325**
Femme Bagneuse (contemporary), #1-5, golden-brn patina, sgn/mk Cire Perdue Valsuani, 15", SBY 10/5/88 .... **2,475**
La Femme Tresse (contemporary), golden patina, sgn/dtd 1953/mk Valsuani, 34", SBY 10/5/88 .... **2,750**
Luce (contemporary), wht marble, sgn twice/dtd 1955, 20" long, SBY 10/5/88 .... **5,500**
Plante (contemporary), gray marble, sgn/dtd 57, 24", SBY 10/5/88 .... **5,225**
Standing Figure (contemporary), wht marble, sgn, 21", SBY 10/5/88 .... **3,850**
Two Birds (contemporary), gr-brn patina, sgn, 18", SBY 10/5/88 .... **3,300**
HANDORFF, Joel (20th C)
Serpent, acrylic on plexiglas, sgn on verso, 72x48", C-E 5/13/88 UE **220**
HANSON, Duane (American, 20th C)

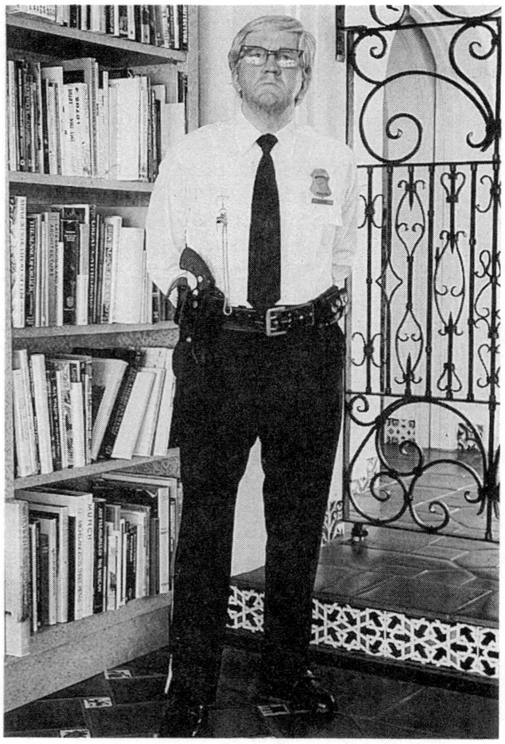

Bank Guard, polyester resin/fiberglass/oil/ mixed media, 1975, life-size, C-NY 5/3/88, $297,000

HARDERS, H.
Untitled, dancer in V-neck tights w/raised arms; polychrome/ivory, gr onyx socle, sgn, ca 1930, 13", SBY 6/10/88.......... **1,320**
HARING, Keith (American, 20th C)
Baby (free-standing sculpture), enamel on steel, sgn/dtd Sept 27 82/inscr, 35x39", SBY 5/2/88 OE.......... **35,750**

HEBALD, Milton Elting (American, 1917-)
Frug Dancers, VII/XII, golden-brn patina, sgn, 16", SBY 3/17/88 ... 1,100
Woman with Flowing Hair (contemporary), #6, golden-brn patina, sgn, 20", lot 298, SBY 6/28/89 ... 1,430
500 Meters, IV, golden-brn patina, sgn/dtd 1962, 19" long, lot 294, SBY 6/28/89 OE ... 1,650
HEBERT, Pierre Eugene Emile (French, 19th/20th C)
Two Boxers, golden patina, separate wood base, sgn, 27", C-NY 5/25/88 ... 9,900
HEIKKA, Earle E. (American, 1910-1941)
Pack Train, 2/20, brn patina, sgn/mk 1940 Dick Flood 1965 Roman Bronze Works, 12", lot 2095, B/B 5/17/89 OE ... 2,750
HEIZER, Michael (American, 1944-)
Circle (East India), rosewood in 8 parts, large circle 59" dia, 4 small circles 30" dia, SBY 2/19/88 ... 15,400
Circle (Houston Deer Island), 2/9, Deer Island granite in 13 parts, aluminum base, 1980-81, 24x3" & 12x3", SBY 2/19/88 ... 19,800
Circle (Maine), 1/3, poplar wood in 11 parts, 1977, largest 28" dia, smallest 14" dia, SBY 2/19/88 ... 6,050
Circle II (Africa), a/p, brauna wood in 9 parts on formica base, 1977, largest circle 33" dia, SBY 5/2/88 ... 15,400
Guenette Deer Island (assemblage), 2/3, Deer Island granite on aluminum base, 1977, 44x37x37", SBY 5/3/88 ... 15,400
North Dakota (sculpture), walnut wood in group of 12 forms, 1977,30/15" dia circles, 4" width forms, SBY 5/3/88 OE ... 14,300
Platform (Blue Pearl), bl pearl granite, 1980, 24x20x8", SBY 5/3/88 ... 6,050
Untitled (circles), 1/3, unfabricated model after Circle (Ghana), largest 48" dia, smallest 24" dia, SBY 2/19/88 ... 3,300
45 Degrees 90 Degrees 180 Degrees (#5), granite/aluminum, wood base, 1982, largest 20x20x10", SBY 2/15/89 ... 14,300
HEPWORTH, Barbara (British, 1903-)
Alabaster Form (abstract), alabaster, 1948-49, 6", SBY 5/11/89 ... 35,200
Figure in a Landscape (Zennor), 5/7, gr patina, intl/mk Morris Singer, 1952, 10" long, SBY 10/7/88 ... 33,000
Horizontal Form (abstract), 5/9, polished bronze, 1968/1969, sgn/mk 1969 MS, 12x18x7", C-NY 5/12/88 ... 28,600
Orpheus (Maquette 2), ed of 8, brass w/string, 1956, 25", SBY 5/11/89 OE ... 104,500
Small Hieroglyph, 1959; 4/10, golden-brn patina, 4", lot 21, WD 5/5/88 ... 4,800
Small Hieroglyph (abstract), 8/10, golden patina, 1959, 4", SBY 2/6/89 ... 9,350
Small Oval (abstract), alabaster, 1963, 9" long, SBY 5/11/89 ... 66,000
Torso (Sunion), carved/polished dk wood mounted on wood base, 1958, 17" (excluding base), SBY 10/7/88 ... 38,500
Two Forms (Atlantic), #6, ed of 10, polished bronze, 1961, 3", lot 162, SBY 2/18/88 ... 16,500
Two Forms (Orkney), 3/9, polished bronze, sgn/dtd 1967/mk Morris Singer, 7", SBY 10/7/88 OE ... 35,750
HERBERT, Emile (French, 19th/20th C)
Thetis (lady in armour w/shield), brn patina, sgn/titled, 15", SBY 6/10/88 ... 495
HERZEL, Paul
Alsatian, rich brn patina, sgn/dtd 61, 9x5", C-E 6/1/88 ... 198
HILBERT, Georges (French, 20th C)
Bulldog (standing figure), granite, sgn/dtd 1936, 16x23", C-NY 6/11/88 OE ... 12,100
HIOLIN, Louis Auguste (French)
Au Loup, male hunter & wolf; rich brn patina, sgn/mk Syndicat des Fondeur on separate tag, 31", C-NY 5/25/88 OE ... 6,600
HISCHINGER
Untitled (4 birds perched on branch), gr patina, stepped circular marble base, sgn, 13", lot 335, C-E 12/8/88 ... 715
HOFFMAN, Malvina (American, 1887-1966)
Bill Working (kneeling figure scrubbing floor), gr-brn patina, wood base, 1923, 9", lot 73, WD 10/5/88 OE ... 22,000
Her Begins New Life (form emerging from hands), tinted plaster, wood base, 1925/1927, 11", lot 75, WD 10/5/88 ... 1,500
La Govotte-Anna Pavlova, wax, sgn, 1915, 14", lot 77, WD 10/5/88 UE ... 5,750
Man Gesturing (full-figure), sgn/mk Bedi-Rassy NYC, ca 1930, life-size, lot 120, C-E 6/1/89 ... 1,430
Matador, gr/golden/brn patinae, sgn/mk Roman Bronze Works, 1953, 14", lot 117, WD 4/13/88 ... 4,750
Oukrainski (portrait statuette incense burner), dk brn patina, wood base, sgn/dtd 1920, 11", lot 72, WD 10/5/88 ... 8,250
Russian Ballet Dancers, brn patina, sgn/mk Roman Bronze Works, 1914, 12", lot 116, WD 4/13/88 OE ... 10,000
Shivering Girl, expressionistic standing girl; gr patina, sgn/inscr RBW 1912, 10", lot 138, RWS 9/29/88 ... 3,600
HOLLAND, Tom (American, 1936-)
Tori (abstract), woven fiberglass, sgn/dtd 1983/titled, 78x54x4", lot 180, SBY 5/3/89 ... 13,200
HOUDON, Jean Antoine; after (French, 1741-1828)
Classical Female Portrait Bust, patinated, circular variegated marble base, reeded columnar stand, lot 790, FAP 11/4/88 ... 1,300
Pair: Companion Busts of Boy & Girl; patinated plaster, circular socle, mk Houdon, 16", lot 302, RWS 6/25/88 UE ... 1,000
Pair: Companion Busts of Toddler Boy Laughing & Screaming; gilt, swivel tripod base, 8", C-E 10/11/88 OE ... 176
Untitled, girl w/upswept hair; waisted gr marble socle, sgn/mk Thiebaut Freres, 17", C-E 10/11/88 OE ... 1,320
HUMPHREY, Ralph (American, 1932-)
Island (wall relief), acrylic/modeling paste on wood, sgn/dtd 1983/84, 60x36x4", lot 91, SBY 2/15/89 ... 7,700
HUMPHRISS, Charles (British, 1867-)
Standing Indian with Shield & War Club, marble base, 19", lot 341, LH 12/4/88 ... 2,200
HUNDERTWASSER, Friedensreich (Austrian, 1929-)
Fall Cloud, Fall in Fog, Fall Out (3-dimensional plexiglas multiple); 92/999, clr scpt, 1979, 11x18x2", SBY 5/12/88 ... 1,430
HUNT, Bryan (American, 20th C)
Colossus, 3/6, limestone base, sgn, 1986, 59", lot 395, C-NY 5/4/89 ... 11,000
Limen (contemporary), copper leaf/lacquered silk paper over spruce, 1979, 9x60x7", lot 272, SBY 2/15/89 OE ... 110,000
Metatech #3, copper foil/silk paper/balsa wood, 1976, 60" long, lot 50, C-NY 5/3/88 ... 82,500
Reclining Linear (abstract), 1/4, gr patina, sgn/dtd 82, 37x42x24", SBY 5/3/88 ... 33,000
Ritual I (contemporary), 3/6, blk/gr patinae, limestone base, sgn/dtd 1986, 72", lot 235, SBY 10/8/88 ... 23,100
Ritual I (contemporary), 3/6, blk/gr patinae, limestone cylinder base, 1986, 72", lot 139, SBY 2/19/88 ... 27,500
Shifted Figure, AP1/1, cast bronze/limestone pedestal, sgn/dtd 82, 21", lot 290, SBY 10/5/89 ... 27,500
HUNT, D. (American Eskimo, 19th C)
Seal Hunt, fossilized walrus ivory/fur/wood, sgn/dtd 87, 14x9", RAB 3/14/89 ... 625

HUNT, Richard (British, 20th C)
Natural Form (contemporary), welded steel, sgn/dtd 69, 23x24x13", C-NY 5/4/88 ... 2,750
Natural Form No 7 (abstract sculpture), welded steel, 1968, 36x23", lot 162, SBY 2/19/88 OE ... 7,700
Untitled (abstract), welded bronze, sgn/stp 78, 72x30", lot 76, C-NY 11/20/88 UE ... 4,400
Untitled (contemporary), golden patina, sgn/dtd 67, 12x15x27", lot 188A, SBY 2/14/89 ... 3,850
Untitled (contemporary), welded steel, sgn/dtd 68, 7x17x9", SBY 10/8/88 ... 2,200

HUNTINGTON, Anna Hyatt (American, 1876-1973)
Mother Bear & Cub at Play, brn patina, sgn, 6" long, SBY 3/17/88 ... 2,970
Two Draft Horses, Winter; #0230, gr-brn patina, sgn/mk Gorham Founders, 7", lot 160, SBY 6/28/89 UE ... 2,530
Yawning Tiger, #292, gr-brn patina, Belgian marble base, sgn/mk Gorham Founders Q492, 14" long, lot 158, SBY 6/28/89 ... 2,200

ILLAVA, Karl (American, 20th C)
Amazon Riding a Horse, blk-brn patina, sgn/mk Roman Bronze Works NY, 13x16", C-NY 6/11/88 ... 1,760

INDIANA, Robert (American, 1928-)
Love, 2/6, polished aluminum, sgn/dtd 66, 12x12x6", lot 192, C-NY 5/4/89 ... 35,200

IPEELIE, Nooveya (Canadian Eskimo)
Walrus, gr soapstone, sgn, 11" long, lot 127, RAB 8/1/89 UE ... 400

IRWIN, Robert (American, 1928-)
Disc (abstract wall relief), sprayed enamel on cast aluminum disc w/2 spotlights, 1967, 60" dia, lot 46, C-NY 5/3/89 ... 93,500
Untitled (contemporary wall relief), acrylic on cast acrylic disc w/4 spotlights, 54" dia, lot 28, C-NY 11/9/89 ... 88,000

Italian School (17th C)
Pair of Candlesticks: Angels (standing/gazing past opposing extended arms); polychrome/gilt wood, 39", C-NY 6/17/89 ... 3,850

Italian School (18th C)
Ave Caesar Mortituri te Salutant (gladiator), octagonal base, titled on base, 26", SLK 9/26/88 ... 1,800
Pair: Angels (winged curly-haired putti w/loose drapery); polychrome/gilt wood, 12", ls/worn, lot 132, C-NY 6/17/89 OE ... 1,980
Winged Angel, wood, 5", severely wormed, lot 137, C-NY 6/17/89 UE ... 110

Italian School (19th C)
Bust of Man (after antique style), gr-blk patina, circular molded wht marble pedestal, 19", lot 125, RWS 6/25/88 ... 1,400
Le Siffleur, Volterra marble, 29", SLK 9/6/88 ... 2,600
Standing Putto (garden figure holds sheaf of wheat), lead, octagonal base on square sandstone socle, RWS 12/10/88 ... 650
Unititled, classical goddess; Volterra marble, 21", SLK 9/26/88 ... 700
Untitled (classical couple), Volterra marble, 17", SLK 11/25/88 ... 850

Italian School (20th C)
My First Corset, lacing her corset; Italian marble, self base, 30", lot 149, C-E 10/11/88 ... 1,430
Untitled, classical goddess on fluted column; Carrara marble, mk Made in Italy, 65", SLK 11/25/88 ... 7,500

JACKSON, Harry (American, 1924-)
Frontiersman-2nd Edition, Pennsylvania Woodsman; #25 & 1750, marble base w/brass tag, 1965, 22", C-NY 2/2/88 ... 6,050
Gunsil (standing cowboy), olive-gr patina, sgn/dtd 66, 20", lot 2920, B/B 6/9/88 ... 6,600
John Wayne, First Working Model; ed of 40, brn patina, sgn/mk WFS Italia, 1981, 25", lot 397, SBY 6/28/89 ... 5,500
Lack of Slack (mounted rider leads tumbling pack horse), #29, sgn/dtd 1973, 16", lot 2923, B/B 6/9/88 ... 6,050
Marshall II, ed of 100, brn patina, realistic rectangular base, sgn/mk WFS MAII 71, 1979, 17", lot 398, SBY 6/28/89 OE ... 9,350
Marshall II, polychrome, sgn/dtd 1979/mk Wyoming Foundry, 17", lot 2922, B/B 6/9/88 ... 11,000
Pennsylvania Woodsman, #14, olive-gr patina, sgn/dtd 1965/titled, 20", Wyoming Foundry, lot 2924, B/B 6/9/88 ... 5,225
Ropin` a Star (working cowboy), #54, dk brn patina, wood base w/brass tag, 1982, 30x23", Wyoming Foundry, C-NY 2/2/88 ... 7,150

JACOBSEN, Robert (Danish, 1912-)
Untitled (abstract), iron sculpture mounted on blk wooden panel, sgn/dtd 1960, 21x17", lot 681, SBY 6/30/88 ... 26,000

JACQUEMART, Andre
Seated Basset & Pup, rubbed brn patina, gr marble base, sgn, 9x11", C-NY 2/23/89 ... 2,420

JEDIEY, Raoul Lamour (19th/20th C)
Untitled, dramatic dancer in voluminous costume; #4, gr-brn patina, blk onyx base, ca 1905, 12", lot 480, SBY 12/12/88 ... 1,100

JEWETT, Maude Sherwood (American, 1873-)
Flowerholder: Male & Female; gr-brn patina, sgn/dtd 1924/mk Gorham Founders QFAZ, ca 1924, 10", lot 2900, B/B 6/9/88 ... 2,475

JOERNING, L.
Two Putti (boy/girl walking & holding hands), golden patina, pk marble base, sgn, 9", C-E 10/11/88 ... 352

JOHNS, Jasper (American, 1930-)
High School Days, 48/60, lead relief/mirror, sgn/dtd 1969, orig aluminum fr, 23x17", Gemini, lot 1076, SBY 5/13/89 ... 31,900

JONCHERY, Charles
Carmen, provocative dancer in revealing dress/shawl; golden-brn patina; circular marble base, sgn, 13", SBY 6/10/88 UE ... 467

JONES, Allen (British, 1937-)
Fourth Man (contemporary), painted wood/plexiglas, 1964, 74", lot 150, SBY 2/15/89 ... 4,950
Green Table (crouched figure supports palette top), fiberglass/resin/leather/glass, 1972, 24x33x57", SBY 11/11/88 OE ... 25,300

JOUVE, Paul (French, 1880-)
Lion Devouring a Boar, reclining cat w/dead prey; blk-brn patina, sgn/mk Alexis Rudier, 38" long, lot 297, SBY 6/8/88 UE ... 9,460
Two Buffalo (battling/locked horns), gr-blk patina, rectangular base, sgn, ca 1905, 22" long, lot 298, SBY 6/8/88 ... 4,825

JUDD, Donald (British, 1928-)
Untitled (contemporary wall relief), pulver on aluminum, 1985, 71x12x12", lot 254, SBY 2/15/89 ... 38,500
Untitled (contemporary wall relief), stainless steel w/turquoise pebbled plexiglas inserts, 6x7x24", C-NY 5/4/88 ... 18,700
Untitled (sculpture), 1/2, galvanized iron, 5x26x9", SBY 5/3/88 OE ... 42,900
Wood-Block (wall relief), #7-L, lt cadmium red oil on wood, stp, dtd 7-78, 21x17x2", lot 234, SBY 2/15/89 OE ... 17,600

JUNGBLUTH, Alfred L.
Elegant Lady (in day costume), #97, sgn, ca 1900, 15", SBY 6/10/88 ... 495

KALISH, Max (American, 1891-1945)
Gold Miner (seated on log), gr patina, 8", Gorham, lot 307, WG 4/23/88 UE 2,000
KANUTH
Bust of a Young Man, shoulder length; lt brn patina, sgn, ca 1900, 10", lot 271, RWS 9/24/88 UE 150
KATZEN, Lila
Echo, steel/stainless steel, 31x32x10", lot 390, C-NY 5/4/89 4,950
KAUBA, Carl (American, 1865-1922)
Die Fromme Helene, girl standing w/hands on hips; blk marble base, sgn/titled, 6", C-E 6/16/88 220
Fighting Game Cocks, 10", lot 956, FAP 12/8/88 UE 550
Hunting Dog, dk brn/golden patinae, sgn, 9" long, lot 273, SBY 4/14/89 UE 935
Untitled (standing cowboy w/rifle under arm), #5745, marble plinth, 16", lot 797, FAP 11/4/88 UE 3,500
KELETY, Alexander (French, 20th C)
Kneeling Girl (nude holds drapery), slvr, fluted oval onyx base, ca 1925, 13", electrified, SBY 3/10/89 5,500
Lamp, formed as stag; blk patina, sgn/dtd 58, 18", lot 9, C-NY 6/10/89 OE 6,050
Male Archer, parcel gilt/dk gr patina, mottled red marble base, sgn/mk Etling Paris, 45", lot 15, C-NY 6/10/89 12,100
Two Birds (in flight as on crest of wave), med-gr patina, square marble base, mk LN Paris JL, 33", lot 331, SBY 3/10/89 3,850
KELLY, Ellsworth (American, 1923-)
Dark Blue Panel (wall sculpture), 8/9, painted aluminum, sgn/mk Gemini GEL Los Angeles, 1982, 32x34x2", SBY 2/19/88 OE 14,300
Diagonal with Curve XIII (wall relief), stainless steel w/mirror finish, 108x47x4", lot 512, C-NY 5/3/89 44,000
White Over Black (abstract), painted aluminum, intl/dtd 63, 72x76x8", lot 45, SBY 5/2/89 OE 577,500
KELLY, James Edward (1855-1933)
Sheridan's Ride, dk brn patina, sgn/titled/mk MJ Power Founder NY, 1879, 19x19", lot 258, SBY 4/14/89 3,575
KENDRICK, Mel (American, 20th C)
Small Cast Iron (abstract), 2/3, cast iron, sgn/dtd 1984-85 on base/mk Canada, 60x9x9", lot 427, C-NY 5/4/89 17,600
KIENHOLZ, Ed (American, 1927-)
Walter Hopps, Hopps, Hopps (free-standing figure); mixed media construction, 1959, 78x34x12", lot 20L, SBY 5/2/89 OE 176,000
KINSBURGER, Sylvain (1855-)
Woman with Muff, in close-fitting dress w/revealing bodice; circular base cast w/roots, sgn, ca 1900, 27", SBY 6/10/88 1,870
KLINGER, Max (German, 1857-1920)
Beethoven (seated three-quarter/clenched fist), gr-brn patina, gr marble base, intl, ca 1902, 18", lot 223, SBY 4/23/88 9,350
KNOWLTON, Win (20th C)
Iron Mercury (contemporary), ed of 2, 1984, 108", lot 279, SBY 2/15/89 OE 22,000
KOCH, John
Pair of Lamps: Companion Seated Man & Lady; terra cotta, wood base, 14", severe cracking/ls, lot 128, C-NY 6/17/89 660
Prometheus, #2, dk brn patina, marble cube base, sgn, 18", lot 125, C-NY 6/17/89 2,090
KOGAN, Moissej (Russian, 1879-1930)
Torse de Femme, 3/6, sgn/mk Valsuani, 20", lot 171, PHL 6/16/88 3,250
KOLBE, Georg (German, 1877-1947)
Die Enkelin (head), golden patina, intl/mk Noack Berlin, 1930/posthumous ed, 9", C-NY 10/6/88 2,200
Kipf Einer Tanzerin (head), brn patina, intl/mk Noack Berlin on base, 11", lot 56, C-NY 2/18/88 OE 16,500
Kleine Pieta, lt brn patina, intl/mk Noack Berlin on right foot, 1929, 15", lot 57, C-NY 2/18/88 9,350
Kniende, #3, golden patina, intl/mk Noack Berlin, 1928/after 1945, 20", lot 75, SBY 2/18/88 11,000
Sitzende (seated nude holds legs), ed of 10, golden patina, sgn/mk H Noack Berlin, 1926, 12", lot 120, SBY 10/7/89 16,500
Sitzende (seated nude), dk brn patina, intl, 1926, 11", lot 74, SBY 2/18/88 11,000
Statuette (standing nude), brn patina, sgn/mk H Noack Berlin on base, 1925/after 1939, 16", lot 50, C-NY 10/5/89 OE 17,600
KOLLWITZ, Kathe (German, 1867-1945)
Die Klage (relief/hands over face), golden-brn patina, sgn/mk H Noack Berlin, 10", lot 122, SBY 10/7/89 OE 13,750
Le Vieux Gaulois (contemporary), 4/11, sgn/mk Atelier, 8", lot 123, SBY 10/7/89 OE 6,050
Mutter Schutzt Ihr Kind I (relief), lt brn patina, sgn/mk H Noack Berlin, 7", lot 121, SBY 10/7/89 OE 8,250
Pieta, ed of 20, brn patina, sgn/mk H Noack Berlin, 1937-38/after 1945, 15", lot 51, C-NY 10/5/89 OE 37,400
Trauer (contemporary head), brn patina, sgn/mk H Noack Berlin, 1938, 10", C-NY 5/12/88 13,200
KOONING, see De Kooning
KOONS, Jeff (American, 20th C)
Bob Hope (caricature figure), stainless steel, mk Esco Products Inc 1979 on base, 1986, 17x6x6", SBY 5/3/88 27,500
KOPYSTIANSKAYA, Svetlana (Russian, 1950-)
Dialogue: N 2 (sculpture); oil/tempera/handwritten text on fld cloth in wooden box, sgn/dtd 1987, 45x61", SBY 7/7/88 OE 17,000
Dialogue: N 3; oil/tempera/handwritten text on pleated & fld linen in wooden box, sgn/dtd 1987, 45x61", SBY 7/7/88 OE 16,000
Story with a Hanger (sculpture), tempera/collage/coat hanger/handwritten text in box, 1982, 32x24", SBY 7/7/88 OE 7,600
Story: N 4 (sculpture); oil/tempera/handwritten text on crumpled cloth in wooden box, sgn/dtd 88, 33x65", SBY 7/7/88 OE 14,000
KORBEL, Mario Joseph (American, 1882-)
Mother & Child, #6, low-grade slvr, sgn/copyright, 5", fitted leather case, C-E 1/12/88 330
KORSCHANN, Charles (Czechoslovakian, 1872-)
Standing Lady with Flowers, golden patina, floral footed base, mk Louchet Foundry, 13", lot 2001, DM 2/19/88 800
KOSTER, E.
Dancing Girl, nude leaning left w/raised leg & arms extended; self base, cylindrical marble pedestal, 18", C-E 6/16/88 550
KOWALCZEWSKI, Katl (German, 1876-)
Amazon Warrior, brn patina, 11", lot 949, FAP 12/8/88 UE 200
KOWALCZEWSKI, P.L.
Dutch Boy, holds stick/stands on rock; golden/dk brn patinae, gr marble base, sgn, 12", C-E 10/11/88 330

KRETSCHMAR
Dr John Hodgen (bust), marble, 24", C-E 1/12/88 UE 242
KRUSE, Max
Nenikhkamen (nude runner), #D729, brn patina, mottled brn marble base, mk Gladenbeck, 16", lot 696, WL 2/26/88 OE 550
KUNO, Shin (20th C)
Untitled (contemporary), polished stainless steel/acrylic on wood mounted on panel, sgn, 1970, 63x51", C-E 5/9/89 OE 2,420
LABATUT, Jules Jacques
David (standing figure), rich brn patina, sgn/mk Thiebaut Freres, 23", C-NY 5/25/88 825
LACHAISE, Gaston (American, 1882-1935)
Bronze Torso of an Acrobat (contemporary nude), brn patina, sgn/dtd 1925, 7", SBY 5/24/89 15,400

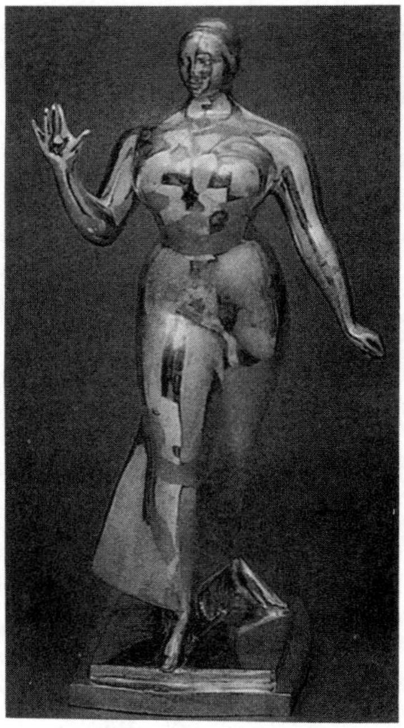

Walking Woman, polished bronze, sgn/mk Roman Bronze Works, 1922, 19", WD 10/5/88 OE, $65,000

LADD, Anna Coleman (American, 1878-1939)
Human Instrument, gr patina, sgn/mk Ideal Castings Co RI, 13", lot 193, RWS 9/8/89 OE 1,400
Pair: Companion Portrait Heads of Man & Lady; gr/brn patinae, blk marble base, 3", RWS 3/16/89 OE 600
Portrait Head of a Young Woman, gr/brn patinae, sgn/mk Kunst Foundry NY, 11", RWS 3/16/89 OE 1,400
LALIBERTE, Alfred (Canadian, 1878-1953)
L'Erminette, sgn/titled, 15", lot 135, FB 5/28/89 2,400
LAM, Wifredo (Cuban, 1902-1982)
L'Oiseau de Feu (abstract bird), 191/500A, polished brass, 10", C-NY 11/21/88 2,860
Pair: L'Oiseau de Feu (abstract bird); 167/500A & 167/500B, polished brass & chrome-plated metal, 10", C-NY 11/21/88 4,950
Pair: L'Oiseau de Feu (abstract bird); 195/500A & 195/500B, polished bronze & chrome-plated metal, 11", C-NY 5/17/88 4,950
Pair: L'Oiseau de Fue (abstract bird); 410/500A & 410/500B, polished brass & chrome-plated metal, 10", C-NY 5/17/89 4,400
LAMBEAUX, Joseph Maria Thomas (Belgian, 1852-1908)
Bust of a Woman, smiling/grape clusters frame face; dk gr patina, sgn, ca 1900, 17", lot 481, SBY 12/12/88 715
Bust: Art Nouveau Woman (head turned to the right); self pedestal base, sgn, 24", C-E 9/16/88 UE 418
Untitled, bust of woman; marble, 11", lot 383, FAP 4/15/88 275
LAMBEAUX, Joseph Maria Thomas; after (Belgian, 1852-1908)
Urn, ovoid, nude/partly cloaked man at shoulder; sgn/mk Tiffany at later date, ca 1900, SBY 6/10/88 1,320
LAMBREAUX, Jeff; see Lambreaux, Joseph
LANCERAY, Eugene Alexandro (Russian, 1848-1866)
Oxen Pulling a Lumber Cart, mk Wolfe Foundry, 20" long, lot 2016, DM 5/13/88 1,850
LANCERAY, Eugene Alexandro; after (Russian, 1848-1866)
Georgian Cavalier, sgn, 24" long, lot 327, LH 10/16/88 3,000
Troika Bearing Three Moujiks, naturalistic base on wood, 12" long, C-L 10/6/89 1,859
LANSON, F. (19th/20th C)
Young Male Singer, holds musical script; brn patina, sgn/dtd 1881, 29", lot 99, C-E 4/19/88 1,320
LAOUST, Andre Louis Adolphe (French, 1843-)
Masquerade (standing figure), lt brn patina, sgn/dtd 1887/titled, 34", SLK 11/25/88 4,000
LAPORTE, Emile; after (French, 1841-1919)
Bust of a Young Lady, waist-length armless figure turned left; circular red marble base, ca 1900, 10", RWS 8/20/88 UE 250
LARCHE, Raoul Francois (French, 1860-1912)
Joan of Arc, #214, parcel gilt, veined red marble base, sgn/mk Siot Paris, 14", SBY 6/10/88 715
Lamp, Loie Fuller, swirling drapery encloses 2 sockets; #1285, gilt, Siot-Decauville seal, 18", C-NY 6/11/88 OE 41,800

LARREGIEU, Fulbert Pierre
Standing Rooster, brn patina, sgn, 5", C-NY 2/23/89 ... 660
LASSAW, Ibram (American, 1913-)
Hliod (contemporary), polychrome brass, sgn/dtd 58, 13", lot 398, SBY 10/7/89 OE ... 5,775
Inscape II, brass, sgn/dtd 77, 21", SBY 10/5/88 OE ... 4,950
Metamorphosis (contemporary), 1955, 72x47x28", lot 12, SBY 2/15/89 ... 23,100
Untitled (contemporary), gilt, sgn/dtd 60, 48x35x22", lot 37, SBY 10/8/88 OE ... 14,300
LATOUR, L.
Bust of a Man, marble, sgn/dtd 1905, RAB 4/25/89 UE ... 250
LAURENS, Henri (French, 1885-1954)
Femme Accoudee (reclining nude), 3/6, terra cotta, 1927, 18" long, SBY 5/11/89 OE ... 16,500
Femme Agenouillee (kneeling nude), 3/4, terra cotta, 1926, intl/#d, 12", SBY 5/11/89 OE ... 121,000
La Musicienne a la Harpe (abstract), 3/6, dk brn patina, intl/mk C Valsuani, 1937, 15", SBY 5/11/88 OE ... 93,500
Tete de Femme aux Boucles d'Oreille (abstract head), 1/6, terra cotta, 1921, sgn/intl/#d, 15", SBY 5/11/89 OE ... 170,500
LAURENT, Robert (American, 1890-1970)
Mother & Child (nude carrying clothed child), wood sculpture, sgn, 12", SBY 3/17/88 OE ... 3,190
LAWLOR, John (1820-1901)
Bust of a Young Lady, wht marble, sgn/dtd 1868, 22", C-NY 5/24/89 ... 2,860
LE DUC, Arthur (French, 1848-1918)
Stallion (standing), rich brn patina, gr marble base, sgn/inscr horse pedigree on separate tag, 16", C-NY 2/23/89 ... 4,180
LE FAGUAYS, Pierre (French, 20th C)
Diana, in tunic w/bow lifted above standing on rocky mound; gr patina, sgn/mk Susse Freres, ca 1925, 27", SBY 6/10/88 ... 1,540
Nymph & Faun, slvr, veined gr marble base, sgn/mk La Stele seal, 20x28", lot 12, C-NY 6/10/89 ... 20,900
Nymphs & Satyrs (relief), gilt, sgn, 15x38", lot 13, C-NY 6/10/89 ... 8,250
Signal Man (medieval archer), parcel slvr/ivory, crenelated marble base, sgn, 16", top of bow missing, C-NY 6/11/88 ... 4,950
Untitled, bare-breasted Egyptian woman on tiptoe holds urn; stepped marble base, sgn/mk France, 15", C-E 12/8/88 ... 1,320
Untitled (nude on toes holds dove aloft in left hand), slvr, veined blk marble base, ca 1935, 30", lot 333, SBY 3/10/89 ... 3,300
Young Dancer (nude on left leg/head back/arms on chest), ivory, gr onyx socle, ca 1930, 8", lot 340, SBY 3/10/89 ... 3,575
LE VERRIER, Max (French)
Bust of a Woman, parcel gilt, wht marble plinth, Belgian marble base, sgn/mk Made in France, 36", C-NY 6/11/88 ... 3,080
Stylized Pierrot, standing w/legs apart & hands in pockets; sgn, 18", C-E 9/16/88 ... 440
LECOURTIER, Prosper
Head of a Bulldog, golden-brn patina, sgn/inscr Punch Tueur de Rats V-a-t-en ville, 13", C-NY 2/23/89 ... 1,760
Pointer Frightened by a Bunny, brn patina, gr onyx base, sgn, 10x11", C-NY 2/23/89 ... 1,100
Setter Howling, golden-brn patina, sgn, 7", C-NY 2/23/89 ... 495
LEDRU, Auguste
Ewer, bulbous ovoid w/face of Neptune spout & nude as handle; brn patina, mk Susse Fres, 25", lot 332, SBY 3/10/89 ... 3,850
Pitcher, nude handle on baluster form body w/molded fish decor; mk Susse Freres, 16", lot 338, RWS 6/25/88 ... 1,600
LEGER, Fernand (French, 1881-1955)
Bateau Blanc (abstract), ed of unknown size, ceramic, sgn/mk 51 Biot on verso, 1951, 13" long, lot 153, SBY 2/18/88 ... 14,300
Composition (abstract), glazed ceramic, mk Ed Originale de F Leger No 3, 12x10", lot 36, SBY 2/14/89 OE ... 8,800
Composition Abstraite, #1, partially glazed ceramic, sgn/mk R Brice Biot AM, 11x10", C-NY 2/16/89 ... 7,700
Composition Abstraite (abstract), 67/250, glazed porcelain, intl/titled/Musse National, 18x13", lot 156, C-NY 2/18/88 ... 4,950
Feuille en Cinq Couleurs (abstract relief), painted/glazed ceramic, sgn/mk Biot, 1951, 10x10", C-NY 5/12/88 ... 14,300
Le Cheval sur Fond Jaune (horse head in relief), ed of 250, partially glazed ceramic, sgn, 18x15", C-NY 2/16/89 OE ... 8,800
Les Danseuses (abstract relief), painted glazed ceramic, sgn/mk 51 Biot (AM), 1951, 11x15", C-NY 5/12/88 ... 8,800
Plate: Visage aux Deux Mains; 111/250, partially glazed porcelain, sgn/titled/mk Biot, 17x15", C-E 5/9/89 OE ... 8,250
Plate: Visage aux Deux Mains; 26/250, partially glazed wht ceramic, ca 1950, sgn, 18x15", lot 649, C-NY 5/10/89 UE ... 1,430
Visage (face), #14, glazed ceramic, mk Ed Originale de F Leger No 14 Ceramiste R Brice Biot, lot 39, SBY 2/14/89 OE ... 12,100
LEMOINE
Dancer, running nude pulling at hem of skirt; brn patina, gr marble base, sgn, 14", C-E 6/16/88 ... 528
LENK, Kaspar Thomas (20th C)
Schichtung, acrylic on aluminum, intl/dtd 64-65, 17x24x6", C-E 5/9/89 UE ... 2,200
LENOCK
Abraham Lincoln (bust), brn patina, 12", lot 1094, DM 3/14/88 ... 650
LENOIR, Pierre
Confidences (fountain figure, women whispering), #10, marble urns/base, mk Perdue AG Paris, 34", lot 224, SBY 4/23/88 OE ... 15,400
LENORDEZ, Pierre (French, 20th C)
Dablan et Jalles, group of horses; brn patina, sgn/titled, 21" long, lot 323, C-E 9/13/88 ... 1,870
LEONARD, Agathon (French, 19th/20th C)
Dancer (in Empire dress w/wide bell sleeves, on one foot), gilt, mk Susse Freres M, ca 1900, 22", lot 302, SBY 6/8/88 ... 3,850
Dancer (in Empire dress w/wide bell sleeves holds tamborine), gilt, mk Susse Freres M, ca 1900, 22", lot 301, SBY 6/8/88 ... 3,850
Dancer (in Empire dress/holds up hem & gazes at other hand), mk Susse Freres M, ca 1900, 18", lot 303, SBY 6/8/88 ... 3,850
Dancer (in flowing gown/drapery, holds tambourine), gilt, sgn/mk Susse Freres, ca 1900, 22", lot 90, SBY 11/17/88 ... 6,050
Dancer (in pleated Empire dress w/long bell sleeves), gilt, sgn/mk Susse Freres A, ca 1900, 9", lot 300, SBY 6/8/88 ... 2,310
LEONARD, Agathon; after (French, 19th/20th C)
Dancing Lady, holds skirt up/hand at chin; sgn A Leonard/mk Susse Freres, late 19th C, 18", lot 225, RWS 9/24/88 ... 4,250
Lady with Tambourine, flowing gown w/bell sleeves, extended arms; gilt, mk Susse Freres, 22", lot 224, RWS 9/24/88 ... 4,000
LERCHE, Hans Stotenberg (German, 19th C)
Vase (Loie Fuller figural), gilt, sgn, Louchet foundry seal, 6", C-NY 6/11/88 ... 1,430

LEVASSEUR, Henri Louis (French, 1853-)
Genie des Arts, rubbed golden patina, sgn/mk Paris, ca 1875, 34", SBY 2/22/89 ... 2,530
LEWITT, Sol (American, 1928-)
A,B,C,D No 7 (2 solid/2 fr cubes on flat grid surface); wht stove enamel on aluminum, 1967, 19x57x57", C-NY 5/3/89 ... 93,500
Incomplete Open Cube, 6/13, wht enamel on aluminum, 1974, 42x42x42", lot 258, SBY 2/15/89 ... 41,250
Modular Structure (contemporary), wht painted wood, 1972, 24x24x39", lot 218, C-NY 5/4/89 ... 41,800
Social Project (contemporary), wht/gray backed enamel on steel in 3 parts, 9x9x9", lot 67, C-NY 11/20/88 ... 5,500
1 2 3 4 5 (sculpture), painted wood, ca 1979, 13x50x17", SBY 5/3/88 OE ... 26,400
LICHTENSTEIN, Roy (American, 1923-)
Brush Stroke III (wall relief), 9/10, epoxy paint/acrylic lacquer/acrylic paint on wood, 1986, 64x27x12", SBY 11/11/88 ... 77,000
Brush Stroke V (sculpture), 9/10, epoxy paint/acrylic lacquer/enamel on cherry wood, 1986, 60x31x14", SBY 5/3/88 OE ... 93,500
Ceramic Sculpture #7 (stack of coffee cups & saucers), glazed ceramic, sgn/dtd 65 in glaze, 10", C-NY 11/9/88 ... 110,000
Modern Head Pendant, unlimited ed, enamel/metal, sgn, 1968, 3x2", C-E 5/9/89 OE ... 3,080
Modern Sculpture with Intersecting Piece, 60/200, plexiglas, 1968, 17", lot 56, PHL 11/15/88 ... 3,750
Modern Sculpture with Three Voids (contemporary), wood/ebonized wood/mirror, sgn/dtd 68, 11x25x9", lot 165, SBY 2/15/89 ... 14,300
Peace Through Chemistry Bronze, 12/38, patinated, sgn, mk Gemini, 1970, 27x43x1", lot 882, SBY 11/5/88 ... 18,700
Salute to Airmail, 43/50, chromium-plated copper, plexiglas base, 1968, 5", International Collector Soc, SBY 5/14/88 ... 1,650
Salute to Airmail, 45/50, gold-plated, blk plexiglas base, intl, 1968, 5", International Collector Soc, SBY 5/14/88 ... 2,200
LIEVERICH, Nicolai Ivanovitch
Hunting Party (Russian equestrian group w/dogs), brn patina, octagonal molded mottled gr base, 13", lot 1162, WL 2/26/88 ... 2,700
LINK, B. Lillian (American, 1880-)
Pair of Bookends: Pan with His Flute; brn patina, sgn/mk Griffoul Newark NJ, 1913, 5", lot 184, RWS 9/8/89 ... 650
LIPCHITZ, Jacques (American, 1891-1973)
Hagar & the Angel, golden patina, sgn/thumbprint, ca 1956-66, 14", SBY 2/6/89 ... 11,000
Hagar II (contemporary), 2/7, gr/bl patinae, sgn/thumbprint on base, 1949, 13", lot 134, C-NY 10/5/89 ... 44,000
Jeune Fille Dansant (abstract), gr patina, intl/thumbprint on base, 1952, 11", lot 112, C-NY 2/18/88 OE ... 11,000
La Corrida (relief), 3/7, dk blk-brn patina, intl/sgn/mk Fonderia Luigi Tommasi Pietrasanta, 1932, 19x24", SBY 10/5/88 ... 5,225
La Femme a la Tresse (surrealistic nude w/long braid), 7/7, gr patina, sgn/thumbprint, 1914/later, 32", SBY 5/11/89 ... 275,000
La Femme au Serpent (surrealistic), 1/7, brn patina, sgn/mk C Valsuani Cire, 1913/later, 24", SBY 5/11/89 ... 264,000
Maquette for Return of the Child, 4/7, brn patina, 1941, sgn/thumbprint, 12", C-NY 5/12/88 ... 13,200
Maquette for Spirit of Enterprise (contemporary), 2/7, gr-brn patina, sgn, 1953, 10", lot 205, SBY 10/7/89 OE ... 9,350
Pierrot a la Mandoline (contemporary), 2/7, dk patina, square wood base, sgn, 1925, 17", lot 4, C-NY 5/3/88 OE ... 176,000
Portrait de Jean Cocteau, 2/3, brn patina, sgn/thumbprint/mk Modern Art Fdry NY, 1920, 14", C-NY 2/16/89 ... 16,500
Slaughterer (contemporary), a/p, 0/0, sgn/inscr Trial Proof, 37", lot 78, SBY 5/30/89 ... 22,000
Study for Bellerophon Taming Pegasus (contemporary), 2/7, gr-brn patina, sgn, 1964, 20", lot 206, SBY 10/7/89 ... 28,600
Study for Our Tree of Life (contemporary), 7/7, dk brn patina, sgn/mk Modern Art Foundry, 1962, 16", SBY 10/7/89 ... 16,500
Terrified One (abstract), 3/7, dk brn patina, sgn/artist fingerprint/mk Modern Art NY, 1936, 15", lot 141, SBY 2/18/88 ... 13,200
Tete (head), 1/7, gr patina, 1914/later, sgn/thumbprint/mk Modern Art Fdry NY, 9", C-NY 5/12/88 ... 29,700
LIPSKI, Donald (20th C)
Grate Book (Building Steam 181), shorthand book/grate/wire, 1984, 9x8", lot 282, SBY 2/15/89 ... 3,300
Propeller (contemporary), propeller/wire, 1983, 23x26", lot 278, SBY 2/15/89 ... 4,125
Untitled (Building Steam 141), shovel handle/bicycle chain/ribbon, 1984, 29", lot 284, SBY 2/15/89 ... 3,300
Untitled (Building Steam 161), wood sticks/stainless steel belt, 1984, 18x6", lot 283, SBY 2/15/89 ... 3,300
LIPTON, Seymour (American, 1903-)
Maquette for Bird (contemporary), golden-brn patina on Monel metal, 15", lot 389, SBY 10/7/89 OE ... 7,700
Maquette for Confessional (contemporary), brn patina on Monel metal, 15", SBY 10/5/88 OE ... 1,540
Maquette for Eyrie (contemporary), golden-brn patina, Monel metal base, 9", SBY 10/5/88 ... 1,210
LOBER, Georg John (American, 1892-)
Doughboy, painted plaster, wood base, 19", C-E 6/1/89 ... 880
LOISEAU-ROUSSEAU, Paul Louis Emile (French)
Baby Boy, nude seated on a cushion; gr patina, sgn/mk Vincennes, 7", lot 325, C-E 9/13/88 ... 385
LONGMAN, Evelyn Beatrice (American, 1874-)
Victory (athlete w/laurels & victory branch), #13, self plinth, sgn/dtd 1908/mk Roman Bronze Works, DM 10/14/88 OE ... 18,000
LONGO, Robert (American, 20th C)
Pair: Songs of Silent Running #4 & #5 (figures in relief); cast aluminum, sgn/dtd 81, 26"/29", lot 299, SBY 2/15/89 ... 23,100
Solid Vision (contemporary), acrylic on paper/plexiglas/wooden frame, 1984, 120x88x8", lot 347A, SBY 5/3/89 OE ... 41,250
LORENZL, J. (Austrian, 20th C)
Dancer, bare-breasted wearing feathered headdress/ribboned skirt; #5044, gilt, marble pedestal, sgn, 15", C-E 6/16/88 ... 462
Dancer, nude covering herself w/mother-of-pearl fan; gilt/abalone, gr onyx plinth, sgn, 15", C-E 6/16/88 ... 715
Dancer, wearing short cape w/bat wing sleeves; gilt, self base w/beading, sgn, 11", C-E 9/16/88 ... 385
Female Jester, standing akimbo; polychrome, variegated onyx pedestal base, sgn, 13", C-E 3/24/88 ... 1,320
Nude Jumping Rope, rope lined w/reindeer bells; gr onyx base, sgn, 6x14", C-E 9/16/88 ... 605
Pair of Bookends: Nude Figurals; 140/105 140 & 140/140 140, rich gr patina, mk Made in Austria, 12", C-NY 6/11/88 OE ... 3,520
Untitled, short-haired nude w/drapery trailing across her hips; gilt, gr onyx socle, ca 1925, 19", SBY 6/10/88 ... 1,100
Woman Applying Lipstick, slvr/polychrome/ivory, gr/blk onyx base, mk F Preiss, 11", C-E 6/16/88 ... 1,045
LORIN, Georges
Woman Dancing (draped nude plays castanets), brn patina, sgn, early 20th C, 16", lot 85, SBY 3/19/88 ... 3,850
LOUCHET, Charles
Vase (floral ovoid shape/one stem forms handle/nude on side), parcel gilt/brn patinae, ca 1900, 24", SBY 3/19/88 OE ... 2,970
LOVET-LORSKI, Boris (American, 1894-1973)
Cretan Dancer (balancing atop bull), polished brass, sgn/dtd 1930, 34" long, SBY 5/24/89 ... 29,700

Danita (head of girl w/long wavy hair), pewter, painted wood base, 16", lot 225, SBY 4/23/88 ... 2,200

LUCCHESI, Bruno (American, 1926-)

Running Woman, dk brn patina, sgn twice, 14", lot 296, SBY 6/28/89 ... 1,320

Untitled (full figure of woman w/purse), polyester resin, 19", C-E 1/12/88 ... 715

LUGERTH, Ferdinand (fl 1885-1915)

Stag (standing), blk patina, gr-veined marble base, sgn/intl/mk Austria, 14", C-NY 5/24/89 ... 1,650

MAC MONNIES, Frederick William (American, 1863-1937)

Diana (standing on one leg), dk brn patina, sgn/dtd 1890/mk copyright 1894, 30", SBY 5/24/89 OE ... 27,500

Nathan Hale, brn patina, sgn/dtd 1890/mk Gruet Jeune Fondeur Avenue de Chatillon Paris, 28", lot 71, WD 10/5/88 OE ... 28,000

Pan of Rohallion, gr-brn patina, sgn/mk Roman Bronze Works NY, ca 1890s, 14", lot 70, WD 10/5/88 OE ... 2,200

MADRASSI, Luca (Italian, 19th C)

Country Lovers, he standing w/arm around her & she gathering her skirt; waisted base, sgn/mk Tiffany, 16", C-E 6/28/88 ... 660

Jupiter & Hebe, brn/golden patinae, self-bronze socle, sgn/Vrai Bronze & Buenos Aires seals, 32", C-NY 5/25/88 ... 2,090

MAILLOL, Aristide (French, 1861-1944)

Baigneuse de Renoir (seated nude), 2/6, gr patina, mk Alexis Rudier Fondeur Paris, 1907, 8", C-NY 5/12/88 OE ... 66,000

Femme Accroupie, 1/6, dk brn/gr patinae, intl/mk Alexis Rudier Fondeur, 1900, 8", SBY 10/7/88 ... 49,500

Feune Fille Assise se Cachant les Yeux, 3/6, brn patina, sgn/mk Alexis Rudier Fondeur, ca 1900, 9", lot 48, SBY 2/18/89 ... 34,100

La Femme au Crabe, dk brn/gr patinae, intl/mk Alexis Rudier Fondeur Paris, 1930, 7", lot 36, SBY 2/18/88 OE ... 33,000

Petite Venus Sans Bras, 2/6, brn patina, sgn/mk Alexis Rudier Fondeur, 1896, 14", SBY 2/6/89 OE ... 88,000

Study for la Mediterranee (nude), 5/6, dk brn/gr patinae, sgn/mk Alexis Rudier, 1902, 8" long, lot 35, SBY 2/18/88 OE ... 44,000

Study for the Mountain, 3/6, dk gr/brn patinae, sgn/mk Alexis Rudier Fondeur Paris, ca 1936-37, 12" long, SBY 2/6/89 OE ... 93,500

Venus dans la Coquille (sculpture), brn/blk glazed terra cotta, 1895, 7", SBY 10/7/88 ... 16,500

MALFRAY, Charles (French, 1887-1940)

Female Figure (standing), 6/8, brn-blk patina, sgn/mk Godard Cire Perdue, 18", C-NY 6/11/88 ... 1,980

Reclining Nude, 2/8, dk brn patina, sgn/inscr/mk E Godard Fond+Paris, 7x19", C-E 5/13/88 OE ... 2,860

MAN-RAY (Emmanuel Radinski)(American, 1890-1976)

Boardwalk (assemblage), a/p, ed of 9, wood/fabric/string, 1917/1973, 23x25", lot 138, SBY 2/14/89 OE ... 9,075

Chess Set, #R32 (on ea king piece), unnumbered ed, 32 red/golden anodized aluminum pieces, 1947, 1-2", SBY 10/5/88 ... 4,675 Non-

Euclidean Object, 8/9, slvr/wood/plastic/wood/steel, 1932/1972-73, 19", lot 139, SBY 2/14/89 ... 4,950

Proverb, 1944; 1/9, slvr, wood base, 1944/1972/73, 12", lot 140, SBY 2/14/89 ... 4,400

Tete aux Mains (contemporary relief/head & hands), 41/90, polished, sgn, 1970, 7", lot 204, SBY 10/7/89 OE ... 2,200

MANE-KATZ (French, 1894-1962)

Double-Bass Player, 7/12, blk patina, sgn, 12", C-E 5/9/89 ... 1,980

Double-Bass Player #0, brn patina, sgn/mk Bedimakki NY, 12", lot 34, C-E 2/13/89 ... 2,420

Flute Player #0, brn patina, sgn/mk Bedimakki NY, 1942/later, 15", C-E 5/9/89 ... 1,870

MANSHIP, Paul Howard (American, 1885-1966)

Baby John Manship (John As Baby), gr-golden patina, inscr/titled, 1928/1967, 79", Paul King Foundry, SBY 1/24/89 ... 990

Madonna & Child, dk brn patina, sgn, ca 1914, 12", SBY 1/24/89 ... 3,575

Sagittarius, golden patina, sgn/dtd 1919, 6" dia, lot 119, C-E 6/1/89 ... 935

Time & Progress: Study for Rockefeller Center; 1/2, gr-brn patina, 1934/1967, 8", Michelucci Foundry, SBY 1/24/89 OE ... 3,025

Wrestlers, 1/2, brn patina, sgn/dtd 1915, ca 1915/1967, 9x16", Michelucci Foundry, SBY 1/24/89 OE ... 8,800

MANZU, Giacomo (Italian, 1908-)

Cristo con Generale (Dalle Serie Cristo Nella Nostra Umanita), brn patina, mk Milano, ca 1942, 28x20", C-NY 10/6/88 ... 27,500

Mother & Child, brn/golden patinae, sgn/mk Fonderia MAF Milano, 1956, 14", SBY 5/11/88 ... 46,750

Pittore con Modella (surrealistic figures), golden-brn patina, mk Manzu Fonderia MAF Milano, 1959, 11", SBY 5/11/89 ... 49,500

Study I of Drapery for Bronze Door of St Laurens Church, Rotterdam; golden patina, sgn, 1967, 23x36", C-NY 5/12/88 ... 24,200

Testa di Sonia (head), dk brn patina, sgn/mk Fonderia MAF Milano, 1957, 10", lot 151, SBY 2/18/88 OE ... 25,300

MARGOULIES, Berta (American, 1907-)

Brother & Sister, terra cotta, sgn twice on base, 21", lot 63, PHL 12/1/88 ... 650

MARIA, Walter; see De Maria

MARIE, Charles

Vicomte du Passage (farmer w/horse & dog), gilt, wood base, late 19th C, 16x31", lot 106, C-E 4/19/88 OE ... 2,860

MARINI, Marino (Italian, 1901-1980)

Acrobate (abstract figure), polychromed bronze, 1954, 19", SBY 10/7/88 OE ... 71,500

Piccolo Cavaliere (surrealistic horse/rider), 4/6, dk gray patina, intl/#d, 1954, 10", SBY 5/11/89 ... 22,000

MARINI, Marino; after (Italian, 1901-1980)

Untitled, wavy-haired maiden in classical dress; square wht pedestal, stepped square plinth, 18", C-E 10/11/88 ... 495

MARIOTON, Eugene (French, 1854-)

Le Couvre-Feu, young man carries lantern/bell; golden-brn patina, square base, sgn, early 20th C, 31", WAD 11/28/88 ... 1,000

MARQUESTE, Laurent Honore

Victory (winged figure), rich gr-brn patina, gr veined marble base, sgn/mk Barbedienne Fondeur, 32", C-NY 5/25/88 ... 1,980

MARQUET, Rene Paul (French, 1875-)

Untitled, young prince holding plumed cap & gem; #4556, gilt/ivory, gr onyx base, sgn, 11", C-E 3/24/88 UE ... 880

MARTEL, Jan & Joel (20th C)

Accordion Player, terra cotta, rectangular plinth, sgn, ca 1925, 15", lot 484, SBY 12/12/88 OE ... 3,300

MARTINS, Maria

Nostalgia (standing nude in grass skirt), sgn/mk Basky Foundry NY, ca 1942, 61", SBY 11/21/88 OE ... 11,550

MARX, Maurice Roger

Cat & Monkey (seated monkey holds struggling cat), brn patina, sgn, ca 1900, 19", lot 93A, SBY 11/17/88 ... 2,750

MASCHERINI, Marcello (Italian, 1906-)

Running Girl, brn-gr/golden patinea, stone base, sgn, 75", lot 107, WD 5/5/88 ... 5,250

MASSEUA, Pierre Felix
Le Secret (standing nude w/head-to-foot drapery, holds box), sgn/mk Decauville, ca 1900, 24", SBY 11/17/88 **6,600**
Le Secret (standing nude w/head-to-foot drapery, holds box), mk Decauville, ca 1900, 11", lot 93, SBY 11/17/88 **1,980**
MASSON, Andre (French, 1896-)
Dans le Foret (contemporary), 2/6, blk patina, sgn/mk Valsuani, 5", lot 207, SBY 10/7/89 OE **14,300**
MASSON, Clovis Edmond (French, 19th C)
Setter Softmouthing a Pheasant, polychrome wht metal, wood base, sgn/mk Salon des Beaux Arts, 14", lot 109, C-E 4/19/88 **660**
MATISSE, Henri (French, 1869-1954)
Henriette I (head), 8/10, brn patina, intl/#d/mk C Valsuani Cire Perdue, 1925, 12", SBY 5/11/89 OE **495,000**
MAZURA
Sparrows (five birds perched on stepped rectangular pedestal), sgn/mk Wien Austria, ca 1920, 8" long, C-E 9/16/88 **770**
MC CONKEY, Murray M. (American, 20th C)
Reclining Male Nude, 22x54", Wichlenski Foundry, SLK 9/26/88 **2,700**
MELANI, S.
Archer, in trailing loincloth w/bow; gr patina on wht metal, gr patina, oval blk onyx base, ca 1930, 24", SBY 6/10/88 **605**
MELGRATH
Head of a Young Man, blk-brn patina, composition cube base, sgn/mk 1960 NZE, 11", lot 129, C-NY 6/17/89 **1,100**
MENE, Pierre Jules (French, 1810-1879)
Arab Falconer on Horseback (on realistic base), med brn patina, sgn, 30", lot 454, WAD 6/12/89 **6,000**
Arab Stallion, brn patina, gr marble base, sgn/mk Arabe, 8", C-NY 5/24/89 **1,870**
Arab Stallion (full figure w/turned head, showing motion), brn patina, sgn, 12x15", C-NY 5/24/89 **3,850**
Arab Stallion (on realistic base), dk brn patina, sgn, 15" long, lot 453, WAD 6/12/89 **1,300**
Brittany Stallion, golden-brn patina, sgn, 14", C-NY 5/24/89 OE **7,700**
Bull, brn patina, sgn/indistinctly dtd, 9x14", C-NY 5/24/89 OE **2,640**
Chasse a la Perdrix (setter/pointer/partidge), rich rubbed brn patina, molded oval base, sgn, 9x17", lot 169, SBY 6/9/89 **2,750**
Cheval a la Barriere, stallion standing next to rustic fence; dk brn patina, mid-19th C, 12", lot 208, SBY 6/9/89 OE **2,640**
Cheval au Palmier, Arabian stallion tied to palm tree; rich rubbed brn patina, sgn/dtd 1877, 11", lot 209, SBY 6/9/89 **2,090**
Cheval de Spahi au Piquet (Arabian stallion), golden-brn patina, sgn, mid-19th C, 11x18", lot 167A, SBY 6/7/89 **2,640**
Chien de Neute avec ses Petits (dog/pups), golden-brn patina, oval molded base, sgn, 8x14", lot 170, SBY 6/9/89 **2,200**
Cow Suckling Its Calf, dk brn patina, rectangular base, sgn, ca 1850, 9x14", lot 175, SBY 6/9/89 **2,200**
Equestrienne, brn patina, sgn/dtd 1865, 18", C-NY 5/24/89 OE **17,600**
Frightened Setter, brn patina, sgn, 8x13", C-NY 2/23/89 **990**
Group Chiens en Defaut (18th-C mounted huntsman w/hounds), coppery-brn patina, sgn, ca 1860, 17x18", lot 165, SBY 6/9/89 **6,325**
Hound Pointing, dk brn patina, gr marble base, sgn, 8x12", C-NY 2/23/89 **1,430**
Hunting Dog (standing pointer w/W on its side), rough rectangular base, sgn, ca 1845, 7x10", lot 172, SBY 6/9/89 **1,540**
Jockey & Horse, marble base, sgn, 18", RAB 8/8/89 **3,400**
Jockey on Horseback, brn patina, sgn, 28x31", lot 2015, DM 5/13/88 **3,000**
L'Accolade (Arab mare & stallion), brn patina, sgn, 13x21", C-NY 5/24/89 **6,050**
Louis XV Huntsman (figure mounted on horse), gilt bronze, sgn/dtd 1874, 25", C-NY 5/24/89 **5,280**
Mare & Foal (group of 2 on naturalistic terrain), rich brn patina, sgn, 18x24", C-NY 5/24/89 **6,600**
Mare & Foal (group of 2), dk brn patina, sgn, 12x20", C-NY 5/24/89 **5,280**
Matador on Horseback, in parade costume; dk brn patina, sgn/mk Susse Freres Editeurs, late 19th C, 36", SBY 6/9/89 **5,500**
Pointer (dog), rich dk brn patina, sgn/dtd 1872, 8x11", C-NY 2/23/89 **1,870**
Pointer Crouching, dk brn patina, sgn, 6x10", C-NY 2/23/89 **1,650**
Pointer Guarding Dead Game, lt brn patina, sgn/dtd 1880, 12x14", C-NY 2/23/89 **3,850**
Pointer Looking Back, rich dk brn patina, gr onyx base, sgn/mk Susse Fres Fond Edtr Paris, 8x11", C-NY 2/23/89 **1,870**
Rooster, dk brn patina, sgn, 3x4", C-NY 2/23/89 OE **660**
Saddled Horse & a Dog (on naturalistic terrain), dk brn patina, sgn, 17x27", C-NY 5/24/89 **7,150**
Scottish Huntsman with Two Deerhounds, golden-brn patina, sgn, 21", C-NY 5/24/89 **2,860**
Seated Griffon, rich brn patina, sgn, 7", C-NY 2/23/89 **825**
Setter, Pointer, & Goose; brn patina, sgn, 10x18", C-NY 2/23/89 **2,640**
Setter (dog), brn patina, gr marble base, 5x6", C-NY 2/23/89 **605**
Setter Pointing, gilt, wood base, sgn, 9", lot 111, C-E 4/19/88 OE **880**
Stag, rich brn patina, sgn, 3x3", C-NY 2/23/89 **462**
Stag & Doe Next to a Tree, brn patina, gr marble base, sgn, 5x8", C-NY 2/23/89 **825**
Two Ducks, brn patina, gr marble base, sgn, 3x5", C-NY 2/23/89 OE **1,100**
Whippet & an Italian Greyhound, rich brn patina, gr marble base, sgn, 6x9", C-NY 2/23/89 **1,760**
MERCIE, Marius Jean Antonin (French, 1845-1916)
Gloria Victus, rich brn patina w/gilt, sgn/mk Barbedienne/Collas Reduction seal, 43", C-NY 5/25/88 OE **17,600**
Gloria Victus (allegorical group), brn patina w/gilt, circular rockery base, sgn/mk Barbedienne, 28", SBY 2/22/89 **7,150**
Victory (winged figure), brn patina, hexagonal red marble base, sgn/mk Thiebault Foundry, 37", C-NY 5/25/88 **2,640**
MEUNIER, Constanin (Belgian, 1831-1905)
Standing Male Figure, rich dk gr patina, sgn, 19", C-NY 5/24/89 **2,860**
MIAULT, Henry; after (French, 20th C)
Platter, 12-sided w/triad of luna moths on stpl ground, lt brn patina, 14" dia, lot 91A, RWS 12/10/88 **650**
MICHIELI, G. (Italian, 19th C)
Liberty with Labor & Family (allegorical group), brn/gr patinae, 17", lot 159, WG 4/23/88 UE **650**
MIDDEGAELS, R.
Untitled (nude poised on right foot holds drapery), ivory, ebony base, sgn, ca 1925, 9", lot 88, SBY 3/19/88 **2,750**
MIKLOS, Gustave (French, 1888-)
Dog, angular stylized standing figure; #27, brn-gr patina, circular base, mk Valsuani, 13" long, lot 94, SBY 11/17/88 **15,400**

MILLER, Carol (American, 1933-)
Clytemnestra with Iphygenia & Orestes (mother w/children), gr patina, sgn, 1979, 39", C-NY 5/17/89 OE 8,250
MILLIOT, F.
La Charge, soldier marching/playing drum; brn patina, late 19th C, 14", lot 98, C-E 4/19/88 770
MINGUZZI, Luciano (1911-)
Contortionist (abstract figure), dk brn patina, intl, 42", SBY 10/7/88........ 14,300
MINUJIN, Marta
Cara (abstract head), blk patina, sgn/dtd 83/mk Fundicion R Buchhass, 16", C-NY 11/21/88........ 8,800
MINUMBOC, Rodolfo
Hommage to Teresa Carrenco, 2/7, total ed of 9, brn patina, sgn/dtd 1988, 52", SBY 11/21/88 6,600
MIRKO
Abstract Sculpture, gr-blk patina, 14", lot 392, SBY 10/7/89 1,980
MOIGNIEZ, Jules (French, 1835-1894)
Cow & Bull, golden-brn patina, sgn, mk w/asterisk, 18" long, C-NY 5/24/89 2,640
Eagle (spreading wings/perched on limb), brn patina, round socle, gr marble plinth, 29", lot 705, WL 2/26/88........ 2,100
Inkwell (formed as dogs emerging from a doghouse), rich brn patina, sgn/mk Parez au Portier, C-NY 2/23/89 2,420
Inkwell (formed as seated hound next to tree), brn patina, sgn, 5", C-NY 2/23/89........ 825
King Charles Spaniel, rich brn patina, sgn, 15x23", C-NY 2/23/89 OE 11,000
Letter Opener (formed as reclining hound), rich brn patina, sgn, 11" long, C-NY 2/23/89 OE........ 1,760
Mare & Dog, golden-brn patina, sgn, 18x23", C-NY 5/24/89........ 4,620
Mare & Stallion, blk patina, sgn, 14x18", lot 210, C-NY 5/24/89 3,520
Mare & Stallion, rich brn patina, sgn, 13x18", lot 213, C-NY 5/24/89........ 2,840
Pheasant (on rocky/floral base), lt brn patina, 20", lot 52, WG 4/23/88 UE 1,200
Pheasant Frightened by a Stoat, golden-brn patina, sgn, 16x31", C-NY 5/24/89........ 2,640
Pointer & a Goose, brn patina, gr onyx base, sgn, 9x12", C-NY 2/23/89 1,540
Running Hound, brn patina, sgn, 3x4", C-NY 2/23/89........ 308
Setter Pointing, gilt, wood base, sgn, 12x17", lot 113, C-E 4/19/88 OE........ 880
Setter Softmouthing a Pheasant, brn patina, wood base, 7x13", lot 115, C-E 4/19/88 OE 660
Stallion (prancing on naturalistic terrain), golden patina, sgn, 8", C-NY 5/24/89 1,320
Standing Sheep, lt brn patina, sgn, 5", C-NY 5/24/89 OE 660
Terrier & a Frog, brn patina, sgn, 2x3", C-NY 2/23/89 418
Three Dogs Playing on Rocks, rich brn patina, gr marble base, sgn, 7x10", C-NY 2/23/89........ 1,210
Two Sheep (ram/ewe on realisic base), chocolate-brn patina, oval self base, sgn, 11x13", lot 157, C-E 11/1/88 1,100
Two Terriers Looking Down an Animal Hole, reddish-brn patina, gr marble base, sgn, 4x5", C-NY 2/23/89 880
Untitled (golden pheasant/lizard in naturalistic setting), self oval base, sgn, 13x30", SLK 11/25/88........ 3,200
MOIGNIEZ, Jules; after (French, 1835-1894)
Pheasant, life-sized on molded base, 28", depatinated, RWS 6/17/89........ 1,200
MOLINS, Charles (Continental, 20th C)
Dancing Girl Wearing a Cat Costume, parcel slvr/cold paint/ivory, brn onyx base, sgn, 16", lot 19, C-NY 6/10/89 7,700
MOLINS, H.
Bookends: Untitled (nude holding train of fabric overhead), blk marble base, sgn, 8", C-E 6/16/88 495
Man Spearing Panther, onyx base, 30" long, lot 387, FAP 4/15/88 688
Untitled (dancer in tight-fitting leotard/fan-shaped cap), bronze/ivory, onyx base, sgn, ca 1925, 15", SBY 6/10/88........ 3,520
MONARD, see De Monard
MOORE, Henry (British, 1898-1986)
Draped Seated Figure Against a Curved Wall, ed of 12, dk brn patina, 1956-57, 9", SBY 5/11/88 OE........ 264,000
Figure in a Shelter, 6/6, sgn, 1983, 72", SBY 5/9/89........ 1,650,000
Hand Relief No 1 (hand clasping smaller hand), ed of 10, gr patina, 1952/1956, 13x14", SBY 2/6/89 29,700
Head of Girl (surrealistic), ed of 9, gr/brn patinae, 1960/1973, 10", SBY 5/11/89 50,600
Maquette for Three Standing Figures (contemporary), ed of 7, 10", lot 157, SBY 2/18/88 82,500
Maquette for Warrior Without Shield, ed of 9, blk patina, 1952-53/1956, 7", SBY 2/16/89 19,800
Mother & Child, Corner Sculpture No 2; ed of 2, golden patina, sgn, 1952, 7", SBY 10/7/88 7,700
Mother & Child, ed of 10, brn-gr patina, 1955/after 1964, 9", C-NY 2/16/89........ 26,400
Mother & Child with Apple, ed of 10, brn patina, 1956, 29", SBY 5/9/89 OE 1,375,000
Oblong Mother & Child, ed of 9, dk brn patina, sgn on base, 1982, 5", lot 175, C-NY 10/5/89 24,200
Reclining Figure, ed of 7, dk brn patina, sgn, 1945, 7" long, SBY 5/11/88 OE........ 104,500
Reclining Figure (Maquette for Elmwood Figure), 1/7, golden/blk patinae, 1945, 7" long, SBY 5/11/89 110,000
Reclining Figure No 7, 6/9, golden-brn patina, sgn/mk Noak Berlin, ca 1978-80, 39" long, SBY 5/9/89 825,000
Reclining Figure: Wedge Base (contemporary); 6/9, sgn, 1977, 7" long, SBY 2/6/89........ 28,600
Reclining Woman No 1, 6/9, brn patina, sgn, 1980, 10", SBY 5/11/88 OE 66,000
Relief: Three-Quarter Mother & Child & Reclining Figure; 7/9, golden-brn patina, sgn, 1977, 7x17", C-NY 2/16/89 14,300
Small Head, ed of 10, brn patina, cube base, 1953, 3", lot 159, C-NY 10/5/89 OE 11,000
Small Mother & Child, 5/9, golden-brn patina, rectangular self base, sgn/dtd, 1982, 4x6", C-NY 2/16/89 28,600
Standing Figure: Pointed Head; 7/9, gr patina, sgn on base, 1983, 8", C-NY 10/6/88........ 9,680
Thin Reclining Woman (surrealistic), ed of 9, brn patina, ca1953, 3x8", C-NY 5/12/88........ 55,000
Torso Shoulders (abstract), 1/9, golden-brn patina, sgn, 1982, 6", C-NY 5/12/88 13,200
Tree Figure, 6/9, gr-brn patina, sgn, 1979, 7", C-NY 10/6/88........ 6,600
Two Seated Girls Against Wall, ed of 12, golden-brn patina, 1960, 20", SBY 5/11/89 165,000
Two Standing Women, 3/9, dk brn patina, sgn, 1983, 6", SBY 10/7/88........ 17,600
Two Standing Women, 8/9, brn patina, sgn/#d on back of base, 1983, 6", C-NY 2/16/89 16,500
Upright Motive Maquette No 9, ed of 9, gr patina, 1955, 11", lot 172, C-NY 10/5/89........ 12,100

Wall Relief: Maguette No 3; ed of 10, gr patina, 1955, 13x19", SBY 10/7/88 22,000
Wall Relief: Maquette No 4; ed of 10, 1955, 13x18", C-NY 2/16/89 14,300

MOORE, Henry; after (British, 1898-1986)
Reclining Female, 2/7, gr marble base, sgn, 13" long, lot 2003, DM 2/19/88 2,500

MORALES, Dario (Colombian, 1944-)
Nude (in repose), sgn/intl/dtd 80/foundry mk, 28", SBY 11/21/88 38,500
Torso, 5/6, stp DM/dtd 80, 13", SBY 5/16/89 15,400

MOREAU, Francois Hippolyte (French, fl 1889-1917)
Chant de l'Alouette, brn patina, pk marble socle, sgn/titled, 15", lot 105, C-E 4/19/88 715

MOREAU, Louis Auguste (French, 1855-1919)
Char de l'Aurore, standing figure w/putto on chariot; parcel gilt, sgn, 34", C-E 6/16/88 4,180
Figaro (figure), 11", lot 499, SLK 4/7/89 200
Genie de la Paix, allegorical figure of Peale; gilt metal, socle base, sgn/mk PAX, 35", C-E 3/22/88 352
Two Women (standing barefooted peasants), gr-brn patina, mottled gr marble base, 28", lot 693, WL 2/26/88 1,800

MOREAU, Louis Auguste; after (French, 1855-1919)
Brise d'Automne, lady w/long windswept tresses & flowing drapery; wht metal, stepped socle base, sgn, 30", C-E 3/22/88 352
Lamp: Warrior (standing w/raised torch & weapon); brn patina on wht metal, moulded rockwork base, sgn, 35", C-E 6/1/88 330
Maiden Amidst Tulips, waisted red-veined circular marble base, sgn, 32", C-E 6/1/88 UE 330

MOREAU, Mathurin (French, 1822-1912)
L'Aurore, semi-nude beside classical column w/vase of flowers; brn patina, red marble plinth, sgn, 25", SLK 5/6/88 1,400
Two Muses, slvr/gilt, 21", lot 327, WG 4/23/89 2,200
Venus, classically draped/gazing into mirror; shaped rectangular base, mounted on slate base, sgn, 19", C-E 10/11/88 1,000
Venus & Cupid, rich brn patina, sgn/mk Susse Fres Paris, 27", C-NY 5/25/88 2,860

MOREAU, Mathurin; after (French, 1822-1912)
Untitled, allegorical figure of a girl reading; brn patina, 23", SLK 9/26/88 2,200

MOREAU-VAUTHIER, Paul
Victorian Lady, gilt, sgn/dtd 1901, 17", SBY 6/10/88 605

MORETTI, G. (Italian, 20th C)
Dante, Carrara marble, sgn/dtd 1911, 43", SLK 5/6/88 1,400

MORICE (19th C)
Napoleon Astride a Horse, golden patina, rectangular blk-veined marble base, sgn, 30", SBY 2/22/89 OE 28,600

MORIS, Louis Marie
Untitled (mounted jockeys jump barriers on rocky base), oval base, sgn, 16" long, lot 211, SBY 6/9/89 2,310

MORRIS, Robert (American, 1931-)
Wall Hanging, cut felt, 1971, 108x120" overall, SBY 2/19/88 17,600

MOSELSIO, Simon (American, 1890-1963)
Cupid Strumming a Mandolin, brn patina, marble pedestal base, sgn/dtd 1912, 7", rpr wing, lot 146, RWS 9/8/89 UE 225

MULLER, Hans (German, 1873-)
Crusader Peter Bischer, brn patina, mottled marble base, 25", lot 701, WL 2/26/88 1,500

MULLER, Karl Hubert Marie (German, 1818-1893)
Lamp (frolicking Pierrot & Columbine), gilt/ivory, gr onyx pedestal, sgn/mk Made in Austria, 9", C-E 9/16/88 UE 770

NADELMAN, Elie (American, 1882-1946)
Female Figure (sculpture), plaster, ca 1944, 11", lot 289, SBY 3/17/88 2,750
Female Figure (sculpture), plaster, ca 1944, 9", lot 290, SBY 3/17/88 2,750
Female Figure (sculpture), plaster, ca 1944, 9", lot 291, SBY 3/17/88 2,750
Female Figure (sculpture), plaster, 13", SBY 3/17/88 OE 8,250
Girl Holding Her Right Foot, #65, painted papier-mache, sgn/typed linen label, 7", C-NY 2/2/88 3,850

NAKIAN, Reuben (American, 1897-)
Bust of Marcel Duchamp, AP, brn patina, sgn/mk Roman Bronze Works, 1943, 22", C-E 5/13/88 OE 11,000
Europa & the Bull, terra cotta, 8", SBY 10/5/88 OE 3,575
Leda & the Swan, 5/10, lt brn patina, sgn, #d on verso, 19" dia, C-E 5/13/88 2,200
Leda & the Swan, 6/10, sgn, 22x10x10", lot 386, SBY 10/7/89 3,575
Leda & the Swan (contemporary), painted ceramic, intl, 8", C-E 5/9/89 3,080
Nymph & Dolphins (contemporary), 6/10, sgn on verso, 13x11", lot 387A, SBY 10/7/89 3,575

NAUMAN, Bruce (American, 1941-)
Untitled (abstract sculpture), resin/fiberglass, 1965, 67", lot 67, SBY 2/19/88 17,600
Untitled (contemporary), painted fiberglass, 1966, 6x77x10", lot 3386, SBY 5/2/88 OE 41,250

NEGRET, Edgar (Colombian, 1920-)
Bridge (abstract), painted metal, ca 1967, 14x51", lot 54, SBY 11/21/88 UE 6,600
Torre Negra (abstract), painted/bolted sheet metal, 1968, 73", lot 33, C-NY 5/17/89 12,100
White Bridge (abstract), painted metal, 1961, 16x41", SBY 11/21/88 5,500

NELSON, Alphonse Henri; after (French, 1854-)
Bust of a Lady, elaborate hairstyle/decollete blouse; gr patina, gr onyx pedestal, sgn, 40", lot 327, C-E 9/13/88 OE 2,420

NEVELSON, Louise (American, 1900-)
Brandeis Multiple, 1/150, orig lucite stand, sgn/dtd 1969 on back, 1968/1969, 4x3", lot 538, C-NY 5/11/88 OE 1,540
Canada Series, 6/6, lucite, stp sgn, 1968, 45x31*1/2*", SBY 5/3/88 OE 27,500
City-Sunscape, 22/150, blk painted wood on metal plaque, sgn, 1973, 13x9", Pace Eds, lot 770, SBY 5/14/88 OE 3,300
Dawn's Landscape XXXVIII (abstract relief), wht painted wood, 1975, 44x26x7", SBY 5/3/88 OE 7,700
Dawn's Wedding Chapel I, painted wood construction, 1959, 90x51x6", lot 43, SBY 5/2/89 OE 253,000
Dream House XXXV (contemporary), painted wood construction, 1972, 77x29x15", SBY 11/11/88 88,000
Moon Phases-Day II, blk painted wood, 1969-76, 36x46x6", SBY 2/19/88 27,500

Night Leaf (contemporary), a/p, 1 of 25, blk opaque plexiglas, 1969, 13x13x2", Pace, lot 752, C-NY 11/1/88 ... 1,650
Rain Forest Column XXI (contemporary), painted wood construction, 1962-64, 92x13x12", SBY 11/11/88 ... 60,500
Seventh Decade Garden VIII (contemporary), blk painted direct-welded aluminum, 1971, 91", SBY 11/11/88 OE ... 143,000
Sky City I (contemporary), painted wood construction, sgn/dtd 57, 93x62x20", SBY 11/11/88 OE ... 203,500
Sky Garden Cryptic VI (contemporary), blk painted wood, 4x11x14", lot 36, C-NY 2/14/89 ... 15,400
Sky Passage (contemporary), 8/150, painted wood/metal plaque, 1976, sgn, 10x6x3", Pace, lot 1177, SBY 5/13/89 OE ... 4,400
Stargate (contemporary wall relief), blk painted wood, 1973, 41x22x3", lot 8, C-NY 5/3/88 ... 38,500
Sunset, 48/125, blk painted wood on metal plaque, 1981, incised sgn, 13x18x3", Pace Eds, SBY 5/14/88 OE ... 3,575
The Dancer, painted plaster, ca 1945, 16x18x8", SBY 10/5/89 ... 22,000
Transparent Sculpture IV, 3/3, plexiglas/metal screws, stp, ca 1967-69, 20x34x31", lot 63, C-NY 2/14/89 ... 12,100
Untitled (abstract), blk painted wood, sgn twice/dtd 1957, 95", lot 131, SBY 5/3/88 ... 46,750
Untitled (contemporary), blk painted wood, sgn, 6x5x2", SBY 11/11/88 OE ... 23,100
Winged Box (wall relief), wht painted wood, sgn/dtd 1960, 18x14x7", lot 90, C-NY 2/14/89 OE ... 20,900

NEWMAN, Howard (20th C)

Avant Garde (contemporary), 7/9, gr patina, sgn/dtd 1986/foundry mk, 14", C-E 5/9/89 ... 3,300
Eve (contemporary), a/p, brn patina, sgn/dtd 1978, 14x12x12", lot 92, C-NY 10/4/89 ... 4,400
Female Torso #5, 8/9, gray patina, sgn/dtd 1983, 8", C-E 5/9/89 ... 2,200
Giulia II (contemporary figure), 2/9, brn patina, sgn/dtd 1988, 13x19x10", lot 313, C-NY 5/4/89 OE ... 9,350
Keeper of the Key (contemporary), 2/8, golden patina, sgn/dtd 1977, 16x13x8", lot 67, C-NY 10/4/89 ... 4,950
Modesty (contemporary), a/p, gray patina, sgn, 1977, 10", C-E 5/9/89 UE ... 550
Oracle (contemporary), 4/6, polished, sgn/dtd 1977, 37x32x15", lot 302, C-NY 5/4/89 UE ... 3,850
Walking Woman (contemporary), 5/8, golden patina, sgn, 1980, 23x11x9", lot 90, C-NY 10/4/89 UE ... 2,640
Winter (contemporary figure), brn patina, 15x8x7", lot 65, C-NY 10/4/89 UE ... 1,320

NOGUCHI, Isamu (American, 1904-)

Appalachian Spring: Rocking Chair (contemporary); 4/6, sgn/dtd 44-85, 41x34x16", SBY 5/2/88 ... 44,000
Black Silhouette (contemporary), anodized aluminum, 1958-59, 96x24x18", SBY 11/11/88 ... 71,500
Ceremonial Object for Marcel Duchamp, marble/glass, stone base, 1963-64, 68x20x11", SBY 11/11/88 OE ... 121,000
Fish for Pebbles (contemporary), granite, sgn, 1978, 13x7", lot 64, C-NY 2/14/89 OE ... 55,000
Head of a Woman, painted plaster, 1930, 19", C-E 5/9/89 OE ... 14,300
Remembrance (abstract in 6 parts), 1/6, brn patina, intl/dtd 44-82, 50x24x9", lot 41, C-NY 5/3/89 OE ... 561,000
Untitled (sculpture), a/p, intl/dtd 84, 22x18x3", SBY 5/3/88 ... 9,900
Worm (sculpture), 1/2, cast iron, sgn, 1956/1967, 6x13x12", SBY 2/19/88 ... 15,400

NORTON, Elizabeth (American, 1887-)

Sleeping Lioness, 1/6, gr/brn patinae, rectangular stone base, sgn, copyright mk on back, 4", RWS 3/16/89 OE ... 2,700

NUNEZ DEL PRADO, Marina (Latin American, 20th C)

Madre y Nino (heads of a mother & child), wht alabaster, sgn on back, 12", C-NY 5/17/89 ... 2,750

OFNER, Josef

Vase (grapes at cylindrical neck/nude sipping at waterfall on side), brn patina, ca 1900, 14", lot 90, SBY 3/19/88 OE ... 11,550

OLDENBURG, Claes (American/Swedish, 1929-)

Bacon & Egg (contemporary), mixed media, sgn/dtd 1961, intl/dtd on verso, 43x35x7", lot 5, SBY 5/2/89 OE ... 495,000
Camera (sculpture), painted plaster, intl/dtd 64/inscr To S-K, 5x7x2", SBY 5/3/88 ... 8,800
Cheescake From Javatime (realistic dessert on saucer), mixed media, 1963, sgn, 2x9x4", lot 2, SBY 5/2/89 OE ... 52,250
Clothespin-4 Ft-Soft Version; painted canvas filled w/kapok on metal hanger/clothespins, 1975, 57x16x4", SBY 11/11/88 ... 60,500
Green Beans, vinyl/painted formica in 18 parts, 1964, ea 2x12x5", lot 15, SBY 5/2/89 OE ... 264,000
Green Ladies' Shoes, muslin/plaster over wire frame, 1962, 12x16x17", lot 7, SBY 5/2/89 OE ... 462,000
Ice Bag, Scale B; kinetic sculpture/mechanical movements/nylon/fiberglass, 1971, 45", lot 195, C-NY 5/4/89 OE ... 41,800
Ice Cream Sandwich, muslin/plaster/wire frame, 1961, 22x22x7", lot 13, SBY 5/2/89 OE ... 407,000
Lightswitch, spray paint on cardboard, 1964, 38x33x12", C-NY 5/4/88 ... 49,500
Miniature Soft Drum Set, 32/200, mixed media, 1969, 10x19x19", Multiples, lot 544, SBY 2/25/88 OE ... 1,980
Plate of Meat, muslin/plaster/wire frame, 1961, 39x53x4", lot 9, SBY 5/2/89 OE ... 396,000
Shrimps on Fork (sculpture), painted plaster/styrofoam on painted wood, ca 1965, 41x30x5", SBY 5/2/88 ... 31,900
Soft Drum Set, 49/200, scpt/canvas/rope, 1969, sgn, 10x19x14", artist/Multiples, lot 551, C-NY 5/11/88 OE ... 3,740
Spectators (abstract), ink/paper collage on corrugated board, intl/dtd 60, 19x14", SBY 11/11/88 OE ... 11,000
Tea Bag, Four on Plexi; 12/125, scpt/collage/vacuformed plexiglas/felt/rope, 1966, Multiples, lot 550, C-NY 5/11/88 OE ... 1,760
Thank You Letter, enamel on canvas, intl/dtd 1962, 5x11x2", SBY 11/11/88 OE ... 24,750
Two Loaves of Bread, One Cut; muslin soaked in plaster over wire frame, painted w/enamel, 1961, lot 286, SBY 5/3/89 OE ... 220,000
Wedding Cake, ed of 8(?), 18 plaster pieces, stp sgn/inscr Wedding Souvenir 1966, 15" dia, ea 6x2x7", SBY 11/11/88 OE ... 126,500

OPIE, Julian (20th C)

Abstract Composition No 63, oil paint/steel, sgn/dtd 83 on verso, 48x42x8", lot 247, SBY 10/5/89 ... 8,800

OPPENHEIM, Dennis (American, 1938-)

Rolling Expolsion (contemporary), steel/aluminum/hardwood/beads, 1984, 36x36x72", lot 226, SBY 2/15/89 OE ... 6,600

ORLOFF, Chana (French, 1888-)

Maternite (contemporary), carved wood, 1914-15, 20", lot 72, C-NY 10/5/89 OE ... 55,000
Mon Fils (full-figure boy), 3/8, brn patina, sgn/mk Susse Fondeur, 1923, 48", SBY 10/7/88 OE ... 42,900
Seated Nude, sgn/dtd 39/mk Alexis Rudier Fondeur, 21", lot 23, SBY 5/30/89 OE ... 28,600

ORTMAN, George (American, 1926-)

Window (wall relief), mixed media, 82x38", C-E 11/17/88 ... 1,540

OSMOND, M.

Bookends: Leaping Gazelles; reddish-brn patina, rectangular gr marble base, sgn, 8", C-E 9/16/88 ... 286

OTTERNESS, Tom (20th C)

Seated Male with Cube, plaster, sgn/dtd 1979, 9", SBY 10/8/88 ... 1,870

PAIK, Nam June (20th C)
I Am the World's Most Famous Bad Pianist, 11 TV monitors in piano fr, 1987, 60x66x32", lot 64, C-NY 5/3/89 OE **110,000**
PAILLET, Charles (French, 1871-)
Cockerel, standing on rockwork base; gilt, rectangular verde antico base, 7", C-E 6/1/88 ..... **165**
Coq (rooster), rubbed golden patina, sgn/mk Barbedienne Fondeur, ca 1919, 37", SBY 2/22/89 ..... **6,875**
PALADINO, Mimmo (Italian, 20th C)
Alla Sicilia (relief), cardboard/fabric/oil/gesso/plaster on paper & canvas, 1980, unfr, 36x42x4", C-NY 5/4/88 OE **27,500**
PANDIANI, Antonio (Italian, 19th C)
Boys Playing with Cat, cat looking at caged mouse; sgn, 20x14x9", lot 2251, DM 5/13/88 ..... **1,500**
PAOLINI, Giulio (20th C)
Intervallo (torso in 2 parts), plaster in 2 parts, 1984-85, 63x32x47" overall, lot 359, SBY 2/15/89 ..... **35,750**
PAOLOZZI, Edouardo (British, 1924-)
Alpha, chrome-plated steel, 1965, 14x42x24", C-E 5/13/88 OE **3,520**
PARIS, Rene (French, 1881-)
Pair: The Start; Two Year Old's Canter (groups of racehorses & jockeys); brn patina, gr marble base, 8", C-NY 5/24/89 OE **6,600**
PARIS, Roland (French, 20th C)
Pierrot, clutches his heart/holds dagger; gilt/ivory, octagonal gr marble plinth, sgn, 11", C-E 6/16/88 OE **1,210**
PARSONS, Edith Barretto Stevens (American, 1878-1956)
Bookends: Puppy Sitting; Puppy Drinking From Saucer; gr-brn patina, sgn/mk Gorham, 6"/4", lot 119, RWS 3/31/88 OE **2,000**
Goose Girl, gr patina, sgn, 59", lot 79, WD 10/5/88 ..... **30,000**

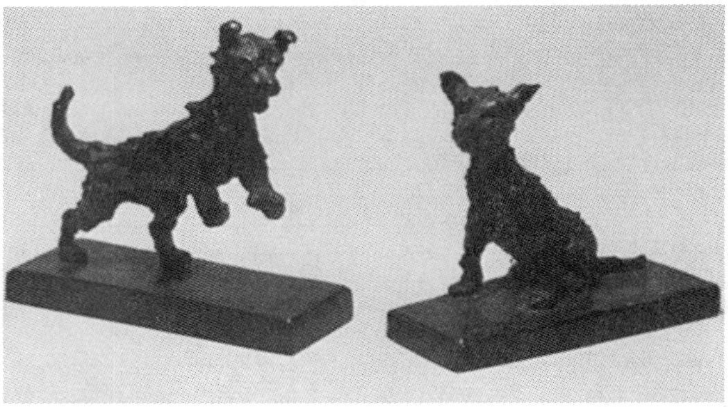

Pair of Bookends: Seated & Bounding Puppies; brn patina, sgn/mk Gorham NY, 1914, 6"/7", RWS 9/8/89 OE, $1,600

Nymph Sleeping Under a Poppy (formed as candlestick), gilt, mk Bonnard Bronze, 1904, 7", lot 122, C-E 6/1/89 UE **715**
Terrior (dog), dk brn patina, sgn, 6x7", C-E 6/1/88 OE **1,045**
PAULOOSIE (Canadian Eskimo)
Loon, gr soapstone, sgn, 9" RAB 8/1/89 UE **300**
PAUTROT, Ferdinand (French, 19th C)
Rooster & a Lizard, reddish-brn patina, sgn, 9x9", C-NY 2/23/89 OE **2,420**
Rooster on a Basket, brn patina, sgn, 7", C-NY 2/23/89 ..... **1,430**
Setter (dog), rubbed brn patina, gr marble base, 4x11", C-NY 2/23/89 ..... **1,430**
Young Eagle on a Rock Ledge, blk patina, sgn, mid-19th C, 10", lot 178, SBY 6/9/89 ..... **880**
PENALBA, Alicia (Argentinian, 1918-)
Sin Titulo (abstract), 7/8, gr patina, sgn, 1978-79, 18", C-NY 5/17/89 ..... **7,700**
Untitled (abstract), 36/300, intl, 10", lot 222A, SBY 11/21/88 ..... **2,750**
Untitled (abstract), 4/4, sgn, ca 1959, 21x47", lot 260, SBY 11/21/88 OE **15,400**
PEPPER, Beverly (American, 1924-)
Penetrative Sculpture (contemporary), painted metal, 16x29", lot 401, SBY 10/7/89 ..... **2,970**
Untitled (contemporary), ed of 2, stainless steel, ca 1969, 73", lot 81, SBY 2/15/89 OE **25,300**
PERELMAGNE, Vladimir (European, 20th C)
Untitled (figure of a lady w/hair piled high wearing fluffy stole), brn patina, sgn/mk Paris 1912, 21", SBY 6/10/88 UE **924**
PERL, Karl
Loie Fuller (wearing revealing bodice/swirling skirts), blk/gr marble base, sgn/foundry seal, ca 1900, 14", SBY 6/10/88 ..... **1,320**
PESCI, Ottilio
Modern Dancer, II, dk brn patina, sgn/mk NY 10 Roman Bronze Works NY, 11", C-E 11/30/88 ..... **528**
PETRILLI (Italian, Florence)
Psyche, bust-length; Carrara marble, red marble plinth, mahogany columnar pedestal, 32" (w/out pedestal), SLK 9/26/88 ..... **3,300**
PEYRE, Raphael Charles (French, 1872-)
Three Putti (entwined together), brn patina, oval molded-edged mottled gr marble base, 23", lot 700, WL 2/26/88 ..... **1,600**
Vase (2 nudes playing hide & seek among iris/slvr iris blossoms at neck), parcel gilt, ca 1900, 19", lot 91, SBY 3/19/88 ..... **3,630**
PFAFF, Judy (American, 20th C)
Circe (abstract wall relief), mixed media collage, 1982, 72x144x6", SBY 11/11/88 ..... **30,250**
PHILIPPE, Louis (19th C)
Greek Revival Kantharos, Bacchic masks in high relief w/vine handles/circular foot, dk brn patina, 7", RWS 12/10/88 OE **425**
PHILIPPE, Paul (French, 20th C)
Adoration, standing female clown; cold paint/ivory, gr marble base, 15", lot 16, C-NY 6/10/89 ..... **4,950**
Radha (in jeweled halter/headress/swirling skirt, arms upheld), polychrome/gilt, marble socle, ca 1925, 22", SBY 3/19/88 ..... **3,300**
Russian Dancer, in pirouette/ruffled dress & dangling belt; waisted pk/wht marble socle, ca 1925, 22", SBY 12/12/88 ..... **2,750**

Russian Dancer (in long ruffled skirt stands on one leg), gilt/ivory, brn onyx socle, sgn, ca 1925, 24", SBY 11/17/88 7,150
Untitled (nude on toes stretches upon awakening), ivory, brn onyx base, sgn, ca 1930, 8", lot 89, SBY 3/19/88 OE 4,400

PHILIPPE, Paul; att (French, 20th C)
Nude Yawning, arms outstretched, gilt, gr marble base, 18", C-E 9/16/88 605

PICASSO, Pablo (Spanish, 1881-1973)
Bacchante, 2/2 & 1708/1692, 23-karat gold, Francois Hugo Marseille hallmark, 1960/1967, 5", fitted case, SBY 10/7/88 22,000
Centaure, 1/2 & 1711/1666, 23-karat gold, sgn/Francois Hugo Marseille hallmark, 1960/1967, 5", case, SBY 10/7/88 20,900
Charger: Nature Morte a la Cuiller; ed of 100, wht ceramic, sgn/mk Madoura, 1952, 13x13", lot 484, C-NY 11/1/88 1,760
Face of a Bearded Man, 2/2, golden patina, 1950, 3", Godard Fondeurs, SBY 2/6/89 11,000
Femme Debout (contemporary), 6/10, lt brn patina, sgn/mk Valsuani, 1945, 8", lot 146, SBY 2/18/88 OE 24,200
Ice Jug: Visage; 48/100, glazed bl/wht ceramic, sgn/mk Madoura, ca 1951, 14", lot 483, C-NY 11/1/88 8,250
Le Joueur de Cymballes, 1/2 & 2388/1694, 23-karat gold, sgn/Francois Hugo hallmark, 1960/1967, 6", case, SBY 10/7/88 20,900
Le Joueur de Pipeaux, 2/2 & 2387/1693, 23-karat gold, sgn/Francois Hugo hallmark, 1960, 6", fitted case, SBY 10/7/88 20,900
Petit Nu (surrealistic nude), 2/10, gr patina, 1945, 7", SBY 5/11/89 OE 93,500
Pitcher: Faune Cavalier; 36/300, glazed ceramic, sgn/mk Madoura Plein Feu, 1952, 9", C-E 5/9/89 5,500
Pitcher: Grand Pichet aux Deux Visages; 38/75, glazed ceramic, mk Madoura/Plein Feu, 30", lot 339, C-NY 5/12/88 OE 41,800
Pitcher: Hibou; glazed ceramic, sgn/mk Madoura Plein Fue, 11", C-NY 10/6/88 OE 4,400
Pitcher: Terre de Faience; 221/300, bl/blk/gray partially glazed ceramic, ca 1945, sgn, 9", lot 175, PHL 6/16/88 3,250
Pitcher: Visage de Femme; painted/partially glazed ceramic, sgn/mk Madoura, 12", C-NY 10/6/88 OE 3,080
Pitcher: Visage; #R137 & 252/350, partially glazed ceramic, sgn/mk Madoura Plein Fue, 1969, 14", C-E 5/13/88 6,600
Pitcher: Visage; 175/200, partially glazed ceramic, sgn/dtd 9-1-69/mk Madoura, 1969, 14", C-NY 10/6/88 6,050
Pitcher: Visage; 39/300, partially glazed ceramic, sgn/mk Madoura, 9" dia, C-NY 10/6/88 2,640
Plate: Masque (happy face); K 121 122/300, partially glazed painted ceramic, sgn/mk Madoura, 8x8", lot 169, C-NY 2/18/88 1,980
Plate: Quatre Danseurs; ed of 450, partially glazed ceramic, 1956, sgn/mk Madoura, 10" dia, lot 65, RWS 9/8/89 2,200
Plate: Satyr; partially dated ceramic, sgn/dtd Picasso 12.7.56 on verso, 1956, 6x6", lot 207, C-NY 2/18/88 8,800
Plate: Tete de Lion; 36/100, glazed ceramic, sgn/mk J 119 Madoura Plein Feu, 1968-69, 17x17", C-E 5/9/89 OE 6,600
Plate: Visage d'Homme; 20/50, partially glazed ceramic, sgn/mk Madoura J 112A, 1968-69, 12x12", C-NY 10/6/88 OE 5,280
Plate: Visage; #212/500, glazed ceramic, sgn/mk Madoura, 10" dia, C-NY 10/6/88 2,310
Platter: Bouquet a la Pomme; ed of 400, partially glazed ceramic, sgn/mk Madoura Plein Feu, 1956, 10" dia, C-E 5/9/89 2,860
Platter: Joueur de Flute et Chevre; ed of 450, glazed ceramic, sgn/mk Madoura Plein Feu, 1956, 10" dia, C-NY 10/6/88 2,090
Platter: Joueur de Flute et Chevre; ed of 450, partially glazed ceramic, sgn/mk Madoura Feu, 1956, 10x10", C-E 5/9/89 OE 2,860
Platter: Paysage (house/crescent moon); #100 140/200, partially glazed ceramic, 1953, 17" dia, lot 164, C-NY 2/18/88 OE 4,950
Platter: Paysage; 165/200, blk/bl/gr/brn/yel/wht on blk slip-glazed ceramic, 1953, 16" dia, lot 485, C-NY 11/1/88 4,950
Platter: Paysage; 88/200, partially glazed ceramic, sgn/mk Madoura Plein Feu, 1953, 17" dia, C-NY 10/6/88 OE 5,280
Platter: Picador (matadors); glazed ceramic, mk Original de Picasso Madoura, 1949, 15" dia, lot 167, C-NY 2/18/88 3,300
Platter: Poissons; 56/200, glazed ceramic, sgn/mk Madoura Plein Feu I.III, 1947, 13x15", C-E 5/9/89 OE 4,620
Platter: Tere de Satyre; F210 & 99/200, partially glazed ceramic, sgn/mk Empreinte Originle, 1956, 17", C-E 5/13/88 OE 4,950
Platter: Tete au Masque; 10/20, slvr repousse/chased on hammered ground, mk Francois/Pierre Hugo, 12" dia, SBY 2/18/88 16,500
Platter: Tete de Chevre de Profil; ed of 50, glazed ceramic, sgn/mk Madoura, 10" dia, lot 482, C-NY 11/1/88 OE 3,410
Platter: Visage (bearded man); #I.121 79/350, glazed ceramic, sgn/mk Madoura, 14" dia, lot 165, C-NY 2/18/88 OE 2,750
Platter: Visage (man w/small mustache); #I.120 119/500, glazed ceramic, mk Madoura, 14" dia, lot 166, C-NY 2/18/88 OE 4,180
Platter: Visage aux Taches; 15/100, partially glazed ceramic, sgn/mk C118 Bis Madoura, 1956, 17", C-E 5/9/89 OE 6,050
Platter: Visage en Carton Ondule; 18/20, slvr repousse/chased on hammered ground, sgn, 1957, 17" dia, C-NY 2/16/89 OE 24,200
Platter: Visage Geometrique aux Traits; 9/20, slvr repousse/chased on hammered ground, 16" dia, lot 170, SBY 2/18/88 11,000
Vase: Arenes; 50/100, unglazed ceramic, sgn/mk Madoura Plein Feu, 1958, 12", C-E 5/9/89 OE 15,400
Vase: Chouette Blanche; 183/350, partially glazed ceramic, sgn/mk Madoura Plein Feu, 1969, 12", C-E 5/9/89 4,180
Vase: Chouette Noire; 53/500, partially glazed ceramic, sgn/mk Madoura Plein Feu, 1969, 12", C-E 5/9/89 OE 4,400
Vase: Chouette Orange; R 146 & 124/500, partially glazed ceramic, sgn/mk Madoura Plein Feu, 12", C-E 5/13/88 OE 5,500
Vase: Chouette Orange; 278/500, partially glazed ceramic, sgn/mk Madoura Plein Feu, 12", C-NY 10/6/88 3,840
Vase: Chouette; 45/200, partially glazed ceramic, sgn/mk Madoura, 11", C-NY 10/6/88 4,400
Vase: Female Form; 63/100, unglazed ceramic, sgn/mk Madoura, 14", lot 75, WD 11/16/88 OE 4,500
Vase: Grande Vase aux Femmes Nues; unglazed terra cotta, sgn/mk Madoura, 1950, 26", lot 149, SBY 2/18/88 77,000
Vase: Grande Vase Carre Hibou; painted/partially glazed ceramic, sgn twice, 1954, 20", SBY 5/11/89 OE 165,000
Vase: Gros Oiseau, Double Visage; #22, ed of 25, terra cotta, sgn/mk Madoura, 1951, 23", lot 150, SBY 2/18/88 OE 41,250
Vase: Gros Oiseau (double-handled); 30/75, painted ceramic, sgn/mk Madoura Plein Feu, 1953, 22", C-NY 5/12/88 38,500
Vase: Hibou Noire (bird); partially glazed ceramic, 100/500, mk Ed Picasso Madoura, 11", lot 168, C-NY 2/18/88 OE 8,250
Vase: Terre de Faience (bird); 135/500, gray-brn/wht/blk ceramic, sgn/mk Madoura, 12", lot 174, PHL 6/16/88 4,250

PICASSO, Pablo; after (Spanish, 1881-1973)
Bearded Man, by Francois Hugo, 20/20, 23-karat gold pendant, 1974, 3" dia, orig case, SBY 10/5/88 4,950
Big Bearded Mask, by Francois Hugo, #1, 23-karat gold pendant, 1972, 3x5", orig case, SBY 10/5/88 10,450
Fish, by Francois Hugo, #1, 23-karat gold pendant, sgn, 1970s, 2x2", SBY 10/5/88 4,125

PICAULT, Emile Louis (French, fl 1863-1909)
Bonaparte (bust), chocolate brn patina, verde antico marble plinth, sgn/titled, 9", lot 156, C-E 11/1/88 528
La Vallance, seated Roman soldier; chocolate-brn patina, self base, mk Salon des Beaux Arts, 25", lot 160, C-E 11/1/88 3,080
Napoleon Bonaparte (bust), rich red/brn patinae, sgn, ca late 19th C, 23", SBY 2/22/89 OE 12,100
Vox Progressi, allegorical group; brn patina, sgn/mk Vox Progressi Ambula Semper Beaux Arts, 46", C-NY 5/25/88 OE 8,800

PICCIRILLI, Attilio (American, 1868-1945)
Boy (head w/wavy hair), rubbed blk patina, rectangular marble base, sgn/mk Zoppo, 19", lot 226, SBY 4/23/88 OE 2,640
Flower of the Alps (standing nude), blk-brn patina, sgn/mk Fecit NY 1916, 25", C-E 11/30/88 2,200

PINTO, Lorraine
Mother & Child, brn patina, veined marble base, sgn, 26", lot 299, PHL 10/28/88 600

PLANCKH, Victor
Head of a Woman Wearing a Turban, blk patina, sgn/dtd, 14", C-E 1/12/88 OE ... 550
PLAZZOTTA, Enzo (Italian, 20th C)
Anthony Dowell Rehearsing for Oberon, 2/9, brn patina, mk Plazzotta, 15", C-E 5/13/88 ... 2,640
Nadia Nerina, Rehearsal II; brn patina, mk Fonderia Luiti Tomassi Pietrasanta, 34", C-E 5/13/88 OE ... 6,820
Reflection, 3/9, brn patina/polished steel, mk Plazzotta, 15", C-E 5/13/88 ... 2,640
PLUTARCH, after
Prosperine, dk brn patina, self base, 21", lot 159, C-E 11/1/88 ... 2,090
POERTZEL, Otto (German, 1876-)
Columbine & Harlequin (dancing), polychrome/ivory, domed gr marble base, ca 1925, 14", SBY 3/10/89 ... 16,500
Flower Seller, North African turbanned child; polychrome/ivory/gilt, tiered marble base, sgn, 13", SBY 6/10/88 ... 825
POLEO, Hector (Venezuelan, 1918-)
Goajira (standing female), 2/7, sgn/dtd 1957-1988, 24", SBY 5/16/89 ... 8,800
POMODORO, Arnaldo (Italian, 1926-)
Disc #1 (abstract), 1/2, bronze on metal base, 1964, 27" dia, 30", SBY 2/19/88 OE ... 66,000
Maquette, GB .02 PA; polished bronze, 4" dia, C-E 5/13/88 OE ... 4,400
Silver Sculpture (Untitled), 1/2, slvr relief mounted on wood, sgn/dtd 68, 13x11", SBY 5/3/88 ... 14,300
Torre a Spirale II (contemporary), #7, ed of 9, gold-plated bronze, titled, 1985, 17x6x6", SBY 11/11/88 ... 13,200
Untitled (Burst Globe), ed of 2, 15", lot 49, SBY 10/6/88 ... 37,400
POMODORO, Gio (Italian, 1930-)
Head, A Unique Piece, 1958 (abstract); 13", lot 230, RWS 3/16/89 UE ... 1,600
PRADIER, Jean Jacques (French, 1792-1852)
Baigneuse, female figure; rich gr-brn patina, sgn/mk Duplan+Salles, 21", C-NY 11/26/88 ... 4,400
Hebe, Jupiter & Hebe; slvr, red veined marble base, sgn/mk Susse Fres, 23", C-NY 11/26/88 ... 11,000
Phryne, allegorical figure of slave girl; rich reddish-brn patina, sgn/mk Susse Fres R, 21", C-NY 5/24/89 ... 3,300
Phryne, standing slave girl; rich gr-brn patina, sgn/mk Susse Fres, 15", C-NY 11/26/88 ... 1,750
PRADIER, Jean Jacques; after (French, 1792-1852)
Lamp (seated maiden w/lyre, 2 scroll arms ending in glass nozzles); spelter, mk Susse Freres, 18", C-E 10/11/88 UE ... 300
PREISS, Johann Philip Ferdinand (German, 1882-1943)
Aphrodite (semi-nude/arms behind head fixing hair), polychrome/ivory, gr onyx base, ca 1925, 9", lot 347, SBY 3/10/88 ... 5,500
Aphrodite Holding a Bowl of Fruit, cold paint/ivory, gr veined marble base, sgn, 9", lot 20, C-NY 6/10/89 ... 4,950
Archer, young huntress standing w/drawn bow; polychrome/ivory, gr onyx base w/4 ivory ball feet, 9", C-E 9/16/88 ... 6,380
Archer (semi-nude w/drawn bow), polychrome/ivory, rectangular gr onyx base, sgn/mk Germany, ca 1930, 10", SBY 11/17/89 ... 11,000
Archer (w/upraised bow & arrow), cold paint/ivory, gr/brn onyx base, sgn/mk Kassler seal, 25", lot 27, C-NY 6/10/89 ... 27,500
Balancing (figure bending backward w/ball), cold paint/ivory, Belgian marble base, sgn, 15", lot 25, C-NY 6/10/89 OE ... 15,400
Bather with Cap on Rock, polychrome/ivory, faceted onyx base, sgn/mk Kassler, ca 1925, 10", SBY 6/8/88 OE ... 34,100
Bookends: Pierot; Pierette; slvr/ivory, brn onyx base, sgn/mk Made in France, 9", C-E 6/16/88 OE ... 2,420
Clock: Bat Dancer (female dancer on clock base), polychrome/ivory, onyx clock base, ca 1925, 15", lot 336, SBY 3/10/89 ... 5,775
Dancer (flowing hair/out-stretched arms/holds tambourine), gilt/ivory, marble base, ca 1930, 14", lot 84, SBY 11/17/88 ... 6,600
Dancing Girl, cold paint/ivory, gr onyx/Belgian marble base, sgn, 10", lot 22, C-NY 6/10/89 ... 4,620
Diver (poised to dive), polychrome/ivory, truncated gr/blk onyx base, sgn/mk Kessler, ca 1930, 10", SBY 6/8/88 OE ... 28,600
Flame Leaper (figure w/torches leaps over flames), cold paint/ivory/amber, marble base, mk Kassler, lot 26, C-NY 6/10/89 ... 33,000
Javelin Thrower, polychrome/ivory, gr/blk onyx rectangular base, sgn, ca 1935, 12", lot 311, SBY 6/8/88 ... 17,600
Space Lady (in slvr-bl dress/elaborate webbed headdress), polychrome/ivory, marble base, ca 1925, 20", SBY 3/10/89 ... 17,600
Spring, classical maiden leaning on wall by fountain; gilt/ivory/marble, sgn, 7", C-E 6/16/88 ... 5,720
Torch Dancer (semi-nude/on one leg), polychrome/ivory, blk/gr onyx pyramidal base, intl, ca 1930, 14", SBY 6/8/88 OE ... 10,450
Torch Dancer (wearing pantaloons), polychrome/ivory, gilt pedestal, blk marble/onyx base, ca 1925, 16", SBY 3/10/89 ... 16,500
Untitled, young dancer en pointe w/extended arms; polychrome/ivory, octagonal gr onyx base, sgn, 7", C-E 12/8/88 ... 1,210
Untitled (nude pinning flowers in long hair), ivory, gr onyx socle, ca 1915, 7", socle cracked, lot 87, SBY 11/17/88 ... 3,300
Woman & Mare (both standing), polychrome/ivory, rectangular bronze/blk onyx base, ca 1930, 17", SBY 11/17/88 ... 16,500
PRICE, Robert (20th C)
Sex (contemporary), wood/aluminum/plexiglas, 1986, 69x83x13", lot 416, C-NY 5/4/89 UE ... 1,100
PRIVAT, Gilbert (French, 1892-1969)
Young Woman Holding Fawn, patinated, sgn, 13", lot 788, FAP 11/4/88 UE ... 350
PUCCINELLI, Raimondo
L'Ondo, gr-brn patina, sgn, 20", lot 196, SBY 10/5/88 UE ... 220
PUERA, Margarita (East European, 20th C)
Figure & Birds, patinated, 23", lot 789, FAP 11/4/88 UE ... 425
PURYEAR, Martin (20th C)
Untitled (contemporary), osage/orange/yel pine/ash woods, 1978, 67", lot 303, SBY 11/11/88 OE ... 44,000
RABIN, Michael (20th C)
Napoleon (abstract), welded steel, intl, 1984-85, 66", lot 264, C-E 5/9/89 ... 1,100
RAUSCHENBERG, Robert (American, 1925-)
Marker (Jammer), weathered board/fabric-covered rattan pole, 1975, 99x9x18", lot 21, SBY 2/19/89 UE ... 44,000
Opal Gospel (mulitiple sculpture), 10 sheets slksc plexiglas in lucite base, 1971, S-18x20", lot 118, PHL 6/16/88 ... 2,250
Revolver (contemporary), ed of 200, 5 plexiglas discs/clr slksc, 1969-70, 9" dia, Multiples/Colorcraft, SBY 2/23/89 ... 1,210
Shoal (Scale), transfer/mirror/fabric collage on wood, sgn/dtd 77/titled, 86x96x38", lot 167, SBY 2/16/89 ... 40,000
Turkey, slksc/paper collage/objects/plexiglas on canvas in 3 panels, 41x37", lot 17, SBY 5/2/89 OE ... 350,000
Untitled (contemporary), wood/fabric/solvent transfer/gouache/plaster/metal tack, 13x15x10", lot 20, C-NY 11/9/88 UE ... 165,000
1/2 Gals AAPCO; cardboard on plywood in 2 parts w/rope, 1971, 89x78x11", lot 3416, SBY 5/2/88 OE ... 26,400

REDER, Bernard (American, 1897-1963)
Birds & Fishes, 2-II, brn patina, sgn/dtd 1955, 25", lot 188, SBY 2/14/89 .... **3,575**
Birds & Fishes, 2-II, sgn/dtd 1955, 25", lot 77, SBY 5/30/89 OE **11,880**
Tambourine, dk brn patina, sgn/dtd 1957, 26", lot 266, SBY 4/14/89 OE **2,475**
REGINATO, Peter (20th C)
Cradle Song (contemporary sculpture), painted steel, 1985, 49x42x33", SBY 10/8/88 .... **6,600**
REMINGTON, Frederic Sackrider (American, 1861-1909)
Coming Through the Rye (equestrian group), rich blk-brn patina, sgn/mk Roman Bronze Works, ca 1902, 31", C-NY 5/25/89 .... **4,400,000**
Mountain Man (equestrian group), brn patina, mottled gr marble base, 12", lot 1152, WL 5/20/88 UE **150**
Mountain Man (equestrian group), brn patina, shaped mottled rouge marble base, 29", lot 1148, WD 5/20/88 .... **1,300**
Rattlesnake (equestrian group), brn patina, mottled gr marble base, 9", lot 1151, WL 5/20/88 .... **225**
Scalp (equestrain group), mottled gr marble base, 12", lot 1150, WL 5/20/88 .... **325**

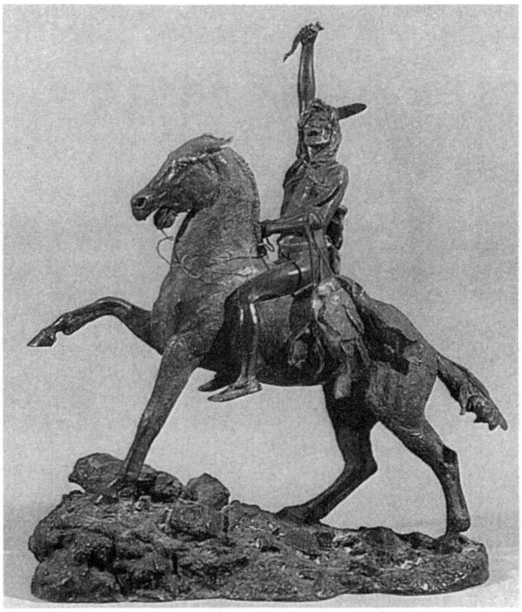
Scalp, #11, dk brn patina, 25", WD 10/5/88 OE, $175,000

Wicked Pony, 10/125, posthumous ed, brn patina, veined gr marble base, 21x20", lot 2048, DM 3/14/88 .... **2,500**
REMINGTON, Frederic Sackrider; after (American, 1861-1909)
Bronco Buster, 22", lot 387B, FAP 4/15/88 .... **632**
Indian Dancer, restrike, marble base, sgn, 19", lot 2095, DM 2/19/88.......... **1,300**
Outlaw, 23", lot 387A, FAP 4/15/88 .... **495**
Rattlesnake, rescast, 29", lot 789, LH 10/16/88 .... **1,500**
RENARD, Marcel (French, 1893-)
Relief of a Woman, stylized nude w/curling hair, arms overhead; gr patina, ca 1930, 31x23", lot 490, SBY 12/12/88 .... **1,540**
REVASSEUR
Liberati, maiden holds onto bell; 24", lot 796, FAP 11/4/88 UE.......... **325**
RICHIER, Germaine (French, 1904-1959)
Guerrier (abstract figure), 4/8, blk patina, sgn/mk C Valsuani, 13", SBY 10/7/88.......... **13,200**
Guerrier aux Bras Croises (abstract figure), 3/6, blk patina, sgn/mk Valsuani, ca 1953, 15", SBY 2/6/89 .... **20,900**
Standing Figure (abstract), ed of 6, golden patina, ca 1946-53, sgn/mk Susse Fondeur Paris, 10", SBY 2/6/89 OE **22,000**
RICKEY, George (American, 1907-)
Column IV (contemporary), stainless steel, 1965, 101x16x16", SBY 11/11/88 OE **71,500**
Column of Seven Triangles with Spirals, plated stainless steel, sgn/dtd 1975, 29", SBY 10/8/88 .... **7,700**
Five Rotors, Two Cubes; stainless steel, sgn/dtd 1973, 17", SBY 10/8/88 .... **6,050**
Five Triangles (contemporary), AP00/15, stainless steel, sgn/dtd 1966, 11x13x2", lot 97, SBY 2/15/89 .... **3,080**
Five Triangles (contemporary), 11/15, stainless steel, sgn/dtd 66, 11x13x2", lot 74, SBY 2/15/89 .... **3,410**
One Up, One Down; stainless steel/lead, blk stone base, sgn/dtd 64, 40x24x3", lot 25, C-NY 10/4/89 OE **13,200**
Space Churn with Cams VI, stainless steel, sgn/dtd 1974, 88", SBY 10/8/88 .... **20,900**
Two Lines (abstract sculpture), 4/5, stainless steel, sgn/dtd 1964, 21", SBY 5/3/88 .... **9,900**
Two Lines Leaning VI, stainless steel, sgn/dtd 1972, 33x30", SBY 10/8/88 .... **9,900**
Two Open Triangles, 1/3, stainless steel, cement base, sgn/dtd 1984, 105", C-NY 11/9/88 OE.......... **46,200**
Untitled (contemporary), stainless steel, 1961, 94", SBY 10/8/88.......... **26,400**
Weathervane, 5/47, aluminum, sgn/dtd 1976, 26x38x6", lot 155, C-NY 11/10/88 .... **6,600**
Weathervane (contemporary), 21/47, stainless steel, sgn, 23x38", lot 80, SBY 2/15/89 .... **5,500**
Weathervane (contemporary), 28/47, stainless steel, marble base, sgn/dtd 1976, 26x38x6", lot 75, C-NY 11/20/88.......... **5,500**
RIGUARD, F. (French, 20th C)
Damascened Female Figure, on knee/right hand upheld & holding ball; parcel slvr/ivory, marble base, 22", C-NY 6/11/88 .... **4,950**
RIPPS, Rodney (American, 20th C)
Shrubs & Weeds (wall relief), 1978, 10x33", lot 326, SBY 2/15/88.......... **2,200**

RIVERA, Manuel (Latin American, 20th C)
Metamorfosis, metal web on wood, sgn/titled/dtd 1962, 47x35", SBY 5/17/88 OE 14,300
RIVERA Jose; see De Rivera
RIVERS, Larry (American, 1923-)
Elephants (wall relief), acrylic/graphite/cardboard nailed to wooden supports on panel, 1960, 26x36x5", C-NY 11/20/88 OE 12,100
RIVIERE, Maurice Giraud
Masked Venetian Harlequin (in voluminous cape), gr patina, sgn/mk Chemann Paris, ca 1925, 26", lot 312, SBY 6/8/88 OE 9,350
RIVIERE, Theodore (French, 1857-1912)
Carthage (Salammbo/Matho), golden patina, gr onyx base, sgn/titled/mk Susse Fes Edts Paris, ca 1900, 17", SBY 6/8/88..... 7,150
RIVOIRE, Raymond Leon (French, 1884-)
Woman & a Hound (tall nude w/spear walks dog), gr/blk patinae, sgn/mk Susse Fes Edts, ca 1925, 22", lot 97, SBY 11/17/88..... 4,950
ROBINSON, John (British, 20th C)
Two Children Walking Hand in Hand, #5, ed of 9, patinated, 29", lot 795, FAP 11/4/88 OE 4,400
ROBUS, Hugo (American, 1885-1964)
Figure in Grief (contemporary), ed of 6, sgn, 1952, 12x14x9", SBY 11/11/88 OE 18,700
Meditating Figure, slvr, sgn, 11", lot 261, SBY 4/14/89 7,700
Seated Woman with Memories, ed of 6, golden-brn patina, square blk bronze base, sgn/mk Battaglia, 1961, 21", SBY 6/28/89..... 3,080
ROCKWELL, Peter Barstow (American, 1936-)
Trip, Tumble, Splash; 1/6, gr patina, intl/dtd 72, 25", RWS 12/10/88 650
RODIN, Pierre Auguste (French, 1840-1917)
Buste de Balzac, dk gr patina, marble base, sgn/mk Alexis Rudier Fondeur, ca 1892-95, 8", SBY 10/7/88 OE 27,500
Eve au Rocher (standing nude), brn patina, 1881, 33", SBY 5/11/88 71,500
Femme Nue Assise, #6, 6/12, brn/gr patinae, sgn/mk Georges Rudier Fondeur, 1886/1964, 6", SBY 10/7/88 9,900
Femmes Damnees, 5/12, brn patina, sgn/mk Musee Rodin, 1885/1977, 11" long, SBY 10/7/88..... 27,500
Figure Volante (floating figure), 7/12, dk brn patina, mk Georges Rudier Fondeur, 1890/1963, 15" long, SBY 5/11/89..... 30,800
Grande Main Gauche (hand), brn/gr patinae, sgn/mk Alexis Rudier Fondeur, 1885, 10", SBY 10/7/88 38,500
Gros Main Droit (a right hand), dk gr patina, sgn/mk Alexis Rudier Fondeur Paris, 13", C-NY 5/12/88 OE..... 77,500
Hand (open/palm up), gr patina, sgn/mk Alexis Rudier, 5", lot 27, SBY 10/7/89 6,600
L'Eternel Printemps, brn patina, sgn/mk Georges Rudier Fondeur, 1884/1966, 20", SBY 10/7/88 OE..... 88,000
La Mort d'Adonis (nude mourning Adonis), 7/12, brn patina, sgn twice/mk Georges Rudier Fondeur, 6x11", SBY 5/11/89..... 28,600
Le Baiser, golden patina, sgn/mk F Barbedienne Fondeur, ca 1903, 10", lot 2, C-NY 2/18/88 28,600
Le Baiser, 1/95, dk brn patina, sgn/mk Barbedienne Fondeur, 1886/1898-1918, 10", SBY 10/7/88..... 27,500
Le Main Droit (a right hand on a base), brn patina, sgn/mk By Mussee Rodin 1957 Rudier Fondeur, 4", C-NY 5/12/88 OE 5,500
Les Premieres Funerailles, #2, br/gr patinae, sgn/mk Alexis Rudier Fondeur, ca 1903, 9", SBY 10/7/88 OE 28,600
Les Sirenes (3 nudes on rock), brn patina, ca 1888, sgn/mk L Perzinka Fondeur Versailles, 17", C-NY 5/12/88 41,800
Lion Blesse (seated roaring lion), marble, ca 1881/1909, 35", SBY 5/11/88 137,500
Main Droite (half-closed hand), dk brn patina, square veined marble base, sgn/mk Alexis Rudier, 4", lot 29, SBY 10/7/89 11,000
Masque d'Hanako (head), gr patina, sgn/mk Alexis Rudier, 1908, 7", lot 28, SBY 10/7/89 OE 13,200
Mere et Deux Enfants (kneeling mother w/children), painted terra cotta, sgn, 11", lot 14, C-NY 2/18/88 OE 19,800
Mignon (Rose Beuret), blk patina, sgn/mk Georges Rudier Fondeur Musee Rodin, ca 1867-68/1973, 16", SBY 10/7/88..... 49,500
Muse of Tragedy, #6, ed of 12, brn patina, sgn/mk Rudier Fondeur, 7", lot 30, SBY 10/7/89 OE..... 9,900
Petit Torse Masculin A (male torso), 9/12, dk brn/golden/gr patinae, square blk marble base, 10", lot 452, WAD 6/12/89 9,000
Seated Lion Weeping, blk patina, sgn/mk Garde Bien, 1881, 13" long, lot 25, SBY 10/7/89 OE..... 17,600
Tete de Balzac, 9/12, blk patina, blk cube base, sgn/mk Georges Rudier Fondeur Paris, 1980, 12", C-NY 10/6/88 19,800
Tete de Damne, #4, ed of 12, brn patina, sgn/mk Susse Paris, 4", lot 26, SBY 10/7/89 OE 8,250
Tete de Genie Funeraire (Etude pour la Tombe de Puvis de Chavannes), ed of 12, brn patina, 1898/1917, 6", C-NY 2/18/88..... 6,050
Triton et Nereide, #4, blk patina, sgn/mk Georges Rudier Fondeur Musee Rodin, ca 1900/1969, 10", SBY 10/7/88..... 18,700
Zuzon (portrait bust), biscuit de Sevres, bronze plinth, marble/bronze base, sgn, 1872, 9", SBY 10/7/88 UE..... 11,000
ROINE, Edouard (20th C)
Portrait Plaque of James Wilson Alexander MacDonald, MCMVI, sgn/mk Henry Bonnard Bronze Co, 1906, 26x18", RWS 8/20/88 325
ROSATI, James (American, 1912-)
Galley, Three Figures; brn patina, rectangular wood base, 1959, 16", lot 155, C-E 2/13/89 OE 6,050
ROSENTHAL, Bernard (American, 1914-)
Untitled (abstract), dk brn patina, sgn/dtd 1965, 25x17", lot 339, SBY 10/5/88..... 990
ROSENTHAL, Ted (American, 20th C)
Bad Suggestion Box (wall relief), enamel/fluorescent paint on welded steel, intl/dtd 83, 29x20", C-E 5/13/88..... 550
ROSENTHAL, Tony (American, 20th C)
Maquette for the Big Fix (contemporary), painted steel, 14x14x10", lot 388, SBY 10/7/89 1,430
ROUSSEAU, after
Lamp (dancing nymph & candle arms w/beaded bulbs), spelter, moulded base, marble plinth, sgn, 21", C-E 10/11/88 350
RUCKI, Jean Lambert (French, 20th C)
Le Baiser (stylistic couple embracing), rich brn patina, sgn/mk Valsuani EA, 19", C-NY 6/11/88..... 6,600
RUSSELL, Charles Marion (American, 1864-1926)
Smoking Up (cowboy on horse), rich dk brn patina, sgn/mk New York Co-Operative Society, 1904, 13", C-NY 2/2/88 OE 39,600
RUSSELL, Charles Marion; after (American, 1864-1926)
Alert (elk), dk brn patina, sgn w/skull, mk Nelli Art Bronze Work LA, 8" long, SBY 1/24/89 UE 550
RUSSELL, Donn (20th C)
Love (contemporary), painted wood/transparent vinyl/plastic ribbon, sgn, 1972, 23x25x5", C-E 5/9/89 550
SAINT-GAUDENS, Augustus (American, 1848-1907)
Portrait Relief of Robert Louis Stevenson, gr-brn patina, sgn/dtd 1887/inscr dedication, 12" dia, SBY 5/24/89 6,600

SAINT-MARCEAUX, see De Saint-Marceaux
SAINT-PHALLE, see De Saint-Phalle
SALMSON, Jean Jules; after (French, 1823-1902)
Pair: Mid-Eastern Couple, male w/sword, female w/water jug; ca 1900, 23", electrified, lot 161, RWS 9/24/88 .... **1,800**
SAMARAS, Lucas (American, 1936-)
Chair Transformation (contemporary), pins/wood, ca 1970, 36", lot 162, SBY 2/16/89 .... **35,750**
Jewel Box, wooden box/glass & plastic jewels/tape measure/straight pins, 4x6x6", lot 140, C-NY 11/10/88 .... **26,400**
SANDOZ, Edouard Marcel (Swiss, 1881-1971)
Grazing Bunny with Raised Ear, sgn/mk Susse Fres Paris, 2", C-E 12/8/88 .... **660**
SANOJA, Miguel (20th C)
Olimpia (abstract figure), blk/golden patinae, sgn, 1988, 24", C-NY 5/17/89 .... **3,520**
SANZEL, Felix (French, 1829-1883)
Satyr (mounted as lamp), dore, sgn on base, 18", lot 950, FAP 12/8/88 .... **900**
SARET, Alan (American, 1944-)
Mainline Polychrome Permutation Cluster, wire sculpture; 1979, 72x36", lot 241, SBY 2/15/89 .... **4,400**
SAUVAGE
Venus de Milo, gr patina, sgn/mk Redito AV, 19th C, 35", depatinated, lot 54, RWS 8/20/88 .... **850**
SCANGA, Italo (20th C)
Monte Cassino: The Plan (contemporary figure); oil on wood construction, 1983, 117x78x36", lot 361, SBY 2/15/89 .... **17,600**
SCHAEFERS, Karin (American/German, 20th C)
Reverie, patinated, marble base, 7", lot 946, FAP 12/8/88 .... **475**
SCHARF, Kenny (20th C)
Answering Machine & Alarm Clock (assemblage), mixed media, ca 1981, lot 142, C-NY 2/14/89 .... **2,200**
Refrigerator (contemporary), refrigerator/mixed media, 60x48x46", lot 384, C-NY 5/4/89 .... **11,000**
SCHMIDT-CASSEL, after (German, 1861-)
Dancer, wearing short tunic & balancing ivory orb; parcel gilt/cold paint/ivory, blk marble base, 18", C-E 6/16/88 UE **440**
SCHMIDT-FELLING
Helmeted Warrior on Horseback, gray marble base, sgn/foundry mk, 1905, 20", C-E 6/16/88 .... **990**
SCHNABEL, Julian (20th C)
Helen of Troy, ed of 2, 1984, 204x36x36", lot 53, C-NY 5/3/88 .... **165,000**
SCHOTT, Walter (German, 1861-1938)
Joueuse de Boules (nude holds crumpled cloth behind/leans to roll ball), gilt, ca 1900, 17", lot 356, SBY 3/10/89 .... **1,210**
SCHUMACHER, Carl
Bust of a Lady, looking at an angle; patinated, shaped gr marble base, sgn, 8", C-E 10/11/88 .... **308**
SCHWATENBERG, S.; after
Standing Male Nude, brn patina, square mottled brn marble base, 12", lot 688, WL 2/26/88 .... **300**
SCRIVER, Robert (American, 1917-)
Winter King (proud elk), 92/110, brn-gr patina, sgn/dtd 1956, 24", lot 2925, B/B 6/9/88 .... **3,575**
SEGAL, George (American, 1924-)
Gazing Woman, American Portrait, 1776-1976; 69/175, wht plastic relief, sgn/dtd 75, 26x19x4", lot 809, C-NY 11/1/88 .... **2,640**
Gazing Woman, 111/175, multiple sculpture, p/s, dtd 75, 27x20", lot 116, LH 5/15/88 .... **2,000**
Gazing Woman, 70/175, multiple sculpture, sgn/dtd, orig bl cloth-covered box, 1976, Transworld Art, SBY 5/14/88 OE **4,125**
Girl on Blanket: Finger to Chin (wall relief); plaster, 1973, 54x36x9", C-NY 11/9/88 .... **77,000**
Hand Over Breast, 25/75, pressed paper, 1982, 14x10x7", Sidney Janis Gallery, lot 950, SBY 11/5/88 OE **3,850**
Machine of the Year, plaster/computers/plastic/metal/glass/flourescent light/wicker/wood, 1982, lot 58, C-NY 5/3/88 OE **187,000**
Seated Woman on Red Chair (profile of nude), painted plaster, 1981, 36x36x20", SBY 2/19/88 OE **66,000**
Self-Portrait with Head & Body (sculpture), plaster/painted wood chair, 1968, SBY 11/10/88 OE **242,000**
SELEY, Jason (American, 1919-)
Eduardo, welded steel, sgn, 1962, 21", C-E 5/13/88 UE **440**
Harp, welded steel, 1965, 16x24", C-E 1/12/88 .... **143**
SERRA, Richard (American, 1943-)
Untitled (Rolled Lead), lead, 1971, 2x17x6", lot 296, SBY 11/11/88 OE **23,100**
SERRANO, Pablo
Aguacate, patinated/polished steel, sgn, 7" long, SBY 10/5/88 .... **495**
El Torro, dk golden patina, intl, 14" long, SBY 10/5/88 OE **357**
SEVERINI, Gino (Italian, 1883-1966)
Arlecchino (abstract sculpture), #2, ed of 5, painted/glazed ceramic, ca 1950, sgn, 14", C-NY 5/12/88 OE **24,200**
SHABANAUD
St Germain des Pres (screen), 4 lacquered wood panels, sgn, ea panel: 68x20", C-E 5/13/88 .... **1,210**
SHAPIRO, Joel (20th C)
Untitled (abstract wall relief), painted wood, sgn/dtd 1979-80, 5x10x3", lot 302, SBY 11/11/88 .... **15,400**
Untitled (contemporary), paint/cast iron, 1975, 4x3x4", lot 299, SBY 11/11/88 .... **27,500**
SHIFRIN, Ray (20th C)
Bell (contemporary), gr patina w/wood & rope, 17", C-E 1/12/88 .... **242**
SHRADY, Henry Merwin (American, 1871-1923)
Bison, golden-brn patina, sgn/mk Roman Bronze Works, 1903, 9x12", lot 157, SBY 6/28/89 .... **6,600**
SIGNORI, Sergio (French, 1906-)
L'Ange Noir (contemporary), blk marble, 20", SBY 10/5/88 OE **2,860**
SILVERMAN, Martin (20th C)
Guardian Angel (contemporary), painted bronze/blk painted metal, wood base, 1981, 77x49x33", lot 154, C-NY 2/14/89 .... **6,600**

SILVESTRE (French, 20th C)
Seated Fawn, 9", lot 391, FAP 4/15/88 OE **742**

SIMEONOVA, Snezhana (East European, 20th C)
Sleeping Man, patinated, 19", lot 786, FAP 11/4/88 UE **300**

SIMMONDS, Charles (20th C)
Number 11 (Ritual Furnace), clay, 1978, 11x30x30", SBY 5/3/88 .... **22,000**
Ritual Place (contemporary), clay, 1979, 7x29x29", lot 262, SBY 2/15/89 .... **11,000**

SINTENIS, Renee (German, 1888-1965)
Boeckchen, II, red-brn patina, sgn, 1915, 4x4", lot 34, SBY 2/14/89 OE **4,950**
Ruckwartsblickendes Fohlen (foal), dk brn patina, sgn, 1919, 4x5", lot 37, SBY 2/14/89 .... **7,150**
Sich Leckendes Fohlen, golden-brn patina, sgn/mk Noack Berlin, 1928, 4x6", lot 33, SBY 2/14/89 .... **7,700**

SMITH, David (American, 1906-1965)
Agricola II, #G2, welded steel, sgn/titled/dtd 1952, 25x41x11", lot 5, C-NY 5/3/88 .... **385,000**
Agricola VII, VII, painted steel/cast iron, sgn, 22x14x10", lot 7, C-NY 5/3/88 .... **209,000**
Dancer (abstract figure), iron, ca 1954, 8", lot 91, SBY 11/11/88 .... **18,700**
Medal for Dishonor: Private Law & Order Leagues; bronze on wood, dtd 1939, 14x15x2", lot 116, C-NY 11/10/88 .... **11,000**
Medallion (abstract), lead, intl, ca 1956, 2x2", SBY 5/3/88 .... **4,400**
Two Wing Circle (contemporary), gr-blk patina, sgn/dtd 1961, 25x17x11", lot 9, C-NY 5/3/88 OE **165,000**
Untitled (Voltri), sgn/dtd 6-62/inscr Dida Rebecca to GCM on base, 21", lot 111, SBY 11/11/88 .... **115,500**
Voltri (Large Circle), welded steel, sgn/titled/dtd 1962, 50x12x10", lot 11, C-NY 5/3/88 .... **220,000**
Voltri III (abstract sculpture), steel, sgn/titled, dtd 6/62, 71", SBY 11/10/88 OE **203,500**
Woman on Horseback (contemporary), sgn/dtd 40, 8", lot 11, C-NY 5/3/89 .... **49,500**

SMITH, Tony (20th C)
Black Box, a/p for ed of 3, corten steel, 23x33x25", SBY 5/3/88 OE **40,700**
Throwback, #5-6, blk painted steel, intl/dtd 76-79, 14x32x16", lot 47, C-NY 5/3/88 .... **44,000**

SNELSON, Kenneth (American, 1927-)
Green Guide, 2/4, aluminum/stainless steel wire, sgn/dtd 75, 17", SBY 10/5/88 OE **8,800**

SOMAINI, Francesco (European, 1926-)
Wave (contemporary), sgn, ca 1960, 26x51x20", SBY 10/8/88 .... **2,475**

SOMME, T.
Centerpiece, bulbous, flower cluster at top/foliage & reclining fairy on sides; patinated, sgn, 20", C-E 12/8/88 .... **495**
Dancer, girl w/raised leg, wearing long skirt & holding scarf; gilt/ivory, circular cream stone base, 13", C-E 6/16/88 .... **1,870**

SORENSON, Carl (19th/20th C)
Pair: Candlesticks (classic wing design w/central bulbous candle cup on circular foot); sgn, ca 1920, 5", RWS 12/10/88 .... **200**

SORTA, Salvador (20th C)
Integraction Surgerente, iron/bronze, sgn/dtd 1962/titled, 69x39", lot 182, SBY 2/14/89 OE **1,210**

SOTO, Jesus Rafael (Venezuelan, 1923-)
Blue et Grande Barre (contemporary), painted wood/metal construction, sgn/dtd 1965/titled, 61x42", SBY 5/16/89 OE **44,000**
Construction (contemporary), painted wood/metal construction, 20x10", SBY 11/21/88 UE **2,090**
Hanging Object (sculpture), oil on wood/metal, 20", C-NY 5/17/89 OE **12,650**
Petite Horizontale-Verticale, painted wood, sgn/dtd 1965, 13x16", SBY 5/17/88 .... **4,400**
Petites Vibrations Rouges, painted wood, sgn/titled/dtd 1965, 20x14", SBY 5/17/88 .... **5,500**
Trapeze (contemporary), 17/100, steel construction, 14x14", SBY 11/21/88 OE **2,475**
Untitled (abstract), metal construction, sgn/dtd 1977/mk Prototipo Ediciones S, 14", SBY 5/16/89 OE **10,450**
7 ET 1 (wall assemblage), metal/wood construction, 1963, 22x51", SBY 5/16/89 OE **33,000**

Spanish School (18th C)
Santa Barbara (standing figure), polychrome/gilt wood, rectangular socle, 23", lt paint ls, RWS 12/10/88 UE **550**

STANKIEWICZ, Richard (20th C)
Untitled (abstract), iron/steel, ca 1958, 20x14x15", lot 115, SBY 5/3/88 .... **18,700**
Untitled (contemporary), welded/rusted steel, intl/dtd 1965-15, 16", lot 344, SBY 10/5/88 OE **6,600**

STEINBACH, Haim (20th C)
Exuberant Relative #3, 2/2, formica/plastic hats/soda & beer cans, sgn/dtd 86/titled, 25x57x15", C-NY 11/9/88 .... **28,600**
Supremely Black (contemporary wall relief), mixed media, 1985, 29x66x13", lot 288, SBY 2/15/89 OE **29,700**

STEINBERG, Saul (American, 1914-)
Lovers & Construction (wall relief), wood/tempera/watercolor/chalk/crayon/pen/stps, 1973, 23x31x2", C-NY 5/4/88 OE **41,800**

STEINER, Michael (20th C)
Star Carr (abstract), sgn/dtd 79/mk Renaissance Art Foundry, 20x22x17", lot 155, C-NY 2/14/89 .... **5,500**

STEINHAUSER, Carl Johann (American, 1813-1879)
Shell Girl (standing figure), marble, sgn/dtd 1840, 53", C-NY 5/25/88 OE **22,000**

STELLA, Frank (American, 1935-)
Bonny Bunch of Roses (wall relief), 1/3, shoe polish/enamel on welded steel, sgn/dtd 75, 23x17x10", C-NY 11/9/88 .... **44,000**
Eskimo Curlew 3X (Second Version), mixed media/honeycomb board, 1976, 54x69x12", lot 76, SBY 5/2/89 .... **253,000**
Estoril, mixed media on tycort, 1981, 72x81x18", SBY 11/8/89 OE **528,000**
Felsztyn IV (abstract wall relief), acrylic/felt/fabric/board/panel, 1971, 103x90x3", lot 37, C-NY 5/3/88 .... **77,000**
Glinne II, mixed media on wood relief, 1972, 118x89", SBY 11/10/88 .... **115,000**
Jungli-Kowwa (abstract relief), mixed media on aluminum/metal tubing/wire mesh, 1978, 86x102x38", SBY 11/10/88 .... **660,000**
Lapa 7 (wall relief), painted metal, 32x51x4", C-NY 11/9/88 .... **110,000**
Misano (abstract), mixed media on tycore, 1981, 67x81x11", lot 46, SBY 5/2/89 OE **418,000**
Playskool Series: Chair; acrylic paint on cast bronze/aluminum/copper/wood dowels/etched magnesium, 31", SBY 11/11/88 .... **44,000**

STONE, Sylvia (Canadian, 1928-)
Origami, acrylic on plexiglas, 1968, 50x98x11", C-E 5/13/88 UE **660**

STRAETEN, see Van Der Straeten
STREETER, see Van Der Streeter
STRUCK, see Von Struck
STRYMANS, Adolphe Joseph (Belgian School, 1866-)
Mermaid with Symbols, patinated, sgn/dtd 1914, no size given, lot 793, FAP 11/4/88 OE **4,600**
SURLS, James (American, 1943-)
Night Dancing (hanging contemporary sculpture), wood, 1985-86, 70x50x40", SBY 10/8/88 .... **16,500**
Walking in Midnight (contemporary), hornbeam/rattan/pine, 1980, 109x48x42", lot 261, SBY 2/15/89 .... **17,600**
SUZOR-COTE, Marc Aurele de Foy (Canadian, 1869-1937)

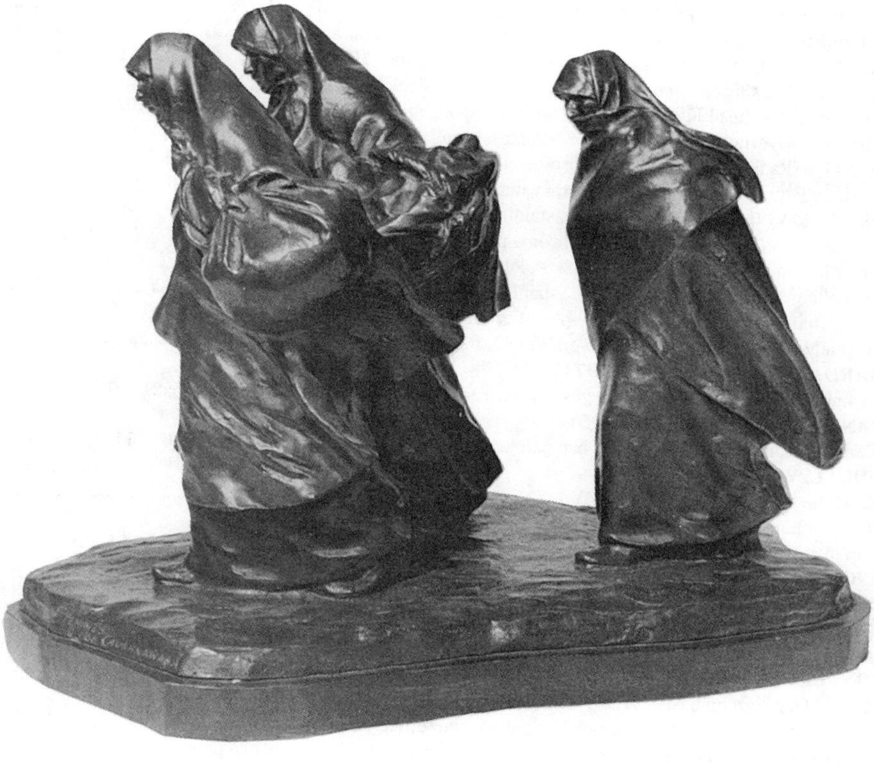

Femmes de Caughnawage, patinated, sgn/dtd 1925/titled, 23", WAD 11/28/88 OE, $19,000

I'Iroquois, 6/24, sgn/titled/dtd 1907, 18", Roman Bronze Works, lot 141, FB 5/28/89 .... **2,800**
Le Defricheur, 4/12, sgn/titled, 25", Roman Bronze Works, lot 142, FB 5/28/89 .... **6,000**
Le Portageur (standing male figure w/pack), sgn/dtd 1922, 16", Roman Bronze Works, lot 138, FB 5/28/89 .... **15,000**
SYKES, Charles (European, 1875-1950)
Spirit of Ecstasy, leaning into the wind; chrome mount, stone base, sgn/mk Rolls Royce Ltd, 1911, 7", C-E 9/16/88 .... **198**
SYPCHYTZ, Samuel; after
Maiden (semi-nude w/drapery about legs), rubbed blk patina/ivory, square plinth/base, 20th C, 16", lot 305, SBY 6/8/88 .... **3,300**
SZCZEBLEWSKI, V.
Mousse Siffleur, 18", lot 954, FAP 12/8/88 OE **1,400**
SZEKESSY, Zolton
Flute Player, V, dk brn patina, 7" long, SBY 10/5/88 .... **330**
TASHA, Carl (American, 20th C)
Woman & Bird (fantasy figure under tree), metal, 24", RAB 8/8/89 .... **600**
TEMELA, Nalinek (Canadian Eskimo, Lake Harbor)
Narwhal with Tusk, bronze-clr soapstone, 1979, 14" long, RAB 8/1/89 .... **400**
TERESCZUK, Paul (Austrian, 20th C)
Group of Children, boy/girl kissing & girl spying; golden-brn patina, intl/mk Real Vienna Bronze, 7", C-E 6/16/88 OE **660**
Lamp, lady leaning back in arms of man; bronze/ivory, gr marble socle, sgn/mk Austria, 30", w/shade, C-E 3/24/88 OE **3,860**
Lamp: Maiden & Rabbits Under Pine Branches; bronze/ivory/cameo glass, sgn/foundry mk/glass sgn, 23", C-E 9/16/88 OE **6,600**
Maiden, standing w/extended arms & wearing long dress; bronze/ivory, gray stone base, sgn/mk Austria, 11", C-E 9/16/88 .... **1,045**
Untitled (boy clown seated by girl holding flower), bronze/ivory, sgn/foundry mk, 5", C-E 3/24/88 .... **440**
Untitled (girl in long dress/hat/parasol), bronze/ivory, sgn/foundry mk, 6", C-E 12/8/88 .... **550**
Untitled (semi-nude dancer w/outstretched arms), gilt/ivory, round marble base, sgn, ca 1910, 11", lot 357, SBY 3/10/89 .... **2,475**
Untitled (standing cloaked maiden w/closed eyes), bronze/ivory, sgn/mk Austria, 7", C-E 3/24/88 OE **1,760**
TERESCZUK, Paul; manner of (Austrian, 20th C)
Untitled, lady on bench removes slipper; brn patina/ivory, rouge marble base, early 20th C, 8" long, SBY 6/10/88 OE **2,200**
THUSS, R.
Sculler, stroking through rippling water; dk golden-brn patina, self base, sgn/mk Argento Wien, 14" long, C-E 9/13/88 .... **330**

TINGUELY, Jean (Italian, 1925-)
Affair of the Heart (abstract assemblage), scrap metal/forged iron/wheels/electric motor, 1963, 71", SBY 11/10/88 OE ... 132,000
Motor-Cocktail, wood/welded metal/steel/3 electric motors painted blk, 1965, 27x19x15", SBY 11/11/88 OE ... 154,000
Untitled (abstract sculpture), painted wood/iron/steel/electric engine, 1987, 59x20x20", lot 675, SBY 6/30/88 ... 80,000
Untitled (Radio WNYR Drawing), assemblage of plexiglas/metal fixtures/radio/motor, 1962, 30x40x9", SBY 5/2/88 OE ... 74,250
Variation Royale Constant, painted steel/wires/electric motor, sgn/dtd 1958/titled, 28x10x26", SBY 5/3/88 OE ... 46,750

TORREANO, John (European, 20th C)
Turquoise (contemporary), oil/glass jewels on wood, 1975, 60x2", lot 417, C-NY 5/4/89 UE ... 1,100
Untitled (Column), oil/glass jewels on wood, 96x8", SBY 11/11/88 ... 4,400

TROVA, Ernest (American, 1929-)
Etc/Troubador #51; patinated, sgn/dtd 1984, 27x13x7", SBY 10/8/88 OE ... 1,320
Etc/Troubador #52; ed of 6, lt brn patina, sgn/dtd 84, 29", lot 441, SBY 10/7/89 ... 3,575
Etc/Troubador #68; 1986, 28x14x8", lot 301, C-NY 5/4/89 ... 3,080
Falling Man Study: Six Figures on a Cube; 4/6, stainless steel, 1964, 16x25x25", lot 104, SBY 2/15/89 ... 15,400
Falling Man/Etc #35; chrome-plated bronze w/painted steel, 1977, 21x23x8", lot 140, SBY 10/8/88 ... 12,100
Falling Man/Overhead Figure, 24"; 5/8, stainless steel, sgn/dtd 1984-85, 33x8x15", SBY 10/8/88 OE ... 27,500
Falling Man/Overhead Figure, 24"; 6/8, stainless steel, stp sgn/dtd 1984-85, 33x8x15", lot 164A, SBY 5/3/88 ... 20,900
Falling Man/Radial Cut Figure; 4/6, chrome-plated bronze, stainless steel base, sgn/dtd 79, 32x16x12", SBY 10/6/88 OE ... 22,000
Pair: Male/Female Dancers (contemporary nudes); 1/3, polished, sgn/dtd 86, 27x8x8", lot 312, C-NY 5/4/89 ... 9,350
Profile Canto VI (contemporary), 10/10, stainless steel, 1972-73, 24", lot 150, SBY 11/11/88 ... 15,400
Reclining Nude (contemporary), 3/6, chrome-plated bronze, dtd 69, 23" long, lot 66, C-NY 10/4/89 ... 6,050
Seated Man on a Wall, sgn/dtd 77, 23x8x8", lot 299, C-NY 5/4/89 ... 4,620
Study Falling Man (One in a Box), #1-1, stainless steel, stp sgn/dtd 1985, 24x42x7", SBY 11/11/88 OE ... 47,300
Study of Double-Hinged Man, chrome-plated bronze, mk 5-6-74, 25x6x6", lot 56, C-NY 10/4/89 OE ... 35,200
Three Lady Poets, 4-6, blk-gr patina, sgn/dtd 82, 16x21x12", lot 439, SBY 10/7/89 ... 3,190

TUNNARD, John (British, 1900-1971)
Composition (abstract), tempera on gesso-prepared masonite, sgn/dtd 46/#d P11, 25x21", SBY 10/7/88 OE ... 22,000

TURCAN, Jean (French, 1846-1895)
Untitled, peasant girl walking w/jar; brn patina, sgn/inscr Salon 1883 1Er Medaille, 30", SLK 11/25/88 ... 2,900

TURNBULL, William (20th C)
Leda, stone base, 1982, 25x11x8", SBY 11/11/88 ... 8,250

TUTTLE, Richard (American, 20th C)
Group of 4: Wien Indonesian Works; wood/wire/watercolor/graphite on cardboard, 1983-84, 12x10x2", SBY 11/11/88 OE ... 12,100

URIANO
Untitled, kneeling man w/ivory bow & dog; patinated metal/ivory, blk stone plinth, sgn, 23" long, C-E 3/24/88 ... 495

VAERENBERGH, G.
Bust of a Victorian Lady, truncated waist; gilt metal/wht marble, variegated gray marble socle, sgn, 24", C-E 10/11/88 ... 2,090

VALTON, Charles (French, 1851-1918)
Attacking Dog, sgn on base, 24x29", lot 388, FAP 4/15/88 UE ... 440
Passez au Large, chained mastiff; rich brn patina, sgn/titled, 19", C-NY 2/23/89 ... 2,860
Two Cavalier King Charles Dogs, curled together on tasseled pillow base; brn patina, sgn, 17x18", lot 121, C-E 4/19/88 ... 715

VAN BIESBROECK, J.
Ouvrier Extenue (male figure), blk patina, sgn/mk Fondienatle Pertermann St Gilles-Bruxelles, 20", C-E 1/12/88 OE ... 1,430

VAN DER STRAETEN, George (Belgian, 1856-)
La Rieleuse (laughing girl), polychrome, rouge marble base, sgn/mk BO, 8", C-E 10/11/88 ... 330

VAN DER STREETER, J. (Dutch, 19th C)
Maiden in a Cap (bust), patinated, variegated gr marble plinth, sgn, 27", lot 794, FAP 11/4/88 ... 1,500

VAN WOUW, Anton (South African, 1862-1945)
Bushman Hunting, sgn/dtd 1902/mk G Nisini Fuse Roma, 1902, 19", lot 107, C-SK 5/25/89 ... 13,780
Man Panning for Gold (prone African native), sgn, 7", lot 106, C-SK 5/25/89 ... 5,500
Mielepap Eater (seated native), dk brn patina, variegated rouge marble base, sgn/mk Nisini, 6", C-SK 6/9/88 OE ... 1,280

VARELA, Abigail (Latin American, 20th C)
Break (seated figure), 2/6, 1985, 9", lot 199, SBY 5/16/89 OE ... 3,850
Caminadora Apurada II (abstract nude), 1/6, reddish-brn patina, sgn, 1988, sgn, 36", C-NY 5/17/89 ... 11,000
Caminadora con Carterita (abstract standing nude), 4/6, brn patina, sgn, 1986, 59", C-NY 11/21/88 ... 11,000

VELA, Vincenzo (Italian, 1820-1891)
Derniers Jours de Napoleon, 876, rubbed golden-brn patina, sgn/dtd 1867/mk Barbedienne, 11", SBY 2/22/89 OE ... 2,420

VERLET, Charles Raoul (French, 1857-1923)
Orpheus (standing figure), #143, rich brn patina, sgn/mk Barbedienne Fondeur/Reduction Mecanique seal, 24", C-NY 5/25/88 ... 1,980

VERTES, Marcel (Hungarian, 1895-1961)
Plate: Homme a Cheval; glazed ceramic, sgn, mk Tapis Vert/B bubino/Vallauris, 12" dia, C-E 5/9/89 ... 275
Plate: Meternite (heads of mother & child); partially glazed ceramic, sgn/inscr, 13x10", C-E 11/17/88 ... 550

VIBERT, Alexandre (French, 19th C)
Urn (C-scroll handle/nude on side fishing with net), rich brn, mk Siot Decauville, ca 1900, 17", lot 98, SBY 3/19/88 OE ... 3,410

VIBERT, Alexandre; after (French, 19th C)
Tray, formed as lily pad w/winged nude in relief; mk Colin & Cie Paris, 9", RWS 12/10/88 UE ... 250

VILLANIS, Emmanuele (Italian, 19th/20th C)
Bust of a Young Woman, long hair bound in scarf; gr-brn patina, mk Bronze Garanti au Tirte, 23", lot 182, RWS 6/25/88 OE ... 1,400
Sibylle, wearing headband/shawl; polychrome, square rouge marble base, sgn/mk Society des Bronzes, 8", C-E 9/16/88 ... 440
Untitled, lady holds hammer/anvil, rests knee on female peasant; gr-brn/brn patinae, ca 1910, 20", lot 495, SBY 12/12/88 ... 1,540

VIRIEUX, Francois Louis; after (French/Italian, 20th C)
Untitled (boy striding forward w/one arm upraised, looking back over his right shoulder), sgn, 39", SLK 11/25/88 1,100
VOCKE, F.H.
Cocker Spaniel (standing), rich warm brn patina, sgn/dtd 1938, 6", lot 174, SBY 6/9/89 605
VOISIN, A. (Continental, 20th C)
Logger, standing male figure; gr-blk patina, sgn/dtd 1934, 18", lot 112, C-E 4/19/88 660
VOLTI, Antoniucci (French, 1915-)
Reclining Nude, 6/9, brn patina, sgn, ca 1956/later, 6x10", C-E 5/9/89 7,700
VON STRUCK, Franz (German, 20th C)
Male Athelete Holding a Ball, blk patina, sgn/mk Guss G Leyrer, 26", lot 2, C-NY 6/10/89 4,400
VONNOH, Bessie Potter (American, 1872-1955)
Daydreams, young women on couch; #14, gr patina, 1899/1903, 9x20", Roman Bronze Works, lot 130, C-E 2/1/89 3,300
Nymph Riding a Dolphin, sgn/mk Gorham Co Agoz, 17", lot 188, WG 4/23/88 15,000
Young Woman (heavily draped standing figure), rich brn patina, sgn/mk Roman Bronze Works, 10", lot 129, C-E 2/1/89 3,960
VOULKOS, Peter (American, 1924-)
Plate (contemporary), ceramic, sgn/dtd 73, 20" dia, lot 198, C-NY 5/4/88 3,300
Plate (contemporary), ceramic, sgn/dtd 78 on verso, 24" dia, lot 58, C-NY 11/20/88 4,400
WALKER, George
Gambler (full-figure man in top hat), veined gr marble base, sgn, 34", lot 1968, DM 2/19/88 3,750
WARHOL, Andy (American, 1928-1987)
Brillo Box (contemporary), oil/stencil on wood, 1964, 17x17x14", lot 193, C-NY 5/4/89 OE 77,000
Campbell's Box, oil/stencil on wood, sgn, 1964, 10x19x10", lot 207, SBY 10/8/88 OE 49,500
Campbell's Soup Can: Chicken with Rice; paint slksc on aluminum, sgn/dtd 66, 4", lot 325A, SBY 5/3/89 OE 22,000
Campbell's Soup Can: Chicken with Rice; painted aluminum, sgn/dtd 66, 4", SBY 2/19/88 OE 11,000
Campbell's Tomato Juice, oil/stencil on wood, 10x9x10", lot 174, S-NY 5/4/88 35,200
Campbell's Tomato Juice, oil/stencil on wood in plexiglas box, 1964, 11x20x10", lot 142, C-NY 11/10/88 49,500
Campbell's Tomato Juice, oil/stencil on wood in plexiglas box, sgn, 11x20x10", lot 142, C-NY 5/3/88 49,500
Kellogg's Corn Flakes Box, unnumbered ed, synthetic polymer slksc on wood, 1964, 25x21x17", lot 171, SBY 10/5/89 44,000
Shoe, gold leaf/paper collage on wood, sgn, ca 1956, 5x9x3", SBY 10/5/89 OE 51,700
Shoe, tempera on wood, ca 1955-57, 5x9x3", lot 50, C-NY 2/14/89 OE 28,600
Shoe (painted butterfly decor), tempera on wood, ca 1950, 5x9x3", lot 169, SBY 10/5/89 OE 46,750
Shoe (painted butterfly decor), tempera on wood, ca 1955-57, 5x8x3", lot 15, C-NY 10/4/89 OE 28,600
Yellow Brillo Box, oil on wood in plexiglas box, sgn, 1964, 13x17x12", C-NY 5/3/88 35,200
WEINMAN, Adolph Alexander (1870-1952)
Chief Blackbird, dk brn patina, bronze base, sgn/mk Roman Bronze Works NY, 16", lot 68, WD 10/5/89 20,000
WEISS, Felix
Bust of Bearded Man, blk variegated marble base, sgn/dtd 1933, 13" without base, lot 379, FAP 4/15/88 220
WESSELMANN, Tom (American, 1931-)
Maquette for a Smoking Cigarette (With a Twist), #33, liquitex on bristol board/wood, sgn/dtd 84, 4x6x2", C-NY 5/4/88 OE 5,250
Maquette for Belt Still Life (contemporary), acrylic on cardboard/plexiglas box, sgn/dtd 80, 15x22x11", SBY 2/15/89 20,900
Maquette for Tulip & Smoking Cigarette, liquitex on ragboard, sgn/dtd 81, 9x11x7", lot 215, SBY 10/5/89 OE 22,000
Tiny Shoe & Tulip #27, #27, liquitex on bristol board, formica base, plexiglas box, 1983, 3x6x3", C-NY 5/4/88 OE 6,050
WESTERMANN, H.C. (American, 1922-)
Horse (sculpture), polychrome laminated pine plywood, sgn/dtd 1962, 49x71x23", SBY 2/19/88 OE 15,400
Shark Board (contemporary), teak/ebony/cedar, stp/sgn, dtd SF 1965 w/anchor motif, 15x30x3", lot 20K, SBY 5/2/89 OE 38,500
Slow, Wood Turning Machine; wht pine, sgn/dtd 66/titled, 27x11x11", SBY 11/11/88 13,200
Untitled (house-shaped sculpture), wood/brass with crate, inscr dedication, 1979, 16x13x11", SBY 2/19/88 OE 9,900
WHITE, Robert Winthrop
Female Nude, plaster, sgn, 7", lot 130, C-NY 6/17/89 66
WIEGHORST, Olaf Carl (American, 1899-1975)
Indian by the Campfire, rich dk brn patina, sgn/mk RBW, 4", C-NY 2/2/88 1,760
WILDER, Louise Hibbard (American, 1898-)
Child with Pursed Lips Standing on Base with Parading Ducks, brn patina, sgn on base, 9", RWS 3/16/89 UE 2,250
WILLIAMS, Roger T. (American, 1903-)
African Venus Disrobed, cast metal, round onyx base, 22x16x8", S/A 9/16/88 850
African Woman with Walking Stick, walnut wood, 16x4x4", S/A 9/16/88 65
Colt Resting, wood, weathered, 13x13x8", S/A 9/16/88 175
Crouching Mountain Lion, maple wood, 6x23x4", S/A 9/16/88 225
Eagle & Eaglets, wood, weathered, 13x13x8", S/A 9/16/88 75
Hippopotamus Mother & Child (plaque), slate, intl/dtd 64, 16" dia, S/A 9/16/88 100
Hound Dog (high-relief plaque), mahogany wood, 19x11x1", S/A 9/16/88 550
Japanese Child Squatting, oak wood, 11x7x9", S/A 9/16/88 110
Lion Cub, cottonwood, cherry plinth, 14x9x10", S/A 9/16/88 450
Mary (plaque), cherry wood, sgn/dtd 1964, 18x13", S/A 9/16/88 200
Mountain Lion at the Ready (plaque), polychrome wood, sgn, 11x24x1", SA 9/16/88 250
Nightmare, gr stone, sgn/dtd 1965, 15x11x10", S/A 9/16/88 100
Nude Dancing, gray stone, 15x8x3", S/A 9/16/88 75
Nude Mounting a Deer, curly maple wood, sgn, 12x7x5", S/A 9/16/88 175
Nude Riding the Sea Snail, w/conch shell; cast metal, onyx base, sgn/dtd 1964, 8x8x5" on 7" base, S/A 9/16/88 1,150
Nude with Bathing Cap, cherry wood, sgn, 13x4x3", S/A 9/16/88 158
Serene African Queen (head & shoulders), stone/brass, gr mottled marble base, 7x7x7", S/A 9/16/88 125

Ticklin' Time, polychrome, intl/dtd 1931, 5x7x8", S/A 9/16/88 320
Vietnam (eagle in cage), cottonwood, sgn, 23x18x12", S/A 9/16/88 500
Wolf Pack Attacking Young Steer, oak wood, sgn, 14x18x18", S/A 9/16/88 400

WILLIAMS, Wheeler (American, 1897-1972)
Spring (draped stylistic nude), gr-brn patina, sgn/dtd 1932/mk Renaissance Art Foundry Norwalk, 40", SBY 5/24/89 14,300

WILMARTH, Christopher (American, 1943-)

Second Roebling #2, glass/steel, intl/dtd 74/titled, 40x40x2", C-NY 11/9/88, $41,800

Stornaway, etched contoured glass/steel, 1974, 42x42x5", lot 183, SBY 5/3/88 49,500
Trench Drawing, glass/steel wire, 1971-72, 17x17x1", C-NY 5/4/88 30,800

WINANT, Alice (Canadian, 20th C)
Fisherman Seated on a Stump, sterling slvr, wood plinth, 15" excluding plinth, lot 339, SLK 2/12/88 400

WITKIN, Isaac (20th C)
Shogun Variation (contemporary), brass/limestone, ca 1978-79, 17x31", SBY 10/5/88 2,750
Study for Untitled Sculpture (abstract), 3/3, steel, sgn/dtd 1976, 8x16", SBY 10/5/88 1,540

WOJNAROWICZ, David
Untitled (Money Pig Skull), mixed media, sgn/dtd 1985 NYC, 14x8x15", lot 316, C-NY 5/4/89 4,400

WOLFE, James (American, 1944-)
Guardian Quartet, welded steel, 1984, 88x55x63", lot 714, LH 5/15/88 1,000

WOTRUBA, Fritz (Austrian, 1907-1975)
Kleine Stehende Figur, 7/7, gr/golden patinae, sgn/mk Guss A Zottl Wien, 1958, 15", lot 173, C-NY 10/5/89 OE 17,600
Liegende Figur (contemporary), dk brn/golden patinae, 1951, 22" long, lot 51, SBY 2/15/89 OE 9,900
Untitled (contemporary figures in relief), dk brn patina, intl, 19x27", lot 50, SBY 2/15/89 5,500

WOUW, see Van Wouw

YANDELL, Enid (American, 1870-1936)
Bacchanal of the Sun (sundial), gr patina, sgn/Henry Bonnard Bronze Co, 31", lot 101, RWS 5/12/89 10,000

YVARAL (20th C)
Interferance (wall relief), blk elastic string/acrylic on panel, sgn/dtd 1967, 35x35", C-E 11/7/88 330

ZACH, Bruno (Austrian, 20th C)
Adagio (dancing couple), dk gr patina, veined blk marble base, 17", lot 185, C-NY 6/11/88 1,980
Ballerina, blk patina, gr marble base, mk Made in Austria, 19", lot 196, C-NY 6/11/88 2,640
Ballerina, onyx base, 6", lot 381, FAP 4/15/88 UE 220
Ballerina (standing in long/full skirt), brn patina, sgn, 16", lot 202, C-NY 6/11/88 1,760
Ballerina (standing), blk patina, veined pk marble base, sgn, 20", lot 195, C-NY 6/11/88 1,650
Dancing Couple, dk gr patina, blk veined marble socle, sgn, 16", C-NY 6/11/88 1,980
Dancing Girl, formed as a vide poche; cold paint, circular veined gray onyx tray, sgn, 7", lot 214, C-NY 6/11/88 OE 880
Dancing Girl, head back/holding out skirts; blk patina, gr onyx vide poche base, sgn/mk Austria, 7", C-E 12/8/88 OE 385
Dancing Girl (in simple flowing gown), gilt, blk marble base, sgn, 19", re-gilted/lacquered, lot 208, C-NY 6/11/88 2,200
Dirty Dancing, gilt, wht onyx base, sgn, lot 194, C-NY 6/11/88 3,300
Embracing Couple (dancers in ecstatic embrace), brn patina, gr marble oval base, ca 1930, 12", lot 105, SBY 11/17/88 4,400
Fashionable Lady, Holding Her Skirt; gr-brn patina, gr marble base, sgn/mk Made in Austria, 13", lot 205, C-NY 6/11/88 1,320
Fashionable Lady with an Umbrella, polychrome, blk marble base, sgn, 25", C-NY 6/11/88 7,700
Fashionable Young Lady, wearing boots/holds umbrella; reddish-brn patina, yel-brn marble base, sgn, 13", C-NY 6/11/88 1,320
Female Bather (standing), polychrome, wht onyx base, sgn, 12", lot 210, C-NY 6/11/88 OE 1,320
Female Bather Wearing a Cap, cold paint, gr onyx base, sgn, 14", lot 206, C-NY 6/11/88 1,320
Female Fencer (bare-breasted), polychrome, veined blk marble base, 29", C-NY 6-11-88 OE 14,300

Female Figure Bending Over Tying Her Shoe, cold paint/parcel gilt, gr onyx base, sgn, 5", lot 212, C-NY 6/11/88 ... 550
Female Figure Wearing a Kimono (bare-breasted), blk lacquered bronze, wht marble base, sgn, 16", lot 207, C-NY 6/11/88 ... 880
Female Jockey (standing), gilt, veined wht marble base, sgn, 17", C-NY 6/11/88 ... 2,420
Figure of Standing Equestrienne, cold paint, blk veined marble base, sgn, 18", C-NY 6/11/88 ... 3,080
Flapper (arms crossed in front/knees together), gr-brn patina, dk gr marble base, ca 1930, 19", lot 102, SBY 11/17/88 ... 3,300
Flapper (in fringed dress/opera gloves), polychrome, rectangular base, mk Argentor Vienna, ca 1925, 33", SBY 11/17/88 ... 11,000
Flapper (semi-nude, in skirt belted w/hearts), cold paint, oval blk marble base, ca 1925, 25", lot 107, SBY 11/17/88 ... 9,350
Girl on a Rearing Horse, rich gr patina, gr marble base, sgn/mk Austria, 15", lot 201, C-NY 6/11/88 ... 2,640
Girl Seated in a Broken Eggshell, cold paint/gilt, marble base, sgn/mk Argentor Vien, 8", lot 197, C-NY 6/11/88 ... 4,180
Girl with a Cigarette (standing figure in pant suit), blk patina, blk marble base, sgn, 28", C-NY 6/11/88 ... 8,250
Girl with a Windblown Skirt, gilt, wht marble base, sgn/mk Argentor Vien, 16", lot 203, C-NY 6/11/88 ... 2,860
Lady Reclining in a Chair, w/separate piece formed as a dress; cold paint, square base, sgn, 3", lot 213, C-NY 6/11/88 ... 330
Male Athlete, blk lacquer/ivory, blk marble base, sgn, 10", lot 216, C-NY 6/11/88 ... 550
Man Smoking (in smoking jacket w/ascot, cigarette in right hand), brn patina, marble socle, ca 1930, 16", SBY 11/17/88 ... 5,775
Music Teacher Holding a Baton, gilt, wht marble base, sgn, 17", lot 209, C-NY 6/11/88 ... 1,760
Pair: Girls in the Wind; patina/ivory, gr veined marble base, sgn, 9", lot 211, C-NY 6/11/88 ... 1,650
Riding Crop (bare-breasted standing figure), golden patina, blk marble base, sgn/mk Austria, 12", C-NY 6/11/88 ... 1,870
Riding Crop (bare-breasted standing figure), rich brn patina/ivory, veined blk marble base, sgn, 12", C-NY 6/11/88 OE ... 9,350
Satyr, brn-blk patina, marble base, sgn, 16", C-NY 6/11/88 ... 1,980
Seated Fashionable Lady Holding a Puppy, rich gr patina, veined blk marble base, sgn/mk Austria, 11", C-NY 6/11/88 ... 1,980
Seated Girl, cold paint, veined blk marble base, sgn/mk Austria, 9", lot 199, C-NY 6/11/88 ... 1,760
Three Dancing Ladies, blk-brn patina, pk marble base, sgn/mk Argentor Vienna, 12x15", lt rpr, lot 200, C-NY 6/11/88 ... 2,090
Untitled, Pierrot holding Columbine in his arms; bronze/ivory, blk marble base, sgn/mk Austria, 16", C-E 9/16/88 OE ... 3,520
Untitled, young flapper in revealing costume; sgn/mk Argentor Vien, blk/gr marble base, ca 1900, 15", SBY 6/10/88 ... 1,100
Untitled (lady in short dress w/flaring skirt carries umbrella), blk patina, oval marble base, 1925, 25", SBY 11/17/88 ... 6,600
Untitled (lady in smoking suit/crossed arms/holds cigarette), blk patina/ivory, ca 1930, 29", lot 109, SBY 11/17/88 ... 13,200
Untitled (woman in smoking suit w/cigarette), blk patina/ivory, oval blk marble base, sgn, 28", lot 289, SBY 6/8/88 ... 20,350
Woman & Parrot, seated nude feeds parrot; lt brn patina/polychrome, red/wht marble base, ca 1920, 9", SBY 12/12/88 ... 1,320
Woman in Coat (nude except stockings/heels/hair comb), brn patina, oval marble base, ca 1930, 17", SBY 11/17/88 ... 5,225
Working Man, brn patina, gr marble base, mk Argentor Vienna on brass tag, 13", lot 215, C-NY 6/11/88 OE ... 880
Young Woman (bows on braids/gartered stockings/removing underwear), brn patina, onyx base, ca 1930, 16", SBY 11/17/88 OE ... 3,630

ZACH, Bruno; after (Austrian, 20th C)

Woman Smoking (in smoking suit), dk brn patina, waisted rectangular verde antico base, 15", lot 104, SBY 11/17/88 ... 3,300

ZADKINE, Ossip (French, 1890-1967)

Arlequin Hurland (contemporary), 2/6, brn patina, sgn/mk Modern Art NY, 1944/later, 37", lot 142, SBY 2/18/88 ... 57,750
Buste de Femme, terra cotta, sgn, 18", lot 56, SBY 2/18/88 ... 8,800
Femme se Tenant le Genou, dk brn patina, sgn, ca 1937, 11x7x9", lot 84, C-NY 2/18/88 OE ... 23,100
L'Eclair (head), wood, sgn/dtd 35, 14", SBY 10/7/88 OE ... 71,500
Le Violoncelliste (seated musician), 2/5, bl-gr patina, sgn/mk Risorglia, ca 1935, 17", lot 183, C-NY 2/18/88 OE ... 41,800
Torse (surrealistic torso), wood, sgn, ca 1935, sgn, 17", SBY 2/6/89 OE ... 79,750

ZELIKSON, Serge (Russian, 1890-)

Untitled (shackled muscular man kneels on rock), gr patina, ca 1920, 23", lot 99, SBY 3/19/88 UE ... 715

ZORACH, William (American, 1887-1966)

Dance (relief), ed of 6, golden patina, sgn/dtd 1920, 9x9", lot 263, SBY 4/14/89 OE ... 3,960
Hands, blk marble base, sgn, 8", lot 123, C-E 6/1/89 OE ... 1,100
Innocence (contemporary standing figure), golden patina, sgn, 14", lot 264, SBY 4/14/89 OE ... 3,575
Mother & Child, blk patina, sgn, 8" long, lot 303, SBY 6/28/89 ... 2,640
Portrait Head, 1/6, gold patina, sgn, 7", RWS 3/16/89 OE ... 2,300
Young Girl (nude), golden-brn patina, sgn, 1921, 9", SBY 3/17/88 ... 18,700

ZUNIGA, Francisco (Costa Rican, 1913-)

Desnudo de Pie (standing nude), III/VI, dk brn patina, sgn/dtd 1971, 21", C-NY 11/21/88 OE ... 28,600
La Abuela (grandmother w/child), I/III, lt brn patina, sgn/dtd 1971, 1970/1971, 30", C-NY 5/17/89 ... 44,000
Madra y Hija (mother & daughter), I/VI, gr patina, sgn/dtd, 1978, 12", C-NY 5/17/89 OE ... 35,200
Mother & Child, IV/VI, sgn/dtd 77, 13", SBY 5/16/89 OE ... 24,200
Mother & Child, VII, sgn/dtd 1960, 19", SBY 11/21/88 ... 17,600
Mujer con Naranja (squatting woman w/orange), AP, brn patina, sgn/dtd 1973, 8", C-NY 11/21/88 ... 5,500
Mujer de Pie (standing woman), III/IV, gr patina, sgn, 16", C-NY 5/17/89 ... 18,700
Nude (squatting), 2/9, sgn, 7", SBY 11/21/88 ... 7,975
Seated Nude, XV/XXVIII, gr patina, sgn/dtd 1974, 14", SBY 11/21/88 ... 9,900
Seated Woman, I/VI, brn patina, sgn/dtd 1977, 14", SBY 11/21/88 ... 13,200
Seated Woman, IV/V, sgn, 13", SBY 5/16/89 OE ... 27,500
Standing Woman, gr-golden patina, sgn, 1962, 16", SBY 5/16/89 ... 12,100
Three Women, III/VI, sgn/dtd 1890, 17", SBY 5/16/89 OE ... 30,800

Paintings, Drawings, and Mixed Media

A.M.C. (American School, 20th C)
Portrait of a Woman (half-length wearing a blue coat), oil on canvas, 23x18", SLK 5/12/88 ..... **350**
A.N.N. (Australian, 19th C)
Sydney Harbour From Garden Island, watercolor heightened w/white, indistinctly initialed, ca 1860, 7x13", C-SK 5/25/89 ..... **735**
A.P. (British, 19th C)
Harbor Scene at Dusk with Multiple Boats, oil on canvas, monogramed/dtd 1888, 12x20", SLK 9/26/88 ..... **360**
A.W. (British, 20th C)
Attentive Sheep Dog, oil on canvas, monogramed/dtd 1902, 11 x15", SLK 5/12/88 ..... **260**
AACHEN, Hans; see Von Aachen
ABBATE, Nicolo; see Dell'Abbate
ABBEMA, Louise (French, 1858-1927)
Private Concert (seated lady playing piano), oil on canvas, sgn, 20x16", RAB 3/27/89 ..... **900**
Suzon et Fly, oil on canvas, sgn/inscr/dtd 1820, 21x31", SBY 12/9/88 ..... **1,860**
ABBETT, Arnold A. (British, 19th C)
Harbor Scene with Passing Tug in the Foreground, watercolor on paper, sgn/dtd 31, 12x17", RAB 8/1/88 ..... **350**
ABBEY, Edwin Austin (American, 1852-1911)
Gentleman Gardner (full-length portrait), pencil on paper, sgn/dtd 1882, 20x16", RWS 5/19/88 OE **800**
Greeting at the Door, watercolor/gouache on paper, sgn/dtd 1883, 11x14", C-E 6/1/88 ..... **660**
Medieval Lady Wearing a Wimple, pastel on paper, sgn/dtd 1895, 19x27", WD 10/5/88 UE **3,000**
Portrait of a Young Lady, gray wash, sgn/dtd, 13x11", WG 9/16/88 ..... **500**
ABDY, Rowena Meeks (American, 1887-1945)
Ravello, oil on canvas, sgn, 35x30", B/B 10/6/88 ..... **6,050**
Village Street, San Juan Bautista; oil on canvas, sgn, 28x42", B/B 10/6/88 OE **13,200**
ABEITTE, F. (French, 1865-1912)
Study of a Zouave, oil on panel, sgn, 11x7", LH 3/20/88 UE **50**
ABEL, Frank (American, 19th/20th C)
Rialto Bridge, Venice; oil on board, sgn, 7x11", B/B 8/10/88 ..... **990**
ABEL-BOULINEAU, N. (French, 20th C)
Figures by a River's Edge, oil on canvas, sgn/inscr Cyzy, 32x46", C-NY 2/23/89 OE **10,450**
ABELA, Eduardo (Cuban, 1892-1966)
Painting No 15 (abstract), mixed media on board, sgn, 16x20", SBY 5/17/88 ..... **2,750**
Painting No 20 (abstract), mixed media on board, sgn, 16x13", SBY 5/17/88 ..... **2,200**
ABRACHEFF, Nicolai (American, 1897-)
Mill Houses on the Water, oil on canvas, sgn, 30x25", SBY 6/24/88 ..... **1,980**
ABRAHAMS, Helen
Interior Kitchen Scene, oil on canvas, sgn, 25x30", C-E 10/18/89 ..... **1,100**
ABREU, Mario (20th C)
Jungle (contemporary), acrylic on canvas, sgn twice/titled Selvas y Lianas, 1988, 63x51", SBY 11/21/88 ..... **6,600**
Jungle & Moon's Bird, acrylic on canvas, sgn twice/titled, 1987, 63x51", SBY 5/17/88 ..... **6,050**
Sun (contemporary scene of dove/snake in landscape before sun), acrylic on canvas, sgn, 1987, 63x51", SBY 5/16/89 ..... **7,150**
ABRY, Leon Eugene Auguste (Belgian, 1857-1905)
Over the Fence (horse w/jockey jumping fence), oil on canvas, sgn/dtd 03, 26x32", SBY 6/9/89 ..... **6,600**
ABSOLON, John (British, 1815-1895)
Italian Girl with a Tambourine, watercolor/gouache over pencil, sgn, 18x13", C-NY 5/25/88 ..... **1,650**
ABSOLON, John; att (British, 1815-1895)
Dancing on the Village Green, oil on canvas, sgn, 12x18", FB 10/17/88 ..... **475**
ACHEFF, William (20th C)
Water Vessels, oil on canvas, sgn 3 times/inscr/copyrighted/dtd 1980, 22x30", SBY 9/23/88 OE **16,500**
ACHENBACH, Andreas (German, 1815-1910)
Looking Out to Sea, oil on canvas, sgn, 15x17", SBY 10/24/89 ..... **8,250**
ACHENBACH, Oswald (German, 1827-1905)
Mountain Trek, oil on panel, sgn, 11x14", SBY 2/22/89 ..... **6,600**
ACHENBACH, Oswald; att (German, 1827-1905)
Gulf of Naples, bears signature, unfr, 16x24", C-E 2/23/88 ..... **935**
ACHILLI, I. (American, 20th C)
Landscape with a Lake in the Middle Distance & Mountains Beyond, oil on canvas, sgn/dtd 1920, 11x14", SLK 2/12/88 ..... **100**
ACHTSCHELLINCK, Lucas (Flemish, 1626-1699)
Extensive Landscape with Figures Walking Along a Path, oil on canvas, 66x96", SBY 6/1/89 OE **24,200**
ACKERSON, Floyd Garrison (American, 1899-)
Landscape, oil on canvasboard, sgn, 25x30", WG 9/16/88 ..... **500**
ADAM, Albrecht (German, 1786-1862)
By the Well, oil on canvas, sgn/dtd, ca 1830s, 19x25", C-NY 2/25/88 OE **26,400**
ADAM, Joseph (British, 1842-1896)
Cattle in Mountains, oil on canvas, sgn, 30x50", FAP 4/15/89 ..... **880**
ADAM, Julius (German, 1852-1913)
Kittens at Play, oil on canvas, sgn, 29x53", FAP 4/15/89 OE **42,350**
Kittens in a Basket, oil on canvas, sgn, 12x18", WD 11/16/88 ..... **25,000**
Playful Kittens, oil on panel, 8x6", SBY 2/22/89 ..... **18,700**

ADAM, Richard Benno (German, 1873-1936)
Picking Up the Scent (hunters on horses w/dogs in a landscape), oil on canvas, sgn/dtd 1906-1907, 26x34", SBY 6/9/89 .... **5,500**
ADAMS, Charles Partridge (American, 1858-1942)
Autumn Haystacks (in grassy meadow, trees beyond), watercolor on paper, sgn/dtd 1896, 10x13", RWS 9/29/88 .... **275**
Coastal Scene (gentle waves along shore), oil on canvas, sgn, 23x30", C-E 6/1/89 .... **3,850**
Sunset Over Marshlands, watercolor on paper, sgn, 9x13", RWS 9/8/89 .... **375**
Twilight West of Denver (low brush opens into expansive landscape), watercolor on paper, sgn, 6x9", RWS 3/31/88 .... **450**
View to the Sierras, Sundown; watercolor/gouache/graphite on paper, sgn, 8x12", RWS 11/10/89 .... **500**
ADAMS, Ed
Sailing Ship in Stormy Seas, oil on canvas, sgn/dtd 1884, 21x26", C-E 10/25/88 .... **1,540**
ADAMS, Jeff (20th C)
Untitled (abstract), oil on plaster on wood, 1987, 40x46", SBY 2/14/89 .... **1,760**
ADAMS, John Clayton (British, 1840-1906)
Distant View of Windsor Castle, oil on canvas, bears signature/dtd 1880, 40x72", SBY 12/9/88 OE **13,200**
ADAMS, Wayman (American, 1883-1959)
American Lady (well-dressed woman seated before a painting), oil on canvas, sgn, orig Harer fr, 46x36", RWS 3/31/88 OE **2,600**
Woman with a Parasol, oil on board, sgn, 20x15", RWS 11/3/88 OE **3,000**
Woman with Parasol (standing in doorway), oil on board, sgn, 20x15", SBY 4/14/89 OE **4,125**
ADAMS, Willis Seaver (American, 1844-1921)
Walk in Mist (figure in landscape), oil on canvas, sgn, 20x16", SBY 3/17/88 .... **1,650**
ADAN, Louis Emile (French, 1839-1937)
Discovery (two figures & goats in a landscape), oil on canvas, sgn, 22x29", B/B 11/9/88 OE **24,750**
Pair: La Musique; La Danse (lady playing guitar, lady dancing); oil on canvas, sgn, 14x10", C-NY 5/24/89 .... **13,200**
ADDY, Alfred (American, 20th C)
Pond Scene, watercolor, sgn/dtd 1907, 21x28", MG 8/27/88 .... **110**
ADEMA, Gerhardus Jan (Dutch, 1898-)
Skating on the Canal, oil on panel, sgn, 8x7", B/B 1/11/89 .... **660**
ADLER, Edmund (German, 1871-1957)
Family Seated in an Interior, oil on canvas laid down on board, sgn, 21x27", SBY 12/9/88 OE **4,400**
Favorite Pets (girl & boy feeding rabbits), oil on canvas, sgn, 27x22", C-NY 2/23/89 .... **5,500**
In Case of the Rain, oil on panel, sgn, 21x17", C-NY 2/25/88 .... **7,150**
Pair: Cheerful Siblings (portraits); oil on panel, sgn, 10x8", C-NY 2/23/89 .... **4,950**
Pet Chick, oil on canvas, sgn, 20x16", LH 10/16/88 .... **5,500**
Snowman (depicts children making a snowman), oil on canvas, sgn, 22x27", DM 5/13/88 .... **7,500**
ADLER, Jankel (Polish, 1895-1949)
Pair: Couple; Seated Figure; ink on paper, stamped twice w/signature, 30x17", 21x15", SBY 10/5/88 .... **2,200**
Seated Figure (abstract), oil on board, sgn, 25x20", SBY 5/30/89 OE **19,800**
Standing Figure (abstract), oil on panel, sgn, 29x21", SBY 5/30/89 .... **13,200**
Still Life of Lobster & Lemon, oil/sand on canvas, sgn, ca 1928, 18x24", SBY 5/30/89 .... **11,000**
Two Figures, oil on canvas, sgn, 1944, 44x34", SBY 10/5/88 OE **29,700**
Woman Holding a Torch (abstract), oil on canvas, sgn, 1948, 51x26", SBY 5/30/89 .... **27,500**
ADNET, Francoise (French, 1924-)
Pair: Seated Girl with Fruit; Still Life; oil on canvas, sgn, 21x13", FB 5/89 .... **1,500**
ADOMEIT, George G. (American, 1879-)
Farm House with Haystacks, oil on board, sgn, 15x20", WG 9/16/88 .... **125**
ADRIAENSSEN, Alexander (Flemish, 1557-1661)
Group of Fish Arranged on Plates, All on a Ledge; oil on canvas, sgn/dtd 1644, unfr, 22x26", C-NY 10/20/88 .... **7,700**
ADRIAN, M. (German, 19th C)
Pair: Setting Out; Fishermen Casting Their Nets; oil on canvas, sgn, 16x26", C-NY 2/23/89 .... **6,050**
ADRIEN, Camille (French, 1834-1901)
Mort de Priam, oil on canvas, indistinctly sgn, 75x102", SBY 2/22/89 .... **33,000**
ADRION, Lucien (French, 1889-1953)
Along the Boulevard, Paris; oil on canvas, sgn, 24x36", WD 5/5/88 UE **2,100**
Bievres en Automne (autumn street scene), oil on canvas, sgn/dtd 38, 21x29", C-E 11/17/88 .... **3,960**
La Cremaillere a Deauville, oil on canvas, sgn, 24x29", C-E 11/17/88 OE **7,700**
Les Champs Elysee, oil on canvas, sgn, 22x26", C-NY 2/18/88 OE **8,250**
Maison et Jardin (landscape w/house & garden), oil on canvas, sgn, 18x24", C-E 11/17/88 .... **1,980**
Place de la Concorde, oil on canvas, sgn, 26x32", C-NY 2/18/88 .... **3,080**
Place de la Concorde, oil on panel, sgn, 23x29", SBY 10/7/89 .... **5,775**
Place du Carrousel, oil on canvas, sgn/inscr, 20x24", C-E 11/17/88 OE **5,500**
Rue d'Harlequin, oil on canvas, sgn/dtd 38, 25x31", B/B 3/17/88 .... **2,090**
Street Scene, oil on canvas, sgn, 24x29", SBY 10/5/88 .... **2,090**
AERTSEN, Pieter (Dutch, 1507-1575)
Kitchen Scene, with Christ in the House of Mary & Martha; oil on panel, 43x47", C-NY 10/20/88 OE **13,200**
Portrait of a Lady, aged 24, half-length, wearing a simple black & brown costume...; oil on panel, 1562, C-NY 1/11/89 OE **88,000**
AERTSEN, Pieter; circle of (Dutch, 1507-1575)
Vegetable Seller, oil on panel, 41x29", C-NY 6/2/88 OE **15,400**
AFFLECK, William (British, 1869-)
Wildflowers (children in meadow w/village beyond), watercolor, sgn, unfr, 16x12", C-NY 2/23/89 OE **18,700**
AFRICANO, Nicholas (American, 20th C)
Her Nose Is Bleeding (two figures), acrylic/wax/oil on canvas, sgn/dtd 1977, 75x83", C-NY 10/4/89 .... **14,300**

Jekyll & Hyde: He Fled From the Scene of These Excesses; oil/acrylic/magna on canvas, sgn/dtd 85, 51x63", SBY 5/3/89 OE **26,400**
Jekyll/Hyde-The Mixture (contemporary); oil/acrylic magna on canvas, sgn/dtd 1982/titled, 52x64", SBY 11/11/88 OE **35,750**
Oysters in Vinegar Again!, oil on masonite, sgn/dtd 1981, 15x27", SBY 10/8/88 ..... **4,400**
Shadow Boxer, oil/acrylic/wax on panel, 48x72", C-NY 5/4/88 OE **19,800**
The Scream (figure on chair), oil/acrylic/magna on canvas, sgn/dtd 1976-77, 89x62", SBY 5/3/89 OE **25,300**
You'll Have To Kill Me First, oil/acrylic/enamel on masonite , artist's frame, sgn/dtd 1980-81, 48x84", SBY 2/15/89 ..... **18,700**

AFRO, Balsadella (Italian, 1912-)
New York (abstract), oil on canvasboard, sgn, ca 1955, 36x17", SBY 10/8/88 ..... **29,700**
Occhio di Vetro, oil on canvas, sgn/dtd 48, 39x27", C-NY 11/10/89 ..... **35,200**
Sperlonga (abstract), oil on canvas, sgn/dtd 60, 29x39", SBY 2/19/88 OE **35,750**
Still Life, oil on board, sgn, 20x14", SBY 2/14/89 ..... **5,775**
Untitled (abstract), charcoal on paper laid down on cardboard, sgn/dtd 1952, 33x26", SBY 10/8/88 ..... **8,800**
Untitled (abstract), gouache on paper, sgn/dtd 1950, SBY 10/8/88 ..... **8,800**
Untitled (abstract), gouache on paper mounted on canvas, sgn/dtd 62, 20x27", SBY 2/19/88 OE **12,100**
Untitled (abstract), watercolor/pastel on paper laid down on cardboard, sgn/dtd 1952, 16x10", SBY 10/8/88 ..... **6,050**

AGAFANOV, E. (Russian)
Russian Troika, oil on canvas, sgn, 23x35", C-L 10/8/88 OE **3,670**

AGAM, Yaacov (Israeli, 1928-)
Blue Star, gouache on paper, sgn/dtd 71, 23x23", WD 5/5/88 OE **6,000**
Communication Night, oil on corrugated wood mounted by the artist, sgn/dtd 74, 13x28", SBY 5/30/89 ..... **22,000**
Study for Pace of Time, oil on corrugated metal mounted by the artist, 20x17", SBY 5/30/89 ..... **30,800**
Untitled (abstract), gouache on board, sgn/dtd 1970, 29x29", SBY 10/5/88 OE **5,225**
Untitled (vertical lineation), gouache on paper, sgn/dtd 70, 30x29", SBY 10/7/89 ..... **4,125**

AGNEW, Clark (American, 19th/20th C)
Portrait of F Scott & Zelda Fitzgerald, oil on canvas, sgn/dtd 28, 36x30", B/B 10/9/88 ..... **5,500**

AGOSTINELLI (French, 20th C)
Le Champs Elysees, oil on board, sgn, 15x18", B/B 9/15/88 ..... **880**

AGOSTINI, Guido (Italian, 19th C)
Sorento (coastal scene w/dwellings on a cliff), oil on canvas, sgn/indistinctly dtd, 17x13", C-E 5/22/89 ..... **3,300**

AGOSTINI, Peter (American, 1913-)
Pair: Three Reclining Figures; Seated Figure; watercolor on paper, sgn/dtd 56, 11x16", 16x9", SBY 2/14/89 UE **990**

AGOSTINI, Tony (American/Italian, 1916-)
Pair: Still Life of Flowers; Still Life of Fruit; oil on canvas, 1 sgn, 1 sgn/inscr, 11x6", 11x14", SBY 10/5/88 ..... **825**

AGRASOT Y JUAN, Joaquim (Spanish, 1836-1907)
Flutist, watercolor over traces of pencil, sgn, 14x9", C-E 10/25/88 UE **286**
Holiday in Valencia, oil on canvas, sgn/dtd 1881, 19x31", SBY 5/23/89 OE **88,000**
Young Mozart, oil on canvas, sgn, 16x26", B/B 3/17/88 ..... **6,050**

AGUILA
Woman Wearing a White Mantilla, oil on panel, sgn/inscr, 21x13", C-E 10/25/88 ..... **1,650**

AGUILAR, Homero
Interior, oil on canvas, sgn/dtd Cali 87, 37x50", C-NY 11/21/88 ..... **4,180**

AHL, Henry Hammond (American, 1869-1953)
Sunset Hour (brilliant sun in dark sky), oil on board, sgn, 6x6", RAB 8/9/88 UE **200**
Sunset Over Marshlands (fiery clouds reflected in water), oil on artist board, sgn, 8x10", RWS 9/29/88 ..... **400**

AHLBORN, Emil (American, 19th/20th C)
Bleak House Peterborough, New Hampshire; oil on canvas, titled/inscr, 21x23", RWS 5/12/89 ..... **400**

AHORN, John (British, 20th C)
Grazing Sheep, watercolor, sgn, 12x18", MG 8/27/88 ..... **100**

AICHLEIN, T. (Continental, 20th C)
Figures Beneath a Tree, watercolor on paper, sgn/dtd 50, 24x19", FAP 4/15/89 UE **110**

AID, George Charles (American, 1872-)
Man of War Under Sail, oil on canvas, sgn, 23x36", SLK 5/11/88 ..... **1,800**

AIKEN, Charles Avery (American, 1872-1965)
Table Top Still Life of Sculpture & Vase, oil on masonite, sgn, 30x25", RWS 4/7/89 ..... **425**

AINSLEY, Dennis (American, 20th C)
Belgian Flower Market, oil on canvas, sgn, 16x20", FAP 4/15/89 ..... **440**
Parisian Street Scene, oil on canvas, sgn, 28x38", SLK 5/12/88 ..... **500**

AIVAZOFFSKI, Ivan Constantinovich (Russian, 1817-1900)
Black Sea (seascape), oil on canvas, sgn twice/dtd 1899 twice/inscr, 40x61", C-NY 2/23/89 ..... **51,700**
Moonlit Coast with Fort & Minaret, oil on canvas, initialed/sgn/dtd 1888, 13x11", C-L 10/8/88 OE **37,180**
Shipping in Rough Waters, oil on canvas, sgn in cyrillic/dtd 1895, 24x39", SBY 2/22/89 OE **58,300**

AIVAZOFFSKI, Ivan Constantinovich; att (Russian, 1817-1900)
Ship Offshore, oil on canvas, sgn/dtd 1900, 8x11", SBY 7/12/89 OE **7,150**

AIZPIRI, Paul (French, 1919-)
Arlequinade (figures), gouache/watercolor/pen/ink on paper, sgn, 29x22", C-E 5/9/89 OE **10,450**
Le Clown, oil on canvas, sgn, 35x27", C-NY 2/13/89 OE **24,200**
Le Clown Musicien, oil on canvas, sgn, 40x29", SBY 10/7/89 OE **48,400**
Pichet et Tapis Rouge, oil on gouache on canvas, sgn, 24x36", C-E 5/13/88 OE **13,200**
Portrait of a Woman with Fan, oil on canvas, sgn, 46x35", SBY 10/7/89 OE **55,000**
Sanary, oil on canvas, sgn twice, 24x29", SBY 10/5/88 OE **14,300**
Still Life of Lantern & Clarinet, oil on canvas, sgn, 33x44", SBY 2/14/89 ..... **24,200**

AKERSDIJK, Jacob (Dutch, 1815-1862)
17th Century Interior with Lady Seated Playing a Mandolin, with Man & Woman Listening; oil on panel, 26x20", SLK 5/9/88 ... 500

AKIMOV, Nikolai Pavlovich (Russian, 1901-1968)
Fashion Design, watercolor/pencil on paper, sgn, ca 1930, 10x6", C-L 10/8/88 ... 560

AKKERINGA, Johan; att (Dutch, 1864-)
Fisherfolk by the Beach, oil on panel, sgn, 7x13", C-E 2/23/88 OE ... 1,980

ALBAN, Samuel
Horses on a Sandy Beach, oil on canvasboard, sgn/indistinctly inscr, 12x16", C-E 5/23/88 UE ... 715

ALBANI, Francesco; att (Italian, 1578-1660)
Expulsion of Hagar, pen/brown ink/wash heightened w/white over red chalk, 15x11", SBY 1/13/89 ... 2,970
Sleeping Child & Study of a Foot, red chalk, 11x8", SBY 1/13/89 ... 4,400

ALBANI, Francesco; circle of (Italian, 1578-1660)
Aurora Bringing the Early Dawn, oil on canvas, unfr, 25x39", SBY 10/21/88 ... 3,850

ALBANI, Francesco; follower of (Italian, 1578-1660)
Pair: Allegories of Summer & Winter; oil on canvas, 14x19", SBY 4/7/88 ... 4,950

ALBANI, Francesco; school of (Italian, 1578-1660)
Cupid Having His Wings Clipped, oil on canvas, 34x28", C-E 4/7/88 ... 935
Diana & Her Nymphs Bathing in a Landscape, oil on canvas, 22x44", C-E 4/7/88 ... 660

ALBERIA, A.
Roman Fountain, oil on canvas, sgn/dtd, 25x38", C-E 10/ 25/88 ... 2,860

ALBEROLA, Jean Michel (20th C)
Petit Africa (abstract), acrylic on marbelized blue paper, dtd 1984, 26x20", C-E 11/14/89 ... 2,200
Suzanne & the Elders Return, oil on canvas, sgn/dtd 1984 twice/inscr Acteon Fecit/titled, 64x59", C-NY 11/10/88 OE ... 9,350

ALBERS, August C.
Group of 4: Four Seasons; oil on panel, 21x24", C-E 1/12/88 OE ... 528

ALBERS, Josef (American, 1888-1976)
Flying, oil on masonite, sgn/dtd 1929 & 39/titled, 24x18", C-NY 11/10/88 OE ... 28,600
Homage to the Square: Arrival; oil on masonite, sgn/dtd 1963/titled, 48x48", C-NY 2/23/89 OE ... 165,000
Homage to the Square: Fusion; oil on masonite, sgn/dtd 1965, 24x24", C-NY 5/4/89 ... 46,200
Pair: Modified Repetition; Biconjugate; oil on paper/oil on blotter paper, sgn, 1943, 12x18" & 17x22", SBY 2/15/89 ... 22,000
Pair: Vice Versa B; Vice Versa C; oil on blotter paper, sgn, 1943, 16x22", 15x22", SBY 2/15/89 OE ... 29,700
Study for Homage to the Square, oil on masonite, initialed/dtd 63, 18x18", SBY 11/11/88 OE ... 27,500
Study for Homage to the Square: Amber; oil on masonite, sgn twice/dtd 64 twice/titled, 30x30", SBY 11/11/88 OE ... 44,000
Study for Homage to the Square: Awake; oil on masonite, initialed/sgn, dtd twice 1957, 18x18", SBY 10/8/88 ... 25,300
Study for Homage to the Square: Desert Dusk; oil on masonite, sgn/initialed/dtd 1958 twice/titled, 30x30", SBY 5/3/88 ... 33,000
Study for Homage to the Square: Gold Miniature; oil on masonite, initialed/dtd 61 twice/titled, 16x16", SBY 5/3/88 ... 20,900
Study for Homage to the Square: Heavy+Bright Under Veil; oil on masonite, sgn/dtd 64, 16x16", C-NY 2/14/89 ... 33,000
Study for Homage to the Square: Mild Signal; oil on masonite, initialed/dtd 66, 18x18", SBY 2/15/89 ... 27,500
Study for Homage to the Square: Nocturne; oil on masonite, initialed/dtd 50-70, 16x16", SBY 10/5/89 ... 30,800
Study for Homage to the Square: Renewed Hope, Encouraged Belief; oil on aluminum, sgn/dtd 55, 24x24", SBY 5/2/88 OE ... 29,700

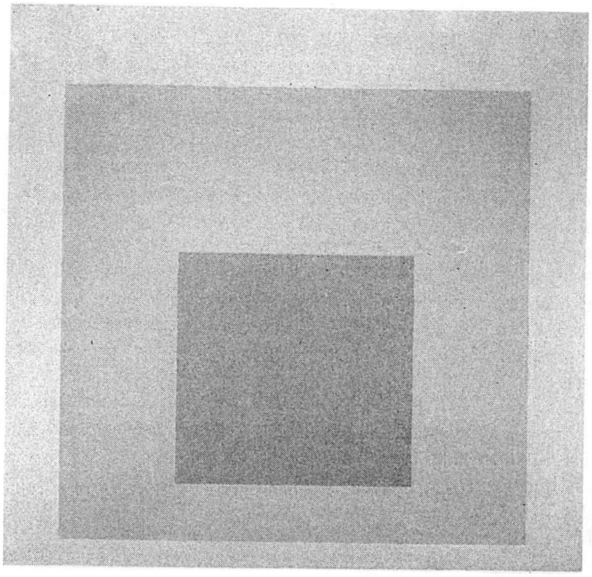

Study for Homage to the Square: Shaded Shade; oil on masonite, monogramed/sgn/dtd 63/titled, 40x40", C-NY 11/10/88 OE, $88,000

Study to Homage to the Square: Portal (abstract); oil on board, sgn twice/dtd 56/titled, 24x24", SBY 2/19/88 OE ... 39,600

LBERT, Arthur (American, 1919-1987)
Boxing Match, pencil/black crayon on paper, sgn, 13x20", SBY 3/17/88 ... 825
Dance Hall, India ink/brown ink/white gouache/red watercolor on paper, sgn twice/inscr Groth, unfr, 15x18", SBY 3/17/88 ... 2,090
Flight by Firelight, oil on canvas, sgn/dtd 1947, 25x46", SBY 5/24/89 OE ... 22,000
Knock Out, oil on board, sgn, 10x17", C-E 11/30/88 UE ... 550

Laughing Faces, pen/ink/watercolor on paper laid down on board, sgn, 6x11", C-E 11/30/88 UE ... 440
Military Parade, India ink/charcoal on paper, sgn/dtd 37, 20x12", SBY 9/23/88 ... 605
Nudist Camp, oil on canvas, sgn, unfr, 36x46", SBY 3/17/88 UE ... 1,980
Pair: Bar Room Fight; Ambulance Scene; oil on board, sgn, 10x18", 13x18", SBY 9/23/88 ... 2,200
Sin (fantasy composition), oil on canvas, sgn, unfr, 45x60", C-E 6/1/89 ... 2,860
Study for Sin, oil on canvas, sgn, unfr, 28x40", SBY 3/17/88 UE ... 1,760
Study for Sin, pen/brown ink/blue ink on paper, sgn, 22x29", C-E 6/1/89 OE ... 1,870
Untitled (line figures doing handstands), enamel on wood, sgn/dtd 83, 12x11", SBY 10/8/88 ... 6,600

ALBERT, E. Maxwell (American, 1890-)
October Landscape, oil on canvas, sgn/dtd 1939, 35x30", C-E 2/1/89 ... 1,320

ALBERT, Ernest (American, 1857-1946)
Among the Hills (landscape w/stream), oil on canvas, sgn, 20x24", C-E 2/1/89 ... 3,300
Bathers #3, oil on masonite, sgn/dtd 84, 24x18", C-NY 11/10/88 ... 19,800
Late Afternoon (snow landscape w/hills & stream), oil on canvas, sgn, 25x30", SBY 1/24/89 OE ... 10,450
October Afternoon, oil on canvas, sgn/dtd 1938, 25x30", C-NY 9/28/89 ... 5,500
Path by the River (autumn landscape), oil on canvas, sgn/dtd 1936, 32x40", C-NY 5/25/89 ... 15,400
Stream in Winter, oil on board, sgn, 12x16", SBY 9/14/89 ... 2,640
White & Lavender (snowy landscape), oil on canvas, sgn/dtd 1938, 32x40", C-NY 3/11/88 ... 10,450
Winter, Dusk; oil on canvas, sgn/indistinctly dtd, 16x20", PHL 12/1/88 ... 1,600

ALBERT, Hermann (20th C)
Return of the Stranger, tempera on burlap in hand-painted fr, sgn/dtd 83, 81x100", C-E 11/17/88 ... 2,970

ALBORI, V.
Italian Genre Scene (gentleman seated next to a woman holding a child), oil on canvas, sgn, 25x31", DM 3/14/88 OE ... 7,500

ALBRIGHT, Adam Emory (American, 1862-1957)
California Terrace, oil on canvas, sgn, 34x26", C-NY 9/30/88 ... 4,400
On the Pier, oil on canvas, sgn, 26x20", C-NY 3/11/88 ... 8,250
Riding High, oil on canvas, sgn, 28x18", C-E 10/18/89 OE ... 3,850
Two Boys Fishing (one stands at shore, another in small boat), oil on canvas, sgn, 24x18", C-E 6/1/89 OE ... 10,450
Two Young Clam Diggers, oil on canvas laid on board, sgn/dtd 1941, 24x36", SBY 9/14/89 ... 4,400

ALBRIGHT, Ivan Le Lorraine (American, 1897-1985)
Interior Scene, watercolor on paper, sgn/dtd 1931, 14x10", SBY 1/24/89 OE ... 2,750

ALBRIZIO, Conrad (American, 20th C)
Green Landscape, oil on canvas, sgn, 26x32", MG 5/28/88 ... 300

ALBRO, Maxine (American, 1903-1966)
Mexican Child with Flowers, oil on canvas, sgn, 20x20", B/B 1/11/89 OE ... 1,320

ALDINE, Marc (Italian, 1917-)
Canal in Venice, oil on canvas, sgn/inscr, 26x20", SBY 12/9/88 ... 2,475

ALDRICH, George Ames (American, 1872-1941)
Autumn Afternoon, Normandy; oil on canvas, sgn/dtd 1908, 32x48", SBY 6/24/88 OE ... 4,400
Cottages by the Stream, oil on canvas, sgn, 30x40", SBY 4/14/89 ... 2,090
In the Old City, oil on canvas, sgn, 30x25", C-NY 3/11/88 ... 2,200
La Chapelle, Seine et Marne; oil on panel, sgn, 20x24", SBY 9/23/88 ... 1,760
Milltown, oil on canvas, sgn, 30x36", C-E 11/30/88 UE ... 495
New England Mill, oil on board, sgn, 14x20", LH 10/16/88 UE ... 600
Stone Bridge Over a River, oil on canvas, sgn, 25x31", B/B 10/9/88 ... 3,575
Village by Moonlight, Normandy; oil on board, 25x30", PHL 12/1/88 ... 1,400
Village in the Distance (river landscape), oil on canvas, sgn, 25x30", C-E 6/1/89 ... 1,980

ALDRIDGE, Frederick James (British, 1850-1933)
Fishermen Returning Home, watercolor, sgn, 16x20", FB 5/28/89 ... 700
Leaving Port (sailing ships in choppy sea), watercolor on paper, sgn, 14x21", WG 4/23/88 UE ... 525
Ships on Rough Seas, watercolor on board, sgn, 9x28", C-E 6/1/88 UE ... 495

ALECHINSKY, Pierre (Belgian, 1927-)
A l'Enseigne Qui Grince (abstract), acrylic on paper laid down on canvas, sgn twice/dtd 1965/titled, 39x61", SBY 6/30/88 ... 60,000
A la Devanture (abstract), acrylic on paper laid down on canvas, sgn/dtd New York 1973/titled, 45x61", SBY 6/30/88 ... 92,000
Bleu de Sevres (abstract), acrylic on paper mounted on canvas, sgn twice/dtd 1977, 41x26", SBY 10/8/88 ... 29,700
La Vie Intime (abstract), oil on canvas, sgn twice/dtd X 1960-I 1963, 36x29", SBY 6/30/88 ... 80,000
Le Depart du Vice-Roi des Indes, acrylic on paper laid down on canvas, sgn/dtd 1967/titled, 54x76", SBY 11/11/88 OE ... 203,500
Le Principe Feminin (abstract figures), acrylic/gouache on paper laid down, sgn/dtd 1970, 61x118", SBY 11/9/89 OE ... 297,000
Paroles d'Eau (abstract), acrylic on paper laid down on canvas, sgn twice/dtd 1982/titled, 41x59", SBY 6/30/88 OE ... 64,000
Point d'Eau (abstract), acrylic on paper laid down on canvas, sgn twice/dtd NY 1981/titled, 39x61", SBY 2/19/88 ... 63,250
Response Poussiereuse (abstract composition), oil on canvas, sgn/dtd 1961, 53x40", SBY 5/3/89 OE ... 143,000
Rien de Plus (abstract), oil on canvas, sgn/dtd 1984, 24x20", C-NY 2/20/88 OE ... 18,700
Telle Sortant du Puits (abstract), acrylic on canvas, sgn twice/dtd 74, 45x61", SBY 6/30/88 ... 60,000
Untitled (abstract), ink/crayon on paper, sgn, 19x24", SBY 2/15/89 ... 4,950

ALEKSANDROVNA, Ol'ga (Russian, 20th C)
Small Boy Playing by a Hearth, watercolor on paper, sgn/dtd 1920, 10x10", C-L 10/8/88 ... 740

ALEXANDER, C. (British, 19th C)
Barnyard Scene, oil on canvas, sgn/dtd 1853, 16x24", SBY 6/8/88 ... 1,320

ALEXANDER, Clifford Grear (American, 1870-1954)
Early Spring, oil on canvas, sgn, 16x24", RWS 11/3/88 OE ... 1,200
Gray Silence (forest landscape), oil on canvas, sgn/dtd 1916, cvd gilt frame, 32x32", RWS 11/3/88 OE ... 4,500

Mountain Trout Brook, Franconia, New Hampshire (landscape); oil on canvas, sgn, 22x18", RWS 3/16/89 700
November (landscape w/stream), oil on canvas, sgn/dtd 1906, 18x24", RWS 5/12/89 2,100

LEXANDER, Francesca (American, 1837-1917)

Madonna & Child, oil/tempera/gold leaf on panel, 12x19", in orig gold trefoil frame, RWS 5/19/88 5,000

LEXANDER, John White (American, 1856-1915)

Alethea, (full-length portrait), oil on canvas, sgn/dtd 95, 64x53", SBY 5/25/88 517,000
Beelzebub & His Boys Dancing Around the Fires of Ishtar, oil on canvas, sgn/dtd 12.85, 90x100", SBY 10/8/88 OE 25,300
Juliette (The Green Dress), oil on canvas, sgn, ca 1897, 47x35", SBY 5/25/88 264,000
Landscape, oil on canvas, sgn, 50x50", SBY 2/14/89 1,760
Looking at Each Other, watercolor/chalk on paper, sgn/dtd 1983, 23x30", C-NY 11/10/88 5,720
Sanctuary (abstract), oil on canvas, 1983, 78x84", SBY 5/3/88 17,600
Untitled (abstract), oil on canvas, sgn/#d, 48x48", C-NY 2/20/88 UE 1,760
Untitled (abstract), oil on canvas, sgn/dtd 82, 64x70", SBY 5/5/89 14,300
Yellow Jacket (contemporary), oil on canvas, sgn/titled, 1984, 42x48", SBY 11/11/88 12,100

LFANI, Domenico

Madonna & Child (in a landscape), oil on panel, 24x18", C-NY 5/31/89 49,500

LFRED, Paul (Canadian)

Autumn, watercolor/bodycolor, sgn, 10x13", C-SK 11/10/88 1,120

LIGNY, Claude (French, 1798-1871)

Italian Landscape with Travelers Outside of Town, oil on pa nel, sgn/dtd, 17x26", SBY 7/12/89 UE 1,650

LIX, Gabriel

Market Road, acrylic on board, sgn, 20x24", SBY 10/7/89 247

LKEN, Henry (British, 19th C)

Derby & London Royal Mail on the Open Road in Winter (stagecoach w/figures), oil on canvas, 13x19", C-NY 5/24/89 8,800
Running Rein (racehorse w/jockey up), oil on canvas, sgn/dtd 1844, 13x16", C-E 5/22/89 3,960

LKEN, Henry Jr. (British, 1810-1894)

Caught in a Water Course (figures walking horses out of water), oil on canvas, sgn, 14x18", B/B 10/9/88 UE 2,750
Water Trap at Steeple Chase (horses & figures in a landscape), oil on canvas, sgn, 14x18", B/B 10/9/88 UE 2,750

LKEN, Henry Thomas (British, 1785-1851)

Gentleman Driving His Four-in-Hand to the Meet Overtaking a Man on His Gray Horse, oil on canvas, 24x17", SBY 6/9/89 UE 9,350
Going to the Races, oil on panel, sgn, 12x18", SBY 6/9/89 OE 40,700
Group of 6: Hunting Scenes; pencil/watercolor on paper, 4 sgn, 10x14" & smaller, SBY 6/9/89 4,950
Halt at an Inn (landscape with coach, horses, & figures), oil on canvas, sgn twice, 25x30", SBY 6/10/88 28,600
Pair: Full Cry; Over the Fence (hunt scenes); oil on canvas, 18x26", SBY 6/9/89 OE 96,250
The Oakley Hunt, oil on canvas, 40x64", SBY 6/9/89 143,000

LKEN, Henry Thomas; follower of (British, 1785-1851)

Group of 4: Fox Hunting Scenes; oil on board, 10x15", SBY 6/9/89 6,050
Over the Wall (hunt scene), oil on canvas, 12x14", SBY 6/9/89 1,430
Picking Up the Scent, oil on canvas, bears signature, 18x24", SBY 6/9/89 2,750

LKEN, Samuel Henry (British, 18th/19th C)

Ipswich to London Coach in Snow, oil on canvas, sgn/dtd 1875, 15x25", SBY 6/10/88 OE 29,700
Preparing for the First Ride, oil on board, sgn, 10x15", SBY 6/9/89 OE 19,800
Set of 4: Steeplechasing; The Start; Water Jump; Taking a Fence; oil on panel, 7x11", SBY 6/9/89 15,400
Taking the Ditch (horses w/riders jumping a stream), oil on panel, sgn, 14x23", SBY 6/9/89 6,600
Terrier with a Ball, oil on canvas, sgn/dtd 1851, 20x24", SBY 6/10/88 8,250

LLAN, David; att (British, 1744-1796)

Portrait of a Young Gentleman, seated, holding a book; oil on canvas, inscr, 30x25", C-NY 6/2/88 1,650

LLAN, David; follower of (British, 1744-1796)

Family in a Park (group portrait), oil on canvas, unfr, 44x33", SBY 7/12/89 1,980

LLAN, M. (British, 19th C)

Cookham Woods on Thames (river landscape), oil on canvas, 20x30", SLK 9/26/88 1,050

LLAN, R.W. (British, 1852-1942)

River Scene with Cottage, oil on canvas, sgn/dtd 90, 16x24", LH 12/4/88 750

LLAUX, Gustave

L'Arrivee de l'Escadre (ships landing), oil, sgn twice/titled, 26x39", C-SK 6/9/88 OE 16,700

LLEMANDE, Ecole

Diptych: Various Religious Scenes; oil on panel, dtd 1951, 52x22", C-M 12/3/88 13,007

LLEN, Boyd (American, 20th C)

Someplace, watercolor on paper, 32x24", B/B 12/8/88 440

LLEN, Junius (American, 1896-1962)

Westchester Creek (industrial scene w/tugboat), oil on canvas, sgn/dtd 1949, 24x34", WD 10/5/88 3,500

LLEN, Thomas (American, 1849-1924)

Dish of Lemons, pastel on paper, initialed, 17x27", RWS 5/12/89 7,000
Marblehead Pasture (cows on dirt road), oil on canvas, sgn/titled, 26x40", RAB 8/8/89 UE 1,200

LLIEVI, Fernando

Collector (man & girl w/still life), charcoal/pastel on paper, sgn/titled, 45x55", SBY 11/21/88 OE 4,400
Marita y los Hombres (portraits of child & two men), pencil/crayon on paper, sgn/titled, 43x52", C-NY 5/17/89 2,640

LLIGRE, F. (French, 19th C)

Figures in a Moorish Stone Archway, oil on canvas, sgn, 28x18", SLK 5/11/88 2,300

LLIS, C. Harry (American, -1938)

Autumnal Landscape (impressionistic forest scene with figures on a road), oil on canvas, sgn, DM 5/89 OE 1,000

ALLORI, Agnolo di Cosimo; see Bronzino, Agnolo di Cosimo
ALLORI, Alessandro; circle of (Italian, 1535-1607)
Standing Soldier Seen From Behind, & Head of Another; black chalk on gray paper, 15x10", SBY 1/13/89 OE ... 6,050
ALLORI, Cristofano (Italian, 1577-1621)
Christ Wearing the Crown of Thorns, oil on canvas, 20x15", SBY 7/12/89 ... 1,760
ALLOU, Gilles (18th C)
Portrait of a Man Holding a Pipe, oil on canvas, sgn/dtd 1715, 29x33", SBY 4/7/88 ... 5,775
ALLSTON, Washington; att (American, 1779-1843)
Portrait of a Gentleman Said To Be Henry Clay, oil on panel, painted in oval, 8x7", C-E 6/1/89 UE ... 2,200
ALLUSTANTE Y PALLARES, Joaquin (Spanish, 19th C)
Flower Seller, oil on panel, sgn, 8x9", C-E 2/23/88 ... 2,200
Lady at the Beach, oil on panel, sgn/dtd, 14x9", C-E 10/25/88 ... 3,520
ALMA-TADEMA, Lawrence (British, 1836-1912)
Death of Galeswinthe, 575 AD-La Victime; oil on panel, sgn/dtd 1865, 13x10", SBY 4/29/88 OE ... 44,000
Hero (woman standing on balcony), oil on panel, sgn, 1898, 15x10", SBY 5/23/89 ... 137,500
Joseph, Overseer of Pharaoh's Granaries; pencil/watercolor on paper, 17x22", SBY 4/29/88 OE ... 14,300
Study for Marguerite, pencil, initialed/inscr, 7x7", C-NY 2/23/89 UE ... 330
ALMA-TADEMA, Lawrence & Laura (British, 19th/20th C)
Five Muslin Hats That Haunted the Glen, pencil, inscr/dtd July 29th 1877, 6x5", C-NY 2/23/89 UE ... 550
ALORDA Y PEREZ, Ramon (Spanish, 19th C)
On the Venetian Lagoon, watercolor, sgn/dtd 1884, 25x39", C-E 5/22/89 ... 1,870
ALOTT, Robert (Austrian, 19th C)
Ladies Gazing at a Ruined Village, oil on panel, sgn, 8x19", C-E 10/25/88 ... 2,200
ALSINA, J. (French, 19th/20th C)
Serenade with a Lyre on the Veranda, oil on canvas, sgn, 22x29", C-E 5/23/88 ... 2,860
ALTAMIRANO, Arturo Pacheco (20th C)
Isla de Tenglo, oil on burlap, sgn/dtd 1969, 24x29", C-NY 5/18/88 ... 3,850
Sombrillas (beach scene), oil on canvas, sgn, ca 1971, 15x26", C-NY 11/21/88 ... 2,200
ALTEN, Mathias (American, 1871-1935)
Portrait (girl in green dress, pink sash), oil on canvas, 27x21", DM 3/14/88 UE ... 250
ALTMANN, Alexandre (Russian, 1885-)
Autumn (landscape), oil on canvas, sgn, 65x33", SBY 5/30/89 ... 13,200
Spring (landscape), oil on canvas, sgn, 65x33", SBY 5/30/89 ... 15,400
ALTOON, John (American, 1925-1969)
Centaur, ink on paper, sgn, 30x20", B/B 12/8/88 ... 880
Centaur with Figures, ink on paper, unfr, 14x21", B/B 12/8/88 ... 467
Cowboys & Indians, ink on paper, inscr/dtd 1968, 30x40", SBY 2/15/89 ... 2,200
Horse, ink on board, sgn, unfr, 16x15", B/B 12/8/88 ... 440
Seated Figures, colored ink on paper, unfr, 7x5", B/B 12/8/88 ... 357
Street People, ink on board, sgn, unfr, 18x15", B/B 5/17/89 ... 660
Untitled (nude figures), pencil/ink/watercolor on paper, inscr, 30x40", SBY 2/15/89 ... 2,200
Washerwoman, ink on board, unfr, 15x8", B/B 12/8/88 ... 357
Woman with Cat, ink on paper, sgn, unfr, 18x12", B/B 12/8/88 ... 770
Woman with Pigeons in the Park, ink on paper, unfr, 18x15", B/B 12/8/88 ... 440
ALTSON, Abbey (British, 19th/20th C)
Idyll on the Terrace, oil on canvas, sgn, 52x39", SBY 2/22/89 ... 22,000
On the Balcony, oil on canvas, sgn/dtd 1903, 36x28", C-NY 5/25/88 ... 9,900
Roses (portrait of young lady wearing crown of roses), sgn/dtd 1900, 18x22", C-SK 6/9/88 ... 1,200
ALVANTEE, E.
Stone Bridge, oil on board, sgn, 9x12", DM 3/14/88 ... 200
ALVAREZ, Luis (Spanish, 1836-1901)
Parlor Scene with Figures Enjoying a Repast, oil on canvas, sgn/dtd 1879, 17x25", DM 5/19/89 OE ... 37,500
AMAN-JEAN, Edmond (French, 1860-1935)
Au Bal Masque, pastel on paper, sgn, 22x19", C-L 6/27/88 ... 18,920
La Robe Rose, pastel, sgn, ca 1898, 38x29", C-L 6/27/88 ... 160,820
AMARAL, Antonio Henrique (Latin American, 20th C)
Battlefield 5 (fork in banana on plate), oil on canvas, sgn/dtd 73, 72x92", SBY 11/21/88 OE ... 28,600
Untitled (contemporary banana), oil on canvas, sgn/dtd 71/inscr Atibaia, 32x51", SBY 11/21/88 ... 2,750
AMAT, Frederic (20th C)
Studio Table, handmade paper/wax/acrylic on wood, 1984, 45x74", C-NY 5/4/89 ... 4,400
AMBROGIANI, Pierre (French, 1907-)
Jardin de Fleurs (garden of flowers), gouache, sgn, 16x19", PHL 11/15/88 ... 800
Vase aux Fleurs (contemporary floral still life), oil on board, sgn, 32x26", PHL 11/15/88 ... 2,600
AMBROIS, Jules Francois Achille
Wooded Path, oil on canvas, sgn/dtd 87, 29x21", C-E 10/25/88 ... 2,420
AMBROS, Raphael; see Von Ambros
AMBROSSI, A.J.
Portrait of Cavalier, oil on canvas, 32x26", DM 3/14/88 ... 950
AMEGLIO, Merio (French, 1897-1970)
Notre Dame, Paris; oil on canvas, sgn, 18x22", B/B 12/8/88 ... 1,045

AMENOFF, Gregory (20th C)	
Echo Pool (abstract), oil on canvas, sgn/dtd 8/81, 13x17", SBY 2/15/89	3,300
Knocking at the Threshold (abstract composition), oil on canvas, sgn/dtd 1982, 78x74", SBY 5/3/89	17,050
Mandorla, oil on canvas, sgn/dtd 1986, 80x80", SBY 2/15/89	15,400
Painting for Summer II (abstract), oil on canvas, initialed/sgn/inscr, dtd twice 81, unfr, 17x21", C-NY 5/4/88	4,180
Radix (abstract), oil on canvas, sgn/dtd 3-83/titled, 82x72", SBY 5/3/88	16,500
Root (abstract composition), gouache/oil sticks/black ink on paper, sgn, dtd 9/83, 43x37", C-NY 5/4/89 OE	3,850
Tempest (abstract), oil on canvas, sgn, dtd 2/83, titled, 78x62", SBY 11/11/88	15,400
Untitled (abstract), acrylic/watercolor/colored oil sticks on paper, sgn/dtd 86, 20x21", C-NY 10/31/89	1,870
Webwork (abstract), oil on canvas, sgn/dtd 1985, 84x90", SBY 10/8/88	17,600
American Indian School (20th C)	
Landscape with Woman & Cornstalks, watercolor/gouache on paper, 16x14", FAP 4/15/89 OE	50
American School (18th C)	
Portrait of Moses Bartram, oil on canvas, 30x25", SBY 1/24/89 OE	1,760
Portrait of Mrs Henry White, small half-length in gray dress; oil on canvas, inscr, unfr, 30x25", C-SK 6/9/88	370
American School (18th/19th C)	
Portrait of a Man, oil on canvas, 20x24", MG 10/28/88	1,000
Portrait of a Young Officer, pastel on paper, 19x15", SBY 1/28/88 UE	1,210
Portrait of Catalina Van Duesen (girl in blue dress holding a flower), oil on canvas, 29x24", SBY 1/28/88	6,875
Relief of Jamestown: Old Times in the New World; oil on panel, 10x14", B/B 10/9/88	3,850
American School (19th C)	
After the Storm (ship silhouetted against clearing sky), watercolor on paper, titled, 12x13", RAB 3/14/89 UE	100
Afternoon Ride (man, woman, & child in horse-drawn chaise), watercolor/ink on paper, 13x8", RWS 10/27/89 OE	3,800
Afternoon Stroll: Hudson River Landscape Scene; oil on canvas, 21x36", RWS 6/10/89 OE	1,200
Along the Coast, oil on board, initialed CB, 7x10", C-E 9/15/88	330
Along the River (house by dammed river, green hills beyond), oil on canvas, indistinctly sgn, 6x10", RAB 8/9/88 UE	250
Along the River (landscape), oil on canvas, 18x28", RAB 3/27/89 UE	900
Along the River (view with house), oil on canvas, illegibly sgn, 6x10", RAB 8/9/88 UE	250
Amasa Wheeler in His Wedding Suit November 1829, Age 21; watercolor/pencil/ink on paper, 6x3", RWS 10/27/89	350
American Eagle on His Nest, oil on canvas, sgn/dtd 1873, 9x19", C-E 6/1/88	770
American Schooner Approaching Port, charcoal/chalk on paper, 18x24", RAB 8/1/88	750
American Ship Entering Port, oil on wood panel, 5x8", RAB 3/14/89 OE	1,700
American Ship M Bartlett Entering Hong Kong, oil on canvas, 20x30", RAB 8/1/88 OE	1,550
American Soldier on the Western Frontier with an Indian Encampment in Background, indistinctly sgn, 11x7", SLK 9/29/88	90
Apple Blossoms (floral-covered branch), oil on canvas, 10x14", WL 5/20/88 OE	1,200
Autumnal Sunset, Catskill Mountains; oil on panel, indistinctly sgn, 12x18", B/B 12/8/88	1,320
Bark Blanche at Sea, oil on canvas, 22x33", RAB 3/14/89	2,750
Barnyard Scene with Chickens, oil on canvas, incomplete inscr/dtd 1884, 13x18", RWS 3/16/89	600
Battle of Lake Erie, War of 1812; oil on canvas, 20x24", SBY 1/28/88	1,980
Battle of the Constitution & the Guerriere (sailing ships), oil on panel, ca 1812-20, 54x26", SBY 1/28/88 OE	22,000
Bird's Eye-View of a Lake-Side Farm, oil on board, 19x25", RWS 6/10/89 OE	2,500
Bird's-Eye View of Charlemont, Massachusetts; oil on canvas, 25x31", RWS 6/10/89	12,000
Black Boy Leaning on a Barrel, oil on canvas, sgn, 10x15", MG 10/28/88 UE	425
Bluenose (ship at sea), colored pencil/graphite on paper, 21x24", C-NY 6/3/89	880
Boone's Knob, Kentucky (extensive landscape); pencil on paper, monogramed, 8x10", WL 5/20/88	600
Bountiful Vista, oil on canvas, 25x32", B/B 5/17/89	880
Boy with Blue Suit with Poodle Pull-Toy & Hoop, oil on canvas, 36x28", SBY 1/28/88 OE	8,525
Breezy Day (coastal seascape), oil on canvas, 16x24", RAB 8/8/89 UE	250
Bridle Falls, Yosemite; oil on canvas, 18x27", FAP 4/15/89 OE	2,860
Camp at Van Cortland Park, oil on canvas, sgn, unfr, 13x22", C-E 4/7/88 UE	385
Chesapeake & the Shannon, oil on canvas, 20x31", SBY 9/14/89	440
Children with Barnyard Friends Along a River, oil on canvas, 25x31", B/B 1/11/89 OE	1,870
Church at Sunset, oil on canvas, sgn, 12x18", NA 11/5/88	350
Cipper Ship Putting Out, oil on canvas, 22x33", RAB 11/10/88 UE	500
Civil War Memorial (draped US flag w/sword & uniforms), oil on canvas, 28x22", C-E 2/1/89 UE	770
Coastal Rhode Island-Near Newport; oil on canvas, 20x39", RAB 8/8/89 UE	1,100
Coastal Scene, oil on canvas, 12x20", SBY 9/23/88 UE	660
Constantinople, the Seraglio Point; oil on canvas, ca 1840, 25x32", SBY 1/28/88 OE	3,575
Dancing Black Man, pen/ink on paper, indistinctly initialed, 1893, 10x8", SWN 12/1/88	275
Death by Wild Horses, oil on canvas, 25x29", SBY 4/29/88 OE	11,550
Deer Hunting, oil on canvas, 30x42", C-E 6/28/88 UE	350
Delaware Gap (landscape), oil on canvas, 24x32", SLK 11/25/88	1,500
Double-Sided: Girl Reading; Boy with Kite; oil on canvas, unfr, 14x18", RAB 8/8/89 UE	300
Easton, Pennsylvania; oil on board, inscr Vue de la ville et Easton dans l'Etats de Pennsylvenia, 11x19", C-NY 1/20/89	4,180
Edge of the Lake, oil on canvasboard, sgn, 20x16", C-E 4/7/88 UE	550
Egg Rock, Looking Towards Nahant From Swampscott (figures on shore, large waves); oil on canvas, 19x30", RAB 8/9/88 UE	1,700
Extensive River Landscape, oil on canvas, 22x36", PHL 12/1/88	550
Family Portrait with Father, Mother & Three Girls: The Shoe-Button Family; oil on canvas, 1840s, 27x34", SBY 1/28/88	33,000
Federal House in a Grove of Trees (primitive), watercolor/ink on paper, 4x5", RWS 10/27/89	1,000
Fishing by the River, oil on panel, 20x24", FAP 4/15/89	330
Fishing in a Landscape, oil on canvas, 20x15", SBY 3/17/88	1,650

Floral Still Life, oil on board, 8x6", RWS 5/12/89	400
Floral Still Life, oil on panel, 16x7", SBY 3/17/88 UE	715
Freed Slave, oil on panel, 10x10", C-E 6/22/88 OE	1,045
Frozen Mill, oil on canvas, dtd 1884, 18x30", MG 12/10/88 UE	100
Galloping Man, oil on canvas, 8x12", LH 10/16/88	300
Glade in Spring, oil on canvas, 20x13", WG 4/23/88 UE	50
Gloucester Harbor (fishing boat being unloaded at dock), oil on academy board, sgn, 6x12", RAB 8/9/88	850
Gloucester Harbor (fishing boat unloading at dock, city skyline beyond), oil on academy board, sgn, 6x12", RAB 8/9/88	850
Harbor Scene at Sunrise, mixed media on heavy cardboard, 17x14", RAB 6/27/89 UE	200
Harmony in Blue & Gold Said To Be Mrs CW Whibley, oil on canvas, bears artist's device, 21x17", C-E 6/1/89	1,100
Harper's Ferry, oil on canvas, 24x30", LH 3/20/88 OE	1,600
Harvesting, oil on canvas, monogramed, 6x12", C-E 10/18/89	1,100
Homestead by the River (landscape), oil on canvas, bears signature JD Barrow/dtd 78, 16x28", RWS 3/16/89 OE	1,700
House in a Valley, oil on canvas, 30x50", C-NY 11/30/88	3,850
House in the Woods (figure in cleared field near trees, house beyond), oil on canvas, 7x12", RAB 8/9/88 UE	100
House in the Woods (figure in field), oil on canvas, 7x12", RAB 8/9/88 UE	100
Impressionistic Landscape, oil on canvas, indistinctly sgn, 20x24", MG 10/28/88	550
Impressionistic Landscape, oil on canvas, 33x34", MG 5/28/88	425
In Memory of Hannah Elizabeth Harrison, watercolor/ink on paper, 15x20", C-NY 1/20/89	3,080
In the Studio, oil on canvas, 15x20", SBY 1/24/89	770
In the Sugar Cane Field, oil on board, 11x6", NA 3/26/88	275
In the Valley, oil on canvas, 12x16", C-E 10/18/89	1,320
Indians & Canoes, oil on canvas, 11x5", C-E 4/7/88 UE	352
Island Farm (distant view painted within oval), oil on artist board, 7x11", RAB 8/9/88 UE	300
Island Farm (small buildings in an open field), oil on artist board, painted in oval, 7x11", RAB 8/9/88 UE	300
Lady at Her Desk, watercolor/pencil on board, unfr, 13x10", C-E 6/1/89	440
Landscape, oil on canvas, 30x42", MG 11/19/88	450
Landscape, oil on canvas, 40x54", C-E 11/30/88	4,180
Landscape (figures, stream & village), oil on canvas laid down on board, 22x36", SLK 11/25/88	1,050
Landscape with Castle, oil on canvas, 21x29", SBY 9/23/88 UE	715
Landscape with Church Steeple in the Distance, oil on canvas, 16x18", C-E 11/30/88 UE	880
Landscape with Figure & Distant Town, oil on canvas, 5x9", SBY 1/24/89	18,700
Life Along the River (figures in various activities), watercolor on paper, new mat & frame, 5x8", RAB 8/9/88	275
Life Along the River (men working by a calm lake), watercolor on paper, 6x8", RAB 8/9/88	275
Little Girl with a Fishbowl, oil on canvas, 45x36", NA 2/24/89 OE	2,000
Looking Up River Towards an Eastern Port, oil on canvas, 25x37", B/B 5/17/89	1,650
Marshy Landscape, oil on canvas mounted on board, 12x16", WG 4/23/88 UE	150
Mast & Spar Shop (in landscape), watercolor on paper, sgn CSG/dtd 89, 10x7", RAB 11/25/88 UE	125
Meadow & Pond, Sunset; oil on canvas, indistinctly sgn, 16x26", RWS 11/3/88 OE	1,500
Meadow Landscape, oil on panel, 12x24", SBY 3/17/88	1,980
Middlebury College, black/white pastel on sandpaper, inscr, 16x21", C-NY 10/1/88	770
Miniature Portrait of a Young Girl, watercolor/gouache on ivory, 3x3", RWS 10/27/89 OE	3,600
Mountain Landscape, oil on canvas, 22x37", RAB 3/27/89 UE	325
Mountain Landscape, oil on canvas mounted on masonite, 21x25", WG 4/23/88 UE	400
My Sister & I (portrait of girls w/doll), pastel on paper, 27x21", RAB 11/25/88 UE	800
Naval Battle, oil on canvas, 27x40", C-E 6/22/88	1,540
New England Mill Town, oil on canvas, 13x26", C-NY 9/30/88	2,420
New Hampshire Landscape, oil on canvas, 20x27", SBY 4/14/89	2,970
New Orleans Street Vendor, oil on board, 8x6", NA 3/26/88	200
New Pearls, oil on panel, 10x8", C-E 6/1/89	880
New Suspension Bridge, oil on canvas, 18x16", B/B 1/11/89	358
New Toy (children in an interior), oil on canvas, initialed/dtd 1870, C-NY 3/11/88	3,850
New York, oil on canvas, 24x30", LH 3/20/88 OE	1,600
Niagara Falls, oil on paper laid down on canvas, 5x8", C-E 11/30/88	2,860
Night Watchman, oil on panel, 16x13", C-SK 11/10/88	1,770
Northumberland & Myrmidon, Conveying Napoleon to the Island of St Helena...; oil on wood panel, 15x22", RAB 3/14/89	1,600
On the Battlefield, oil on canvas, 41x33", LH 9/10/89	750
Outing Party, oil on canvas, 30x44", SBY 9/23/88 UE	385
Pair: Brother & Sister; watercolor on paper, 10x8", C-NY 10/1/88	6,050
Pair: Indians in a Rocky Mountain Landscape; Sunset in the Rocky Mountains; oil on board, 1 sgn, 19x25", SBY 9/23/88 OE	3,300
Pair: Landscapes; oil on academy board, 6x9", RAB 11/25/88 UE	125
Pair: Mother with Young Daughter in Blue Dress; Father with Son Holding a Red Volume; oil on canvas, 41x26", SBY 4/29/88	17,600
Pair: On the Whippany River Moris Co, NJ; Walk Along the River's Edge; oil on board, sgn/dtd, 8x6", RWS 9/8/89 OE	1,900
Pair: Outing; Summer Landscape with Cows & Bridge; watercolor on paper, 10x14", 12x15", SBY 9/14/89	1,210
Pair: Portraits of a Lady & a Gentleman (half-length); oil on canvas, 29x23", SBY 3/17/88 OE	7,700
Pair: Portraits of a Lady & a Gentleman; oil on canvas, 25x30", MG 10/28/88	1,000
Pair: Portraits of a Lady & a Gentleman; oil on canvas, 30x25", SBY 1/24/89	1,430
Pair: Portraits of a Lady & a Gentleman; oil on canvas, 30x25", B/B 3/22/89	3,025
Pair: Portraits of a Lady & a Gentleman; watercolor/pen/pencil on paper, 10x8", C-NY 6/3/89 UE	1,100
Pair: Portraits of Husband & Wife in Dark Formal Attire; oil on canvas, 17x14", RAB 11/25/88 UE	450
Pair: Portraits of Jacob Schnell & Mary Schwartz Schnell; oil on canvas, 29x24", LH 10/16/88	600

Pair: Portraits of Robert Myers & Mary Colgate Stewer Shoemaker; oil on canvas, 30x25", LH 10/16/88 OE	1,900
Pair: Still Life of Strawberries; Still Life of Butterfly & Currants; oil on cardboard, 7x9", RAB 3/27/89	450
Pioneers, oil on canvas, 14x19", C-E 9/30/88 OE	30,800
Portrait of a Black Man Reading the State Newspaper, oil on canvas, 16x20", MG 10/28/88	900
Portrait of a Boy, oil on canvas, 31x25", C-NY 6/3/89	3,080
Portrait of a Boy (standing, full-length in a landscape), oil on canvas, 40x30", C-E 6/1/89	1,650
Portrait of a Boy with a Dog, oil on canvas, 30x24", SBY 3/17/88	1,540
Portrait of a Boy with His Toy Horse, oil on canvas, 28x23", C-NY 6/3/89	2,860
Portrait of a Boy with Whip, oil on canvas, 16x12", LH 3/20/88 OE	4,800
Portrait of a Bride, oil on canvas, 30x26", SBY 6/28/89	990
Portrait of a Child in Velvet Costume w/Black & White Puppy, Play Ball, & Whip; oil on canvas, 44x30", SBY 4/29/88	5,225
Portrait of a Creole Lady, New Orleans (Neoclassical style); oil on canvas, ca 1830-40, 35x28", NA 11/5/88	3,250
Portrait of a Family, watercolor/ink on paper (now pasted to board), 15x18", C-NY 1/20/89	3,850
Portrait of a Gentleman, half-length, in Indian costume...; oil on canvas, indistinctly inscr, 22x16", C-SK 11/10/88 OE	5,580
Portrait of a Gentleman, oil on canvas, 18x14", LH 5/15/88	1,000
Portrait of a Gentleman, oil on canvas, 27x22", NA 2/6/88	850
Portrait of a Gentleman, oil on canvas, 30x25", FAP 4/15/89	825
Portrait of a Gentleman, oil on canvas, 30x25", FAP 4/15/89 OE	1,320
Portrait of a Gentleman, oil on canvas, 30x25", LH 10/16/88	400
Portrait of a Gentleman (seated at table w/cup & carafe), oil on canvas mounted on panel, 35x27", SBY 3/17/88 OE	4,620
Portrait of a Gentleman (wearing dark blue jacket before a landscape), watercolor/ink/gilt paper, 5x4", RWS 10/27/89	700
Portrait of a Gentleman at His Work Desk, oil on canvas, unfr, 30x25", RWS 10/25/89	3,000
Portrait of a Gentleman Said To Be Captain Isaac Hull, oil on canvas, sgn/dtd 183(?), 29x25", C-E 6/1/89 UE	1,100
Portrait of a Girl, oil on canvas, 31x25", C-NY 6/3/89	2,860
Portrait of a Girl in a White Dress, oil on canvas, oval, 24x20", B/B 5/17/89 OE	1,210
Portrait of a Girl with Vase of Flowers, oil on canvas, indistinctly sgn/dtd Jan 1802, 9x13", C-E 1/12/88 OE	770
Portrait of a Lady, oil on canvas, 30x24", SBY 3/17/88	990
Portrait of a Lady, three-quarter length in floral gown in rich interior; oil on canvas, 1895, 46x40", RWS 8/20/88	600
Portrait of a Lady at a Desk, Said To Be Miss Ambroisia; oil on canvas, 18x14", C-E 9/15/88 UE	385
Portrait of a Lady Presumed To Be Mary Wyllis Marshall, Nee Ambler; oil on canvas, 30x25", SBY 9/14/89	1,320
Portrait of a Young Naval Officer, oil on canvas, 30x25", SBY 1/24/89	1,760
Portrait of an American Politician, holding copy of Washington's Farewell Address; oil, unfr, 32x27", C-SK 6/9/88 OE	2,410
Portrait of an Astronomer, oil on canvas, 82x41", SBY 4/29/88	37,400
Portrait of an Early Victorian Lady Wearing Glasses, oil on canvas, 26x22", RAB 6/27/89 UE	225
Portrait of an Officer, watercolor/pastel on paper, 9x7", C-NY 10/1/88 UE	550
Portrait of Four Children with School Slate & Book, oil on canvas, 36x30", SBY 4/29/88	10,450
Portrait of General John Pegram, oil on canvas, 30x25", C-E 1/12/88 UE	330
Portrait of George Washington, oil on canvas, 29x23", C-E 10/18/89 OE	4,180
Portrait of George Washington, oil on panel, 10x8", C-E 6/20/89	715
Portrait of George Washington, oil on panel, 7x6", SBY 6/28/89 OE	600
Portrait of George Washington (bust-length), oil on canvas painted in oval, 30x26", SBY 3/17/88 OE	2,475
Portrait of Hannah Lawrence Fairfield, oil on canvas, 24x20", LH 10/16/88 UE	200
Portrait of Isabel Homer Pegram, oil on canvas, initialed/dtd 1877, 30x25", C-E 1/12/88 UE	385
Portrait of Judge Emil George Stone of New Orleans, oil on canvas, sgn, 40x50", MG 12/10/88	800
Portrait of Lillian Wolverton, oil on canvas, 34x27", SBY 6/28/89	1,650
Portrait of Lucinda Petit, oil on canvas, 15x17", MG 10/28/88	300
Portrait of Mrs Henry Vallette & Child, Laura; oil on canvas, 29x24", LH 10/16/88 OE	1,100
Portrait of Young McDowell Brothers, Joseph Sebastian & Keith Marshall; oil on canvas, 36x29", NA 2/24/89	3,000
Proposal (couple in landscape), oil on canvas, 24x30", C-E 6/1/89	1,100
Queen of the West, oil on canvas, dtd 1869, 261x92", B/B 12/8/88	2,090
Rabbits in a Flower Garden, oil on canvas, indistinctly sgn, 16x19", RAB 3/27/89 UE	200
Raspberries Spilling From a Straw Basket, oil on canvas, 13x18", WD 10/5/88 OE	8,750
Red Fan (portrait of a woman), oil on canvas, 24x18", C-E 11/30/88	1,760
Regatta Scene, oil on canvas, indistinctly sgn, 20x30", SBY 1/28/88	4,070
River Landscape (primitive), oil on canvas, 28x44", SLK 11/25/88	400
River Landscape with Boats & Figures, oil on canvas, 16x23", SBY 9/23/88 OE	4,400
River View, oil on canvas laid down on panel, 40x54", C-E 2/1/89	4,400
River View at Sunset, oil on canvas, 18x24", C-NY 10/1/88	715
Riverscape with Fishermen, oil on canvas, 18x26", RAB 1/31/89	700
Riverside Campsite, study of camping life; oil on canvas, orig frame, 24x36", RAB 11/25/88 UE	650
Scene on the Delaware (cows in water, hills beyond), oil on canvas, bears initials/dtd 56, unfr, 28x48", SBY 9/14/89	8,525
School Children on a Beach, oil on canvas, 10x16", WG 4/23/88 OE	5,500
Seascape, oil on canvas, unfr, 26x42", SBY 6/28/89	1,320
Serene Tropical Lake Scene, oil on canvas, 30x42", B/B 6/15/89	4,675
Shepherdess in a Hilly Landscape Carrying a Lamb Accompanied by a Sheep, oil on canvas, 30x25", SLK 2/12/88	375
Ship Francis of Salem, gouache on paper, 17x23", SBY 1/24/89	2,310
Ship of Flags, oil on canvas, 14x19", C-E 6/22/88 OE	1,980
Ship Servia, watercolor on paper, 13x22", C-NY 1/20/89	4,620
Shipping Off the Coast, oil on canvas, 33x50", B/B 3/22/89	1,980
Sinking of the Cumberland by the Iron Clad Merrimack, oil on canvas, inscr, 29x36", SBY 1/24/89	2,200
Sloop Blazing Star of New York & US Frigate Essex 1812, watercolor/gouache/ink on paper, dtd 1812, 14x10", RWS 10/27/89	2,750

Sprigs of Strawberries Enclose Geometric Device (fraktar drawing), watercolor/ink on paper, 10x14", RWS 10/27/89 OE	1,500
Square-Rigger in Stormy Seas, oil on canvas, 47x70", SBY 4/29/88	8,800
Squirrel Eating Corn, oil on canvas, 17x21", C-E 10/18/89	1,100
Still Life of Apples, oil on canvas, 13x18", RAB 8/8/89 UE	350
Still Life of Flowers (roses in tole bowl w/Pilsner glass & fan), oil on canvas, 14x18", RAB 3/27/89	400
Still Life of Fruit, Green Glass, & Pitcher; oil on canvas, indistinctly sgn, 20x30", RWS 11/10/89	1,900
Still Life of Fruit, Meat, Corn, Wine & Money; oil on canvas, 25x30", SBY 6/28/89	605
Still Life of Fruit & Nautical Shell, oil on canvas, 30x25", B/B 9/15/88	990
Still Life of Fruit & Wine, oil on canvas, unsgn, 16x13", RWS 3/16/89 OE	950
Still Life of Fruit on a Ledge, oil on board, 20x16", B/B 12/8/88	2,200
Still Life of Fruit on a Ledge, oil on canvas, 30x44", B/B 3/22/89 OE	9,350
Still Life of Game, oil on canvas, 30x25", SBY 4/14/89	880
Still Life of Pipe & Pouch, oil on canvas, bears signature/dtd 1899, 12x8", SBY 6/24/88 OE	2,750
Stream Fishing (farm scene w/children fishing), oil on canvas, bears signature, 36x47", C-E 2/1/89 UE	990
Studying Nature, girl holds butterfly to moss rose; watercolor/pencil on paper, 17x13", RAB 11/25/88 UE	275
Sunday Best, oil on canvas, arched top, 24x20", C-SK 11/10/88	3,350
Sunset, oil on canvas, indistinctly sgn/dtd 1886, 20x40", C-E 6/1/88	605
Sunset Walk, Long Island; oil on canvas, sgn/dtd 71, 10x20", RWS 11/10/89	800
Tending the Flocks, placid summer landscape; oil on canvas, unfr, 18x24", RAB 5/17/88	450
The CB Jones at Full Sail, oil on canvas mounted on masonite, 20x27", SBY 6/24/88 OE	7,150
The Mary A Ivin Entering a Harbor (sailing vessel), oil on canvas, 26x36", SBY 6/24/88 OE	16,500
The Sam Skolfield (sailing vessel), oil on canvas mounted on masonite, 16x23", SBY 6/24/88 OE	6,875
Thieves Observed (genre scene with squirrels & cat), oil on canvas, 20x16", RWS 10/27/89	1,000
Three Boys with Cherries, oil on canvas, 27x22", C-NY 11/30/88	1,650
Three Shipwrecked Sailors Beckoning Rescue, oil on canvas, ca 1870, 21x29", SBY 4/29/88 OE	9,350

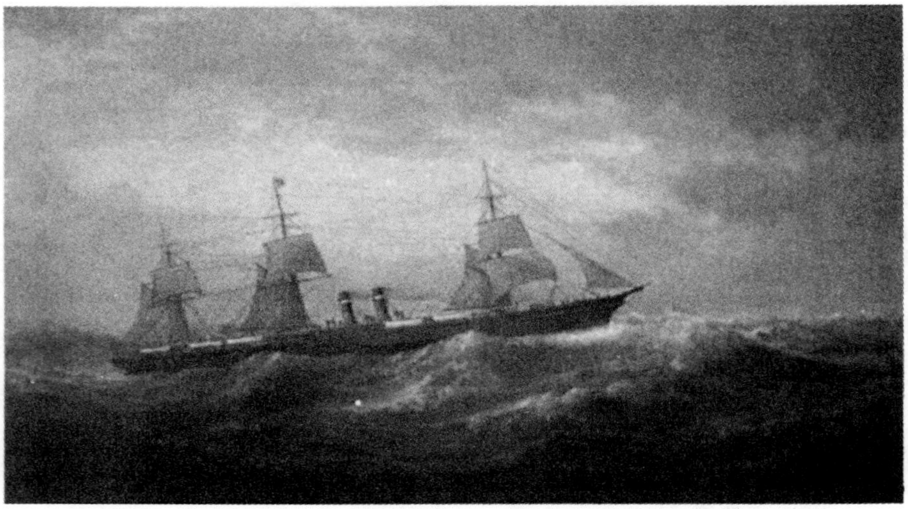

Three-Masted Ship, oil on canvas, 36x61", C-E 2/1/89 OE, $8,800

Travelers on a Bridge (in extensive landscape), oil on canvas, 24x32", C-E 6/1/89 UE	1,100
Tropical Rain Forest, oil on canvas, 12x8", SBY 6/24/88 UE	440
Trotters, oil on canvas, initialed JW, 14x24", C-E 2/1/89	660
Trumpeting Angel, pen/blue ink, 11x20", C-NY 10/31/89	715
Tucker's Landing-Marblehead (cottages/shacks on cliffs above harbor), oil on board, initialed FWS, 9x12", RAB 3/27/89	750
View From Westpoint, charcoal on paper, dtd 1820, 26x20", FAP 4/15/89	165
View of Bethlehem, Pennsylvania; oil on zinc, 9x13", C-NY 10/1/88	1,430
View of Red Hook, New York; oil on canvas, 20x30", SBY 4/14/89	1,430
View of the Valley, oil on canvas, 15x21", C-E 10/18/89	2,420
Watching the Sailboats Along the Edge of the River, oil on canvas, 23x31", FAP 4/15/89 OE	1,870
Waterfall, purple mountain in distance; oil on canvas, 35x48", RAB 9/8/88 OE	1,200
Watermelon on the Fence (young black boy eating watermelon), oil on canvas, 15x24", MG 10/28/88	550
Wedding Day, pastel on paper, 49x35", NA 10/1/88	450
Whaleships in the Arctic, oil on canvas, 25x35", RAB 8/1/89 UE	1,000
Windmill in a Fall Landscape, oil on canvas, 18x21", C-E 4/7/88 UE	275
Winter Evening (distant village), oil on board, sgn, 9x11", RAB 8/9/88 OE	900
Winter Evening (snowy field, village with lights in the distance), oil on board, indistinctly sgn, 9x11", RAB 8/9/88 OE	900
Winter Landscape, oil on canvas, indistinctly sgn/dtd 89, 20x24", FAP 4/15/89 OE	2,530
Woman Holding Roses, oil on canvas, 25x19", FAP 4/15/89	248
Wooded River Clearing with Red Flowers, oil on board, indistinctly sgn, 9x12", C-E 2/16/88	352
Young Skater, oil on panel, dtd 80, 10x5", RWS 8/20/88	550
4th of July, New York; pencil on paper, 13x18", C-E 4/7/88 OE	1,430

American School (19th/20th C)

Character Study of a Man, oil on canvas laid down on board, 11x9", SBY 6/24/88	1,760
Haying Fields (haystacks in field, road & trees at edge), oil on canvas, sgn, 16x20", RWS 9/29/88	550
In the Park (girl playing with a hoop), oil on panel, ca 1907, 4x6", RWS 9/29/88	700
Interior Scene (w/woman looking in mirror), oil on canvas, 33x26", RWS 5/12/89 OE	4,750
Jungle Flower (still Life), oil on board, bears signature, 12x9", SBY 4/14/89 UE	550
Newspaper Vendor & Boy Seated on Stool, watercolor, 13x9", FAP 4/15/89	440
Pair: Boy Carrying Bucket; Boy Reclining on a Rock; watercolor, 8x12", 12x8", FAP 4/15/89	358
Pair: Street Urchins; watercolor, 13x10", 8x12", FAP 4/15/89	440
Portrait of a Setter in the Field, oil on canvas, sgn/dtd 1909, unfr, 24x38", RWS 11/10/89	3,500
Portrait of Whaler Adeline Gibbs on Her Beam Ends, oil on canvas, orig frame, 27x36", RAB 11/10/88	1,000
Seated Nude, oil on canvas, 30x22", B/B 5/17/89 OE	2,750
Sewing (at) Dusk, oil on canvas, sgn Margaret S Perkin, unfr, 36x28", RWS 3/16/89 OE	1,000
The Pollockrip in Rough Waters (sailing vessel), oil on canvas mounted on board, 24x34", SBY 6/24/88	1,760
Wooded Pasture, oil on canvas, 20x27", RWS 9/8/89 UE	475

American School (20th C)

American Tragedy (murdered man/crowd in street), tempera on gessoed panel mounted on masonite, sgn, 25x35", RWS 9/29/88	700
Architects Rendering 7th & Market, watercolor on paper, monogramed FD, 22x24", FAP 4/15/89 UE	330
Artist's Studio (two figures painting in a cluttered studio), oil on canvas, 16x20", RAB 8/9/88 UE	250
Ash Can Scene, oil on canvas, sgn, 17x14", RWS 11/10/89	475
At the Beach, oil on panel, 9x10", C-E 11/30/88	1,320
Beached Boat in the Moonlight, watercolor on paper, initialed CCC, 16x12", RAB 3/27/89 UE	100
Black Boy Playing an Instrument, oil on canvas, sgn/dtd 1921, 19x29", MG 10/28/88 UE	350
City in Bloom, oil on canvas, dtd 1922, 22x17", RWS 9/8/89	325
Collecting Wood in the Forest, oil on canvas, indistinctly sgn, 20x30", C-E 9/15/88 UE	462
Confidential Chat, oil on canvas, 9x7", RWS 5/12/89 OE	1,300
Contemplation, orange/white kitten on green background; oil on canvas laid down on cardboard, 13x11", RAB 3/27/89 UE	100
Cool & Calm, Ocean Side of Peaks Island in Winter; oil on canvasboard, sgn/dtd 1927, 9x12", RWS 9/8/89	300
Country Lane, oil on canvas, 31x35", LH 9/10/89	500
Days End (landscape w/stream), oil on canvas laid down, unfr, 21x26", B/B 1/11/89	605
Diary, oil on canvas laid down on board, 30x22", C-E 11/30/88 UE	715
Fight for the Waterhole, watercolor, 13x18", SLK 5/12/88	175
Figures on a Mountain Top, watercolor on paper, 6x8", FAP 4/15/89 UE	82
Fishing at Sunset, oil on panel, indistinctly sgn, 13x19", B/B 1/11/89	880
Gibson Girl, oil on canvas, 36x24", FAP 4/15/89	385
Girl Playing with a Dog on a Beach, oil on panel, 7x10", C-E 11/8/88	880
Gloucester Harbor Scene (figures on wharf), oil on canvas, sgn, 24x30", RWS 9/29/88 UE	450
Grassy Hill, Distant Shores; oil on canvas, 20x24", RWS 9/8/89 UE	200
Harbor Inlet, oil on board, indistinctly sgn Oswald/dtd 1924, 10x13", RWS 8/12/89 OE	450
He Refused To Be Entangled in the Concerns of Fairyland (boy & characters), ink on paper, sgn, 17x13", RWS 9/29/88 OE	1,700
He Was a Young American (youth stands at table w/hand on book), oil on canvas, 23x21", RWS 5/19/88 UE	300
Hockey Game (Rochester Americans Playing Montreal Canadians), oil on particle board, illegibly sgn, 22x48", RWS 9/29/88	800
Horse & Groom, oil on masonite, bears initials REA, 14x16", C-E 6/28/88 UE	110
Hounds, oil on canvas, 22x36", C-E 2/3/88	770
Houses on the Bay, oil on canvas, bears signature, 9x12", C-E 2/16/88 OE	660
Impressionist French Quarter Scene, oil on board, 15x19", MG 10/28/88	250
In the Park, oil on panel, 8x12", C-E 10/18/89	605
Landscape with Figures, oil on canvas, indistinctly sgn, 25x30", C-E 6/1/88	1,100
Lily Pond (impressionistic landscape), oil on board, sgn, 16x11", RWS 3/31/88	275
Mountain Valley in Autumn, oil on canvas, 18x24", B/B 9/15/88 UE	468
Nautical Scene with Moon, oil on canvas, 16x20", C-E 9/15/88	440
New England Harbor View, oil on canvas, sgn, 28x25", RWS 3/16/89	500
Orchard Sunrise, Connecticut; oil on canvas, monogramed, 16x20", RWS 11/10/89	550
Ozark Landscape, oil on masonite, monogramed/dtd 1928, 16x2O", SLK 11/25/88	225
Persian Dancer, ink/watercolor on paper, sgn/titled, unfr, 12x9", RWS 8/20/88 UE	45
Picnic on the Beach (impressionistic beach w/figures), oil on canvas mounted on cardboard, 16x18", RWS 3/31/88	800
Pine Cabinet with Blue Willow China, oil on canvas, 48x60", C-E 6/28/88	950
Portrait of a Girl with Flowers, oil on canvas, bears initials ST, unfr, 53x26", C-E 6/28/88 UE	242
Portrait of a Woman Playing the Violin, oil on canvas, 52x38", B/B 1/11/89	550
Pumpkin Patch, oil on canvas, 14x24", RWS 12/10/88	450
Purple Mountains on the Desert Edge, oil on canvasboard, 18x24", B/B 1/11/89	385
Purple Skirt (lady seated in profile), oil on canvas, 25x18", C-E 6/1/89 OE	4,620
Rocky Coastline, oil on canvas, bears signature, unfr, 12x20", B/B 1/11/89	770
Saved Before Nightfall (girl by fallen horse found by cowboys), oil on canvas, sgn/dtd 1908, 31x40", RAB 8/9/88 UE	350
Seaside House, oil on canvas, indistinctly sgn/inscr, 17x21", C-E 11/30/88 OE	8,250
Ship America of Salem, watercolor/gouache on paper, sgn, 14x20", WL 5/20/88 UE	350
Ship in New York Harbor, oil on canvas, 24x36", FAP 4/15/89 OE	2,530
Snow Drifts (winter landscape), oil on masonite, titled, 20x26", RAB 8/8/89 UE	550
Snow Squalls (winter landscape), oil on canvas, 25x30", RWS 11/10/89	850

American School (20th C)

Southwestern Mexican Village Scene (man w/burros, village/mountains beyond), oil on canvas, sgn, 20x18", RWS 3/31/88 UE	350

American School (20th C)

Spanish Mission, oil on canvas, indistinctly sgn, 18x24", C-E 6/1/88 1,045
Spring Landscape with Cottages, oil on board, indistinctly sgn, 18x21", FAP 4/15/89 550
Spring Pastures (horses in field w/flowers, fox in foreground), oil on canvas, sgn, 24x30", RWS 9/29/88 OE 850
Spring Reflections: Walk by a Lake; oil on canvas, sgn Jon, 20x26", FAP 4/15/89 110
Stick of Candy, oil on canvas laid down on board, indistinctly sgn, 10x8", C-E 11/30/88 715
Still Life of Flowers, oil on canvas, sgn, 20x24", FAP 4/15/89 OE 715
Still Life of Lemon, Salmon & Copper Pots; oil on canvas, 21x29", SBY 9/14/89 550
Still Life of Peonies & Pears, oil on canvas, sgn WB Hazelton/dtd 24, 30x24", RWS 3/16/89 OE 2,500
Sunflowers, oil on panel, 40x26", B/B 9/14/89 880
Sword Lily (Oriental lady w/two panthers on footbridge beside flower garden), oil on canvas, 28x20", RWS 3/31/88 800
Through the Window (ornate turn-of-century stove, girl at window), oil on artist board, sgn, 26x19", RWS 3/31/88 UE 200
Tulips, watercolor on paper, 12x15", SBY 6/24/88 OE 2,200
View Down to the Sea, oil on canvas, 24x30", RWS 11/10/89 1,600
View in the Adirondacks, oil on canvas, 8x12", B/B 12/8/88 3,025
View of a Pennsylvania Farm, Autumn; oil on board, 5x7", RWS 12/10/88 OE 750
View of the Artist's Studio (interior w/paintings), oil on canvas, sgn, 14x11", RWS 3/16/89 OE 700
View of the Steamship Archer & Chinese Junk in a Storm, oil on canvas, 10x23", C-E 4/26/88 440
View of the Summer Cottage, oil on panel, indistinctly sgn/dtd 1910, 17x34", RWS 11/3/88 850
When Knights Were Bold (knight & lady riding in forest), watercolor/pastel/gouache on paper, sgn, 6x11", RWS 3/31/88 UE 125
Who Died, graphite on paper, 11x8", WG 10/19/88 UE 20
Winter Day in Bucks County, oil on canvas, bears indistinct signature/inscr, 24x30", C-E 2/3/88 1,430
Winter Landscape, oil on canvas, 24x30", SBY 9/14/89 2,420
Winter Reflections (golden stream, landscape/buildings beyond), oil on canvas, indistinctly sgn, 21x24", RWS 3/31/88 OE 900
Woman Seated by a Window, oil on canvas, on Boston stretcher, 16x12", RWS 5/19/88 OE 3,000
Wood Nymph, nude seated on rock contemplates butterfly; pastel on paper, 30x20", RAB 3/27/89 450

American/Canadian School (20th C)

Details From a Garden, watercolor on paper, sgn, 40x27", RWS 5/12/89 500

AMES, Ezra (American, 1768-1836)

Pair: Man & Woman (portraits); oil on canvas, 25x20", C-NY 12/2/88 3,520

AMES, May (American, 19th C)

Autumn Landscape, oil on canvas, sgn/dtd 1908, 24x36", WG 4/23/88 UE 250

AMICK, Robert Wesley (American, 1879-1969)

Railroad Workers (urban scene of men at railroad construction site), ink/crayon on paper, sgn, 14x10", RWS 3/31/88 UE 225

AMIEZ (French, 19th or 20th C)

Hay Cart in an Extensive Landscape, oil on panel, sgn, 5x7", SLK 2/12/88 100

AMIGONI, Jacopo (Italian, 1675-1752)

Allegorical Figure of a Woman Standing in a Landscape, oil on canvas, 35x26", SBY 6/2/89 52,250
Portrait of a Young Lady with Flowers in Her Hair, oil on canvas, 23x17", SBY 6/1/89 12,100

AMIGONI, Jacopo; circle of (Italian, 1675-1752)

Putti in a Landscape, oil on canvas, 34x25", SBY 7/12/89 2,200

AMOROSI, Antonio (Italian, 1660-1736)

Guitar Player, oil on canvas, 39x29", C-NY 5/31/89 44,000
Portrait of a Boy, oil on canvas, 15x12", SBY 4/7/88 2,750
Portrait of a Young Woman Sewing, oil on canvas, 11x10", SBY 6/8/88 2,750
Woman Winding Wool, oil on canvas, unfr, 23x18", C-NY 6/2/88 3,520

AMOROSI, Antonio; circle of (Italian, 1660-1736)

Woman & Three Children with Baskets of Fruits & Vegetables & a Table with Game, oil on canvas, 16x21", SBY 4/7/89 1,980

AMORSOLO, Fernando (Phillipino, 20th C)

Harvest, oil on canvas, sgn/dtd 1929, 32x32", C-E 2/23/88 OE 7,480
Island Travelers (figures afoot with animals on path in landscape), oil on board, sgn/dtd 1936, 20x26", B/B 10/9/88 2,750
Parade Scene, oil on canvas, sgn/dtd 1945, 16x20", B/B 3/22/89 3,575
Village Scene, oil on canvas, sgn/dtd 1945, 16x20", B/B 3/22/89 3,575
Wash Day at the River, oil on board, sgn/dtd 1953, 24x34", B/B 6/15/89 5,500

ANA, Chiara (American, 20th C)

Bouquet of Flowers, watercolor on paper, 28x21", WG 4/23/88 OE 375

ANDERS, Ernst (German, 1845-1911)

Newborn (woman holding small baby in an interior), oil on canvas, sgn, 35x22", WD 3/23/88 3,000

ANDERS, Robert (American)

Sailboats at Sea, oil on canvas, sgn, 26x38", C-E 6/20/89 715

ANDERSEN, Carl Christian (Danish, 1849-1906)

Christianborg Slot Efter Branden, oil on canvas, sgn/dtd 12 Oct 1884, 23x30", SBY 10/24/89 24,200

ANDERSON, C.W. (American, 20th C)

Spring in Virginia (mare & foal in a landscape), oil on canvas, sgn/dtd 49, 20x24", SBY 6/9/89 UE 1,650

ANDERSON, Doug (20th C)

Everytime You Change We Change (abstract composition), oil/acrylic/metalic paint, sgn/dtd 1985, 70x60", SBY 10/5/89 UE 2,750

ANDERSON, Karl (American, 1874-1956)

Lily Pads, oil on canvas, 29x27", SBY 6/24/88 UE 1,980

ANDERSON, Laurie (American, 20th C)

New York Times Horizontal/China Times Vertical, woven newsprint mounted on paper, sgn/dtd 1971/79, 30x22", SBY 10/8/88 1,760

ANDERSON, Lennart (American, 1928-)
Head of Gabriele, oil on board, 11x9", C-NY 6/17/89 OE ... 2,420
Street Scene, oil on board laid down on masonite, dtd 1959, 10x12", C-NY 6/17/89 OE ... 5,500
ANDERSON, Oscar (American, 1873-)
Gloucester Beach, oil on canvasboard, sgn, 7x8", RWS 11/10/89 ... 800
ANDERSON, T.M. (American, 20th C)
Bouquet, oil on canvas, sgn, 15x22", LH 12/4/88 UE ... 30
ANDERSON, Victor Coleman (American, 1882-1937)
Flying Machine (aerial view), oil en grisaille on canvas laid down on board, sgn/dtd 12, 18x28", C-E 2/1/89 OE ... 3,300
Keeping the Little Ones Dry (young girl w/hen & chicks), oil on board, sgn, 20x16", RWS 11/10/89 ... 4,000
Picket Fence, oil on canvas, sgn, 24x30", WD 10/5/88 ... 5,000
ANDERSON, Walter (20th C)
Trash Fish, watercolor, 11x9", MG 5/28/88 ... 1,100
ANDRADE, Magda (Venezuelan, 1808-)
Trees in Spring, oil on canvas, sgn, 24x28", WG 4/23/88 UE ... 300
Village de Chantilly, oil on panel, sgn, 9x13", RWS 11/3/88 ... 550
ANDRE, Albert (French, 1869-1954)
Fillettes Jouant, oil on canvas, sgn twice/titled, 18x26", SBY 10/7/88 OE ... 36,300
Interieur, Femme Ecrivant (seated woman writing in an interior); oil on canvas, sgn, 13x16", SBY 2/16/89 ... 15,400
Interieur, Porte Ouverte; oil on canvas, sgn, 1935, 22x18", SBY 10/6/89 ... 24,750
Interieur (seated lady in interior), oil on panel, sgn, 15x11", SBY 2/16/89 ... 23,100
Paysage (landscape with building, stone wall, & tree), oil on canvas, sgn, 13x16", C-NY 10/6/88 ... 14,300
Paysage du Midi, watercolor/pencil on paper laid down, sgn, 8x11", WD 5/5/88 UE ... 600
Place Pigalle (view of street from balcony), oil on canvas, sgn, 27x24", C-NY 10/6/88 ... 44,000
Roquemaure (garden view of estate), oil on canvas, sgn, 1935, 18x22", C-NY 2/16/89 OE ... 26,400
Study for Provencal Landscape, watercolor over pencil on paper, sgn, 8x11", SBY 2/14/89 ... 880
Vase de Caquelicots (floral still life), oil on canvas, sgn, 26x21", C-NY 2/16/89 ... 24,200
ANDREA, Mariano
Serenade (allegorical), oil on panel, sgn/dtd 39, 15x11", NA 10/1/88 ... 650
ANDREAE, Tobias
Morning Walk, oil on canvas, sgn, 33x30", C-E 2/23/88 OE ... 5,280
ANDREENKO, Mikhail (Russian, 1894-)
Blue Composition (abstract), gouache on paper, sgn, 9x12", C-L 10/8/88 OE ... 2,416
Composition (abstract), gouache on paper, sgn, 13x18", C-L 10/8/88 ... 1,120
Standing Nude (contemporary male figure), gouache on paper, sgn, 20x10", C-L 10/8/88 OE ... 4,090
ANDREIS, Alex; see De Andreis
ANDREOTTI, Federico (Italian, 1847-1930)
Cavaliers (interior scene with drinking & singing), oil on panel, sgn, 12x16", NA 5/13/89 ... 6,250
Dance (nymph dances while others play instruments), oil on canvas, sgn, 19x25", SBY 10/24/89 ... 19,800
Letter (portrait), oil on canvas, sgn, 25x17", C-NY 2/25/88 OE ... 16,500
Love Poem, oil on board, sgn, 13x21", WD 1/11/89 ... 1,200
Tavern Scene, oil on panel, sgn, 12x16", C-NY 5/25/88 ... 3,850
ANDREWS, George H. (British, 1816-1898)
Oregon Trail (wagon train), pencil/watercolor/bodycolor, sgn/dtd 1860, 7x23", C-SK 5/25/89 ... 2,390
ANDREWS, Henry (British, 1816-1869)
Banquet by a Lake, oil on canvas, sgn, 30x36", C-NY 2/25/88 OE ... 10,450
Fete Galante, oil on canvas, sgn, 20x26", C-NY 2/25/88 ... 5,500
ANDREWS, James (19th C)
Summer's Bounty, watercolor on paper, sgn/dtd 1845, 15x11", C-E 10/25/88 UE ... 605
ANDRIEU, Mathurin Arthur
Burning Ship on the Rhode Island Coast, oil on panel, sgn/dtd 1873, 8x15", C-E 11/30/88 ... 1,650
ANDRIEU, Pierre (French, 1821-1892)
Still Life of Fruit, oil on canvas, sgn/dtd 1870, 14x17", WL 5/20/88 ... 500
ANDSELL, Richard (British, 1815-1885)
Good Friends (girl leaning on a brick wall w/cows & dog at her feet), oil on canvas, sgn, 36x28", SBY 6/9/89 ... 27,500
ANESI, Paolo (Italian, 1700-1761)
View of St Peter's, Rome, with Travelers on a Path in the Foreground; oil on canvas, 20x27", C-NY 6/2/88 OE ... 24,200
ANGAS, Charlie
Owners Up (A Horserace), pen/ink/watercolor, monogramed/dtd 1882/inscr/titled, 6x8", C-SK 6/9/88 ... 650
ANGELI, A. (Italian, 20th C)
Untitled, interior of Moorish courtyard; oil on canvas, sgn, 36x21", SLK 2/11/89 ... 100
ANGELIS, Pieter (1685-1734)
Gathering of Peasants Eating & Drinking Before a Cottage, oil on canvas on board, sgn/dtd 1725, 18x24", SBY 4/7/88 OE ... 8,250
Market with Booths in a Field Outside Village, Peasants Arriving...; oil on canvas, unfr, 78x54", C-M 12/3/88 ... 27,872
ANGELIS, Pieter; school of (1685-1734)
Card Players in an Interior, oil on canvas, 22x19", C-NY 4/8/88 ... 3,300
Peasants Dancing, oil on canvas, 11x13", B/B 9/15/88 ... 715
ANGELUCCIO, att
Classical River Landscape with Figures by a Waterfall, a Monastery in the Distance; oil on canvas, 27x39", C-NY 10/20/88 ... 13,200
ANGLADA-CAMARASA, Hermen (Spanish, 1873-1959)
View in Mallorca, oil on panel, sgn/inscr, 9x9", SBY 5/23/89 OE ... 50,600

ANGLADE, Gaston (French, 1854-)
Boys with Goats Outside a Village, oil on canvas, sgn, 15x18", B/B 9/15/88 — 1,650
Mountainous Landscape, oil on canvas, sgn, 22x26", C-E 5/22/89 — 2,200

Anglo-American School (19th C)
Still Life of Grapes & Peaches, oil on canvas, sgn, 10x15", RWS 5/12/89 OE — 1,100

Anglo-Chinese School (19th C)
British Paddle Steamer in Chinese Waters, oil on canvas, unfr, 18x24", C-SK 6/9/88 — 650
Bund, Shanghai; no media given, 20x40", C-SK 5/25/89 UE — 1,650
Pair: On the Pearl River; pencil/watercolor heightened w/bodycolor, 13x189", C-SK 5/25/89 — 1,840
Praya Grande, Macao, with Junks & a British Paddlesteamer Offshore; bodycolor, 7x9", C-SK 5/25/89 — 770
Praya Grande, Macao with Junks & Other Shipping Offshore; oil on glass, 13x19", C-SK 5/25/89 — 920
Praya Grande, Macao; bodycolor, 8x11", C-SK 5/25/89 — 515
Sketch of Graham's Island by Mr HA Hervey, July Anno Domini A83A; oil on canvas, inscr, unfr, 13x11", C-SK 6/9/88 — 930
Three-Masted Wood-Screw Frigate Off Hong Kong, oil on canvas, 18x24", C-SK 5/25/89 — 2,760

Anglo-Dutch School (18th C)
Portrait of a Lady, oil on canvas, ca 1700, 40x32", SBY 12/9/88 — 1,210

Anglo-Flemish School (17th C)
Portrait of a Gentleman, w/figures traveling along country roads beyond; oil on round panel, ca 1600, 8", SBY 4/7/89 — 14,300

ANGO, Jean Robert (fl 1759-1769)
Delphic Sibyl, red chalk, bears signature/dtd 22.8 1767, 17x14", SBY 1/13/89 OE — 4,400

ANGZHI, Zhu (Chinese, 1764-)
Landscape After Wang Meng (hanging scroll), ink/color on silk, sgn, 56x19", SBY 5/31/89 OE — 4,675

ANIVITTI, Filippo (Italian, 1876-)
Flower Market at the Foot of the Spanish Steps, watercolor over traces of pencil, sgn, 12x9", C-NY 2/23/89 — 1,320

ANKER, Albert
Double-Sided: Studies of Babies; pencil on paper, sgn recto, 8x13", C-E 5/23/88 — 880

ANQUETIN, Louis (French, 1861-1932)
Seine Near Rouen, oil on canvas, sgn/dtd 92, 26x32", WD 5/5/88 — 8,000

ANSCHUTZ, Thomas Pollock (American, 1851-1912)
Farmer & His Son at Harvesting, oil on canvas, sgn/dtd 1879, 24x17", C-NY 5/26/88 OE — 1,540,000
Indians on the Ohio, oil on canvas, ca 1907, 30x22", SBY 5/25/88 — 16,500

ANSDELL, Richard (British, 1815-1885)
Return From Stalking, oil on canvas, 48x67", SBY 6/10/88 OE — 137,500

ANTES, Horst (German, 1936-)
Gray Head with Green Nose (abstract), gouache/charcoal on paper, sgn/dtd 69, 22x18", SBY 5/3/88 — 15,400
Untitled (abstract nude), mixed media on vellum, sgn, 11x17", SLK 4/7/89 — 550

ANTOLINEZ, Francisco
Pair: Landscape with Flight Into Egypt; Landscape with Christ & Woman of Samaria; oil on canvas, 19x30", C-NY 1/15/88 — 9,350

ANTONIANI, Pietro
Bay of Naples with Mount Vesuvius, oil on canvas, 72x26", C-NY 10/20/88 OE — 52,800

ANTONIO, Cristobal; see Di Antonio, Christobal

ANTUNEZ, Nemesio (Chilean, 1918-)
Untitled (abstract), oil on canvas, dtd 1962/inscr, 26x40", SBY 5/16/89 — 2,200

Antwerp School (16th C)
Christ & Woman Taken in Adultery, oil on panel, shaped top, ca 1530, 38x28", C-NY 4/6/89 OE — 9,900
Christ & Woman Taken in Adultery, oil on panel, shaped top, ca 1530, 38x28", C-NY 4/8/88 — 5,500
Pair: Saint Catherine of Alexandria; Saint Barbara; tempera on panel, ca 1530, 24x8", SBY 4/7/89 — 44,000
Saint Lucy & the Resurrection of Christ, oil on double-sided panel, a wing of an altar piece, 30x9", SBY 4/7/89 — 2,640
Triptych: Virgin & Child w/Sts Barbara & Catherine & Holy Trinity; oil on panel/shaped top, 37x23", 37x10"; SBY 6/1/89 — 44,000

Antwerp School (18th C)
Kitchen Still Life with Figures, oil on canvas, unfr, ca 1700, 64x82", SBY 10/13/89 OE — 37,400

ANUSKIEWICZ, Richard (American, 1930-)
Blue in a Stimulus (abstract), oil on canvas, sgn, 50x28", SBY 10/7/89 — 3,300
Cypress Extract (composition w/squares), acrylic on masonite, sgn/dtd 1964, 36x36", SBY 2/14/89 — 3,025
Quadrivalent (geometric design), liquitex on board, sgn/dtd 1966/#d 130, 24x24", SBY 10/7/89 — 3,850
Soft Corner Vermillion (square), acrylic on canvas, sgn/dtd 1978/#d 544, 43x43", WD 5/5/88 — 3,400
Untitled (geometric composition), acrylic on canvas, sgn/dtd 1971, 60x60", SBY 2/15/89 OE — 13,200
Untitled (linear composition), acrylic/masonite, sgn/dtd 1964, 18x32", C-E 11/17/88 — 1,980

APOL, Louis (Dutch, 1850-)
Brook Before a Farmhouse, watercolor heightened w/white, sgn/indistinctly dtd, 14x21", RWS 5/12/89 — 1,600

APPEL, Charles P. (American, 1877-)
City Harbor at Dusk, oil on canvas, sgn, 18x24", SBY 6/24/88 — 5,225
Glowing Light, oil on canvas, sgn, 16x20", C-E 9/15/88 — 1,650
Man in Rowboat, oil on canvas, sgn/dtd 1926, 30x24", C-E 6/1/88 — 3,520
New York Harbor, oil on canvas, sgn, 11x18", DM 9/16/88 — 2,250

APPEL, Charles P.; att (American, 1877-)
Sunset Landscape, oil on canvas mounted on masonite, sgn/dtd 1920, 10x14", SBY 9/23/88 — 660

APPEL, Karel (Dutch, 1921-)
Abstractions with Bird, oil on canvas, sgn/dtd 75, 22x28", SBY 2/19/88 OE — 23,100
Appel Circus (abstract), acrylic on paper mounted on canvas, sgn, 34x24", SBY 10/5/89 — 12,100
Bird Like a Hand (abstract), acrylic/crayon on paper, sgn/dtd 73, 23x30" SBY 10/8/88 — 8,800

Birds (abstract), oil on canvas, sgn/dtd 51, 34x39", SBY 6/30/88	180,200
Black-Eyed Animal, acrylic on paper laid down on canvas, sgn/inscr/dtd 78, 22x30", C-E 5/13/88	4,620
Dancing Head, oil on canvas, sgn, 1966, 46x35", SBY 11/9/89 OE	77,000
Enfants avec Oiseaux (children w/birds, abstract), acrylic on canvas, sgn/dtd 1969, 48x63", SBY 10/5/89	55,000
Enfants Interrogeant (abstract), mixed media collage on cardboard, sgn/dtd 49, 84x65", SBY 6/30/88	124,100
Faces Together (abstract), gouache on paper, sgn/dtd 78, 22x30", SBY 2/15/89 OE	12,100
Figures (abstract), oil on canvas, sgn/dtd 74, 20x30", SBY 5/3/88 OE	20,900
Fish in Grass (abstract), oil on canvas, sgn/dtd 1971, 35x46", SBY 10/8/88	17,600
Flying Head (abstract), acrylic on paper laid down on linen, sgn/dtd 78, 22x30", SBY 10/5/89	8,800
He Wants To Be King (abstract), acrylic on paper, sgn/dtd 1969, 26x23", C-NY 2/14/89 OE	20,900
Head (abstract), acrylic on canvas, sgn/dtd 74, 20x16", C-NY 2/14/89 OE	26,400
Head (abstract), oil on canvas, sgn, 1976, 10x8", SBY 10/5/89 OE	12,100
Head (abstract), oil on canvas, sgn/dtd 53, 38x28", SBY 6/30/88 OE	210,000
Head Like Animal, acrylic on paper laid down on canvas, sgn/inscr/dtd 78, 23x30", C-E 5/13/88	7,700
Head of a Woman (in profile), charcoal/pastel on rice paper, sgn/dtd 47, 15x11", SBY 5/16/89 OE	16,500
Le Grand Oiseau (abstract), acrylic on canvas, sgn twice/dtd 73, 77x99", SBY 6/30/88	64,000
Les Visages, acrylic on paper mounted on panel, sgn, 29x43", C-NY 11/10/88	24,200
Man Wearing Hat (contemporary), gouache/India ink/crayon on paper, sgn, ca 1960, 19x22", SBY 5/3/89	13,200
Once I Was the Sun, acrylic on paper laid down on canvas, sgn/dtd 78, 23x30", C-E 5/13/88	7,150
Owl (abstract), oil on canvas, sgn, 1966, 21x26", SBY 11/9/89	35,750
Paysage Avec Animeaux, gouache/colored crayons on paper, sgn/dtd 3 times 59, 22x30", C-NY 5/4/88	12,100
Personnage, oil on canvas, sgn/dtd 67, unfr, 119x80", C-NY 11/10/88	99,000
Personnage (abstract), gouache/crayon on paper, sgn/dtd 58, 30x22", WD 5/5/88	9,500

Personnage et Soleil, oil on canvas, sgn/dtd 1958, 32x39", PHL 11/15/88 OE, $65,000

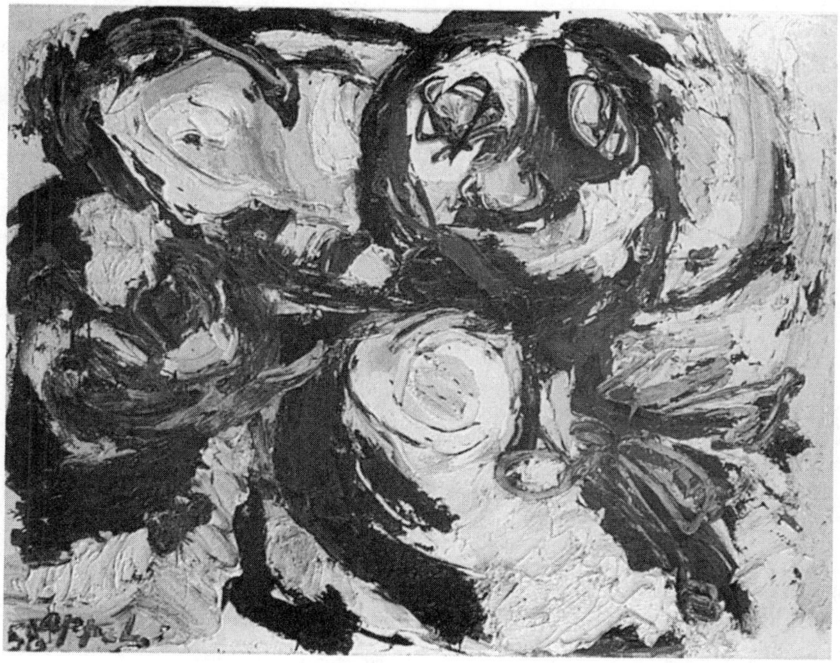

Running Horse (abstract), acrylic on paper, sgn/dtd 1977, 22x30", SBY 2/15/89	11,000
See Me Running Again, acrylic on paper laid down on canvas, sgn/dtd 78, 23x30", C-E 5/13/88	7,150
Tetes dans Tempette (abstract), oil on canvas, sgn/dtd 1960/titled, 38x57", SBY 2/19/88	45,100
The Kiss (abstract), oil on canvas, sgn, 1966, 36x29", SBY 10/5/89	49,500
Two Heads in the Wind (abstract), gouache/crayon on paper, sgn/dtd 59, 20x25", SBY 2/15/89 OE	16,500
Untitled (abstract figures), gouache/tempera/crayon/collage on paper, sgn/dtd 66, 23x35", SBY 5/3/88	8,250
Untitled (abstract), acrylic on canvas, sgn, 1973, 16x9", C-NY 10/4/89	18,700
Untitled (abstract), acrylic on canvas, sgn, 1977, 16x20", C-NY 5/4/88 OE	20,900
Untitled (abstract), acrylic on paper, sgn, ca 1978-79, 15x20", C-NY 5/4/89	14,300
Untitled (abstract), acrylic on paper laid down on canvas, sgn, 19x20", SBY 10/8/88	7,150
Untitled (abstract), acrylic on paper mounted on canvas, sgn/dtd 1973, 26x32", SBY 10/8/88	11,000
Untitled (abstract), acrylic on paper mounted on canvas, sgn, 1976, 19x30", C-NY 5/4/89	24,200
Untitled (abstract), acrylic on paper mounted on canvas, sgn, 1973, unfr, 30x23", C-NY 10/4/89	17,600
Untitled (abstract), acrylic on paper mounted on canvas, sgn/dtd 73, unfr, 31x19", C-NY 10/4/89	19,800
Untitled (abstract), acrylic/metallic paint/pencil on paper, sgn, 26x20", SBY 5/3/89	14,300
Untitled (abstract), oil on canvas, sgn, ca 1969, 42x27", C-NY 5/4/89	55,000
Untitled (abstract), oil on canvas, sgn twice/dtd 1953 twice, 51x38", SBY 2/19/88 OE	71,500
Untitled (abstract), oil on canvas, sgn/dtd 54, 42x35", C-NY 5/4/88 OE	66,000
Untitled (abstract), oil on paper mounted on canvas, sgn/dtd 73, 22x30", SBY 2/19/88 OE	7,700

Untitled (abstract), oil/paper collage on printed paper, sgn twice, ca 1959, 25x18", SBY 10/8/88 OE 13,200
Waiting for the Colorful Rain, acrylic on paper laid down on canvas, sgn/inscr/dtd 78, 23x30", C-E 5/13/88 5,280

APPERT, George (French, 20th C)
Birds Singing, oil on canvas, sgn, 24x11", C-E 10/25/88 2,090
Birds Swimming, oil on canvas, sgn, 25x11", C-E 10/25/88 2,860

APPIAN, Louis (French, 1862-1896)
Male Nude, standing, right hand on a staff; black chalk on laid paper, stamped, 25x19", C-NY 10/26/88 OE 2,420

ARAKAWA, Shusaku (Japanese, 1936-)
An Old Story (Explosion) From Explosion (Large Story), oil on canvas, 1967, 81x63", SBY 5/3/89 49,500
Kiss (abstract), acrylic/black felt-tip pen/graphite on canvas, sgn/dtd 1968, 49x72", C-NY 2/20/88 15,400
Untitled (abstract), acrylic/black felt-tip pen/graphite/coat hanger on canvas, sgn/dtd 1963, 91x63", C-NY 5/4/88 OE 57,200
Untitled (abstract), watercolor/pen/black ink/graphite on paper, sgn/dtd 63, 24x18", C-NY 2/14/89 4,180

ARAPOFF, Alexis (Russian, 1904-1948)
Man & His Dog, oil on canvas, sgn/dtd 27, 36x23", C-E 5/9/89 5,500

ARBEIT, Eugene (French, 1825-)
Wooded River Landscape, oil on canvas, indistinctly sgn, 10x15", SBY 6/8/88 1,980

ARBUCKLE, Franklin (Canadian, 1909-)
Old House, Montreal; oil on board, sgn, 12x16", FB 10/30/89 1,320

ARBUCKLE, George Franklin (Canadian, 1909-)
Dry Country Near Taxco, oil on board, sgn, 12x16", WAD 6/12/89 400
Northern Lumbering Town, Haliburton, Ontario; oil on board, sgn, 20x24", FB 10/17/88 1,400

ARCHIPENKO, Alexander (Russian, 1887-1964)
Personnage Cubiste, India ink on paper, sgn/inscr Paris, 12x8", SBY 10/5/88 OE 9,900

ARCIMBOLDO, Giuseppe; follower of (Italian, 1527-1593)
Portrait of King Herod: An Allegory; oil on parchment laid down on board, 12x9", SBY 4/7/89 OE 15,400

ARCIMBOLDO, Giuseppe; school of (Italian, 1527-1593)
King Herod (body formed by interwoven figures of nude infants), oil on parchment mounted on panel, 11x8", RWS 5/19/88 1,600

ARCOS Y MEGALDE, Santiago (Chilean, -1912)
Looking Across the Valley, oil on canvas, sgn/dtd 82, 29x20", SBY 6/8/88 2,200

ARDEN, V. (Belgian, 19th C)
Steer on a Road, oil on canvas, sgn/dtd 1849, 30x26", B/B 1/11/89 UE 385

ARDISSONE, Yolande (French, 1872-)
Village Grec, oil on canvas, sgn, 30x36", WD 5/5/88 1,100

ARDON, Mordecai (Israeli, 20th C)
Fields in the Emek (abstract), oil on canvas, sgn/dtd 64, 22x18", SBY 5/30/89 OE 37,400
Stones of the Ancient Wall (green composition), oil on canvas, sgn/dtd 62, 32x39", SBY 5/30/89 46,200
Stones of the Negev (abstract), oil on canvas, sgn/dtd 64, 22x16", SBY 5/30/89 OE 30,800

ARELLANO, see De Arellano

ARENTZ, Arent (Dutch, 1586-1635)
Landscape with Elegant Figures, Peasants, & Fishermen Along Riverbank; oil on panel, bears monogram, 6x8", SBY 6/3/88 44,000

ARIENTIA, Gustavo Lopez
Desde la Mesa, oil on canvas, sgn twice/dtd 85, 55x71", C-NY 11/21/88 3,300

ARIKHA, Avigdor (1929-)
Composition (abstract), gouache on paper laid down on panel, sgn/dtd 59, 28x20", SBY 5/30/89 OE 7,700
Mount of the Temple & the Dome of the Rock, India ink on paper, sgn/dtd 14 IX 67, 15x18", SBY 10/5/88 2,750

ARISTALL, Joshua; att
Girl with Dog, watercolor, sgn/dtd 1807, 11x9", C-E 9/15/88 110

ARIZA, Gonzalo (Colombian, 1912-)
Clouds & Rocks (contemporary), oil on canvas, sgn/inscr Nubes Y Rocas, ca 1950s, 28x20", SBY 11/21/88 UE 5,500
Coffee Plantation, oil on canvas, sgn, 1987, 36x36", SBY 5/17/88 OE 11,000
Mist in the Afternoon (landscape), oil on canvas, sgn, 1988, 63x36", SBY 5/16/89 25,300

ARMAN
Violins, black ink/pencil on paper, sgn/dtd 83, 38x24", SBY 10/7/89 5,775

ARMAND-DUMARESQ, Edouard (French, 1826-1895)
Still Life of Musical Instrument, Globe, Artist's Palette & Bust; oil on canvas, sgn, unfr, 39x51", SBY 12/9/88 1,760

ARMENTIA, Gustavo Lopez
Mundane Relationships, oil on canvas, sgn/dtd 87, 79x79", SBY 11/21/88 3,850

ARMET Y PORTANEL, Jose (Spanish, 19th C)
Caserio Rural (rural hamlet), oil on canvas, sgn, 23x45", SBY 2/22/89 OE 27,500

ARMFIELD, Edward (British, 19th C)
Terriers Ratting, oil on canvas, sgn, 25x30", SBY 6/9/89 3,025
Two Terriers, oil on canvas, sgn, 22x30", MG 8/27/88 525

ARMFIELD, George (British, 1808-1893)
Day's Bag, oil on canvas, 14x18", SBY 6/9/89 5,225
Eyeing the Prey (fox watching rabbits in a landscape), oil on canvas, 25x30", SBY 6/9/89 4,950
Flushing Mallards, oil on canvas, sgn, in painted circle, 24x24", SBY 6/10/88 OE 12,100
Fox & Terriers at Play, oil on canvas, sgn, 16x20", SBY 6/9/89 3,300
Guarding the Day's Bag (dogs with game in a landscape), oil on canvas, 14x18", B/B 10/9/88 UE 4,400
Pair: Eyeing the Quarry; Two Spaniels; oil on board, sgn, 5x8", B/B 10/9/88 3,300
Pair: Terriers Getting Into Mischief; Teasing; oil on canvas, 1 sgn/dtd 1854, 1 sgn/dtd 1851, 12x14", SBY 6/9/89 6,050
Playful Terriers, oil on canvas, sgn/dtd 1871, 12x16", SBY 6/9/89 2,750

Spaniels in an Interior, oil on canvas, sgn, 28x35", SBY 6/10/88 ... 7,150
Terriers & Fox in a Landscape, oil on panel, sgn, 8x10", C-E 10/25/88 ... 1,540
Terriers Getting Into Mischief, oil on canvas, sgn/dtd 1881, in painted circle, 22x21", SBY 6/10/88 ... 4,125
Terriers Ratting, oil on canvas, 28x36", C-E 5/22/89 ... 5,500
Three Cairns Rabbiting, oil on canvas, sgn/dtd 1844, 28x36", SBY 6/9/89 ... 16,500
Three Terriers, oil on canvas, sgn, 8x10", MG 8/27/88 ... 850

ARMFIELD, George; att (British, 1808-1893)
After the Hunt, oil on canvas, in a painted oval, 17x21", SBY 6/9/89 OE ... 2,970
Pair: Tug O' War; King for the Day (dogs); oil on canvas, 12x16", SBY 6/10/88 ... 3,575

ARMFIELD, George; manner of (British, 1808-1893)
Good Friends (portrait of four dogs), oil on canvas, in a painted circle, unfr, 34" dia, SBY 6/9/89 ... 1,210
Terriers Ratting, oil on canvas, bears signature, 24x36", SBY 7/12/89 UE ... 1,650

ARMFIELD, Maxwell (British, 1882-1972)
Madison Square Park, oil on canvas, monogramed, 34x30", C-NY 9/28/89 OE ... 17,600
Salome with the Head of John the Baptist, watercolor/pencil/pen/ink, sgn w/monogram, ca 1903, 11x8", C-L 6/27/88 ... 15,136
Windy Day, California (contemporary depiction); oil on canvas, monogramed, 20x24", C-NY 9/28/89 ... 4,400

ARMIN, Emil (Austrian, 1895-1983)
At the Well, watercolor, sgn, dtd 1931, 12x16", LH 10/16/88 OE ... 250

ARMITAGE, Thomas Liddall (British, 18th/20th C)
When We Were Young (girls digging at the seashore), oil on canvas, sgn/dtd 1891, 36x24", C-NY 5/24/89 ... 33,000

ARMLEDER, John (20th C)
Untitled (canvas w/vertical line, electric guitars on both sides), mixed media, 1986, 99x121", SBY 10/5/89 OE ... 27,500

ARMOUR, S.E.
Autumn Wooded Scene, oil on canvas, sgn, 35x41", MAG 4/24/88 ... 600

ARMSTRONG, Rolf (American, 1881-1960)
Young Lovely, pastel on paper, sgn, 14x11", SBY 3/17/88 ... 1,100

ARMSTRONG, William W. (American, 1822-1914)
Algoma in Choppy Water, watercolor, sgn/dtd 1867, 19x26", WAD 6/12/89 OE ... 13,500
Indian on a Lakeside Trail, oil on canvas, sgn/dtd 86, unfr, 50x30", B/B 10/6/88 ... 880
Lake View with Indian Camp, watercolor, inscr/dtd August 15th 86, 11x15", WAD 6/12/89 ... 1,300
Mountainous Lake Landscape, oil on board, sgn, 19x24", PHL 12/1/88 ... 2,800
Red Rock, Nipigon Bay; pen/ink/watercolor, sgn/dtd 1867/titled, 12x19", C-SK 6/9/88 ... 1,020

ARNEGGER, Alois (Austrian, 1879-1967)
Alpine Peaks in Winter Sun, oil on canvas, sgn, 28x32", SBY 7/12/89 OE ... 4,950
Autumn Landscape with Figure, oil on canvas, 28x36", FAP 11/4/88 ... 225
Italian Villa & Summer Gardens by a Lake, oil on canvas, sgn, 29x40", C-E 5/22/89 ... 3,520
Lake Como, oil on canvas, sgn, 23x31", DM 10/14/88 ... 900
Mediterranean Coastal Scene, oil on canvas, sgn, 24x36", FAP 11/4/88 ... 600
On Lake Como, oil on canvas, sgn, 35x48", SBY 7/12/89 ... 4,400
Snow Scene with Mountains, oil on canvas, sgn, 16x24", LH 12/4/88 OE ... 800
Varenna, Lake Como; oil on canvas, sgn/dtd 1957, 40x28", LH 10/16/88 ... 700
Villa Garden, oil on canvas, sgn, 24x32", B/B 9/14/89 ... 1,760

ARNETT, J.A. (Dutch, 19th/20th C)
Floral Still Life with Bird Nest, oil on panel, sgn, 20x16", B/B 1/11/89 OE ... 1,100

ARNOLD, George (British, 1763-1841)
Three Spaniels in a Landscape, a Manor House Beyond; oil on canvas, sgn/dtd 1798, 28x36", SBY 6/9/89 ... 14,300

ARNOLD, Reginald Ernst (British, fl 1876-1896)
All's Fair in Love & War, oil, sgn, 20x36", WD 1/11/89 ... 1,800
Courting in a Music Room, oil on canvas, sgn, 28x36", C-E 5/23/88 ... 3,520

ARNOLDI, Charles Arthur (American, 1946-)
Altair (abstract), acrylic on canvas, sgn/dtd 1978, unfr, 84x74", SBY 10/7/89 ... 11,550
Carat (abstract), acrylic/flashe on wood, sgn/dtd 1981, 96x94x9", SBY 10/8/88 UE ... 17,600
Linnie (abstract), sgn/dtd 1978, unfr, 40x32", SBY 10/5/88 OE ... 6,050

ARNOUX, Michel (French, 1833-1877)
Reading Lesson (two small girls w/book in an interior), oil on panel, sgn, 13x10", RWS 5/19/88 ... 1,400
Story Hour (interior, two children w/book), oil on panel, sgn, 13x10", C-E 2/21/89 ... 3,850

ARNULL, George (British, 19th C)
Ascot Races-Coming In; oil on board, 11x14", SBY 6/9/89 ... 15,400
Racecourse with Sam Basden in Red Silks Up, oil on canvas, sgn/dtd 1891, 18x24", SBY 6/9/89 ... 5,500

ARONSON, Boris (American, 1900-)
Fiddler on the Roof-Design for the Decor; pen/ink/gouache/collage, sgn/dtd 64, 15x26", SBY 10/5/88 UE ... 1,100

ARP, Jean; & TAUBER, Sophie
Duo (abstract), collage/gouache on paper, monogramed, 1947, 12x9", C-NY 2/18/88 OE ... 7,700

ARP, Jean Hans (French, 1887-1966)
Composition (abstract), brown contact paper/pencil on paper, sgn, 12x8", C-NY 2/16/89 OE ... 10,450
Untitled (abstract), watercolor/pencil on board, sgn/dtd August 1963, 16x11", SBY 2/16/89 ... 7,700

ARPA Y PEREA, Jose (Spanish, 1862-1903)
Abdication of Charles V, oil on canvas, sgn, 17x25", B/B 3/22/89 ... 5,225
Sta Maira Cuixcoma-Puebla (extensive landscape); oil on canvas, sgn/titled, 15x21", C-NY 5/17/89 ... 4,400

ARRIAGA, Juan Antt (18th C)
Childhood of Christ, oil on canvas, sgn/dtd 1735, 24x45", WD 10/19/88 OE ... 2,100

ARRIETA, Jose Agustin (Latin American)
Vista de la Mina de La Sierra de Loreto, Real del Monte (landscape); oil on canvas, 19x28", C-NY 11/12/88 30,800
Vista del Patio (figures/horse & buggy in courtyard), oil on canvas, 20x18", C-NY 11/21/88 OE 38,500
ARSHILE, Gorky
Portrait of a Tree, oil on canvas, 24x14", ca 1927, 24x14", SBY 10/8/88 27,500
ARTER, Charles J. (American, -1929)
Peasant Girl by a Tree, oil on canvas laid down on masonite, sgn, 15x21", C-E 5/23/88 770
ARTHURS, Stanley Massey (American, 1877-1950)
Seashore, oil on canvas, sgn, 20x26", C-E 2/1/89 1,540
ARTS, Alexis (Canadian, 1940-)
First Snow, Howick; oil on board, sgn/dtd 1976, 16x20", FB 10/30/89 825
Gathering Fire Wood, oil on canvas, sgn, 16x20", FB 5/28/89 400
Winter Forest Scene, oil on board, sgn/dtd 1976, 12x16", FB 28/89 280
ARTS, Dorus T. (Dutch, 1901-1961)
Fisherman's Return, oil on canvas, sgn, 12x16", FB 5/28/89 900
Winter Homested, oil on canvas, sgn, 12x16", FB 5/28/89 OE 1,300
ARTSCHWAGER, Richard (American, 1924-)
Buildings & Grounds (contemporary), acrylic on celotex, sgn/dtd 73/titled, 32x48", SBY 11/11/88 60,500
Chair/Chair/Table (contemporary), liquitex on celotex, sgn/dtd 80, 25x23", C-NY 2/14/89 OE 71,500
City of Man #2 (abstract), acrylic/charcoal on celotex in oak frame, 1982, 75x55x12", SBY 5/3/89 104,500
City of Man III (abstract), acrylic on celotex/formica/mahogany, 1982, 51x48x6", SBY 11/11/88 77,000
Interior (Southeast), acrylic on celotex on 3 panels, 1973,44x52", 32x52", 24x52", SBY 5/2/88 OE 176,000
Rug (abstract), graphite on paper, sgn/dtd 77, 33x23", SBY 11/11/88 UE 4,400
Untitled (abstract), charcoal on paper, 25x19", lot 227, SBY 2/15/89 UE 1,870
Untitled (abstract), liquitex on celotex, sgn/dtd 1969, 9x10", C-NY 11/10/88 18,700
Untitled (abstract), liquitex on celotex, 1974, 22x17", C-NY 11/10/88 28,600
Untitled (contemporary depiction of chair at table), charcoal on paper, sgn/dtd 87, 25x19", C-NY 10/4/89 6,050
Untitled (figure at table viewed from above), charcoal/graphite on paper, sgn/dtd 78, 19x25", C-NY 5/4/89 5,500
Untitled (lineation), liquitex on celotex, aluminum frame, 1970, 28x24", C-NY 5/3/88 60,500
Untitled (woven design), liquitex on celotex, 17x14", C-NY 5/4/89 41,800
Upper Right Hand X (contemporary), charcoal on paper, sgn/dtd 69, 19x25", C-NY 5/4/89 8,800
Volcano III, charcoal on paper, sgn/dtd 82, 19x25", C-NY 11/10/88 4,400
ARTZ, Constant (Dutch, 1870-1951)
Ducks by a Pond, oil on canvas, sgn, 20x28", C-E 2/23/88 3,520
Ducks on the Shore, watercolor/gouache on paper, sgn, 15x20", C-NY 5/24/89 OE 4,400
ARTZ, David Adolf Constant (Dutch, 1837-1890)
Feeding the Baby, oil on canvas, sgn, 20x26", SBY 6/8/88 4,675
Kitchen Hearth, oil on canvas, sgn, 24x30", SBY 6/8/88 5,500
The First Step, oil on canvas, sgn/dtd 1872, 41x59", SBY 10/24/89 8,250
ARVILLAND (American, 19th C)
Elodia A Kennedy, New York; watercolor on paper, indistinctly sgn/titled, 21x33", RAB 8/1/88 2,500
Portrait of the American Bark Carie Wyman, watercolor on paper, sgn, 16x22", RAB 8/1/88 800
ASCENZI, E. (Italian, 19th/20th C)
Courtyard Scene, oil on canvas, sgn, 22x11", LH 5/15/88 160
Pottery Merchant, watercolor w/gum arabic, sgn/inscr, 34x24", C-E 2/23/88 1,650
ASCHENBRENNER, T.
Sultan's Choice, oil on canvas, sgn/dtd 1906, 24x18", C-E 11/8/88 750
ASCHER, Georges
Vase of Flowers, oil on canvas, sgn, 29x24", SBY 5/30/89 2,750
ASHBROOK, Paul
Mexican Street Scene, oil on canvas, sgn, 30x22", C-E 2/3/88 OE 1,320
ASHLEY, Clifford W. (American, 1881-1947)
Sperm Whales (pod of whales in sea), oil on canvas, sgn, orig frame, 24x49", RAB 11/10/88 4,000
ASHLEY, Frank N. (American, 1920-)
Epsom 200th Derby, Pulling Up; watercolor on paper, sgn, 30x22", SBY 6/10/88 2,750
Parade of the Welsh Guard, pen/watercolor/gouache on paper, sgn, 10x24", SBY 6/9/89 2,750
Three Huntsmen, pencil/watercolor/gouache on paper, sgn, 14x10", SBY 6/9/89 3,960
ASHTON, William (British, 19th/20th C)
Hay Wain on a Country Road at Dusk, oil on canvas laid down, sgn, 18x22", B/B 12/8/88 550
ASOMA, Tadashi
Nude & Screen, acrylic on canvas, sgn/dtd 66, 50x58", C-E 5/13/88 1,760
ASSELIN, Maurice (French, 1882-1947)
Flower Arranger, oil on canvas, sgn/dtd 26, 52x26", C-E 10/18/89 1,320
ASSELYN, Jan (Dutch, 1610-1652)
Cavalry Skirmish in a Landscape, oil on panel, sgn/dtd 1634, 12x19", SBY 6/3/88 18,700
Travelers Halted by an Inn, oil on canvas, 18x21", SBY 6/2/89 25,300
ASSERETO, Gioacchino (Italian, 1600-1649)
Christ Healing the Blind Man, oil on canvas, 45x57", C-NY 5/31/89 OE 110,000
Pieta, oil on canvas, 51x62", C-NY 1/15/88 OE 77,000
ASTI, Angelo (French, 1847-1903)
Portrait of a Sensual Woman, oil on canvas, sgn, 20x16", FAP 11/4/88 1,800

Portrait of Actress Mary Frayne, oil on canvas, sgn, 24x19", WG 9/16/88 3,200
Portrait of the Actress Mary Frayne, oil on canvas, sgn, ca 1880, SBY 2/22/89 7,700

ASTUDILLO, Ever (20th C)
Untitled (interior of movie theatre), pencil on paper, sgn/dtd 1980, 20x28", SBY 5/16/89 1,100

ATALAYA, Enrique (Spanish, 19th C)
Bare-Chested Soldier, watercolor over pencil on paper, sgn/inscr/dtd 1880, 17x8", SBY 6/8/88 UE 495

ATKINSON, William Edwin (Canadian, 1862-1926)
Old Street in St Brieno, Brittany, France; oil on board, sgn/dtd 1918, 10x8", WAD 6/12/89 180

ATL, Geraldo Murillo (Mexican, 1875-1964)
Sol Poniente (extensive view w/sun shining through tree), oil on canvas, sgn, 1962, 20x28", C-NY 5/17/89 OE 52,800

ATLAN, Jean (French, 1913-1960)
Chaldee (abstract), oil/tempera on canvas, sgn twice/dtd 59 twice, 46x29", SBY 6/30/88 OE 360,400

ATTONSON, E. (Canadian)
Canadian Lake Landscape, pencil/watercolor, sgn/dtd 1925, 12x7", C-SK 11/10/88 75

AUBER, Christiane (French, 20th C)
View Along the Seine, oil on canvas, sgn, 9x11", RWS 8/12/89 275

AUBERT, Jean Ernest (French, 1824-1906)
Cupid's Magic Lantern, oil on canvas, sgn, 39x28", SBY 12/9/88 6,325

AUBRY, Emile (French, 1880-1964)
Bather, oil on canvas, sgn, 26x21", SBY 7/12/89 2,640

AUBRY, Etienne; manner of (French, 1745-1781)
Domestic Interior, oil on canvas, framed as an oval, 11x13", WD 1/25/89 UE 1,500

AUDUBON, John James; att (American, 1785-1851)
Portrait of a Man Said To Be Robert Best, oil on panel, 22x19", LH 10/16/88 UE 275

AUDUBON, John Woodhouse (American, 1812-1868)
Scottish Highlander, oil on canvas, inscr/dtd 1831, 45x31", SBY 12/9/88 3,850

AUERBACH, Frank (American/German, 1931-)
Head of EOW (abstract), oil on board, 1963, 14x12", SBY 6/30/88 84,000
Primrose Hill (abstract), oil on board, 1980, 58x48", SBY 6/30/88 OE 250,200
Untitled (abstract), pencil/crayon on paper, sgn, 9x12", SBY 2/15/89 4,400

AUGUSTI, Chesare (Italian, 19th C)
Young Artist Painting Grandmother's Portrait, oil on canvas, sgn, 28x30", B/B 10/9/88 3,300

AUKELL, T. (Continental School, 20th C)
Ship at the Wharf, watercolor on paper, sgn, 10x15", MG 11/19/88 UE 100

AULT, George Copeland (American, 1891-1948)
A Lily, watercolor/pencil on paper, sgn/dtd 28, 20x15", C-NY 9/28/89 3,300
Kitchen Door (view of table, shelves, & sink), pencil on tan paper, sgn/dtd 29, 18x10", C-NY 9/28/89 1,980
Summer Landscape, oil on canvas, sgn/dtd 34, 16x30", SBY 9/23/88 OE 10,725
Truro Hills, oil on canvas, sgn/inscr/dtd 1921, 16x20", C-NY 5/26/88 OE 28,600
Walking by the Shed on a Winter Night, oil on canvas, sgn/dtd 43, 20x16", SBY 3/17/88 OE 33,000

AUMONT, Auguste Louis; att (Danish, 1805-1879)
Portrait of a Gentleman, oil on canvas, sgn, 8x7", RWS 6/17/89 UE 175

AURELI, Giuseppe (Italian, 1858-1929)
Bathing Beauty, watercolor/pen/brown ink over traces of pencil, sgn/dtd 1881, 20x28", C-E 5/22/89 8,580
Pair: Boudoir Scenes; watercolor on paper, sgn/dtd 1894, 17x11", B/B 12/8/88 OE 2,200
Pair: Harem Scenes; watercolor on paper, sgn, 11x17", B/B 10/9/88 OE 9,900
Roman Children by the Tiber, watercolor/gum Arabic over pencil, sgn/dtd 1883, 21x15", C-NY 2/25/88 1,430
Una Lettuza Interessante alla Corte di Enrico III di Francia, watercolor on paper, sgn/inscr, 32x47", SBY 2/22/89 7,700
Waterbearer (young lady, full-length), watercolor/gouache on paper, sgn, 21x14", B/B 5/17/89 715

AUSSANDON, Joseph Nicolas Hippolyte (French, 1836-)
La Nymphe a Corot (draped nude weeping), oil on canvas, sgn, 40x36", SBY 10/24/89 24,200

AUSTEN, Alexander (British, 19th/20th C)
Chess Game, oil on canvas, sgn, 10x12", B/B 9/15/88 880
Fine Wine (two men at table in an interior), oil on canvas, sgn, 10x12", B/B 9/15/88 880
Pair: Woman Darning; Man Smoking a Pipe; oil on canvas, sgn, 12x10", C-E 2/21/89 UE 1,320

AUSTEN, Winifred (British, -1964)
Pair: Tree Sparrows; Chickadees; watercolor on paper, monogramed, 7x8", 6x9", SBY 7/12/89 1,870

AUSTIN, Darrel (American, 1907-)
Fishing at Moonlight, oil on canvas, sgn/dtd 1958, 10x14", C-E 9/15/88 UE 440

AUSTIN, R.S. (British, 19th C)
Ship Approaching Shore, oil on canvas, sgn/dtd 1894, 20x14", FAP 4/15/89 440

Australian School (18th C)
Pair: Fame; Charity; pen/brown ink/brown wash, star wm, ca 1720, 10x7", 9x7", C-NY 1/12/88 OE 4,180

Australian School (19th C)
Government House, Sydney; watercolor, unfr, ca 1860, 8x12", C-SK 11/10/88 590
Larra (extensive view of Australian estate), oil on canvas, ca 1860, 17x34", C-SK 6/9/88 22,300
Pair: Double Bay, Sydney; Sydney From Vaucluse; oil on board, ca 1860, 9x14" & smaller, C-SK 11/10/88 6,510
Pair: Macwhirts, Killarney, Queensland; Nundah, Queensland; oil on canvas, inscr, unfr, 9x12", C-SK 6/9/88 OE 1,300
Shepherd Resting on a Riverbank, pencil/watercolor, inscr Nr Adelaide S Australia, 10x14", C-SK 6/9/88 600
Sydney Harbor, watercolor, ca 1860, 7x12", C-SK 6/9/88 1,020
Sydney Harbour, pencil/watercolor, ca 1860, 11x18", C-SK 11/10/88 2,230

Two Aborigines Surveying a Landscape, pencil/charcoal, 14x10", C-SK 6/9/88 OE 1,020

Australian School (20th C)

River at Sunset, oil on canvas, indistinctly sgn/dtd 1911, unfr, 12x25", C-SK 6/9/88 340

Austrian School (15th C)

Death of Saint Coloman of Stockerau, oil on panel, 33x22", SBY 10/21/88 9,350

Austrian School (18th C)

Apotheosis of a Saint, oil on canvas, unfr, 34x28", C-NY 10/20/88 UE 550
Elegant Woman & Her Dog, oil on canvas, 31x25", SBY 6/8/88 1,540
Port Scene with Trompe l'Oeil Border, oil on canvas, 17x15", SBY 6/8/88 2,640
Portrait of a Lady, oil on canvas, sgn, 15x12", WD 1/25/89 750
Portrait of a Royal Child, with an Orb, Sceptre, & Coronet on a Table Beside Him; oil on canvas, 36x27", SBY 10/21/88 OE 6,050
Portrait of an Elegant Lady, oil on canvas, 31x25", SBY 6/8/88 660
St Stanislaus of Krakow Within a Painted Arch, oil on canvas, 19x12", SBY 10/21/88 OE 8,250

Austrian School (19th C)

Deer in a Wooded Landscape, oil on panel, 16x12", C-E 10/25/88 UE 330
Delivering Offerings to the Gods, oil on canvas, indistinctly sgn & dtd, 18x24", WD 3/23/88 UE 550
Goatherd on a Mountain Path, oil on masonite, 25x29", NA 2/24/89 UE 325
Hoher Markt, Vienna; oil on panel, inscr, 16x10", C-E 10/25/88 1,320
Resting Shepherdess (in a landscape, building beyond), oil on tin, 7x9", WG 4/23/88 UE 125
Shepherdess with Dog, oil on tin, 7x9", WG 4/23/88 300

Austrian School (20th C)

Pair: Rabbis (portraits); oil on wood panel, sgn, 7x10", MG 11/19/88 UE 200

AVED, Jacques Andre Joseph (French, 1702-1766)

Portrait of a Financier, oil on canvas, 45x35", SBY 1/12/89 11,000

AVED, Jacques Andre Joseph; circle of (French, 1702-1766)

Portrait of a Gentleman, bust-length, wearing a black coat with epaulets...; oil on canvas, 22x19", C-NY 4/6/89 UE 440

AVED, Jacques Andre Joseph; school of (French, 1702-1766)

Portrait of a Gentleman Said To Be the Author Bernard de Fontenelle...; oil on canvas, 40x32", C-NY 5/31/89 OE 1,980

AVEDISIAN, Edward (American, 1936-)

Feu d'Artifice (abstract), acrylic on panel, sgn/dtd 1971, 48x30", C-E 11/14/89 462
Untitled (abstract), acrylic on canvas, unfr, 86x100", C-E 11/17/88 1,320
Untitled (contemporary), acrylic on canvas, 55x55", C-E 5/9/89 UE 110

AVERKAMP, Hendrick; circle of (Dutch, 1585-1663)

Seaport with Vessels & Peasants Attending a Market, pen/ink/wash/watercolor, loss at edges, 9x15", C-NY 1/11/89 OE 6,050

AVERY, Milton (American, 1893-1965)

Across the Bay, Provincetown; black marker/black ballpoint pen, sgn/dtd 1957, unfr, 9x11", SBY 1/24/89 1,870
Aquarium (fish in rectangular bowl), oil on board, sgn/dtd 1945, 13x22", SBY 5/24/89 22,000
Artist Painting by the Sea, watercolor on paper, sgn/dtd 1944/titled, 30x22", SBY 5/3/88 OE 55,000
Baby Carriage by Sea (contemporary), watercolor/gouache on paper, sgn/dtd 1944, 30x22", SBY 5/24/89 OE 68,750
Band Stand by Sea (contemporary), oil on canvasboard, sgn/dtd 1959, 20x24", C-NY 5/4/89 82,500
Bather, oil on board, sgn, 12x10", SBY 1/24/89 OE 17,600
Bathers on the Beach, watercolor on paper, sgn/dtd 1948, 22x30", SBY 5/25/88 OE 47,300
Beach Quartet, oil/charcoal on canvasboard, sgn, 1934, 19x15", SBY 5/25/88 33,000
Dark Sea-Pale Beach; watercolor on paper, sgn/dtd 1944, 22x31", C-NY 11/10/88 OE 52,800
Double-Sided: Figures on a Beach; Landscape; watercolor/pencil on paper, sgn/dtd 1948, 22x30", SBY 5/25/88 24,200
Dune Grasses & Yellow Sea (contemporary landscape), watercolor on paper, sgn/dtd 1957, 20x26", SBY 5/3/89 OE 24,750
Figural Studies, watercolor on paper, sgn, 6x7", B/B 3/22/89 1,760
Five Sketches (Beach Series), pen/ink on paper, sgn, 17x14", C-NY 5/4/88 OE 6,600
Forest Clearing, pen/ink on rice paper, sgn/dtd 1953, 18x24", SBY 2/15/89 4,125
Gaspe, oil on canvas, sgn, ca 1939, 28x36", SBY 5/25/88 66,000
Gull with Fish, gouache on cardboard, sgn/dtd 1950, 10x27", SBY 1/24/89 OE 17,600
Hillsides, oil on canvasboard, sgn, 18x24", C-NY 3/11/88 20,900
Landscape (primitive), oil on canvas, sgn, ca 1935, 28x36", C-NY 2/20/88 OE 57,200
Letter Writer, lithocrayon on board, sgn twice/inscr, 9x8", C-NY 9/30/88 1,650
Mother & Child, oil on canvas, sgn/dtd 1944, 36x20", C-NY 5/25/89 82,500
Nude Recumbent, flobrush/blue ballpoint pen on paper, sgn/dtd 1945, 13x17", SBY 6/28/89 3,300
Nude Standing, oil/graphite on panel, sgn twice/inscr/dtd 1945, 17x9", C-NY 5/4/88 9,900
Nude with Nets (study for The Blue Nude), marker/ballpoint on paper, sgn/dtd April 11 1972, 14x17", SBY 4/14/89 OE 7,700
Old Church, gouache/pencil on paper, sgn, 18x24", C-NY 3/11/88 OE 14,300
Orchard & Mountain (contemporary), oil on canvas, sgn twice/dtd 1962 twice/titled, 36x50", SBY 5/24/89 UE 82,500
Pale Profile, oil on board, sgn/dtd 1954, orig frame, 8x6", RWS 3/16/89 9,500
Pigeons in the Park (contemporary), oil on canvasboard, sgn/dtd 1961, 18x14", SBY 5/24/89 19,800
Pool Bather, oil on paper, sgn/dtd 1962, 35x23", SBY 11/9/89 14,300
Portrait of a Girl on a Victorian Chair, oil on canvas, sgn twice/inscr, ca 1945, 24x18", SBY 5/25/88 22,000
Quarry Birch, oil on canvas, sgn/dtd 1950, 36x28", SBY 5/25/88 OE 88,000
Reclining Nude, oil on masonite, sgn, 9x19", SBY 5/24/89 11,000
Red Sail (contemporary), oil on canvas, sgn twice/dtd 1960 twice/titled, 30x40", SBY 5/24/89 OE 68,750
Rocks & Sea (abstract), oil on canvas, sgn/dtd 1944, inscr, 28x36", C-NY 12/2/88 52,800
Sally on the Beach, watercolor/gouache/charcoal on paper, sgn, 15x22", C-NY 12/2/88 24,200
Sandbar with Avery (contemporary), oil on canvas, sgn/dtd 1957, 36x45", C-NY 2/20/88 OE 181,500
Sea Grasses & Blue Sea (contemporary), oil/watercolor/black wash on paper, sgn/dtd 1958, 23x31", SBY 5/24/89 OE 104,500

Seated Nude, crayon/pencil/ink on paper, sgn/dtd 1956, 16x13", SBY 9/23/88 ... 4,180
Seated Woman (in profile), gouache on paper, sgn/dtd 1963, 30x22", C-NY 9/28/88 ... 17,600
Siesta (still life of violin & ceramics on orange cloth), oil on canvas, sgn/dtd 1949, 22x27", RWS 3/31/88 OE ... 11,000
Spring (whimsical landscape), gouache on paper, sgn, 17x23", SBY 9/14/89 ... 9,900
Still Life with Peppers & Grapes, oil on board, sgn, 20x24", C-NY 5/25/89 ... 20,900
Swimmers & Float, gouache/pencil on paper, sgn/dtd 1944, 23x31", C-NY 5/25/89 ... 38,500
Towering Tree, crayon/chalk/black felt-tip pen on paper, sgn/dtd 1953, 24x12", C-NY 11/10/88 ... 5,500
Tulips in a Teapot, oil on canvasboard, sgn/dtd 1958, 24x18", SBY 5/25/88 OE ... 41,250
Untitled (standing nude), ballpoint pen on paper, sgn, 11x8", C-NY 5/4/89 OE ... 2,420
Vase & Decanter, oil on canvasboard, sgn/dtd twice 1949, inscr, 20x16", C-NY 5/3/88 OE ... 71,500
White Rooster, gouache/watercolor on paper, sgn, 22x29", SBY 5/25/88 OE ... 22,000
Woman with Rebozo, oil on canvas, sgn/dtd 1947, 44x32", C-NY 5/25/89 ... 198,000

AVERY, Sally Michel (American, 20th C)
Lavender Beach, oil on canvas, sgn/dtd 1970, 39x30", RWS 5/12/89 ... 2,250
White Horse, oil on canvasboard, sgn/dtd 1976, 9x12", C-E 11/30/88 UE ... 495

AVIANI, Frencesco; att (Italian, 1662-)
Belshazzar's Feast in a Baroque Loggia, oil on canvas, 45x38", C-NY 5/31/89 ... 11,000

AVIGNON, school of (French, 15th C)
Assumption of the Virgin, oil on gold ground on panel, 45x45", C-NY 1/11/89 UE ... 22,000
Christ on the Road to Cavalry, on gold ground/oil on panel, carved frame w/Gothic tracery, 25x16", C-NY 10/20/88 ... 8,250

AYOTTE, Leo (Canadian, 1909-1976)
Bord du St Laurent (Banks of St Laurent), oil on canvas, sgn/dtd 1972, 16x20", FB 5/28/89 ... 2,500
Cabin at Val Morin, oil on canvas, sgn/dtd 1973, 16x20", FB 4/25/88 ... 2,500
Le Marais Bleu, oil on canvas, sgn/dtd 1973, 20x24", FB 5/28/89 ... 2,300
Les Vagues, oil on canvas, sgn/dtd 1974, 16x20", FB 5/28/89 ... 2,600
Nature Morte aux Pommes (still life w/apples), oil on panel, ca 1942, sgn, 16x20", FB 4/25/88 ... 2,400
Riviere Metis (river scene), oil on canvas, sgn/dtd 1972, 16x20", FB 4/25/88 OE ... 2,400
Trees on Country Road by the Lake, oil on canvas, sgn/dtd 1963, FB 5/28/89 ... 2,300

AYRTON, Michael (British, 1921-1975)
View of a Village by an Inlet, oil on masonite, sgn/dtd 56, 20x24", PHL 6/16/88 ... 2,500

AZENTOWICZ, Theodor (Polish, 1859-1938)
Omnibus, oil on panel, sgn, 14x18", SBY 5/23/89 OE ... 38,500

BABA (Corneliu)
Harlequin, oil on canvas, sgn/dtd 70, 28x23", C-E 4/7/88 UE ... 605

BABER, Alice (American, 1928-)
Green Door to the Wind, acrylic on canvas, sgn/inscr/dtd 1976, 30x40", C-E 5/13/88 UE ... 550

BACARDY, Don
Portrait of Robert Mapplethorpe, pen/black ink wash on paper, sgn, inscr w/title, dtd 2/9/79, 29x23", C-NY 10/31/89 OE ... 16,500

BACCHUS, Eliza R.; att (American, 1857-1959)
View of Mt Shasta, oil on board, 8x16", WG 9/16/88 UE ... 75

BACCI, Edmondo (European, 1913-)
Avenimento #242, oil on canvas, sgn, 74x50", SBY 10/7/89 ... 2,860
Avenimento 22 (abstract), mixed media on board, 1967, 14x19", C-NY 5/4/89 OE ... 1,650
Pair: Untitled (abstract hand); colored pencils on paper, sgn/dtd 1958, 1955, 9x13", 17x14", C-NY 5/4/89 OE ... 4,180

BACH, Guido (German, 1828-1905)
Young Girl with a Basket, oil on canvas, sgn, 13x10", C-E 10/25/88 ... 2,860

BACHE, Otto (Danish, 1839-1914)
Spaniel & a Pug, oil on canvas, sgn/dtd 1885, 26x38", SBY 2/22/89 ... 17,600
Spaniel & a Pug, oil on canvas, sgn/dtd 1885, 26x38", SBY 6/10/88 ... 13,750

BACHER, Otto (American, 1856-1909)
Cedar Creek, Virginia, Sept 1885 (Civil War); pen/ink on paper, sgn/inscr, unfr, 17x21", C-E 11/30/88 ... 275

BACHMANN, Adolphe (Swiss, 19th/20th C)
Grand Canal, Venice; oil on canvas, sgn, 20x26", C-E 5/23/88 OE ... 2,090

BACHMANN, Alfred (German, 1863-)
View of Hagia Sophia From the Bosphorus, oil on canvas, sgn, 26x32", PHL 6/16/88 ... 2,500

BACKER, Jacob Adriaensz (Dutch, 1609-1651)
Portrait of a Young Girl, bust-length, wearing a brown dress...; oil on panel, 19x16", C-NY 5/31/89 ... 9,900

BACKER, Jacob Adriaensz; circle of (Dutch, 1609-1651)
Feast of the Gods, oil on panel, unfr, 32x38", C-NY 1/11/89 ... 10,450

BACKHUYSEN, Ludolf; manner of (Dutch, 1631-1708)
Shipping in Stormy Seas, oil on canvas, 14x17", SBY 7/12/89 ... 660

BACKHUYSEN, Ludolf; school of (Dutch, 1631-1708)
Shipping in a Choppy Sea, oil on canvas, monogramed, unfr, 17x24", C-NY 4/6/89 OE ... 6,050

BACKUS, A.E. (American)
Beach Scene, oil on canvas, sgn, 31x27", FB 5/28/89 UE ... 950

BACKVIS, Francios (French, 19th C)
Pheasant & Floral Still Life, oil on canvas, sgn/dtd 1887, 39x28", C-E 5/22/89 ... 4,950
Still Life of a Vase of Roses, oil on canvas, indistinctly sgn, 40x26", SBY 5/23/89 OE ... 18,700

BACON, Charles Roswell (American, 1868-1913)
Farmhouse with Figures in a Landscape, oil on canvas, sgn, 36x45", SBY 1/24/89 ... 3,850
Pinchbeck Hill (sheep on rocky meadow w/stream), oil on canvas, sgn, 24x34", RWS 9/29/88 UE ... 100

BACON, Francis (British, 1909-)
- Study for Figure I, oil on linen, 1953, 78x54", C-NY 5/3/88 — 935,000
- Study for Figure in a Room (crouching nude), oil on canvas, sgn/dtd 1953, 78x54", SBY 5/2/89 OE — 2,090,000
- Study for Portrait of Van Gogh II, oil on canvas, 1957, 78x56", SBY 5/2/89 OE — 5,830,000
- Triptych: May-June (sequential view of George Dyer's death); oil on canvas, sgn/dtd 1973, 78x58", SBY 5/2/89 OE — 6,270,000
- Triptych: Three Studies for a Portrait (Peter Beard); oil on canvas, sgn/dtd 1975, 14x12", C-NY 11/9/88 — 825,000

BACON, Henry (American, 1839-1912)
- Classroom (interior scene), oil on panel, sgn/dtd 1868, 11x9", C-NY 5/25/89 — 9,900
- La Bretagne, oil on board, sgn/dtd 29 Oct 1890, 11x14", RWS 11/10/89 — 7,500
- Pay Attention (father scolding child in church congregation), oil on canvas, sgn, 16x13", C-NY 5/25/89 — 9,900
- Shepherdess Watching Her Flock, watercolor on paper, sgn, 12x19", SBY 4/14/89 — 880

BACON, Irving R. (American, 1875-1962)
- Dordrecht, Holland; oil on board, sgn, 13x18", DM 10/14/88 UE — 400

BACON, Peggy (American, 1895-)
- In the Forest, pen/ink wash on paper, sgn/inscr, 14x11", C-E 6/1/88 UE — 385
- Rabbit, pen/ink on paper, sgn, 3x5", WG 10/19/88 — 250

BADER, Wilhelm Johann (1855-)
- Figure in a Mountainous Landscape, oil on panel, sgn/dtd 1896, 25x19", C-L 6/27/88 — 6,054

BADER (19th C)
- Pair: Charpentier de la Troisieme Demi Brigade Helvetique 1800; watercolor on paper, sgn, 16x10", WG 4/23/88 UE — 75

BADGER, C.H. (American, 20th C)
- Ducks Alighting, oil on board, sgn/dtd 28, 30x40", LH 12/4/88 — 300

BADGER, Joseph; att (American, 1708-1765)
- Portrait of Edward Gray, oil on canvas, 30x26", SBY 4/14/89 — 1,430

BADGER, S.F.M. (American, 19th/20th C)
- Catboat Under Way, oil on canvas, sgn/dtd 95, 22x36", RWS 5/12/89 OE — 12,100
- Portrait of Schooner Lizzie Ann (ship), oil on canvas, sgn, modern frame, 22x36", RAB 11/10/88 — 7,000

BAECHLER, Donald (20th C)
- Don's Dilemma II (Cowboy), enamel on paper, 46x35", SBY 2/15/89 OE — 4,950
- Oum Kalsoum (abstract head), acrylic on canvas, sgn/dtd 1983, 60x60", SBY 2/15/89 UE — 4,400
- Oum Kalsoum (abstract head), acrylic on canvas, sgn/dtd 1983, 60x60", C-NY 5/4/89 — 12,100
- Suitcase Painting, acrylic/linen collage on linen, initialed/inscr/dtd 87, unfr, 79x79", C-NY 5/4/88 — 14,300

BAEDER, John (European, 19th C)
- Ho-Jo, Rt 2, Williamstown, Massachusetts; oil on canvas, sgn/dtd 79 twice/titled, 30x48", SBY 11/11/88 — 27,500

BAES, Firmin (Belgian, 19th C)
- Odalisque, pastel on stretched canvas, sgn twice/inscr, 28x24", C-NY 2/25/88 OE — 2,640

BAGG, Henry Howard (American, 1852-1928)
- Yosemite Falls, oil on canvas, sgn, 46x16", B/B 10/6/88 — 1,320

BAGLIONE, Cavaliere Giovanni (Italian, 1571-1644)
- Woman Giving Alms to a Pilgrim & a Woman in Labor with Attendants, chalk/pen/ink/wash squared in chalk, C-NY 1/11/89 — 1,430

BAHIEU, Jules G. (Belgian, 19th C)
- Shipping Off a Jetty in Stormy Seas, oil on canvas, sgn/dtd 1876, 17x32", C-E 5/23/88 — 1,870

BAIL, Franck Antoine (French, 1858-1924)
- Maid Pouring Water (before display of plates in cabinet along wall), oil on canvas, sgn, 22x18", PHL 10/28/88 — 5,000
- Maid Watering Flowers, oil on canvas, sgn, 26x21", PHL 6/16/88 — 6,500
- Maid Watering Flowers (vase of flowers on table), oil on canvas, sgn, 26x21", SBY 10/24/89 — 15,400

BAIL, Joseph (French, 1862-1921)
- Le Marmiton, oil on canvas, sgn, 29x24", SBY 10/24/89 OE — 33,000
- Storing Pickles, oil on canvas, sgn, 29x24", SBY 6/8/88 OE — 8,800

BAILEY, Clarence E. (American, 19th C)
- Guardians of the North (ship & large iceburg), oil on canvas, sgn/1915, 30x42", RAB 8/9/88 UE — 900
- New Hat (study of a young girl), oil/pencil on paper, sgn/dtd 1914, 10x12", RAB 8/9/88 — 650

BAILEY, Forest R. (American, 20th C)
- Parade, oil on canvas, sgn/dtd 1967, 48x54", LH 12/4/88 UE — 160

BAILEY, Frederick Victor (British, 20th C)
- Still Life of Flowers & Insects, oil on panel, monogramed, 36x28", B/B 3/22/89 OE — 9,900

BAILEY, T. (American, 20th C)
- Evening Departure (ship & lighthouse silhouetted against sky), oil on canvas, sgn, 16x20", RAB 8/1/88 — 550
- Fair Day at Sea, full-rigged ship in calm seas, oil on canvas, sgn, 24x36", RAB 8/1/88 UE — 1,000
- Fishing Schooner Marie, Glouster, Massachusetts; oil on canvas, sgn/titled, 23x29", RAB 11/10/88 — 500
- Full Sail at Night (masted ship at sea), oil on canvas, sgn, orig frame, 24x31", RAB 11/25/88 UE — 400
- Racing Sloop, oil on canvas, sgn, unfr, 20x25", RAB 3/14/89 UE — 350
- Under Shortened Sail (clipper at sea), oil on canvas, sgn, 23x31", RAB 8/1/89 UE — 500
- Witch of the Wave, oil on canvas, sgn/titled, orig frame, 24x32", RAB 8/1/88 — 1,100

BAILEY, Walter Alexander (American, 1894-)
- Looking into the Bay, oil on canvas, sgn, 16x20", C-E 6/1/89 UE — 352

BAILEY, William (American, 1930-)
- Pencil on Paper (still life), pencil on paper, sgn/dtd 1986, 19x15", SBY 5/3/89 — 30,800
- Still Life Trevi (various pieces of stoneware), oil on canvas, sgn/dtd 1982, 26x21", SBY 5/3/89 — 132,000
- Still Life with Slate Green Wall (various pieces of stoneware & egg), oil on canvas, sgn/dtd 1976, 24x30", SBY 5/3/89 — 137,500
- Still Life-Monterchi (assorted pottery pieces on a table); oil on canvas, sgn/dtd 81, 38x51", SBY 11/10/88 — 253,000

BAILLY, David; att (Dutch, 1584-1657?)
Vanitas: Still Life with a Bust, Books...; oil on panel, bears monogram of Harmen van Steenwyck, 19x24", SBY 4/7/89 ... 7,700
BAINES, Henry (Canadian, 1866-)
Niagara Falls, watercolor, initialed/dtd 6/11/64, 7x10", WAD 11/30/89 ... 350
BAINES, Thomas (British, 1822-1875)
Pair: Caloblepas Gnoo-the Gnoo; Baasland Harte Beeste; pencil/chalks/watercolor, inscr, 6x6" & smaller, C-SK 5/25/89 ... 1,650
Study of Leaves, watercolor, inscr/dtd 1849, 10x7", C-SK 5/25/89 ... 550
BAIRD, Nathaniel Hughes (British, 1865-)
March Day on the Sussex Downs (men plowing with teams of horses), oil on canvas, monogramed, 20x30", PHL 10/28/88 ... 6,000
BAIRD, William Baptiste (American, 1847-)
Hen Feeding Her Chicks (brick wall beyond), oil on panel, sgn, 8x6", C-E 6/1/89 ... 3,300
Mares & Foals Grazing on the Edge of the Sea, oil on canvas, sgn/inscr, 21x32", SBY 6/10/88 ... 3,575
Mountain Lake (deer beside lake), oil on canvas, sgn/dtd 1879, 22x32", RAB 8/8/89 ... 4,500
Nice, oil on canvas laid down on board, sgn, 13x9", C-SK 11/10/88 OE ... 3,530
River Scene, oil on canvas, sgn, 21x32", LH 3/20/88 ... 2,600
Saint Raphael, oil on canvas, sgn, 13x18", C-SK 11/10/88 ... 1,860
BAISHI, Qi (Chinese, 1864-1957)
Chicks (hanging scroll), ink on paper, sgn/dtd 1947, 42x13", SBY 5/31/89 OE ... 10,450
Moth & Oil Lamp (hanging scroll), ink/color on paper, sgn, 13x13", SBY 5/31/89 ... 7,150
Rooster & Chicks (hanging scroll), ink/color on paper, sgn, 44x16", SBY 5/31/89 ... 7,700
Squirrel with Grapes (hanging scroll), ink/color on paper, sgn, 39x13", SBY 5/31/89 OE ... 7,150
Vegetables (fan painting), ink/color on paper, sgn, 7x20", SBY 5/31/89 ... 5,225
BAJ, Enrico (Italian, 1924-)
Due Fidanzatti, mixed media on canvas, sgn, 16x20", SBY 10/7/89 OE ... 29,700
Due Fidanzatti, oil on canvas/mixed media collage, sgn, no size given, SLK 4/7/89 ... 2,700
Head (abstract), mixed media collage, sgn, 16x16", SBY 2/14/89 OE ... 7,150
BAKALOWICZ, Ladislaus (Polish, 1833-1904)
Au Bal Masque, oil on panel, sgn/inscr, 39x28", C-NY 5/25/88 ... 3,300
Court Jester, oil on panel, sgn/inscr, 10x12", C-E 5/23/88 ... 2,200
Un Rapt (figures with swords in an interior), oil on canvas, sgn, 13x17", FB 5/28/89 UE ... 900
BAKER, Carlton (American, 20th C)
Leaping Sperm Whale, pastel on paper, sgn/dtd 1960, 18x13", RAB 11/10/88 UE ... 100
BAKER, E.
Fishing Boats, oil on canvas, sgn/dtd 74, 13x19", C-E 5/23/88 ... 1,210
BAKER, Elisha J. (American, 19th C)
Sailboats, oil on board, sgn/dtd 70, 8x13", C-E 6/1/88 ... 990
BAKER, Ernest (American, 19th C)
Catboats Under Sail, oil on canvas, sgn/dtd 81, 30x26", RAB 8/8/89 UE ... 2,300
BAKER, George Herbert (American, 1878-1943)
Autumnal Landscape, oil on board, sgn, 28x31", SLK 5/11/88 ... 900
BAKER, George O. (American, 1882-)
Pensive Moment, oil on canvas, sgn/dtd Paris 1911, 29x24", B/B 12/8/88 ... 1,650
BAKER, Gladys (American, 1821-1880)
Whale Goes Down, oil on board, sgn, 20x24", C-E 6/22/88 ... 880
Whale Hunt, oil on board, sgn, 20x24", C-E 6/22/88 ... 715
BAKER, O.F. (American, 19th C)
Rock Point, Long Island; no media given, sgn, 16x24", WG 4/23/88 UE ... 150
Seascape (sailboat in distance w/crashing waves on shore), oil on canvas, sgn, 22x36", RAB 8/8/89 UE ... 350
BAKER, Roger (20th C)
Boy with Pigeons, oil on masonite, sgn/dtd 1956, 8x10", C-NY 6/17/89 OE ... 220
Chester Kallman, pencil on paper, sgn, 6x4", C-NY 6/17/89 ... 55
Seaffolding I, oil on canvasboard, sgn/dtd 1955, 6x8", C-NY 6/17/89 ... 110
BAKER, Samuel Colwell (American, 1874-1964)
Mission Church in the Desert, oil on masonite, 25x36", B/B 9/14/89 UE ... 1,100
BAKER, Thomas of Bath; att
River Landscape with Mount Snowdon, Wales, & Figure on Horseback; oil on canvas, 18x25", C-E 6/1/88 ... 660
BAKER, Thomas of Leamington (British, 1809-1869)
Cartland Crags Bridge Near Lanard, Scotland, on the Mousewater River; oil on canvas, sgn/dtd 1845, C-NY 5/25/88 UE ... 2,200
BAKHUYSEN, Ludolf (Dutch, 1631-1708)
Fleet of Dutch Three-Deckers Off the Coast, Villagers on Shore; oil on canvas, sgn/dtd 1705, 27x38", C-NY 10/20/88 OE ... 44,000
Shipping in a Stormy Sea Off a Coast, oil on canvas, sgn/dtd 1665, 16x25", SBY 4/7/89 ... 7,700
BAKHUYZEN, Alexandre H. (Dutch, 1830-)
Figures on a Frozen River, oil on panel, sgn, 20x28", C-E 5/22/89 ... 3,300
BAKST, Leon (Russian, 1866-1924)
Pierrot & Columbine, charcoal/watercolor/gouache, 12x9", C-E 6/16/88 ... 220
BALDOCK, Charles E. (British, fl 1900-1905)
Cow in Pasture, watercolor, sgn, 14x10", LH 12/4/88 ... 275
BALDOCK, James Walsham (British, 1844-1899)
Two Horses & Chickens, oil on panel, sgn, 9x7", LH 9/10/89 ... 900
BALDOCK, James Walsham; circle of (British, 1844-1899)
Chestnut Hunter with a Spaniel in a Landscape, oil on canvas, 24x29", WD 1/25/89 ... 2,200

BALE, Charles Thomas (British, 19th C)
Still Life of Fruit, Jug, & Dead Game on a Wooden Table; oil on canvas, sgn, 19x14", C-E 5/23/88 1,045
Still Life of Fruit & Game Birds, oil on canvas, sgn, 30x20", SBY 6/8/88 1,760
BALE, Edwin R.J. (British, 1842-)
Ships Moored in a Harbor, oil on board, sgn, 14x32", WG 9/16/88 UE 550
BALENCIAGA
Fashion Design, charcoal/watercolor on paper, sgn/#d 199, 39x26", SBY 4/23/88 1,430
BALESTRA, Antonio (Italian, 1660-1740)
Allegory of Summer, oil on canvas, 44x60", C-NY 1/11/89 20,900
Dead Abel, oil on canvas, 48x59", C-NY 1/11/89 20,900
BALESTRA, Antonio; circle of (Italian, 1660-1740)
Mystic Marriage of Saint Catherine, oil on canvas, unfr, 29x24", C-NY 4/8/88 660
BALINK, Hendricus Cornelius (American, 1882-1963)
Peonies in a Blue Vase, oil on canvas, sgn/inscr, 21x24", C-NY 9/30/88 UE 550
BALL, Adrien Joseph Verhoeven (Belgian, 1824-1882)
Woman at Her Spinning Wheel in an Interior, oil on cradled panel, sgn/dtd 1846, 22x18", B/B 3/22/89 4,675
BALL, Thomas Raymond
Figure in Spring Landscape, oil on board, sgn, 10x8", C-E 9/15/88 UE 440
BALL, Wilfred (British, 1853-1917)
Stone Church, watercolor on paper, sgn/dtd 83, 11x14", FAP 11/4/88 110
BALLA, Giacomo (Italian, 1871-1958)
Linee di Velocita + Vortice di Spazio (abstract), pencil on paper, inscr/sgn, ca 1914, 18x23", C-NY 5/12/88 OE 30,800
BALLANTYNE, John (British, 1815-1897)
Elorna Howard Bell at 14 (profile portrait), oil on canvas, sgn/dtd 1891, 16x12", B/B 9/14/89 825
Scottish Gentleman Standing with Dog, oil on canvas, sgn, 30x25", DM 10/14/88 10,000
BALLANTYNE, Keith
Out for a Stroll (child playing dress-up, doll in stroller, large dog at side), oil on canvas, sgn, 26x33", PHL 10/28/88 1,400
BALLARD, Richard
Eden, oil on paper, sgn/dtd Nov 82, 48x60", SBY 10/5/88 880
BALLAVOINE, Jules Frederic (French, fl 1880-1901)
L'Hiver (portrait of woman in profile w/snowy rooftops beyond), oil on panel, sgn, 13x10", SBY 5/23/89 35,200
Summer Afternoon by the River (w/woman seated on fence), oil on canvas, sgn, 26x18", C-NY 2/23/89 6,600
Sylvia, portrait, oil on canvas, sgn, 16x14", SBY 12/9/88 8,525
BALLESIO, Federico (Italian, 19th C)
Pottery Merchant, pencil/watercolor on paper, sgn/inscr, 21x30", SBY 6/8/88 UE 4,675
BALLIO, H.C. (Italian, 19th C)
Portrait of a Woman, oil on canvas, sgn, 14x18", MG 10/28/88 UE 150
BALLIQUANT, N. (French, 19th C)
Sheep in a Barn, oil on canvas laid down on board, sgn, 21x26", WD 1/11/89 550
BALTEN, Pieter; att (Flemish, 1525-1598)
Village Kermesse with a Theatre & a Procession, oil on panel, 50x63", SBY 6/1/89 OE 176,000
BALTHUS (Balthasar Klossowski de Rola)(French, 1908-)
Femme Couche (reclining woman w/seascape beyond), oil on canvas, sgn/dtd 1947, 21x26", SBY 5/10/89 550,000
BAMA, James (American, 1926-)
Butch Kelley, Bronc Rider; oil on masonite, sgn twice/inscr/dtd 76, 30x24", SBY 5/25/88 36,300
Wilbur Bunn, Old Time Rancher; oil on masonite, sgn/dtd 76, inscr/titled, 16x14", SBY 6/24/88 OE 9,350
BAMBERGER, Fritz (German, 1814-1873)
Extensive View with a Ruined Fort, oil on canvas laid down on board, sgn/dtd 1865, 22x28", C-NY 2/25/88 6,600
BAMBOIS, Camille
Femme au Bord de la Riviere, oil on canvas laid down on masonite, sgn, 24x20", C-NY 10/6/88 13,200
BANCHIERI, Giuseppe (Italian, 1920-)
City, oil on canvas, sgn/dtd 58, 29x27", LH 10/16/88 UE 100
Serenade, oil on canvas, sgn, 20x16", C-E 5/23/88 3,080
BANCROFT, Milton (American, 1867-)
Two Seated Classical Women, pencil on paper, 12x16", C-E 1/12/88 55
BANDALL, Nal (American, 20th C)
Swamp Scene, oil on canvas, sgn/dtd 43, 16x20", MG 5/28/88 125
BANDECK, Fritz Muller (German, 19th/20th C)
Sommermorgen (summer morning, deer by stream in landscape), oil on canvas, sgn, 34x44", C-E 2/21/89 1,650
BANDINELLI, Baccio (Italian, 1493-1560)
Seated Male Nude Holding a Staff, red chalk over stylus, 17x10", SBY 1/13/89 19,800
BANDINELLI, Baccio; att (Italian, 1493-1560)
Head of a Horse, brown ink on paper, bears signature, 8x8", WD 1/25/89 OE 6,000
BANDING, Chen (Chinese, 1877-1970)
Figures in a Landscape (hanging scroll), ink/color on paper, sgn/dtd 1943, 32x12", SBY 5/31/89 2,750
Flowers (hanging scroll), ink/color on paper, sgn, 40x16", SBY 5/31/89 990
BANG, Hieronymus; att
Study of Putto with a Sphinx, black chalk/pen/black/gray ink/gray wash, inscr, 5x13", C-NY 1/12/88 UE 165
BANGDA, Dong (Chinese, 1699-1769)
Pine & Rock (hanging scroll), ink on paper, sgn/dtd 1759, 50x22", SBY 5/31/89 8,250
BANISTER, Patti
Portrait of a Girl, oil on board, 8x10", NA 11/5/88 325

BANK, J.O. (British, 19th C)
Flowers From the Woods, oil on canvas, sgn, 20x16", C-NY 5/25/88 6,050
BANKS, B. (American, 20th C)
Still Life of Fruits, oil on canvas, sgn/dtd 1962, 21x26", LH 9/10/89 180
BANKS, Robert (British, 20th C)
Back Alley in Florence, watercolor over pencil, sgn/#d 587, 28x20", C-NY 10/26/88 1,540
Facade of a Church & the Hotel Virgilio, watercolor, sgn/#d 609, 19x26", C-NY 5/25/88 1,100
Square, with Clock Tower & Vine-Covered Dining Terrace; watercolor over pencil, sgn/#d 608, 19x26", C-NY 10/26/88 1,320
Venetian House Behind a Small Arched Bridge, watercolor over pencil, sgn/#d 600, 28x20", C-NY 5/25/88 2,640
View in Sienna, watercolor, sgn/dtd 91, 27x20", C-NY 5/25/88 OE 5,280
BANKS, William
Mary Queen of Scots Receiving Flowers, oil on canvas, sgn/dtd 1880, 28x38", C-E 2/23/88 3,300
BANNARD, Walter Darby (American, 1934-)
Amazon #1 (abstract), acrylic on canvas, sgn, 66x99", SBY 5/3/89 OE 2,860
Canyon Head #1 (abstract), acrylic on canvas, sgn/dtd 1968, 30x45", SBY 2/14/89 UE 770
Grave East, acrylic on canvas, sgn/dtd 1971, 77x103", C-E 11/17/88 1,100
Iron Cleaving (abstract), acrylic on canvas, sgn/dtd 1975, 69x41", C-E 11/17/88 1,980
Powder #I (square composition), alkyd resin on canvas, sgn/dtd 1963, 64x63", C-E 11/17/88 1,100
Remembrance of Terracina (abstract), acrylic on canvas, sgn, 1978, 34x67", C-E 11/14/89 1,650
Scottish Phantom (abstract), oil on canvas, sgn/dtd 1972, 31x62", SBY 2/14/89 935
Viridine, acrylic on canvas, sgn/inscr/dtd 1976, 54x26", C-E 5/13/88 UE 220
BANNISTER, Edward M.
Gathering Clouds, oil on canvas, sgn/dtd 81, 9x12", C-E 10/18/89 1,650
BANTING, Frederick Grant (Canadian, 1891-1941)
Bylot Inlet, Baffin Island; oil on panel, sgn, 9x11", FB 4/25/88 400
BAOSHI, Fu (Chinese, 1904-1965)
Figure in Landscape (hanging scroll), ink/color on paper, sgn, 41x24", SBY 5/31/89 8,800
Lady, ink/color on paper, sgn/dtd 1944, 25x14", SBY 5/31/89 7,700
BAQUERO, Mariano (Spanish, 19th C)
Carriages at the Park of Buen Retiro, Madrid; watercolor on paper, sgn/dtd 1883, 39x54", SBY 10/24/89 41,250
BAR, Bonaventure; see De Bar, Bonaventure
BARABAN-CAHAGNET, Blanch Marie (French, 20th C)
Floral Still Life on Tablecloth, oil on canvas, sgn, 19x22", B/B 9/14/89 1,210
BARBAGELATA, Giovanni
Saints Julian the Hospitaller & Catharine of Alexandria, tempera on panel, 22x17", SBY 10/13/89 OE 22,000
BARBARINI, Emil (Italian, 19th C)
Figures on a Wooded Lane, oil on canvas, sgn, 27x42", SBY 6/8/88 3,025
BARBARINI, Franz (Austrian, 1804-1873)
Figures at a Spring Before an Alpine Chalet, oil on panel, sgn, 16x20", PHL 10/28/88 UE 157
BARBASAN, Mariano (Spanish, 1864-1924)
Vista Rural de los al Rededores de un Peublo de Roma, oil on canvas, sgn/dtd 96, 30x52", SBY 2/22/89 38,500
BARBER, Alfred R. (British, 19th C)
Escaped: Two Rabbits & a Guinea Pig; oil on canvas, sgn/dtd 1880, 14x9", C-NY 5/24/89 OE 18,700
BARBER, C.J.
Young Girl Reading, oil on panel, initialed, 13x12", C-E 10/25/88 UE 2,200
BARBER, Charles Burton; att (British, 1854-1894)
First Come, First Served; oil on canvas, bears signature/dtd 1881, 48x60", C-NY 2/25/88 4,400
BARBER, George (1910-)
Study for the Bronx Post Office Mural Competition, oil on canvas, inscr/#d 29, 30x30", SBY 9/23/88 OE 1,760
BARBERA, Camillo Gioja
Prayers at Votive Alter, oil on canvas, sgn/dtd 1888, unfr, 22x40", C-E 7/26/88 UE 550
BARBIER, Nicolas Francois (1768-1826)
Study for a Medallion with a Warrior, red chalk, 4" dia, SBY 1/13/89 OE 1,375
BARBIER L'AINE, see Le Barbier L'Aine
BARBIERI, Giovanni Francesco; see Guercino, Giovanni
BARBUDO, Salvador Sanchez (Spanish, 1858-1919)
Presentation of the Princess, oil on canvas, sgn/inscr, 24x40", C-NY 5/25/88 OE 68,200
BARCELO, Miguel (Spanish, 17th C)
Untitled, gouache/charcoal/collage on paper, sgn/dtd V.83, 25x31", SBY 10/7/89 OE 16,500
Villanova (figure in boat), ink/watercolor/oil/sand on paper, sgn/dtd IV 84, 19x28", SBY 10/5/89 OE 14,300
BARCHUS, Eliza R. (American, 1857-1959)
Golden Sunset at Mount Ranier, oil on canvas, sgn, 20x23", B/B 1/11/89 550
Landscape with Mount Rainier, oil on board, 10x12", SLK 11/25/88 200
Mt Shasta, oil on board, sgn, 7x9", SBY 4/14/89 OE 1,100
Multnomah Falls, Columbia River; oil on canvas, sgn, 22x12", B/B 10/6/88 770
View of Mt Rainier, oil on board, 9x12", B/B 1/11/89 UE 330
BARCLAY, J. (American, 19th C)
Peasant Girl Holding a Dog, watercolor on paper, sgn, 14x10", C-E 10/25/88 1,210
BARCLAY, McClelland (American, 1891-1943)
Courtship, oil en grisaille on canvas, sgn, 32x22", C-E 10/18/89 1,870

Girl Seated with Two Scottish Terriers, oil on canvas, sgn, 33x26", DM 9/16/88 OE **4,000**
Girl Standing with Automobile, Sailboats in Background; oil on canvas, sgn, 33x24", DM 9/16/88 OE **4,000**
Hummingbird Girl, oil on canvas, sgn, 40x20", C-E 10/18/89 ..... **1,650**
Latest Magazine, oil en grisaille on canvas, sgn, 26x22", C-E 10/18/89 OE **2,640**
Opening Gifts, oil on canvas, sgn, 32x18", C-E 10/18/89 OE **2,420**
Quarrel, oil on canvas, sgn, 40x30", SBY 9/23/88 ..... **1,870**

BARD, James (American, 1815-1897)
Mattano (steamboat on river), oil on canvas, sgn/dtd 1859, 30x50", SBY 1/28/88 OE **132,000**

BARDI, Louis; after
Aurora, oil on canvas, inscr, 31x62", SBY 7/12/89 ..... **2,090**

BARDONE, Guy (French, 1927-)
Le Nappe Bleu (the blue tablecloth), oil on canvas, sgn/dtd 65, 64x51", LH 5/15/88 ..... **1,500**

BARDUT-DAVRAY, Luc
Dormeuse, oil on canvas, sgn, 18x15", C-E 5/23/88 ..... **2,420**

BARDWELL, Thomas (British, fl 1735-ca 1780)
Portrait of a Gentleman & Lady in Historical Costume (three-quarter length), oil on canvas, 50x51", SBY 4/7/89 ..... **6,050**

BARE, E. (French, 19th C)
Farm in Winter, oil on canvas, sgn, 26x38", FB 5/28/89 ..... **1,200**
Reverie (lad w/cows & chickens in farmyard), oil on canvas, sgn/dtd 1872, 24x17", C-E 5/22/89 OE **5,280**

BARE, Ed W. (19th C)
Collecting Mussels, oil, sgn, 23x43", WD 1/11/89 UE **1,600**

BARGUE, Charles (French, -1883)
Three Horses, a Pig & a Man by a Building; pencil, initialed twice/artist's Vente stamp, 6x8", C-NY 2/25/88 ..... **2,200**

BARIG, L. (Continental, 19th C)
Caught Napping, oil on canvas, sgn, 16x20", B/B 1/11/89 ..... **522**

BARILARI, Enrique (Latin American, 20th C)
Untitled (three figures w/ochre background) acrylic on canvas, 1987, 62x47", SBY 5/17/89 OE **8,250**
Untitled (two seated nudes looking at a portrait), oil on canvas, 47x55", SBY 5/17/88 UE **550**

BARKER, Benjamin the younger; att (Bristish, 1776-1838)
Figures in a Pastoral Landscape, oil on canvas, sgn/dtd 1807, 33x42", B/B 10/9/88 OE **5,225**

BARKER, John (British, 19th C)
Lakeside Cottage, oil on canvas, sgn, 28x36", LH 12/4/88 ..... **2,500**

BARKER, Thomas (British, 1769-1847)
Blind Man Seranading Three Girls in the Roman Forum, oil on canvas, indistinctly sgn/dtd 1797, 29x38", SBY 10/21/88 OE **7,150**
Peasants Resting on a Country Road, oil on canvas, sgn, 21x25", B/B 12/8/88 ..... **3,300**

BARKER, Wright (British, 19th C)
Shepherd & Flock on a Path in Winter, oil on canvas, sgn, 28x36", C-NY 2/25/88 ..... **8,250**

BARLACH, Ernst (German, 1870-1938)
Baurerin Holz Tragend, charcoal on paper, sgn, 13x10", SBY 10/5/88 OE **7,425**
Personlichkeit, charcoal/brown wax crayon/pen/brown ink on paper, 10x12", C-NY 5/11/89 ..... **11,000**

BARLAND, Adam (British, 1843-1881)
Mountain Stream at Lanberis, Wales; oil on canvas, sgn, 30x50", SBY 12/9/88 OE **5,500**

BARLOW, John Noble (American, 1861-1937)
Close of the Day Near Bray-on-Thames, oil on canvas, sgn, 28x13", C-E 10/25/88 ..... **2,200**

BARLOW, Myron (American, 1873-1937)
Letter, oil on canvas, sgn, 39x36", C-NY 9/30/88 ..... **8,800**
New Shoes (peasant woman showing shoes to friend), oil on canvas, sgn, 30x30", C-NY 9/28/89 ..... **8,800**
Strong Cup of Tea (three women seated at a table), oil on canvas, sgn, 39x39", SBY 9/23/88 ..... **14,300**
Young Girl Leaning on Table, pastel, sgn, 30x30", DM 2/19/88 ..... **5,000**

BARNARD, Edward Herbert (American, 1855-1909)
Along the Coast, oil on canvas, sgn, 17x21", C-E 11/30/88 OE **4,180**

BARNARD, Frederick
Letter (woman writing the letter), oil on canvas, initialed, 23x18", C-NY 5/25/88 ..... **5,280**

BARNARD, William Henry (British, 1769-1817)
Punting, ink wash, 7x12", SBY 7/12/89 UE **99**

BARNES, Edward Charles (British, 19th C)
Mother & Daughter by the Sea, oil on canvas, initialed, 36x28", C-NY 5/25/88 ..... **4,620**
Peeling Turnips (peasant woman outside cottage leaning against chair), oil on canvas, 30x20", C-E 2/21/89 UE **1,320**

BARNES, Ernest Harrison (American, 1873-)
Autumn Watermeadow, oil on canvas, sgn, 24x30", RWS 9/8/89 ..... **475**
Moonlight, Autumn (in lavender tones); oil on canvas, sgn/dtd 1917, 20x24", RWS 9/8/89 ..... **750**
Moonlight (tonal landscape), oil on canvas, sgn, 25x30", RWS 9/8/89 ..... **475**

BARNES, Gertrude Jameson (American, 1865-)
Pair: Grapes, Peaches, Oranges, Plums; oil on board, sgn, 9x12", C-E 11/30/88 ..... **1,650**

BARNES, Wilfred Molson (Canadian, 1882-1955)
Brook, oil on board, sgn, 8x10", FB 10/17/88 ..... **200**
Hill Top, oil on board, sgn, 8x10", FB 10/17/88 ..... **300**
Pond in the Woods, oil on panel, sgn, 6x9", FB 4/25/88 ..... **350**
Sunlit Forest, no media given, sgn, 17x20", WAD 11/30/89 OE **14,000**

BARNETT, Will (American, 1911-)
Anticipation (black cat peering through banister), oil on canvas, sgn twice/dtd 80, 43x37", SBY 2/19/88 OE **25,300**

Big Black, oil on canvas, 42x47", C-E 6/1/88 2,420

BARNEY, Frank A. (American, 1862-1954)

Moonlight, oil on canvas, sgn, 14x18", C-E 2/1/89 UE 770

BARNOIN, Henri Alphonse (French, 1882-1935)

Marche de Quimper, Bretagne (village market scene); oil on canvas, sgn, 15x18", C-NY 5/24/89 9,350

Washerwoman at a Riverbank, oil on canvas, sgn, 21x26", WD 11/16/88 5,250

BARNSLEY, James MacDonald (Canadian, 1861-1929)

Landscape in Morning Light, watercolor, sgn, 4x5", WAD 6/12/89 240

BAROCCI, Federico; after (Italian, 1526-1612)

Noli Me Tangere, oil on canvas laid down on board, unfr, 53x36", SBY 12/9/88 OE 6,325

Rest on Return From the Flight into Egypt, by Joachim Wtewael (1566-1638), oil on copper, unfr, 15x11", SBY 6/2/89 OE 220,000

BAROCCI, Federico; att (Italian, 1526-1612)

Study of an Arm & a Foot, chalks on blue paper, 14x10", SBY 1/13/89 OE 13,200

BAROCCI, Federico; follower of (Italian, 1526-1612)

Saint Francis of Assisi Receiving the Stigmata, oil on canvas, 19x24", SBY 4/7/89 3,575

BARON, Henri Charles Antoine (French, 1816-1885)

Jeune Femme a la Guitare (ladies w/guitar), oil on canvas, sgn/dtd 1838, 16x13", C-NY 2/23/89 4,180

Three Women Fetching Water From a Spring, oil on panel, sgn, 9x7", C-E 2/21/89 1,760

BARONE, Antonio (American, 1889-)

Little Mother, oil on canvas, sgn/dtd 1914, 45x36", C-NY 5/26/88 6,600

BARR, William (American, 1867-1933)

Gaffer's Cottage, Scotland; oil on canvas, sgn, 18x24", RWS 5/12/89 OE 3,400

Landscape, oil on canvas, 18x24", LH 10/16/88 UE 250

BARRAGAN, Luis (20th C)

Pintura (abstract), oil on canvas, sgn, ca 1966-68, 71x41", C-NY 5/17/89 3,300

BARRAU, Laureano (Spanish, 1864-)

Red Parasol (woman seated on donkey under red parasol), oil on canvas, sgn, 56x44", SBY 2/22/89 55,000

BARRAUD, Henry (British, 1811-1874)

Grooms with Hunters Outside a Stable, oil on canvas, 26x42", SBY 6/10/88 19,800

Strawberry Roan & a Bay Hunter in a Landscape, oil on canvas, 42x60", SBY 6/10/88 39,600

BARRAUD, William (British, 1810-1850)

Hunter in a Landscape, oil on canvas, sgn/dtd 1845, 25x30", C-NY 3/22/89 8,800

BARRE, Martin (20th C)

60.T.39 (abstract), oil on canvas, sgn/dtd 1960, 77x38", C-E 11/17/88 UE 24,200

BARREDA, Ernesto (Chilean, 1927-)

Soledad (child standing in doorway), oil on canvas, sgn/titled/inscr No 2, 32x32", C-NY 5/17/89 2,860

Untitled (lady strolling sunny garden), oil on canvas, sgn/dtd 87, 39x47", SBY 11/21/88 6,050

BARRERA, Antonio (Colombian, 1948-)

Atardecer Amazonico (landscape), oil on canvas, sgn/dtd 1985/titled, 32x39", C-NY 11/21/88 7,150

Dawn (extensive view), oil on canvas, sgn twice/dtd 86/titled Amanecer, 51x77", SBY 5/16/89 16,500

Dawn (landscape), oil on canvas, sgn twice/dtd 87/titled Amanecer, 51x77", SBY 11/21/88 15,400

Rio Bogota, oil on canvas, sgn twice/dtd 1986, 45x57", SBY 5/17/88 OE 12,100

BARRETT, George Sr. (British, 1728/32-1784)

Couple Resting by a Waterfall in a Mountainous River Landscape, oil on canvas, sgn/dtd, 42x56", C-NY 6/2/88 OE 60,500

Pair: Landscape with Cows & Sheep; Sheep Grazing on the Bank of a Lake; oil on canvas, unfr, 34x49", SBY 10/21/88 OE 46,200

BARRETT, William S. (American, 1854-1927)

Coast of Maine (view across waves to a rising full moon), charcoal on paper, 5x7", RWS 9/29/88 UE 50

Rockport Harbor, Maine; watercolor/gouache on paper, sgn, 5x8", RWS 11/10/89 500

BARROW, Edith (British, -1920)

Basket of Lilacs, watercolor/pencil laid down on board, sgn/dtd 1920, 13x25", C-E 6/1/89 550

BARROW, John Dobson (American, 1827-1907)

The Gorge (landscape), oil on canvas, sgn, 25x30", C-NY 9/30/88 2,860

BARSCH, Wulf Erich (20th C)

Das Zeichen, oil on paper, sgn/dtd 83/titled, 25x38", SBY 5/3/88 1,650

BARSE, George Randolph Jr. (American, 1861-1938)

Oasis, oil on canvas, sgn/dtd 1886, 26x35", SBY 1/24/89 OE 8,250

BARSTOW, G.M. (American, 19th C)

Lake View, oil on canvas, sgn/dtd 65, 48x72", SBY 1/24/89 660

BARTHOLDI, Frederic Auguste

Statue of Liberty, watercolor/pencil on paper laid down on board, initialed, 5x8", C-NY 9/28/89 OE 12,100

BARTHOLOME-ESTEBAN, Murillo; att (Spanish, 1618-1682)

St Catherine, oil on canvas, 33x26", S/A 2/18/89 7,500

BARTHOLOMEW, William Newton (American, 1822-1898)

Old Windmill at Chatham, oil on canvas, sgn/dtd 87/titled, 14x10", RAB 11/25/88 1,300

Wreck of the Grecian Dec 6, 1885; oil on wood panel, sgn/dtd 87/titled, 9x13", RAB 11/25/88 450

BARTLEBACH, Hans

Pair: Man with a Pipe; Woman Wearing a Hat; oil on panel, 7x6", C-E 11/8/88 UE 650

BARTLETT, Dana (American, 1882-1957)

Arizona Desert, oil on canvas, sgn, 25x30", B/B 10/6/88 1,870

Autumn Landscape, oil on canvas, sgn, 24x20", B/B 8/10/88 770

Eucalyptus Trees, oil on canvas, sgn, 24x20", B/B 10/6/88 4,400

From the Land of Omar, oil on board, 30x40", B/B 10/6/88 1,980
Palos Verdes Trees, oil on canvas, sgn, 25x30", B/B 10/6/88 1,210

BARTLETT, Frederic Clay (American, 1873-)
Strollers on a Sunday Afternoon, oil on canvas, sgn, 27x31", WD 4/13/88 1,700

BARTLETT, Jennifer (American, 1941-)
At Sands Point #2 (contemporary landscape), oil on canvas, 12x24", SBY 11/11/88 15,400
At Sands Point #33, oil on canvas, painted in 1985-1986, unfr, 60x60", C-NY 5/4/88 66,000
At Sands Point #34, oil on canvas, 1985-86, 60x72", SBY 10/8/88 29,700
Diptych: In the Garden II, #3; oil on canvas & conte crayon on paper, 1981, 48x72", SBY 11/10/88 OE 99,000
Fixed Variable (5 rows, ea w/5 squares of various designs), 25 baked enamel plates, ea 12x12", ca 1974, C-NY 2/20/88 33,000
In the Garden #74, graphite/colored pencil on paper, 20x26", SBY 2/15/89 9,350
Study for Tidal Wave 3 (Row 1, Plate 1); enamel/silkscreen/baked enamel on steel plate, unfr, 12x12", SBY 2/14/89 2,530

BARTOL, Joel
Sailboats on a Lake, oil on canvas, sgn/dtd 1872, 20x30", C-E 11/8/88 550

BARTOLI, Jacques (French, 1920-)
Autour de la Table, oil on canvas, sgn, no size given, FAP 11/4/88 1,900

BARTOLINI, Frederico (Italian, 19th/20th C)
Arab Men at Leisure, watercolor on paper, sgn, 21x15", C-NY 5/24/89 7,150
Mosque Scene (Arabs washing feet to enter mosque), watercolor, sgn, sgn, 14x21", DM 10/14/88 2,750
Negotiation, oil on canvas, sgn, 31x19", SBY 5/23/89 49,500

BARTOLO, see Di Bartolo

BARTOLOMMEO, Fra; att (Italian, 1472-1517)
Double-Sided: Head of a Monk; Angel's Head; black chalk on gray paper, 10x7", SBY 1/13/89 OE 46,750

BARTOLOMMEO, Fra; studio of (Italian, 1472-1517)
Lying in State & Ascension of Saint Anthoninus, oil on panel, inscr w/Latin couplets on reverse, 20x22", C-NY 5/31/89 8,250

BARTON, Arthur B. (American, 1842-1914)
Approaching Storm (landscape), oil on canvas, sgn, 20x33", RAB 3/27/89 UE 1,000

BARTON, Loren (American, 1893-1975)
Late Afternoon, watercolor on paper, sgn, 21x30", B/B 1/11/89 770

BARUCCI, Pietro (Italian, 1845-1917)
Cattle Watering in an Extensive Italian Landscape, oil on canvas, sgn, 18x40", C-NY 2/23/89 4,400
Crossing the Marsh, oil on canvas, sgn/inscr, 22x34", C-NY 2/25/88 8,250
Gypsy Caravan, oil on canvas, sgn/inscr, 29x52", C-NY 5/24/89 19,800
Untitled, pastoral landscape w/amorous couple; oil on canvas, sgn, 24x46", SLK 4/7/89 7,000
Untitled (peasant family & parson riding in an Italian landscape), oil on canvas, 24x37", SLK 4/7/89 5,500

BARWICK, John (British, fl 1835-1876)
Bay StallionSaid To Be the Property of Lord Willoughby d'Eresby...; oil on canvas, sgn/dtd 1840, 27x36", SBY 6/10/88 10,450

BARYE, Antoine Louis (French, 1796-1875)
Stalking Lion, watercolor/pen/brown ink heightened with white on paper, 6x6", SBY 6/1/89 8,250
Studies of Deer, oil on paper laid down on canvas, estate stamp, 9x12", C-E 10/25/88 2,200
Tiger Walking, pastel/watercolor on paper, sgn, 11x14", SBY 7/12/89 OE 88,000
Two Leaping Stags in Landscape, oil on panel, sgn/stamped w/Vente Baryl seal, #d 360, 9x13", SBY 12/89/88 3,850

BARZANTI, Licinio (Italian, 1857-1944)
Harvesters, oil on canvas, sgn, 11x24", C-E 10/25/88 UE 880

BAS, see Van Den Bas

BASALDELLA, Afro (20th C)
New York (abstract composition), oil on paper, sgn/dtd 1953, 39x26", C-NY 5/4/89 OE 33,000

BASAR (European, 20th C)
Woman with a Parasol on a Bamboo-Lined Path, watercolor on paper, sgn, 10x19", LH 9/10/89 UE 60

BASCHENIS, Evaristo; follower of (1617-1677)
Still Life of Lutes, Violin, Guitar, Recorder, Books, & Paper; oil on canvas, 28x40", SBY 10/21/88 OE 22,000

BASCHENIS, Evaristo; studio of (1617-1677)
Still Life with a Lute & Violins, oil on canvas, unfr, 38x51", SBY 6/1/89 OE 99,000

BASCOM, Andrew J. (American, 19th C)
Portrait of a Man, 1837; oil on canvas, sgn/dtd 1837, 30x25", RWS 8/20/88 450

BASELITZ, Georg (German, 1938-)
Curly Head with Hatchet, oil on canvas, initialed/dtd 67, 64x51", SBY 5/2/89 OE 385,000
Der Bote (abstract figure), oil on canvas, sgn twice/dtd 4.III.84 twice/titled, 98x79", SBY 11/11/88 OE 121,000
Der Bote (abstract), oil on canvas, initialed/dtd 13 VII 84, 98x79", SBY 5/2/88 115,500
Die Flasche II (abstract), oil on 5 canvas panels, sgn/dtd Nov 80/titled on panel I, 28x99", SBY 11/11/88 OE 110,000
Untitled (abstract), crayon/watercolor on paper, sgn/dtd 15 Nov.73, 23x17", C-NY 2/20/88 3,080
Untitled (abstract), gouache on paper, dtd 8.III.79, 34x24", SBY 2/15/89 OE 17,600
Untitled (abstract), graphite/watercolor on paper, sgn/dtd 3 Dec.73, 19x14", C-NY 2/20/88 3,080
Untitled (abstract), watercolor on paper, initialed/dtd 18.VI.83, 24x17", SBY 10/8/88 OE 6,875
Untitled (abstract), watercolor on paper, sgn/dtd VI.83, 24x17", SBY 10/8/88 4,620
Untitled (head drinking from bottle), gouache on paper, sgn/dtd 12 VIII 81, 24x17", SBY 10/5/89 5,500
Zeichnung und Radierung, charcoal/graphite on paper, initialed/dtd 64, 9x12", C-NY 5/4/88 3,850
Zwei Hunden (contemporary), ink on paper, sgn/dtd 1967, 28x20", SBY 11/11/88 9,900

BASING, Charles (American, 1865-1933)
Low Tide at the Beach (seascape), watercolor on paper, sgn, 12x15", RAB 3/27/89 UE 200

BASKELL, William Frederick (American, 1866-1951)

Haystacks in the Marsh (haystacks on an inlet at sunset), watercolor on paper, sgn, 9x16", RAB 8/9/88 OE 900

BASKIN, Leonard (American, 1922-)

Man, watercolor/ink on paper, sgn, unfr, 28x20", C-E 2/3/88 OE 1,210
Man with Hand on Heart, watercolor/ink on paper, sgn, unfr, 28x20", C-E 2/3/88 OE 1,650
Peddlar, pen/black ink/pencil on paper, sgn/dtd 1958, 18x24", C-E 6/1/89 OE 1,540
Self-Portrait, watercolor/India ink on paper, sgn/monogramed/dtd 1975, 24x15", SBY 4/14/89 1,485

BASQUIAT, Jean Michel (European, 20th C)

Aaron, graphite on paper, 11x9", C-E 11/14/89 OE 8,250

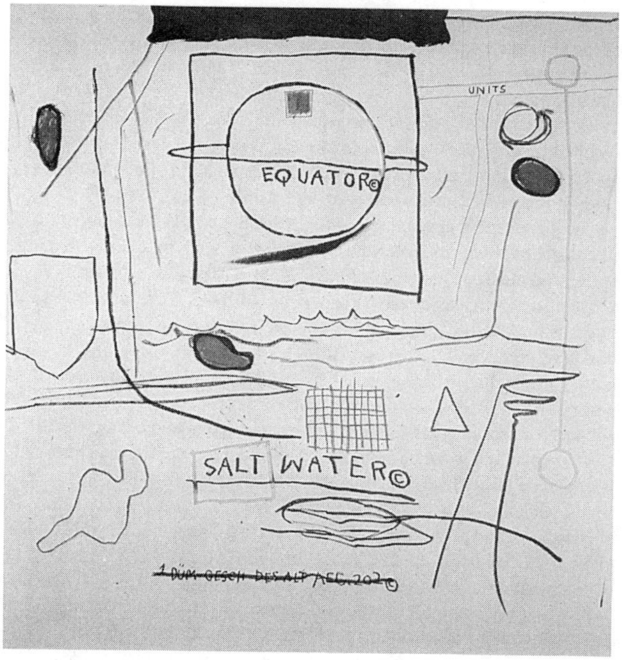

Big Sun, acrylic/oil sticks on canvas, sgn/dtd 1984, unfr, 66x60", C-NY 10/4/89 OE, $159,500

Birks (abstract head framed in white), mixed media, sgn/titled/dtd 85, 48x40", SBY 10/5/89 OE 176,000
Danny Rosen (abstract composition), acrylic/oil stick/paper collage on canvas, sgn/dtd 1983, 88x48", SBY 5/3/89 OE 181,500
Diptych: Untitled (abstract cow & figure); oil stick on paper, 1982, 30x22", SBY 2/15/89 OE 17,600
Dos Cabezas (two heads), acrylic on canvas w/wood supports, sgn/dtd 1982/titled, 61x61", SBY 5/2/88 OE 99,000
Equals (abstract composition), oil/crayon on canvas on artist's stretcher, sgn/dtd Sept 1982, 67x67", SBY 5/3/89 OE 220,000
Exercisio, acrylic/colored crayon on canvas, sgn/dtd 1984 Kipahulu/titled, unfr, 72x96", C-NY 11/10/88 OE 41,800
Famous Negro Athletes, oil sticks on newsprint, 36x29", C-NY 10/4/89 OE 20,900
Flypaper (abstract), acrylic/oil sticks on canvas, initialed/dtd 82, 60x12", C-NY 5/4/89 66,000
Greenish Skin, colored chalk/green crayon/gouache on paper, sgn/titled, 1983, 22x30", C-NY 11/10/88 OE 9,900
Group of 12: Untitled (abstracts); 9: oil sticks on paper, 3: crayon on paper, 17x14", C-NY 5/4/89 OE 159,500
In Italian (abstract), acrylic on 2 canvas panels hinged together w/5 smaller canvases, sgn/dtd 1983, 89x80", SBY 5/2/88 60,500
La Hara (abstract figure), acrylic/oil stick on wood, sgn/titled/dtd NYC 81, 72x48", SBY 10/5/89 341,000
Man Struck By Lightening-2 Witnesses; oil stick/acrylic on canvas w/wood supports, sgn/dtd 1982, 72x72", SBY 10/8/88 OE 60,500
Masque (abstract composition), oil on canvas, sgn, 56x49", SBY 5/3/89 OE 286,000
MCVIIV9 (contemporary), colored oil sticks on paper, 1979, 14x11", C-NY 5/4/89 OE 11,000
Number 1 (abstract), collage with oil/sprayed enamel/paper/felt-tip pen/crayon on canvas, 1981, 56x34", C-NY 5/3/89 OE 308,000
Orange Sports Figure (abstract composition), oil/acrylic/oil stick on canvas, 1982, 60x48", SBY 2/15/89 OE 126,500
Pair: Untitled (abstracts); pencil on paper, ea initialed/1 dtd 1986, 10x11", 12x12", C-E 11/14/89 OE 5,280
Pair: Untitled (Venus & Plato); ink on paper, 30x22", SBY 2/15/89 OE 9,350
Peso Neto, acrylic/oil stick on 4 panels, 1982, ea 21x21", C-NY 11/10/88 OE 52,800
Plush Safe-He Think (contemporary); oil/oil stick on board, 1981, 28x27", SBY 2/19/88 5,500
Porter (contemporary), oil/oil stick/color xerox collage on canvas, sgn, 84x52", SBY 5/3/89 OE 231,000
Red Rabbit (contemporary), oil/acrylic/oil stick on canvas, sgn/dtd 1982/titled, 69x64", SBY 11/11/88 OE 110,000
Set of 3: Untitled (the words Power Tools, scribbled head); graphite on paper, sgn/dtd 80, 24x18", C-NY 10/4/89 13,200
Set of 4: Untitled (abstract of red car, splash of black); 3 crayon, 1 acrylic/crayon on paper, 18x12", C-NY 10/4/89 12,100
Texas (abstract), collage/oil on wood, sgn/dtd 1983, 27x25", SBY 2/19/88 7,150
Thin Foil (abstract), acrylic/oil sticks/crayons on canvas, sgn/dtd 1984, unfr, 68x86", C-NY 5/3/89 OE 286,000
Thirty-Sixth Figure (abstract), acrylic on canvas, sgn/titled, 1983, 60x48", SBY 2/19/88 17,600
Top Tee, acrylic/colored xerox on canvas, sgn/dtd 82, unfr, 12x9", C-E 11/14/89 OE 13,200
Trunk, oil/crayon on canvas on wood stretchers, sgn/dtd 1982, 72x72", SBY 10/5/89 198,000
Untitled, oil stick on paper, sgn/dtd 82, 30x22", SBY 2/15/89 OE 17,600
Untitled (abstract, man with fish), acrylic/colored crayons on canvas, unfr, 1981, 78x68", C-NY 11/9/88 OE 110,000
Untitled (abstract composition), crayon/gouache/collage on paper, sgn, 1985, 22x30", SBY 5/3/89 OE 46,750
Untitled (abstract composition), crayon/pencil on paper, sgn/dtd 1986, 30x22", SBY 5/3/89 OE 52,250
Untitled (abstract composition), oil stick on paper, 1981, 17x12", SBY 2/15/89 16,500

Untitled (abstract composition), oil stick on paper, 1981, 20x24", SBY 2/15/89 11,000
Untitled (abstract composition), oil stick on paper, 30x23", SBY 5/3/89 OE 25,300
Untitled (abstract composition), oil/paper/crayon/masking tape on canvas, sgn, 1980, 19x25", SBY 2/15/89 28,600
Untitled (abstract cow w/goat printed three times), oil stick on paper, 17x14", SBY 10/5/89 6,050
Untitled (abstract figure & bird), oil stick on paper, sgn, 22x30", SBY 10/5/89 33,000
Untitled (abstract figure holding sword & bone), oil stick/paint on paper, 1981, 30x22", SBY 10/8/88 OE 12,100
Untitled (abstract figure w/sword), gouache/oil stick on paper, 1982, 16x13", SBY 5/3/89 OE 18,700
Untitled (abstract figure), acrylic/oil sticks/colored xerox on canvas, sgn/dtd 85, unfr, 86x68", C-NY 5/4/89 OE 143,000
Untitled (abstract figure), oil stick/ink wash on paper, sgn/dtd 81, 30x22", SBY 10/5/89 OE 48,400
Untitled (abstract figures), oil stick on paper, sgn/dtd St Martin 1982, 17x14", SBY 10/5/89 11,000
Untitled (abstract head), oil stick on paper, 20x16", SBY 10/5/89 8,800
Untitled (abstract head), oil stick/gouache on paper, sgn, 1985, 15x19", SBY 10/5/89 OE 18,700
Untitled (abstract head), watercolor/oil stick on paper, 1982, 24x18", lot 145, C-NY 2/14/89 OE 10,450
Untitled (abstract head), watercolor/oil stick on paper, 1982, 24x18", lot 147, C-NY 2/14/89 OE 8,800
Untitled (abstract male figure in red), oil stick on paper, 1982, 30x22", SBY 5/3/89 OE 35,750
Untitled (abstract monster-like figure), colored marker on paper, initialed, 21x12", SBY 10/5/89 8,800
Untitled (abstract portrait), colored oil sticks on paper, 1982, 43x30", C-NY 11/10/88 OE 26,400
Untitled (abstract skull), colored oil sticks on paper, sgn, 10x16", C-NY 2/14/89 OE 5,500
Untitled (abstract w/face & words), crayons on paper, 1984, 30x22", C-NY 2/20/88 2,200
Untitled (abstract), collage of colored xerox/carpet/acrylic/oil stick on canvas, sgn/dtd 1982, 30x24", C-NY 5/4/89 79,200
Untitled (abstract), colored chalk on paper, 22x30", C-NY 11/10/88 OE 6,050
Untitled (abstract), colored oil sticks/acrylic on paper, sgn/dtd Oct 6 1983, 28x39", C-NY 5/4/89 OE 57,200
Untitled (abstract), gouache/colored chalks/crayons/paper collage on paper, sgn, 30x22", C-NY 5/4/88 3,960
Untitled (abstract), mixed media on canvas, sgn/dtd NYC 87, 18x36", C-NY 5/4/89 OE 143,000
Untitled (contemporary ghost, bat, & man in mask by campfire), oil stick on paper, 30x22", SBY 5/3/89 OE 38,500
Untitled (contemporary studies), oil stick/pencil/color xeros on paper, sgn/dtd 1986, 30x42", SBY 5/3/89 OE 36,300
Untitled (contemporary), oil/spray paint/varnish/black felt-tip pen on canvas, 40x30", C-NY 2/14/89 OE 88,000
Untitled (half-length figure in hat, words Buena Suerte, $, Bacon, Top Tee), oil sticks, 30x23", C-NY 10/4/89 OE 28,600
Untitled (lead dust), colored oil sticks on paper, 1982, 22x30", C-NY 5/4/89 OE 22,000
Untitled (red skull), oil stick on paper, 12x18", SBY 10/5/89 9,900
Untitled (scribbled abstract standing figure), oil sticks on paper, sgn, 30x23", C-NY 10/4/89 16,500
Untitled (scribbled abstract), oil sticks on paper, sgn/dtd 1981, 13x18", C-NY 10/4/89 OE 27,500
Untitled (scribbled composition), acrylic/white chalk on paper, unfr, 14x23", C-E 11/14/89 13,200
Untitled (scribbled head w/letters AOF), oil sticks on paper, 30x23", C-NY 10/4/89 19,800
Untitled (scribbled head), colored oil sticks on paper, sgn, 1982, 30x22", C-NY 5/4/89 OE 28,600
Untitled (Self-Portrait, The King), oil/acrylic/oil stick/collage/wood/mirror, 1981, 47x35", SBY 11/11/88 OE 93,500
Untitled (skeleton studies), acrylic/watercolor/colored pencils/chalks/pencil, sgn/dtd 86, 30x22", C-E 11/17/88 OE 9,900
Untitled (skull w/hat, 1960, words poison, German, foal crossed out), graphite on paper, sgn, 11x11", C-NY 10/4/89 7,150
Untitled (skull), oil stick/marker/pencil on paper, sgn, 26x20", SBY 5/3/89 OE 28,600
Untitled (skull-like head), oil stick on paper, 14x11", SBY 5/3/89 OE 13,200
Untitled (three heads, ax, & inscriptions), colored felt-tip pens on paper, 22x16", C-E 11/17/88 OE 4,950
Untitled (three heads), oil stick on paper, sgn, 1981, 20x16", SBY 10/5/89 11,000
Untitled (two male figures), oil stick on galvanized steel, 71x23", C-NY 2/14/89 OE 20,900
Venus, acrylic/crayon/paper collage on 3 attached panels, sgn/dtd 1982/titled, unfr, 84x54", C-NY 11/10/88 OE 104,500
Wall Segment, colored crayons/gesso on wall segment w/aluminum plates, 42x28", C-E 11/17/88 OE 11,000

BASSANI, P.
Roosters & Hens in a Farmyard, oil on panel, sgn, 12x10", C-E 11/8/88 935

BASSANO, Jacopo (Italian, 1515-1592)
Noli Me Tangere, brush/brown ink heightened w/white on beige paper, 12x9", SBY 1/13/89 9,900
Supper at Emmaus, oil on canvas, 38x50", C-NY 1/11/89 OE 440,000

BASSANO, Jacopo; att (Italian, 1515-1592)
Orpheus Charming the Animals, oil on canvas, unfr, 46x48", C-NY 6/2/88 20,900
The Transfiguration, oil on canvas, 62x41", SBY 6/1/89 OE 49,500

BASSANO, Jacopo; circle of (Italian, 1515-1592)
Christ at the House of Martha & Mary, oil on canvas, unfr, 21x26", SBY 4/7/88 5,500

BASSANO, Jacopo; manner of (1515-1592)
Pair: Supper at Emmaus; Return of Saint Roch; oil on canvas, 53x68", SBY 10/13/89 OE 33,000

BASSANO, Leandro (Italian, 1557-1662)
Saint Francis in Contemplation, oil on canvas, 52x38", C-NY 10/12/89 4,400

BASSANO, Leandro; att (Italian, 1557-1662)
Christ in the House of Simon the Pharisee, oil on canvas, 42x70", SBY 6/1/89 UE 15,400

BASSANO, Leandro; circle of (Italian, 1557-1622)
Portrait of a Bearded Man, oil on canvas, 27x21", SBY 7/12/89 3,025

BASSANO, Leandro; school of (Italian, 1557-1622)
Winter, oil on canvas, 35x46", C-NY 6/2/88 OE 5,500

BASSEPORTE, Madeleine Francoise (1701-1780)
Still Life of Flowers in a Glass Vase, gouache on vellum, 11x8", SBY 1/13/89 16,500

BASSIRE, Dale (American, 1892-)
Autumn Landscape, oil on canvas, sgn, 31x36", B/B 5/17/89 OE 1,210

BASTANIER, Hans (German, 20th C)
Mother & Child, oil on panel, sgn/inscr/dtd 1927, 35x24", C-E 5/23/88 1,100

BASTERT, Nicolas (Dutch, 1854-1939)
Op De Hei, oil on panel, sgn twice/inscr No 1 on label on reverse, 14x22", SBY 12/9/88 2,310
BASTIANI, Lazzaro di Jacopo (Italian, ca 1425-1512)
Madonna of Humility, tempera on gold ground on arched panel, 22x14", SBY 6/2/89 52,250
BASTIDE
La Tiolette, oil on canvas, sgn, 35x40", C-E 2/23/88..... 4,400
BASTIEN, Alfred Theodore Joseph (Belgian, 1873-1955)
Floral Still Life, oil on board, sgn, 29x38", C-E 2/21/89 3,850
BASTIEN-LEPAGE, Jules (French, 1848-1884)
Rajane dans Mimi, oil on canvas, sgn, 1880, 15x26", SBY 5/23/89 9,900
BATCHELLER, Frederick S. (American, 1837-1889)
After a Day's Hunt, oil on canvas, sgn/dtd 78, 16x24", C-NY 9/30/88 4,400
Still Life of Lily of the Valley, oil on canvas, sgn/dtd 63, 16x14", RWS 5/12/89 UE 950
Strawberries in a Basket, oil on canvas, sgn, 12x16", WD 4/13/88 UE 6,000
BATEMAN, James (British, 1815-1849)
His Favorite Toy (dog), oil on canvas, sgn, 17x21", SBY 6/10/88 3,300
BATES, David (British, 1840-1921)
Early Morning on the Lledr, oil on canvas, sgn/dtd 1898, 20x30", PHL 10/28/88 6,500
Farmstead Warwick (sheep, figures, hay wagon in landscape), oil on canvas, sgn twice/titled, 18x24", C-NY 2/23/89 8,250
Marshland by the Colne, Withington; watercolor on paper, sgn/titled, 11x14", C-NY 5/24/89 1,760
Mountain Pathway, oil on canvas, sgn/dtd twice 1897, 36x24", SBY 6/8/88 4,675
On Malvern Common (landscape w/sheep), watercolor heightened w/white & scraping out on paper, sgn, 10x15", C-NY 5/24/89 1,320
On the Avon, Near Kenilworth; oil on canvas, twice sgn/dtd 1895, 16x23", SBY 2/22/89 7,150
BATHIEU, J.
Shepherd with His Flock Returning Home, oil, sgn, 26x36", WD 1/11/89..... 1,300
BATHUS (Balthasar Klossowski de Rola)(French, 1908-)
Double-Sided: Study for The Street (2nd version); drawing; pen/ink wash, 8*1/2*x7", WG 10/9/88 OE 1,850
BATON, Claude (French, 20th C)
Amsterdam Street Scene, oil on canvas, sgn, 20x24", B/B 9/14/89 OE 2,090
BATONI, Pompeo (Italian, 1708-1787)
Portrait of Young Man, leaning on books, bust of Diana behind; oil on canvas, in painted oval, 32x25", C-NY 6/2/88..... 110,000
BATONI, Pompeo; circle of (Italian, 1708-1787)
Education of the Virgin, oil on canvas, unfr, 45x37", C-NY 10/20/88 OE..... 12,100
BATOWJKI, Stanilas Kaczor
Serenade by the Hearth, oil on canvas, sgn, 39x59", C-E 10/25/88..... 3,520
BATTAGLIA, Alessandro (Italian, 1870-1940)
Faraway Thoughts (woman in a landscape), oil on canvas, sgn/dtd 1919, 30x29", C-NY 2/25/88 9,350
BATTAGLIA, Clelia Bompiani (Italian, 1848-1927)
By the Fountain, watercolor on paper, sgn, 29x21", SBY 6/8/88 1,100
Flower Vendors (two girls with flowers in a cityscape), watercolor on paper, sgn, 21x14", B/B 10/9/88 4,675
Italian Flower Sellers, watercolor, sgn/inscr, 21x15", C-NY 10/26/88 1,650
Roman Girl, watercolor over pencil on paper, sgn/inscr, 21x14", C-E 2/23/88 715
BATTISTELLO, see Caracciolo, Giovanni
BATTLES, Blake D. (American, 1887-1972)
Trees by a Riverside, watercolor, sgn/dtd 1922, 14x19", WG 9/16/88..... 300
BAUCHANT, Andre (French, 1873-1958)
Fleurs Champetres, oil on canvas, sgn/dtd 1928, 40x32", C-NY 10/6/88 OE 34,100
Paysage aux Paysans (landscape w/peasants), oil on canvas laid down on board, sgn/dtd 1928, 9x13", C-NY 2/16/89 11,000
Still Life of Tulips, oil on canvas, sgn/dtd 1956, 15x19", SBY 10/7/89 OE 17,600
Trois Oiseaux sur un Branche (three birds on a branch), oil on paper, sgn/dtd 1930, 11x15", C-NY 10/5/89..... 9,900
Two Women in a Landscape, oil on canvas, sgn/dtd 1946, 12x18", SBY 10/5/88..... 15,400
Violettes et Mugets (floral composition); oil on canvas, sgn, 8x10", SBY 2/14/89 4,950
BAUCHE, Leon Charles
Ducks by a Pond, oil on canvas, sgn 1909, 12x14", C-E 5/23/88 880
BAUDERON, Louis (French, 1809-)
Girl Playing Lute with Flowers in Her Hair, oil on canvas, sgn/inscr/dtd 1888, 38x25", C-E 5/23/88..... 2,420
Madonna of the Flowers (still life), oil on canvas, sgn/dtd 1858, 32x25", RWS 5/19/88 600
BAUDESSON, Nicolas (French, 1611-1680)
Still Life of Flowers in a Basket on a Ledge, oil on canvas, 20x24", SBY 4/7/89 7,700
BAUDOUIN, Albert (French, 19th/20th C)
Peaceful River, oil, sgn, unfr, 18x33", WD 1/11/89..... 600
BAUDRY, Paul (French, 1828-1886)
Nymph with Putti, oil on panel, sgn, 18x13", C-E 10/25/88 1,650
Putto Sitting on a Cloud, black/red chalk on beige paper, sgn/inscr, 10x8", C-NY 2/25/88 OE 2,420
BAUER, Rudolf (German, 1889-1953)
Bommb (abstract), oil on canvas, sgn, 1920, 29x41", SBY 10/6/89 38,500
Composition (abstract), pastel on paper, sgn, 17x14", C-NY 5/12/88..... 4,180
Con Rosso (abstract), oil on board, sgn twice, 1918, 29x40", SBY 2/16/89 OE 45,100
Concentric (abstract), oil on board, sgn, 1925, 29x40", SBY 2/16/89 36,300
Heavy & Light (abstract), oil on board, sgn twice, 1921, 29x41", SBY 2/16/89 OE 49,500
Improvisation (abstract), pastel on newsprint, sgn, 7x9", RWS 9/8/89..... 1,500

Komposition 27 (Spitzen), oil on masonite, inscr/dtd 1927, 40x28", WD 5/5/88 ... **18,000**
Larghetto (abstract composition), oil on canvas, sgn, ca 1918-1920, 46x38", SBY 10/6/89 ... **30,800**
Spiritual Pleasures (abstract), oil on canvas, sgn twice, ca 1935-38, 51x51", SBY 2/16/89 OE ... **90,750**
Untitled (composition w/lines), pencil/pastel on paper, sgn, 1921, 8x11", PHL 11/15/88 ... **4,000**

BAUER, Willi (German, 1923-)
Market Scene, oil on canvas, sgn, 25x37", LH 5/15/88 OE ... **275**
Snow, oil on canvas, sgn, 27x31", LH 5/15/88 ... **90**

BAUFFE, Victor (Dutch, 19th C)
Canal Scene, oil on canvas, sgn, 34x25", LH 5/15/88 OE ... **1,100**
Tree in the Meadow, oil on canvas, sgn, 17x12", FB 10/17/88 ... **375**

BAUGIN, Lubin (French, 1612-1633)
Madonna & Child, oil on panel, monogramed, 13x10", SBY 6/1/89 ... **71,500**

BAUM, Carl (American, 19th C)
Pair: Still Lifes of Fruit; oil on canvas laid down on board, oval, 24x20", C-E 6/1/88 ... **6,820**
Still Life of Fruit, oil on canvas, sgn/dtd 1863, unfr, 30x25", SBY 4/14/89 ... **5,500**

BAUM, Walter Emerson (American, 1884-1956)
Black Bass Inn, Lumberville, Pennsylvania; oil on board, sgn/inscr w/artist's name, 12x16", WD 4/13/88 ... **3,400**
Farmhouse, oil on canvas, 6x9", C-E 1/12/88 UE ... **242**
Fieldstone House, Buck's County; oil on canvas laid down on board, sgn, 16x20", WD 4/13/88 ... **3,000**
Fishing Fleet, oil on canvasboard, sgn twice/inscr/dtd 1938, 16x20", C-NY 9/30/88 ... **2,200**
Garden Wall, oil on canvasboard, 12x14", C-E 1/12/88 UE ... **132**
Landscape with Stream, oil on canvas, sgn, 30x34", DM 3/14/88 OE ... **3,500**
Lane (landscape w/road), oil on canvas, sgn twice/titled on verso, 25x30", SBY 3/17/88 ... **4,675**
Lehigh County Village, oil on canvas, sgn twice/inscr, 25x30", C-NY 9/30/88 ... **5,500**
Old Mill, oil on board, sgn/dtd 1926, 12x14", C-E 10/18/89 ... **2,860**
Pennsylvania Brook, no media given, on artist board, sgn, 16x20", WD 10/5/88 UE ... **2,700**
Pennsylvania Mill (rural river landscape), oil on canvas, sgn, ca 1928, 32x40", C-NY 5/25/89 ... **16,500**
Ridge Valley Brook, oil on canvasboard, sgn, 16x20", C-E 11/30/88 ... **2,200**
Saucon, oil on canvas, sgn/inscr, 20x24", C-NY 9/30/88 OE ... **19,800**
Snowy Scene on a Pennsylvania Hillside, oil on masonite, sgn, ca 1940s or 50s, 9x12", C-E 2/1/89 ... **1,430**
St Nicholas Square, Philadelphia; oil on canvas, sgn, 20x24", C-E 6/1/89 ... **3,300**
Stream Through Forest, oil on board, initialed, 10x12", C-E 1/12/88 UE ... **308**
White Birch Row, oil on canvas, sgn, 16x20", C-E 2/1/89 ... **1,650**
Winter (snowy landscape), oil on canvasboard, sgn, 12x16", WL 5/20/88 ... **1,200**
Winter Hills, oil on canvas, sgn, no size given, FAP 11/4/88 ... **5,000**
Winter Landscape (w/stream & village), oil on board, sgn twice/dtd 1931, 40x50", SBY 5/24/89 ... **16,500**
Winter Landscape (winding stream), oil on board, sgn, 25x30", B/B 10/9/88 OE ... **5,500**
Winter Scene (stream running through hilly landscape), watercolor on paper laid down on board, sgn, 12x16", C-E 6/1/89 ... **2,200**
Winter Street Scene, oil on canvasboard, sgn twice/inscr, 16x20", 16x20", SBY 3/17/88 OE ... **2,530**

BAUMANN (19th C)
Telling a Secret, oil on canvas, sgn, 10x8", C-E 2/23/88 ... **1,540**

BAUMGARTNER, H. (Swiss, 19th C)
Crossing an Alpine Stream (figures in landscape w/cottage), oil on canvas, sgn/dtd 52, 11x17", C-E 2/21/89 ... **2,200**
Woodsman & Family in an Alpine Landscape, oil on canvas, sgn, 27x38", SBY 10/24/89 ... **13,200**

BAUMGARTNER, Johann Wolfgang & studio; att
Set of 4: Scenes From the Lives of St Gregory, Clothide, Boniface, & St Mark; oil on canvas, 11x8", SBY 10/13/89 ... **6,600**

BAUMGARTNER, John Jay (American, 1865-1946)
Fawn in a Winter Landscape, gouache on paper, sgn/dtd 1928, 10x14", B/B 10/6/88 ... **880**

BAUMGARTNER, Warren W. (American, 1894-1963)
Interior with Figures in Oriental Dress, oil on canvas, sgn/dtd 24, 30x27", SBY 3/17/88 ... **880**

BAUMGRAS, Peter (American, 1827-1904)
Pair: Still Lifes of Treasures From the Deep; oil on cardboard, sgn/dtd 1877, 22x9", RWS 5/12/89 ... **1,000**

BAUMHOFFER, Walter M. (American, 1904-)
Signing the Declaration, oil on board, sgn, 36x28", C-E 11/30/88 ... **3,300**

BAUR, Johann Wilhelm (German, -1640)
Army Gathering on a Quay by an Elaborate Palace, gouache on vellum, 14x18", SBY 1/13/89 ... **7,700**

BAURE, Carl Ferninand (Austrian, 1879-1954)
Group of 4: Trotters on a Course; Thoroughbreds Down the Stretch; oil on canvas, 8x11", C-E 2/21/89 ... **4,950**

BAXTER, B. (American, 20th C)
Lighthouse, oil on artist board, sgn, 13x18", NA 10/1/88 ... **150**

BAXTER, Elijah Jr. (American, 1849-1939)
Solitude (lady in white sitting at river bank), oil on canvas, sgn, 12x6", RWS 9/29/88 OE ... **1,400**

BAYES, Alfred Walter (British, 1869-1956)
Courtship, oil on canvas, sgn, 31x22", C-E 2/23/88 ... **1,870**

BAYEU, Ramon (Spanish)
Vegetable Seller (cartoon for a series of tapestries), oil on canvas, 41x70", C-NY 1/11/89 ... **57,200**

BAYLINSON, A.S. (American, 1882-1950)
Lilacs & Baby's Breath in a Blue Vase, oil on canvas, sgn/dtd 1948, 24x20", C-E 10/18/89 UE ... **440**
Mixed Bouquet in Blue Vase, oil on canvas, sgn/dtd 1946, 24x20", C-E 10/18/89 UE ... **440**
Nude, oil on board, sgn/dtd 1919, 13x10", C-E 6/1/88 OE ... **2,860**

AYNE, Walter McPherson (British, 1795-1859)
Cottage at Rittenhouse Farm, Pennsylvania, 1838; oil on canvas, sgn, 14x21", FAP 11/4/88 3,000
AYNES, Frederick Thomas (British, 19th C)
Grapes & Plums, watercolor, sgn, 9x11", C-NY 5/25/88 550
AYUOLA, F.
Caricature of a Man Smoking a Pipe, oil on panel, sgn, 15x12", C-E 7/26/88 UE 264
AZAINE, Jean (French, 1904-)
Banlieu Printaniere (abstract), oil on canvas, sgn/dtd twice 1953, 46x32", SBY 2/18/88 OE 605,004
Composition, black ink/watercolor/tempera on paper, sgn/dedicated/dtd 52, 5x8", SBY 10/5/88 OE 1,540
Noel 1952, gouache on paper mounted on paper, sgn/dtd twice 1952, 8x6", SBY 10/5/88 1,100
Verre et Fleurs, oil on board, sgn, 14x11", SBY 2/14/89 OE 15,400
AZIOTES, William (American, 1912-1963)
Bather Form (abstract), oil on canvas, sgn/dtd 1947, 24x30", SBY 2/15/89 49,500
Blue Curtain (abstract), pastel/graphite on gray toned paper, sgn twice/dtd 1951, 19x13", SBY 10/8/88 23,100
Chameleon (abstract), oil on canvas, sgn twice/dtd 1953/titled, 18x14", SBY 11/10/88 52,250
Mirage, oil on canvas, sgn/dtd 1960, 48x36", 11/9/89 165,000
Untitled (abstract composition), gouache on paper laid down on canvas, sgn, ca 1944, 9x12", SBY 5/3/89 OE 12,100
Untitled (abstract composition), ink on paper, sgn, ca 1947, 8x6", SBY 5/3/89 OE 3,850
Untitled (abstract composition), ink on paper, sgn, ca 1947, 8x11", SBY 5/3/89 OE 3,850
Untitled (abstract composition), ink on paper, sgn, 1947, 8x11", SBY 5/3/89 3,575
Untitled (abstract), watercolor/graphite on paper, sgn, 7x9", C-NY 2/14/89 OE 26,400
Water Reflections (abstract), pastel/pencil on paper, sgn, 1953, 38x25", SBY 2/19/88 OE 66,000
EACH, Thomas (American, 1738-1806)

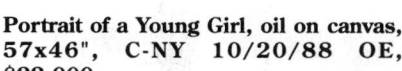

Portrait of a Young Girl, oil on canvas, 57x46", C-NY 10/20/88 OE, $22,000

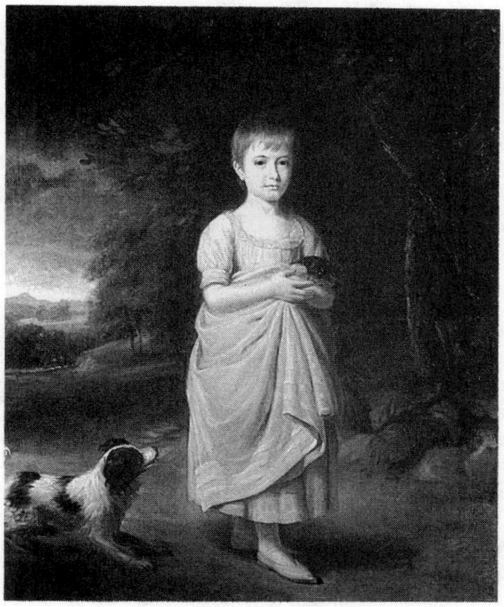

Portrait of the Burnaby Children of Leicestershire, in a landscape; oil on canvas, sgn, 31x44", C-NY 1/15/88 5,500
EAL, Gifford (American, 1879-1956)
City Impression, oil on board, sgn/dtd 09, 12x16", C-NY 3/11/88 2,750
Hauling in the Nets, Rockport, Summer 1923; brush/ink/gray wash/pencil on paper, sgn/dtd 1923, 13x19", RWS 5/19/88 550
Old Houses, gouache/pencil on brown paper, 12x18", C-NY 3/11/88 OE 4,620
Rockport Harbor, Night #2; gouache on paper, sgn, 9x12", SBY 6/28/89 1,760
Strolling by the Ruins, gouache/watercolor on paper, sgn/dtd 09, 15x20", SBY 9/14/89 1,650
Strolling Players, oil on masonite, sgn, 10x12", SBY 6/28/89 2,750
Summer Outing (elegant figures w/horse-drawn carriages, estate on hillside), oil on canvas, sgn, 24x30", C-NY 9/28/89 OE 72,600
EAL, Jack (American, 1931-)
Still Life of Flowers, oil on canvas, sgn, 30x24", C-NY 2/14/89 OE 9,350
EAL, Reynolds (American, 1867-1951)
At the Circus (tents & figures in landscape), graphite/pastel on paper, sgn/dtd 1936, 11x14", RWS 5/19/88 650
Circus Scene, watercolor on paper, sgn, 11x15", SBY 1/24/89 OE 6,875
EC Benedict's House, oil on board, 6x10", C-E 2/3/88 550
Edgartown, Sunday, Aug 14, 1938 (waterfront buildings & boats); watercolor/pencil on paper, 6x9", RAB 8/9/88 OE 1,100
Fowey Rocks & Light, Shark Channel; watercolor/graphite on paper, sgn/dtd 1941, 7x10", RWS 11/10/89 UE 275
Inside Circus Tent, Sparks; graphite/crayon on paper, sgn/dtd 1931, 6x8", RWS 11/10/89 UE 300
Marine Scene (sailing & power boats in open ocean), watercolor/gouache/pencil on paper, sgn/dtd 1943, 7x10", RWS 9/29/88 450
Nobska Light NE Gale Storm Signal, 1938; watercolor/graphite on paper, sgn, 7x11", RWS 11/10/89 UE 425
On the High Sea (two boats at full sail), oil on canvas, sgn/dtd 1921, 30x48", C-E 6/1/89 6,820
Pixie Greenport, oil on board, 6x10", C-E 2/3/88 935
Road to Langsville, watercolor/pencil on paper, sgn/dtd 1919/titled, 14x21", SBY 3/17/88 1,100

Savalton, New York (Back of Newburgh); oil on canvas, sgn/dtd 1915, 26x36", SBY 5/25/88 ... 29,70
SF in Gloucester, graphite/crayon on paper, initialed/dtd 1928, 6x9", RWS 11/10/89 UE ... 40
South Rondout, tempera on board, sgn/dtd 1914, 26x36", SBY 5/25/88 OE ... 25,30
Sparks Circus (elephants, figures & tents in landscape), pastel/crayon/graphite on paper, sgn, 10x13", RWS 5/19/88 ... 70
Swimming on East Side of Chappaquiddick Island, Martha's Vineyard; watercolor on paper, 6x9", RAB 8/9/88 ... 60
Table Mountain-Capetown Jan 23-34; watercolor/pencil on paper, sgn, 7x10", RAB 8/8/89 ... 40
Town by a River, oil on canvas, sgn/dtd 1920, 29x36", SBY 5/25/88 ... 13,20
Vegetable Boat Vender (boats in sea), watercolor on paper, sgn/dtd 1941, 7x10", RWS 3/16/89 ... 75
Watching the Sailboats, watercolor/gouache/graphite/ink on paper, sgn/dtd 1947, 7x10", RWS 11/10/89 ... 75

BEALE, Mary; att
Portrait of a Gentleman, seated half-length...; oil on canvas, in painted oval, 30x25", C-NY 4/6/89 UE ... 1,10

BEALIEU, Paul Vanier (Canadian, 1910-)
L'Oiseleur (boy, half-length, in black sweater with dove), oil on canvas, sgn/dtd 1956, 36x29", FB 5/28/89 ... 11,50
Paysage d'Automne (autumn landscape), gouache, sgn, 11x15", FB 5/28/89 ... 45

BEALIEU, Robert (Canadian)
General Store, Rural Quebec; pastel, sgn, 20x24", FB 4/25/88 ... 55

BEALL, Cecil Calvert (American, 1892-)
Bathers (nudes drying off after a bath), oil on masonite, sgn, 18x22", RAB 8/9/88 UE ... 70
Bathers (three nudes), oil on masonite, sgn, 18x22", RAB 8/9/88 UE ... 70
Portrait of Abraham Lincoln (bust-length, battle of Gettysburg as backdrop), oil on board, sgn, 20x16", RAB 8/9/88 UE ... 20
Portrait of Abraham Lincoln (bust-length, ruins beyond), oil on board, sgn, 20x16", RAB 8/9/88 UE ... 20

BEAMAN, Waldo Gamaliel (American, 1852-1937)
June Pinks on Railing...; oil on canvas, sgn, 34x22", RWS 8/20/88 ... 32

BEAMENT, Thomas Harold (Canadian, 1898-1984)
Laurentian Autumn, oil on board, sgn, 12x16", FB 5/28/89 ... 30
Laurentian River in Winter, oil on canvas, sgn, 20x24", FB 5/28/89 ... 40
Snowfall Across the Lake, Laurentians; oil on board, sgn, 12x16", WAD 6/12/89 ... 70
Spring Pattern, oil on canvas, sgn, 24x28", FB 4/25/88 ... 1,50
Still Life, Flowers in a Glass; oil on board, sgn, 10x7", FB 5/28/89 ... 50

BEAN, Caroline Van Hook (American, 20th C)
Little Church Around the Corner, watercolor/gouache on paper, sgn, 15x10", C-E 9/15/88 ... 71
Orchard Street, gouache/pencil on paper, sgn/dtd 1918/titled, 18x12", C-E 9/15/88 OE ... 2,75

BEARD, James Henry (American, 1812-1893)
Baby with Dog, oil on canvas, sgn/dtd 1875, unfr, 22x27", C-E 6/1/88 ... 3,30
Circus Announcement, oil on canvas, sgn/dtd 1866, 17x14", SBY 9/23/88 ... 7,15
Puppy's Supper (close-up of puppy w/food & water bowls), oil on canvas, sgn/dtd 1873, 13x18", SBY 9/14/89 ... 8,52

BEARD, William Holbrook (American, 1823-1900)
Ajax Defying the Lightening (owl in tree), oil on canvas, bears signature, 11x9", SBY 1/24/89 UE ... 3,85
Fable of the Fox & the Heron, oil on board, 8x7", SBY 9/14/89 ... 2,31
Help a Feller, Can't Ye (bear swinging from a limb); oil on canvas, inscr/titled, 13x11", SBY 9/23/88 ... 7,70
Kindred Spirits (a drunk monkey), oil on board, inscr w/artist's name, framed as an oval, 8x7", WD 4/13/88 ... 3,20
Sailor's Delight (sailor & mermaid under water), oil on canvas, sgn/dtd 1891, 30x17", C-NY 5/25/89 ... 7,70

BEARDEN, Romare (American, 1914-)
Adoration, ink/watercolor on paper, 13x18", SBY 10/7/89 ... 1,32
Prologue to Troy #2 (contemporay figures in landscape), acrylic/collage on paper, sgn, 1972, 56x46", SBY 5/3/89 OE ... 66,00
Spring Planting (contemporary), collage on board, sgn, 1969, 36x48", SBY 11/11/88 ... 38,50
Summer Song, paper collage on composition, sgn, 1967, 40x30", SBY 11/9/89 OE ... 60,50
Two Women (abstract), paper collage/gouache/watercolor/graphite on canvas, 1968, 44x56", C-NY 5/4/88 OE ... 46,20
Untitled (abstract seated figure), paper/fabric collage on board, sgn, 1972, 21x14", SBY 10/5/89 OE ... 17,60

BEARDSLEY, Aubrey (British, 1872-1898)
Title Page for The Girl From the Farm, pencil/India ink on paper, titled, 7x4", C-NY 6/11/88 ... 1,98

BEARDSLEY, M.H. (20th C)
Children Saying Grace, watercolor, 14x10", WG 4/23/88 UE ... 32

BEARE, George (British, fl 1744-1749)
Portrait of a Lady Said To Be Mrs Ann Burney, oil on canvas, 29x24", SBY 6/2/89 ... 37,40

BEATON, Cecil (British, 1904-1980)
Costume Design, gouache/pencil on paper, sgn, 15x11", SBY 10/7/89 ... 88
Portrait of Ina Claire, watercolor/charcoal on paper, 24x19", B/B 9/15/88 OE ... 2,47
Portrait of Ina Claire, watercolor/charcoal on paper, 24x19", B/B 1/11/89 ... 71
Portrait of Ina Claire, watercolor/graphite on paper, sgn, 23x17", B/B 9/15/88 OE ... 1,04

BEATTY, Frank T. (American, 1899-)
Seascape, aqua water against brown rocks; watercolor on paper, sgn/dtd 1928, 8x10", RAB 8/8/89 UE ... 5

BEATTY, John Wesley (American)
End of the Day, oil on canvas, sgn/dtd XX, 20x30", C-E 6/1/88 ... 1,32

BEATTY, John Williams (Canadian, 1869-1941)
On the North Shore (stand of trees), oil on board, sgn, 13x10", WAD 11/30/89 ... 1,40
Wood Interior, Choats Woods, Port Hope; oil on board, sgn/dtd 1936, 9x11", WAD 6/12/89 ... 1,30

BEAUBRUN, circle of
Portrait of a Lady, holding flowers in a landscape; oil on canvas, unfr, 29x39", C-NY 10/20/88 OE ... 4,18

BEAUBRUN, school of
Portrait of a Lady, bust-length, wearing black dress with white collar...; oil on canvas, 22x18", C-NY 4/6/89 UE ... 1,10

EAUCHAMP, Robert (American, 1923-)
Devil's Foot (abstract figures), oil on canvas, sgn/dtd 81, unfr, 59x75", C-E 11/14/89 ..... **2,640**
Untitled, oil on canvas, sgn/dtd 62, 52x53", C-E 5/13/88 ..... **2,200**
EAUGUREAU, Francis H. (American, 1920-)
Canyon del Muerto (cavalry raiding Indian camp), oil on canvas, sgn, 34x46", B/B 3/22/89 ..... **3,300**
EAULEY, William (American, 1874-)
St Paul's, oil on canvas laid down on panel, 16x12", C-E 6/1/88 UE **770**
EAULIEU, Paul Vanier (Canadian, 1910-)
Abstract, watercolor, sgn/dtd 1958, 13x20", FB 10/30/89 ..... **1,100**
Abstract, watercolor, sgn/dtd 1964, 13x20", FB 10/30/89 ..... **1,210**
EAULIEU, Robert (Canadian)
O'Grady's Cycle, pastel, sgn, 28x22", FB 10/17/88 ..... **400**
EAUMONT, Arthur Edwaine (American, 1879-1956)
Double-Sided: Harbor Activity; oil on board, sgn, 10x13", RAB 8/8/89 UE **850**
Harbor View with Moored Boats, oil on canvas, sgn, 12x16", RWS 9/8/89 OE **1,400**
Pair: Old Bridge; Moonlight Winter Landscape; oil on canvas laid down on board, sgn, 6x7", 6x8", C-E 1/12/88 UE **143**
Set of 4: Landscapes; 3 oil on canvas, 1 oil on board, sgn, 5x6" & smaller, C-E 4/7/88 ..... **605**
Winter Dry Dock, oil on board, sgn, 10x14", RWS 9/8/89 OE **1,200**
EAUMONT, Charles (American, 19th C)
Pair: Summer & Autumn; oil on canvas, sgn, 22x12", SBY 4/14/89 ..... **825**
EAUMONT, Claudio Francesco (Italian, 1694-1766)
Double-Sided: Sacrifice of Iphigenia; Virgin & Child with Female Saints or Angels; pen/ink & chalk, 16x13", C-NY 1/11/89 ..... **2,860**
EAUMONT, Lillian Adele (American, 1880-1922)
Satin Gown (full-length portrait of lady in white satin gown), oil on canvas, sgn/dtd 1906, 48x36", RWS 3/31/88 ..... **1,900**
EAUQUESNE, Wilfred Constant (French, 1847-1913)
Combat at Woerth, oil on canvas, sgn, 15x18", SBY 7/12/89 ..... **3,300**
Reconnaissance: Portrait of a Soldier; oil on canvas, sgn, 18x11", RWS 6/17/89 UE **475**
EAVIS, Richard (British, 1824-1896)
Arab Caravan, oil on canvas, sgn, 16x22", C-E 5/23/88 ..... **3,520**
Dedouin Feeling His Way Across a Morass, oil on canvas, sgn/dtd 87, 18x14", SBY 6/8/88 ..... **2,860**
Pushing the Haywagon, oil on canvas, sgn, 12x20", C-E 2/21/89 ..... **2,860**
ECHI, Luigi (Italian, 1830-1919)
Friar's Visit, oil on canvas, sgn, 24x34", SBY 2/22/89 OE **31,900**
Friar's Visit, oil on canvas, sgn, 46x32", SBY 6/8/88 ..... **9,075**
ECHTLE, Robert (American, 1932-)
Hawaii Malibu-Max at Kilauea (exiting car), watercolor on paper, initialed/dtd 74 twice/titled, 10x15", SBY 11/11/88 OE **8,800**
69 Ford (in suburban landscape), watercolor on paper, initialed/dtd 73, 10x16", SBY 11/11/88 OE **6,600**
ECK, Joel (20th C)
Untitled (abstract interior, landscape), acrylic on canvas, sgn/dtd 1982, 96x61", SBY 10/7/89 ..... **1,100**
ECK, Rosemary (American, 1923-)
Abstract, oil on canvas, sgn, 24x36", C-E 1/12/88 UE **330**
Face, oil on canvas, 28x34", C-E 11/30/88 ..... **660**
ECKER, Frederick W. (American, 1888-1973)
California White Water, watercolor on paper, sgn, 12x15", B/B 1/11/89 ..... **302**
Landscape with Farmhouse, oil on canvasboard, sgn, 11x15", RWS 8/12/89 OE **550**
Lola at Will Rogers State Beach, oil on canvas laid down, sgn, 16x20", B/B 10/6/88 ..... **522**
Sand Pit in the Forest, oil on canvas, sgn, 14x18", B/B 9/15/88 ..... **220**
Texas Landscape, oil on canvas, sgn, 18x22", B/B 1/11/89 UE **330**
ECKER, Maurice (American, 1889-)
Ploughed Gardens, oil on canvas, sgn, 18x22", C-E 10/18/89 UE **935**
Woman of Tehuanteper, oil on canvas, sgn/dtd 1946-49, 24x20", C-E 10/18/89 UE **770**
ECKER, W. (British, 19th/20th C)
View of a Village Through the Trees, oil on canvas, sgn/dtd 1900, 37x35", B/B 5/17/89 ..... **1,045**
ECKLEY, William (American, 20th C)
Jungle Ordeal (composition w/text & zipper), watercolor/collage on paper, sgn/dtd 1980, 30x42", SBY 2/14/89 ..... **880**
ECKMAN, Jessie Mary (American, 1856-1929)
Still Life of Flowers & Books on a Table, oil on canvas, sgn, 16x20", B/B 5/17/89 ..... **770**
ECKMAN, William (American, 20th C)
Nude (back), pencil on paper, sgn, 19x25", SBY 2/15/89 ..... **3,850**
Study for Diana (standing nude), pencil on paper, sgn/dtd 1972, 23x18", SBY 11/11/88 ..... **4,125**
ECKMANN, Max (American, 1884-1950)
Der Eismann II, pen/black ink on paper, sgn/dtd 1944/titled, 14x9", C-NY 5/11/89 OE **15,400**
ECKWITH, Arthur (American, 1860-1930)
Landscape with Mountain in the Distance, oil on canvas laid down, sgn, 13x16", B/B 5/17/89 UE **357**
Stream in the California Foothills, oil on board, sgn, 14x16", B/B 1/11/89 ..... **440**
ECKWITH, James Carroll (American, 1852-1917)
Le Donjon de Polignac (view of city), oil on canvas, sgn/dtd 1911, 20x24", SBY 6/28/89 ..... **7,150**
Portrait of a Lady, oil on canvas, sgn, 32x26", SBY 9/23/88 ..... **3,575**
Portrait of Mrs Gould Jennings (Nee Mary Crimmins), oil on canvas, sgn, 27x22", SBY 9/23/88 ..... **4,125**
EDA, Francesco (Italian, 1840-1900)
Lady with a Parrot, oil on canvas, sgn, 21x11", C-E 2/23/88 ..... **1,650**

BEDA, Giulio (Italian, 1879-)
Rocky Landscape with Houses in the Distance at Dusk, oil on canvas, sgn, 18x23", C-E 2/23/88 1,98
BEDER, Jack (Canadian, 1909-)
River & Landscape, gouache, sgn, 17x22", FB 5/28/89 UE .... 3(
Street in Montreal, oil on panel, sgn/dtd 1963, 16x20", FB 4/25/88 .... 7C
BEDINEFIELD
Black Horse, oil on canvas, sgn, 13x17", LH 10/16/88 .... 8C
BEDINI, A. (Italian, 19th C)
Young St John the Baptist, oil on canvas, sgn, 17x13", DM 5/13/88 .... 3C
BEECHEY, Richard Brydges (British, 1808-1895)
Magillicuddys Reeks (figures & cart on road, village beyond), oil on canvas, sgn/dtd 1878, 24x36", PHL 10/28/88 .... 6,0C
BEECHEY, school of
Officer on Horseback Brandishing a Saber, oil on canvas, 51x40", C-NY 4/8/88 6,05
BEECHEY, William (British, 1753-1839)
Lady Mary Ann Pigot (portrait, seated, wearing white dress, holding a letter), oil on canvas, 50x40", C-NY 4/8/88 .... 6,6C
Portrait of a Lady, full-length, wearing a white dress, in a landscape; oil on canvas, 73x45", C-NY 10/20/88 .... 4,0C
Portrait of a Lady, Seated Half-Length, in a White Dress Wrapped in a Veil; oil on canvas, oval, 35x28", C-NY 10/12/89 2,86
Portrait of Lord William Douglas, oil on canvas, 24x29", MG 5/28/88 65
Portrait of Mrs William Fletcher Norton, seated next to a window; oil on canvas, 43x39", SBY 10/21/88 3,02
Portrait of Thomas Kite, wearing jacket, white waistcoat & cravat; oil on canvas, inscr/dtd 1826, 30x25", C-NY 10/20/88 .... 3,3C
BEECHEY, William; att (British, 1753-1839)
Portrait of a Gentleman, half-length...; oil on canvas, 30x25", C-NY 4/6/89 .... 1,1C
BEECHEY, William; circle of (British, 1753-1839)
Portrait of Mrs Lloyd Robinson, half-length, wearing white dress & red shawl; oil on canvas, 30x24", SBY 4/7/88 1,76
BEELT, Cornelis (fl 1660-1702)
Figures on the Beach at Schevengingen, oil on panel, sgn, 18x25", SBY 10/13/89 .... 13,2C
BEER, John (British, fl 1895-1915)
Left at Home (portrait of a hound sitting on straw), oil on panel, sgn/dtd 05, 36x14", SBY 6/9/89 2,47
BEERS, Julie Hart (American, 1835-1913)
Birch Tree, oil on panel, sgn, 16x6", C-E 9/15/88 UE 11
BEERSTRATEN, Jan Abrahamsz (Dutch, 1622-1666)
Winter Landscape with Figures Along a Highway, oil on canvas, 28x37", SBY 10/21/88 7,15
BEERT, Osias (Flemish, 1596-1624)
Still Life of Fruit in a Wan-Li Bowl, oil on panel, 21x29", SBY 1/12/89 OE 902,0C
Still Life of Strawberries, Raspberries, Capers, & Cherries, an Artichoke...; oil on panel, 19x31", C-NY 1/11/89 .... 110,0C
BEERT, Osias; att (Flemish, 1596-1624)
Still Life of a Covered Cup, Lemon Slices on a Pewter Plate, Berries...; oil on panel, 19x26", SBY 4/7/88 .... 14,3C
BEEST, see Van Beest
BEET, see De Beet
BEGA, Cornelis Pietersz (Dutch, 1620-1664)
Interior with Two Peasants, oil on panel, sgn, unfr, 11x8", SBY 4/7/88 1,65
Peasants at a Village Market, oil on copper, sgn, 13x16", SBY 6/2/89 .... 60,5C
Peasants in an Interior, oil on canvas, sgn, 23x21", SBY 1/12/89 .... 27,5C
Peasants in an Interior, oil on panel, sgn, 10x8", C-NY 10/20/88 .... 2,2C
BEGEYN, Abraham Jansz; att (1637-1697)
Pastoral Landscape with a Sleeping Shepherd & His Flock, oil on canvas, indistinctly sgn, 15x21", SBY 10/13/89 1,65
BEICH, Joachim Frans; circle of (German, 1665-1748)
Herders Resting with Their Flock on Path in Rocky River Landscape...; oil on canvas, unfr, 33x47", C-NY 5/31/89 .... 11,0C
BEIHLE, August (American, 1885-1979)
Road to a Mountain Lake, watercolor/gouache on paper, 15x20", WG 4/23/88 UE 4C
BEIHONG, Xu (Chinese, 1895-1953)
Pair: Couplet in Xing Shu (Running Script, hanging scrolls); ink on paper, sgn/dtd 1938, 40x13", SBY 5/31/89 1,98
BEINEKE, Fitz (German, 1842-1907)
Children Playing on a Log, oil on canvas, sgn, 23x29", SBY 6/8/88 .... 4,4C
BEJARANO, Manuel Cabral (Spanish, 19th/20th C)
Carmen y Don Jose, oil on canvas, sgn/dtd 1849, 24x30", C-NY 2/25/88 OE 15,4C
BEL GEDDES, Norman
Decor Design for Ermine, watercolor/gouache on artist board, sgn, 10x15", SBY 10/7/89 3,08
Decor Design for Ermine, watercolor/gouache on artist board, stamped, 10x15", SBY 10/7/89 2,53
Pair: Two Costume Designs for Ermine; watercolor/gouache on artist board, sgn/dtd 1920, 15x10", SBY 10/7/89 2,97
Belgian School (19th C)
Game of Cards, oil on panel, bears signature/dtd 1833, unfr, 23x20", SBY 12/9/88 UE 2,64
Letter, oil on panel, 15x12", C-E 2/23/88 1,65
Nymphs, oil on canvas, sgn, 19x25", C-E 11/8/88 71
Pair: Flowers in Urns; oil on canvas, 60x39", WD 10/19/88 6,75
Portrait of a Woman, combing her hair wearing a lace-trimmed dress; oil on canvas, 10x9", C-E 4/7/88 55
Young Woman in Gray Dress with a White Bonnet (bust-length profile portrait), oil on canvas, 18x12", SLK 2/12/88 12
Belgian School (19th/20th C)
In From the Rain (nude standing by fireplace), oil on canvas, indistinctly sgn/dtd, 46x31", SBY 10/24/89 6,60
BELIMBAU, Adolfo (Italian, 1845-)
Young Woman in Garden, oil on canvas, sgn, 14x22", FAP 11/4/88 OE 1,20

ELKIN, Arnold (Canadian/Mexican, 1930-)

Oracle (abstract), acrylic on canvas, sgn/dtd 1975, 65x80", SBY 5/17/88 OE ... 5,775

ELKNAP, Zedekiah (American, 1781-1858)

Child in White with Doll, oil on canvas, 26x24", RWS 10/27/89 ... 25,000

Portrait of Two Children, oil on canvas, ca 1830, 25x30", C-NY 1/20/89 OE ... 82,500

ELKNAP, Zedekiah; att (American, 1781-1858)

Pair: Portraits of Mary Ann Hazard & Josiah Fisk Everett; oil on panel, ca 1835, 24x19", RWS 6/10/89 OE ... 5,000

Portrait of a Lady, oil on board, ca 1830, 26x20", C-NY 1/20/89 ... 4,620

ELL, A.D. (British, 20th C)

Clipper & Boats in a Harbor, watercolor/gouache, sgn/dtd 1938, 15x20", C-NY 5/25/88 ... 1,100

ELL, Arthur George (British, 1849-1916)

Rue de Marche, Dieppe; oil on panel, sgn, 16x13", SBY 6/8/88 ... 2,860

ELL, Caroline M.

Sailboats in Drydock, oil on board, 14x16", NA 11/5/88 ... 225

Sailboats in the Harbor, oil on board, sgn, 13x15", NA 11/5/88 ... 550

ELL, Cecil C. (American, 1906-1970)

Battery (figures & seascape w/ship), watercolor/gouache on paper, sgn/dtd 44, 22x30", SBY 3/17/88 ... 1,650

Brooklyn Bridge, oil on masonite, sgn, 1968, 15x30", SBY 1/24/89 ... 2,090

Fight Crowd, oil on masonite, sgn twice/dtd 1958/titled/inscr Slide 51K, 30x40", SBY 3/17/88 ... 5,500

Group of 3: Newspaper Vendor; On the Bowery; Street Scene; 2 oil on masonite & 1 ink wash/crayon on paper, SBY 1/24/89 ... 1,650

Late Afternoon, Brooklyn Bridge; oil on masonite, sgn twice/dtd 37/titled, 22x30", SBY 3/17/88 ... 1,760

Life Class (class studying as teacher works with skeleton), pen/ink on paper, sgn, 1932, 11x15", WG 10/19/88 ... 600

Orchard Street, Chicken Market; oil on panel, sgn/dtd (1938?) or 39, 30x40", SBY 4/14/89 OE ... 8,800

Penn Station (interior w/crowd of people), charcoal/watercolor on paper, sgn, 22x29", SBY 3/17/88 ... 1,980

ELL, Charles (American, 1874-1935)

Art Angel (angel w/pallet & fantasy figures), oil on canvas, sgn, 1986, 72x60", C-NY 5/4/89 UE ... 38,500

Gumball #7 (close-up of gum machine & jar of peanuts), oil on canvas, sgn, 60x70", SBY 11/11/88 OE ... 121,000

Pace Bantam (photo-real view of slot machine), watercolor on paper, sgn/dtd 82, 12x16", C-NY 5/4/89 OE ... 14,300

ELL, Clara Louise (American, 1886-)

The Studio Window, oil on canvas, sgn, 30x24", SBY 4/14/89 OE ... 2,970

ELL, Edward August (American, 1862-1953)

Dancers, oil on canvas, sgn, 22x33", C-NY 12/2/88 ... 8,800

In the Study (lady seated at writing desk in interior), oil on panel, sgn, 24x18", SBY 3/17/88 OE ... 6,600

Reflecting (lady seated at desk), oil on panel, sgn, 18x12", SBY 1/24/89 OE ... 13,200

ELL, George C. (American, 19th C)

Greenwood Lake-New York End (landscape); watercolor on paper, sgn/dtd 1883, 17x36", RAB 8/8/89 UE ... 1,300

ELL, John (British, 19th C)

Lake View with Villa & Figures, oil on canvas, sgn, 24x36", SBY 7/12/89 ... 4,400

ELL-SMITH, Frederic Marlett (Canadian, 1846-1923)

On the St Lawrence, watercolor, sgn/dtd 81, 6x11", WAD 6/12/89 ... 400

Promenade, watercolor, sgn/dtd 1892, 9x13", WAD 11/30/89 OE ... 3,600

Rainy Streets, London; watercolor, sgn/dtd 1920, 9x13", WAD 11/30/89 OE ... 4,000

Rainy Westminster, watercolor, sgn, no size given, WAD 11/30/89 ... 3,600

River Through the Mountains, watercolor, sgn, 13x10", FB 5/28/89 ... 450

Rocky Shore, watercolor, sgn, 9x14", WAD 6/12/89 ... 750

St Dunstans, Fleet Street; watercolor, sgn/dtd 1919, 11x8", WAD 11/30/89 OE ... 3,200

View of Mountains From Bridge, watercolor, sgn, 13x10", FB 5/28/89 ... 650

ELLANGE, Joseph Louis Hippolyte (French, 1800-1866)

French Cavalry Pursuing Arab Warriors, watercolor heightened w/white over black chalk, sgn, 10x14", C-NY 2/25/88 ... 1,320

Napoleon et le Petit Messager, oil on canvas, sgn, 22x26", SBY 2/22/89 OE ... 52,250

ELLANGER, Camille Felix (French, 1853-1923)

Daphnis & Chloe, oil on canva, sgn/dtd 1893, 58x43", WD 5/5/88 ... 20,000

Idylle (Daphnis et Chloe), oil on canvas, sgn/dtd 1893, 57x43", SBY 2/22/89 OE ... 137,500

ELLANO, A. (Italian, 19th C)

Reprimand (man & boys in an interior), oil on canvas, sgn, 20x32", C-NY 2/23/89 OE ... 9,350

ELLE, Alexis Simon (French, 1674-1734)

Portrait of a French Princess of the Blood, in a fleur-de-lys embroidered gown; oil on canvas, 41x49", C-NY 6/2/88 UE ... 10,450

ELLE, Charles; see De Belle

ELLE, Marcel (French, 19th/20th C)

Le Viaduct d'Auteuil, oil on board, sgn/dtd 1922, 15x18", SBY 10/7/89 ... 3,300

ELLECOUR, Etienne Prosper Berne (French, 19th C)

Messenger, oil on panel, sgn/dtd 1897, 11x15", C-E 2/23/88 ... 1,980

ELLEFLEUR, Leon (Canadian, 1910-)

Estival, gouache, sgn/dtd 1989, 17x23", FB 10/30/89 ... 4,180

ELLEI, Gaetano (Italian, 1857-1922)

Pipesmoker, oil on canvas, sgn, 15x11", PHL 6/16/88 ... 850

ELLEMONT, Leon (French, 1866-1961)

Breton Women at Church, oil on canvas, sgn/dtd 1904, 50x82", C-E 5/23/88 ... 3,300

ELLENGE, Michel Bruno (French, 1726-1793)

Flowers in a Crystal Vase with Insects, a Peach & Currants on a Ledge; oil on canvas, 10x8", SBY 4/7/89 OE ... 12,100

ELLERMAN, Ferdinand (German, 1814-1889)

La Cueva del Guacharo, Venezuela (tropical landscape); oil on canvas, sgn/dtd 1880, 38x50", SBY 11/21/88 ... 49,500

BELLET, Auguste Emile (European, -1911)
Serenade, oil on canvas, sgn, 25x33", C-E 10/25/88 OE 6,6
Woman with Red Hair Wearing a Pink Ribbon, oil on canvas, sgn, 25x20", C-E 10/25/88 OE 3,3
BELLEUSE, Pierre Carriere (19th C)
Newstand, oil on canvas, sgn, unfr, 20x24", C-E 10/25/88 2,2
Portrait of a Lady, with cherries & roses in her hat & on her bodice; pastel, sgn/dtd 1871, oval, 24x20", C-E 10/25/88 1,3
BELLEVOIS, Jacob; circle of (Dutch, 1621-1675)
Shipping in a Choppy Sea, oil on panel, 14x22", C-NY 10/20/88 5,5
BELLI, Giovacchino (1756-1822)
Design for a Single Candlestick, pen/brown ink/gray wash over black chalk, 13x8", SBY 1/13/89 1,1
Two Designs for Full-Length Figures: St James & St Paul; pen/ink/wash over black chalk, 13x9", SBY 1/13/89 7
Two Designs for Ink Stands w/Separate Studies for Various Fittings Below, pen/ink/wash over chalk, 13x8", SBY 1/13/89 OE 3,3
Two Designs: Two-Handled Oval Tray & Tray w/Choice of Two Different Galleries; pen/ink/wash, 13x8", SBY 1/13/89 7
BELLIAS, Richard (French, 1921-)
Banquet d'Ete, oil on canvas, sgn, 21x18", LH 12/4/88 5
Vase de Cristal (floral still life), oil on canvas, sgn/dtd 1961, 39x29", SBY 10/7/89 2,2
BELLINI, Giovanni; circle of (Italian, 1430-1516)
Entombment of Christ, oil on panel, 8x14", C-NY 1/15/88 11,0
Portrait of a Youth with a Black Cap, oil on panel, 6x5", SBY 10/13/89 7,7
BELLINI, Giovanni; school of (Italian, 1430-1516)
Madonna & Child, oil on panel, 19x16", C-NY 4/6/89 OE 14,3
Madonna & Child Before a Parapet, oil on canvas, 23x17", C-NY 10/20/88 5,5
BELLIS, Hubert (Belgian, 1831-1902)
Still Life of Roses, oil on canvas, sgn, 30x20", B/B 3/17/88 4,9
BELLMER, Hans (French, 1902-)
Akt (loose drawing of a nude, seated), pencil on graph paper, sgn/blindstamp, 9x7", C-NY 10/6/88 3,9
Double-Sided: Composition; Figure; pencil on pink paper, 12x10", C-E 5/9/89 OE 7,1
BELLOLI, Andrei Franzovich (Russian, -1881)
La Baigneuse (seated nude), oil on canvas, sgn/dtd 1872, WD 11/16/88 15,5
BELLOTTI, Pietro; circle of (Italian, 1627-1700)
Philosopher Holding a Manuscript & a Seedling, oil on canvas, dtd 1670, 31x25", C-NY 10/20/88 UE 2,2
BELLOTTO, Bernardo (Italian, 1720-1780)
Architectural Capriccio w/Self-Portrait...in Costume of Venetian Nobleman; oil on canvas, ca 1765, 61x44", SBY 6/1/89 OE 1,870,
Capriccio with a Roman Triumphal Arch, oil on canvas, 41x54", SBY 1/12/89 OE 40,7
San Giorgio Maggiore, Venice; oil on canvas, 18x28", SBY 1/12/89 35,2
BELLOTTO, Bernardo; after (Italian, 1720-1780)
View of Dresden From the Right Bank of the Elbe Below the Augustusbrucke, oil on canvas, 37x64", C-NY 1/11/89 OE 93,5
BELLOTTO, Bernardo; studio of (Italian, 1720-1780)
Piazza del Campidoglio, Santa Maria d'Aracoeli, & the Cordonata, Rome; oil on canvas, 35x58", SBY 1/12/89 OE 192,5
BELLOWS, Albert Fitch (American, 1829-1883)
Cattle Watering, oil on canvas, within a painted arch, sgn, 9x7", SBY 6/24/88 OE 1,5
Cows in a Country Setting, oil on canvas, 9x16", DM 9/16/88 1,7
Midday (landscape w/figures & water), oil on canvas, sgn, 30x48", C-NY 12/2/88 OE 39,6
Pair: Morning & Evening; oil on canvas/oil on canvas laid down on board, sgn, 27x22", C-NY 12/2/88 OE 33,0
Quiet Nook (figures in landscape), watercolor on paper mounted on board, sgn twice/dtd 1869, 17x14", SBY 1/24/89 2,0
BELLOWS, George Wesley (American, 1882-1925)
Barnyard & Chickens, oil on panel, bears signature/initialedESB, 18x22", C-NY 12/2/88 OE 110,0
Bridge & Swimming Hole, Woodstock; conte crayon on buff paper, bears signature/initialed, 12x12", C-E 11/30/88 1,8
Caricature of Mary Cheney Platt, black crayon on paper, sgn/dtd 1920, authenticated by sitter, 13x9", SBY 6/28/89 8
Early Standing Nude, oil on canvas, sgn, 1906, 71x35", SBY 4/29/88 14,8
Fisherman, oil on canvas, sgn, 1917, 30x44", SBY 5/25/88 OE 1,430,
Introducing Georges Carpentier: The Dempsey-Carpentier Fight; pencil/conte crayon, sgn, 21x28", C-NY 5/25/89 OE 220,0
Nude Reclining, charcoal/crayon on paper, 10x13", C-NY 5/26/88 OE 17,6
Old Farmyard, Toodleums; oil on canvas, sgn by artist's wife/inscr Toodluums (sic) Old Farmyard, 36x58", SBY 5/24/89 181,5
Proposal, pen/black ink on paper laid down on paper, sgn, 12x11", C-NY 9/30/88 6,6
Salvation Army Lassie, Girl with Bonnet; conte crayon on paper, bears signature, 1924, 12x8", SBY 6/28/89 3,4
Through the Trees, Monhegan Island, Maine; oil on panel, sgn, 15x20", C-NY 9/30/88 25,3
BELLOWS, George Wesley; att (American, 1882-1925)
Crashing Waves on Rocky Coastline, oil on board, bears signature, 18x22", B/B 12/8/88 3
BELMONT, I.J.
In the Garden, oil on canvas, sgn, 30x40", C-E 6/28/88 UE
BELOT, H.
Fancy Dress, oil on canvas, sgn, 11x7", C-E 2/23/88 1,6
BELVEDERE, Andrea (Italian, 1642-1732)
Flowers in a Glass Vase Beside a Silver Ewer, on a Ledge; oil on canvas, inscr, 25x17", C-NY 4/8/88 41,8
BEMBO, Giovanni Francesco (Italian, 16th C)
Portrait of a Man, half-length, wearing a black costume & hat...; oil on canvas, 16x19", C-NY 1/11/89 OE 63,8
BEMELMENS, Ludwig (German, 20th C)
Grinzing, Outside Vienna; watercolor on paper, sgn, 17x24", B/B 12/8/88 7
BEMMEL, see Von Bemmel

ENASSIT, Emile Louis (French, 1853-1902)
Soldiers in the Snow, oil on panel, sgn, 14x11", SBY 6/8/88 .... **1,980**
Troops in a Winter Forest, oil on panel, sgn, 14x11", C-E 2/23/88 .... **1,045**
ENDINER, Alfred (American, 1899-)
Traveling Uphill on Horseback, watercolor on paper, initialed, FAP 4/15/89 UE **110**
ENEDITO-VIVES, Manuel (Spanish, 1875-1963)
Woman with Water Jug, oil on canvas laid down on board, sgn, 16x10", C-E 2/21/89 OE **4,400**
ENEKER, Gerrit Albertus (American, 1882-1934)
Sloop by the Pier, pastel on paper, sgn/dtd 1905, 9x7", RAB 3/27/89 UE **300**
Sunny Day, Provincetown (girl in white dress & straw hat), oil on canvas, sgn/dtd 1912, 24x20", C-NY 5/25/89 .... **23,000**
ENGER, W.E. (British School)
Landscape, watercolor, sgn, 12x17", FB 5/28/89 .... **140**
ENGSTON, Billy Al (American, 20th C)
Plato de Moreno, paper collage/watercolor on paper, intitialed/dtd 1982, 23x30", C-E 5/9/89 .... **1,100**
ENHOLD
Quail in a Highland Landscape, oil on canvas, indistinctly sgn, 20x30", SBY 6/9/89 .... **2,860**
ENLLIURE Y GIL, Jose (Spanish, 1855-1914)
Mischievous Choirboys, oil on canvas, sgn, unfr, 42x22", SBY 10/24/89 OE **55,000**
ENN, Ben (American, 1884-1984)
Bathers, oil on canvas, sgn/dtd 33, 14x16", C-E 11/8/88 UE **700**
Coffee Pot, oil on canvas, sgn/inscr/dtd 57, 20x24", C-E 6/1/88 .... **935**
Conversation, oil on canvas, sgn/dtd 71/titled, 30x24", C-E 11/8/88 .... **550**
Dice Game, oil on canvas, sgn/dtd 68, 30x36", C-E 11/8/88 .... **750**
Flowers & Newspapers, oil on canvas, sgn/dtd 72/titled, unfr, 27x22", C-E 9/15/88 .... **1,650**
Jetty, oil on canvas, sgn/dtd 41/titled, unfr, 16x20", C-E 9/15/88 .... **990**
Portrait of a Woman (bust-length), oil on canvas, sgn/dtd 26, 23x28", SBY 6/28/89 .... **1,760**
Recreation, Riverside Drive; watercolor on paper, 16x18", C-E 11/30/88 .... **550**
Still Life, oil on board, sgn/dtd 58, 10x12", SBY 3/17/88 .... **440**
Street, New York City; no media given, sgn twice/dtd 48 twice, titled/inscr New York W 24th St, 24x20", SBY 3/17/88 .... **2,860**
Three Boys, oil on canvas, sgn twice/dtd/titled, 20x16", C-E 11/8/88 .... **660**
Village Fisherman (men w/boats along shore), oil on canvas, sgn/dtd 28, 25x30", C-E 6/1/89 OE **4,180**
Yellow Flowers, sgn/inscr/dtd, 25x18", C-E 6/1/88 .... **880**
ENNETT, Frank Moss (British, 20th C)
Bit of Winter Sunshine (three men drinking in an interior), oil on canvas, sgn/dtd 1935, 20x16", C-E 5/22/89 .... **4,950**
Whist (four gentleman playing cards), oil on canvas, sgn/dtd 1936, 20x16", C-E 5/22/89 .... **7,150**
ENNETT-BROWN, Mae (American, 20th C)
Kabuki Dancers & Flowers (flowers in bowl beside Japanese doll), oil on canvas, sgn, 30x25", RAB 8/9/88 UE **700**
ENOIS, Alexandre (Russian, 1870-1960)
Costume Design for Loubova: Sadko; watercolor/pencil on paper, sgn/dtd 1930, 12x8", C-L 10/8/88 OE **1,670**
Costume Design for Sadko (full-length man), watercolor/pencil on paper, sgn/dtd 1930, 12x8", C-L 10/8/88 OE **1,860**
Costume Design for Sadko: A Russian Serving Girl; watercolor/pencil on paper, sgn/dtd 1930, 12x9", C-L 10/8/88 .... **1,860**
Costume Design for the Countess: Rigoletto; pencil/India ink/watercolor, sgn/inscr/dtd 1938, 14x10", SBY 10/5/88 OE **1,430**
Le Saint Vieillard: Sadko; watercolor/pen/ink on paper, sgn/dtd 1930/titled, 12x9", C-L 10/8/88 OE **1,020**
Mountainous Landscape, watercolor on paper, sgn twice/dtd 1916 twice, about 11x16", C-L 10/8/88 OE **2,600**
Novgorod, A Design for a Curtain: Sadko; watercolor/gouache/pen/ink on paper, sgn/dtd 1930, 16x24", C-L 10/8/88 OE **2,416**
Petrouchka: Butterweek Fair (pre-Lenten fair w/church beyond); watercolor/pen/ink on paper, sgn, 10x15", C-L 10/8/88 .... **4,090**
ENOIS, Nicolai (Russian, 1901-)
Decor Design for the Sorochinsky Fair, watercolor/charcoal on paper, sgn, 16x25", SBY 10/7/89 .... **1,100**
ENOIT, Pierre J. (1782-1854)
Coutume Surinamois (lady in tropical landscape), watercolor, sgn twice/inscr/titled, unfr, 9x7", C-SK 6/9/88 OE **890**
Pont de Bosch-Negre, sur la Saramaca a Surinam; watercolor heightened w/gum arabic, sgn, 6x8", C-SK 5/25/89 .... **370**
ENSO, Giulio (Italian, ca 1601-1668)
Mars & Venus Surprised by Vulcan, pen/brown ink/wash, 17x12", SBY 1/13/89 .... **5,500**
Mars Chastising Cupid, pen/brown ink/wash, 3x5", SBY 1/13/89 .... **1,320**
ENSON, Ambrosius (Flemish, fl 1519-1550)
Portrait of a Man Holding a Pair of Gloves, oil on panel, sgn/dtd 1546, 22x18", SBY 4/7/88 .... **13,200**
ENSON, Ambrosius; att (Flemish, fl 1519-1550)
Madonna & Child with a Parrot, oil on panel, 15x11", SBY 10/13/89 OE **16,500**
ENSON, Ambrosius; circle of (Flemish, fl 1519-1550)
Portrait of an Ecclesiastic Praying, oil on panel, 18x14", SBY 1/12/89 .... **22,000**
ENSON, Ambrosius; follower of (Flemish, fl 1519-1550)
Love Feast (couples gathered around a table), oil on panel, 32x38", SBY 6/1/89 OE **41,250**
ENSON, Eugene (American, 1839-1908)
Allegory: Eternal Spring (two figures in landscape); oil on canvas, monogramed/dtd 83, 25x71", RWS 5/19/88 .... **4,750**
Panoramic View of Venice From the Harbor, oil on canvas, sgn/indistinctly dtd Venice 187(?), 11x33", SBY 4/14/89 OE **4,125**
ENSON, Frank Weston (American, 1862-1951)
Adirondack Campsite (two tents), watercolor on paper, sgn/dtd 25, 25x30", RAB 8/9/88 OE **7,500**
Ducks at Dawn, black ink/wash/pencil on paper, sgn, 18x25", SBY 1/24/89 OE **8,250**
Eagle Alighting, watercolor on paper laid down on board, sgn, 20x27", WD 10/5/88 UE **2,200**
Firelight, oil on canvas, sgn/dtd 93, 40x30", SBY 5/25/88 UE **165,000**
Gorge in Autumn (landscape), watercolor/pencil on paper mounted on cardboard, sgn/dtd 28, 16x14", RWS 3/16/89 OE **2,750**

Grouse (bird on tree branch), watercolor on paper, sgn/dtd 30, 19x15", SBY 5/24/89 OE 22,0
Hawk & Teal, gray wash/India ink on paper, sgn, 25x21", SBY 1/24/89 11,0
Herons by an Inlet, India ink/wash on paper, sgn, 25x18", SBY 4/14/89 4,51
Portrait of a Lady, oil on canvas, sgn/dtd 1907, 44x36", C-NY 12/2/88 110,0
River at Sunset, watercolor on paper, sgn, 7x14", B/B 1/11/89 2,47
Widgeon Alighting, gray wash/India ink on paper, sgn/dtd 35, 24x20", SBY 1/24/89 OE 12,0

BENSON, John P. (American, 1865-1947)

Fleet in Morning Fog, three ships pass in mist; oil on canvas, sgn/dtd 1912, 26x54", RWS 8/20/88 1,0

BENSON, Nesbitte (American, 20th C)

Festivities on Beach, oil on board, initialed/dtd 1920, 6x8", FAP 4/15/89 19

BENSON, Tressa Emerson (American, 1896-)

Carnival, watercolor/pen/ink on paper, sgn, 12x16", C-E 6/1/88........ 1,10
Daguerreotype Dandies (portrait of three seated men in landscape), oil on canvas, sgn, 36x44", SBY 4/14/89........ 1,65
Fireplace, gouache on paper, sgn, 14x20", C-E 2/3/88 UE 33

BENTLEY, James (20th C)

Just a Murmer, oil on masonite, sgn/dtd 1960, 20x29", C-E 6/28/88 UE........ 10

BENTLEY, Lester (American, 1908-1972)

Ossing (quiet street scene), oil on panel, sgn, 20x26", MAG 9/18/88 60

BENTON, Harry Stacy (American, 1877-)

Woman at Fountain, oil on canvas, sgn, 30x20", LH 12/4/88 UE........ 13

BENTON, Thomas Hart (American, 1889-1975)

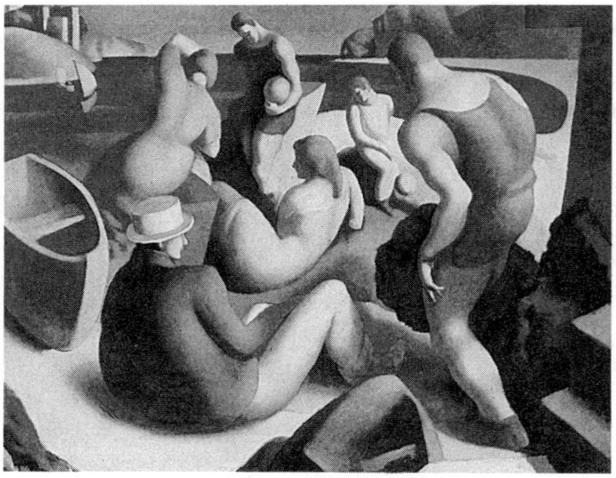

Beach, oil on canvas, sgn, 1920-21, 40x50", C-NY 5/25/89 OE, $495,000

Central Park, watercolor/pencil on paper, sgn/inscr, 15x18", C-NY 9/30/88 7,70
Construction Workers (contemporary), oil on canvas mounted on masonite, sgn twice/inscr, 10x11", SBY 3/17/88........ 7,15
Cotton Pickers, oil/pencil on paper laid down on board, sgn/dtd 44, 8x10", C-NY 9/28/89 55,00
Double-Sided Pair: Views of Manhattan & Houses; pencil on paper, 10x8" & smaller, C-E 11/30/88 UE 99
Double-Sided: July Hay; Studies of Clouds; oil on tin, sgn, 1942, 12x8", SBY 5/25/88 OE 143,00
Farmer (portrait, half-length in profile), oil on paper, 1925, 10x9", SBY 4/14/89 2,20
Fish (abstract), oil on tin, 60x48", C-NY 12/2/88 38,50
Grand Tetons, oil on tin, sgn/inscr, 10x12", C-NY 5/26/88 49,50
Landscape #28, oil/pencil on paper laid down on paper, 9x11", C-NY 12/2/88 OE 22,00
Male Torso, India ink on paper, 11x9", SBY 9/23/88........ 93
Mountain Stream (landscape), oil on board, sgn twice/dtd 1972/titled/inscr, 11x14", SBY 5/24/89 OE 46,20
Navajo Sand (Indian on mount tending sheep in hilly landscape), oil tempera on masonite, sgn, 19x24", C-NY 5/25/89........ 187,00
New Fence (workers repairing fence in a landscape), tempera on canvas laid down, sgn/dtd 45, 9x13", C-NY 5/25/89........ 99,00
Old Maple Tree, pen/ink wash/pencil on paper, sgn/inscr, 11x8", C-E 11/30/88 2,64
Palisades of the Hudson, oil on canvas, sgn, ca 1918-20, 24x24", C-NY 9/28/89 35,20
Palisades of the Hudson, oil on canvas, sgn, 24x24", C-NY 12/2/88 44,00
Sea Phantasy I, oil on metal backed w/panel, 1920s, 63x46", SBY 5/25/88 50,60
Small Town Life, pencil on paper, 5x6", WL 5/20/88........ 1,80
Spring Storm (horse running in meadow, lightning in angry sky), tempera on board, sgn, 19x27", WG 4/23/88 170,00
Study for Cultural Progress (mural), pencil/pen/ink on paper, 7x24", SBY 3/17/88........ 7,15
Sunday Morning, oil en grisaille on paper, unfr, 17x23", C-NY 9/30/88 7,15
Train in the Desert (landscape), oil on canvasboard, sgn, 13x19", SBY 5/24/89 40,70
Two Figures at a Picnic, oil on paper, 7x8", C-NY 9/30/88 2,97
Two Figures at a Picnic (modernistic depiction), oil on paper, 7x8", C-E 6/1/89 9,35
Two Steers & Windmill, watercolor on paper, sgn/inscr, 15x22", C-NY 5/26/88 26,40
Waterfront, oil on paper, 11x7", C-NY 9/30/88 3,08
Workers, oil/India ink on paper laid down on board, 12x10", SBY 9/23/88 6,60

BENVENUTI, E. (Italian, 19th/20th C)

Rialto Bridge on the Grand Canal, watercolor on paper, sgn, 7x12", B/B 1/11/89 UE 49

BERANGER, Jean Baptiste Antoine Emile (French, 1814-1883)
Hoping for Pearls, oil on panel, sgn/dtd 1879, 11x9", C-NY 5/25/88 .... **4,400**
BERAUD, Jean (French, 1849-1936)
Cancan au Cafe de Paris, oil on panel, sgn, 22x14", SBY 5/23/89 .... **170,500**
Coquelin aine dans le Bourgeois Gentilhomme de Moliere, oil on panel, sgn, 18x15", SBY 10/24/89 .... **19,800**
La Lettre, oil on panel, sgn/dtd 1908, 18x15", SBY 2/22/89 .... **143,000**
Le Bal Public (view of Paris night life), oil on canvas, sgn/dtd 1880, 30x49", C-NY 5/24/89 OE **860,000**
Les Grands Boulevards: Le Theatre des Varietes; oil on canvas, sgn, 15x22", SBY 5/23/89 .... **220,000**
Outside the Cafe Americain on the Boulevard des Capucines, oil on panel, sgn, ca 1890-95, 15x22", C-NY 2/23/89 OE **220,000**
Une Avenue Parisienne (street scene), oil on canvas, sgn, ca 1880, 16x23", C-NY 2/23/89 OE **418,000**
Une Parisienne (Parisian street scene), oil on canvas, sgn, 14x10", SBY 2/22/89 .... **93,500**
Une Place Ensoleille (sunny street scene), oil on panel, sgn, 9x13", C-NY 2/23/89 .... **60,500**
BERCHEM, Nicolaes (Dutch, 1620-1683)
Herdsmen with Cows & Sheep in a Wooded Landscape, oil on canvas, bears signature, 22x19", C-NY 6/2/88 .... **9,900**
BERCHEM, Nicolaes; manner of (Dutch, 1620-1683)
Shepherd in an Extensive Landscape, oil on canvas, 17x21", SBY 12/9/88 .... **1,100**
BERCHERE, Narcisse (French, 1819-1891)
Arabian Caravan, oil on panel, sgn, 15x24", RWS 11/10/89 .... **3,100**
Arabs at Work in the Fields, oil on canvas, sgn, 13x19", SBY 12/9/88 .... **2,750**
BERCHMANS, Emile
Portrait of a Young Girl, in a red dress, seated; pastel on stretched canvas, sgn/dtd 99, 26x27", C-NY 10/26/88 OE **2,420**
BERCKHEYDE, Gerrit Adrianensz (1638-1698)
Game of Skittles in a Garden, oil on canvas, 21x26", SBY 6/3/88 .... **19,800**
BERCOT, Paul (French, 20th Century)
Les Bergers, oil on canvas, sgn/dtd 51, 44x58", LH 10/16/88 UE **300**
BEREA, Dimitri (European, 1908-1975)
Le Peintre avec Fleurs (painting w/flowers), oil on canvas, sgn/dtd 59, 18x22", C-E 11/17/88 UE **440**
BERGAMINI, Francesco (Italian, 1815-1883)
Donkey Ride, oil on canvas, sgn, 24x16", SBY 2/22/89 .... **7,150**
Mischievous Altarboys, oil on panel, sgn, 18x22", C-NY 2/25/88 OE **11,000**
BERGAMO, school of (17th C)
Interior with a Bracket Clock, a Statue of Joshua, & Other Items; oil on canvas, bears signature, 39x53", C-NY 1/15/88 .... **70,400**
BERGER, Nick
Fisherman's Church, watercolor/pen/black ink/pencil on paper, sgn, 13x20", C-E 6/1/89 UE **550**
BERGERON, Eugene (French, 19th C)
Two Figures by a River in a Wood, oil on canvas, sgn, 18x24", PHL 10/28/88 .... **1,900**
BERGLER, Joseph (1753-1829)
Pair: Portrait of a Scholar; Woman Sewing; oil on canvas, sgn/dtd 1789, 27x23", SBY 10/13/89 .... **5,500**
BERGMAN, Anna-Eva
Untitled (abstract), oil on canvas, initialed/dtd 1960, 43x66", C-E 11/14/89 .... **2,640**
BERGMANN, Julius Hugo (German, 1861-1940)
Leading the Flock (woman leading geese in a landscape), oil on canvas, sgn, 37x45", SBY 2/22/89 .... **6,600**
BERGUE, Tony Francis; see De Bergue
BERJON, Antoine; att (French, 1754-1843)
Pair: Floral Still Lifes; oil on panel, oval, 16x12", C-E 5/22/89 .... **7,700**
BERKE, Ernest (American, 1921-)
Trappers Shoring Their Canoes, oil on canvas, sgn/dtd 1962, 22x32", SBY 3/17/88 OE **4,125**
BERKES, Antal (Hungarian, 1874-)
After the Rain, Montmartre; oil on canvas, sgn/dtd 1925, 20x28", B/B 3/22/89 .... **1,650**
Street Scene, oil on canvas, sgn, 20x28", B/B 3/17/88 .... **1,760**
BERKOWITZ, Leon (American, 20th C)
Untitled 1975, acrylic on canvas, 100x74", B/B 8/10/88 OE **3,575**
BERLANT, Tony (20th C)
Queen of Clubs, mixed media, 1980, 24x24", SBY 10/5/89 .... **5,500**
Self-Portrait in Landscape, metal collage on panel, sgn/dtd 1984, 54x95", C-NY 5/4/89 .... **17,600**
BERLIN, Harry (American, 1886-)
Harvesting the Sea (fishermen in small boat), oil on canvas, sgn/dtd 09, 22x16", RAB 11/25/88 UE **250**
BERMAN, Eugene (Russian, 1899-1972)
Antique Archives, watercolor/gouache/ink on paper, initialed/dtd 1948, 10x13", SBY 10/7/89 .... **2,310**
Antique Column (Trompe l'Oeil), gray wash/watercolor on paper, initialed, 1936, 40x30", C-NY 10/6/88 OE **7,700**
Appian Summer, oil on canvas, initialed/sgn/inscr, dtd twice 1967, 39x32", C-E 6/1/88 UE **1,100**
Architectural Capriccio, brush/ink/watercolor heightened w/white gouache on board, sgn/dtd 1949, 17x12", SBY 2/14/89 .... **2,310**
Black Goat Hill, oil on canvas, initialed/dtd 1960, sgn/inscr/dtd 1960, 22x18", C-NY 3/11/88 .... **1,100**
Brutus, watercolor/pen/black ink, sgn/dtd 1964, 5x7", C-E 10/18/89 UE **440**
By the Seashore, brush/pen/Indian ink on paper, dtd 1935, C-NY 10/6/88 .... **605**
Costume Design for Nero in quo Vadis, watercolor/India ink on paper, initialed/dtd 1943, 12x10", SBY 10/7/89 .... **1,760**
Decor Design for Concerto Barocco, gouache/watercolor/India ink on paper, initialed/dtd 45, 10x12", SBY 10/7/89 .... **1,650**
Decor Design for Roma, watercolor/gouache/India ink on paper, initialed/dtd 1955, 16x22", SBY 10/7/89 .... **1,650**
Desolate Trees with Ruins in a Landscape, gouache on paper, 9x12", C-NY 10/6/88 OE **1,045**
Figure Among Ruins, pen/brush/India ink on blue paper, unfr, 13x10", C-NY 10/6/88 .... **495**
Figure with Masks, pen/black ink/ink wash heightened w/white gouache on paper, inscr, 13x9", C-NY 10/6/88 OE **1,760**

Figures Among Ruins, pen/black ink on paper, initialed/dtd 34, 13x9", C-NY 10/6/88 ... 495
Figures Before a Classical Arch, oil on canvas, sgn/dtd 1932, 36x29", SBY 2/14/89 OE ... 10,450
Figures in Ruined Arch, pen/brush/India ink on paper, unfr, 11x7", C-NY 10/6/88 OE ... 935
Fisherman with Nets, pen/black ink on paper, initialed/dtd 1934, 12x9", C-NY 10/6/88 ... 440
Five Heads, watercolor/black ink on paper laid down on board, initialed/dtd 43, 17x13", SBY 10/5/88 ... 825
Fountain, black ink/gray & brown wash/collage heightened w/white gouache on paper, initialed/dtd 49, 13x9", SBY 2/14/89 ... 1,870
Gypsy Family, watercolor/pen/black ink on yellow paper, initialed/dtd 1937, 13x10", C-NY 10/6/88 ... 1,430
L'Opera de Quatre Sous, l'Ecurie; watercolor/pen/ink on paper, initialed/dtd 1937, 11x14", C-NY 10/6/88 OE ... 1,760
Laguna Veneta (pool in landscape), gouache/watercolor on paper, initialed/dtd 1935, 9x12", C-E 6/1/89 ... 935
Landscape in Provence, pen/brown ink/brown wash on paper, sgn/dtd 1933, 20x15", SBY 10/5/88 UE ... 660
Landscape with Ruins, gouache/watercolor on paper, initialed/dtd 1960, 13x9", SBY 10/7/89 ... 1,760
Le Bon Samaritain, oil on canvas, sgn/dtd 1930, 38x31", SBY 2/14/89 ... 4,125
Little Girl, watercolor/gouache/ink on paper, initialed/dtd 1948, 9x12", SBY 10/7/89 ... 2,970
Maison d'Olivia, la Nuit des Rois; watercolor/pen/black ink on paper, titled/dtd 1938, 14x11", C-NY 10/6/88 OE ... 2,420
Neo-Romantic Landscape, gouache/watercolor/pen/black ink on paper, sgn/dtd 1937, 11x15", C-NY 10/6/88 OE ... 3,300
Nobilissima Visione, oil/India ink on canvasboard, initialed/dtd 1941, 20x16", SBY 10/7/89 ... 3,300
Padova de Prato Della Valle, oil on canvas, sgn/dtd, 27x20", SBY 2/14/89 ... 2,090
Provencal Landscape-Les Baux; pen/black ink on paper, sgn/dtd 1933, 20x15", C-NY 10/6/88 ... 550
Ruins with Volcano by the Sea, watercolor/gouache on paper, initialed/dtd 1938, 10x14", C-NY 10/6/88 OE ... 770
Seated Muse, oil on canvas, initialed/dtd 1941, 37x27", C-NY 10/6/88 UE ... 1,700
Set of 4: Ruines Romaines; brush/India ink on blue-gray paper, 6x10", C-NY 10/6/88 OE ... 1,210
Sleeping Figures in Village Street, pen/brush/India ink on violet paper, unfr, 9x13", C-NY 10/6/88 ... 550
The Little Fortune, red/gray wash/ink on paper, initialed/dtd 1942, 16x10", SBY 10/7/89 ... 1,045
Vine d'en Port de Mar en Wines (View of Seaport in Ruins), oil on canvas, sgn/dtd 1933, 24x20", C-E 10/18/89 ... 3,520
Winter, oil on canvasboard, sgn/dtd 1967, 12x16", C-E 10/18/89 ... 715

BERMAN, Leonid (Russian, 1898-1976)
Deux Pecheurs de Nazare, Portugal; oil on canvas, sgn/dtd twice, 47, wood frame, 18x26", C-NY 10/6/88 ... 6,600
Lagune Venitienne (two figures wading), oil on canvas, sgn/dtd 48, 36x28", SBY 2/14/89 ... 3,025
Mussel Gatherers, oil on canvas, sgn/dtd 38, 11x18", C-NY 6/17/89 ... 1,650
Mussel Growers, Chatelaillon; oil on canvas, sgn/dtd 50, 32x50", SBY 2/14/89 ... 1,760
Pecheurs Tirant Leur Barque (small boats at sea), oil on canvas, sgn/dtd 47, 22x31", SBY 2/14/89 UE ... 1,100
Sand Hills, oil on canvas, sgn/dtd 38, 17x39", C-NY 10/6/88 ... 5,500

BERMAN, Saul (20th C)
Hobo (man seated on crate, figures beyond), oil on canvas, sgn/dtd 1932, 21x24", C-E 6/1/89 OE ... 7,150

BERMAN, W.E. (American, 19th C)
Workhorses, oil on canvas, sgn, 23x37", B/B 12/8/88 ... 2,090

BERMUDEZ, Cundo (Cuban, 1914-)
Interior, oil on canvas, sgn, 35x24", C-NY 5/18/88 ... 4,620
La Habana Vieja (contemporary cityscape), oil on masonite, sgn/dtd 41, 21x25", C-NY 6820 OE ... 7,150
La Sobremesa (After Dinner), oil on board, sgn, 1945, 28x34", SBY 5/17/88 OE ... 31,900
Untitled (abstract w/figures), oil on canvas, sgn/dtd 76, 36x46", SBY 11/21/88 OE ... 13,200
Woman (contemporary figure in interior), oil on canvas, sgn, 30x24", SBY 11/21/88 OE ... 7,700

BERNARD, Emile (French, 1868-1941)
Auto-Portrait, oil on board laid down on panel, sgn/dtd 29, 27x21", C-NY 2/13/89 ... 3,080
Nature Morte (still life w/fruits on floral cloth), oil on board laid down on cradled panel, sgn, 22x26", C-NY 10/5/89 ... 11,000

BERNARD, Francois (French, 1814-)
Portrait of a Naval Officer (in full uniform on ship deck), oil on board, sgn/indistinctly dtd, 12x10", RAB 1/18/89 UE ... 650

BERNARD, Joseph (French, 1864-1933)
Pair: Wooing; Engagement; oil on panel, sgn, 23x15", C-E 2/21/89 ... 6,820

BERNATH, Aurel
Christmas, oil on canvas, 32x45", C-E 9/15/88 ... 935

BERNE, Sydney (Canadian, 1921-)
Farm Setting in Winter, oil on canvas, sgn, 20x24", FB 10/17/88 ... 275

BERNE-BELLECOUR, Etienne Prosper (French, 1838-1910)
Cavalryman Mending His Vest, oil on panel, sgn/dtd 1896, 15x10", RWS 5/12/89 ... 3,000
French Cavalryman Removing His Gloves, oil on panel, sgn/dtd 1903, 15x11", SBY 7/12/89 ... 2,640
L'Attaque, oil on canvas, sgn/dtd 1874, 24x41", SBY 10/24/89 OE ... 27,500
Officer of the Garde Mobile on Reconnaissance, Franco-Prussian War; oil on panel, sgn, 13x10", SBY 6/8/88 ... 2,640
Reminiscence, oil on panel, sgn/dtd 1882, 14x9", SBY 10/24/89 ... 7,150

BERNEKER, Louis Frederick (American, 1876-1937)
Garden (nymphs in a garden), oil on canvas, sgn, 24x20", RWS 9/8/89 ... 1,100
Under Brooklyn Bridge, oil on canvas, sgn, 8x10", C-NY 3/11/88 OE ... 4,180

BERNIER, Geo (Belgian, 1862-1918)
Cows Grazing in a Field, oil on panel, sgn, 9x12", B/B 12/8/88 ... 880

BERNINGHAUS, Oscar Edmund (American, 1874-1952)
Anheuser-Busch Pack Mule, oil on canvas, 53x150", C-NY 9/28/89 ... 30,800
Anheuser-Busch Wagon Train, oil on canvas, 53x218", C-NY 9/28/89 ... 19,800
Horses in Front of Kit Carson's House, oil on board, sgn, 35x40", SBY 5/25/88 ... 31,900
Indian Encampment, oil on canvas, sgn, 25x78", SBY 5/25/88 ... 15,400
Indian on Horseback, oil on canvas, indistinctly sgn, 24x30", SBY 5/25/88 ... 41,250
Indian on Horseback (in desert landscape, mountains beyond), oil on canvas, 24x30", C-NY 5/25/89 ... 38,500

Indian Village, oil on board, sgn, 8x11", SBY 6/24/88 OE	11,550
Rabbit Hunt (landscape with riders & mountains), oil on canvas, sgn, 20x25", SBY 5/24/89	27,500
Retrato de Nina con Paloma (portrait of girl w/doves in landscape), oil on canvas, sgn, 24x18", C-NY 11/21/88 OE	7,700
Stagecoach, oil on canvas, 53x161", SBY 5/25/88 UE	57,750
Stagecoach (in landscape), oil on canvas, 53x161", SBY 5/24/89	14,300
Street in Taos, oil on canvas, sgn, 22x28", SBY 5/25/88	30,800
Taos Valley Ranch (landscape), oil on canvas, sgn, 35x40", SBY 5/24/89	26,400
BERNINI, Gian Lorenzo; follower of	
Portrait of a Boy (possibly self-portrait), black/red chalk on buff paper, ca 1613-14, 7x5", SBY 1/13/89 OE	5,500
BERNSTEIN, Theresa Ferber (American, 20th C)	
Boats in a Harbor, oil on canvas, sgn, 25x29", WG 9/16/88	1,200
Coney Island, oil on board, sgn/indistinctly dtd, 14x21", SBY 9/14/89	3,080
Gloucester Harbor (cityscape w/boats & water), oil on canvas, sgn, 12x17", RWS 9/8/89	1,100
Harbor View, oil on board, sgn/dtd 20, 15x20", SBY 6/28/89	8,800
Lunch Counter at S Klein's in Union Square in the 1930s, watercolor on paper, sgn, 22x30", WD 4/13/88	2,000
New England Town: Gloucester; oil on board, sgn, 16x20", WD 4/13/88	3,800
Parisian Street Scene, oil on canvas, sgn/dtd 23, 30x37", SBY 9/23/88	7,150
Polish Village on the Russian Border, oil on board, initialed/dtd 22, 16x20", WD 4/13/88	3,000
Return of the Army, oil/graphite on board, 15x20", RWS 5/12/89	2,500
School Children, oil on board, sgn, 6x8", SBY 3/17/88 OE	4,400
School Children (abstract), oil on board, sgn, 6x8", SBY 3/17/88 OE	4,400
Sheep Meadow, Central Park, New York; oil on canvas, partially sgn, 20x25", RWS 5/12/89	3,500
Still Life of Wildflowers, oil on cardboard, sgn, 20x16", RWS 5/12/89	1,000
Street Market Scene, oil on canvas laid down on board, sgn, unfr, 23x20", C-E 6/1/88 UE	1,320
Summer, Gloucester, 1921 (detailed village landscape); oil on canvas, sgn, 27x35", RWS 5/19/88 UE	3,000
BERNT, Rudolf (Austrian, 1844-)	
Figures in Front of a Temple, watercolor on paper, sgn/dtd 1889, 14x7", C-NY 5/24/89 UE	550
BERRESFORD, Virginia (American, 1904-)	
Coral Reef (underwater view of fish & plants), watercolor on paper, sgn/dtd 45, 14x10", RAB 8/9/88 UE	150
BERRETTINI, Pietro; follower of (Italian, 1596-1669)	
Rebecca Receiving Eliezer at the Well, oil on canvas, unfr, 64x96", SBY 10/13/89 OE	15,400
BERRIO, T.	
Man Playing Violin, oil on canvas, sgn, 25x21", C-E 7/26/88	495
BERRUGUETE, Alonso; circle of	
Deposition, oil on panel, 37x37", C-NY 4/6/89	3,300
BERRY, Carroll Thayer (American, 1886-1978)	
Bath Iron Works (industrial scene w/billowing smoke), oil on canvas, sgn, 26x29", RWS 3/31/88	800
BERRY, Nathaniel L. (American, 1859-)	
Breaking Clouds Along the Shore, oil on board, sgn/dtd 1912, 6x12", RAB 11/25/88 UE	400
Marshes in Haying Time, oil on canvas, sgn, 20x30", RWS 9/29/88 UE	1,100
BERRY, Patrick Vincent (American, 1843-1914)	
Farm Scene, oil on canvas, sgn, 16x24", C-E 6/1/88	1,650
Foothills of the Blue Ridge Mountains, oil on canvas, sgn, 18x30", SBY 6/28/89	4,950
Pair: Haying Fields Before a Storm; Edge of the Field; oil on board, 10x12", RWS 5/12/89	550
Pastoral Landscape, oil on canvas, sgn, 16x24", RAB 8/8/89	1,350
Scene in Orange County (cows fording stream beside meadow), oil on canvas, sgn, 14x11", RWS 9/29/88	950
Wooded Riverbank, oil on board, sgn, unfr, 14x18", C-E 2/16/88 OE	715
BERSON, Adolph (American, 1880-1970)	
Sausalito Houseboat, oil on board, sgn, 11x9", B/B 9/15/88	358
BERTALAN, Albert (Hungarian, 20th C)	
Couple Seated Under Green Trees, oil on canvas, sgn, 26x24", MG 5/28/88	1,250
Still Life of Shells, Bottle, & Pitcher; oil on canvas, sgn, 24x29", MG 5/28/88	1,100
Street Scene, oil on canvas, sgn, 19x24", MG 5/28/88	1,150
BERTHELEMY, Antoine the younger; att (1631-1669)	
Assumption of the Virgin: Study for a Dome Decoration; oil on canvas, 25" dia, SBY 6/2/89 OE	12,100
BERTHELEMY, Jean Simon (French, 1743-1811)	
Reclining Bacchante Playing the Cymbals, oil on canvas, sgn/dtd 1778, 25x31", SBY 1/12/89 OE	181,500
BERTHELSEN, Johann (American, 1883-1969)	
Brooklyn Bridge in Snow, oil on canvasboard, sgn, 16x12", SBY 1/24/89	1,540
Central Park, sgn, 20x18", C-E 2/3/88	1,100
Central Park in Spring, oil on canvas, sgn, 16x20", SBY 3/17/88	2,530
Central Park in Winter, oil on canvasboard, sgn, 17x17", B/B 3/22/89	1,430
Chrysler Building (snowy street scene), oil on canvas, sgn, 16x12", C-E 2/1/89	1,870
Grace Church, oil on canvasboard, sgn, 8x6", C-E 2/3/88	880
Grand Central Station (snowy scene w/figures), oil on canvasboard, sgn, 18x12", SBY 3/17/88	2,090
Hansom Carriage on Fifth Avenue (street scene), oil on canvasboard, sgn, 17x17", B/B 3/22/89	1,980
Moonlight, Washington Square; oil on canvasboard, sgn, 12x9", B/B 3/17/88	2,475
New York City Street Scene in Snow, oil on canvas laid down on board, sgn, 19x15", SBY 9/14/89	1,650
New York City Street Scene in Winter, oil on canvasboard, sgn, 20x16", B/B 3/17/88	3,300
Pair: New York Winter; oil on canvasboard, sgn, 12x9", B/B 6/15/89 UE	1,870
Park Avenue at 52nd Street, oil on canvasboard, sgn, 16x12", SBY 6/28/89 OE	3,080

Plaza Hotel in Winter, oil on canvasboard, sgn, 20x16", B/B 6/15/89 ... 2,200
Plaza Square, oil on canvas, sgn, 16x12", C-E 2/3/88 ... 2,200
United Nations, oil on canvas, sgn/dtd 1964, 24x30", WD 4/13/88 ... 2,100
Vase of Flowers, oil on canvasboard, sgn, 18x14", C-E 6/1/88 ... 1,430
View of Trinity Church From Wall Street, oil on canvas, sgn, 16x13", B/B 3/17/88 ... 2,475
Wall Street, oil on canvas laid down on board, sgn, 20x18", C-E 2/3/88 ... 1,760
Washington Square at Night, oil on canvas, sgn, 20x24", WD 10/5/88 OE ... 7,250
Washington Square in Winter, oil on canvasboard, sgn, 21x17", C-E 2/1/89 ... 2,200
Washington Square Park, oil on board, sgn, 12x16", C-E 2/3/88 ... 1,210
Washington Square Park, oil on canvas, sgn, 22x28", C-E 11/30/88 ... 2,200
Winter, New York; oil on canvas laid down, sgn, 20x16", B/B 3/17/88 ... 3,025
Winter in New York, oil on canvas, sgn, 16x12", B/B 3/17/88 ... 1,760
Winter in the Park, New York City; oil on canvas, sgn, 16x12", RWS 9/8/89 UE ... 1,900
Woodland Scene, oil on panel, sgn, 8x10", RWS 3/16/89 ... 325
43rd Street at 5th Avenue in Winter (figures in snowy cityscape), oil on canvas laid down, sgn, 12x9", B/B 10/9/88 ... 2,200
5th Avenue Looking North From 23rd Street, oil on canvasboard, sgn, 12x9", B/B 3/17/88 ... 2,090

BERTHOT, Jake (American, 1939-)
Eye Arch & the River, oil on linen, sgn/dtd 81, 20x18", SBY 10/7/89 ... 5,500
October Group #4, enamel/graphite on paper, sgn/dtd 73, 30x22", C-E 5/9/89 OE ... 770
Untitled (abstract), enamel/graphite on paper, initialed/dtd 74, 21x19", C-NY 5/4/89 ... 1,100
Untitled (abstract), enamel/graphite on paper, sgn/dtd 72, 22x30", C-NY 2/20/88 ... 2,420
Untitled (abstract), enamel/pencil on paper, initialed/dtd 74, 14x16", C-E 11/14/89 OE ... 2,420
Untitled (abstract), oil on canvas mounted on wood, sgn, 1973, unfr, 36x36", C-NY 5/4/89 ... 8,250

BERTI, A.
Farmer, oil on canvas, sgn, 29x21", C-E 5/3/88 ... 440

BERTIN, Roger (French, 1915-)
Le 14 Juillet a Paris (festive gathering), oil on canvas, sgn, 21x26", WD 11/16/88 ... 4,500

BERTINIZZI, G. (Italian, 20th C)
Venice, watercolor on paper, sgn, 12x19", FAP 4/15/89 UE ... 132

BERTON, A. (British, 19th/20th C)
Taking the Fence, oil on canvas, sgn, 24x36", SBY 6/8/88 ... 1,650

BERTON, L.
Arabs on Horseback, oil on canvas, sgn, 23x32", C-E 5/23/88 ... 4,620

BERTOUNESQUE, Andre (Canadian)
Strolling Along the Beach, oil on board, sgn, 16x20", FB 10/30/89 ... 468

BERTZIK (Northern European, 19th C)
Woman Standing with a Bouquet of Flowers with Birch Forest & Village Beyond, oil on panel, sgn, 28x17", SLK 5/11/88 ... 5,000

BESCHEY, Balthasar (Flemish, 1708-1776)
Flight Into Egypt, oil on panel, 20x15", C-NY 10/20/88 ... 2,200
Lady Receiving a Visitor After the Birth of Her Child, Maids in Attendance; oil on panel, sgn, 28x34", C-NY 6/2/88 ... 16,500
Minerva Visiting the Muses, oil on panel, sgn, 25x32", C-NY 6/2/88 ... 11,000
Virgin & Child with Infant St John & Angels Gathering Fruit, oil on panel, 26x19", C-M 6/16/89 ... 12,225

BESNARD, Albert (French, 1849-1934)
Two Girls Embracing, pastel on paper laid down on canvas, sgn, 20x24", C-E 11/17/88 OE ... 4,620

BESSE, Raymond (French, 1899-)
European Street Scene, oil on canvas, sgn, 29x36", B/B 5/17/89 UE ... 412

BESSER, Arne
Ice Cream Parlor, oil on canvas, sgn, 40x30", C-NY 2/13/89 ... 1,980

BEST, Arthur W. (American, 1859-1935)
Marin Summer Landscape, oil on canvas, sgn, 14x19", B/B 10/6/88 ... 715

BEST, Hans (German, 19th/20th C)
Reading the Morning Paper, oil on board, sgn/dtd 16, 24x19", B/B 12/8/88 OE ... 4,400

BEST, Harry Cassie (American, 1863-1936)
Stand of Redwood Trees, oil on canvas, sgn, 36x18", B/B 1/11/89 ... 522

BEST, Mary Ellen (British, 1809-1891)
Royal Apartment in the Berg, Nuremberg; pencil/watercolor on paper, unfr, 11x15", SBY 2/22/89 UE ... 2,750

BETTERA, Bartolommeo; att (fl 1600)
Still Life of Two Violins, Guitar, & a Lute with Globes; oil on canvas, 25x32", SBY 6/3/88 ... 13,200

BETTS, E.F. (American, 20th C)
Cinderella, oil on canvas, sgn, 25x18", SBY 4/14/89 OE ... 6,050

BETTS, Harold Harrington (American, 1881-)
Landscape (hilly terrain w/path, stream, & cabin), oil on canvas, sgn, 32x37", LH 3/20/88 OE ... 1,700
Pueblo Scene, oil on canvas, 22x28", C-E 4/7/88 ... 605
Spanish Bayou, oil on canvas, sgn, 36x39", NA 11/5/88 ... 1,000
Wooded River Scene, oil on canvas, sgn, 26x30", LH 12/4/88 ... 800

BETTS, Louis (American, 1873-1961)
Boy in Blue, oil on canvas, sgn, 30x25", LH 10/16/88 UE ... 750
Still Life of Teakettle, Coffee Cup, & Porcelain Pitcher; oil on board, sgn, 24x20", B/B 10/9/88 ... 11,000
Turquoise Wrap (nude viewed from behind, draping herself in a wrap), oil on canvas, sgn/#d 116, 40x30", RWS 3/31/88 UE ... 3,500
Woman in a Yellow Bonnet, oil on canvas, sgn, 13x10", B/B 3/17/88 ... 4,125
Woman with Red Parasol, oil on canvas, sgn, 13x10", B/B 3/17/88 ... 5,500

BEUL, see De Beul

BEUYS, Joseph (German, 1921-1986)

Diary, March-December 1974; 35 pages of appointment calendar mounted on board, 1975, 29x49", SBY 5/2/88 OE **60,500**
Dreams, ink/rubber stamp on paper, sgn/dtd 1955, 6x8", SBY 10/5/89 ..... **9,350**
Filzwinkel am Hirschdenkmal, tempera on paper, sgn/dtd 1963/titled, 8x6", C-NY 11/10/88 ..... **12,100**
Korperstudien, graphite on paper, sgn twice/dtd 1948/inscr dedication, 13x10", C-NY 11/10/88 ..... **28,600**
Painting Version 1-90, oil/fat on Rives Buttem, torn hole on panel, sgn/titled, 37x29", C-NY 11/10/88 ..... **28,600**
Untitled (abstract), oil on paper cutout mounted on paper, sgn/dtd 1962/inscr, 28x20", SBY 5/2/88 OE **34,100**
Untitled (abstract), oil on paper mounted on paper, sgn/dtd 62/inscr, 28x20", SBY 5/2/88 OE **55,000**
Untitled (abstract), oil/photo transfer on metal-backed sheet on sheet between glass, sgn, 1978, 27x22", SBY 5/2/88 OE **63,250**
Untitled: Five Works (abstract): i; ii; iii; iv; v; chalk/photo-sensitized canvas, sgn/dtd 72, 36x36", SBY 5/2/88 OE **121,000**

BEVORT, Jean (Dutch, 20th C)

Cafe Scene, oil on panel, sgn, 15x12", B/B 1/11/89 ..... **495**
Dutch Canal in a Winter Snow, oil on canvas, sgn, 28x20", B/B 1/11/89 ..... **412**

BEYLE, Pierre Marie (French, 1838-1902)

Whaling in Newfloundland, oil on canvas, sgn/dtd 1887, 42x57", SBY 6/28/89 ..... **5,500**

BEYSCHLAG, Robert (German, 1838-1903)

Young Girl Sewing Young Boy's Back Pocket (landscape background), oil on canvas, sgn, 24x20", DM 9/16/88 OE **7,000**

BEZOMBES, Roger (French, 1913-)

Fetes a Venise, oil on plywood, sgn/inscr Paris, 26x32", SBY 10/7/89 ..... **5,775**
La Table Verte, oil/gouache on board, sgn/#d, 20x24", SBY 2/14/89 OE **2,750**
Matadors, oil on panel, sgn twice/inscr, 13x17", SBY 10/5/88 ..... **880**

BIALA, Janice (American/Russian, 20th C)

Boat on Seine (gray), oil on canvas, 1969, 35x46", RWS 9/8/89 UE **650**

BIANCHI, Pietro (Italian, 1694-1740)

Venus Discovering the Dead Adonis, oil on canvas, 53x39", C-NY 1/11/89 ..... **11,000**

BIBERSTEIN, Franz (American/Swiss 1850-1930)

Cottage in the Woods, oil on board, 12x10", B/B 12/8/88 ..... **357**
Mount Sir Donald, oil on canvas on academy board, sgn/dtd 1908, 12x16", S/A 2/18/89 ..... **300**

BIBIENA, Ferdinando; circle of (Italian, 1657-1743)

Stage Design: Fountains & a Domed Arcade; pen/brown ink/gray wash, 8x7", SBY 1/13/89 ..... **1,760**

BIBIENA, Giuseppe Galli (Italian, 1696-1756)

Interior of a Palace: Design for the Stage; pen/brown ink, eagle wm, 10x8", C-NY 1/11/89 ..... **1,650**
Monumental Stairway: Design for the Stage; pen/brown ink, 11x8", C-NY 1/11/88 ..... **1,650**

BICHARD, A.

Set of 12: Illustrations for the Adventures of Baron Munchausen; watercolor/gouache, sgn, unfr, 11x10", C-NY 2/25/88 OE **16,500**

BICHER, Alfred Thompson (American, 1837-1908)

Group of 3: Seascapes; 2 India ink on paper & 1 watercolor/ink wash on blue paper, sgn, ea 4x8", SBY 1/24/89 OE **2,475**

BICKERSTAFF, George (American, 1897-)

Majestic Mountains, oil on panel, sgn, 24x30", B/B 1/11/89 ..... **495**
Mountain Sunset, Olympic Range, Seattle, Washington; oil on canvas, sgn, 20x30", WL 5/20/88 ..... **450**

BICKFORD, Nelson Norris (American, 1846-1943)

The Tease (a cockatoo & two cats in an interior), oil on canvas, sgn, 25x20", WD 4/13/88 ..... **4,600**

BICKNELL, Albion Harris (American, 1837-1915)

Drummer & the Fife Player, oil on canvas, sgn, 15x21", SBY 6/24/88 ..... **2,860**
Flowers in a Vase, oil on canvas, sgn twice, 38x24", SBY 6/24/88 ..... **5,500**

BICKNELL, Evelyn M. (American, 1857-)

Coastal Scene, watercolor on paper, sgn, 11x17", FAP 4/15/89 ..... **192**
Harbor View, Castine, Maine; oil on canvasboard, 8x11", RWS 11/10/89 ..... **600**

BICKNELL, Frank Alfred (American, 1866-1943)

Autumn Afternoon on the River, oil on canvas, sgn/dtd 1885, 27x23", WD 4/13/88 ..... **1,200**
Bermuda, watercolor/gouache/pencil on paper, sgn/inscr, 5x9", C-E 6/1/88 OE **1,430**
Hamburg Cove, Lyme, Connecticut; oil on canvas, sgn/titled, 12x16", RWS 8/12/89 ..... **4,500**
Miss Florence Garden, oil on canvas, sgn, 16x20", C-E 11/30/88 OE **24,200**
Winter Evening, oil on masonite, sgn, 12x16", C-NY 9/30/88 ..... **3,080**

BIDDLE, George (American, 1885-1973)

Clown with the Pig, oil on masonite, sgn/dtd 1948, 20x16", C-E 11/30/88 UE **880**
Mother & Child (in landscape), oil on canvas, sgn/dtd 1915, 28x24", SBY 9/14/89 ..... **7,700**

BIDLO, Mike (American, 20th C)

Campbell's Chili Beef Soup, acrylic on canvas, sgn, unfr, 20x16", C-E 5/9/89 ..... **2,420**
Campbell's Onion Soup, acrylic on canvas, sgn, unfr, 20x16", C-E 5/9/89 OE **5,500**
Not Morandi (Natura Morta), 1939; oil on linen, sgn/dtd 1939/1985, 17x23", SBY 2/15/89 ..... **2,475**
Not Morandi (Natura Morta), 1957; oil on canvas, sgn/dtd 1957.1986, unfr, 12x17", C-E 11/14/89 ..... **2,860**
Not Morandi (Natura Morta), 1958; oil on canvas, sgn/dtd 1958/1985, unfr, 10x12", C-E 11/14/89 OE **4,620**

BIEDERMAN, James (American, 20th C)

Untitled (abstract composition), charcoal/pastel on paper, sgn/dtd July 1980, 73x18", SBY 2/15/89 ..... **4,400**

BIEDERMANN, Edward

300th Anniversary Celebration of the Founding of Jamestown, gouache/watercolor/pencil, initialed, 19x29", C-NY 9/28/89 ..... **6,600**

BIEGEL, Peter (British, 1913-)

Long Walk, Return From Ascott (a commission by the Queen); oil on canvas, sgn, 18x24", SBY 6/9/89 ..... **7,700**

BIEHLE, August F. (American, 1885-1979)
Road to Berlin Heights, gouache on paper, sgn, 17x23", WG 4/23/88 UE **1,200**
View of Berlin Heights, gouache on paper, sgn, 18x24", WG 4/23/88 UE **1,300**
BIEHN, Joseph
Young Boy Eating a Banana, oil on canvas masonite, sgn/dtd 1896, 10x7", C-E 6/1/88 .... **605**
BIELER, Andre C. (Canadian, 1896-)
Foster's Lock on the Rideau, oil on board, sgn/dtd 1979, 9x12", FB 5/28/89 .... **1,700**
Sion, watercolor, sgn/dtd 1925, 18x25", FB 5/28/89 .... **750**
BIERHALS, Otto
Penn Station, oil on masonite, sgn, 29x24", C-NY 9/30/88 .... **8,250**
BIERSTADT, Albert (American/German, 1830-1902)
Blue & Orange Butterfly, watercolor/gouache on paper, sgn/dtd Feb 23/91, unfr, 5x8", WD 4/13/88 OE **13,500**
Blue Mountain & Lake, oil on paper, 10x15", C-NY 12/2/88 UE **7,700**
Breaking Spray (coastal scene), oil on paper laid down, sgn, 13x18", C-NY 5/25/89 .... **29,700**
Butterfly, watercolor/gouache/pencil on paper laid down on board, sgn, ca 1873, 7x10", C-NY 12/2/88 OE **20,900**
Cloud Study-Mountain Tops-Lake Tahoe, California; oil on paper laid down on board, initialed, 14x19", C-NY 5/26/88 OE **30,800**
Coastal Scene, oil on paper laid down on board, sgn, 13x19", C-NY 12/2/88 .... **7,700**
Hunter in Oaks, California; oil on paper mounted on paper, sgn, 22x16", SBY 4/29/88 .... **27,500**
Landscape with Ruins, oil on paper, sgn, 8x13", SBY 9/14/89 .... **5,225**

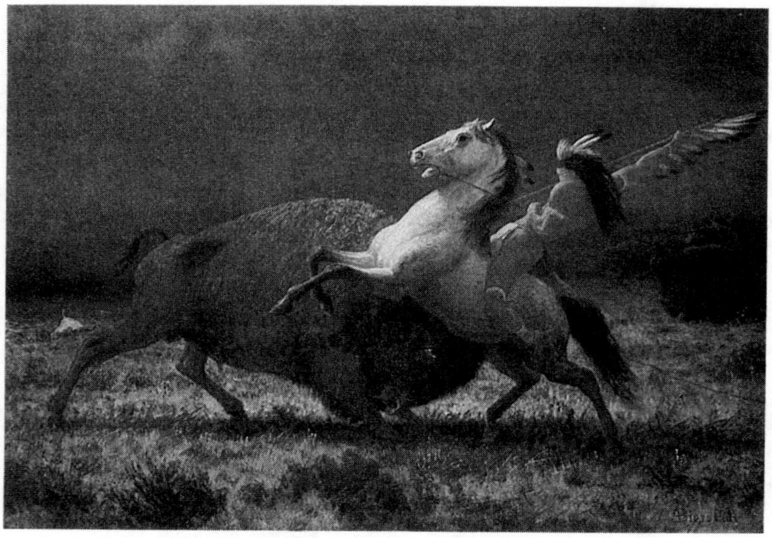

Last of the Buffalo, oil on canvas, sgn, 26x36", C-NY 5/26/88 OE, $1,870,000

Long's Peak, Estes Park, Colorado; oil on canvsa, sgn w/monogramed signature, 26x36", SBY 5/25/88 .... **82,500**
Lowing at Dusk, oil on paper laid down on canvas, initialed, 11x16", C-NY 5/26/88 OE **22,000**
Moose in the Snow, oil on paper laid down on masonite, sgn, 14x18", C-E 10/18/89 .... **3,190**
Morteratsch Glacier, Upper Engadine Valley, Pontresina; oil on canvas, sgn/dtd 1895/inscr, 72x120", SBY 5/24/89 .... **990,000**
Mount Vesuvius & the Bay of Naples, oil on paper laid down, sgn, 6x13", B/B 3/22/89 .... **12,100**
Mountain Canoeing, oil on paper laid down on canvas, initialed, 8x11", C-NY 5/25/89 OE **71,500**
New England Study Near Glen House, Thompson's Cascade; oil on paper, inscr, 12x13", C-NY 12/2/88 .... **4,400**
Peaks, Clouds, & Firs; oil on paper, 7x10", C-NY 12/2/88 .... **4,400**
Rising Mist (cows drinking in pond in a landscape), oil on canvas, sgn, 20x30", C-NY 12/2/88 .... **44,000**
Sierras at Inyo, California (extensive mountain landscape); oil on board, 14x19", B/B 10/9/88 .... **8,250**
Study for the Landing of Columbus in the Bahamas (Watkins Island), oil on paper, initialed, 14x19", C-NY 5/26/88 .... **14,300**
Sunlit Forest, oil on paper laid down on canvas, 26x19", C-NY 3/11/88 .... **46,200**
Sunset, oil on paper laid down on canvas, 8x11", C-NY 12/2/88 UE **14,300**
Sunset in the Rockies, oil on canvas, sgn/dtd 1866, 26x36", C-NY 5/25/89 .... **990,000**
Turbulent Clouds, White Mountains, New Hampshire; oil on paper, inscr, 9x11", C-NY 12/2/88 OE **13,200**
Two Ships (The Santa Maria), oil on paper mounted on masonite, sgn, 14x19", SBY 4/14/89 UE **7,150**
Upland Pasture (close-up of sheep), oil on paper laid down on canvas, initialed, ca 1855-57, 13x19", C-NY 9/28/89 .... **8,800**
Upland Pastures (landscape), oil on board, sgn, 14x19", SBY 1/24/89 .... **10,450**
Valley Floor, oil on paper laid down on board, sgn, 13x19", C-NY 5/26/88 OE **44,000**
Waterfall & Rainbow: Niagara; oil on paper laid down on board, sgn, 20x14", C-NY 5/26/88 .... **27,500**
Western Landscape at Sunset, oil on board, sgn, 7x10", SBY 5/25/88 OE **88,000**
Woodland Scene, Early Autumn; oil on paper laid down on canvas, sgn, 26x19", C-NY 5/26/88 .... **35,200**
Yosemite Valley, California; oil on board, monogramed, 14x22", SBY 5/24/89 .... **14,300**
Yosemite Valley (w/deer at water's edge), oil on paper laid down, sgn, 11x15", C-NY 5/25/89 OE **176,000**
BIERSTADT, Albert; after (American/German, 1830-1902)
Yosemite (extensive landscape), oil on canvas, 33x46", B/B 5/17/89 .... **880**
BIEVRE, see De Bievre
BIGARI, Vittorio Maria (Italian, 1692-1776)
Design for a Hanging with a Relief of a Royal Saint, chalk/pen/brown ink/brown & gray wash, 17x10", C-NY 1/11/89 OE **2,860**

Design for an Urn, black chalk/pen/brown ink/brown wash, wm encircled device, 14x10", C-NY 1/11/89 UE 1,540
Immaculate Conception, oil on canvas, oval, 23x17", SBY 10/13/89 3,850
Saint Luke Painting the Virgin & Child, oil on canvas, within painted Trompe l'Oeil arch, unfr, 24x30", SBY 1/12/89 33,000

BIGARI, Vittorio Maria; att (Italian, 1692-1776)
Antique Duel, brown ink on paper, bears signature/#d 149, 11x8", WD 1/25/89 OE 2,200

BIGELOW, Daniel Folger (American, 1823-1910)
Coastal Scene with Sailboats, oil on board, sgn, 16x24", LH 9/10/89 UE 100
Cows in a Valley, oil on canvas, sgn, 24x34", C-E 9/15/88 715

BIGG, William Redmore; att (British, 1755-1828)
Portrait of Master Worley, half-length, wearing red coat w/a yellow collar; oil on panel, 31x25", C-NY 10/25/88 8,250

BIGGI, Felice Fortunato; circle of
Putto with a Still Life of Flowers in an Overturned Basket, oil on canvas, 28x38", SBY 10/13/89 4,675

BIGGS, Walter (American, 1886-1968)
Fallen Tree (fallen white tree in a green forest), watercolor on paper, sgn/dtd 53, 21x30", RAB 8/9/88 OE 1,500
Girls in Yellow Automobile (well-dressed girls in car, girl in doorway), oil on canvas, 25x34", RAB 8/9/88 OE 6,000
Hunting Year (interior scene), oil on canvas, indistinctly sgn, 28x40", C-E 2/1/89 3,080

BIHAN, D.L. (British, fl 1850s)
Niagara Falls with City of Buffalo in Distance, oil on canvas, sgn, 30x50", SBY 9/14/89 6,050

BILCOQ, Marie Marcc Antoine (French, 1755-1838)
Pair: Figures in a Wine Cellar; Figures in a Tavern; oil on panel, sgn/dtd 1788, 9x7", C-NY 10/20/88 OE 12,100

BILIBIN, Ivan Iakovlevich (Russian, 1876-1942)
Costume Design for A Man of the People in The Tale of Tsar Sultan, watercolor/pencil/ink, 1936, 9x6", C-L 10/8/88 UE 2,420

BILIVERTI, Giovanni; att (Italian, 1576-1666)
Saint Dominic of Bologna Receiving the Rosary From the Madonna, oil on canvas, 54x43", SBY 10/21/88 3,575

BILIVERTI, Giovanni; circle of (Italian, 1576-1666)
Saint Catherine of Alexandria, oil on canvas, 28x23", SBY 4/7/88 OE 5,500

BILL, Max (Swiss, 1908-)
Lineare Farbspanning, oil on canvas, sgn/dtd 1942/49-1979, 13x13", SBY 11/9/89 OE 23,100
System of Six Similar Rows of Color Forming a Pythagorean Triangle, oil on canvas, sgn/dtd 1978, 39x39", SBY 5/2/88 OE 88,000
Transcoloration III (geometric), oil on canvas, sgn/dtd 1965-66, sgn/titled, 48x24", SBY 2/19/88 OE 14,300
Yellow Quarter (geometric composition), oil on canvas, sgn/dtd 1959, 25x25", SBY 2/15/89 OE 23,100

BILLET, Etienne (French, 1821-88)
Turkish Women by a Well, oil on panel, sgn, 19x26", SBY 10/24/89 9,350

BILLET, Pierre (French, 1837-1922)
Gleaners, oil on canvas, sgn/dtd 1881, 24x20", C-NY 5/25/88 OE 9,350

BILLINGS, Moses (19th C)
Portrait of George Canfield Bickensdorfer, oil on canvas, sgn/dtd 1857, 31x25", C-NY 1/20/89 3,850

BILLOU, Paul L. (French, 1821-)
An Afternoon Walk, oil on canvas, sgn, 20x16", WG 9/16/88 UE 400

BIMBI, Bartolommeo (Italian, 1684-1725)
Still Life of Various Fruits in a Landscape, oil on canvas, 35x46", SBY 4/7/77 OE 34,100

BIMMERMANN, Caesar (German, 19th C)
Wounded Stag (in winter landscape), oil on canvas, sgn/dtd 1889, 31x25", C-E 5/22/89 4,950

BINDER, Alois (German, 19th C)
The Toast, oil on canvas, sgn/dtd, 20x16", C-E 10/25/88 1,980

BINDER, John
Along the Coast, oil on canvas, sgn, 24x30", C-E 9/15/88 UE 330

BINET, Georges (French, 1865-1949)
Marche aux Fleurs (flower market scene), oil on canvas, sgn, 13x16", C-E 5/9/89 OE 7,480
Village au Bord d'une Riviere (landscape), oil on canvas, sgn, 12x16", C-E 5/9/89 OE 3,520

BINFORD, Julian (1908-)
San Francisco Bridge, oil on canvas, sgn, 23x25", C-E 10/18/89 3,300

BIODI, Nicola; att (Italian, 19th C)
Young Girl with Her Pet Lamb, oil on canvas, 17x22", C-E 2/21/89 2,420

BIPSHAM, Henry Collins
Farm Animals, oil on canvas, sgn, 22x36", C-E 6/1/88 880

BIRCH, Samuel John Lamorna (British, 1869-1955)
Fishing at the Old Farm, oil on canvas, sgn/dtd 1896-98, 25x34", SBY 5/23/89 13,200

BIRCH, Thomas (American, 1779-1851)
American Warships Anchored at Port Mahon, Spain; oil on panel, sgn, 16x24", B/B 3/17/88 55,000
Eagles Nest, oil on canvas, 9x19", NA 2/24/89 1,050
English Setter, oil on panel, sgn/dtd twice, 1813, unfr, 9x11", C-NY 9/30/88 3,300
Shipwreck, oil on canvas, sgn/dtd 1928, 20x28", C-NY 12/2/88 13,200
Winter Sleigh Ride (extensive landscape w/figures), oil on canvas, sgn, 20x30", C-NY 5/25/89 39,600

BIRCH, Thomas; att (American, 1779-1851)
Ships in a Harbor, oil on canvas, 20x30", SBY 4/14/89 OE 3,850

BIRCHALL, William Minshall (British, 20th C)
American Four Master (ship at sea), watercolor on paper, sgn/dtd 1924/titled, 10x15", RAB 8/1/88 1,000
Lizzie-HMS Queen Elizabeth; watercolor heightened w/white, sgn/dtd 1917, 9x12", C-E 2/23/88 440

BIRD, Edward; circle of (British, 1772-1819)
Domestic Interior, oil on panel, unfr, 17x22", C-E 5/23/88 UE 1,430

BIRDSALL, Bryon (American, 20th C)

Distant Mountains, watercolor on paper, sgn/dtd 76, 19x14", B/B 8/10/88 ... 880
EL Bartlett, watercolor on paper, sgn/dtd 1977, 20x20", B/B 8/10/88 ... 935
Forest McKinley, watercolor on paper, sgn/dtd 1977, 14x14", B/B 8/10/88 OE ... 1,430
McKinley Snow, watercolor on paper, sgn/dtd 1977, 12x19", B/B 8/10/88 ... 1,320
Melting Snows, watercolor on paper, sgn/dtd 1976, 15x15", B/B 8/10/88 ... 1,045
Midnight Passage, watercolor on paper, sgn/dtd 1977, 14x14", B/B 8/10/88 ... 990
Midnight Sun, watercolor on paper, sgn/dtd 1976, 14x20", B/B 8/10/88 ... 880
Moonlit Mountains, watercolor on paper, sgn/dtd 1976, 20x20", B/B 8/10/88 OE ... 2,200
Mountain Contrast, watercolor on paper, sgn/dtd 1977, 17x18", B/B 8/10/88 OE ... 1,870
Mountain in the Lake, watercolor on paper, sgn/dtd 1977, 29x22", B/B 8/10/88 OE ... 3,300
Mountain Slopes, watercolor on paper, sgn/dtd 1977, 16x9", B/B 8/10/88 ... 1,980
Pair: Mountain Light; Nellie Lake; watercolor on paper, sgn/dtd 1977, framed as 1 oval, 11x11", B/B 8/10/88 ... 1,210
Path Through the Forest, watercolor on paper, sgn/dtd 1976, 19x13", B/B 8/10/88 ... 935
Prince William Moon, watercolor on paper, sgn/dtd 1977, 15x15", B/B 8/10/88 OE ... 1,320
Silent Sound (island scene), watercolor on paper, sgn/dtd 1977, 12x18", B/B 8/10/88 ... 825
Snowy Landscape, watercolor on paper, sgn/dtd 1976, 20x20", B/B 8/10/88 ... 1,430
Sunlight Through the Woods, watercolor on paper, sgn/dtd 1975, 16x16", B/B 8/10/88 ... 990
Winter Scene, watercolor on paper, sgn/dtd 1976, 14x14", B/B 8/10/88 ... 990
Winter Shadows, watercolor on paper, sgn/dtd 1976, 14x20", B/B 8/10/88 ... 660

BIRNEY, William Verplanck (American, 1858-1909)

His Fortune, oil on canvas, sgn, 18x24", C-NY 11/30/88 ... 715
Story Gains in the Telling (three gentlemen in an interior), oil on canvas, sgn, 18x24", C-NY 5/25/89 ... 7,150
Watching the Ants (young girl in garden), oil on canvas, sgn, 10x8", C-NY 5/26/88 OE ... 10,450

BIROLLI, Renato (Italian, 1906-1959)

Canto Popolare Fiammingo #2, oil on canvas, sgn/dtd 1957-58,35x58", SBY 10/7/89 OE ... 34,100
Vista de una Piazza (view of town square), oil on canvas, sgn/dtd 47, 16x20", C-E 11/17/88 ... 3,520

BIRREN, Joseph Pierre (American, 1865-1933)

Chip Hill, oil on canvas, sgn, 24x27", SBY 9/14/89 ... 6,600
Patio of the Lions, Alhambra; oil on board, sgn, 16x20", LH 3/20/88 ... 475

BIRTLES, Harry (British, 1838-1907)

Figures Seated in a Doorway, oil on canvas, initialed/dtd 1871, 15x12", C-E 2/21/89 ... 880

BISCHOFF, Franz Arthur (American, 1864-1929)

California Farm, oil on board, sgn, 8x10", B/B 1/11/89 OE ... 1,210
California Forest Clearing, oil on canvas, sgn w/estate stamp, 18x24", B/B 10/6/88 ... 6,050
Canna Lillies, oil on board, sgn, 26x19", SBY 5/24/89 ... 38,500
Shadows in the Canyon, oil on board, sgn, 7x10", B/B 1/11/89 ... 1,045
Summer Days-California Woodlands; oil on canvas, sgn, 26x41", B/B 6/15/89 OE ... 24,750
View of the Arroyo Seco From the Artist's Studio (landscape), oil on canvas, sgn, 24x34", SBY 5/24/89 OE ... 34,100

BISHOF, S. (American)

Winter Scene, watercolor, 30x20", LH 12/4/88 UE ... 50

BISHOP, Isabel (American, 1902-)

Seated Nude, pen/gray wash, sgn, 8x6", SBY 9/14/89 ... 3,740
Studies of Two Girls, pen/brush/ink on paper, sgn, 14x10", C-NY 3/11/88 ... 1,650
Two Figures on a Subway, pen/brush/black ink on paper, sgn, 8x6", C-NY 6/17/89 ... 3,850

BISHOP, Richard (American, 1887-)

Canvasbacks in Alaska, oil on canvasboard, sgn/dtd 1941, 12x16", B/B 6/15/89 UE ... 1,650
Mallards in Great Bear Marsh, Utah; oil on canvasboard, sgn, 12x16", B/B 6/15/89 ... 1,760

BISON, Giuseppe Bernardino (Italian, 1762-1844)

Capriccio with Classical Buildings, pen/ink/wash over black chalk, sgn, 5x6", SBY 1/13/89 ... 1,320

BISPHAM, Henry Collins (American, 1841-1882)

Cows Resting, oil on canvas, sgn/dtd 1872, 18x32", C-E 6/1/88 ... 880
Horse Carriage, oil on canvas, sgn/dtd 1877, 24x40", C-NY 12/2/88 OE ... 16,500
Lion's Head, oil on canvas, sgn/dtd 1884, 54x64", C-E 9/15/88 ... 1,320
Man in Carriage Drawn by Two Horses, oil on canvas, sgn/dtd 1876, unfr, 25x40", SBY 6/9/89 ... 9,350

BISSCHOP, Abraham (1670-1731)

Pair: Allegories of Autumn & Summer; oil on canvas, sgn/dtd 1722, 93x64", SBY 10/13/89 OE ... 126,500

BISSCHOP, Jan; see De Bisschop

BISSELL, Kate E. (19th C)

Lemon & Lace, oil on canvas, sgn/dtd 1894, 18x22", C-E 2/3/88 OE ... 3,850

BISSI, C.S.

Dancers, oil on canvas, sgn, 19x27", LH 3/20/88 OE ... 425

BISSIER, Jules (French, 1893-1965)

A 15 Juni 62 My (abstract), watercolor on paper, sgn/dtd 1962, 5x10", SBY 2/15/89 OE ... 15,400
12 April 61 (abstract), watercolor on paper, sgn/dtd, 5x10", SBY 2/15/89 OE ... 13,200
13 Juni 65, oil on primed linen, sgn/dtd 13 Juni 65, 9x11", SBY 11/9/89 ... 30,250
13-4-58 (abstract), oil on primed linen mounted on canvas, sgn/dtd 13-4-58, 8x8", SBY 2/15/89 OE ... 22,000
17 Marz 60 (abstract), oil on primed linen, sgn/dtd 17 Marz 60, 8x9", SBY 10/5/89 ... 17,600
17 XI 60 (abstract), oil on primed linen, sgn/dtd 17 XI 60, 7x8", SBY 10/5/89 ... 20,900
19 Sept 60 (abstract w/bottle shapes), oil on primed linen, sgn/dtd 60, 18x22", SBY 2/15/89 OE ... 33,000
2 January 59, oil/tempera on linen, sgn/dtd 59/titled, 7x8", SBY 2/19/88 OE ... 11,000

25-II-60 (abstract), oil on primed linen, sgn/titled, 1960, 7x9", SBY 11/11/88 OE — 18,700
26 Dec 58 (abstract), tempera on primed linen, sgn/dtd 26 Dec 58 B, 8x9", SBY 10/8/88 OE — 15,400
28 Juni 63 (abstract), watercolor on paper, sgn/dtd 28 June 63, 10x12", C-NY 5/4/89 OE — 14,300
29.8.57, oil/tempera on canvas, sgn/titled, 7x7", C-NY 11/10/88 OE — 10,450
30 Oct 63 (abstract), watercolor on paper, sgn/dtd 30 Oct 63, 9x12", C-NY 5/4/89 OE — 14,300
4 Juni 58 (abstract), oil on primed linen mounted on canvas, sgn/dtd, 7x9", SBY 2/15/89 OE — 22,000

BISSON, Lucienne (European, 20th C)
Spring Blossoms, oil on canvas, sgn, 21x29", C-E 9/15/88 — 880
View From a Garden Wall, oil on canvas, sgn, unfr, 20x24", C-E 9/15/88 — 880

BISTTRAM, Emil (American, 1895-1976)
Abstract, watercolor on paper, sgn/dtd 58, 30x22", C-NY 5/26/88 — 2,750
City Patterns (abstract), oil on canvas, sgn/dtd 60, 45x40", C-NY 9/30/88 — 4,620
Composition No 18, oil on masonite, sgn/dtd 63/titled, 32x39", SBY 3/17/88 — 3,025
Flamenco, oil/enamel on canvas, sgn/dtd 60, 40x25", C-NY 3/11/88 — 3,300
Flight into the Subtle World (contemporary), oil on canvas, sgn/dtd 61, 48x36", SBY 3/17/88 — 2,750
Nude (cubistic sketch), pencil on paper, unfr, 17x12", C-NY 9/28/89 — 1,210

BITTAR, Pierre (French School)
Harbor Pointe at Harbor Springs From Bluff Overlooking the Bay, no media given, sgn, 22x26", DM 9/16/88 — 6,500

BITTINGER, Charles (20th C)
Lamp (woman holding fan), oil on canvas laid down on board, sgn/dtd 1911, 32x25", C-NY 5/26/88 — 4,400

BITZOL (19th C)
After the Bath (nude towelling dry), oil on masonite, sgn, 30x23", WG 4/23/88 — 350

BIU, Hing
Interior, acrylic on canvas, 36x48", C-E 11/14/89 — 440

BIVA, Henri (French, 1848-1928)
Verdant Landscape, oil on canvas, sgn, 51x44", SBY 5/23/89 — 22,000

BIXBEE, William Johnson (American, 1850-1921)
On the Swift River, Tamworth, New Hampshire; oil on canvas, sgn, 20x16", RAB 8/9/88 — 800
Rocky Coast, watercolor on paper, sgn, 14x20", RAB 3/27/89 UE — 225
Smoky Weather, Tamworth, New Hampshire; oil on board, sgn, 11x15", RAB 8/9/88 OE — 1,900

BIZZELLI, Giovanni (1556-1612)
Saint Apollonia, oil on canvas, 26x20", SBY 6/3/88 — 8,800
SS Gregory, Romuald, & Blaise; pen/brown ink/wash on paper, 11x10", SBY 1/13/89 — 4,400

BLAAS, see Von Blaas

BLACHE, Christian Vigilius (Danish, 1838-1920)
Shipping Off the Coast, oil on canvas, sgn/dtd 1902, C-E 10/25/88 — 2,200

BLACK, La Verne Nelson (American, 1887-1938)
Indian on Horseback, oil on canvas, sgn, 14x14", SBY 6/24/88 — 7,150

BLACK, Mae (American, 1932-)
Desert Dune, oil on canvasboard, sgn, 9x11", B/B 1/11/89 — 192

BLACK, Olive Parker (American, 1868-1948)
Cattle Watering in a Summer Landscape, oil on board, sgn, 10x12", SBY 6/28/89 — 935
Green Pasture, oil on canvas, sgn, 16x24", WL 5/20/88 — 3,300
New England Stream, Early Autumn; oil on canvas, sgn, 16x24", RWS 11/3/88 — 2,100
Pond Before a Farm, Spring; oil on canvas, sgn, 16x24", RWS 5/12/89 OE — 2,100
Summer Landscape, oil on canvas, sgn, 16x24", C-NY 9/30/88 — 2,200
Summer Landscape, oil on canvas, sgn, 24x30", SBY 6/24/88 — 5,500
Summer Landscape with River, oil on canvas, sgn, 20x30", SBY 9/23/88 — 3,300

BLACKMAN, Walter (American, 1847-1928)
Sailing, oil on canvas, 14x22", C-E 6/1/89 — 1,210
Woman with a Jug, oil on canvas, sgn, 54x37", C-E 6/1/89 — 3,850

BLAINE, Nell (American, 1922-)
Stone Oven & Settee, oil on canvas, sgn, 20x27", C-E 11/14/89 — 2,860
Woods at Saratoga, watercolor on paper, sgn/dtd 9.14.62, 12x16", SBY 10/7/89 — 660

BLAIR-BRUCE, William (Canadian, 1859-1906)
Bulldogs, oil on canvas, sgn/dtd 1903, 30x36", SBY 6/9/89 — 4,125

BLAKE, George
St Andrew Gold Course, watercolor/pencil on paper, sgn/dtd 20, 13x18", C-E 9/15/88 — 286

BLAKE, Leo B. (American, 1887-)
Vermont Church Scene, oil on canvas, sgn, 24x20", LH 10/16/88 OE — 3,500
Vermont Covered Bridge, Winter, with Team of Horses...; oil on canvas, sgn, 25x30", S/A 2/18/89 — 3,000

BLAKE, Thomas C. (American, 20th C)
Mountain Landscape, oil on canvas, sgn, 28x38", LH 9/10/89 UE — 150

BLAKELEY, Dudley Moore
Croton Reservoir, New York's Water Supply; oil on canvas, sgn/dtd 1933, 14x18", C-E 11/30/88 — 880

BLAKELOCK, Ralph Albert (American, 1847-1919)
Autumn Landscape, oil on canvas, sgn, 16x24", SBY 3/17/88 — 8,800
Enchanted Pool (night view w/moon shining through trees on pond), oil on canvas, sgn, 29x36", SBY 5/24/89 — 49,500
Evening Landscape, oil on canvas, sgn w/arrowhead insignia, 16x24", SBY 9/14/89 — 6,600
Forest Scene with Figure, oil on board, sgn, ca 1882, 7x4", C-NY 3/11/88 — 3,850
Golden Sunset, no media given, 17x24", SBY 6/28/89 — 2,750

Indian Seated by Wigwam, oil on panel, initialed, 7x10", NA 10/1/88 800
Landscape with Figures by a Lake, oil on canvas, sgn, 10x15", SBY 3/17/88 1,650
Landscape with Indians, oil on canvas, sgn, 20x30", C-E 10/18/89 2,860
Moonlight, oil on panel, sgn, 14x20", LH 12/4/88 UE 1,200
Pioneer Home, oil on canvas, sgn twice/titled, 17x33", SBY 1/24/89 5,500
Silvery Moon, oil on board, bears signature, 18x24", C-E 1/12/88 UE 1,430
Sunset Beyond the Woods, oil on panel, sgn, 8x10", B/B 1/11/89 1,540
Valley & Stream, oil on canvas, sgn, 5x7", C-NY 3/11/88 2,420

BLAKELOCK, Ralph Albert; att (American, 1847-1919)
Emerald Pool, oil on canvas, 16x24", SBY 6/24/88 1,210
Indian Encampment, oil on canvas, bears signature, 20x30", B/B 1/11/89 3,575
Indian Encampment in a Landscape, oil on canvas laid down on masonite, sgn, 22x27", SBY 6/28/89 1,650
Indian Encampment in the Moonlight, oil on canvas, 17x22", S/A 3/12/88 1,343
Sunset Landscape with Indians, oil on panel, sgn w/artist's arrowhead insignia, 10x14", SBY 6/24/88 1,980

BLANCH, Arnold (American, 1896-1968)
Harbour Town, gouache on board, sgn, ca 1952, 13x17", C-E 2/1/89 440
Nude Reading the Newspaper, oil on canvas, sgn, 15x22", C-E 11/30/88 1,650
Outside the City, oil on canvas, sgn, 22x36", RWS 9/8/89 OE 2,200

BLANCHARD, Antoine (French, 1910-)
Avenue de l'Opera a Paris (street scene), oil on canvas, sgn/titled, 13x18", C-E 5/9/89 OE 5,500
Champs Elysee, oil on canvas, sgn, 20x24", MG 10/28/88 2,000
Pair: L'Arc de Triomphe; Rue de Rivoli; oil on canvas, sgn, 13x18", SBY 10/7/89 7,700
Paris (people & carriages, city lights reflecting on wet streets), oil on canvas, sgn, 20x24", RAB 8/9/88 2,100
Paris Boulevard Scene, oil on canvas, sgn, 24x20", B/B 12/8/88 OE 2,750
Paris Street Scene, oil on board, sgn, 11x14", FAP 4/15/89 660
Paris Street Scene, oil on canvas, sgn, 13x18", LH 5/15/88 OE 1,300
Paris Street Scene, oil on canvas, sgn, 13x18", RAB 3/27/89 UE 1,300
Paris Street Scene, oil on canvas, sgn, 18x21", LH 5/15/88 OE 2,000
Paris Street Scene, oil on canvas, sgn, 20x24", DM 5/13/88 OE 2,250
Paris Street Scene, oil on canvas, sgn, 20x24", DM 9/16/88 OE 3,250
Paris Street Scene, oil on canvas, sgn, 24x30", DM 9/16/88 OE 3,500
Porte Saint Denis, oil on canvas, sgn, 18x22", B/B 12/8/88 3,025
Rue de Paris, oil on canvas, sgn, 20x24", MG 10/28/88 2,100
Rue de Paris, oil on canvas, sgn/inscr, 13x18", C-E 11/17/88 2,090
View of Notre Dame, oil on canvas, sgn, 18x22", B/B 12/8/88 1,870

BLANCHARD, Emile
Connecticut Landscape, oil on board, sgn, 12x15", C-E 9/15/88 UE 220

BLANCHARD, Jacques; school of (French, 17th C)
Gentleman in Brown Doublet & White Ruff Collar, oil on canvas, 22x17", RWS 5/19/88 2,300

BLANCHARD, Remy (20th C)
Untitled (stag head), acrylic/tempera/fabric on board, sgn/dtd 81, 23x30", C-E 5/9/89 715

BLANCHE, Jacques Emile (French, 1861-1942)
Miss Elsa Maxwell's Party Showing Lady Peel at the Right, oil on canvas, sgn, 32x39", C-NY 5/24/89 OE 40,700
Pivoines (floral still life), oil on canvas, sgn, 36x29", SBY 10/24/89 55,000
Rialto Bridge, pastel on canvas, sgn, 20x25", C-NY 5/24/89 OE 15,400
Still Life of Pink & White Peonies, oil on canvas, sgn/dtd 97, 31x27", C-NY 5/24/89 OE 24,200

BLANCO, Dionisio (20th C)
Images of Planters Before the False Mirror, oil on canvas, sgn/dtd 88/inscr Santo Domingo, 30x40", SBY 11/21/88 3,575
Sembralor con Pose de Espantajo (field hand posed as scarecrow), oil on canvas, sgn/dtd 89/titled, 41x30", SBY 5/16/89 2,200
Untitled (planters in misty landscape), oil on canvas, sgn/dtd 88, 40x30", SBY 5/16/89 UE 1,650

BLANES, Juan Luis
Uruguayan Gaucho (in a landscape), oil on canvas, sgn, 8x6", C-SK 11/10/88 1,120

BLANEY, Dwight (American, 1865-1944)
Over the Hills & Far Away (trees & snowy slopes), watercolor on paper, sgn/dtd 1923, 14x20", RWS 3/31/88 600

BLARENBERGHE, see Van Blarenberghe

BLAS, G.
Woman with a Basket of Flowers, oil on panel, sgn/inscr, 18x13", C-E 2/23/88 1,210

BLASHFIELD, Edwin Howland (American, 1848-1936)
Indian Maiden, charcoal/white chalk, sgn, 36x24", C-NY 9/30/88 2,860
Pensive, red conte crayon on paper laid down on board, sgn/inscr, 28x21", C-NY 9/30/88 2,200
Pipers in Ancient Rome, oil on canvas, sgn/dtd 1880, 37x26", WD 3/23/88 4,000

BLASS, Eugene; see De Blass

BLATAS, Arbit (American, 1909-)
Paris Autumn, oil on canvas, sgn, 21x32", C-E 2/1/89 1,650
Still Life (flowers & objects), oil on canvas, sgn, C-E 6/1/88 1,320
Still Life with Pomegranates, oil on canvas, sgn, 22x26", SBY 10/7/89 1,760

BLAUVELT, Charles F. (American, 1824-1900)
Foot Bath (boy bathing feet in landscape), oil on canvas, sgn, 27x22", SBY 9/14/89 2,310
Still Life of Apples & Grapes, oil on canvas, sgn/dtd 1856, 12x14", B/B 3/22/89 1,870
Studying Hard, oil on canvas, sgn, 12x9", C-NY 9/30/88 2,200

BLAZEBY, J. (British, 19th C)
Red Ox & a Roan Ox, oil on canvas, sgn/dtd 1868, C-E 5/22/89 ... 3,300
BLECKNER, Ross (American, 20th C)
Fence (abstract), oil on canvas, sgn/dtd 1985, 20x16", C-NY 5/4/89 OE ... 46,200
Not Being Born (abstract), watercolor on paper, sgn/dtd 1987, 16x12", SBY 10/5/89 ... 12,100

One Wish, oil on canvas, sgn/inscr/dtd 1986, unfr, 48x40", C-NY 5/3/88 OE, $187,000

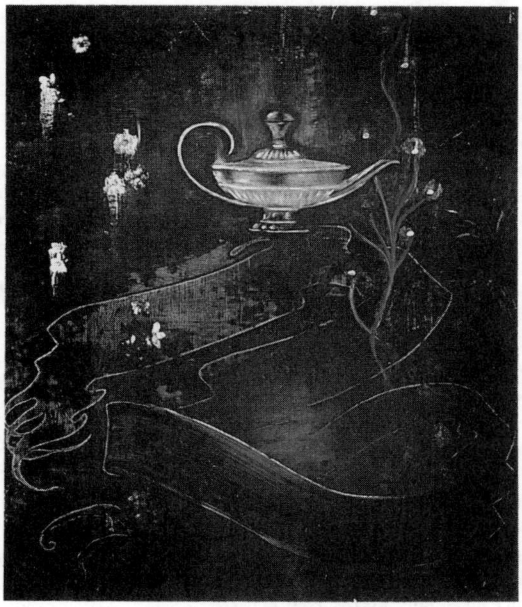

Place's: Elsewhere (abstract); acrylic on canvas, sgn/inscr/dtd 1974, unfr, 65x69", C-NY 5/4/88 ... 8,800
Recurring Triangle (hummingbird & flowers), oil on linen, sgn/dtd 1987/titled, 48x40", SBY 11/11/88 ... 88,000
Study for Brother's Swords (vertical lineation), oil on canvas, sgn/dtd 1986, 26x26", SBY 5/3/89 ... 33,000
Sun (abstract), acrylic on canvas, sgn/inscr/dtd 1982, unfr, 76x64", C-NY 11/9/88 ... 66,000
Untitled (abstract), oil/charcoal on paper, sgn/dtd 75, 38x22", C-NY 2/20/88 ... 3,520
Untitled (abstract), watercolor on paper, sgn/dtd 12/87, 16x12", C-NY 5/4/89 OE ... 12,100
Untitled (contemporary), oil/crayon on canvas, sgn/dtd 2/1976, 20x16", C-NY 2/20/88 ... 3,300
X-Friends (abstract), oil on canvas, sgn/dtd 1985, 18x14", SBY 2/15/89 ... 23,100
BLEENER, Carle J. (American, 1864-1952)
French Begonias, oil on canvas, sgn twice/titled/inscr, 20x24", SBY 3/17/88 ... 4,675
BLEKER, Dirck (1622-1672)
Fortune Teller, oil on canvas, sgn/dtd 1647, 53x43", SBY 10/21/88 ... 34,100
BLENNER, Carle John (American, 1864-1952)
Bouquet of Pansies (bust-length portrait of woman w/flowers), oil on canvas, sgn, 20x24", RWS 5/19/88 ... 1,000
Irises, Peonies, & Daffodils in an Ornate Vase; oil on canvas, sgn, 30x25", WD 5/5/88 ... 2,300
Looking Glass, oil on canvas, sgn, 24x20", C-NY 6/26/88 ... 11,000
Midsummer's Bounty (floral still life), oil on canvas, sgn, 30x59", C-NY 5/26/88 ... 9,350
Pair: Glimpse of the Ocean at Nantucket; Summer Haystacks; oil on board, sgn/inscr, 8x10", SBY 3/17/88 ... 1,870
Portrait of a Lady, oil on panel, sgn, 12x10", B/B 3/17/88 ... 1,100
Purple Dress (portrait of a young woman), oil on panel, sgn, 10x8", C-E 10/18/89 ... 715
Ready To Swim, oil on canvas, sgn, 25x35", C-NY 9/30/88 ... 5,500
Still Life of Peonies & Iris, oil on canvas, sgn, 30x25", C-NY 9/30/88 UE ... 5,500
Study of Sunlight (haystacks in field in late afternoon sun), oil on canvas, sgn, 11x16", RWS 3/31/88 ... 1,200
Yellow & Purple Iris in a Vase, oil on canvas, sgn, 25x36", C-E 2/16/88 ... 1,210
Young Woman with a Rose in Her Hair, oil on panel, indistinctly sgn, 10x8", SBY 4/14/89 ... 1,320
Young Woman with Roses (bust-length portrait), oil on artist board, sgn, 10x14", RWS 5/19/88 OE ... 2,100
BLENT, C. (American, 19th C)
Country Mill, oil on canvas, sgn, 30x50", NA 2/6/88 ... 4,250
BLEULER, Johann Heinrich (Swiss, 1758-1823)
Battle on a Bridge Over a Chasm, watercolor/gouache/pen/brown ink, sgn/inscr, 16x22", C-NY 10/26/88 OE ... 4,950
BLEULER, Louis (Swiss, 19th C)
Swiss View, gouache on paper, inscr, 20x28", SBY 6/8/88 ... 3,190
View of Coblence, gouache, sgn, inscr twice, 16x22", C-NY 10/26/88 OE ... 3,080
BLEUMNER, Oscar F. (American, 1867-1938)
Family Affair (street scene), watercolor/pencil on paper, monogramed/dtd 12, 7x9", RWS 5/19/88 UE ... 1,000
Fowl Play (chickens in yard, farmhouse beyond), watercolor/pencil on paper, monogramed, 9x11", RWS 5/19/88 UE ... 1,000
BLINKS, Thomas (British, 1860-1912)
Ancient Britons (portrait of six dogs), oil on canvas, sgn, 18x28", SBY 6/9/89 OE ... 20,900
Hunting Scene (two spaniels in a wooded area), oil on canvas, sgn/dtd 90, 20x30", DM 10/14/88 ... 11,000
Over the Hedge (fox hunt scene), oil on canvas, sgn/dtd 91, 14x18", C-NY 5/24/89 OE ... 13,200

Steady (two setters on point), oil on canvas, sgn/dtd 01, 14x19", SBY 6/9/89 OE 25,300
Two Pointers on a Moor, oil on canvas, sgn, 16x20", SBY 6/10/88 7,700
Ware Away, The Cattistock (fox hunt scene); sgn, 10x14", C-NY 5/24/89 7,150

BLISS, C.W. (American, 19th/20th C)
Summer Landscape with Figures & Water, oil on academy board, sgn, 11x14", S/A 2/18/89 300

BLOCH, Alexandre (French, 19th/20th C)
Soldier with Bicycle, oil on board, sgn/dtd 1898, 10x6", SBY 6/8/88 UE 880

BLOCH, Julius Thiengen (American, 1888-1966)
Dispossessed Farmer, oil on canvas, sgn, 48x36", C-E 6/1/89 UE 1,045
Woman in a Mauve Dress, oil on canvas, sgn, 16x12", FAP 4/15/89 1,100

BLOCK, Eugenius; see De Block

BLOCK, J.
Blowing Bubbles, oil on canvas, 20x14", C-E 4/7/88 660

BLOEMAERT, Abraham (Dutch, 1564-1651)
Double-Sided: Studies of Head of Bearded Man; Studies of Putti; red chalk/verso: black/red chalk, 11x8", SBY 1/13/89 18,700
Farm & Church by a River, pen/brown ink w/later gray/colored wash heightened w/white, ink fr lines, 6x11", C-NY 1/12/88 2,420

BLOEMAERT, Abraham; circle of (Dutch, 1564-1651)
Annunciation to the Shepherds, oil on metal, 17x14", SBY 4/7/88 4,400

BLOEMEN, see Van Bloemen

BLOM, Gustav Vilhelm (Danish, 1853-)
Candlelight Dance, oil on canvas, initialed/dtd 1886, 48x70", WD 5/5/88 3,600

BLOMFIELD, Charles (British, 1848-1926)
Pair: Otukapuarangi (Pink Terrace); Te Tarata (White Terrace); oil on canvas, 20x30", C-SK 5/25/89 11,940

BLOMMERS, Bernardus Johannes (Dutch, 1845-1914)
Domestic Interior, watercolor/gouache heightened w/white on paper, sgn, 12x15", SBY 6/8/88 OE 8,525

BLONDEL, Merry Joseph (French, 1781-1853)
Antiigone Washing the Body of Polynices, oil on canvas, bears David signature/indistinctly sgn, 62x77", C-NY 5/31/89 OE 39,600
Minerva & Neptune Contesting Before Jupiter, oil on board, sgn, 12x17", LH 10/16/88 1,800

BLONDIN, Charles (French, 20th C)
Provincial Flower Market, oil on canvas, sgn, 13x18", B/B 1/11/89 550

BLOODGOOD, Morris (American, 20th C)
Sun-Lit Mist, oil on panel, sgn/dtd 1947, 16x20", WG 9/16/88 UE 175

BLOOM, Hyman (American, 1913-)
Chandelier II, oil on canvas, 1945, 72x42", SBY 9/23/88 8,800
Dissolving (abstract), oil on canvas, initialed/dtd 74, 32x69", SBY 9/23/88 UE 1,320
Older Jew with Torah, oil on canvas laid down on masonite, 42x32", SBY 6/24/88 OE 12,100
Rabbi, gouache/ink on paper, 19x17", SBY 9/23/88 1,760
Waterfall II, ink/gouache on paper, initialed, 22x17", SBY 9/23/88 UE 550

BLOOMER, Hiram Reynolds (American, 1845-1910)
At Barbazon (landscape), oil on canvas, sgn/dtd 1878, unfr, 15x12", C-SK 5/25/89 920
Sierra Lake Landscape, watercolor on paper, sgn, 6x10", B/B 1/11/89 248

BLOOMERS, Bernardus Johannes (Dutch, 1845-)
Mother & Child (on path in landscape), oil on canvas, sgn, 27x23", PHL 10/28/88 OE 26,000

BLOOMFIELD, Harry (British, 19th/20th C)
Floral Still Life of Yellow & Crimson Dahlias, oil on board, sgn, 26x20", SBY 10/7/89 2,420

BLOWER, David (American, 20th C)
Fishing on Jumba Beach, watercolor on paper, sgn, 14x21", B/B 12/8/88 1,210

BLUEMNER, Oscar Florianus (American, 1867-1938)
#1, Bloomfield, NJ (willow, cottage & fields in sketched landscape); pencil on tan paper, monogramed, 5x6", RWS 9/29/88 325
Boat House, Branch Brook Park (sketch for painting); charcoal on paper, monogramed/inscr, 5x6", RWS 11/3/88 275
Copper Mill, Soho (foliage & industrial buildings in landscape); charcoal on paper, monogramed, 5x6", RWS 9/29/88 400
Double-Sided: Seated Female Nude; Alpine Winter Landscape; watercolor, monogramed, 23x14", PHL 6/16/88 500
East 182nd Street, Bronx, New York; colored crayon on paper, sgn/dtd June 13-10, 5x6", SBY 6/28/89 UE 1,100
Pair: Patterson, New Jersey; Irvington, New Jersey; charcoal/pencil on paper, dtd 18 & 20, 5x7"; 3x6", C-E 6/1/89 1,430
Riverhead (landscape w/dwelling fence, trees), watercolor on paper, monogramed/dtd July 18-03, 10x7", SBY 9/14/89 1,430
Soho (Silverdale), New Jersey; pencil on paper, sgn/dtd Nov 10-14, 5x7", SBY 6/28/89 UE 825
Space Motivė, a New Jersey Valley; charcoal/graphite on paper laid down on board, 1918, 31x41", C-NY 9/28/89 OE 52,800
View of Bloomfield, conte crayon on paper, monogramed/dtd Jan 8-17/#d 5P S, 5x6", SBY 9/14/89 522

BLUHM, Norman (American, 1920-)
Crow's Nest, oil on canvas, sgn/dtd 65 twice, inscr, 51x38", C-E 5/13/88 OE 4,400
Untitled, acrylic on canvas, sgn/dtd 60 twice, unstretched, C-E 5/13/88 2,420
Untitled (abstract), acrylic on canvas, sgn/dtd 74, 24x36", C-E 11/14/89 OE 3,520
Untitled (abstract), oil on canvas, sgn/dtd 53, 36x20", SBY 2/14/89 3,850

BLUM, Edith C. (American, fl 1930s)
Pink Blouse (bust-length portrait), oil on canvas, sgn, 22x18", SBY 6/28/89 1,320

BLUM, Maurice (French, 1832-)
Friendly Dispute, oil on panel, sgn, 10x13", WD 3/23/88 UE 450

BLUM, Robert Frederick (American, 1857-1903)
Flora de Stephano (shoulder-length portrait), pencil on paper, sgn, 21x10", SBY 6/28/89 3,410
Japanese Lady (full-length portrait), colored ink/watercolor on board, sgn, 17x9", SBY 6/28/89 UE 2,750
Japanese Lady (shoulder-length portrait), colored ink/watercolor on board, sgn, 17x9", SBY 6/28/89 UE 2,750

Lantern (Oriental lady w/stringed instrument by hanging lantern), watercolor on paper, sgn, 13x9", WL 5/20/88 OE 3,500
Portrait of Flora de Stephano, pastel on paper, sgn, 18" dia, SBY 5/24/89 44,000
Repose, pastel on paper, monogramed signature, 10x12", SBY 5/25/88 55,000
San Marco, watercolor on paper, sgn/inscr/dtd V88, 10x13", C-NY 12/2/88 11,000
Still Life of Fruit & Objects, watercolor on paper, sgn, 14x21", C-E 2/3/88 605
Woman with a Pink Bow (portrait), watercolor/gouache/pencil on paper, sgn, 18x14", B/B 6/15/89 44,000

LUM-SIEBERT, Ludwig (German, 1853-)
Farm Scene with Woman & Child Feeding Geese, oil on canvas, sgn, 24x20", SLK 5/11/88 6,250

LUME, Edmund (British, 1844-)
The Confession, oil on canvas, sgn, 99x70", B/B 3/17/88 3,575

LUME, Peter (American, 1906-)
Edge of Ravine, charcoal on paper, sgn/dtd 1938, 15x12", SBY 9/14/89 3,080
Toadstools, pencil on paper laid down on paper, sgn/dtd 1938, 11x11", SBY 9/14/89 2,860

LUNT, John S.; att (American, 1798-1835)
Mother Wearing a White Mantle with Little Girl & Infant Boy, oil on canvas, 26x20", SBY 4/29/88 28,600

LYTHE, David Gilmour (American, 1815-1865)
Hideout (five characters in an interior), oil on canvas, sgn, 22x27", C-NY 5/25/89 60,500

OARDMAN, William (American, 1825-1865)
Hudson River Landscape, oil on canvas, sgn, 33x49", C-NY 9/28/89 5,500

OBAK, Bruno Joseph (Canadian, 1923-)
Afternoon Shadows, oil on canvas, sgn/dtd 1980, 22x30", FB 5/28/89 3,000
Wild Flowers, watercolor, sgn/dtd 76, 22x15", WAD 6/12/89 550

OCCARD, Baron E.
Still Life with Flowers, oil on canvas, sgn, 20x12", FB 4/25/88 180

OCCHI, Faustino; circle of (Italian, 1659-1742)
Pair, Fantasies of Animal: Who Eats More Than Us; Who Has a More Beautiful Voice...; oil, inscr, 35x47", SBY 1/12/89 30,800

OCCHI, Faustino; follower of (Italian, 1659-1742)
Scene with Various Demons & the Temptation of Saint Anthony, graphite/pen/ink/colored washes, 18x24", SBY 12/9/88 OE 2,530

OCHNER, Mel (American, 1940-)
Probe (abstract), oil on canvas, 1985, 88x56", SBY 5/3/88 19,800

OCK, Frederick William (American, 1876)
Fishing Shed, Algoma, Wisconsin; oil on board, sgn, no size given, SBY 9/14/89 2,420

OCK, Theophile; see De Bock

OCKLIN, Arnold; after (Swiss, 1827-1901)
Der Heilige Hain, oil on canvas, 39x63", SBY, 6/8/88 OE 9,900

ODDINGTON, att
Fisherman on the Bank of a River in an Extensive Landscape, oil on canvas, 12x20", C-E 11/8/88 UE 650

ODDINGTON, Edwin (English, 19th C)
On the River Trent, oil on canvas, sgn, 17x31", MG 7/30/88 UE 350

ODDINGTON, Henry John (British, 1811-1865)
Along a Country Lane, oil on canvas, 23x32", SBY 10/24/89 7,700
View of Norton Hall, Near Daventry, North Hamptonshire, England; oil on canvas, sgn/dtd 1848, 30x25", C-NY 5/24/89 9,350

ODEMAN, Willem (Dutch, 1806-1880)
Cattle Watering in a Rural Landscape, oil on canvas, sgn, 24x32", SBY 2/22/89 4,400

ODIN, A. (19th C)
Elegant Lady in an Interior (full-length), oil on canvas, sgn, 20x15", C-E 2/21/89 1,870

ODINE, W.A. (American, 20th C)
Head of Man (cubistic school), pastel, sgn, 20x14", S/A 2/18/89 75

ODLEY, Josselin (French, 20th C)
Basque Church in the Snow, oil on canvas, sgn/dtd 34, 20x15", B/B 8/10/88 715

OEH, H. (English, 19th C)
Sunlit Landscape with a Boy & Dog Standing Beside a Stream, oil on canvas, sgn/dtd 1892, 20x30", SLK 9/27/88 850

OEHME, Karl Theodor (German, 1866-)
Waves Crashing on the Shore, oil on canvas laid down, sgn/dtd 1902, 16x21", B/B 3/17/88 2,200

OEHNER, Alexander (European, 20th C)
Untitled, garden urn w/flowers in landscape, oil on canvas, 34x33", SLK 11/25/88 750

OEL, Pieter (Flemish, 1622-1674)
Floral Still Life with a Parrot, oil on canvas, sgn, 36x49", SBY 4/7/88 28,600

OEMM, Ritta (Dutch, 1868-?)
Still Life of Roses, watercolor, sgn, 20x16", NA 11/5/88 375
Two Dolls, oil on canvas, sgn, 24x21", C-E 5/23/88 UE 660
Two Dolls Holding Flowers, oil on canvas, sgn, 20x16", C-E 11/8/88 UE 200
Two Dolls Holding Hands, oil on canvas, sgn, 20x16", C-E 11/8/88 UE 300

OERNER, Edward A. (American, 20th C)
Figure, watercolor/ink, sgn, 12x5", S/A 2/18/89 45
Judgment of Paris, watercolor/pen/ink, sgn, 10x13", S/A 2/18/89 30
Nostalgia No 3, casein, sgn, 8x10", 2/18/89 45
Nude Seated, oil on masonite, sgn, 24x24", S/A 2/18/89 325

OERS, Marianne (20th C)
Foil 8 (still life of foil boxes), watercolor on paper, sgn/dtd 1973/titled, 23x30", SBY 11/11/88 OE 2,750

BOESEN, Johannes (Danish, 1847-1916)
View of Horsens Fiord, oil on canvas, monogramed, 12x17", B /B 1/11/89 880
Wooded Stream, oil on canvas, sgn, 25x19", C-E 2/23/88........ 1,980

BOEUFF, see Le Boeuff

BOEVER, see De Boever

BOGDANI, Jakob (Hungarian, 1660-1724)
Exotic Birds in a Forest, oil on canvas, 27x51", SBY 6/3/88 11,000
Melons, Grapes, Peaches & Plums, with Parakeets, on a Ledge; oil on canvas, indistinctly sgn, 24x20", C-NY 1/15/88........ 35,000
Melons & Other Fruit on a Table, with a Flask of Wine; oil on canvas, 23x27", C-NY 1/15/88 OE 10,450
Peaches, Grapes, a Melon, Jug, Roemer & Plant on a Table, Draped with a Rug; oil on canvas, 50x40", C-NY 4/8/88 OE 38,500
Still Life of Tulips, Roses, Morning-Glory, & Other Flowers in an Elaborate Vase...; oil on canvas, 33x27", SBY 6/2/89 57,750

BOGDANOV-BJELSKY, Nikolai Petrowitch (Russian, 1868-1945)
By Lantern Light, oil on canvas, sgn/#d 10, 30x25", SBY 12/9/88 OE 8,800

BOGDANY, Jakob; att (Hungarian, 1660-1724)
Fruit on a Silver Plate..., Filbert & Flowers on a Ledge; oil on canvas, bears Ruysch signature, 30x25", C-NY 5/31/89 28,600

BOGERT, George Hirst (American, 1864-1923)
Grand Canal, Venice; oil on canvas, sgn, 22x29", LH 10/16/88 UE 450
Red Sails, oil on artist board, sgn, 12x9", NA 5/13/89 850
Venetian Sunset, oil on canvas, sgn, 28x40", B/B 8/10/88 990
Venice Harbor Scene, oil on canvas, inscr XXX Bogert, 28x40", C-E 9/15/88 935

BOGGIO, Emilio (French, 1857-1920)
Etude de Pommier en Fleur (blossoming apple tree), oil on canvas, sgn/dtd 1915/titled, 15x18", C-NY 11/21/88 8,800
La Moisson (landscape), oil on panel, sgn, 6x14", C-NY 5/18/88........ 2,860
Portrait of Madame Dupnis, oil on canvas, sgn/titled/#d 332, ca 1913-14, 57x47", C-NY 5/17/89 OE 28,600

BOGGS, Frank (American/French, 1855-1926)
Espalion, oil on board, sgn, 15x18", SBY 9/23/88........ 2,200
Gloucester Harbor, watercolor/charcoal on paper, 14x20", C-E 6/1/88 OE........ 2,420
Honfleur, oil on canvas, sgn/inscr/dtd 1898, 13x18", C-NY 9/30/88 5,500
Les Quais de la Seine (The Banks of the Siene), oil on canvas, sgn, 24x29", C-NY 12/2/88 28,600
Louvre & the Arc du Caroussel, oil on canvas, sgn/inscr, 24x29", C-NY 5/26/88 11,000
Pair: Le Moulin de la Galette; Marche aux Fleurs a la Conciergerie; oil on canvas, sgn, 48x22", C-NY 5/25/89........ 33,000
Paris Street Scene, watercolor/pencil on paper, sgn, 13x10", C-E 6/1/89 715
Parisian Boulevard (busy street scene), oil on panel, sgn, 13x16", WD 10/5/88 UE 3,200
River Traffic at Greenwich, oil on canvas, sgn/inscr, 11x16", C-NY 5/25/89 OE 8,800
Sailing on the High Seas, oil on canvas, sgn, 10x12", B/B 3/17/88 3,025
Steam Tug with Sailing Ship Under Tow, oil on canvas, sgn, 26x20", SBY 4/14/89 UE 3,080

BOGH, Carl Henrik (Danish, 1827-1893)
Pigs & Magpies in a Farmyard, pencil/watercolor on paper, sgn/dtd 1877, 8x11", SBY 6/9/89 3,300
Pigs in a Pen After a Meal, oil on canvas, sgn/dtd 1873, 16x21", SBY 6/10/88 OE 13,200
Sunny Farmyard, oil on canvas, sgn/dtd 1877, 17x22", SBY 6/9/89 13,200

BOHDE, George W.
Chased by Indians, oil on canvas, sgn/dtd 1878, 27x40", WG 9/16/88........ 1,000

BOHM, Max (American, 1868-1923)
Raising of Lazarus, oil on board, sgn, 14x10", B/B 6/15/89 UE 550

BOHM, Pal (Hungarian, 1839-1905)
Marketplace, oil on cradled panel, sgn, 13x19", C-E 10/25/88 OE 2,860

BOHROD, Aaron (American, 1907-)
Blue Roses & Peanut Birds, oil on panel, sgn, 5x7", S/A 2/18/89 1,500
Canadian Oil Derrick, gouache on paper, sgn, 18x14", B/B 8/10/88........ 1,045
Chicago Tenements, pen/ink/watercolor/pastel on paper laid down on board, 8x12", C-E 4/7/88 440
Chicago Tenements, watercolor/gouache on paper, sgn/dtd 31, 15x13", B/B 8/10/88 990
Circus People, oil on board, sgn/dtd 34, 36x48", LH 12/4/88 UE........ 7,000
Drunk (man passed out on street), oil on board, sgn, 11x15", C-NY 9/30/88 2,750
Female Nude, gouache on paper, sgn, 13x9", B/B 9/15/88........ 605
Peaceable Kingdom, oil on masonite, sgn, 18x24", SBY 6/28/89 6,600
Peas in a Pod, oil on masonite, sgn, 10x14", SBY 9/23/88........ 2,530
Portrait of a Man Wearing Glasses, watercolor/gouache/pen on paper, sgn, 16x12", C-E 6/1/88 770
Seven Beauties, oil on masonite, sgn, 1978, 26x34", SBY 6/28/89 7,700
South of the Loop (view of poor neighborhood), gouache on board, sgn, 12x16", C-E 6/1/89 OE 6,600
Three or Four Nudes, oil on board, sgn, 16x12", SBY 4/14/89 UE........ 1,430
Valley, gouache on paper laid down on board, sgn, 15x20", C-E 11/30/88 1,320
Winter Landscape by Moonlight (buildings, skating figures), oil on masonite, sgn, 19x30", SBY 6/28/89 5,500

BOICHARD, Jean Alcide Henri; att (French, 1817-?)
Fitting (girl & seamstress in an interior), oil on panel, sgn, 19x26", RWS 5/12/89........ 2,800

BOILLY, Jules Leopold (French, 1796-1874)
Portrait of Anna Demenynch, nee Simon; black/colored chalk, sgn/dtd 1835, oval, 14x11", C-NY 10/26/88 880
Portrait of Camille Jean Baptiste Corot, brown wash over pencil, sgn/inscr/dtd 1822, 9x6", C-NY 5/25/88 OE........ 11,000

BOILLY, Jules Leopold; att (French, 1796-1874)
Portrait of Natis, bust-length; black chalk heightened w/white chalk, inscr, 11x8", C-NY 2/23/89 UE 1,100

BOILLY, Louis Leopold (French, 1761-1845)
Portrait of a Lady, oil on canvas, 8x6", SBY 10/24/89 7,150

Scullery Maid Playing with a Cat, oil on panel, sgn, 11x8", SBY 1/12/89 33,000
Young Woman at Her Toilet, no media given, 24x18", C-M 6/16/89 32,600
OILLY, Louis Leopold; circle of (French, 1761-1845)
Billiard Players (many figures in an interior), oil on canvas, 22x32", SBY 6/1/89 UE 30,800
OIS, see Du Bois
OISROND, Francois (20th C)
Untitled (abstract), gouache/oil on canvas, sgn/dtd 83, unstretched, 85x52", C-E 5/13/88 OE 2,860
Untitled (contemporary), acrylic on canvas, sgn/dtd 83, 60x99", C-NY 2/14/89 2,310
Untitled (contemporary), acrylic/tempera on newsprint, sgn/dtd 81, 20x26", C-E 5/9/89 OE........ 1,100
OISSIER, Gaston Maurice Emile (French, 18th/20th C)
Promenade des Anglais (beach scene), oil on canvas, sgn, 38x77", C-NY 2/23/89 35,200
OIT, Edward Darley (American, 1840-1916)
Early Morning Seascape, watercolor on paper, sgn/dtd 93, 10x14", RAB 8/8/89 UE........ 450
Garden Path, watercolor on paper, sgn/dtd 1911, 14x20", RWS 5/19/88 1,100
OITARD, Francois; att (French, 1670-1716)
Triumph of Amphitrite, pen/brown ink/brown/gray wash, inscr, 10x16", C-NY 1/12/88 OE........ 1,430
OIZARD, C.U. (American, 19th/20th C)
Circus Parade, oil on canvas, sgn, 20x30", DM 9/16/88 1,600
Country Store (gathering around a potbellied stove), oil on canvas, sgn, 20x30", DM 9/16/88 1,500
OL, Ferdinand; att (Dutch, 1616-1680)
Baron General Menno Van Coehoorn (three-quarter length portrait), oil on canvas, 46x37", B/B 3/22/89 5,500
Portrait of a Man, seated at a table; oil on canvas, sgn/inscr/dtd 1659, bearing a coat-of-arms, 39x32", SBY 6/3/88 OE........ 23,100
OL, Ferdinand; manner of (Dutch, 1616-1680)
Man Playing Flute, oil on canvas, 28x25", SBY 7/12/89 2,750
OL, Ferdinand; school of (Dutch, 1616-1680)
Portrait of a Gentleman, bust-length, wearing a black coat & hat; oil on canvas, 26x21", C-NY 4/6/89 OE 4,180
OLAND, Charles (Continental, 19th C)
Good Friends (horse & pup), oil on canvas, sgn, 24x30", SBY 6/9/89 OE 18,700
OLDINI, Giovanni (Italian, 1842-1931)
Le Lavandaie, oil on panel, sgn/dtd 74, 13x20", C-NY 2/25/88........ 715,000
On the Terrace, watercolor on paper, sgn/dtd 1905, 17x11", SBY 5/23/89 OE 57,750
Portrait of Josefina Errazuriz Holding a Cat, oil on canvas, sgn/dtd 1910, 74x42", C-NY 5/25/88 352,000
Summer Stroll (elegant lady in landscape), oil on canvas, sgn, 22x14", C-NY 2/23/89 1,650,000
OLDUC, Blanche (Canadian, 1907-)
Bataille d'Oreillers, oil on board, sgn, 12x20", FB 5/28/89 600
Chapelet en Famille Apres Souper, oil on board, sgn, 12x20", FB 5/28/89 850
Grand-Pere Amuse son Petit-Fils, oil on board, sgn, 12x16", FB 5/28/89 OE 750
Hacher, Tabac pour Providion d'Hiver; oil on board, sgn, 14x21", FB 5/28/89 850
Lavage a Braie St Paul, oil on board, sgn, 15x15", FB 5/28/89 500
Lecture de Testament, oil on board, sgn, 13x21", FB 5/28/89 600
Magasin General, oil on board, sgn, 10x22", FB 5/28/89........ 950
Priere de Mois de Mai a la Croix du Chemin, oil on board, sgn, 11x19", FB 5/28/89 OE........ 1,100
Procession Fete-Dieu (festival of Corpus Christi); oil on board, sgn, 14x32", FB 5/18/89 UE 500
Repos du Midi, la Saison des Foins; oil on board, initialed, 9x14", FB 5/28/89 800
Visite du Cure dans le Salon, oil on board, sgn, 11x19", FB 5/28/89 OE........ 1,100
OLDUC, Yvonne (Canadian, 1905-)
Winter Village Scene, oil on board, sgn/dtd 1935, 16x30", FB 10/17/88 1,500
OLE, Jeanne (French, fl 1870-83)
L'Enfant au Bilboquet, oil on canvas, sgn, 39x24", SBY 10/24/89 OE........ 17,600
OLIN, Alex (19th C)
Still Life of Peonies, Pansies, & White Hyacinths; oil on canvas, sgn/inscr/dtd 1894, 39x26", C-E 2/23/88 2,310
OLINGER, Franz Joseph (American, 20th Century)
Hurricane Weather (bending palm trees), oil on canvas, sgn/dtd 27 XIII, 42x50", SBY 6/28/89 2,420
ologlnese or Roman School (ca 1700)
Holy Family (Mary & Joseph w/Christ Child in portrait), oil on canvas, 26x30", SBY 4/7/89 11,000
olognese School (16th C)
Flight into Egypt, oil on canvas, 22x33", SBY 10/13/89........ 4,125
Holy Family with Saint Catherine, oil on panel, 26x21", C-NY 4/6/89 OE........ 8,800
Holy Family with Saint John the Baptist & a Donor, oil on panel, 24x20", SBY 4/7/88 OE........ 6,600
Mystic Marriage of Saint Catherine with Saints Francis of Assissi & Joseph, oil on panel, 20x15", SBY 4/7/89........ 9,350
Portrait of a Lady, oil on canvas, 37x27", SBY 7/12/89 2,750
Portrait of an Elderly Man, Probably Meant To Be a Prophet of the Old Testament; oil on canvas, 36x29", SBY 10/13/89........ 6,050
olognese School (17th C)
Angel Playing a Lute, black chalk/stumping w/touches of white chalk on gray paper, 8x25", SBY 1/13/89 OE........ 16,500
Annunciation to the Shepherds, chalk/pen/ink/wash on brown arched paper, loss in corners, 22x15", C-NY 1/11/89 OE 24,200
Christ Mocked, black chalk/pen/brown ink, 4x6", C-NY 1/12/88........ 385
Ecce Homo, red chalk squared in black chalk, encircled bird wm, 14x8", C-NY 1/11/89 715
Head of a Man, oil on canvas, 18x18", SBY 7/12/89 OE........ 8,800
Head of a Youth with a Garland of Fruit on His Head, black chalk heightened w/white on buff paper, 16x14", SBY 1/13/89........ 46,750
Last Supper, black chalk/pen/brown ink/brown wash on gray paper, 13x20", C-NY 1/11/89 1,430
Madonna & Child with Saint Francis, oil on canvas, 30x24", WD 10/19/88 OE 10,500

Madonna & Child with Saints Francis & Claire, oil on copper, 14x11", C-NY 4/6/89 1,540
Mocking of Christ, oil on canvas, oval, 29x25", SBY 4/7/88 2,475

Bolognese School (18th C)
Education of the Virgin, oil on canvas, 30x25", SBY 6/8/88 UE 385
Pair: Moses Drawing Water From the Rock; Israelites Gathering the Manna; oil on canvas, 42x58", SBY 10/13/89 10,450
Pair: Prophet Elijah Fed By Ravens; Saint Jerome in the Wilderness; oil on copper, 12x10", SBY 10/21/88 1,320
Saint Among Plague Victims, pen/brown ink/brown wash heightened w/white on slate preparation, 12x14", C-NY 1/12/88 1,870

BOLOTOWSKY, Ilya (American, 1907-)
Blue Horizontal (geometric composition), oil on wood panel, initialed/dtd 68, 6x13", SBY 2/15/89 OE 7,700
Double Red Tondo (red circle w/verticle lines), oil on canvas, sgn/dtd 70, 47" dia, SBY 5/3/89 OE 19,800
Horizontal Tondo, acrylic on canvas, sgn/dtd 64, unfr, 32" dia, C-NY 5/4/88 7,150
Miniature Black, Red, & White Diamond (geometric composition); acrylic on wood panel, sgn/dtd 71, 11x11", SBY 2/15/89 OE 7,150
Red Tondo, oil on wood, sgn/dtd 81, 9" dia, SBY 10/5/89 OE 8,800
Red Tondo, 1971 (geometric composition); acrylic on wood panel, sgn/dtd 71, 8", SBY 2/15/89 OE 7,150
Rhomb in Reds & Blue (abstract), acrylic on wood, sgn/dtd 1975, 16x9", C-NY 2/14/89 OE 4,620
Scarlet Diamond (geometric abstract), acrylic on canvas, sgn twice/dtd 1981 twice/titled, 42x42", SBY 2/19/88 13,750
Single Line Tondo (geometric composition), acrylic on canvas, sgn/dtd 71, 32", SBY 2/15/89 8,250
Small Diamond (geometric composition), oil on wood panel, initialed/dtd 69, 8x8", SBY 2/15/89 OE 7,700
Small Horizontal Lines, oil on canvas, sgn/dtd 64-65, 12x24", SBY 5/3/89 OE 8,800
Tondo in Red & Yellow (lineation in circle), acrylic on canvas, 1974, 39" dia, SBY 11/11/88 OE 12,100
Untitled (lines within a circle), oil on canvas, sgn/dtd 70, unfr, 31" dia, C-E 11/14/89 4,400
Variation in Red, Diamond; acrylic on canvas, sgn/dtd 74, 63x63", C-NY 10/4/89 OE 18,700
Vertical Ellipse, Blue, Red, & White; acrylic on canvas, sgn/dtd 1972, 51x36", SBY 10/5/89 17,600
White Horizontal with Blue, Red, & Yellow; acrylic on canvas, sgn/dtd 73, 30x65", SBY 10/5/89 17,600
Yellow Tondo (geometric composition), oil on wood, sgn/dtd 81, 9", SBY 2/15/89 OE 7,150

BOLTRAFFIO Giovanni Antonia (Italian, 1467-1516)
Virgin & Child, oil on panel, 24x18", SBY 6/1/89 121,000

BOMBERG, David (British, 1890-1957)
Palestine Restoration Fund Poster (a study), watercolor/gouache/pencil, inscr, 1923, 15x10", SBY 5/30/89 7,150

BOMBLED, Charles (French, 1862-1927)
Northwind, watercolor, sgn, 10x22", MG 5/28/88 1,300

BOMBOIS, Camille (French, 1883-1970)
Afternoon by the River, oil on cradled panel, sgn, 5x7", SBY 10/5/88 3,575
Au Bord de la Riviere (landscape), oil on panel, sgn, 3x4", C-E 5/9/89 OE 3,520
Bessy-sur-Cure, oil on canvas, sgn/titled, 6x9", C-E 5/9/89 9,020
Bouquet de Fleurs (still life), oil on cradled panel, sgn, 7x5", C-E 5/9/89 6,600
Charlie Chaplin, oil on canvas, sgn, 15x18", WD 5/5/88 OE 14,000
Chatillon-sur-Seine (village scene on the Siene), oil on canvas, sgn/dtd 1959, 40x32", C-NY 5/11/89 OE 121,000
Infants dans le Bois, oil on board, sgn, 8x11", WD 11/16/88 3,000
L'Eglise et l'Armancon a Cheny, Yonne (river landscape w/figures & church); oil on canvas, sgn, 11x16", C-NY 10/5/89 OE 24,200
La Marne a Gournay (figure fishing from bank, bridge in distance), oil on canvas, sgn, 6x9", C-NY 10/5/89 10,450
La Route Pres du Bois (road between house & forest w/figures), oil on canvas, sgn, 1930, 26x36", C-NY 2/18/88 19,800
Le Canal de Bourgogne (w/man fishing), oil on canvas, sgn, 18x15", C-NY 2/16/89 OE 28,600
Le Lac, oil on canvas, sgn, 8x11", SBY 2/16/89 OE 23,100
Les Laumes-Telesia et le Pont Romain (bridge, building & figure in a landscape); oil on panel, sgn, 6x10", C-E 5/9/89 9,020
Les Lavandieres (river landscape w/washerwoman on shore, figure in boat), oil on canvas, sgn, 11x14", C-NY 10/5/89 27,500
Les Pecheurs (fishermen in boat by shore), oil on canvas, sgn, 24x22", WD 11/16/89 24,000
Quiet Street, oil on canvas, sgn, 18x25", WD 11/16/88 71,000
Scene de Village, oil on canvas, sgn, 32x26", C-NY 2/18/88 19,800

BOMPARD, Maurice (French, 1857-1936)
Gondolas on a Venetian Canal, oil on canvas, sgn, 22x18", B/B 3/17/88 3,300
Rue de Montagne, oil on canvas, sgn, 22x18", C-E 3/22/88 UE 330

BOMPIANI, Augusto (Italian, 1852-1930)
Good Counsel, watercolor on paper, sgn/inscr, 21x14", SBY 6/8/88 UE 770
Italian Boys at a Fountain, watercolor, sgn, 22x15", C-NY 5/25/88 2,420
Pair: Young Girl & Boy; watercolor on paper, sgn/inscr, 22x14", 20x14", SBY 6/8/88 UE 605

BOMPIANI, Roberto (Italian, 1821-1908)
Minstrel, oil on canvas, sgn, 25x20", RWS 11/10/89 1,100
Roman Woman Adorning the Bust of Her Father, oil on canvas, sgn/dtd 1876, 31x15", SBY 2/22/89 5,500

BONANOMI
La Sorlie de l'Eglise, oil on canvas, sgn, 32x40", C-E 6/28/88 UE 55

BONAVIA, Carlo (Italian, 1740-1756)
View of a Rocky Mediterranean Coastline with Fishermen Casting Their Nets into a Stormy Sea, oil, 29x38", SBY 1/12/89 11,000

BONAVIA, Carlo; circle of (Italian, 1740-1756)
Pair: Coastal Landscapes with Shipping; oil on canvas, 15x20", C-NY 6/2/88 7,700

BONAY, M.
Vase of Flowers, oil on canvas, sgn, 29x36", GAI 6/17/89 50

BONE, Muirhead (British, 1876-1953)
Clyde Near Dalmarimode, pencil on paper, sgn/titled, 6x8", C-E 9/15/88 385
Night, Morningside Park, New York; charcoal, sgn/titled on mat, 14x11", C-E 9/15/88 495
Winter Near Aylmerton, Norfolk; charcoal/chalk on paper, sgn, 11x16", C-E 2/21/89 UE 440

BONECHI, Matteo (ca 1672-after 1754)
Allegory of Justice & Prudence, oil on canvas, unfr, 12x10", SBY 10/13/89 2,750
Assumption of San Gaetano, oil on canvas, 29x23", C-NY 1/15/88 6,600

BONEVARDI, Marcelo (Argentinian, 1929-)
Painting 33-1959 (abstract), oil on canvas, sgn/dtd 1959, 32x25", C-NY 5/18/88 2,420
Sky Watcher (contemporary), burlap/wood construction, sgn/dtd 65/titled, 30x46", SBY 5/16/89 9,350

BONFILS, Gaston (French, 19th Century)
At the Antique Shop (three gentlemen in interior), oil on canvas, sgn, 26x32", WF 11/16/88 UE 1,900

BONHEUR, Juliette Peyrol (French, 1830-1891)
Sheep in a Summer Landscape, oil on canvas, sgn, 16x28", SBY 7/12/89 2,200

BONHEUR, Rosa (French, 1822-1899)
Doe & Fawn in a Thicket, oil on canvas, sgn/dtd 68, 26x23", SBY 2/22/88 17,600
Horses in a Landscape, oil on panel, sgn, 10x16", C-NY 2/25/88 OE 11,000
Stag in a Landscape, oil on cradled panel, sgn/dtd 1897, 9x7", SBY 6/9/89 4,400
Study of an Ox, watercolor heightened w/gum Arabic & white, sgn, 14x10", C-NY 5/25/88 1,430
Two Stags in a Clearing in Winter, oil on canvas, sgn/stamp w/Vente seal, 18x15", C-NY 5/25/88 OE 10,120

BONHEUR, Rosa; att (French, 1822-1899)
Horses in a Landscape, oil on canvas, bears signature, 17x28", C-E 2/23/88 1,650

BONHOMME, Leon (French, 1870-1924)
Nu au Canape, watercolor/chalk on paper, sgn/dtd 1919, 4x5", C-E 5/9/89 OE 1,870

BONINGTON, Richard Parkes; manner of
Ayr Bridges, oil on canvas, 18x24", SBY 7/12/89 UE 550

BONITO, Giuseppe (Italian, 1707-1789)
Musical Party (group in an interior), oil on canvas, 41x61", SBY 6/1/89 352,000
Pair: Companion Portraits of a Man & Lady (possibly Eleonora Palma); oil on canvas oval, 40x30", C-NY 1/11/89 48,400

BONNAR, James King (American, 1885-1961)
At the Docks (lobster pots on dock, boats tied up, water & village beyond), oil on canvas, sgn, 16x20", RAB 8/9/88 UE 300
Group of 3: East Gloucester; Gloucester Boats; Winter in New England; 2 watercolor/1 gouache, ca 9x11", RWS 3/16/89 OE 1,200
North Shore Village (village with tree-lined street & white clapboard buildings), oil on board, sgn, 16x20", RAB 8/9/88 375
Old Wharf, East Gloucester; oil on canvasboard, sgn, 20x24", RWS 3/16/89 OE 1,500
Old Wharf at East Gloucester, oil on canvasboard, sgn, 20x24", RWS 3/16/89 OE 900
So This Is Vermont, oil on canvas, sgn/inscr, 25x30", SBY 9/23/88 2,860
Vermont Farm, oil on canvas, sgn, 25x30", RWS 9/8/89 800

BONNARD, Pierre (French, 1867-1947)
Apres la Repas (artist's wife, Martha, setting a table), oil on canvas, sgn, 1925, 46x44", C-NY 11/14/88 OE 7,480,000
Avant le Depart, Champ de Courses (horse racing scene); oil on panel, sgn/dtd 94, 10x13", C-NY 11/16/88 264,000
B: Study for Abecedaire; pen/chalk on paper, stamped initials/inscr B, 7x7", SBY 10/5/88 1,980
Bord de Seine a Vernon (Shores of the Seine at Vernon), oil on canvas, ca 1916, 8x12", SBY 5/10/89 52,250
Double-Sided: Boat; Still Life; India ink/gray wash on paper, initialed, unfr, 9x8", SBY 2/14/89 4,675
Double-Sided: Etude pour 'Les Demoilelles Natanson'; charcoal on buff paper, stamped initials, 9x11", C-NY 2/18/88 1,870
Double-Sided: Nude Studies; ink on paper, stamped initials, 6x4", SBY 10/5/88 935
Enfant et Chats (child w/cats in interior), oil on canvas, sgn, ca 1906, 25x18", C-NY 11/14/88 OE 825,000
Femme Brune au Collier Blanc Devant un Radiateur, oil on canvas, stamped signature, ca 1920, 25x21", SBY 11/11/88 495,000
Femme dans sa Baignoire (woman bathing in tub), pencil on paper, sgn, 1941, 13x10", SBY 11/12/88 OE 30,800
Femme et Bebe, pencil/black ink on paper, stamped initials, ca 1893, 6x10", SBY 10/5/88 1,100
Femme Mettant ses Bas (lady putting on stockings), oil on paper laid down on canvas, sgn, ca 1908, 26x19", SBY 5/9/89 550,000
Femme Nue a la Chaise (nude woman on a chair), oil on canvas, stamped signature, ca 1917, 31x18", SBY 11/11/88 880,000
Femme Nue Debout (sketch of standing nude), pencil on paper, stamped signature, 20x12", SBY 5/10/89 35,200
Fleurs, pencil on paper, stamped initials, 5x4", SBY 10/5/88 605
Fleurs sur une Cheminee (floral still life), oil on canvas, sgn, 1913, 32x21", C-NY 11/14/88 OE 913,000
Jeune Femme au Torse Denude (study of young woman w/nude torso), oil on board, 1892, 11x9", C-NY 10/5/89 OE 50,600
Jeune Fille et Chien (sketch of girl & dog), pencil on canvas, ca 1947, 19x23", SBY 5/10/89 17,600
Jeunes Femmes au Jardin (young woman in garden), oil on canvas, stamped signature, 1918, 36x41", SBY 11/12/88 OE 319,000
L'Eglise dans la Vallee, oil on cradled panel, stamped, ca 1915, 9x11", SBY 5/11/88 OE 99,000
La Mer, watercolor/gouache/pencil on paper, stamped signature, 5x6", SBY 11/12/88 22,000
La Seine a Vernon, watercolor/pencil on paper laid down on canvas, ca 1920s, 13x10", SBY 11/12/88 30,250
La Toilette, watercolor on thin buff paper, ca 1930s, 11x9", SBY 2/18/88 4,400
Landscape, pencil/white gouache on paper, stamped initials, 5x6", SBY 10/5/88 OE 2,750
Le Bebe, watercolor/wash/India ink/pencil on thin paper backed with paper, ca 1892, 9x7", SBY 11/2/88 OE 30,800
Le Boeuf et l'Enfant, oil on canvas, sgn, 1946, 37x47", SBY 5/11/88 OE 341,000
Le Bouquet de Roses, oil on canvas, sgn, ca 1936, 14x12", SBY 5/11/88 OE 214,500
Le Cannet (landscape), pastel/watercolor/pencil on paper mounted on canvas, 10x13", SBY 5/11/88 OE 187,000
Le Cheval (sketch of a horse & figures), brush/ink over pencil on paper, 1892, 10x9", SBY 5/10/89 OE 18,700
Le Mer (seascape), watercolor/pastel on paper mounted on canvas, ca 1944, 11x10", SBY 5/11/88 OE 170,500
Le Toit Rouge (landscape w/view of red roof), oil on canvas, stamped signature, 1894, 13x20", C-NY 5/11/89 242,000
Les Fraises (The Strawberries), oil on canvas, sgn, 1910, 25x20", SBY 11/11/88 715,000
Mi-Careme, charcoal on paper, 13x10", SBY 10/5/88 OE 2,750
Nature Morte aux Fruits dans le Soleil (still life), oil on canvas, ca 1931, 13x24", SBY 5/9/89 OE 1,815,000
Pair: Landscape; Study of Woman in Profile; pencil on buff paper, initialed, 5x7", C-E 11/17/88 1,100
Pair: Still Life on a Table; Harbor Scene; pencil on paper, stamped initials, 4x5", 6x5", SBY 2/14/89 OE 4,675
Par la Fenetre-Pelotes de Couleur sur Table, crayon/pencil, stamped signature, ca 1938-46, 13x18", SBY 10/7/88 OE 44,000

Paysage, watercolor/pencil on paper, stamped signature, 5x6", SBY 2/16/89 ..... **14,850**
Paysage aux Arbres Verts, oil on cradled panel, stamped, ca 1921, 15x18", SBY 5/11/88 OE **88,000**
Paysage de Cagnes, oil on canvas, sgn, 1916, 14x17", SBY 5/11/88 ..... **170,500**
Petite Nature Morte, pencil on paper, stamped initials, 6x4", SBY 10/5/88 OE **1,430**
Portrait d'Andree Bonnard, oil on canvas, stamped, 1890, 32x18", 32x18", SBY 5/11/88 OE **407,000**

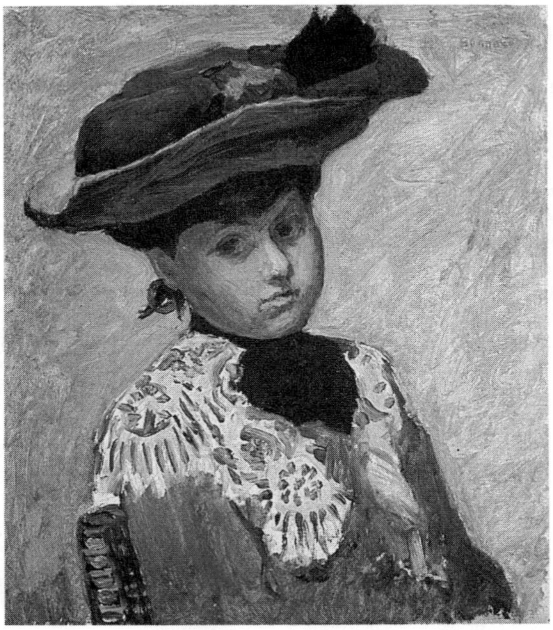

Portrait de Jeune Femme, oil on canvas on board, sgn, ca 1905, 19x16", C-NY 11/14/88 OE, $528,000

Portrait de Vivette Terrasse (young girl reading book), oil on canvas, sgn, ca 1906, 14x13", SBY 5/10/89 OE **341,000**
Races, pencil on paper, stamped initials, 4x3", SBY 10/5/88 ..... **715**
Still Life on a Table, pencil on paper, stamped initials, 4x5", SBY 10/5/88 ..... **1,540**
Tete d'Homme (head study of a man wearing a cap, facing left), ink/pencil on paper, studio stamp, 5x8", WG 10/19/88 OE **1,800**
Through a Window (Rough Sketch), oil on canvas, sgn, 1910, 27x12", SBY 5/10/89 OE **242,000**
Vue du Cannet, oil on cradled panel, stamped, ca 1943, 19x16", SBY 5/11/88 OE **352,000**

BONNAT, Leon Joseph Florentin (French, 1834-1922)
Jeune Fille Italienne (three-quarter length portrait), oil on canvas, sgn/indistinctly dtd, 37x28", SBY 2/22/89 ..... **8,800**
Mother & Daughter (portrait), oil on canvas, sgn/dtd 1905, 57x45", C-NY 2/23/89 ..... **17,600**

BONNEMAISON, see De Bonnemaison

BONNER, L.K. (American, 20th C)
Mustang Round-Up, oil on canvas, sgn, 36x47", WG 4/23/88 UE **600**

BONNET, Franz; see De Bonnet

BONNY, James (European, 19th C)
Feeding Chickens by a River, oil on canvas, sgn, 20x30", C-E 2/23/88 OE **1,540**

BONONE, Carlo; att (Italian, 1569-1632)
Holy Family with the Infant Saint John the Baptist, oil on canvas, unfr, 20x16", SBY 1/12/89 OE **17,600**

BONTECOU, Lee (American, 1931-)
Untitled (abstract), soot on linen, sgn/dtd 1963, 17x18", SBY 2/14/89 ..... **1,650**
Untitled (contemporary), pencil on black paper, sgn/dtd 1970, 24x18", C-E 5/9/89 OE **1,760**

BONVICINO, Alessandro; att (Italian, 1498-1554)
Portrait of a Perlate of the Court of Leo X, oil on canvas, 39x32", SBY 6/1/89 ..... **66,000**

BONVIN, Francois (French, 1817-1887)
Portrait de Madame Mosselman, oil on panel, sgn/dtd 69, 11x8", SBY 7/12/89 OE **9,625**
Standing Female Nude, pen/brown ink on light brown laid paper, sgn/dtd 56, 10x6", C-NY 2/25/88 ..... **660**

BOOG, Carle Michel (American, 1877-1967)
Old New York (wintery street scene w/figures, wagon, & horse), oil on canvas, sgn, 30x40", C-NY 12/2/88 ..... **9,350**
Onions (still life of onions & vases), oil on board, sgn, 8x10", C-E 10/18/89 ..... **1,100**
Prospect Park Lake, Brooklyn, in the 1920s; watercolor on paper, sgn, 13x19", WD 4/13/88 ..... **6,000**

BOOG, Frank Myers (American)
Dutch Canal, oil on canvas laid down on panel, sgn, 12x22", C-E 2/1/89 ..... **4,620**

BOOGAARD, Willem Jacobus (Dutch, 1842-1887)
Pair: In the Stable; oil on panel, 1 sgn/dtd 1880, 1 sgn/dtd 1886, 11x16", SBY 6/9/89 ..... **12,100**
Stable Boy with Dray Horses, oil on panel, sgn/dtd 1877, 8x112", B/B 9/14/89 ..... **1,430**
Still Life of Fruit, Morning Glories, & Wild Rose; oil on canvas, sgn/dtd 1864, 25x19", SBY 5/23/89 ..... **15,400**

BOONEN, Arnold; circle of (Dutch, 1669-1729)
Portrait of a Young Boy, holding a flower, with a dog in a landscape; oil on canvas, 39x30", C-E 4/7/88 ..... **3,300**

BOONEN, Arnold; school of (Dutch, 1669-1729)
Lady Playing a Mandolin Attended by a Servant, oil on canvas, 17x14", C-NY 10/20/88 ..... **1,650**

BORDELET, Louis (fl 1647)
Village Wedding Feast with Peasants Dancing & a Church Beyond, oil on canvas, sgn/dtd 16, unfr, 32x62", C-M 12/3/88 .... **29,730**
BORDONE, Paris; att (Italian, 1500-1571)
Venus & Cupid (portraits in landscape), oil on canvas, 39x36", SBY 6/1/89 OE **99,000**
BORDUAS, Paul Emile (Canadian, 1905-1960)
Abstract, green ink, sgn/dtd 1956, 13x9", FB 10/30/89 .... **14,300**
Abstract, ink, sgn/dtd 1950, 11x9", FB 10/30/89 .... **11,000**
Abstract, watercolor/ink/gouache, sgn/dtd 1954, 8x10", FB 10/30/89 .... **12,100**
Harlequin, gouache, 22x17", FB 10/30/89 .... **41,800**
La Coulee, oil on canvas, sgn, 23x30", WAD 11/30/89 OE **125,000**
Petit Jardin, oil on board, ca 1935, 6x7", FB 10/30/89 .... **8,250**
Still Life of Vase, Apple, & Candle; watercolor, sgn, 18x11", FB 10/17/88 UE **4,800**
BOREIN, Edward (American, 1872-1945)
Cowboy, ink/wash on paper, sgn/dtd 14, 20x12", C-NY 12/2/88 .... **6,050**
Cowboys Riding, watercolor on paper, sgn, 8x10", C-NY 12/2/88 .... **9,900**
Double-Sided: Stagecoach; Two Cowboys Riding; watercolor/verso: pencil/ink; sgn, 8x10", SBY 6/24/88 .... **4,125**
Herding Cattle, watercolor on paper, sgn, 8x9", C-NY 12/2/88 OE **11,000**
Mounted Rurale, watercolor on paper, 15x12", B/B 9/15/88 .... **4,400**
Resting on the Trail (cattle herder on horse), watercolor/pencil on paper, sgn, 6x8", C-NY 9/28/89 .... **6,050**
Set of 5: Scenes of Cowboys & Steers; India ink on paper, 1 sgn, 8x10" & smaller, SBY 9/23/88 .... **2,860**
The Meeting (three cowboys on horses in the desert), watercolor on paper laid down on board, sgn, 9x12", C-NY 9/28/89 .... **11,000**
Tied Patience (three horses tethered by cabin in snow), gouache on board, initialed/dtd 1933, 15x18", C-NY 9/28/89 .... **4,620**
Wyoming Trailboss, watercolor/gouache/pencil on paper, sgn, 5x5", SBY 4/14/89 .... **2,750**
BOREN, James (American, 1921-)
Conversation, watercolor on paper, sgn/inscr/dtd 1973, 21x28", SBY 9/23/88 .... **1,870**
Heading for Water, watercolor on paper, sgn/inscr/dtd 1971, 24x39", SBY 9/23/88 .... **2,310**
In Bracketville, watercolor on paper, sgn/inscr/dtd 1972, 14x21", SBY 9/23/88 OE **3,025**
Resting, watercolor on paper, sgn/inscr/dtd 1972, 14x21", SBY 9/23/88 .... **1,045**
Riders of the Picosa, watercolor on paper, sgn/inscr/copyrighted/dtd 1974, 24x38", SBY 9/23/88 .... **3,025**
Two Horses Beneath a Tree, watercolor/gouache on paper, sgn/inscr/copyrighted/dtd 1978, 17x21", SBY 9/23/88 UE **1,045**
West Texas, watercolor on paper, sgn/inscr/copyrighted/dtd 1974, 25x38", SBY 9/23/88 .... **2,530**
When the Train Runs Late, watercolor/gouache on paper, sgn/inscr/copyrighted/dtd 1978, 21x29", SBY 9/23/88 OE **6,600**
Where the Living Is Easy, watercolor on paper, sgn/inscr/dtd 1972, 24x39", SBY 9/23/88 .... **3,190**
BOREN, Wen (Chinese, 1502-1575)
Mountain Abode, ink on paper, sgn, 45x10", SBY 5/31/89 .... **4,675**
BORENSTEIN, Sam (Canadian, 1908-1969)
Farm Buildings by the River Crossing, gouache, sgn, 14x22", FB 10/17/88 UE **500**
Still Life, oil on board, sgn, 24x18", FB 4/25/88 .... **2,200**
Still Life with Vase, Flowers, Plate, Pipe, Etc...; oil on canvas, sgn, 22x26", FB 10/30/89 .... **1,650**
Street Scene (abstract), oil on canvas, sgn/dtd 1959, 19x31", FB 10/30/89 .... **3,740**
Village in Winter, oil on board, sgn/dtd 1963, 12x16", FB 5/28/89 .... **2,600**
BORES, Francisco
Nature Morte sur une Table (still life on a table), oil on canvas, sgn/dtd 44, 18x22", C-E 5/13/88 OE **11,000**
Study of a Nude, ink on paper, sgn/dtd 42, 11x8", SBY 10/7/89 .... **1,045**
Woman Disrobing, black marker on paper, sgn/dtd 59, 25x19", SBY 10/7/89 .... **1,760**
BORG, Carl Oscar (American, 1879-1947)
Campfires Under the Stars (camp scene in an extensive landscape), gouache on paper, sgn, 13x9", B/B 10/9/88 .... **2,750**
Chateau Gaillard, France; pencil/watercolor, sgn/dtd 1913, 13x15", C-SK 6/9/88 .... **744**
Clouds Brewing at Sea, oil on canvasboard, sgn, 10x14", B/B 10/6/88 .... **825**
Indian Lookout, gouache on board, sgn, 12x16", B/B 10/6/88 .... **2,750**
Oil Rig, watercolor on board, sgn/dtd 1929, 12x15", B/B 10/6/88 .... **1,650**
The Debate, watercolor, sgn/inscr, 15x22", C-SK 11/10/88 .... **1,580**
Woman & Child in a Doorway, gouache on paper, sgn/dtd 1923, 13x18", B/B 3/22/89 .... **3,575**
BORGES, Jacobo (Venezuelan, 1931-)
Still Life (abstract), oil on canvas, sgn/dtd 72, 40x51", SBY 11/21/88 .... **18,700**
Untitled (abstract), oil on canvas, sgn/dtd 51, 29x36", SBY 11/21/88 OE **66,000**
BORGET, Auguste; circle of
Guayaquil, Ecuador (village/river in landscape); pencil, indistinctly sgn/titled/inscr, unfr, 7x12", C-SK 6/9/88 OE **130**
BORGIANI, Orazio; att (Italian, 1578-1616)
Presentation in the Temple, oil on canvas, unfr, 56x45", SBY 6/3/88 .... **6,600**
BORIE, Adolphe
Blue Feathered Hat (portrait of a lady), oil on canvas, sgn, 20x16", C-NY 9/28/89 .... **7,700**
Tulips & Hyacinths, oil on canvas, inscr w/title/#d 105, 20x16", C-E 10/18/89 .... **2,860**
White Calla Lilies (still life), oil on canvas, 30x25", C-NY 9/28/89 .... **3,300**
BORIONE, Bernard Louis (French, 1865-)
Cardinal Inspecting His Commission (interior view), oil on panel, sgn, 16x13", C-E 5/22/89 UE **1,210**
Man & Woman in a Bedroom, watercolor on paper, sgn/dtd 1907, 14x10", C-E 5/23/88 UE **715**
Recital (figures in an elegant interior), watercolor, sgn, 20x24", PHL 10/28/88 .... **3,250**
Wake Up for Chocolate!, watercolor, sgn/inscr, 17x13", C-NY 2/25/88 .... **93,500**
BORKOVE, H.
Eastern European Village, oil on canvas, sgn/dtd 1876, 32x27", C-E 5/23/88 .... **2,860**

BOROFSKY, Jonathan (European, 20th C)
Counting to Infinity (13 sheets), ballpoint pen/felt-tip pens/pencil/Xerox on paper, sgn, 11x9", C-NY 10/4/89 ... 4,180
Double-sided: Study for Running Man at 2547776 (hand); graphite/oil on paper, sgn/inscr, 12x9", C-NY 2/20/88 ... 3,850
Light Where the Painting Is, Painting Where the Light Is at 2,590,213; oil w/stage light, ca 1978-80, SBY 11/11/88 ... 27,500
Man with Briefcase at 2,833,991 (contemporary); acrylic airbrushed on paper, #d, 1982-83, 97x43", SBY 5/3/89 OE ... 46,750
Set of 3: Untitled; ball-point pen/pencil/cellophane tape/pen/black ink on paper, 13x7" & smaller, C-E 11/17/88 ... 1,980
Untitled (self-portrait at 2645205 & 2607003), crayon on paper w/ink on vellum overlay, 12x9", SBY 10/5/89 ... 6,050
Untitled #2 at 2,397,211; oil on canvas, 1976, 20x24", C-NY 11/10/88 OE ... 13,200
We All Influence Each Other (2719922), gold paint/graphite/ink on paper, 1982, 8x6", SBY 2/15/89 ... 7,150
2,810,556 Untitled (contemporary); pen/ink/pencil on paper/paper patch/rubber cement, #d 2810556, 12x9", SBY 11/11/88 ... 6,600

BORONDA, Lester D. (American, 1886-1953)
Salinas River Looking West, oil on board, sgn/dtd 45, 16x20", B/B 10/6/88 ... 1,045

BORRANI, Odoardo (Italian, 1834-1905)
Promenade in the Garden, oil on canvas, sgn, 17x14", C-NY 2/23/89 OE ... 154,000

BORSTEL, R.A. (British, 19th/20th C)
Speedonia, a Clipper Off Sydney Heads; oil on canvas, sgn/dtd 1918, 20x30", C-SK 11/10/88 ... 1,210

BORTNYIK, Sandor (European, 20th C)
Bokszolok (two fighters in the ring), gouache on paper, sgn, 9x12", C-NY 5/11/89 ... 17,600

BORTOLUZZI, Camillo 'Millo' (Italian, 1868-)
Fetching Water From an Alpine Pond, oil on canvas, sgn, 15x22", C-E 2/21/89 ... 2,750
Venetian Fishing Boats, oil on panel, sgn, 11x18", C-E 2/21/89 ... 2,200

BORTSOME, Filippo; att
Cove at Trouville, gouache, indistinctly sgn/dtd 68, 9x16", C-NY 10/26/88 UE ... 770

BOSA, Louis (American, 1905-)
Canoe on a Beach (w/crowd of bathers), oil on panel, sgn, 8x10", C-E 6/1/89 ... 935
City Street, oil on board, sgn, 7x10", C-E 10/18/89 ... 880

BOSBOOM, Johannes (Dutch, 1817-1891)
Figures in a Church, pen/brown ink/gray & brown wash on paper, initialed, 8x7", C-E 10/25/88 OE ... 1,540

BOSCO, Pierre (French, 1909-)
Untitled, oil on canvas, sgn, 47x24", PHL 6/16/88 ... 900

BOSELLI, Felice; circle of (Italian, 1650-1732)
Poultry Seller (man with various dead fowl before him), oil on canvas, 53x74", C-NY 4/6/89 OE ... 8,800

BOSLEY, Frederick Andrew (American, 1881-1941)
Peace at Home, oil on canvas, sgn/dtd AD-MDCCCCXV, 72x60", C-NY 5/26/88 ... 12,100
Purity (portrait of lady seated, hands cupped around knees), oil on canvas, sgn, 50x46", SBY 9/14/89 ... 2,310

BOSMAN, C. (Dutch, 19th/20th C)
Putti in an Arcadian Landscape, oil on canvas, sgn/dtd 1818, 26x36", B/B 8/10/88 UE ... 385

BOSMAN, Richard (American, 20th C)
Climbing Sailor (sailor climbing cliff, viewed from above), acrylic on paper, sgn, 1980, 30x22", SBY 5/3/88 ... 2,750
Rower (young man in row boat), oil on canvas, sgn/dtd Spring 84, 48x72", SBY 2/14/89 ... 6,875

BOSS, Henry Wolcott (American, 1820-1916)
Sailing Off a Rocky Coast, oil on canvas, sgn/dtd 90, 24x36", SBY 3/17/88 OE ... 5,225

BOSSCHAERT, Ambrosius (Flemish, 1570-1645)
Floral Still Life in a Porcelain Vase with Exotic Shells on a Ledge, oil on copper, monogramed, 11x8", C-NY 6/2/88 ... 550,000

BOSSCHAERT, Jean Baptiste (Flemish, 1667-1746)
Still Life of Tulips, Carnations, Anemone, & Other Flowers in Vase on Ledge; oil on canvas, sgn, 32x26", SBY 10/13/89 OE ... 42,900

BOSSCHAERT, Jean Baptiste; att (Flemish, 1667-1746)
Roses, Hyacinth, Carnations, Daffodils & Other Flowers in a Terra Cotta Urn; oil on canvas, 33x26", C-NY 10/12/8 OE ... 14,300

BOSSCHAERT, Jean Baptiste; manner of (Flemish, 1667-1746)
Still Life of Flowers in a Sculpted Urn, oil on canvas laid down on board, 44x45", SBY 4/7/88 ... 4,675

BOSSCHAERT, Johannes (Dutch, 1565-1621)
Basket of Flowers on a Table, oil on panel, sgn, 12x20", C-NY 6/2/88 OE ... 198,000

BOSSE, Abraham (French, 1602-1676)
Allegory on the Birth of Louis XIV, black chalk w/touches of pen/brown ink, 8x17", SBY 1/13/89 ... 1,650

BOSSE, Abraham; circle of (French, 1602-1676)
Elegant Couples in a Garden, & Figures Dining in a Gazebo; pen/brown ink/gray wash, 4x7", C-NY 1/12/88 OE ... 4,180

BOSSUET, Francois Antoine (Belgian, 1800-1889)
Tour de l'Or, Seville; oil on canvas, sgn/dtd 1878, 20x28", SBY 5/23/89 ... 23,100

BOSTOCK, Mabel Winifred
Cape Province Farm, oil on canvas laid down, sgn, 12x16", C-SK 11/10/88 ... 370
Drachenstein Mountain, South Africa; oil on canvas, inscr/dtd 1912, 11x15", C-SK 11/10/88 ... 240

BOSTON, Frederic James (American, 1855-1932)
An Extensive River Landscape, oil on canvasboard, sgn, 12x16", PHL 6/16/88 UE ... 300
Cottage in a Landscape, oil on canvas laid down on board, 12x16", C-E 6/1/89 UE ... 550
Meadow, oil on canvas, sgn, 12x16", C-E 2/3/88 ... 990
Pailsades Looking Towards New York (coastal landscape), oil on canvas, sgn, 40x49", C-E 6/1/89 UE ... 1,100
Woman Picking Flowers, oil on canvas, sgn, 30x20", C-E 6/1/88 ... 1,650
Woman with Yellow Roses in Her Hair, oil on canvas, sgn, 18x14", C-E 6/1/88 ... 1,100

BOSTON, Joseph H. (American, -1954)
Landscape Scene, oil on canvas, sgn, 16x12", RWS 11/3/88 OE ... 1,500

BOTELLO, Angel (20th C)
Cabeza de Muchacha (head of a young girl), oil on canvas, sgn, 24x20", C-NY 11/21/88 ... 2,200
Checkers Players in San Juan (contemporary), oil on panel, sgn, ca 1975, 16x12", SBY 5/16/89 ... 7,700
Mother & Child (contemporary), oil on panel, sgn, ca 1970, 48x37", SBY 5/16/89 OE ... 31,900
Two Figures (contemporary), oil on panel, sgn, 42x54", SBY 5/16/89 ... 23,100
Untitled (half-length nude w/hand on face looking at bird), oil on masonite, sgn, ca 1948, 23x19", SBY 11/21/88 ... 9,900
Woman, oil on board, sgn, ca 1966, 48x17", SBY 5/17/88 ... 14,300

BOTERO, Fernando (Colombian, 1932-)
A Marie France (portrait), watercolor on paper, sgn, 1975, 23x17", SBY 5/16/89 ... 36,300
After Mantegna, oil on canvas, sgn/dtd 80, 93x108", SBY 5/17/88 OE ... 341,000
Basket of Fruit (still life w/fruit & pitcher), sanguine on canvas, sgn/dtd 75, 64x71", SBY 11/21/88 ... 121,000
Bath of the Vatican (caricature figures in a bathtub), oil on canvas, sgn twice/dtd 69/titled, 58x72", SBY 5/16/89 ... 247,500
Bird (caricature of bluebird in a tree), pastel on paper, sgn/dtd 68, 41x32", SBY 11/21/88 ... 50,600
Caballo (horse), pencil on paper laid down on board, sgn, 1980, 14x17", C-NY 5/18/88 ... 18,700
Double-Sided: Nina; Still Life with Fruit; watercolor, sgn, 1952, 19x16", SBY 11/21/88 UE ... 25,300
El Alguacil (The Constable, man on horse in arena), oil on canvas, sgn, 1981, 67x48", C-NY 5/18/88 ... 242,000
Fallen Bull (contemporary view in landscape), oil on panel, sgn/dtd 56, 34x54", SBY 11/21/88 ... 37,400
Family (caricature figures in interior), pencil on paper, sgn/dtd 80, SBY 11/21/88 OE ... 23,100
Family (oil sketch for another painting), oil on canvas, sgn/dtd 67, 14x13", SBY 11/21/88 ... 30,800
Juanita (nude), oil on canvas, sgn/dtd 79, 76x51", C-NY 11/21/88 ... 31,900
L'Atelier (still life in artist's studio), oil/collage on canvas stretched over masonite, sgn, 77, 35x28", C-NY 5/17/88 ... 110,000
Man Smoking (portrait), oil on canvas, sgn/dtd 73, 54x37", SBY 5/16/89 OE ... 159,500
Nina con Muneca (girl w/doll), pencil on paper, sgn/dtd 1971, 16x14", C-NY 11/21/88 ... 9,900
Pair: Houses; watercolor on paper, 1 sgn/dtd 52, 14x14", 15x20", SBY 11/21/88 ... 16,500
Pear, oil on canvas, sgn/dtd 67, 12x11", SBY 11/21/88 ... 26,400
Pineapples (still life), oil on canvas, sgn twice/dtd 68 twice/titled, 66x73", SBY 5/16/89 ... 137,500
Political Prisoner, oil on canvas, sgn/dtd 72, 50x36", SBY 5/17/88 ... 88,000
Princess Margarita After Velasquez, oil on canvas, sgn twice/dtd 78 twice/titled, 84x76", C-NY 5/17/89 ... 440,000
Profile of a Girl, oil on canvas, sgn/dtd 62, 52x48", SBY 5/17/88 ... 104,500
Rosita (standing nude w/cat), pencil on paper, sgn/dtd 71/titled, 17x13", C-NY 5/17/89 OE ... 26,400
Rosita Sentada (portrait), pencil on paper, sgn/dtd 70, 17x14", C-NY 5/18/88 ... 11,000
Rubens' Wife (caricature), oil on canvas, sgn/dtd 63, 50x50", SBY 11/21/88 ... 110,000
Spanish Conquistador, oil on canvas, sgn, ca 1981, 78x50", SBY 5/16/89 ... 297,000
Still Life (w/fruit & wine glass), ink wash/black & white chalk/gouache on board, sgn, 1960s, 26x20", SBY 4/29/88 OE ... 14,850
Still Life of Fruit, pastel on paper, sgn/dtd 68, 22x21", SBY 11/21/88 ... 37,400
Studio of Sanchez Cotan (contemporary), oil on canvas, sgn/dtd 1963, 52x58", SBY 5/16/89 ... 104,500
Three Sisters (three ladies in interior), pencil on paper, sgn/dtd 70/titled, 16x12", SBY 5/16/89 OE ... 27,500
Un Cardenal (impressionistic portrait of a Cardinal), oil on canvas, sgn/dtd 67, 22x22", C-NY 5/18/88 ... 52,800
Woman (portrait), oil on canvas, sgn, 1954, 26x20", SBY 11/21/88 ... 41,800

BOTH, Andries Dirksz (Dutch, 1608-1650)
Diablerie: Satire on Doctors; pen/brown ink, 7x11", SBY 1/13/89 OE ... 12,100
Diablerie: Scribe Attended by Monsters; pen/brown ink, 7x11", SBY 1/13/89 OE ... 14,300

BOTH, Jan (Dutch, 1618-1652)
Italianate Landscape with Travelers on a Path, oil on canvas, sgn, 25x33", SBY 6/2/89 ... 88,000

BOTH, Jan; att (Dutch, 1618-1652)
Double-Sided: Seated Boy From Behind; Head of a Horse; black chalk w/touch of gray wash, 4x5", SBY 1/13/89 OE ... 7,150

BOTKE, Jessie Arms (American, 1883-1971)
Fish, oil/gold leaf on canvas mounted on board, sgn, 25x30", B/B 10/6/88 OE ... 16,500
Two White Peacocks in a Garden, oil on canvas laid down, 30x25", B/B 10/6/88 ... 7,700

BOTKE, Jessie Arms; after (American, 1883-1971)
Cockatoos, oil on masonite, 24x30", LH 5/15/88 ... 500

BOTTANI, Giuseppe (European, 1717-1784)
Nude with a Pole, red/black chalk, inscr, 22x15", C-NY 1/12/88 ... 1,045

BOTTESIRA, A. (Italian, 19th C)
Study of a Peasant Woman Seated in a Chair Spinning Yarn, oil on canvas, sgn, 19x14", SLK 2/12/88 ... 550

BOTTICELLI, Sandro; studio of (Italian, 15th/16th C)
Madonna & Child with a Franciscan Saint, Possibly San Giovanni Gualberto; oil on panel, 28x19", C-NY 5/31/89 ... 55,000

BOTTICINI, school of (Italian, 15th C)
Madonna & Child with the Infant St John the Baptist, oil on panel, circular, unfr, 33x33", C-E 1/15/88 OE ... 15,400

BOTTON, see De Botton

BOUAT, H.
Tulips, Roses, Morning Glory, Chrysanthemums, & Others in an Urn on Ledge; oil on canvas, sgn, 48x38", C-NY 10/20/88 OE ... 11,000

BOUCHARD, Lorne Holland (Canadian, 1913-1978)
Back Field, St Placide; oil on board, sgn/dtd 1969, 5x6", FB 10/17/88 ... 500
Dead End Street, Montreal North; oil on board, sgn/dtd 1962, 12x16", FB 5/28/89 ... 1,300
Farmhouse & Barn, oil on board, sgn/dtd Aug 20th 1975, 12x13", FB 4/25/88 ... 1,200
Frosty Morning, oil on board, sgn, 8x10", FB 5/28/89 OE ... 1,200
Frosty Morning, St Francis River, Near Drummondville; oil on board, sgn, 6x7", FB 10/17/88 OE ... 1,700
Quebec Street, oil on board, sgn/dtd 1969, 12x6", FB 5/28/89 OE ... 1,100
Winter Harbor, Douglas Town, Gaspe Coast; oil on panel, sgn/dtd 1940, 5x7", FB 10/17/88 ... 1,800
Winter Road, oil on panel, sgn, 25x32", FB 10/17/88 UE ... 4,200

BOUCHARDON, Edme; att (French, 1698-1762)
Head of an Oriental, red w/white chalk on buff paper, Crown wm, inscr, 10x10", C-NY 1/11/89 .... **5,500**
Triton Defending a Nymph From a Sea Monster (after Raphael), red chalk, 8x12", SBY 1/13/89 .... **660**

BOUCHE, Louis (American, 1896-1969)
Harlem River, oil on canvas, sgn/dtd 1944, 10x11", C-NY 9/28/89 .... **1,100**
New York Harbor, oil on canvas, sgn/dtd 1943, 20x24", SBY 6/28/89 .... **3,300**
Snow-Fifth Avenue, oil on canvas, sgn, 22x16", SBY 4/14/89 .... **935**

BOUCHER, Alfred (French, 1850-1934)
Figures on a Path by a Field of Poppies & Heather with a Village Beyond, oil on canvas, sgn, 40x59", C-NY 2/23/89 OE **13,200**

BOUCHER, Francois (French, 1703-1770)
Annunciation, black chalk offset, inscr arch, 12x7", C-NY 1/12/88 OE **7,150**
Birth of Venus, oil on canvas, sgn/indistinctly dtd, 12x16", SBY 1/12/89 .... **132,000**
Double-Sided: Studies of Cleopatra & Her Attendant Laonica; black chalk w/touches of white, 11x8", SBY 1/13/89 .... **2,090**
La Petite Laitiere, oil on canvas, oval, 16x12", C-NY 1/15/88 .... **330,000**
Seated Female Nude, red & white chalk over black chalk on buff paper, 14x11", SBY 1/13/89 .... **159,500**
Venus Ordering Arms for Aeneas, brown/white chalk on light brown paper, sgn/dtd 1767, 12x8", C-NY 1/11/89 OE **41,800**
Virgin & Child, oil on canvas, sgn/dtd 1768, oval, 22x18", C-NY 1/15/88 .... **85,000**

BOUCHER, Francois; & Assistants (French, 1703-1770)
Dark Odalisque, oil on canvas, inscr, 44x57", SBY 6/3/88 .... **550,000**

BOUCHER, Francois; & Studio (French, 1703-1770)
Watermill of Quiquengrogne at Charenton, oil on canvas, sgn, 38x51", SBY 1/12/89 .... **77,000**

BOUCHER, Francois; att (French, 1703-1770)
Head of a Young Girl, pastel on paper, 10x8", WD 1/25/89 OE **10,000**

BOUCHER, Francois; circle of (French, 1703-1770)
Children Playing Blind-Man's Bluff, en grisaille/oil on canvas, unfr, 27x54", SBY 10/21/88 .... **2,200**
Italianate Landscape with a Young Man Teaching a Girl To Play the Flute, oil on canvas, 31x25", SBY 10/21/88 OE **11,000**
Jupiter & Callister, oil on canvas, 32x51", C-NY 6/2/88 OE **71,500**

BOUCHER, Francois; follower of (French, 1703-1770)
Landscape with a Shelter by a River, black chalk, 10x10", SBY 1/13/89 OE **6,325**

BOUCHER, Francois; manner of (French, 1703-1770)
Fete Champetre, oil on canvas, 33x53", SBY 10/21/88 .... **5,775**
Pair: Putti Dancing; Putti Catching Birds; oil on canvas, arched top, unfr, 19x57", SBY 4/7/88 .... **3,025**
Three Putti, oil on shaped canvas, inscr 1733, 28x43", SBY 7/12/89 .... **3,025**

BOUCHER, Francois; school of (French, 1703-1770)
Putti Playing in a Garden, oil on canvas, oval, 29x25", C-NY 4/8/88 .... **2,200**
Venus Reclining Before a Curtain Attended by Cupid, oil on canvas, unfr, 35x54", C-NY 10/20/88 .... **3,300**

BOUCHER, Francois; style of (French, 1703-1770)
Pair: Scenes with Rustic Lovers; oil on canvas, 76x50", B/B 12/8/88 OE **20,900**
Revelation of Psyche, oil on canvas, 15x14", B/B 9/15/88 OE **1,650**

BOUCHER, Joseph Felix (French, 1853-1935)
Les Cypres d'Amalfi, oil on canvas, 30x25", FAP 4/15/89 .... **2,090**

BOUDEWYNS, Adriaen Frans; & SCHOEVAERDTS, Mathys (Flemish)
Peasants Resting by a Fountain in a Mountainous River Landscape, oil on canvas, 21x27", C-NY 10/20/88 OE **14,300**

BOUDEWYNS, Adriaen Frans; att (Flemish, 1644-1711)
Landscape with Peasants, Cows, & Sheep; oil on canvas, 26x31", SBY 10/21/88 .... **2,200**
Travelers in an Extensive Country Landscape, oil on panel,12x17", SBY 7/12/89 .... **2,970**
Travelers on a Path in a Mountainous River Landscape, oil on panel, 20x26", C-NY 4/8/88 .... **12,100**

BOUDEWYNS, Adriaen Frans; school (Flemish, 1644-1711)
Landscape with Travelers, oil on panel, bears initials, 10x13", C-NY 6/2/88 .... **3,850**

BOUDIN, Eugene (French, 1824-1898)
Antibes, les Rochers de l'Ilette et les Fortifications (coastal view); oil on canvas, sgn, 1893, 20x30", SBY 5/10/89 .... **440,000**
Baie en Bretagne, oil on canvas, sgn/dtd 72, 15x23", SBY 5/11/88 OE **115,500**
Berck, le Depart des Barques (seascape w/boats departing); oil on canvas, sgn/dtd 79, 26x36", C-NY 11/16/88 .... **143,000**
Camaret le Mole, oil on canvas, sgn/dtd 73, 22x35", C-NY 2/16/89 .... **110,000**
Crinolines sur la Plage (beach scene), watercolor/pencil on paper on board, sgn/dtd 1866, 6x11", C-NY 11/14/88 OE **60,500**
Douarnenez, Bateaux dans la Baie (boats on the bay); oil on canvas, sgn/dtd 1897, 22x36", C-NY 5/11/88 .... **209,000**
Douarnenez, Bateaux de Peche a Quai; oil on cradled panel, sgn, 1855, 14x23", SBY 5/11/88 .... **55,000**
Environs de Trouville, la Moisson; oil on canvas, sgn/dtd 78, 14x23", SBY 5/11/88 .... **63,250**
Etude de Vaches (study of cows), oil on canvas, ca 1880-85, 14x18", SBY 10/6/89 .... **19,800**
Etudes de Figures, watercolor over pencil on paper laid down on board, stamped initials, 6x9", C-NY 11/15/88 OE **18,700**
Femmes sur la Plage, Trouville (ladies on beach); pencil/watercolor on paper laid down, initialed, 4x5", PHL 11/15/88 .... **6,000**
Jour de Foire au Pays Bigouden, watercolor/pencil on paper, sgn/dtd 64, 6x10", SBY 10/27/89 .... **15,400**
La Havre, le Bassin de la Barre (port scene); oil on cradled panel, sgn/dtd 94, 15x22", SBY 5/10/89 .... **170,500**
La Moisson au Faou (man & woman harvesting), watercolor/pencil on paper, sgn, 1870-71, 6x8", C-NY 10/5/89 .... **11,000**
La Seine a Quillebeuf, oil on canvas, sgn/inscr, ca 1892-94, 19x26", SBY 5/11/88 .... **126,000**
La Touques a Saint-Arnoult, oil on canvas, sgn/dtd 91, 20x29", SBY 5/11/88 OE **68,750**
Le Havre, l'Avant-port au Soleil Couchant (harbor scene at sunset); oil on canvas, sgn/dtd 1870, 26x36", C-NY 5/11/88 .... **330,000**
Le Havre, la Fete Des Regates; oil on panel, sgn/dtd 69, 9x15", SBY 10/27/89 OE **770,000**
Le Havre, un Bassin (port scene); oil on cradled panel, sgn/dtd 90, 13x16", C-NY 5/11/88 .... **121,000**
Le Havre, un Bassin (ships in port); oil on panel, sgn/dtd 92/inscr, 11x14", C-NY 5/11/89 OE **154,000**
Le Parc Cordier a Trouville (park w/figures), oil on canvas, sgn, ca 1880-85, 20x24", SBY 11/12/88 .... **220,000**

Le Port de Marseilles (busy port scene), oil on canvas, sgn, 24x46", SBY 10/6/89 OE ... 242,000
Les Canots sur la Plage, watercolor on paper, sgn/dtd 70, 5x10", WD 5/5/88 ... 15,000
Les Crinolines, watercolor/pencil on paper, stamped initials/dtd 70, 5x11", SBY 10/27/89 ... 38,500
Lex Bateaux (sailing vessel), watercolor/pencil on paper, initaled, 8x8", B/B 10/9/88 OE ... 8,800
Marche a Trouville (people gathered at market place), oil on cradled panel, sgn, 13x16", C-NY 11/16/88 ... 176,000
Plage Pres de Trouville (beach scene), oil on canvas, sgn/dtd 70, 12x18", SBY 11/12/88 OE ... 176,000
Plougastel, le Rivage au Bord de la Baie (view of a bay); oil on canvas, sgn, 1870-73, 13x22", C-NY 5/12/88 ... 49,500
Rotterdam, un Coin du Bassin; oil on canvas, sgn/dtd 77, 20x29", SBY 5/10/88 ... 154,000
Scene de Plage (Beach Scene), oil on panel, sgn/dtd 68, 8x14", SBY 11/11/88 ... 357,500
Scene de Plage (Beach Scene), oil on panel, sgn/dtd 75, 5x10", SBY 5/10/89 OE ... 308,000
Scene de Ville (impressionistic village scene), oil on paper, stamped initials, 5x5", SBY 10/6/89 ... 22,000
Scene du Port, watercolor over pencil on paper mounted on paper, stamped initials, 7x8", C-NY 10/6/88 OE ... 19,800
Sur la Plage, watercolor/pencil on paper, sgn/dtd 1867, 6x10", SBY 11/12/88 OE ... 39,600
Trouville, la Plage a Maree Basse; oil on canvas, sgn/dtd 78, 20x29", SBY 10/27/89 ... 495,000
Trouville, oil on canvas, sgn/inscr/dtd, 21x29", RWS 11/3/88 OE ... 180,000

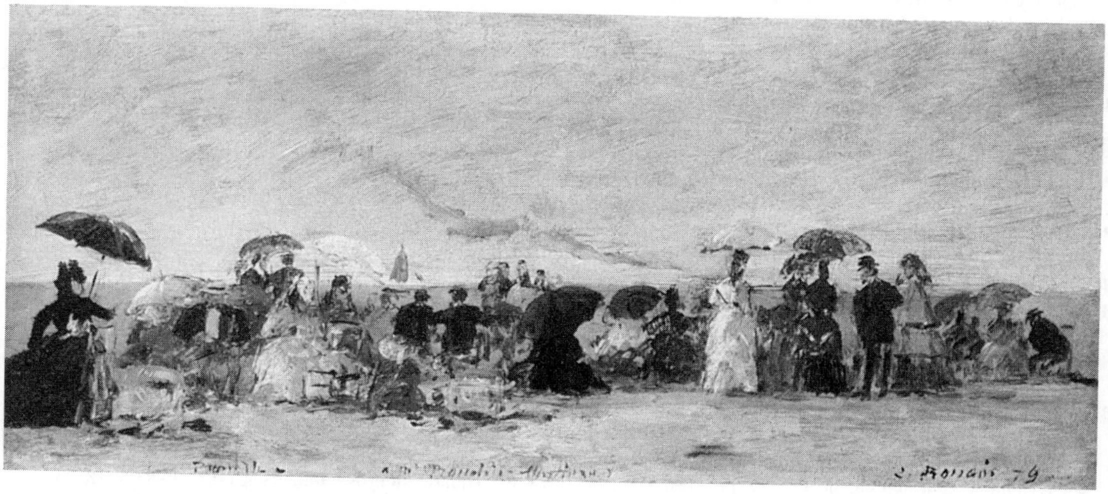

Trouville, Scene de Plage; oil on cradled panel, sgn/dtd 79 titled, 6x14", C-NY 11/14/88, $352,000

Trouville, Scene de Plage; oil on panel, sgn/dtd 81, 8x13", SBY 10/27/89 ... 660,000
Un Coup de Mistral a Antibes, oil on canvas, sgn/dtd 93, 22x35", SBY 5/11/88 ... 176,000
Venise, Eglise San Giorgio (Venice canal scene); oil on canvas, sgn/dtd 25 Juin, 1895, 14x22", C-NY 5/11/88 ... 528,000
Venise. Vue Prise de San Giorgio; oil on canvas, sgn/dtd 95, 20x29", SBY 10/27/89 ... 1,540,000
Voiliers au Port (port scene), watercolor/pencil on thin paper, inscr, ca 1870-75, 8x11", SBY 10/7/88 ... 8,250
Voiliers au Port (sailing boats in port), brush/black ink on paper, stamped initials, 5x8", C-NY 2/18/88 ... 5,280
Voiliers au Port (sailing boats in port), oil on panel, sgn/inscr, 11x9", C-NY 11/16/88 ... 110,000
Washerwomen on a River Bank, oil on panel, sgn, ca 1888-95, 24x35", SBY 5/9/89 OE ... 407,000

BOUDRY, Alois (Belgian, 19th C)
Still Life of Zinnias in a Blue Vase with Fruit on a Table, oil on canvas, sgn/inscr 81, 26x18", C-E 5/23/88 ... 2,860

BOUDUC, April (European, 19th/20th C)
Oxen Pulling Carts, oil on canvas, sgn, 12x20", WG 9/16/8870 ... 86

BOUGH, Sam (British, 1822-1878)
Lord Ard (lake scene w/hills beyond), oil on canvas laid down on board, sgn/dtd 1845, 15x24", C-E 5/22/89 ... 3,960

BOUGH, Sam; att (British, 1822-1878)
Riverscape, oil on canvas, sgn/indistinctly dtd, 22x38", B/B 9/14/89 ... 1,320

BOUGHTON, George Henry (American, 1833-1905)
At the Hearth (two seated figures), oil on panel, sgn/dtd 1887, 26x24", C-E 2/21/89 ... 3,300
Falling Leaves (woman in profile by brick wall), oil on canvas, initialed, 24x16", C-NY 9/28/89 OE ... 33,000
Hester & the Clergyman, watercolor/gouache on board, sgn, 11x7", C-NY 3/11/88 ... 4,620
Music Lesson, oil on canvas, initialed, 54x43", SBY 5/25/88 ... 17,600
Painted Near Albany, 1853 (winter landscape); oil on canvas, 15x24", C-NY 5/26/88 ... 4,400
Spring (girl in a landscape), oil on canvas, initialed/inscr, 18x12", SBY 6/24/88 ... 6,875
Warming Themselves by the Hearth, oil on cradled panel, sgn/inscr/dtd 1887, 26x24", C-E 2/23/88 OE ... 2,530
Widow's Acre, oil on canvas, sgn/dtd 1879, 22x30", SBY 1/24/89 ... 1,650
Woman in the Snow, pastel on paper, sgn, 17x11", DM 3/14/88 ... 1,600
Young Lady with Muff, gouache on board, sgn twice, 19x14", SBY 1/24/89 ... 2,200

BOUGUEREAU, Elisabeth Jeanne Gardner (French, 1851-1922)
Souvenir de Bouguereau, oil on canvas, 50x29", C-NY 2/25/88 ... 24,200

BOUGUEREAU, William Adolphe (French, 1825-1905)
Allant au Bain (woman & child in a landscape), oil on canvas, sgn/dtd 1887, 69x32", C-NY 5/24/89 ... 165,000
Enfants Endormis (two small children sleeping in a bed), oil on canvas, sgn, ca 1868, 15x22", SBY 2/22/89 ... 38,500
Jeune Fille Mangeant la Soupe (portrait), oil on canvas laid down on board, sgn, 16x13", C-NY 2/23/89 ... 44,000
L'Eveil du Coeur; or, The Heart's Awakening; oil on canvas, sgn/dtd 1892, 63x43", C-NY 5/24/89 ... 242,000
La Grande Soeur (portrait of a young girl holding a child), oil on canvas, sgn/dtd 1865, 40x29", C-NY 2/23/89 ... 132,000

La Liseuse (portrait), oil on canvas, sgn/dtd 1895, 46x32", SBY 5/23/89 165,000
Mignon Pensive, oil on canvas, sgn/dtd 1869, 39x32", SBY 4/29/88 71,500
Moissoneue (L'Italienne a la Fontaine), oil on canvas, sgn/dtd 1868, 42x34", SBY 5/23/89 132,000
Pet Bird (girl holding bird in an interior), oil on canvas laid down, sgn/dtd 1867, 32x26", WD 5/5/88 67,500
Printemps (woman & child ina landscape), oil on canvas laid down on board, sgn/dtd 1904, 21x12", C-NY 5/24/89 22,000
Tete d'Ange (portrait), oil on canvas, sgn/dtd 1883, 18x15", SBY 2/22/89 41,250
Un Moment de Repros, oil on canvas, sgn/dtd 1900, 59x29", C-NY 5/25/88 OE 132,000
Une Petite Fille, oil on canvas, sgn/dtd 1886, 14x11", C-NY 2/25/88 35,200
Young Girl, Three-Quarter Length; oil on canvas, sgn/dtd 1902, 46x29", C-NY 5/24/89 55,000
Younger Generations, depicting young girl with a puppy; oil on canvas, sgn, 20x17", MAG 4/24/88 17,000

BOUILLON, Michel (fl mid-17th C)
Still Life of Peaches, Currants, Figs, & Glasses on a Ledge; oil on copper, sgn/dtd 1653, 15x11", SBY 10/21/88 OE 41,800
Still Life of Various Fruits & Flowers Set in a Landscape, oil on canvas, sgn/dtd 1674, 34x55", SBY 10/13/89 28,600

BOULANGER, Garciela Rodo (South American, 20th C)
Girl with a Cat, oil on canvas, sgn/dtd 1969/titled, 26x21", SBY 5/16/89 OE 11,000
Juggler, oil on canvas, sgn twice/titled/dtd 1975, 32x26", SBY 5/17/88 15,400
Promenade (two contemporary figures on bulls), oil on canvas, sgn/dtd 1966/#d No 8, 29x24", SBY 5/16/89 6,600
Three Rhinoceroses, oil on canvas, sgn/dtd 1980, 51x64", SBY 5/17/88 30,800
Walk with a Cat (contemporary), oil on canvas, sgn/dtd 1969, 36x29", SBY 11/21/88 9,350

BOULANGER, Gustave Clarence Rodolphe (French, 1824-1888)
Reception of an Emir (also known as C'est un Emir'), oil on canvas, sgn/dtd 1871, 26x19", SBY 2/22/89 33,000
Tale of 1001 Knights, oil on canvas, sgn, 19x28", C-NY 5/25/88 OE 33,000

BOULARD, Auguste (French, 1825-1897)
Dreaming Away (portrait of a woman with one bare breast), oil on panel, sgn/dtd 1888, 24x29", B/B 5/17/89 UE 550

BOULINEAU, Aristide (French, 19th C)
Playful Afternoon at the Beach, oil on canvas, sgn, 11x16", C-E 5/23/88 2,310

BOULLOGNE, see De Boullogne

BOULT, Francis Cecil (British, fl 1877-95)
Through the Gate (fox hunt scene), oil on canvas, sgn/dtd 1887, 20x36", SBY 6/10/88 6,875

BOUN, V. (American, 19th C)
Man Shaving, oil on canvas, sgn, 12x8", SBY 1/24/89 770

BOUNACCORSE, Perino; circle of (Italian, 1500-1546)
Double-Sided: Standing Man Wearing Cloak & Wreath; Seated Female Figure; pen/brown ink, 11x8", SBY 1/13/89 990
Frieze of Dragons, Lions, & Other Beasts; black chalk/pen/brown ink/brown wash heightened w/white, 4x11", C-NY 1/12/88 1,650
Martyrdom of Saint Agatha, black chalk/pen/brown ink/brown wash, squared in brown ink, inscr, 11x8", C-NY 1/12/88 1,210

BOUNACCORSI, see Del Vaga

BOUNDEY, Burton Shepard (American, 1879-1962)
Still Life of Yellow Roses, oil on canvas, sgn, 16x20", B/B 10/6/88 660

BOUQUET, Andre (French, 19th C)
Winter Village Street, oil on canvas, sgn, 15x18", SBY 10/7/89 935

BOUQUIER, Gabriel (18th C)
Terrace of the Villa Mattei, Rome; pen/gray ink/watercolor, sgn/dtd 1778, 7x10", C-NY 1/12/88 OE 2,090

BOURDELLE, Emile Antoine (French, 1861-1929)
La Musicienne, pencil/watercolor on paper, sgn, 6x5", WD 5/5/88 900

BOURDON, Sebastian; att (French, 1616-1671)
Portrait of a Nobleman, oil on panel, oval, 24x20", SBY 6/1/89 OE 20,900

BOURDON, Sebastian; circle of (French, 1616-1671)
Saint John the Baptist (portrait in a landscape), oil on canvas, 24x20", SBY 4/7/89 3,300

BOURGAIN, Gustave (French, -1921)
Napoleon's Entry into Cairo, oil on canvas, sgn/indistinctly dtd, 59x48", SBY 2/22/89 99,000

BOURGEOIS, Albert (Canadian, 1876-1962)
Sunlit Forest Scene, watercolor, sgn, 22x30", FB 5/28/89 800

BOURGES, Pauline-Elise Leonide (French, 1838-1910)
Boy & Young Sister with Basket of Produce & Flowers Walking Down Garden Path, oil on wood panel, 11x14", DM 9/16/88 1,750

BOURGOIN, Clarence (Canadian, 1946-)
Au Repos, oil on canvas, sgn/dtd 1989, 20x24", FB 10/30/89 900
Nika'l et Ses Amis (two small boys with dog in tire in landscape), oil on canvas, sgn/dtd 1989, 30x36", FB 5/18/89 OE 1,100

BOURGOIN, Francois Jules (French, fl 1796-1812)
Kingston Racetrack, Overlooking Port Royal, Jamaica; oil on cradled panel, indistinctly sgn, 25x36", SBY 6/10/88 26,400

BOUT, Pieter; & BOUDEWYNS, Adriaen Frans (Flemish)
Italianate Wooded Landscape with Shepherds & Travelers, oil on panel, 11x15", C-NY 4/8/88 OE 11,000

BOUTELLE, Dewitt Clinton (American, 1817-1884)
Trout Fishing, oil on canvas, sgn/dtd 1876, 50x40", C-NY 12/2/88 17,600

BOUTER, Cornelis (Dutch, 1888-1966)
Family Gathering, oil on canvas, sgn, 17x21", C-E 5/23/88 5,500
Midday Meal, oil on canvas, sgn, 20x24", C-E 10/25/88 4,180
Mother & Children in an Interior, oil on canvas, sgn/dtd 48, 20x24", SBY 12/9/88 OE 3,520
New Doll, oil on canvas, sgn, 22x18", SBY 12/9/88 4,400

BOUTERWEK, Friedrich (German, 1806-1867)
Recontre d'Isaac et de Rebecca, oil on canvas, sgn/dtd 1841, 69x84", SBY 5/23/89 20,900

OUTON, C. (European, 20th C)
Interior with Mother & Child, oil on canvas, sgn, 25x30", LH 12/4/88 OE 3,000
OUTTATS, Frederik the elder (17th C)
Temptation in the Garden of Eden, oil on panel, 15x31", SBY 4/7/89 19,800
OUTTATS, Jacob; att (fl 1700)
Orpheus Charming the Animals (in a landscape), oil on panel, 11x30", C-M 6/16/89 16,300
OUTTATS, Johann Baptiste (fl 1706-1735)
Shipping Off a Beach with Figures on a Windy Day, oil on canvas, sgn/dtd 1719, 17x28", SBY 4/7/88 3,575
OUVARD, Antoine (French, -1956)
Canal Scene in Venice, oil on canvas, sgn, 18x24", C-E 2/23/88 3,960
Grand Canal, Venice; oil on canvas, sgn, 10x14", C-E 5/22/89 3,850
Santa Maria Salute, Venice; oil on canvas, sgn, 10x13", C-E 5/22/89 3,300
Venetian Canal Scene, oil on canvas, sgn, 10x13", C-E 5/22/89 3,300
Venetian Canal Scene, oil on canvas, sgn, 20x25", SBY 7/12/89 4,675
Venetian Canal Scene (figures in gondola, houses lining canal), oil on canvas, sgn, 29x39", PHL 10/28/88 4,000
Venetian Canal Scene with the Alghieri Bridge in Background, oil on canvas, sgn, 19x24", B/B 3/22/89 OE 7,150
Venetian Canal with San Torini in the Background, oil on canvas, sgn, 25x19", B/B 3/22/89 OE 8,250
Venice, oil on canvas, sgn, 9x11", C-E 10/25/88 2,420
OUVARD, Hughes; see De Bouvard
OUVARD, Noel A. (French, 1912-1975)
Venice (water & buildings in landscape), oil on canvas, sgn, 20x26", DM 5/89 2,250
OUVIER, Auguste (French, 19th C)
Portrait of a Lady, seated, half-length, in blue dress & gold chain, gouache/oil on ivory, 5x4", C-E 6/1/88 330
OUVIER, Joseph (19th C)
Echoes of the Sea, oil, sgn/dtd 1852, fr as an oval, 16x15", WD 1/11/89 900
OUVIER, Jules
Annunciation, watercolor on paper, sgn, 15x12", C-E 5/23/88 1,210
OVERIE, L. (Belgian, 1888-)
Multiple Figures on a Beach, watercolor, sgn, 21x29", SLK 5/11/88 1,200
OWEN, Paul
Shield #1, mixed media, 26x51", C-NY 10/31/89 OE 1,870
OWER, Alex (American, 1875-1952)
Maine Landscape, watercolor on paper, sgn, 14x20", FAP 4/15/89 302
OWER, J. (American, 19th C)
Cabin in Winter Landscape, oil on board, sgn/dtd 1888, 18x14", C-E 4/26/88 330
Still Life of Two Peaches & Two Strawberries, pastel on paper, sgn, 8x9", SBY 1/28/88 UE 1,100
Wilderness Lake by Moonlight, lone deer waters at moonlit lake; pastel on paper, sgn/dtd 1901, 24x20", RAB 8/8/89 UE 200
OWER, Lucy Scott (American, ca 1864-1934)
Sailboat & Dinghy Anchored at Shore with Two Female Figures, oil on canvas, sgn, 12x16", SLK 2/12/88 70
OWERS, Edward (American, 1822-1870)
Portrait of a Woman, oil on canvas, 24x20", WL 5/20/88 450
OWIE, Frank Louville (American, 1857-1936)
Winter Landscape Scene, oil on canvas, sgn, 18x22", RWS 3/31/88 800
OWLER, Thomas William (British, 1812-1869)
British Regiment Approaching a River, pencil/watercolor/gum arabic, unfr, 12x20", C-SK 6/9/88 7,436
Cape Sunset (landscape w/river & villages), pencil/watercolor/gum arabic, ca 1858, unfr, 12x20", C-SK 6/9/88 8,920
Table Bay (coastal view w/ships), pencil/watercolor heightened w/white, inscr/dtd 1863, 13x20", C-SK 5/25/89 UE 1,100
WMAN, M.E. (American, 19th/20th C)
Waiting for a Bite, oil on canvas, sgn, 19x26", FAP 4/15/89 770
XER, Stanley (American, 1926-)
Crestedhushofsputteredsoul, oil on canvas, sgn/inscr/dtd 77, 69x17", C-E 5/13/88 1,100
Wanderingdawns (contemporary), oil on canvas, titled, 64x64", C-E 5/9/89 OE 3,520
YD, Elizabeth Frances (Scotch, fl 1896-1935)
Pair: Haying in the Sunshine; oil on canvas, sgn/dtd 08, WD 3/23/88 1,000
YD, Rutherford (American, 1884-1951)
Harriet Knitting, oil on canvas, estate stamp, ca 1910-15, 30x22", SBY 1/24/89 6,600
YD, S. (British, 19th C)
Highland River Landscape, oil on canvas, sgn, 20x30", SLK 9/26/88 250
YDEN, Dwight Frederick (American, 1860-1933)
Summer Landscape, rutted roads along field w/trees in distance; oil on canvas, sgn/dtd 1912, 15x22", RAB 8/8/89 UE 250
YLE, A. (British, fl 1884-1889)
View in Sutton Park (landscape), oil on canvas, sgn/titled, 24x20", SLK 4/7/89 450
YLE, Charles Wellington (American, 1861-1925)
Shoreline of Lake Pontchartrain, Lewisburg; oil on canvas, sgn, 20x36", NA 5/13/89 OE 4,000
YS, Thomas Shooter; att (British, 1803-1874)
Fishing Boat & Figures, watercolor, sgn/dtd 1829, 8x12", FB 4/25/88 UE 900
ZE, Honore (British, 1830-1908)
Dawn, First Day of Ramaddan; oil on canvas, sgn, unfr, 42x66", SBY 5/23/89 16,500
ZE, Joseph; att (French, 1744-1826)
Portrait of an Artist in a Red Coat, pastel on paper laid down, 22x18", SBY 1/12/89 5,500

BRABE, Dosio
Allegorical Scene with Female Nude & Bull by the Seashore, oil on canvas, sgn, 28x37", DM 5/89 ... 300
BRACHT, Eugen (Swiss, 1842-1921)
Die Papenberge am Regenstein Harz', oil on canvas, sgn/inscr/initialed/dtd 1883, 20x39", C-NY 5/25/88 ... 7,700
BRACK, Emil (German, 1860-1905)
Couple in Interior, watercolor heightened w/gouache, sgn, 29x22", C-NY 10/26/88 ... 2,860
BRACKENBURG, Richard (1650-1702/03)
Ladies Fighting in an Interior with Others Watching, oil on canvas, 21x25", SBY 4/7/88 ... 5,225
BRACKETT, Sidney Lawrence (American, 19th/20th C)
Captive Audience (kittens after a fish in a bowl), oil on canvas, sgn, ornate gilt gesso frame, 29x22", RWS 9/8/89 OE ... 2,500
Feeding Time (puppies in landscape), oil on canvas, sgn, 10x14", SBY 3/17/88 UE ... 825
Where There's Smoke (kittens & lit cigar on table's edge), oil on canvas, sgn, gilt gesso frame, 29x22", RWS 9/8/89 OE ... 2,500
BRACKMAN, Robert (American, 1898-1980)
Back View of a Seated Nude, pastel on paper, sgn, 17x24", C-E 2/1/89 ... 1,430
Fruit Study, oil on canvas, sgn, 9x15", B/B 10/9/88 ... 2,200
In Autumn Light #7, oil on canvas, sgn twice, 20x12", C-E 11/30/88 ... 2,200
Seated Woman Fixing Her Hair, pastel on light brown paper, sgn, 18x20", SBY 4/14/89 ... 1,705
Self-Portrait, oil on canvas, sgn, 10x8", C-E 2/1/89 OE ... 1,430
Still Life (fruit), oil on canvas, sgn, unfr, 8x10", SBY 4/14/89 ... 1,430
Still Life of Fruit, oil on board, sgn, 10x14", C-E 11/30/88 ... 1,100
Study #9 (girl standing, nude from waist-up), oil on canvas, sgn, 10x8", C-E 2/1/89 ... 1,045
Study of Two Nudes, pastel on paper, sgn, 18x24", SBY 9/14/89 ... 1,760
BRACQUEMOND, Felix (French, 1833-1914)
Monkey & Birds in a Landscape, watercolor over pencil on paper, initialed/inscr, 12x16", SBY 12/9/88 OE ... 4,400
BRACQUEMOND, Pierre (French, 1870-)
Portrait de Coudurier de Chassaigne, oil on panel, sgn/dtd 1909, 13x10", B/B 5/17/89 ... 880
BRADBURY, Bennett (American, 20th C)
North Cliffs at Noteleys Ledge, oil on canvas, sgn, 20x30", SLK 2/11/89 ... 1,050
BRADBURY, Gideon Elden (American, 1833-1904)
Still Life of Garden Flowers, oil on canvas, sgn/dtd 1874, 21x27", RAB 8/8/89 ... 3,500
BRADE, J. (American, 20th C)
Fishing, oil on canvas, unfr, sgn, 20x26", WL 5/20/88 ... 375
BRADFORD, H.
Seascape, oil on canvas, sgn, 20x16", DM 2/19/88 ... 250
BRADFORD, William (American, 1823-1892)
Arctic Glow, oil on canvas, sgn, ca 1885, 18x20", SBY 5/25/88 ... 26,400
Backing Down to Meet the Pilot, watercolor/mixed media on paper, sgn/dtd 1887, 7x13", RAB 3/14/89 ... 4,500
Dory with Fishermen & Boats, oil on canvas, sgn/dtd 1861, 20x30", C-NY 12/2/88 ... 52,800
Fisherman in an Approaching Storm, oil on canvas, sgn/dtd 1863, 20x30", C-NY 5/26/88 OE ... 90,200
Mary of Boston Returning to Port, oil on canvas, sgn/dtd 1857, 20x30", SBY 5/25/88 OE ... 68,750
New Bedford, Massachusetts, 1864 (ship in heavy seas); watercolor on paper, sgn/titled, 9x12", RAB 8/1/88 ... 850
Running for a Harbor Near Newfoundland, oil on canvas, sgn/dtd 77, 20x30", C-NY 12/2/88 ... 17,600
Ships Off the Coast of Newfoundland, charcoal/pencil on paper, sgn, 18x30", WD 10/5/88 UE ... 3,000
Ships Off the Coast of Newfoundland, oil on canvas, en grisaille, sgn, 18x30", SBY 6/28/89 ... 4,950
Sierra Landscape, oil on panel, sgn, 14x21", SBY 4/14/89 UE ... 6,600
Storm Over Labrador, oil on paper laid down on canvas, 12x18", C-NY 5/26/88 OE ... 16,500
BRADLEY, Basil (British, 1842-1904)
Cows Watering, watercolor/pastel/charcoal on paper, sgn/dtd 1884, 14x24", C-E 2/23/88 ... 1,760
BRADLEY, F.G. (British, 19th C)
Ships by the Cliffs, oil on canvas, sgn/dtd 1887, 12x18", WG 9/16/88 UE ... 175
BRADLEY, John (American, fl 1832-1847)
Pair: Gentleman Holding a Newspaper; Woman with a Handerchief; oil on canvas, sgn/dtd 1832, 12x11", RWS 10/27/89 ... 2,500
BRAEKELEER, see De Braekeleer
BRAITH, Anton (German, 1836-1905)
Flock of Sheep Along a Mountain Path, oil on canvas, sgn/dtd 1889, 28x24", B/B 3/22/89 ... 33,000
BRAITH, Anton; manner of (German, 1836-1905)
Cows & Goats in a Landscape, oil on canvas, bears signature, unfr, 49x61", C-E 5/23/88 OE ... 2,640
Peasants Dancing in a Tavern, oil on panel, bears indistinct signature, 15x20", C-NY 4/8/88 ... 8,250
BRAKENBURGH, Richard (1650-1702)
Peasants Making Merry in a Tavern, oil on canvas, sgn, 15x19", SBY 10/13/89 ... 4,950
BRALEY, Clarence E. (American, 19th C)
Early Spring Landscape, pastel on paper, sgn, 10x23", RAB 3/27/89 UE ... 200
Fishing Boats at Sunset, pastel on paper, sgn, 19x15", RAB 8/9/88 UE ... 600
Guardians of the North (derelict ship against iceburg), oil on canvas, sgn/dtd 1914-15, 30x42", RAB 8/9/88 UE ... 900
New Hat (bust-portrait of girl in black hat with a red bow), oil/pencil on paper, sgn/dtd 1914, 10x12", RAB 8/9/88 ... 650
Sunset at Sea (small fishing boat & distant sailboats), pastel on paper, sgn, 8x28", RAB 8/9/88 UE ... 300
BRAMER, Leonard (Dutch, 1596-1674)
Coronation of the Virgin, oil on panel, ca 1620, 42x37", SBY 6/1/89 ... 33,000
Triumphal Entry into Jerusalem, watercolor on vellum, inscr, 5x4", C-NY 1/11/89 OE ... 1,320
BRAMER, Leonard; circle of (Dutch, 1596-1674)
Christ & the Money Changers, oil on panel, 18x15", C-E 4/7/88 OE ... 1,870

RANCACCIO, Carlo (Italian, 1861-1920)
La Place Clichy, Paris; oil on canvas, sgn/inscr, ca 1908, 15x18", SBY 7/12/89 8,800
Poultry Feeding Outside a Farmhouse, oil on canvas, sgn/inscr, unfr, 21x25", C-NY 5/24/89 7,700
Rainy Day in Paris, oil on artist board, sgn/dtd Paris 1910, 6x9", SBY 12/9/88 OE 6,600
View of Sorento From the Coast, oil on canvas, sgn/inscr Paris Sorrento, 32x40", C-NY 2/23/89 22,000
View of the Bay of Naples, oil on canvas, sgn/inscr Naples, 19x30", C-NY 2/23/89 9,350

RANCUSI, Constantin (American, 1876-1957)
Portrait d'une Femme, tempera/pencil on board mounted on canvas, sgn, ca 1918, 25x16", SBY 11/11/88 385,000

RAND, Johann Christian; att (Austrian, 1722-1795)
Figures in an Extensive Country Landscape, oil on panel, 9x10", SBY 7/12/89 990

RAND, Myra (American, 19th C)
Still Life of Lilacs in a Bowl, oil on canvas, sgn/dtd 96, 39x28", B/B 9/15/88 660

RANDAO, Wilson (20th C)
Compostion No 3, oil on canvas, sgn twice/dtd New York 1982/titled, 74x48", C-NY 11/21/88 2,860

RANDEIS, Antonietta (Bohemian, 1849-)
Il Cordile del Palazzo Vecchio, Florence (courtyard scene), oil on board, sgn, 10x6", C-E 2/21/89 1,650
Il Ponte Vecchio, Florence (buildings & water in landscape), oil on board, sgn, 7x9", C-E 2/21/89 OE 6,380
Pair: Ponte E Castel S Angelo, Roma; Palazzo Ducale, Venezia; oil on board, sgn, ea 7x10", SBY 2/22/89 OE 16,500
Palazzio on Canale de Trovaso, Venice (canal scene); oil on board, sgn, 10x6", C-E 2/21/89 OE 3,300
Santa Maria Delle Salute & the Dogana, oil on canvas, sgn, 15x27", SBY 6/8/88 OE 6,050
Veduta dal Giardino Boboli, Florence (cityscape), oil on board, sgn, 7x9", C-E 2/21/89 OE 6,380

RANDES (German, 19th C)
Peasants with a Team of Horses in a Field, oil on board, sgn, 14x20", SLK 9/28/88 1,400

RANDI, Domenico; att (1683-1736)
Pastoral Landscape with a Donkey, oil on canvas, 36x52", SBY 6/1/89 8,250

RANDI, Giacinto (Italian, 1623-1691)
Biblical Couple, Possibly Judah & Tamar; oil on canvas, oval, 40x30", SBY 10/13/89 OE 20,900

RANDI, Giacinto; circle of (Italian, 1623-1691)
Bacchus & a Satyr, oil on panel, unfr, 11x8", C-NY 4/6/89 UE 1,320
St John the Baptist, oil on canvas, 29x20", C-NY 4/6/89 UE 1,540

RANDI, Giacinto; school of (Italian, 1623-1691)
St John the Baptist (a fragment), oil on canvas, unfr, 27x24", C-E 6/1/88 OE 2,420

RANDNER, Karl C. (American, 1898-1961)
Grand Canyon, oil on canvas, sgn/dtd 40, 30x36", LH 5/15/88 950
Grand Canyon, oil on canvas, sgn/dtd 53, 25x28", B/B 5/18/89 UE 880
Stream Near Old Lyme, Connecticut; oil on canvas, 12x15", NA 2/24/89 350
Winter Scene, oil on canvas, sgn, 19x25", LH 10/16/88 OE 1,800

RANDT, Carl (Swedish, -1930)
Snow Covered Forest, oil on canvas laid down on board, sgn/dtd 1918, 53x40", C-NY 5/23/89 5,500
Snowy Landscape at Sunset, oil on canvas, sgn/dtd 1930, 37x49", C-E 10/25/88 3,080

RANDT, Warren (American, 1918-)
Iris & Poppies (still life of flowers on table), oil on canvas, sgn, 30x40", RWS 9/8/89 1,100

RANDTNER, Fritz (Canadian, 1896-1969)
People Standing (abstract), mixed media, sgn/dtd 1942, 9x6", FB 10/14/88 1,100
Reprisal Bombing, mixed media, sgn/dtd 1942, 9x12", FB 10/17/88 UE 700
Still Life, mixed media, no size given, WAD 11/30/89 700
Still Life (flowers, fruit, pitcher on table), mixed media, 1934, 6x6", FB 10/17/88 UE 600

RANGWYN, Frank (British, 1867-1943)
Side Canal, Venice; oil on panel, initialed, 15x12", C-NY 5/25/88 7,150

RANK, Rockwell (American, 20th C)
Evening at Ponta da Sol, oil on canvas, sgn, 20x30", SBY 3/17/88 UE 660

RANNAN, Peter (British, 20th C)
Northern Street Scene, oil on panel, sgn, 12x10", PHL 6/16/88 500

RAQUAVAL, Louis (French, 1856-1919)
Les Marliques Circa 1893 (canal scene), oil on panel, sgn, 18x15", B/B 10/9/88 UE 4,400
Paris, La Bourse; oil on canvas, sgn, 20x24", C-NY 2/18/88 OE 3,300

RAQUE, Georges (French, 1882-1963)
Compotier Pain et Verre (modern still life w/bread & fruit), oil on canvas, sgn/dtd 41, 9x21", SBY 5/10/89 341,000
La Nappe Rouge (abstract still life), oil on canvas, sgn/dtd 35, 9x13", C-NY 5/11/89 OE 396,000
Le Double Bouquet (abstract), oil on canvas, 1952, 40x40", SBY 5/10/88 660,000
Le Tir a l'Arc (maquette for cover plate), ink/collage on hand made fibrous paper, sgn/dtd Avril 58, 9x6", SBY 10/6/89 16,500
Les Dahlias Rouges, oil on burlap, 1956, sgn, 18x15", SBY 2/16/89 OE 170,500
Les Marguerites II, oil on canvas, sgn, 1944, 8x13", SBY 5/11/88 71,500
Les Pommes, pastel on paper laid down on board, sgn, 9x16", C-NY 5/11/89 OE 253,000
Milarepa (finished study for an etching), gouache on paper, 1949, 12x19", SBY 5/10/89 OE 44,000
Nature Morte a la Corbeille de Fruits, oil on canvas, sgn/dtd 27, 12x29", SBY 11/12/88 OE 528,000
Nature Morte aux Raisin (abstract still life), oil on paper laid down, 1919, 11x14", C-NY 5/11/88 330,000
Nature Morte de Citrons (still life of lemons), oil on canvas, sgn, 8x10", SBY 11/12/88 OE 99,000
Oiseau (bird), India ink on paper, sgn, ca 1958, 9x7", SBY 10/6/89 19,800
Oiseau (mosiac), initialed, 1962, 22x42", C-NY 10/6/88 OE 37,400
Pichet Noir et Limande (still life), oil on canvas, sgn/dtd 42, 20x24", SBY 11/12/88 OE 297,000

Still Life: Two Apples; pastel/charcoal on buff paper, sgn, ca 1925, 7x13", SBY 5/10/89 OE 137,500

BRASILIER, Andre (French, 1929-)

Bouquet de Tulips Devant la Fenetre, oil on canvas, sgn, 32x26", SBY 10/7/89 OE 45,100
Le Cheval Noir et Blanc (black & white horse w/figure), oil on canvas, sgn, 1963, 22x18", SBY 10/5/88 OE 13,200

BRASZ, Arnold Franz (American, 1888-)

The Buggy Ride, Spring of 72; oil on canvas, sgn, 17x22", B/B 12/8/88 550

BRATBY, John (British, 1924-)

Reclining Nude, oil on canvas, sgn/dtd 1962, 50x30", SBY 10/7/89 2,860

BRAUN, Maurice (American, 1877-1941)

Autumn Colors, oil on board, sgn, 8x10", C-E 10/18/89 UE 2,860
Autumn in California, oil on canvas, sgn twice/inscr, 12x16", C-E 6/1/88 OE 3,080
Autumn Landscape, oil on canvas laid down, sgn, 10x14", B/B 10/6/88 1,320
By the Sea, oil on canvas, sgn, 18x28", C-NY 9/28/89 11,000
California Dunes, oil on canvas, sgn, 25x30", B/B 10/6/88 6,600
Country Road, oil on canvas, sgn, 12x18", B/B 10/6/88 2,750
Lake Hodges (landscape), oil on canvasboard, sgn/titled, 10x8", SBY 3/17/88 2,310
Marine Scene/Pacific (waves crash on rocks in late afternoon light), oil on canvas, sgn, 16x20", RWS 3/31/88 OE 3,250
Marshland After the Storm, watercolor on paper, sgn/dtd 22, 7x6", B/B 1/11/89 440
Summer Landscape, oil on canvas, sgn, 12x18", B/B 10/6/88 3,025
Summers Skies, oil on canvas, sgn, 18x24", B/B 10/6/88 9,350
Toward the Dessert, oil on canvas, sgn, 25x30", B/B 6/15/89 16,500

BRAUN, Maurice; att (American, 1877-1941)

Spring Trees (early buds on trees in landscape), oil on canvas, bears signature, 24x30", B/B 9/14/89 OE 1,870

BRAUNER, Victor (French, 1903-1966)

Ce Qui m'Appartient, oil on canvas, sgn/dtd 1950, 32x26", SBY 5/11/88 OE 110,000
Infrascape (abstract), encaustic on board, sgn/dtd II 1957, 26x20", SBY 11/12/88 OE 99,000
L'Evasion (abstract head in profile), oil on canvas, ca 1945, 26x21", SBY 10/6/89 121,000
La Lumiere Silencieuse (abstract), oil on canvas, sgn/dtd 1964/titled, 32x26", SBY 11/12/88 82,500
Psychoscaph (contemporary composition), oil on canvas, sgn/dtd 1948/titled, 22x18", C-NY 5/11/89 121,000
The Dream Reve, watercolor/India ink on buff paper, sgn, 12x18", SBY 5/10/89 OE 24,200
Untitled, encaustic on board laid down on panel, sgn/dtd 1949, 24x29", SBY 5/11/88 OE 148,500

BRAUNTUCH, Troy (20th C)

Untitled, white chalk on black paper, sgn/dtd 1980, 45x28", C-E 5/13/88 UE 550
Untitled (abstract), white chalk on black paper, sgn/dtd 81, 82x28", C-NY 2/20/88 3,300
Untitled (compositions), pencil on 2 sheets of black paper, 46x64", SBY 10/5/89 4,950
Untitled (sculptured head on table), white pencil on black paper, 1981, 83x30", SBY 11/11/88 OE 9,350

BRAVO, Cladio (Chilian, 1936-)

Amarillo, Rojo y Azul (yellow/red/blue composition); oil on canvas, sgn/dtd 1973, 79x47", C-NY 11/21/88 93,500
Bailarina (seated ballerina), watercolor/pencil on paper, sgn/dtd 1953, 11x8", C-NY 11/21/88 4,400
Bodegon y Paisaje (interior w/painter's easle, view through window), oil on canvas, sgn/dtd 1986, 51x43", C-NY 5/17/89 143,000
Cactus & Sponges, pastel on paper, sgn/dtd 1985, 27x39", SBY 5/17/88 39,600
Copa de Cristal con Huevos de Marmol (still life), oil on canvas, sgn/dtd 1962, 36x27", C-NY 5/18/88 49,500
El Musico Ciego (portrait of blind musician), oil on canvas, sgn/dtd 1956, 29x24", C-NY 11/21/88 OE 26,400
Girl with Mirror (nude in landscape), oil on canvas, sgn/dtd MCMLXXI, 1971, 63x51", SBY 5/16/89 148,500
Grisaille Package, oil on canvas, sgn/dtd 1970, 64x45", SBY 5/17/88 85,250
La Chaise le Corbusier (interior view), oil on canvas, sgn/dtd 1977, 38x51", C-NY 11/21/88 132,000
Landscape, oil on canvas, sgn/dtd MCMLIX, 37x23", SBY 5/16/89 12,100
Naturaleza Muerta con Frutas, oil on canvas, sgn/dtd 1982, 18x22", C-NY 5/18/88 OE 71,500
Package, pastel on paper, sgn/dtd MCMLXVI, 25x20", SBY 11/21/88 OE 63,250
Portrait of Mohammed (seated on shelf in artist's studio), oil on canvas, sgn/dtd MCMLXXIV, 79x59", SBY 11/21/88 126,500
Self-Portrait, oil on canvas, sgn/indistinctly dtd 1964(?), 29x21", SBY 5/16/89 16,500
Still Life (urn/flowers/mushrooms in landscape), oil on canvas, sgn/dtd MCMLIX, 37x23", SBY 5/16/89 OE 25,300
Still Life of Watches, oil on canvas, sgn/dtd MCMLXIV, 23x27", SBY 11/21/88 34,100
Untitled (male winged figure w/electric guitar & bird in cloud), pencil on card, sgn/dtd MCMLXX, 18x18", SBY 5/16/89 UE 3,850
Untitled (pinball machine w/man peering from behind door), oil on canvas, sgn/dtd MCMLXXIII, 67x47", SBY 5/16/89 UE 88,000

BRAY, Albert; see De Bray

BRAY, Arnold (American, 20th C)

Green Hills, Marin Landscape; oil on canvas, sgn/dtd 28, 24x30", B/B 9/15/88 ..... 41[illegible]
Inlet Along the California Coast, oil on canvas, sgn/dtd 23, 24x30", B/B 10/6/88 990
Pair: Female Portraits; oil on canvas, 30x24", B/B 8/10/88 ..... 30[illegible]
View of Fort Point, oil on canvas, sgn, 24x30", B/B 10/6/88 ..... 46[illegible]

BRAYER, Yves (French, 1907-)

Le Tajo a Tolede (landscape), oil on canvas, sgn, 29x36", C-E 5/9/89 OE 12,100
Odalisque, oil on canvas, sgn, 14x11", B/B 1/11/89 1,100

Brazilian School (19th C)

Bay of Rio de Janeiro, oil on canvas, 17x24", C-SK 5/25/89 ..... 4,78[illegible]

BREAKSPEARE, William A. (British, 1855-1914)

Classical Maiden, oil on panel, sgn, 4x9", SBY 12/9/88 ..... 1,21[illegible]
Lady Reclining on a Stone Bench in a Garden, oil on canvas, sgn, 10x14", C-E 2/21/89 3,300
Pretty Serving Maid, oil on canvas, sgn, 30x20", SBY 6/8/88 3,300

REANSKI, see De Breanski

RECKENRIDGE, Hugh Henry (American, 1870-1937)

Landscape, pastel on paper, sgn, 28x36", C-E 6/1/88 ... 1,760
Quarry, oil on canvas mounted on board, sgn, 13x10", RWS 11/10/89 UE ... 475

REDAEL, Peeter; circle of (Flemish, 1629-1719)

Village Scene with Peasants & Animals, oil on canvas, unfr, 18x24", SBY 10/13/89 ... 17,600

REDT, Ferdinand Max (German, 1860-)

Watercarrier, oil on board, sgn/inscr, 15x11", C-E 5/23/88 ... 1,760

REEDWELD, H.

Ducks by a Lake, oil on canvas, 17x20", C-E 9/15/88 ... 550

REKELENKAMP, Quiryn (Dutch, 1620-1668)

Man Cutting Fish, with Children Watching; oil on panel, indistinctly initialed, unfr, 15x19", C-NY 1/15/88 OE ... 22,000

REKELENKAMP, Quiryn; circle of (Dutch, 1620-1668)

Woman Sitting at a Spinning Wheel, oil on panel, unfr, 31x24", C-NY 4/6/89 ... 7,700

REKELENKAMP, Quiryn; school of (Dutch, 1620-1668)

Woman Spinning in an Interior, oil on canvas, 14x10", C-E 6/1/88 ... 1,760

RELL, J. Peru (Spanish, 19th/20th C)

Entering a Spanish Marketplace, oil on canvas, sgn/dtd Valencia 1920, 30x38", C-NY 2/23/89 OE ... 8,800

REMEN, see Von Bremen

RENDENBERG, Wilhelm (German, 1824-1901)

Alpine Landscape with Figures & Boats on a Foreground Stream, oil on canvas, sgn, 19x27", SLK 5/12/88 ... 375

RENEISER, Stanley Grontevent (American, 1890-)

Desert North of Sante Fe, watercolor on paper, sgn/dtd, 15x22", B/B 1/11/89 UE ... 275

RENNER, Carl Christian (American, 1838-1888)

Birches in a Forest Glade, oil on canvas, sgn/dtd 1833-1884, 30x50", SBY 1/24/89 ... 7,150
Landscape at Sunset, oil on canvas, sgn/dtd 1877, 16x27", MAG 3/27/88 ... 650
Landscape with Brook, oil on canvas, sgn/dtd 1883, 22x40", WG 4/23/88 OE ... 1,800
Wash Day in the Woods, oil on canvas, sgn/dtd 1866, 12x22", NA 2/24/89 ... 1,900

RENNIR, Carl (British, 1850-1920)

English Landscape with Hunter & His Dog, oil on canvas, sgn, 28x21", C-E 10/25/88 ... 2,200

RENTON, Jules (French, 1827-1905)

Water Carrier (portrait of woman w/water jug), oil on canvas, sgn/dtd 1881, 32x24", SBY 5/23/89 OE ... 41,250

RERETON, Robert; style of (British, 1835-1847)

Horses & Colt (in a landscape), oil on canvas, sgn/dtd 1823, 26x36", B/B 10/9/88 ... 4,950

RESCIA, see Bonvicino, Alessandro

RETHAUER, C.G. (American, 20th C)

Spring Landscape, oil on canvas, sgn, 13x17", SLK 2/12/88 ... 150

RETLAND, Thomas (British, 1802-1874)

Gentleman with His Gray Hunter, oil on canvas, sgn/dtd 1844, 25x30", SBY 6/9/89 ... 7,700

RETON, Andre

Decalcomanie, black gouache decalcomanie on blue paper, inscr, 1936, 11x8", C-NY 10/6/88 OE ... 7,150
Decalcomanie, black gouache decalcomanie on paper, inscr, 11x9", C-NY 10/6/88 OE ... 6,050

RETON, Jacqueline

Decalcomanie, black gouache decalcomanie on paper, inscr, 1936, 13x10", C-NY 10/6/88 ... 4,180

RETON, Jules Adolphe (French, 1827-1905)

Beside the Lily Pond, oil on canvas, sgn/dtd 1879, unfr, 28x39", SBY 4/29/88 OE ... 17,600
La Fin du Travail, oil on canvas, sgn, 12x10", WD 5/5/88 OE ... 9,000
La Saint Jean (festival with dancing around bonfire), oil on canvas, sgn/dtd 1875, 44x77", SBY 6/1/89 ... 484,000
Le Femme a l'Ombrelle, Baie de Douarnenez (artist's wife, Elodie); oil on canvas, sgn/dtd 1871, 26x36", SBY 2/22/89 OE ... 1,650,000
Le Rappel des Glaneuses, oil on canvas, ca 1855-60, unfr, 26x39", SBY 10/24/89 OE ... 35,750
Ronde de la Saint Jean, a Courrieres (peasant women dancing); oil on canvas, sgn, ca 1875, 11x19", SBY 10/24/89 ... 38,500
Siesta, oil on canvas, sgn, 13x22", C-NY 2/25/88 ... 7,150
Travers Champs (landscape depicting potato harvesters), oil on canvas, sgn/dtd 1887, SBY 2/22/89 ... 165,000
Young Girl Watching the Cows, oil on canvas, sgn/dtd 1872, 19x24", SBY 10/24/89 ... 115,500

RETON, Yvon (Canadian, 1942-)

Riviere Jenne, oil on canvas, sgn/titled, 16x20", FB 10/30/89 ... 412

RETT, Harold Matthew (American, 1880-)

Flirtation, oil on board, sgn, unfr, 40x30", SBY 9/23/88 UE ... 1,320
Mother & Daughter (in interior), watercolor & pencil on paper, sgn, 25x15", C-E 2/1/89 ... 715

REU, Jorg the elder (16th C)

Bridal Chamber with an Empress & Her Attendants, pen/black ink/brown & orange wash, 8" dia, C-NY 1/12/88 OE ... 77,000

REU, Jorg the elder; att (16th C)

Portrait of Hans Hermann, half-length, in fur-lined coat & cap...; oil on panel, inscr, 15x12", C-NY 1/11/89 UE ... 13,200

REUGHEL, Pieter the younger

Kermesse, oil on panel, 25x36", C-NY 1/11/89 OE ... 275,000

REVOORT, James Renwick (American, 1832-1918)

Americas Cup Race, oil on canvas, sgn, 24x17", SBY 9/14/89 ... 1,980
Morning on the Hackensack Meadows, oil on canvas, sgn twice/dtd 1863/titled, 7x13", SBY 1/24/89 OE ... 2,090

REWER, Nicholas Richard (American, 1857-1949)

Hills of Cheyenne, oil on canvas, sgn, 24x34", B/B 6/15/89 ... 4,400
Street Urchen (boy holding coins), oil on canvas, sgn, 24x20", RAB 8/9/88 UE ... 150

BREWER, R.J. (American, 20th C)
Mountain Lake Scene, oil on panel, sgn/dtd 37, 21x25", LH 9/10/89 UE 150
BREWERTON, George Douglas (American, 1820-1901)
Fort Sumter, mixed media on board, sgn/dtd 1862, 18x35", B/B 12/8/88 OE 3,025
Off Grand Manan, Maine; watercolor/chalk on paper, sgn, 27x21", SBY 6/28/89 1,100
Seascape, Grand Manan, Maine; watercolor/chalk on paper, sgn, 24x36", SBY 6/28/89 1,650
Sunset at Grand Manan, Maine; pastel on arched board, 23x10", SBY 1/24/89 1,430
BREWSTER, Anna Richards (American, 1870-1952)
Across the Hill Luxor, Egypt, 1912 (view to the cliffs of Luxor); oil on canvas mounted on masonite, 4x13", RWS 3/31/88 225
Autumn Lake, oil on canvasboard, initialed, 7x14", RWS 3/16/89 450
Autumn Lake (landscape), oil on canvasboard, initialed, 7x14", RWS 3/16/89 450
Delphi, Greece, 1912 (view of mountains surrounding Delphi); oil on canvas mounted on masonite, sgn, 9x14", RWS 3/31/88 600
Mosque in Tunis, oil on canvas, 18x24", C-E 2/3/88 880
Olympia, Greece, 1912 (valley w/mountains beyond); oil on canvas mounted on masonite, 7x12", RWS 3/31/88 OE 700
Pair: Street Scene with Carriages; Outside the Great Hall of William Rufus, oil on canvas on board, 6x8", SBY 6/24/88 1,320
Pair: View of Blois; View of Pau; oil on canvas laid down on board, 6x8", SBY 6/24/88 1,320
Pair: View to the Coast; Old Orchard; oil on artist board, 1 sgn, 1 ca 1915, 5x8", 9x13", RWS 9/29/88 UE 275
BREWSTER, John Jr. (American, 1766-1854)
Comfort Starr Mygatt & His Daughter Lucy Mygatt (Adams), oil on canvas, sgn/dtd 1799, 54x39", SBY 1/28/88 852,500
Portrait of a Man in a Yellow Vest, oil on canvas, 29x26", C-E 6/20/89 OE 4,950
BREYDAEL, Karel (Flemish, 1678-1733)
Battle Scene Before a Castle, oil on panel, sgn/indistinctly dtd, 17x19", SBY 10/21/88 4,950
Battle Scene Before a Castle, oil on panel, sgn/indistinctly dtd, 17x19", SBY 4/7/89 4,675
BRIANCHON, Maurice (French, 1899-1979)
Caleche dans un Sous-Boius (landscape w/carriage & figures), oil on canvas, sgn/dtd 1941, 26x36", C-NY 10/6/88 44,000
Maree Basse (low tide, figures on beach, orange sky), oil on canvas, sgn, 20x16", C-NY 10/5/89 60,500

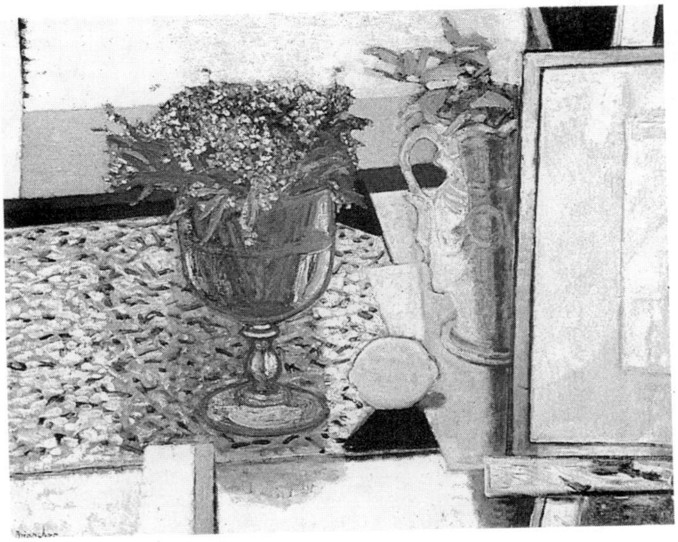

Nature Morte aux Myosotis, oil on canvas, sgn, 24x29", C-NY 10/5/89 OE, $110,000

Nu aux Bas Rouges (nude w/red stockings), watercolor over pencil on paper, sgn, 11x11", C-NY 2/18/88 3,520
BRIANTE, Ezelino (Italian, 1901-1970)
Fishing Boats Along the Coast of Naples, oil on board, sgn, 11x13", B/B 12/8/88 1,210
BRICHER, Alfred Thompson (American, 1837-1908)
Afternoon, Southampton Beach; oil on canvas, monogramed, 20x36", C-NY 12/2/88 77,000
Afternoon on the Hudson, oil on canvas, sgn/dtd 67, 20x42", SBY 5/25/88 77,000
At Low Tide (seascape), oil on canvas, sgn, 9x18", SBY 3/17/88 OE 9,350
At the Shore, oil on paper, sgn/dtd 1871, 6x12", SBY 5/25/88 OE 60,500
Autumn Cabin (lake scene), oil on canvas, sgn/dtd 65, 10x19", C-NY 5/26/88 20,900
Bathers at Long Branch, New Jersey; watercolor/gouache/pencil on paper, monogramed, 10x22", C-NY 12/2/88 22,000
Coastal Scene, Maone; watercolor/pencil on paper, sgn/#d 29, 26x10", RWS 5/19/88 2,800
Coastal Scene, watercolor on paper, sgn/#d 131, 10x22", SBY 3/17/88 2,530
Coastal Scene with Boats, watercolor on paper, sgn, 10x24", SBY 6/28/89 3,080
Coastal Scene with Sunset & Sailboats, watercolor on paper, sgn, 10x22", SBY 4/14/89 4,675
Coastal View, watercolor/gouache on paper, sgn, unfr, 11x27", SBY 6/28/89 3,850
Cushings Island, Casco Bay, Maine (coastal scene); watercolor/pencil on paper, sgn/#d 2, 15x21", RWS 3/16/89 OE 4,500
Deserted Boatyard, watercolor/Chinese white/pencil on paper laid down on board, sgn, 10x22", C-NY 5/25/89 OE 24,200
Double-Sided: Indian Viewing a Mountain Lake; Lady in Ball Gown; pencil on paper, 6x4", RAB 8/8/89 400
Drying the Sails, Oyster Boats, Patchogue, Long Island; watercolor/pencil, initialed, 21x10", C-NY 5/25/89 17,600
Headlands & Breakers-Grand Manan Maine (seascape); oil on canvas, monogramed, 28x53", SBY 5/24/89 UE 33,000
Marine Scene (gentle waves on rocks), watercolor/gouache on paper, sgn, 21x10", RWS 9/8/89 UE 500
Massachusetts Coast, watercolor & pencil heightened w/white on tan paper, sgn, 11x22", SBY 6/28/89 3,630

Merrimack at Plymouth, New Hampshire; pencil on paper, dtd July 7-68/titled, 5x9", RAB 8/8/89	350
Mount Washington, New Hampshire; oil on canvas, 9x19", C-NY 3/11/88	7,700
New England Beach Scene, watercolor/gouache, sgn, 15x21", WL 5/20/88 OE	3,300
Pleasant Afternoon, watercolor on paper, monogramed, dtd July 27/80, 14x21", SBY 5/25/88	65,500
Quiet Shore, oil on canvas laid down on masonite, monogramed, 24x50", C-NY 3/11/88	28,600
Rocky Coastline with Pines, watercolor on paper, initialed, 4x10", RWS 3/16/89	650
Rough Seas, oil on canvas, monogramed, 17x36", C-NY 12/2/88	30,800
Rounding the Point (seascape), oil on canvas, initialed, 30x63", C-NY 5/26/88	41,800
Seascape, watercolor on paper, sgn, 9x21", RAB 8/8/89	1,600
Surf & Rocks, Grand Manan; black wash on paper, sgn, 3x6", SBY 6/28/89	770
View of Lake at Sunrise, oil on canvas, sgn/dtd 1872, 10x9", C-NY 12/2/88	16,500
View of the Ocean, oil on canvas, sgn w/initials in monogram, 18x38", C-NY 12/2/88	28,600
RIDAHAM, Lester Burbank	
Roudez Vous des Chochers (figures in an interior), oil on canvas, dtd 1932, 38x63", WG 4/23/88 UE	1,200
RIDGES, Fidelia (American, 1834-1924)	
Lake with Birds & Lily Pads, gouache on paper laid down on board, sgn/dtd 1873, 8x12", SBY 9/14/89	1,320
RIDGMAN, Frederick Arthur (American, 1847-1928)	
Apollon Enlevant Cyrene, oil on canvas, sgn/dtd 1872, 34x54", SBY 10/24/89 OE	63,250
Arab Tribesman Resting, oil on panel, sgn/dtd 1822, 7x9", C-SK 5/25/89	1,650
Bazaar Scene, oil on canvas, sgn, 26x23", SBY 6/28/89 OE	11,000
Dolce far Niente, oil on canvas, sgn/inscr opus/CCCL, ca 1897, 20x24", SBY 5/23/89	38,500
Eastern Courtyard, oil on canvas, sgn, 17x23", SBY 10/24/89	13,200
Eastern Veranda, oil on canvas, sgn, 24x36", SBY 2/22/89	49,500
Fellahin & Child, The Bath; oil on canvas, sgn, 24x32", C-NY 5/25/88	24,200
Harem Girl (full-length portrait in landscape), oil on canvas, sgn/dtd 1887, 49x28", B/B 3/22/89	16,500
Head of a Gypsy (in profile), oil on canvas, sgn/dtd 1887, 13x10", SBY 9/14/89	9,350
In the Harem, oil on canvas, sgn/dtd 1875, 30x25", SBY 4/29/88 OE	90,750
Orange Seller (woman squatting by basket of oranges), oil on panel, sgn/dtd 1875, 11x9", C-SK 5/25/89 OE	7,720
Pharaoh's Army Engulfed by the Red Sea, oil on canvas, sgn/dtd 1900, 45x83", SBY 2/22/89 UE	9,900
Procession of the Bull, oil on canvas, SBY 6/8/88 UE	2,420
Reclining by a Stream, oil on canvas, sgn, 20x36", SBY 2/22/89	13,200
Within the Seraglio (girl seated in doorway petting cat), oil on canvas, sgn/dtd 1879, 22x29", C-NY 12/2/88	17,600
Young Woman by a Fruit Tree, oil on canvas, sgn/inscr, 26x20", SBY 9/23/88 UE	1,870
RIDGMAN, Frederick Arthur; att (American, 1847-1928)	
Eastern Beauty, oil on board, 20x31", WD 1/11/89	1,500
RIEVA, Manuel Villegas (Spanish, 19th C)	
Spanish Courtyard Scene, oil on canvas, sgn/dtd 1890, 20x28", LH 3/20/89 OE	3,000
RIGANTI, Nicholas P. (American, 1895-)	
Landscape with Figures by a Pond, oil on canvas, sgn, 28x38", C-E 2/3/88	1,320
Venetian Canal, oil on canvas, sgn, 20x26", NA 3/26/88 OE	950
Venetian Scene, View From Landing at San Marco to Saint Giorgio Maggiore; oil on canvas, sgn, 18x40", RWS 11/3/88 UE	500
RIGGS, Lamar (American, 20th C)	
Ibeza, gouache on paper, sgn, 30x41", PHL 6/16/88	1,000
RIGGS, Lucius A. (American, 1852-1931)	
Flying Scud (ship), watercolor on paper, titled, 17x23", RAB 11/25/88	500
Portrait of an American Warship (probably the Constitution), watercolor on paper, sgn, 17x23", RAB 8/1/88	500
Staffordshire (ship), watercolor on paper, sgn/titled, 18x23", RAB 11/25/88	400
Whaleship Gazelle, watercolor on paper, sgn, 17x22", RAB 8/1/89	1,000
Whaleship Pocahontas, watercolor on paper, sgn, 16x23", RAB 8/1/89	800
RIGHT, Harry (British, fl 1867-1892)	
Kingfisher, watercolor/gouache on paper, sgn, 16x12", SBY 6/10/88	3,025
Music in the Woods, watercolor on paper, sgn/dtd 1880, 17x12", SBY 7/12/89	1,430
RIGHT, Henry (British, 1814-1873)	
Outside the Church Garden, watercolor on paper heightened w/white, initialed, 13x10", C-E 2/23/88	550
RIGHTON	
Soldier with Medals, watercolor on paper, sgn/dtd 1820, unfr, 7x6", C-E 2/16/88 OE	176
RIL, Paul (Flemish, 1554-1626)	
Mountainous Landscape with a River in a Gorge & a Fort on an Overhanging Rock, pen/brown ink, 7x11", SBY 1/13/88	15,400
Mountainous Landscape with Wildlife Gathered Around a Cascade, oil on canvas, dtd 1619, 27x38", SBY 6/2/89	77,000
Mountainous Wooded Landscape with a Peasant by a Bridge Over a Torrent, oil on canvas, 35x26", C-NY 1/11/89	30,800
Traveler Resting in a Wooded Clearing in a Mountainous River Landscape, oil on canvas, 24x19", C-NY 1/11/89	11,000
RISCOE, Franklin D. (American, 1844-1903)	
Fishermen's Return, oil on canvas, sgn/dtd 75, 30x50", WD 10/5/88	4,250
Gettysburg, oil on canvas, sgn/dtd 1864/inscr On the Edge of the Wheatfield, 24x20", C-E 10/18/89	3,300
Pier, oil on board, sgn, 11x14", C-E 11/30/88	1,100
Sailing in a Haze, oil on canvas, sgn, 12x20", SBY 6/24/88 OE	3,850
Sailing Ships at Sea, oil on board mounted on board, sgn, 7x8", FAP 4/15/89 OE	2,310
Seascape, oil on canvas, sgn/inscr Atlantic City, 12x20", RWS 3/16/89 OE	1,700
Ship Approaching Cliffs During Storm, oil on board, sgn/dtd 82, 12x18", FAP 11/4/88	850
Ships on a Stormy Sea, oil on canvas, sgn, 28x50", SBY 6/24/88	8,250
Shipwreck & Rescue, oil on canvas, sgn/dtd 1897, 22x37", C-NY 9/30/88	4,620

Sunset on a Palm Tree, oil on canvas, sgn, 30x50", FAP 11/4/88 OE 4,000

BRISCOE, Franklin D.; att (American, 1844-1903)

At Sea, oil on canvas, 20x30", C-E 10/18/89 4,400
Sailing Near a Harbor (ships at sea), oil on canvas, 29x38", SBY 3/17/88 1,760

BRISSET, Emile (French, -1904)

Calvary Charge, oil on canvas, sgn, 32x39", SLK 5/11/88 1,600

BRISTOL, John Bunyan (American, 1826-1909)

Cows Watering, oil on canvas, sgn, 24x40", C-E 6/1/88 3,300
End of Day, oil on canvas, 10x16", C-E 11/30/88 4,620
Figures Along the River, oil on canvas, sgn, 18x30", B/B 3/17/88 7,150
Glimpse of Lake Champlain, oil on canvas, sgn, 18x30", C-NY 3/11/88 7,150
Landscape South Bennington, Vermont; oil on canvas, sgn, 12x22", C-E 6/1/89 2,640
Pair: Cottage on Summer Day; Rooftops; oil on canvas, 9x14", 8x12", SBY 6/24/88 OE 5,500
Pair: Landscape with Church; Landscape with Fields & Trees; oil on canvas, 6x12", 7x13", SBY 6/24/88 OE 3,300
View of a Church in a River Landscape, oil on canvas, sgn, 14x22", PHL 12/1/88 1,300
View of Silver Bay, Lake George; oil on canvas, sgn, 18x30", SBY 9/14/89 7,150
Warm Sunset, oil on canvas, sgn, 7x12", C-E 11/30/88 OE 4,400
Woman Reading Beneath a Tree, oil on board, 15x10", SBY 6/24/88 OE 2,860
Woman Strolling with Parasol, oil on board, sgn/inscr, 8x15", SBY 6/24/88 OE 3,300

BRISTOW, Edmund (British, 1787-1876)

Bridge Over a Stream with a Castle in the Distance, oil on panel, initialed, 9x13", C-E 11/8/88 990
Clewer Point on the Thames, two boys fishing; oil on canvas, 20x16", SLK 4/7/89 1,600
Stella, a Bay Racehorse, in a Landscape; oil on canvas, sgn, 16x20", SBY 6/9/89 11,000
Village Blacksmith, oil on canvas, sgn, oval, 14x14", C-E 10/26/89 2,200

BRISTOW, Edmund; att (British, 1787-1876)

Huntsman's Return (exterior view of tavern w/horse, game, & dog), oil on canvas, 27x25", B/B 3/22/89 5,500

British School (18th C)

Gentlemen Meeting by a Dock in a Harbor Town...; black chalk/pen/ink/watercolor, 18x24", C-NY 1/11/89 880
Interior with Smokers Seated at Table & an Artist by His Easel, oil on panel, 12x15", SBY 12/9/88 OE 7,425
Pair: Brown & White Speckled Owl; watercolor on paper, 20x14", SBY 12/9/88 OE 5,775
Pair: Young Gentlemen; oil on panel, oval, 10x8", SBY 6/8/88 1,100
Portrait of a Gentleman Holding a Cat, oil on canvas in a painted oval, 30x25", SBY 7/12/89 1,320
Portrait of a Lady, oil on canvas, 26x21", SBY 6/8/88 UE 385
Portrait of a Lady Holding Flowers, oil on canvas, 45x32", B/B 12/8/88 1,760
Portrait of a Lady in a Landscape, oil on canvas, 9x7", SBY 12/9/88 OE 2,750
Portrait of a Lady Said To Be the Duchess of Tuscany (seated w/dog), oil on canvas, 46x34", SBY 7/12/89 1,760
Portrait of a Young Boy with His Dog, oil on canvas, 30x25", SBY 6/8/88 1,870
Portrait of a Young Girl with a Dog, oil on canvas, 48x40", SBY 7/12/89 3,080
View of Greenwich, oil on canvas, 21x29", SBY 7/12/89 1,980
Wooded Landscape, oil on canvas, 18x24", SBY 7/12/89 880

British School (19th C)

Ariadne of Newcastle, watercolor on paper, titled/inscr, 13x17", SBY 7/12/89 770
Bark Mead Approaching Port (ship), oil on canvas, 20x28", RAB 11/10/77 1,500
British Sporting Scene, watercolor on paper, indistinctly sgn, 6x11", B/B 9/15/88 UE 275
Caught Off Guard, oil on panel, 16x12", SBY 6/8/88 990
Columbus & Isabella (court scene), oil on canvas, 23x34", FAP 4/15/89 522
Cottage by a River, oil on canvas, bears signature/dtd 1868, 20x27", SBY 12/9/88 UE 715
Country Gentleman & His Hounds (in nighttime landscape), oil on canvas, 25x30", B/B 3/22/89 3,025
Cricket Match at Lords, London; oil on canvas, 17x28", SBY 6/10/88 OE 25,300
Equestrienne, oil on canvas, 20x24", SBY 6/8/88 1,980
Family in an Interior, oil on canvas, 16x23", B/B 9/15/88 1,100
Fishermen Off the Coast, oil on canvas laid down, unfr, 17x20", B/B 5/17/89 OE 1,210
Fishing in the Stream, oil on panel, 8x9", SBY 7/12/89 715
Gamekeeper's Pantry, oil on canvas, 25x19", RWS 8/20/88 475
Gathering in the Highlands, oil on canvas, 28x36", SBY 7/12/89 OE 6,600
Good Ship Atlanta (clipper on high seas), oil on canvas, 18x24", B/B 3/22/89 2,200
Gustavus, a Gray Colt, Winner of the Derby in 1821; oil on canvas, 21x25", SBY 7/12/89 110
Hackney Horses & Groom in a Landscape, oil on paper laid down on canvas, dtd 1824, 15x20", SBY 6/8/88 UE 1,430
Mountain Valley with Rushing Water, oil on canvas, 14x21", LH 9/10/89 400
Pair: Shooting Scenes; oil on canvas, 38x38", SBY 6/10/88 7,150
Picnic in the Countryside, oil on canvas, 45x60", B/B 3/17/88 4,950
Plaid Frock & Stockings: Young Girl with a Cat Pull-Toy; watercolor/gouache/varnish on paper, 7x6", RWS 6/10/89 1,000
Portrait of a Girl, bust-length facing forward in lace shawl; oil on canvas, 19x15", SLK 11/25/88 1,050
Portrait of a Girl & Boy, oil on canvas, 42x32", SBY 4/7/88 UE 2,475
Portrait of a Lady, in Regency period gown; oil on canvas, 33x23", RWS 8/20/88 OE 1,800
Portrait of a Lady in a Red Shawl, pastel on paper, 29x25", B/B 12/8/88 825
Portrait of a Man Said To Be Bertram 4th Earl of Ashburnham, oil on canvas, inscr, 30x25", SBY 12/9/88 1,870
Portrait of a Member of the British Royal Family, oil on canvas, 30x20", B/B 1/11/89 OE 1,320
Portrait of a Naval Officer (three-quarter length, sea beyond), oil on wood panel, orig frame, 12x10", RAB 8/1/88 950
Portrait of a Shepherd Boy, oil on canvas, ca 1800, 21x17", SBY 7/12/89 440
Portrait of a Stud, Sergent; oil on canvas, 26x32", B/B 3/22/89 1,430

Quiet Harbor (ships docked in harbor inlet), watercolor on paper, 9x13", RAB 3/27/89 UE ... 250
Rescue, figures near dory along stormy coast w/ship in distance; oil on canvas, indistinctly sgn, 8x14", RAB 3/27/89 OE ... 1,700
Resting by the Wayside, oil on panel, initialed, 19x15", B/B 9/15/88 ... 770
Sailor's Young Apprentices, oil on canvas, 15x13", RWS 6/17/89 ... 750
Spaniel in a Landscape, oil on canvas, 24x32", SBY 12/9/88 ... 935
Stormy Coastal Scene, oil on canvas, 20x30", B/B 6/15/89 ... 1,100
Surprise Catch (humorous scene of fisherman & eel), oil on canvas, 24x20", RAB 9/8/88 UE ... 1,050
Travelers in a Wooded Landscape with Trees & Stream, oil on panel, initialed, ca 1800, 21x27", SBY 7/12/89 ... 2,970
Twilight Landscape, oil on canvas, initialed twice/dtd 1879, 7x6", RAB 3/27/89 ... 400
Two Travelers Resting on a Path, oil on canvas, 14x12", LH 9/10/89 ... 425
View of Gravesend on the Thames, oil on canvas, bears signature/inscr/dtd 1859 twice, 32x51", SBY 12/9/88 OE ... 6,050
West Highland White Terrier in a Landscape, oil on canvas, bears signature, 20x25", SBY 7/12/89 ... 1,430
Young Girl & Dog (standing before bay window), watercolor/gouache/varnish on paper, 8x6", RWS 6/10/89 UE ... 475
Young Girl Holding a Rabbit, oil on canvas, 26x21", B/B 9/14/89 OE ... 1,980

itish School (19th/20th C)

First Salute to the Stars & Stripes-John Paul Jones, 1778; oil on canvas, 76x92", SBY 6/8/88 UE ... 3,080
Pair: Coaching Scenes; oil on panel, 13x22", SBY 6/9/89 ... 2,090
Portrait of a Military Officer (half-length), oil on canvas, 30x25", B/B 5/17/89 ... 825
Resting Hounds, watercolor on paper, indistinctly sgn, unfr, 10x15", B/B 9/15/88 OE ... 1,760
Scottish Highland Scene, oil on canvas, sgn/dtd 1905, 12x16", B/B 5/17/89 ... 1,210
Ships at Sea, oil on panel, 7x10", FAP 4/15/89 ... 495

RITO, Ramon Vasquez (Latin American, 20th C)

Como Rozando Azules (coastal view w/mountain range), oil/marble dust on canvas, sgn, 45x64", C-NY 11/21/88 ... 6,600
Se Oculto la Esperanza (seascape), oil on canvas, sgn/dtd 88/titled, 51x77", SBY 5/16/89 ... 9,350
Seascape, oil on canvas, sgn/dtd 85, 45x58", SBY 5/17/88 ... 7,700

RITTON, Harry (Canadian, 1878-1958)

Harvest Moon, oil on board, sgn, 9x12", WAD 6/12/89 ... 800

RIZZI, Francesco (1574-1623)

Two Children Eating an Apple in an Interior, oil on canvas laid down on panel, 16x14", SBY 4/7/89 ... 2,200

ROCHART, Constant Joseph (French, 1816-1899)

Portrait of a Young Girl in a Vineyard, pastel on paper, sgn/dtd 1881, 32x25", B/B 6/15/89 ... 4,400

ROCK, H.M.

Molony's Lament, pen/ink, sgn/dtd 1896, 6x7", SWN 6/15/89 ... 193

ROCKHURST, Gerald Leslie (British, 1890-)

Anais (portrait), oil on canvas, sgn, 20x18", SBY 6/8/88 ... 1,870

ROCKLEHURST, S.

Village Street, watercolor/pencil, sgn/dtd 56, 20x16", C-E 9/15/88 UE ... 165

ROCQUY, see Le Brocquy

ROCZIK, Wenceslas (Bohemian, 1851-1901)

Cavalier with Sword, oil on canvas, sgn, 40x29", C-E 2/23/88 UE ... 1,650
Gathering Vegetables, oil on canvas, sgn, unfr, 13x17", C-E 5/22/89 ... 1,980

RODERSON, Morris (American, 1928-)

Kabuki Lady, watercolor/mixed media on paper, sgn/dtd 65, 35x17", B/B 1/11/89 ... 880
Lament for Ignacio Sanchez II, watercolor/pastel/pencil on paper, sgn/dtd 66, 35x35", SBY 6/24/88 OE ... 3,575
Reimei Kurama Yama, oil on canvas, sgn/dtd 62-63, 73x56", C-E 11/14/89 ... 1,650

ROE, Vern (American, 20th C)

Afternoon by the Sea (two girls seated on hillside), oil on masonite, sgn, 16x20", RAB 8/8/89 ... 1,700
Afternoon Sail, oil on board, sgn, 10x14", RAB 11/24/89 ... 575
Afternoon Sail (two sailboats in choppy sea), oil on board, sgn, 18x28", RAB 8/9/88 ... 1,200
Catboats at Sunset, oil on board, sgn, 16x20", RAB 11/24/89 ... 650
Catboats Off the Coast, oil on artist panel, sgn, 16x20", RAB 3/14/89 ... 800
Catboats Racing, oil on artist panel, sgn, orig frame, 11x15", RAB 8/1/88 ... 800
Catboats Sailing, oil on artist board, sgn, 16x20", RAB 3/14/89 UE ... 700
Catboats Under Sail, oil on board, sgn, 16x20", RAB 3/27/89 UE ... 650
Children at the Sea, oil on artist board, sgn, 11x14", RAB 11/25/88 OE ... 1,200
Children at the Seashore, oil on board, sgn, 11x14", RAB 11/24/89 ... 700
Children by the Sea, oil on masonite, sgn, 11x14", RAB 3/27/89 UE ... 550
Fair Day for Sailing, oil on board, sgn, 18x28", RAB 8/1/89 UE ... 700
Flowers by the Sea (two girls looking out to sea), oil on board, sgn, 11x14", RAB 8/9/88 OE ... 1,500
Friendship Sloop Under Sail, oil on board, sgn, 16x20", RAB 3/27/89 ... 800
Impressionistic View of a Young Girl Picking Berries Along a Shore, oil on masonite, sgn, 16x20", RAB 11/24/89 UE ... 650
Late Afternoon on the Bay, oil on board, sgn, 16x20", RAB 8/8/89 ... 1,000
Picking Flowers by the Sea, oil on board, sgn, 16x20", RAB 11/24/89 ... 750
Picking Flowers by the Sea (two girls overlooking sea), oil on artist board, sgn, 18x24", RAB 11/25/88 ... 2,250
Picnic by the Sea (two girls in landscape), oil on board, sgn, 16x20", RAB 8/8/89 ... 1,400
Summer Fun (children with pails & shovels at water's edge), oil on board, sgn, 11x14", RAB 8/9/88 OE ... 1,300
Summer Sail (sailboats on blue water), oil on board, sgn, 16x20", RAB 8/8/89 ... 850
Summer Sailing, gold-hulled catboat in blue water; oil on artist board, sgn, 10x14", RAB 11/25/88 ... 800
Yachts Sailing on a Fair Day, oil on artist board, sgn, orig frame, 22x28", RAB 8/1/88 ... 1,200

OMBERG (American, 20th C)

Summer Afternoon (lady sewing under tree near cottage), oil on canvas, sgn, 14x18", RAB 3/27/89 UE ... 200

BROMBO, E.
Still Life of Carafe & Apples, acrylic on canvas, sgn, 24x32", C-E 6/28/88 UE ... **8,800**
BROMLEY, Franc C. (American, 19th C)
Niagara Falls, oil on canvas, sgn, 30x48", LH 12/4/88 OE ... **2,000**
BROMLEY, Valentine Walker (British, 1848-1877)
Rest Beside a Stream, oil on canvas, sgn, 14x18", SBY 12/9/88 UE ... **1,650**
BROMLEY, William (British, fl 1835-88)
The New Boat, oil on panel, sgn, 31x35", SBY 10/24/89 ... **9,350**
BRON, Achille (French, 19th/20th C)
La Cote (coastal view), oil on canvas, sgn, 19x34", NA 2/24/89 ... **1,200**
BRONZINO, Angelo di Cosimo; circle of (Italian, 1503-1572)
Madonna & Child with the Infant Saint John the Baptist, oil on panel, 37x28", C-NY 4/8/88 ... **7,700**
Portrait of a Lady, bust-length, wearing ornate dress w/white lace collar; oil on panel, unfr, 28x21", C-NY 4/8/88 ... **6,050**
Portrait of Cosimo de Medici I, bust-length, wearing a black costume...; oil on panel, unfr, 23x17", C-NY 4/6/89 ... **2,200**
BRONZINO, Angelo di Cosimo; manner of (Italian, 1503-1572)
Portrait of a Gentleman Said To Be Cosimo I De Medici, oil on canvas, unfr, 23x17", SBY 12/9/88 ... **1,870**
BROOK, Alexander (American, 1898-)
Blue Ribbon (nude woman), oil on canvas, sgn, 14x6", C-E 11/30/88 ... **1,045**
BROOKE, Percy (British, 20th C)
Broken Pipe, watercolor, sgn, 16x12", SLK 2/12/88 ... **175**
BROOKE, Richard Norris (American, 1847-1920)
Children & Ducks (in a landscape), oil on canvas, sgn, 25x30", SBY 6/24/88 OE ... **12,100**
BROOKES, Samuel Marsden (American, 1816-1892)
Trout Beside a Stream, oil on canvas, sgn/dtd 1869, 16x20", B/B 10/6/88 ... **7,150**
BROOKS, Adele Richards (American, 1873-)
Pair: Across the Harbor; Wisconsin; oil on board; oil on canvasboard; sgn, 16x14", 15x12", RWS 9/8/89 ... **500**
BROOKS, Frank Leonard (Canadian, 1911-)
Bendale, oil on board, sgn/dtd December 1941, 12x16", WAD 6/12/89 ... **400**
Martins Lake Near North Bay, oil on board, sgn/dtd 34, 9x11", WAD 11/30/89 ... **300**
Winter Farm, gouache, sgn/titled, 14x7", FB 10/17/88 ... **140**
BROOKS, Henry Howard
Daffodils, Pansies & Periwinkle (still life); oil on masonite, sgn, 18x15", C-NY 9/28/89 ... **3,520**
BROOKS, Jacob (British, 1877-)
Eating Porridge, oil on canvasboard, sgn/dtd 1904, 14x18", C-E 10/25/88 ... **1,100**
BROOKS, James D. (American, 1906-)
Beri (abstract), oil on canvas, sgn, 1956, 62x66", SBY 10/5/89 ... **41,250**

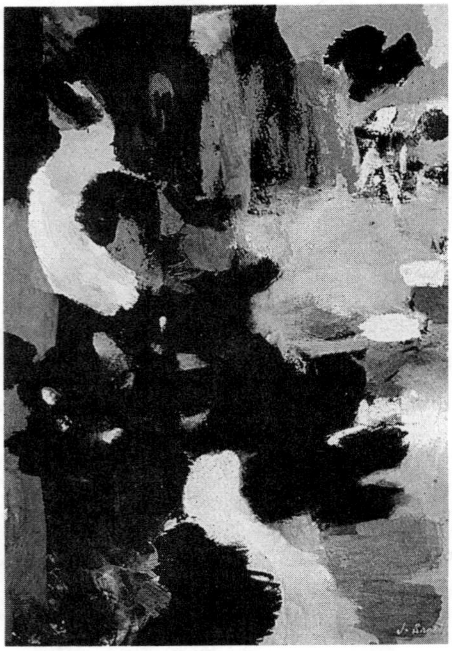

Huron, oil on canvas, sgn/dtd 1957, 48x33", C-NY 10/4/89, $35,200

Ingie (abstract), oil on canvas, sgn twice/dtd 1957/titled, 52x27", SBY 2/19/88 ... **6,875**
Saskia (abstract), oil on canvas, sgn/dtd 1959, 43x48", C-NY 2/14/89 OE ... **33,000**
Untitled (abstract), ink/acrylic on paper, sgn/dtd 67, 23x30", SBY 2/14/89 ... **1,870**
Untitled (abstract), oil on canvas, sgn/dtd 4-1954, 32" dia, SBY 10/8/88 ... **7,150**
BROOKS, Maria (British, fl 1869-1890)
Down Piccadilly, Returning From Covent Garden Market One June Morning, 1882; oil on canvas, sgn, 38x50", SBY 2/22/89 ... **110,000**
BROOKS, Nicholas Alden (American, 20th C)
Pair: Scenes of Lake George; oil on canvas, sgn/dtd 09, 12x18", C-E 11/30/88 UE ... **1,100**

Rounding the Point, oil on canvas, sgn/inscr/dtd 1900, 10x16", C-NY 9/30/88 ... 2,200

ROSHARD (French, 20th C)

Paysage (modernistic landscape), oil on canvas, sgn, 20x24", B/B 9/14/89 UE ... 825

ROUGHTON, George Henry (American, 1833-1905)

Winter in the City (half-length portrait of woman in hat & coat), oil on canvas, initialed, 34x25", C-SK 5/25/89 UE ... 1,010

ROUGIER, Adofphe (German, 1870-)

French Coastal Fishing Village, oil on canvas, sgn, 17x22", B/B 12/8/88 ... 2,475

ROUILLET, Pierre Andre (French, 1857-1914)

Independence Day, oil on canvas, sgn/dtd 1890, 38x51", SBY 5/23/89 ... 104,500

ROUWER, Adraien (Flemish, 1606-1638)

Doctor Tending to a Wounded Peasant, oil on panel, 10x8", SBY 6/3/88 ... 55,000

ROUWER, Adraien; circle of (Flemish, 1606-1638)

Interior Scene with a Doctor Operating on the Foot of a Peasant, oil on panel, initialed, unfr, 11x9", SBY 4/7/89 ... 7,700

Peasant Eating, oil on panel, octagonal, 5x4", SBY 12/9/88 OE ... 3,190

ROUWER, Gien (Dutch, 20th C)

Autumn Canal Scene, oil on canvas, sgn, 20x28", B/B 12/8/88 ... 715

ROWN, A.E.D.G. Stirling (British, 19th/20th C)

Pair: Congonie & Buccleugh Horse Races; oil on canvas, sgn, 16x20", LH 12/4/88 OE ... 8,500

ROWN, Alexander K. (British, 1849-1922)

Scottish Fen Scene, watercolor, initialed, 16x22", MG 11/19/88 ... 350

Thatched Cottages in a Country Landscape, oil on canvas, initialed, 44x34", C-E 5/22/89 ... 2,860

ROWN, Anna Wood (American, 20th C)

Woman Seated, Wearing a Hat; oil on canvas, sgn, unfr, 22x18", WL 5/20/88 UE ... 200

ROWN, Benjamin Chambers (American, 1865-1942)

Pathway in the Desert Foothills, oil on board, sgn, 12x16", B/B 10/6/88 ... 3,025

Rising Fog, river landscape; oil on canvas laid down on board, sgn/titled, 22x30", SLK 4/7/89 ... 6,250

Untitled (lush valley in landscape), oil on canvas, sgn, 18x24", SLK 4/7/89 ... 15,000

When Sycamores Are Green (mountain valley landscape), oil on canvas, sgn/titled, 30x40", SLK 4/7/89 ... 24,000

ROWN, Carlyle (American, 1919-1964)

Dramatic Marine Still Life, watercolor/gouache/pen/black ink on paper, sgn/dtd 47, 16x13", C-NY 10/6/88 ... 825

Embracing Couple, gouache/watercolor on paper, sgn/dtd 48, 14x11", C-NY 10/6/88 ... 1,320

Harvester with Butterfly, gouache on paper, sgn/dtd 48, 25x12", C-NY 10/6/88 ... 1,980

Icarus, watercolor on paper, sgn/dtd 48, unfr, 17x19", C-NY 10/6/88 ... 385

Poppies, gouache on paper, sgn/dtd 48, 18x22", C-NY 10/6/88 OE ... 1,430

Portrait, gouache on paper, sgn/dtd 48, 22x18", C-NY 10/6/88 ... 385

Portrait of a Young Girl, watercolor heightened w/white chalk on paper, sgn/dtd 48, 14x11", C-NY 10/6/88 ... 385

Reclining Youth, gouache/watercolor on paper, sgn/dtd 48, 14x18", C-NY 10/6/88 ... 1,760

Sleeping Farm Hand, gouache on paper, sgn/dtd 48, 18x22", C-NY 10/6/88 ... 990

Triple Portrait, gouache on paper, sgn/dtd 48, 17x22", C-NY 10/6/88 ... 1,100

ROWN, Carroll

Wild Field, oil on canvas, sgn/dtd 05, 17x28", LH 10/16/88 UE ... 200

ROWN, Catherine Madox; att

Arab Woman Reclining, oil on panel, monogramed, 18x22", lot 412, C-E 5/23/88 ... 1,650

Arab Woman Reclining, oil on panel, monogramed, 18x22", lot 80, C-E 2/23/88 ... 1,650

ROWN, Charles; att (American, 1848-)

Portrait of a Gentleman, oil on canvas, 30x25", FAP 4/15/89 UE ... 275

ROWN, F.

Fisherman on a Lake, oil on canvas, sgn, 21x30", C-E 11/8/88 ... 550

ROWN, Frank A. (American, 1876-)

Seascape (waves crashing on rocky shore), oil on canvas, sgn/dtd 1927, 15x18", RWS 3/31/88 ... 600

ROWN, Fred C.

End of the Harvest (still life of apples), oil on board, sgn, 8x11", C-NY 5/26/88 ... 11,000

ROWN, G. (American, 19th C)

Violinist, oil on canvas, sgn, 18x12", FAP 4/15/89 ... 440

ROWN, George Elmer (American, 1871-1946)

Solitude, oil on canvas, sgn, 53x64", C-E 7/26/88 OE ... 2,200

ROWN, George Loring (American, 1814-1889)

Hauling in the Nets (figures on beach at sunset), oil on canvas, sgn/dtd 1861, 26x40", RWS 9/29/88 OE ... 700

Italian Landscape, pencil on paper, sgn/dtd 1852, unfr, 9x11", C-NY 12/2/88 OE ... 2,090

Mount Pelligrino & the Harbor of Palermo, Sicily; oil on canvas, sgn/inscr/dtd 1865, 34x60", C-NY 5/26/88 OE ... 13,200

Naples Harbor, oil on canvas, sgn/inscr/dtd 1867, 28x48", C-NY 5/26/88 ... 7,150

View of Lake of Maggiore, the Town of Lugano, & the Alps in the Distance; oil on canvas, 1877, 28x40", RWS 12/10/88 OE ... 8,250

View of Livermore Falls, Three Miles From Plymouth, New Hampshire; oil on paper, sgn/dtd 1868, 11x15", RAB 11/25/88 UE ... 1,700

View of Our Garden at Medford, oil on canvas, sgn/inscr/dtd 1862, 18x24", C-NY 3/11/88 ... 4,400

ROWN, H.E. (American, 19th C)

Battle of Lookout Mountain (Civil War), pen/ink on paper, sgn/inscr, 12x16", C-E 5/27/88 OE ... 825

ROWN, Harrison Bird (American, 1831-1915)

Coast of Maine (coastal seascape), oil on canvas, sgn/dtd 77, 13x25", SBY 3/17/88 UE ... 1,210

Coastal Cliff (coastal seascape w/pounding surf), oil on canvas, sgn/dtd 77, 13x11", SBY 3/17/88 UE ... 550

ROWN, Horace (American, 1876-)

Vermont Village, cluster of white houses in green mountain valley; oil on canvas, estate stamp, unfr, 27x24", RAB 8/8/89 ... 700

BROWN, James (American, 1934-)
#9 Sinbad (abstract composition), acrylic/crayon/graphite on paper, sgn/dtd 1985 NYC, 40x60", C-NY 5/4/89 OE ... **19,800**
Black & White Mask (contemporary), oil/enamel on canvas, sgn/dtd 1983, 72x48", SBY 5/3/89 OE ... **66,000**
Large Wooden Head (contemporary), oil/enamel/pencil on canvas, 1983, 60x96", SBY 11/11/88 OE ... **35,750**
Portrait of Alexandria Sutherland (abstract), acrylic/oil stick on linen, sgn/dtd 1983, 28x30", SBY 10/5/89 OE ... **20,900**
Untitled (abstract composition), oil/oil stick/charcoal on canvas, sgn/dtd 1983, 29x30", SBY 5/3/89 OE ... **23,100**
Untitled (abstract figure w/crosses), gouache on 2 sheets of corrugated cardboard, ca 1985, 45x25", C-E 11/17/88 OE ... **3,300**
Untitled (abstract head w/figure beyond), acrylic enamel/crayons/graphite, sgn/dtd 1983, 61x55", C-NY 10/18/89 OE ... **101,200**
Untitled (abstract), gouache/colored chalks on colored paper, sgn/initialed/dtd 1985, unfr, 30x22", C-NY 5/4/88 OE ... **3,080**
Untitled (abstract), graphite on paper, sgn/inscr/dtd 1948, unfr, 40x59", C-NY 5/4/88 OE ... **4,950**
Vases, graphite on paper, initialed/dtd VIII V & New York 1985 on reverse, 20x13", C-NY 10/31/89 ... **1,870**

BROWN, Joan (American, 1938-)
Cocker Spaniel with Cloud at Night, oil on canvas, sgn/dtd Sept 2, 1963, 34x30", B/B 12/8/88 OE ... **6,050**
Ira Yeager, oil on canvas, dtd 1965, 16x16", B/B 12/8/88 ... **660**
Study of a Pickle, oil on paper, sgn/dtd 1966, 12x8", B/B 1/11/89 ... **468**
Things on Flying Carpet (abstract), oil on canvas, sgn, dtd 6/59, 56x60", C-NY 2/20/88 OE ... **3,850**
Yellow Box, acrylic on canvas, inscr/dtd 1971, 16x22", B/B 12/8/88 ... **935**

BROWN, John Appleton (American, 1844-1902)
Landscape, oil on canvas, sgn/dtd 74, 24x18", SBY 6/24/88 ... **1,430**
Shipwrecked, oil on canvas, sgn, 18x24", MG 5/28/88 UE ... **475**
White Island Light, New Hampshire (lighthouse); pastel on brown paper, sgn, 18x14", RWS 9/8/89 OE ... **1,900**

BROWN, John George (American, 1831-1913)
Bandaging His Paw (shoeshine boy wrapping dog's paw), oil on canvas, sgn/dtd 1901, 24x18", SBY 3/17/88 ... **8,800**
Cleaning the Catch (three fishermen in landscape), oil on canvas, sgn/dtd 1877, No 24, 25x20", C-SK 5/25/89 ... **47,760**
Collecting Wild Flowers, oil on canvas, sgn/dtd 1863, 8x6", C-NY 3/11/88 ... **5,500**
Crossing the Brook (view of young girl in landscape), watercolor/pencil on paper, sgn/dtd 1877, 22x16", C-NY 9/28/89 OE ... **38,500**
Extra (young boys selling newspapers on street corner), oil on canvas, sgn/inscr, 25x30", C-NY 12/2/88 ... **66,000**
Favorite Red Dress (portrait of little girl in landscape), oil on canvas, sgn/dtd 1861, 10x8", C-NY 9/30/88 ... **8,250**
Grandmother's Favorite (portrait of grandmother & child), oil on canvas, sgn, 30x24", DM 5/13/88 ... **9,000**
Liberated Woman (full-length portrait), oil on canvas, sgn/dtd 1895, 42x32", C-NY 5/26/88 ... **55,000**
No Customers, oil on canvas, sgn, 24x16", B/B 3/17/88 ... **7,700**
Portrait of a Man, oil en grisaille on canvas, sgn, 8x6", C-E 2/1/89 ... **880**
Portrait of a Young Boy Wearing a Hat, watercolor/pencil on paper, sgn/dtd 1890, 5x3", C-NY 12/2/88 OE ... **2,860**
Quiet Reflections (portrait of a girl), oil on canvas, sgn/dtd 1864, 14x10", SBY 9/23/88 ... **10,450**
See What I Got (girl holding flowers), oil on canvas, sgn/dtd 1879, 14x10", SBY 9/23/88 ... **5,775**
Shoeshine Boy, oil on canvas, sgn, unfr, 24x17", B/B 3/17/88 ... **4,950**
Shoeshine Boy, pastel on canvas, sgn/dtd 1899, 32x24", rpr tr, RWS 8/20/88 UE ... **550**
Shoeshine Boy with Dog, oil on canvas, sgn/inscr Copyright, 24x17", SBY 5/24/89 ... **9,900**

BROWN, John George; after (American, 1831-1913)
Three (Scape) Graces, by Tivoli, oil on canvas, sgn, 31x25", C-SK 6/9/88 ... **1,300**

BROWN, John Lewis (British, 1829-1890)
Figures in a Horse-Drawn Carriage, oil on paper board, sgn/inscr twice, dtd 1863, 9x23", C-NY 5/25/88 ... **4,400**

BROWN, Joseph
Harbor Scene, watercolor on paper, sgn/dtd 92, 12x19", C-E 4/7/88 UE ... **462**

BROWN, M.E.D. (American, 1810-1896)
View on the Mohawk Near Little Falls, oil on canvas, sgn/dtd twice, 1854, 40x50", SBY 6/24/88 ... **11,000**

BROWN, Paddand
Colonial Monument in Malaya, oil on canvas, 17x25", C-SK 11/10/88 UE ... **3,720**

BROWN, Paul (American, 1893-1958)
Horse & Groom, pencil on paper, sgn/dtd 39, 9x10", C-E 9/15/88 ... **275**
Meeting in the Road, pencil on paper, sgn, 8x14", C-E 9/15/88 ... **220**
Over His Heels, colored pencil on paper, sgn, 12x16", C-E 6/1/89 UE ... **165**
Pair: Schwartz Backs One; Hopping Hooks Roark; chalks heightened w/white on paper, sgn/dtd 29, 10x15", SBY 6/9/89 ... **4,125**
Sleigh-Drawn Carriage, pencil on paper, sgn, 6x12", C-E 9/15/88 ... **220**

BROWN, R.G. (British, fl 1844-59)
Setter & Two Retrievers in a Landscape, oil on canvas, sgn/dtd 1854, 22x29", SBY 6/10/88 ... **3,300**

BROWN, Roger (American, 1941-)
American Sycamore (contemporary), acrylic on canvas, 96x72", SBY 10/5/89 ... **14,300**
Diner, oil on wood with metal strips, 1973-74, 8x24", SBY 10/8/88 OE ... **8,800**
Dusk (composition), acrylic on canvas, 72x72", SBY 10/5/89 ... **26,400**
Flying in Formation (contemporary composition), oil on canvas, 72x72", SBY 5/3/89 UE ... **11,000**
Jonah & the Whale, acrylic on canvas, 1982, 36x72", SBY 5/3/88 ... **11,000**
Nostalgic History (contemporary), acrylic on canvas, dtd 1971, 34x48", SBY 2/15/89 ... **14,300**
Storm's Path, oil on canvas, 1974, 52x70", SBY 10/8/88 ... **18,700**

BROWN, Roy (American, 1879-1956)
Winter Fields (sheep grazing in field dotted w/snow), oil on canvas mounted on masonite, sgn, 20x30", RWS 9/29/88 UE ... **350**

BROWN, W. Warren (Canadian, 1881-)
Owl's Head, Maine (boats at sea, lighthouse on bluff, full moon); oil on canvas, sgn, 14x28", RAB 8/9/88 ... **1,500**
Still Life of Peach, Melon, & Grapes; oil on board, sgn/dtd 1866, 10x8", C-E 9/15/88 ... **495**
Stroll Along the River (two figures), oil on canvas, sgn, 16x24", RAB 8/9/88 OE ... **1,400**
Winter's Sunset (figures in snowy field, house beyond, deep yellow sky); oil on canvas, sgn, 16x20", RAB 8/9/88 OE ... **1,500**

BROWN, Walter Francis (American, 1853-1929)

Seaside Sunset (rocky coast & sailboats in last minutes of light), watercolor on paper, sgn/dtd 97, 10x14", RAB 8/9/88 ... 225

BROWN, William Mason (American, 1828-1898)

Autumnal Tints, oil on canvas, sgn/initialed/inscr, 12x18", SBY 5/25/88 ... 8,800
Early Autumn on the Susquehannah (river landscape), oil on panel, initialed, ca 1875, 12x18", C-NY 5/25/89 ... 35,200
Fall Landscape with River Beyond, oil on canvas, sgn, 12x18", SBY 6/28/89 OE ... 28,680
Peaches (still life), oil on canvas, monogramed, 16x20", SBY 5/25/88 ... 10,450
Setting Sun (extensive landscape), oil on panel laid down on board, sgn, 10x12", C-E 6/1/89 ... 6,600
Still Life of Grapes, Flowers & Peach; oil on canvas, initialed, 9x7", SBY 6/28/89 ... 3,300
Still Life of Grapes, Plums, & Peaches in a Basket; oil on canvas, monogramed, 20x16", SBY 5/24/89 OE ... 25,300
Strawberries (in landscape), oil on canvas, monogramed, 10x11", SBY 1/24/89 UE ... 3,300
Sunrise, oil on board, sgn/inscr, 12x11", C-NY 5/26/88 ... 11,000
Table Top Still Life, oil on canvas, sgn, 16x20", SBY 5/25/88 ... 13,200

BROWN, William Mason; after (American, 1828-1898)

Still Life of Fruit, oil on canvas, 15x20", C-E 9/15/88 ... 550

BROWN, William Mason; att (American, 1828-1898)

Landscape with Cottage, oil on canvas, sgn, unfr, 14x20", SBY 3/17/88 ... 1,870

BROWN, Woodley R. (British, 19th C)

Pair: River Landscapes with Figures; oil on canvas, dtd London 1850, 9x12", SLK 11/25/88 ... 1,200

BROWNE, Byron (American, 1907-1961)

Abstract, gouache on paper, sgn/dtd 1954, unfr, 26x20", C-E 4/7/88 ... 990
Abstract, watercolor/India ink/gouache/collage on paper laid down on board, 13x19", SBY 3/17/88 OE ... 4,675
Abstraction, tempera on paper, sgn/dtd 1951, 20x26", SBY 1/24/89 ... 1,650
Artist & His Model, pastel/charcoal on paper, sgn/dtd 1957, unfr, 20x26", C-E 4/7/88 UE ... 528
Boats & Beach, gouache/pen/ink on paper, sgn/dtd 1954, 20x26", C-E 6/1/89 ... 1,980
Bull Fight, ink/ink wash on paper, sgn/dtd 1959/inscr For Ebie, unfr, 20x26", C-E 3/22/88 UE ... 352
Central Park, oil on canvas, sgn/dtd 1858 twice, inscr, 14x18", SBY 9/23/88 OE ... 2,750
Clown (abstract), oil on board, sgn/dtd 1959, 18x14", C-E 10/18/89 ... 1,980
Corrida, oil on canvas, sgn/dtd twice, 1958, 48x36", SBY 6/24/88 ... 3,410
Dancing Figures (fantasy figures, 6 studies on 1 sheet); gouache on paper, sgn, 20x25", SBY 4/14/89 ... 4,125
Fallen Horse (caricature drawing), pencil/ink/crayon on paper, sgn, 15x16", SBY 4/14/89 OE ... 4,125
Head of Woman, oil on board, sgn/dtd 1939, 28x24", SBY 6/28/89 OE ... 6,050
Huntsman, oil on panel, sgn/dtd 47, no size given, B/B 1/11/89 ... 1,870
Milton Avery Drawing, Feb 8-1956 (nude viewed from behind); brown/red chalk on paper, sgn, 26x20", SBY 4/14/89 OE ... 1,980
Odalisque (reclining nude), India ink/pencil on paper, sgn/dtd 1939, 10x20", SBY 6/28/89 ... 1,540
Pair: Seated Nudes; pastel/pencil on paper, sgn/dtd 1957, 26x20", C-E 2/3/88 ... 770
Portrait in Blue, tempera on paper, sgn/dtd 1952, 26x20", SBY 9/23/88 ... 1,430
Roaring Lion (caricature drawing), pencil/gouache/India ink on paper, sgn, 18x19", SBY 4/14/89 ... 1,210
Seated Figure with Guitar (expressionistic depiction), oil on canvas, sgn/dtd September 1958, 26x20", C-NY 9/28/89 ... 4,400
Set of 3: Woman with a Crown of Leaves (3 drawings of same model); pencil on paper, sgn/dtd 1954, 26x20", C-E 4/7/88 UE ... 462
Skaters in Central Park, oil on canvas, sgn twice/inscr/dtd 1960, 20x26", SBY 3/17/88 ... 2,200
The Black Clown, oil/sand on canvas, sgn/dtd 1950, 26x20", C-NY 9/28/89 ... 5,280
The Jack, gouache on paper, sgn/dtd 1952, unfr, 26x70", C-E 2/3/88 ... 1,320
White Tablecloth (abstract still life), oil on canvas, sgn, 24x30", SBY 4/14/89 OE ... 10,175

ROWNE, C.F. (American, 19th/20th C)

River Scene with Boat, oil on canvas, sgn, 20x28", LH 10/16/88 OE ... 6,500

ROWNE, Dorothea (American, 20th C)

Eastern Point Light (lighthouse & buildings on rocky coast), oil on canvas, sgn, 25x30", RAB 8/9/88 UE ... 650

ROWNE, George Elmer (American, 1871-1946)

Beach at Provincetown, oil on panel, bears estate stamp, 10x13", C-E 4/7/88 UE ... 418
Brittany Landscape, bears estate stamp, 10x14", C-E 4/7/88 UE ... 385
Fields in Brittany, oil on board, 15x18", C-E 1/12/88 ... 242
From My Window, Paris (view of buildings & grounds); oil on canvas laid down, sgn, 11x13", B/B 5/17/89 ... 715
Gypsy Woman with Water Jugs (exterior scene), oil on canvas, sgn, 51x62", SBY 1/24/89 ... 2,750
Houses on Square in Spain, watercolor on paper, sgn, 21x28", C-E 4/7/88 ... 462
Interior Toledo, watercolor on paper, sgn/inscr/dtd 1922, 14x20", C-E 4/7/88 ... 385
Jungfrau, oil on canvas, sgn/inscr/dtd 1907, 32x40", RWS 11/3/88 UE ... 800
Landscape with Moon in Distance, oil on panel, bears estate stamp, 14x11", C-E 6/1/88 OE ... 990
Morning in the Garden, oil on board, 15x18", C-E 1/12/88 UE ... 154
Pair: Kairovan; Landscape; oil on board; oil on panel; sgn,11x14" & smaller, C-E 2/3/88 ... 1,430
Pathway to Forest, oil on board, 10x14", C-E 4/7/88 UE ... 352
Poplars in the Morning, oil on panel, 18x15", C-E 6485 ... 440
Portuguese Sailor, oil on canvas, sgn, no size given, FAP 11/4/88 ... 400
Redhead Drake in Flight, oil on canvas, sgn, 25x30", C-E 11/30/88 ... 1,650
Seaside Village, oil on canvas, sgn/dtd 1902, 25x30", C-NY 3/11/88 OE ... 7,150
Slave Market, oil on board, sgn, 14x14", C-NY 3/11/88 ... 1,320
Small River, oil on panel, bears estate stamp, 12x16", C-E 6/1/88 ... 770
Summer in Brittany, oil on panel, 10x14", C-E 9/15/88 ... 880
Trees in Fall, oil on board, bears estate stamp, 15x18", C-E 4/7/88 ... 825
Venice Scene, oil on board, bears estate stamp, 11x14", C-E 6/1/88 OE ... 1,210
Village Street, Brittany; oil on panel, bears estate stamp, 11x14", NA 2/24/89 ... 500

Woman in Green, oil on panel, bears estate stamp, unfr, 18x15", C-E 6/1/88	935
BROWNE, Hablot Knight (British, 1815-1882)	
Set of 10: (hunt scenes); crayon/gouache on paper, ea 9x13", SBY 6/9/89	2,750
BROWNE, Margaret Fitzhugh (American, 1884-1972)	
Still Life of Dahlias, oil on canvas, sgn, 30x22", RWS 5/19/88	3,000
BROWNE, Richard (Australian, 19th/20th C)	
Killigrant (native), bodycolor, inscr, unfr, 12x9", C-SK 6/9/88	6,500
Magil, Corroboree Dance (native w/spear); bodycolor, indistinctly inscr, unfr, 9x9", C-SK 6/9/88	7,800
Native Man of NS Wales with a Death Spear in Right Hand...; watercolor/bodycolor, inscr, 11x15", C-SK 6/9/88	2,790
Ninge, Ninge, Native of New South Wales...; watercolor/bodycolor, 11x16", C-SK 6/9/88 OE	40,900
BROWNELL, Peleg Franklin (Canadian, 1857-1946)	
Old Road, Late Autumn; oil on board, sgn/dtd 1904, 12x17", FB 10/17/88	850
Seated Woman, Tonal Portrait; oil on canvas, sgn/dtd 85, 24x20", RWS 5/12/89	750
Trilliums (flowers in a landscape), pastel, initialed, 12x9", C-SK 11/10/88	590
BROWNS, Benjamin Chambers (American, 1865-1942)	
Gathering Clouds, oil on canvas, sgn, 22x30", B/B 10/6/88	3,850
BROWNSCOMBE, Jennie Augusta (American, 1850-1936)	
Cherry Tree, gouache en grisaille on board, monogramed/dtd 1875, 10x9", C-E 10/18/89	880
Flora's Frolic (girls frolicking in a field), oil on canvas, sgn, 17x33", C-NY 5/26/88	9,350
Florentine Girl XVI Century, watercolor on paper, sgn, 10x13", B/B 3/17/88	1,430
Mater Familias (child holding puppy, pulling wagon in landscape), gouache on paper, sgn, 8x10", SBY 6/28/89 UE	1,870
Portrait of a Lady, half-length in elegant gown; oil on canvas, sgn, 33x24", RWS 8/20/88 UE	150
Woman Playing a Guitar (full-length portrait), watercolor/pen/pencil/heightened with white, unfr, 12x9", B/B 10/9/88 UE	1,210
BROZIK, see De Brozik	
BRUCE, Edward (American, 1879-1943)	
Ranch in the Mountains, oil on canvas, sgn, 24x29", SBY 1/24/89	3,300
BRUCKMAN, Lodewijk (American/Dutch, 1913-)	
Abstract Still Life (clasped hands, crown of thorns, & rocks), oil on canvas, sgn/dtd 50, 21x16", RAB 8/8/89 UE	400
Neptune's Treasures (shell & coral weave through encrusted chain links), oil on canvas, sgn/dtd 59, 22x14", RWS 9/29/88	1,000
Shirt (portrait of young man in red, white & blue striped shirt), oil on canvas, sgn/dtd 54-55, 38x27", RAB 8/8/89	2,800
BRUDER, Harold	
Pair: City Street Scenes; gouache on paper, sgn/1 dtd 76, 10x12", 7x10", C-NY 6/17/89	330
Weeping Figure, acrylic on canvas, sgn/dtd 5/72, 12x12", C-NY 6/17/89	66
BRUEGHEL, Abraham; school of	
Pomegranates, Grapes, & Figs in a Landscape; oil on canvas, 14x18", C-NY 4/8/88 OE	8,250
BRUEGHEL, Jan the elder (Flemish, 1568-1625)	
Wooded Landscape with Figures & Animals on a Path, a Castle on a Mountaintop Beyond; oil on panel, 11" dia, SBY 6/2/89	99,000
BRUEGHEL, Jan the elder; style of (Flemish, 1568-1625)	
Coastal Village Scene, oil on panel, 8x10", B/B 9/15/88	1,320
BRUEGHEL, Jan the younger (Flemish, 1601-1678)	
Allegory of Music, oil on canvas laid down on panel, 1640s, 34x64", C-NY 6/2/88	33,000
BRUEGHEL, Jan the younger; att (Flemish, 1601-1678)	
Madonna & Child in a Wooded Landscape, oil on panel, 18x26", C-NY 1/11/89	30,800
Still Life of Flowers in a Vase, a Coffer of Coins & Jewelry, a Garland of Blossoms...; oil on panel, 20x27", SBY 4/7/89	28,600
Travelers on a Path in an Extensive Wooded Landscape, oil on panel, 13x17", C-NY 1/11/89	49,500
BRUEGHEL, Pieter III (1589-after 1608)	
Collection of Tithes, oil on panel, 28x42", SBY 10/13/89	33,000
BRUEGHEL, Pieter the elder; follower of (Flemish, 1525-1569)	
Noah's Ark, brown ink on paper, 11x8", WD 10/19/88	5,000
BRUEGHEL, Pieter the younger (Flemish, 1564-1637)	
Landscape with a Village Church, Figures & Sheep on a Path; oil on panel, 14x22", C-NY 1/15/88	88,000
Payment of the Tithe, oil on panel, 21x33", C-NY 1/11/89	55,000
Return From the Kermesse, oil on panel, sgn, 16x23", SBY 1/12/89 OE	858,000
BRUEGHEL, Pieter the younger; att (Flemish, 1564-1637)	
Man Eating Ribs on a Barrel by a House, oil on panel, 7" dia, C-NY 10/20/88 OE	52,800
BRUEGHEL, school of (Flemish, 16th/17th C)	
Lovers by a Statue of Diana, oil on panel, 26x11", C-E 4/7/88	550
Musical Couple, oil on panel, unfr, 19x18", C-NY 10/20/88 OE	3,960
BRUENECH, George Robert (Canadian, 1851-1941)	
Evening Near Gloucester, England; watercolor, sgn, 5x9", WAD 6/12/89	120
BRUESTLE, Bertram George (American, 1902-)	
At the River, oil on board, sgn, 12x16", C-E 2/1/89 OE	3,300
Landscape, oil on board, sgn, 8x10", C-E 6/1/88 OE	1,980
BRUESTLE, George M. (American, 1872-1939)	
Autumn Farm (open field at dusk, farm reflected in pond beyond), oil on board, sgn, 10x14", RWS 9/29/88	800
Autumn Farm Scene, oil on panel, sgn, 11x15", NA 10/1/88 UE	450
Haystacks (large stacks in open landscape), oil on panel, sgn, 9x13", NA 2/24/89	650
New England Hillside (landscape), oil on board, sgn/dtd 1917, 12x16", SBY 3/16/89 OE	1,600
New England Landscape, oil on canvas, sgn/dtd 1920, 12x16", RAB 8/8/89	1,400
Receding the Clouds, oil on academy board, sgn, 8x10", RWS 11/3/88	850
Spring Thaw, oil on board, sgn, 8x10", RWS 5/19/88	850

BRUGO, Guiseppe (Italian, 19th/20th C)
Classical Balcony, oil on board, sgn, 24x12", SBY 7/12/89 UE 1,100
BRULLOFF, Alexandre (Russian, 1798-1877)
Portrait of a Lady (standing, three-quarter length), gouache on paper, sgn, 8x7", RAB 8/9/88 UE 200
BRUN, Charles; see Le Brun
BRUN, Christopher; see Le Brun
BRUN, Louis Auguste; style of (Swiss, 1758-1815)
Pair: Portraits of a Lady & a Gentleman; oil on composite, sgn, 8x6", B/B 9/14/89 UE 822
BRUN, Louise Elizabeth Vigee; see Le Brun
BRUNEL DE NEUVILLE, A.A. (French, 1852-1941)
Kitten Chaos (mischievous kittens on table), oil on canvas, sgn, 26x32", C-NY 2/23/89 7,700
Overturned Basket with Gooseberries & Peaches on a Ledge, oil on canvas, sgn, 21x26", C-NY 2/23/89.......... 4,950
Still Life of Plums, Lemons, Gooseberries, & Vessels on a Ledge; oil on canvas, sgn, 26x37", C-NY 2/23/89 6,050
BRUNERI, E.
Fishing in the Venetian Lagoon, oil on canvas, sgn, 14x21", NA 3/26/88 UE 500
BRUNERY, Francois (Italian, fl 1898-1909)
Non Abbiate Paura (three religious figures in elegant interior), oil on panel, sgn, 24x20", SBY 10/24/89 23,100
BRUNI, Umberto (Canadian, 1914-)
Cascades de la Riviere du Nord, Mont Rolland; oil on canvas, sgn/dtd 1980, 16x20", FB 10/30/89 825
L'Erabliere, St Jacques de Montcalm; oil on board, sgn/dtd 1980, 12x14", FB 10/30/89 880
Un Jour d'Automne, Baie St Paul; oil on board, sgn/dtd 1978, 12x14", FB 10/17/88 550
BRUNIN, Leon (Belgian, 1861-1949)
Calm After the Storm, oil on panel, sgn, 3x9", C-E 2/23/88 770
Library (interior w/woman at window), oil on cradled panel, sgn/dtd 87, 24x19", RWS 5/19/88 OE 6,500
BRUNO, Ertz (American, 1873-1965)
Cardinal, watercolor, sgn/dtd 1916, 17x10", MAG 4/24/88 260
BRUSCA, Jack (20th C)
Metallurgy, acrylic on canvas, sgn/inscr/dtd 1968, 32x24", C-E 5/13/88 UE 110
BRUSH, George de Forest (American, 1855-1941)
In the Garden, oil on zinc panel, sgn/dtd 1923, 20x9", SBY 5/25/88 46,200
Portrait of a Woman Wearing a Hat, oil on panel, sgn/dtd 1886, 8x6", SBY 6/28/89 OE 17,050
BRUSKIN, Grisha (Russian, 1945-)
Alephbet: N 15 (surrealistic figures); oil on canvas, sgn/dtd 1985, 46x38", SBY 7/7/88 OE 150,000
Fundamental Lexicon (surrealistic figures), oil on 32 canvases, sgn/dtd 1986, overall 87x120", SBY 7/7/88 OE 440,000
Memorial (surrealistic figures), oil on canvas, sgn/dtd 1983, 40x47", SBY 7/7/88 OE 64,000
Monuments (surrealistic figures), oil on canvas, sgn/dtd 1982, 49x43", SBY 7/7/88 OE 64,000
Pair: Alephbet: N 3 & N 4 (surrealistic figures); oil on canvas, sgn/dtd 1984, 43x38", SBY 7/7/88 OE 170,000
Partner (surrealistic figures), oil on canvas, sgn/dtd 1982, 47x38", SBY 7/7/88 OE 28,000
BRUYN, Bartholomaeus the elder (German, 1493-1556)
Portrait of a Lady, aged 23, wearing a green & black costume...; oil on arched panel, dtd 1530, 17x13", C-NY 1/11/89 33,000
BRUYN, Bartholomaeus the elder; att (German, 1493-1556)
Portrait of a Bearded Man Wearing a Fur Trimmed Hat, oil on panel, arched top, 17x13", SBY 10/13/89 11,000
BRUYN, Bartholomaeus; circle of (German, 16th/17th C)
Triptych: Donors Before Altars; Crucifixion in Center; oil on panel, 39x28", 2: 39x14", C-NY 4/6/89 OE 19,800
BRUYN, Cornelis Johannes; see De Bruyn
BRUZZI, Stefano (Italian, 1835-1911)
Plough Team, oil on canvas, sgn/dtd 1872, 14x24", C-NY 5/25/88 38,500
BRYANT, Everett Lloyd (American, 1864-1945)
Daisy in a Pitcher, oil on canvas, sgn, 20x16", C-E 10/18/89 2,200
Still Life on a Table (jar, glass & vase of flowers), oil on canvas, sgn, 20x24", B/B 5/17/89 UE 605
BRYCE, Gilbert (British, 19th C)
Thoughts (lady seated on landing, reflecting), oil on canvas, sgn, 20x31", SBY 6/8/88 UE 2,200
BRYER, see De Bryer
BRYERS, Duane (American, 1911-)
Red River Crossing, oil on canvas, sgn/copyrighted/dtd 80, 24x36", SBY 9/23/88 2,530
BRYMNER, William (Canadian, 1855-1925)
By the Forest, watercolor, sgn/dtd 1893, 15x11", FB 10/30/89 880
BRYNJOLF, Gorgen (Danish, 1931-)
Flora, oil on canvas, sgn, 1965, 26x20", LH 10/16/88 UE 30
Interior, Sal; oil on canvas, sgn, 1964, 29x36", LH 10/16/88 UE 100
BUBKOVSKII, G. (Russian, fl 1854)
Motherly Love (women w/child in interior), no media given, sgn/dtd 1854, 29x23", C-L 10/8/88 OE 10,230
BUCCI, Ermocrate (Italian, 19th C)
Bunny Family, oil on panel, sgn, 14x10", WD 3/23/88 1,400
BUCCIARELLI, Danielle (Italian, 19th Century)
Flirtation, watercolor, sgn, 21x15", FB 4/25/88 700
BUCHBINDER, Simeon (German, 19th C)
Astronomer (man seated at a table studying maps), oil on panel, sgn, 8x10", C-NY 5/24/89 7,150
BUCHEL, Charles (American, 20th C)
View of a House by a Lake, oil on masonite, sgn, 30x24", PHL 6/16/88 650

BUCHET, Gustave (Swiss, 1888-1963)
Composition, oil on canvas, sgn/dtd 1918, 11x14", SBY 10/5/88 OE 6,325
BUCHHOLTZ, T.T. (Russian, 1857-?)
Boyar Marozoff Discovers the Love of His Wife, Helene, For Prince Serebrjani; oil on canvas, sgn, 38x65", B/B 3/17/88 5,225
BUCK, Carl
Subway Repairs, oil on board, sgn/dtd 33, 22x30", C-E 10/18/89 2,420
BUCK, Claude (American, 1890-)
Still Life with Fuchsias, oil on board, sgn, 21x16", B/B 10/6/88 1,100
BUCK, William Henry (American, 1840-1888)
Gulf Coast Road (man in horse-drawn carriage, park pavilions beyond), oil on canvas, sgn/dtd 89, 12x20", NA 5/13/89 30,000
BUCKLER, Charles E. (American, 1869-)
Cabin in the Snow, oil on canvasboard, sgn, 12x16", RWS 9/8/89 UE 250
Valley in June, oil on canvas, sgn, 28x36", C-E 2/3/88 880
Valley Stream, oil on canvas, sgn, 24x30", B/B 12/8/88 440
White Stream, oil on canvas, sgn, 16x20", RWS 5/12/89 UE 400
Winter's Creek, oil on canvasboard, sgn, 12x16", RWS 9/8/89 UE 275
BUCKLEY, Charles F. (British, 1841-1869)
June Near Keswick, Cumberland; watercolor on parchment, sgn, 22x29", WG 4/23/88 2,000
BUCKLEY, John Michael (American, 1891-1958)
WPA New England Village, Winter (woman on snowy path by church); oil on canvas, sgn, 25x30", RWS 9/29/88 550
BUCKLEY, Stephen (20th C)
Woven Red Wax, wax encaustic on canvas woven on wooden supports w/metal, sgn/dtd 1976, 40x48x3", SBY 10/8/88 6,325
BUEL, see De Buel
BUERGERNISS, Carl (American, 1877-)
Contemplating a Swim, sgn, unfr, 16x20", C-E 6/1/88 UE 770
BUFF, Conrad (American, 1886-1975)
Desert Cactus, oil on board, sgn, 12x16", B/B 1/11/89 1,870
Desert Peaks, oil on board, sgn, 12x16", B/B 10/6/88 2,200
Sentinel Rock, Arizona; oil on board, sgn, 16x24", B/B 10/6/88 2,750
BUFFET, Bernard (French, 1928-)

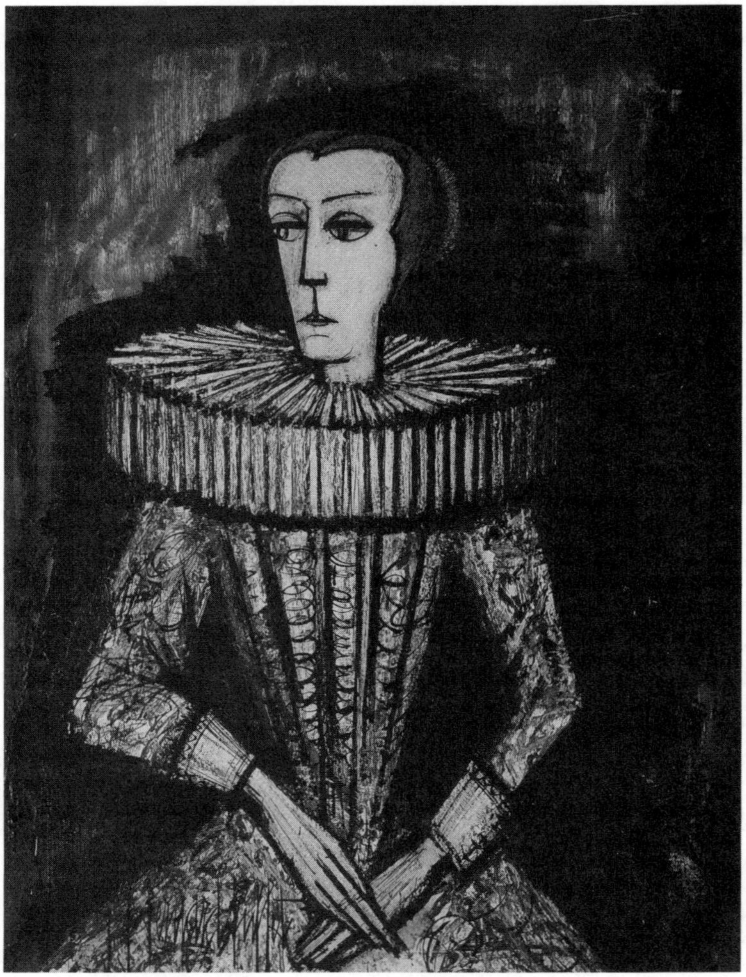

Grande Dame (half-length portrait), oil on canvas, sgn/dtd 59, 52x39", C-NY 10/5/89 OE $209,000

Clown Fond Jaune, oil on canvas, sgn/dtd 66/#d 3, 52x32", C-NY 5/12/88 OE	63,800
Cocconelle, oil on canvasboard, sgn, 9x6", SBY 10/7/89 OE	41,250
Dahlias et Eventail (floral still life), oil on canvas, sgn/dtd 64, 46x29", SBY 10/7/88 OE	82,500
Dahlias Rouges (floral still life), oil on canvas, sgn/dtd 67, 26x22", C-NY 5/11/89 OE	132,000
Eglise de Bretagne (landscape w/church), oil on canvas, sgn/dtd 65, 32x40", SBY 10/7/88 OE	93,500
Esquisse pour La Passion (sketch for La Passion), pencil on paper, sgn/dtd 54, 30x22", C-NY 10/5/89 OE	15,400
Etand, Environs des Ponts Neufs, Bretagne; oil on canvas, sgn/dtd 64, 33x46", C-NY 11/16/88 OE	88,000
Femme Nue (nude), oil on canvas, sgn/dtd 79, 51x32", C-NY 2/18/88	27,500
Fleurs, oil on canvas, sgn/dtd 1965, 32x26", SBY 10/6/89 OE	385,000
Fleurs dans un Cafetiere, oil on canvas, sgn/dtd 59, 26x20", SBY 10/6/89	209,000
Garage du Moulin (front view of gas station w/car & figure), oil on canvas, sgn/dtd 54, 66x76", SBY 11/12/88	143,000
Iris Bleus (floral still life), oil on canvas, sgn/dtd 66, 36x58", SBY 5/11/88	**79,750**
Iris Bleus dans un Vase Chinois (floral still life), oil on canvas, sgn/dtd 67, 52x38", C-NY 5/11/89 OE	**165,000**
L'Homme Pendu (nude man standing), pencil on tracing paper laid on paper, initialed, 12x4", SBY 10/7/89	**3,850**
L'Interieur, oil on canvas, sgn/dtd 56, 39x52", SBY 10/6/89 OE	**220,000**
L'Oiseau (bird), oil on canvasboard, sgn, 8x10", SBY 10/7/89 OE	**44,000**
La Bretonne, oil on canvas, sgn/dtd 56, 58x35", C-NY 11/16/88	**44,000**
La Jacinthe Blanche, oil on canvas, sgn/dtd 1976, 26x22", SBY 2/16/89	**82,500**
La Plage, charcoal on paper, sgn/indistinctly inscr, 9x14", SBY 10/5/88 OE	**4,125**
La Plage, oil on canvas, sgn/dtd 61, 16x36", SBY 10/7/88 OE	**59,400**
La Plage a Marseilles, oil on canvas, sgn/dtd 59, 22x29", SBY 2/18/88 OE	**52,250**
La Terre-Neuvas (view of ship), oil on canvas, sgn/dtd 68, 24x29", C-NY 5/11/89 OE	**101,200**
Le Canal, oil on canvas, sgn/dtd 55, 35x58", SBY 5/10/89	**247,500**
Le Chemin de Fer, pencil on paper, sgn/dtd 53, 20x25", C-NY 10/6/88 OE	**15,400**
Le Clown, oil on canvas, sgn/dtd 66, 26x20", C-NY 10/6/88	**44,000**
Le Monocycle, watercolor/brush/India ink/pencil on paper laid down on canvas, sgn, 26x20", C-NY 5/11/89	**24,200**
Le Peintre (The Painter, half-length sketch), pen/India ink on paper, mounted, sgn/dtd 1948, 26x19", C-NY 10/5/89 OE	**24,200**
Le Phare (ship at dock), oil on canvas, sgn, 29x36", SBY 10/7/88 OE	**71,500**
Le Pupitre (school desk w/spilled bottle of ink), oil on canvas, sgn/dtd 56, 26x18", SBY 11/12/88	**99,000**
Le Repas (still life w/orange & white tablecloth), oil on canvas, sgn/dtd 57, 29x36", SBY 10/6/89 OE	**253,000**
Le Studio, oil on canvas, sgn/dtd 53, 18x24", SBY 10/6/89 OE	**209,000**
Le Voilier (sailboats), oil/pencil/black crayon on paper laid down on canvas, sgn/dtd 59, 20x26", SBY 10/6/89	**110,000**
Les Bluets (floral still life), oil on canvas, sgn/dtd 53, 19x28", SBY 10/6/89	**209,000**
Les Corneilles, oil on canvas, sgn/dtd 55, 39x51", SBY 10/6/89 OE	**341,000**
Les Falaises Crayeuses, oil on canvas, sgn/dtd 58, 37x51", SBY 2/16/89	**110,000**
Man Standing, pencil on paper, sgn, 15x6", SBY 10/7/89 OE	**12,650**
Nature Morte (still life w/oil lamp), pencil on paper, sgn/dtd 51, 20x26", SBY 10/6/89 OE	**24,200**
Nature Morte (still life w/stemmed glass, fruit), oil on canvas, sgn/dtd 52, 11x16", SBY 10/6/89 OE	**77,000**
Nature Morte (still life w/white dish & six cherries), mixed media, sgn/dtd 50, 9x12", SBY 10/6/89 OE	**71,500**
Nature Morte (still life), oil on canvas, sgn/dtd 59, 26x20", C-NY 5/11/89	**104,500**
Nature Morte (still life), oil on canvas, sgn/dtd 67, 35x46", SBY 2/16/89 OE	**121,000**
Nature Morte a la Citrouille (still life), oil on canvas, sgn/dtd 55, 39x52", C-NY 11/16/88	**88,000**
Nature Morte au Fromage (still life), gouache/watercolor/pen/India ink/pencil, sgn/dtd 60, 20x26", C-NY 2/18/88 OE	**16,500**
Nature Morte au Melon, oil on canvas, sgn/dtd 53, 20x26", SBY 10/6/89 OE	**176,000**
Nature Morte au Poisson (still life w/fish), oil on canvas laid down on panel, sgn/dtd 48, 33x49", SBY 10/6/89 OE	**198,000**
Nature Morte au Poisson et Citrons (still life of fish & lemons), oil on canvas, sgn/dtd 53, 20x26", C-NY 10/5/89 OE	**121,000**
Nature Morte au Poissons (still life w/fish), oil on canvas, sgn/dtd 60, unfr, 38x77", SBY 2/16/89 OE	**143,000**
Nature Morte aux Artichaux, oil on canvas, sgn/inscr/dtd 56, 38x77", C-NY 10/6/88 OE	**132,000**
Nature Morte aux Cerises (still life), oil on canvas, sgn/dtd 62, 24x29", SBY 2/16/89 OE	**126,500**
Nature Morte aux Figues, oil on canvas, sgn/dtd 51, 13x22", C-NY 10/6/88 OE	**35,200**
Nature Morte aux Figues (still life w/figs), oil on canvas, sgn/dtd 56, 29x36", SBY 10/6/89 OE	**253,000**
Nature Morte avec Fleurs (floral still life), gouache/India ink on board, sgn/dtd 63, 26x19", SBY 2/16/89 OE	**30,800**
Pavots et Delphiniums, oil on canvas, sgn/dtd 64, 46x35", SBY 5/11/88 OE	**126,500**
Paysage, oil on canvas, sgn/dtd 67, 26x39", SBY 10/7/88	**34,100**
Pichet de Fleurs (floral still life), oil on canvas, sgn/dtd 53, 24x15", C-NY 10/6/88	**52,800**
Portrait de Femme (portrait of a woman), oil/pencil on masonite, sgn/dtd 50, 26x20", C-NY 2/18/88	**12,100**
Portrait de Femme III, oil on canvas, sgn/dtd 55, 26x20", SBY 2/16/89 OE	**60,500**
Pot de Fleurs, oil on canvas, sgn/dtd 63, 32x22", SBY 10/6/89 OE	**253,000**
St Tropez, les Yachts; oil on artist board, sgn, 16x13", SBY 10/6/89 OE	**93,500**
Tete de Torero, oil on canvas, sgn/dtd 67, 29x20", SBY 5/11/88 OE	**60,500**
Tete de Veau (head of cow), oil on canvas, sgn/dtd 57, 45x64", C-NY 11/16/88	**35,200**
Tete de Veau (still life w/head of cow), oil on canvas, sgn/dtd 54, 77x38", SBY 10/6/89	**79,750**
Torreador, oil on canvas, sgn/dtd 58, 51x38", C-NY 10/6/88 OE	**79,200**
Torreador, oil on canvas, sgn/dtd 58, 63x20", SBY 2/16/89	**96,250**
Tulips (floral still life), oil on canvas, sgn/dtd 58, 39x26", SBY 5/10/89	**176,000**
Vase de Fleurs, gouache/watercolor/crayon/charcoal/pencil/pen/India ink, sgn/dtd 62, 26x20", C-NY 2/18/88 OE	**20,900**
Vase de Fleurs, oil on canvas, sgn/dtd 61, 26x18", SBY 10/6/89 OE	**264,000**
Vase de Fleurs, oil on canvas, sgn/dtd 64, 26x20", SBY 10/6/89 OE	**231,000**
Vase de Fleurs, oil on masonite, sgn/dtd 70, 32x26", SBY 5/10/89	**110,000**
Vase de Fleurs (abstract floral still life), oil on canvas, sgn/dtd 65, 32x26", C-NY 10/5/89 OE	**165,000**

Vase de Fleurs (still life), oil on canvas, sgn/dtd 62, 46x35", SBY 11/12/88 OE 110,000
Vase de Fleurs (still life), oil on canvas, sgn/dtd 64, 29x24", SBY 10/7/88 OE 55,000
Vierzon, les Maisons et les Jardins (garden view of estate); oil on canvas, sgn/dtd 1975, 35x51", C-NY 5/12/88 71,500
Voies de Garage (train yard), oil on canvas, sgn/dtd 1982, 35x52", SBY 10/7/88 OE 66,000

BUGGIANI, Paolo
Festa d'Estate, oil on burlap, sgn/inscr, dtd twice 61, 51x64", C-E 5/13/88 OE 1,870

BUGIARDINI, Giulio (Italian, 1475-1554)
Portrait of Pope Clement VII (seated in profile), oil on panel, 36x29", SBY 6/1/89 UE 99,000

BUGZESTER, Max
Village, oil on canvas, sgn, 12x9", SBY 2/14/89 1,045

BUHLER, Augustus W. (American, 1853-1920)
Low Tide, Gloucester Harbor; oil on board, sgn/dtd Dec 31, 9x12", RAB 8/8/89 UE 1,000

BULL, Charles Livingston (American, 1874-1932)
Family of Mountain Goats, ink/watercolor on paper, sgn, 21x18", RAB 8/9/88 UE 600

BUNCH, C.V. (Scandinavian, 20th C)
Old Passing the New, oil on canvas laid down, sgn/dtd 1921, 10x14", B/B 1/11/89 715

BUNDY, E.W. (British, 19th C)
Figures in a Landscape, oil on canvas, sgn, 28x36", SBY 7/12/89 2,090

BUNDY, Edgar; att (British, 1862-1922)
One That I Brought Up of a Puppy, watercolor, bears signature/dtd 1899, 16x21", FB 5/28/89 300

BUNDY, Horace; att (American, 1814-1883)
Portrait of Mrs Silas Wright, oil on canvas, ca 1830, 25x21", SBY 1/28/88 5,225

BUNDY, John Elwood (American, 1853-1933)
Evening Approach, oil on canvas, sgn/dtd 1917, 22x30", WG 9/16/88 2,200
Evening in the Woods, oil on canvas, sgn/dtd 1921, 16x20", B/B 3/17/88 1,650
Landscape with a Stream, oil on canvas, sgn/dtd 00, 18x26", C-E 10/18/89 2,200

BUNN, George (British, fl 1890s)
Dutch Sailing Vessels, oil on canvas, sgn/dtd Antwerp 89, 16x24", RWS 6/17/89 UE 400
Fisherfolk by the Sea, oil on canvas, sgn/dtd 96, 23x32", C-E 2/23/88 UE 935

BUNNER, Andrew Fisher (American, 1841-1897)
Venetian Canal, watercolor, sgn/dtd 1883, 11x15", PHL 10/28/88 UE 275
Venice, oil, sgn, 12x24", WD 1/11/89 2,000

BUONACCORSI, Pietro; att (Italian, 1500-1546/47)
General Receiving a Baton From a Seated Man, pen/brown ink over black chalk, 16x12", SBY 1/13/89 6,600

BURBANK, Addison Buswell (American, 1895-)
Road in Brittany, oil on canvas, sgn, 20x16", RWS 11/10/89 950

BURBANK, Elbridge Ayer (American, 1858-1947)
Chief Geronimo Apache, oil on canvas mounted on board, sgn/dtd 1898/titled, 14x11", SBY 1/24/89 1,045
Chief Stinking Bear, oil on canvas, sgn/dtd 1899/inscr Sioux & Pine Ridge SD, 30x20", SBY 1/24/89 3,575
Chief Stinking Bear (portrait), oil on canvas, sgn/dtd 1899, 30x20", SBY 4/14/89 4,675
Ton-Had-Dle-I-C-O Kiowa (portrait), oil on canvas, sgn/dtd 1899, 13x10", SBY 6/24/88 OE 2,860

BURCHARD, Pablo
House in the Country, oil on canvas, sgn, ca 1935, 38x38", SBY 11/21/88 OE 7,150

BURCHFIELD, Charles Ephraim (American, 1893-1967)
Barber Shop (exterior), watercolor/pencil on paper, sgn/dtd 1918, 9x12", SBY 6/28/89 7,150
Bluejay on a Fence, watercolor/pencil on paper, sgn/dtd 1916, 12x9", SBY 6/28/89 OE 6,050
Clock & Candles, pencil on paper, initialed/dtd 1917, 7x4", SBY 9/23/88 715
Clouds at Sunset, watercolor/pencil on paper laid down on board, sgn/dtd 1917, 15x21", C-NY 9/30/88 6,600
Community Park, pencil on board, monogramed/dtd 1937, 19x25", C-NY 9/28/89 4,180
Dandelions, watercolor/pencil on paper, sgn/dtd 1916, 14x20", SBY 6/24/88 9,350
Farmyard, watercolor/pencil on paper, sgn, 9x12", C-NY 9/28/89 7,700
February Dusk (snowy landscape), watercolor/pencil on paper laid down on board, sgn/dtd 1918, 15x21", C-NY 5/25/89 60,500
March Day, Gowanda; watercolor/gouache/charcoal/chalk on paper laid down, initialed, 26x36", C-NY 5/25/89 8,800
Railroad Signal Switch, watercolor/ink on paper, monogramed/dtd 1936, 7x6", SBY 6/24/88 OE 3,300
Shacks & Boats in a Yard, 1933; watercolor on paper, sgn, 10x9", RAB 8/9/88 UE 3,000
Spring Landscape, 1931; watercolor on paper, initialed, 21x29", WD 10/5/88 4,200
Summer Morning (Dutchman's Salem), gouache/watercolor/pencil on tan paper, sgn, 1917, 14x20", C-NY 9/28/89 9,350
Sunset (sun setting, expressionistic depiction), gouache on paper, sgn/dtd 1917/#d B-169, 22x18", C-NY 9/28/89 46,200
Wheatfields (landscape w/stacks), gouache/watercolor/colored crayon on paper, sgn/dtd 1917, 18x21", SBY 5/24/89 OE 46,750
Wild Bleeding Hearts (woodland landscape), watercolor on paper, monogramed/dtd 1961, 39x32", SBY 5/24/8 143,000
Winter Sun (Victorian house), watercolor/gouache/charcoal/pastel on paper, monogramed/dtd 1961, 17x14", SBY 5/24/89 27,500
Woman in a Garden, watercolor/gouache/pencil on paper laid down on board, sgn/dtd 1915, 12x9", C-NY 9/30/88 9,900

BURDICK, Horace Robbins (American, 1844-1942)
Lonesome Pine (landscape), oil on canvas, sgn, ca 1910, 12x16", RWS 5/19/88 950
Mountain Lake, watercolor on paper, sgn, 6x9", RAB 8/9/88 200
Summer Landscape (green trees lining a calm lake), oil on cardboard, sgn, 8x9", RAB 8/9/88 200

BURDICK, Horace Robbins; att (American, 1844-1942)
Sunlight in Shadow, Landscape with Two Figures; oil on board, sgn, 9x13", RWS 11/10/89 UE 200

BURFIELD, James M. (British, fl 1865-1883)
Broken Tea Set, oil on panel, sgn, 11x8", SBY 12/9/88 990

BURGDORFF, Ferdinand (American, 1881-)
Southwest Coastline with Sailboats, oil on board, sgn/dtd 1963, 18x24", DM 3/14/88 UE 550
Virginia City, Nevada; oil on board, sgn/dtd 1929, 24x27", SBY 6/24/88 825
Western Landscape, oil on canvas, sgn twice, dtd 1925/inscr Bohemian Club San Francisco California, 20x35", SBY 3/17/88 1,045
BURGERS, Hendricus Jacobus (Dutch, 1834-1899)
Past Bedtime (mother holding child in an interior), oil on panel, sgn/dtd 1871, 11x8", B/B 10/9/88 3,300
Young Girl Reading (on bench by stone wall), oil on canvas, sgn/dtd 73, 13x9", SBY 10/24/89 18,700
BURGESS, Arthur James Wetherall (Australian, 1879-)
Sun Glitter on the Sea (ship in the distance), watercolor, sgn, 11x15", C-SK 11/10/88 890
BURGESS, John Bagnold (British, 1830-1897)
Fruit Girl, oil on canvas, sgn, no size given, FAP 11/4/88 UE 450
Girl with a Fan (portrait), oil on canvas, initialed/dtd 1872, 29x21", C-E 5/22/89 7,150
BURGESS, John Bagnold; att (British, 1830-1897)
Spanish Beauty (bust-length portrait), oil on canvas laid down on board, bears signature/dtd 1875, 19x15", C-E 2/21/89 1,320
BURGESS, Ruth Payne (American, -1934)
Portrait of a Seated Girl Holding a Rose (full-length), oil on canvas, sgn/dtd 1904, 54x40", WL 5/20/88 1,300
Portrait of a Young Boy in Costume, oil on canvas, sgn/dtd 1904, unfr, 64x40", SBY 6/24/88 1,430
BURGH, see Van Der Burgh
BURGHART, C. (American, 19th/20th C)
Repairing Boats in a Dry Dock, oil on canvas, sgn, 24x34", B/B 9/15/88 1,320
BURKHARD, Henri (American, 1892-)
Figure Study, charcoal/pastel on paper, sgn/dtd 62, 24x18", C-NY 3/11/88 UE 1,100
BURKHARDT, Hans (American, 1904-)
Abstract Figure, pastel on paper, sgn/dtd 1971, 26x19", B/B 8/10/88 385
BURLEIGH, Charles H.H. (British, 1875-1956)
Afternoon Tea (interior of English tea shop at teatime), oil on canvas, sgn, 24x20", C-NY 2/23/89 OE 24,200
BURLEIGH, Sidney Richmond (American, 1853-1931)
Along the Rhode Island Coastline, watercolor/gouache/charcoal on gray paper, sgn, 7x10", RWS 11/10/89 950
Sand & Dunes, watercolor on paper, sgn, 7x10", C-E 2/3/88 UE 220
Windrush (row of trees dividing grassy fields), watercolor/pencil on paper mounted on cardboard, sgn, 7x10", RWS 9/29/88 700
BURLIN, Harry Paul (American, 1886-1969)
Horse with Saddle, watercolor on paper, sgn, 8x10", C-E 9/15/88 495
Music From the Heavens, oil on masonite, sgn, 32x39", SBY 9/23/88 1,760
BURLINGAME, Charles Albert (American, 1860-1930)
Summer Landscape, oil on canvas, sgn/dtd 02, 12x16", C-E 6/1/89 495
Tree-Lined Rocky Brook, oil on canvasboard, sgn, 16x20", B/B 5/17/89 880
BURLIUK, David (American, 1882-1967)
Afternoon Siesta (woman & chickens), oil on board, sgn/dtd 1947, 14x11", SBY 6/28/89 1,650
At the Pub, watercolor/gouache/ink on paper, sgn/dtd 1946, 11x15", C-E 9/15/88 OE 1,210
Birds of the Windy Night (figures, buildings & unicorn, many birds overhead), oil on canvasboard, sgn, 8x10", C-E 6/1/89 1,540
Bourgeois Riding in State (abstract composition), oil on canvas, sgn, 1922, 51x69", SBY 11/12/88 OE 275,000
Bradenton Beach, Florida (figures in foreground, houses beyond); oil on canvas, sgn/dtd 1951, 11x17", C-E 6/1/89 2,090
Captain Olsen's Place, oil on canvas, sgn/dtd 1949 twice/titled, 20x30", SBY 3/17/88 2,640
Card Games, oil on canvas, sgn, 13x18", C-E 11/30/88 1,650
Cubistic Still Life, oil on canvas, sgn, 15x14", C-E 6/1/89 3,080
Daisies & Wildflowers, oil on panel, sgn, 19x13", C-E 6/1/88 1,100
Edgartown, oil on canvas, sgn, 15x19", SBY 3/17/88 OE 2,090
Figures in a Park, watercolor on paper, 12x15", B/B 4/14/89 715
Flowers by the Sea, oil on canvas, sgn, 20x30", C-E 10/18/89 2,200
Flowers in a Field, oil on board, sgn, 24x20", C-E 2/3/88 2,200
For the Phantoms of Unknown Tales, oil on canvas, sgn/dtd 1960, 24x20", C-NY 3/11/88 1,760
Fort Matanzas, watercolor/pen/ink on paper, sgn/inscr, 12x16", C-E 11/30/88 UE 440
Gleize Bridge on the Vigueuret Canal, oil on canvas, sgn/dtd France 1949, 15x24", SBY 9/14/89 4,125
Gorky & Friend (contemporary landscape w/couple, cow & sunflowers), oil on canvas, sgn/dtd 1949, 36x52", PHL 12/1/88 8,000
Hampton Bays Train Station, watercolor on paper, sgn/dtd 1945, 12x15", FAP 4/15/89 770
Headless Barber, oil/collage on canvas, ca 1912, 21x24", SBY 11/12/88 OE 52,250
Homestead, oil on board, sgn, 8x10", C-E 2/1/89 1,100
Horse & Cow, oil on canvas, sgn, 8x10", PHL 12/1/88 700
Ixtapun, Mexico; watercolor/pen/ink on paper, sgn/dtd 1947/titled, 12x15", C-E 11/8/88 UE 480
London Bridge, oil on canvas, sgn, 16x20", C-E 10/18/89 880
Night Rider (The Death Rider), oil on burlap, sgn in cyrillic, ca 1911-12, 36x25", SBY 11/12/88 55,000
Old Captain, oil on canvas, sgn/dtd 1948, 8x6", C-E 6/1/89 UE 1,320
Old Man with Dog, oil on board, sgn, 8x10", C-E 2/3/88 OE 1,540
Park Landscape, oil on canvas, sgn/dtd October 21, 1945; 12x16", MG 5/28/88 500
Peasants with Ducks, oil on panel, sgn/dtd 27, 14x26", C-NY 3/11/88 2,420
Piers (industrial view), watercolor/pencil on paper laid down on board, sgn, 15x19", C-E 2/1/89 1,100
Portrait of the Artist's Wife, oil on canvasboard, sgn/dtd 4?, 11x9", C-E 6/1/89 825
Prudent Advise, oil on masonite, sgn, 10x8", C-E 2/1/89 1,430
River Landscape with Mountains, oil on canvas, sgn, ca 1910, 16x26", C-L 10/8/88 5,950
Sleigh Ride, oil on board, sgn, 5x10", C-E 2/1/89 1,210

Southhampton, oil on canvas, sgn, 22x13", C-E 6/1/88 — 2,200
Still Life of Flowers, oil on canvas, sgn, 14x19", SBY 9/23/88 UE — 1,540
Still Life of Flowers, oil on canvas, sgn/dtd 1944, 16x15", FAP 4/15/89 — 1,540
Street in Gloucester, Massachusetts; oil on canvas, sgn/dtd 1930, 14x20", SBY 6/24/88 OE — 2,310
Summer (floral still life by window, woman hanging clothes on line), oil on canvas, sgn/dtd 48, 27x20", C-E 6/1/89 — 3,520
Sunflowers, oil on canvas, sgn, 38x24", C-NY 3/11/88 — 3,960
Teatime, oil on canvasboard, sgn/dtd 1956, 8x10", SBY 9/23/88 — 715
View of the Harbor, Green Port, Long Island; watercolor on paper, sgn/dtd 1945, no size given, FAP 4/15/89 — 880

BURN, E. (American, 19th/20th C)
Bay Horse in a Landscape, oil on canvas, sgn/dtd 1899, 24x30", SBY 6/8/88 OE — 2,860

BURNE-JONES, Edward Coley (British, 1833-1898)
Flora (full-length, standing), pastel on paper, 60x23", SBY 6/1/89 UE — 82,500
Head of a Girl, pencil, initialed, 11x7", C-NY 2/25/88 OE — 24,200
Studies of the Artist's Son, Philip, As a Young Boy, ca 1875; pencil, 9x7", C-NY 2/23/89 — 22,000

BURNS, J. (American, 19th C)
Brun House, Prospect Park, New York; oil on canvas, sgn/dtd NY 1870, 36x54", SBY 1/24/89 OE — 4,400

BURNS, M.J. (American, 19th C)
Shell Bursting on the Alabama (Civil War), oil on paper laid down on board, sgn/inscr, 17x22", C-E 5/27/88 OE — 2,420

BURNS, Milton J. (American, 1853-1933)
Fisherfolk Gathering After the Catch, oil on canvasboard, sgn, 14x20", B/B 3/17/88 — 2,200

BURNS-WILSON, Robert (American, 1851-1916)
Classical Garden Scene, watercolor/gouache on paper, sgn, 15x21", SBY 4/14/89 — 990

BURPEE, William Partridge (American, 1846-)
In the Dunes, oil on canvas, sgn, 20x24", SBY 4/14/89 — 2,750
Summer, North Africa (walkway under the shade of an arbor); watercolor/pencil on paper, sgn, 14x18", RWS 9/29/88 — 275
Winter Solstice (snow-covered landscape), pastel on paper, sgn, 5x9", RWS 3/31/88 — 350

BURR, Alexander Hohenlohe (British, 1837-1899)
Games with Grandfather (w/children & dog watching in an interior), oil on canvas, sgn/dtd 1875, 16x24", C-NY 5/24/89 — 4,950

BURR, George Brainard (American, 1876-1939)
Double-Sided: Path by a River; Fall Landscape; oil on canvas, 20x25", SBY 9/23/88 — 5,500
Memories (woman seated, daydreaming), oil on canvas, 25x20", SBY 6/24/88 — 1,760

BURR, George Elbert (American, 1859-1939)
Spanish Peaks, Sunrise; oil on canvas, sgn/dtd 1919, 14x20", SBY 1/24/89 OE — 6,050

BURRELL, Alfred Ray (American, 1877-1952)
Landscape with Flowering Cherry Trees, oil on canvas, sgn, 16x20", B/B 9/14/89 UE — 550

BURRILL, E. Jr. (American, 19th/20th C)
Waiting for Their Feeding Time (chickens in yard, cows watch from barn window), oil on canvas, sgn, 14x20", RWS 9/29/88 — 450

BURROUGHS, John; school of (20th C)
Landscape (primitive), oil on canvas, sgn, ca 1935, 28x36", C-NY 2/20/88 OE — 57,200

BURT, James (American, fl 1835-1849)
T Ebenezer's Mill, oil on canvas, 22x30", C-NY 5/26/88 — 4,950
Trenton Falls, Mowhawk River, New York; oil on canvas, sgn/dtd 1839, 22x30", RWS 10/27/89 — 2,600

BURTON, Frederick (British, 1816-1900)
Old Farmhouse, oil on canvas, sgn/dtd 1886, 20x30", B/B 5/17/89 — 1,100

BURTON, Ralph W. (Canadian, 1905-1983)
Barns at Ashton, Ontario; oil on panel, sgn/dtd 1979, 11x14", FB 10/17/88 — 300
Bleached Rocks, oil on board, sgn, 11x14", FB 10/30/89 — 308
Church at Brittania Bay, oil on board, sgn, 14x11", FB 10/30/89 — 495
Forest Scene, oil on board, sgn, 10x14", FB 10/30/89 — 412
Old Log House, Marlborough Township, Ontario; oil on panel, sgn/dtd 1968, 14x11", FB 10/17/88 — 325
Spring at Farmer's Rapids, Quebec; oil on panel, sgn/dtd 1954, 11x14", FB 4/25/88 — 375

BUSCH, Clarence Francis (American, 1887-)
Moment's Pause, oil on canvasboard, sgn/titled, 16x12", C-E 1/12/88 — 352
Three Muses (nudes in a landscape), oil on canvas, sgn, 38x30", WD 4/13/88 — 1,800

BUSCHER, Franz (American, 19th C)
My Old Kentucky Home, oil on canvas, 22x32", SBY 1/24/89 — 3,300

BUSH, Jack (Canadian, 20th C)
Hymn (abstract), acrylic on canvas, sgn/dtd 1971, 78x49", SBY 10/5/89 — 52,250
Untitled (abstract), acrylic on canvas, sgn/dtd 1966, 90x70", SBY 2/15/89 — 49,500

BUSH, Norton (American, 1834-1894)
Misty Sunrise Over a Lagoon, oil on canvas, monogramed/sgn/dtd 1886, 20x36", B/B 1/11/89 — 1,540
Tropical Lagoon Scene at Sunset, oil on canvas, sgn/dtd 1882, 12x20", B/B 10/9/88 — 3,025

BUSH, Norton; att (American, 1834-1894)
Sunset in the Tropics, River Scene; oil on board, 5x9", RWS 3/31/88 UE — 300

BUSLL, Jared
Meeting on the Path, oil on canvas, sgn/dtd 1850, 20x24", C-E 4/7/88 UE — 440

BUSSE, Gustave
Pair: Cows in a Pasture; Cows by a Stream, pencil with ink washes on paper, sgn/inscr, 5x7", 4x6", C-E 10/25/88 — 176

BUSSIERE, Gaston (French, 1862-1929)
Deux Enfants aux Couronnes de Fleurs (two nude girls w/floral crowns), oil on canvas, sgn, 26x19", SBY 10/24/89 — 8,800

BUSSON, Georges Louis Charles (French, 1859-1919)
Equipage de Bonnelles-Rambouillet a Madame la Duchesse d'Uzes, oil on canvas, sgn, 28x19", SBY 6/10/88 OE 5,775
BUTHE, Michael (20th C)
Untitled, gouache/blue crayon/gold leaf/graphite on paper, sgn/dtd 83, 13x9", C-E 5/13/88 605
BUTLER, Elizabeth Southerden (English, 19th C)
Lifeguards (skirmish), oil on panel, monogramed, 12x10", C-E 2/21/89 UE 1,100
BUTLER, Howard Russell (American, 1856-1934)
Beaching Boats at Hale, oil on canvas, sgn/dtd 1886, 15x22", C-NY 3/11/88 OE 6,050
Colma, Mexico; oil on canvas, ca 1883, 22x36", C-NY 3/11/88 4,400
Haystacks, oil on canvas, sgn, 21x28", C-NY 3/11/88 UE 3,300
Low Tide at St Ives (beach scene w/ships in distance), oil on canvas, sgn, 15x22", C-E 2/1/89 2,420
Restless Pacific (waves crashing on rocky coast), oil on canvas, sgn, 40x50", C-NY 5/25/89 13,200
Summer by the Sea, oil on canvas, sgn, 8x14", C-E 2/1/89 OE 4,400
BUTLER, Manley (American, 20th C)
Transportation Company Landing, Marblehead; oil on canvasboard, sgn/inscr/dtd twice, 10x14", C-E 2/3/88 352
BUTLER, Mary (American, 1865-1946)
Western Mountain Landscape, oil on canvas, sgn, 20x28", RWS 3/16/89 OE 1,400
BUTLER, Theodore Earl (American, 1876-1936/37)
Fisherman, pastel, sgn, 9x16", LH 12/4/88 1,000
Reading (girl seated in an interior), oil on canvas, sgn/dtd 90, 29x24", DM 9/16/88 25,000
BUTLER, Thomas (British, fl 1750-1759)
Scope, a Bay Racehorse with Jockey Up; oil on canvas, inscr, 21x25", SBY 6/9/89 6,050
The Meet (hunt scene in extensive landscape w/estate), oil on canvas, 48x79", SBY 6/9/89 UE 66,000
BUTMAN, Frederick A. (American, 1820-1871)
Group of 3: Figures in Landscape; 2 oil on canvas/1 oil on board, 2 sgn/1 initialed, 2 9x12", 1 10" dia, SBY 1/24/89 OE 5,500
BUTTERFIELD, W. Cortland (American, 20th C)
Female Nude (seated, turned to side), oil on canvas, sgn, 36x24", B/B 9/14/89 UE 550
BUTTERSAY (20th C)
Newspaper Delivery, oil on canvas, sgn/dtd 1941, 14x12", C-E 6/28/88 UE 100
BUTTERSWORTH, James E. (American, 1817-1894)
Alice, oil on canvas, sgn, 28x42", SBY 5/25/88 60,400
British Frigate Off Dover, oil on canvas, sgn, ca 1842, 25x30", C-NY 5/25/89 37,400
Clipper Ships at Sea, oil on panel, sgn, 9x12", SBY 9/14/89 12,100
Flying Cloud Off the Needles (coastal view, ship on stormy sea), oil on panel, sgn, 12x18", WD 10/5/88 50,000
Racing Cutters Close Hauled, oil on canvas, sgn, 20x30", PHL 12/1/88 OE 125,000
Racing Yachts, oil on canvas, initialed, 20x24", RAB 8/1/89 OE 41,000
Ships Off Castle Garden, oil on panel, sgn, 8x12", SBY 6/28/89 OE 17,600
Strong Breeze Reposing the Vigilant & Valkyrie Under Snug Canvas Running Free, oil on board, sgn, 9x12", C-NY 2/12/88 30,800
United States Ship of the Line Ohio, oil on canvas, 26x38", C-NY 12/2/88 46,200
Vigilant & Valkyrie Bending to Windward in a Strong Breeze, oil on board, sgn/inscr, 9x12", C-NY 2/12/88 OE 30,800
Yacht Race, oil on board, sgn, 14x24", C-NY 12/2/88 88,000
Yacht Race, oil on canvas, sgn, 18x24", SBY 5/25/88 42,900
Yacht Race Off Sandy Hook, oil on academy board, sgn, 8x12", RAB 8/1/89 27,500
BUTTERSWORTH, Thomas; circle of (British, fl 1798-1827)
Shipwreck, oil on tin, 19x23", C-NY 6/2/88 3,300
BUTTNER, Hans (German, 19th C)
Hunting Party, oil on canvas, sgn/inscr, 15x12", C-NY 2/25/88 12,100
BUTTON, Albert Prentice (American, 1872-)
Autumn Landscape (stream meanders through golden glade), oil on artist board, sgn, 14x14", RWS 9/29/88 UE 275
Canoeing (three figures in canoe), watercolor/pencil on paper, sgn, 5x4", RWS 5/19//88 500
Dunes-Annisquam (golden foreground, dunes w/marine scene beyond); oil on artist board, sgn, 5x6", RWS 3/31/88 1,000
Pheasant Hunting (hunter & dog in landscape), watercolor/pencil on paper, sgn, 5x6", RWS 5/19/88 425
The Fair, watercolor/ink on paper, sgn, 5x6", RWS 9/8/89 250
BUTTON, John (American, 1929-)
Breaking Clouds, gouache on paper, sgn, 10x13", C-NY 6/17/89 330
Evening Landscape, oil on canvas, sgn, 32x36", C-E 5/13/88 UE 660
Set of 3: Landscapes; watercolor on paper, ea sgn/1 dtd 1907, 9x12" & smaller, C-E 4/7/88 OE 825
BUZZI, A. (Italian, 20th C)
New Arrival (family figures w/new baby in an interior), watercolor on paper, sgn, 15x21", WG 4/23/88 OE 1,050
BUZZI, Federico
Lesson From Grandmother, oil on canvas, sgn/dtd 1870, 24x17", C-E 5/23/88 1,870
BYLANDT, see De Bylandt
BYRD, Henry (American, fl 1866-1884)
Portrait of Charles Caffin, New Orleans; oil on canvas, sgn/dtd 1900, 38x50", MG 10/28/88 1,900
BYRON, Michael
Untitled (abstract), watercolor on paper, initialed, 1985, 7x10", C-NY 10/4/89 550
C.R.
Running Brook in an Extensive Landscape, oil on canvas, initialed, 1858, 38x51", C-E 10/25/88 2,750
CABAILLOT, Camille Leopold Dit Lasalle (French, 1839-)
Gazing Out a Window, oil on panel, sgn/dtd 1878, 17x13", C-E 10/25/88 3,300

CABALLERO, Luis (South American, 20th C)
Sin Titulo (nude male w/figures supporting him from behind), charcoal on paper, 1982, 77x51", C-NY 5/18/88 ... 13,200
Untitled (reclining male), charcoal on paper, sgn/dtd 83, 30x42", SBY 11/21/88 ... 2,750
CABALLERO, Maximo (Spanish, 19th/20th C)
Card Game, oil on canvas, sgn/dtd 1899, 32x40", C-NY 2/25/88 OE ... 18,700
Confrontation in the Guard Room, oil on canvas, sgn, 24x36", WD 3/23/88 OE ... 7,500
Une Histoire d'Armour, oil on canvas, sgn/dtd 1901, 24x29", C-NY 5/25/88 OE ... 22,000
CABANEL, Alexandre (French, 1823-1889)
Arab Beauty (portrait), oil on canvas, sgn/dtd 1871, 29x24", C-NY 2/23/89 ... 15,400
Listening to the Voice of Echo (portrait of lady), oil on canvas, sgn, 30x24", C-NY 2/23/89 ... 7,150
CABANEL, Alexandre; att (French, 1823-1889)
Allegory of Spring (figures in a landscape), oil on canvas, framed as semi-circle, 35x83", B/B 9/14/89 ... 1,980
CABANYES, see De Cabanyes
CABEL, Arent; see Arentz, Arent
CABIE, Louis Alexandre (French, 1853-1939)
Bridge Over a Rocky Brook, oil on canvas, sgn/dtd 1898, 35x52", C-E 5/23/88 ... 2,420
CABOT, Edward Clarke (American, 1818-1901)
Nantucket Sound (white-capped waves, sailboats & landscape beyond), watercolor on paper, ca 1883, 13x20", RAB 8/9/88 UE ... 300
CABRAL, R. (American, 20th C)
Yacht Race Off Newport, oil on canvas, sgn, 30x20", RAB 8/1/88 ... 850
CABRERA, Miguel (Mexican, 1695-1768)
Inmaculada (religious), oil on canvas, sgn, ca 1780, 17x12", C-NY 5/17/89 OE ... 12,100
CABRERA, Ricardo Lopez (Spanish, 1864-1950)
By the Window, oil on canvas, sgn, unfr, 31x22", SBY 5/23/89 ... 9,900
CACCIARELLI, Victor (Italian, 19th C)
Discussion Over Tea, watercolor on paper, sgn/inscr, 21x15", SBY 6/8/88 ... 825
Gentleman, watercolor on paper, sgn/inscr, 14x11", C-E 2/23/88 UE ... 660
Last Chess Game, watercolor/gouache over traces of pencil, sgn, 22x15", C-NY 10/26/88 ... 1,320
Pretty Maid (serving two gentlemen in elegant interior), oil on canvas, sgn, 19x13", PHL 6/16/88 UE ... 2,200
Receiving the Cardinal, watercolor/gouache over pencil, sgn, 15x10", C-NY 10/26/88 UE ... 770
CACCIERELLI, Umberto (Italian, 19th C)
Gentlemen Drinking Tea, oil on canvas, sgn, 10x14", C-E 2/21/89 ... 3,080
CACHOUD, Francois Charles (French, 1866-1943)
Moonlit Country Lane with Figure, oil on canvas, sgn, 26x32", FB 4/25/88 UE ... 4,000
River Landscape, oil on canvas, sgn, 29x36", SBY 12/9/88 ... 2,200
Strolling on a Starry Night, oil on canvas, sgn/dtd 1906, SBY 12/9/88 ... 2,750
CADDY, Alexander E. (19th/20th C)
Indian River Landscape, oil on canvas, sgn/dtd 1903, 22x18", C-SK 5/25/89 ... 510
CADENASSO, Giuseppe (American, 1854-1918)
A Forest Home, oil on canvas, sgn, 25x30", B/B 10/6/88 ... 1,650
After the Storm, Aladeda (trees & water-soaked field), oil on canvas, sgn, 25x30", RAB 8/9/88 ... 1,200
Marin Lake Scene, oil on canvas, sgn, 18x30", B/B 10/6/88 ... 8,250
Marin Landscape, oil on canvas laid down, sgn, 27x36", B/B 10/6/88 ... 2,475
Pond at Dusk, pastel on paper, sgn, 15x22", B/B 1/11/89 OE ... 2,090
CADES, Giuseppe; att (1750-1799)
Design for a Frontispiece: Group of Musicians; pen/brown ink/wash, 9x12", SBY 1/13/89 ... 2,475
CADMUS, Paul (American, 1904-)
Double-Sided: Seated Nude; Reclining Nude; crayon/pencil & crayon on paper, sgn/#d 165 S, 25x19", SBY 4/14/89 ... 3,300
Idle Afternoon, pen/black ink on buff paper, sgn, 8x10", C-NY 3/11/88 OE ... 9,900
Male Nude, colored crayons on hand-toned paper, sgn/inscr, 20x16", SBY 6/24/88 ... 6,050
Male Nude (viewed from behind), crayons heightened w/white on colored paper, sgn/#d B 32, 18x10", SBY 9/14/89 ... 7,700
Nude Kneeling at Table Reading (male), pencil/case on colored paper, sgn/#d TS 8, 11x15", SBY 9/14/89 ... 2,420
Seated Male Nude, black/brown/white chalk on prepared paper, sgn/#d NM127, 15x10", SBY 9/14/89 ... 1,320
Standing Nude (male, viewed from behind, hand on hip), pen/ink/casein on paper, sgn/#d A17, 13x10", SBY 9/14/89 ... 3,080
Two Dancers Resting, conte crayon/pastel on tan paper, sgn/#d NM 133, 17x25", C-NY 3/11/88 OE ... 7,700
CADY, Arthur (American, 20th C)
Telephone (pay phone on brick background), watercolor/gouache/graphite on paper, sgn/dtd 1969, 24x18", RWS 9/8/89 OE ... 325
CADY, Henry N. (American, 1849-)
Beach at Sunset, oil on canvas, sgn, 27x22", C-NY 9/30/88 ... 4,620
CADY, Sam (20th C)
Roof with Skylight, oil on shaped canvas, sgn/dtd 1979, 31x63", C-E 5/9/89 ... 550
Surburban House with Pool, Winter Afternoon; oil on canvas laid down on panel, sgn/dtd 80, 6x20", C-E 11/17/88 ... 550
CAFE, Thomas Watt (British, 1856-)
New Bead Necklace (classical lady admiring her necklace in mirror), oil on panel, sgn, 10x7", B/B 6/15/89 ... 1,430
CAFFE, Nino (Spanish, 1909-)
Ottobrata (religious figures dining at long table in landscape), oil on panel, sgn, 16x27", SBY 2/14/89 ... 8,800
Partita al Golf, oil on panel, sgn, 9x19", B/B 2/17/88 ... 2,750
Partita al Golf, oil on panel, sgn, 9x20", SBY 10/5/88 ... 4,675
Piccolo Autoritratto Col Piviale (artist in his studio), oil on panel, sgn, 14x10", C-E 11/17/88 OE ... 2,860

Pioggia de Marzo, oil on panel, sgn, 9x12", C-E 11/17/88 OE 4,950
Ponticello Celeste, oil on panel, sgn, 13x18", B/B 3/17/88 2,750
Ponticello Celeste, oil on panel, sgn, 13x18", SBY 10/5/88 4,675
Red & the Black, oil on canvas, sgn, 16x28", SBY 10/5/88 5,775
Sera (religious figures in repose on beach), oil on panel, sgn, 8x14", SBY 2/14/89 UE 2,090
Stranieri in Visita (figures at entrance to nunnery), oil on panel, sgn/dtd 61, 8x15", SBY 2/14/89 1,650
Visita al Vescovo di Urbino, oil on panel, sgn, 12x28", B/B 3/17/88 2,750
Visita al Vescovo di Urbino, oil on panel, sgn, 12x28", SBY 10/5/88 8,800

CAFFERTY, James Henry (American, 1819-1969)

Boys Fishing, oil on canvas, 16x20", C-NY 5/26/88 4,400
Peaches on a Table Top, oil on board, sgn/dtd 1862, 5x7", SBY 9/23/88 OE 3,572

CAFFI, Margherita; circle of (Italian, 18th C)

Pair: Tulips, Carnations, Narcissi, & Other Flowers in Sculpted Urns; oil on canvas, 25x29", C-NY 1/15/88 OE 35,200

CAFFIERI, Hector (British, 1847-1932)

Fishing Party, oil on canvas, sgn/dtd 1875, 14x20", SBY 6/8/88 6,600

CAFFYN, Walter Wallor (British, -1898)

Old Stone Bridge, oil on canvas, sgn/dtd 1898, 30x50", SBY 5/23/89 UE 4,950

CAGLI, Corrado (Italian, 1910-)

Acquisgrana (abstract), oil on canvas, sgn/dtd 58, 30x40", SBY 2/14/89 3,850

CAGNACCI, Guido (Italian, 1601-1681)

Pan (portrait), oil on canvas, 34x34", C-NY 1/11/89 55,000

CAHOON, Charles D. (American, 1861-1951)

Cape Cod Pine, oil on canvas, sgn/titled, 10x12", RAB 11/25/88 750
Cape Cod Sand Dune (landscape), oil on canvas, sgn, 10x12", RAB 11/25/88 850
Cape Cod Sand Dune (ocean beyond), oil on canvas, sgn, original gilt frame, 12x17", RAB 8/8/99 1,750
Cave of the Winds, Niagara Falls (cascading water on gray rocks); oil on canvas, sgn, 39x31", RAB 8/9/88 5,250
Chickadee on a Branch, oil on canvas, sgn, 12x20", RAB 8/9/88 1,500
Gay Head, Massachusetts (rolling hills, distant lighthouse & houses); oil on artist board, sgn, 9x12", RAB 8/9/88 4,500
Gay Head Mews, sheep graze on a path by stone wall; oil on canvas, sgn/titled, 16x24", RAB 11/25/88 3,250
Homeward Bound (ship at sea), oil on canvas, sgn, 20x26", RAB 8/9/88 UE 3,500
Is This Yours? (small boy holding egg up to chicken), oil on canvas, 17x12", RAB 8/9/88 3,750
Long Pond at Pleasant Lake, Robin Hood Hill; oil on cardboard, sgn/titled, 5x11", RAB 8/8/89 1,300
Marine Scene (three-masted ship at sea), oil on canvas, sgn, 30x25", RWS 9/8/89 OE 2,000
Ocean Sunset, oil on canvas, sgn, 9x12", RAB 11/25/88 550
Ocean Sunset (crashing surf, distant sailboat), oil on canvas, sgn, 24x60", RAB 8/9/88 UE 1,250
Old Fisherman, dressed in foul weather gear; oil on masonite, sgn, 9x12", RAB 11/25/88 OE 1,300
Portrait of a Two-Masted Schooner with Black Hull Under Full Sail, oil on artist board, sgn, 11x11", RAB 11/25/88 2,250
Road Home (landscape), oil on canvas, sgn, 10x17", RAB 8/8/89 OE 6,500
Scene in South Sandwich, Pond Behind Frank Ewer's Old Homestead That Burned; oil on cardboard, 7x9", RAB 11/25/88 1,100
Stage Harbor, Chatham, Massachusetts (fishing shacks along harbor); oil on board, sgn, 14x18", RAB 11/25/88 2,750
Summer Afternoon (creek & fields in extensive landscape), oil on artist board, sgn, 9x12", RAB 8/9/88 3,250
Sunset Landscape, oil on board, sgn, 10x11", RAB 3/27/89 UE 1,200

CAHOON, Charles D.; att (American, 1861-1951)

Late Autumn Sunset, oil on artist board, 9x12", RAB 8/9/88 900
Late Autumn Sunset (red sunset filtering through bare trees), oil on artist board, 9x12", RAB 8/9/88 900

CAHOON, Martha (American, 20th C)

And What Is So Rare As a Day in June? (sailor & girl with banner in field), oil on masonite, sgn, 10x12", RAB 8/9/88 OE 900
Butterflies & Shells (group of shells on shore, two butterflies above), oil on masonite, sgn, 10x14", RAB 8/9/88 UE 300
Cape Cod 1915 (primitive), crayon/pen on paper, sgn/dtd 1989, 9x12", RAB 11/24/89 UE 200
Frosty's Finishing Touches, pen/pencil/crayon on cardboard, sgn/dtd 1986, 10x12", RAB 11/25/88 650
Little Girl with Doll in a Landscape (primitive), crayon/pen on paper, sgn/dtd 1988, 12x9", RAB 11/24/89 300
Play Time (primitive), crayon/pen on paper, sgn/dtd 1989, 8x10", RAB 11/24/89 375
Running Free (horse trots through landscape), sgn/dtd 84, 12x14", RAB 8/9/88 UE 500
Running Free (horse trotting through landscape), oil on masonite, sgn/dtd 84, 13x14", RAB 8/9/88 UE 500
Shells & Shore (shells & pine cone on tree-lined shore), oil on masonite, sgn, 10x14", RAB 8/9/88 UE 400

CAHOON, Ralph (American, 1910-1982)

Cape Cod Skin Divers (w/mermaids), oil on masonite on 2 panels, sgn/inscr Pinxt, 21x27", RAB 8/8/89 6,500
Duck Hunting (sailor, three mermaids, clipper ship & balloon), oil on masonite, sgn, oval frame, 16x20", RAB 8/9/88 12,000
Fanciful Balloon Flight, oil on masonite, sgn, 28x22", RWS 9/8/89 5,500
I Found Her in the Water, Honey! (sailor holds mermaid, woman holds towel); oil on masonite, sgn, 12x15", RAB 11/25/88 5,000
Mermaids in a Circus Act, oil on masonite, sgn, 18x24", SBY 3/17/88 6,050
Monday at Cotuit (mermaid hanging laundry on line, harbor scene beyond), oil on masonite, sgn, 10x8", RAB 8/9/88 OE 10,500
Sailor's Fantasy (sailor/mermaids in landscape), oil on masonite, sgn/dtd Jan 1958, 18x24", RAB 8/8/89 UE 1,700
Ship Mermaid (masted ship, mermaids w/name plate, balloon in distance), oil on masonite, sgn, 18x22", RAB 8/8/89 6,500
Shipwreck (sailor, globe & mermaid on chest in landscape), oil on masonite, sgn, 14x18", RAB 8/8/89 8,000
South Pacific Yacht Club, whalers approaching whale w/four mermaids on back; oil on beaverboard, 14x28", RAB 11/24/89 5,500
Still Life of Fruit, oil on masonite, sgn/titled, 22x28", RAB 11/25/88 11,000
Still Life of Fruit in a Chinese Lowestoft Bowl, oil on beaverboard, 20x24", RAB 11/24/89 5,000
Susanna & the Elders (sailors spying on bathing lady), oil on board on 3 panels, sgn, 7x3", RAB 8/8/89 UE 2,500

CAILLE, Leon Emile (French, 1836-1907)
Ironing & Studying (interior scene w/mother & daughter), oil on canvas, sgn/dtd 1890, 18x15", WD 11/16/88 UE **3,000**
Ironing Day, oil on paper laid down on board, sgn, 9x6", WD 3/23/88 OE **2,000**
Mother & Child, oil on board, sgn/dtd 1886, 9x6", C-E 10/25/88 .... **3,300**
Mother with Children, oil on panel, sgn, 14x11", SBY 7/12/89 .... **4,125**
CAILLEBOTTE, Gustave (French, 1836-1894)
Paysage en Normandie (landscape in Normandy w/house), oil on canvas, sgn, 1884, 25x29", SBY 11/12/88 .... **484,000**
CAIN, Georges Jules Auguste (French, 1856-1919)
Elegant Lady in the Salon, oil on canvas, sgn, 18x15", C-E 2/23/88 OE **3,080**
Selling Wares to the Gentleman (interior scene), oil on canvas, sgn/dtd 1879, 20x24", C-NY 2/23/89 .... **4,950**
Two Favorite Ladies (in street escorted by a gentleman), oil on canvas, sgn/dtd 1892, 22x17", C-NY 2/23/89 .... **4,400**
CALABRIA, Ennio (Italian, 1937-)
Fummatori al Tavolo Verde, oil on canvas, sgn twice/dtd 1959, 30x37", C-E 5/9/89 .... **2,310**
CALAME, Alexandre (Swiss, 1810-1864)
Angler Fishing in a Mountain Stream, oil on cradled panel, sgn/dtd 1861, 16x23", B/B 3/17/88 .... **10,450**
CALANDRUCCI, Giacinto (Italian, 1646-1707)
Angel Healing the Blind Tobit, black chalk, inscr/#26, 10x15", C-NY 1/11/89 .... **605**
CALDER, Alexander (American, 1898-1976)
Arrangements in Black & Orange, watercolor on paper, sgn/dtd 62, 27x40", SBY 10/5/89 OE **9,900**
Bird of Destiny (abstract composition), India ink/ink wash/watercolor on paper, sgn/dtd 66, unfr, 30x43", SBY 10/7/89 .... **5,775**
Black & Yellow Bow Tie, gouache on paper, sgn/dtd 67, 29x43", C-E 11/17/88 OE **9,900**
Black Letter A (abstract), gouache/black ink on paper, initialed/dtd 61/titled, 15x22", SBY 2/19/88 OE **7,700**
Butterflies with Sun (abstract composition), gouache on paper, sgn/dtd 66, 42x29", SBY 10/7/89 OE **14,300**
Caterpillar on Spiral (abstract), gouache on paper, sgn/dtd 66, 30x42", SBY 10/8/88 OE **13,200**
Circus Studies (110 sheets, 3 folding boxes), watercolor/ink/pencil on paper, unfr, various sizes, C-E 11/17/88 OE **17,600**
Circus Train (line drawing), India ink on paper, sgn/dtd 1932/inscr dedication, 30x22", SBY 5/11/88 OE **52,800**
Cirque (The Circus), gouache on paper, sgn/dtd 74, 43x15", SBY 10/5/89 OE **18,700**
Colored Spiral, gouache on paper, sgn/dtd 70, 29x43", SBY 2/15/89 OE **17,600**
Composition, watercolor on paper laid down on masonite, sgn/dtd 4?, 23x31", SBY 10/7/89 .... **4,950**
Composition (abstract), gouache/ink wash on paper, sgn/dtd 46, 15x19", SBY 2/16/89 OE **7,700**
Composition on Yellow Ground, oil on canvas, initialed, ca 1945-50, 29x39", SBY 10/5/89 OE **55,000**
Coo (abstract), gouache on paper, sgn/dtd 66, 29x43", SBY 10/5/88 .... **4,125**
Double-Sided: Go Fetch; Spatial Composition; India ink on stiff card (wax crayon on verso), 28x15", SBY 2/18/88 .... **9,350**
Double-Sided: Gymnast (line drawing); India ink on paper, sgn/dtd 1932, 22x30", SBY 5/11/88 .... **8,250**
Drawings (31 sheets & 3 folding boxes, figures & animal studies), mixed media, various sizes, C-E 11/17/88 OE **8,250**
Emerging Globes (composition w/line & circles), gouache on paper, sgn/dtd 71, 23x31", C-NY 5/4/89 .... **9,900**
Equilibrium, gouache on paper, sgn/dtd 74, 30x43", SBY 10/5/89 .... **8,250**
Eye of the Nautilus, gouache on paper, sgn/dtd 67, 23x31", SBY 10/5/89 .... **6,600**
Fox & Huntsmen From Aesop's Fable, ink on paper, sgn, 9x7", WD 5/5/88 .... **1,700**
Green Boomerang (abstract composition), gouache on paper, sgn/dtd 70, 21x29", SBY 10/7/89 .... **9,900**
Himself (contemporary mountains & birds), gouache on paper, sgn/dtd 63, 14x21", SBY 10/7/89 .... **9,075**
L'Etoile (red, white, & blue sun), gouache/brush/black ink on paper, sgn/dtd 75, 30x43", C-NY 10/4/89 .... **11,000**
La Pie de Sache, gouache on paper, monogramed/inscr/dtd 74, unfr, 44x15", C-E 5/13/88 .... **5,500**
Les Discs, gouache on paper, sgn/dtd 70, 30x43", C-E 5/13/88 OE **8,250**
Nocturne, gouache on paper, monogramed/inscr/dtd 73, 18x43", C-E 5/13/88 OE **5,720**
On the Beach (abstract w/circles), gouache/brush/black ink on paper, sgn/dtd 65, 30x43", C-NY 10/4/89 .... **8,250**
Over the Horizon (abstract composition), gouache on paper, initialed/dtd 60, 41x30", SBY 10/7/89 .... **13,200**
Overpass (abstract), gouache on paper, sgn/dtd 75, 29x41", SBY 10/5/88 .... **8,250**
Paw Print in the Blue, gouache on paper, sgn/dtd 63, 23x31", C-E 5/13/88 .... **5,720**
Portrait of Jean Paul Sartre, India ink on paper, sgn, ca 1948, 8x6", SBY 10/7/88 OE **7,700**
Profile, gouache on paper, sgn/dtd 65, 29x42", SBY 10/5/88 OE **9,900**
Rearing Horse & Nude, pen/ink on paper laid down on board, ca 1944, 20x27", SBY 10/7/88 OE **12,100**
Red Dots on Green, gouache on paper, sgn/dtd 65, 21x29", SBY 10/5/88 .... **6,600**
Red Sun, Yellow Boomerang (abstract composition); gouache on paper, sgn/dtd 62, 30x42", C-E 11/14/89 .... **12,100**
Rodeo, India ink on paper, sgn/dtd 1932, 22x30", SBY 2/18/88 OE **19,800**
Shapes with Butterfly, oil on canvas, sgn, ca 1955, 32x46", SBY 11/11/88 OE **55,000**
Soucoupes Volontes, Chinese ink on paper, sgn/dtd 68, 43x30", LH 5/15/88 .... **1,400**
Spiral (composition), gouache on paper, sgn/dtd 71, 29x43", SBY 10/7/89 .... **6,600**
Still Life on Beach (abstract composition), gouache on paper, sgn/dtd 47, 23x31", RWS 11/10/89 .... **7,000**
Stilt Walker & Acrobats in Center Ring, India ink on paper, sgn/dtd 1932, 14x19", SBY 10/7/88 .... **17,600**
Stripes & Beams, watercolor/black ink on paper, sgn, 1944, 23x31", C-E 11/17/88 OE **5,280**
Sunflower (w/star, moon, dice, & snake), gouache on paper, initialed/dtd 61, 15x22", SBY 2/15/89 OE **10,450**
Tightrope Walker (line drawing), India ink on paper, sgn/dtd 1932, 22x30", SBY 5/11/88 .... **14,850**
Trainer & Equestrian, gouache on paper, monogramed/dtd 76, 23x15", C-E 5/13/88 OE **6,050**
Trapeze Artist Inside the Big Top, India ink on stiff card, sgn/dtd 1932, 22x15", SBY 2/18/88 OE **19,800**
Untitled, gouache on paper, sgn/dtd 49, unfr, 22x30", C-E 5/13/88 OE **7,700**
Untitled, gouache on paper, sgn/dtd 69, 29x43", C-E 5/13/88 .... **6,050**
Untitled (abstract composition), black ink/gouache/watercolor on paper, sgn/dtd 70, 29x43", SBY 10/7/89 OE **17,600**
Untitled (abstract composition), gouache on paper, sgn/dtd 64, 30x43", SBY 10/7/89 .... **8,800**

Untitled (abstract composition), gouache on paper, sgn/dtd 63, 40x27", SBY 10/7/89 4,950
Untitled (abstract composition), gouache on paper, sgn/dtd 69, 22x30", SBY 10/7/89 OE 17,600
Untitled (abstract composition), gouache on paper, sgn/dtd 70, 43x24", C-E 11/14/89 OE 17,600
Untitled (abstract composition), gouache/brush/black ink on paper, sgn/dtd 68, 29x43", C-E 11/14/89 OE 14,300
Untitled (abstract composition), oil on canvas, 1948, 12x18", SBY 10/5/89 OE 41,250
Untitled (abstract figures), gouache on paper, sgn/dtd 68, 30x43", C-NY 5/4/88 4,950
Untitled (abstract), black ink/watercolor/gouache on paper, sgn/dtd 49, 16x23", SBY 2/14/89 OE 11,550
Untitled (abstract), gouache on paper, sgn/dtd 42, 23x31", SBY 11/11/88 24,200
Untitled (abstract), gouache on paper, sgn/dtd 50, 30x42", SBY 2/15/89 OE 24,200
Untitled (abstract), gouache on paper, sgn/dtd 66, 30x42", SBY 2/15/89 OE 14,300
Untitled (abstract), gouache on paper, sgn/dtd 70, 29x43", SBY 2/15/89 OE 20,900
Untitled (abstract), gouache on paper, sgn/dtd 70, 30x43", SBY 2/19/88 OE 7,975
Untitled (abstract), gouache on paper, sgn/dtd 71, 29x43", SBY 10/5/88 7,425
Untitled (abstract), gouache on paper, 20x26", C-NY 10/4/89 8,250
Untitled (abstract), gouache/brush/black ink on paper, sgn/dtd 66, 23x31", C-NY 5/4/89 OE 13,200
Untitled (abstract), gouache/ink on board, sgn/dtd 61, 38x30", C-NY 2/14/89 OE 11,000
Untitled (abstract), gouache/ink on paper, sgn/dtd 42/inscr Para Josep y monchat del amigo Sandy, 30x22", SBY 11/11/88 25,300
Untitled (abstract), gouache/watercolor on paper, sgn/dtd 56, 22x30", SBY 10/7/89 OE 19,800
Untitled (abstract), watercolor on paper, sgn/dtd 47, 23x31", SBY 2/19/88 OE 12,100
Untitled (composition), brush/black ink/gouache on paper, sgn/dtd 76, 30x43", C-NY 5/4/89 8,250
Untitled (composition), watercolor/ink on paper, sgn/dtd 46, unfr, 12x9", SBY 10/7/89 5,500
Untitled (contempory), pen/ink on paper, ca 1942, 22x30", SBY 2/19/88 4,950
Untitled (drawing w/two pyramids, circles, & other symbols), gouache on paper, sgn/dtd 75, 30x43", B/B 6/15/89 4,950
Untitled (fish & hawks), gouache/brush/black ink on paper, sgn/dtd 75, 23x31", C-NY 5/4/89 8,250
Untitled (geometric composition), gouache on paper, sgn/dtd 62, 29x42", SBY 2/15/89 OE 14,300
Untitled (man-beast, sun, & moon), oil on canvas, sgn/dtd 51, 24x16", C-NY 2/14/89 OE 38,500
Untitled (nude juggler, line drawing), pen/black ink on paper, sgn, 12x9", C-NY 10/4/89 OE 9,350
Untitled (pyramids w/circles), gouache on paper, sgn/dtd 76, 30x43", C-NY 5/4/89 OE 18,700
Untitled (surrealistic forms), crayon/pen/watercolor on paper, ca 1942, 22x29", SBY 11/11/88 20,900
Untitled (woman & dog); black ink/gouache on paper, sgn/dtd 49, 22x14", SBY 2/14/89 OE 34,100
Untitled (zoo animals), gouache on paper, initialed/dtd 75, 23x31", C-NY 5/4/88 OE 6,600
X Marks the Spot, gouache on paper, sgn/dtd 68, 43x29", C-NY 5/4/88 OE 10,450

CALDER, Alexander; after (American, 1898-1976)

Acrobat (tapestry), maguey fiber, initialed/dtd 75/#d 39/100, 97x72", C-NY 2/13/89 3,080
Circus (tapestry), maguey fiber, sgn/dtd 75, 18/100, 86x57", C-E 11/14/89 OE 3,520
Lombrizi (abstract tapestry), maguey fiber, initialed/dtd 75/#d 41-10, 72x96", Bon Art, C-E 11/17/88 3,080
Lombrizi (tapestry), maguey fiber mounted on wooden stretcher, 56x85", C-E 11/14/89 3,850
Sillons Noirs (wool tapestry), 6/6, sgn in weave/Pinton Tapisserie d'Aubusson label/#33, 62x45", C-E 11/14/89 OE 11,000
Star (tapestry), maguey fiber, initialed/dtd 75, 80/100, 58x84", C-E 11/14/89 OE 6,600
Star (tapestry), maguey fiber, initialed/dtd 75/#d 39/100, 73x96", C-NY 2/13/89 2,640
Star (tapestry), maguey fiber, initialed/dtd 75/#d 41-100, 72x96", Bon Art, C-E 11/17/88 1,870
Untitled (tapestry), maguey fiber, initialed/dtd 74/#d 57/100, 57x85", C-E 11/17/88 1,320
Zebra (tapestry), maguey fiber, initialed/dtd 75/#d 52/100, 72x96", C-E 11/17/88 1,870

CALDER, Alexander; att (American, 1898-1976)

Bubbles, gouache on paper, sgn/dtd 71, 23x30", B/B 12/8/88 1,045

CALDINI, A. (Italian, 20th C)

Untitled (Neopolitan harbor scene), oil on canvas, sgn, 24x36", SLK 2/11/89 400

CALDWELL, Edmund (British, 1852-1930)

Gazelles, pencil/watercolor heightened w/white, sgn, 8x12", C-SK 11/10/88 1,020

CALDWELL, Georgia Leigh (American, 20th C)

Winter Landscape, oil on canvas, sgn, 20x24", LH 12/4/88 130

CALIARI, Paolo; follower of (called Veronese)(1528-1588)

Extensive Landscape with Mythological Scene, oil on panel, unfr, 21x30", SBY 6/8/88 1,100
Penitent Madgalen (three-quarter length, seated), oil on canvas, 49x47", SBY 6/1/89 UE 11,000

CALIARI, Paolo; manner of (called Veronese)(1528-1588)

Return of the Prodigal Son, oil on canvas, 15x22", SBY 6/8/88 UE 550

CALIFANO, John (American, 1864-1924)

Caring for the Barnyard Animals, oil on canvas, sgn, 35x52", B/B 6/15/89 2,090
Coastal Scene, oil on canvas, sgn, 13x15", DM 2/19/88 400
Country House, oil on canvas, sgn, 20x26", C-E 1/12/88 UE 385
Golden Autumn, oil on canvas, sgn, 24x36", DM 2/19/88 1,000
In a Canyon, oil on canvas, sgn, 16x20", C-E 11/8/88 1,100
Market Scene, oil on board, sgn, 13x15", DM 2/19/88 400
Mediterranean View, oil on canvas, sgn, 24x36", SBY 6/8/88 2,750
Shepherd with Goats Amidst Ruins, oil on canvas, sgn, 48x36", B/B 3/22/89 4,125
Shepherds` Rest in the Italian Alps, oil on canvas, sgn, 54x70", B/B 10/9/88 UE 14,300
Venetian Canal Scene (gondolas & figures in water, buildings beyond), oil on canvas, sgn, 10x32", C-E 6/1/89 1,980

California School (19th C)

Pair: Blue Wing Tavern, Sonoma; Stone House, Sonoma; pencil, indistinctly monogramed, 8x14", 8x11", B/B 10/6/88 605

California School (20th C)
Dredger, Sacramento River; oil on canvas, indistinctly sgn, 27x32", B/B 10/6/88 1,650
Laguna Beach, oil on canvas, indistinctly sgn, 14x20", C-E 2/3/88 1,980

CALIGA, Issac Henry (American, 1857-)
Seated Nude, oil on canvas, sgn, 27x22", SBY 4/14/89 1,100

CALISCH, Moritz (Dutch, 1819-1870)
Madonna & Child, oil on canvas, sgn/dtd 1864, 45x35", RWS 6/17/89 650

CALLCOTT, Augustus Wall (British, 1779-1844)
Boats in a Harbor, oil on canvas, initialed/dtd 1808, unfr, 41x60", SBY 6/8/88 OE 4,620
Daily Chores by the Riverside, oil on canvas, sgn, 22x31", RWS 6/17/89 600

CALLOT, Giacomo; manner of
Village Scene with Peasants Thatching a Roof, oil on canvas, 19x15", C-E 4/7/88 OE 1,320

CALLOT, Jacques; follower of (French, 1592-1635)
Set of 3: Commedia Dell'Arte Groups; pen/brown ink/gray wash, inscr, 3x8", C-NY 1/12/88 1,100

CALLOW, John (British, 1822-1878)
Gale Coming-Running into Ramsgate, oil on canvas laid down on masonite, sgn, 19x29", SBY 7/12/89 2,310

CALLOW, John; att (British, 1822-1878)
Marine Scene, oil on canvas, sgn, 12x24", RWS 6/17/89 UE 225

CALLOW, John; manner of (British, 1822-1878)
Shipping Off the Coast, oil on canvas, 20x31", C-E 5/23/88 770

CALLOW, William (British, 1812-1908)
Cross at Salisbury While Under Repair, oil on panel, sgn/inscr, 10x14", SBY 12/9/88 OE 3,520

CALS, Adolphe Felix (French, 1810-1880)
La Lecture, oil on canvas, sgn/dtd 1874, 9x7", SBY 7/12/89 4,980

CALVAERT, Denys (Dionisio) (Flemish, 1540-1619)
Annunciation, pen/brown ink/wash heightened w/white over black chalk, 14x9", SBY 1/13/89 OE 10,450

CALVAERT, Denys (Dionisio); att (Flemish, 1540-1619)
Madonna & Child in Majesty Surrounded by Putti & Angels Playing Instruments, oil on panel, 35x26", SBY 10/21/88 7,700
Saint Agnes, oil on canvas, 70x48", SBY 4/7/88 5,225

CALVAERT, Denys (Dionisio); school of (Flemish, 1540-1619)
Holy Family, oil on panel, 24x20", C-NY 4/8/88 3,300

CALVERT, Elizabeth (American, 20th C)
Set of 7: Murals Depicting the History of Natchez Trail; oil on canvas, 47x92", MG 6/25/88 UE 800

CALVES, Leon Georges (French, 1848-)
Peasant Girl with Her Flock, oil on canvas, sgn, 32x22", RWS 5/12/89 1,200

CALVET, Henri Bernard
Still Life of Fruit, Jug, & Bowl; oil on canvas, sgn, 15x22", C-E 5/23/88 1,320
Still Life of Jug & Fruit, oil on canvas, sgn, 13x18", C-E 5/23/898 OE 1,650

CALZADA, Humberto (Cuban, 1944-)
Heirloom (contemporary interior w/view), acrylic on canvas, sgn twice/dtd 85/titled, 60x45", C-NY 5/17/89 4,950
Light of the West, oil on canvas, sgn twice/dtd 82, 48x36", SBY 5/17/88 6,600
Waiting for News (view through several doorways), acrylic on canvas, sgn/dtd 1979, 55x38", SBY 11/21/88 UE 4,400

CAMACHO, Jorge (Cuban, 1934-)
Bird Hunters, oil on canvas, sgn, 72x58", SBY 5/17/88 2,750
La Boiteuse Lubrique (morbid figure), oil on canvas, sgn/dtd 62/titled, 40x32", SBY 5/16/89 2,475

CAMASSEI, Andrea; att (Italian, 1601-1648)
Flora Surrounded by Putti Holding Garlands of Flowers in a Landscape, oil on canvas, 77x114", C-NY 4/6/89 OE 33,000

CAMBIASO, Luca (Italian, 1527-1585)
Aeneas Carries His Father From Burning Troy, pen/brown ink, 16x11", SBY 1/13/89 7,425
Assumption of the Virgin, pen/brown ink, bears inscription, 11x6", SBY 7/12/89 1,870
Holy Family & the Infant Saint John the Baptist by Candlelight, oil on canvas, unfr, 50x43", C-NY 1/15/88 18,700
Nailing to the Cross, pen/brown ink/wash, 25x11", SBY 1/13/89 12,100

CAMBIASO, Luca; att (Italian, 1527-1585)
Adoration of the Shepherds, pen/brown ink/gray wash squared in black chalk, 15x9", SBY 1/13/89 2,200

CAMBIASO, Luca; follower of (Italian, 1527-1585)
Death of Cleopatra, pen/brown ink/wash, 11x16", C-NY 1/11/89 2,860
Mother with Two Children, Two Others Picking Apples; pen/brown ink/brown wash, inscr, 12x8", C-NY 1/12/88 1,100

CAMERON, Donald (Scottish, 19th C)
Shepherd with Sheep on a Mountain Path, sgn, 30x20", SLK 9/26/88 500

CAMERON, Hugh (British, 1835-1918)
Rest in the Field, oil on canvas, sgn/dtd 1878, 28x36", SBY 6/8/88 OE 16,500

CAMILLA
Portrait of a Spanish Man, pencil, sgn, 20x14", LH 3/20/88 50

CAMILLE, Jean Baptiste; school of (French, 1796-1875)
Landscape with Figures, oil on canvas, 20x36", RWS 8/12/89 2,100

CAMOIN, Charles (French, 1879-1965)
Anemones (floral still life), oil on canvas, sgn, 14x11", PHL 11/15/88 11,000
Blonde au Miroir (reclining nude), oil on canvas, sgn, 1904, 25x32", C-NY 10/5/89 OE 41,800
Cabanon dans les Vignes a Saint-Tropez (landscape), oil on canvas, sgn, 1858, 21x29", C-NY 2/18/88 OE 14,300
Femme Debout au Miroir (woman standing at mirror), oil on canvas, sgn, 14x10", C-NY 10/6/88 14,300
Fleurs des Champs (floral still life), oil on canvas, sgn, 15x18", C-NY 5/12/88 12,100

La rue Bouterie a Marsielle (street scene), oil on canvas, sgn, 1904, 32x26", C-NY 2/16/89 OE ... 71,500
La Table de la Cuisine a la Cantine (still life), oil on panel, sgn, 1941, 10x8", C-NY 5/12/88 ... 6,050
Le Pont du Gard (view of bridge over river), oil on canvas, stamped signature/titled, 1953, 20x26", C-NY 5/12/88 OE ... 26,400
Le Repos du Modele (partially nude woman reclining on bed), oil on canvas, atelier stamp, ca 1904, 26x32", C-NY 2/16/89 ... 30,800
Marie la Corse (portrait), oil on canvas, sgn, ca 1950, 22x18", C-NY 2/18/88 OE ... 16,500
Nature Morte (still life), oil on canvas, sgn, 24x29", SBY 2/16/89 ... 38,500
Nature Morte a la Bouteille de Chianti (still life), oil on canvas, sgn, ca 1910, 18x21", C-NY 2/18/88 ... 17,600
Nu Allonge sur un Lit (nude lying on bed), oil on canvas, sgn, 26x32", C-NY 10/5/89 ... 44,000
Place des Lices (village street scene), oil on canvas, sgn, ca 1935, 24x36", C-NY 2/18/88 OE ... 20,900
Portrait de Femme, pastel on paper laid down on board, sgn/indistinctly dedicated, 18x13", C-NY 10/6/88 ... 5,500
Ramateulle Entre les Pins (landscape), oil on canvas, sgn, ca 1959, 26x32", SBY 11/12/88 ... 28,600
Saint-Tropez (port scene), oil on canvas, sgn, 15x21", C-NY 5/12/88 ... 18,700
Still Life, oil on board, sgn, 11x13", SBY 2/14/89 OE ... 4,675
Tete de Jeune Fille (bust portrait of young girl), oil on canvas, sgn, 18x13", SBY 10/7/89 ... 12,100
Two Peasants, oil on board, sgn, 11x14", B/B 6/15/89 ... 1,650

CAMP, Jeffery (American, 20th C)
Rainbow Jumper (beach scene), oil on board, sgn, 7x10", RWS 11/10/89 ... 750

CAMP, Joseph; see De Camp

CAMPAGNOLA, Domenico; follower of (Italian, 1484-1550)
Group of Figures & Children, After the Relief The Miracle of the Miser's Heart; pen/brown ink, 9x7", C-NY 1/11/89 ... 1,320

CAMPAGNOLA, Enrico (Italian, 1911-)
Seascape with Beached Boats (contemporary), oil on canvas, sgn, 20x24", RWS 3/16/89 UE ... 300

CAMPAIGNE, see De Champaigne

CAMPBELL, Blendon (American, 1872-)
Allegorical Figure, oil on canvas, sgn/dtd 1906/indistinctly inscr, 22x18", SBY 3/17/88 ... 1,100

CAMPBELL, George F. (American, 20th C)
Spanish Treasure Fleet, Portobello Harbor; oil on canvasboard, sgn/inscr, 21x25", C-E 5/23/88 ... 1,100

CAMPBELL, Percy
Lake St Clair, Tasmania; en grisaille, sgn twice/inscr, C-SK 6/9/88 ... 110

CAMPBELL, R. (American, 20th C)
Boy & His Friend (young boy walking w/his dog & carrying fish), oil on canvas, sgn/dtd 1948, 34x45", MG 10/28/88 ... 1,000

CAMPBELL, Steven (20th C)
Goats, oil on canvas, unfr, 103x95", C-NY 5/4/88 OE ... 22,000
Man with a Floured Head Impersonation a Burning Dovecoat, oil on canvas, 1985, 110x91", SBY 10/5/89 UE ... 9,350
Searching for Fossils at Night, oil on canvas, 1984, unfr, 111x102", C-NY 10/4/89 ... 13,200
Study for a Portrait of an Agoraphobic Portraying a Claustrophbic, oil on canvas, 1986, 80x97", SBY 10/8/88 ... 19,800
Untitled (contemporary), gouache on paper, 1984, 20x15", SBY 2/15/89 ... 3,850

CAMPBELL, William Addison (American, 1914-)
Fishing Boat, oil on paper, sgn, 11x15", B/B 9/15/88 UE ... 88

CAMPI, Giulio; att (Italian, 1502-1572)
Portrait of a Bearded Man, half-length, wearing a black costume & cap; oil on panel, 30x24", C-NY 5/31/89 UE ... 13,200

CAMPI, Giulio; workshop of (Italian, 1502-1572)
David Seated with a Gamba & Two Putti...; chalk/pen/ink/wash on paper laid down on canvas, 17x12", C-NY 1/11/88 OE ... 2,200

CAMPIGLI, Massimo (Italian, 1895-1971)
Due Donne Sedute (two seated women), charcoal on paper, sgn/dtd 52, 24x19", C-NY 2/18/88 OE ... 11,000
Idolo su Sfondo Verde, oil on canvas, sgn twice/dtd 64, 32x20", C-NY 11/16/88 ... 77,000
Le Tessitrici, oil on canvas, sgn/dtd 59, 38x58", SBY 5/11/88 ... 253,000
Scalinata de Piazza di Spagna, oil on canvas, sgn/dtd 55, 36x22", SBY 5/10/89 ... 176,000
Trois Femmes, charcoal on paper, sgn/inscr, 8x5", C-E 5/13/88 ... 1,980

CAMPOS, Florencio Molina (South American, 20th C)
Mate Bajo el Ombu (caricature figures/landscape), oil on canvas laid down, sgn/dtd 43, 16x20", C-NY 5/17/88 OE ... 10,450

CAMPOTOSTO, Henry (Belgian, 1910-)
Young Girl Knitting (three-quarter length portrait in a landscape), oil on panel, sgn/dtd 1880, 9x7", B/B 3/22/89 ... 1,650

CAMPRIANI, Alceste (Italian, 1848-1933)
Figures on the Terrace of the Palazza Sant'Anna, Naples; pastel, sgn/inscr, 19x25", C-NY 5/25/88 ... 2,420
Hunting For Duck in a Marshy Landscape Near Naples, oil on panel, sgn, 9x20", C-NY 2/25/88 OE ... 20,900

CAMUS, Blanche Augustine (French, 19th/20th C)
En Hiver sous les Oliviers, oil on canvas, sgn/inscr, 21x26", C-E 5/13/88 ... 2,420
La Maternite, oil on canvas, sgn, 45x46", SBY 5/23/89 ... 16,500
Mere et Enfents (mother & children in landscape), oil on panel, sgn, 15x18", C-E 5/13/88 OE ... 3,300

CAN, Kun; att
Landscape (hanging scroll), ink/color on paper, sgn, 53x12", SBY 5/31/89 ... 14,300

Canadian School
Beach Scene Near Perce Rock, oil on board, 11x14", FB 5/28/89 ... 550
Canadian Lake Scene, oil on canvas, indistinctly sgn, ca 19th C, unfr, 19x27", C-SK 11/10/88 ... 520
Going to Church at Dusk, oil on canvas, 13x16", FB 4/25/88 OE ... 500
Montreal, pencil/watercolor w/scratching, inscr, ca 19th C, unfr, C-SK 5/25/89 ... 180
Mountain Village & Steamboat, watercolor, 20x14", WAD 6/12/89 ... 350
Niagara Falls, oil on board, 16x26", WAD 6/12/89 ... 800
Waterfalls in a Forest Landscape, oil on canvas, 14x22", FB 5/28/89 ... 280

CANAL, Giovanni Antonio; see Canaletto, Antonia

CANALETTO, Antonia (Italian, 1697-1768)
Men Playing Cards & Studies of Boats, chalk/pen/ink, bird wm, inscr/#d 52, 8x11", C-NY 1/11/89 OE ... **16,500**
Old Somerset From the River Thames, London; oil on canvas, 31x46", C-NY 6/2/88 UE ... **990,000**
View of San Marco From the Lagoon, oil on canvas, 24x31", WD 1/25/89 OE ... **29,000**
CANALETTO, Antonia; att (Italian, 1697-1768)
Rio dei Mendicanti, oil, 45x29", WD 1/25/89 ... **26,000**
CANALETTO, Antonia; manner of (Italian, 1697-1768)
View of the Grand Canal, Venice; oil on canvas, 27x39", SBY 7/12/89 ... **2,640**
CANALETTO, Antonia; school of (Italian, 1697-1768)
Grand Canal, Venice, with the Bucintoro; oil on canvas, 17x25", C-NY 4/6/89 OE ... **26,400**
Grand Canal, Venice (busy cityscape), oil on canvas, 14x20", C-NY 4/6/89 OE ... **9,900**
Quay from the Harbor of St Mark's, oil on canvas, 18x24", WD 10/19/88 OE ... **4,500**
Salute & Dogana From the Campo Santa Maria Zobenigo, oil on canvas, 23x38", LH 10/16/88 ... **5,000**
View of Venice, oil, 22x30", WD 1/25/89 OE ... **10,000**
CANALETTO, Antonia; studio of (Italian, 1697-1768)
View of the Riva Degli Schiavone, Venice; oil on canvas, 29x46", SBY 1/12/89 ... **198,000**
CANALETTO, Antonia; workshop of (Italian, 1697-1768)
Rialto Bridge, Venice; oil, 45x29", WD 1/25/89 ... **22,000**
CANAVERAL Y PEREZ, Enrique (Spanish, 19th C)
Mediterranean Courtyard, oil on panel, sgn, 7x11", SBY 2/22/89 OE ... **7,700**
CANCIO, Carlos (20th C)
Untitled (man holding nude child), oil on canvas, sgn/dtd 1988, 43x32", SBY 5/16/89 OE ... **6,600**
CANDIA, Domingo (Latin American, 20th C)
El Arbol (The Tree, in abstract landscape), oil on canvas, sgn, ca 1975, 36x51", C-NY 5/17/89 ... **10,450**
CANDMAN, E.S. (18th C)
Marie Cecile de Montenach, oil on canvas, sgn/dtd 1746, unfr, 32x25", FB 4/25/88 OE ... **850**
CANE, see Le Cane
CANEDALLE, R.
Subway (crowded interior view), oil on canvas, sgn/dtd 79, 22x42", C-E 2/1/89 ... **1,100**
CANELLA, G. (Italian, 1788-1847)
Man Smoking a Pipe, oil on panel, sgn, 9x7", C-E 1/12/88 UE ... **143**
CANEVARI, Carlo (Italian, 20th C)
Jam Session, oil on board, sgn, 12x23", WD 5/5/88 ... **1,500**
CANO, Alonso; att (Spanish, 1601-1667)
Portrait of Benedictine, holding a prayer book; oil on canvas laid down on masonite, 43x34", C-NY 6/2/88 ... **3,300**
CANO, Alonzo; circle of (Spanish, 1601-1667)
Saint Joseph Holding the Infant Christ, oil on canvas, oval, 49x43", C-NY 4/8/88 ... **6,600**
CANTAGALLINA, Remigio; circle of
Rest on the Flight into Egypt, with the Infant Saint John the Baptist & an Angel; ink anchor wm, 10x16", C-NY 1/11/89 ... **660**
CANTARINI, Simone (Italian, 1612-1648)
Saint John the Evangelist, oil on copper, 16x12", SBY 4/7/88 ... **3,575**
CANTARINI, Simone; att (Italian, 1612-1648)
Saint John the Baptist, red chalk, 12x9", SBY 1/13/89 ... **1,980**
CANTATORE, Domenico (Italian, 1906-)
Portrait of a Young Woman, oil on board, sgn, 18x12", SBY 10/5/88 ... **1,320**
Still Life of Books, Notebooks, & Candlestick; oil on panel, sgn, 13x19", SBY 10/5/88 ... **2,475**
CANTIENI, Graham (Canadian, 20th C)
Knossos, oil on canvas, sgn/dtd 1986, 64x81", FB 10/30/89 ... **3,300**
CANTU, Federico (Mexican, 1908-)
El Guitarrista, watercolor/crayon on paper, sgn, 26x20", C-NY 5/18/88 UE ... **330**
Man & Horse (nude before horse), oil on canvas, sgn/dtd 34, 16x20", SBY 5/16/89 OE ... **2,420**
CAPIELLO, Leonetto (French, 1875-1942)
Mme Gyp, collage laid down on paper, sgn, 13x10", C-E 11/17/88 UE ... **55**
CAPLIN, Alfred Gerald; see Capp, Al
CAPONE, Gaetano (Italian, 1845-1920)
Standing Woman (three-quarter length portrait), oil on canvas, sgn, 18x12", C-E 6/1/89 ... **1,045**
Sunset (figure on path in a landscape), oil on canvas, sgn/dtd 1918, 20x24", C-E 6/1/89 OE ... **2,860**
Venetian Canal Scene, oil on canvas, sgn, 30x20", SBY 6/8/88OE ... **3,850**
CAPORALI, Bartolomeo; att
Annunciation, tempera on panel, 21x21", C-NY 5/31/89 OE ... **74,800**
CAPP, Al (American, 1909-)
Animated L'il Abner (portrait in profile), ink/pencil/crayon on paper, sgn, 14x11", RWS 9/29/88 ... **350**
CAPP (American, 20th C)
Impressionistic View of Hudson, oil on canvas, sgn/dtd 45, 37x43", FAP 4/15/89 UE ... **550**
CAPPIELLO, Suzanne (French, 20th C)
Still Life of a Bouquet of Flowers in a Glass Vase, oil on panel, sgn, 12x10", SBY 12/9/88 ... **2,475**
CAPRON, Jean-Pierre (French, 1921-)
Crepuscule Mediterranean, oil on canvas, sgn, 18x22", DM 9/16/88 ... **1,500**
CAPUTO, Ulysse (Italian, 1872-1948)
View of Venice, oil on canvas, sgn/dtd 1902, 12x22", C-NY 5/25/88 ... **1,100**
Young Girl Reading in the Sunlight, oil on panel, sgn, 10x13", C-E 2/21/89 ... **4,400**

CARABAIN, Jacques Francois (Belgian, 1834-1892)
La Plage a Vietri (Italie), oil on canvas, sgn/titled/inscr, 26x42", SBY 5/23/89 18,700
Town Square, oil on canvas, sgn, 31x23", C-NY 2/25/88 6,600
Village Marketplace (street scene), oil on canvas, sgn, 31x25", RWS 3/31/88 OE 9,000
CARACCIOLO, Giovanni B. (Italian, 1570-1637)
Head of a Woman, Probably a Female Saint: a Fragment; oil on canvas, 18x15", SBY 10/13/89 5,775

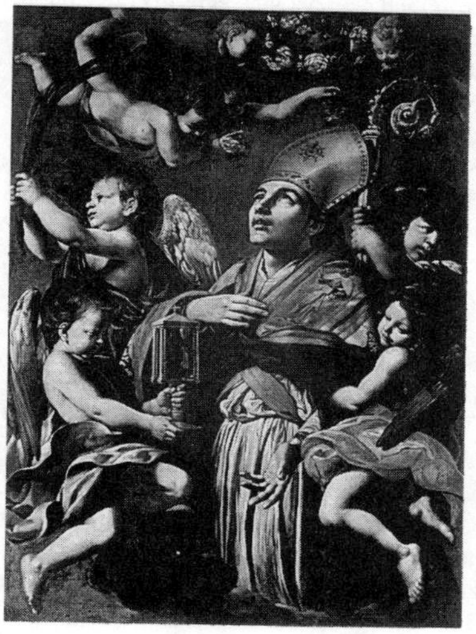

Saint Januarius in Glory, oil on canvas, monogramed, 66x48", C-NY 1/11/89, $121,000

CARACCIOLO, Giovanni B.; circle of (Italian, 1570-1637)
Head of a Young Boy, pen/brown ink, 7x6", C-NY 1/12/88 660
CARAUD, Joseph (French, 1821-1905)
Visitor (interior scene of seated lady w/standing suitor), oil on canvas, sgn/dtd 1881, 29x36", C-NY 2/23/89 17,600
CARAVAGGIO, Cecco; see Del Caravaggio
CARAVAGGIO, Michaelangelo; see Da Caravaggio
CARAVAGGIO, see Polidoro
CARBINO, Jon
In Battle, oil on canvas, sgn, 12x16", C-E 11/8/88 825
CARDENAS, Santiago (Colombian, 1937-)
Gray Jacket (on hanger against white wall), oil on canvas, sgn, ca 1976, 75x65", SBY 11/21/88 10,450
CARDI, Lodovico Cigoli; att (Italian, 1559-1613)
Saint Dominic Receiving From the Madonna, oil on canvas, unfr, 50x43", B/B 3/22/89 4,400
CARDON, Claude (British, 19th C)
Feeding the Chickens, watercolor on paper, sgn, 11x15", C-NY 5/24/89 1,100
CARELLI, Gabriel (Italian, 1820-1880)
Road by a Fortress in an Italian Landscape, watercolor, sgn/indistinctly inscr, 4x15", C-NY 2/23/89 1,650
CARGNEL, Vittore Antonio (Italian, 1872-1931)
Portrait of a Pensive Woman, oil on canvas, sgn/dtd 1901, 19x14", B/B 5/17/89 770
CARILLO, Lilia (Mexican, 1929-)
Abstract, mixed media on canvas laid down on board, sgn/dtd 61, 16x18", SBY 11/21/88 OE 5,225
Ensayo de Vuelo (abstract), oil on canvas, sgn/dtd 57, 13x16", C-NY 5/18/88 3,850
CARL, Ewan B. (American, 19th C)
Dawn, oil on canvas, sgn, 12x18", B/B 8/10/88 660
CARLANDI, Onorato (Italian, 1848-1939)
Freshly Picked Bouquet, watercolor on paper, sgn/inscr, 25x14", SBY 12/9/88 550
CARLEBUR, Francois (Dutch, 1821-1893)
Boats in an Estuary, oil on canvas, sgn, 30x44", C-E 5/23/88 4,620
CARLES, Arthur Beecher (American, 1876-1952)
Dancers, Circa 1927 (abstract); oil on canvas, 40x34", C-NY 5/26/88 44,000
Still Life of Flowers, oil on canvas, sgn, 20x16", SBY 5/25/88 OE 23,100
Summer Landscape, oil on panel, 6x9", C-E 10/18/89 UE 1,980
CARLETON, Anne (American, 1878-1968)
Toilers, oil on canvas, sgn twice/inscr/titled, 22x30", SBY 9/23/88 1,540
CARLETTI, Alicia (Argentinian, 1946-)
Garden (young girl wearing high heels in garden), watercolor on paper, sgn/dtd 82, 48x36", SBY 11/21/88 2,200
CARLEVARIJS, Luca (Italian, 1665-1731)
Piazza San Marco, Venice, with the Loggetta; oil on canvas, 15x26", C-NY 5/31/89 93,500
CARLIER, Jules (Belgian, 19th/20th C)
In Her Garden (lady in garden near cottage), gouache on paper, sgn, 11x14", RAB 11/25/88 UE 125
CARLIN, Andrew B.
Samuel Taylor Middleton w/Great White Pyrennes Hound Seated in a Landscape, oil, sgn/dtd 1852, 41x46", RWS 10/27/89 8,000

CARLONE, Carlo; circle of (Italian, 1686-1776)
God Receiving the Virgin, oil on canvas, 14x11", SBY 4/7/88 1,650

CARLSEN, Dines (American, 1901-1966)
Autumn Fire (landscape), oil on canvas, 27x29", DM 9/16/88 4,500
Brass Kettle, oil on canvas, sgn/dtd 1926, 30x25", SBY 9/23/88 OE 18,700
Cloisonne & Laurel (still life), oil on canvas, sgn/dtd 1935, 25x30", C-NY 5/26/88 14,300
Still Life with Wine Glasses, oil on board, sgn, 29x25", SBY 3/17/88 UE 3,850
Violets (still life w/violets, pitcher, & plate), oil on masonite, sgn, 17x14", SBY 4/14/89 3,575
White African Violet, oil on panel, sgn twice, inscr/titled, 20x16", SBY 6/24/88 UE 1,540

CARLSEN, Soren Emil (American, 1853-1932)
Anchored on the Shore, oil on canvas, sgn/dtd 81, 18x24", C-NY 5/26/88 UE 7,700
Autumn Trees, oil on canvas, sgn, 20x16", LH 10/16/88 4,750
Cracked Ice, oil on canvas, sgn/dtd 1894, 22x27", C-NY 5/26/88 35,200
Crashing Waves, oil on canvas laid down on masonite, sgn, 20x24", C-NY 3/11/88 9,900
Hanging the Laundry To Dry, watercolor on paper, sgn/dtd 91, 19x13", B/B 3/17/88 4,675
House in the Trees, oil on canvas, 5x10", RWS 9/8/89 700
In the Woods, oil on canvas, sgn/dtd 76, 12x16", B/B 10/6/88 1,045
Landscape, oil on canvas, sgn, 10x14", C-NY 5/26/88 6,600
Meeting of the Seas (landscape), oil on canvas, sgn/dtd 1919/inscr Gray of the Storm, 47x58", SBY 5/24/89 37,400
Nature Morte (still life), oil on canvas, sgn/dtd 1895, 36x50", C-NY 5/26/88 14,300
Open Sea, oil on canvas, sgn, 25x30", RWS 11/3/88 9,000
Portrait of the Artist's Wife (half-length), oil on canvas, sgn, 19x14", C-E 6/1/89 UE 1,430
Rocks & Surf, oil on canvas, 7x9", C-E 2/3/88 1,540
Root Cellar, oil on canvas, sgn/dtd 84, 17x31", C-NY 9/30/88 15,400
Ruby Reflection (still life), oil on canvas laid down on masonite, sgn/dtd 95, 15x16", C-NY 5/26/88 22,000
Sand Hills, Qqunquit, Maine; oil on canvas laid down on board, sgn, 6x9", C-E 6/1/89 OE 1,210
Self-Portrait, oil on canvas, 32x24", SBY 1/24/89 2,200
Still Life (bowl, glasses, & pitcher), oil on canvas, sgn/dtd 91, RWS 11/10/89 18,000
Still Life of Copper Pots, oil on canvas, sgn/dtd 94, 16x15", SBY 6/24/88 7,975
Still Life of Dead Game, oil on canvas, sgn/dtd 91, 25x35", SBY 3/17/88 UE 5,500
Still Life of Fish, oil on canvas, sgn, 25x35", SBY 9/23/88 8,800
Still Life of Fish & Radishes, oil on canvas, sgn, 15x19", SBY 9/14/89 9,075
Still Life of Oriental Vase, oil on canvas, sgn/dtd 1884, 30x20", C-NY 12/2/88 19,800
Still Life with Cock & Pitcher, watercolor on paper, sgn/dtd 93, 12x10", C-NY 9/28/89 7,150
Summer Mist, oil on canvas, sgn/dtd 1882, 31x40", C-NY 5/26/88 38,500
Trees on a Hillside, Woodchuck Burrow, Falls Village, Connecticut; oil on panel, artist stamp, 18x15", C-NY 5/26/88 3,850
Valley, Moonlight (landscape); oil on canvas, sgn, 34x32", SBY 5/24/89 27,500
View of the Sound, oil on canvas, bears artist's stamp, 20x24", C-NY 9/30/88 6,600
Woman Sewing, oil on board, inscr/dtd Nov 5th 1919, 14x10", SBY 6/28/89 4,400

CARLSEN, Soren Emil; after (American, 1853-1932)
Autumnal Landscape, oil on board, 19x14", FAP 4/15/89 275

CARLSEN, Soren Emil; manner of (American, 1853-1932)
Still Life of Flowers, oil on canvas, sgn, 22x14", FAP 4/15/89 770

CARLSON, Carl A. (American, 20th C)
Park Bench Twosome (couple embracing under full moon), watercolor on paper, sgn/dtd 35, 24x19", RAB 8/9/88 UE 125
Walking in Central Park, watercolor on paper, sgn/dtd 35, 25x19", RAB 8/9/88 250
Walking in Central Park (figures on path), watercolor on paper, sgn/dtd 35, 25x19", RAB 8/9/88 250

CARLSON, John Fabian (American, 1875-1945)
From the Hills (snowy rural landscape), oil on canvas, sgn, 18x24", SBY 4/14/89 OE 8,800
Hickory Hill, Colorado, 1921; oil on canvasboard, 4x6", RWS 9/8/89 UE 700
Melted Snow, oil on board, sgn, 8x10", SBY 4/14/89 2,475
Monarchs of the Stream (large trees in landscape), oil on canvas, sgn, 30x40", C-NY 5/25/89 UE 9,900
Opal Waters, oil on canvasboard, sgn, 12x16", C-E 10/18/89 3,520
Pair: Landscapes; oil on board, sgn, 4x6", C-E 6/1/88 1,210
Sanctuary (forest scene), oil on canvas, sgn, 30x40", C-NY 5/26/88 8,800
Sunlit Groves (snowy landscape), oil on canvasboard, sgn, 11x11", SBY 3/17/88 OE 2,530
Templed Hills (snowy hills in blue shadows), oil on canvas, sgn, 49x59", C-NY 9/28/89 22,000
Thawing Stream, oil on canvas, sgn, 30x40", C-NY 5/25/89 13,200
Trees & Snow Covered Lake, oil on canvas, sgn, 18x24", C-NY 3/11/88 5,500
Woodland Brook, Big Indian, New York; oil on canvas, sgn, ca 1919, 20x26", C-NY 3/11/88 6,050

CARMICHAEL, John Wilson (British, 1800-1868)
Moro Castle, Cuba; oil on canvas, 39x64", RWS 4/7/89 6,500
Portrait of the Brig Sophie, oil on canvas, sgn, 17x30", RAB 3/14/89 3,250

CARMICHAEL, John Wilson; att (British, 1800-1868)
Shipwreck, oil on canvas, 18x24", SBY 6/8/88 UE 2,750
Village Off a Lake, oil on canvas, sgn, 11x19", C-E 5/23/88 UE 550

CARMICHAEL, John Wilson; circle of (British, 1800-1868)
Shipwreck Off New Marseden Castle, oil on canvas, sgn, 24x36", RAB 11/25/88 UE 950

CARMIENCKE, Johan Hermann (American, 1810-1867)
Hyde Park (view of bay w/sailboats), oil on canvas, sgn, 7x10", C-E 2/1/89 OE 3,300
Landscape with Cows, oil on canvas, sgn/dtd 1860, 24x36", C-E 6/1/88 3,520

Niagara Falls, oil on canvas, sgn/indistinctly dtd 1859, 24x32", SBY 1/24/89 ... 7,150

CARNICERO, Antonio (1748-1814)

Portrait of the Son of the Duke of Osuna, oil on canvas, sgn/dtd 1811, 48x32", SBY 10/13/89 OE ... 57,750

CARO, Anthony (British, 1924-)

As You Art (Number 24), graphite/acrylic/paper on Tycore, sgn/dtd 1981, titled, 38x24", C-NY 11/10/88 ... 5,500

CAROLUS-DURAN, Emile Auguste (French, 1837-1917)

Dans le Parc (In the Park), oil on canvas, 33x47", SBY 5/23/89 ... 11,000

CARON, J. (Continental School, 19th/20th C)

Impressionistic River Landscape with Middle Distant Village, oil on panel, sgn/dtd 1914, 14x20", SLK 5/9/88 ... 250

CARON, Paul Archibald (Canadian, 1874-1941)

Laurentian Hamlet, oil on canvas laid down on board, sgn, 12x16", WG 4/23/88 ... 450
Place Royal, Montreal; pencil, sgn, 8x10", FB 4/25/88 UE ... 70
Portrait of a Woman (bust-length), oil on board, 11x13", FB 10/17/88 UE ... 60
Portrait of a Young Girl, pastel, sgn, 16x10", FB 4/25/88 ... 500
Winter in Quebec (horse-drawn sleigh with figure, house & village beyond), oil on canvas, sgn, 17x22", FB 5/28/89 ... 4,000

CARONE, Nicolas (1917-)

Anvil Heart, oil on canvas, sgn twice/dtd 1956/titled, 25x30", SLK 4/7/89 ... 125

CAROT, Jules Etienne

Still Life of Flowers & Sheet Music, oil on canvas, sgn, 29x36", C-NY 5/25/88 ... 4,400

CARPENTER, Ellen Maria (American, 1836-1909)

Woodland Stream, oil on canvas, 19x14", RAB 8/9/88 UE ... 200

CARPENTER, Fred Green (American, 1882-1965)

David & Saul, oil on canvas, sgn/dtd 1929, 35x29", SLK 9/27/88 ... 800
Mediterranean Harbor Scene, oil on canvas, 31x45", SLK 9/27/88 ... 1,400
Young Lady in a Garden, oil on canvas, sgn/dtd 1921, 30x24", SLK 9/27/88 ... 750

CARPENTER, Margaret (British, 1793-1872)

Master Browlow Bettie Mathew, oil on canvas, 30x25", C-E 10/25/88 ... 4,950

CARPENTER, Margaret; att (British, 1793-1872)

Rinaldo & Armida (two figures in a landscape), oil on canvas, 27x36, SBY 4/7/89 ... 3,025

CARPENTER, Percy (British, -1858)

Lady by Her Horse on a Plantation, pencil/watercolor, sgn/dtd Singapore August 1853, oval, 22x16", C-SK 6/9/88 OE ... 17,660

CARPENTERO, Henri Joseph Gommarus (Belgian, 1820-1874)

Reading the News (figures around table as man reads paper), oil on canvas, sgn/dtd 1861, 14x11", PHL 10/28/88 UE ... 1,100

CARPENTIER, Madeleine (French, 1865-)

Deux Enfants Joant au Bord de l'Eau (two children fishing), oil on canvas, sgn, 33x18", C-E 5/22/89 ... 1,980

CARPI, see Da Carpi

CARPIONI, Giulio the elder (Italian, 1611-1674)

Death of Adonis, oil on canvas, 55x60", SBY 1/12/89 ... 28,600

CARR, J.A. (Canadian, 20th C)

Race on the High Seas, Yacht & Ocean Liner; oil on academy board, sgn/dtd 1919, 10x12", RWS 6/17/89 UE ... 275

CARR, Lyell (American, 1857-1912)

Following the Scent, oil on canvas, sgn, 25x20", C-E 11/30/88 ... 1,540
John Twachtman Home, Old Post Road; oil on canvas, sgn/dtd 10x14", NA 5/13/89 ... 800

CARR, M. Emily (Canadian, 1871-1945)

West Coast Scene, watercolor, initialed, 6x9", FB 4/25/88 OE ... 3,800

CARR, Samuel S. (American, 1837-1908)

Children on Their Way Home From School (in landscape), oil on canvas, sgn/dtd 84, 8x18", SBY 5/24/89 ... 14,300
Coming Storm, oil on canvas, indistinctly sgn, 6x10", C-E 6/1/88 ... 2,090
Gathering Nuts (children in a landscape), oil on canvas, sgn, 10x8", C-NY 5/26/88 OE ... 8,800
Getting Ready for Market (girl playing w/doll, toy wagon & horse), oil on canvas, sgn, 24x18", C-NY 5/25/89 OE ... 82,500
Landscape Scene with Sheep, oil on canvas, sgn, 12x18", RWS 11/3/88 OE ... 2,100
Landscape with Sheep, oil on canvas, sgn, 12x18", RWS 9/8/89 ... 1,900
Prospect Park, oil on canvas, sgn, 16x24", C-NY 9/30/88 ... 6,600
Sheep Grazing, oil on canvas, sgn, 12x18", B/B 3/22/89 ... 2,750
Sheep in a Landscape, oil on canvas, sgn, 16x24", B/B 9/14/89 ... 1,210
Woman with Bucket, oil on canvas, sgn, 24x14", C-NY 9/30/88 UE ... 4,400

CARRACCI, Agostino; after (Italian, 1557-1602)

Head of a Woman, red chalk, 10x7", C-E 1/12/88 ... 286

CARRACCI, Agostino; att (Italian, 1557-1602)

Portrait of a Man, bust-length, wearing black costume with white collar & hat; oil on canvas, 23x20", C-NY 1/15/88 ... 13,200

CARRACCI, Annibale; circle of (Italian, 1560-1609)

Portrait a Male Nude, three-quarter length with head turned & holding a staff(?)...; chalk, 12x9", C-NY 1/11/89 ... 2,530

CARRACCI, Annibale; follower of (Italian, 1560-1609)

Christ & the Woman of Canaan, oil on canvas, unfr, 51x39", SBY 4/7/88 ... 2,750

CARRACCI, Annibale; studio of (Italian, 1560-1609)

Pieta, oil on canvas, 77x62", SBY 4/7/88 ... 8,800

CARRACCI, Lodovico; school of (Italian, 1583-1618)

Charity, oil on copper, 16x12", C-NY 4/8/88 OE ... 14,300

CARRACCI, Ludovico; circle of (Italian, 1583-1618)

Man Kneeling by a Basket, Bowl of Fruit, & Other Objects; black chalk/pen/brown ink/brown wash, 8x11", C-NY 1/12/88 ... 550

CARREE, Michiel (Dutch, 1657-1747)
Herdsmen Watering Their Flock in a Landscape, oil on canvas, 21x24", C-NY 4/6/89 ... 6,600

CARRENO, Mario (Cuban, 1913-)
Fisherwoman (contemporary), oil on canvasboard, sgn/dtd 45, 24x20", SBY 11/21/88 ... 8,800
Sin Titulo (abstract composition), oil on canvas, sgn/dtd 56, C-NY 11/21/88 ... 7,700
Sugar Cane Cutters (contemporary), oil on panel, sgn/dtd 43, 65x48", SBY 11/21/88 OE ... 121,000
Untitled (abstract), oil on canvas, sgn/dtd 53, 41x31", SBY 5/16/89 ... 16,500
Untitled (abstract), oil on canvas, sgn/dtd 77, 47x66", SBY 5/17/88 UE ... 3,300

CARRENOS, T. Dairy (19th C)
Senora with Fan, oil on panel, sgn/dtd Madrid 1873, 9x7", LH 5/15/88 ... 325

CARRIER-BELLEUSE, Pierre (French, 1851-1932)
Danseuse (dancer in costume, full-length), pastel on linen, sgn/dtd 1898, 46x24", SBY 10/24/89 ... 27,500
In the Railway Carriage, oil on canvas, sgn/dtd 1879, unfr, 21x37", C-NY 2/25/88 ... 13,200
L'Arlequin aux Danseuses, pastel, sgn/dtd 1876, 78x47", C-L 6/27/88 OE ... 94,600
Portrait of Two Young Girls, pastel on linen, sgn/dtd 1909, 36x29", SBY 5/23/89 ... 7,700

CARRIERA, Rosalba; follower of (Italian, 1675-1757)
Portrait of an Elegant Lady, pastel on paper, 25x19", SBY 12/9/88 ... 1,650

CARRIERA, Rosalba; follower of (1675-1757)
Portrait of a Lady as Fame, or Nymph at the Court of Apollo; pastel on paper laid down on canvas, 28x22", SBY 10/13/89 ... 8,800

CARRIERE, Eugene (French, 1849-1906)
Les Filles de l'Artiste (the artist's daughters), oil on canvas, sgn, unfr, 21x15", C-E 2/21/89 UE ... 1,100
Portrait of the Artist's Wife, oil on canvas, sgn/dtd 1905, 18x15", SBY 2/22/89 OE ... 19,800

CARRIERE, Eugene; att (French, 1849-1906)
Portrait of a Seated Woman, charcoal on paper, stamped, 10x7", B/B 9/15/88 ... 165

CARRILLO, Lilia (Mexican, 1930-1974)
Composicion (abstract), oil on canvas, sgn/dtd 58, 20x29", C-NY 11/21/88 ... 5,280

CARRINGTON, James Yates (British, 1857-1892)
Children by a Lake, oil on canvas, sgn/dtd 18XX, 17x26", C-E 11/8/88 ... 1,540
Two Young Girls by a Brook, oil on canvas, sgn/dtd 1882, 25x16", SBY 7/12/89 ... 2,090

CARRINGTON, Leonora (British, 1917-)
Car of Silence, gouache on paper, sgn/dtd 1946, 13x18", C-NY 10/6/88 ... 9,350
Cow Bird, watercolor/brush/pen/black ink on paper, sgn, 13x19", C-NY 5/17/89 ... 5,500
Dead Queens of Cockerham (surrealistic), gouache on paper, sgn/titled, ca 1950s, 15x12", SBY 5/16/89 ... 5,775
Double-Sided: Looking into the Future; pencil on paper, sgn on verso, 13x11", C-NY 10/6/88 OE ... 1,045
El Grito (abstract), oil on board, sgn/dtd 1951, 16x35", C-NY 10/6/88 OE ... 35,200
Fantastic Figure on Horseback, gouache/ink on paper, sgn, 13x9", SBY 5/16/89 OE ... 6,050
Horses (images of horses' heads on black background), oil on masonite, sgn, ca 1970, 14x12", SBY 5/16/89 ... 18,700
How True My Love (abstract bat figures), oil on board, sgn, 27x12", C-NY 10/6/88 OE ... 17,600
Mystical Figure, pencil on paper, sgn/dtd 1946, 13x8", C-NY 10/6/88 OE ... 1,430
Pair: Portrait of Edward w/Squirrel; Standing Lady w/Bird; pencil on paper, sgn, unfr, 7x10", 17x12", C-NY 10/6/88 ... 770
Sueno Crepuscular, oil on canvas, sgn/dtd 1959, 28x15", C-NY 5/18/88 ... 24,200
Tuesday (surrealistic), tempera on panel, sgn/dtd 1946, 22x33", C-NY 10/6/88 ... 132,000
Under a Bad Omen (figures), pencil on paper, sgn, 1979, 17x12", C-NY 5/17/89 ... 2,420
Untitled (abstract), oil on canvas, sgn, 18x19", SBY 5/17/88 OE ... 20,900
Ur of the Chaldees (surrealistic), oil on canvas, 36x22", C-NY 10/6/88 OE ... 23,100
Virtue of Certain Birds (abstract), oil on canvas, sgn/dtd 1960, 28x20", SBY 11/21/88 ... 17,600
Weeper of the Blue Sky (surrealistic), brush/ink/watercolor/gouache on paper, sgn/titled, 12x9", SBY 5/16/89 ... 3,850

CARROLL, Beryl (American, 20th C)
Group of 3: Floral Still Lifes; watercolor, sgn, 15x11", WG 9/16/88 UE ... 210
Pair: Forested Landscapes; watercolor, sgn, 11x14", 11x18", WG 9/16/88 UE ... 100

CARROLL, John (American, 1892-1959)
Head of a Sailor, oil on canvas, sgn, 20x16", DM 2/19/88 ... 650
Woman in Blue, oil on canvas, sgn/dtd 17, 22x24", LH 10/16/88 OE ... 1,200

CARSMAN, Jon (American, 20th C)
April Shadows (contemporary landscape w/buildings), acrylic on canvas, sgn/dtd 73, 60x50", C-E 11/14/89 ... 1,430
Nick on the Roof, oil on canvas, unfr, 72x49", C-E 6/1/88 ... 1,100

CARSON, W.A.
Pair: Landscapes, rocky falls or Indian & teepee in woods; oil on canvas, sgn, 18x28", lot 360, GAI 6/17/89 ... 470

CARTER, Clarence H. (American, 20th C)
Untitled, man & woman at lawn party or races; watercolor on paper, sgn/dtd 34, 15x22", lot 309, GAI 6/17/89 ... 2,600

CARTER, Dennis Malone (American, 1827-1881)
Painful Parting (man & woman saying good-bye), oil on canvas, sgn/dtd 1867, 24x20", SBY 6/24/88 ... 2,530
4th of July (couple fishing from boat on river), oil on canvas, sgn/dtd 1876, 18x27", C-E 2/1/89 ... 4,620

CARTER, Gary (American, 1939-)
Expedition Pass, oil on masonite, sgn 3 times/inscr twice/copyrighted, 30x22", SBY 9/23/88 ... 6,600
Solitary Life, oil on masonite, sgn/#d 16, 20x32", SBY 9/23/88 ... 5,225

CARTER, R. (British, 1839-1911)
Full Sail, oil on panel, sgn, 12x10", NA 3/26/88 UE ... 200
Gloucester Fishing Boats, oil on panel, sgn, 10x12", NA 3/26/88 UE ... 200

CARTER, Sydney (British, 19th/20th C)
Good Book, oil on canvas, sgn, 30x20", SBY 7/12/89 UE 4,400
Good Book, oil on canvas, sgn/dtd 1900, unfr, 30x20", C-SK 11/10/88 930
CARTER, William Sylvester (American, 20th C)
Street Walker (figures in cityscape), oil on board, sgn, 16x20", B/B 5/17/89 UE 1,210
Three Bad Cats (three male figures), pastel on paper, sgn, 23x17", B/B 5/17/89 825
CARTON, Norman (American, 20th Century)
Southern Journey, oil on canvas, sgn, 1956, 60x46", LH 10/16/88 UE 70
CARTWRIGHT, Isabel Branson (American, 1885-)
Cornelius (ship docked in harbor), oil on board, sgn/dtd 1919, 24x20", RWS 5/19/88 OE 5,000
CARTWRIGHT, W.P. (British, 19th C)
On the Thames at Streatley, oil on canvas, sgn/dtd, 16x26", PHL 10/28/88 UE 200
CARUCCI, Jacopo (Italian, 1493-1558)
Head of the Madonna, oil on panel, 18x21", C-NY 1/11/89 385,000
CARVER, Franklin H. (American, 20th C)
The Cove, oil on canvas, sgn/dtd 36, 24x30", FAP 4/15/89 UE 275
CARVILL, V.F. (French, 19th/20th C)
Portrait of the French Ship France Marie of Marseilles, watercolor on paper, sgn/dtd 1911, 22x25", RAB 3/14/89 UE 800
CASANODAY, Arcadio (Spanish, 19th C)
Rainy Day in Paris (busy street scene), oil on canvas, sgn/dtd 88, 15x24", SBY 10/24/89 7,700
CASANOVA, A.
Lutenist, watercolor over traces of pencil, sgn, 22x14", C-E 10/25/88 990
CASANOVA, Francesco (Italian, 1729-1802)
Military Skirmish, oil on canvas, 20x28", C-NY 1/11/89 OE 12,100
CASANOVA, Francesco; circle of (Italian, 1729-1802)
Battle with Turks, oil on canvas, 17x18", SBY 7/12/89 OE 2,475
CASAS, Ramon (Spanish, 1866-)
Lady in Red, charcoal/chalk on paper, sgn, 27x19", C-E 2/23/88 660
CASCELLA, Michele (Italian, 1892-1989)
La Torre Eiffel (view of Eiffel Tower), oil on canvas, sgn/#d/dtd Paris 31, 24x20", SBY 2/14/89 2,750
Montmartre (quiet street scene), watercolor/gouache on paper, sgn, 13x18", B/B 9/14/89 1,045
Rue Danton (street scene), watercolor/gouache/pen/ink on paper, sgn, 14x19", B/B 5/17/89 1,320
CASCIARO, Giuseppe (Italian, 1863-1941)
Dal Castello Ischia, oil on canvas, sgn/dtd 1917/indistinctly inscr, 34x51", C-NY 5/24/89 11,000
Veduta di Capri (View of Capri), oil on canvas, sgn/inscr, 17x26", C-NY 5/24/89 UE 4,400
CASE, Edmund E. (American, 1840-1919)
Old Road at Annisquam, oil on canvas, sgn, 12x17", RWS 5/12/89 900
CASER, Ettore (American, 1880-1944)
Tending to Her Garden (portrait), oil on canvas, sgn, 34x36", SBY 1/24/89 UE 1,320
CASILE, Alfred (French, 1847-1909)
Feeding Chickens, oil on canvas laid down on board, sgn/inscr, 18x12", C-E 4/7/88 550
CASILEAR, John William (American, 1811-1893)
Cows in a Landscape, oil on canvas, monogramed/dtd 81, 18x27", SBY 5/25/88 OE 22,000
Hudson River Scene, oil on paper laid down on panel, sgn, 10x8", C-E 11/30/88 1,320
Solitude (man fishing in river), oil on canvas, sgn twice/indisctinctly dtd, 7x14", C-E 11/30/88 1,980
CASILEAR, John William; att (American, 1811-1893)
Landscape with Ruins & Figures, oil on canvas, 11x13", SBY 3/17/88 UE 1,320
CASNELLI, Victor (American, 1865-1961)
Portrait of an Indian, watercolor on paper, sgn, 7x5", B/B 1/11/89 880
CASOLANI, Alessandro; att (Italian, 1552-1606)
The Virgin, black chalk, 10x4", SBY 1/13/89 3,025
CASSANA, Giovanni Agostino; att (Italian, 1658-1720)
Pair: Poultry with a Porcupine; Rabbit with Fruit; oil on canvas, 53x29", C-NY 10/20/88 OE 35,200
CASSANA, Niccolo; att (Italian, 1659-1714)
Pair: Dog with Goats; Donkey with Sheep & Sleeping Shepherd; oil on canvas, 44x59", SBY 10/21/88 16,500
CASSATT, Mary (American, 1844-1926)
Augusta Reading to Her Daughter (portrait in landscape), oil on canvas, sgn, 1910, 46x35", SBY 5/9/89 3,080,000
Baby Lying on His Mother's Lap Reaching To Hold a Scarf, pastel on paper, sgn, ca 1914, 30x25", SBY 5/9/89 1,100,000
Clarissa, Turned Left, with Her Hand to Her Ear; pastel on paper, initialed, 1895, 26x20", SBY 11/11/88 UE 522,500
Conversation (portrait of two women), pastel on paper laid down on canvas, sgn, ca 1896, 26x32", C-NY 5/11/88 4,510,000
Double-Sided: Sketch for Young Woman in a Small Winged Hat Holding a Cat; watercolor, stamped, 1914, 19x13", SBY 4/29/88 29,700
Femme se Penchant sur un Bebe, pastel/charcoal on tan paper laid down on board, 22x18", C-NY 12/2/88 UE 71,500
Group of 3: Sketches; pencil, Mathilde X Collection stamp, 1 10x7", 2 5x9", SBY 3/17/88 1,650
Head of a Young Woman, pastel on paper, ca 1895, 12x11", C-NY 5/11/89 OE 52,800
Leontine in a Pink Fluffy Hat (portrait), pastel on paper, 1898, 15x10", SBY 5/24/89 41,250
Madame H de Fleury & Her Child, oil on canvas, sgn, 29x24", SBY 5/25/88 OE 2,090,000
Mother & Child, watercolor on paper, sgn, 17x14", C-NY 5/26/88 9,350
Mother & Child (portraits), pastel on paper, sgn, ca 1913, 28x21", SBY 5/24/89 660,000
Mother with Left Hand Holding Sara's Chin, oil/pastel on canvas, 33x27", C-NY 5/25/89 286,000
Roman Girl Smiling, oil on canvas, sgn, ca 1872, 19x16", SBY 5/25/88 18,700
Sara Holding Her Dog (portrait), oil on canvas, sgn, ca 1901, 30x23", SBY 11/11/88 2,750,000

Sketch of Francoise, pastel on paper, sgn, 19x17", SBY 5/24/89 ... 44,000
Sketch of Vernon Lee Wearing a Pince-Nez, watercolor/pencil/crayon on paper, sgn, 10x7", C-NY 5/25/89 OE ... 41,800
Slight Sketch of the Head of a Woman in a Large Hat, pencil on gray paper, 5x3", C-NY 3/11/88 ... 1,650
Study for a Woman in Black at the Opera, pencil on paper, stamped, ca 1880, 5x9", PHL 12/1/88 ... 4,000

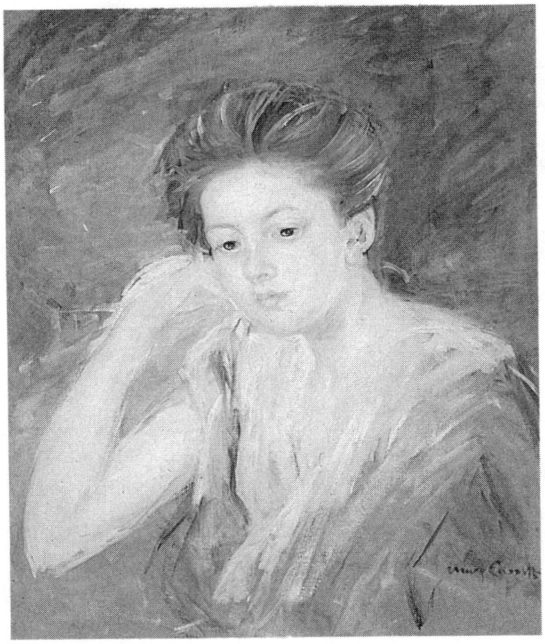

Young Girl Leaning on Her Right Hand, oil on canvas, sgn, 24x20", C-NY 5/25/89, $319,000

CASSEL, J. (American, 20th C)
Young Lady with Horse, oil on canvas mounted on board, sgn/dtd 1906, 25x17", RWS 12/10/88 UE ... 300

CASSELL, Frank (British, 19th C)
Playful Terriers, oil on canvas, sgn/dtd 1874, 18x25", C-E 10/25/88 UE ... 825

CASSIDY, Ira Diamond Gerald (American, 1879-1934)
Navaho Medicine Man, watercolor on paper, sgn w/insignia, 28x18", SBY 5/25/88 OE ... 20,900
New Mexico Adobe, watercolor on paper, sgn, 8x12", SBY 6/24/88 OE ... 2,860
Path to the Watering Hole, oil on canvas, sgn, 25x30", SLK 9/28/88 ... 8,500

CASSON, A.J. (Canadian, 1898-)
Country Houses by the River Side, oil on panel, 7x9", RWS 11/3/88 OE ... 4,600

CASTALDO, Amalyia (American, 1906-)
Little Roses in a Chinese Vase, oil on canvas, sgn, 20x12", C-E 6/1/88 UE ... 330
Pink Roses, oil on canvas, sgn, 10x12", C-E 6/1/88 UE ... 418
Portrait of a Young Girl, oil on canvas, sgn, 30x25", C-E 9/15/88 UE ... 220
Red Roses, oil on canvas, sgn, 12x10", C-E 6/1/88 UE ... 385
Red Shoes, oil on canvas, unfr, 19x13", C-E 9/15/88 ... 165
Young Girl in Yellow Dress, oil on canvas, unfr, 24x20", C-E 9/15/88 UE ... 110

CASTALGNE, Andre (French, 19th/20th C)
Venetian Procession, oil on board, sgn/dtd 1904, 24x36", SBY 6/8/88 ... 2,860

CASTAN, Pierre Jean Edmond (French, 1817-1892)
Good News, young woman reads letter to elderly mother; oil on board, sgn/dtd 186(?)/titled, 13x11", RAB 11/25/88 UE ... 3,250
Happy Hours, young couple watch their children play; oil on board, sgn/dtd 1872, 11x9", RAB 11/25/88 UE ... 3,750

CASTANEDA, Alfredo (Spanish, 1938-)
At the Beginning of the Trip (two figures on horse), oil on canvas, sgn/dtd 71, 32x32", SBY 11/21/88 ... 9,350
Donde Podriamos no Estar Ausentes? (surrealistic), oil on canvas, sgn/dtd 86, 26x26", C-NY 5/17/89 OE ... 26,400
Este Despertar Creciente, oil on canvas, sgn/dtd 1980, 47x62", C-NY 5/18/88 OE ... 41,800
Hablemos de Nosotros (two-headed figure in circle), gouache/pencil/collage on paper, sgn/dtd 82, 9" dia, C-NY 5/18/88 ... 2,200
Mirror, oil on board w/mirror & photograph, sgn/dtd 71, 20x20", SBY 5/17/88 ... 2,640
Parejisima (surrealistic portrait of a couple), mixed media on paper, 7" dia, SBY 11/21/88 OE ... 4,125
Vocation of Ezekiel (surrealistic), oil on canvas, sgn/dtd 86 twice, 47x47", SBY 11/21/88 OE ... 23,100

CASTEELS, Pieter (Flemish, 1684-1749)
Still Life of Tulips, Peonies, Iris, & Other Flowers in a Vase...; oil on canvas, sgn/dtd 1733, 29x24", SBY 6/2/89 OE ... 45,100
Tulips, Poppies, Lilacs, Fruit Blossoms, Daffodils, in a Vase; oil on canvas, sgn/dtd 1727, 45x36", C-NY 4/8/88 OE ... 52,800

CASTEELS, Pieter; school of (Flemish, 1864-1749)
Two Herons in a Landscape, oil on canvas, #d 70, 22x15", WD 1/25/89 ... 1,700

CASTEL, Mosse (Israeli, 1909-)
Poesie Hittit (abstract), oil/sand on canvas, sgn twice/dtd 1963, 51x38", SBY 10/8/88 OE ... 8,800
Untitled (abstract), gold paint/sand on panel, sgn/dtd 1972, 29x21", C-E 11/17/88 OE ... 3,740
Untitled (abstract), mixed media on canvas, sgn/dtd 1966, 29x21", PHL 11/15/88 ... 3,000

ASTEL (French, 20th C)
Provincial Village Square, oil on canvas, sgn/dtd 34, 21x26", B/B 5/17/89 522
ASTELLAN, Federico (American, 1914-)
Lover's Dream (contemporary), oil on canvas, sgn, 17x21", SBY 6/28/89 OE 10,175
ASTELLANOS, Julio (Latin American)
Fall of the Evil Angels (contemporary), pen/India ink on thin card, 16x11", SBY 5/16/89 2,530
ASTELLI, Luciano (20th C)
Indianer III (contemporary view of two heads), acrylic on canvas, sgn/dtd 1982/titled, 63x79", SBY 5/3/88 OE 28,600
ASTELLI, see Spadino, Giovanni Paolo
ASTELLO, Giovanni Battista (Italian, 1547-1637)
Adoration of the Shepherds, black chalk/pen/brown ink/brown-gray wash on blue paper, dtd 1583, 10x8", C-NY 1/12/88 8,800
ASTELLO, Giovanni Battista; circle of (ca 1547-1637)
Adoration of the Shepherds, oil on copper, 11x9", SBY 10/13/89 OE 7,700
ASTELLO, Valerio (Italian, 1625-1659)
Legend of Saint Genevieve of Brabant (figures in cave, landscape beyond), oil on canvas, 65x101", SBY 6/1/89 OE 1,100,000
ASTELLO, Valerio; school of (Italian, 1625-1659)
Christ on the Mount of Olives, oil on canvas, 26x20", WD 1/25/89 OE 3,000
ASTELLO, Valerio; style of (Italian, 1625-1659)
Washerwoman in a Classical Landscape, oil on canvas, 49x46", B/B 8/10/88 3,300
ASTER, James (American, 20th C)
Totts Gap, oil on panel, dtd 11-7-36, 12x16", SBY 4/14/89 770
ASTEX-DEGRANGE, see Degrange, Adolphe Louis
ASTILLO, Jorge (Spanish, 20th C)
Frutero, oil on canvas, sgn/dtd 78, 20x29", C-NY 2/13/89 OE 7,700
Interior en Berlin, oil on canvas, sgn/dtd 76, 39x32", C-NY 2/13/89 OE 14,300
Mesa Blanca, oil on canvasboard, sgn/dtd 83 NY, 36x24", C-NY 2/13/89 OE 13,200
Seated Woman, oil on canvas, sgn/dtd 63, 36x29", C-E 11/17/88 OE 6,380
Still Life of Fruit, watercolor on paper, sgn/dtd 63, 26x38", C-E 11/17/88 OE 3,300
ASTLEDON, George F. (American, fl 1917-1936)
Bayou Scene, oil on board, sgn, 8x10", MG 5/28/88 475
ASTRES, Edouard (Swiss, 1838-1902)
Road by the Church (village scene), oil on canvas, sgn, 31x49", C-NY 2/23/89 22,000
ATALAN, Ramos (Chilean, 20th C)
Straits of Magellan, oil on canvasboard, sgn, 19x23", C-SK 5/25/89 460
atalan School (ca 1500)
Santiago de Campostela, oil on panel, 57x23", WD 10/19/88 5,000
ATES, J. (American, 19th C)
Pair: Untitled, pheasants in landscapes; oil on canvas, sgn, 38x15", SLK 2/11/89 400
ATHELIN, Bernard (French, 19th C)
Bouquet de Pavots, oil on canvas, sgn/dtd 62, 48x24", SBY 10/5/88 OE 9,900
Marche aux Grandes Arbres, oil on canvas, sgn/dtd 65, 57x38", SBY 10/5/88 OE 14,300
Nu au Bouquet, oil on canvas, sgn/dtd twice 1963, 51x38", SBY 10/5/88 OE 12,100
Scene de Port, oil on canvas, sgn/dtd 57, 36x24", C-E 5/9/89 5,720
ATHERWOOD, Frederick (British, 1799-1854)
Ruins of Thebes, watercolor heightened w/white & gum Arabic, sgn, 11x15", C-NY 5/25/88 2,420
ATLIN, George (American, 1794-1872)
Group of Deer, oil on canvas, sgn, 19x27", C-NY 12/2/88 71,500
Well Point with Drill, watercolor/gouache/pen/black ink/pencil on paper, sgn/dtd 1828, 12x19", C-NY 1/20/89 41,800
West Point with a View of the Hudson River, watercolor/gouache/pen/ink/pencil on paper, sgn, 1828, 12x19", C-NY 1/20/89 38,500
TOK, Lottie Meyer (American, 20th C)
Road to the Sea, watercolor on paper mounted on cardboard, sgn, 23x31", RWS 11/10/89 150
TS, Jacob (Dutch, 1741-1799)
Frozen Canal in a City with Skaters & Figures Loading Barrels, chalk/pen/ink/wash, sgn/dtd, 9x12", C-NY 1/11/89 OE 3,080
Poultry Seller Holding a Basket of Fruit at a Window...; chalk/pen/gray ink/watercolor, sgn/inscr, 15x11", C-NY 1/11/89 6,050
UCHOIS, Eugene Henri (French, 1850-1911)
Basket of Flowers, oil on canvas, sgn, 18x22", SBY 2/22/89 7,700
Cofret a Bijoux, oil on canvas, sgn, 24x32", SBY 5/23/89 12,650
Fleurs (floral still life in a landscape), oil on canvas, sgn, 21x26", C-NY 5/24/89 11,000
Still Life of a Vase of Peonies, a Blue Porcelain Jar, & a Musical Score; oil on canvas, sgn, 29x37", C-NY 2/23/89 8,250
Still Life of Autumn Flowers, oil on canvas, sgn, 21x29", C-NY 5/25/88 6,050
Still Life of Pansies & Literary Objects on a Table, oil on panel, sgn, 21x16", C-NY 5/25/88 OE 15,400
Still Life of Rabbit & Vine, oil on canvas, sgn, 26x21", RWS 5/12/89 850
Still Life of Roses & Wildflowers on a Ledge with a Fan, oil on canvas, sgn, 26x22", C-NY 2/23/89 4,950
Still Life of Wildflowers, oil on canvas, sgn, 18x22", SBY 10/24/89 9,350
Still Life of Wildflowers, oil on canvas laid down, 22x26", B/B 3/22/89 5,225
Still Life of Wildflowers in a Blue Vase, oil on canvas, sgn, unfr, 26x20", C-E 2/23/88 2,640
Wildflowers, oil on canvas, sgn, 16x26", SBY 10/24/89 7,700
UHOIS, H. (Dutch, 20th C)
Still Life of Fish, oil on canvas, sgn, 28x40", FAP 11/4/88 1,300
ULLERY, see De Caullery

CAVALCANTE, Lito (20th C)
Birth of Maria (abstract), mixed media/acrylic on canvas, sgn/dtd 1980, 66x48", SBY 11/21/88 — 2,750

CAVALCANTI, see Di Cavalcanti

CAVALERI, Ludovicio (Italian, 1867-1942)
Street Scene Near Lake Como, oil on wood panel, sgn/dtd 1912, 31x31", RAB 8/8/89 — 1,800

CAVALLINO, Bernardo (Italian, 1622-1654)
Pair: Lot & His Daughters; The Drunkeness of Noah; oil on panel, 16x15", SBY 1/12/89 OE — 1,925,000

CAVALLINO, Bernardo; circle of (Italian, 1622-1654)
Continence of Scipio, oil on canvas, 41x52", C-NY 1/11/89 — 15,400

CAVALLINO, Bernardo; school of (Italian, 1622-1654)
The Visitation, oil on canvas, unfr, 31x38", C-E 1/12/88 — 385

CAVALLON, Giorgio (American, 1906-)
Untitled (abstract composition), oil on canvas, sgn/dtd 1956, 72x48", SBY 11/9/89 OE — 99,000
Untitled (abstract), oil on canvas, sgn twice/dtd 58, 30x26", C-NY 11/10/88 OE — 20,900
Untitled (abstract), oil on canvas, sgn/dtd 6.60 & 6.6.60/titled, 52x78", SBY 11/11/88 OE — 44,000
Untitled (abstract), oil on masonite, sgn/dtd 55, 24x24", SBY 2/15/89 OE — 17,600

CAVELL, Frank E. (Canadian, 1909-)
Hauling Logs on a Winter's Day, oil on canvas, sgn, 25x29", WAD 6/12/89 — 500

CAVINESS, M. (American, 20th C)
Sun River Country, oil on canvas, sgn/dtd, 5x7", MG 11/19/88 — 90

CAWSE, John (British, 1779-1862)
Ribbon Vendor, oil on canvas, sgn/dtd 1848, 25x30", B/B 5/17/89 — 1,650

CAWTHORNE, Neil (British, 1836-)
Paddock, Leicester (horse racing scene); oil on canvas, sgn/dtd 69, 20x30", SBY 6/10/88 — 3,850
Set of 4: (Four Seasons Horse Scenes); oil on canvas, sgn, 2 20x26", 2 20x28", SBY 6/9/89 — 14,300

CAYEUX (French, 19th C)
French Village, watercolor, sgn/dtd 76, 10x14", C-E 2/21/89 UE — 385

CAYLEY, Neville Henry Peniston (Australian, 1853-1903)
Bird on a Branch, pencil/watercolor heightened w/white, sgn, 9x13", C-SK 5/25/89 — 275

CAZES, J.P.; circle of
Rest on the Flight into Egypt, oil on canvas, 13x16", C-NY 6/2/88 — 2,090

CAZIN, Jean Charles (French, 1841-1901)
Chaumiere au Crepuscle, oil on canvas, sgn, 20x17", SBY 7/12/89 — 2,750
Farmhouses in the French Countryside, oil on panel, sgn, 9x113", C-E 2/21/89 UE — 1,100
Landscape with Windmills, oil on cradled panel, sgn, 8x13", SBY 6/8/88 — 3,080
Thatched Roofs at Dusk, oil on canvas, sgn, 19x15", C-E 5/23/88 — 2,750
Windmill in a Landscape, oil on canvas, sgn, 19x16", C-E 5/23/88 — 2,090

CECCOBELLI, Bruno (20th C)
Chiostro, oil on paper on panel, sgn/dtd 1983, 78x93x9", SBY 2/15/89 UE — 7,700
The Sessi (abstract), acrylic/sand on paper, 90x65", C-NY 10/4/89 — 12,100
Untitled (abstract), tempera on brown paper, 47x32", SBY 2/15/89 — 3,300

CELIS, Perez (20th C)
Memoria de Metales II (abstract), oil on canvas, sgn/dtd Paris 80, 32x40", C-NY 11/21/88 — 6,600
Resonance, oil on canvas, sgn twice/dtd 1987, 48x54", SBY 5/17/88 OE — 13,200
Terrestrial Substances (abstract), oil on canvas, sgn/dtd New York 1984, 66x60", SBY 11/21/88 — 11,000

CELMINS, Vija
Small Desert (close-up view of pebbled ground), graphite on paper, 1974-75, 12x15", C-NY 5/4/89 — 19,800

CELOMMI, Pasquale (Italian, 1860-)
Broken Dish, oil on canvas, sgn, 22x31", C-NY 2/25/88 OE — 11,000
Fishing Boats at Sunset, oil on canvas, sgn, 26x45", C-E 5/23/88 — 6,050
Sunlit Coastal Scene with Fisherfolk, oil on canvas, sgn, 16x27", SLK 9/28/88 — 2,700

CERAMANO, Charles Ferdinand (Belgian, 1829-1909)
Sheep Grazing, oil on canvas, sgn, unfr, 13x18", B/B 3/17/88 — 2,200
Shepherd & His Flock at Dusk, oil on canvas, sgn, 29x24", SBY 12/9/88 — 6,325
Shepherdess & Her Flock, oil on canvas, sgn, 22x33", C-E 10/25/88 — 4,180
Shepherdess with Flock, oil on panel, sgn, 14x11", LH 3/20/88 — 600

CERANO, see Crespi, Giovanni Battista

CERCONE, Ettore (Italian, 1850-1896)
Egyptian Guides Assisting an Elegant Traveler, oil on canvas, sgn/dtd 88, 28x21", C-NY 2/23/89 OE — 13,200

CERIA, Edmond (French, 1884-1955)
Environs de Toulon, oil on canvas, sgn, 15x24", B/B 8/10/88 — 1,100

CERQUOZZI, Michelangelo; & CODAZZI, Viviano (17th C)
Landscape with Elegant Figures Entering a Palace with a Carriage Waiting...; oil on canvas, unfr, 43x57", SBY 6/2/89 — 42,900

CERQUOZZI, Michelangelo; circle of (Italian, 1602-1660)
Peasants Disporting Along a River Bank, oil on canvas, 26x14", SBY 4/7/89 — 3,300

CERQUOZZI, Michelangelo; school of (Italian, 1602-1660)
Army Encampment by a Harbour, oil on canvas, 31x47", C-NY 10/20/88 — 5,500

CERRINI, Giovanni Domenico (Italian, 1609-1681)
Joseph Interpreting Dreams, oil on canvas, 69x58", SBY 6/6/88 — 44,000

ERUTI, Giacomo (1698-1767)
Portrait of an Elderly Lady Dressed in Black Holding a Book, oil on canvas, 28x23", SBY 10/13/89 OE 20,900
ESARI, Giuseppe (Italian, 1580-1640)
Studies of Two Horses, black/red chalk, inscr/#d 36, 17x12", C-NY 1/12/88 44,000
ESTARO, see Del Cestaro
EUVAS, Jose Luis
Misterio en Tanger (portrait), pen/black & brown ink/wash on paper, sgn twice/dtd 68 twice, 10x7", C-NY 11/21/88 UE 495
EZANNE, Paul (French, 1839-1906)
Clocher dans les Arbres (church steeple among the trees), pencil on paper, ca 1892-96, 20x13", C-NY 5/11/89 55,000
Dans la Vallee de l'Oise (impressionistic landscape), oil on canvas, 1873-74, 29x37", C-NY 11/14/88 5,060,000
Etude d'Arbres (Study of Trees), watercolor over pencil on paper, ca 1900, 12x19", C-NY 5/11/89 55,000
L'Amour en Platre (statuette of a cupid), oil on linen, ca 1867, 22x14", SBY 5/10/89 OE 352,000
La Cote du Galet, a Pontoise (extensive landscape); oil on canvas, 24x30", SBY 5/10/88 OE 9,240,000
Mars (standing male nude), pencil on paper, ca 1879-82, 12x9", C-NY 5/11/89 26,400
Nereide et Tritons (mythological scene), oil on canvas, sgn, ca 1867, 10x13", C-NY 5/11/89 OE 319,000
Paysage (landscape), pencil/traces of watercolor on paper mounted at edges, ca 1882-86, 20x13", C-NY 5/12/88 88,000
Pont sur la Seine (Bridge Over the Seine), watercolor/pencil on paper, ca 1880-85, 17x22", C-NY 5/11/89 OE 275,000
Puits et Route Tournante dans le Parc de Chateau Noir, watercolor over pencil, ca 1900, 21x17", C-NY 11/15/88 OE 858,000
Saint-Henri et la Baie de l'Estaque (landscape), oil on canvas, ca 1877-79 or 1882-85, 26x33", SBY 5/10/88 OE 6,820,000
HAB, Victor (Argentinian, 1930-)
On the Run (abstract figure w/red background), collage/oil on canvas, sgn/dtd 87, 70x59", SBY 11/21/88 OE 17,600
Untitled (abstract), oil on canvas, sgn/dtd 1962, 36x24", SBY 5/16/89 4,125
HABAS, Maurice (French, 1862-1947)
Figures in a Coastal Landscape, oil on board, sgn, 20x25", SBY 12/9/88 5,225
HABAS, Paul (French, 1869-1937)
Young Girl Bathing, oil on panel, sgn, unfr, 10x13", C-E 10/25/88 2,090
HABRIER, G.
Cavaliers & Gypsy Girl, oil on canvas, sgn, 20x24", RAB 1/18/89 375
IADWICK, Lynn (British, 1914-)
Composition, watercolor on paper, sgn/dtd 65, 19x25", SBY 2/14/89 1,650
IADWICK, William (American, 20th C)
Connecticut Landscape, oil on board, sgn, 14x18", C-NY 12/2/88 14,300
Houses by a Stream, oil on board, sgn, 14x18", C-SK 6/9/88 OE 7,440
Landscape with Trees, oil on board, 14x18", SBY 6/28/89 UE 1,540
Spring Thaw (landscape w/house), oil on canvas, sgn, 30x30", C-NY 5/25/89 15,400
IAFFEE, Oliver Newberry (American, 1881-1944)
Boy & Horse (contemporary), watercolor/pencil on paper, sgn, 9x13", RAB 8/8/89 475
IAGALL, Marc (Russian/French, 1887-1985)
Adam et Eve, pen/black ink/gray wash on paper, sgn/titled, 30x22", C-NY 5/12/88 OE 165,000
Adam et Eve, varnished gouache/pastel/brush/black ink on paper laid down on canvas, sgn, 1956, 15x11", C-NY 5/11/89 OE 341,000
Arlequin a la Lune Jaune, gouache/crayons on paper, sgn, 1969, 26x20", C-NY 5/11/89 OE 770,000
Artist & Rooster, India ink/tempera on title page of Chagall by Charles Estienne, sgn/dtd 1951, 7x5", SBY 10/7/88 OE 11,550
Artist in Profile with a Palette, blue pastel on paper laid down on board, sgn/inscr, 17x13", SBY 10/7/88 8,250
Artist Painting the Lovers, gouache/tempera, sgn, 1981, 18x15", SBY 5/30/89 OE 308,000
Au-Dessus de Vitebsk, gouache/watercolor/pencil on tan paper, sgn, ca 1925, 14x19", SBY 11/12/88 OE 522,500
Auto-Portrait avec Lauries, pen/brown ink/colored chalks on paper, sgn/dtd Paris 1959, 9x16", C-E 5/9/89 OE 4,620
Bouquet dans l'Atelier, pastel/colored wax crayons over pencil on paper, sgn, 1975, 24x19", C-NY 11/15/88 OE 440,000
Bouquet de Fleurs, gouache/colored wax crayons/pen/brush/India ink, sgn, 22x16", C-NY 11/15/88 OE 220,000
Bouquet de Fleurs (floral still life), colored wax crayons on paper, sgn, 1950, 19x13", C-NY 5/12/88 72,600
Bouquet Devant le Village, oil on masonite, sgn twice, 1976, 18x22", SBY 5/11/88 OE 550,000
Country Wedding, watercolor/gouache/ink wash on paper laid down on canvas, sgn, 34x24", SBY 5/11/88 319,000
Double Portrait with a Glass of Wine, gouache/pastel on paper, sgn/dtd 1919, 14x9", SBY 11/12/88 OE 797,500
En Bleu (two lovers in blue), gouache/pastel on paper, sgn, ca 1962, 31x31", SBY 5/11/88 OE 462,000
Epicerie a Vitebsk (interior view of general store), gouache on board, sgn/dtd 1911, 10x12", C-NY 5/11/88 OE 132,000
Femme a la Fenetre, gouache/watercolor/ink wash on paper, sgn/dtd 1953, 26x20", SBY 11/12/88 110,000
Femme et Cog (woman & rooster), black ink on paper, sgn, 6x5", C-NY 5/12/88 OE 12,100
Femme Nue au Bouquet de Fleurs (abstract), tempera on board, sgn/inscr, 1980, 22x18", C-NY 11/16/88 330,000
Fleurs (floral still life), oil on canvas, sgn, ca 1925, 36x29", SBY 11/11/88 OE 990,000
Fleurs et Corbeille de Fruits, pen/ink/gray wash on paper, sgn, ca 1949, 19x25", SBY 11/12/88 OE 71,500
Girl on Rooster Flying Over Village, pen/ink/watercolor on paper, sgn, 13x10", SBY 5/10/89 82,500
Green Cockerel with Lovers Over Paris, oil on canvas laid down on panel, sgn, ca 1950, 10x13", SBY 5/30/89 253,000
Homme a Cheval et Maternite, gouache/brush/ink/pencil on paper laid down on canvas, sgn, 12x9", SBY 11/12/88 96,250
King David & Bathsheba, pastel on paper laid down on board, sgn/inscr, 17x13", SBY 10/7/88 OE 29,700
L'Ane Rouge, gouache/pastel on paper laid down on canvas, sgn, ca 1958-59, 30x30", SBY 11/12/88 OE 473,000
L'Echelle de Jacob, tempera on paper laid on board, sgn, 24x20", SBY 5/11/88 396,000
L'Enlevement d'Europe, gouache on paper, sgn, ca 1927, 20x26", SBY 11/12/88 181,500
L'Oiseau au Dessus du Village (bird in tree over village), watercolor/ink wash on paper, sgn, ca 1940-50, SBY 5/10/89 49,500
La Chevre a Beaver Lake (The Goat at Beaver Lake), gouache on paper, sgn, 24x20", C-NY 5/11/89 440,000
La Chevre au Bouquet (goat w/bouquet), red crayon on paper, sgn, 12x9", C-NY 10/5/89 OE 23,100
La Mariee au Coucher de Soliel (wedding night), oil on canvas, sgn, ca 1936, 19x20", SBY 5/9/89 OE 1,650,000
La Promenade, oil on canvas, sgn, ca 1975, 32x26", C-NY 5/11/88 616,000

La Sirene (Nice), pastel/gouache on paper, sgn, 1960, 31x22", C-NY 5/11/89 OE ... 682,000
Le Cheval Jaune (Yellow Horse), pastel/ink wash/watercolor on Japan paper, sgn, ca 1966, 22x15", SBY 5/11/88 OE ... 159,500
Le Cirque (The Circus), gouache/watercolor/crayons/pastel/pencil on paper, 27x21", C-NY 5/11/89 ... 297,000
Le Clown au Bouquet, oil on canvas, sgn, ca 1970-74, 22x18", SBY 11/11/88 OE ... 880,000
Le Coq Rouge, pastel/gouache/brush/black ink on paper laid down on board, sgn, 21x19", C-NY 11/15/88 OE ... 418,000
Le Couple, pastel/pen/black ink on paper, sgn/dtd New York 1966, 13x10", C-NY 2/16/89 ... 7,700
Le Couple aux Fleurs, gouache/pastel/brush/India ink on paper, sgn, 1950, 12x10", C-NY 5/11/89 OE ... 148,500
Le Lion s'en Allant en Guerre (an illustration), gouache on red paper, sgn, 1926-27, 20x17", SBY 5/10/89 ... 165,000
Le Paysan Allonge (fantasy), oil on canvas, sgn/dtd 1962, 37x36", SBY 5/9/89 ... 2,420,000
Le Peintre, Amoureux et Coq; crayons/brush/pen/ink on frontispiece of a book, sgn/dtd Vence 1957, 7x12", SBY 10/6/89 ... 20,900
Le Peintre, pen/India ink on paper, sgn/inscr/dtd 1971, 10x7", C-NY 10/6/88 ... 1,980
Le Peintre a Son Chevalet, pen/inks/watercolor on the frontispiece of a book, sgn/dtd Chicago 1946, 10x7", SBY 10/6/89 ... 13,200
Le Soir (The Night), oil on canvas, sgn, 36x29", SBY 11/11/88 ... 1,045,000
Les Acrobats, watercolor/pastel/pencil on paper, sgn, ca 1927, 14x10", SBY 5/11/88 OE ... 154,000
Les Amoureux au Claire de Lune, watercolor/ink wash on paper, sgn/dtd 1952, 6x5", SBY 10/6/89 OE ... 26,400
Les Amoureux, watercolor/gouache/crayons/pastel/pen/black ink, sgn, 16x13", C-NY 2/16/89 OE ... 220,000
Les Amoureux (The Lovers), gouache on paper mounted at edges on board, sgn, ca 1935, 7x5", C-NY 5/12/88 OE ... 77,000
Les Amoureux (The Lovers), oil on canvas, sgn, 1964, 18x15", SBY 5/10/89 OE ... 660,000
Les Amoureux et le Coq (The Lovers & the Rooster), India ink/pastel on laid paper, sgn, 11x18", SBY 5/11/88 ... 60,500
Les Deux Bouquets de Fleurs, oil on canvas, sgn/dtd 1954, 59x47", SBY 11/12/88 OE ... 770,000
Les Pommes de Pin, Peyra-Cava; oil on canvas, sgn/dtd `930, 29x24", SBY 5/10/88 ... 528,000
Lovers & a Bouquet of Flowers, watercolor/gouache/pencil on paper, ca 1935-38, 26x21", SBY 5/10/89 OE ... 407,000
Lovers in Front of Large Bouquet of Roses, watercolor/India ink on paper, sgn, ca 1959, 28x18", SBY 5/11/88 ... 231,000
Lovers with Flowers, gouache/watercolor/crayons, sgn, 1979, 26x20", SBY 5/30/89 ... 264,000
Lovers with Flowers (on program page of Die Zauberflote), pen/India ink, sgn/dtd 1967, 24/II N.Y., 10x6", SBY 5/30/89 ... 7,700
Marin a Toulon (sailor & his girl at Toulon), gouache on blue paper, sgn/inscr, 1926, 25x19", SBY 5/10/89 ... 198,000
Maternite avec Pere Noel, gouache/watercolor/ink wash/pencil on paper laid down on canvas, sgn, 15x12", SBY 11/12/88 ... 104,500
Memories of Vitebsk, oil on board, sgn, ca 1935, 29x23", SBY 5/10/88 OE ... 1,155,000
Moses & the Ten Commandments, crayon over pencil, sgn/inscr/dtd Vence 1959, 18x13", SBY 5/30/89 ... 33,000
Moses Holding the Tablets of the Law, pen/brown ink, sgn, ca 1941-46, 13x10", SBY 5/30/89 ... 8,800
Nature Morte aux Poissons (Still Life of Fish), gouache on paper laid down on paper, sgn, 20x25", SBY 5/11/88 OE ... 165,000
Nude, watercolor/gouache on paper laid down on board, sgn/inscr, ca 1912-13, 12x9", SBY 5/10/89 OE ... 77,000
Pan, watercolor on paper, sgn, 1964, 27x28", C-NY 5/11/89 OE ... 225,500
Pastorale, colored wax crayons/brush/black ink on paper mounted at edges on board, sgn, 13x10", C-NY 10/6/88 ... 20,900
Peintre, Ange et Amoureux; tempera/pastel/ink/pencil on masonite, sgn/dtd 1980, 16x13", C-NY 5/12/88 ... 220,000
Peintre dans son Village, watercolor/brush/ink/pencil on paper, sgn, 1982, 30x22", C-NY 11/15/88 ... 104,500
Rue d'un Village Russe (village street scene), gouache/watercolor/pencil on paper, sgn, 1914, 18x22", C-NY 5/11/89 ... 440,000
Self-Portrait, pen/blue ink on an envelope, sgn/dtd 1979, 4x7", SBY 5/30/89 OE ... 4,400
Self-Portrait (drawn on catalog for artist's 1st exhibit in Israel), pen/brown ink, sgn/dtd 1951, 9x6", SBY 5/30/89 OE ... 3,850
Self-Portrait with Flowers, oil on canvas, sgn, 1969-70, 26x21", SBY 5/30/89 ... 385,000
Talmud Scholar with Red Donkey, watercolor/gouache/ink wash on paper, sgn/dtd 1950-56, SBY 5/10/89 OE ... 319,000
Tete de Cheval, Soldat Assis, et l'Oiseau Noir sur un Cochon; pen/ink on paper, ca 1927-30, 5x9", SBY 10/7/88 OE ... 12,100
Tree of Arts, gouache/ink wash on paper laid down on paper, sgn, ca 1959, 13x10", SBY 5/11/88 ... 63,250
Vase de Fleurs, gouache/pastel/brush/black ink/wash on Japan paper, sgn/inscr, 1958, 40x26", C-NY 11/15/88 ... 198,000
Vase de Fleurs (floral still life), watercolor/gouache/pencil on paper, sgn, 25x19", SBY 5/10/89 ... 187,000
Vase de Fleurs sur la Nappe Bleue (floral still life), colored wax crayons/pencil on paper, sgn, 8x8", C-NY 5/12/88 ... 24,200
Vase de Roses (floral still life), gouache over black chalk on paper, sgn, 1940-50, 13x10", C-NY 2/18/88 ... 46,200
Vase of White Roses, pen/ink/brush/gray wash/pastel on paper, sgn/dtd 1949, 22x28", SBY 5/10/89 ... 82,500
Vitebsk, le Vieil Homme sur le Village, brush/black ink w/traces of gouache on paper, sgn twice, 10x8", C-NY 11/15/88 OE ... 41,800

CHALEYE, Jean (French, 1878-1960)
Melange des Fleurs, oil on canvas, sgn, 29x40", SBY 10/24/89 ... 6,050
Spring Landscape with River Winding Through a Mountain Valley, oil on board, sgn, 28x21", SLK 5/11/88 ... 70

CHALLENER, Frederick Sproston (Canadian, 1869-1959)
Franciscan Patriarch of Mount Carmel Monastery, Palestine; oil on panel, sgn/dtd 1898, 16x13", WAD 6/12/89 ... 60

CHALMERS, George Paul (British, 1833-1878)
Wooded River Before the Storm, oil on canvas, sgn, 22x36", C-E 4/7/88 UE ... 55

CHALON, Henry Bernard (British, 1770-1849)
Asking the Way, oil on canvas, sgn, 30x38", SBY 6/10/88 UE ... 16,50
Colonel with William Scott Up at Doncaster, oil on canvas, sgn/dtd 1829, 29x40", SBY 6/10/88 ... 41,25
Fang with P Connelly Up at a Winning Post, oil on canvas, sgn/dtd 1832, 25x30", SBY 6/10/88 ... 31,90
Tethered Hunter (horse & dog in a landscape), oil on canvas, 25x30", SBY 6/9/89 ... 9,90

CHALON, Henry Bernard; att (British, 1770-1849)
Groom with a Chestnut Hunter & a Hound by the Entrance to a Manor, oil on canvas, 27x39", SBY 6/10/88 UE ... 5,50

CHALON, Henry Bernard; manner of (British, 1770-1849)
Fight, oil on canvas, 32x46", C-E 2/23/88 ... 1,65

CHAMBERLAIN, Elwynn (American, 1928-)
Burial of a Hero, egg tempera on canvas, 26x14", C-NY 3/11/88 OE ... 12,10

CHAMBERLAIN, Helen (American, 20th C)
Path Through Tall Trees, oil on canvasboard, sgn, 14x14", MG 5/28/88 ... 12
Young Girl in a Blue Dress, oil on board, sgn, 19x22", MG 5/28/88 ... 55

:HAMBERS, C. Bosseron (American, 1883-)
Saint, oil on canvas, sgn, 36x31", SBY 9/23/88 1,430
:HAMBERS, Charles Edward (American, 1883-1942)
Dinner Time (two men & woman in kitchen), oil on canvas, sgn, 36x27", C-E 6/1/89 OE 1,500
Shoot Out, oil en grisaille heightened with gouache on canvas, sgn, 30x30", C-E 6/1/88 2,420
'HAMBERS, George W. (American, 19th C)
In the Tennessee Mountains (woman hoes tobacco, sheds beyond), oil on canvas, sgn/dtd 1887, unfr, 47x63", SBY 6/28/89 OE 30,800
HAMBERS, George W.; att (American, 19th C)
View of Greenwich From the Thames, oil on canvas, 20x30", SBY 12/9/88 OE 5,225
HAMBERS, Richard Edward Elliot (Irish, 1863-1944)
Along the Nile (figures/desert/mountains in landscape), watercolor on paper, sgn/titled, 10x16", RAB 8/8/89 UE 150
S Ute Reservation, watercolor, sgn/dtd 1891, 18x14", NA 2/24/89 175
Zuni Indian in Full War Paint, Back View; watercolor on paper, monogramed/dtd 1891, 11x9", WL 5/20/88 OE 1,100
HAMBERS, Thomas (American, 1805-1866)
Early Morning, oil on canvas, sgn/dtd 1864, 14x18", B/B 12/8/88 880
Pair: Fanciful Landscapes; oil on canvas, 18x24", RWS 10/27/89 OE 33,000
HAMBERS, Thomas; att (British, 1724-1789)
Firing the Salute (British warship entering fortified port), oil on canvas, unfr, 18x25", RAB 11/25/88 UE 3,500
HAMP, L.A. (American, 20th C)
Profile of a Woman Wearing a Brightly-Colored Scarf, oil on canvas, sgn/dtd 1913, 20x15", SLK 2/12/88 375
HAMPNEY, Benjamin (American, 1817-1909)
Figure on a Path Along a River, oil on canvas, 10x8", C-E 11/8/88 OE 2,640
Rocky Brook, oil on panel, sgn twice, indistinctly inscr/dtd 1883, unfr, 14x10", SBY 9/23/88 1,980
Rocky Meadow, oil on canvas, sgn, 10x15", C-E 2/3/88 2,200
Still Life of Apples & Grapes, oil on canvas, sgn, 6x10", RWS 10/27/89 950
Woodland Stream (New England landscape), oil on canvas, 14x20", RWS 9/8/89 OE 9,000
HAMPNEY, Benjamin; att (American, 1817-1909)
Watching the Herds, oil on canvas, inscr Landscape by Champney 1852 NH artist, 14x20", RWS 3/16/89 OE 1,500
HAMPNEY, James Wells (American, 1843-1903)
At the Well (couple conversing), oil on board, sgn, 24x18", B/B 3/22/89 3,025
Garden of Versailles, watercolor/pencil on paper, sgn/dtd 1893, 15x21", C-NY 5/25/89 4,400
Nature's Poetry (woman in forest), oil on canvas, sgn, 12x20", C-NY 5/26/88 3,300
Saucy Jane (portrait of a girl in red bonnet), oil on canvas, sgn, 12x10", RWS 5/12/89 550
HANDLER, Mildred (American, 20th C)
Betsy Ross (woman sitting, flag in hand), oil on canvas, sgn, 26x18", WL 5/20/88 UE 300
HANDLER, Winthrop; att (American, 1747-1790)
View of a City (Florence viewed from San Miniato), oil on wood panel, ca late 18th C, 51x32", RWS 10/27/89 OE 230,000
HANEY, Lester Joseph (American, 1907-)
Lake Superior, oil on canvas, sgn/dtd 36, 26x36", LH 5/15/88 UE 325
Rocky Coastline with Crashing Surf, oil on canvas, sgn, 25x30", B/B 12/8/88 OE 1,870
HANGSHOU, Wu (Chinese, 1844-1927)
Gourds (hanging scroll), ink/color on paper, sgn, 58x16", SBY 5/31/89 4,125
Lotus After Zhu Da (hanging scroll), ink on paper, sgn/dtd 1919, 43x12", SBY 5/31/89 OE 8,250
Pipa (hanging scroll), ink/color on paper, sgn/dtd 1910, 33x14", SBY 5/31/89 OE 11,000
IAORAN, Feng (Chinese, 1882-)
Figure by a Willow (hanging scroll), ink/color on paper, sgn, 41x20", SBY 5/31/89 1,760
IAPELAIN-MIDY, Roger (French, 1904-)
Low Tide: Ile de Re; oil on canvas, sgn/dtd 1952, 13x22", WD 5/5/88 1,000
Nature Morte au Carre Rouge (still life), oil on canvas, sgn, 36x29", SBY 2/14/89 OE 6,325
IAPIN, Bryant (American, 1859-1927)
Honeycomb, Peaches, & Grapes; oil on canvas, 16x24", C-NY 12/2/88 13,200
Impressionistic Landscape, oil on canvas, sgn/dtd 1908, 17x13", RAB 8/8/89 UE 350
Isle of Man, oil on canvas, sgn/inscr/dtd 1913, 14x21", C-E 11/30/88 UE 660
Seascape, watercolor on paper, sgn/dtd 1925, 9x15", RAB 3/27/89 UE 300
Still Life of Apples, oil on artist's palette, sgn, unfr, 15x10", RAB 8/8/89 UE 1,300
Still Life of Fruit (on table top), oil on canvas, sgn/dtd 15, orig fr, 10x16", RAB 11/25/88 OE 3,500
Still Life of Plums, oil on canvas, sgn/dtd 1919, 18x24", RWS 5/12/89 6,500
IAPIN, C.H. (American, 19th/20th C)
Evening at Lake Lonely, Adirondacks (landscape with mountain beyond); oil on canvas, sgn, 14x12", B/B 9/14/89 UE 550
IAPIN, Francis (American, 1899-1965)
Pewter & Apples (on table top), oil on canvas, sgn, 24x20", RWS 9/29/88 UE 475
IAPIN, James (American, 1887-)
Building the Stack, pencil/watercolor on paper, sgn/dtd 26, 9x14", SBY 4/14/89 550
IAPLIN, Charles (French, 1825-1891)
After the Masked Ball (maid w/serving tray), oil on canvas, sgn, 32x19", SBY 10/24/89 OE 71,500
Jeune Femme Deshabille (portrait of young bare-breasted woman), oil on canvas, sgn, 17x11", SBY 10/24/89 9,350
La Jeune Fille aux Colombes, oil on canvas laid down on panel, sgn/dtd 74, 31x19", SBY 2/22/89 20,900
Opal Necklace, pastel on paper laid down on canvas, sgn, 18x18", SBY 2/22/89 5,500
Pair: Putti Frolicking in the Clouds; oil on canvas, sgn, 18x45", C-NY 5/25/88 UE 5,500
Pet Dove (portrait of a girl with dove), oil on canvas, sgn, 14x11", SBY 2/22/89 4,400
Portrait of a Young Girl (bare-breasted), oil on canvas, 28x19", SBY 10/24/89 24,750

Portrait of an Elegant Lady (three-quarter length), oil on canvas, sgn/dtd 1888, 51x38", C-E 5/22/89 OE 24,200

CHAPMAN, Carlton Theodore (American, 1860-1926)

All Hands to the Rigging (ship floundering on stormy sea), oil on canvas, sgn/titled, 20x30", RAB 3/27/89 800

Low Tide (ships at shore), watercolor on paper, sgn, 10x17", RAB 8/8/89 UE........ 300

Old Salt, bearded man in foul-weather gear rests against boom; oil on canvas, sgn/dtd 1883, 20x13", RAB 3/27/89 UE........ 500

CHAPMAN, Charles Shepard (American, 1879-1962)

Cotton Gin (work house w/slaves), oil on board, sgn, 20x44", SBY 1/24/89........ 4,950

Portrait of a Lady, dressed in robe w/billowing collar; oil on masonite, sgn, 24x18", RAB 8/8/89........ 850

CHAPMAN, Conrad Wise (American, 1842-1910)

Beach at Le Havre, oil on panel, sgn/indistinctly dtd, 9x16", SBY 5/25/88 11,000

Valle y Ciudad de Mexico desde Chapultepec (landscape), watercolor on paper, dtd 1873, 8x19", C-NY 11/21/88 OE 7,700

CHAPMAN, John Gadsby (American, 1808-1889)

Italian Village (boy on donkey w/grapes, girl w/basket of grapes on head), oil on canvas, 17x13", RWS 9/8/89 OE 800

CHAPMAN, John Linton (American, 19th C)

Erie Canal, New York, Lock 36 at Little Falls; oil on canvas, sgn, 10x14", WD 4/13/88 6,000

Via Apia (view of ruins), oil on canvas, sgn/dtd 1870, 10x25", SBY 9/14/89 2,640

CHAPMAN, Theodore Carlton (American, 1860-1926)

Activity on the Beach, oil on canvas, sgn, 26x36", FAP 4/15/89 3,630

CHAPNEY, Benjamin (American, 1817-1909)

Forest Pond & Distant Pastures (New England landscape), oil on canvas, initialed/dtd 1856, 14x20", RWS 9/8/89 OE 7,700

New Hampshire River View (on the Saco), oil on canvasboard, sgn/dtd 79, 9x17", RWS 9/8/89 OE 2,500

View at Intervale, New Hampshire; oil on canvas, 13x20", RWS 9/8/89 850

CHAPOVAL, Youla (French/Russian, 1919-1951)

Untitled (contemporary), watercolor/gouache on paper, sgn/dtd V 1950, 15x11", C-E 5/9/89 1,650

CHAPPELL, Reuben (British, 1870-1940)

Eliza J, Bangor Capt Asa Slocum: Schooner in Full Sail; oil on canvas, sgn/titled, 20x30", RWS 6/10/89 3,200

Kinnaird of Liverpool, oil on canvas, sgn, 20x32", SBY 7/12/89 2,420

CHARCHOUNE, Serge (Russian, 1888-)

Composition (abstract), oil on canvas, sgn, 13x16", SBY 10/7/89 OE 22,000

Composition (abstract), oil on masonite, sgn, 15x18", lot 149, SBY 2/16/89........ 33,000

Composition (abstract), oil on masonite, sgn/dtd VII 43, 13x18", lot 148, SBY 2/16/89 33,000

Double-Sided: Cubist Still Lifes; oil on canvas, sgn, 16x25", SBY 10/7/89 OE........ 77,000

CHARDIN, Jean Baptiste Simeon (French, 1699-1779)

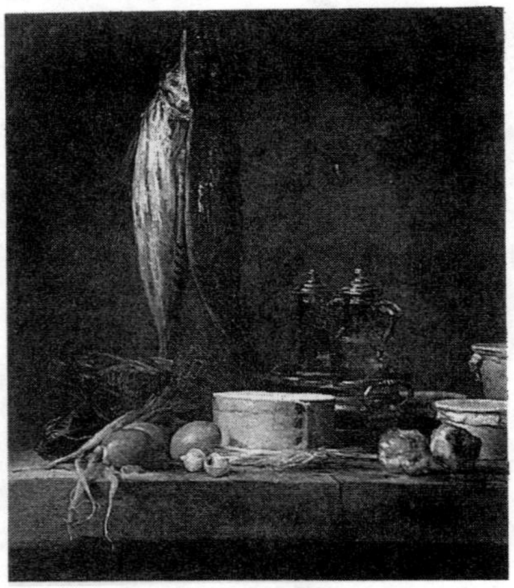

Fish, Vegetables, Pots & Cruets on a Table; oil, sgn/dtd 1769, 25x22", WD 1/25/89, $2,300,000

CHARLEMAGNE, Adolphe Jossifovich (Russian, 1826-1901)

Winter Scene in St Petersburg, gouache/pencil on board, 11" oval, C-L 10/8/88 OE 4,830

CHARLEMONT, Eduard (Austrian, 1848-1906)

Helping Hand, oil on panel, sgn, 21x16", SBY 5/23/89 7,700

Mother & Child Sketching in the Park, oil on canvas, sgn/dtd 1886, 112x47", C-NY 5/25/88........ 17,600

Reading of the Letter (interior scene w/three men), oil on panel, sgn/dtd 84, 9x8", SBY 7/12/89 7,150

CHARLESON, Malcolm Daniel (Canadian, 1888-)

Fond Memories (men viewing trophies in an interior), oil on canvas, sgn/dtd 56, 26x26", B/B 5/17/89 660

CHARLET, Emile (Belgian, 1851-)

Stag on a Promontory in a Snowy Wooded Landscape, oil on canvas, sgn, 35x28", SLK 5/11/88 1,200

CHARLET, Frantz (Belgian, 1862-1928)

Toy Boat (two children & man w/toy boat in courtyard), oil on canvas, sgn, 29x36", SBY 10/24/89 OE 28,600

CHARLET, Nicholas Toussaint (French, 1792-1845)

Les Tirailleurs, oil on canvas, sgn, 9x7", SBY 6/8/88 660

CHARLOT, Jean (French, 1898-1979)

Amantes (abstract couple), oil on canvas laid down on board, sgn, ca 1930-35, 6x6", C-NY 11/21/88 1,320

Trenzando el Pelo (Braiding the Hair), oil on canvas, sgn, ca mid-1930s, 48x24", C-NY 5/17/89 OE........ 28,600

HARLOT, Louis (French, 1878-1951)
Paysage, oil on panel, sgn, 18x22", SBY 10/5/88 — 1,430
HARMAN, Frederick Montague (American, 1894-1986)
Evening Stroll, couple walks road in moonlight; watercolor on paper, sgn, 23x27", RAB 3/27/89 UE — 150
Lazy Afternoon (man in small boat at dock under the shade of a tree), watercolor on paper, sgn, 16x20", RAB 8/9/88 — 400
On the Lake (couple/boat on water), watercolor on paper, sgn, 23x31", RAB 3/27/89 UE — 90
Wet Evening, lights from lunch counter reflect on wet road; watercolor on paper, sgn/titled, 23x30", RAB 3/27/89 — 500
HARPENTIER, Michel (French, 20th C)
Under the Volcano (detailed volcanic field, two figures in foreground), oil on panel, sgn, 15x21", RWS 3/31/88 — 1,100
HARPIN, Albert (French, 1842-1924)
Sheep in a Manger, oil on panel, sgn, 6x9", B/B 8/10/88 — 660
HARPIN, C.D. (French, 19th/20th C)
Young Lady with Apple Blossoms, oil on panel, sgn/dtd Paris 1901, 16x12", C-E 2/16/88 — 1,760
HARPIN, F.
Pair: Elegant Ladies; oil on canvas, sgn, unfr, 23x15", C-E 9/15/88 — 990
HARRETON, Victor (French, 1864-1937)
Automne, Crouzol; oil on board, sgn, 15x18", SBY 2/16/89 — 22,000
Jardin a Goiches (landscape), oil on board, sgn, 21x26", C-E 5/9/89 OE — 41,800
La Cabane a Jassat (Auvergne), Effet de Soleil sur Neige; oil on board, sgn, 24x29", SBY 10/6/89 — 30,250
La Terrasse, Automne (table & chairs under tree, house beyond); oil on canvas, sgn, 29x36", C-NY 10/5/89 OE — 49,500
Paysage Sous la Neige (winter landscape), oil on canvas, sgn, 18x24", C-NY 10/5/89 — 14,300
Printemps, oil on board, sgn, 15x18", RWS 5/12/89 OE — 9,000
Village d'Auvergne en Hiver (winter village scene), oil on board, sgn, 15x18", C-NY 2/23/89 OE — 12,100
HARTON, Ernest (British, 19th C)
Valparaiso, Chile (extensive landscape); oil on canvas, sgn/dtd 1857, 25x34", C-SK 11/10/88 — 31,600
Vista General de Panama (view of Panama), oil on canvas, sgn/dtd 1852, 28x42", C-NY 11/21/88 — 49,500
HARTRAND, Esteban (Spanish, 19th C)
Atardecer Cubano (landscape), oil on canvas, sgn/dtd 1879, 11x14", C-NY 5/18/88 OE — 5,500
Paisaje Cubano (Cuban landscape), oil on canvas, sgn/dtd 1882, 7x12", C-NY 11/21/88 OE — 3,520
Paisaje Cubano (landscape), oil on canvas, sgn/dtd 1882, 30x48", C-NY 5/18/88 — 10,450
HASE, Henry (American, 1853-1889)
Peasant Women on the Beach, watercolor on paper, sgn, 10x16", RWS 6/17/89 — 500
HASE, Jessie Kalmbach (American, 1879-1970)
Birch Trees Along a River, oil on canvas, sgn, 20x24", B/B 3/22/89 — 1,650
HASE, Louisa (American, 20th C)
Blind (abstract), oil on canvas, initialed/sgn/inscr/dtd 84, unfr, 48x42", C-NY 5/4/88 — 4,180
Blue Pose (abstract composition), oil on canvas, sgn/dtd 1979, 78x72", SBY 10/5/89 — 12,650
Emerald Sea (abstract), acrylic on canvas, sgn twice/dtd 1983, 72x84", SBY 10/8/88 — 10,450
Endless Sea (contemporary), oil/encaustic on canvas, sgn/dtd 1979/titled, 70x80", SBY 5/3/88 — 11,000
Entwine (abstract composition), oil on canvas, sgn/dtd 80, unfr, 72x96", C-NY 10/4/89 — 6,600
Island, oil/encaustic on canvas, sgn twice/dtd 1980/titled, 70x90", SBY 5/3/88 — 8,800
Purple Sunset (abstract), oil on canvas, initialed/sgn/dtd twice 1983, unfr, 36x72", C-NY 5/4/88 — 4,620
Red Sea (fantasy composition), oil on canvas, sgn/dtd 1983, 84x108", SBY 5/3/89 — 16,500
Temptation (Saint Anthony), oil on canvas, sgn/dtd 79, unfr, 78x72", C-NY 2/20/88 — 6,600
Thicket (abstract composition), acrylic on canvas, sgn/dtd 80, 70x80", SBY 10/5/89 — 8,250
Triptych: Glen (contemporary depiction of a grove of trees); oil on canvas, sgn/dtd 1981, unfr, 72x108", C-NY 10/4/89 — 7,700
Untitled (abstract), oil on paper, 1980, 28x40", SBY 10/8/88 — 3,300
Untitled (arms & hands in abstract), oil on paper, 1979, 22x30", SBY 2/14/89 — 2,860
Untitled (composition w/peaks), charcoal/pastel on paper, sgn/dtd 1972, 30x33", SBY 10/7/89 — 1,870
Untitled (contemporary), oil on canvas, sgn/dtd 1980, unfr, 18x24", SBY 2/14/89 OE — 3,300
Waterfall, oil on canvas, sgn/dtd 1980, 84x24", SBY 10/8/88 — 8,800
ASE, Sidney March (American, 1877-1957)
Chucking Clams, oil on board, sgn, 16x20", C-E 11/30/88 — 2,090
Evening, oil on canvas, sgn, 25x30", C-NY 9/30/88 — 7,700
Gray Weather (rocky coastline w/boat on water), oil on canvas, sgn, 20x24", C-E 6/1/89 UE — 1,650
ASE, William Merritt (American, 1849-1916)
Along the Path at Shinnecock (figures in landscape), oil on panel, sgn, ca 1896, 12x18", SBY 5/24/89 — 1,100,000
Coastal Landscape, oil on panel, sgn, 10x15", C-NY 5/25/89 — 28,600
Dowager, oil on canvas, sgn/dtd Muncheon 1874, 37x29", C-E 10/18/89 — 8,800
Feeding Baby, oil on panel, sgn/inscr, 21x15", C-NY 5/25/89 — 60,500
Old Venetian Houses (impressionistic), oil on panel, ca 1913, 8x12", C-NY 5/25/89 — 17,600
Portrait of a Woman, oil on canvas, sgn, 20x16", C-NY 12/2/88 — 19,800
Portrait of Helen, oil on panel, sgn/inscr, 12x9", C-NY 9/30/88 — 11,000
Portrait of Mrs Chase, pastel on paper, sgn, 10x11", SBY 5/24/89 — 187,000
Portrait of Mrs Chase (three-quarter length, seated), oil on canvas, sgn, ca 1910, 53x44", C-NY 5/25/89 — 44,000
Prospect Park, pencil on paper, 9x13", WD 4/13/88 — 2,700
Still Life (fish on table), oil on canvas, sgn, 30x36", C-NY 5/26/88 — 33,000
Still life of Fish, oil on canvas, sgn, ca 1905-15, 29x36", SBY 5/24/89 — 18,700
Summer Rowing Party, oil on panel, sgn, 17x29", C-NY 5/26/88 — 77,000
ASE, William Merritt; att (American, 1849-1916)
Portrait of Thomas Edison, pen/ink on paper, sgn/sgn by sitter, 17x7", SBY 3/17/88 — 715

CHASHNIK, Ilya Grigorevich (Russian, 1902-1929)
Suprematist Architecture (abstract), watercolor on paper, ca 1925, 6x6", C-L 10/8/88 ... 11,150
Untitled (abstract composition), watercolor/gouache on paper, 1923, 10x7", SBY 5/11/88 OE ... 38,500
CHASSELAT, Pierre
Woman Seated in an Armchair, black/white chalk on buff paper, 12x10", C-NY 1/11/89 OE ... 9,900
CHASSERIAU, Theodore (1819-1856)
Portrait of a Lady, bust-length; oil on panel, 15x12", C-M 6/16/89 ... 21,189
CHASSON, Pierre (French, 20th C)
Parisian Street Scene, oil on canvas, sgn, 25x30", B/B 10/9/88 UE ... 1,430
CHATEIGNON, Ernest (French, 19th C)
Harvesters, oil on canvas, sgn, 15x22", SBY 6/8/88... 2,750
CHATELET, Claude Louis (1753-1794)
Cascade dell Marmore, Near Terni; oil on paper laid down on canvas, 38x25", SBY 10/13/89 ... 44,000
Set of 3: Two Landscapes with Waterfalls; Landscape with Covered Bridge; pen/ink/wash, 8x11", 11x8", SBY 1/13/89 OE ... 12,100
CHATELET, Claude Louis; att (1753-1794)
Figures Catching Fish Near Falls in an Italianate Landscape, oil on canvas, unfr, 24x29", SBY 10/13/89... 3,625
CHATTEL, see Van Rossum Du Chattel
CHATTERTON, Clarence K. (American, 1880-1973)
Beach Politicians (three figures seated on crates), oil on paper laid down on canvas, sgn, 16x22", C-E 6/1/89 ... 4,400
Cottage, watercolor/gouache on paper, sgn, 14x20", C-E 9/15/88 UE ... 440
Fair Days, oil on board, sgn, 12x16", C-NY 12/2/88 OE ... 16,500
Street Scene, Newburgh, NY (buildings, people, elevated railway on snowy day); oil on canvas, sgn, 20x25", RAB 8/9/88 UE... 3,500
CHAUDET, Jeanne Elisabeth (1767-1832)
Portrait of Madame Augustin, nee Madeleine Pauline du Cruet de Barailhon (1781-1865); oil, sgn, 22x18", C-M 6/16/89 OE... 57,048
CHAVANNES, E. (Haitian, 20th C)
Marche, tempera on board, sgn, 12x15", WG 9/16/88 UE... 100
CHAVANNES, Pierre Puvis; see De Chavannes
CHAVET, Victor Joseph (French, 1822-1906)
Tea Time, oil on cradled panel, sgn, 9x7", SBY 12/9/88... 1,540
CHAVEZ, Gerardo (French, 20th C)
Untitled (surrealistic abstract), oil on canvas, sgn/dtd 64, 44x38", SBY 5/16/89 OE ... 13,200
CHAZAL, Antoine; att (French, 1793-1854)
Roses in a Glass, oil on canvas, 13x10", C-E 5/22/89 OE ... 4,620
CHELMINSKI, Jan V. (Polish, 1851-1925)
Lady Riding on the Beach, oil on canvas, sgn, 22x19", C-E 5/22/89 ... 3,080
CHEMIAKINE, Mihail (Russian, 1934-)
Fantasy Figures, colored pencil/pen/black ink on paper, sgn/dtd 1979, 12x12", C-E 5/9/89 ... 3,740
CHEN, Hilo (American, 1942-)
Blossom-16 Glory Lily, gouache on paper, sgn/#d 8302, 27x32", C-NY 2/13/89 ... 495
CHENEY, Russell (American, 1881-1945)
Vermont Valley (landscape), oil on canvas, sgn/dtd 16/titled, 24x30", RAB 3/27/89 UE... 600
CHENG, Zhu (Chinese, 1826-1900)
Parrot (hanging scroll), ink/color on paper, sgn, 51x20", SBY 5/31/89 ... 880
CHERET, Jules (French, 1836-1932)
Baroness Vitta, pastel on paper, sgn, 17x11", C-E 6/16/88 ... 2,200
Comedy & The Dance (impressionistic), pastel on linen, sgn, 33x21", C-NY 6/10/89... 16,500
Dancers (impressionistic), pastel on linen, sgn, 17x25", C-NY 6/10/89 ... 16,500
Seated Woman, charcoal on paper, sgn/dtd 1.10.20, 15x9", SBY 10/5/88 ... 605
CHERON, Louis (French, 1660-1725)
Hercules & the Centaur, red chalk/gray wash, monogramed HF, armorial cartouch wm, 9x6", C-NY 1/12/88 OE ... 1,100
CHERRY (20th C)
Self-Portrait, oil on canvas, 23x20", LH 9/10/89 UE ... 90
Spanish Lady, oil on canvas, sgn, 29x24", LH 9/10/89 UE ... 60
CHERUBINI, Andrea (Italian, 19th C)
A Little Music (shepherd with instrument, mountains, & goats), oil on canvas, sgn/dtd 1806, 9x6", RAB 8/9/88... 250
Little Music (shepherd plays instrument in landscape as two goats listen), oil on canvas, sgn/dtd 1806, 9x6", RAB 8/9/88... 250
Street Scene, oil on board, sgn, 4x5", LH 3/20/88 UE ... 70
CHERUBINI, Carlo (Italian, 1897-)
Racehorses, oil on canvas, sgn/dtd 63, 16x20", DM 9/16/88 ... 1,100
CHERUBINO (1553-1615); or ALBERTI, Giovanni (1558-1601)
Two Partially-Draped Male Nudes (a study), red/black chalk, 15x10", SBY 1/13/89 OE... 13,200
CHEVALIER, Nicholas (Australian, 1828-1902)
Homestead in High-Country, South Island; pencil/watercolor heightened w/bodycolor, sgn, 1866, 10x20", C-SK 5/25/89 UE ... 1,650
CHEVALIER, Peter (20th C)
Lied der Muschel (contemporary), acrylic on canvas, sgn/dtd 84, 87x94", C-NY 2/14/89... 9,350
Untitled (abstract), colored chalks/gouache on paper, sgn/dtd 83, 17x24", C-E 5/13/88 UE ... 550
Untitled (abstract), pastel/charcoal/watercolor on paper, sgn/dtd 84, 24x18", SBY 10/5/88 ... 880
CHEVILLIARD, Vincent Jean Baptiste (French, 1841-1904)
Love Story, oil on board, sgn, 10x14", SBY 7/12/89... 6,600
CHI, Chen (American/Chinese, 1912-)
Evening Chat (two figures in conversation under street light), watercolor on paper, sgn, 14x6", RAB 8/9/88 OE ... 875

HI-CHUNG, Hu (20th C)
Playmates, oil on canvas, sgn 3 times/titled, 50x60", SBY 9/23/88 UE 220
HIA, Sandro (European, 20th C)
Boy & Dog (contemporary), oil on canvas, sgn, 1984, 52x39", SBY 2/19/88 28,600
Boy Spinning Net, pencil/colored pencil on paper, sgn, 11x9", SBY 2/15/89 3,300
Dance of the Chairs with Flies (abstract w/two figures dancing), oil on canvas, sgn, 1981, 77x63", SBY 5/3/88 38,500
Fresh Flesh Gilgamesh (male nudes encircle figure), pastel on paper, sgn/dtd 87, 60x104", SBY 10/5/89 OE 41,250
La Pentola dell'Oro, oil on canvas, sgn/dtd 1980, unfr, 64x51", C-NY 10/4/89 82,500
Man with Dogs, pastel/charcoal on paper, sgn/inscr/dtd 81, 14x13", SBY 10/8/88 OE 3,575
Three Pupils, oil/black crayon on paper mounted on masonite in hand-painted frame, sgn, 1981-82, 87x101", C-NY 11/10/88 44,000
Untitled (contemporary), acrylic/wooden boat on canvas, sgn/dtd 82, 25x25x5", C-NY 5/4/89 OE 33,000
Untitled (contemporary), oil/paper collage on 2 joined sheets of paper, sgn/dtd 81/inscr To Andy, 60x42", SBY 5/2/88 OE 71,500
Untitled (figure from behind, arm outstretched); oil stick/crayons/chalks on paper, sgn/dtd 83, 18x14", C-NY 10/4/89 6,600
Untitled (nude figure), pastel on paper, 1983, 59x39", SBY 10/5/89 18,700
Untitled (two male figures embracing), oil/graphite on paper, sgn/dtd 84, 12x9", C-NY 10/4/89 5,500
Waterbearer (man carrying large fish on his back), oil on canvas, sgn/dtd 1981, 75x53", SBY 11/11/88 82,500
HIALIVA, Luigi (Swiss, 1842-1914)
Barnyard Fowl, oil on cardboard, sgn, 16x24", SBY 5/23/89 4,950
Cart Full of Puppies (exterior scene of women & child w/puppies), oil on canvas, sgn, unfr, 23x17", C-NY 2/23/89 OE 16,500
HIARA, John (American, 20th C)
Bouquet of Flowers, watercolor on handmade paper, sgn, 25x19", WG 9/16/88 UE 25
HIERICI, Gaetano (Italian, 1838-1920)
Interior Genre Scene (mother & little girl talking), oil on canvas, sgn, 18x23", RWS 11/10/89 12,100
HIERICI, Gaetano; after (Italian, 1838-1920)
Mischievous Children, oil on canvas, inscr, 23x33", C-E 5/23/88 3,300
HIGOT, Eugene (French, 1860-1927)
Fishing by a Stream, oil on canvas, sgn/inscr, 32x18", C-E 2/23/88 2,750
ilean School (19th C)
French Cavalry Officer & His Mount, an Encampment Beyond; oil on canvas, 21x15", C-SK 5/25/89 1,100
HIMENTI, Jacopo (Italian, 1554-1640)
Bishop Holding a Chalice, oil on canvas, 29x25", SBY 10/21/88 2,750
HIMENTI, Jacopo; att (Italian, 1554-1640)
Standing Robed Figure Seen From Behind, red chalk, 15x9", SBY 1/13/89 OE 2,475
inese School (19th C)
Ancestral Portrait of an Official, watercolor on paper, 45x28", WL 5/20/88 250
Approaching Hong Kong, oil on canvas, 20x26", RAB 3/14/89 2,000
British Ship Off Coast, oil on canvas, 20x25", RWS 10/27/89 6,000
Chinese Junk (w/Hong Kong in background), oil on canvas, orig Chippendale frame, 18x24", RAB 11/25/88 1,100
Eurasian Girl, oil on canvas, 16x13", C-E 2/16/88 OE 880
Flower Pagoda Whampoa Hong Kong, oil on canvas laid down on cardboard, titled, 13x17", RAB 1/31/89 UE 200
Hong Kong, detailed view of the port ca 1860-70, oil on canvas, orig Chippendale frame, 18x31", RAB 11/25/88 52,500
Pagoda Anchorage on the Min River, oil on canvas, Chinese sgn, titled, orig frame, 18x31", RAB 11/25/88 OE 40,000
Pair: Harbor Views with Junks; Commercial Shipping; oil on canvas, oval, 18x13", WD 1/25/89 OE 5,500
Portrait of a Seagoing Junk, oil on canvas, 9x12", RAB 1/31/89 UE 200
Portrait of a Young Girl, oil on canvas, 16x13", RAB 11/25/88 UE 100
Portrait of Lady Holding a Fan, oil on canvas, 24x18", WD 1/25/89 UE 500
Scene in a Small Harbor, oil on fine fabric or canvas, 15x26", RAB 1/31/89 UE 300
Shanghai (view of city), oil on canvas, Chinese sgn, orig Chippendale frame, 18x30", RAB 11/25/88 OE 70,000
Very Early View of Hong Kong (panoramic view), oil on canvas, ca 1850, 11x20", RAB 3/14/89 5,000
View of Boca Tigris (many boats), oil on canvas, 17x29", RAB 8/9/88 2,750
View of Macao From a Verandah (two figures on expansive columned porch), oil on canvas, 11x20", RAB 8/9/88 UE 2,000
inese School (20th C)
Oriental Man, pencil/watercolor on paper, 12x10", C-E 2/16/88 UE 55
IINNERY, George (British, 1774-1852)
Bathers, oil on canvas, inscr, unfr, 8x11", C-SK 5/25/89 16,530
Chinese Figures by a Beached Boat, pen/brush/brown ink, inscr/dtd 2 12.1841, 5x8", C-SK 5/25/89 1,560
Cow in a Landscape, pencil/watercolor, 6x7", C-SK 5/25/89 1,190
Fulton Family Around a Piano, pen/brown ink on paper, 5x6", C-NY 5/24/89 3,520
Two Chinese Farmers Tending a Cow, pencil/watercolor, indistinctly inscr, 7x10", C-SK 5/25/89 OE 6,980
INNERY, George; circle of (British, 1774-1852)
Portrait of a Gentleman, seated three-quarter length, in an interior...; oil on canvas, 11x10", C-SK 5/25/89 OE 1,560
INNERY, George; school of (British, 1774-1852)
Chinese War Junk Chasing Piratical Junks, oil on canvas, sgn, 18x23", WD 1/25/89 UE 2,200
Hongs of Canton, ca 1840-45 (boats in harbor, cityscape beyond); oil on canvas, 15x27", WL 5/20/88 16,000
IRICO, see De Chirico
ITTENDEN, Alice Brown (American, 1859-1944)
Basket with Chrysanthemums, oil on canvas, sgn/dtd 1889, 24x40", B/B/ 10/6/88 17,600
Cut Roses, oil on panel, sgn/dtd 1888, 14x24", B/B 10/6/88 6,050
Still Life of Pink Roses, oil on canvas laid down, sgn, 16x12", B/B 3/22/89 2,200
ITTENDEN, Alice Brown; att (American, 1859-1944)
Turquoise Vase of Pink Roses, oil on board, 6x9", B/B 1/11/89 605

CHOCARNE-MOREAU, Paul Charles (French, 1855-1931)	
Bishop Painting Kittens, oil on canvas, sgn/dtd 1929, 26x22", SBY 12/9/88	2,750
CHOCHON, Andre (French, 20th C)	
Twins in Pigtails, oil on board, sgn, 13x16", B/B 9/15/88	550
CHONG, Manuel Neto	
When Your Dream of Light Fills Me with Memories, oil on canvas, sgn/dtd 84, 40x30", SBY 5/17/88	2,750
CHONG, Wang (Chinese, 1494-1533)	
Loan Agreement in Xing Shu (running script, hand scroll), ink on paper, sgn/dtd 1528, 10x9", SBY 5/31/89	14,300
CHOQUET, Rene	
Man with a Horse-Drawn Wagon Crossing a Bridge, oil on canvas, sgn, unfr, 54x74", C-E 2/23/88	935
CHOULTSE, Ivan F. (Russian, fl 1800-1920)	
Old Mission, oil on board, sgn/dtd 21, 13x11", WL 5/20/88 OE	2,100
Seacoast Near Capri, oil on canvas, sgn, 22x26", C-L 10/8/88	6,500
Snowscape, oil on canvas, sgn/dtd 81, 29x39", C-L 10/8/88 OE	13,000
Winter Idyll, oil on canvas, sgn, 26x32", C-NY 2/25/88	9,350
Winter Morning Landscape, oil on canvas, sgn, 25x25", B/B 10/9/88 OE	7,700
Winter Sunrise, oil on canvas, sgn, 26x32", SBY 2/22/89	7,700
CHRISTENSEN, Anthonore (Danish, 1849-1926)	
Morning-Glories, oil on board, sgn w/monogram, 12x9", SBY 2/22/89	4,400
CHRISTENSEN, Dan (American, 1942-)	
Birch Brown (abstract), enamel/acrylic on canvas, sgn/dtd 1971, 81x45", C-E 11/17/88	550
Bold Fluff, acrylic on canvas, sgn/dtd 1972, 93x48", C-E 11/17/88 UE	770
Shagwong, acrylic on canvas, sgn/dtd 1974, 91x36", C-E 11/17/88 UE	440
Study for 5x8 PTG, graphite on paper, sgn/dtd 1967, 10x14", SBY 2/15/89 OE	715
Untitled (abstract), enamel on canvas, sgn/dtd 1970, 76x12", C-E 11/17/88	880
CHRISTENSEN, Ronald Julius (American, 20th C)	
Landscape (abstract), acrylic on board, sgn, 24x43", FAP 4/15/89	165
CHRISTENY (Continental, 20th C)	
Coming to the Rescue of a Burning Ship, oil on canvas, sgn, 26x36", B/B 9/14/89 UE	880
CHRISTIANSEN, Nils H. (Swedish, 1876-1903)	
Farmyard, oil on canvas, monogramed, 13x19", B/B 1/11/89	605
Winter in a Village, oil on canvas mounted on board, sgn, 30x13", DM 2/19/88	1,200
CHRISTO (Javacheff)(Bulgarian, 1935-)	
Abu Dhabi Mastaba (Project for United Arab Emirates), mixed media on board, sgn/dtd 1977, 12x12", C-NY 5/4/88	6,050
Abu Dhabi Mastaba (Project for United Arab Emirates), mixed media, sgn/dtd 1979/titled, 32x24", SBY 11/11/88	18,700
Abu Dhabi Mastaba (Project for United Arab Emirates), mixed media on paperboard, sgn/dtd 1978, 31x24", SBY 5/3/89 OE	35,750
Abu Dhabi Mastaba (Project for United Arab Emirates), mixed media on paperboard, sgn/dtd 1978, 28x22", SBY 5/3/89 OE	35,750
Double Store-Front, oil/crayon/paper collage on paper, sgn/dtd 64, 22x30", SBY 10/8/88	40,700
Gates (Central Park, NY City Project), crayon/graphite/fabric/string/map, sgn/dtd 84, 11x28" & 22x28", SBY 10/8/88	51,700
Handle with Care, stencil/acrylic on canvas, stamped signature, 38x10", SBY 5/3/88	46,200
Houston Mastaba (1,250,000 Stacked Oil Drums), acrylic/crayons/charcoal/tape on board, sgn/dtd 77, 15x11", C-NY 2/20/88	6,050
Package on Dolly, charcoal/pencil/string/cloth/staples on paperboard, sgn/dtd 1974/titled, 22x28", SBY 11/11/88	19,800
Package on Handtruck (Project), fabric/string/charcoal/gouache/graphite on paper, sgn/dtd 1973, 28x22", SBY 5/3/88	29,700
Package on Handtruck (Project), mixed media, sgn/dtd 1981, 28x22", C-NY 5/4/89	35,200
Package on Handtruck (Project), mixed media on board, 28x22", C-NY 2/14/89 OE	41,800
Packed a Girl (Project for Temporary Sculpture for Duration of 6 Hours), mixed media, sgn, 1967, 22x28", SBY 11/11/88 OE	31,900
Packed Coast (Project for Australia Near Sydney), mixed media, sgn/dtd 1969, 28x22", SBY 11/11/88	18,700
Packed Coast (Project for Australia Near Sydney), mixed media, sgn/dtd 69, 28x22", SBY 11/11/88 OE	28,200
Packed Coast (Project for Australia Near Sydney), mixed media/collage on paperboard, sgn/dtd 1969, 28x22", SBY 5/3/88 OE	77,000
Packed Coast (Project for Australia Near Sydney), mixed media on paper board, sgn/dtd 1969, 28x22", SBY 2/15/89 OE	46,750
Pont Neuf, Wrapped (Project for Paris); architectural drawing/crayon/charcoal, sgn, 79, 15x96" & 41x96", SBY 11/11/88 OE	110,000
Pont Neuf, Wrapped (Project for Paris); charcoal/crayon/paper collage on paper in 2 parts, sgn/dtd 1981, SBY 2/19/88 OE	56,100
Pont Neuf, Wrapped (Project for Paris); crayon/graphite/fabric/collage in 2 parts, sgn/dtd 1985, 33x28", SBY 6/30/88	36,000
Pont Neuf, Wrapped (Project for Paris); mixed media on board, sgn/dtd 1985, 14x22", C-NY 2/14/89 OE	28,600
Pont Neuf, Wrapped (Project for Paris); mixed media on paperboard, sgn/dtd 1984, 11x28" & 22x28", SBY 5/3/89 OE	99,000
Pont Neuf, Wrapped (Project for Paris); photograph/map/cloth/string/charcoal, sgn/dtd 1979, 28x22", SBY 11/11/88 OE	31,900
Project for Documenta IV-Kassel; graphite/crayon/fabric/string on paper, sgn/dtd 1967-68, 29x22", SBY 11/11/88 OE	22,000
Running Fence (Sonama/Marin Cos, CA Project), map/crayon/graphite on paper, sgn/inscr/1976, 15x96" & 42x96", C-NY 5/8/88	55,000
Running Fence (Sonoma/Marin Cos, CA Project), chalk/charcoal/graphite on paper, sgn/dtd 1976, 28x22", SBY 5/3/88	22,000
Running Fence (Sonoma/Marin Cos, CA Project), graphite/charcoal/pastel/paper collage, sgn/dtd 1976, 22x28", SBY 10/8/88	33,000
Running Fence (Sonoma/Marin Cos, CA Project), mixed media, sgn/dtd 1976, 22x28", SBY 10/5/89 OE	60,500
Running Fence (Sonoma/Marin Cos, CA Project), mixed media, sgn/dtd 1979, 22x28", SBY 11/11/88	17,600
Store Front (Project), collage w/enamel/charcoal/paper/cellophane tape, sgn/dtd 64, 26x20", C-NY 10/4/89 OE	93,500
Store Front (Project), watercolor/pencil on paper, sgn/dtd 65, 27x21", SBY 5/3/89 OE	71,500
Surrounded Islands (Project for Biscayne Bay, Miami), collage/fabric/crayon/charcoal, sgn/dtd 1981, 28x22", C-NY 5/4/89	46,200
Surrounded Islands (Project for Biscayne Bay, Miami), mixed media, sgn/dtd 1983, 11x28" & 22x28", SBY 10/8/88	57,200
Surrounded Islands (Project for Biscayne Bay, Miami), mixed media, sgn/dtd 1982, 57x96", SBY 5/3/88	82,500
Surrounded Islands (Project for Biscayne Bay, Miami), mixed media, sgn, 1982, 2 parts: 11x28", 22x28", SBY 10/5/89 OE	143,000
Two Lower Manhattan Packed Buildings (Project) 2 Broadway & 20 Exchange Place; mixed media, 22x17", SBY 11/11/88 OE	38,500
Umbrellas (Project for Japan & Western USA), mixed media, sgn/dtd 1986/titled, 31x27", SBY 11/11/88 OE	66,000
Valley Curtain (Project for Colorado), collage/mixed media on board, sgn/dtd 72, 28x22", C-NY 11/10/88 OE	33,000

Valley Curtain (Project for Colorado), mixed media, sgn/dtd 1972/titled, 28x22", SBY 11/11/88 25,300
Valley Curtain (Project for Colorado), mixed media on paperboard, sgn/dtd 72/titled, 36x96" & 36x96", SBY 11/11/88 99,000
Valley Curtain (Project for Colorado), paper collage/fabric/graphite/paint, sgn/dtd 1972, 28x22", SBY 11/11/88 OE 28,600
Wall (Project for a Wrapped Roman Wall), collage/mixed media on board, sgn/dtd 1973/titled, 22x28", C-NY 11/10/88 OE 26,400
Wrapped Floor & Staircase (Project for Wide White Space Gallery, Anvers), mixed media, 28x22", SBY 11/11/88 OE 34,100
Wrapped Monument ot Vittorio Emanuele (Project for Piazza Duomo, Milano), collage, sgn/dtd 1970, 28x22", C-NY 11/10/88 30,800
Wrapped Reichstag (Project for Berlin), crayon/graphite/schematic map, sgn/dtd 79, 15x96" & 41x96", SBY 2/15/89 OE 104,500
Wrapped Reichstag (Project for Berlin), map/charcoal/crayon on paperboard, sgn/dtd 1985, 15x65" & 42x65", SBY 11/11/88 46,750
Wrapped Reichstag (Project for Berlin), map/fabric/string/pastel/charcoal, sgn/dtd 1978, 11x28" & 22x28", SBY 11/11/88 27,500
Wrapped Reichstag (Project for Berlin), mixed media on paperboard, sgn/dtd 1981, 11x28" & 22x28", SBY 2/15/89 OE 55,000

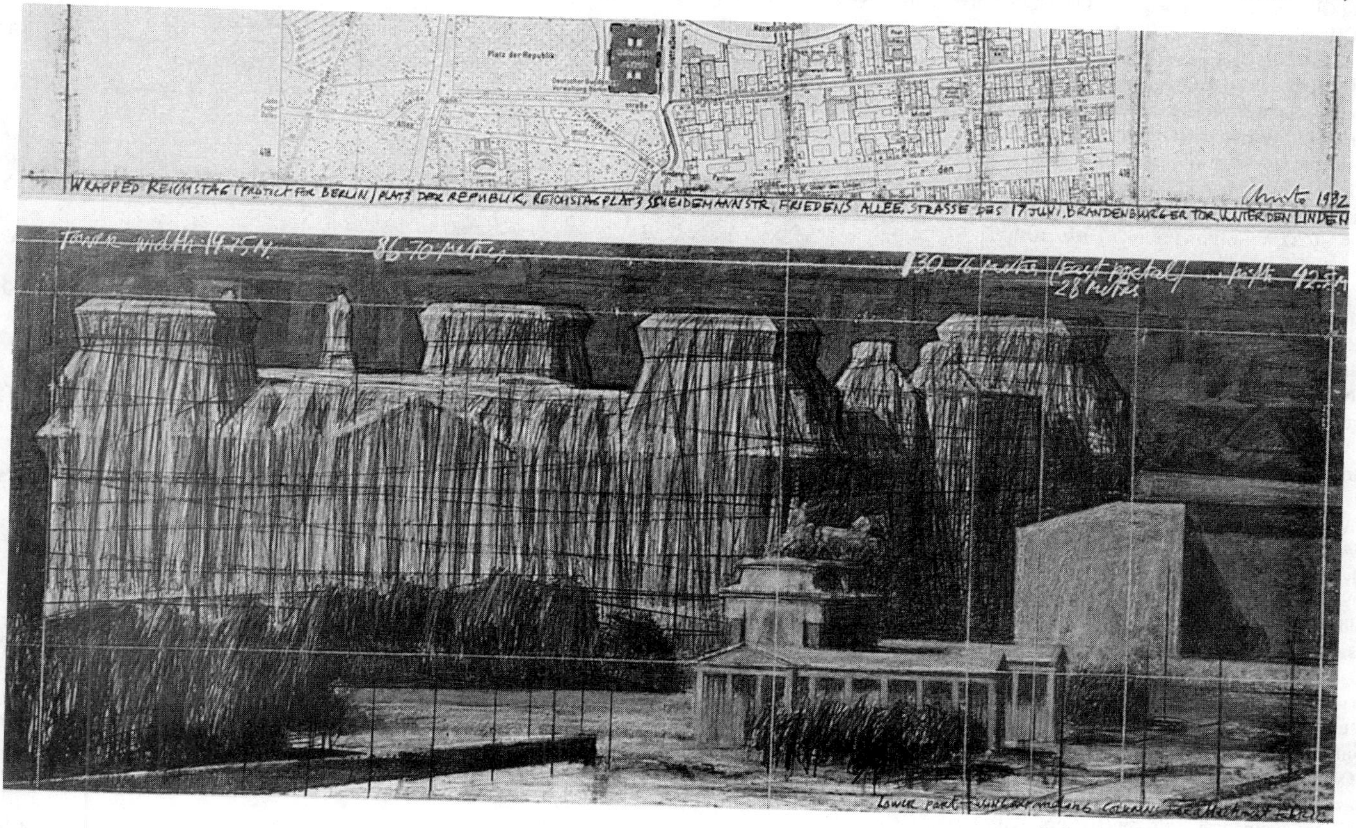

Wrapped Reischtag (Project for Berlin), mixed media on board, sgn/dtd 1982, 15x97", 43x97", C-NY 5/3/89, $132,000

Wrapped Table with a Package (Project), charcoal/crayon/collage/cloth/string/cloth, 24x29", SBY 11/11/88 OE 30,800
Wrapped Walkways (Project for JL Loose Park, KC, MO), mixed media, sgn/dtd 1978, 15x65" & 42x65", SBY 5/3/88 33,000
Wrapped Walkways (Project for JL Loose Park, KC, MO), mixed media, 28x22" & 28x22", SBY 11/11/88 OE 26,400
Wrapped Walkways (Project for JL Loose Park, KC, MO), oil/graphite/photo, sgn/inscr/dtd 1978, 15x10", C-NY 5/4/88 5,500
Wrapped Walkways (Two Parks Project), Sonsbeek 1971; mixed media on paperboard, sgn/dtd 70/titled, 28x22", SBY 11/11/88 12,100
Yellow Store Front, wood/cloth/plastic/paint on wood, sgn/dtd 1965-66, 29x24", SBY 11/11/88 22,000

HRISTY, Howard Chandler (American, 1872-1952)

After the Storm, oil on canvas, sgn/dtd 1936, 42x30", SBY 6/24/88 OE 13,200
At the Party, study of three women & man conversing; charcoal on paper, 39x30", RAB 8/8/89 UE 550
Evangeline, pen/ink wash on paper, sgn/dtd 1905, 37x26", C-E 11/30/88 1,320
Good Day for Skating, oil on canvas, sgn/inscr/dtd 1923, 37x28", C-NY 9/30/88 OE 24,200
New Hat (lady taking hat out of box), oil on canvas, sgn, unfr, 33x27", C-NY 9/28/89 4,400
Nude Reclining, oil on canvas, sgn, 16x21", C-NY 9/28/89 OE 22,000
Nudes at the Beach, oil on canvas, sgn/dtd 1930, 40x50", SBY 5/25/88 OE 115,500
On the Riverbank (lady in a boat, two children on the bank), oil on canvas, sgn/dtd 1946, 35x30", SBY 5/24/89 35,200
Portrait of a Lady, oil on canvas, sgn/dtd 1922, 50x39", C-E 2/1/89 3,300
Portrait of John Drew, watercolor on watercolor board, sgn, 11x8", RWS 11/3/88 UE 175
Portrait of Sylvia Kress Abry, oil on canvas, sgn, 55x40", SBY 9/14/89 9,900
Recital, watercolor heightened with gouache on board, sgn/dtd 1914, 37x53", C-E 4/7/88 OE 3,190
Same Old Yarn (couple), watercolor/gouache/pencil on board, sgn/dtd 1918, 35x25", C-NY 9/28/89 7,700

UIKOV, Ivan (Russian, 1935-)

Fragment of a Sky (abstract), Alkit enamel on board, sgn/dtd 86, 85x59", SBY 7/7/88 20,000
Random Choice I (abstract), Alkit enamel on board, sgn/dtd 1987, 67x59", SBY 7/7/88 24,000

UMLEY, John (American, 1928-)

Mary's Creek, watercolor/gouache on board, sgn, 15x24", C-NY 3/11/88 660

CHURCH, Frederic Edwin (American, 1826-1900)
Home by the Lake (Scene in the Catskill Mountains), oil on canvas, sgn/dtd 1852, 32x48", SBY 5/24/89 OE ... 8,250,000
On Otter Creek (landscape w/covered bridge), oil on canvas, indistinctly sgn, 18x24", SBY 5/24/89 ... 242,000
CHURCH, Frederick Stuart (American, 1842-1924)
Dancing Bear (girl & bear dancing in landscape), oil on canvas, sgn/dtd NY 1914, 16x22", SBY 3/17/88 ... 1,870
Fairy & the Swans, oil on canvas, sgn/dtd NY 1915, 16x22", C-E 10/18/89 ... 1,980
Little Miss & Her Pony, oil on canvas, sgn/dtd 1916, 46x44", SBY 4/14/89 ... 3,300
Sorceress, oil on canvas, sgn/dtd NY 89, 20x36", SBY 1/24/89 OE ... 6,600
The Tourist (Cupid w/flock of cranes), gouache on paperboard, sgn, 13x27", PHL 12/1/88 UE ... 1,500
Young Girl at the Shore, oil on canvas, sgn/dtd 1901, 12x18", C-E 11/30/88 OE ... 6,600
Young Girl with Lotus Blossoms & Flamingos, oil on canvas, sgn/inscr/dtd 1916, 22x41", SBY 9/23/88 UE ... 1,650
CHURCH, H. (European, 20th C)
Trespasser (shepherdess w/sheep talking to Cupid), graphite on paper, sgn/dtd 1906, 12x16", WG 10/19/88 UE ... 45
CHURCHILL, Alfred Vance (American, 1864-)
Amberley Church, Sunset; oil on board, sgn, 12x16", RAB 8/9/88 ... 450
CHURCHILL, Winston (British, 1874-1965)
Red-Roofed House at Mimizan, oil on canvas, initialed, ca 1920s, 24x20", SBY 2/18/88 OE ... 44,000
CIALLI, G.
Young Beauty Surrounded by Baskets of Flowers & Fruit, oil on canvas, sgn, 24x18", C-NY 2/25/88 OE ... 16,500
CIAMMARCO, Camillo (Italian, 19th/20th C)
Portrait of an Old Woman, oil on board, sgn, 12x9", PHL 10/28/88 UE ... 250
CIAPPA, Carlo (Italian, 19th/20th C)
Idillio, oil on canvas, sgn/dtd 1900, 24x18", SBY 7/12/89 ... 2,200
CICERO, Carmen (American, 1926-)
Bird of Prey, oil on canvas, sgn/dtd 56, 47x60", LH 5/15/88 ... 700
CIDONCHA, Rafael
Modern Sweets (still life of desserts), oil on canvas, sgn/dtd 1988, 39x64", SBY 11/21/88 ... 3,300
CIGNANI, Carlo; circle of (Italian, 1628-1719)
Adam & Eve, oil on canvas, 49x40", SBY 10/21/88 ... 1,870
Holy Family with the Infant Saint John the Baptist, oil on canvas, unfr, 51x39", C-NY 4/6/89 ... 4,400
Roman Charity, oil on canvas, oval, 43x34", C-NY 10/20/88 ... 5,280
CIGNAROLI, Scipione (Italian, 1715-1766)
Hilly Landscape with Figures by a Pool, pen/brown ink/brown wash, inscr, 6x9", C-NY 1/12/88 ... 1,430
CIKOVSKY, Nicolai (American, 1894-1934)
Fields & Hills of Long Island, oil on canvas, sgn, 34x46", SBY 6/24/88 ... 3,850
First Lesson, oil on canvas, sgn, 26x22", SBY 9/23/88 ... 1,870
Hillside Landscape, oil on canvas, sgn, 24x30", SBY 4/14/89 ... 1,870
Portrait of a Boy, standing half-length; oil on canvas, sgn, 34x28", C-E 9/15/88 UE ... 715
Seated Nude, oil on canvasboard, sgn, unfr, 20x16", C-E 1/12/88 ... 308
Young Woman Seated on a Sofa, oil on canvas, sgn/dtd 47, 24x20", SBY 9/23/88 ... 2,640
CILFONE, Gianni
Thawing Brook, oil on canvas, sgn, 25x30", C-E 10/18/89 UE ... 990
CIMAROLI, Giovanni Battista (Italian, 18th C)
Extensive Mountainous River Landscape with a Bridge, oil on panel, 13x15", SBY 4/7/88 ... 4,400
Landscape in the Veneto with Figures, Cows, Sheep Along a River; oil on canvas, 17x25", SBY 10/21/88 ... 3,300
CIMAROLI, Giovanni Battista; circle of (Italian, 18th C)
Figures Amongst Classical Ruins by a Harbor, oil on canvas, 31x41", PHL 6/16/88 OE ... 3,750
CIMIOTTI, Gustave (American, 1875-)
Banning, California (farm/mountains in landscape); oil on wood panel, sgn twice/titled, 4x10", RAB 8/8/89 ... 500
Banning, California (landscape w/freight train & mountains); oil on wood panel, sgn twice/titled, 4x10", RAB 8/8/89 ... 400
Plough (man ploughing w/horses, barns & mountains beyond); oil on board, 12x15", MG 11/19/88 UE ... 300
Road Near Taos, oil on board, sgn, 11x15", FAP 4/15/89 ... 742
CINALLI, Ricardo
Fight (male nude torso w/centaur & man in background), pastel on layered tissue paper, sgn/dtd 87, 86x77", SBY 11/21/88 ... 4,400
CINGOLI, see Da Cingoli
CIPOLLA, Fabio (Italian, 1854-)
Tryst on Horseback, oil on panel, sgn/dtd 1874, 14x11", WD 10/19/88 ... 1,400
CIPPER, Giacomo Francesco; att (ca 1670-1736)
Three Men Gathered Around a Table, oil on canvas, 33x54", SBY 4/7/89 OE ... 14,300
Young Peasant Woman, oil on canvas, 36x28", SBY 10/13/89 ... 4,400
CIPRIANI, Giovanni Battista (Italian, 1727-1785)
Saint John the Baptist Preaching in the Wilderness, pen/gray ink/gray wash, 8x8", C-NY 1/12/88 ... 330
Venus on a Chariot, & an Eagle; black chalk, bears inscription, 9x7", C-NY 1/12/88 UE ... 110
CIPRIANI, Giovanni Battista; att (Italian, 1727-1785)
Head of a Youth, pastel on paper, 8x6", SBY 1/13/89 ... 2,090
Jupiter & Callisto (bathers in a landscape), oil on canvas, 40x50", SBY 4/7/89 ... 8,800
CIRINO, Antonio (American/Italian, 1889-1983)
High Elms of Vermont, 1977; oil on board, sgn, 13x15", RWS 11/10/89 ... 1,000
Lost Stream (landscape), oil on board, sgn, 18x20", RWS 3/16/89 ... 1,300
New England Harbor Scene, oil on canvas, sgn, 25x30", SBY 9/14/89 ... 3,300

Stream in Winter, oil on canvasboard, sgn, 8x10", RWS 5/12/89 1,100
Winter in the City, oil on canvasboard, sgn, unfr, 8x10", RWS 11/10/89 OE 2,200
RY, Michel (French, 1919-1944)
Barques a Etretat (coastal view w/boats on beach), oil on canvas, sgn/dtd 56, 42x42", C-E 11/17/88 3,520
Hiver en Pays de Vaud Suisse, oil on canvas, sgn/dtd 62, 36x42", FAP 4/15/89 OE 4,400
ITADINI, Pier Francesco (Italian, 1616-1681)
Portrait of a Lady, half-length, wearing a coral dress, trimmed w/lace & bows...; oil on canvas, 30x23", C-NY 5/31/89 17,600
ITADINI, Pier Francesco; att (Italian, 1616-1681)
Wreath of Roses, Tulips, Morning Glory, Narcissus, Irises, Lilies, & Other Flowers; oil on canvas, 37x32", C-NY 1/15/88 14,300
ITADINI, Pier Francesco; follower of (Italian, 1616-1681)
Portrait of a Lady, oil on canvas, oval, 19x15", SBY 6/8/88 1,760
AESSENS, Anthonie; att (Flemish, 1536-1613)
Holy Family, with Other Relations; oil on panel, 20x26", C-NY 6/2/88 6,600
AESSENS, Anthonie; circle of (Flemish, 1536-1613)
Martyrdom of Female Saint with Other Scenes of Martyrdom & Temptation Beyond; oil on panel, unfr, 23x21", C-NY 4/6/89 8,800
AESZ, Anthony I (Dutch, 1592-1635)
Still Life of Lilies, Irises, Variegated Tulips, Carnations, Peonies...; oil on panel, 28x19", SBY 1/12/89 28,600
AGHORN, Joseph C. (American, 1869-)
Blacksmith Shop, watercolor on paper, sgn, 18x28", B/B 1/11/89.......... 522
Boating Party (figures in boat on calm river), oil on canvas, sgn, 30x25", RWS 9/29/88 OE 1,300
Cabin John (flat boat on river in landscape), no media given, sgn/titled, 28x44", SBY 3/17/88 1,760
AGUE, Richard (American, 19th C)
Back of City Park, New Orleans; oil on canvas, sgn, 22x36", MG 3/26/88.......... 10,500
Tropical Landscape, oil, sgn, unfr, 20x26", C-SK 6/9/88 OE 7,800
AIR, Charles (French, 19th/20th C)
Sheep Feeding in Barn, oil on canvas, sgn, 26x32", SBY 7/12/89 1,100
AIRE, Marie (Canadian, 1939-)
Famille d'Ours, oil on canvas, sgn/dtd 1977, 24x30", FB 5/28/89 2,600
AIRE, Vincent (European, 1855-1928)
Pair: Still Lifes of Fruit; oil on canvas, sgn, 10x12", B/B 6/15/89 2,750
Still Life of Flowers in a Basket, oil on canvas, sgn, 24x20", B/B 10/9/88 UE 5,500
AIRIN, Georges Jules Victor (French, 1843-1919)
Pipe Dreams, oil on canvas, sgn, 24x37", C-NY 2/25/88 7,700
Scene de Harem, oil on canvas, sgn, 40x24", SBY 4/29/88 52,250
Self-Portrait, oil on canvas, sgn/dtd 1871, WD 3/23/88.......... 1,100
AIRIN, Pierre Eugene (French, 1897-)
Maison le Faller, Pont Aven; oil on canvas, sgn, 29x20", SBY 10/5/88.......... 2,750
APP, William H. (American/Canadian, 1879-1954)
Nude in a Landscape, oil on board, sgn, 39x26", B/B 10/6/88 9,350
Reclining Nude, oil on canvas, ca 1913, 15x18", FB 4/25/88 OE 1,200
Reclining Nude, oil on canvas, 15x18", C-E 9/15/88.......... 990
Sunlit Street Scene, oil on board, sgn/dtd 1912, 24x20", FB 5/28/89 2,600
ARE, George (British, 19th C)
Pair: Grapes, Plums, Raspberries on a Bank; Violets & Bird Nest on a Bank, oil on canvas, sgn, 12x10", C-E 2/23/88 OE 4,620
ARE, J. (British, 19th/20th C)
Still Life of Flowers & Fruit, oil on canvas, sgn, 10x14", WL 5/20/88 650
ARE, Oliver (British, 19th C)
Pair: Still Lifes of Fruit on a Ledge; oil on board, sgn, 1 dtd 1900, 12x9", C-E 2/21/89 OE 4,400
Still Life, Fruit; oil on panel, sgn/dtd 99, 5x7", FB 4/25/88 450
Still Life of Grapes, Plums, Pears, & Bird's Nest on a Mossy Bank; oil on canvas, sgn, 25x30", C-E 2/23/88.......... 3,960
Still Life of Grapes, Raspberries, & Peaches; oil on canvas, sgn, 12x10", C-E 2/23/88 2,200
ARK, Albert James (British, fl 1890-1943)
Pair: Tower-B Dillon Up; Lord Chatham-J McKenna Up; oil on canvas, sgn/dtd 1909, 25x30", SBY 6/10/88 13,200
Silver Leaf in a Loose Box (horse in his stall), oil on canvas, sgn/dtd 1898, unfr, 18x24", C-E 2/21/89 3,300
ARK, Alson Skinner (American, 1876-1949)
California Coast, oil on artist board, 1922, 7x9", DM 9/16/88 OE.......... 2,750
Early Autumn, St Lawrence; oil on canvas, bears signature, 14x17", B/B 10/6/88.......... 3,850
Impressionistic Landscape, oil on canvas laid down, sgn/dtd 21, 15x18", B/B 10/6/88 3,025
Steamboat on Icy Chicago River, oil on canvas laid down on masonite, sgn/dtd 06, 18x22", C-E 10/18/89 OE 8,800
ARK, Anne (19th C)
Parsonage, Gurukhpore; watercolor, inscr/dtd 1823, 7x12", C-SK 5/25/89.......... 275
ARK, Benton Henderson (American, 1895-1964)
During the Hunt, oil on canvas, sgn/dtd 1937, 30x46", B/B 3/22/89 4,400
Picking Up the Scent (horse & rider w/dogs in a landscape), oil on canvas, sgn, 30x46", SBY 6/9/89.......... 9,075
Roping a Stray (cowboy), oil on canvas, sgn, 32x26", SBY 6/28/89.......... 1,980
Young Seymour's Success (man & woman in dressing room), oil en grisaille on board, 17x25", C-E 6/1/89 935
ARK, C. Myron (American, 1876-1925)
Campsite (tent staked in lush river valley), watercolor on paper, sgn/dtd 94, 13x18", RWS 9/29/88 425
Cape Cod Sand Dune, oil on canvasboard, sgn, 10x15", RAB 8/8/89 350
Sails in Venice Harbor, oil on canvas, sgn/dtd 1912, 20x30", RAB 8/9/88 600

USS Constitution (masted ship), oil on canvas, sgn/dtd 1922, 43x32", RAB 8/8/89 .... **2,250**
USS Constitution Underway, oil on canvas, sgn, 20x27", RWS 9/8/89 OE **1,800**
USS Constitution Underway, oil on canvas, sgn, 20x30", RWS 3/16/89 OE **1,200**

CLARK, C.A. (American, 19th/20th C)
Still Life of Roses, oil on canvas, sgn/dtd 1889, 20x29", B/B 5/17/89 .... **412**

CLARK, Eliot Candee (American, 1883-1980)
Creek Running Through Landscape, oil on canvas, sgn, 20x24", C-E 11/30/88 .... **1,980**
Flying Clouds, oil on board, sgn 3 times/titled/dtd 1926, 18x20", SBY 6/24/88 .... **770**
Hill with Shrubs, oil on canvasboard, estate stamp/sgn/dtd 1925, 12x14", SBY 6/24/88 .... **660**
Immensity, oil on canvasboard, sgn, ca 1940, 12x16", WL 5/20/88 .... **850**
Kent, Connecticut, 1920s (landscape); oil on board, monogramed/estate stamp, 20x30", SBY 3/17/88 .... **2,750**
Savannah Harbor, oil on canvas, sgn, 20x24", SBY 6/28/89 OE **4,400**
Study: Autumn, Kent, Connecticut; oil on board, sgn twice/dtd 1923/titled, 14x18", SBY 1/24/89 UE **550**
Sunset over Venice (shadows of buildings & boats offset by a sunset sky), oil on board, sgn, 8x10", RAB 8/9/88 .... **450**
View From Van Dyck Studios, oil on masonite, sgn/bears artist's estate stamp, 30x25", C-E 11/30/88 UE **2,420**

CLARK, Homer (American, 19th/20th C)
Horse in a Field, oil on canvas, sgn/dtd 1924, 24x29", WG 9/16/88 UE **350**

CLARK, James (British, 1858-1943)
Joining the Hunt, oil on canvas, sgn, unfr, 30x50", SBY 6/9/89 .... **15,400**
Young Girl with a Doll, oil on canvas, indistinctly sgn, 40x31", SBY 6/8/88 UE **4,400**

CLARK, P. (19th C)
Schuylkill River at Gray's Ferry, watercolor/gouache on paper, 14x20", SBY 9/14/89 .... **990**

CLARK, Walter (American, 1848-1917)
Blossoming Trees, oil on panel, sgn/estate stamp, 13x16", SBY 1/24/89 .... **1,870**
Blowing Trees, oil on canvas, sgn, 14x20", SBY 4/14/89 .... **880**
Burning Bush, oil on board, 9x13", SBY 4/14/89 .... **1,210**
Coastal Inlet, oil on canvas, estate stamp, 16x20", SBY 1/24/89 OE **2,750**
Cows in a Landscape, oil on board, sgn, 12x16", SBY 6/28/89 OE **8,800**
Flowering Trees in Spring, oil on canvas, 14x20", SBY 6/28/89 .... **1,650**
Girl Walking on a Woodland Path (landscape), oil on canvas, sgn/dtd 84, 11x16", SBY 3/17/88 .... **1,650**
Hilly Landscape with Cottages, oil on canvas, sgn, unfr, 20x24", SBY 4/14/89 OE **5,500**
Landscape with River, oil on canvas, 20x27", WG 9/16/88 .... **800**
Stream in Dappled Sunlight, oil on panel, 12x16", SBY 6/28/89 .... **1,650**

CLARK, William (British, fl 1827-1841)
Busy Harbor (sailing ships in misty harbor), oil on canvas, 18x14", RAB 8/9/88 .... **900**
Cruise at Sunset (small steamboat with many passengers, view of a warship beyond), oil on canvas, 10x11", RAB 8/9/88 UE **900**
Misty Morning (sailboats), oil on canvas, 9x14", sm hole in sky, RAB 8/9/88 UE **600**
Storm at Sea Ending, partially dismasted vessel in rough seas; oil on canvas, sgn/dtd 1871, 20x30", RAB 8/1/88 UE **2,100**
Survivor of the Storm, sailing vessel w/anchor holding it into the wind; oil on canvas, sgn, 20x30", RAB 8/1/88 UE **2,000**

CLARKE, John Clem (American, 1936-)
Abstract with Subject #12 (Bronco), oil on canvas, sgn/dtd 72, unfr, 69x90", SBY 2/14/89 UE **2,200**
Boucher-Birth of Venus; oil on canvas, sgn/dtd 68, unfr, 58x68", C-E 5/9/89 .... **1,870**
Judgement of Paris III, acrylic on canvas, sgn/inscr/dtd 69, unfr, 90x64", C-E 5/13/88 .... **2,200**
Lady Godiva II, oil on canvas, sgn/dtd 69, unfr, 67x78", C-E 11/14/89 .... **2,200**
Vermeer-An Artist in His Studio, acrylic on canvas, sgn/inscr/dtd 68, unfr, 58x42", C-E 5/13/88 .... **2,200**

CLARKE, Joseph Clayton (British, 19th/20th C)
Set of 55: Works depicting characters from books of Charles Dickens; watercolor/pen/ink, sgn, 9x6", C-E 2/21/89 .... **1,100**

CLAUS, William A.J. (American, 1862-)
Houses by the Beach in Provincetown, oil on board, sgn, 8x10", RWS 11/10/89 .... **500**

CLAUSADES, see De Clausades

CLAUSEN, Franciska (Danish, 20th C)
Composition, gouache on paper laid down on board, sgn/dtd 27, 10x9", SBY 10/6/89 .... **12,100**
Composition, gouache on paper laid down on board, sgn/dtd 27, 9x9", SBY 10/6/89 OE **15,400**

CLAUSEN, George (British, 1852-1944)
Hayrick & Trees, watercolor/gouache over black chalk, initialed, 14x10", C-E 10/25/88 .... **660**

CLAVE, Antoni (Spanish, 1913-)
Boy with Birdcage (abstract), oil on paper mounted on board, sgn, ca 1950, 14x11", SBY 10/5/89 .... **44,000**
Carmen, Costume Design for Mlle Belinda; black ink/wash/gouache on paper, sgn, 19x21", SBY 2/14/89 OE **36,300**
Chaise au Panier (abstract floral & fruit still life on chair), oil on canvas, sgn, 1946, 32x40", C-NY 10/5/89 OE **99,000**
Composition (abstract), oil/paper collage on paper mounted on canvas, sgn, 1957, 21x29", SBY 10/5/89 OE **49,500**
Hommage a Domenikos Theotokopoulos (abstract figure), oil on canvas, sgn/dtd 1964, 63x44", SBY 5/10/89 OE **187,000**
La Sagrada Familia (composition of the sacred family), oil on canvas, sgn, 1948, 36x32", C-NY 2/18/88 OE **52,800**
Le Banc de Gaudi (abstract), oil on canvas, sgn twice/titled, 51x58", SBY 11/12/88 OE **110,000**
Le Picador, gouache/ink wash on paper, sgn, 1948, 29x22", SBY 10/6/89 .... **66,000**
Le Roi, oil/gouache/brush/black ink on paper laid down on panel, sgn, ca 1957, 30x22", C-NY 11/16/88 OE **110,000**
Maternite, oil on masonite, sgn/dtd 1941, 18x15", C-NY 10/5/89 OE **49,500**
Paysage (abstract landscape), oil on canvas, sgn, ca 1953-57, 19x23", SBY 5/3/88 OE **35,750**

CLAVER, Fernand (French, 20th Century)
La Madeleine, Paris; oil on canvas, sgn, 19x24", FB 4/25/88 .... **800**

CLAXTON, Marshall (British, 1812-1881)
Hindu Nautch Girl in a Railway Carriage, oil on board, sgn twice/dtd 1855 & Calcutta 1856/inscr, 18x14", C-SK 6/9/88 .... **4,830**

CLAYES, see Des Clayes

CLAYS, Paul Jean (Belgian, 1819-1900)

Boats in the Harbor, oil on canvas, sgn/dtd 1871, 30x44", SBY 5/23/89 17,600
Fishing Boats in a Harbor, oil on canvas, sgn, 32x24", C-NY 2/25/88 3,850
Sailboats in a Dutch Harbor, oil on panel, sgn, 20x24", C-E 10/25/88 2,750
Shipping Off Hellevortsluis, Zeeland, Holland; oil on canvas, sgn, 28x40", WD 5/5/88 6,000
Zuyder Zee (maritime scene), oil on canvas, sgn, 36x26", SBY 2/22/89 7,700

CLEAVES, W.P. (American, 20th C)

Mountain Valley, Summer; oil on canvas, sgn, 18x26", RWS 11/3/88 900

CLEEMPUT, Paul

Grist Mill, Built in 1843, Cascade, Ohio (folk art); sgn, 22x30", GAI 9/1/89 275
Pair: Farm Scene; Putnam County Fair, Ottawa, Ohio, 1980; oil on canvas, sgn, 23x31", 22x29", GAI 9/1/89 450

CLEENEWERCK, Henry (French, 19th C)

Hunter in the Cuban Jungle-Sunrise; oil, sgn/dtd Paris 1869, 38x33", C-SK 6/9/88 OE 14,870
Porto d'Anzio, oil on canvas, sgn/dtd 1875, 13x28", SBY 6/8/88 4,070

CLEM, Robert Verity (American, 20th C)

Chickadees (two birds on pine bough), watercolor on paper, sgn/dtd 1955, 12x10", RAB 8/9/88 375

CLEMENS, Paul (American, 1911-)

Nude in an Interior, oil on canvas mounted on masonite, sgn/dtd 42, 43x33", SBY 2/14/89 8,800

CLEMENT, Francisco; see San Clement

CLEMENT-RENE, Paul Henry (French, 20th C)

Pair: Corner of the Henhouse; The Perch; oil on board, sgn, 11x13, 8x10", B/B 5/17/89 935

CLEMENTE, Francesco (European, 20th C)

Cane (contemporary), gouache on paper mounted on canvas, 1979, 41x60", SBY 2/15/89 OE 29,700
Four Panels: untitled (allegory); enamel on sheet metal, 48x36", C-NY 5/3/89 198,000
Funo-Smoke, pigment on plaster, 1981, 10x20", SBY 10/5/89 41,250
Horizon (contemporary), pastel on paper, 1980, 24x18", SBY 11/11/88 22,000
Libero, Libera (contemporary); watercolor/charcoal on paper, sgn, 1981, 12x9", SBY 5/3/89 12,100
Non Nolde (abstract), oil on canvas, sgn/titled twice, 1981, 14x28", SBY 11/11/88 OE 44,000
Numbers (green bananas, a hand, & head), pastel on paper, 1980, 24x18", SBY 2/15/89 OE 60,500
Page From a Sketchbook, ink/watercolor on paper, 8x10", SBY 10/5/88 OE 1,100
Una Sola, gouache on paper laid down on canvas, 1979, 40x60", SBY 10/5/89 38,500
Untitled (abstract, man & mountain), pastel on paper, 1982, 27x31", SBY 2/15/89 28,600
Untitled (abstract figure), colored chalks on paper, 1983, 26x19", C-NY 5/4/89 15,400
Untitled (abstract figures), pastel on paper, 1983, 26x19", SBY 2/15/89 OE 55,000
Untitled (abstract), colored chalks on paper, sgn, 12x12", C-NY 5/4/88 OE 22,000
Untitled (abstract), colored chalks/charcoal on paper, sgn, 12x12", C-NY 5/4/88 OE 9,350
Untitled (abstract), gold enamel/gouache/brush/black ink on paper mounted on canvas, 1979, 41x61", C-NY 11/10/88 11,000
Untitled (abstract), pastel on paper, 1985, 26x19", SBY 10/5/89 33,000
Untitled (abstract), watercolor on paper, inscr Rene Ricard your 7 Lukie mates, 1981, 12x18", C-NY 11/10/88 OE 24,200
Untitled (contemporary), oil on canvas, 1983, 78x93", SBY 2/15/89 OE 286,000
Untitled (contemporary), pastel on paper, sgn/inscr For Andy Warhol, ca 1982, 24x18", SBY 5/2/88 OE 44,000
Untitled (contemporary), watercolor on paper, 1983, 18x24", SBY 5/3/89 7,700
Untitled (contemporary), watercolor on paper, 1985, 20x14", SBY 5/3/89 7,700
Untitled (contempory), pastel on paper, 1986, 26x19", SBY 5/3/89 OE 55,000
Untitled (head), pastel on paper, 1985, 26x19", SBY 5/3/89 27,500
Untitled (imaginary composition), pastel on paper, 1983, 26x19", SBY 2/15/89 33,000
Untitled (lips, hand, & fork), pastel/watercolor/acrylic on paper, 1980, 15x18", SBY 11/11/88 18,700
Untitled (portrait of Robert Mapplethorpe), watercolor, sgn/dtd NY City MCMLXXVI March, 14x20", C-NY 10/31/89 OE 46,200
Untitled (surrealistic composition), pastel on paper, 1983, 26x19", SBY 11/11/88 OE 66,000
Untitled (two heads), oil on canvas, sgn, 1983, 78x93", SBY 5/2/89 OE 220,000
Women & Men #12 (abstract composition), watercolor on paper on 3 sheets, 1985-86, 43x20", SBY 10/5/89 63,250

CLEMINSON, Robert (British, fl 1865-1868)

Collecting the Game (two dogs w/dead game), oil on panel, indistinctly sgn/dtd 1868, 12x15", SBY 6/9/89 880
Hounds & Dead Game in a Valley, oil on canvas, sgn, 30x50", C-E 5/23/88 OE 3,080
Setter & Two Spaniels in a Highland Landscape, oil on canvas, sgn, 30x50", SBY 6/10/88 3,850
Spotting the Prey (two hunting dogs in a landscape), oil on canvas, sgn, 12x15", SBY 6/9/89 1,650

CLERCK, see De Clerck

CLERGET, Hubert

Laundry in the Hotel Colbert, watercolor/pen/brown ink/pencil on lt tan paper, sgn/inscr, 9x12", C-NY 10/26/88 880

CLERICI, Fabrizio (Italian, 1913-)

Minotaur Publicly Denouncing His Mother, watercolor/gouache on paper, sgn/dtd 1968, 25x39", B/B 8/10/88 2,090

CLERISSEAU, Jean Louis; circle of (French, 18th C)

Travelers Resting by Classical Ruins, pen/brown ink/bodycolor, 14x12", C-NY 1/12/88 OE 3,520

CLIFTON, F.C.

Bay Horse in a Stable, oil on canvas, sgn/dtd 97, 18x22", C-E 11/8/88 550

CLIME, Winfield Scott (American, 1881-1958)

Building of the Poseidon, a Harbor Scene; oil on canvasboard, sgn, 9x11", RWS 9/8/89 800

CLINEDINST, May Spear (American, 1859-1931)

Greener Pastures (verdant farming scene, mountains beyond), watercolor on paper, sgn, 14x18", RWS 3/31/88 UE 225
Harbor View, New England (expressionistic coastal scene w/figures at pier); watercolor on paper, 14x20", RWS 3/31/88 UE 250

CLOAR, Carroll (American, 1913-)
Faculty & Honor Students, Lewis School; tempera on masonite, sgn twice, inscr/dtd 1966, 28x40", C-NY 3/11/88 OE 11,000
CLOISIEN, R. (English, 18th C)
Chickens, oil on canvas, 10x11", MG 3/26/88 UE 450
CLOSE, Chuck (American, 20th C)
Georgia (portrait of young girl in pigtails), stamp pad ink on paper, 1980, 43x31", SBY 2/19/88 OE 44,000
Lisa P (portrait), ink/graphite on paper, sgn twice/dtd 1974 twice/titled twice, 30x22", SBY 11/11/88 15,400
Nat/Horizontal, Vertical, Diagonal (portrait); watercolor/graphite on paper, sgn/dtd 1973/titled, 30x22", SBY 11/11/88 19,800
Sandy (head portrait), ink/graphite on paper, sgn/dtd 1974, 26x22", SBY 10/5/89 16,500
CLOSKY
Untitled (fantasy composition), acrylic/enamel on canvas, sgn, 1984, 66x65", C-NY 5/4/89 1,210
CLOSSON, William Baxter Palmer (American, 1848-1926)
After the Day's Labor (harbor scene), oil on canvasboard, sgn, 10x10", RWS 11/10/89 850
Striking Profile, pastel on brown paper, sgn, 19x13", C-NY 5/26/88 4,400
CLOUET, Francois; circle of (French, 1510-1572)
Portrait of a Gentleman, half-length, wearing a doublet with gold braiding; oil on panel, 14x10", C-NY 10/20/88 5,500
Portrait of a Lady Said To Be Marchesa de Bergis, oil on panel, 12x9", C-NY 1/11/89 OE 33,000
Portrait of Rene de Birague, Chancellor of France; oil on panel, bears inscription, 14x10", SBY 10/21/88 8,800
CLOUET, Francois; manner of (French, 1510-1572)
Portrait of Two Women, oil on panel, 11x8", C-E 4/7/88 OE 770
CLOUET, Francois; school of (French, 1510-1572)
Portrait of Jesuit Preist, standing, half-length...; oil on panel, 14x10", C-NY 5/31/89 UE 1,650
CLOUGH, George L. (American, 1824-1901)
Angler (figure in a river landscape), oil on canvas, sgn, 24x36", SBY 1/24/89 7,700
Boats on the Hudson, oil on board, sgn, 17x24", SBY 6/28/89 1,430
Hunter in a Landscape, oil on canvas, sgn, 23x16", C-E 2/1/89 990
CLOUGH, Prunella (British, 20th C)
Bone (abstract composition), oil on canvas, 16x11", SBY 10/7/89 2,970
CLOUTIER, Albert (Canadian, 1902-1965)
St Lawrence Yacht Club, oil on board, sgn, 20x24", FB 4/25/88 350
CLOWES, Daniel (British, 1774-1828)
Mister Rutson's Favorite Horse, Pat, in a River Landscape; oil on canvas, sgn/dtd 1824, 33x45", SBY 6/9/89 11,000
CLYMER, John Ford (American, 1907-)
Artic Heather, tempera on board, sgn/inscr, 10x14", SBY 9/23/88 OE 3,300
Caribou in the Frozen North, oil on canvas, 24x40", SBY 6/28/89 OE 14,300
Red Dust, oil on canvas, sgn/copyrighted/dtd 77, 20x40", SBY 9/23/88 OE 51,700
River Landscape, oil on canvas, sgn, 20x24", DM 2/19/88 750
COALE, Griffith Baily (American, 1890-)
Fishing Boats, Venice; oil on canvas, sgn, 26x22", SBY 6/24/88 2,090
COATES, Edmund C. (American, 1816-1871)
Dobb's Ferry on the Hudson, oil on canvas, 48x75", C-NY 3/11/88 OE 12,100
East Hampton, oil on canvas, sgn/dtd 1853, 22x27", C-NY 9/30/88 5,280
Fishing Boats at Sea, oil on canvas, sgn/dtd 1852, 24x28", SBY 6/24/88 5,225
Flatboat on the Hudson, oil on canvas, sgn/dtd 1871, 24x32", WD 4/13/88 3,200
COBB, Ann M. (American, 19th C)
Moulin Pres de Stanz (landscape w/buildings), watercolor on paper, sgn/dtd March 24th 1833, 17x24", RAB 5/23/89 UE 300
COBB, Darius (American, 1834-1919)
Early Autumn Landscape (forest bordering small lake), oil on canvas, sgn, 20x30", RAB 8/9/88 425
COBELLE, Charles
Rue de la Paix, Paris; oil on canvas, sgn, 20x24", SBY 10/7/89 2,420
COBURN, Frank (American, 1866-1931)
Under the Umbrella-Rainy Day on the Streets of San Francisco; oil on canvas, sgn, 20x15", RWS 5/12/89 OE 3,200
COBURN, Frederic Simpson (Canadian, 1871-1960)
Fisherman & an Artist (figure studies), pencil, sgn/dtd 93, 17x12", WAD 6/12/89 700
Logging in Winter (two teams pulling sled), oil on canvas, sgn/dtd 1933, 12x14", FB 10/17/88 11,000
Winter Eastern Township Landscape w/Horse & Log Sleigh, oil on canvas, sgn/dtd 1927, 21x19", FB 10/17/88 15,000
Winter Logging Team in a Birch Tree Forest, oil on canvas, sgn/dtd 1925, 9x13", FB 10/17/88 7,800
COCCAPANI, Sigismondo; att (Italian, 1583-1642)
Bishop Saint Being Given a Mitre by Two Children, Perhaps Saint Nicholas of Myra; oil on canvas, 36x27", SBY 4/7/89 OE 5,500
COCCORANTE, Leonardo; manner of (Italian, 18th C)
Capricio of Classical Architecture, oil on canvas, unfr, 19x25", C-E 6/1/88 OE 4,400
COCCORANTE, Leonardo; school of (Italian, 18th C)
Architectural Capriccio, oil on canvas, 46x36", C-E 4/7/88 OE 4,180
Landscape with Ruins, oil on canvas, 32x43", C-E 1/12/88 1,650
Shipwreck by a Harbour, oil on canvas, 37x49", C-NY 10/20/88 8,800
COCHIN, Charles N. the younger; manner of (French, 18th C)
Pair: Elegant Lady & Gentleman, seated; red/white chalk, 10x8", 10x7", SBY 7/12/89 825
COCHRAN, Allen Dean (American, 1888-1935)
Catskills, Near Woodstock, New York; oil on canvas, sgn/dtd 1915, 24x30", RWS 5/19/88 5,000
Harbor Scene, oil on canvas laid down on board, sgn, 16x19", SBY 9/14/89 1,980
Snow Scene, oil on canvas, sgn, 24x30", SBY 4/14/89 OE 8,250

Tannery Brook, oil on canvasboard, sgn, 1942, 12x16", SBY 9/23/88 UE ... 605
Winter Forest Scene, oil on canvas, sgn, 24x30", WG 4/23/88 OE ... 3,100
Winter Landscape, oil on canvas, sgn, 24x30", WG 9/16/88 ... 3,000

COCK, Zavier; see De Cock

COCKCROFT

Angeles Pyrenees, oil on canvas, sgn/dtd 1923, 32x40", C-E 9/15/88 ... 715

COCTEAU, Jean (French, 1889-1963)

Esquisses, blue ballpoint pen on paper laid down on paper & mounted on canvasboard, sgn, 11x8", C-E 11/17/88 ... 825
Etude pour La Chapelle a Villefranche (line drawing), black crayon/colored pencils, sgn/dtd 26, 19x24", C-NY 2/18/88 OE ... 8,250
Harlequin, colored crayons on paper, sgn, unfr, 14x11", SBY 10/5/88 UE ... 1,650
Les Danseurs (The Dancers), pencil on paper, sgn, 9x11", B/B 3/22/89 ... 1,320
Minotaure, pen/India ink w/red wax crayon on paper, sgn, 11x8", C-NY 2/13/89 ... 1,980
Pair: Opium; Tete d'Homme en Profil; blue ballpoint pen on paper, sgn/dtd, 8x5", 7x5", C-E 11/17/88 ... 2,860
Reclining Male Nude, pencil on paper, stamped w/initials, unfr, 11x8", SBY 10/5/88 OE ... 2,860
Seated Sailor, pencil on paper, stamped with initials, unfr, 11x8", SBY 10/5/88 ... 1,870
Self-Portrait, red/blue/green crayon, sgn, 8x5", FAP 4/15/89 OE ... 1,045
Tete d'Homme, colored wax crayons/pencil/collage on tan paper, sgn, 9x8", C-NY 10/6/88 ... 2,420
Tete d'Homme (man's head in profile), colored markers on paper, sgn, 24x19", C-NY 2/18/88 OE ... 3,850
Tete d'Homme en Profil, pen/black ink/blue chalk on paper, sgn/inscr/dtd 32, 11x9", C-E 5/13/88 OE ... 3,960
Tete d'Homme en Profil (man's head in profile, line drawing), colored pencils, sgn/stamped/dtd 1951, 7x5", C-E 11/17/88 ... 1,760

CODAZZI, Viviano (Italian, 1611-1672)

Architectural Capriccio of Ancient Ruins with the Adoration of the Magi, oil on canvas, 40x50", SBY 10/21/88 OE ... 31,900
Peasants Dancing & Making Merry Among Classical Ruins, oil on canvas, 27x38", SBY 10/13/89 OE ... 30,800

CODAZZI, Viviano; att (Italian, 1611-1672)

Set of 4: Architectural Capriccio with Figures; oil on canvas, 29" dia, SBY 10/13/89 OE ... 22,000

CODAZZI, Viviano; circle of (Italian, 1611-1672)

Capriccio of Classical Ruins with Figures, oil on canvas, 39x53", C-NY 10/12/89 ... 3,300

CODAZZI, Viviano; follower of (Italian, 1611-1672)

Capriccio with the Arch of Titus & the Farnese Gardens, oil on canvas, 60x46", SBY 4/7/89 ... 10,450

CODDE, Pieter (Dutch, 1599-1678)

Interior with Elegant Figures Making Music, oil on panel, 16x21", SBY 6/2/89 OE ... 110,000

CODDE, Pieter; school of (Dutch, 1599-1678)

Elegant Figures in an Interior, oil on panel, 18x22", C-NY 4/6/89 OE ... 3,300

CODRON, Jef (French, 19th C)

Still Life of White & Yellow Roses, oil on canvas, sgn, 48x61", C-NY 2/23/89 ... 7,150

COELLO, Alonso Sanchez; att (Spanish, 1515-1590)

Portrait of King Philip II of Spain, standing, three-quarter length; oil on canvas, 47x34", C-NY 5/31/89 ... 33,000

COELLO, Alonso Sanchez; school of (Spanish, 1515-1590)

Portrait of a Young Lady in a Court Costume, oil on canvas, 76x40", SBY 7/12/89 ... 2,200

COFFERMANS, Marcellus (Flemish, 16th C)

Madonna & Child, oil on panel w/arched top, 6x4", C-NY 1/11/89 ... 19,800

COFFIN, George Albert (American, 1856-1922)

Shipwreck, ink/ink wash/gouache on paper, sgn/dtd 1900, 16x15", C-E 2/3/88 ... 660

COFFIN, William Anderson (American, 1855-1925)

Grove of Trees, oil on canvas, sgn, 20x30", C-E 10/18/89 ... 1,320
October in New England (extensive landscape), oil on canvas, sgn/dtd 1899, 30x40", C-SK 11/10/88 ... 15,800
Snowy City Streets, oil on canvas laid down on board, sgn/dtd 1879, 12x9", C-E 2/1/89 OE ... 6,820

COGGESHALL, K.M. (American, 20th C)

Untitled (old courthouse in St Louis), oil on canvas, sgn, 20x24", SLK 2/11/89 ... 125

COGNEE, Philippe (French, 20th C)

Untitled (abstract portrait), acrylic on paper mounted on canvas, sgn/dtd 84, unfr, 35x43", C-NY 11/10/88 OE ... 3,080

COGNIET, Leon (French, 1794-1880)

Bataille d'Heliopolis (Basse-Egypte, battle at Heliopolis), oil on canvas, sgn, 29x23", SBY 2/22/89 UE ... 30,250

COHEN, Bernard

Yellow Space/Interior, oil on masonite, 36x48", C-E 11/17/88 UE ... 330

COHEN, Lewis (American, 1857-1915)

Plaza Hotel From Central Park, oil on board, sgn, unfr, 10x21", C-E 2/3/88 OE ... 1,540
Reflecting Pond, oil on board, unfr, 12x16", C-E 2/3/88 UE ... 440

COHLE, A.E. (British, 19th C)

Highlighted Landscape, oil on canvas, sgn, 20x34", SLK 2/12/88 ... 350

COIGNARD, James (French, 1925-)

Otage en Zone Vert (abstract), acrylic/collage on paper, sgn, 21x17", WD 5/5/88 ... 1,800
Presence Horizontale (abstract), acrylic/collage on canvas, sgn, 31x38", WD 5/5/88 ... 2,000

COL, Jan David (Belgian, 1822-1900)

Retour de Chasse (interior scene after a hunt), oil on canvas, sgn/dtd 1885/titled, 39x33", C-NY 5/24/89 OE ... 28,600

COLACICCO, Salvatore (Italian, 20th C)

Man of War at Cowes, Isle of Wight; oil on panel, sgn, unfr, 24x37", B/B 9/14/89 UE ... 715

COLB, F. (American, 20th C)

Still Life of Pink Flowers, oil on canvas, sgn, 27x21", MG 11/19/88 UE ... 200

COLE, George (British, 1810-1883)

Harvesters in an Extensive Landscape, Harting Coombe, Sussex; oil on canvas, sgn/dtd 1873, 20x30", C-NY 2/23/89 OE ... 19,800

COLE, George Vicat (British, 1833-1893)
Surrey, England; oil on canvas, sgn, 21x31", C-E 5/23/88 ... 4,400
COLE, George Vicat; att (British, 1833-1893)
Afternoon Rest in a Wheatfield, oil on canvas, sgn, 26x32", C-E 5/23/88 ... 3,300
Pair: Feeding the Ducks; Cows Grazing; oil on canvas, bears signature, 14x25", C-E 2/25/88 ... 1,870
Peasant by a River Landscape, oil on canvas, 14x18", C-E 4/7/88 OE ... 1,430
COLE, Joseph Foxcroft (American, 1837-1892)
Driving the Flock Home, oil on canvas, sgn, 22x32", RWS 12/10/88 ... 950
Landscape with Herder & Cattle, oil on canvas, 34x47", RWS 5/19/88 ... 5,500
Normandy Pastoral, oil on canvas, sgn/dtd 1890, 14x18", C-NY 9/30/88 ... 3,300
Paddock (cows & horses beside old building), oil on canvas, sgn/dtd 1877, 18x26", RWS 9/8/89 UE ... 600
Street Scene Pierrefitte, oil on canvas, sgn/dtd 1877, 12x16", C-NY 9/30/88 ... 3,520
COLE, Philip Tennyson (British, fl 1878-1889)
Portrait of Benjamin Disraeli, Earl of Beaconsfield; oil on canvas, sgn/inscr, 50x36", SBY 12/9/88 UE ... 1,540
COLE, Thomas (American, 1801-1848)

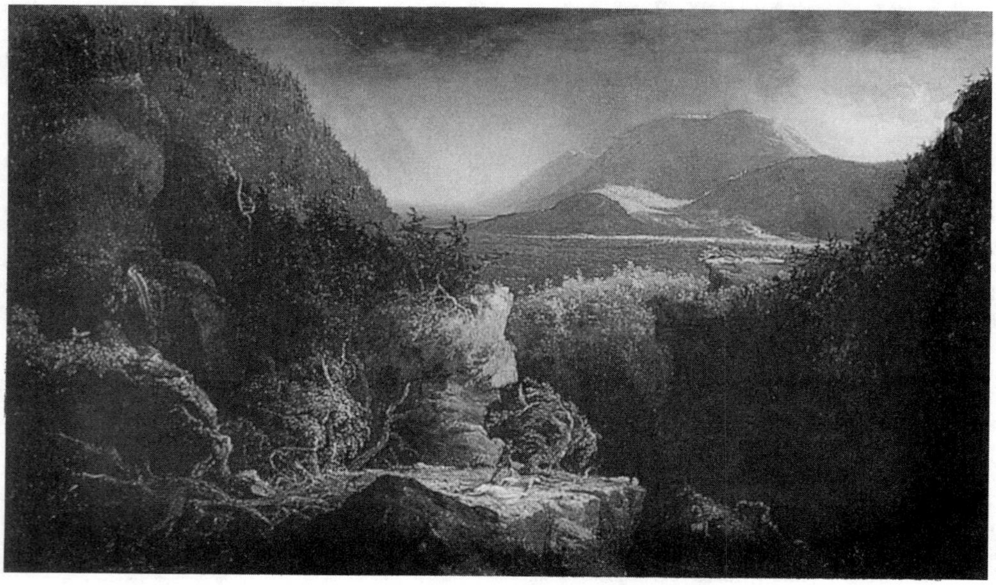

Last of the Mohicans, oil on panel, sgn/dtd 1826, 26x43", C-NY 5/26/88 OE, $1,045,000

Ruins at Taormina (study for a major work), oil on canvas, 12x16", C-NY 5/25/89 UE ... 28,600
COLE, Thomas; after (American, 1801-1848)
The Voyage, oil on canvas, 22x29", B/B 12/8/88 ... 1,320
COLEMAN, C. (Italian, 19th C)
The Well (figures in a landscape), oil on canvas laid down, sgn/indistinctly dtd, 31x60", B/B 9/14/89 UE ... 1,320
COLEMAN, Charles Caryl (American, 1840-1928)
A Capri Pergola, oil on canvas, monogramed/sgn/dtd 1912, 40x33", B/B 3/17/88 OE ... 60,500
An Old Mill Caprili, oil on canvas, monogramed/dtd 1898, 19x31", B/B 3/17/88 OE ... 20,900
Engaging in Gossip (women in an interior), oil on canvas, initialed/dtd 1884, 17x26", B/B 10/9/88 ... 18,700
Harvesting Scene, oil on canvas, monogramed/dtd 1923, 42x89", B/B 3/17/88 ... 9,350
Night Owl, oil on canvas, sgn w/initials in monogram/dtd 1879, 59x11", C-NY 12/2/88 ... 16,500
Outside the Walls, oil on paper laid down on canvas, initialed/dtd Roma 1868, 7x14", C-E 10/18/89 ... 2,860
Rome, oil on canvas, monogramed/dtd 1888, 23x37", C-SK 11/10/88 OE ... 13,010
Ruins in the Wake of Mount Vesuvius, gouache on paper, indistinctly dtd, 18x24", B/B 3/17/88 ... 4,400
Scene in Capri, oil on panel, sgn w/monogramed initials/inscr, 6x25", C-NY 12/2/88 ... 16,500
The Watercarrier, oil on canvas, monogramed/inscr Capri, 36x16", B/B 3/17/88 ... 11,000
Vintage Time, oil on canvas, monogramed/dtd Capri 1923, 24x16", B/B 3/17/88 OE ... 14,300
Woman Leaning Against a White Stucco Wall, oil on canvas, monogramed/Copyright CCC ??, 24x19", B/B 3/17/88 ... 11,000
Women Relaxing in the Shade of the Vines, Capri; oil on canvas, monogramed/dtd 1898, 23x34", B/B 3/17/88 OE ... 93,500
COLEMAN, Charles Caryl; att (American, 1840-1928)
Study of a Dog, oil on artist board, sgn, 9x7", RAB 3/27/89 UE ... 100
COLEMAN, Enrico (Italian, 1846-1911)
Herding Horses Along a Road in the Italian Countryside, watercolor, sgn, 18x26", C-NY 2/23/89 OE ... 10,450
Herding Horses in the Compagna, watercolor, sgn/inscr, 8x18", C-NY 10/26/88 OE ... 8,250
Letter (seated lady before folding screen reading letter), watercolor on paper, sgn, 17x11", RAB 8/8/89 UE ... 350
COLEMAN, F. (Italian, 1851-)
Court Scene, oil on canvas, sgn, 25x26", LH 10/16/88 ... 1,700
COLEMAN, Glenn O. (American, 1887-1932)
Humming Birds, watercolor/gouache on paper, sgn, 8x10", C-E 11/30/88 ... 770
COLEMAN, Harvey (American, 1884-1959)
Evening Shadows on a Sierra Lake, oil on canvas, sgn, 20x24", B/B 1/11/89 ... 660

COLEMAN, Loring W. (American, 20th C)
Spring in November (hilly landscape), oil on canvasboard, sgn, 8x10", RWS 9/8/89 425
COLEMAN, Mary Darter (American, 1894-)
California Landscape in Autumn, oil on canvas, sgn, 16x20", B/B 9/15/88 468
Rolling Hills, oil on board, sgn, 16x20", B/B 8/10/88 550
COLEMAN, Michael (American, 1946-)
Barnyard Romance, oil on panel, sgn, 12x6", B/B 9/15/88 UE 110
Blackfeet Camp, gouache on paper, sgn, 18x26", SBY 5/25/88 13,750
Checking the Nest, oil on board, sgn, 12x10", B/B 9/15/88 248
Chicken in Backyard at Dusk, oil on board, sgn, 20x26", SBY 9/14/89 3,300
Dawn's First Glow, oil on board, sgn, 14x11", B/B 9/15/88 UE 110
Edge of the Forest, oil on board, sgn, 20x16", B/B 9/15/88 UE 248
Forest Interior, oil on canvas laid down, sgn, 11x9", B/B 9/15/88 UE.......... 110
Indian Encampment, oil on canvas, sgn/dtd 1.9.7.3, 14x20", B/B 3/22/89 4,400
Indian Encampment, watercolor on paper, sgn/copyrighted, 13x17", SBY 6/28/89 7,700
Summer Landscape, gouache on paper, sgn/dtd 1978 III, 14x18", SBY 6/28/89 9,350
Twin Tree Stumps, oil on panel, sgn, 11x17", B/B 9/15/88 358
COLEMAN, William Stephen (British, 1829-1904)
A Treat for the Goldfish, oil on canvas, sgn, 23x29", SBY 10/24/89.......... 8,800
Mischief with the Goldfish (sisters feed fish cookies), oil on canvas, sgn, 23x29", RAB 3/27/89 6,500
Young Girl Looking at a Fish Bowl, oil on canvas, sgn, 32x17", B/B 3/22/89 OE 10,450
COLERIDGE, Francis George (Canadian, 19th C)
Rainbow Over Niagara Falls (From Canadian Side), watercolor, sgn/dtd 1867, 13x20", WAD 6/12/89.......... 1,200
COLI, Giovanni; & FILIPPO, Gherardi (Italian, 17th C)
Christ on the Road to Cavalry, oil on canvas, unfr, 30x38", C-NY 4/8/88 2,200
COLIN, Gustave Henri (French, 1828-1910)
Le Toreador, oil on panel, sgn/dtd 79, 18x15", SBY 7/12/89 1,650
Seated Woman on a Park Bench, oil on canvas, sgn, 32x26", C-E 2/23/88 OE 2,970
Village Road, oil on canvas, sgn, 12x17", B/B 3/17/88 2,750
COLIN, Paul (French, 1892-)
Josephine Baker, oil on canvas, sgn, 22x18", SBY 4/23/88 OE 3,850
COLINSON, J. (British, 19th C)
Ships Along the Coast, oil on canvas, sgn, 10x14", WG 9/16/88 UE.......... 200
COLLANTES, Francisco; school of (Spanish, 1599-1656)
Wooded Landscape with Riders on a Path, oil on canvas, bears signature, 19x25", C-NY 10/20/88 3,080
COLLE, G. (Italian, 19th C)
Grand Canal, Venice; watercolor on paper, sgn, unfr, 11x16", C-E 5/23/88 UE 440
View of San Marco & the Campinile, watercolor, sgn, 14x10", C-E 2/21/89 605
COLLE, Michel Auguste (French, 1872-1949)
Cathedrale de Toul, oil on canvas, sgn/dtd 1909, 63x42", SBY 5/23/89 6,600
COLLIAN, V. (French, 1867-)
Four Peasants Picking Grapes, watercolor, sgn, 16x12", DM 3/14/88 325
COLLIER
Dutch Interior Landscape, oil on panel, sgn, 15x11", LH 10/16/88.......... 160
COLLIER, Alan Caswell (Canadian, 1911-)
Near Bells Rapid, oil on board, sgn, 12x16", WAD 11/30/89 850
On Bay of Chaleur, Stonehaven, New Brunswick; oil on board, sgn, 12x16", WAD 6/12/89 700
COLLIER, Evert (Dutch, -1702)
Vanitas Still Life with Armour & Chest Filled with Jewels, oil on canvas, sgn/dtd 1669, 33x46", SBY 6/3/88.......... 35,200
COLLIER, Imogen (British, 19th/20th C)
Pair: Duchess & Miss Barrie (racehorses); oil on canvas, sgn/dtd 1899, 12x15", SBY 6/8/88 1,980
COLLIER, John (British, 1850-1934)
Land Baby, oil on canvas, sgn/dtd 1921, 42x34", LH 10/16/88 UE 3,800
Portrait of Field Marshall BF Haines...; oil on canvas laid down on masonite, sgn/dtd 1891, 66x42", SBY 2/22/89 9,900
COLLIN, Louis Joseph Raphael (French, 1850-1916)
Young Arcadian Lovers, oil on canvas, sgn, 18x13", SBY 7/12/89.......... 3,300
COLLINA, Alberto (Italian, 19th C)
Reading to the Cardinal (interior scene), watercolor, sgn, 22x15", C-E 2/21/89.......... 550
COLLINS, Earl (American, Contemporary)
Portrait of the Clipper Ship Sea Witch, oil on canvas, sgn, 24x36", RAB 8/1/89 850
COLLINS, Sewell (American, 1876-)
Pair: A is for Adams; J is for Jefferson (poems); ink/watercolor/gouache/pencil on paper, sgn, 13x11", RWS 3/31/88 325
COLLINS, William (English, 1788-1847)
Children on the Isle of White Shore, oil on canvas, sgn/dtd 1835, 29x37", C-E 5/22/89 1,980
COLLINSON, J. (Continental School, 19th C)
Before the Race (trainer & horse), oil on board, sgn, 20x27", SBY 6/9/89 6,600
COLMAN, Samuel (American, 1832-1920)
Man in Native Dress, watercolor/gouache/pencil on paper, 11x6", SBY 6/28/89 605
Overlooking the City & Harbor, watercolor/pen/brown ink on paper laid down on board, sgn/dtd 1876, 12x22", C-NY 9/30/88 1,980
Study of Mt Tacoma, oil on canvas, sgn, 10x21", WD 4/13/88.......... 2,500
View of Lake Placid From Whiteface Mountain, Adirondacks; oil on canvas, sgn/dtd 1869, 16x30", C-NY 12/2/88 OE 35,200

View of Lincoln, England (cityscape); watercolor on paper, dtd 1876, 5x10", WL 5/20/88 UE 400

COLOMBEL, Nicolas (French, 1644-1717)

Noli Me Tangere, oil on canvas, 35x42", C-NY 10/20/88 4,400

COLOMBO, Virgilio (Italian, 19th C)

Peasant Girl Carrying Hay, watercolor on paper, sgn, 13x9", B/B 12/8/88 605

Colonial School (18th C)

Panel Depicting Four Saints, oil on canvas, 25x17", MG 3/26/88 UE 475

Colonial School (19th C)

Eimeo: Tahiti, the Residence of Mr & Mrs Elijah Armitage, 1820-1836; pencil/watercolor, 12x19", C-SK 11/10/88 1,670
Set of 4: South African Landscapes; pencil/watercolor heightened w/white, unfr, 10x15", C-SK 11/10/88 UE 150

COLT, John N. (20th C)

Abstract, mixed media on paper, sgn/dtd 1963, 19x25", S/A 2/18/89 25

COLT, Morgan (American, 1876-1926)

Ocean, Red Bank, New Jersey; oil on canvasboard, sgn, 12x16", C-NY 3/11/88 4,620

COLUNGA, Alejandro (Latin American, 20th C)

At the Movies (contemporary), oil on canvas, sgn/dtd 73/inscr Cabron & En el cine club, 40x32", SBY 11/21/88 7,150
Crazy Boy Playing with a Toy (surrealistic), mixed media on paper, sgn twice/dtd 82, #d 4/5, 26x24", SBY 5/16/89 2,750
Front & Back (surrealistic), mixed media on paper, sgn/dtd 1984/titled Caro e Nalga, 24x18", SBY 11/21/88 1,870
Moon Blowing Stars (surrealistic), oil on canvas, sgn/dtd 1988 twice/titled, 40x38", SBY 5/16/89 OE 20,900
Untitled (abstract), oil on canvas, sgn/dtd 1987, 80x63", SBY 5/17/88 OE 23,100

COLVIN

Picking Berries, oil on canvas, sgn, 30x20", C-E 10/25/88 1320 1,320

COMAN, Charlotte Buell (American, 1833-1924)

Cottage in a Landscape, oil on canvas, sgn, 16x20", C-E 11/30/88 UE 880
Cottage in a Landscape, oil on canvas, sgn, 17x21", C-E 11/30/88 2,640
Landscape with Cottage in the Distance, oil on canvas, sgn, 17x21", C-E 11/30/88 2,090

COMBAS, Robert (20th C)

Comando-Suicide! (expressionistic composition), oil/acrylic canvas, sgn, 1983, unfr, 76x61", C-E 11/14/89 OE 14,300
I Love the Beat, acrylic on fabric, unfr, 93x54", C-NY 11/10/88 OE 6,050
Reglement de Compte, acrylic on shaped canvas stretched over wood, sgn/dtd 83, unfr, 43x57", C-NY 5/4/89 OE 11,000
Untitled (contemporary), colored felt-tip pens on paper, sgn/dtd 82, 12x8", C-E 5/9/89 OE 3,080
Untitled (expressionistic composition), acrylic on canvas, sgn/dtd 84, unfr, 53x43", C-E 11/14/89 OE 14,300

COMERRE, Leon Francois (French, 1850-1916)

Ballerina's Dream, pen/black ink/watercolor, sgn twice, 23x15", C-NY 5/25/88 880
Favorite (three-quarter length portrait of a lady), oil on canvas, sgn, 48x30", SBY 2/22/89 30,250
Portrait of a Young Girl (half-length), oil on canvas, sgn, 26x20", B/B 3/22/89 4,675
The Sultan's Favorite, oil on canvas, sgn, 43x28", SBY 10/24/89 26,400

COMERRE-PATON, Jaqueline (French, 1859-)

At the Spring, oil on canvas, sgn, 50x72", SBY 10/24/89 13,200

Company School (ca 1790)

Mausoleum of Itimad-Ud-Daula, Agra; pencil/pen/black ink/watercolor, inscr/#d 97, 12x18", C-SK 5/25/89 90

COMPARD, Emile (French, 1900-)

Le Port, oil on canvas, sgn twice/inscr, 32x26", C-E 5/13/88 880

COMPTE-CALIX, Francois Claudius (French, 1813-1880)

Spanking (woman spanking child in a landscape w/figures beyond), oil on canvas, sgn, 32x24", C-NY 5/24/89 UE 7,700

COMPTON, Edward Theodore (British, 1849-1921)

Alpine Vista, Switzerland; oil on canvas, sgn, 19x31", C-NY 5/25/88 OE 11,000

COMTOIS, see Le Comtois

CONANT, Lucy Scarsborough (American, 1867-1921)

Country Haze, gouache on brown paper, sgn, 14x18", RWS 11/10/89 250

CONDAMY, see De Condamy

CONDO, George (American, 20th C)

Canard sur Guillotine, graphite/orange pencil on paper, sgn/dtd 1985, 12x9", C-E 5/9/89 OE 2,200
Improvisation IV: Animal Farm (abstract); oil/paper collage on canvas, sgn/dtd 84, 14x11", SBY 2/15/89 5,500
Three Dimensional Exercise #1 (abstract), oil on canvas, unfr, 60x48", C-NY 2/14/89 27,500
Untitled, watercolor/India ink on paper, dtd 11.84, 11x14", SBY 10/5/88 1,100
Untitled (abstract composition), oil on canvas, sgn/dtd 83-6-16, 48x36", SBY 2/15/89 22,000
Untitled (abstract man), oil on canvas, 18x14", SBY 10/8/88 7,975
Untitled (abstract), oil on canvas, sgn/dtd 83, 30x30", C-NY 11/10/88 OE 26,400
Untitled (abstract), oil on canvas, sgn/dtd 83, 46x47", SBY 5/3/89 OE 35,750
Untitled (contemporary), watercolor on paper, 26x20", C-E 5/9/89 OE 3,850
Untitled (fantasy composition), oil on canvas, dtd 11-83, 10x10", SBY 2/15/89 5,225
Untitled (fantasy drawing), watercolor/black ink on paper, dtd 11.84, 11x14", C-NY 5/4/89 OE 6,600
Untitled (head w/sad expression), oil on canvas, sgn/dtd 84, 13x9", C-NY 5/4/89 9,900

CONE, Marvin D. (American 1891-1965)

Saloon Interior-Charlie's Bar, oil on composition board, sgn, 13x15", LH 10/16/88 5,000

CONEGLIANO, see Da Conegliano

CONNARD, Philip (British, 1875-1958)

Windswept (figures & dog on knoll looking over valley), oil on canvas, sgn, 30x40", SBY 10/24/89 14,300

CONNAWAY, Jay Hall (American, 1893-1970)

Against the Wind (contemporary landscape), oil on canvas, sgn, 9x16", RWS 3/16/89 OE 1,800

Landscape (stream leads to view of trees & mountain range), oil on board, sgn/dtd 27, 12x15", RWS 3/31/88 ... 650
Monhegan Surf 1946 (waves crashing over rocky shore), oil on board, sgn, 16x20", RWS 9/29/88 ... 900
Squeaker Cove, Monhegan, Maine (waves crashing over rocks); oil on canvasboard, sgn, 16x20", C-E 2/1/89 ... 3,080
Sunlit Spray, oil on board, sgn/dtd 44/titled, 18x24", RAB 3/27/89 UE ... 600

CONNELL, Edwin D. (American, 1859-)
Summer Landscape with Church, oil on canvas, sgn, 18x24", SBY 9/14/89 ... 3,575

CONNELLY, Chuck (American, 20th C)
Merry-Go-Round, oil on canvas, sgn/dtd 1984, unfr, 63x71", C-NY 5/4/88 ... 3,850
Milk Shaker (contemporary), oil on canvas, sgn/dtd 85, 66x109", SBY 2/19/88 ... 6,050
Study for Weather of the World, oil on canvas, sgn/dtd 1986, unfr, 9x22", C-E 5/13/88 UE ... 550

CONNER, Bruce (American, 1909-)
Black Collage, mixed media collage on masonite, sgn/dtd 1959, 12x9", SBY 10/5/89 OE ... 9,350
Hearts, mixed media on board, 22x17", SBY 10/5/89 ... 15,400
Saturday Night Collage, mixed media on composition board in wood & glass box, sgn/dtd 1959, 23x16x4", SBY 10/5/89 ... 12,100

CONNER, John Anthony (American, 1932-)
Mojave Desert Landscape, oil on canvas, sgn, 20x24", B/B 1/11/89 ... 468
Palm Springs Desert Landscape, oil on board, sgn, 20x24", B/B 10/6/88 ... 770
Purple Desert Mountain, oil on board, sgn, 16x14", B/B 10/6/88 ... 495

CONNER, John Ramsey (American, 1867-1952)
Husbandry (two figures in a landscape), oil on canvas, sgn/dtd 1939, 30x25", WL 5/20/88 UE ... 250

CONRADI, H.
Grand Canal, Venice; oil on canvas, sgn, 15x31", C-E 5/23/88 ... 2,640

CONSTABLE, John; att (British, 1776-1837)
Flatford Mill From the Lock, oil on canvas, 18x26", FB 10/11/88 ... 1,100

CONSTABLE, John; follower of (British, 1776-1837)
Landscape with Church, oil on canvas, 32x45", SBY 6/8/88 ... 990

CONSTABLE, John; school of (British, 1776-1837)
Farmhouse with an Extensive Landscape, oil on canvas, 21x31", C-E 1/12/88 UE ... 605
Hilly Landscape with a Traveler in the Foreground, oil on canvas, 13x20", C-NY 10/12/89 ... 1,100

CONSTANT
Vase of Flowers, watercolor/pen/colored ink on paper, sgn, 31x22", C-E 6/28/88 ... 352

CONSTANT, Benjamin (French, 1845-1902)
Blue Turban (portrait of a woman), oil on canvas, sgn, 22x18", SBY 2/22/89 ... 6,600
Head of a Woman, left profile, pen/black ink/brown wash, sgn/dtd 1892, 9x7", C-NY 2/25/88 ... 990
Moor Sitting by a Fire, oil on canvas, sgn, 26x37", C-E 10/25/88 ... 3,080
Portrait of a Seated Woman, oil on canvas, sgn, 46x26", LH 5/15/88 ... 9,000

CONSTANT, David Adolf
Mealtime, oil on canvas, sgn, 32x46", C-E 10/25/88 ... 5,500

CONSTANTIN, S. (European, 19th C)
Pleasant Roadside Pause (elderly couple in landscape), oil on canvas, sgn, 29x40", RAB 3/27/89 UE ... 400
Untitled, fisherfolk beginning the day; oil on canvas, 23x31", SLK 11/25/88 ... 2,000

CONSTANTINEAU, Fleurimond (Canadian, 1905-1981)
Campement Indian de Fort Rupert, Baie James (Indian encampment); oil on board, sgn/dtd 1970, 20x32", FB 5/89 ... 260
L'Iglou de Voyage, Maricourt, Nouveau Quebec; oil on board, sgn/dtd 1968, 10x12", FB 10/30/89 ... 302
Paysage de Godthab, Groenland; oil on board, sgn/dtd 1973, 10x12", FB 10/30/89 ... 330
Rue St-Paul, Montreal; oil on board, sgn/dtd 1936, 14x18", FB 4/25/88 ... 280

CONSTANTINI, Guiseppe (Italian, 19th C)
Little Vanity & the Old Mirror, oil on panel, sgn/dtd 1877, 11x15", SBY 6/8/88 OE ... 6,050

CONTCHAROVA, Natalia (Russian, 1881-1962)
Bouteille (still life), oil on canvas, sgn/dtd 1911, 16x10", C-NY 2/18/88 ... 4,950
Composition-I (abstract), oil on panel, initialed, 8x4", C-L 10/8/88 ... 4,460
Composition-II (abstract), oil on panel, 8x4", C-L 10/8/88 ... 4,460
Cubist Figure, colored crayon on paper, sgn, ca 1916-18, 14x10", C-L 10/8/88 OE ... 12,640
L'Espagnole (full-length portrait of Spanish woman in profile), oil on canvas, sgn, 45x23", C-NY 2/16/89 OE ... 38,200
Le Coq d'Or; The Backdrop From Act III; peinture a la detrempe on canvas, 1914, 36ft-4x58ft, C-L 10/8/88 ... 13,000
Spanish Portrait (of a lady), black crayon on paper, sgn/dtd 1915, 13x10", C-L 10/8/88 ... 4,460

CONTI, Antonio (18th C)
Trompe l'Oeil Composition with a Map...; brown ink/watercolor, sgn/dtd 1760, 18x24", SBY 4/7/88 OE ... 3,575

CONTI, Francesco; circle of
Allegory of the Four Continents, oil on canvas, 23x54", C-NY 10/20/88 ... 7,700

CONTI, Gino
Children Playing with a Bird, oil on canvas, sgn, 28x38", C-E 5/23/88 ... 2,750

CONTI, Primo (Italian, 1900-)
Reclining Nude, oil on canvas, sgn/dtd 1947, 12x16", SBY 10/7/89 ... 4,400
Table in an Artist's Studio, oil on canvas, sgn/dtd 1947, 20x26", SBY 10/7/89 ... 2,750

CONTI, Tito (Italian, 1842-1924)
Cavalier, oil on cradled panel, sgn/dtd 1874, 14x9", C-E 10/25/88 UE ... 715
Cavalier Playing a Lute, oil on panel, sgn/indistinctly inscr, 13x10", C-E 10/25/88 ... 3,520

Continental School, after Raphael (1510-1512)
Madonna de Gran Duca, oil on canvas, 32x22", MG 12/10/88 UE ... 500
Madonna Della Sedia, oil on canvas, 28" dia, MG 12/10/88 UE ... 450

Continental School (17th C)

Portrait of Lorenzo, oil on canvas, 23x19", RWS 7/8/89 ... 550
Still Life of Fruit & Other Objects, oil on canvas on beaverboard, unfr, 34x45", RAB 11/25/88 OE ... 16,000

Continental School (18th C)

Bouquet of Flowers in an Ornate Urn, oil on canvas laid down, unfr, 54x39", B/B 3/22/89 ... 9,350
Fishing Along the River (two figures in landscape), oil on board, 4x6", RAB 8/8/89 ... 1,200
House of Cards, oil on canvas, painted faux marble fr, 32x29", RWS 6/17/89 OE ... 3,000
Lovers (bust-length portrait of couple), oil on board, 10x8", RAB 8/8/89 ... 600
Madonna & Child with Attendents, oil on canvas, 37x31", WG 4/23/88 UE ... 500
Portrait of a Child with Fruit & Flowers, oil on canvas, indistinctly inscr/dtd 1716, 26x19", SBY 12/9/88 ... 1,045
Portrait of a Lady, oil on canvas, ca 1700, 32x26", SBY 7/12/89 ... 1,650
Portrait of Young Boy with Cat, oil on canvas, indistinctly sgn, 16x12", WG 4/23/88 UE ... 500
Study of Religious Figures, oil on panel, 11x15", FAP 4/15/89 ... 632
Temptation, sleeping man tormented by semi-nude women; oil on canvas, 36x29", RAB 3/27/89 ... 1,200

Continental School (18th/19th C)

Bear Baiting, oil on panel, 10x13", B/B 5/17/89 UE ... 247
Classical Ruins, oil on canvas, 18x23", FAP 4/15/89 OE ... 3,190

Continental School (19th C)

Allegorical Figure, oil on canvas laid down on panel, indistinctly sgn/dtd 1866, oval, 16x13", C-E 5/23/88 ... 660
Alpine Scene, oil on panel, indistinctly sgn, 7x10", B/B 12/8/88 ... 412
Barnyard Fowl, oil on board, indistinctly sgn, 4x4", SBY 7/12/89 OE ... 1,320
Beautiful Water Bearer, oil on canvas, 72x56", B/B 1/11/89 OE ... 3,300
Beauty in a Classical Garden, oil on canvas, ornate gilt fr, 31x25", RWS 5/12/89 ... 1,600
Birth of Christ, figures surround the Christ Child w/angels above; oil on canvas, 22x14", RAB 3/27/89 ... 450
Capture of Christ, group of men surround Christ before stone building; oil on canvas, 18x15", RAB 8/8/89 UE ... 125
Carnival in Rome, oil on canvas, 35x27", SBY 2/22/89 ... 7,150
Cavalier Having a Drink, oil on board, oval, 9x7", FAP 4/15/89 ... 330
Children Dancing, oil on canvas, 10x14", PHL 6/16/88 ... 425
Christ with the Elders, oil on canvas, 40x60", B/B 6/15/89 ... 3,300
Circumcision of Christ, oil on canvas, 26x33", B/B 1/11/89 OE ... 1,045
Classical Landscape (figures & deer in landscape), oil on canvas, 20x15", RAB 3/27/89 ... 1,100
Clipper in Full Sail, oil on canvas, 10x14", B/B 5/17/89 OE ... 1,320
Concert, oil on panel, indistinctly sgn, 13x17", C-E 9/15/88 ... 880
Cottages in a Landscape, oil on canvas, sgn, 10x15", C-E 11/8/88 ... 300
Country Estate (landscape), oil on canvas, 14x20", RAB 8/8/89 OE ... 1,200
Country Genre Scene, Country Road (cattle in a landscape), oil on canvas, 18x22", WG 4/23/88 UE ... 300
Couple with a Dog, oil on canvas, 28x19", MG 10/28/88 OE ... 3,100
Courtly Love, oil on panel, monogramed, 28x23", SBY 7/12/89 UE ... 1,980
Courtyard with Garden & Chickens, oil on canvasboard, bears signature Otto Pfeiffer, 11x9", RWS 3/16/89 OE ... 800
Cows in the Shade, oil on canvas, 26x40", C-E 6/28/88 ... 1,320
Cupid with His Bow, oil on canvas, 9x11", MG 12/10/88 UE ... 150
Ducks Wading, oil on canvas, unfr, 18x25", C-E 5/23/88 ... 1,650
Elaborate Still Life, oil on canvas, 37x40", C-E 5/3/88 ... 825
Elaborate Still Life of Flowers in a Vase, oil on metal, 28x22", C-E 2/23/88 ... 1,650
Final Lesson (young man studying at his desk), oil on canvas, indistinctly sgn/dtd 1899, unfr, 27x39", SBY 7/12/89 ... 1,650
First Snow (village in landscape), oil on board, 9x12", RAB 8/8/89 ... 2,000
Floral Still Life, oil on panel, 14x10", LH 9/10/89 OE ... 1,100
Flower Girl, oil on canvas, 26x19", FAP 4/15/89 ... 495
Fortified Chinese Town, oil on canvas, 20x32", C-SK 11/10/88 OE ... 16,730
Frederick the Great, oil on canvas, framed as an arch, 47x29", C-E 11/8/88 ... 1,430
Girl at the Well (girl in red/white/green dress with copper jug at well), oil on board, sgn WMF, 12x10", RAB 8/8/89 UE ... 125
Goat Herder with Dog, ink/wash on paper, 7x10", C-E 2/16/88 ... 55
Holy Family, oil on canvas, 39x31", B/B 9/15/88 OE ... 3,025
In the Picture Gallery, oil on canvas, 26x32", SBY 10/24/89 ... 6,600
Indians on Horseback, oil on canvas, unfr, 54x67", SBY 4/29/88 ... 23,100
Landscape with Figures, oil on canvas, 28x40", SBY 7/12/89 ... 1,430
Landscape with Mountains, Travelers, & a Ruin; oil on panel, 6x9", SBY 12/9/88 ... 660
Landscape with Old Woman, oil on board, unfr, 10x7", C-E 1/12/88 ... 242
Lesson, oil on canvas, 28x40", C-E 5/23/88 ... 1,870
Madonna (portrait), oil on canvas, oval, 28", SLK 2/12/88 ... 175
Madonna with Christ as Papal Figure, oil on canvas, 50x38", MG 10/28/88 ... 2,200
Maids Interlude, oil on canvas, indistinctly sgn, 27x19", WG 4/23/88 ... 425
Man & Woman in an Interior, oil on canvas, 29x24", SBY 12/9/88 OE ... 1,760
Mary with Jesus, oil on canvas, sgn, 30x40", MG 3/26/88 ... 500
Miser (elderly man in tall black hat), oil on canvas laid down on board, 11x8", RAB 8/8/89 ... 550
Mother & Child in an Interior, oil on canvas, 13x10", B/B 9/15/88 UE ... 440
Native Woman in the Jungle, oil on canvas, indistinctly sgn, unfr, 27x41", C-SK 11/10/88 ... 710
North Italian Riverscape, oil on canvas, 17x26", RAB 11/25/88 ... 600
Off To Battle (uniformed officer w/other figures in interior), oil on canvas, 38x60", RAB 8/8/89 UE ... 2,000
Old Stone Church (in landscape), oil on canvas, 12x14", RAB 8/8/89 ... 750

Pair: David & Bathesheba; pastel on woven paper, 9x13", B/B 1/11/89 1,320
Pair: Elaborate Still Lifes of Flowers in an Urn; oil on canvas, 81x40", C-E 5/23/88 5,280
Pair: Landscapes with Villages; oil on panel, oval, 25x35", B/B 5/17/89 UE 660
Pair: Portraits Depicting an Elderly Man & a Young Man; oil on canvas, 8x7", MG 10/28/88 700
Pair: Tavern Scenes; oil on canvas, 13x24", C-E 2/23/88 OE 1,210
Pair: Untitled (children playing dice; lady feeding parrot); oil on tin, unfr, 8x7", RAB 6/27/89 OE 800
Pair: Woman Spinning Flax; Goat Herder; oil on canvas, unfr, 17x13", FAP 4/15/89 358
Peasant Girl with Sheaf of Wheat, oil on canvas, sgn, gilt gesso frame, 19x13", RWS 9/8/89 UE 450
Piazza San Marco, oil on canvas, 19x24", SBY 6/8/88 OE 2,530
Playing with the Baby, oil on canvas, indistinctly sgn, 22x31", C-E 9/15/88 990
Portrait of a Woman Holding a Peach, oil on canvas, 41x39", MG 10/28/88 2,700
Portrait of a Woman in a Black Ball Gown, oil on canvas, 90x65", B/B 3/22/89 3,025
Portrait of a Young Girl, pastel, 18x22", LH 5/15/88 375
Portrait of a Young Girl & Her Dog, oil on canvas, 36x28", B/B 5/17/89 OE 1,210
Portrait of a Young Girl by Candlelight, pastel on paper, 18x15", B/B 12/8/88 605
Portrait of an Elderly Lady in a Red Shawl, oil on canvas, oval, 25x20", B/B 1/11/89 440
Portrait of an Officer, oil on canvas, 30x25", SBY 6/8/88 1,540
Portrait of Franz Schubert, oil on canvas, 27x22", SBY 7/12/89 4,125
Rabbits & Pigeon in a landscape, oil on canvas, indistinctly sgn, 15x19", RAB 3/27/89 750
Rowboat on a Wooded River, oil on canvas, 9x12", C-E 9/15/88 UE 330
Saint Sebastian, oil on paper, 17x10", B/B 1/11/89 468
Samson & Goliath, mixed media, 35x31", FAP 4/15/89 UE 192
Sheep in a Meadow, oil on wood panel, indistinctly sgn, unfr, 21x26", RAB 3/27/89 2,100
Still Life of Flowers & Fruit, oil on canvas, 38x28", RAB 3/27/89 500
Still Life of Lobster & Tankard, oil on canvas, 30x23", MG 10/28/88 1,100
Still Life of Roses in an Oriental Vase, oil on canvas, indistinctly initialed, 19x15", C-E 5/23/88 1,760
Still Life of Tea Service (w/flowers on a table), oil on canvas, 23x28", WG 4/23/88 525
Study of a Hand, charcoal on paper, initialed/dtd 1889, oval, 20x16", C-E 4/7/88 UE 110
Summer Landscape, oil on canvas laid down on board, 25x29", RAB 1/18/89 UE 400
Summer Landscape with Cows Watering Along River, oil on canvas, indistinctly sgn/dtd, 23x31", SBY 7/12/89 1,320
Venice Scene, oil on canvas, 34x51", lot 252, RAB 4/25/89 OE 425
Village Scene, oil on panel, indistinctly inscr, 11x15", SBY 12/9/88 605
Watching the Herd (couple w/sheep in a landscape), oil on panel, 29x41", B/B 6/15/89 2,200
Woman Playing Mandolin to Lover, oil on board, 57x38", FAP 4/15/89 798
Young Boys at Picnic, oil on board, 8x7", FAP 4/15/89 UE 440

Continental School (19th/20th C)

City Snowfall, oil on board, indistinctly sgn, 9x11", RWS 11/10/89 1,000
Monk Reading Above the Sea, watercolor on paper, sgn, 6x4", FAP 4/15/89 82
Portrait of a Gentleman with White Collar, oil on canvas, indistinctly sgn, 10x8", B/B 1/11/89 550
Seated Pekinese, oil on canvas, 25x30", SBY 6/8/88 UE 770
Tavern Scene, oil on canvas, 25x37", SBY 7/12/89 330

Continental School (20th C)

Bridge in Summer, oil on canvas, sgn/dtd 1908, 21x18", RWS 5/12/89 OE 850
Children Beside a Garden Pond, oil on canvas, 12x15", B/B 1/11/89 UE 192
Impressionist View of Coast, oil on board, indistinctly sgn, 16x11", FAP 4/15/89 UE 100
Pair: Mediterranean Harbor Views; gouache on paper laid down, 8x11", FAP 4/15/89 798
Sentry (uniformed figures/officer on horseback in winter landscape), oil on canvas, 8x11", RAB 3/27/89 UE 300
Venetian Canal Scene (boats w/apartments & buildings in background), oil on board, sgn, 33x25", RWS 3/31/88 950
Victorian Maiden, oil on canvas, 28x16", FAP 4/15/89 302

CONWAY, Fred (American, 1900-1972)

Untitled, street scene in Maux, France; watercolor, sgn/titled, 15x19", SLK 2/11/89 2,000
Urban Scene, watercolor, sgn, 16x20", SLK 9/26/88 300

CONWAY, John Severinus (American, 1852-1925)

Colosseum, oil on canvas, sgn/dtd 84, 28x42", WD 10/5/88 5,500
Reclining Nude, oil on canvas, sgn/inscr, 15x24", C-NY 9/30/88 3,520

CONYERS, Alfred (American, 20th C)

Rockport, Massachusetts, 1945; graphite on artist board, sgn/dtd 1945, 12x18", WG 10/19/88 50

COOK, Howard (American, 20th C)

Merchant, charcoal on paper, sgn, 11x7", C-E 6/1/89 OE 990
Waterfall, pastel on paper, sgn, 29x20", B/B 12/8/88 880

COOK, John A. (American, 1870-1936)

Sailboats at Sunset, watercolor on paper, sgn, 20x15", C-E 2/1/89 605

COOK, Nelson (American, 1817-1892)

Portrait of a Gentleman, study of handsome man in black suit, seated; oil on canvas, sgn/dtd 1852, 29x25", RAB 11/24/89 500

COOKE, Edward William (British, 1811-1880)

Beach Scene with Ships, oil on panel, sgn, 7x10", LH 9/10/89 OE 550
Tower of Francis I at Havre, watercolor/gouache/pencil on paper, sgn/dtd 64/inscr, 8x9", C-NY 5/24/89 1,540

COOKE, George (American, 1793-1849)

Shipping in Coastal Waters, oil on canvas, sgn, 20x30", SLK 9/27/88 700

COOKE, George; att (American, 1793-1849)

Mount Parnassus, oil on canvas, inscr, 32x46", SBY 6/24/88 UE 1,760

COOKESLEY, Margaret Murray (English, 19th C)
Nubian Beauty (draped nude standing by large vase), oil on canvas, sgn/dtd 1886, 16x12", C-E 2/21/89 3,520
COOKMAN, Charles Edwin (American, 1856-1913)
Violinist, oil on canvas, sgn/dtd 1880, 14x9", C-E 2/16/88 495
COOL, Delphine; see De Cool
COOLE, Brian (American/British, 19th/20th C)
American Sailing Ship, oil on canvas, sgn, 16x24", LH 12/4/88 1,300
American Sailing Ship, oil on canvas, sgn, 16x30", LH 12/4/88 OE 1,700
Erie (19th C style portrait of American frigate), watercolor on plywood, sgn/titled, 15x21", RAB 3/14/89 400
Fleet of Warships at Sea, oil on canvas, sgn, 20x30", LH 12/4/88 OE 357
Three-Masted Man of War Entering a Harbor, oil on canvas, sgn, 20x30", SLK 9/28/88 1,200
COOLIDGE, Cassius Marcellus (American, 1844-1934)
Portrait of Girl Feeding Her Doll, oil on canvas, sgn, 41x32", SBY 9/14/89 4,400
COOLIDGE, Rosamond (American, 1884-)
Bridge, Fenway Promenade Bridge; oil on canvasboard, sgn, 8x10", RWS 11/10/89 UE 200
COOMANS
Artemis & Cupid, oil on canvas, sgn/dtd 1883, 24x20", LH 10/16/88 OE 2,200
COOMANS, Auguste (Belgian, 1855-)
Sheep & Chickens in a Pasture, oil on board, sgn, 17x23", WD 3/23/88 UE 800
COOMANS, Pierre Olivier Joseph (Belgian, 1816-1889)
After the Bath, oil on canvas, sgn/dtd 1858, 41x33", SBY 10/24/89 UE 3,850
Harvest of Plums, oil on panel, sgn/dtd 1874, 19x14", C-NY 2/25/88 OE 11,000
Homer (figures in landscape), oil on canvas, sgn/dtd 1877, 24x36", RWS 5/19/88 OE 7,000
COOMBS, Delbert Dana (American, 1850-1936)
Driving the Herd Home (farmer & dog w/cattle, landscape beyond), oil on canvas, sgn/dtd 1915, 16x14", RWS 3/31/88 UE 450
Study of Cows, oil on canvas, sgn/dtd 1921, 32x27", RWS 5/12/89 1,200
COONAN, Emily (Canadian, 1885-1971)
Landscape of Land & Sea, oil on panel, sgn, 10x14", FB 4/25/88 425
COOPER, Abraham (British, 1784-1868)
Out for Coursing (three gentlemen, two on horses w/dogs in a landscape), oil on canvas, 28x36", B/B 6/15/89 OE 17,600
COOPER, Alfred Heaton (American, 1864-1929)
Steamship in Icy Waters, watercolor/gouache on board, sgn, 15x22", RWS 11/10/89 450
COOPER, Astley David Montague (American, 1856-1924)
Landscape with Buffalo & Dead Indian, oil on canvas, sgn, 31x48", SBY 6/28/89 1,870
Portrait of an Indian with Shield, oil on canvas, sgn, 24x20", SBY 1/24/89 770
COOPER, Colin Campbell (American, 1856-1937)
An Afternoon Stroll, gouache/watercolor on paper, sgn/dtd 1916, 18x22", B/B 3/22/89 OE 14,300
At Clisson, France (landscape with bridge & buildings); oil on panel, sgn, 7x12", B/B 10/9/88 2,750
Cafes Along the Water, oil on canvas laid down on board, sgn, 15x18", C-E 6/1/89 OE 3,850
Cathedral Interior, watercolor/charcoal on paper laid down on board, sgn, 18x15", C-E 6/1/89 660
Central Park in Winter, oil on canvas, sgn, 26x21", SBY 5/25/88 OE 44,000
Man, Horse, & Cart on Country Road; watercolor on paper mounted on board, sgn, 13x19", FAP 11/4/88 750
New England Farm, oil on canvas laid down on board, sgn/dtd 1903, 23x29", C-NY 9/30/88 5,500
North African Market Scene (busy street scene), oil on board, sgn, 10x14", B/B 10/9/88 2,750
Portrait of Thomas Lipton, watercolor/gouache/charcoal on paper, sgn/dtd 1914, 16x12", B/B 8/10/88 495

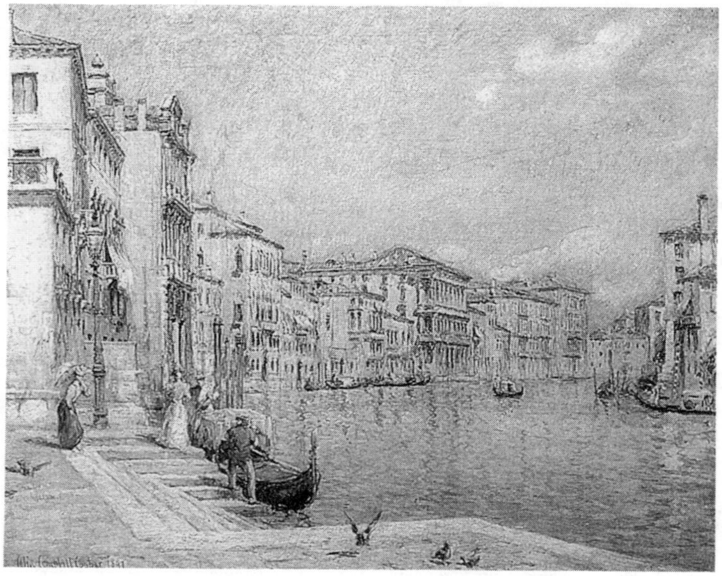

Steps of the Academy, Venice; oil on canvas, sgn/dtd 1897, 21x25", WD 10/5/88, $55,000

COOPER, Edwin (British, 1785-1833)
Gray Hunter with a Bay Pony in a Paddock, oil on canvas, 24x33", SBY 6/9/89 ... 4,400
COOPER, Emma Lampert (American, 1860-1920)
Pair: River Landscapes; oil on canvasboard, sgn, 15x21", B/B 3/22/89 ... 2,200
COOPER, Henry (British, 20th C)
Cottage by a Stream, oil on canvas, sgn, 21x31", C-E 2/16/88 ... 605
Fishing the Stream, oil on canvas, sgn, 16x24", SBY 6/8/88 ... 1,100
COOPER, M. (American, 19th/20th C)
Indian Camp on a Lake, oil on canvas, sgn/inscr, 18x15", SBY 6/24/88 OE ... 880
COOPER, Richard (British, 18th/19th C)
Cabin in the Woods, oil on canvas, sgn, 16x20", LH 10/16/88 ... 475
COOPER, Rita (Dutch, 20th C)
Woman in a Field of Spring Flowers, oil on canvas, sgn, 24x36", B/B 1/11/89 ... 1,210
COOPER, Thomas George (British, fl 1857-1896)
Highland Rams, oil on canvas, sgn/dtd 1893, 36x24", SBY 12/9/88 UE ... 1,540
COOPER, Thomas Sidney (British, 1803-1902)
Canterbury Sheep, oil on panel, sgn/dtd 1870, 12x16", B/B 3/22/89 ... 3,850
Carthorse & Sheep by a Box, oil on panel, sgn/dtd 1873, 10x8", C-NY 5/... 4,620
Cow & Sheep by a Coast, oil on panel, sgn/dtd 1863, 13x21", C-NY 2/25/... 9,900
Cows & Sheep in a Landscape, watercolor over traces of pencil, sgn/dtd ... 13x17", C-NY 2/25/88 ... 1,870
Flock of Sheep in a Landscape, oil on canvas, sgn/dtd 1872, 24x36", C-NY ... /88 ... 8,250
Old Mill, oil on canvas, sgn/dtd 1834, 20x28", C-NY 2/25/88 OE ... 11,000
Pastoral Landscape with Cows, oil on canvas, sgn/dtd 1893, 24x36", DM ... 13,000
Sheep & Cow Watering, oil on panel, sgn/inscr/dtd 1875, 9x12", C-E 5/23 ... 3,960
Summer Afternoon (cows at water's edge), oil on panel, sgn/dtd 1882, 9x... C-NY 2/23/89 ... 4,950
COOPER, Thomas Sidney; att (British, 1803-1902)
Highland Sheep (close-up in landscape), oil on board, sgn, 8x10", C-E 2/2... 9 UE ... 1,430
COOPER, Thomas Sidney; follower of (British, 1803-1902)
Sheep in a Landscape, oil on panel, bears signature, 11x16", C-E 3/22/88 ... 880
COORMAN, C.E.
Pond, oil on canvas, sgn/dtd 1884, 10x20", C-E 10/18/89 ... 3,080
COPE, Charles West (British, 1811-1890)
Othello Relating His Adventures, oil on canvas, sgn w/monogram/dtd 1855, 42x55", C-E 5/23/88 ... 4,620
COPE, George (American, 1855-1929)
Elk in Clearing, oil on canvas, sgn/dtd 07, 27x22", SBY 3/17/88 ... 3,740
COPE, Gordon Nicholson (American, 1906-1970)
Maroon Creek, Aspen, Colorado; oil on board, sgn/dtd 1932, 30x36", B/B 6/15/89 UE ... 3,850
COPELAND
Still Life of Flowers, Hat & Gloves; oil on canvas, sgn, 24x20", LH 12/4/88 ... 120
COPELAND, Alfred Bryant (American, 1840-1909)
Concert (soldier singing before group, lady at piano), oil on canvas, sgn/dtd 1894, 30x37", RAB 8/9/88 ... 1,600
Curious (English Setter sniffing rooster perched on cage), oil on canvas, 6x8", RAB 8/9/88 ... 475
Paris, oil on board, sgn/dtd 1877, 9x14", WD 5/5/88 OE ... 8,750
COPLEY, John Singleton (American, 1737-1815)
Study of a Child, charcoal/white chalk on gray-brown paper, sgn twice/dtd June 25 1752/inscr, unfr, 12x17", C-SK 6/9/88 ... 1,580
COPLEY, William (American, 1919-)
Chelsea Girls, acrylic on canvas, sgn/dtd 73/#d 24, unfr, 45x58", C-E 11/17/88 OE ... 4,620
I Remember Cuba (expressionistic composition), acrylic on canvas, sgn/dtd 63, 32x25", C-E 11/14/89 OE ... 3,520
La Reine Midas, Iris Joyeuse; acrylic/sand on canvas, sgn/dtd 61, 39x32", C-E 11/14/89 ... 3,080
Migilla Gorilla (contemporary), acrylic on canvas, sgn/dtd 66, 77x59", SBY 11/11/88 OE ... 19,800
Think Mort aux Vaches, black crayon on paper, sgn/dtd 65, 14x10", SBY 10/7/89 ... 330
Tomb of the Unknown Whore (contemporary), oil on canvas, sgn/dtd 65, 46x65", SBY 11/11/88 ... 9,900
Untitled (bare-breasted native woman), oil/mixed media on canvas, sgn/dtd 1959, 45x35", SBY 11/11/88 OE ... 9,350
Untitled (contemporary), oil on canvas, sgn/dtd 60, 24x29", SBY 10/8/88 UE ... 2,750
Untitled (contemporary), oil/lace collage on canvas, sgn/dtd 62, 30x40", SBY 10/5/89 ... 7,700
Untitled (woman wearing garter, looking through camera), acrylic on canvas, sgn/dtd 74, 46x35", SBY 2/15/89 ... 3,300
COPP, William S. (American, 1891-)
Threshing (men working in field), oil on canvas, sgn, 36x32", RWS 9/8/89 ... 700
COPPEDGE, Fern Isabel (American, 1888-1951)
Fishing Fleet, Gloucester; oil on canvas, sgn twice/inscr/titled, 8x10", SBY 3/17/88 ... 1,210
Landscape with Foreground Buildings & Rolling Hills, oil on canvas, sgn, 9x11", SLK 2/12/88 ... 375
Little Stone House (winter landscape), oil on canvasboard, 16x13", SBY 3/17/88 OE ... 2,310
Lobster Cove (dock scene), oil on canvas, sgn twice/inscr New Hope PA/titled, 25x30", SBY 3/17/88 ... 3,740
Pennsylvania Hills Near New Hope, oil on canvas, sgn/inscr, 20x24", C-NY 9/30/88 ... 3,080
Spring at St David's (landscape), oil on canvas, sgn/titled, 16x16", SBY 3/17/88 ... 2,200
Village on the Delaware River, New Hope, Pennsylvania; oil on canvas, sgn, 25x30", C-NY 9/30/88 ... 3,850
Winter Mist on the Canal, oil on canvas laid down on board, sgn, 14x16", WG 4/23/88 OE ... 2,200
COPPER, Colin Campbell (American, 1856-1937)
Afternoon in the Tuileries, oil on canvas, sgn/dtd Paris 1896, 18x26", WD 10/5/88 UE ... 18,000
COPPINI, G. (Italian, 19th C)
Still Life of Birds, oil on board, sgn/dtd 1874, oval, 11x9", SBY 12/9/88 ... 1,100

COQUES, Gonzales; manner of (Flemish, 1614-1684)
Portrait of a Woman, standing, three-quarter length, holding flowers; oil on canvas, 40x32", C-NY 4/8/88 3,850

COQUES, Gonzales; school of (Flemish, 1614-1684)
Portrait of a Young Nobleman, oil on panel, 18x14", RWS 5/12/89 750

CORBELLINI, Luigi (Italian/French, 1901-1968)
Girl with a Bird, oil on canvas, sgn, 22x18", DM 5/13/88 650
Girl with Lute, oil on canvas, sgn, 30x21", SBY 10/7/89 3,190
Harlequin Bleu, oil on canvas, sgn, 14x11", FAP 4/15/89 468
Paris Street Scene, oil on canvas, sgn, 20x25", B/B 1/11/89 330
Winter Afternoon on a Paris Street, oil on canvas, sgn, 26x20", B/B 1/11/89 UE 440

CORBETT, Edward (American, 1919-1971)
Untitled (abstract), pastel/charcoal on paper, sgn/dtd 51, 25x19", SBY 2/19/88 OE 770

CORBETT, Josephine Gilmer
Daydreaming, oil on canvas, sgn, 30x24", C-E 11/30/88 1,650

CORBOULD, Aster (British, 19th C)
Suffolk Farm (buildings & cattle in an extensive landscape), oil on canvas, sgn/dtd, 24x42", B/B 10/9/88 1,650

CORBUSIER, see Le Corbusier

CORCOS, Lucille (American, 1908-1973)
Poker Game, tempera/ink on board, sgn/dtd 47, 12x16", WD 4/13/88 2,000

CORCOS, Vittorio (Italian, 1859-1933)
In the Garden (lady seated on bench, flowers in lap), oil on canvas, sgn/dtd 92, 42x30", SBY 10/24/89 23,100

CORDERO, Francisco (Mexican, 19th C)
Spring Landscape, oil, sgn, 14x26", WD 1/11/89 1,800

CORELLI, Augusto (Italian, 1853-1910)
Arab Sentry (leaning against a wall), watercolor over pencil, sgn, 21x13", C-NY 10/26/88 1,100

CORIA, Benjamin
Reclining Female Nude, oil on canvas, sgn/dtd 1925, 26x46", C-SK 11/10/88 OE 3,900

CORINTH, Lovis (German, 1857-)
Pair: Domestic Scenes; graphite on paper, 11x17", 16x12", B/B 1/11/89 880

CORIS, Nicholas; see De Coris

CORMACK, Neil (fl 1818-1837)
Lion Attacking an Ox, pencil/watercolor, ca 1820, unfr, 18x26", C-SK 5/25/89 1,650

CORMON, Fernand Anne Piestre (French, 1854-1924)
Artist's Daughter Fishing, oil on canvas, sgn/indistinctly dtd, 22x26", C-NY 2/25/88 4,620
La Modele (portrait), oil on canvas, sgn/dtd 1905, 24x29", SBY 2/22/89 27,500

CORNEILLE, Cornelius Guillaume Van Beverloo (Spanish, 1922-)
Blue Bird (abstract), on paper, sgn/dtd 69, 19x19", SBY 10/7/89 10,450
Jardin Errant, gouache/pencil over lithography on paper, sgn/dtd 62, unfr, 13x10", C-E 11/17/88 OE 4,620
Les Petales du Soleil, oil on canvas, sgn/dtd twice 70, inscr, 40x32", C-NY 5/4/88 OE 22,000

CORNEILLE DE LYON, & Studio (Flemish, -1574)
Portrait of Count Charles de la Rochefaucauld (bust-length), oil on panel, C-NY 6/2/88 OE 99,000

CORNEILLE DE LYON, att (Flemish, -1574)
Portrait of a Bearded Man, bust-length, wearing black jacket & feathered cap; oil on panel, 7x5", C-NY 6/2/88 33,000
Portrait of a Lady, wearing blue costume & gold necklace, holding a dog; oil on panel, 6x6", C-NY 6/2/88 OE 209,000
Portrait of a Man, wearing a dark doublet & cap, oil on copper, 7x6", C-NY 1/15/88 OE 13,750

CORNEILLE DE LYON, school of (Flemish, -1574)
Portrait of a Gentleman, half-length, wearing a black costume & hat; oil on panel, inscr, 8x6", C-NY 10/20/88 5,500

CORNEILLE DE LYON (Flemish, -1574)
Portrait of a Gentleman, bust-length, wearing a black costume & cap; oil on panel, 7x6", C-NY 1/11/89 35,200

CORNELIUS (Continental, 19th C)
Ships in Amsterdam Harbor, oil on canvas, sgn/dtd 89, 26x36", B/B 5/17/89 2,200

CORNELL, Joseph (American, 1903-1972)
La Fenetre de Fanny Cerrito, paper collage on board, sgn/titled/inscr, ca 1962-65, 12x9", SBY 5/3/88 OE 10,175
Lapis Lazuli (WB Yeats), paper collage w/coin on board, sgn, 12x9", C-NY 5/4/89 OE 15,400
Storm That Never Came, pencil/paper collage on board, sgn/dtd 1953, 12x9", SBY 10/5/89 20,900
Through the Doorway, paper collage/graphite on board, sgn/dtd 1965, 12x9", C-NY 5/4/89 OE 24,200
Time Transfixed (contemporary), plaster/paint/collage on board, sgn/titled, 12x9", SBY 11/11/88 OE 12,100
Untitled (Hotel Neptune), mixed media, box construction, sgn, ca 1954, 18x11x4", SBY 5/3/88 27,500
Untitled (Porcelain Figurine Series), paper collage on masonite, sgn, ca 1964-66, 12x9", SBY 11/11/88 OE 11,000

CORNIL, Gaston (French, 1883-)
Foire du Trone, oil on canvas, sgn, 52x64", SBY 5/23/89 23,100

CORNOYER, Paul (American, 1864-1923)
After the Rain, Central Park South; oil on board, sgn/incised, 8x10", SBY 6/28/89 OE 13,20
Charles River, Boston; oil on canvas, sgn, 32x36", SBY 9/23/88 7,70
Gloucester (street scene), oil on canvas, sgn, 27x22", C-NY 5/26/88 30,80
Gloucester at Evening, oil on board, sgn, 6x8", C-E 10/18/89 1,10
Portrait of a Young Girl in Red, oil on canvas, sgn, 15x13", C-E 4/7/88 66
Rainy Sunday (street scene), oil on canvasboard, sgn, 1910, 10x8", B/B 5/17/89 88
Twilight in Gloucester, oil on canvas, sgn, 18x24", C-NY 3/11/88 20,90
Venetian Reflections, oil on canvas, sgn, 22x27", C-NY 5/25/89 8,80
Venice, oil on canvas, sgn/dtd 95, 10x12", C-NY 9/30/88 8,80

Venice (canal scene), oil on canvas, sgn/dtd 1914, 28x60", C-NY 5/25/89 28,600

CORNOYER, Paul; att (American, 1864-1923)

River Landscape, oil on canvas, sgn/dtd 96, 16x22", SLK 5/9/88 750

CORNWELL, Dean (American, 1892-1960)

Aviator Charting His Course, oil on canvas, sgn, 25x29", SBY 9/14/89 3,025
Holding Their Own, sgn/dtd 1916, 35x24", C-E 6/1/88 3,850
Kitchen Still Life, oil on canvas, sgn/inscr Painted in London, 1925; 25x30", SBY 4/14/89 OE 2,860
Portrait of an Indian, pencil/conte crayon on paper, sgn, 17x14", C-NY 3/11//88 UE 275
Portrait of Peggy, oil on masonite, sgn, 22x18", SBY 4/14/89 770
Village on the Hillside, oil on board, sgn, 17x21", WG 9/16/88 800

CORONA, Leonardo; att (1561-1605)

Immaculate Conception, w/Adam & Eve & Pair of Saints; pen/brown ink/gray wash over black chalk, 11x7", SBY 1/13/89 7,700

CORONEL, Pedro (Mexican, 1923-1985)

La Oquedad de su Espacio (abstract), oil/sand on canvas, sgn/dtd Mexico 1980, 79x98", C-NY 5/17/89 OE 88,000
Untitled (abstract), oil on canvas, sgn/inscr Mex 81, 1981, 32x32", C-NY 5/18/88 11,000

CORONEL, Rafael (Mexican, 1932-)

Cabeza III (Head III), oil on canvas, sgn/titled, 1965, 32x18", C-NY 5/17/89 UE 1,760
El Vagabundo (portrait of vagabond in profile), acrylic on canvas, sgn, 1974, 40x50", C-NY 5/17/89 20,900
Hombre de Guanajuato (portrait of a man), acrylic on Fabriano paper, sgn, 17x39", C-NY 5/18/88 5,280
La Nina y el Nino (portrait of two children), oil on canvas, sgn/dtd 1965, 55x40", C-NY 5/17/89 18,700
La Perversa, oil on canvas, sgn, 1972, 59x79", SBY 5/17/88 OE 35,200
Leonardo in a Red Background (portrait), oil on canvas, sgn, 1982, 49x40", SBY 5/16/89 OE 33,000
Mailman (portrait), acrylic/pencil on paper, sgn, ca 1983, 40x28", SBY 5/16/89 3,850
Mujer Indigena (portrait of native woman), acrylic/pencil on Fabriano paper, sgn, 40x28", C-NY 5/18/88 4,180
Pair: La Pintora; Portrait of Tiepolo's Mother; pencil/acrylic on paper, sgn/dtd 69 Mexico, 25x20", C-NY 6820 3,850
Portrait of a Man, oil on canvas, sgn, 20x40", SBY 5/16/89 6,600
Three Brothers (portrait), oil on canvas, sgn/dtd 68/titled, SBY 11/21/88 19,800
Two Figures (head portraits), oil on board, sgn, 1965, 11x19", SBY 11/21/88 3,575
Untitled (five male religous figures), oil on canvas laid down on masonite, sgn, 1966, 47x39", SBY 5/16/89 19,800
Untitled (man's head w/closed eyes), oil on canvas, sgn, 16x17", SBY 5/16/89 4,400
Untitled (seated woman w/dog), oil on masonite, sgn, 14x24", SBY 5/16/89 4,400

COROT, Jean Baptiste Camille (French, 1796-1875)

Double-Sided: Punt in a River Landscape; Study of a Tree in a Landscape; black chalk, stamped, 7x10", C-NY 10/26/88 OE 11,000
Effet du Lune avec de Grands Arbres et un Clocher Loitain, oil on canvas, sgn, ca 1885-50, 14x10", SBY 5/23/89 OE 88,000
Figures Along a Shore in a Wooded Landscape, oil on canvas, sgn, 10x13", C-NY 2/25/88 49,500
Fontainebleau-le Chaos (landscape w/figure), oil on canvas, sgn, ca 1860-65, 18x22", SBY 10/24/89 275,000
La Chevriere Italienne (landscape w/figure), oil on canvas, sgn, 19x15", C-NY 2/3/88 OE 176,000
La Cueillette au Bord du Chemin (landscape w/figures), oil on cradled panel, sgn, ca 1960-65, 15x18", SBY 5/23/89 OE 341,000
Le Marais au Clocher Lointain (landscape w/figure & cow), oil on canvas, sgn, ca 1860-65, 14x18", SBY 10/24/89 220,000
Le Sentier sur un Plateau (Bretagne), oil on paper laid down on canvas, sgn, ca 1850-55, 10x15", C-NY 2/25/88 OE 66,000
Le Vallon (figures in a clearing), oil on canvas, sgn, 1871, 22x19", SBY 10/24/89 330,000
Les Petits Denicheurs (landscape w/figures, one climbing a tree); oil on canvas, sgn, 29x40", C-NY 10/25/89 OE 1,375,000
Les Sorcieres, oil on canvas, sgn, 1871, 11x10", SBY 10/24/89 OE 38,500
Maisons de Pecheurs au Bord de la Mer (Trouville ou Honfleur), oil on canvas, sgn, ca 1845, 13x18", SBY 10/24/89 OE 209,000
Paysage a la Tour Blanche, Souvenir de Crecy; oil on paper laid down on canvas, sgn, 10x12", SBY 10/24/89 115,500
Promeneur sur un Sentier (landscape w/figure), oil on canvas, sgn, 9x15", SBY 5/23/89 OE 121,000
Saule et Aulnes (landscape w/resting figures), oil on canvas, sgn, 15x19", C-NY 2/3/88 OE 214,500
Souvenir de Noise-Le-Grand (figure in a landscape), oil on canvas, sgn, 13x9", WD 11/16/89 OE 110,000
Ville-d'Avray-Sur les Hauteurs: Paysans Travaillant dans les Champs; oil on canvas, sgn, 17x27", SBY 2/22/89 OE 550,000

COROT, Jean Baptiste Camille; style of (French, 1796-1875)

Pastoral Forest Scene, oil on canvas, bears signature, 26x32", B/B 5/17/89 605

CORPORA, Antonio (Italian, 1909-)

Inundation (abstract), oil on canvas, sgn/dtd 1949, 32x40", SBY 10/5/88 OE 8,800
Voyage sur l'Atlantique, oil on canvas, sgn/dtd 51, 39x32", SBY 10/5/88 OE 8,250

CORRADI, Konrad (Swiss, 1813-1878)

Town in an Alpine Valley, watercolor/gouache, sgn, 13x18", C-NY 2/23/89 1,980

CORRADINI, C. (Italian, 19th C)

Artist at Work, oil on panel, sgn/dtd 1882, 14x19", SBY 12/9/88 2,200

CORREA, Benito Rebolledo (Chilean, 1880-1964)

Children at the Beach, oil on canvas, sgn/dtd 1915, unfr, 21x27", C-NY 5/25/88 6,050
Children on the Beach at Sunset, Valencia; oil on canvas, sgn, ca 1909, 38x52", SBY 10/24/89 14,300
Young Boy at a Water Barrel, oil on canvas, sgn, 21x17", C-NY 2/23/89 6,600

CORREA, Juan

Flight into Egypt, oil on canvas, sgn, 63x39", C-NY 5/31/89 OE 22,000

CORREGGIO, Antonio; see Da Correggio

CORRELLI (Italian, 19th C)

Group of 3: Bay of Naples, gouache, sgn, 9x16" & smaller, C-E 2/21/89 880

CORRODI, Hermann David Salomon (Italian, 1844-1905)

Caravan (figures in a landscape with building beyond), oil on canvas, sgn, 39x26", B/B 10/9/88 14,300
Coastal Scene with a Sentinel's Post, oil on canvas, sgn/inscr Roma, 26x50", C-NY 2/23/89 OE 12,100
Praying to Mecca, oil on canvas, sgn/inscr, 40x26", C-NY 5/25/88 OE 26,400

Ruins in the Roman Campagna, oil on canvas, bears signature, 26x50", SBY 7/12/89 OE 2,860
The Balcony, Venice (lady calling from balcony); oil on panel, sgn/inscr Roma, 20x12", SBY 10/24/89 6,050
Venice in the Evening: A Visit to the Shrine; oil on canvas, sgn/inscr, 27x50", C-NY 2/25/88 4,400

CORRODI, Salomon (Swiss, 1810-1892)
View of the Vatican, watercolor on paper, sgn/dtd Roma 1848, 12x18", RAB 8/8/89 UE 2,100

CORSARA (Italian, 19th C)
Study of a Man Holding a Jar on His Shoulder & Smoking a Pipe, oil on canvas, sgn, 17x11", SLK 2/12/88 100

CORSI, Sante (Italian, 19th C)
Interior of the Pitti Palace, oil on canvas, twice sgn/inscr, 42x57", SBY 5/23/89 9,900

CORSINI, Raffael (Italian, 19th C)
Brig Ottoman of Boston Commanded by Capt John Atkins, March 28th, 1839; watercolor on paper, sgn, 18x25", RAB 8/1/89 6,500

CORSINI, Raffael; manner of (Italian, 19th C)
Hebe of Boston, David Cushman Jr, Mate, Entering in the Bay of Smyrna, 1831; watercolor, 17x22", RAB 11/25/88 5,000

CORTE, see De la Corte

CORTES, Edouard Leon (French, 1882-1969)
Booksellers Along the Seine, oil on canvas, sgn/#d, 13x18", SBY 2/14/89 OE 17,600
Booksellers Along the Seine with a View of Notre Dame, oil on canvas, sgn, 13x18", C-NY 5/24/89 14,300
Boulevard Bonne Nouvelle, Paris; oil on canvas, sgn, 18x36", SBY 2/22/89 44,000
Boulevard de la Madeleine, en Hiver; oil on canvas, sgn, 13x18", SBY 5/23/89 16,500
Bustling Paris Street at Twilight, oil on canvas, sgn, 18x22", C-NY 2/23/89 OE 24,200
Carriage sur le rue Rivoli (street scene), oil on canvas, sgn, 18x22", B/B 6/15/89 16,500
Champs Elysee with a View of the Arc de Triomphe, oil on canvas, sgn, 13x18", C-NY 5/24/89 13,200
Champs Elysees, oil on canvas, sgn, 13x18", C-NY 2/25/88 OE 20,900
Champs Elysees (busy street scene), oil on canvas, sgn, 13x18", B/B 3/22/89 19,800
Champs Elysees at Dusk, oil on canvas, sgn, 13x18", B/B 6/15/89 13,200
Chickens Feeding, oil on canvas, sgn, 13x19", C-E 5/23/88 3,300
Crossing the Boulevard, oil on canvas, sgn, 18x22", C-NY 5/25/88 OE 24,200
Evening in Paris, oil on canvas, sgn, 15x20", WD 5/5/88 OE 12,000
Evening in Paris (busy street scene), oil on canvas, sgn, 18x22", C-NY 2/23/89 OE 25,300
Flower Stalls by the Madeleine, oil on canvas, sgn, 13x18", C-NY 5/24/89 13,200
Knitting, oil on board, sgn, 9x7", C-E 2/23/88 OE 5,720
L'Opera (busy night street scene), oil on canvas, sgn, 13x18", SBY 10/7/89 20,900
L'Opera (street scene w/view of the opera house), oil on canvas, sgn, 13x18", C-NY 5/24/89 15,400
LaMadeleine in Paris on a Snowy Winter's Eve, oil on canvas, sgn, 13x18", C-NY 2/23/89 14,300
La Madeleine (busy street scene), oil on canvas, sgn, 13x18", SBY 2/14/89 OE 17,600
La Madeleine en 1910, oil on canvas, sgn, 13x18", SBY 5/23/89 14,300
La Madeleine Under Snow, oil on canvas, sgn, 13x18", SBY 10/7/89 OE 23,100
Le Quai du Louvre (Paris street scene), oil on canvas, sgn, 13x18", SBY 2/22/89 17,600
Louvre Zuay, pastel on paper laid down on stretched canvas, 18x26", C-NY 5/25/88 OE 15,400
Marche aux Fleurs a la Madeleine, oil on canvas, sgn, 13x18", SBY 2/22/89 26,400
Montmartre (street scene), oil on canvas, sgn, 13x18", B/B 3/22/89 8,800
Notre Dame (snowy street scene), oil on canvas, sgn, 14x18", SBY 10/7/89 20,900
Notre Dame de Paris, oil on canvas, sgn, 13x18", SBY 2/22/8 9 17,600
Pair: La Madeleine; Quai du Louvre; oil on canvas, sgn, unfr, 9x13", SBY 10/5/88 OE 18,700
Pair: Parisian Street Scenes; oil on panel, sgn, 7x9", SBY 2/14/89 19,800
Paris at Dusk, oil on canvas, sgn, 13x18", WD 5/5/88 7,250
Paris at Dusk (busy street scene), oil on canvas, sgn, 18x22", B/B 3/22/89 22,000
Paris at Dusk (street scene with autos & many figures), oil on canvas, sgn, 18x21", B/B 10/9/88 24,750
Paris in the Snow, oil on canvas, sgn, 13x18", WD 5/5/88 9,250
Paris in Winter with a View of the Madeleine, oil on canvas, sgn, 13x18", C-NY 2/23/89 17,600
Paris Street Scene, oil on canvas, sgn, 13x18", B/B 10/9/88 OE 18,700
Paris Street Scene, oil on canvas, sgn, 13x18", B/B 10/9/88 OE 10,500
Paris Street Scene, oil on canvas, sgn, 13x18", C-NY 2/23/89 13,200
Paris Street Scene, oil on canvas, sgn, 13x18", C-NY 5/25/88 OE 15,400
Paris Street Scene, oil on canvas, sgn, 13x18", SBY 10/7/89 22,00
Paris Street Scene, oil on canvas, sgn, 18x22", DM 9/16/88 OE 11,00
Paris Street Scene at Sunset, oil on canvas, sgn, 13x18", C-NY 5/25/88 OE 18,70
Parisian Street Scene with Cafe, oil on canvas, sgn, 20x26", SBY 10/7/89 OE 26,40
Parisian Street Scene with Carriages, oil on canvas, sgn, 13x18, SBY 2/14/89 16,50
Place de la Bastille, Paris; oil on canvas, sgn, unfr, 13x18", SBY 5/23/89 11,00
Place de la Concorde, le Soir; oil on canvas, sgn, 13x18",SBY 2/22/89 25,30
Place de la Concorde, oil on canvas, sgn, 13x18", C-NY 2/25/88 OE 17,60
Place de la Concorde, oil on canvas, sgn, 13x18", C-NY 5/24/89 15,40
Place de la Concorde, oil on canvas, sgn, 13x18", C-NY 5/25/88 11,00
Place de la Concorde, oil on canvas, sgn, 13x18", SBY 5/23/89 14,30
Place de la Republique, Paris (busy street scene); oil on canvas, sgn, 13x18", C-NY 2/23/89 15,40
Place Vendome, Paris; oil on canvas, sgn, unfr, 13x18", SBY 5/23/89 11,00
Place Vendome (busy street scene), oil on canvas, sgn, 13x18", C-NY 2/23/89 15,40
Port St Denis, Paris (street scene); oil on panel, sgn/dtd 1906, 10x13", C-NY 2/23/89 13,20
Port St Denis, Paris; oil on canvas, sgn, 13x18", C-NY 2/25 /88 OE 15,40
Rue Capucine, Paris (street scene); oil on canvas, sgn, 19x26", B/B 6/15/89 24,75

Rue Royale with a View of the Madeleine, oil on canvas, sgn, 13x18", C-NY 5/24/89 ... 18,700

Rue Royale-La Madelaine et les Trois Quartiers; oil on canvas, sgn, 20x26", C-NY 5/25/88 OE ... 33,000

Snowy Day, Port St Martin, Paris; oil on canvas, sgn, 13x18", C-NY 2/23/89 ... 15,400

Winter Scene, Paris; oil on canvas, sgn/#d, 13x18", SBY 2/14/89 OE ... 15,400

CORVI, Domenico; circle of

Virgin Mary (portrait), oil on canvas, 9x7", SBY 10/13/89 ... 5,500

CORWIN, Charles Abel (American, 1857-1938)

Indians at the Ford (four Indians on horseback at stream), oil on canvas, sgn, 30x41", RAB 8/8/89 UE ... 1,100

CORZAS, Francisco (Mexican, 1936-)

Desastre en Nicaragua (abstract), oil on canvas, sgn/dtd 1962, 53x92", C-NY 5/18/88 ... 24,200

Portrait of a Man, watercolor on paper, sgn/dtd 71, 12x10", SBY 11/21/88 ... 2,200

Presence (nude w/other figures), oil on paper laid down on masonite, sgn/dtd 70, 18x25", SBY 11/21/88 ... 5,225

Untitled (reclining nude), oil on canvas, sgn/dtd 1976, 48x67", SBY 5/16/89 ... 49,500

Untitled (two figures), oil on canvas, sgn/dtd 67, 51x67", SBY 11/21/88 OE ... 37,400

COSENZA, Guiseppe (Italian, 1847-)

Neopolitan Lovers in a Boat, oil on canvas, sgn, 18x30", C-E 2/21/89 ... 3,850

COSGROVE, Stanley M. (Canadian, 1911-)

Arbres (landscape w/trees), oil on canvas, sgn, 25x32", FB 4/25/88 ... 7,000

Head of a Young Woman, oil on canvas, sgn, 16x12", FB 10/17/88 ... 9,000

Nude, charcoal, sgn, 18x13", FB 4/25/88 ... 1,400

Reclining Nude, sanguine, sgn, 11x14", FB 10/30/89 ... 1,650

Still Life of Jug & Vase of Flowers, oil on board, sgn, 12x16", FB 10/30/89 ... 5,060

View of the Lake, oil on canvas, sgn, 25x32", FB 10/30/89 ... 9,900

Winter Landscape, oil on board, sgn, 12x16", FB 5/28/89 ... 3,800

Woodland Landscape, oil on canvas, ca 1955, 20x24", FB 4/25/88 ... 7,000

COSSIERS, Jan; att (Flemish, 1600-1671)

Drunken Silenus, oil on canvas, 45x59", SBY 4/7/88 ... 4,125

COSSON, Marcel (French, 1878-1956)

Club Scene (two ladies seated at table playing checkers), oil on canvas, sgn, 24x29", SBY 10/7/89 OE ... 14,300

Parisian Bar Scene, oil on canvas, sgn, 24x20", SBY 10/5/88 OE ... 9,350

COSTA, E.

Woman Arranging Flowers, oil on canvas, sgn, 29x17", C-E 5/23/88 ... 2,640

COSTA, Giovanni (Italian, 1833-1903)

Young Woman Holding Flowers, oil on canvas, sgn, 25x20", SBY 12/9/88 OE ... 4,400

COSTA, Lorenzo; circle of (ca 1460-1535)

Madonna & Child, Distant Landscape Beyond; oil on panel, 17x14", SBY 10/13/89 OE ... 9,900

COSTA, Olga

December (poinsettias), oil on canvas, sgn/dtd 85, 43x43", SBY 5/17/88 UE ... 1,980

Tehuana Sentada (seated woman), gouache on paper, sgn/dtd 49, 24x19", C-NY 11/21/88 ... 7,150

COSTA, Oreste (Italian, 1851-)

Room in the Pitti Palace, oil on canvas, sgn twice/inscr Firenze Via Romana 8, 44x32", C-NY 5/23/89 OE ... 26,400

Unrequited Love, oil on canvas, sgn, 22x29", SBY 5/23/89 OE ... 22,000

COSTANZI, Placido; att (Italian, ca 1590-1659)

Angel with Hagar & Ishmael (in a landscape), oil on canvas, 51x37", SBY 6/1/89 UE ... 23,100

COSTE, Jean Baptiste (French, 18th/19th C)

Classical Landscape with Figures, watercolor/gouache/India ink on paper laid down, sgn/dtd 1816, 25x34", SBY 7/12/89 ... 2,090

COSTIGAN, John Edward (American, 1888-1972)

Bathers, oil on canvas, sgn, 24x30", SBY 9/23/88 ... 6,050

Figures in a Wooded Landscape, gouache/watercolor on paper, sgn, 20x26", SBY 4/14/89 ... 2,970

Group of Bathers (thick impasto, figures wading in water), oil/acrylic on artist board, sgn, 12x16", RWS 3/31/88 ... 2,400

COSWAY, Richard (British, 1742-1821)

Portrait of a Lady, oil on canvas, 30x25", SBY 6/8/88 UE ... 990

Portrait of a Woman as Terpischore, reclining on a terrace; oil on canvas, oval, sgn, 28x36", C-NY 4/6/89 OE ... 7,700

Portrait of a Young French Boy, oil on canvas, 22x18", S/A 2/18/89 ... 10,750

COSWAY, Richard; manner of (British, 1742-1821)

Portrait of Mrs Johnson, oil on canvas, 29x24", SBY 12/9/88 ... 990

COSWAY, Richard; school of (British, 1742-1821)

Two Ladies Reading (in a landscape), oil on canvas, 15x12", C-NY 6/17/89 ... 550

COTE, Bruno (Canadian, 1940-)

Boileau, pastel, sgn, 1988, 8x10", FB 5/28/89 ... 200

En Descendant a Petite Riviere St Francis, oil on board, sgn/dtd 1979, 35x42", FB 10/17/88 ... 600

COTES, Francis (British, 1725-1770)

Lady Charlotte Boyle, Marchioness of Hartington; oil on canvas, inscr, 27x21", SBY 7/12/89 ... 2,090

Portrait of Miss Stuart, half-length, in profile; pastel on paper laid down on canvas, 29x24", C-NY 1/11/89 ... 7,150

COTES, Francis; circle of (British, 1725-1770)

Portrait of a Lady, oil on canvas, 30x24", SBY 12/9/88 ... 1,320

Portrait of a Lady, seated, half-length, wearing blue dress/black shawl; oil on canvas, 30x25", C-NY 4/8/88 ... 5,500

Portrait of a Lady Dressed in an Ermine-Lined Robe & Her Child, oil on canvas, 49x30", SBY 7/12/89 ... 1,540

COTTET, Charles (French, 1863-1924)

Cathedral de Moulins, oil on panel, sgn, 24x20", B/B 8/10/88 ... 660

Steamboat at Dock: White Smoke; oil on canvas laid down on board, sgn, 23x31", WD 11/16/88 UE ... 4,000

COTTINGHAM, Robert (American, 1935-)

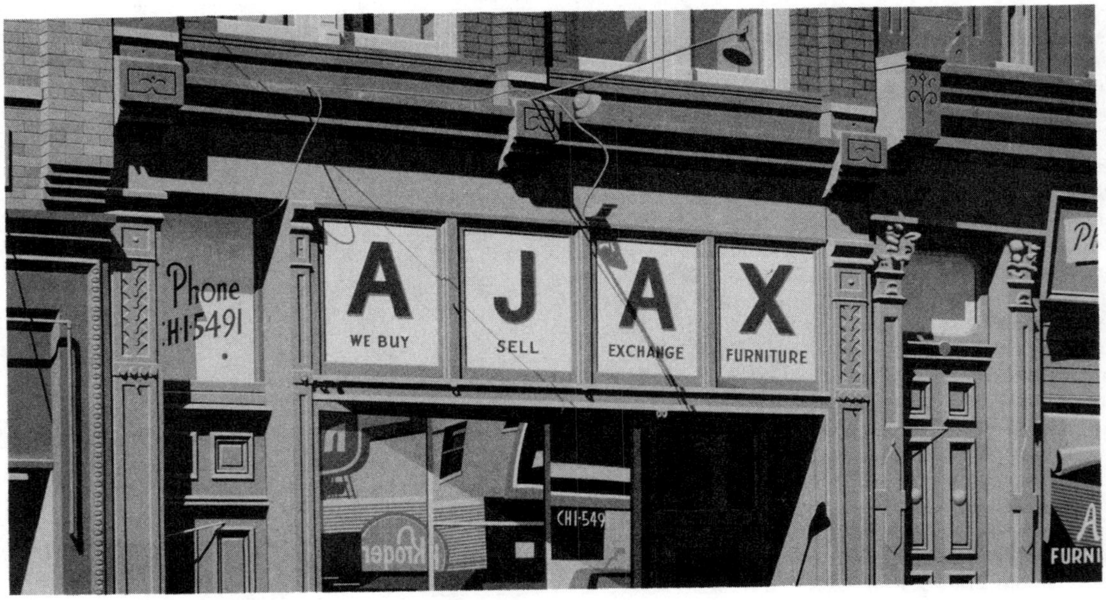

Ajax, acrylic on paper, sgn/dtd 1983, 25x40", C-NY 5/4/89 OE, $26,400

Art (close-up of neon sign), oil on canvas, sgn/dtd 1971, 78x78", SBY 5/3/89 OE 198,000
Barrera-Rosa's, watercolor on paper, sgn/dtd 1983/titled, 18x28", C-NY 11/10/88 OE 16,500
JC, graphite on vellum, sgn/dtd 1982/titled, 19x24", C-NY 11/10/88 OE 6,050
JC (storefronts), acrylic on paperboard, sgn/dtd 1982, 17x24", SBY 10/5/89 24,750
Miller High Life (sign), oil on canvas, sgn/dtd 1977, 78x78", SBY 10/8/88 23,100
Old Crow (storefront), acrylic on canvas, sgn/inscr/dtd 98, 25x33", C-NY 5/4/88 OE 20,900
Ral's, watercolor on paper, sgn/dtd 1983/titled, 20x25", C-NY 11/10/88 UE 4,400
Ritz Bar (realistic view of entrance to bar), watercolor on paper, sgn/dtd 1986, 21x21", C-NY 5/4/89 OE 9,350
The Spot (realistic neon sign on brick building), oil on canvas, 1979, 32x32", SBY 2/19/88 OE 40,700
Wichita (air traffic control tower), acrylic on board, sgn/dtd 1985, 30x40", C-NY 5/4/88 20,900

COTTON, John Wesley (American, 1868-1931)
Near the Salton Sea; oil on canvas laid down on board, sgn/titled/inscr, 13x19", SBY 6/28/89 1,430

COTTON, Mariette
Portrait of a Lady, oil on canvas, sgn, 30x25", C-E 6/1/88 UE 880

COTTON, William (American, 1880-1958)
Peggy (portrait of a young girl), oil on canvas, sgn, 15x12", C-E 10/18/89 OE 6,600

COUGH, George L.
Sailing on Rough Seas (clipper ships in storm), oil on board, monogramed, 10x14", C-E 6/1/89 1,100

COULDERY, Horatio Henry (British, 1832-1893)
Goldfish Bowl, oil on canvas, sgn, unfr, 12x16", SBY 12/9/88 5,500
Proud of Her Litter (cats), oil on canvas, sgn, 17x25", C-NY 2/25/88 8,800
Waiting for Their Master (two dogs sitting on cushion), oil on canvas, sgn, 24x20", SBY 6/10/88 OE 9,350

COULON, B.
Dressing at the Boudoir, oil on panel, sgn, 17x12", C-E 5/23/88 1,760

COULON, George D. (American, fl 1822-1904)
George Washington's Tomb, oil on board, sgn/dtd 98, 9x6", NA 3/26/88 1,200
Pair: Mallard Duck; Red Snapper; pastel on paper mounted on canvas, ea sgn/1 dtd 93, 16x32", MG 6/25/88 2,700
Swamp Cabin (in a landscape), gouache, sgn/dtd 92, no size given, NA 11/5/88 3,200

COULTER, William Alexander (American, 1849-1936)
Clipper Ship in Choppy Seas, oil on canvas, sgn, 23x27", B/B 10/6/88 2,750
Sailing Vessels Off the Coast, oil on canvas, indistinctly sgn, 11x17", B/B 10/6/88 1,760
Ships at Golden Gate, oil on canvasboard, sgn, 10x14", B/B 10/6/88 3,575
View of Alcatraz, San Francisco Bay; oil on canvas laid down on board, sgn, 12x20", C-E 10/18/89 3,300

COURBET, Gustave (French, 1819-1877)
La Plage, Soleil Couchant (beach scene after sunset); oil on canvas, sgn/dtd 67, 22x26", SBY 10/24/89 OE 308,00
La Vague (The Wave), oil on canvas, sgn, ca 1874, 45x57", SBY 5/23/89 715,00
Le Chasseur d'Eau (hunter by the water in a landscape), oil on canvas, sgn, 1873, 24x29", SBY 5/23/89 OE 275,00
Le Dormoir au Bord de la Mer, oil on canvas, sgn, 29x37", C-NY 2/25/88 60,50
Le Paysage du Gue (man carrying woman through stream), oil on canvas, sgn, 10x8", C-NY 2/23/89 OE 88,00
Paysage (landscape), oil on canvas, sgn, ca 1877, 15x27", SBY 10/24/89 132,00
Portrait d'Alphonse Bon, oil on panel, sgn, 1849, 18x13", SBY 2/22/89 165,00

COURBET, Gustave; & ORDINAIRE, Marcel (French, 19th C)
Ruisseau de la Breme (landscape), oil on canvas, bears signature, 1872, 25x32", SBY 2/22/89 OE 44,00

COURBET, Gustave; & Studio (French, 1819-1877)
Paysage de Riviere (landscape), oil on canvas, bears signature/dtd 69, 21x25", SBY 2/22/88 33,000
COURBET, Gustave; manner of (French, 1819-1877)
Deer in a Mountainous Landscape, oil on canvas, bears signature, 24x29", C-E 11/8/88 880
Study of a Rabbit, oil on canvas, 20x10", SBY 7/12/89 1,045
COURBET, Gustave; school of (French, 1819-1877)
Jeune Femme Endorme (sleeping woman), oil on canvas, 19x17", C-E 6/28/88 UE 110
COURBET (French, 20th C)
Untitled, street scene, oil on board, sgn, 24x20", SLK 11/25/88 225
COURTAT, Louis (French, -1909)
Gathering Woodland Flowers, oil on canvas, sgn, 32x38", SBY 2/22/89 13,200
Portrait of a Girl with Her Toy Hoop, oil on canvas, sgn/dtd 1882, 26x21", SBY 10/24/89 8,250
COURTOIS, Gustave Claude Etienne (French, 1853-1923)
Cows Watering by a Trough, oil on canvas, sgn, 26x37", C-E 10/25/88 UE 1,540
La Bayadere, oil on canvas, sgn/dtd 1882, 32x21", SBY 2/22/89 33,000
Sultry Beauty (portrait), oil on canvas, sgn/dtd 1883, 16x13", C-E 5/22/89 5,280
COURTOIS, Jacques; att (French, 1621-1676)
Battle Scene (men on horses in fierce combat), oil on canvas, 12x20", C-NY 4/6/89 2,090
COURTOIS, Jacques; circle of (French, 1621-1676)
Battle Scene, oil on canvas, 26x22", SBY 7/12/89 OE 5,775
COUSE, Eanger Irving (American, 1866-1936)
Card Player (wounded Indian lying by campfire), oil on canvas, sgn, 1897, 31x45", SBY 5/25/88 19,800
Fisherfolk Along the Beach, watercolor over pencil on paper, sgn, 15x21", SBY 6/24/88 OE 3,850
Indian by Fireside, oil on canvas, sgn, 24x29", SBY 5/25/88 38,500
Indian Girl Wrapped in a Blanket, oil on canvas, sgn, 10x8", SBY 5/25/88 OE 14,300
Indian Wrapped in Blanket, oil on canvas, sgn, 12x6", SBY 5/25/88 5,500
Lone Hunter (Indian in forest landscape), oil on canvas, sgn, 20x24", C-NY 5/26/88 30,800
Moonlight Meditation, oil on canvas, sgn, 36x30", SBY 5/25/88 34,100
Night Signals (Indian by campfire beating drum), oil on canvas, sgn, 24x29", C-NY 5/25/89 33,000
Pair: Gray House; Red Roof; oil on canvasboard, sgn, 7x9", C-NY 3/11/88 3,520
Peasants on the Beach, oil on canvas, sgn, 24x29", WL 5/20/88 5,100
Portrait of Fanny Walker Kamm, oil on canvas, sgn/dtd 97, 9x12", B/B 3/22/89 3,300
Putting on the War Shoes (two young Indians in wooded area), oil on canvas, sgn, 24x29", SBY 5/25/88 28,600
Set of 3: Dog; Lamb; Cow; oil on canvas, ea sgn, 1 dtd 27/08, 2 7x9", 1 9x7", B/B 3/22/89 6,600
Set of 4: Landscapes with Pink Horizons; oil on canvas, ea sgn, 7x9", B/B 3/22/89 4,400
Set of 4: Landscapes; oil on canvas, sgn, 3 9x7", 1 7x9", B/B 6/15/89 3,575
Set of 4: Landscapes; oil on canvas, sgn, 7x9", B/B 3/22/89 3,300
Set of 4: Landscapes; 3 oil on canvas, 1 oil on board, 3 sgn, no size given, B/B 6/15/89 3,300
Set of 4: Portraits of Women; oil on canvas, sgn, 1 7x6", 3 9x7", B/B 3/22/89 4,400
Set of 4: Portraits of Women; One of a Young Girl; oil on canvas, 3 sgn, 12x10" & smaller, B/B 3/22/89 4,400
Set of 4: Seashore Scenes; 3 oil on canvas, 1 oil on board, ea sgn, 27x19" & smaller, B/B 6/15/89 3,300
OUSENS, Henry (American, 19th C)
Quack (Indian men in interior), oil on canvas, sgn/dtd Sept 1887/inscr, 22x29", C-SK 6/9/88 1,487
OUSIN, Charles (French, 19th/20th C)
Venetian Canal Scene, oil on canvas, sgn, 20x25", FB 10/17/88 5,200
OUSTOU, Jean (1719-1791)
Trompe l'Oeil Overdoor w/Portrait Bust in Relief of Comte de Caylus...; oil, indistinctly sgn, 24x50", C-M 6/16/89 10,595
OUTTS, Alice (American, 1880-1973)
Playtime (Indian children in basket w/pup & kitten), oil on canvas, sgn/dtd 12, 8x10", C-NY 5/25/89 4,400
OUTTS, Gordon (American, 1880-1937)
San Jacinto Mountains Near Palm Springs, oil on canvas, sgn, 24x28", B/B 10/6/88 1,430
Sunset Landscape, oil on canvas, sgn, 30x40", C-E 4/7/88 UE 462
The Harvest, oil on canvas, sgn/dtd 1906, 22x36", B/B 10/6/88 3,300
Western Landscape, oil on canvas, sgn, 14x18", C-E 2/1/89 2,200
OUTURE, Thomas (French, 1815-1879)
Head of a Young Girl, black/white chalk on (faded) blue paper, sgn twice/dtd 1854, 18x14", C-NY 2/23/89 OE 8,250
Opening of the Cask (woman opening a cask as a man is exiting the room), oil on canvas, sgn, 23x20", DM 10/14/88 2,000
Pair: Head of a Young Girl; oil on canvas, 1876, 16x13", SBY 10/24/89 19,800
Rabbits & Plucked Chicken: a Recipe; pen/black ink, initialed, 12x8", C-NY 10/26/88 1,540
UTURIER, Philibert Leon (French, 1823-1901)
Dressing the Game (girl dressing game), oil on canvas, sgn, 79x138", SBY 10/24/89 16,500
VARRUBIAS, Miguel (Mexican, 1904-1957)
Art Critic, pastel/gouache/watercolor/pencil on paper, sgn/dtd 1939, 14x18", WD 5/5/88 1,100
Balinese Woman, gouache on paper, 1934, 15x11", SBY 5/17/88 4,950
Cabeza de Nina (Head of a Girl), watercolor/brush/ink/pencil on paper, sgn, 11x8", C-NY 5/17/89 2,200
Caricature of Clare Boothe Luce, crayon on paper, ca 1933, 8x5", SBY 5/17/88 UE 1,650
Caricature of Clare Boothe Luce, gouache on paper, sgn, ca 1933, 16x11", SBY 5/17/88 UE 1,650
El Critico de Art, pastel/pencil/gouache/pen/ink on illustration board, sgn/dtd 39, 15x21", C-NY 11/21/88 OE 7,700
Tehuanas (two women in landscape), watercolor on paper, sgn, 15x11", C-NY 5/17/89 8,250
X, David (British, 1873-1859)
Barden Tower on the Wharf Above Bolton Abbey, watercolor, sgn/inscr/dtd 1832, 10x14", C-NY 10/26/88 5,280

Haystacks, oil on canvas laid down on board, sgn/dtd 1843, 11x14", C-NY 6/17/89 ... 2,640
Shepherd with His Flock in an Extensive Landscape, oil on canvas, sgn/dtd 1859, 22x30", C-E 10/25/88 OE ... 6,050

COX, Frank (American, 19th/20th C)
Landscape, oil on panel, sgn, 11x19", NA 10/1/88 ... 850

COX, Louise (American, 1865-)
Young Boy in a Sailor Suit, oil on canvas, sgn/dtd 1912, 25x17", WD 4/13/88 UE ... 3,100

COX, Palmer (American, 1840-1924)
Bugaboo Bill-The Giant Waiting; ink on paper, sgn/titled, 8x7", RAB 8/8/89 UE ... 150
Giraffe Feeding, pencil on paper, sgn, 9x7", RAB 8/8/89 UE ... 100

COX, Timmy (20th C)
Boss John on a Good Horse, oil on canvas, sgn/copyrighted/dtd 1980, 18x24", SBY 9/23/88 ... 1,430

COXCIE, Michel; att
Christ Child in Glory Surrounded by Adoring Angels, oil on panel, unfr, 49x49", SBY 10/13/89 ... 7,700

COXE, Reginald Cleveland (American, 1855-)
In Gloucester Harbor (sailboats & dory), oil on canvas, sgn, 18x30", RAB 8/9/88 ... 2,750

COYPEL, Charles Antoine (French, 1692-1752)
Painting Ejecting Thalia, oil on canvas, sgn/dtd 1732, 26x32", SBY 6/1/89 ... 77,00
Portrait of a Gentleman in a Brown Coat with a Red Embroidered Vest & a Leopard Muff, oil on canvas, 39x31", SBY 4/7/89 ... 9,90
Portrait of a Woman Said To Be Actress Lecouvreur, bust-length...; pastel on paper laid down, 17x14", C-NY 4/6/89 OE ... 4,95

COYPEL, Noel Nicholas; after (French, 1628-1707)
Saint James the Greater Being Led to His Execution, oil on canvas, 32x26", C-NY 4/6/89 ... 2,86

COYPEL, Noel Nicholas; circle of (French, 1628-1707)
Mercury Placing the Infant Bacchus in the Care of the Maenads, oil on canvas, 21x25", SBY 10/13/89 ... 7,70

COYPEL, Noel Nicholas; studio of (French, 1628-1707)
Emperor Trajan Giving Audience, oil on canvas, 50x48", SBY 6/2/89 ... 23,10

COZENS, Alexander (British, ca 1717-1786)
Highland Landscape with a Lake, brush/black ink/brown wash over black chalk, 4x5", SBY 1/13/89 OE ... 2,09

COZZA, Francesco (1605-1682)
Hagar & the Angel, oil on canvas, 30x22", SBY 6/2/89 ... 74,25

COZZENS, Frederick Schiller (American, 1856-1928)
Bark at Sea (ship w/tug & ship in background), watercolor on paper, sgn/dtd 96, 13x21", RAB 8/1/88 ... 2,50
Out to Sea, watercolor/pencil on paper, sgn/dtd 05, 14x18", C-E 6/1/89 ... 88
Rescue (sailboat & two figures in dinghy), watercolor/pencil on paper, sgn/dtd 05, 14x18", C-E 6/1/89 ... 1,54
Sailboats by the Beach, watercolor/pencil on paper, sgn/dtd 05, 14x18", C-E 6/1/89 OE ... 2,20
Sailing at Sea, watercolor on board, sgn/dtd 08, unfr, 15x24", SBY 9/14/89 ... 1,87
Schooner Yachts Tempest & Fortuna Putting Out to Sea, watercolor on paper, sgn/dtd 01, modern frame, 12x21", RAB 8/1/88 UE ... 3,00
Seascape with Ships in Choppy Waters, watercolor on paper, sgn/dtd 07, 12x22", SBY 6/28/89 ... 1,32
Set Sail, watercolor/pencil on paper, sgn/dtd 05, 14x18", C-E 6/1/89 ... 88
Ship Riding a Storm, watercolor on paper, sgn/dtd 1909, 12x15", WG 4/23/88 ... 75
Shipping Off the Coast, watercolor on paper, sgn/dtd 07, 13x24", RAB 8/1/88 ... 2,25
Shipping Off the Coast (seascape of long beach w/ship), watercolor on paper, sgn/dtd 07, 13x24", RAB 8/1/89 OE ... 4,00
Twilight Along the Shore, watercolor on paper, sgn/dtd 92, 13x21", RAB 3/27/89 ... 1,30

CRADOCK, Marmaduke (British, 1660-1717)
Peacock, Cockerel, Turkey, & Other Birds, on Terrace in an Ornamental Garden; oil on canvas, 31x51", C-NY 4/8/88 ... 15,40

CRAIG, Frank (British, 1874-1918)
Plaisirs Sensuels-Cote d'Azur; oil on canvas, no size given, FAP 4/15/89 OE ... 2,31

CRAIG, Thomas Bigelow (American, 1849-1924)
Brookside, oil on cradled panel, sgn twice/dtd 1896, 16x20", SBY 9/23/88 ... 1,0
Cattle Along a River, oil on canvas laid down, sgn/dtd 87, 12x17", B/B 12/8/88 ... 1,5
Cows Grazing, watercolor on paper, sgn, unfr, 14x22", B/B 9/15/88 ... 5
Day in Early Summer (cows drinking at stream), oil on canvas, sgn/dtd 1900, 10x14", C-E 6/1/89 ... 9
Driving the Herd to Pasture, watercolor/gouache/graphite on paper, sgn, 12x21", RWS 9/8/89 UE ... 2
Grazing Cattle, watercolor on paper, sgn/inscr Ama, 18x24", C-E 9/15/88 UE ... 1
In the Meadow, watercolor on paper, sgn, 18x28", SBY 1/24/89 ... 1,1
Landscape with Cattle at Stream, watercolor on paper, sgn, 14x20", WG 9/16/88 UE ... 3
October Sunlight, oil on canvas, sgn/inscr/dtd 1888, 18x14", C-NY 3/11/88 ... 2,7
Panther Mountain From Woodland Valley, Ulster Co, New York; oil on canvas, sgn twice/dtd 1897, 20x30", SBY 3/17/88 OE ... 2,8
Returning From Hillside Pasture, oil on canvas, sgn, 16x20", C-E 2/1/89 ... 1,8
Sheep Grazing, watercolor on paper, sgn, unfr, 16x24", B/B 9/15/88 ... 5

CRAIG, William (American, 1829-1875)
Waterfall in the Adirondacks (w/2 figures), watercolor heightened w/wht over pencil, sgn/dtd 1874, 14x18", C-E 2/21/89 ... 7

CRALI, Tullio
La Place Dauphine (building), oil on canvas, sgn/dtd Paris 53, 18x22", C-E 5/9/89 ... 3,0

CRAM, H. (?)(American or British, 20th C)
Portrait of the Steamship Vita, oil on academy board, sgn, 6x12", RAB 3/14/89 ... 2

CRANACH, Lucas the elder (German, 1472-1553)
Lucretia, oil on panel, sgn, 33x22", C-NY 1/11/89 ... 220,
Lucretia, oil on panel, sgn/dtd 1529, 23x15", SBY 6/1/89 ... 715,
Lucretia, oil on panel, 23x18", SBY 6/3/88 OE ... 352,
Melancholia (sad woman in interior w/many lively nude children), oil on panel, 21x30", C-NY 5/31/89 ... 88,

ANACH, Lucas the elder; att (German, 1472-1553)
ucretia, oil on panel, sgn, 23x14", SBY 10/13/89 44,000
ANACH, Lucas the elder; manner of (German, 1472-1553)
Portrait of Catarina Von Bora, Wife of Martin Luther; oil on panel, 15x11", SBY 1/12/89 4,950
Portrait of Martin Luther, oil on panel, bears inscription, 15x10", SBY 1/12/89 14,300
ANACH, Lucas the younger; & Studio (German, 1515-1586)
Head of the Virgin, oil on canvas, 13x10", C-NY 1/11/89 15,400
ANACH, Lucas; school of
Mercenary Love (portrait of woman w/child, landscape beyond), oil on panel, 1541, unfr, 12x9", C-M 6/16/89 4,890
ANCH, Christopher Pearce (American, 1813-1892)
River View of Upstate New York, oil on canvas laid down on board, sgn/dtd 1843, 25x33", WD 4/13/88 3,400
ANCH, Christopher Pearce; att (American, 1813-1892)
Fisherman in a Woodland Stream, oil on canvas, sgn, 22x14", RWS 5/19/88 850
ANE, Robert Bruce (American, 1857-1937)
Apple Orchard, oil on canvas, sgn, 24x36", C-NY 3/11/88 14,300
Autumn Landscape, oil on canvas, sgn, 18x24", SBY 1/24/89 4,400
Autumn Landscape, oil on canvas, sgn, 20x28", SBY 9/23/88 8,800
Autumn Landscape, oil on canvas, sgn, 25x30", B/B 10/9/88 2,750
Autumn Landscape, oil on canvas, sgn/indistinctly dtd, 14x18", B/B 3/17/88 3,300
Cherry Blossoms (landscape w/path), oil on canvas, sgn, 16x25", C-E 6/1/89 OE 18,700
Cottage by the Lake Shore Ogunquit, oil on board, sgn, 9x12", PHL 6/16/88 OE 1,300
December Morning, oil on canvas, sgn, 14x20", C-NY 3/11/88 4,620
Early Autumn, oil on canvas, sgn, 14x20", SBY 6/28/89 6,325
Fall Landscape, oil on canvas, sgn, 14x20", SBY 9/14/89 3,300
House in a Landscape, oil on canvas, sgn/dtd 1912, 12x20", C-E 6/1/89 2,200
Indian Summer, oil on canvas mounted on panel, sgn, 22x30", SBY 9/23/88 8,250
Misty Summer Morning, oil on canvas, sgn, 22x30", C-E 2/3/88 OE 8,250
Moonlight on the Waterfront, oil on canvas, sgn, 25x35", SBY 6/28/89 3,300
Old Wood Lot, oil on canvas, sgn, 28x36", C-NY 9/30/88 8,800
Path to the Pond, oil on canvas, sgn, 12x16", C-E 10/18/89 2,420
Road in the Village, oil on canvas, sgn, 16x20", B/B 10/9/88 4,400
Snowy Landscape, oil on canvas, sgn, 18x24", WD 10/5/88 7,250
Spring Blossoms, oil on canvas, sgn, 14x20", C-NY 9/28/89 OE 12,100
Starlit Night, oil on canvas, sgn, 25x30", C-NY 9/30/88 7,700
Sudbury, Vermont; oil on canvas, sgn, 36x40", SBY 6/24/88 OE 13,200
Summer at Newport, New York (landscape); oil on panel, sgn, 10x13", B/B 3/22/89 2,750
The Old Wood Lot, oil on canvas, sgn, 18x24", SBY 4/14/89 OE 11,000
Tramping by the Lake, oil on panel, sgn, 6x7", WD 4/13/88 2,900
Untitled, moonlit river landscape w/farmhouse; oil on canvas, sgn, 23x30", SLK 4/7/89 2,000
Valley of the Mohawk, oil on canvas, sgn, 14x20", C-E 2/1/89 2,310
Winter Sunset (rural landscape), oil on canvas, sgn, 16x24", C-NY 5/25/89 OE 17,600
Young Lady in a Blue & Pink Dress, oil on board, sgn, 19x15", C-E 10/25/88 4,180
ANE, Walter (British, 1845-1915)
Outside the Church of the Gapuchins, Rome; gouache on paper, monogramed/dtd 1871, 30x12", SBY 4/29/88 6,600
Skeleton in Armour: Study Illustrating Figure at a Banquet Table; gouache on brown paper, inscr, 9x41", C-NY 2/25/88 OE 8,250
Skeleton in Armour: Study Illustrating Viking Ships Battling a Storm; gouache on paper, inscr, 9x73", C-NY 2/25/88 OE 20,900
ANE, Wilbur
Hay Stack, oil on canvasboard, sgn/inscr, 14x12", C-E 11/30/88 UE 220
ANSTON, Toller (Canadian, 1949-)
Floral Princess, no media given, sgn/dtd 84, 40x30", WAD 6/12/89 1,200
Flying Fish, gouache, sgn/dtd 77, 30x20", WAD 6/12/89 700
AWFORD, Ralston (American, 1906-1978)
Nassau 1 (geometric abstract), oil on canvas, sgn, 20x30", C-NY 12/2/88 49,500
anford Tanks, watercolor/pen/black ink/pencil on paper laid down on board, sgn, 11x16", C-NY 9/28/89 15,400
Wing Fabrication #2, oil on canvas, sgn, 1947, 12x22", SBY 5/25/88 52,400
AWLEY (Irish, 19th C)
Two Women Examining a Teacup, oil on paper on board, 10x13", WG 9/16/88 UE 250
AYER, see De Crayer
ECO, Gennaro; att
Architectural Capriccio, oil on canvas, unfr, 21x40", C-NY 4/8/88 OE 6,600
EDI, see Di Credi
EMONINI, Leonardo
a Bagnante Che si Spoglia, oil on canvas, initialed/dtd 52, sgn/dtd 52-53, 32x19", C-E 11/17/88 OE 10,450
e Bagnante (the bather), oil on canvas, sgn/dtd 51, 14x20", C-E 11/17/88 OE 4,620
Mama et Due Bambini en Barque (mother & children in boat), oil on canvas, sgn/dtd 51, 38x74", C-E 11/17/88 OE 19,800
Maternite, oil on canvas, sgn/dtd 51, 24x18", C-E 11/17/88 4,620
EO, Leonard (Canadian, 1925-)
Interior Scene with Figures, oil on canvas, sgn, 16x20", FB 4/25/88 300
ESPI, Giovanni Battista (Italian, 1557-1633)
Ceres, oil on canvas, unfr, 69x41", C-NY 4/8/88 OE 20,900
Martyrdom of Saint Lucy, oil on canvas, unfr, 36x55", C-NY 4/8/88 17,600

CRESPI, Giuseppe Maria (Italian, 1665-1747)
Portrait of a Young Woman with a Gun & a Bird Trap, red chalk, 9x8", SBY 1/13/89 OE 52,
CRESPI, Luigi; & Studio (Italian, 1710-1779)
Set of 4: Allegories of the Seasons; oil on canvas, 37x29", SBY 4/7/88 OE 33,
CRESPI, Luigi; circle of (Italian, 1710-1779)
Saint Francis, oil on canvas, inscr, oval, 14x12", C-NY 10/20/88 UE 1,
CRESSWELL, William Nichol (Canadian, 1822-1888)
Coastal View with Distant Lighthouse, watercolor, sgn/dtd 1883, 7x11", WAD 6/12/89 ....
Encampment & Falls, watercolor, sgn/dtd 1867, 12x20", WAD 6/12/89 3,
Pair: Desert Island; Ship Wreck; watercolor on paper, sgn/dtd 1882, 12x20", C-E 6/1/88 1,
River Settlement, watercolor, sgn/dtd 1867, 12x20", WAD 6/12/89 2,
CRESWICK, Thomas (British, 1811-69)
Cottage & Figures by a Lake, oil on canvas, bears signature, in a painted circle, 20" dia, SBY 12/9/88 UE ....
CRETI, Donato (Italian, 1671-1749)
Portrait of a Man Said To Be Count Caylus, black chalk/pen/brown ink/lt brown wash, wm, oval, 6x5", C-NY 1/12/88 2,
Virgin & Child with Infant St John Within a Mandorla, & Two Heads; pen/brown ink, 9x7", SBY 1/13/89 1,
CRETI, Donato; after (Italian, 1671-1749)
Portrait of a Musician, seated, holding a violin; oil on canvas, 18x15", C-E 6/1/88 1,
CRETI, Donato; att (Italian, 1671-1749)
Double-Sided: Figure Studies; Rape of Proserpinna; black ink over chalk/red chalk, unfr, 16x20", WD 1/25/89 ....
Mars & Venus, pen/brown ink on paper laid on heavy paper, ca 1740, 13x8", SWN 6/15/89 ....
CRETI, Donato; circle of (Italian, 1671-1749)
St John the Baptist (seated in a landscape), oil on canvas, 30x20", SBY 4/7/89 OE 11,
CREWE, Thomas (British, 19th C)
Portrait of an Italian Peasant, charcoal/white highlight on paper, sgn/dtd 1852, 24x16", B/B 12/8/88..........
CRILEY, Theodore Morrow (American, 1880-1930)
Figure Along the Stream, oil on canvas, estate monogram & stamp, 16x13", RWS 9/8/89 1,
CRIPPA, Roberto (Italian, 1921-1972)
Composition, mixed media collage mounted on wood, sgn/dtd 60/#d 5 on backing, 64x51", SBY 10/5/88 OE 6,
CRISP, Arthur Watkins (American, 1881-)
Allegory of Spring, oil on canvas mounted on panel, sgn, 25x30", RWS 4/22/89 ....
Springtime, oil on canvas laid down on board, sgn, 25x21", WD 3/23/88 UE 1,
CRISS, Francis (American, 1901-1973)
Romans (classical depiction), oil on masonite, sgn, 24x36", C-NY 9/28/89 5,
Romans (toga-clad Romans in interior), oil on masonite, sgn, 24x26", SBY 3/17/88 4,
Subway (caricature figures on subway), oil/pencil on canvas laid down, sgn/dtd 31, 9x6", C-NY 5/25/89 4,
View of Brooklyn Heights, oil on canvas, sgn, 24x30", C-E 10/18/89 OE 18,
CRIVELLI, Angelo Maria
Pair: Birds in a Landscape; oil on canvas, 17x24", SBY 10/13/89 8,
CRIVELLI, Vittorio (fl 1481-1501)
Christ Arising From the Sepulchre, oil on panel with gilt, shaped/carved frame, 25x15", SBY 10/21/88 OE 36,
CRIVELLONE, att
Turkey & Other Fowl on a Ledge, oil on canvas, 36x26", C-NY 4/6/89 OE 9,
CROCKER, Charles Matthew (1877-1950)
Phantom Mood, oil on canvas, sgn, 48x36", B/B 10/6/88 3,
CROCKFORD, Duncan (Canadian, 20th C)
Mount Eisenhower Near Banff, Alberta; acrylic on canvas, sgn/dtd 1974 twice/titled, 24x30", SBY 3/17/88 1,
CROCKWELL, Spencer Douglass (American, 1904-1968)
Tailor (man threading needle), watercolor/gouache/oil/gum arabic on masonite, sgn, unfr, 19x24", SBY3/17/88 UE.......... 1,
CROEGAERT, Georges (French, 1848-)
Flirtation (couple on shore, man waving to figures in boat), oil on panel, sgn/dtd 1885, 29x19", SBY 10/24/89 88,
Objects d'Arts et des Bijoux (still life), oil on canvas, sgn/inscr, 16x13", C-NY 5/24/89 11,
Taking Dictation, oil on panel, sgn/inscr Paris, 22x18", SBY 10/24/89 8,
Winning Hand, oil on panel, sgn, 22x18", SBY 5/23/89 UE 13,
CROFT, Louis Scott
Landscape, oil on masonite, sgn, 12x16", C-E 6/28/88 UE ....
CROME, John Berney (British, 1794-1842)
Moonlit River Landscape, oil on canvas, 25x30", SBY 12/9/88 3,
CROME, William Henry (British, 1806-1873)
Wooded Landscape with an Extensive Inner Estuary, oil on canvas, sgn/dtd 1846, 27x41", C-NY 5/25/88 3,
CRONE, Marvin D. (American, 1891-1964)
Farm in the Hills, oil on canvas, sgn, 16x32", SBY 5/24/89.......... 19,
CROOKE, Ray Austin (Australian, 1922-)
Chasing Ducks, Thursday Island (landscape); oil on paper laid down on panel, sgn, 12x9", C-SK 6/9/88.......... 1,
CROPSEY, Jasper Francis (American, 1823-1900)
Autumn, Lake George; oil on canvas, sgn/dtd 1881, 8x14", C-NY 9/28/89 9,
Autumn (landscape), oil on canvas, sgn/dtd 98, 12x20", C-NY 3/11/88 OE.......... 22,
Autumn on the Delaware River (cows at water's edge), oil on canvas, sgn/dtd 1890, 7x13", C-NY 9/28/89 14,
Autumn on the Wanaque, oil on canvas, sgn/dtd 1877, 10x8", C-SK 5/25/89 15,
Autumn Pastoral, oil on canvas, sgn/dtd 1889, 14x24", SBY 5/24/89 16,
Boating on the Hudson, oil on canvas, sgn/dtd 1887, 14x12", WD 10/5/88.......... 15,

Clearing Through the Trees, oil on canvas, sgn/dtd 1869, 8x12", C-NY 12/2/88 OE 37,400
Coast of Dorset (in a storm), oil on canvas, sgn/dtd 1858, 22x37", SBY 5/24/89 52,250
Deer in an Autumn Landscape, oil on canvas, sgn/dtd 1854, 7x10", B/B 6/15/89 OE 14,300
Figures by a Lake, oil on canvas, initialed/dtd 1873, unfr, 5x9", SBY 3/17/88 8,800
Greenwood Lake, New Jersey; oil on canvas, sgn/dtd 1866, 21x35", SBY 5/25/88 OE 85,250
Greenwood Lake at Twilight, oil on canvas, initialed/dtd 1873, 6x10", C-NY 9/30/88 OE 25,300
Hackensack Meadows in the Autumn (w/meandering stream), watercolor/pencil on paper, sgn/dtd 1894, 13x22", C-NY 9/28/89 17,600
House in the Mountains, pencil/watercolor heightened w/white gouache, initialed/dtd 1884, unfr, 5x7", SBY 6/24/88 2,200

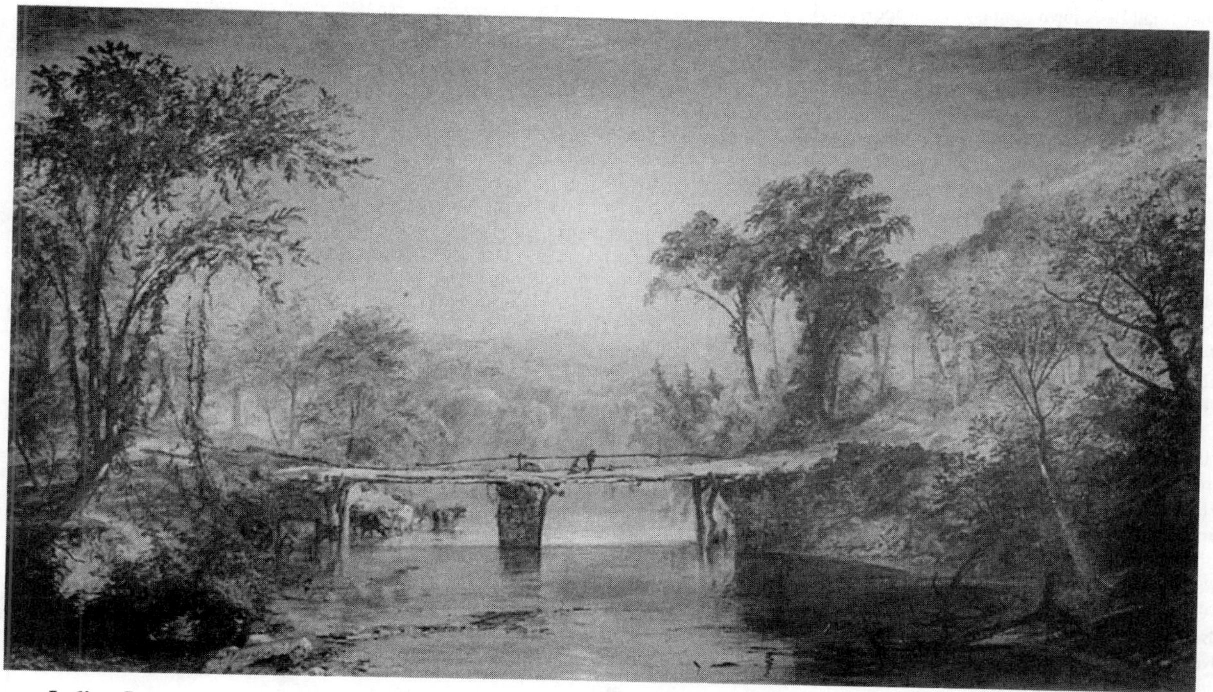

Indian Summer on the Delaware River, oil on canvas, sgn/dtd 1862, 24x41", C-NY 5/25/89 OE, $209,000

Lake View in Fall, watercolor/gouache/pencil on paper, sgn/dtd 1889, 17x27", C-NY 12/2/88 OE 26,400
Landscape, pencil/white gouache on paper, sgn/dtd 1845, unfr, 8x12", SBY 6/24/88 OE 4,950
New Hampshire Scenery, oil on canvas, initialed, 5x9", WD 4/13/88 7,000
O'er the Hills & Far Away, watercolor/gouache/pencil on paper, sgn twice, inscr/dtd 1892, 13x21", SBY 9/23/88 OE 11,000
Old Homestead of Isaac Cooley, Greenwood Lake, Passaic Country, NJ; oil on canvas, sgn/dtd 1863, 10x16", SBY 5/25/88 OE 66,000
Ramparo River, oil on canvas, sgn/dtd 1891, 24x44", SBY 5/25/88 39,600
Rocky Coast, oil on cardboard laid down on plastic mount, sgn, 10x16", RAB 8/8/89 2,250
Sailing on the Hudson, oil on canvas laid down on board, sgn/dtd 1889, 7x12", C-NY 12/2/88 OE 26,400
Shepstow Castle on the Wye (landscape w/ruins), oil on canvas, sgn/dtd 1854, 19x28", SBY 5/24/89 OE 25,300
Summer Walk (figure & cattle in landscape), watercolor on paper, sgn, 8x12", SBY 1/24/89 6,050
Sunset Over the River, watercolor on paper, sgn/dtd 1899, 18x14", C-NY 9/30/88 UE 1,760
Three Indians Stalking Deer, oil on canvas, sgn/dtd 1860, 15x24", SBY 5/25/88 35,200

CROSBY, Ray (American, 20th C)
Workhorse, red tugboat in East River w/Manhattan & Brooklyn Bridge; oil on canvas, sgn/titled, 24x30", RAB 8/8/89 1,100

CROSBY, Raymond (American, 1876-)
Night Street Scene, pencil on paper, 7x5", C-E 1/12/88 110

CROSIO, Luigi (Italian, 1835-1915)
Going to Market, oil on canvas, sgn, 14x10", C-NY 5/25/88 5,500

CROSMAN, John Henry (American, 1897-)
Beach Plums (flowering bushes on a sandy beach), oil on canvas, 26x32", RAB 8/9/88 UE 800
Still Life of Roses (in a green vase on a white cloth), oil on canvas, sgn, 20x24", RAB 8/9/88 2,250

CROSS, Henri Edmond (French, 1856-1910)
L'Epave (pointillistic coastal landscape w/figure & boat), oil on canvas, sgn/dtd 99, 24x32", SBY 5/9/89 467,500
La Ronde (Study for La Clairiere), oil on canvas, sgn, ca 1906-07, 18x22", SBY 11/12/88 264,000
Mediterranee par Vent d'Est (pointillistic coastal landscape), oil on canvas, ca 1902, 23x32", SBY 5/9/89 605,000
Pins au Bord de la Mer (Pine Trees by the Sea), watercolor on paper, stamped initials, 9x12", SBY 5/11/88 OE 15,400
Une Route au Bord de la Mer, watercolor/charcoal on paper, stamp initialed, 5x12", SBY 2/16/89 2,750

CROSS, Henry H. (American, 1837-1918)
Herd of Bison: Braving the Attack; oil on canvas, sgn/dtd 1879, 26x39", SBY 9/14/89 1,980
Lady Hilary, a King Charles Spaniel (portrait in a red chair); oil on panel, sgn, 1890, 13x17", SBY 6/9/89 18,700
Lion, oil on canvas, sgn/dtd 1884, 45x30", C-E 5/23/88 UE 1,540
Marcus Daly Training Prodigal, oil on canvas, sgn, 90x120", SBY 6/9/89 20,900

Marcus Daly's Child of the Mist (horse), oil on canvas, sgn/dtd 1892, 90x108", SBY 6/9/89 UE 18,700

CROSS, Penni Anne (American, 1939-)

Pink Striped Blanket, pastel on paper, sgn/inscr, 17x24", SBY 9/23/88 OE 3,575

CROSS, Watson

Oil Refiners, watercolor/pencil on paper, sgn, dtd 41, 15x22", C-E 2/1/89 OE 2,200

CROSZ, George

Im Lokal (abstract), India ink on thin paper, sgn twice/dtd 15 & 1917, inscr No 40, 13x8", SBY 2/16/89 OE 17,600

CROW, Gonzalo Endara (Latin American, 20th C)

Asi Aparecieron (fantasy village w/floating apples, train & fish), acrylic on canvas, 39x55", C-NY 11/21/88 OE 13,200
For This They Shall Be Known (fantasy landscape), acrylic on canvas, sgn/dtd 87, 32x47", lot 160, SBY 11/21/88 9,900
Here They Shall Live Forever, acrylic on canvas, sgn/titled/dtd 1987, 47x32", SBY 5/17/88 OE 14,300
Iban Buscando los Montes (village scene w/floating train & eggs), acrylic on canvas, 1987, 32x47", C-NY 5/18/88 OE 16,500
Paisaje Andino (fantasy village w/birds & floating eggs), acrylic on canvas, sgn/dtd 88, 32x47", C-NY 5/17/89 9,350
Untitled (fantasy village scene w/train & fish in sky), acrylic on canvas, sgn/dtd 87, 32x49", SBY 5/16/89 13,200
Untitled (village with figures in landscape), oil on board, sgn/dtd 83, 24x32", SBY 5/17/88 4,95

CROWNINSHIELD, Frederic (American, 1845-1918)

Classical Ruins, oil on canvas, sgn/dtd 1912, 30x21", SBY 1/24/89 3,02

CROWTHER, H. (British, 20th C)

Terriers Watteau Orlando & Watteau Nanette, oil on canvas, sgn/dtd 1932, 12x15", PHL 10/28/88 47

CRUICKSHANK, William (Canadian, 1849-1922)

Fallen Nest, watercolor, matted in an oval, 7x8", WAD 6/12/89 UE 35
Pair: Bird's Nest & Flowers on a Mossy Bank; gouache, sgn, 7x10", C-NY 5/25/88 4,62
Pair: Bird's Nest & Flowers on a Mossy Bank; watercolor on ivory, sgn, ovals, 5x6", C-E 5/23/88 1,04

CRUIKSHANK, George (British, 1792-1878)

Titania & Bottom the Weaver, A Midsummer Night's Dream; watercolor over traces of pencil, sgn, 4x5", C-E 5/22/89 66

CRUPPE, Charles Paul (American, 1860-1940)

Homeward Way, Road to Noordwyck, Holland; oil on canvas, sgn, 20x24", SBY 1/24/89 2,47
Indian Summer Landscape, oil on canvas, sgn, 16x20", SBY 3/17/88 1,21
Roadside Pasture, oil on canvas laid down on cardboard, sgn/titled, 12x16", RAB 8/8/89 1,50

CRUYS, Cornelis (European, ca 1644-1660)

Still Life of Grapes on Silver Tazza, a Silver Salt Cellar...& Other Objects; oil on panel, 28x23", SBY 6/2/89 49,50

CSAKY, Joseph (Hungarian/French, 1888-1971)

Scene de Cirque (contemporary circus scene), watercolor/gouache over pencil, sgn, 9x8", C-NY 2/18/88 OE 6,60

CSOSZ, John (20th C)

Birdge Over the River, oil on canvas, sgn/dtd 1921, 17x22", WG 4/23/88 UE 32
Dancing in the Forest, gouache on paper, sgn, 20x14", WG 4/23/88 UE 10

CUARTAS, Gregorio (Colombian, 1938-)

Head of a Man, watercolor on paper, sgn/dtd 71, 20x18", SBY 11/21/88 UE 77
Landscape with Cypresses, oil on canvas, 1987, 51x51", SBY 11/21/88 6,05
Naturaleza Muerta IV (still life), watercolor on paper, sgn/dtd 78, 30x23", C-NY 5/18/88 88
Pair: Naturaleza Muerta con Jarra y Servilleta; Naturaleza Muerta con Cebollas; watercolor, 1977, 22x30", C-NY 11/21/88 93
Still Life, oil on canvas, sgn/dtd 1982, 12x12", SBY 11/21/88 1,10

CUBELLS Y RUIZ, Enrique Martinez; att

On the Beach (elegant ladies on beach), oil on canvas laid down on board, monogramed, 24x21", SBY 10/24/89 11,0

CUCARO (20th C)

Creature Force, acrylic on canvas, sgn, 24x48", LH 12/4/88 .....

CUCCHI, Enzo (Italian, 1950-)

Heroe of the Adriatic Sea (contemporary), oil on canvas, dtd 1977-80/titled, 51x81", SBY 5/3/88 49,5
La Casa dei Barbari (contemporary), oil on canvas, sgn/dtd 1982, unfr, 124x84", C-NY 5/4/89 OE 121,0
Passeggiata Barbara (contemporary), oil/objects on canvas, sgn/dtd 1982/titled, 68x35", SBY 5/3/88 41,2
Tetto (abstract), oil stick/graphite/varnish on paper, sgn/dtd 1984, 18x7", C-NY 10/4/89 4,6
Untitled (abstract), oil/metal object on canvas, sgn/dtd 1982/inscr Rittrato per Andy Warhol, 32x40x8", SBY 5/2/88 OE 66,0
Untitled (contemporary), charcoal on paper, sgn/dtd 1984, 14x19", SBY 5/3/89 OE 5,2

CUCUEL, Edward (American, 1875-1951)

Awakening (draped nude seated on bed), oil on canvas laid down on panel, sgn, 28x32", C-NY 9/28/89 18,7
Bustard, black/white chalk on faded blue paper, 12x13", SBY 1/13/89 10,4
Down the Garden Path (lady w/parasol), oil on canvas, sgn, 21x30", C-NY 9/28/89 OE 17,6
Farewell (elegant couple dining), oil on canvas, sgn, 43x36", C-NY 5/25/89 35,2
Gitta Cucuel, the Dancer; oil on canvas, sgn/inscr, 48x37", C-NY 3/11/88 OE 14,3
Hot Day (draped nude, lady in dress resting in shade), oil on canvas, sgn, 35x39", C-NY 9/28/89 19,8
Morning in New York Harbor, oil on canvas, sgn twice/inscr, 26x32", C-NY 12/2/88 41,8
Polo Set, Palm Beach; oil on canvas, sgn, 30x25", SBY 6/9/89 36,3
Portrait of Evechen Meyerweissflog, oil on canvas, sgn twice/dtd Sept 1934/inscr, 32x26", C-SK 6/9/88 UE 2,2

CUERRIER, Raymond

Artichaux et Crane (still life), oil on canvas, sgn/dtd 60, 58x45", SBY 2/14/89 2,2

CUEVAS, Jose Luis (Mexican, 1934-)

A la Memorie De (To the Memory Of), pen/ink on paper, sgn/dtd 55, 10x24", B/B 5/17/89 UE 1,1
Assassins, black ink/wash on paper, sgn/dtd NY May 1973, 31x42", SBY 5/17/88 4,6
Autorreatrato (self-portrait in caricature), watercolor/India ink/brush on paper, sgn twice/dtd 73, 12x9", C-NY 5/17/89 3,8
Barrio Chino II, watercolor/pen/black ink/pencil on paper, sgn/dtd 1981/titled, 22x30", C-NY 5/18/88 UE 4,9
Police Station, watercolor on paper, sgn/titled/dtd 68, 28x39", SBY 5/17/88 4,4

Untitled (four figures standing on each other's heads), ink/watercolor on canvas, sgn, 21x5", SBY 11/21/88	3,080
JGAT, Xavier (Argentinian, 20th C)	
Rock & Roll Rhumba (man & woman in foreground, many musicians beyond), oil on canvasboard, sgn, 25x39", B/B 5/17/89	935
JILLARD	
Portrait of a Young Girl, oil on canvas, sgn, 20x15", FB 4/25/88	110
JLBERTSON, Josephine (American, 1852-1939)	
A Sandy Beach, oil on canvasboard, sgn, 10x14", B/B 10/6/88	605
Carmel by the Sea, oil on canvas, sgn/dtd 1914, 20x14", B/B 10/6/88	1,320
JLIN, Alice Mumford (American, 1890-)	
Double-Sided: Seated Woman; Quiet Shore; oil on panel, initialed, 8x12", RWS 8/20/88 UE	150
JLLEN, Maurice Galbraith (Canadian, 1866-1934)	
Snow: Storm Near North River, Quebec; oil on canvas, sgn, ca 1923, 18x15", B/B 5/17/89	17,000
JLOSILA, B.	
Pair: Venetian Parlor Interior Courting Scenes (impressionistic/contemporary); oil on canvas, sgn, 19x28", DM 5/13/88	900
JLVER, Charles (American, 1908-1967)	
Gila Woodpecker, watercolor on board, sgn, 20x24", DM 9/16/88	900
JLVERHOUSE, Johann Mongels (Dutch, 1820-1891)	
Death of De Soto (men in boats lower body into water), oil on canvas, 28x44", WD 10/5/88	4,600
Robbers' Retreat, oil on canvas, sgn/dtd 1875, 30x50", C-NY 12/2/88 UE	6,600
Skating by Moonlight, oil on canvas, sgn/dtd 1873, 24x40", SBY 6/28/89 OE	5,500
Vegetable Market at Night, oil on canvas, sgn/dtd 1878, 24x20", RWS 11/3/88 OE	9,000
Venice Night Scene, oil on canvas laid down on board, sgn/dtd 1848, 30x56", LH 10/16/88	5,000
JMING, Beatrice (American, 1903-)	
November in New London, Connecticut; oil on canvas, sgn, 23x30", C-E 9/15/88 OE	1,210
JMMING, Arthur (American, 19th C)	
Cliffs & Sea (seascape), watercolor/gouache on paper, sgn/dtd 1877, 9x16", RAB 3/27/89 UE	150
Gray Day (windswept tree on beach), oil on board, sgn, 7x10", RAB 8/9/88	700
Isle of Shoals Lighthouse (coastal landscape), oil on canvas, sgn/dtd 1895, 24x37", RAB 8/8/89 UE	1,400
Summer Beach (pines & grass shading sandy beach), watercolor on paper, sgn/dtd 1897, 12x19", RAB 8/9/88	500
JMMINGS, Marjorie (American, 20th C)	
California Mountains, watercolor on porcelain, sgn, 6x6", B/B 12/8/88	660
JMMINGS, Vera (New Zealand, 1891-1949)	
Maori Chieftainess, oil on canvas, sgn/indistinctly dtd, 14x12", C-SK 11/10/88	1,770
Portrait of a Maori Chief, oil on canvas, sgn, 12x10", C-SK 6/9/88	705
Portrait of a Young Maori Woman, oil on canvas, sgn, 10x8", C-SK 11/10/88	780
JNDELL, Nora Lucy Mowbray (British, 1889-1948)	
Cliffs, Houserock Valley, Navaho, Colorado; watercolor, sgn/dtd 36, 11x15", C-SK 6/9/88	240
Looking Across Houserock Valley, Navaho, Colorado; oil on board, sgn/dtd 37, 16x20", C-SK 6/9/88	1,020
San Francisco Peaks, Arizona; oil on canvasboard, sgn, 14x18", C-SK 11/10/88	280
JNEO, Rinaldo (American, 1877-1939)	
Billowy Clouds Above the Bay, oil on panel, inscr The Emporium, San Anselmo, California, 20x45", B/B 10/6/88	2,750
JPRIEN, Frank William (American, 1871-1948)	
Pair: Sunset Over the Sea; oil on board, sgn, 10x12", B/B 10/6/88	1,980
JRFI, S. (French, 19th/20th C)	
Woman in Bonnet Carrying Yellow Book, oil on canvas, sgn, 16x11", FAP 4/15/89	825
JRRADI, Francesco (Italian, 1570-1661)	
Portrait of a Standing Man Looking to the Right, chalk, 16x9", C-NY 1/11/89	1,430
Study of a Standing Man Holding a Book, red/white chalk on buff paper, #d 99, 15x8", SBY 1/13/89	7,150
JRRAN, Charles Courtney (American, 1861-1942)	
After the Storm (figures in a landscape), oil on canvas laid down, sgn/dtd 1916-19, 30x40", C-NY 5/25/89 OE	99,000
By the Lily Pond (elegant lady by pond), no media given, sgn/dtd 1908, 17x10", SBY 5/24/89	39,600
Dawn of Spring, oil on canvas, sgn/inscr twice, dtd 1902/1902-29, 18x32", SBY 9/23/88	7,700
Female Nude Under a Waterfall, oil on canvas, sgn/dtd 1903, 20x9", SBY 6/24/88	3,300
Goldfish (maid in flowing gown by fish bowl), oil on canvas, sgn/dtd 1911, inscr, 30x20", C-NY 12/2/88	49,500
In the Barnyard (man w/pitchfork resting, cow & chickens), oil on canvas, sgn/dtd 1891, 9x12", C-NY 5/25/89	26,400
Peonies (still life), oil on canvas, sgn/dtd 87, 12x9", SBY 5/24/89 OE	34,100
Peris, Fairies Among White Roses; oil on canvas, sgn/dtd 1898, 18x32", RWS 11/10/89	21,000
Standing Nude with Drape (Art Nouveau), oil on canvas, inscr, 16x10", DM 9/16/88	1,200
View of the Jungfrau, oil on canvas, sgn/dtd WENGEN 1900, 18x22", SBY 4/14/89	5,775
JRRIE, Mrs. S.C. (British, 19th C)	
Coming Storm (landscape), oil on canvas, 30x51", C-E 2/21/89 UE	550
JRRIER, Cyrus Bates (American, 1868-1946)	
California Sunset, oil on canvas, sgn/dtd 1940, 20x30", B/B 1/11/89	550
JRRIER, Edward Wilson (American, 1857-1918)	
Chinatown, San Francisco; oil on canvas, sgn/dtd 1903 & 19??, 12x18", C-NY 9/28/89	2,750
JRRIER, Joseph Frank (American, 1843-1909)	
Rain Clouds (dark clouds over landscape w/house & pond), pastel on heavy gray paper, sgn, 1890s, 6x8", RWS 3/31/88 OE	1,500
JRRIER, Mary Ann	
Apples & Mail (still life), oil pastel on board, sgn/dtd 87, 52x60", SBY 11/11/88 OE	41,250
JRRIER, Walter Barron (American, 1879-1934)	
Rip Tide, oil on canvas, sgn/dtd 1925, 20x26", B/B 1/11/89	550

CURRY, Elizabeth E. (Canadian 1864-1941)
Sunlit Forest, oil on board, sgn, 14x17", FB 4/25/88
CURRY, John Steuart (American, 1897-1946)
Circus Scene, watercolor on paper, sgn/dtd 1931, 11x15", SBY 9/23/88 .... **8,**
Self-Portrait, oil on canvas laid down on board, sgn/inscr/dtd 1935, 30x25", C-NY 5/26/88 .... **28,**
CURTER, J.
Venetian Canal, oil on canvas, sgn/dtd 29, 28x22", C-E 6/28/88 UE
CURTIS, George (American, fl 1840-1885)
Ships at Sunset, oil on canvas, sgn, 12x18", SBY 6/24/88 OE **5,**
CURTIS, James Waltham (Australian, 19th/20th C)
On the Road (horse-drawn coach, tent, & figures along a road), oil on canvas, sgn, 16x27", C-SK 11/10/88 OE **11,**
CURTIS, Ralph Wormsley (American, 19th/20th C)
River Scene, pencil/watercolor, sgn/dtd 1880, 9x13", C-SK 5/25/89 .... **1,**
CURTISS, Sprague (American, 19th C)
Canale Della Salute, watercolor on paper, sgn/titled, 10x5", RAB 8/8/89 UE
Mont St Michel, watercolor on paper, sgn/titled, 6x11", RAB 8/8/89 UE
CUSACHS Y CUSACHS, Jose (Spanish, 1851-1908)
Portrait of Alfonso III on Horseback, oil on canvas, sgn/dtd 1900, unfr, 79x71", SBY 2/22/89 OE **93,**
Soldiers on Horseback, oil on canvas, sgn/dtd 1892, 30x54", SBY 10/24/89 .... **137,**
Two Cavaliers, oil on canvas, sgn, 22x31", B/B 5/17/89 OE **3,**
CUSATI, Gaetano
Pair: Still Lifes of Various Flowers in Urns Standing on Marble Ledges; oil on canvas, 40x26", SBY 4/7/88 .... **18,**
CUSTIS, Eleanor Parke (American, 1897-)
Arab Scene, watercolor/gouache on paper, sgn, 22x18", C-E 6/1/88
CUSTODIS, Hieronimus; circle of (Flemish, 16th C)
Portrait of a Lady, aged 24, standing, three-quarter length...; oil on canvas, dtd 1582, 41x35", C-NY 5/31/89 UE **77,**
CUTHBERT, V.
Low Tide, oil on canvas, 22x18", C-E 2/16/88 UE
CUTTS, Gertrude Spurr (Canadian, 1858-1941)
Bridge on Bettws-y-Coed, oil on artist board, sgn, 6x10", WAD 6/12/89
Stone Tower Ruins, oil on canvas, sgn, 7x10", WAD 6/12/89
Summer Landscape, oil on canvas, sgn, 24x18", WAD 11/30/89 .... **1,**
CUTTS, William Malcom (Canadian, 1857-1943)
Vicarage Farm, oil on canvas, sgn, 18x26", WAD 11/30/89
CUVILLON, see De Cuvillon
CUYP, Aelbert (Dutch, 1620-1691)
Cowherds & Shepherds Tending Their Flocks on a Bluff...; oil on canvas, sgn/dtd 1646, 40x51", C-NY 1/11/89 UE **46,**
Fishing Boats by the Shore on a Calm Moonlit Sea, oil on canvas, 19x23", SBY 4/7/89 UE **18,**
CUYP, Aelbert; att (Dutch, 1620-1691)
Traveler Asking Directions, oil on panel, initialed, 11x15", WD 1/25/89 OE **3,**
CUYP, Aelbert; manner of (Dutch, 1620-1691)
Extensive Landscape with Elegant Figures on Horseback, oil on canvas, 42x35", SBY 6/1/89 OE **25,**
CUYP, Benjamin Gerritsz (Dutch, 1612-1652)
Adoration of the Shepherds, oil on panel, ca late 1630s-40s, 27x35", SBY 6/1/89 .... **35,**
Calvary Skirmish with a Battle Raging in the Distance, oil on panel, 8x11", SBY 10/13/89 .... **3,**
Soldiers Playing Cards in a Stable, oil on panel, sgn, oval, 16x22", SBY 10/21/88 .... **10,**
Troopers Playing Cards in an Encampment, oil on panel, 16x24", C-NY 5/31/89 OE **18,**
CUYP, Jacob Gerritsz (Dutch, 1594-1651)
Portrait of a Bearded Man, Said To Be Mayor of Dordrecht; oil on panel, sgn/inscr/dtd 1649, 28x25", SBY 6/3/88 .... **24,**
Cuzco School (18th C)
El Buen Pastor (shepherd w/flock in landscape), oil on canvas, 24x32", C-NY 11/21/88 UE
Last Judgement, oil on canvas, ca 1700, 72x57", lot 41, C-NY 1/15/88 .... **5,**
Last Judgement, oil on canvas, ca 1700, 72x57", lot 49, C-NY 10/20/88 .... **6,**
Madonna & Child, oil on canvas, unfr, 56x42", C-SK 5/25/89 .... **5,**
Pair: Scenes of Angels Mourning the Assumption; oil on canvas, 15x12", 19x13", B/B 1/11/89 OE **2,**
Virgin of the Rosary of Pomata, oil on canvas, 26x21", SBY 5/17/88 .... **7,**
CYGAN, Z. (Polish, 20th C)
Untitled, troikas in a snowy winter landscape; oil on canvas, sgn, 24x36", SLK 2/11/89
CYGNE, B.J. (French, 20th C)
Parasol, oil on canvas, sgn, 24x36", LH 12/4/88
CYRUS-FARNUM, H.
Lady in Straw Hat, oil on canvas, sgn/dtd Paris 96, 29x20", C-E 7/26/88
CZACHORSKI, see De Czachorski
CZERNUS, Tibor
Ecrerisses et Cageot (still life w/lobsters & basket), oil on canvas, 1981, 18x26", SBY 10/7/89 .... **4,**
Vendeuse de Mangues (market scene), oil on canvas, sgn/dtd 1979, 45x58", SBY 10/7/89 .... **14,**
CZESCHKA, Carl Otto (Austrian, 1878-1960)
Greek Warriors Setting Out To Battle, oil on canvas, 10x25", C-L 6/27/88 UE **3,**
D'ACOSTA, H. Walker (Spanish, 19th C)
Elegant Party Returning Home, oil on panel, sgn/inscr Paris, 10x15", C-NY 2/23/89 .... **7,**

D'AGOTY, Pierre Edouard Gautier (1775-1871)
Portrait of a Young Girl Beside a Silver Urn with Flowers, oil on canvas, 12x8", SBY 10/21/88 3,850
D'AGUILAR, M.
Effet du Matin, oil on canvas, sgn/dtd 77, 24x36", LH 5/15/88 250
Paysage d'Auvergne, oil on canvas, sgn twice/dtd 77, 24x36", LH 5/15/88 225
D'ANVERS, Cavalier; see Breydael, Karel
D'AOUST, Enrique (Mexican, 20th C)
Muchacha con Flores, oil on canvas, sgn/dtd 62, 54x44", B/B 6/15/89 3,850
D'ARCANGELO, Alan (American, 1930-)
Barrier #3, acrylic on canvas, 70x60", SBY 10/7/89 OE 18,150
Constellation, graphite on canvas, sgn/dtd New York City 1971/titled, 36x36", C-E 5/9/89 990
Landscape, acrylic on canvas, sgn/inscr dtd 1968, 40x36", C-E 5/13/88 OE 1,100
D'ARLES, Jean Henri (French, 1734-1784)
Rocky Coastline at Dawn with Fishermen Landing Their Catch Near Fortress, oil on canvas, unfr, 35x72", C-M 12/3/88 OE 48,310
D'ARPINO, Cavaliere; circle of
Female Martyr Saint, oil on canvas, unfr, 30x22", C-NY 10/20/88 1,540
D'ARTHOIS, Jacques; circle of (Flemish, 1613-1686)
Horse & Rider in a Parkland Setting, oil on panel, 19x25", SBY 7/12/89 UE 1,650
Hunters Stopping To Talk to Gypsies Along a Road, oil on panel, 20x28", SBY 10/21/88 OE 14,300
D'AVENNES, Emile Prisse
Tomb of Petamenophis, Thebes; pen/brush/black ink/watercolor over pencil, wm J Whatman, 15x10", C-NY 10/26/88 1,100
D'AZIGBOR, E. (French, 19th C)
Woman (bust-length portrait facing forward wearing dress/high collar), oil on canvas, sgn/dtd 1890, 22x18", SLK 2/12/88 120
D'ESPAGNAT, Georges (French, 1870-1950)
Baigneuse, oil on canvas, initialed, 24x40", C-NY 10/6/88 24,200
Bouquet d'Anemones (floral still life), oil on canvas, initialed, 18x15", C-NY 2/16/89 24,200
Deux Jeunes Filles au Bord de la Mer (two young girls by the sea), oil on canvas, initialed, 35x39", C-NY 2/18/88 27,500
Femme Assise, red chalk on paper, initialed, 10x8", C-NY 2/13/89 440
Femme dans un Paysage (reclining woman in landscape), oil on canvas, initialed, 23x29", C-NY 2/16/89 24,200
Femme Nue Allongee (reclining nude), oil on canvas, initialed, 32x26", C-NY 2/16/89 15,400
Femme Nue Lisant, oil on canvas, initialed, 24x20", SBY 10/7/88 16,500
Fleurs, oil on canvas, initialed, 18x15", SBY 2/18/88 10,450
Jeunes Filles (two young women in an interior), oil on canvas, initialed, 19x15", C-NY 2/16/89 15,400
La Tasse de Cafe (woman seated at table), oil on canvas, initialed, 32x39", C-NY 2/16/89 44,000
Landscape with Church, oil on canvas, sgn, 13x17", SBY 10/7/89 8,250
Le Port de Camaret, Bateaux de Pecheurs (port scene), oil on canvas, initialed, 19x24", C-NY 5/12/88 30,800
Les Baigneuses (The Bathers), watercolor over pencil on paper, initialed, 5x7", C-E 11/17/88 440
Marie, oil on canvas, initialed, 26x21", SBY 2/18/88 22,000
Mme d'Espagnat Assise a la Robe Bleu (artist's wife seated), oil on canvas, initialed, 40x32", C-NY 2/16/89 24,200
Nature Morte, Fruits; oil on canvas, initialed, 20x24", SBY 2/18/88 24,200
Nature Morte aux Fleurs (floral still life), oil on canvas, initialed, 37x29", C-NY 10/6/88 35,200
Nature Morte aux Fleurs et aux Fruits (floral still life w/fruit), oil on canvas, initialed, 22x18", C-NY 2/16/89 28,600
Nature Morte Avec Portrait de Renoir (still life of fruit/portrait), oil on canvas, initialed, 32x26", C-NY 5/12/88 OE 49,500
Paysage a Cagnes (landscape w/two children & house), oil on canvas, initialed, 26x32", C-NY 5/11/89 77,000
Petit Jardin de Sicile (woman & child in garden scene), oil on canvas, initialed, 26x43", C-NY 5/11/89 55,000
Portrait de Femme, oil on canvas, initialed, 16x13", C-NY 10/6/88 6,050
Portrait de Jeune Fille (lady, half-length, in bonnet, holding rose), oil on canvas, initialed, 25x25", C-NY 10/5/89 22,000
Portrait de Jeune Fille (portrait of a girl, seated), oil on canvas, initialed, 25x32", C-NY 10/6/88 28,600
Vase de Fleurs (floral still life in interior), oil on canvas, initialed, 23x28", SBY 10/6/89 OE 41,250
Vase de Fleurs (floral still life), oil on canvas, initialed, 28x24", C-NY 5/12/88 OE 52,800
Vase de Fleurs (floral still life), oil on canvas, initialed, 18x15", SBY 10/7/88 8,250
Vase de Fleurs (floral still life), oil on canvas, initialed, 26x21", C-NY 11/16/88 44,000
HEUR, Cornelis Joseph; att
Elegant Figures Resting in a Landscape, oil on canvas, bears indistinct signature, 30x21", C-NY 4/8/88 1,980
HONDECOETER, see De Hondecoeter
OYLY, Charles; circle of (British, 1741-1845)
Pair: Mountain Waterfall; Ghats at Benares; oil on board, 12x8", C-SK 5/25/89 2,200
A, Zhu (Bada Shanren) (Chinese, 1624-1704)
Xing Shu, Transcription of Poem by Bai Juyu (running script, hanging scroll); ink, sgn/dtd 1703, 59x17", SBY 5/31/89 OE 99,000
A CARAVAGGIO, Michelangelo; follower of (Italian, 16th C)
Deposition, oil on canvas, unfr, 40x45", SBY 12/9/88 935
Virgin & Child, oil on canvas, 35x27", SBY 4/7/88 3,575
A CARPI, Girolamo; circle of (Italian, 1501-1556)
Group of Soldiers Leaving a Tent, Palisade Behind; black chalk/pen/brown ink, outsides indented, 12x9", C-NY 1/12/88 UE 165
A CINGOLI, Messer Ulisse Severino (Italian, 19th C)
Study of a Tree, Rocks, & Distant Landscape with Boats; pen/ink/wash heightened w/white, 11x7", SBY 1/13/89 OE 25,300
A CONEGLIANO, Cima; studio of
Madonna & Child Before a Curtain, a landscape beyond; oil on panel, 22x17", C-NY 5/31/89 OE 30,800
A CORREGGIO, Antonio Allegri; after (Italian, 1494-1534)
Madonna Adoring the Christ Child, oil on canvas laid down on board, 31x26", SBY 12/9/88 1,870
Noli Me Tangere, oil on canvas, 51x40", C-NY 10/12/89 2,200

DA EMPOLI, Jacopo; after (Italian, 1554-1640)
Marriage by Proxy of Henry IV of France & Marie de Medici; oil on panel, 10x13", C-NY 4/6/89 UE 990

DA PONTE, Francesco; follower of (17th C)
Allegory of the Months of May & June, oil on panel, 21x29", SBY 10/21/88 6,600

DA PONTE, Jacopo; see Bassano

DA RIPATRANSONE, Padre Francesco
Three Birds, Three Butterflies, Cherries, Plums, & a Rose; chalk/bodycolor, sgn/dtd 1662, C-NY 1/11/89 4,620

DA SAN FRIANO, Maso; circle of
Portrait of a Lady, seated half-length, wearing a red & black costume...; oil on canvas, 28x24", C-NY 1/11/89 15,400

DA SANTACROCE, Francesco di Simone (Italian, ca 1443-1508)
Adoration of the Magi, oil on panel, 30x46", SBY 6/2/89 UE 38,500

DA SANTACROCE, Girolamo (Italian, 16th C)
Annunciation, oil on panel, pointed top, 10x13", SBY 10/13/89 17,600

DA SANTACROCE, Girolamo; school of (Italian, 16th C)
Sacra Conversazione (four figures in a landscape), oil on panel, 13x17", C-NY 4/6/89 2,86

DA SILVA, Jose (European, 1909-)
Natureza Morta con Frutas Tropicais (still life of tropical fruit), oil on canvas, sgn, 26x32", C-NY 5/18/88 UE 2,20

DA SILVA, Maria Elena Vieira (20th C)
Children with Flags (contemporary), India ink/watercolor on paper, sgn, 9x6", SBY 10/7/89 OE 8,25
Figures in an Interior, colored wax crayons on paper, sgn/dtd 39, 13x9", C-NY 5/12/88 OE 35,20
La Jardin (abstract), gouache on paper, sgn/dtd 58, 20x25", C-NY 5/12/88 OE 63,80
Untitled (abstract), gouache/pen/black ink on paper, sgn, 9x7", C-NY 11/15/88 24,20

DA TIVOLI, Rosa (German, 1657-1706)
Shepherd with His Flock & a Boy on a Donkey, oil on canvas, circular, 16" dia, C-NY 10/12/89 3,52

DA TIVOLI, Rosa; school of (German, 1657-1706)
Goatherd with His Flock, oil on canvas, unfr, 25x26", C-E 6/1/88 2,09

DA VERONA, Liberale; att
Saint Sebastian, metalpoint/brush/gray wash heightened w/white on greenish preparation, inscr, 7x4", C-NY 1/12/88 OE 33,00

DA VINCI, Leonardo; after (Italian, 1452-1519)
Madonna & Child Contemplating Carnations, oil on panel, 12x9", C-NY 1/11/89 OE 8,25
Mona Lisa, oil on panel, 30x23", C-E 6/1/88 1,65
Mona Lisa, oil on panel, 29x22", C-NY 10/20/88 OE 5,50

DA VISSO, Paolo
Madonna & Child Enthroned, God the Father with the Holy Spirit Above; oil on gold ground on panel, 22x11", C-NY 1/11/89 46,20

DABO, Leon (American, 1868-1960)
Circle Line on the Hudson (river landscape), oil on canvas, sgn/monogramed, 25x20", SBY 4/14/89 OE 9,0
Figure by a Shore, oil on canvas, sgn twice/monogramed, 15x18", C-E 2/3/88 OE 4,95
Grove (stand of trees), oil on canvas laid down on board, sgn w/artist's device, 10x12", C-NY 9/28/89 3,85
Mother & Child Looking Towards Sea, oil on canvas, 30x34", FAP 4/15/89 OE 25,20
Pair: Trouville, 1938 II; Dieppe; oil on board, sgn/dtd 1938, 6x7", SBY 6/28/89 1,70

DADO (20th C)
Herouval (surrealistic), oil on canvas, sgn/dtd 67 & 68, 90x57", C-E 11/17/88 OE 18,7
La Police Vegetale, oil on canvas, sgn/dtd 69, 51x77", C-NY 2/13/89 OE 22,0
Personnage Assis Ciel Bleu (surrealistic), oil on canvas, sgn/dtd 65 & 66, 51x39", C-E 11/17/88 OE 13,2

DAGGY, Richard
Pair: Poultry in a Landscape; watercolor on paper, 1 sgn/dtd 37, 18x21", FAP 4/15/89 UE 2

DAGNAN, Isadore (French, 1794-1873)
Franco-Prussian Battle; oil on canvas, initialed, 36x26", B/B 4/20/88 3

DAGNAN-BOUVERET, Pascal Adolphe Jean (French, 1852-1929)
Hopgrower's Daughter (portrait), oil on canvas, sgn, 40x29", C-NY 2/23/89 4,4

DAGNAUX, Albert Marie Adolphe (French, 1861-1933)
Avenue du Bois-de-Boulogne, Club des Pannes; oil on canvas, sgn, 84x120", SBY 5/23/89 550,0

DAHL, Johannes Siegwald (German, 1827-1902)
King Charles & a Whippet with a Macaw, oil on canvas, sgn/dtd 1858, 47x34", SBY 6/9/89 25,3
Two Dogs Amused by a Parrot, oil on canvas, sgn/dtd 1891, 14x9", SBY 12/9/88 2,4

DAHL, Michael (Swedish, 1656-1743)
Portrait of a Lady Said To Be Barbara Villiers, Duchess of Cleveland; oil on canvas, 22" dia, C-NY 4/8/88 3,8
Portrait of a Woman, wearing blue-green dress & white blouse; oil on canvas, oval, 30x25", C-NY 4/8/88 2,4

DAHL, Michael; att (Swedish, 1656-1743)
Portrait of a Lady (three-quarter length wearing brown dress seated in landscape), oil, unfr, 48x41", SBY 10/13/89 5,5

DAHLAGER, Jules (American, 20th C)
Deserted Cabin, Near Ketchikan, Alaska; oil on canvasboard, sgn/dtd 1940, 6x8", B/B 5/17/89 OE 1,6
Lake Connell, Near Ketchikan, Alaska; oil on canvas, sgn/dtd 40, 6x8", B/B 5/17/89 9
Mount McKinley, oil on board, sgn/dtd 1929, 7x5", B/B 5/17/89 OE 1,3
Mountain Scene, oil on canvasboard, sgn/dtd 1932, 6x8", B/B 5/17/89 .... [illegible]
Native Runner (full-length portrait of Eskimo man), oil on board, sgn/dtd 1935, 15x10", B/B 5/17/89 .... [illegible]
Reflections, Bell Arm, Behm Canal, SE Alaska; oil on board, sgn, 6x8", B/B 5/17/89 OE 1,0

DAHLGREEN, Charles W. (American, 1864-1955)
Jackson Branch (autumn landscape), oil on masonite, sgn, 24x30", RWS 5/12/89 1,
Morning (wooded landscape), oil on board, sgn, 22x26", B/B 9/14/89 UE ....
White River, Ozarks; oil on panel, sgn, 32x29", LH 3/20/88 OE 1,

DAINGERFIELD, Elliott (American, 1859-1932)
Farmyard, Spring; watercolor on paper, sgn, 7x10", RWS 11/10/89 UE ... 150
Floral Still Life, oil on canvas, sgn/dtd NY 1881, 24x14", SBY 1/24/89 ... 2,750
Golden Sunset on the Lake, oil on canvas, sgn, 24x34", NA 2/24/89 ... 7,000
Mountain Landscape (two figures dwarfed by mountain range), oil on artist board, sgn, 7x9", RWS 3/31/88 ... 375

DAINI, Augusto (Italian, 19th C)
Flirtation, watercolor, sgn, 22x15", C-NY 2/25/88 ... 1,210

DAIO, David (20th C)
Breaker, acrylic on canvas, sgn/dtd 1972, 66x150", SBY 2/1/489 ... 1,320

DAKEN, Sidney Tilden (American, 1876-1935)
Fallen Leaf Lake, oil on board, sgn, 16x20", B/B 12/8/88 ... 715
North California Alps, Indian & Cathedral Peak; oil on canvas, sgn, 16x20", C-E 11/30/88 UE ... 770
View of Mount Tamalpais, oil on canvas, sgn, 18x24", B/B 8/10/88 ... 550

DAKIN, J. (British, 19th/20th C)
Angler by a Pond, oil, initialed/dtd 1893, 25x37", WD 1/11/89 ... 950

DAL SOLE, Giovan Gioseffo (Italian, 1654-1719)
Mary Magdalene Annointing Christ's Feet, en brunaille/oil on panel, oval, 14x10", SBY 6/8/88 UE ... 550

DALBY, David (British, 1794-1836)
Jerry, Winner of the 1824 St Leger with B Smith Up; oil on canvas, sgn/inscr w/horse's name, 23x30", SBY 6/10/88 ... 22,000
St Patrick (racehorse w/jockey up), oil on canvas, sgn/indistinctly dtd, 25x30", SBY 6/9/89 ... 17,600

DALBY, John (British, fl 1838-1953)
Mishap at a Ditch (rider being thrown into water in a landscape), oil on canvas, sgn, 9x13", SBY 6/9/89 ... 4,070

DALE, Stanley (American, 20th C)
Boat Yard, oil on canvas, sgn/dtd 1918, 18x22", WG 4/23/88 ... 175

DALI, Salvador (Spanish, 1904-1989)
Amazones, pen/India ink/pencil on paper, sgn/dtd 1937, 21x31", C-NY 11/15/88 ... 33,000
Bathroom Soliloquies (man in bathtub in surrealistic composition), India ink on artist board, 12x8", SBY 4/29/88 OE ... 23,100
Battle of Tetuan II, oil/gouache/watercolor on paper, sgn/dtd 1960, 9x16", SBY 10/6/89 OE ... 71,500
Chanel: Grand Central Powder Room; India ink on stiff card, 7x8", SBY 4/29/88 OE ... 10,450
Christ Child, oil on canvas, sgn/dtd 1956, 7x6", SBY 5/11/88 OE ... 115,500
Clowns in Clover (abstract), India ink/ink wash on artist board, sgn, 5x6", SBY 4/29/88 OE ... 8,250
Dance of the Flower Maidens (design for a china plate), watercoler/pencil on card, sgn/dtd 1942, 13" dia, SBY 5/20/89 ... 60,500
Double-Sided: Atomic Head; Studies; black ballpoint pen on paper, sgn/dtd 1954, 8x9", C-NY 5/11/89 OE ... 23,100
Double-sided: Study for Inventions of the Monsters; pencil on paper, sgn, ca 1937, 14x10", C-NY 10/5/89 ... 9,900
Dream of Venus VI, watercolor/India ink/pencil on paper, 1939, 13x14", SBY 11/12/88 OE ... 41,250
El Sombrero de Tres Picos (surrealistic depiction), gouache on brown paper, sgn/dtd 1949, 11x14", SBY 11/16/89 OE ... 176,000
Eleanor (portrait in surrealistic composition), India ink on paper laid down, sgn, 12x9", SBY 4/29/88 OE ... 22,000
Escargot sur un Feuille, black felt-tip pen on paper, sgn, 9x14", C-NY 2/13/89 OE ... 2,860
Etude Anamorphique, pen/black ink over pencil on paper, bears signature, 7x8", C-NY 10/5/89 ... 4,400
Grand Opera (surrealistic illustration for the Ziegfield Theatre), oil on canvas, sgn/dtd 1957, 37" dia, SBY 11/12/88 ... 330,000
L'Hirondelle Immobile, oil on canvas, sgn/dtd 1956, 18x14", SBY 5/11/88 ... 154,000
Le Cavalier, pen/ink/thickened sepia ink wash on thin card, sgn/dtd 1952, 17x22", SBY 11/12/88 OE ... 46,750
Man Bites Pencil (abstract), India ink over pencil on artist board, sgn, 6x7", SBY 4/29/88 OE ... 9,350
Nativite, watercolor/pen/brown ink over pencil on board, sgn/dtd 1950, 20x26", C-NY 11/15/88 ... 68,200
Noblesse of the Triumpher & the Vanquished, brush/reddish-brown ink on paper, sgn/dtd 1950, 40x30", C-NY 5/11/89 ... 86,900
Pair: Horse & Rider with Trainer; Fantastic Object; pen/ink on paper, 4x6", 8x8", SBY 10/6/89 ... 3,300

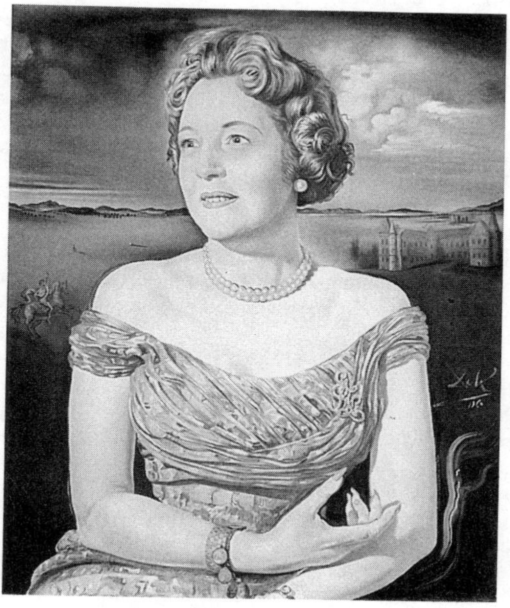

Portrait de la Comtesse Ghislaine d'Oultremont, oil on canvas, sgn/dtd 1960, 29x24", C-NY 5/11/89 OE, $286,000

Portrait of Billy Rose (in a surrealistic composition), India ink on stiff card, sgn/dtd 1947, 10x6", SBY 4/29/88 OE 14,300
Rocking Chair, India ink on artist board, 9x9", SBY 4/29/88 OE 12,100
San Juan de la Cruz (portrait of kneeling figure), India ink on sketchbook paper, sgn/dtd 1951, 10x8", SBY 5/11/88 OE 11,000
Surrealist Landscape, gouache on board, sgn, ca 1963-64, 56x21", SBY 5/11/88 115,500
Toreador (shoulder-length portrait), watercolor/gouache on paper, sgn, 20x16", SBY 10/6/89 44,000
Tristan & Isolde, oil on canvas, sgn/dtd 1941, velvet-lined frame, 25x31", C-NY 10/6/88 OE 462,000
Untitled (sketch of woman from behind), pen/ink/white chalk on tan paper, sgn/dtd 1937, 26x20", SBY 5/10/89 82,500
Untitled (surrealistic composition), India ink/watercolor/gouache on paper, sgn/dtd 1944, 13x18", SBY 11/16/89 OE 253,000
Untitled: Melting Clock with Biomorphic Form; India ink/pencil on paper, ca 1930-33, 5x6", SBY 5/10/89 49,500
Virgin & Child, pen/brown & black inks/watercolor/gouache heightened w/gold paint, sgn/dtd 1947, 14x15", SBY 5/10/89 55,000
What the Countryside Will Look Like in 1987, pen/India ink on paper, sgn, ca 1937, 11x15", C-NY 5/11/89 30,800

DALLAIRE, Jean Philippe (Canadian, 1916-1965)
Abstract Study of a Woman, oil on board, sgn/dtd 1939, 11x9", FB 10/17/88 8,000
Poeme Chinois, oil on paper, sgn/dtd 1962, 5x8", FB 10/30/89 2,640
Poissons (fish), oil on board, sgn/dtd 1960, 15x20", FB 4/25/88 7,200
Still Life, gouache, sgn/dtd 1951, 7x5", FB 4/25/88 OE 3,400

Dalmation School (14th C)
Crucifixion, oil on panel w/gold ground, shaped top, 14x12", C-NY 5/31/89 13,200

Dalmation School (17th C)
Agony in the Garden, oil on panel, 19x17", C-NY 4/6/89 28,607

DAM, Vu Cao
Combat de Coqs, oil on canvas, sgn/dtd 64, 21x26", C-NY 2/13/89 440

DAMOYE, Pierre Emmanuel (French, 1847-1916)
Champs de Coquelicots, oil on canvas, sgn/dtd 1902, 26x39", SBY 2/22/89 28,600
Extensive Wheatfield, oil on panel, sgn, 13x24", C-E 10/25/88 OE 4,400
La Jetee a Houlgate, oil on canvas, sgn/dtd 91, 26x44", SBY 7/12/89 3,57
Landscape with Windmill in the Distance, oil on panel, sgn/dtd 79, 13x24", SBY 12/9/88 OE 4,12

DAMSCHROEDER, Jan Jac Matthys (German, 1825-1905)
Fisherman's Family, oil on canvas, sgn, 14x22", C-NY 2/25/88 7,70
Kitchen Interior with Figures, oil on canvas, sgn twice/dtd 1882, 27x32", SBY 6/8/88 4,95
Return Home (family in interior), oil on canvas, sgn/dtd 1877, 26x32", B/B 9/14/89 OE 3,30
Stolen Moment, oil on canvas, sgn twice/inscr/dtd 1885, 21x28", C-NY 5/25/88 3,85
Traveling Circus, oil on canvas, sgn, 26x32", C-NY 5/24/89 6,05

DANA, C.G. (American, 19th/20th C)
Manchester, Massachusetts, Harbor; oil on cardboard, sgn/dtd 1901, 10x13", RAB 8/8/89 60

DANCE, Nathaniel; after (British, 1734-1811)
Portrait of Captain Cook, oil on board, oval, 4x3", C-SK 5/25/89 1,19
Portrait of Captain James Cook, watercolor on ivorine, 3" dia, C-SK 6/9/88 OE 71

DANCE, Nathaniel; school of (British, 1734-1811)
Portrait of a Gentleman (seated in a Windsor Chair, in a landscape), oil on canvas, 36x28", C-NY 4/8/88 1,98

DANDINI, Cesare
Saint Michael, oil on copper, oval, 4x3", C-NY 10/12/89 6,05

DANDINI, Pietro (Italian, 1646-1712)
Sacrifice of Iphigenia, oil on canvas, 43x62", C-NY 10/20/88 OE 35,20

DANERI, Eugenio (20th C)
Magnolias (still life), oil on board, sgn, ca 1960, 20x16", SBY 11/21/88 6,60

DANIELL, William (British, 1769-1837)
Indian Mausoleum in the Mysore with Banyan Tree, gray wash, inscr, unfr, 6x8", C-SK 6/9/88 65
View of Esplanade Row From the Chouringhee Road, Calcutta; pencil/watercolor, 19x27", C-SK 5/25/89 5,88
View of Gyah, Bahar; oil on canvas, 25x30", C-SK 5/25/89 OE 20,21

DANIELS, Andries (1580-)
Crucifixion in a Garland Surround of Mixed Flowers, oil on panel, 24x19", C-M 6/16/89 9,78
Virgin & Child in a Garland Surround of Mixed Flowers, oil on panel, 26x20", C-M 6/16/89 9,78

DANIELS, George Fisher (American, 1821-)
Panoramic Landscape with Distant Town, oil on canvas, sgn, 10x19", SBY 1/24/89 2,7

Danish School (19th C)
Christianstead St Croix (island inlet landscape w/ships/village), bodycolor, inscr, ca 1810, 15x11", C-SK 6/9/88 OE 2,7
Henriette von Schimmelmann (bust-length wearing blue/white dress), oil on canvas, inscr/dtd 1814, 28x22", SLK 5/11/88 1,2
Rio de Janeiro (coastal view), oil w/bodycolor, inscr, 12x14", C-SK 6/9/88 OE 1,8

Danish School (20th C)
Fisherman, oil on canvas, sgn/dtd Kalledosoe 1936, 17x21", MG 5/28/88 2

DANKOWSKI, F.W. (European, 19th C)
Lakeside Country Palace, oil on canvas, sgn, 8x19", RWS 6/17/89 4

DANLOUX, Henri Pierre (French, 1753-1809)
Portrait of John King, Esq; oil on canvas, inscr, 45x23", SBY 6/3/88 16,5

DANLOUX, Henri Pierre; circle of (French, 1753-1809)
Portrait of a Lady in a Turban & Fur-Edged Coat, oil on canvas, 20x16", SBY 7/12/89 1,0
Portrait of a Young Lady, oil on canvas, oval, 38x31", SBY 4/7/89 UE 5,5

DANNENBERG, Alice (Russian/French, 1861-)
Le Bebe (baby w/doll in highchair), oil on canvas, sgn, 22x19", SBY 12/9/88 1,3

NNER, Sara Kolb (American, 1894-1969)
In the Park, Santa Barbara; oil on canvas, sgn, 24x20", B/B 10/6/88 2,200
NNHAUSEN, E.G.
Hour of Prayer, oil on canvas, sgn, 24x30", LH 3/20/88 UE 40
NSAERT, Leon (Belgian, 1830-1909)
Christening Party, oil on panel, sgn, 31x38", C-NY 10/25/89 7,150
Dance (gathering in interior), oil on panel, sgn, 28x36", C-NY 2/23/89 5,280
OFEN, Ye (Chinese, 19th C)
Landscape (hanging scroll), ink/color on paper, sgn, 38x13", SBY 5/31/89 2,200
OJI, att (Shitao)(Chinese, 1641-1707)
Landscape (hanging scroll), ink/color on paper, sgn/dtd 1698, 37x17", SBY 5/31/89 5,500
Set of 4: Landscapes (album leaves); ink/color on paper, 1 sgn, 8x13", SBY 5/31/89 UE 13,200
OJI (Shitao)(Chinese, 1641-1707)
Hermitage on Mount Tongpo (hanging scroll), ink on paper, sgn/inscr w/poem, 33x17", SBY 5/31/89 52,250
OZHOU, Huang (Chinese, 1585-1646)
Calligraphy in Xing Shu (Running Script, handscroll), ink on silk, sgn, 10x86", SBY 5/31/89 7,150
PHNIS, Nassos (Greek, 1914-)
#9-68 (geometric design), epoxy on canvas, sgn, unfr, 136x136", C-E 11/17/88 OE 4,620
Untitled, plastic paint on paper mounted on board, 11x14", SBY 2/14/89 OE 1,870
QIAN, Zhang (Chinese, 1899-1983)
Sitting Alone by the Lake (hanging scroll), ink/color on paper, sgn/dtd 1932, 49x24", SBY 5/31/89 4,950
RBOUR, Marguerite Mary (French, 19th C)
Sunny Day at the Beach, oil, sgn, 18x25", WD 1/11/89 2,200
RET, Ernesto; att (Italian, 17th C)
Pair: Horse Fair with Gentleman...; Peasants Drinking...; oil on canvas, bears signature, 28x43", C-NY 4/6/89 OE 20,900
RIEN, Andre
Lady After Her Bath, oil on canvas, sgn, 24x30", WG 4/23/88 UE 900
RLEY, Felix Octavius Carr (American, 1822-1888)
Chief of the Little Osages, oil on canvas, sgn/titled, 7x6", LH 5/15/88 OE 1,200
Entry of Washington into New York, oil on canvas, 71x107", SBY 6/28/89 OE 36,300
Liberation, ink wash/pencil on paper, sgn/inscr, 15x11", C-E 11/30/88 UE 440
Liberation, pen/black ink/wash/pencil on paper, sgn, 15x11", C-E 2/1/89 550
RLEY, Jane Cooper; att (American, 1807-1877)
Portrait of a Young Girl, oil on canvas, oval, 21x17", B/B 12/8/88 770
RRAH, Sophie Towne (American, 19th/20th C)
Kitten Sleeping on a Pillow, oil on panel, 8x14", FAP 12/8/89 UE 225
RRO, Peter (20th C)
Indian Maiden Drawing Water by the River, oil on canvas, sgn, 16x22", SBY 9/14/89 330
RVEY (19th C)
Still Life of Fruit, watercolor, sgn/dtd 1888, 5x7", LH 5/15/88 70
SBURG, Andrew Michael (American, 1887-1979)
Pueblo Village (modernistic depiction), oil on canvas, sgn, 20x24", C-NY 5/25/89 OE 121,000
SHOU, Du (Chinese, fl 1610-)
Orchids & Rock (horizontal scroll), ink on paper, sgn/dtd 1627, 12x43", SBY 5/31/89 6,050
STUGUE, Maxime (French, 19th C)
Avenue du Bois de Boulogne a Paris, oil on canvas, sgn, 21x29", SBY 5/23/89 6,600
TTLER
Impressionistic Landscape Scene (figures walking through a wooded area), oil on canvas, sgn, 24x36", DM 3/14/88 400
UBIGNY, Charles Francois (French, 1817-1878)
Boeufs pres des Graves de Villerville, oil on canvas, sgn, 1874, 20x32", SBY 2/22/89 7,700
Figures Pulling in Nets, red chalk, artist's estate stamp, 6x9", C-NY 5/25/88 990
Landscape of a Pond, oil on panel, sgn, 7x17", WG 4/23/88 3,800
Les Pecheurs d'Anguilles, oil on cradled panel, sgn/dtd 1864, 7x12", SBY 5/23/89 18,700
Marecage au Soleil Levant (landscape), oil on board, sgn, 14x23", WD 11/16/88 OE 6,500
Point du Jour, L'Oise, Ile de Vaux; oil on canvas, sgn/dtd 1869, 32x57", SBY 2/22/88 OE 82,250
Sunny Plain (w/figures), oil on canvas laid down on board, sgn/dtd 1861, 7x12", WD 5/5/88 UE 3,400
Village au Bord de l'Oise (landscape), oil on board, sgn/dtd 1874, 16x27", RWS 8/12/89 OE 3,600
UBIGNY, Charles Francois; att (French, 1817-1878)
Landscape with Rustic Cottage, pencil w/touches of Chinese white/black strokes, sgn, ca 1840, 4x6", SWN 6/15/89 495
Sunlit Village Street, oil on panel, sgn, 8x9", SBY 12/9/88 UE 1,980
Wooded River Landscape, oil on canvas, partial signature, 14x30", WAD 6/6/88 2,600
UBIGNY, Karl Pierre (French, 1846-1886)
Au Bord de Riviere (river landscape), oil on panel, sgn, 11x19", C-E 2/21/89 UE 1,650
Bateau dans la Mer...(ships at sea), oil on canvas, sgn, 29x59", RWS 8/12/89 OE 19,000
Bord de Riviere, oil on panel, sgn/dtd 73, 14x23", RWS 8/12/89 OE 1,200
Path Through a Woods, oil on panel, sgn, 11x14", C-NY 2/25/88 UE 2,200
Peasants in a Wooded Landscape, oil on canvas, sgn, unfr, 14x16", C-E 5/23/88 1,650
Rocky Landscape, oil on canvas, sgn, 13x18", WD 3/23/88 UE 750
Twilight Over a Peaceful Landscape, oil on canvas, sgn, 16x22", C-E 5/22/89 5,500
UCHOT, Gabriel (French, 1927-)
Au Grenier, oil on canvas, sgn, 32x46", SBY 10/7/89 1,980

Clown, oil on canvas, sgn, 39x20", C-E 2/16/88 ... 71

La Salle a Manger du Chateau, oil on canvas, sgn/dtd 51, 26x32", SBY 10/5/88 ... 1,65

DAUDIN, Henry Charles (French, 1861-)

Nude in an Interior, oil on canvas, sgn, 20x25", FAP 11/4/88 ... 4,00

DAUGHERTY, James Henry (American, 1886-1974)

Magic Garden, colored chalks on paper, initialed/dtd July 20 71, 12x17", C-E 11/17/88 UE ... 22

Untitled (abstract), pastel on paper, initialed/dtd 68, 17x14", SBY 9/23/88 ... 1,87

DAUMIER, Honore (French, 1808-1879)

Don Quixote et Sancho Pansa, oil on panel, initialed, ca 1850-52, 14x20", C-NY 11/16/88 OE ... 308,00

Don Quixote et Sancho Se Rendant aux Noces de Gamaches, oil on canvas, sgn, 1850, 16x12", SBY 5/10/88 ... 275,00

Le Buveur Chantant (portrait), oil on panel, sgn, ca 1856, 9x6", SBY 5/23/89 OE ... 38,00

Le Chasseur Buvant (hunter & dog in landscape, oil on panel, initialed, ca 1850, 14x11", SBY 2/18/88 ... 93,50

DAUMIER, Honore; att (French, 1808-1979)

Scene de Menage, watercolor, initialed, 9x8", FB 5/28/89 ... 50

DAVENPORT, W.S. (American, 19th/20th C)

Stone Church, oil on canvas, sgn/dtd XXVII, 26x32", RAB 8/8/89 UE ... 32

DAVEY, Randall (American, 1887-1964)

Along the Coast, oil on panel, sgn, 13x13", C-E 11/30/88 UE ... 82

At the Starting Post (racing scene), oil on canvas, sgn, unfr, 20x24", SBY 6/9/89 ... 13,20

Blacksmith, oil on masonite, sgn, 16x20", C-NY 3/11/88 ... 2,42

Flowers on the Table, encaustic on masonite, sgn, 22x30", C-NY 3/11/88 ... 1,87

Girl in Red Shawl, oil on canvas, sgn, 34x25", SBY 4/14/89 ... 9,35

Horse in a Landscape, watercolor/pencil on paper, sgn, 17x20", C-E 2/1/89 ... 1,10

Seated Nude, oil on masonite, sgn, 19x14", C-E 10/18/89 ... 1,65

Seated Nude, oil on masonite, sgn, 19x14", C-NY 3/11/88 UE ... 60

Semi-Nude, Isabel; oil on canvas, sgn, 30x20", C-NY 3/11/88 ... 2,42

Trotters, encaustic on masonite, sgn, 15x20", C-E 2/1/89 ... 2,20

Woman Selling Fish, oil on paper mounted on fiberboard, sgn, 21x14", C-E 2/3/88 ... 1,21

Young Girl, Blue Top; oil on canvas, sgn, 24x20", C-NY 3/11/88 UE ... 82

DAVID, Gerard (Flemish, 1450-1523)

Rest on the Flight into Egypt, tempera/oil on wood, unfr, 18x14", C-NY 1/11/89 ... 33,00

DAVID, Jacques Louis; after (French, 1748-1825)

Paris & Helene (in classical setting), oil on canvas, 22x26", B/B 3/22/89 OE ... 6,60

Portrait of Napoleon, oil on canvas, sgn/dtd 1856, by F Grund, 65x50", C-E 2/21/89 ... 2,42

DAVIDSON, Charles Grant (American, 1866-1945)

Apple Blossom Time, watercolor/gouache on paper, sgn, 10x16", RAB 3/27/89 UE ... 5

Autumn Landscape (quiet brook), watercolor on paper, sgn, 12x11", RAB 8/9/88 ... 22

Autumn Landscape (stands of trees beside quiet brook), watercolor on paper, sgn, 12x11", RAB 8/9/88 ... 22

Birches in the Field (trees in a field by small stream), watercolor on paper, sgn, 10x13", RAB 8/9/88 ... 25

DAVIDSON, J.O. (American, 19th C)

Arrival of the Monitor at Hampton Roads (Civil War), pen/ink on paper, sgn/inscr, 3x6", C-E 5/27/88 OE ... 82

Boat Attack on Fort Sumner (Civil War), tempera on paper laid down on board, sgn/inscr, 12x15", C-E 5/27/88 OE ... 2,09

Chase in the Fog (Civil War), tempera on board, sgn/inscr, 12x14", C-E 5/27/88 OE ... 33

Confederate Gunboat Stonewall Jackson (Civil War), pen/ink on paper, sgn/inscr, unfr, 7x10", C-E 11/30/88 OE ... 1,21

Confederates Deserting the Underwriter (Civil War), pen/ink on paper, sgn/inscr, 7x15", C-E 5/27/88 OE ... 4,40

Constellation & Vengeance (Civil War), tempera on board, sgn/inscr, 14x11", C-E 5/27/88 OE ... 88

Destruction of the Arkansas, Vicksburg (Civil War); tempera on board, inscr, 11x14", C-E 5/27/88 OE ... 99

Farragut's Squadron at New Orleans (Civil War), tempera on board, sgn/inscr, 6x13", C-E 5/27/88 OE ... 2,64

Fort St Phillip Under Attack (Civil War), tempera on board, sgn/inscr, 8x10", C-E 5/27/88 OE ... 1,87

Pair: Wachusett Ramming the Florida; US Hospital Ship Red Rover (Civil War); tempera, sgn, unfr, 15x11", C-E 11/30/88 ... 82

Porter's Gunboat Fleet Passing Vicksburg Batteries (Civil War), tempera on paper, sgn/inscr, 14x17", C-E 5/27/88 OE ... 1,21

Rebuilding Merrimack (Civil War), pen/ink on paper, sgn/inscr, 4x7", C-E 5/27/88 OE ... 2,64

Sailor on Mast, Initial T (Civil War); pen/ink on paper, sgn/inscr, 16x14", C-E 5/27/88 OE ... 33

Sinking of the Alabama (Civil War), no media given, sgn/inscr, 10x14", C-E 5/27/88 OE ... 2,86

Sinking of the USS Oneida (Civil War), tempera on board, sgn/inscr, 9x11", C-E 5/27/88 OE ... 88

DAVIE, Alan

Bird Noises #2 (abstract), gouache on paper mounted on board, sgn/dtd July 1963, 20x30", SBY 5/3/88 OE ... 4,95

White Anchor (abstract composition), enamel on paper laid down on board, sgn/dtd 57, 11x21", C-E 11/14/89 OE ... 3,85

DAVIES, A.G. (New Zealand)

Set of 24: New Zealand Landscapes; pencil, sgn/dtd 1894, unfr, 6x8" & smaller, C-SK 11/10/88 ... 33

DAVIES, Arthur Bowen (American, 1862-1928)

A Night in Spring (female figures in landscape), oil on canvas, sgn, 18x30", SBY 4/14/89 ... 2,20

Alchemy (nude woman in a landscape), oil on canvas, sgn, 18x30", C-NY 5/26/88 ... 7,70

Bathers, watercolor/pastel/charcoal on brown paper, sgn, 19x13", C-NY 3/11/88 ... 1,32

Boy with Snake, oil on canvas, sgn, 15x8", C-NY 9/30/88 ... 1,98

Classic Dance, pastel on paper, 13x16", C-E 11/30/88 UE ... 55

Coastal Town with Mountains, watercolor/pencil/crayon/colored pencil on blue paper, sgn, 12x10", C-E 6/1/88 ... 93

Columbine, oil on canvas, sgn, unfr, 16x13", C-E 10/18/89 UE ... 1,54

Contemplation, pastel on tan paper, 10x13", C-NY 6/17/89 ... 1,21

Dancing Figure, watercolor/gouache/pencil on paper, sgn, 9x10", C-E 2/3/88 OE ... 1,76

Desert Scene, oil on canvas, sgn, 26x39", C-NY 3/11/88 UE ... 1,65

Ducks Near a Cottage, watercolor/gouache/pencil on paper laid down on board, sgn, 13x19", C-E 6/1/89
Enlightenment of Education, mixed media on cardboard, 16x22", WD 4/13/88 1,650
Evening on the Beach, watercolor/pastel/pencil on paper, sgn/dtd 1927, 10x12", C-E 10/18/89 1,700
Girl in White, pastel on tan paper, 8x14", C-NY 6/17/89 OE 770
Green Pavilions (figures in landscape), oil on canvas, sgn, 6x15", C-E 6/1/89 2,420
Johnson's Island Prisoner of War Camp (Civil War), pen/ink on paper, initialed/inscr, 9x12", C-E 5/27/88 OE 2,090
Landscape, oil on board, 6x10", C-E 4/7/88 UE 1,320
Landscape, watercolor on paper, sgn/inscr/dtd 1925, 11x15", SBY 6/24/88 OE 605
Mighty Forest, oil on canvas stretched over panel, sgn/inscr, 18x42", C-NY 3/11/88 OE 2,200
Nude, pastel on paper, stamped signature, 9x12", SBY 4/14/89 6,050
Nude Dancer, charcoal heightened w/white on prepared paper, sgn, 17x12", SBY 9/14/89 385
Nudes in an Extensive Landscape, oil on canvas, sgn, 36x66", SBY 1/24/89 1,100
Pair: Rockland County; Storm Over Hudson; oil on board/oil on panel, 5x9", C-E 11/30/88 14,300
Rockland Lake From the South Shore, oil on panel, 5x10", C-E 10/18/89 UE 935
Sicilian Idyll, oil on canvas, sgn, 16x11", C-NY 9/30/88 OE 605
Singing Sea (nudes by the sea in a landscape), oil on canvas, sgn, 7x15", C-NY 6/17/89 7,700
Springtime, the Dreamer; oil on canvas, sgn, 18x30", C-NY 9/30/88 2,640
Three Figures: A Study; charcoal/colored chalks on paper, 24x18", SBY 1/24/89 OE 5,500
Tidal Pool (waves wash over rocks in a small inlet), oil on cardboard, sgn, 5x9", RWS 9/29/88 UE 1,980
Tryst at Twilight, oil on canvas, sgn, 18x23", SBY 9/14/89 200

DAVIES, J. (British, 19th C) 4,950
Sketching Party, oil on canvas, sgn/dtd 1866, 18x24", SBY 6/8/88

DAVIES, James Hey (British, 1848-) 1,045
Pair: Rural River Landscapes (views near Poynton, Chesire); oil on canvas, 14x21", SLK 11/25/88

DAVIES, Norman Prescott (British, 1862-1915) 1,400
Organ Grinder, oil on canvas, sgn 1889, 20x27", RWS 11/3/88

DAVIES, William Steeple 2,500
Racing on the Mississippi, watercolor/gouache on paper, sgn/inscr, 9x12", C-E 11/30/88 OE

DAVIHOT (French, 20th C) 1,430
Melancholy Clown, oil on canvas, sgn, 31x15", WG 9/16/88

DAVILA, Jose Antonio (Venezuelan, 1935-) 750
Everything Has Its Shadow (contemporary), sgn/dtd Caracas 1975/titled, 69x59", SBY 11/21/88
Marina de Margarita, oil on canvas, sgn, 1975, 32x36", C-NY 5/18/88 3,300
Ofrendas III (still life), acrylic on canvas, sgn/inscr, 39x39", C-NY 5/18/88 4,400
Quienes Somos? (abstract), acrylic on canvas, sgn twice/dtd 1976/titled, 53x47", C-NY 11/21/88 18,700
Second Tower of Babel (still life of boxes/fruits), oil on canvas, sgn/dtd 88, 48x48", SBY 11/21/88 4,400
Sixteenth Encounter (still life of fruit/box/cat/butterfly), acrylic on canvas, sgn, 47x59", C-NY 5/17/89 12,100

DAVIS, Alexander Jackson (American, 1803-1892) 13,200
West Point of the Capitol, Washington DC; pencil/pen/black ink/ink wash on paper, sgn, 5x7", C-E 6/1/89

DAVIS, Brad (20th C) 880
Fisher & Lotus/Night (contemporary), acrylic/polyester collage on canvas, sgn/dtd 1979-80/titled, 48x36", SBY 5/3/88

DAVIS, Charles F. (British, 19th/20th C) 6,050
Portrait of a Horse, oil on canvas, sgn/dtd 1902, 16x20", B/B 12/8/88 OE

DAVIS, Charles Harold (American, 1856-1932) 1,430
Dunes, oil on canvas, sgn, 20x27", C-NY 9/30/88
Fall Landscape, oil on canvas, sgn, 13x16", C-E 11/30/88 5,280

DAVIS, Floyd MacMillan (American, 20th C) 1,980
Wartime Goodbye (bride & groom with other figures among ruins), ink, sgn, no size given, NA 5/13/89 UE

DAVIS, G.H. (British, 20th C) 525
Famous Ship Mayflower Recreated From Authentic Records...; gouache/ink on board, sgn/dtd 1955, 19x30", RWS 6/17/89

DAVIS, Gene (American, 1920-) 400
Amber Sonata (vertical lineation), acrylic on canvas, sgn/dtd 1965, 94x49", C-NY 10/4/89 OE
Black Tulip (vertical lineation), acrylic on canvas, sgn/dtd 1979, 41x68", C-NY 10/4/89 28,600
Butterfly (vertical lineation), acrylic on canvas, sgn/dtd 1979, 49x34", C-E 11/14/89 6,600
Hot Seat, acrylic on canvas, sgn/dtd 1979/titled, unfr, 70x91", C-NY 11/10/88 7,150
Mohawk (vertical lineation), acrylic on canvas, sgn/dtd 1970, C-NY 2/20/88 OE 15,400
Untitled, colored felt-tip pens on paper, sgn/dtd 1981, 13x18", C-E 11/17/88 16,500
Untitled (vertical lineation), acrylic on canvas, sgn/dtd 1971, unfr, 121x3", C-NY 10/4/89 715
Untitled (vertical lineation), acrylic on canvas, sgn/dtd 1972, 32x24", C-E 11/17/88 8,800
Untitled (vertical lineation), acrylic on canvas, sgn/dtd 1972, 34x25", C-E 11/17/88 4,620

DAVIS, Gladys Rockmore (American, 1901-1967) 4,620
From the Ballet ALEKO, oil on canvas, initialed, 12x20", SBY 9/14/89
Portrait of the Artist's Daughter Deborah, pastel on paper, initialed, 24x18", SBY 9/23/88 UE 1,760

DAVIS, H.W. 440
Sunset Near Boulogne, oil on canvas, sgn, 15x17", C-E 5/23/88 OE

DAVIS, Joseph H. (fl 1832-1837) 4,620
Portrait of Sally B Buzell (standing in profile in interior), pencil/ink/watercolor, 1834, 11x10", RWS 10/27/89 OE
Portrait of Tobias Bunker (standing in profile in interior), pencil/watercolor/ink, inscr/1834, 11x8", RWS 10/27/89 21,000

DAVIS, Leonard Moore (American, 1864-1938) 7,500
Alaskan Glacier, oil on canvas, sgn, 36x54", B/B 1/11/89
Basket of Roses, oil on canvas, 18x28", LH 10/16/88 770
500

Pair: Alaskan Scenes; oil on board, both sgn/inscr, dtd 1913 & 1917, 6x10", C-E 6/1/88 UE **462**

DAVIS, M.A. (American, 19th C)

Still Life of Violets, oil on canvas, sgn, 6x10", RAB 8/9/88 .... **500**

DAVIS, Richard Barrett (British, 1782-1854)

Derviche, a Bay Racehorse, with a Groom & Terrier; oil on canvas, 25x30", C-E 10/26/89 .... **3,080**
James John Farquharson with the Blackmore Vale Hunt, oil on canvas, sgn, 40x50", SBY 6/9/89 .... **66,000**
Pair: Fox Hunting Scenes; 1 oil on board/1 oil on canvas, sgn/dtd 1833, 12x14", SBY 6/10/88 .... **3,850**

DAVIS, Ron (American, 1935-)

Diamond Slab (contemporary), acrylic/colored chalks on canvas, sgn/dtd 1975, 84x64", C-NY 5/4/89 .... **16,500**
Five Plane (contemporary), acrylic on linen, 1973, 20x48", SBY 11/9/89 .... **6,050**
Untitled (geometric composition), vinyl on acetate on board, 1968, 8x20", C-NY 5/4/89 .... **1,210**
Violet (contemporary abstract), watercolor on paper, 1972, 38x26", SBY 11/9/89 OE **4,950**

DAVIS, Stuart (American, 1894-1964)

At the Library, crayon/ink/pencil on paper, sgn, 16x19", SBY 9/14/89 .... **4,950**
Fire by the Bridge, watercolor/pen/black & brown ink/pencil, sgn/dtd 1912, 11x8", C-NY 5/25/89 .... **8,800**
Gloucester Landscape with Rooster & Ducks, oil on canvas, sgn, ca 1915, 18x23", SBY 6/24/88 .... **17,600**
Group of 3: Auction Room; Book Auction; At the Museum; watercolor on paper, sgn/dtd 1910, ea 8x12", SBY 3/17/88 OE **34,100**
Marine Abstract, gouache/watercolor/pencil on paper, sgn, ca 1932, 17x22", C-NY 5/25/89 OE **71,500**
On the Waterfront (harbor w/two figures), oil on canvas, sgn, 30x38", SBY 6/28/89 .... **8,800**
Underpass #1 (abstract), gouache/pencil on paper, sgn/inscr, 12x16", C-NY 5/26/88 .... **71,500**
Yellow Cafe, oil on canvas, sgn, 12x17", C-NY 12/2/88 OE **52,800**

DAVIS, Theodore R. (American, 1840-1894)

Army Transports at the Cairo Levee (Civil War), watercolor on paper, 7x13", C-E 5/27/88 OE **1,650**
Battle of Champion's Hill (Civil War), pen/ink on paper, inscr, 6x14", C-E 5/27/88 .... **440**
Building Gunboats & Motor Boats (Civil War), ink/wash on paper, inscr, 5x10", C-E 5/27/88 .... **605**
Carmody Mans the Barbette Battery, Fort Sumpter (Civil War); pen/ink on paper, inscr, unfr, 10x13", C-E 11/30/88 OE **825**
Charleston Under Fire (Civil War), pen/ink on paper, inscr, 10x20", C-E 5/27/88 OE **2,640**
Decoration Day in Chattanooga (Civil War), pen/ink on paper, sgn/inscr, 7x8", C-E 5/27/88 OE **605**
Effect of Shell Fire, Vicksburg (Civil War); pen/ink on paper, inscr, unfr, 7x9", C-E 11/30/88 OE **275**
Evacuation of Fort Moultrie (Civil War), pen/ink on paper, sgn/inscr, 6x11", RWS 5/27/88 OE **880**
Explosion of the Vicksburg Mine (Civil War), pen/ink on paper, sgn/inscr, 10x14", C-E 5/27/88 OE **2,200**
Firing on the Star of the West (Civil War), pen/ink on paper, sgn/inscr, 7x10", C-E 5/27/88 OE **2,090**
First Conference, Grant & Pemberton Discuss Terms (Civil War); pen/ink on paper, inscr, 7x8", C-E 5/27/88 OE **825**
Generals Sherman & Thomas at Kennesaw Mountain (Civil War), pen/ink on paper, inscr, 11x10", C-E 5/27/88 OE **1,540**
Hazen's Assault on Brown's Ferry (Civil War), pen/ink on paper, sgn/inscr, 10x16", C-E 5/27/88 UE **385**
Hospital Ship DA January (Civil War), pen/ink on paper, sgn/inscr, 6x10", C-E 5/27/88 .... **330**
Incident at New Hope Church, Bad Confederate Fix for a Sharpshooter (Civil War); pen/ink, initialed, 12x5", C-E 5/27/88 .... **770**
Incident in the Vicksburg Campaign (Civil War), pen/ink on paper, inscr, 6x8", C-E 5/27/88 OE **715**
Last Days of the Vicksburg Siege (Civil War), pen/ink on paper, sgn/inscr, 12x20", C-E 5/27/88 .... **880**
Military Funeral, Vicksburg (Civil War); pen/ink on paper, sgn/inscr, 7x11", C-E 5/27/88 .... **495**
Openings of the Civil War (Civil War), watercolor on paper, sgn/inscr, 5x15", C-E 5/27/88 OE **2,750**
Pensacola Harbor From the Bar (Civil War), pen/ink on paper, sgn/inscr/dtd 1861, 6x11", C-E 5/27/88 OE **2,420**
Quartermaster's Dock, Fortress Monroe (Civil War); pen/ink on paper, inscr, 5x11", C-E 5/27/88 OE **770**
White House, Federal Lines, Vicksburg (Civil War); pen/ink on paper, sgn/inscr, 8x13", C-E 5/27/88 .... **550**
Wooden Mortar in the Saps, Vicksburg (Civil War); pen/ink on paper, sgn/inscr, 12x8", C-E 5/27/88 .... **825**

DAVIS, W.T. (American, 20th C)

Landscape with Red Houses, oil on canvas, sgn/dtd 1926, 24x20", FAP 4/15/89 .... **632**

DAVIS, Warren B. (American, 1865-1928)

At the Pool (nude woman leaning over rock), oil on canvas laid down on board, sgn, 8x10", C-E 6/1/89 .... **4,620**
Music (three dancing nudes), oil on canvas, sgn, 16x12", C-NY 9/28/89 .... **3,080**
The Green Glade, oil on canvas, sgn, 18x14", C-NY 9/28/89 .... **2,200**

DAVIS, William Henry (British, -1865)

Dark Roan Bull, oil on canvas, sgn/dtd 1859, 25x30", C-NY 5/24/89 .... **7,700**
Roan Heifer in a Landscape, oil on canvas, sgn/dtd 1849, 18x24", C-E 5/22/89 .... **3,080**

DAVIS, William M. (American, 1812-1873)

Farmyard, oil on canvas, sgn, 14x22", C-NY 9/28/89 OE **16,500**
Lighthouse, gouache on paper laid down on board, sgn, 15x21", C-NY 9/30/88 .... **3,300**
Port Jefferson, watercolor/gouache on board, sgn, 13x19", C-NY 3/11/88 OE **9,350**
Still Life of Hanging Game, oil on canvas, sgn, 16x12", RAB 8/8/89 UE **250**

DAVIS, William R. (American, 20th C)

Bishops & Clerks Light Off Hyannis Port-Sunset; oil on canvas, sgn, 15x22", RAB 8/8/89 OE **5,250**

DAVISON, Robert (19th C)

Boats & Harbor in a Calm, oil on canvas, sgn twice/dtd 1893, 76x68", C-SK 6/9/88 .... **930**
Shipping in an Estuary, South America; oil on canvas, sgn twice/dtd 1893/inscr, 40x34", C-SK 6/9/88 UE **465**

DAVOL, Joseph B. (American, 1864-1923)

Beach Scene, oil on canvas, sgn, 17x21", RWS 11/10/89 .... **1,000**

DAWES, Edwin (American, 1872-1945)

Sweet Water #2, gouache/pencil on board, sgn/dtd 47, 22x30", C-E 2/1/89 UE **440**

DAWSON, Henry (British, 1811-1878)

Mountain Pass, oil on canvas, sgn, 12x22", C-E 2/21/89 .... **1,980**
Nottingham From Woolford Hill (extensive landscape), oil on canvas, sgn/indistinctly dtd, 31x40", C-E 5/22/89 .... **6,380**

DAWSON, Henry; att (British, 1811-1878)
Figure by a Stream Before a Country House, oil on canvas, bears signature & date, 24x36", PHL 10/28/88 1,700
DAWSON, John Wilfred (American, 1888-)
Rocky River, watercolor on paper, sgn/dtd 1934, 8x12", RAB 8/9/88 UE 100
Rocky River (jagged rocks along river lined with steep green hills), watercolor on paper, sgn/dtd 1934, RAB 8/9/88 UE 100
DAWSON, Montague (British, 1895-1973)
Arial & Taeping (in rough seas), oil on canvas, sgn, 40x50", C-NY 2/23/89 OE 176,000
China Trader on the Open Sea (masted ship), oil on canvas, sgn, 24x36", C-NY 2/23/89 OE 55,000
Clipper Ship Fanny Forrester, oil on canvas, sgn, 24x36", DM 5/13/88 27,500
Constitution, oil on canvas, sgn, 28x42", SBY 5/23/89 25,300
Dawn-The Norman Court (ship at sea); oil on board, sgn, 16x20", C-NY 2/23/89 24,200
Enemy Bimber in Thunderstorm, oil on canvas, 20x30", C-E 5/22/89 3,960
Flagship of the Line, oil on canvas, sgn, 19x29", SBY 2/22/89 26,400
Flowing Sea, watercolor, sgn, 20x30", C-NY 10/25/89 OE 16,500
Fully-Rigged Tall Ship, oil on canvas, sgn, 42x28", C-NY 2/25/88 24,200
Homecoming, The Clipper Ship, South Australia; oil on canvas, sgn, 28x42", SBY 2/22/89 63,250
Off the Storm Bound Horn (Cape Agulhas & Africa behind her), oil on artist board, 12x16", DM 5/13/88 13,000
On the High Sea (masted ship), oil on canvas, sgn, 20x24", SBY 10/24/89 OE 20,900

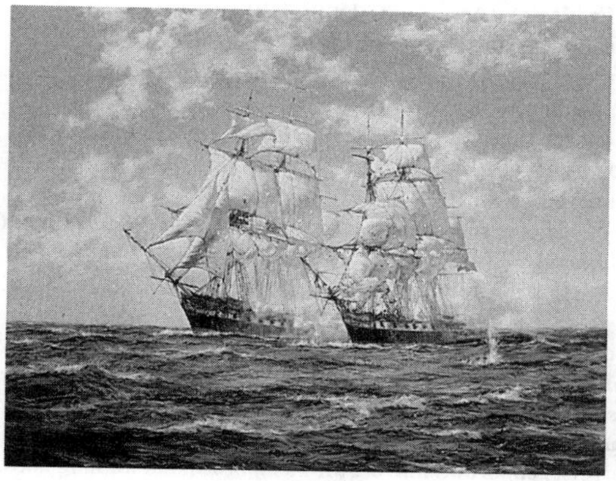

President & Little Belt, British & American Frigates Engaged in Battle; oil on canvas, sgn, 40x50", C-NY 5/25/88 OE, $159,500

Rescue Launch, en grisaille/oil on canvas, sgn, 24x20", C-E 2/23/88 1,540
Santa Maria (ship), oil on canvas, sgn, 28x42", SBY 5/23/89 16,500
Ship, Marco Polo, Running Before the Wind; oil on canvas, sgn, 30x40", SBY 5/23/89 110,000
Sun-Flecked Foam, The Barnabas Webb of Thomaston (ship at sea); oil on canvas, sgn, 1942, 20x30", C-NY 5/24/89 55,000
The Pilot Rescued by the British Submarine, Mustang; oil on board/en grisaille, sgn, 15x22", SBY 10/24/89 12,100
Winged Hunter (sailing scene), watercolor/gouache on paper, sgn, 17x26", B/B 10/9/88 17,600
Yachting Competition, watercolor/gouache/pen/brown ink/pencil on paper, sgn, 11x19", C-NY 5/24/89 OE 15,400
DAWSON-WATSON, Dawson (American, 1864-1939)
Cotton Picker (three-quarter length), oil on canvas, inscribed, 40x30", SBY 6/28/89 1,100
Harvested Pasture, oil on canvas, sgn, 18x22", C-NY 9/28/89 2,750
Mother & Daughter Gathering Wood in Winter, oil on canvas, sgn/dtd Giverny 1890, 65x52", SBY 3/17/88 5,775
DAY, Francis (American, 1863-)
Bathers (figures in woodland glade rest beside river), oil on academy board, bears signature, 14x18", RWS 9/29/88 UE 425
In the Woods (two nudes), oil on panel, sgn/inscr, 15x9", C-E 2/3/88 825
Love Affair, oil on canvas, sgn/dtd 1906, 30x24", C-NY 9/30/88 OE 13,200
Quiet Time (mother & child in interior), oil on panel, 16x18", RWS 9/29/88 5,500
Story Read by Candlelight (woman & child in dimly lit interior), oil on canvas, sgn, 40x30", B/B 9/14/89 UE 7,150
DAY, Larry (American)
Outing: Hommage to Le Nain; oil on canvas, sgn, 54x50", FAP 4/15/89 1,650
DAYEZ, Georges (French, 1907-)
Femme se Coiffant, oil on canvas, sgn/dtd 55-56, 25x31", SBY 2/14/89 OE 5,500
View of Toledo, Spain; oil on canvas, sgn, 11x9", SBY 10/7/89 660
DAYNES-GRASSOT-SOLIN, Suzanne (French, 1884-)
Flamenco Dancer, oil on canvas, sgn/dtd 1910, 50x38", C-NY 2/23/89 OE 14,300
DE ANDREIS, Alex (Belgian, 19th/20th C)
Cavalier, oil on canvas, sgn, 32x27", C-E 5/23/88 1,430
Cavalier, oil on canvas, sgn/dtd 1924, 31x24", C-E 10/25/88 1,650
Cavalier in a Green Cape, oil on canvas, sgn, 32x26", B/B 9/15/88 1,870
Game of Chess (interior scene w/figures), oil on canvas, sgn, 26x33", C-NY 2/23/89 5,280
The Loyalist, oil on canvas, 13x10", WAD 6/6/88 600
DE ANDREIS, Alexis (French, 19th C)
Artist Admiring His Work, oil on panel, sgn, 23x29", SBY 12/9/88 1,760
Pair: Soldier & Gentleman; oil on canvas, sgn, 32x26", SBY 7/12/89 1,430
DE ARELLANO, Juan (Spanish, 1614-1676)
Still Life of Tulips, Carnations, Morning-Glory, Daffodils, an Iris...; oil on canvas, 25x20", C-NY 1/11/89 44,000

Virgin of the Rosary Appearing to Saint Dominic Guzman, oil on canvas, sgn, 50x39", SBY 10/13/89 9,900
DE ARELLANO, Juan; circle of (Spanish, 1614-1676)
Lilies, Tulips, Carnations, & Other Flowers in a Vase on a Ledge; oil on canvas, 27x21", C-NY 10/20/88 UE 2,640
DE ARELLANO, Juan; follower of (Spanish, 1614-1676)
Still Life of Flowers in a Basket on a Ledge, oil on canvas, unfr, 37x30", SBY 4/7/88 5,225
DE ARELLANO, Juan; school of (Spanish, 1614-1676)
Still Life of Lilies, Tulips, Carnations, & Other Flowers in a Vase...; oil on canvas, 27x21", C-NY 1/11/89 OE 9,350
DE BACKER, Francois Joseph Thomas (fl 1812-1872)
French Shepherd Telling the Story of His Life, oil on canvas, sgn/dtd 1858, 28x34", C-E 10/26/89 6,600
DE BAR, Bonaventure (French, 1700-1729)
Fete Champetre, oil on canvas, 15x18", C-NY 6/2/88 4,400
DE BEET, Cornelius (American, 1779-1840)
Still Life of Fruit, Flowers, & Game; oil on panel, sgn/dtd 1819, 24x17", SBY 6/24/88 13,200
DE BELLE, Charles Ernest (Canadian, 1873-1939)
Jean Filles (young girls), pastel, initialed, 18x14", FB 5/28/89 1,400
Landscape, pastel, initialed, 10x13", FB 5/28/89 850
Pair: Winter Woodland Scenes; pastel, initialed, 10x13", WAD 11/30/89 450
Portrait of a Girl, oil on canvas, initialed, 24x19", FB 5/28/89 850
Winter Landscape, oil on board, initialed, 18x13", FB 5/28/89 800
DE BERG RICHARDS, Frederick (American, 1822-1903)
Coastal Scene, Atlantic City Coast; oil on canvas, sgn, 15x30", C-E 2/1/89 1,980
River Landscape with Sunset, oil on canvas, sgn, 22x36", SBY 9/23/88 OE 5,500
DE BERGUE, Tony Francis (French, 1820-)
Church Procession, oil on canvasboard, sgn, 27x23", C-E 5/23/88 1,045
Reading the Dispatch, oil on panel, sgn, 10x7", DM 3/14/88 1,000
DE BEUL, Franz (Belgian, 1849-1919)
Barn Interior with Sheep & Shepherdess, oil on canvas, sgn, 32x36", SBY 7/12/89 OE 2,475
DE BEUL, Laurent (Belgian, 1821-1872)
Sheep at Rest, oil on panel, sgn/dtd 1871, 15x21", C-E 3/22/88 OE 1,320
DE BIE, Cornelis
Hagar & the Angel, oil on canvas, 32x25", C-NY 10/12/89 2,860
DE BIEVRE, Marie (Belgian, 1865-)
Still Life of Roses & Raspberries, oil on canvas, sgn/dtd 87, 16x20", B/B 3/22/89 5,500
DE BISSCHOP, Jan (Dutch, 1628-1671)
Barges Loaded with Barrels, pen/brown ink/brown wash/brown ink framing lines, #d f18, 4x6", C-NY 1/11/89 OE 3,300
DE BLAAS, Eugene (Austrian, 1843-1931)
Affectionate Glance (woman standing w/hands on hips), oil on cradled panel, sgn/dtd 1909, 51x25", SBY 2/22/89 88,000
Le Plaisir (lady leaning against stone wall daydreaming), oil on cradled panel, sgn/dtd 1900, 33x19", SBY 2/22/89 OE 88,000
Le Travail (lady carrying water), oil on cradled panel, sgn, 33x19", SBY 2/22/89 OE 110,000
Pair: Portrait of a Brother; Portrait of a Sister; oil on canvas, sgn/dtd 1886, ea 19x17", SBY 2/22/89 OE 49,500
DE BLAAS, Guilo (American/Italian, 1880-1934)
Lido (beach scene), watercolor/pencil/bodycolor heightened w/white, sgn/dtd 1929, unfr, C-SK 6/9/88 650
DE BLIECK, Daniel (Dutch, 17th C)
Church Interior with Figures, oil on panel, sgn/dtd 1655, 18x12", C-NY 10/12/89 8,800
DE BLOCK, Eugenius Frans (American, 19th C)
Portrait of John C Calhoun, oil on canvas, sgn/dtd Brau 1851, 40x32", C-E 2/1/89 770
DE BOCK, Theophile Emile Achille (Dutch, 1851-1904)
Cattle in a River Landscape, oil on canvas, sgn, 21x33", C-NY 2/25/88 6,050
Cottages on a Lake, oil on canvas, sgn, 12x17", C-E 10/25/88 1,980
DE BOEVER, Jean Francois (Belgian, 1872-1949)
Charmeuse, oil on canvas, sgn, 30x34", B/B 6/15/89 3,575
DE BONNEMAISON, Jules (French, 1809-)
Le Comte de Bonnemaison a la Chasse, oil on canvas, sgn, 25x36", SBY 6/10/88 6,600
DE BONNET, Franz
Flowers in a Sculptured Urn on a Marble Ledge, oil on canvas, sgn, 30x25", WD 3/23/88 700
DE BOTTON, Jean Isy (French, 1898-1978)
Composition (abstract), oil on canvas, sgn/dtd 59, 20x26", PHL 11/15/88 650
Coronation Naval Revue (contemporary), oil on canvas, sgn/dtd 37, 26x32", PHL 11/15/88 850
Invitation au Voyage, oil on canvas, sgn/inscr/dtd, 29x36", PHL 11/15/88 500
La Chute d'Icare, oil on canvas, sgn/dtd 65, 32x26", PHL 11/15/88 500
La Force du Destin-Mozart, oil on canvas, sgn/dtd 1968, 26x39", PHL 11/15/88 600
La Tamise, au de Hampton; oil on canvas, sgn, 15x18", PHL 11/15/88 UE 325
Les Champs de Course a Deauville (night street scene), oil on canvas, sgn/dtd 1969-70/#d 1554, C-E 11/17/88 1,100
Les Fleurs du Mal, oil on canvas, sgn/dtd 1973, 29x24", PHL 11/15/88 500
Madonna & Child with the Infant Saint John the Baptist, oil on panel, 42x26", SBY 6/1/89 52,250
No 1665 Theme & Variations on Beethoven's Eroica, oil on canvas, sgn, 1973, 48x48", LH 10/16/88 950
Notre-Dame de Paris, oil on canvas, sgn/dtd twice, 1939, inscr, unfr, 22x28", C-E 5/13/88 UE 660
Paris, les Courses a Auteuil (horseracing scene); oil on canvas, sgn/dtd Paris 1967-68/#d 1171, 16x24", C-E 11/17/88 990
Paris-Montmartre: Le Lapin Agile avec le Pere Frede et Bilboquet; oil on canvas, sgn/dtd 1935-1970, 21x29", C-E 5/13/88 600
River Landscape, oil on canvas, sgn, 20x20", PHL 11/15/88 800
Rythme de la Mer, oil on canvas, sgn/inscr/#d 748, 15x22", C-E 5/12/88 550

View on the River Thames, oil on canvas, sgn, 13x16", PHL 11/15/88 UE 200

DE BOULLOGNE, Bon (French, 17th/18th C)

Latona, oil on canvas, 51x40", C-NY 1/15/88 OE 19,800

DE BOULLOGNE, Bon; circle of (French, 17th/18th C)

Deluge (figures in anguish), oil on canvas, 38x52", C-NY 4/6/89 2,860

DE BOUVARD, Hughes (Austrian, 1879-1959)

Gondolas on a Venetian Canal, oil on canvas, sgn, 10x13", C-E 2/21/89 3,300
Grand Canal, Venice; oil on canvas, sgn, unfr, 20x26", C-E 5/22/89 3,520

DE BRAEKELEER, Adrien Ferdinand (Belgian, 1818-1904)

Armor Shop, oil on panel, sgn/dtd 1851, 25x32", C-NY 5/24/89 OE 23,100

DE BRAY, Jan (Dutch, 1626-1697)

Portrait of a Lady, oil on canvas, 39x31", SBY 10/21/88 7,150

DE BRAY, Jan; follower of (Dutch, 1626-1697)

Portrait of a Gentleman in Black, oil on canvas, indistinctly dtd, 39x32", SBY 4/7/89 UE 1,980

DE BREANSKI, Alfred Jr. (British, 1877-1957)

Autumn, Morning, the Straits of Balmaha-Loch Lomond; oil on canvas, sgn, 25x30", C-E 2/21/89 OE 4,950
Conway Shore From Marine Drive, Landudno, North Wales; oil on canvas, sgn, 12x18", B/B 5/17/89 825
English Lakes, Fleetwith Pike & Buttermere; oil on canvas, sgn, 24x36", WG 4/23/88 UE 1,600
Loch Leven, oil on canvas, sgn, 12x20", C-E 10/25/88 UE 1,100
Old Bridge of Dee, Invercauld; oil on canvas, sgn, 20x30", FB 5/89 2,100
River & Holy Trinity Church Stratford Upon Avon, oil on canvas, 18x24", WG 4/23/88 UE 1,400

DE BREANSKI, Alfred Sr. (British, 1852-1928)

Autumn Evening, Burnham Wood; oil on canvas, sgn twice, 24x36", SBY 12/9/88 6,875
Below the Falls of Glenfinlas, oil on canvas, sgn/inscr/dtd, 16x24", C-NY 5/25/88 3,500
Ben Lomond NW, oil on canvas, sgn, 20x12", C-E 2/23/88 OE 1,540
Borders of Argyle, oil on canvas, sgn, 20x30", C-E 5/23/88 3,080
Fishing by a Stream, oil on canvas, sgn/dtd 1876, 20x31", C-E 2/23/88 3,520
Glen Douglas (landscape w/lake, figure, & sheep grazing), oil on canvas, sgn/titled, 20x30", SBY 5/23/89 OE 19,800
Landscape with a Young Fisherman, oil on canvas, sgn, 24x18", C-NY 2/25/88 UE 1,980
Loch Lomond (landscape w/figures by the loch), oil on canvas, sgn, 12x20", PHL 6/16/88 1,400
Lodore, oil on canvas, sgn twice, 20x30", SBY 12/9/88 OE 9,075
Man Fishing in a Stream with a Cathedral Beyond, oil on canvas, sgn, 20x30", C-E 10/25/88 OE 5,280
Marlow Lock-Autumn Evening; oil on canvas, bears signature, inscr #2 on label on verso, 30x50", SBY 2/22/89 14,300
Old Bridge (stream w/rushing water, figures on bridge), oil on canvas, sgn/dtd 1873, 20x37", C-E 5/22/89 7,480
Old Cottage Near Barmouth, North Wales; oil on canvas, sgn/inscr/dtd 99, 20x31", C-E 4/7/88 UE 418
Pastoral River Scene, oil on canvas, sgn/dtd 1896, 21x17", B/B 3/22/89 2,090
Sunrise Near Arrochar NB, oil on canvas, sgn, 12x20", C-E 5/23/88 1,980
Sunset on the Loch, oil on canvas, sgn, 30x50", SBY 10/24/89 23,100
Sunset on the Loch, oil on canvas laid down on masonite, sgn, 30x50", SBY 2/22/89 OE 25,300
Sunset Over a Highland Loch, oil on canvas, sgn, 30x50", SBY 2/22/89 OE 29,700
Ullawater From Pooley (cattle watering in landscape with mountains beyond), oil on canvas, sgn, 16x22", FB 5/28/89 2,000
Windsor Castle (in the distance w/dwellings & swans on a pond), oil on canvas, sgn, 16x22", B/B 3/22/89 2,750

DE BRESCIA, Moretto; see Bonvicino, Alessandro

DE BROZIK, Wenceslas (Bohemian, 1851-1901)

Pair: Resting Cows; oil on canvas, 1 initialed/1 sgn, 7x11", SBY 2/21/89 1,320
Portrait of a Bishop, seated; oil on canvas, sgn, 18x16", C-E 2/21/89 1,320
Portrait of the Artist's Wife (half-length), oil on panel, sgn, 33x24", C-NY 2/23/89 3,300

DE BRUYN, Cornelis Johannes (Dutch, 1763-1828)

Roses, Morning-Glories, Pansies, & Other Flowers in a Vase on a Ledge; oil on panel, sgn, 14x12", SBY 1/12/89 22,000

DE BRYER, C. (Flemish, 17th C)

Still Life of Fruits on a Ledge with a Gold-Mounted Nautilus Shell, oil on canvas, sgn, 30x25", SBY 6/3/88 UE 38,500

DE BYLANT, A.

Shepherdess with Her Flock, oil on panel, sgn, 24x19", C-E 5/23/88 2,420

DE CABANYES, Alejandro (Spanish, 1877-)

Tranquildad de Playa, oil on canvas, sgn, 26x42", SBY 6/8/88 2,750

DE CAMP, Joseph (American, 1858-1923)

New England Landscape, oil on canvas, sgn, 12x16", PHL 10/28/88 OE 2,100

DE CAMP, Joseph; after (American, 1858-1923)

Portrait of a Woman, oil on canvas, bears signature, 30x25", C-E 2/16/89 242

DE CAMP, Ralph Earl (American, 1858-1936)

Mountain View (mountain landscape w/deer drinking at stream), oil on canvas, sgn/dtd 1915, 20x30", RWS 3/31/88 UE 700

DE CAULLERY, Louis (French/Flemish, 16th/17th C)

Crucifixion, oil on panel, unfr, 40x26", C-NY 4/8/88 3,300
Elegant Feast in an Interior, oil on panel, 19x26", SBY 10/21/88 13,200
Elegant Figures in a Hall Listening to Musicians, oil on panel, 16x22", SBY 10/13/89 OE 22,000

DE CAVALCANTI, Emiliano (Latin American, 19th/20th C)

Mulata con Autoretrato (figures), brush/pen/India ink/blue ink on paper, sgn, ca 1959, 11x7", C-NY 5/17/89 3,300

DE CHAMPAIGNE, Philippe; circle of (Flemish, 1602-1674)

Nun in Prayer (portrait), oil on canvas, 29x23", C-NY 5/31/89 UE 3,080

DE CHAMPAIGNE, Philippe; manner of (Flemish, 1602-1674)

Portrait of a Theologian Said To Be Monsieur Arnauld, Doctor of the Sorbonne; oil on panel, oval, 7x5", SBY 6/3/88 OE 3,850

DE CHAMPAIGNE, Phillipe; follower of (Flemish, 1602-1674)
Portrait of a Man in Armour Said To Be Louis II De Bourbon, oil on canvas, dtd 1647, 24x20", SBY 10/13/89 2,200
DE CHAVANNES, Pierre Puvis (French, 1824-1898)
Portrait of a Man, black chalk on laid paper, sgn/inscr, 19x13", C-NY 2/25/88 2,200
Three Seated Ladies, charcoal/gray wash on paper, sgn/stamped Lugt 217a, 5x7", SBY 12/9/88 1,100
DE CHAVANNES, Pierre Puvis; after (French, 1824-1898)
Pantheon Murals, by Edwin Howland Blashfield, oil on canvas, sgn, 21x28", C-E 11/30/88 3,080
DE CHIRICO, Giorgio (Italian, 1888-1978)
Arbres dans la Chambre (Equinoxe), oil/pencil on canvas, sgn/dtd 1926, 36x29", SBY 5/11/88 OE 517,000
Cavalli, oil on canvas, sgn, 11x16", SBY 2/18/88 OE 50,600
Cavallo E Zebra in Riva al Mare, oil on canvas, sgn, ca 1930, 29x36", SBY 5/11/88 OE 319,000
Dionysus (standing male figure), watercolor/brush/black ink/pencil, sgn, 13x8", C-NY 2/18/88 6,600
Due Cavalli (two horses, loosely painted), oil on canvas, sgn, ca 1926-27, 18x15", C-NY 11/16/88 143,000
L'Archeologia e l'Architettura, gouache on board, sgn, 21x16", C-NY 11/15/88 110,000
La Pernice (still life of dead fowl in a landscape), oil on canvas, sgn, ca 1948, 20x24", SBY 11/12/88 68,750
Pair: Horse with One Figure Seated; Horse with Two Figures; pen/ink/pencil on paper, 1930s, 4x6", SBY 5/10/89 OE 28,600
Personaggi in Riva al Mare (contemporary), oil on canvas, sgn/dtd 1926, 45x34", SBY 5/9/89 OE 660,000
Piazza d'Italia, oil on canvas, sgn twice, ca 1955, 16x12", SBY 5/11/88 88,000
Piazza d'Italia, oil on canvas, sgn twice, ca 1960, 12x16", SBY 5/11/88 88,000
Roses, oil on artist board, sgn, 33x34", DM 9/16/88 8,500
Testa di Donna (portrait), oil on board, sgn/dtd 1957/inscr Copa da Bassano, unfr, 8x5", SBY 10/7/88 16,500
Visita ai Bagni Misteriosi, oil on canvas, sgn, 1935, 15x18", SBY 5/11/88 OE 220,000
DE CHIRICO, V. Colombo (Italian, 1888-1978)
New Arrival, watercolor/gouache, sgn, 12x8", C-NY 10/26/88 3,080
DE CLAUSADES, P.T.
Extensive View of the Shore, oil on canvas, sgn, unfr, 22x40", C-E 5/23/88 2,420
DE CLERCK, Hendrick; follower of (Flemish, 1570-1629)
Fishermen Repairing Their Boat by the Sea, oil on canvas, 14x18", SBY 12/9/88 3,080
DE COCK, Xavier (Belgian, 1818-1896)
Shepherd in the Forest with His Flock, oil on panel, sgn/dtd 1880, 15x23", SBY 7/12/89 9,900
DE CONDAMY, Charles Fernand (French, 19th C)
Stag Hunt, watercolor over pencil on paper, sgn, 12x19", C-E 10/25/88 990
DE COOL, Delphine (French, 1830-)
Favorite (full-length portrait of a woman), oil on canvas, sgn/dtd 1877, 58x79", SBY 2/22/89 13,200
DE CORIS, Nicholas
Cottages by a Canal, oil on canvas, sgn, 24x30", C-E 2/23/88 1,430
DE CRAYER, Gaspar; att (Flemish, 1584-1669)
Madonna & Child, oil on panel, 41x29", SBY 10/13/89 13,200
Portrait of the Archduke Albert (full-length, standing), oil on canvas, 77x51", SBY 6/1/89 30,800
DE CUVILLON, Louis Robert (French, 1848-)
Sweet Dreams (designed for a fan), watercolor/gouache, sgn, 10x19", C-E 2/21/89 UE 440
DE CZACHORSKI, Ladislas (Polish, 1850-1911)
Elegant Couple by a Window, oil on canvas, sgn/dtd 1889, 36x24", C-NY 2/23/89 OE 8,800
DE DIEGO, Julia
Basic Energy, oil on board, sgn/inscr w/title, no size given, C-E 10/18/89 OE 3,080
DE DOMINICI, Antonio (ca 1730-before 1800)
Pair: Allegory of Justice; Allegory of Faith; oil on panel, on gold ground; 27x43", SBY 4/7/88 6,875
DE ERDELEY, Francis (American, 1904-1959)
Holocaust, pen/ink on paper, sgn/dtd MCMXXX, 28x21", B/B 1/11/89 UE 385
Two Men, oil on canvas, sgn, 16x20", B/B 5/17/89 OE 5,500
DE ESCURIAZ, Diego (fl 1587-1589)
Design for the Hood of a Cape: The Last Supper; pen/ink/wash heightened w/white, 20x16", SBY 1/13/89 5,225
DE ESCURIAZ, Diego; att (fl 1587-1589)
Visitation: Scene From the Life of a Saint; brown wash heightened w/white on blue-gray paper, 18x7", SBY 1/13/89 3,025
DE ESTE, Francesco Bossi (fl ca 1800)
Pair: Trompe l'Oeil Still Lifes with Fruits, Cat, Chocolate Pot...; oil on canvas, sgn/1 dtd 1800, 21x27", SBY 4/7/89 OE 37,400
DE FERRARI, Lorenzo (Italian, 1644-1726)
Adam & Eve with the Infants Cain & Abel, oil on canvas, 36x37", SBY 1/12/89 OE 30,800
Ecstasy of a Saint: Design for Ceiling; black chalk, wm, arched top, 16x10", C-NY 1/12/88 3,080
DE FEURE, Georges (French, 1868-1929)
Woman in a Landscape (autumn), mixed media on paper, sgn/dtd 46, in orig carved & gilt-wood frame, 36x48", SBY 11/17/88 OE 165,000
DE FLEURY, J. Vivien (British, 19th C)
River Near Naples, oil, sgn/dtd 1870, 24x38", WD 1/11/89 2,000
DE FONTAINEBLEAU, Ecole
Le Jugement de Paris, oil on canvas, 46x76", C-M 12/3/88 13,007
DE FOREST, Henry J.(Canadian, 1860-1924)
View of the Waugauus River, oil on canvas, sgn/dtd 1893, 24x36", B/B 10/9/88 UE 2,475
DE FOREST, Lockwood (American, 1850-1932)
Tranquil Waters, oil on board, initialed/dtd 1909, 10x14", B/B 9/15/88 880
DE FOREST, Roy (American, 1930-)
Life on the Bull (imaginary view w/figure, bull, dogs in lanscape), acrylic on canvas, sgn, 1976, 66x72", C-NY 5/4/89 OE 23,100

Swiss Gentledog (contemporary), acrylic on canvas, sgn/dtd 1973, 66x72", C-NY 2/20/88 OE ... 12,100
The Wizard of Oz (fantasy), watercolor/acrylic/spray enamel/colored chalk/charcoal, sgn/dtd 84, 30x42", C-NY 5/4/89 OE ... 6,050

DE FOREST BRUSH, George; see Brush

DE FOY SUZOR-COTE, see Suzor-Cote

DE FRANCA, Manuel J.; att (American, 19th C)
Portrait of Malvina Sedam Curtis, oil on canvas, sgn/dtd 1863, 29x24", LH 10/16/88 UE ... 375

DE FRANCESCHI, Mariano (Italian, 1849-1896)
Figures in an Italian Village, oil on panel, sgn, 16x9", C-E 2/21/89 ... 2,420
Peasant Girl Amongst Ancient Ruins, watercolor, sgn, 22x25", C-E 2/21/89 ... 550
Scent of Incense, watercolor, sgn/inscr, 30x21", C-NY 5/25/88 ... 1,760

DE FRICK, Paul (French, 1864-1935)
Terrace on the Sea, oil on canvas, sgn, 18x22", B/B 9/14/89 UE ... 880

DE FROMANTIOU, Hendrik (Dutch, 1633-1694)
Game & Hunting Implements on a Ledge, oil on canvas, 24x19", C-NY 5/31/89 ... 22,000

DE GALLARD, Michel (French, 20th C)
Composition (abstract), oil on canvas, sgn, 52x38", SBY 2/14/89 ... 3,300

DE GARTHE, William Edward (Canadian)
Fishing Boats at Dusk, oil on board, sgn, 7x9", WAD 11/30/89 ... 350

DE GAVARDIE, Jean (French, 1909-1961)
La Table de Toilette, oil on canvas, sgn, 36x23", WD 5/5/88 UE ... 1,200

DE GEEST, Juliaen Franciscus (-1699)
Portrait of a Gentleman Holding a Skull: A Vanitas; oil on panel, sgn/dtd 1662, 17x14", SBY 10/13/89 ... 5,500

DE GEETERE, Georges (19th C)
Harem Guard, oil on canvas, sgn/inscr/dtd 1885, 80x47", C-NY 5/25/88 ... 17,600

DE GESNE, Jean Victor Albert (French, 1834-1903)
Un Cerf au Bois, oil on canvas, sgn, 40x52", SBY 6/9/89 ... 3,300

DE GHIZE, Eleanor (American, 1896-)
Front Porch, oil on canvas, sgn, 24x36", SBY 1/24/89 UE ... 1,320

DE GILLABOZ
Set of 3: Studies of Swiss Plants; watercolor, 2 inscr, 19x13", C-E 4/7/88 ... 880

DE GRAILLY, Victor; att (French, 1804-1889)
Dream of Arcadia, oil on canvas, 23x36", B/B 8/10/88 ... 2,200
Niagara Falls, oil on canvas, ca 1830, 16x22", LH 10/16/88, OE ... 3,400

DE GRAILLY, Victor; school of (French, 1804-1899)
Back-Lit Scene of Herders Watering Their Cattle, oil on canvas, sgn, 20x25", WG 4/23/88 ... 2,000

DE GRANDMAISON, Nickola (Canadian, 1892-1978)
Portrait of a Young Girl, pastel, sgn/dtd 1946, 14x11", FB 4/25/88 ... 1,650

DE GREBBER, Pieter Franz (Dutch, 1600-1692)
Allegory: Young Boy Drinking From a Glass Held by a Woman; oil on canvas, 35x27", SBY 10/21/88 ... 6,050
Allegory: Young Boy Drinking From a Glass Held by a Woman; oil on canvas, 35x27", SBY 4/7/88 ... 4,125

DE GREFF, Adriaen; att (Flemish, 1670-1715)
Still Life of Hanging Game Birds, oil on canvas, bears signature/dtd 1665, 48x37", SBY 6/8/88 OE ... 4,675

DE GRIMBERGHE, Edmond Comte (German, 1856-1920)
L'Odalisque (woman reclining behind barred window), oil on canvas, sgn, 49x67", C-NY 5/23/89 OE ... 35,750

DE GROOT, Frans Arnold Breuhaus (Dutch, 1824-1872)
Activity by the Docks, oil on canvas laid down on masonite, sgn, 40x55", SBY 2/22/89 ... 25,300
Mountainous Landscape with Waterfall, oil on canvas, sgn/indistinctly dtd, unfr, 31x24", C-E 4/7/88 UE ... 110

DE GROUX, Charles (Belgian, 1825-1870)
Figure by a Church, oil on canvas laid down on board, sgn, unfr, 10x13", PHL 10/28/88 UE ... 500

DE GROUX, Henry (Belgian, 1867-1930)
Diana (goddess), pastel on board, sgn, 26x19", SBY 6/8/88 UE ... 1,650

DE GRUYTER, Jacob Willem (Dutch, 1817-1880)
Ships at Sea, oil on panel, sgn, 11x18", C-E 5/23/88 ... 880

DE GUASTAVINO, Clement Pujol (French, fl 1880-1889)
Arabs Outside a Mosque, oil on panel, sgn, 22x18", SBY 10/24/89 ... 17,600
Jeune Femme Nourrissant des Cygnes, oil on canvas, sgn, 25x21", SBY 10/24/89 ... 9,900
Outdoor Concert, oil on canvas laid down on panel, sgn/indistinctly dtd, 15x22", C-NY 10/25/89 ... 30,800

DE GYSELAAR, M. (fl 1813-1820)
Pair: Anemones; watercolor over pencil, 1 sgn/dtd 1813, 9x7", SBY 1/13/89 ... 880
Spray of Convolvulus, watercolor over pencil, sgn/dtd 1820, 9x7", SBY 1/13/89 ... 660

DE HAAS, Johannes H. Leonardus (Dutch, 1832-1908)
Cows on a Country Path, oil on panel, sgn, 12x19", C-E 10/25/88 ... 3,300

DE HAAS, Johannes H. Leonardus; style of (Dutch, 1832-1908)
Cows in a Landscape with Stream, oil on panel, sgn, 12x22", WG 9/16/88 ... 250

DE HAAS, Mauritz Frederick Hendrik (Dutch, 1832-1895)
Coastal Sunset (w/figures & boats), oil on canvas, sgn, 20x34", C-NY 5/25/89 ... 13,200
Fishermen Along the Coast, oil on canvas, sgn, 14x24", B/B 6/15/89 ... 4,400
Fishermen Along the Coast, oil on canvas, sgn, 14x24", SBY 1/24/89 ... 2,750
Fishing at Sunset, oil on canvas, sgn/dtd 75, 12x20", C-NY 9/28/89 ... 7,700
Fishing Boats in Rough Seas, oil on canvas, sgn, 14x22", RAB 8/8/89 ... 6,000
Moonlight Coast Off Holland, oil on canvas, sgn, 26x20", B/B 3/22/89 ... 5,500

Night Sail, oil on canvas, estate stamp, 12x9", SBY 6/28/89	990
Sailing at Sunset, oil on canvas, sgn/dtd 74, 25x40", C-NY 5/25/89	35,200
Ships at Sea, oil on canvas, sgn, 12x17", FAP 4/15/89	688
Three Mile Harbor, Long Island; oil on canvas, sgn, 12x19", SBY 9/23/88	2,640
Twilight's Catch (fishermen in dories, sailboats beyond), oil on canvas, sgn, 14x24", C-NY 9/28/89	11,000
DE HAGEMANN, Godefroy (French, -1877)	
Shepherd with Dog Tending Sheep in Woods, oil on canvas, sgn, 47x63", SBY 7/12/89	4,125
DE HAMILTON, Franz; att	
Cockatoo, a Parrot, Another Bird & a Gibbon on a Chain with Fruit in a Park; oil on canvas, 36x52", C-NY 10/12/89	6,600
DE HAMILTON, Johann Georg	
Arabian Steed in a Landscape, oil on canvas, sgn/dtd 1724, 18x23", C-NY 10/12/89	6,600
DE HAMILTON, Karl Wilhelm	
Reptiles, Butterflies & Insects by a Raspberry Plant in a Landscape; oil on panel, 14x11", C-NY 10/12/89	9,350
DE HASPE, Francois (Belgian, 1874-)	
Untitled, expansive landscape w/middle distant village; oil on canvas, sgn/dtd 1901, 23x29", SLK 4/7/89	850
DE HAVEN, Franklin (American, 1856-1934)	
After Rain (road running through fields, barn beyond), oil on panel, sgn, 8x12", RWS 9/29/88 UE	200
Approaching Storm, oil on canvas, sgn/dtd 1907, unfr, 24x30", SBY 6/24/88 UE	660
Autumn (trees & fields along winding river), oil on canvas, sgn, 28x40", RAB 8/9/88	2,750
Clouds & Sunshine (landscape), oil on canvas, sgn twice/dtd 1889/titled, 14x20", SBY 3/17/88	1,320
Landscape, oil on canvas, sgn, 29x41", DM 9/16/88	1,800
Maranacook Lake, Maine; oil on canvas, sgn, 37x26", SBY 4/14/89	2,090
Rocky Coast, oil on canvas, sgn, 24x30", SBY 3/17/88	1,650
Running Brook, oil on canvas, sgn, 28x40", C-E 6/1/88	2,420
Silent Pool, oil on canvas, sgn twice/inscr/titled, 24x30", SBY 1/24/89	1,925
Trees in the Autumn Twilight, oil on canvas, sgn/dtd 1887, 16x24", B/B 10/9/88 OE	4,125
Woodland Landscape with Stream, oil on canvas, sgn, 30x24", SBY 3/17/88	1,650
DE HEEM, Cornelis (Dutch, 1631-1695)	
Fruit, Ears of Corn & Filberts Hanging From a Nail with a Blue Ribbon; oil on canvas laid down, 11x8", C-NY 5/31/89	104,500
Fruit on a Pewter Plate on a Ledge Draped with a Green Cloth, oil on panel, sgn, 9x14", C-NY 5/31/89	220,000
Peaches, Grapes, Cherries, Roemer, & a Pewter Plate on a Ledge; oil on canvas, sgn, 18x15", C-NY 1/15/88 OE	242,000
Still Life of Flowers, Cherries, Peaches, Plums, a Half-Peeled Lemon...; oil on panel, sgn, 15x11", SBY 1/12/89	49,500
Still Life of Flowers in a Glass Vase on a Shelf, oil on panel, sgn, 18x13", SBY 6/3/88 OE	143,000
DE HEEM, David Davidsz (Dutch, 1610-1669)	
Still Life of Flowers, oil on canvas, sgn, 17x14", SBY 1/12/89	22,000
DE HEEM, Jan Davidsz (Dutch, 1606-1684)	
Banquet Still Life, oil on canvas, sgn/dtd 1642, 61x82", C-NY 1/15/88	6,600,000
DE HEEM, Jan Davidsz; manner of (Dutch, 1606-1684)	
Still Life of a Bowl of Fruit, Overturned Tazza, Standing Covered Cup, & a Roemer; oil on panel, 23x29", SBY 10/21/88	6,600
Tulips, Roses, & Other Flowers in a Glass Vase on a Ledge with a Snail; oil on copper, 14x11", C-M 6/16/89 OE	11,409
DE HEEM, Jan Jansz (Dutch, 1650-1695)	
Still Life of Silver Gilt Cup, Pewter Flagon, Peaches...; oil on canvas, initialed, 34x48", C-M 12/3/88	222,973
DE HEUSCH, Jacob	
Rocky Mediterranean Inlet with Stevedores Cooking at a Campfire in the Foreground, oil on canvas, 19x38", C-NY 1/15/88	28,600
DE HEUVEL, Theodore Bernard (Flemish, 1817-1906)	
Game with Nuts, oil on panel, sgn, unfr, 25x31", WD 5/5/88	5,500
DE HONDECOETER, Gillis Claesz (Dutch, 1575-1638)	
Extensive Rocky Landscape with a Distant View of a Town, sgn in monogram/dtd 1619, 10x15", SBY 10/21/88	22,000
DE HONDECOETER, Melchior (Dutch, 1636-1695)	
Peacocks & Other Birds by a Lake, oil on canvas, sgn, 67x85", SBY 6/1/89	242,000
Still Life of Brace of Rabbits, Small Birds & Hunting Equipment in a Landscape; oil, monogramed, 22x19", SBY 1/12/89	49,500
DE HOOCH, Pieter (Dutch, 1629-1681)	
Woman Seated by a Window with a Child in a Doorway, oil on canvas, 22x27", C-NY 1/11/89 OE	132,000
DE HOOG, Bernard (Dutch, 1867-1943)	
A Mother's Love, oil on panel, sgn, 12x10", C-E 10/26/89	2,860
Friendly Visit, oil on canvas, sgn, 31x26", C-NY 5/25/88	4,400
Interior Genre Scene (mother & child peeling potatoes w/kettle over a fire), oil on canvas, sgn, 22x27", DM 9/16/88	4,000
Interior Scene, oil on canvas, sgn, 11x9", RWS 5/12/89 OE	2,000
Interior Scene with Mother & Children, oil on canvas, sgn, 16x20", FB 10/30/89	8,800
Mother & Child, oil on canvas, sgn, 18x16", FB 4/25/88	4,500
Mother & Child, oil on canvas, sgn, 19x25", FB 4/25/88	7,500
Mother's Little Helper, oil on canvas, sgn, 20x26", C-NY 5/25/88	8,250
Pair: Domestic Felicity; oil on canvas, sgn, 12x10", C-NY 5/25/88	7,700
Sewing Lesson, oil on canvas, sgn, 20x16", C-E 10/26/89	8,800
Still Life of a Vase of Roses & Daisies, oil on board, sgn, 14x11", SBY 5/23/89 OE	23,100
The Little Family, oil on canvas, sgn, 38x46", WAD 6/6/88 OE	38,000
The Little Lecturer, oil on canvas, sgn, 22x18", WAD 6/6/88	11,000
DE IVANOWSKI, Sigismund (American?, 1875-1944)	
Lady in Blue, oil on canvasboard, 12x16", C-NY 9/30/88	2,860
Portrait of the Artist's Wife, Helen; oil on canvas, 73x33", SBY 3/17/88	11,000
Window Shopping (figures peering in windows), oil on canvas, 20x32", C-NY 9/28/89	6,050

DE JOHGH, Ludolph (Dutch, 1616-1679)
Portrait of a Man, in a dark costume & lace collar; oil on canvas, indistinctly sgn/dtd, 28x25", C-NY 1/15/88 ... 6,600
DE JONG, Jacobus Sterre (Dutch, 1866-1920)
Family Gathering, oil on canvas, sgn, 13x16", C-E 10/25/88 ... 1,210
Mother & Daughter Peeling Carrots, watercolor, sgn, 23x18", C-E 10/26/89 ... 770
DE JONGERE, Marius (Dutch, 1912-)
Dutch Coastal View with Windmill, oil on canvas, sgn, 24x36", SBY 7/12/89 OE ... 2,475
DE JONGH, Gabriel Cornelis (Dutch, 1913-)
In the Transkei, oil on canvas, sgn, unfr, 10x12", C-SK 5/25/89 ... 550
Table Mountain, Cape Town; oil on canvasboard, sgn, 18x24", C-SK 5/25/89 ... 700
DE JONGH, Oene Romkes (Dutch, 1812-1896)
Amsterdam Canal Scene in Winter, oil on canvas, sgn, 22x18", C-E 10/25/88 ... 2,420
Dutch Winter Street Scene, oil on canvas, sgn, 25x31", SBY 6/8/88 ... 4,125
Market Scene, oil on canvas laid down on masonite, sgn, 27x21", C-E 5/23/88 ... 1,320
Skating on the Canal (winter cityscape), oil on canvas, sgn, 22x18", WG 4/23/88 ... 1,600
DE JONGH, Tinus (Marthinus Johannes)(Dutch, 1885-1942)
Mill in Cape Province, oil on canvas, sgn/inscr/dtd 1934, 16x20", C-SK 5/25/89 ... 340
Table Mountain, oil on canvas, sgn, 10x12", C-SK 5/25/89 ... 1,100
Table Mountain (landscape), oil on canvas, sgn, 10x13", C-SK 6/9/88 ... 840
DE JUAN, Ronaldo (Argentinian, 1930-)
Orgasm, oil on canvas, sgn/twice dtd 60, 51x38", C-E 5/13/88 ... 605
DE KEMPENER, Pieter; circle of (1503-1580)
Crucifixion (Christ & two men on crosses, women at Christ's feet, figures beyond), oil on canvas, 36x33", SBY 4/7/89 ... 2,640
DE KEYSER, Thomas; att (Dutch, 1596-1667)
Portrait of a Man on Horseback, oil on canvas, 37x31", SBY 1/12/89 UE ... 5,500
DE KEYSER, Thomas; circle of (Dutch, 1596-1667)
Portrait of a Gentleman Said To Be Eduard Mole (bust-length); oil on copper, oval, 6x5", C-NY 6/2/88 ... 1,650
DE KONINCK, David
Fruit in a Basket with Grapes & Mushrooms on a Ledge, a Dog & Cat in a Landscape; oil on canvas, 25x34", C-NY 6/2/88 ... 13,200
DE KONINGH, Leendert the elder (Dutch, 1777-1849)
Cattle Along the Banks of a Dutch River, oil on panel, sgn, unfr, 12x15", C-E 2/21/89 ... 1,760
DE KOONING, Elaine (American, 1920-)
John F Kennedy & Friend, charcoal on paper, initialed/sgn/dtd 63, 25x19", C-NY 3/11/88 OE ... 3,300
Man in a Hotel Room (rough sketch), oil on canvas, initialed, 32x22", SBY 2/14/89 OE ... 9,900
Squeeze Play (abstract), oil on canvas, sgn, 30x30", SBY 10/7/89 ... 8,250
Untitled, gouache on paper mounted at top corners on paper, initialed, 11x14", C-E 5/13/88 ... 990
Untitled, oil on masonite, initialed, 8x12", C-E 5/13/88 ... 1,540
Untitled, oil on paper, initialed, 15x20", C-E 5/13/88 OE ... 1,870
Veronica (abstract), oil on masonite, sgn/dtd 59, 36x48", SBY 2/15/89 ... 4,950
DE KOONING, Willem (American, 1904-)
Cedar Street (abstract), oil/ink/charcoal on heavy wove paper mounted on board, sgn, ca 1956, 23x30", SBY 11/10/88 OE ... 385,000
Daily News, oil on newspaper laid down on board, sgn, 15x21", WD 5/5/88 ... 2,000
East Hampton IV, oil on canvas, sgn, 1977, 30x36", SBY 11/9/89 OE ... 880,000
Five Women (abstract), graphite on paper, sgn, 18x29", C-NY 5/3/89 OE ... 374,000
Head, oil on newsprint mounted on wood panel, sgn, 23x15", SBY 11/9/89 ... 88,000

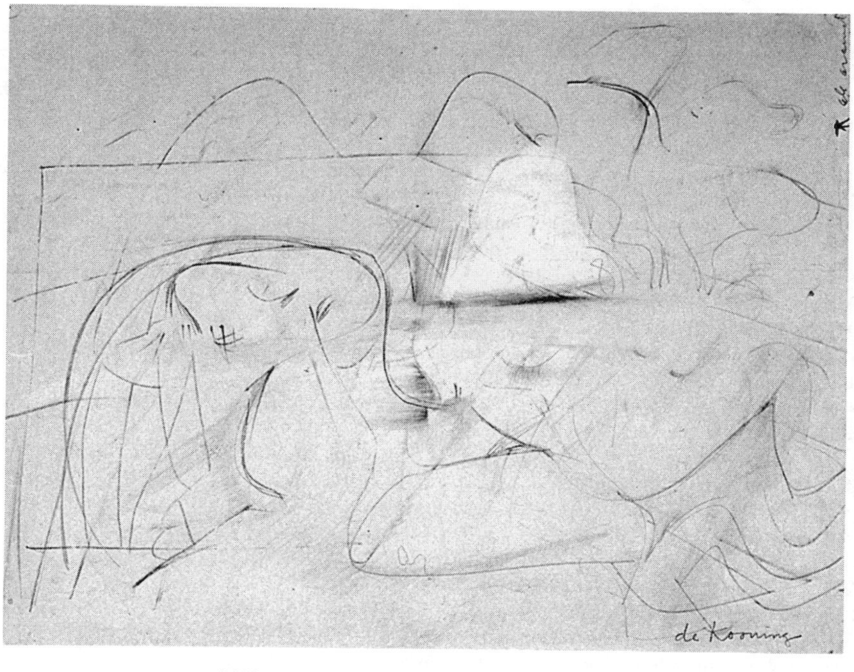

Landscape, chalk/graphite on paper, sgn, ca 1948, 11x14", C-NY 5/3/89 OE, $148,500

Pair: Untitled: Two Figure Studies (abstract); ink/brush on vellum mounted on canvas, sgn, ca 1960, 22x8", SBY 5/3/88 15,400
Red Lips (abstract figure), pencil/crayon on paper, sgn, 10x8", SBY 5/3/88 OE 12,100
Seated Man, pencil on paper, sgn, ca 1938-42, 9x7", SBY 10/8/88 19,800
Steeplechase with Jim Lisle Taking Water Hazar, oil on board, 12x16", MAG 11/30/89 500
Study for Marshes (abstract), oil/charcoal on paper mounted on panel, sgn, ca 1946, 29x23", SBY 5/2/88 462,000
Study of a Man's Arm, pencil on paper, ca 1927-35, 12x6", SBY 10/8/88 6,600
Study of Woman's Head, pencil on paper, sgn, ca 1927-35, 9x7", SBY 10/8/88 OE 3,960,000
Two Men: Study for Clam Diggers (abstract figures); oil on paper mounted on masonite, sgn, 23x29", SBY 5/2/89 715,000
Two Women (abstract figures), pastel/charcoal/pencil on paper, sgn, 1954, 15x15", SBY 5/2/89 OE 715,000
Two Women (abstract), pastel/charcoal/pencil on paper, sgn/dtd 54, S-22x26", SBY 11/10/88 797,500
Two Women (abstract), pen/ink on paper, sgn/dtd 1959, 23x19", C-NY 2/14/89 60,500
Two Women IV (abstract), graphite/colored chalks/charcoal/gouache on paper, sgn, 1952, 16x20", C-NY 11/9/88 1,870,000
Untitled (abstract figures), charcoal on paper, sgn, 10x8", C-NY 10/4/89 16,500
Untitled (abstract woman), oil on vellum laid down on paperboard, sgn, ca 1964, 19x24", SBY 2/15/89 OE 60,500
Untitled (abstract), charcoal on paper, sgn, ca 1965, 11x15", SBY 5/3/88 OE 8,250
Untitled (abstract), charcoal on paper, sgn, ca 1969, 9x11", C-NY 2/1/489 10,450
Untitled (abstract), charcoal on paper, sgn, 11x9", C-NY 2/14/89 13,200
Untitled (abstract), charcoal on paper, sgn, 1975, 11x8", SBY 10/5/89 13,750
Untitled (abstract), charcoal on paper, sgn, 1980, 23x18", C-NY 5/4/89 16,500
Untitled (abstract), charcoal on paper, sgn/dtd 1980, 11x9", SBY 2/15/89 14,300
Untitled (abstract), charcoal on vellum, sgn, ca 1965, 23x18", SBY 5/3/88 9,350
Untitled (abstract), charcoal on vellum mounted on board, ca 1975, 42x28", SBY 5/3/88 18,700
Untitled (abstract), charcoal/oil on vellum, sgn, ca 1975, 53x41", SBY 5/2/88 60,500
Untitled (abstract), ink/brush on paper, sgn, ca 1954, 22x17", SBY 5/3/89 68,750
Untitled (abstract), oil on newspaper laid down on canvas, sgn, 23x29", SBY 10/8/88 OE 34,100
Untitled (abstract), oil on newspaper laid down on canvas, sgn, 1972, 23x29", SBY 2/15/89 24,200
Untitled (abstract), oil on newspaper laid down on canvas, sgn, ca 1975, 29x23", SBY 2/15/89 OE 60,500
Untitled (abstract), oil on newsprint mounted on board, sgn, ca 1973, 24x30", C-NY 10/4/89 68,200
Untitled (abstract), oil on newsprint mounted on canvas, sgn, 1970, 23x30", C-NY 5/4/88 OE 33,000
Untitled (abstract), oil on newsprint mounted on masonite, sgn, 29x23", C-NY 11/10/88 OE 66,000
Untitled (abstract), oil on paper, sgn, ca 1957, 8x7", SBY 5/3/89 OE 143,000
Untitled (abstract), oil on paper, sgn, 22x18", SBY 2/15/89 OE 15,400
Untitled (abstract), oil on paper, 1955-56, 8x7", C-NY 5/3/89 OE 143,000
Untitled (abstract), oil on paper mounted on canvas, sgn, ca 1965, 46x18", C-NY 11/9/88 209,000
Untitled (abstract), oil on paper mounted on canvas, sgn, ca 1965, 23x18", SBY 5/3/89 OE 99,000
Untitled (abstract), oil/charcoal on paper, sgn, ca 1944-45, 21x20", SBY 11/10/88 231,000
Untitled (abstract), oil/paper/graphite on paper mounted on canvas, sgn/dtd 51, 22x30", C-NY 5/3/89 440,000
Untitled (black abstract on white), oil on paper, sgn, ca 1959, 17x14", SBY 10/5/89 15,400
Untitled (contemporary abstract), charcoal on vellum, sgn, ca 1975, 14x17", SBY 11/9/89 33,000
Untitled (contemporary abstract), oil on paper mounted on canvas, sgn, ca 1965, 46x18", SBY 11/9/89 OE 440,000
Untitled (contemporary abstract), oil on vellum mounted on canvas, sgn, 22x19", SBY 11/9/89 OE 82,500
Untitled (man in water, abstract), oil on paper laid down on canvas, sgn, 1977, 41x32", SBY 11/10/88 132,000
Untitled (Study for Figure in Watermill Landscape), oil on newspaper mounted, sgn, 1966, 23x30", SBY 11/9/89 OE 291,500
Untitled (Woman, abstract), oil on canvas, sgn/dtd 66, 48x36", SBY 11/8/89 OE 935,000
Untitled (Woman Series), oil on paper, inscr dedication, ca 1959, 11x9", SBY 11/11/88 11,000
Untitled (2 abstract figures), charcoal on tracing paper, sgn/inscr To Perrault, ca 1965, 19x24", SBY 5/2/88 OE 16,500
Untitled #7 (abstract), oil on paper laid down on canvas, sgn, 1957-58, 13x11", SBY 2/15/89 OE 159,500
Untitled II (abstract), oil on canvas, sgn, 1977, 77x88", SBY 11/8/89 OE 1,980,000
Untitled III (abstract), oil on canvas, 1976, 70x80", SBY 11/8/89 OE 3,520,000
Woman (abstract), colored crayons/graphite/paper collage mounted on board, sgn, ca 1952, 20x14", SBY 10/8/88 63,250
Woman (abstract), oil on paper mounted on panel, sgn, 1966, 24x19", C-NY 5/3/88 OE 132,000
Woman (abstract), oil on vellum mounted on canvas, sgn, 1965, 19x24", SBY 5/3/89 88,000
Woman (abstract), oil/enamel/graphite/paper collage on paper, mounted by the artist, sgn, ca 1952, 16x13", C-NY 5/3/88 286,000
Woman (abstract), pencil on paper, sgn, ca 1965, 10x8", SBY 10/8/88 OE 11,000
Woman (contemporary abstract), oil on paper mounted on canvas, sgn, ca 1967-68, 23x19", SBY 11/9/89 OE 561,000
Woman in the Garden (abstract), oil on paper laid down on canvas, sgn, 1967, 23x19", SBY 11/11/88 OE 181,500
Women Seated & Standing (abstract composition), pastel/charcoal on paper, sgn, 1952, 21x24", SBY 5/2/88 1,210,000
Yellow Woman (abstract), tempera/oil/graphite/charcoal on paper, sgn, 9x6", C-NY 11/9/88 OE 715,000

DE LA CORTE, Gabriel (1648-1694)
Pair: Still Lifes of Flowers in Elaborate Vases; oil on canvas, indistinctly sgn, 16x10", SBY 10/21/88 OE 132,000

DE LA FOSSE, Charles Alexander (French, 1829-1900)
An Amusing Thought, oil on canvas, sgn, 37x26", SBY 7/12/89 6,050

DE LA FRESNAYE, Roger (French, 1885-1925)
Interieur, pen/black ink on paper mounted at the edges on board, sgn/dtd 1921, 7x10", C-NY 11/15/88 19,800

DE LA HAYE, Reinier (ca 1640-after 1695)
Portrait of an Elegant Lady Holding a Rose & Lily, Seated at a Table; oil on canvas, 19x15", SBY 10/13/89 OE 35,200

DE LA HYRE, Laurent (French, 1606-1656)
Sacrifice of Abraham, oil on arched-top canvas, initialed, 45x35", C-M 12/3/88 OE 297,297

DE LA HYRE, Laurent; att (French, 1606-1656)
Classical Figures Opening a Tomb, brush/oil/brown wash heightened w/white, 8x11", SBY 1/13/89 OE 20,900

DE LA HYRE, Laurent; circle of (French, 1606-1656)
Capriccio of Classical Ruins with Figures, oil on canvas, 29x36", C-NY 4/8/88 6,600

DE LA MAR, David (French, 19th/20th C)
Shepherdess with Goat, oil on canvas, sgn, 29x19", RWS 5/12/89 UE 550
DE LA MARCHE, Nathalie (19th C)
View of Rome with Architectural Fragments on the Palatine, black chalk/pen/ink/wash, sgn/dtd 1821, 15x22", C-NY 1/11/89 OE 4,620
DE LA PENA, Narcisse; see Diaz De La Pena
DE LA ROCHE, Charles Ferdinand (French, 19th C)
Keeping Watch on a Cold Winter's Eve, oil on panel, sgn, unfr, 10x12", B/B 1/11/89 OE 1,210
DE LA ROUERE, Pietro Lonte (Italian, 19th/20th C)
Huntress, oil on panel, 54x32", FAP 11/4/88 OE 5,750
DE LA RUE, Louis Felix (French, 1731-1765)
Miraculous Draught of Fishes, black chalk/pen/black ink/watercolor, sgn/inscr/dtd 1764, 11x15", C-NY 1/12/88 OE 1,540
Mythological Scene, black chalk/pen/black ink/lt brown wash, 6x7", C-E 4/7/88 UE 55
DE LA SERNA, Ismael (Spanish, 1899-)
Composicion de un Interior (abstract interior composition), sgn/dtd 36, 26x21", SBY 10/7/89 OE 23,100
Nature Morte avec Deux Citrons (still life), oil on masonite, sgn/dtd 27, 26x20", C-E 5/9/89 OE 13,600
DE LA VEGA, Jose (Spanish, 19th C)
Corrida en Sevilla (bull fight scene), oil on canvas, sgn/inscr, 17x25", B/B 6/15/89 1,980
DE LA VILLEON, Emmanuel (French, 1858-1944)
Accacias Fleuris, oil on panel, sgn, 14x11", SBY 10/7/89 6,600
Automne (Nievre), oil on canvas, sgn, 1915, 20x29", SBY 10/6/89 22,000
Pair: Le Lavoir; L'Hiver Salvan; oil on board, sgn/inscr, 4x5", C-NY 5/13/88 2,420
DE LAAR, Jan Hendrik; see Van De Laar
DE LACROIX, see Lacroix de Marseille
DE LAFOSSE, Charles Alexander (French, 1829-1900)
Woman Standing Beside a Buffet & Cleaning a Pewter Charger, oil on canvas, sgn, 19x12", SLK 9/28/88 1,400
DE LAIRESSE, Gerard; circle of (Flemish, 1641-1711)
Putti Wrestling a Goat in a Landscape, oil on canvas, 15x18", SBY 4/7/88 1,870
DE LALL, Oscar (Canadian, 1903-1971)
Laurentian Winter Landscape, oil on canvas, sgn, 20x26", FB 10/17/88 950
Marine (seascape), oil on canvas, sgn, 24x32", FB 4/25/88 UE 800
St Adele, Quebec (autumn landacape); oil on board, sgn, 22x28", FB 5/28/89 800
DE LARGILLERE, Nicolas; att (French, 1656-1746)
Gentleman in Armour, oil on canvas, 29x22", WG 9/16/88 UE 300
DE LARGILLERE, Nicolas; school of (French, 1656-1746)
Portrait of a Gentleman, standing, small three-quarter length...; oil on canvas, 25x20", C-NY 4/6/89 4,620
Portrait of a Lady, seated three-quarter length, wearing a white dress...; oil on canvas, 55x43", C-NY 4/6/89 OE 13,200
Portrait of a Lady, wearing a white dress w/a blue ribbon & red shawl; oil on canvas, 34x26", C-NY 6/2/88 3,300
DE LASZLO DE LOMBOS, Philip Alexius (British, 1869-1937)
Portrait of a Lady with a String of Pearls, oil on canvas, sgn/dtd 1927, unfr, 42x29", SBY 2/22/89 OE 12,100
DE LATOUCHE, Gaston (French, 1854-1913)
La Salutation de Pierrot, oil on canvas, 67x93", SBY 10/24/89 55,000
Le Bain (two women bathing in stream), oil on canvas, sgn, 48x48", SBY 2/22/89 19,800
Les Amants et les Cygnes, La Promenade d'Automne; pastel on paper, sgn/dtd 96, 29x24", C-L 6/27/88 66,220
Souper de Chasse, oil on cradled panel, sgn, 30x32", SBY 5/23/89 13,200
The Picnic, oil on panel, sgn/dtd 93, 23x30", B/B 6/9/88 OE 30,250
Two Studies of Women, oil on wood panel, about 6x6", LH 10/16/88 600
Woman with Swans, watercolor/gouache, bears signature, 29x20", C-NY 10/25/89 1,760
DE LAVAULT, Albert Tibule Furcy
Washerwoman by a Wooded River at Dusk, oil on canvas, sgn, 36x59", C-E 5/23/88 2,200
DE LEEUW, Alexis (Belgian, 1848-)
Figures in a Winter Landscape, oil on canvas, sgn, 16x24", SBY 12/9/88 4,675
Shepherd & His Flock in a Snowy Wooded Landscape, oil on canvas, sgn, 24x36", C-E 10/25/88 4,180
DE LEMPICKA, Tamara (Polish, 1898-)
Back of Female Nude, oil on canvas, sgn, 30x20", C-E 11/17/88 OE 14,300
Blue Composition (contemporary), oil on canvas, sgn, 36x24", C-E 5/9/89 OE 5,280
Cubist Madonna & Child, oil on canvas, unfr, 20x16", SBY 2/14/89 OE 7,700
Deux Jeunes Filles Lisant (close-up of two young ladies reading), oil on canvas, 11x14", C-NY 10/5/89 17,600
Femme avec Guirlande de Fleurs (portrait), oil on panel, sgn/dtd 1925, 12x9", C-NY 10/6/88 33,000
Femme Avec une Cigarette (portrait), gouache over pencil on paper, sgn/dtd 1937, 12x10", C-NY 5/12/88 OE 33,000
Femme Nue (modernistic draped nude), oil on canvas, 1974, 32x21", SBY 10/6/89 OE 41,250
Girl with a Crock Jar, oil on canvas, 1961, 24x20", C-NY 2/18/88 3,850
Gray & Pink Composition (contemporary), oil on canvas, unfr, sgn, 30x24", C-E 5/9/89 OE 8,800
Gray & Yellow Composition (abstract), oil on canvas, sgn, 26x40", C-E 5/9/89 OE 8,580
Head of a Young Girl in a Blue Veil, oil on canvasboard, 7x5", C-E 11/17/88 OE 17,600
Head of Mme Alan Bolt, pencil on paper, ca 1930, 14x18", C-NY 2/18/88 OE 12,100
La Bella Donna (seated woman wearing cape w/book in lap), pencil on paper, ca 1934, 19x12", C-NY 2/18/88 1,870
Le Couple (portrait), oil on canvas, 20x16", C-NY 10/6/88 16,500
Le Turban Vert (portrait of two women, one w/green turban), oil on panel, sgn, 1930, 16x13", SBY 11/12/88 220,000
Les Deux Amies (two nudes), oil on panel, sgn, 1927, 29x15", C-NY 5/12/88 297,000
Main Surrealiste (surrealistic hand), oil on canvas, 27x20", C-NY 10/5/89 14,300

Orange Turban, oil on canvas, 1974, 11x9", SBY 10/7/89 OE 14,300
Oranges in a Basket, oil on canvas mounted on board, sgn, 15x19", SBY 10/7/89 OE 22,000
Pair: Nude Model; Figures Embracing; pencil on paper, 1st ca 1924, 2nd ca 1930, 12x9", 9x6", C-NY 2/16/89 3,080
Paysage Surrealiste (surrealistic landscape), oil on canvasboard, sgn, 14x11", C-NY 10/5/89 12,100
Paysanne, oil on canvas, ca 1938, 10x6", SBY 5/11/88 57,750
Portrait d'Arlette Boucard, oil on panel, sgn, 1930, 36x22", SBY 11/12/88 220,000
Portrait du Pierre de Montaut, charcoal on paper, 1928-29, 32x24", C-NY 10/5/89 18,700
Portrait of Madame M (modern depection), oil on canvas, sgn, 1933, 39x26", SBY 11/16/89 990,000
Portrait of Mrs Alan Bott (modernistic full-length view), oil on canvas, sgn/dtd Paris 1930, 64x38", SBY 5/10/89 1,320,000
Saint Antoine (bust-length, wrists crossed on chest), oil on panel, sgn, 1936, 14x11", C-NY 10/5/89 20,900
Self-Portrait, oil on canvas, 14x11", C-NY 2/16/89 OE 46,200
Skyscrapers, oil on panel, initialed, 1930, 14x11", C-NY 5/12/88 41,800
Still Life of Drapery & Pearls (abstract cubist composition), oil on canvas, unfr, 20x16", SBY 2/14/89 OE 8,250
Still Life of Fish, oil on canvas, sgn, 13x26", C-E 11/17/88 OE 5,280
Still Life of Mask, Plume & Cards; oil on board, sgn, 22x15", SBY 10/7/89 OE 29,700
Still Life of Teapot, oil on canvas, unfr, 22x17", C-E 5/9/89 OE 5,500
Study of Hands, oil on canvas, unfr, 8x10", C-E 5/9/89 OE 2,860
Tete de Jeune Fille (head of young lady), oil on canvas, unfr, 12x9", C-E 11/17/88 OE 4,400
Vase de Fleurs (floral still life), oil on canvas, sgn, 16x12", C-NY 10/6/88 OE 33,000
Vase of Flowers, oil on canvas, sgn, 30x20", C-E 11/17/88 OE 9,900
Vase of Roses, oil on canvas, 1955, 20x16", C-NY 2/16/89 22,000

DE LEON, Amanda
Girl in Window, oil on masonite, sgn, 12x10", C-E 10/18/89 UE 44

DE LEON Y ESCOSURA, Ignacio (Spanish, 1834-1901)
Armory Shop, oil on panel, sgn/dtd 1878, 13x17", SBY 5/23/89 30,800
Figures in an Elegant Interior, oil on panel, sgn/dtd 1879, 15x22", C-NY 5/25/88 OE 24,200
Presentation at Court, oil on canvas, sgn/dtd 1873, 18x24", C-NY 10/25/89 26,400

DE LESIO, A.
Seated Peasant Woman, watercolor on paper, sgn, 22x16", C-E 5/23/88 660

DE LILLE, Louis Watteau; manner of
Pair: Figures Drinking by Tavern; Figures Dancing by a Stream; oil on canvas, cartouch shaped, 39x35", C-NY 4/8/88 OE 18,700

DE LOMBOS, Philip; see De Laszlo De Lombos

DE LONGPRE, Paul (American/French, 1855-1911)
Bouquet of Lavender Lilacs & Yellow Roses, pastel on paper mounted on stretched linen, sgn/dtd 1903, 29x21", B/B 10/6/88 2,200
Bouquet of White Lilacs & Pink Roses, pastel on paper mounted on stretched linen, sgn/dtd 1903, 29x21", B/B 10/6/88 2,200
Poinsettia, watercolor/pencil on paper, sgn, 26x18", C-NY 9/28/89 4,950
Rhododendrons, watercolor on paper, sgn/dtd 1895, 18x13", B/B 10/6/88 3,300
Roses & a Bumblebee, watercolor/pen/blk ink/pencil on paper laid down on board, sgn/dtd 1900, 20x14", C-E 2/1/89 OE 4,180

DE LONGPRE, Raoul M. Fils (American/French, 19th/20th C)
Bouquet of Pink & White Roses, pastel on paper, sgn/dtd 78, 27x20", B/B 3/22/89 2,200
Bouquet of Pink Roses & White Lilacs, gouache on paper, sgn, 20x28", SBY 9/14/89 2,200
Bouquet of Wildflowers, watercolor/gouache/pencil on paper, sgn, 29x21", SBY 3/17/88 1,980
Cut Roses & Lilacs with Shears, gouache on paper laid on board, sgn, 29x37", C-NY 9/30/88 8,800
Lilacs (still life), oil on board, sgn, 27x35", B/B 10/9/88 11,000
Pink & White Roses with Lilacs, watercolor/gouache on paper, sgn, 26x20", SBY 9/23/88 2,420
Pink & Yellow Roses, black chalk/watercolor/gouache on paper, 27x20", SBY 6/24/88 2,090
Pink Roses & White Lilacs, pastel on paper laid down on board, sgn, 21x29", C-NY 9/30/88 3,850
Spring Bouquet (still life), gouache on paper, sgn, 27x20", WL 5/20/88 OE 2,400
Yellow Roses & Lilacs, watercolor/gouache on paper, sgn, 29x37", SBY 3/17/88 OE 6,050

DE LOOSE, Basile (Dutch, 1809-1885)
Busy Schoolroom, oil on board, sgn/dtd 1862, 31x24", C-NY 10/25/89 8,800

DE LORNE, Anthonie; circle of
Interior of the Laurenskerk, Rotterdam, with People Gathering for a Service; oil on canvas, 26x32", SBY 1/12/89 24,200

DE LOUTHERBOURG, Jacques P. (French, 1740-1812)
Destruction of Pharoah's Host, oil on canvas, sgn/dtd 1792, 50x40", C-NY 5/31/89 OE 121,000
Shipwreck, oil on panel, 20x28", WD 10/19/88 3,500
Study of a Tree, black chalk on brown prepared paper, 22x15", SBY 1/13/89 1,980

DE LOUTHERBOURG, Jacques P.; circle of (French, 1740-1812)
Rustic Suitors Disputing in a Mountainous River Landscape, oil on canvas, 41x50", WD 10/19/88 OE 4,750

DE LOUTHERBOURG, Phillip James; circle of
Landscape with Gothic Ruin & Figure by a Stream, oil on canvas, 23x30", SBY 7/12/89 1,870

DE LUTERO, Giovanni (Italian, 1479-1542)
Allegory with a Male & Female Figure, Seated Against a Dark Background; oil on canvas, unfr, 71x86", C-NY 1/11/89 4,070,000

DE LYON, Corneille; school of
Portrait of a Gentleman, Bust-Length, Wearing a Black Coat with Fur Collar & a Hat; oil on panel, 6x5", C-NY 10/12/89 2,860

DE MADRAZO Y GARRETA, Raimundo (Spanish, 1841-1920)
After the Ball (seated lady in a ball gown), oil on canvas, sgn, 33x25", C-NY 2/23/89 OE 132,000
Broken Bowl (lady seated in a landscape looking at broken bowl), oil on panel, sgn, 12x7", SBY 2/22/89 27,500
Music Lesson (two gentlemen playing music, two ladies listening), oil on canvas, sgn, 20x30", SBY 2/22/89 154,000
Portrait of Mrs James Leigh Coleman, oil on canvas, sgn/dtd Paris 86, 58x38", lot 191, C-NY 10/25/89 14,300
Portrait of Mrs James Leigh Coleman, oil on canvas, sgn/dtd Paris 86, 58x38", lot 190, C-NY 10/25/89 33,000

DE MAGRATH, Georges Achille (French, 19th C)
View of the Gardens & the Chateau de St Cloud, watercolor on paper, 17x13", SBY 10/24/89 ... 2,530
DE MAINE, Harry (American, 1880-1951)
Rocky Neck, Gloucester, Massachusetts; gouache on paper, sgn, 16x19", RWS 11/10/89 ... 700
DE MAINERI, Gian Francesco (fl 1491-1505)
Christ Carrying the Cross, oil on panel, unfr, 27x23", SBY 6/3/88 OE ... 154,000
DE MAJO, Paolo
Saint Nicholas of Bari & the Miracle of the Three School Children, oil on canvas, 40x30", C-NY 10/20/88 ... 2,200
DE MARCO, M. (American, 20th C)
Portrait of Mr Ogilvie with the Terminal Tower in the Distance, oil on canvas, sgn/dtd 1929, 38x28", WG 4/23/88 UE ... 150
DE MARIA, Nicola (Italian, 1954-)
Pensieri Generosi Delle Donne, gouache/acrylic/chalks on paper mounted on canvas, sgn/dtd 1984, 43x59", C-NY 2/20/88 ... 28,600
Regno Dei Fiori, watercolor/crayon/gold & silver paint/pen on paper, sgn/dtd 1983, 12x16", C-NY 11/10/88 OE ... 8,800
DE MARIA, Walter (20th C)
Dark Green-Light Green Line, green pencil on 2 sheets of paper, sgn/dtd 1977/inscr, 29x47", C-NY 11/10/88 OE ... 14,300
DE MARTINO, Eduardo
Regatta a Buenos Ayres, Nel Nuova Porto Madero, 1892; pencil/watercolor w/white, sgn, 11x24", C-SK 6/9/88 OE ... 4,090
DE MATTEIS, Paolo (1662-1728)
Iris Making the Earth Abundant, no media given, 51x61", C-M 6/16/89 ... 32,600
DE METZ, Francois Louis Lanfant (French, 1814-1892)
Artist in His Studio, oil on panel, sgn, 8x6", C-E 2/23/88 ... 1,540
Ladies Caught Bathing (in a landscape), oil on board, sgn, 6x10", C-E 2/21/89 ... 2,640
Lecon de Musique, oil on panel, sgn, 8x11", C-NY 5/25/88 OE ... 9,350
Village Upstarts, oil on panel, sgn, 9x19", WD 5/5/88 ... 6,250
DE MEYER, Hendrik the elder; att (Dutch, 1600-1690)
Shipping on River Moss with the Gothic Tower of the Church of Dordrecht in Background, oil on panel, 15x20, SLK 9/28/88 ... 1,700
DE MEYER, Hendrik the younger (Dutch, 1737-1793)
Peasants Drinking & Merrymaking Outside a Tavern, oil on canvas, sgn/dtd 1795, 18x25", C-NY 1/11/89 ... 16,500
Peasants Picking Grapes & Conversing Outside a Cottage, oil on canvas, 18x25", C-NY 10/12/89 ... 15,400
DE MIRANDA, Juan Garcia; att
Portrait of a Lady Said To Be Queen Maria Gabriela de Savoya, Wife of Philip V, King of Spain; oil, 30x22", SBY 7/12/89 ... 3,025
DE MOMPER, Joos (Flemish, 1564-1635)
Extensive River Landscape with Figures on a Road & a View of a Town, oil on canvas, 35x64", SBY 6/3/88 ... 40,700
Extensive River Landscape with Figures Resting by a Grotto, oil on panel, 19x31", SBY 6/3/88 UE ... 16,500
Travelers in a Mountainous Landscape, oil on panel, 18x30", SBY 6/2/89 OE ... 176,000
DE MOMPER, Joos; circle of (Flemish, 1564-1635)
Autumn: Figures Harvesting a Field; oil on panel, unfr, 29x48", C-NY 1/15/88 ... 63,800
DE MOMPER, Philips
Pilgrims Arriving at a Grotto Chapel in an Extensive Mountainous Landscape, oil on panel, 29x41", C-NY 1/11/89 ... 26,400
DE MONFORT, E. (19th C)
Emperor Maximillian in Mexico, pencil/chalk/watercolor/bodycolor on blue paper, sgn/dtd 1880, 19x24", C-SK 6/9/88 OE ... 1,580
DE MONFREID, Georges Daniel (French, 1856-1929)
Portrait of the Artist's Wife with a Cup of Tea, oil on board, initialed/dtd 1906, 32x25", C-E 2/21/89 OE ... 9,900
DE MONVEL, Bernard Boutet (French, 1884-1949)
Le Parc (elegant gathering in a park), oil on canvas, sgn/dtd 1908, 32x81", PHL 6/16/88 ... 8,500
DE MONVEL, Louis-Maurice Boutet (French, 1851-1913)
School Children, watercolor/pencil on paper, sgn, 10x6", RWS 11/3/88 OE ... 2,600
DE MOOR, Carel (Dutch, 1656-1738)
Parapet Portrait of a Young Lady Seated, Holding a Basket of Flowers; oil on panel, 11x9", SBY 4/7/89 ... 6,600
Portrait of a Lady in a Parkland Setting, oil on canvas, sgn, 21x17", SBY 4/7/88 OE ... 8,250
DE MOOR, Carel; circle of (Dutch, 1656-1738)
Gentleman & His Wife, with a Child, a Formal Garden Beyond; oil on canvas, 54x66", C-NY 4/8/88 ... 6,600
DE MORALES, Luis (Spanish, 1509-1586)
Ecce Homo, oil on panel, 19x15", C-NY 1/11/89 OE ... 15,400
DE MOUCHERON, Frederik (Dutch, 1633-1686)
Landscape with Figures & Cattle Near a Forest, oil on canvas, unfr, 20x27", SBY 7/12/89 ... 2,200
DE MOUCHERON, Isaac (Dutch, 1667-1744)
Banquet with Elegant Figures & Peasants in a Ruined Pavilion, oil on canvas, 43x59", SBY 10/21/88 OE ... 24,200
Classical Capriccio with Figures Resting by a Tomb, a Castle Beyond; pen/brown ink/watercolor, 8x6", C-NY 1/11/89 OE ... 4,400
Figures by an Ornamental Lake, pen/brown ink/watercolor, sgn/dtd 1736, 9x13", SBY 1/13/89 OE ... 13,200
DE MOUCHERON, Isaac; follower of (Dutch, 1667-1744)
Extensive Landscape with Figures & Ruins, oil on canvas, 27x33", SBY 10/13/89 ... 4,675
DE MURA, Francesco (Italian, 1696-1782)
Madonna & Child, oil on copper, oval, 8x11", C-NY 6/2/88 ... 8,250
Putti Playing with Parrots & Other Birds, oil on canvas, 38x55", SBY 6/3/88 ... 66,000
Putti with Game, oil on canvas, 38x55", SBY 1/12/89 ... 24,200
DE MURA, Francesco; att (Italian, 1696-1782)
Holy Family with the Infant Saint John the Baptist, oil on canvas, 36x24", C-NY 10/20/88 OE ... 5,500
DE MURA, Francesco; circle of (Italian, 1696-1782)
Deathbed of a Female Saint Visited by Christ, Mary, & Angels; oil on canvas, sgn/dtd 1707, unfr, 26x21", C-NY 10/20/88 ... 1,760

DE MURA, Francesco; follower of (Italian, 1696-1782)
Adoration of the Shepherds, oil on slate, oval, 9x10", SBY 10/21/88 ... 2,200
DE MURA, Francesco; school of (Italian, 1696-1782)
Tobias & the Angel, oil on canvas, 31x25", C-NY 4/8/88 ... 2,200
DE MUTTONI, Pietro (Italian, 1605-1678)
King Saul Listening to the Harp of David, oil on canvas, 30x25", WD 10/19/88 ... 5,000
Portrait of a Youth, half-length, wearing red jacket & plumed hat, arms crossed; no media given, 25x19", C-M 6/16/89 ... 6,520
Three Men Gambling with Dice, oil on canvas, 29x57", SBY 4/7/88 OE ... 17,600
Young Couple, oil on canvas, 19x15", C-NY 1/15/88 ... 7,700
DE MUTTONI, Pietro; att (Italian, 1605-1678)
Bravo with a Sword, oil on canvas, 26x19", C-NY 10/12/89 ... 7,700
DE MUTTONI, Pietro; circle of (Italian, 1605-1678)
Warrior with a Severed Head, Elderly Couple Looking on; oil on canvas, unfr, 33x40", C-NY 10/12/89 ... 6,600
DE MYRBACH-RHEINFELD, Baron Felicien (German, 1853-)
Hussars Rounding Up Cattle, watercolor/pencil on paper, sgn, 15x24", C-NY 5/24/89 ... 3,080
DE NAGY, Ernest (German, 20th C)
Gloucester Harbor, oil on canvas, sgn, 15x19", C-E 6/1/88 UE ... 550
DE NATHAN, Raoul
Peasant Meal, oil on canvas, sgn, 38x46", C-E 7/26/88 UE ... 950
DE NEALE MORGAN, Mary (American, 1868-1948)
City Hall Columns, San Francisco, 1906; watercolor on paper, sgn, 13x9", B/B 10/6/88 ... 990
Cypresses Along the Monterey Coast, gouache on paper, sgn, 12x10", B/B 10/6/88 ... 825
Late Afternoon, Point Lobos, Old Guards; oil on board, sgn, 11x16", B/B 10/6/88 ... 1,980
Near Point Lobos, Monterey; pastel on paper, sgn, 6x10", B/B 1/11/89 ... 220
Tree in a Flowering Meadow, watercolor on paper, sgn, 9x9", B/B 1/11/89 ... 468
DE NETER, Laurentius (German, 1600-)
Elegant Figures Playing Backgammon, & a Woman with a Mandolin; oil on panel, 13x15", C-NY 4/6/89 ... 6,600
DE NEUVILLE, Alfred Arthur Brunel (French, fl 1879-1907)
Cats (portrait of five cats in an interior), oil on canvas, sgn, 10x13", DM 5/13/88 ... 1,000
Cautious Spectators (kittens), oil on canvas, sgn, 32x26", C-NY 2/25/88 ... 5,500
Five Playful Kittens, oil on canvas, sgn, 21x25", WAD 6/6/88 ... 4,400
Kittens by a Bowl of Milk, oil on canvas, sgn, 21x26", C-NY 5/24/89 ... 5,280
Mischief Makers (three kittens w/saucer of milk), oil on canvas, sgn, 21x25", B/B 10/9/88 ... 7,700
Playful Kittens, oil on canvas, sgn, 22x26", C-E 2/23/88 OE ... 3,850
Still Life of Currants & Plums, oil on canvas, sgn, 21x26", RWS 5/19/88 ... 2,300
Still Life of Fruit, oil on canvas, sgn, 16x18", FAP 4/15/89 ... 1,155
Still Life of Game, oil on canvas, sgn, 29x36", RWS 11/10/89 ... 2,500
Still Life of Plums, Peaches, & Grapes; oil on canvas, sgn, 21x26", SBY 7/12/89 ... 6,050
DE NEUVILLE, Alphonse Marie (French, 1835-1885)
Color Sargeant (full-length portrait), oil on canvas laid down on board, sgn/dtd 1876, 13x9", C-E 5/22/89 ... 3,850
Hussars (army on horseback in landscape), oil on canvas, sgn, 18x15", C-NY 5/24/89 ... 8,800
On the March, oil on canvas, sgn/dtd 1880, SBY 2/22/89 ... 13,200
Sergent du Genie, oil on panel, sgn/dtd 1871, 22x14", SBY 7/12/89 ... 1,760
Soldier Smoking, oil on panel, sgn, 11x8", SBY 6/8/88 ... 2,420
Storming the Baracade, oil on canvas, sgn, 11x9", C-E 10/26/89 ... 2,420
DE NITTIS, Giuseppe (Italian, 1846-1884)
Woman Crocheting, oil on panel, sgn, 7x6", C-NY 2/23/89 ... 24,200
DE NOME, Francois; circle of (Italian, 16th/17th C)
Death of Dido: Architectural Fantasy; oil on canvas, 37x52", SBY 10/21/88 OE ... 23,100
DE NOTER, David Emile (Belgian, 1825-1912)
Nature Morte (still life w/flowers, fruits & vegetables), oil on panel, sgn, 12x10", SBY 10/24/89 ... 10,450
Still Life of Assorted Fruits & Vegetables, oil on panel, sgn/dtd 56, 12x10", C-NY 10/25/89 ... 8,800
Woman Eating Cherries, oil on canvas, 32x26", B/B 6/9/88 ... 18,700
DE PAEZ, Jose (Joseph)(European, 18th C)
Assumption of the Virgin, Surrounded by Saints; oil on copper, circular, sgn, 7" dia, C-NY 10/12/89 ... 4,400
Casta: De Espanol y Mestiza, Castisa (shop scene); oil on copper, titled/#d 2, ca 1780, 12x16", C-NY 11/21/88 OE ... 12,100
Nuestra Cenora de la Misericordia (madonna/child/cherubs), oil on canvas, sgn, ca 1780, 25x20", C-NY 11/21/88 OE ... 8,800
Saint Emigdio Martyr in Glory Surrounded with Angels Above...; oil on copper, sgn/inscr, 17x13", C-SK 11/10/88 ... 3,720
Saint Joseph Holding the Christ Child, oil on copper, sgn/inscr, 15x12", C-E 4/7/88 UE ... 770
San Emigdio Martir (religious), oil on copper, sgn, 17x13", C-NY 5/17/88 ... 6,600
DE PAREDES, Vincenta (Spanish, 19th C)
Entertaining the Baby, watercolor on paper, sgn, 12x18", SBY 7/12/89 ... 1,100
Flirtation (peasant couple in courtyard), oil on canvas, sgn, 37x26", SBY 10/24/89 ... 16,500
George Washington & His Cavalry Charge, watercolor/pen/ink on paper, sgn, 8x12", C-E 5/23/88 ... 385
Revelers at a Dining Table, oil on panel, sgn/indistinctly dtd, 9x12", B/B 3/17/88 ... 2,090
Royal Procession, oil on canvas, sgn, 20x26", SBY 7/12/89 ... 7,150
DE PAULA FERG, Franz (Austrian, 1689-1740)
Fishermen in a Cove, oil on panel, unfr, 9x11", C-NY 4/8/88 ... 3,300
Gathering of Peasants in a Courtyard, Some Drinking & Others Washing Clothes; oil on canvas, 13x9", SBY 4/7/88 OE ... 4,125
Hunting Party in a Landscape, oil on copper, unfr, 12x14", C-NY 1/11/89 ... 22,000
Village Fair (figures & tents in an extensive landscape), oil on panel, indistinctly sgn, 11x16", C-NY 5/31/89 ... 17,600

DE PAULA FERG, Franz; circle of (Austrian, 1689-1740)
Travelers Resting by Classical Ruins in a Mountainous River Landscape, oil on canvas, unfr, 14x17", C-NY 10/12/89 3,850
DE PENALOSA Y SANDOVAL, att (-1936?)
Santa Justa (full-length portrait), oil on canvas, 31x22", SBY 6/1/89 OE........ 13,200
DE PENNE, Charles Oliver (French, 1831-1897)
Bloodhounds Resting in a Landscape, oil on panel, sgn, 13x9", RWS 4/7/89 500
Hounds Waiting for Their Master (in a landscape), oil on panel, sgn, 18x15", SBY 6/9/89 OE........ 13,200
Huntsmen with Beagles in a Woodland Clearing, oil on canvas, sgn, 26x31", SBY 6/10/88 12,100
Scene de Chasse a Course, oil on canvas, sgn/dtd 1883, 46x68", SBY 6/9/89 33,000
Waiting for the Hunt, oil on panel, sgn, 12x17", SBY 6/10/88........ 6,600
DE PEREDA, Antonio; att (Spanish, 1599-1669)
Madonna & Child, oil on canvas, 31x25", SBY 6/1/89 OE 35,200
DE PEREDA, Antonio; circle of (Spanish, 1599-1669)
Basket of Flowers, Cabinet, Plate with Beads, Book & a Fan, Dog on a Cushion; oil on canvas, 40x52", C-NY 10/12/89 OE 19,800
DE PEREDA, Antonio; school of (Spanish, 1599-1669)
Flowers in a Silver Urn on a Ledge, Flanked by Drapes; oil on canvas, 28x34", C-NY 5/31/89........ 7,150
DE PIETERE, Edmond Joseph (Belgian, 1826-1888)
Homeward Bound, oil on canvas, sgn, 27x21", WAD 6/6/88........ 2,500
DE POGEDAIEFF, Georges (Russian, 1897-1950)
King Lear, Three Costume Designs; watercolor/gouache, sgn/dtd 31, 17x22", SBY 10/5/88 OE........ 1,210
DE PONTE, Gerolamo; after (1566-1621)
Spring, oil on panel, 19x29", SBY 4/7/88 OE 9,900
DE POORTER, Willem (Dutch, 1608-1648)
Betrothal Scene From the Old Testament, oil on canvas, 23x33", C-NY 4/8/88 OE 3,300
Portrait of a Gentleman, three-quarter length, wearing an elegant costume & turban; oil on panel, 28x23", C-NY 1/22/89 15,400
DE POOTER, J.
Les Peintres Animaliers, oil on canvas, sgn/dtd 1889, 39x54", C-NY 5/25/88 7,700
DE PRADES, Alfred (British, 1795-1865)
Chase (horse & rider rushing up hill), oil on board, sgn/dtd 1879, 25x18", C-E 5/22/89 3,520
Pair: At the Crossroads in the Snow; Coaching Scenes; oil on canvas, sgn/dtd 1885, 18x32", SBY 6/10/88 OE 9,350
DE PRADES, Alfred; att (British, 1795-1865)
Flying Dutchman, oil on canvas, bears apocryphal signature/dtd 1829, 18x27", WD 10/19/88........ 5,250
DE PREVAL, Christiane (French, 1876-)
La Salle a Manger au Tapis Rouge, oil on canvas, sgn, 16x20", SBY 7/12/89 1,100
DE PURY, Edmond Jean (Swiss, 1845-1911)
Street Urchin (portrait of a girl seated on curb beside jar), oil on canvas, sgn/dtd 1897, 44x32", WD 11/16/88........ 4,500
DE QUIROS, Bernaldo (Argentinian, 1881-1968)
Corral de Palo a Pique, oil on canvas, sgn, 30x34", C-NY 5/18/88 9,900
DE RETZ, Eudes Alfred Francois (French, 1857-)
Landscape with Figures, oil on canvas, sgn, 32x44", RWS 11/10/89........ 2,200
DE RIBCOWSKY, Dey (American, 1880-1935)
Amsterdam Avenue North From Beacon, oil on canvas, sgn, 31x23", NA 10/1/88 OE 3,100
Coastal Inlet (sailboats in distance, small boat on shore), oil on canvas, sgn/dtd 17, 30x40", RWS 9/8/89 1,900
Gorge, oil on canvas, sgn/dtd 1930, 30x40", RWS 9/8/89 UE 650
Marine Scene (waves crash on rocks in late afternoon sunlight), oil on canvas, sgn/dtd 1912, 30x40", RWS 9/29/88........ 700
Sunset Over the Pacific, oil on canvas, sgn, 20x24", B/B 10/6/88........ 1,430
Venetian Scene, oil on canvas, sgn/dtd 16, 20x30", RWS 9/8/89 850
View of Cairo, oil on canvas, sgn, 40x64", B/B 10/6/88 1,320
Waves Breaking on a Rocky Shore, oil on canvas, sgn, 30x36", WL 5/20/88 850
DE RIBERA, Jusepe; circle of (Spanish, 1588-1656)
Good Samaritan, oil on canvas, 55x77", C-NY 1/11/89 OE........ 35,200
DE RIBERA, Jusepe; follower of (Spanish, 1588-1656)
Archimedes of Syracuse, oil on canvas, 51x38", SBY 1/12/89 OE 38,500
DE RIBERA, Jusepe; manner of (Spanish, 1588-1656)
Saint Joseph, oil on canvas, 26x21", SBY 12/9/88 OE 3,190
St Francis of Assisi, oil on canvas, unfr, 49x40", SBY 6/8/88 OE........ 1,760
St Paul Writing, oil on canvas, bears signature/dtd 1628, 29x39", SBY 7/12/89 UE........ 220
DE RIBERA, Jusepe; school of (Spanish, 1588-1656)
Aristotle, oil on canvas, 43x35", C-NY 1/15/88 OE 11,550
Penitent Saint Peter, oil on canvas, 30x26", C-NY 4/6/89 OE 4,400
Saint Jerome (man praying), oil on canvas, 38x29", C-NY 4/6/89 OE 12,100
DE RING, Pieter (Dutch, 1615-1660)
Still Life of Grapes, Oranges, Oysters, Roemer, & Ring on Draped Ledge; oil on canvas, sgn, unfr, 24x19", SBY 6/2/89........ 49,500
Strawberries in a Wan-Li Bowl, Glass of Wine, Shrimps, & Fruits on a Table; oil on canvas, sgn, 23x20", C-NY 1/15/88 UE 26,400
Tazza, Pears, Plums, a Wan-Li Bowl...(still life); oil on canvas, sgn w/ring, 37x30", C-NY 1/15/88 OE 242,000
DE RING, Pieter; att (Dutch, 1615-1660)
Grapes, Lemons, Oysters, Crayfish on a Silver Plate; oil on panel, bears artist's device, 17x15", C-NY 6/2/88 OE........ 28,600
DE ROOY, Johannes Embrosius Wetering (Dutch, 1877-)
Village Scene, oil on canvas, sgn, 24x20", SBY 12/9/88........ 1,430
DE ROSSI, Francesco; called Salviati (1510-1563)
Virgin & Child w/St Anne & Infant St John, Christ w/Cross in Oval Above; pen/ink/heightened wash, 9x7", SBY 1/13/89 49,500

DE ROUCY TRIOSON, Anne Louis Girodet (French, 1767-1824)
Study for the Sleep of Endymion, oil on canvas, 19x24", C-NY 10/25/89 ..... **16,500**
DE ROUSSEAUX, Jacques; manner of (Dutch, 1600-1628)
Democritus & Heraclitus, oil on canvas, 20x26", SBY 9/12/89 ..... **1,320**
DE SAINT-ANDRE, Simon Renard (1613-1677)
Allegory of the History of Gaul (still life), oil on canvas, 35x29", SBY 1/12/89 ..... **187,000**
DE SAINT-AUBIN, Gabriel Jacques; school of
Gentleman Declaring His Love for a Young Woman in a Bedroom, oil on panel, initialed, 33x15", C-M 6/16/89 ..... **13,855**
DE SAINT-AUBIN, Louise Amelie Legrand (1798-)
Portrait of a Lady, half-length, wearing black dress, in a landscape; oil on canvas, sgn/dtd 18?, 26x21", C-M 12/3/88 OE **10,220**
DE SAINT-MEMIN, Charles B.; style of (French, 1770-1852)
Profile Portrait of a Woman in a Lace Bonnet (bust-length), charcoal on paper, dtd 1802, 16x12", WL 5/20/88 ..... **700**
DE SAINT-PHALLE, Niki (American, 1930-)
Hand (abstract), painted polyester, stamped w/signature/#d 1/7, 1985, 13x17", SBY 10/5/88 ..... **2,750**
Nana, gouache/felt-tip pen/paper cutouts on board, 1965-68, 40x27", C-E 5/9/89 OE **15,400**
Paris Love, gouache/felt-tip pen/paper cutouts on board, 1965-68, unfr, 40x27", C-E 5/9/89 OE **13,200**
DE SALAZAR Y MENDOZA, Jose Francisco Xavier; att
Portrait of Major William Gordon Forman, oil on canvas, indistinctly sgn/dtd N Orleans 1801, 40x31", SBY 3/17/88 ..... **15,400**
DE SANCHES, Harriet (American, 20th C)
City Park, oil on canvas, sgn, unfr, 14x12", SBY 3/17/88 ..... **1,540**
DE SCHRYVER, Louis Marie (French, 1862-1942)
Ballerina (full-length portrait), oil on canvas, sgn/dtd 1882, 25x21", B/B 3/22/89 ..... **4,400**
Young Beauty (portrait), oil on canvas, sgn/dtd 1902, 24x20", C-NY 2/23/89 ..... **11,000**
DE SEGONZAC, Andre; see Dunoyer De Segonzac
DE SENECOURT, Charlotte (French, 19th C)
Violet Seller, oil on panel, sgn, 12x9", SBY 7/12/89 ..... **3,850**
DE SILVESTRE, Louis; school of (French, 1675-1760)
Portrait of Queen Maria Leczinska, standing, three-quarter length...; oil on canvas, 55x41", C-NY 4/6/89 ..... **4,180**
DE SIMONE, Tomasco (Italian, fl 1851-1907)
Santanna (steam yacht at sea), gouache on paper, sgn/titled, 17x25", RAB 3/14/89 ..... **850**
DE SIMONI, A. (Italian, 19th C)
Returning Home, oil on canvas, sgn/inscr, 18x40", C-E 5/23/88 OE **4,180**
DE SOUZA-PINTO, Jose Julio (Portuguese, 1856-1939)
La Baignade, oil on canvas, sgn/dtd 1895, 32x26", SBY 5/23/89 ..... **46,750**
DE STAEL, Nicolas (Russian, 1914-1955)
Bouteilles (abstract still life of bottles), oil on canvas, sgn, 1952, 21x28", SBY 6/30/88 ..... **380,000**
Composition, oil on canvas, 1946, 32x23", SBY 4/29/88 ..... **57,750**
Composition on Black Ground, collage on black paper, sgn/dtd 53, 21x17", C-NY 2/18/88 OE **20,900**
Nature Morte (abstract still life), oil on canvas, stamped signature, 1955, 25x32", C-NY 5/11/88 ..... **330,000**
Untitled (abstract), oil on canvas, sgn, ca 1950, 8x11", SBY 10/5/89 OE **198,000**
DE STROBEL, Daniele (1873-)
San Giorgio, pastel on canvas, sgn, oval, 28x38", C-L 6/27/88 ..... **10,406**
DE SZYSZLO, Fernando (Peruvian, 1925-)
Abstraction, oil on canvas, sgn, ca 1971-72, 59x47", SBY 5/17/88 ..... **4,950**
El Innomerbrable (abstract), oil on canvas, sgn/dtd 80/inscr Orrantia/titled, 59x59", SBY 5/16/89 ..... **15,400**
Mar de Lurin (abstract composition), oil on canvas, sgn, 1988, 59x59", C-NY 11/21/89 ..... **14,300**
Puka Wamani II (abstract), acrylic on canvas, sgn/dtd 69, 47x47", C-NY 5/18/88 ..... **6,600**
Puriq Runa XII, acrylic on canvas, sgn twice/dtd 76, 39x32", SBY 5/17/88 ..... **3,575**
Ritual Table, acrylic on canvas, dtd 1986/titled, 74x54", SBY 11/21/88 ..... **16,500**
Ritual Table (abstract), oil on canvas, sgn/dtd 1986/titled Mesa Ritual, 47x40", SBY 11/21/88 ..... **7,150**
Travesia (abstract), oil on canvas, sgn/dtd 73/titled, 58x46", SBY 5/16/89 OE **17,600**
Untitled (abstract), oil on board, sgn/dtd 1954/inscr Golfe Juan, 10x14", SBY 5/16/89 ..... **1,760**
Untitled (abstract), oil on canvas, sgn, 30x24", SBY 5/16/89 OE **6,600**
Villac Umu, acrylic/charcoal/pastel on paper, sgn twice/dtd 86/titled, 59x47", C-NY 11/21/88 ..... **8,800**
Villac Umu (abstract), acrylic on canvas, sgn twice/dtd 1986, 57x37", SBY 5/17/88 OE **17,600**
Visitante (abstract), oil on canvas, sgn/dtd Orrantia 88/titled, 59x47", C-NY 5/17/89 OE **22,000**
DE TENGNAGEL, Frederik Michael Ernst F. (Danish, 1781-1849)
Winter Landscape, oil on canvas, sgn/dtd 1827, 27x38", SBY 2/22/89 ..... **8,800**
DE THIERRENS, Jacques Favre
Jeune Fille Allonge (young girl lying on bed), oil on canvas, sgn, 24x29", C-E 5/13/88 OE **2,200**
DE THULSTRUP, Thure (American, 1849-1930)
Battle at Shiloh: Buell's Troops Arriving at Pittsburgh Landing (Civil War); tempera, sgn/inscr, 13x11", C-E 5/27/88 ..... **550**
Battle of Malvern Hill (Civil War), pen/ink on paper, sgn/inscr, 12x17", C-E 5/27/88 OE **1,320**
Field Hospital at Savages Station (Civil War), pen/ink on paper laid down, sgn/inscr, 11x14", C-E 5/27/88 ..... **440**
Hauling Down State Flag, New Orleans (Civil War); no media given, sgn/inscr, unfr, 13x16", C-E 11/30/88 OE **1,540**
DE TOMMASI, Publio
Figures in a Tavern, watercolor, sgn/dtd 91, 24x40", C-NY 2/25/88 ..... **3,300**
DE TOULOUSE-LAUTREC, see Toulouse-Lautrec
DE TOURS, Georges Moreau; att (French, 1848-1901)
Battle Scene, oil on canvas, bears signature, 24x36", C-E 10/26/89 ..... **1,540**
DE TROY, Francois (French, 1645-1730)
Portrait of a Lady Seated at a Table & Holding a Book, oil on canvas, 31x40", SBY 4/7/88 ..... **6,050**

Vertumnus Wooing Pomona, oil on canvas, sgn, 60x47", SBY 1/12/89 ... 132,000

DE VALDES NICA LEAL, Juan (1622-1690)

Immaculate Conception, oil on canvas, sgn/dtd 1682, 81x57", SBY 1/12/89 OE ... 79,750
The Good Shepherd, oil on canvas, 23x27", C-NY 10/12/89 OE ... 16,500

DE VANY FORESTALL, Thomas (Canadian, 1936-)

Airing the Wash, watercolor, sgn, 15x20", WAD 11/30/89 ... 1,400

DE VILALLONGA, Jesus Carlos (Canadian, 1927-)

Portrait of a Lady Holding a Fan (standing), oil on board, sgn/dtd 1961, FB 10/17/88 ... 900

DE VLAMINCK, Maurice (French, 1876-1958)

Apres l'Orage (After the Storm), oil on canvas, sgn, 18x22", C-NY 11/16/88 ... 93,500
Avant l'Orage, brush/ink/gouache on paper, sgn, ca 1930, 15x18", SBY 2/16/89 ... 40,700
Bateau a la Riviere (boat on a river), oil on canvas, sgn, 1911, 24x29", C-NY 5/12/88 OE ... 192,500
Bouquet de Fleurs (floral still life), oil on canvas, sgn, 18x13", SBY 10/6/89 OE ... 137,500
Bouquet de Fleurs (floral still life), oil on canvas, sgn, 29x24", SBY 11/12/88 ... 165,000
Chaumiere sous l'Orage (Cottage in the Storm), oil on canvas, sgn, 15x18", SBY 5/10/89 ... 93,500
Eglise du Village (village church), oil on canvas, sgn, 13x16", SBY 11/12/88 ... 77,000
Falaises au Bord de la Mer (stormy coastal scene), oil on canvas, sgn, 24x29", C-NY 2/16/89 OE ... 82,500
Fete de Village (village street scene), watercolor on paper, sgn, 18x25", SBY 5/10/89 ... 44,000
Fleurs dans un Vase (floral still life), oil on canvas, sgn, 22x15", C-NY 5/12/88 OE ... 110,000
Gerbe de Fleurs Rouges (floral still life), oil on canvas, sgn, 24x18", C-NY 11/16/88 ... 165,000
Guillaume Apollinaire au Bord de la Seine, or Lile de la Grenouillere; oil on canvas, sgn, 1906, 21x26", SBY 5/10/88 OE ... 797,500
Houses on a Hillside, watercolor/gouache on paper, sgn, 17x21", SBY 11/12/88 ... 44,000
Jardin Public a La Carriere St Denis (public garden at La Carriere), oil on canvas, sgn, ca 1904, 21x26", SBY 5/9/89 ... 1,100,000
L'Etang du Village (landscape w/pond by a village), oil on canvas, sgn, ca 1917, 24x29", SBY 11/12/88 ... 176,000
L'Inondation, oil on canvas, sgn, 23x31", SBY 5/11/88 OE ... 154,000
La Charrette, oil on canvas, sgn, 22x26", SBY 5/11/88 OE ... 137,500
La Chaumiere, gouache/ink wash on paper, sgn, 16x19", SBY 11/16/89 ... 77,000
La Ferme, oil on canvas, sgn, 21x26", SBY 5/11/88 OE ... 121,000
La Ferme (farm scene), oil on canvas, sgn, 29x36", SBY 11/12/88 ... 165,000
La Ferme sous la Neige, oil on canvas, sgn, 20x26", SBY 5/11/88 OE ... 159,500
La Maison de Coin (the corner house), gouache on paper, sgn, 19x25", C-NY 10/6/88 ... 30,800
La Petite Route (landscape), brush/ink/watercolor/gouache on paper, sgn, ca 1945-46, 8x13", SBY 2/16/89 OE ... 20,900
La Route de la Village (landscape of a village road), oil on canvas, sgn, 24x29", C-NY 5/12/88 ... 176,000
La Seine (river landscape), oil on canvas, sgn, 1914, 24x29", SBY 11/12/88 OE ... 242,000
Le Poisson (The Fish), oil on canvas, sgn, 20x26", C-NY 10/6/88 ... 41,800
Le Pont Chatou (river landscape w/bridge), oil on canvas, sgn, 1908, 18x22", SBY 5/10/89 ... 192,500
Le Pont de Chatou (The Bridge at Chatou), oil on canvas, sgn, 1905-06, 29x40", C-NY 5/11/88 OE ... 4,400,000
Le Retour (stormy landscape), oil on canvas, sgn, 15x18", C-NY 5/11/89 ... 110,000
Le Sentier (rural landscape w/path leading to house), oil on canvas, sgn, 24x29", SBY 5/10/89 ... 121,000
Le Village, gouache/ink wash on paper, sgn, 18x21", SBY 11/16/89 ... 38,500
Le Village, oil on canvas, sgn, 29x36", SBY 5/11/88 OE ... 154,000
Le Village apres l'Orage, oil on canvas, sgn, 23x29", C-NY 10/6/88 OE ... 137,500
Le Village au Clocher (street scene), oil on canvas, sgn, ca 1925, 26x32", C-NY 5/12/88 ... 165,000
Les Meules d'Automne, brush/ink/watercolor/gouache on paper, sgn, ca 1945-46, 8x13", SBY 2/16/89 OE ... 23,100
Les Saules, brush/ink/watercolor/gouache on paper, sgn, 18x21", SBY 11/12/88 ... 44,000
Les Toits Rouges, oil on canvas, sgn, ca 1912, 26x32", SBY 5/11/88 OE ... 220,000
Louvilliers-les-Perche (Eure-et-Loire, village scene w/stormy sky), oil on canvas, 1938, 26x32", C-NY 11/16/88 ... 187,000
Maison au Toit Rough, sous la Neige; oil on canvas, sgn, 26x32", C-NY 11/16/88 ... 242,000
Maison dans un Paysage (houses in a landscape), ink wash/watercolor/gouache on paper, sgn, 16x19", SBY 10/6/89 OE ... 22,000
Maisons dans le Champs, gouache/watercolor/India ink on paper, sgn, 22x15", SBY 2/18/88 ... 15,400
Nature Morte, Cruche et Pommes de Terre; oil on canvas, sgn, 20x26", C-NY 10/6/88 ... 59,400
Nature Morte (floral still life), oil on canvas, sgn, 22x18", SBY 11/12/88 ... 148,500
Nature Morte (still life w/white plate, bowl & knife), oil on board laid down, sgn, 1921, 19x22", SBY 10/6/89 ... 49,500
Nature Morte (still life), oil on canvas, sgn, 32x39", SBY 11/12/88 ... 154,000
Nature Morte aux Fleurs (floral still life), oil on canvas, sgn, 18x15", SBY 5/10/89 ... 132,000
Paysage, gouache/pen/India ink on paper, sgn, 15x18", C-NY 11/15/88 OE ... 49,500
Paysage, oil on artist board, sgn, 1919, 12x16", SBY 11/12/88 ... 319,000
Paysage, oil on canvas, sgn, 24x28", SBY 11/12/88 ... 121,000
Paysage (landscape w/buildings), watercolor/ink wash/gouache on paper, sgn, 18x22", SBY 10/7/88 ... 20,900
Paysage (landscape), oil on canvas, sgn, 15x18", SBY 5/10/89 ... 104,500
Paysage (stormy landscape), gouache/watercolor/pen/black ink on paper, sgn, 8x8", C-NY 5/11/89 OE ... 24,200
Paysage aux Arbres (landscape with trees), oil on canvas, sgn, 21x26", SBY 5/10/89 ... 198,000
Paysage aux Arbres (wooded landscape), oil on canvas, sgn, 22x26", SBY 5/10/89 ... 132,000
Paysage avec Maisons (landscape w/house), sgn, 20x23", C-NY 5/11/89 OE ... 99,000
Paysage de la Beauce, oil on canvas, sgn, 25x31", SBY 5/11/88 ... 159,500
Paysage en Hiver (winter landscape), brush/ink/watercolor/gouache on paper, sgn, ca 1930, 15x18", SBY 2/16/89 OE ... 41,250
Paysage en Hiver (winter landscape), oil on canvas, sgn, 21x29", C-NY 5/12/88 ... 165,000
Paysage et Riviere (river landscape w/figure in boat), gouache/brush/black ink on paper, sgn, 18x23", C-NY 10/5/89 OE ... 38,500
Personnage dans la Ville, gouache/watercolor/brush/pen/black ink on board, sgn, 18x22", C-NY 2/16/89 ... 46,200
Place de l'Eglise, gouache on paper, sgn, 18x21", C-NY 11/15/88 OE ... 60,500

Plaine dans la Beauce (landscape w/haystacks & village beyond), oil on canvas, sgn, ca 1920-26, 29x36", SBY 5/10/89 OE **253,000**
Port de Cassis (port scene), oil on canvas, sgn, ca 1920, 26x40", C-NY 5/12/88 ..... **159,500**
Port de Cassis (port scene), oil on canvas, sgn, 1920, 26x40", C-NY 5/12/88 ..... **159,500**
Road Through the Village, brush/ink/watercolor/gouache on paper, sgn, 15x18", SBY 11/12/88 OE **48,400**
Roses dans un Vase (floral still life), oil on canvas, sgn, sgn, 22x15", C-NY 11/16/88 ..... **110,000**
Route de Village, gouache/ink wash on paper, sgn, 18x22", SBY 11/16/89 ..... **77,000**
Route de Village (village road), brush/ink/watercolor/gouache on paper, mounted on canvas, sgn, 15x19", SBY 10/6/89 ..... **44,000**
Route de Village (village road), gouache/pen/India ink over pencil on paper, sgn, 16x24", C-NY 10/5/89 ..... **37,400**
Route du Village (quiet village street), oil on canvas, sgn, 21x25", SBY 11/12/88 ..... **176,000**
Rue a Auvers-sur-Oise, Animee d'un Personnage; oil on canvas, sgn, 22x26", C-NY 11/16/88 ..... **132,000**
Rue de Village (street scene), watercolor on paper, sgn, 16x19", B/B 10/9/88 OE **18,700**
Rue de Village (village scene), oil on canvas, sgn, 1914, 21x26", C-NY 2/16/89 OE **308,000**
Rue de Village sous la Niege (village night scene w/figure), gouache on paper, sgn, 12x17", SBY 5/11/88 OE **57,750**
Scene de Rue, oil on canvas, sgn, 24x29", SBY 5/11/88 ..... **187,000**
Scene de Village (village scene), gouache/watercolor/brush/black ink on buff paper, sgn, 18x22", C-NY 5/12/88 ..... **35,200**
Scene de Ville, gouache/ink wash on paper laid down on board, sgn, 18x22", SBY 11/16/89 ..... **44,000**
Soir d'Hiver (stormy landscape), oil on canvas, sgn, 1924, 24x29", C-NY 5/11/89 ..... **198,000**
Vase de Fleurs (floral still life), oil on canvas, sgn, ca 18x13", SBY 10/7/88 OE **110,000**
Vase de Fleurs (floral still life), oil on canvas, sgn, 18x15", C-NY 10/5/89 ..... **104,500**
Vase de Fleurs (floral still life), oil on canvas, sgn, 1955, 22x15", C-NY 11/16/88 ..... **132,000**
Vase de Fleurs (floral still life), oil on canvas, sgn, 22x15", C-NY 10/6/88 ..... **110,000**
Vase de Fleurs (floral still life), oil on canvas, sgn, 22x18", SBY 5/11/88 OE **121,000**
Vase de Fleurs (floral still life), oil on canvas, sgn, 26x20", C-NY 2/16/89 OE **176,000**
Vase de Fleurs (floral still life), oil on canvas, sgn, 26x20", SBY 5/10/89 ..... **187,000**
Village au Bord de la Riviere (village by a river), oil on canvas, sgn, 24x29", C-NY 11/14/88 ..... **187,000**
Village en Hiver (village in winter), oil on canvas, sgn, 15x18", C-NY 11/16/88 ..... **63,800**
Village en Hiver (village in winter), oil on canvas, sgn, 18x22", C-NY 5/12/88 ..... **143,000**

DE VOGEL, Cornelis Jan; & VERBOECKHOVEN, Eugene (19th C)
Cattle & Sheep Watering in an Extensive River Landscape, oil on canvas, sgn by both artists, 27x40", C-NY 2/23/89 ..... **12,100**

DE VOLL, F. Usher (American, 1873-1941)
Summer Street Scene, oil on board, estate stamp, 9x11", RAB 3/27/89 UE **225**

DE VOS, Maerten (Flemish, 1532-1603)
Jeremiah Cast into the Dungeon of Malchiah, pen/brown ink/wash over traces of black chalk, 7x10", SBY 1/13/89 ..... **5,225**

DE VOS, Maerten; circle of (Flemish, 1532-1603)
Martyrdom of St Lawrence, pen/brown ink/wash heightened w/white, 4x4", SBY 1/13/89 OE **1,100**

DE VOS, manner of (Flemish, 16th/17th C)
Portrait of a Young Gentleman, falconing with dogs, in a landscape; oil on canvas, 40x30", C-E 4/7/88 ..... **1,650**

DE VOS, Paul; att (Flemish, 1596-1678)
Fable of the Fox & the Herons (jar of food between fox & herons in a landscape), oil on canvas, 62x45", SBY 4/7/89 ..... **10,450**

DE VRIENDT, Julian (Belgian, 1842-1935)
Studying the Sculpture, oil on canvas, sgn/dtd 1877, 22x17", C-E 5/23/88 ..... **1,870**

DE VRIES, Paul Vredemann (Flemish, 1567-1630)
Interior of a Gothic Cathedral with Christ & Other Figures, oil on panel, monogramed/dtd 1607, 44x58", SBY 6/1/89 OE **52,250**

DE VRIES, Roelof Jansz (Dutch, 1631-1681)
Landscape with a Figure Driving a Herd Along a Road, a Ruined Building Beyond; oil on panel, 15x21, SBY 4/7/89 UE **7,150**

DE VRIES, Sophia (Dutch, 1915-)
Cows Grazing by a Canal, oil on canvas, sgn, 20x32", B/B 12/8/88 ..... **880**

DE WAEL, Cornelis; att (Flemish, 1592-1667)
Group of Figures Conversing, pen/brown ink/gray wash, inscr, 3x6", C-NY 1/12/88 ..... **385**
Travelers by a Fountain, pen/brown ink, 4x5", SBY 1/13/89 ..... **770**

DE WARVILLE, Felix Saturnin Brissot (French, 1818-1892)
Hunters in a Landscape, oil on canvas, sgn, 10x13", SBY 12/9/88 ..... **2,310**
Shepherd & Flock on a Roadway, oil on canvas, sgn, 25x36", WAD 6/6/88 ..... **2,000**

DE WET, Jacob Willemsz (Dutch, 1610-1671)
Christ Among the Doctors, oil on panel, sgn/dtd 1635, 19x26", C-NY 5/31/89 ..... **9,350**
Shadrach, Meshach & Abed-Nego in the Fiery Furnace; oil on panel, 24x33", SBY 4/7/89 ..... **4,400**

DE WET, Jacob Willemsz; att (Dutch, 1610-1671)
Sacrificial Scene, oil on panel, 22x33", SBY 6/8/88 ..... **2,090**

DE WINT, Peter; follower of (British, 1784-1849)
Figures on a Hill Viewing a Distant Landscape, oil on canvas, 49x73", SBY 12/9/88 OE **6,875**

DE WIT, Jacob (Dutch, 1695-1754)
Putti & Hounds Beside a Dead Stag: An Allegory of Hunting; oil on canvas, sgn/dtd 1733, 52x40", SBY 1/12/89 OE **16,500**

DE WIT, Jacob; att (Dutch, 1695-1754)
Pair: Allegory of Fire & Water; Allegory of Air; en grisaille/oil on canvas, circular, unfr, 31" dia, C-NY 10/12/89 ..... **2,860**
Pair: Allegory of Spring; Allegory of Autumn; en grisaille/oil on canvas, oval, unfr, 32x46", C-NY 10/12/89 ..... **8,250**
Pair: Putti Fishing; Putti Harvesting; en grisaille/oil on canvas, circular, unfr, 36" dia, C-NY 10/12/89 ..... **6,050**

DE WIT, Jacob; circle of (Dutch, 1695-1754)
Five Putti Playing in a Landscape, oil en grisaille on canvas, 37x52", C-NY 4/6/89 ..... **3,300**
Pair: Apollo & Daphne; Pyramus & Thisbe; oil on canvas, 29x36", C-NY 4/8/88 ..... **4,400**

DE WITTE, Emanuel; att (Dutch, 1617-1692)
Frozen River with Figures, oil on panel, indistinctly sgn, 20x22", FB 10/17/88 OE **3,200**

DE YONG, Joe (American, 1894-1975)
Caballero of Old California, pen/ink on paper, sgn, 14x19", NA 10/1/88 ... **400**
Mountain Landscape with Waterfall, oil on canvas, sgn/dtd 1913, 16x24", SBY 3/17/88 ... **1,045**
Pair: Flathead River at Belten; Sunset on the Peaks, McDonald Lake; oil on canvas, sgn/1 dtd 1921, 10x15", B/B 8/10/88 ... **1,210**

DE ZUBIAURRE, Ramon (Spanish, 1882-)
Fisherfolk in a Harbour Town, oil on canvas, sgn, 16x14", C-NY 10/25/89 ... **14,300**

DE ZUBIAURRE, Valentin (Spanish, 1879-1963)
Sailboats Off a Rocky Coast at Dusk, oil on canvas, sgn, 15x18", C-NY 2/23/89 OE ... **10,450**
Spanish Peasant (portrait in a landscape), oil on canvas, sgn, 24x18", B/B 3/22/89 OE ... **10,450**

DE ZURBARAN, Francisco (Spanish, 1598-1664)
Fray Guillermo de Sagiano, oil on canvas, 25x17", C-NY 1/15/88 OE ... **24,200**
Regina Angelorum, oil on canvas, 43x34", SBY 6/3/88 ... **57,750**

DE ZURBARAN, Francisco; & Studio (Spanish, 1598-1664)
Saint Francis of Assisi Receiving the Stigmata, oil on canvas, sgn, 98x66", SBY 6/2/89 OE ... **253,000**

DE ZURBARAN, Francisco; circle of (Spanish, 1598-1664)
Immaculate Conception, oil on canvas, 74x47", SBY 4/7/88 OE ... **14,300**

DE ZURBARAN, Francisco; manner of (Spanish, 1598-1664)
Procession of Monks Holding Tapers, oil on canvas, 19x33", SBY 12/9/88 ... **1,100**

DE ZURBARAN, Francisco; studio of (Spanish, 1598-1664)
Cardinal Niccolo Albergati, oil on canvas, 49x19", SBY 6/2/89 ... **26,400**
Saint Francis of Assisi in Meditation, oil on canvas, 71x43", SBY 6/2/89 ... **41,800**

DEAKIN, Edwin (American, 1838-1923)
Castle Cluny, oil on canvas, sgn/dtd 1883, 36x24", B/B 1/11/89 ... **2,090**
Harvesting Fields Near Mt Tamalpais, oil on canvas, sgn, 20x30", B/B 10/6/88 ... **1,760**
Pair: Floral Still Lifes; watercolor on paper, sgn/dtd 1857, 11x9", B/B 10/6/88 ... **715**
Rubicon Valley, California; oil on canvas, sgn/dtd 1874, 30x50", B/B 6/15/89 ... **4,950**
Rue Notre Dame, Paris; oil on board, inscr/dtd 1878, 10x7", B/B 8/10/88 ... **1,100**

DEAN, Peter (20th C)
Star Gazers (surrealistic figure), oil on canvas, sgn/dtd 1981, unfr, 60x50", C-E 11/14/89 ... **1,320**

DEAN, Walter Lofthouse (American, 1854-1912)
Boston (view of city from harbor), oil on canvas, initialed/dtd 1879, 8x16", RWS 9/29/88 OE ... **950**
Wharves & Warehouses, Gloucester Harbor; oil on canvas, sgn, 20x24", RWS 5/12/89 ... **3,250**

DEANE, William Wood (British, 1825-1873)
Extensive View of a Mountainous Landscape, watercolor on paper, sgn/dtd, 25x36", C-E 5/23/88 ... **550**

DEARING, Roger
Seascape with House on Point, oil on canvas, sgn, 22x30", C-E 6/28/88 UE ... **55**

DEARTH, Henry Golden (American, 1864-1918)
Still Life of Vases on a Table, oil on canvas, sgn, 21x25", C-E 6/1/89 OE ... **2,200**

DEAS, Charles; school of (American, 1818-1867)
Long Jakes (man on horseback in a landscape), oil on canvas, 32x24", RWS 5/12/89 ... **7,000**

DEBAT-PONSON, Edouard Bernard (French, 1847-1913)
Rest in the Fields, oil on canvas, sgn, 28x39", SBY 2/22/89 UE ... **9,350**

DEBLOIS, Francois B. (Canadian, 1829-1913)
Summer Landscape, oil on canvas, sgn/dtd July 80, 12x18", RAB 8/8/89 ... **1,500**

DEBONNET, Maurice G. (American, 1872-)
Harbor Scene (boats & fishermen at dock), oil on board, sgn, 14x14", RWS 3/31/89 ... **250**

EBRAS, Louis
Cavalier & a Maiden, oil on canvas, sgn, 22x18", C-E 9/15/88 ... **880**

DEBROCK, Eugene (19th C)
Skaters on a Frozen Pond, oil on board, sgn/dtd 1871, 15x17", C-E 10/25/88 ... **1,100**

DECAISNE, Henri (Belgian, 1799-1852)
Letter (figures around a table in an interior), oil on panel, sgn, 22x28", C-NY 5/25/88 ... **4,400**

DECAMPS, Alexandre Gabriel (French, 1803-1860)
Pheasant Shooting, oil on canvas, sgn, 13x18", C-E 5/23/88 ... **2,860**
Untitled (Arab village/figures along a river bank), oil on board, sgn, 13x16", SLK 4/7/89 ... **3,100**

DECKER, Cornelis Gerritsz; att (fl 1640-1678)
Landscape with Figures & a Cart Along a Country Road, oil on panel, 18x25", SBY 4/7/89 ... **5,225**

DECKER, Jean Charles
Horse & Riders, oil on canvas, sgn, 32x39", FB 10/30/89 ... **2,200**

DECKER, Joseph (American, 1853-1924)
Portrait of a Young Lady, gouache on paper, sgn, 14x11, RAB 8/9/88 UE ... **500**
Portrait of a Young Lady (three-quarter length), gouache on paper, sgn, 14x11", RAB 8/9/88 UE ... **500**
Still Life of Plums & Melons, oil on canvas, sgn/dtd 1896, 12x18", SBY 5/24/89 UE ... **19,800**

DECKER, Robert M. (American, 1847-)
Spring (landscape), oil on canvas, sgn, 20x34", C-E 6/1/88 ... **3,740**
Sunset Beyond a Wintry Landscape, oil on canvas, sgn, 9x11", B/B 4/20/88 ... **1,045**

DECLOCHE, Paul Joseph
Holy Family in Joseph's Workshop, oil on panel, sgn/inscr, 15x17", SBY 12/9/88 UE ... **715**

DEFAUX, Alexandre (French, 1826-1900)
Barn Interior with Sheep & Chickens, oil on canvas, sgn, 24x36", SBY 12/9/88 UE ... **3,575**
Venetian Scene, oil on canvas laid down, sgn/dtd 1858, 19x29", B/B 4/20/88 ... **1,650**

View of a Town, oil on canvas, sgn/dtd 1858, 19x26", SBY 6/8/88 UE 2,860

DEFFNER, Ludwig (German, 19th/20th C)

Pair: Flowers in Vases; oil on masonite, sgn, 10x7", WD 1/11/89 1,400
Pair: Still Lifes; oil on masonite, sgn, 10x7", SBY 6/8/88 990

DEFREGGER, Franz Von

Return From the Hunt, oil on canvas, sgn, 31x37", C-NY 2/25/88 OE 137,500

DEGAS, Edgar (French, 1834-1917)

Amazone sur un Cheval, pencil on paper, atelier stamp, 10x7", SBY 2/16/89 OE 23,100
Buste de Femme (portrait), pastel on tan paper mounted on board, stamped signature, ca 1880-85, 20x20", SBY 5/11/88 OE 605,000
Chanteuse de Cafe-Concert (singer, Mlle Dumay); pastel on joined paper over monotype, sgn, 1878, 7x6", C-NY 5/11/89 OE 1,100,000
Cheval a l'Ecurie, counterproof of another study of horse; charcoal, stamped signature, ca 1885-89, 10x13", SBY 11/16/89 19,800
Copie d'Apres le Mariage Mystique de Sainte Catherine de Tintoret, oil on canvas, ca 1859-60, 9x12", SBY 10/7/88 OE 47,300
Danseuse, La Jambe Droite Levee; charcoal on tan paper laid down on board, stamped signature, 12x9", SBY 11/12/88 OE 71,500
Danseuse (dancer taking a bow), charcoal on paper, stamped, 18x15", C-NY 5/12/88 OE 143,000
Danseuse en Scene (dancing figure), charcoal heightened w/white/brown chalk, atelier stamp, 19x20", C-NY 5/12/88 5,500
Danseuses (dancers), pastel on paper, sgn, 25x17", SBY 11/15/89 2,310,000
Danseuses Russes (Russian Dancers), pastel on paper, stamped signature, 1895, 21x28", SBY 11/11/88 OE 1,265,000
Deux Danseuses en Maillot, charcoal on buff paper laid down at edges on board, stamped, ca 1885, 17x21", C-NY 11/15/88 77,000
Etude de Danseuse (Study of a Dancer), pastel/charcoal on paper, stamped signature, 13x9", C-NY 5/11/89 OE 99,000
Femme a sa Toilette (woman bathing over wash bowl), pastel, stamped signature, 1892, 26x19", SBY 5/10/88 OE 1,210,000
Femme Mettant son Corset (lady putting on a corset), pastel on paper, sgn, ca 1883, 20x20", SBY 5/9/89 OE 638,000
Femme Nue se Coiffant, charcoal/pastel on paper mounted on board, stamped signature, 19x25", C-NY 5/11/89 OE 374,000
Femme s'Essuyant, charcoal/pastel on laid paper, stamped signature, ca 1888-92, 18x24", SBY 11/12/88 66,000
Femme se Peignant, pastel on buff paper, sgn, ca 1889-92, 19x15", SBY 11/16/89 825,000
Jeune Femme Debout, Vue de Face (sketch of standing woman); charcoal on buff paper, stamped, 20x13", PHL 11/15/88 30,000
Jockey a Cheval (jockey on horse), pencil on paper, atelier stamp, Lutg #657, 8x9", SBY 5/10/89 OE 46,750
La Toilette Apres le Bain, pastel on canvas, stamped signature, ca 1886-90, 35x28", SBY 5/10/88 495,000
Le Baisser du Rideau (The Lowering of the Curtain), pastel on joined paper, sgn, 1880, 21x29", SBY 11/11/88 7,975,000
Mont St Michel, black chalk on paper, atelier stamp/dtd 1885, 15x11", C-NY 10/6/88 OE 10,450
Quatre Danseuses (Four Dancers), pastel on paper, sgn, ca 1903, 33x29", SBY 11/11/88 1,760,000
Quatre Danseuses au Foyer de la Danse (four dancers), pastel on joined paper, sgn, ca 1890, 19x24", SBY 11/15/89 1,870,000
Tete de Femme (Portrait de Mdme Ernest May), pastel on paper, stamped signature, Lugt #658, ca 1881, 16x12", SBY 5/10/89 26,400
Trois Danseuses, charcoal on tan paper laid down on board, stamped signature,26x23", SBY 11/12/88 OE 225,500
Trois Danseuses (Jupes Jaunes, Corsages Rouges), pastel on joined paper, stamped signature, 1900s, 26x20", SBY 11/11/88 1,650,000
Vetements sur une Chaise (clothes on chair), pastel on paper mounted at edges on board, 1887, 18x12", C-NY 5/12/88 OE 38,500
Woman Standing at Table, pencil, sgn, 11x7", S/A 2/18/89 3,000

DEGRANGE, Adolfe Louis (French, 1840-)

Flowers (still life), oil on canvas, sgn, 24x37", C-E 2/21/89 UE 2,200

DEHN, Adolf (American, 1895-1968)

America (East), watercolor, sgn, oval format, 21x21", LH 5/15/88 400
America (Midwest), watercolor, sgn, oval format, 21x21", LH 5/15/88 400
America (South), watercolor, sgn, oval format, 21x21", LH 5/15/88 400
America (West), watercolor, sgn, oval format, 21x21", LH 5/15/88 400
Blimp, watercolor/ink on paper, sgn, 13x17", C-E 2/3/88 1,320
Central Park, watercolor/gouache on paper, sgn, 19x27", SBY 9/14/89 4,950
Central Park (extensive view w/figures), watercolor/gouache on paper, sgn/dtd 1946, 20x28", SBY 3/17/88 4,950
Evening on the Marches, ink/ink wash on paper, sgn/dtd 83, 15x21", C-E 2/3/88 660
Farm Scene, watercolor, sgn, 13x20", WG 9/16/88 UE 1,400
Figures at a Viennese Cabaret, pen/ink on paper, sgn/dtd 24, unfr, 13x15", SBY 6/28/89 2,310
Gray Hudson (snowy river landscape), gouache/pencil on paper, sgn/dtd 48, 19x30", C-NY 9/28/89 4,620
Long Peak, Estes Park (extensive landscape); watercolor/pen/black ink/pencil on paper, sgn/dtd 1940, 20x28", C-E 6/1/89 880
Marron Lake, Colorado; watercolor on paper, sgn twice/inscr/dtd 1946, 23x30", C-NY 3/11/88 2,200
Mini Mini 9 (abstract), gouache on paper, sgn, 4x7", RWS 3/16/89 600
Minnesota Farm, watercolor/pen/ink on pencil, 15x22", C-E 2/1/89 OE 3,520
One Has To Enjoy Themselves, pen/ink, sgn/titled, ca 1926, 10x14", SWN 12/1/88 935
Rural Farm Scene, pen/ink on paper, sgn/dtd 1932, unfr, 12x20", C-E 12x20", C-E 6/1/88 880
Sailing on Lake Cowan, Ohio; watercolor on paper, sgn/dtd May-June 1964/titled, 20x29", SBY 3/17/88 1,760
South (beach scene w/palm trees, docked boat), watercolor/pencil on paper, shaped as circle, sgn, 23x26", C-E 2/1/89 UE 605
Study of Two Figures: Gossip & Watermelons; watercolor on paper, sgn/dtd 44, 12x16", SBY 9/23/88 2,420

DEI CONTI, Bernardino

Portrait of a Young Man, half-length, wearing a block costume w/fur trim & hat; oil on panel, 30x23", C-NY 5/31/89 24,200

DEI CROCIFISSI, Simone (fl 1330-1339)

Coronation of the Virgin, gold ground/tempera on panel, 44x22", SBY 6/1/89 OE 484,000

DEI CROCIFISSI, Simone; manner of (fl 1330-1339)

Crucifixion, on gold ground/oil on panel, shaped as a cross, 41x29", C-NY 10/20/88 OE 4,180

DEI PIETRI, Pietro Antonio; att (Italian, 1663-1716)

Studies of Two Angels & Two Putti, black/red/white chalk, encircled fleur-de-lys wm, 15x10", C-NY 1/11/89 OE 2,200

DEIBL, Anton (German, 1833-1883)

Children Eating Grapes, oil on canvas, sgn/dtd 1867, 23x27", C-E 10/26/89 3,300

DEL BIMBO, see Bimbi

EL CARAVAGGIO, Cecco
Guardian Angel with Saints Ursula & Thomas, oil on canvas, 82x42", C-NY 6/2/88 OE 71,500
EL CESTARO, Jacopo (Italian, fl 18th C)
Martyrdom of a Saint, oil on canvas, unfr, 27x18", SBY 10/21/88 13,200
EL CESTARO, Jacopo; circle of (Italian, fl 18th C)
Young Couple Eating Spaghetti in a Landscape, oil on canvas, 35x35", C-NY 4/8/88 OE 14,300
EL GARBO, Raffaellino; manner of (Italian, 16th C)
Madonna & Child with the Infant Saint John the Baptist, oil on panel, 27" dia, C-NY 5/31/89 68,200
EL MARLE, Felix (French, 1936-)
Fugue (abstract), pastel on paper, indistinctly stamped w/initials, 1925, 22x8", SBY 10/5/88........ 2,750
EL MORO, Battista Angolo (Italian, 1514-1575)
Monk Preaching to King & Queen & Other Figures, pen/ink/brush/wash heightened w/white, 9x12", SBY 1/13/89 5,500
EL MORO, Battista Angolo; att (Italian, 1514-1575)
Female Figure Holding a Cross & Chalice, pen/brown ink/wash over black chalk heightened w/white, 6x6", SBY 1/13/89........ 660
St Catherine of Alexandria, brush/brown wash heightened w/white, 7x4", SBY 1/13/89........ 880
EL PIOMBO, Sebastiano; circle of (Italian, 1485-1547)
Madonna of the Veil (Madonna covering sleeping Christ child), oil on panel, 50x37", SBY 6/1/89 UE 44,000
EL PO, Giacomo (Italian, 1652-1726)
Rachel at the Well, oil on canvas, sgn, 70x91", SBY 1/12/89 OE 154,000
EL RIO, Marcelo
La Mujer en la Selva (woman in forest), oil on canvas, sgn, 32x40", LH 3/20/88 UE 30
EL SARTO, Andrea; after (Italian, 1487-1530)
Annunciation, oil on canvas, bears monogram, 70x51", C-NY 4/8/88........ 3,520
Portrait of a Lady Known as Lucrezia del Fede, oil on canvas, 29x22", SBY 6/8/88 UE 1,320
St Giovanni (portrait), oil on linen, 36x27", NA 5/13/89........ 2,000
EL SARTO, Andrea; circle of (Italian, 1487-1530)
Portrait of a Young Man, three-quarter length; black chalk on pink-washed paper, 8x7", SBY 1/13/89........ 15,400
EL SARTO, Andrea; manner of (Italian, 1487-1530)
Holy Family with Saint John the Baptist, oil on canvas, 30x24", SBY 6/8/88 412
EL SARTO, Andrea; school of (Italian, 1487-1530)
Madonna & Child with Infant John the Baptist, oil on canvas mounted on panel, 22x18", RWS 12/10/88 OE 1,100
Madonna & Child with Two Angels in a Landscape; oil on canvas, 39x32", C-NY 1/15/88 OE 5,500
Saint James with Two Figures in a Landscape, oil on panel, 22x16", C-E 4/7/88 OE........ 1,760
Study of the Head of the Virgin, oil on canvas, Italian tabernacle frame, 16x12", RWS 11/3/88 OE........ 3,000
EL TINTORE, Simone; att (Italian, fl 1630-1670)
Silver Urns with Flowers & Fruit, sculpted urn with flowers, & birds in courtyard; oil on canvas, 64x70", C-NY 4/6/89 OE........ 28,600
EL TINTORE, Simone; manner of (Italian, fl 1630-1670)
Still Life of Fruits Including Apples, Figs & Lemons on a Ledge; oil on canvas, 18x31", SBY 4/7/89 OE 44,000
EL TORRE, Giulio (Italian, 1856-1932)
Pair: Seamstresses (portraits); oil on panel, sgn/dtd 87, 9x6", C-E 2/21/89 6,600
EL VAGA, see Buonaccorsi
LACROIX, Eugene (French, 1798-1863)
Church Interior with Arches, brown/blue-gray wash over pencil, stamped initials, 9x7", C-NY 2/23/89 OE........ 13,200
Circassian Holding a Horse by Its Bridle, oil on canvas, sgn, ca 1858, 13x16", SBY 10/24/89 473,000
La Captivite a Babylone: Dessin a la Mine de Plomb; pencil on paper, stamped initials, 9x11", WD 5/5/88 OE 11,000
Pommiers et Chaumiere de Normandie, brown wash on lt brown paper, stamped, 6x8", C-NY 10/25/89 OE 19,800

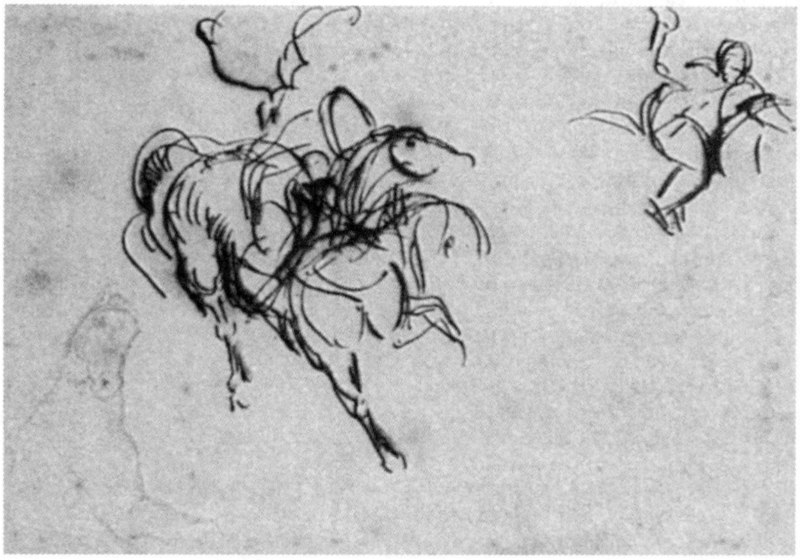

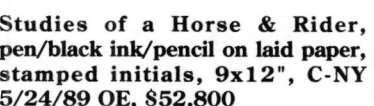

Studies of a Horse & Rider, pen/black ink/pencil on laid paper, stamped initials, 9x12", C-NY 5/24/89 OE, $52,800

Studies of a Young Jewess in Tangier, watercolor over pencil, stamped initials/Spanish inscr, 6x7", C-NY 2/23/89........ 4,950
Studies of Figures & Animals, black chalk on laid paper, wm: wreath around shield/stamped ED, 10x15", C-NY 2/25/88 OE 4,180

Study of Christ Carrying the Cross, pencil on calque laid down, stamped initials, 12x8", C-NY 5/24/89 5,500
Study of the Interior of a Church, watercolor on paper, stamped initials, indistinctly inscr, unfr, 6x4", C-NY 5/24/89 4,950
Young Girl Carrying a Rake & a Hoe, brown ink on paper, stamped initials, 4x3", WD 5/5/88 650

DELACROIX, Henri Eugene (French, 1845-1930)
Egyptian Street Scene, oil on canvas, sgn, 18x30", SBY 6/8/88 2,310

DELAGE, Pierre (European, 20th C)
Pair: Discussion with a Cardinal; Two Gentlemen Conversing; oil on board, sgn, 18x15", C-E 10/25/88 3,300

DELAHOGUE, Alexis Auguste (French, 1867-1930)
Caravan Venant du Sud, El Kantara; oil on panel, sgn/inscr, dtd twice 1910, 9x22", SBY 6/8/88 2,090

DELANCE, Paul (French, 19th/20th C)
Stroll in the Park, oil on board, sgn, 11x7", MG 5/28/88 325

DELANO, Gerard Curtis (American, 1890-1972)
Old West Passes (with the Coming of the Railroad), oil on canvas, sgn/stamped, 36x30", SBY 5/25/88 14,300
On the Trap Line (A Northlands Indian with Dog Team of Huskies), oil on canvas, sgn/inscr/#d 31, 22x40", SBY 3/17/88 OE 17,600

DELAUNAY, Robert (French, 1885-1941)
Rythme, Relief (abstract); oil on canvas, sgn/dtd 1936, 39x28", SBY 5/11/88 220,000

DELAUNAY, Sonia (French, 1885-)
Auto-Portrait (abstract), gouache on paper, 13x8", SBY 5/10/89 OE 36,300
Choco (poster theme developed for Berensdorf Chocolate), pastel on thin paper, sgn/dtd 1916, 10x8", SBY 5/10/89 OE 17,600
Composition (abstract), gouache on paper, sgn/dtd 1942/#d 2 285, 11x9", SBY 2/16/89 7,150
Composition (abstract), gouache/watercolor/pencil on paper, sgn/dtd/#d 51-249, 11x9", SBY 2/16/89 OE 15,400
Composition Carres Bleus et Rouges, gouache/pencil on paper, sgn/dtd 20-12-72, 21x15", C-NY 5/12/88 OE 12,100
Composition en Carres (composition w/colored squares), gouache on paper, sgn/#d N-198, 9x10", C-NY 10/5/89 8,250
Costume Simultane, watercolor/pencil on paper, sgn/dtd 1924, 16x11", SBY 11/16/89 25,300
Costume Simultane (abstract figure), gouache on paper, sgn/dtd 1916/#d 479, 11x7", C-NY 10/5/89 OE 20,900
French Street Scene, oil on canvas, 1918, 22x18", LH 12/4/88 UE 300
Le Marche au Minho (abstract), oil on paper laid down on canvas, sgn/dtd 1916, 37x51", SBY 11/12/88 OE 341,000
Portrait de Jeune Fille, oil on canvas, 1907, 26x20", C-NY 11/16/88 24,200
Project de Couverture Pour L'Album I (abstract), watercolor/gouache on paper, 1916, 9x9", SBY 10/6/89 OE 31,900
Robe Jaune (Yellow Dress, abstract figures), pastel on paper, sgn/initialed/dtd 1926/#d 520 SD 26, 13x10", C-NY 10/5/89 2,860
Rythme Couleur, gouache/colored crayons on paper, sgn/dtd 10-11-70, 26x18", lot 267, SBY 10/6/89 14,300
Rythme Couleur, gouache/colored crayons on paper, sgn/dtd 1970, 27x21", lot 266, SBY 10/6/89 14,300
Rythme Couleur, gouache/pencil on paper, sgn/dtd 1970, 26x20", SBY 10/6/89 8,800
Rythme Couleur (abstract), gouache/colored crayons on paper, sgn/inscr Grave 1943-1946-1948, 23x19", SBY 2/18/88 OE 25,300
Rythme Couleur No 7 (abstract), gouache/colored crayons on paper affixed to board, sgn/dtd 1942, 7x9", SBY 2/18/88 7,150
Tete de Femme (Head of a Woman), gouache on paper, ca 1925, 9x8", SBY 11/16/89 OE 19,800
Two Figures in Interior, watercolor/gouache over pencil on paper, sgn/dtd 1923, 10x11", SBY 5/10/89 33,000
Untitled (abstract), watercolor/gouache on paper, sgn/stamped, unfr, 10x8", SBY 10/5/88 1,870

DELBOS, Julius (American, 1879-)
Still Life of Fruit, oil on canvas, sgn, 15x18", B/B 1/11/89 605
Still Life of Mushrooms, oil on canvas, sgn, 15x18", B/B 1/11/89 605
Walking Along the Shore, oil on board, sgn, 10x13", C-E 9/15/88 UE 286

DELBRIDGE, Thomas James; att (American, 1894-)
General's Wife, oilon canvas, 36x27", LH 9/10/89 200

DELESSARD, Auguste Joseph (French, 1827-1890)
Spotted Bull Terrier, oil on canvas, initialed, 29x36", SBY 6/9/89 2,860

DELFF, Cornelis Jacobsz (Dutch, 1571-1643)
Still Life of Vegetables & Fowl in a Basket, Fish on a Plate...; oil on panel, 27x37", C-NY 1/11/89 OE 30,800

DELFGAAUW, Gerard Johannes (Dutch, 1882-1947)
Rotterdam Harbor, oil on canvas, sgn, 16x24", LH 12/4/88 1,500

DELFOSSE, Marie Joseph Georges (Canadian, 1869-1939)
Bonsecours Church, oil on board, sgn, 11x14", FB 4/25/88 OE 900
Island Reflection, watercolor, sgn, 13x19", WAD 11/30/89 425
Marche Bonsecours, oil on canvas, 10x14", FB 10/17/88 1,500
Old Gentleman, pencil, initialed, 6x4", FB 5/28/89 180
Portrait of a Woman, pastel, initialed/dtd 1910, 19x14", FB 10/88 320
Portrait of Senator McDougle, charcoal, sgn, 21x15", FB 10/17/88 UE 110
View of a Church, mixed media, atelier stamp, 9x7", FB 10/30/89 165

DELL'ABBATE, Niccolo (Italian, 1512-1571)
Portrait of a Lady (three-quarter length, hand on hip), oil on canvas, ca 1548, 44x37", SBY 6/1/89 OE 297,000

DELLA PORTA, Baccio; see Bartolommeo, Fra

DELLA ROCCA, Giovanni (Italian, 1788-1858)
Flirtation, oil on canvas, sgn, 27x17", C-E 1/12/88 1,430
Flirtation, oil on canvas, sgn, 27x17", C-E 10/25/88 1,320

DELLE ROVERE, Giovanni Mauro (Italian, 1575-1640)
Procession with the Arrival of a Cardinal, pen/brown ink/wash over black chalk, 10x8", SBY 1/13/89 1,760

DELLENBAUGH, Frederick Samuel (American, 1853-1935)
Man in Workshop (man at grinding wheel in detailed interior), oil on canvas, sgn/dtd 1887, 25x32", C-E 6/1/89 OE 13,200

DELOBBE, Francois Alfred (French, 1835-1920)
Flirtation (young peasant in a landscape), oil on canvas, sgn, 14x11", B/B 6/15/89 3,300
Floral Still Life, oil on canvas, sgn, 36x26", SBY 7/12/89 OE 12,100

ELORME, Anthonie (Dutch, 1627-1673)
Church Interior with Figures, oil on panel, sgn/dtd 1640, 36x48", SBY 4/7/88 UE 4,400
ELORT, Charles Edouard (French, 1841-1895)
Casque, oil on canvas, sgn/dtd 1872, 22x14", SBY 7/12/89 5,500
ELPY, Hippolyte Camille (French, 1842-1910)
Au Bord de l'Oise, oil on panel, sgn, 18x28", SBY 5/23/89 8,250
Docks at Dieppe, oil on canvas, sgn, 49x79", C-NY 10/25/89.... 55,000
Lavandiere a la Riviere (laundress at the river), oil on panel, sgn/dtd 92, stamped HCD on verso, 13x24", SBY 2/22/89 9,900
Lavandiere au Bord de la Riviere, oil on panel, sgn/dtd 1901, inscr HCD on verso, 16x28", SBY 2/22/89 13,200
Lavandiere au Soleil Couchant, oil on panel, sgn/dtd 90, stamped HCD on verso, 9x16", SBY 2/22/89 6,050
Lavandiere pres d'un Groupe de Maisons, oil on panel, sgn, inscr HCD on verso, 19x25", SBY 2/22/89 16,500
On the Oise (river landscape), oil on panel, sgn, 16x28", C-NY 2/23/89 11,000
River Landscape, oil on panel, sgn/dtd 98, 17x28", SBY 10/24/89 11,000
River Landscape with Washerwomen, oil on board, sgn/dtd 01, 16x28", WD 11/16/88 7,500
Sunset, At the River's Edge; oil on panel, sgn/dtd 04, 16x28", C-NY 5/25/88 9,350
Sunset on the Loire, oil on panel, sgn/dtd 72, 14x24", C-NY 2/25/88 4,400
Washerwoman by a River, oil on panel, sgn, 11x20", C-NY 2/25/88 4,950
Winter Landscape, oil on panel, sgn, 26x34", SBY 2/22/89.... 7,700
ELPY, Lucien Victor (French, 1898-)
Le Port, oil on board, sgn, 9x11", C-E 5/13/88.... 330
ELSAUX, Jeremie (Belgian, 1852-1927)
View of a Canal in Ghent (Gand), oil on canvas, sgn/dtd 1-1, 14x22", B/B 6/15/89 UE 1,870
ELSIGNORE, Littorio (Canadian, 1938-)
Le Retour, oil on canvas, sgn/dtd 1989, 20x24", FB 10/30/89 715
ELVAUX, Paul (Belgian, 1898-)
La Comedie du Soir or Les Belles de Nuit, oil on canvas, sgn/dtd 36, 39x39", C-NY 10/6/88 OE 605,000
Queen (nude), India ink/gray & brown wash on paper, initialed/dtd 11-2-48, 14x11", SBY 5/11/88 OE 52,250
EMARNE, Jean Louis (French, 1754-1829)
Coach Stopping Before a Walled Inn, oil on panel, 16x22", SBY 10/21/88 22,000
EMETROPOULOS, Charles P. (American, 1912-1976)
Christian Science Mother Church, Boston, Massachusetts (busy street scene); watercolor on paper, 20x28", RAB 8/9/88 500
Downtown, Boston; gouache on paper, sgn/dtd 41, 13x10", RAB 8/9/88.... 700
Under the Boston El (busy street scene), watercolor on paper, 23x17", RAB 8/9/88 UE 300
EMING, Edwin Willard (American, 1860-1942)
Calling Moose, oil on canvasboard, monogramed, 12x16", RWS 5/12/89.... 3,250
Indian Competition, oil on canvas, sgn w/artist's insignia, 32x60", SBY 9/23/88 OE.... 9,900
Mary Ogden Piggo & Her Brother Alfred Ogden on Horseback, oil on panel, sgn, 9x12", C-E 10/18/89 1,430
Pioneer on Horseback, gouache on paper, initialed, 4x6", B/B 12/8/88.... 715
Shooting Buffalos, oil en grisaille heightened w/gouache on board, sgn, 25x20", C-E 6/1/88.... 660
Stagecoach at Plymouth, Massachusetts; oil on panel, sgn, 24x120", RAB 8/8/89 3,500
The Hunt (Indians hunting in autumn landscape), oil on panel, monogramed, 16x48", C-NY 2/3/88 7,150
EMING, Edwin Willard; att (American, 1860-1942)
Dog Howling at the Moon, oil on panel, 18x12", MAG 4/24/89.... 500
EMONT, Adrien (French, 1851-1928)
Farewell, oil on canvas, sgn, 31x45", WD 3/23/88 UE 1,200
EMONTE, Bruno (Brazilian, 20th C)
Ariramba Grande da Mata Virgem (Macho), watercolor on paper, sgn/dtd 1987, 29x16", C-NY 5/18/88 UE.... 1,430
Pair: Papagaio de Cara Roxa; Ariramba Grande da Mata Virgem (Macho); watercolor, sgn, 1987, about 28x17", C-NY 5/17/89.... 3,080
Papagaio de Cara Roxa (parrot), watercolor on paper, sgn/dtd 1987, 28x18", C-NY 5/18/88 1,430
EMONTE, Rosalia (Brazilian, 20th C)
Butterfly, gouache on paper, sgn/dtd 1987, 22x14", B/B 9/14/89.... 880
Herron, gouache on paper, sgn/dtd 1987, 29x22", B/B 9/14/89 1,045
Papilio Scarmander (butterflies), watercolor on paper, sgn/dtd 1987, 22x15", C-NY 5/18/88 1,650
Parrot, gouache on paper, sgn/dtd 1987, 27x18", B/B 9/14/89 UE.... 605
EMONTE, Yvonne
Gato Mourisco Ruivo (cat), watercolor on paper, sgn/dtd 1987, 22x15", C-NY 5/18/88.... 1,650
EMUTH, Charles (American, 1883-1935)
Animal Tamer Presents (illustration for play), watercolor/pencil on paper, sgn/dtd 1918, 13x8", C-NY 5/25/89 OE 99,000
Cabaret, watercolor/pencil on paper, sgn/inscr/dtd 1919, 8x10", SBY 5/25/88 OE.... 308,000
On Leave (caricature of couple w/soldier on scale, woman wanting to leave), watercolor/pencil, 13x10", C-NY 5/25/89 18,700
On the Beach (figures), watercolor/pencil on buff paper, sgn, 8x11", C-NY 5/25/89 12,100
Pair: Head of a Woman; Man with Hat; pencil on paper, 10x6" & smaller, C-E 11/30/88 UE 550
River Landscape, watercolor on paper laid down on board, sgn, 9x13", C-NY 5/25/89 8,250
Study for Black & White Ball, pencil on paper, 10x8", SBY 6/28/89 7,700
Trees #5 (landscape), watercolor on paper, sgn/titled, ca 1912-15, 10x14", SBY 5/24/89 OE 23,100
Vaudeville Figure, watercolor/pencil on paper, sgn, 13x8", C-NY 5/25/89 60,500
ENEUVILLE, Henry Edmund (French, fl 1925-1928)
Farmyard with Chickens & Roosters, oil on canvas, 12x9", SLK 9/29/88 475
ENIS, Maurice (French, 1870-1943)
Arc de Constantin, Rome (figures in park setting, arc & building); oil on canvas, sgn, 1928, 14x22", C-NY 10/5/89 20,900
Deux Jeunes Filles sur le Balcon de Silencio (girls on balcony), oil on canvas, sgn, ca 1908, 13x10", C-NY 10/5/89.... 26,400

L'Annonciation, oil on canvas, sgn/dtd 1930, 21x29", C-E 5/13/88 OE 12,100
Le Balcone (artist's two daughters on balcony), oil on canvas, sgn/dtd MAVD 1913, 29x18", C-NY 2/16/89 OE 46,200
Saint-Tropez (Petit Decor), oil on board laid down on cradled panel, monogramed, ca 1906-13, 9x15", SBY 2/16/89 22,000
Set of 3: Three Sections of La Bacchanale du Tigre Royal; oil on canvas laid down, 1920, 36x14" & smaller, C-NY 2/18/88 12,100
Viaducq des Fonds Saint-Leger, Saint-Germain-en-Laye; oil on board, sgn, ca 1902, 11x9", C-NY 10/6/88 OE 10,450

DENNER, Balthasar (German, 1685-1749)
Portrait of an Elderly Lady Wearing a Fur-Trimmed Coat, oil on panel, 16x13", SBY 10/13/89 7,700
Portrait of an Old Man, oil on panel, 15x13", SBY 6/8/88 935

DENNINGHOFF, H. (Continental, 19th C)
Pair: Anemones; Wild Fox Glove & Butterfly with a Castle Beyond; oil on canvas, sgn, 34x18", C-E 2/21/89 1,760

DENNIS, J. (American, 19th C)
Ship on the Beach, watercolor on paper, sgn/dtd 91, 24x15", MG 11/19/88 UE 125

DENNY, Gideon Jacques (American, 1830-1886)
Wreck of the King Phillip at Ocean Beach, oil on canvas, sgn/dtd 1878, 16x28", B/B 10/6/88 6,050

DENNY, Gideon Jacques; att (American, 1830-1886)
Ships Off the California Coast, oil on canvas, sgn/dtd 1880, 14x24", B/B 10/6/88 880

DENOYER DE SEGONZAC, Andre (French, 1884-1974)
Paysage, India ink/watercolor on paper, sgn, 22x30", SBY 10/27/89 37,400

DENTON, Troy (American, 20th C)
Buffalo Hunters, oil on canvas, sgn, 24x48", B/B 5/17/89 OE 1,320

DENTZ, T. (American, 20th C)
View of Broadway, oil on canvas, sgn, 24x20", SBY 9/14/89 1,540

DER, John (Canadian, 20th C)
Drift Fishing the Weed Line, oil on board, sgn/dtd 1984, 20x24", WAD 6/12/89 900

DER GROOT, Jan (Dutch, 20th C)
Dutch Interior with Women & Child, oil on canvas, sgn, 21x25", WAD 6/6/88 1,200

DERAIN, Andre (French, 1880-1954)
Black Feather Boa (full-length portrait of artist's niece), oil on canvas, sgn, ca 1935, 64x38", SBY 5/9/89 467,500
Bouquet de Fleurs (floral still life), oil on canvas laid down on cradled panel, sgn, 23x16", SBY 11/12/88 OE 82,500
Femme a Demi-Habillee, oil on canvas, sgn, 21x12", C-E 5/13/88 OE 9,350
Femme Assise (woman seated, half-length), oil on panel, sgn, ca 1924, 17x11", SBY 10/6/89 66,000
Femme Nue Allonge (reclining nude), pencil on paper, sgn, 10x13", C-NY 2/18/88 1,320
Figure Study, ink on paper, initialed, 12x8", RWS 11/3/88 UE 100
Landscape, sepia ink wash on paper, sgn, 14x20", SBY 10/7/89 3,960
Le Jeune Prince (a young prince), watercolor on paper, stamped Atelier Andre Derain, 8x10", C-E 11/17/88 OE 3,300
Le Modele (seated nude, full-length portrait), pencil on wove paper, sgn, 25x18", B/B 10/9/88 3,300
Le Mont Olympe (mountainous landscape), oil on canvas, sgn, ca 1930, 13x16", C-NY 2/18/88 OE 23,100
Le Roi (The Ring), blue gouache over chalk on paper, stamped Atelier Andre Derain, 9x8", C-E 11/17/88 OE 3,080
Le Sentier dans la Foret (a path through the forest), oil on canvas, sgn, 21x26", C-NY 2/18/88 25,300
Nature Morte (still life), charcoal on laid paper laid down on board, 1912, 19x12", SBY 2/16/89 9,350
Nature Morte (still life), oil on canvas, sgn, 32x21", SBY 11/12/88 63,250
Nature Morte (still life), oil on canvas, sgn, 8x19", SBY 10/7/88 OE 22,000
Nature Morte a la Table (abstract), oil on canvas, stamped signature, ca 1903, 26x20", C-NY 11/16/88 70,000
Oliviers en Provence (provencial landscape w/olive trees), oil on canvas, sgn, 1926-28, 21x26", C-NY 11/14/88 OE 143,000
Paysage, oil on canvas, sgn, 13x16", SBY 2/18/88 33,000
Paysage (hilly landscape w/houses), oil on canvas, sgn, 1929, 13x16", C-NY 2/18/88 OE 24,200
Paysage de Provence (landscape), oil on panel, sgn, ca 1930, 21x26", C-NY 10/5/89 OE 110,000
Portrait de Eve Curie, oil on canvas, sgn, ca 1935-36, 18x15", C-NY 2/18/88 OE 28,600
Portrait de Femme, oil on artist board, sgn, ca 1948-49, 19x14", SBY 10/7/88 22,000
Portrait de Femme (bust portrait of woman), oil on canvas, sgn, ca 1928-29, 9x7", SBY 10/7/89 OE 26,400
Portrait de Jeune Femme, red chalk on paper, sgn, 24x19", C-NY 2/13/89 3,850
Portrait de Mme Francis Carco, oil on panel, sgn, 1923, 13x11", SBY 2/18/88 11,000
Reclining Nude, red chalk on paper, atelier mark, 19x25", SBY 10/7/89 1,100
Standing Nude, charcoal on gray-green paper, studio stamp, 12x10", SBY 2/14/89 OE 1,870
Still Life (abstract), oil on canvas, atelier stamp, 9x9", SBY 10/5/88 3,575
Still Life of Fruit, oil on canvas laid down on board, sgn, 6x11", SBY 10/7/89 OE 26,400
Tere de Femme (portrait), oil on canvas, sgn, ca 1934-35, 17x14", SBY 10/7/88 26,400
Tete de Femme, charcoal on paper, sgn, 22x18", SBY 10/5/88 2,200
Vase de Fleurs (floral still life), oil on canvas, sgn, 1928-30, 19x14", C-NY 5/12/88 44,000
Vase de Fleurs (floral still life), oil on canvas, sgn, 25x19", C-NY 5/12/88 OE 66,000

DERCUM, Elizabeth
Still Life, Vase of Flowers on Table; oil on canvas, 22x24", C-E 10/18/89 UE 440

DERICKS, Louis (French, 19th C)
Deux Femmes dans une Clairere (two women in a clearing), oil on canvas, sgn/dtd 64, 31x39", SBY 2/22/89 OE 60,500

DERY, Alex (20th C)
Boats in the Harbor, pastel on paper, sgn/dtd 63, 16x22", WG 4/23/88 UE 160

DERYKE, William
Cleopatra, oil on canvas, sgn, 25x34", C-NY 10/20/88 6,600

DES CLAYES, Berthe (Canadian, 1877-1968)
Autumn River Scene, pastel, sgn, 10x12", FB 4/25/88 1,200
Fall Landscape, pastel on board, sgn, 14x14", C-E 11/30/88 825

In the Village, pastel, sgn, 8x10", FB 4/25/88 OE 2,500
Spring at Melbourne, Quebec; pastel, sgn, 8x11", FB 4/25/88 1,200
:S FONTAINES, Andre (French, 1869-)
Beach at Trouville, pastel on paper, sgn, 10x14", C-NY 5/24/89 OE 6,600
Summer Landscape, oil on canvas, sgn, 15x21", lot 669, MAG 6/22/88 OE 2,200
Summer Landscape, oil on canvas, sgn, 15x21", lot 670, MAG 6/22/88 OE 2,600
:SAR, Louis Paul (American, 1867-1952)
Return of the Flock, oil on canvas, sgn/dtd 1896, 18x23", LH 10/16/88 OE 4,200
:SATNICK, Mike (American, 1943-)
Boy with Feathered Red Banner, oil on masonite, sgn/dtd 80, 22x28", SBY 6/28/89 UE 440
:SBOUTIN, Marcelin Gilbert (French, 1823-1902)
Jeune Fille Assise, oil on canvas, sgn, 37x28", SBY 5/23/89 UE 11,000
:SCHAMPS, Gabriel (French, 1919-)
Pair: Notre Dame Cathedral; Flower Seller; oil on masonite, sgn, 6x7", FAP 12/8/89 200
:SCHAMPS, Louis (French, 1846-1902)
Peasant Girl Seated by a Table, oil on canvas, sgn/dtd 1891, 37x30", C-E 11/8/88 1,100
Watching Over Her Grandchildren, oil on canvas, sgn, 50x40", C-E 10/25/88 3,520
:SFONTAINES, F.B.
Pair: Summer River Landscape; Frozen Winter Landscape; 1 canvas laid down on masonite, sgn, 22x26", WD 10/19/88 1,600
SGOFFE, Blaise Alexandre (French, 1830-1901)
Still Life of Fruit, Glass of Wine, & Bronze Vessel on a Ledge; oil on panel, sgn/dtd 1863, 21x24", C-NY 10/25/89 16,500
Still Life of Urns & Illuminated Manuscript on a Draped Table, oil on canvas, sgn, 22x15", SBY 2/22/89 9,900
SHAYES, Charles Felix Edouard (French, 1831-)
Flowing Brook, oil on panel, sgn/dtd 1872, 12x21", C-E 5/22/89 1,650
Les Chines des Etangs de Cernay du Ville Seine et Oise France, oil on canvas, sgn/dtd 1873, 23x29", RWS 11/10/89 2,300
SHAYES DE COLLEVILLE, Jean Baptiste Henri (1729-1765)
Belshazzar's Feast, oil on canvas, unfr, 22x18", C-M 6/16/89 16,300
:SIDERIO, see De Nome
:SIRE-LUCAS, Louis Marie (French, 1869-1949)
Le Pardon de St Cadoc, oil on canvas, sgn, 24x37", SBY 6/8/88 3,850
:SMAREES, George; circle of (Swedish, 1697-1776)
Portrait of a Child Said To Be Archduke Joseph Von Hapsburg, oil on canvas, 31x25", SBY 10/21/88 OE 6,050
SNOYER, Francois
Cafe Scene (modernistic depiction), watercolor/pencil on paper, sgn, 9x11", SBY 10/7/89 2,200
:SPIAU, Charles (French, 1975-1946)
Bending Nude, brown chalk on paper laid down on paper, 9x12", SBY 10/7/78 1,100
SPORTES, Alexandre Francois (French, 1661-1743)
Peaches in a Vessel, Plums in a Basket, Brass Pitcher & Game; oil on canvas, sgn/dtd 1717, 44x37", C-NY 1/15/88 79,200
Portrait of Compte d'Armagnac (holding gun, in landscape w/dog & game), oil on canvas, sgn/dtd 1706, 67x75", SBY 6/1/89 286,000
SPORTES, Alexandre Francois; circle of (French, 1661-1743)
Still Life of Ducks on a Ledge, oil on canvas, 14x19", SBY 4/7/88 3,850
SPORTES, Alexandre Francois; studio of (French, 1661-1743)
Ormolu-Mounted Marble Sideboard w/Garlands of Flowers & Laden w/Ewers...; oil, arched top, unfr, 110x83", C-M 6/16/89 OE 48,899
SPORTES, Claude Francois; manner of (1695-1774)
Parrot Hanging From Its Perch with a Cat...Mirror Behind; oil on canvas, bears signature/dtd 173(?), SBY 4/7/89 OE 8,800
SSAR, Louis Paul; att (American, 1867-)
Woodcutters, oil on canvas, sgn, 24x29", SBY 1/24/89 1,760
SVARREAUX, Raymond (French, 1876-1961)
Charge of Col de l'Ariboisiere, Battle of Moskowa; oil on canvas, sgn/dtd 1903, 29x24", C-E 5/23/88 OE 4,400
SVARREUX-LARPENTEUR, James (American, 1847-)
Shepherd with His Flock, oil on canvas, sgn, 29x24", B/B 3/22/89 3,300
TAILLE, Jean Baptiste Edouard (French, 1848-1912)
Arab on Horseback, pen/ink, sgn, 8x10", C-E 10/26/89 770
Artilleur a Cheval, oil on canvas, sgn/dtd 1870, 59x41", SBY 2/22/89 28,600
Attack (soldiers fighting), oil on canvas, sgn, unfr, 47x50", SBY 6/8/88 3,300
Drunken Soldiers, oil on canvas, 10x12", NA 11/5/88 OE 4,400
Le Dragon d'Espagne, oil on canvas, sgn/dtd 1870, 59x41", SBY 2/22/89 22,000
Mounted First-Empire Dragoons in Front of a Country House; oil on canvas, sgn/dtd 1897, 26x18", SBY 2/22/89 13,200
Napoleon with His Troops, watercolor on paper, sgn/dtd 1907, 25x16", SBY 2/22/89 22,000
TREVILLE, Richard (American, 19th/20th C)
Lake Tahoe (extensive landscape), oil on canvas, sgn, 14x24", B/B 5/17/89 550
TREVILLE, Richard; att (American, 19th/20th C)
Mount Tamalpais, oil on board, 8x16", B/B 1/11/89 220
TROY, Leon (French, 1857-1955)
Paysage de Neige, oil on canvas laid down on masonite, sgn, 21x26", C-E 5/9/89 1,760
TTI, Cesare Auguste (Italian, 1847-1914)
Confirmation Procession, oil on canvas, sgn/dtd 89, 48x35", SBY 10/24/89 39,600
Gypsy Woman & Child, oil on canvas, sgn/dtd 77, 29x19", SBY 10/24/89 19,800
Halt Along the Way, oil on canvas, sgn/dtd Paris 88, 21x29", C-NY 10/25/89 18,700
Halt for Refreshment, oil on canvas, sgn, 17x22", SBY 7/12/89 5,500
Report (two men conversing in an interior), watercolor on paper, sgn/inscr Roma, 10x13", SBY 7/12/89 UE 1,980

Troubador (portrait of man with musical instrument), oil on canvas, sgn, 37x29", PHL 10/28/88 6,000

DETTMAN, Walter (British, 20th C)
On the North Sea, oil on canvas, sgn, 24x36", PHL 10/28/88 UE 200

DETWILLER, Frederick K. (American, 1882-1953)
New York City From Fort Lee, New Jersey; oil on canvas, sgn, 1920, 16x12", RWS 9/8/89 UE 425

DEULLY, Eugene Auguste Francois (French, 1860-)
La Marche aux Fleurs (flower market), oil on canvas, sgn, 21x32", SBY 2/22/89 29,700

DEUTSCH, David (20th C)
Interior/Receptical (contemporary), oil on paper mounted on canvas, unfr, 81x97", C-NY 5/4/89 11,000

DEVAUX, Jules Ernest (French, 1837-)
Rainy Day's Entertainment, oil on panel, sgn, unfr, 18x15", RWS 11/10/89 2,400

DEVENTER, Willem Antoine (Dutch, 1824-1893)
Coastal Sunset, oil on panel, 17x25", SBY 12/9/88 3,850

DEVIS, Arthur; circle of (British, 1708-1787)
Portrait of a Young Man, Full-Length, Wearing Gray Breeches, in a Landscape; oil on canvas, 29x23", C-NY 10/12/89 1,650

DEVIS, Arthur; school of (British, 1708-1787)
Portrait of an Officer (full-length, standing), oil on canvas, 20x15", C-NY 4/6/89 3,520

DEVRIENT, W. (Continental, 19th C)
Portrait of a Lady (three-quarter length), pastel, sgn, 12x10", C-E 2/2/189 990

DEWEHRT, Friedrich (German, 1808-)
Peasant Family in a Doorway, oil on panel, sgn/dtd 1853, 22x17", B/B 9/14/89 2,200

DEWEY, Charles (American, 1849-1937)
Shepherdess with Her Flock, oil on canvas, 21x16", SBY 1/24/89 1,430

DEWING, Thomas Wilmer (American, 1851-1938)
Lady in White, oil on panel, sgn, ca 1901, 20x16", SBY 5/25/88 165,000
Pandora, oil on canvas, sgn, 24x18", B/B 3/17/88 OE 594,000

DEWIT, Jacob; manner of (Dutch, 19th C)
Putti with Grapes in a Basket, oil on canvas, 21x49", C-E 2/16/88 1,430

DEXTER, William (Australian, 1818-1860)
Pair: Goldfinches by a Nest; Blue Tits by a Nest; watercolor/bodycolor w/gum arabic, sgn, oval, 8x11", C-SK 5/25/89 1,470
Still Life of Fruit, a Teapot & Mixed Flowers in a Vase...; watercolor/pencil, sgn/dtd 1846, 18x14", C-SK 6/9/88 1,580

DEYGAS, Regis Jean Francois
Arrivee de Sigurd en Irlande, oil on canvas, sgn/dtd 1903, 58x88", C-E 5/23/88 OE 9,900

DEYNUM, Jean Baptiste; circle of
Portrait of a Scientist, oil on canvas, 16x13", SBY 12/9/88 UE 1,430

DEZA, Oscar Mario (20th C)
Sucecion Dinamica Sobre Plano Estatico Gris, acrylic on canvas, sgn/dtd 1984, 39x28", C-NY 5/18/88 1,430

DI ANTONIO, Cristobal (Spanish, 19th C)
Beauty with Irises (portrait), oil on panel, 22x18", C-E 2/21/89 2,200

DI BARTOLO, Andrea (Italian, 1389-1428)
Madonna of Humility with Four Attending Angels, tempera on panel on gold ground, 34x22", SBY 1/12/89 OE 74,250

DI CAVALCANTI, Emiliano (Peruvian, 1897-1967)
Composicao Tropical (Tropical Composition), brush/India ink/watercolor on paper, sgn, ca 1920-21, 9x7", C-NY 5/17/89 4,400
Dois Saltimbancos (abstract), watercolor/gouache/pen/ink on paper, sgn, 12x9", C-NY 11/21/88 1,650
Estudo de dois Desnudos (study of two nudes), pen on paper, sgn/dtd Paris 1956, 16x13", C-NY 11/21/88 1,210
Flowers (fruit/birds & landscape beyond), oil on canvas, sgn, 1954, 32x26", SBY 5/16/89 38,500
Macumba, oil on canvas, sgn/dtd 1958, 26x39", SBY 5/17/88 29,700
Moca (nude woman seated), pencil on paper, initialed, 12x8", C-NY 5/18/88 1,650
Mulata, India ink on paper, sgn, 14x9", C-NY 5/18/88 2,860
Mulata con Papagayo, India ink/brush & ink/pencil on paper, initialed, 11x8", C-NY 5/18/88 OE 2,200
Nude with a Dove, oil on canvas, sgn/dtd 1961, 24x32", SBY 5/17/88 34,100

DI COCCO, Francesco (American/Italian, 1900-)
Surrealistic Landscape, gouache on paper, 16x21", B/B 9/15/88 302

DI CREDI, Lorenzo; follower of (Italian, 1459-1527)
Madonna & Child with an Attendant Angel, oil on panel, circular, unfr, 26x26", C-NY 1/15/88 OE 14,300

DI FREDI, Bartolo
Saint Lucy, tempera on gold on arched wood, 29x21", C-NY 1/11/89 121,000

DI GIOVANNI, Girolamo de Benvenuto
Madonna & Child with Saints Michael & Catherine, oil on panel on gold ground, arched top, 22x16", C-NY 5/31/89 60,500

DI LIONE, Andrea (1610-1685)
Tobit Burying the Dead (man praying as bodies are being interred), oil on copper, 25x35", SBY 6/1/89 OE 99,000

DI LORENZO, Fiorenzo
Madonna & Child Surrounded by a Mondorla of Seraphim, oil on panel, unfr, 28x29", C-NY 1/15/88 12,100

DI NICCOLO, Lorenzo
Madonna & Child Enthroned, Surrounded by Saints...; oil on gold ground on arched panel, inscr, 34x20", C-NY 1/11/89 93,500

DI PAPI, Cristofano; att
Portrait of Cardinal Niccolo Ridolfi, half-length; oil on panel, 26x20", C-NY 4/6/89 UE 5,500

DI PIETRO, Sano (1406-1481)
Saint Margaret of Antioch (full-length, standing), gold ground/tempera on panel, arched top, 40x17", SBY 6/1/89 77,000

DI PORCIA, Francesco Apollodoro (16th C)
Portrait of Ercole Sassonia, oil on canvas, SBY 6/1/89 OE 49,500

I ROSA, Herve (20th C)
Jalousie, acrylic on canvas, sgn/dtd 84/titled, unfr, 74x54", C-NY 11/10/88 OE ... 2,420

I SUVERO, Mark (20th C)
Untitled (abstract composition), colored felt-tip pens on paper, sgn/dtd Nov 65, 17x14", C-E 11/17/88 ... 1,760

I TITO, Santi; studio of (Italian, 1536-1603)
Portrait of a Lady, bust-length, wearing an embroidered dress; oil on canvas, inscr, 23x17", SBY 1/11/89 OE ... 15,400

IAMOND, Martha (20th C)
Untitled (abstract), acrylic on canvas, sgn/dtd 1973, unfr, 84x72", C-E 11/17/88 ... 1,320

IAO, David (20th C)
Untitled X, acrylic on canvas, sgn/dtd 1968, 88x88", C-E 11/17/88 UE ... 275

IAQUE, Ricardo (French, 19th C)
Elegant Lady & Child with Hoop, oil on canvas, sgn, 20x15", SBY 6/8/88 ... 2,640

IAZ DE LA PENA, Narcisse Virgile (French, 1807-1876)
Children Playing with a Lizard, oil on panel, sgn/dtd 64, 15x18", SBY 5/23/89 ... 13,200
Entrance du Bas-Breau (forest view), oil on canvas, sgn, dtd N Diaz 64, 20x28", LH 3/20/88 ... 4,200
Faggot Gatherer (in wooded landscape), oil on panel, 15x11", C-E 2/21/89 ... 1,870
Faggot Gatherer in a Wood, oil on panel, sgn/dtd 69, 14x12", C-NY 2/25/88 ... 4,950
Figure in a Woodland Clearing, oil on panel, sgn/dtd 72, 17x22", C-NY 2/23/89 OE ... 30,800
Forest of Fontainebleau, oil on canvas, sgn/dtd 67, 32x44", C-NY 2/3/88 ... 9,900
Forest Pool with Female Figure, oil on panel, sgn, 12x16", WD 11/16/88 ... 5,250
Gypsies by a Woodland Pool, oil on panel, sgn, 17x14", SBY 5/23/89 ... 12,100
In the Forest, oil on canvas, sgn/dtd 68, 33x44", C-NY 2/3/88 ... 14,300
In the Park, oil on canvas, sgn, 36x42", SBY 6/8/88 ... 6,600
La Source, Foret de Fontainebleau (forest landscape); oil on panel, sgn/stamped, 12x18", SBY 2/22/89 ... 7,150
Landscape Scene, oil on cradled panel, sgn, 11x16", RWS 8/12/89 ... 10,000
Landscape with Pond, oil on panel, sgn, 10x14", SBY 12/9/88 ... 4,675
Landscape with Pond, oil on panel, sgn, 9x13", B/B 3/17/88 ... 3,300
Spaniel in a Wooded Landscape, oil on canvas, 10x8", C-E 6/28/88 ... 462
Still Life of Flowers, oil on canvas, sgn, unfr, 12x9", SBY 6/8/88 ... 4,125
Sunlit Clearing in the Forest at Fontainebleau, oil on canvas, sgn/dtd 68, 33x44", SBY 2/22/89 ... 27,500
Two Girls & a Dog, oil on panel, sgn, 13x9", SBY 7/12/89 ... 6,050
Venus & Cupid, oil on panel, sgn, 10x7", B/B 9/15/88 ... 2,750
Women of the Seraglio, oil on canvas, sgn/dtd 60, 18x26", SBY 10/24/89 ... 37,400
Wooded Clearing, oil on panel, sgn, 11x8", C-E 10/25/88 ... 2,860
Wooded Landscape, oil on panel, sgn, 10x14", C-E 2/23/88 UE ... 1,760
Wooded Landscape with a Stream, oil on cradled panel, sgn, 8x10", C-E 10/25/88 ... 3,850
Wooded Landscape with Figure, oil on canvas, sgn/dtd 55, 10x12", WD 11/16/88 ... 3,500
Woodgatherer, oil on panel, sgn, 9x13", B/B 3/17/88 ... 6,600
Woodland Clearing, oil on canvas, sgn, 30x37", SBY 10/24/89 ... 13,200

IAZ DE LA PENA, Narcisse Virgile; att (French, 1807-1876)
Faggot Gatherer in a Clearing, oil on panel, sgn, 22x29", C-NY 10/25/89 ... 14,300
Pool in the Forest, oil on panel, bears signature, 9x12", SBY 6/8/88 UE ... 1,430
Twig Gatherer in a Wooded Landscape, oil on canvas, bears signature, 22x19", C-E 5/23/88 ... 3,850

ICK, James L. (American, 1834-1868)
Always at Mischief, oil on canvas, sgn/dtd Brooklyn 1867/titled, 10x12", SBY 1/24/89 ... 1,430

ICK, Robert H. (American)
Indians in Taos Pueblo, oil on canvas, sgn, 18x24", SLK 5/9/88 ... 250

ICKINSON, Anson (American, 1779-1852)
Portrait of a Naval Officer, mixed media on ivory mounted on pasteboard, sgn/dtd 1826, 4x3", RAB 5/17/88 ... 350

ICKINSON, Edwin (American, 1891-1978)
Cafe Tortoni-Le Havre; pencil on paper, sgn/inscr/dtd 1920, 8x5", C-NY 3/11/88 ... 880
Fragment Head & Drapery (Esther H Sawyer), oil on canvas, sgn/dtd 1931, inscr 1973, 18x16", C-NY 5/26/88 ... 12,100
Landscape by RR (impressionistic), oil on canvas, sgn/dtd 1936, 26x30", C-NY 5/26/88 ... 26,400
Pont des Artes, pencil on paper, sgn/inscr/dtd 1920, 5x8", C-NY 3/11/88 ... 1,210
Study Window, Buffalo; pencil on paper, sgn/inscr/dtd 1939, 13x11", C-NY 9/30/88 ... 3,300
Tibi's Luncheon, pencil on paper, sgn/inscr/dtd 1934, 7x18", C-NY 3/11/88 ... 2,310

ICKINSON, Preston (American, 1891-1930)
Island Landscape (w/beached boats & factory beyond), pastel on paper, sgn/dtd 30, 12x19", SBY 5/24/89 ... 18,700
Watertower at High Bridge, pastel/gouache/charcoal on board, sgn, 24x18", C-NY 5/26/88 ... 28,600

ICKINSON, R. (American, 20th C)
Desert Landscape, watercolor on paper, sgn, 7x10", B/B 1/11/89 ... 330

ICKINSON, Sidney (American, 1890-)
Young Painter, no media given, sgn/dtd 1917, 40x34", C-E 1/12/88 ... 1,430

ICKSEE, Frank (British, 1853-1928)
Group of 11: Scenes from Romeo & Juliet; gouache en grisaille, all initialed/3 dtd 82, 12x17", C-NY 2/23/89 OE ... 264,000
Portrait of a Woman (in profile, viewed from behind), oil on canvas, 8x6", C-E 2/21/89 ... 4,180

ICKSEE, Herbert Thomas (British, 1862-1942)
On the Albert, watercolor/gouache, sgn/dtd 1940, 18x27", C-NY 10/31/89 OE ... 7,700
Polar Bear, black/white chalk on tan paper, 16x24", C-NY 10/26/88 ... 770
Wild Cat & a Snake, black chalk heightened w/white, 18x26", C-NY 10/31/89 ... 1,210

DIDIER, Jules (French, 1831-1892)

Figures on a Country Lane, oil on canvas, sgn, 18x22", B/B 3/17/88 ... **3,025**

DIDIER-POUGET, William (French, 1864-1959)

Brume et Rosee du Matin-Cruyeres en Fleurs (landscape); oil on canvas, sgn/inscr, 21x26", SBY 12/9/88 UE ... **2,750**

Field of Flowers, oil on canvas, sgn, unfr, 40x53", SBY 12/9/88 ... **4,675**

DIEBENKORN, Richard (American, 1922-)

Coffee (lady seated by window drinking coffee), oil on canvas, initialed/dtd 1959, 58x52", SBY 5/2/89 ... **1,430,000**

Corner of Studio (contemporary), oil on canvas, sgn twice/dtd 1961 twice/titled, 46x48", SBY 11/10/88 ... **737,000**

Girl in the Sun, oil on panel, initialed/sgn, dtd twice 57, 12x7", SBY 10/8/88 ... **30,800**

Girl with a Cup (contemporary), oil on canvas, initialed/dtd 60, 25x21", SBY 11/10/88 ... **242,000**

Girl with Flowered Background (contemporary), oil on canvas, sgn twice/dtd 62 twice/titled, 40x34", SBY 11/10/88 ... **440,000**

July (contemporary view of man seated on bench), oil on canvas, 1957, 59x54", SBY 5/2/88 OE ... **1,155,000**

Ocean Park #120 (abstract), oil/charcoal on canvas, initialed/inscr/sgn, dtd twice 1977/79, 55x93", C-NY 5/3/88 ... **308,000**

Ocean Park #7 (abstract), oil/charcoal on canvas, initialed/sgn/inscr, dtd twice 1968, 92x80", C-NY 5/3/88 ... **330,000**

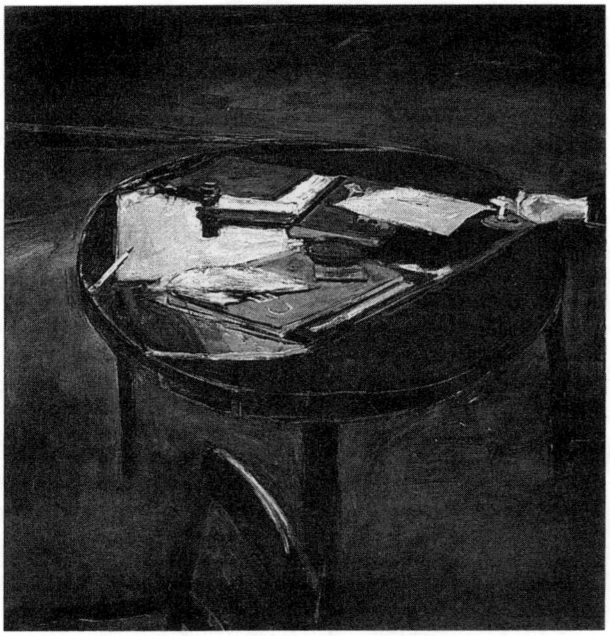

Round Table, oil on canvas, initialed/dtd 62, 70x64", C-NY 11/7/89, $792,000

Seated Girl, graphite on paper, initialed/dtd 62, 17x12", SBY 11/11/88 OE ... **30,250**

Seated Woman with Cigarette, graphite on paper, initialed, 1965, 17x13", SBY 11/9/89 ... **22,000**

Untitled (abstract), charcoal/gouache on paper, initialed/dtd 71, 29x23", SBY 10/5/89 ... **126,500**

Untitled (abstract), gouache/charcoal on paper, initialed/dtd 74, 30x22", C-NY 11/10/88 OE ... **66,000**

Untitled (contemporary still life), ink/wash on paper, initialed/dtd 64, 17x14", SBY 10/5/89 OE ... **104,500**

Untitled (half-figure), ink on paper, initialed/dtd 60, 11x16", SBY 5/3/88 ... **8,800**

Untitled (lineation), gouache/watercolor/charcoal on paper, initialed/dtd 79, 30x22", C-NY 11/10/88 ... **93,500**

Untitled (Ocean Park, abstract), gouache/colored crayons on paper, initialed/dtd 71, 25x18", C-NY 5/4/89 OE ... **77,000**

Untitled (red/yellow/blue lineation), oil/acrylic/crayon on paper, initialed/dtd 79, 29x22", SBY 11/11/88 OE ... **159,500**

Untitled #17 (abstract), acrylic/crayon on paper, initialed/dtd 84, 38x25", SBY 5/2/88 ... **143,000**

Untitled #30 (abstract), gouache/crayon on paper, initialed/dtd 81, 26x25", SBY 2/19/88 ... **71,500**

Untitled #35 (abstract), gouache/crayon on paper, initialed/dtd 81, 25x38", SBY 5/3/88 ... **99,000**

Untitled #6 (abstract), acrylic/crayon on paper, initialed/dtd 83, 36x26", SBY 5/3/88 OE ... **104,500**

Woman with Hat & Gloves (contemporary), oil on canvas, initialed/dtd 63, 34x36", SBY 11/8/89 ... **880,000**

DIEFENBACH, Karl Wilhelm (German, 1851-1931)

Adrift in Stormy Seas, oil on canvas, sgn/dtd 1900, unfr, 26x36", C-E 10/26/89 ... **1,100**

DIEHL, Arthur Vidal (American, 1870-1929)

Along Penosbscot Bay (landscape), oil on board, sgn/dtd 1928, 17x30", RWS 3/16/89 OE ... **2,300**

Autumn Landscape, oil on cardboard, sgn, 6x8", RAB 3/27/89 ... **300**

Cape Cod Dunes, oil on board, sgn, 6x10", RAB 8/9/88 ... **700**

Cape Cod Sand Dune, cart tracks in white sand to blue water; oil on cardboard, sgn, 8x10", RAB 8/8/89 ... **650**

Connecticut Coast, oil on cardboard, sgn/titled, 12x18", RAB 8/8/89 ... **1,600**

Cottage by the Salt Marshes, oil on canvas, sgn/dtd 1901, 20x30", RWS 11/10/89 OE ... **2,300**

Heavy Surf, oil on cardboard, sgn, 7x18", RAB 8/9/88 ... **500**

In the Breeze-Truro, Massachusetts (seascape); watercolor on paper, sgn/dtd 1913/titled, 7x13", RAB 3/27/89 ... **350**

In Venice (street scene), oil on particle board, sgn/titled, 5x5", RWS 3/16/89 OE ... **700**

Mediterranean Courtyard, oil on board, sgn, 20x16", RWS 5/12/89 ... **400**

Moonlight Sail, oil on canvas, sgn, 10x8", C-E 2/3/88 ... **770**

Night Fishing (two figures in dory), oil on canvas, sgn, 6x12", RAB 3/27/89 ... **750**

Night Fishing (two figures in dory), oil on canvas, sgn, 6x12", RAB 8/9/88 OE ... **550**

Pair: Dunes; Boat at the Pier (coastal scenes); oil on canvas/oil on board, sgn, 6x12", 5x5", RWS 11/10/89 900
Provincetown, Morning (village w/figures at fishing shack); oil on board, sgn, 14x12", RWS 3/31/88 OE 1,000
Provincetown Harbor at Sunrise, oil on canvas, sgn/dtd 1915, 12x25", RAB 8/8/89 1,650
Provincetown Sand Dunes, oil on board, sgn/dtd 1918, 16x27", RAB 8/9/88 1,750
Provincetown Sand Dunes, oil on cardboard, sgn, 6x12", RAB 3/27/89 475
Spanish Courtyard, oil on board, sgn/dtd 1922, 12x20", RAB 3/27/89 1,150
Still Life of Poppies, oil on board, sgn, 18x23", RAB 8/8/89 UE 1,800
Under Full Sail, oil on board, sgn/dtd 1926, 30x18", RAB 3/27/89 UE 850
Venetian Backwater, oil on canvas, sgn/dtd 1908, 12x18", C-SK 5/25/89 1,010
Village Scene (figures in street), oil on board, sgn, 5x6", RWS 9/8/89 OE 550
Waterfront Activity at Low Tide, oil on board, sgn, 5x4", RAB 11/25/88 275

DIELMAN, Frederick (American, 1847-1935)
Afternoon Chat, oil on panel, sgn/dtd 81, 6x5", C-E 2/23/88 OE 4,950
Young Woman in a Field of Flowers, watercolor/gouache on board laid down on board, sgn/dtd 99, 18x12", SBY 1/24/89 6,600

DIELMANN, F. (American, 1847-1935)

DIEPRAAN, A. (Dutch, 1622-1670)
Man Smoking a Pipe, oil on panel, 9x7", FAP 12/8/89 1,150

DIERCKX, Pierre Jacques
Cooking by the Hearth, oil on canvas, sgn, 27x31", C-E 10/25/88 UE 1,430

DIES, Albert Christophe (Austrian, 1755-1822)
Castello Nuovo, Naples; watercolor on paper, sgn/dtd 1786, 19x27", B/B 4/20/88 1,045

DIETERLE, Georges Pierre (French, 1844-)
Ships by Moonlight, oil on canvas, sgn, 52x76", SBY 6/8/88 UE 2,640

DIETERLE, Marie (French, 1856-1935)
Cattle in a Landscape, pencil/brown wash on paper heightened w/white, sgn, 14x11", SBY 12/9/88 UE 1,100
Cattle Watering, oil on canvas, sgn, 19x25", C-E 2/21/89 OE 4,620
Cows & Sheep by a Stream, oil on canvas, sgn, 28x3", C-E 1/12/88 OE 1,760
Cows Grazing, oil on canvas, sgn, 16x24", C-E 5/23/88 2,640
Cows Grazing in a Spring Landscape, oil on canvas, sgn, 31x41", C-E 5/23/88 3,190
Cows Wading, oil on canvas, sgn, 11x15", C-E 10/25/88 2,640

DIETRICH, Adelheid (American, 1827-)
Still Life of Dog Roses, Larkspur, & Bell Flowers in a White Cup; oil on canvas, sgn/inscr/dtd 1858, 10x8", SBY 5/25/88 27,500
Still Life of Flowers, oil on canvas, laid down on masonite, sgn/dtd 1869, 13x17", C-NY 12/2/88 OE 44,000
Still Life of Grapes, Peach, & Flower Blossoms; oil on canvas, sgn/inscr/dtd 1859, 9x11", SBY 5/25/88 17,050

DIETRICH, Christian Wilhelm E. (German, 18th C)
Rinaldo & Armida, oil on canvas, sgn/dtd 1758, 28x22", SBY 10/13/89 27,500

DIETRICH, Christian Wilhelm E.; circle of (German, 18th C)
Portrait of a Couple Said To Be Henry IV & Gabrielle, oil on panel, 24x23", SBY 12/9/88 2,970

DIETTERLIN, Bartholomeus (ca 1590-)
Elegant Figures Riding in Landscape with Shepherds & Ruins, pen/ink/gouache on vellum, sgn/dtd 1638, 5x7", SBY 1/13/89 4,950

DIETZSCH, Barbara Regina (German, 1706-1783)
Two Quinces on a Branch, gouache, 11x8", SBY 1/13/89 OE 16,500

DIEU, Antoine (French, 1662-1727)
Adoration of the Golden Calf, red chalk/pen/gray ink/wash, wm crowned coat-of-arms, 12x7", C-NY 1/12/88 2,860

DIGHTON, Denis (1792-1827)
Portrait of Sunung-Gise, North American Indian Chief; pencil/watercolor, sgn, 15x17", C-SK 5/25/89 6,430

DIGNAM, Mary Ella Williams (Canadian, 1860-1938)
November Muskoka, oil on panel, sgn/dtd 1917, 6x9", WAD 11/30/89 160
Old Cross, Church Yard, Lucerne; oil on panel, sgn, 9x6", WAD 6/12/89 140
Open Book, oil on canvas, sgn/dtd 88, 14x18", C-E 2/1/89 880

DIGNIMONT, Andre (French, 1891-1965)
Femme sur la Terrasse, watercolor/gouache over pencil on paper, sgn, 15x18", C-E 5/13/88 1,320

DILL, Lesley (20th C)
Standing in the Water (contemporary), oil/paper/canvas collage on paper, 1983, 72x42", SBY 2/15/89 UE 550

DILLE, J.H. (American, 1820-)
Still Life of Peaches, oil on canvas, sgn/dtd 1901-02, 13x19", S/A 2/18/89 1,400

DILLENS, Adolphe Alexandre (Belgian, 1821-1877)
Family Amongst Haystacks in the Field, oil on canvas, sgn, 40x50", SBY 5/23/89 16,500

DILLER, Burgoyne (American, 1906-1965)
First Theme #1 (contemporary), crayon on paper, initialed, ca 1964, 14x13", SBY 11/9/89 OE 14,850
First Theme #2 (contemporary), crayon on paper, initialed, ca 1964, 15x16", SBY 11/9/89 OE 19,800
Untitled (squares within squares), graphite/colored pencil on paper, initialed/dtd 62, 8x8", SBY 11/11/88 OE 7,150

DILLON, Frank (British, 1823-1909)
Doum Palm, Upper Egypt (landscape); watercolor on paper, sgn/dtd 21st Feb 1855, 10x15", RAB 8/8/89 850

DILLON, Julia McEntee (American, 1834-1919)
Basket of Flowers, oil on canvas, sgn, 29x36", C-E 2/3/88 OE 9,020

DINE, Jim (American, 1935-)
Bird Mask (standing female nude), pastel/charcoal/watercolor on paper, sgn/dtd 1978, 46x32", SBY 11/9/89 OE 46,750
Child's Room #4 (toy on a blue wall), oil/objects on canvas, sgn/dtd 1962, 72x60", SBY 5/2/88 88,000
Double Venus, gouache/pastel/charcoal/fabric collage on paper, sgn/dtd 1983, 48x34", SBY 5/3/89 OE 99,000
Four Hearts, watercolor on paper, sgn/dtd 1969, 19x15", SBY 5/3/88 OE 28,600

Gray Charterhouse Painting No 3, oil on canvas, sgn/dtd 1981, 28x36", SBY 11/9/89 OE ... 154,000
Head of Christ, oil on canvas, sgn/dtd 1956, 20x14", WG 4/23/88 ... 3,000
Heart (abstract composition), gouache/pastel/charcoal on paper, sgn/dtd 1981, 58x60", SBY 5/3/89 OE ... 110,000
Heart Drawing, watercolor/graphite on paper, sgn/dtd 1970, 24x36", C-NY 11/10/88 ... 18,700
Heart Drawing M (abstract), enamel paint/marker on paper, sgn/dtd 1970, 24x36", SBY 5/5/89 OE ... 18,700
Hearts, acrylic on 57 canvases, 1969, ea canvas 8x6", SBY 11/8/89 OE ... 660,000
Hearts (contemporary), watercolor on paper, sgn/dtd 1972, 23x29", SBY 11/11/88 ... 28,600
Jessie Seated in 1979 (portrait), charcoal/crayon/graphite on paper, sgn/dtd 1979, 50x38", C-NY 2/14/89 OE ... 20,900
Jessie with a Shell XI (abstract), pastel/watercolor/charcoal on paper, sgn/dtd 1982/titled, 43x31", SBY 5/3/88 OE ... 46,750
Kandinsky (abstract), oil/paper collage/fabric collage on cardboard, 1957, 51x35", SBY 10/8/88 ... 8,800
Large Abstract, California 1956; oil on canvas, 50x43", WG 4/23/88 ... 4,000
Little Black Screwdriver (abstract), oil/screwdriver on canvas, sgn/dtd 1962, 16x12", C-NY 2/23/89 ... 49,500
Little Black Tools, tools/oil on canvas, sgn/dtd 1962, 36x24", C-NY 5/3/88 OE ... 82,500
Pair: Broom; White Tie with Big Copper Knot; mixed media on paper, sgn/dtd 1958 & 1961, 21x15", 24x18", C-NY 2/20/88 ... 4,950
Palette, oil/cloth/graphite/paper collage on paper, sgn/dtd 1964, 48x36", SBY 11/11/88 ... 30,250
Palm Tree (contemporary), acrylic/oil/sand/fabric on canvas, sgn/dtd 1982, 136x108", C-NY 5/3/89 ... 82,500
Pitchfork (contemporary), acrylic/colored chalks/charcoal on paper, sgn/dtd 1975, 52x21", C-NY 5/4/89 ... 66,000
Red Robe (Self-Portrait Study), mixed media, sgn/dtd 1964, 48x35", C-NY 11/7/89 OE ... 154,000
Shoes with Black Cherries, paper collage/cloth/black ink/acrylic on paper, sgn/dtd 1965/titled, 23x18", C-NY 11/10/88 ... 4,950
Shower #5, gouache/crayon/graphite on 2 sheets of paper mounted on board, sgn/dtd 1962/titled, 37x23", C-NY 11/10/88 ... 11,000
Tie (contemporary), gouache on paper, sgn/dtd 1961, 32x18", SBY 11/9/89 OE ... 28,600
Tie (contemporary), watercolor/charcoal on paper, sgn/dtd 1961, 18x24", C-NY 5/4/89 ... 20,900
Toothbrush & Tumbler #3, gouache/graphite on paper, sgn/dtd 1962/titled, 29x23", C-NY 11/10/88 ... 12,100
Top-Sided: Double Heart (abstract); gouache on paper, initialed, 25x20", SBY 10/8/88 OE ... 7,150
Untitled (abstract w/yellow heart), watercolor on paper, sgn, 12x11", SBY 11/9/89 OE ... 17,600
Untitled (Hammer), pencil on paper, sgn/dtd 1973 NYC, 22x29", SBY 5/3/88 OE ... 9,350
Untitled (Hatchet), pastel/charcoal on paper, sgn/dtd 1973 NYC, 28x22", SBY 11/11/88 ... 9,900
Visiting with Charcoal II (man's torso in a robe), charcoal on paper, sgn/dtd 1980, 59x41", SBY 11/11/88 ... 27,500
16 Sheets: March, Without You (abstract); watercolor on paper, sgn/#d consecutively/dtd 1969, 23x29", C-NY 5/3/89 OE ... 385,000

DINGLE, John Darley (Adrian)(Canadian, 1911-1974)
Ancient Spectator, Spain; oil on board, sgn, 15x8", WAD 11/30/89 ... 300
Boat Races, Lower Slaughter, Gloucester; oil on board, sgn, 8x15", WAD 11/30/89 ... 300
Boy Climbing Fence, oil on canvas, sgn/dtd 68, 24x32", WAD 11/30/89 ... 1,000
Cape Anne, pen/ink, sgn/dtd 69, 6x13", WAD 11/30/89 ... 300
Dockside Delivery, Gloucester Harbour; oil on board, 9x12", WAD 11/30/89 ... 500
Evening Mooring, Atlantic Coast; oil on board, sgn, 20x34", WAD 11/30/89 ... 1,550
Fishing Boats in Drizzle, oil on board, sgn, 20x34", WAD 11/30/89 ... 950
From Sand to Sea, Mousehole, Cornwall; oil on board, sgn, 8x15", WAD 11/30/89 ... 325
Men of the Sea, oil on board, sgn, 15x8", WAD 11/30/89 ... 375
Moppet on the Rock (East Coast), oil on board, sgn, 15x8", WAD 11/30/89 ... 225
Street in Sienna, Italy; oil on board, sgn, 9x12", WAD 11/30/89 ... 325

DINGLE, Thomas (British, 19th C)
Landscape with Shepherd & His Flock, oil on canvas laid down, sgn, 24x36", B/B 5/17/89 ... 1,430

DINNERSTEIN, Harvey
Hudson River View, oil on board, 8x10", C-NY 6/17/89 ... 605

DIRANIAN, Serkis (Turkish, 19th/20th C)
Rocky Landscape with a Town Beyond, oil on canvas, sgn, 13x18", C-E 10/26/89 ... 2,090
Seated Lady at Tea Time, oil on canvas, sgn, 18x13", SBY 7/12/89 OE ... 5,500
White Boa (lady wearing boa in front of mirror in an interior), oil on cradled panel, 26x19", SBY 12/9/88 ... 6,875

DIRK, Nathaniel (American, 1895-1961)
Landscape with Distant Village, watercolor on paper, sgn, 14x20", SBY 4/14/89 ... 550
Marine Fiesta, watercolor on paper, sgn/inscr/titled, 17x23", SBY 6/24/88 OE ... 1,650

DISCART, Jean (French, 19th C)
In the Harem, oil on canvas, sgn/inscr Tanger, 45x24", SBY 10/24/89 ... 18,700

DISLER, Martin (20th C)
Untitled (abstract), acrylic on paper, sgn/dtd 82, 60x120", SBY 10/8/88 OE ... 6,325

DISNEY, Walt; studio of (American, 20th C)
Goofy As a Knight on Horseback, black/colored chalk on tan paper, 1946, 6x8", RWS 9/29/88 ... 225

DITTMANN, Edmund (German, 1873-)
Children Caught Poaching a Rabbit, oil on board, sgn, 8x12", WG 4/23/88 UE ... 2,000
Harbor Scene, oil on canvas, sgn, 16x24", SBY 6/8/88 ... 3,300

DIVITY, Alberto (Italian, 20th C)
Paris Street Scene, oil on canvas, sgn, 24x36", DM 5/13/88 ... 350

DIX, Harry
Brooklyn View, oil on canvas, sgn, 11x17", C-E 4/11/88 UE ... 308

DIX, Otto (German, 1891-1969)
Frauenkopf (head of woman), watercolor/ink/wash/pencil on thin stiff card, sgn/dtd 1922/#d 147, 13x11", SBY 5/10/89 OE ... 74,250
Madame (caricature portrait), gouache/watercolor/silver paint/pencil, sgn/dtd/#d 24/327, 16x12", SBY 10/6/89 OE ... 23,100
Mord (figure of dead woman), watercolor/brush/ink over pencil, sgn/dtd 1922/#d DIX 22-153, 19x14", C-NY 5/12/88 OE ... 85,800
Vergewaltigung (woman being attacked), gouache/watercolor/brush/black ink over pencil, sgn/dtd 27, 22x15", C-NY 5/12/88 ... 79,200

IXON, Charles (British, 1872-1934)
Swansea Sands, South Wales; watercolor heightened w/gouache on paper, sgn/dtd 1890, 8x31", SBY 6/8/88 UE 770
IXON, Francis Stillwell (American, 1879-1967)
Manchester, Vermont (stream running through snowy hills); oil on panel, sgn, 9x10", RWS 9/29/88 OE 900
New England Evening, Arlington, Vermont; oil on canvas, sgn, 12x16", RWS 11/10/89 650
IXON, G. (American, 19th/20th C)
Clipper Ship at Full Sail, oil on canvas, sgn, 28x41", SBY 3/17/88 660
IXON, M.R. (American, 19th C)
Two Girls Reading (interior scene), oil on canvas, sgn, 24x18", SBY 1/24/89 2,200
IXON, Maynard (American, 1875-1946)
Adobe Ranch House, oil on canvas laid down, initialed/dtd July 07, 13x10", B/B 6/9/88 7,700
Arizona Ranch, oil on canvas laid down, sgn/dtd Dec 1940, 12x16", B/B 10/6/88 OE 13,200
Cattle Drive, pastel on linen over board, sgn/dtd 1939, 50x36", B/B 6/9/88 17,600
Chaparrel & Mountains, pencil on paper, initialed/dtd July 1900, 9x12", B/B 10/6/88 1,100
Figures in a Surry, pen/ink w/highlights on paper, sgn/dtd March 95, 10x13", B/B 10/6/88 2,200
Heading for the Pueblo, watercolor/pencil on paper, sgn, 13x14", SBY 6/24/88 6,050
Herring Hotel, Texas; watercolor/pencil on stationery, initialed, 8x5", WG 9/16/88 800
Indian on Horseback, pen/ink on paper, initialed/inscr/dtd 1931, 23x12", SBY 9/23/88 OE 2,530
Kiva Poles, oil on canvas, sgn, 25x30", B/B 6/15/89 33,000
Moonlight on Mojave, oil on canvasboard, sgn/dtd 1928, 16x20", B/B 10/9/88 9,900
Peace Talk, gouache/charcoal on board, sgn/dtd 1935, 10x20", SBY 9/23/88 4,950
Pistola Stood Above Her, Laughing Up at the Sun, Sole Witness of His Triumph; gouache, sgn, 22x15", B/B 10/6/88 8,800
Riders with Wagon & Oxen, gouache/pencil on paper, sgn/dtd 1930, 19x17", SBY 9/23/88 6,600
Rolling Hills, oil on canvas, sgn/dtd 1921, 12x18", B/B 10/9/88 8,800
Romance, mixed media on paper, initialed/dtd 41, 9x7", B/B 10/6/88 880
Shaver, California; charcoal heightened w/white on paper, initialed/dtd July 1906, 9x11", B/B 10/6/88 2,475
Showing Concern (two men in landscape), gouache/pen/ink on paper, sgn, 15x14", B/B 5/17/89 1,210
Still Life of Green Jug, watercolor on paper, monogramed/dtd October 23-99, 12x9", B/B 10/6/88 1,650
Tempe, Arizona; pencil on paper, sgn/dtd Sept 1900, 9x11", B/B 10/6/88 4,125
The Black Bucker, pencil on paper, initialed/dtd 1942, 4x4", B/B 12/8/88 935
The Navajo, oil on canvas laid down, sgn/dtd 1918, 42x63", B/B 6/9/88 192,500
Walls of Monument Valley, oil on canvasboard, sgn/dtd August 1922, 16x20", B/B 10/6/88 OE 24,750
Wild Horses of Nevada, graphite on paper, initialed/sgn/dtd 1927, 7x11", B/B 1/11/89 1,100
Wild Horses on the Plain, pencil on paper, initialed/dtd 1927, 7x11", B/B 10/6/88 3,025
IZIANI, Antonio (1737-1797)
Wooded Landscape with Figures & Animals by a Lake, oil on canvas, 28x36", SBY 6/3/88 19,800
IZIANI, Gaspare (Italian, 1689-1767)
Adoration of the Shepherds, oil on canvas, 21x12", C-NY 1/15/88 OE 33,000
Martyrdom of Saint Stephen, oil on canvas, 26x17", SBY 10/21/88 OE 24,200
Moses & the Daughters of Jethro, pen/brown ink/wash over red chalk, 6x12", SBY 1/13/89 OE 10,450
IZIANI, Gaspare; circle of (Italian, 1689-1767)
Maid Attending Two Men & a Soldier in a Tavern, oil on canvas, 38x52", C-NY 10/20/88 OE 24,200
River Landscape with Figures Pulling a Barge & Others Conversing on the Bank, oil on canvas, 21x41", SBY 12/9/88 OE 2,200
O, Giovanni
Adoration of the Shepherds, oil on canvas, 56x65", SBY 10/21/88 OE 35,200
O, Giovanni; follower of
Adoration of the Shepherds, oil on canvas, 24x32", SBY 7/12/89 OE 3,575
OBSON, William (British, 1610-1646)
Sunset Mountain, oil on canvas, sgn, 21x28", C-E 4/7/88 660
OBSON, William Charles Thomas (British, 1817-1898)
Young Girl, standing, nude, holding a jug; black chalk, sgn/dtd 1882/indistinctly inscr, 29x20", C-NY 5/25/88 OE 4,400
OBUJINSKY, Mstislav (American/Russian, 20th C)
Anne of England, Kennsington Palace; gouache on board, sgn/dtd 1941, 12x17", C-E 11/17/88 880
Chapel in Vilna, gouache/pen/black ink on gray paper laid down on board, sgn/dtd 1907, 12x9", C-NY 2/13/89 660
ODD, Louis (British, 19th C)
Boston Harbor, 1779; oil on panel, sgn, 19x32", C-NY 3/11/88 7,700
ODD, Robert (British, 1748-1846)
Ships at Sea, oil on canvas, 28x45", FAP 4/15/89 UE 3,080
ODGE, John Wood (American, 1807-1893)
Listening to the Fairies, watercolor on paper, sgn, 18x13", FAP 11/4/88 150
Revenge of the Flowers, watercolor on paper, sgn, 14x20", FAP 11/4/88 290
ODGE, William Deleftwich (American, 1867-1935)
Blowing the Horn, watercolor/gouache on paper laid down on board, sgn, 36x24", C-E 11/30/88 1,045
Givette in Giverny (figure in landscape), oil on board, sgn, 40x25", SBY 5/24/89 8,250
Guinevere, gouache on silk, sgn, 33x27", C-E 11/30/88 OE 4,180
OESJAN, Adriaan
Trompe l'Oeil of Printed Sheets, Playing Cards...; pen/ink/watercolor/gum arabic, sgn/dtd 1767, 16x13", C-NY 1/11/89 OE 4,400
OHANOS, Steven (American, 1907-)
Avocados, gouache/watercolor/pencil on paper, sgn/inscr/dtd 1936, 10x14", C-E 6/1/88 990
OIKER, E. (Continental, 19th C)
Still Life of Grapes & Butterfly, gouache on paper, sgn, 9x13", RAB 8/9/88 400

DOILLON, Maydeleine (French, 20th C)
Still Life of Bottle & Onions, oil on canvas, sgn/dtd 1907, 24x29", FAP 4/15/89 UE **385**
DOKOUPIL, Jiri Georg (Czechoslovakian/German, 1954-)
Anfang, acrylic on canvas, initialed/dtd 83/titled, 27x24", C-NY 11/10/88 .... **2,640**
Mountain Climber & the Mountain (abstract), acrylic on canvas, sgn/dtd 1983 Koln, 39x39", C-NY 5/4/89 OE **7,700**
Untitled (abstract composition), oil on canvas, sgn/dtd 1983, 60x60", SBY 10/5/89 .... **5,775**
DOLAN, G.H.
Gossiping, oil on canvasboard, sgn, 18x14", C-E 9/15/88 UE **220**
DOLCI, Carlo (Italian, 1616-1686)
Adoration of the Magi, oil on canvas, sgn/dtd 1649, 46x36", SBY 6/2/89 OE **176,000**
Flight into Egypt, oil on canvas, 13x21", SBY 6/3/88 .... **18,700**
Saint Joseph & the Infant Jesus (in a landscape), oil on canvas, 58x47", SBY 6/1/89 OE **121,000**
DOLCI, Carlo; after (Italian, 1616-1686)
Martydom of Saint Andrew, oil on canvas, 49x39", SBY 10/13/89 .... **4,950**
DOLCI, Carlo; circle of (Italian, 1616-1686)
Portrait of a Lady, bust-length, viewed from behind...; black/white chalk on gray paper, 16x12", C-NY 1/12/88 .... **880**
Saint Carlo Borromeo, oil on canvas, 16x13", C-NY 10/12/89 .... **6,600**
Saint Elizabeth of Hungary, oil on canvas, 28x23", C-NY 10/12/89 .... **9,350**
DOLCI, Carlo; follower of (Italian, 1616-1686)
Head of an Angel, oil on canvas, in painted oval, unfr, 26x20", SBY 7/12/89 .... **1,100**
DOLCI, Carlo; school of (Italian, 1616-1686)
Portrait of the Poet Tasso, oil on canvas, 14x18", C-NY 10/12/89 .... **7,700**
DOLE, William (American, 1917-)
Second Ceremonial, collage on paper, sgn/dtd 1978, 12x23", SBY 10/5/88 OE **1,760**
South of Garden Grove, collage, sgn/dtd 1976, 17x26", SBY 10/5/88 .... **1,650**
DOLL, Anton (German, 1826-1877)
Figures in a Frozen Winter Landscape, oil on canvas, sgn/inscr, 12x22", C-NY 5/24/89 .... **14,300**
Skaters & Washerwomen in a Frozen Landscape, oil on canvas, sgn/inscr, 12x22", C-NY 5/24/89 .... **17,500**
DOLLMAN, John Charles (British, 1851-1934)
Enchantress (woman with leopards in a landscape), oil on canvas, sgn/dtd 1922, 44x72", SBY 6/1/89 OE **40,700**
Temptation of Saint Anthony, oil on canvas, sgn/dtd 1897, 44x69", SBY 2/22/89 .... **14,300**
DOLPH, John Henry (American, 1835-1903)
Cat & Kittens, oil on canvas, sgn, 14x20", LH 12/4/88 OE **4,400**
Forgotten Cigar (three kittens watching cigar), oil on canvas laid down on board, sgn, 10x13", C-E 2/1/89 OE **2,200**
Outskirts of the Village (mountainous landscape w/cows watering), oil on canvas, sgn/dtd 9-65, 20x30", C-NY 5/25/89 .... **9,350**
Pair: Family of Chickens; Family of Ducks; oil on canvas, sgn/inscr, 7x10", SBY 6/24/88 .... **6,600**
Playful Kittens in a Cradle, oil on canvas, sgn, 20x24", SBY 9/14/89 .... **6,875**
Puppies in a Basket, oil on canvas, 18x22", C-E 2/3/88 .... **2,860**
Rooster in a Barnyard (w/chickens), oil on canvas, sgn/dtd 1871, 12x16", SBY 3/17/88 OE **3,850**
DOMELA, Cesar (Dutch, 1900-)
Composition (abstract), gouache over pencil on board, sgn twice/dtd 1956, 29x17", C-NY 5/12/88 .... **7,700**
DOMENICHINO, school of (Italian, 17th C)
Susannah & the Elders, oil on canvas, unfr, 39x30", C-NY 4/8/88 .... **2,200**
DOMERGUE, Jean Gabriel (French, 1889-1962)
Portrait of Jeune Fille Nue (half-length nude), oil on masonite, sgn, 13x9", C-E 11/17/88 OE **4,620**
DOMINGO, Roberto (Spanish, 1867-)
Bullfight, charcoal/watercolor on paper, sgn, 10x19", C-E 10/25/88 .... **880**
Group of 5: Bullfights; 4 ink/pencil on paper, 1 pencil/watercolor on paper, sgn, from 6x9" to 9x13", SBY 5/17/88 .... **3,850**
DOMINGO Y MARQUES, Francisco (Spanish, 1842-1920)
Figures in a Wooded Landscape, oil on canvas, sgn, unfr, 9x15", B/B 3/17/88 .... **6,600**
Musketeer with Violin, oil on canvas laid down on cradled panel, sgn/dtd 93, 24x18", SBY 12/9/88 OE **8,800**
DOMINICI, see De Dominici
DOMINIQUE, John Augustus (American, 1893-)
California Landscape, oil on canvas, sgn, 22x30", B/B 1/11/89 .... **880**
Landscape Near Ojai, oil on board, indistinctly sgn/dtd, 12x16", B/B 9/15/88 .... **495**
Southern California Stream, oil on canvas, sgn/dtd 64, 13x18", B/B 9/15/88 .... **495**
DOMINQUEZ, Oscar (Spanish, 1906-1958)
Untitled (globe & other objects), oil on canvas, sgn/dtd 43, 25x20", SBY 2/18/88 .... **44,000**
DOMMERSEN, Cornelis Christian (Dutch, 1842-1928)
Montelbaans Tower, Amsterdam; oil on canvas, sgn/dtd 1902, 15x12", SBY 6/8/88 .... **3,850**
DOMMERSEN, Pieter Christian (Dutch, 1834-1908)
Skating on a Frozen River, oil on canvas, sgn/dtd 1874, 21x17", FB 5/28/89 OE **7,500**
Unloading Cargo in Heavy Seas, oil on canvas laid down, sgn, 20x30", B/B 5/17/89 .... **2,200**
DOMMERSEN, William (Dutch, -1927)
Game of Skittel in Holland, oil on canvas, sgn/dtd 81, initialed/inscr/dtd 81, 11x15", C-E 2/23/88 .... **2,530**
Pair: Fisherfolk on the Shore; oil on panel, sgn, 8x10", B/B 3/22/89 .... **1,650**
Pair: Modena, Italy; A View of Perugia; oil on canvas, sgn/inscr, 16x24", C-E 5/23/88 .... **3,300**
DOMOTO, Hisao (20th C)
Opening Night (abstract), oil on canvas, 1958, 23x32", SBY 10/7/89 .... **6,600**
DONA, Lydia (20th C)
Can I Live (abstract composition), oil/acrylic on canvas, sgn/dtd 1985, unfr, 90x72", C-E 11/14/89 UE **1,100**

Deceptive Speeds (abstract composition), oil on canvas, sgn/dtd 1986, unfr, 112x108", C-E 11/14/89 UE	550
I Am Shifting Ground on the Margins of Understandings (abstract), oil/acrylic on canvas, 1985, 90x72", C-NY 5/4/89 OE	7,700
ONADONI, Stephano (Italian, 1841-1911)	
Arc de Triomphe, watercolor on paper, sgn, 10x15", B/B 9/15/88	770
Roman Ruins, watercolor on paper, sgn, 11x15", C-E 10/25/88 OE	990
View of Italian Ruins, watercolor on paper, sgn, 13x20", FAP 11/4/88 UE	150
ONAHUE, Vic (American, 20th C)	
Cooling Hooves From a Night in Town, oil on canvas, sgn/titled, 24x30", SBY 6/28/89 UE	330
Settlement Ahead, oil on canvas, sgn, 12x18", SBY 9/14/89	935
ONATI, Enrico (American, 1909-)	
Arabian Knight (abstract), oil/sand on canvas, sgn twice/dtd 1957/titled, 50x50", SBY 2/19/88	8,800
Black Line Cut, oil/sand on canvas, sgn/dtd 1953, 16x12", SBY 10/7/89	3,850
Curtain Call II (abstract), oil/sand on canvas, sgn/dtd 1971, 43x39", C-NY 2/14/89	5,500
Curtain Call VII (abstract), oil/sand on canvas, sgn/dtd 1971, 45x39", SBY 10/5/89	7,150
Mystere I (abstract), oil/sand on canvas, sgn, 50x50", SBY 10/8/88	9,350
Mystere III, oil/sand on canvas, sgn/dtd 1966, 30x34", SBY 10/7/89	6,600
Reincarnation (abstract composition), oil/sand on canvas, sgn/dtd 1971, 50x40", SBY 2/15/89	4,125
SPQR, oil/sand on canvas, sgn/dtd 1963, 40x43", SBY 10/7/89	6,600
ONATI, Lazzaro (Italian, 1926-)	
Fecundita, oil on panel, sgn, 34x43", LH 9/10/89	1,300
Figura con Cavalli, oil on panel, sgn/dtd 66, 14x16", B/B 1/11/89	715
Pair: Female Nudes; brush/black ink on printed page, sgn/dtd 54, sgn, 14x10", C-NY 2/13/89	440
ONCKER, Herman Mijnerts (Dutch, 1620-1660)	
Family Geneology Seated in an Amphitheater, in a Landscape; oil on canvas, sgn w/monogram, C-NY 4/8/88	7,700
ONDUCCI, Giovanni Andrea (Italian, 1575-1655)	
Saint Elizabeth Visiting the Virgin, oil on canvas, 32x27", SBY 10/13/89	5,500
ONDUCCI, school of (Italian, 16th/17th C)	
Adoration of the Golden Calf, oil on canvas, unfr, 26x38", C-E 1/12/88 OE	495
ONNATO, H.	
Parade, oil on canvas, sgn, 13x18", C-NY 5/25/88	4,400
ONNELL, James M. (Canadian, 19th C)	
Pair: Town in Winter; The Log Sleigh; pencil/watercolor, sgn/dtd 51, 14x18", C-SK 11/10/88	520
ONOGHUE, Lyn (Canadian, 1953-)	
Study for a Portrait of Paul Hutner (sketch), charcoal, sgn, 29x23", WAD 6/12/89	200
ONOHO, Gaines Ruger (American, 1857-1916)	
Bridge of Sighs, Late Evening; oil on canvas, sgn, unfr, 23x35", NA 2/6/88 UE	275
Lilly Hill, Autumn Sundown; oil on canvas, sgn, unfr, 21x44", NA 2/6/88	425
Storm Over Valley of Loing, oil on canvas, sgn/dtd 1903, 45x68", C-NY 3/11/88	15,400
ONOUY, Alexandre Hyacinthe (1757-1841)	
Italianate Landscape with Figure & Animals & in the Distance...; oil on canvas, sgn/dtd 1790, 31x44", SBY 1/12/89 OE	20,900
OORN, Jeane (Dutch, 20th C)	
Untitled, children playing in the ocean; oil on panel, sgn, 10x12", SLK 4/7/89	950
ORAZIO, Piero (Italian, 1927-)	
Emesa VII, acrylic on linen, sgn/dtd 1976/titled, unfr, 20x47", C-NY 11/10/88 OE	9,900
Untitled, watercolor on paper, sgn/dtd 1964, 13x10", C-NY 2/13/89	880
ORCY, Albert (French, 19th C)	
Young Nymph (portrait), oil on panel, sgn, 7x5", C-E 2/21/89 UE	220
ORE, Gustave (French, 1832-1883)	
Andromeda, oil on canvas, sgn/dtd 1869, 101x68", SBY 2/22/89 OE	577,500
Crowd in a Vaulted Interior, pencil, stamped Atelier G Dore, 17x13", C-NY 2/25/88	1,045
Ecce Homo!, oil on canvas, sgn/dtd 1877, 230x139", SBY 2/22/89	77,000
Les Vagabonds (poor family w/dog standing by wall), oil on canvas, sgn, 78x38", SBY 10/24/89	88,000
Moses in the Bullrushes, oil on canvas, sgn, 36x51", SBY 5/23/89	55,000
Paolo & Francesca da Rimini, oil on canvas, sgn, 1863, 111x77", SBY 2/22/89 OE	605,000
Two Figures by a Woodland Stream, watercolor on paper, sgn/dtd 1876, 18x12", SBY 7/12/89	1,760
ORIAN, E.	
Still Life of Flowers & a Bowl, oil on board, sgn, 11x7", WG 9/16/88	225
ORN, Vincent (American, 20th C)	
Twilight From the Beach, oil on canvas laid down on board, sgn, 8x10", FAP 12/8/89 UE	100
OU, Gerrit (Gerard)(Dutch, 1613-1675)	
Rest on the Flight into Egypt, oil on panel, 30x25", SBY 1/12/89	330,000
OU, Gerrit (Gerard); manner of (Dutch, 1613-1675)	
Pair: Dentist & the Scribe; oil on panel, 10x8", SBY 6/8/88	1,100
OU, Gerrit (Gerard); style of (Dutch, 1613-1675)	
Reading by Candlelight, oil on canvas, 19x14", B/B 9/15/89	550
OUGHERTY, James Henry (American, 1889-1974)	
Enclosure, charcoal/pastel, initialed/dtd Jan 31, 66, 8x9", PHL 6/16/88	400
OUGHERTY, Parke Curtis (American, 1867-)	
Road in Twilight (landscape), oil on panel, sgn, 14x18", RWS 3/16/89 UE	350
OUGHERTY, Paul (American, 1877-1947)	
California Coast, oil on canvas, sgn, 20x30", SBY 3/17/88	2,420

Harbor Scene, oil on board, sgn/indistinctly dtd, 13x16", SBY 1/24/89 OE ... 1,540
Summer Landscape, oil on canvas, sgn/dtd 1900, 12x16", B/B 10/6/88 ... 825
Waves Breaking on a Rocky Shore, oil on panel, sgn, 15x18", B/B 3/22/89 ... 3,300

DOUGHTY, Thomas (American, 1763-1856)
Landscape with Footbridge & Figures, oil on canvas, sgn/dtd 1835, 27x35", C-NY 5/25/89 ... 28,600

DOUGLAS, Edward Algernon; att (British, 19th C)
Hunting Scene with Riders & Dogs, oil on panel, 12x10", RWS 12/10/88 ... 1,300

DOUGLAS, Edwin (British, 1848-1914)
Brothers of the Brush (portrait of two terriers), oil on canvas, sgn/dtd 1906, 27x23", SBY 6/9/89 ... 27,500

DOUGLAS, James (Scottish, 19th C)
Princess Street Gardens (city park), watercolor, sgn, 12x18", C-NY 2/23/89 ... 1,320

DOUGLAS, Walter (American, 1868-)
Feeding Roosters, oil on canvas, sgn, unfr, 16x16", C-E 2/1/89 ... 990
Feeding Roosters, oil on panel, sgn, 5x7", C-E 11/30/88 ... 825

DOUGLAS, William Fettes (British, 1822-1891)
Outside Church, oil on canvas, sgn, 26x36", SBY 6/8/88 UE ... 1,980

DOVASTON, Margaret (British, 20th C)
Old Campaigners, oil on canvas, sgn, 18x24", WAD 6/6/88 ... 6,000

DOVE, Arthur Garfield (American, 1880-1946)
Breezy Day (abstract), watercolor/black crayon on paper, 1931, 5x7", SBY 9/23/88 ... 6,600
Derrick, watercolor/pencil on paper laid down on board, sgn, 1933, 3x5", C-NY 9/28/89 ... 4,950
Italian Child Combing Her Hair, watercolor/pencil on paper laid down on board, sgn, 1933, 5x7", C-NY 9/28/89 ... 4,400
Poison, charcoal/watercolor/gouache/pencil on board, sgn/inscr, 27x20", C-E 11/30/88 UE ... 770
Runway, oil on canvas, sgn, 18x24", SBY 5/25/88 ... 34,100
Untitled, pastel on paper, sgn, 5x8", B/B 3/17/88 ... 9,350

DOVMAND, Christine (Danish, 1803-1872)
Still Life with Potted Flowers, oil on canvas, sgn/dtd 1870, 17x15", SBY 2/22/89 ... 9,900

DOW, Arthur Wesley (American, 1857-1922)
Autumn Sketch (atmospheric landscape w/river beyond), oil on canvas, ca 1907, 14x27", RWS 3/31/88 ... 3,400
Sunset (contemporary), oil on canvas, sgn, 14x20", RWS 3/16/89 ... 2,700

DOWALSKOFF, J.A. (Russian, 19th C)
Green Parlor, pencil/watercolor/gouache on paper, sgn w/cyrillic, dtd 1856, 8x12", SBY 2/22/89 ... 11,000

DOWNES, Rackstraw (20th C)
Portland From Back Cove (landscape), graphite on buff paper mounted on paperboard, sgn/dtd 83, 19x46", C-NY 5/4/89 ... 4,180
Searsport Docks with the Unloading of the SS Unger, oil on canvas, initialed, 1980, 15x53", SBY 2/15/89 ... 25,300

DOWNING, Thomas (American, 1928-)
Phased Red (five circles in a line on plain background), no media given, 1965, 77x77", C-E 11/17/88 ... 880
Untitled (geometric composition w/circles), acrylic on canvas, 72x72", C-E 11/17/88 ... 880

DOYEN, Gustave (French, 1837-)
Gathering Wildflowers, oil on canvas, sgn, 39x26", SBY 6/8/88 UE ... 3,300

DRAKE, Peter (20th C)
O For M (contemporary allegory), oil on canvas, 1985, 74x48", C-NY 5/4/89 ... 3,300

DRAKE, William H. (American, 1856-)
Confederate Headquarters of the 52nd Illinois, Corinth, Mississippi; pen/ink, sgn/inscr, 14x18", C-E 5/27/88 ... 550

DRATZ-BARAT, Charles (French, 20th C)
Sunlit Landscape with Flowers Blooming Beside a Path Which Runs Along a River, oil on canvas, sgn, 18x24", SLK 5/11/88 ... 1,600

DREHER, N.
Family Portrait, sgn/dtd 1889, 47x59", C-E 2/23/88 OE ... 5,500

DREIER, Katherine S. (American, 1877-1952)
Joy & Sorrow (abstract), oil on canvas, sgn/dtd 1936, 34x24", C-NY 9/30/88 ... 3,850
Mercedes; or, The Chinese Cloak; oil on canvas, sgn twice/titled, no size given, SBY 3/17/88 OE ... 6,600

DREVIN, Alexander (Russian, 1889-1938)
Flood (landscape), oil on canvas, ca 1928, 27x32", SBY 7/7/88 OE ... 40,000
Garage in the Steppe (contemporary landscape w/building & man on tractor), oil on canvas, ca 1932, 26x35", SBY 7/7/88 OE ... 60,000

DREW, Clement (American, 1806-1889)
Commencement of the Yacht Race Off Marblehead, June 29th, 1886...; oil on canvas, sgn/titled, 14x24", RAB 11/10/88 UE ... 7,600
View Near Bass Rock House Cape Ann, oil on wood panel backed w/paper, sgn/dtd 1880, 4x6", RAB 3/14/89 ... 950

DREW, Clement; att (American, 1806-1889)
Sailing Vessels Outside Boston Harbor, oil on canvas, 20x30", RWS 10/27/89 ... 5,500

DREW, Elbert G. (American, 19th/20th C)
Old Cottage (in green landscape), oil on canvas, sgn, 14x17", RAB 8/9/88 UE ... 150

DREW, George W. (American, 1875-1968)
Cherry Blossom, Connecticut; oil on canvas, sgn, 24x36", B/B 6/15/89 ... 3,025
Cottage by a Pond, oil on canvas, sgn, 20x30", C-E 2/3/88 ... 990
Cottage on a Pond, oil on canvas, sgn, 24x36", C-E 10/18/89 ... 1,870
Day of Pleasure (man fishing from boat, a cottage beyond), oil on canvas, sgn, 20x30", B/B 3/22/89 ... 1,980
House by a Pond, oil on canvas, sgn, 21x31", C-E 2/3/88 UE ... 1,540
Landscape Scene with House, oil on board, sgn, 6x10", RWS 11/3/88 ... 500
New England River Scene, oil on canvas, sgn, 5x8", LH 3/20/88 ... 475
Old Home, Connecticut (sunny view of house at water's edge, ducks); oil on canvas, sgn, 20x30", RWS 3/31/88 ... 1,000
Old New England House, oil on canvas, sgn, 24x36", C-E 11/30/88 ... 2,640

Pair: Cottages by a Stream; oil on canvasboard, sgn, 12x16", C-E 6/1/88 ... 1,045
Pair: Landscape & Seascape; oil on canvas, sgn, 9x13", 12x9", C-E 6/1/88 UE ... 660
Pair: Turn in the Road; Boy Fishing; oil on canvas laid down/oil on canvasboard, sgn, 10x14", C-E 6/1/88 ... 1,980
Red Oak, oil on canvas, sgn, 19x13", NA 10/1/88 ... 1,050
Windy Day, oil on canvas, sgn, 19x13", NA 10/1/88 ... 1,050

DREWES, Werner (American, 1899-)
Abstraction, oil on unstretched canvas, sgn w/artist's device/dtd 43, 6x10", C-E 6/1/89 OE ... 4,950
Boat in Moonlight (contemporary depiction), oil on board, sgn/dtd 31, 16x18", C-E 6/1/89 ... 4,180
Forest Clearing, oil on canvas, sgn/dtd 509, #d 826 on reverse, 30x38", C-E 6/1/88 ... 3,080
It Can't Happen Here, watercolor/pen/black ink on paper, sgn, unfr, 9x12", C-NY 3/11/88 ... 1,210
Meteors, oil on canvas, sgn/dtd 7-2, 32x42", C-E 6/1/88 ... 3,080

DREYFUS, Bernardo (Nicaraguan, 1940-)
La Fete (contemporary), acrylic on canvas, sgn twice/dtd 1985/titled, 32x39", C-NY 11/21/88 ... 4,400

DRISCOLL, Robert E. (American, 20th C)
Shield's Corner, Osterville, Massachusetts (house in winter); watercolor on paper, sgn/dtd 1967, 14x21", RAB 8/9/88 UE ... 200

DROLLING, Martin (French, 1752-1817)
Beggarwoman & Her Child Approaching a Lady at a Well Outside a Cottage, oil on panel, sgn/dtd 1796, 6x9", C-NY 5/31/89 ... 13,200
Kitchen Interior with Mother & Daughter Sewing & Another Child Playing with Kitten, oil on canvas, 24x31", SBY 10/21/88 ... 12,100
Landscape with Travelers on a Country Road Beside a Walled Garden, oil on canvas, sgn/dtd 1816, 15x20", SBY 10/13/89 OE ... 46,750

DROLLING, Martin; att (French, 1752-1817)
Astronomer in His Study, oil on paper mounted on canvas, 8x6", RWS 5/12/89 UE ... 200

DROLLING, Martin; circle of (French, 1752-1817)
Peasants & Rustic House by a Stream, oil on panel, 8x10", SBY 7/12/89 ... 1,760

DROMMETER, Magda (Russian, 1880-1945)
Portrait of Ol'ga Afanas'evna Glebova-Sudeikina, oil on panel, sgn/dtd 1923, 27x28", C-L 10/8/88 ... 4,460

DROOCHSLOOT, Joost Cornelisz (Dutch, 1586-1666)
Gathering of Peasants Eating & Drinking Beside Buildings, oil on canvas, 35x41", SBY 4/7/88 ... 13,200
Town Square with Figures, oil on panel, sgn in monogram, 19x25", SBY 10/21/88 ... 9,900

DROOCHSLOOT, Joost Cornelisz; att (Dutch, 1586-1666)
Family Members Seated in an Amphitheater, oil on canvas, 25x40", NA 2/6/88 ... 2,100

DROUAIS, Francois Hubert; att (French, 1727-1775)
Portrait of a Boy Wearing a Three-Corner Hat, oil on canvas, sgn/dtd 1756, 18x15", SBY 4/7/88 OE ... 23,100
Portrait of a Lady with Fan (half-length, seated, in blue ruffled dress), oil on canvas, 40x29", RAB 8/8/89 UE ... 1,800

DROUAIS, Francois Hubert; follower of (French, 1727-1775)
Portrait of a lady (three-quarter length), oil on canvas, 36x28", SBY 4/7/89 ... 2,750

DROUAIS, Francois Hubert; school of (French, 1727-1775)
Portrait of a Young Girl, in pink & blue dress, holding a dog & ring; pastel, 21x18", C-NY 1/12/88 OE ... 2,640
Russian Nobleman, oil on canvas, bears signature/dtd, 40x32", C-E 4/7/88 OE ... 2,860

DROUAIS, Francois Hubert; studio of (French, 1727-1775)
Portrait of a Lady Dressed as a Pilgrim, oil on canvas, 32x25", SBY 10/21/88 ... 9,350

DROUIN, J.; & Petit E. (French, 19th C)
Three Masted Ships on High Seas, oil on canvas, sgn/dtd 1875, 21x29", C-E 10/25/88 ... 2,640

DRUMMOND, J. (British, 19th C)
Little Girl Reading, oil on canvas, sgn, unfr, 24x20", C-E 9/15/88 ... 660

DRYSDALE, Alexander John (American, 1870-1934)
Bayou Oak, oil on academy board, sgn/dtd 1912, 18x24", NA 3/26/88 ... 1,000
Bayou Scene, oil on board, sgn/dtd 1909, 12x18", MG 5/28/88 ... 1,400
Bayou Scene, watercolor, sgn/dtd 1932, 20x20", MG 3/26/88 ... 500
Bayou St John, Moonlit Bridge; oil on academy board, sgn/dtd 1911, 18x24", NA 2/6/88 ... 4,200
City Park, New Orleans; watercolor, sgn, no size given, MG 1/14/89 ... 700
Hut in the Marsh, watercolor on paper, sgn/dtd 1915, 19x29", SBY 9/23/88 ... 1,430
Impressionistic Bayou Scene, oil on canvas, sgn/dtd 1909, 10x17", MG 12/10/88 ... 1,000
Impressionistic Bayou Scene, watercolor, sgn, 16x20", MG 10/28/88 ... 550
Impressionistic Bayou Scene, watercolor, sgn, 16x42", MG 11/19/88 ... 1,100
Live Oak, oil on canvas, sgn, 10x14", NA 10/1/88 ... 650
Live Oak, watercolor on paper, sgn/dtd 1915, 19x29", SBY 9/23/88 ... 1,320
Live Oak by the Bayou, watercolor, sgn/dtd 1933, 15x20", NA 2/6/88 ... 1,100
Live Oaks, oil wash, sgn, 6x20", NA 3/26/88 ... 850
Live Oaks on Bayou, oil wash, sgn, 15x40", NA 10/1/88 ... 450
Louisiana Bayou, oil wash, 20x30", NA 3/26/88 ... 1,450
Louisiana Live Oak, oil wash, sgn, 20x30", NA 2/24/89 ... 650
Louisiana Live Oak, oil wash, 10x30", NA 2/24/89 ... 850
Louisiana Live Oak (landscape with stream), oil wash, dtd 1923, 25x30", NA 5/13/89 ... 1,600
Louisiana Marsh, watercolor, sgn/dtd 1916, 10x29", NA 2/6/88 ... 1,700
Lovers, Suicide & Dueling Oak; oil wash, sgn/dtd 1922, 20x29", NA 10/1/88 ... 950
Mist on the Bayou, oil wash, sgn, 6x20", NA 10/1/88 ... 425
Moss Laden Oaks, oil on academy board, sgn/dtd 1911, 12x18", NA 3/26/88 ... 2,300
Moss Trees, New Orleans; oil on canvas, sgn/dtd 1912, 18x24", MG 1/14/89 ... 900
North Louisiana Landscape, oil on canvas, sgn/dtd, 15x19", NA 11/5/88 ... 1,200
Pair: Bayou Scenes; watercolor, sgn/dtd 1921, 14x28", MG 12/10/88 ... 1,800
Skiff Docked in the Reeds, oil on canvas, sgn/dtd 1910, 24x28", NA 10/1/88 ... 2,700

Sunset on the Bayou, oil wash, sgn, 10x30", NA 10/1/88 UE ... 225
Willow Tree in Bayou Mist, watercolor on paper, sgn/dtd 1914, 15x19", RWS 5/12/89 ... 700

DRYSDALE (Australian, 19th/20th C)
Jacaranda Time-Pictoria; watercolor on paper, sgn, 10x7", FAP 4/15/89 UE ... 275

DU, Qian (Chinese, 1763-1844)
Pair: Landscapes (fan paintings); ink/color on paper, sgn/dtd 1842, 9x23", SBY 5/31/89 OE ... 6,050

DU DOMINICIUS, Achille (Italian, 19th C)
Gathering Wildflowers, oil on canvas, sgn, 42x31", C-E 10/26/89 ... 6,600

DU MELEZET (fl mid-17th C)
Still Life of Fraises du Bois (strawberries) in a Late Ming Blue & White Bowl, oil on panel, 14x22", SBY 6/2/89 ... 550,000

DU MONT, Franccois Sr.; att (French, 1751-1831)
Portrait of the Artist, oil on canvas, sgn, 24x19", RWS 6/17/89 ... 250

DU NOUY, Lecomte; att
Portrait of a Rabbi, no media given, bears signature, unfr, 9x5", C-E 2/16/88 ... 132

DU VAUNES, A. (American, 19th/20th C)
Forest Clearing, oil on canvas, sgn, 19x25", B/B 8/10/88 UE ... 440

DUBOIS, Gaston (Continental, 19th/20th C)
Elaborate Floral Still Life, oil on canvas, sgn, 40x28", C-E 10/26/89 ... 8,250

DUBOIS, Guy Pene (American, 1884-1958)
Abandoned, gouache on paper laid down on board, sgn/dtd 41, 11x9", C-E 11/30/88 OE ... 2,420
Circus Tent (two ladies & a gentleman seated at table outside of tent), oil on panel, sgn, 20x25", C-NY 9/28/89 OE ... 137,500
Late Hour (interior), oil on canvas, 16x20", C-NY 5/26/88 ... 14,300
Nanette in Her Sunday Clothes (portrait of seated lady), oil on canvas, sgn, 57x45", SBY 5/24/89 ... 34,100
Nude Pulling Her Hair Back, pencil on paper, sgn, 18x12", C-E 11/30/88 ... 1,045
Nude with Red Bow, oil on masonite, sgn/dtd 48, 17x12", C-E 2/1/89 ... 3,850
Portrait of a Lady, oil on canvas, sgn/dtd 41, 32x26", SBY 4/29/88 ... 15,400
Portrait of a Woman, oil on canvas, sgn/dtd 22(?), 22x18", SBY 4/14/89 ... 6,875
Three Nudes, pencil on paper, sgn, 21x15", C-NY 3/11/88 ... 1,980
Woman in a Purple Dress, oil on canvas, sgn/dtd 39, 20x16", B/B 6/15/89 UE ... 16,500

DUBOIS, Yvonne Pene (20th C)
Fifth Avenue From the Heckscher Building, oil on canvas, sgn/dtd 1945-53, 36x30", C-NY 9/30/88 ... 2,750

DUBOURG, Louis Fabricius (Dutch, 1693-1775)
Putti Blowing Bubbles, red chalk, indistinct Pro Patria (?) wm, initialed/dtd 1740, 7x5", C-NY 1/11/89 OE ... 1,320

DUBRAY, Jean Paul (French, 19th/20th C)
Man with the Golden Hair, mixed media heightened with chalk, sgn/dtd 01, 12x10", S/A 3/12/88 ... 200

DUBUFFET, Jean (French, 1901-1985)
Arabe au Baton (Arab w/staff), crayons/pencil on paper laid down on board, sgn/dtd 48, 13x9", C-NY 5/11/89 ... 18,700
Arabe et Chameau, gouache on paper laid down on board, sgn/dtd 48, 17x22", C-NY 11/15/88 OE ... 77,000
Arabe et Chameau (Arab & camel), watercolor/gouache on paper, sgn/dtd 48, 17x22", SBY 5/10/89 OE ... 88,000
Arabe et Palmiers sous le Soleil, colored crayon on paper, sgn/dtd 48, 9x13", SBY 11/12/88 ... 17,600
Arabes avec Traces de Pas, gouache/India ink on paper, sgn/dtd 48/inscr Arabes aux empreintes, 12x16", SBY 11/12/88 ... 52,250
Arbre Logologique, colored felt-tip pens on paper collage on board, initialed/dtd 71, 30x17", C-NY 11/10/88 OE ... 55,000
Bedoin et Chameau sous le Soleil, colored wax crayons on paper, sgn/dtd 48, 13x10", C-NY 5/12/88 ... 22,000
Bolero (abstract), acrylic on paper mounted on canvas, initialed/dtd 84, 39x79", SBY 11/8/89 ... 363,000
Canon I (abstract), black marker on paper, initialed/dtd 64/titled Canon, 12x8", SBY 11/11/88 ... 11,000
Chameau Couche (resting camel), colored crayon/pencil on paper laid down on board, sgn/dtd 48, 10x13", SBY 5/11/88 ... 23,100
Congres (abstract), acrylic on paper mounted on canvas, initialed/dtd 82, 27x40", SBY 10/8/88 ... 104,500
Dame au Teint Vineux (woman's head in pink w/purple background), oil on board, sgn/dtd Mai 50, 29x24", SBY 5/10/89 OE ... 495,000
Dentiste, incised India ink on gesso, sgn/dtd 47/inscr dedication, 14x13", SBY 5/11/88 OE ... 148,500
Deux Arabes, gouache on paper, sgn/dtd 48, 13x15", C-NY 11/12/88 ... 44,000
Deux Bedouins avec Chameau Entrave, peinture a la colle on paper, sgn, 1948, 16x13", SBY 11/12/88 OE ... 38,500
Deux Nomades (Two Nomads), gouache on paper, ca 1948-49, 15x21", C-NY 5/11/89 OE ... 121,000
Escalier (abstract composition), marker on paper, sgn/dtd 67, 38x14", SBY 5/3/89 ... 71,500
Escalier Coupe D'un Palier (contemporary), marker/vinyl/collage laid down on canvas, sgn/dtd 67, 62x27", SBY 11/9/89 OE ... 121,000
Escalier pour Queneau, marker/vinyl on paper, sgn/dtd 67, 19x12", SBY 10/8/88 ... 19,800
Euclid's Sand (abstract), acrylic on canvasboard, sgn/dtd twice 1975, 18x14", SBY 10/8/88 OE ... 52,250
Frise Moustache, viburnum fruit/wild convolvulus/burdock/mixed media on paper, sgn/dtd 59, 26x13", SBY 11/12/88 ... 220,000
L'Echelle III, colored felt-tip pens on paper, initialed/dtd 66/inscr, 10x7", C-NY 11/10/88 OE ... 16,500
L'Effraye (frightful figure), oil/mixed media on canvas, 36x29", SBY 5/10/89 ... 495,000
L'Homme au Papillon (Man with Butterfly), oil on canvas, sgn twice/dtd 1949, 46x35", SBY 5/9/89 ... 742,500
L'Oisif (The Isle, abstract figure on green background), oil on canvas, sgn/dtd 54, 36x29", SBY 6/30/88 ... 420,000
La Cantatrice, marker on paper, initialed/dtd 66, 10x7", SBY 11/9/89 ... 24,200
La Chaumiere (abstract), marker on paper, initialed/dtd 66, 10x6", SBY 10/5/89 ... 16,500
La Clef (abstract composition), marker on paper, initialed, dtd 66, 10x6", SBY 5/3/89 OE ... 24,200
La Scenique de l'Hourloupe III (abstract), marker/vinyl on paper, initialed/dtd 64, 26x39", SBY 5/3/88 ... 82,255
Le Chemin Sinueux (abstract), oil on canvas, sgn/dtd 57, 35x46", SBY 5/10/88 ... 440,000
Le Cruchon (abstract composition), marker on paper, initialed/dtd 66, 10x6", SBY 5/3/89 OE ... 19,800
Le Cuisinier (contemporary), felt marker on paper, initialed/dtd 66, 10x7", SBY 11/9/89 ... 19,800
Le Petit Jardinier (The Little Gardener, contemporary); oil on canvas, sgn/dtd Octobre 55, 29x36", SBY 5/2/89 OE ... 616,000
Le Soleil les Decolore (The Fading Sun), oil on canvas laid down on masonite, April 24, 1947, 51x38", C-NY 11/15/88 ... 528,000
Les Implications Quotidiennes (abstract composition), acrylic/paper collage, initialed/dtd 76, 72x65", SBY 11/8/89 OE ... 907,500

Les Versatiles (abstract composition in red, white & blue), oil on canvas, sgn/dtd 1964, 52x64", SBY 5/2/89 OE	770,000
Maast a Criniere (Portrait de Jean Paulhan), oil on canvas, Sept 1946, 43x36", SBY 6/30/88	1,121,000
Maison de Campagne, oil on canvas, sgn/dtd VIII 44, 32x22", SBY 11/15/89 OE	1,870,000
Masque Coiffe d'un Chapeau, felt-tip pen/paper collage on Kraft paper, sgn/dtd 73/titled, 10x8", C-NY 11/10/88	7,700
Massif (abstract), colored felt-tip pens/collage on brown paper, initialed/dtd 71, 11x11", C-NY 5/12/88	11,000
Memoration X (abstract), ink/collage on paper, intl/dtd 78, 20x28", SBY 11/11/88 OE	41,800
Memoration XVII (abstract), black ink/paper collage on paper, initialed/dtd 78, 20x28", SBY 10/8/88	25,300
Mire (abstract), acrylic on paper mounted on canvas, initialed, dtd 83, 27x40", SBY 5/3/89 OE	104,500

Monsieur d'Hotel, oil/sand on canvas, sgn/dtd 47, 47x35", C-NY 11/7/89 OE, $2,530,000

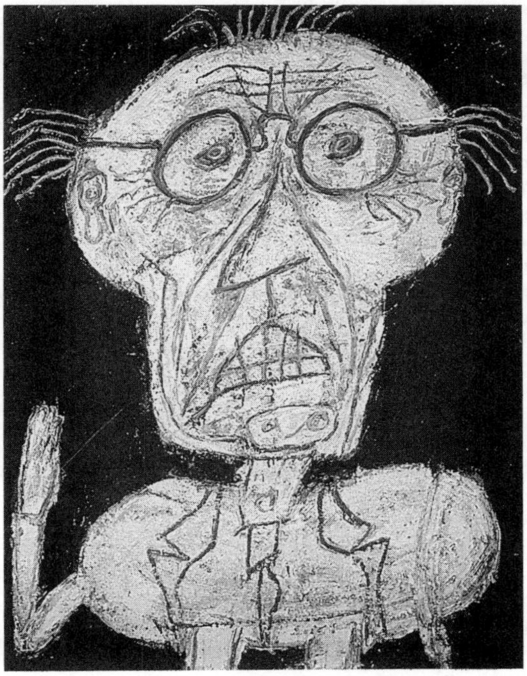

Motif, black felt-tip pen on paper collage on board, initialed/dtd 74, 8x9", C-NY 11/10/88	6,600
Motif, colored felt-tip pen/paper collage on Kraft paper, sgn/dtd 71/titled, 9x10", C-NY 11/10/88	9,350
Obelisque (abstract), marker/paper collage on brown paper, initialed/dtd 71, 13x7", SBY 10/5/89	10,450
Pair: Still Lifes of Red Grapes; oil on canvas, sgn, 22x27", C-E 10/18/89	935
Parachiffre (abstract), acrylic on paper laid down on canvas, sgn/dtd 75, 27x40", SBY 2/15/89 OE	74,250
Parachiffre XLVII (abstract), vinyl paint/acrylic on paper mounted on canvas, initialed/dtd 75, 27x40", SBY 10/8/88	66,000
Paris Plaisir V (contemporary), gouache/collage on paper, initialed/dtd 62, 26x32", SBY 11/11/88 OE	209,000
Partition (abstract), acrylic/paper collage on paper, initialed/dtd 79, 22x14", SBY 11/11/88 OE	55,000
Paysage avec Chien (abstract landscape w/dog), collage w/lithographic elements, sgn/dtd 1958, 16x12", SBY 5/11/88 OE	66,000
Paysage avec Personnage (abstract landscape w/figure), gouache on paper, 1946, 12x9", SBY 5/11/88 OE	48,400
Paysage Mineralogique (abstract), oil on canvas, sgn twice/dtd 55 twice/titled, 47x37", SBY 5/9/89 OE	605,000
Paysage Vert (abstract), oil on canvas, sgn/dtd 44, 26x32", SBY 11/11/88	495,000
Personnage, marker in bristol board collage mounted on Kraft paper, initialed/dtd 71, 13x7", SBY 11/9/89	30,250
Personnage, marker on bristol board collage mounted on Kraft paper, initialed, dtd 71, 13x6", SBY 5/3/89 OE	35,750
Personnage (abstract), colored marker/paper collage on Kraft paper, sgn/dtd 72, 14x9", SBY 2/19/88	16,500
Personnage (abstract), ink on paper, initialed/dtd 64, 11x8", SBY 10/5/89	9,350
Personnage (abstract), pen/colored ink on paper, initialed/dtd 63, 9x5", SBY 10/8/88	12,100
Personnage (abstract), red/blue marker on paper, initialed/dtd 64/titled, 11x8", SBY 5/3/88 OE	22,000
Personnage Assis au Journal (scribbled drawing of figure w/newspaper), ink, initialed/dtd Juin 60, 13x10", SBY 5/2/89 OE	52,250
Personnage de Profil (abstract), paper collage/colored felt-tip pens on paper, initialed/dtd 72, 15x7", C-NY 5/4/89 OE	26,400
Personnage IV (abstract), tempera on paper, initialed/dtd 64, 11x8", SBY 10/5/89	14,300
Personnages 12 (contemporary), ballpoint pen on paper, initialed/dtd 63, 8x5", SBY 11/9/89	18,700
Polymorphie I (Maquette pour Practicable Massif aux Barbes), marker/collage on Kraft paper, 1971, 10x14", SBY 5/3/88	19,800
Ponge feu Follet Noir (abstract), oil on canvas, 1947, 51x38", SBY 11/11/88	825,000
Porte de l'Oasis avec Traces de Pas dans le Sable, crayon on paper, sgn twice/dtd 48, 14x10", C-NY 5/11/89	20,900
Promeneuse au Parapluie (abstract female figure), oil on canvas, 1945, 36x26", SBY 11/11/88	1,430,000
Recit VI (abstract), black felt-tip pen on paper collage on board, initialed/dtd 74, 13x17", C-NY 2/14/89	13,200
Rubbing Piece #6, charcoal on folded paper mounted on board, initialed/dtd 73, 30x39", C-NY 11/10/88	2,860
Site Avec 11 Personnages (eleven abstract figures), black felt-tip pen on paper, initialed, 17x14", C-NY 2/14/89	18,700
Site Avec 3 Personnages (abstract), acrylic on paper laid down on canvas, sgn/dtd 82, 26x20", SBY 6/30/88	66,000
Site Avec 3 Personnages (abstract), acrylic on paper laid down on canvas, initialed/dtd 81, 20x26", SBY 6/30/88	50,000
Situation LXXV (abstract), black felt-tip pen/paper collage on paper, initialed/dtd 79, 14x10", C-NY 5/4/89 OE	35,200
Situation LXXVII, black felt-tip pen/collage on paper, initialed/dtd 79, 14x10", C-NY 10/4/89	24,200
Situation LXXXCIII (Avec Arbre et Oisseau), black felt marker/collage on paper, initialed/dtd 79, 14x10", SBY 5/3/88	15,400

Situation XLI (contemporary abstract w/figures), ink/paper collage on paper, initialed/dtd 78, 14x10", SBY 11/9/89 ... **25,300**
Situation XLIII (abstract), ink/paper collage on paper, initialed/dtd 78, 14x10", SBY 11/11/88 ... **19,800**
Situation XXVI (abstract composition), ink/paper collage on paper, initialed/dtd 78, 14x10", SBY 10/5/89 ... **16,500**
Situation XXXI (contemporary), ink/paper collage on paper, initialed/dtd 78, 14x10", SBY 11/9/89 OE ... **25,300**
Tete (abstract head), watercolor/gouache on paper, sgn/inscr/dtd 1953, 26x19", SBY 5/10/89 OE ... **101,750**
Tete Bleuissante (abstract head), oil on paper laid down, sgn/dtd 1954, 26x20", C-NY 5/11/88 OE ... **308,000**
Tour, color felt-tip pen on paper collage on board, initialed/dtd 74, 21x11", C-NY 11/10/88 ... **30,800**
Trepidation (abstract), oil on paper laid down on canvas, initialed/dtd 84, 27x39", SBY 10/8/88 ... **57,750**
Trois Chameaux (Three Camels), gouache/brush/India ink on paper, sgn/dtd 48, 12x16", C-NY 5/11/89 ... **44,000**
Vache, pen/ink on paper, sgn/dtd 54, 13x10", SBY 10/8/88 OE ... **53,900**
Vache (cow), ink on paper, sgn/dtd 54, 8x5", SBY 11/11/88 OE ... **14,300**

DUC, Victor; see Le Duc

DUCHAMP, Marcel (American/French, 1887-1968)
Amtlich, collage on writing paper mounted on board, sgn/dtd 1930, 12x9", SBY 4/29/88 OE ... **26,400**
Variation on the Optical Disc No 6, watercolor/pencil, 1938, 10" dia, SBY 4/29/88 OE ... **26,400**

DUCHAMP, Suzanne (French, 1898-1963)
Portrait de JC (in profile), oil on canvas, sgn/dtd 56, 22x18", C-E 11/17/88 ... **2,420**

DUCHEMIN, Victoire (French, fl 1864-1879)
Nature Morte aux Fleurs, oil on canvas, sgn/dtd 1877, 13x15", SBY 12/9/88 ... **1,870**

DUCK, Jacob (Dutch, 1600-1660)
Guardroom Interior, oil on panel, sgn, 13x16", C-NY 6/2/88 ... **33,000**
Guardroom Interior with an Officer Surrounded by Sleeping Soldiers, oil on panel, sgn, 18x27", C-NY 1/15/88 OE ... **220,000**

DUCKMANNS, J. (Continental, 19th C)
Floral Still Life on a Ledge, oil on canvas laid down on panel, 20x25", C-E 5/22/89 ... **4,180**

DUDLEY, Frank V.
Late Autumn Valley, oil on canvas, sgn, 45x60", C-E 10/18/89 ... **4,180**

DUESSEL, Henry A. (American, 19th/20th C)
Heavy Surf (seascape), oil on canvas, sgn, 22x36", RAB 3/27/89 ... **500**
Seascape (ships in background), oil on canvas, sgn, 22x36", RWS 8/20/88 ... **700**

DUEZ, Ernest (French, 1834-1896)
La Promenade au Bord de Mer, Presume Sarah Bernhardt; pastel on paper, sgn/dedicted, ca 1890, 10x15", C-L 6/27/88 OE ... **6,054**

DUFAUG, G.A. (French, 19th C)
Bustling Street Scene, oil on canvas, sgn, 24x37", C-NY 5/24/89 OE ... **20,900**

DUFF, John T. (American)
Yosemite Falls, oil on canvas, 35x24", C-E 2/1/89 ... **1,320**

DUFFAUT, Prefete (Haitian, 1929-)
Jacmel Haiti (harbor view), oil on masonite, sgn, 24x20", RWS 9/8/89 ... **1,000**
Porte Haitien, oil on masonite, sgn/dtd 6-71, 24x36", C-NY 5/18/88 UE ... **1,540**

DUFFIELD, William (British, 1816-1863)
Still life of Grapes, Peaches, Plums, & a Pineapple; oil on panel, sgn/dtd 1861, 12x17", C-NY 5/25/88 ... **5,500**

DUFNER, Edward (American, 1871-1957)
Chimney Builders, oil on canvas, sgn, 25x30", SBY 6/24/88 ... **4,675**
Dorothea Arranging Flowers, oil on canvas, sgn, 45x35", SBY 6/24/88 ... **11,000**
End of the Storm, oil on board, sgn, 24x19", C-E 10/18/89 ... **825**
Garden Club (women sewing), oil on board, sgn, 8x10", LH 12/4/88 ... **2,600**
Little Girl Fishing, watercolor on paper, sgn, 10x7", C-E 6/1/88 ... **1,320**
Low Tide, oil on canvas, sgn/dtd 1906, 25x32", C-E 10/18/89 ... **5,500**
Summer Breezes (landscape w/figures), oil on canvas, sgn, 19x23", WD 4/13/88 ... **6,250**
Summer Light & Shade (figures in landscape), oil on canvas, sgn, 20x24", SBY 5/24/89 ... **15,400**
Under the Birches, oil on canvas, sgn twice, 25x30", SBY 5/25/88 OE ... **30,800**

DUFRESNE, Charles
Nature Morte a la Guitare (still life), oil on canvas, sgn, 41x41", C-NY 10/6/88 ... **17,600**

DUFY, Jean (French, 1888-1964)
Animation aux Abords du Fleuve, gouache/watercolor on paper laid down on board, sgn, ca 1955, 15x27", SBY 2/16/89 ... **9,900**
Au Champ de Courses a Longchamp, gouache/watercolor on paper, sgn, ca 1950, 18x23", SBY 2/16/89 OE ... **18,700**
Au Cirque, Danse Espagnol; watercolor/gouache on paper laid down on canvas, sgn, ca 1935, 19x25", SBY 2/18/88 OE ... **13,200**
Bateau a Vapeur (figures on pier viewing steamship, smaller boats), watercolor on paper, sgn, 1930, 16x21", SBY 10/6/89 ... **16,500**
Bateau de Peche, watercolor/gouache/pen/ink on paper laid down on board, dtd 1924, 22x18", C-NY 10/6/88 ... **2,860**
Bateaux a Voiles dans un Port (port scene), watercolor/gouache on paper, sgn, ca 1935, 19x25", SBY 10/6/89 OE ... **17,600**
Bateaux au Port (port scene), oil on canvas, sgn, 18x24", C-NY 2/16/89 ... **16,500**
Bateaux dans le Port (modernistic port scene), oil on canvas, sgn/dtd 1920, 15x18", SBY 10/6/89 ... **22,000**
Bateaux dans un Port, pencil on paper, sgn, 9x9", C-NY 2/13/89 ... **1,540**
Bateaux de Peche a Honfleur (ships in harbor), gouache/watercolor on paper, sgn/dtd 47, 14x25", SBY 10/7/88 ... **9,460**
Bateaux et Voiliers au Port, watercolor over pencil on paper laid down on board, sgn/dtd 24, 22x18", C-NY 10/6/88 ... **6,820**
Bois de Boulogne, oil on canvas, sgn, 15x24", SBY 10/6/89 ... **38,500**
Bois de Boulogne, oil on canvas, sgn, 20x26", SBY 2/16/89 OE ... **36,300**
Bois de Boulogne, oil on canvas, sgn, 24x32", SBY 2/16/89 OE ... **47,300**
Bouquet, watercolor/gouache on paper, stamped signature, 15x11", SBY 10/7/89 ... **5,500**
Bouquet de Fleurs, gouache/watercolor over pencil on board, sgn, 30x28", C-NY 2/16/89 ... **18,700**
Bouquet de Roses, pen/ink/watercolor heightened w/white gouache on paper, sgn/dtd 1951, 7x4", SBY 2/14/89 ... **1,430**
Campagne Normande, pen/ink on paper, sgn, 10x16", SBY 2/16/89 ... **6,050**

Cavaliers et Caleches, au Bois; gouache/watercolor on paper, sgn, ca 1955, 19x24", SBY 2/16/89 OE
Cavaliers et Caleches, Vers le Bois; watercolor/gouache on paper, sgn, ca 1955, 8x11", SBY 2/16/89 OE 14,300
Chambre des Deputees, oil on canvas, sgn, 22x18", SBY 2/16/89 OE........ 8,800
Chevaliers au Course (whimsical racing scene), oil on canvas, sgn, ca 1960, 18x22", C-NY 10/5/89 38,500
Clowns, oil on canvas, sgn/dtd 26, 20x26", SBY 2/18/88 22,000
Clowns, varnished gouache on paper laid down on canvas, sgn, 10x7", C-NY 10/6/88........ 16,500
Clowns Musiciens au Cirque, watercolor/gouache on paper, sgn, ca 1935, 18x24", SBY 2/18/88 OE 5,500
Clowns Musiciens au Cirque, watercolor/gouache on paper, sgn, ca 1935, 18x24", SBY 10/7/88........ 16,500
Composition avec Vase de Fleurs (floral still life w/chair), gouache/watercolor on board, sgn, 17x23", C-NY 2/16/89 12,100
Composition Florale, watercolor on paper laid down on board, sgn/dtd 24, 21x17", SBY 2/14/89........ 11,000
Concert (formal symphony in concert hall), oil on canvas, sgn, 15x18", SBY 10/7/88........ 2,420
Coquilles sur la Plage, watercolor/gouache on paper, stamped signature, ca 1930, 14x27", SBY 10/6/89 22,000
Cottage in the Country, watercolor on paper, sgn/dtd 24, 17x21", B/B 10/9/88........ 7,150
Danseuses Espagnoles, oil on canvas, sgn/dtd 29, 18x22", SBY 10/6/89........ 3,300
Double-Sided: Les Voiliers; Scene de Mer (landscape & ships in port); watercolor, sgn/dtd 1907, 11x13", SBY 10/7/88 27,500
Fleurs et Feuilles, gouache on paper laid down on board, sgn, 15x19", C-E 5/13/88 3,575
Honfleur, watercolor/pen/colored inks on paper laid down on paper, sgn/dtd 1924, 18x20", C-NY 10/6/88 3,300
Interieur (modernistic interior scene w/open window), oil on canvas, sgn/dtd 1920, 29x24", SBY 10/6/89 OE 5,060
L'Arc de Triomphe (whimsical depiction), gouache on paper, sgn, 20x26", C-NY 10/5/89........ 52,250
L'Ochestre, watercolor over pencil on paper, sgn/dtd 24, 14x19", C-NY 10/6/88 16,500
L'Orchestre, gouache on paper laid down on board, sgn, ca 1945, 18x23", C-NY 10/5/89........ 13,200
La Bouille, pencil on paper, stamped w/signature, 18x24", SBY 10/5/88 13,200
La Chasse, oil on canvas, sgn, 18x22", SBY 2/18/88........ 880
La Claise a Preuilly (landscape), oil on canvas, sgn, 18x26", C-NY 2/16/89 OE 20,900
La Place de la Concorde, oil on canvas, sgn, 18x26", C-NY 2/18/88 16,400
La Place de la Concorde, oil on canvas, sgn, 9x15", C-NY 10/5/89........ 24,200
La Seine, Sainte Chapelle (whimsical depiction), oil on canvas, sgn, ca 1960, 18x22", C-NY 10/5/89........ 11,550
La Seine a Paris, oil on canvas, sgn, 13x16", SBY 2/16/89 OE........ 33,000
La Village, oil on canvas, sgn, 11x18", WD 5/5/88 24,200
La Ville de Paris (Paris river scene w/bridge), gouache on paper, sgn, ca 1940, 9x15", C-NY 2/18/88 OE........ 2,800
Le Boite de Jazz (orchestra playing at dance), watercolor/gouache on paper, sgn, 17x23", SBY 10/6/89........ 15,400
Le Cirque, oil on canvas, sgn, 20x26", SBY 2/16/89........ 16,500
Le Cirque, oil on canvas, sgn, 22x18", SBY 2/18/88 OE 25,300
Le Grand Palais et le Petit Palais, Paris; oil on canvas, sgn, 20x26", C-NY 2/16/89 OE........ 17,600
Le Palais (view of palace), gouache on paper laid down on board, sgn, 19x23", C-E 5/9/89........ 28,600
Le Pont, pencil on paper, stamped signature, 13x20", C-E 5/9/89 18,700
Les Champs Elysee, gouache on paper, sgn, ca 1950, 19x25", C-NY 10/5/89 880
Les Voiliers au Basin (modernistic port scene), oil on canvas, indistinctly sgn, ca 1917, 25x31", SBY 10/6/89 18,700
Musician Clowns at the Circus, watercolor/gouache on paper laid down on board, sgn, ca 1935, 25x19", SBY 10/6/89 OE 22,000
Musiciens de Cirque, oil on canvas, sgn, 11x9", C-NY 10/6/88........ 16,500
Nature Morte, oil on canvas, sgn/dtd 1921, 18x15", SBY 2/16/89 OE 7,590
Nature Morte (abstract still life), gouache over pencil on paper, sgn, ca 1920, 18x16", C-NY 10/5/89........ 27,500
Nature Morte avec Fleurs (still life), pen/ink on paper, stamped signature, 21x14", C-E 5/9/89........ 16,500
Nature Morte Devant la Fenetre, oil on canvas, sgn/dtd 24, 15x18", C-NY 2/16/89 OE........ 550
Nature Morte et Vase de Fleurs, gouache on dk gray paper laid down on board, sgn, ca 1930, 24x17", SBY 2/18/88........ 12,100
Pair: Grenade; blue ballpoint pen on paper, stamped w/signature/inscr, 12x17", 10x17", C-E 5/13/88........ 4,950
Pair: L'Eglise; Le Port de Piree; pencil on paper, stamped signature, 15x11", 11x17", C-NY 2/13/89........ 1,320
Pair: La Ferme (The Farm); pencil on paper, stamped signature, 12x19", 11x18", C-E 11/17/88 OE........ 550
Pair: La Ferme; Vue d'un Village Arabe; pencil on paper, stamped signature, 10x17", 11x15", C-E 5/9/89........ 1,430
Pair: Nature Morte; Le Port; pencil on paper, sgn, 11x16", 11x15", C-E 5/9/89 OE........ 990
Pair: Rhodes; Marche Marocain; pencil on paper, stamped signature, 11x17", 11x14", C-E 11/17/88 1,430
Pair: Rhodes; pencil on paper, stamped signature, 11x17", C-NY 2/13/89........ 715
Pair: Rhodes; pencil on paper, stamped w/signature/inscr, 11x16", C-E 5/13/88 OE........ 550
Pair: Still Life of Flowers; oil on canvas, sgn, 10x6", 9x6", SBY 2/14/89 OE 1,210
Pair: Studies of Men & Animals; 1 pen/blue ink, 1 pen/black ink, stamped signature, 11x15", C-E 11/17/88........ 9,350
Pair: Village Pres d'un Canal; pencil on paper, stamped w/signature, 10x16", C-E 5/13/88 825
Palais du Louvre, oil on canvas sgn, 8x15", SBY 10/7/89 1,100
Parc Bois de Boulogne, oil on canvas, sgn, 18x26", SBY 2/18/88........ 11,550
Paris, aux Abords du Bois du Boulogne; gouache on paper laid down on board, sgn, ca 1950, 18x24", C-NY 2/18/88 OE 27,500
Paris, La Seine au Pont des Arts et l'Institut; gouache/watercolor on paper, sgn, ca 1945, 19x24", SBY 10/7/88 OE 22,000
Paris, Montmartre Rue Lepic vers le Sacre-Coeur (street scene); gouache/watercolor on paper, sgn, 18x24", SBY 10/7/88 OE........ 13,200
Paris, Vers la Porte Dauphine; gouache on paper laid down on board, sgn, ca 1960, 18x25", C-NY 10/6/88........ 14,300
Paris vers les Bois de Boulogne, gouache on paper, sgn, 8x14", C-E 11/17/88 16,500
Paris: Rue Animee (street scene); oil on canvas, sgn, 26x32", C-NY 2/18/88 5,280
Pastoral Scene, crayon, stamped signature, 9x12", LH 12/4/88........ 26,400
Paysage aux Peupliers (landscape with poplar trees), oil on canvas, stamped twice, ca 1930, 22x18", C-NY 10/6/88........ 450
Peniche au Bord de l'Eau (boats along a river), watercolor on paper, sgn, 16x20", WD 11/16/88 7,700
Phare a Trouville (sailboats on calm seas near harbor entrance), gouache on paper, sgn, 6x8", RAB 8/9/88 UE 7,000
Phare a Trouville (sailboats), gouache on paper, sgn, 6x8", RAB 8/9/88 UE 2,100
Place de Clichy, oil on canvas, sgn, 18x22", C-NY 2/16/89 2,100
Place de la Concorde, oil on canvas, sgn, 9x22", SBY 10/7/89........ 26,400
9,900

Place Lafayette, Eglise Saint-Vincent de Paul; oil on canvas, sgn, ca 1935, 15x18", C-NY 10/5/89 18,700
Preuilly-sur Claise (village landscape w/figure in a field), oil on canvas, sgn/dtd 1928, 15x18", C-NY 10/5/89 12,100
Projet pour un Decor de Theatre, pen/ink/watercolor on paper, sgn, 1930, 20x16", SBY 2/16/89 6,050
Rue Lepic et Vue de Sacre Coeur, Montmarte; oil on canvas, sgn, 22x18", C-NY 10/6/88 28,600
Sailboats in Port, watercolor on paper, sgn/dtd 1924, 16x24", SBY 10/7/89 5,500
Scene de Cirque, brown ink on paper, stamped w/artist's signature, 14x20", SBY 10/5/88 825
Scene de Port, watercolor/gouache on paper, sgn, ca 1935, 15x19", SBY 10/6/89 11,000
Set of 3: Roses; Flowers; Urn; 1 black ballpoint pen/1 pencil/1 black chalk, stamped, 15x15" & smaller, C-E 11/17/88 OE 1,430
Set of 3: Roses; pencil on paper, stamped w/signature, 18x12", 9x11", & 11x8", C-E 5/13/88 715
Sevilla (landscape), blue pen on paper, estate stamped, 10x16", B/B 5/17/89 UE 715
Square St Pierre, oil on canvas, sgn, 13x16", C-NY 10/6/88 20,900
Tete de Femme (portrait), watercolor/pencil on paper laid down on canvas, 18x15", C-E 5/9/89 2,640
Venise, watercolor on laid paper laid down on board, sgn/dtd 1926/titled, 19x25", SBY 2/16/89 4,950
Viennese Riding School, watercolor/gouache/pencil on paper, sgn, 20x26", SBY 10/7/88 16,500
Voiliers a Deauville, watercolor/gouache on paper, sgn, ca 1935, 27x21", SBY 2/18/88 9,350
Voiliers sur la Plage Pres d'Honfleur (beached sailboats), oil on canvas, sgn, 16x20", SBY 10/6/89 22,000
Vue de Cintra (sketch of building), blue pen on paper, stamped signature, 12x15", C-E 5/9/89 418
Vue de Paris, gouache on paper, sgn, 18x24", C-NY 2/16/89 7,700
Vue de Paris: Pont Neuf; watercolor/gouache on paper, sgn, 19x25", SBY 10/6/89 25,300

DUFY, Raoul (French, 1877-1953)

Anemones au Vase Bombe (floral still life), watercolor/gouache on paper, sgn/dtd 1942, 20x26", SBY 5/10/89 OE 132,000
Arrangement of Flowers Against Vertically Stripped Background, gouache/watercolor, bears monogram, 24x19", FAP 11/4/88 1,300
Au Bord de la Mer (the seashore), pen/India ink on paper, sgn/dtd 1922, 18x22", C-NY 10/5/89 7,150
Bal du 14 Juillet a Vence, pen/ink/watercolor on paper laid down on board, sgn/dtd 1920, 19x26", SBY 11/12/88 OE 40,700
Bateaux en Mer (boats at sea), gouache/watercolor on paper, sgn, ca 1925, 20x26", C-NY 10/5/89 66,000
Bateaux Pavoises, watercolor/gouache on paper, sgn, 20x26", SBY 2/18/88 OE 46,750
Bateaux Pavoises a Deauville, gouache/watercolor on paper, sgn, 20x26", C-NY 11/15/88 104,500
Butterflies, ballpoint pen/watercolor on paper, sgn/inscr, SBY 10/5/88 1,320
Carnaval a Nice, oil on canvas, sgn, 11x22", SBY 10/6/89 OE 170,500
Chevaux, Jockeys et Personnages Sous Bois; watercolor/gouache on paper, sgn, 20x26", SBY 10/27/89 176,000
Country Village, crayon/oil/charcoal on paper, sgn, 18x23", B/B 6/9/88 20,900
Depiquage Rouge (farming scene), oil on canvas, sgn, ca 1945, 13x16", SBY 5/10/89 82,500
Elegantes a Epsom (elegant gathering at racecourse), gouache/water color sgn/dtd 39, 20x26", SBY 5/10/89 231,000
Epsom, le Defile Des Partants; watercolor on paper, ca 1937, 20x26", SBY 10/27/89 170,500
Epsom, Les Turfistes dans les Tribunes (racetrack viewed from stands); watercolor, sgn, 1939, 20x26", C-NY 5/12/88 143,000
Femme a la Coquille, gouache on sheets of paper mounted on canvas, sgn, ca 1925, 89x73", SBY 5/11/88 126,500
Grand Bouquet (floral still life), oil on canvas, sgn/dtd 1932, 59x59", SBY 5/9/89 825,000
Jeux de la Mer (Fun at the Sea), gouache on paper, sgn, ca 1928, 15x22", SBY 5/10/89 OE 121,000
L'Avenue du Bois (w/horse-drawn carriages), oil on canvas, sgn, ca 1909, 21x25", C-NY 5/11/88 209,000
L'Estaque, oil on canvas, sgn, 1913, 18x22", SBY 2/16/89 93,500
La Corrida (The Bullfight), oil on canvas, stamped signature, ca 1949, 19x24", C-NY 5/11/89 192,000
La Cote Normande (landscape), oil on canvas, ca 1903, 21x26", C-NY 5/11/89 35,200
La Manoir du Vallon, oil on canvas, sgn/dtd 1934, 18x22", SBY 5/11/88 OE 132,000
La Moisson a Langres (view of field w/village in distance), oil on canvas, sgn, 13x16", C-NY 11/16/88 68,200
La Paddock (racecourse scene), oil on canvas, sgn, 1925-26, 34x50", C-NY 5/11/88 OE 935,000
La Peintre Axilette et sa Famille, oil on linen laid down on panel, sgn, 1906, 17x15", SBY 5/11/88 88,000
La Pelouse, watercolor/gouache on paper, sgn, 19x26", SBY 11/12/88 OE 220,000
La Peniche, watercolor/pencil on paper, sgn/dtd 1901, 19x24", SBY 2/16/89 33,000
La Plage de St Adresse (modernistic depiction of beach), oil on canvas, sgn, 1908-09, 26x32", C-NY 11/15/88 242,000
La Visite de l'Escadre Anglaise au Havre, gouache/watercolor on paper, sgn, ca 1927-29, 20x26", C-NY 5/11/89 OE 220,000
Le Boeuf sur le Toit, gouache/pen/black ink/colored wax crayons on paper, sgn, 10x14", C-NY 11/15/88 22,000
Le Casino de Nice, la Nuit; watercolor on paper, sgn, 20x26", C-NY 11/15/88 71,500
Le Champ de Courses a Ascot, watercolor on paper, sgn, 20x26", C-NY 11/15/88 OE 209,000
Le Champ de Courses a Ascot (racecourse scene), watercolor/gouache on paper laid down, sgn, 19x24", SBY 5/10/89 187,000
Le Chateau (country estate), watercolor on paper, sgn, 1937, 19x25", C-NY 2/16/89 OE 71,500
Le Depart (the start of race), watercolor on paper, sgn, ca 1930, 22x30", SBY 5/10/89 154,000
Le Harras: La Prairie Normande; watercolor on paper, sgn, ca 1928-29, 20x26", SBY 11/12/88 44,000
Le Port de New York, watercolor/gouache on paper laid down on board, sgn/dtd 1937, 10x13", SBY 2/18/88 19,800
Le Quai de Honfleur (figures on a warf, lighthouse & boats beyond), oil on canvas, sgn, 1928, 18x22", C-NY 11/15/88 264,000
Le Quai-Marseilles, oil on canvas, sgn, 1903, 18x22", SBY 2/16/89 OE 214,500
Le Vignoble (The Vinyard), watercolor/gouache on paper laid down on board, sgn, ca 1936, 22x26", SBY 5/10/89 OE 110,000
Les Ballets du Monte Carlo, watercolor on 3 pieces of paper, initialed, 1933, 20x15", SBY 11/12/88 OE 93,500
Les Bateaux, watercolor/gouache on paper laid down on board, sgn, 20x26", SBY 11/12/88 44,000
Les Jetees de Trouville-Deauville (figures on a jetty), oil on canvas, sgn, 1927, 15x18", SBY 5/10/89 214,500
Les Musiciens (after painting of same title), woven wool tapestry, sgn, 1951, 69x84", edition of 8, SBY 10/6/89 35,750
Marigny, watercolor w/traces of gouache/charcoal on paper, atelier stamp, ca 1912, 18x16", C-NY 11/15/88 OE 41,800
Maroc, Fes; pencil on paper laid down on board, sgn, 1926, 19x25", SBY 2/16/89 OE 19,800
Nu Debout (Etude pour les Affluents de la Seine), oil on panel, stamped signature, ca 1940, 16x10", SBY 10/7/88 44,000
Nu Debout au Chevalet (nude model in artist's studio), oil on canvas, sgn, ca 1929, 22x18", SBY 5/10/89 253,000
Pablo Casals, pen/ink/watercolor/gouache on paper, stamped signature, ca 1946, 10x15", SBY 5/11/88 OE 30,250
Pair: Palm Trees at Cannes; Venetian View; pencil on tracing paper, unfr, 8x6", 8x12", SBY 2/14/89 3,025

Paris (fantasy view), oil on canvas, sgn/dtd 1937, 76x59", SBY 5/9/89 OE
Paysage de Munich, oil on canvas, sgn, 1909, 18x22", SBY 5/11/88 1,815,000
Paysage du Midi, watercolor on paper, affixed to board, sgn, 1921, 20x26", SBY 10/6/89 90,200
Personnages sur la Plage, gouache/pencil on paper, atelier stamp, 14x17", SBY 10/27/89 33,000
Place a Cannes, pencil on tracing paper, 8x11", SBY 2/16/89 49,500
Portrait de Femme, oil on canvas, sgn, ca 1931, 32x26", SBY 11/12/88 OE 2,750
Queue-les-Yvelines (horses at the edge of village), watercolor over pencil, sgn, ca 1928, 19x25", C-NY 10/5/89 OE 121,000
Reception a Marrakech, gouache on paper, 20x26", C-NY 5/11/89 53,900
Rowers on a River, watercolor on paper, sgn, 19x25", SBY 2/18/88 OE 99,000
Sainte-Adresse, l'Eglise; oil on canvas laid down on board, sgn, 1909, 13x10", SBY 10/6/89 44,000
Sainte-Adresse, oil on canvas, sgn, 1924, 21x26", SBY 5/11/88 OE 44,000
St James's Palace, oil on canvas, sgn/dtd 1936/titled, 13x16", C-NY 5/11/89 181,500
Tribune et Paddock a Chantilly, gouache/watercolor on paper, sgn, 20x25", SBY 11/16/89 132,000
Voiliers (sailboats), pen/brown ink on paper, stamped signature, 17x21", C-NY 10/5/89 341,000
Vue de Monte-Carlo, pencil on paper laid down on board, sgn, ca 1932, 19x25", SBY 2/16/89 6,050
Vue de Vence, pastel on paper, sgn, 18x23", SBY 11/12/88 11,550

DUFY, Raoul; after (French, 1877-1953) 55,000
Orchestre Mexicain (wool tapestry), w/Atelier Paymond PicaudAubusson monogram, #5/6, 1951, 69x84", C-NY 10/5/89

DUFY, Raoul; att (French, 1877-1953) 23,100
Procession, oil on canvas, bears signature, 9x12", LH 12/4/88 OE

DUGHET, Gaspard; att (Italian, 1615-1675) 1,800
Italianate Landscape with a Shepherd & Sheep, oil on canvas, 22x28", SBY 6/1/89 OE
Italianate Landscape with Figures, Waterfall, & Ruins; oil on canvas, 22x32", SBY 10/21/88 OE 7,700

DUGHET, Gaspard; circle of (Italian, 1615-1675) 4,125
Stormy Landscape with Travelers by a Cliff, oil on copper, circular, 10" dia, C-NY 10/12/89

DUGHET, Gaspard; follower of (Italian, 1615-1675) 1,870
Extensive Landscape, oil on canvas, 29x38", SBY 7/12/89
Extensive Wooded Landscape with Classical Figures, oil on canvas, 30x39", C-NY 4/6/89 1,980
Figures Resting by a Cascade in a Mountainous Landscape, oil on canvas, 25x36", C-NY 10/20/88 8,800
Italianate Landscape with a Figure on a Road, oil on canvas,19x26", SBY 4/7/89 5,280
Pair: Italianate Landscapes with Pastoral Figures; oil on canvas, 37x54", C-NY 1/15/88 OE 16,500
Pair: Italianate Landscapes; 1 red chalk/1 red chalk counterproof, 6x11", SBY 7/12/89 33,000
Pair: Shepherds on a Path in Extensive Wooded Landscape; Hunting Party on Path...; oil on canvas, 19x25", C-NY 1/11/88 825

DUGUAY, Rodolphe (Canadian, 1891-1973) 22,000
Paysage (landscape), oil on board, sgn, 8x10", FB 10/17/88 OE
Summer Landscape, oil on board, sgn/dtd 13/6/36, 9x11", FB 10/30/89 800
Un Coin de Nicolet, oil on canvas, sgn, 13x15", FB 5/28/89 770
Wood Cutter, charcoal, sgn, 24x18", FB 10/17/88 1,900

DUGUERRE, Louis Jacques Mande (French, 1787-1851) 325
Figures in the Church of St Jean, Ehiers; brown wash heightened w/white over pencil, sgn, 9x7", C-NY 10/25/89 OE

DUJARDIN, Karel; att (Dutch, 1622-1678) 6,600
Nanny Goat & Her Young in an Italianate Landscape, oil on canvas laid down on panel, 11x8", SBY 4/7/89

DUJARDIN, Karel; circle of (Dutch, 1622-1678) 4,400
Annunciation to the Shepherds, oil on canvas, 29x24", C-NY 4/8/88 OE

DUKE, Albert (British, 1847-1904) 4,180
Two Dogs, oil on panel, 7x10", LH 9/10/89

DULAC, A. 425
Rue de Village (village road), oil on canvas, sgn, C-E 11/17/88

DULAC, Edmund (French, 1882-1953) 440
Autumn (mythological scene), watercolor/gouache/metallic gold paint, sgn, arched top, 14x11", C-NY 10/26/88
Feng Bird (Oriental), pencil/gouache on board, sgn/inscr, 12x11", SBY 12/9/88 OE 26,400
Spring (mythological scene), watercolor/gouache/metallic gold paint, sgn, arched top, 14x11", C-NY 10/26/88 OE 8,250
Summer (mythological scene), watercolor/gouache/metallic gold paint, sgn, arched top, 14x11", C-NY 10/26/88 OE 19,800
Urashima (Oriental), pencil/watercolor/gouache on paper, sgn/inscr, 12x11", SBY 12/9/88 OE 39,600
Winter (mythological scene), watercolor/gouache/metallic gold paint, sgn, arched top, 14x11", C-NY 10/26/88 OE 8,250

DULL, John J. (American, 1862-) 26,400
Arch Bridge, watercolor on paper, sgn, 9x11", FAP 12/8/89 UE
Dogwood Tree in Blossom, pastel, sgn, 11x10", FAP 12/8/89 125

DUMAS, Antoine (Canadian, 1932-) 225
La Voie Maritime, oil on canvas, sgn/dtd 1973, 18x36", FB 10/30/89
Taking a Break, oil on canvas, sgn, 22x28", FB 10/30/89 3,740

DUMOND, Frank Vincent (American, 1865-1981) 3,740
Mystic Vision, oil on canvas, sgn, 22x16", C-NY 9/30/88
Walt Whitman Picking Lilacs, oil on canvas, 24x30", C-NY 5/25/89 2,200

DUMONT, Pierre (French, 1884-1936) 6,600
Still Life of Fruit with Blue & White Pitcher, oil on canvas, sgn/dtd 08, 24x29", SBY 10/5/88 OE

DUMOULIN (Belgian, 19th C) 7,150
Untitled (fisherman/family in landscape w/windmills), oil on canvas, sgn, 13x18", SLK 4/7/89

DUNBAR, Harold C. (American, 1882-1953) 750
Autumn Landscape, oil on canvas, sgn/dtd 08, 11x14", RWS 5/19/88
1,500

Cape Cod Dunes (coastal landscape), oil on board, sgn, 25x46", RAB 8/8/89 400
Double-Sided: Twin Sisters of Cape Cod; Cape Cod Cottage; oil on wood panel, sgn, unfr, 19x66", RAB 3/27/89 UE 400
Early Spring (landscape), oil on board, 5x7", RAB 11/25/88 UE 200
Harding Beach Point, oil on masonite, sgn/dtd 1949, 21x21", RAB 8/9/88 600
Moret sur Loing (stone house by dam with rushing water), watercolor on paper, sgn/dtd 1913, 10x14", RAB 8/9/88 350
Peonies (still life), oil on canvas, sgn/dtd 1934, 34x30", SBY 4/14/89 UE 770
Poppies, Beach, & Sea, Carmel, California; oil on board, sgn/dtd 1950, 20x22", RAB 8/9/88 700
Return to the Lighthouse (man in rowboat, Royal Copenhagen Christmas plate style), oil on board, sgn, 11x15", RAB 8/9/88 250
Riverscape (water cutting through winter landscape), oil on canvas, sgn, 10x12", RAB 8/9/88 UE 300

DUNCAN, Edward (British, 1803-1882)
Grazing Flock by a Country House, watercolor on paper, sgn/dtd 1864, 7x10", B/B 1/11/89 715
Sailbats on High Seas, watercolor heightened w/gouache, 9x14", C-E 2/21/90 1,210

DUNCAN, Geraldine Birch (American, 1883-1972)
California Hills, oil on canvas, sgn, 28x23", B/B 8/10/88 1,100

DUNCANSON, Robert S. (American, 1821-1871)
Woman & Star, oil on canvas, sgn, oval, 29x36", C-E 6/1/89 2,200

DUNCKHAM, H. (British, 19th C)
Castle of Spier, Switzerland; oil on panel, sgn/dtd 1836, 12x16", SBY 7/12/89 770

DUNEI, L.
Mandolin Player, oil on panel, sgn, 14x18", DM 2/19/88 UE 150

DUNHAM, Carroll (20th C)
E (abstract), ink/gouache/charcoal/crayon on wood veneer, sgn/dtd 11-4-85, 21x13", SBY 2/15/89 5,500
P (abstract), mixed media on maple veneer, sgn/dtd 1985, 48x36", SBY 5/3/89 33,000
Pool (abstract), casein/acrylic/dry pigment/charcoal/pen on birch panel, 1982, 49x30", SBY 5/3/89 38,500
Untitled (abstract), casein/graphite on wooden panels, laminated to panel, sgn/dtd 1984, unfr, 69x46", C-NY 5/3/88 OE 66,000
Untitled (abstract), charcoal/graphite on wood veneer, dtd 11/29/83, 19x15", C-NY 11/10/88 12,100
Untitled (abstract), gouache/charcoal/crayons/pen/ink on wooden veneer taped to paper, sgn/dtd 1985, 15x10", C-NY 5/4/88 8,250
Untitled (abstract), gouache/graphite on paper, dtd April 1980, 30x22", C-NY 11/10/88 5,500

DUNLAY, Thomas R. (American, 20th C)
Summer Meadow, Williamstown; oil on canvas, sgn/dtd 78, 16x20", RWS 5/12/89 5,500

DUNN, Harvey Thomas (American, 1884-1952)
By Way of the Torch (rural landscape w/couple in old car), oil on canvas, monogramed, 34x38", SBY 5/24/89 19,800
Old Miner (sitting on bed, oil lamp on washstand), oil on canvas, monogramed/dtd 24, 30x40", C-NY 9/28/89 8,800
San Antonio, oil on canvas, sgn/dtd 1911, 30x40", SBY 5/25/88 OE 52,250
Women Having Coffee (interior scene), oil on canvas, sgn/dtd 43, 38x30", B/B 3/22/89 OE 24,750

DUNNING, Robert Spear (American, 1829-1905)
Peaches in a Glass Bowl, oil on canvas, sgn, 11x13", C-NY 9/28/89 8,800
Sunset, Taunton River Near Fall River, Somerset, Massachusetts; oil on canvas, sgn/dtd 1880, 6x11", RWS 11/10/89 2,000
Winter Walk (two figures in rural landscape), oil on canvas, sgn, 7x11", RWS 9/8/89 800

DUNNINGTON, A. (British, 19th C)
Homeward Bound (herdsmen w/sheep in a landscape), oil on canvas, sgn/dtd 1889, 24x36", B/B 6/15/89 1,100

DUNOYER DE SEGONZAC, Andre (French, 1884-1974)
Figure with a Dog in a Landscape, oil on canvas, sgn, 24x32", SBY 10/7/89 15,400
Ile-de France (landscape w/stream & white house), oil on canvas, sgn, 32x22", C-NY 10/5/89 22,000
Jeune Femme a la Rose, crayons/pencil on paper, sgn, 17x13", SBY 10/27/89 38,500
La Table sur la Terrasse (view of table on a terrace), oil on canvas, sgn, 18x22", SBY 5/10/89 27,500
Les Canotiers sur la Marne (river landscape w/boaters), watercolor/pen/black ink, sgn, 21x31", C-NY 2/18/88 22,000
Les Poires, oil on panel, sgn, 10x13", SBY 10/27/89 15,400
Les Tomates, India ink/watercolor/pencil on paper, sgn, 12x18", SBY 10/27/89 OE 46,200
Nature Morte (still life w/cheese, carrots, bottle of wine on table), oil on canvas, sgn, 24x32", C-NY 10/5/89 OE 48,400
Nature Morte a la Soupiere de Moustiers (still life), India ink/watercolor/pencil on paper, sgn, 23x31", SBY 2/16/88 19,800
Still Life of Cabbage, Tureen, & Bottle of Wine; oil on canvas, sgn/dtd 1955, 21x26", SBY 2/14/89 14,300
Vignes au Printemps (vineyards in springtime), watercolor/pen/black ink on paper, sgn, 23x31", C-NY 10/5/89 30,800
Voiture Ravitaillement Anglais, watercolor/pen/ink on paper mounted on board, sgn/dtd 1916, 10x8", C-E 5/9/89 OE 1,980
Vue de Grimaud (landscape), pen/brush/India ink on paper, sgn, 16x23", C-NY 10/5/89 2,860

DUNSMORE, John Ward (American, 1856-1945)
Needlework, oil on panel, sgn/dtd 1909, 8x11", C-E 11/8/88 650

DUNSTAN, Bernard (England, 1920-)
Breakfast Table, oil on board, initialed, 11x8", C-E 10/26/89 3,300

DUNTON, William Herbert 'Buck' (American, 1878-1936)
Bronc Rider, oil on canvas, sgn/dtd 08, 29x19", C-NY 5/26/88 41,800

DUNTZE, Johannes Bertholomaus Duntze (German, 1832-1895)
Geinangerfjord, oil on canvas, sgn/dtd 1873, 24x36", C-NY 5/25/88 8,800
Mill by a Norwegian Fjord, oil on canvas, sgn/dtd 1872, 33x51", WD 11/16/88 OE 12,000

DUO, Wang (Chinese, 1592-1652)
Calligraphy in Cao Shu (cursive script, hand scroll), ink on silk, sgn/dtd 1646, 10x93", SBY 5/31/89 OE 44,000

DUPAS, Jean (French, 1882-)
Poster Study for XVME Salon des Artistes Decorateurs, pencil/ink/watercolor/gouache, sgn/1924, 17x12", SBY 4/23/88 OE 12,100
Woman & Birds, pencil on paper, initialed/dtd 1924, fr, 13x17", SBY 4/23/88 OE 4,675
Zolma Poster Study, pencil/ink/gouache on paper, sgn/dtd 1929, 17x14", SBY 4/23/88 OE 6,050

DUPATY, Charles (fl 1788-1796)
Portrait of a Gentleman Wearing Red Jacket & Yellow Waistcoat, Writing; oil, sgn/dtd 96/an.4, 27x21", C-M 12/3/88 4,645

DUPLESSIS, J.S. (French, 1725-1802)
Portrait of the Baron Trescatel, oil on canvas, 32x26", B/B 5/17/89 605

DUPOND, Marcel (French, 1907-1954)
Boats by the Sea, oil on canvas, sgn/dtd 1945, 23x32", WG 9/16/88 UE 50

DUPONT, Gainsborough (British, 1754-1797)
Portrait of Mother & Infant, oil on panel, arched top, sgn/dtd 86(?), 7x5", SBY 7/12/89 1,100

DUPONT, Gainsborough; att (British, 1754-1797)
Portrait of a Lady Said To Be Mrs Paul Jodrell, half-length...; oil on canvas, 30x25", C-NY 4/6/89 2,860
Portrait of an Artist in His Studio, oil on canvas, 23x19", SBY 4/7/89 3,850

DUPONT, Louise (French, 19th C)
Still Life of Flowers in a Vase & a Wedgwood Plate, oil on canvas, sgn, 17x15", C-E 2/21/89 UE 1,650

DUPRAT, Albert Ferdinand (Italian, 1882-)
Overlooking the Canal, oil on panel, sgn, 19x26", C-E 10/25/88 1,540

DUPRAY, Henry Louis (French, 1841-1909)
French Cavalry Officers, oil on canvas, sgn, 22x17", SBY 6/8/88 825
Guards of the First Republic, oil on panel, sgn, 13x9", SBY 6/8/88 1,210
La Voiture Du Cure, oil on canvas, sgn, 14x11", SBY 6/8/88 1,870
Mounted Soldiers, oil on panel, sgn, 10x6", SBY 6/8/88 825
Pair: Cavalry Charge & Cavalry at Rest; oil on cradled panel, sgn/dtd 1887 & 1881, 13x18", C-E 2/23/88 2,420

DUPRE, Francois (French, 1803-1871)
Walking Her Dog, oil on canvas, sgn, 9x11", RAB 3/27/89 UE 225

DUPRE, Jules (French, 1811-1889)
Cattle Watering in a Wooded Landscape, oil on panel, sgn, 9x16", C-NY 2/25/88 4,400
Figures & a Dog Outside a Cottage, oil on panel, sgn, 17x22", C-NY 2/23/89 OE 15,400
Landscape, oil on canvas, sgn, 24x29", SBY 6/8/88 2,420
Marine Scene, oil on canvas, sgn, 20x26", C-NY 5/25/88 OE 20,900
Mills (windmills on canal), oil on panel, sgn, 8x9", WD 11/16/88 OE 7,500
Morning (landscape w/man in boat), oil on canvas, sgn, 16x13", C-NY 2/3/88 8,800
Returning Home From the Fields, oil on canvas, sgn, 8x13", C-E 10/26/89 4,400
River Landscape with Fishermen, oil on canvas, sgn, 18x30", WD 5/5/88 5,000
Ship on a Stormy Sea, oil on canvas, sgn, 13x16", C-NY 10/25/89 6,600
Ships on Rough Seas, oil on canvas, sgn, 15x22", RWS 8/12/89 OE 11,000
Windmill in the Open Fields, oil on panel, sgn, 7x10", C-E 10/26/89 4,180
Wooded River Landscape, oil on panel, sgn, 13x11", C-E 5/22/89 UE 1,320
Wooded River Landscape at Sunset, oil on panel, sgn, 8x10", C-NY 2/23/89 6,050

DUPRE, Jules; att (French, 1811-1889)
Cows Watering, oil on canvas, initialed, 18x15", C-E 2/21/89 1,650
Landscape, oil on canvas, 15x18", SBY 6/8/88 UE 1,100
Shepherd with His Flock, oil on canvas, 18x22", C-E 10/26/89 1,320

DUPRE, Julien (French, 1851-1910)
Feeding Time (woman & child feeding chickens), oil on canvas, sgn, 26x32", SBY 2/22/89 OE 44,000
Harvesters, oil on canvas laid down, sgn, 18x24", B/B 6/9/88 OE 24,750

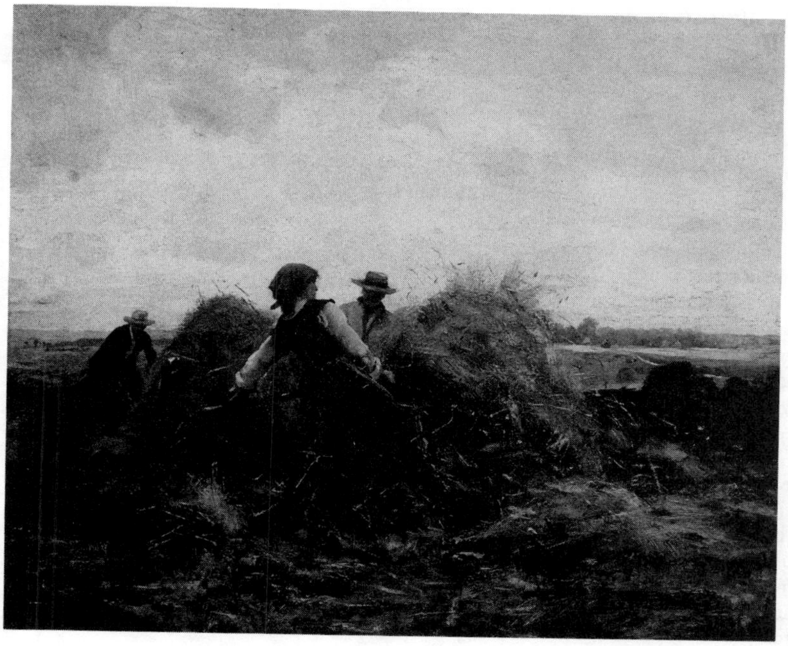

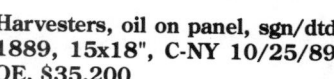

Harvesters, oil on panel, sgn/dtd 1889, 15x18", C-NY 10/25/89 OE, $35,200

La Bergere (shepherdess & sheep in an extensive landscape), oil on canvas, sgn, 21x25", B/B 10/9/88 ... 6,600
La Laitiere, oil on canvas, sgn, 26x32", SBY 10/24/89 OE ... 52,250
Le Berger (herdsman & dog watching over sheep), oil on canvas, sgn, 56x79", SBY 10/24/89 OE ... 170,500
Les Faucheurs, oil on canvas, sgn, 18x22", SBY 5/23/89 ... 37,400
Midday Repast (man & woman in a landscape resting & eating), oil on canvas, sgn, 22x26", C-NY 10/25/89 ... 41,800
Milkmaid with Her Cows on a Summer Day, oil on canvas, sgn, 26x32", C-NY 10/25/89 ... 41,800
Pond with Birch Trees, oil on canvas, sgn/dtd 1900, 18x26", B/B 10/9/88 ... 5,500
Returning From the Fields (woman & child leading cattle), oil on canvas, sgn/dtd 1895, 49x59", C-NY 10/25/89 OE ... 82,500
Shepherd & His Flock, oil on canvas, sgn, 26x33", C-NY 10/25/89 ... 39,600
Vachere Menant ses Vaches a la Riviere (peasant girl w/cows by river), oil on canvas, sgn, 16x24", SBY 10/24/89 ... 28,600

DUPRE, Leon Victor (French, 1816-1879)
After the Storm, oil on panel, sgn/dtd 69, 7x11", B/B 6/9/88 ... 1,540
Cows Grazing at River's Edge, oil on panel, sgn, 9x13", WL 5/20/88 UE ... 850

DUPUIS, Pierre (French, 1833-)
Reclining Nude in a Landscape, oil on canvas laid down on board, sgn, 19x31", SBY 7/12/89 ... 1,650

DUPUIS, Pierre; att (French, 1833-)
Portrait of a Young Boy (bust-length, resting cheek on shoulder), oil on board, sgn/dtd 1905, 14x10", B/B 9/14/89 ... 550

DUPUY, L. (French, 19th C)
Gathering Nuts by the River, oil on canvas, sgn, 15x21", SBY 7/12/89 ... 1,045

DUPUY, Paul Michel (French, 1869-1949)
Figures on a Veranda by the Beach, oil on canvas, sgn/dtd 1916, 24x32", C-E 2/21/89 OE ... 66,000

DURAND, Asher Brown (American, 1796-1886)
Picnic in the Country, oil on canvas, sgn/dtd 1863, 28x42", SBY 5/25/88 ... 137,500
Stream Crossing, oil on canvas, initialed, 16x24", C-E 6/1/88 ... 5,610

DURAND, Asher Brown; att (American, 1796-1886)
Double-Sided: Trees; Cottage; pencil on paper, sgn, 11x9", FAP 4/15/89 ... 522
Landscape Study, oil/pencil on canvas, 17x24", SBY 9/14/89 ... 2,860

DURAND, Carolus
Bearded Knight, oil on masonite, sgn, 36x51", C-E 2/23/88 ... 1,760

DURAND, Francisque (French, 19th C)
Afternoon Outing on the River, oil on canvas laid down, sgn/dtd 1851, 20x24", SBY 6/8/88 UE ... 1,870

DURAND-BRAGER, Jean Baptiste Henri (French, 1814-1879)
View of a Harbor, oil on canvas, sgn, 14x26", C-NY 2/23/89 ... 4,620

DURANTI, Fortunato (Italian, 1787-1863)
Bishop Blessing a Knight, pen/brown ink/brown wash, 7x10", C-NY 1/12/88 ... 330

DUREAU, George (American, 20th C)
Male Nude, charcoal/crayon, sgn, 41x33", NA 2/24/89 ... 900

DUREN, Terence Romaine (American, 1907-)
Backyard in Shelby, watercolor on paper, sgn, 9x12", C-E 2/1/89 ... 770

DURGIN, Lyle (American, 19th/20th C)
Portrait of a Woman (three-quarter length, standing), oil on canvas, sgn/dtd 87, 52x32", RWS 9/8/89 ... 1,500

DURIE (French, 20th C)
Woman in 18th Century Attire Seated on a Veranda, oil on canvas, sgn, 31x62", SLK 2/12/88 ... 225

DUROCHER, Renee (Canadian, 1939-)
Family, mixed media, sgn/dtd 1983, 22x26", FB 10/17/88 UE ... 350

DURRIE, George Henry (American, 1820-1863)
Portrait of Phebe Ann Lawrence, oil on canvas, sgn/dtd 1842, 30x25", SBY 1/28/88 ... 3,300
Seven Miles to Salem (snowy farm scene), oil on canvas, sgn/dtd 1863, 26x36", C-NY 5/25/89 OE ... 385,000
Winter Farmyard, oil on board, sgn/dtd 1862, 8x13", C-NY 9/28/89 ... 16,500

DURRIE, George Henry; att (American, 1820-1863)
Watering Horses (man & two horses at trough in landscape), oil on board, 11x14", C-E 6/1/89 ... 3,850

DURRIE, John (American, 1818-)
Pair: Apples, Grapes, & Nuts; Peaches & Grapes; oil on canvas, sgn/dtd 51, 7x10", 8x11", C-NY 12/2/88 OE ... 19,800

DURUY, P. (French, 19th/20th C)
Two Maidens in a Neoclassical Garden, watercolor on paper, sgn, 9x12", B/B 5/17/89 ... 550

DUSART, Cornelis (Dutch, 1660-1704)
Peasants Drinking & Smoking Outside a Tavern, oil on panel, 18x15", C-NY 1/11/89 ... 18,700

DUSART, Cornelis; att (Dutch, 1660-1704)
Drinker Being Served by a Barmaid Under a Trellis Before a Tavern, oil on panel, unfr, 8x6", C-NY 1/11/89 ... 12,100
Man Smoking a Pipe Holding a Bowl, black/red chalk/brown ink framing lines, 4x4", C-NY 1/11/89 ... 990

DUSART, Cornelis; manner of (Dutch, 1660-1704)
Man Seated at a Table Holding a Pipe, oil on panel, 8x7", SBY 12/9/88 ... 440

Dutch School (16th C)
Castle of Abcoude, pen/brown ink/watercolor, inscr, ca 1700, 4x6", C-NY 1/11/89 OE ... 880

Dutch School (17th C)
Bacchus, oil on panel, 21x17", LH 10/16/88 UE ... 850
Boaters on an Estuary, oil on canvas, unfr, 15x21", C-E 1/12/88 UE ... 1,265
Cavalry Skirmish, oil on canvas, unfr, 17x27", SBY 12/9/88 ... 550
Child Holding a Draped Globe in a Landscape: An Allegory; oil on panel, inscr, unfr, 12" dia, SBY 6/2/89 OE ... 19,800
Classical Figures & Sheep Along a Wooded Road, a Town in the Distance; oil on canvas, 49x45", SBY 4/7/89 OE ... 22,000
Cottage Interior with a Man Descending Steps, Boy Below; black chalk/gray wash, in framing lines, ca 1650, 8x9", C-NY 1/12/88 ... 6,050

Extensive Landscape with a Village, pen/brown ink/gray wash, 6x9", SBY 7/12/89 ... 550
Flora (bust-length, holding bouquet of mixed flowers), oil on panel, ca 1650, 26x20", SBY 6/1/89 UE ... 14,300
Interior with Three Elderly Women & a Girl, oil on canvas, 15x13", SBY 4/7/88 ... 1,650
Landscape with a Man on a Path & a Windmill, chalk/wash/ink framing lines, bears monogram VR, 7x12", C-NY 1/11/89 OE ... 1,210
Landscape with Cows & Figures, oil on canvas, ca 1800, 12x14", SBY 7/12/89 ... 660
Landscape with Figures on Horseback on Road in Forest & Man on Foot with Dog, oil on canvas, 1686, 21x29", S/A 2/18/89 ... 900
Landscape with Figures Standing Beside Classical Ruins, oil on panel, inscr/dtd Elsheimer 163(?), 6x9", SBY 12/9/88 ... 825
Pair: Companion Portraits of a Young Boy & Girl in Landscapes; oil on canvas, 44x35", C-NY 1/11/89 ... 7,700
Pair: Mussel Seller; Cutler, a Vendor of Chestnuts Nearby; oil on canvas, 27x33", SBY 4/7/88 OE ... 15,400
Portrait of a Boy Dressed in Classical Costume As an Archer, oil on canvas, 22x18", SBY 10/21/88 ... 2,475
Portrait of a Boy in a Hat, black chalk on vellum, initialed/dtd (16)36, 6x5", SBY 1/13/89 ... 550
Portrait of a Gentleman, bust-length, in armor; oil on panel, 15x12", C-NY 4/8/88 ... 2,200
Portrait of a Gentleman Said To Be Henry Halswell, oil on canvas, 23x19", SBY 10/13/89 ... 3,850
Portrait of a Gentleman Said To Be Sir Walter Raleigh, bust-length; oil on canvas, in painted oval, 24x19", C-NY 4/8/88 ... 1,210
Portrait of a Woman in a White Ruff & Cap, oil on panel, 15x13", SBY 10/13/89 OE ... 6,600
Portrait of D Van Maris, Aged 6; oil on panel, inscr w/sitter's name & age/dtd 1647, 27x20", WD 1/25/89 ... 650
Sailing in Rough Seas, oil on panel, bears signature W Velde/dtd 1679, unfr, 17x22", C-E 6571 OE ... 2,860
Saint John the Evangelist, oil on panel, 28x21", SBY 6/3/88 ... 7,150
Scene From the Life of Christ, oil on panel, 13x18", SBY 12/9/88 ... 1,540
Sense of Smell (portrait of a woman holding a flower), oil on canvas, oval, 33x26", SBY 4/7/88 OE ... 7,700
Still Life of Fruit, oil on canvas, 30x25", S/A 3/12/88 ... 40,000

Dutch School (18th C)

Alpine Landscape with Herdsman Driving Cattle Across Stone Bridge Spanning a Waterfall, oil, 10x15", SBY 10/13/89 ... 6,600
Blacksmith Shop, oil on panel, bears signature/dtd 165(?), 19x25", C-NY 10/12/89 ... 3,300
Country Scene with Two Figures, oil on board, 4x6", WG 4/23/88 ... 425
Elegant Horseman Pausing To Speak with Man & Child Walking on a River Road, oil on canvas, 48x66", SBY 10/13/89 ... 14,300
Flower Vendors by a Canal, pencil/wash on paper, 8x12", WD 10/19/88 ... 500
Gaberlunzie Man & the Beggars, oil on panel, 17x10", C-NY 4/8/88 ... 1,100
Goats, Sheep, & Donkey; graphite/brown wash on paper, 7x10", C-NY 6/17/89 ... 242
Italian Landscape with Peasants, oil on canvas, 19x26", LH 10/16/88 ... 3,200
Landscape with Lake & Figures, oil on panel, 7x9", SBY 12/9/88 UE ... 550
Landscape with Men Repairing a Ship, Town on River Beyond; oil on panel, unfr, 9x12", SBY 10/13/89 ... 1,320
Oriental Figures in a Classical Landscape, oil on canvas, 25x30", SBY 12/9/88 UE ... 935
Pair: Figures by a Mill; Figures in a Seaside Village; oil on panel, 8x10", B/B 3/17/88 ... 4,400
Pair: Portraits of Family Groups in Garden Landscapes; oil on canvas, 22x18", SBY 10/13/89 ... 6,600
Park with Two Statues, black chalk/gray wash, 11x9", C-NY 1/12/88 OE ... 715
Pastoral Landscape, oil on canvas, 17x22", SBY 12/9/88 ... 825
Portrait of a Man, oil on copper, 7x9", MG 5/28/88 ... 250
Rocky Landscape with Peasants & Cattle, black/white chalk, 12x14", SBY 1/13/89 OE ... 5,225
Skating Scene: an Allegory of Youth & Old Age; oil on panel, 14x12", SBY 4/7/88 OE ... 4,675
Still Life of Grapes, Plums, & Peaches; oil on canvas, 15x13", SBY 4/7/88 OE ... 8,250
Tobias & the Angel, oil on panel, 20x24", SBY 6/8/88 ... 880

Dutch School (19th C)

Chickens Feeding, oil on canvas, indistinctly sgn, 15x19", C-E 5/23/88 OE ... 2,640
Confrontation (street scene w/men, cart, & dogs), oil on canvas, indistinctly sgn/dtd 1832, 20x24", C-E 2/21/89 ... 2,750
Dramatic Marine Scene with Galleons & Sailing Vessels, oil on panel, sgn Abraham Van Rhijn, 16x20", RWS 4/7/89 OE ... 1,500
Fishing Boats on a Moonlit Shore, oil on canvas, indistinctly sgn/dtd 1888, 30x50", C-E 2/23/88 ... 1,650
Gentleman (half-length portrait, wearing a white ruff), oil nn canvas, unfr, 31x25", C-E 2/16/88 ... 440
Harbor Scene, oil on canvas, sgn, 28x18", MG 10/28/88 ... 450
HMS Dragon 74 Guns & Espiegle 18 Guns (ships), oil reverse painted on glass, sgn/titled, 17x20", RAB 11/10/88 ... 2,000
Horse Trader, oil on panel, 10x12", RWS 11/3/88 ... 400
Interior Depicting a Couple Seated Beside the Hearth, He Smoking Pipe, She Knitting; oil on canvas, 18x14", SLK 2/12/88 ... 450
Interior with Multiple Figures Depicting a Man Having a Tooth Pulled, oil on canvas, 11x10", SLK 2/12/88 ... 275
Lady Reading a Letter, Being Attended by a Maid; oil on panel, 21x17", C-E 6/1/88 ... 1,320
Pair: Coastal Scene; Ships in High Seas; oil on canvas, sgn/dtd 1847, 25x34", RWS 5/19/88 OE ... 2,600
Portrait of a Gentleman, bust-length, wearing a black costume with a white collar; oil on panel, 16x13", C-NY 10/20/88 ... 1,760
Portrait of a Lady in a Seventeenth Century Costume, oil on canvas, 45x39", WD 10/19/88 OE ... 3,250
Putting the Baby To Sleep, oil on canvas, indistinctly sgn, 22x28", C-E 2/23/88 ... 1,650
Skaters on a Frozen Canal, oil on canvas, indisctinctly sgn, 16x24", C-E 11/8/88 ... 1,870
Still Life of Grapes, Nuts, Peeled Lemon, Cherries, an Oyster, Bread, a Roemer...; oil on canvas, 15x19", SBY 7/12/89 ... 1,760
Street Vendor, oil on canvas, 18x14", C-E 4/7/88 ... 660
Tax Collector at the Tavern (figures in an interior), oil on canvas panel, 12x17", WG 4/23/88 UE ... 675
The Clam Diggers, oil on canvas, indistinctly sgn, 32x20", B/B 12/8/88 ... 990
Winter Scene with Skaters on a Frozen Stream, oil on canvas, 20x24", SLK 2/12/88 ... 175

Dutch School (20th C)

Dutch Township, oil on canvas, 13x18", C-E 6/28/88 ... 600
Portrait of a Man in 1600s Costume Standing Beside a Table, oil on canvas, bears signature, 20x16", C-E 4/7/88 ... 264
Tavern Scene, oil on board, 7x10", SLK 2/12/88 ... 80
Untitled, pheasants in a field; oil on canvas, 27x38", SLK 2/11/89 ... 175

DUTERTRE, Andre

Elegant Young Man in a Riding Costume, pencil/gray wash/red chalk, 11x7", C-NY 5/25/88 ... 1,210

DUVAL (Continental, 19th C)
Peasant Family Setting Out, oil on panel, sgn/dtd 1833, unfr, 8x12", C-E 2/21/89 ..... **1,540**
DUVENECK, Frank (American, 1848-1919)
Boy in Blue (portrait), pastel on board, sgn, after 1888, 10x8", C-NY 3/11/88 ..... **4,400**
DUVENECK, Frank; att (American, 1848-1919)
Old Woman, no media given, 10x7", WD 4/13/88 ..... **750**
DUVERGER, Theophile Emmanuel (French, 1821-)
Plucking the Chicken, oil on canvas, sgn, 12x15", C-E 10/26/89 ..... **2,200**
DUVIEUX, Henri (French, 19th C)
View of Venice, oil on canvas, sgn, 20x37", B/B 6/15/89 OE **9,350**
DUVIVIER (19th C)
Design & Plan for a Bridge, pen/black ink/watercolor over pencil, sgn/dtd 1857, 14x17", SBY 1/13/89 ..... **1,650**
DUYSTER, Willem Cornelisz; att (Dutch, 1600-1635)
Soldiers in a Guardroom, oil on panel, 17x19", SBY 1/12/89 ..... **46,750**
DVORAK, Franz (Austrian, 1862-)
I Want My Cake (child after a fall, losing her cake to baby chicks), oil on canvas, sgn/dtd 93, 11x15", B/B 3/22/89 ..... **4,950**
DWIGHT, Mabel (American, 1876-1955)
Still Life of Fruit, oil on canvas, 19x22", C-E 6/1/88 ..... **715**
DYASON, E.H. (British, 20th C)
Ships at Sea, oil on panel, sgn/dtd 09, 11x16", LH 9/10/89 ..... **400**
DYBSKY, Evgeni (Russian/Rumanian, 1955-)
Empty Avenues in the Park (abstract), oil on canvas, sgn/dtd 1985, 47x59", SBY 7/7/88 ..... **10,400**
Landscape with Architecture (abstract), oil on canvas, sgn/dtd 1986, 47x59", SBY 7/7/88 ..... **6,000**
Landscape with Falling Stars (abstract), oil on canvas, sgn/dtd 1985-86, 59x79", SBY 7/7/88 ..... **6,000**
Problems of Construction (abstract), oil on canvas, sgn/dtd 1987, 32x40", SBY 7/7/88 ..... **7,600**
DYCK, see Van Dyck
DYCKMANS, Josephus Laurentius (Dutch, 1811-1888)
Busy Housewife, oil on panel, sgn/dtd 1846, 14x12", WAD 6/6/88 ..... **2,600**
DYCKZKOWSKI, Eugene M.
Cary Street Houses, oil on canvas, sgn, 32x40", C-NY 9/30/88 ..... **7,700**
DYE, Charlie (American, 1906-1973)
Cutting Out Mexican Cows, oil on masonite, sgn, 30x40", C-NY 5/26/88 OE **18,700**
Over the Rope, oil on masonite, sgn w/insignia, 18x24", SBY 5/25/88 ..... **16,500**
Stranger in Town, oil on masonite, sgn w/insignia, 24x30", SBY 5/25/88 OE **46,200**
DYE, Clarkson (American, 1869-1955)
Old Pump, Columbia, California; oil on linen laid down, sgn/dtd 94, 18x23", B/B 10/6/88 ..... **2,750**
Palms, Death Valley; oil on board, sgn/dtd 1945, 20x24", B/B 10/6/88 ..... **990**
Santa Barbara Mission, oil on canvas, sgn, 20x30", B/B 5/17/89 ..... **1,540**
DYER, Hezekiah Anthony (American, 1872-1943)
Apple Blooming Time...Abbot Run Reservoir, Cumberland, Rhode Island; watercolor/gouache, sgn, 22x30", RWS 3/16/89 OE **1,000**
Caudebec, gouache on paper, sgn, 8x11", RWS 11/10/89 ..... **600**
Cliffs by the Ocean, gouache on board, sgn, 16x20", C-E 2/3/88 ..... **715**
Italian Landscape, gouache/watercolor on paper laid down on board, sgn, 12x16", C-E 6/1/89 ..... **605**
Venace, watercolor/gouache on paper laid down on board, sgn/inscr, 14x10", C-E 2/3/88 OE **1,320**
DYF, Marcel (French, 1899-1985)
Danseurs Espagnols (Spanish couple dancing), oil on canvas, sgn, 18x15", C-E 11/17/88 ..... **2,860**
En Deshabiller, oil on canvas, sgn, 22x19", WD 5/5/88 UE **4,000**
Femme Assise avec un Livre (woman seated w/book viewed from behind), oil on canvas, sgn, 15x18", C-E 11/17/88 OE **5,500**
Floral Still Life with Blue Vase, oil on canvas, sgn, 22x18", B/B 3/22/89 OE **9,900**
Flowers in a Glass on a Table, oil on canvas, sgn, 22x18", WD 5/5/88 ..... **5,250**
Gypsy Camp, oil on canvas, sgn, unfr, 18x22", SBY 10/5/88 ..... **4,950**
Landscape with Trees & Mountains, oil on canvas, sgn, 29x36", SBY 2/14/89 OE **8,250**
Le Centre du Village (village scene), oil on canvas, sgn, 21x15", C-E 11/17/88 ..... **2,420**
Le Port (port scene), oil on canvas, sgn, 18x22", C-NY 5/13/88 ..... **5,500**
Marche aux Fleurs, oil on canvas, sgn, 18x22", SBY 10/5/88 OE **9,350**
Peonies in a White Porcelain Pitcher, oil on canvas, sgn, 35x29", SBY 10/5/88 ..... **10,450**
Portrait of a Young Woman with Mandolin, oil on canvas, sgn, 29x24", SBY 10/5/88 OE **9,900**
Sailboats in a Calm, oil on canvas, sgn, unfr, 18x22", B/B 6/9/88 ..... **4,400**
Young Girl Combing Her Hair, oil on canvas, sgn, 18x22", WD 5/5/88 ..... **7,750**
Young Girl in Disarray, oil on canvas, sgn, 22x18", WD 5/5/88 OE **6,500**
Young Girl Seated at Table, oil on canvas, sgn, 22x18", SBY 10/7/89 ..... **5,775**
Young Girl with Hat, oil on canvas, sgn, 22x18", SBY 10/7/89 ..... **6,600**
DYKE, Samuel P. (American, fl 1855-1870)
Landscape with Barn, oil on canvas, sgn, 24x41", B/B 9/14/89 UE **990**
DYKMAN, Howard
In the Valley, oil on canvas, sgn, 22x31", C-E 9/15/88 UE **110**
DYSHLENKO, Yuri (Russian, 1936-)
Dirty Provocation: Dig Deeper (abstract); acrylic on canvas, sgn/dtd 1988/inscr Penta/titled, 59x38", SBY 7/7/88 UE **4,000**
Dirty Provocation: Espionage in an Area of Comfort (abstract); acrylic on canvas, sgn/dtd 88, 59x38", SBY 7/7/88 UE **4,000**
Dirty Provocation: Scandalous Details (abstract); acrylic on canvas, sgn/dtd 88/inscr Penta, 59x38", SBY 7/7/88 UE **4,000**
Dirty Provocation: What Were They Doing There? (abstract); acrylic on canvas, sgn/dtd 88/inscr Penta, 59x38", SBY 7/7/88 ..... **6,400**

ZIGURSKI, Alexander (American/Yugoslavian, 1910-)	
Below Big Sur, oil on canvas, sgn, 20x16", B/B 1/11/89	825
Pacific Sunset, oil on board, sgn, 23x47", B/B 10/6/88	1,430
Seascape at Sunset, oil on canvas, sgn, 36x48", lot 2147, DM 5/13/88	1,300
Seascape at Sunset, oil on canvas, sgn, 36x48", lot 2148, DM 5/13/88 UE	1,500
Sunset on the California Coast (seascape), oil on canvas, sgn, 16x20", RAB 8/9/88 UE	300
ZUBAS, Friedel (German, 20th C)	
Breaking Free (abstract), acrylic on canvas, sgn/dtd 1984-85, 40x40", SBY 10/8/88	5,500
Echo (abstract), oil on canvas, sgn/dtd 62, 21x20", SBY 10/7/89	4,125
Gray Abbey, oil on canvas, sgn twice/dtd 66, 95x72", C-E 5/13/88	3,080
Gray Beginning (abstract), magna on canvas, sgn/dtd 1975, 40x40", SBY 2/15/89	8,800
Gray Over Red (abstract), acrylic on canvas, sgn/dtd 71, 24", SBY 2/15/89	3,575
Heartland (abstract), acrylic on canvas, sgn/dtd 1983, 40x40", SBY 2/15/89	7,700
Henge (abstract), oil on canvas, sgn/inscr/dtd 1965, 69x84", C-NY 5/4/88/4/88	8,800
Klingsor's Promise (contemporary), acrylic on canvas, sgn/dtd 1975, 72x72", SBY 11/9/89	22,000
Melander's Bliss (abstract), acrylic on canvas, sgn/dtd 1983, 40x40", SBY 2/15/89	7,150
Mesita Run, acrylic on canvas, sgn/dtd 1976/titled, 40x40", C-NY 11/10/88 OE	10,450
Other Desert (abstract), acrylic on canvas, sgn/dtd 1974, 72x72", SBY 5/3/89	19,800
Red Over Blue (abstract), acrylic on canvas, 1973, 39x39", SBY 2/19/88 OE	14,300
Shonto (geometric abstract), magna on canvas, sgn/dtd 70, unfr, 24" dia, SBY 2/14/89	1,100
Untitled (abstract), acrylic on canvas, sgn, dtd twice 1969/1985, 24" dia, SBY 10/8/88	2,750
Untitled (abstract), acrylic on canvas, sgn/dtd 80, 72x72", SBY 10/5/89 OE	30,250
Untitled (abstract), dyes on handmade paper, sgn/dtd 81, 30x24", SBY 2/14/89	2,420
Untitled (abstract), oil on canvas, sgn, 82x47", C-E 11/17/88	2,640
Untitled (abstract), oil on canvas, sgn/dtd 65, 46x92", SBY 10/8/88	7,700
AKINS, Thomas (American, 1844-1916)	
Portrait of Professor William D Marks, oil on canvas, ca 1886, 76x54", SBY 5/24/89	165,000
ARL, George (British, 19th C)	
Seated Female Nude, oil on canvas, sgn, 36x28", B/B 5/17/89	1,320
ARL, Maud (British, 1864-1943)	
English Terriers on the Moor, oil on canvas, sgn, 46x22", SBY 6/10/88	8,250
French Poodle, sgn/dtd 1906, 24x20", SBY 6/10/88	5,500
German Shepherd in a Landscape, oil on canvas, sgn/dtd 1917, 66x50", WL 5/20/88	750
Little Blue Heron in Flight, oil on board, sgn, 1927, 35x60", SBY 10/24/89	15,400
Portrait of a Lady, oil on canvas, sgn/dtd 97, 84x48", SBY 6/8/88	4,950
ARL, Ralph; att (American)	
Portrait of a Man Said To Be John Jay, oil on canvas, 30x25", SBY 9/14/89	2,310
ARLE, Charles (British, -1893)	
English Garden in Springtime, watercolor/gouache over pencil, sgn, 14x30", C-NY 10/25/89 OE	3,520
ARLE, Lawrence Carmichael (American, 1845-1921)	
Butterfly, watercolor on paper, sgn/dtd 93, 13x10", SBY 3/17/88	660
Peddler, watercolor, sgn/dtd 1883, 28x20" LH 12/4/88 OE	1,600
Returning Home, oil on board, sgn, 11x14", C-E 11/8/88 UE	600
ARLY, Miles J. (American, 1886-)	
Winter, Northern Michigan (landscape); oil on canvas, sgn/dtd Dec 29th, 1931, 19x22", RAB 8/8/89 UE	150
ARNIST, Florence Reinhold (American, 20th C)	
California Landscape, oil on canvas, sgn/dtd 1946, 30x36", B/B 5/17/89	660
AST, Alfred (British, 1849-1913)	
Shady Pool, oil on canvas, sgn, 12x16", B/B 10/9/88	1,980
AST, Herbert (British, 19th C)	
Near Haslemere, Surrey; oil on canvas, sgn, 12x16", FB 4/25/88 OE	700
ASTMAN, Emily (American, 19th C)	
Lilac Veil (portrait of a young woman), watercolor/graphite on paper, 1830, 14x20", RWS 10/27/89	2,900
ASTMAN, William Joseph (American, 1888-1950)	
Monte Carlo, oil on canvas laid down on board, sgn/dtd 1922/titled, 25x25", C-E 9/15/88 UE	330
ATON, Alfred J. (American, 19th C)	
Early Autumn/Lovers Ramble/Watkins Glen/New York; oil on canvas, sgn/dtd 1895/titled, 20x16", RAB 3/27/89 UE	150
ATON, Charles Warren (American, 1857-1937)	
A Winter Scene, watercolor on paper, sgn/dtd 1888, 14x20", SBY 4/14/89	1,980
Berry Picking (girls picking berries, men at work in forest), watercolor on paper, sgn/dtd 81, 6x8", RAB 8/9/88 UE	125
Canal Bruges, oil on canvas, sgn, 18x16", C-E 9/15/88 UE	770
Connecticut Landscape, oil on canvas, sgn, 12x16", SBY 4/14/89	1,320
Connecticut Pine Trees, oil on canvas, sgn, 24x20", C-E 6/1/88	4,400
Evening Landscape, oil on canvas, sgn, 20x30", SBY 1/24/89	3,300
Glacier National Park, Montana; oil on canvas, sgn, 20x24", SBY 4/14/89 UE	1,320
Group of Pines, watercolor on paper, sgn, 16x20", C-E 2/1/89 UE	880
Landscape, oil on canvas, sgn, 12x16", SBY 1/24/89 UE	660
Landscape, watercolor/pencil on paper laid down on masonite, sgn, 11x15", C-E 6/1/89 UE	660
November (landscape), oil on canvas, sgn, 20x24", SBY 4/14/89 OE	6,050
Pair: Lake Como; oil on board, both sgn/1 inscr, 8x10" & smaller, C-E 6/1/88	1,100
Pastoral Landscape, oil on canvas, sgn, 16x22", B/B 6/15/89	3,025

Rocky Coast, watercolor/pencil on paper, sgn, 10x15" UE **440**
Sheep in Landscape, oil on canvas, sgn/indistinctly dtd 18(?), 20x30", C-E 2/3/88 ..... **4,400**
Stream Landscape, watercolor on board, sgn/dtd 1893, 12x15", C-E 11/30/88 ..... **1,430**
Sunset in Pine, oil on canvas, indistinctly sgn, 12x16", C-E 2/3/88 ..... **1,650**
Twilight, oil on canvas, sgn/dtd 1888, 12x16", SBY 9/23/88..... **4,400**

EATON, Hugh M. (American, 1865-1924)
Gunboats Tyler & Lexington at the Battle of Shiloh (Civil War), pen/ink on paper, sgn/inscr, 12x16", C-E 5/27/88..... **880**

EATON, I.F. (American, 19th C)
November (boys hunting birds), watercolor on paper, sgn/dtd 81, 10x7", RAB 8/9/88 ..... **400**

EBERHARD, Heinrich
Bildnis (abstract figure), oil on board, sgn/dtd 1923, 24x19", SBY 10/7/89 ..... **2,530**
Gesprach (three contemporary figures in interior), oil on board, sgn/dtd 1923, 20x24", SBY 10/7/89 ..... **2,200**
Village (cubist village landscape), oil on board, sgn/dtd 1916, 18x23", SBY 10/7/89 ..... **2,420**

EBERLE, Adolf (German, 1843-1914)
Love Letter, oil on cradled panel, sgn, 19x16", WAD 6/6/88 OE **19,000**

EBERT, Anton (Austrian, 1845-1896)
Gift of the Rose (portrait of lady w/two children), oil on canvas, sgn/dtd Wien 1887, 44x31", C-NY 2/23/89 ..... **7,700**

EBERT, C. (American/German, 19th C)
Untitled, deer in winter landscape; oil on canvas, sgn, 1898, 10x15", SLK 2/11/89 ..... **4,500**

EBERT, Carl (German, 1821-1885)
Fishing & Laundering in a Stream, oil on panel, sgn, 9x13", SBY 7/12/89 OE..... **8,250**
Mill in the Woods, oil on board, sgn, 10x15", SBY 7/12/89 ..... **7,700**

EBERT, Charles H. (American, 1873-1959)
Giverny (impressionistic landscape), oil on canvas, 25x30", C-NY 5/25/89 OE **24,200**
The Village Pump, oil on canvas, sgn, 25x30", C-NY 9/28/89..... **8,800**

EBHARD, G. (American, (19th C)
Sunset on the River, oil on canvas laid down on cardboard, sgn, 15x20", RAB 3/27/89 ..... **300**

ECHEVERRIA, Enrique (Mexican, 1923-1972)
Manit (abstract), oil on canvas, sgn/dtd 70, 32x24", C-NY 5/18/88 ..... **3,080**

ECHTLER, Adolf (German, 1843-1914)
Meditation (portrait of a girl holding a rosary), oil on canvas, sgn, 26x17", WD 11/16/88 ..... **3,500**

ECKBERG, John E. (American, 20th C)
Winter River (snow scene w/stream & trees), oil on canvas, sgn, orig frame, 22x26", RWS 9/29/88 UE **375**

ECKENFELDER, Friedrich (German, 1861-)
Plough-Team, oil on canvas, sgn, 35x50", C-NY 2/25/88 ..... **13,200**

ECKERMANS, Alice (European, 19th/20th C)
Fragments (young girl & boy gazing upward), oil on canvas, sgn/dtd 1893, 30x24", SBY 12/9/88..... **1,980**

EDAM, M.
Courting Scene (lady serving cavalier), oil on wood panel, sgn, 21x17", DM 10/14/88 ..... **1,700**

EDE, F.C.V. (Dutch, 20th C)
Grazing Cows, watercolor on paper, sgn, 14x18", B/B 1/11/89 UE..... **138**

EDE, Frederic (American, 1865-1907)
Fishing by the Stream, oil on canvas, sgn, 22x27", SBY 9/14/89..... **2,530**
French Landscape with House & Figure by the River, oil on canvas, sgn, 19x18", DM 2/19/88 ..... **2,500**

EDELFELT, Albert (Finnish, 1854-1905)

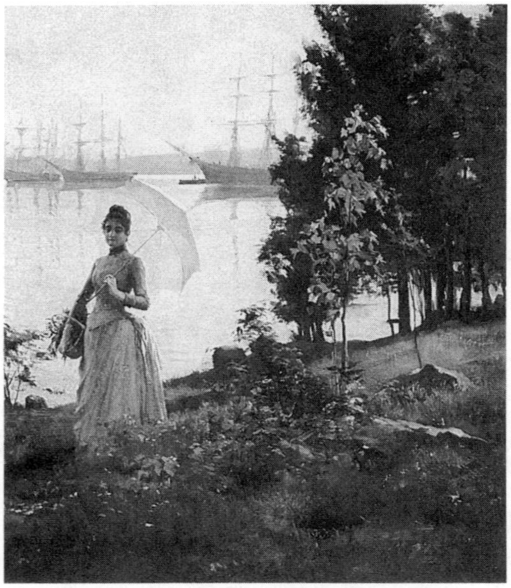

Woman with a Parasol, oil on canvas, sgn, 1887, 22x18", B/B 3/17/88 OE, $418,000

EDEN, John

Untitled Abstraction, oil/encaustic/paper collage on canvas mounted on panel, sgn, 1986, 9x12", C-NY 10/31/89 220

EDGERLY, Beatrice; att (American, 20th C)

Hugh, Portrait of a Young Man; watercolor on ivory, sgn/dtd 18, orig carved oak frame, 8x3", RWS 4/22/89 OE 900

EDLICH, Stephen (American, 1944-)

Reflections on a Season's Landscape (abstract), mixed media, sgn/dtd 1981.1982, 72x48", C-E 11/14/89 3,080
Studio View (abstract), paper & wood collage/charcoal on canvas, sgn/dtd January 1982, 44x30", C-E 11/14/89 880
Untitled (contemporary), acrylic/white chalk/paper collage on paper, gilt frame, 1980, 87x107", C-E 5/9/89 3,850
Untitled 48, mixed media, sgn/dtd 1977, 60x40", C-E 11/14/89 OE 5,500

EDMONDS, Francis William (Edmunds)(American, 1806-1863)

Barking Up the Wrong Tree (interior w/figures), oil on canvas, initialed/inscr, 16x20", C-NY 12/2/88 16,500

EDMONDSON, William S. (American, 1868-1951)

Landscape (meadow w/trees beyond), oil on board, sgn, 7x11", WG 4/23/88 175

EDRIDGE, Henry (British, 1769-1831)

Portrait of a Lady, full-length, in a black dress & white hat...; pencil/gray wash/watercolor, 13x9", C-NY 1/11/89 UE 550
Portrait of Colonel John Drinkwater-Bethume...; pencil/lt gray wash, 10x7", C-NY 1/11/89 1,650
Portrait of Edward, Viscount Lascelles...; black & red chalk/lt gray wash/pencil, 10x8", C-NY 1/11/89 OE 2,420

EDRIDGE, Henry; att (British, 1769-1831)

Portrait of a Gentleman Said To Be Charles Mall Pybus, MP; oil on canvas, 21x17", WD 1/25/89 OE 2,000

EDSON, Allan (Canadian, 1846-1888)

Farm Scene, oil on canvas, sgn/dtd 84, 15x25", C-E 10/18/89 2,860
Farm Scene, watercolor, sgn/dtd 1883, 10x17", FB 4/25/88 600
Un Jour de Decembre (winter landscape), oil on canvas, sgn/dtd 1884-85, 29x24", FB 5/28/89 8,500

EDUARDO, Jorge

Veneza, Villa Adriana; oil on masonite, sgn/dtd 88, 64x27", C-NY 11/21/89 11,000

EDWARD-MILLER, Richard

Summer Bouquet (still life), oil on canvas, sgn, 14x18", C-NY 5/25/89 8,800

EDWARDS, George Wharton (American, 1859-1950)

Fete Day, Paris; oil on canvas, sgn, 30x30", WD 4/13/88 OE 26,000
Flemish Lacemaker, gouache/pastel/pencil on brown paper laid down on board, sgn, 17x13", C-NY 9/28/89 9,900
Old Bridge & Washing Boats on the Seine, Paris; oil on canvas, sgn twice/inscr, 24x20", SBY 6/24/88 UE 3,850
Tea Time, watercolor/pencil heightened with gouache on paper laid down on board, sgn/dtd 1904, 17x23", C-NY 9/30/88 3,300

EDWARDS, H. (Canadian)

Pair: Logging in Muskoka; oil on canvasboard, sgn, 8x10", WAD 6/12/89 UE 100

EDWARDS, Harry C. (American, 1868-1922)

Federal Observation Balloon Being Shelled Across Chickahominy (Civil War), pen/ink/gouache, inscr, 9x12", C-E 5/27/88 OE 1,430
Protecting Her Cub, oil on canvas, sgn/copyrighted 1917, 36x24", SBY 1/24/89 OE 1,430

EDWARDS, J. (British, 19th C)

Snowy Winter Landscape, oil on canvas, sgn/dtd 1881, unfr, 20x30", SLK 9/27/88 750

EDWARDS, Lionel (British, 1878-1966)

Cottesmore, Ranksboro Gorse (fox hunt scene); oil on canvas, sgn, 20x30", SBY 6/10/88 OE 13,200
Taking Out the Hounds, oil on panel, sgn, 17x27", SBY 6/10/88 OE 19,800
Thoroughbred in Open Field, oil on canvas, sgn/dtd 51, 13x17", C-E 2/21/89 2,090

EDZARD, Dietz (German, 1893-1963)

At the Opera, oil on board, sgn, 13x6", SBY 10/5/88 OE 3,575
At the Party, oil on canvas, sgn, unfr, 28x22", WD 5/5/88 4,000
Au Cafe Concert (woman & other figures in an interior), oil on canvas, sgn/dtd 1942, 32x26", B/B 10/9/88 OE 8,800
Au Theatre (lady in profile at theatre), oil on canvas laid down on masonite, sgn, 27x24", C-E 11/17/88 OE 8,250
Bouquet sur Fond Jaune, oil on canvas, sgn, 22x18", SBY 10/5/88 OE 9,350
Cafe Scene, oil on canvas, sgn, 29x24", SBY 10/5/88 8,800
Caprice, oil on canvas, sgn, 29x24", C-E 5/9/89 OE 18,700
Chanteurs d'Operette, 1947 (couple watching opera), oil on canvas, sgn, 26x32", SBY 10/7/89 OE 18,700
Danseuse a l'Evantail, oil on canvas, sgn, 32x21", SBY 10/7/89 9,625
Fete au Grand Canal, oil on canvas, sgn, 16x13", B/B 4/20/88 1,045
Fete au Grand Canal (holiday on the Grand Canal), oil on canvas, sgn, 16x13", C-E 11/17/88 OE 8,250
Head of a Singer, oil on canvas, sgn, 16x11", SBY 10/7/89 1,575
In the Garden, oil on canvas, sgn, unfr, 22x18", SBY 10/5/88 OE 11,000
Jeune Femme avec Parasol (Young Woman with Parasol), oil on canvas, sgn, 11x9", C-E 11/17/88 935
La Repetition (three girls rehearsing a dance), oil on canvas, sgn, 1961, 17x9", C-E 11/17/88 OE 5,280
Le Grand Defile (girl watching parade), oil on canvas, sgn, 26x32", SBY 10/5/88 OE 11,000
Les Courses (racetrack), oil on canvas, sgn, 21x29", C-E 5/9/89 11,000
Pernod, oil on canvas, sgn, 30x23", SBY 10/7/89 7,040
Pink & Red Roses, oil on panel, sgn, 10x6", SBY 2/14/89 1,210
Prima Ballerina, oil on canvas, sgn, 26x19", B/B 10/9/88 OE 7,150
Rose pour la Fiancee, oil on paper laid down on canvas, sgn, 16x8", SBY 10/7/89 2,090
Roses, oil on canvas, sgn, 7x11", SBY 2/14/89 1,540
Still Life of Pink Rose & Sheet Music, oil on board, sgn, 13x6", SBY 10/7/89 1,760
Sur la Scene, oil on canvas, 24x20", C-E 5/13/88 3,080
Vase de Fleurs, oil on canvas, sgn, 9x7", C-E 5/9/89 OE 1,760
Vase de Fleurs, oil on canvas, sgn/inscr, No 240 on reverse, 29x21", SBY 10/5/88 5,225
Vendeuse de Fleurs, oil on board, sgn, 51x24", SBY 10/7/89 8,250

Woman with Flowers in Her Hair, oil on canvas, sgn, 16x13", SBY 10/7/89 .... **3,850**
Young Girl at a Cafe Along the Seine, oil on canvas, sgn, 26x22", WD 5/5/88 .... **3,200**
Young Woman & Children in a Park, oil on canvas, sgn, unfr, 18x15", B/B 3/22/89 OE........ **6,050**

EDZGVERADZE, Giya (Russian, 1953-)
Derby (abstract), oil on canvas, sgn/dtd 1983, 71x67", SBY 7/7/88 .... **5,600**
Jacob's Dream (abstract), oil on canvas, sgn/dtd 87, 79x63", SBY 7/7/88 OE **10,000**
Simple Secret (abstract), oil on canvas, sgn/dtd 1986, 71x79", SBY 7/7/88 .... **6,400**

EERELMAN, Otto (Dutch, 1839-)
Afternoon at the Beach, watercolor/gouache, sgn, 19x29", C-NY 10/25/89 OE **20,900**

EGERTON, Daniel Thomas (British, -1842)
Presa de Pozuelas (landscape), oil on canvas, sgn twice/dtd 1835/titled, 9x12", C-NY 11/21/88 OE **15,400**
Ravine of the Desert, oil on canvas, sgn twice/dtd 1838 twice/titled, 14x18", C-NY 11/21/88 .... **26,400**

EGERTON, Daniel Thomas; att (British, -1842)
Pair: Mexican Street Scenes; pencil/watercolor heightened with white, 6x8", C-SK 6/9/88 OE........ **2,045**

EGGENHOFFER, Nick (American, 1897-)
Lewis & Clark on the Yellowstone, gouache on paper, sgn, 15x25", SBY 5/25/88 OE **22,000**
Sheriff Wins, pen/black ink on board, sgn, 14x10", C-E 11/30/88 .... **1,320**

EGGLESTON, Benjamin (American, 1867-1937)
Brooklyn Bridge, oil on canvas, sgn, 48x38", SBY 1/24/89 OE **7,700**
Man Reading The Times (newspaper), oil on board, sgn, 11x15", SBY 1/24/89 .... **4,125**
Portrait of a Woman, oil on panel, sgn/dtd 95, 9x6", RWS 9/8/89 .... **1,500**
Portrait of a Young Lady, three-quarter length; oil on canvas, sgn, 50x36", PHL 12/1/88 UE **1,200**
Seated Woman with Fan in a Garden Setting, oil on canvas, sgn, 24x18", B/B 6/15/89........ **2,750**

EGLAN, Max (American, 1825-)
Man Sitting by a Stream, oil on canvas, unstretched, 7x12", C-E 2/3/88........ **385**
River Landscape, Men in Rowboat; oil on board, 7x12", FAP 4/15/89 .... **880**

EGOROV, A. (Russian)
View of Riga on the Baltic Sea, oil on panel, sgn, 11x13", C-L 10/8/88 .... **1,120**

EHNINGER, John Whetton (American, 1827-1889)
Portrait of a Gentleman, oil on canvas, sgn, 12x10", RAB 8/8/89 UE **300**

EHRET, Georg Dyonis (British, 1710-1770)
Branch of Double Red Camellia, watercolor/bodycolor on vellum, sgn/inscr, 21x15", C-NY 1/12/88........ **6,600**

EICHENS, Edward
Portrait of Three Girls, pencil/watercolor, sgn/inscr, wm Whatman Turkeymill 1832, 8x7", C-NY 5/25/88 .... **660**

EICHHOLTZ, Rebecca (American, 19th/20th C)
Foot of Sommes Sound, oil on canvas, sgn, 10x15", B/B 5/17/89 UE **935**

EICHINGER, Erwin (Austrian, 19th C)
Settling the Debt (interior scene w/figures), oil on panel, sgn/inscr Wien, 16x19", C-NY 2/23/89 OE **11,000**
Toper, oil on board, sgn, 13x10", WD 3/23/88 UE **1,000**

EICHINGER, Oswald (German, 1915-)
Still Life of Bananas, Apples & Mug; oil on panel, sgn, 13x11", LH 10/16/88 UE........ **800**
Still Life of Plums, oil on panel, sgn, 13x11", LH 10/16/88 .... **900**

EICHINGER, Otto (Austrian, 1922-)
Still Life of a Bowl of Cherries & Beer Stein, oil on panel, sgn, 13x11", C-E 5/23/88 .... **1,650**

EICHOLTZ, Jacob (American, 1776-1842)
Mrs Pierre Louis Laguerenne (portrait), oil on canvas, 30x25", C-NY 5/26/88 .... **2,200**
Portrait of Captain Jacob da Costa, oil on canvas, 23x18", SBY 1/24/89........ **2,200**

EICHOLTZ, Jacob; att (American, 1776-1842)
Portrait of Jeremiah & Sarah Lynard (early 19th C, bust-length), watercolor on paper, 5x4", C-NY 10/1/88 UE **550**

EICHSTAEDT, Rudolph (German, 1857-1924)
Bach Playing Before Frederick the Great, oil on canvas, sgn, 48x64", SBY 12/9/88 .... **3,300**

EICKELBERG, William Hendrik (Dutch, 1845-1920)
Fisherfolk by a Jetty in Stormy Seas, oil on canvas, sgn, 13x24", C-E 2/23/88 .... **1,650**
On a Winter Road, oil on panel, sgn, 12x16", SBY 7/12/89 .... **2,475**

EILSHEMIUS, Louis Michel (American, 1864-1941)
Autumn Mood, oil on board, sgn, 20x30", C-E 9/15/88 .... **935**
Barn in a Landscape, oil on canvasboard, sgn, 16x20", C-E 6/1/89........ **1,320**
Bather by a Stream, oil on paper mounted on masonite, sgn, 16x10", SBY 1/24/89 OE **1,760**
Bathers by a Woodland Fall, oil on paper mounted on panel, sgn, 8x5", RWS 5/12/89 .... **700**
Bathers in a Landscape, oil on board, sgn, 9x9", SBY 6/24/88 .... **1,100**
Boaters on a Lake, oil on masonite, sgn/dtd 1919, 18x31", SBY 1/24/89 .... **1,100**
Bust of Nude Woman, oil on paper mounted on board, sgn, 18x9", C-E 6/1/88 .... **880**
Coming Ashore, oil on board, sgn, 18x18", C-E 11/30/88 .... **1,870**
Dancing Bathers, oil on board, sgn/dtd 1910, 15x21", C-E 10/18/89 .... **1,430**
Four Nudes Bathing in a River, oil on board laid down on masonite, sgn/dtd 1919, 18x22", C-NY 3/11/88 .... **1,760**
Lady with Yellow Flowers in a Landscape, oil on masonite, sgn/dtd 1908, 15x22", SBY 3/17/88 OE........ **2,750**
Les Anbunet et Claire de Lune (landscape), oil on board, 18x14", SBY 3/17/88........ **770**
Moonlight Sail, oil on board, sgn, 13x10", C-E 6/1/88 .... **770**
Night in the City, pencil on paper, sgn, 7x5", C-E 6/1/89 .... **330**
Nude Bather, oil on board, sgn, 13x18", C-E 6/1/88 OE **1,650**
Nude by a Stream, oil on board, sgn, 12x11" oval, SBY 1/24/89 .... **440**

Nude in a Landscape, oil on paper mounted on masonite, sgn, 39x30", SBY 1/24/89	2,475
Nude Picking Blossoms, oil on canvas, sgn/dtd 1890, 13x8", SBY 4/14/89	1,980
Nude Swimming, oil on board, sgn, 9x17", C-E 11/30/88	825
Nude Washing Her Hair, oil on board, sgn, 8x6", C-E 2/3/88	495
Nymph, oil on masonite, sgn twice/inscr, 30x25", C-E 11/30/88	2,860
Nymphs Dancing by Moonlight, oil on board laid down on masonite, sgn/dtd 1908, 26x38", C-NY 3/11/88	4,950
Pair: Sail Boat Along the Shore; Landscape with Fisherman; oil on panel, sgn, 5x6", SBY 3/17/88	825
Pair: Square in Biskra; Sundown; watercolor/charcoal on paper, ea sgn/1 inscr, 10x13", C-E 2/3/88 OE	2,200
Palms at Biskra, oil on canvas, sgn/dtd 1891, 13x10", C-NY 6/17/89	990
Portrait of a Woman with Golden Hair, oil on board mounted on fiberhead, sgn, 20x18", C-E 2/3/88 OE	1,870
Reclining Nude, oil on board, sgn, 22x22", C-E 11/30/88	2,860
Samoan Bathers, oil on board, sgn, 16x20", C-E 9/15/88 OE	880
Shallow Waters, oil on board, sgn/dtd 1918, 20x29", C-E 11/30/88 OE	3,080
Summer Day, watercolor/pencil on paper, sgn, 10x13", C-E 2/3/88	550
Three Nudes Near a Stream, oil on canvas, sgn, 15x21", C-NY 3/11/88 OE	3,080
Two Bathers, oil on masonite, 9x8", SBY 6/28/89 OE	1,650
Two Men in a Boat, oil on paper mounted on board, sgn/dtd 1919, 8x13", C-E 6/1/88 UE	220
Two Nudes by a Waterfall, oil on board, sgn/dtd 1918, 23x23", B/B 9/15/88 UE	990
Two Nymphs, oil on board laid down on masonite, sgn/dtd 1908, 26x40", C-NY 3/11/88	6,050
Two Women in a Rowboat, oil on canvas, sgn, 11x13", C-E 10/18/89	1,320
Woman in a Swing, oil on board mounted on panel, sgn, 13x8", C-E 2/3/88 OE	1,540
1969 in Red, Green, & Yellow Flourescent Light; colored pencil/graphite on graph paper, sgn, 17x22", C-NY 11/10/88 OE	12,100
ISELE, Charles Christian Carl (American, 20th C)	
Black Canyon of the Gunnison, Colorado; oil on canvas, sgn, 30x48", B/B 5/17/89	1,870
ISEN, Francois (ca 1695-1778)	
Pair: Tavern Scenes with Guards Smoking & Drinking & Guards Brawling; oil on canvas, sgn/dtd 1770, 13x17", SBY 4/7/89	13,200
ISENDIECK, Suzanne (German, 1908-)	
Bouquet de Fleurs a la Fenetre, oil on canvas, sgn, 9x14", FB 10/17/88	2,000
Champ de Coquelicots, oil on canvas, sgn, 19x23", WD 5/5/88	1,200
Coiffure de Bal Champetre (portrait of a girl), oil on canvas, sgn, 21x10", SBY 10/5/88	2,750
Dans les Dunes, oil on canvas, sgn, 16x13", C-E 11/17/88 OE	2,420
Ete a Ramatelle (modernist landscape), oil on canvas, sgn, 26x22", B/B 6/15/89	3,300
Femme et Enfant au Bord de l'Eau, oil on canvas, sgn, 21x26", SBY 10/5/88	4,125
Fete a Issambres, oil on canvas, sgn, 22x18", FAP 11/4/88	2,500
Girl at the Lake, oil on canvas, sgn, 22x18", FB 10/30/89	5,500
Jeune Femme au Jardin, oil on canvas, sgn/#d 488, 22x18", C-NY 2/13/89	2,860
Jeune Garcon Deguis en Pierrot, oil on canvas, sgn, 18x13", C-E 11/17/88	1,760
La Chanteuse, oil on canvas, sgn, 29x24", B/B 6/9/88	4,675
Le Trac (three-quarter length portrait of elegant lady), oil on canvas, 24x14", SBY 2/14/89	2,475
Mother & Daughter on a Beach, oil on canvas, sgn, 26x21", SBY 10/7/89	4,125
Parasol a Ranayuelle, oil on canvas, sgn, 26x22", FAP 11/4/88	2,400
Petite Fille d'Honeur Romaine, oil on canvas, sgn, 14x11", FAP 11/4/88	1,000
Young Girl Holding Flowers, oil on canvas, sgn, 18x15", FB 5/28/89	3,500
Young Girl with Parasol, oil on panel, sgn, 11x9", FB 4/25/88	1,900
ISENHUT, Ferencz (Hungarian, 1857-1903)	
Backgammon Game, oil on canvas, sgn/dtd 86, 30x22", SBY 10/24/89	33,000
ISENSHITZ, Willy (French, 1889-1974)	
Canal St Martin, oil on canvas, sgn/dtd 1956, 32x40", WG 9/16/88	950
ISLER, Georg (Austrian, 1939-)	
Interieur mit Drei Figuren, oil on canvas, sgn/dtd 65-66, 24x32", C-E 11/17/88	1,870
Interieur mit Eintretendem III, oil on canvas, sgn/dtd 66, 32x24", C-E 11/17/88	935
ISMANN, Johann Anton; att	
Landscape with a City on a Harbor, oil on canvas, 32x51", SBY 10/13/89	14,300
KENAES, Jahn (Norwegian, 1847-1920)	
Talking to the Dolls, oil on canvas, sgn/dtd 1915, 26x19", SBY 6/8/88	4,950
KVALL, Knut (Swedish, 1843-1912)	
Reading Lesson, oil on panel, sgn, 30x24", C-NY 10/25/89	44,000
Waiting for Her Suitor (lady peering out window), oil on panel, sgn, 33x26", PHL 6/16/88	8,000
LDRED, E.W.	
Pair: Lendgay Castle; A Castle; oil on canvas, 1 sgn, 7x10", C-E 6/28/88	110
LDRED, Lemuel D. (American, 1848-1921)	
Fishing Off Grand Manan, oil on paper, sgn, 4x6", RAB 11/24/89	1,200
Fishing Village, pencil on paper, sgn, 7x11", RAB 8/9/88	300
Fishing Village (study of small village at water's edge), pencil on paper, sgn, 7x11", RAB 8/9/88	300
Fishing with Nets, oil on canvas, sgn, 12x20", C-E 11/30/88	2,640
Harbor Inlet, oil on canvas, sgn/dtd 74, 16x26", RWS 11/3/88 OE	10,000
Landscape, oil on canvas, sgn/dtd 1878, 22x36", C-E 10/18/89	1,980
Low Tide (figure/dory in coastal seascape), oil on cardboard, sgn/dtd 74, 4x8", RAB 8/8/89 OE	5,000
New England Coastal Scene, oil on canvas, sgn, 12x20", RAB 11/24/89	3,000
No 15 Fishing Settlement, NS (fishing boats, village beyond); oil on board, sgn/dtd 1880, RAB 8/9/88	6,500
Venetian Canal in Morning Light (canal scene, San Marco/palaces beyond), oil on canvas, sgn/dtd 81, 16x13", RWS 3/31/88	800

Venice Harbor (seascape), oil on canvas, sgn/dtd 83, 16x26", RAB 8/8/89 6,500

ELIAERTS, Jean Francois (Belgian, 1761-1849)
Still Life of Grapes, Peaches, & Cherries in Basket on Ledge...; oil on canvas, sgn/dtd 1829, 27x22", SBY 1/12/89 OE 57,750

ELIASOPH, Paula (American, 1895-1983)
Transportation (abstract composition), oil on canvas, sgn, 1940, 20x32", SBY 4/14/89 3,850

ELKINS, Henry Arthur (American, 1847-1884)
Rocky Mountains, oil on canvas, sgn/dtd 1883, 36x60", B/B 3/22/89 5,500
The Russian River, oil on canvas, sgn, 14x18", B/B 10/6/88 550
Western Landscape, oil on canvas, sgn, 25x46", WG 9/16/88 1,500

ELKINS, Henry Arthur; att (American, 1847-1884)
Mountain Landscape, oil on panel, 22x36", FAP 11/4/88 500

ELLENSHAW, Peter (20th C)
Seascape, oil on canvas, 25x50", DM 5/13/88 UE 3,000

ELLIOT, Charles Loring; att (American, 1812-1868)
Pair: Portraits of a Lady & a Man; oil on canvas/oil on canvas laid down on board, unfr, 21x17" oval, SBY 3/17/88 935

ELLIOT, Emily Louise Orr (Canadian, 1867-1952)
Still Life of Flowers, oil on canvas, sgn, 30x25", WAD 6/12/89 700

ELLIS, Edwin (British, 1841-1895)
Watering Hole (figures in a landscape), watercolor heightened w/gouache, sgn, 13x20", C-E 5/22/89 440

ELLIS, William (British, 1747-1810)
Otaheite, pencil/brush/ink/gray wash, inscr, unfr, 12x18", C-SK 11/10/88 1,770

ELLIS, William; att (British, 1747-1810)
View on the Coast of the Island of Dominica, gray wash, unfr, 11x15", C-SK 6/9/88 460

ELLIVAL, Charles
Interior of a Parlor, oil on canvas, initialed, 15x22", C-E 2/23/88 OE 2,090

ELLSWORTH, Clarence Arthur (American, 1885-1961)
Land of the Buffalo, oil on canvas, sgn/dtd 1930, 24x36", SBY 6/24/88 1,430

ELLSWORTH, James Sanford (American, 1802-1974)
Pair: Mr & Mrs Marcum; watercolor on paper, sgn by Mrs Marcum, orig veneer frame, 3x4", C-NY 10/1/88 OE 7,150

ELLY, Gerald (British, 1879-1972)
Ma Seyn Me (full-length portrait of woman in an interior), oil on canvas, sgn/dtd 1951, 42x32", SBY 2/22/89 OE 30,800

ELMER, Edwin Romanzo
White Magnolias in a Glass Pitcher, oil on canvas, ca 1890, 17x15", C-NY 9/28/89 7,700

ELMER, Steven; circle of (British, -1796)
Flushing a Pheasant, oil on canvas, 30x36", SBY 6/10/88 UE 3,300

ELSCHEIMER, Adam; circle of (German, 1578-1620)
Tobias & the Angel (in a landscape), oil on copper, 5x7", SBY 6/1/89 UE 22,000

ELWELL, D. Jerome (American, 1857-1912)
Breezy Day, Dordrecht, Holland (sailboats & windmill); watercolor on paper, sgn/dtd 12:95, 14x21", RAB 8/9/88 UE 250
The Grand Canal, Venice; oil on canvas, sgn/dtd 1900, 10x14", PHL 12/1/88 800
View Taken on Charles River, oil on canvas, sgn/dtd 9:77, 20x42", RWS 9/8/89 OE 1,300

EMBRY, Norris
Untitled (abstract figures), tempera/brush/India ink on paper, sgn, 13x19", C-E 11/14/89 1,540

EMERIC (French, 1920-)
Les Eternelles, oil on canvas, sgn, 1965, 58x45", LH 10/16/88 UE 50

EMERSON, Edith (American, 1888-)
Red Head, oil on board, sgn, 14x11", FAP 12/8/89 UE 175

EMERSON, Louis (American, 20th C)
Street in Gloucester, oil on canvasboard, sgn, 12x16", WG 9/16/88 UE 250

EMERSON, William Otto (American, 1856-)
Still Life of Pears, oil on canvas, sgn, 13x28", B/B 8/10/88 385

EMERY, James (American, 19th C)
Sunset on the Hudson River, oil on canvas, sgn, 30x24", RAB 11/25/88 UE 500

Emilian School (17th C)
Assumption of Saint Catherine, oil on canvas, unfr, 37x25", SBY 4/7/88 4,950

EMMET, Lydia Field (American, 1886-1952)
Two Sisters (portrait), pastel on canvas, sgn/dtd 97, 22x24", SBY 6/24/88 5,500

EMMONS, Alexander H. (American, 1816-1879)
Heavenward Gaze, oil on canvas, sgn/dtd 1876, 24x20", FAP 11/4/88 UE 180

EMMS, John (British, 1841-1912)
After the Hunt, oil on canvas, sgn, 35x51", SBY 6/10/88 OE 77,000
After the Hunt, watercolor, sgn/dtd 1899, 15x20", NA 11/5/88 2,100
After the Hunt (portrait of four tired hounds), oil on canvas, sgn/dtd 1887, 49x36", SBY 6/9/89 38,500
At the Blacksmith's, oil on canvas, sgn/dtd 1898, 30x45", SBY 6/9/89 18,700
Awaiting Dinner (dogs in an interior), oil on canvas, sgn, 16x22", SBY 6/10/88 OE 16,500
Before the Hunt, oil on canvas, sgn/dtd 1896, 24x36", SBY 6/10/88 22,000
Black Horse in a Stall, oil on canvas, sgn, 21x26", SBY 6/10/88 4,125
Cattle in a Landscape, oil on canvas, sgn/dtd 79, 9x12", C-E 10/25/88 UE 1,650
Chicken & Rooster in a Landscape, oil on canvas, sgn, 15x13", C-E 10/25/88 2,530
Cow Eating Hay, oil on board, sgn/dtd 75, 9x14", C-E 10/26/89 2,090
Milking Time, oil on canvas, sgn/dtd 88, 28x36", SBY 6/10/88 17,600

Quex (dog), oil on canvas, sgn/inscr w/dog's name/dtd 1904, 14x18", SBY 6/10/88	5,720
Rough Journey Home, oil on canvas, sgn/dtd 83, 34x46", SBY 6/10/88	55,000
Still Life of Canteloupe & Nuts, oil on canvas, sgn, 7x9", C-E 10/25/88 UE	1,500
The Kill (hunter, horse, & fox hounds after the prey), oil on canvas, sgn, 18x25", SBY 6/10/88	6,600
Waiting for the Master (horse & dog by steps), oil on canvas, sgn, 15x19", SBY 6/9/89	11,000
Wire Haired Terrier, oil on canvas, sgn/dtd 1897, 14x16", SBY 6/10/88	4,950
:MMS, John; manner of (British, 1841-1912)	
Tug of War (pups playing w/mother watching), oil on canvas laid down on board, 21x17", SBY 6/9/89	2,475
:MPAIN, Joseph	
Japanese Doll, oil on canvas, sgn, 24x18", C-E 2/23/88	2,200
:MPOLI, Jacopo da; see Chimenti, Jacopo	
:NCKE, Fedor (German, 1851-)	
Portrait of Mrs Learner B Harrison, oil on canvas, sgn/dtd 1897, 27x21", LH 10/16/88 UE	275
Two Sisters (portrait in a landscape), oil on canvas, sgn/dtd New York Dec, 1877, 46x34", C-NY 2/23/89	10,450
:NDER, Axel Hjalmar (Norwegian, 1853-1920)	
Sleigh Ride (girl sledding down a hill), oil on panel, sgn, 12x9", C-NY 2/23/89 OE	24,200
:NDER, Edouard (Australian, 1822-1883)	
Sleeping on Duty, oil on panel, sgn, 12x10", B/B 9/15/88	1,430
:NDER, Maria (Russian, 1895-1955)	
Untitled (abstract), watercolor on paper, ca 1932, 9x12", SBY 7/7/88 OE	9,000
:NDER, Thomas (Austrian, 1793-1875)	
Afternoon Stroll Through the Park, oil on canvas, sgn, 15x10", C-E 2/21/89 UE	2,420
:NDER, Thomas; att (Austrian, 1793-1875)	
Fazenda dos Jezuitas, Ponte dos Jezuitas, Santa Cruz, Near Rio de Janeiro; oil, 15x24", C-SK 6/9/88	5,580
:NGEL, Johann Friedrich (German, 1844-)	
Tyrolean Boy with Knapsack, oil on panel, sgn, 13x10", WAD 6/6/88	5,500
:NGELHARDT, Georg (German, 1823-1883)	
Alpine Mill House, oil on canvas, sgn/dtd 1864, 47x39", SBY 2/22/89	11,000
:NGELHART, Joseph (Austrian, 1864-1941)	
Figures on a Paris Street, gouache/watercolor/charcoal on board, sgn/dtd 92, 5x7", C-E 2/25/88 OE	1,100
NGLAN, Max (American, 1925-)	
River Landscape at Dusk, oil on canvas, sgn, 20x28", FAP 4/15/89	1,072
NGLEHARDT, Edna Palmer (American, 19th/20th C)	
Winter Landscape, oil on canvas, sgn, 25x30", WG 9/16/88	900
NGLISH, Frank F. (American, 1854-1922)	
Along the Road, Sunset; watercolor/gouache on paper, sgn, 27x15", RWS 8/20/88	425
Clearing Timber, watercolor on paper, sgn, 23x35", WG 4/23/88	2,500
Farmhouse with Flowering Cherry, watercolor on paper, sgn, 18x40", WG 4/23/88	2,100
Greetings on a Country Path, watercolor/gouache on paper, sgn, 13x26", C-E 9/15/88 OE	2,310
Harvest Time, watercolor/gouache, sgn, 19x28", FAP 4/15/89	1,210
Hay Wagon, watercolor heightened w/white on paper, sgn, 17x27", RWS 4/7/89 UE	450
Horsecart, watercolor on paper, sgn, 15x32", C-E 9/15/88 OE	2,310
Landscape, watercolor on paper, sgn, 23x39", LH 10/16/88 OE	2,200
Log Carriers (man leading team of horses pulling logs), watercolor on board, sgn, 39x17", C-E 2/1/89 OE	2,860
Pumpkin Patch (man w/horse & wagon in field w/dog), watercolor on paper, sgn, 14x20", RWS 9/8/89	1,300
Road Home (man/dog lead ox cart in landscape), watercolor/gouache on paper, sgn, 18x28", RAB 3/27/89 UE	300
Steamboat on the Brandywine River, watercolor on paper, sgn, 12x21", FAP 11/4/88	800
Team of Horses on a Country Road by a Stream, watercolor/gouache on paper, sgn, 18x28", SBY 1/24/89	1,430
Windmill & Sailboats, watercolor on paper, sgn, 12x21", C-E 11/30/88	1,100
NGLISH, T.H. (19th C)	
Snowy Winter Street Scene, oil on canvas, monogramed/dtd 1920, 31x44", SLK 5/9/88	175
nglish School (16th C)	
Portrait of a Gentleman Said To Be Lord Burleigh, Aged 34; oil on canvas, inscr/dtd 1590, 42x35", C-NY 10/20/88 OE	12,100

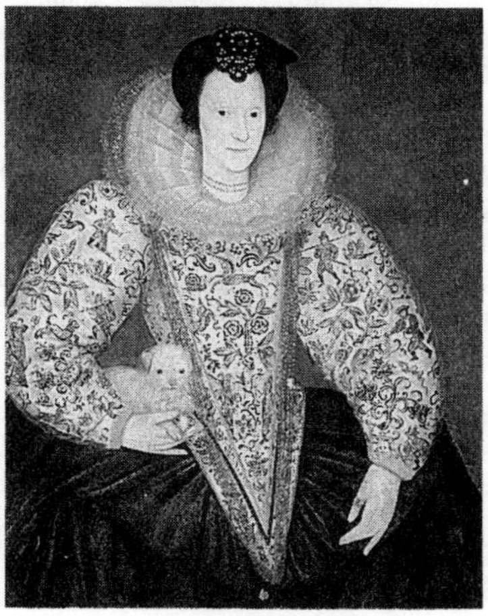

Portrait of a Lady, wearing embroidered & beaded dress, holding a lap dog; tempera on panel, 44x35", C-NY 6/2/88, $6,600

English School (17th C)

- Portrait of a Lady, oil on canvas, 14x12", LH 10/16/88 ... **225**
- Portrait of Queen Elizabeth I, half-length, holding the septre & orb; oil on canvas, 27x20", SBY 10/21/88 OE ... **5,500**

English School (18th C)

- Arcadian landscape with Temple & Figure, oil on canvas laid down on board, 16x22", C-E 6/1/88 ... **1,430**
- Card Game, watercolor, sgn, 12x18", MG 12/10/88 UE ... **300**
- Country Squire, oil on canvas, 32x25", LH 10/16/88 OE ... **800**
- Landscape with Figure, no media given, 10x8", WG 9/16/88 ... **80**
- Men Pushing a Boat Off a Beach, pencil/pen/brown ink/watercolor, crowned shield wm, ca 1790, 9x13", C-NY 1/12/88 OE ... **1,210**
- Milkmaid, oil on canvas, framed in an oval, 9x11", MG 7/30/88 UE ... **200**
- Pair: Girl Offering Cherries to a Bird; Young Boy Offering Cherries to a Dog; oil on canvas, 44x35", SBY 10/21/88 ... **6,600**
- Pair: Portraits of a Lady & a Gentleman (three-quarter length); oil on canvas, 49x39", SBY 4/7/89 OE ... **8,800**
- Pastoral Scene, oil on canvas, 28x38", LH 5/15/88 ... **2,500**
- Portrait of a Gentleman (seated in giltwood chair, w/classical column in background), oil on canvas, 30x25", SLK 5/9/88 ... **350**
- Portrait of a Girl Holding a Peach, oil on canvas, 36x28", SBY 4/7/88 ... **2,750**
- Portrait of a Lady Holding Her Child, oil on canvas, 30x25", WD 1/25/89 ... **5,000**
- Portrait of a Man, half-length, in a wig, wearing a brown coat; oil on canvas, 30x25", C-E 4/7/88 ... **770**
- Portrait of JMW Turner (said to be a self-portrait), oil on canvas, 23x20", WG 4/23/88 UE ... **2,000**
- Portrait of King George I, wearing robes of state & the order of St George; oil on canvas, 56x47", C-NY 10/20/88 ... **2,200**
- Portrait of Robert, Viscount Hampden; oil on board, sgn/dtd 75, oval, 14x11", WL 5/20/88 UE ... **200**

English School (19th C)

- Angler & Cattle by a River, oil on canvas, 8x12", PHL 10/28/88 UE ... **375**
- Boaters in a River Near a Thatched Cottage, oil on canvas, 14x13", C-E 2/16/88 ... **198**
- Boy & Girl with Dog in Landscape, oil on canvas, 20x15", C-E 3/22/88 OE ... **1,760**
- Bridgetown, Barbadoes From the Icehouse; pencil/bodycolor, initialed/dtd 1867, 7x10", C-SK 11/10/88 ... **520**
- Busy Harbor Scene with Multiple Three Masted Ships at Anchor, watercolor, 10x14", SLK 5/9/88 ... **850**
- Busy Harbor Scene with Multiple Three Masted Ships at Anchor, watercolor, 10x14", SLK 2/12/88 ... **1,200**
- Cathedral Overlooking a Cobblestone Street, watercolor on paper, sgn/dtd 1908, 21x14", C-E 10/25/88 UE ... **220**
- Cherub with a Cross, oil on panel, 5x8", MG 12/10/88 ... **175**
- Children Fishing, oil on canvas, 16x24", C-E 5/23/88 ... **660**
- Children in a Landscape, oil on canvas, ca 1820, 48x60", C-E 1/12/88 ... **2,530**
- Coastal Scene with Fisherfolk & Boats, oil on panel, 9x11", SLK 9/29/88 ... **150**
- Country Lane (w/figures), watercolor, indistinctly sgn/dtd 1879, 9x12", C-E 5/22/89 ... **1,100**
- Cow on a Path, oil on canvas, 22x30", C-E 11/8/88 ... **990**
- Elaborate Still Life in an Urn, oil on canvas, 30x25", C-E 2/23/88 ... **2,750**
- Extensive River View with Castle in the Distance, oil on canvas, indistinctly sgn, 11x15", C-E 5/23/88 ... **880**
- Fairies with an Owl & Other Creatures, black chalk/pencil/watercolor on lt tan paper, 21x13", C-E 2/21/89 ... **660**
- Farm Scene, oil on canvas, 7x8", MG 5/28/88 ... **275**
- Figure by a Stream Before a Cottage, oil on canvas, 12x18", PHL 10/28/88 ... **600**
- Full Cry, oil on canvas laid down on board, 26x41", WD 1/25/89 OE ... **5,750**
- Gentleman (half-length, holding a book), oil on canvas, 30x25", C-E 2/16/88 ... **418**
- Group of 3: Thingvalla Landscapes, Iceland; oil on shaped canvas, 1 dtd 1878/#d, unfr, 10x14", C-SK 6/9/88 ... **297**
- Heavenly Procession (descending angels), watercolor/gouache/pencil/pen/black ink, unfr, 16x10", C-NY 2/23/89 ... **1,210**
- Herdsman with His Flock by a River, oil on canvas, 19x25", C-E 4/7/88 UE ... **715**
- Horses Grazing, oil on canvas laid down on board, 20x34", C-E 5/23/88 ... **1,650**
- Huntsman & His Hound, oil on canvas, 25x34", C-E 2/23/88 OE ... **3,300**
- Indian Port, watercolor/bodycolor, 10x31", C-SK 11/10/88 ... **930**
- Indian Scene, oil on canvas, 17x28", C-SK 11/10/88 ... **1,210**
- Indians Grading & Packaging Pekoe Tea, oil on canvas, sgn w/monogram GP, 26x36", C-SK 6/9/88 ... **930**
- Inside the Garden Wall (two women conversing), oil on canvas, 25x21", RWS 4/7/89 ... **475**
- John the Baptist with Jesus, oil on canvas, 15x19", MG 5/28/88 UE ... **325**
- Lady in the Woods, oil on canvas, indistinctly sgn, 20x31", MG 7/30/88 ... **375**
- Lady Wearing a Plumed Hat, oil on canvas, 30x25", C-E 2/23/88 ... **715**
- Landscape with Children Beside a Pond with Farmyard & Buildings Beyond, oil on canvas, 20x24", SLK 9/27/88 ... **900**
- Landscape with Figures, oil on canvas, 36x51", LH 5/15/88 ... **550**
- Lion, oil on canvas, 36x30", C-E 2/23/88 OE ... **4,620**
- Madonna & Child Enthroned Surrounded by Saints & Angels: Small Alterpiece w/Wings; oil on metal, 18" high, WD 1/25/89 OE ... **1,700**
- Maiden with a Plate of Fruit & a Greyhound, oil on canvas, 45x28", C-E 5/23/88 OE ... **2,640**
- Mountain & Lake Landscape at Sunset, watercolor on paper, 5x10", SLK 2/12/88 ... **175**
- Old Man & His Friends, oil on board, initialed, 10x16", MG 3/26/88 ... **1,000**
- On the Shelf, oil on canvas, 15x20", WD 3/23/88 ... **3,250**
- Paddle Streamer Ho Nan, Hong Kong, Canton & Macao Steamboat Co, Ltd; oil on canvas, ca 1850, 20x28", C-E 4/7/88 OE ... **2,640**
- Pair: Landscapes with Fishermen Beside Streams; oil on canvas, 18x14", SLK 5/9/88 ... **700**
- Pair: Portrait of Sam Salter; Portrait of Hannah Salter; oil on panel, 12x10", RWS 12/10/88 ... **750**
- Panoramic View of a Valley in Kashmir, pencil/watercolor, 13x64", C-SK 11/10/88 ... **590**
- Pansies & Bird's Nest on a Mossy Bank, oil on canvas, indistinctly signed/dtd 1860, 11x9", C-E 2/21/89 ... **3,300**
- Pasture Around the Tyrolean Alps, oil on canvas, 23x29", WL 5/20/88 ... **1,000**
- Peasants on a Path Returning Home, initialed, unfr, 21x35", C-E 2/23/88 ... **935**
- Portrait of a Boy in a Lace Collar, oil on canvas, ca 1830, 18x15", C-E 1/12/88 OE ... **495**
- Portrait of a Cavalier, oil on board, oval, 27x23", C-E 4/7/88 UE ... **440**
- Portrait of a Dog (floating on a raft), oil on canvas, 44x30", SLK 9/27/88 ... **1,900**

Portrait of a Gentleman, oil on canvas, 30x25", WD 1/25/89	1,000
Portrait of a Gentleman, oil on panel, 20x16", LH 5/15/88	275
Portrait of a Gentleman, Three Quarter-Length, Standing in a Landscape; oil on canvas, 50x40", SBY 10/21/88	2,750
Portrait of a Gentleman Said To Be John Calcott Horsley, oil on canvas, 31x25", WD 3/23/88	1,000
Portrait of a Gentlewoman with Her Dog, oil on canvas, 45x29", NA 5/13/89	950
Portrait of a Horse, oil on canvas, 24x16", MG 5/28/88	175
Portrait of a Lady (long bust-length), oil on canvas, 26x21", PHL 10/28/88 UE	750
Portrait of a Lady Wearing a Bonnet, pencil w/traces of black conte chalk/wash, ca 1810, 6x5", SWN 12/1/88 UE	193
Portrait of a Man (bust-length), oil on board, monogramed, 11x9", WL 5/20/88 OE	900
Portrait of a Seated Gentleman, oil on canvas, 49x38", MG 3/26/88	900
Portrait of a Seated Gentleman, pastel, 14x11", LH 3/20/88	140
Portrait of a Woman in a Roman Dress, oil on canvas, 21x17", C-E 2/16/88	264
Portrait of a Young Boy in a Top Hat, oil on board, 20x25", MG 7/30/88	775
Portrait of Woman in 17th-C Costume, oil on canvas, 20x16", C-E 6/1/88	880
Profile of a Young Man Wearing a Hat with a Red Plume, oil on canvas laid down on board, 12x10", SLK 2/12/88	100
Promenade in the Park, watercolor/gouache on paper, 21x29", C-E 10/25/88	715
Quebec (viewed from the sea w/ships), pen/ink/watercolor on laid paper, wm PRADO w/fleur-de-lys, 9x13", C-SK 6/9/88	557
Regatta, oil on canvas, 23x35", C-E 5/22/89	2,860
River Landscape with Castle, oil on canvas, initialed, 12x24", FAP 4/15/89 UE	577
Riverscape, oil on canvas, sgn, 12x18", MG 8/27/88 UE	100
Robbers on the Road, watercolor, 5x8", MG 2/27/88 UE	60
Scottish Heather, oil on canvas, indistinctly sgn, 28x40", MG 8/27/88 UE	225
Set of 4: Country Houses & a Church; ink on paper, 3x4", SLK 6/26/88	300
Settling Accounts (interior genre subject), oil on canvas, 24x36", SLK 5/11/88	1,500
Sheep Resting Under Trees, oil on canvas, 16x24", C-E 9/15/88	880
Shipwreck, oil on canvas, 24x32", C-E 2/23/88	1,100
Sitting Pretty (portrait of a young girl & her dog), oil on canvas, 30x25", RWS 4/7/89	750
St Helena, pencil/watercolor heightened w/bodycolor, unfr, 14x21", C-SK 5/25/89	280
Still Life of Peaches, oil on panel, 8x9", RWS 5/19/88	800
Study of a Terrior, oil on board, bears signature, 11x14", PHL 10/28/88	475
Study of a White Stallion, oil on panel, 10x14", C-E 5/23/88 UE	165
Study of a Young Italian Boy Smoking a Cigarette (half-length), oil on canvas, sgn/dtd 1888, 12x10", SLK 2/12/88	50
Summer Days (landscape w/pond & figures), oil on canvas, momogramed, 18x30", WD 5/5/88	3,600
The Proposal, oil on canvas, bears signature, 41x28", PHL 6/16/88 UE	140
Three-Masted Clipper Ship at Sea, oil on canvas, 26x42", C-NY 2/23/89 OE	7,700
Traveler on a Country Path, oil on board, 19x18", C-E 4/7/88	1,430
Two Figures in Cottage Garden, oil on canvas, 28x14", C-E 2/16/88	418
Victorian Interior with Girl Seated in Study with Two Dogs, oil on canvas, sgn/dtd 1877, 26x18", SLK 5/11/88	1,400
View From Wooded Kloof, in Drakensberg Mountains...; watercolor, inscr, unfr, 7x10", C-SK 6/9/88	240
View of Paris, oil on canvas, 22x32", C-E 10/25/88 OE	9,350
Village, watercolor/gouache on paper, indistinctly sgn/dtd 1880, 17x23", C-E 11/8/88 UE	132
White Horse in a Landscape, oil on canvas, indistinctly sgn, 28x35", WD 3/23/88	1,500
Winter Farm Scene with Horses & Other Farm Animals, oil on panel, 12x20", SLK 9/26/88	600
Young Girl with a Pink Rose, pastel on paper, oval 13x11", C-E 5/3/88	242
Young Girl with Autumn Leaves, oil on canvas, 24x20", C-E 7/26/88	660
Young Girl with Basket, oil on board, 8x10", MG 6/25/88	400
Young Girl with Her Dog (in a landscape), oil on canvas, 30x25", WL 5/20/88 OE	3,200
Young Lady Wearing a Crown of Laurel Leaves, oil on canvas, framed as an oval, 24x20", C-E 11/8/88	1,000
nglish School (20th C)	
Coastal Scene, watercolor, 11x21", MG 5/28/88	140
Landscape with Boy & Girl Fishing in a Stream, oil on canvas, indistinctly sgn, 16x22", SLK 5/9/88	225
Racehorse with a Jockey Up, oil on canvas, 26x33", C-E 2/23/88	1,980
Seascape, oil on canvas, 23x40", MG 8/27/88 UE	150
Shipping Off the Harbor, oil on panel, bears signature, 24x36", C-E 2/23/88	2,750
Ships on High Seas, oil on canvas, indistinctly sgn, 27x39", C-E 2/16/88	550
NIKO, Zulij (Hungarian, 20th C)	
Still Life of Pink Roses, oil on canvas, sgn/dtd 77, 10x8", WG 9/16/88 UE	30
NJOLRAS, Delphin (French, 1857-)	
The Rose (portrait of seated nude smelling a rose), pastel on canvas, sgn, 28x20", C-NY 5/24/89 OE	8,250
Two Ladies Reading by Lamp Light, oil on canvas, sgn, 18x22", SBY 6/8/88	6,875
NNEKING, John Joseph (American, 1841-1916)	
Autumn Landscape, oil on canvas, sgn/dtd 00, 22x30", SBY 1/24/89 OE	7,700
Autumn Landscape, oil on canvas, sgn/dtd 97, 30x22", C-NY 5/25/89	19,800
Autumn Sunset, Hyde Park; oil on canvas, sgn, 22x35", RWS 11/10/89 OE	8,750
Autumn Sunset, oil on board, sgn, 8x9", SBY 9/23/88	1,320
Autumn Sunset, oil on canvas, sgn, 18x24", C-NY 3/11/88	4,400
Autumn Twilight, oil on canvas mounted on masonite, sgn, 60x68", C-NY 5/26/88	39,600
Autumn Woods, Sunset; oil on canvas, sgn, 39x50", RWS 11/3/88 UE	5,500
Blossom Time, oil on board, sgn, 8x12", C-NY 9/30/88	4,950
Blue Shawl (portrait of a woman), oil on canvas, sgn/dtd 1920, 30x30", C-NY 5/26/88	4,400
Country House by a River's Edge, oil on canvas, bears signature, 24x30", SBY 1/24/89	7,150

Figure in a Winter Marsh, Sunset; oil on canvas, sgn/dtd 83, 10x12", RWS 9/8/89 ... 900
Harbor Scene-Low Tide (sailing ship on shore); oil on artist board, sgn/dtd 84, 8x11", RWS 5/19/88 ... 3,600
Hunters in the Snow, oil on panel, 8x13", C-NY 5/26/88 ... 12,100
Indian Summer, oil on canvas, sgn/inscr, 19x24", C-NY 5/26/88 ... 11,000
Indian Summer, Sunset; oil on canvas, sgn/dtd 98, 22x30", SBY 9/14/89 ... 4,070
Landscape Scene with Boat on Shore, oil on canvasboard, sgn/dtd 77, 9x7", RWS 5/12/89 ... 1,200
Loading the Hay Wagon, oil on canvas, sgn/indistinctly dtd 96(?), 22x33", WD 4/13/88 ... 12,000
Marshes at Dusk, oil on canvas, sgn/dtd 88, 16x22", RWS 11/10/89 ... 6,500
Mountain Vista, Early Autumn; oil on panel, sgn, 18x24", RWS 5/19/88 ... 3,200
New England Hillside, oil on canvas, sgn/dtd 02, 18x24", C-NY 9/30/88 OE ... 11,000
New England Village in Autumn Twilight, oil on board, sgn, 5x7", RWS 11/3/88 ... 1,500
November (landscape w/cows), oil on canvas, sgn/dtd 79, 32x39", C-NY 12/2/88 ... 52,800
Old Farm, oil on canvas, sgn, unfr, 9x19", RAB 8/8/89 UE ... 700
Old Red Mill, oil on board, sgn/inscr, 10x14", C-NY 9/30/88 OE ... 8,800
Pair: Pasture Scenes; oil on board, unfr, 7x5", RWS 11/10/89 ... 550
Peaceful Valley (cows grazing & watering), oil on canvas, sgn/dtd 77, 12x18", C-NY 5/25/89 ... 7,150
Sheep in a Pasture at Ogunquit, Maine; oil on canvas, 18x24", SBY 9/23/88 ... 3,850
Summer Landscape, oil on canvasboard, sgn/dtd 1898, 9x12", MAG 4/24/88 ... 900
Sunset, oil on board, sgn, 14x16", C-NY 9/30/88 ... 2,530
Sunset, oil on board, 9x12", WD 3/23/88 ... 1,200
Winter (snowy landscape w/figures & buildings), oil on canvas, 18x25", C-NY 5/25/89 UE ... 9,350

ENNEKING, Joseph Elliot (American, -1946)
Apple Blossom, oil on canvas, sgn, 12x24", MG 10/28/88 ... 550
Appletree-E Gloucester, Massachusetts; oil on canvasboard, sgn, 14x12", RWS 11/3/88 ... 950
Mills Along the River (believed to be along the Merrimack River, Massachusetts), oil on canvas, 14x18", RWS 9/29/88 OE ... 1,700
New England Homestead (house beyond trees), oil on canvas, sgn/dtd 1916, 17x21", RWS 5/19/88 OE ... 2,000
Paul's Bridge in Readville, Massachusetts; oil on panel, sgn/dtd 68, 8x10", RWS 5/19/88 ... 650

ENNIS, George Pearce (American, 1884-1936)
Hunting Party at Klachau, watercolor/charcoal on paper, sgn, 16x20", SBY 4/14/89 ... 660
Repairing the Boat (family scene by dwelling), oil on canvas, sgn, 25x30", SBY 4/14/89 ... 1,430
Rising Fog (men conversing by docked boat), oil on canvas, sgn, 24x29", SBY 4/14/89 OE ... 3,850
Smugglers Cove, oil on canvas, sgn, 25x30", C-NY 9/30/88 ... 4,950
St Andrews Light (lighthouse w/sailboats on water beyond), oil on canvas, sgn, 35x36", C-NY 9/28/89 ... 7,150

ENNIS, Gladys Atwood (American, 19th/20th C)
Counterpoint (abstract composition), oil on canvas, sgn, 26x32", RWS 9/8/89 UE ... 250

ENRIQUEZ, Carlos (South American, 20th C)
Sugar Cane Cutters (three caricature nudes), oil on canvas, sgn, ca 1950s, 30x24", SBY 11/21/88 ... 4,400

ENSER, John F. (American, 1898-)
Autumn, oil on board, sgn, 12x16", RAB 8/9/88 ... 325
Autumn (forest landscape), oil on board, sgn, 12x16", RAB 8/9/88 ... 325

ENSOR, James (Belgian, 1860-1940)
Judith et Holopherne (biblical scene), oil on canvas, sgn/dtd 79, 21x26", C-NY 5/11/89 ... 71,500
La Tentation de St Antoine, pencil on paper mounted at edges on board, sgn/dtd 1901, 8x11", C-NY 11/15/88 OE ... 24,200
Mon Atelier (My Studio), colored pencils on paper, sgn/dtd 31 XII 1930, 11x8", SBY 11/16/89 ... 34,100

EPP, Rudolf (German, 1834-1910)
Lady Wearing a Mantilla (portrait), oil on panel, sgn, 11x8", C-NY 2/23/89 ... 6,050
Lady with a Guitar, oil on canvas laid down on board, sgn, 9x7", C-NY 5/25/88 ... 6,050
Lesson, oil on canvas, sgn/dtd 1877, 30x25", LH 10/16/88 ... 13,000
Red Sleeve, oil, sgn, 15x10", WD 1/11/89 OE ... 4,500

EPSTEIN, Henri (Polish, 1891-)
Port Scene, oil on canvas, sgn, 18x26", SBY 5/30/89 ... 6,600
Reclining Nude, oil on canvas, sgn, 20x24", SBY 5/30/89 ... 4,070
Village Street, oil on canvas, sgn/dtd 1934, 16x24", SBY 5/30/89 OE ... 8,800

EPSTEIN, Jacob (British, 1880-1959)
Roses, watercolor on paper, sgn, 22x17", SBY 10/5/88 ... 1,100

EPSTEIN, Jehudo (Polish, 1870-1946)
Well on a Spring Terrace, oil on canvas laid down, sgn/dtd 99, 14x17", B/B 1/11/89 ... 825

ERDELEY, see De Erdeley

ERDMANN, Otto (German, 1834-1905)
Adieu (elegant couple in an interior), oil on canvas, sgn/dtd 1872, 27x21", SBY 7/12/89 ... 3,300

ERDOSSY, Bela (Hungarian, 1871-1928)
Hay Wagons (harvest scene), oil on canvas, sgn, 24x32", B/B 5/17/89 ... 495
Village Square, oil on panel, sgn, 6x8", C-E 10/25/88 UE ... 770

ERIKSEN, Vigilius; after (Russian, 1722-1782)
Portrait of Catherine II, at the time of her coup d'etat; pencil/watercolor on paper, 7x9", C-L 10/8/88 ... 650

ERMELS, Johann Franciscus
Figures Among Classical Ruins in a Mountainous River Landscape, oil on canvas, 18x23", C-NY 10/12/89 ... 9,900

ERNESTO, Monsu; see Daret

ERNI, Hans (Swiss, 1909-)
Two Charwomen, oil on canvas, sgn/dtd 53, 40x59", LH 10/16/88 ... 9,500
Two Figures (nude man & woman seated), mixed media, sgn, 31x40", LH 5/15/88 OE ... 11,500

RNST, Jimmy (American, 1920-)
Alarm, oil on canvas, sgn/inscr/dtd 49, 18x18", C-NY 3/11/88 .... **2,460**
Elements (contemporary fantasy), oil on canvas, sgn, 24x20", SBY 6/28/89 OE **8,250**
On the Edge of Night, oil on canvas, sgn/dtd twice 43 & 42, inscr, 8x9", C-E 11/30/88 OE **1,045**
Pair: Black; collage, acrylic/ink/panel on masonite, sgn/dtd 59, 36x12", C-E 11/30/88 .... **2,860**
Untitled (abstract), oil en grisaille on canvas, sgn/dtd 45, 10/5/88 .... **1,650**

RNST, Max (German, 1891-1976)
Abstract, pen/ink, sgn, 11x9", S/A 3/12/88 .... **775**
Comedie et Tragedie (Comedy & Tragedy), pastel on paper, sgn, 1973-74, 18x14", C-NY 5/11/89 .... **23,100**
Descente dans la Vallee (abstract), oil on canvas, sgn twice/dtd 49 twice/titled, 22x18", SBY 11/12/78 OE **143,000**
Dormeuse (abstract), oil on canvas, sgn/dtd 1955, 22x18", C-NY 5/11/89 .... **258,500**
Enfant, Cheval, Fleur et Serpent (abstract); oil on canvas, sgn/dtd 1927, 28x32", SBY 11/11/88 .... **660,000**
L'Eclipse, oil/blue crayon/monotype on paper laid down by artist on board, sgn, orig frame, 8x6", C-NY 5/11/89 .... **31,900**
Moon II, sgn/dtd 44/titled, 26x32", C-NY 5/12/88 OE **297,000**

RNST, Rudolf (Austrian, 1854-1920)
Awaiting the Tiger, oil on panel, sgn, 39x28", SBY 2/22/89 OE **93,500**
Departure, oil on canvas, sgn/dtd 1881, 31x24", SBY 5/23/89 .... **16,500**
Hammam, oil on panel, sgn, 19x24", SBY 5/23/89 .... **132,000**
In the Alhambra, oil on panel, sgn/dtd 88, 24x19", SBY 10/24/89 OE **93,500**
Le Marchand de Fleurs, oil on panel, sgn, 22x17", SBY 10/24/89 .... **57,750**
Les Captives, oil on panel, sgn, 15x18", C-NY 10/25/89 .... **59,400**
Moroccan Street Musician, oil on cradled panel, 14x8", SBY 6/8/88 UE **1,980**
Rug Merchant, oil on panel, sgn/dtd 88, 24x19", SBY 5/23/89 .... **44,000**

RTE, Romain de Tirtoff (Russian, 1892-)
Abondance, ou Une Ombre au Tableau; gouache on board, sgn/#d N4487, 15x11", SBY 4/23/88 OE **16,500**
American Millionaire, Costume Design for Louisiana; gouache/metallic paint on paper, sgn/dtd 17, 14x10", SBY 2/14/89 OE **14,300**
Autumn-Design for a Harper's Bazaar Cover; India ink on board, sgn/inscr/stamped/dtd/# 4, 11x9", SBY 10/5/88 .... **3,575**
Costume Design, portrait, gouache/silver paint on paper, sgn/inscr, 14x10", SBY 10/5/88 OE **13,200**
Design for the October 1927 Cover of Harper's Bazaar, gouache on board, sgn/#d 127/dtd VII-1927, 15x12", SBY 4/23/88 OE **16,500**
Illustration for the Widow, gouache on board, sgn/#d N1955/dtd 1931, 15x11", SBY 4/23/88 .... **3,025**
Kiss Me Again: Design for the Decor; gouache on paper, sgn/#d 1345/dtd 1928, 11x15", SBY 4/23/88 OE **9,350**
L'Oiseaux Merveillieux, gouache/gold/silver paint on paper, sgn/stamped/dtd II-1927, 22x14", SBY 10/5/88 OE **19,800**
La Cake-Walk for the Decor, gouache on paper, sgn/inscr/dtd 1975/#18409 on reverse, SBY 10/5/88 .... **4,400**
La Princesse Lointaine-Costume Design; gouache/silver paint on paper, sgn/inscr/dtd IX-1929, unfr, 15x11", SBY 10/5/88 .... **7,150**
Lucky Doll: Costume Design for the Four-Leaf Clover; gouache/gold paint on paper, sgn/#d 1066, 15x11", SBY 4/23/88 OE **13,200**
Lucky Doll: Costume Design for the Lucky Star; gouache/gold paint on paper, sgn/#d 1069, 15x11", SBY 4/23/88 OE **23,100**
Lucky Doll: Costume Design for the New Moon; gouache/gold paint on paper, sgn/#d 1071/dtd 1926, 15x11", SBY 4/23/88 OE **20,900**
Lucky Doll: Costume Design for the Wishbone; gouache/gold paint on paper, sgn/#1067/dtd 1926, 15x11", SBY 4/23/88 OE **22,000**
Masque Hilaire (comical figure in frilly dress & bonnet), gouache on paper, sgn/stamped, 15x10", C-E 6/16/88 .... **1,650**
Modes Excentriques, gouache/gold paint on paper, sgn/dtd III-1918/#d 11120, 13x10", SBY 10/7/89 .... **15,400**
Pair: Illustrations for the Gold Wizard; gouache on board, sgn/#d 1.760/dtd 1930, 14x11", SBY 4/23/88 .... **1,675**
Restless Sex-Costume Design for a Dying Warrior; gouache/silver/gold paint, sgn/stamped, unfr, 1919, 11x7", SBY 10/5/88 .... **5,500**
Sketches of Mlle Gaby Deslys, Costume Design for Finale; gouache on paper, sgn/stamped/#d/dtd 1919, SBY 2/14/89 OE **19,800**
Sketches of Mlle Gaby Deslys, Costume Design for the Bride;gouache on paper, sgn/dtd 1919, 13x10", SBY 2/14/89 OE **14,300**
Sketches of Mlle Gaby Deslys, Costume Design for 2nd Dame Noire; gouache on paper, sgn/dtd III-19, 12x9", SBY 2/14/89 OE **12,100**
Sketches of Mlle Gaby Deslys, Costume Design for 2nd Party Dress; gouache on paper, sgn/dtd 18, 15x11", SBY 2/14/89 OE **14,300**
Sketches of Mlle Gaby Deslys, Deshabille Costume Design; gouache on paper, sgn/#d/dtd 1919, 13x10", SBY 2/14/89 .... **10,450**
Tete de Mannequin (head of mannequin), gouache on paper, sgn/#d N1750/dtd IV 1930, 16x11", SBY 4/23/88 OE **4,400**

RTZ, Bruno (American, 1873-1965)
Blue Birds, watercolor, sgn/dtd 1909, 12x9", S/A 2/18/89 .... **350**
Bluejay, watercolor, sgn/dtd 1918, 15x7", MAG 4/24/88 .... **300**
Cardinal Bird & Maple Leaf, watercolor, sgn, 17x13", S/A 2/18/89 .... **300**
Depiction of a Red-Headed Woodpecker, oil on panel, sgn, 10x7", MAG 6/22/88 .... **200**
Kingfisher, watercolor, sgn, 13x20", S/A 2/18/89 .... **200**
Scarlet Tangaer & Friends, watercolor, sgn/dtd 45, 13x20", S/A 2/18/89 .... **300**

RTZ, Edward Frederick (American, 1862-)
Summertime (lady w/parasol in a boat on the water), oil on canvas, sgn, C-E 2/3/88 .... **6,050**

RUBELLIN, J. (French, 19th C)
Still Life of a Bowl of Fruit on a Marble Table, oil on canvas, indistinctly sgn, 32x26", SBY 2/22/89 .... **14,300**

SCHARD, Charles (French, 1748-1810)
Figures Among Ruins, gouache on paper, sgn, 9x15", SBY 7/12/89 .... **550**

SCHKE, see Von Eschke

SCOBAR, Daniel
Vineyard of Errazuriz-Panquehue, Chile; oil on canvas, sgn/dtd 96, 42x62", C-NY 5/25/88 .... **22,000**

SCOSURA, Ignacio Leon (Spanish, 19th C)
Connoisseur (man studying a portrait), oil on panel, sgn/dtd 1867(?), 8x6", SBY 12/9/88 .... **2,750**

SCURIAZ, see De Escuriaz

SILOD, L.
Bramercy Park, oil on canvas, sgn, 40x28", LH 10/16/88 .... **300**

SPINOSA, Professor (Spanish, 19th/20th C)
Coquette, oil on panel, sgn, 10x14", B/B 9/15/88 .... **1,980**

ESPOSITO, Gaetano (Italian, 1858-1911)
Peasant Girl with a Horse, oil on canvas, sgn, 40x22", C-NY 10/25/89 OE **28,600**
ESPOY, Angel (American, 1869-1963)
Spring in the Mountains (rider on path), oil on canvas, sgn, 25x30", C-NY 9/28/89 ..... **3,080**
Sunset, oil on board, sgn, 8x10", B/B 10/6/88 ..... **715**
Sunset on the Surf, oil on canvas, sgn, 24x36", B/B 9/14/89 UE **770**
Sunset Pastoral Scene, oil on board, sgn, 11x14", B/B 10/6/88 ..... **1,100**
ESSIG, George Emerick (American, 1838-)
Coastal Scene, sgn, 15x28", C-E 2/1/89 OE **1,540**
Marshy Landscape (house in distance), watercolor/pencil on paper laid down on board, sgn, unfr, 10x17", C-E 6/1/89 ..... **880**
Moonlight Harbor, oil on canvas, sgn, 20x36", C-E 6/1/88 ..... **1,540**
Waves Breaking on Shore, watercolor on paper, sgn, 9x16", FAP 11/4/88 ..... **320**
ESTALL, William Charles (British, 1857-1897)
Figures in a Landscape, oil on panel, 15x11", PHL 10/28/88 OE **475**
ESTE, see De Este
ESTES, A. Fowles (American, 20th C)
Calm Day (seascape w/ships in distance), oil on canvas, sgn/dtd 1906, 11x14", RAB 3/27/89 UE **250**
ESTES, Florence (American, 1860-1926)
Landscape-Cork Trees in Spain; oil on canvas, sgn, 39x46", DM 10/14/88 UE **600**
ESTES, Richard (American, 1936-)
Baby Doll Lounge (contemporary cityscape), oil on canvas, initialed/dtd 78, 36x60", C-NY 5/3/88 ..... **550,000**
Cadillac, oil on canvas, 1967, 40x50", C-NY 5/4/88 ..... **38,500**
Figure Studies of Children & a Fountain, gouache/India ink on board, 10x14", SBY 10/5/88 ..... **1,100**
Food, watercolor on paper, sgn, 12x14", C-NY 11/10/88 OE **16,500**
Holland Hotel (photo-real street scene), oil on canvas, 1984, 45x72", SBY 5/2/89 ..... **539,000**
Revolving Doors, oil on masonite, sgn, 1968, 30x48", SBY 5/2/88 ..... **165,000**
Softball Game, oil on canvas, sgn/dtd 1967, 43x50", SBY 11/9/89 ..... **33,000**
U-Ban (subway), acrylic/oil on canvasboard, sgn/dtd 1980, 14x20", SBY 11/9/89 ..... **93,500**
Untitled (view out 3 windows of high rises w/interior reflections), oil on canvas, sgn, 1969, 35x44", SBY 2/19/88 ..... **29,700**
Woolworth's (interior view of store), gouache on board, sgn/dtd 1973, 15x24", SBY 11/10/88 ..... **49,500**
ESTEVE, Agustin; see Esteve y Marques
ESTEVE, Maurice (French, 1904-)
Ferme Normande, oil on canvas, sgn twice/dtd 43, 26x32", SBY 5/11/88 OE **79,500**
L'Arbre au Rivage (abstract), oil on canvas, sgn twice/dtd 49 twice/titled, 26x36", SBY 6/30/88 OE **180,100**
Meditation, oil on canvas, sgn/dtd twice 1944, 32x26", SBY 5/11/88 OE **104,500**
Table Rouge aux Fruits (abstract still life), oil on canvas, sgn twice/dtd 1943 twice/titled, 29x36", SBY 6/30/88 OE **100,000**
ESTEVE Y MARQUES, Agustin (Spanish, 1753-1809)
Portrait of a Boy & His Dog, oil on canvas, 36x38", SBY 4/7/89 OE **77,000**
Portrait of the Third Countess of Superunda (three-quarter length), oil on canvas, 32x41", SBY 6/1/89 ..... **44,000**
ESTEVE Y MARQUES, Agustin; studio of (Spanish, 1753-1809)
Pair: Portraits of Charles IV & Maria Luisa of Parma, King & Queen of Spain; oil on canvas, oval, 49x36", SBY 4/29/88 OE **10,450**
ETIENNE, Francois Theophile
Monks Playing Chess, oil on panel, sgn, 13x16", C-E 2/23/88 UE **1,100**
ETIENNE, Yves (Haitian, 20th C)
Cap Haitien, oil on board, sgn, 16x24", WG 9/16/88 UE **75**
ETNIER, Stephen (American, 1903-)
Pumpkin Field, oil on board, 24x32", C-E 11/30/88 OE **1,980**
ETTING, Emlen
Leaves & Fruit, oil on canvas, sgn, 16x28", C-E 10/18/89 ..... **1,650**
ETTY, William (British, 1787-1849)
Bacchus, oil on panel, 23x28", SBY 7/12/89 ..... **3,410**
Nude Fixing Her Hair, oil on panel, 26x19", SBY 7/12/89 ..... **3,300**
Nude Holding a String of Flowers, oil on panel, 27x20", B/B 9/14/89 UE **1,045**
Venus & Her Satellites (The Toilet of Venus), oil on panel, unfr, 32x44", SBY 2/22/89 OE **38,500**
ETTY, William; att (British, 1787-1849)
The Coral Finder, oil on canvas, 13x17", WAD 6/6/88 ..... **1,600**
EUBANKS, Tony (1939-)
Hard Work, Mighty Little Pay (cowboys branding cattle); oil on masonite, sgn/copyrighted, 23x30", SBY 9/23/88 ..... **2,420**
EUGENE, Henry N. (French, 19th C)
Ancient Street with Figures, oil on canvas, sgn/dtd 1885, 14x12", FB 4/25/88 ..... **1,100**
EULER, Carl (German, 1815-)
Approaching Storm, oil on canvas, sgn, unfr, 26x30", C-E 2/21/89 ..... **1,320**
EURICH, Richard (British, 1903-)
Akenaten & Gourds, oil on canvas, sgn/dtd 73, 11x17", C-E 6/28/88 OE **2,200**
Sunbathing on the Jetty, oil on canvas, sgn, 21x24", C-E 10/25/88 OE **7,150**
European School (17th C)
Still Life of Birds & Fish, oil on panel, 8x10", FB 5/28/89 ..... **550**
European School (18th C)
Evening Landscape, oil on canvas, unfr, 18x24", FB 4/25/88 OE **500**
Pair: Portrait of a Lady; Portrait of a Gentleman; oil on canvas, 29x24" oval, FB 4/25/88 ..... **650**
Perseus Slaying Medusa, oil on canvas, unfr, 17x14", LH 9/10/89 ..... **600**

Portrait of a Lady, oil on canvas, 29x25", FB 4/25/88	350
Religious Subject, oil on canvas, sgn, 33x25", FB 4/25/88	250
Woman with Anchor, oil on canvas, illegible signature, 34x25", FB 4/25/88	700
European School (19th C)	
Boy with Dog, oil on canvas, 18x15", FB 4/25/88	280
Coastal Scene with Stone House on a Cliff, oil on canvas, 30x25", SLK 5/12/88	230
Evening Landscape, oil on panel, 9x18", FB 5/28/89	150
Figure at the Window, oil on canvas, laid down on panel, 10x7", FB 5/28/89 OE	325
Head of Turk (bust-length portrait in profile), oil on canvas, 24x18", WG 4/23/88 UE	900
Interior of a Church, oil on panel, 18x13", LH 10/16/88 UE	170
Landscape with River, oil on canvas, indistinctly sgn, 24x34", WG 4/23/88 UE	250
Pair: Ladies' Portraits; oil on ivory, unsgn, 2x2", FB 4/25/88	130
Portrait of a Lady, oil on canvas, sgn, 16x13", FB 5/28/89 OE	800
Portrait of a lady, oil on copper, 11x9", FB 4/25/88	420
River Landscape with Figure, oil on canvas, bears Daubigny Signature, 12x18", SLK 5/12/88	900
St Jerome, oil on copper, 9x7", LH 10/16/88	190
Still Life of Fruit, oil on canvas, 19x16", FB 5/28/89	1,200
Traveler Pausing at the Inn, oil on panel, 16x12", WG 4/23/88	250
Village Scene, oil on canvas, sgn, 19x26", FB 4/25/88 OE	650
Windmill on River, oil on board, 10x17", LH 9/10/89 UE	150
European School (20th C)	
Portrait of an Elderly Woman, oil on tin, monogramed/dtd 1914, 16x12", WG 4/23/88 UE	125
EVANS, De Scott (American, 1847-1898)	
Blossoms of Spring (bust-length portrait of woman from behind), oil on canvas, sgn/dtd 1893, 20x16", C-E 2/1/89	2,860
Entanglement, oil on canvas, sgn, 24x36", C-E 6/1/88 UE	2,310
Hanging Apples, oil on canvas, 12x10", SBY 5/25/88 UE	10,450
Oranges & Grapes, oil on canvas, sgn/dtd 91, 10x12", C-NY 5/25/89 OE	19,800
EVANS, De Scott; att (American, 1847-1898)	
Doctor's Prescription (Trompe l'Oeil still life), oil on canvas, 9x6", C-NY 9/28/89	18,700
EVANS, Jessie Benton (American, 1866-1954)	
Desert Basin-Morning; oil on canvas, sgn, 25x31", RWS 3/16/89	650
EVERGOOD, Philip (American, 1901-1973)	
Aggressive Bird & Frightened Frog, oil on canvas, sgn/dtd 53, 12x20", SBY 6/28/89	1,210
Balls on the Beach, oil on canvas, sgn, 14x18", SBY 4/14/89	2,860
Big Peter & the Oranges, oil on canvas, sgn/dtd twice, titled/#d 15, 30x36", SBY 9/23/88	5,500
Boy with Book, pencil/sepia wash on paper, sgn/dtd 1961, C-NY 3/11/88	1,100
Caucus (group of many faces), oil on canvas, sgn/dtd LXII, 24x20", C-E 6/1/89	5,280
Child Sitting in a Chair, watercolor on paper, sgn, 6x6", C-E 2/3/88	495
Cup of Tea, brush/black/sepia ink/pencil on paper, sgn/dtd 1939, sgn/inscr, 17x14", C-NY 3/11/88	1,650
Dead Sparrow, oil on masonite, sgn/dtd 1965, 10x14", C-E 6/1/89	1,210
Father & Son, brush/sepia ink/wash on tan paper, sgn/dtd LXII, 23x18", C-NY 3/11/88	1,320
Girl Combing Her Hair, India ink/gray wash on paper, sgn/dtd LXII, 17x14", SBY 3/17/88	1,760
Girl with the Mona Lisa Smile, pencil w/yellow wash on paper, sgn/dtd 1965, 20x16", SBY 9/14/89	2,640
Hundredth Psalm (critical interpretation of KKK), oil on canvas, sgn, 16x20", C-NY 5/26/88	6,600
Jerry's Purtie Log Cabin, gouache on paper laid down on masonite, sgn/dtd 35, 14x20", SBY 3/17/88 OE	16,500
Rachel with Flowers, oil on canvas, sgn/dtd LXII, 26x22", C-NY 5/26/88	5,500
Self-Portrait (man in hat, brush in hand), oil on canvas, sgn, 15x22", C-E 6/1/89 OE	3,740
Street & Cathedral Scene, watercolor on paper, sgn/dtd, 17x26", C-E 6/1/88 UE	660
Susanna & the Elders, oil on canvas, sgn/dtd 58 in Roman numerals, 20x18", SBY 6/28/89	3,300
Waterbabies, gouache/watercolor on joined paper, sgn/dtd 50, 28x18", SBY 3/17/88	1,870
Zebra Man, pen/black ink/pencil on paper, sgn, 26x20", C-E 6/1/89 OE	715
EVERSEN, Adrianus (Dutch, 1818-1897)	
Dutch Town Scene (church in background, figures walking), oil on canvas, sgn, 21x18", DM 9/16/88	14,000
Street Scene in Amsterdam, oil on canvas laid down on board, sgn, 22x28", C-NY 2/25/88	28,600
Sunlit Street on Market Day, oil on canvas, sgn, unfr, 22x18", SBY 2/22/89 OE	24,200
EWEN, William Paterson (Canadian, 1925-)	
Alert (abstract), oil on canvas, initialed/dtd 1961, 28x30", FB 4/25/88 OE	4,200
Square Sunset (abstract), oil on canvas, sgn, ca 1964, 36x46", FB 10/17/88 OE	11,000
EXTER, Alexandra (Ekster)(Russian, 1882-1949)	
Costume Design: The Hunter; gouache on paper, #d 87/inscr, ca 1930, 18x12", C-L 10/8/88	6,690
Dancing Figures, gouache on thick paper, 16x12", C-L 10/8/88	5,950
Prancing Horse (in abstract landscape), oil on canvas, 13x16", C-L 10/8/88 OE	11,150
EYDELL, W.A.	
October Landscape, oil on canvas, sgn, 22x32", C-E 11/30/88 UE	1,100
EYDEN, William T. (American, 1859-1919)	
Autumn Road (dirt road among fall foliage), oil on cardboard, sgn/dtd 1901, 22x32", RAB 8/8/89 UE	200
EYRE, Gladstone (Australian, 1863-1933)	
Off the Coast of New South Wales, pencil/watercolor heightened w/white, sgn, 10x22", C-SK 11/10/88 OE	650
FABBI, Alberto (Italian, 1858-1906)	
Water Carrier (man & woman beside doorway), oil on panel, sgn/dtd 1888, 16x11", B/B 10/9/88	4,400

FABBI, Fabio (Italian, 1861-1946)
Harem Courtyard, oil on canvas, sgn, 24x32", SBY 6/8/88 .... **8,800**
Harem Dance, oil on canvas, sgn, 26x34", C-E 5/23/88 OE **13,200**
Harem Dancer, watercolor over pencil, sgn, 18x12", C-E 10/25/88 .... **1,430**
Harem Dancer, watercolor/pen/colored ink over pencil on paper, sgn, 16x10", C-NY 5/24/89 .... **2,200**
Harem Dancers, oil on canvas, sgn, 36x54", SBY 2/22/89 .... **41,250**
Mantilla (three-quarter length portrait of Spanish lady), pen/ink on paper, sgn/monogramed, 9x6", WL 5/20/88 .... **400**
Old Flirt, oil on canvas, sgn, 12x8", C-E 10/26/89 .... **2,860**
Opium Smoker, oil on canvas, sgn, 67x39", SBY 7/12/89 .... **6,600**
Per la Bambina, oil on canvas laid down on board, sgn, 52x37", C-NY 5/25/88 .... **3,520**
Reflecting Pool, watercolor, sgn, 17x12", C-E 10/26/89 .... **550**
Slave Market, oil on canvas, sgn/dtd 1910, 34x24", SBY 5/23/89 .... **13,200**
Women with a Rug Merchant, watercolor/gouache/pen/white ink over pencil, sgn, 19x10", C-NY 2/25/88 OE **2,860**

FABER, Jean (French, 20th C)
Marche, oil on canvas, sgn, 9x11", MG 10/28/88 .... **350**
Marche, oil on canvas, sgn, 9x11", MG 5/28/88 .... **300**

FABIEN, Henri
Mrs Tait McKenzie, oil on canvasboard, sgn/inscr/dtd 1923, 18x24", C-E 6/1/88 .... **990**

FABRES Y COSTA, Antonio Maria (Spanish, 1854-)
Young Snake Charmer, oil on panel, sgn, 18x22", SBY 5/23/89 .... **29,700**

FABRIS, Pietro (Italian, 18th C)
Temples of Oaestum From the Southeast, watercolor/bodycolor, sgn, 11x23", C-NY 1/11/89 OE **26,400**
View of Naples From the East with the Certosa di San Martino Above, watercolor/bodycolor, 11x23", C-NY 1/11/89 OE **31,900**
View of Naples with the Castel d'Elmo From the Chaiji, watercolor/bodycolor, 12x23", C-NY 6746 OE **23,100**
View of Naples with the Chaiji Looking Towards Posilipo, watercolor/bodycolor, sgn/dtd 1773, 12x22", C-NY 1/11/89 OE **27,500**

FABRITIUS, Karel; circle of
Portrait of a Bearded Man Wearing a Cap, oil on panel, 20x16", C-NY 6/2/88 OE **6,050**

FABRY, Emile (Belgian, 1865-1966)
Le Poete, pastel on paper, sgn/inscr/dtd 1915, 22x7", C-L 6/27/88 OE **32,164**

FACCHINETTI, Nicolau Antonio (Italian, 19th C)
Island of Paqueta, The Bay of Rio de Janeiro; oil on paper laid down on board, sgn/dtd 1878, 8x15", C-SK 6/9/88 OE **17,600**

FACCINI, Pietro
Saint Jerome in the Wilderness, oil on copper, 19x14", C-NY 10/12/89 OE **71,500**

FACHINATTI, C.
Genre Scene, Mother & Child (by fireside w/hen); oil on canvas, sgn, 28x22", DM 3/14/88 .... **1,500**

FAED, Thomas; att (Scottish, 1826-1900)
Bedtime, oil on canvas, sgn, 12x10", RWS 6/17/89 UE **300**

FAES, Peter; att (Belgian, 1750-1814)
Still Life of Crown Imperial, Tulips, Daffodils, Hollyhocks...; oil on canvas, bears signature, 33x25", C-NY 1/11/89 OE **20,900**
Tulips, Carnations, Bluebells, & Other Flowers in a Glass Vase; oil on panel, bears signature, 9x7", WD 3/23/88 .... **2,900**

FAHEY, James (British, 1804-1885)
After the Haying, watercolor/gouache on paper, sgn/dtd 1859, 21x34", SBY 6/8/88 .... **1,760**

FAHNESTOCK, Wallace Weir (American, 1877-)
Bright Autumn, oil on canvasboard, sgn, 9x12", RWS 11/10/89 UE **400**
October Landscape, oil on canvas, sgn, unfr, 20x24", RAB 8/8/89 UE **400**
Winter Afternoon, Dorset, Vermont (landscape); oil on artist board, sgn, 8x10", RWS 5/19/88 .... **750**

FAIRINETTI, C. (Italian, 19th/20th C)
Farmgirl with Goat & Sheep, oil on canvas, sgn, 16x22", C-E 2/21/89 .... **1,540**

FAIRMAN, James (American, 1826-1904)
Coilantingle Ford, oil on canvas, sgn, 23x36", LH 12/4/88 .... **3,000**
Jerusalem From the Mount of Olives, oil on canvas, sgn, 32x46", C-NY 3/11/88 OE **18,700**
Rocky Coast at Sunset (water crashing along rocky shore, steep cliffs beyond), oil on canvas, sgn, 24x36", RAB 8/9/88 .... **1,800**
Sunset, oil on canvas, sgn, 23x36", B/B 9/14/89 UE **550**

FAIRMAN, James; att (American, 1826-1904)
Old Castle Garden, View to a Lakeside Palace; oil on board, sgn, 19x32", RWS 6/17/89 UE **200**

FAIRWEATHER, Ian (Austrian, 1663-1708)
Untitled (abstract), oil on board, monogramed, 14x14", C-SK 6/9/88 .... **5,950**

FAISTENBERGER, Anton; att (Austrian, 1663-1708)
Preocession on Path in a Mountainous Landscape, oil on canvas, 29x38", C-NY 5/31/89 OE **8,250**
Stormy Italianate Landscape, oil on canvas, 14x19", C-NY 4/8/88 .... **2,640**

FAIVRE, Antoine Joseph Etienne (French, 1830-1905)
Delft Basin, oil on panel, sgn/dtd 1873, 17x11", B/B 3/17/88 .... **6,600**

FALCHETTI, Giuseppe (Italian, 1840-)
Floral Still Life, Grapes, Peach, & Butterfly on a Ledge; oil on canvas, sgn, 30x25", C-E 5/22/89 UE **1,980**
Flowers in an Urn on a Ledge, oil, sgn, 31x25", WD 1/11/89 OE **2,400**

FALCIATORE, Filippo (fl 1728-1768)
Pair: Elegantly Dressed Man Outside Tavern; Elegant Figures Taking a Snuff in Parkland; oil, 26" dia, SBY 1/12/89 OE **121,000**

FALERO, Luis Riccardo
Chosen One, oil on canvas, sgn/dtd 1877, 30x16", C-E 2/23/88 OE **9,680**

FALK, Robert (Russian, 1886-1956)
House in the Forest (landscape), oil on canvas, sgn, ca 1920, 21x32", C-L 10/8/88 .... **11,150**

Fall River, Massachusetts, School (19th C)
Still Life of Fruit, oil on canvas, 8x12", RAB 8/9/88 450
Still Life of Roses, oil on canvas, 14x18", RAB 8/9/88 UE 300
Still Life of Roses (in bowl & on tabletop), oil on canvas, 14x19", RAB 8/9/88 UE 300

FANCELLI, Pietro; att (Italian, 1764-1850)
Design for a Dome & Decorative Frieze, pen/black ink/colored wash over black chalk, 10x14", SBY 1/13/89 440

FANFANI, Enrico (Italian, 19th C)
Connoisseur, oil on canvas, sgn, 28x33", C-E 5/23/88 1,100

FANIEL, Alfred (Canadian, 1879-1950)
Pair: Figures in a Landscape; oil on canvas, sgn/dtd 1915, 19x13", FB 10/17/88 325

FANNING, William Sanders
Landscape: Rolling Hillside; oil on canvas, sgn, 23x20", NA 2/24/89 550

FANTIN-LATOUR, Henri (French, 1836-1904)
Asters & Fruits on a Table, oil on canvas, sgn/dtd 68, 22x22", SBY 5/9/89 1,870,000
Auto-Portrait, oil on canvas, sgn, 1861, 9x6", SBY 5/23/89 12,100
Baigneuse (seated nude), oil on canvas, sgn, 13x15", C-NY 2/23/89 OE 41,800
Bouquet of Roses, oil on canvas, sgn, 8x9", SBY 2/16/89 OE 88,000
Chrysanthemes, oil on canvas, sgn/dtd 77, 13x16", SBY 11/12/88 OE 159,500
Deux Peches et Deux Prunes, oil on canvas, sgn, 1899, 6x8", SBY 11/12/88 71,500
Fleurs de Printemps (still life of spring flowers), oil on canvas, sgn/dtd 79, 15x12", SBY 5/10/88 198,000
Fruits (still life, grapes in basket, apples on table), oil on canvas, sgn/dtd 90, 16x20", SBY 10/6/89 OE 154,000
Gros Vase de Dahlias et Fleurs Variees (floral still life), oil on canvas, sgn, ca 1875, SBY 5/9/89 990,000
Hommage a Delacroix, oil on canvas, sgn, 1964, 12x11", SBY 5/23/89 55,000
Hortensias, Giroflees, Deux Pots de Pensees (floral still life); oil on canvas, sgn/dtd 79, 22x30", C-NY 11/14/88 OE 3,080,000
La Poete (impressionistic figures), oil on canvas, sgn, 11x9", C-NY 5/24/89 39,600
Panier de Dahlias (floral still life), oil on canvas, sgn, 1891, 18x23", SBY 11/11/88 1,430,000
Pieds d'Alouette (floral still life), oil on canvas, sgn/dtd 88, 29x24", SBY 5/9/89 1,100,000
Repos de la Sainte Famille, oil on canvas, sgn, 1896, 14x14", SBY 10/24/89 27,500
Roses (still life), oil on canvas, sgn/dtd 85, 19x17", SBY 5/10/88 OE 605,000

Roses dans un Vase, oil on canvas, sgn/dtd 1892, 16x14", C-NY 5/11/88, $385,000

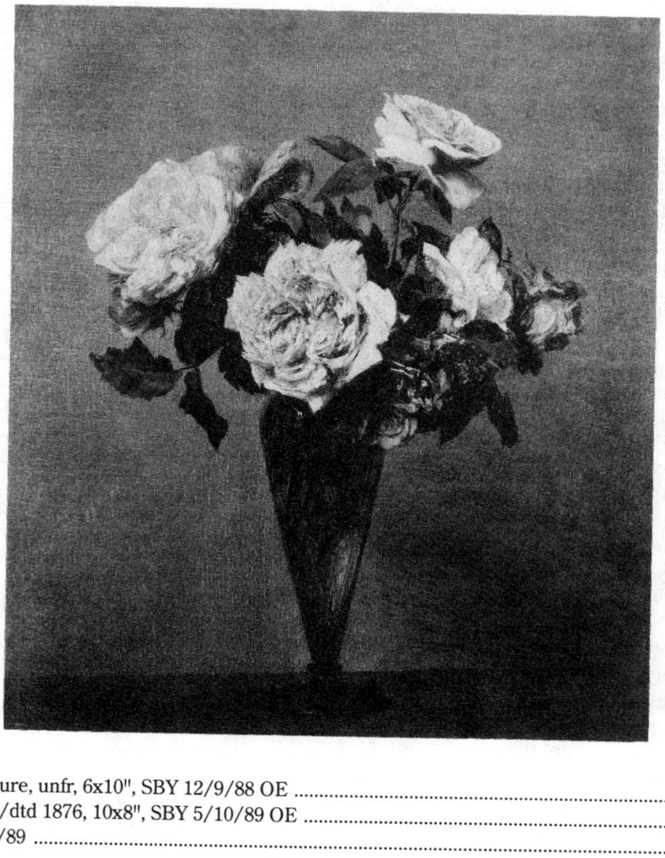

Set of 4: Nude Studies; pencil on tracing paper, stamped signature, unfr, 6x10", SBY 12/9/88 OE 2,750
Tete de Jeune Fille (portrait of artist's wife), oil on canvas, sgn/dtd 1876, 10x8", SBY 5/10/89 OE 198,000
Toilette de Venus, oil on canvas, sgn, 1904, 10x12", SBY 10/24/89 22,000

FANTIN-LATOUR, Theodore (1805-1872)
Portrait of a Girl, seated half-length, wearing nightdress, holding spaniel; pastel on paper, sgn, 22x19", C-M 6/16/89 19,559

FANTIN-LATOUR, Victoria Dubourg (French, 1840-)
Still Life of Grapes & Apple on a Table, oil on canvas, sgn, 7x14", C-NY 10/25/89 22,000
Still life of White Flowers, Peaches, & Plums on a Table; oil on canvas, sgn/inscr 8305, 16x18", C-NY 2/23/89 OE 49,500

FARETO, Pietro
Pair: Still Life of Fruit; Still Life of Fish & Vegetables; oil on canvas, sgn, ovals, 27x22", C-E 2/23/88 3,300

FARINA, Isidoro (Italian, 19th C)
Red Parasol (portrait of a woman seated in a landscape), oil on canvas, sgn, unfr, 37x25", C-NY 10/25/89 17,600
FARINATI, Paolo (Italian, 1524-1606)
St John the Evangelist (preparatory study for an etching), pen/brown ink/wash, dtd 1567, 11x7", SBY 1/13/89 OE 49,500
FARLEY, Richard Blossom, (American, 1875-)
Pintail Ducks in Flight, oil on canvas, sgn, 24x16", RWS 9/8/89 UE 800
FARM, Gerald (American, 1935-)
Birthday at the Saloon, oil on masonite, sgn/copyrighted/dtd 1978, 30x40", SBY 9/23/88 3,575
FARMER, Edna (American 20th C)
Grand Staircase, watercolor, sgn, 29x19", LH 10/16/88 UE 500
FARNDON, Walter (American, 1876-1964)
Gloucester Harbor, oil on canvas, sgn, unfr, 26x32", B/B 9/14/89 OE 3,300
Quiet Cove, oil on canvas, sgn, 26x32", C-NY 9/30/88 3,850
FARNSWORTH, Jerry (American, 1895-1983)
Susan (portrait), oil on canvas, sgn twice/dtd Aug 1960/inscr Painted at Truro, 20x16", SBY 3/17/88 UE 330
Young Man From Arkansas (portrait), oil on canvas, sgn twice/titled, 40x30", SBY 3/17/88 1,100
FARNUM, Herbert Cyrus (American, 1866-)
Club Carillion, oil on canvas, sgn, 22x32", SBY 6/28/89 4,950
Jim's Barn-Dudley (barn in landscape); oil on canvas mounted on cardboard, sgn, 10x14", RWS 3/16/89 550
FARNY, Henry F. (American, 1847-1916)
Buffalo Grazing at Dusk, gouache on paper, sgn/dtd 1913, 5x17", C-NY 5/26/88 28,600
Obsidian Mountain in the Yellowstone (Indians in snowy landscape), gouache on paper, sgn/dtd 97, 23x17", SBY 5/24/89 203,500
Water Carriers, watercolor/gouache/pen/black ink on paper, sgn/dtd 88, 8x16", C-NY 5/25/89 29,700
FARQUHARSON, Joseph (British, 1846-1935)
On the Coast, Connemara, Ireland; oil on canvas, sgn, 13x27", C-E 5/22/89 2,200
View of Connemara, Ireland; oil, sgn, 13x28", WD 1/11/89 1,500
Winter Landscape, oil on canvas, sgn/dtd 1910, 20x30", FB 10/30/89 OE 4,400
FARRE, Henri (American, 1871-1934)
Harriet B Hopkins with a Parasol, oil on canvas laid down on board, initialed/dtd 1922, 23x16", C-E 6/1/89 1,980
Portrait of Harriet B Hopkins (three-quarter length, in landscape), oil on canvas, initialed, 1922, 60x38", C-E 6/1/88 4,400
Still Life of Pink & White Roses, oil on canvas, sgn, 20x16", C-E 6/1/89 OE 4,620
FARRER, Henry (American, 1843-1903)
Afterglow (sunset in river landscape), watercolor on paper laid down, sgn/dtd 1899, 25x37", C-NY 9/28/89 OE 17,600
Figure in a Landscape, watercolor on paper, sgn, 12x17", SBY 3/17/88 OE 2,090
Landscape with Cottage Overlooking Pond, watercolor on paper, sgn/dtd 1890, 8x13", SBY 9/14/89 3,575
Pair of Birds, watercolor/pen/black ink/ink wash on paper, sgn/dtd 1867, 10x8", C-NY 5/25/89 OE 18,700
Reflecting Pond, watercolor/pencil on paper laid down on board, sgn/dtd 1901, 21x26", C-E 6/1/89 2,420
FARRIER, Edgar G. (British, 1827-1902)
Unexpected Return, oil on panel, sgn, 36x48", SBY 7/12/89 UE 3,300
FARRIER, Robert (British, 1796-1879)
Prophecy You'll Marry a Rich Young Lady, oil on canvas, 24x20", DM 3/14/88 900
FARRINGTON
Along Verdugo Road, oil on board, sgn, 12x16", MAG 4/24/88 100
FARSKY, Otto (American, 19th/20th C)
Landscape with Farmhouse, oil on canvas, sgn, 19x27", LH 9/10/89 300
Pensive (portrait of Mary Fassett), oil on canvas, sgn/dtd 1933, 40x36", C-E 11/30/88 3,850
Summer Landscape, oil on canvas, sgn, 17x21", B/B 10/6/88 412
FASCE, F. (Italian, 19th C)
Conversation (couple chat in barnyard), watercolor on paper, sgn, 18x24", RAB 8/8/89 425
FASSETT, Truman E. (American, 1885-)
Spanish Dancer (full-length portrait), oil on canvas, sgn, 40x32", C-NY 5/26/88 14,300
FATTORI, Giovanni (Italian, 1825-1908)
Charge of the Brigade, oil on board, sgn, 4x8", MG 5/28/88 1,700
FAUCONNET, Guy Pierre (1882-1920)
Sleeping Shepherd, oil on canvas, sgn, ca 1915-20, 38x51", C-L 6/27/88 17,974
FAUGERON, Adolphe (French, 1866-)
Naiad, oil on canvas, sgn, 58x38", C-NY 10/25/89 9,900
FAULKNER, Frank (British, 20th C)
Cave (abstract), acrylic on canvas, sgn/dtd 1982, 84x60", SBY 10/8/88 7,700
Untitled, acrylic on canvas, sgn/dtd 1979, 49x65", SBY 10/7/89 2,750
FAULKNER, John (British, 19th C)
Extensive British Landscape, oil on canvas, sgn, 17x32", DM 1/15/88 1,500
Woodland Retreat, oil on canvas, sgn, 84x109", B/B 3/17/88 4,125
FAURE, Marie (American, 19th/20th C)
City Park, New Orleans; oil on canvas, sgn/dtd 1906, 14x24", NA 2/6/88 1,200
FAURET, Jean Joseph Leon
L'Applaudissement, oil en grisaille on canvas, sgn, 29x24", C-E 2/23/88 1,650
FAURNIER, Alex (French, 19th/20th C)
Cattle in a Landscape, oil on canvas laid down on board, sgn/dtd 1911, 16x20", SBY 7/12/89 OE 1,870
FAUTEAU, Henriette (20th C)
Abstract, acrylic on paper, sgn/dtd 1964, 24x15", FB 5/28/89 250

FAUTRIER, Jean (French, 1898-1964)
Construction, Tableau a 4 Cotes (abstract); oil/pigment on paper laid down on canvas, sgn/dtd 58, 18x21", SBY 6/30/88 ... 116,000
Construction (abstract), oil/pigment on paper laid down on canvas, sgn/dtd 58, 32x39", SBY 6/30/88 ... 190,000
FAVAI, Gennardo (Italian, 1879-1958)
Venetian River View, oil on board, sgn, 10x12", FAP 4/15/89 ... 715
FAVORY
Portrait de Jeune Fille, gouache/chalk/pencil on paper, 24x18", C-E 3/22/88 ... 242
FAVRETTO, Giacomo; att (Italian, 1849-1887)
Vandalismo, Poveri Antichi; oil on canvas, bears signature, 30x20", C-E 10/25/88 OE ... 7,700
FAZZINI, Achille (20th C)
Self-Portrait, brush/ink/touches of gray wash, sgn/dtd 1937, 11x9", SWN 6/15/89 ... 495
FEBVRE, Edouard (French, 20th C)
Scene de Montmartre (quiet street scene), oil on board, sgn, 20x26", C-E 11/17/88 ... 825
FECHIN, Nicolai (American, 1881-1955)
Portrait of Rose KL Davis, oil on canvas, sgn/dtd 52, 20x16", SBY 3/17/88 ... 9,350
Rio Grande (impressionistic landscape), oil on canvas, stamped signature, 15x13", SBY 3/17/88 OE ... 11,000
Tuppy with Cat (portrait of a woman), oil on canvas, sgn, 30x25", C-NY 5/25/89 ... 121,000
FECHIN, Nicolai; att (American, 1881-1955)
Portrait of an Indian, oil on board, 12x9", B/B 9/15/88 ... 1,045
FECTEAU, Marcel (Canadian, 1927-)
La Minerve, Laurentians; oil on board, sgn/dtd 1981, 12x16", FB 10/30/89 ... 770
Winter Landscape with Cabin, oil on board, sgn/dtd 1980, 10x12", FB 4/25/88 ... 280
FEDER, Adolphe (French, 1886-1943)
Famille a Table, oil on canvas, sgn/dtd 1940, 32x39", C-E 11/17/88 OE ... 2,860
Village Street, oil on canvas, sgn, 24x29", SBY 5/30/89 OE ... 5,500
FEDERICO, Cavalier Michele (Italian, 1884-)
Cliffs on the Coast of Capri, oil on canvas laid down, sgn, 25x44", B/B 4/20/88 ... 1,540
FEDERLE, Helmut
Frau Mit Hut (geometric composition), pencil/brown crayon on lined yellow paper, initialed/dtd 82, 13x8", C-E 11/14/89 ... 1,320
FEELEY, Paul (American, 1913-)
Untitled #7 (abstract), acrylic on canvas, sgn/dtd 60, 70x47", C-NY 5/4/88 ... 7,700
FEHER, Joseph (American, 1908-)
Hualala Volcano, Kailua, Hawaii, TH; oil on canvas, sgn/dtd 1940, 20x24", RWS 5/12/89 ... 350
FEININGER, Lyonel (American/German, 1871-1956)
An der Kuste (abstract landscape scene), oil on canvas, sgn twice/dtd 20/titled, 14x16", C-NY 11/16/88 ... 132,000
Belgische Eisenbahn (train cars, engine, figures, & buildings), oil on canvas, sgn/dtd 1911, 29x36", SBY 5/10/89 ... 495,000
Brigantine Off the Coast (cubist depiction), oil on canvas, sgn/dtd 1939, 18x31", SBY 10/6/89 OE ... 264,000
Church on the Cliffs, IV; watercolor/pen/ink on paper, sgn/dtd 5 VII 53/#d IV, 13x19", SBY 11/16/89 OE ... 31,900
Church on the Cliffs, VI; watercolor/pen/ink on paper, sgn/dtd 7 July, 1953/#d VI, 13x19", SBY 11/16/89 ... 17,600
Church Spire, charcoal/gray wash on paper, sgn/dtd 51, 10x6", SBY 10/6/89 ... 4,950
Cityscape with Locomotive, watercolor/charcoal on paper, sgn/dtd 30.IX.43, 10x13", SBY 10/6/89 OE ... 14,300
Composition: City Houses; oil on canvas, sgn/dtd 1952, 16x24", SBY 5/11/88 ... 77,000
Connecticut Hills (contemporary), pen/ink/watercolor on laid paper, sgn/dtd 1952/titled, 13x9", SBY 5/11/88 ... 11,000
Crest & Image, oil on canvas, sgn, 1952, 20x30", SBY 5/11/88 ... 46,750
Die Kirche Von Heringsdorf (church), watercolor/pen/black ink on paper, sgn/dtd 1916, 12x9", C-NY 2/16/89 OE ... 35,200
Dune, pen/ink/watercolor on laid paper, sgn/dtd 8-8-32, 12x18", SBY 10/6/89 OE ... 16,500
Dune (abstract), pen/ink/watercolor on laid paper, sgn/dtd 8 8 32/titled, 12x18", SBY 10/7/88 OE ... 12,100
Fishing Cutter (abstract), oil on canvas, sgn twice/dtd 1940/titled, 14x21", SBY 11/12/88 ... 60,500
French Brigantine, watercolor/India ink on paper, sgn/dtd 18.VIII.42, 10x12", SBY 10/6/89 OE ... 25,300
Harbor Scene (abstract), pen/ink/watercolor on paper, sgn/dtd 1952, 7x10", SBY 10/7/88 OE ... 8,800
Harbor Scene (contemporary), pen/ink/watercolor/gold leaf on laid paper, sgn/dtd 46, 8x12", SBY 5/11/88 OE ... 25,300
Houses by the River I, oil on canvas, sgn, 19x30", SBY 5/10/89 OE ... 187,000
Hove To, pen/ink/watercolor on laid paper, sgn/dtd 2I.9.37./titled, 11x10", SBY 11/12/88 OE ... 22,000
Kirche von Treptow AR, pen/ink/watercolor on laid paper, sgn/dtd 1933/titled, 15x19", SBY 11/12/88 OE ... 44,000
Locomotive: HP 300; India ink on paper, sgn/dtd Sat Aug 8 08, 6x9", SBY 10/6/89 ... 7,150
Locomotive: Old Prussian Freightloco; charcoal/India ink on paper, sgn/dtd 1945, 10x13", SBY 10/6/89 OE ... 15,400
Manna-Hata, oil on canvas, sgn, 1952, 28x18", C-NY 5/11/89 OE ... 121,000
Mid-Manhattan, gouache/watercolor/pen/black ink on paper, sgn/dtd 52, 19x13", C-NY 5/11/89 OE ... 33,000
Mid-Manhattan, watercolor/charcoal/pen/black ink on paper, sgn/titled/dtd 10.VII.55, 19x12", C-NY 5/12/88 OE ... 17,600
Mirage III (Coast of Nevermore), oil on canvas, sgn/dtd 1944, 15x30", SBY 5/11/88 ... 49,500
Never-Never-More Land (fantasy landscape), pen/ink/watercolor on laid paper, sgn/dtd 6.6.52, 11x19", SBY 5/11/88 OE ... 22,000
Oh, 'Just Curiosity!,' watercolor/India ink on paper, sgn/dtd 1945, 9x11", SBY 10/6/89 ... 8,800
Old Sea, watercolor/pen/ink on paper, sgn/dtd 28 XII 52, 12x19", SBY 11/16/89 ... 18,700
Recollection II (contemporary), watercolor/pen/ink on paper, sgn/dtd 1955, 12x19", C-NY 2/18/88 ... 15,400
Recollection III (contemporary), pen/ink/watercolor on Ingres paper, sgn/dtd 30 VIII 55/titled, 12x19", SBY 5/11/88 ... 8,800
Scheunen I, watercolor/pen/black ink on paper, sgn/dtd 1926, 12x19", C-NY 5/11/89 OE ... 20,900
Seascape, watercolor/charcoal/pen/black ink on paper, sgn/dtd 12.VII. 53, 13x19", C-NY 5/12/88 ... 9,350
Skerry Cruisers Racing (abstract), pen/ink/watercolor on laid paper, sgn/dtd 1943, 12x19", SBY 10/7/88 OE ... 18,150
Stadt mit Sonne (view of house w/purple sun), watercolor/pen/black ink, sgn/titled/dtd d.23.III.21, 8x11", C-NY 5/12/88 ... 26,400
Starlit Night (ships at sea), watercolor/pen/black ink on paper, sgn/dtd 1936, 12x18", C-NY 5/11/89 OE ... 33,000
Topaz Sun II (abstract composition), watercolor/pen/black ink/traces of graphite, sgn/dtd 17.7.47, 9x11", C-NY 10/5/89 ... 17,600

Two Ghosties (abstract line figures), ink/pastel on paper, sgn, 7x4", SBY 10/7/89 8,800
Village Scene, crayon on paper, dtd Aug 3 10, 7x8", SBY 5/10/89 17,600
Watchtower (contemporary), watercolor/pen/ink on laid paper, sgn/dtd 25, SBY 5/11/88 OE 11,000
Westward Ho!, pen/ink/watercolor on laid paper, sgn/dtd 1936/titled, 9x12", SBY 11/12/88 OE 18,700
Wolke I (contemporary coastal view w/boat), pen/ink/watercolor on laid paper, sgn/dtd 1922, 11x16", SBY 5/11/88 OE 25,300

FEININGER, Theodore Lux (American, 1910-)
Elliot House Figure Composition (contemporary), acrylic on canvas, initialed/inscr, 24x22", RWS 3/16/89 OE 800

FELDHUTTER, Ferdinand (German, 1842-1898)
Alpine Lake Scene, oil on canvas, sgn/dtd 1894, 22x29", S/A 2/18/89 2,700
Pair: Mountain Stream; Chalet by a Mountain Lake; oil on panel, sgn, 10x6", B/B 6/9/88........ 5,225
Tyrol, oil on canvas, sgn, 25x43", WD 3/23/88 4,000

FELDMANN, Wilhelm
Haystacks, oil on canvas, sgn/inscr, 28x38", C-E 5/23/88........ 990

FELGUEREZ, Manuel (South American, 20th C)
Iconografia Personal (abstract), oil on canvas, sgn/dtd NY 66, 45x50", C-NY 11/21/88 9,350

FELICIAN, H. (Italian, 19th C)
Arab Merchants, oil on canvas, sgn, 26x37", C-E 5/22/89 2,860

FELLIG, Arthur H.; see Weegee

FENDI, Peter; att (Austrian, 1796-1842)
Interior of a Church, Facing the Alter; watercolor, sgn, 12x18", C-E 2/16/88........ 330

FENETTI, F.M. (American, 19th C)
Still Life of Carnations (multicolored flowers in yellow vase), oil on canvas, sgn, 30x24", RAB 8/9/88 UE 1,400

FENGHAN, Gao (Chinese, 1683-1748)
Calligraphy in Xing Shu (running script, hanging scroll), ink on paper, sgn/dtd 1747, 59x21", SBY 5/31/89 OE........ 9,350

FENGMIAN, Lin (Chinese, 1900-)
Cranes (hanging scroll), ink/color on silk, sgn/dtd 1925 (?), 55x16", SBY 5/31/89 OE........ 7,150

FENN, Harry (American, 1845-1911)
Battle of Belmont (Civil War), watercolor on paper, inscr, 9x14", C-E 5/27/88 OE 935
Carondelet Passing Island Number Ten (Civil War), watercolor on paper, inscr, 10x12", C-E 5/27/88 OE 935
Casemates, Fort Negley, Nashville (Civil War); pen/ink on paper, inscr, 12x12", C-E 5/27/88 550
Confederate Fortifications at Manassas Junction (Civil War), pen/ink on paper, initialed/inscr, 7x12", C-E 5/27/88 OE 880
Confederate Lines in Rear of Vicksburg (Civil War), pen/ink on paper, unfr, inscr, 7x12", C-E 11/30/88........ 660
Depot & Hotel, Corinth, Mississippi (Civil War); pen/ink on paper, inscr, 8x13", C-E 5/27/88 OE 990
Fight in the Crater, Vicksburg (Civil War); pen/ink on paper, inscr, 9x13", C-E 5/27/88 550
Gunboats at Fort Donelson (Civil War), watercolor on paper, inscr, 11x14", C-E 5/27/88 OE 2,200
Headquarters of General Thomas Grant, Chattanooga (Civil War); pen/ink/wash, initialed/inscr, 15x16", C-E 5/27/88 OE........ 1,320
Lily Pond, watercolor on board, monogramed, 7x21", C-NY 9/30/88 4,400
Lookout Mountain (Civil War), pen/ink on paper, initialed/inscr, 13x21", C-E 5/27/88........ 330
National Cemetery & Frayser's Farm (Civil War), watercolor on paper, initialed/inscr, 10x11", C-E 5/27/88 825
Perryville: Spring That Watered Bragg's Army (Civil War); pen/ink on paper, initialed/inscr, 9x9", C-E 5/27/88........ 275
Pontoon Bridge Over the Rappahannock (Civil War), pen/ink on paper, inscr, 8x11", C-E 5/27/88 700
Provost Marshal's Office, Corinth, Mississippi (Civil War); watercolor on paper, inscr, 7x13", C-E 5/27/88 OE 3,080
Ross House, Chattanooga (Civil War); pen/ink on paper, initialed/inscr, 9x12", C-E 5/27/88 440
Seige of Vicksburg, Explosion of the Vicksburg Mine (Civil War); pen/ink, inscr, 10x15", C-E 5/27/88........ 880
Wilderness Church (Civil War), watercolor on paper, inscr, 8x10", C-E 5/27/88 770

FENN, Walter J. (American, 20th C)
Houses in Corinth, Mississippi (Civil War); pen/ink on paper, sgn/inscr, unfr, 19x13", C-E 11/30/88 220

FENNELL, Nora H. (American, 19th/20th C)
Mission Dolores, oil on canvas, sgn, 11x18", B/B 10/6/88........ 1,100

FENTON, Walter Scott
Bridal Veil Falls, Telluride, Colorado; oil on canvas, sgn, 24x36", C-E 6/1/89........ 1,100

FENYES, Adolphe (Hungarian, 1867-1945)
Reading by the Shade of an Umbrella, oil on canvasboard, sgn, 22x21", B/B 3/22/89 4,400

FEOLLI, John (American, 19th C)
Portrait of a Woman in a Black Dress, oil on canvas, sgn/dtd 1903, 30x25", WL 5/20/88 UE........ 150

FERAT, Serge (Russian, 1881-1958)
Les Jumeaux (mother w/twins), gouache/pen/black ink on paper, sgn/dtd 1929, 7x5", C-E 11/17/88 1,100

FERBER, Herbert (American, 1906-)
Couple at No 40, gouache on paper, sgn/dtd 40, 15x12", SBY 1/24/89 550
Untitled, acrylic on paper, sgn/dtd 52, 30x22", C-E 5/13/88 495

FERENZ, Anton Johan (Hungarian, -1874)
Pair: Gentleman & an Elegant Lady; oil on canvas, sgn/dtd, 12x9", SBY 6/8/88 2,200

FERG, see De Paula Ferg

FERGUSON, C.
Arabian Riders, oil on canvas, sgn, 23x31", LH 10/16/88 OE........ 500

FERGUSON, Henry A. (American, 1842-1911)
Venetian Scene (sailboats on water), oil on canvas, sgn, 12x23", C-E 6/1/89 1,650

FERGUSSON, William J. (British, 19th C)
Going to the Boat, watercolor on paper, sgn/dtd 1867, 9x13", C-E 2/21/89........ 440

FERNANDEZ, Agustin (Cuban, 1928-)
Composicion, gouache/watercolor/pencil on paper laid down on canvas, sgn, 25x28", C-NY 11/21/89 3,520

Sin Titulo (abstract), oil on canvas, sgn/dtd 60, 43x43", C-NY 5/17/89 3,850
Snake Describes a Circle Around the Dreamer, oil on canvas, sgn/dtd 86/inscr #2 anaconda serie, 52x42", SBY 11/21/88 17,600
Untitled (abstract), oil on canvas, sgn/dtd 1986, 50x55", SBY 5/17/88 16,500

FERNANDEZ, Alejo; att
Pair of Altar Shutters: Old Testament figures, full-length; gold ground, oil on panel, 61x16", C-NY 4/6/89 OE 24,200

FERNANDEZ, Eduardo Pelayo (Spanish, 1850-)
Summer Idyll, oil on panel, sgn/dtd 83, 19x13", C-NY 10/25/89 14,300

FERNANDEZ, Rafa (Latin American, 1935-)
Visit (three women in interior, figure in doorway), oil on canvas, sgn/dtd 87, 32x39", SBY 5/17/88 3,850

FERNANDI, Francesco (Italian, 18th C)
Adoration of the Magi, oil on canvas, 29x34", SBY 4/7/89 9,350

FERNELEY, John E. Sr. (British, 1781-1860)
Bay Hunter with a Spaniel in a Landscape, oil on canvas, sgn/dtd 1825, 34x44", SBY 6/10/88 55,000
Bay Hunter with Robert Day Up, Belgrave Hall, Leicester; oil on canvas, sgn/dtd 1807, SBY 6/10/88 165,000
Cur, Chestnut Racehorse w/Jockey on Newmarket Heath, Racehorse Exercising Beyond; oil, sgn/dtd 48, 40x50", SBY 6/9/89 308,000
Dark Brown Stallion in a Paddock, a Village in the Distance; oil on canvas, sgn/dtd 1851, 34x42", SBY 6/10/88 29,700
Edward Hartopp's Three Hunters: Moonshine, Corporal, & Scraptoft...; oil on canvas, sgn/dtd 1844, 44x70", SBY 6/9/89 71,500
Gentleman Holding Dangerous, the Winner of the 1833 Derby; oil on canvas, 29x37", C-NY 5/24/89 37,400
Jolly Roger, oil on canvas, sgn/dtd 1808, 28x36", SBY 6/10/88 14,300
Outside Allington Hall, oil on canvas, sgn/dtd 1847, 34x42", SBY 6/10/88 49,500
Portrait of the Racehorse Harkaway, Winner of the 1838 Goodwood Cup; oil on canvas, sgn, 1840, 28x34", C-NY 5/24/89 OE 39,600
Red Setter in a Landscape, oil on canvas, sgn/dtd 1810, 20x24", SBY 6/9/89 UE 5,500
Saddled Chestnut Hunter Beside a Stable, oil on canvas, sgn, 33x41", SBY 6/9/89 49,500
Thomas Crosby's Racehorse, Pussy, at Finishing Post; oil on canvas, sgn/dtd 1834, 32x42", SBY 6/10/88 176,000
Two Horses: Bockett & Crusader with Grooms, in a landscape; oil on canvas, 1851, 45x58", SBY 6/10/88 165,000

FERNELEY, John Jr. (British, 1815-1862)
Pair: Shorthorn Bull in a Barn; Shorthorn Cow in a Landscape; oil on canvas, sgn/1 dtd 1843, 20x25", SBY 6/10/88 8,800

FERNELEY, John Jr.; att (British, 1815-1862)
Crib Biter Being Groomed in a Stall, oil on canvas, bears signature, 18x22", SBY 6/9/89 1,760

FERRANTI, Carlo (Italian, 19th C)
Grape Gatherer, watercolor on paper, sgn, unfr, 30x22", B/B 9/15/88 1,320
Italian Peasants on a Road, watercolor, sgn/inscr twice, 21x15", C-E 10/25/88 OE 1,760
Musical Recital, oil on canvas, sgn, 18x25", C-E 10/26/89 2,750
Returning Home From the Vineyard, watercolor, sgn, 21x14", PHL 10/28/88 750

FERRARI, A. (Italian, 19th/20th C)
Plowing (man plowing field), oil on board, sgn, 8x11", SBY 12/9/88 OE 2,200

FERRARI, Lorenzo; see De Ferrari

FERREN, John (American, 1905-)
Abstract, oil on paper laid down on board, sgn/initialed, dtd twice 32, C-NY 9/30/88 2,420
Fleur du Mal, watercolor on paper, sgn/dtd 52, 26x20", C-E 10/18/89 1,100
Untitled (abstract), oil on canvas, sgn/dtd 63, 16x17", C-E 11/14/89 1,100

FERRER, Joaquin (20th C)
Untitled (abstract), oil on canvas, dtd Paris 1970, 32x32", SBY 5/16/89 1,870

FERRER, Jose; circle of (1746-1815)
Pair: Mixed Flowers in Brass Urn; Basket on Draped Ledges; oil on panel, 7x11", C-M 12/3/88 8,361

FERRETTI, Giovanni Domenico; att
Harlequin & Columbine, oil on canvas, 28x23", C-NY 10/12/89 6,600

FERRI, Ciro; att (Italian, 1634-1689)
Madonna & Child with Infant Saint John the Baptist in a Landscape, oil on canvas, 39x47", C-NY 4/6/89 3,300

FERRIER, Richard (Canadian, 1929-)
Muskoka Lake, acrylic on board, sgn, 12x16", WAD 11/30/89 150

FERRIERES, Martin (French, 19th/20th C)
Dahlias Pompons, oil on panel, sgn, 26x19", LH 12/4/88 900
Voiliers, le Port (sailing boats coming into port); oil on canvas, sgn, 20x29", C-NY 2/18/88 OE 17,600

FERRIS, Jean Leon Jerome (American, 1863-1930)
Her Weight in Gold (historical), oil on canvas, sgn/inscr, ca 1921, 25x35", C-NY 5/25/89 13,750
Home for Christmas, 1784; oil on canvas, sgn/inscr, 26x36", C-NY 12/2/88 16,500

FERRO, G. (French, 20th C)
Les Maisons sur la Colline, oil on board, sgn/dtd 53, 11x9", MG 5/28/88 200

FERRON, Marcelle (Canadian, 1924-)
Abstract, mixed media on paper, sgn/dtd 1961, 25x19", FB 10/30/89 1,650
Abstract, oil on canvas, sgn/dtd 1956, 19x30", FB 10/30/89 8,800
Sans Titre (abstract), oil on canvas, sgn/dtd 1960, 32x40", FB 10/17/88 6,000

FERRONE, Gianfranco (Italian, 1927-)
Landscape, oil on canvas, sgn/dtd 57, 25x28", LH 10/16/88 UE 200

FERRONI, Egisto (Italian, 1835-1912)
Peasant with a Mandolin, oil on canvas, sgn, unfr, 32x14", C-E 5/23/88 UE 660

FERY, John (American, 1865-1934)
Buck & Two Does in a Wooded Landscape, oil on canvas, sgn, 9x13", B/B 9/14/89 1,320
Moose on a Lake Shore, oil on canvasboard, sgn, 14x24", SBY 3/17/88 1,430

FETI, Domenico; after (Italian, 1589-1624)
Story of Hero & Leander, by David Teniers the younger (1610-1690); oil on canvas, monogramed, 24x32", SBY 6/2/89 .... **55,000**
FETI, Domenico; att (Italian, 1589-1624)
La Melancolie (lad at desk staring at skull, a dog & open book on floor), oil on canvas, #d 55, 59x44", C-M 12/3/88 .... **92,900**
Saint Roche (full-length portrait, holding walking stick, dog at side), oil on canvas, 58x29", C-NY 4/6/89 OE **14,300**
FETTING, Rainer (20th C)
Am Gerat (abstract), oil on canvas, sgn/dtd 84, unfr, 60x72", C-NY 10/4/89 .... **15,400**
Der Wolfs Junge (contempory depiction of male figure & wolf), oil on canvas, sgn/dtd 83, 90x72", SBY 5/3/89 OE **27,500**
Gabi on Green Sofa, oil on canvas, sgn/dtd 86/titled, unfr, 72x90", C-NY 11/10/88 OE **20,900**
Green Mountain Indian (green nude figure w/blue abstract background), powder paint on cotton, 1982, 98x95", SBY 2/15/89 .... **14,300**
Halluzination (abstract head w/red eyes), acrylic/wood on canvas, sgn/dtd 84, 90x72", SBY 10/5/89 .... **34,100**
Holsbild (abstract), oil on canvas & wood, sgn/dtd 83/titled, 90x72x4", SBY 2/19/88 OE **24,200**
Man with the Candle, oil/wood on canvas, sgn/dtd 84/titled, 90x81", C-NY 11/10/88 OE **30,800**
Mann V Axt (Grun II), acrylic on canvas, sgn/inscr/dtd 81, 87x63", C-NY 5/4/88 OE **12,100**
Red Head (abstract), oil/wood on canvas, sgn/dtd 84, 91x72x4", SBY 2/15/89 .... **23,100**
Ricky III, oil on canvas, sgn/dtd 81, 87x67", SBY 11/9/89 .... **20,900**
FEUCHSEL, Herman (American, 1833-1915)
Reminiscence, a Hudson River Scene; oil on canvas, sgn/dtd NY 1883, 10x21", RWS 11/10/89 OE **9,000**
FEUDEL, Arthur (American, 1857-)
Bit of Old Holland, oil on canvas, sgn, 20x24", C-E 9/15/88 UE **715**
FEUDEL, Constantin (German, 1860-)
Gentleman Playing a Lute, oil on canvas, sgn, 41x32", C-E 10/25/88 .... **1,100**
FEURE, see De Feure
FEYEN-PERRIN, Francois Nicolas Augustin (French, 1826-1888)
Le Repos de la Faneuse, oil on canvas, sgn, 77x44", SBY 2/22/89 .... **9,900**
Retour de la Peche aux Huitres (people returning w/baskets of oysters), oil on canvas, sgn, 52x39", C-NY 2/23/89 .... **6,600**
FIAMMINGO, Paolo; circle of (Flemish, 1540-1596)
Elegant Figures in a Forest Landscape, oil on canvas, unfr, 28x37", C-NY 10/20/88 OE **3,300**
FICHEL, Benjamin Eugene (French, 1826-1895)
Chess Game, oil on panel, sgn/dtd 1859, 9x6", C-E 10/25/88 .... **3,520**
Reading the News, oil on panel, sgn/dtd 1866, 13x16", C-NY 10/25/89 .... **7,150**
Scholar at Work, oil on panel, sgn/dtd 1857, 9x6", C-E 10/26/89 .... **6,600**
FICHERELLI, Felice; circle of (Italian, 1605-1660)
Rape of Lucretia, oil on canvas, 46x62", SBY 4/7/89 UE **5,500**
FICHT, C.O. (American, 19th C)
Columbia River Above the Dalles, oil on masonite, sgn, 9x14", SBY 4/14/89 .... **550**
FIDLER, Anton (Austrian, fl 1825-1855)
Still Life of Basket of Fruit & Birds, oil on canvas, sgn/dtd 1854, 23x29", SBY 2/22/89 .... **11,000**
FIDLER, Harry (British, -1935)
Milking the Cows, oil on canvas, sgn/inscr, unfr, 16x20", SBY 12/9/88 OE **4,675**
FIELD, Edward Loyal (American, 1856-1914)
Autumn Landscape, oil on canvas, sgn, 16x20", WL 5/20/88 OE **1,300**
Farm by the River, watercolor on paper, sgn, 12x21", B/B 12/8/88 .... **385**
FIELD, Erastus Salisbury (American, 1805-1900)
Ark of the Covenant, oil on canvas, 21x29", C-SK 5/25/89 .... **1,290**
Boy in Red with Yellow Rattle, oil on canvas, 12x9", RWS 10/27/89 .... **18,000**
FIELD, Frances
Stasis, pastel on paper, initialed, 11x14", SBY 2/14/89 OE **440**
FIELD, Isabel Jane (New Zealand, 19th/20th C)
Lake Landscape, South Island; watercolor heightened w/white, sgn/dtd 1901, 15x25", C-SK 11/10/88 .... **4,090**
FIELDING, Copley (British, 1787-1855)
Alnwick Castle, watercolor on paper, sgn/dtd 1843, 13x20", B/B 9/15/88 .... **935**
Fall Landscape, watercolor on paper, sgn/dtd 1839, 8x11", B/B 9/15/88 .... **550**
Watching the Herd, watercolor on paper, sgn, 7x10", B/B 12/8/88 .... **605**
FIELDING, Copley; manner of (British, 1787-1855)
Boats at Sunset, watercolor & gouache, bears signature/dtd 1825, 8x15", C-E 2/21/89 .... **990**
FIELDING, Ernest (British, 19th C)
Putti in a Garden, oil on canvas, sgn, 20x16", B/B 12/8/88 OE **2,750**
FIELDING, George (British, 19th C)
Forest Path Along the Stream, oil on canvas, sgn, 30x25", NA 5/13/89 .... **900**
FIENE, Ernest (American, 1894-1965)
Apple Blossoms, oil on board, sgn/dtd 25, 12x16", C-E 6/1/88 .... **1,100**
Colonial Village, oil on relined canvas, sgn, 23x28", FAP 12/8/89 .... **1,300**
Cottages in a Hilly Landscape, oil on panel, sgn/dtd 1917, 16x12", SBY 6/28/89 .... **880**
Early Summer, oil on canvas, sgn, 10x16", C-E 11/30/88 .... **3,080**
Evening Light-Woodbury Village; oil on canvas, sgn, 20x28", C-E 6/1/89 .... **3,080**
Oriental Poppies in Persian Pot, oil on canvas, sgn, 20x16", SBY 6/28/89 .... **1,045**
Pittsburgh (snowy cityscape at night), oil on canvas, sgn, 30x36", C-NY 5/25/89 OE **28,600**
Red Poppies (still life, contemporary depiction), oil on canvas, sgn, 24x18", C-E 6/1/89 .... **1,045**
Still Life of Pink & White Peonies, oil on board, sgn, 14x10", RWS 11/10/89 .... **600**
Under the El (modernistic city scene), oil on canvas, sgn, 24x36", C-NY 5/25/89 .... **19,800**

Winter Evening: Connecticut (view of church); oil on canvas, sgn, 32x38", SBY 9/14/89 2,420

FIERAVINO, Francesco; circle of (Italian, 1640-)

Still Life of Fruit & an Ornate Silver Urn on a Draped Table, oil on canvas, unfr, 31x26", SBY 12/9/88 3,080

FIERAVINO, Francesco; school of (Italian, 1640-)

Gold Plate, Ewer, & Game on a Table; oil on canvas, unfr, 29x39", C-NY 10/20/88 1,650

FIERRO, Pancho (19th C)

Group of 3: Vendedores Peruanos (Peruvian Vendors); watercolor/pen/ink on rice paper, ca 1830, 9x6", C-NY 5/17/89 OE 3,850

FIEUX, Robert (American, 20th C)

Eel River, Cape Cod; oil on canvas, sgn/dtd 66, 20x24", RAB 8/9/88 650

FIGARI, Pedro (Uruguayan, 1861-1938)

A la Fiesta (festive gathering under full moon), oil on board, sgn, 21x27", C-NY 11/21/89 33,000
Agotamiento (After the Dance), oil on board, sgn/#d 259/stamped 69/inscribed 1727, 16x13", SBY 5/17/88 13,200
Baile Criollo, oil on board, sgn/#d 104, 24x32", C-NY 11/21/89 44,000
Baile Criollo (Dancing Creole), oil on board, sgn, 19x25", C-NY 5/17/89 44,000
Candombe (gathering of people), oil on board, titled/inscr Serie B No 116, 16x9", SBY 5/16/89 9,350
Confraternidad (people meeting), oil on board, sgn/dtd 1932/#d XII Ei, 19x25", C-NY 5/18/88 35,200
Country Dance (gathering in landscape), oil on board, sgn/dtd 1921/titled, 14x20", SBY 11/21/88 13,200
El Hermano (The Brother), oil on board, sgn, 14x20", C-NY 5/18/88 17,600
Gato, oil on board, sgn/#167, 21x32", SBY 5/17/88 49,500
House of the Witch Doctor, oil on board, sgn/dtd 1921/inscr No 71 Serie XXV DG, 13x16", SBY 5/16/89 OE 17,600
La Conquista del Chaco (caravan in landscape), oil on board, sgn twice/#d 43 Serie VXIII Ai, 14x20", C-NY 11/21/88 13,200
La Consulta (The Consultation), oil on board, sgn/#d 142 Serie VIII Ch/titled, 20x28", C-NY 5/17/89 UE 20,000
La Familia (three figures in an interior), oil on board, sgn/titled/inscr, 13x20", C-NY 11/21/88 7,150
La Media Cana (festive gathering in landscape), oil on board, sgn/titled, 20x28", SBY 11/21/88 55,000
La Naticia, no media given, series label No 37 Serie XVP1, ca 1920s, 16x23", SBY 5/16/89 19,800
La Receta, oil on board, sgn/dtd 1932, 19x25", C-NY 11/21/89 16,500
Mientras la Bocha Rueda (men playing boccie), oil on board, sgn/inscr Serie B No 101, ca 1918, 10x20", SBY 5/16/89 9,350
Nostalgias Africanas (Candombe), oil on board, sgn/titled/inscr No 116 Serie XIIEd, 19x25", C-NY 5/17/89 28,600
Pericon, oil on board, sgn twice/dtd 1922, 14x20", C-NY 5/18/88 OE 20,900

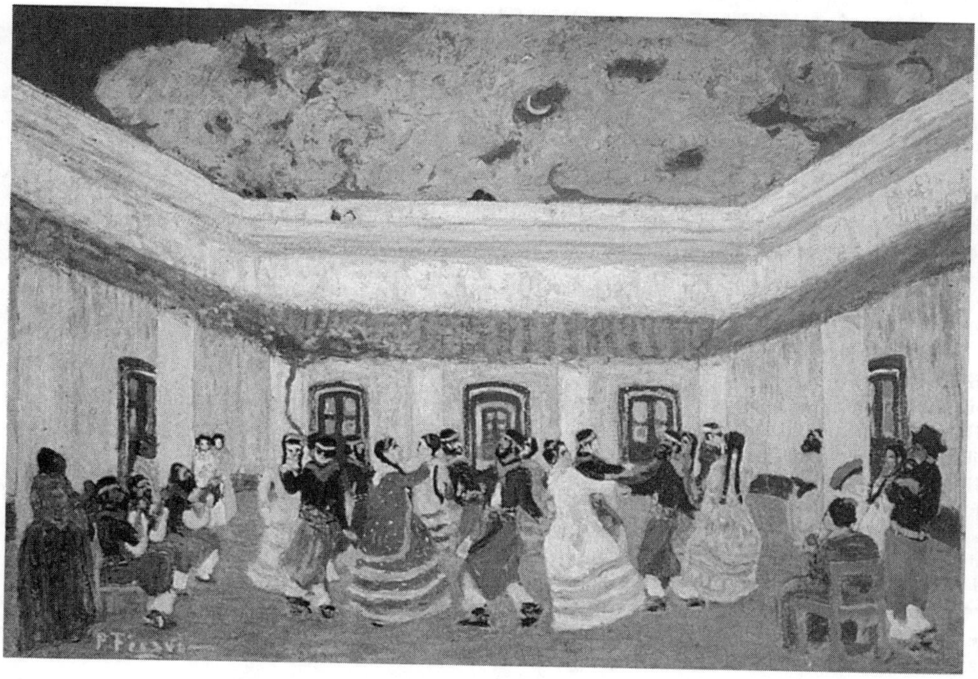

Percion en el Patio, oil on board, sgn, 27x39", C-NY 11/21/89, $82,500

Pericon en el Patio (people dancing on a patio), oil on board, sgn, 27x39", C-NY 5/18/88 57,200
Presentation (impressionistic figures in interior), oil on board, sgn, 11x9", SBY 11/21/88 5,500
Quitanderas (wagon/figures in landscape), oil on panel, sgn/inscr No 75 Serie XII C/#d 180, 19x24", SBY 5/16/89 9,350
Reunion Colonial (gathering in interior), oil on board, sgn, 27x39", C-NY 11/21/88 UE 30,250
Teniendome a Mi (three figures), oil on board, sgn/#d 48 Serie XIII Da/titled, 15x20", C-NY 5/17/89 9,900
Untitled (figures in church interior), oil on board, sgn, 19x25", SBY 11/21/88 9,900

GINO, Ambrogio (Italian, 1548-1608)

Double-Sided: Cupid & Psyche; Two Portrait Studies; pen/brown ink over red chalk, 8x6", SBY 1/13/89 UE 1,650

GURA, Hang (Australian, 20th C)

Extensive Alpine Landscape, oil on canvas, sgn, 24x30", WG 9/16/88 250

LATOV, Nikolai (Russian, 1951-)

Dyptich: The Roads (abstract); oil on 2 canvases, sgn/dtd 1987, 79x57", SBY 7/7/88 OE 18,000
Minotaure (abstract), oil on canvas, sgn/dtd 1987, 79x59", SBY 7/7/88 OE 22,000

FILLON, Arthur (French, 1900-)
Le Canal Saint Martin et le Petit Chemin de Fer (canal scene), oil on canvas, sgn, 18x22", C-E 11/17/88 1,760
FILOSA, Giovanni Battista (Italian, 1850-1935)
Contemplation-Woman Seated on a Balcony; watercolor on paper, sgn/dtd 1884, 10x7", RWS 6/17/89 500
Gathering Spring Flowers, watercolor/gouache over traces of pencil, sgn/dtd 1874, 19x30", C-NY 2/25/88 1,870
Pair: Letter; A Confidence; watercolor on paper, sgn/2nd dtd 1885, ea 19x12", SBY 2/22/89 8,800
FINCK, Hazel
Found, A Lost Buddy (two sailors under lamppost in a landscape); oil on canvas, sgn, ca 1941, 25x30", C-NY 5/25/89 8,800
FINCKEN, James Horsey (American, 1860-1943)
Landscape-Darby Creek (Outside Philadelphia, Pennsylvania); oil on board, sgn/titled, 6x8", RAB 8/8/89 UE 200
FINDERS, Frank (American, 19th/20th C)
Happy Thought 1912, watercolor, sgn/dtd 1912, 26x20", S/A 3/12/88 750
FINES, Eugene Francois (French, 1826-)
Blowing Bubbles, oil on canvas, sgn, 27x18", SBY 7/12/89 1,980
FINI, Leonor (Italian, 1885-)
Cat Woman, pen/brush/black ink/watercolor on paper, sgn, 10x9", C-NY 10/6/88 OE 4,620
Composition with Figures on a Terrace, oil on canvas, sgn/dtd 1938, 39x32", C-NY 10/6/88 OE 154,000
Deux Figures (two figures), pen/ink, sgn, 12x10", PHL 11/15/88 900
Exotic Female Head, pen/black ink on paper, sgn, 6x4", C-NY 10/6/88 OE 1,540
Exotic Female Head, pen/black ink on paper, sgn, 9x7", C-NY 10/6/88 OE 1,870
Exotic Male Nude, pen/black ink heightened w/orange chalk on gray paper, sgn, 20x12", C-NY 10/6/88 1,760
Fantastic Head (abstract), watercolor/pen/black ink on paper, sgn, 14x10", C-NY 10/6/88 1,760
Green Sphinx-Spring; watercolor/pen/black ink on paper, sgn, 12x8", C-NY 10/6/88 OE 4,400
Head of a Girl, pen/black ink/brush/gray wash on paper, sgn, 8x12", C-NY 10/6/88 880
Head of a Young Woman, watercolor on paper, sgn, 13x11", SBY 10/5/88 2,750
La Sphinge, watercolor/pen/black ink over pencil on paper, sgn, unfr, 15x11", C-E 11/17/88 OE 3,520
La Statue, watercolor/pen/black ink on paper, sgn, 16x12", C-E 11/17/88 1,980
Pale Sphinx-Winter; watercolor/pen/black ink on paper, 12x9", C-NY 10/6/88 3,080
Pink Sphinx-Autumn; watercolor/pen/black ink on paper, sgn, 12x9", C-NY 10/6/88 OE 6,050
Retrato de un Joven (portrait of man's head), oil on canvas, 14x11", C-NY 5/17/89 11,000
Sphinx, watercolor/pen/black ink on paper, sgn, 14x10", C-NY 10/6/88 OE 6,600
Woman with Cat, watercolor/India ink on paper, sgn, 17x13", SBY 10/5/88 1,540
FINK, Aaron (American, 20th C)
Green Cherry (green field reveals single image of a cherry), oil on canvas, sgn/dtd 1985, 50x36", RWS 3/31/88 UE 1,600
Poker Player (man w/cards on red & black field), oil on canvas, sgn/dtd 1986, 30x24", RWS 3/31/88 UE 1,500
FINKERNAGEL, E. (European, 19th C)
View of Rome From the Tiber, oil on canvas, sgn/dtd, 41x53", C-E 2/23/88 OE 4,180
FIRMIN-GIRARD, Marie Francois (French, 1838-1921)
Feeding Swans at a Lake, oil on canvas, sgn, 11x16", SBY 2/22/89 23,100
Quiet Afternoon (woman knitting), oil on canvas, sgn/dtd 1917, 22x18", C-NY 5/25/88 6,600
FIRUSHON, Emil
Portrait of a Lady, oil on canvas, sgn/dtd 1912, 33x24", NA 3/26/88 UE 225
FISCHBACH, Johann (Austrian, 1797-1871)
After the Shoot, oil on cradled panel, sgn/dtd 1842, 30x24", C-E 2/23/88 3,740
FISCHEL, Eric
Untitled (abstract), oil on paper, sgn/dtd 86, 27x35", SBY 5/3/88 OE 38,500
FISCHER, Adolph (German, 1860-)
Twilight Lake View, oil on canvas, sgn, unfr, 25x27", SBY 6/8/88 UE 770
FISCHER, Anton Otto (American, 1882-1962)
Confrontation, oil on canvas, initialed/dtd 1933, 22x26", C-E 2/1/89 715
Discussion, oil on canvas, sgn/dtd 1940, 23x18", C-E 6/1/89 660
Midnight Intruder (man on stairs w/gun, shining flashlight in intruder's eyes), oil on canvas, sgn/dtd 1940, C-E 2/1/89 605
Salt-Water Diplomacy, oil on canvas, initialed/titled, 18x28", SBY 3/17/88 880
Six Men Leaving Ship, oil on canvas, sgn/dtd 1934, 24x36", B/B 6/15/89 1,980
The Campbell (ship at sea), oil on canvas, sgn, 18x26", SBY 3/17/88 2,090
The Fight (two men fighting in ship's interior), oil on canvas, sgn/dtd 1930, 22x22", C-E 6/1/89 935
Windmills, boy/dog in landscape; oil on canvas, sgn, 22x18", SLK 11/25/88 800
FISCHER, C.
Niagara (ship) Bound for Japan, Early 19th C; oil on canvas, sgn, unfr, 36x48", C-NY 1/20/89 OE 17,600
FISCHER, Carl (Danish, 19th/20th C)
Courtship (peasant couple seated on bench in a landscape), oil on canvas, sgn, 18x22", B/B 3/22/89 1,650
FISCHER, Ludwig Hans (German, 1848-1915)
Roman Temple Facade, oil on canvasboard, sgn, 14x11", SBY 7/12/89 4,400
FISCHL, Eric (American, 20th C)
Savior Self, oil on paper, sgn/dtd 80, 24x58", C-NY 11/10/88 49,500
Untitled (interior w/TV on table & nude couple on bed), oil wash on coated paper, sgn/dtd 82, 24x40", SBY 5/3/89 52,250
Untitled (male nude from behind), charcoal on paper, sgn/dtd 86, 24x18", SBY 11/9/89 11,000
Untitled (man's profile in silhouette), gouache/pencil on paper, sgn/dtd 1977, 24x23", SBY 2/19/88 4,125
Untitled (nude couple in contemporary landscape), oil on paper, 1984, 20x24", SBY 2/15/89 OE 46,750
Untitled (nude sitting on beach, viewed from behind), oil on paper, sgn, 35x46", SBY 5/3/89 OE 77,000
Untitled (pair of scissors), gouache/pencil on paper, sgn/dtd 77/inscr, 26x20", SBY 2/19/88 3,850

Untitled (posterior view of nude in outdoors), oil on canvas, sgn/dtd 86, 11x9", SBY 5/3/88 ... 11,000
Untitled (Study for Bayonne), oil on paper, sgn/dtd 85, 16x12", SBY 5/3/88 ... 24,200
Untitled (Study for Fort Worth), oil on paper laid down on linen, sgn/dtd 85, 46x35", SBY 11/11/88 ... 49,500
Untitled (Study for Whitney Poster), oil on paper, sgn/dtd 84, 16x13", SBY 5/3/88 ... 27,500
Untitled (two young bathers in pool), acrylic/ink on paper, sgn/dtd 86, 9x11", SBY 5/3/89 ... 11,000
Untitled (woman on raft), oil on paper, sgn/dtd 86/inscr, 11x14", SBY 11/11/88 ... 22,000
Untitled (woman), charcoal on paper, sgn/dtd 85, 60x42", C-NY 5/4/88 ... 38,500

FISEN, Engelbert

Triumph of a Roman General, Apollo, Minerva, Neptune, & Others Presenting Wreaths; oil on canvas, 54x71", C-NY 6/2/88 OE ... 28,600

FISH, Janet (American, 1938-)

Mixed Fruit (in produce tray w/shrinkwrap), pastel on paper, sgn/dtd 1973, 22x38", SBY 11/11/88 ... 8,800
Six Glasses of Water, pastel on paper, sgn/dtd 1974, 22x37", SBY 10/8/88 ... 19,800
Skowhegan Water Glass I, pastel on paper, sgn/dtd 1974, 27x18", SBY 2/15/89 OE ... 9,350
Skowhegen 7 Glasses Painted, pastel on brown-toned paper, sgn/dtd 1974, 30x25", SBY 10/5/89 OE ... 19,800
Skowhegen 7 Glasses Painted, pastel on brown-toned paper, sgn/dtd 1974, 29x24", SBY 5/3/88 OE ... 11,500
Tequila Bottles (still life), oil on canvas, sgn/dtd 1974, 66x54", SBY 11/11/88 OE ... 104,500
Untitled (still life of peaches & roses), pastel on paper, sgn/dtd 69, 18x24", SBY 10/5/89 ... 5,500

FISHBEIN, J.B.

Cliffs, oil on canvas, sgn/dtd 64, 42x30", C-NY 6/17/89 UE ... 220
Market Place, oil on masonite, initialed/dtd 67, 8x6", C-E 1/12/88 ... 121

FISHER, A.

Cattle Watering, oil on canvas, sgn, 16x24", DM 1/15/88 ... 600

FISHER, Alvan (American, 1792-1863)

Landscape Scene with Figures, oil on canvas, sgn/dtd 1835, 25x36", RWS 11/3/88 ... 4,250
Pair: Views of Harvard College; brush/pen/ink on paper laid down on board, 1 sgn/dtd 1821, ea 9x14", C-NY 5/26/88 OE ... 22,000
Under the Bridge, oil on canvas, sgn/dtd twice 1828, 30x25", RWS 11/3/88 OE ... 24,000

FISHER, Anton Otto (American, 1882-1962)

Sailing into Sunset, oil on canvas, sgn, 26x28", C-E 4/7/88 ... 1,650
Sailing Ship (ship at sea), oil on canvas, sgn, 10x28", SBY 3/17/88 ... 1,045

FISHER, Ben (Welsh, -1939)

Cows Grazing by a Stream, oil on canvas, sgn/London canvas stamp, 16x24", RWS 3/16/89 ... 300

FISHER, D. (British, 19th C)

Beach Scene, oil on canvas, sgn/dtd 1880, 9x14", FB 10/30/89 ... 522

FISHER, Edgar H. (British, 1870-1939)

Mare & Her Colt in a Landscape, oil on panel, sgn, 16x19", LH 9/10/89 ... 1,200

FISHER, Elizabeth Clay (American, 1910-)

Portrait of the Artist's Grandmother Sewing, oil on canvas, estate stamp on verso, 30x26", C-E 9/15/88 UE ... 110

FISHER, Harrison C. (American, 1875-1934)

Red Cross, pastel on canvas, sgn/dtd 1918, 44x30", C-NY 3/11/88 OE ... 24,200
Sunday Best (portrait of a woman), gouache/charcoal on board, sgn, 27x20", C-E 10/18/89 ... 1,980

FISHER, Horace (British, -1893)

Young Girl Picking Flowers, oil on canvas, sgn, 50x35", C-NY 5/24/89 ... 6,600

FISHER, Hugo Antoine (American, 1867-1917)

Autumn Landscape, watercolor on paper, 21x29", B/B 9/14/89 UE ... 715
Cattle Grazing, watercolor on paper, sgn, 17x25", B/B 8/10/88 ... 358
Winter Sleigh, watercolor/gouache, 26x36", FAP 4/15/89 ... 1,045

FISHER, Hugo Melville (American, 1878-1946)

Country Road with Cottage, oil on canvas, sgn, 34x36", WG 4/23/88 UE ... 875

FISHER, J. (British, 19th C)

Farmer's Wife & the Raven, scene from Gay's fable; oil on canvas, sgn/dtd 1855/titled, 21x28", RAB 5/17/88 ... 900

ISHER, Paul

Jardin Mexicano (Mexican garden), watercolor/pencil on paper, initialed, 7x10", C-NY 11/21/89 ... 2,860

ISHER, Samuel Melton (British, 1860-1939)

The Mirror (lady admiring reflection in mirror), oil on canvas laid down on masonite, sgn, 53x41", SBY 10/24/89 ... 15,400

ISHER, Vernon (20th C)

Line Up, acrylic on 2 sheets of paper incised w/text & mounted on backboard, 26x55", C-NY 10/4/89 ... 6,820
Parachute, acrylic on laminated paper, 1976, 90x92", SBY 2/15/89 OE ... 17,600

ISHER, William Mark (American, 1841-1923)

Cattle by a River in an Extensive Landscape, oil on canvas, sgn, 18x24", PHL 10/28/88 ... 3,250
Changing Pastures (sheep in a mountainous landscape), oil on canvas, sgn, 11x14", SBY 7/12/89 UE ... 660
Landscape Scene with Barn, oil on particle board, sgn, 22x28", RWS 11/3/88 ... 950

ISKE, Gertrude (American, 1879-1961)

Amusement Park, oil on canvas, sgn, 36x48", C-NY 12/2/88 OE ... 52,800

TLER, William Crothers (American, 1857-1915)

Late Afternoon (landscape), oil on canvas, sgn/inscr NY, 12x16", SBY 3/17/88 ... 935
Sunset, gouache on blue-gray paper laid down on board, sgn/dtd 19(?), 9x13", C-NY 9/30/88 ... 1,760

TZGERALD, Edward

Hearts (Tromp l'Oeil still life), oil on canvas, initialed/dtd 76, 13x12", C-NY 6/17/89 ... 550
John Koch, pencil/Chinese white on paper, initialed/dtd 76, 9x12", C-NY 6/17/89 ... 165

ACK, Audrey (American, 1931-)

Banana Split Sundae, colored chalks/graphite on paper, sgn, 1985, 23x30", C-NY 5/4/89 ... 5,500

Coconut Lemon Cake, acrylic on canvas, 1974, 24x30", SBY 2/19/88 OE ... 56,100

Time To Save (still life of flowers/fruit/timepieces/insects), oil on canvas, sgn/dtd 1979, 80x64", SBY 11/11/88 OE ... 104,500

FLAGG, Charles N. (American, 1948-1916)

Still Life, study of a quill, art glass bowl, & brass bird-form letter holder; oil, sgn/dtd 87, 16x13", RAB 11/24/89 ... 1,000

Still Life of Pipe, Wine, & Book; oil on canvas laid down on masonite, sgn/dtd 1880, 13x16", C-E 11/8/88 ... 660

FLAGG, H. Peabody (American, 1859-)

Extensive Landscape, oil on canvasboard, sgn/dtd 1922, 10x8", PHL 10/28/88 UE ... 275

Sheep Grazing, oil on canvas, sgn, 12x16", FB 10/17/88 ... 300

FLAGG, James Montgomery (American, 1877-1960)

Pink Veil, watercolor, sgn/dtd 1900, oval, 16x14", C-SK 11/10/88 ... 520

The Fight, watercolor on paper, sgn, 22x28", B/B 6/15/89 ... 1,650

Warm Hearth, watercolor/gouache/pencil on paper laid down on board, sgn, 15x22", C-NY 9/30/88 ... 1,320

FLAGG, Jared Bradley (American 1820-1899)

Portrait of Mrs William Woolsey Scarborough (Sara Van Buren) & Child, oil on canvas, sgn, 35x29", LH 10/16/88 ... 2,800

FLAHERTY, James Thorp (American, 19th/20th C)

Southern Pennsylvania (landscape with house & stream), oil on canvas, sgn/dtd 1881, 14x24", C-NY 3/11/88 OE ... 4,400

FLAMENG, Francois (French, 1856-1923)

Ile Pointeaux, oil on canvas, sgn/titled, 29x36", SBY 2/22/89 OE ... 49,500

Napoleon After the Battle of Waterloo, oil on cradled panel, sgn, 17x24", SBY 2/22/89 ... 18,700

FLAMM, Albert (German, 1823-1906)

On the Steps of a Monument, oil on canvas, sgn, 32x40", C-E 10/26/89 ... 9,350

FLANNERY, Vaughn (American, 20th C)

Schooling Steeplechasers, oil on panel, sgn twice, 14x20", C-E 6/1/88 ... 1,540

FLAXMAN, John; att (British, 1753-1826)

Greek Play Scene No 1, pen/ink on paper, 6x9", WG 10/19/88 UE ... 100

Greek Play Scene No 2, pen/ink on paper, 8x13", WG 10/19/88 UE ... 100

FLECK, Joseph Amedeus (American, 1892-1977)

Portrait of an Indian Girl (in profile), oil on canvas, sgn/dtd Taos NM 24(?), 24x20", SBY 4/14/89 ... 5,500

Taos, July; oil on masonite, sgn/dtd Taos July 20, 28x35", C-NY 5/25/89 ... 18,700

FLEGEL, George; att

Rabbit, Rooster & Pigeons in a Park; oil on canvas, 39x54", WD 1/25/89 OE ... 5,250

FLEM (American?, 19th C)

River Landscape with Sheep, oil on canvas, sgn, 12x9", WG 4/23/88 UE ... 150

FLEMALLE, Bertholet; att

Scene From Roman History, oil on canvas, 29x40", C-NY 10/12/89 OE ... 28,600

FLEMING, A. (British, 20th C)

Grand Canal, Venice; oil on board, sgn, 16x20", B/B 1/11/89 ... 660

Hong Kong Harbor, oil on canvasboard, sgn, 16x20", B/B 1/11/89 ... 605

Paris Flower Market, oil on canvasboard, sgn, B/B 9/15/88 ... 1,100

FLEMING, Alexander M. (Canadian, 1878-1929)

Bronze of an October Day, Caledon; oil on canvas, sgn/dtd 1918, 24x30", WAD 11/30/89 ... 1,000

Flemish School (15th C)

Portrait of a Gentleman, Holding a Glove; oil on panel, unfr, 38x27", ca 1600, SBY 10/13/89 ... 5,500

Flemish School (16th C)

Adoration of the Shepherds, oil on panel, 11x8", WD 10/19/88 ... 5,000

Double-Sided: Madonna & Child with St Benedict; Scull in Painted Rope Border; oil on panel, 14x12", SBY 10/21/88 ... 17,600

Madonna & Child, oil on panel, a fragment, 22x7", C-NY 4/6/89 OE ... 4,620

Madonna & Child (in an interior, landscape beyond viewed through window), oil on panel, 20x15", WD 1/25/89 ... 11,000

Madonna & Child with the Infant St John the Baptist & St Francis of Assisi, oil on panel, inscr, 19x13", SBY 10/21/88 ... 2,475

Portrait of a Gentleman, Half-Length, Wearing a Dark Costume & Cap; oil on panel, 12x10", C-NY 10/12/89 ... 5,500

Portrait of a Lady, wearing a jeweled dress & hat w/veil; oil on panel, 7x4", C-E 6/1/88 OE ... 2,200

Flemish School (17th C)

Adam & Eve, oil on panel, 32x24", WD 1/25/89 OE ... 5,000

Adoration of the Magi (many figures in an interior, star shines from above), oil on copper, 14x11", C-NY 4/6/89 ... 6,600

Christ Crowned with Thorns (bust-length portrait), oil on copper, 13x10", C-NY 4/6/89 UE ... 1,100

Church by a River with Figures, oil on panel, 20x29", SBY 6/8/88 OE ... 3,300

Cumean Sibyl, oil on canvas, inscr, 41x32", C-NY 4/8/88 ... 1,760

Eve Presenting the Apple to Adam, oil on canvas, ca 1600, 19x29", SBY 10/21/88 ... 5,225

Feast Scene, oil on canvas, 22x26", SBY 12/9/88 ... 770

Flowers with Swags of Fruits & Vegetables in a Courtyard, w/Figures Returning; oil on canvas, unfr, 170x84", C-NY 6/2/88 ... 30,800

Gypsy Fortune Teller, oil on canvas, 26x20", SBY 12/9/88 OE ... 1,980

Head of a Satyr, After the Antique; black chalk w/touches of white heightening, 10x8", SBY 1/13/89 ... 650

Italianate Harbor with Men O` War, One Firing a Salute; oil on canvas, 30x45", C-NY 4/6/89 OE ... 17,600

Madonna & Child, oil on panel, 28x19", SBY 1/12/89 OE ... 15,400

Mythological Scenes, oil on panel, 3x8", C-E 4/7/88 ... 2,640

Pair: Portraits of an Old Peasant & His Wife; oil on panel, 1 initialed CV, 6x5", SBY 12/9/88 ... 4,400

Portrait of a Man & Woman, oil on canvas, 46x36", SBY 1/12/89 ... 33,000

Rebecca at the Well, oil on canvas, 26x32", C-NY 10/20/88 ... 3,850

St John the Baptist, oil on copper, in ornate 19th-C frame, 11x9", WD 10/19/88 ... 3,000

St John the Baptist, oil on copper, 9x7", WD 1/25/89 ... 1,100

Still Life of Fish & Shells, oil on canvas, 19x28", WD 10/19/88 ... 1,300

Susanna & the Elders in an Architectural Capriccio, oil on canvas, 19x30", WD 1/25/89 OE **6,250**
Victory Crowning Mars, oil on canvas, 17x14", C-NY 4/6/89 .... **1,650**

emish School (18th C)
Cavalry Skirmish, oil on canvas laid down on panel, oval, 25x19", C-E 4/7/88 UE **242**
Cupid, oil on canvas, ca 1700, 25x30", SBY 6/8/88 .... **1,980**
Figures in a Classical Italianate Landscape, oil on canvas, 14x19", C-E 4/7/88 .... **715**
Flowers in an Urn on a Ledge, oil on canvas, 49x38", WD 1/25/89 OE **20,000**
Ice Skaters on a Frozen Pond in a Winter Landscape, oil on canvas, 23x36", WD 10/19/88 OE **2,600**
Landscape with Peasants, Bulls, & Sheep; oil on canvas, bears signature, 6x8", C-E 4/7/88 .... **770**
Landscape with Peasants Fishing, oil on cradled panel, 22x30", B/B 3/22/89 .... **4,125**
Mother & Her Children Outside a Farmhouse, oil on canvas, 17x23", C-NY 4/6/89 .... **2,530**
Mythological Subject-Nymphs Dancing Around a Figure & Being Transformed into a Tree; oil on canvas, 30x37", SBY 7/12/89 .... **3,300**
Parrot Perched on a Grapevine, oil painted in oval on canvas, unfr, 34x29", SBY 6/2/89 OE **19,800**
Portrait of a Woman, oil on canvas, 20x15", SBY 7/12/89 .... **1,320**
Putti Amorini, oil on cradled panel, 24x31", B/B 3/22/89 .... **3,850**
Putti with Flowers & Fruit, oil on canvas, 61x41", WD 1/25/89 OE **42,500**
River Landscape with Figures on a Bridge, oil on panel, 9x13", C-NY 4/6/89 .... **1,760**
Shepherdess with Livestock Amidst Ruins, oil on canvas, 31x25", B/B 9/14/89 .... **1,320**
Stags in the Woods, oil on canvas, 18x26", WD 10/19/88 UE **500**
Still Life of Flowers in a Blue & White Vase, oil on canvas, 25x20", B/B 3/17/88 .... **3,300**
Still Life of Flowers in a Garden in Urn on a Ledge, a Mountainous Landscape Beyond; oil on canvas, 48x36", SLK 2/12/88 .... **900**
Still Life of Tulips, Roses, Morning-Glories, & Other Flowers in Vase, oil on canvas, unfr, ca 1700, 27x23", SBY 12/9/88 .... **3,575**
Study of Butterflies & Insects with a Mouse, Snail, & Frog; oil on panel, inscr, 12x21", SBY 10/21/88 .... **4,950**
Travelers on a Path in a Mountainous River Landscape, oil on canvas, 29x37", C-NY 4/6/89 .... **3,520**
Two Heads: Joos de Momper & Bacchus; black chalk, ca 1700, 10x6", SBY 1/13/89 .... **990**
Wooden Cottage & Figures in an Extensive Landscape, oil on canvas, unfr, 28x36", C-E 4/7/88 .... **1,980**

emish School (19th C)
Floral Still Life, oil on canvas, 18x14", B/B 12/8/88 .... **3,300**
Floral Still Life of Fruit, oil on canvas, bears signature, 21x17", B/B 12/8/88 .... **3,025**
Jovial Monkey & a Nun, oil on canvas, 18x23", SLK 2/12/88 .... **120**
Still Life of Books, oil on canvas, indistinctly sgn, 20x24", C-E 4/7/88 OE **880**

ETCHER, Aaron Dean (American, 1817-1902)
Portrait of a Young Man Wearing a Black Coat & White Stock, oil on panel, ca 1835, 34x26", SBY 1/28/88 OE **4,620**

ETCHER, E.H. (British, 19th C)
Harbor Scene at Sunrise, 30x49", SBY 12/9/88 .... **2,860**

ETCHER, George (Canadian, 1914-)
Lake Muskoka, oil on board, sgn, 20x30", WAD 6/12/89 OE **900**
Spring Thaw, oil on board, sgn, 24x36", WAD 6/12/89 .... **750**
Warming Sun Near Markham, oil on board, sgn, 24x36", WAD 11/30/89 .... **1,150**

EURY, Francois Antonine Leon (French, 1804-1858)
Village in Southern France, oil on canvas, sgn, 15x24", SBY 12/9/88 .... **2,475**

EURY, J. Vivien; see De Fleury

IEHER, Karl (Austrian, 19th/20th C)
Tyrolean Vista, gouache/oil, sgn/dtd 1904, 11x16", C-E 2/21/89, UE **220**

INCK, Govaert (Dutch, 1615-1660)
Angel Disappearing Before Manoah & His Wife, oil on panel, ca 1635, 44x40", SBY 6/1/89 UE **23,100**
Portrait of a Girl, wearing a pink dress, holding a fan; oil on panel, 28x22", C-NY 6/2/88 .... **28,600**
Portrait of Young Man Holding Short Sword in an Elaborate Sheath, oil on canvas, inscr/dtd 1644, 40x34", SBY 1/12/89 OE **407,000**

INCK, Govaert; att (Dutch, 1615-1660)
Young Man in Armor with a Red Beret (portrait), oil on canvas, 22x18", C-NY 1/15/88 .... **11,550**

INCK, Govaert; circle of (Dutch, 1615-1660)
Shepherdess, Seated Holding a Letter, in a Landscape; oil on panel, 19x15", C-NY 1/11/89 OE **9,020**

INCK, Govaert; manner of (Dutch, 1615-1660)
Portrait of Rembrandt, oil on canvas, 19x15", SBY 4/7/89 OE **30,250**

INT, William Russell (British, 1880-1969)
Ambrosine, red chalk on laid paper, sgn twice, inscr/dtd 1962, 14x9", C-NY 5/25/88 .... **3,300**
Granary, watercolor on paper, sgn, 13x22", SBY 2/22/89 OE **46,750**
Jennifer (portrait), red chalk on paper, sgn, 8x12", SBY 6/8/88 .... **3,025**
July Morning on the Loire, watercolor on paper, sgn twice, unfr, 11x15", SBY 12/9/88 .... **1,540**
Lap of the Tide, St Malo; watercolor on paper, sgn, 15x22", SBY 2/22/89 .... **35,750**
Marble Portico (lady in interior), watercolor, sgn twice/dtd June-July 1926/inscr, 20x27", C-NY 2/23/89 OE **49,500**
Model Called Paulette, red chalk on pink laid paper, wm, sgn twice/dtd 65/#d 131, 12x7", C-NY 5/25/88 .... **1,100**
Mrs Belleroughton, the Head Mistress, circa 1870; red chalk on heavy cream paper, sgn/titled, 12x16", C-NY 5/24/89 .... **2,420**
No 1 Bull Fight-Banderillero; watercolor on paper, twice sgn/titled, 22x31", SBY 2/22/89 OE **41,250**
Novembre, St Jeanett, Provence; watercolor, sgn/dtd Nov 16, 1962, 8x11", C-NY 10/25/89 .... **2,200**
On the Gareloch (landscape w/figures at water's edge), watercolor, sgn twice/titled/inscr No 2, 19x26", C-NY 2/23/89 OE **19,800**
Pensive Model, red chalk on paper, sgn, 13x8", SBY 6/8/88 OE **3,190**
Pontaix, watercolor, sgn twice, inscr/dtd 1962, 11x15", C-NY 5/25/88 .... **2,750**
Reclining Female Nude, red/brown chalk on laid paper, sgn, wm PS in a cartouche, 8x11", C-NY 2/25/88 OE **2,750**
Reclining Female Nude, sanguine on paper, indistinctly sgn, 8x16", B/B 1/11/89 OE **3,025**

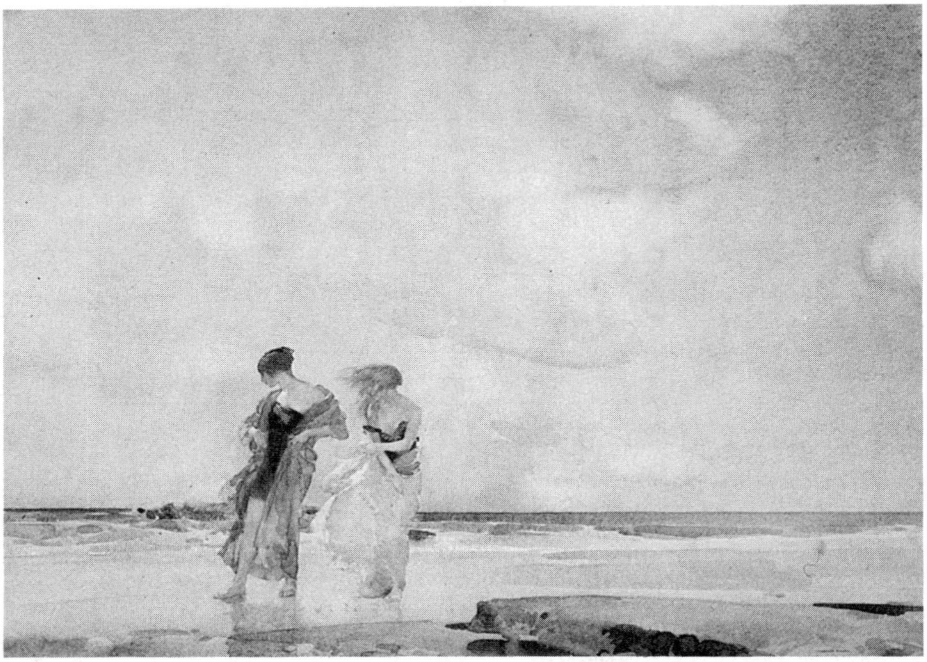

Shivers, watercolor, sgn/titled/inscr, 20x27", C-NY 2/23/89 OE, $35,200

Sunday Evening Gossip at a Provencal Farm, watercolor, sgn twice/inscr/dtd 19.5.63, 14x11", C-NY 5/25/88 .... **5,500**
Toil at Dawn, oil on canvas, sgn, 37x39", C-NY 2/25/88 UE **9,900**
Under the Ramparts, St Malo, High Tide; watercolor on paper, sgn/titled/inscr, 10x13", SBY 2/22/89 OE **44,000**
Waitress, Cafe des Pommes; red chalk on blue paper, sgn twice/inscr, 11x7", C-NY 5/25/88.......... **2,860**

FLOCH, Joseph (Polish, 1894-)
Figure at the Gates to a House, oil on canvas, sgn, 15x24", PHL 6/16/88 .... **1,000**
Rest (figure sleeping in bed), oil on canvas, sgn, 1965, 49x36", C-E 10/18/89 OE **7,700**

FLOCKENHAUS, Heinz (German, 20th C)
Beach at Winter, oil on panel, sgn, 10x20", C-E 10/26/89.......... **3,300**
Snowy Path at Sunset, oil on panel, sgn, 12x17", C-E 10/25/88 .... **2,200**

FLORA
Head of a Woman, ink/gouache on silk, sgn, 20x14", SBY 4/23/88 OE **2,310**

Florentine School (14th C)
Crucifixion, with Madonna & St John Evangelist & Two Angels; tempera on panel on gold ground, 23x11", C-NY 4/6/89 OE.......... **8,250**

Florentine School (15th C)
Madonna with the Infant Christ Holding a Goldfinch, oil on canvas, on gold ground, 25x18", C-NY 4/8/88 OE **16,500**
Nativity with Young Saint John the Baptist, tempera on panel, within an engaged frame, 37x22", SBY 10/13/89 .... **6,050**
Pair: Portraits in Profile of Boy & Man Before Barrel Vaults; oil on panel, 19x18", C-NY 4/6/89 OE.......... **19,800**

Florentine School (16th C)
Charity: Design for the Decoration of a Spandrel; red chalk, inscr, 17x10", C-NY 1/12/88 OE **2,640**
Design for a Wall Decoration with Male Figures, pen/brown ink/wash over black chalk, 10x16", SBY 1/13/89.......... **880**
Double-Sided: Study of Roman Portrait Bust; Diana & Gods in Celestial Sphere; red/black chalk, 10x7", SBY 1/13/89 OE **1,320**
Holy Family, oil on panel, 29x24", WD 1/25/89 .... **4,250**
Martyrdom of a Saint, black chalk/brown wash, 8x10", SBY 1/13/89.......... **2,200**
Penitent Magdalene, oil on panel, 28x21", SBY 10/13/89.......... **5,775**

Florentine School (17th C)
Esther Before Ahasuerus, oil on canvas, 41x53", C-E 6/1/88 .... **1,045**
Male Academy, Kneeling, Leaning Forward on a Post; red chalk, 10x15", SBY 1/13/89 .... **715**
Male Academy, Seated on a Block; red chalk, 15x10", SBY 1/13/89 .... **550**
Male Academy, Standing, Hands Behind His Head; red chalk, 15x10", SBY 1/13/89 .... **605**
Male Academy, Standing, Holding a Staff; red chalk, 15x10", SBY 1/13/89 .... **770**
Saint John the Baptist, oil on canvas, inscr, 37x48", SBY 10/21/88 .... **4,950**

Florentine School (18th C)
Young Woman with a Dog (portrait), oil on canvas, 27x22", SBY 4/7/89.......... **2,475**

Florentine School (19th C)
Untitled (interior of wine cellar w/five monks about table), oil on canvas, monogramed CR, 18x25", SLK 2/11/89 .... **500**

Florentine School (20th C)
Profile Portrait of a Woman, oil on panel, arched top, 16x10", SBY 7/12/89.......... **880**

FLORES, Pedro Victor (Spanish, 1897-)
Harlequin, oil on canvas, sgn, 24x20", B/B 6/15/89.......... **2,090**

FLORES (Spanish, 20th C)
Don Quixote, oil on canvas, sgn, 1945, 29x24", LH 10/16/88 UE **100**

FLORIA, Walter (American, 1878-1909)
Portrait of a Distinguished Gentleman, oil on canvas laid down on board, sgn/dtd 1906, 30x25", WG 9/16/88 UE.......... **400**

FLORIS, Frans (Flemish, 16th/17th C)

Moses Nursed by His Mother, oil on panel, 38x36", C-NY 5/31/89 OE 33,000

FLORIS, Frans; follower of (Flemish, 16th/17th C)

Mary Magdalene Washing the Feet of Christ in the House of Simon the Pharisee, oil on panel, 28x42", SBY 10/13/89 6,600

FLORY, Arthur (American, 20th C)

Fence Movements, oil on canvas, sgn, 30x36", FAP 12/8/89 OE 925

Lobster Pot Floats, oil on canvas, sgn, 20x24", FAP 12/8/89 400

FLOZY, P. (20th C)

Interior Scene, oil on canvas, sgn, 18x15", LH 12/4/88 UE 50

FOCARDI, Elisina

Sultan's Choice, oil on canvas, sgn/inscr/dtd 1907, 26x30", C-E 4/7/88 1,540

FOERSTER, Herbert (American, 20th C)

After the Rain, oil on canvas, 17x21", FAP 4/15/89 412

Maine Coast by Portland Light, oil on canvas, 20x23", FAP 4/15/89 248

FOGG, C.P. (American, 19th C)

Still Life of Strawberries (outdoor still life), oil on canvas, sgn/dtd 1889, 12x22", RWS 8/20/88 UE 175

FOGILSON, (American, 20th C)

Western Landscape, gouache/watercolor on paper, sgn, 10x12", FAP 4/15/89 165

FOLDES, Peter (20th C)

Untitled (abstract), tempera on fabric laid down on board, sgn/dtd 1960, 57x45", SBY 2/19/88 1,320

Vivez a la Sauvage en Vacances, ink/gouache on paper, sgn/dtd 62, 40x28", SBY 10/8/88 1,980

FOLINSBEE, John Fulton (American, 1892-1972)

Harbor View (buildings along water), oil on artist board, sgn, 8x10", RWS 5/19/88 800

New Hope Paper Mill, oil on board, sgn, 8x10", C-NY 9/30/88 4,620

Sailboats in Dock, oil on canvas, sgn, 25x30", WD 10/5/88 OE 11,000

Winter Sunset (winter landscape), oil on canvas, sgn/titled, 16x20", SBY 3/17/88 OE 8,250

FONG, Lai (American/Chinese, 19th/20th C)

American Ship Entering Hong Kong, oil on canvas, sgn, orig Chippendale frame, 24x31", RAB 11/25/88 20,000

Merzey Off Calcutta, oil on canvas, sgn/dtd 1898, 26x35", B/B 3/17/88 4,675

FONSECA, John Joseph (19th C)

Colonial House, Madras; pencil/watercolor, sgn/dtd 1872, 11x17", C-SK 5/25/89 310

FONT, Constantin (French, 1890-)

Pastorale (draped nude w/herdsmen & goat in landscape), oil on canvas, sgn/dtd 1919, 57x46", C-NY 2/23/89 6,050

FONTAINE, see La Fontaine

FONTAINEBLEAU, Ecole; see De Fontainebleau

FONTAINES, see Des Fontaines

FONTANA, Lavinia (Italian, 1552-1614)

Madonna with the Sleeping Infant Christ, & Saints Joseph & Anne...; oil on canvas, 57x47", C-NY 1/11/89 12,100

FONTANA, Lavinia; circle of (Italian, 1552-1614)

Portrait of a Lady in an Elaborate White Dress, oil on panel, 38x29", SBY 10/21/88 OE 16,500

FONTANA, Lucio (Italian, 1899-1969)

Concetto Spaziale (abstract), oil/colored glass pebbles/mixed media on canvas, sgn/dtd 55, 32x26", SBY 6/30/88 210,000

Concetto Spaziale (abstract), tempera on canvas, sgn/titled/inscr Attesse 1+1-SSAO, 1960, 37x54", SBY 5/2/88 OE 132,000

Concetto Spaziale (dk red canvas w/six slash marks), waterpaint on canvas, sgn/dtd 1959, 39x50", SBY 6/30/88 140,000

Concetto Spaziale (white canvas w/one slash mark), waterpaint on canvas, sgn, 39x39", SBY 6/30/88 88,000

Concetto Spaziale (white canvas w/six vertical slash marks), waterpaint on canvas, sgn, 1964-65, 32x26", SBY 6/30/88 100,000

Concetto Spaziale (white canvas w/six vertical slash marks), waterpaint on canvas, sgn, 1963, 15x18", SBY 6/30/88 54,000

Untitled (abstract), torn paper, sgn, 1965, SBY 5/3/89 OE 23,100

ONTANA, Roberto (Italian, 1844-1907)

Portrait of a Woman, oil on canvas, 12x16", LH 9/10/89 OE 2,900

ONTANESI, Francesco

Interior of a Barn with a Skinned Calf, black chalk/pen/brown ink/brown wash, #d 128, 10x12", C-NY 1/11/89 495

OOTE, M.K. (American, 20th C)

Garden Scene with Statuary & Red Poppies, oil on canvasboard, sgn/dtd 1909, 13x9", SBY 3/17/88 1,760

OOTE, Mary (American, 19th C)

Lady in Pink, oil on canvas, sgn, 50x36", LH 10/16/88 UE 950

OOTE, Will Howe (American, 1874-1965)

Arizona Gold Mine, oil on canvasboard, sgn, 12x16", C-E 10/18/89 605

Elvira (portrait of seated woman leaning on elbow), oil on canvas, sgn, 30x24", SBY 4/14/89 OE 9,900

Irises (still life), oil on canvas, sgn, 24x24", SBY 4/14/89 OE 9,900

Jamaica Girl in White (portrait), oil on canvas, inscr July 26 1978/#d Jamaica #24, 1935, 30x30", SBY 3/17/88 5,500

West Indian Girl (portrait in profile), oil on canvasboard, sgn, 16x12", SBY 4/14/89 1,320

ORABOSCO, Girolamo (Italian, 1675-)

Portrait of a Lady As Saint Ursula, oil on canvas, C-NY 6/2/88 22,000

Portrait of a Man As David with the Head of Goliath, oil on canvas, 31x24", C-NY 10/20/88 OE 6,600

ORAIN, Jean Louis (French, 1852-1931)

Au Salon (nudes), oil on paper laid down on canvas, sgn/dtd 1921, 22x26", SBY 10/24/89 14,300

Femme Assise, pencil/chalk on paper laid down on board, sgn, 16x21", C-E 5/9/89 OE 1,980

Le Buffet, pen/brush/black ink, sgn/inscr, 12x9", C-NY 2/25/88 1,100

Le Lever, oil on canvas, sgn, 24x29", SBY 5/23/89 OE 44,000

On ne Peut Pas Etre et Avoir Ete (two women in an interior), ink/crayons, sgn, 7x15", PHL 11/15/88 OE 5,500

Pair: En Soiree; Reclining Nude; pen/ink on paper, sanguine/black & white pastel, sgn, 6x4", 9x16", SBY 10/7/89 2,200

FORBES, Charles Stuart (American, 1860-)

Bridge at Florence, Italy; oil on board, unfr, 11x8", WL 5/20/88 UE 175
Bridge Over a Venetian Canal, watercolor, unfr, 9x12", NA 2/6/88 UE 140
Bridge Over the Seine, oil on panel, sgn/dtd 1919, 9x11", WL 5/20/88 600
Grays Inn, Queen Anne's County, Maryland; watercolor, initialed/dtd June 90, 5x9", NA 2/6/88 240
Pair: Fishing Boat in Venetian Lagoon; Fishing Fleet Leaving the Venetian Lagoon; oil on panel, unfr, 6x7", NA 2/6/88 325
Pair: Pont Neuf, Paris; View of a Parisian Bridge; oil on panel, dtd 97, unfr, 5x7", NA 3/26/88 UE 175
Pair: Tree-Lined Road with Church; Misty Seascape; oil on panel, 1 unfr, 5x6", 7x10", SBY 6/28/89 550
Sailboat in the Venetian Lagoon, watercolor, dtd 94, unfr, NA 3/26/88 UE 100
Sailing Boat, Venice (view along banks of the Grand Canal); oil on panel, 7x11", RWS 3/31/88 400
Salute at Venice, oil on canvas, unfr, 20x18", WL 5/20/88 250
Venice: Grand Canal from the Lagoon: oil on wood panel, 8x11", NA 5/13/89 425

FORBES, Edwin (American, 1839-1895)

Abandoning Winter Camp, Falmouth (Civil War); gouache on paper, initialed/inscr, 7x11", C-E 5/27/88 825
Cemetery Gate, Gettysburg (Civil War); pencil on paper, sgn/inscr, unfr, 11x15", C-E 11/30/88 OE 1,320
Christmas Dinner (man at campfire), oil on canvas, sgn/dtd 1891, 16x24", C-NY 12/2/88 UE 7,700
Confederate Assault on Cemetery Hill (Civil War), pencil on paper, initialed/inscr, 10x14", C-E 5/27/88 OE 1,980
Confederate Assault on Culp's Hill (Civil War), no media given, initialed/inscr, 11x16", C-E 5/27/88 OE 1,320
Crossing the Rappahannock (Civil War), gouache on paper, initialed/inscr, 7x11", C-E 5/27/88 OE 495
Federal Artillery at Spotsylvania, PA/Centre of Position... (Civil War); pen/ink, initialed, 10x14", C-E 5/27/88 OE 2,200
Germanna Ford on the Rapidan (Civil War), pencil on paper, initialed/inscr, 8x12", C-E 5/27/88 OE 2,420
Hancock's Corps on the Brock Road (Civil War), pencil on paper, initialed, 8x12", C-E 5/27/88 660
March of Longstreet's Corps Through Throughfare Gap (Civil War), ink/wash, initialed/inscr, 5x8", C-E 5/27/88 OE 1,540
Outriders (soldier on horseback in landscape), pencil on paper, sgn/dtd 1885, 12x16", C-NY 12/2/88 3,300
Pastoral Scene, oil on canvas, sgn/dtd 1893, 20x30", C-NY 12/2/88 UE 3,300
Reading Hooker's Address to the Army (Civil War), watercolor heightened w/white, initialed, unfr, 8x13", C-E 11/30/88 OE 880
Rescuing Wounded From Burning Woods (Civil War), watercolor on board, initialed/inscr, 8x12", C-E 5/27/88 660
Retreat of the Army of Virginia (Civil War), watercolor on paper, sgn/inscr, 5x8", C-E 5/27/88 OE 660
Second Battle of Bull Run (Civil War), watercolor on paper, sgn/inscr, 6x12", C-E 5/27/88 OE 1,870
2nd Line, Chancellorsville (Civil War); watercolor on board, sgn/inscr, unfr, 8x13", C-E 11/30/88 770

FORBES, Elizabeth Adela (Stanhope)(Canadian, 1859-1912)

Old Salt (portrait), oil on board, oval, 21x18", C-NY 5/25/88 UE 1,650

FORBES, Kenneth Keith (Canadian, 1892-1980)

Red Feather (portrait of a woman w/hat & cane), oil on canvas, sgn/dtd 1909, 24x18", FB 4/25/88 650
Still Life with Reflection, oil on board, sgn/dtd 1919, 16x20", WAD 6/12/89 620

FORBES, Leyton (British, 20th C)

Old Forge, Cockington Village, Near Torquay, Devon; watercolor/gouache on paper, sgn/titled, 15x26", C-NY 5/24/89 2,420

FORBES, Stanhope Alexander (British, 1857-1947)

Antiquarian, oil on canvas, sgn, 16x20", C-NY 5/25/88 6,600
By an English Cottage Door (view of facade of country home), oil on canvas, sgn, 20x25", WG 4/23/88 OE 26,000
Midday Meal, oil on canvas, 27x20", C-NY 5/25/88 9,350
Santa Maria Della Salute, oil on canvas, sgn, 30x24", C-NY 5/25/88 9,350

FORBES, Stanhope Alexander; att (British, 1857-1947)

Contemplation (woman reading at desk in an interior), oil on canvas, sgn/inscr No 39, 27x24", SBY 2/22/89 13,200

FORD, F.T. (British, 19th C)

Fort Royal, St Malo; watercolor, sgn/dtd 1846, 13x24", FB 5/28/89 600

FORD, Gordon Onslow

Beanstalk (abstract), parles paint on canvas, sgn/dtd 60-61, 120x36", SBY 10/8/88 13,200

FORD, Henry Chapman (American, 1828-1894)

Mission Scene, watercolor on paper, sgn, 13x20", B/B 10/6/88 1,540

FORD, James (20th C)

Untitled (study for Urban Cave painting), latex/plaster on panel, sgn/dtd 1980, unfr, 36x48", C-NY 10/31/89 220

FOREST, see De Forest

FORGET, Sylvain (Canadian)

L'Amorce d'Une Communication, oil on canvas, sgn/dtd 86, 22x22", WAD 11/30/89 2,400

FOROBOSCO, Girolamo; att

Portrait of a Noblewoman, oil on canvas, 31x27", SBY 6/8/88 OE 1,870

FORREST, Charles Ramus (Canadian/British, 19th C)

Bridge of Oudanulla, Bengal; pencil/watercolor, inscr/dtd 1807, 11x18", C-SK 11/10/88 1,210

FORSTER, George (American, fl 1860-1890)

Fruit Piece with Birds Nest & Lizard, oil on panel, sgn/dtd twice, 1844, inscr, 11x8", C-NY 12/2/88 7,700
Fruit Still Life, oil on panel, sgn/dtd 1869, 16x21", C-NY 5/26/88 8,800
Queen Anne Cherries, oil on canvas, sgn/dtd 1890, 9x14", C-NY 12/2/88 4,400
Still Life (fruit in a landscape), oil on panel, sgn/dtd 1860, 17x22", SBY 5/25/88 UE 12,650
Still Life of Fruit, oil on canvas, sgn/dtd 1894, 9x11", RAB 3/27/89 3,200
Still Life of Grapes & Glass of Wine, oil on canvas, sgn/dtd 1878, 8x10", C-NY 9/30/88 6,050

FORSTER, John Wycliffe (Canadian, 1850-1938)

Indian Girl at Prayer, oil on canvas laid down, sgn, 16x9", WAD 11/30/89 370

FORSYTHE, Victor Clyde (American, 1885-1962)

Silence (landscape), oil on masonite, sgn, 12x17", SBY 6/24/88 1,210

FORT, Theodore (French, 19th C)
Spaniel & a Ploughhorse Outside a Barn, watercolor/pencil, sgn, 4x5", C-E 10/26/89 550
FORTE, Luca; manner of (Italian, fl ca 1640-1670)
Pair: Still Lifes of Pomegranates, Pears, Grapes, Apples, Cherries & Melon; oil on canvas, 38x52", SBY 4/7/89 OE 35,200
FORTE, Vincente (Argentinian, 1912-)
Viejo Instrumento (abstract still life), oil on canvas, sgn twice/dtd 68/titled, 28x39", C-NY 5/17/89 4,620
FORTI, Ettore (Italian, 19th C)
Embarkment of a Roman Queen, oil on canvas, sgn/inscr Roma, 32x55", C-NY 2/23/89 OE 49,500
Figures on a Veranda with Vesuvius Beyond, oil on canvas, sgn/inscr, 24x40", C-NY 2/25/88 OE 12,100
Pompeiian Maiden & Swan, oil on canvas, sgn, unfr, 40x24", SBY 10/24/89 14,300
Selling His Wares (man showing rugs to two ladies in an interior), oil on canvas, sgn/dtd, 21x33", C-NY 5/24/89 UE 19,800
FORTIN, Marc Aurele (Canadian, 1888-1970)
Back Yard Scene with Clothesline, oil on board, sgn, 7x8", FB 5/28/89 OE 3,600
Dock Side, Montreal; oil on board, 12x12", FB 4/25/88 1,500
Grand Orme, Ste Rose; oil on panel, sgn, 5x3", FB 10/17/88 1,900
Hochelaga in Winter, oil on board, sgn, 34x40", FB 10/30/89 154,000
Landscape at Ste Scholastique, Quebec (three houses); oil on board, sgn, 20x24", FB 10/17/88 42,000
Le Bateau Rouge, oil on board, sgn, 8x8", FB 5/28/89 1,500
Pont Jacques Cartier (view from back yards of Jacques Cartier bridge), watercolor, sgn, ca 1934, 14x20", FB 4/25/88 5,000
Vue Hochelaga (village), oil on board, sgn, ca 1935, 23x31", FB 10/17/88 56,000
FORTUNA, A.
Beached at Sunset, oil on canvas, sgn, 14x21", C-E 11/8/88 UE 600
FORTUNEY (French, 19th/20th C)
Flower Stall, pastel on paper, sgn, 20x12", SBY 6/8/88 1,100
FORTUNY Y CARBO, Mariano (Spanish, 1838-1874)
La Salida de la Iglesia de San Gines de Madrid, watercolor on paper, authenticated, ca 1867-68, 5x8", SBY 10/24/89 14,300
Seated Lady, watercolor on paper, sgn/inscr, 11x8", SBY 6/8/88 OE 4,675
FORTUNY Y DE MADRAZO, Mariano (Spanish, 1949-)
Venetian Canal Scene, oil on panel, sgn, 18x14", B/B 6/15/89 5,500
FOSBURGH, James W. (American, 1910-)
Billy, oil on canvas, sgn/dtd 54, 30x26", C-E 6/28/88 605
FOSCHI, Francesco (Italian, 18th C)
Winter Landscape with Figures Collecting Wood, oil on canvas, 14x18", C-NY 4/8/88 7,700
Winter Landscape with Figures on a Path & Houses on a Hill, oil on canvas, 18x24", SBY 4/7/88 OE 7,700
FOSCHI, Francesco; school of (Italian, 18th C)
Elegant Figures Skating on a River, oil on canvas, 9x12", C-NY 10/20/88 1,100
FOSS, Cornelia
Landscape, oil on canvas, sgn, 11x14", LH 5/15/88 UE 80
FOSSATI, Domenico (1743-1784)
Architectural Capriccio with Piazza & Monumental Fountain, pen/ink over black chalk, 7x8", SBY 1/13/89 3,025
FOSSOUX, Claude (French, 20th C)
Dans le Jardin, oil on canvas, 26x22", SLK 11/25/88 1,100
FOSTER, Ben (American, 1852-1926)
Autumn Moon (landscape), oil on canvas, sgn, 24x24", SBY 6/28/89 UE 1,100
Delphiniums, oil on canvas, 25x22", SBY 9/23/88 4,400
Landscape, Stumps, a Forest Cut Down; oil on canvas, 12x16", WG 4/23/88 UE 550
Landscape (meadow & trees, mountain beyond), oil on canvas, sgn, 12x15", C-E 6/1/89 3,300
Landscape with Stream, oil on canvas, sgn, 36x30", WG 4/23/88 UE 1,500
Reflecting Pond, oil on canvas, sgn, 20x36", C-E 4/7/88 1,210
Road Through the Pines, oil on canvas, sgn twice/stamped/titled, 18x22", SBY 9/23/88 880
Summer Landscape, oil on canvas, sgn, 12x15", C-E 2/3/88 715
Summer Landscape, oil on canvasboard, sgn, 19x24", SBY 9/23/88 UE 660
Valley at Dusk, oil on canvas, sgn, 25x25", WD 10/5/88 UE 2,200
FOSTER, Charles (American, 1850-1931)
Cow Grazing in Mountain Pasture (landscape), oil on canvas, sgn, 18x21", RWS 3/16/89 UE 450
Open Fields & Distant Valleys, oil on canvas, sgn, unfr, 16x24", RWS 9/8/89 300
FOSTER, Myles Birket (British, 1825-1899)
Fisher Folk by a Coastal Cottage, watercolor/bodycolor on paper, monogramed, 9x8", WG 4/23/88 2,500
FOSTER, Richard
Street Scene, watercolor on paper, sgn, 10x13", C-E 6/28/88 UE 176
FOSTER, Will F. (American, 1882-1953)
Night the Contract Was Signed, oil on canvas, sgn/dtd 08, 26x35", LH 10/16/88 800
Portrait of a Female Nude with Fan, oil on canvasboard, initialed, 17x13", B/B 5/17/89 OE 1,650
Portrait of a Seated Female Nude, oil on canvas, estate stamped, 42x32", B/B 5/17/89 OE 1,210
Portrait of a Young Woman in Profile, oil on canvas laid down, initialed, 12x9", B/B 9/14/89 1,100
Portrait of Mrs Foster, oil on canvas, 50x40", B/B 5/17/89 OE 770
Seated Woman with Parasol, oil on canvas, unfr, 34x30", B/B 5/17/89 OE 1,100
Study of a Female Nude with Parasol & Hat, oil on canvas, sgn, 40x32", B/B 5/17/89 OE 1,100
Study of Female Nude, oil on canvas, estate stamp, 42x29", B/B 5/17/89 467
FOSTER, Willet S. (American, 1885-1940)
Crane on the Dock, oil on panel, indistinctly sgn, 8x11", B/B 10/6/88 385

FOUBERT, Emil Louis (French, 1840-1910)
Pair: Diana & Acteon; Venus & Mercury Appearing to Apollo; oil on canvas laid down, sgn, 28x14", B/B 6/9/88 ... **3,575**
The Flower Seller, oil on canvas, sgn, 19x15", C-E 10/26/89 ... **6,600**
FOUJITA, Tsuguharu (Japanese, 1886-1968)
Auto-Portrait avec Chats, oil/gold paint on canvas, sgn twice/dtd 1930, 26x20", C-NY 11/16/88 OE ... **616,000**
Chat, watercolor/pen/black ink on paper, sgn twice/dtd 1932, 17x13", C-NY 11/15/88 ... **38,500**
Chat (cat), oil on canvas, sgn twice/dtd 1931, 14x11", C-NY 11/16/88 ... **110,000**
Chat (portrait of a cat), sgn/dtd 1940, 13x16", C-NY 5/11/8 9 ... **187,000**
Chat aux Tulipes (cat w/tulips), oil on linen, sgn/dtd 1957, 18x15", SBY 11/12/88 ... **242,000**
Deux Nus, pastel/pencil on tan paper mounted at edges on board, sgn twice, 25x47", C-NY 11/15/88 ... **165,000**
Elle Epluchant des Pommes de Terre, oil on canvas laid down on masonite, sgn, 14x10", C-NY 5/12/88 OE ... **462,000**
Femme Endormie, watercolor/pen/brush/black ink on paper mounted at edges on board, sgn twice, 10x14", C-NY 11/15/88 ... **46,200**
Femme Nue Allongee (reclining nude), pencil heightened w/white chalk on paper laid down on paper, 18x41", C-NY 5/11/89 ... **60,500**
Femme Nue Assise (seated nude), pencil/white chalk on paper laid down on board, sgn/dtd 1931, 24x22", C-NY 5/11/89 ... **88,000**
Filette Blonde (portrait of a young girl), oil on canvas, sgn twice/dtd 1926, 10x8", C-NY 11/16/88 ... **110,000**
Fleurs: Two Panel Screen (floral design); oil on canvas, sgn/dtd 1940, 21x16", SBY 5/10/89 ... **275,000**
Girl in a Red Dress, ink/watercolor on paper, sgn, 11x8", WD 5/5/88 ... **52,500**
Homme Nu, pencil on tan paper mounted at the edges on panel, sgn twice, 48x33", C-NY 11/15/88 ... **33,000**
Jeune Femme Allongee au Chat (reclining nude w/cat), oil on canvas, sgn/dtd Paris 1939, 19x24", SBY 11/12/88 OE ... **742,500**
Jeune Femme Pensive, watercolor/chalk/pen/ink on paper laid down on board, sgn/dtd 1931, 16x12", C-NY 5/11/89 ... **60,500**
Jeune Fille, black ink/watercolor on paper, sgn/dtd 1951, 10x7", C-NY 11/15/88 OE ... **115,500**
Jeune Fille au Chat (young girl with cat), pen/ink/gray wash on paper laid down on board, sgn, 14x9", SBY 5/11/88 OE ... **88,000**
Jeune Fille au Chat (young girl with cat), pen/ink/gray wash on paper laid down on board, sgn, 13x9", SBY 5/11/88 OE ... **71,500**
Jeune Fille avec Oiseau (young girl w/bird), pen/ink/watercolor/gray wash on paper, sgn/dtd 1932, 12x9", SBY 5/10/89 ... **82,500**
Kiki (portrait), oil on canvas, sgn/dtd 1927, 24x20", C-NY 5/11/88 OE ... **495,000**
L'Homme au Chapeau, pencil drawing, sgn/inscr, 11x8", LH 5/15/88 OE ... **950**
Les Deux Petites Amies (portrait of two young girls), oil on canvas, sgn twice/dtd 1918, 26x21", SBY 11/12/88 ... **352,000**
Mexican Peasant (head in profile), pen/ink/watercolor/gray wash on buff paper, sgn/dtd 1933, 14x12", SBY 10/6/89 ... **24,200**
Modonna & Child, gouache/watercolor/gold leaf on paper, sgn twice, 13x9", SBY 5/11/88 OE ... **137,500**
Nu Allonge, pen/ink/watercolor/wash on paper, sgn twice/dtd 1931, 20x28", SBY 11/12/88 OE ... **286,000**
Nu en Buste, pencil on buff paper, sgn twice, 12x11", SBY 2/18/88 ... **6,600**
Pair: Peruvian Landscapes; pen/black ink/watercolor on paper, 1 sgn/dtd 1932, unfr, 9x6", SBY 10/7/89 ... **3,575**
Pair: Urban Scenes; pen/ink/wash on buff paper, sgn twice, 10x14", 11x14", SBY 10/7/88 ... **5,500**
Paris Street Scene with Metro, pen/ink/wash/watercolor on paper, sgn/dtd 1925, 10x13", SBY 10/6/89 OE ... **55,000**
Petite Fille au Chat (portrait of girl w/cat), watercolor/pen/ink on paper laid down, sgn/inscr, 9x7", SBY 5/10/89 OE ... **154,000**
Portrait d'Enfant (portrait of a child), pen/ink/wash on paper laid down on board, sgn/dtd 1929, 14x11", SBY 5/10/89 ... **30,250**
Portrait de Jeune Fille, pen/ink/gray wash/blue & pink water color traces on paper, sgn/dtd 1934, 17x13", SBY 5/10/89 OE ... **82,500**
Portrait de Jeune Fille (portrait of a young girl), oil on canvas, sgn/dtd 59, 13x9", C-NY 2/18/88 OE ... **220,000**
Portrait de Jeune Fille (portrait of a young woman), pen/ink/chalk on paper, sgn, 13x13", C-NY 5/11/89 ... **44,000**
Portrait of a Lady, watercolor/wash/pencil on buff paper laid down on board, sgn twice/dtd 1932, 25x18", SBY 5/11/88 OE ... **110,000**
Portrait of a Young Man, pencil on paper, indistinctly sgn, unfr, 11x8", SBY 10/7/89 OE ... **10,450**
Portrait of Dalzell Hatfield, watercolor/pencil on rice paper, sgn twice/dtd 1933, 17x15", SBY 2/18/88 OE ... **12,100**
Portrait of Madelaine Foujita (in profile), pen/ink/watercolor on rice paper, sgn/dtd 1932, 11x8", SBY 10/6/89 ... **33,000**
Portrait of Young Woman (in profile), pen/ink/gray wash on paper, sgn/dtd 1926, 9x7", SBY 10/6/89 OE ... **28,600**
Portrait Study of Polianski, India ink on paper laid down on paper, sgn/dtd 1926, 6x5", SBY 10/7/89 ... **2,200**
Seated Nude, pencil sketch, sgn, 13x7", DM 5/13/88 OE ... **650**
Tete de Femme (head of a woman), pen/brush/black ink, sgn/dtd 1926, 13x10", C-NY 2/18/88 UE ... **12,100**
Tete de Jeune Fille, brush/black ink/gray wash on paper, sgn, 10x8", C-NY 5/12/88 ... **35,200**
Tete de Jeune Fille, pen/black ink/watercolor on paper, sgn/dtd 1930, 11x9", C-NY 10/6/88 ... **14,300**
Two Women (in profile), pen/ink/gray wash on paper, laid down, sgn/dtd 1926, 10x9", SBY 10/6/89 ... **49,500**
Two Young Women in Profile, pen/ink/watercolor on 2 panels of concertina sketchbook, sgn/dtd 1930, 9x14", SBY 5/10/89 OE ... **37,400**
View of Hailar (Manchuria), oil on canvas, sgn/dtd 20.9.15, 20x24", SBY 10/6/89 OE ... **93,500**
Young Girl Holding a Cat, ink/watercolor on paper, sgn, 9x7", WD 5/5/88 ... **65,000**
Young Girl with Flaxen Hair, oil on canvas, sgn/dtd 1957, 13x10", WD 5/5/88 OE ... **250,000**
FOULQUIER, Francois Joseph
Design for an Urn on a Ledge, black chalk/pen/brown ink/gray-brown wash/watercolor, sgn/inscr, 16x10", C-NY 1/11/89 ... **1,650**
FOUQUAYS, see Le Fouquays
FOURIE, Albert Auguste (French, 1854-)
Young Woman Seated on a Wooded Path, oil on canvas, sgn/dtd 08, 37x30", C-NY 2/23/89 ... **8,800**
FOURNIER, Alexis Jean (American, 1865-1948)
House on an Embankment, oil on academy board, sgn/dtd 87, unfr, 12x18", C-NY 10/31/89 ... **770**
My Studio-So Lee, oil on panel, sgn/inscr, unfr, 5x8", RWS 11/3/88 ... **800**
FOURNIER, Alfred Victor (French 19th/20th C)
Springtime in the Orchard, oil on canvas, sgn/dtd 1907, 20x24", PHL 6/16/88 ... **950**
FOURNIER, Louis Edouard Paul (French, 1857-)
Portrait of a Young Woman Wearing a Hat, bust-length; black chalk on laid paper, partial wm, 22x16", C-NY 2/25/88 ... **1,320**
FOURNIER, Victor Edmond Charles (French, 1872-1904)
Bringing in the Catch, oil on canvas, sgn/dtd 1911, 86x108", SBY 6/8/88 ... **6,600**
FOUSSIER, Jean Victor (French, 19th/20th C)
Mediterranean Port Scene, oil on panel, sgn, 16x20", LH 9/10/89 ... **550**

FOWLER, Daniel (Canadian, 1810-1894)
Allington Castle, watercolor/pencil, sgn/dtd August 2nd, 1838, 9x13", WAD 6/12/89 .... **500**
Classical Bridge, Florence; charcoal, 5x7", WAD 6/12/89 .... **200**
FOWLER, Frank (American, 1852-1910)
Two Friends, oil on canvas, 15x12", C-NY 9/30/88 .... **2,860**
FOWLER, Robert (Scottish, 1853-1926)
Girl Amid Pink Blossoms (half-length portrait), oil on canvas, sgn, 20x12", NA 5/12/89........ **1,300**
FOWZER, J. (American, 19th/20th C)
Redwood Forest Path Along the Mendicino Coast, oil on canvas, sgn/dtd 1915, 59x35", B/B 9/15/88 .... **550**
FOX, G. (British, 19th C)
Knotty Point (two gentlemen playing chess), oil on board, sgn, 8x11", B/B 5/17/89 .... **1,430**
Pair of Pointers (in a landscape), oil on canvas, sgn, 20x30", WG 9/16/88 .... **575**
FOX, John Richard (Canadian, 1927-)
Dresser, oil on canvas, sgn, 22x27", FB 4/25/88 .... **1,900**
La Bouteille Rose, oil on canvas, sgn, 32x24", WAD 11/30/89 .... **1,600**
Still Life of Fruit, Bottle, & Pottery; oil on board, sgn/dtd 1948, 18x21", FB 10/30/89 .... **1,210**
FOX, John S. (British, 1860-)
River Landscape with Cattle Watering & Distant Hills, oil on canvas, sgn, 16x24", SLK 5/12/88 .... **450**
River Landscape with Figures & Cattle, oil on canvas, sgn, 16x24", SLK 5/12/88........ **475**
FOX, R. Atkinson (Canadian, 19th C)
Wooded River Landscape, oil on board, sgn, 14x20", C-E 6/1/88 .... **990**
FOY, F.M.
Sailing by Moonlight, oil on canvas, sgn, 6x8", WD 3/23/88........ **300**
FOY, Gray (20th C)
Fantastic Tree, pencil on paper, sgn/dtd 1950, 13x10", C-NY 6/17/89 .... **1,540**
FOY, Marc-Aurele de; see Suzor-Cote
FRAGIACOMO, Pietro (Italian, 1856-1922)
Armonie Verdi, oil on board, sgn, 31x46", C-NY 2/25/88 .... **10,450**
Boating in Venetian Waters, oil on panel, sgn, 9x19", SBY 12/9/88 OE........ **4,125**
FRAGONARD, Alexandre Evariste (French, 1780-1850)
Magician, oil on canvas, sgn, 24x29", C-NY 5/24/89........ **33,000**
FRAGONARD, Jean Honore (French, 1732-1806)
Pair; Woman Wading in a Pool; Man Leaning Against Stone Wall; oil on panel, unfr, 7x5", C-NY 4/6/89 OE........ **2,090**
Rest of the Holy Family on the Flight into Egypt, oil on canvas, oval, 75x87", SBY 6/1/89 .... **352,000**
Shepherd Seated on a Rock, with His Flock & a Bull in a Landscape; oil on canvas, 15x18", C-NY 6/2/88 UE........ **132,000**
St Michael Finds Silence at the Gates of the House of Sleep, black chalk/brown & gray wash, 15x10", SBY 1/13/89 .... **110,000**
FRAGONARD, Jean Honore; circle of (French, 1732-1806)
Nude Woman with a Youth by a Tree, red chalk, indistinct wm, inscr, 9x7", C-NY 1/11/89 .... **990**
FRAGONARD, Jean Honore; manner of (French, 1732-1806)
Head of a Young Boy, oil on canvas, oval, 27x23", SBY 7/12/89 .... **1,100**
FRAGONARD, Jean Honore; school of (French, 1732-1806)
La Gimblette (18th-C copy after lost painting by Fragonard), oil on canvas, 16x18", C-NY 5/31/89 OE **16,500**
Wooded Landscape w/Young Herdsman Running To Help Peasant Girl Tripped by a Donkey, no media given, 17x26", C-M 6/16/89 .... **8,965**
FRAILLION, Paul (French, 19th/20th C)
Lake Reflection, oil on canvas, sgn/dtd 1895, 10x16", B/B 9/14/89 .... **1,430**
FRANCA, see De Franca
FRANCANZANO, Francesco (after 1612-1656?)
Saint Peter, oil on canvas, 26x29", SBY 6/3/88 OE **35,750**
FRANCE, Eurilda Loomis (American, 1865-1931)
Bouquet (girl w/umbrella in a landscape), oil on canvas, sgn/dtd France 1894, RWS 11/10/89 .... **8,000**
Still Life of Grapes & Oranges, oil on canvas, sgn, 34x22", C-E 6/1/88 .... **1,540**
FRANCE, Jesse Leach (American, 1862-after 1926)
Road to the Village, oil on canvas, sgn, 12x19", RWS 3/16/89 UE **275**
FRANCES Y PASCUAL, Placido (Spanish, 1840-)
Summons, oil on panel, sgn/dtd 1879, 18x26", SBY 12/9/88 OE **8,250**
FRANCESCHI, see De Franceschi
FRANCESCHINI, Marc Antonio (Italian, 1648-1729)
Pair: Cumaean; Delphic Sybils; oil on canvas, oval, 39x30", C-NY 1/15/88 .... **8,800**
Saint Catherine of Siena with the Infant Christ, oil on canvas, unfr, 26x38", C-E 1/12/88 .... **385**
FRANCESCHINI, Marc Antonio; circle of (Italian, 1648-1729)
Perseus & Andromeda, oil on canvas, 39x69", C-NY 4/8/88 .... **4,400**
Saint Anthony of Padua, oil on canvas, 15x12", C-NY 10/20/88UE........ **1,540**
FRANCHERE, Joseph Charles (Canadian, 1866-1921)
Falls at Lac Marios, oil on board, sgn, 10x14", FB 4/25/88........ **900**
Ile Perrot, oil on canvas, sgn, 14x22", FB 5/28/89........ **1,000**
La Gaspesie, oil on canvas, sgn, 23x35", FB 10/30/89 .... **2,640**
La Poudriere, oil on canvas, sgn, 29x39", FB 10/30/89 .... **23,100**
Vaches au Repos, oil on board, sgn, 9x13", FB 10/30/89........ **605**
FRANCHINI, Antonio (Italian, 19th C)
Figures Conferring in a Piazza, oil on canvas, sgn, 21x27", SBY 7/12/89 .... **1,760**

FRANCHOYS, Peter (1606-1681)
Portrait of an Architect, oil on panel, 28x22", SBY 1/12/89 .... **6,600**
FRANCIA, Francesco; manner of (Italian, 1450-1518)
Annunciate Virgin, oil on canvas, 23x17", WD 1/25/89 OE **1,700**
FRANCIA, Giacomo (Italian, 1486-1557)
Madonna & Child, oil on panel, 21x16", C-NY 6/2/88 .... **22,000**
Madonna & Child with the Infant Saint John the Baptist, oil on canvas, 24x20", C-NY 5/31/89 OE **49,500**
FRANCIS, John F. (American, 1808-1886)
Apples & Biscuits, oil on panel, sgn, 12x15", C-NY 12/2/88 UE **9,900**
Apples & Chestnuts, oil on canvas, sgn/dtd 78, 11x14", C-NY 5/26/88 .... **13,200**
Wine Taster's Table, oil on canvas laid down on masonite, sgn/dtd 1858, 25x30", C-NY 5/25/89 OE **264,000**
FRANCIS, John Jesse (American, 1889-)
Sheep in a Meadow, watercolor on paper, sgn, 14x17", RAB 8/9/88 UE **200**
Sheep in a Meadow (under a full moon), watercolor on paper, sgn, 14x17", RAB 8/9/88 UE **200**
FRANCIS, Sam (American, 1923-)
Blue (abstract), watercolor on paper, sgn/dtd 1956, 31x23", SBY 11/10/88 OE **165,000**
Manborne (contemporary abstract), acrylic on paper, 1985, 69x48", SBY 11/9/89 OE **192,500**
Passing Through (abstract), acrylic on paper mounted on linen, 1973, 30x22", SBY 5/3/88 OE **60,500**
Plenty, acrylic on paper, sgn/dtd 1985, 19x16", SBY 11/9/89 OE **24,200**
Saturated Blue (abstract), oil on canvas, 1953, 77x45", SBY 11/10/88 .... **962,000**
Self-Portrait, acrylic on paper, sgn/titled, 1985, 41x30", C-NY 11/10/88 .... **31,900**
Silvio Set One (abstract composition), oil on canvas, 1963, 48x40", SBY 11/8/89 OE **990,000**
Towards Disappearance I (abstract), oil on canvas, unfr, 1957-58, 108x126", C-NY 11/9/88 .... **1,320,000**
Triptych: Untitled (abstract); acrylic on canvas, sgn/dtd 1986, unfr, ea 13x10", C-NY 11/10/88 OE **63,800**
Untitled, acrylic on paper, sgn/dtd 1978, 10x16", C-NY 2/13/89 .... **7,150**
Untitled (abstract composition), acrylic on canvas, 1977, 72x84", SBY 5/2/89 OE **154,000**
Untitled (abstract composition), acrylic on paper, sgn/dtd 1970, 41x28", SBY 11/9/89 OE **60,500**
Untitled (abstract composition), acrylic on paper, 1975, 14x17", SBY 11/9/89 .... **33,000**
Untitled (abstract), acrylic on canvas, sgn, 1983, 12x12", SBY 10/5/89 OE **35,750**
Untitled (abstract), acrylic on canvas, sgn/dtd 1967, unfr, 55x19", C-NY 5/4/89 OE **99,000**
Untitled (abstract), acrylic on canvas, sgn/dtd 1980, 28x114", SBY 11/9/89 OE **374,000**
Untitled (abstract), acrylic on canvas, sgn/dtd 1983, unfr, 24x48", C-NY 2/14/89 .... **63,800**
Untitled (abstract), acrylic on canvas, sgn/dtd 1984, unfr, 36x36", C-NY 5/4/89 OE **99,000**
Untitled (abstract), acrylic on canvas, sgn/dtd 1986, 36x139", C-NY 2/14/89 OE **198,000**
Untitled (abstract), acrylic on canvas, 1979, 120x96", SBY 2/19/88 .... **110,000**
Untitled (abstract), acrylic on canvas, 1984, 72x36", SBY 10/5/89 OE **264,000**
Untitled (abstract), acrylic on paper, ca 1974, 27x40", C-NY 5/4/89 UE **22,000**
Untitled (abstract), acrylic on paper, sgn, 1977, 12x9", SBY 10/5/89 OE **19,800**
Untitled (abstract), acrylic on paper, sgn, 1980, 20x14", C-NY 2/14/89 .... **19,800**
Untitled (abstract), acrylic on paper, sgn, 30x22", C-NY 10/4/89 OE **30,800**
Untitled (abstract), acrylic on paper, sgn/dtd Los Angeles 1983, 15x22", SBY 5/3/88 .... **26,400**
Untitled (abstract), acrylic on paper, sgn/dtd Tokyo 1974, 22x30", SBY 11/9/89 OE **88,000**
Untitled (abstract), acrylic on paper, sgn/dtd 1970, 22x30", C-NY 2/14/89 OE **30,800**
Untitled (abstract), acrylic on paper, sgn/dtd 1971, 22x30", SBY 2/15/89 OE **35,200**
Untitled (abstract), acrylic on paper, sgn/dtd 1973, 20x14", SBY 11/11/88 OE **55,000**
Untitled (abstract), acrylic on paper, sgn/dtd 1973 LA, 22x30", SBY 10/8/88 OE **39,600**
Untitled (abstract), acrylic on paper, sgn/dtd 1974 Tokyo, 30x22", C-NY 11/10/88 OE **38,500**
Untitled (abstract), acrylic on paper, sgn/dtd 1975, 12x15", SBY 2/15/89 OE **28,600**
Untitled (abstract), acrylic on paper, sgn/dtd 1976, 22x30", SBY 5/3/89 OE **49,500**
Untitled (abstract), acrylic on paper, sgn/dtd 1976, 22x30", C-NY 5/4/89 .... **28,600**
Untitled (abstract), acrylic on paper, sgn/dtd 1977, 29x41", SBY 5/3/89 .... **77,000**
Untitled (abstract), acrylic on paper, sgn/dtd 1978, 19x24", C-NY 5/4/89 .... **38,500**
Untitled (abstract), acrylic on paper, sgn/dtd 1978, 24x36", C-NY 5/4/89 OE **71,500**
Untitled (abstract), acrylic on paper, sgn/dtd 1979, 19x14", SBY 5/3/89 OE **27,500**
Untitled (abstract), acrylic on paper, sgn/dtd 1982, 19x29", SBY 10/8/88 .... **35,750**
Untitled (abstract), acrylic on paper, sgn/dtd 1986, 36x24", SBY 10/5/89 OE **99,000**
Untitled (abstract), acrylic on paper, sgn/dtd 1986, 41x30", SBY 2/15/89 OE **85,250**
Untitled (abstract), acrylic on paper, 1983, 37x37", SBY 5/3/89 OE **82,500**
Untitled (abstract), acrylic on paper, 30x22", C-NY 5/4/89 OE **60,500**
Untitled (abstract), acrylic on paper laid down on board, 1957, 40x27", SBY 11/11/88 .... **176,000**
Untitled (abstract), acrylic on paper laid down on canvas, 1978, 37x73", SBY 11/11/88 OE **110,000**
Untitled (abstract), acrylic on paper laid down on Japan paper, ca 1979, 41x29", SBY 5/2/88 OE **46,750**
Untitled (abstract), acrylic on paper mounted on Japan paper, ca 1979, 29x41", SBY 5/2/88 OE **44,000**
Untitled (abstract), acrylic on paper mounted on Japan paper, ca 1979, 29x41", SBY 5/3/89 OE **60,500**
Untitled (abstract), gouache on paper, initialed/dtd 1961 Bern, 18x22", C-NY 5/4/89 OE **88,000**
Untitled (abstract), gouache on paper, sgn/dtd 1956, 18x22", C-N 5/3/89 OE **198,000**
Untitled (abstract), gouache on paper, sgn/dtd 1957, 27x40", C-NY 11/9/88 .... **66,000**
Untitled (abstract), gouache on paper, sgn/dtd 1966, 15x11", SBY 2/15/89 OE **17,600**
Untitled (abstract), gouache on paper, sgn/dtd 1973, 22x30", SBY 5/3/89 OE **60,500**
Untitled (abstract), gouache on paper laid down on paper, 1961, 17x13", SBY 11/11/88 .... **27,500**
Untitled (abstract), gouache/acrylic on paper, sgn/dtd 59, 20x27", C-NY 5/4/89 OE **154,000**

Untitled (abstract), oil on canvas, sgn/dtd 1953, 32x24", SBY 2/15/89 OE	341,000
Untitled (abstract), oil on canvas, sgn/dtd 1953 San Francisco, 18x11", SBY 2/19/88	24,200
Untitled (abstract), oil on canvas, sgn/dtd 1958, 40x29", SBY 5/2/89	484,000
Untitled (abstract), oil on canvas, 1962, 51x77", SBY 5/2/89	605,000
Untitled (abstract), oil on paper, sgn/dtd 1963 LA, 17x12", SBY 10/8/88 OE	33,000
Untitled (abstract), oil on paper mounted on canvas, 1959, 66x44", SBY 11/9/89 OE	231,000
Untitled (abstract), oil/acrylic on paper laid down on ragboard,sgn/dtd Tokyo 1963, 73x38", SBY 11/11/88 OE	137,500
Untitled (abstract), oil/gouache on paper, sgn/dtd LA 1962, 17x20", SBY 10/8/88 OE	60,500
Untitled (abstract), tempera on paper, sgn/dtd 1960 Paris, 16x13", C-NY 5/4/89 OE	35,200
Untitled (abstract), watercolor on paper, ca 1957, 29x38", SBY 10/5/89	220,000
Untitled (abstract), watercolor on paper, ca 1959, 39x27", SBY 5/3/89	132,000
Untitled (abstract), watercolor on paper, sgn/dtd Tokyo 1974, 22x30", SBY 2/19/88	23,100
Untitled (abstract), watercolor on paper, sgn/dtd 1954/inscr, 11x9", SBY 11/11/88 OE	33,000
Untitled (abstract), watercolor on paper, sgn/dtd 1957, 22x15", SBY 11/10/88	110,000
Untitled (abstract), watercolor on paper, sgn/dtd 1957, 27x40", C-NY 11/7/89 OE	352,000
Untitled (abstract), watercolor on paper, sgn/dtd 53, 26x20", C-NY 5/3/88	77,000
Untitled (abstract), watercolor on paper, sgn/inscr/dtd 1973, 22x30", SBY 10/8/88	37,400
Untitled (abstract), watercolor on paper mounted on board, sgn/dtd 1966, 20x26", C-NY 11/10/88	28,600
Untitled (contemporary abstract), gouache on paper, sgn/dtd Tokyo 1972, 30x22", SBY 11/9/89	66,000
Untitled (contemporary), paper collage/gouache on paper, sgn, 1959, 25x19", C-E 5/9/89 OE	20,900

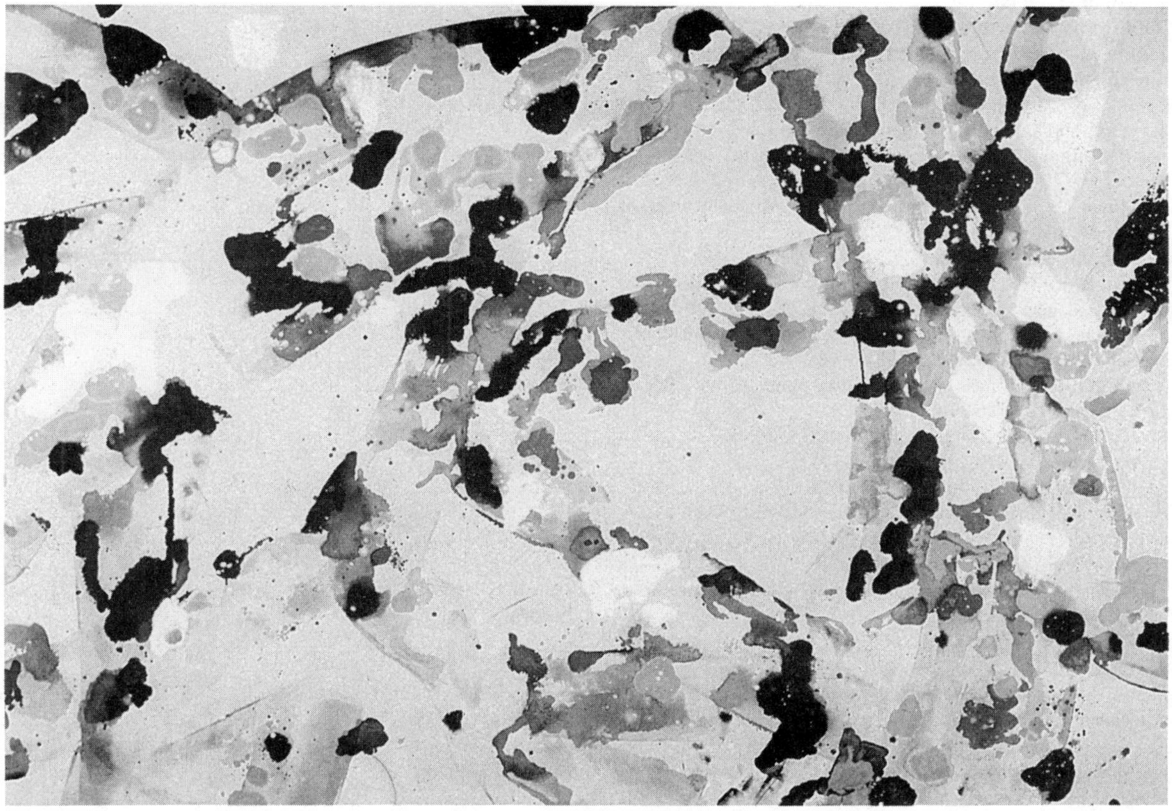

Untitled #7, acrylic on canvas, 84x121", C-NY 5/3/89 OE, $253,000

RANCIS, Thomas Edward (British, 1899-1912)	
Summer Flowers, the Old Cottage; oil on canvas laid down, sgn, 29x25", B/B 6/15/89	1,650
RANCISCO, John Bond (American, 1863-1931)	
California Landscape, oil on canvas, sgn, 16x20", B/B 10/6/88	2,090
Old Shack, oil on a cigar box top, sgn, 6x8", B/B 10/6/88	1,210
RANCK, Albert Jacques (Canadian, 1899-1973)	
Backyard on Robert Street, watercolor, sgn/dtd 64, 6x5", WAD 11/30/89	1,760
Lane Off Isabella Street, watercolor, sgn/dtd 65, 5x7", WAD 6/12/89	1,700
RANCKEN, Frans II (Flemish, 1581-1642)	
Allegory of Pursuits of Mankind Showing History, the Arts, Sciences, Religion, & War; oil on panel, 38x58", SBY 1/12/89	18,700
Belshazzar's Feast, oil on copper, 26x33", SBY 4/7/77 OE	6,325
Costume Ball, oil on panel, indistinctly dtd 1608, 19x28", C-NY 1/11/89	38,500
Council of Trent & the Doctrine of Transubstantiation, oil on copper, 13x17", SBY 10/13/89	4,400
Death Courting the Miser, oil on copper, 9x7", C-NY 10/12/89 OE	26,400
Death Courting the Miser, oil on panel, unfr, 9x7", C-NY 10/20/88 OE	15,400

Parting of the Red Sea, oil on panel, 16x22", SBY 10/21/88 UE **8,800**

FRANCKEN, Frans II; circle of (Flemish, 1581-1642)
Adoration of the Shepherds, oil on panel, 14x12", C-NY 10/12/89 ..... **2,200**
Christ on the Road to Calvary, oil on copper, 13x18", SBY 4/7/88 ..... **3,850**
Crucifixion with the Madonna, Saint Mary Magdalene & Saint John the Evangelist; oil on panel, 16x13", C-NY 10/12/89 ..... **5,500**
Elegant Party in an Interior, oil on canvas, 23x34", C-NY 4/8/88 ..... **4,400**
Lucretia (standing nude pointing dagger at her midriff), oil on panel, sgn/dtd 1529, 23x15", SBY 6/1/89 ..... **715,000**
Pentecost (radiant light shines over figures), oil on copper, 8x10", C-NY 4/6/89 ..... **2,200**

FRANCKEN, Frans II; follower of (Flemish, 1581-1642)
Feast of Herod, oil on panel, 30x40", SBY 7/12/89 ..... **4,675**

FRANCKEN, Frans III (Flemish, 1607-1667)
Adoration of the Magi, oil on panel, 21x26", SBY 10/21/88 OE **10,450**

FRANCKEN, Frans; school of
Madonna & Child Adored by Angels, oil on cradled panel, unfr, 21x14", SBY 6/8/88 OE **3,080**

FRANCKEN, Hieronymous II (Flemish, 1611-)
Abigail Offering Food to David & His Troops (figures in a landscape), oil on copper, 20x28", SBY 4/7/89 OE **8,250**

FRANCO, Siron
Expulsao do Paraiso, oil on compressed board, sgn/dtd 76, 36x47", C-NY 11/21/89 ..... **8,250**
Personagem Indeciso (contemporary portrait), oil on canvas, sgn twice/dtd 86/titled, 28x24", C-NY 5/17/89 OE **5,280**

Franco-Flemish School (16th C)
Standing Male Saint Holding a Crozier at Prayer, oil on panel, shaped top, ca 1500, 19x9", C-NY 5/31/89 UE **3,080**

Franco-Flemish School (17th C)
Mocking of Christ, oil on canvas, 13x17", SBY 4/7/88 UE **1,980**
Portrait of a Lady in a Cartouch Surrounded by Flowers, oil on canvas, 16x13", SBY 4/7/89 ..... **4,125**

FRANCOIS, Ange (Flemish, 1800-1869)
In the Garret, oil on panel, sgn, 12x15", C-NY 5/25/88 ..... **5,500**

FRANCOIS, Pierre Joseph Celestin (Belgian, 1759-1851)
Themistocle, Banni d'Athenes, se Rend Suppliant Chez Admete,...; oil on panel, sgn/dtd 1832, 30x24", SBY 2/22/89 ..... **16,500**

FRANCUCCI, Innocenzo (Italian, 1494-1550)
Holy Family with Infant Saint John the Baptist & Saint Elizabeth, oil on panel, 25x19", SBY 10/13/89 ..... **19,800**

FRANDZEN, Eugene M. (American, 20th C)
Green Forest, oil on canvas, sgn, 30x24", B/B 5/17/89 UE **550**

FRANGIAMORE, Salvatore (British, 1853-1915)
Flowers for the Cardinal, oil on canvas, sgn/inscr, unfr, 22x30", C-NY 2/25/88 OE **18,700**
Isabella Orsini Listening to the Sons of Tasso, oil on canvas, sgn/inscr, 24x20", C-NY 5/25/88 OE **15,400**

FRANGIPANE, Niccolo; circle of (Italian, 1555-1600)
Smiling Boys (portrait), oil on canvas laid down on masonite, 15x18", SBY 6/8/88 ..... **1,760**

FRANK, Eugene C. (American, 1885-1914)
Landscape with Mountain, oil on canvas, sgn, 23x36", C-E 6/1/88 ..... **935**

FRANK, Gerald A. (American, 1889-)
Pink Camellia, oil on canvas, sgn, 27x26", LH 10/16/88 OE **1,250**
Still Life of Flowers in a Vase, oil on canvas, sgn, 30x30", B/B 6/9/88 ..... **1,430**
The Balcony, oil on canvas, 30x30", B/B 6/15/89 ..... **2,200**

FRANK, J. (European, 19th C)
Midnight Sail (moonlight scene w/sailing ship on choppy seas), oil on canvas, sgn/dtd 1885, 22x14", DM 5/13/88 ..... **350**

FRANK, Josef (European, 19th C)
Cardinal in His Study, oil on canvas, sgn, 10x15", C-E 2/21/89 UE **1,100**

FRANK-WILL (French, 1900-1951)
L'Arc de Triomphe, watercolor/black chalk over pencil on paper laid down on board, sgn/inscr, 18x22", C-E 5/13/88 ..... **4,620**
L'Opera a Paris, watercolor/black chalk/pencil on paper laid down on board, sgn/inscr, 9x12", C-E 5/13/88 OE **1,870**
Le Marche a la Madeleine, watercolor/black chalk on paper laid down on board, sgn/inscr, 18x23", C-E 5/13/88 OE **4,650**
Le Mont St Michel, watercolor/black chalk/pen/black ink on paper, sgn/inscr, 19x25", C-E 5/13/88 ..... **2,640**
Parisian Street Scene, oil on canvas, sgn/dtd 26, 24x29", SBY 10/5/88 ..... **5,225**
Place Blanche a Paris, watercolor/black chalk on paper, sgn/inscr, 9x12", C-E 11/17/88 OE **3,080**
Procession Militaire a la Place Vendome, watercolor/black chalk on paper laid on board, sgn/dtd 28, 20x26", C-E 5/13/88 ..... **3,520**

FRANKE, Albert Joseph (German, 1860-1924)
After Dinner Conversation (interior scene), oil on panel, sgn, 12x8", C-NY 2/23/89 UE **4,400**
Chess Players, oil on panel, sgn, 10x7", C-NY 2/25/88 ..... **6,050**
Chess Players, oil on panel, sgn, 9x7", FAP 4/15/89 ..... **3,740**
Man Reading, oil on panel, sgn, 7x5", FAP 4/15/89 ..... **1,540**
Play Reading, oil on panel, sgn, 9x11", FAP 4/15/89 ..... **3,850**
Spanish Dancer (barroom scene), oil on panel, sgn, 14x19", SBY 2/22/89 ..... **6,050**

FRANKENSTEIN, Godfrey N.; att (American, 1820-1873)
Under the Spreading Chestnut Tree, oil on paperboard mounted on board, 9x11", SBY 1/24/89 ..... **1,650**

FRANKENTHAL, school of (German, 17th C)
Betrayal of Christ, oil on copper, 7x6", SBY 10/21/88 ..... **3,850**
Saint John the Baptist Preaching in the Wilderness, oil on canvas, 19x25", SBY 4/7/89 ..... **4,950**

FRANKENTHALER, Helen (American, 1928-)
August Deep (abstract), acrylic on canvas, sgn/dtd 78, 95x168", SBY 10/5/89 ..... **60,500**
Cave Memory (abstract), oil on canvas, sgn twice/titled, 1959, 37x41", SBY 11/11/88 ..... **110,000**
China (abstract), acrylic on canvas, sgn, 1972, 105x81", C-NY 5/3/88 OE **187,000**

Cloud Edge (abstract composition), oil on canvas, 1969, 67x51", SBY 11/9/89 159,500
Cravat (abstract), acrylic on canvas, sgn/dtd 73, 63x59", C-NY 5/3/89 OE 220,000
Eight in a Square, acrylic on canvas, sgn, 1961, 40x41", SBY 11/9/89 88,000
Face of the Landscape, acrylic on paper, sgn, 23x16", SBY 5/3/88 20,900
Figures in a Landscape (abstract composition), oil on primed canvas, sgn, 1960, 57x73", SBY 11/8/89 165,000
Ginger Box (abstract), acrylic on canvas, sgn/dtd 1975, 68x106", C-NY 5/3/89 104,500
Green & Beyond (abstract), acrylic on canvas, sgn/dtd twice 1979, 52x62", SBY 10/8/88 OE 40,700
Higher Threshold (abstract), acrylic on canvas, sgn/dtd 1972, 35x62", SBT 2/15/89 OE 71,500
Logging (abstract), acrylic on canvas, dtd 1967, 94x97", C-NY 5/3/89 132,000
March (abstract), acrylic on canvas, 89x48", C-NY 2/14/89 71,500
New Year's Series IV (abstract), acrylic/pastel on paper, sgn/dtd 79, 23x31", SBY 10/8/88 OE 18,700
One O'Clock (abstract), acrylic on canvas, 1966, 94x76", SBY 11/10/88 82,500
Orange Shapes in Frame (abstract), acrylic on canvas, 93x74", C-NY 11/7/89 OE 649,000
Passage (abstract landscape), acrylic on canvas, 1981, 45x124", SBY 11/11/88 OE 99,000
Reunion (abstract), acrylic on canvas, sgn twice/inscr/dtd 1969, 67x36", C-NY 11/9/88 OE 99,000
Untitled (abstract), acrylic on brown-toned paper, sgn/dtd 81, 19x26", SBY 2/15/89 OE 19,800
Untitled (abstract), acrylic on canvas laid down on masonite, 1952, 7x15", SBY 11/9/89 9,350
Untitled (abstract), acrylic on paper, sgn/dtd 65, 18x24", C-NY 10/4/89 13,200
Untitled (abstract), acrylic on paper, sgn/dtd 77, 30x19", SBY 10/8/88 OE 13,200
Untitled (abstract), oil on paper, sgn/dtd 61, 16x21", SBY 2/19/88 OE 60,500
Virgo (abstract), acrylic on canvas, sgn, 1969, 106x67", SBY 2/19/88 44,000

FRANKLIN (Continental, 19th C)
Portrait of a Man in Arab Dress, watercolor, sgn/dtd 1847, 11x8", C-E 10/26/89 935

FRANQUE, Joseph; att
Hercules (nude, full-length, seated with face resting on hand), oil on canvas, unfr, 77x57", SBY 6/1/89 UE 13,200

FRANQUELIN, Jean Augustin (French, 1798-1839)
In the Bedroom, oil on canvas, sgn, 18x15", SBY 2/22/89 OE 93,500

FRASCASSI, Cesare; att (Italian, 1838-1868)
Group of 6: Virgin Mary & Saints; black/white chalk on 1 mount, 8" dia, 27x35" overall, C-NY 2/23/89 UE 1,100

RASER, John Arthur (Canadian, 1838-1898)
Autumn Landscape, watercolor, sgn, 18x26", WAD 11/30/89 OE 3,000
Landscape with Mountains, watercolor, sgn, 8x12", FB 5/28/89 360

RASER, Thomas Douglas (American, 1885-1955)
Coast of Monterey, Carmel; oil on canvas, sgn/dtd 1945, 10x14", B/B 10/6/88 1,650

RAUENFELDER, F.J. (Dutch, 20th C)
Chickens Grazing, oil on panel, sgn, 7x10", C-E 5/23/88 990

RAZIER, Kenneth (American, 1867-1949)
Hudson Highlands (landscape), oil on canvas, sgn, 25x30", C-NY 5/25/89 OE 19,800

REDENTHAL, David (American, 1914-1958)
Brooklyn Bridge, watercolor on paper, sgn, 9x12", SBY 6/24/88 OE 1,760
Times Square, watercolor on paper laid down on board, sgn, 1951, 12x18", C-E 5/9/89 OE 3,080

REDERIC, Leighton (British, 1830-1896)
Antigone (portrait), oil on canvas, ca 1882, 24x20", SBY 2/22/89 154,000

REDERIC, Leon Henri Marie (Belgian, 1856-1940)
By the Windmill, Summer; oil on canvas, sgn/dtd 1903, 52x28", SBY 5/23/89 14,300

REDERICO, Cavilier Michel (Italian, 1884-)
Early Morning, Ile de Capri; oil on canvas, sgn, 12x16", FB 5/28/89 700

REDI, see Di Fredi

REDOU, Jean Martial (French, -1795)
Two Boys Drinking with Straws, pastel on paper, sgn, 17x21", SBY 7/12/89 4,950

REEDMAN, Maurice
Santa Ross Rocks, oil on canvas, sgn, 34x22", C-E 10/18/89 UE 660

REEMAN, Don (American, 1908-1978)
Late Editions, oil on canvas laid down on masonite, sgn, 24x28", C-NY 12/2/88 13,200
New York Street Scene, oil on board, sgn, 24x19", SBY 1/24/89 2,200

REEMAN, George; att (1789-1868)
Miniature Portrait of Lydia Freeman, bust-length; watercolor on ivory, 4x3", RWS, 10/27/89 600

EER, Frederick Warren (American, 1849-1908)
Letter, oil on canvas, sgn/dtd 84, 10x16", NA 11/5/88 8,500
Portrait of a Gentlewoman, watercolor, sgn, 9x13", NA 5/13/89 1,050

EEZOR, George Augustus (British, fl 1861-1879)
Kitchen Hearth, oil on canvas, sgn/dtd 74, 17x21", SBY 12/9/88 OE 3,850

EILICHER, Jane (American, 20th C)
Green & Gray (landscape), pastel on paper, sgn, 39x50", RWS 9/8/89 UE 950

EMIET, Emmanuel (French, 1824-1910)
Stallion, Badge #82; oil on canvas, sgn, 10x20", WG 9/16/88 325

ENCH, Jared (American, 1905-)
Nude, pastel/watercolor on blue paper, sgn, ca 1956, 20x9", C-NY 3/11/88 2,750

nch School (16th C)
Drunken Silenus Surrounded by Maenads & Baby Satyrs, oil on canvas, ca 1700, 58x45", SBY 10/13/89 7,700
Lovers (portrait), oil on canvas, 36x32", C-NY 1/11/89 OE 82,500

Madonna & Child, tempera/oil on panel, unfr, 26x20", SBY 1/12/89 ... 6,600
Portrait of Bearded Man, half-length, wearing costume with white collar; oil on panel, dtd 1599, 15x11", C-NY 4/6/89 UE ... 1,100
Reclining Nude, black/white chalk on gray paper, wm, ca 1760, 16x22", C-NY 1/11/89 ... 1,760
Study of the Head of a Warrior Seen From Below, black/white chalk on blue paper, ca 1700, 5x4", SBY 1/13/89 OE ... 1,925

French School (17th C)

Birth of Benjamin, gouache on paper, 10x12", WD 1/25/89 OE ... 2,400
Carnations, Roses...in a Sculpted Vase on a Pedestal; oil on canvas, 24x18", C-NY 4/6/89 ... 4,950
Portrait of a Lady Said To Be the Actress Madame Bejart, oil on canvas, initialed/dtd 1956, oval, 32x28", C-NY 4/8/77 ... 880
Portrait of a Nobleman, oil on panel, 25x19", SBY 6/8/88 ... 660
Rocky Landscape with Travelers, oil on canvas, 25x18", SBY 10/13/89 ... 4,675
Still Life of an Elaborate Glass Goblet, a Jug with Flowers; oil on canvas, 24x30", SBY 4/7/89 OE ... 99,000

French School (18th C)

A Fete Champetre, oil on canvas, bears signagure of Bonaventura de Bar, ornate gilt frame, 41x59", SBY 4/7/89 OE ... 25,300
Albatross, a Heron, a Rooster in a Feedpen & a Hen, in a Landscape; pen/ink/wash, inscr, 8x12", C-NY 1/11/89 ... 660
Alexander the Great Before Erato & Minerva, oil on canvas, 12x10", C-NY 10/20/88 UE ... 1,100
Allegory of Sculpture, oil on canvas, 32x26", SBY 7/12/89 ... 2,200
Arranging Flowers, oil on canvas, 14x11", C-E 3/22/88 ... 715
Atrium of the Roman Palace with Figures, chalk/pen/ink/wash/watercolor, Strasburg wm, ca 1785, 15x21", C-NY 1/11/89 ... 3,850
Barge on a River by a Fortress, black chalk/watercolor, inscr/wm Strasbourg Lily & Van der Lay, 21x17", C-E 4/7/88 OE ... 1,430
Biblical Scene, black chalk, ca 1725, 7x5", SBY 1/13/89 ... 770
Bishop Blessing a Mother & Two Children, black/white chalk on gray paper, inscr, ca 1700, 9x6", C-NY 1/12/88 ... 110
Cottage with a Thatched Roof, red chalk on paper, ca 1760, 7x8", C-NY 6/17/89 ... 660
Country Landscape with Hay Wagons, oil on cradled panel, indistinctly sgn/dtd, 20x26", RWS 3/31/88 ... 2,200
Diogenes, pen/black ink/brown & gray wash over black chalk, monogramed/dtd 1771, 8x7", SBY 7/12/89 UE ... 550
Equestrain Portrait of King Louis XVI As a Boy, overlooking battle; oil on canvas, 14x19", SLK 11/25/88 ... 600
Exotic Tropical Bird Perched on a Branch, oil on canvas, oval, 16x12", SBY 10/13/89 OE ... 35,750
Extensive Landscape with a Hermit, red chalk, 7x9", SBY 7/12/89 ... 660
Figures in an Ornamental Park, gouache heightened w/white, 7x9", SBY 1/13/89 ... 10,450
Holy Family, black chalk on paper, 9x7", C-NY 6/17/89 ... 418
Military Officer Said To Be Solongue, Emperor & Grand Admiral of Haiti; oil on canvas, 23x17", C-NY 10/20/88 OE ... 15,400
Mill in a Valley Below Cliffs, black chalk/pen/gray ink/gray wash, inscr, ca 1760, 16x22", C-NY 1/11/89 ... 1,100
Pair: Allegorical Depictions of Liberty; gouache on paper, 12x17", WD 1/25/89 OE ... 3,250
Pair: Bacchantes; oil on panel, ovoid, 17x11", C-E 2/16/88 OE ... 1,540
Pair: Hunting Dogs Attacking a Bear & a Lion; oil on canvas, 32x47", SBY 10/21/88 ... 3,300
Pair: Portraits of a Young Boy & Girl; oil on canvas laid down, oval, ca 1700, 11x10", SBY 1/12/89 OE ... 16,500
Pair: River Landscapes with Figures by Ruins; pen/brown ink/wash, ca 1700, 5x3", SBY 7/12/89 ... 1,210
Pair: Still Life of Tulips, Roses, Carnations...; bodycolor/gold on vellum laid on board, 9x7", C-NY 1/11/89 OE ... 6,820
Portrait of a Gentleman, Half-Length, in a Red & Blue Costume with Gold Trim; oil on canvas, 32x26", C-NY 10/12/89 OE ... 13,200
Portrait of a Lady Said To Be Mme Lavilliere, oil on canvas, 30x25", SBY 10/21/88 ... 3,025
Portrait of a Man in Blue, oil on canvas, 34x28", LH 9/10/89 ... 475
Portrait of a Prince (wearing red sash & standing beside a table), oil on canvas, 40x29", SLK 5/9/88 ... 1,450
Portrait of a Turkish Gentleman, pastel on paper, 27x21", SBY 4/7/89 OE ... 24,220
Portrait of Marie Josephe de Saxe, Dauphine de France; oil on canvas, 32x26", SBY 6/8/88 ... 1,760
Sea Battle, oil on canvas, 26x42", WD 10/19/88 OE ... 7,250
Still Life of Flowers, oil on canvas, oval, 20x16", SBY 7/12/89 ... 1,430
Still Life of Flowers in a Vase, with Fruits on a Table & a Draped Column Beside; oil on canvas, 31x26", SBY 4/7/88 ... 3,850
Still Life of Roses & Peonies, oil on canvas, 36x30", RWS 5/19/88 ... 9,000
Triumph of Bacchus, oil on canvas, 34x65", SBY 6/1/89 ... 6,600
Young Boy Purchasing a Drink in a Courtyard, oil on canvas, 16x13", SBY 7/12/89 ... 1,210

French School (19th C)

Academic Nude, seated on a block; black chalk, 20x17", C-NY 5/25/88 ... 1,760
An Unwilling Guest, oil on canvas, 37x60", SBY 7/12/89 ... 2,900
Bacchic Revels, oil on panel, indistinctly sgn/dtd 1829, 26x20", SBY 10/24/89 ... 11,550
Cherry Seller, oil on panel, 15x18", C-E 2/23/88 ... 3,740
Comforting a Weakened Man, oil on canvas, 32x39", FAP 4/15/89 UE ... 192
Cottage Interior, oil on board, 8x11", PHL 10/28/88 UE ... 170
Cows by a Stream, oil on canvas, bears signature, 27x34", SBY 6/8/88 ... 2,310
Crowning of Psyche by Cupid, oil on canvas, 43x32", SBY 4/29/88 ... 16,500
Dans l'Atelier, oil on board, 13x10", C-E 5/23/88 ... 1,210
Detail of the Portal of the Pantheon, Rome; pen/ink/gray wash on paper, 27x20", SBY 6/8/88 ... 330
Diana the Huntress, black chalk heightened w/white chalk on laid paper, 21x15", C-NY 2/25/88 ... 770
Floral Still Life with Basket, oil on canvas, ca 1800, 18x24", SBY 6/8/88 ... 522
Flower Sellers, oil on canvas, indistinctly sgn, 18x13", C-E 5/23/88 OE ... 7,150
Judith with Head of Holofernes, oil on canvas, 32x24", C-E 11/8/88 ... 825
Mischievous Kittens, oil on canvas, initialed, 32x24", C-E 10/25/88 ... 1,650
Napoleon III Reviewing the Troops in the Place Vendome, oil on canvas, 30x43", SBY 12/9/88 ... 6,600
On the Coast, oil on canvas, bears signature, 18x30", SBY 6/8/88 OE ... 2,310
Pair: Commedia Dell'Arte Characters in Garden Landscapes; oil on panel, ca 1800, 14x12", SBY 10/21/88 ... 2,750
Paysage (landscape), oil on canvas, 35x45", C-E 2/16/88 ... 715
Portrait of a Lady, half-length, wearing black dress & lace veil; black/white chalk, ca 1810, 23x15", C-NY 1/12/88 OE ... 1,210
Portrait of a Lady, oil on canvas, 22x19", LH 5/15/88 ... 750

Portrait of a Man Said To Be Robert Fulton, black chalk, inscr Fulton inventeur, 7x6" oval, C-NY 2/23/89 ... 1,430
Portrait of Marquise de Collert, oil on canvas, oval frame, 29x24", LH 5/15/88 OE ... 850
Portrait of the Baron of Chantilly, in judicial robes, three-quarter length; oil on canvas, 51x39", C-E 4/7/88 OE ... 1,045
Shepherd Tending His Flock, oil on canvas, bears signature, 25x30", SBY 7/12/89 ... 660
Still Life of Fruit & Nuts, oil on canvas, ca 1800, 25x38", SBY 7/12/89 ... 4,290
Study of a Woman's Head, oil on paper laid down, 18x15", SBY 7/12/89 OE ... 4,675
Turkish Port Scene, oil on cradled panel, 10x14", C-E 4/7/88 OE ... 825
Twelve Medallions: Greek & Roman Profiles; pencil, cut out & mounted together, inscr, 10x14", C-NY 10/26/88 ... 1,650
Two Nude Bathers, oil on panel, 7x5", C-E 10/25/88 ... 825
Unusual Sight (peasants stop work to gaze at balloon), gouache on paper laid down on board, 33x27", RAB 3/27/89 OE ... 1,150
View of Rome, black/white chalk on blue paper, ca 1800, 11x16", C-NY 1/12/88 UE ... 550
Voyage Autour d'Une Etoile, pen/ink/watercolor, 12x9", MG 5/28/88 ... 250
Walk Through the Woods, oil on canvas, 11x7", NA 10/1/88 ... 200

French School (20th C)
Academic Nude, standing; black/white chalk on laid paper, dtd 22, 23x18", C-NY 5/25/88 OE ... 6,600
Champs Elysees, oil on canvas, bears signature, 20x24", C-E 2/16/88 ... 605
Collecting Water at the Well, oil on canvas, 24x20", B/B 9/15/88 ... 358
Fauve Landscape, oil on canvas, 20x26", B/B 1/11/89 ... 825
Portrait of a Man, half-length, wearing a wide-brim hat; oil on canvas laid down on masonite, 23x18", C-E 4/7/88 UE ... 110

FRENTZ, Rudolph (German, 1831-1888)
Two Retrievers in a Landscape, oil on canvas, sgn/dtd 1870, 53x66", SBY 6/10/88 ... 5,500

FRENZEL, Oscar (German, 1855-)
Cows by a Wooded Watering Hole, oil on canvas, sgn, 23x38", B/B 10/9/88 ... 2,750

FRENZENY, P. (American, 1840-1902)
Portrait of Jonathan Phipps, oil on canvas, sgn, 30x25", FAP 4/15/89 ... 275

FREQUENEZ, Paul Leon (French, 1876-)
Parc de St Cloud in the Snow, oil on canvas, sgn, 61x79", C-NY 10/25/89 ... 22,000

FRERE, Charles Theodore (French, 1814-1888)
Along the Nile, oil on canvas, sgn, 38x51", SBY 2/22/88 OE ... 82,500
Arab Caravan at Dusk, oil on panel, sgn, 10x16", C-NY 5/25/88 ... 7,150
Arab Caravan Outside City Walls, watercolor on paper, sgn, 11x18", WL 5/20/88 ... 600
Arab Woman by an Oasis, oil on panel, sgn, 10x13", C-E 10/25/88 ... 3,520
Caravan Train to Jerusalem, oil on canvas, sgn, 14x24", SBY 10/24/89 ... 33,000
Caravane au Soleil Couchant, oil on panel, sgn/inscr, 9x16", SBY 5/23/89 ... 7,150
Caravane en Marche, Desert d'Arabie; oil on panel, sgn twice/titled on reverse, 8x16", SBY 12/9/88 ... 4,125
Figures on a Street in a Small Town, watercolor over pencil, sgn, unfr, 18x12", C-E 10/26/89 ... 440
Halte a l'Oasis, oil on canvas, sgn, 17x28", SBY 5/23/89 ... 29,700
Haute Egypte, oil on panel, sgn/dtd 1871, 8x13", C-E 10/26/89 ... 7,150
Le Matin (Haute Egypte), oil on panel, sgn/dtd 1875, 8x13", C-E 10/26/89 ... 9,350
Les Chameliers Buvant le The, oil on canvas, sgn/dtd 1855, 26x22", SBY 5/23/89 ... 22,000
Pair: Market Place; Along the Nile; oil on panel, sgn, ea 10x13", SBY 5/23/89 OE ... 16,500
Seated Arab Woman, black chalk on brown paper, sgn/inscr, unfr, 9x7", C-E 2/23/88 UE ... 110
Traveler (full-length portrait in a landscape), oil on cradled panel, sgn, 15x10", B/B 3/22/89 ... 2,200
Watering Hole Outside the City, oil on panel, sgn, 10x16", C-NY 5/25/88 OE ... 8,250

RERE, Edouard (French, 1819-1886)
Pair: Little Cook; Home From School; oil on panel, sgn/dtd 1877, 10x8", WAD 6/6/88 ... 13,500
Peasant Boy with a Cart, oil on panel, sgn/dtd 54, 13x9", PHL 10/28/88 UE ... 425

RERICHS, William Charles Anthony (American, 1829-1905)
Coming Ashore, oil on canvas, sgn, 36x60", C-NY 5/26/88 ... 6,600
Figures in a Wooded Landscape, oil on canvas, initialed, 22x36", C-NY 9/30/88 OE ... 10,450
Lake in Autumn, oil on canvas, initialed, 22x36", C-NY 9/30/88 ... 8,800
Mountain Landscape, oil on canvas, sgn, 22x36", LH 10/16/88 OE ... 900
Red Sunset Over Crashing Waves, oil on canvas, sgn, 28x47", C-E 6/1/89 UE ... 880

ERICHS, William Charles Anthony; att (American, 1829-1905)
Brook Through the Valley, oil on canvas laid down on board, 24x20", RAB 3/27/89 UE ... 600
Overlook Near the Falls, two Indians on cliff overlooking falls; oil on canvas, 24x16", RAB 3/27/89 UE ... 500

ESENMAIER, Helene (20th C)
Side View of the Construction: Back & Forth; chalk/enamel/charcoal/pencil/paper collage, 1975, 38x25", C-E 5/9/89 ... 715

ESNAYE, see De La Fresnaye

EUD, Lucian (British, 1922-)
Head of a Man, oil on canvas, sgn/dtd 1966, 18x15", SBY 6/30/88 OE ... 500,500
Seated Figure (nude), oil on canvas, 1980-82, 14x9", SBY 6/30/88 OE ... 400,400

EUND, Harry Louis (American, 1905-1979)
Seine, Paris 1930; oil on canvas mounted on board, sgn/dtd 1930, 10x13", RWS 9/8/89 ... 900

EYBERG, Conrad (German, 1842-)
Battle Scene, oil on canvas, sgn/dtd 1874, unfr, 23x40", lot 281, SBY 6/8/88 ... 2,310
Battle Scene, oil on canvas, sgn/dtd 1874, unfr, 23x40", lot 264, SBY 12/9/88 ... 1,760

IANO, see Da San Friano

IANT, Emile (French, 1863-1932)
'ortrait of Abel Combarieu, pencil, sgn/inscr/dtd 1903, 20x15", C-NY 5/25/88 ... 550

FRICK, Paul; see De Frick

FRIED, Pal (Hungarian, 1893-1976)

Angele (ballerina), oil on canvas, sgn/titled, 24x30", SLK 4/7/89 70
Ballerina Tying Her Slipper, oil on canvas, sgn, 25x30", B/B 5/17/89 2,20
Monique, oil on canvas, sgn, 24x29", B/B 1/11/89 52
Mother & Child, oil on canvas, sgn, 30x24", WG 4/23/88 1,30
Nude Female, oil on canvas, sgn, 29x23", WG 4/23/88 90
Portrait of a Female Nude, oil on canvas, sgn, 30x24", DM 3/14/88 1,20
Sleeping Beauty, oil on canvas, sgn, 24x30", C-E 11/8/88 UE 55
Sleeping Nude, oil on canvas, sgn, 24x32", C-E 2/1/89 88
Two African Women, oil on canvas, sgn, 30x24", WG 4/23/88 1,30

FRIEDENSON, Arthur (British, 1872-1955)

Warehouse Church, oil on board, sgn/dtd 1912, 12x16", C-E 2/23/88 1,32

FRIEDLAENDER, Friederich (Austrian, 1825-1901)

Argument (two men seated at table), oil on panel, sgn, 10x7", C-E 2/21/89 2,20

FRIEDLANDER, Camilla (Austrian, 1856-1928)

Antiquitaten, oil on panel, sgn, 13x10", C-E 10/26/89 4,40

FRIEDMAN, Arnold (American, 1879-1946)

Portrait of His Son, oil on canvas, 22x16", C-E 4/7/88 OE 4,18

FRIELICHER, Jane (20th C)

Goldenrod & Grapes (still life w/landscape beyond), oil on canvas, sgn/dtd 1966, 43x42", SBY 2/15/89 28,60

FRIEND, Washington F. (British, 20th C)

Quebec From the Fall of Montmorency, watercolor heightened w/white, sgn/dtd 1871, 23x37", C-SK 11/10/88 OE 11,15

FRIESEKE, Frederick Carl (American, 1874-1939)

Bowl of Flowers, watercolor on paper, sgn/dtd 28, 12x16", SBY 6/24/88 4,40
Floral (still life), oil on panel, sgn/dtd 1927, 14x11", C-NY 5/25/89 OE 38,50
Flower Garden (impressionistic, elegant lady in field of flowers), oil on canvas, sgn, 32x32", SBY 5/24/89 440,00
French Scene, oil on panel, sgn, 11x14", C-NY 5/26/88 7,15
Lady at the Mirror, oil on canvas, sgn, ca 1922, 32x32", SBY 5/25/88 198,00
Nude in a Glade, oil on board, sgn/inscr, 14x11", C-NY 3/11/88 OE 22,00
Nude Reclining on a Sofa, charcoal/watercolor on paper, sgn/dtd 28, 10x13", RWS 11/10/89 UE 2,70
On the River, oil on canvas, sgn, ca 1908-09, 26x32", SBY 5/2/25/88 638,00
Seated Woman (portrait), oil on canvas, sgn/dtd 25, 36x28", SBY 5/24/89 35,20
Symphony in Yellow (full view of lady wearing yellow dress), oil on panel, sgn/dtd 1902, 18x14", C-NY 5/25/89 99,00
Venus au Soliel, oil on canvas, sgn, 16x20", SBY 5/25/88 60,50
Woman Sewing in the Garden, oil on canvas, sgn, 32x32", C-NY 5/26/88 88,00

FRIESLAND, school of (17th C)

Pair: Portrait of a Man, Aged 32; Portrait of a Woman, Aged 30; oil on panel, sgn/inscr/dtd 1627, 41x32", C-NY 1/15/88 22,00

FRIESZ, Emile Othon (French, 1879-1949)

L'Automne (three children gathering nuts), oil on canvas, sgn/dtd 1939, 29x24", C-NY 10/5/89 28,60
Landscape with Hill Town, oil on canvas, sgn/dtd 25, unfr, 18x21", SBY 2/14/89 OE 11,50
Le Baigneuses (bathers), oil on canvas, sgn, 15x18", C-E 5/9/89 OE 12,65
Le Pont de Crozant (bridge in extensive landscape), oil on canvas, sgn, 14x22", B/B 10/9/88 3,02
Les Jarres, oil on canvas, sgn, 1930, 18x15", SBY 2/16/89 OE 39,60
Maison et Jardin, watercolor/chalk on paper, stamped signature, 25x19", C-E 5/9/89 2,09
Nature Morte (still life), oil on canvas, sgn, 16x13", SBY 10/7/88 5,77
Paysage du Midi (landscape at midday), oil on canvas, sgn, ca 1906, 26x20", C-NY 5/12/88 82,50
Paysage en Provence, oil on canvas, sgn, 26x21", SBY 2/16/89 15,40
Paysake Provencal, oil on masonite, sgn, 21x26", SBY 10/5/88 6,60
Personnages dans une Piscine, oil on board, sgn, 16x20", SBY 2/16/89 16,50
Still Life of Lavender Roses, oil on panel, sgn, 16x13", SBY 10/7/89 8,80
Une Foret (landscape), chalk on paper, initialed, 20x16", C-E 5/9/89 1,04
Vue du Port de Peche (port scene), oil on canvas, sgn, 20x24", WD 11/16/88 5,50

FRIGERIO, R. (Italian, 19th/20th C)

Street Urchins, oil on canvas, sgn, 12x16", B/B 4/20/88 1,98
Untitled, interior scene of elderly man/boy; oil on canvas, sgn, 27x19", SLK 2/11/89 3,00

FRISCH, Johann Christoph (German, 1738-1815)

Village by a River, oil on canvas, sgn, 12x18", C-E 2/23/88 1,10

FROELICH, Paul

Bowmans Hill, watercolor on rag paper, sgn, 19x25", C-E 10/18/89 UE 33

FROMANTIOU, see De Fromantiou

FROMENTIN, Eugene (French, 1820-1876)

Arab Camp at d'Jelfa, black chalk on lt squared buff paper, artist's Vente stamp/dtd, 11x17", C-NY 10/26/88 1,76
Arab Horsemen Crossing a Ford, oil on panel, sgn/dtd 75, 13x16", SBY 10/24/89 OE 44,00
Arabs on the March, oil on panel, sgn/dtd 75, 13x16", SBY 10/24/89 OE 55,00
Barnyard Scene with Sheep, Farm Hand, Chicken, Etc; oil on canvas, sgn, 26x19", S/A 2/18/89 1,00
Centaures & Centauresses s'Exercant au Tir de l'Arc, oil on canvas, sgn, 79x54", C-NY 5/25/88 UE 15,40
Le Simoon (Arab horsemen in a desert windstorm), oil on canvas, sgn, 22x26", C-NY 5/24/89 99,00

FROMKES, Maurice (American/Russian, 1872-1931)

Castillian Peasants, oil on canvas, sgn, 40x30", LH 12/4/88 2,00

FROST, Arthur Burdett (American, 1851-1928)
Accusation, pen/ink/ink wash/Chinese white on paper, sgn, 12x10", C-E 11/30/88 UE ... 330
Hanging Woodcocks, oil on canvas, sgn/dtd 1899, 17x14", SBY 4/14/89 OE ... 3,850
Hello He Called to the Major Cheerily, gouache/en grisaille on board, sgn/dtd 1901, titled twice, 13x9", SBY 9/23/88 ... 1,045
Inspection (men in an interior), watercolor en grisaille, sgn, 16x18", RWS 5/19/88 UE ... 750
Untitled, duck hunter in a blind, watercolor, sgn, 13x20", SLK 2/11/89 ... 8,000

FROST, Arthur Burdett; after (American, 1851-1928)
Pair: Carnival; Country Store; oil on canvas, sgn/inscr, 20x30", SBY 6/24/88 OE ... 1,980

FROST, F.
Composer's Fancy, oil on masonite, sgn, 8x10", C-E 11/30/88 UE ... 770
Peonies, oil on masonite, sgn, 8x10", C-E 11/30/88 ... 935

FROST, John; att (American, 1890-1937)
Mojave Desert, oil on board, sgn/dtd 1925, 18x22", RWS 9/8/89 ... 950

FROST, William Edward (British, ?-1877)
Nymphs Bathing, oil on canvas, oval, 22x22", C-E 10/26/89 ... 1,100

FROTHINGHAM, James; att (American, 1786-1864)
Portrait of Nancy Leeds Thayer, oil on panel, 27x22", SBY 9/23/88 ... 1,100

FRULLI, Giovanni Battista
Assassination of Julius Caesar, pen/brown ink/gray wash, inscr, 8x12", C-NY 1/12/88 ... 385

RY, Elizabeth (American, 20th C)
North African Casbah, oil on canvas, sgn, 31x21", B/B 1/11/89 UE ... 330

RY, Marshall
Cooling Off, oil on canvas, sgn, unfr, 24x30", C-E 6/28/88 UE ... 220

U, Zhang (Chinese, 1546-after 1631)
Landscape (hanging scroll), ink/color on silk, sgn/dtd 1613, 54x24", SBY 5/31/89 ... 3,300

UCHS, Richard (German, 1852-)
Madonna & Child, oil on canvas, sgn/dtd 92, 22x16", B/B 5/17/89 ... 1,650

UECHSEL, Hermann (American, 1833-1915)
Dream of New England (realistic landscape), oil on canvas, 35x46", SBY 5/24/89 OE ... 40,700
Evening on the Hudson, oil on canvas, sgn/inscr NY, 26x34", SBY 6/28/89 UE ... 7,700
On the Hudson, oil on canvas laid down on board, sgn/dtd NY 83, 18x30", C-E 6/1/88 OE ... 9,860
River Landscape, oil on canvas, sgn/dtd 69, 12x20", SBY 6/24/88 OE ... 14,850

UERTES, Louis Agassiz (American, 1874-1927)
Coming In (ducks on a marsh), watercolor/gouache on paper, sgn/dtd 1919, 22x29", SBY 5/24/89 ... 14,300
Flamingoes, gouache on board, sgn, 14x24", SBY 1/24/89 OE ... 17,600
Flying Ducks Over a Marsh, watercolor on cardboard, 16x24", WD 10/5/88 UE ... 9,250
Wild Wings (flock of geese flying over wheat field), watercolor on cream wove paper, sgn/dtd 1919, 14x21", RWS 11/10/89 ... 5,500

UGER, Friedrich Heinrich (German, 1751-1818)
Poseidon, oil on canvas, 58x44", C-NY 1/11/89 UE ... 22,000

ULLER, George (American, 1822-1884)
American Ship, Mollie, Standing Off Damaged Paddlewheel Steamer James M; oil on canvas, sgn, 40x60", NA 5/12/89 ... 25,000
Landscape Scene, oil on canvas, sgn/dtd 1889, 22x28", RWS 6/17/89 UE ... 200
Portrait of Miss Wynne, oil on canvas, 25x21", SBY 6/24/88 ... 990
Volunteer (two sloops at sea), oil/woven silk on silk, sgn/titled, 9x17", RAB 8/1/89 ... 900

JLLEYLOVE, John (British, 1845-1908)
Busy Street, London; watercolor, sgn, 10x8", C-E 5/22/89 ... 660

JLOP, Karoly (American/Hungarian, 1898-1963)
Arrival in the Harbor, oil on canvas, sgn, 30x30", SBY 2/14/89 OE ... 3,300
Figures in an American Interior, watercolor on paper, sgn, 25x21", B/B 10/6/88 ... 3,025

JLTON, R. (British, 18th C)
Portrait of a Young Man Said To Be the Honorable John Ponsonby, pastel on paper, 29x24", SBY 12/9/88 ... 1,210

JLTON, Samuel (British, 1855-1941)
Portrait of a Cocker Spaniel, oil on canvas, sgn, 20x16", C-E 10/26/89 ... 1,760

NKE, Anton (Dutch, 1869-1955)
Still Life of Canteloupe, Strawberries, & Grapes; oil on canvas, sgn, 16x23", SBY 12/9/88 UE ... 1,980

NKE, B. (German, 1902-)
German Landscape with Road, oil on board, sgn, 15x19", DM 5/19/89 OE ... 550

NNEKOTTER, Jan (1929-)
Street Scene, oil on board, sgn, 10x8", FB 4/25/88 ... 220

RINI, Francesco (Italian, 1604-1946)
Saint Ursala, oil on canvas, 36x30", C-NY 10/20/88 ... 33,000

RINI, Francesco; follower of (Italian, 1604-1946)
Saint Catherine of Alexandria, oil on canvas, unfr, 26x21", SBY 7/12/89 ... 1,100

RNER (19th C)
Woman & Child Asleep by an Arch, pencil heightened w/white, sgn/dtd 1849, 9x6", C-E 10/25/88 ... 110

RNIS, Harly (British, 19th C)
Pair: Prostitute; Tailor Shop; pen/ink, 11x7", LH 12/4/88 ... 250

RST, August (Italian, 19th/20th C)
Pair: Floral Still Life w/Grapes; Floral Still Life w/Birds Nest; oil on panel, sgn, 20x16", 16x12", B/B 9/14/89 OE ... 24,575
Still Life With Flowers in a Vase & Butterflies, oil on cradled panel, sgn, 24x20", B/B 9/14/89 ... 1,100

FUSSELL, Charles Lewis (American, 1840-1909)
Our Old Colonial Home, oil on canvas laid down on board, sgn/dtd 1901, 8x12", SBY 1/24/89 .... **2,20**
FUSSELL, Katherine Barker
Violet Teapot, oil on canvas, sgn, 26x19", C-E 10/18/89 UE **44**
FUZHEN, Gu (Chinese, 1634-1716 or later)
Quietly Farming in the Mountain Village (hanging scroll), ink/color on paper, sgn, 71x37", SBY 5/31/89 .... **14,30**
FYT, Jan (Flemish, 1611-1661)
Still Life of Animals & Game in a Landscape, oil on canvas, sgn/dtd 1649, 54x79", SBY 6/3/88 .... **132,00**
FYT, Jan; circle of (Flemish, 1611-1661)
Game, Fowl, a Hare, & Hunting Implements in a Landscape; oil on canvas, 33x40", C-NY 10/12/89 .... **10,45**
Still Life of Basket of Fruit, a Basket of Vegetables, & a Parrot; oil on canvas, 41x58", SBY 4/7/88 OE **27,50**
GABANI, Giuseppe (Italian, 1846-1899)
Arabs on Horseback, watercolor, sgn, 21x29", C-NY 2/25/88 OE **6,05**
Oriental Horseman (two riders in landscape), watercolor on paper, sgn, 29x20", WG 4/23/88 .... **45**
GABRIEL, F. (French, 19th/20th C)
Floral Still Life of Fruit, oil on panel, sgn, 16x12", SBY 7/12/89 .... **3,02**
Floral Still Life of Roses, Delphinium, & Honeysuckle; oil on panel, sgn, 16x12", SBY 7/12/89 .... **2,75**
Still Life of Flowers, oil on panel, sgn, 16x12", SBY 12/9/88 .... **3,85**
GABRIEL, J. (Italian, 19th C)
Venice, Doges Palace Beyond; oil on canvas, sgn, 26x31", C-E 2/21/89 .... **88**
GABRIEL, Paul Joseph Constantin (Dutch, 1828-1903)
Paysage Canal Hollandis (canal scene), oil on canvas, sgn, 15x24", C-E 2/21/89 .... **1,98**
GABRIELLI (Continental, 19th C)
Elk Crossing Stream, oil on canvas, sgn, 34x27", SBY 6/8/88 UE **1,32**
GABRINI, Pietro (Italian, 1856-1926)
Arriving by Boat, oil on canvas, sgn, 26x40", SBY 2/22/89 .... **6,60**
Fisherfolk by the Sea, oil on canvas, sgn, 35x24", C-E 10/25/88 OE **4,62**
Grand Canal (Venice), oil on canvas laid down on board, sgn, 26x41", C-NY 5/24/89 .... **17,60**
Offering, oil on canvas, sgn/dtd 1907, 54x40", SBY 7/12/89 .... **5,50**
Piazza Barbarini with the Temple of Vesta, oil on canvas, sgn, 31x49", C-NY 2/25/88 OE **16,50**
Reclining Nude Male, charcoal on paper, sgn, 10x16", C-E 10/25/88 .... **88**
Woman in a Garden, watercolor over pencil, sgn/inscr, 16x10", C-E 5/22/89 .... **60**
GADSBY, William Hippon (British, 1844-1924)
Sunday Evening (two little girls sitting on bench, one asleep), oil on canvas, sgn, 27x22", SBY 12/9/88 .... **4,67**
GAEDT
Britenburg, watercolor/gouache, sgn/inscr/dtd 1843, 19x29", C-NY 5/25/88 .... **1,87**
GAEL, Barent (Dutch, 1620-1703)
Travelers at a Village Well, oil on panel, indistinctly sgn, unfr, 16x22", SBY 10/13/89 .... **7,15**
GAEL, Barent; att (Dutch, 1620-1703)
Encampment with Skaters on a Frozen River, black chalk/pen/brown ink/gray wash, inscr, 4x6", C-NY 1/11/89 OE **1,32**
GAETANO, Scipione Pulzone (Italian, 16th C)
Portrait of Cardinal Ferdinando de Medici, Later Third Grand Duke...; oil on canvas, sgn/1580, 73x47", C-NY 5/31/89 OE **286,00**
GAGE, Jane (American, 20th C)
Loading Steel (shipping scene), oil on canvas, sgn, 30x36", WG 4/23/88 UE **90**
GAGEN, Robert Ford (Canadian, 1847-1926)
Mountain Landscape, watercolor, sgn/dtd 1901, 24x18", WAD 11/30/89 OE **2,60**
GAGILIARDINI, Julien Gustave (French, 1846-1927)
Harbor Scene, oil on canvas, sgn, 15x22", SBY 7/12/89 .... **4,95**
GAGNI, P. (European, 20th C)
Place de Madeleine, oil on canvas, sgn, 19x23", LH 9/10/89 .... **60**
St Germain de Pres, oil on canvas, sgn, 9x12", LH 9/10/89 .... **27**
GAGNON, Clarence A. (Canadian, 1881-1942)
Boat, gouache, bears atelier stamp, 4x5", FB 10/30/89 .... **2,86**
Le Village en Hiver (winter village scene), oil on canvas, sgn, ca 1913, 24x32", FB 4/25/88 UE **15,00**
Sylvie, oil on board, sgn, 20x16", FB 10/17/88 .... **30**
GAGNON, Martin (Canadian, 1931-)
Joies d'Hiver (winter merriment), oil on canvas, sgn/dtd 1980, 16x20", FB 4/25/88 .... **36**
GAGNON, Rene (Canadian, 1927-)
Anse Creuse, oil on board, sgn, 48x40", FB 4/25/88 UE **90**
Cote Nord, oil on board, sgn, 8x10", FB 10/17/88 .... **9**
Landscape, oil on board, sgn, 20x24", FB 4/25/88 .... **38**
GAINES, Charles (20th C)
Walnut Tree Orchard (3 panels), 1 photo on board, 2 pen/ink on graph paper, 1976, ea 22x18", C-NY 11/10/88 OE **2,64**
GAINSBOROUGH, Thomas (British, 1727-1788)
Portrait of a Gentleman in a Red Coat, oil on canvas, in painted oval, 30x25", SBY 6/3/88 .... **34,10**
Portrait of Frances, Mrs Alexander Champion (half-length); oil on canvas, in painted oval, 30x25", SBY 6/2/89 .... **110,00**
Portrait of J Banks, Esquire; oil on canvas, ca 1760, 50x40", SBY 1/12/89 .... **33,00**
GAINSBOROUGH, Thomas; after (British, 1727-1788)
Horse-Drawn Cart with Figures Crossing Stream in Wooded Landscape, oil on canvas, bears signature, 24x18", SLK 9/27/88 .... **80**
The Blue Boy, oil on canvas, 30x21", NA 10/1/88 .... **25**

AINSBOROUGH, Thomas; circle of (British, 1727-1788)
Cows in a Landscape, oil on canvas, 22x28", SBY 4/7/88 ... **1,320**
Wooded River Landscape with Sheep, Cattle & Herdsman; chalk/wash on paper laid down on cardboard, 10x13", WD 10/19/88 OE ... **950**
AINSBOROUGH, Thomas; follower of (British, 1727-1788)
Portrait of a Lady Believed To Be Mrs Baderly (half-length), oil on canvas, inscr/dtd 1790, 30x25", SBY 7/12/89 ... **550**
AINSBOROUGH, Thomas; manner of (British, 1727-1788)
Cottage Door, oil on board, 12x11", C-NY 6/17/89 ... **495**
Portrait of a Lady, half-length, in blue dress, by a column in a landscape; oil on canvas, 30x25", C-E 4/7/88 OE ... **1,100**
Woman in a White Gown (portrait), oil on canvas, 35x29", MG 5/28/88 ... **700**
AINSBOROUGH, Thomas; school of (British, 1727-1788)
Portrait of a Woman in Profile, oil on canvas, 30x25", LH 12/4/88 UE ... **475**
AISSER, Jakob Emmanuel (German, 1825-1899)
Cavaliers in a Tavern, oil on panel, sgn, 12x10", SBY 6/8/88 ... **2,750**
First Communion (figures in an interior), oil on panel, sgn, unfr, 9x7", B/B 10/9/88 ... **2,475**
Game of Cards, oil on canvas, sgn, 28x22", C-E 2/21/89 ... **2,860**
Pair: Her Damaged Dignity; Gossip; oil on panel, sgn, 12x15", C-E 5/23/88 ... **7,150**
ALBRAITH-CORNELL, Betty (Canadian, 1917-)
Evening Fog, Peggy's Cove, NS; oil on board, sgn, 22x30", FB 10/30/89 ... **715**
ALE, George (American, 1893-1951)
Sugar Brig & Privateer-Cup Defender; watercolor on paper, sgn/dtd 1930/titled, 9x6", RAB 8/8/89 UE ... **100**
ALIEN-LALOUE, Eugene (French, 1854-1941)
Along the Seine, gouache/pen/brown & red ink over black chalk, sgn, 7x11", C-NY 10/26/88 ... **13,200**
Au Bord de la Seine (people walking along the Seine, Paris), pencil/gouache on paper, sgn, 12x7", SBY 2/22/89 ... **6,875**
Figures on a Parisian Street, gouache/pen/black & brown ink over pencil, sgn, 8x12", C-NY 2/25/88 OE ... **14,300**
Figures on a Parisian Street at Dusk, gouache, sgn, 7x12", C-NY 2/23/89 ... **7,700**
Figures on a Parisian Street at Dusk, gouache/black chalk/pen/brown ink, sgn, 10x9", C-NY 5/25/88 ... **11,000**
French Village on a River, oil on canvas, sgn, 17x24", C-NY 2/25/88 ... **6,050**
Harbor at Trouville, oil on canvas, sgn, 18x26", SBY 10/24/89 ... **11,000**
La Place de la Republique, pencil/gouache on paper, sgn, 10x18", SBY 5/23/89 ... **16,500**
La Place Saint Michel (Paris street scene), watercolor/gouache on paper, sgn, 10x13", SBY 2/22/89 ... **12,100**
Le Lion de Belfort, gouache, sgn, 11x19", C-NY 10/26/88 ... **15,400**
Le Quai de la Seine, pencil/gouache on paper, sgn, 8x13", SBY 5/23/89 ... **9,350**
Le Quai de la Seine (Paris street scene), pencil/gouache on paper, sgn, 8x13", SBY 2/22/89 ... **12,100**
Le Theatre du Gymnase, Paris; gouache, sgn, 7x12", C-NY 5/25/88 OE ... **28,600**
Les Quais a Paris, gouache, sgn, 11x19", C-NY 10/26/88 ... **19,800**
Les Quais a Paris (busy street scene w/art market), watercolor on paper, sgn, 10x18", B/B 3/22/89 OE ... **17,600**
Les Quais et Notre-Dame a Paris, gouache on paper, sgn, 7x12", SBY 10/24/89 ... **14,300**
Marche aux Fleurs, La Madeleine (French flower market); pencil/gouache on paper, sgn, 8x12", SBY 2/22/89 ... **12,100**
Marche aux Fleurs (flower market), gouache over black chalk, sgn, 8x12", C-NY 2/23/89 OE ... **12,100**
Moonlit River Landscape, oil on canvas, sgn, 12x16", C-NY 2/23/89 ... **6,600**
Paris at Dusk (street scene with figures & horse-drawn carriages), gouache on paper, sgn, 8x12", B/B 10/9/88 OE ... **9,900**
Parisian Street Scene with a Flower Vendor, watercolor/gouache/chalk on gray-green paper, sgn, 7x12", C-NY 2/23/89 OE ... **12,100**
Place d'Anvers, Paris; pen/ink/gouache on paper, sgn, 8x13", SBY 10/24/89 ... **16,500**
Place de la Republique (busy street scene), gouache on paper, sgn, 11x15", WD 11/16/88 ... **15,000**
Place du Theatre Francais, gouache, sgn, 7x13", C-NY 5/25/88OE ... **26,400**
Place St Michel (busy street scene), gouache on cardboard, 9x12", WD 11/16/88 ... **6,500**
Porte St Denis (busy street scene), gouache on paper, 8x12", WD 11/16/88 ... **14,000**
Snowy Evening in Paris, gouache over black chalk, sgn, 13x8", C-NY 10/26/88 ... **9,350**
St Germain des Pres (street scene), gouache/watercolor/black chalk, sgn, 8x13", C-NY 2/23/89 ... **9,900**
View Along the Seine with Notre Dame Beyond, watercolor/gouache/black chalk, sgn, 8x13", C-NY 2/23/89 ... **9,350**
View of the Seine with Notre Dame in the Distance, oil on canvas, sgn/dtd 1882, 22x15", C-NY 2/23/89 ... **9,250**
Village Lane, oil on canvas, sgn, 38x61", B/B 4/20/88 ... **4,400**
Village Scene with Washerwomen at a River, oil on board, sgn, 18x20", B/B 3/22/89 ... **4,950**
ALINDEZ, P. (Spanish, 19th C)
Spanish Beauty (portrait), oil on canvas, sgn, 24x15", B/B 6/15/89 ... **1,430**
ALL, Francois (French, 1912-1945)
Along the Promenade at Argenteuil, oil on board, sgn, 13x16", WD 5/5/88 ... **1,900**
Along the Seine (portrait of a girl on a bridge), oil on canvas, sgn, 26x31", SBY 10/5/88 ... **5,775**
Apres le Bain, oil on canvas, sgn, 11x9", C-NY 2/13/89 ... **3,080**
Au Bord de la Seine, Paris (barges docked, figures on shore along the Siene); oil on canvas, sgn, 9x11", C-E 11/17/88 OE ... **4,400**
Au Bord de la Seine, Paris; oil on masonite, sgn/inscr, unfr, 15x18", C-E 5/13/88 OE ... **2,420**
Auteuil Avant la Course (equestrians), oil on canvas, sgn, 20x24", WD 11/16/88 ... **9,750**
Beach Scene, oil on canvas, sgn/inscr Acarnon, 11x18", SBY 10/5/88 ... **3,575**
Beach Scene with Figures, oil on canvas, sgn, 11x19", FB 4/25/88 ... **4,200**
Dans le Parc (figures in park), oil on canvas, sgn, 9x11", C-E 5/9/89 OE ... **3,850**
Day at the Shore, oil on canvas, sgn, 9x10", SBY 10/5/88 ... **2,750**
Dejeuner sur l'Herbe, oil on canvas, sgn/indistinctly inscr, 19x24", C-E 5/9/89 ... **7,150**
Edude du Piano (girl playing piano), oil on canvas, sgn, 18x15", FB 5/28/89 ... **7,500**
Figures on a Quay, Honfleur; oil on canvas, sgn, 9x11", PHL 11/15/88 OE ... **2,000**
Girl with Parasol, oil on canvas, sgn, 11x9", SBY 10/5/88 ... **4,125**
Jeune Femme au Cafe (young woman at cafe), oil on canvas, sgn, 11x9", C-E 11/17/88 OE ... **4,620**

Jeune Femme au Miroir, oil on canvas, sgn, 18x13", WAD 6/6/88 ... 4,60
Jeune Femme au Miroir (young woman in profile seated at mirror), oil on canvas, sgn, 11x9", C-E 11/17/88 OE ... 3,08
Jeune Fille au Bouquet de Fleurs (seated woman w/bouquet of flowers), oil on canvas, sgn, 18x15", SBY 10/5/88 ... 4,12
La Place du Tertre a Montmartre (figures in landscape), oil on canvas, sgn/inscr Paris, 1952, 9x11", C-E 5/9/89 OE ... 3,74
La Plage d'Arrachon, oil on masonite, sgn/inscr, 9x14", C-E 5/13/88 OE ... 3,74
La Plage d'Arrachon (beach scene), oil on canvas, sgn/inscr, 9x11", C-E 11/17/88 ... 3,52
Le Pont des Arts a Paris (landscape), oil on canvas, sgn, 16x20", C-E 5/9/89 OE ... 6,82
Les Saltimbanques (a circus family w/horse & wagon), oil on canvas, sgn, 36x48", SBY 10/7/89 ... 8,80
Mother & Child, oil on board, sgn, 13x15", SBY 10/7/89 ... 5,77
Pair: At the Cafe; oil on canvas, sgn, 11x9", WD 5/5/88 ... 6,50
Paris in the Spring, oil on canvas, sgn, 9x11", WD 5/5/88 ... 1,40
Place du Terte (street scene), oil on panel, sgn, 13x16", C-E 11/17/88 OE ... 2,42
St Denis (river scene w/figures on walkway), oil on canvas, sgn, 20x24", WD 11/16/88 ... 7,50
Stroll by the Sea, oil on masonite, sgn, 8x10", FAP 12/8/89 ... 1,90
Sunday in the Park, oil on canvas, sgn, 9x11", WD 5/5/88 ... 2,10
Sur la Plage (at the beach), oil on canvas, sgn, 9x11", C-NY 2/13/89 OE ... 3,30
Vue de Notre Dame de Paris (street scene), oil on canvas, sgn/dtd Paris 62, 13x16", C-E 5/9/89 OE ... 3,96
Woman Fixing Her Hair, oil on canvas, sgn, 24x20", B/B 3/22/89 OE ... 9,35
Young Girl Reading in an Interior, oil on canvas, sgn, 19x22", WD 5/5/88 ... 3,80
Young Woman Knitting in a Meadow, oil on masonite, sgn, 9x11", SBY 10/5/88 ... 1,98

GALLAGHER, John
Bermuda Moonlight, St George, 1959; oil on canvas, sgn, 1959, 24x30", MAG 4/24/88 UE ... 15

GALLAGHER, Michael
Dance Mad 125 (abstract), acrylic on canvas, sgn/dtd 79, unfr, 78x102", SBY 10/7/89 ... 3,57

GALLAGHER, Sears (American, 1869-1955)
Pair: Lone Tree; Mountain Meadow (Vermont landscapes); oil on canvas mounted on cardboard, sgn, 8x10", RWS 3/16/89 OE ... 70

GALLARD, see De Gallard

GALLATIN, Albert Eugene (American, 1882-1952)
Connected Triangles (geometric composition), oil on canvas, sgn/dtd March 1951, 24x20", C-NY 5/25/89 OE ... 16,50

GALLEGOS Y ARNOSA, Jose (Spanish, 1859-1902)
Geographers (four men studying map & globe in an interior), oil on panel, sgn/dtd 1902, 9x12", C-NY 5/24/89 OE ... 66,00
Waiting for His Eminence, oil on panel, sgn/dtd 1902, 9x12", C-NY 5/24/89 OE ... 46,20

GALLI, Guiseppe (Italian, 1868-1953)
Character Study of a Man Wearing a Striped Red Shirt, Vest, Cap, & Holding Wine; oil on canvas, sgn, 8x6", SLK 2/12/88 ... 7
Village Lawyer, oil on panel, sgn, 16x22", WAD 6/6/88 ... 5,50

GALLIARI, att
Stage Design: Exotic Plants, Nymphs, & Putti; watercolor heightened w/gold over black chalk, 13x20", SBY 1/13/89 ... 99
Stage Design: Figures in the Foreground, The Saved & The Damned; watercolor w/gold heightening, 13x20", SBY 1/13/89 ... 1,10
Stage Design: Oriental Temple in a Landscape; pen/black ink/watercolor over black chalk, 9x13", SBY 1/13/89 ... 1,10

GALLIARI, Bernardino (Italian, 1707-1794)
Stage Design: Vaulted Interior; pen/brown ink/wash, 11x16", SBY 1/13/89 ... 3,85

GALLIARI, Fabrizio (Italian, 1709-1790)
Interior of a Mausoleum: Design for the Stage; chalk/ink/wash, wm, #d 45, 9x12", C-NY 1/11/89 ... 1,65

GALLIARI, G. (Italian, 1760-1823)
Stage Design: Garden with a Nymphaeum & Putti with Gardens; watercolor over black chalk, sgn, 11x13", SBY 1/13/89 ... 1,54
Stage Design: Garden with a Topiary Temple, Altar, Fountains, & Putti w/Garlands; watercolor, sgn, 11x13", SBY 1/13/89 ... 1,54

GALLIARI, G.; att (Italian, 1760-1823)
Stage Design: Ruins of a Colonnade, Obelisk, & Trees; pen/ink/colored wash over black chalk, 9x15", SBY 1/13/89 ... 3,30

GALLO, Vincent (20th C)
Come to My Neighborhood (abstract), oil on metal, sgn/dtd 1985, 43x33", SBY 10/5/89 ... 2,20
Red Flower IX (abstract), acrylic on canvas, sgn/dtd 86, 111x20", SBY 10/5/89 ... 33,00
So So Many Times (abstract), oil on metal, sgn/dtd July 1985, 37x49" SBY 2/15/89 ... 5,22

GALLON, Robert (British, 1845-1925)
Gathering Twigs by a River, oil on canvas, sgn, 20x30", C-E 2/23/88 ... 2,20
House by a Waterfall, oil on canvas, sgn/dtd 84, 13x24", C-E 10/26/89 ... 2,86

GALVAN, Jesus Guerrero (Mexican, 1910-1973)
Nina con Palomas (portrait of seated girl w/doves), oil on canvas, sgn/dtd 1971, 40x32", C-NY 5/17/89 OE ... 28,60

GAMACHE, Cecile (Canadian)
Going for a Sleigh Ride, oil on canvas, sgn, 12x16", FB 5/28/89 ... 32

GAMARRA, Jose (Latin American, 20th C)
Antepasados (landscape of water creature/horse/ruins beyond), oil on canvas, sgn twice/dtd 1980, 46x35", C-NY 5/17/89 OE ... 17,60
Pintura P.64105 (abstract), oil on canvas, sgn/dtd 1964, 51x64", SBY 5/17/88 ... 4,40

GAMBARA, Lattanzio; att (Italian, ca 1530-1574)
Scene of Classical Sacrifice, pen/brown ink/brown-gray wash, 3x6", SBY 1/13/89 ... 88

GAMBARTES, Leonidas
Yuyera (a sorceress), chromogesso on board, sgn, 32x24", C-NY 5/17/89 ... 9,35

GAMBEY, Andre (French, 19th C)
Foundry at Night, oil on canvas, sgn/dtd 1873, 11x9", SBY 6/8/88 ... 88

GAMBINO (Italian, 20th C)
Two Lovers (contemporary), oil on canvas, sgn/dtd 1961, 28x40", MG 5/28/88 UE ... 6

AMBLE, John M. (American, 1863-1934)
Tranquility (desert scene), oil on canvas, sgn, 36x48", B/B 3/22/89 4,675
AMBLE, Roy C. (American, 1887-1972)
Camping, Wagonside; oil on board, sgn/estate stamp, 8x9", RWS 3/16/89 275
Mother & Child in a Courtyard, oil on board, sgn, 8x7", DM 3/14/88 500
Oyster Gatherers, oil on board, sgn, 9x7", DM 3/14/88 325
Portrait of an Old Soldier, oil on canvas, sgn/monogramed, 30x25", SLK 11/25/88 1,100
AMBRINI, P. (Italian, 1865-1926)
Lovers at Sea, watercolor, sgn, 21x29", DM 5/19/89 1,800
AMOS
Sulla Strada, oil on canvas, sgn/dtd 64, 23x27", LH 5/15/88 UE 40
AMPENRIEDER, Karl (German, 1860-)
Prinzessin Elvira von Bayern mit Freudin (two women in an interior), oil on canvas, sgn/dtd 86, 36x44", SBY 2/22/89 29,700
ANDOLFI, Gaetano (Italian, 1734-1802)
Male Nude Sleeping on a Rock, red chalk, 17x12", SBY 1/13/89 3,850
ANDOLFI, Mauro (Italian, 1764-1834)
Nine Heads, Including That of Saint Francis; pen/brown ink,8x10", C-NY 1/11/89 OE 4,620
Portrait of Three Girls, pen/black/brown ink/gray/blue/pink wash, in a drawn circle, 12x10", SBY 1/13/89 9,350
Sheet of Studies of Heads, pen/brown ink, 8x10", SBY 1/13/89 7,150
ANDOLFI, Mauro; att (Italian, 1764-1834)
Aeneas & Charon, black chalk/pen/brown ink/brown washes, inscr, 13x19", C-NY 1/12/88 OE 3,520
ANDOLFI, Ubaldo (Italian, 1728-1781)
Seated Male Nude, red chalk heightened w/white chalk, 15x11", SBY 1/13/89 OE 9,350
ANNON, Florence V.
Pair: Still Life of Flowers in a Vase; Morning-Glories; watercolor on paper, sgn, 24x30", 22x27", C-E 10/18/89 UE 165
ANSO, Emil (American, 1895-1941)
Corner of the Garden, watercolor on paper, 14x10", SBY 3/17/88 825
Girl in an Old-Fashioned Chaise, pencil on paper, sgn, 18x15", RWS 11/3/88 OE 600
Nude Sitting in Chair, oil on canvas, sgn, 30x24", C-E 11/30/88 OE 4,180
Reclining Nude, charcoal with pencil on paper, sgn/dtd 29, 9x12", PHL 10/28/88 400
Reclining Nude, oil on canvas, sgn, 14x22", SBY 4/14/89 1,760
Reclining Nudes with High Heels, conte crayon/pencil, sgn, ca 1930, 14x21", SWN 6/15/89 523
Rue Blondel, watercolor/pen/ink on paper, sgn, 10x13", C-E 11/30/88 OE 1,760
Seated Nude, pencil, sgn, ca 1930, 19x13", SWN 6/15/89 715
Sleeping Nude, oil on canvas, sgn/dtd 34, 15x12", C-E 11/30/88 880
Still Life of Goblet, oil on paper, sgn, 14x18", FAP 11/4/88 UE 300
Two Women, ink wash on paper, sgn, 13x18", C-E 4/7/88 825
Young Girl Reading on a Couch, pencil/ochre chalk on white wove Arches paper, sgn, 15x20", RWS 5/19/88 UE 200
ANTNER, Bernard (French, 1930-)
Winter Pond, pastel on paper, sgn/dtd 68, 15x11", B/B 9/14/89 880
ARABEDIAN, Charles
Ruins VII (two male nudes), acrylic on canvas, 1981-82, 72x72", SBY 2/15/89 11,000
ARAT, Francis (French, 19th C)
Crossing the Place, oil on panel, sgn/dtd 1890, 13x9", C-NY 5/25/88 3,300
Pair: Paris Street Scenes; oil on panel, sgn/dtd 1890, 13x9", C-NY 5/25/88 OE 15,400
Park in Paris with Sacre Coeur in the Distance, watercolor/charcoal/gouache on brown paper, sgn, 8x11", C-E 2/23/88 OE 1,100
ARBER, Daniel (American, 1890-1958)
Green Mansions (close view of tree branches & leaves), no media given, sgn twice/titled, 1934, 53x57", SBY 5/24/89 OE 154,000
Manchester, Vermont (mountainous landscape); oil on board, sgn, 14x22", C-NY 5/25/89 17,600
Pennsylvania Quarry From a High View, watercolor on paper remounted on linen, sgn/dtd 1909, 12x9", SWN 12/1/88 990
Portrait of a Woman, charcoal on paper, sgn, 25x18", C-E 6/1/88 OE 1,045
Portrait of Bonnie (seated child), oil on canvas, sgn, 22x18", SBY 6/28/89 13,200
Sally (lady seated, hands folded), charcoal/chalk on buff paper, sgn/dtd 1933, 22x18", C-NY 9/28/89 1,100
Tohickon Bridge, oil on board, sgn/dtd 1923, 18x20", C-NY 9/28/89 OE 23,100
ARBO, see Del Garbo
ARCIA, Joaquin Torres (Uruguayan, 1874-1949)
Arte Constructivo (contemporary), oil on board, initialed/dtd 42, 24x32", SBY 5/16/89 68,750
Composition in Red, Black, & White; oil on board, initialed/dtd 38, 21x17", SBY 5/16/89 44,000
Composition with Five Colors on White Background (contemporary), oil on board, dtd 1943, 28x20", SBY 5/16/89 OE 82,500
Constructive Structure with Fragmented Forms (contemporary), oil on board, initialed/dtd 43, 20x28", SBY 5/16/89 66,000
Figuras Universales a Cinco Tonos Agrisados, oil on board, sgn/dtd 1943, 20x28", SBY 5/17/88 71,500
Still Life (contemporary), oil on board, sgn/dtd 47, 16x18", SBY 5/16/89 37,400
Still Life of Flowers (contemporary), oil on board, sgn/dtd 47, 20x16", SBY 11/21/88 24,200
Still Life with Guitar (abstract), gouache on paper, sgn/dtd 35, 19x32", SBY 5/16/89 60,500
Three Figures (abstract), oil on board, initialed/dtd 46, 16x18", SBY 5/16/89 68,750
ARCIA Y MENCIA, Antonio (Spanish, fl 1871-1915)
Favorite, watercolor over traces of pencil on paper, sgn, unfr, 27x19", C-NY 5/24/89 6,050
ARCIA Y RAMOS, Jose (Spanish, 1852-1912)
Red Parasol (portrait of a woman), oil on canvas, sgn, 35x26", SBY 2/22/89 19,800
Spanish Cabaret, oil on panel, sgn, 11x7", C-NY 5/24/89 28,600

GARCIA Y RODRIGUEZ, Manuel (Spanish, 1863-1925)
Day's Journey, oil on canvas, sgn/dtd 1911, 22x30", SBY 2/22/89 27,500
Estangue du un Jardin Sevillano, òil on panel, sgn/dtd 1902, 8x10", SBY 5/23/89 7,150
Feeding Poultry in a Courtyard, oil on canvas, sgn, 11x14", C-NY 10/25/89 8,250
Figures Around a Fountain, oil on canvas, sgn/dtd 1921, 30x35", C-NY 5/25/88 6,600
Figures in a Spanish Courtyard, oil on board, sgn/dtd Granada 1919, 11x13", C-NY 2/23/89 8,800
Figures in a Spanish Courtyard, oil on board, sgn/dtd 1919, 11x13", C-NY 10/25/89 7,700
Fuente Arabe-Jardines del Alcazar Sevilla; oil on panel, sgn/titled, unfr, 8x12", SBY 5/23/89 7,700
Hacienda at la Jara (couple standing at gate to hacienda), oil on panel, sgn/inscr, 18x12", B/B 6/15/89 9,350
In the Gardens of the Royal Alcazar, Seville; oil on canvas, sgn/dtd/inscr 9-V-1912, 13x17", SBY 2/22/89 16,500
Jardin Sevillano, oil on panel, sgn/dtd 1902, 8x10", SBY 5/23/89 8,250

GARDANNE, August (French, 19th C)
Pair: Soldier & Horses in a Landscape; oil on canvas, sgn, 11x9", FAP 4/15/89 1,925

GARDELLI (Italian, 20th C)
Portrait of a Gentleman Smoking a Pipe, oil on panel, sgn, 12x7", B/B 5/17/89 605

GARDEUR
French Soldier, oil on canvas, sgn, 8x7", C-E 9/15/88 UE 330

GARDINER, J.H (American, 20th C)
Champion of the Seas (ship), watercolor on paper, sgn/dtd 89/titled, 15x22", RAB 8/1/189 UE 700

GARDNER, Beatrice
Flowers, oil on canvas, indistinctly sgn, 16x20", C-E 4/7/88 UE 275

GARDNER, Walter
Taking a Swim, oil on canvas, sgn, 22x28", C-E 10/18/89 UE 825

GARET, Jedd (American, 20th C)
Mom & Dad (abstract composition), acrylic on canvas, sgn/dtd 1983, 73x57", SBY 10/5/89 UE 3,850
Third Style, white pastel on black paper, 1983, 33x25", SBY 10/5/88 1,650
Unique Swim (contemporary), oil on canvas, sgn/dtd 1985/titled, 24x36", SBY 2/19/88 2,750

GARIBALDI, Joseph (French, 1863-)
A Village in Provence, oil on canvas, sgn, 40x28", SBY 10/24/89 6,050
Fishing Village, oil on panel, sgn, 11x14", B/B 4/20/88 1,045

GARINEI, Giovanni
Good Vintage, oil on canvas, sgn/dtd 1884, 18x22", C-E 5/23/88 2,860

GARINO, Angelo (Italian, 1860-)
Holy Procession in Piedmont, oil on board, sgn, 15x21", WD 11/16/88 UE 900

GARLAND, George (American, 20th C)
Let's Bury the Hatchet (girl/brave on horse), watercolor/gouache/ink on paper mounted on board, sgn, 22x29", RWS 3/31/88 325

GARLAND, Henry (British, fl 1854-1890)
Border Foray, oil on canvas, sgn, 40x78", SBY 7/12/89 4,125

GARLING, Frederick
Sudney Cove (port scene), pencil/watercolor, 12x18", C-SK 11/10/88 UE 1,670

GARNER, Olga C.
Pair: Quamby Bluff, North Tasmania, Westfield Angus Stud; Mount Olympus; oil, sgn, 20x30", C-SK 11/10/88 1,770

GARNERAY, Jean; att (French, 1755-1837)
Female Nude Before a Landscape, oil on panel, bears signature, 16x22", PHL 10/28/88 500

GARNIER, H.
Village, oil on canvas, sgn, 16x24", C-E 1/12/88 OE 462

GARNIER, Jules Arsene (French, 1847-1889)
Courting Couple, oil on canvas, dtd 1880, 31x19", C-NY 5/25/88 7,700
Le Droit du Seigneur, oil on canvas, sgn/dtd 1872, 27x49", SBY 10/24/89 19,800

GARRI, Giorgio; att
Two Putti Arranging Flowers in an Urn, An Elegant Garden Beyond; oil on canvas, 37x50", SBY 10/13/89 OE 24,200

GARRIDO, Eduardo Leon (Spanish, 1856-1906)

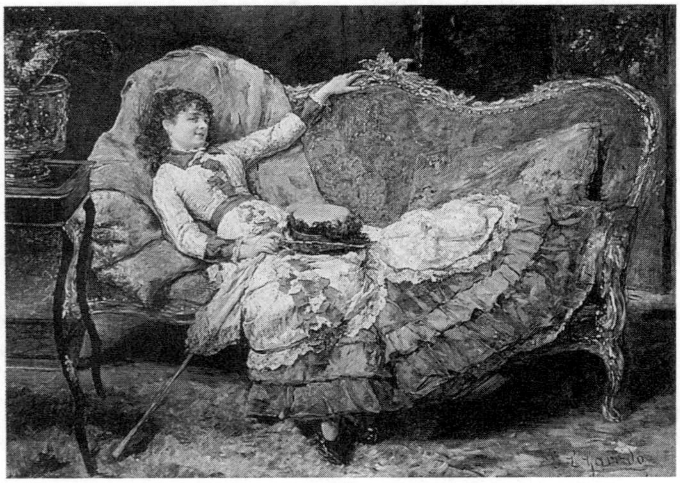

Elegant Lady in a Red Dress, oil on canvas, sgn, 34x46", C-NY 10/25/89, $77,000

:legant Lady with Her Dog, oil on panel, sgn, 16x13", C-NY 5/24/89	28,600
;erenade (lady serenading another, figure behind red drape), oil on panel, sgn, 21x26", SBY 10/24/89 OE	39,600
RRIDO, Leandro Ramon (Spanish, 1868-1909)	
)ancing Reflections, oil on canvas, sgn/dtd 1891, 26x18", B/B 6/9/88	1,870
RSIDE, Thomas H. (Canadian, 1906-1980)	
\utumn River Scene in the Mountains, oil on canvas, sgn, 12x16", FB 5/28/89	1,100
Vorth River in Winter, pastel, sgn, 22x30", FB 10/30/89	2,640
₹ed Sleigh, oil on board, sgn, 7x10", FB 5/28/89	700
Vinter Pool, Sunset; pastel on tan paper, sgn, 12x16", RWS 5/12/89	1,200
RTH, John (American, 1889-1971)	
onquil Lady, oil on paper laid down on canvas, sgn, 20x16", B/B 10/6/88	1,210
RTHE, see De Garthe	
RTNER, L. (European, 19th C)	
'isherfolk by the Sea, oil on canvas, sgn, unfr, 35x48", C-E 2/23/88 OE	4,180
RZI, Luigi (Italian, 1638-1721)	
\potheosis of a Bishop Saint, oil on canvas, 45x25", C-NY 4/8/88	4,180
RZI, Luigi; att (Italian, 1638-1721)	
)ouble-Sided; Partially Draped Male Nude; Reclining Male Nude; 1 black/white chalk, 1 red chalk, 17x11", SBY 1/13/89	1,650
RZOLINI, Guiseppi (Italian, 1850-1938)	
Aarket Scene, oil on panel, sgn, 10x15", WL 5/20/88 OE	700
SPARD, Leon (American, 1882-1964)	
'orest, oil on board, sgn, 13x15", C-NY 5/26/88 UE	4,950
;ate to Gobi, Peking; oil on canvas laid down on board, sgn, 13x15", C-NY 5/26/88	14,300
Aan Resting on Rickshaw #2, oil on board, sgn, 10x9", C-E 6/1/89	2,420
Aongolian Girl, oil on board, indistinctly sgn/stamped signature, 20x15", SBY 5/25/88 OE	23,100
'easant Houses, oil on board, sgn, 5x7", C-E 6/1/89 OE	2,640
;ouks in Tunis, oil on canvas laid down on board, sgn/dtd 1931, bears artist's estate stamp, 12x13", C-NY 5/26/88	15,400
;treet Scene, Tunis; oil on canvas laid down on board, sgn/dtd 1930, 13x13", SBY 9/23/88	10,450
'eam 13 Russia (horses in harness), oil on board, sgn, 5x7", C-E 6/1/89	1,760
'isiting Apaches, oil/pencil on linen board, stamped w/signature/estate stamp, 12x23", SBY 5/25/88	11,000
SPARO, Oronzo (American, 1903-)	
Aission (adobe building), oil on canvasboard, sgn/dtd 1951, 16x20", B/B 5/17/89	715
SSEL, Lucas van; see Helmont, Lucas van Gassel	
SSER, Henry Martin (American, 1909-1981)	
:ountry Town, watercolor/pencil on paper, sgn, 13x16", C-E 6/1/89 UE	440
)istant Pastures (fence running to mountains, house in distance), watercolor/pencil on paper, sgn, 8x10", RWS 3/31/88 UE	100
'actory Town (view from hilltop), oil on canvas, unfr, 25x30", SBY 3/17/88	3,850
'ruit Still Life #4, oil on canvasboard, sgn, 22x28", C-E 2/1/89 UE	3,850
Iarbor View, oil on board, sgn/dtd 68, 21x30", SBY 4/14/89	1,045
Iarlem Palladium, oil on paper, sgn twice/titled, 12x17", SBY 3/17/88 OE	550
Aale Nude, oil on canvas, sgn/inscr, unfr, 38x30", C-E 4/7/88 UE	7,150
Vew England Harbor, watercolor/pencil on paper, sgn, 21x29", SBY 3/17/88	330
'air: Gloucester Views; pencil on paper, 1 sgn/other inscr Gloucester, unfr, ea ca 14x20", SBY 3/17/88 UE	1,870
'air: Service Station; Portrait of Mrs Gasser; oil on masonite/oil on board, sgn, 9x12" & smaller, C-E 6/1/88	605
'air: Venetian Scenes; watercolor on board, sgn/inscr, 1 stamped, 8x10", 10x8", SBY 9/23/88	935
'rayer Meeting, oil on canvasboard, sgn, 12x16", SBY 9/23/88	1,320
:ailroad Tracks & Telephone Poles, watercolor/charcoal/pencil on paper, sgn, 15x24", C-E 6/1/88	3,575
:enslerville, New York (dwelling on a hillside w/two figures); oil on board, sgn, 16x20", SBY 4/14/89	1,650
:iver Bank, watercolor mounted on cardboard, sgn, 8x10", NA 11/5/88	1,760
et of 3: Army Life Scenes; watercolor/pencil on paper, sgn, 8x5" & smaller, C-E 6/1/88 UE	300
et of 4: Landscape Studies; watercolor on paper, sgn, 10x15" & smaller, SBY 4/14/89	440
hacks on a Slope, watercolor/gouache on board, sgn, 16x23", C-E 6/1/89	2,090
panish Steps, watercolor/pencil/pen/black ink on paper laid down on board, sgn/inscr, 16x22", C-E 11/30/88	825
'ournament (locker room scene), watercolor on paper, sgn, 12x16", SBY 9/23/88	1,980
'urner's Grocery, watercolor/gouache/pencil on paper laid down on board, sgn, 20x25", C-NY 3/11/88 OE	3,960
Vinter Housetops, watercolor on board, sgn/inscr, 15x22", C-E 11/30/88 UE	4,950
Vintry Coast, watercolor/gouache on paper laid down on board, sgn, 21x28", C-NY 3/11/88	715
	2,310
STINEAU, Maria (British, 19th C)	
'rawing Room, watercolor heightened w/white on paper, sgn, 11x19", SBY 6/8/88 UE	385
TCH, Lee (American, 1902-1968)	
:radel Stone, oil on fabric/mixed media collage mounted on wood, sgn/dtd 64, 34x72", SBY 9/14/89	6,050
;aster Morning, oil on canvas, sgn, 22x40", SBY 6/24/88	6,600
'ew York, 1955 (abstract); oil on canvas, sgn, 14x27", C-NY 5/25/89	6,600
trata Tapestry, stone/sand/fabric/wood collage, sgn/dtd 64, 23x45", SBY 9/14/89	3,025
TTIE, Annibale (Italian, 1828-1909)	
;alileo Galilei Before the Inquistion, oil on canvas, sgn, 32x44", C-E 2/16/88	605
JCCIMANNI, Alessandro (American)	
ainy Streets, New York; oil on canvas, sgn/dtd 94, 20x14", C-NY 5/25/89 OE	24,200
JCHET, C. (French, 19th C)	
'erbal Exchange Between Two Military Men, watercolor/pen/ink on paper, sgn, 9x7", B/B 9/15/88	330

GAUDEZ-CHENNEVIERE, Cecile Delphine (French, 1851-)
Menuet, watercolor/gouache, sgn, 11x22" fan shape, C-NY 2/23/89 ..... **1,980**
GAUERMANN, Friedrich (Austrian, 1807-1862)
Der Dorfbrunn, oil on cradled panel, sgn/dtd 1836, 29x38", SBY 10/24/89 OE **308,000**
Huntsman Returning Home, oil on canvas, sgn/inscr Der Regen, 13x16", C-NY 2/23/89 OE **14,300**
GAUFFIER, Louis (French, 1761-1801)
Angel Releasing Saint Peter From Prison, oil on paper laid down on canvas, sgn/dtd 1788, 8x5", SBY 10/13/89 OE **52,250**
GAUGENGIGL, Ignaz Marcel (German, 1855-1932)
Hat (figures in a landscape), oil on panel, sgn/inscr, 10x7", C-NY 5/26/88 ..... **13,200**
GAUGUIN, Paul (French, 1848-1903)
A Flanc de Coteau (landscape), oil on canvas, sgn/dtd 1884, 26x18", C-NY 5/11/88 OE **374,000**
Buste de Jeune Fille Nue (nude bust of young girl), oil on panel, 1882, 10x8", SBY 5/10/89 OE **907,500**
Double-Sided: Man in Top Hat; Studies of a Woman; recto: chalk on blue gray, verso: red/black chalk, 9x11", SBY 2/18/88 ..... **8,800**
Double-Sided: Nativity (Fragment); Head of a Marquesan; gouache monotype, ca 1902, 12x11", SBY 11/12/88 ..... **77,000**
Etude pour le Christ Jaune, pencil on yellow paper mounted at edges to board, initialed, 1889, 10x6", C-NY 11/14/88 ..... **60,500**
Etudes (sketches of heads), charcoal/sanguine on laid paper, 1884, 9x11", SBY 5/10/89 OE **18,700**
Jeune Bretonne (portrait), oil on canvas, initialed/dtd 89, 18x15", SBY 11/15/89 ..... **2,090,000**
La Lisiere de la Foret (II) (figure & mule near edge of forest), oil on canvas, sgn/dtd 85, 26x32", C-NY 11/15/88 ..... **682,000**
Oviri, pen/watercolor over watercolor monotype on paper laid down on card, artist seal, 1894, 12x8", SBY 11/12/88 ..... **220,000**
Parau Hina Tefatou (Words of Moon & Earth), pen/brown ink/gray wash/charcoal on paper, ca 1891-93, 9x8", SBY 5/11/88 OE **99,000**
Pointillistic Still Life (still life of fruit & peppers w/bowl & pot), oil on canvas, dtd 89, 12x16", SBY 5/10/89 ..... **495,000**
Portrait of the Artist's Wife (Mette Gauguin), charcoal/brown wash on blue paper, 6x5", SBY 11/16/89 ..... **44,000**
Village sous la Neige (village snow scene), oil on canvas, sgn, 1894, 30x26", SBY 11/11/88 OE **2,310,000**
GAUL, Arrah Lee (American, 1888-1980)
D'Agulvar Street, Hong Kong; oil on canvas, sgn, 30x25", C-E 10/18/89 ..... **1,100**
GAUL, Gilbert (American, 1855-1919)
At the Stream, oil on canvas, 14x20", DM 5/13/88 UE **1,300**
Carving a Pumpkin, oil on canvas, sgn, 24x18", C-E 11/30/88 UE **1,100**
Chimney Smoke, oil on board, sgn, 12x16", C-E 11/30/88 ..... **2,200**
Explorers (river scene w/men fishing from boat), oil on canvas laid down on board, sgn, 12x16", C-E 10/18/89 ..... **1,760**
Molly Pitcher at the Battle of Monmouth, 1778; oil on board, sgn, 34x44", SBY 5/24/89 ..... **9,900**
New Jersey Farmhouse, oil on canvas, sgn, 14x20", C-E 6/1/88 ..... **3,300**
Sailboats at Shore, oil on board, sgn, 12x15", C-E 6/1/89 OE **3,520**
Seated Indian, oil on canvas, sgn, 25x30", SBY 5/25/88 ..... **22,000**
Soldier in the Battlefield, oil on canvas, 26x16", SBY 4/14/89 ..... **7,700**
GAULD, David (British, 1865-1936)
Cattle Coming Through the Woods, oil on canvas, sgn, 16x24", B/B 4/20/88 ..... **2,750**
GAULEY, Robert David (American, 1875-1943)
City on a Cliff, watercolor on paper, sgn/dtd 1883, 10x14", C-E 11/30/88 UE **121**
Looking Toward Verena From Menaggio, oil on canvas, sgn/dtd 1882, 15x21", C-E 11/30/88 UE **990**
GAULLI, Giovanni Battista (Italian, 1639-1709)
Portrait of a Young Ecclesiastic (half-length), oil on canvas, indistincty inscr, in painted oval, 28x23", C-NY 1/15/88 ..... **8,800**
GAULLI, Giovanni Battista; after (Italian, 1639-1709)
Solomon & the Queen of Sheba, oil on canvas, 22x33", C-E 4/7/88 OE **1,760**
GAULLI, Giovanni Battista; att (Italian, 1639-1709)
Portrait of a Cardinal, red/black/white chalk on buff paper, #d 1151, 11x6", SBY 1/13/89 ..... **7,700**
GAULOIS, Jules
Travelers on a Path in a Mountainous River Landscape, oil on canvas, sgn, 26x38", C-NY 4/8/88 ..... **8,800**
GAUME, Henri Rene (French, 1834-)
Lady Reading, oil on panel, sgn/dtd 68, unfr, 8x6", C-E 2/21/89 OE **5,720**
GAUSSEN, Adolphe
Rochers au Bord de la Mer (rocky coastline), oil on panel, sgn, 13x16", C-E 11/17/88 ..... **770**
GAUT, Joseph
Paurini te Whiti, Rangatira-O-Ngatingarengare (portrait); oil on canvas, sgn/dtd 89, 28x22", C-SK 6/9/88 ..... **2,790**
GAUTIER, Amand (19th C)
Portrait of Diana, the Huntress; sgn/inscr/dtd 1884, 27x18", C-E 10/25/88 ..... **1,210**
GAUVREAU, Gilles (Canadian, 1924-)
Etude en Bleu et Vert (study in blue & green), oil on board, sgn, 9x11", FB 4/25/88 ..... **325**
GAUVREAU, Pierre (Canadian, 1922-)
Abstract, pen/ink, sgn/dtd 1947, 11x17", FB 10/30/89 ..... **3,960**
GAVARDIE, see De Gavardie
GAY, Edward B. (American, 1837-1928)
After the Rain, oil on canvas, sgn, 16x27", C-E 6/1/88 ..... **1,650**
Along the Shore Off Long Island, oil on panel, sgn, 13x21", C-E 11/30/88 UE **715**
Autumn Landscape, oil on panel, sgn/dtd 1887, 16x24", SBY 9/23/88 ..... **2,475**
Country Path, oil on board, sgn, 16x12", SBY 6/24/88 ..... **2,640**
Dusk (landscape), oil on canvas, sgn, 18x24", C-E 6/1/89 UE **1,870**
Edge of the Orchard, oil on canvas, sgn, 20x24", C-NY 3/11/88 ..... **2,200**
Fall Landscape, oil on canvas, sgn/dtd 1914, 34x43", C-NY 12/2/88 ..... **7,700**
Flowering Dogwood, oil on canvas, sgn/dtd 1881, 37x13", WD 4/13/88 ..... **2,000**
Forest Scene, oil on canvas, sgn, 40x36", DM 1/15/88 ..... **800**

Harvest Field, oil on canvas, sgn, 28x36", FAP 11/4/88	3,000
Harvesting Hay (figures in extensive landscape), oil on canvas, sgn/dtd 1878, 18x36", SBY 4/14/89	2,860
Long Island Beach Scene with Figures, oil on canvas, sgn/dtd 1880, 20x36", C-NY 9/28/89	6,050
Marsh Landscape with Boats, oil on canvas, sgn/dtd 1910, unfr, 33x43", SBY 3/17/88	2,200
Noll at Napanach, Ulster Co (landscape); oil on board, sgn/dtd 05/titled, 12x16", RAB 3/27/89	1,000
Pair: Twilight on East Chester Creek; Boats by a Creek; oil on panel, sgn, 8x13", 7x12", SBY 4/14/89 OE	3,850
Romantic Twilight, oil on panel, sgn, 16x13", C-E 2/3/88	2,200
Sailing Off the Coast, oil on canvas, sgn, 6x10", C-E 6/1/88	935
Spring Landscape, oil on canvas, sgn, 10x10", C-E 11/8/88 UE	440
Town Dock, East Chester; oil on canvas, sgn, 18x15", C-NY 3/11/88 OE	4,180
Tropical Sunset, oil on panel, sgn, 16x14", B/B 5/17/89	1,100
View From Gayland Cragsmoor, New York (landscape), oil on canvas, sgn, 18x24", RWS 5/19/88	1,200
Winter Woods, no media given, sgn, 25x30", C-E 2/16/88	770
Wooded River Landscape, oil on canvas, sgn, unfr, 24x30", C-SK 11/10/88	1,580
Wooded Stream, oil on canvas, sgn, 13x8", C-E 6/1/88	1,045
GAY, George Howell (American, 1858-1931)	
Beach Coast with Waves, watercolor on paper, sgn, 18x28", lot 311, GAI 6/17/89	320
Good Trout Brook, watercolor on paper, sgn, 10x20", B/B 1/11/89 UE	358
Land's End (seascape), watercolor on paper, sgn, 14x23", RAB 8/8/89	1,000
Low Tide at Bass Rocks, Gloucester, Massachusetts; watercolor on paper, sgn, 10x20", RAB 8/9/88	1,200
Maine Rocks, oil on panel, sgn, 9x10", NA 5/13/89	800
November Day (landscape), oil on canvas, sgn/dtd 29, 20x24", RAB 3/27/89	1,000
Rocky Surf, oil on board, sgn/dtd 1930, 11x15", NA 5/13/89	950
Seascape, watercolor on paper, sgn, 15x26", RAB 3/27/89 UE	350
Seascape, watercolor on paper, sgn, 9x20", RAB 3/27/89 UE	900
Storm Moving Out to Sea, watercolor/gouache on paper, sgn, 19x19", RWS 9/8/89	325
GAY, Walter (American, 1856-1937)	
Artist's Bedroom, oil on board, sgn, 13x16", C-E 11/30/88	2,420
Cottage Craft (woman at spinning wheel), oil on canvas, sgn, 35x26", C-NY 12/2/88	17,600
Fencing Lesson (figures in a courtyard), oil on canvas, sgn, 27x43", C-NY 9/28/89	8,800
French Interior, oil on canvas, sgn, 22x18", C-NY 12/2/88 OE	22,000
Game of Cards in the Carriage House, oil on panel, sgn, 14x11", SBY 9/14/89	5,225
In the Garden (girl viewed from behind), oil on canvas, sgn/dtd 1878, 18x15", C-NY 5/25/89	13,200
Interior with Clock Garniture, oil on panel, sgn, 22x18", B/B 10/9/88 OE	9,350
Pair: Daisies with Buttercups; Golden Rod with Red Berries; oil on panel, sgn/bears signature, 25x8", RWS 3/16/89 UE	1,000
Pink & White Flowers, oil on panel, sgn, 18x7", SBY 9/23/88 UE	1,430
Print Connoiseurs, oil on panel, sgn/dtd Paris 1881, 22x18", C-E 10/18/89	3,300
Shuttered Interior with a Daybed, oil on panel, sgn, 21x25", B/B 10/9/88 OE	8,250
AZE, Harold (American, 20th C)	
Fairy Garden, watercolor/pen/gray ink heightened w/white, sgn/dtd 1930, 13x10", C-NY 2/25/88 OE	3,850
ECHTOFF, Leonid (American, 19th/20th C)	
Arab Street Scene, pastel, sgn, 9x7", FAP 11/4/88	160
Blue Vase, oil on canvas, sgn/dtd 40, 25x30", B/B 12/8/88	2,200
EDDES, Andrew; att (British, 1783-1844)	
Portrait of a Little Girl Seated in a Landscape, oil on canvas, 41x33", C-NY 2/23/89	5,500
EDLEK, Ludwig (Austrian, 1847-)	
Ambush, oil on panel, sgn/dtd 1880, 14x27", C-NY 5/24/89	7,150
Cossak Outpost, oil on panel, sgn, 8x11", SBY 6/8/88	3,300
Fortune Teller, oil on canvas, indistinctly sgn, 10x23", WD 3/23/88	1,100
Rest Along the Way (horses w/wagon, & figures resting in a landscape), oil on panel, sgn/dtd 880, 12x25", C-NY 5/24/89	7,150
EEST, see De Geest	
EETERE, Georges Francois de; see De Geetere	
EETS, Willem (Belgian, 1838-)	
Polishing Brass & Copper (girl on knees in an interior), oil on canvas, sgn, 36x54", C-NY 5/24/89 OE	13,200
EGOUX, J.	
Carting Hay, oil on canvas, sgn/dtd 1907, 28x42", C-E 10/25/88	880
EHRIG, Jacob (German, 1846-1922)	
Boats Returning to Shore, oil on canvas, sgn, unfr, 18x20", SBY 12/9/88	1,100
EHRING, Louis H. (American, 1900-)	
Rolling Fields of Summer (landscape), oil on board, sgn, 10x14", RAB 3/27/89 UE	150
Spring in Vermont (landscape), oil on board, sgn, 10x13", RAB 3/27/89 UE	125
IBEL, Casimir (German, 1839-1896)	
Transporting Wine (figures & horse with loaded cart in a landscape), oil on canvas, sgn/dtd 1893, 16x24", B/B 9/14/89	1,210
IGER, Richard (Austrian, 1870-)	
Clowning at the Ball, oil on canvas, sgn, 23x31", SBY 12/9/88	935
Eastern Beauty Holding a Parrot, oil on canvas, sgn, 32x24", C-E 10/25/88	3,080
IGER, Robert	
Young Lady Reading, oil on canvas, sgn, 24x20", C-E 5/23/88	4,950
LHAY, Edouard (French, 1856-)	
Reflection (women looking in mirror in an interior), oil on canvas, sgn, 26x21", C-NY 5/24/89	9,350
Wedding Procession, oil on canvas, sgn, 13x16", C-E 10/25/88 UE	1,540

GELIBERT, Jules Bertrand (French, 1834-)
Chasse au Canard, oil on canvas, sgn/dtd 1891, 18x24", SBY 6/10/88 **2,750**
GELLA, Gugliemo
Taste of Wine, watercolor on paper laid down on board, sgn, 12x16", C-E 5/23/88 **605**
GELLEE, Claude (Lorrain) (French, 1600-1682)
Landscape w/Two Men Walking in Foreground, Seated Figure & Cattle Beyond; pen/ink/wash over chalk, 8x11", SBY 1/13/89 UE **26,400**
GELLEE, Claude (Lorrain); after (French, 1600-1682)
Harbor Scene, oil on canvas, unfr, 40x53", SBY 7/12/89 OE **3,300**
Mediterranean Harbor Scene, oil on canvas, unfr, 33x44", SBY 12/9/88 **1,760**
Pastoral Scene, oil on canvas, 41x55", SBY 12/9/88 **1,760**
GELLEE, Claude (Lorrain); circle of (French, 1600-1682)
Landscape with Classical Figures Along a Road, oil on canvas, 20x26", SBY 10/21/88 OE **7,150**
GELLEE, Claude (Lorrain); manner of (French, 1600-1682)
Pair: Extensive River Landscapes with Figures; oil on canvas, 17x23", SBY 7/12/89 OE **7,150**
GELMUYDEN, R.E. (Dutch, 19th/20th C)
Young Woman Sharing a Letter on the Beach, watercolor on paper, sgn, 19x28", B/B 6/15/89 **2,200**
GEN-PAUL (French, 1895-1975)
Clown & Violin, gouache/colored crayon on paper, 24x19", PHL 6/16/88 **1,000**
GENGE, Charles (British, -1929)
Lilacs in a Vase, oil on canvas, sgn, 36x24", C-E 10/25/88 **1,760**
GENIN, Lucien (French, 1894-1958)
La Place de Triomphe (traffic around the Arc de Triomphe), gouache on paper, sgn, 20x24", RWS 9/29/88 **500**
Le Marche (street scene w/figures), oil on canvas, sgn, 21x26", C-E 5/13/88 OE **6,050**
Le Sacre-Coeur a Montmartre; gouache on paper, sgn/inscr, 16x13", C-E 11/17/88 OE **1,540**
Pont Neuf, watercolor/gouache/pencil on paper, sgn, 9x15", B/B 1/11/89 **440**
GENIS, Rene (French, 1922-)
Still Life of Flowers, Pitcher, & Seashells; oil on canvas, sgn, 24x32", SBY 10/5/88 OE **3,300**
Vieux Sardiniers a Douarenez, oil on canvas, sgn, 21x32", SBY 10/7/89 **4,125**
GENN, Robert (Canadian, 1936-)
Evening Gold, oil on panel, sgn, 8x10", FB 4/25/88 **340**
Gentle, oil on board, sgn, 8x10", WAD 11/30/89 **225**
GENNISON, Jules Victor (Belgium, 1805-1860)
Church Interior, oil on canvas, sgn, 16x13", C-E 2/23/88 **3,850**
Genoese School (17th C)
Boar Attacked by a White Mastiff, oil on canvas, 70x80", C-NY 4/8/88 **17,600**
Drunken Silenus & Other Figures, red chalk, 5x6", SBY 1/13/89 **3,300**
Holy Family with a Bowl of Milk, oil on canvas, 43x29", WD 1/25/89 OE **5,250**
Shepherds in an Extensive Wooded River Landscape with a Village & Mountains...; oil on canvas, 19x25", SBY 4/7/88 OE **3,960**
Genoese School (19th C)
Putti with a Heart Transfixed by an Arrow, chalk/pen/ink/wash/squared in chalk, ca 1700, 16x12", C-NY 1/11/89 OE **990**
GENOVES, Juan (Spanish, 1930-)
Cinco Minutos, acrylic/oil on canvas, sgn/dtd 69, 36x79", C-E 11/14/89 OE **6,600**
GENTH, Lillian (American, 1876-1953)
Nude in the Woods, oil on canvas, sgn, 30x39", C-NY 9/28/89 **7,700**
GENTILINI, Franco (Italian, 1909-)
Ritratto di Donna (portrait of a woman), oil on panel, sgn, 28x20", C-E 11/17/88 **2,860**
GEOFFROY, Henry Jules Jean (French, 1853-1924)
Training Lesson (girl offering her dog a treat), oil on canvas, sgn, 40x24", S/A 2/18/89 **12,000**
GEORG, Edouard
Un Bouquet Bonnet (still life), oil on canvas, sgn twice/dtd 56/titled, 22x13", C-E 5/9/89 OE **6,820**
GEORGE, Vesper (American, 1865-1934)
Gentleman Playing a Piano, oil on canvas, sgn/dtd 94, 27x33", RWS 5/12/89 **6,500**
Rockport 1929, watercolor on paper, sgn/titled, 14x17", RAB 8/8/89 UE **500**
GEORGES
Reclining Female Nude, pencil on paper, sgn/dtd 62, 17x13", C-NY 6/17/89 OE **220**
GEORGI, Friedrich Otto (German, 1819-1874)
Les Deux Majestes, oil on canvas, sgn/dtd 1863, 26x36", SBY 10/24/89 **31,900**
Ruins at Phylae, oil on canvas, sgn/dtd 1864, 25x38", C-E 10/26/89 **8,250**
GERARD, Marguerite; school of (French, 1761-1837)
Portrait of a Woman Said To Be Mademoiselle de la Michodiere, Reading at Table; oil on canvas, 24x20", C-NY 10/12/89 OE **22,000**
GERARD, Rolf
Portrait of Beatrice Lillie, oil on canvas, 16x20", SBY 10/7/89 **6,325**
GERARD, Theodore (Belgian, 1829-1895)
Day's Delivery, oil on canvas, sgn/dtd 95, 27x21", C-NY 10/25/89 **7,700**
Day's Delivery (woman knocking on door), oil on canvas, sgn/dtd 94, 27x21", C-NY 5/24/89 UE **8,800**
Farmer's Children, oil on panel, sgn twice/dtd 1861, 33x23", SBY 5/23/89 **33,000**
GERE, Charles March (British, 1869-)
Cotswold Village, watercolor over pencil, 6x5", C-NY 5/25/88 **1,045**
GERHARDT, Eduard (German, 1813-1888)
Das Haus der Famlie Moro (Othello) in Venedig, oil on canvas, sgn/inscr twice, dtd 1859, 21x17", C-E 2/23/88 **5,720**

GERICAULT, Theodore (French, 1791-1824)

Landscape with Aqueduct, oil on canvas, 1818, 99x87", SBY 6/1/89 OE ... 2,420,000
Study of a Lion Attacking a Horse; Study of a Snarling Lion; pencil on calque on 2 joined sheets, 11x8", C-NY 5/24/89 OE ... 33,000

GERICAULT, Theodore; manner of (French, 1791-1824)

Portrait of a Man in a Red Turban, oil on canvas, bears signature, 23x18", C-E 5/22/89 ... 2,730

GERICAULT, Theodore; school of (French, 1791-1824)

Raft of the Medusa, oil on canvas, 5x9", SBY 7/12/89 OE ... 1,870

GERMAIN, Jacques (French, 20th C)

Composition, oil on canvas, sgn/dtd 60, 32x40", SBY 10/7/89 ... 9,350
Untitled (abstract), oil on canvas, sgn/dtd twice 53, 45x58", SBY 10/5/88 OE ... 8,250

GERMAIN, Thomas; att

Merman & a Mermaid in a Compartment Set in Rocaille Decoration, black chalk, 6x10", C-NY 1/11/89 OE ... 1,540

German School (15th C)

Presentation in the Temple, oil on panel, ca 1480, 38x28", C-NY 1/11/89 ... 33,000

German School (16th C)

Banquet of Anthony & Cleopatra, oil on panel, initialed/dtd 1577, 20x34", C-NY 10/20/88 OE ... 8,250

German School (17th C)

Church Interior with Figures, oil on panel, unfr, 30x24", C-NY 10/20/88 OE ... 7,150
Festival Interior Scene (crowned woman & jester at table), oil on canvas, 25x30", DM 5/19/89 ... 3,500
Four Apostles, oil on copper, 13x10", C-NY 4/8/88 ... 3,300
Peasants Drinking & Dancing Before a Tavern, oil on panel, initialed/dtd 1749, 6x10", C-NY 4/6/89 ... 3,520
Portrait of a Man Said To Be Sebastianus Schmidius, oil on canvas, 10x7", C-E 6/1/88 ... 2,600
Portrait of Nobleman Wearing Order of Golden Fleece...King Christian II of Denmark; oil on panel, 8x6", SBY 4/7/89 UE ... 1,925
Salvator Mundi, with Herdsmen Fighting Wild Boar Beyond; chalk/pen/ink/wash, crayfish wm, 8x6", C-NY 1/11/89 OE ... 1,210
Set of 12: The Months (Latin names), Flowers in Pottery Vases; black chalk/watercolor, ca 1630, ea 13x8", C-NY 1/12/88 ... 28,600

German School (18th C)

Artist Painting a Portrait of an Officer, oil on canvas, unfr, 43x35", C-NY 10/20/88 ... 2,200
Cavalry Skirmish, oil on canvas, 17x14", C-NY 10/20/88 ... 1,870
Elegant Couples at Table on a Terrace Overlooking a Formal Garden, gouache on vellum, ca 1700, 5x7", SBY 1/13/89 ... 4,400
Figures in a Rocky Landscape, oil on canvas, unfr, 26x32", SBY 6/8/88 ... 1,870
Landscape with Travelers Along a Road, River & Castles Beyond; oil on canvas, 28x24", SBY 10/13/89 ... 3,080
Pair: Elegant Figures at a Winery; Nymphs Dancing in a Landscape; gouache on paper, 8x14", WD 1/25/89 OE ... 3,000
Pair: Landscape with Palace; Landscape with Ruins; pen/black ink, 8x10", 8x14", SBY 1/13/89 UE ... 165
Pair: Portrait of Lady & Gentleman (half-length); oil on canvas/oil on panel, 18x13", C-NY 4/6/89 ... 1,650
Peasants on a Road by an Inn, oil on canvas, unfr, 18x24", SBY 12/9/88 ... 2,860
Portrait of Catherine the Great, Seated Half-Length, in Royal Dress; oil on canvas, 37x30", C-NY 10/12/89 ... 2,640
Portrait of Charles VI, Holy Roman Emperor; oil on canvas, inscr, ca 1700, 49x40", SBY 6/8/88 ... 3,960
Portrait of Woman Taking Snuff, oil on canvas, 24x18", C-E 6/1/88 ... 935
Prodigal's Return, oil on canvas, unfr, 35x29", SBY 6/8/88 ... 605
Vertumnus & Pomona, oil on canvas, unfr, 99x55", SBY 6/8/88 ... 2,200
Young Girl, seated on cushion, holding a finch, with attendant behind a curtain; oil on canvas, 39x32", C-NY 4/8/88 ... 3,850

German School (19th C)

Barber, oil on canvas, initialed, 16x13", C-E 5/23/88 ... 935
Bedouin Boy, oil on canvas, indistinctly initialed/dtd 1851, 56x43", C-NY 5/25/88 OE ... 28,600
Brace of Hare for the Friars, oil on canvas, 21x35", NA 3/26/88 ... 800
Drinkers in a Tavern, oil on canvas, unfr, 40x51", C-E 4/7/88 ... 880
Figures by a Watermill in an Alpine Landscape, oil on canvas, indistinctly sgn, 38x31", PHL 6/16/88 UE ... 1,000
Interior Depicting Children Playing with Pets, oil on panel, 9x6", SLK 2/12/88 ... 200
Landscape with Figure Before a Cottage, Mountainous Terrain Beyond; oil on canvas, 19x23", SBY 7/12/89 ... 1,980
Landscape with Ruins, oil on canvas, 16x21", SBY 6/8/88 UE ... 495
Mother & Her Children Standing in a Doorway, oil on panel, 14x11", B/B 9/15/88 OE ... 1,760
Old Gentleman with Guest, oil on canvas, sgn, 21x17", B/B 1/11/89 ... 1,870
Pair: Cavalry Scene; Lion Attacking Dog; oil on board, inscr, 8x10", B/B 6/15/89 ... 1,650
Pair: Flowers in Urns on Marble Ledges; oil on copper, 13x11", WD 10/19/88 OE ... 9,500
Pair: Seated Ladies; oil on canvas, 12x11", C-E 5/23/88 OE ... 2,090
Peasants in a Wagon, oil on canvas, unfr, 17x23", C-E 11/8/88 ... 1,320
Playing the Zither, oil on canvas, unfr, 32x28", C-E 5/23/88OE ... 4,180
Portrait of a Lady Letting Down Her Hair, oil on canvas, 18x15", WG 4/23/88 UE ... 1,200
Portrait of a Young Couple in a Landscape, oil on canvas, 25x21", B/B 3/22/89 ... 2,200
Portrait of Young Man with Felt Hat, oil on canvas, 20x13", S/A 3/12/88 ... 500
Puppies Playing, oil on panel, 18x13", PHL 10/28/88 ... 800
Spinning Wheel, oil on canvas, indistinctly sgn/dtd 1865, 21x25", C-E 10/25/88 ... 1,320
Still Life of Mouse & Objects on a Table, oil on canvas, 16x13", C-E 10/25/88 ... 2,860
Too Much Wine, oil on canvas mounted on academy board, sgn, 10x8", S/A 2/18/89 ... 1,250
Travelers Being Entertained by the Innkeeper's Family, oil on canvas, 21x42", C-E 2/21/89 ... 330

German School (19th/20th C)

Caravan Watering at an Oasis, oil on canvasboard, 64x99", B/B 5/17/89 ... 2,475
Landscape with Frozen River, oil on board, initialed LR, 9x19", LH 9/10/89 ... 225
Portrait of Herr Helmer, oil on canvas, 22x27", MG 10/28/88 UE ... 325
Traveling Children, oil on canvasboard, sgn, 14x14", LH 9/10/89 ... 300
Woman & Child in a Garden, oil on panel, 9x13", B/B 1/11/89 ... 330

German School (20th C)
Blast Furnaces (interior scene), oil on cardboard, sgn/inscr O Kuhler Dusseldorf, 14x19", RWS 3/16/89 OE **600**
Mainzener Brucke (view of bridge), oil on canvas, indistinctly sgn, 41x76", B/B 5/17/89 .... **2,200**
Still Life of Wild Flowers, oil on canvas, sgn, 25x22", RWS 11/3/88 .... **700**

GERNEZ, Paul Elie (French, 1888-1948)
Fleurs, pastel on paper, sgn, 28x23", SBY 10/5/88 OE **18,700**

GEROME, Francois (French, 20th C)
L'Avenue des Champs Elysees a Paris, oil on canvas, sgn/inscr, 23x29", C-E 5/13/88 .... **880**

GEROME, Jean Leon (French, 1824-1904)
Colossus of Memnon, oil on canvas, sgn/dtd MDCCCLVII, 26x32", SBY 10/24/89 .... **440,000**
La Priere dans de Desert, oil on cradled panel, sgn, 1864, 13x23", SBY 2/22/89 .... **165,000**
Le Premier Baiser du Soleil (view of several pyramids), oil on canvas, 7x10", C-NY 2/23/89 .... **7,150**
Lion on the Watch, oil on canvas, sgn, ca 1900, 28x51", SBY 5/23/89 .... **181,500**
Louis XI Feeding Pigeons at Plessis-Les-Tours, oil on canvas, sgn, ca 1860, 18x12", SBY 2/22/89 OE **49,500**
Oriental Man, standing, hands folded, wearing a long coat; red chalk, initialed, 13x9", C-NY 5/25/88 .... **990**
Sculpturae Vitam Insufflat Pittura or Atelier de Tanagra, oil on canvas, sgn, ca 1893, 25x36", SBY 2/22/89 .... **99,000**
Standing Arab Holding a Staff, pencil on paper, sgn, 11x8", C-E 10/25/88 .... **550**
Standing Boy with a Staff, black chalk on lt tan paper, inscr, 14x9", C-NY 2/25/88 OE **4,950**
Standing Man, wearing a long coat; red chalk, initialed, 13x9", C-NY 5/25/88 .... **1,320**
Standing Man Wearing a Long Coat Playing a Triangle, red chalk, initialed, 13x9", C-NY 2/23/89 .... **1,320**
Standing Russian Soldiers, red chalk, initialed, 13x9", C-NY 10/25/89 .... **2,200**
Study of an Arab Woman, standing; black chalk, sgn, 14x9", C-NY **1,320**
Study of Ars (portrait), pencil on lt gray-beige paper, inscr, 11x12", C-NY 2/23/89 .... **1,100**
Une Journee Chaud au Caire (Devant la Mosquee), oil on canvas, sgn, 26x18", SBY 10/24/89 .... **71,500**

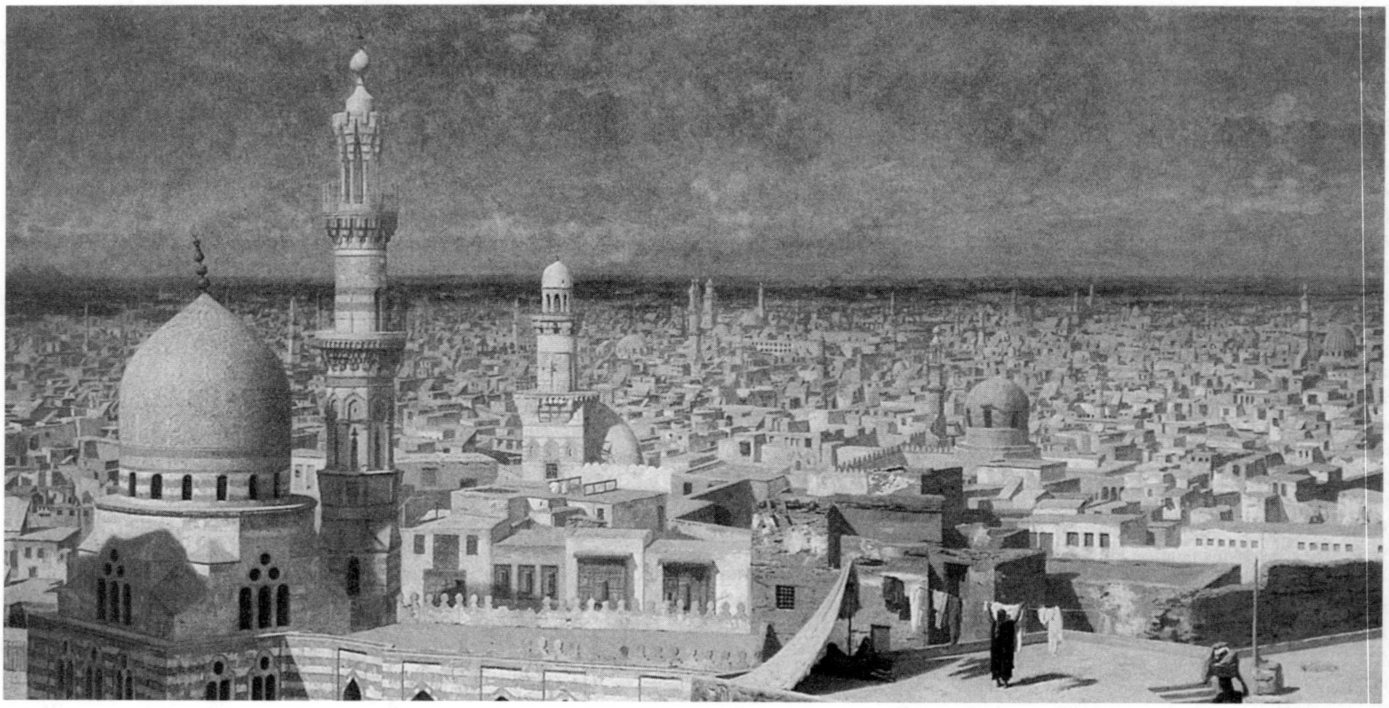

View of Cairo, oil on canvas, sgn, 28x51", C-NY 10/25/89, $550,000

GEROME, Jean Leon; circle of (French, 1824-1904)
Awakening in the Harem (kneeling nude), oil on canvas, 21x26", C-E 2/21/89 OE **17,600**

GEROME, Jean Leon; studio of (French, 1824-1904)
Cock Fight (two draped nudes with two gamecocks), oil on canvas, 16x22", SBY 6/1/89 UE **12,650**

GEROMEX, F.
Port St Denis, oil on canvas, sgn/inscr, 9x22", C-E 6/28/88 UE **198**

GERRY, Samuel Lancaster (American, 1813-1891)
Coastal Pastures, Marblehead (rocky shore, sailing ships beyond); oil on canvas, 9x18", RWS 5/19/88 .... **1,100**
Cows Watering (landscape), oil on canvas, sgn, 12x20", SBY 1/24/89 .... **2,310**
Hudson River Scene (mountains & waterfalls), oil on canvas, sgn/dtd 1855, 35x28", DM 3/14/88 .... **1,200**
In the Mountains, oil on canvas, sgn, 14x10", RAB 8/8/89 UE **700**
Madison Falls, New Hampshire; oil on canvas, sgn, 18x12", RWS 2/22/89 .... **800**

GERVAIS, Paul Jean (French, 1859-1936)
Bacchanale (orgy), oil on canvas, unfr, 86x145" SBY 2/22/89 .... **26,400**

GERVELLI
Blue Mosque Cairo, watercolor on paper, sgn, 18x11", C-E 5/23/88 .... **1,210**

GERVEX, Henri (French, 1852-1929)
Elegant Man on a Terrace, oil on canvas, sgn/dtd 85, 46x36", C-NY 10/25/89 49,500
GERZSO, Gunther (Mexican, 1915-)
Amarillo-Azul-Verde (Yellow-Blue-Green, composition), oil on masonite, sgn, 1974, 22x23", C-NY 11/21/89 28,600
Azul-Blanco-Verde (Blue-White-Green, composition), oil on masonite, sgn/dtd 1982, 13x18", C-NY 11/21/89 24,200
Azul-Rojo-Verde-Amarillo (abstract), acrylic on paper, sgn/dtd 77/titled, 23x19", C-NY 5/17/89 OE 16,500
Azul-Verde-Ocre (abstract), oil on masonite, sgn/dtd 70/titled, 22x32", C-NY 11/21/88 30,800
Mythology (abstract), oil on canvas, sgn/dtd 61/titled, 21x32", SBY 11/21/88.......... 14,300
White Woman (abstract), oil on masonite, sgn/dtd 61, 26x20", SBY 11/21/88 13,200
GESINUS-VISSER, Bob
Le Port, oil on canvas, sgn, 32x39", C-E 5/13/88 660
GESNE, see De Gesne
GESSI, Giovanni Francesco; att (Italian, 1588-1649)
Martyred Innocents, oil on canvas, 27x35", SBY 10/13/89 4,400
GESSI, Giovanni Francesco; school of (Italian, 1588-1649)
Lucretia (half-length portrait), oil on canvas, 37x29", C-NY 4/6/89 1,430
GESSNITZER, T.C. (German, 19th C)
Pair: Dutch Canal Scenes; oil on canvas, sgn, 22x27", MG 10/28/88 2,600
GEST, Margaret Ralston
City, oil on canvas, sgn, 38x28", C-E 10/18/89 OE 2,420
GETMAN, William (American, 1917-1972)
Abstract, oil on canvas, sgn, 32x38", C-SK 11/10/88 200
GEZA, Peske
Young Girl with Dog, oil on canvas, sgn, 36x40", C-E 10/25/88 1,320
GHENDINI (20th C)
Don Quixote, acrylic on board, sgn, 24x29", LH 9/10/89.......... 170
GHEZZI, Guiseppe; att (Italian, 1634-1721)
Sacrifice of Iphigenia, oil on canvas, 68x88", C-NY 4/8/88.......... 19,800
GHIGLION-GREEN, Maurice (French, 1913-)
Sur la Colline, oil on paper laid down on board, sgn, 7x10", C-E 5/9/89 1,045
GHIKAS, Panos George
Red & Blue Abstraction, oil on canvas, sgn/dtd 52, 48x37", C-E 11/14/89 OE.......... 2,860
GHIRLANDAIO, Ridolfo (Italian, 1483-1561)
Portrait of Young Lady, half-length, wearing a black & white dress by window; oil on panel, 24x20", C-NY 1/11/89 OE 19,800
GHIRLANDAIO, Ridolfo; manner of (Italian, 1483-1561)
Portrait of a Young Man, oil on panel, 16x9", WD 1/25/89 OE 2,200
GHISLANDI, Vittore; circle of (Italian, ca 1632-1683)
Portrait of a Cleric, oil on canvas, 29x24", SBY 4/7/88 5,500
GHISOLFI, Giovanni (Italian, 1632-1683)
Architectural Capriccio of Classical Ruins with Figures & Landscape Beyond, oil on canvas, unfr, 51x46", SBY 4/7/88 22,000
GHISOLFI, Giovanni; circle of (Italian, 1632-1683)
Architectural Capricco with Figures by a Harbor, oil on canvas, 38x53", C-NY 10/12/89 4,400
Pair: Architectural Capriccio of Ruins with Figures; oil on canvas, oval, 29x23", SBY 4/7/88 OE 8,250
GHISOLFI, Giovanni; follower of (Italian, 1632-1683)
Classical Ruins with Figures, oil on canvas, 30x37", SBY 10/21/88 OE.......... 9,900
GHISOLFI, Giovanni; manner of (Italian, 1632-1683)
Classical Scene with Bathing Maidens, oil on canvas, 30x44", SBY 12/9/88.......... 1,045
GHISOLFI, Giovanni; school of (Italian, 1632-1683)
Pair: Architectural Ruins with Figures; oil on canvas, hexagonal, 19x26", C-NY 10/20/88 OE.......... 8,250
GHIZE, see De Ghize
GIACHI, E. (Italian, 19th C)
Monk Singing, oil on canvas, sgn, 12x9", C-E 4/7/88 UE.......... 220
GIACOMETTI, Alberto (Swiss, 1901-1966)
Annette Debout, blue ballpoint pen on paper, sgn/dtd 1959, 15x10", SBY 11/12/88 49,500
Diego dans l'Atelier (sketch of Diego in the studio), oil on canvas, sgn/dtd 1954, 46x31", SBY 11/15/89 OE..........3,190,000
Double-Sided: Standing Nude; Sketch of Interior; pencil on paper, sgn, 8x5", SBY 11/16/89 OE.......... 47,300
Femme s'Appuyante (Etude pour Pomme Endormie), pen/ink on paper, sgn, 9x8", C-NY 2/18/88 10,450
Medallion, Tree, & Chandelier; red ballpoint pen on paper, ca 1960, 15x22", SBY 10/6/89 11,000
Nature Morte avec Fruit, pencil on paper, sgn, ca 1954, 20x14", SBY 11/12/88 OE 38,500
Portrait de Diego, pencil on BFK Rives paper, sgn, 20x13", SBY 11/16/89 OE.......... 68,750
Portrait of a Woman (Bella Kransne), pencil on BFK Rives paper, sgn/dtd 1953, 20x13", SBY 5/11/88 OE.......... 45,100
Standing Couple, black crayon on paper laid down on board, sgn/dtd 1949, 20x13", WD 5/5/88 OE 16,500
Studies of Heads, red/black pen on outside covers of Le Mecure de France, sgn/inscr, 1964, 9x11", SBY 5/10/89 OE.......... 68,750
Teapot (still life sketch), pencil on BFK Rives paper, sgn/dtd 1963, 20x13", SBY 5/11/88.......... 27,500
Tete d'Homme (head study), blue ballpoint pen on newspaper, 12x9", C-NY 10/5/89 8,800
Tete d'Homme (sketch of man's head), ballpoint pen on paper, sgn/dtd 1963, 20x13", SBY 5/10/89.......... 27,500
Walking Man (sketch), pencil on paper, sgn/dtd 1950, 25x19", SBY 5/11/88.......... 24,200
GIACOMUCCI, (Italian, 19th C)
Herding the Livestock, oil on canvas, sgn, 26x39", B/B 1/11/89 385
GIAMPETRINO
Salome with the Head of Saint John the Baptist, oil on panel, 20x26", C-NY 1/11/89 13,200

GIANGIANNI (Italian, 19th/20th C)
Marina of Capri, watercolor, sgn, ca 1911, 5x7", LH 10/16/88 OE ... **400**
GIANI, Feliceo; att (Italian, 1760-1823)
Diana & Endymion, oil on paper laid down on board, 21x15", C-NY 4/6/89 OE ... **39,600**
GIANNI, Gian (Italian, 19th C)
Pair: Grand Harbor; Malta; oil on board, 1 sgn/dtd 1879, 10x19", SBY 6/8/88 ... **5,500**
Pair: The Bay of Naples; oil on canvas, sgn/dtd 1867, 30x41", SBY 10/24/89 ... **11,000**
GIANNI, M. (Italian, 19th C)
Pair: View of the Bay of Naples; On the Amalfi Drive; gouache, sgn, 5x13", C-E 10/26/89 ... **715**
View of Naples with Vesuvius Beyond, gouache, sgn, 10x14", C-E 10/26/89 ... **935**
GIAQUINTO, Corrado (Italian, 1703-1765)
Adoration of the Magi, oil on canvas, ca 1750, 60x45", SBY 6/1/89 OE ... **253,000**
Pair: Ruth the Gleaner; Rebecca the Shepherdess; oil on canvas, 15x19", SBY 4/7/89 ... **38,500**
GIAQUINTO, Corrado; att (Italian, 1703-1765)
Moses Striking Water From the Rock, oil on canvas, arched top, unfr, 30x16", C-NY 4/8/88 ... **6,820**
GIAQUINTO, Corrado; circle of (Italian, 1703-1765)
Venus Appearing to Aeneas in the Guise of a Huntress, oil on canvas, 77x50", SBY 6/1/89 UE ... **12,100**
GIARDIELLO, J. (Italian, 19th/20th C)
Children Playing Cards on the Seashore, oil on canvas, sgn, 18x26", C-E 2/21/89 OE ... **7,150**
Pillared Veranda Overlooking Capri, oil on canvas, sgn, 20x29", C-E 10/25/88 ... **1,540**
GIBBS, George (American, 1870-1942)
Marigolds (woman tending flower beds), pastel on mounted paper, sgn, 33x22", RWS 5/12/89 ... **3,250**
GIBERT, Jean Amedee (French, 1869-)
Le Villa Medicis (landscape), oil on canvas, sgn/dtd 1903, 11x16", B/B 9/14/89 UE ... **440**
GIBSON, Charles Dana (American, 1867-1944)
Confrontation, pen/ink laid down on board, sgn, 20x21", C-E 6/1/88 ... **1,430**
Council of War in the Days To Come, pencil/pen/ink on paper, sgn, 19x27", B/B 5/17/89 ... **1,980**
I Often Wonder Why You Never Got Married, pen/black ink/pencil on paper laid down on board, sgn, 19x29", C-NY 9/30/88 ... **4,400**
I Often Wonder Why You Never Got Married, pen/ink/pencil on paper laid down on paper, sgn, 19x29", C-E 2/1/89 UE ... **1,100**
In the Meantime, Plate 9 From the Education of Mr Pipp; pencil/pen/ink on paper, sgn, 18x30", B/B 10/9/88 OE ... **5,500**
Letter (woman seated in an interior), oil on canvas, sgn, 22x26", SBY 6/24/88 UE ... **1,650**
Ride Through Central Park Zoo, pen/ink/pencil on buff paper, sgn, 18x27", C-NY 5/26/88 ... **4,400**
GIBSON, George (American, 1810-1860)
Pair: Scenes in the Wilderness (Civil War); watercolor on paper, sgn/inscr, 17x11", C-E 5/27/88 ... **385**
GIEBERICH, Oscar H. (American, 1886-)
Windy Day, windblown trees near white house w/water beyond; oil on canvas, sgn, 18x24", RAB 8/8/89 UE ... **350**
GIES, Joseph W. (American, 1860-1935)
Lady Playing a Mandolin, oil on canvas, sgn/inscr/dtd 89, 16x13", SBY 6/8/88 ... **2,090**
Quiet Contemplation (woman sits in garden, man on steps beyond), oil on canvas, sgn, 30x23", RWS 5/19/88 ... **2,200**
Woman & Dog Seated Beside a Fence in Spring Landscape, oil on canvas, sgn, 17x14", SLK 5/9/88 ... **450**
GIFFORD, Charles Henry (American, 1839-1904)
Cuttyhuck Island, Massachusetts, in 1971; oil on canvas, 11x17", RAB 11/24/89 ... **11,000**
Dunluce Castle, County of Antrim, Ireland (coastal seascape); oil on canvas, sgn/dtd 1881, 26x44", RAB 8/8/89 OE ... **18,000**
Fishing Off Gay Head, watercolor on paper, sgn/dtd 1877, 9x11", RAB 3/27/89 ... **2,750**
Fishing Village, oil on canvas, sgn/dtd 79, RAB 8/8/89 OE ... **4,500**
Fishing Village (activity on beach), oil on canvas, sgn/dtd 1979, 6x10", small hole in canvas, RAB 8/9/88 ... **3,200**
Fishing Village (busy water scene, village & cliffs beyond), oil on canvas, sgn/dtd 79, 6x10", RAB 8/9/88 ... **3,200**
Highland Light North Truro Cape Cod, oil on canvas, sgn, 9x15", RAB 11/24/89 UE ... **1,250**
Hurricane Watch (stormy coastal scene w/figures & cottage), oil on canvas, sgn/dtd 97, 18x30", RWS 3/31/88 ... **8,250**
New Bedford Harbor (seascape w/ships), oil on canvas, sgn/dtd 1858, 17x25", RAB 8/8/89 OE ... **8,250**
Storm Clearing-Elizabeth Islands; oil on canvas, sgn/dtd May 1871, 16x25", RAB 8/8/89 OE ... **15,000**
Sunrise, Coast of Maine; oil on canvas, sgn/dtd 1876, unfr, 9x14", RAB 8/9/88 ... **5,750**
GIFFORD, Charles Henry; att (American, 1839-1904)
Shipwreck (most likely a study for a larger work), oil on canvas, 12x20", RAB 11/24/89 UE ... **450**
GIFFORD, John (British, 19th C)
At the End of the Day (dogs, dead rabbits & birds in a landscape), oil on canvas, sgn, unfr, 50x40", SBY 6/10/88 ... **5,500**
Day's Bag (hunting dogs resting in a landscape), oil on canvas, sgn, 50x40", C-NY 10/25/89 ... **5,500**
Highland Shooting, The Day's Bag (dogs & dead birds in a landscape); oil on canvas, sgn, 50x40", SBY 6/9/89 ... **6,600**
GIFFORD, Robert Swain (American, 1840-1905)
European Fishing Boat, watercolor on paper laid down on mat, initialed, 2x4", RAB 8/8/89 ... **300**
Lone Tree in an Autumn Field, oil on canvas, sgn/dtd 89, 18x26", B/B 6/15/89 ... **3,300**
Ocean Sunset, oil on board, sgn/dtd 62, 4x9", RAB 8/8/89 OE ... **2,100**
On the Lagoon, Venice; oil on canvas laid down on masonite, sgn/dtd 1880, 24x40", SBY 6/28/89 ... **2,860**
GIFFORD, Sanford Robinson (American, 1823-1880)
Constantinople, oil on canvas, initialed/dtd 1869, 7x12", SBY 5/25/88 UE ... **12,100**
Hound in the Woods, oil on canvas, 16x11", C-E 2/1/89 ... **2,420**
In the Wilderness, Twilight; oil on canvas, sgn/dtd 1861, 12x22", SBY 5/25/88 ... **363,000**
La Riviera di Ponete, Genoa; oil on canvas, initialed/inscr Rome, 10x14", SBY 5/24/89 ... **13,200**
On the Bronx River, oil on canvas, sgn twice/dtd 1862, 12x10", SBY 5/25/88 ... **13,750**
Summer Verandah (view of lake & hills w/figures), oil on canvas, sgn/dtd 62, 5x9", C-NY 12/2/88 OE ... **46,200**
Tombs of the Mamluks, Cairo; oil on canvas, ca 1870s, 12x26", C-NY 5/25/89 ... **110,000**

GIFFORD, Sanford Robinson; att (American, 1823-1880)
Coastal Scene, oil on canvas, bears signature, no size given, FAP 11/4/88 UE 550

GIGLI, R. (Italian, 19th C)
Arch of Constantine, Rome; watercolor over traces of pencil, sgn, 30x21", C-E 10/26/89 2,420
Peasants on a Path, watercolor on paper, sgn, 18x12", C-E 11/8/88 320
Roman Forum, watercolor, sgn, 14x21", C-E 10/26/89 1,870
Tourists Taking In the Sights at the Forum, Rome; watercolor, sgn, 20x14", C-E 10/26/89 1,320

GIGNOUX, Regis Francois (American/French, 1816-1882)
American Landscape (Majesty of the Mountains), oil on canvas, sgn, 36x50", SBY 5/24/89 UE 34,100
Ice Harvesting, oil on canvas, sgn, 9x13", C-NY 9/30/88 7,700
Indian Summer, oil on canvas, sgn/dtd 1855, 39x56", SBY 5/25/88 22,000
Niagara Falls in the Winter, oil on panel, 23x30", B/B 1/11/89 2,475
West Point (coastal view w/figures, boats & mountains beyond), oil on canvas, sgn, painted oval, 20x24", C-NY 9/28/89 7,150

GIHON, Clarence Montfort (American, 1871-1929)
Bal du Quatorze Jullet, Boulevard du Montparnasse; oil on board, sgn/dtd 1921, 9x11", SBY 1/24/89 2,530
La Cite et le Pont Neuf (river landscape w/bridge & city beyond), oil on board, sgn, 9x11", C-E 2/1/89 OE 3,300
La Maisonde Jeanne d'Are a Chinon dans la Touraine (Indre-et-Lorie), oil on board, sgn, 9x11", C-E 2/1/89 1,320

GILBERT, Alfred (British, 1854-)
Vanity (woman looking in the mirror), watercolor/gouache, sgn/dtd 1908, 25x15", C-NY 10/25/89 2,200

GILBERT, Arthur (British, 1819-1895)
Forest Interior, oil on canvas, sgn, 12x23", RAB 8/9/88 650
Moonlight Off the Irish Coast, oil on canvas, sgn, 14x20", WD 3/23/88 1,100
Mountain Glade, oil on canvas, sgn, 13x23", RAB 8/9/88 600

GILBERT, Arthur Hill (American, 1894-)
Cloudy Day on the Seine, oil on canvas, sgn/dtd 1927, 32x40", B/B 10/6/88 OE 18,700
Doud's Hill, Big Sur (landscape); oil on canvas, sgn, 25x30", SBY 3/17/88 OE 2,640

GILBERT, C. Ivar (American, 20th C)
Floral Still Life, gouache on paper, sgn, 15x22", RAB 3/27/89 UE 150
Going a Mile Down in the Grand Canyon (horses descending path), oil on canvas, sgn, 30x32", WD 10/5/88 UE 1,800

GILBERT, John (British, 1817-1897)
Ferdinand & the Spirits (taken from Tempest, Act I, Scene II), watercolor/gouache, sgn, 19x15", C-E 5/22/89 770

GILBERT, Victor Gabriel (French, 1847-1933)
At the Flower Market, oil on canvas, sgn, 19x15", C-NY 10/25/89 15,400
Au Marche, oil on canvas, sgn, 29x24", SBY 5/23/89 13,200
Au Marche aux Fleurs, oil on canvas, sgn, 19x15", C-NY 5/25/88 11,550
Lady in a Garden, pastel on paper, sgn/dtd 1887, 36x29", C-NY 10/25/89 55,000
Le Gouter des Enfants, oil on canvas, sgn/dtd 1922, 22x26", SBY 2/22/89 14,300

GILCHRIST, Philip Thomas (British, 1865-1956)
An Artist's Dog, oil on canvas, 24x22", SBY 7/12/89 UE 990
Nearing Port, oil on canvas, sgn/dtd 04, 24x36", SBY 7/12/89 3,300

GILCHRIST, William Wallace Jr. (American, 1879-1926)
Coast of Maine, watercolor/pencil/gouache on paper, sgn, 19x13", RWS 11/3/88 UE 700
In Her Boudoir (interior scene/charcoal sketch on reverse), oil on canvas, sgn/dtd 1918, 24x19", C-NY 5/25/89 28,600
Kindergarden, oil on canvasboard, initialed, 8x14", C-NY 5/26/88 OE 11,000
Portrait of Artist's Daughter (girl along woodland path), oil on canvas, artist's estate stamp, 84x46", RWS 9/29/88 OE 7,000
Quahog Bay, Maine; watercolor/pencil/gouache on paper, sgn, 20x13", RWS 11/3/88 UE 500
Studio Interior, 1920; oil on canvas, sgn/dtd 20, 28x36", C-NY 5/26/88 35,200
Vitiv Kirk, Wien (view of St Stephen's Cathedral in morning mist); pencil on paper, sgn/dtd 1913, 14x10", RWS 9/29/88 325

GILDER, Robert Fletcher (American, 1856-1940)
Brook on a Winter's Morning, oil on canvas, sgn, 14x18", B/B 9/15/88 385
Desert Clouds, oil on canvas, sgn/inscr Tucson, 30x24", C-E 11/8/88 UE 700

GILE, Seldon Conner (American, 1877-1947)
Green Meadows & Barns, oil on canvas, sgn/dtd 14, 11x14", B/B 10/6/88 6,050

GILES, Geoffrey Douglas (British, 1857-1923)
Rose Bird Jockey Up, oil on panel, sgn/dtd X3, 11x14", C-E 11/8/88 715

GILES, R.H. (British, 19th C)
Study of Two Young Girls, watercolor, sgn, 14x11", FB 5/28/89 UE 600

GILL, Edmund (British, 1820-1894)
Landscape at Noon, oil on panel, sgn/dtd twice, 1847, inscr, 12x17", C-E 5/23/88 2,750

GILLABOZ, see De Gillaboz

GILLEMANS, Jan Pauwel the elder (Flemish, 1618-1675)
Garland of Fruits Hanging From Blue Ribbon, oil on canvas, sgn, unfr, 13x15", SBY 4/7/88 9,900
Still Life of Fruit, Lobster, Fish, & Meat Pie w/Birds, & 3 Statues in Niches; oil on canvas, sgn, 25x28", SBY 4/7/88 OE 33,000
Still Life with a Swag of Fruit Including Grapes & Other Fruits Hanging From an Urn, sgn/1656, 26x34", SBY 4/4/89 OE 16,500

GILLESPIE, Gregory (American, 1936-)
Back to School, oil on paper laid down on panel, sgn/dtd 1971, 11x15", C-NY 3/11/88 3,520
Three People in a Courtyard, oil on panel, 7x6", C-NY 6/17/89 OE 8,800

GILLIG, Jacob (Dutch, 1636-1701)
Bass on a Ledge, oil on panel, 16x13", C-NY 10/20/88 1,650
Still Life of a Barrel of Fish, oil on panel, 12x16", SBY 6/8/88 OE 2,860

GILLOT, Claude (French, 1673-1722)
Clown Holding a Tambour, pen/brown ink/red wash, 6x4", C-NY 1/12/88 OE **3,850**
GILPIN, Sawrey (British, 1733-1807)
Master of the Hounds on a Gray Hunter, oil on canvas, sgn/indistinctly dtd, 20x24", SBY 6/9/89 ..... **11,000**
Saddled Gray Hunter with a Caballero in a Mountainous Landscape, oil on canvas, 25x29", SBY 6/9/89 ..... **11,000**
GIMENO, Andres (Spanish, 1879-)
Bullfight, oil on panel, indistinctly sgn/dtd 1905, 9x11", C-E 10/25/88 ..... **1,320**
GIMIGNANI, Ludovico; circle of (Italian, 1643-1697)
Venus Restaining Mars From Killing Adonis, oil on canvas, 26x30", SBY 4/7/89 OE **8,800**
GINGRAS, Gilles (Canadian, 1932-)
Brome, oil on canvas, sgn/dtd 1986, 16x20", FB 10/30/89 ..... **770**
Le Vent (The Wind), oil on canvas, sgn/dtd 1977, 20x30", FB 10/17/88 ..... **650**
Riviere du Nord, oil on canvas, sgn/dtd 1984, 20x24", FB 10/17/88 ..... **900**
GINOUX, F.E. (19th C)
Mandan Village, sgn twice/titled/inscr Indian Scene on the Upper Missouri, 30x46", SBY 3/17/88 OE **1,210**
GIOJA, Belisario (Italian, 1829-1906)
Entertainment in the Harem, oil on canvas laid down on masonite, sgn, 36x54", SBY 2/22/89 ..... **88,000**
Painting Lesson, watercolor heightened w/gouache over traces of pencil, sgn/inscr, 21x14", C-NY 10/26/88 ..... **2,750**
Ready To Draw, watercolor on paper, sgn, 16x23", C-E 5/23/88 ..... **715**
GIONO, Wilson Brandao (20th C)
Full-Bloom (abstract), oil on canvas, sgn twice/dtd NYC 88 twice/titled, 48x36", C-NY 5/17/89 ..... **3,300**
GIORDANO, Felice (Italian, 1880-)
Seaside Villa, oil on canvas, sgn, 24x30", SBY 7/12/89 ..... **1,760**
GIORDANO, Luca (Italian, 1632-1705)
Adoration of the Shepherds, black chalk/gray wash, 17x12", SBY 1/13/89 UE **4,000**
Europa & the Bull, oil on canvas, 54x72", C-NY 1/15/88 ..... **22,000**
Martydom of Saint Placido, oil on canvas, unfr, 27x15", SBY 4/7/88 OE **10,450**
Philosopher, oil, 39x35", WD 1/25/89 OE **42,500**
Stoic Philosopher (in profile, half-length), oil on canvas, 44x34", C-NY 5/31/89 ..... **12,100**
Virgin Appearing to Cardinal, oil on canvas, sgn, 54x77", SBY 6/3/88 ..... **22,000**
GIORDANO, Luca; & Studio (Italian, 1632-1705)
Finding of Moses, oil on canvas, 49x59", SBY 10/21/88 OE **25,300**
GIORDANO, Luca; att (Italian, 1632-1705)
Biblical Sacrifice, en grisaille/oil on canvas, unfr, 36x23", C-NY 6/2/88 ..... **8,800**
Temptation of Christ, oil on canvas, 39x33", SBY 6/3/88 OE **11,000**
GIORDANO, Luca; manner of (Italian, 1632-1705)
Bethsheba, oil on panel, bears indistinct signature, 30x21", WD 1/25/89 ..... **6,250**
GIORDANO, Luca; school of (Italian, 1632-1705)
Bacchic Figure, oil on canvas, a fragment, unfr, 19x16", C-NY 10/20/88 UE **440**
GIOVA, Benedetto (Italian)
Religious Scene, oil on canvas, sgn, 30x41", FB 5/28/89 ..... **800**
GIOVANE, Palma; att (Italian, 16th C)
Saint John the Baptist in the Wilderness, oil on canvas, 26x32", SBY 7/12/89 ..... **4,950**
GIOVANE, Palma; circle of (Italian, 16th C)
Dead Christ with a Saint, oil on canvas, 30x24", C-E 4/7/88 UE **220**
GIOVANNI, Girolamo de Benenuto; see Di Giovanni
GIOVANNI, Migliara; att (1785-1837)
View of Venice with Santa Maria Della Salute at the Right, oil on canvas, 7x11", SBY 10/13/89 OE **18,700**
GIPS, Cornelis
Extensive Canal with a Windmill, oil on tin, sgn/dtd 1869, 10x12", C-E 10/25/88 ..... **1,045**
GIRARD, Marie Fermin; see Firmin-Girard
GIRARDET, Edouard Henri (Swiss, 1819-1880)
Knitting Lesson, oil on canvas, sgn/dtd 1873, 19x15", lot 394, B/B 6/9/88 ..... **6,600**
Knitting Lesson (peasant couple in interior), oil on canvas, sgn/dtd 1873, 19x15", lot 4558, B/B 9/14/89 ..... **1,650**
Women in a Forest, oil on canvas, sgn, 14x34", B/B 12/8/88 ..... **825**
GIRARDET, Eugene Alexis (French, 1853-1907)
Almeh, oil on canvas, sgn, 26x36", SBY 5/23/89 ..... **44,000**
Caravanes de Sel dans le Desert, oil on canvas, sgn, 20x40", SBY 2/22/89 OE **77,000**
Cheikhet son Ane, oil on panel, sgn, 16x10", SBY 10/24/89 ..... **7,700**
GIRARDOT (French, 19th/20th C)
Polo Player, oil on panel, sgn/dtd 1902, 13x9", SBY 6/10/88 ..... **2,475**
GIRIN, David Eugene (French, 1848-1917)
Le Printemps, oil on canvas, sgn, 26x21", SBY 5/23/89 ..... **13,200**
GIRODET-TRIOSON, Ann Louis; studio of (French, 1767-1824)
Theseus & Ariadne, oil on canvas, bears signature, 88x69", SBY 6/1/89 UE **23,100**
GIROGIONE, school of
David with Head of Goliath, oil on panel, unfr, 39x30", C-NY 4/6/89 UE **2,200**
GIROUST, Jean Antoine Theodore (1753-1817)
Group Portrait of Mademoiselle d'Orleans, Receiving Harp Lesson From Contesse de Genlis...; oil, 98x73", C-M 6/16/89 ..... **521,585**
GIRTEN, Thomas; att (British, 1775-1802)
Landscape with Country Church, watercolor, sgn/dtd 1801, 9x13", LH 12/4/88 ..... **300**

GISSING, Roland (Canadian, 1895-1967)

Distant Mountains, watercolor, sgn, 12x14", WAD 6/12/89 UE 300
Rocky Mountain View, oil on board, sgn, 12x16", WAD 11/30/89 850
Spray Lakes Valley (Near Banff), oil on board, sgn/dtd 1926, 18x20", WAD 11/30/89 450

GISSON, Andre (French, 1910-)

Arc de Triomphe, oil on canvas, sgn, 24x36", C-NY 2/13/89 3,850
At the Gallery (two ladies seated in front of paintings), oil on canvas, sgn, 20x24", SBY 10/7/89 6,600
Aux Bords de la Riviere, oil on canvas, sgn/dtd 58, 9x12", C-NY 2/13/89 1,650
Boating Pond (figures in landscape), oil on canvas, sgn, 24x30", SBY 2/14/89 OE 7,425
Carousel, oil on canvas, sgn, 16x20", B/B 3/22/89 3,575
Dans le Parc, oil on canvas, sgn, 20x16", C-NY 2/13/89 2,420
European Street Scene, oil on canvas, sgn, 24x36", LH 5/15/88 2,200
Figures in a Landscape, oil on canvas, sgn, 9x12", B/B 3/22/89 19,870
Figures in a Meadow, oil on canvas, sgn, 12x16", DM 10/14/88 2,250
Figures on a Beach, oil on canvas, sgn, 16x20", B/B 6/15/89 2,200
Figures on a Seashore, oil on canvas, sgn, 20x24", B/B 3/22/89 4,400
Jeune Fille, oil on canvas, sgn, 12x16", C-NY 2/13/89 1,870
L'Arc de Triomphe, oil on canvas, sgn, 20x16", B/B 10/9/88 1,760
La Madeleine a Paris (busy street scene), oil on canvas, sgn, 13x16", C-E 11/17/88 3,080
Landscape, oil on canvas, sgn, 24x36", FB 5/28/89 1,900
Lily Pond, oil on canvas, sgn, 10x12", SBY 10/7/89 2,200
Mere et Enfant dans la Campagne, oil on canvas, sgn, 9x12", C-E 5/13/88 OE 4,620
Merry-Go-Round at an Amusement Park, oil on canvas, sgn, 23x35", B/B 3/22/89 2,200
Mother & Child, oil on canvas, sgn, 12x16", FAP 11/4/88 OE 2,700
Mother & Child at a Carnival, oil on canvas, sgn, 20x24", SBY 10/7/89 3,300
Notre-Dame de Paris (busy street scene), oil on canvas, sgn, 12x16", C-E 11/17/88 1,320
Nude (three-quarter length, viewed from behind, in a landscape), oil on canvas, sgn, 14x11", LH 9/10/89 1,500
Pair: L'Arc de Triomphe; Parisian Street Scene; oil on canvas, sgn, 12x16", SBY 10/5/88 2,475
Pair: Le Pont Alexandre III; La Rive Gauche a Paris; oil on canvas, sgn, 12x16", C-NY 2/13/89 OE 2,860
Paris Scene, oil on canvas, sgn, 12x24", lot 309, LH 10/16/88 UE 750
Paris Scene, oil on canvas, sgn, 12x24", lot 316, LH 10/16/88 900
Paris Scene, oil on canvas, sgn, 24x12", lot 310, LH 10/16/88 UE 550
Paris Street Scene, oil on canvas, sgn, 24x36", lot 381, FB 5/28/89 2,500
Paris Street Scene, oil on canvas, sgn, 24x36", lot 411, C-E 5/23/88 2,640
Paris Street Scene (Arc de Triomphe in distance), oil on canvas, sgn, 12x40", lot 189, RAB 8/9/88 UE 1,600
Portrait of Girl in Landscape (in profile), oil on canvas, sgn, 9x12", SBY 10/7/89 2,200
Rue de Paris (street scene), oil on canvas, sgn, 12x24", C-E 5/9/89 3,080
Sitting on the Banks of the River (figure in landscape), oil on canvas, sgn, 16x20", SBY 2/14/89 OE 4,400
Still Life of Three Vases with Flowers, oil on canvas, sgn, 20x24", B/B 10/9/88 4,400
Street Scene Paris (impressionistic), oil on canvas, sgn, 24x36", S/A 3/12/88 2,700
Sunday in the Park, oil on canvas, sgn, 30x24", B/B 4/20/88 2,200
Sur la Plage (at the beach), oil on canvas, sgn, 24x30", C-NY 2/13/89 2,860
Vase of Flowers, oil on canvas, sgn, 14x10", B/B 5/17/89 605
Waders in Kennebunkport, oil on canvas, 11x14", B/B 12/8/88 3,300
Walking on the Beach (figures on beach, extensive view of cloudy sky), oil on canvas, sgn/dtd 63, 24x30", B/B 9/14/98 1,650
Woman on a Flower-Adorned Veranda, oil on canvas, sgn, 16x20", B/B 10/9/88 1,980
Young Girl in Park, oil on canvas, sgn, 16x20", FAP 11/4/88 OE 2,600

GIUNTA, Joseph (Canadian, 1911-)

Autumn, Quebec; oil on board, sgn/dtd 1971, 24x20", FB 10/30/89 3,190
Bonsecours Market, Montreal; oil on board, sgn, 24x20", FB 10/30/89 1,650
Forest Scene with River, oil on canvas, sgn, 20x24", FB 5/28/89 1,300
January, Laurentians, Quebec; oil on board, sgn, 12x16", lot 234, FB 10/30/89 935
January, Laurentians, Quebec; oil on board, sgn, 12x16", WAD 6/12/89 375
Paris Canal Scene, oil on board, sgn, 8x10", lot 77, FB 10/30/89 660
Paris Street Scene, oil on board, sgn, 8x10", lot 76, FB 10/30/89 OE 825
Place Jacques Cartier, oil on board, sgn/dtd 1952-53, 20x24", FB 5/28/89 OE 4,200
Still Life, oil on board, sgn/dtd 1962, 20x24", FB 10/17/88 OE 5,000
Washing Day, oil on canvas, sgn/dtd 1930, 20x28", FB 10/30/89 990
Winter Laurentians, oil on board, sgn, 12x16", FB 10/30/89 935

GIUSIANO, Eduardo (20th C)

Passenger, acrylic on canvas, sgn/titled/dtd 1987, 32x38", SBY 5/17/88 UE 1,980

GIUSTI, Guglielo (Italian, 1824-)

Grotto di Pozzuoli, gouache, sgn, 15x11", C-E 10/25/88 880

GIUSTO, Faust (Italian, 19th C)

Place de la Republique, Paris; oil on canvas, sgn, unfr, 18x26", C-NY 2/25/88 OE 10,450
Return From the Vineyards, oil on canvas, sgn, 33x20", C-E 10/26/89 6,050

GJOEDESEN, A. (Danish, 19th/20th C)

Portrait of a Fisherman, oil on canvas, sgn/dtd 1889, 14x12", B/B 1/11/89 550

GLACKENS, William James (American, 1870-1938)

Anemones (still life), oil on canvasboard, initialed, 16x13", C-NY 5/25/89 20,900
Apples, oil on board, bears signature, 10x12", C-NY 12/2/88 OE 19,800

Art Class, pencil on buff paper, sgn, ca 1890, 11x9", C-E 2/1/89 ... 990
Asters in a Blue Vase (still life), oil on canvas, sgn, 16x12", C-NY 5/25/89 OE ... 41,800
Bathers, oil on canvas, sgn, 12x16", SBY 5/25/88 ... 71,500
Beach Scene with Boats, charcoal on paper, sgn, 5x8", SBY 9/23/88 ... 3,850
Blue Vase & Spring Flowers, oil on canvas, initialed, 26x14", C-NY 5/26/88 ... 25,300
Courtroom, pen/brush/ink/pencil/Chinese white on paper, sgn/inscr, 13x14", C-NY 3/11/88 ... 2,860
Dinner Party, pen/brush/ink/pencil/collage on paper, sgn, 12x12", C-NY 3/11/88 OE ... 2,420
Double-Sided: Washington Square; A Cafe Scene; pastel/pencil on tan paper, sgn, 10x15", C-NY 9/28/89 ... 22,000
Ferry at Samois, charcoal on paper mounted on board, sgn/inscr, 5x7", SBY 6/24/88 ... 770
Figures on a Ship Deck (sketch), pencil on paper, sgn, 12x9", C-E 6/1/89 OE ... 4,620
Figures Strolling, charcoal/tan paper laid down on board, sgn, ca 1905, 10x20", C-NY 5/25/89 ... 7,150
Gentleman's Pose, charcoal on tan paper, 9x6", C-NY 6/17/89 UE ... 770
Girl with Straw Hat (half-length portrait in profile), oil on canvas, initialed, 11x7", C-NY 5/25/89 ... 46,200
Head of a French Girl, oil on canvas, 15x12", C-NY 12/2/88 ... 27,500
Lacing Her Shoe (seated lady in red dress), oil on canvas, sgn, 13x10", C-NY 5/25/89 OE ... 104,500
Mardi Gras, brush/ink/pencil/gouache/Chinese white on board, sgn, 13x20", C-NY 5/26/88 ... 4,180
Mrs Wilson's Soothing Syrup, charcoal/ink wash/gouache on board, sgn/inscr, 11x10", C-NY 9/30/88 ... 1,760
Neantiction (surrealistic), oil on canvas, sgn, 31x24", C-NY 11/21/88 ... 22,000
Poppies, Lilies, & Blue Flower; oil on canvas, ca 1915, 18x15", SBY 5/25/88 ... 20,900
Portrait of a Young Woman (in profile), oil on canvas laid down, initialed, 13x11", C-NY 5/25/89 OE ... 18,900
Red-Haired Model (half-length nude), oil on canvas, sgn, 24x20", C-NY OE ... 93,500
Seemed To Be All Red Hair (man standing before door), ink on paper, sgn, 7x5", WL 5/20/88 UE ... 500
Still Life of Apples, oil on board, sgn, 10x12", WG 9/16/88 UE ... 6,000
Study for Family Group (impressionistic), oil on canvas, initialed, 13x18", C-NY 12/2/88 ... 27,500
Temple Gold Medal Nude (nude in interior), oil on canvas, sgn, 1924, 32x22", SBY 5/24/89 OE ... 275,000
The Boss, Inspector McCue (full-length portrait); ink wash on paper, sgn, 11x9", WL 5/20/88 ... 800
Village Disturbance, charcoal/gouache/white chalk on board, sgn, 14x22", C-NY 9/30/88 ... 4,620
Washington Square, pencil on paper, 13x14", C-NY 3/11/88 OE ... 4,180
Winter in the City, ink, sgn, 19x15", FAP 12/8/89 ... 1,150

GLANDSDORFF, Hubert (Belgian, 1877-1963)

Still Life of Roses, oil on canvas, sgn/dtd 40, 24x20", B/B 10/9/88 ... 5,500

GLANTZMAN, Judy (20th C)

Red Shorts (abstract), oil on shaped canvas, 40x34", C-NY 2/14/89 UE ... 1,100

GLARNER, Fritz (Swiss, 1899-1972)

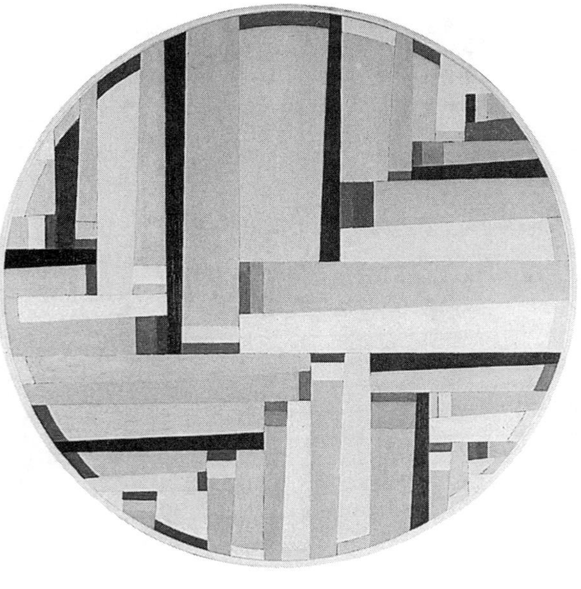

Relational Painting, Tondo #56; oil on masonite, sgn/inscr/dtd 1962, 49" dia, C-NY 11/9/88 OE, $330,000

Studies: Center-Points; Sketch for Relational Painting; sgn/dtd 46, charcoal/graphite, unfr, ea 11x9", C-NY 2/20/88 OE ... 7,700

GLASCO, Joseph (American, 1925-)

Pink Landscape, tempera/watercolor/pen/black ink on paper, sgn/dtd 1958, 11x15", C-E 11/17/88 ... 550
Standing Man, oil/pen/black ink/charcoal on paper, 24x19", C-E 11/17/88 ... 220
Two Women with a Mirror, oil/sand on canvas, sgn/dtd 1950, 56x36", C-E 11/17/88 ... 1,320

GLAUBER, Johannes (Jan)(Dutch, 1646-1726)

Arcadian Landscape with Figures, oil on canvas, 36x49", C-NY 10/12/89 ... 13,200

GLAZUNOV, Ilya (Russian, 1930-)

Ivan the Terrible (contemporary portrait), oil/collage on canvas, sgn/dtd 1974, 60x31", SBY 7/7/88 ... 56,000
Legend of the City of Kitege (contrast of mythical/skyscraper cities), oil on canvas, sgn, 1986, 78x39", SBY 7/7/88 ... 52,000
Snow Storm (Russian woman in blue coat in snowy landscape), oil on canvas, sgn/dtd 1978, 71x37", SBY 7/7/88 ... 48,000
Third Cock (contemporary red rooster at dawn in blue landscape), oil on canvas, sgn/dtd 1987, 39x57", SBY 7/7/88 ... 28,000

GLEITSMANN, Raphael (American, 1910-)
Blue Wall (contemporary depiction of a church), oil on panel, sgn/dtd 1950, 28x32", WG 9/16/88 UE 2,000
Winter Dusk, oil on board, sgn, 10x14", WG 9/16/88 600

GLEIZES, Albert (French, 1881-1953)
Composition (abstract), oil on burlap, sgn/dtd 43, 46x62", C-NY 5/12/88 68,200
Composition (abstract), oil on canvas, sgn, 1921, 29x24", C-NY 5/12/88 OE 52,800
Composition (abstract), oil on canvas, sgn/dtd 1935, unfr, 29x24", SBY 2/16/89 OE 66,000
Composition (Madonna & Child), casein on canvas, sgn/dtd 1930, 57x45", SBY 11/12/88 132,000
Composition (Peinture No 2), oil on panel, sgn twice/dtd 22/titled, 35x28", C-NY 5/12/88 50,600
Le Dejeuner, sepia/pen/black ink over pencil on paper laid down on board, sgn/dtd 08, 9x14", C-E 11/17/88 1,100
Sur une Theme de Cirque, gouache on board, sgn/dtd 14, 27x21", SBY 11/12/88 OE 126,500

GLENDENING, Alfred Augustus Jr. (British, fl 1861-1903)
Cattle & Fishermen by the Stream, oil on canvas, initialed/dtd 1869, 30x50", SBY 10/24/89 9,900
Fittleworth, Essex; oil on canvas laid down on masonite, sgn/dtd 1908, 24x42", SBY 6/8/88 4,675
Flower Market in a French Town, watercolor/gouache on paper, sgn w/monogram, dtd 1899, 24x36", C-NY 5/24/89 OE 14,300
Harvesters (shocking wheat), oil on canvas, sgn, 16x26", C-NY 2/23/89 9,900
Mill House, oil on canvas, sgn/dtd 97, 18x32", SBY 2/22/89 11,000
Pair: River Landscapes; oil on canvas, sgn/dtd 1895 & 1896, 16x12", SBY 6/8/88 OE 7,150
Summer Afternoon, oil on canvas, monogramed/dtd 1897, 18x24", C-E 2/23/88 OE 3,080
White Dove, watercolor heightened w/white, monogramed/dtd 1895, 18x9", C-NY 10/26/88 4,950

GLENN, Robert (Canadian, 1936-)
Landscape Near Lillooes, oil on boards, sgn, 8x10", FB 4/25/88 300

GLINTENKAMP, Hendrik (American, 1887-1946)
Sunset, watercolor on paper, sgn, 11x15", SBY 9/23/88 825

GLOVER, John (British, 1767-1849)
Traveler in a Rugged Mountain Landscape, oil on canvas, 30x46", SBY 12/9/88 990

GLUCKMANN, Grigory (American/Russian, 1898-)
Corps de Ballet, oil on panel, sgn, 20x26", SBY 10/5/88 4,950
Pink Leotard, oil on panel, sgn, 36x24", B/B 6/15/89 12,100
Quiet Moment, oil on board, sgn, 22x16", B/B 6/9/88 7,700
Reclining Nude, oil on panel, sgn/dtd 'Paris' 1929-30, 22x29", SBY 10/5/88 15,400

GNOLI, Domenico (Italian, 1933-1970)
Buste en Vert (woman's bust in green dress), oil/sand on canvas, sgn/dtd 1964, 36x36", SBY 6/30/88 104,000
Capigliatura Machia (a man's head of hair), oil/sand on canvas, 53x79", SBY 6/30/88 144,000

GOATER, Walter H. (American, 19th C)
Wharf Boat, Cairo, Illinois (Civil War); pen/ink on paper, initialed/inscr, unfr, 8x11", C-E 11/30/88 110

GOBERT, Pierre (French, 1662-1744)
Lady's Toilet, oil on canvas, 34x26", WD 1/25/89 OE 15,000

GOBERT, Pierre; manner of (French, 1662-1744)
Portrait of Mme Declermont, oil on canvas, 30x25", SBY 6/8/88 OE 2,310

GODARD, Gabriel (American, 1933-)
Glaneuses Bleues, oil on canvas, sgn/dtd 64, 36x29", PHL 11/15/88 800

GODCHAUX, Roger (French, 1878-)
Pair: Asters; Roses; oil on canvas, sgn, ea 59x16", SBY 2/22/89 14,300
View of Constantinople, oil on canvas, sgn, 38x59", C-NY 10/25/89 9,900

GODDARD, George Bouverie (British, 1832-1886)
Racehorse in a Landscape, oil on canvas, sgn/dtd 1861, 28x36", SBY 6/10/88 OE 15,400

GODDARD, Margaret E.
Roses in a Vase, oil on panel, sgn/dtd 1880, 14x9", C-E 11/30/88 1,540

GODOY, A.T. (American, 20th C)
Canal Street, New Orleans; oil on canvas, sgn, 21x27", MG 5/28/88 475
Haynes Boulevard on Lake Ponchartrain, New Orleans; oil on canvas, sgn, 21x27", MG 10/28/88 UE 225
On the Mississippi River Docks, oil on canvas, sgn, 21x27", MG 5/28/88 300

GODWARD, John William (British, 1861-1922)
Contemplation (portrait), oil on panel, sgn/dtd 1904, 8x5", C-NY 5/25/88 6,380

GOEBEL, Paul
Red Barn in a Landscape, oil on canvas, 13x16", C-E 2/1/89 UE 495

GOEBL-WAHL, Camilla (Austrian, 1871-1965)
Wild Flowers & Fruit Before a Window, oil on board, sgn, 23x28", B/B 6/9/88 1,760

GOENEUTTE, Norbert (French, 1854-1894)
L'Elegante (three-quarter length portrait of a woman), pencil/watercolor/gouache on paper, sgn, 18x13", SBY 5/23/89 14,300

GOERG, Edouard (French, 1893-1969)
Le Timide Amoureux se Cache dans les Fleurs, oil on canvas, sgn/dtd 48, 18x15", C-E 11/17/88 6,600

GOERLICH (American, 19th C)
Flowers & Fruit on a Marble Ledge, oil on canvas, sgn, 24x18", SBY 1/24/89 1,650

GOETZ, Henri (American, 1909-)
Abstract Compositions, pastel on board/oil on board, sgn, 11x14", 10x13", B/B 9/14/89 OE 3,575

GOHL, E.H. (American, 1862-)
Peonies in a Vase, watercolor on paper, sgn/dtd 1914, 28x23", C-E 7/26/88 UE 380

GOINGS, Ralph (American, 1928-)
Breakfast Menu (still life of condiments on restaurant table), watercolor on paper, sgn/dtd 79, 10x12" SBY 2/15/89 OE 15,400

Laundry (interior of coin-operated laundry), watercolor/graphite on paper, sgn/dtd 74, 11x15", C-NY 2/14/89 9,350
Smith's Ford Custom (parked at shopping center), watercolor on paper, sgn/dtd 74/titled, 10x14", SBY 11/11/88 OE 13,200
Sundaes-Shakes (view of drive-in at shopping center); oil on canvas, sgn twice/dtd 1972 twice, 35x48", SBY 11/11/88 OE 77,000

GOLD, Albert (American, 1906-)
Workers in a Stable Yard, oil on masonite, sgn, 22x14", SBY 9/23/88 UE 330

GOLDBERG, Glenn (American, 20th C)
Black Lantern (contemporary), oil on wood, sgn/dtd 1984, 66x49", SBY 11/19/89 OE 23,100
Black Rose (abstract line drawing), oil/enamel on wood, 1985, 66x49", SBY 5/3/89 OE 14,300
Garden (abstract), oil/enamel on wood, 1985, 96x70", C-NY 5/4/89 OE 15,400
Third Winter (abstract line drawing), oil/enamel on wood, 1985, 66x49", SBY 5/3/89 OE 14,300
Young American (abstract), oil/enamel on wood, 1985, 96x70", C-NY 5/4/89 OE 18,700
22 (soldier's helmet), acrylic/varnish/nails on masonite, sgn/dtd 1983, 14x10", C-E 11/14/89 880

GOLDBERG, Michael (American, 1924-)
Apples, oil/colored chalks/paper collage on canvas, sgn/dtd 63, unfr, 24x30", C-E 11/14/89 1,320
August 1, 1960 (abstract); oil on paper, sgn, 11x14", SBY 10/5/88 UE 715
Bourgeois Still Life (abstract), oil on canvas, sgn twice/dtd 1955, 79x62", SBY 10/8/88 OE 25,300
Flowers (abstract), oil on canvas, sgn/dtd 65, 45x40", SBY 2/14/89 4,400
Landscape, Southampton Bypass (abstract); oil on canvas, sgn/dtd 67, 45x50", C-NY 2/20/88 UE 2,860
Untitled, oil on board mounted on masonite, sgn, 14x11", C-E 5/13/88 1,650

GOLDSCHMIDT, Henrique (South American, 20th C)
Rio de Janeiro, watercolor/bodycolor, sgn, 6x8", C-SK 5/25/89 180

GOLDSMITH, Callander (English School, fl 1880-1910)
Pair: Hunt Scenes; oil on board, sgn/dtd September 25 79, 48x", MG 3/26/88 1,100

GOLDSMITH, Walter H. (British, 19th C)
Siren Playing a Lyre, oil on canvas, sgn, 30x40", WG 4/23/88 2,400

GOLDSTEIN, Jack (American, 1945-)
Untitled (abstract), acrylic on canvas, 1981, unfr, 96x72", C-NY 11/10/88 4,620
Untitled (contemporary), acrylic on canvas, 1983, unfr, 96x132", C-NY 2/14/89 8,800

GOLDTHWAIT, Harold (British, 19th/20th C)
A Wooded River Landscape, oil on canvas, sgn, 20x30", PHL 6/16/88 1,000

GOLDTHWAITE, Anne (American, 20th C)
Bermuda Pines, oil on canvas, sgn, 25x21", C-E 10/18/89 660

GOLLINGS, William Elling (American, 1878-1932)
Indian Encampment in Winter, oil on canvas, sgn, 17x20", B/B 3/17/88 8,250

GOLLMAN, Julius (German, -1898)
Departed Soul (body floating in water, dog watching from bank), oil on canvas, sgn/dtd 1862, 22x19", C-E 2/21/89 UE 330

GOLUB, Leon (American, 1922-)
Head V (contemporary), oil on canvas, sgn, ca 1961, 28x27", C-NY 5/4/89 4,180
Head XXV (abstract), oil on canvas, sgn, ca 1958, 27x24", SBY 10/8/88 6,600
Untitled (Franco), acrylic on linen, sgn/dtd 1975, 24x21", SBY 2/15/89 7,150

GOMEZ, Gabriel (Spanish, 19th C)
Mother & Child Waiting in a Vestibule, oil on panel, sgn, 11x8", B/B 6/9/88 4,125

GOMEZ Y PLASENT, Vincente
Grand Canal Venice, oil on canvas, sgn, 10x14", C-E 5/23/88 OE 6,050

GONGSHOU, Hu (Chinese, 1823-1886)
Landscape (hanging scroll), ink/color on paper, sgn, 54x15", SBY 5/31/89 990

GONTARD, R.D. (French, 19th/20th C)
Sultan's Delight, oil on canvas, sgn, 32x51", MG 6/25/88 UE 1,750

GONTIER, Pierre Camille (French, 19th C)
First Blossoms of Spring, oil on canvas, sgn, 36x29", C-NY 2/23/89 4,400

GONZAGA, Pietro (Italian, 1751-1831)
Interior of a Mausoleum, black chalk/pen/brown ink/brown wash squared in black chalk, 8x11", C-NY 1/11/89 880

GONZALES, Eva (French, 1849-1883)
Sur le Banc (wooded scene w/woman seated on bench reading), oil on canvas, sgn, ca 1878, 16x13", C-NY 5/11/89 154,000

GONZALES, Xavier (American/Mexican, 20th C)
Hong Kong, mixed media on paper, initialed, dtd 59, 27x41", LH 10/16/88 UE 100

GONZALEZ, Juan Antonio (Spanish, 1842-)
The Wait, oil on panel, sgn/dtd VI 75, 16x13", B/B 3/17/88 OE 8,250

GOODALE (American, 20th C)
Inner Passage, Alaska; oil on canvas, sgn, 16x20", B/B 12/8/88 935

GOODALL, Frederick (British, 1822-1904)
Le Bon Cure (the kind parson among the village children), oil on canvas, sgn/dtd 1845, 24x31", C-NY 5/24/89 7,700
Pair: Bedouin's Pasture; Drawing Water on the Nile; oil on canvas, sgn w/monogram, dtd 1885 & 1884, 15x36", SBY 12/9/88 3,300
Pyramids of Gizeh After Sundown, oil on canvas, sgn w/monogram, inscr/titled/dtd 1884, SBY 2/22/89 5,500

GOODALL, John Strickland (British, 1908-)
Naughty Nancy, watercolor/gouache on paper, sgn, 6x7", WL 5/20/88 400

GOODBY, Frank H. (American, 20th C)
Sailing Before the Wind, watercolor, sgn/dtd, 5x10", S/A 2/18/89 150

GOODELL, Ira Chaffee (1800-ca 1875)
Angelo Newton Goodell, Expert in Phonographic Writing; oil on canvas, 44x34", SBY 1/28/88 24,200

GOODMAN, J. Reginald
Extensive Landscape, watercolor on paper laid down on board, sgn/inscr, 14x20", C-E 5/23/88 UE **330**
GOODMAN, Robert Gwelo (British, 1871-)
Hex River Mountains, pencil/watercolor, initialed, 8x12", C-SK 11/10/88 UE **220**
GOODNOUGH, Robert (American, 1917-)
Black Shapes, oil/acrylic on canvas, sgn/dtd twice, 1969, inscr, 30x30", C-E 5/13/88 .... **825**
Cowboy #4 (cubist abstract), oil on canvas, sgn/dtd 58, 19x15", SBY 2/14/89 .... **1,320**
Double Group (two groups of geometric shapes), oil/acrylic over pencil on canvas, sgn/dtd 1979, 24x60", C-E 11/14/89 OE **5,500**
Figures (abstract), oil on canvas, sgn, 1956, 36x36", C-E 11/14/89 OE **18,700**
Flying Horses (abstract), oil on canvas, sgn, 71x59", SBY 10/7/89 OE **12,650**
Green, Blue, Gray (abstract); oil/acrylic on canvas, sgn/dtd twice 1973, 36x60", SBY 10/5/88 .... **1,320**
Movement of Horses V, oil on canvas, sgn/dtd 60 twice/titled, 20x30", C-E 5/9/89 OE **4,950**
Pastel & White (abstract), acrylic/oil on canvas, sgn/dtd 1968, 62x62", SBY 10/7/89 .... **2,530**
Pastel Movement (abstract composition), acrylic/oil on canvas, sgn/dtd 1971, 36x36", SBY 10/7/89 .... **3,300**
Pastel White, Pale Blue (abstract); acrylic/collage on canvas, sgn twice/dtd 1981, 48x64", SBY 10/5/88 .... **1,760**
Seated Woman, charcoal/pastel on paper, sgn/dtd 1973, 20x26", SBY 5/16/89 .... **7,150**
Spring Landscape, oil on canvas, sgn/dtd 56, 24x28", C-E 11/17/88 OE **3,520**
Summer I, oil on canvas, sgn, 20x20", C-E 11/17/88 OE **2,200**
Summer II (abstract), oil on canvas, sgn, 20x20", C-E 11/17/88 OE **2,420**
Summer III, oil on canvas, sgn, 20x22", C-E 11/17/88 .... **1,980**
Summer IV, oil on canvas, sgn, 22x20", C-E 11/17/88 OE **2,200**
Untitled, acrylic on canvas, sgn/dtd 57, 42x48", SBY 10/7/89 .... **1,980**
Untitled (abstract), oil on canvas, sgn/dtd 63-64, 82x106", SBY 2/14/89 OE **9,625**
Untitled (abstract), paper/canvas collage/oil on canvas, sgn, 19x18", C-E 11/17/88 OE **2,200**
Untitled (geometric composition), oil on canvas, sgn/dtd 62-63, 79" dia, SBY 10/7/89 OE **6,600**
Untitled (studies of figures), oil/pencil on paper, sgn/dtd 61, 24x18", C-E 11/14/89 OE **1,540**
Variations on a Theme VI/Green Gray; oil/acrylic on canvas, sgn/dtd 1969-70, 76x76", C-E 11/14/89 .... **3,520**
Vertical KR (abstract), acrylic/charcoal on canvas, sgn/dtd 64, 76x14", C-E 11/14/89 OE **8,800**
GOODRIDGE, Sarah (American, 1788-1853)
Portrait of a Lady, wearing blue dress w/white lace collar & comb in hair; oil on ivory, 3x3", RWS 6/10/89 UE **600**
GOODWIN, Albert (British, 1845-1932)
Backs at Cambridge, watercolor/gouache over pencil, sgn/inscr/dtd 1911, 10x15", C-NY 10/26/88 .... **14,300**
Bristol Docks, pencil/oil on paper, sgn/indistinctly inscr, 11x15", C-NY 2/25/88 OE **6,050**
Sentinel (under banyan trees), watercolor/gouache/pen/black ink on lt brown paper, sgn/inscr, 11x15", C-NY 10/26/88 .... **7,150**
Sunset, Bosham, Sussex; gouache, sgn/dtd 1917, 13x20", C-NY 10/25/89 .... **3,300**
GOODWIN, Arthur Clifton (American, 1864-1929)
Bench by the Frog Pond, Boston Common; pastel on ochre paper, sgn/dtd 07, 12x19", RWS 11/10/89 .... **16,000**
Brooklyn Bridge, charcoal/pastel on paper, sgn/dtd 26, 12x15", SBY 4/14/89 .... **1,760**
Buttress, East Cambridge Viaduct; pastel on board, sgn twice, inscr, 13x19", C-NY 9/30/88 .... **3,300**
Canton, Massachusetts; pastel on brown paper, sgn, 19x24", RWS 11/3/88 UE **800**
Central Park in Winter, oil on canvas, sgn/titled/#d G95, 30x36", SBY 5/24/89 .... **19,800**
Copley Square, Boston (cityscape), oil on canvas, sgn/titled, 30x41", RAB 8/8/89 .... **25,000**
Factory on the Neponset, pastel on board, sgn/inscr/dtd 1910, 19x24", C-NY 9/30/88 UE **1,320**
Frog Pond, Twilight; pastel on brown paper, sgn, 12x17", RWS 5/12/89 .... **2,400**
House on the Neponset River, pastel on tan paper, sgn, 21x24", RWS 5/12/89 .... **3,250**
Ladycliffe Academy, pastel on tan paper, sgn/inscr, 20x24", RWS 11/3/88 .... **1,300**
Louis Kronberg in His Studio, oil on canvas, sgn, 22x28", RWS 11/10/89 .... **15,000**
Northwest Wind, Misty Harbor Scene; pastel on tan paper, sgn twice/titled, 12x18", RWS 3/16/89 OE **4,200**
Old Chatham Hills (landscape), pastel/pencil on tan paper, sgn, 18x23", RWS 3/16/89 .... **1,900**
Our Own Doorway (landscape with houses), pastel on board, sgn, 18x22", C-E 10/18/89 UE **308**
Park Street Church in Snow (street scene), oil on canvas, sgn/dtd 1913, 25x30", C-NY 5/25/89 .... **19,800**
Quincy Market, Winter; oil on canvas, sgn, 25x30", RWS 5/12/89 .... **10,000**
Spuyten Duyvil, Upper New York; oil on canvas, sgn twice/inscr/titled, 30x36", SBY 9/23/88 .... **11,000**
Storm King Highway, pastel on tan paper, sgn/inscr, 20x24", RWS 11/3/88 .... **1,300**
T Wharf South Side Looking Towards Ames Building, pastel on tan paper, sgn, 13x20", RWS 5/12/89 .... **6,000**
Tremont Street, Pelham Hotel, Boston; oil on canvas, sgn, 22x28", C-NY 5/26/88 .... **16,500**
Washington Square, New York, in Winter (view of the arch); oil on board, sgn, 28x23", RAB 8/9/88 .... **8,500**
Wharf in Winter, Boston; oil on canvas, inscr, 14x18", RWS 5/12/89 .... **12,000**
Winter, Boylston Street at Copley Square, Boston; oil on canvas, sgn, 30x36", RWS 11/10/89 .... **25,000**
GOODWIN, Philip Russell (American, 1882-1935)
Buck in Landscape, oil on canvas, 12x16", C-E 11/30/88 .... **3,520**
Intruder, oil on canvas, sgn, 30x20", FAP 11/4/88 UE **200**
Sundown Over a Mountain Lake, oil on canvasboard, sgn, 4x8", RWS 9/8/89 .... **350**
GOODWIN, Richard Labarre (American, 1840-1910)
Autumn Landscape with Bridge, watercolor on paper, sgn, no size given, FAP 4/15/89 OE **138**
Lilacs in a Vase, oil on canvas, sgn, 24x18", C-NY 9/30/88 .... **2,200**
Still Life of Peaches, oil on canvas, sgn, 25x17", B/B 6/9/88 .... **2,200**
Strawberries, oil on canvas, sgn, 12x16", SBY 9/23/88 .... **2,530**
Study of Hanging Game & Hunting Pouch, oil on canvas, sgn/dtd 1889, 40x28", repaired, RAB 8/9/88 UE **4,750**
GORBATOFF, Constantin (Continental, 20th C)
Fishing Boats Along a Canal, View of Pskov; oil on panel, 12x13", B/B 1/11/89 .... **2,200**

GORCHOV, Ron (American, 1930-)
Study: Philosophy; oil on shaped canvas, sgn/dtd 1981, 34x44", C-E 11/17/88 .... **2,860**
Untitled #4 (abstract), oil on canvas, sgn/dtd 1-25-74, 32x24", SBY 2/15/89 .... **1,540**
GORDON, Hortense Mattice (Canadian, 1889-1961)
Garden Hat, watercolor, sgn/dtd 1942, 17x24", WAD 6/12/89 .... **180**
Merok, Norway; oil on canvasboard, sgn/dtd 55, 12x14", WAD 6/12/89 .... **225**
GORDON, John Watson; att (British, 1788-1864)
Portrait of a Young Gentleman Said To Be a Member of the Forbes Family, oil on canvas, 30x25", SBY 10/21/88 OE **5,500**
Young Artist en Plein Air, oil on canvas, 36x28", C-E 2/23/88 .... **1,210**
GORDON-FRAZER, Charles E.
Duatto, New Guinea (tropical landscape); oil on canvas, sgn, 20x16", C-SK 11/10/88 .... **3,720**
Gully, Tasmania (dense tropical landscape); oil on board, inscr, 18x14", C-SK 11/10/88 .... **4,090**
GORE, William Henry (British, 20th C)
Playmates (child & dog playing w/newspaper in an interior), oil on canvas, sgn, 25x20", C-NY 5/24/89 .... **11,000**
GORGER, Arnold Marc (Dutch, 1866-1933)
Tree-Lined Stream, oil on canvas, sgn, 30x38", LH 10/16/88 .... **4,800**
GORKA, Paul (American, 20th C)
Surrealistic View of Pigeons on Rooftop, oil on canvas, 41x60", FAP 4/15/89 .... **1,155**
GORKY, Arshile (American, 1904-1948)
Abstract (still life), oil on canvas, ca 1928, 13x35", SBY 2/15/89 .... **38,500**
Abstraction, graphite on paper, 11x8", C-NY 11/10/88 .... **5,500**
Composition, oil on canvas, ca 1946, 11x14", SBY 11/9/89 .... **55,000**
Delicate Game (abstract composition), oil on canvas, sgn/dtd 46, 34x44", SBY 5/2/89 .... **880,000**
Double-Sided: Figure Studies; India ink on paper, 5x8", lot 261, SBY 10/5/88 .... **2,200**
Double-Sided: Figure Studies; India ink on paper, 5x8", lot 260, SBY 10/5/88 .... **2,750**
Double-Sided: Figures; Horse; pen/black ink on paper, sgn, 7x5", C-E 11/14/89 .... **2,640**
Double-Sided: Portrait (recto); Still Life (verso); pencil on paper, 20x16", C-E 5/9/89 .... **5,500**
Double-Sided: Portrait of Graham; Seated Nude; pen/ink on paper, sgn/dtd 1933, 14x20", SBY 2/14/89 .... **4,675**
Double-Sided: Untitled (abstract); pencil on tan paper, 1934, 11x8", C-E 11/17/88 .... **1,980**
Family, pen/black ink on paper laid down on board, unfr, 7x5", C-E 5/9/89 OE **4,180**
Head (contemporary), oil on panel, 16x12", C-NY 2/14/89 .... **38,500**
Horse & Horse's Head, pen/black ink on paper, 6x9", C-E 5/13/88 OE **1,100**
Landscape, Gaylordsville (contemporary); oil on canvas, ca 1937, 22x18", SBY 10/5/89 .... **27,500**
Leonore Gallett Portnoff Playing a Musical Instrument, India ink on paper, sgn, 13x10", SBY 10/5/88 .... **3,300**

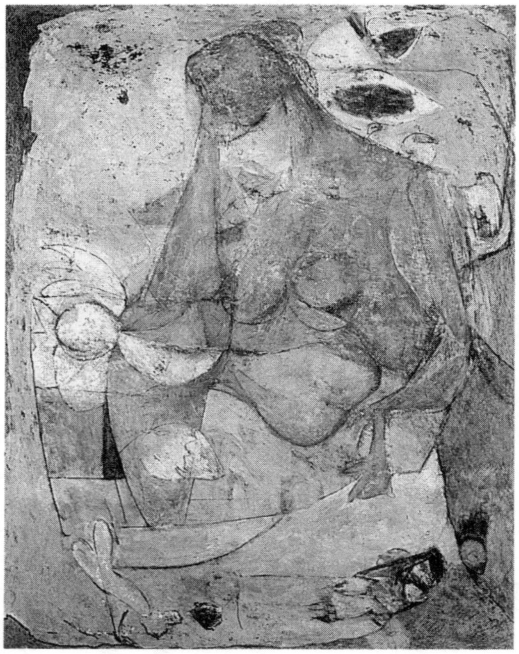

Mother & Child, oil on canvas, 1937, 47x36", C-NY 5/3/89 OE, $242,000

Portrait of David Burliuk, pen/black ink over traces of pencil on paper, sgn, 13x9", C-E 11/14/89 .... **1,870**
Portrait of the Artist's Sister (abstract), oil on canvas mounted on masonite, 1937, 34x23", C-NY 11/9/88 OE **132,000**
Portrait of the Artist's Wife, pen/black ink on paper, ca 1930, 14x10", C-NY 5/4/89 OE **13,200**
Reclining Nude, pen/black ink on paper mounted on board, 4x5", C-E 5/9/89 OE **3,300**
Two Figures & a Horse, pen/black ink on paper, 5x9", C-E 5/9/89 .... **1,650**
Untitled (abstract composition), ink/gouache on toned paper laid down on panel, ca 1945-46, 10x7", SBY 5/2/89 .... **46,750**
Untitled (abstract landscape), pencil/crayon on paper, ca 1940, 6x9", SBY 10/8/88 .... **14,300**
Untitled (abstract), graphite/crayon on paper, sgn, 1945, 19x13", SBY 10/5/89 OE **30,250**
Untitled (abstract), oil on canvas, sgn/dtd 1930, 23x30", SBY 10/5/89 OE **77,000**

Untitled (abstract), oil on masonite, sgn, 24x18", C-NY 11/10/88 ... 71,500
Untitled (abstract), pen/ink on paper, 8x11", SBY 10/5/88 ... 3,025
Untitled (fantasy drawing), pencil & crayon on paper, 1946, 19x25", SBY 5/2/89 ... 264,000
Untitled (head in profile), graphite on paper, sgn/dtd XXXVI, 1936, 9x6", C-NY 5/4/89 OE ... 4,620

GORMAN, R.C. (American, 1933-)
American Indian, charcoal/pastel on board, sgn, 36x50", C-E 4/7/88 OE ... 4,620
Indian Woman, acrylic on paper, sgn/dtd 1982, 32x40", C-E 9/15/88 OE ... 4,180

GORSON, Aaron Henry (American, 1872-1933)
Evening, Factories on the River; oil on canvas laid down on masonite, sgn/dtd 23, 34x44", C-NY 5/25/89 ... 17,600
Industrial Scene, Pittsburgh; oil on canvas, sgn/dtd 28, 20x24", C-NY 5/26/88 OE ... 13,200
Mills At Night, oil on canvas, sgn/inscr, 16x11", C-NY 5/26/88 ... 5,500
Monongahela River, Pittsburgh, Jones & Laughlin Steel Plant; oil on canvas, sgn/inscr, ca 1923, 34x45", SBY 5/24/89 ... 17,600
Paris Street Scene, pencil on paper, sgn, 16x12", C-E 2/16/88 UE ... 55
Pittsburgh Factories (riverscape w/bridge & factories by water), oil on canvas, 16x19", C-NY 9/28/89 ... 9,350

GORTER, Arnold Marc (Dutch, 1866-1933)
Autumn Landscape, oil on canvas, sgn, 17x22", C-E 10/26/89 ... 2,750
Autumn Landscape, oil on canvas, sgn, 26x33", SBY 6/8/88 ... 4,400
Autumn Tints, oil on canvas, sgn, 23x30", C-E 10/26/89 ... 4,180
Cattle Grazing by a Pond, oil on canvas, sgn, 30x40", WD 3/23/88 ... 5,500
Cattle Grazing in a River Landscape, oil on canvas, sgn, 30x39", PHL 6/16/88 ... 3,750
Cattle Grazing in a Wooded River Landscape in Autumn, oil on canvas, initialed, 18x22", C-NY 5/25/88 ... 3,850
Changing Pasture, Holland; oil on canvas, sgn, 26x34", FB 10/30/89 ... 3,300
Cows Grazing in an Autumn Landscape, oil on canvas, sgn, 20x16", C-E 10/25/88 UE ... 2,200
Cows Grazing Near a Stream, oil on canvas, sgn, 24x33", B/B 3/17/88 ... 4,125
Curve in the River, oil on canvas, sgn, 22x16", SBY 7/12/89 ... 3,750
Early Autumn, oil on canvas, sgn, 20x169", C-E 10/26/89 ... 3,520
Homeward Bound (herder & cows in a landscape), oil on canvas, sgn, 20x26", B/B 6/15/89 ... 3,575
Late Afternoon, oil on canvas, sgn, 16x19", C-E 10/26/89 ... 1,320
Maiden with Cows in Summer Landscape, oil on canvas, sgn, 28x36", SBY 7/12/89 OE ... 6,050
Peasant Woman with Her Herd of Cattle, oil on canvas, sgn, 23x30", C-E 10/26/89 ... 4,400
Shepherd's Flock on a Woodland Path, oil on canvas, sgn, 42x58", SBY 5/23/89 ... 7,700
Sunshine & Shadow, oil on canvas, sgn, 22x18", FB 4/25/88 OE ... 3,200
Wooded Landscape, oil on canvas, sgn, 30x40", SBY 12/9/88 ... 3,300

GORTZIUS, Geldorp (17th C)
Portrait of a Gentleman, oil on panel, dtd 1612, 32x25", C-NY 1/11/89 ... 30,800

GOSLING, William (British, 1824-1833)
Rowboat on a Lake, oil on canvas, sgn, 18x34", C-E 5/23/88 ... 1,980

GOSSELIN, Ferdinand Jules Albert (French, 1862-)
Le Pont-Vaille du Loing; oil on canvas, sgn, 25x33", LH 10/16/88 OE ... 5,000

GOTHELF, Louis (American, 1901-)
Summer Landscape, oil on board, sgn/dtd 1927, 24x28", DM 10/14/88 ... 475

GOTTLIEB, Adolph (American, 1903-1974)
Arabesque, India ink/gouache on board, sgn/dtd 1967, 19x24", SBY 10/5/88 ... 8,800
Black Emblems (abstract composition), oil on canvas, sgn/dtd 1971, 84x90", SBY 5/2/89 ... 176,000
Black Sun (abstract), oil on masonite, sgn twice/inscr/dtd 1947, 24x20", C-NY 11/9/88 ... 63,800
Counterpoise (abstract), oil on canvas, sgn, 1959, 108x90", SBY 5/2/88 ... 170,500
Dusk, oil on canvas, titled/dtd 1972, 60x48", SBY 11/9/89 ... 110,000
Green Turbulence (abstract), acrylic on canvas, sgn/dtd 1968, 94x157", C-NY 5/3/89 ... 352,000
Labyrinth, oil on canvasboard, sgn/dtd 55, 8x10", SBY 2/19/88 ... 6,600
Marine (abstract in green w/three red dots), watercolor/acrylic on canvas, sgn/dtd 1970, 9x12", SBY 10/5/89 OE ... 13,200
Ochre & Gold (abstract), oil on canvas, sgn/inscr/dtd 1971, 90x72", C-NY 5/3/88 ... 220,000
Pink, Blue, Black (abstract); oil on canvas, sgn/dtd 1957, 84x41", SBY 5/2/88 ... 165,000
Return (abstract), oil on canvas, sgn/inscr/dtd 1962, 48x72", C-NY 5/3/88 OE ... 198,000
Rising (abstract), acrylic on paper laid down on board, sgn/dtd 1970, 40x30", SBY 2/15/89 OE ... 66,000
Ritual Object (abstract composition), oil on canvas, sgn/dtd 1948, 30x24", WD 11/16/88 OE ... 55,000
Small Burst (abstract in red & black), watercolor on paperboard, sgn/dtd 1961, 15x10", SBY 10/5/89 OE ... 28,600
Sorcerer (abstract), oil on canvas, sgn, 1948, 38x30", SBY 1/11/88 ... 90,750
Study for Ancestral Image (abstract), oil/sand on canvasboard, sgn twice/dtd 1948/titled, 10x8", SBY 11/11/88 ... 20,900
Three Clouds (abstract), ink on paper, sgn, 1956, 21x30", SBY 10/8/88 ... 13,200
Three Figures (abstract), gouache/ink on brown paper, sgn, ca 1950, 18x23", SBY 10/8/88 ... 19,800
Three Umbers (abstract), oil/acrylic on canvas, sgn/dtd 1972/titled, 40x30", SBY 11/11/88 ... 93,500
Unstill-Life II (abstract), oil on masonite, sgn twice/dtd 1955/titled, 20x24", SBY 5/3/88 OE ... 27,500
Untitled (abstract), acrylic on paper, sgn/dtd 1967, 19x24", SBY 2/15/89 OE ... 19,800
Untitled (abstract), acrylic on paper, sgn/dtd 70, 12x9", SBY 5/3/89 OE ... 33,000
Untitled (abstract), ink/watercolor on paper, sgn/dtd 1950, 19x24", SBY 10/8/88 ... 13,200
Untitled (abstract), oil on canvasboard, sgn/dtd 1956, 9x12", SBY 10/8/88 ... 7,700
Untitled (sunburst abstract), gouache/ink on paper, sgn/inscr/dtd 1961, 22x16", SBY 2/15/89 OE ... 66,000

GOTTLIEB, Harry (American, 1895-)
Unloading the Catch, oil on canvasboard, sgn, 20x24", PHL 6/16/88 ... 800
Village Scene, oil on canvas, sgn, 24x30", C-E 6/1/88 OE ... 2,200

GOTTSCHALK, Max (American, 20th C)
Spring Landscape with Middle Distant Building, oil on canvasboard, sgn, 17x19", SLK 2/12/88 ... 140
GOTTWALD, Fredrick C. (American, 1860-)
Italian Village by a Lake, no media given, sgn, 27x21", WG 4/23/88 OE ... 3,500
Rocks, oil on canvas, sgn, 22x26", C-E 11/8/88 UE ... 100
GOTZ (German, 1874-)
Bavarian Man (seated at table, pipe in one hand, stein in other), oil on canvas, sgn, 22x18", WG 4/23/88 UE ... 90
GOTZINGER, Hans (Austrian, 1867-)
Woman Playing a Mandolin in an Interior, watercolor on paper, sgn/dtd 1914, 22x28", WD 3/23/88 UE ... 600
GOUBIE, Jean Richard (French, 1842-1899)
Her Lover's Return (lady on horseback looks to ship at sea), oil on canvas, sgn, 15x18", RAB 3/27/89 ... 24,000
Looking Out to Sea (young woman on a horse w/binoculars), oil on canvas, sgn, 15x18", C-NY 10/25/89 ... 28,600
GOUGELET, J. (French, 19th/20th C)
Pair: Two Cavaliers & a Lady; watercolor on paper, sgn, 42x29", B/B 6/15/89 ... 1,650
GOUILLET, Jules (French, 1826-)
Still Life of Fruit, oil on canvas laid down, sgn/dtd 1858, 27x33", B/B 10/9/88 ... 4,400
GOULD, Walter (American, 1829-1893)
Egyptian Dancer, watercolor, initialed/dtd 63, 7x5", C-E 11/30/88 OE ... 1,760
GOUPIL, Jules Adolphe (French, 1839-1883)
Pretty Maid (three-quarter length profile portrait), oil on panel, sgn, 36x22", SBY 2/22/89 ... 8,800
Trusted Confidant, oil on canvas, sgn, 18x15", C-E 10/26/89 ... 4,180
GOUPIL, Leon Lucien (French, 1834-1890)
Queen Katherine of Arragon, Before the Vision; oil on panel, sgn/dtd 1867, 13x10", SBY 7/12/89 UE ... 1,650
GOURDAULT, Pierre (French, 1880-1915)
Musiciens Arabes, oil on artist board, sgn/dtd 1913, 15x20", SBY 12/9/88 ... 2,200
GOURGUE, Jean Enguerrand (Haitian, 20th C)
Village Scene, oil on masonite, sgn, 40x18", RWS 9/8/89 ... 900
GOWER, George; follower of (British, 1540-1596)
Portrait of a Gentleman Traditionally Called a Member of the Dacre Family, oil on panel, dtd 1571, 30x24", SBY 4/7/89 ... 16,500
GOYA, Francisco; follower of (Spanish, 1746-1828)
Portrait of an Elegant Lady (three-quarter length, seated in chair, landscape beyond), oil on canvas, 34x24", SBY 4/7/89 ... 3,025
GOYEN, Jan van; see Van Goyen, Jan
GOZZARD, J.W. (Continental, 19th C)
Fishermen, oil on canvas, sgn, 12x16", RAB 11/24/89 UE ... 200
GOZZARD, William (Continental, 19th C)
Rainy Day, oil on canvas, sgn, 29x17", SBY 6/8/88 OE ... 2,200
GRABACH, John R. (American, 1880-1981)
Brooklyn Bridge, watercolor/pencil on paper laid down on board, sgn, 12x13", SBY 9/23/88 ... 1,870
Connecticut River Near Deerfield, oil on canvas, sgn, 42x48", SBY 5/25/88 ... 14,300
Deutschland (steamship), oil on canvas, sgn, 29x31", SBY 9/23/88 ... 9,900
Every Man's Home Is His Castle (cityscape w/figures, tenaments, & dwellings), oil on canvas, sgn, 36x42", SBY 5/24/89 ... 12,100
Fishing Boats, oil on canvas mounted on masonite, sgn, unfr, 14x18", SBY 3/17/88 ... 2,475
Free Enterprise (interior of sweat shop), oil on canvasboard, sgn, ca 1930, 12x16", SBY 3/17/88 ... 9,900
Man with Shovel (Snow in Irvington), oil on canvas, sgn, 42x48", SBY 5/25/88 ... 22,000
March Snow (fenced neighborhood landscape), oil on canvas, sgn, 36x42", SBY 1/24/89 ... 18,700
Nude Study, oil on canvas, sgn, 23x14", C-E 6/1/88 ... 2,200
Rainy Night, Central Park; watercolor heightened w/white on paper, sgn twice, 21x26", SBY 3/17/88 ... 2,860
Still Life (flowers, vase, horse figurine), watercolor on paper, sgn, 18x23", SBY 4/14/89 ... 1,210
Summer in Newark, watercolor on paper, sgn, 24x26", C-E 11/30/88 ... 2,860
Under the L, New York (busy street scene); oil on panel, sgn, 14x18", B/B 10/9/88 ... 9,350
View of Central Park, watercolor/gouache on paper, sgn, unfr, 24x20", SBY 9/23/88 ... 2,200
Waiting for the Bus in a Snow Storm, watercolor/pencil on paper, sgn, 18x24", C-E 2/1/89 ... 1,320
Winter Sleigh Ride, watercolor/gouache/pencil on board, sgn, 16x19", C-E 6/1/89 ... 880
GRABWINKLER, Paul (Austrian, 1880-)
Nude with Monkey, colored crayons on paper, sgn/inscr, 16x16", C-L 6/27/88 ... 9,081
Portrait of a Lady in Profile (bust-length), watercolor on paper, initialed, 12x9", B/B 10/9/88 ... 8,250
GRACE, A.L. (British, 19th C)
Jolly Huntsman, oil on canvas, sgn, 16x12", WAD 6/6/88 ... 550
GRACIANO, Covis
Tiguras Dancando (two figures dancing), pen/black ink on paper, sgn/dtd 46, 14x10", C-NY 11/21/88 ... 1,100
GRADFORD, T. (American)
Expulsion of Adam & Eve From Paradise, oil on canvas, sgn/dtd 1800, 10x8", SLK 2/12/88 ... 160
GRAEB, Karl George Anton (German, 1816-1884)
Berlin Street Scene, oil on canvas, sgn/dtd 1867, 28x21", SBY 7/12/89 OE ... 15,400
GRAECEN, Edmund William
Girl with Parasol, oil on canvas, sgn, 30x30", C-NY 5/26/88 ... 48,400
GRAF, Carl C. (American, 1890-)
Field of Flowers, oil on canvas, sgn, 28x30", C-NY 9/30/88 ... 4,400
Morning Wet with the Haze & Dew, oil on board, 24x26", C-NY 9/30/88 ... 3,300
GRAF, Ilma
Gentleman Seated Reading, oil on canvas, sgn/dtd 1906, unfr, 40x32", C-E 10/25/88 ... 1,430

GRAF, Paul (Swedish, 1866-1903)
Break Time, oil on panel, sgn/dtd 94, 18x13", C-E 10/26/89 UE ... 220
GRAFF, Anton; att (German, 1736-1813)
Portrait of a Nobleman, oil on canvas, 17x22", SBY 7/12/89 ... 1,650
GRAFF, Anton; circle of (1736-1813)
Portrait of the Artist, oil on canvas, 21x17", SBY 10/13/89 ... 11,000
GRAGONY (French, 20th C)
Untitled (night street scene in Paris), oil on canvas, 24x20", SLK 11/25/88 ... 100
GRAHAM, Colin D. (Canadian, 20th C)
Population Density, tempera, sgn/dtd 1980, 11x17", FB 10/17/88 UE ... 220
GRAHAM, George (British, 19th C)
Town View, oil on canvas, sgn, 40x51", SBY 6/8/88 OE ... 6,270
GRAHAM, James Lillie (Canadian, 1873-1965)
Village in Winter, oil on canvas, sgn, 23x29", FB 5/28/89 ... 4,600
GRAHAM, John D. (American, 1890-1961)
Abstract Landscape, oil on canvas, sgn, 13x22", SBY 2/14/89 ... 3,850
Daffodils in a Vase, oil on canvas, sgn, 20x16", SBY 10/8/88 ... 6,600
Double-Sided: Nude Bather on Beach; Still Life of Fruit; oil on canvas, sgn/dtd 26, 16x20", SBY 6/24/88 UE ... 4,400
Harlequin (portrait), oil on canvas, 1944, 25x20", SBY 11/11/88 ... 74,250
Head of a Woman, oil on canvas, sgn/dtd twice 1925, 23x18", SBY 5/25/88 ... 11,000
Head of a Woman: Red Eyes; oil on masonite, ca 1950, 16x13", SBY 11/9/89 ... 60,500
Leda & the Swan, oil on panel, sgn/inscr, 24x20", C-NY 5/3/88 ... 165,000
Portrait of Ultra Violet, graphite on paper, sgn, 11x9", C-NY 5/4/88 ... 6,600
Pystis Sophia, graphite/white pencil on vellum, sgn/inscr/dtd LV, 17x14", C-NY 11/9/88 ... 82,500
Untitled (seated nude), oil on canvas, sgn/dtd Paris 9/28, 36x25", C-NY 5/4/89 ... 20,900
Untitled (still life), oil on canvas, 20x25", SBY 11/9/89 ... 22,000
GRAHAM, Kathleen M.H. (Canadian, 1913-)
Arctic III, Mountains, Seas, & Cliffs (Dorset Line No 6); acrylic/chalk, sgn/dtd 75, 22x30", WAD 11/30/89 ... 600
GRAHAM, Robert MacDonald
Mrs Greenberry & Ragan (two figures seated looking at photos), egg tempera on panel, 36x48", C-NY 12/2/88 ... 33,000
GRAHAM, Ruth (Canadian)
Digby, New Brunswick; oil on board, sgn, 32x40", FB 10/30/89 ... 495
GRAHAM, Thomas Alexander Ferguson (British, 1840-1906)
Looking Into Her Future, oil on canvas, sgn, 48x38", SBY 7/12/89 UE ... 1,980
GRAILLY, see De Grailly
GRAIN, Peter Sr.; att (American, ca 1786-)
Ruins Near Frescati, Italy; oil on canvas, sgn/dtd 1830, 34x26", RWS 5/19/88 UE ... 950
GRAION, C. (Continental, 20th C)
Untitled, still life of flowers in vase; oil on canvas, sgn, 22x32", SLK 2/11/89 ... 650
GRAN, Daniel; att (1694-1757)
Angel Bearing Monstrance Appearing Before Religious Figure, Probably St Norbert of Magdeburg; oil, 24x18", SBY 10/13/89 ... 3,575
GRANDMAISON, see De Grandmaison
GRANER, Ernst
Portico of a Cathedral, watercolor on paper, sgn/dtd 17, 21x9", C-E 2/23/88 OE ... 935
GRANER Y ARUFFI, Luis (Spanish, 1867-1929)
Nightfall at a Waterside Village, oil on canvas, sgn, 44x64", C-E 2/21/89 OE ... 17,600
Sailing by Moonlight, oil on panel, sgn/dtd 1924, 18x22", C-E 11/30/88 OE ... 5,500
Sea Coast, oil on canvas, sgn, 22x30", NA 5/13/89 ... 900
Ships Docked at Port, Evening; oil on canvas, sgn, 52x79", C-E 2/21/89 OE ... 18,700
GRANSOW, Helmut (Canadian, 1921-)
Deserted Boat, oil on board, sgn/dtd 1973, 36x48", FB 5/28/89 ... 2,400
Ete Laurentien (Laurentien summer scene), oil on board, sgn, 24x36", FB 4/25/88 ... 1,600
GRANT, Catherine Harley (American, 1897-1954)
Portrait of a Lady, oil on canvas, sgn, 30x25", NA 5/13/89 ... 450
GRANT, Charles (American, -1939)
Seascape, oil on canvas, sgn, 14x21", B/B 1/11/89 ... 302
GRANT, Clement Rollins (American, 1849-)
Rest in the Park (portrait of a young woman), watercolor/graphite/gouache on paper, sgn, 11x8", RWS 11/10/89 ... 850
GRANT, Donald (American, 20th C)
Early Breakfast (three deer at water's edge), oil on canvas, sgn, 26x36", SBY 3/17/88 ... 2,200
GRANT, Duncan Edmond (Canadian, 1846-1924)
Winter's Afternoon, no media given, sgn/dtd 79, 30x24", WAD 11/30/89 ... 3,000
GRANT, Durnell (American, 20th C)
Contrathemis, paper collage/colored pencil on tissue paper, initialed/dtd 41, 9x11", lot 328B, C-NY 5/26/88 UE ... 825
Contrathemis, paper collage/colored pencil on tissue paper, initialed/dtd 41, 9x11", lot 328C, C-NY 5/26/88 ... 2,420
Contrathemis, paper collage/pencil/colored pencil on tissue paper, initialed/dtd 41, 9x11", lot 328A, C-NY 5/26/88 UE ... 880
Line Study, brush/pen/ink/gouache/watercolor on paper, initialed/dtd 42, 20x15", lot 328E, C-NY 5/26/88 UE ... 1,650
GRANT, Frederic M. (American, 1886-)
Radio & Communications Building, the Century of Progress Fair, Chicago; oil on canvas, sgn, 33x31", B/B 10/9/88 ... 3,300
Summer Flowers, oil on canvas, sgn, 22x24", C-NY 3/11/88 UE ... 1,320
Treasure (figures w/treasure on beach, ships beyond), oil on canvas, sgn, 30x36", SBY 9/14/89 ... 2,200

GRANT, Gordon Hope (American, 1875-1962)
Boats in a Harbor, watercolor on paper, sgn, 15x21", SBY 6/24/88 ... 1,320
Clipper Ship Under Sail, watercolor on paper, sgn, 10x14", RAB 8/9/88 ... 800
Dry Dock, watercolor on paper, sgn, 15x21", C-E 2/3/88 OE ... 2,200
East Indiaman (sailing ship), oil on canvas, sgn, 36x36", WD 4/13/88 ... 3,200
Harbor Scene, watercolor on paper, sgn, 14x21", SBY 4/14/89OE ... 2,530
Hull Down (ship in distance), oil on canvasboard, sgn/titled, 8x12", RAB 3/27/89 ... 1,100
Imaginary Toy Ship, pen/ink on board, sgn/dtd 1911, 22x28", C-E 6/1/88 UE ... 352
Sailboats & Houses, watercolor on paper, sgn, 15x21", C-E 2/3/88 ... 1,870
Sailing Ships, watercolor on paper, sgn, 13x19", SBY 3/17/88 ... 990
Set of 3: Figural Studies; pen/ink on paper, sgn, no sizes given, WG 10/19/88 UE ... 240
Set of 3: Figure Studies; pen/ink on paper, sgn, 9x6", WG 10/19/88 UE ... 270

GRANT, J. Jeffrey (American, 1883-1960)
Ye Red Lobster (village scene w/figures before lodging house), watercolor on paper, sgn, 12x14", RWS 3/31/88 UE ... 300

GRANT, William James (British, 1829-1866)
Eugene Beauharnais Refusing To Give Up His Father's Sword, oil on canvas, sgn w/monogram, dtd 1858, 32x39", SBY 2/22/88 ... 17,600

GRASDORP, Willem (Dutch, 1678-1723)
Still Life of Lilies, Morning-Glory, Roses, Poppies, a Tulip...; oil on canvas, sgn, 25x22", C-NY 1/11/89 OE ... 198,000

GRASSI, Nicola; att (Italian, 1662-1748)
Baptism of Christ, oil on canvas, bears signature/dtd 1694, oval, unfr, 23x17", C-NY 10/20/88 ... 7,700

GRASSI, Nicola; circle of (Italian, 1662-1748)
Christ with an Apostle, en grisaille/oil on canvas, unfr, 29x21", SBY 6/8/88 UE ... 880

GRATZ, Rudolf
Young Grape Picker, sgn/dtd 75, 30x25", C-E 2/23/88 ... 3,300

GRAU, Enrique (Colombian, 1920-)
Portrait of Lucretia, gouache on paper, sgn/dtd 70/inscr Para Lucrecia, 41x31", SBY 11/21/88 ... 6,600
Untitled (abstract), gouache on paper, sgn/dtd 58, 24x19", SBY 5/17/88 ... 5,500

GRAU-SALA, Emile (Spanish, 1911-1975)
At the Racecourse, oil on panel, sgn/dtd 1957, 18x15", SBY10/7/89 OE ... 30,800
Bathers on a Beach, oil on canvas, sgn/dtd 1952, 24x29", WD 11/16/88 OE ... 26,000
Course de Chevaux, oil on canvas, sgn/dtd Paris 67, 18x22", C-NY 2/13/89 OE ... 24,200
Jeune Fille a la Fenetre (young girl at the window), oil on canvas, sgn/dtd 70, 21x29", C-E 11/17/88 OE ... 22,000
La Charette aux Fleurs, oil on canvas, sgn twice/dtd 1964, 21x26", C-E 5/13/88 OE ... 8,250
Le Cirque (The Circus), oil on canvas, sgn, 18x24", C-E 5/13/88 OE ... 12,100
Le Cirque (The Circus), pastel on paper laid down on board, sgn/dtd Paris 1937, 30x24", C-E 11/17/88 OE ... 12,100
Le Cirque (The Circus), pastel on red paper laid down on masonite, sgn, 26x20", C-E 11/17/88 OE ... 24,200
Le Paddock a Deauville, oil on canvas, sgn twice/titled, 15x18", C-E 5/9/89 OE ... 35,200
Lecon de Piano (Piano Lesson), oil on canvas, sgn/dtd 66, 24x29", B/B 6/15/89 OE ... 24,750
Park Scene, pastel on canvas, sgn, 32x32", SBY 10/7/89 OE ... 24,200
Port d'Honfleur, 1951; pen/ink/tempera on paper, sgn/dtd 51, 16x22", B/B 6/15/89 OE ... 9,900
Still Life with Standing Woman, oil on canvas, sgn/dtd 1961, 49x39", PHL 6/16/88 OE ... 9,500
Terraces a Barcelone, oil on canvas, sgn/dtd 1963, 29x36", C-E 11/17/88 OE ... 46,200

GRAUER, William C. (American, 1896-1985)
Mexican Mosaics, acrylic on masonite, sgn, 21x24", WG 4/23/88 UE ... 150

GRAUMANN, Julius
Village Square, oil on canvas, sgn/dtd 1918, 11x13", C-E 11/8/88 ... 850

GRAVELOT, Hubert (French, 1699-1773)
Death of Darius, King of Persia; pen/black ink/watercolor, 7x4", SBY 1/13/89 ... 935

GRAVES, Abbott Fuller (American, 1859-1936)
Connoisseur (seated man examining glass of wine), oil on canvas, sgn, 24x20", SBY 3/17/88 ... 4,070
Flower Sellers (seated in an interior readying flowers for market), oil on canvas, sgn, 20x24", C-NY 5/25/89 ... 49,500
House & Flowers, watercolor/pencil on paper laid down on board, 15x12", C-NY 9/30/88 ... 1,100
Pair: Jamaican Scenes; oil on canvas, sgn, 8x12", C-NY 9/30/88 ... 3,850
Peace & Sunshine (potted flowers at open doorway), oil on canvas, sgn, 25x30", C-NY 5/25/89 OE ... 30,800
St Episcopal Church, Cape Arundel, Maine; oil on canvas, sgn, 20x30", RWS 5/19/88 ... 9,500
Still Life of Peonies, oil on canvas, sgn, 36x42", SBY 5/24/89 ... 57,750
Wiscasset House (house in landscape), oil on canvas, sgn, 30x25", 30x25", SBY 5/24/89 ... 11,000

GRAVES, Morris (American, 1910-)
Cliff, watercolor/white chalk on brown paper laid down on canvas, 54x28", C-NY 3/11/88 ... 5,500
Eagle, gouache on rice paper, sgn, 26x30", C-E 3/22/88 OE ... 2,420
Head (animal), tempera on paper, sgn/dtd 51, 16x12", SBY 6/24/88 ... 5,225
Minnow, tempera on paper, sgn/dtd 67, 8x11", SBY 6/24/88 ... 3,080
Mouse, pencil on paper, sgn/dtd 34, 14x19", SBY 1/24/89 OE ... 3,300
Rooster, watercolor/gouache/pencil on paper, sgn, 16x12", C-NY 5/26/88 ... 6,600
Seeking To Nest (bird w/twig in mouth), black ink wash on paper laid down on paper, sgn, 17x29", C-E 2/1/89 OE ... 1,650
Spring Jardiniere, watercolor/gouache on rice paper, sgn/titled, 18x15", SBY 6/24/88 ... 6,050
Still Life (flowers in a mug), pastel on rice paper, unfr, 14x9", SBY 9/23/88 ... 2,640
Study of Birds, black ink on buff paper, 16x26", SBY 6/24/88 ... 1,760
Swanriver Daisie, black ink/brown wash/gouache on paper, titled/inscr, 19x13", SBY 6/24/88 ... 3,740

GRAVES, Nancy (American, 1940-)
Clue (abstract), oil on canvas, sgn/dtd 77, 64x76", SBY 10/5/89 ... 23,100

Kata (abstract), watercolor on paper, sgn/dtd 3-10-80, 61x44", SBY 10/5/89 OE 19,800
Mlaek (abstract), oil on canvas, sgn/dtd 1978, 82x64", SBY 2/15/89 27,500
Veig (abstract), watercolor/pastel/oil stick/pencil on paper, sgn/dtd 7-77, 30x23", SBY 5/3/89, OE 14,300
Zolen (abstract), oil on canvas, 1978, 71x53", SBY 10/8/88 20,900

GRAY, Charles A. (American, 1858-)
Lily Pond, oil on canvas, sgn, 24x18", WG 9/16/88 1,200

GRAY, Cleve (American, 1918-)
Conjunction #150 (abstract), acrylic on canvas, sgn/dtd 76, 74x56", C-E 11/14/89 OE 13,200
Masquerade at Esna (abstract), acrylic on canvas, sgn/dtd 77, 50x72", SBY 10/5/88 1,980

GRAY, George (British, 19th C)
Children Playing in a Brook, oil on canvas, sgn, 19x33", C-E 2/23/88 1,760
River Landscape with Figures Beside a Stream, Stone Bridges & Cottages Beyond; watercolor, sgn, 20x13", SLK 5/12/88 150

GRAY, Henry Percy (American, 1869-1952)
California Oaks, watercolor on paper, sgn/dtd 1919, 10x14", B/B 10/6/88 9,900
Californian Landscape, oil on canvas laid down, sgn/indistinctly dtd 1929, 32x69", C-SK 5/25/89 OE 77,150
Eucalyptus Grove, watercolor on paper, sgn/dtd 1926, 21x29", B/B 10/6/88 19,800
View of Mt Tamalpais, watercolor on paper, sgn, 11x15", B/B 10/6/88 8,800
View of Mt Tamalpais, watercolor/pencil on paper, sgn, 12x16", B/B 10/6/88 OE 14,300

GRAY, Jack Lorimer (American/Canadian, 1927-1981)
Aloft in the Prow, watercolor on paper, sgn, 15x21", WD 10/5/88 OE 5,000
Coastal Fishing Scene, oil on board, sgn, 22x30", FB 5/28/89 3,600
First Dory Out, oil on canvas, sgn twice/titled, 30x50", SBY 1/24/89 OE 8,800
Lobster Fisherman Laying His Traps, oil on canvas, sgn, 24x36", B/B 10/9/88 4,950
Lobstermen (in boat on rough sea), oil on canvas, sgn, 26x36", WD 10/5/88 OE 12,000
Nova Scotia Fishing Scene, oil on board, sgn, 22x30", FB 5/28/89 OE 6,000
Off the Banks, Nova Scotia; oil on board, sgn, 22x30", FB 5/28/89 OE 6,000
Pulling in Traps, oil on canvas, sgn, 24x36", B/B 3/17/88 OE 8,250
SS Brasil (cruise ship), oil on canvas, sgn/dtd 58, 27x40", WD 10/5/88 UE 3,000
Sword Fishing, Brown's Bank; oil on canvas, sgn twice/dtd Sept 1962/inscr dedication, 16x24", SBY 3/17/88 6,050

GRAY, Jim
Pull Boys, Pull (harpooning a whale); watercolor/gouache on board, 15x23", C-NY 3/11/88 1,650

GRAY, Mary Chilton (American, 20th C)
Still Life of Objects, oil on canvas, sgn/dtd 23, 24x18", C-E 6/1/88 1,045

GRAYSON, L.
White Horse in a Landscape, oil on canvas, sgn/dtd 1899, 22x28", C-E 7/26/88 UE 440

GRAZIANI, Ercole the elder; att (Italian, 1651-1726)
Infant Moses Proving His Innocence of Treason Against the Pharaoh by Eating Live Coals, oil, unfr, 52x67", SBY 6/2/89 18,700

GRAZIANI, Ercole the younger (Italian, 1688-1765)
Scene From the Life of a Saint, oil on canvas, unfr, 50x30", SBY 4/7/88 4,675

GREACEN, Edmund William (American, 1877-1949)
Flowers in a White Vase, oil on canvas, sgn/estate stamp, 24x20", SBY 6/24/88 5,500
Parasol (portrait of a woman), oil on canvas, sgn, 26x21", C-NY 5/26/88 16,500
Portrait Study of a Woman, oil on canvas, sgn/dtd 1926, 24x20", SBY 4/14/89 1,650
Stream in Winter (landscape), oil on canvas mounted on masonite, sgn/indistinctly dtd, unfr, 24x29", SBY 1/24/89 8,800
Winter Woods, oil on canvas, sgn, 30x40", C-NY 12/2/88 11,000

GREASON, William (American, 1884-)
Low Tide (docks/buildings), oil on board, sgn/inscribed Provincetown Massachusetts, 13x10", SBY 6/28/89 1,210
Lowtide (quiet pier in Provincetown, Massachusetts), oil on cardboard, sgn/inscr, 13x10", RWS 9/29/88 650
Still Life of Pears, oil on canvas, initialed/dtd 90, 18x12", C-E 6/1/88 1,540

GREATOREX, Katherine Honora (American, 1851-)
Pair: Hollycocks; oil on canvas, sgn/dtd 1879, 57x19", C-NY 9/30/88 11,000

GREAVES, Walter (British, 1846-1930)
Waterfall in British Lake District, oil on canvas, sgn/dtd 78, 12x18", B/B 1/11/89 935

GREBBER, see De Grebber

GRECHOFF, L. (20th C)
Golden Autumn, oil on canvas, dtd 1936, 25x20", LH 10/16/88 225

GRECO, Emilio (Italian, 1913-)
Donna Seduta, pen/India ink on paper, sgn/dtd 1960, 26x19", C-E 5/13/88 825
Testa di Donna, pen/black ink on paper, sgn/dtd 1961, 20x14", C-E 5/13/88 605
Testa di Donna (portrait), pen/India ink on paper laid down on board, sgn/dtd Roma 1961, 27x20", C-E 5/9/89 OE 3,300

GRECO, El (Spanish, 1547-1614)
Espolio (Disrobing of Christ), oil on canvas, 39x22", SBY 6/3/88 OE 48,000
Saint Francis of Assisi & Fra Leone Contemplating Mortality, oil on canvas, 66x38", SBY 10/21/88 OE 99,000

GRECO, El; manner of (Spanish, 1547-1614)
Crucifixion, oil on canvas, 41x25", SBY 6/8/88 OE 2,310

GRECO, El; school of (Spanish, 1547-1614)
Saint Francis in Ecstasy, oil on canvas, 18x14", C-NY 6/2/88 OE 24,200

GRECO, El; studio of (Spanish, 1547-1614)
Landscape Near Toledo, oil on canvas, 15x6", C-NY 4/8/88 OE 13,200
Saint Francis Contemplating a Skull with Brother Leo, oil on canvas, 40x30", C-NY 10/20/88 19,800

GREEN, A.R.; att (British, 20th C)
Domestic Interior with Three Figures & a Dog, oil on canvas,multiple imperfections, 12x16", SLK 2/12/88 ... **25**
GREEN, Charles (British, 1840-1898)
Bookie (crowd placing bets), watercolor heightened w/white on paper laid down, initialed, 12x10", B/B 5/17/89 OE ... **2,750**
Sailor's Wedding, watercolor on paper, sgn/dtd 1895, 20x35", SBY 2/22/89 ... **8,250**
GREEN, Charles Edwin Lewis (American, 1844-1915)
Along the River's Edge (trees along water), oil on paper, sgn, 9x14", RWS 5/19/88 ... **1,100**
Along the Shore, oil on canvas, sgn, 14x18", C-E 6/1/88 OE ... **3,520**
In the Lynn Woods, oil on canvas, sgn, ca 1900, 27x36", RWS 5/19/88 ... **6,500**
Still Life of Oil Painting & Wine Bottle, oil on cardboard, sgn/dtd 84, 6x7", RAB 8/8/89 UE ... **700**
Swampscott Harbor, oil on artist board, sgn, 12x17", RAB 8/8/89 UE ... **700**
GREEN, Florence Topping (American, 20th C)
Old Dock, oil on canvas, sgn/dtd 1913/inscr 104FXX Long Beach, 26x15", C-E 11/8/88 UE ... **300**
GREEN, Frank Russell (American, 1856-1940)
Cottages Nestled in Autumn Hills, oil on board, sgn, 8x10", FAP 4/15/89 ... **440**
GREEN, George (American, 1943-)
Val-Setz (abstract), acrylic on canvas, sgn/dtd 1981, unfr, 60x96", C-NY 10/4/89 OE ... **16,500**
Whistle Pink (abstract), acrylic on canvas, 1980, 66x66", SBY 2/19/88 OE ... **11,000**
GREENAWAY, Kate (British, 1846-1901)
Cinderella (carrying pumpkin), watercolor, initialed, 11x8", C-NY 2/23/89 OE ... **17,600**
Sisters on a Winter Walk, pencil, 15x11", C-NY 10/26/88 ... **1,980**
Summer (little girl & boy sitting on a bench holding umbrella), watercolor/ink on paper, 7x5", RWS 11/10/89 OE ... **2,300**
GREENAWAY, Roy (Canadian, 1891-1972)
English Village, oil on board, sgn, 20x24", WAD 6/12/89 UE ... **200**
GREENBAUM, Joseph (American, 1864-1940)
Catalina Island, oil on canvas, sgn, 22x28", B/B 10/6/88 ... **2,475**
GREENBLAT, Rodney Alan (20th C)
Bad Day for the Devil, enamel/acrylic on panel, 1983, 23x30", SBY 2/15/89 ... **4,950**
Boom (contemporary), gouache/crayon on paper in acrylic painted wooden frame, initialed, 1986, 20x22", C-NY 2/14/89 ... **1,870**
Magic Fish (contemporary), oil/seashells on board in gilt frame, initialed, 1984, 17x21", C-NY 2/20/88 ... **2,090**
Untitled (abstract), acrylic on panel in gilt frame, initialled, 17x21", lot 356, C-NY 11/10/88 OE ... **2,860**
Untitled (abstract), acrylic on panel in gilt frame, initialled, 17x21", lot 358, C-NY 11/10/88 ... **2,640**
Valu-Days (contemporary), acrylic/felt/plastic on panel, initialed, 1986, 12x14", C-NY 2/14/89 ... **1,760**
GREENE, Balcomb (American, 1904-)
Classical Forms (abstract), pencil/paper collage, sgn/dtd 37 twice, #d 24/36, SBY 3/17/88 OE ... **4,400**
GREENE, Gertrude (American, 1911-1956)
Black, Tan & White Collage; pencil/paper, sgn/dtd 38-18, 12x8", SBY 6/28/89 ... **3,575**
Collage (abstract), pencil/paper collage, sgn/dtd 38-1, 12x8", SBY 3/17/88 ... **3,575**
Collage in Green, White & Black; pencil/paper, sgn/dtd 39-8, 12x8", SBY 6/28/89 OE ... **5,225**
GREENE, H.S. (American, 20th C)
Grand Banks Fishing Schooner (sun sets on boats), oil on canvas, sgn, 20x16", RAB 8/8/89 UE ... **100**
GREENE, J. Barry (American, 1895-1966)
Gloucester Pastoral (with village & sea beyond), oil on canvas, sgn, 24x29", B/B 9/14/89 ... **1,045**
Late Summer, Annay; oil on canvasboard, sgn/dtd 1937, 15x18", B/B 8/10/88 ... **468**
Reclining Female Nude, oil, sgn, 24x32", WD 1/11/89 ... **1,100**
Sunny Day (landscape), oil on canvas, sgn/dtd 1924, unfr, 26x32", SBY 1/24/89 ... **770**
GREENE, J.G. (American, 19th C)
Caroline, Tucker, New Yorker, JR Congdon, Master (ship); watercolor on paper, sgn/titled, 19x26", RAB 8/1/88 ... **2,000**
GREENE, Leroy (American, 20th Century)
Western Frolic (mountainous landscape w/horses), oil on canvas, sgn/dtd 57, 20x24", SBY 6/28/89 ... **1,210**
GREENE, Stephen (American, 1917-)
Light (abstract), oil on canvas, sgn/dtd 1979, 48x48", C-E 11/14/89 ... **1,100**
Untitled (abstract), oil on canvas, 14x8", C-E 11/14/89 ... **715**
GREENE, Thomas Garland (Canadian, 1875-1955)
Orchard in Bloom, watercolor, sgn, 11x14", WAD 6/12/89 ... **140**
GREENE, Walter L. (American, 19th/20th C)
Watering Hole (fowl in landscape), watercolor heightened w/white on paper, sgn/dtd 97, 11x15", RWS 3/16/89 ... **350**
GREENE, William Bradford (American, 1871-1945)
Marigolds (vase of flowers), oil on board, sgn, 13x13", RAB 8/9/88 UE ... **300**
GREENLEAF, Jacob I. (American, 1887-1968)
Sail Loft at the Cove (shanty/figures near harbor), oil on canvas, sgn, 16x20", RAB 8/8/89 UE ... **550**
Spring Landscape (New England farmhouse & blooming apple tree), oil on board, sgn, 20x16", RAB 8/9/88 UE ... **100**
Spring Landscape (New England farmhouse shaded by trees), oil on board, sgn, 10x15", RAB 8/9/99 UE ... **400**
GREENWOOD, Joseph H. (American, 1857-1927)
Autumn Marshes, oil on canvas, sgn/dtd 23, 21x28", RWS 5/19/88 OE ... **4,000**
Blue Hills (haystack w/farm scene beyond), oil on board, sgn/dtd 20, 12x16", RWS 3/31/88 ... **1,400**
Marshlands in Autumn (impressionistic landscape w/pond in foreground), oil on board, 7x11", RWS 3/31/88 ... **800**
Rising Hill with Light Snow Cover (panorama of snow-covered wooded slopes), oil on panel, 6x8", RWS 3/31/88 UE ... **300**
GREFF, Adrien; see De Greff
GREFF, Eleanor; see De Ghize

GREGG, Paul (American, 20th C)
His Spirit, oil on canvas, sgn/dtd 1925, 24x22", MAG 6/22/88 ... 350

GREGOR, Harold (American, 1929-)
Illinois Barn Series #16 (realistic), oil on canvas, sgn, 43x66", SBY 9/14/89 ... 1,650
Illinois Farmscape #24, oil on acrylic on canvas mounted on canvas, sgn/inscr/dtd 1977, 15x19", C-E 5/13/88 UE ... 1,100
Illinois Landscape #43 (realistic), oil/acrylic on canvas, sgn/dtd 1980, 60x84", C-NY 10/4/89 ... 11,000
Illinois Landscape #46, oil/acrylic on canvas, sgn/dtd 1981, 60x82", C-NY 2/20/88 ... 7,700

GREGORY, Angela
Double-Sided: Portrait of a Gentleman; Another Portrait; oil on board, 20x16", NA 10/1/88 ... 550

GREGORY, Charles (British, 19th/20th C)
Rip Van Winkle's Return, watercolor/gouache, sgn, 12x9", C-NY 5/25/88 ... 660
Summer's Afternoon, oil on canvas, monogramed, 12x18", C-E 10/26/89 ... 8,250

GREGORY, George (British, 1849-1938)
A Hulk, oil on canvas, sgn/dtd 1888, 24x38", C-E 10/26/89 ... 2,200
Sailing on the River, oil on canvas, sgn/dtd 1885, 16x26", C-E 10/26/89 ... 2,640

GREINEAR, M.
Bathing the Puppy, oil on canvas, sgn/dtd 1866, 14x11", C-E 11/8/88 UE ... 500

GREINER, Art (American, 20th C)
Tiger, graphite on paper, sgn, dtd 1927, 5x5", WG 10/19/88 UE ... 20

GREISSINGER, F. (American, 20th C)
Seascape, oil on canvas, sgn, 20x40", FAP 12/8/89 ... 150

GREITZER, Jack (American, 1910-)
Blue Vase with Flowers, India ink/watercolor/gouache on paper, sgn/dtd 1931, 17x13", SBY 6/28/89 OE ... 7,975

GRENDERARD, Lucien Henri (French, 1880-1965)
Ciel Agite (rural landscape), oil on paper laid down on board, sgn/#d, 11x13", C-E 2/21/89 UE ... 660

GREPPI, Antonio (Italian, 19th C)
Face of Great Character, oil on canvas, sgn, 19x13", WAD 6/6/88 ... 700

GRESL, Gary John (American, 20th C)
Protoforms Dissolving with Frog Fields, oil on canvas, sgn/dtd 1984, 47x47", MAG 9/18/88 ... 200

GRESLEY, Gabriel; circle of (French, 1712-1756)
Trompe l'Oeil of Playing Cards, Letters, Sketches, a Ribbon, a Butterfly...; oil on canvas, 30x39", C-NY 1/11/89 OE ... 33,000

GRESPO, Helaine
Still Life of Apples (contemporary), oil on canvas, sgn/dtd 69, 22x22", MG 10/28/88 UE ... 125

GRETZNER, Harold (American, 1902-1977)
Old Victorian, watercolor on paper, sgn, 19x24", B/B 10/6/88 ... 1,045

GREUVERBROECK, Alessandro (Italian, 17th C)
Mediterranean Port, oil on canvas, sgn, 22x45", FAP 12/8/89 OE ... 4,000

GREUZE, Jean Baptiste (French, 1725-1805)
Head of a Sleeping Child, black/red/white chalk on buff paper, sgn, 11x9", C-NY 1/11/89 ... 30,800
Portrait of a Lady, Head & Shoulders; red chalk, sgn/#d 8-N 56, 17x13", SBY 1/13/89 OE ... 39,600
Portrait of a Young Peasant Girl, oil on canvas, 13x20", RWS 12/10/88 UE ... 425
Young Girl Embracing a Dove, oil on canvas, 25x20", SBY 6/3/88 ... 187,000

GREUZE, Jean Baptiste; after (French, 1725-1805)
Bible Reading (figures around a table in an interior), oil on canvas, 29x36", B/B 9/14/89 UE ... 605
Laundress, oil on panel, 18x13", C-NY 6/2/88 ... 2,860
Portrait of a Young Child, oil on canvas, 16x13", C-E 4/7/88 ... 880
Tame Canary, oil on canvas, oval, 23x19", PHL 10/28/88 ... 700
Village Bride, sanguine chalk on paper, 14x11", WD 10/19/88 ... 1,100

GREUZE, Jean Baptiste; att (French, 1725-1805)
Portrait of a Young Woman, oil on canvas, 22x21", FB 5/28/89 ... 1,100

GREUZE, Jean Baptiste; manner of (French, 1725-1805)
Portrait of a Girl in Hooded Fur-Lined Robe, oil on canvas, 23x19", SBY 7/12/89 ... 3,025
Two Children with a Cat, oil on canvas, 26x26", WD 1/25/89 ... 2,600

GREUZE, Jean Baptiste; school of (French, 1725-1805)
Pair: Girl Holding Basket of Fruit; Girl in a White Blouse & Green Dress; oil on canvas, 18x15", C-NY 4/8/88 ... 3,300
Young Girl Holding a Basket, oil on canvas, inscr #39, 16x13", C-NY 10/12/89 ... 2,640

GREY, Steve (20th C)
Wichita Falls Depot, watercolor on paper, sgn, 21x29", SBY 9/23/88 UE ... 110

GRIFFIER, Jan II (-1750)
Extensive River Landscape with Figures, Cottages & Tents on the Bank; oil on canvas, sgn, 17x24", SBY 10/21/88 OE ... 17,600

GRIFFIN, Thomas Bailey (American, 1861-)
Autumn Landscape, oil on canvas, sgn, 30x25", LH 10/16/88 OE ... 3,000
Fall Forest, oil on canvas, sgn, 16x24", C-E 6/1/89 ... 935
Fall Landscape with Stream, oil on canvas, sgn, 16x24", C-E 2/1/89 ... 1,760
Hunting Dogs, oil on canvas mounted on masonite, sgn/dtd 99, 16x24", SBY 6/24/88 ... 1,045
Running Brook, oil on canvas, sgn, 30x25", C-E 9/15/88 ... 935
Running Stream, oil on canvas laid down on masonite, sgn, 16x20", C-E 2/3/88 ... 1,760
Storm Clouds (river landscape w/mountain beyond, angry sky), oil on canvas, 16x20", C-E 6/1/89 ... 2,640
Stream, oil on canvas, sgn, 16x24", lot 35, C-E 6/1/88 ... 1,650
Stream, oil on canvas, sgn, 16x24", lot 38, C-E 11/30/88 ... 1,540

GRIFFIN, Thomas Bartholomew
On the Scent (dogs in landscape), oil on canvas, sgn, 24x36", C-E 6/1/89 ... 3,300
GRIFFIN, Walter (American, 1861-1935)
Apple Blossom Time (orchard in bloom), pastel on thick wove tan paper, sgn/dtd 1904, 11x14", RWS 5/19/88 ... 1,000
Apple Blossom Time (trees in bloom), pastel on thick wove tan paper, sgn/dtd 1904, 11x14", RWS 9/8/89 ... 900
French Countryside, oil on canvasboard, sgn, 9x11", C-NY 9/28/89 ... 3,850
Stroudwater, Maine (coastal view), oil on canvas, sgn, 24x30", C-NY 9/28/89 ... 5,500
Woman with Cows, oil on canvas, sgn, 26x30", B/B 3/17/88 ... 7,150
Woman with Cows (buildings beyond), oil on canvas, 26x30", B/B 10/9/88 ... 3,300
GRIFFITH, Grace (Allison)(American, 1885-1955)
Sheep Grazing in a Landscape, watercolor on paper, sgn/dtd 23, 16x19", B/B 10/6/88 ... 715
GRIFFITH, Julius Edward Lindsay (Canadian, 1912-)
Morning Rush, Montreal; watercolor, sgn, 22x30", WAD 6/12/89 ... 550
Squeeze Right, watercolor, sgn, 10x13", WAD 6/12/89 ... 110
GRIFFITH, Marie Osthaus
Roses, oil on canvas, sgn, 34x50", C-E 2/1/89 OE ... 12,100
GRIFFITH (American, 20th C)
Fire House (two men at table, dog sleeping, kittens playing), oil on gesso panel, sgn, 24x30", B/B 3/22/89 ... 1,650
GRIFFITHS, Wilf Frank (Canadian)
Bakers Sugar Shack, oil on board, sgn, 10x12", WAD 11/30/89 ... 325
Near Parry Sound, oil on board, sgn, 10x12", WAD 11/30/89 ... 200
Pair: River on Way to Markdale; Michipiloten River, Wawa; oil on board, sgn, 8x10", WAD 11/30/89 ... 200
Trees & Creek Killarney, oil on board, sgn, 10x12", WAD 11/30/89 ... 280
Winter at Moose Creek, Haliburton; oil on board, sgn, 10x12", WAD 11/30/89 ... 460
GRIGGS, Samuel W. (American, 1827-1898)
Still Life of Trout (on bank beside tree trunk), oil on canvas, sgn, 14x31", RAB 8/9/88 UE ... 450
GRIGORESCU, Nicolas (Romanian, 1838-1970)
Trees in a Forest, oil on canvas, sgn, 20x18", C-E 5/22/89 ... 4,400
GRIGORIEV, Boris Dmitrievich (Russian, 1886-1939)
Borisella, gouache on paper mounted on paper, sgn/dtd 1930/titled, 11x17", C-E 5/9/89 ... 2,090
Hommes de l'Ile de Paquetes-Bresil (figures in landscape); watercolor/gouache/pencil on paper, 15x20", C-E 5/9/89 ... 1,045
Motherhood (portrait of mother holding child), oil on canvas, sgn/artist label, 30x25", C-L 10/8/88 OE ... 27,890
View Over a Country Town, oil on canvas, sgn/dtd 24, 27x29", C-L 10/8/88 OE ... 20,450
GRIMALDI, Giovanni Francesco (Italian, 1606-1680)
Apollo & Daphne in a Landscape, pen/brown ink over traces of black chalk, 8x12", SBY 1/13/89 ... 2,200
GRIMALDI, Giovanni Francesco; circle of (Italian, 1606-1680)
Hilly Wooded Landscape, with a Warrior Subduing a Lion; pen/brown ink, 7x12", C-NY 1/12/88 OE ... 1,045
GRIMBERGHE, see De Grimberghe
GRIMM, Paul (American, 1891-1974)
America the Beautiful, oil on masonite, sgn, 30x40", C-E 11/30/88 ... 1,760
Lake Hodges, Del Dios; oil on canvasboard, sgn, 16x20", B/B 10/6/88 ... 2,750
Southern California Desert Landscape, oil on canvas laid down, sgn, 20x24", B/B 5/17/89 ... 495
Southern California Landscape, Fertile Valley; oil on board, sgn, 12x16", B/B 12/8/88 ... 495
GRIMMER, Abel (1573-1619)
Winter Landscape, oil on panel, 12x12", SBY 1/12/89 ... 66,000
GRIMMER, Abel; circle of (1573-1619)
Shepherds with Their Flock Resting by a Stream, a Village Beyond; oil on panel, 10x16", C-NY 6/2/88 ... 8,800
GRIMMER, Abel; manner of (1573-1619)
Hunters in the Snow, oil on panel, 11x16", WD 1/25/89 ... 2,400
GRIMOU, Alexis; circle of (French, 1678-1733)
Young Man Playing a Flute, oil on canvas, 27x22", SBY 4/7/88 OE ... 3,850
GRIMSHAW, Atkinson (British, 1836-1893)
Pair: River by Ilford Village; Ruins by a Church; oil on canvas, sgn, 16x24", B/B 3/17/88 ... 16,500
St Paul's & Southwark Bridge, London; oil on canvas, sgn/dtd 1886, 20x30", RAB 8/9/88 ... 13,000
GRINNELL, Roy (American, 1934-)
Pair: Battle Paint; After the Hunt; oil on canvas, sgn/copyrighted, 12x9", 12x16", SBY 1/24/89 ... 1,650
Someone's Trackin' Us (figures w/horses in landscape), oil on canvas, sgn/copyrighted/dtd 81, 20x30", SBY 1/24/89 ... 1,760
Traps for the Beaver Hunt (trappers in a snowy landscape), oil on canvas, sgn/dtd 79, 30x48", SBY 1/24/89 ... 3,300
GRIS, Juan (Spanish, 1887-1927)
Compotier et Livre (modern still life w/book, knife, & dish of fruit), oil on canvas, sgn/dtd 25, 13x16", SBY 5/10/89 OE ... 352,000
Conversation, ink wash/blue crayon over pencil on paper, sgn, 15x9", SBY 2/18/88 OE ... 6,600
Guitar on the Table (abstract), oil on canvas, sgn/dtd 4-13, 24x29", C-NY 5/11/88 ... 1,870,000
La Femme au Tableau (abstract portrait), oil on canvas, sgn, 1924, 24x20", SBY 5/10/88 ... 286,000
Le Supreme Argument..., crayon/pencil/wash/gouache on thin trace paper, sgn, 14x11", SBY 2/16/89 OE ... 19,250
Nature Morte (abstract still life), oil on cradled panel, sgn/dtd 7-16, 25x32", SBY 11/15/89 ... 2,640,000
Verres sur une Table (abstract), oil on paper collage on canvas, 1913-14, 23x15", SBY 5/10/88 OE ... 1,540,000
GRISET, Ernest Henry (French, 1844-1907)
Gathering of Dogs, watercolor/gouache, monogramed, 4x6", C-NY 10/25/89 ... 1,320
Set of 8: Monkey Capers; pen/brown ink/watercolor/crayon heightened w/white, sgn, unfr, 7x6", C-NY 5/25/88 OE ... 8,250
GRISON, Francoise Adolphe (French, 1845-1914)
The Toast (man making a toast), oil on canvas, sgn, 32x26", SBY 5/23/89 ... 22,000

Un Depart Clandestin, oil on panel, sgn, 9x6", C-E 2/23/88 OE
GRISWOLD, Casimir Clayton; att (American, 1824-1918) 3,300
Near Newport, Rhode Island (coastal scene); oil on panel, 12x20", RWS 3/16/89 OE
GRIVAZ, Eugene (French, 1852-1915) 1,700
Three Women in Fashionable Bathing Costumes, watercolor on paper, sgn/dtd 1896, 15x12", B/B 12/8/88 OE
GRIVEAU, Lucien; att (French, 19th C) 3,575
Village Street, oil on canvas, 20x29", C-E 10/26/89
GROB, Conrad (Swiss, 1828-1904) 3,300
Teasing the Kittens (lady seated on steps), oil on canvas, sgn/dtd 1900, 46x33", WD 11/16/88 OE
GROENEWEGEN, see Van Groenewegen 15,000
GROLL, Albert Lorey (American, 1866-1952)
Desert Landscape, oil on board, sgn, 12x16", C-E 11/30/88
Evening, New Mexico (extensive landscape); no media given, sgn, 10x14", C-E 6/1/89 UE 1,100
Mountain Pool, oil on canvas, sgn, 26x30", C-E 10/18/89 935
GROLLERON, Paul Louis Narcisse (French, 1848-1901) 1,650
Apres la Battaille, oil on canvas, sgn, 39x52", SBY 5/23/89 OE
Army Officer Smoking a Pipe, oil on panel, sgn, unfr, 5x4", C-E 5/23/88 25,300
Break Time, oil on panel, sgn, 13x10", C-E 10/26/89 715
Portrait of a Zouave, oil on panel, sgn/dtd 1882, 11x8", SBY 6/8/88 3,080
Soldier Lighting His Pipe, oil on panel, sgn, 13x8", C-E 2/21/89 3,080
GROMAIRE, Marcel (French, 1862-1971) 1,980
Femme Nue Assise (seated nude), pen/ink on paper, stamped signature, 13x10", C-E 5/9/89 OE
Maison avec Arbres, India ink/watercolor on paper, sgn/dtd 1927, 13x10", SBY 2/18/88 4,400
Modele dans l'Atelier, pen/ink/watercolor on paper, sgn/dtd 1949, 17x13", SBY 10/7/88 OE 3,300
Moulins en Hollande (contemporary), oil on canvas, sgn twice/dtd 1949 twice/titled, 15x18", SBY 10/7/88 OE 17,600
New York, L'Eglise Noire (contemporary cityscape w/church); oil on canvas, sgn/dtd 1951, 22x18", C-NY 5/11/89 OE 30,250
New York, La Nuit (contemporary); oil on canvas, sgn twice/dtd 1951 twice/titled, 25x32", SBY 10/7/88 OE 44,000
Standing Nude, pen/ink on paper, sgn/dtd 1966, 14x10", SBY 10/7/89 88,000
Toilette (abstract nude), pen/ink/watercolor on paper, sgn/dtd 1948, 17x13", SBY 10/7/88 OE 3,850
Vieille Femme Assise (old woman, seated), oil on canvas, sgn/dtd 1920, 39x32", C-E 11/17/88 14,300
RONDARD, Philippe (French, 19th/20th C) 8,250
Sharing a Meal (woman, child, & dog in an interior), oil on board, sgn, 10x14", C-E 5/22/89
RONLAND, Theude (German, 1817-1876) 1,650
Still Life with Lobster & Game, oil on canvas, sgn/dtd 1848, SBY 2/22/89
ROOM, Emily (American, 20th C) 13,200
Zinnias, watercolor, 22x15", S/A 2/18/89
ROOMS, Red (American, 1937-) 150
Don't Draw in Bed (Matisse), graphite on paper, sgn/dtd 75, 22x31", C-NY 11/10/88 OE
Elephants (theater stage set), acrylic on plywood, sgn, 1978, 142x64", C-NY 5/4/89 17,600
Founders (of United Artist's Studio), colored inks/collaged paper, sgn/dtd 66, 37x39", SBY 10/8/88 13,200
I Nailed Wooden Suns to Wooden Skies, watercolor/gouache/collage on paper, sgn/dtd 1972, 23x31", SBY 11/11/88 38,500
Jackson Pollock (portrait), pastel/graphite on board, sgn/dtd 86, 9x9", SBY 5/3/88 13,200
Mimie Drawing Red Drawing Mimie, pen/ink on paper, sgn, 11x8", SBY 2/14/89 OE 5,500
Miss Astro 1969: Costume Design for Skowhegan Costume Ball; watercolor/gouache/pencil, sgn/dtd 69, 23x17", SBY 5/10/88 3,575
Morris Louis, the Pouring (contemporary); colored pencil on paper, sgn/dtd 86, 90x120", SBY 5/3/89 2,750
Porno Bookstore (contemporary), gouache on paper, sgn/dtd 1976, 50x38", SBY 5/3/88 OE 55,000
Self-Portrait As a Beer Mug, watercolor on cardboard, sgn, 1977, 25x17", SBY 11/9/89 27,500
Untitled (portrait of a man), pastel on paper, sgn/dtd 1978, 35x23", SBY 10/8/88 19,250
Vlamincked (cariacture of three men, bicycle, & cat), gouache/pencil on paper, sgn/dtd 75, 42x30", SBY 2/14/89 OE 3,850
OOT, see De Groot 15,400
OOTVELT, see Van Grootvelt
OPPER, William (American, 1897-1977)
ig Business Pushing Uncle Sam Into a Canyon, ink/crayon/whiting/graphite on paper, sgn, 18x13", RWS 9/8/89
e Profundis, oil on canvas, sgn/inscr in Hebrew, 30x20", SBY 9/23/88 850
igh Jump, charcoal/brush/ink on paper, sgn, 13x18", C-NY 3/11/88 7,975
udge (caricature portrait), oil on masonite, sgn, 1937, 12x12", SBY 3/17/88 OE 880
Member of the NAM, pen/brush/ink on paper, sgn, 26x20", C-NY 3/11/88 2,640
arty Man, pastel on paper, sgn, 17x13", SBY 9/23/88 2,640
pain (two figures in landscape), wash/watercolor on paper, sgn, 14x20", SBY 6/28/89 880
weat Shop, oil on canvas, sgn/artist's stamp, 18x30", C-NY 5/26/88 UE 880
ntouchables (caricature depiction of what appears to be political figures), oil on canvas, sgn, 40x50", C-NY 5/25/89 11,000
OS, Jean Antoine; school of (French, 1771-1835) 24,200
ortrait of a French General (compositional study), oil on canvas, 16x13", RWS 11/10/89 UE
OS, Jean Louis (French, 1793-1879) 700
t the Foot of Popocatepetl (mountainous landscape), oil on canvas, sgn/dtd 20 Mai 1833, 13x18", SBY 11/21/88
OSE, D.C. (American, 19th C) 25,300
ishing Along the River, oil on canvas, sgn, 15x26", C-E 6/1/89
ooking Into the Valley, oil on canvas, sgn, 26x36", C-E 2/1/89 1,320
ehama Mills, oil on canvas, sgn/dtd 1869, 22x32", B/B 12/8/88 1,430
OSS, Chaim (American, 1904-) 1,760
ancing Girls, watercolor/pencil on paper, sgn, 8x30", C-E 2/3/88
495

Fishermen's Return, pencil/ink/watercolor, sgn/dtd 1947, 9x21", PHL 12/1/88 OE ... 1,00
Group of 3: Park Scene; Two Acrobats; Trapeze Artists; India ink wash/pencil, sgn/dtd, 21x15" & smaller, SBY 6/28/89 ... 2,09
Jerusalem, watercolor/pencil on paper laid down on board, sgn/dtd 57, 15x23", C-E 6/1/89 OE ... 1,32
Jerusalem (view from distance), watercolor/pencil/brown ink on paper, sgn/dtd Jerusalem 57, 15x23", SBY 3/17/88 ... 1,10
Pair: On the Beach; The Boardwalk; ink/watercolor on paper, ea sgn, 1 dtd 40, 15x23", 10x15", SBY 4/14/89 ... 3,02
Study of Seated Nude, ink/wash, sgn, 14x9", PHL 10/28/88 UE ... 30

GROSS, Mario
Honest Harry, oil on canvas, sgn/dtd 1974, 20x28", FB 4/25/88 ... 45

GROSS, Peter Alfred (American, 1849-1914)
Canal by the Village, oil on canvas, sgn/dtd 1899, 19x26", RWS 6/17/89 ... 65

GROSSENHEIDER, Richard Philip (American, 1911-1975)
Two Flying Squirrels, watercolor/India ink over pencil on paper, sgn, 14x11", SBY 1/24/89 OE ... 2,75

GROSSIER, Maurice
View of Isthmea, Morning; oil on canvas, sgn/dtd 63, 15x24", C-NY 6/17/89 ... 1,76

GROSSMAN, Joseph B.; att (American, 1899-)
Pair: Landscapes (expressionistic roads & streams w/rural scenes beyond), oil on canvas, sgn, 16x20", RWS 3/31/88 UE ... 32

GROSSMAN, M. (American, 20th C)
Baccanalian Scene, oil on canvas, sgn, 32x38", WG 4/23/88 ... 42

GROSZ, George (American/German, 1893-1959)
Alkoholfreis, brush/ink on heavy paper, sgn/#d 23/estate stamp & #3 54 2, ca 1920, 20x16", SBY 5/11/88 ... 7,70
Arbeiterversamhneg (caricature drawing of a speaker before a crowd), pen/ink on primed canvas, 24x19", SBY 10/7/89 ... 4,95
Auf Spesenkonto (figures in interior), pen/ink on paper, sgn, 24x18", SBY 10/7/88 ... 8,80
Aus Gutem Hause, India ink on paper, sgn/estate stamp/#d 3 92 1, 1926, 26x21", SBY 4/29/88 OE ... 11,55
Berlin Bar Scene, watercolor on paper, bears signature, 12x8", B/B 5/17/89 OE ... 6,05
Blue & Gold Lake, watercolor on paper, sgn, 16x20", C-NY 3/11/88 ... 2,75
Cafe, India ink on paper, sgn/dtd 1918, 16x12", SBY 11/16/89 OE ... 42,90
Chaos, pen/India ink on paper, sgn/#d 3-1-1, 12x18", C-NY 10/5/89 OE ... 13,75
Chinatown, watercolor on paper, sgn/inscr 34 Bayside L Id, 23x16", SBY 5/24/89 ... 16,50
Corned Beef & Cabbage, watercolor/brush/black ink on paper, stamped/#d 1-112-2, 1933, 13x26", C-NY 5/12/88 ... 4,40
Der Einkauf, pen/India ink on paper, sgn/dtd 1926, 19x25", C-NY 10/5/89 ... 8,80
Die Elternhabensorgen Vignette, brush/pen/India ink over pencil, sgn/titled/dtd 1931/#d 8, 23x18", C-NY 5/12/88 ... 3,08
Die Spaziergange, watercolor/pencil on paper, sgn/dtd 1929/inscr Berlin, 18x23", SBY 11/12/88 OE ... 38,50
Double Sided: Upheaval of the Nothingness; Study of a Nude; watercolor, sgn on recto, ca 1947-48, 19x26", C-NY 5/12/88 ... 7,70
Double-Sided: Das Volk Hat Gesiegt; pen/ink on paper, sgn, ca 1924, 20x16", SBY 2/18/88 ... 5,50
Draped Nude Reading: Portrait of Eva; oil/watercolor on paper, sgn, 19x24", SBY 10/7/88 ... 6,05
Drei Soldaten (soldiers firing guns), pen/ink on paper, sgn/estate stamp/#d 31172, 1930, 24x18", SBY 10/7/88 ... 3,02
Ehepaar (couple taking a walk), watercolor on paper, sgn, 27x21", C-NY 10/6/88 OE ... 37,40
Eine Traurige Geschichte (drunken man w/woman & baby), watercolor/gouache/brush/ink, sgn/dtd 37, 23x18", C-NY 2/18/88 OE ... 14,30
Erotische Szene (nude in erotic pose), no media given, estate stamp/dtd 31.1.22, 13x12", PHL 11/15/88 ... 5,00
From Pommerania (country village scene), pen/brush/India ink on paper, sgn/dtd 1930, 18x24", C-NY 5/11/89 UE ... 7,70
Hommage a Courbet (seated nude pulling clothing over her head), oil on canvas, 1938, 20x16", SBY 10/7/88 ... 11,0
Im Cafe, pen/ink on paper, sgn, ca 1918, 13x8", SBY 10/6/89 OE ... 28,6
Interrogation, pen/ink/watercolor on paper, sgn, 1938, 18x22", SBY 10/6/89 ... 38,5
Karnival (sketched figures dancing), pen/ink on paper, ca 1924, 18x18", SBY 10/6/89 OE ... 12,1
Landscape on Long Island, watercolor on paper, sgn twice/dtd 49, 14x17", C-NY 10/6/88 ... 2,5
Midday, Cos Cob; watercolor/pencil on paper, inscr, 16x20", C-E 11/30/88 UE ... 1,9
New York Harbor, oil on board, sgn twice, 31x23", C-NY 12/2/88 OE ... 33,0
No Hiding Place (foggy forest), pencil/watercolor on paper, sgn/dtd 46, 14x20", C-E 10/18/89 OE ... 1,54
Reclining Female Nude, India ink/pencil on paper, sgn/estate stamp/#2 46 4, 16x23", SBY 10/7/89 ... 2,2
Reclining Nude, pencil on paper, sgn, 12x16", SBY 10/5/88 ... 1,4
Restaurant (group of people in a restaurant), watercolor on paper, sgn, 1932, 17x26", SBY 10/6/89 OE ... 33,0
Roter Pfeffer, brush/ink over pencil on paper, sgn/dtd 1932/titled/#d 3 123 6, 24x18", SBY 11/12/88 OE ... 16,5
Seated Nude, pen/ink/pencil on paper, sgn/artist stamp/#d, 11x9", SBY 2/14/89 ... 1,32
Seated Nude with Drapery, charcoal on paper mounted at the edges on paper, sgn/dtd 38, 25x19", C-NY 10/6/88 ... 4,4
Seated Woman in Profile, ink wash on paper, sgn/dtd 1924, 26x21", SBY 10/7/89 ... 2,2
Secret, pen/black ink on paper, sgn twice, ca 1936, 25x19", C-NY 10/6/88 ... 2,8
Shoeshine, brush/ink/watercolor on laid paper, sgn/titled, ca 1932-33, 25x19", SBY 2/16/89 OE ... 24,2
Sitzender Akt (female nude, seated), graphite on buff paper, sgn/dtd 1916, 13x11", C-NY 10/6/88 ... 2,7
Sitzender Akt (posterior view of seated nude), pastel on paper, sgn, 23x16", C-NY 2/16/89 ... 5,2
Standing Nude, watercolor on paper, stamped signature/estate stamp, 20x16", SBY 10/5/88 ... 4,4
Stehender Akt (posterior view of nude), watercolor/black chalk on tan paper, sgn, 1946, 24x18", C-NY 10/6/88 ... 8,2
Still Life, Apples & Fruit; oil on canvasboard, sgn, 24x20", SBY 10/7/89 ... 16,5
Strandleben, brush/ink on paper, sgn/dtd 1925-26/#d 8/inscr Abbildung Simplicussimus, 25x19", SBY 2/16/89 ... 7,7
Strandleben (beach scene), watercolor on paper, sgn/#d 7, ca 1926, 19x26", SBY 5/10/89 ... 31,9
Strassenszene (street scene w/three figures), pencil on paper, sgn/dtd/stamped/#d 4-156-5, 1912, 11x9", C-NY 5/12/88 ... 4,9
Street Battle, watercolor on paper laid down on board, sgn/dtd Bayside L Isl 1934, 22x17", SBY 3/17/88 ... 4,9
Street in the City, watercolor/ink on paper, estate stamp, 15x20", SBY 2/14/89 OE ... 5,5
Street Scene (four figures), pen/ink/watercolor on paper, sgn/dtd 33, 10x14", SBY 10/6/89 ... 18,7
Three Figures, New York Street Scene; watercolor on paper, sgn/dtd 33, 25x18", SBY 5/25/88 OE ... 23,6
Truro, watercolor on paper, sgn/inscr/dtd 39, 9x12", C-E 11/30/88 ... 2,4
Veteran's Day, New York (disabled selling poppies); watercolor/brush/ink, sgn, 1933, 18x25", SBY 10/7/88 ... 10,4

Wandervogel (figures from behind, two w/guitars), pen/ink on paper, sgn, ca 1925, 25x20", SBY 10/6/89 8,800
We Want War (Keiner Kann Sie Aufhalten), brush/black ink on brown paper, sgn/stamped, #d 4/13/2, 1937, C-NY 5/12/88 2,420
Weiblicher Akt (posterior view of nude woman), black chalk on tan paper, 28x19", C-NY 10/6/88 2,640
Zwei Manner, pen/India ink on paper, 1924, 12x10", C-NY 10/6/88 OE 4,180
Zwei Nackte Frauen (two nudes), charcoal on paper, stamped signature, #d 4/188/2, 1939, 19x25", C-NY 10/5/89 OE 44,000

ROTTGER, Arthur (Polish School, 1837-1867)
Soldier on Horseback, oil on canvas, sgn/dtd 1886, 24x29", FB 10/30/89 2,530

ROUARD, John E. (American, 19th C)
Pemigawasset, figures on grassy riverbank/in boat; oil on canvas, sgn/dtd 1882, 10x14", RAB 11/25/88 3,000

ROUX, see De Groux

ROVE, Maria (Danish, 19th C)
Basket of Flowers, oil on canvas, sgn/dtd 1841, 14x17", SBY 2/22/89 9,900

ROVER, Dorothy Reno (American, 1908-1975)
Portrait of a Woman, oil on canvas, sgn/dtd 36, 14x12", B/B 1/11/89 825

ROVER, Oliver Dennett (American, 1861-1927)
Alessandro My Gondolier (canal scene), oil on canvas, sgn/dtd 1928, 34x41", SBY 4/14/89 1,760
Campo San Giovanni e Paulo (cityscape), oil on board, sgn/dtd 1923/titled, 12x16", SBY 3/17/88 OE 2,310
Grand Canal, Venice; oil on canvas, sgn/dtd 1923, 24x31", SBY 9/23/88 4,400
Sailing in the Summer, oil on canvas, 13x16", C-E 6/1/89 UE 715

RUBACS, Carlo (German, 19th C)
View of the Doges Palace, oil on canvas, sgn, 31x46", C-NY 10/25/89 18,700

RUBER, Carl (Austrian, 1803-1845)
Studies of Flowers: Delphinium Consolida, Coronilla Coronata, Echium Vulgare, Orchis Bifolia; unfr, 21x14", C-NY 2/23/89 1,100
Studies of Flowers: Orobanche Elation, Polygola Major Varietas, Campanula Sibirica, Arum Maculatum; 21x14", C-NY 2/23/89 1,100

RUENWALD, Gustavus (19th C)
Niagara Falls (landscape), oil on canvas, before 1833, 25x34", SBY 1/28/88 25,300
Table Rock, Niagara Falls; oil on canvas, before 1833, 25x34", SBY 1/28/88 25,300

RUEZE, Jean Baptiste; after (French, 1725-1805)
Tame Canary, oil on canvas, oval, 23x19", PHL 10/28/88 700
Two Sisters From the Marriage Contract, oil on canvas, oval, 13x9", SBY 7/12/89 1,760

RUFFAUT, Georges (French, 1857-1882)
Tranquil Moment, oil on panel, 14x20", NA 2/24/89 UE 600

RUGER, T.R.
Pioneers, pencil/charcoal/ink wash heightened w/white, sgn, 9x13", C-E 2/16/88 110

RUND, Johann (Austrian, 1808-1887)
Sneaking a Taste, oil on canvas, sgn/dtd 79, 12x16", B/B 6/9/88 3,575

RUND, Norbert (German, 1717-1767)
Pair: Travelers Resting by a Fountain in a Mountainous Landscape; oil on panel, 11x9", C-NY 6/2/88 11,000

RUND, Norbert; att (German, 1717-1767)
Mountainous River Landscape with Figures...; bodycolor on paper laid down on canvas, 7x10", C-NY 1/11/89 660

RUNENWALD, Jakob (German, 1822-1896)
Entertaining the Baby, oil on canvas, sgn/dtd 1870, 42x31", SBY 2/22/89 OE 46,200

RUNWALD, Isaac (Swedish, 1889-1946)
The Picnic, oil on canvas, sgn, 27x39", B/B 6/9/88 UE 3,850

UPPE, Charles Paul (American, 1860-1940)
Autumn Landscape, oil on board, 11x8", DM 9/16/88 750
Beached Fishing Boats, watercolor/gouache on paper, sgn, 16x21", RWS 9/8/89 850
Beached Ship, oil on canvas, sgn, 30x40", SBY 9/23/88 5,225
Boats in Gloucester Harbor, watercolor on paper, sgn, 14x21", B/B 12/8/88 660
Boats on the Dutch Coast, oil on canvas, sgn, 10x17", SBY 4/14/89 2,090
Coastal Scene, oil on canvas, sgn, 20x30", DM 9/16/88 1,700
Cottage by a Stream in Winter, oil on canvas, sgn, 25x30", B/B 10/9/88 3,300
Cows Grazing by a Stream, oil on canvas, sgn, 25x30", B/B 10/9/88 3,300
Dordrecht, watercolor heightened w/gouache on board, sgn/inscr, 15x23", C-E 6/1/88 1,045
Dutch Canal Scene, oil on canvas, sgn, 18x22", C-E 6/1/88 1,430
armer in a Hay Field, oil on canvas laid down on board, sgn, 13x16", C-E 11/30/88 1,760
armers in the Field, oil on canvas, sgn, 33x36", B/B 3/17/88 5,500
igures by Beached Vessel, watercolor on paper, sgn, 19x15", RWS 3/16/89 OE 860
igures in a Fall Landscape, oil on canvas, sgn, 14x20", PHL 12/1/88 1,200
oggy Sunrise, oil on canvas, sgn, 24x30", B/B 6/15/89 9,900
orest Scene, tempera & watercolor, sgn, 14x18", LH 3/20/88 600
From Fishing, watercolor/gouache/pencil on paper laid down on paper, sgn, 19x15", C-E 11/8/88 660
the Harvest Fields (girl seated by fence row), oil on canvas, sgn, 13x18", C-E 6/1/88 2,860
coming Tide at Bass Rocks Mass Near Gloucester (figures along rocky shore), oil on canvas, sgn, 36x41", RWS 3/31/88 OE 4,200
te October (landscape), oil on canvas, sgn/dtd 1912, 23x30", C-E 6/1/89 UE 3,520
other & Child on the Seashore, oil on canvas, sgn, 52x36", SBY 9/23/88 7,150
ovember Day, Holland (landscape); watercolor on paper, sgn twice/titled, 18x26", RAB 3/27/89 1,000
ctober Afternoon, oil on canvas, sgn, 33x48", RWS 11/3/88 OE 7,500
d Mill at Voorburg, Holland; oil on canvas, sgn, 24x20", SBY 6/24/88 UE 1,650
ir: Nude Lady; Standing Man; oil on canvas laid down on board, oil on board, sgn, 17x10" & smaller, C-E 6/1/88 UE 440
ading Lesson, oil on board, sgn, 10x8", C-E 6/1/89 1,045

- Sailboat at Day Dock, oil on canvas, sgn, 13x20", NA 2/24/89 ... 1,600
- Sailboats on Land, oil on canvas, sgn, 13x20", C-E 6/1/88 ... 1,430
- Sheep Grazing by a Pond, oil on board, sgn, 14x20", WD 4/13/88 ... 2,400
- Shepherd with Flock of Sheep, watercolor/gouache on paper, sgn, 18x22", SBY 6/24/88 OE ... 2,090
- Smoking a Pipe Before the Fire, oil on canvas mounted on panel, sgn, 19x15", RWS 5/12/89 ... 950
- Swimming in Holland, oil on canvasboard, sgn, 8x10", RWS 5/12/89 OE ... 1,500
- Windmill in Hague, watercolor on board, sgn/inscr, 13x23", C-E 6/1/88 ... 462
- Winter Stream, oil on canvas, sgn, 25x30", B/B 3/22/89 ... 8,800
- Woman Peeling Fruit in a Sun-Dappled Yard, oil on canvas, sgn, 1898, 18x15", SBY 9/14/89 ... 2,475

GRUPPE, Emile Albert (American, 1896-1978)

- After the Storm (shoreline w/house on hill), oil on canvas, sgn, 20x24", SBY 4/14/89 ... 2,200
- At Dock, oil on canvas, sgn, 24x20", SBY 9/14/89 ... 3,300
- Australian Pines (pines at shoreline), oil on canvas, sgn, 30x25", RWS 3/31/88 UE ... 1,100
- Autumn Trees, oil on canvas, sgn, 25x30", RWS 11/3/88 ... 3,000
- Bass Rocks, oil on board, sgn, 11x14", LH 10/16/88 ... 700
- Bass Rocks, oil on canvas, sgn, 20x24", C-E 2/3/88 ... 1,320
- Bass Rocks (beach), oil on canvas, sgn/inscr 1928, 20x24", RWS 11/3/88 OE ... 26,000
- Bass Rocks (Gloucester, Massachusetts), oil on canvas, sgn/titled, 30x35", RAB 8/8/89 UE ... 3,000
- Bass Rocks (rocky coastal scene), oil on canvas, sgn/inscr, 20x24", RWS 11/3/88 ... 2,000
- Beachcombers at Sunset (buildings in foreground, figures on shore beyond), oil on canvas, sgn, 28x41", B/B 10/9/88 ... 3,575
- Beech Tree in the Snow, oil on canvas, sgn, 25x30", B/B 3/17/88 ... 3,575
- Birch Trees, oil on canvas, sgn, 30x36", C-E 10/18/89 ... 4,950
- Bird's Eye View of Motif I (harbor scene w/buildings & ships), oil on canvas, sgn, 30x36", RWS 5/19/88 ... 3,750
- Cambridge, Vermont; oil on canvas, sgn, 24x36", C-E 11/30/88 ... 6,600
- Cape Ann, Afternoon; oil on canvas, sgn, 25x30", RWS 5/12/89 UE ... 2,500
- Church in an Autumn Landscape, oil on canvasboard, sgn, 16x12", SBY 3/17/88 ... 1,980
- Cloudy Day, Gloucester, Arnold's Wharf, Seine Nets Drying; oil on canvasboard, sgn, 16x20", RWS 9/8/89 ... 1,400
- Coming Storm, oil on canvas, sgn, 30x36", SBY 9/14/89 ... 2,750
- Drying the Sails (docked boats), oil on canvas, sgn, 24x20", SBY 4/14/89 OE ... 5,775
- East Gloucester, Rocky Neck (boats in harbor, fishing shacks beyond); oil on board, sgn, 12x18", RAB 8/9/88 ... 3,250
- Evening Light, Vermont; oil on canvas, sgn twice/titled, 20x24", SBY 1/24/89 ... 3,025
- Fishing Boats, Gloucester; oil on canvas, sgn, 24x20", B/B 3/22/89 ... 2,200
- Fog, Gloucester; oil on canvas, sgn twice/dtd 1954, 30x36", SBY 6/24/88 OE ... 5,500
- Gloucester Harbor, oil on canvas, sgn, 24x20", SBY 9/14/89 ... 5,775
- Gloucester Harbor in Winter, oil on canvas, sgn/dtd Nov 1968, 30x36", RAB 8/8/89 ... 5,250
- Gloucester Morning, oil on canvas, sgn, 20x24", LH 10/16/88 OE ... 6,750
- Gulls in a Harbour, oil on canvasboard, sgn, 12x16", C-E 2/1/89 ... 1,870
- Harbor Scene, oil on canvas, sgn, 24x21", SBY 3/17/88 ... 3,300
- Lamoille River, Jeffersonville, Vermont; oil on canvas, sgn, 25x30", SBY 9/14/89 ... 2,200
- Landing, oil on canvas, sgn/inscr, 25x30", C-NY 9/30/88 ... 9,350
- Mending the Nets, oil on canvas, sgn, 16x20", RWS 5/12/89 ... 3,600
- Pleasant Valley Road (landscape), Vermont; oil on canvas, sgn/titled, 30x40", SBY 1/24/89 ... 5,500
- Road to Waterville, Vermont; oil on canvas, sgn, 25x30", SBY 6/28/89 ... 5,775
- Rocky Coastal Scene with Breaking Waves (impressionistic), oil on canvas, 24x29", DM 9/16/88 ... 1,750
- Rocky Shoreline, oil on canvas, 20x24", NA 2/24/89 ... 1,900
- Seagulls, oil on canvas, sgn, 24x20", DM 3/14/88 ... 80
- Smith's Cove, Gloucester; oil on canvas, sgn, 20x24", RWS 11/10/89 UE ... 4,000
- Spring Thaw (landscape w/stream), oil on canvas, sgn/dtd 1947, 25x30", SBY 4/14/89 ... 2,75
- Storm, Gloucester (crashing waves); oil on canvas, sgn, 30x36", SBY 4/14/89 ... 3,30
- Sugaring, Vermont; oil on canvas, sgn, 30x36", RWS 5/12/89 OE ... 9,00
- Sunset, Gloucester Harbor; oil on canvas, sgn/inscr, unfr, 30x36", RWS 11/3/88 ... 6,00
- Tide Coming In (waves washing along shore), oil on canvas, sgn, 20x36", C-E 6/1/89 ... 2,09
- Vessels Off a Rocky Shore, oil on canvas, sgn, 30x36", RWS 5/12/89 UE ... 2,40
- View Across the Valley (extensive landscape), oil on canvas, sgn, 20x18", SBY 4/14/89 ... 1,98
- Winter Hills (farm in snowy landscape), oil on canvas, sgn/dtd 1947, 20x24", SBY 4/14/89 OE ... 4,67
- Winter Landscape, oil on canvas, sgn, 16x20", SBY 1/24/89 OE ... 2,53
- Winter Stream, oil on canvasboard, sgn/dtd 1940, 12x16", SBY 4/14/89 ... 1,87
- Woodland Stream, oil on canvas laid down on board, sgn, 8x10", PHL 10/28/88 ... 32

GRUST, F.G. (Dutch, 19th/20th C)

- Interior Scene with Mother & Children Before a Hearth, oil on canvas, sgn, 26x30", MAG 6/22/88 ... 90

GRUYTER, see De Gruyter

GSELL, Laurent (French, 1860-1944)

- Promenade in the Park (prim lady w/umbrella, figures beyond), oil on canvas, sgn, 24x18", C-E 5/22/89 ... 8,80
- Senegalese Encampment, oil on canvas, sgn/dtd 1913, 21x26", SBY 6/8/88 ... 2,20

GU, Xu (Chinese, 1824-1896)

- Fish, fan painting; ink/color on paper, sgn, 7x19", SBY 5/31/89 ... 4,4
- Landscape with Pagoda (hanging scroll), ink/color on paper, sgn, 29x16", SBY 5/31/89 OE ... 25,3

GUARDI, Francesco (Italian, 1712-1793)

- Capriccio with a Ruined Arch & Figures, oil on panel, 8x6", SBY 1/12/89 OE ... 85,2
- Pair: Isola di San Michele; Rio dei Mendicanti; oil on canvas, 6x9", SBY 10/27/89 OE ... 275,0
- Pair: Landscape with Figures Beside a Ruined Arch; Walled Garden of a Church; oil on panel, 8x10", SBY 6/2/89 OE ... 231,0

ıir: Views of Molo, Palazzo Ducale; Libreria, Santa Maria Della Salute, Venice; oil on canvas, 10x14", SBY 10/27/89 OE 506,000
ıazza di San Marco, Venice; oil on canvas, 1770-80, 10x17", SBY 10/27/89 OE 418,000
ꞏaside Fortress on Fire, oil on canvas, 7x10", SBY 6/3/88.......... 38,500
ıew of Island of San Christoforo w/Islands of San Michele & Murano in the Distance, oil on canvas, 25x38", SBY 10/27/89 4,400,000

ARDI, Francesco; att (Italian, 1712-1793)

ıpriccio Landscape, oil on canvas, 4x6", SBY 10/21/88 OE 6,600
adonna & Child, oil on canvas, 27x20", C-NY 10/20/88 OE.......... 12,100

ARDI, Francesco; circle of (Italian, 1712-1793)

ıpriccio with Cottages by the Water, oil on panel, 7x6", SBY 10/13/89 UE 2,200
ıir: Architectural Cappriccio by the Water; oil on canvas, 6x9", SBY 10/13/89 OE 35,750

ARDI, Francesco; manner of (Italian, 1712-1793)

editerranean Port with Figures, oil on shaped canvas, 18x47", SBY 12/9/88.......... 935
ıir: Views of Venice; oil on canvas, 10x7", C-NY 6/17/89 1,320
ꞏnetian Street Scene, oil on canvas, 19x14", SBY 6/8/88.......... 2,310
ıew of the Canal at Mestre, oil on canvas, 17x27", SBY 12/9/88 OE.......... 4,125

ARDI, Giacomo (Italian, 1764-1835)

ıew of the Palazzo Ducale, Venice, From the Lagoon with Boats & Figures; oil on canvas, unfr, 22x32", SBY 4/7/88 OE.......... 40,700
ıew of the Piazza San Marco, Venice; bodycolor, sgn/inscr, 5x9", C-NY 1/11/89 3,080

ARDI, Giacomo; att (Italian, 1764-1835)

ınnareggio, Venice; oil on canvas, 9x12", C-NY 6/17/89 1,430
ıpriccio, oil on canvas, 7x6", C-NY 6/17/89.......... 1,100
ıir: Piazza San Marco; Ducale Palace at Venice; wash on paper, unfr, 15x19", WD 1/25/89 OE 8,500

ARDI, Giacomo; manner of (Italian, 1764-1835)

azza S Marco, Venice; pen/brown ink, 10x14", SBY 7/12/89.......... 1,870

ARDI, Giacomo; style of (Italian, 1764-1835)

ıir: Venetian Canal Scenes; gouache on paper w/highlights, sgn, 4x7", B/B 9/15/89.......... 1,100

ARDI, Giovanni Antonio; att (Italian,1698-1760)

strologer, oil on canvas, 28x22", SBY 4/7/88 3,025

ARDI, manner of

ıir: Church of San Giorgio; Classical Ruins; oil on canvas, shaped tops, 29x17", WD 1/25/89 OE 8,750
ıir: Two Views of Venice; oil on canvas, ovoid, 20x15", C-E 2/16/88 OE 2,860

ARDI, school of

rand Canal at Carrareggio at the Church of San Geremia, oil on canvas, oval, 23x32", WD 10/19/88 4,000
ındscape with a Tree, pen/brown ink/wash on paper, 5x8", C-NY 6/17/89 UE 264
ıew of the Arsenal, Venice; oil on canvas, 12x16", C-NY 10/12/89 OE.......... 12,100

ARDY, H. (American, 20th C)

ntitled, figures in wooded landscape; watercolor, sgn, 16x14", SLK 2/11/89 350

ASTAVINO, see De Guastavino

AY, see Le Guay

AYASAMIN, Oswaldo (Ecuadorian, 1919-)

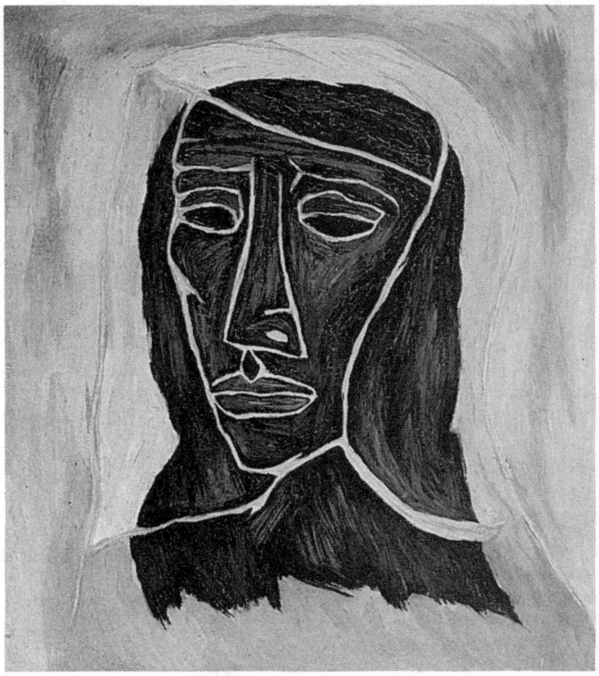

Cabeza de Indio, oil on canvas, sgn, 1950, 23x20", C-NY 5/18/88 OE, $13,200

hrist (abstract), oil on panel, sgn, 1950s, 43x47", SBY 5/17/88.......... 17,600
gures (sketch), black ink on paper, sgn, 26x20", SBY 11/21/88 2,640

Flores (abstract floral still life), oil on canvas, sgn/inscr Para Susy con Carino, 35x24", C-NY 11/21/88 ... 9,35
Marimbas (abstract), oil on board, sgn, 13x20", C-NY 11/21/88 ... 4,95
Mujer Pensativa (abstract portrait of a woman), oil on board, sgn, 30x22", C-NY 5/18/88 ... 15,40
Untitled (mournful figure), oil on canvas, sgn, ca 1964, 51x23", SBY 5/16/89 ... 8,80

GUBIN, Selma (American, 1903-1974)
Urban Landscape, oil/gouache on paper, sgn/dtd 39, unfr, 13x20", SBY 4/14/89 ... 1,10

GUDIASHVILI, Lado
Two Dancers in Georgian Costume with a Doe, pencil with traces of red chalk, sgn/dtd Paris 1923, 20x13", SBY 10/7/89 ... 1,65

GUDIN, Henriette (French, 19th C)
Pair: A Day's Catch; oil on panel, sgn, 6x8", C-E 10/26/89 ... 5,50

GUELDRY, Ferdinand Joseph (French, 1858-)
Repairing the Skull (three figures by river bank), oil on canvas, sgn/dtd 95, 16x18", SBY 10/24/89 ... 19,80

GUERCINO, Giovanni Francesco (1591-1666)
Andromeda Standing in the Sea, pen/brown ink/wash, 10x8", SBY 1/13/89 OE ... 31,90
Christ Crowned with Thorns, red chalk, 8x7", SBY 1/13/88 OE ... 82,50
Cupid Holding a Bow & Arrow, red chalk, 8x9", SBY 1/13/89 ... 24,20
Landscape with a Man Seen From Behind, seated on a stone, taking off his shirt; pen/ink, 7x8", SBY 1/13/89 OE ... 57,75
Portrait of Grand Duke Paul Petrovich (future tsar Paul I), oil on canvas, 29x23", C-L 10/8/88 ... 13,00
Prophet Isaiah (portrait), oil on canvas, 81x28", C-NY 5/31/89 ... 71,50
Saint John the Evangelist, red chalk, inscr, encircled bird wm, 4x7", C-NY 1/12/88 ... 6,60

GUERCINO, Giovanni Francesco; circle of (1591-1666)
Mother Seated with Her Child Seen From Behind, pen/brown ink/gray wash, 11x8", C-NY 1/11/89 OE ... 2,09

GUERCINO, Giovanni Francesco; school of (1591-1666)
Trial of Moses, oil on canvas, 46x71", C-NY 4/6/89 ... 15,40

GUERIN, Armand (Swiss, 1913-)
L'Institute de Paris, oil on board, sgn, 25x30", SBY 10/7/89 ... 2,53
Street Scene, oil on masonite, sgn, unfr, 9x10", SBY 10/5/88 UE ... 22

GUERIN, Charles (French, 1875-1939)
La Robe Bleue, oil on canvas, sgn/dtd 1895, 57x35", C-E 2/23/88 ... 1,76

GUERIN, Joseph (American, 1889-)
New York Harbor with Statue of Liberty in Distance, watercolor on paper, sgn, 23x31", C-E 2/3/88 UE ... 41

GUERIN, Jules (American, 1866-1946)
High Bridge, New York City; graphite/oil en grisaille on canvasboard, sgn/dtd Oct 1902, 18x26", RWS 11/10/89 ... 1,80
Water Carriers, watercolor/pencil on paper, sgn, 10x13", C-E 11/30/88 ... 66

GUERIN, Pierre Narcisse; att (French, 1774-1883)
Pyrrhus & Polites, depicted w/Greek warriors, accusing Polites, his sister pleads; oil on canvas, 45x57", SBY 10/24/89 ... 17,60

GUERMACHEFF, Michel Markinovich (Russian, 1867-)
Snowy Mountains, oil on canvas, sgn, 26x32", C-E 9/15/88 ... 66
Winter Evening Sunlight, oil on canvas, sgn, 21x18", WAD 6/6/88 ... 2,50

GUERRA, Achille (Italian, 1832-)
Artist & His Admirers, oil on canvas laid down on board, sgn, 18x32", C-NY 5/24/89 UE ... 5,50

GUERRA, Carlos Hernandez (20th C)
Paisaje de Guanipa (landscape), acrylic on canvas, sgn, 51x77", C-NY 5/18/88 ... 6,05
Paisaje en Ocre (landscape), oil on canvas, sgn, 51x77", C-NY 5/17/89 ... 5,50

GUERRERO, Jose (American/Spanish, 1915-)
Putnam's House, Danvers, Massachusetts, A Winter Scene; oil on board, sgn/titled, 15x18", RWS 3/16/89 ... 1,50

GUERRESCHI, Giuseppe (Italian, 1929-)
Bovisa, oil on canvas, sgn/dtd 1956, 39x19", LH 10/16/88 UE ... 10
Ceclista, oil on canvas, sgn/dtd 1954, 47x31", LH 9/10/89 OE ... 1,70
Man on a Bicycle, gouache, sgn, 18x9", LH 12/4/88 UE ... 4

GUIDI, Giuseppe (Italian, 20th C)
Afternoon of Leisure, oil on canvas, sgn, 17x23", C-E 10/26/89 ... 5,50
Connoisseur, watercolor heightened with white/gum arabic, sgn/inscr, 21x14", C-NY 10/26/88 ... 2,64
Family Checkers, watercolor over pencil, sgn/inscr, 21x29", C-NY 5/25/88 ... 1,76
Game of Checkers (gathering of two elegant couples in interior), oil on canvas, sgn/inscr, 24x34", C-E 5/22/89 ... 5,72
Women in a Harem, watercolor, sgn, 21x14", C-NY 10/25/89 ... 6,05

GUIDOBONO, Bartolomeo; att (Italian, 1657-1709)
Bacchanal with Putti & Satyrs in a Wooded Landscape, oil on canvas, 10x37", C-NY 6/2/88 OE ... 5,50

GUIGNAROLA
Papal Portrait, oil on canvas, sgn, 15x11", LH 5/15/88 ... 30

GUILLAUMET, Gustave (French, 1840-1887)
Bergeres Arabes, oil on canvas, sgn, 28x37", C-NY 5/25/88 ... 6,60
Portrait of a Moroccan Woman, oil on canvas, unfr, 15x12", B/B 4/20/88 ... 66
Water Carriers Outside a Walled Town, oil on canvas, sgn, 12x19", C-NY 5/25/88 ... 6,05

GUILLAUMIN, Armand (French, 1841-1927)
Agay, pastel on paper, sgn/inscr/dtd 95, 18x25", SBY 10/5/88 ... 5,50
Agay au Pied du Dramont (coastal scene w/sailboat), oil on canvas, sgn, 26x32", C-NY 2/16/89 OE ... 77,00
Baie d'Agay, le Semaphore; oil on canvas, sgn, ca 1895, 30x40", SBY 5/11/88 ... 55,00
Bateaux au Pont Charenton (river landscape), pastel on tan paper laid down on board, sgn, 12x18", SBY 5/10/89 ... 26,40
Bords de la Creuse, Matin (river landscape); oil on canvas, sgn, ca 1896, 24x32", SBY 11/12/88 ... 60,50
Cottage, gouache/watercolor on tan paper, sgn, ca 1928, 15x19", SBY 2/18/88 ... 18,70

Crozant-la Rouche de L'echo; oil on canvas, sgn, 1899, 26x32", SBY 2/18/88 38,500
Environs d'Auvers (landscape w/figures), oil on canvas, sgn/dtd 79, 20x25", C-NY 11/16/88 OE 99,000
L'Allier a Saint Julien Des Chazes (hilly river landscape), oil on canvas, sgn/dtd 23 Octobre 91, 29x37", SBY 5/10/89 99,000
Landscape Near Paris, pencil on paper, initialed/dtd 78, 7x11", RWS 11/3/88 UE 100
Le Barrage de Genetin a Crozant (river landscape), oil on canvas, sgn, 1917, 20x26", SBY 10/6/89 55,000
Le Moulin Brigand, Ruines de Chateau de Crozant (landscape); oil on canvas, sgn, ca 1900, 20x24", C-NY 5/11/89 30,000
Le Plateau Bromant a Pontgibaud (Puy de Dome), landscape, oil on canvas, sgn/dtd 1890, 26x32", C-NY 11/16/88 OE 8,800
Le Rocher Gaupillat au Trayas (seascape w/coastline), oil on canvas, sgn, ca 1913, 26x32", SBY 2/18/88 35,750
Le Trayas (coastal scene), oil on canvas, sgn, 1907, 25x31", C-NY 11/16/88 59,400
Le Village de Crozant, oil on canvas, sgn, 26x32", SBY 2/18/88 OE 63,250
Les Moulins de Saardam, Hollande; oil on canvas, sgn, ca 1904, 24x29", SBY 2/18/88 44,000
Luxembourg Gardens, Paris; oil on canvas, sgn, ca 1898, 22x32", SBY 11/12/88 77,000
Moulin Bouchardon, Crozant (landscape with stream & dwelling); oil on canvas, sgn, ca 1905, 19x23", C-NY 5/12/88 46,200
Moulin Bouchardon, Crozant; oil on canvas, sgn, ca 1895, 26x32", SBY 2/18/88 OE 68,750
Moulins en Hollande (landscape w/windmills), oil on canvas, sgn, ca 1904, 21x25", C-NY 11/16/88 55,000
Paysage, Daniette (extensive landscape); oil on canvas, sgn, ca 1885, 24x29", C-NY 5/11/89 OE 204,500
Paysage aux Environs de Rouen, oil on canvas, sgn, ca 1898, 21x26", SBY 10/7/88 33,000
Paysage de Crozant, oil on canvas, sgn/inscr Crozant 1906, 26x32", SBY 10/7/88 57,750
Paysage de l'Ile de France, oil on canvas, ca 1897, 24x20", C-NY 11/15/88 2,090,000
Paysage de l'Ile de France, oil on canvas, sgn/dtd 90, 32x26", SBY 5/11/88 148,500
Pont Charraud sous la Neige (winter landscape), oil on canvas, sgn, 26x31", SBY 5/10/89 63,250
Rochers a Agay (rocky coastal scene), oil on canvas, sgn, 1893, 21x27", C-NY 5/12/88 33,000
Route a Damiette, oil on canvas, sgn/dtd 85, 26x32", SBY 5/11/88 OE 99,000
Rue de la Scie, Pontcharra (landscape w/figures); oil on canvas, sgn/dtd 1901, 29x24", C-NY 5/11/89 82,500
Vallee de la Sedelle, oil on canvas, sgn/inscr Crozant 1920, 13x16", SBY 2/16/89 38,500

UILLEMET, Jean-Baptiste Antoine (French, 1843-1918)
River Landscape, oil on canvas, sgn, 15x22", SBY 12/9/88 4,400

UILLEMINET, Claude (French, 1821-1860)
Chickens, Duck, & Guinea Hen in a Yard; oil on panel, sgn, 13x9", WAD 6/6/88 900
Upheaval in the Hen House, oil on canvas, sgn, 17x23", RWS 4/7/89 OE 4,700

UILLERMO, Juan (European, 20th C)
Pescada con Gallo, oil on canvas, sgn, 40x32", WG 4/23/88 1,700

UILLONET, Octave Denis Victor (French, 1872-1967)
Ascot Races, oil on canvas, initialed, 86x143", SBY 6/10/88 UE 26,400
Henley Regatta, oil on canvas, initialed, 85x144", SBY 6/10/88 UE 26,400
Hyde Park Rotten Row (landscape w/horses & riders), oil on canvas, initialed, 87x146", SBY 6/10/88 UE 14,300
Roses (still life), oil on canvas, sgn, 24x18", C-E 11/17/88 1,430

UILLOU, Alfred (French, 19th C)
Pecheuses de Crevettes (young girl & boy fishing for shrimp), oil on canvas, sgn/dtd 1874, unfr, 47x84", C-NY 5/24/89 52,800
White Lace (portrait of girl's head draped in white lace), oil on panel, sgn, 12x8", RWS 9/8/89 OE 1,300

UIRAMAND, Paul (French, 1926-)
Le Tapis Bleu, watercolor, 1978, 26x20", LH 10/16/88 900

UISE, J. (American, 20th C)
Portrait of the Ship Reynard, oil on wood panel, sgn, 11x17", RAB 8/1/88 550

UIZHEN, Li; style of (Chinese, 10th C)
Auspicious Birds (hanging scroll), ink/color on silk, bears signature, 79x40", SBY 5/31/89 UE 1,925

ULBRANDSEN, Olaf (Norwegian, 1873-)
Portrait of the Freighter Elmdene, oil on artist board, sgn/dtd 1902, 16x24", RAB 11/10/88 475

LLAGHER, Christian; att (American, 1762-1826)
Portrait of Sarah Woodhull Forman, oil on canvas, ca 1797, 37x27", SBY 3/17/88 2,200

NDLACH, Max (American, 20th C)
Landscape, oil on panel, sgn, 40x30", LH 10/16/88 UE 650

NOT
Afternoon Walk (couple in landscape), oil on panel, sgn, 20x15", C-E 5/23/88 1,045

NTHER, Georg (German, 1886-)
Still Life of Carnations, oil on board, sgn, 25x38", B/B 3/22/89 2,750

ORD, A. (19th/20th C)
Arabian Infantry, oil on canvas, sgn, 12x24", MG 6/25/88 UE 600

RIG, Fischer; see Fischer, Adolph

RPPE, Emile Albert (American, 1896-1978)
Pompano Fisherman (expressionistic scene w/fishermen surf casting), oil on artist board, sgn, 16x20", RWS 3/31/88 UE 1,600

RRY, William (American, 19th C)
Still Life of Box of Strawberries, oil on canvas, sgn, 9x13", RWS 5/19/88 UE 350

RSCHNER, Herbert (1901-)
Flamingos at Play, oil on canvas, 1938, 42x76", C-E 6/16/88 UE 220

SSOW, Bernard (American, 1881-1957)
Chess Players in a Park, oil on canvasboard, sgn, 12x16", WD 4/13/88 1,600
Figures in a Summer Landscape, oil on canvas, sgn, 25x30", SBY 4/14/89 2,200
Hudson Tubes, oil on canvas, sgn, 24x30", SBY 4/14/89 2,200
Interior, oil on canvas, sgn twice/titled, 34x30", SBY 3/17/88 2,750
Interior (music room beyond), oil on canvas, sgn twice/titled, 34x30", SBY 3/17/88 2,750

New York Dock Scene, charcoal/pastel on paper, sgn, 16x21", C-E 6/1/88 UE ... 55
Street Scene, oil on board, sgn, 8x10", MG 5/28/88 ... 42
Street Scene, oil on canvas, sgn, 12x8", MG 5/28/88 ... 47
The Window (potted plant, cat on sill peering out window), oil on canvas, sgn, 25x22", SBY 4/14/89 ... 2,20

GUSSOW, Carl (German, 1843-1907)
Old Scholar (portrait), oil on panel, sgn/dtd 1881, 17x13", B/B 5/17/89 ... 1,54

GUSTIN, Paul M. (American, 1886-)
Morning Mist, oil on canvas, sgn, 18x24", B/B 4/20/88 ... 82

GUSTON, Philip (American, 1912-)
Change No 1 (abstract), oil on paper laid down, sgn/dtd 1959, 23x29", SBY 5/2/89 OE ... 143,00
Clock Face, acrylic on panel, sgn/dtd 1968, 18x20", SBY 11/9/89 ... 55,00
Dark Room (contemporary), oil on canvas, sgn/dtd 1978, 68x80", SBY 5/2/88 ... 220,00
Drawing No 2 (abstract), pen/black ink on paper, sgn/dtd 61, 18x24", C-NY 2/14/89 ... 6,05
Late April II (abstract), oil on paperboard laid down on masonite, sgn twice/dtd 1961/titled, 30x40", SBY 5/3/88 ... 45,10
Orders (contemporary), oil on canvas, sgn/dtd 1978, 79x97", SBY 5/2/89 OE ... 528,00
Room III (abstract), oil on paper mounted on masonite, sgn/twice/inscr/dtd 1960, 30x37", C-NY 11/9/88 OE ... 121,00
Shower (contemporary), ink on paper, sgn/dtd 76, 16x21", SBY 11/11/88 OE ... 33,00
Sun Up (abstract), oil on paper laid down on masonite, sgn/dtd 1959, 22x30", SBY 10/5/89 OE ... 93,50
Tivoli, gouache on board, sgn, 22x30", C-NY 11/10/88 OE ... 71,50
Untitled, crayon on paper, sgn/dtd 69, 16x19", SBY 2/15/89 OE ... 24,75
Untitled (abstract composition), charcoal on paper mounted on board, sgn/dtd 71, 19x24", C-NY 5/4/89 ... 52,80
Untitled (abstract), ink on paper, sgn, 1954, 18x24", SBY 5/3/89 OE ... 66,00

GUTE, Herbert Jacob (American, 1908-1977)
Easy Does It (men working to raise circus tent pole), egg tempera on board, sgn, 26x19", RWS 9/29/88 OE ... 95
Hiker (portrait of hunter in landscape), polytempera on cardboard, sgn, 17x14", RWS 5/19/88 UE ... 37
Plowend (close-up of man w/hands on plow), polytempera on board, 15x11", RWS 5/19/88 UE ... 32

GUTHERZ, Carl (Czechoslovakian, 1844-1907)
Seated Girl, oil on canvas laid down on panel, sgn/inscr/dtd 1883, 18x12", SBY 12/9/88 ... 1,65

GUTIERREZ, Ernesto (Spanish, 19th/20th C)
Hilly Landscape, oil on canvas, sgn, 19x22", C-E 2/21/89 ... 2,20

GUTIERREZ, Francisco A. (Mexican, 1915-)
Cape (abstract), gouache/pencil on paper, sgn/dtd 1936/titled, 14x9", SBY 11/21/88 OE ... 1,98

GUTTMAN, Bernhard (German, 1869-)
Portrait of a Woman with a Fan, oil on canvas, sgn/dtd 1917, 16x13", WG 9/16/88 ... 1,40

GUTTUSO, Renato (Italian, 1912-)
Gleaners (contemporary), black ink/wash on paper laid down on board, 9x12", SBY 2/14/89 UE ... 66

GUY, Seymour Joseph (American, 1824-1910)
Cool Drink From the Stream (girl holds cabbage leaf for brother to drink), oil on canvas, sgn, 20x16", RAB 3/27/89 ... 21,00
Portrait of a Lady, oil on canvas, initialed/dtd 1866, 10x8", C-NY 9/28/89 ... 5,50

GUYS, Constantin (French, 1802-1892)
Carriage Ride, pen/ink wash on paper, 8x12", B/B 6/15/89 ... 2,47
Elegant Figures Riding in a Carriage, ink/wash on paper laid down, 10x13", SBY 7/12/89 ... 1,04
Injured Bullfighter Manuel Ezuna, pencil/pen/ink on paper, inscr, 7x10", SBY 12/9/88 ... 1,54
Sandhurst Cadets, ink/watercolor on paper, 4x2", SBY 6/8/88 ... 46

GWATHMEY, Robert (American, 1903-)
Field Worker (contemporary), oil on canvas, sgn, 16x13", SBY 4/14/89 OE ... 11,55
Man with a Hoe (contemporary), oil on canvas, sgn, 15x12", SBY 4/14/89 OE ... 8,52
Reflections (caricature of old woman before mirror), oil on canvas, sgn, 27x32", WD 10/5/88 ... 10,00
The Blues Man, oil on canvas, sgn, 10x8", C-NY 9/28/89 ... 6,38

GWYN, Woody (20th C)
New Mexico Highway, acrylic on canvas, sgn, 72x72", C-E 5/13/88 OE ... 4,62

GYORGY, Nemeth
Pair: Village in Winter; oil on panel, sgn, 10x14", C-E 2/23/88 ... 82

GYSELAAR, see De Gyselaar

GYSELS, Pieter (Flemish, 1621-1690)
Peasants & Travelers on a Road Passing Through a Village, Windmill on the Left; oil on panel, 8x10", SBY 10/13/89 ... 17,60

GYSELS, Pieter; att (Flemish, 1621-1690)
Figures Disembarking From a Ferryboat by a Village, oil on panel, 10x13", C-NY 1/15/88 OE ... 30,80
Horse Carts & Peasants on a Road Through a Village in a Wooded Landscape, oil on copper, 8x11", SBY 4/7/88 ... 9,35

GYSELS, Pieter; circle of (Flemish, 1621-1690)
Landscape with Traffic Along a Country Road, an Estuary Beyond; oil on copper, indistinctly sgn, 6x7", SBY 4/7/89 ... 26,40
Village Square with a Horse-Drawn Cart & Other Peasants, oil on copper, 5x6", SBY 4/7/88 OE ... 25,30

GYSELS, Pieter; manner of (Flemish, 1621-1690)
Peasants Farming, oil on panel, 6x11", C-E 4/7/88 OE ... 1,65

H.A.S. (19th C)
Set of 4: Sydney (harbor view); pencil/watercolor, initialed/dtd 1861, 7x12", C-SK 5/25/89 ... 92

HAAG, Carl (Swedish, 1820-1915)
Historical Judgement Hall at Jerusalem, el Mahgameh; pencil/watercolor on paper, sgn/dtd 1859, 14x20", SBY 10/24/89 ... 13,20
Widow Visiting the Tomb of Her Husband, watercolor, sgn/dtd 1874, 10x14", MG 6/25/88 ... 90

HAAG, Jean Paul (French, 19th C)
Domino Game, oil on panel, sgn, 11x8", PHL 10/28/88 ... 3,25

ANEN, Casparis (Dutch, 1778-1849)
till Life of a Vase of Flowers & Various Objects on a Dressing Table, oil on panel, sgn, 23x23", SBY 5/23/89 OE 25,300
APANEN, John Nichols (American, 1891-)
Vinter Brook (snow-covered pines & running water), oil on artist board, sgn/dtd 31, 20x24", RWS 9/29/88 300
ARDT, J. (Dutch, 20th C)
eaport Village (group at water's edge), watercolor heightened w/gouache, 9x14", C-E 2/21/89 1,210
ARLAM, school of (Dutch, 17th C)
'ortrait of a Man, oil on copper, oval, 6x4", SBY 4/7/88 4,400
AS, Johannes Hubertus Leonardus; see De Haas
AS, Richard (20th C)
26 Broadway (view of building front), graphite on board, sgn, 1972, 20x15", SBY 11/11/88 2,750
AXMAN, Pieter Alardus (Dutch, 1814-1887)
lind Fiddler, oil on canvas, sgn/dtd 67, 24x19", WD 3/23/88 3,500
BENSCHADEN (German, 1813-1868)
et of 5: Two Donkeys Playing; Barnyard Animals; pencil on paper, 5x5", C-E 10/25/88 UE 330
BIE, L. (British, 18th C)
heep, oil on canvas, 10x11", MG 3/26/88 UE 450
CKAERT, Jacob Philip (German, 1737-1807)
xtensive Italianate Landscape, oil on canvas, sgn/dtd 1777, unfr, 32x43", SBY 6/2/89 OE 85,250
CKER, Arthur (British, 1858-1919)
nd There Was a Great Cry in Egypt, oil on canvas, sgn/dtd 97, 36x60", C-L 6/27/88 OE 22,704
bjects on a Tabletop, oil on canvas, sgn, unfr, 26x21", B/B 4/20/88 1,760
CKER, Arthur; att (British, 1858-1919)
ittle Flower Girl, oil on canvas, bears signature, 20x16", C-E 5/23/88 1,760
CKER, Deiter (20th C)
ie Brucke (contemporary nude), oil on canvas, sgn/dtd 25/2/1983, 76x11", SBY 5/3/89 OE 15,400
rau 2 (portrait), gouache on paper, sgn/dtd 85/titled, 39x48", SBY 2/19/88 3,080
Ion Dieu 9 (nude girl w/abstract objects), charcoal on paper, sgn/dtd 83, 42x31", C-E 5/13/88 1,540
chwarze Botin, watercolor/gouache/charcoal on paper, sgn/dtd 84, 31x42", C-E 11/14/89 OE 4,400
CKER, Horst (German, 1842-1906)
lpine Valley, oil on canvas, sgn/inscr, 36x53", C-NY 5/24/89 OE 19,800
CKER (American, 19th C)
chooner on a Stormy Night, oil on canvas, sgn, 24x36", SBY 1/24/89 3,300
CKERT, Jacob Philippe (German, 1737-1807)
acob at Bethel Anointing the Altar of Stones, oil on canvas, 63x57", C-NY 10/20/88 OE 8,800
orthern Italian Landscape with Herdspeople & Their Animals in the Foreground, oil on canvas, 50x76", SBY 10/21/88 37,400
ark with Lake & Classical Temple, Figures Resting on Bank...; oil on canvas, sgn/dtd, 26x39", C-NY 5/31 OE 93,500
CKERT, Jacob Philippe; follower of (German, 1737-1807)
astoral Figures in an Extensive Landscape, a Citadel Beyond; oil on cradled panel, 17x21", SBY 12/9/88 OE 2,090
DDON, Arthur Trevor (British, 1864-1941)
fternoon on the Terrace, oil on canvas, sgn, 20x30", SBY 7/12/89 3,850
Iarket Day in France, oil on canvas, sgn, 26x36", WAD 6/6/88 4,000
ENGER, Merio (Continental, 19th/20th C)
eacock & Fowl, oil on panel, sgn, 7x9", B/B 12/8/88 OE 1,540
eacock & Turkey, oil on panel, sgn, 6x8", B/B 9/15/88 OE 1,760
ENSBERGEN, Willem; manner of (Dutch, 1680-1755)
loral Still Life, oil on panel, 27x21", FAP 11/4/88 2,700
GBORG, August Wilhelm Nickolaus (Swedish, 1852-1925)
otato Gatherers, oil on canvas, sgn, 40x32", C-NY 2/23/89 30,800
GEDORN, Friedrich (German, 1814-1889)
raia Luisa, Rio de Janeiro (rocky coastal scene w/boats); oil w/bodycolor, sgn/inscr, 15x24", C-SK 6/9/88 OE 4,800
GEMANN, Godefroy; see De Hagemann
GEMANN, Oskar H. (German, 1888-)
ortrait of a Boy, oil on canvas, sgn/dtd 1948, 16x12", LH 10/16/88 400
ortrait of a Gentleman, oil on canvas, sgn/dtd 1912, 35x30", B/B 4/20/88 770
GEN, A. (Continental, 20th C)
katers on a Pond, oil on board, 19x24", B/B 1/11/89 412
GERUP, Nels (American, 1864-1922)
each Scene, oil on canvas, sgn/dtd 1915, 12x24", B/B 9/15/88 OE 1,100
alifornia Coast, oil on board, sgn, 19x25", B/B 12/8/88 440
ands End, oil on canvas, sgn, 18x31", B/B 12/8/88 770
Ionterey Coastal Scene, oil on canvas, sgn/dtd 1901, 29x48", B/B 10/6/88 2,475
Ioonlit Seascape, oil on canvas, sgn, 18x30", FAP 11/4/88 600
eascape, oil on canvas, sgn, 20x30", B/B 9/14/89 1,100
eascape at Dusk, oil on canvas, sgn, 19x34", B/B 10/6/88 880
unset Through the Golden Gates, oil on canvas, sgn, 20x30", B/B 9/15/88 358
GGERTY, Isabel (American, 20th C)
aystacks (landscape), oil on canvas, sgn, 20x24", SBY 4/14/89 OE 2,750
GHE, Louis (Belgian, 1806-1885)
nniversary Toast, watercolor heightened w/gouache, sgn/dtd 1868, 24x36", C-NY 10/26/88 4,620

HAGUE, Michael
Father Christmas, pen/black/brown/white ink/watercolor heightened w/white, sgn, 14x19", C-NY 2/25/88 .... **3,52**
Koala, watercolor/pen/black ink, initialed, 15x10", C-NY 5/25/88 .... **1,21**

HAHN, George (German, 1841-1889)
Morning Prayers, oil on cradled panel, sgn, 21x15", C-E 5/23/88 .... **3,52**
Wedding Flotilla, oil on canvas, sgn, 12x18", SBY 5/23/89 .... **9,90**

HAHN, Gustave Adolph (German, 1811-1872)
Brawling Outside a Tavern, oil on canvas, sgn, 12x18", FAP 11/4/88 .... **1,40**
Wedding on a River Boat, oil on canvas, sgn, 12x18", FAP 11/4/88 .... **2,30**

HAHN, William (American, 1829-1887)
Portrait of a Lady, bust-length, in a black dress...; oil on canvas, sgn/dtd 1862, 23x17", C-SK 11/10/88 .... **71**

HAIER, Joseph (Austrian, 1816-1891)
Serenade, oil on canvas, sgn/dtd 1876, 29x39", B/B 9/14/89 UE **88**

HAIG, Mabel George (American, 1884-)
Laguna Beach Scene, watercolor on paper, sgn/dtd 1923, 6x9", B/B 9/15/88 .... **24**

HAIGH, Alfred G. (British, 1870-1963)
Racehorse in a Loosebox, oil on canvas, sgn/dtd 1897, 16x20", SBY 6/9/89 .... **1,43**

HAINES, Frederick Stanley (Canadian, 1879-1960)
Eastern Townships, oil on canvasboard, sgn, 16x20", WAD 6/12/89 .... **1,20**
Pickerel River, oil on board, sgn, 16x20", WAD 6/12/89 .... **90**

HAINES, Marie (American, 20th C)
Possum Hunt, gilt/painted gesso panel, sgn, 39x24", RWS 12/10/88 .... **27**

HAINES, Richard (American, 1906-)
Net Menders, oil on canvas, sgn/dtd LVIII, 16x16", B/B 8/10/88 .... **44**

HAINS, Raymond (20th C)
Untitled (abstract), paper collage mounted on canvas, sgn/dtd 1975, 30x41", SBY 2/19/88 .... **6,60**

HAITE, George C. (British, 1855-)
Floral Still Life, oil on canvas, sgn/dtd 90, 33x15", B/B 9/15/88 .... **33**

HALBERG-KRAUSS, Fritz (German, 1874-1951)
Hay Wain, oil on canvas, sgn/inscr, 15x24", C-NY 2/25/88 .... **3,85**
Shepherd with His Flock, oil on panel, sgn/dtd 1920, 8x13", B/B 3/22/89 .... **3,30**
Springtime by a Lake, oil on canvas, sgn, 40x52", C-E 2/21/89 .... **5,28**

HALE, Ellen Day (American, 1855-1940)
Floral Arrangement, oil on canvas, sgn/dtd 1934, 24x18", RWS 5/12/89 .... **3,00**
Robin (full-length portrait of boy standing, reading a book), oil on canvas, 50x26", C-NY 5/25/89 .... **11,00**
Roman Bride (draped figure in full veil), oil on canvas, inscr Ellen Day Hale 1855-1949 Collection, 70x37", RWS 3/16/89 .... **2,00**
Young Woman with Guitar & Dog, watercolor/gouache on blue paper, estate stamp, 13x17", RWS 3/16/89 .... **1,80**

HALE, Lilian Westcott (American, 1881-1963)
Church, charcoal/pencil on paper, 29x23", WL 5/20/88 UE **25**

HALE, Phillip Leslie (American, 1865-1931)
Summer Visitor (woman in sunny garden), oil on canvas, sgn/indistinctly dtd, 30x25", SBY 5/25/88 .... **132,00**
Trees, oil on canvas, 22x18", SBY 6/28/89 .... **7,15**

HALEY, Robert Duane (American, 1892-1959)
Out for a Spin (girl at wheel of an antique roadster), oil on canvas, sgn/dtd 08, 12x16", RAB 8/9/88 OE **2,75**

HALFFERICH, Willem (Dutch, 20th C)
Summer's Day at the Beach (figures on beach & in water), oil on board, sgn, 16x26", C-E 2/21/89 .... **2,09**

HALL, E.W. (American, 1835-1910)
Children at Play in Winter, oil on canvas, sgn, 18x24", FAP 11/4/88 .... **17**

HALL, George Henry (American, 1825-1913)
Flowers in White Vase, oil on canvas, sgn/dtd 1860, 14x12", SBY 6/28/89 .... **9,35**
Morning-Glories, oil on board, sgn/dtd 1857, 6x9", SBY 3/17/88 UE **2,09**
Still Life of Flowers, oil on canvas, sgn, 36x20", C-E 11/8/88 UE **62**
Young Woman in an Arched Window, oil on canvas, sgn/dtd 1873, 24x16", C-NY 2/23/89 UE **1,54**

HALL, Harry (British, 1814-1882)
Canezou, Bay Racehorse, with Frank Butler Up; oil on canvas, 28x36", SBY 6/9/89 .... **7,70**
Flying Dutchman, oil on canvas, sgn/dtd 1849, 28x36", SBY 6/10/88 .... **27,50**
George Mure of Herringswell, Master of East Suffolk Hunt, on Bay Hunter, w/Huntsmen & Hounds; oil, 41x60", SBY 6/9/89 .... **220,00**
Marquis de Montgomery's Chestnut Filly, La Toucques, at Chantilly; oil on canvas, sgn/dtd 1863, 28x42", SBY 6/10/88 .... **46,75**
Mr Cartwright's Bay Colt, Maurice Daly with Boyce Up; oil on canvas, sgn, 26x35", SBY 6/9/89 .... **17,60**
Prince Charlie w/John Osborne Who Rode Him To Win the Two Thousand Guineas, 1872; oil, sgn/dtd 1874, 30x40", SBY 6/9/89 .... **22,00**
Queen Bertha, a Bay Racehorse, in a Stall; oil on canvas, sgn/inscr with horse's name, 20x24", SBY 6/9/89 .... **3,02**

HALL, Henry R. (British, -1902)
Highland Cattle, Loch Genachar; oil on canvas, sgn, 20x30", DM 5/13/88 .... **60**
Highland Cattle, Loch Scaraig; oil on canvas, sgn, 20x30", DM 5/13/88 .... **60**

HALL, J. (19th/20th C)
Cart Horses, watercolor on cardboard, sgn, 7x10", MG 5/28/88 .... **15**

HALL, M. (British, 19th/20th C)
Moroccan Sultan, watercolor, sgn, 5x7", MG 6/25/88 UE **20**

HALLAM, Joseph Sydney (Canadian, 1889-1953)
On the Road to Arundel, Quebec; oil on board, sgn, 12x16", WAD 11/30/89 .... **27**
Ploughing, oil on board, sgn, 12x16", WAD 6/12/89 .... **45**

HALLBERG, Charles (Continental, 19th/20th C)
Gothenberg Harbor, oil on canvas, sgn, 16x24", B/B 9/15/88 UE ... 330
HALLE, Noel (French, 1711-1781)
Assumption of the Virgin, oil on canvas, arched top, unfr, 102x66", SBY 1/12/89 ... 20,900
HALLER, G. (British, 19th C)
Pair: Wooded Landscapes with Figures; oil on canvas, sgn, 21x13", SLK 9/26/88 ... 900
HALLETT, Hendricks A. (American, 1847-1921)
American Fleet in Action During the Spanish-American War, pastel on paper, sgn, 24x38", RAB 3/14/89 ... 850
Seascape (black-hulled boats on a choppy green sea), watercolor on paper, sgn, 13x17", RAB 8/9/88 UE ... 125
Seascape (sailboats), watercolor on paper, 13x17", RAB 8/9/88 UE ... 225
HALLETT, W. (American, 19th C)
Sunset, Long Island (seascape); oil on canvas, sgn/indistinctly dtd, 10x12", RAB 11/25/88 UE ... 700
Sunset, Long Island; oil on canvas, sgn/indistinctly dtd, 10x12", RAB 8/8/89 UE ... 350
HALLOCK, Ruth Mary (American, 1876-)
Finger Lakes, oil on board, sgn, 12x16", FAP 12/8/89 ... 450
IALLWORTH, R. (American, 19th/20th C)
Old Windmill, Nantucket; oil on canvas, sgn/dtd 91, 9x12", MG 10/28/88 ... 300
IALM, George R. (American, 19th C)
15-Inch Gun (Civil War), pen/ink on board, sgn/inscr, unfr, 6x8", C-E 11/30/88 ... 220
IALPERT, Samuel T. (American, 1884-1930)
Commerce Along the River, oil on canvas, 18x24", C-NY 9/30/88 ... 2,750
Nude Model in Chair, watercolor/pen/ink/pencil on paper, sgn, 15x10", C-E 9/15/88 UE ... 187
Tabletop Still Life with Fruit, oil on cardboard mounted on plywood, sgn, 15x18", RWS 5/12/89 ... 2,600
IALS, Dirck (Dutch, 1591-1656)
Cavaliers Playing Backgammon in a Tavern, oil on panel, sgn/dtd 1631, 18x27", C-NY 10/12/89 OE ... 71,500
IALS, Dirck; circle of (Dutch, 1591-1656)
A Merry Company, oil on canvas, 20x26", C-NY 10/12/89 ... 3,300
IALS, Frans; after (Dutch, 1580-1666)
Portrait of Jacob Josias Van Bredehoff, oil on panel, inscr, 29x24", LH 10/16/88 ... 1,300
IALS, Frans; follower of (Dutch, 1580-1666)
Portrait of the Magistrate Dirk Schatter, oil on canvas, 30x24", SBY 1/12/89 ... 11,000
Young Man Playing a Lute, oil on canvas, 35x28", SBY 4/7/88 OE ... 4,400
ALS, Harmen Franz (Dutch, 1611-1669)
Serving Girl Being Seduced by a Youth, oil on panel, monogramed/dtd 1648, 16x13", SBY 10/21/88 ... 28,600
ALSALL, William Formby (American, 1841-1919)
Ocean Sunset (boats near rock), oil on canvas, sgn, 10x14", RAB 8/8/89 UE ... 500
Point Loma (seascape), oil on canvas, sgn/titled, 14x28", RAB 11/25/88 ... 600
Shipping Off the Coast (two vessels by rocky coast), oil on canvas, sgn/dtd 83, 30x46", RAB 8/9/88 UE ... 2,500
Sunset, Long Island (beached square-rigger, small sailboat beyond); oil on canvas, sgn, 10x12", RAB 8/9/88 ... 1,600
AMBOURG, Andre (French, 1909-)
Aux Courses (racecourse w/horses & figures), oil on canvas, 5x9", DM 9/16/88 ... 2,500
L'Heure des Regates, Marie Mouvante a Trouville; oil on canvas, sgn, 24x29", SBY 10/7/89 OE ... 26,400
La Cathedrale de Saint Marc a Venise, oil on canvas, sgn, 8x20", C-E 11/17/88 OE ... 6,600
La Maree Montante sur la Touques (ships at sea), oil on canvas, sgn/titled, 6x11", C-E 5/9/89 OE ... 8,250
La Monte dans la Carriere (jockey & horses), oil on canvas, 4x7", DM 9/16/88 ... 2,000
Les Pecheurs Vers la Large (fishing boats at sea), oil on canvas, sgn, 9x21", B/B 3/22/89 ... 6,600
Sailboats at Deauville, oil on canvas, sgn/initialed, 5x7", SBY 2/14/89 ... 6,600
AMBRIDGE, Jay (American, 1867-1924)
Schoolgirls' Outing (street scene), watercolor/pencil/gouache on tan paper, sgn, 22x36", RWS 9/29/88 ... 1,000
AMILTON, Edward Wilbur Dean (American, 1864-)
Girl in Pink, oil on canvas, sgn/dtd 1906, 43x32", RWS 11/10/89 ... 7,500
Sheep Pastures, Morning Mist; watercolor/gouache on paper, sgn, 14x20", RWS 11/10/89 UE ... 300
AMILTON, Gavin; school of (British, 1723-1798)
Judgement of Paris (three figures in a landscape), oil on canvas, unfr, 29x43", B/B 9/14/89 ... 1,430
MILTON, Gawen (British, 1697-1737)
Elegant Company Gaming in an Interior, oil on canvas, 23x21", SBY 6/3/88 OE ... 16,500
Portrait of a Family (six figures in an interior), oil on canvas, 23x26", SBY 6/1/89 ... 38,500
MILTON, Hamilton (American, 1847-1928)
Playground (children playing in the yard), oil on canvas, sgn/dtd 1876, 20x36", C-NY 9/30/88 ... 3,300
Storm Clouds (in a mountainous landscape), oil on canvas, sgn, 17x14", C-E 6/1/89 ... 1,100
MILTON, James (American, 1819-1878)
After the Storm on the Coast of Newfoundland (ships on rough seas), oil on canvas, sgn/dtd 1860, 29x44", SBY 5/24/89 ... 14,300
Gleam of Hope (disabled boat in water, ship in distance), oil on canvas, sgn/dtd 1876, 20x30", B/B 3/22/89 ... 2,750
On the Beach at Atlantic City: The Winds Off Shore; oil on canvas, initialed, ca 1860s, 20x40", WD 10/5/88 ... 3,600
Prometheus Chains (seascape), oil on canvas, sgn/inscr, 17x27", C-E 6/1/88 OE ... 4,180
Seascape Viewed From the Shore at Dusk, oil on canvas, sgn/dtd 1885, 15x25", C-NY 3/11/88 OE ... 6,050
Ship in Heavy Seas, oil on canvas, sgn/dtd 1874, unfr, 20x30", SBY 4/14/89 ... 1,100
Shipwreck Along a Rocky Shore, oil on canvas, sgn/dtd 1872/inscr, 12x20", SBY 3/17/88 OE ... 2,750
Winter, Stevenstons Cottage; oil on canvas, sgn/dtd 1958, 19x13", FB 4/25/88 ... 1,000
MILTON, James Whitelaw (British, 1860-1932)
Helensburgh Town Hall, Demolished 1878; oil on panel, sgn, 10x13", WAD 6/6/89 ... 900

HAMILTON, Richard (British, 1922-)
Swinging London 67 (Robert Fraser/Mick Jagger handcuffed in police van), silkscreen/pastel, 28x35", SBY 6/30/88 .... **48,000**
HAMILTON, see also De Hamilton
HAMILTON, William R. (American, 1810-1865)
View of a New York Farm Compound, oil on paper mounted on canvas, sgn/dtd 1856, 18x24", RWS 6/10/89 OE **2,500**
HAMMERAS, Ralph (American, 1939-)
View Through the Eucalyptus, oil on board, sgn, 24x18", B/B 10/6/88 .... **1,100**
HAMMERSTAD, John H. (American/Norwegian, 19th C)
Winter Twilight, oil on canvas, sgn, 18x26", DM 1/15/88 .... **700**
HAMMOND, Arthur J. (American, 1875-1947)
Boats at the Pier, Gloucester; oil on board, sgn, 12x16", RWS 11/10/89 .... **800**
Wooded Glade, oil on panel, sgn, 10x14", C-SK 11/10/89 .... **930**
HAMMOND, George F. (British, 19th/20th C)
Crashing Waves (on rocky coast), watercolor on paper, sgn/dtd 1917, 26x30", WG 4/23/88 UE **400**
HAMMOND, John A. (Canadian, 1843-1939)
Castle Overlooking River, oil on canvas, sgn, 9x12", WAD 11/30/89 .... **750**
Cattle in a Meadow, Landscape; oil on canvas, 18x31", FB 5/28/89 UE **750**
Evening Over the Meuse River, Belgium; oil on board, sgn/dtd 1928, 5x9", WAD 6/12/89 .... **1,300**
Field, BC; oil on board, sgn/dtd 1902, 6x9", FB 5/28/89 .... **475**
Fisherman in Morning Light, oil on panel, sgn/dtd 1896, 9x13", WAD 6/12/89 OE **1,600**
Landscape with River & Boats, oil on board, sgn, 14x17", FB 5/28/89 .... **1,200**
Marine Scene, oil on panel, sgn, 9x6", FB 5/28/89 OE **750**
River Landscape with Figures, oil on board, sgn, 14x17", FB 4/25/88 .... **950**
Sachville, New Brunswick; oil on board, sgn/dtd 1914, 6x14", FB 5/28/89 .... **475**
St Johns Harbor, New Brunswick; oil on board, sgn, 12x24", WAD 6/12/89 .... **2,000**
Tantamire Marshes, New Brunswick; oil on board, sgn, 21x30", WAD 6/12/89 .... **2,400**
Venetian Scene, oil on board, sgn/indistinctly dtd, 5x8", WAD 6/12/89 .... **650**
Windmills Under Heavy Skies, oil on board, sgn/dtd, 18x24", WAD 11/30/89 .... **4,000**
HAMMOND, Richard Henry (American, 1854-)
Still Life of Fruits & Vegetables, oil on canvas, sgn/dtd 1912, 18x20", LH 10/16/88 UE **600**
HAMON, Jean Louis (French, 1821-1874)
Old China Shop, Pompeii (ladies examining wares); no media or size given, ca 1860, SBY 6/1/89 OE **67,850**
HAMON, Roland (20th C)
Rue a Montmartre (street scene), oil on canvas, sgn/dtd Paris 1980, 18x22", C-E 11/17/88 .... **462**
HAMPE, Ernst Heinrich Wilhelm (German, 1806-1862)
Pair: Monks in Wine Cellars; oil on canvas, sgn, 9x7", SLK 11/25/88 .... **1,200**
HAMPEL, Carl (Australian, -1942)
Zinnias (still life), oil on canvas, sgn, 27x34", C-SK 6/9/88 .... **835**
HAMPEL, Sigmund Walter (Austrian, 1868-1949)
Mozart, pen/ink on paper, sgn/inscr, 13x19", C-L 6/27/88 OE **30,272**
Mozart, pen/ink/pencil on paper, sgn/inscr/dtd MCMXXXIII, 12x8", C-L 6/27/88 OE **21,758**
Temptation of St Anthony, watercolor/pencil/pen/black ink heightened w/gold on paper, sgn, ca 1900, 13x12", C-L 6/27/88 .... **12,298**
Vision, oil on panel, ca 1903-05, 27x33", C-L 6/27/88 .... **30,272**
Young Mozart, pen/ink/pencil on paper, sgn/inscr twice, 11x7", C-L 6/27/88 .... **6,054**
HAMPTON, John W. (American, 1918-1976)
Pony Guard, oil on canvas, sgn 3 times/inscr/dtd 1973, 20x30", SBY 9/23/88 OE **4,400**
HAMZA, Johann (German, 1850-1927)
Critical Patron, oil on panel, sgn, 13x10", C-NY 2/25/88 .... **9,900**
Elegant Lady Crossing a Brook, oil on panel, sgn, 11x9", C-NY 10/25/89 .... **9,350**
Plate of Fruit (portrait of child holding a plate of fruit), oil on canvas, sgn, 19x15", SBY 7/12/89 .... **1,925**
HANAU, Jean (French, 1899-)
Still Life of Lilacs & Goldenrod in a Vase, oil on board, sgn/dtd 1926, 23x19", C-E 10/26/89 UE **440**
HANCOCK, Charles (British, 1795-1868)
Chestnut Mare & a Dog in a Landscape, oil on canvas, sgn/dtd 1841, 29x37", SBY 6/10/88 .... **13,200**
Near Hampstead Heath, oil on panel, sgn/dtd 1849, 9x12", B/B 4/20/88 .... **1,045**
HANGER, Max (German, 1874-)
Roosters & Chickens Feeding, oil on panel, sgn, 5x7", C-E 5/23/88 .... **1,430**
HANISCH, Alois (Austrian, 1866-1937)
Scarecrow by the Farm, oil on canvas, sgn, 13x18", C-E 10/26/89 .... **2,200**
HANJE (Dutch, 20th C)
Begonia Pots, oil on canvas, sgn, 24x32", B/B 1/11/89 .... **660**
HANKEY, William Lee (British, 1869-1952)
Calm Day, oil on canvas, sgn, 28x36", SBY 7/12/89 OE **15,400**
Market Day, oil on canvas, indistinctly sgn, 28x34", SBY 2/22/89 .... **16,500**
Marketing the Tunny, Concarneau (selling fish on the docks); oil on canvas, sgn, 25x30", C-NY 5/24/89 UE **5,500**
Ready for Fishing (view of fishing boat w/town beyond), oil on board, sgn, 9x12", C-E 5/22/89 .... **3,300**
Young Woman on a Road Through a Village in Brittany, watercolor, sgn/dtd 99, 11x15", C-NY 5/25/88 .... **3,850**
HANKS, Jervis F. (American, 1799-)
Portrait of a Man (seated, three-quarter length), oil on panel, sgn/dtd 1834, 24x33", C-NY 1/20/89 .... **1,430**
HANNA, Thomas King (American, 1872-1957)
Art Class, oil on canvas, sgn/dtd 1916, 18x29", C-NY 5/26/88 .... **7,700**

Western Sky (extensive landscape), oil on board, sgn, 25x30", B/B 9/14/89 OE

HANNAH, Duncan (American, 1952-) 3,025

Mediterranean, oil on canvas, initialed/sgn/dtd 6-81, 44x32", SBY 10/8/88 UE

Mr Man, oil on canvas, initialed/sgn/dtd 1981, 40x50", SBY 10/8/88 UE 3,025

Runabout by Rialto (boat on water, buildings behind), oil on canvas, sgn/dtd 1980, 24x36", SBY 2/15/89 5,500

HANNEMAN, Adriaen; att (Dutch, 1601-1671) 2,750

Portrait of Jean Roose, half-length, wearing a black costume with a white collar; oil on canvas, C-NY 4/6/89

HANNIS (19th C) 7,150

Still Life of Fruit, oil on canvas, sgn, 22x36", SBY 9/23/88

HANSCH, Anton (Austrian, 1813-1876) 1,540

Rushing Brook in a Mountainous Landscape, oil on canvas, 24x17", C-E 2/23/88

IANSCH, Anton; att (Austrian, 1813-1876) 935

Alpine Stream, oil on canvas, 23x17", PHL 10/28/88 OE

IANSEN, Armin Carl (American, 1886-1957) 2,500

Bucking Horse, watercolor/ink on paper, initialed/dtd 53, 4x4", B/B 8/10/88

Dock Workers (men working with barrels on dock), sanguine on paper, sgn, 13x9", B/B 9/14/89 UE 468

Harbor Scene, oil on board, 15x20", B/B 10/6/88 1,100

On an Iceland Fishing Boat, oil on board, sgn, 16x20", B/B 10/6/88 3,300

IANSEN, Hans (British, 1853-1923) 16,500

Interior of a Mosque, watercolor, sgn, 10x14", MG 6/25/88

IANSEN, Herman Wendelborg (American, 1854-1924) 850

A Ride for Life (hunter on horseback shooting a wolf), watercolor on paper, sgn, 21x30", C-NY 2/3/88

Attack on the Wagon Train, oil on canvas, sgn, 37x51", SBY 5/25/88 9,900

Crow War Party, watercolor on buff paper laid down on board, sgn, 20x30", C-NY 2/3/88 57,750

Leader of the Herd (horse on mound, herd behind), watercolor on paper, sgn, 19x29", C-NY 9/28/89 14,300

Roping the Steer, watercolor on buff paper, sgn, 24x36", C-NY 2/3/88 6,050

Yosemite From the Valley Floor, oil on canvas, sgn/dtd 1884, 10x14", B/B 10/6/88 20,900

ANSEN, Leon (Australian, 1918-) 2,475

Street Scene with Wide Street, oil on panel, sgn/dtd 1949, 14x23", WG 9/16/88 UE

ANSON, Peter (American, 1877-) 100

Extensive Landscape, oil on canvas laid down on panel, sgn/dtd 1874, 22x36", PHL 10/28/88 UE

APSMANS, M. (American, 20th C) 600

Shepherd with His Flock, watercolor on paper, sgn, 46x33", FAP 4/15/89 UE

ARDING, James Duffield (British, 1798-1863) 660

View of Lake Como, watercolor, 9x15", C-NY 10/26/88

ARDING, John L. (American, 1835-1882) 1,320

Portrait of a Young Woman Said To Be Lola Montez, oil on canvas, sgn, 36x30", SBY 6/28/89 OE

ARDWICK, Melbourne H. (American, 1857-1916) 1,540

Daydreams (mother & child on shore, ships passing by), watercolor on paper, sgn, 13x19", RWS 3/31/88

Favorite Toy (mother & child in interior), watercolor/gouache on paper, sgn, 23x27", RWS 9/29/88 700

Lady by the Sea, watercolor/pencil heightened w/gouache, 20x13", C-E 6/1/88 650

Peeling the Potatoes (lady peeling potatoes, girl watching), oil on canvas, sgn, 18x24", C-E 2/1/89 1,650

Sailing in Rough Seas, watercolor on paper, sgn, 19x25", C-E 4/7/88 1,430

Summer Reflection (landscape with pond), watercolor on paper, sgn, 13x19", RWS 3/16/89 UE 825

ARDY, Heywood (British, 1842-1933) 300

Passing the Hunt (gentlemen in carriage w/huntsmen & hounds), oil on canvas, sgn, 20x30", SBY 6/9/89

Stirrup Cup (fox hounds, horses, hunters, w/lady in a landscape), oil on canvas, sgn, 20x30", SBY 6/10/88 27,500

Stop at the Inn (exterior scene of huntsmen & serving girl), oil on canvas, sgn, 18x24", C-NY 2/23/89 OE 22,000

31,900

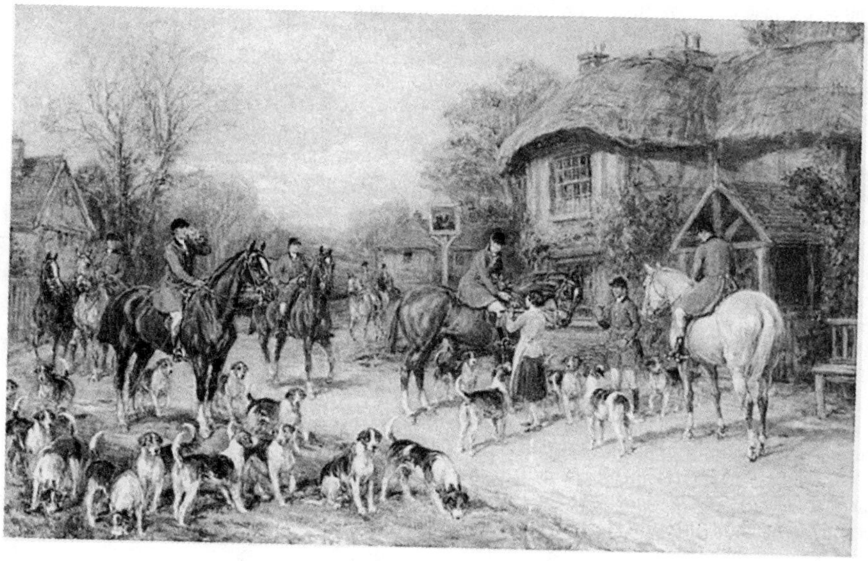

The Meet, oil on canvas, sgn, 20x30", PHL 10/28/89 OE, $35,000

HARDY, Thomas Bush (British, 1842-1897)
- Harbor Scene with Paddle Wheel Tug, oil on canvas, 12x24", RAB 8/1/88 UE **600**
- Mouth of the Medway, watercolor/gouache/pen/brown ink w/scraping out, sgn/dtd 1874, 18x28", C-NY 10/25/89 OE **6,600**

HARE, George (British, 1857-)
- Borzo by a Chair (portrait of a Russian wolfhound), oil on canvas, sgn, 43x27", C-NY 5/24/89 OE **14,300**

HARE, John (American, 19th or 20th C)
- Clearing Weather (boats docked at harbor), oil on canvas, sgn, 24x30", C-E 6/1/89 UE **1,760**
- Fishing Docks, oil on canvas, sgn, 24x30", RAB 8/9/88 .... **1,500**
- Fishing Docks (sail & power boats, large weathered fish houses), oil on canvas, sgn, 24x30", RAB 8/9/88 .... **1,500**
- Gloucester Schooner (dock scene), oil on canvas, sgn twice/inscr Sayville NY/titled, 24x30", SBY 3/17/88 .... **1,980**
- Pair: Church by the River; Landscape with Barn; watercolor, sgn, 10x12", FAP 4/15/89 UE **165**

HARE, Nathaniel; att
- Portrait of a Lady in Blue, oil on canvas, 31x25", SBY 12/9/88 OE **3,850**

HARGENS, Charles (American, 1893-)
- Way West (man walking beside oxen-drawn wagon), oil on canvas, sgn, 33x27", B/B 10/9/88 .... **3,575**

HARGREAVES, E. (American, 20th C)
- Boats in a Harbor, watercolor/pen/pencil on paper, sgn, 6x11", B/B 9/15/88 .... **302**
- Rural American Village, watercolor/pen/pencil on paper, sgn, 8x10", B/B 9/15/88 .... **302**
- View of Fort Point From Seacliff, watercolor/pencil on paper, sgn, 12x19", B/B 10/6/88 .... **935**

HARING, Keith (American, 1958-)
- Meatloaf Drawing for Meals on Wheels, watercolor/gouache/brush/ink, sgn/dtd August 24 1987, 31x41", C-E 11/14/89 OE **39,600**
- Smile with Three Eyes, black ink on hand-colored paper, sgn/dtd 83, unfr, 16x21", C-NY 5/4/88 OE **6,600**
- Untitled (abstract composition in red, purple, & yellow), acrylic on muslin, sgn/dtd 1984, 60x60", SBY 10/5/89 OE **126,500**
- Untitled (abstract head w/pointed cat-like ears), brush/black ink on paper, sgn/dtd Sept 21-82, 39x50", C-NY 10/4/89 OE **33,000**
- Untitled (abstract line figure), enamel on wood, sgn/dtd 83, 12x11", SBY 10/8/88 .... **3,190**
- Untitled (abstract), brush/black enamel on steel, sgn/dtd 1981, 40x25", C-NY 5/4/88 OE **7,150**
- Untitled (abstract), brush/black ink on paper, sgn/dtd Oct 13-81/inscr dedication, 38x46", C-NY 11/10/88 .... **4,180**
- Untitled (abstract), brush/black ink on paper, sgn/dtd Sept 23-81, 22x30", C-NY 11/10/88 .... **3,520**
- Untitled (abstract), ink on paper, 1981, 39x50", SBY 2/14/89 OE **4,125**
- Untitled (contemporary), acrylic on muslin, sgn/dtd April 20, 1984, 60x60", SBY 2/15/89 .... **26,400**
- Untitled (contemporary), acrylic on paper, sgn/dtd Nov 1-85, 22x30", C-NY 5/4/89 OE **14,300**
- Untitled (contemporary), acrylic on wood, sgn/dtd 82, 8x32", C-NY 2/14/89 OE **5,280**
- Untitled (contemporary), brush/black ink on paper, sgn/dtd March 1982, 23x29", C-NY 5/4/89 OE **20,900**
- Untitled (contemporary), brush/black ink on vellum, sgn/dtd 1981, 41x45", C-NY 2/14/89 OE **9,900**
- Untitled (contemporary), colored felt-tip pens on paper, 22x30", C-NY 5/4/89 OE **9,350**
- Untitled (contemporary), ink on paper, sgn/dtd Jan 21-82, 30x43", C-NY 5/4/89 OE **8,800**
- Untitled (contemporary), vinyl on tarp, sgn/dtd Friday January 13 1984, 73x73", SBY 5/2/88 OE **27,500**
- Untitled (figure w/radio head), black felt-tip pen on paper, sgn/dtd 84, 26x20", C-NY 10/4/89 OE **18,700**
- Untitled (three eyes w/nose & mouth), vinyl ink on tarpaulin, 1982, 108x108", SBY 11/11/88 OE **38,500**
- Untitled-From the Nuclear Sex Series (abstract); ink on paper, sgn twice/dtd 1981, 38x50", lot 409, SBY 10/5/88 .... **2,750**
- Untitled-From the Nuclear Sex Series; ink on paper, sgn twice/dtd 81, 38x50", lot 411, SBY 10/5/88 OE **3,300**

HARLAMOFF, Alexis (Russian, 1842-)
- Gypsy Holding a Bunch of Flowers in Her Right Hand (portrait), oil on canvas, sgn/dtd 1907, 50x34", C-L 10/8/88 .... **26,960**
- Portrait of a Neapolitan Girl, oil on canvas, sgn, 14x10", SBY 10/24/89 .... **8,250**
- Portrait of Princess Youssupoff, oil on canvas, sgn/dtd 1904, 19x13", C-NY 2/23/89 .... **7,150**
- Young Woman Holding a Book (portrait), oil on canvas, sgn, 26x20", C-L 10/8/88 .... **16,730**

HARLES, Victor Joseph (American, 1894-)
- Composition (abstract), oil on canvasboard, sgn, 12x9", C-NY 9/28/89 .... **3,520**
- Composition 2 (abstract), oil on canvasboard, 19x14", C-NY 9/28/89 .... **2,200**
- Cottage Scene, oil on canvasboard, sgn, 16x20", LH 3/20/88 OE **350**

HARLEY, George Willis (British, 19th/20th C)
- A View of Windsor Castle, oil on canvas, sgn, 14x38", PHL 6/16/88 .... **800**

HARLOW, George Henry (British, 1787-1819)
- Portrait of a Lady, seated half-length, wearing a red dress, holding a rose; oil on canvas, 30x26", C-NY 4/6/89 .... **6,050**
- Portrait of Mrs Maria Whitmore nee Stainforth, pencil/watercolor on paper, 9x7", WD 10/19/88 OE **1,300**

HARLOW, George Henry; att (British, 1787-1819)
- Portrait of a Young Girl (bust-length), oil on board, 14x12", PHL 10/28/88 .... **5,000**

HARLOW, Louis Kenney (American, 1850-1913)
- Peaceful Reflections (autumn landscape), watercolor on paper, sgn, 12x23", RAB 3/27/89 UE **200**
- Seascape (figures on shore, sailing ships beyond), watercolor on paper, sgn, 13x19", RWS 3/313/88 UE **225**

HARMON, Charles Henry (American, 1859-1936)
- Autumn in Humboldt, oil on canvas, sgn, 16x12", B/B 1/11/89 .... **522**
- Geneva Peak, Colorado; oil on canvas, sgn, 16x24", B/B 12/8/88 .... **935**
- Seascape with Rocks & Gulls, oil on canvas, sgn/dtd 1912, 16x28", B/B 5/17/89 .... **990**

HARMS, Alfred (American, 19th/20th C)
- Deer in the Shade of a Bay Tree, oil on canvas, sgn/dtd 1919, 23x29", B/B 1/11/89 .... **825**

HARNETT, William Michael (American, 1848-1892)
- Still Life of Apples, Grapes, & Almonds; oil on canvas, sgn/dtd 1876, 10x14", SBY 5/25/88 UE **44,000**
- Still Life of Mug, Pipe, & New York Herald; oil on canvas, monogramed/dtd 1879, 14x12", SBY 5/25/88 OE **170,500**
- Tobacco & Pipe, oil on canvas, monogramed/dtd 1877, 6x8", C-NY 12/2/88 OE **143,000**

RNEY, Paul E. (American, 1850-1915)
'armyard with Chickens, oil on canvas laid down on board, sgn/dtd 19, 8x10", SLK 5/12/88 675
ROLD, E.
Iarbor Scene, oil on canvas mounted on masonite, sgn, 16x26", LH 5/15/88 600
RPIGNIES, Henri Joseph (French, 1819-1916)
utumn Morning, Pool of Bleneau, Yonne; oil on canvas, sgn/dtd 1903, 26x32", C-NY 2/3/88 14,300
Chateau de Beauvoir (landscape), oil on canvas, sgn/titled, 12x17", RWS 8/12/89 OE 17,000
Coastal View, watercolor on paper, sgn, 7x10", C-E 2/23/88 550
igure on a Path by a River, oil on canvas, sgn/dtd 92, 15x18", C-NY 2/25/88 OE 15,400
isherman at the River's Edge, Sunset; oil on canvas, 26x32", SBY 7/12/89 3,300
talian Landscape, watercolor on board, sgn, ca 1850-60, 7x10", SWN 6/15/89 715
a Bourboule, oil on canvas, sgn/dtd 81/inscr, 9x12", SBY 5/23/89 7,700
es Eyzies (landscape), watercolor/pencil, sgn/dtd 98/titled, 5x9", C-NY 2/23/89 2,640
Aediterranean Cove, oil on canvas, sgn, 19x14", WAD 6/6/88 4,200
Aoonlit Landscape, oil on canvas, sgn, 11x7", B/B 3/22/89 1,210
'aysage, oil on paper laid down on panel, sgn, 8x10", C-E 10/26/89 1,320
'echeurs au Bord de la Riviere (fishermen by a river), oil on canvas, sgn, 24x44", RWS 8/12/89 UE 10,000
Restful Afternoon (couple in landscape), oil on canvas, sgn/indistinctly dtd, 22x13", C-NY 2/23/89 8,250
River Landscape, oil on canvas, sgn/dtd 98, 26x32", WG 9/16/88 9,000
Setting Sun on the Banks of the Allier, oil on panel, sgn/dtd 1904, 21x29", C-NY 5/25/88 14,300
Study of a Wooded Landscape, watercolor, sgn/dtd 1915, 7x5", C-NY 10/26/88 825
RRIMAN, Phyllis
'air: Green Valley; Winter Landscape; pastel on paper, 4x7", C-NY 6/17/89 88
RRINGTON, James
Iats, watercolor, sgn, 22x30", LH 5/15/88 200
RRIS, Charles Gordon (American, 1891-)
Church Yard, no media given, sgn/dtd 1888, 19x18", WG 9/16/88 UE 350
Delivering Milk in Winter, oil on canvas, sgn/dtd 1937, 20x24", WG 9/16/88 UE 750
New England-Country Road, Winter (landscape); oil on canvasboard, sgn, 12x14", RWS 3/16/89 1,100
Rhode Island Farm in Spring, oil on canvas, sgn, 25x30", RWS 9/8/89 UE 900
Sketching in the Dunes, watercolor/pencil on paper, sgn, 8x10", RWS 3/16/89 UE 125
Winter Birches, watercolor/gouache on paper, sgn, gold leaf frame, 14x21", RWS 5/12/89 700
RRIS, Edwin (British, 19th C)
'eaceful Moments, oil on canvas, sgn, 36x24", C-NY 5/25/88 UE 2,200
'ortrait of Dorothy, oil on canvas, sgn/dtd 1904, 48x28", C-NY 5/25/88 22,000
Yellow Shawl (portrait), oil on canvas, sgn, 15x12", C-NY 5/25/88 UE 2,200
RRIS, H.J. (20th C)
Sailing Off Portland Lighthouse, Maine; oil on canvas, sgn/dtd 1911, 27x22", S/A 2/18/89 2,000
RRIS, Henry (British, 1805-1865)
Bridge on the Usk, oil on canvas, sgn, 18x34", SBY 12/9/88 1,760
RRIS, Lawren S. (Canadian, 1885-1970)
At St John's, Newfoundland; oil on panel, sgn/dtd ca 1921, 11x14", FB 4/25/88 19,000
RRIS, R. (British, 18th C)
Two Children with Fruit, oil on canvas, sgn/dtd 1730, unfr, 50x40", WL 5/20/88 5,000
RRIS, Robert (Canadian, 1849-1919)
'ortrait of a Gentleman, oil on board, initialed, 9x7", WAD 6/12/89 750
RRIS, Sam Hyde (American, 1889-1977)
andscape, oil on canvas, sgn, 10x12", DM 9/16/88 OE 1,100
RRISON, Allan (Canadian, 1911-)
Still Life of Basket of Fruits, oil on canvas, sgn/dtd 1979, 20x16", FB 10/30/89 1,540
RRISON, C.P. (19th C)
'ortrait of Franklin Pierce, oil on canvas, sgn/dtd 1853, 36x29", SBY 9/23/88 1,540
RRISON, Lowell Birge (American, 1854-1929)
Along the Road, oil on canvas, sgn/dtd 1887, 18x22", C-NY 5/26/88 18,700
Blue Sails, pastel on brown paper, sgn, 30x40", C-NY 3/11/88 3,850
umberjacks (rolling logs in winter landscape), oil on canvas, sgn, 22x31", B/B 3/22/89 3,025
Madison Square, Rainy Night (quiet street scene); oil on canvas, sgn, 25x30", C-NY 5/25/89 19,800
Moonlit Houses in the Snow, oil on canvas, sgn, 28x36", SBY 5/25/88 16,500
Red Mill, oil on canvas, sgn, 24x30", SBY 5/25/88 37,400
Snowy Path, oil on canvas, sgn, 22x31", LH 10/16/88 8,500
Winter Twilight, oil on canvas, sgn/inscr, 24x30", C-NY 3/11/88 13,200
RRISON, Ted (Canadian, 1926-)
Tutshi & Skaters, Carcross; acrylic on board, sgn/dtd 1973, 21x27", FB 4/25/88 1,500
RRISON, Thomas Alexander (American, 1853-1930)
Dunes, oil on canvas, sgn, 28x40", SBY 6/24/88 4,400
Ocean Sunset, oil on canvas, sgn, 16x24", B/B 9/14/89 UE 1,100
Wave (sun setting over ocean view), oil on canvas, sgn, 16x16", SBY 6/24/88 5,500
RT, F.J. (American, 19th/20th C)
Unloading Cotton (figures & steamship at pier), oil on board, sgn, 19x25", B/B 9/14/89 UE 77
RT, George Overbury (American, 1868-1933)
Carnival, New Orleans; watercolor/charcoal on paper, sgn/inscr/dtd 1924, 11x15", C-E 2/3/88 715

Street Scene, Paraquay; sgn/inscr/dtd 1918, 8x13", C-E 2/3/88 495

HART, James McDougal (American, 1828-1901)

Autumn Farm (cows grazing), oil on canvas, sgn/dtd 67, 9x18", C-NY 5/25/89 **12,100**

Cattle in a Landscape, oil on canvas, sgn/dtd 1889, 16x21", SBY 1/24/89 **3,300**

Cattle on a Woodland Path, oil on canvas, sgn, 24x14", SBY 1/24/89 **1,100**

Cows Watering, oil on canvas, sgn, 12x16", B/B 3/22/89 **1,650**

Deer by Lake, oil on canvas, sgn/dtd 1873, 16x26", C-NY 12/2/88 **23,100**

Pastoral Landscape with Cows, oil on board, sgn, 8x12", B/B 3/17/88 **3,300**

Small Patch of Sunlight (forest view), oil on canvas, sgn/dtd 1870, 14x23", C-NY 12/2/88 **12,100**

Valley Vista, oil on canvas, sgn/dtd 68, 11x20", C-NY 9/30/88 OE **13,200**

HART, James McDougal; att (American, 1828-1901)

Cows by a Stream, oil on canvas laid down on masonite, indistinctly sgn, 20x15", C-E 6/1/88 **1,210**

HART, Mary E. (American, -1899)

Vineyard Haven-July 26th, 1891; watercolor on paper, sgn, 6x12", RAB 11/25/88 UE **100**

HART, Mary Theresa (American, 1872-1921)

Still Life of Flowers, oil on canvas, sgn, 12x10", SBY 6/24/88 UE **1,650**

Still Life of Flowers, sgn, 14x17", PHL 12/1/88 **550**

HART, William M. (American, 1823-1894)

Autumn Landscape (herder w/cows in middle distance), oil on canvas, sgn, 14x11", SBY 9/14/89 **4,125**

Brooklet (cows wading in stream in a landscape), oil on board, sgn, ca 1885, 7x6", C-E 10/18/89 **2,420**

Catskill Landscape with Mountains in the Distance, oil on canvas, initialed, 8x13", C-E 2/1/89 **5,280**

Cattle in a Landscape, oil on canvas, sgn, 9x12", SBY 4/14/89 UE **1,870**

Cows in Pasture, oil on panel, sgn, no sz given, FAP 4/15/89 OE **5,060**

Cows Watering in a Mountainous River Landscape, no media given, initialed, 7x7", WD 4/13/88 **3,000**

Gathering Hay, oil on canvas, 26x37", C-E-2/1/89 **3,850**

Group of 4: Windmill; Rocks; Summer Landscape; Fall Landscape; oil on canvas, sgn/#d, ea 3" dia, SBY 1/24/89 **7,700**

Harvest Scene-Valley of the Delaware; oil on canvas, ca 1868, 11x19", SBY 5/24/89 OE **39,600**

Mount George, oil on panel, sgn/dtd 1894, 5x8", C-E 2/1/89 OE **2,860**

Mountain Landscape, oil on canvas, sgn, 24x22", SBY 6/24/88 **2,530**

Romantic Landscape (river through the mountains, sheep & shepherd on path), oil on canvas, 38x54", DM 2/19/88 **8,500**

Sail Boats on Lake George, oil on canvas, sgn, 6x13", C-E 2/1/89 OE **7,700**

HARTIGAN, Grace (American, 1922-)

Bony Labyrinth (abstract), acrylic on canvas, sgn/dtd 67, unfr, 52x63", C-NY 5/4/89 **6,050**

Bushmill (abstract), paper collage/gouache on paper, sgn/dtd 58, 22x28", SBY 10/8/88 **3,850**

Crowning of the Poet, oil on canvas, sgn/dtd 85, 72x78", C-NY 5/4/88 UE **4,950**

Pair: Untitled (abstract); gouache/pencil on paper, sgn, 12x9", SBY 2/14/89 OE **2,310**

Untitled, acrylic/collage on paper, sgn/dtd 56, 22x28", SBY 10/7/89 **5,500**

HARTING, Lloyd (American, 1910-1976)

Navajo Goat Herders, watercolor on paper, sgn, 21x30", B/B 5/17/89 **550**

River Belle Steamboat, watercolor, sgn, 22x29", MG 10/28/88 **950**

HARTL, Leon (American, 1889-1973)

Foliage in October, oil on canvas, sgn/dtd 67, 25x36", C-E 6/28/88 UE **50**

HARTLAND, Henry Albert (British, 1840-1893)

Cutting Peat in a Bog, watercolor, sgn, 14x28", C-NY 5/25/88 **825**

HARTLAND, L. (British, 19th C)

Ships in an English Harbor, watercolor, sgn, 12x20", WG 9/16/88 UE **325**

Ships Near a Rocky Coastline, watercolor, sgn, 12x20", WG 9/16/88 UE **125**

HARTLEY, Marsden (American, 1878-1943)

Apples on a Plate, oil on canvas, ca 1926, 9x11", C-NY 5/25/89 **14,300**

Bird Study, India ink on paper, sgn/dtd 41, unfr, 14x17", SBY 1/24/89 OE **6,600**

Mont St Victoire, Afternoon; brush/black ink/pencil on tan paper, sgn, 21x29", C-NY 5/25/89 OE **24,200**

Mt Katahdin No 4, charcoal on brown paper, ca 1940, 11x14", C-NY 3/11/88 **3,080**

HARTLEY, Richard V. (20th C)

Circus (people approaching large tents), oil on canvasboard, sgn/dtd 1935, 22x28", C-E 6/1/89 **1,540**

HARTMANN, Bertram (American, 1882-1960)

Autumn (modern depiction), oil on canvas, sgn, 24x30", C-NY 9/28/89 **4,950**

Bright Flowers in a Glass Vase, watercolor on paper, sgn, 30x22", SBY 6/28/89 **1,540**

Exotic Fantasy, oil on canvas, sgn/dtd 13, 21x34", C-L 6/27/88 OE **32,164**

Farm Scene, watercolor/pencil on paper, sgn/dtd 1936, 15x23", C-E 6/1/89 UE **220**

New York Canyon, watercolor on paper, sgn twice/titled, unfr, 22x15", SBY 3/17/88 OE **2,530**

New York Canyon (view of tall buildings), watercolor on paper, sgn, ca 1935, 22x15", C-NY 9/28/89 **3,300**

Storm over New York From 13th Street, oil on canvas, sgn/dtd 1943, unfr, 27x36", SBY 9/14/89 **4,015**

Two Natures, oil on canvas, sgn/dtd 1913, 30x39", C-L 6/27/88 OE **62,436**

HARTMANN, George (American, -1934)

Orioles Win the Series, oil on canvas, sgn, 14x18", C-NY 9/30/88 **1,650**

HARTON, William (American, 1872-1936)

Children by the Sea, group playing Ring Around the Rosy at beach; pencil on paper, 7x10", RAB 8/8/89 **1,200**

HARTSHORNE, Howard Morton (American, 19th/20th C)

Game of Chess (w/two older gentlemen), oil on canvas, sgn/dtd 1908, 77x77", SBY 9/14/89 **5,225**

HARTUNG, Hans (French, 1904-)

Composition, black ink/ink wash on paperboard, sgn/dtd 61, 20x29", SBY 11/9/89 OE **38,500**

Composition, oil on paper, sgn/dtd 61, 20x29", SBY 11/9/89 OE 52,250
T 47-21 (abstract), oil on board, sgn/dtd 47, 15x25", SBY 6/30/88 84,000
T 48-17 (abstract), oil on canvas, sgn/dtd 48, 38x51", SBY 6/30/88 OE 212,200
Untitled (abstract), acrylic on board, sgn/dtd 77, 9x7", WD 11/16/88 5,500
Untitled (abstract), charcoal/crayon on paper, sgn/dtd 53, 19x29", SBY 2/15/89 OE 44,000
Untitled (abstract), charcoal/crayon on paper, sgn/dtd 54, 19x29", SBY 2/15/89 OE 41,250
Untitled (abstract), crayon on paper, sgn/dtd 25.3.64, 19x15", SBY 10/8/88 OE 7,150
Untitled (abstract), oil on paper, sgn/dtd 53, 19x28", SBY 5/3/89 OE 77,000
Untitled (abstract), pastel on paper, sgn/dtd 49, 20x15", SBY 6/30/88 34,000

HARTUNG, M. (Continental, 19th C)
Study of a Horse, oil on canvas, sgn, 12x10", PHL 10/28/88 UE 150

HARTWELL, Nina Rosabel (American, 19th/20th C)
Lady Arranging Flowers, oil on canvas, sgn/indistinctly dtd, 51x38", SBY 1/24/89 OE 19,800

HARTWICK, Gunther (American, fl 1845-1860)
Landscape Scene, lake & road w/mother, mountain in background; oil on canvas, sgn, unfr, 28x35", DM 1/15/88 900
Winter's Pleasures (landscape w/figures ice skating), oil on panel, 30x42", C-NY 5/26/88 9,350

HARTWICK, Gunther; att (American, fl 1845-1860)
Winter Scene (landscape w/buildings & figures on frozen pond), oil on canvas, 25x30", SBY 3/17/88 3,850

HARTWICK, Herman (American, 1853-1926)
Birches in the Fall, oil on canvas, sgn, 20x27", C-NY 9/30/88 3,080

HARTWIG, Heinie (American, 1937-)
Acorn Pickers, oil on panel, sgn, 24x31", B/B 1/11/89 990
By the Lake, oil on board, sgn, 6x9", NA 10/1/88 475
Clipper Ship at Sunset, oil on panel, sgn, 13x24", B/B 1/11/89 375
Indian Encampment (figures & tepees in extensive landscape), oil on board, 17x22", PHL 10/28/88 750
The Way It Was, oil on panel, sgn, 12x16", NA 10/1/88 OE 1,150
Untitled, Indian encampment w/tepees; oil on masonite, 12x24", SLK 2/11/89 300
Way It Was, oil on panel, sgn, 12x24", FAP 4/15/89 467

HARVEY, Eugene (American, 19th C)
Return (fishing boat returning European coastal village), oil on canvas, sgn, 15x25", RAB 8/9/88 500
Return (sail boat in rough seas approaching coastal town), oil on canvas, sgn, 15x25", RAB 8/8/89 500
The Return (fishing boat, coastal village), oil on canvas, sgn, 15x25", RAB 8/9/88 500

HARVEY, George (British, 1806-1876)
Old Gloucester Harbor, watercolor on paper laid down on board, sgn/dtd 82, 7x14", C-E 2/1/89 1,980

HARVEY, George Wainwright (American, 1835-1920)
Boats in Harbor, Venice; pastel/pencil on paper, sgn, 24x19", C-E 6/1/88 1,100
Distant Sailing, pastel on paper, sgn, 16x24", WG 9/16/88 UE 300
Figures on the Shore, Dieppe; watercolor on paper, sgn, 13x20", RWS 11/10/89 550
Huckle Berry Hill, Annisquam, Massachusetts (landscape); oil on canvas, 18x22", RWS 3/31/88 950
Sailing Along the Coast, watercolor/pencil on board, sgn/dtd 83, 12x19", C-E 11/30/88 UE 550

HARVEY, Gerald (American, 1933-)
Breaking Light, oil on canvas, sgn twice/copyrighted/dtd 1983, titled/#d 4924, 24x36", SBY 9/23/88 OE 17,600
Drifting Through (man on horse drifting through town), oil on canvas, sgn/dtd 1974, 24x36", SBY 9/23/88 7,150
In Morning Light, sgn/dtd 1983, 20x16", SBY 9/23/88 OE 6,050
In the Land of the Walking Rain, oil on canvas, sgn/inscr/copyrighted/dtd 1978, 24x36", SBY 9/23/88 OE 14,300
New Land (man on horse w/mule packs in landscape), oil on canvas, sgn/dtd 1977, 20x24", SBY 9/23/88 3,740
Snowy Trail, oil on canvas, sgn/copyrighted/dtd 1977, 20x36", SBY 9/23/88 OE 8,800
Teton Encampment, oil on canvas, sgn/dtd 1982, titled/copyrighted, 48x40", SBY 9/23/88 OE 29,700
Winter Softness (man on horseback w/mule pack in landscape), oil on canvas, sgn/dtd 83/#d 4925, 16x12", SBY 9/23/88 OE 5,060

HARWOOD, James Taylor (American, 1860-1940)
Red Boat of Spain (freighter docked in harbor), oil on canvas, sgn/dtd 28, 20x30", RWS 9/29/88 OE 2,000

HASBROUCK, Dubois Fenelon (American, 1860-1934)
Mill Pond (figure in boat on pond), oil on artist board, sgn/dtd 89, 18x10", RAB 3/27/89 UE 250
Winter, Twilight (landscape); oil on canvas, sgn/dtd NY 98, 12x16", RWS 3/16/89 OE 2,600
Winter Morning (landscape), oil on artist board, sgn/dtd 89/titled, 18x10", RAB 3/27/89 425
Woodland Stream in Winter, watercolor on paper, sgn/dtd 1914, 18x26", SBY 3/17/88 1,430

HASELTINE, William Stanley (American, 1835-1900)
Coastal Landscape, oil on canvas, sgn/dtd 59, 24x37", C-NY 12/2/88 UE 11,000
Fishing Boats, Venice; oil on canvas, sgn/dtd 82, 14x27", C-NY 9/28/89 14,300
New England Woods, oil on canvas, 8x14", C-E 6/1/88 1,320
View of a Mediterranean Coastal Town, oil on canvas, sgn/dtd 1878, 33x56", C-NY 12/2/88 UE 9,900

HASLEHUST, E.W. (Scottish, 19th/20th C)
Bridge to the River Afton, watercolor on paper, sgn, 15x20", B/B 1/11/89 935
Cityscape Near a River, watercolor on paper, initialed, 14x20", B/B 1/11/89 550

HASLER, William N. (American, 1865-)
Lowlands, oil on canvasboard, sgn, 12x16", C-E 2/3/88 550

HASLIM, James (20th C)
Bob & Marilyn Haslim, oil on canvas, 1981, 92x80", SBY 2/19/88 16,500

HASPE, see De Haspe

HASS, A. (Dutch, 19th/20th C)
Shore Scene with Boats, watercolor, sgn, 16x20", LH 9/10/89 500

HASSALL, John (British, 1868-1948)
Red Indian, charcoal drawing, sgn, 26x20", LH 12/4/88 UE ... 90

HASSAM, Frederick Childe (American, 1859-1935)
Autumn Hilltop, New England (landscape); oil on canvas, sgn/dtd 1906, 24x23", SBY 5/24/89 ... 137,500
Banks of the Seine, oil on canvas, sgn/dtd 1888, 9x11", WD 4/13/88 ... 135,000
Battery Park, pencil/white chalk on brown paper, dtd 1916, 13x7", C-NY 9/30/88 ... 5,720
Bridge at Posilippo, Naples; oil on canvas, sgn/dtd 1899, 25x30", C-NY 12/2/88 ... 165,000
Idle Hours (beach scene w/man on barrel, man mending net), watercolor on paper, sgn/dtd 1882, 10x15", C-NY 9/28/89 ... 33,000
In an East Hampton Garden (three ladies conversing), oil on canvas, sgn/dtd June 7 1931, 31x40", SBY 5/24/89 ... 170,500
In the Garden, watercolor/Chinese white/pencil on paper laid down, sgn, ca 1889, 6x11", C-NY 5/25/89 OE ... 28,600
Lady Walking Down Fifth Avenue (snowy street scene), oil on canvas, sgn/dtd 1902, 16x12", SBY 5/24/89 ... 352,000
Landscape, oil on canvas on masonite, sgn, 14x10", S/A 2/18/89 ... 10,500
Les Grands Boulevards, Paris (street scene); oil on canvas, sgn twice/dtd 1897 twice, 18x30", SBY 5/24/89 ... 1,045,000
Mill Pond, Cos Cob; oil on canvas, sgn/dtd 1902, 26x18", SBY 5/25/88 OE ... 253,000
Mill Site & Old Tidal Dam, Cos Cob (landscape); oil on canvas, sgn twice/dtd 1902 twice, 24x26", SBY 5/24/89 OE ... 154,000
Mrs Hassam's Garden at East Hampton (still life in a landscape), sgn/dtd 1934, 41x29", SBY 5/24/89 OE ... 275,000
Old House, East Hampton; oil on canvas, sgn twice/dtd 1917 twice, 21x30", SBY 5/24/89 OE ... 154,000
Outside the Cafe on the Grand Boulevard, gouache/charcoal on brown paper, sgn/dtd 1898, 15x11", SBY 5/25/88 OE ... 63,800
Paris at Twilight, oil on canvas, sgn/dtd 1887, 26x21", C-NY 12/2/88 OE ... 550,000
Paris Street, oil on canvas, sgn/dtd 1889, 13x18", SBY 5/24/89 ... 330,000
Paris Street in Winter, oil on panel, sgn/dtd twice, 1889, 6x4", SBY 5/25/88 ... 63,250
Path in the Woods, oil on panel, sgn/dtd 1907, 6x10", C-NY 5/25/89 ... 19,800
Pont Neuf, oil on panel, sgn/dtd twice 1910, 6x7", SBY 5/25/88 UE ... 66,000
Posillipo, Italy; oil on canvas, sgn/dtd 1897, 26x21", C-NY 5/25/89 ... 187,000
San Pietro, Venice; watercolor on paper, sgn/titled, ca 1883, 8x11", SBY 5/24/89 ... 42,900

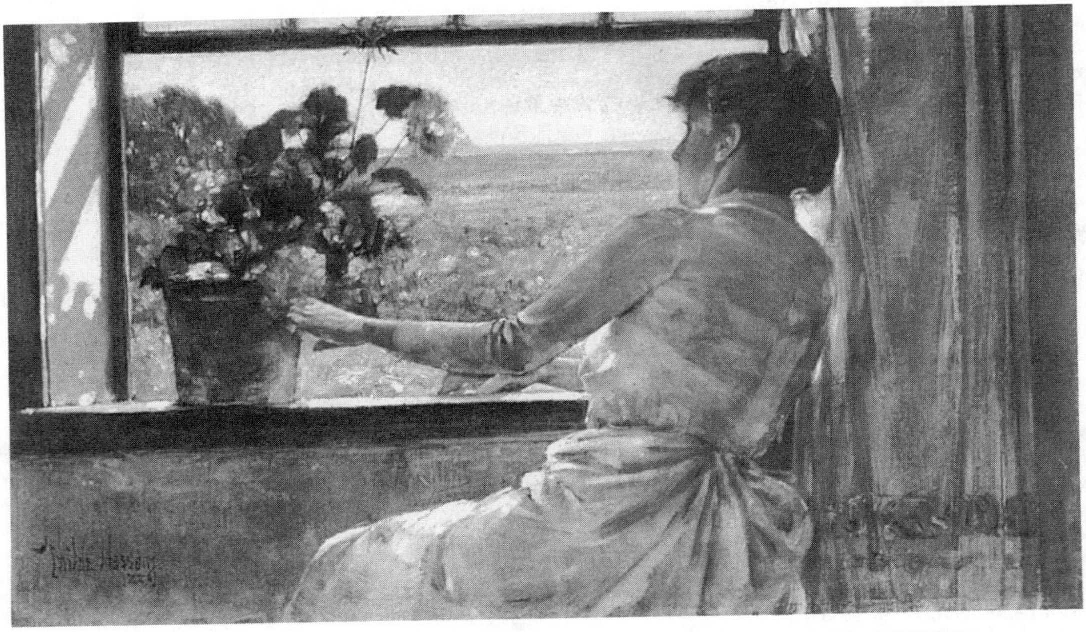

Summer Evening, oil on canvas, sgn/dtd 1886, 12x20", C-NY 5/25/89, $572,000

Woodcutters (Old Elm), oil on canvas, sgn/dtd 1903, 18x22", C-NY 12/2/88 ... 187,000

HASSELBAR
Adirondack Silver Birches, oil on canvas, sgn, 20x29", NA 2/6/88 UE ... 275

HASSELL, Hilton McDonald (Canadian, 1910-)
Fishing Boats, Parkers Cover, Nova Scotia; oil on board, sgn, 12x18", WAD 11/30/89 ... 575
Over Orange Hulls, oil on board, sgn, 10x16", WAD 11/30/89 ... 300

HATCH, Emily Nichols (American, 19th/20th C)
Mary's Garden, oil on artist board, sgn/dtd 1914, 7x9", RWS 12/10/88 ... 900

HATFIELD, Joseph Henry (American, 1863-1928)
Stream Through the Salt Marshes, oil on canvas, sgn, 15x18", RWS 5/12/89 OE ... 2,300

HATHAWAY, Bruce (British, 20th C)
Figure Beside a Summer Cottage, oil on canvas, sgn, 30x40", B/B 12/8/88 ... 1,320

HATHAWAY, George M. (American, 1852-1903)
Schooner Nellie Sailing Off the Coast, oil on canvas, sgn/dtd 1891, 11x22", RAB 3/14/89 OE ... 3,500
Ship & Tug Off Coastline, watercolor on paper, sgn, 6x10", RWS 6/10/89 ... 1,100
Ship Off Rocky Coast, watercolor on paper, sgn, 6x10", RWS 6/10/89 ... 900

HAU, Eva (Russian, 19th C)
Figures in a Picture Gallery, Possibly the Uffizi; watercolor/gouache, sgn/indistinctly dtd, 8x10", C-NY 10/25/89 ... 12,100
Interior of an Elegant Pink & Green Music Room, watercolor/gouache, sgn, 11x17", C-NY 10/25/89 ... 13,200

HAU, Woldemar Ivanovich (Russian, 1816-1895)
Portrait of Seated Officer, pen/brush/ink/watercolor, sgn/dtd 1837, 9x7", C-L 10/8/88 .... **1,950**
HAUNOLD, Karl Franz Emanuel (Austrian, 1832-1911)
Mountain Lane with Figures, oil on canvas laid down on board, sgn/inscr, 12x21", SBY 6/8/88 OE **6,325**
HAUSCH, Alexander Fiodorovich (Russian, 1873-)
Light Night in Finland, oil on canvas, sgn, 28x56", SBY 5/23/89 UE **6,050**
HAUSCHILD, Maximilian (German, 1810-1895)
The Return of General Morosini From the Turkish Wars, oil on canvas, sgn, 50x58", B/B 3/17/88 .... **6,600**
HAUSER, John (American, 1859-1913)
Chief Fire Cloud, Sioux (bust-length portrait in full regalia); oil on board, sgn/dtd 1912, 12x8", RWS 3/31/88 .... **3,400**
Chief's Pow Wow (Indians/ponies & village in background), oil on canvas, sgn/dtd 1904, 18x28", SBY 5/24/89 .... **13,200**
Indian with Shotgun Standing by His Horse, gouache on board, sgn/dtd 1911, 12x8", DM 2/19/88 UE **2,750**
HAUSHALTER, George M. (American, 1862-)
House by a Stream, oil on board, sgn, 12x15", SBY 9/14/89 .... **990**
HAVARD, James (American, 20th C)
Brahma Run (abstract), acrylic on board, sgn/dtd 83, 31x81", C-NY 2/14/89 .... **12,100**
Buccaneer Jumbie Dancer (abstract), acrylic on canvas, sgn/dtd 79, unfr, 60x47", C-NY 5/4/89 OE **33,000**
BVI (abstract), acrylic on canvas, unfr, 72x36", C-NY 2/14/89 .... **19,800**
Cane Garden Bay (abstract), acrylic on canvas, sgn/dtd 77/titled, 52x48", SBY 2/19/88 .... **19,800**
Cheyenne (abstract), acrylic on canvas, sgn/dtd 77, 95x63", SBY 10/5/89 .... **41,250**
Chippewa (abstract), acrylic on canvas, sgn/dtd 1977, 60x66", SBY 10/8/88 OE **30,800**
Clam Digger/Hopi Mask #895 (abstract); acrylic/paper collage on ragboard, sgn/dtd 85, 40x32", SBY 2/15/89 .... **7,700**
Crow Bed, acrylic on canvas, sgn twice/dtd 77/titled, unfr, 46x46", C-NY 11/10/88 .... **17,600**
Diptych: Brahma Night Ride (abstract); acrylic on canvas, sgn/dtd 81, unfr, 72x96", C-NY 2/14/89 .... **28,600**
Diptych: North West Swell; acrylic on canvas, sgn/dtd 80, unfr, 60x60", C-NY 5/4/89 OE **24,200**
Ghost Dance Shirt No 421 (abstract), acrylic on canvas, sgn/dtd 77/titled, 35x35", SBY 5/3/88 .... **12,100**
Gold Coast (abstract), sheet acrylic/colored crayons on board, sgn/dtd 80, 32x20", C-E 11/14/89 OE **9,350**
Green Bank BVI (abstract), acrylic on canvas, sgn/dtd 80, 24x28", SBY 2/15/89 OE **11,000**
Kachina, acrylic on canvas, sgn/inscr/dtd 76, unfr, 48x48", C-NY 5/4/88 OE **23,100**
Sand Dog (abstract), acrylic on canvas, sgn twice/dtd 80 twice/titled, 60x48", SBY 2/19/88 .... **11,550**
Santa Fe Sun Brahma (abstract), acrylic on canvas, sgn/dtd 80, 60x72", SBY 10/5/89 .... **25,300**
Sequoya Letter, acrylic laquer on paper, sgn/inscr/dtd 71, 28x24", C-E 5/13/88 .... **825**
Sioux (abstract), acrylic on canvas, sgn/dtd 76, unfr, 48x48", C-NY 10/4/89 .... **22,000**
Soshhoni (abstract), acrylic/charcoal on canvas, sgn/inscr/dtd 77, unfr, 96x72", C-NY 5/4/88 OE **49,500**
Triptych: Brangus (abstract); acrylic on canvas, sgn/dtd 81, unfr, 66x113", C-NY 5/4/89 OE **82,500**
Untitled (abstract), acrylic on canvas, sgn/dtd 80, unfr, 60x36", C-NY 5/4/89 .... **13,200**
Untitled (abstract), acrylic on canvas, sgn/dtd 81, 54x48", SBY 2/15/89 OE **12,100**
Untitled (abstract), acrylic/charcoal on board, sgn/dtd 76, 40x35", C-NY 10/4/89 .... **5,500**
Untitled (abstract), mixed media mounted on board, sgn/dtd 85, 70x40", C-NY 5/4/89 OE **44,000**
Untitled (abstract), oil/crayon on cardboard, 1985, 29x41", SBY 10/8/88 .... **4,950**
Untitled #4 (contemporary composition), acrylic on canvas, sgn/dtd 75, 96x48", SBY 11/9/89 .... **38,500**
Virgin Gorda (abstract), acrylic on canvas, sgn/dtd twice 79/titled, 66x60, SBY 5/3/88 OE **23,100**
HAVELL, Edmund; att (British, 1819-1894)
Boating on a Lake, oil on canvas, 19x25", C-E 2/23/88 .... **1,650**
HAVELL, Robert Jr. (American, 1793-1878)
Upper Hudson, oil on canvas, initialed, 8x14", SBY 9/23/88 .... **2,750**
HAVEN, see De Haven
HAVERS, Alice (British, 1850-1890)
Children's Games, oil on canvas, sgn, 18x13", C-E 5/23/88 OE **3,520**
HAWLEY, Hughson (American, 1850-1936)
Appomattox Court House (Civil War), pen/ink on paper, sgn/inscr, unfr, 10x14", C-E 11/30/88 OE **605**
Near Larchmont, New York (landscape); watercolor/gouache on paper, sgn/dtd 1885, 14x19", RWS 12/10/88 .... **500**
HAWLEY, Reginald A. (American, 20th C)
Evening Light, oil on canvas, sgn, 16x20", FAP 12/8/89 UE **225**
HAWORTH, Bobs Cogill (Canadian, 1904-)
Landscape with Grazing Horses, watercolor, sgn, 20x24", WAD 6/12/89 .... **1,000**
HAWORTH, Peter (Canadian, 1889-)
Bon Echo, oil on panel, sgn, 11x14", C-SK 11/10/88 .... **350**
Fall Tapestry, oil on board, sgn, 20x25", WAD 11/30/89 UE **250**
Old Buggy, watercolor, sgn, 23x16", WAD 6/12/89 .... **750**
HAWTHORNE, Charles Webster (American, 1872-1930)
First Mate (portrait of a man seated), oil on board, 48x48", C-NY 12/2/88 .... **44,000**
Fish Mongers, oil on canvas, indistinctly sgn, unfr, 51x38", C-NY 12/2/88 .... **17,600**
Landscape, deep woods in spring greens, oil on canvas, sgn, 21x16", RAB 8/8/89 OE **2,000**
Lovers (portrait of a couple standing, half-length), tempera on panel, 40x40", SBY 3/17/88 OE **4,125**
Portrait of a Woman, oil on canvas, sgn, 24x22", C-NY 9/28/89 .... **4,400**
Portrait of Sir William Richmond, oil on canvas, sgn, 40x39", SBY 3/17/88 .... **6,050**
Red Dress (portrait), oil on board, sgn, 14x14", C-NY 3/11/88 .... **7,700**
Tennis Player (full-length portrait of man), oil on board, sgn, 72x47", WD 10/5/88 .... **8,000**
HAWTHORNE, Charles Webster; att (American, 1872-1930)
Beach Scene with Nude Bather, oil on canvas, sgn/inscr, 17x21", SBY 9/23/88 .... **3,300**

Children in the Park, oil on canvas, 21x24", SBY 1/24/89 ... 3,575

HAY, Bernard (British, 1864-)

Along the Amalfi Coast, oil on canvas, sgn/dtd 1904, 16x10", C-E 10/26/89 ... 5,500
Capri, oil on canvas, sgn, 16x10", SBY 12/9/88 ... 2,090

HAYDEN, Charles H. (American, 1856-1901)

Palm Trees, oil on canvas, sgn, 14x18", C-E 11/30/88 UE ... 1,100
Plowing the Field, oil on canvas, sgn/dtd 1900, 14x18", C-E 11/30/88 ... 2,640

HAYDEN, Henri (Polish, 1883-1970)

Carrousel (in park), oil on paper mounted on board, sgn, 15x18", C-E 5/9/89 ... 2,200
Corbeille et Potiche (basket & porcelain vase), gouache on paper laid down on board, sgn/dtd 63, 16x22", C-E 11/17/88 OE ... 2,200
Nature Morte en Violet (Still Life in Violet), gouache on paper laid down on board, sgn/dtd 66, 15x22", C-E 11/17/88 OE ... 2,200
Paysage Vert, oil on masonite, sgn/dtd 65, 13x18", SBY 10/5/88 ... 3,300
Vue sur Mollien, gouache on board, sgn/dtd 64, 15x21", SBY 10/5/88 ... 2,750

HAYE, see De La Haye

HAYES, Claude (British, 1852-1922)

Foddering Sheep in Winter Snow, oil on board, sgn, 33x29", WAD 6/6/88 ... 6,200
Sheep in a Landscape, watercolor, sgn, 21x29", FB 10/17/88 ... 1,100
Sheep with Shepherd, watercolor, sgn, 26x39", FB 10/17/88 ... 2,300
Shepherd & His Flock, oil on board, sgn, 34x30", C-NY 2/25/88 ... 3,300

HAYES, Edwin (British, 1820-1904)

Ships Off the Pier, oil on canvas, sgn, 22x32", B/B 9/14/89 ... 2,750
Wind on Shore, Ostend (figures & boat); oil on canvas, sgn/dtd 58, 24x43", C-E 2/21/89 OE ... 12,100

HAYES, Woodie (American, 20th C)

Western Landscape, oil on canvas laid down on board, sgn, 1946-47, 17x28", LH 12/4/88 ... 40

HAYEX, Francesco; circle of

Hagar & Ishmael, oil on canvas, 36x32", C-E 5/23/88 ... 770

HAYLLER, Jessica (British, fl 1880-1915)

Portrait of a Child, oil on board, sgn/dtd 1880, 10x8", SBY 12/9/88 UE ... 660

HAYNES-WILLIAMS, John (British, 19th C)

Interior View of Fontainbleau-Marie Antoinette's Bedroom; oil on canvas, sgn, 21x31", lot 3907, B/B 12/8/88 ... 1,980
Interior View of Fontainbleau-Marie Antoinette's Boudoir; oil on canvas, sgn, 20x31", lot 3906, B/B 12/8/88 UE ... 220
Interior View of Fontainbleau-The Gilded Reception Room; oil on canvas, sgn, 20x30", B/B 12/8/88 ... 2,200

HAYS, Barton S. (American, 1826-1914)

Apples & Peaches (still life), oil on canvas, sgn, 14x21", C-E 6/1/89 ... 2,420
Grapes & Blackberries (still life), oil on canvas, sgn, 10x15", SBY 1/24/89 OE ... 2,640
Ripe Apples (still life), oil on canvas, 11x14", C-E 2/1/89 OE ... 1,540
Still Life of Large Apples, oil on canvas, sgn, 14x22", C-E 2/1/89 OE ... 1,870

HAYS, Bret (British, 1880-1940)

Seascape, oil on canvas, sgn/dtd 91, 30x50", LH 10/16/88 UE ... 1,500

HAYS, George Arthur (American, 1854-)

Cow & Calf in Water Meadow (cows in landscape), oil on canvas, sgn/dtd 98, 12x16", RWS 3/16/89 ... 800
Cows in Pool, oil on canvas, sgn, 1915, 10x14", RWS 9/8/89 ... 700
Landscape with Cows, oil on canvas, sgn, 9x12", RWS 5/12/89 ... 600
Landscape with Grazing Flock, oil on canvas, sgn, 12x19", RWS 5/12/89 ... 1,000
Ploughing, oil on canvas, sgn, 14x17", RAB 11/24/89 ... 800
Watering Hole, Landscape with Cows; oil on canvas, sgn, 13x18", RWS 11/10/89 ... 550
Woonsocket Hill, a Summer Morning (cattle in mountain meadow); oil on canvas, sgn, 25x30", RWS 9/29/88 ... 950

HAYTER, John (British, 1800-1895)

Call to Arms (figures in an interior), oil on canvas, sgn/dtd 1882, 24x20", WL 5/20/88 ... 1,200

HAYTER, Stanley William (British, 1901-1988)

Abstract Figure, ink/watercolor on paper, sgn/dtd July 28/Aug 3-47, unfr, 29x23", SBY 10/7/89 ... 5,500
Abstract Studies, pen/ink/colored wash on paper, sgn/dtd 44, 22x34", PHL 11/15/88 OE ... 2,100
Backwash, oil on canvas, sgn/dtd 64/titled, 39x39", C-E 5/9/89 OE ... 10,450
McGovern (contemporary), gouache on paper, initialed/dtd 72, unfr, 31x23", C-E 5/9/88 OE ... 3,950
Untitled, watercolor/brush/black ink on paper, sgn/dtd May 13-14-1947, 23x35", C-NY 2/13/89 ... 4,620
Untitled (abstract), acrylic on canvas, sgn, 18x26", SBY 2/14/89 ... 4,950

HAYWARD, Peter (American, 1905-)

Delancy Street, oil on canvas, sgn, 24x30", FAP 12/8/89 ... 250

HEAD, Cecil (American, 1906-)

Still Life, oil on canvas, sgn/dtd 1932, LH 9/10/89 OE ... 2,700
Still Life, oil on canvas, sgn/dtd 1932, 25x30", LH 10/16/88 OE ... 2,600

HEADE, Martin Johnson (American, 1819-1904)

Great Florida Sunset, oil on canvas, sgn/dtd 1887, 53x96", SBY 5/25/88 ... 1,650,000
Hummingbirds, oil on canvas, 16x12", lot 67, SBY 5/25/88 OE ... 104,500
Hummingbirds, oil on canvas, 16x12", lot 68, SBY 5/25/88 ... 99,000
Hummingbirds & Passion Flowers, oil on canvas, sgn, 20x12", SBY 5/24/89 OE ... 1,100,000
Magnolias on Light Blue Velvet, oil on canvas, initialed, 15x24", C-NY 5/26/88 ... 264,000
Orchids, Passion Flowers, & Hummingbird; oil on canvas, sgn, ca 1875-85, 20x14", SBY 5/25/88 ... 385,000
Orchids & Hummingbird, oil on panel, sgn/dtd 72, 16x20", C-NY 5/26/88 OE ... 550,000
Orchids & Hummingbirds in a Brazilian Jungle, oil on canvas, sgn, 17x21", C-NY 5/25/89 ... 418,000
Red Rose with Ruby Throat (hummingbird), oil on board, sgn, 12x10", SBY 5/24/89 OE ... 66,000

Still Life of Glass of Roses, oil on canvas, sgn/dtd 1880, 17x15", C-NY 5/26/88 ... 30,800
Tropical Greenery (jungle landscape), oil on canvas, sgn/dtd 1875, 18x15", SBY 1/24/89 ... 8,800
Two Hummingbirds by an Orchid, oil on canvas, sgn, ca 1890, 13x20", SBY 5/24/89 ... 319,000
Two Hummingbirds in a Landscape, oil on canvas, ca 1863-65, 12x10", SBY 5/25/88 ... 96,250
Two Small Hummingbirds Above an Orchid, oil on canvas, sgn/dtd 1893, 22x14", SBY 5/25/88 ... 220,000

HEALY, George Peter Alexander (American, 1808-1894)
Portrait of a Woman, oil on canvas, sgn/dtd 1863, 27x22", B/B 4/20/88 ... 1,045

HEAPHY, Thomas Frank (British, 1775-1835)
Distressed Poet, oil on canvas, sgn w/monogram, dtd 1866, 38x26", C-NY 5/25/88 ... 7,150

HEBERER, Charles (American, 19th C)
Robert Burns & Highland Mary (couple by a stream), oil on canvas, sgn/dtd 1895, 40x50", B/B 3/22/89 ... 3,850

HEBERT, Adrien (Canadian, 1890-1967)
Coquillages Nicolas, oil on canvas, sgn, 18x30", FB 5/28/89 ... 4,600
Montreal Docks, oil on canvas, sgn, 19x25", WAD 6/12/89 ... 2,000
Paysage d'Ete (summer landscape), watercolor, sgn/dtd 1919, 11x19", FB 4/25/88 UE ... 500
Street Scene, crayon, sgn, 15x12", FB 4/25/88 ... 130

HEBERT, Jules (Swiss, 1812-1897)
Study for Leaning Male Nude, pencil on paper, dtd 1844, unfr, 11x8", B/B 9/14/89 UE ... 605
Study for Seated Male Nude, pencil on paper, sgn/dtd 1850, unfr, 7x10", B/B 9/14/89 UE ... 550

HEBERT (American, 20th C)
Girl in Blue (portrait in landscape), oil on canvas, sgn/dtd 63/titled, RAB 8/8/89 UE ... 275

HECHT, Victor David (American, 1873-)
Seated Woman in White Dress, oil on canvas, sgn, 50x36", SBY 6/28/89 ... 3,190

HECKEL, Erich (German, 1883-1970)
Die Brucke Bei Le Puy, watercolor over black chalk on paper mounted on paper, sgn/dtd 26, 20x25", C-NY 10/6/88 ... 9,020
Double-Sided: Bauernhof (pencil study for farmhouse); watercolor/pencil on paper, sgn/dtd 14, 16x20", SBY 10/6/89 ... 7,150
Wanderzirkus, watercolor on paper, sgn/dtd 48, 17x12", SBY 10/7/89, OE ... 12,100

HEDA, Gerrit Willemsz (Dutch, 1642-1702)
Still Life of Pewter Plates, a Tazza, a Nautilus Cup...; oil on panel, sgn/dtd 1646, 24x32", C-NY 1/11/89 OE ... 352,000

HEDA, Willem Claesz (Dutch, 1594-1680)
Still Life of Silver Ewer, Silver Gilt-Covered Cup...; oil on canvas, sgn/indistinctly dtd, 41x45", SBY 1/12/89 OE ... 451,000

HEDA, Willem Claesz; follower of (Dutch, 1594-1680)
Still Life of Fruits on a Draped Table with Glass & a Flagon, oil on panel, bears signature/dtd, 36x29", SBY 4/7/88 OE ... 14,300

HEEM, see De Heem

HEEREMANS, Thomas (Dutch, fl 1660-1697)
Elegant Couple Outside a Tavern, oil on canvas, 32x26", C-NY 10/12/89 ... 7,150
Ferryboats Docked Before a Tavern, oil on canvas, sgn/dtd 1691, 40x56", C-NY 5/31/89 ... 52,800
Ferryboats Docking by a Tavern, oil on canvas, sgn, 26x32", C-NY 10/20/88 ... 28,600
Figures Before an Inn on a Frozen River, oil on panel, 15x12", C-NY 10/12/89 ... 7,700
Fishermen Unloading Their Catch on the Beach at Terheide, oil on panel, sgn/dtd 1675, 12x15", SBY 10/13/89 ... 16,500
Skater on a River by a Town Hall, oil on panel, sgn/dtd 1665, 16x23", C-NY 10/12/89 ... 14,300
Village by a River with Figures in Boats, oil on panel, sgn/dtd 1692, 10x12", SBY 4/7/88 ... 9,350

HEEREMANS, Thomas; circle of (Dutch, fl 1660-1697)
Landscape with Houses & Traffic on a Canal, the City of Dordrecht in the Distance; oil on panel, 22x32", SBY 4/7/89 ... 4,125

HEERSCHOP, Hendrik (Flemish, 1620-1672)
Geographer, oil on canvas, 19x24", WD 10/19/88 ... 5,750

HEESAKKER, Thomas (Dutch, 20th C)
Old Master Style Floral Still Life, oil on canvas, sgn, 24x20", B/B 1/11/89 ... 1,430

HEFFNER, Karl (German, 1849-1925)
Boats Moored on a Calm Lake, oil on canvas, sgn, 28x38", SBY 12/9/88 ... 4,400
Pond, oil on canvas, sgn, 46x66", SBY 2/22/89 ... 14,300
Quiet Autumn Evening, oil on canvas, sgn, 28x38", SBY 7/12/89 ... 4,400
View of the Village Across an Estuary, oil on canvas, sgn, 27x37", B/B 3/17/88 ... 7,150

HEGI, Johann S. (Swiss, 1814-1896)
Calle de Mexico Cerca de la Catedral (Mexican street scene), watercolor on paper, sgn, 7x10", C-NY 11/21/88 OE ... 4,950

HEHIANCHI, J.L.
View of Roman Antiquities, oil on canvas, sgn/inscr, 30x40", C-E 5/23/88 OE ... 6,050

HEICKE, Joseph (Austrian, 1811-1861)
Arab Encampment, oil on panel, sgn/dtd 844 (sic), 18x22", C-E 2/21/89 ... 2,420

HEIL, Charles Emile (American, 1870-)
Landscape Scene (cow grazing, buildings beyond), oil on canvas, sgn, 16x12", RWS 9/29/88 ... 200

HEILBUTH, Ferdinand (French, 1826-1889)
Elizabethan Lovers in a Wood, watercolor/gouache, sgn/dtd 1868, 9x13", C-NY 10/25/89 ... 1,100
Portrait of Edmond de Goncourt, pastel on paper, sgn/dtd 1850, 16x13", SBY 5/23/89 ... 16,500

HEILMAYER, Karl (German, 1829-1908)
Grand Canal, Venice; oil on canvas laid down on masonite, sgn/dtd 1874, 30x56", C-E 2/23/88 OE ... 6,050

HEIM, Francois Joseph (French, 1787-1865)
Portrait of the Painter Charles Thevenin, seated; pencil, sgn/inscr, 8x5", C-NY 10/26/88 ... 1,100

HEINE, Friedrich Wilhelm (American, 1845-1921)
Portrait of a Young Lady, oil on academy board, sgn, 12x9", S/A 3/12/88 ... 400
Sunset Scene with Cattle Watering Near a Lake, oil on board, sgn/dtd 1920, 12x18", MAG 6/22/88 ... 400

HEINE, Thomas Theodore (German, 1867-1948)
Evening Walk (Abend Spaziergang), oil on copper, ca 1902, oval, 23x32", C-L 6/27/88 ... **37,840**
HEINISCH, Karl Adam (German, 1847-1923)
Landscape with Farm & Animals, oil on canvas, sgn, 20x28", SBY 12/9/88 OE ... **8,250**
HEINS, D. (German, 1725-1779)
Portrait of a Young Man, Feeding a Cherry to a Parrot, with a Spaniel; oil on canvas, sgn/dtd 1741, 50x44", C-NY 1/15/88 ... **16,500**
HEINSIUS, Johann Ernst (German, 1740-1812)
Portrait of a Lady in Pink with an Elaborate Headdress, oil on canvas, sgn/dtd 1788, 26x21", SBY 10/21/88 ... **3,850**
HEINSIUS, Johann Ernst; circle of (German, 1740-1812)
Portrait of a Lady Playing the Guitar & a Gentleman Holding a Violin, oil on canvas, 45x38", SBY 4/7/89 OE ... **11,000**
HEINTZ, Joseph; school of (Swiss, 16th/17th C)
Adam & Eve, oil on canvas, unfr, 32x39", C-E 1/12/88 ... **1,100**
HEINZE, Adolphe (American, 1887-)
Landscape, oil on canvas, sgn, 28x33", LH 12/4/88 ... **600**
HEISS, J.S.C. (American, 19th C)
Rushing Stream, watercolor on paper, sgn/dtd, 16x22", FAP 4/15/89 ... **468**
HEITER, Michael M. (American, 1883-)
Alexandre Bridge on the Seine, oil on canvas, sgn, 30x34", WD 4/13/88 UE ... **700**
View of Colmar, oil on canvas, sgn, 25x31", WD 4/13/88 UE ... **700**
HEITKAMP, Irving (American, -1917)
In the Harbor, oil on canvas, sgn, 16x20", FAP 12/8/89 ... **1,200**
HEITLAND, Wilmot Emerton (American, 1893-)
Indian Market, watercolor/pencil on paper, sgn/inscr/dtd 1921, 21x26", C-NY 9/30/88 ... **1,210**
Venetian Brooklyn, watercolor/pencil on paper, sgn/dtd 1922, 22x24", C-NY 9/30/88 ... **1,320**
HEIZER, Michael (American, 1944-)
Actual Size: Empty Containers; photo offset/acrylic/spray paint/crayon on zinc pl, sgn/dtd 75-85, 37x45", SBY 2/19/88 ... **3,025**
Actual Size: Empty Film Boxes; photo offset/pencil/spray paint/crayon on zinc plate, 36x44", SBY 2/19/88 ... **2,970**
Match Drop Dispersal, incised graphite, 3x55x45", C-NY 10/31/89 ... **30,800**
Matchbooks, etching/black ink on zinc plate, sgn/dtd 72, 36x44", C-NY 11/10/88 ... **1,870**
Pair: Untitled Drawings (abstract); brush/black ink/charcoal on paper, sgn, ca 1975, 16x12", C-NY 11/10/88 ... **1,650**
Russian Constructivist Painting, polyvinyl latex on canvas, unfr, 1974, 96" dia, C-NY 11/10/88 ... **22,000**
Simple Curves, black ballpoint pen on paper, titled/dtd 1968, 19x25", C-NY 10/31/89 OE ... **5,280**
Untitled #1 (Brick Red), polyvinyl latex on canvas, 1976, 72x72", SBY 2/19/88 ... **4,950**
Untitled #2 (abstract), polyvinyl latex on canvas, 1975, 96" dia, SBY 2/19/88 UE ... **4,950**
Untitled #3 (abstract), polyvinyl latex on canvas, 1975, 96x96", SBY 2/19/88 ... **4,950**
Untitled #5 (solid color), polyvinyl latex on canvas, sgn/dtd, 1975, 120x72", SBY 10/8/88 ... **7,150**
Untitled #6 (Aquamarine), polyvinyl latex on canvas, sgn/dtd 76/titled, 99x83", SBY 5/3/88 OE ... **9,350**
Untitled #7 (Red), polyvinyl latex on canvas, 1974, 111x156, SBY 2/19/88 ... **6,600**
Untitled #9 (contemporary), polyvinyl latex on canvas, sgn/dtd 1975/titled, 96" dia, SBY 5/3/88 OE ... **17,600**
HEKKING, Joseph Antonio (American/German, fl 1859-1885)
Mountain Landscape with Stream (man in boat, cows grazing, mountains beyond), oil on canvas, sgn, 10x14", RWS 9/29/88 ... **3,500**
HELD, Al (American, 1928-)
C Series No 13 (composition), ink on paper, 1969, 24x35", SBY 11/11/88 ... **4,400**
Circle & Two Squares, oil on canvas, sgn/dtd 67, 70x48", SBY 5/2/89 OE ... **154,000**
Group of 3: G Series 1; G Series 4; G Series 8; India ink on paper, 1970, 23x35", SBY 5/3/88 OE ... **14,300**
H Series 12 (abstract), India ink on paper, sgn, dtd 62, 18x24", SBY 5/3/89 OE ... **3,850**
Noah's Dream I (geometric composition), pencil on paper, 1971, 23x70", SBY 11/11/88 OE ... **9,900**
Out (abstract), acrylic on canvas, sgn/dtd 66, 36x36", C-NY 10/4/89 ... **52,800**
Padua (geometric abstract), acrylic on canvas, 1981, 72x48", SBY 2/19/88 ... **36,300**
Untitled (abstract), acrylic on canvas, sgn/dtd 60, 60x42", C-NY 5/3/89 OE ... **209,000**
Untitled (abstract), brush/black ink on paper, sgn/dtd 67, 23x35", C-NY 5/4/88 OE ... **4,400**
Untitled (abstract), brush/black ink on paper, sgn/dtd 67, 23x35", C-NY 5/4/89 ... **8,800**
Untitled (abstract), gouache on paper, sgn/dtd 60, 18x24", C-NY 2/14/89 ... **6,050**
Untitled (abstract), gouache on paper, sgn/dtd 61, 24x18", C-NY 5/4/88 OE ... **14,300**
Untitled (abstract), oil on canvas, sgn/dtd 58, 30x34", SBY 10/8/88 ... **20,900**
Untitled (contemporary composition), graphite on paper, sgn/dtd 1983, 33x62", SBY 11/9/89 ... **27,500**
Untitled (geometric composition), acrylic on canvas, sgn/dtd 61, 82x66", SBY 5/2/88 ... **110,000**
Untitled (geometric composition), graphite on paper, sgn/dtd 75, 27x40", SBY 5/3/89 OE ... **12,100**
Volta II (geometric abstract in black & white), acrylic on canvas, sgn/dtd 76, unfr, 84x84", C-NY 5/3/89 OE ... **319,000**
HELD, John Jr. (American, 1889-1958)
Three Christmas Cowboys, watercolor on paper, sgn/dtd 38, 11x19", C-E 11/8/88 ... **990**
HELDNER, Collette Pope (American, 20th C)
Old Creole Courtyard on Decatur Street, oil on masonite, sgn, 20x16", MG 10/28/88 ... **1,800**
HELDNER, Knute (American, 1886-1952)
Bayou Country, oil on canvas, sgn, 24x30", B/B 9/15/88 ... **825**
Bayou Lafourche, oil on canvas, sgn, 30x36", NA 11/5/88 ... **2,500**
Bayou Scene, oil on canvas, sgn, 14x18", MG 5/28/88 ... **750**
Bayou Scene, oil on canvas, sgn, 54x36", MG 5/28/88 ... **5,500**
Birch Trees, oil on canvas, sgn, 30x35", C-E 10/18/89 ... **1,100**
Clouds Over Swamp, oil on canvas, sgn, 14x16", B/B 9/15/88 ... **358**
Couple Dancing, oil on canvas, sgn, 8x14", NA 5/13/89 ... **475**

Forest Pool, oil on board, sgn, 15x17", NA 2/6/88 550
Moonlight Bayou, oil on canvas, sgn, 16x20", NA 2/6/88 OE 1,200
Swamp Garden, oil on board, sgn, 8x10", MG 10/28/88 1,200
Twilight on the Lake, oil on canvas, sgn/dtd 21, 34x30", C-E 10/18/89 2,860

HELFERICH, Willem (Dutch, 20th C)
By the Seashore, oil on canvas, sgn, 27x39", C-E 5/22/89 UE 1,760
Summer Day at the Beach, oil on board, sgn, 32x47", C-E 10/26/89 3,080

HELIKER, John Edward (American, 1909-)
Coastal Landscape, oil on board, sgn, 11x10", C-NY 6/17/89 1,100
San Ruffino, gouache/pen/ink on board, sgn, 20x13", SBY 1/24/89 UE 330
Tabletop Still Life, watercolor/pencil on paper, sgn, 11x10", C-NY 6/17/89 605

HELION, Jean (French, 1904-)
Figure Debout (standing abstract figure), watercolor/brown ink on paper, 12x9", WD 11/16/88 7,000
Nu aux Raisins, oil on canvas, initialed/sgn, dtd twice 53, 24x36", SBY 2/18/88 14,300

HELLBUSCH, H. (19th/20th C)
Haystacks (extensive landscape), oil on canvas, sgn, 29x39", SBY 4/14/89 2,200

HELLEMANS, Jean Pierre (Belgian, 1787-1945)
Dead Hare, Blue Tit, & Grouse with an Urn on a Ledge; oil on canvas, sgn/dtd 1833, 34x29", C-NY 2/25/88 7,700

HELLER, Eugenie M. (American, 20th C)
Irises (close-up garden view), oil on canvas, sgn/dtd 1904, 27x53", C-NY 9/28/89 4,400

HELLESEN, Thorvald (Scandinavian, 1888-1937)
Composition aux Rayures, oil on paper laid down on board, sgn, 14x9", SBY 10/5/88 3,850

HELLEU, Paul Cesar (French, 1859-1927)
Breste de Nus, charcoal w/red & white highlights on paper, sgn, 23x18", B/B 6/9/88 2,750
Elegante (sketch of woman), black/red chalk heightened w/white on paper, sgn, 30x19", SBY 10/24/89 14,300
Le Femme aux Fleurs, pastel on linen, sgn, 49x36", SBY 5/23/89 220,000
Portrait of a Lady, waist-length, wearing fur-collared coat & gloves; pastel, sgn, 29x24", C-NY 10/26/88 33,000
Portrait of a Woman in Profile, black/red/white chalk, sgn/inscr, 20x16", C-NY 10/26/88 1,760
Portrait of the Artist's Daughter, Ellen, bust-length; black/red chalk on paper, sgn, 15x12", C-NY 5/24/89 OE 26,400
Protrait of a Lady Wearing a Feathered Hat, black/red/white chalk, sgn/inscr Warren, 26x21", C-NY 2/23/89 19,800
Reclining Nude, black/red/white chalk, sgn, 20x14", C-NY 10/26/88 4,400
Studies of Ellen, the Artist's Daughter; black/red/white chalk, sgn, 13x18", C-NY 10/26/88 13,200
Woman in a Hat, black/red chalk heightened w/white, sgn, 29x22", C-NY 10/26/88 2,640

HELLEU, Paul Cesar; att (French, 1859-1927)
Woman with a Plumed Hat, charcoal/red chalk on paper, bears signature, 23x16", C-E 5/23/88 825

HELLWAG, Rudolf (German, 1867-1942)
Ships at Anchor, oil on canvas laid down, sgn, 16x21", B/B 9/15/88 UE 550

HELMER, Philipp (German, 1846-1912)
Fall Landscape, oil on board, sgn, 16x21", B/B 4/20/88 770
Farmhouse in a Landscape, oil on canvas, 11x16", B/B 4/20/88 770

HELMONT, Lucas van Gassel; circle of (Flemish, 1480-1570)
Christ on the Road to Calvary in a Fantastical River Landscape with a Castle, oil on panel, 9x15", C-NY 6/2/88 OE 15,400

HELSBY, Alfredo
Paisaje (landscape), oil on canvas, sgn, 18x24", C-NY 11/21/89 2,860
Paisaje con Arco Iris (landscape w/rainbow), oil on canvas, sgn, 20x25", C-NY 11/21/88 2,200

HEMING, Arthur (Canadian, 1870-1940)
Peril of Winter (two men on snowshoes, one has fallen), oil on board, sgn, 11x15", FB 10/17/88 2,500

HEMMRICH, Georg (German, 19th C)
Harvesters, oil on panel, sgn, 4x8", C-E 10/25/88 1,320

HEMY, Bernard Benedict (British, 19th C)
Fishing Vessel on Rough Seas, oil on canvas, sgn, 24x36", C-E 10/26/89 1,650

HEMY, Charles Napier (British, 1841-1917)
Figures in an English Country Garden by a Stream, watercolor/gouache, initialed/dtd 1890, 13x19", C-NY 5/25/88 4,400
In Spite of Wind & Weather (boats at sea), oil on canvas, sgn twice/dtd 1911/titled, 40x60", C-NY 5/24/89 26,400

HENDERSON, Charles Cooper (British, 1803-1877)
Pair: Leeds to London Royal Mail; Louth Coach in Heavy Snow; oil on canvas, 1 monogramed, 13x23", SBY 6/9/89 18,700
The Inverness, oil on canvas, initialed/dtd 63, 28x36", B/B 6/9/88 11,000

HENDERSON, Joseph (Scottish, 20th C)
Fisherfolk, oil on panel, sgn, 10x16", SLK 5/12/88 225

HENDERSON, Joseph Morris (British, 1863-1936)
Children Playing on a Rocky Beach, oil on canvas, sgn, 24x36", C-E 5/22/89 3,850

HENDERSON, William (British, fl 1874-1892)
Pair: Beagle in a Landscape; oil on canvas, 1 sgn/dtd 1881, 12x15", SBY 6/10/88 4,400

HENDERSON, William Penhallow (American, 1877-1943)
Sunset on Downs, oil on canvas, unfr, 16x20", SBY 6/24/88 UE 220

HENDON, Cham (20th C)
Portrait of Mayor Koch in His Office, acrylic on canvas on two panels, 1981, unfr, 68x116", C-NY 2/13/89 2,200

HENDRIKS, Gerardus (Dutch, 19th C)
Sailboats at Sunset, oil on canvas, sgn, 19x24", B/B 12/8/88 1,210

HENDRIKS, Willem (Dutch, 1828-1891)
Apple Blossom Time, oil on canvas, sgn, 12x16", FB 10/30/89 825

Autumn River Landscape, oil on canvas, sgn, 20x24", C-E 10/25/88 UE 2,200
Cows Grazing by a Stream, oil on canvas, sgn, 22x26", C-E 2/23/88 2,200
Springtime, Holland (farm scene); oil on canvas, sgn, 20x30", FB 5/28/89 1,400
Winter Landscape, oil on canvas, sgn, 12x16", FB 10/30/89 825

HENGKE, Chen (Chinese, 1876-1923)
Abundance (hanging scroll), ink/color on paper, sgn/dtd 1922, 37x17", SBY 5/31/89 OE 3,300

HENLEY, Lionel Charles (British, 1843-)
The Tiff (man & woman in an interior), oil on canvas, sgn/dtd 1883(?), 18x24", SBY 12/9/88 2,475

HENNAH, John Edward (British, 1897-)
Near Phwllheli, North Wales (panoramic view); oil on canvas, sgn, 21x30", B/B 9/14/89 UE 715

HENNECK, G. (Continental, 19th C)
Venetian Canal, oil on canvas, sgn, 18x22", WG 9/16/88 250

HENNER, Jean Jacques (French, 1829-1905)
An Auburn-Haired Woman in Profile, oil on panel, sgn, 13x9", C-E 5/22/89 4,620
Diana at Her Bath, oil on panel, sgn, 13x10", SBY 2/22/89 3,575
Jeune Femme Rousse dans un Paysage (nude in landscape), oil on canvas, sgn, 37x27", C-NY 5/25/88 7,150
Nude Woman in a Wooded Landscape, oil on canvas, sgn, 22x16", C-E 6/28/88 1,320
Portrait of a Girl with Auburn Hair, oil on canvas, sgn, 22x15", SBY 10/24/89 OE 22,000
Portrait of a Girl with Red Hair, oil on panel, sgn, 11x8", S/A 2/18/89 3,000
Portrait of a Schoolgirl, oil on canvas, sgn, 24x18", B/B 6/9/88 2,200
Portrait of a Woman, oil on canvas, sgn, 18x15", SBY 6/8/88 2,750
Portrait of a Woman with Red Hair, oil on canvas laid down, sgn, 14x10", B/B 6/9/88 1,650
Portrait of a Young Girl in Profile, oil on board, sgn, 10x7", C-E 10/26/89 4,950
Prisoner of the Rocks, oil on panel, sgn, 16x10", C-E 10/26/89 2,640
Profile of a Young Girl, oil on panel, sgn, 11x9", B/B 6/9/88 1,650
Reclining Nude in a Landscape, oil on canvas, sgn, 11x16", C-E 10/26/89 4,950
Reclining Nude in a Landscape, oil on canvas, 15x22", C-E 2/23/88 1,760
Reclining Nude Woman in a Landscape, oil on panel, sgn, 9x13", C-E 2/23/88 OE 2,200
Red-Haired Beauty (portrait), oil on canvas, sgn, 16x13", C-NY 5/24/89 4,400
Red-Haired Beauty in a Scarlet Velvet Dress, oil on canvas, sgn, 23x19", C-NY 2/23/89 4,400
Solitude (portrait of a woman kneeling, nude from waist up), oil on canvas, sgn, 36x26", C-NY 5/24/89 11,000
St Catherine, black chalk, 4x2", C-NY 5/25/88 880
Woman in Red, oil on cradled panel, sgn, 16x13", SBY 5/23/89 OE 14,300
Young Beauty (portrait in profile), oil on panel, sgn, 11x9", C-NY 2/23/89 4,950

HENNESSEY, Frank (Canadian, 1893-1941)
Lenore, pastel, sgn/dtd 1923, 24x18", FB 10/30/89 330

HENNESSEY, Timothy
Two Banners, each painted cloth, 160x160", 94x68", SBY 2/14/89 UE 165

HENNESSY, Richard (20th C)
Untitled (abstract), acrylic on canvas, sgn/dtd 72, 84x60", SBY 2/14/89 OE 1,980

HENNESSY, William John (American/Irish, 1839-1917)
Portrait of a Young Woman (bust-length), oil on canvas mounted on board, unfr, 18x13", WL 5/20/88 750
Study of a Woman's Head From Behind, oil on canvas, sgn/inscr, unfr, 18x12", SBY 6/24/88 990

HENNINGS, Ernest Martin (American, 1886-1956)
At the Fountain, St Jeanette; oil on canvas, sgn, 30x25", C-NY 12/2/88 15,400
Portrait of a Woman, shoulder-length in white top; oil on canvas, 18x15", MAG 6/22/88 3,000
Portrait of an Old Man, oil on canvas, sgn, 24x20", SBY 3/17/88 2,860
Way Home, watercolor/gouache on paper, sgn, 18x30", SBY 9/23/88 OE 18,700

HENNINGSON, Henning (Danish, 19th/20th C)
Funen Straits, oil on canvas, initialed, 26x36", B/B 1/11/89 990

HENRI, Michel (French, 1928-)
Les Voiliers (The Sailboats), oil on canvas, sgn, 13x16", C-E 11/17/88 935

HENRI, Robert (American, 1865-1929)
Azores (mountainous coastal view), oil on panel, sgn/dtd June 1908, 5x7", C-NY 9/28/89 2,860
Boats in Cove, oil on board, sgn, 8x10", SBY 3/17/88 OE 5,500
Bullfighter, pen/sepia ink on paper, sgn/dtd 1900, 9x7", WL 5/20/88 525
Female Nude, pen/ink, embossed w/estate stamp, 6x5", NA 2/6/88 OE 1,100
Figures on the Pont Des Arts, Paris (impressionistic); oil on board, sgn/dtd May 1898, 4x6", SBY 9/14/89 7,150
Full-Length Female Nude Before a Curtain, black crayon, estate stamp, 18x11", NA 2/24/89 750
Irish Cottage, oil on panel, 13x16", C-NY 12/2/88 7,700
Jimmie Gerry (portrait), oil on canvas, sgn/#d 98-L, 24x20", C-NY 12/2/88 71,500
Ladies & Swans, pen/ink on paper, sgn/monogramed, 4x6", WL5/20/88 400
Lady in Black & White, brush/ink on paper, sgn/artist's estate stamp, 7x5", WL 5/20/88 625
Lady in Studio, pencil on paper, bears signature/initialed, 11x8", C-E 2/3/88 935
Lady with Bouffant Hair (profile portrait), brown ink on paper, sgn, 9x6", RWS 3/31/88 UE 275
Landscape, pencil on paper, bears signature/initialed, 4x7", C-E 2/3/88 385
Landscape with Figure in Pink, oil on canvas, sgn/titled, 18x12", SBY 5/24/89 OE 36,300
Listening Boy, oil on canvas, sgn twice, 24x20", SBY 5/25/88OE 176,000
Man & Open Book (drawing), pencil, sgn w/embossed estate stamp, 10x7", NA 10/1/88 550
Nude Before a Mirror, ink wash, artist's stamp, 4x9", RWS 5/19/88 OE 900
Nude Seated with Elbow on Knee, pen/ink/gray wash on paper, sgn/artist's estate stamp, 6x9", WL 5/20/88 UE 350

Nude Woman on Sofa, pencil on paper, bears signature/initialed, 8x10", C-E 11/30/88 OE ... 3,300
Oh Mr Taft, You Said a Wrong Woid!; pen/ink on paper, sgn/artist's estate stamp, 6x9", WL 5/20/88 ... 700
Places Where They Might Be (sun shining on forest foliage), pastel on paper, sgn/#d 171, 12x20", SBY 4/14/89 ... 1,870
Quai de Boulogne (impressionistic street scene), oil on panel, sgn, 6x10", C-NY 5/25/89 ... 17,600
Red Top (portrait of red-headed child, arms folded), oil on canvas, sgn/#d 138F, 1910, 24x20", SBY 5/24/89 OE ... 165,000
Revelers (two figures, one drinking), pen/ink on paper, sgn/monogramed, 5x5", WL 5/20/88 ... 450
Rocks & Sea (Near Black Head), oil on panel, sgn twice, inscr/titled, 1903, 8x10", SBY 9/23/88 OE ... 6,600
Self-Portrait, pencil on paper, estate stamp/titled, 11x9", RAB 8/8/89 UE ... 200
Sketch of a Woman, charcoal on paper, bears signature/initialed, 11x8", SBY 6/24/88 ... 825
Standing Nude, pen/ink on paper, sgn/monogramed, 5x4", WL 5/20/88 UE ... 325
Sunset, oil on panel, sgn, 12x15", C-E 2/3/88 ... 2,090
The Bather, pen/ink, embossed w/estate stamp, 5x6", NA 2/6/88 OE ... 1,100
Two Distinguished Artists (three cartoon drawings), pen/ink on paper, artist's stamp, 8x11", RWS 5/19/88 UE ... 250
Volendam, Gray House; oil on panel, sgn, 8x10", C-NY 9/28/89 ... 5,500

HENRICH, A.M. (American, 20th C)
Young Woman Pinning Red Flower on Her Gown, oil on canvas, sgn, 32x27", MG 5/28/88 OE ... 2,200

HENRION, Armand Francois Joseph (French, 1875-)
Clown, oil on board, sgn, 9" dia, WD 3/23/88 ... 1,000

HENRY, Edward Lamson (American, 1841-1919)
A Philadelphia Doorway (dog lying in doorway, figure at gate), oil on panel, sgn/dtd 82, 10x8", C-NY 9/28/89 ... 13,200
At the Well, oil on paper mounted on panel, sgn/indistinctly dtd twice, 13x10", SBY 1/24/89 ... 9,900
Esopus Canal, pen/brush/black ink/Chinese white/pencil on paper, sgn, 9x13", C-NY 9/28/89 ... 3,080
Itinerant Peddler Displaying His Wares, oil on canvas, sgn/dtd 87, 19x29", WD 10/5/88 OE ... 77,500
Korppel & Old Church, oil on board, inscr, 10x14", SBY 6/24/88 UE ... 1,980
Old House, watercolor/pencil/gouache on paper laid down on board, sgn/dtd 73, 10x14", C-E 10/18/89 ... 2,200
Protecting the Groceries (boy w/basket, dog peering through fence), oil on panel, sgn/dtd 86, 14x11", C-NY 5/25/89 ... 28,600
Reading the News, oil on panel, sgn/dtd twice, 1865, inscr, 8x6", SBY 5/25/88 ... 25,300
Sabbath Morning (ladies in interior), oil on paper laid down on board, sgn/dtd 1874, 7x6", C-NY 5/25/89 ... 13,200
Scene Along the Delaware & Hudson Canal, 1907; oil on panel, sgn/dtd 1907, 7x11", C-NY 12/2/88 ... 28,600
Strolling Along the River (landscape), oil on panel, sgn, 12x8", SBY 3/17/88 ... 5,500
9:45 AM Accommodation, Stratford, Connecticut; oil on board, sgn twice/inscr/dtd 1864, 10x18", C-NY 12/2/88 OE ... 192,500

HENRY, Michel (French, 1928-)
Les Bleuets, oil on canvas, sgn, 51x35", B/B 1/11/89 ... 715
Still Life of Flowers, Fruit, & Blossom; oil on canvas, sgn, 32x40", P 11/15/88 ... 1,200

HENSEL, D.
Temptation, oil on canvas, sgn, 34x40", MAG 9/18/88 UE ... 400

HENSHALL, J. (British, fl 1848-1863)
Quay at Rouen, oil on canvas, dtd 1853, 38x32", SBY 2/22/89 ... 6,600

HENSHALL, John Henry (British, 1856-1928)
Daydreaming Repose, watercolor on paper, sgn/dtd 1890, 22x22", B/B 6/15/89 OE ... 7,700

HENSHAW, Frederick Henry (British, 1807-1891)
Eagle Peak, British Columbia; oil on panel, sgn/dtd 1860, 9x12", C-SK 5/25/89 ... 550
Out for a Stroll, oil on canvas, initialed, 17x24", WD 3/23/88 ... 700
The Mill in the Mountains, oil on panel, indistinctly sgn, 9x12", B/B 12/8/88 ... 412

HENSHAW, Frederick Henry; att (British, 1807-1891)
Deer Crossing a Path, oil on canvas, sgn, 24x36", B/B 9/14/89 ... 1,100

HENSHAW, Glenn Cooper (American, 1881-1946)
Gloucester Boats, pastel on paper, sgn, 18x13", RWS 9/8/89 ... 650
Landscape, oil on canvas, sgn/dtd 06/inscr, 16x20", SBY 1/24/89 ... 1,210

HENSON (20th C)
Adobe House, watercolor on paper, sgn, 17x23", SBY 9/23/88 ... 110
Branding Cattle, oil on canvas, sgn, 22x28", SBY 9/23/88 ... 495
Roping the Steer, oil on canvas, sgn, 24x36", SBY 9/23/88 ... 440

HENSTENBURGH, Herman (Dutch, 1667-1726)
Still Life of Plums, Cherries, an Apple, a Bunch of Grapes...; bodycolor on vellum, sgn, 14x11", C-NY 1/11/89 OE ... 39,600

HENTSCHEL (Continental, 20th C)
Medieval Allegory, pen/ink on paper, sgn, 12x9", B/B 5/17/89 ... 412

HEPWORTH, Barbara (20th C)
Construction: Gouache & String; gouache/string on board, sgn/dtd 1940, 11x15", SBY 11/16/89 ... 44,000

HERBERT, Rene (Canadian, 1932-)
L'Hiver, Ste Anne; oil on canvas, sgn/dtd 1977, 20x24", FB 10/17/88 ... 500

HERBERTE, Edward Benjamin (British, 1857-1893)
At the Smithy's Before the Meet, oil on canvas, sgn/dtd 1878, 28x37", WD 1/25/89 ... 7,250
Pair: Meet; Full Cry (hunters & horses in a landscape); oil on canvas, sgn/dtd 1885, 12x20", SBY 6/10/88 ... 17,600
Pair: Taking the Jump; Over the Ditch; oil on canvas, sgn/dtd 1876, 12x18", SBY 6/10/88 ... 4,125
Set of 4: Meeting; Finding the Scent; Over the Fence; The Kill; oil on canvas, sgn/dtd 1883, 12x20", C-E 10/25/88 OE ... 18,150

HERBIN, Auguste (French, 1882-1960)
Composition Abstraite, gouache/watercolor/pen/black ink on paper, ca 1925, 15x10", C-NY 10/6/88 ... 8,250
Composition: Sculpture; oil on canvas, sgn, 32x26", SBY 2/18/88 ... 48,400
Le Pont, oil on canvas laid down on aluminum, sgn, 26x22", SBY 2/18/88 ... 11,000
Paysage au Bord de la Seine (La Seine a la Roche-Guyon), oil on canvas, sgn, ca 1903, 21x29", C-NY 5/11/89 ... 30,800

Portrait de Madame Herbin, oil on canvas, sgn, 1912, 32x26", C-NY 5/11/89 ..... **41,800**
Trois Oppositions Polaires (abstract composition), gouache/pencil on paper, sgn, 1941, 14x11", C-NY 5/11/89 OE **24,200**

HERBO, Fernand (French, 1905-)
Harbor Scene, oil on canvas, sgn, 33x40", SBY 2/14/89 ..... **8,250**

HERBO, Leon (Belgian, 1850-1907)
Reading Hour (lady reclining on pillow with book), oil on panel, sgn, 22x27", B/B 5/17/89 OE **1,950**
Spanish Lady, oil on canvas, sgn, 14x11", C-E 10/25/88 ..... **1,980**
Young Maiden, oil on panel, sgn/inscr/dtd 1882, 15x11", C-E 2/23/88 ..... **1,540**

HERBST, Frank C. (American, 20th C)
Mush, watercolor, sgn, 16x11", C-E 2/3/88 ..... **1,320**

HEREAU, Jules (French, 1879-1939)
Horses About To Be Led Onto a Boat, oil on canvas, sgn/dtd 1877, 32x40", C-E 5/22/89 ..... **5,060**

HERERA, G. (Continental, 20th C)
Untitled, three figures in farmyard on sunny spring day; oil on canvas, sgn, 27x22", SLK 11/25/88 ..... **1,100**

HERKOMER, Herman Gustave (American, 1862-1935)
Portrait of Mrs Albert Vickers, oil on panel, sgn/dtd 1898, 14x9", SBY 6/24/88 UE **550**

HERLAND, Emma (French, 1856-1947)
Plumeuses de Poulets-Apres Midi d'Ete Bretagne (three women cleaning chickens); oil on canvas, sgn, 43x52", C-NY 2/23/89 ..... **8,800**

HERMANN, Emil (German, 19th/20th C)
Untitled, interior of art gallery w/dustman sleeping; oil on canvas, sgn, 15x11", SLK 11/25/88 ..... **500**

HERMANN, H. (Continental, 19th C)
Still Life of Roses & Butterflies, oil on panel, sgn, 11x8", C-E 10/26/89 ..... **2,750**

HERMANN, Leo (French, 1853-?)
Directoire Dandy, oil on canvas, sgn, 10x7", C-E 10/26/89 ..... **1,650**
Two Cardinals Feeding Fish, oil on canvas, sgn, 16x19", C-E 10/26/89 ..... **8,800**

HERMANN, Ludwig (German, 1812-1881)
Extensive River Town, oil on canvas, sgn/dtd 1870, 13x18", C-E 10/25/88 OE **5,280**

HERMANN, Walther
Lucerne, Switzerland; watercolor/gouache/pencil on paper, 10x7", C-E 2/23/88 ..... **275**
Pisa, watercolor/gouache/ink/pencil on paper, initialed/inscr/dtd 1856, 8x10", C-E 2/23/88 ..... **220**
Tyrolian Village, watercolor/gouache/ink/pencil on paper, initialed/dtd 1856, 7x9", C-E 2/23/88 ..... **220**

HERMANNS, Heinrich (German, 1862-1942)
View of a Dutch Port From the Water, watercolor, sgn/dtd 96, 7x15", C-E 10/26/89 ..... **1,045**

HERMANSEN, Olaf August; att (Danish, 1849-1879)
Floral Still Life, oil on canvas, initialed/dtd 1848, 18x15", C-NY 10/25/89 ..... **14,300**

HERNANDEZ, J.
Nude Bathers by the Sea, oil on canvas, sgn/dtd 1911, unfr, 22x27", C-E 10/25/88 ..... **1,540**

HEROLD A. (20th C)
Fawn & Satyr, oil on academy board, sgn/dtd 1918, 12x10", WG 4/23/88 UE **300**

HERPFER, Carl (German, 1836-1897)
Musician's Dilemma, oil on canvas, sgn, 46x36", SBY 5/23/89 ..... **15,950**

HERPIN, Leon Pierre (French, 1841-1880)
Sandy Beach with a Lighthouse, oil on canvas, sgn/dtd 1877, 15x18", C-NY 2/23/89 ..... **3,850**
Ville d'Vray (shoreline view), watercolor, sgn/dtd 69, 5x7", C-E 5/22/89 ..... **1,320**
Ville l'Aveay, watercolor/pencil on paper, sgn/dtd 69/titled, 5x7", RWS 3/16/89 ..... **550**

HERRARA, Francisco the Younger (Spanish, 1622-1685)
Dream of Saint Joseph, oil on canvas, ca 1670s, 82x77", SBY 6/1/89 OE **396,000**

HERRER, Cesar (Hungarian, 1868-1919)
Scene on a Venetian Canal, oil on canvas, sgn, 23x13", WAD 6/6/88 ..... **3,000**

HERRICK, Henry W. (American, 1824-1906)
Old Mill Stream (landscape), watercolor on paper, sgn/dtd 1891, 15x20", RAB 3/27/89 UE **100**

HERRING, John Frederick Jr. (British, 1815-1907)
Bringing in the Hay (farmyard scene w/animals), oil on canvas, sgn, 22x36", C-NY 5/24/89 ..... **20,900**
Carthorses, Pigs, & Poultry by a Water Trough; oil on canvas, sgn, 12x18", SBY 6/10/88 ..... **11,550**
Carthorses & Ducks in a Farmyard, oil on canvas, sgn/dtd 1864, 12x18", SBY 6/10/88 ..... **9,350**
Country Life (farm animals in a landscape), oil on canvas, sgn, 28x36", C-NY 5/24/89 ..... **22,000**
Farmyard by a Stream in Summer (w/horses, cows, pigs, & ducks), oil on canvas, sgn, 26x42", SBY 6/9/89 ..... **44,000**
Farmyard Scene, oil on canvas, sgn, 24x36", SBY 6/10/88 ..... **30,800**
Farmyard Scene, oil on canvas, sgn, 28x36", FB 10/30/89 ..... **15,400**
Farmyard Scene, oil on canvas, sgn/dtd 185(?), 16" dia, SBY 6/10/88 ..... **6,325**
Farmyard Scene with Horses, Pigs, Ducks, & Chickens; oil on canvas, sgn, 24x36", SBY 6/10/88 ..... **39,600**
Farmyard with a Village Church in the Distance, oil on canvas, sgn, 35x52", SBY 6/10/88 ..... **19,800**
Gentleman with Two Whippets in the Lake District, oil on canvas, 21x17", SBY 6/9/89 ..... **1,760**
Horses, Cows & Poultry in a Barn; oil on canvas, 20x30", WAD 6/6/88 ..... **3,500**
Horses in a Stable, oil on canvas, sgn, 15x20", DM 10/14/88 ..... **8,500**
In the Farmyard (horses, cows, pigs, & chickens in a landscape), oil on canvas, sgn, 24x36", SBY 6/9/89 OE **44,000**
Mr S Baton's Plenipotentiary with Jockey Up a Six Mile Bottom, Newmarket; oil on canvas, sgn/dtd 1832, SBY 6/9/89 ..... **4,400**
Old Farmstead (w/horses, pigs, & chickens), oil on canvas, sgn, 24x36", SBY 6/9/89 ..... **30,800**
Pair: Farmyard Scenes; watercolor heightened w/white on paper, sgn, 8x12", SBY 6/10/88 OE **3,410**
Plow Team, oil on board, sgn, 10x14", SBY 6/9/89 ..... **5,500**
Set of 3: Cavalry; watercolor heightened w/white on paper, sgn, 8x12", SBY 6/10/88 ..... **1,980**

Stable Companions, oil on canvas, sgn, 16x24", SBY 6/9/89 13,200
Winter Farmyard (w/horses, pigs, & ducks), oil on canvas, sgn, 28x36", SBY 6/9/89 37,400

HERRING, John Frederick Jr.; manner of (British, 1815-1907)
End of the Hunt, oil on canvas, 20x30", FAP 4/15/89 1,870

HERRING, John Frederick Sr. (British, 1795-1865)
Chestnut in the Grounds of a Country House, oil on canvas, sgn/dtd 1820, 22x30", SBY 6/9/89 17,600
Cotherstone, Bay Colt in a Stall; oil on canvas, sgn/dtd 1843, 27x35", SBY 6/19/89 60,500
Dapple Gray Mare in a Landscape, oil on canvas, sgn/dtd 24, 10x13", SBY 6/9/89 14,850
Doctor Fop (two dogs in a landscape), oil on canvas, sgn/dtd 1850, 22x27", SBY 6/10/88 OE 104,000
Edward Petre's Bay Filly Matilda w/Jockey Jem Robinson Up & John Scott, Trainer; oil, sgn/dtd 1828, 24x30", SBY 6/9/89 85,250
Gray in a Stable with Ducks & Goats, oil on canvas, sgn/dtd 1843, 39x52", SBY 6/10/88 137,500
Harnessed Coach Horse with a Spotted Terrier in a Loosebox, oil on canvas, sgn/dtd 1822, 22x30", SBY 6/10/88 OE 28,600
Hon E Petre's Rowton with W Scott Up & Trainer at Doncaster, oil on canvas, sgn/dtd 1829, 22x30", SBY 6/10/88 63,250
Horses & Farmyard Scene, oil on canvas, sgn, 11x15", MG 11/19/88 UE 1,300
Lop-Eared Rabbits, oil on canvas, sgn, in painted circle, 16x16", SBY 6/10/88 18,700
Mare & Foal by the Stable, oil on panel, sgn/dtd 1854, 12x15", SBY 6/9/89 18,700
Nutwith in a Loosebox, oil on canvas, sgn, 13x17", B/B 6/9/88 OE 14,300
Priam Beating Lord Exeter's Augustus at Newmarket, 1831; sgn, 28x42", SBY 6/9/89 495,000
Racehorse Actaeon in a Loosebox, oil on panel, sgn/dtd 1840, 10x12", C-NY 10/25/89 13,200
Stableyard at Meopham Park, oil on canvas, sgn/dtd 1847, 28x38", SBY 6/10/88 99,000
Two Setters in a Landscape, oil on panel, sgn/dtd 1820, 11x15", SBY 6/9/89 17,050
Waiting for the Fairy, oil on canvas, sgn/dtd 1841, 24x33", C-NY 10/25/89 28,600

HERRING, John Frederick Sr.; att (British, 1795-1865)
Chestnut Stallion, Hawk; oil on canvas, bears signature, 20x24", FB 4/25/88 2,800

HERRING, John Frederick Sr.; circle of (British, 1795-1865)
Racehorse with Jockey Up, a Gentleman & a Groom; oil on canvas, 25x30", C-NY 2/23/89 7,700

HERRING, John Frederick Sr.; manner of (British, 1795-1865)
Bay Racehorse by a Stream, oil on panel, 6x8", C-E 3/22/88 OE 1,210
Set of 4: On the Hunt; oil on board, bears signature, 6x9", C-E 5/22/89 2,750

HERRING, John Frederick Sr.; studio of (British, 1795-1865)
Don John with Jockey Up, oil on canvas, sgn/dtd 1839, inscr w/horse's name, 25x31", SBY 6/10/88 10,450

HERRMANN, Leo (French, 1853-)
Two Lawyers Greeting Each Other on Stairs, oil on panel, sgn, unfr, 22x19", SBY 7/12/89 1,100

HERRMANNSTORFER, J. (German, 1817-1901)
Mountains Lake Idyll (figures in a boat w/mountains beyond), oil on canvas, sgn, 24x30", B/B 6/15/89 2,475

HERSESHEIMER, Ella S.
Still Life of Fish & Potatoes, oil on canvas, sgn, 20x24", C-E 11/30/88 2,200

HERTER, Adele (American, 1869-1946)
Still Life of Carnations, oil on panel, sgn, 20x15", RWS 9/29/88 OE 850
White Petunias (arranged in oriental vase), oil on panel, sgn, 21x16", RWS 9/29/88 OE 2,900

HERTER, Albert (American, 1871-1950)
Eastern Blossoms, watercolor on board, sgn/dtd 94, unfr, 10x14", C-NY 9/30/88 OE 4,400
Japanese Maiden with Flowers, watercolor on paper, sgn dtd 189, 9x7", SBY 6/28/89 1,650

HERVE, Jules Rene (French, 1887-1981)
Feeding the Pigeons, oil on canvas, sgn, 13x16", B/B 3/22/89 3,300
In the Park, oil on canvas, sgn, 18x22", B/B 3/22/89 6,600
Jardin de Tuilleries, oil on canvas, sgn, 26x32", LH 9/10/89 3,600
Luxembourg Gardens, oil on canvas, sgn, 9x11", SBY 10/7/89 3,740
Paris Park Scene, oil on canvas, sgn, 18x22", SBY 10/7/89 6,050
Paris Street Scene with a Sidewalk Procession, oil on canvas, sgn/#d 50429, 22x18", C-E 10/26/89 4,400
Pont des Arts Paris, oil on canvas, sgn, 9x11", PHL 11/15/88 1,100
Promenade Pres de Notre Dame, oil on canvas, sgn, 26x32", SBY 2/22/89 11,000
Sunday Afternoon Along the River Banks, oil on canvas, sgn, 26x32", RWS 5/12/89 3,500
Wedding Portrait, oil on canvas, sgn, 26x32", B/B 10/9/88 OE 7,700

HERVIER, Louis Adolphe (French, 1818-1879)
Feeding Chickens, oil on panel, sgn, 15x18", C-E 10/25/88 1,650

HERWEGEN-MANINI, Veronica Maria (German, 1851-)
Confessional (figures in interior), oil on canvas, sgn, 25x16", C-E 2/21/89 UE 880

HERZOG, Frans Max (American, 19th/20th C)
Three Figures in a Cathedral, gouache on board, sgn, no size given, FAP 4/15/89 330

HERZOG, Herman (American/German, 1832-1932)
Crashing Stream, oil on canvas laid down on masonite, sgn, 16x20", C-E 6/1/88 5,500
Crashing Waves on the Maine Coast, oil on canvas, sgn, 22x27", C-NY 9/30/88 4,180
Crossing the Stream, oil on canvas, sgn, 16x20", C-NY 3/11/88 8,800
Deer in Florida Marches, oil on canvas, sgn, 15x11", C-E 2/3/88 OE 5,280
Deer in the Clearing, oil on canvas, sgn, 17x23", C-NY 3/11/88 6,600
Ducks Rising, oil on canvas, sgn, 22x26", C-E 11/30/88 7,150
Ducks Rising, oil on canvas, sgn, 22x26", C-NY 3/11/88 9,900
Falls, Yosemite Valley; oil on canvas, sgn, 25x20", SBY 6/28/89 9,350
Figures & Mill by a Mountain Stream, oil on panel, sgn/dtd 1875, 17x23", SBY 6/28/89 4,950
Florida Marsh Scene, oil on canvas, sgn, 16x13", SBY 4/14/89 OE 8,525

Florida Palms (marshy landscape), oil on canvas, sgn, 15x18", C-NY 5/25/89 OE 24,200
Haying (pitching hay into horse-drawn wagon in landscape), oil on canvas, sgn/dtd 1932/inscr, 18x22", SBY 3/17/88 3,520
In Before the Storm (boat fighting to get to shore, figures on pier), oil on canvas, sgn/dtd 18, 20x30", C-NY 9/28/89 8,800
Matterhorn, Switzerland; oil on canvas, sgn, 30x40", C-NY 5/26/88 33,000
Milking Time, oil on canvas, sgn, 18x22", C-NY 9/30/88 5,500
Mill by a Stream, oil on canvas, sgn, 16x22", SBY 1/24/89 3,520
Moonlit Harbor, oil on panel, sgn, 9x13", C-NY 12/2/88 OE 18,700
Mountain Travelers, oil on canvas, initialed/dtd 1867, 38x56", C-NY 5/25/89 33,000
Mountain View, watercolor on paper laid down on board, sgn/dtd 01, 9x12", C-NY 3/11/88 4,400
Mountain Vista, oil on canvas, sgn, 15x18", C-NY 3/11/88 7,150
Norwegian Waterfall in Gool Near Hallingdal, oil on canvas, sgn, 17x24", WD 4/13/88 3,000
On a Glacier Lake, oil on canvas, sgn, 14x20", C-NY 9/30/88 7,700
Rapids, oil on canvas, sgn, 14x16", C-E 6/1/89 4,620
Rocky Shore Off Crabtree Point, Maine; oil on canvas, sgn, 10x15", SBY 3/17/88 OE 5,225
Securing the Anchor, oil on canvas, sgn/dtd 1876, 15x22", C-NY 12/2/88 17,600
Shipping Off a Jetty in Stormy Seas, oil on canvas, sgn/dtd 1865, 37x54", C-NY 2/23/89 28,600
Storm Coming Up Over the Ausable River (water rushing by mining shacks), oil on canvas, sgn, 22x27", C-NY 5/25/89 11,000
Stormy Coast, oil on canvas, sgn, 17x21", SBY 9/23/88 2,530
Sunset with Elk, oil on canvas, sgn, 12x18", C-NY 5/26/88 OE 24,200
Upper Yosemite Falls, oil on canvas laid down, bears signature, 30x22", B/B 12/8/88 4,400
Venetian Canal Scene, oil on canvas, sgn, 28x34", SBY 3/17/88 5,500
Woodland Scene, oil on canvas, sgn, 18x26", WD 4/13/88 3,200

HESS, A. (20th C)
Chinese Scene, oil on canvas, sgn, 13x22", LH 12/4/88 300

HESS, Sara M. (American, 1880-)
El Captain, oil on canvas, sgn, 25x30", C-E 2/3/88 1,650
Mountain Landscape, oil on canvas, sgn, 19x24", NA 11/5/88 950
Still Life of Flowers, oil on board, sgn, 16x16", C-E 2/3/88 880

HESSE, Eva
Untitled (composition), black ink/colored ink/crayon/pencil on paper, sgn/dtd 65, 20x26", SBY 11/9/89 16,500

HESSE, Hans Meyer
Damstadt, oil on canvas, sgn/inscr/dtd 1916, unfr, 35x57", C-E 10/25/88 2,310

HETSCHER, C. (German, 19th C)
Interior of Physician's Office, oil on metal, unfr, 10x9", SLK 5/12/88 625

HETZEL, George (American, 1826-1906)
Hudson River Valley, oil on board, sgn, 17x26", FAP 11/4/88 OE 4,750

HEULLANT, Felix Armand (French, 1834-)
Display of Seashells (gathering under make-shift canopy by a river), oil on canvas, sgn, 30x36", C-E 5/22/89 7,480

HEURLIN, Magnus Rusty (American, 19th/20th C)
Imiaks Under Sail, oil on canvas, sgn/dtd 1952, 40x60", B/B 8/10/88 33,000

HEUSCH, see De Heusch

HEUSTIS, Louise Lyons (American, 1878-)
Floral Still Life, oil on canvas, sgn, 17x20", SBY 6/24/88 770

HEUVEL, see De Heuvel

HEWARD, Prudence (Canadian, 1896-1947)
Eastern Townships Landscape, oil on board, sgn, 12x14", WAD 6/12/89 1,900

HEYDENDAHL, Friedrich Joseph (German, 1844-1906)
Winter Landscape, oil on canvas, sgn, 16x24", SBY 7/12/89 2,750

HEYER, Arthur (German, 1872-1931)
Playful Kittens, oil on canvas, sgn, 19x25", C-E 2/23/88 3,080
Proud Mother (white mother cat w/four white kittens), oil on canvas, sgn, 23x31", SBY 6/9/89 4,950
Three White Kittens, oil on canvas, sgn, 24x32", SBY 12/9/88 OE 5,500
White Long-Haired Cat, oil on canvas, sgn/dtd 11, 22x27", SBY 12/9/88 2,090

HEYERMANS, Jean Arnould (Belgian, 1837-)
Three Children, oil on canvas, sgn, 1878, 26x22", LH 10/16/88 3,400

HEYLIGERS, Hendrik (Dutch, 1877-1915)
Mother & Daughter Doing Laundry (in landscape), oil on canvas, sgn, 24x28", B/B 3/22/89 4,950

HEYN, August (German, 1837-)
War Widow, oil on canvas, sgn/dtd 1871, 34x39", SBY 7/12/89 OE 5,500

HIBBARD, Aldro Thompson (American, 1886-1972)
Autumn Woods, oil on canvasboard, sgn, 18x25", RWS 11/3/88 UE 550
Canadian Rockies, Lake Louise; oil on canvasboard, sgn, 17x20", RWS 5/12/89 3,000
Coastal Scene, oil on board, sgn, 8x10", C-E 11/30/88 1,100
Covered Bridge Swiftwater, New Hampshire; oil on canvasboard, sgn/inscr, 18x24", RWS 11/3/88 3,600
Farm Valley, Autumn; oil on canvas, sgn/artist's estate stamp, 24x30", RWS 11/3/88 2,300
Fishing Boats at Gloucester Harbor, oil on canvas, sgn, 20x24", C-E 6/20/89 1,045
Hillside Village, oil on canvas laid down on board, sgn, 17x21", C-NY 9/28/89 4,180
Jeffersonville, Vermont; oil on canvas, sgn, 24x32", C-NY 9/28/89 9,350
Late Spring, No 69-83; oil on canvas, sgn, 20x40", SBY 1/24/89 9,900
Maple Sugar Shack, oil on canvas laid down on board, sgn, 18x25", C-NY 9/30/88 4,950

Mount Washington, oil on canvas laid down on board, sgn, 17x20", C-E 10/18/89

Mt Mansfield, Stowe, Vermont; oil on canvas laid down on board, sgn, 18x21", C-E 6/1/88 2,860

Quick Notes of a Yoke of Oxen (oxen in winter scene), oil on artist board, artist's estate stamp, 17x23", RWS 5/19/88 UE 4,400

River Valley, oil on canvas, sgn, 25x30", C-E 11/30/88 450

Snow-Laden Spruce, oil on canvas, sgn, 30x36", C-NY 3/11/88 OE 6,600

Vast Landscape, oil on canvas, bears signature, 25x30", C-E 10/18/89 8,800

Vermont Landscape, oil on canvas mounted on board, sgn, 16x20", SBY 9/23/88 2,860

Wardsboro Brook, Vermont; oil on canvas, sgn, 24x32", WD 4/13/88 3,630

Winter Brook (icy stream running through glade), oil on artist board, sgn, 18x24", RWS 9/29/88 2,900

Winter Stream, oil on board, sgn/titled, 9x12", RAB 8/8/89 1,700

Woodland Brook, oil on canvas, sgn twice/titled/#d 62-13, 22x30", SBY 9/23/88 2,000

HIBEL, Edna (American, 1917-) 4,675

Mother & Child, oil on canvas laid down on masonite, sgn, 24x20", SBY 3/17/88 OE

HICKAM, Richard 5,500

Seated Woman, oil on canvas, sgn, 60x60", C-E 5/13/88 UE

HICKEY, Thomas; att (British, 1741-1824) 550

Portrait of a Gentleman Believed To Be George Earl Macartney, oil on canvas, 30x25", SBY 7/12/89 OE

HICKS, George Elgar (British, 1824-) 3,300

Mrs Baxendale & Her Children (portrait in landscape), oil on canvas, sgn/dtd 1887, 83x67", C-NY 2/23/89 UE

HICKS, George H. (American, 19th/20th C) 33,000

Chicago River (cityscape), oil on board, sgn, 12x20", SLK 11/25/88

HICKS, Morley (American, 1877-1959) 1,150

Landlubbers Dream 108, oil on academy board, sgn, 8x10", S/A 2/18/89

Prague Houses & River No 307, oil on academy board, sgn/dtd 1928, 20x24", S/A 2/18/89 75

Sand Island Duck No 1071, oil on academy board, sgn, 24x20", S/A 2/18/89 250

HICKS, Morley; att (American, 1877-1959) 275

Monisson Church, 1945; oil on academy board, sgn/#d 1232/dtd 1945, 8x11", S/A 2/18/89

Prahg River, Czechoslovakia, 1928; oil on academy board, sgn/#d 248/dtd 1928, 9x11", S/A 2/18/89 75

Summer Landscape, oil on academy board, 10x12", S/A 2/18/89 125

HICKS, Richard Clayton (American, 20th C) 150

Chinese Wall, oil on board, sgn, 12x16", FAP 12/8/89

HICKS, Thomas (American, 1823-1890) 175

Rustic Interior, oil on canvas, sgn twice/dtd 1862/inscr, 13x17", SBY 5/24/89

Young Maidens & Chaperones, oil on canvas laid down on board, sgn/dtd 69, 19x15", WD 3/23/88 8,800

HIDALGO, Linares Fernandez (Spanish, 1880-) 900

Mosque Scene, oil on canvas, sgn, 33x14", B/B 9/15/88

HIDER, Frank (British, 19th C) 550

Near Land's End (rocky coastal landscape), oil on canvas, sgn/titled, 14x18", RAB 3/27/89 UE

Wild Rocks & Rising Sea, oil on canvas, sgn/titled, 14x18", RAB 3/27/89 UE 700

HIERSCH-MINERBI, Joachim (Van Hier)(Austrian, 1834-1905) 600

Barques de Peche au Coucher de Soleil, oil on canvas, sgn, 24x36", WD 5/5/88

HIGGENSON, Stephen 3,200

US Frigate Constitution, 44 Guns; watercolor on paper, sgn/dtd 1799, 17x22", RAB 8/1/88 OE

HIGGINS, Eugene (American, 1874-1958) 800

Family on a Boat, pastel on paper laid down on board, sgn, 10x8", C-E 2/1/89

In the Doorway, oil on board, sgn, 9x6", C-E 2/1/89 1,210

Old Man & the Setting Sun, oil on board, sgn/dtd 1919, 15x11", C-E 10/18/89 990

Ox Cart, oil on canvas, sgn, 16x20", C-E 2/1/89 990

Peasants on Path, pen/ink/watercolor on paper, sgn/inscr, 8x10", C-E 6/1/88 1,100

Tree of Life (woman & child by tree in a landscape), oil on canvasboard, sgn, 11x11", SBY 3/17/88 550

Weary (beggar seated on sidewalk), oil on canvas, sgn, 1905, 31x22", C-NY 9/30/88 OE 1,320

HIGGINS, G. (American, 19th C) 6,600

Sheep in Autumnal Landscape with Distant Mountains, oil on canvas, sgn, 24x36", SLK 2/12/88

HIGGINSON, Dudley Clark (American, 1908-) 325

Untitled, winter landscape w/figures walking along road; oil on canvas, sgn, 23x29", SLK 2/11/89

HIGHMORE, Joseph (British, 1692-1780) 200

Portrait of a Boy with a Pet Squirrel, oil on canvas, 29x24", SBY 10/21/88 OE

Portrait of a Lady Said To Be Mrs Elizabeth Purley Holding a Letter, oil on canvas, 50x40", C-NY 1/15/88 10,450

HIGHMORE, Joseph; follower of (British, 1692-1780) 6,600

Portrait of a Gentleman Said To Be Charles Brimsley (wearing red coat), oil on canvas, 30x26", SLK 9/27/88

HIGHMORE, Joseph; style of (British, 1692-1780) 650

Portrait of a Lady, oil on canvas, 43x32", B/B 6/15/89 UE

HIGHSTEIN, Jene (20th C) 1,760

Untitled (abstract), acrylic/chalks on paper, initialed/dtd 82, 38x50", C-E 11/14/89 OE

HILAIRE, Camille (French, 1916-) 2,420

Jockeys (contemporary depiction), oil on canvas, sgn, 28x36", NA 10/1/88

HILDEBRANDT, Eduard (German, 1818-1869) 4,250

The Doge's Palace From the Grand Canal, Venice; oil on panel, sgn, 10x13", B/B 12/8/88 OE

HILDEBRANDT, Howard Logan (American, 1872-1958) 2,750

FLoral Still Life, oil on canvas, sgn, 27x22", SBY 1/24/89

Landscape with Cows in a Meadow, oil on board, sgn, 12x15", C-E 6/1/88 1,320

770

On the Wharf, oil on board, sgn, 11x14", LH 9/10/89 650
Picture Gallery, oil on panel, sgn, 7x9", C-E 2/1/89 1,430
Still Life of Flowers, oil on canvas, sgn, 16x12", RAB 8/8/89 UE 1,150
Trimming Sails, oil on canvas, sgn, 25x30", C-NY 3/11/88 3,850

HILDEBRANT, Eduard (German, 1818-1869)
Ship on Rough Seas, oil on canvas, sgn/dtd 1850, 11x15", C-E 10/26/89 2,420

HILDER, Richard; circle of (British, 1815-1848)
In the New Forest, oil on canvas, 14x18", LH 9/10/89 OE 950

HILDITCH, George; att (British, 1803-1857)
Windsor Castle, oil on canvas, 30x45", C-E 10/25/88 4,400

HILER, Hilaire (American, 1898-)
Cafe Brasserie du Dome, oil on canvas, sgn/dtd 1928, 18x25", SBY 6/24/88 OE 3,080
Castles in Spain, oil on canvas, sgn twice, dtd 1931 & 1924, 29x21", C-NY 9/30/88 4,180

HILL, Edward Rufus (American, 1852-1908)
Hunter & Dogs, a Woodland Scene; oil on board, sgn/dtd 99, 7x5", RWS 9/29/88 OE 1,800
Ravine Brook, White Mountains, New Hampshire; oil on canvas, sgn/inscr, 15x11", RWS 3/16/89 750

HILL, George Snow
Old Book Seller (w/three other figures), oil on canvas, sgn, 26x22", C-E 6/1/89 825

HILL, Howard (American, fl 1860-1870)
Atlantic Flyway (hunters/dogs near lake), oil on canvas, sgn, 18x33", RAB 8/8/89 2,200
Ducks & Chickens by the Watering Hole, oil on canvas, sgn, 10x8", RWS 9/8/89 1,300
Family of Grouse, oil on canvas, sgn, 32x24", SBY 1/24/89 8,250
Grouse in a Landscape, oil on canvas, 24x32", SBY 3/17/88 4,125
Pair of Grouse in a Landscape, oil on canvas, 24x32", SBY 4/14/89 3,300
Quail & Her Chicks (in a landscape), oil on canvas, sgn, 14x16", SBY 3/17/88 OE 4,950
Quail Decoying a Hunting Dog, oil on canvas, sgn, 14x20", SBY 4/14/89 2,200

HILL, James John (British, 1811-1882)
Harvester (portrait), oil on canvas, sgn/dtd 1855, framed as an oval, 27x24", C-E 2/23/88 2,860

HILL, James John; att (British, 1811-1882)
Refill, oil, inscr artist's name/dtd 1860, 22x16", WD 1/11/89 1,400

HILL, James Stevens (British, 1854-1921)
Robin's Nest with Apple Blossoms, oil on canvas, sgn, 10x14", B/B 1/11/89 1,100

HILL, John Henry (American, 1839-1922)
Shoshone Falls, Idaho; oil on canvas, sgn/dtd 1870-86, 36x48", SBY 6/28/89 3,080

HILL, John William (American, 1812-1879)
Figures by the Sea, watercolor on paper, sgn/dtd 1859, 9x13", SBY 6/24/88 OE 3,190
Hudson River Near Albany, watercolor/gouache on paper, sgn/inscr Hudson Near Albanyon, 12x19", SBY 1/24/89 2,090

HILL, Thomas (American, 1829-1908)
Alpine Scene, oil on canvas, sgn, 14x10", B/B 10/6/88 3,025
Merced River, Yosemite Valley; oil on panel, sgn, 11x9", B/B 10/6/88 3,850
Pair: Stroll Through the Woods; Mountain Stream, oil on canvas, sgn/dtd 1876, 21x13", C-NY 12/2/88 UE 8,800
Riders Among the Giant Redwoods, oil on canvas, sgn, 34x26", B/B 10/6/88 5,500
Riders in the Redwood Forest, oil on canvas, sgn/dtd 1906, 30x40", B/B 6/9/88 55,000
River Landscape, oil on board, sgn/dtd 1870(?), 13x19", SBY 1/24/89 OE 7,700
Sierra Landscape, oil on board, sgn, 14x21", B/B 10/6/88 8,800

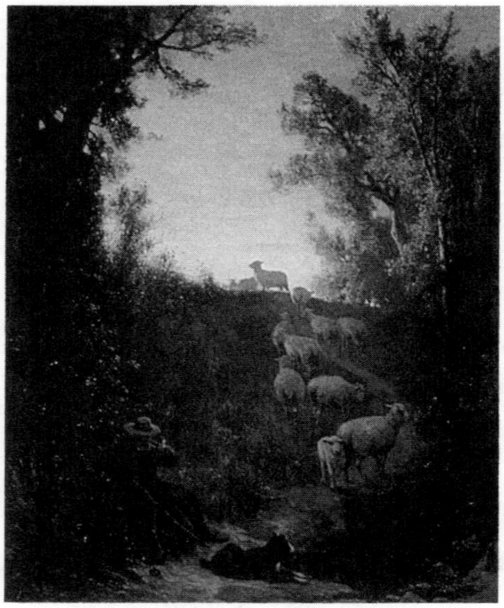

Shepherd with His Evening Pipe, oil on canvas, sgn, 27x22", B/B 10/6/88, $15,400

Sierra River Scene, oil on canvas, sgn, 12x9", B/B 10/6/88

Sisson's Inn, Near Mt Shasta; oil on board, sgn, 14x21", B/B 10/6/88 ... 3,850

Spaniels Beside a Basket of Flowers in an Idyllic Landscape, oil on canvas laid down, sgn, 29x36", B/B 10/6/88 ... 15,400

The Golden Gate, San Francisco Bay; oil on card mounted on canvas, sgn, 15x22", NA 3/26/88 ... 5,500

View of Yosemite Valley, oil on canvas, sgn, 25x18", B/B 10/6/88 ... 19,000

View of Yosemite Valley From the Fallen Monarch, oil on panel, sgn, 8x11", B/B 10/6/88 ... 20,900

Yosemite Valley (landscape w/waterfall), oil on canvas, sgn/dtd 1888, 30x20", SBY 1/24/89 ... 6,600

Young Shepherdess with Her Flock, oil on canvas, sgn, 20x32", B/B 10/6/88 ... 7,150

HILL, Thomas Virgil T. (American, 1871-1922) ... 12,100

Vernal Falls, oil on canvas, sgn, 20x16", B/B 10/6/88

HILL, Thomas; att (American, 1829-1908) ... 2,200

Yosemite Valley with Bridal Veil Falls, oil on canvas, 43x54", RWS 11/3/88

HILLBOM, Henrik (American, 1863-) ... 4,250

Brook in Winter (meandering stream lined w/trees), oil on canvas, sgn/dtd 39, 25x30", RWS 9/29/88

Pair: Autumnal Silence; Shady Woods (landscapes); oil on canvas, sgn/dtd 04, 20x16"; RWS 9/29/88 UE ... 425

HILLIARD, William Henry (American, 1836-1905) ... 500

Canal Scene, oil on canvas, sgn, 18x24", C-E 2/3/88

Path into the Woods, oil on canvas mounted on board, sgn, 15x10", SBY 4/14/89 ... 1,320

HILLINGFORD, Robert Alexander (British, 1825-1904) ... 660

Disaster at the Ball Given by the Austrian Embassy in Paris, 1810; oil on canvas, sgn/dtd 1810, 45x68", SBY 2/22/88 UE

Duel, oil, sgn, 21x30", WD 1/11/89 ... 27,500

Elopement, oil on canvas, sgn, 30x20", SBY 7/12/89 UE ... 2,000

Marguerite & Mephistopheles, oil on canvas, initialed, 15x12", C-E 10/26/89 ... 1,650

HILLS, Anna Althea (American, 1882-1930) ... 1,650

Landscape, oil on board, sgn, 14x20", B/B 10/6/88

HILLS, Laura Coombs (American, 1859-1952) ... 1,100

Gelley Flowers #29, pastel on board, sgn, 12x18", RWS 11/3/88 OE

Hollycocks in the Sunshine, pastel on tan paper, sgn, 21x14", RWS 5/12/89 OE ... 19,000

Pale Pansies, pastel on ochre paper, sgn, 10x12", RWS 11/10/89 ... 41,000

Still Life of Pink Dahlias, pastel on paper, sgn, 21x18", SBY 6/28/89 ... 7,500

White Camellia, pastel on ochre paper, sgn, 13x10", RWS 11/10/89 ... 4,400

White Jar of Flowers, pastel on tan paper, sgn, 24x20", RWS 5/12/89 ... 6,500

White Petunias in a Silver Ballister Cup, pastel on tan paper, sgn, 22x17", RWS 3/16/89 OE ... 21,000

Yellow Pansies, pastel on board, sgn/inscr, 11x13", C-NY 5/26/88 ... 7,750

HILLS, Robert (British, 1769-1844) ... 3,300

Herd of Deer at Rest in a Wood, watercolor, sgn, 19x32", C-NY 2/25/88 OE

HILLYER, David (British, 1850-1890) ... 7,700

View Near Guildford, Surrey; oil on canvas, sgn, 24x43", WD 5/5/88 UE

HILTON, John William (American, 1904-) ... 1,400

Coyote Canyon, oil on canvasboard, sgn/dtd 51, 12x16", B/B 10/6/88

HILTON, William (American, 1829-1909) ... 1,210

Portrait of a Gentleman, standing, wearing brown jacket, in a landscape; oil on canvas, 50x40", C-NY 4/8/88

HILVERDINK, Eduard Alexander (Dutch, 1846-1891) ... 7,700

Village Street in Winter, oil on panel, sgn/dtd 1860, 12x9", C-E 2/23/88 OE

HINCKLEY, Thomas Hewes (American, 1813-1896) ... 2,750

Cattle & Sheep in a Summer Landscape, oil on canvas, sgn/dtd 1857, 32x44", SBY 6/28/89

Flushing the Covey, Setters & Quail; oil on canvas, sgn/dtd 1880, 22x36", RWS 11/10/89 ... 7,700

Two Pointers in a Landscape, oil on canvas, sgn/dtd 1847, unfr, 30x40", SBY 6/9/89 ... 6,000

HINES, Theodore (British, 19th C) ... 4,400

Medmenham Abbey on Thames (depicts house in background, swans in foreground), oil on canvas, sgn, 20x30", DM 5/13/88

HINKLE, Clarence Keiser (American, 1880-1960) ... 2,200

Bird Sanctuary, Santa Barbara; oil on panel, sgn, 17x19", B/B 10/6/88

Jesus Asleep on the Boat, oil on board, sgn, unfr, 30x24", B/B 12/8/88 ... 880

Laguna Beach, oil on board, sgn, 11x14", B/B 10/6/88 ... 935

Lone Pines in the Mountains, watercolor on paper, sgn, 15x21", B/B 12/8/88 ... 7,700

Mission Creek, Santa Barbara (landscape); oil on board, sgn, 30x24", B/B 10/9/88 ... 935

Outside the Artist's Studio, colored crayon on paper, sgn, 13x18", B/B 12/8/88 ... 5,500

Tabletop Still Life, oil on board, sgn, 20x24", B/B 10/6/88 ... 935

Villefranche, oil on panel, sgn, 11x14", B/B 10/6/88 ... 3,300

HINMAN, Charles (American, 1932-) ... 2,200

Capillary Action, acrylic on canvas, sgn/dtd 73, 79x59", SBY 10/5/89

Phenomena Tidal Guard, oil on canvas, sgn/dtd 1966-67, 40x26", C-E 11/14/89 OE ... 9,900

Red-Green (geometric composition), acrylic on canvas, sgn/dtd 64, unfr, 67x82", C-E 11/14/89 ... 14,300

Untitled, acrylic on shaped canvas, sgn/dtd 64, 52x66x14", C-E 5/13/88 UE ... 2,640

Untitled (geometric composition), acrylic on shaped canvas, sgn/dtd 64, 88x84", C-E 11/17/88 ... 1,430

HINTERREITER, Hans (American, 20th C) ... 3,850

Opus 10 (composition), tempera on paper, initialed/dtd 1951, 15x11", C-NY 2/14/89

Opus 101 (design in a circle), tempera on paper, initialed/dtd 1944, 12" dia, PHL 11/15/88 OE ... 3,850

Opus 105A (composition), acrylic on canvas, sgn/dtd 1959-82, 28x38", C-NY 2/14/89 ... 5,500

Study 1941 (abstract design), tempera on paper, sgn/dtd 4.41, 8x8", PHL 11/15/88 OE ... 6,050

5,000

HINTZE, Johann Ferdinand Julius (German, 1849-1877)
Time Has Run Out, oil on panel, sgn/dtd 1874, 14x17", C-E 10/26/89 4,400
HIRRSINGER, J. (German, fl 1906)
Portrait of a Lady, oil, sgn, 52x37", WD 1/11/89 850
HIRSCH, Alphonse (French, 1843-1884)
Les Engants Camando dans le Jardin d'Hiver de leur Hotel Particulier, oil on canvas, sgn, 1875, 45x58", C-NY 5/24/89 OE 55,000
HIRSCH, Joseph (American, 1910-1981)
Allegory (elevated seated nude before three men in classical scene), oil on canvas, sgn, 1977-78, 56x60", SBY 5/24/89 24,200
Bathers, oil on canvas, sgn, 35x40", C-NY 5/26/88 OE 8,800
Delegate (portrait), oil on masonite, sgn, 16x12", C-NY 3/11/88 2,750
Dreaming Nude, oil on canvasboard, sgn, 17x36", C-NY 5/26/88 3,300
Lady with Red Background, oil on canvas, sgn, 24x20", C-NY 3/11/88 6,050
Portrait of a Painter, oil on canvas, sgn, 36x16", C-E 6/1/88 2,750
HIRSCHBERG, Carl (American, 1854-1923)
Big Brother (boy w/his baby sister on his shoulder in a landscape), oil on canvas, sgn, unfr, 32x27", C-E 10/18/89 1,980
Home Again (lady picking flowers from garden, house in background), indistinctly sgn/dtd 1909, 31x29", RWS 5/19/88 1,400
Ripe Cherries (mother & two daughters picking cherries), oil on canvas, sgn, unfr, 30x20", C-E 10/18/89 1,760
Three Jolly Tars, oil on canvas, sgn, 28x20", PHL 6/16/88 UE 4,500
HIRST, Claude Raguet (American, 1855-1942)
Bedtime Reading (still life of books & candle), watercolor on paper, sgn/inscr NY, 6x11", SBY 3/17/88 UE 2,090
Don Quixote (still life of books, pipe & other objects), watercolor on paper, sgn/inscr, 11x11", SBY 6/28/89 14,300
Don Quixote (still life of books & vase on a table), oil on canvas, sgn, 12x9", SBY 5/25/88 OE 27,400
Gentleman's Table (still life w/cards, pipes & various objects), oil on canvas, sgn, 18x32", C-NY 9/28/89 OE 44,000
Oliver Goldsmith's Poems, oil on canvas, sgn/inscr, 8x10", C-NY 5/26/88 OE 26,400
HIRT, Heinrich (German, 19th C)
Buying Apples in the Rain, oil on canvas, sgn, 27x22", WD 5/5/88 16,000
HITCHCOCK, George (American, 1858-1916)
Dutch Street Scene with Figures, oil on canvas, sgn/indistictly dtd, 25x21", SBY 6/24/88 OE 4,675
Siren, oil on panel, sgn/inscr/dtd 1902, 10x6", C-NY 9/30/88 6,600
HITCHCOCK, Lucius Wolcott (American, 1868-1942)
Music Hath Charms, oil on board, sgn/dtd 11, 24x19", SBY 6/24/88 UE 770
Taking Her Leave (figures in interior scene), oil on canvas, sgn/dtd 15, unfr, 26x34", SBY 3/17/88 1,870
HITZ, Conrad (Swiss, 1798-1866)
Portrait of a Young Girl with an Urn, oil on canvas, sgn/dtd 1851, 36x30", C-E 5/22/89 3,300
HOANG (Japanese, 20th C)
Winter Scene, acrylic on canvas, sgn/dtd 1987, 17x24", LH 5/15/88 40
HOARE, William; att (British, 1706-1799)
Portrait of a Lady Believed To Be Elizabeth Lovett (half-length), oil on canvas, 30x25", SBY 7/12/89 1,980
HOBART, Clark (American, 1868-1948)
Nymphs Beside a Pond, oil on canvas, sgn, 14x16", B/B 10/6/88 1,870
HOBBEMA, Meindert; att (Dutch, 1638-1709)
Farmers Herding Cattle Below Threatening Skies, oil on panel, 30x42", SBY 1/12/89 44,000
HOBBEMA, Meindert; manner of (Dutch, 1638-1709)
Old Mill House in a Landscape, oil on panel, 22x26", SBY 12/9/88 2,750
HOBBS, George Thompson (American, 1846-)
Figure in the Forest, oil on canvas, sgn/inscr/dtd 04, 14x20", C-E 6/1/88 1,100
Still Life of Stein & Pretzels, oil on panel, sgn, 14x10", C-NY 5/26/88 5,280
HOCKNEY, David (British, 1937-)
Adhesiveness (abstract), oil on board, sgn/inscr/dtd 1960, 50x40", C-NY 5/3/88 165,000
Bedroom, crayon/pencil on paper, initialed/dtd 66, 14x17", SBY 5/2/89 OE 132,000
Clean Boy (male nude from behind), pencil on paper, sgn/dtd 64, 18x24", SBY 11/9/89 16,500
Daisies (still life), pen/ink on paper, initialed/dtd 78, 17x14", SBY 11/11/88 OE 30,250
Deep & Wet Water (composition), acrylic on canvas, sgn/dtd 1971, 60x60", SBY 11/8/89 OE 1,430,000
Demonstration of Versatility-Swiss Landscape in a Scenic Style; oil on canvas, 1961, 20x24", SBY 6/30/88 OE 90,000
Different Kinds of Water Pouring into a Swimming Pool, Santa Monica; acrylic on canvas, 1965, 72x60", SBY 5/2/89 OE 506,000
Early Morning, Sainte-Maxime; acrylic on canvas, sgn/dtd 1969, 48x60", C-NY 11/9/88 352,000
Fire Island Pines (exterior view w/figure), colored pencil on paper, sgn/dtd Aug 75/titled, 17x14", SBY 11/11/88 OE 74,250
Geography Book Illustration for a Simple Heart, colored pencil on paper, initialed/dtd 1973, 14x17", SBY 10/8/88 17,600
Gitanes (contemporary still life), pen/ink on paper, initialed/dtd Carennac Aug 70, 17x14", SBY 11/11/88 16,500
Grand Procession of Dignitaries in the Semi-Egyptian Style, oil on canvas, sgn/dtd 1961, 84x144", SBY 5/2/89 OE 2,200,000
Henry, Grand Hotel, Calvi (seated man w/cigar); crayon/pencil on paper, initialed/dtd 1972, 17x14", SBY 5/2/89 OE 209,000
House on Miller Place (contemporary), colored oil sticks on paper laid down on board, sgn/inscr, 14x17", SBY 11/11/88 30,800
Lemon & Two Limes (contemporary), colored pencil on paper, initialed/dtd 70, 17x14", SBY 11/11/88 30,250
Marinka Nude (seated), colored pencil on paper, initialed/dtd 77, 17x14", SBY 5/3/89 OE 77,000
Mark Strand Hotel Rangoon, pen/black ink on paper, dtd 4th Dec 1971, 17x14", C-NY 5/4/89 26,400
Mo on Gray Bed (posterior view of reclining nude on bed), colored pencil on paper, sgn/dtd 1966, 16x20", SBY 5/2/88 OE 20,900
Patrick & George, ink on paper, sgn/dtd NY 60, 14x17", SBY 11/9/89 12,100
Peking (landscape), watercolor on paper, initialed, dtd 81, 14x17", SBY 5/3/89 OE 38,500
Peter, Carrennac (nude); pen/black ink on paper, initialed/dtd Aug 67, 14x17", C-NY 2/20/88 3,850
Peter Having a Wash, watercolor on paper, initialed/dtd Paris 67, 16x13", SBY 11/9/89 19,800
Plastic Sheet Floating in a Pool (contemporary), oil on canvas, sgn/ca 1977, 25x34", C-NY 2/20/88 165,000

Portrait of Andy Warhol, colored pencil/pencil on paper, initialed/inscr Andy Paris 1974, 26x20", SBY 5/2/88 OE 330,000
Portrait of John St Clair, colored pencil on paper, initialed/dtd 3rd April 1972, 14x17", SBY 10/5/89 OE 33,000
Portrait of Robert Mapplethorpe, pen/black ink on paper, sgn/dtd New York June 1st 1971, 17x14", C-NY 10/31/89........ 77,000
Portrait of Shinro, colored pencils/crayon on paper, sgn, 12x12", C-NY 5/4/89 22,000
Portrait of the Artist's Mother, pen/ink on paper, monogramed/dtd 73, 17x14", C-NY 5/4/88 11,000
Room, Manchester Street (man with cigarette standing in an interior); acrylic on canvas, 95x95", C-NY 5/3/89 880,000
Singer (abstract), colored pencils/graphite on paper, initialed/dtd 63, 13x10", C-NY 5/4/88 29,700
Teeth Cleaning, W 11 (contemporary); oil on canvas, sgn/dtd March 1962, 72x48", SBY 5/3/89........ 187,000
Washington (abstract), charcoal/white chalk/pen/black ink on paper mounted on paper, sgn/dtd 61, 18x24", C-NY 5/4/89........ 18,700
Wayne & Graham (two male nudes), pen/ink on paper, initialed/dtd 69, 14x17", SBY 11/11/88 OE 13,200

HODGDON, Sylvester Phelps (American, 1830-1906)
Harbor, Sunset; oil on canvas, sgn/dtd 1878, 30x48", RWS 6/17/89 OE 1,600
Pair: Seascape; City of Boston at Sunset; oil on board, sgn, 8x12", RAB 11/24/89........ 500
Sailing Off Rocky Cliff, oil on canvas, sgn/dtd 1879, 20x30", RWS 11/10/89 2,000

HODGKIN, Howard (British, 20th C)
Architecture (abstract), textile dyes on handmade paper, sgn/dtd 1978, 28x36", SBY 10/8/88........ 15,400
Counting the Days (abstract), oil on wood panel/frame, sgn/dtd 1979-82, 22x25", SBY 11/8/89 OE 440,000
Garden of the Bombay Museum (contemporary), oil on wood panel, sgn/dtd 1978-82, 48x56", SBY 5/2/89 OE 506,000
Guest (abstract), oil on panel, sgn, 1972, 23x29", SBY 6/30/88 OE 148,100
Passion (abstract), oil on wood, sgn/dtd 1980-84/titled, 13x22", SBY 2/19/88 66,000
Venetian Glass (contemporary), oil on wood panel/frame, sgn/dtd 1984-87, 13x17", SBY 11/9/89 132,000

HODGKINS, Frances (New Zealander, 1869-1947)
Drawing Water, watercolor/bodycolor, sgn/inscr, 14x19", C-SK 5/25/89 11,940
Portrait of a Girl, watercolor, initialed/dtd 95, 13x9", C- SK 6/9/88 11,150

HODGSON, John Even (British, 1836-1895)
In the Garden, oil on panel, sgn/dtd 1888, 18x24", SBY 7/12/89 3,850

HOEDRIENG (Continental, 19th C)
Still Life of Mushrooms, oil on panel, sgn, 10x16", B/B 1/11/89 660

HOEFFLER, Adolf (German, 1825-1898)
Hay Cart at the Edge of a Forest, oil on canvas, sgn/dtd 1862, 26x37", SBY 7/12/89 3,850

HOEL, Arthur (American, 20th C)
Pamet River, Cape Cod, July 1911; oil on artist board, sgn/titled, tramp art frame, 6x9", RAB 11/25/88 UE 175

HOERMAN, Carl (American, 1885-)
Grand Canyon, oil on canvas, sgn, 43x49", NA 2/6/88 2,300

HOET, Gerard; att (Dutch, 1648-1733)
Mars Attending Venus at Her Toilet, oil on canvas, 36x50", SBY 4/7/89 5,500

HOEY, see Van Hoey

HOFBAUER, Ferdinand (Austrian, 1801-1864)
Shipwreck, oil on canvas, sgn, 29x40", C-NY 10/25/89........ 6,600

HOFEL, Johann Nepomuk (German, 1786-1864)
Napoleon & Josephine (portrait), oil on canvas, sgn/dtd 1825, 33x40", C-NY 2/23/89 8,800

HOFER, Carl (German, 1878-1955)
Portraet Eines Jungen Mannes (portrait of lad holding bowl of fruit), oil on canvas, initialed, 31x24", SBY 2/14/89 OE........ 27,500

HOFER, Heinrich (German, 1825-1878)
Travelers on a Snowy Road, oil on panel, sgn/dtd 1874, 8x12", SBY 12/9/88 OE........ 4,400

HOFER, M. (German, 19th C)
Cabin in the Mountains, oil on canvas, sgn/dtd 1886, 16x12", DM 5/89 1,100

HOFFBAUER, Charles C.J. (American, 1875-1957)
Il Carnivale di Venezia, pastel on mounted tissue, sgn, 24x29", RWS 5/12/89 5,000
Military Parade Through the Arc de Triomphe, watercolor/gouache/pencil on paper, sgn, 13x9", RWS 5/19/88 UE 325
Military Reception (military men & other people in plaza), watercolor on paper, sgn, 8x10", RWS 3/31/88 UE........ 200
On the Beach, oil on canvas, sgn/dtd 07, 25x32", RWS 11/3/88 OE 130,000
Pair: Equestrian Battle, Winter; In the Trenches; watercolor/gouache/pencil on paper, sgn, 11x12", 7x11", RWS 3/16/89 OE........ 425
Pair: Terrain-Gun Emplacement; Cannon in a Field; watercolor/gouache on paper, sgn, 11x15", 8x11", RWS 3/31/88 UE 200
Rainy Night in New York, oil on canvas, sgn, 12x16", C-NY 3/11/88 4,400

HOFFMAN, Arnold (American, 1886-)
Friendship, oil on canvas, sgn, 42x22", DM 5/13/88........ 1,600
Friendship (portrait of a girl w/pet), oil on canvas, sgn, 42x22", DM 5/13/88 1,600

HOFFMAN, Frank B. (1888-1958)
Riders in the Hills, India ink/watercolor on paper, sgn, 21x20", SBY 9/23/88 OE 1,980

HOFFMAN, Ronald (American, 20th C)
Sacred Lotus, three misty figures rise from lotus blossoms; oil on canvas, sgn/titled, 40x36", RAB 3/27/89 UE 100

HOFFMANN, Charles C. (1821-1882)
View of Benjamin Rever Farm, Lower Heidelberg Township, Berks County, PA; oil on canvas, sgn/1879, 25x34", SBY 1/28/88 30,800

HOFFMANN, J. (Austrian, 20th C)
Pair: Primitive Landscapes with Farm Buildings, oil on canvas, 16x21", SLK 2/12/88........ 220

HOFFMANN, Oskar Adol'fovich Gofman (Russian, 1851-1913)
Baltic Breakfast (man seated at table), oil on board, sgn/dtd 1892, 9x6", C-L 10/8/88 1,490

HOFLER, Max (Continental or British, 20th C)
Pair: Thames Valley Landscapes; oil on masonite, 21x24", SBY 12/9/88........ 1,320

HOFMANN, A. (German, 19th C)
Pair: Ducks, Geese, Roosters & Hens by Stream; Peacocks, Ducks, Roosters; oil on panel, sgn, 7x10", C-E 2/21/89 3,850
HOFMANN, Ansen (Scandanavian, 19th C)
Flamenco Dancer (figures watching beyond), oil on canvas, sgn, 28x22", C-E 2/21/89 UE 1,650
HOFMANN, Earl (American, 20th C)
Loew's Century (landscape w/buildings), oil on board, sgn, 9x12", SBY 1/24/89 OE 2,090
HOFMANN, Hans (American, 1880-1966)
Avis (abstract), oil on canvas, sgn/dtd 59, 72x60", SBY 5/2/89 550,000
Awakening (contemporary composition), oil on canvas, sgn/dtd 11.12.47, 60x40", SBY 11/8/89 275,000
Blue Glory (abstract), oil on canvas, sgn/dtd 50, 36x32", SBY 11/11/88 170,500
Capriccio No V (abstract), oil on cardboard, sgn, 1959, 22x26", SBY 10/8/88 OE 12,100
Composition (abstract), oil on board, sgn twice/dtd 52, 8x10", SBY 2/19/88 14,300
Double-Sided: Untitled Lecture Drawing; charcoal on paper, sgn, 25x19", SBY 2/14/89 1,650
Flight (abstract), oil on board, sgn/titled, ca 1947-49, 55x40", SBY 5/2/88 77,000
Genius Logic (Pervading Spirit), oil on canvas, sgn/dtd 63, 48x36", SBY 5/3/89 192,500
Germania III (abstract), oil on canvas, sgn/dtd VII.27.49, 48x50", SBY 11/11/88 41,250
Gloria in Excelsis (abstract), oil on canvas, sgn twice/dtd 1963 twice/titled, 50x40", SBY 11/10/88 594,000
Golden Light (abstract), oil on paper mounted on board, sgn/dtd 58, 11x14", SBY 10/5/89 28,600
Green Beast (abstract), gouache on paper, sgn/dtd VII, 1945, 29x23", C-NY 5/4/89 44,000
Joyful Celebration (abstract), gouache on paper, 1962, 23x29", C-NY 5/4/88 OE 38,500
L'Obstacle, oil on board mounted on masonite, sgn/dtd 49, 17x14", C-NY 11/10/88 OE 35,200
Landscape (abstract), casein on panel, sgn/dtd 40, 24x30", C-NY 5/4/89 63,800
Landscape (abstract), oil on board, sgn/dtd 37, 30x40", SBY 5/3/88 57,750
Landscape (abstract), oil on panel, 1942, 24x30", SBY 10/8/88 55,000
Le Dragon (abstract), oil on board, 1947, 23x22", SBY 11/9/89 88,000
Miracle (abstract), gouache on paper, sgn/dtd 44.23.45, 29x23", C-NY 5/4/88 OE 49,500
Mirage II, oil on canvas, sgn/dtd 1963, 50x40", SBY 11/8/89 506,000
Nocturn (abstract), oil on canvas, sgn twice/inscr/dtd 1952, 60x48", C-NY 5/3/88 319,000
On the Sound (abstract), oil on board mounted on canvas, sgn/dtd 47, 18x24", SBY 11/9/89 OE 132,000
Provincetown, Town & Harbor (abstract); oil on panel, sgn/dtd 36, 25x30", C-NY 5/4/89 77,000
Provincetown Harbor (abstract), oil on board, sgn/dtd 1983/titled, 30x36", SBY 5/3/88 OE 110,000
Ravine (abstract), oil on composition board, sgn/dtd 1954, 24x36", SBY 10/5/89 OE 242,000
Red, Brown, Blue: Chromatic Series 1 (abstract); gouache on paper, sgn/dtd 62, 18x24", C-NY 2/20/88 8,800
Scotch & Burgundy (abstract), oil on board, sgn, 1951, 61x41", SBY 11/10/88 OE 407,000
Search for the Real (abstract), gouache, ca 1949, 12x10", PHL 11/15/88 3,250
Shapes (abstract), tempera/crayon/watercolor on paper, sgn, 1947, 26x22", SBY 10/8/88 28,600
Simultan (abstract), oil on plywood, sgn/dtd 53, 35x30", SBY 11/11/88 88,000
Source (abstract), oil on canvas, sgn/dtd 62, 50x40", SBY 5/2/88 660,000
St Tropez vue sur les Montagnes de St Raphael, black ink/graphite on paper, sgn/dtd III 4 29, 11x14", C-NY 10/4/89 OE 8,800
Study for Fruit Bowl (abstract), ink/oil on paper, sgn/dtd 50, 17x14", SBY 10/8/88 7,700
Untitled (abstract composition), oil on paper, initialed, 1945, 18x22", SBY 11/9/89 24,200
Untitled (abstract landscape w/buildings), crayon & ink on paper, sgn/dtd VIII 26 41, 14x17", SBY 5/3/89 23,100
Untitled (abstract landscape), oil on board, ca 1937, 25x30"SBY 2/15/89 46,750
Untitled (abstract), crayon on paper, initialed/dtd VII.28.42, 14x17", C-NY 5/4/89 OE 8,250
Untitled (abstract), crayon on paper, sgn, 1943, 18x24", C-NY 5/4/89 41,800
Untitled (abstract), crayon/ink on paper, sgn/dtd June 2 43, 11x14", SBY 11/11/88 13,200
Untitled (abstract), gouache on board, sgn/dtd 48, 26x22", C-NY 11/10/88 10,450
Untitled (abstract), gouache on paper, sgn/dtd 1944, 22x30", C-NY 2/20/88 16,500
Untitled (abstract), gouache on paper, sgn/dtd 54, 14x11", C-NY 5/4/88 8,250
Untitled (abstract), gouache on paperboard, sgn/dtd 45, 22x26", SBY 10/5/89 OE 33,000
Untitled (abstract), gouache/chalk/brush/black ink on paper, sgn, 1941, 12x9", lot 6904, C-NY 10/4/89 16,500
Untitled (abstract), gouache/crayon/pen & black ink on paper, sgn, 1943, 18x24", lot 6806, C-NY 5/4/89 OE 55,000
Untitled (abstract), gouache/ink/crayon on paper, sgn, 1943, 18x24", SBY 10/8/88 OE 66,000
Untitled (abstract), gouache/pen/black ink on paper, sgn/dtdXI.14.46, 18x23", C-NY 5/4/88 OE 11,000
Untitled (abstract), ink on paper, sgn/dtd 39, 17x14", SBY 2/15/89 OE 7,700
Untitled (abstract), oil crayon on paper, sgn, 1943, 18x24", SBY 5/3/88 30,250
Untitled (abstract), oil on board, 10x8", C-NY 5/4/89 30,800
Untitled (abstract), oil on canvas, sgn/dtd V.10.50, 60x40", SBY 11/10/88 319,000
Untitled (abstract), oil on panel, ca 1951, 24x30", C-NY 5/4/89 OE 88,000
Untitled (abstract), oil on panel, sgn, 20x24", sgn, ca 1948, 20x24", C-NY 2/14/89 60,500
Untitled (abstract), oil on panel, sgn/dtd 45, 43x31", SBY 11/9/88 OE 165,000
Untitled (abstract), oil on paper, sgn/dtd 1963, 14x11", SBY 10/8/88 31,900
Untitled (abstract), oil on paper, sgn/dtd 61, 13x11", SBY 5/3/89 28,600
Untitled (abstract), oil on paper, sgn/dtd 62, 24x19", SBY 5/3/89 35,750
Untitled (abstract), oil on paper, sgn/dtd 63, 11x14", SBY 5/3/89 18,700
Untitled (abstract), oil on paper board mounted on canvas, 1962, 32x24", SBY 11/11/88 OE 66,000
Untitled (abstract), oil on paper laid down on canvas, 1960, 14x11", SBY 5/3/88 OE 31,900
Untitled (abstract), oil on paper mounted on canvas, sgn/dtd 61, 26x22", SBY 11/9/89 OE 71,500
Untitled (abstract), oil/gesso on cardboard, sgn/dtd VIII.28.45, 22x26", SBY 10/8/88 OE 55,000
Untitled (abstract), watercolor/ink on paper, sgn/dtd VIII 20 46, 18x24", SBY 11/9/89 27,500
Untitled (contemporary sketch of head), black ink/graphite on board, sgn, dtd 13/I, ca 1932, 13x10", C-NY 10/4/89 4,400

Untitled (contemporary sketch of head), charcoal on paper, ca 1932, 19x15", C-NY 10/4/89 3,850
Untitled (view of balcony w/landscape beyond), watercolor on paper, sgn, 1941, 12x10", SBY 5/3/88 OE 17,600
Untitled Self-Portrait (abstract), watercolor on paper, 1935, 11x9", SBY 10/8/88 OE 10,450
Untitled Self-Portrait (abstract), watercolor on paper, 1935, 11x9", SBY 10/8/88 13,200
Untitled Sketch (abstract composition), gouache/crayon on paper, initialed, dtd 43, 18x24", SBY 5/3/89 OE 49,500
Vue sur les Quatre Meres, gouache/black ink/graphite on paper, sgn/dtd II 7 29, 11x14", C-NY 10/4/89 OE 7,700
White Flash (abstract), oil on panel, sgn twice/dtd 54 twice/titled, 25x20", SBY 11/11/88 OE 71,500
X (abstract), oil on canvas, sgn/dtd 55, 60x48", SBY 11/10/88 363,000

)FMANN, Heinrich (German, 19th C)
Untitled, man standing leaning on staff; oil on board, sgn, 24x15", SLK 4/7/89 700
Untitled, study of girl facing left; oil on canvas, sgn, 25x20", SLK 4/7/89 1,400

)GAN, Thomas (American, 19th C)
Camp, Military Telegraphs Corps (Civil War); pen/ink on board, sgn/inscr, 8x10", C-E 5/27/88 OE 495
Pair: Camp Kitchen; General Burnside's Headquarters (Civil War); pen/ink, sgn/inscr, 10x13" & smaller, C-E 5/27/88 770

)GARTH, William; after (British, 1697-1764)
Rakes Progress, oil on canvas, 13x17", RWS 8/12/89 325

)GARTH, William; circle of (British, 1697-1764)
Pair: Portrait of a Gentleman with Hunting Horn; Lady Holding Apples; oil on copper, 9x7", SBY 7/12/89 2,750

)GUET, Charles (French, 1821-1870)
Busy Marketplace, oil on canvas, sgn/indistinctly dtd, 18x15", C-NY 2/23/89 6,050

)GUET, Louis; att (German, 19th C)
Boats Along the Coast, oil on board, initialed, 5x7", B/B 6/9/88 1,210

)IN, Claude Jean Baptiste (French, 1750-1817)
Lady Seated with Her Pet Spaniel in a Park, oil on panel, 14x13", SBY 1/12/89 14,300

)IT, Albert Gallatin (American, 1809-1956)
Portrait of George Washington, oil on canvas, 96x60", SBY 6/28/89, UE 10,000

)LBEIN, Hans; manner of (German, 15th/16th C)
Portrait of Edward VII, oil on panel, 10x8", SBY 12/9/88 1,870
Portrait of Thomas More, oil on panel, unfr, 18x13", SBY 12/9/88 OE 2,860

)LBERG, Richard A. (American, 1889-1942)
Fisherman, oil on cardboard, sgn twice, 20x16", RAB 8/8/89 1,000
Fisherman's Shack, oil on particle board, sgn, 20x16", RWS 5/12/89 900
Winter Stream, oil on canvas, initialed/indistinctly dtd, 12x15", B/B 3/22/89 OE 7,700

)LD, Ben (British, 19th C)
Owl (perched on limb), oil on board, sgn/dtd 1883, 17x19", WL 5/20/88 UE 225

)LDEN, Schuyler
Southern Meadows, oil on canvas, sgn/dtd 1891, 18x26", C-E 6/1/88 OE 2,750

LDENSEN, Peter (American, 20th C)
Scituate (summer landscape w/figures by river, houses beyond), watercolor on paper, sgn/dtd 1930, 12x18", RWS 3/31/88 UE 200

LDREDGE, Ransome Gillet (American, 1836-1899)
Indian Encampment in the Mountains, oil on canvas, sgn, 42x70", B/B 12/8/88 660
Indian Encampment Under the Oaks, oil on panel, sgn, 10x12", B/B 1/11/89 1,100

LDREDGE, Ransome Gillet; att (American, 1836-1899)
Indian Encampment (tepees & figures in extensive landscape), oil on canvas, 30x50", B/B 5/17/89 UE 522

LDSTOCK, Alfred Worsley (Canadian, 1820-1901)
At les Grand Calumets on the Ottawa (encampment by river), pastel, sgn, 13x21", FB 10/17/88 OE 3,000
Grand Falls, Nameanker River; pastel, sgn, 12x21", FB 10/17/88 1,900
On Beancour River, Quebec District; pastel, sgn, 13x22", FB 10/17/88 2,200
View of Niagara Falls, pastel, sgn, 17x26", WAD 6/12/89 2,600

LFFERICH, Wilhelm
Beach Scene, oil on panel, sgn, 22x36", C-E 10/25/88 2,200
Children at the Beach, oil on panel, sgn, 22x36", C-E 5/23/88 1,650

LGUIN, Santiago Uribe (20th C)
Untitled (abstract), mixed media, 1987, 55x39", SBY 11/21/88 UE 1,320

LINGS, Clark (American, 20th C)
Noontime-Malaga Spain; oil on canvas, sgn, 30x20", SLK 2/11/89 450

LLAENDER, A. (Continental, 19th/20th C)
In Coro, oil on canvas, sgn, 25x33", SBY 7/12/89 2,090

LLAMS, Florence Mabel (British, 1877-1963)
Robin, English Bulldog; oil on panel, sgn, 20x16", SBY 6/9/89 2,750

LLAND, Francis Raymond (American, 1886-1934)
Pittsburgh (snowy scene w/smoke stacks), oil on canvas, sgn/dtd 1919, 36x42", C-NY 5/25/89 11,000

LLAND, James (British, 1799-1870)
Venetian Bridge, oil on board, 8x11", B/B 5/17/89 935

LLAND, John (British, 19th C)
Fisherfolk by the Coast with a Castle in the Distance, oil on canvas, sgn, 16x24", C-E 2/25/88 2,860
Fisherfolk with Castle in the Distance, oil on canvas, sgn, 16x24", FB 10/17/88 5,000
Harbor Scene, oil on canvas, sgn, 14x21", DM 2/19/88 650

LLAND, Tom (American, 1936-)
SP#91938, epoxy on cardboard/paper, 20x4x5", B/B 12/8/88 3,575
Untitled (abstract), acrylic/oil stick/varnish on paper construction, sgn/dtd 82, 25x29", SBY 10/8/88 4,400

HOLLANDER, Gino (20th C)
Head of a Youth, acrylic on canvas, sgn/dtd 72, 59x59", C-E 11/17/88 ... 715
Untitled (abstract), acrylic on canvas, sgn/dtd 72, 58x58", C-E 11/17/88 ... 605
HOLLOSY, Simon
Entertaining the Troops, oil on canvas, sgn/inscr, 26x38", C-E 2/23/88 ... 3,520
HOLLOWAY, Charles (American, 1859-1941)
Pursuit of Pleasure, oil on canvas, sgn, in a painted arch, 20x40", SBY 9/23/88 ... 990
HOLLOWAY, Edward Stratton (American, -1939)
Summer Landscape, oil on canvasboard, sgn, 12x16", C-E 11/8/88 UE ... 250
HOLLOWAY(?), F. (American, 19th C)
Niagara Falls As Seen From Below & Near To the American Ferry, oil on canvas, ca 1846, SBY 1/24/89 ... 5,775
HOLLOWELL, Robert
Portrait of a Lady, oil on canvas, sgn/dtd 34, 29x21", C-E 11/30/88 ... 660
HOLLYER, Gregory (British, 19th/20th C)
Stable Interior with Sheep, oil on board, sgn, 6x10", RWS 12/10/88 UE ... 175
HOLMAN, Louis Arthur (American, 1866-1939)
Lake in Autumn (landscape), oil on cardboard, sgn, 5x8", RWS 9/29/88 ... 250
HOLMBOE, Thorolf (Norwegian, 1866-1935)
Coastal View, oil on canvas, sgn/dtd 1897, 32x59", SBY 6/8/88 ... 1,870
Winter Landscape, oil on canvas, sgn, 29x22", SBY 6/8/88 UE ... 1,100
HOLMES, Basil
Afternoon Near Sevenoaks, Kent; oil on canvas, sgn, 20x27", C-NY 5/25/88 OE ... 10,450
HOLMES, Ralph William (American, 1876-1963)
California Hills, oil on canvasboard, sgn, 16x20", B/B 10/6/88 ... 770
Farm at the Base of the California Foothills, oil on canvasboard, sgn, 16x20", B/B 10/6/88 ... 880
Green Hills, oil on canvas, sgn, 24x28", B/B 8/10/88 ... 660
Southern California Foothills, oil on canvas, sgn, 28x32", B/B 12/8/88 ... 2,475
Spring Landscape, oil on board, sgn, 15x20", FAP 12/8/89 OE ... 950
View of the Grand Canyon, oil on board, sgn, 18x20", B/B 10/6/88 ... 1,045
HOLMSTED, Marie H. (Canadian, 1857-1911)
Thundering Falls, watercolor, sgn, 7x11", WAD 6/12/89 ... 300
HOLMSTEDT, J. (Scandinavian, 19th/20th C)
Norwejian Fjord in Summer, oil on canvas, sgn, 15x23", SBY 7/12/89 UE ... 440
HOLSOE, Carl Vilhelm (Danish, 1863-1935)
Reading, oil on canvas, sgn/inscr #39, 27x24", SBY 2/22/89 ... 27,500
Silver Bowl (still life on table in front of oil painting), oil on canvas, sgn, 31x27", SBY 10/24/89 ... 17,600
HOLST, Laurits B. (Danish, 1848-1934)
Monterey Coast, oil on canvas, sgn/dtd 1870, 15x29", SBY 1/24/89 ... 1,540
HOLSTAYN, Josef (Austrian, 20th C)
Flowers & a Porcelain Bowl in a Chiche, oil on canvas, sgn, 29x25", WD 3/23/88 UE ... 3,250
Opulent Still Life in a Niche with a Butterfly, oil on panel, sgn/inscr, 24x20", C-E 10/25/88 ... 4,950
Still Life of Flowers, Bird's Nest, & Grapes in a Niche; oil on canvas, sgn/inscr, 30x24", C-E 2/23/88 ... 7,150
Still Life of Flowers, Peaches, & a Blue Vase in a Niche; oil on canvas, sgn/inscr, 30x24", C-E 2/23/88 ... 6,050
HOLSTEYN, Pieter the younger (Flemish, 16th/17th C)
Pair: Tulips; watercolor/bodycolor, inscr, 13x8", C-NY 1/12/88 OE ... 9,350
Pair: Tulips; watercolor/bodycolor, inscr/wm WR, 12x8", C-NY 1/12/88 OE ... 12,100
Pair: Tulips; watercolor/bodycolor, inscr/wm WR, 12x8", C-NY 1/12/88 ... 7,700
Pair: Tulips; watercolor/bodycolor, inscr/wm WR, 12x8", C-NY 1/12/88 OE ... 10,450
Pair: Tulips; watercolor/bodycolor, inscr/wm WR, 13x8", C-NY 1/12/88 ... 7,150
Pair: Tulips; watercolor/bodycolor, inscr/wm WR, 13x8", C-NY 1/12/88 OE ... 8,800
HOLT, E.F. (British, 19th C)
Hilly Landscape, oil on board, initialed/dtd 1884, 7x11", C-E 2/23/88 ... 1,320
Rocking the Baby Asleep, oil on canvas, sgn/dtd 1860, 17x22", C-E 2/23/88 ... 4,400
HOLTY, Carl Robert (American, 1900-1973)
Abstract, watercolor/pencil on paper laid down board, initialed, 12x9", C-E 6/1/89 OE ... 3,080
Abstract Forms, oil on masonite, initialed, 7x9", C-E 10/18/89 ... 1,100
Abstract Landscape, pastel on paper, sgn, unfr, 24x27", C-E 6/1/88 ... 1,320
Abstraction, oil on masonite, sgn, 12x9", C-E 11/30/88 ... 935
Body Check (contemporary, two figures), oil on canvas, sgn/dtd 1944, 44x55", SBY 6/28/89 ... 4,675
Cienega II, oil on canvas, sgn, 44x30", B/B 12/8/88 ... 825
Dancers, oil on canvas, sgn, unfr, 30x38", C-E 11/30/88 OE ... 4,400
Dawn Rider (contemporary view of rider & horse), oil on canvas, sgn/dtd 1947, 30x38", SBY 4/14/89 ... 3,080
Europa (abstract composition), oil on canvas, sgn/dtd 46(?), 18x14", SBY 4/14/89 ... 1,540
Group of 3: Abstractions; brush/black ink on paper laid down on board, sgn/dtd 1936, 7x10" & smaller, C-E 2/1/89 ... 1,210
Group of 3: Abstractions; brush/black ink on paper laid down on board, sgn/dtd 56, 7x10" & smaller, C-E 2/1/89 ... 990
Gypsy (contemporary portrait of man), oil on masonite, sgn/dtd 47, 14x11", SBY 4/14/89 ... 1,540
Harlequin (contemporary), oil on masonite, sgn/dtd 46, 30x24", SBY 6/28/89 ... 2,090
Moonlight, gouache on paper laid down on board, initialed/dtd 28, 16x21", C-NY 3/11/88 ... 1,100
Set of 3: Figurative & Geometric Abstraction; brush/ink on paper laid on board, sgn, 7x9" & smaller, C-E 11/30/88 OE ... 1,650
Set of 3: Figurative & Geometric Abstraction; brush/ink on paper laid down on board, sgn, 7x10" & smaller, C-E 11/30/88 ... 660
The Grove, oil on masonite, sgn/dtd 1948, 14x18", SBY 4/14/89 ... 3,190

The Victor (abstract of fencing match), oil on masonite, sgn/dtd 45, 30x24", SBY 1/24/89	7,700
Untitled (abstract composition), paper laid down on board, sgn/dtd 42, 9x7", WD 10/5/88 OE	3,500
OLUB, Georg (Austrian, 1861-1919)	
Spring Landscape, oil on canvas, sgn/dtd 1916, 20x30", FAP 11/4/88 OE	900
OLZER, Joseph (Austrian, 1824-1876)	
Dachstein (river valley landscape), oil on canvas, sgn, 27x37", C-NY 2/23/89	8,800
OMER, Winslow (American, 1836-1910)	
Beetle & Wedge (four boys playing in landscape), pencil on paper, ca 1870s, inscr, 9x7", C-NY 5/25/89	28,600
Building Fort Ethan Allen, South of Chainbridge; pencil/ink wash on paper, initialed/inscr, 10x13", C-NY 12/2/88	7,150
Cavalry Officer, charcoal on paper, initialed/dtd 63, 9x8", B/B 3/22/89	27,500
Early Morning, pen/ink on paper, 1870s, 4x5", SBY 9/23/88	4,950
Fishing Schooner, Nassau; watercolor/gouache/pencil on paper, sgn/inscr, 15x21", C-NY 5/26/88	660,000
Fort Lion (figures in a landscape), pencil on cream paper, ca 1860s, 7x10", WL 5/20/88 OE	22,000
Garden in Nassau, watercolor/gouache/pencil on paper, sgn/dtd 85, 15x30", C-NY 5/26/88 OE	660,000
Girl on a Swing, charcoal/white gouache on paper, sgn/dtd 75, 16x12", SBY 5/25/88	66,000
Honeymoon (couple in landscape), pencil/Chinese white on gray paper, initialed, 1875, 9x11", C-NY 5/25/89	121,000
Horse & Plowman, Houghton Farm; watercolor on paper, sgn, ca 1878, 6x11", SBY 5/25/88	55,000
In the Mountains, charcoal with white highlight on paper, initialed, 9x13", B/B 3/17/88	60,500
Plains of Abraham, watercolor/pencil/gouache en grisaille on paper, sgn/dtd 1895, 14x20", C-NY 5/26/88	22,000
Return to Camp (man in canoe), watercolor/gouache/pencil on paper, sgn/dtd 1892, 15x24", C-NY 5/26/88	440,000
Rowing at Prout's Neck (girl in boat), watercolor/pencil on paper laid down, sgn/dtd 87, 14x20", C-NY 5/25/89	550,000
Summer Cloud, watercolor on paper, sgn/dtd 1881, 14x20", SBY 5/25/88	572,000
Volante on a Mountain Road, Cuba; watercolor on paper laid down on board, sgn/dtd 1885, 13x20", C-NY 5/25/89	60,500
OMEXT, H.M. (Dutch, 19th C)	
Reading Lesson (girl & boy seated on beach against exterior wall), watercolor/gouache on paper, sgn, 12x8", B/B 9/14/89	1,210
OMITZKY, Peter (20th C)	
Rooftop Newark #1, oil on canvas, sgn/dtd 74, 40x30", SBY 10/7/89	1,100
Turnpike, Bergen; oil on canvas, sgn/dtd 75, 22x28", SBY 10/5/88	1,100
ONDECOETER, Melchior; see De Hondecoeter	
ONDIUS, Abraham (Dutch, 1625-1695)	
Boar Hunt (dogs attacking wild boar in landscape), oil on canvas, sgn, 61x76", SBY 6/1/89	33,000
ONDIUS, Gerrit (American, 1891-1970)	
Fruit Stalls, New York City (people in street market scene); oil on canvas, sgn, 30x40", RWS 9/8/89 UE	1,000
ONE, Nathaniel (British, 1718-1784)	
Portrait of a Lady, seated, an oval portrait of a man behind; oil on canvas, unfr, 30x25", C-NY 6/2/88	4,400
Portrait of Mary Edwards, half-length, wearing a blue dress; oil on canvas, inscr, 30x25", C-NY 1/11/89	3,850
ONGSHOU, Chen (Chinese, 1598-1652)	
Children Worshipping the Buddha (hanging scroll), ink/color on silk, sgn, 48x22", SBY 5/31/89	23,100
ONIGBERGER, E. (Continental, 20th C)	
Reclining Nude, oil on canvas, sgn/dtd 30, 36x26", B/B 1/11/89	605
OOCH, Pieter; see De Hooch	
OOG, Bernard; see De Hoog	
OOPER, Edward (American, 1882-1967)	
Sultry Day (houses w/coastal view beyond), watercolor on paper, sgn, 14x19", SBY 5/24/89	137,500
OOPER, John Horace (British, 19th C)	
Man in a Punt, oil on canvas, sgn, 24x36", C-E 5/23/88	2,200
OOVEN, Herbert Nelson (American, 1897-)	
Impressionistic Landscape, oil on board, sgn, 14x16", FAP 4/15/89 OE	935
Wooded Path (impressionistic landscape), oil on board, 24x29", FAP 4/15/89	908
OPE, C.H. (American, 19th C)	
Fruit with Morning-Glories, oil on canvas, monogramed/sgn/dtd 1863, unfr, 16x20", C-E 2/1/89	1,650
OPE, James (American, 1818-1892)	
Rainbow Falls, Watkins Glen, New York; oil on canvas, sgn, 12x10", C-NY 5/25/89	4,400
OPE, Robert (British, 1869-1936)	
Woman in Blue with Parasol, oil on canvas, sgn, 20x16", C-E 2/23/88	3,080
OPE, Thelma Paddock (American, 1898-)	
Convoy, oil on canvas laid down, sgn, 24x35", B/B 9/15/88	385
OPKIN, Robert (American, 1832-1909)	
Clipper Ship, oil on canvas, sgn, 36x66", LH 10/16/88 OE	1,500
Oyster Gatherers, oil on canvas, sgn, 16x14", DM 10/14/88	1,200
Sailing Vessels Off Cape Wrath, oil on canvas, sgn, 11x22", DM 10/14/88	850
Stormy Coastline Scene (sea wall, lighthouse & sailboats), oil on canvas, sgn, 8x22", DM 5/19/89	1,000
OPKINS, Budd (American, 1931-)	
Montpelier (abstract), oil on canvas, sgn/dtd 62, 41x52", C-E 11/14/89	1,320
Untitled, oil on canvas, sgn/dtd 57/#d 11, 13x10", C-E 11/14/89	880
Untitled (abstract), oil on canvas, sgn/dtd 72, 19x25", SBY 10/5/88	1,100
Untitled (contemporary), oil/paper collage on paper, sgn/dtd 59, 14x11", C-E 5/9/89 OE	1,100
Untitled (contemporary), paper collage/brush/black ink/acrylic on paper laid down on board, 1968, 11x11", C-E 5/9/89 OE	1,210
OPKINS, C.	
Riverscape, oil on canvas, sgn/dtd 1880, 20x30", RAB 1/18/89 UE	250

HOPKINS, Frances Anne (Canadian, 1856-1919)
Forest in the Backwoods of Canada, watercolor heightened w/white, initialed, 15x22", C-SK 11/10/88 OE **10,220**
Mountainous River Landscape, oil on canvas, initialed, 6x8", C-SK 11/10/88 ..... **410**

HOPKINSON, Charles Sydney (American, 1869-1962)
Portrait of a Baby (seated, playing w/ribbon), oil on canvas, 33x28", SBY 5/24/89 ..... **11,000**
Rolling Hills in Autumn, New Zealand; watercolor on paper, sgn/dtd 48, 15x22", RWS 11/10/89 OE **11,000**
Studio Porch, Manchester, Massachusetts (figures viewed from interior); oil on canvas, ca 1906, 23x26", C-NY 5/25/89 OE **12,100**

HOPPE, C.A.W. (German, 19th C)
Still Life of Apple & Wrapper, oil on canvas, sgn/dtd 1860, 12x9", SBY 6/8/88 ..... **1,320**
Still Life of Roses, oil on canvas, sgn/dtd 1865, 20x16", SBY 6/8/88 ..... **2,475**
Still Life of Roses, Peonies, & Morning-Glories on a Mossy Bank; oil on canvas, sgn/dtd 1865, 21x17", C-E 10/25/88 ..... **2,860**

HOPPER, Edward (American, 1882-1967)
Double-Sided: Steam Fire Engine; Male Figure Studies; charcoal on paper, sgn, 19x24", C-NY 3/11/88 ..... **10,450**
Figure Standing on a Bridge, pen/ink/watercolor on paper, sgn/dtd 99, 22x14", SBY 9/23/88 ..... **4,125**
Moongazer, brush/black ink/gouache/pencil on paper, initialed/inscr/dtd 1923, 7x9", C-E 11/30/88 ..... **3,080**
Portrait of a Man, oil on panel, sgn, 16x12", C-NY 5/25/89 ..... **88,000**
Souvenir de Noel, 1922; gouache/pencil on paper, sgn/inscr/dtd 1922, 7x8", C-E 11/30/88 ..... **3,850**
Study of a Woman Knitting, pencil on paper, 10x8", C-NY 3/11/88 OE **8,800**

HOPPIN, Thomas Frederick (American, 1816-1872)
Country Tavern, oil on canvas, sgn/dtd 1853, 18x24", RWS 4/7/89 ..... **1,700**

HOPPNER, John (British, 1758-1810)
Portrait of a Gentleman, seated half-length, wearing a black coat & white jabot; oil on canvas, 30x25", C-NY 4/6/89 ..... **3,850**
Portrait of Lady Harrington, Countess of Clair, half-length...; oil on canvas, 30x25", C-NY 4/6/89 ..... **3,850**
Portrait of Sarah Erle Drax Grosvenor (half-length, stormy landscape beyond), oil on canvas, 36x28", SBY 4/7/89 ..... **6,050**

HOPPNER, John; circle of (British, 1758-1810)
Portrait of a Boy, oil on canvas, 30x25", SBY 7/12/89 ..... **1,760**
Portrait of a Lady, oil on canvas, 30x25", SBY 7/12/89 ..... **3,575**

HOPPNER, John; school of (British, 1758-1810)
Portrait of a Lady Said To Be Jane Elizabeth Countess of Oxford, oil on canvas, 31x25", C-E 4/7/88 ..... **1,045**

HORACIO (Mexican, 1912-)
Nina Con Canasta de Frutas, oil on canvas, sgn, 24x18", C-NY 11/21/89 ..... **5,500**
Nina con Panuelo de Puntillas, oil on canvas, indistinctly sgn, 26x18", C-NY 5/18/88 ..... **2,200**
Nino Con Mascotas, oil on canvas, sgn, 24x18", C-NY 11/21/89 OE **6,050**
Pair: Portraits of a Girl & a Boy; oil on canvas, sgn, 24x18", SBY 11/21/88 OE **17,600**
Portrait of a Young Girl in a Kitchen, oil on canvas, sgn, 24x18", SBY 11/21/88 OE **8,250**
Retrato de Nino con Perro (portrait of boy w/dog in interior), oil on canvas, sgn, 13x18", C-NY 11/21/88 OE **6,600**
Retrato de Rita Anguiano Sevilla (full-length portrait), oil on canvas, sgn/inscr, 24x18", C-NY 5/17/89 OE **8,250**
Young Girl Overlooking the Prado Square, oil on canvas, sgn, 24x18", B/B 12/8/88 ..... **4,950**
Young Girl with Fish & Fruit, oil on canvas, sgn, ca 1940s, 24x18", SBY 5/16/89 OE **8,800**

HOREMANS, Jan Joseph (Flemish 1682-1759)
Naughty Child, oil on panel, sgn, 10x9", SBY 7/12/89 ..... **1,980**
Pair: Recital; Visit to the Doctor; oil on panel, sgn, 10x9", SBY 10/13/89 OE **23,100**

HOREMANS, Jan Joseph; att (Flemish 1682-1759)
Afternoon in the Country, oil on canvas, bears signature, 20x24", B/B 9/14/89 ..... **825**
Naughty Child, oil on panel, 10x9", C-E 1/12/88 ..... **770**

HOREMANS, Jan Joseph; manner of (Flemish 1682-1759)
Family in an Interior by a Fire, oil on panel, 18x14", C-E 4/7/88 UE **1,100**

HOREMANS, Jan Joseph; school of (Flemish 1682-1759)
Drunkard Leaving a Tavern & Children Merry-Making with a Cat, oil on canvas, 34x40", C-E 4/7/88 ..... **1,100**

HORIK, Vladimir (Canadian, 1949-)
Au Bord de la Riviere Malbaie, oil on board, sgn, 12x16", FB 10/30/89 OE **880**

HORLOR, George William (British, fl 1849-1891)
A Draft Horse, a Heifer, a Ram, & an Ewe in a Pasture; oil on canvas, sgn/dtd 1844, 16x24", SLK 9/28/88 ..... **2,500**
Protectors (dogs guarding sheep in a landscape), oil on canvas, sgn/dtd 1872, 16x24", SBY 6/9/89 ..... **11,000**

HORLOR, Joseph (British, 19th C)
English Landscape, oil on canvas, sgn/dtd 55, 11x21", DM 3/14/88 ..... **2,000**

HORLOR (British, 19th C)
Highlands Landscape with Figures Outside of a Millhouse, oil on canvas, sgn, 25x36", SLK 9/27/88 ..... **1,600**

HORNAK, Ian (American, 1944-)
Marcia's House, Vermont, 1981; oil on canvas, sgn, 42x60", RWS 9/8/89 UE **850**

HORNBROOK, R.L. (19th C)
Rio de Janeiro, pen/ink/watercolor, inscr, 12x18", C-SK 5/25/89 ..... **550**

HORNBY, Lester George (American, 1882-1956)
Automne dans le Bois de Boulogne, oil on board, sgn/dtd 57, 13x15", C-E 10/18/89 UE **1,320**
Gloucester Harbor, pencil on paper, sgn, 9x12", WG 10/19/88 UE **125**

HORNYANSKY, Nicholas (Canadian, 1896-1965)
Stone House, watercolor, sgn, 8x10", WAD 6/12/89 ..... **300**

HORST, Gerrit Willemsz (Dutch, 1612-1652)
Allegory of Music, oil on canvas, 48x38", SBY 6/3/88 OE **88,000**

HORTER, Earl (American, 1881-1940)
Landscape House in Green Field, oil on canvas, 15x19", FAP 4/15/89 ..... **550**

Study of a Nude, conte on brown paper, sgn/dtd 36, FAP 4/15/89 ... 1,100

Tabletop Abstraction, oil on panel, sgn, 20x24", C-NY 9/28/89 OE, $66,000

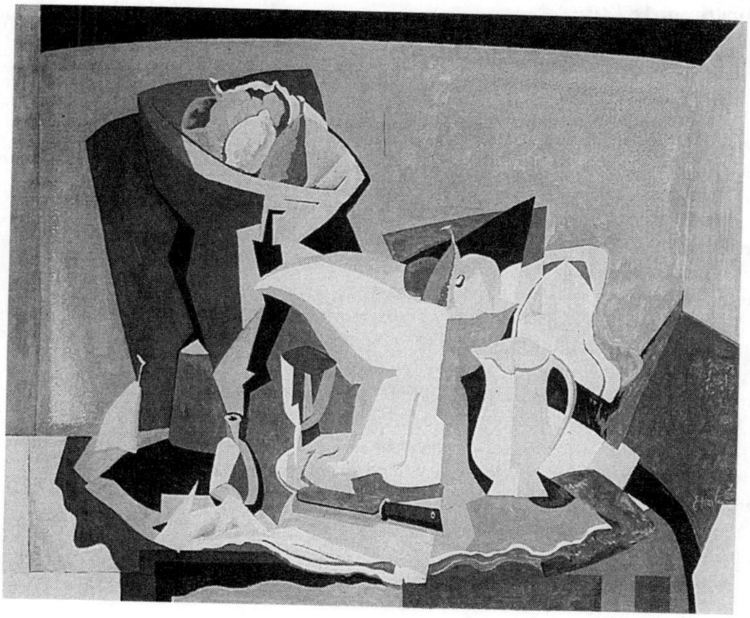

HORTIG, Hans

Russian Village in Winter, oil on board, sgn, 14x20", C-E 10/25/88 ... 1,650

IORTON, William Samuel (American, 1865-1936)

Broadstairs Beach, oil on panel, sgn, 15x18", C-NY 9/30/88 OE ... 24,200

Children Paddling at the Beach, crayon on paper, stamped signature/titled, 7x9", RAB 3/27/89 UE ... 275

Claudette Colbert & Clark Gable (Art Deco), oil on artist board, 24x17", DM 2/19/88 ... 700

Dutch Woman in an Interior, pastel on paper, sgn, 11x17", SBY 1/24/89 ... 880

European Street Scene, gouache on paper, sgn, 17x12", RAB 3/27/89 UE ... 300

Floral Still Life, oil on board, sgn/dtd 1934, 24x28", C-NY 3/11/88 ... 2,420

Group of 4: Figures by a Boat Basin; Men Hauling Boat; Figure Studies; City Buildings; charcoal, sgn, 8x9", SBY 6/28/89 ... 2,090

Hecksher Tower Sunset, pastel on paper laid down on board, sgn, 19x25", C-NY 9/30/88 ... 4,400

New Growth (study of tree trunks), crayon on buff paper, artist's estate stamp, 13x9", RWS 5/12/89 UE ... 300

New York, oil on canvas, sgn, 36x42", SBY 9/23/88 ... 13,200

Pink Bridge, Sonning on the Thames Upriver From London; pencil on paper, sgn, 7x10", RAB 8/9/88 ... 400

Place St Pierre, Pontarlier, France; oil on canvas, sgn/dtd 1924, 26x31", SBY 9/23/88 ... 11,000

Rowing the Ship, oil on canvas, sgn, 25x30", B/B 10/9/88 UE ... 3,850

Trees in Winter, oil on board, sgn/dtd 1922, 14x17", SBY 1/24/89 ... 2,530

ORVATH (Hungarian, 19th/20th C)

Sharing a Meal Among Friends, oil on canvas, sgn, 22x26", FAP 4/15/89 ... 412

ORWOOD, Charles (British, 20th C)

Day at the Beach (groups of bathers on beach), oil on masonite, sgn, 8x12", RWS 3/31/88 ... 400

OSKINS, Gayle (American, 1887-1962)

Bandit & Cowboy, oil on canvas, sgn, 30x21", C-E 2/1/89 OE ... 4,950

Desperation, oil on canvas, sgn, 30x25", FAP 4/15/89 ... 1,210

OUBEN, Henri (Belgian, 1858-1910)

Landscape with Farm Hands & Wagons, oil on canvas, sgn, 25x32", WG 4/23/88 ... 1,600

OUQUET, Charles (French, 19th C)

After the Storm (shipwreck scene), oil on canvas, sgn/dtd 59, 29x45", LH 9/10/89 UE ... 900

OUSSER, Yvonne McKague (Canadian, 1898-)

Sleep Walker, oil on board, sgn, 30x24", FB 10/30/89 ... 3,080

OUSTON, William (American, 19th C)

Seascape, oil on canvas, sgn/dtd 1881, 15x27", SBY 6/24/88 ... 4,400

OUSTOUN, Donald MacKay (Canadian, 1916-)

Toward the Bay, oil/lucite on canvas, sgn, 24x30", WAD 11/30/89 ... 1,800

OVENDEN, Thomas (American, 1840-1895)

Portrait of a Young Girl, oil on canvas, sgn/dtd 1882, 12x10", SBY 6/28/89 OE ... 8,800

Returned Home with Day's Catch (interior), watercolor on paper laid down on board, sgn/dtd 1880, 15x18", C-E 5/22/89 OE ... 5,500

Sailor's Return, oil on canvas, sgn/inscr/dtd 1892, 36x57", C-NY 9/30/88 ... 17,600

Study for the Hands of the Enemy, pencil on paper, 13x11", SBY 6/28/89 ... 1,045

OVENER, Johannes (Dutch, 20th C)

Ballet Dancer Tying Her Slipper, oil on canvas, sgn, 28x20", B/B 1/11/89 ... 825

OVER, Edward

Shipping Off Istanbul at Night, oil on canvas, sgn/dtd 80, 30x50", C-NY 5/25/88 ... 4,180

HOW, Kenneth G. (American, 1883-)
In Portsmouth Harbor (docks & warehouses in morning mist), oil on canvas, sgn, 25x30", RWS 3/31/88 .... **3,200**
HOWARD, B.K. (American, 1872-)
Double-Sided: Florence Griswold House...1907; Moneylender (allegorical); oil on canvas, sgn, 31x28", RWS 3/31/88 OE **3,100**
HOWARD, Hugh Huntington (American, 1860-1927)
Haystacks at Sunset, oil on canvas, sgn, 16x20", WG 4/23/88 UE **425**
Sailboat on Calm Water, oil on canvas, sgn, 16x23", WG 9/16/88 .... **400**
HOWARD, John Langley (American, 1902-)
Rolling Fields, watercolor on paper, sgn/dtd 1931, unfr, 14x20", B/B 10/6/88 .... **990**
HOWARD, Marion (American, 1883-)
Birch Grove, Autumn; oil on canvas, sgn/dtd 1949, 24x23", RWS 5/19/88 .... **800**
HOWARD, Newton (American, 20th C)
Molai (contemporary), watercolor, sgn/dtd 1942, 16x10", MG 5/28/88 .... **170**
HOWE, W.H. (American, 1846-)
Pair: Horse & Cart in a Landscape; Field Bordered by Trees; oil on panel, sgn, 12x16", SLK 5/9/88 .... **850**
Pastoral Landscape, watercolor, sgn/dtd 79, 13x17", LH 5/15/88 .... **650**
HOWEL, Arthur A. (American, 20th C)
Pamet River, Truro, Massachusetts; oil on board, sgn, 8x10", RAB 11/25/88 UE **100**
HOWELL, Felicie Waldo (American, 1897-)
Across the Moors, Washington St, Marblehead; oil on canvas, sgn/dtd 1923, 16x20", RWS 11/3/88 OE **2,600**
Approaching Showers (boats in Gloucester harbor), gouache on tan paper, sgn/dtd 1921, 24x18", RWS 5/12/89 OE **9,500**
Buttercups & Blue Things (still life), oil on canvas, sgn/dtd 1920, 24x20", RWS 5/19/88 .... **1,500**
California Shore Scene, oil on canvasboard, sgn, 12x14", RWS 5/12/89 .... **1,900**
Garden Flowers, oil on canvas, sgn/dtd 1920, 20x24", RWS 3/16/89 .... **2,400**
October (houses on hillside in detailed landscape), oil on canvas, sgn/dtd 1920, 30x40", RWS 5/19/88 .... **19,000**
October (view of East Gloucester from Rocky Neck), oil on canvas, sgn/dtd 1920, 30x40", SBY 5/24/89 .... **27,500**
HOWELL, Frank (American, 20th C)
Memory (imaginary landscape w/figure, written ruminations), watercolor on paper, sgn/dtd 1983, 9x12", RWS 3/31/88 .... **700**
HOWELL, Samuel (19th C)
Portrait of a Man, half-length, holding a stick; oil on canvas, inscr/dtd 1825, 30x25", C-NY 4/8/88 .... **880**
HOWITT, John Newton (American, 1885-1958)
Winter Sleigh Ride, oil on canvas, sgn, 33x47", FAP 12/8/89 UE **500**
HOWLAND, Alfred Cornelius (American, 1838-1909)
Figures on a Country Path, oil on canvas, sgn/dtd 1865, 11x16", B/B 10/9/88 .... **4,950**
HOWLAND, J.D. (19th C)
Forsyth Farm, Ohio; oil on canvas, sgn, 18x27", C-NY 1/20/89 .... **6,050**
HOWORTH, Charles Henry
Pair: New Zealand Landscapes; oil on canvas, sgn, 16x24", C-SK 6/9/88 .... **745**
HOYLAND, John (British, 1934-)
Cathay (abstract), acrylic on canvas, sgn/dtd 7-7-81, 90x100", SBY 2/15/89 OE **9,075**
Pair: Composition VI; Composition VII; acrylic on paper, sgn/dtd 69, 22x30", SBY 10/7/89 .... **4,950**
Pair: Composition X; Composition IV (abstract); acrylic on paper, sgn/dtd 69, 30x22", 22x30", SBY 10/7/89 .... **5,500**
Turn Turn (abstract), acrylic on canvas, sgn/dtd 30-8-83, 100x90", C-NY 5/4/89 .... **6,600**
Untitled (abstract), acrylic on canvas, sgn twice, 1970, 72x66", SBY 2/19/88 .... **4,400**
Untitled (abstract), acrylic on canvas, sgn/dtd 13.2.69, 96x36", C-E 11/17/88 OE **8,250**
Untitled (abstract), acrylic on canvas, sgn/dtd 3.3.70, 40x96", C-E 11/17/88 OE **9,900**
HOYOLL, Philip (German, 1816-)
Very Wise Politicians (girl & cat in an interior), oil on canvas, sgn/inscr, 12x10", SBY 6/8/88 .... **1,760**
HOYOS, Ana Mercedes (Colombian, 1942-)
Bodegon (contemporary still life), oil on canvas, sgn/dtd 85, 47x47", C-NY 11/21/89 OE **18,700**
La Palangana de Zeni (still life of bowl of fruit on crate), oil on canvas, sgn twice/dtd 88, 95x47", C-NY 5/17/89 .... **10,500**
Palenquera, oil on canvas, sgn/dtd 89, unfr, 40x79", B/B 6/15/89 .... **11,000**
Palenquera (clothed native torso w/bowl of fruit), oil on canvas, sgn/dtd 88, 59x59", SBY 5/16/89 OE **24,200**
Palenqueras 4:44 (still life of bowls of fruit w/partial figures), oil on canvas, sgn, 1987, 59x59", SBY 11/21/88 OE **16,400**
4:44 PM (still life), oil on canvas, sgn, ca 1986, 47x47", SBY 5/17/88 OE **8,250**
HOYT, Edith (American, 1894-)
Demolition of the Charity Hospital, Paris; oil on canvas, 26x39", SBY 4/14/89 UE **2,750**
HUA, Pu (Chinese, 1834-1911)
Bamboo & Rock (hanging scroll), ink on paper, sgn/dtd 1872, 53x26", SBY 5/31/89 .... **1,980**
Prunus, ink on paper, sgn, 58x16", SBY 5/31/89 .... **1,320**
HUAI, Guan (Chinese, 18th C)
Landscape (hand scroll), ink/color on paper, sgn, 6x53", SBY 5/31/89 .... **4,400**
HUBACEK, William (American, 1866-1958)
Potting Bench (still life of flowers in pots), oil on canvas, sgn, 28x22", C-NY 12/2/88 OE **14,300**
HUBBARD, Lydia M.B. (American, 1849-1911)
Still Life of Daisies & Black-Eyed Susans, oil on canvas, sgn/dtd July 98, 28x23", SBY 4/14/89 .... **1,980**
HUBBARD, Richard William (American, 1816-1888)
Bucolic Pastures, oil on canvas, sgn/dtd 1879, 13x12", RWS 11/10/89 .... **3,000**
On the Battenkill, Manchester, Vermont; oil on canvas, sgn/dtd 74, 12x20", WD 10/5/88 UE **3,500**
River Scene with Figures & Boat, oil on canvas, sgn, 14x13", SBY 1/24/89 OE **3,850**

UBBARD, Sigismund Ivanowski
Pair: Shelter Island Heights; North Folk, Long Island; oil on board, 12x10", 9x10", C-E 10/18/89 OE 4,180
UBBELL, Charles H. (American, 20th C)
Dog Fight-US Navy; oil on canvas, sgn, 28x39", NA 11/5/88 650
UBBELL, Henry Salem (American, 1870-1949)
Cradle Song, oil on canvas, sgn, 24x17", B/B 6/15/89 OE 6,600
UBER, E. (Dutch, 19th C)
Harvest Scene, oil on canvas, sgn, unfr, 20x26", DM 5/19/89 OE 1,300
UBER, Helene G. (American, 20th C)
Old House, oil on board, sgn, 12x16", FAP 12/8/89 UE 125
UBER, Leon Charles (French, 1858-1928)
Four Playful Kittens in an Interior, oil on canvas, sgn, 19x15", SBY 7/12/89 4,950
Gift of Kittens (kittens in a basket w/flowers), oil on canvas, sgn, 19x24", C-NY 5/24/89 14,300
Kittens Frolicing by a Brass Bucket, oil on canvas, sgn/dtd 1914, 32x26", C-NY 2/23/89 17,600
Playful Kittens, oil on canvas, sgn, 15x22", B/B 3/22/89 4,400
UBERLIN, C. (29th C)
Good Book Before Bed, oil, sgn/dtd 1857, 13x16", WD 1/11/89 UE 300
UBERT, Laurent
Study for a Decorative Frieze with Demons, red/black chalk, 12x18", SBY 1/13/89 792
UBLIN, Emile (French, 1830-)
Looking Glass, oil on canvas, sgn/dtd 1868, 29x24", SBY 6/8/88 3,850
UBNER, Carl Wilhelm (German, 1814-1879)
Family Gathering, oil on panel, sgn/dtd 1874, 12x15", C-E 2/23/88 2,200
Fond Remembrances, oil on canvas, sgn/dtd 1870, 36x31", SBY 2/22/89 4,950
UDON, Normand (Canadian, 1929-)
Bagotteville, Quebec; oil on board, sgn/dtd 1948, 14x18", FB 10/17/88 450
UDSON, Charles Bradford (American, 1865-)
Untitled, mountain sunrise; oil on canvas, sgn, 21x36", SLK 4/7/89 500
UDSON, Charles William (American, 1871-1943)
Primeval Pines (forest landscape), oil on canvas, sgn, 20x40", B/B 10/9/88 1,650
UDSON, Grace Carpenter (American, 1865-1937)
Charmer of the Flowers (portrait), no media given, sgn/dtd 16/#d 456, 20x16", C-NY 2/3/88 8,800
Culin: Indian Child with Apple (portrait); oil on canvas, sgn/dtd 16/#d 471, 20x15", C-NY 2/3/88 17,600
Indian Girl in a Mendocino Landscape, oil on board, sgn, 10x8", SBY 10/6/88 4,125
Mendocino Landscape, oil on board, sgn, 10x8", B/B 10/6/88 2,750
Rain Mother: The Passing of Makila Madtha; oil on canvas, sgn/dtd 16/#d 484, 24x18", C-NY 2/3/88 22,000
Shai: War Eagle (Indian girl & boy gazing upwards); oil on canvas, sgn/dtd 16/#d 478, 27x20", C-NY 2/3/88 28,600
UDSON, Kenneth (American, 1904-1988)
Complex, acrylic on masonite, sgn, 1973, 48x36", SLK 2/11/89 350
UDSON, Thomas (British, 1701-1779)
Portrait of a Gentleman, in a brown jacket, & white waistcoat with gold trim; oil on canvas, 49x39", C-NY 10/20/88 OE 20,900
UDSON, Thomas (British, 1844-1920)
Rough Pastures, oil on panel, sgn, 11x15", B/B 6/9/88 2,200
UDSON, Thomas; att (British, 1701-1779)
Portrait of a Woman in a White Satin Dress, oil on canvas, 50x40", B/B 3/17/88 2,475
UDSON, Thomas; circle of (British, 1701-1779)
Portrait of Lady Colomb, seated half-length, in a beige dress; oil on canvas, 37x29", C-NY 4/6/89 OE 4,180
UDSON, Thomas; follower of (British, 1701-1779)
Portrait of a Lady Wearing a White Dress, oil on canvas, oval, 29x23", SBY 4/7/88 1,650
UDSON, William Jr. (American, 1787-)
Portrait of a Mr Todd of Newburyport, Massachusetts, half-length; oil on canvas, sgn/dtd 1850, 30x25", RWS 8/20/88 700
dson River School (19th C)
Hudson River View, oil on canvas, 24x32", C-NY 10/1/88 3,850
Mountain Lake with Sailboats, oil on canvas, 8x14", WG 4/23/88 UE 500
Summer View of River & Mountains, oil on canvas, 22x36", RAB 5/23/89 800
Summer View of the River, oil on canvas, 18x24", RAB 5/17/88 OE 1,300
UERTAS, Segundo (American)
Cactus (contemporary), oil on canvas, sgn, 20x25", WG 10/28/88 375
UET, Christophe (fl 1735-died 1759)
Pair: Hounds Hunting Fowl in a Landscape; oil on canvas, 39x58", SBY 6/2/89 77,000
UET, Jean Baptiste (French, 1745-1811)
Pair: Landscape with Shepherd & His Flock; River Landscape with a Herdsman Fishing; bodycolor, sgn, 7x11", C-NY 1/11/89 23,100
Pair: Shepherdess & Herdsman w/Animals by Cottage; Hawking Party by a Ruin; oil on panel, sgn, 1763, 28x22", C-M 6/16/89 29,339
Rustic Landscape with Peasants & Livestock at a Stream, oil on canvas, sgn/dtd 1786, oval, 23x19", SBY 4/7/89 34,100
Shepherd & Shepherdess with Their Flock in a Landscape, oil on canvas, sgn/dtd 1786, oval, 23x19", C-NY 4/8/88 19,800
UET, Jean Baptiste; att (French, 1745-1811)
Two Seated Figures, red chalk, 9x11", LH 12/4/88 400
UET, Jean Baptiste; circle of (French, 1745-1811)
Figures in an Italianate Landscape with an Arched Bridge Over Small Falls, oil on canvas laid down, 18x53", SBY 10/13/89 6,600
Shepherd & Shepherdess with Flowers Seated by a Fountain, oil on canvas, unfr, 32x29", C-NY 10/20/88 OE 17,600
Shepherdess with Her Children Resting in a Landscape, pen/brown ink/brown wash, inscr, 7x10", C-NY 1/11/89 770

Sleeping Shepherdess & a Young Man Releasing a Bird From a Cage, oil on canvas, 23x50", C-NY 10/12/89 4,400
Woman Making an Offering to Venus, Accompanied by Cupid & a Putto, in a Landscape; oil on canvas, 36x27", C-NY 10/12/89 4,400

HUET, Jean Baptiste; follower of (French, 1745-1811)
Girl in a Straw Hat, pastel on paper, 16x12", SBY 12/9/88 OE 660
Pastoral Landscape with Shepherd & Maiden, oil on canvas, 35x30", SBY 10/13/89 4,400

HUET, Jean Baptiste; school of (French, 1745-1811)
Allegory of Spring, oil on canvas, 53x39", C-E 4/7/88 1,100

HUET, Jean Baptiste; style of (French, 1745-1811)
Lovers Idyll, oil on canvas, 14x24", B/B 1/11/89 1,045

HUGENTOBLER, E.J. (American, 20th C)
Street Scene, Bergerac, France; oil on board, sgn/dtd 1955, 12x16", B/B 8/10/88 440

HUGGINS, William (British, 1820-1884)
In the Stable, oil on canvas, sgn/dtd 1866, 23x26", WD 5/5/88 4,200

HUGGINS, William John (British, 1781-1845)
British Sailing Vessel, oil on canvas, sgn, 16x22", SBY 6/8/88 3,300

HUGH, W. (British, 19th C)
Still Life of Branches of Fruit on a Mossy Bank, oil on canvas, sgn/dtd 1875, 30x25", SBY 7/12/89 3,300

HUGHES, Edwin (British, 19th C)
Tired Out (portrait of an armorer), oil on canvas, sgn/dtd 1875, 16x12", RWS 5/12/89 UE 700

HUGHES, Edwin; att (British, 19th C)
Gentleman Reading, oil on canvas, sgn, 10x7", C-E 6/28/88 UE 330

HUGHES, John Joseph (British, 19th C)
Ducks in a Pond by Cottages, oil on canvas, sgn, 18x30", C-E 11/8/88 1,430

HUGHES, Talbot (British, 1869-1942)
Croquet Player (elegant lady), colored pencil on paper, sgn/dtd 1905, 14x10", C-NY 5/24/89 1,870
Game of Chance, oil on panel, sgn/dtd 1891, 20x24", C-NY 10/25/89 OE 18,700
The Retrieved (man handing lady her hat in a landscape), oil on canvas, sgn, 36x28", DM 5/13/88 6,500

HUGHES, William (British, 1842-1901)
Still Life with Dead Game & Fruit, oil on canvas, sgn/dtd 1872, 28x36", C-NY 2/25/88 5,280

HUGHES-STANTON, Herbert (British, 1870-1937)
Brunden, Near Dolgelly, North Wales; oil on canvas, sgn, 18x26", WAD 6/6/88 2,200

HUGNUT, Georges
Decalcomanie, black gouache on paper, inscr, 13x10", C-NY 10/6/88 2,420

HUGO, Jean (French, 1894-)
La Nouvelle (villagers waiting for the bull to arrive), tempera on canvas, sgn, 1930, 24x20", C-NY 2/18/88 13,200

HUGUET, Victor Pierre (French, 1835-1902)
Arab Caravan Crossing a Bridge, oil on canvas, sgn, 21x26", SBY 10/24/89 9,350

HUI, Wang (Chinese, 1632-1717)
Landscape After Dong Yuan & Juran (hanging scroll), ink on silk, sgn/dtd 1701, 25x9", SBY 5/31/89 UE 5,500

HULDAH, Cherry Jeffe (American, 20th C)
Ballerina on Stage, oil on canvas, sgn/dtd 1954, 26x21", WL 5/20/88 1,500
Park Scene (mother holding a poodle, her young daughter by her side), oil on canvas, sgn, 23x31", DM 5/13/88 1,600

HULINGS, Clark (American, 1922-)
Bread Wagon, Belmonte, Spain; oil on masonite, sgn/dtd 1968, 22x26", SBY 9/23/88 OE 31,900
Mule with Plaid Blanket, oil on canvas, sgn/copyrighted/dtd 1976, 24x36", SBY 9/23/88 OE 36,300

HULK, Abraham Jr. (British, 1851-1922)
Figure Before a Village in a Landscape, oil on canvas, sgn, 16x24", PHL 10/28/88 600
Oak-Lined Path, oil on canvas, sgn, 40x30", SBY 6/8/88 UE 3,300

HULK, Abraham Sr. (Dutch, 1813-1897)
Country Lane Near Surrey, oil on canvas, sgn, 28x36", C-E 2/21/89 2,420
Estuary with Boats, oil on panel, sgn, 7x10", FB 10/17/88 OE 4,200
Evening on a Dutch Coast, oil on canvas, sgn, 12x19", WD 3/23/88 5,000
Pair: Fishing Boats on Turbulent Seas; oil on canvas, 1 sgn, 19x24", SBY 7/12/89 6,050

HULK, Johannes Frederick (Dutch, 1829-1911)
Harbor Inlet with Barques & Figures, oil on panel, sgn, 11x8", RWS 5/12/89 1,900

HULK, John Frederick (Dutch, 1855-1913)
Dutch Canal Scene, oil on panel, sgn twice, 12x16", SBY 12/9/88 2,310

HULK, William F. (British, 19th C)
Three Running Setters, oil on canvas, sgn, 25x34", B/B 3/22/89 3,300

HULL, John
Site of the Temple (figures in landscape), acrylic on canvas, sgn/dtd 84, 36x48", C-E 5/9/89 1,100

HULME, Frederick William (British, 1816-1884)
Chalfont Street, Peters-Bucks; oil on canvas, sgn, 24x36", C-E 10/26/89 3,850
Evening (figures & dog on a rural road), oil on canvas, sgn, 15x25", B/B 3/22/89 2,200
Farm Scene, oil on canvas, sgn/dtd 1881, 24x20", FB 5/28/89 5,600
Road Home, oil on canvas, sgn/dtd 1881, 24x20", C-NY 5/25/88 3,300

HULTBERG, John (American, 1922-)
Land Maze, gouache/watercolor on paper, sgn, 22x30", SBY 6/24/88 OE 660
On a Stage (abstract), gouache/watercolor/chalks on paper, sgn/inscr/dtd 1957, 22x30", C-E 5/13/88 715
Underground, gouache/black crayon/ink/wash on paper, sgn, 27x41", SBY 2/14/89 8,254
Untitled, acrylic/gouache/black wax crayon on paper, sgn/dtd 1961, 20x25", C-NY 2/13/89 1,045

Untitled (abstract), oil on canvas, sgn, 30x36", C-E 11/17/88 ... **880**
UMANN, O. Victor (American, 20th C)
October Evening, Worcester, Massachusetts, 1934; oil on board, sgn/titled, 10x14", RAB 8/8/89 ... **450**
UMBOURG, Adolf (Austrian, 1847-)
Monks in a Monastery Interior, oil on panel, sgn, 15x12", C-E 2/21/89 UE ... **1,540**
Reading the Paper, oil on canvas, 16x13", C-E 2/23/88 ... **1,760**
UMPHREY, Ralph (American, 1932-)
Orange, acrylic on canvas, sgn/initialed/dtd 1964, unfr, 66x61", C-E 11/17/88 ... **1,540**
Over Green, acrylic on canvas, sgn/dtd 1970/titled, unfr, 61" dia, C-E 5/9/89 ... **660**
UNAEUS, Andreas Herman (Danish, 19th C)
Hilly Landscape, oil on canvas, inscr by grandson, 20x25", C-E 2/21/89 UE ... **1,100**
UNDERTWASSER, Friedensreich (Austrian, 1929-)
Die Sonne von Calabrien (abstract), egg/oil/watercolor/polyvinyl/hemp on paper, sgn/dtd 1968/#d 677, 32x20", SBY 6/30/88 ... **72,000**
Le Beau Flou Spiraloid aux Fenetres dans la Fente, mixed media on paper mounted on linen, sgn, 1957, 19x22", SBY 6/30/88 ... **44,000**
ungarian School (19th C)
Tyrolean Peasant by a Winding River, oil on canvas, indistinctly sgn/dtd 1901, 28x24", C-E 2/23/88 ... **990**
UNLEY, Katherine Jones (American, 1883-1964)
View of the Grand Canyon, oil on canvas, sgn, 16x20", B/B 10/6/88 ... **660**
UNN, Tom (British, 19th C)
Woman in the Woods, watercolor on paper, sgn, 11x15", B/B 4/20/88 ... **413**
UNT, Bryan (American, 1947-)
Black Falls XXIII (abstract), graphite/linseed oil on paper, sgn/dtd 79, 82x21", SBY 10/8/88 ... **14,300**
Crux (abstract), black oil stick/linseed oil/brown chalk/graphite on paper, sgn/dtd 83 & 1.4.83, 30x23", C-NY 5/4/89 ... **6,600**
Pair: Reclining Figure (Night); Reclining Figure (Day); mixed media, sgn/dtd 6.82, 12x15", C-NY 5/4/89 ... **6,600**
Set of 3: Trio; crayon/linseed oil/graphite on paper, sgn/dtd 7.7.83, 30x23", C-NY 2/14/89 ... **17,600**
Twin Falls II, graphite/linseed oil on paper, sgn/dtd 78, 30x23", SBY 11/9/89 ... **6,600**
Untitled (abstract), black oil stick/linseed oil/chalk/graphite on paper, sgn/dtd 1.1.83, 30x23", C-NY 5/4/89 ... **6,600**
Untitled (abstract), oil stick/linseed oil/pencil on paper, dtd May 10 1979 NYC, 30x23", SBY 2/19/88 ... **6,325**
UNT, Charles (British, 1803-1877)
Country Fair (many people), oil on canvas, sgn/dtd 1854, 18x24", WD 11/16/88 OE ... **13,500**
Reading Lesson (gathering of children & tutor), oil on canvas, sgn, 17x22", B/B 3/22/89 ... **4,675**
UNT, Charles Day (American, 1840-1914)
Heart of the Adirondacks, oil on canvas, sgn/dtd 1907, unfr, 36x52", C-E 6/1/88 ... **1,540**
Paddy's Courtship, oil on canvas, sgn/dtd 96, 30x20", WAD 6/6/88 ... **7,500**
Pond at Sunset, oil on canvas, sgn, 22x36", B/B 8/10/88 ... **660**
UNT, Charles; after
Children's Games, oil on canvas, bears signature, 10x14", C-E 7/26/88 ... **660**
UNT, Edgar (British, 1876-1953)
Calves & Poultry in a Barnyard, oil on board, sgn, 12x16", C-NY 2/25/88 OE ... **10,450**
Pair: Barnyard Fowl; oil on canvas, sgn/dtd 1907, 12x10", SBY 6/9/89 ... **26,400**
Pigeons, Guinea Pigs, & Lop-Eared Rabbit by a Hutch; oil on canvas, 12x16", C-NY 2/23/89 OE ... **24,200**
UNT, Edward Aubrey (British, 1855-1922)
Boating on the River, oil on canvas, sgn/dtd 87, 32x48", SBY 7/12/89 ... **4,400**
New Pasha, oil on canvas, sgn/dtd 1901, 46x67", C-E 10/25/88 ... **5,280**
Pair: Desert Caravan; Camel by a Fountain; watercolor on paper, sgn, 10x14", 15x10", C-E 10/25/88 UE ... **330**
Sails on High Seas, oil on canvas, sgn, 41x51", C-E 10/25/88 OE ... **4,400**
Venetian Fishing Boats, oil on canvas, sgn, 15x27", SBY 6/8/88 ... **1,650**
View of Venice, watercolor on paper, sgn, 10x14", C-E 10/25/88 UE ... **330**
UNT, Esther Anna (American, 1875-1951)
Oriental Girl with Incense, watercolor on paper, sgn, 12x9", B/B 10/6/88 ... **1,760**
UNT, Lynn Bogue (American, 1878-1960)
Ducks on Wing, oil on board, sgn, 14x10", B/B 8/10/88 ... **1,320**
Rainbow Trout (jumping trout diving into blue-green stream), oil on board, sgn, 9x7", RWS 3/31/88 ... **1,800**
UNT, Richard
Untitled #5, drawing, 42x30", LH 5/15/88 UE ... **100**
UNT, Thomas (American, 1882-1938)
Unloading at the Docks, oil on canvas, sgn, 24x30", NA 11/5/88 ... **650**
UNT, Walter (British, 1861-1941)
Ponies, a Calf, & Poultry in a Farmyard; oil on canvas, sgn/dtd 1925, 20x30", C-NY 5/24/89 ... **14,300**
UNT, William Henry; att (British, 1827-1910)
Beached Fishing Boats, pencil, 3x4", NA 2/6/88 ... **110**
UNT, William Holman
Portrait of Thomas Bull, an Innkeeper, in the Isle of Wight; oil on canvas, sgn, 21x17", C-NY 2/25/88 ... **3,300**
UNT, William Howes (British, 1806-1879)
Still Life of Grapes, watercolor on paper, sgn, 7x10", FAP 11/4/88 ... **625**
UNT, William Morris (American, 1824-1879)
#11 Spring Watertown (landscape), oil on canvas, initialed, 14x25", RWS 5/19/88 OE ... **4,750**
Blackguard Mercury (boy in winged hat), charcoal on paper, sgn/dtd 1873, 11x7", RWS 5/19/88 OE ... **1,100**
Florida (everglade scene), oil on canvas, sgn/dtd 1875, 25x39", C-NY 12/2/88 OE ... **24,200**
Playing Field Hospital (two children in an interior), oil on paper laid down on board, 13x10", C-NY 5/25/89 ... **15,400**

Study for Columbus the Discoverer, ink/wash/white gouache on board, unfr, 10x16", SBY 9/23/88 .... **3,850**

HUNTER, Clementine (American, 1880-)

Baptism, oil on board, sgn, 18x24", MG 5/28/88 .... **600**
Black Mask, oil on canvasboard, monogramed, 16x20", NA 3/26/88 OE **1,200**
Funeral (primitive depiction of procession outside of church), oil on artist board, sgn, 15x25", NA 5/13/89 OE **2,300**
Pecan Harvest, oil on canvasboard, monogramed, unfr, 12x24", NA 3/26/88 .... **425**
Saturday Night (primitive), oil on board, sgn, 16x24", NA 11/5/88 .... **475**
Still Life, Flowers in a Red Jug; oil on canvasboard, monogramed, 20x16", NA 2/6/88 .... **650**
Still Life, Pitcher of Zinneas (primitive); oil on canvas, monogramed, 20x16", NA 2/6/88 OE **900**
Tobacco Planters, oil on canvas, monogramed, unfr, 15x30", NA 3/26/88 .... **450**
Uncle Tom in the Garden (primitive), oil on board, sgn, 16x20", NA 11/5/88 .... **600**
Washday, oil on canvasboard, monogramed, unfr, 12x16", NA 2/6/88 .... **800**
Wedding Day, oil on board, sgn, 18x24", MG 5/28/88 .... **950**

HUNTER, Frances Tipton

Woman in the Window, oil on canvas, sgn, 26x20", C-E 6/1/89 UE **550**

HUNTER, Frederick Leo (American, 1858-1945)

Glory of the Seas, clipper ship in calm seas w/sails set; oil on canvas, sgn/dtd 1927, orig frame, 24x37", RAB 8/1/88 .... **800**
Wooded Landscape & River Scene, oil on canvas, sgn/dtd 1916, 29x27", MAG 9/18/88 .... **1,400**

HUNTER, George Sherwood (British, -1920)

Piazza San Marco on the Grand Canal, oil on canvas, sgn/dtd 87, 12x24", C-E 10/25/88 .... **2,200**
West Groot Fishing Village, oil on canvas, sgn, 7x14", WG 9/16/88 UE **700**

HUNTER, John Young (British, 19th/20th C)

Romance (portrait of reclining woman), oil on canvas, sgn, 60x50", SBY 5/23/89 .... **82,500**
Spanish Dancer, watercolor, sgn, 29x21", C-NY 10/25/89 .... **1,100**

HUNTINGTON, Daniel (American, 1816-1906)

Figures in a Rocky Landscape, oil on canvas, sgn/dtd 1854, 8x11", B/B 12/8/88 .... **1,760**
Fisherman (in a rocky coastal scene), oil on canvas, sgn/dtd 74, unfr, 14x24", C-SK 11/10/88 .... **1,580**
Greek Girl with Lekythos, oil on canvas, sgn/dtd 1849, 30x25", RWS 11/3/88 .... **1,600**
Portrait of a Man Said To Be Nathaniel Platt Bailey, oil on canvas, sgn/dtd 1871, unfr, 34x27", SBY 3/17/88 UE **770**
Portrait Study of Abraham Lincoln, oil on canvas, unfr, 36x29", SBY 6/28/89 UE **1,200**
Rapids (close-up view), oil on canvas, sgn, 17x25", C-E 6/1/89 .... **1,760**

HUNTINGTON, Dwight W.

Camp of Standing Bear, gouache on paper, initialed/dtd 93, 9x12", C-NY 5/25/89 .... **3,080**
Pair: Winter Trail; Spring Landscape; gouache, 1 initialed/dtd 95, 5x5", 11x11", C-NY 5/25/89 UE **1,100**
Vigil (Indian encampment), watercolor/pen/black ink/pencil on paper, initialed/dtd 95, 5x10", C-NY 5/25/89 UE **1,100**

HUNTINGTON (American, 19th/20th C)

Schooner JW Doane (ship), pastel on paper, sgn/indistinctly dtd, 16x22", SBY 3/17/88 UE **495**

HURD, L. Fred (American, 19th C)

Coast, watercolor on paper, sgn, 22x28", WL 5/20/88 .... **1,100**

HURD, Peter (American, 1904-1984)

First Snow, oil on masonite, sgn, 30x36", C-E 6/1/89 .... **5,500**
Landscape with Stream & Mountains, watercolor/gouache/India ink on paper, sgn, 12x16", SBY 6/24/88 .... **2,640**
Pair: San Patricio Dam; Sketch for Summer Eve; watercolor/pen/black ink on paper, 9x10", 9x12", C-NY 3/11/88 .... **2,200**
Sailing in a Cove, charcoal/pencil on paper, sgn/dtd 1949, 7x11", C-E 9/15/88 .... **550**
Still Life of Books & Geraniums, oil on canvas, dtd 1924, 16x20", RWS 5/19/88 UE **350**

HURD, Richard (American, 20th C)

Portrait of Julie Harris (seated, full-length), oil on canvas, sgn/dtd 70, 48x36", RAB 8/9/88 UE **200**

HURLSTON, J. (19th C)

Two Orientals on a Track, oil on metal, sgn/dtd 1867, 11x9", C-SK 5/25/89 .... **1,010**

HURT, Louis B. (British, 1856-1929)

Grazing Cattle, oil on canvas, sgn, unfr, 16x24", B/B 3/22/89 OE **13,200**
Highland Cattle, oil on canvas, sgn, 23x18", B/B 6/9/88 .... **6,600**
Highland Cattle, Sunshine After Rain; oil on canvas, sgn, 23x35", WAD 6/6/88 .... **4,500**
Highland Cattle Grazing, oil on canvas, sgn/dtd 1897, 24x40", B/B 3/22/89 OE **35,750**
Rest by a Rosshire Loch, oil on canvas, sgn/dtd 1888, 51x41", SBY 7/12/89 OE **12,100**

HUS, Zultan

Girl with a Rabbit, oil on panel, sgn, 15x11", C-E 10/25/88 UE **660**

HUSER, A.C.

Peasant on a Country Path in Winter, oil on canvas, sgn/dtd 84, 33x27", C-E 11/8/88 .... **3,300**

HUTCHENS, Frank Townsend (American, 1869-1937)

Landscape, oil on canvas, sgn, 12x18", LH 12/4/88 .... **470**
Winter Scene (woodland scene in the winter w/figure), oil on canvas, sgn, 34x25", DM 5/13/88 UE **1,750**

HUTCHINS, A.; att (American, 20th C)

Spring Morning Landscape, oil on board, sgn, 16x21", RWS 3/16/89 .... **500**

HUTCHINSON, Frederick William (American, 1874-1937)

Old Settlement (path in foreground leads to village scene), oil on canvas, sgn, 12x16", RWS 3/31/88 OE **750**
Women on a Porch, St Urbain; oil on canvas, sgn, 12x16", FB 10/17/88 OE **1,800**

HUTCHINSON, George (American, fl 1930s)

Album: Bengal Cottage Scenery, 1833, Ninety-Five Drawings; pen/ink, overall 11x8", C-SK 5/25/89 .... **1,270**

HUTCHINSON, Robert Gemmell (British, 1855-1936)

At the Races, Glasgow; oil on canvas, sgn, 15x20", SBY 5/23/89 .... **9,350**

Young Sailor (lad sailing boat in tub of water, other children watching), oil on canvas, sgn, 44x30", B/B 3/22/89 OE	8,250
UTTY, Alfred Heber (American, 1877-1954)	
Little Meeting House at Shady (church in landscape), watercolor on paper, sgn, ca 1940s, 16x21", RWS 3/16/89	550
UVE, Jean Jacques (French, 1742-1808)	
Design for a Waterfall in the Garden of Mme Elizabeth, Sister of Louis XVI; pen/ink/wash, sgn, 17x11", SBY 1/13/89	3,300
UYGENS, Leon	
Building a Dock, oil on canvas, sgn, 20x26", C-E 2/23/88 UE	880
UYSMANS, Cornelis (Flemish, 1648-1727)	
Figures in a Landscape, oil on canvas, 23x27", SBY 6/8/88	4,840
UYSMANS, Cornelis; circle of (Flemish, 1648-1727)	
Rocky Landscape with Figures, oil on canvas, 23x34", C-E 6/1/88 OE	5,280
UYSMANS, Jacob (Flemish, 1633-1696)	
Portrait of a Lady, wearing red & white dress & green shawl; oil on canvas laid down on board, 30x25", C-NY 10/20/88	1,870
Portrait of Edward Henry Lee, First Earl of Litchfield & His Wife...As Children; oil on canvas, 74x70", SBY 6/1/89 OE	11,000
YETT, Will J. (American, 1876-)	
Cotswolds, oil on canvas, sgn/dtd 10, 17x23", B/B 9/14/89	990
YLANDER (19th C)	
Dutch Canal at Moonlite, oil on panel, sgn/dtd 1878, 20x32", C-E 2/23/88 OE	2,640
YON, Georges Louis (French, 1855-)	
Cavalry Battle in a French Town, oil on canvas, sgn, 24x16", SBY 6/8/88	1,100
YPPOLITE, Hector (Haitian, 1889-1948)	
Maitresse Elizabethe (portrait), oil on masonite, ca 1945, 31x24", SBY 11/21/88	31,900
Two Priestesses with Vase (primitive), oil on masonite, sgn, ca 1945, 27x20", SBY 11/21/88	27,500
YRE, see De La Hyre	
)NS, Frederick Timpson (South African, 1802-1887)	
Xhosa Woman & Child by a River, oil/watercolor on board, sgn/dtd 1864, 13x12", C-SK 6/9/88	1,766
COVLEFF, Alexandre (French, 1887-)	
Diana the Huntress, oil on canvas, sgn/dtd 1928, unfr, 39x20", C-E 5/9/89 OE	3,520
Femme a Son Travail (portrait), tempera on paper, 30x21", C-E 5/9/89 OE	2,970
Reclining Nude, red chalk w/traces of charcoal on buff paper, sgn/dtd 1935, 36x59", C-E 11/17/88	1,100
CURTO, Francesco (Canadian, 1908-)	
Fishing by the Stream, oil on board, sgn/dtd 1970, 8x10", FB 10/30/89	1,320
L'Hiver aux Eboulements, oil on canvas, sgn/dtd 1975, 16x20", FB 10/17/88	2,600
Le Vieux Quai de Quebec, oil on board, sgn/dtd 1971, 10x12", FB 5/28/89	1,300
Les Eboulements, oil on board, sgn/dtd 1981, 10x12", FB 5/28/89	850
Les Eboulements, oil on canvas, sgn/dtd 1975, 10x12", FB 10/17/88	1,000
Scene de Quebec, oil on canvas, sgn/dtd 1961, 30x20", FB 5/28/89	2,400
Vieille Ferme, Les Emboulements; oil on canvas, sgn/dtd 1975, 20x24", FB 10/30/89	2,200
Village sur la Cote de Beaupre, Quebec; oil on canvas, sgn/dtd 1960, 16x20", FB 10/30/89	1,650
KOVLEV, Alexander Evegen'evich (Russian, 1887-1938)	
Study of Two Male Torsos, red/black pencil, dtd 1905/Chinese blue stamp, about 11x8", C-L 10/8/88 OE	2,420
KULOV, Georgii (Russian, 1884-1928)	
Pair: Costume Design for an Oarsman; Sailor in Signor Formica; watercolor/pen/ink, sgn/dtd 1922, 12x10", C-L 10/8/88	3,720
NELLI, Arcangelo (Brazilian, 1922-)	
Sin Titulo, oil/pencil on canvas, sgn, 1982, 51x39", C-NY 11/21/89	5,500
Untitled (abstract), oil on canvas, sgn/dtd 1980, 39x32", SBY 11/21/88 OE	4,675
NNELLI, Alfonoso (American, 1888-1965)	
Maria & Bill Hart (original design for poster), tempera on board, sgn, ca 1915, 38x28", LH 12/4/88	1,100
BETSON, Julius Caesar (British, 1759-1817)	
Children at Play, oil on panel, indistinctly sgn, 15x12", C-NY 4/8/88 OE	13,200
Cottage with Peasants, oil on canvas, sgn/dtd 1809, 24x31", B/B 6/15/89 UE	1,100
No 56 Cottage in Berkshire, oil on canvas, sgn/inscr, C-E 5/23/88	1,760
BETSON, Julius Caesar; att (British, 1759-1817)	
Stonebreakers in Quarry, oil on artist board, 6x9", C-NY 6/17/89	1,100
:ART, Louis (French, 1888-1950)	
Caught in a Breeze, pastel/charcoal on paper, sgn, 16x13", B/B 9/15/88	935
Dancing Ballerina, watercolor/charcoal on paper, 18x12", DM 10/14/88	850
Girls with Swans, oil on canvas, sgn, ca 1940, 13x16", C-E 6/16/88	5,060
Harlequin & Ballerina, watercolor, sgn, 14x17", LH 5/15/88 OE	1,700
Lady Seated, pastel on paper, sgn, 13x16", DM 10/14/88	550
Lady with Parasol (full-length sketch), watercolor/pen/ink on paper, sgn, 6x4", B/B 9/14/89	825
New York, oil on canvas, sgn, ca 1925, 23x18", SBY 6/16/88	4,950
Portrait of a Young Woman (seated, holding a hat), charcoal heightened w/pastel on paper, sgn, 18x13", RWS 3/31/88 OE	1,200
Reclining Lady, pastel/charcoal on paper, sgn, 17x20", DM 10/14/88	1,200
Reclining Nude, watercolor on paper, 10x17", FAP 4/15/89 UE	468
Seated Lady with Poodle, pastel on paper, sgn, 17x20", DM 10/14/88	1,200
Standing Ballerina, pastel on paper, sgn, 19x12", DM 10/14/88	1,100
Standing Ballerina, watercolor/charcoal on paper, sgn, 18x12", DM 10/14/88	750
Standing Female, pastel on paper, 23x14", DM 10/14/88	550
Windy Day (sketch of woman), charcoal/pastel, sgn, 17x13", FB 10/17/88	1,100

ICART, Louis; att (French, 1888-1950)
Pensive Woman, watercolor, signed, ca 1945, 14x9", lot 448, C-E 9/20/89 UE **352**
ICAZA, Ernesto (Mexican, 1866-1935)
Lazando un Toro (riders roping bull in landscape), oil on canvas laid down on board, ca 1912, 8x12", C-NY 11/21/88 OE **7,700**
IGLER, Gustav (Austrian, 1842-1908)
Balling the Yarn, oil on canvas, sgn/dtd 1874, unfr, 36x29", C-E 2/23/88 OE **5,720**
ILLES, Aladar Edvi (Hungarian, 1870-1911)
Pet Goat (girl with a goat), oil on board, sgn, 10x14", C-E 2/23/88 .... **2,750**
ILSLEY, Frederick Julian (American, 1855-1933)
A Sea Turn (red dingy beached beside rocks & small shacks), oil on canvas, sgn/dtd 1932, 14x14", RWS 3/31/89 .... **225**
ILSTED, Peter Vilhelm (Danish, 1861-1933)
In a Sunlit Garden, oil on board, sgn w/monogram, 11x12", SBY 2/22/89 .... **24,200**
Looking Out the Window, oil on canvas, sgn w/monogram, dtd 1908, 25x24", SBY 2/22/89 .... **63,250**
IMHOF, Joseph A. (American, 1871-1955)
Osceola, the Rising Sun; oil on board, sgn/inscr, 28x22", SBY 6/24/88 UE **660**
IMMENDORF, Jorg (German, 20th C)
Cafe Deutschland Erbe, oil on canvas, sgn/dtd 83, unfr, 59x79", C-NY 5/4/88 .... **24,200**
Cafe Deutschland Horerwunsch, oil on canvas, sgn/dtd 83, unfr, 60x79", C-NY 11/10/89 OE **28,600**
Mige Freunde (abstract), oil on canvas, sgn/dtd 1983, 79x59", SBY 2/15/89 OE **33,000**

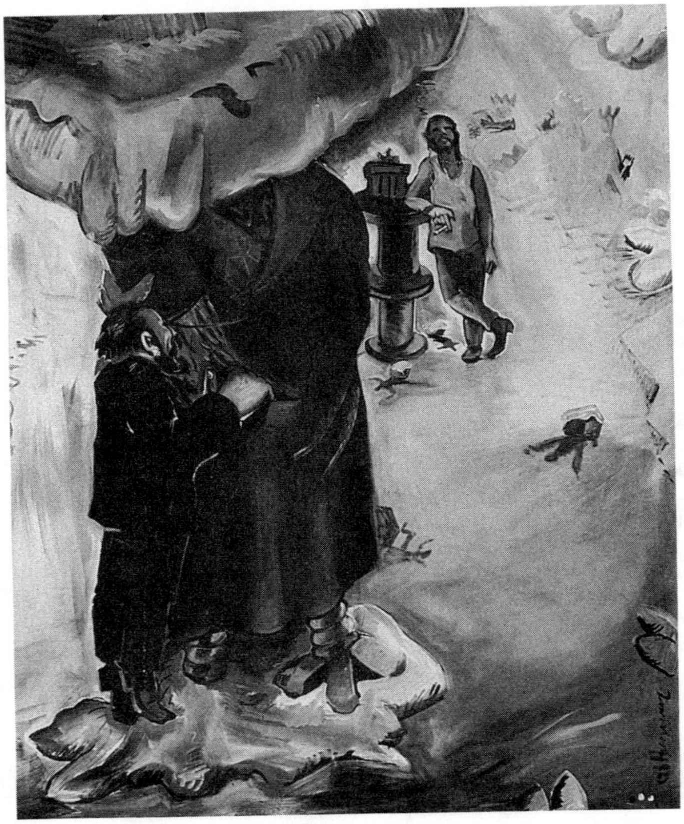

Westralf, oil on canvas, sgn/dtd 1980, 98x79", C-NY 11/7/89 OE, $495,000

3 Partei Tag (abstract), oil on paper laid down on canvas, sgn/inscr/dtd 81, 41x36", SBY 5/3/89 OE **17,600**
IMMERMAN, David (American, 20th C)
Portrait of a Woman, oil on canvas, 9x7", SLK 9/26/88 .... **900**
IMPERIALI, att
Four-Fold Screen: Coriolanus & Daughters of Volumnia; oil on canvas, unfr, 76x24" overall, C-NY 4/6/89 .... **14,300**
IMRE, Greguss (Hungarian, -1910)
Portrait of Francis II Rak Oczi Listening to Czinka Panna, 1735; oil on canvas, sgn, 63x93", LH 3/20/88 UE **3,200**
INDIANA, Robert (American, 1928-)
Diptych: Love; oil on canvas, stamped RI Aspen 1968, unfr, 12x24", C-NY 10/4/89 OE **82,500**
Lillian Russel (full-length portrait), colored graphite rubbing on paper, sgn/dtd 1966, 26x20", C-NY 2/20/88 .... **1,760**
Love, oil on canvas, sgn, 48x48", SBY 5/5/89 OE **104,500**
INDONI, Filippo (Italian, 19th C)
Arab Guard, watercolor, sgn, 20x14", C-NY 5/25/88 .... **1,320**
Dancing in a Wheatfield, watercolor on board, sgn, 21x14", C-E 10/25/88 .... **880**
Faggot Gatherers, oil on canvas, sgn, 26x19", C-E 2/21/89 UE **2,200**
Game of Checkers, watercolor over pencil, sgn, 22x31", C-NY 10/26/88 OE **12,100**
Winning the Derby, watercolor/gouache on paper, sgn/dtd 47, 14x21", C-E 10/25/88 UE **385**
Young Couple, watercolor on paper, sgn, 20x14", SBY 6/8/88 .... **990**

INDUNO, Girolamo (Italian, 1827-1890)
Peasant Family (walking along road), pencil/watercolor on paper, sgn, unfr, 12x9", SBY 10/24/89 OE 16,500

INGALLS, Eileen (American, 20th C)
At Delray Beach, watercolor on paper, sgn, 22x30", WG 4/23/88 200

INGHAM, A. (20th C)
Two Hackneys in Autumnal Landscape, oil on canvas, sgn, 14x24", SLK 2/12/88 260

INGRAM, William Ayerst (British, 1855-1913)
View of New York Harbor, watercolor on paper, sgn, unfr, 10x15", WL 5/20/88 UE 150

INGRES, Jean Auguste Dominique (French, 1780-1867)
La Sainte Vierge, pencil on paper, sgn/dtd 1862/inscr, 10x9", SBY 2/22/89 OE 25,300
Raphael & the Fornarina, oil on canvas laid down on panel, 27x21", SBY 6/1/89 1,430,000
Reclining Odalisque, crayon on paper, 85x89", C-M 6/16/89 OE 52,158

INMAN, John O'Brien (American, 1828-1896)
Nap Time (girl in repose by cottage wall), oil on board, sgn/indistinctly dtd, 12x15", B/B 3/22/89 OE 7,700

INNERST, Mark (20th C)
By a Window, spray paint/graphite on brown paper, initialed, 1981, 26x19", C-NY 5/4/89 OE 10,450

INNESS, George Jr. (American, 1853-1926)
Farmyard with Man & Woman, oil on canvas, sgn, 24x60", C-NY 5/26/88 11,550
Man Walking Down a Path, oil on canvas, sgn, 18x24", B/B 6/9/88 4,125
Pair: Farmyard Scene; Tending the Sheep; oil on canvas, sgn/dtd 1879, unfr, 58x18", C-NY 9/30/88 UE 2,200
Twilight on the River, oil on canvas, sgn, 18x20", MG 10/28/88 2,150

INNESS, George Sr. (American, 1825-1894)
Bringing the Boat Ashore, oil on canvas, sgn, 8x12", B/B 10/9/88 10,450
Coming Storm (landscape), oil on cradled canvasboard, sgn/titled, ca 1878, 8x15", SBY 1/24/89 4,400
Cows Grazing at Sunset, oil on canvas, sgn, 9x14", C-NY 5/26/88 17,600
Cromwell's Bridge (landscape), oil on canvas, sgn/dtd 1875, 20x30", SBY 5/24/89 OE 132,000
Delaware Water Gap (landscape), oil on canvas, monogramed/dtd 1857, 32x52", SBY 5/24/89 935,000
Harvest Scene in the Delaware Valley (landscape), oil on canvas, sgn/dtd 1867, 30x45", SBY 5/24/89 495,000
In the Orchard, Milton; oil on canvas, sgn/dtd 1881, 20x30", C-NY 12/2/88 UE 20,900
In the Woods, oil on board, sgn, ca 1880, 12x18", C-NY 9/28/89 6,600
Near Montclair, New Jersey; oil on paper laid down on canvas, sgn, 19x29", C-NY 9/30/88 5,500
North Conway, New Hampshire (landscape); oil on panel, sgn/indistinctly dtd, ca 1875, 22x28", SBY 5/24/89 16,500
Road to the Village, Milton; oil on panel, sgn/dtd 1880, 22x34", WD 4/13/88 55,000
Seated Monk in a Landscape, oil on board, sgn, 12x18", C-NY 12/2/88 OE 22,000
Spring Landscape (stream & stand of trees w/houses), oil on canvas, sgn/indistinctly dtd, ca 1865, 12x18", C-NY 9/28/89 22,000
Summer Landscape, oil on canvas, sgn/dtd Aug 4 69/inscr Morristown NJ, 6x10", SBY 3/17/88 OE 11,000
Sunburst, oil on canvas, sgn/dtd 1886, 20x30", C-NY 12/2/88 20,900
Sunset at Milton, oil on panel, sgn/dtd 1885, 16x24", C-NY 5/26/88 24,200

INNESS, George Sr.; att (American, 1825-1894)
Autumn Sunset, oil on paper, 7x9", FAP 12/8/89 500
Close of Day, oil on canvas, bears signature, 20x28", B/B 8/10/88 OE 5,225
Moonlit Scene, oil on panel, sgn/dtd 1890, unfr, 16x24", MAG 6/22/88 OE 2,100
On the Connecticut River Near Bellows Falls, Vermont; oil on board, 7x14", RWS 9/8/89 OE 4,100

INNOCENTI, Camilio (Italian, 1871-1961)
Reading Hour (seated lady relaxing in an interior), oil on panel, sgn, 5x8", B/B 6/15/89 2,200

INNOCENTI, Gugliemo (Italian, 19th C)
Charmeuse (man performing w/tame pigeons), oil on board, sgn, 37x29", C-NY 5/24/89 7,700

INSLEY, Albert (American, 1842-1937)
Looking Towards Clarkstown, New York; oil on canvas, sgn, 12x18", SBY 6/24/88 880
Nanuet Fields, oil on canvas, sgn, 12x18", C-E 6/1/89 2,090
North Shore, Staten Island, New York (boats in dock); oil on canvas, sgn/titled, 12x18", RAB 3/27/89 800
Single Tree on William Bennett Hill, oil on canvas, sgn, 12x19", C-E 11/30/88 1,650
Summer Landscape, oil on canvas, sgn, 12x18", SBY 9/23/88 OE 2,750
Tree-Lined Stream in Spring, oil on canvas, initialed, 18x12", B/B 9/15/88 715
Two Landscape Studies: Stone Wall, Wood Fence; 1 oil on canvas, sgn/dtd 1875, 8x11", WL 5/20/88 OE 1,500

INUKAI, Kyohei (American, 1934-)
Down the Path, oil on canvas, sgn/dtd 11, 42x57", C-NY 9/28/89 4,400
Portrait of a Woman, oil on canvas, sgn/dtd 32, 60x48", C-NY 5/26/88 18,700
Yellow House, oil on canvas, sgn, 14x20", C-E 10/18/89 2,750

IRELAND, Edouard A. (German, 1830-1869)
Woman Winding Yarn, oil on panel, 8x10", SBY 6/8/88 UE 990

IRELAND, Tayler (British, fl 1894-1921)
Country Road, watercolor, sgn, 21x13", FB 10/17/88 600
Path Through the Forest, watercolor, sgn, 21x13", FB 10/17/88 550

IROLLI, Vincenzo (Italian, 1860-1942)
Children with Turkeys, oil on canvas, sgn, 38x19", C-NY 5/25/88 OE 88,000
Flirtation (couple in exterior scene), oil on board, sgn, 25x18", C-NY 2/23/89 OE 88,000
Italian Beauty, oil on panel, sgn, 17x11", WAD 6/6/88 6,600
Little Girl on a Terrace, oil on canvas, sgn, 25x28", C-NY 10/25/89 99,000
Summer (portrait of a girl in sunny exterior), oil on panel, sgn, 13x8", SBY 2/22/89 OE 15,400
Young Girl Gathering Flowers in the Sunshine, oil on canvas sgn, 23x25", C-NY 10/25/89 88,000

Young Girl Seated in Garden Observing a Snail, watercolor on cardboard, sgn, 20x16", WG 9/16/88 5,000

IROLLI, Vincenzo; att (Italian, 1860-1942)
Portrait of a Peasant Girl, oil on canvas, bears signature, 25x14", SBY 7/12/89 3,850

IRVINE, Sadie (American, 20th C)
Boy Playing the Violin, graphite on paper, 8x10", MG 5/28/88 UE 375
Boy Sitting on the Table, graphite on paper, 8x10", MG 5/28/88 UE 600
Lady on Washington Avenue Selling Pralines, graphite on paper, 8x10", MG 5/28/88 1,600
Little Girl in a Hat, graphite on paper, 8x10", MG 5/28/88 UE 275

IRVINE, Wilson Henry (American, 1869-1936)
Arrival of Spring, oil on canvas, sgn, 24x27", C-NY 3/11/88 6,820
Artist's Daughter (seated), oil on canvas, sgn, 30x25", SBY 6/28/89 UE 1,650
Artist's House, oil on masonite, sgn, 12x16", C-E 10/18/89 2,860
Blue Landscape, watercolor/gouache on paper laid down on board, sgn, 14x17", C-E 11/30/88 1,100
Brittany Village, oil on canvas, sgn, 18x24", SBY 9/14/89 5,500
Coast, watercolor/gouache on paper, sgn, 14x18", C-E 11/30/88 UE 550
Knock on the Door (lady, half-length in an interior), oil on canvas, sgn, 30x25", C-NY 5/25/89 22,000
Nude Beside a Stream, watercolor/white highlight on paper, sgn, 14x14", B/B 10/9/88 UE 2,200
Sunflowers, oil on canvas, sgn, 25x30", NA 2/6/88 4,250
Wooded River Landscape, oil on canvas, sgn, 25x30", NA 3/26/88 5,600

IRVING, I.
Before the Storm, oil on panel, sgn/dtd 1877, 12x16", NA 10/1/88 650

IRWIN, Robert (20th C)
Apricot (apricot background, one horizontal line at top, two at bottom), acrylic on canvas, 1964, 83x85", C-NY 11/7/89 198,000

IRWIN, William Hyde (American, 1903-)
Marietta, oil on canvas, sgn/dtd 1932, 26x20", B/B 10/6/88 1,210

ISABEY, Louis Gabriel Eugene (French, 1803-1886)
Beacon (figures in a stormy landscape), oil on canvas, initialed, 32x26", B/B 6/15/89 UE 4,400
Cardinal's Reception, oil on canvas, sgn, 21x23", C-NY 10/25/89 8,800
Ghaumiere au Bord d'Une (figure & house in landscape), oil on canvas, 13x10", RWS 8/12/89 9,000
L'Auguille d'Etretat, oil on panel, bears signature, 10x15", SBY 12/9/88 3,300
La Barque de Secours, oil on canvas, sgn, 13x20", SBY 2/22/89 6,050
Squall (ships on stormy seas), oil on canvas, sgn, 16x23", C-NY 5/24/89 10,450
Woman in an Interior, oil on canvas, stamped w/Vente stamp, 10x8", SBY 7/12/89 1,100

ISABEY, Louis Gabriel Eugene; att (French, 1803-1886)
Cardinal's Processing Through the Gates of a City, oil on canvas, sgn, 11x14", C-E 5/22/89 1,650

ISABEY, Louis Gabriel Eugene; manner of (French, 1803-1886)
Fisherfolk by the Sea, oil on canvas, bears signature, 16x24", C-E 4/7/88 550

ISEMBERT, Emile (French, 1846-1921)
La Famille de l'Artiste sur la Plage, Bretagne, vers 1890 (beach scene); oil on canvas, sgn, 22x39", C-NY 5/24/89 16,500

ISENBRANT, Adriaen; circle of (Flemish, 1485-1551)
Madonna & Child, oil on panel, 14x12", C-NY 1/11/89 OE 11,000

ISENBURGER, Eric (American, 1902-)
Backyard, oil on canvas, sgn, 15x18", C-E 6/1/88 935

ISHIDA, S.
Japanese Village (street scene), oil on canvas, sgn, 24x35", C-SK 6/9/88 OE 3,720

ISKOWITZ, Gershon (Canadian, 1921-)
Trio (abstract), oil on canvas, sgn/dtd 65, 60x48", WAD 11/30/89 UE 6,500

ISOLA, Giancarlo (Italian, 1927-)
Abstract Window Scene, oil on canvas, sgn/dtd 67, 39x27", LH 9/10/89 OE 4,200
Roccia dei Gabbiani (abstract), acrylic on canvas, sgn/dtd 68, 47x36", RWS 5/12/89 750
Sailboats in Harbor, oil on canvas, sgn, 27x39", LH 9/10/89 UE 300

ISRAEL, Daniel (Austrian, 1859-1901)
Oriental Beauty (portrait), oil on panel, sgn/inscr, unfr, 6x5", SBY 12/9/88 880
Pair: Young Peasant Girl; Young Arab Boy; oil on board, sgn, oval, 7x7", C-E 10/26/89 1,100

ISRAEL, Marvin (American, 1924-)
Untitled (contemporary composition), acrylic/colored chalk on paper, 1968, 42x30", C-E 11/14/89 UE 440

ISRAELS, Isaac (Dutch, 1865-1934)
Nieuwe Kerkte Amsterdam, oil on canvas, sgn, 38x31", C-NY 5/25/88 8,250
Oosterpark (father & three daughters on bench), watercolor on paper, sgn, ca 1890-94, 13x19", SBY 10/24/89 OE 29,700

ISRAELS, Josef (Dutch, 1824-1911)
Children Playing at the Beach, oil on panel, sgn, 9x13", C-E 2/21/89 OE 10,450
Family Eating, Dutch Interior; oil on canvas, sgn, 32x38", SBY 5/30/89 OE 52,800
Frugal Meal (family seated at table, cat watching), oil on canvas, 32x38", WD 11/16/88 OE 18,000
Grief, oil on canvas, indistinctly sgn/dtd, 14x18", SBY 12/9/88 OE 2,200
Mother & Child, oil on canvas, sgn, 24x19", SBY 5/23/89 OE 12,100
Mother & Daughter by the Hearth, oil on canvas, sgn, 14x10", RWS 5/12/89 1,100
Op Weg Naar Huis (peasant returning from the fields), oil on panel, sgn, 8x13", RWS 5/12/89 2,000
Peeling Potatoes, oil on canvas, sgn, 19x15", WAD 6/6/88 12,500
Washerwoman, oil on canvas, sgn, 11x14", C-E 2/23/88 3,080
Woman Warming Her Hands by a Fire, watercolor on paper, indistinctly sgn, 11x7", B/B 9/15/88 1,870

ISRAELS, Josef; att (Dutch, 1824-1911)

Portrait of a Boy, oil on cradled panel, 21x18", LH 9/10/89 650

ISSUPOFF, Alessio (Russian, 1889-1957)

Boats Docked in the Bay of Naples with Vesuvius Erupting, oil on board, sgn, 10x13", B/B 5/17/89 OE 1,100
The Race, oil on panel, sgn, 12x16", B/B 12/8/88 OE 2,750

ISTRATI, Alexander (French, 1915-)

Composition in Green & Blue, oil on canvas, sgn/dtd twice, 1957, 31x16", C-E 5/13/88 OE 1,045

Italian School (15th C)

Adoration of the Child, oil on panel, 25x17", C-NY 1/15/88 OE 28,600

Italian School (16th C)

Circumcision, oil on panel, unfr, 22x16", SBY 12/9/88 990
Design for a Fountain, pen/brown ink/wash over traces of black chalk, 15x10", SBY 1/13/89 UE 165
Design for a Monumental Frame, pen/black ink/gray wash over black chalk, 20x14", SBY 1/13/89 275
Double-Sided: Design for an Elaborate Window Frame; pen/ink/wash over traces of black chalk, 11x8", SBY 1/13/89 660
Portrait of a Scholar Holding a Book, oil on canvas, 30x23", C-E 6/1/88 935
Study of a Nude Seen From Behind, black chalk/pen/brown ink/wash on paper, 11x6", C-NY 6/17/89 OE 660
Three Designs for Ornamental Frames, pen/brown ink/wash over black chalk, 8x5", 6x9", 4x7", SBY 1/13/89 660
Tobias & the Angel, oil on panel, ca 1500, 19x14", C-E 4/7/88 495

Italian School (17th C)

Angels Appearing Before the Infant Christ in the Manger, oil on canvas, unfr, 18x25", C-E 4/7/88 OE 3,080
Assumption of the Virgin, oil on canvas, unfr, 37x29", C-NY 4/8/88 UE 550
Biblical Scene, oil on canvas, 22x19", SLK 5/12/88 950
Christ & Woman of Samaria, oil on canvas, 42x52", C-NY 4/6/89 UE 1,100
Christ on the Road to Emmaus, oil on panel, 11x26", C-E 4/7/88 242
Clemency of Titus, black & brown wash on paper, unfr, 6x12", WD 1/25/89 1,400
Design for an Altar, pen/brown ink/wash over traces of black chalk, 7x6", SBY 1/13/89 440
Design for an Elaborate Window Frame, pen/brown ink/wash over black chalk, 8x4", SBY 1/13/89 330
Landscape with a Ruined Farmhouse & Figures, oil on canvas, 8x12", C-E 6/1/88 OE 1,210
Martydom of a Saint, black chalk/brown wash on blue paper, 8x9", C-NY 6/17/89 440
Pair: Still Life of Flowers in a Vase with Sculpted Grotesques...; oil on canvas, 30x24", C-NY 1/11/89 OE 143,000
Reclining Muse, oil on canvas, 29x28", C-E 4/7/88 935
Sacrifice of Isaac, oil on canvas, unstretched, 39x54", C-E 6/1/88 UE 850
Sacrifice of Isaac, oil on canvas, 53x35", C-E 4/7/88 880
Set of 8: Figures in Landscapes Representing Letters of the Alphabet; pen/brown ink, ea 4x4", SBY 7/12/89 OE 3,190
St Francis Kneeling in Prayer, red/white chalk on brown washed paper, 15x11", SBY 1/13/89 1,540
St John, oil on canvas laid down on panel, 13x10", SBY 7/12/89 1,870
St John the Baptist in the Wilderness, oil on copper, oval, 6x5", SBY 12/9/88 880
St Paul, oil on canvas, 25x15", C-E 1/12/88 UE 440
St Peter with Rooster in Landscape, oil on copper, 9x6", SBY 7/12/89 2,090
Study for a Catafalque, pen/ink/wash over traces of black chalk, ca 1600, 30x18", SBY 1/13/89 OE 2,860

Italian School (18th C)

Archangel Michael Smiting a Demon, oil on canvas laid down, 48x41", B/B 1/11/89 468
At Prayer, oil on canvas, 19x24", LH 5/15/88 325
Cain Being Accused by God, oil on canvas, 29x39", SBY 4/7/89 6,600
Capriccio with Figures in a Vast Colonnade, gouache on paper, 12x16", SBY 1/13/89 2,200
Death of Alexander, oil on canvas, 36x46", C-E 6/1/88 2,200
Extensive Italianate Landscape with Peasants, oil on canvas, 28x38", SBY 7/12/89 OE 5,500
Figures by a River Beside a Villa in a Mountainous Landscape, oil on canvas, 18x28", C-NY 4/6/89 2,860
Flowers in a Basket & Ceramic Pots, no media given, 26x43", WD 1/25/89 OE 16,000
Harbor Scene with Figures, oil on canvas, 21x28", SBY 6/8/88OE 1,045
Holy Family with the Infant Saint John the Baptist, oil on canvas, 30x49", C-E 4/7/88 OE 1,650
Hunter Beside Classical Architecture, oil on canvas, 19x25", LH 10/16/88 850
Italian Port Scene, gouache on paper w/highlights, 4x6", B/B 9/15/88 OE 935
Jesus, Mary, & Joseph; oil on canvas, 21x19", LH 5/15/88 UE 150
Judgement of Paris, black chalk/pen/brown ink/brown wash, ca 1780, 7x10", C-NY 1/12/88 418
Kohlrabi, Leeks, Carrots, Artichokes, & Apples on a Ledge; oil on canvas, 19x38", C-NY 6/2/88 6,820
Landscape with Peasants, brown ink/brown wash over pencil, indistinctly sgn/dtd 1798, 11x17", SBY 7/12/89 275
Male Academy, kneeling, leaning forward on a rock; black chalk/stumping heightened w/white chalk, 18x15", SBY 1/13/89 1,430
Male Academy, reclining; black/white chalk on blue-green paper, 20x16", SBY 1/13/89 2,090
Male Academy, standing, leaning on a pedestal; black chalk heightened w/white chalk, 20x16", SBY 1/13/89 880
Melon & Flowers, oil on canvas, 20x26", WD 1/25/89 OE 5,250
On the Flight into Egypt, oil on canvas, 11x14", B/B 1/11/89 OE 1,760
Pair: Carnival Revellers in Masks; oil on canvas, unfr, 23x17", C-E 4/7/88 OE 3,740
Pair: Floral Still Lifes; oil on canvas laid down on board, 4x7", SBY 12/9/88 OE 1,870
Pair: Rustic Landscapes; oil on canvas, 105x40", SBY 7/12/89 OE 11,000
Pair: Still Life of Birds; Still Life of Fruit; oil on canvas, 18x23", SBY 7/12/89 2,750
Pair: Still Life of Flowers; oil on canvas, 28x21", C-E 1/12/88 OE 1,760
Pastoral Landscape with Waterfall, Ruins, & Shephard with Goats; oil on panel, 14x28", SBY 7/12/89 1,980
Portrait of a Gentleman, seated, half-length, wearing dark coat, playing guitar; oil on canvas, 36x28", C-M 12/3/88 2,230
Portrait of an Artist, oil on canvas, 29x23", WD 10/19/88 4,500
Portrait of Princess Catarina Pilo, oil on canvas, inscr/dtd 1713, 30x25", SBY 12/9/88 3,300

River Crossing (figures in an extensive landscape), oil on canvas, 19x28", B/B 10/9/88 ... 2,090
Riverscape with Boats & Figures, oil on canvas, 16x25", SBY 6/8/88 OE ... 4,070
Shepherd & Shepherdess Resting in a Mountainous River Landscape, oil on canvas, unstretched, 21x29", C-E 4/7/88 ... 4,840
Still Life of Flowers, oil on canvas, 11x31", LH 5/15/88 UE 150 ... 642
Still Life of Peonies, Poppies, Tulips, & Other Flowers in a Vase; oil on canvas, 30x25", C-E 4/7/88 ... 1,320
Still Life of Spoonbill, Woodcock, & Game Birds; oil on canvas, 38x28", SBY 6/3/88 ... 18,700
View of the Grand Canal, oil on canvas laid down on masonite, SBY 7/12/89 OE ... 2,475

Italian School (19th C)
Antiquarian, oil on canvas, 29x22", WD 3/23/88 ... 4,250
Arch of Constantine, watercolor, 26x33", FAP 4/15/89 ... 770
Biblical Subject, oil on canvas, 30" dia, SLK 2/12/88 ... 600
Brig Duxbury Otis Baker Mate Bound Out (In) to the Harbor of Palermo, watercolor on paper, 17x24", RAB 8/1/88 ... 6,000
Busy Port Scene (buildings in background, choppy seas), oil on wood panel, 11x24", RAB 8/1/88 OE ... 1,400
Conversation, oil on canvas, 15x20", C-E 6/28/88 ... 462
Fishing in the Bay of Naples at Sunset, gouache, 17x25", PHL 10/28/88 OE ... 1,200
Floral Still Life, oil on canvas, 36x32", SBY 7/12/89 ... 1,320
Gathering Before the Villa Valmarana, oil on canvas, 24x40", C-E 1/12/88 OE ... 2,090
Geography Lesson, watercolor on paper, indistinctly sgn, 9x12", RWS 6/17/89 ... 500
Head of the Virgin, oil on panel, 17x14", C-E 4/7/88 ... 880
Italian Port Scene, oil on canvas, unfr, 16x21", B/B 5/17/89 UE ... 357
Lesson in the Garden (group w/dog), oil on canvas laid down on board, 16x12", C-E 2/21/89 OE ... 8,250
Letter, oil on canvas, 31x25", C-E 5/23/88 ... 1,650
Opulent Still Life of Flowers in a Basket, oil on canvas, 12x10", C-E 10/25/88 ... 770
Pair: Bacchus & Ariadne; Aurora; gouache on paper, ca 1800, 17x13", 18x13", SBY 1/13/89 ... 3,575
Portrait Head of a Classical Figure, oil on panel, 10x8", SLK 2/12/88 ... 90
Portrait of a Young Man in Armor Holding a Baton, oil on canvas, 37x28", SBY 7/12/89 ... 1,650
Praying Woman, oil on board, 11x11", LH 9/10/89 ... 160
Promenade Along the Canal, a Venetian Scene; oil on board, 13x10", RWS 6/17/89 ... 300
Reading the Paper, oil on canvas, indistinctly sgn, 9x12", C-E 10/25/88 ... 880
Rocky Landscape with a Temple by the Sea, watercolor over pencil, ca 1800, 15x23", SBY 1/13/89 ... 880
Roman Ruins, oil on canvas, sgn/dtd 1888, 13x22", C-E 5/23/88 OE ... 2,640
Ruth & Boaz in a Landscape, oil on canvas laid down on masonite, 41x53", C-E 4/7/88 OE ... 4,180
Shepherds Amidst Roman Ruins, oil on canvas, 15x22", B/B 12/8/88 ... 935
Still Life of Flowers, oil on canvas, ca 1800, 33x51", SBY 6/8/88 OE ... 3,080
Still Life of Fruit & Flowers by an Urn, a Classical Landscape Beyond; bears signature, 30x70", SBY 7/12/89 ... 2,860
View of Camparola, pencil/watercolor on paper, 7x9", C-E 2/16/88 OE ... 66
Village by a Mountainous Lake, oil on canvas laid down on board, unfr, 19x33", C-E 10/25/88 ... 1,650
Virgin Mary with the Christ Child, oil on canvas, 12x10", C-E 1/12/88 OE ... 330

Italian School (20th C)
Bay of Naples, oil on canvas, sgn, 11x16", FAP 5/15/89 ... 275
Design for a Stained Glass Dome with Four Different Views, watercolor, ca 1900, 22x29", lot 39, SBY 7/12/89 ... 1,320
Interior Design with Two Walls & a Ceiling, watercolor, ca 1900, 17x22", lot 40, SBY 7/12/89 ... 1,320
Interior Design with Two Walls & a Ceiling, watercolor, ca 1900, 19x23", lot 41, SBY 7/12/89 ... 1,320
Judas Receiving the Tribute Money, oil on panel, 11x10", SBY 12/9/88 ... 825
Market Scene, watercolor on paper, sgn/dtd indistinctly, 16x20", B/B 5/17/89 ... 247
Pair: By the Garden Fountain; Masquerade Ball; oil on canvas, indistinctly sgn, 14x18", RWS 4/7/89 ... 850

Italo-Flemish School (16th C)
Mars & Venus with Andromeda in the Distance, pen/brown ink/wash, 7x9", SBY 1/13/89 OE ... 2,475

ITAYA, Foussa (Japanese, 1919-)
Deux Coqs avec Deux Chiens (Two Roosters with Two Dogs), oil on canvas, sgn/inscr Paris, 22x18", C-E 11/17/88 ... 660
Femme a la Fenetre, oil on canvas, sgn/dtd 1956, 20x24", C-E 5/9/89 ... 550

IVANOVITCH, Paul (Austrian, 1859-)
Barde Serbe, oil on canvas, sgn/dtd 91, 40x60", SBY 10/24/89 ... 8,800

IVANOWSKI, Sigismund; see De Ivanowski

IVES, Percy (American, 1864-1928)
Portrait of Frederick Buhl, oil on canvas, 27x22", DM 10/14/88 ... 500

IVEY, James (American, 19th/20th C)
Mountain Landscape, watercolor on paper, sgn, 17x25", LH 9/10/89 ... 200

IZQUIERDO, Maria (Mexican, 1906-1955)
Circus, gouache on paper, ca 1940, 16x22", SBY 5/17/88 ... 13,200
Naturaleza Muerta (still life of guitar/camera on chair), oil on canvas, sgn/dtd 31, 24x19", C-NY 5/17/89 OE ... 99,000
Poppies (still life), oil on canvas, sgn/dtd 45, 26x34", SBY 5/16/89 ... 46,750
Retrato del Turista (Retrato de Henri de Chatillon), oil on canvas, indistinctly sgn, 1940, 63x75", C-NY 5/18/88 OE ... 55,000
Tributo a Pablo Neruda, gouache on paper, sgn/dtd 1949, 12x10", C-NY 5/18/88 ... 14,300
Vacas (mountainous landscape w/animals), gouache on paper, sgn/dtd 59, 10x12", C-NY 11/21/89 ... 16,500

J.A. (Austrian, 19th/20th C)
Castle on a Hill, gouache on paper, initialed, 16x17", PHL 10/28/88 ... 600

JACK, Richard (Canadian, 1866-1952)
Ducks in a Pond, oil on canvas, sgn/dtd 1901, 24x20", FB 4/25/88 ... 900
Peonies, oil on board, sgn, 20x24", FB 10/17/88 ... 1,500
Pool, Kennibunk Beach, Maine; oil on board, sgn, 20x24", FB 10/17/88 ... 800

JACKMAN, Theodore (American, 19th/20th C)
- Rosa Ponselle As Carmen, oil on canvas, sgn, 52x47", C-E 11/15/88 ... 770

JACKSON, Alexander Young (Canadian, 1882-1974)
- Abandoned Farm, Combermere, Ontario; oil on board, sgn/dtd October 1960, 11x14", FB 10/30/89 ... 6,600
- Creek at Lake Millette, Quebec; oil on panel, sgn/dtd 1959, 11x14", FB 5/28/89 ... 7,500
- Farm at Clyde River, oil on panel, sgn/dtd March 1960, 11x14", FB 4/25/88 ... 5,000
- Farm at Wilno, Ontario; oil on board, sgn/dtd October 1966, 11x14", WAD 6/12/89 ... 5,000
- La Cloche Hills, Algoma Lake, 1938; oil on panel, sgn, 11x14", WAD 6/12/89 ... 12,000
- Mine Shaft, Cobalt; oil on board, sgn, 9x11", WAD 11/30/89 ... 13,500
- Rocky Shore, oil on board, sgn, 10x13", WAD 6/12/89 ... 8,000

JACKSON, George; att (British, 19th C)
- Young Man with Black Hunter & Bull Mastiff in a Park, a Manor House Beyond; oil on canvas, 23x30", SBY 6/10/88 ... 4,510

JACKSON, Harry (American, 1924-)
- Self-Portrait, oil on canvas, sgn/dtd 55, 12x10", SBY 1/24/89 OE ... 5,500

JACKSON, John (British, 1778-1831)
- Portrait of Sir George Philips, half-length; oil on canvas, 36x28", C-E 4/7/88 ... 1,210

JACKSON, Lee (American, 1909-)
- Paddock, oil on masonite, sgn, 10x20", C-E 11/30/88 ... 660

JACKSON, Martin (American, 1871-)
- Angel Wrestling with Jacob, oil on canvas, sgn, 35x46", FAP 4/15/89 ... 1,045

JACKSON, Stephanie
- Brewster's Blue, colored chalks on paper, sgn/dtd 76, 24x35", C-E 5/13/88 UE ... 132

JACKSON, William Franklin (American, 1850-1936)
- Deer in a Forested Landscape, oil on panel, sgn/dtd 72, 20x14", B/B 9/15/88 ... 440

JACOB, Max (French, 1876-1944)
- Interieur sous le Directoire, gouache on paper, sgn/dtd 32, 17x24", SBY 10/7/89 ... 2,530

JACOBI, Marcus (Swiss, 1891-1969)
- Cottage in a Mountainous Landscape, oil on board, sgn, 16x25", C-E 5/23/88 ... 1,320

JACOBI, Otto Reinhold (Canadian, 1812-1901)
- Dense Foliage, watercolor, sgn/dtd 1889, 8x7", WAD 11/30/89 ... 160
- Falls on the River, oil on canvas, sgn/dtd 1884, 14x20", WAD 11/30/89 ... 1,500
- Forest Glen, watercolor, sgn/dtd 1874, 7x9", FB 5/28/89 ... 400
- Forest Landscape with Cabins & Mountains, watercolor, sgn/dtd 1872, 14x19", FB 5/28/89 ... 1,000
- Lac et Montagne (lake & mountain scene), watercolor, sgn/dtd 1878, 7x11", FB 10/17/88 ... 500
- Morning on the Upper Ottawa, oil on canvas, sgn/dtd 1868, 38x68", WAD 11/30/89 OE ... 27,000
- Mountain Landscape with Dense Foliage, oil on canvas, sgn/dtd 1863, 18x15", WAD 6/12/89 ... 1,150
- Rushing Water, watercolor, 17x10", WAD 11/30/89 ... 400

JACOBS, F. (19th C)
- Planning the Evening Meal, oil on panel, sgn/dtd 1868, artist's seal, 24x19", C-NY 2/25/88 ... 4,400

JACOBS, Martin (20th C)
- Firenze, watercolor on paper, sgn/dtd 1982, 18x19", C-E 6/28/88 UE ... 140

JACOBS, William (American, 1897-)
- Chicago Street Scene, gouache on board, sgn/dtd 50, 19x23", LH 12/4/88 ... 180
- Landscape with a Stream, oil on canvas, sgn, 14x17", LH 12/4/88 OE ... 300

JACOBSEN, Antonio (American, 1850-1921)
- Ailsa, oil on canvas, sgn/inscr/dtd 1878, 22x36", C-NY 3/11/88 ... 14,850
- Atalanta (ship at sea), oil on board, sgn/dtd 1911/inscr, 22x36", SBY 1/24/89 ... 7,700
- Clipper Charles H Marshall, oil on board, sgn/dtd, 14x20", SBY 6/28/89 ... 4,125
- Clipper Flying Cloud 1851, oil on panel, sgn/dtd 1918, 12x20", FAP 4/15/89 ... 3,950
- El Siglo (steamship at sea), oil on board, sgn/inscr/dtd 1910, 16x28", C-E 6/1/88 ... 6,050
- Five-Masted Schooner Diria, oil on panel, sgn/dtd 1918, 20x35", SBY 1/28/88 ... 5,500
- Full Sails, oil on board, sgn/dtd 1915, 30x22", C-NY 3/11/88 ... 7,700
- Harvest Queen (sailing ship), oil on board, sgn/dtd 1917, 14x20", SBY 6/28/89 OE ... 5,225
- Hekla (steamship), oil on canvas, sgn/dtd 1899, 22x36", lot 1630, SBY 1/28/88 ... 12,650
- Hondo (steamship), oil on canvas, sgn/dtd 1889, 22x36", lot 1631, SBY 1/28/88 ... 15,400
- Lakeshore View, oil on canvas, sgn, 26x37", SBY 6/8/88 ... 770
- M Moran Tugboat, oil on canvas, sgn/inscr/dtd 1901, 22x36", C-NY 9/30/88 OE ... 38,500
- New York, oil on canvas, sgn/dtd 1904, 14x22", C-E 11/30/88 ... 4,180
- Orlando V Wooten, a Four-Masted Schooner; oil on board, sgn/dtd 1914, 28x48", SBY 1/28/88 ... 9,075
- Pilot Boat New York: Delivering Pilot to American Liner New York Off Sandy Hook; oil on canvas, 21x35", SBY 1/28/88 OE ... 23,100
- Pilot Boat Steamer, New York (steamboat); oil on canvas, sgn/dtd 1898, 22x36", SBY 1/28/88 ... 8,800
- Portrait of the American Liner Oceana, oil on heavy artist panel, sgn/dtd 1915, orig frame, 20x36", RAB 11/10/88 ... 11,000
- Portrait of the British Freighter Craigendoran at Sea, oil on academy board, sgn/dtd 1907, 10x16", RAB 8/1/88 ... 3,750
- Portrait of the City of St Louis (ship), oil on academy board, sgn/dtd 1910, 22x36", RAB 8/1/89 ... 7,000
- Portrait of the Italian Freighter Cera, oil on canvas mounted on heavy pasteboard, sgn/dtd 1909, 16x31", RAB 8/1/88 ... 4,750
- Portrait of the Ocean-Going Tug Wallace B Flint, oil on canvas, sgn/dtd 1895, modern frame, 22x36", RAB 8/1/88 UE ... 5,500
- Rescue (on a stormy sea), oil on canvas, sgn/dtd 1902, 18x30", SBY 6/24/88 ... 7,425
- Riviera (steamship), oil on canvas, sgn/dtd 1906, 22x36", SBY 1/28/88 UE ... 7,150
- Ship Governor Goodwin of New York Under Shortened Sail, oil on artist panel, sgn/dtd 1916, 12x20", RAB 11/10/88 ... 6,500
- SS John Englis, 1897 (ship); oil on canvas, sgn/dtd 1897, 24x42", C-NY 1/20/89 ... 6,050
- SS Saint Ronams, 1883 (ship); oil on canvas, sgn/dtd 1883, 22x36", C-NY 1/20/89 ... 14,300

Steamship, City of Alexandria; oil on canvas, sgn/dtd 1900, 18x30", C-NY 9/28/89 ... 4,400
Steamship Riviera, oil on canvas, sgn, 22x36", C-NY 6/3/89 ... 11,000
Three-Masted Rigger, Great Western; oil on board, sgn/dtd 1916, 18x30", C-NY 9/28/89 ... 11,000
Yacht Race Off Sandy Hook, oil on academy board, sgn/dtd 1906, 10x16", RAB 8/1/88 ... 8,000

JACOBSEN, Antonio; att (American, 1850-1921)
Steamship City of New York (ship at sea), oil on canvas, 19x36", SLK 4/7/89 ... 4,500

JACOBSEN, Egill (Danish, 1910-)
Untitled (abstract), oil on canvas, sgn/dtd 1946, 26x30", SBY 6/30/88 ... 20,000

JACOBSEN, Sophus (Norwegian, 1833-1912)
Moonlit Bay, oil on canvas, indistinctly sgn, 30x50", SBY 5/23/89 ... 16,500
Moonlit Seascape, Cottage by Lake; oil on canvas, 28x42", FAP 11/4/88 ... 2,100

JACOBSZ, Lambert; follower of (1598-1636)
Judah Giving His Ring & Staff to Tamar, oil on canvas, 36x29", SBY 10/21/88 ... 2,750

JACOMIN, Alfred (French, 1842-1913)
Un Coup de Jarnac, oil on panel, sgn, 18x15", WAD 6/6/88 ... 1,600

JACQUAND, Claude (French, 1804-1878)
Mater Dolorosa, oil on panel, 8x11", B/B 4/20/88 ... 770

JACQUE, Charles Emile (French, 1813-1894)
By the Haystack at Dusk, oil on canvas, sgn, 26x21", SBY 5/23/89 UE ... 15,400
End of the Day (shepherdess leading flock into a barn), oil on canvas, sgn, 22x18", C-NY 2/23/89 OE ... 38,500
Flock of Sheep Near a Wood, oil on canvas, sgn, 21x29", C-NY 2/25/88 ... 12,100
La Bergere (shepherdess watching sheep watering), oil on canvas, sgn, 26x32", SBY 10/24/89 OE ... 40,700
Le Berger (herdsmen w/flock of sheep), oil on canvas laid down on panel, bears signature, 25x33", SBY 10/24/89 ... 20,900
Poultry in a Barnyard, oil on board, sgn, 6x9", C-E 5/23/88 ... 1,430
Sheep in a Pasture, oil on panel, sgn, 11x18", WD 11/16/88 UE ... 2,000
Shepherd, Sheep & Lamb; oil on canvas, sgn, 42x30", C-NY 2/3/88 OE ... 41,800
Shepherd & Flock, oil on canvas, sgn, 32x26", C-NY 2/3/88 ... 18,700
Shepherd & Maiden Attending Their Flock, oil on canvas, sgn/dtd 71, 30x26", B/B 6/9/88 OE ... 22,000
Shepherd Tending His Flock, oil on panel, sgn, 11x14", C-E 5/22/89 ... 4,620
Shepherd with His Flock Leaving His Barn, black chalk on paper, sgn, 11x16", B/B 10/9/88 ... 1,760
Shepherd with His Flock Outside a Cottage, oil on cradled panel, sgn, 16x12", C-E 2/23/88 ... 1,650
Shepherd with His Flock Outside a Cottage, oil on panel, sgn, 16x12", C-E 10/26/89 ... 2,750
Shepherdess & Her Flock, oil on canvas, sgn, 26x34", SBY 10/24/89 ... 33,000
Shepherdess & Her Flock by a Stream, oil on canvas, sgn, 10x13", C-NY 10/25/89 ... 6,600
Shepherdess Watering Her Flock, oil on canvas, sgn, 19x15", SBY 10/24/89 ... 20,900
Shepherdess with Her Flock & a Sheepdog on the Edge of a Forest, oil on canvas, sgn, 32x26", SBY 2/22/89 ... 38,500
Shepherdess with Her Flock & Sheepdog, black chalk heightened w/white on paper, sgn/dtd 79, 14x19", SBY 12/9/88 ... 4,400
Swineherd, oil on canvas, sgn/dtd 1890, 27x40", C-NY 10/25/89 ... 22,000
Tending Her Flock, oil on panel, sgn, 10x16", C-NY 5/25/88 ... 10,450
Woman Tending Sheep, oil on canvas, sgn, 26x32", LH 3/20/88 UE ... 1,200

JACQUET, Gustave Jean (French, 1846-1909)
Elegant Lady in a Black Hat, oil on panel, sgn/dtd 1878, 42x28", C-NY 10/25/89 ... 13,200
Music Lesson, oil on panel, sgn, 13x9", LH 10/16/88 UE ... 5,500
Portrait de Femme, oil on panel, sgn, 13x9", SBY 5/23/89 ... 5,500
Portrait of a Lady in a Purple Dress, oil on canvas, sgn, 12x10", C-E 2/21/89 ... 4,320
Portrait of a Mediterranean Beauty (bust-length), oil on canvas, sgn, 21x17", B/B 10/9/88 ... 1,980
Portrait of a Young Girl Wearing a Black Velvet Cap, oil on canvas, sgn, 12x9", C-E 2/21/89 OE ... 5,280
Study of French Soldiers at Rest, pencil, sgn twice, unfr, 10x14", C-NY 10/26/88 ... 3,850
Woman with Red Hair (portrait), oil on cradled panel, sgn, 18x13", C-E 2/23/88 ... 1,320
Young Maiden with a Blue Satin Ribbon in Her Hair, oil on cradled panel, sgn, 14x10", C-E 10/25/88 ... 3,850

JACQUET, Henry Leon (French, 1856-)
Vestiges d'Anciens Monumens Romains (ruins in landscape), gouache on paper, sgn/titled, RAB 8/8/89 ... 1,750

JACQUETTE, Yvonne (American, 1934-)
East 12th Street (view of street lights), graphite on paper, sgn/dtd 73, 26x20", SBY 11/11/88 ... 990
Telephone #2 (telephone pole, clouds, & sky), acrylic on canvas, 1971, 60x80", SBY 2/15/89 ... 7,700

JAFFE, Lee (20th C)
Portrait of Sacco & Venzetti, mixed media on canvas, 1983, 140x136", C-NY 5/4/89 UE ... 462
Silver Skins (depicting animal skins), silver/aluminum/gold leaf/mink/fox on canvas, 1983, 104x73", C-NY 5/4/89 UE ... 110

JAKOBS, Paul Emil (German, 1802-1866)
Harem Beauty at Her Toilette, oil on canvas, sgn/dtd 1839, 50x39", SBY 10/24/89 ... 88,000

JAMBOR, Louis (American, 1884-1955)
Heave-Ho (men struggling to get horses across river), oil on board, sgn, 10x14", RAB 8/9/88 ... 450
Sunshine Sonata (three figures in sunny interior), oil on canvas, sgn, 31x36", B/B 10/9/88 ... 27,500
The Outing, oil on canvas, sgn, 55x44", B/B 6/9/88 ... 20,900

JAMES, A.
On the Lake at Wollgelley, oil on canvas, sgn/inscr, 20x30", C-E 10/25/88 ... 1,540

JAMES, Alexander R. (American, 1890-1941
Portrait of Mrs Martin Fisher, Santa Barbara; oil on canvas, sgn/dtd 1918/inscr, 37x29", LH 10/16/88 UE ... 300

JAMES, David (British, 1881-1898)
Corner Breaker, oil on canvas, twice sgn/dtd 92, 19x28", SBY 2/22/89 OE ... 9,350
In Mounts Bay, oil on canvas, sgn/dtd 93, 25x50", C-E 10/26/89 ... 4,400

Rocky Coast, oil on canvas, sgn/dtd 84, 25x42", C-NY 5/25/88 3,520
MES, John Seymoure
Grandmother & Small Child, oil on canvas, sgn/dtd 86, 22x17", C-E 9/15/88 OE 1,540
MES, John Wells (American, 1873-)
Lifting Fog (landscape), oil on board, sgn/dtd 1910, 11x14", C-E 6/1/89 770
MES, Phyllis Hipwell (Canadian)
Mother & Child, charcoal, sgn, 21x16", WAD 11/30/89 110
MES, Sandra (American, 20th C)
Seascape Ogunquit, Maine; oil on masonite, sgn, orig frame, 24x30", RAB 11/25/88 UE 300
MES, William (American, 19th/20th C)
Back Pasture, Dublin, New Hampshire; oil on canvas, sgn/dtd 1924, 24x30", RWS 9/29/88 OE 650
MES, William (British, fl 1754-died 1771)
Bucintoro Returning to the Molo on Ascension Day, oil on canvas, 37x60", SBY 6/2/89 110,000

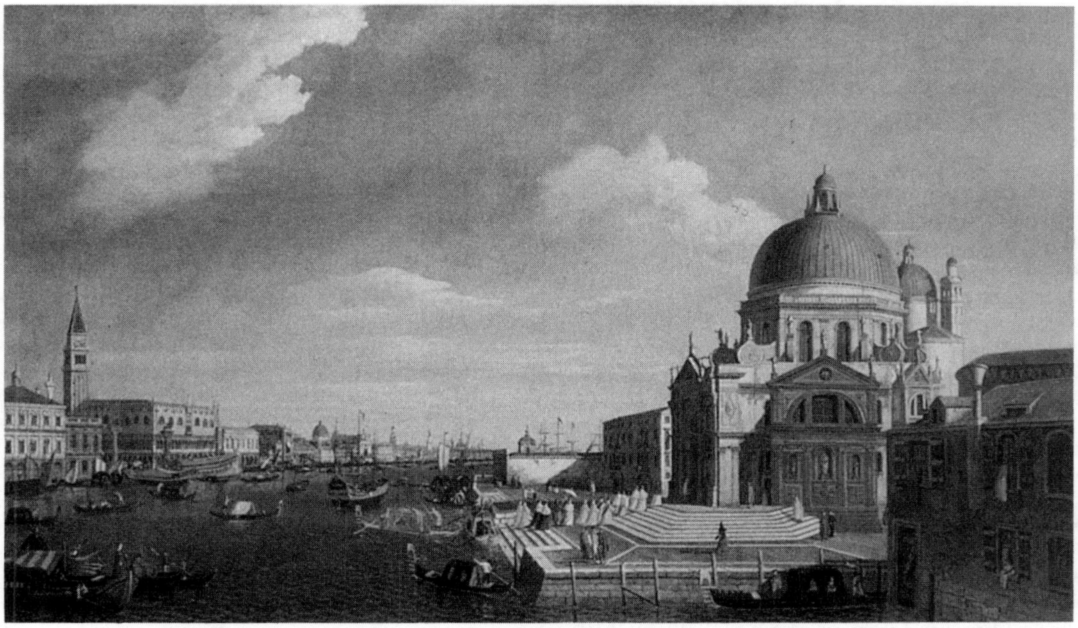

Ducal Procession Entering Santa Maria della Salute, the Grand Canal, Venice; oil on canvas, 30x35", C-NY 1/11/89 OE, $93,500

MESON, Demetrios G. (American, 1919-)
Scene Backstage at a Theatre with One Ballerina on Stage & Another in the Wings, sgn/dtd 48, unfr, 38x19", SLK 2/12/88 70
Study of a Dancer Seated in a Chair, oil on canvas, sgn/dtd 48, unfr, 34x23", SLK 2/12/88 260
MESON, F.E. (British, 19th C)
Evening Glow, oil on canvas, sgn, 20x31", WL 5/20/88 UE 200
MESON, N.B. (British, 19th/20th C)
Pair: River Landscapes with Cattle; oil on board, 9x12", SLK 2/12/88 300
MIESON, Alexander (Scottish, 1873-)
Loch Lomond, oil on canvas, sgn, 16x24", FB 10/17/88 350
MIESON, Ron (Canadian, 1916-)
House & Shed, oil on board, sgn, 14x18", FB 10/30/89 605
MISON, Philip (American, 1925-)
Buttonwood (tree in snowy landscape), watercolor on paper, sgn, 14x21", SBY 4/14/89 OE 2,860
Cottage Behind a Hill, watercolor on paper, sgn, 18x30", SBY 3/17/88 1,760
Daisies, gouache/watercolor on paper, sgn, 20x26", C-E 11/30/88 2,420
Herders with Their Flock Fording a Stream in a Landscape, oil on canvas, 26x32", C-NY 4/6/89 OE 3,520
White House in the Snow, watercolor on paper, sgn, 10x18", WD 4/13/88 1,000
MSEM, Jean
Deux Femmes, oil on canvas, sgn, 14x11", SBY 2/14/89 OE 7,150
NCE, Paul Claude (French, 1840-)
Vase of Pink & White Peonies on a Window Sill, oil on canvas, sgn/dtd 1883, 36x32", SBY 7/12/89 OE 9,900
NCK, Angelo (German, 1868-)
A Cavalry Officer & His Mount, oil on panel, sgn/dtd 17, 14x12", B/B 12/8/88 1,320
Cavalry Officer at Full Gallop, oil on canvas, sgn/dtd 1916, 20x21", B/B 12/8/88 825
NCO, Marcel (French, 1895-)
Landscape (abstract), oil on panel, sgn/dtd 40, 19x27", SBY 10/7/89 8,250
Refugees Leaving Spain, oil on panel, sgn, ca 1936, 20x28", SBY 5/30/89 14,300
Still Life (abstract), oil/collage on board, sgn, ca 1920-25, 20x14", SBY 5/30/89 11,000

Three Seated Arabs (caricature portraits), watercolor/brush/India ink over pencil, sgn/dtd 1950, 13x16", SBY 5/30/89 ... 3,52
Two Figures Smoking, oil on canvas, sgn, 29x40", SBY 10/7/88 OE ... 29,70

JANESCH, Albert (Austrian, 1889-)
Peonies & Poppies (still life), oil on panel, 34x29", C-NY 2/23/89 ... 5,28

JANKEY, William Lee (British, 1869-1952)
Brittany Harbor, oil on canvas, sgn, 20x24", FB 5/28/89 OE ... 14,00

JANNECK, Franz Christoph; att (Austrian, 1703-1761)
Musical Comedy (seated lady w/sheet music, two gentlemen w/instruments), oil on canvas, 41x46", SBY 4/7/89 OE ... 16,50

JANOUSEK, Frantisek (European, 1890-)
Biomorphic Forms in Landscape, oil on panel, sgn/dtd 35, 24x29", SBY 10/7/89 ... 3,30
Exploded Figure in Space, oil on canvas, sgn/dtd 38, 27x24", SBY 10/7/89 ... 2,75
Two Biomorphic Forms, oil on board, sgn/dtd 38, 19x28", SBY 10/7/89 ... 2,53

JANSEM, Jean (French, 1920-)
Bust of Young Girl in Profile, pen/India ink over watercolor on paper, sgn, 26x20", C-E 11/17/88 OE ... 2,64
Deux Enfants (two children), oil on canvas, sgn, 32x39", SBY 10/5/88 OE ... 12,10
Femme Nue Assise, pen/black ink on paper, sgn, 26x20", C-NY 2/13/89 ... 1,43
Femme Nue Assisse (seated nude from behind), pen/brush/India ink on paper, sgn, 26x20", C-E 11/17/88 OE ... 1,87
Girl in Orange Jacket, oil on canvas, sgn, 40x20", SBY 10/7/89 OE ... 24,20
Girl in Yellow (seated on bench), oil on canvas, sgn/dtd 63, 58x35", SBY 10/7/89 OE ... 37,40
Jeune Femme Assise (young woman seated), pen/black ink on paper, sgn, 26x20", C-NY 2/13/89 ... 1,98
Jeune Femme en Profil, pen/ink on paper, sgn, 26x20", C-E 5/9/89 ... 2,09
Jeune Fille (nude), pen/ink/gouache on paper, sgn, 26x20", C-E 5/9/89 OE ... 2,31
Jeune Fille Debout (young girl standing), pen/India ink over watercolor on paper, sgn, 26x20", C-E 11/17/88 OE ... 1,87
Jeune Fille Vue de Dos (figure before fireplace), pen/ink on paper, sgn, 26x21", C-E 5/9/89 ... 1,54
Jeune Fille Vue de Dos (view of young girl from behind), pen/black ink on paper, sgn, 26x20", C-NY 2/13/89 ... 1,54
Man with Pushcart, oil on canvas, sgn, 22x18", SBY 10/7/89 OE ... 17,60
Man with Two Children, oil on canvas, sgn/dtd 58, 77x38", SBY 10/7/89 OE ... 31,90
Mother & Child, oil on canvas, sgn, 23x12", PHL 6/16/88 ... 1,80
Nature Moret au Pot Blanc (floral still life w/white pot), oil on canvas, sgn/dtd 63, 59x75", LH 3/20/88 ... 5,00
Still Life, oil on canvas, sgn, 29x36", SBY 2/14/89 OE ... 17,60
Still Life (contemporary), oil on canvas, sgn, 29x20", PHL 6/16/88 ... 2,00
Two Seated Women, oil on canvas, sgn, 21x26", SBY 10/7/89 OE ... 18,70
Venetian Canal, oil on canvas, sgn/dtd 66, 38x64", SBY 2/14/89 OE ... 27,50
Woman Cleaning, oil on canvas, sgn, 26x20", SBY 10/7/89 OE ... 22,00
Young Girl in Profile (nude), pen/black ink over watercolor on paper, sgn, 26x20", C-E 11/17/88 OE ... 1,87

JANSEN, Joseph (German, 1829-1905)
An Alpine Lake, oil on canvas, sgn/dtd 1896, 37x52", SBY 2/22/89 ... 6,60
End of the Day, oil on canvas, sgn, 38x51", SBY 5/23/89 ... 11,00
Monastery by an Alpine Lake, oil on canvas, sgn, 37x51", PHL 10/28/88 UE ... 6,50
Shepherds in a Landscape, oil on canvas, sgn, 38x57", SBY 2/22/89 UE ... 11,00

JANSEN, Willem George Frederik (Dutch, 1871-1949)
Windmill on the Water, oil on board, sgn, 5x7", C-E 2/16/88 ... 3
Woman Tending Vegetable Garden, oil on canvas, sgn, 18x15", RWS 5/12/89 ... 1,40

JANSSENS, Abraham; circle of (Flemish, 1575-1632)
Woman Holding a Roemer in a Stand & a Young Man Carving a Fowl, oil on canvas, unfr, 48x41", C-NY 10/20/88 ... 3,52

JANSSENS, Hieronymous (Flemish, 1624-1693)
Elegant Company at Banquet with Couple Dancing, Group of Musicians & Landscape; oil on canvas, 24x36", SBY 4/7/89 OE ... 15,40

JANSSON, Alfred (American/Swedish, 1863-1931)
Colorful Forest Scene, oil on canvas, sgn/dtd, 17x26", LH 5/15/88 OE ... 2,20

Japanese School (19th C)
Portrait of an American Steam Warship of the Mid-Nineteenth Century, watercolor on paper, 10x14", RAB 8/1/88 UE ... 50

JAPY, Louis Aime (French, 1840-1916)
River Landscape with a Shepherdess & Her Flock, oil on canvas, sgn, 26x32", C-NY 2/25/88 ... 7,70
Shepherdess in a Meadow, oil on panel, sgn, 16" L, C-E 10/25/88 UE ... 99

JARDINES, Jose Maria (Spanish, 1862-)
Mountain Village, oil on canvas, sgn, unfr, 22x10", C-E 5/23/88 OE ... 2,86
On the River, oil on canvas, sgn, 15x21", C-E 10/26/89 ... 2,42
Shepherd & Shepherdess with Their Flock, oil on canvas, sgn, 20x26", C-E 10/25/88 UE ... 1,87
Village in the Mountainside, oil on canvas, sgn, 22x11", C-E 5/23/88 OE ... 3,30
Young Girl at Her Balcony, oil on canvas, sgn, 16x10", C-E 10/26/89 ... 2,20

JAROCKI, Wladyslav (Polish, 20th C)
Peasant Girl, oil on canvas, sgn/dtd 1924, 39x34", LH 10/16/88 OE ... 1,40

JARVIS, George (British, 19th/20th C)
Two Cavaliers (seated at table), oil on panel, sgn, 12x16", B/B 3/22/89 ... 3,02

JARVIS, John Wesley (American, 1780-1840)
Portrait of Eleazor Bullard, oil on canvas, sgn/dtd 1838, unfr, 30x25", C-E 10/18/89 ... 2,64

JARVIS, John Wesley; att (American, 1780-1840)
Portrait of an Officer, long bust-length, in dress uniform; oil on canvas, 26x20", PHL 12/1/88 ... 2,40

JAUDON, Valerie (American, 1945-)
Avalon (geometric composition), oil/metallic paint on canvas, sgn/dtd 1976, unfr, 72x108", C-NY 2/20/88 ... 7,70
Bay Springs (contemporary), oil on canvas, sgn/dtd 1976, 72x72", SBY 11/9/89 OE ... 41,80

Brazil (a composition of arches), acrylic on canvas, sgn/dtd 82, 36x36", C-NY 5/4/89	8,250
Canton (composition), oil on canvas, 1979, 71x72", SBY 11/9/89	17,600
Grand Gulf, graphite on paper, sgn/dtd 1975/titled, 18x17", C-E 5/9/89 OE	2,420
Mantrose, oil on canvas, sgn/dtd 1983, 94x116", SBY 10/5/89 OE	37,400
Ovett (geometric design), oil on canvas, 1978, 36x36", SBY 2/15/89	3,850
Sartartia (design in red), oil on linen, 1985, 90x138", C-NY 5/4/89 OE	28,600
Tatum Lake (geometric design), oil on canvas, sgn, 1978, 72x72", SBY 2/15/89 OE	11,000
JAUREZ, Nicholas Rodriguez	
Scenes From the Life of Santa Libania, oil on canvas, sgn/inscr, 66x47", C-NY 1/15/88 OE	24,200
JEAN, Marcel	
Decalcomanie, black gouache decalcomanie on paper, inscr, 1936, 13x10", C-NY 10/6/88	2,420
JEANNIOT, Pierre Georges (French, 1848-1934)	
Night View of the Seine, oil on canvas, sgn/dtd 1892, 20x24", C-E 10/26/89	2,090
JEANRON (French, 19th C)	
Landscape with Children Fishing, oil on wood panel, sgn, 9x14", DM 5/89	700
JEAURAT, Etienne; att (French, 1699-1789)	
Studies of a Standing Woman Seen From the Back & a Seated Woman, chalk on gray paper, #d 20, 9x13", C-NY 1/11/89 OE	4,950
JEGOROV, A. (European, 20th C)	
Winter Sleigh Scene, gouache, sgn, 10x13", LH 3/20/88 UE	200
JENKINS, George H. (British, 20th C)	
Lake View, watercolor on paper, sgn/dtd 02, 8x11", FAP 4/15/89	330
Sunset & Moonrise, the River Lyd; oil on canvas, sgn, 24x40", B/B 5/17/89	880
JENKINS, Paul (American, 1923-)	
Phenomena, watercolor on paper, sgn, 45x30", SBY 10/7/89 OE	6,600
Phenomena a Pour Skunk Keander (abstract), watercolor on paper, sgn twice/dtd Paris 1963, 15x11", SBY 10/5/88	1,100
Phenomena a Sound of Surf, watercolor on paper, sgn twice/inscr/dtd 1979, 43x31", C-E 5/13/88	1,980
Phenomena Alter Dome (abstract), oil on canvas, sgn twice/dtd 1975/titled, 60x50", SBY 2/19/88	12,100
Phenomena April Wind Off March, watercolor on paper, sgn twice/inscr/dtd 1964, 23x30", C-E 5/13/88	2,200
Phenomena Belly to Belly, watercolor on paper, sgn/dtd 1977, 44x31", C-E 11/14/89 OE	4,950
Phenomena Black Is Magic, watercolor on paper, sgn, 22x30", SBY 2/14/89	1,980
Phenomena Bonjour Jeanne Claude et Christo, acrylic on canvas, sgn, 60x50", SBY 10/8/88	11,000
Phenomena Broad Arrow Mark, oil on canvas, sgn/dtd 1961, 46x35", SBY 2/14/89	5,775
Phenomena Broadside, watercolor on paper, sgn twice/dtd 1973/titled, 30x42", C-E 5/9/89 OE	3,740
Phenomena Byron's Hunch (abstract), watercolor on paper, sgn twice/dtd 1978, 43x31", SBY, 10/5/88	2,750
Phenomena Cajun Entrance, acrylic on canvas, sgn/dtd 1968, 16x20", SBY 2/14/89	3,520
Phenomena Careening Grid, acrylic on canvas, sgn/dtd 1979, 25x62", C-E 11/17/88	7,700
Phenomena Catherine Wheel, watercolor on paper, sgn/dtd 1981, 43x31", C-E 11/17/88	3,850
Phenomena Chase Dragon Red, acrylic on canvas, sgn twice/inscr/dtd 1966, 21x26", C-E 5/13/88	3,850
Phenomena Chippwa Mound (abstract), acrylic on canvas, sgn/dtd 1978, 36x97", SBY 2/15/89 OE	17,600
Phenomena Circle Over, watercolor on paper, sgn twice/dtd 1969/titled, 23x31", C-E 5/9/89 OE	3,520
Phenomena Continental Drift, watercolor on paper, sgn twice/inscr/dtd 1972, 30x42", C-NY 5/4/88	3,300
Phenomena Cosmic Spine, watercolor on paper, sgn/dtd St Croix 1980, 31x43", C-E 11/14/89 OE	6,600
Phenomena Cry Tri-Color (abstract), acrylic on canvas, sgn twice/inscr/dtd 1968-69, 75x49", C-NY 5/4/88	17,600
Phenomena Cusp of Aries, oil on shaped canvas, sgn/dtd 1974-77, 71x98", SBY 2/14/89	11,000
Phenomena Eagle Dwell (abstract), acrylic on canvas, sgn/dtd 1968, 72x35", SBY 2/15/89 OE	17,600
Phenomena Eden March, acrylic on canvas, sgn/dtd 1963, 36x36", C-E 11/17/88	3,520
Phenomena Eminence Grise, acrylic on canvas, sgn/dtd 1962, 77x51", C-NY 2/20/88	9,900
Phenomena Este's Land, watercolor on paper, sgn twice/inscr/dtd 1974, 31x22", C-E 5/13/88	1,320
Phenomena Eyes of the Dove, oil on canvas, sgn/dtd 1964, 20x16", SBY 2/14/89	4,180
Phenomena Far Is Near (abstract), acrylic on canvas, sgn/dtd 1983, 53x38", C-E 11/17/88	6,600
Phenomena Fire Curtain, acrylic on canvas, sgn/dtd Yew York 1985-86, 78x120", C-NY 2/20/88	19,800
Phenomena for 1923, watercolor on paper laid down on board, sgn, ca 1962, unfr, 20x22", SBY 2/14/89	1,100
Phenomena Function Star Throw: Anatomy of a Cloud; acrylic on canvas, sgn/dtd 1977, 36x50", C-NY 10/4/89	4,950
Phenomena Grace Three, watercolor on paper, sgn twice/inscr/dtd 1975, 30x22", C-E 5/13/88	2,750
Phenomena Greek Chorus (abstract), acrylic on canvas, sgn/dtd 1981, 78x58", C-NY 5/4/88	14,300
Phenomena Guardian Watch, watercolor on paper, sgn/dtd 1977, 43x31", C-E 11/14/89 OE	5,500
Phenomena High Sound Larnac, watercolor on paper, sgn/dtd 1973, 42x30", C-E 11/17/88	2,200
Phenomena Insistance of Orange, oil on canvas, sgn/dtd 1977, 76x87", C-E 11/14/89 OE	46,200
Phenomena Invocation of Solstice (abstract), acrylic on canvas, sgn twice/dtd 1970 Paris/titled, 38x77", SBY 2/19/88	7,425
Phenomena Joanne's Wish, watercolor on paper, sgn, 32x22", C-E 11/14/89 OE	4,400
Phenomena Katherine Wheel Horoscope, oil on canvas, sgn twice/dtd 1971, titled, 84x70", C-NY 11/10/88 OE	22,000
Phenomena Lantern Line, watercolor on paper, sgn twice/dtd 1979/titled, 42x30", C-E 5/9/89	3,520
Phenomena Long Horn Bluff (abstract), watercolor on paper, sgn, 42x29", WD 5/5/88 UE	2,000
Phenomena Loop the Sun, acrylic on canvas, sgn/dtd 1981, 78x67", SBY 10/5/89 OE	25,300
Phenomena Lunar Moth, acrylic on canvas, sgn/dtd 1967, 60x48", SBY 10/5/89	23,100
Phenomena Meeting, watercolor on paper, sgn/dtd Paris 1964, 15x11", C-E 11/17/88	880
Phenomena Near Gander (abstract), acrylic on canvas, sgn/dtd 1965, 36x40", SBY 2/15/89	13,200
Phenomena Nearing Spring Solstice, acrylic on canvas, sgn twice/inscr/dtd, 26x40", C-NY 5/4/88	6,600
Phenomena Nimbus, oil on canvas, sgn/dtd 1969, unfr, 39x39", SBY 10/7/89 OE	22,000
Phenomena Nimbus Sounds (abstract), acrylic on canvas, sgn/dtd 1976, 38x54", C-NY 2/14/89	7,150
Phenomena Not Far From Shore, oil on canvas, sgn twice/dtd New York 1965/titled, 22x47", C-E 5/9/89 OE	15,400

Phenomena Now (abstract), watercolor on paper, sgn/dtd New York 1965, 15x11", SBY 2/14/89	1,100
Phenomena on Weather Eye (abstract), acrylic on canvas, sgn/dtd 1968, 33x33", SBY 5/3/89	8,250
Phenomena Point of Return, acrylic on canvas, sgn/dtd Paris 1966, 35x46", SBY 10/5/89 OE	10,450
Phenomena Rain King (abstract), acrylic on canvas, sgn/dtd, 77x149", SBY 2/15/89 OE	44,000
Phenomena Rain Palace Regent (abstract), acrylic on canvas, sgn/dtd 1979, 77x79", SBY 10/5/89	24,200
Phenomena Rake Still Life (abstract), acrylic on canvas, sgn, 1981, 52x78", SBY 10/5/89	16,500
Phenomena Round the Horn, acrylic on canvas, sgn/dtd twice 1974, 50x60", SBY 10/8/88	7,700
Phenomena Round the Horn, acrylic on canvas, sgn/dtd 1974, 50x60", C-NY 10/4/89	12,100
Phenomena Samothrace (abstract), oil on canvas, sgn twice/inscr/dtd 1967, 72x48", C-NY 5/4/88	9,350
Phenomena Shoulder to the Sun, oil on canvas, sgn/dtd 1951, 78x58", SBY 2/14/89	11,000
Phenomena Spellbound 5, watercolor on paper, sgn/dtd Paris 1964, 30x22", SBY 10/7/89	5,500
Phenomena Standfast, oil on canvas, sgn/dtd 1965, 47x22", C-E 11/17/88	4,400
Phenomena Star Finder (abstract), acrylic on canvas, sgn/dtd 1984, 80x12", C-NY 2/14/89 UE	6,600
Phenomena Star Throw Mader (abstract), watercolor on paper, sgn/dtd 1971, 43x31", SBY 2/14/89 UE	2,200
Phenomena Susi Hart (abstract), acrylic on canvas, sgn twice/dtd 1969, 64x51", SBY 10/8/88	15,400
Phenomena Tibetan Ascent, oil on canvas, sgn/dtd 1972, 48x26", C-E 11/17/88	5,500
Phenomena Tibetan Valley, watercolor on paper, sgn/dtd 1982, 41x60", C-E 11/17/88	4,400
Phenomena to Votress, watercolor on paper, sgn twice/dtd Paris 1963/titled, 15x11", C-E 5/9/89	2,200
Phenomena Trail by Fire, watercolor on paper, sgn twice/inscr/dtd 1975, 42x30", C-E 5/13/88	1,760
Phenomena Triple Arch, oil on canvas, sgn twice/dtd Paris 1962/titled, 11x18", C-E 5/9/89 OE	3,300
Phenomena Veil of Vespers (abstract), acrylic on canvas, sgn twice/dtd 1970/titled, 61x55", SBY 2/19/88	20,900
Phenomena Welsh Ancestor, acrylic on canvas, sgn/dtd 1974, 30x44", C-NY 10/4/89	8,800
Phenomena Wind Compass: Anatomy of a Cloud; acrylic on canvas, sgn/dtd 1977, 50x36", C-NY 10/4/89	4,950
Phenomena Wind Tunnel (abstract), acrylic on canvas, sgn/dtd 1978, 77x116", SBY 10/8/88	23,100
Phenomena Winds Burn Haze (abstract), acrylic on canvas, sgn/dtd 1979, 77x41", C-NY 5/4/89	19,250
Phenomena Winston's Signal, watercolor on paper, sgn twice/dtd 1975/titled, 30x23", C-E 5/9/89	2,200
Phenomena with Whiteness Passing, watercolor on paper, sgn/dtd, New York 1961, 30x22", SBY 2/14/89	1,100
Phenomena Yellow Cross Over, oil on canvas, sgn/dtd 1968, unfr, 26x40", SBY 10/7/89 OE	22,000
Phenomena Yellow Solstice (abstract), acrylic on canvas, sgn twice/dtd New York 1964/titled, 50x36", SBY 2/19/88	7,150
Phenomena Yellow Thread (abstract), acrylic on canvas, sgn/dtd Paris 1962, 18x11", SBY 10/5/88	1,540
Phenomenon Big Sun Traces (abstract), acrylic on canvas, sgn twice/dtd 1968/titled, 72x60", SBY 11/11/88	18,700
Phenomenon View Finder, watercolor on paper, sgn, 42x30", SBY 2/14/89	4,400
Phenomenon Wind Reed, acrylic on canvas, sgn/indistinctly dtd, 37x21", SBY 10/5/88	4,400
JENNER, Isaac Walter	
Pair: Sunset, West Coast; Brighton Beach; oil on canvas, oil, ea 7x16", C-SK 11/10/88	1,860
JENNEY, Neil (American, 1945-)	
Angles & Curves, oil/graphite on canvas, painted wooden frame, 1971, 58x56", C-NY 5/3/88	165,000
Atmosphere (contemporary), oil on panel with painted wood frame, sgn/dtd 1975 & 1985, 33x79", SBY 5/2/89 OE	154,000
Bag & Can (contemporary), acrylic on canvas w/painted wood frame, titled, 1970, 47x46", SBY 11/10/88	176,000
Felis Catus (cat on green background), acrylic on canvas w/painted wood frame, titled, 46x67", SBY 10/5/89	198,000
Husband & Wife (on green background), oil on canvas in painted wood frame, sgn, 1969, 56x76", C-NY 11/9/89 OE	308,000
Man & Thing, oil on canvas stretched on panel in painted wooden frame, sgn/dtd 1969, 71x44", C-NY 11/9/88	242,000
Plowed & Plower (contemporary), acrylic on canvas w/painted wood frame, titled on frame, 1969, 59x77", SBY 11/10/88	242,000
Scent & Pup (dog on green background), acrylic on canvas, 1970, 34x49", SBY 5/2/88	148,500
Schmuck & Schlemiel (two figures, green background), oil on canvas in painted frame, sgn/dtd 1969, 59x80", C-NY 5/3/89	264,000
JENNINGS-BROWN, H.W. (British, 19th C)	
Before the Recital, oil on canvas, sgn/dtd 1885, 51x73", SBY 2/22/89	22,000
JENS, Heinrich Engelbert Reynt (Dutch, 1817-1878)	
Elegant Figures in an Interior, oil on canvas, sgn, 22x27", SBY 7/12/89	1,980
JENSEN, Alfred (Dutch, 1859-1935)	
Acrobatic Rectangle, Per Eight; oil on canvas, sgn/dtd 1967, 70x44", SBY 10/8/88	41,250
Atlantis, Per II (contemporary composition); oil on canvas, sgn/dtd 1965, 50x50", SBY 11/9/89	66,000
Calling Back the Soul (contemporary), oil on canvas, sgn/inscr/dtd 1960, 76x50", C-NY 11/9/88	49,500
Copan (contemporary), oil on canvas, sgn/dtd 1969/titled, 51x51", SBY 11/11/88 OE	46,750
Diagram Oct 15, oil on brown-toned paper, sgn/dtd 1959/titled/inscr, 21x23", SBY 11/11/88	17,600
Exploding Square II (colored squares), oil on paper laid down on board, sgn/titled, 1958, 28x28", SBY 11/11/88	25,300
Hommage aux Prix Nobel (Hommage to Nobel Peace Prize 1947), oil/brush/ink on board, sgn, ca 1970, 30x20", C-NY 5/3/89	22,000
Hommage aux Prix Nobel (Hommage to Nobel Peace Prize 1947) oil/brush/ink on board, sgn, 1959-60, 30x20", C-NY 5/3/89	22,000
Incomplete Color Scale, oil on canvas, sgn/dtd 1963, 50x26", SBY 2/15/89	35,750
Portrait of the Moon (abstract), oil on canvas, 1961, 54x44", C-NY 5/4/88	38,500
Thirty-Seventh Time Inc Project Diagram, oil on paper laid down on canvas, sgn/dtd Feb 1 59, 12x16", SBY 11/11/88	9,900
Thirty-Seventh Time Inc Project Diagram, oil on paper mounted on canvas, sgn/dtd Feb 1 59, 12x16", SBY 11/9/89	12,100
Untitled (abstract), oil on paper, sgn/dtd 1959, 11x9", C-NY 10/4/89	5,500
JENSEN, Bill (American, 20th C)	
Untitled (abstract), charcoal on vellum, sgn/dtd 1978, 16x16", C-NY 11/10/88	3,520
JENSEN, George (American, 1878-)	
Stream in Winter, oil on canvas, sgn, 22x30", RWS 9/8/89 UE	425
JENSEN, Johan Laurents (Danish, 1800-1856)	
Pink Roses, oil on panel, sgn, 7x5", SBY 5/23/89 OE	16,500
Still Life of a Basket of Fruit & a Wreath of Asters, Dahlias...; oil on canvas, sgn/dtd 1826, 31x46", SBY 2/22/89	99,000
Still Life of a Rose & Violets on a Marble Ledge, oil on panel, sgn/dtd 1843, 9x12", SBY 2/22/89	17,600

Still Life of Pink Roses on a Marble Ledge, oil on panel, inscr on verso, 6x9", SBY 5/23/89 .... **8,800**
Still Life of Poppies & Other Flowers, oil on canvas, sgn, 20x15", SBY 2/22/89 OE **63,250**
Still Life of Primroses on a Marble Ledge, oil on panel, sgn/dtd 1838, 7x9", SBY 10/24/89 .... **19,800**
Still Life of Roses, Carpenteria, & Assorted Flowers in a Glass Vase, oil on panel, sgn, 13x10", C-NY 2/25/88 OE **13,200**
Violets, gouache on paper, sgn, 4x6", SBY 5/23/89 .... **22,000**

:NSEN, Louis (American, 20th C)
Landscape with Lake, oil on canvas, sgn, 19x22", LH 12/4/88 .... **275**

:NSON, Holger H. (American, 20th C)
Landscape (cabin at foot of mountain), oil on canvas, sgn, 30x34", LH 3/20/88 OE **1,700**

:RN-MUNTHE, Gerhard Arij Ludvig Morgenst
Shipping Off the Coast, oil on panel, sgn, 8x9", C-E 2/23/88 .... **495**

:RNBERG, Olaf (Swedish, 1855-1935)
Young Shepherd with Flock, oil on canvas, sgn, 23x25", SBY 6/8/88 .... **990**
Wheat Harvesting, oil on canvas, sgn, 24x18", SBY 6/8/88 .... **1,320**

:RNBERG, Olaf August Andreas (Swedish, 1826-1896)
Fjord, oil on canvas, sgn, 15x20", C-E 5/23/88 .... **2,860**

:RVAS, Charles; att (British, 1675-1739)
Portrait of a Lady, half-length, wearing red & white dress; oil on canvas, oval, 30x25", C-NY 4/8/88 .... **1,100**

:TTEL, Eugene (Austrian, 1845-1901)
Clamming, oil on panel, sgn, 13x25", C-E 10/25/88 OE **7,700**

:WELL, Elizabeth G. (American, 1874-1956)
Gloucester Harbor, oil on cardboard, estate stamp, 18x16", RAB 8/8/89 UE **800**
Ogunquit Harbor (sailboat in harbor), oil on canvas, estate stamp, 14x16", RAB 8/8/89 .... **350**

:WETT, Matthew Harris; att
Portrait of a Man Said To Be Robert Pope, oil on canvas, 30x25", SBY 6/28/89 OE **1,210**

:X, Garnet W. (American, 1895-1979)
In New Hampshire (village scene, church spire in distance), oil on canvas, sgn/dtd 1928, 20x24", RWS 3/31/88 OE **1,100**

, Yu (Chinese, 1738-1823)
Lady Wenji Returning to China (hanging scroll), ink/color on silk, sgn/dtd 1814, 43x33", SBY 5/31/89 .... **1,925**

A, Cai (Chinese, fl 1680-1760)
Landscape (hanging scroll), ink/color on paper, sgn, 69x41", SBY 5/31/89 .... **8,250**

AN, Wang (Chinese, 1598-1677)
Landscape After Dong Yuan (hanging scroll), ink on paper, sgn, 22x11", SBY 5/31/89 .... **11,000**

ANFU, Gao (Chinese, 1879-1951)
Prunus (hanging scroll), ink/color on paper, sgn/dtd 1941, 37x13", SBY 5/31/89 .... **2,750**

AYAN, Chen (Chinese, 1529-after 1625)
Magpies in Prunus Trees (hanging scroll), ink on paper, sgn/dtd 1618, 80x37", SBY 5/31/89 .... **17,600**

CHA, Joseph (American, 20th C)
Bahamas (figures on bow of boat), watercolor on paper, sgn, 15x22", WG 4/23/88 .... **375**

MENEZ Y ARANDA, Jose (Spanish, 1837-1903)
Los Dos Pintores (two painters in landscape, model in distance), gouache on paper, sgn/dtd 1886, 12x17", SBY 10/24/89 .... **29,700**

MENEZ Y ARANDA, Luis (Spanish, 1845-1928)
Returning From Market, oil on panel, sgn/dtd 1890, unfr, 18x12", SBY 5/23/89 .... **8,250**
Woman Wearing a Red Shawl Standing in a Doorway, watercolor, sgn/dtd Paris 1893, 16x12", SLK 2/12/88 .... **850**

MINEZ Y MARTIN, Juan (Spanish, 1858-)
Cavalier Resting, oil on panel, sgn/dtd 1887, 15x7", C-NY 10/25/89 OE **30,800**

QIAN, Wang (Chinese, 1907-)
Landscape After Guo XI (hanging scroll), ink on paper, sgn/dtd 1937, 36x20", SBY 5/31/89 OE **4,400**

XIONG, Lao (Chinese, 20th C)
Landscape (hanging scroll), ink/color on paper, dtd 1988, 53x26", SBY 5/31/89 .... **1,210**

OCHEMZ, P.F. (Dutch, 20th C)
Sailboats Docked on a Dutch Beach, oil on panel, sgn, 20x28", B/B 5/17/89 UE **330**

OCHMUS, Harry (German, 1855-1915)
Feeding the Horses, oil on canvas, sgn, 40x48", C-NY 10/25/89 .... **11,000**
Outside the Village Inn, oil on canvas, sgn/inscr, 41x55", C-NY 5/25/88 OE **24,200**
Still Life of Melons, Grapes, Figs, & Other Fruit w/Basket of Flowers in a Landscape; oil, unfr, 39x60", SBY 10/13/89 OE **77,000**

OHANSEN, Andres D. (American/Danish, 20th C)
Flowers & a Pitcher, watercolor on paper, sgn, 22x28", C-E 2/3/88 UE **110**

OHGH, see De Johgh

OHN, Augustus (British, 1878-1961)
Seated Female Nude, pencil on tan paper, sgn, 13x8", RWS 11/3/88 UE **250**

OHNS, Jasper (American, 1930-)
Colored Alphabet, oil/encaustic & paper collage on panel, 1959, 12x11", C-NY 5/3/89 .... **3,520,000**
Diver (abstract), oil/mixed media on 5 canvas panels, stenciled JJ 62, unfr, 90x170", C-NY 5/3/88 .... **4,180,000**
Figure 3, sculpmetal/paper collage on canvas, sgn/dtd 61, 26x20", C-NY 11/9/88 .... **825,000**
Flag, encaustic/collage on canvas, initialed/inscr/dtd 65, 8x11", C-NY 5/3/88 OE **660,000**
Gray Numbers, oil on canvas, sgn/dtd 59-61/inscr dedication, 6x4", C-NY 2/23/89 .... **286,000**
Gray Rectangles, encaustic on canvas, 1957, 60x60", SBY 11/10/88 OE **4,290,000**
High School Days (drawing of shoe), charcoal/graphite/paper collage on paper, 40x30", SBY 5/2/88 OE **34,100**
Land's End (contemporary composition), ink/watercolor on plastic, sgn/dtd 10 Jan 77, 36x25", SBY 11/8/89 .... **990,000**
Light Bulb, pencil/graphite wash on paper, 1958, 7x9", SBY 5/2/88 OE **242,000**

Screen Piece (abstract), oil on canvas, sgn/dtd 1967/titled, 72x50", SBY 5/2/88 OE **660,000**
Screen Piece II, oil on canvas, sgn/dtd 1968/titled, 72x50", SBY 11/12/88 OE **1,375,000**
Untitled (Study for Skin), oil imprint w/powdered graphite on paper, stamped signature, ca 1973, 10x8", SBY 5/2/88 OE **26,400**
White Flag, encaustic/newsprint on 3 attached canvases, sgn/dtd 1955-58/titled, 52x79", C-NY 11/9/88 .... **7,040,000**

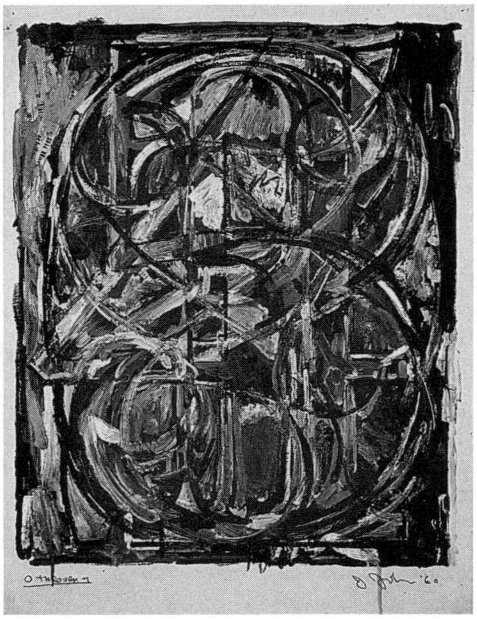

0 Through 9, oil/paper collage on paper mounted on masonite, sgn/dtd 60, 30x22", C-NY 11/7/89, $2,970,000

HNSON, Arthur Clark (American, 1897-)
Mr Daniel Huntley (half-length portrait), oil on canvas, sgn/dtd 1925, 38x28", RWS 3/16/89 UE **100**

JOHNSON, Ben (American, 1902-)
Man & Razor, charcoal/colored crayons on paper, sgn/dtd March 69, 21x15", SBY 2/14/89 .... **660**
Woman Smoking, charcoal/gouache on paper, sgn/dtd 69, 22x15", SBY 2/14/89 .... **660**

JOHNSON, Buffie (American 1912-)
True North, oil on canvas, sgn, 40x60", LH 10/16/88 UE **80**

JOHNSON, Clarence R. (American, 1894-1981)
New Hope, Pennsylvania, by the River; oil on canvas, sgn, ca 1927, 28x30", SBY 5/25/88 OE **45,100**

JOHNSON, David (American, 1827-1908)
Clearing, Mt Lafayette, New Hampshire (landscape); initialed/dtd 1887-88/titled, 27x41", SBY 5/24/89 UE **16,500**
Cottage in a Forest Landscape, oil on board, initialed/dtd 79/inscr Redwood NY, 8x6", SBY 3/17/88 UE **1,650**
Figure in a Landscape, oil on board, 3x4", C-E 2/1/89 OE **2,640**
Fisherman on the Rocks, oil on canvas, initialed, 5x7", B/B 6/15/89 UE **880**
Marlborough, oil on canvas, initialed/dtd 1870, 11x19", C-NY 5/26/88 .... **13,200**
Near Noroton, Connecticut (coastal scene); oil on canvas, sgn twice/dtd 1875 twice, 16x23", SBY 5/24/89 OE **132,000**
Ocean Beach, New Jersey; oil on canvas, sgn/dtd 1876 twice, 10x18", C-NY 9/30/88 OE **13,200**
On Esopus Creek, oil on board, sgn/dtd twice, 1876, inscr, 6x9", C-NY 9/30/88 .... **3,850**
View of the Falls (figures in landscape), oil on panel, initialed, 8x11", C-NY 5/25/89 .... **14,300**

JOHNSON, Frank Tenney (American, 1874-1939)
Bringing in the Horses, oil on canvas, sgn/dtd 1936, 30x40", SBY 5/25/88 .... **71,500**
Camping on the Oregon Trail, oil on canvas, sgn, 30x38", B/B 6/15/89 .... **44,000**
Covered Wagon on the Santa Fe Trail, oil on canvas, sgn/dtd 1933, 20x30", SBY 5/25/88 .... **30,250**
Mexican Ponies, oil on canvas, sgn/titled, 12x16", SBY 6/28/89 .... **16,500**
Old Timer, oil on canvas, sgn/dtd 1920, 18x14", SBY 5/25/88 .... **16,500**
Pair: Studies of Nudes; charcoal on paper, 23x14", B/B 12/8/88 UE **605**
Woodland Landscape, watercolor on paper, sgn/indistinctly dtd, 29x21", SBY 1/24/89 .... **2,750**
Wyoming Landscape, oil on board, 12x16", LH 9/10/89 OE **750**

JOHNSON, Franz (Canadian, 1888-1949)
Early Spring, oil on board, sgn, 15x18", FB 4/25/88 .... **3,200**

JOHNSON, Guy (American, 1927-)
Accident, oil on panel, sgn twice/inscr, 16x13", C-E 5/13/88 .... **880**

JOHNSON, James (American, 1925-1963)
Composition (1962-1963), oil on canvas, 49x40", WG 9/16/88 UE **300**

JOHNSON, Jonathan Eastman (American, 1824-1906)
Edwin Booth As Hamlet (full-length, standing), charcoal/white chalk on paper, initialed/dtd 1845, 20x15", C-NY 9/28/89 .... **8,250**
Golden October, Catskill (cabin in autumn landscape); oil on canvas, initialed/dtd 1869, 10x15", C-SK 5/25/89 .... **5,880**
Portrait of Mrs Cross of Milford, Pennsylvania; oil on board, initialed, 15x13", SBY 6/24/88 .... **1,870**

HNSON, Jonathan Eastman; att (American, 1824-1906)
Man Reading, charcoal on paper, initialed, 15x11", C-E 7/26/88 ... 330
Portrait of a Standing Gentleman, pencil on brown paper mounted on rag paper, initialed, ca 1900, 20x13", SWN 6/15/89 ... 3,960
HNSON, Lester (American, 1919-)
City Classic #1 (group of people), pastel on paper, sgn, 29x41", SBY 10/7/89 ... 8,250
City Scene Ave 6 (figures), chalks on paper, sgn, 30x22", C-NY 10/4/89 ... 4,950
City Women, oil on canvas, sgn, 1974, 40x30", SBY 5/3/89 ... 18,700
Four Men (heads), oil on canvas, 1961, 56x68", SBY 2/15/89 ... 19,800
Lower Broadway (group of men dressed in suits/hats), oil on canvas, sgn, 60x50", SBY 11/11/88 ... 22,000
Oldster (contemporary, half-length), oil/sand on canvas, sgn/dtd 1962, 60x27", C-NY 2/20/88 ... 7,700
One Green Man, canvas mounted on masonite, sgn/dtd 1963, 47x43", C-NY 2/20/88 OE ... 15,400
Street Scene, People Walking No 5; oil on canvas, sgn, 1978, 60x50", SBY 11/9/89 ... 19,800
Street Scene with Buildings #4, oil on canvas, sgn, 1974, 30x40", SBY 2/19/88 ... 11,000
Street Scene-People Walking #2; oil on canvas, sgn, 1977, 50x40", SBY 10/8/88 OE ... 23,100
Temptation of Saint Anthony, oil on canvas, unfr, 32x49", C-E 4/7/88 ... 1,320
Three Men (contemporary, dark heads on light background); oil on canvas, 1960, 54x68", SBY 5/5/89 ... 18,700
Two Women with Men (contemporary), oil on canvas, sgn, 1974, 50x40", SBY 10/5/89 ... 16,500
Untitled, brush/black ink/black crayon on paper laid down on panel, sgn/dtd 1961, 40x26", lot 188, C-E 5/13/88 UE ... 880
Untitled (dark-colored head with abstract background), oil on paper, sgn/dtd 1961, 40x27", C-NY 2/14/89 OE ... 4,180
Untitled (figures), oil on canvas, sgn, 50x40", C-NY 5/4/88 OE ... 19,800
Untitled (street scene), watercolor/pastel on paper, sgn, ca 1975, 29x40", SBY 10/8/88 OE ... 8,250
Untitled (3 women & a man), oil on canvas, sgn, ca 1982, 40x50", SBY 10/8/88 OE ... 27,500
Walking (abstract), oil on canvas, sgn/inscr/dtd 1965, 34x22", C-NY 5/4/88 ... 4,620
Young Man Before a Fence, oil on canvas, sgn/dtd 1963, 24x36", C-NY 5/4/88 ... 6,600
2 Winter Heads, oil on canvas, sgn/dtd 1964, 22x28", SBY 2/15/89 OE ... 16,500
HNSON, Marshall (American, 1850-1921)
Beating to Windward (tall ship in choppy water), oil on canvas, sgn, 18x24", needs restoration, RAB 8/9/88 OE ... 2,900
Mayflower Sighting Cape Cod, oil on canvas, sgn/titled, 18x24", RAB 11/25/88 ... 4,250
Sailing Ship on High Seas, watercolor on paper mounted on cardboard, sgn, 16x20", RWS 11/10/89 ... 1,200
Wrecked on Sambyo NS, stormy scene w/patch of sun illuminating wreck; oil on canvas, sgn/dtd 85, 24x36", RAB 11/10/88 ... 2,250
HNSON, Marshall; att (American, 1850-1921)
Marine Scene (Cape Cod), oil on canvas, 18x24", RWS 9/8/89 UE ... 1,000
HNSON, Reuben LeGrande (American, 1850-1919)
Landscape with Geese, oil on canvas, sgn, 11x14", WL 5/20/88 OE ... 2,900
Resting Cows, oil on canvas, sgn, 24x30", C-E 9/15/88 ... 880
Sheep Grazing in a Pasture, oil on canvas, sgn, 22x30", WL 5/20/88 OE ... 2,400
HNSON, Sidney Yates (British, 19th C)
Rocky Coastline Scene, oil on canvas, sgn/dtd 1900, 18x32", DM 5/19/89 ... 500
Seascape, oil on canvas, sgn/dtd 1909, 131x61", B/B 12/8/88 ... 660
HNSTON, Frank Hans (Canadian, 1888-1949)
Forest Interior, oil on board, sgn, ca 1925, 14x10", FB 10/30/89 ... 3,080
Fraser River Canyon, tempera, sgn, 40x30", WAD 6/12/89 ... 7,500
HNSTON, Henrietta (American, -1728)
Portrait of a Man, small bust-length; pastel on pale blue paper, sgn twice/indistinctly dtd, 12x9", C-SK 6/9/88 OE ... 7,800
Portrait of a Man, small bust-length; pastel on pale blue paper, sgn/dtd South Carolina Ano 1726, 12x9", C-SK 6/9/88 OE ... 4,830
HNSTON, John Bernard (American, 1847-1886)
Napping While the Herd Grazes, oil on masonite, sgn, 16x22", RWS 11/10/89 UE ... 200
HNSTON, John R. (American, 19th C)
Boy & Girl by a Country Fence, oil on canvas, sgn/dtd 1890, 20x36", C-E 2/16/88 ... 990
Fall Landscape with Stream, oil on canvas, sgn, 19x35", C-E 11/30/88 UE ... 990
HNSTON, W.R. (European, 19th C)
Shipwreck Rescue, oil on canvas, sgn, 30x50", C-E 10/25/88 ... 1,980
HNSTONE, Henry James (British, 1835-1907)
Backwater of the River Murray, South Australia; oil on canvas, sgn, 24x36", C-NY 10/25/89 ... 19,800
Shepherdess, watercolor on paper, sgn, 10x7", SBY 6/8/88 OE ... 6,050
Shepherdess with Dog, watercolor on paper, sgn, 10x7", SBY 6/8/88 OE ... 4,125
Woodgatherer, watercolor on paper, sgn, 10x7", SBY 6/8/88 OE ... 6,050
INER, Harvey (American, 1852-1932)
Light in the Forest, oil on canvas, 16x27", NA 2/24/89 ... 950
Stream Through a Stand of Birchwood, oil on canvas, sgn, 26x46", B/B 9/14/89 OE ... 2,750
LI, Antonio (Italian, 1700-1777)
Piazza San Marco, Venice, Looking East From South of the Central Line; oil on canvas, 21x38", SBY 6/1/89 ... 176,000
LLY, C.E. (Continental, 18th/19th C)
Two Ships at Sea, oil on panel, sgn/dtd 1901, 11x15", WG 9/16/88 ... 575
NAS, Leroy F. (American, 1897-)
Moonlight & Clouds, oil on canvas, sgn, 20x24", MAG 6/22/89 ... 350
NES, Allen (British, 1937-)
Black Shadow (contemporary), oil on canvas, 1964, 48x84", SBY 5/3/89 ... 22,000
NES, Charles (British, 1836-1892)
Sheep at Twilight, oil on canvas, sgn/dtd 1890, 24x42", SBY 7/12/89 ... 5,500

JONES, D. Paul (American, 1860-)
Still Life, Vase of Flowers; oil on canvas, sgn/dtd 23, 20x16", NA 2/6/88 UE ... 400
JONES, Daniel Adolphe Robert (Belgian, 1806-1874)
Sheepdog with Mountain Rams & Lamb, oil on panel, sgn, 17x23", SBY 12/9/88 ... 5,225
JONES, Francis Coates (American, 1857-1932)
Garland of Yellow Roses, portrait, oil on canvas, 16x13", C-NY 3/11/88 ... 4,620
In the Parlor, oil on canvas, sgn, 27x22", C-NY 3/11/88 OE ... 23,100
Meditation, oil on canvas, sgn, 20x14", B/B 6/15/89 ... 22,000
Sunny Day (portrait of a young woman on the beach), oil on canvas, sgn, 12x10", WD 4/13/88 OE ... 24,000
Woman at Teatime, oil on canvas, sgn, unfr, 30x36", LH 5/15/88 OE ... 42,000
JONES, Frederick (American, 1914-)
Figural Study, watercolor, 17x13", MAG 4/24/88 ... 250
JONES, Grace Church (American, 20th C)
Mountain Landscape, oil on canvas, sgn, 16x24", RAB 3/27/89 UE ... 100
JONES, H.F. (British, 19th C)
Going to the Derby, oil on canvas, sgn/dtd 1866, 10x30", C-E 5/22/89 OE ... 6,380
JONES, Henry Wanton (Canadian, 1925-)
Still Life, oil on board, sgn, 10x12", FB 10/17/88 ... 475
Still Life of Cactus, oil on board, sgn/dtd 1982, 14x12", FB 10/17/88 ... 400
Vase & Paper Bag, oil on board, sgn/dtd 1983, 14x16", FB 10/17/88 ... 850
JONES, Herbert H. (British, 19th/20th C)
Dog Rose (horse in stable), oil on canvas, sgn/dtd 1902 & 1903, 12x16", SBY 12/9/88 ... 1,760
JONES, Hugh Bolton (American, 1848-1927)
Arab Market Scene, oil on board, sgn/dtd 1882, 12x18", B/B 6/15/89 ... 2,750
Autumn Landscape, oil on canvas, 18x24", SBY 6/24/88 ... 2,750
Broken Fence (landscape), oil on canvas, sgn, 20x30", C-NY 12/2/88 ... 9,350
Brook in Autumn, oil on canvas, sgn, 24x40", C-NY 12/2/88 ... 30,800
Brook-Morning (landscape); oil on canvas, sgn, 30x36", SBY 5/24/89 ... 13,200
Brookside Pasture, oil on canvas, sgn, 16x24", C-NY 12/2/88 ... 22,000
Early Spring (landscape), oil on canvas, sgn, 16x24", C-NY 5/26/88 OE ... 30,800
Fresh Spring (landscape), oil on canvas, sgn, 16x24", C-NY 12/2/88 ... 8,800
Landscape with Ducks, oil on canvas, sgn/dtd NY 1868, 18x36", C-NY 9/28/89 ... 24,200
Landscape with House, oil on canvas, sgn, 17x24", B/B 3/22/89 ... 4,675
Lush Spring, oil on canvas, sgn, 14x20", C-NY 9/30/88 ... 4,400
Pond in a Landscape, watercolor on paper, sgn, 14x17", B/B 3/22/89 ... 3,025
Winter Landscape at Sunset, oil on board, sgn, 16x24", MAG 4/24/88 OE ... 6,500
JONES, Jessie B.
Dusk at the Bridge, oil on canvas, sgn, no size given, C-E 9/15/88 ... 935
JONES, Joe (American, 1909-1963)
Girl Reading (at small table in an interior), oil on canvas, sgn, 24x20", C-E 6/1/89 ... 4,620
The Smile, oil on canvas, sgn, 16x13", C-E 6/1/89 ... 1,320
JONES, Mary Bacon (American, 1868-1924)
Summer Landscape, oil on canvas, sgn, 15x18", SBY 4/14/89 OE ... 1,870
JONES, Paul (British, 19th C)
Pair: Close Encounter; Great Huntsman; oil on panel, sgn/dtd 1877, 8x6", B/B 10/9/88 ... 4,125
Pair: Farmyard Scenes; oil on canvas, sgn/dtd 1879, 12x9", B/B 6/15/89 ... 2,090
JONES, Richard (British, 1767-1840)
Stephen Denstone of Stanwardine Hill, Shropshire; oil on canvas, 36x43", SBY 6/10/88 ... 33,000
JONES, Richard; att (British, 1767-1840)
Bay Hunter with Spaniels in a Landscape, oil on canvas, 10x14", SBY 6/10/88 OE ... 3,410
JONES, Samuel John Egbert (British, 1820-1849)
Pair: Catch; Patience (men fishing in streams); oil on canvas, 12x14", SBY 6/9/89 OE ... 23,100
JONES, Susan (American, 1897-)
Grapes (still life), oil on canvas, sgn, 10x14", RWS 5/12/89 ... 225
JONGERE, see De Jongere
JONGH, see De Jongh
JONGKIND, Johan Barthold (Dutch, 1819-1891)
Landscape with Windmill, oil on canvas, sgn, 7x8", WAD 6/6/88 ... 1,600
Pair: Harbor Scenes; pencil/watercolor on paper framed together, sgn, 5x6", WD 5/5/88 ... 2,200
JONNEVOLD, Carl (American, 1856-1930)
Berkeley Woods, oil on canvas, sgn, 16x20", B/B 10/6/88 ... 1,760
Marin Summer Landscape, oil on canvas, sgn, 18x22", B/B 1/11/89 ... 770
Sunset After the Storm, oil on canvas, sgn, 16x20", B/B 10/6/88 ... 1,210
JONNIAUX, Alfred (Belgian, 1882-)
Portrait of an Elegant Parisian Lady, oil on canvas, sgn, 79x40", B/B 6/15/89 OE ... 18,700
Portrait of Kathleen, oil on canvas, sgn, 24x20", DM 2/19/88 ... 550
JONSON, Cornelis (Dutch, 1593-1664)
Portrait of a Gentleman, Standing, three-quarter length; oil on panel, initialed, 15x12", C-NY 4/6/89 OE ... 9,900
Portrait of a Man Wearing a Black Costume & White Ruff, oil on panel, initialed/dtd 1625, 31x25", C-NY 10/12/89 OE ...
JONSON, Cornelis; att (Dutch, 1593-1664)
Portrait of a Gentleman, half-length, in armour & white lace collar; oil on panel, 31x26", C-NY 6/2/88 ... 7,150

Portrait of a Gentleman, oil on canvas, inscr, 29x22", SBY 1/12/89 11,000
Portrait of a Gentleman, oil on canvas, inscr/dtd 1655, 46x37", SBY 6/8/88 2,750
Portrait of a Little Girl in a Pink Dress with Her Pet Dog, oil on canvas, sgn/dtd 1652, 43x35", SBY 6/2/89 OE 143,000
Portrait of a Man Said To Be Edward Cornewall, Esquire, half-length; oil on canvas, 30x24", SBY 4/7/88 OE 6,875
Portrait of William, 2nd Viscount Grandison, in Military Garb; inscr, 49x39", SBY 10/21/88 UE 4,400

)NSON, Cornelis; circle of (Dutch, 1593-1664)
Portrait of a Young Lady, bust-length, wearing white & black dress; oil on panel, oval, 25x19", C-NY 10/20/88 1,760

)NSON, Cornelis; school of (Dutch, 1593-1664)
Portrait of a Cleric, Aged 79, in Clerical Robe Holding a Book; oil on canvas, inscr/dtd 1670, 28x24", C-NY 4/8/88 1,210

)NSON, Raymond
The Temple, oil on canvas, sgn/dtd 1918, 16x20", C-E 10/18/89 UE 1,650

)ORS, Eugene (Belgian, 1850-)
Still Life of Apples, Pears, & Two Jugs of Wine on a Table; oil on canvas, sgn, 25x30", C-E 5/22/89 3,300

)OSTENS, Paul (Belgian, 1889-1960)
Untitled (abstract), collage on board, ca 1917, 13x12", C-NY 10/6/88 OE 6,380

)RDAENS, Jacob; & Studio (Flemish, 1593-1678)
Infant Jupiter Fed by the Goat Amalthea, oil on canvas, 73x87", SBY 10/21/88 55,000

)RDAENS, Jacob; circle of (Flemish, 1593-1678)
Profile Head of a Man, oil on panel, 19x14", SBY 12/9/88 1,320

)RDAENS, Jacob; manner of (Flemish, 1593-1678)
Peasants Merry-Making in an Interior, oil on canvas, 43x61", C-NY 4/8/88 OE 4,400

)RDAENS, Jacob; school of (Flemish, 1593-1678)
Mary & Martha, oil on canvas, 79x52", C-NY 10/20/88 UE 1,100

)RDAENS, Jacob; studio of (Flemish, 1593-1678)
Triumph of Bacchus, oil on canvas, unfr, 80x60", SBY 4/7/88 7,700

)RDAN, Samuel (1803/04-after 1831)
Portrait of Young Woman Wearing Pink Shawl Posed Before an Open Window, oil on canvas, 29x23", SBY 1/28/88 UE 2,640

)RGENSEN, Christian (American, 1860-1935)
Quiet Creek, oil on paper, sgn, 10x13", RAB 8/9/88 UE 100
Quiet Creek (mirror-like stream banked by green trees), oil on paper, sgn, 10x13", RAB 8/9/88 UE 100

)RGENSON, Nels
Hudson River View, oil on canvas, sgn/dtd 1910, 14x20", C-E 6/1/89 1,980

)RISSEN, Willem
Pair: Mother & Child Reading; Mother & Her Boy Reading; oil on canvas, sgn, 16x21", C-E 5/23/88 3,300

)SEPH, Jacques Francois; see Swebach-Desfontaines, Jacques

)SEPH, Julian (American, 20th C)
Afternoon in the Park, oil on canvas, sgn/dtd 46, 35x28", SBY 9/14/89 3,025
Fifth Avenue, oil on canvas, sgn, 39x31", C-E 10/18/89 3,300

)ULLIN, Amadee (American, 1862-1917)
Back Bay Marsh Scene, oil on canvas laid on panel, sgn, 11x14", B/B 10/6/88 1,045
Yeong Wo Joss House, San Francisco (two men in interior); oil on canvas, 20x26", WD 10/5/88 3,000

)UVE, Paul (French, 1880-)
S Paraskevi Salonique, pencil/pen/ink on paper, sgn/dtd 1916, 19x25", SBY 3/10/89 1,540
View of Notre Dame, oil on canvas, sgn, 37x26", SBY 3/10/89 2,310
View of Riems Cathedral, oil on canvas, sgn/titled, 31x22", SBY 3/10/89 2,310

)UVENET, Jean Baptiste (French, 1644-1717)
Saint Paul, oil on canvas, 30x26", C-NY 10/20/88 1,650

)UVENET, Jean Baptiste; circle of (French, 1644-1717)
Seated Nude, red chalk, wm CAB with heart, inscr, 11x15", C-NY 1/11/89 2,200

)UVENET, Jean Baptiste; follower of (French, 1644-1717)
Latona Turning the Lyceans into Frogs, oil on canvas, 49x39", SBY 6/1/89 8,800

)Y, John (Canadian, 1925-)
Tired Old Iron, watercolor, sgn/dtd 67, 17x23", WAD 11/30/89 250

)Y, Thomas Musgrove (British, 1812-1866)
Going to School (two elegant girls w/small dog in coastal landscape), oil on canvas, sgn/dtd 1860, 36x25", C-NY 2/23/89 19,800

)YCE, Marshall W. (American, 20th C)
Helmsman (man in slicker at wheel of sailboat in storm), oil on masonite, sgn, 18x24", RAB 8/9/88 700

JAN, see De Juan

JAREZ, Jose
Birth of the Virgin (many figures in an interior), oil on copper, indistinctly sgn, 40x33", C-NY 4/6/89 16,500

JAREZ, Roberto (20th C)
Vieja Luna (abstract), acrylic on canvas, sgn/dtd NYC 1982, 57x73", SBY 5/3/88 UE 4,400

JDD, Donald (American, 1928-)
Group of 5: Untitled Drawings (lineations); graphite on paper, sgn/dtd 74, ea 23x31", C-NY 11/10/88 13,200

JDSON, Alice (American, -1948)
Harbor Scene, oil on canvas, sgn, 16x20", SBY 1/24/89 880
Stream by a Farmhouse, oil on canvas, sgn, 20x24", SBY 3/17/88 OE 2,750
Winding Road, oil on canvas, sgn/titled, 20x24", SBY 3/17/88 1,320

JDSON, William Lees (American, 1842-1928)
California Landscape, oil on canvas, sgn, 17x23", B/B 10/6/88 2,750
English Country House by a Lily Pond, watercolor on paper, sgn, 17x22", B/B 1/11/89 825

Golden Sky, watercolor on paper, sgn, 11x16", B/B 1/11/89 330

JULIANA Y ALBERT, Jose (Spanish, 19th C)

Blessing, watercolor on paper w/traces of pencil, sgn, 15x10", C-E 5/23/88 OE 1,100
Venetian Gondoliers Across From the Doge's Palace, oil on panel, sgn, 17x28", SBY 2/22/89 OE 11,000

JULIEN, Henri Octave (Canadian, 1852-1908)

Le Porteur d'Eau, ink, embossed stamp, 14x10", FB 5/28/89 750
Return From Market (man on horse-drawn sled), oil on board, sgn/dtd 1903, 12x18", FB 10/17/88 OE 18,000

JULIEN (20th C)

Portrait of a Clown, oil on board, 22x38", MG 11/19/88 UE 350

JULLIARD, Jacques Nicolas (1715/19-1790)

Jupiter & Callisto, oil on canvas, sgn/dtd 1770, 21x25", SBY 4/7/88 9,350

JUN, Su (Chinese, 18th C)

Landscape After Huang Gongwang (hanging scroll), ink/color on paper, sgn/dtd 1767(?), 44x29", SBY 5/31/89 2,475

JUNG, Charles Jacob

Pair: Winter Afternoon; Winter Morning; oil on canvas laid down on masonite, sgn, 29x35", C-E 10/18/89 3,850

JUNGWIRTH, Joseph (Austrian, 20th C)

Blumen Zu Waidhofen, oil on canvas, sgn/dtd 46, 28x20", SBY 7/12/89 2,090

JUNIOR, Joseph D. Strong (American, 1852-1899)

Mt Shasta From the Valley, oil on canvas, sgn/dtd 1880, 14x24", B/B 1/11/89 522

JURUTKA, Josef

Still Life of Books, Inkwell, & Money on a Red Table Cloth; oil on panel, sgn, 20x25", C-E 2/23/88 3,080

JUTZ, Carl (German, 1838-)

Ducks at the Water's Edge, oil on panel, sgn/dtd 74, 5x7", C-NY 2/23/89 OE 18,700

KABAKOV, Ilya (Russian, 1933-)

Answers of the Experimental Group, oil/Alkit enamel/handwritten text in ink, sgn/dtd 1970-71, 48x146", SBY 7/7/88 OE 40,000
The Answers...(contemporary); oil/Alkit enamel/handwritten text in ink on board, sgn/dtd 1970-71, 58x120", SBY 7/7/88 24,000
Where Are They?, oil/Alkit enamel/handwritten text in black ink on board, sgn/dtd 1970-71, 58x138", SBY 7/7/88 32,000
Where Are You? (contemporary), colored pencil/handwritten text on paper on 36 sheets, sgn, album: 19x13", SBY 7/7/88 OE 24,000

KACZ, Komiomi (Hungarian, 1880-)

Interior Scene (elegantly furnished room), oil on canvas, sgn, 29x23", WG 4/23/88 700

KADAR, Bela (Hungarian, 1877-1956)

Bride (portrait), gouache on brown board, sgn, 18x12", C-E 5/9/89 2,640
City at Night, watercolor/charcoal on paper, sgn, 9x11", SBY 2/14/89 OE 3,575
Composition with Rider & Birds, gouache, sgn, 23x33", SBY 5/30/89 3,300
Egyptian Composition, oil on canvas, sgn, 20x24", C-NY 2/18/88 1,980
Embrace, gouache on paper, sgn, 36x24", C-NY 10/6/88 OE 8,800
Faces Against a Backdrop of Classical Ruins, watercolor on paper, 25x16", WG 4/23/88 UE 600
Figures & Horses in a Stable Yard (contemporary), ink/watercolor on paper, sgn, 12x19", SBY 10/7/89 1,100
Four Figures, watercolor on paper, sgn, 12x8", WD 5/5/88 UE 700
Group of 3: Tigers; Wrestlers; Hill Town; pen/ink on paper, unfr, 12x8" or smaller, C-E 1/12/88 OE 440
Head Design, gouache, sgn, unfr, 12x9", PHL 11/15/88 500
Hungarian Couple, gouache on paper, sgn, 32x23", SBY 2/18/88 3,850
Lovers (2 abstract figures), ink wash on paper, 17x11", WG 4/23/88 500
Milkmaid with Cows (contemporary composition), gouache on paper, sgn, 17x24", SBY 10/6/89 13,200
Mountain Village, watercolor on tan paper, sgn, 7x10", C-E 5/13/88 990
Nude at the Window, watercolor/pencil on paper, sgn, 18x12", C-E 5/9/89 3,080
Nudes with Circus Animals, pen/ink/watercolor on paper, sgn, unfr, 12x19", C-E 1/12/88 528
Pair: Horses at the Mill; Abduction; pencil on paper, pen/black ink on paper, sgn, 6x8", 8x9", C-E 5/13/88 715
Pair: In the Grips of a Giant; Composition with Figures, ink/wash; ink on paper, sgn, 11x8", 9x11", SBY 10/5/88 880
Pair: Three Nudes in Interior; Reclining Nude; gouache on paper; watercolor/India ink on paper, sgn, 12x8", SBY 2/14/89 1,760
Reclining Nude (modernistic), gouache/pencil on paper, laid down on board, sgn, 29x39", SBY 10/6/89 14,300
Standing Figure (abstract composition), ink/watercolor heightened w/bodycolor, sgn, unfr, 14x10", PHL 11/15/88 700
Standing Figure & Abstract Figure, gouache on paper, sgn, 29x27", SBY 10/5/88 UE 1,210
Standing Nude with Fruit Bowl, gouache on paper, sgn, 40x29", SBY 11/12/88 OE 26,400
Standing Nude with Fruit Bowl (modernistic), gouache on paper, sgn, 40x29", SBY 10/6/89 22,000
Stripper's Dream, gouache on paper laid down on canvas, sgn, 33x25", C-NY 2/16/89 OE 6,050
Stripper's Dream (nude standing before a crowd), gouache on paper laid down on canvas, sgn, 33x25", C-NY 10/5/89 6,600
Two Figures with Column & House, gouache on paper, sgn, 1929-30, 23x31", SBY 10/5/88 UE 1,650
Two Women, brush/sepia wash on paper, sgn, unfr, 34x24", C-NY 2/13/89 1,760
Woman Holding a Dove, brush/ink/wash on paper laid down on board, sgn, 34x24", C-E 5/9/89 1,540
Young Boy with a Hat, gouache on paper laid down on canvas, sgn, 30x23", C-NY 2/16/89 OE 5,280
Young Woman Before a Crowd, watercolor, sgn, unfr, 12x9", PHL 11/15/88 600

KADISHMAN, Menashe (American, 20th C)

Head of a Sheep (contemporary), acrylic/oil on canvas, sgn/dtd 1984, unfr, 51x38", C-NY 5/4/89 11,000

KAELIN, Charles Salis (American, 1858-1929)

Boats in a Harbor, pastel on paper, sgn, 15x16", SBY 6/24/88 OE 5,775
Boats in a Harbor (houses beyond), oil on canvas, sgn, 16x16", C-E 6/1/89 OE 3,520
Harbor, pastel on gray paper, sgn, 10x11", C-NY 3/11/88 4,400
Jagged Coastline, pastel on gray paper, sgn, 15x17", RWS 11/10/89 OE 2,000
Rockport Harbor, oil on canvas, sgn, 21x24", C-E 10/18/89 4,400
Sailboats at Their Moorings, pastel on paper, sgn, 17x14", SBY 1/24/89 UE 1,650

Waves on the Coast, oil on board, sgn, 8x10", LH 12/4/88 700
Winter Woods, pastel on gray paper, sgn, 16x18", C-E 6/1/89 UE 1,650
EMMERER, Frederik Hendrik (Dutch, 1839-1902)
The Apple Harvest, oil on canvas, sgn, 22x13", B/B 3/17/88 11,000
ESEN, H.R. (Continental, 19th C)
Fixing Her Corsage, oil on canvas, sgn/dtd 95, 40x30", C-E 10/26/89 5,500
GY, Wilhelm (Swedish, 1889-1960)
Portrait of the Artist's Wife (holding bowl of fruit), oil on panel, sgn/dtd 1933, 20x16", MAG 6/22/88 OE 2,300
HLO, Frida (Mexican, 1910-1954)
Autorretrato con Diego en mi Pecho (self-portrait w/Diego & dog), oil on masonite, ca 1953-54, 24x16", C-NY 11/21/88 143,000
Ella Juega Sola o Nina con Mascara de la Muerte, oil on tin, sgn/dtd 38, 6x4", C-NY 11/21/89 OE 242,000
La Tierra Misma o Dos Desnudos en la Jungla (woman comforting another), oil on tin, sgn/dtd 39, 10x12", C-NY 11/21/89 OE 506,000
Portrait of Cristina (younger sister of artist), oil on panel, sgn/dtd 1928, 31x24", SBY 11/21/88 198,000
Tu Suegra Cantina, watercolor on paper, sgn/dtd Julio 18 1927, 8x10", SBY 5/16/89 30,800
Tunas, oil on tin, 1938, 8x10", SBY 5/17/88 74,250
HN, Wolf (American/German, 1927-)
Adams Farm Marlboro II, oil on canvas, sgn, 52x66", C-NY 12/2/88 9,350
Beach Houses, pastel on paper, sgn, 13x16", SBY 2/14/89 OE 2,310
Blue at the Racetrack, oil on canvas, sgn/dtd 1977, 22x40", SBY 10/8/88 UE 4,400
Charity, oil on canvas, 46x62", C-NY 10/20/88 4,950
Crabapple Trees in Tennessee (in yard w/birdhouse on pole), oil on canvas, sgn, 1981, 36x52", C-NY 9/28/89 11,000
Flowers in a Vase, pastel on paper, sgn, 11x8", SBY 1/24/89 OE 1,760
Green Airstrip II, oil on canvas, sgn/dtd 1983, 36x52", SBY 10/8/88 12,100
Hidden Beaver Pond, oil on canvas, sgn, 14x18", C-E 11/30/88 OE 2,420
Landscape with Pond, pastel on paper, sgn/dtd 86, 24x31", SBY 6/28/89 2,090
Late Fall, Panoramic Landscape; oil on canvas, sgn, 37x52", C-NY 5/26/88 OE 18,700
Long Farmstead (landscape), oil on canvas, sgn/dtd 1980/#d, 22x28", SBY 2/14/89 5,500
March in Vermont II (landscape), oil on canvas, sgn, 24x30", C-NY 5/25/89 4,950
Neighbor Shed, oil on canvas, sgn, 26x44", C-E 11/30/88 OE 13,200
New England Barn, oil on canvas, sgn/dtd 1985, 32x52", C-NY 9/30/88 10,450
Rhoads Farm, oil on canvas, sgn, 16x30", SBY 6/28/89 2,860
Saint Anthony of Padua Adoring the Infant Christ, oil on canvas, inscr, 84x57", C-NY 10/20/88 UE 2,420
Salt Marsh (landscape), oil on canvas, sgn/dtd 1977/titled, 36x52", SBY 2/19/88 OE 11,000
Spot of Blue Sky, oil on canvas, sgn, 32x55", C-NY 9/30/88 7,700
Street Scene, pastel on paper, sgn/dtd 1950, 8x10", SBY 2/14/89 825
Summer Flowers in a Glass Vase, oil on canvas, initialed, 34x25", C-NY 5/25/89 6,050
The Yellow Field (landscape), oil on canvas, sgn/dtd 1973/#d 113, 40x52", SBY 2/15/89 13,200
Thurber Farmyard in the Afternoon, oil on canvas, sgn, 1981, 22x46", C-NY 9/28/89 6,050
Tree Sentinels (landscape), oil on canvas, sgn/dtd 85, 53x63", C-NY 12/2/88 13,200
View of Edgartown, pastel on paper, sgn/dtd Edgartown 1971, 9x11", SBY 1/24/89 935
ISER, Richard (German, 1868-1941)
Upper Bavaria (pastoral landscape), oil on canvas, sgn, 24x32", B/B 10/9/88 1,760
KE, T. (American, 20th C)
Child in a Pastoral Setting, oil on canvas, sgn, 12x18", SLK 2/12/88 175
LLMEYER, Minnie (Canadian, 1882-1947)
Fishing Boats, Concarneau, France; oil on board, sgn, 9x7", WAD 6/12/89 280
LMYKOV, Ivan Leonidovich (Russian, 1866-1925)
Coastal Scene, oil on canvas, sgn, 40x33", C-L 10/8/88 OE 5,580
LTENMOSER, Karl (Kasper)(German, 1806-1867)
Flirtation, oil on canvas, sgn/dtd 1866, 33x27", C-NY 2/25/88 OE 11,000
LTSCHARSCH (Austrian, 20th C)
Village Archway, oil on board, sgn/dtd 1921, 19x14", LH 9/10/89 90
MPF, Arthur; after (German, 1864-1950)
Punjabi Soldier (three-quarter length portrait), sgn & indistinctly inscr After A Kampf, 34x20", B/B 9/14/89 UE 605
MY, Barnard (American, 20th C)
Autumn, oil on canvas, sgn, 36x24", LH 10/16/88 UE 70
Forest with Pond, oil on canvas, sgn, 24x36", LH 10/16/88 UE 50
Mediterranean Port, oil on canvas, sgn, 18x24", LH 10/16/88 UE 300
Rocky Coast, oil on canvas, sgn, 24x36", LH 10/16/88 UE 50
Springtime, oil on canvas, sgn, 36x24", LH 10/16/88 UE 60
NDINSKY, Wassily (Russian, 1866-1944)
Composition, India ink on paper mounted on stiff card, initialed/dtd 32/#d 22, 16x11" overall, SBY 5/10/89 OE 48,400
Composition, pen/ink over pencil on paper mounted on board, initialed/dtd 40, 6x9", SBY 11/16/89 OE 30,800
Composition (abstract), pen/ink/watercolor n paper, initialed/dtd 18, 12x18", SBY 5/10/89 OE 330,000
Composition No 1, brush/ink/watercolor on paper, monogramed/dtd 15, 13x9", SBY 11/12/88 156,750
Double-Sided: Park von Saint Cloud; oil on board, inscr, 1906, 10x13", SBY 11/12/88 OE 192,500
Drei Saulen, oil on board, monogramed/dtd K 43/#d 719, 16x23", C-NY 5/11/88 319,000
Geflecht von Oben, No 231 (composition); gouache/watercolor/pen/ink on paper, monogramed/1927, 13x19", C-NY 5/11/89 OE 440,000
Grau-Grun-Braun #138, watercolor/gouache/India ink on paper, initialed/dtd 1924/#d 138, 14x10", SBY 11/16/89 OE 440,000
Herbstlandschaft (abstract landscape), oil on canvas, sgn/dtd 1911, 28x39", SBY 5/9/89 3,960,000
Kallmunz mit Burg, oil on canvas, inscr, 1903, 13x10", SBY 5/11/88 OE 275,000

L'Entourage Blanc (fantasy drawing), gouache on paper, monogramed/dtd 39, 20x14", C-NY 5/11/89 OE **209,000**
La Ligne Volontaire, gouache on paper laid down on board, initialed/dtd 36, 19x14", C-NY 11/15/88 .... **165,000**
Landschaft mit dun Klem Baum (abstract landscape), oil on board, 1908, 13x16", C-NY 5/11/88 .... **440,000**
Petits Plans, gouache on black still card mounted on board, initialed/dtd 1936, 20x13", SBY 11/16/89 OE **203,500**
Plumpe Flache (abstract), watercolor/India ink on paper mounted on black paper, initialed/dtd 28, 13x19", SBY 5/11/88 .... **176,000**
Study for Mit Gruner Dame (relates to a lost glass painting), pen/ink on paper, 1917, 13x16", SBY 5/10/89 .... **29,700**
Untitled (abstract), watercolor/pen/black ink on paper laid down on board, monogramed, 1915, 11x13", C-NY 5/11/89 OE **209,000**
Untitled: The Black Line; India ink/watercolor on paper, initialed/dtd 22, 13x19", SBY 11/16/89 OE **440,000**
Vasilevskoie-Barn with Pony; oil on artist board, sgn/#d 45, 1903, 9x13", SBY 5/10/89 .... **143,000**

KANE, John (American, 1860-1934)
Girl with Collie (primitive), oil on canvas, sgn/dtd 1931, 11x14", SBY 1/24/89 .... **8,250**
Grandma at Fireside (Grandma & the Children), primitive, oil on canvas, sgn, ca 1928-29, 8x10", SBY 1/24/89 .... **3,850**
Playing Doctor (children at play), primitive, oil on canvas, sgn, 16x20", SBY 1/24/89 .... **9,350**

KANNEMANS, Christian Cornelis (Dutch, 1812-1884)
Boats Tossed in Rough Waters Near Shore, oil on panel, sgn, unfr, 17x23", SBY 7/12/89 .... **2,750**

KAPLAN, Edith Jaffrey (American, 20th C)
Anna Ironing, oil on board, sgn, 29x23", FAP 12/8/89 UE **250**

KAPPES, Alfred (American, 1850-1894)
News From the Old Sod (man reads newspaper), oil on canvas, sgn/dtd 79/titled, 16x13", RAB 8/8/89 UE **1,000**

KAPPS, Karl
Lady in Yellow Coat, gouache on board, sgn/dtd 91, 7x4", C-E 9/15/88 .... **330**

KARFUNKLE, David (American, 19th C)
Landscape with Cherry Blossoms & Weeping Willow, oil on canvas, sgn, 16x20", C-E 2/1/89 UE **330**

KARLOUSZKY, Bertalan (Hungarian, 1858-1939)
Nude (standing, full-length, viewed from behind), oil on canvas, sgn, 26x20", WG 4/23/88 UE **650**

KAROLY, Andrew (20th C)
Whaling, pencil, sgn/dtd 1971, 11x16", SWN 12/1/88 .... **275**

KARS, Georges (Czechoslovakian, 1882-)
Still Life of Teapot & Fruit, oil on canvas, sgn, 26x32", SBY 5/30/89 OE **9,900**

KARSSEN, A.N.M. (Continental, 20th C)
Figures in a Frozen Winter Landscape, oil on panel, sgn, 28x30", C-E 2/21/89 .... **1,650**

KASHETSKY, Herzl (Canadian, 1950-)
Send van Gogh Flowers, ink, sgn/dtd 1980, 16x12", FB 4/25/88 .... **200**
Studio, Still Life, oil on board, sgn/dtd 1981, 24x15", FB 4/25/88 .... **750**

KASSAY, K.
Floral Still Life of Zinnias, oil on canvas, ca 1925, 36x24", DM 9/16/88 .... **200**

KASYN, John (Canadian, 1926-)
Back of Gerrard Street, oil on masonite, sgn, 9x7", WAD 6/12/89 .... **900**
Wellesley Street, watercolor, sgn, 8x5", WAD 6/12/89 .... **800**

KATE, see Ten Kate

KATO, E.
Japanese Landscape in Winter, watercolor/gouache on paper, sgn, 12x19", RAB 11/24/89 .... **350**

KATZ, Alex (American, 1927-)
Ada (profile view), oil on board, sgn/dtd 63, 12x12", SBY 2/15/89 .... **9,350**
Ada in Red T-Shirt, oil on masonite, sgn/dtd 80, 12x9", SBY 10/8/88 .... **9,900**
Barbara (portrait of seated lady), pencil on paper, sgn/dtd 1971, 30x23", SBY 11/11/88 OE **7,700**
Beach Scene, Yellow Flower II; oil on masonite, sgn/dtd 86, 9x12", SBY 11/9/89 OE **17,600**
Dog at the End of Pier, watercolor/collage on paper, sgn, 1960, 8x11", SBY 5/3/88 .... **6,600**
Doug (portrait), pencil on paper, sgn/dtd 77, 22x15", SBY 10/5/89 OE **6,050**
Interior, oil on masonite, sgn/dtd 1950, 18x14", SBY 11/19/89 OE **33,000**
Ivy (contemporary still life composition), oil on masonite, sgn, ca 1951, unfr, 10x12", C-E 11/14/89 OE **6,050**
January (window view of building across the way), oil on canvas, sgn/dtd, 49x42", C-NY 5/4/89 OE **85,800**
Jean & Mare (close-up of young lady w/horse), oil on masonite, sgn, 1976, 12x14", C-NY 10/4/89 OE **15,400**
Portrait (woman seated in blue dress, child in red standing at her knee), oil, sgn/dtd 61, 46x59", SBY 10/5/89 .... **22,000**
Portrait of Al Held, oil on masonite, sgn, ca 1963, 17x24", SBY 11/9/89 .... **15,400**
Red Band, oil on aluminum painted on both sides, 1978, 18x48", SBY 10/5/89 .... **35,750**
Rex #1, oil on canvas, 1975, 49x49", C-NY 5/4/89 .... **44,000**
Ruth (three-quarter length, standing in robe), oil on canvas, 1979, 72x48", SBY 2/15/89 .... **49,500**
September (head in profile against blue sky), oil on masonite, sgn, 1964, 12x14", SBY 10/5/89 .... **13,200**
Slab City, oil on canvas, sgn/dtd 63, 48x49", C-NY 11/10/88 OE **30,800**
Superb Lilies (abstract depiction), oil on masonite, sgn, 1966, 9x12", C-NY 10/4/89 .... **6,600**
Tiger Lily #1 (close-up view), oil on canvas, sgn/dtd 68, 32x49", SBY 5/3/89 OE **35,750**
Untitled (close-up of young man's head in landscape), oil on panel, sgn/dtd 70, 16x12", C-NY 10/4/89 .... **8,800**
Untitled (heads of woman & boy w/cityscape beyond), oil on canvas, sgn/dtd 65, 35x63", C-NY 2/20/88 .... **11,000**
Untitled (landscape), paper collage, sgn, ca 1956-60, 5x7", SBY 2/15/89 OE **7,150**
Untitled (red building in landscape), oil on panel, ca 1960, 8x10", SBY 5/3/89 .... **6,600**
Untitled (seascape), paper collage, sgn, ca 1956-60, 8x5", SBY 10/8/88 .... **4,070**
Vase of Flowers (contemporary composition), oil on masonite, sgn, ca 1951, 10x10", C-E 11/14/89 OE **5,720**
Vincent, oil on aluminum painted on both sides, 1979, 18x15", SBY 10/5/89 .... **18,700**
William Dunas (portrait), oil on canvas, 1971, 49x72", SBY 11/11/88 OE **60,500**
2:30, I (woman's head in profile w/scarf); graphite on paper, sgn/dtd 73, 24x31", C-NY 5/4/89 OE **8,800**

IZ, Raymond Alexander (American, 1895-1974)	
'arrot & Trainer, oil on board, initialed, 42x32", NA 2/24/89 UE	350
U, Georg (German, 1870-)	
/illage Service, oil on canvas, sgn, 28x19", PHL 10/28/88 UE	600
UFFMANN, Angelica (Swiss, 1740-1807)	
self-Portrait, oil on panel, inscr, 7x6", SBY 6/8/88 OE	5,775
UFFMANN, Angelica; att (Swiss, 1740-1807)	
'ortrait of a Lady, seated, half-length holding a portfolio; oil on canvas, 30x25", C-NY 4/8/88	1,540
UFFMANN, Angelica; follower of (Swiss, 1740-1807)	
)avid Playing for Saul, oil on copper, bears signature, 8x18", SBY 7/12/89	1,210
UFFMANN, Angelica; school of (Swiss, 1740-1807)	
'erpsichore, oil on canvas, 16x12", C-E 4/7/88	462
UFFMANN, Hugo Wilhelm (German, 1844-1915)	
3avarian Peasant Girl, oil on panel, sgn, 21x9", C-NY 2/25/88	17,600
'ardplayer's Dispute, oil on panel, sgn/dtd 75, 8x9", C-NY 2/25/88	13,200
UFFMANN, Robert C. (American, 20th C)	
anus, oil on canvas, 24x20", C-E 10/18/89 UE	55
UFMAN, John Francois (American/Swiss, 1870-)	
shoe Shine Boy, oil on canvas mounted on panel, sgn/dtd 1897, 22x13", RWS 11/10/89 UE	900
UFMAN, Stuart (American, 1926-)	
'wo Figures in a Garden, oil on panel, sgn/dtd 68, 9x6", C-E 2/16/88	132
UFMANN, Adolf (Austrian, 1848-1916)	
'igure by a Wooded Lake, oil on canvas, sgn, 18x22", C-E 5/23/88	3,740
lightfall Along the River, oil on canvas, sgn, 20x32", C-E 10/26/89	5,500
shepherdess with Sheep in a Spring Landscape, oil on canvas, sgn, 43x38", PHL 10/28/88	4,750
/illage Street, oil on canvas laid down on board, sgn, 22x26", WD 1/11/89	950
UFMANN, Ferdinand (American, 1864-after 1934)	
'ucalyptus in Spring (landscape), oil on canvas, sgn/titled, 30x25", SBY 3/17/88	1,210
ndian Summer in the High Sierras (landscape), oil on canvas, sgn/titled, SBY 3/17/88 UE	1,100
'ranqulity, Late Afternoon, Southern Pacific Coast; oil on canvas, sgn, 30x36", B/B 10/6/88	12,100
UFMANN, Karl (Austrian, 1843-1901)	
'ardinal Reading, oil on panel, sgn, 6x9", C-E 5/23/88 UE	495
leopolitan Port Scene, oil on canvas, sgn, 18x23", C-E 5/22/88	2,970
ULA, Lee Lufkin (American, 1865-1957)	
3lue & Gold (portrait of a young woman), oil on canvas, sgn, 29x29", RWS 11/3/88 OE	8,000
'hoosing an Accessory, oil on canvas, sgn, 29x24", C-NY 9/30/88	7,700
ULA, William Jurian (American, 1871-1953)	
)ownstream (a landscape), watercolor on paper, sgn/dtd 1894, 21x14", RWS 9/8/89	650
Iouse by the Sea, watercolor on paper, sgn/dtd 1894, 12x19", RWS 11/10/89	600
Aillstream, Ipswich, New Hampshire; oil on canvas, sgn/inscr, 35x46", C-NY 5/26/88	52,800
'wilight, watercolor/charcoal on board, sgn, 18x22", C-NY 3/11/88	2,090
'iew Through a Mountain Pass to a Distant Lake, watercolor/graphite on paper, sgn, 7x10", RWS 5/12/89 UE	225
Vinter Landscape, oil on board, sgn/inscr, 12x15", SBY 3/17/88 OE	1,980
'our House in 1920 (white farmhouse in autumn), oil on artist board, sgn/dtd 1920, 12x15", RWS 9/29/88	700
ULBACH, Anton (German, 20th C)	
'ortrait of Lola Montez, oil on canvas, sgn, 66x38", B/B 3/22/89	2,750
ULBACH, Hermann (German, 1846-1909)	
lun with Child, oil on board, 12x9", LH 10/16/88	13,000
US, Max (German, 1891-)	
3eggar Interrupts the Festivities, oil on canvas, sgn, 29x38", WG 9/16/88 UE	550
VANAGH, Joseph (Irish, 1856-1918)	
Aother & Child, oil on canvas, sgn, 21x16", C-E 10/25/88	1,320
VEL, Martin (French, 19th/20th C)	
'arasol (portrait), oil on canvas, sgn, 37x29", C-NY 5/25/88	6,600
'oung Lady Contemplating by a River Bank, oil on canvas, sgn, 32x26", C-E 2/23/88 OE	4,400
Y, Louis (Canadian, 1919-)	
rctic Hunter Carving, oil on canvas, sgn, 20x16", WAD 11/30/89	200
YE, Otis (American, 1885-1974)	
'oins on Rembrandt, tempera over etching on paper, sgn, rounded at top, 14x10", SBY 6/28/89	2,000
)ollar Bill & Coins, tempera, coins on etched bill, sgn, 6" long, SBY 6/28/89	2,860
ey to Success (Trompe l'Oeil), oil on canvas mounted on panel, sgn, 8x10", SBY 5/25/88	24,200
ove of Money (Trompe l'Oeil still life), sgn twice, SBY 5/24/89 OE	28,600
'arget Practice (Trompe l'Oeil still life), oil on panel, sgn, 15x18", SBY 5/24/89 OE	45,100
'rompe L'Oeil, oil on canvas mounted on panel, sgn, 13x10", SBY 5/25/88 OE	20,900
AMMERER, Frederik Hendrik	
etter, oil on panel, sgn, 11x8", C-E 2/23/88	2,860
ANE	
)epicts Ballerina in Black Leotard, Blue Ground; oil on canvas, sgn, 7x21", DM 9/16/88	400
'ortrait of Ballerina, Gray & Pink Ground; oil on canvas, sgn, 7x21", DM 9/16/88	400
ARNS, Jerry (20th C)	
'ear of Music (three contemporary heads), acrylic on canvas, initialed/dtd 1986, unfr, 74x122", C-NY 5/4/89	17,600

KEELER, Burton (American, 20th C)
Still Life of Flowers, oil on canvas, sgn, 24x20", LH 5/15/88 ... 250

KEELHOFF, Franz (Belgian, 1820-1893)
Pastoral Landscape, oil on canvas, 24x36", SLK 9/28/88 ... 2,800

KEIFER, Anselm
Der Eingeborene (contemporary), photograph/paper collage/branches/lead, titled/inscr New York, 38x27", SBY 11/11/88 OE ... 165,000

KEIL, Bernhard (Danish, 1624-1687)
Young Woman Playing a Guitar, oil on panel, circular, 15" dia, SBY 4/7/88 OE ... 15,400

KEIL, Bernhard; follower of (Danish, 1624-1687)
Huntsman at Rest (portrait of man w/gun & dog), oil on canvas, 38x28", SBY 4/7/89 ... 4,400

KEIRINCX, Alexander (Flemish, 1600-1652)
Hunting Scene in an Extensive Wooded River Landscape, oil on canvas, 47x63", SBY 10/21/88 ... 44,000

KEISERMAN (Continental, ca 1800)
Set of 4: Views of Roman Monuments; watercolor on paper, sgn, 7x9", SBY 7/12/89 ... 3,850

KEISTER, Roy (American, 1886-)
Settling Down (two cowboys on horses in a landscape), oil on canvas, sgn, 20x40", B/B 6/15/89 UE ... 1,430

KEITH, Castle (American, 19th/20th C)
Dutch Village, oil on canvasboard, sgn/dtd 07, 10x14", C-E 2/3/88 OE ... 935
Sailboats Along a Dutch Canal, oil on canvas, sgn/dtd 1910, indistinctly inscr, 20x24", B/B 6/15/89 ... 1,980
View Along the Canal (figures in autumn landscape), watercolor on paper, sgn, 10x15", RWS 3/31/88 ... 650
Woman at the Piano, oil on canvas, sgn, 16x22", B/B 3/17/88 ... 2,200

KEITH, W. Castle (American, 19th/20th C)
Cottage Across the Pond, oil on board, sgn, 8x13", RWS 11/10/89 UE ... 150
Cottage at Sunset, oil on canvas, sgn/dtd 1900, unfr, 20x34", C-E 6/1/88 ... 1,100
Evening Grazing, oil on canvas, sgn, 11x15", RWS 11/10/89 ... 350

KEITH, William (American, 1839-1911)
Autumn Twilight (cow in the water), oil on canvas, sgn/inscr SF, 20x30", C-NY 9/28/89 ... 3,300
Cattle at a Stream in a Moonlit Landscape, oil on canvas, sgn/dtd 1892, 20x30", PHL 12/1/88 ... 4,000
Cows in a Clearing, oil on board, sgn, 6x10", B/B 10/6/88 ... 1,980
Figures by a Pool at Sunset, oil on canvas, sgn, 17x22", B/B 10/6/88 ... 3,300
Figures in a Forest, oil on canvas, sgn, 16x24", B/B 10/6/88 ... 3,025
Figures in a Wooded Landscape, oil on canvas, sgn, 16x20", PHL 12/1/88 ... 1,600
Golden California, oil on canvas, sgn, 20x30", B/B 10/6/88 ... 3,575
Heart of the Oaks (figures by a stream in a landscape), oil on canvas, sgn, 20x24", B/B 3/22/89 ... 4,125
Moonlit Forest, watercolor on paper, sgn, unfr, 16x24", B/B 10/6/88 ... 1,100
River Scene at Dusk, oil on board, sgn, 11x15", B/B 9/15/88 OE ... 2,200
Santa Clara Mountains, oil on canvas laid down, sgn, 10x16", B/B 10/6/88 ... 4,125
Spring Storm Clearing Across the Valley, oil on board, sgn, 10x16", B/B 10/6/88 ... 6,600

KEITH, William; att (American, 1839-1911)
Golden Glow, oil on canvas, bears signature, 20x30", B/B 1/11/89 ... 2,475

KELDERMAN, Jan (Dutch, 1911-)
Path by a River, oil on panel, sgn, 12x16", C-E 5/23/88 UE ... 385
Snowy Canal, oil on panel, sgn, 16x24", C-E 10/25/88 UE ... 495

KELLER, Adolphe
Vue de Saint-Tropez (cityscape), oil on canvas, sgn, 29x37", SBY 2/16/89 ... 13,200

KELLER, Arthur Ignatius (American, 1867-1924)
Indians, pen/ink wash heightened w/gouache on board, 19x19", C-E 11/30/88 UE ... 440

KELLER, Dora
Lailio-Cattleyea-Glaucus, watercolor on buff paper, sgn/dtd 1932, 22x28", C-NY 2/3/88 ... 440
Pair: Cypripedium Doris Stanton; Cypripedium Royal Geo; watercolor, sgn/dtd 1934-33, 23x18", C-NY 2/3/88 ... 550
Pair: Cypripedium-Stadium; Cypridedium-Doris Stanton; watercolor on buff paper, sgn/1933, 1 unfr, 23x18", C-NY 2/3/88 ... 605
Pair: Laelio-Cattleya Cantalo; Laelio-Cattleya; watercolor, sgn/1 dtd 1934, 1 unfr, 23x18", 23x19", C-NY 2/3/88 ... 880

KELLER, Edgar Martin (American, 1868-1932)
Charles River in Winter, oil on canvas, sgn/dtd 1923, 36x49", B/B 10/9/88 ... 5,22

KELLER, Ferdinand (German, 1842-1922)
Flora (portrait of a young woman picking flowers), oil on canvas, sgn/dtd 1883, 70x39", C-NY 10/25/89 ... 22,00
View of Rio de Janeiro, oil on canvas, sgn/dtd 1863, 13x18", SBY 5/16/89 ... 7,15

KELLER, Henry George (American, 1870-1949)
Lake Erie Shoreline, oil on canvas, sgn, 13x24", WG 4/23/88 UE ... 50
Plowing Time (man working team of horses), watercolor on paper, sgn, 9x15", WG 4/23/88 ... 55
Rural Landscape in Late Winter (w/bare trees & icy water), oil on canvas laid down on board, sgn, 8x9", WG 4/23/88 UE ... 15
View to the Heights, gouache on board, monogramed, 20x16", WG 9/16/88 UE ... 12
Washerwoman in an Impressionistic Landscape, gouache/watercolor on paper, monogramed, 11x14", B/B 1/11/89 ... 55

KELLER, R. (Dutch, 20th C)
Pair: Snowy Winter Scenes with Skaters on Ponds; oil on panel, 8x10", SLK 9/26/88 ... 95

KELLOGG, C.B. (American, 20th C)
Western Mission, gouache on paper, sgn, 10x14", B/B 1/11/89 UE ... 33

KELLY, Ellsworth (American, 1923-)
Abstract Composition, ink/gouache on paper, initialed/inscr, 11x9", SBY 5/3/88 ... 9,35
Black & White (composition), oil on canvas, sgn/dtd 1976, 91x99", SBY 5/2/89 ... 209,00
Black Triangle with White (abstract), oil on canvas, 107x114", C-NY 5/3/89 ... 715,00

Blue Red (contemporary), oil on canvas, 1965, 65x150", SBY 11/10/88 ..... **264,000**
Brooklyn Bridge (abstract), ink on paper, dtd 1958/titled, 12x9", SBY 11/11/88 ..... **6,050**
Galerie Maeght (abstract), ink on paper, sgn/dtd 64, 14x10", SBY 11/11/88 OE **27,500**
Green (geometric), oil on canvas, 72x88", C-NY 11/7/89 OE **495,000**
Leaf (line drawing), pen/ink on paper, sgn/dtd 1970 twice, 23x29", SBY 11/11/88 OE **35,750**
Lily, graphite on paper, initialed/dtd 23 July 83, 14x11", C-NY 10/31/89 ..... **12,100**
Orange Blue I (abstract), oil on canvas, sgn/dtd 65, 60x54", SBY 5/2/89 OE **363,000**
Red-Orange White (Rogue, abstract), oil on canvas, initialed/dtd 56, 34x38", SBY 11/10/88 ..... **176,000**
Tropical Plant-Santo Domingo; pen/black ink on paper, initialed/sgn/inscr/dtd 1981, 24x18", C-NY 5/4/88 OE **22,000**
Two Lilies (line drawing), pencil on paper, sgn/dtd Aug 8, 1980, 22x30", SBY 5/3/89 OE **28,600**
Two Panels: Red Blue Green Yellow; oil on canvas, initialed/dtd 65, 88x54x88", C-NY 11/7/89 ..... **660,000**
Untitled, ink on paper, sgn/dtd Oct 1984, 10x14", SBY 2/15/89 OE **7,700**
Untitled (abstract), oil on canvas, 1959, 47x25", SBY 11/10/88 ..... **154,000**
Yellow Black (abstract), oil on canvas on 2 panels, 1972, 96x71", SBY 11/10/88 OE **319,000**
Yellow Curve I (yellow diamond form), oil on canvas, sgn/dtd 1972, 67x134", SBY 11/8/89 OE **687,500**

KELLY, Grace V. (American, 1877-1950)
Horse on the Hill, watercolor on paper, sgn, 9x13", WG 4/23/88 UE **100**
Landscape with a Japanese Garden, gouache on paper, monogramed, 15x20", WG 4/23/88 UE **300**
Landscape with Hay Wagon, gouache on paper, monogramed, 14x21", WG 4/23/88 UE **100**
Lone Carroree, watercolor, sgn, 28x32", WG 9/16/88 UE **100**
Still Life of Fruit, oil on canvasboard, monogramed, 16x20", 16x20", WG 4/23/88 ..... **650**

KELLY, John D. (Canadian, 1862-1958)
First Brewery in Canada, watercolor, sgn/dtd 1922, 10x13", FB 4/25/88 ..... **170**

KELLY, Leon (American, 1901-)
Absinthe Drinker (woman w/head in hands at table), black ink/watercolor/gouache on paper, sgn, 21x16", SBY 1/24/89 ..... **1,760**
Barnagat Bay Fishery, India ink/watercolor on paper, sgn/titled, ca 1956, 18x24", SBY 3/17/88 ..... **1,100**

ELMAN, Benjamin (American, 1887-)
Swan on a Spring Pond, oil on canvas, sgn, 33x27", B/B 12/8/88 ..... **1,100**

ELPE, Paul (American, 1902-1985)
Composition (geometric), watercolor/pencil on paper, sgn/dtd 1930, 10x8", SBY 10/6/89 ..... **9,350**
Composition #335 (geometric), watercolor on paper, sgn/dtd 33, 12x8", SBY 9/14/89 ..... **14,300**

ELSEY, C. (American, 19th C)
Small Girl with a Bunch of Grapes in a Landscape, oil on canvas, sgn/dtd 1854, 34x27", RAB 7/12/88 OE **5,250**

EMMER, Hans (ca 1495-after 1554)
Christ & the Adultress, oil on panel, ca 1525, 25x38", SBY 6/1/89 OE **242,000**

EMPENER, see De Kempener

EMPF, Anna Gumlich (German, 1860-)
Still Life of Flowers, oil on canvas, sgn, 20x16", B/B 4/20/88 ..... **550**

EMPSON, Julie Hart (American, 1835-1913)
Study of Violets, oil on paper, sgn, 8x5", PHL 12/1/88 ..... **110**

ENDALL, Sergeant (American, 1869-1938)
Connecticut Snow (landscape), pastel on brown paper, sgn, 12x19", SBY 3/17/88 OE **4,950**

ENDRICK, Albert H. (British, 19th C)
Road to Sussex (figures & dwelling in a landscape), oil on canvas, sgn, 32x48", B/B 6/15/89 ..... **2,750**

ENDRICK, Charles (American, 19th C)
Sap Roller (Civil War), pen/ink on paper, sgn/inscr, 13x15", C-E 5/27/88 ..... **110**

ENNEDY, Cecil Napier (British, 1905-)
Approach of Zeus, oil on canvas, sgn, 51x34", C-E 2/23/88 ..... **1,980**

ENNEDY, H. Arthur (British, 19th C)
Orpheus, oil on canvas, sgn/dtd 1878, 27x16", SBY 4/29/88 OE **10,450**

ENNEDY, S.J. (American, 1877-)
French Country Scene Depicting Trees Along a Pond, oil on canvas, sgn, 18x21", MAG 6/22/88 ..... **550**
French Country Scene with Haystacks & Cottage, oil on canvas, sgn, 15x18", MAG 6/22/88 ..... **800**
Portrait of a Man, oil on canvas, 16x11", MAG 6/22/88 ..... **500**
Still Life of Two Floral Bouquets & a Candlestick on a Table, oil on canvas, sgn, 25x36", MAG 6/22/88 UE **250**

NNEDY, William; att (American, 1818-)
Portrait of a Woman (bust-length), oil on board, 15x11", SLK 9/28/88 ..... **2,900**

NNEY, C. (American, 19th/20th C)
Mountain Scene with Cabin & Lake, oil on masonite, sgn/#d 44, 17x57", SBY 4/14/89 ..... **605**

NSETT, John Frederick (American, 1816-1872)
Bash-Bish Falls, oil on canvas laid down on board laid down on panel, in painted oval, 19x16", C-NY 12/2/88 OE **68,200**
Bergen Park, Colorado (mountainous landscape); oil on canvas, 1870, 10x14", C-NY 5/25/89 UE **13,200**
Brook (landscape), oil on canvas laid down on board, initialed, #d 1054, 8x11", C-E 2/1/89 ..... **2,420**
Covered Wagon (in landscape), oil on paper laid down on canvas, initialed, 11x14", C-NY 5/25/89 OE **17,600**
Kearsage Mountain (figure & dog on wooded path), oil on paper laid down on canvas, sgn, 12x14", C-NY 5/25/89 ..... **19,800**
Middlebury, Vermont (landscape); pencil on paper heightened w/white, inscr/dtd July 22 1851, 9x13", SBY 1/24/89 ..... **5,775**
Mountain Overlook, oil on canvas, 9x20", C-NY 5/25/89 ..... **5,500**
Old Man Mountain, Franconia Notch White Mountains, New Hampshire; oil/pencil on canvas, 1850s, 12x20", RWS 5/19/88 UE **5,000**
Rhode Island Landscape, oil on canvas, 14x24", C-NY 3/11/88 UE **11,000**
Rhode Island Meadow, oil on canvas, 14x24", C-NY 12/2/88 OE **60,500**
Sketch, Catskill; oil on paper laid down on canvas, inscr, 10x15", C-NY 5/25/89 ..... **11,000**

View From Narragansett, oil on canvas laid down on masonite, C-NY 5/25/89 28,60
White Mountains, oil on canvas, 11x17", SBY 9/23/88 4,95

KENT, A. (19th C)
Landscape with Two Figures, oil on canvas, sgn, 16x20", WG 4/23/88 UE 15

KENT, Rockwell (American, 1882-1971)
Children's Mother (nude, viewed from behind), pencil, sgn/titled, ca 1920, 15x11", SWN 12/1/88 66
Christmas, Adirondacks (winter landscape); gouache/watercolor/pencil on board, 11x15", C-NY 5/26/88 7,15
Christmas Eve (Winter landscape), watercolor/gouache/pencil on paper, 12x15", C-NY 5/26/88 5,50
Generator of Jobs (allegory depicting the might & power of coal), oil on canvas, sgn, 38x44", SBY 4/14/89 OE 23,10
Motherhood (expressionistic nude figures in landscape), oil on canvas, sgn/dtd 1913, 32x42", C-NY 9/28/89 22,00
Mountainous Landscape, pen/ink on cardboard, sgn, 6x8", WG 10/19/88 40
Policeman Stopping Car, pen/black ink on board, bears artist's estate stamp, unfr, 11x16", C-E 11/30/88 1,10
Russian Mother, watercolor/gouache/brush/ink/pencil on board, sgn/dtd 1943, 13x17", C-NY 5/26/88 6,60
Scene From Faust, pen/ink on paper, 7x11", B/B 6/9/88 1,04
Single Tree, pen/black ink on paper, 6x5", C-E 6/1/89 55
View of the Ausable River, oil on canvas, sgn/dtd 1945, 20x24", SBY 6/28/89 19,80

KENYON, Henry R. (American, 1861-1926)
Landscape with Stream, oil on board, sgn, 10x12", C-E 11/30/88 1,10
Pair: Marshes; Near the Sea (wetlands & woodlands); oil on academy board, 11x14", 9x12", RWS 9/29/88 45

KEOGH, Tom
Portrait of a Young Girl, pencil on paper, sgn/dtd 50, unfr, 12x13", C-NY 10/6/88 33

KEPES, Gyorgy (American/Hungarian, 1906-)
Amber Scape (abstract), oil/mixed media on canvas, sgn, 72x61", LH 5/15/88 OE 1,90
Shy Mirage 1967 (abstract), oil/sand on canvas, sgn/dtd 1967, 19x24", RWS 3/16/89 1,00
Souvenir for Children (abstract), oil/sand on canvas, sgn/dtd 1965, 20x24", C-E 11/14/89 1,10

KERKAM, Earl (American, 1890-1965)
Group of 8: Nude Studies; mixed media, sgn, 1 dtd 51, average size 17x12", SBY 2/14/89 UE 1,98
Pair: Self-Portrait; Head of Young Woman; oil on board, sgn, 1 unfr, 15x11", 12x8", SBY 2/14/89 OE 2,42

KERLING, Anna E. (Dutch, 1862-)
Still Life of Fruit & Wildflowers, oil on panel, sgn, 16x12", C-E 10/26/89 5,50

KERN, Hermann Arman (Hungarian, 1839-1912)
In the Forge, oil on canvas, sgn/initialed/dtd 1906, 17x21", SBY 7/12/89 3,85
Reading the Newspaper, oil on panel, sgn, 10x9", C-E 10/25/88 1,43

KEROVINC, Constantin
Snow Queen, gouache on canvasboard, 22x17", C-E 2/1/89 99

KERRN, Hansine Sophie Joachimine (Danish, 1826-1860)
Bouquet of Lilacs, Hibiscus, a Pansy & Crabapple Blossom on a Marble Ledge; oil on canvas, sgn, 11x14", SBY 2/22/89 6,60

KERRY, Thomas
Deserted Barn, oil on board, sgn, 22x26", LH 5/15/88 UE 11

KESSLER, August (German, 1826-1906)
Twilight in the Forest, oil on panel, sgn, 7x10", B/B 9/15/88 99

KESSLER, Michael (20th C)
Inside Wood, wood/acrylic on masonite, sgn/inscr, 27x23", C-E 4/7/88 UE 44

KETTLE, Tilly (British, 1735-1786)
Portrait of a Gentleman, half-length, wearing brown jacket; oil on canvas, indistinctly sgn, 34x28", C-NY 10/20/88 UE 44
Portrait of Mrs Baldwin, oil on canvas, ca 1763, 29x24", SBY 6/2/89 37,40

KEVER, Jacob Simon Hendrik (Dutch, 1854-1922)
Bag of Potatoes, oil on canvas, sgn, 16x24", C-E 10/26/89 1,98
Mother & Child in an Interior, oil on canvas, sgn, 23x28", B/B 10/9/88 5,22
Naptime, oil on canvas, sgn, 18x15", C-NY 10/25/89 4,95
Rocking the Baby, oil, sgn, 31x23", WD 1/11/89 OE 4,25
Still Life of Peonies, oil on canvas, sgn, 32x35", C-NY 10/25/89 OE 17,60

KEY, Adriaen Thomasz the younger (Flemish, 1544-1590)
Portrait of a Nobleman (shoulder-length), oil on panel, 18x15", SBY 6/1/89 OE 18,70

KEY, Adriaen Thomasz the younger; att (Flemish, 1544-1590)
Portrait of a Gentleman (three-quarter length, ruffled collar & cuffs), oil on canvas, 40x30", SBY 4/7/89 OE 44,00

KEY, John Ross (American, 1832-1920)
Bridge & Stream, figures cross bridge reflected in placid stream; charcoal on paper, sgn/dtd 77, 15x9", RAB 3/27/89 40
Cliffs By the Sea, oil on canvas, sgn, 14x20", C-NY 9/30/88 2,86
Figures in a California Landscape, oil on canvas, sgn, 16x30", SBY 3/17/88 OE 12,10
Lake Landscape at Sunset, oil on canvas, sgn/dtd 1871, 20x40", SBY 5/24/89 OE 31,90
Mount Washington Valley, oil on canvas, sgn/dtd 72, 12x26", RAB 8/8/89 OE 8,50
River View with Barges, oil on canvas, sgn/dtd 77, 16x26", SBY 3/17/88 4,67
Sunset Over Ruins, oil on canvas, sgn, 14x24", RWS 5/19/88 OE 3,50
Wild Azalea & Blackberry, oil on canvas, sgn, 26x14", RWS 3/16/89 OE 1,60

KEY, Willem (Flemish, 1520-1568)
Four Doctors of the Church, oil on canvas, 49x41", C-NY 1/15/88 6,60

KEY, Willem; att (Flemish, 1520-1568)
Portrait of a Gentleman, dressed in black coat with fur-trimmed collar; oil on panel, 16x12", SBY 10/13/89 4,67

KEYSER, see De Keyser

:YZOK, M.
Loosing the Hounds, oil on canvas, sgn, 19x27", WG 4/23/88 255
:ZDI-KOVACS, E.K. (Laszlo)(Russian, 1864-1942)
Landscape with Cow, oil on canvas, sgn, 24x30", WG 4/23/88 U 150
INOPFF, Fernand (1858-1921)
Jeune Homme en Habit Renaissance, charcoal on paper, 1914, 6x4", C-L 6/27/88 15,136
La Meduse Endormie, pastel on paper, sgn twice, 1896, 12x5", C-L 6/27/88 OE 227,040
La Tiare d'Argent, pastel on paper, sgn, in silver foil frame, 1909, 10" dia, C-L 6/27/88 OE 321,640
Portrair de Jeune Femme, oil on canvas laid down on board, 6x4", C-L 6/27/88 30,272
IODASEVICH, Valentina (Russian, 1894-1970)
Design for Decorating Petrograd for the 7 November 1932 Celebrations, watercolor/pencil/gouache, C-L 10/8/88 2,230
AERSKOU, Frederick (Danish, 1805-1891)
Danish Landscape, oil on canvas, sgn/dtd 1853, 23x33", SBY 7/12/89 9,350
DD, Harry M.
Ponte Vecchio, Florence; watercolor/pencil on paper, sgn/inscr w/title, 18x14", C-E 10/18/89 UE 330
EFER, Anselm (German, 1945-)
Brunhilde Schalft (abstract), oil on photographic paper, inscr, 1978, 23x31", C-NY 5/4/88 OE 77,000
Dein Blondes Haar, Margarette (Your Blonde Hair, Margarette); oil/straw on canvas, sgn/dtd 1981, 47x57", SBY 11/8/89 220,000
Des Malers Atelier (abstract), paint on photograph, 1984, 22x26", SBY 5/3/88 30,900
Grosse Eisenfaust Deutschland, oil on photographic paper, inscr, 1978, 32x23", C-NY 5/4/88 35,200
Johannis-Nacht (abstract), oil/straw/epoxy on photographic paper, inscr, 1978, 23x33", C-NY 5/4/88 OE 90,200
Johannis-Nacht (abstract), oil on paper mounted on canvas, 1978, 48x60", SBY 5/2/88 143,000
Yggsdrasil I (abstract), oil on linen, inscr, unfr, 1978, 51x66", 51x66", C-NY 5/3/88 418,000
ENBUSCH, William (American, 1914-)
Autumn Field #1, crayon on paper, sgn/dtd 71, 8x10", C-NY 6/17/89 110
Bayberry Island, crayon on paper, sgn, 8x8", C-NY 6/17/89 550
ENHOLZ, Edward (American, 1927-)
Untitled, mixed media on wood, sgn, 12x72", B/B 12/8/88 2,200
ESEL, Conrad (German, 1846-1921)
Lute Player (portrait of a woman in an interior), oil on canvas, sgn, 40x30", SBY 2/22/89 16,500
Oriental Dancer (nude), pastel, sgn, 28x12", WG 9/16/88 UE500 500
HN, William Landon (American, 1898-1957)
Americans, Man & Wife of Norwegian Heritage (portrait of couple in landscape); oil on canvas, sgn, 36x26", RAB 8/9/88 4,700
KOINE, Michel (Russian, 1892-1968)
Card Players, oil on masonite, sgn, ca 1958-60, 21x26", SBY 5/30/89 9,350
La Ferme, oil on canvas, sgn, 21x28", C-NY 2/13/89 7,150
Landscape (impressionistic), oil on panel, sgn, 14x18", SBY 10/5/88 3,850
Landscape with Figures, oil on canvas, sgn, 40x48", SBY 10/7/89 OE 31,900
Paysage en Bourgogne, oil on canvas, sgn, 18x22", C-E 5/9/89 9,680
LBURNE, George Goodwin (British, 1839-1924)
Admiring the Baby, oil on canvas, sgn, unfr, 50x36", C-NY 10/25/89 12,100
Break From Shooting, oil on canvas, sgn, 12x18", SBY 6/9/89 3,850
Hunt Scene (two dogs & three hunters in an open field), oil on panel, sgn/dtd 93, 7x10", DM 2/19/88 3,700
Hush (elegant mother/children in interior), watercolor, sgn twice/titled, 11x15", C-NY 2/23/89 3,300
King!, watercolor/gouache w/scraping out, sgn, 11x15", C-NY 5/25/88 3,850
Pair: Happy Days (man & woman in fishing boat); watercolor over pencil heightened w/white, sgn, 7x11", C-NY 5/25/88 OE 7,150
Winner Pours the Wine, watercolor heightened w/white over pencil, sgn, 11x8", C-NY 10/25/89 1,760
LGOUR, Andrew Wilkie (Canadian, 1868-1930)
Pair: Thanksgiving in the Woods, Val Morin; October, Sweetsburg; oil on board, sgn, 5x7", FB 10/17/88 675
LPUN, Legh Mulhall (1853-1919)
Haystacks, watercolor on paper, sgn/dtd 09, 20x28", C-E 4/7/88 935
MBALL, Charles Frederick (American, 1835-1907)
Pastoral Scene (summer landscape w/cow at water's edge), oil on canvas, sgn/dtd 1873, 21x31", RWS 3/31/88 1,600
Rocky Grove, Spring (rocks & trees in landscape); oil on canvas, sgn/dtd 1897, 20x30", RWS 5/19/88 OE 4,000
NG, Albert Francis (American, 1854-1945)
Basket of Cherries, oil on canvas, sgn, 10x14", SBY 6/24/88 3,410
Brown Bag of Apples, oil on canvas, sgn, 12x18", C-NY 12/2/88 6,600
Lobster, Oyster, Fish, Bottles of Beer, & Basket of Vegetables; oil on canvas, sgn, 18x27", SBY 9/23/88 3,575
Still Life of Watermelon, Blueberries, & Other Fruits; oil on canvas, sgn, 18x24", SBY 6/28/89 9,350
NG, Charles Bird (American, 1785-1862)
Apples, Pears, Plums, & Grapes; oil on canvas, 25x30", C-NY 5/25/89 55,000
Portrait of Big Buffalo, a Chippewa; oil on panel, sgn/inscr/dtd 1826, 18x14", SBY 5/25/88 63,250
Portrait of Timpooche, Barnard, a Yuchi Warrior; oil on panel, 1825, 18x14", SBY 5/25/88 121,000
Wakechai (Crouching Eagle), a Sauk Chief; oil on panel, inscr, 1824, 18x14", SBY 5/25/88 66,000
NG, F.W. (American, 19th C)
Landscape with Farm, oil on canvas, sgn, 18x32", WG 9/16/88 1,300
NG, George W. (American, 1836-1922)
Autumn Afternoon (cows in pasture, canoeists on river), oil on canvas, sgn, 20x30", RWS 9/29/99 1,000
Country Manor House (landscape), oil on canvas, sgn, 29x40", B/B 3/22/89 3,300
NG, Gordon (British, 20th C)
Finding the Scent, oil on canvas, sgn, 24x36", PHL 10/28/88 950

KING, Hamilton (American, 1871-)
- Snow on the Dunes, sgn/inscr, 25x35", C-E 6/1/88 UE — 308

KING, Henry John Yeend (British, 1855-1924)
- Morning Interlude (two figures in a landscape), oil on canvas, sgn, 24x36", SBY 5/23/89 — 7,700
- Picking Apple Blossoms, oil on canvas, sgn, 36x28", C-NY 10/25/89 — 12,100
- Picking Bluebells, oil on board, sgn, 15x21", WAD 6/6/88 — 2,600
- Sporting Offer, oil on canvas, sgn, 34x24", WAD 6/6/88 — 3,800

KING, Paul (American, 1867-1947)
- Autumn Gold (wooded landscape w/mountains beyond), oil on canvas, sgn, 25x30", RWS 5/19/88 — 3,000
- Birches (landscape w/stream), oil on canvas, sgn, 16x20", C-NY 12/2/88 — 9,900
- Coast of Maine, Chester Harbor; oil on canvas, sgn, 25x31", C-NY 9/28/89 — 7,150
- Fishing Boats, Brittany; oil on canvasboard, sgn twice/inscr Stony Brook NY/titled, 16x12", SBY 3/17/88 OE — 2,200
- Fishing Boats at Concarneau, oil on canvas, sgn twice/inscr Concarneau/titled, 12x16", SBY 3/17/88 — 1,540
- Returning Fishermen, oil on canvas, sgn/dtd 1929, 25x30", C-NY 9/28/89 — 8,800
- Ships in San Sebastian Harbor, oil on canvas, sgn, 51x60", C-NY 12/2/88 UE — 11,000
- Snow Flurry, Lake Placid; oil on board, sgn/dtd 1921, 16x20", SBY 9/14/89 — 4,675
- Winter in the Adirondacks (wooded landscape), oil on canvas, sgn, 69x101", C-NY 5/25/89 — 13,200

KING, Tony (British, 20th C)
- Yellow & Orange Diamond Panel, acrylic on canvas, sgn/dtd 74, unfr, 48x48", C-NY 2/14/89 — 2,530

KINGMAN, Dong (American, 1911-)
- Chinatown, San Francisco; watercolor on paper, sgn/inscr in Chinese, 21x14", SBY 4/14/89 — 4,400
- Crucibles of Industry, watercolor/gouache on paper laid down on board, sgn, 19x15", C-NY 9/30/88 — 3,300
- Festival in Chinatown (costumed figures watch Chinese dragons), watercolor on paper, sgn, 26x40", RWS 9/29/88 OE — 3,700
- Hong Kong Harbor, watercolor on paper, sgn, 22x29", B/B 3/17/88 — 6,050
- How To Paint & Take a Bath, watercolor on paper, sgn/dtd Mar 44, 10x13", B/B 10/6/88 — 1,540
- Milwaukee, watercolor on paper, sgn, 22x17", SBY 9/23/88 — 3,300
- New Years Celebration in Hong Kong Harbor, watercolor/gouache on paper, sgn, 26x39", B/B 3/22/89 — 4,400
- Panoramic Cityscape, watercolor on paper, sgn/inscr in Chinese, 22x29", WBY 6/28/89 — 7,425
- Statue at Market Scene, watercolor on paper laid down on board, sgn, 15x22", C-E 6/1/89 — 1,870
- Telegraph Hill, San Fancisco; watercolor on paper, sgn/dtd 1949, 22x15", SBY 6/28/89 — 6,600
- View of Istanbul, watercolor on paper, sgn/dtd 54, 15x22", SBY 6/28/89 — 2,420
- Waterfront Temple (sampans & figures in foreground), watercolor on paper laid down on board, 23x15", C-E 6/1/89 UE — 1,100

KINGMAN, Eduardo (South American, 20th C)
- Dos Ninos (two boys), oil on canvas, sgn twice/dtd 59/titled, 40x32", C-NY 5/17/89 — 4,950
- El Payaso (clown), oil on canvas, sgn/dtd 40, 53x30", C-NY 11/21/88 — 6,050
- Mendigos, oil on canvas, sgn/dtd 74, 40x52", C-NY 11/21/89 — 7,700
- Nino con Quena, pastel on paper, sgn/dtd 41, 24x18", C-NY 5/18/88 UE — 1,100
- Untitled (lady wearing red shawl holding doll in a landscape), oil on canvas, sgn, 1941, 23x21", SBY 5/16/89 — 7,150
- Untitled (two women in interior), oil on canvas, sgn/dtd 1941, 24x39", SBY 11/21/88 OE — 7,700

KINGS, Haynes (British, 1831-1904)
- Returning to Market, oil on canvas, sgn/dtd 1863, 16x13", WG 4/23/88 UE — 600

KINLEY, Peter (British, 20th C)
- Flowers, oil over pencil on paper laid down on board, sgn, 1960, 12x10", C-E 11/17/88 OE — 605
- Studio Interior, oil on canvas, sgn/dtd 1959/#d 115, 50x34", C-E 11/17/88 UE — 550

KINNAIRD, Frederick Gerald (British, 19th C)
- Children with Bundles of Bracken, oil on canvas, sgn, 29x36", LH 10/16/88 — 2,400

KINNAIRD, Henry J. (British, fl 1880-1891)
- Old Bridge Near Eshing, Surrey; watercolor on paper sgn, 13x20", B/B 1/11/89 OE — 1,320
- Sussex Cornfield, watercolor/gouache on paper, sgn/titled, 10x18", C-NY 5/24/89 — 2,310
- Thames Below Goring, oil on canvas, sgn, 18x23", C-E 2/21/89 — 3,080
- Threshing Near Steyning, Sussex; watercolor on paper, sgn, unfr, 14x10", SBY 7/12/89 — 2,420
- View Near Lancing, Sussex; watercolor heightened w/gouache, 18x28", C-NY 10/26/88 OE — 4,950

KINNAIRD, Wiggs (British, 19th C)
- On the River Chalmer Essex, watercolor, sgn/inscr, 14x21", C-E 10/25/88 — 880
- Thames Near Marsh Lock, watercolor, sgn/inscr, 14x21", C-E 10/25/88 — 990

KINNEAR, John H. (Canadian)
- Old Dock Buildings, Vancouver; oil on board, sgn/dtd 68, 12x13", WAD 6/12/89 — 240

KINSEY, Alberta (American, 1875-1955)
- French Quarter Courtyard, oil on artist board, sgn, 22x17", NA 2/24/89 — 300
- French Quarter Courtyard, oil on canvas, sgn, 17x23", MG 5/28/88 — 275
- Vieux Carre Courtyard, oil on board, sgn, 17x15", NA 11/5/88 — 500

KINZEL, Josef (Austrian, 1852-1925)
- Overlooking the Garden, oil on canvas, sgn, 32x23", SBY 2/22/89 — 11,000
- Seated Man (in an interior alcove by window), oil on canvas, sgn, 29x22", B/B 3/22/89 OE — 66,007
- Toper, oil on board, sgn/inscr Wien, 11x8", WD 3/23/88 — 1,000

KIPNISS, Robert (American, 1931-)
- Barn (building & trees amid open landscape), oil on canvas, sgn, 33x35", C-E 6/1/89 — 1,320
- Courtyard, oil on board, sgn, 1974, 17x22", LH 9/10/89 OE — 850
- Courtyard, oil on canvas, sgn/inscr, 16x20", LH 5/15/88 OE — 750
- Hideaway House, oil on canvas, sgn, 48x36", LH 5/15/88 OE — 2,800
- Red Roof, oil on canvas, sgn, 40x30", LH 5/15/88 OE — 1,900

RCHNER, Ernst Ludwig (German, 1880-1938)

rtist with Two Models in His Studio, graphite on paper, Busler Nachlas Stamp, 17x13", B/B 6/9/88	11,000
Ballspiel (two nudes), pen/black ink on buff paper, estate stamp, 10x8", C-NY 10/6/88	2,420
)er Stadtturm (landscape w/buildings), oil on canvas, sgn, ca 1911, 38x33", C-NY 5/11/88	200,000
'rauen in Landschaft, colored wax crayons on paper, stamped, ca 1923, 15x19", C-NY 11/15/88	13,200
iroup of Four Persons, black crayon on yellow paper, stamped kDa/Bi 59, 15x19", SBY 2/18/88	5,500
Iomecoming Peasants, watercolor/pencil on paper, Nachlass stamp, inscr A Da/Bc 27, ca 1924-25, 20x14", SBY 5/11/88	27,500
itzender Frauenakt (seated nude), colored chalks/wax crayons on tan paper, ca 1907, 18x15", C-NY 5/12/88 OE	26,400
'anzgruppe Mary Wigman, watercolor/colored crayons/ink wash on paper, sgn, ca 1926, 12x16", SBY 2/18/88	8,800
'aufe (Bauerngruppe vor Berghaus), charcoal on paper, sgn/dtd 20, estate stamp, 16x20", C-NY 10/6/88	7,700
Veiblicher Akt, Teilweise im Badetuch (woman nude from waist up); pencil on paper, 1912, 23x18", C-NY 2/16/89	7,700
wei Akte (sketch of pair of nudes), pencil on buff paper backed w/rice paper, sgn, ca 1911-13, SBY 10/7/88 UE	1,100

RCHNER, Otto (German, 1887-)

Reading by Candlelight, oil on panel, sgn, 9x7", DM 2/19/88 UE	350

RK, Thomas (British, -1797)

'he Visit, oil on canvas, oval, 17x14", WG 9/16/88 UE	500
'outh Visited by Love, oil on canvas, oval, 18x14", WG 9/16/88	650

RKEBY, Per (Danish, 1938-)

Jntitled (abstract), oil on canvas, sgn/dtd 1981, 73x90", SBY 11/11/88 OE	26,400
Jntitled (abstract), oil on linen, 1980, 79x118", SBY 2/15/89 OE	39,600

RKPATRICK, Frank Le Brun (American, 1853-1917)

n the Museum, oil on canvas, sgn twice/inscr, 20x30", C-E 2/3/88	1,760

RKPATRICK, Frank Le Brun; att (American, 1853-1917)

'illing Up, oil on canvas, sgn, unfr, 18x26", C-E 6/1/88	1,100

SELEV, Aleksandr Aleksandrovich (Russian, 1838-1911)

'air: Riverscape in Summer; Shore of the Black Sea; oil on board/panel, 1 sgn/dtd 1906, 6x10", C-L 10/8/88	7,060
'illage Road, oil on canvas, sgn/dtd 1890, 16x22", NA 5/13/89 OE	6,100

SLING, Moise (French, 1891-1953)

pres le Bain (posterior view of nude bathing), oil on canvas, sgn/dtd 1919, 36x29", C-NY 2/16/89 OE	66,000
Bouquet (floral still life), oil on canvas, sgn/dtd 1948, 18x15", SBY 5/10/89	209,000
Bouquet de Marquerites (floral still life), oil on canvas, sgn/dtd Paris 1948, 26x20", SBY 5/10/89	209,000
'emme en Gris (portrait of a woman), oil on canvas, sgn, 1942, 16x13", C-NY 5/11/89	90,200
'emme Nue Allongee (back of reclining nude), oil on canvas, sgn, 24x39", C-NY 10/6/88 OE	85,800
'emme Nue Assise (seated nude), oil on canvas, sgn, 1925, 32x24", C-NY 5/12/88 OE	165,000
'emme Nue Assise (seated nude), oil on canvas, sgn, 1938, 22x17", C-NY 5/11/89	82,500
'emme Nue Couche (reclining nude), oil on canvas, sgn, 1923, 28x39", SBY 5/10/89	275,000
'lowers in a White & Terra Cotta, oil on canvas, sgn, 22x15", SBY 5/30/88 OE	187,000
eune Suedoise, oil on canvas, sgn, 11x9", SBY 2/18/88	44,000
onquils et Roses (floral still life), oil on canvas, sgn/dtd Paris 1947, 22x15", SBY 5/10/89	154,000
iki au Decollete (portrait of a woman), oil on canvas, sgn, 22x15", C-NY 10/6/88 OE	88,000
a Fenetre du Resturant, oil on canvas, sgn twice/dtd 1916 twice, 35x46", SBY 2/16/89	143,000
Aargueritttes dans un Vase Blanc (floral still life), oil on canvas, sgn/dtd 1948, 25x20", C-NY 11/16/88 OE	242,000
Jature Morte aux Fruits (still life), oil on canvas, sgn/dtd 914, 26x32", SBY 10/7/88 OE	88,000
Jue Assise (seated nude), oil on canvas, sgn, 8x6", C-NY 5/12/88 OE	33,000
)rta (landscape w/buildings in distance), oil on canvas, sgn, 1922, 24x29", SBY 10/7/88	50,600
'aysage de Sanary (hilly landscape), oil on canvas, sgn/dtd 1948, 22x18", SBY 5/10/89 OE	154,000
'ortrait de Jeune Femme, oil on canvas, sgn, 1920, 16x13", C-NY 5/11/89	93,500
'ortrait de Jeune Fille (portrait of young lady), oil on canvas, sgn/dtd 1941, 16x13", C-NY 10/5/89 OE	143,000
'ortrait of Agadati, pencil, sgn/dtd Paris 1925, 13x10", SBY 5/30/89 OE	4,400

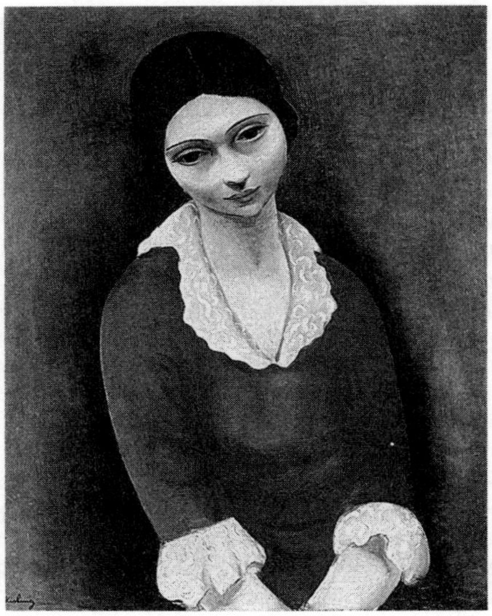

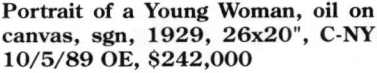

Portrait of a Young Woman, oil on canvas, sgn, 1929, 26x20", C-NY 10/5/89 OE, $242,000

Roses, oil on canvas, sgn, 1927, 29x21", SBY 5/11/88 OE ... 132,000
Toulon, oil on canvas, sgn/dtd 1937, 15x22", SBY 2/18/88 OE ... 31,900
Vase de Fleurs (floral still life w/red background), oil on canvas, sgn, 1942, 16x14", SBY 10/6/89 OE ... 101,750
Vase de Fleurs (floral still life), oil on canvas, sgn, 18x22", C-NY 2/16/89 ... 132,000
Vase de Mimosa (still life), oil on canvas, sgn/dtd 1949, 13x16", C-NY 5/12/88 OE ... 66,000
Vase of Flowers, oil on canvas, sgn, 9x6", SBY 5/30/89 OE ... 39,600
Vase of Lilies, oil on canvas, sgn, 1931, 22x18", SBY 5/30/89 OE ... 176,000
Vue d'Amsterdam (view of Amsterdam), oil on canvas, sgn/dtd 1935, 15x22", C-NY 5/12/88 OE ... 63,800

KISS, Erno (Hungarian, 20th C)
Set of 12: Landscapes & Figure Studies; graphite on paper, various sizes, WG 10/19/88 UE ... 45

KISS, Rudolphe
Lake Scene, oil on canvas, sgn/dtd 1935, 30x33", C-E 6/1/89 UE ... 605
Looking Over the Balcony, oil on canvas, sgn/dtd 1932, 30x33", C-E 6/1/89 UE ... 605

KITAJ, R.B. (American, 1932-)
The Messianist (contemporary), oil on canvas, sgn/dtd 1985, 1985-1986, 72x24", SBY 5/2/88 ... 99,000

KITCHELL, Hudson Mindell (American, 1862-1944)
Autumn Landscape, oil on canvas, sgn/dtd 1918, 27x40", B/B 4/20/88 ... 2,750
Landscape at Sunset, oil on canvas, sgn, 20x30", SBY 3/17/88 UE ... 660
Wooded Landscape, oil on canvas, sgn, 12x10", WD 3/23/88 ... 700

KITE, J. Milner (British, 1862-)
Western Landscape, oil on canvas, sgn, 21x28", C-E 6/28/88 ... 550

KITINGER
Nightlife, New Orleans; watercolor, sgn, 13x10", NA 3/26/88 ... 190

KLANKE
Orchids, oil, sgn/dtd Sao Paolo 52, 35x31", C-SK 6/9/88 ... 836

KLAPPER, Siegfried (German, 1918-)
Flasche Mit Zitrone (cubist still life), oil on canvas laid down on board, sgn/dtd 57, 10x16", SBY 10/7/89 ... 2,420

KLARWEIN, Mati
Real Estate (of Private Property), oil on canvas laid down on masonite, titled/dtd 76-77, 31x31", C-E 11/17/88 ... 550

KLAUS, Joseph (Belgian, 19th C)
Pair: Still Life of Roses; Still Life of Asters; oil on canvas, sgn, 22x18", B/B 10/9/88 OE ... 8,800

KLEE, Paul (Swiss, 1879-1940)
Alphabet Aioek, black paste on paper mounted on card, sgn/dtd 1938/#d p7, 11x8", SBY 11/16/89 OE ... 49,500
Auf der Wiese (wided-eyed girl w/other whimsical figures) watercolor on paper, sgn/dtd 1923/#d 93, S-9x12", SBY 5/11/88 ... 742,500
Baltrum (Gegen Langeook), pencil on paper mounted on board, sgn/dtd 1923/#d 264, 5x12", SBY 11/16/89 ... 25,300
Barbarische Komposition, watercolor on 2 pieces of paper mounted on board, sgn/dtd 1916/#d 68, 12x9", SBY 11/12/88 OE ... 253,000
Bei Vergehender Zeit (head), watercolor/gouache/black crayon on paper, sgn/dtd 1940, S-12x8", SBY 5/11/88 ... 88,000
Blitzschlag, watercolor/black ink transfer on joined paper laid down on paper, sgn, 1920, 12x8", C-NY 5/12/88 ... 82,500
Blume Im Maerz, watercolor/ink on paper mounted on board, sgn/dtd 1913/#d N.6, S-13x8", SBY 11/12/88 OE ... 143,000
Braut und Brautigam im Herbst des Lebens (semi-abstract figures), oil on paper, sgn, 1933, 8x13", C-NY 5/11/89 OE ... 330,000
Campanula (Canterbury Bell Flower), oil on paper, sgn, 13x18", SBY 5/11/88 OE ... 11,000
Der Sauerbaum (abstract), watercolor on joined paper mounted on paper, sgn, 1939, 17x11", C-NY 5/12/88 OE ... 101,200
Die Dorfverruckte, pen/ink on paper mounted on board, sgn/dtd 1920/#d 55, 5x8", SBY 11/16/89 ... 46,750
Die Eingeschlafene, watercolor on paper mounted on stiff card, sgn/dtd 1939/titled, S-11x8", SBY 11/12/88 OE ... 88,000
Die Vorrede des Streiters, pencil on paper laid down by artist on paper, sgn/dtd 22, 9x6", C-NY 11/15/88 OE ... 35,200
Edelklippe, watercolor on thin sketchbook paper, sgn, 1933, 12x17", SBY 11/12/88 OE ... 93,500
Face of a Flower, watercolor on 2 joined sheets of paper w/black wash border, sgn/dtd 1922/#d 57, 17x9", SBY 11/15/89 OE ... 1,320,000
Figurale Blatter (abstract), gouache over pencil on paper mounted on paper, sgn, 1938, 15x10", C-NY 5/12/88 ... 71,500
Garten der Zahlembaume (Number-Trees), watercolor/pencil on paper on board, sgn/dtd 1918, 10x9" overall, SBY 5/10/89 OE ... 148,500
Garten in Heissen Zeit (fantasy painting of garden), oil on paper, sgn, 1938, 10x14", SBY 5/11/88 OE ... 176,000
Gelander am See, pastel/ink wash on linen mounted on board, sgn/dtd 1937/#d S 4, 4x13", SBY 11/15/89 OE ... 198,000
Hain (composition), watercolor on paper mounted on board, sgn/dtd 1932/#d K4, 25x19", SBY 11/15/89 ... 297,000
Haus am Hugel, gouache on brown wrapping paper, sgn/dtd 1935/#d P10, 7x20", SBY 11/16/89 OE ... 165,000
Hieroglyph mit Fisch und Vogel, pencil on paper mounted on board, sgn/dtd 1917/#d 142, 6x9", SBY 11/16/89 OE ... 66,000
Hohlen Ausblick (abstract), watercolor on paper mounted on board, sgn/dtd 1929/#d UE 1, 11x13", SBY 11/15/89 ... 440,000
Junger Pierrot, watercolor/pen/black ink on paper laid down on board, dtd 1918/#d 31, 10x2", C-NY 5/12/88 ... 33,000
Kurbis Flasche, gouache on tan paper mounted on board, sgn/dtd 1934, 20x17", C-NY 11/15/88 ... 22,000
Landschaft mit Wolf, pencil on paper mounted by the artist on board, sgn, 1929, 14x18", C-NY 5/11/89 OE ... 38,500
Landschaftsteile Gesammelt (fantasy landscape), watercolor on laid paper, sgn/dtd 1935/#d M 18, 14x19", SBY 5/11/88 ... 82,500
Latomie (abstract), watercolor on paper, sgn, 1939, 11x8", C-NY 5/11/89 ... 82,500
Leichte Wendung, watercolor on linen w/2 joined horizontal strips of fabric, sgn/dtd 1937/#d L 6, 12x7", SBY 11/15/89 ... 121,000
Les Amoureux, brush/ink/ink wash on heavy paper, sgn, 24x18", SBY 11/12/88 ... 82,500
Metaphysisches Blatt aus der Vogelwelt (symbolic bird drawing), pen/ink on paper, sgn/dtd 1917, S-6x10", SBY 5/11/88 ... 29,700
Mit Stacheln, pen/ink on paper mounted on board, sgn/dtd 1927/#d B7, 8x12", SBY 11/16/89 ... 44,000
Modell 106, im Farbiger Polyphonie; watercolor on paper, sgn, 18x25", SBY 11/16/89 OE ... 742,500
Munchen Frachtbahnhof (industrial scene), pen/black ink on paper, sgn/dtd 1911/#d 110, 5x9", C-NY 10/5/89 OE ... 26,400
Nicht Ohne Herz, pen/ink on laid paper mounted on board, sgn/dtd 1928, #d M 3, 12x12", SBY 4/29/88 ... 23,100
Pflanze, watercolor on paper mounted by artist on board, sgn/dtd 1915, 10x7", C-NY 11/15/88 OE ... 49,500
Rita, black colored paste on paper mounted on thin stiff card, sgn/dtd 1937/#d V19, S-11x7", SBY 5/11/88 OE ... 36,300
Schlussbild Einer Tragikomodie, oil transfer/watercolor on chalk primed paper, sgn/dtd 1923/#d 144, 10x14", SBY 4/29/88 ... 286,000
Schupper II (study for an oil, Creator II), oil transfer on printing paper, sgn/dtd 1930, S-15x9", SBY 5/11/88 OE ... 71,500

Secret Hieroglyphs, charcoal/white gesso over newsprint on paper, indistinctly sgn, 1937, 19x13", SBY 11/15/89 .... **357,500**
Seltsamejagd (abstract), watercolor on linen & burlap, sgn/dtd 1937/#d R12 on stretcher, 332x21", SBY 5/10/88 .... **770,000**
Sonnenfinsternis (abstract), watercolor/pen/black ink on paper laid down on paper, sgn, 1918, 8x5", C-NY 5/12/88 .... **71,500**
Von Klein zu Gross (abstract figures), pen/ink on paper laid down on board, sgn/dtd 1922/#d 238, 11x9", C-NY 5/12/88 .... **28,600**
Zu Weit Gehender Spuk (Spook Going Too Far), pen/ink on paper mounted on board, sgn/dtd 1932, S-8x12", SBY 11/12/88 .... **26,400**
Zwei Bluten (abstract), pen/ink/pencil on paper mounted on board, sgn/dtd 1927/titled/#d 315, S-12x10", SBY 2/16/89 .... **20,900**

KLEEMAN, Ron (American, 1937-)
Christmas Tree Series Greenlight, no media given, sgn/dtd 1971, 48x48", SBY 10/7/89 .... **3,850**
Monaco, March in May (racecar & driver), acrylic on canvas, sgn/dtd 1972, 68x90", SBY 10/8/88 .... **22,000**
XX on Xmas, acrylic on canvas, sgn/dtd Sept 1983, 15x20", C-NY 2/13/89 .... **880**

KLEIN, Yves (French, 1928-1962)
Ant 170 (abstract), blue pigment in synthetic resin on paper laid down on canvas, sgn/dtd 1960, 66x49", SBY 6/30/88 OE **370,000**
F 94 le Feu de l'Esprit et l'Empreinte de l'Amitie, charred paper on card on panel, sgn/dtd 1961, 39x26", SBY 6/30/88 .... **100,000**
M105 (contemporary), green pigment in synthetic resin on linen laid down on wood panel, ca 1955-56, 7x5", SBY 5/2/88 OE **23,100**
M106 (contemporary), red pigment in synthetic resin on linen laid down on wood panel, sgn/dtd 56, 5x11", SBY 5/2/88 OE **61,600**

KLEINERT, A. (German/Austrian, 20th C)
Portrait of a Gentleman ((head study of spectacled man with beard & hat), pastel on board, sgn/dtd 1914, RAB 8/9/88 .... **225**
Portrait of a Woman (bust-length), oil on canvas, sgn/dtd 1913, 13x9", RAB 8/9/88 UE **300**

KLEINHART, Joseph Edgar (Austrian, 1859-)
Afternoon Pastime, oil on canvas, sgn/dtd 1885, 20x16", C-E 2/23/88 OE **3,250**

KLEINMEYER, B.
Arabian Scene, oil on canvas, sgn, 23x31", C-E 10/25/88 .... **1,430**

KLEINSCHMIDT, Paul (German, 1883-1949)
Der Tunnel (landscape w/rail tunnel, river & village), oil on canvas, indistinctly sgn, ca 1929, 28x33", SBY 10/7/89 OE **19,800**
Praying Mountain (abstract), oil on canvas, sgn, 1957, 23x30", C-NY 9/28/89 .... **4,620**

KLEITSCH, Joseph (American, 1885-1931)
L'Arc de Carousel, Paris, 1927; oil on canvas, sgn/dtd 1927, 18x21", B/B 10/6/88 .... **20,900**
Portrait of Mrs Guy Bates Post, oil on canvas, sgn/dtd 1918, 40x28", B/B 10/6/88 .... **5,500**
Tuilleries Gardens in Paris 1927, oil on canvas, sgn/dtd 1927, 18x21", B/B 10/6/88 .... **22,000**

KLENGEL, Johann Christian (German, 1751-1824)
Cowherd with His Flock Near a Lake, a Ruined Castle...; chalk/pen/ink/wash, wm IV, sgn/dtd 1779, 12x17", C-NY 1/11/89 .... **1,650**

KLEPPER, Max Francis
Clean Pair of Heels, watercolor heightened w/white, sgn, 18x26", C-SK 11/10/88 .... **840**

KLEYN, Lodewyk Johannes (Dutch, 1817-1897)
Extensive View of a Dutch Village, oil on panel, sgn, unfr, 17x23", C-E 10/25/88 OE **9,350**
Figures on a Frozen River, oil on panel, sgn, 11x16", SBY 7/12/89 .... **8,800**
On the Frozen Lake, oil on panel, sgn, 15x21", SBY 10/24/89 .... **25,300**

KLIMT, Gustav (Austrian, 1862-1918)
Frauenakt (female nude), pencil on paper, 23x15", C-NY 10/6/88 .... **5,280**
Stehende, die Rechte Wange an die Hande Gelegt; pencil on buff paper, ca 1900, 18x13", C-NY 5/11/89 OE **24,200**
Stehender Madchenakt Nach Links (standing nude), pencil on paper, 1910, 22x15", SBY 5/11/88 OE **20,900**
Study for Oil Portrait of Fritza Riedler, black chalk on buff paper, 1904-05, 18x12", SBY 5/10/89 .... **28,600**

KLINCK, Arthur (American)
River Landscape, oil on masonite, sgn, 24x30", SLK 2/12/88 .... **110**

KLINE, Franz (American, 1910-1962)

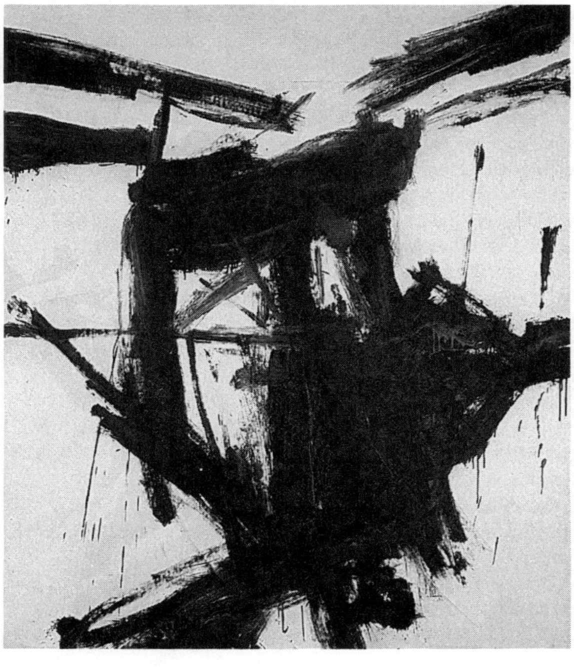

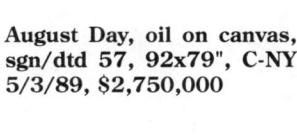

August Day, oil on canvas, sgn/dtd 57, 92x79", C-NY 5/3/89, $2,750,000

Bigard (abstract), oil on canvas, sgn/dtd 1961, 92x68", SBY 5/2/89 1,430,000
Black Center (abstract), oil on paper mounted on panel, sgn/dtd 57, 9x11", C-NY 5/4/89 OE 99,000
Blue Horizontal (abstract), oil on paper laid down on paperboard, sgn/dtd 59, 9x10", SBY 5/3/88 22,000
Composition, crayons/pen/black ink on paper, initialed, 7x8", C-E 11/14/89 1,320
Composition (abstract), oil on canvas, sgn/dtd 53, 42x38", SBY 5/2/89 880,000
Dance Hall, ink/pencil on paper, ca 1941, 5x7", SBY 10/5/89 UE 3,025
Double-Sided: Untitled (abstract w/teapot); oil on plywood, sgn, 17x20", SBY 11/9/89 46,750
Hampton (black on white abstract), oil on canvas, sgn/dtd 54, 44x38", SBY 5/2/89 1,210,000
Horse, pen/black ink on paper mounted at top edge on board, initialed, 7x5", C-E 5/9/89 990
Kitten, brush/black ink on paper, initialed, 11x9", C-E 5/9/89 OE 2,640
Leda (composition), oil on canvas, sgn, 1950, 30x25", SBY 11/8/89 660,000
Lehigh (abstract), oil on canvas, 81x114", C-NY 11/9/88 OE 2,310,000
Male Model in Studio, gouache/pen/black ink on gray paper mounted at edges of board, sgn/dtd 49, 8x12", C-E 5/13/88 OE 2,420
Marionette, oil on canvas, sgn, 16x13", C-E 11/17/88 6,050
New Space No 1 (abstract), oil/graphite on paper mounted on panel, 1954, 23x30", C-NY 5/3/88 154,000
Ninth Street (abstract), oil on canvas, sgn, 60x78", SBY 5/2/88 OE 1,870,000
Number 3 (abstract), gouache/black ink on newsprint mounted on board, 1954, 11x9", C-NY 5/4/89 OE 99,000
Orange & Black (abstract), oil on paper, sgn twice/dtd 58, 19x24", SBY 2/19/88 55,000
Pair: Leo the Lion; Louie; charcoal on paper, sgn, ca 1940, 9x12", SBY 10/5/89 2,750
Pair: Lumber Man Jack; John the Moving Man; charcoal/gouache on paper, sgn, ca 1940, 12x9", SBY 10/5/89 2,750
Pair: Two Cats; Woman Standing at Window; brush/ink, crayons/brush/ink, 1 initialed, 11x7", 6x5", C-E 11/14/89 OE 4,180
Portrait of a Woman, pen/black ink on paper, initialed, 6x6", C-E 5/9/89 880
Portrait of the Artist's Wife, pencil on paper, sgn, 14x12", C-NY 2/13/89 OE 3,850
Red Painting (abstract), oil on canvas, 1961, 110x78", SBY 5/2/89 OE 1,760,000
Sabro IV (abstract), oil on canvas, sgn/dtd 60 twice/titled, 107x80", SBY 11/10/88 1,100,000
Scudera (abstract), oil on canvas, sgn/dtd 61, 111x79", C-NY 5/3/89 2,860,000
Seated Woman, gouache/gray paper laid down on board, sgn/dtd 49, 10x10", C-E 5/13/88 OE 2,640
Self-Portrait, oil on canvas mounted on board, sgn, ca 1945, 10x8", SBY 10/5/89 OE 17,600
Sketches of Cats, pencil on paper, sgn, 8x10", C-E 11/14/89 OE 3,080
Street Scene, pen/black ink/ink wash/pencil on paper, sgn, 9x11", C-NY 2/13/89 OE 1,760
Third Avenue (contemporary composition), oil on canvas, 1954, 38x25", SBY 11/8/89 1,210,000
Two Seated Figures, gouache on paper, initialed/dtd 46, 10x9", C-E 11/14/89 OE 5,280
Untitled, gouache on paper, 15x14", C-NY 2/13/89 10,450
Untitled, 1950 (abstract); oil on masonite, sgn twice, 18x25", C-NY 11/9/88 220,000
Untitled (abstract composition), ink on paper, sgn, ca 1958, 10x8", SBY 11/9/89 38,500
Untitled (abstract), brush/black ink on paper, 18x21", C-E 11/14/89 OE 24,100
Untitled (abstract), brush/black ink/crayon on paper, sgn, 1957, 14x17", C-NY 5/4/89 55,000
Untitled (abstract), gouache on paper, 14x17", C-E 11/14/89 OE 34,100
Untitled (abstract), India ink on paper, sgn/dtd 54, 11x9", SBY 5/3/89 OE 63,250
Untitled (abstract), India ink on paper, sgn/dtd 54, 9x11", SBY 5/3/89 OE 154,000
Untitled (abstract), ink on paper, ca 1950, SBY 5/3/89 UE 18,700
Untitled (abstract), ink on telephone book paper, ca 1952, 11x9", SBY 2/15/89 19,800
Untitled (abstract), ink on telephone book paper mounted on paper board, sgn/dtd 53, 9x11", SBY 5/3/89 27,500
Untitled (abstract), ink/oil on paper, sgn, 1956, 20x15", SBY 2/15/89 60,500
Untitled (abstract), oil on black paper board, sgn, 8x11", SBY 10/8/88 UE 16,500
Untitled (abstract), oil on canvas, sgn/dtd 61, 79x59", SBY 5/2/88 797,500
Untitled (abstract), oil on canvas, 1955, 35x31", SBY 11/10/88 467,000
Untitled (abstract), oil on canvas, 87x68", SBY 11/11/88 OE 126,500
Untitled (abstract), oil on paper, sgn, 1958-59, 15x20", SBY 5/3/89 UE 55,000
Untitled (abstract), oil/enamel on canvas, 1954, 83x67", SBY 11/10/88 1,870,000
Untitled (abstract), tempera on paper, 17x14", SBY 10/8/88 UE 14,300
Untitled (contemporary), brush/black ink on paper, sgn/dtd 50, 21x18", C-E 5/9/89 OE 24,200
Untitled (contemporary), brush/black ink on paper, 7x10", C-E 5/9/89 OE 15,400
Untitled (contemporary), gouache on paper, sgn, 14x15", C-E 5/9/89 OE 17,600
Untitled (house & birdbath in landscape), oil on masonite, sgn twice/inscr, 13x17", SBY 2/19/88 OE 6,875
Untitled (Study for Wanamaker Block), oil on paper mounted on board, ca 1955-56, 12x11", SBY 11/10/88 OE 198,000

KLINE, William Fair (American, 1870-1931)
Romantic Scene of Women in the Forest, oil on canvas, sgn/dtd 1906, 17x25", WG 4/23/88 400

KLINGSBOGL, Rudolf (Austrian, 1881-)
Interior with Clergymen Gathered Around a Table, oil on canvas, sgn, 22x27", SLK 9/27/88 350
Toper, oil on board, sgn, unfr, 19x13", WD 1/11/89 1,000

KLINKER, Orpha M. (American, 1891-1964)
Trees Along the Northern California Coast, oil on board, sgn/dtd 27, 10x14", B/B 9/15/88 358

KLIUN, Ivan (Russian, 1873-1943)
Man Walking (abstract), watercolor on paper, initialed, 8x6", C-L 10/8/88 5,580

KLODNICKI, Taddeus (American/Polish, 1904-1982)
Pair: Old Scollay Square; On the Boston Common; watercolor on paper, sgn, 14x22", 17x23", RWS 3/31/88 600

KLOSSOWSKI, Erich (German, 1875-)
Bateaux sur le Lac, watercolor/pencil on paper, sgn, 8x11", WD 5/5/88 850

KLUGE, Constantine (French, 1912-)
Berest, oil on canvas, sgn, 32x32", DM 2/19/88 2,500

Champs Elysees, oil on canvas, sgn, 24x36", SBY 10/7/89	4,950
Chateau, oil on canvas, sgn, 29x40", SBY 10/5/88	6,600
La Seine en Hiver (river in winter), oil on canvas, sgn, 51x77", SBY 2/14/89	2,750
River Gauche (figures on paved walkway beside river, bridge beyond), oil on canvas, sgn, 20x29", WL 5/20/88	1,300
Scene de Port (port scene), oil on canvas, sgn, 32x32", C-E 5/13/88	3,740
UMPKE, Anna Elisabeth (American, 1856-1942)	
Peasant Girl Knitting in a Landscape, oil on canvas, sgn/dtd Paris 1887, unfr, 56x69", C-E 2/1/89	4,400
UTH, R. (American, 1854-1921)	
Windmill in the Snow, oil on canvas, sgn/dtd 98, 18x31", C-E 2/16/88	715
NAPP, Charles W. (American, 1822-1900)	
Cows Crossing the Stream, oil on canvas, initialed, 10x14", C-E 6/1/89	770
Cows in a Fall Landscape, oil on canvas laid down on board, sgn, 24x40", C-E 6/1/88	5,720
Figures by the Shore, oil on canvas, sgn, 20x36", C-E 2/3/88 OE	8,800
Golden Morning (mountainous landscape w/cows watering), oil on canvas, sgn, 28x50", C-NY 5/25/89 OE	26,400
Landscape, oil on canvas, sgn/dtd 76, 18x32", SBY 6/24/88	2,090
Landscape with Figures, oil on canvas, sgn, 14x22", WL 5/20/88	650
Meadow View From Sketches, oil on canvas, sgn/dtd 1894, 17x27", C-E 10/18/89	1,760
Mountain Lake at Sunset (landscape), oil on canvas, initialed/dtd 1863, 30x48", SBY 1/24/89	11,000
NAPP, K. (German, 20th C)	
Still Life of Flowers in a Vase, oil on masonite, sgn, 25x20", C-E 5/23/88	550
NATHS, Karl Otto (American, 1891-1971)	
Abstract, pastel on paper, sgn, 9x6", C-E 6/1/89	825
Abstract Interior, crayon on paper, bears estate stamp, 8x5", C-E 6/1/89	990
Barker (abstract of announcer at side-show act), oil on canvas, sgn twice/dtd 1968/titled, 40x50", SBY 3/17/88	7,150
Danish Pastry, oil on canvas, sgn/dtd 1964, 30x42", C-E 10/18/89	6,050
Landscape, watercolor/crayon on paper, sgn/estate stamp/titled, 11x18", RAB 8/8/89 UE	325
Lilacs, oil on canvas, sgn twice/inscr/dtd 1963, 42x30", SBY 9/23/88	6,875
Portrait of a Man (abstract), pen on paper, estate stamp, 6x4", RAB 8/8/89 UE	80
Standing Nude, pen/black ink on paper, bears artist stamp, 11x9", C-E 6/1/89 UE	220
Still Life (abstract), oil on canvas, sgn/dtd 1966, 42x30", C-E 6/1/89	7,150
NAUS, Ludwig (German, 1829-1910)	
Birthday Party (children, dog, & cats in a landscape), oil on panel, sgn, 23x36", C-NY 5/24/89	49,500
Head of Young Girl, oil on board, sgn, 9x7", LH 10/16/88 OE	5,500
Young Girl with Her Dog, oil on canvas, sgn, unfr, 13x10", B/B 6/9/88	8,250
Zigeuner im Walde, Vom Ortsschulzen Uber Ihre Legitimation Ausgefragt; oil on canvas, sgn/dtd 1855, 44x60", SBY 10/24/89	41,250
NAUS, Ludwig; att (German, 1829-1910)	
Pair: Urchin with Turnips; Farm Boy with Carnation; oil on canvas, sgn, 31x22", WAD 6/6/88	2,600
NELL, William Callcott (British, 19th C)	
Ships in a Storm, oil on canvas, sgn/dtd 1868, 13x21", LH 3/20/88	1,500
Shipwreck, oil on canvas, sgn/dtd 1877, 12x24", FB 5/28/89	1,900
NELLER, Godfrey (German/British, 1646-1723)	
Portrait of an English Gentleman, oil on canvas, sgn, 30x25", S/A 2/18/89	3,000
Portrait of Henry Jermyn, 1st Earl of St Albans; oil on canvas, bears inscription, 30x25", SBY 6/3/88 OE	20,900
Portrait of Miss Anne Heathcote, oil on canvas, inscr, 49x39", SBY 6/8/88	2,970
NELLER, Godfrey; att (German/British, 1646-1723)	
Portrait of a Boy, standing, with a parrot in a landscape; oil on canvas, 50x41", C-NY 6/2/88	6,050
Portrait of a Lady in Blue Gown, oil on canvas, 50x40", LH 5/15/88 OE	4,000
Portrait of a Lady Said To Be Member of Vasasour Family, oil on canvas, ca 1860, 32x38", LH 10/16/88 UE	1,100
Portrait of Marie Princesse d'Orange et Reine d'Angleterre, watercolor/crayon, dtd 1688, 10x8", FB 5/28/89	450
NELLER, Godfrey; circle of (German/British, 1646-1723)	
Charles Seymoir, 6th Duke of Somerset; oil on canvas, 29x24", WAD 6/6/88	2,200
Portrait of a Gentleman (half-length, in blue jacket/white jabot), oil on canvas, inscr, 31x25", C-NY 4/8/88	1,100
Portrait of Queen Anne, seated, brown/white dress & ribbon of the Order of the Garter; oil on canvas, 50x40", C-NY 4/8/88	1,870
Portrait of the Duke of Schonberg, oil on canvas, inscr, unfr, 30x25", SBY 6/8/88 OE	1,100
NELLER, Godfrey; follower of (German/British, 1646-1723)	
Portrait of a Lady, oil on canvas, bears signature, 49x40", SBY 6/8/88 UE	1,320
Portrait of a Lady (full-length), oil on canvas, 79x53", SBY 7/12/89	1,320
NELLER, Godfrey; manner of (German/British, 1646-1723)	
Portrait of a Woman Said To Be the Duchess of Bedford, oil on canvas, unfr, 50x40", C-E 4/7/88	418
NELLER, Godfrey; school of (German/British, 1646-1723)	
Portrait of a Lady, oil on canvas, 31x26", B/B 5/17/89	770
Portrait of a Lady Holding a Flower, oil on canvas, 43x34", C-E 1/12/88 UE	605
Portrait of a Young Girl, seated, holding two cherries in a landscape; oil on canvas, unfr, 30x25", C-NY 4/8/88	1,100
Portrait of William Dawsonne, oil on canvas, unfr, 49x40", WD 1/25/89	1,100
NIGHT, A. Roland (British, 19th C)	
Oxford-Cambridge Mail, oil on canvas, sgn/dtd 1879, 25x40", WD 10/19/88	5,000
NIGHT, Daniel Ridgway (American, 1839-1924)	
Apple Blossoms (lady in landscape), oil on canvas, sgn/inscr, 31x26", C-NY 2/25/88	28,600
Burning Brush (w/three peasant women & boy), oil on canvas, sgn, 21x26", SBY 9/14/89	11,550
Courtship (couple in garden setting), oil on canvas, sgn, 18x15", C-NY 9/28/89 UE	8,250
Girl Knitting by a Garden Gate, oil on canvas, sgn/inscr, 22x19", SBY 5/25/88	22,000

Golden Sunset (young girl going to a river), oil on canvas, sgn/inscr Paris, 22x18", SBY 5/24/89 ... 15,400
In the Field, pencil, 19x14", C-NY 5/25/88 ... 990
Old Gallant (man retreiving lady's dropped hankerchief), oil on panel, sgn/dtd Paris 1872, 24x19", SBY 1/24/89 ... 3,575
Path to the Garden (two women w/flower cart), oil on canvas, sgn/inscr, 27x32", C-NY 12/2/88 ... 34,000
Picking Blossoms, oil on canvas, sgn/inscr, 46x35", C-NY 5/26/88 OE ... 71,500
Stopping for Conversation, oil on canvas, sgn, unfr, 26x32", B/B 3/17/88 UE ... 17,600
Three Women in a Landscape, watercolor on paper, sgn, 10x14", SBY 4/14/89 ... 1,870
Woman Picking Flowers, oil on canvas, bears signature, 26x22", C-E 7/26/88 ... 605
Young Girl Standing Near Lake, oil on canvas, sgn, 21x18", PHL 5/89 ... 47,500

KNIGHT, Daniel Ridgway; after (American, 1839-1924)
Girl with Pitcher (full-length, by lake), oil on canvas, bears signature/dtd Paris 1923, 32x25", SBY 6/28/89 ... 6,050
L'Arpel au Passeur, oil on panel, sgn, 49x66", FAP 11/4/88 ... 1,850

KNIGHT, F. (British, 19th C)
Seascape, oil on canvas, sgn, 10x14", lot 1019, LH 10/16/88 ... 650
Seascape, oil on canvas, sgn, 10x14", lot 1020, LH 10/16/88 OE ... 850

KNIGHT, Louis Aston (American/British, 1837-1948)
Canal in Venice, oil on canvas, sgn, 32x26", C-NY 10/25/89 UE ... 4,400
Connoisser, oil on panel, sgn, 12x8", C-E 5/23/88 UE ... 770
Cottage by the Water, oil on canvas, sgn/inscr, 26x32", C-NY 5/25/88 ... 8,250
Cottage in Normandy, oil on canvas, sgn/inscr, 18x22", SBY 6/24/88 ... 7,150
Cottage on a River, oil on canvas, sgn/inscr Paris, 32x26", C-NY 2/23/89 ... 15,400
Cottages Along a River in Normandy, oil on canvas, sgn/inscribed Paris, 33x36", SBY 6/28/89 ... 6,600
Country Stream in Spring, oil on canvas, sgn, 32x26", B/B 9/15/88 ... 6,050
Drawbridge at Dordrecht, oil on canvas, sgn, 18x22", B/B 3/17/88 ... 2,200
Falls, oil on masonite, sgn/inscr, 18x22", C-E 11/30/88 UE ... 2,200
Flowering Apple Tree on a River Bank, oil on canvas, sgn/inscr Paris, 32x26", C-NY 2/23/89 OE ... 20,900
Flowering Vine Along a Winding Stream with a Country Church Beyond, oil on canvas, sgn/inscr, 45x33", C-NY 5/24/89 OE ... 28,600
Flowers By a River Bank, oil on canvas, sgn, 18x22", B/B 6/9/88 ... 4,400
French River Landscape, oil on canvas, sgn, 26x33", C-NY 10/25/89 ... 8,800
La Prairie au Bord de Fleuve (river landscape), oil on canvas, sgn, 40x59", C-NY 5/25/89 ... 22,000
Lifeboat, watercolor on paper, sgn/inscr/dtd 1929, 10x14", SBY 6/24/88 ... 330
Montmartre (cityscape), oil on canvas, sgn/inscr Paris, 14x11", C-NY 9/28/89 ... 3,080
Norfolk, oil on canvas, sgn/inscr, 18x22", C-E 11/30/88 ... 1,540
Old Mill in Summer (landscape), oil on canvas, sgn/inscr Paris, 26x32", SBY 3/17/88 OE ... 9,350
On the Risle River, Normandy; oil on canvas, sgn/inscr Launay, 26x32", C-NY 2/23/89 ... 19,800
Pastoral River Scene, watercolor/gouache on paper, sgn, 14x10", B/B 12/8/88 ... 880
Pink Hawthorne Tree by a River in Normandy, oil on canvas, sgn, 46x35", SBY 10/25/89 ... 30,800
River Landscape by Moonlight, oil on canvas, sgn/inscribed Paris, 26x32", WD 10/5/88 UE ... 3,200
Roses Along the Rivers Edge, oil on canvas, sgn, 26x32", C-NY 5/25/89 ... 8,800
The Watermill, oil on canvas, sgn, 26x32", B/B 3/17/88 ... 11,000
Venice, oil on canvas, sgn/inscr, 46x35", C-NY 5/26/88 ... 14,300
Venice at Night, watercolor/gouache on paper mounted on canvas, sgn, 32x26", SBY 6/24/88 ... 3,850
View of Rouen (cityscape), oil on canvas, sgn twice/inscr Marche Place de la Haut Vieux Tour Rouen, 22x19", SBY 3/17/88 ... 5,500
View of the Seine, oil on canvas, sgn twice/dtd July 1929/inscr, 22x18", SBY 3/17/88 OE ... 8,250

KNIGHT, William Henry (British, 1823-1863)
Huntsman with His Greyhounds, oil on canvas, sgn/dtd 1850, 30x25", C-NY 2/23/89 OE ... 13,200

KNIJF, Wouter (ca 1607-1693)
A Ferryboat Approaching a Landing by a Walled Town, oil on panel, 16x20", C-NY 4/6/89 OE ... 11,000
Landscape with a Castle on a Canal, oil on panel, sgn in monogram/dtd 1647, 19x25", SBY 10/21/88 ... 23,100

KNIP, William Alexander (Dutch, 1883-1967)
Boats at Vollendam, oil on canvas, sgn/titled, 16x32", RAB 8/8/89 ... 1,000

KNOBLAUET, F.L. (19th C)
Vase with Carnations, oil on canvas laid down on board, sgn, 28x24", DM 9/16/88 ... 300

KNOEBEL, Imi
Untitled (abstract), collage w/paper/acrylic on paper, sgn/dtd 77, 39x28", C-NY 5/4/89 ... 3,850

KNOLL, Waldemar (Russian, 1839-1909)
Worontsov Bridge in Caucasus, pencil/watercolor on paper, sgn/inscr, 9x13", C-L 10/8/88 ... 1,300

KNOLLE, Helene Friedriks (American, 20th C)
Market, colored graphite on paper, initialed/dtd August 29, 1930, 9x14", MG 5/28/88 ... 700

KNOOP, August (German, 1856-1900)
Connoisseurs, oil on panel, 13x10", C-E 5/23/88 ... 1,540

KNOPF, Herman (Austrian, 1870-)
Going to Market, oil on canvas, sgn, 30x25", B/B 5/17/89 ... 1,760

KNOWLES, C.B. (British, 19th C)
Proposal, oil on canvas, sgn, 24x30", B/B 10/9/88 ... 4,675

KNOWLES, Elizabeth A. McGillivary (Canadian, 1886-1929)
Unwelcome Visitor, oil on ivory, sgn/dtd 1914, 2x2", WAD 11/30/89 ... 475

KNOWLES, Elizabeth C. (American, 20th C)
Still Life of Oranges, watercolor on paper, sgn/dtd 1905, 9x10", FAP 4/15/89 ... 138

KNOWLES, Farguhar McGillivray (American/Canadian, 1859-1932)
Coastal Scene with Sailboats, oil on board, sgn, 8x12", WAD 11/30/89 ... 280

lm Trees, oil on board, sgn, 9x10", WAD 11/30/89	325
ishing Shacks Along the Coast, watercolor on paper, sgn/dtd 1889, 11x20", RAB 8/9/88	500
akeside Birches, oil on board, 7x5", WAD 11/30/89	300
air: Village Road & Figures; Village at Dusk; oil on board, sgn/dtd , 5x7", WAD 11/30/89	1,100
uebec Village, oil on canvas, sgn, 18x14", WAD 11/30/89	2,200
eashore, oil on board, sgn/dtd 189(?), 7x13", C-E 2/1/89 OE	1,650
unlit Farmyard, oil on canvas, sgn, 28x20", WAD 11/30/89	2,000
OWLES, George Sheridan (British, 1863-1931)	
eeding the Doves, oil on canvas, sgn/dtd 1903, 30x20", SBY 5/23/89	16,500
ady with a Young Girl (seated on a bench, in a landscape), oil on panel, sgn, 24x19", FB 5/28/89 OE	10,200
OX, James (American, 1866-)	
Vooded Landscape with Fallen Logs, oil on board, sgn/dtd 1922, 12x14", SBY 6/24/88 OE	4,400
OX, James; att (American, 1866-)	
Moonrise, oil on board, sgn/dtd 1919, 12x14", RWS 11/10/89 UE	425
OX, Susan Ricker (American, 1874-1960)	
rashing Waves, oil on board, sgn, 10x12", C-E 3/22/88 UE	154
ady in a Summer Dress, pastel/pencil on paper, sgn/dtd 1905, 26x20", WL 5/20/88 UE	600
CH, Berthe (American, 1899-1975)	
ing St, Rockport, Massachusetts; oil on canvas, sgn/titled, 18x24", RWS 3/16/89 UE	150
CH, John (American, 1909-1978)	
sleep (man prone on stomach w/cigarette in hand), pencil/wht chalk on gray paper, sgn/inscr #2, 10x13", C-NY 9/28/89	6,380
acchanal, oil on canvas, sgn, 71x83", C-NY 9/28/89	16,500
athers (three nudes in a landscape), oil on canvas, sgn, 32x40", C-NY 6/17/89 OE	13,200
ouquet for Dora (lady seated, arms resting on table w/vase of flowers), oil on masonite, sgn, 4x5", C-NY 6/17/89	1,210
ocktail Party (gathering of the artist's friends in the arts), oil on canvas, sgn, 40x50", C-NY 5/25/89 OE	363,000
onversation, oil on canvas, sgn/dtd 75, 36x24", C-NY 12/2/88	71,500
ay, Papa, & George; pencil on tan paper, sgn, 7x9", C-NY 6/17/89	220
the Museum (figures seated on bench, man beyond viewing sculpture), oil on canvas, sgn, 40x55", C-NY 5/25/89	71,500
amplight with Dora (lady seated by lamp in an interior), oil on masonite, sgn, 8x10", C-NY 5/25/89 OE	16,500
Mary & Michael (portrait of two children), oil on canvas, sgn, 16x20", C-NY 9/30/88	7,700
Mother & Two Children (reading paper, baby asleep, brother watching), oil on canvas, sgn, 30x25", C-NY 6/17/89	4,400
Music Lesson (man & woman in interior), oil on canvas, sgn, 30x25", C-NY 12/2/88	71,500
On the Stairs (lady in white dress climbing stairs), oil on canvas laid down, sgn, 13x10", C-NY 9/28/89	7,480
Portrait of a Lady, oil on canvas, sgn, 21x17", WD 10/5/88 UE	1,100
Portrait of an Old Man, oil on canvas, sgn, 14x12", C-NY 6/17/89	990
Portrait of Dora, oil on canvas, sgn, 12x10", B/B 6/9/88	880
Portrait of Dora, oil on canvas, sgn/dtd 34, 17x14", C-NY 6/17/89	1,210
Portrait of Dora, pencil/white chalk on paper, sgn/dtd 74, 8x6", C-NY 6/17/89 UE	440
Portrait of Dora Koch Before the Piano, oil on canvas, sgn, 30x26", C-NY 6/17/89 OE	24,200
Portrait of My Mother, oil on canvas, sgn/dtd 65, 24x20", C-NY 9/28/89 OE	22,000
Portrait of My Wife, oil on canvas, sgn, 12x11", C-NY 6/17/89 UE	990
Portrait of the Artist's Father, oil on canvas, sgn/dtd 1951, 24x20", C-NY 9/28/89	5,500
Portrait of the Artist's Mother, oil on canvas, sgn, 24x20", C-NY 6/17/89	2,860
Rehearsal (two figures at piano, one from behind w/cello, lady reading music), oil on canvas, sgn, 31x25", C-NY 5/25/89	49,500
Self-Portrait, oil on canvas, sgn, 16x12", C-NY 6/17/89 UE	1,650
Self-Portrait, oil on canvas, sgn/dtd 68, 20x16", C-NY 5/25/89 OE	8,800
Self-Portrait, pencil/Chinese white on gray paper, initialed/inscr for Dora, 7x6", C-NY 6/17/89	660
Study in Allegory, oil on canvas, sgn, 9x12", C-NY 6/17/89 UE	462
Summertime, oil on canvas, sgn, 36x40", B/B 6/9/88	8,800
The Window (lady looking out window, man sitting in chair, reflecting), oil on canvas, sgn, 20x16", C-NY 9/28/89	16,500
Woman Dressing (nude viewed from behind), pencil on tan paper, sgn, 14x9", C-NY 6/17/89	462
CH, Ludwig (Austrian, 1866-1934)	
Polo Match (two riders battling for the play), oil on canvas, sgn/dtd 1922, 36x28", C-NY 2/23/89	15,400
EHLER, Henry (American, 1927-)	
Three Studies, Jockey in Red; oil on canvas, sgn, 20x30", SBY 6/9/89 OE	19,800
EHLER, Paul R. (American, 1866-1909)	
Landscape, nocturnal river landscape; pastel, sgn, 13x18", SLK 11/25/88	350
Winter's Evening in New York, pastel on board, sgn, 8x10", FAP 11/4/88 OE	1,600
EKKOEK, Barend Cornelis; circle of	
River Landscape with Village in the Distance, oil on canvas, 25x36", C-E 5/23/88 OE	2,640
EKKOEK, Hermanus Jr. (Dutch, 1836-1909)	
Locks & Windmill at an Entrance to a Town, oil on canvas, sgn, 34x44", SBY 7/12/89	5,500
Merchant Ships on a Dutch Canal, oil on canvas, sgn, 18x24", C-E 2/21/89	2,860
Shipping Off a Jetty, oil on panel, sgn/dtd 86, 12x16", C-E 5/23/88	2,640
EKKOEK, Hermanus Sr. (Dutch, 1815-1882)	
Preparing for the Storm (maritime scene), oil on panel, 17x24", SBY 2/22/89	7,150
EKKOEK, Jan Hermanus Barend (Dutch, 1840-1912)	
Unloading Seaweed, oil on canvas, sgn, 13x20", C-NY 5/25/88	7,150
EKKOEK, Johannes Hermanus (Dutch, 1778-1851)	
River Landscape, oil on panel, sgn, 7x10", C-E 10/25/88	2,860
Sailing the Stormy Seas, oil on panel, sgn, 15x20", SBY 2/22/89 UE	7,700

KOEKKOEK, Marianus Adrianus (Dutch, 1807-1870)

On the Maas (landscape with cottage & figures in a boat), oil on canvas, sgn/dtd 1864, 24x31", SBY 2/22/89 — 16,500

KOEN, Felix N. (19th C)

US Frigate Constitution with US Frigate America, 19th August, 1812; watercolor/ink, sgn, 8x10", C-NY 6/3/89 — 1,980

KOENIGER, Walter (American, 1881-)

Forest Stream, oil on canvas, sgn, unfr, 16x21", C-E 11/30/88 — 660

Mountain Stream in Winter, oil on canvas, 35x37", SBY 9/14/89 — 6,050

Summer Landscape with Birch Trees, oil on canvas, sgn, 32x32", SBY 1/24/89 — 3,850

Vermont Winter Landscape, oil on canvas, 35x37", SBY 9/14/89 — 5,775

Winter Thaw, oil on canvas, sgn, 20x24", C-E 6/1/88 UE — 1,320

Winter Thaw, oil on canvas, sgn/dtd 28, 38x45", C-NY 12/2/88 OE — 17,600

Woodland Stream in Winter, oil on canvas, sgn/dtd 27, 32x32", SBY 9/23/88 — 5,500

KOENTZ, W. (19th C)

Winter Landscape, oil on canvas, sgn, 20x24", WG 4/23/88 UE — 125

KOERNER, William Henry Dethlef (American, 1878-1938)

Illustration for White Men (a short story by GA Chamberlin), oil on canvas, sgn/dtd 1918, 28x36", SBY 1/24/89 OE — 7,425

Self-Portrait, oil on canvas, sgn/dtd 1922, 30x36", C-E 11/30/88 UE — 1,320

KOESTER, Alexander Max (German, 1864-1932)

Beute (group of ducks splashing in water), oil on canvas, sgn, 39x67", SBY 10/24/89 — 264,000

Ducks, oil on canvas, sgn, 22x33", C-NY 2/25/88 OE — 71,500

Ducks in a Pond, oil on canvas, bears signature, 22x32", C-E 5/23/88 — 1,650

Enten im Grass-Sonn (group of ducks in the sunshine), oil on canvas, sgn, 21x29", SBY 10/24/89 — 55,000

Enten im Teich, oil on canvas, sgn, 20x31", C-NY 10/25/89 OE — 104,500

Enten in Wasser Unter Birken (close-up of ducks in water), oil on canvas, sgn, 31x51", C-NY 5/24/89 — 187,000

Feeding Ground, oil on canvas, sgn, 25x31", SBY 5/23/89 OE — 110,000

Gansegutterung, oil on canvas, sgn/dtd 90, unfr, 26x90", C-NY 10/25/89 — 60,500

KOETS, Roelof; att (Dutch, 1592-1655)

Overturned Silver Cup & Peach on a Silver Plate...on a Table with a Cloth; oil on panel, 25x35", C-NY 5/31/89 — 33,000

Still Life of Fish, Bread, Peeled Lemon, Grapes in a Basket, Gilt Cup...; oil on panel, sgn, 30x43", SBY 1/12/89 — 99,000

Still Life with a Ham, Salmon with Herbs, Roll, Bowl of Broth, Stoneware Jugs...; oil on panel, 23x30", SBY 4/7/89 — 6,600

KOFFERMANS, Marcellus

Coronation of the Virgin, oil on copper, ornate frame w/marble columns, initialed/dtd 1570, 19x14", SBY 1/12/89 OE — 82,500

Crucifixion (Christ being nailed to cross, figures beyond), oil on panel, 7x6", C-NY 5/31/89 — 18,700

KOGAN, Anna (Russian, 1902-1974)

White Suprematism with Circle (abstract), oil on canvas, sgn, 1923, 22x25", C-L 10/8/88 — 26,030

KOGAN, Nina (Russian, 1887-1942)

Composition (geometric), gouache/pencil on paper, 12x9", SBY 10/6/89 — 16,500

KOGL, Benedict (German, 1892-1969)

Set of 3: Kittens; oil on canvas laid down on board, sgn, 6x7" & smaller, C-E 5/22/89 — 3,850

KOHL, Clemens

Youth Sleeping on a Rock, red chalk, crowned coat of arms & PB wm, sgn, 18x23", C-NY 1/11/89 OE — 1,650

KOHLEN, Carl (German, 19th C)

Black Cat on a Green Sofa, oil on canvas, sgn, 30x40", B/B 9/15/88 — 3,575

KOHN, Bill (American, 20th C)

Techos Tres, acrylic on canvas, sgn/dtd 1980, 48x60", LH 9/10/89 UE — 100

KOHRL, Ludwig (German, 1858-)

Accident, oil on panel, sgn/dtd 1890, 9x7", SBY 12/9/88 — 1,430

Interior Scene with Four Figures Playing Card Game, oil on canvas, sgn, 16x12", MAG 3/27/88 — 1,000

KOKKEN, Henri (Belgian, 1860-)

Vase of Roses, oil on canvas, sgn, 28x22", SBY 12/9/88 — 7,425

KOKO-MIKOLETZKY, Friedrich Albin (Austrian, 1887-)

Valluga in the Lechtaler Alps at Sunset, oil on canvas, sgn, 28x40", B/B 6/9/88 — 1,100

KOKOSCHKA, Oskar (American, 1886-1980)

Begegnung-Studie Fur Eine Bach-Kantate; black chalk on paper, 12x17", C-NY 2/16/89 — 8,250

Dresden, Neustadt I (cityscape seen from a river); oil on canvas, initialed, 32x44", SBY 5/9/89 OE — 2,970,000

Girl Resting on Her Elbows, brush/black ink on paper, sgn, ca 1921, 17x26", C-NY 11/15/88 — 9,900

Hunters (interior scene), oil on canvas, initialed, 1944, 25x30", SBY 11/12/88 OE — 176,000

Pierrot et Vielle Femme, brown ink on paper laid down on board, initialed, 8x7", SBY 10/5/88 OE — 4,400

Portrait of Claire Waldorff, blue pastel on buff paper, initialed, ca 1916, 17x12", C-NY 11/15/88 — 22,000

Prague: View From the Moldau Pier II; oil on canvas, initialed, 33x45", SBY 11/15/89 — 990,000

Stillben: Blumen am Fenster (floral still life w/beach beyond), oil on canvas, initialed, 1925-26, 29x39", SBY 5/10/89 — 374,000

Soldier, crayon drawing, initialed, 9x8", LH 5/15/88 — 2,000

KOLAR, Jiri (French, 1914-)

Chagalloland (abstract), paper montage/fabric on panel, sgn/dtd 73, 21x16", C-E 11/14/89 OE — 4,180

Dvouhlave Jaro, montage mounted on board, sgn/inscr/dtd 70, 11-12x16", C-E 5/13/88 — 990

Fifteen Collages, paper collage on paper, initialed, unfr, 15x11" & smaller, C-E 11/17/88 OE — 2,640

Four Paper Collages, colored pencils/paper on paper & board, initialed/1 dtd 62, unfr, 17x11" & smaller, C-E 11/17/88 — 1,870

Two Collages: Untitled; paper collage on printed paper, initialed, unfr, 9x5", 10x7", C-E 11/17/88 — 715

KOLESNIKOFF, Sergei (Russian, 1889-)

Church Procession, oil on canvas, sgn, 24x32", C-E 10/25/88 — 2,750

igures From Outside a Church, oil on canvas, sgn, 29x39", C-E 5/22/89 3,520
isherman on a River, oil on canvas, sgn/dtd 1945, 49x63", C-E 5/22/89 3,300
LITZ, Louis (German, 1845-1914)
attle Scene, oil on canvas, sgn/dtd 1873, unfr, 46x68", SBY 6/8/88 2,310
oblemen Riding Toward a Castle, oil on canvas, sgn/dtd 1868, 28x41", C-E 10/26/89 5,280
LLMAN, Karl Ivanovich (Russian, 1788-1846)
oujik Resting at the Garden Fence, pencil/watercolor, sgn/dtd 1842, 8x7", C-L 10/8/88 1,490
easant Family in an Izba Interior, pencil/watercolor, 9x12", C-L 10/8/88 OE 3,900
hree Peasant Women Gathering Herbs, pencil/watercolor, dtd 1842, 10x8", C-L 10/8/88 1,860
Voman & Child Paying a Visit to an Old Peasant, pencil/watercolor, 6x8", C-L 10/8/88 1,490
LLOCK, M. (American, 19th C)
Aill on Edge of Forest, oil on board, 13x15", FAP 4/15/89 412
LLWITZ, Kathe (German, 1867-1945)
aby in Mothers Arms, charcoal on paper, sgn/dtd 1922, 18x23", RWS 11/10/89 7,000
lande (two studies of right hand), charcoal on paper, sgn, 18x23", C-NY 5/11/89 6,600
NER, Max
ed-Haired Lady, oil on canvas, sgn/dtd 96, 22x18", C-E 11/8/88 UE 300
NINCK, see De Koninck
NINGH, see De Koningh
NO, Micao (Japanese, 20th C)
eclining Nude, oil on canvas, sgn/dtd XXXII, 13x16", SBY 2/14/89 6,600
NRAD, Adolf
clipse of the Sun, oil on canvasboard, sgn, 8x10", C-E 6/1/89 935
OL, Willem Gillesz (Dutch, 1608-1666)
ishermen Displaying Their Catch at the Shore, oil on panel, sgn/dtd 1648, 16x26", SBY 10/21/88 UE 16,500
andscape with Figures on a Frozen River & a Walled City Beyond, oil on panel, sgn/indistinctly dtd, 24x34", SBY 4/7/89 33,000
ONING, see De Kooning
PF, Maxim (Austrian, 20th C)
Red Cranes, oil on canvas, sgn, 30x37", LH 10/16/88 UE 400
PMAN, Benjamin (American, 1887-1965)
Music Room (man playing piano, another looking over his shoulder), oil on canvas, sgn/dtd 45, 23x31", RWS 11/10/89 UE 475
Scholars, oil on canvas, sgn, 27x22", SBY 1/24/89 770
PPENOL, Cornelis (Dutch, 1865-1946)
At the Beach, oil on panel, sgn, 19x28", WD 5/5/88 3,600
Children Playing in a Boat, oil on panel, sgn, 20x25", B/B 12/8/88 OE 1,430
Pair: At the Shore; oil on panel, sgn, 11x15", 12x16", SBY 7/12/89 OE 7,150
Untitled (busy sandy beach/cabanas/flying flags), oil on canvas, sgn, 24x40", SLK 4/7/89 1,600
PY, P.R.
Fall Landscape, pastel on board, sgn, 8x9", C-E 4/7/88 550
PYSTIANSKAYA, Svetlana (Russian, 1950-)
Landscape (contemporary), oil/tempera/handwritten text on canvas, sgn/dtd 1988, 49x65", SBY 7/7/88 OE 80,000
Landscape: N 4 (contemporary); tempera/handwritten text on canvas, sgn/dtd 1988, 49x63", SBY 7/7/88 OE 52,000
PYSTIANSKY, Igor (Russian, 1954-)
Compact Composition: N 2 (4-part work); oil on canvas, sgn/dtd 1987, 61x77", SBY 7/7/88 8,000
Construction 7 (4-part work); oil on canvas, sgn/dtd 1987, overall: 83x118x70", SBY 7/7/88 16,000
Dyptich: N 4 (seated nude in landscape); oil on canvas, sgn/dtd 1988, ea 77x61", SBY 7/7/88 OE 22,000
Interior 4 (6-part work); oil on canvas, sgn/dtd 1987, overall: 83x106x76", SBY 7/7/88 OE 24,000
Restored Painting: N 5 (portrait of a lady); oil on canvas, sgn/dtd 1987, 77x61", SBY 7/7/88 OE 80,000
Restored Painting: N 7 (landscape); oil on canvas, sgn/dtd 1987, 61x77", SBY 7/7/88 OE 44,000
rean School (18th/19th C)
Hanging Scroll: Diety Seated on a Hillside with Dragon; watercolor on cloth, frame, 53x31", WL 5/20/88 OE 1,400
RNBECK, Herman Julius (German, 1839-1920)
The Harvest, oil on board, sgn, 10x17", C-E 5/23/88 2,200
ROVINE, Alexis (Russian, fl 1927)
Still Life of Roses & Chrysanthemums, oil on canvas, sgn/dtd Paris 1927, 32x26", C-L 10/8/88 8,370
ROVINE, Constantin (Russian, 1861-1939)
Ballerina in Her Boudoir, oil on canvas, sgn/dtd 1923, 33x25", C-L 10/8/88 OE 26,000
Boulevard des Italians, oil on linen, sgn/dtd 1902, WG 9/16/88 14,500
Parisian Street Scene, oil on panel, sgn/inscr, 16x13", SBY 10/5/88 OE 2,860
Scene de Paris, oil on board, sgn/dtd Paris 1902, 10x14", C-NY 2/13/89 1,100
ROVINE, Constantin; att (Russian, 1861-1939)
Rites of Spring, oil on canvas, sgn, 29x37", C-E 5/22/89 OE 7,700
SA, Emile Jr. (American, 1903-1968)
Hills of Malibu, oil on canvas, sgn, 24x34", B/B 6/15/89 UE 4,675
Silver Lustre, oil on canvas, sgn, 28x32", B/B 10/6/88 4,125
SA, Emile Sr. (American, 1876-1955)
Granddaughter of the Artist, oil on board, 20x16", B/B 10/6/88 1,100
SLER, Franz Xavier (Austrian, 1864-)
Portrait of a Man in a White Turban, oil on board, sgn/dtd 1901, 8x6", C-E 10/26/89 1,760
Portrait of a Young Arab Boy, oil on canvas, sgn, 24x16", C-E 10/26/89 2,200
SSAK, see Von Kossak, Woicieck

KOSSUTH, Egon Josef (German, 1874-)
Portrait of Fedor, oil, sgn/dtd 1916, 30x20", WD 1/11/89 1,600

KOSTABI, Mark (American, 1960-)
Accumulation, oil on canvas, sgn/insr/dtd 1986, unfr, 60x84", C-NY 5/4/88 7,700
Baptism (contemporary nun w/umbrella, pitcher & bowl), oil on canvas, sgn/dtd 1988, unfr, 48x36", C-NY 10/4/89 5,500
Beauty, Wit, Sensuality, Intensity & Style (two figures); acrylic on canvas, sgn/dtd 1984, unfr, 71x48", C-N 2/14/89 9,350
Co-Ops/Condos; oil on canvas, sgn/dtd 1987, 90x68", SBY 2/15/89 4,950
Conversation (contemporary), oil on canvas, sgn/dtd 1982, unfr, 48x36", C-NY 5/4/89 4,400
Dinosaurs, acrylic on canvas, sgn/dtd 10-28-83, unfr, 48x72", C-NY 5/4/89 5,720
Edge of Night (figure teetering on edge), oil/silkscreen on canvas, sgn/dtd 1988, unfr, 48x36", C-NY 10/4/89 8,250
Hyper-Mediated Universe, oil on canvas, sgn/dtd 1984, 72x48", SBY 2/15/89 6,050
Just Say No, oil on canvas, sgn/dtd 1988, unfr, 68x68", C-NY 10/4/89 OE 10,450
Pair: Cash Not Trash (Perpetual Vision); Media Shower; mixed media/xerography, sgn, 9x11", 11x9", C-E 11/17/88 1,100
Service (contempory figure with top of head on platter), acrylic on canvas, sgn/dtd 1985, 72x48", C-NY 2/14/89 6,050
Singin` in the Rain (contemporary figures & umbrellas), oil on canvas, sgn/dtd 1982, 46x34", C-NY 10/4/89 9,900
The Staff of Life, oil on canvas, sgn/dtd 1987, unfr, 60x72", C-NY 5/4/89 4,950
Untitled (woman at computer holding phone), oil on canvas, sgn/dtd 11.24.83, 46x66", C-NY 2/20/88 4,950

KOSUTH, Joseph (American, 1945-)
Drawing for Not Documentation, graphite on paper, sgn/dtd 1966, 11x11", C-NY 5/4/89 OE 2,860

KOUNELLIS, Jannis (European, 1936-)
Untitled (two x's & an arrow), tempera on paper, sgn/dtd 1961, 28x39", SBY 11/11/88 22,000

KOUPAL, Marie (19th/20th C)
Seated Peasant Girl, oil on canvas, sgn/dtd 88, 29x22", LH 9/10/89 190

KOVNER, Saul (American, 1904-1982)
Art Magazines, oil on canvas, sgn/dtd 34, 26x32", C-NY 9/30/88 UE 1,650

KOWALSKI, Ivan Ivanovich
Sunrise: Wooded River Landscape; pastel, sgn, 22x15", C-NY 10/26/88 1,100

KOWALSKI, Leopold Franz (French, 1856-)
La Main Chaude-Who Touched? (French Game), oil on canvas, sgn, 57x87", SBY 2/22/89 132,000

KOZAKIEWICZ, Anton (Polish, 1841-)
Knife Sharpener, oil on panel, sgn/dtd 1885, 13x17", FB 10/30/89 OE 10,450
Pair: Rustic Flirtation; oil on panel, sgn, 8x6", C-NY 2/25/88 5,500

KRABBE, Hendrik Maarten (Dutch, 1868-1931)
Playing with a Doll, oil on canvas, sgn, 36x28", C-E 10/25/88 3,300

KRAEMER, Peter (German, 1857-1941)
At the Inn, watercolor w/traces of pencil on paper, sgn/inscr, 9x11", C-NY 5/24/89 OE 2,640
Group of 4: A Pipe Smoker; Musician & Drinkers; watercolor/pencil on paper, sgn/inscr, about 10x9", C-NY 5/24/89 OE 8,800
Group of 6: Hunters and a Mountaineer; watercolor/pencil on paper, sgn/inscr, about 9x7", C-NY 5/24/89 8,250
Group of 6: Hunters; A Pipe Smoker; A Beer Drinker; watercolor/pencil on paper, sgn/inscr, about 10x7", C-NY 5/24/89 OE 11,000
Group of 6: Woodcutters; Mountaineers; Hunters; watercolor/pencil on paper, sgn/inscr, about 11x8", C-NY 5/24/89 OE 11,000
Newspaper Vendor, watercolor, sgn, 7x9", FAP 4/15/89 1,815
Pair: Good Business; Bad Business; watercolor w/traces of pecil on paper, sgn/inscr, 7x6", C-NY 5/24/89 4,180
Pair: Hunters; watercolor w/traces of pencil on paper, sgn/inscr, 9x8", C-NY 5/24/89 4,950
Pair: Tyrolean Musicians (portraits); oil on canvas, sgn/inscr, 11x8", C-NY 5/24/89 7,150
Portrait of Hindenberg, watercolor/pencil on paper, sgn/dtd 1915, 7x6", C-NY 5/24/89 1,650

KRAFFT, Carl R. (American, 1884-1938)
Encampment with Conestoga Wagon, oil on canvas, sgn, 18x20", LH 12/4/88 OE 2,400
Old Mill in Winter, oil on canvas, sgn, 25x30", LH 10/16/88 OE 4,600

KRAMER, R.
Oxen-Drawn Carriage, oil on canvas, sgn, 13x16", C-E 5/23/88UE 660

KRANTZ, F. (French, 19th C)
Spilled Ink, oil, sgn, 15x21", WD 1/11/89 1,600

KRASNER, Lee (American, 1911-)
Dark Easter (abstract), oil on canvas, sgn/dtd 56, 58x38", SBY 2/15/89 OE 85,250
Nude Study From Life (abstract), charcoal on paper, sgn/dtd 38, 24x20", SBY 2/15/89 20,900
Seed #16 (abstract), gouache on paper, 1969, 17x13", SBY 2/15/89 16,500
Study for Mosaic at 2 Broadway, New York (abstract); oil/duck cloth collage on paper, 1959, 36x36", SBY 11/11/88 33,000
Untitled I (abstract), gouache on paper, sgn, 1962, 13x18", SBY 11/11/88 20,900

KRASNOPEVTSEV, Dimitri (Russian, 1925-)
Niche (contemporary), oil on masonite, sgn twice/dtd 1982 twice/titled, 29x23", SBY 7/7/88 OE 8,000
Still Life with Flower & Table: N 17 (contemporary); oil on masonite, sgn/dtd 88/titled/inscr, 22x13", SBY 7/7/88 OE 6,400
Three Amphoras (still life), oil on masonite, sgn twice/dtd 84 twice/titled/inscr, 30x24", SBY 7/7/88 OE 15,000

KRAUS, August (German, 1852-1917)
Toast in a Wine Cellar, oil on panel, sgn, 7x9", C-E 10/25/88 2,640

KRAUS, Friederich (German, 1826-1894)
Pearl Necklace, oil, sgn/dtd 1884, 33x26", WD 1/11/89 UE 1,200

KRAUS, Georg Melchior (German, 1737-1806)
Portrait of a Young Woman Leaning on a Hurdy-Gurdy, oil on canvas, sgn/indistinctly dtd, 11x9", SBY 10/13/89 8,250

KRAUSE, Lina (German, 1857-)
Pair: Floral Still Lifes; oil on panel, sgn, 12x10", C-E 2/21/89 OE 10,450
Still Life of Flowers, Butterflies, & a Bee on a Ledge; oil on panel, sgn, 17x13", C-E 10/25/88 3,520

KRAUSKOPF, Bruno (German, 1892-)

Port Scene, watercolor/gouache on paper, sgn, 19x25", SBY 10/7/89 1,870

KREMEGNE, Pinchus (Russian, 1890-)

Ceret (view of hillside village), oil on canvas, sgn, 15x18", SBY 2/14/89 5,225

Double-Sided: Two Women Plaiting Their Hair; Portrait of a Woman; oil on canvas, sgn/dtd 1915, 21x29", SBY 5/30/89 9,900

Interior, oil on canvas, sgn twice, 21x26", SBY 10/5/88 6,050

La Foret a Ceret, oil on canvas, sgn, 26x36", SBY 10/5/88 5,775

Landscape with Farm, oil on canvas, sgn, ca 1925, 18x25", SBY 5/30/89 8,800

Paysage (landscape), oil on canvas, sgn, 21x26", C-NY 2/16/89 OE 9,900

Paysage a Ceret, oil on canvas, sgn/inscr, 18x26", SBY 10/5/88 4,950

Pommes, Oranges et Grenades (still life); oil on canvas, sgn, 18x22", SBY 2/14/89 6,050

KREMEGNE, Pinchus; after (Russian, 1890-)

Paysage de Riviere Avec Barques (river landscape w/boats), oil on canvas, bears signature, 22x28", C-E 2/16/88 UE 242

KREMEGNE, Pinchus; att (Russian, 1890-)

Landscape, oil on canvas, sgn, 23x29", C-E 4/7/88 OE 3,080

KRENN, Edmund (Autstian, 1846-1902)

The Tinker, oil on canvas, sgn/dtd 1883, 44x35", B/B 3/22/89 11,000

KRENZ, A. (American, 20th C)

Harvest Sunset, oil on academy board, sgn, 8x12", FAP 12/8/89 UE 100

KRETSCHMER, W.

Pair: Bridge Over a Stream Near a Hillside Village; Village Entrance; pencil on paper, sgn, 7x9", C-E 10/25/88 UE 242

KRETZINGER, Clara Josephine (American, 1883-)

Woman with Potted Plant (three-quarter length portrait), oil on canvas, sgn/dtd 23, 29x24", SBY 9/14/89 7,975

KREUTZER, B. (German, 1873-)

Docking Boats in the Snow, oil on canvas laid down on panel, sgn, 12x22", WD 3/23/88 UE 1,100

KREYSSIG, Hugo (German, 1873-)

Tree-Lined Path, oil on canvas, sgn, 18x26", C-E 5/23/88 UE 660

KRIEGHOFF, Cornelius (Canadian, 1912-1872)

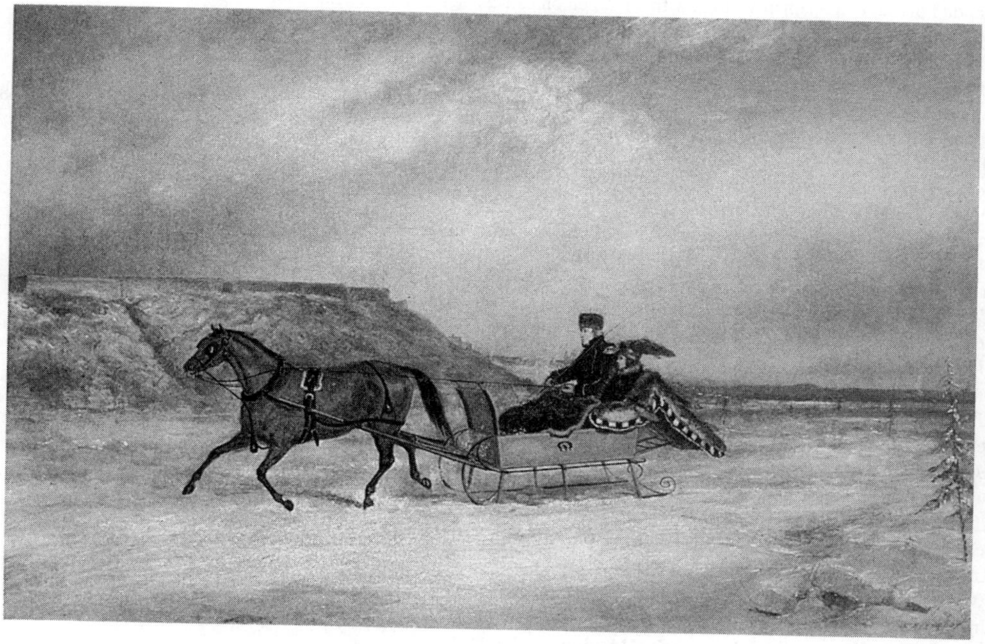

Captain Alfred Torrens & His Wife Caroline Aimee (nee Price) on the Ice in Front of the Citadel at Quebec, oil on canvas, sgn, ca 1854, 12x18", C-SK 6/9/88, $118,300

Pair: Indian Hunters; watercolor/pencil on paper laid down on board, sgn, 5x7", C-NY 3/11/88 12,100

Winter Landscape with Figure, oil on canvas, 8x12", WG 4/23/88 850

KRIEGHOFF, Cornelius; after (Canadian, 1912-1872)

Canoe in Fast Water, watercolor, sgn, 8x11", WAD 11/30/89 350

KRIEGHOFF, Cornelius; manner of (Canadian, 1912-1872)

Pair: Ice Harvest; The Ice Road; watercolor w/scratching out, 5x9", C-SK 6/9/88 706

KRIEGHOFF, Cornelius; school of (Canadian, 1912-1872)

Ice Cutting, oil on canvas laminated on board, bears signature, 12x18", FB 4/25/88 4,600

KRIEHUBER, Josef (Austrian, 1800-1876)

Little Girl in Pink with a Book & Toys (portrait), watercolor over pencil, sgn, oval, 9x10", C-NY 10/26/88 OE 2,640

Portrait of a Young Woman with Roses, watercolor heightened w/gold/white over pencil, sgn/dtd 1837, 9x7", C-NY 10/26/88 2,860

KRIMMEL, John Lewis (Johann Ludwig)(American, 1787-1821)

Francis Thomas (portrait), watercolor/gouache/pencil on paper, sgn/dtd 18(?), 5x4", C-NY 5/26/88 8,800

KRIPPENDORF, William H. (Dutch, 19th/20th C)

Sunlit Autumn Landscape, oil on board, sgn, 16x20", WG 9/16/88 UE 100

KROHG, Per (Norwegian, 1889-1949)
Seated Woman (w/man leaning on her chair & table from behind), sgn/dtd 27, 18x15", C-E 11/17/88 ... 935
KROLL, Leon (American, 1884-1974)
Blooming Trees (in a landscape), oil on canvas, sgn/dtd 1910, 21x26", SBY 4/14/89 OE ... 13,200
Dennison Road (girl w/guitar in a landscape), oil on panel, sgn/dtd 1961, artist's estate stamp, 30x25", RWS 5/12/89 ... 22,000
Female Nude Seated in an Armchair, watercolor/gouache/charcoal on paper, sgn, unfr, 19x24", B/B 9/14/89 OE ... 2,750
La Garde (landscape w/figures), oil on canvas, sgn, 27x36", C-NY 9/30/88 OE ... 8,250
Manhattan Rhythms, oil on canvas, sgn, 48x36", C-NY 9/30/88 OE ... 93,500
Nude in the Woods, oil on board, sgn, 18x16", C-E 6/1/89 ... 4,620
Portrait of a Woman, charcoal/pastel on green paper, sgn, 14x10", SBY 6/24/88 UE ... 550
Portrait of a Woman in Bonnet, oil on canvas, sgn, 30x25", FAP 11/4/88 ... 1,000
Portrait of Sonia Burthon, oil on canvas laid down on board, sgn, 24x21", C-E 10/18/89 ... 1,320
Reclining Female Nude, black chalk on thin laid Japan paper, sgn, unfr, 14x21", RWS 11/3/88 ... 650
Reclining Nude, pastel on paper, 10x17", B/B 5/17/89 ... 2,090
Seated Female Nude with Legs Crossed, red chalk on thin laid Japan, sgn, unfr, 20x14", RWS 3/16/89 UE ... 300
Springtime in Central Park, oil on masonite, sgn, 18x28", SBY 4/14/89 OE ... 25,300
Study of the Upper Torso of a Seated Female Nude, charcoal on newsprint, sgn, 14x11", RWS 5/12/89 ... 300
Sunlit Forest, oil on canvas, sgn, 30x36", SBY 3/17/88 ... 3,025
Tess Kroll Pergament, the Artist's Sister; oil on canvas, sgn/dtd 1912, 49x36", C-NY 9/30/88 ... 25,300
KROLL, Leon; att (American, 1884-1974)
Study for Federal Building, oil on canvas, sgn, 22x15", WL 5/20/88 ... 500
KRONBERG, Louis (American, 1872-1964)
Ballerina with Fan, oil on canvas, sgn/dtd 1918, 36x28", B/B 12/8/88 ... 1,100
Ballet Dancer, pastel on board, sgn/initialed/dtd 1940, 20x13", C-NY 3/11/88 ... 2,860
Ballet Girl (full-length portrait), pastel on paper, sgn/dtd 1914, 26x19", RWS 9/8/89 ... 1,800
Behind the Scenes (two dancers in orange & green), sgn/monogramed/dtd Boston 1920, 34x30", RWS 11/10/89 ... 3,000
Dancer in Green, no media given, sgn/dtd 1939, 28x21", SBY 6/28/89 ... 1,540
Dancing Ballerina (classic pose wearing Spanish attire), oil on canvas, sgn, 22x15", RAB 8/21/89 OE ... 1,700
End of the Ballet, oil on canvas, sgn, 28x24", RWS 11/10/89 UE ... 2,500
Lalinda-Portrait of a Spanish Woman with a Fan; oil on canvas, sgn twice/dtd Barcelona 1923/inscr, 37x29", RWS 3/16/89 ... 700
Louise Against the Light at the Window, pastel on textured board, sgn, 24x20", WD 4/13/88 ... 600
Mlle Yvonne a l'Eventail, pastel on textured board laid down, sgn, 28x22", WD 4/13/88 ... 1,600
Ode to Degas, pastel on fan-shaped paper, sgn, 8x14", RWS 3/16/89 ... 600
Signorita DaCosta (half-length portrait, Spanish lady seated on a balcony), oil on canvas, sgn/dtd 1933, RWS 3/31/88 UE ... 500
Woman in a Pink Kimono, oil on canvas, sgn/dtd 1904/#d 5665, 22x12", RWS 3/16/89 OE ... 4,250
KRONBERGER, Carl (Austrian, 1841-1921)
Piety, oil on panel, sgn, 7x5", SBY 2/22/89 ... 6,050
KRONENGOLD, Adolph (American, 20th C)
French Quarter, Charter Street, New Orleans, Louisiana; acrylic on board, sgn, 29x40", RAB 8/8/89 UE ... 500
KROYER, Peder Severin (Danish, 1851-1909)
Artist & His Wife on the Beach at Skagen, oil on canvas, sgn/dtd 1899, 38x26", SBY 5/23/89 ... 374,000
KRUGER, Eugen (German, 1832-1876)
Deer in a Wooded Clearing, oil on canvas, sgn, 39x52", SBY 6/8/88 ... 3,300
KRUGER, Richard (American, 20th C)
Surf, oil on canvas, sgn, 28x36", LH 12/4/88 UE ... 275
KRUMEYER (American, 20th C)
Lettuce Pickers, oil on canvas, sgn, 24x30", FAP 12/8/89 ... 375
KRUPP, F.
Ducks in a Pond, oil on canvas, sgn, 18x28", DM 1/15/88 ... 1,200
KRUSE, Alexander (American, 1890-)
Scale, crayon on paper, initialed, 1926, 24x18", WG 10/19/88 UE ... 150
KRUSHENICK, Nicholas (American, 1929-)
Five Silver Dogs, acrylic on canvas, sgn/dtd 1969, unfr, 84x74", C-E 5/9/89 OE ... 3,080
Untitled (abstract composition), acrylic on canvas, sgn/dtd July 1965, 28x22", C-E 11/14/89 OE ... 3,850
KRYZHITSKII, Konstantin Iakovlevich (Russian, 1858-1911)
Lake Landscape with Mountains Beyond, oil on canvas laid down on board, sgn/dtd 98, 35x56", C-L 10/8/88 ... 9,300
KUBA, Ludvik (Czechoslovakian, 1863-1956)
Jan Kubelik in Concert at Smetana Hall, Prague; oil on canvas, sgn/dtd 1920, 70x59", WD 11/16/88 ... 6,750
KUDRIASHEV, Ivan (Russian, 1896-1972)
Suprematist Compostion (abstract), watercolor on paper, sgn/dtd 20, 8x14", C-L 10/8/88 ... 3,720
KUEHNE, Max (American, 1880-1968)
Autumn Still Life, oil on panel, sgn, 30x35", SBY 9/23/88 OE ... 6,050
Cliffs in Cornwall, oil on canvasboard, sgn/dtd 1913, 24x30", RWS 11/10/89 ... 750
Cornish Cliffs, Hillside & Sea; oil on canvas laid down on board, sgn, 24x30", NA 5/13/89 UE ... 800
Gloucester Docks, oil on board, sgn/dtd 1918, 8x10", C-NY 9/28/89 ... 2,200
Gloucester Harbor, oil on canvas, sgn/dtd 1926, 20x24", SBY 9/23/88 OE ... 18,700
Market Square, Segovia Spain; no media given, sgn/dtd 17, unfr, 30x29", C-E 10/18/89 ... 1,760
Over the Bay Provincetown (rooftop view of houses, bay beyond), oil on panel, sgn, 7x9", C-E 2/1/89 ... 3,300
Street at Burgos, Spain; sgn/dtd 1923, unfr, 20x24", SBY 6/24/88 UE ... 550
View of Rockport, oil on board, sgn, 13x16", C-E 10/18/89 ... 4,180
Village Store (many figures standing outside of large building), oil on masonite, sgn, 18x23", WL 5/20/88 OE ... 5,000

KUGHLER, Francis Vandeveer (American, 1901-)
Spring in a Glass Case (collection of birds in glass case), oil on canvasboard, sgn/titled, 16x12", SBY 3/17/88 UE ... 550
KUHN, Justus Engelhardt; after (American)
Portrait of Master Digges, oil on canvas, 53x37", SBY 9/14/89 ... 3,410
KUHN, Walt (American, 1880-1949)
Bareback Rider (three-quarter portrait), oil on canvas, sgn/dtd 1926/titled, 40x30", SBY 5/24/89 ... 192,500
Beach Scene, oil on canvas, sgn, 10x10", DM 3/14/88 ... 650
Clown with Camera, pen/black ink/watercolor on paper, sgn, 5x10", C-E 10/18/89 OE ... 3,850
Cow Girl-New Mexico; pencil on paper, 16x13", SBY 9/14/89 OE ... 17,600
Cowboys & a Christmas Star, watercolor/ink on paper, sgn/dtd 1940, 5x7", B/B 8/10/88 ... 330
Dancer with Red Plume (full-length), gouache on paper laid down on paper, 25x13", C-NY 9/28/89 ... 8,800
Eye Opener (man drinking at the bar), oil on canvas, sgn/dtd 1906, 24x34", SBY 5/25/88 ... 22,000
First Tanner in America (man tanning, soldier watching), oil on masonite, initialed, 30x40", C-E 2/1/89 UE ... 1,870
Girl in a Clown Suit, oil on canvas, sgn/dtd 1944, 22x20", SBY 5/25/88 ... 33,000
Girl with Cornucopia (portrait), oil on canvas, sgn/dtd 1937, 41x30", C-NY 12/2/88 UE ... 44,000
Green Plums, oil on canvas, sgn/dtd 1923, 8x10", SBY 5/25/88 ... 16,500
Magnolias & Jonquils (in a landscape), watercolor/gouache on board, sgn/dtd 1927, 22x28", C-NY 5/26/88 ... 15,400
Miss X, oil on canvas, sgn/dtd 1932, 32x26", SBY 4/14/89 OE ... 19,800
Mrs Elizabeth Bliss Parkinson (portrait), oil on canvas laid down on board, sgn/dtd 1944, inscr, C-NY 12/2/88 ... 9,900
Performer (portrait), oil on canvas, sgn/dtd 1936, 40x30", C-NY 5/26/88 ... 50,600
Rooster 1944, watercolor/pen/ink on paper, sgn, 9x8", B/B 9/15/88 ... 248
Roosters, black ink/charcoal on paper, unfr, 12x9", SBY 6/28/89 OE ... 9,350
Ruth with Green Headcloth (portrait), oil on canvas, sgn/dtd 1927, 15x12", C-NY 5/26/88 ... 13,200
Sailboats, oil on canvas, sgn, 10x10", DM 3/14/88 ... 650
Set of 7: Mystery of Edwin Drood, Seven Character Illustrations; pen/ink/watercolor, sgn, 7x4", C-E 2/23/88 ... 605
Show Girl, oil on canvas, 13x18", C-NY 9/30/88 ... 4,620
Show Girl in Dressing Room, pencil on paper, indistinctly sgn/initialed, 9x7", C-E 2/3/88 ... 935
Still Life of Flowers in a White Vase, oil on panel, sgn, 15x12", C-E 6/1/89 ... 4,400
Studio Corner (lady at table seated), oil on canvas, sgn twice/dtd 1932 twice/titled, 40x46", SBY 5/24/89 ... 159,500
Study of a Child with a Blue Scarf Around the Neck (bust-length), oil on canvas, sgn, 15x10", SLK 5/12/88 ... 50
Summer Evening, oil on canvas, sgn/dtd 1906, 22x65", SBY 5/25/88 ... 31,900
Tree-Lined Country Stream, oil on canvas, sgn/dtd 1885, 13x10", B/B 1/11/89 ... 1,100
Trude (full-length portrait), watercolor on paper, sgn/dtd 1931/inscr dedication, 19x14", SBY 5/24/89 ... 8,800
Vase with Flowers, pen/brush/black ink on paper, sgn/dtd 1922, 8x6", C-NY 9/28/89 ... 4,400
KUITCA, Guillermo
First Hours Without Laura, Good Morning Heartache; acrylic on canvas, sgn/dtd 1985, 55x63", SBY 5/17/88 ... 5,500
Yo Como una Noche, acrylic on canvas, sgn/dtd 1985, 79x118", SBY 11/21/88 ... 11,000
KULIK, Karl (1654-1713)
Artist & Other Figures in a Picture Gallery, oil on canvas, indistinctly sgn, 30x37", SBY 10/13/89 ... 37,400
KUMMER, Julius Herman (American, 1817-1869)
Mountainous Landscape, oil on canvas, sgn/dtd X9, 12x17", C-E 10/25/88 UE ... 880
KUNIYOSHI, Yasuo (American, 1893-1953)
Broken Objects, casein on board, initialed, 1952, 19x24", SBY 5/25/88 ... 99,000
Cripple Creek, Colorado; gouache on gessoed masonite, sgn/dtd 1941, 10x16", C-NY 9/28/89 ... 57,200
Double-Sided: Execution Scene; Nude; pencil on paper/red ink on paper, sgn/dtd 1943, 16x12", SBY 3/17/88 OE ... 1,980
Figs, casein on board, sgn, 12x16", C-NY 5/26/88 ... 55,000
Four Peaches, oil on canvas, sgn/dtd 35, 12x16", C-NY 5/26/88 OE ... 44,000
Park Ridge, Beautiful Chicago; gouache on board, sgn/dtd 34, 15x19", C-NY 9/30/88 ... 4,400
Smoker, pen/black ink/ink wash on paper laid down on board, sgn, 6x10", C-NY 9/30/88 OE ... 5,720
Still Life of Bananas, oil on canvas, 15x19", C-NY 9/30/88 ... 12,100
Still Life of Cucumber & Lemons, India ink/wash over pencil, sgn/dtd 22, 8x11", SBY 6/28/89 OE ... 8,525
Vase with Flower (still life), India ink on paper, sgn/dtd 1922, 3x6", SBY 3/17/88 OE ... 3,850
Village Street, India ink/gray wash on paper, sgn/dtd 21, 12x10", SBY 3/17/88 OE ... 18,700
KUNST, Pieter Cornelisz (1490-)
Faith (or Ecclesia), pen/black ink, 9x7", SBY 1/13/89 ... 4,400
Justitia, pen/black ink, 9x7", SBY 1/13/89 UE ... 3,850
KUNSTLER, Mort (American, 1931-)
Snow Herder, oil on masonite, sgn, 24x19", SBY 6/24/88 ... 2,090
KUNTZ, Roger (American, 1926-)
Arches (viaducts over a roadway), oil on canvas, sgn, 40x50", SBY 2/14/89 OE ... 3,850
At Queens College (building in landscape), oil on canvas, dtd 1981/#d, 18x24", SBY 2/14/89 ... 3,575
KUNZ, Ludwig Adam (Austrian, 1857-1929)
Exotic Birds & Flowers, oil on shaped canvas, sgn/dtd 1893, 45x38", C-NY 5/25/88 OE ... 8,250
KUPETZKI, Johann; school of (German, 1667-1740)
Pair: Portraits of a Man; oil on panel, unfr, 12x9", C-NY 4/8/88 ... 1,100
KUPFERMAN, Moshe (Israeli, 20th C)
Composition (abstract), oil on canvas, sgn/dtd 71, 39x32", SBY 5/30/89 OE ... 5,280
KUPKA, Frank (Czechoslovakian, 1871-1957)
Composition (abstract), gouache/pastel on paper, sgn, 18x14", WD 5/5/88 UE ... 6,000
Composition Spirale, gouache on paper laid down on paper, 9x6", C-E 5/9/89 ... 4,950

KURILOFF, Edna (American/Russian, 1889-1979)
Still Life with Flowers & Grapes, oil on canvas, sgn, 24x30", WG 9/16/88 UE ... 160

KURLAND, Bruce
Kitchen Still Life, oil on canvas, initialed, 10x8", C-NY 6/17/89 OE ... 1,760

KURTZ, Elaine (American, 1928-)
Untitled (abstract), tempera on canvas, sgn/dtd 78, 22x51", C-E 11/14/89 UE ... 44

KUSHNER, Robert (American, 1949-)
Hamman (seated male w/arms wrapped around knees), India ink/plastic/fabric collage, sgn, 1982, 47x32", SBY 5/3/88 ... 4,950
Waterfall, acrylic on cotton with tassels, 1976, overall: 76x174", SBY 2/15/89 ... 15,400

KUWASSEG, Charles Euphrasie (French, 1838-1904)
Dutch Village at the Ford (detailed landscape), oil on canvas, sgn, 16x24", B/B 10/9/88 ... 12,100
Figures & Town by a River, oil on canvas laid down on board, sgn/dtd 1870, 12x18", SBY 12/9/88 OE ... 4,125
Fishermen in a Cove, oil on panel, initialed, 7x14", B/B 6/9/88 ... 2,200
Italian Figures & Town by a Lake, oil on canvas, sgn/dtd 1868, 20x26", SBY 7/12/89 ... 6,050
River Town, oil on panel, bears signature, 9x16", C-E 5/23/88 ... 2,420
Town in an Alpine Pass, oil on canvas, sgn/dtd 1875, 13x10", SBY 7/12/89 ... 4,400
View of Rocamadour, France; oil on canvas, sgn/dtd 1877, 23x40", C-NY 5/24/89 ... 17,600

KWATHS, Karl
Abstract (green, yellow, orange), oil on canvas, sgn, 12x11", C-E 2/3/88 UE ... 770

L.A. (19th C)
Verdant Landscape with Cattle, oil on canvas, monogramed, 16x22", SLK 5/12/88 ... 120

L'ARCHEVEQUE, Andre (Canadian, 1923-)
Erosion, oil on board, sgn/dtd 1980, 14x23", FB 4/25/88 ... 1,900
Jour Rose, oil on canvas, sgn/dtd 1980, 16x20", FB 10/30/89 ... 2,090
Soir d'Hiver, oil on canvas, sgn/dtd 1989, 10x14", FB 10/30/89 ... 1,320

L'ARTEOUS (Russian, 20th C)
Costume Design: A Courtier; gouache/gold paint on paper, sgn/dtd 922, 14x10", C-L 10/8/88 OE ... 2,970
Costume Design: A Gypsy; gouache on paper, sgn/dtd 921, 15x9", C-L 10/8/88 OE ... 2,970
Costume Design: Lady in Purple Cloak; gouache on paper, sgn/dtd 922, 14x10", C-L 10/8/88 ... 4,090

L'ENGLE, William (American, 1884-1957)
Celli 1936, oil on canvasboard, unfr, 20x16", RWS 3/16/89 ... 300
Fish Composition (still life of fish), oil on canvas, sgn, 16x20", RWS 9/29/88 ... 600
North Truro-Fishermen Around a Stove; watercolor on paper, initialed/dtd 1925, 13x19", RWS 3/15/89 OE ... 800
Pair: Danse Group; Study for Danse Group; oil & watercolor, sgn/dtd, 20x16", 6x4", RWS 3/16/89 OE ... 500
Snow Fence (figures building fence in landscape), watercolor/pencil on paper, 14x20", RWS 3/16/89 OE ... 450
Snow Fence (three men setting a fence in autumn landscape), oil on canvas, sgn/dtd 40, 24x30", RWS 9/29/88 OE ... 1,100

LA CORTE, see De la Corte

LA FARGE, John (American, 1835-1910)
October, Clearing Off After the Rain; oil on panel, 1870, 10x8", SBY 5/25/88 ... 19,800
Seated Woman (full-length in profile), watercolor/gouache/pencil on paper laid down, sgn/dtd 1889, 9x7", C-NY 5/25/89 ... 8,800
Southern Tip of Oahu, Hawaii (seascape); watercolor/gouache on paper, 7x9", SBY 1/24/89 ... 4,400
Still Life, Study of Silver, Glass, & Fruit, 1859; oil on canvas, 13x19", RWS 11/10/89 OE ... 100,000
Wild Roses & Waterlily, watercolor/gouache on paper, sgn/dtd 1886, 14x11", C-NY 12/2/88 ... 28,600

LA FONTAINE, Charles
At the Spring (portrait of a girl in a landscape), oil on canvas, sgn, C-NY 2/25/88 ... 4,950

LA FONTAINE, Thomas Sherwood (British, 1915-)
Tim Langley & the Berkeley Hunt (study for larger oil), oil on panel, 11x14", SBY 6/9/89 ... 6,600

LA FRESNAYE, see De la Fresnaye

LA GRANDE, P. (French, 20th C)
Interior with Figures, oil on canvas, sgn, 12x21", SLK 9/29/88 ... 400

LA HAYE, Reinier; see De La Haye

LA HOTAN, Robert
At the Table, oil on canvas, sgn, 12x14", C-NY 6/17/89 UE ... 55

LA HYRE, see De La Hyre

LA MAR, David; see De La Mar

LA MARCHE, Nathalie; see De La Marche

LA MARTINIERE, Marie Francoise Constance (1775-1821)
Self-Portrait with the Artist's Father, oil on canvas, 89x71", SBY 1/12/89 ... 132,000

LA NOUE, Terence (American, 1941-)
Luxor (abstract), acrylic/rhoplex/tobacco cloth on canvas, sgn/dtd 81, 95x84", SBY 2/15/89 ... 6,050

LA PENA, Narcisse; see Diaz De La Pena

LA PIRA (Italian, 19th/20th C)
Pair: Naples Scenes; watercolor on paper, sgn, 8x13", 12x21", B/B 12/8/88 ... 1,320

LA POINTE, Jean Paul (Canadian, 20th C)
Liberte Hivernale, oil on canvas, sgn, ca 1986, 24x30", FB 10/17/88 ... 400

LA ROCHE, Charles; see De La Roche

LA RUE, see De La Rue

LA RUERE, Pietro; see De La Ruere

LA SERNA, Ismael; see De La Serna

LA VEGA, Jose; see De La Vega

LA VILLEON, see De La Villeon

LAAR, Jan Hendrik; see Van De Laar

LABASQUE, Henri (European, 1865-1937)

Jardin au Printemps (a garden in springtime), oil on canvas, sgn, ca 1904, 20x24", C-NY 11/16/88 ... 71,500
Nu au Tapis Rouge (seated nude), oil on canvas, sgn, 29x22", C-NY 11/16/88 ... 165,000

LABAUDT, Lucien Adolph (American/French, 1880-1943)

Bedouin Tents Before Hagia Sophia, oil on canvas, sgn, unfr, 16x12", RWS 11/10/89 UE ... 325

LABELLE, Fernand (Canadian, 1934-)

L'Hiver, Tout Est Calme (winter scene); oil on canvas, sgn, 30x40", FB 4/25/88 ... 650
The Way to My Studio, oil on canvas, sgn, 20x24", FB 4/25/88 UE ... 425

LABOR, Charles (French, 1813-1900)

Units of American Fleet in Villefranche-Sur-Mer, 1875; oil on canvas, sgn/dtd 1875/titled, 28x50", C-NY 5/24/89 ... 15,400

LABOURER, Jean Emile (French, 1877-1943)

Jeune Fille Devant une Port (young woman in landscape), oil on cradled panel, sgn, 15x18", RWS 5/19/88 OE ... 18,000

LABRANCHE, Gilles (Canadian, 1947-)

Coin Guy et Sherbrooke (snowy street scene); oil on canvas, sgn/dtd 1988, 30x36", FB 10/17/88 ... 1,100
St Andre & Mariane St Montreal, oil on canvas, sgn/dtd 1989, no size given, FB 5/28/89 OE ... 1,700

LABRUZZI, Carlo (Italian, 1786-1818)

After the Harvest: Shepherds with Their Flocks (3 studies on 1 page); pen/ink on wove paper, 15x9", B/B 9/14/89 UE ... 605

LACAZE, Germaine

Children in a Garden, oil on canvas, sgn/stamped, 39x32", SBY 10/5/88 OE ... 3,300

LACHAISE, Eugene A. (American, 1857-1925)

Geisha Girl, oil on canvas, sgn/dtd 1890, 31x36", C-NY 10/25/89 ... 11,000

LACHAISE, Gaston (American, 1882-1935)

Double-Sided: Female Nude Wearing Headdress; pencil/ink, pencil on paper, 21x17", SBY 2/14/89 ... 3,850
Female Nude, pencil on paper, sgn, 24x18", SBY 6/24/88 UE ... 2,200
Study of a Female Nude, charcoal on buff paper, sgn, 10x8", SBY 6/24/88 ... 2,420

LACHENWITZ, F. Sigmund (German, 1820-1868)

Dogs Fighting in a Landscape, oil on canvas, sgn, 35x60", C-E 2/23/88 ... 2,750

LACHMAN, Harry (American/French, 1886-1974)

Figures Outside a Building, oil on board, sgn, 14x11", B/B 1/11/89 ... 2,200

LACKTMAN (20th C)

Landscape with Road, oil on canvas, sgn, 26x34", LH 12/4/88 ... 160

LACOMBE, Georges (French, 1868-1916)

La Baie (view of a bay), oil on canvas, ca 1895, 20x25", C-NY 5/12/88 ... 143,000

LACOMBLE, Adolphe

Reflecting Pond, oil on canvas, sgn, 11x16", C-E 5/23/88 ... 1,320

LACRETELLE, Jean Edouard (French, 1817-1900)

Racehorse Harvester with Arthur Yates Up, oil on canvas, sgn, 28x36", SBY 6/9/89 ... 13,200

LACROIX, Paul (American, fl 1855-1870)

Study of Cherries, oil on board, sgn, 4x6", SBY 6/24/88 ... 5,225

LACROIX DE MARSEILLE, Charles (French, 1720-1782)

Harbor by Cliffs with Fishermen & a Ship at Anchor in the Distance, oil on canvas, sgn/dtd 1760, 30x51", SBY 6/2/89 ... 55,000

LADBROOKE, John Berney; att (British, 1803-1879)

Untitled, wooded landscape w/figures & cottages along road & distant windmill, oil on panel, 13x19", SLK 2/11/89 ... 625

LADELL, Edward (British, 1821-1886)

Still Life of Fruit, Wine, & Compote on a Table; oil on canvas, 17x13", C-E 5/23/88 ... 1,650

LADOROJAY, Vasily S. (Russian, 20th C)

Shy Bride, oil on panel, sgn, 24x36", B/B 1/11/89 ... 605

LADOUCEUR, Jean Paul (Canadian, 1921-)

L'Effeuilleur, Laval (landscape); watercolor, sgn, ca 1981, 21x28", FB 10/17/88 UE ... 650
La Souche Bleu, St Bruno; watercolor, sgn/dtd 1979, 20x28", FB 5/28/89 ... 850
Theme #112, watercolor, sgn/dtd 28/21/71, 25x18", FB 4/25/88 UE ... 475
Un Bouquet de Soucis (bouquet of marigolds), watercolor, sgn, 28x21", FB 5/28/89 ... 550

ADURNER, Adol'f Ignatievich (Russian, 1796-1856)

Grand Duke Konstantin Nikolaevich Taking Oath of Allegiance in Georgievskii Hall...; oil on canvas, 12x20", C-L 10/8/88 ... 14,870
Presentation of Grand Duke Konstantin Nikolaevich to the Pavlovski Regiment, oil on board, 7x10", C-L 10/8/88 UE ... 3,530
Troop of the Caucasian Guard at Full Gallop, Female Spectators Watching From Tents; oil on board, 6x9", C-L 10/8/88 UE ... 2,790
Troops of the Imperial Guard at Attention, Parading the Military Mascot on Admiralty Square; oil, 7x10", C-L 10/8/88 UE ... 2,790

AFITTE, Louis (French, 1770-1828)

Gemini: Lady with a Sickle & a Dove; black chalk, sgn, 10x8", C-NY 1/11/89 ... 3,080
Libra: Lady Holding a Scale with Grapes & a Goat Chewing a Vine Tendril; black chalk, sgn, 10x7", C-NY 1/11/89 ... 2,860

AFON, Francois (French, 19th C)

Nymphs in a Wooded Landscape, oil on canvas, sgn, 14x22", C-E 2/22/88 ... 935

AFOSSE, see De Lafosse

AFRAMBOISE, Robert (Canadian, 1921-)

Tendress et Chaleur (young girl in profile holding cat), oil on canvas, sgn/dtd 1987, 24x20", FB 4/25/88 ... 1,000

AGACE, Paule (Canadian)

Standing Figure in a Sunlit Room, oil on canvas, sgn, 33x40", FB 5/28/89 ... 450

AGLENNE, Jean Francis (French, 1899-)

Still Life of Wildflowers, oil/wash/pencil on board, sgn, 9x11", RWS 3/16/89 ... 650

LAGNDT, H. (19th C)
Portrait of a Girl with a Laurel Wreath, oil on canvas, sgn/dtd 1849, 31x26", C-E 10/25/88 ... 3,300

LAGORIO, Mariia Aleksandrovna (Italian/French, 1893-1979)
Harvest (portrait of a woman w/grain bundle on her head), oil on canvas, sgn, 46x32", C-L 10/8/88 OE ... 5,200
Last Moments (lady holding water jar), oil on canvas, sgn, 46x32", C-L 10/8/88 ... 4,830

LAGRANGE, Jacques (French, 1917-)
Composition aux Assiettes, oil on canvas, sgn, unfr, 29x39", C-E 5/13/88 ... 770
Tea Time: Abstract Design; oil on canvas, sgn, 15x24", FAP 4/15/89 ... 412

LAGRENEE, Louis Jean Francois (1725-1805)
Galatee se Jouant sur les Eaux avec les Tritons, oil on canvas, sgn/dtd 1757, 44x53", SBY 6/2/89 ... 44,000

LAGRENEE, Louis Jean Francois; att (1725-1805)
Hercules Leading Alcestis From the Underworld Back to Her Husband Admetus, oil on canvas, 47x71", SBY 6/3/88 ... 60,500

LAGUE, Achille (French, 1861-1944)
L'Entree du Village, Printemps; oil on canvas, sgn/dtd 1919, 21x29", SBY 10/7/88 ... 17,600

LAHNER, Emile (French, 1893-1980)
Composition II 1946, oil on board, sgn, 22x20", B/B 5/17/89 ... 660
Still Life of Fruit, oil on canvas, sgn, 15x17", B/B 5/17/89 ... 660
Vieille Eglise Romane en Dordogne, oil on canvas, sgn, 22x18", B/B 4/20/88 ... 275

LAIRESSE, see De Lairesse

LALANGER, Nicolay Tysland (American, 1832-1896)
Sheep Grazing by a Lake, oil on canvas, sgn, 18x30", WL 5/20/88 ... 825

LALAUZE, Alphonse (French, -1872)
Sous-Officer du 4Eme Chasseur a Cheval, oil on panel, sgn, 13x9", SBY 6/8/88 UE ... 1,100

LALIBERTE, Normand (1925-)
Birds, oil on glass, sgn/dtd 1978, 24x18", FB 4/25/88 ... 800

LALL, see De Lall

LAM, Jennett (Brinsmade)(American, 1911-)
Pair: Sky Chair; Ghost Chair (folding deck chairs); oil on canvas, sgn, ca 1963, 12x12", 14x16", SLK 4/7/89 ... 175

LAM, Wifredo (Cuban, 1902-1982)
Composicion con Idolos (Composition with Idols), pastel/charcoal on paper, sgn/dtd 1972, 19x26", C-NY 5/17/89 OE ... 1,430
Composition (fantasy figures), oil/charcoal on canvas, 1959, 24x32", C-NY 5/17/89 OE ... 35,200
El Pez (The Fish), crayon on paper, sgn/dtd 1973/inscr, 10x 24, C-NY 5/18/88 ... 2,860
Femme Cheval (Female Horse, abstract), oil/charcoal on linen, sgn/dtd 1950, 39x32", C-NY 11/21/89 OE ... 143,000
Femme et Oisseau (woman & bird, abstract figures), pastel on paper, sgn, 1969, 24x23", C-NY 11/21/89 ... 29,700
Figura (abstract), oil on canvas, sgn/dtd 1955, 51x40", C-NY 11/21/88 ... 165,000
Figura (abstract), oil on canvas, sgn/dtd 1969, 32x24", C-NY 11/21/88 ... 33,000
Figura Totemica con Luna (abstract), brush/pen/ink/collage on paper, sgn/dtd 1954, 10x8", C-NY 11/21/88 ... 4,400
Figuras en el Balcon (abstract), gouache/pastel on paper, 43x30", C-NY 5/18/88 ... 44,000
Foresta, charcoal/watercolor/gouache on paper laid down on canvas, sgn/dtd 1962, 30x22", C-NY 5/18/88 ... 11,000
Here on Earth (imaginary composition), oil on canvas, sgn/dtd 1955, 42x39", SBY 11/21/88 ... 77,000
Homme Juene (abstract portrait), gouache/watercolor on paper laid down on board, sgn/dtd 1938, 22x16", C-NY 11/21/88 ... 15,400
Idolo (abstract), oil on canvas, sgn/dtd 1967, 24x20", C-NY 5/18/88 ... 41,800
Je m'En Vais (imaginary figures), ink on paper, sgn/dtd Paris-Sept 1953, 25x19", SBY 11/21/88 ... 8,250
La Cortina (abstract figure), pastel/charcoal on paper laid down on board, sgn/dtd 1942, 42x34", C-NY 11/21/89 ... 52,800
La Ventana (view from window), oil on canvas, 1936, 38x30", C-NY 5/17/89 ... 121,000
Le Rideau Grenade (contemporary), oil on paper laid down on canvas, sgn/dtd 1944, 45x32", C-NY 11/21/89 ... 187,000
Mujer (abstract of a woman), oil on canvas, sgn/dtd 1974/#d AB-29-9-3-76, 10x14", C-NY 5/18/88 ... 9,900
Mujer y Gato (abstract portrait), pastel/watercolor on paper laid down on linen, ca 1936-39, 21x17", C-NY 11/21/88 ... 19,800
Mujer-Pajaro (abstract), oil on canvas, sgn, dtd 1957, 36x29", C-NY 5/18/88 ... 82,500
Mujeres Recostadas (2 reclining nudes), pastel/gouache on paper laid down on linen, ca 1936-37, 38x47", C-NY 11/21/88 ... 71,500
Pair: Manos con Luna; Manos Cruzadas (line drawings); pen/ink on paper, 6x8", C-NY 11/21/88 ... 2,860
Pajaro Quieto, crayon on paper, sgn/dtd 1973, 13x19", C-NY 5/18/88 ... 3,520
Seated Woman (abstract), oil on canvas, sgn/dtd 1951, 48x41", SBY 5/17/88 ... 198,000
Sin Titulo (abstract figure), oil on canvas, sgn/dtd 1959, 26x32", C-NY 11/21/88 ... 121,000
Sin Titulo (abstract), oil on canvas, stamped signature, ca 1958, 83x66", C-NY 5/17/89 ... 132,000
Sin Titulo (fantasy figures), oil on canvas, sgn/dtd 1962, 20x28", C-NY 5/17/89 ... 35,200
Sin Titulo (fantasy figures), oil on canvas, sgn/dtd 1970, 20x28", C-NY 5/17/89 OE ... 38,500
Spanish Civil War, gouache on paper, ca 1936, 83x93", SBY 5/17/88 OE ... 12,100
Untitled (abstract), charcoal/pastel on paper, sgn/dtd 1959, SBY 5/17/88 ... 9,350
Untitled (abstract), watercolor/charcoal on paper, sgn/dtd 1968, 40x26", SBY 4/29/88 OE ... 29,700
Untitled (imaginary figures), oil on canvas, sgn twice/dtd 1970 twice, 20x16", SBY 11/21/88 ... 16,500
Untitled (imaginary figures), oil on canvas, sgn/dtd 1973, 12x16", SBY 11/21/88 ... 11,000

LAMATTE, Bernard
Conversation, oil on canvas, stamped/initialed/inscr/atelier stamp/#d 27 on reverse, 15x18", SBY 10/5/88 ... 1,430

LAMB, Frederick Mortimer (American, 1861-1936)
Afternoon Light, oil on cardboard, sgn, 14x17", RWS 5/12/89 OE ... 800
Cautious (red fox in small clearing, surrounded by snow-laden branches), oil on board, 24x21", RAB 8/9/88 ... 800
Loading Firewood, a Winter Landscape Scene; pastel on paper, sgn, 19x12", RWS 3/16/89 ... 660
On the Trail-Dogs in an Autumnal Landscape Scene; oil on canvas, sgn, 12x18", RWS 3/16/89 ... 1,400
Portrait of a Spitz, oil on canvas, sgn/dtd 1904, unfr, 20x28", RWS 3/16/89 OE ... 1,800
Riverscape, large tree shades placid river; oil on board, sgn, 10x13", RAB 8/8/89 ... 525

Silent Night (winter scene with distant house), oil on board, sgn, 25x30", RAB 8/9/88 ... 3,500
Summer Landscape, green trees/fields under blue sky; oil on cardboard, sgn, 16x20", RAB 8/8/89 UE ... 300
Summer Landscape Scene, pastel on linen, sgn, 19x25", RWS 3/16/89 UE ... 500
Summer Landscape Scene with Cattle Grazing, pastel on paper, sgn, 18x21", RWS 3/16/89 UE ... 450
Summer River, oil on cardboard, sgn, 10x13", RAB 8/8/89 UE ... 250
Summer Waterfall, watercolor on paper, sgn/dtd 1900, 10x14", RAB 8/9/88 ... 575
West Bridgewater, Massachusetts (landscape); oil on canvas, unfr, 31x25", RAB 8/8/89 UE ... 350
Winter Shadows, oil on board, sgn, 13x17", WG 9/16/88 UE ... 450

LAMBDIN, George Cochran (American, 1830-1896)
Blowing Bubbles (seated young girl), oil on canvas, sgn/dtd 1858, 29x23", C-NY 12/2/88 ... 16,500
Flowers, watercolor/pencil on paper, sgn, 12x9", C-E 2/3/88 UE ... 220
Roses, oil on canvas, sgn, 18x23", C-E 2/1/89 ... 2,640
Roses, oil on canvas, sgn/dtd 82, 30x20", SBY 6/24/88 ... 11,550
Roses, oil on panel, sgn/dtd 80, 28x12", C-E 2/3/88 ... 2,420
Roses, watercolor on paper, sgn/dtd 1881, 19x11", B/B 4/20/88 OE ... 3,025
Roses (still life), oil on panel, sgn/dtd 78, 24x12", SBY 4/29/88 ... 8,250
Still Life of Pink & Yellow Roses, oil on panel, sgn, 27x19", SBY 6/28/89 ... 2,310
Still Life of Roses, oil on panel, sgn/dtd 1874(?), 16x8",SBY 4/14/89 OE ... 9,350
Still Life of Roses, oil on panel, sgn/dtd 1876, 24x12", RWS 11/10/89 ... 8,000
Still Life of Roses (in oriental baluster vase), oil on canvas, sgn/dtd 1872, 16x12", RWS 9/29/88 OE ... 15,000
Still Life of Roses & Fuchsia, oil on canvas, sgn/dtd 1873, 14x10", RWS 5/12/89 OE ... 20,900
Woman with a Fan, oil on canvas, sgn, 36x24", B/B 4/20/88 ... 2,090

LAMBDIN, James Reid (American, 1807-1889)
Portrait of General Ambrose Burnside, oil on canvas, 30x24", FAP 11/4/88 OE ... 1,050

LAMBERT, Camille Nicolas (Belgian, 1876-)
Canal in Venice (buildings & gondolas in waterscape), oil on canvas, sgn, 18x30", C-E 2/21/89 UE ... 1,210

LAMBERT, Ferdinand Alexis (French, 1868-)
Landscape with Water, Building, Figures & Boats, a Village in the Background; oil on canvas, sgn, 30x25", S/A 2/18/89 ... 750

LAMBERT, G. (American)
Untitled, harbor scene; oil on canvas, sgn, 24x30", SLK 4/7/89 ... 350

LAMBERT, George (French, 1919-)
Evening Along the Seine in the Pointillist Manner, oil on canvas, sgn, 21x26", B/B 12/8/88 ... 1,045

LAMBERT, T.R. (American, 1905-1960)
Hunter's Camp, oil on canvas, sgn/dtd 1941, 8x11", DM 3/14/88 ... 1,100

LAMBERT-RUCKI, Jean (French, 1888-1967)
La Femme aux Violets (woman with violets), oil on panel, sgn, 30x23", SBY 4/23/88 ... 12,100

LAMBERTI (Italian, 19th C)
In the Harem, watercolor heightened w/white over pencil, sgn, 24x17", C-NY 2/23/89 OE ... 4,620

LAMBINET, Emile Charles (French, 1815-1877)
Raking in the Sunshine, oil on canvas, sgn, 10x13", WD 5/5/88 ... 1,700

LAMBRECHTS, Jan Baptiste (Flemish, 1815-1877)
Group Seated at Table Taking Refreshments, oil on canvas, 34x27", C-NY 4/6/89 ... 4,950
Pair: Before & After the Supper; oil on canvas, unfr, 22x18", SBY 10/21/88 UE ... 3,850
Pair: Tavern Interiors with Peasants Seated at Tables of Food & Drink; oil on canvas, 15x12", 14x11", SBY 4/7/88 ... 5,500
Tavern Interior with Revelers, oil on canvas, indistinctly sgn, 22x19", WD 10/19/88 ... 2,600

LAMBRECHTS, Jan Baptiste; manner of (Flemish, 1815-1877)
Pair: Outside the Tavern; Playing Cards; oil on canvas laid down on panel, 15x12", SBY 7/12/89 OE ... 3,575

LAMBRECHTS, Jan Baptiste; school of (Flemish, 1815-1877)
Indoor Market, oil on canvas, 16x13", C-E 4/7/88 UE ... 550

LAMBRICH, E.A.C. (Belgian, 1830-1887)
The Farewell, oil on panel, sgn, 29x21", DM 1/15/88 ... 2,500

LAMDON, James Northcote (19th C)
Filleys Land, oil on board, sgn/dtd 1879, 9x12", C-E 6/1/88 ... 660

LAMI, Eugene Louis (French, 1800-1890)
Elegant Figures in a Park, pencil heightened w/watercolor & gouache, initialed, 5x8", C-NY 5/25/88 ... 1,980
La Queue du Chat, watercolor on paper, initialed/inscr/dtd 1885, 5x6", SBY 6/8/88 ... 1,100

LAMONT, Louis (American, 20th C)
Maureen, pastel, sgn/dtd 87, 13x10", FAP 12/8/89 ... 125

LAMOTTE, Bernard (French, 1903-)
La Place de la Concorde, oil on canvas, sgn, 13x22", C-NY 2/13/89 ... 528
Nature Morte (still life), oil on canvas, sgn, 28x23", C-E 11/17/88 ... 1,100
Notre Dame, Paris; oil on canvas, sgn/dtd 1954, 18x21", WG 9/16/88 UE ... 200
Nude with Still Life, India ink/gouache on paper, sgn, 25x18", SBY 10/5/88 UE ... 660
Screen: Bords de Riviere (river landscape); oil on canvas laid down on 3 hinged panels, 114x114", C-E 11/17/88 OE ... 22,000

LAMPE, L. (Belgian, 19th C)
Brooch (full-length portrait of a lady w/dog in an interior), oil on canvas, sgn, 28x22", B/B 6/15/89 UE ... 1,650

LAMPLOUGH, Augustus Osborne (British, 1877-1930)
Arab Warrior Riding a Camel, watercolor on board, sgn, 24x30", B/B 6/9/88 ... 1,760
Colassi at Thebes, the Nile in Flood; watercolor on paper, inscr, 9x25", C-E 2/23/88 ... 660
Rue de la Citadelle, Cairo; watercolor, sgn/dtd 1904, 14x10", FB 4/25/88 ... 800
Street Scene, watercolor, sgn, 14x8", FB 5/28/89 ... 375

LAMY, Pierre Desire Eugene Franc (French, 1855-1919)
Chestnut Hunter with Rider, oil on canvas, sgn, 20x30", SBY 6/9/89 .... **8,800**
LANAY
Montmartre, Rue Norvious (French street with cafe & figures); watercolor, sgn, 9x12", DM 2/19/88 OE **250**
LANAZIN (Continental School, 19th C)
Artists in Paris, oil on canvas, indistinctly sgn/inscr, 48x66", SBY 5/23/89 OE **44,000**
LANCEROTTO, Egisto (Italian, 1847-1916)
Young Woman in a Vineyard, oil on canvas, sgn, 43x31", SBY 10/24/89 .... **22,000**
LANCKOW, Ludwig (German, 19th C)
Canal Scene at Sunset, oil on canvas, sgn/dtd 80, 26x21", WG 4/23/88 .... **1,300**
Still Life of Fruit & a Glass of Champagne on a Table, oil on board, sgn/dtd 1888, 13x17", C-E 10/26/89 .... **2,750**
LANCON, Auguste Lancon (French, 1836-1887)
Tigers at Rest, oil on canvas, sgn/dtd 1882, 16x20", C-E 2/21/89 .... **2,420**
LANCON, Edouard Michel (French, 1854-)
Une Fete de Printemps, oil on canvas, sgn, 35x56", C-E 10/26/89 .... **7,150**
LANCRET, Nicolas (French, 1690-1743)
Couple Seated on the Ground, Looking at a Songbook; black/white chalk on light brown paper, 9x11", SBY 1/13/89 .... **93,500**
Figures in a River Landscape Preparing To Depart on a Boat, oil on canvas, 17x23", SBY 4/7/88 .... **8,800**
L'Oiseau Prisonnier, oil on canvas, 17x21", SBY 1/12/89 .... **33,000**
Les Deux Amis (the two friends), oil on canvas, unfr, 11x15", SBY 10/13/89 .... **22,000**
Study of a Gentleman Leaning Forward, red chalk, 8x4", SBY 1/13/89 OE **17,600**
LANCRET, Nicolas; att (French, 1690-1743)
Fete Champetre, oil on canvas, 20x24", B/B 1/11/89 .... **1,045**
LANCRET, Nicolas; follower of (French, 1690-1743)
Fete Champetre, bodycolor on vellum, 17x25", C-NY 1/12/88 OE **2,420**
Pair: Elegant Figures Playing Tric-Trac in a Park; Lady Serving Tea to a Clergyman; oil on canvas, 25x32", SBY 4/7/89 .... **7,700**
LANCRET, Nicolas; school of (French, 1690-1743)
Fete Champetre, oil on tin, 16x18", C-NY 4/8/88 .... **1,540**
LAND, Louis
Fresh Cherries (still life), oil on canvas, sgn/dtd 77, 20x16", C-E 6/1/89 .... **1,045**
LANDAU, Zygmunt (Polish, 19th C)
Portrait d'une Femme avec Fruit, oil on canvas laid down on board, sgn/dtd 1923, 31x22", C-E 5/13/88 UE **495**
Route sur la Montagne, oil on canvas laid down on board, sgn/dtd 1923, 25x31", C-E 5/13/88 .... **990**
LANDELLE, Charles Zacharie (French, 1812-1908)
Maiden of Marrakesh, oil on canvas, sgn, 54x33", SBY 2/22/88 OE **27,500**
LANDFIELD, Ronnie (American, 20th C)
Flashing in the Light (abstract line composition), acrylic on canvas, sgn/dtd 1974, 46x96", C-E 11/17/88 .... **1,430**
LANDIS, H.W. (American, 19th/20th C)
Old Violin, oil on canvas, sgn twice/dtd 1903, 36x22", SBY 6/24/88 .... **1,430**
LANDRIANI, Paolo (Italian, 1755-1839)
Atrium of the Palace with Colonades, black chalk/pen/brown ink/brown & gray wash, Pro Patria wm, 9x11", C-NY 1/11/89 .... **605**
LANDSEER, Charles (British, 1799-1879)
Titania Crowns Bottom, oil on canvas laid down, sgn, 24x36", B/B 6/15/89 .... **6,600**
LANDSEER, Charles; circle of (British, 1799-1879)
Horseplay Outside the Vintner, oil on canvas, 26x38", SBY 6/8/88 .... **4,675**
LANDSEER, Edwin Henry (British, 1802-1873)
Heads of Sheep & Cattle, oil on panel, initialed/dtd 1828, 19x24", SBY 6/10/88 .... **41,250**
Portrait of Brunette, a Favorite Horse, the Property of Lord Henniker; oil on canvas, sgn, 1823, 28x36", SBY 6/9/89 .... **27,272**
Study of a Goat, oil on paper laid down on masonite, 6x9", SBY 6/10/88 OE **8,250**
LANDSEER, Edwin Henry; after (British, 1802-1873)
Hawking, oil on canvas, bears signature/dtd 80, 27x35", SBY 6/9/89 .... **4,125**
Le Chien Interesse (dog sitting up looking at two monkeys on a chair), oil on panel, sgn, 26x21", SBY 6/9/89 .... **6,050**
Pair: Dignity; Impudence (Terrier puppies); oil on canvas, no size given, MG 10/1/88 UE **475**
LANE, Fitz Hugh (American, 1804-1865)

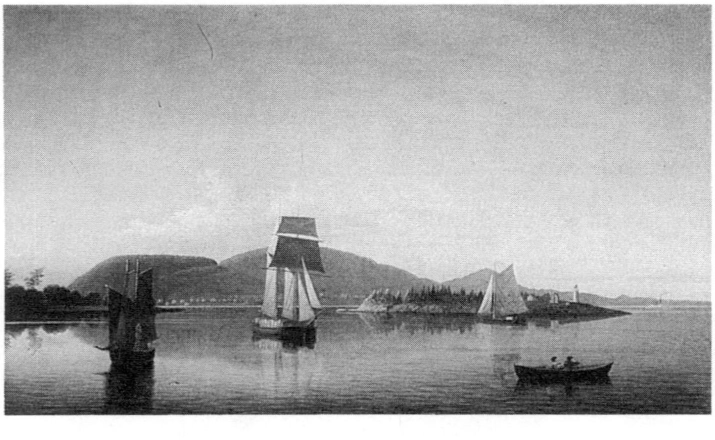

Camden Mountains From the South Entrance to Harbor, 19x30", C-NY 12/2/88 OE; $770,000

LANE, Francis (American, 20th C)
Marin Landscape with Mount Tamalpais in the Distance, oil on canvas, sgn, 33x47", B/B 8/10/88 UE 440
LANE, Leonard (Canadian, 20th C)
Fine Breeze, oil on canvas, sgn, 26x36", LH 10/16/88 1,500
LANE, Lois (American, 1948-)
Untitled #157 (abstract), oil on canvas, 1985, 108x84", SBY 5/3/88 4,675
LANE, Martella Cone (American, 1875-1964)
Sierra Landscape, oil on panel, sgn, 20x24", B/B 9/15/88 248
LANE, Susan Minot (American, 1832-1893)
Miss Theodosia (lady knitting in Windsor chair by roaring fire), charcoal on paper, sgn/dtd 1878, 13x11", RAB 8/9/88 UE 300
LANFAIR, Harold Edward (American, 1898-)
Back Porch, watercolor on paper, sgn, 14x20", B/B 1/11/89 660
The Fairgrounds, watercolor on paper, sgn, 14x20", B/B 12/8/88 935
LANFANT DE METZ, Francois (French, 1814-1892)
La Lecon de Musique (children playing musical instruments in interior), oil on board, sgn, 9x6", C-NY 2/23/89 3,300
LANFRANCHI, Alessandro (1662-1730)
Pair: Aaron & Moses Performing Miracles Before Pharoah; oil on canvas, 15x20", SBY 4/7/88 5,500
LANFRANCO, Giovanni; att (Italian, 1580-1647)
Miracle of the Loaves & the Fishes, oil on canvas, 57x87", C-NY 1/15/88 13,200
LANFRANCO, Giovanni; circle of (Italian, 1580-1647)
Crucifixion, oil on copper, 11x9", SBY 6/8/88 770
LANG, A.B.
Mountain Scene (mountaineer on white stallion, grizzly bear in distance), oil on canvas, sgn, 38x20", DM 3/14/88 125
LANG, Albert (German, 1847-)
Munich Skyline, gouache/pencil on paper, sgn/dtd 1910, 13x18", B/B 4/20/88 605
Still Life of Flowers, oil on board, 16x20", B/B 8/10/88 1,320
LANG, Louis (American, 1814-1893)
Chinese Amah & Child, oil on board, sgn/dtd 1862, 14x10", C-E 1,320
Young Girl Studying, oil on canvas, sgn/dtd 1853, in painted oval, 37x40", C-NY 12/2/88 3,850
LANGDALE, Markaduke A. (British, 1905-)
Still Life of Roses, oil on canvas, sgn/dtd 1879, 24x18", B/B 3/17/88 1,650
LANGENDYK, Dirk (Dutch, 1748-1805)
Attack on a Convoy, pen/brown ink/gray wash, 10x13", SBY 1/13/89 OE 4,400
Attack on a Convoy, pen/brown ink/gray wash, 14x20", SBY 1/13/89 OE 4,675
Battle Scene with Troops Storming a Bridge, pen/black/gray/brown wash over black chalk, sgn, 13x20", SBY 1/13/89 OE 6,875
Cavalry Battle in a Field, pen/brown ink over traces of graphite, indistinctly sgn/dtd, 6x9", SBY 1/13/89 OE 4,125
Cavalry Leaving an Arsenal on a Quai, pen/ink/wash over traces of chalk, sgn/dtd 1799, 5x7", SBY 1/13/89 OE 2,200
Cavalry Passing Through a Town Gate, pen/ink/gray wash over traces of black chalk, sgn/dtd 1789, 5x8", SBY 1/13/89 2,200
Figures Watching a Battle in a Distant Field, pen/ink/gray wash over traces of black chalk, sgn, 10x14", SBY 1/13/89 7,425
Landing of the British Fleet at Kuikduin, pen/ink/gray wash over black chalk, sgn/dtd 1799, 18x23", SBY 1/13/89 OE 14,300
Military Encampment on a Hillside, pen/ink/gray wash over traces of black chalk, sgn/dtd 1800, 6x9", SBY 1/13/89 2,310
Military Field Bakery, pen/brown ink/gray wash over traces of black chalk, sgn/dtd 1785, 5x7", SBY 1/13/89 OE 2,200
Soldiers Storming a Walled Town by Moonlight, pen/brown ink/gray wash over black chalk, sgn/dtd 1790, 4x7", SBY 1/13/89 2,200
LANGEVELD, Frans (Dutch, 1877-1939)
Heading Home, oil on canvas, sgn/dtd 07, 21x29", WD 3/23/88 UE 1,200
LANGEVIN, Claude (Canadian, 1942-)
Arriere Cour a Ste Agathe, oil on canvas, sgn, 12x16", FB 10/30/89 468
Overlooking the Lake, oil on canvas, sgn, 24x30", FB 10/30/89 1,045
Promenade du Matin, oil on canvas, sgn, 16x20", B/B 12/8/88 825
LANGFORD, E
Tree-Lined Coastal Cliffs, oil on canvas, sgn, 24x30", NA 3/26/88 325
LANGHFLOWER, A.B.
Still Life of Pineapple & Fruit, oil on canvas, sgn/indistinctly dtd, 6x10", C-E 6/28/88 UE 242
LANGLEY, Edith May (American, 19th/20th C)
By the Light of the Fire, oil on canvas, sgn, 39x29", B/B 6/15/89 2,750
LANGLEY, Edith May; att (American, 19th/20th C)
Woman in Green Dress, oil on canvas, 36x29", B/B 6/15/89 2,200
LANGLEY, William (British, 19th C)
Coastline with Sea Gulls, oil on canvas, sgn, 16x24", DM 2/19/88 OE 900
Cottage By a Mountain Stream, oil on canvas, sgn, 20x30", B/B 6/9/88 2,200
Docked Longboat, oil on canvas, sgn, unfr, 12x20", C-E 6/28/88 UE 200
LANGLOIS
Terriers (in a landscape), oil on canvas, sgn, 19x30", NA 11/5/88 2,000
LANGLOIS, C. (British, 19th C)
Pair: Albert on the Moor; Terrier Running; oil on canvas, sgn, 20x30", SBY 6/8/88 UE 1,430
LANGLOIS, Jerome Martin (French, 1779-1838)
Diana & Endymion, oil on canvas, 13x10", C-NY 10/12/89 7,150
Diane et Endymion, replica of painting of same title now destroyed; oil on canvas, 125x83", SBY 10/24/89 OE 440,000
LANGLOIS, Mark W. (British, 19th C)
Children & Dog in Cottage, oil on canvas, initialed, 23x19", WAD 6/6/88 1,800
LANGNETIN, Paul Francois Berthoud Dit Gilbert
Entrance to a Village, gouache on paper laid down on board, sgn, 20x24", C-E 10/25/88 UE 198

LANOUX, B.
Two Pointers by a Lake, oil on canvas, sgn, 26x22", C-E 5/23/88 OE **3,080**
LANSIL, Walter Franklin (American, 1846-1925)
Midnight Arrival, oil on canvas, sgn/dtd twice, 1883, inscr, 34x50", C-E 2/23/88 .... **3,300**
Morning on Grand Canal, Venice (sailboats & waterside buildings); oil on canvas, sgn/dtd 1909, 22x29", RAB 8/9/88 .... **1,250**
Pilot Meeting Steamer Off Highland Light, oil on canvas, sgn/dtd 1902/titled, 14x23", RAB 3/27/89 .... **1,000**
LANSIL, Walter Franklin; att (American, 1846-1925)
Venice, End of Day (sailboats in harbor); oil on canvas, 12x16", RAB 8/9/88 .... **1,100**
LANSKOY, Andre (Russian/French, 1902-1976)
Decision Pris a Minuet (abstract), oil on canvas, sgn/dtd 57, 38x57", SBY 10/8/88 OE **66,000**
Group of Performers, oil on canvas, sgn/dtd 25, 26x32", SBY 10/7/89 .... **14,300**
Ressemblance Impreme (abstract), oil on canvas, sgn twice/inscr/dtd 63, 39x29", C-NY 5/4/88 OE **36,300**
LAPARRA, William Julien Emile Edouard
Ravages of War, oil on canvas, sgn, 30x61", C-E 5/23/88 UE **330**
LAPCHINE, Georges (Russian, 20th C)
Beach Scene, oil on canvas, sgn, 10x17", FB 10/30/89 .... **1,045**
LAPICQUE, Charles (French, 1898-)
Les Regates, oil on canvas, sgn/dtd twice 1943, 39x29", SBY 10/5/88 OE **28,600**
Nuit sur la Lagune, oil on canvas, sgn/dtd twice, 55, inscr, 15x22", C-E 5/13/88 OE **18,700**
LAPIERRE, Louis Emile (French, 1817-1886)
Fishing Boats Returned Home, oil on canvas, sgn/dtd 1867, 25x40", C-E 2/21/89 .... **2,860**
LAPIERRE, Viateur (Canadian, 1917-)
Erabliere dans le Rang Chicot a St Eustache, oil on canvas, sgn/dtd 1973, 20x24", FB 10/17/88 UE **450**
LAPINE, Christian Andreas Gottfried (Canadian, 1868-1952)
Sketching at a Draughting Table, watercolor over pencil, sgn/dtd June 20, 1918; 13x9", WAD 6/12/89 .... **375**
LAPIRA, Pasto (Italian, 19th C)
Paestum (view), gouache on paper, sgn, 16x23", SBY 6/8/88 .... **1,430**
LAPIRA (Italian, 19th C)
Napoli da Mare, gouache on paper, sgn/titled, 21x29", C-NY 5/24/89 OE **6,050**
Napoli da Mare (boats on water, volcano erupting beyond), gouache, sgn, 17x25", PHL 10/28/88 OE **2,300**
North Italian Coast, gouache on paper, sgn/dtd La Pira 1890, 8x12", RAB 8/8/89 .... **600**
LAPORTE, George Henry (German, 1799-1873)
Fox Hunt, oil on canvas, 12x23", C-E 5/23/88 OE **3,300**
LAPORTE, George Henry; att (German, 1799-1873)
Over the Fence, oil on canvas, sgn/dtd 1832, 17x21", WAD 6/6/88 .... **3,800**
LAPORTE, George Henry; circle of (German, 1799-1873)
Off to the Meet, oil on canvas, 20x24", SBY 6/10/88 UE **3,300**
LAPOSTOLET, Charles (French, 1824-1890)
Harbor Scene, oil on panel, sgn/inscr, 13x16", SBY 6/8/88 OE **5,500**
Pair: Harbor Views; oil on panel, sgn, 13x16", SBY 6/8/88 OE **13,200**
LARA, Georgina (British, fl 1862-1871)
Pair: Scenes From Rural Life; oil on board, sgn, 12x9", SBY 7/12/89 .... **3,300**
Pair: Travelers by a Roadside Inn; oil on canvas, 1 sgn, 10x18", C-NY 2/23/89 .... **8,250**
Rustic Village, oil on canvas, 20x30", SBY 12/9/88 .... **3,850**
Travelers at a Country Inn, oil on canvas, sgn, 10x18", C-E 2/21/89 .... **2,200**
Wayside Inn, oil on canvas, sgn, 12x18", C-E 2/23/88 .... **2,750**
LARGILLIERE, see De Largilliere
LARIMER, Ruth (American, fl 1920-1930)
Colorado Desert, oil on canvasboard, sgn, 7x9", B/B 9/15/88 .... **192**
LARIONOV, Mikhail (Russian, 1881-1964)
Composition, black ink/wash on paper, initialed, 8x10", SBY 10/5/88 .... **1,210**
Jour et Nuit (still life), watercolor/pencil on paper, sgn/dtd 1910/titled, 17x22", C-L 10/8/88 .... **1,670**
Portrait of Sergei Diaghilev, pencil on paper, sgn, ca 1920, 11x8", C-L 10/8/88 .... **5,200**
LARRAZ, Julio (Cuban, 1944-)
Alpha Centaure (still life), oil on canvas, sgn, 1983, 60x72", SBY 11/21/88 .... **25,300**
Ant View (still life of pear as seen by an ant), oil on canvas, sgn, 1982, 24x28", C-NY 11/21/88 OE **11,000**
Melt Down, oil on canvas, sgn/dtd 79, 68x48", SBY 5/17/88 OE **28,600**
LARRUE, Guillaume (French, 1851-)
Fountain, Autumn; oil on canvas, sgn, 20x24", SBY 5/23/89 .... **7,150**
Lady Sewing, oil on canvas, sgn/inscr, 18x15", DM 2/19/88 .... **1,500**
LARSEN, Harold E.
Abstract, collage, sgn, 20x30", LH 5/15/88 OE **180**
LARSEN, W.
Hunter with Hounds in a Clearing, oil on canvas, sgn, 18x24", WD 10/19/88 .... **1,300**
LARSSON, Carl (Swedish, 1853-1919)
Sunflowers (portrait of artist's daughter), pen/ink/watercolor/gouache on paper, initialed, 1893, 18x10", SBY 10/24/89 .... **330,000**
LASABTIER
Medieval Interior, oil on canvas, sgn, 30x25", C-E 5/23/88 .... **1,650**
LASCANO, Juan (Latin American, 20th C)
Desnudo (three-quarter length standing nude), acrylic on canvas, sgn/dtd 80, 47x37", C-NY 11/21/89 OE **25,300**

La Ventana (nude standing by window), acrylic on canvas, sgn/dtd 86, 51x40", C-NY 11/21/88 OE 15,400
ASCAUX, Elie (French, 1888-)
Le Viaduc (The Viaduct), oil on canvas, sgn, 22x26", C-E 11/17/88 OE 1,980
Recostada (reclining nude), oil on canvas, sgn/dtd 88, 51x51", C-NY 5/17/89 20,900
ASKER, Joe
Morning-Glories, watercolor/pencil on paper, sgn, 11x17", C-NY 6/17/89 UE 110
ASKER, Jonathan (American, 1919-)
Cave Painting (abstract composition), acrylic on canvas, sgn/dtd 1983, 66x48", SBY 10/5/89 14,850
Forest (abstract), oil on panel, sgn/dtd 1982, unfr, 12x10", C-E 11/14/89 1,760
Heart in a Whirl (abstract), oil on canvas, 1981, 48x60", C-NY 5/4/89 OE 12,100
The Oddness Factor (abstract composition), oil on canvas, 1985, 59x71", C-NY 5/4/89 16,500
ASLO, Patricia
Double Rings, pastel, sgn, 24x18", LH 5/15/88 UE 30
ASSALLE, M. (20th C)
Cattle Drinking Water, oil on canvas, sgn/dtd 1978, 18x22", DM 5/19/89 400
ASSONDE, Omer T. (American, 1903-1980)
Big Sur, Mariposa Bridge (western landscape of river w/large bridge beyond); oil on canvas, sgn, 25x30", RWS 3/31/88 OE 600
Empire Gates (elegant 19th century ironwork in abstract style), oil on canvas, sgn, 25x30", RWS 3/31/88 500
Fish Market, oil on canvas, sgn, 25x30", WG 4/23/88 UE 825
Mill Dam, oil on canvas, sgn, 20x24", WG 4/23/88 UE 500
ASTMAN, Pieter (Dutch, 1583-1633)
Judgement of Midas, oil on panel, 33x39", SBY 6/1/89 UE 57,750
ASTMAN, Pieter; follower of (Dutch, 1583-1633)
Stoning of Saint Stephen, black chalk/pen/brown ink/brown wash heightened w/white, 5x4", C-NY 1/12/88 UE 165
ASZLO DE LOMBOS, see De Laszlo de Lombos
ATHANGUE, Henry (British, 1859-1929)
Regatta in the Fountain, oil on canvas, sgn, 28x31", C-NY 5/25/88 OE 52,800
ATHROP, Francis (American, 1849-1909)
Mending Her Scarf (young girl seated in wicker chair, sewing), oil on canvas, sgn, 41x34", RAB 8/8/89 UE 750
ATHROP, William Langson (American, 1859-1938)
Grandfather's Naughty Child (in impressionistic landscape), oil on canvas, sgn, ca 1920, 19x20", C-NY 5/25/89 UE 5,500
Landscape in Pennsylvania, oil on canvas, sgn, 36x40", C-NY 9/28/89 6,050
Oyster Bay, Long Island; oil on canvas, sgn, 1933, 16x20", C-E 2/1/89 2,860
Oyster Bay, Long Island; oil on canvas, sgn/dtd 1933, 14x18", WD 4/13/88 1,800
Pair: Northport Bay; oil on masonite, initialed/inscr/dtd 34 & 36, 9x20", C-NY 12/2/88 OE 18,700
Pennsylvania Quarry, oil on canvas, sgn, 12x14", C-E 11/30/88 1,045
Rocky Shore, Lloyd's Harbor, Long Island; oil on masonite, sgn, 16x20", C-NY 5/25/89 UE 2,200
Summer Fields, oil on masonite, sgn/dtd 34, 16x20", WD 10/5/88 UE 2,500
atin American School (19th/20th C)
San Isedro as Husbandman, oil on canvas, 35x26", RWS 4/7/89 UE 300
ATOIX, Gaspard (British, fl 1882-1903)
Plains Indian on Horseback, watercolor heightened w/white, sgn, 20x15", C-SK 5/25/89 OE 4,410
ATORTUE, P.
Haitian Village Scene, oil on masonite, sgn, 36x48", SBY 10/7/89 1,980
ATOUCHE, see De Latouche
ATOUR, Adrian (French, 20th C)
Woman Walking Down Dirt Road, oil on canvas, sgn/dtd 1900, 20x30", FAP 4/15/89 605
AUCK, R.E.
Along the River, oil on canvas, sgn/dtd 1894, 20x36", NA 10/1/88 850
AUDA, Richard (Czechoslovokian, 1873-1929)
Peasants Tilling a Field, oil on canvas, sgn/dtd 92, 29x32", B/B 8/10/88 UE 605
AUDER, Charles James (British, 1841-1920)
View of an English Town, watercolor/gouache over pencil, sgn, 20x13", C-NY 10/25/89 OE 3,080
View of Naples, oil on canvas, sgn, 24x36", SBY 10/24/89 6,600
View of the Royal Exchange, watercolor heightened w/gouache, sgn, 8x13", C-NY 10/26/88 2,750
AUDY, Jean (Belgian, 20th C)
Urn of Roses (still life), oil on arched canvas, sgn, 51x60", C-NY 2/23/89 8,800
AUFMAN, Sidney (American, 1891-)
Trees, oil on canvas, sgn, 40x30", C-E 11/30/88 OE 2,420
AUGEE, Georges (French, 1853-)
After the Day's Work Is Done, oil on canvas, sgn, 22x19", SBY 12/9/88 1,540
Harvest Scene, oil on canvas, sgn, 32x26", SBY 7/12/89 9,075
Le Jeune Bergere (girl w/sheep), oil on canvas, sgn, 15x22", C-E 2/21/89 OE 4,180
AUGIER, Guy (French, 20th C)
Paris Street Scene, oil on canvas, sgn, 15x18", LH 10/16/88 275
AUR, Yvonne Marie Yo (French, 1879-)
Friendly Confrontation (pups & kittens in an interior), oil on canvas, sgn, 29x24", B/B 10/9/88 5,500
AURENCE, Sydney (American, 1865-1940)
Along the Alaskan Coast, watercolor on paper, sgn, 10x21", SBY 9/14/89 4,400
Beached Fishing Boats, oil on canvas, sgn/dtd 1894, 14x21", B/B 3/17/88 4,400
Boat in a Pond, oil on panel, sgn, 12x16", B/B 3/22/89 2,750

Boats of Venice, watercolor on paper, sgn, 8x11", B/B 6/15/89 1,650
Boats Off the Coast, oil on canvas, sgn/dtd 94, 14x20", B/B 3/17/88 3,300
Docked Sailboats, oil on board, sgn, 12x16", B/B 6/15/89 2,200
Figures on the Shore of Lake Como, watercolor on paper, sgn, 10x14", B/B 6/15/89 1,100
Fishing Boats at Sunset, watercolor/gouache on paper, sgn, 11x19", B/B 6/9/88 3,025
Haystack in a Spring Field, oil on canvas, sgn, 11x17", B/B 6/15/89 2,200
In the Cascade Mountains, oil on canvasboard, sgn, 10x12", B/B 6/15/89 5,500
In the North Arm of Burrad Inlet, watercolor/gouache on paper, sgn, 3x7", B/B 4/20/88 605
Indian Cache, Susitna River, Alaska (small hut on poles along river bank); oil on board, sgn, 8x10", B/B 10/9/88 OE 7,150
Misty Mountain, watercolor on paper, sgn, 12x15", B/B 3/22/89 6,050
Mount McKinley, oil on board, sgn, 16x12", B/B 3/22/89 7,700
Mount McKinley, oil on board, sgn/dtd Sept 1919, 20x30", B/B 8/10/88 OE 60,500
Mount McKinley, oil on canvas, sgn, 40x30", B/B 8/10/88 OE 71,500
Mount McKinley, oil on canvas, sgn/dtd 19(c)24, 72x132", B/B 8/10/88 187,000
Mount McKinley (landscape), oil on canvas, sgn, 20x16", SBY 5/24/89 11,000
Mount Mckinley Through the Mist (landscape), oil on canvas, sgn, 20x15", SBY 5/24/89 19,800
Mountain Cabin, watercolor/gouache on paper, sgn, 10x7", B/B 6/9/88 1,320
Mountain Landscape, oil on canvas, sgn, 40x30", SBY 5/25/88 33,000
Mountain Landscape, oil on panel, sgn, circular, 6x6", B/B 3/22/89 1,320
Northern Lights, oil on canvas, sgn, 15x20", B/B 3/22/89 6,600
Off to Market (figures in a landscape), watercolor on paper, sgn, 12x37", B/B 3/22/89 3,300
Orange Glow (landscape), oil on board, sgn, 10x14", B/B 6/15/89 4,950
Parents with Their Newborn at Rest, watercolor on paper, sgn, 12x37", B/B 3/22/89 3,300
Starting a Fire, oil on canvas laid down, sgn, 24x18", B/B 3/17/88 9,900
Stoking the Coals (figure by campfire in a landscape), oil on canvas, sgn, unfr, 16x20", B/B 3/22/89 8,800
The Cache, oil on canvas, sgn, 20x16", B/B 3/17/88 6,050
The Hunt (man in winter landscape), oil on board, sgn, 10x8", B/B 10/9/88 4,400
Through the Morning Midst (shadowy view of a moose in a landscape), oil on board, sgn, 16x8", B/B 10/9/88 6,600
View of Ruins at Night, oil on canvas, sgn, 20x16", B/B 6/15/89 4,950

LAURENCE, Sydney; att (American, 1865-1940)

Cheated (nude girl sitting by a tree), oil on canvas, sgn, 16x8", SBY 6/24/88 4,125

LAURENCIN, Marie (French, 1885-1956)

Auto-Portrait, oil on board, sgn, ca 1916, 18x14", SBY 11/12/88 176,000
Auto-Portrait, watercolor/pencil on paper laid down on board, sgn/dtd 1912, 7x6", SBY 11/12/88 33,000
Buste de Jeune Femme Nue (portrait of a nude, bust-length), oil on canvas, sgn, 18x15", C-NY 5/11/89 297,000
Cour du Chateau de Crans (courtyard scene), pencil/colored crayon on paper, sgn/dtd 1935, unfr, 7x10", SBY 2/14/89 1,650
Creoles (II), oil on canvas, sgn/dtd 1929, 32x24", SBY 5/11/88 OE 638,000
Deux Femmes au Balcon, watercolor/pencil on paper, sgn, 13x10", SBY 11/12/88 38,500
Deux Femmes dan la Foret (two women in the forest), oil on canvas, sgn, ca 1918, 29x24", C-NY 11/16/88 OE 297,000
Deux Femmes dans un Jardin (two ladies in a garden), watercolor/pencil on paper, sgn, 10x14", C-NY 10/5/89 60,500
Deux Jeunes Femmes, oil on canvas, sgn, 16x13", SBY 11/12/88 OE 187,000
Diane (mythological figure in a landscape), oil on canvas, sgn/dtd 1921, 26x32", SBY 5/10/89 297,000
Femme a la Rose, oil on canvas, sgn/dtd 1930, 18x22", SBY 5/11/88 OE 374,000
Femme au Buste Nu (portrait), oil on canvas, sgn/dtd 1928, 15x18", C-NY 11/16/88 242,000
Femme au Turban (seated lady wearing a turban), oil on canvas, sgn/dtd 1922, 17x15", SBY 5/10/89 220,000
Femme en Chapeau, watercolor over pencil on paper, sgn, 13x10", SBY 11/16/89 77,000
Femme et Chat (woman w/cat), watercolor over pencil on paper, sgn, ca 1908, 10x8", C-NY 2/16/89 26,400
Femme Nue Allonge (reclining nude), oil on canvas, sgn, 10x13", C-NY 10/5/89 93,500
Femmes a la Guitare (two ladies & a guitar), oil on canvas, sgn/atelier stamp, 22x18", C-NY 5/12/88 297,000
Five Dancers, pastel on paper, sgn/dtd 1937, unfr, 13x18", SBY 2/14/89 OE 24,200
Fleurs avec Guitare, oil on canvas, sgn, 22x19", C-NY 11/16/88 82,500
Francine (bust-length portrait), watercolor on paper, sgn/#d, 13x10", WD 11/16/88 47,500
Friese Decorative: Jeunes Filles dans un Paysage; watercolor on paper laid down on board, sgn, 5x12", C-NY 2/16/89 24,200
Groupe de Femmes et Enfants, colored pencil on paper, sgn, 10x13", SBY 2/16/89 OE 22,000
Heroine (portrait), oil on canvas, sgn, ca 1927, 18x15", C-NY 11/16/88 220,000
Jeune Femme Assise (young woman, seated), oil on canvas, sgn/dtd 1944, 18x15", C-NY 5/11/89 220,000
Jeune Femme au Chapeau, pencil/colored wax crayons on paper, estate stamp, 10x8", C-NY 11/15/88 16,500
Jeune Femme au Perroquet (portrait of girl w/parrot), watercolor over pencil, sgn, 9x7", C-NY 2/16/89 OE 66,000
Jeune Femme au Ruban Blue (young lady w/blue ribbon), watercolor/pencil on paper, sgn, 13x10", C-NY 5/11/89 77,000
Jeune Fille a la Mantille (portrait of a girl), oil on canvas, sgn, 10x9", C-NY 5/11/89 OE 264,000
Jeune Fille Assise, watercolor/pen/brown ink over pencil on paper, sgn, 12x10", C-NY 5/12/88 82,500
Jeune Fille au Bouquet (portrait of a young girl w/bouquet), oil on canvas, sgn, 22x18", SBY 5/10/89 341,000
Jeune Fille au Bras Leve, oil on cradled panel, sgn, 13x10", SBY 2/16/89 OE 118,250
Jeune Fille au Chapeau Bleu, watercolor over pencil on paper, sgn, 13x10", SBY 11/16/89 66,000
Juene Fille Assise, watercolor/pencil laid down on board, sgn, 12x10", SBY 11/12/88 71,500
L'Echarpe Rose, oil on canvas, sgn, 13x10", SBY 5/11/88 OE 209,000
L'Enfant au Chiot Blanc (head of child w/white puppy), oil on board, sgn, ca 1921, 4" dia, C-NY 10/5/89 OE 24,200
La Chevelure Fleurie (portrait of young woman w/flowers in hair), oil on canvas, sgn, 18x15", SBY 11/12/88 286,000
La Vie au Chateau (modernistic), oil on canvas, sgn, 1925, 45x64", SBY 5/9/89 OE 1,430,000
Lavandiere au Bord de la Riviere a Theou (woman doing laundry by the river), oil, estate stamp, 9x11", C-NY 2/18/88 16,500
Le Prince Charmant (Prince Charming), oil on canvas, sgn/titled, 1912, 30x23", C-NY 11/16/88 104,500

Michele Verly, oil on board, sgn/dtd 1942, 11x9", SBY 2/18/88 OE **101,750**
Pauline Laurencin (mother of the artist), oil on paper laid down, sgn, ca 1904-05, 14x11", SBY 10/6/89 OE **46,750**
Portrait de Deux Jeunes Filles (portrait of two girls), oil on canvas, ca 1937, 18x15", C-NY 5/11/89 .... **374,000**
Portrait de Femme, pencil on paper, stamped initials, 16x12", SBY 10/7/88 .... **5,500**
Portrait de Femme, pencil/heightened with colored pencils on paper, sgn/dtd 8 Aout 1950, 8x7", SBY 10/6/89 .... **5,500**
Portrait de Femme, watercolor over pencil on paper, sgn, 11x10", SBY 11/16/89 .... **88,000**
Portrait de Femme (portrait of a woman), oil on canvas, sgn, 16x13", SBY 10/6/89 .... **187,000**
Portrait de Femme (portrait of a woman), pencil on paper, estate stamp, 12x9", C-NY 2/18/88 .... **3,080**
Portrait de Jeune Femme, oil on panel, sgn/dtd 1939, 11x8", C-NY 5/11/89 .... **132,000**

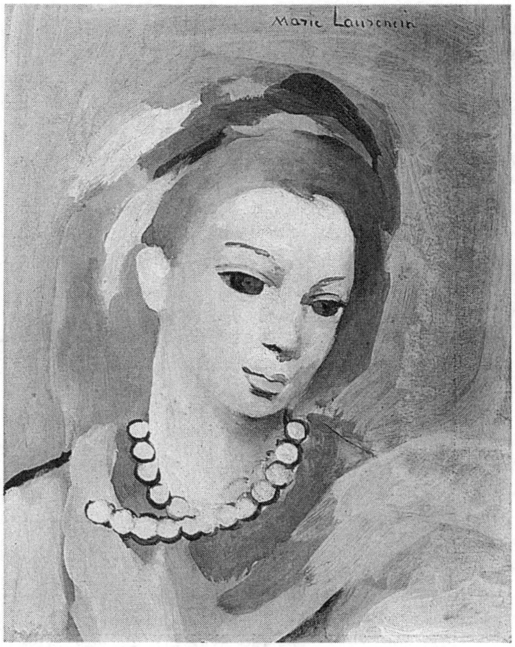

Portrait de Jeune Fille, oil on canvas, sgn, 14x10", C-NY 11/16/88 OE; $385,000

Portrait of a Young Girl, watercolor on paper, initialed, oval, 3x3", WD 5/5/88 .... **900**
Set of 12: Illustrations for La Dame aux Camelias; watercolor/pencil on paper, 11 sgn, 1936, 7x6", C-NY 11/14/88 OE **1,100,000**
Tete de Femme (head of a woman), oil on canvasboard, initialed, 11x9", C-NY 5/12/88 UE **38,500**
Tete de Jeune Fille, colored pencils over pencil on paper, sgn/estate stamp, 13x9", C-NY 11/15/88 .... **41,800**
Tete de Jeune Fille, watercolor over pencil on paper, sgn, 11x10", SBY 11/16/89 .... **77,000**
Tete de Jeune Fille, watercolor/pencil on paper, sgn, 12x10", SBY 11/12/88 .... **38,500**
Three Young Girls, watercolor on paper, sgn, 17x14", WD 11/16/88 OE **95,000**
Trois Jeunes Filles (portrait of three young women), oil on canvas, sgn, 13x22", SBY 11/12/88 OE **330,000**
Trois Jeunes Filles a la Guitare (three girls w/guitar), watercolor/pen/India ink on paper, sgn, 8x11", C-NY 5/11/89 .... **46,200**
Two Girls, colored crayons on buff paper, sgn/dtd 1937, unfr, 18x13", SBY 10/5/88 OE **6,600**
Two Women in a Landscape, pencil on paper, sgn/#d, 8x5", SBY 2/14/89 .... **4,400**

LAURENCIN, Marie; att (French, 1885-1956)
Portrait of a Girl, watercolor, bears signature, 6x5", FB 10/30/89 .... **715**

LAURENSON, Edward Louis (British, 1868-)
Carrying Turf in Achill Islands (landscape), oil on wood panel, sgn/titled, 13x17", RAB 3/27/89 UE **275**
Road to Kylemore Counemara (landscape), oil on wood panel, sgn/titled, 13x18", RAB 3/27/89 UE **275**
Shepherd of Firle Beacon (shepherd/flock on hillside), oil on canvas laid down on cardboard, sgn, 13x17", RAB 3/27/89 UE **500**

LAURENT, Ernest Joseph (French, 1859-1929)
Gypsy Couple (portraits in profile), oil on canvas, sgn/dtd 1887, 37x26", C-NY 2/23/89 .... **15,400**
Seated Woman, oil on canvas, sgn w/monogram, 22x18", SBY 5/23/89 UE **5,500**

LAURENT, Felix (French, 1821-1908)
Harem Dancer, oil on canvas, sgn/dtd 1863, 26x22", C-E 10/26/89 OE **19,800**

LAURENT, John (American, 20th C)
Robert Laurent's House, Cape Neddick, Maine (winter landscape); oil on masonite, initialed, 18x32", RAB 8/9/88 .... **500**

LAURENTY, L. (French, 19th C)
Fisherwoman, oil on canvas, sgn, 26x36", RWS 11/3/88 .... **1,000**

LAURI, Filippo; att (Italian, 1623-1694)
Pair: Allegories of Summer & Winter; oil on panel, 5x7", SBY 6/8/88 .... **2,750**

LAURITZ, Jack (American, 20th C)
Paradise Valley, Arizona; oil on canvas, sgn, 24x32", B/B 1/11/89 .... **715**

LAURITZ, Paul (American, 1889-1975)
Autumn Trees, watercolor on paper, sgn, 21x24", B/B 10/6/88 .... **468**
California Foothills, oil on canvas laid down, sgn, 16x20", B/B 10/6/88 .... **2,475**
Moonlight Trail, Alaska; oil on canvas, sgn/inscr, 30x24", C-NY 3/11/88 .... **3,080**

Mountain Stream, oil on board, sgn, 34x48", B/B 10/6/88 3,575
Mountainous Landscape, oil on canvas, sgn, 29x23", SBY 9/14/89 2,860
Winter in California (snow landscape), oil on canvas, sgn, 28x32", SBY 1/24/89 OE 8,250
Wooded Riverbank, watercolor on paper, sgn, 14x19", B/B 10/6/88 715

LAURON, Albert Frederic (French, 1841-)
Flowers by a Garden Fence, oil on canvas, sgn, 32x26", B/B 6/15/89 4,400

LAUTER, Flora (American, 1874-)
Landscape, oil on board, sgn, 28x35", SLK 2/11/89 325

LAUX, August (American, 1847-1921)
Apples & Grapes, oil on canvas, sgn, 10x14", C-NY 9/30/88 4,950
Blacksmith, oil on canvas, sgn, 20x30", C-E 6/1/88 1,210
Chickens & Terrier in a Barn, oil on canvas, sgn, 12x16", SBY 9/14/89 3,575
Chickens Feeding, oil on canvas, sgn, 10x14", C-E 6/1/89 UE 660
Chickens Feeding, oil on panel, sgn, 6x9", DM 5/13/88 1,300
Kittens, oil on canvas, sgn, 12x16", C-E 2/3/88 OE 2,860
Peaches & Grapes (still life), oil on canvas, sgn, 12x16", C-NY 9/28/89 OE 4,400
Raspberries, oil on canvas, sgn, 10x14", C-NY 5/25/89 9,900
Raspberries, oil on canvas, sgn, 11x14", C-E 6/1/88 1,430
Still Life of Oranges, oil on canvas, sgn, 10x16", RAB 8/9/88 UE 2,000
Still Life of Peaches, oil on canvas, sgn, 16x20", RAB 3/27/89 UE 2,000
Strawberries, oil on canvas, sgn, 10x14", C-NY 5/25/89 OE 11,000

LAVALLE, John (American, 1896-1971)
Castellane (figures in plaza in early morning), watercolor/pencil on paper, sgn/dtd 1925, 18x14", RWS 9/29/88 400
Portrait of a Young Girl (three-quarter length profile), oil on particle board, sgn/dtd 1923, 36x30", RWS 9/29/88 OE 1,400
The Kill (bullfighting scene w/matadors & bull), oil on masonite, sgn/dtd 1949, 6x8", RWS 9/29/88 425

LAVALLEE, Denyse (Canadian, 20th C)
Nouveau Mexique, oil on canvas, sgn/dtd 1988, 30x40", FB 10/30/89 1,320

LAVALLEN, Julio (South American, 20th C)
Untitled (posterior view of standing nude), charcoal/pastel/acrylic on canvas, sgn/dtd 1986, 47x44", SBY 5/17/88 3,850

LAVALLEY, Jonas Joseph (American, 1858-1930)
Still Life of Grapes & Strawberries, oil on canvas, sgn, 10x14", C-E 11/30/88 1,540

LAVAULT, Albert; see De Lavault

LAVERTY, Elizabeth Stevens (American, 1899-)
Manayunk, watercolor/pencil on paper, sgn/dtd 34, 14x20", FAP 4/15/89 138

LAVERY, John (British, 1856-1941)
Lady in White (Portrait of Lady Lyle), oil on canvas, sgn/dtd 95, 50x41", SBY 2/22/89 14,300

LAVILLE, Joy (British, 1923-)
Couple in Their Room, acrylic on canvas, sgn, 1987, 32x39", SBY 5/17/88 9,350
Pajaro Azul (Blue Bird), pastel on paper, sgn, 13x19", C-NY 11/21/88 2,750
Seated Woman & Her Reflection (contemporary), acrylic on canvas, sgn/dtd 86, 47x59", SBY 11/21/88 11,000
Seated Woman with Book (contemporary), acrylic on canvas, sgn, 1985, 55x47", SBY 5/16/89 11,000
Untitled (dog & seated woman in chair in landscape), pastel on paper, sgn/dtd 87, 24x16", SBY 5/17/88 3,300
Woman on the Beach (contemporary), acrylic on canvas, sgn, 47x55", SBY 11/21/88 11,000

LAVOLPE, Nicola (19th C)
Fishing Village, oil on canvas, sgn/dtd 1862, 17x29", C-E 5/23/88 OE 2,640

LAWLEY, J. Douglas (Canadian, 20th C)
On the Move at Sable Island (horses running through pasture), oil on canvasboard, sgn, 20x24", RWS 5/12/89 UE 350

LAWMAN, Jasper Holman (American, 1825-1906)
Mrs O'Doud's Grocery Store (rural village scene), oil on canvas, sgn/dtd 1868, 22x37", WD 4/13/88 OE 48,000

LAWRENCE, Edna W. (American, 1898-)
Young Girl Reading in Bed, graphite on board, sgn, 20x30", RWS 11/10/89 UE 300

LAWRENCE, Jacob (American, 1917-)
Halloween Play, gouache on paper, sgn/inscr/dtd 1950, 22x30", C-NY 9/30/88 OE 41,800
Street Scene, Nigerian Series (contemporary); watercolor/gouache on paper, sgn/dtd 64/titled, 30x22", SBY 5/24/89 OE 44,000
The Wedding (expressionistic depiction), tempera on gessoed board, sgn/dtd 48, 20x24", C-NY 9/28/89 44,000

LAWRENCE, Jean Paul
Scholar, oil on panel, initialed, 15x11", C-E 3/22/88 UE 462

LAWRENCE, Thomas (British, 1679-1830)
Portait of Hart Davis Jr (half-length, a stormy sky beyond), oil on canvas, 30x25", SBY 1/12/89 OE 110,000
Portrait of Lady Hicks (half-length, wearing red dress in a landscape), oil on canvas, oval, 29x23", SBY 1/12/89 OE 23,100
Portrait of Sir Samuel Shepherd (1760-1840), oil on canvas, 49x40", SBY 6/3/88 OE 85,200

LAWRENCE, Thomas; & Studio (British, 1679-1830)
Portrait of a Lady, bust-length, carrying a basket on her head; oil on canvas, 25x19", SBY 10/21/88 4,400

LAWRENCE, Thomas; after (British, 1679-1830)
Portrait of Sir Henry Torrens, oil on canvas, 28x36", FAP 11/4/88 800

LAWRENCE, Thomas; att (British, 1679-1830)
Portrait of Cornelis van der Geest, after Van Dyck; oil on canvas, 32x25", WD 10/19/88 OE 6,000
Portrait of Miss Cecilia Siddons (three-quarter length portrait facing forward), oil on canvas, 30x25", SLK 4/7/89 4,750
Portrait of Mrs Meredith, pencil on paper, 9x7", B/B 1/11/89 2,200
Portrait of Nathan Mayer Rothschild, oil on canvas, 20x16", FB 4/25/88 475
Portriat of King George IV, oil on canvas laid down, 36x28", B/B 10/9/88 1,980

LAWRENCE, Thomas; circle of (British, 1679-1830)
Diana, Countess of Bedford; oil on canvas, 30x25", WG 9/16/88 ... 1,000
Portrait of a Gentleman, oil on canvas, 36x28", SBY 7/12/89 ... 2,090

LAWRENCE, Thomas; follower of (British, 1679-1830)
Portrait of Miss Kimble, oil on canvas, 17x13", SBY 6/8/88 ... 1,210

LAWRENCE, Thomas; manner of (British, 1679-1830)
Head of a Woman, oil on canvas, 16x13", SBY 7/12/89 OE ... 3,300

LAWRENCE, Thomas; school of (British, 1679-1830)
Portrait of a Lady, seated, half-length in blue dress holding lorgnette; oil on canvas, 30x25", C-E 6/1/88 OE ... 1,540
Portrait of Sir John Moore, bust-length, in uniform; oil on canvas, 30x25", C-NY 1/15/88 ... 3,850

LAWRIE, Alexander S. (American, 1828-1917)
View From a Hill, oil on canvas, sgn/dtd 1870, 14x24", C-NY 5/26/88 ... 8,800

LAWSON, Alexander (British, 19th/20th C)
Cattle at Water's Edge, oil on canvas, 16x26", NA 2/24/89 ... 650

LAWSON, Ernest (American, 1873-1939)
Central Park & Temple Beth-El, oil on canvas, sgn, 16x25", C-NY 12/2/88 UE ... 13,200
Country Road to Spuyten Duyvil, New York; oil on canvas, sgn, 18x14", C-NY 5/26/88 OE ... 26,400
Country Scene, Winter; oil on canvas, ca 1910, 20x24", SBY 5/25/88 ... 27,500
Country Village (impressionistic landscape w/village), oil on canvas, sgn, 20x24", SBY 5/24/89 OE ... 68,750
Early Spring (river landscape w/bridge & town beyond), oil on canvas, sgn, 25x30", C-NY 5/25/89 OE ... 176,000
Fall Landscape, oil on canvas laid down on panel, sgn, 16x20", C-NY 3/11/88 OE ... 14,300
Feeding the Baby (interior scene), oil on canvas, sgn, 31x26", C-NY 5/24/89 ... 30,800
Grant's Tomb (in a landscape), oil on canvas, sgn, 25x30", C-NY 12/2/88 ... 121,000
New England Hills, oil on canvas, sgn, 16x20", SBY 6/24/88 ... 10,450
Old Mill, Wilton, Connecticut; oil on canvas, sgn, 25x30", C-NY 12/2/88 ... 55,000
Orchard, oil on canvas, sgn, 16x20", SBY 6/28/89 ... 4,950
Stone Walls & Autumn Fields, New England; oil on canvas, sgn, 21x24", RWS 11/3/88 ... 21,000
Tug Boat on a River, pastels, sgn, 9x11", PHL 6/16/88 ... 4,000
Winding Road, New England; oil on canvas, 8x10", C-NY 9/30/88 ... 4,950
Winter, Harlem River; oil on canvas, sgn, 18x24", SBY 5/25/88 ... 44,000
Winter Landscape, oil on canvas, sgn, 20x24", RWS 5/12/89 ... 45,000
Winter Landscape with Waterfall, oil on canvas, sgn, 20x24", SBY 4/14/89 OE ... 30,800

LAWSON, Ernest; att (American, 1873-1939)
Landscape with Farmhouse, pencil, sgn, 12x9", SWN 12/1/88 ... 193

LAWSON, Francis Wilfried (British, 1842-1935)
On Thames` Bank, oil on panel, sgn/dtd 1922, 12x18", RWS 8/12/89 ... 600

LAZANO, Margarita (Latin American, 20th C)
Columbian Flowers (still life in landscape), oil on canvas, sgn, 1988, 47x41", SBY 5/16/89 ... 7,150

LAZAREV, Victor
Russian Sleigh Ride in the Winter, oil on canvas, sgn, 28x37", C-E 11/8/88 ... 1,700

LAZERGES, Jean Baptiste Paul (French, 1845-1902)
Arab Encampment Under a Starry Sky, oil on canvas, sgn/dtd 1900, 23x29", C-NY 10/25/89 ... 7,700
Arab Guards Resting Their Horses, oil on panel, sgn, 7x11", C-E 2/21/89 UE ... 660
Noonday in the Town of Blidah, Algeria; oil on canvas, sgn/dtd 88, 37x48", C-NY 2/3/88 ... 7,700

LAZZARINI, Gregorio; circle of (Italian, 1655-1730)
Temptation of Saint Anthony Abbott, oil on canvas laid down on masonite, 33x38", C-NY 4/8/88 ... 3,300

LAZZELL, Blanche (American, 1878-1956)
Abstract Composition, pencil on paper, sgn/dtd 1928, 10x8", SBY 6/24/88 ... 1,650
Cubist Composition, charcoal on paper, sgn/dtd 1927, 11x9", C-NY 9/28/89 ... 2,090
Flowers (modernistic still life), oil on incised panel, initialed, ca 1920, 12x11", C-NY 5/25/89 OE ... 15,400
No 6 Boats Early Dawn, watercolor on cardboard, sgn/dtd 33, 8x8", RWS 5/12/89 ... 900
Tulips (modernistic still life), oil on incised panel, initialed, ca 1920, 12x12", C-NY 5/25/89 OE ... 14,300

LE BARBIER L'AINE, Jean Jacques F. (French, 1738-1826)
Allegory on the Occasion of a 50th Wedding Anniversary, oil on canvas, sgn/dtd 1813, 30x24", SBY 4/7/88 ... 9,900

LE BOEUFF, Pierre (French, 19th C)
Malines Cathedral, watercolor on paper, sgn, 12x15", B/B 5/17/89 ... 440

LE BROCQUY, Louis (British, 1917-)
Woman, oil on canvas, sgn/dtd 1960, 64x38", C-E 11/17/88 OE ... 16,500

LE BRUN, Christopher (20th C)
Parnassus (abstract), oil on canvas, 1981, 90x126", SBY 11/11/88 ... 20,900
Xanthus (contemporary), oil on canvas, 1981, 84x120", SBY 11/11/88 OE ... 33,000

LE BRUN, Louise Elizabeth Vigee; after
Mother & Child, oil on canvas, 49x37", SBY 6/8/88 OE ... 715

LE BRUN, school of
Triumph of Alexander the Great, oil on canvas laid down on panel, 28x37", C-NY 10/20/88 OE ... 7,150

LE CAVE, Peter (British, 18th/19th C)
Sheltering From the Storm, watercolor/pen/gray ink on paper, sgn/dtd 1805, 15x19", C-NY 5/24/89 ... 880

LE COMTOIS, Henry
Courtship, oil on canvas, sgn, 37x29", C-E 2/23/88 ... 1,980

LE CORBUSIER (Charles Edouard Jeanneret)(French, 1887-1965)
Duex Musiciennes au Violon et a la Guitare (abstract), brush/ink/chalk on paper, sgn, ca 1937, 8x10", SBY 5/11/89 ... 11,550

Femme Nue (abstract nude), watercolor on paper mounted at the edges on board, initialed/dtd L-C 57, 8x11", C-NY 10/5/89 ... 6,050
La Main et le Silex Vert, oil on canvas, sgn/dtd 30-32, 32x39", SBY 5/11/88 OE ... 148,500

LE DUC, Victor Viollet (French, 1848-1901)
Bords de Riviere, oil on panel, sgn, 9x13", SBY 7/12/89 ... 1,320
By the River, oil on canvas, sgn, 24x36", SBY 7/12/89 OE ... 6,600

LE FOUQUAYS (French, 20th C)
Hiding in a Corner, oil on canvas, sgn, 23x29", MG 5/28/88 ... 150

LE GUAY, Etienne Charles (French, 1762-1846)
Portrait of a Young Man, half-length, in profile to the right; chalk/wash, sgn/dtd 1790, 4" dia, C-NY 1/11/89 ... 1,650

LE MASSON, Paul (French, 1898-1980)
Pair: Village in the Snow; Gypsy Caravan; oil on masonite, sgn, 12x13", WD 11/16/88 ... 3,000

LE MERCIER, Charles; att
Village with Figures, gouache, ca 1835, 9x11", SWN 12/1/88 ... 303

LE NAIN, Louis; circle of (French, 1593-1648)
Three Ages, oil on canvas, 18x23", SBY 6/3/88 OE ... 34,100

LE NAIN, Mathieu; circle of (French, 1607-1677)
Portrait of a Young Girl, half-length, wearing a blue & gold dress...; oil on canvas, 22x16", C-NY 4/6/89 ... 3,080

LE NAIN, school of (French, 16th C)
Portrait of a Gentleman Said To Be Henri II, Duc de Montmorency (1595-1632); oil on canvas, 24x20", C-NY 5/31/89 OE ... 14,300

LE PHO (French, 1907-)
Les Pivoines, oil on board, sgn, 16x11", LH 12/4/88 UE ... 500

LE PRINCE, Jean Baptiste (French, 1734-1781)
Children Playing Blind Man's Bluff, oil on canvas, 31x35", C-NY 4/8/88 OE ... 4,950
Couple Embarking From Ornamental Park as Ladies Listen to Galant Playing Guitar, oil, sgn/dtd 1775, 103x97", C-M 12/3/88 ... 120,777
Fisherman & a Woman with a Baby by a Stream Near a Cottage, oil on canvas, sgn, 35x59", C-NY 10/12/89 OE ... 26,400

LE ROUX, Jacques (French, 20th C)
Nouvelle Guinee, oil on canvas, sgn, 36x29", SBY 10/5/88 UE ... 495

LE ROY, Harold (American, 20th C)
Still Life of Peaches, oil on canvasboard, sgn, 8x10", C-E 2/16/88 UE ... 33

LE SAUTEUR, Claude (Canadian, 1926-)
Incertitude (figure in modernistic landscape wearing green hat & hat), oil on canvas, sgn/dtd 1980, 20x40", FB 5/89 ... 5,000
Jardinage, oil on canvas, sgn/dtd 1976, 12x16", FB 10/30/89 ... 2,090
La Chaise (chair w/still life of fruit, portrait behind), oil on canvas, sgn/dtd 1979, 20x16", FB 10/17/88 ... 3,600
Soleil Levant (rising sun), oil on canvas, sgn/dtd 1978, 16x20", FB 4/25/88 ... 2,100

LE SIDANER, Henri (French, 1862-1939)
Automne a Nemours, oil on canvas, sgn, 23x28", SBY 10/6/89 ... 88,000
Bateaux sur la Lagune a Venise, oil on panel, sgn/dtd 1892, 10x14", SBY 5/11/88 ... 31,900
Bridge Near Bruges, oil on canvas, sgn, 19x22", FB 5/28/89 OE ... 88,000
Hampton Court Place, oil on canvas, sgn, 25x40", SBY 2/18/88 ... 46,750
L'Atelier de L'Artiste (Gerberoy) (artist's studio), oil on panel, sgn, 13x18", C-NY 10/6/88 ... 35,200
L'Eglise, Treguier (Church, study for a larger painting); oil on panel, sgn, 1913, 10x13", C-NY 10/5/89 ... 15,400
L'Etang, oil on panel, sgn, 9x7", C-E 5/9/89 ... 11,000
La Table sous la Tonnelle (Le Rendez-vous), oil on canvas, sgn, 1932, 44x38", C-NY 5/11/89 ... 440,000
Le Jardin en Automne, oil on panel, bears inscr A Schoeller Amicalement, 14x11", SBY 2/16/89 ... 33,000
Le Pont, oil on canvas, sgn, 26x32", WD 5/5/88 OE ... 92,500
Le Village sous la Neige (winter village scene), oil on canvas, sgn, 24x29", SBY 10/7/88 ... 71,500
Les Barques au Crepuscule, oil on canvas, sgn, 24x29", SBY 10/7/88 ... 57,750
Les Piliers, Gerberoy (view of a country home), oil on canvas, sgn, 1901, 23x32", C-NY 5/12/88 ... 85,800
Maison a Nemours (view of house at night), pastel on canvas, ca 1930, 23x32", C-NY 5/12/88 ... 60,500
Maisons au Bord d'un Canal (Houses Along the Canal), oil on canvas, sgn, 25x24", SBY 10/7/88 OE ... 66,000
Maisons sur le Canal, Nemours (pointilistic landscape); oil on canvas, sgn, 1920, 28x36", C-NY 5/11/89 ... 154,000
Moulin a Crepuscule (view of a mill at dusk), oil on canvas, sgn, 14x22", C-NY 5/12/88 ... 55,000
Paysage a Moret, le Pont (waterfront scene w/bridge), oil on canvas, sgn, 1918, 26x32", C-NY 11/16/88 ... 165,000
Petite Place de la Ville (view of village square w/fountain), oil on canvas, sgn, 26x32", SBY 5/10/89 ... 96,250
Pruniers en Fleurs (view of blossoming plum tree w/flowers), oil on canvas, sgn, 26x32", SBY 5/10/89 ... 176,000
Village sous la Neige (wintery village at night), pastel on canvas, sgn, 21x26", SBY 10/6/89 ... 49,500
Ville au Clair du Lune (village in the moonlight), oil on panel, sgn, 1923, 13x16", C-NY 10/5/89 ... 38,500

LE SUEUR, Eustache (French, 1616-1655)
Study of Figure for Marcus Curtius Throwing Himself into the Abyss, black chalk on buff paper, 17x9", SBY 1/13/89 OE ... 49,500

LE SUEUR, Eustache; circle of (French, 1616-1655)
Crucifixion of Saint Peter, black chalk/lt brown wash, inscr, 8x13", C-NY 1/12/88 ... 825

LE VA, Barry (American, 1941-)
Center Points & Blocks (abstract), ink/colored pencil on paper, sgn/dtd 1974, 36x59", SBY 2/15/89 ... 17,600

LEA
Falling Leaves, watercolor/India ink/pencil on paper, sgn/dtd 50, 27x18", SBY 10/7/89 ... 330

LEADER, Benjamin Williams (British, 1831-1923)
An Angler in a River Landscape Near Godalming, oil on canvas, sgn/dtd 1892, 20x30", PHL 6/16/88 UE ... 2,000
Autumn Evening After the Rain, oil on canvas, sgn/dtd 1886, 30x48", C-NY 2/23/89 OE ... 52,800
Autumn Gold, oil on canvas, sgn/dtd 1900, 20x30", SBY 12/9/88 ... 5,225
Country Scene with Thatched Cottages, oil on canvas, 16x21", WG 9/16/88 UE ... 100
Figures Walking in a Twilight Landscape, oil on canvas, sgn/dtd 97, 20x30", C-E 2/21/89 ... 3,080

On Gomshall Common, Surrey; oil on canvas, sgn/dtd 1906, 16x24", FB 10/30/89 2,090
River Landscape, oil on canvas, sgn/dtd 1884, 24x42", C-NY 2/23/89 UE 8,800
Rushing River, oil on canvas, sgn/dtd 1890, 16x26", B/B 4/20/88 1,100
:ADER, Benjamin Williams; att (British, 1831-1923)
Christ Church, Hants (figures in boat & on bank, dwellings & church beyond); oil on canvas, 16x24", C-E 5/22/89 1,650
:ADER, Charles (British, 19th C)
Fishing in North Wales, oil on canvas, sgn, 18x14", SBY 7/12/89 UE 660
Lake & Mountain Scene, oil on canvas, sgn, 16x24", WAD 6/6/88 850
:ADER, Mrs. Benjamin Eastlake (British, fl 1883-1902)
Windswept Shore (coastal seascape), oil on canvas, sgn, 14x26", RAB 3/27/89 UE 175
AKE, Gerald (American, 1885-1975)
Ocean Racer Ticonderoga, oil on canvas, sgn, 20x36", RAB 8/9/88 UE 450
Two Sisters (portrait w/landscape beyond), oil on canvas, sgn, 26x21", DM 1/15/88 1,400
AR, Edward (British, 1812-1888)
Coastal Scene at Laggia, pen/brown ink/watercolor heightened w/white, inscr/dtd 1864, 6x10", C-NY 2/25/88 1,760
Crescenza, watercolor/gouache/pen/brown ink on blue paper, sgn/dtd 1844/titled, 3x5", C-NY 5/24/89 6,050
Desert at Madourah, pencil/pen/brown ink, dtd twice 1858, numbered twice, 5x14", C-NY 2/25/88 1,100
Monaco, watercolor/gouache heightened w/gum arabic, sgn w/monogram, 5x7", C-NY 5/25/88 OE 7,700
Study of a Bearded Vulture, watercolor/pencil on paper, sgn, 9x13", SBY 6/8/88 4,400
View in the Roman Compagna, watercolor/gouache/pen/brown ink on blue paper, sgn/dtd 1844/inscr, 3x5", C-NY 5/24/89 6,050
View Near Palermo, watercolor/pencil/pen/ink, dtd 12 July 1847/#d 239, 10x17", C-NY 10/25/89 OE 7,700
AR, John (American, 20th C)
Men at Construction Site, watercolor on paper, sgn, 19x28", FAP 11/4/88 475
AVER, Charles (British, 19th C)
Wooded Path, oil on board, sgn/dtd 1869, 9x12", C-E 2/23/88 UE 308
AVER, Noel Harry (British, 1889-1951)
Fishing Boats in Harbor, watercolor heightened with bodycolor, sgn, 7x10", PHL 6/16/88 UE 600
Mosque Scene with Figures & Camel, watercolor on paper, sgn, 20x14", DM 5/89 1,600
Old Mosque at Baghdad, watercolor on paper, sgn, 14x10", DM 5/89 1,000
Roman Gateway, watercolor on paper, sgn, 14x10", DM 5/19/89 1,000
Sacred Gate, watercolor/gouache, sgn/inscr, unfr, 15x11", C-NY 2/25/88 1,980
Street Scene in Old Tunis, watercolor on paper, sgn, 20x14", DM 5/19/89 1,600
AVERS, Lucy A. (British, fl 1887-1898)
Barnyard Friends (four pups looking over a gobbler), oil on canvas, sgn, ca 1890, 35x40", SBY 6/9/89 UE 3,025
AVITT, Agnes (American, 1859-)
Birches (woodland path bisects grove of trees), watercolor on paper, sgn/dtd 1901, 21x15", RWS 3/31/88 UE 400
AVITT, Edward Chalmers (American, 1842-1904)
Apples, oil on canvas, sgn/dtd 1888, 12x10", SBY 6/24/88 UE 2,750
Apples (still life), oil on canvas, sgn/dtd 1900, 14x18", C-NY 5/26/88 4,180
Branch of Purple Plums, oil on canvas, sgn/dtd 1887, 26x13", SBY 9/14/89 2,310
Egyptian Still Life, oil on canvas, sgn/dtd 1870, 16x20", C-NY 5/25/89 6,600
Peaches in a Basket with Grapes & Pears on a Ledge, oil on canvas, sgn, 26x30", WD 4/13/88 3,600
Roses & Crystal (still life), oil on canvas, sgn/dtd 1902, 20x12", RWS 5/19/88 OE 1,100
Still Life of Currants, oil on canvas, sgn/dtd 1904, 6x8", RWS 9/8/89 475
Still Life of Grapes, oil on canvas, sgn/dtd 1895, 15x22", RWS 5/19/88 2,200
Still Life of Grapes & Urn, oil on canvas, sgn/dtd 1878, 20x16", C-E 10/18/89 4,950
Still Life of Plums, oil on canvas, sgn/dtd 1885, 8x10", RWS 5/12/89 1,500
Still Life of Sea Bass, oil on canvas, sgn/dtd 1897, 36x16", RWS 5/12/89 850
AVITT, John F. (American, 20th C)
Bully Haye's Brig Leonore, watercolor on paper, sgn, modern frame, 10x14", RAB 8/1/88 850
Preliminary Sketch Schooner Half-Moon for CY Morse, Esq 8/27/62; watercolor on paper, sgn, 12x16", RAB 11/25/88 400
BADANG
La Branche Morte, oil on canvas, sgn twice/inscr, 40x20", C-E 5/13/88 484
BAS, Leonie
Pair: Winter in Paris; oil on panel, sgn, 6x9", C-E 5/23/88 1,320
BASQUE, Henri (French, 1865-1937)
Cueillant des Fleurs, oil on canvas, sgn, 1923, 22x18", SBY 2/18/88 77,000
En Barque les Andelys, watercolor over pencil on paper laid down on board, sgn, 15x22", C-NY 10/6/88 8,250
Femme a l'Ombrelle dans un Barque (woman in boat), oil on canvas, sgn, ca 1915, 29x37", C-NY 11/16/88 OE 275,000
Femme Assise Pres d'une Fenetre, watercolor/charcoal on paper, sgn, 13x10", SBY 2/16/89 OE 12,100
Femme Assise sur la Plage (seated woman on beach), oil on canvas, sgn, ca 1922, 21x26", C-NY 2/16/89 OE 52,800
Femme Nue a sa Toilette, oil on canvas, sgn, 26x21", SBY 2/16/89 77,000
Femme nue Allongee (reclining nude), charcoal on paper, sgn, 18x27", C-NY 2/18/88 3,300
Fillettes Jouant dans un Jardin (two girls jumping rope in garden), oil on canvas, sgn, 1899, 32x26", C-NY 5/12/88 187,000
Interieur a la Harpe, oil on canvas, sgn/dtd 09, 29x36", SBY 5/11/88 181,500
Jeune Fille aux Fleurs (young woman seated at table w/flowers), oil on canvas, sgn, 22x26", SBY 11/12/88 99,000
Jeune Fille Courant sur la Pelouse (young girl running in the grass), oil on canvas, sgn, 18x15", C-NY 10/6/88 5,720
La Fille de L'Artiste (figure seated at easel, painting), oil on canvas, sgn, 20x10", C-NY 10/5/89 33,000
La Promenade Printaniere (springtime landscape w/woman & child), oil on canvas, sgn, ca 1913, 20x24", SBY 11/12/88 82,500
La Toilette (Nu s'Habillant), oil on canvas, sgn, 37x20", C-NY 2/16/89 OE 44,000
La Voile Bleue, Prefailles (ladies in garden viewing sailboats); oil on canvas, sgn, 1922, 29x39", SBY 5/10/89 198,000

Le Pont sur la Marne (bridge over the Marne), oil on canvas laid down on board, sgn, 15x24", C-NY 2/16/89 UE ... 28,60
Madame Vian Assise dans un Parc, oil on canvas, sgn, ca 1900, 51x50", SBY 5/11/88 OE ... 907,50
Nature Morte Aux Pommes, oil on canvas, sgn, 24x26", C-NY 10/6/88 OE ... 46,20
Nu a la Fontaine (landscape w/nude at fountain), oil on canvas, sgn, 17x20", C-NY 5/12/88 ... 41,80
Nu Allonge (reclining nude), oil on canvas, sgn, 15x22", C-NY 10/5/89 OE ... 126,50
Nu Allonge (reclining nude), oil on canvas, sgn, 25x32", C-NY 2/16/89 OE ... 330,00
Nu Assis, oil on canvas, sgn, 23x20", C-NY 2/16/89 OE ... 154,00
Nu des dos Devant la Fenetre, oil on canvas, sgn, 24x18", SBY 10/7/88 ... 44,00
Nu Devant une Fenetre (nude standing in front of window), oil on canvas, sgn, 1926-28, 18x15", C-NY 2/16/89 OE ... 115,50
Nudes Bathing, watercolor/pencil on paper, sgn, 17x12", SBY 10/7/89 ... 1,32
Paysage (landscape), watercolor over pen/black ink on paper, sgn, 8x10", C-NY 10/5/89 ... 6,05
Paysage du Midi (landscape w/two figures & mountain), oil on canvas, sgn, 1911, 36x29", C-NY 11/16/88 ... 110,00
Phare (The Lighthouse), oil on canvas, sgn, 22x18", C-NY 10/5/89 ... 38,50
Portrait de Mlle Marthe Lebasque, oil on canvas, sgn, 1926, 22x18", C-NY 2/16/89 ... 41,80
Portrait de Mlle Suzanne Bergaud, oil on canvas, sgn, 1924, 32x26", C-NY 2/16/89 OE ... 41,80
Standing Female Nude, pencil on tracing paper, stamped signature, 19x7", SBY 10/7/89 ... 99
Trois Femmes a la Plage (three ladies on the beach), oil on canvas, sgn, 38x51", C-NY 10/5/89 ... 99,00
Un Apres-Midi dans le Parc (Afternoon in the Park), oil on canvas, sgn, 20x24", SBY 11/12/88 ... 110,00

LEBASQUE, Marthe (French, 19th/20th C)

Tabletop Still Life of Theatre Masks, oil on canvas, sgn, 32x26", WD 5/5/88 ... 4,00
View From a Window: Winter Rooftops; oil on canvas, sgn, 32x21", WD 5/5/88 ... 3,00

LEBDUSKA, Lawrence H. (American, 1894-1966)

Cantering Horses, oil on canvas, sgn/dtd 46, 12x14", C-E 2/3/88 ... 99
Elephant Hole (elephant in the water w/panther stalking), oil on panel, sgn, 18x24", SBY 1/24/89 UE ... 88
Group of 4: Underwater Fish Series; oil on panel, sgn/#d, 3 unfr, ca 12x14", SBY 1/24/88 ... 1,87
Kangaroo, oil on board, sgn/dtd 60, 17x13", C-E 2/3/88 UE ... 66
Pair: Pink, Blue, & Purple Horses; Elephants; oil on board, sgn, 1st dtd 9-60, 14x18", 16x20", SBY 1/24/89 UE ... 99
Pair: Shepherdess; Rhinoceri; oil on board, ea sgn/1 dtd 9-60, 20x16", C-E 10/18/89 ... 1,32
Peasant Couple (in a landscape), oil on masonite, sgn/dtd 1919, unfr, 30x24", SBY 1/24/89 ... 1,32
Peasant Couple & Horses by the Sea (folk art style), oil on canvas, sgn/dtd 37, 18x22", SBY 9/14/89 ... 1,32
Picnic, oil on masonite, sgn/dtd 42, 14x18", C-E 6/1/89 ... 1,10
Plowing the Field, oil on masonite, sgn/dtd 42, 16x22", SBY 9/23/88 ... 66
Three Pandas, oil on canvas, sgn, 30x36", SBY 1/24/89 ... 1,87
Tiger & Bear (in landscape), oil on masonite, sgn, 21x24", SBY 4/14/89 ... 1,65
Underwater World, oil/seashells on panel, sgn, 18x24", SBY 1/24/89 ... 82
Unknown Fish, oil on canvas, sgn/dtd 10-60, 16x20", C-E 2/3/88 ... 1,32
Vase of Flowers, oil on canvas, sgn, 3x18", C-E 4/7/88 UE ... 33
Zebras & Antelopes, oil on masonite, sgn, 18x24", SBY 1/24/89 OE ... 2,75

LEBEDEV, Vladimir (Russian, 1891-1967)

Cabaret Dancer (contemporary), watercolor/pen/ink on gray paper, 11x8", C-L 10/8/88 OE ... 1,86
Robber (contemporary), watercolor/pen/ink on paper, 12x11", C-L 10/8/88 OE ... 2,60

LEBON, Maurice (Canaidan)

View of Church From the Park in Autumn, oil on canvas, sgn, 20x24", FB 5/28/89 ... 50

LEBOURG, Albert (French, 1849-1928)

Autumn Landscape, oil on panel, sgn, 12x16", LH 9/10/89 ... 3,80
Environs de Rouen, Temps de Neige; oil on canvas, sgn, 15x22", SBY 10/7/88 OE ... 39,60
L'Allier a Pont du Chateau, oil on canvas, sgn, 18x30", C-NY 10/6/88 ... 26,40
La Route d'Hondouville, Effet de Givre (provincial landscape); oil on canvas, sgn, 26x20", C-NY 5/12/88 ... 30,80
La Seine et le Faubourg Saint-Sever, Etude de Ciel; oil on canvas, sgn, 11x16", SBY 10/7/88 ... 15,40
Le Degel Apres le Neige aux Environs de Rouen (landscape), oil on canvas, sgn/dtd 1902, 18x34", C-NY 5/12/88 ... 22,00
Le Havre (seascape w/boats & shoreline in distance), oil on canvas, sgn/titled, 15x28", SBY 10/7/88 OE ... 15,95
Le Palais Alberien au Bord de la Seine, oil on canvas, sgn/dtd 1889/inscr, 15x28", SBY 2/16/89 ... 82,50
Le Port de Rouen, oil on canvas, sgn, 16x26", SBY 10/7/88 ... 23,10
Le Port de Rouen, Temps Gris (port scene); oil on canvas, sgn/inscr, ca 1885, 12x23", C-NY 11/16/88 ... 44,00
Le Quai du Louvre au Printemps, oil on canvas, sgn/inscr/dtd 1907, 18x29", C-NY 10/6/88 OE ... 46,20
Le Village sur la Seine aux Environs de Rouen (landscape), oil on canvas, sgn, 15x24", C-NY 5/12/88 ... 14,30
Les Bords de L'Allier au Soleil Couchant, oil on board, sgn/dedicated, 11x14", C-NY 10/6/88 ... 9,90
Les Bords de la Seine a Puteaux (river landscape), oil on canvas, sgn, 16x29", C-NY 5/11/89 OE ... 82,50
Les Bords du lac de Geneve, a Saint-Gingolph; oil on canvas, sgn, 22x32", SBY 10/6/89 ... 66,00
Maisons a l'Entree du Pont de Neuilly, oil on canvas, sgn, 16x26", C-NY 5/12/88 ... 23,10
Port et la Cathedrale de Rouen (impressionistic harbor landscape), oil on canvas, sgn/dtd 1892, 14x24", C-NY 5/12/88 OE ... 49,50
River & Landscape with Boats, oil on canvas, sgn, 18x34", FB 10/30/89 ... 61,60
View of the Rhone, oil on canvas, sgn, 20x36", B/B 10/9/88 ... 27,50
Vue Prise sur la Seine au Port du Louvre (figures along the Seine), oil on canvas, sgn/dtd 1900, 16x26", C-NY 10/5/89 ... 38,50

LEBRET, Paul (French, 19th/20th C)

Architecutural Design of a Great Hall Interior, watercolor/pencil on paper, sgn/dtd 1914, 35x32", SBY 7/12/89 ... 2,09

LEBRUN, F.

Cows Grazing in a Wooded Landscape, oil on canvas, sgn, 25x33", C-E 1/12/88 ... 52

LEBRUN, Fredrico

Turkey Dinner, brush/ink on board, sgn/dtd 58, 14x32", C-NY 3/11/88 ... 1,10

BRUN, M.
Mother & Child in an Embrace, oil on canvas, 27x22", C-E 11/8/88 550
BRUN, Rico (American, 1900-1964)
Two Nude Figures, watercolor on paper, sgn/dtd 1956, 19x24", C-E 11/30/88 660
BUSKA, Lawrence H. (American, 1894-1966)
Wayside Shrine, oil on canvas, sgn, 14x18", C-E 2/3/88 495
COCQ, Adrien (French, 1832-1887)
Summer Landscape, oil on canvas, sgn/inscr/dtd 1876, 31x32", SBY 6/8/88 2,200
COMTE, Paul Emile (French, 1877-1950)
Fishing Boats in a Harbor, oil on canvas, sgn, 38x44", SBY 6/8/88 OE 11,000
French Country Landscape with Figures & Plough Horse, watercolor on paper, sgn, 13x19", SBY 7/12/89 1,045
French Market Scene, oil on canvas, sgn, 24x29", C-NY 5/24/89 9,900
Harbor Scene, oil on canvas, sgn, unfr, 24x36", SBY 7/12/89 6,600
L'Entree du Parc (landscape), oil on canvas, sgn/dtd 1928, 25x32", C-E 2/21/89 4,180
River Landscape, oil on canvas, sgn, 28x36", SBY 2/14/89 8,250
Spanish Street Scene, oil on canvas, sgn, 24x30", SBY 12/9/88 2,200
COMTE-VERNET, Charles Emile Hippolyte (French, 1821-1900)
Femme Fellah Portant son Enfant (Egypte), oil on canvas, sgn/dtd 1872, 23x16", SBY 5/23/89 57,550
COQUE, Alois (Czechoslovakian, 1891-1981)
Chez Pierre, oil on board, sgn, 20x24", B/B 9/14/89 1,540
Notre Dame, Paris; oil on canvas, sgn/dtd 1976, unfr, 18x24", SBY 2/14/89 2,475
Prague, oil on canvas, sgn/dtd 1971, 20x24", B/B 9/14/89 UE 1,100
Rue Chevalier de la Barre, Montmartre; oil on canvas, sgn/dtd 1975, 18x24", C-E 11/17/88 1,650
Une Rue a Montmartre, oil on canvas, sgn, 18x22", C-E 5/13/88 1,980
Village in Winter, oil on masonite, sgn, unfr, 18x24", SBY 2/14/89 OE 6,050
DAIN, Bruce (Canadian, 1928-)
Rue St Louis, Beaupre, Quebec; oil on board, sgn/dtd 1976, 14x20", FB 10/30/89 770
DBUSKA, Lawrence (American, 1894-)
Morning Promenade, oil on masonite, sgn, 12x15", SBY 3/17/88 715
DFORD, Freda Wedder (American, 20th C)
Winter's Thaw, oil on upson board, sgn, 8x12", FAP 12/8/89 UE 225
DOUX, Jean Philiberte (French, 1767-1840)
Portrait of a Young Lady, bust-length, turned to the left; red/black chalk, 18x14", C-NY 1/11/89 OE 7,150
DOUX, Jean Philiberte; att (French, 1767-1840)
Portrait of a Young Boy, bust-length, wearing a red jacket & white shirt; oil on canvas, 10x8", C-NY 4/6/89 4,620
DUC, Ozias (Canadian, 1864-1955)
Antigonish, Nova Scotia; watercolor, initialed/dtd 1903, 7x5", FD 10/17/88 950
DUC, Paul (Belgian, 1876-1943)
Untitled, bright garden scene w/flowers; oil on canvas, sgn/dtd 1910, 28x32", SLK 4/7/89 4,000
E, Bertha Stringer (American, 1873-1937)
Sand Dunes, oil on board, sgn, 7x7", B/B 1/11/89 440
Sand Dunes on Monterey Coast, oil on canvas, sgn, 14x22", B/B 12/8/88 1,210
Trees Along the Coast, oil on board, sgn, 7x10", B/B 5/17/89 467
E, Frederick Richard (British, 1798-1879)
Highland Pathway (extensive landscape), oil on canvas, indistinctly sgn, 9x12", B/B 5/17/89 UE 357
Traveler Crossing a Stone Bridge, oil on canvas, sgn/dtd 1828, 28x36", SBY 12/9/88 1,760
E, George E. (American, 20th C)
Two-Masted Schooner at Anchor, oil on canvas, sgn, 24x20", RAB 3/14/89 300
E, Henry Charles
Spring Landscape, oil on panel, sgn, 12x14", C-E 6/1/88 605
E, Robert E. (American, 1899-)
REA Express, oil on canvas, sgn/inscr, 36x42", B/B 6/15/89 6,600
E, William
Le Retour de Cythere, oil on canvas, sgn, 41x39", C-NY 5/25/88 9,350
EMANS, Antonius (Dutch, 1631-1673)
Vanitas Still Life Homage to the Admiral Marten Herperts, oil on canvas, sgn/inscr/dtd 1655, 33x27", SBY 10/21/88 OE 46,200
EMANS, Johannas; & LEEMANS, Antonius (Dutch, 17th C)
Pair: Floral Still Lifes; oil on canvas, sgn, 50x41", FAP 4/15/89 OE 9,350
EUW, Alexis; see De Leeuw
EBVRE, Claude; circle of (French, 1632-1675)
Portrait of a Gentleman Said To Be Jean Baptist Colbert, oil on canvas, 25x19", SBY 7/12/89 UE 770
EBVRE, Jules Joseph (French, 1836-1911)
L'Amour Blesse, oil on canvas, sgn, 75x49", SBY 10/24/89 26,400
La Cigale (nude standing by wall), oil on panel, sgn, 16x8", SBY 6/1/89 UE 8,800
La Fiancee, oil on canvas, sgn, 1882, 62x52", SBY 2/22/89 35,200
Le Parc de St Cloud, oil on canvas, sgn, 32x46", SBY 5/23/89 13,200
Reclining Nude, oil on panel, sgn, 6x13", C-NY 10/25/89 OE 28,600
EBVRE, Robert (French, 1755-1830)
Portrait of a Lady, seated, half-length; oil on canvas, sgn/dtd 1805, 46x35", C-NY 5/31/89 OE 33,000
EBVRE, Robert; att (French, 1755-1830)
Portrait of a Gentleman, seated by a table with books; pastel on paper laid down on canvas, 36x29", C-NY 6/2/88 13,200

LEFLER, Franz (Czechoslovakian, 1831-1898)
Children's Bacchanale, oil on canvas, sgn, 54x45", SBY 5/23/89 ..... **16,50**
Young Anglers, oil on canvas, sgn, 54x45", SBY 5/23/89 ..... **16,50**
LEFORT, Jean (French, 1875-)
Le Pont Neuf (river landscape w/bridge), oil on canvas, sgn, 13x16", C-E 11/17/88 ..... **44**
LEFTWICH, George R. (British, fl 1875-1880)
Fred Archer Up at the St Leger, oil on canvas, sgn, 29x44", SBY 6/10/88 ..... **27,50**
LEGANGER, Nicolay Tysland (American, 1832-1894)
Ausable River, New York, 1891; oil on canvas, sgn, 30x50", RWS 11/3/88 OE **2,40**
LEGEAY, Jean Laurent (French, 1710-1786)
Pair: Capriccio of Classical Ruins & Trees; red chalk, 13" dia, C-NY 1/11/89 OE **6,60**
LEGENDRE, Maurice (French, 20th C)
Pont Alexandre III, Paris; oil on canvas, sgn, 18x22", WAD 6/6/88 ..... **35**
LEGER, Fernand (French, 1881-1955)
Composition (abstract), oil on canvas, sgn/dtd 32, 36x24", SBY 11/11/88 ..... **440,00**
Composition (abstract), oil on canvas, sgn/dtd 38, 15x19", SBY 5/10/89 ..... **187,00**
Composition (abstract), oil on canvas, sgn/dtd 38, 26x22", SBY 5/10/89 ..... **159,00**
Composition (abstract), oil on canvas, sgn/dtd 39, 15x18", SBY 5/10/89 ..... **143,00**
Composition a la Danseuse, oil on artist board, sgn/dtd 34, 18x15", SBY 5/10/89 ..... **143,00**
Composition Abstrait, pencil on paper, initialed/dtd 43, 14x11", SBY 11/12/88 ..... **17,60**
Composition aux Deux Fleurs (abstract), oil on canvas, sgn twice/dtd 50, 21x26", C-NY 11/16/88 UE **143,00**
Composition aux Gants Jaunes (abstract), oil on canvas, sgn twice/dtd 34, 26x21", C-NY 11/16/88 ..... **198,00**
Composition aux Trois Personnages, pencil on tracing paper, initialed, 7x10", C-NY 11/15/88 ..... **26,40**
Composition avec Figures (composition w/figures), oil on canvas, sgn/dtd 31, 25x18", SBY 5/9/89 ..... **440,00**
Contrastes de Formes, watercolor on paper, initialed, ca 1918, 13x9", SBY 11/12/88 OE **242,00**
Deux Femmes Drapes, gouache/pencil on buff paper, initialed/dtd 29/inscr, 7x10", SBY 11/12/88 ..... **38,50**
Double-Sided: Workmen's Heads: Studies for Les Constructeurs; mixed media, initialed, ca 1950-51, 25x20", SBY 11/12/88 ..... **71,50**
End of the Trail II, watercolor on paper, sgn/dtd 1962, 17x22", WL 5/20/88 ..... **85**
Esquise pour la Mere et l'Enfant, gouache/ink wash/pencil on paper, dtd 1952/titled, 17x11", SBY 11/12/88 OE **93,50**
Etude pour l'Anniversoire, gouache/brush/ink over pencil on paper, initialed, 28x22", C-NY 2/18/88 ..... **57,20**
Etude pour le Grand Dejeuner, pencil on paper, initialed/dtd 21, 6x8", C-NY 11/15/88 ..... **35,20**
Fantaisies sur Fond Rouge (abstract), oil on canvas, sgn/dtd 43, 18x14", SBY 11/12/88 ..... **187,00**
Femme au Collier de Perles, Marie l'Acrobate; gouache/ink wash on paper, initialed/dtd 48, 21x16", SBY 5/11/88 OE **214,50**
Feuille Rouge (Red Leaf, abstract), gouache/watercolor/pencil on paper, initialed/dtd 50/#d 52, 12x16", SBY 5/11/88 OE **29,70**
L'Anniversaire (couple w/city in background), gouache/brush/black ink over pencil, stamped, 1950, 30x22", C-NY 5/12/88 ..... **85,80**
La Couverture Bleue dans le Paysage, oil on canvas, sgn/dtd 51, 22x15", SBY 5/10/89 ..... **143,00**
La Danseuse au Cheval (abstract), oil on canvas, sgn twice/dtd 53, 36x26", SBY 11/11/88 ..... **605,00**
La Racine Jaune, oil on canvas, sgn, ca 1943-44, 26x36", SBY 11/15/89 OE ..... **1,210,0(**
La Ville: Le Fumeur; ink wash/white gouache over pencil on paper, initialed, ca 1954-55, 13x10", SBY 4/29/88 OE **60,50**
Le Chapeau sur la Chaise (The Hat on the Chair), oil on canvas, sgn/dtd 52, 26x20", SBY 5/10/88 ..... **275,00**

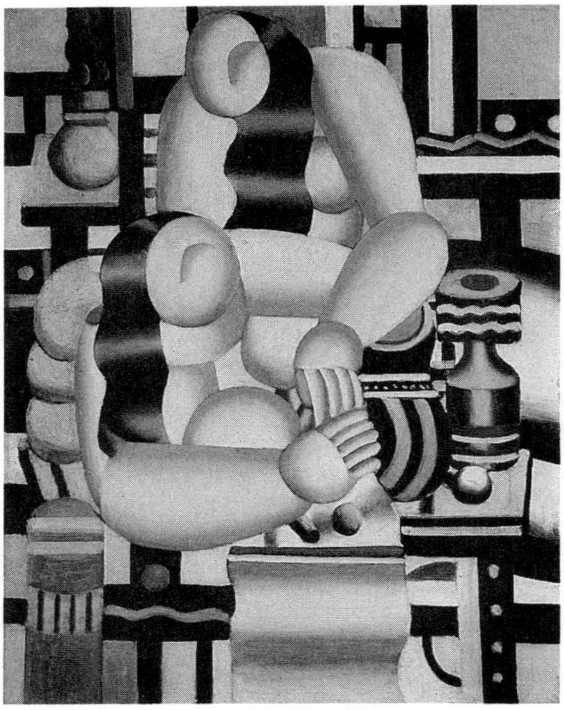

Le Dejeuner, oil on canvas, 1921, 26x20", C-NY 5/11/88; $2,200,000

Le Dejeuner (sketch of three women), pencil on paper, 9x13", SBY 5/10/89 ..... **22,00**

Le Plongeur Noir (abstract), oil on canvas, sgn/dtd 43, 33x26", C-NY 11/16/88 ... 209,000

Le Profil Noir (abstract), oil on canvas, sgn/dtd 28, 26x36", SBY 5/10/88 ... 440,000

Le Tournesol (abstract), gouache/ink wash/pencil on buff paper on board, initialed/dtd 51, 22x19", SBY 2/16/88 ... 24,200

Le Tronc d'Arbre Rouge, gouache/ink wash on paper, initialed/dtd 37, 12x14", SBY 11/16/89 ... 40,700

Les Deux Amoureux, oil on canvas, sgn/dtd 52/inscr Ler Etat, 26x20", SBY 11/11/88 OE ... 550,000

Les Oiseaux sur l'Echelle, gouache/ink wash on buff paper laid down on board, initialed/dtd 43, 11x18", SBY 11/12/88 OE ... 55,000

Les Plongeurs (abstract figures), gouache/black ink on buff paper, initialed/dtd/titled, 1941, 18x16", C-NY 5/12/88 OE ... 66,000

Les Plongeurs (abstract), gouache/India ink over pencil on paper, initialed/dtd FL 42, 12x10", C-NY 5/12/88 ... 46,200

Mandoline et Pommes, gouache/ink wash on paper laid down on board, initialed/dtd 6.38, 13x10", SBY 11/12/88 OE ... 23,100

Mere et Enfant, gouache/ink wash over pencil on paper, 8" dia, SBY 11/16/89 ... 27,500

Nature Morte, gouache/watercolor/ink wash/pencil on squared paper, initialed/dtd 1926, 15x10", SBY 11/16/89 OE ... 264,000

Nature Morte (abstract still life), oil on canvas, sgn/dtd 1932, 11x18", C-NY 5/11/88 ... 176,000

Nature Morte (abstract still life), oil on canvas, sgn/dtd 1929, 36x26", C-NY 5/11/88 OE ... 462,000

Nature Morte (abstract still life), watercolor/pencil on buff paper, initialed/dtd, 1924, 7x9", C-NY 5/12/88 ... 8,250

Nature Morte (abstract still life), watercolor/pencil on paper, sgn w/initials/dtd, 1927, 7x6", C-NY 5/12/88 OE ... 26,400

Nature Morte a la Mandoline, India ink/pencil on paper, initialed/dtd 42, 15x11", SBY 11/16/89 ... 20,900

Nature Morte a la Pipe, oil on canvas, sgn/dtd twice 38, 21x26", SBY 5/11/88 ... 198,000

Nature Morte au Citron (abstract still life), oil on canvas, sgn/dtd 1939, 26x20", C-NY 5/11/88 ... 220,000

Nature Morte au Vase, gouache/ink wash on paper squared for transfer, initialed/dtd 50, 9x12", SBY 11/16/89 ... 55,000

Nature Morte aux Deux Couteaux (still life), oil on canvas, sgn/dtd 52/titled, 20x26", SBY 5/9/89 ... 330,000

Nature Morte avec Visage (Still Life with Face), gouache/pen/ink/pencil, initialed/dtd FL 19, 1925, 12x9", C-NY 5/12/88 ... 143,000

Nature Morte sur Fond Jaune, gouache over pencil on paper, initialed/dtd 36, 23x16", C-NY 11/15/88 ... 66,000

Paix et Pardon (study for the cover), gouache/ink wash on buff paper, stamped initials, 11x8", SBY 5/11/88 OE ... 36,300

Project for a Ceramic Mural (abstract), gouache/ink wash/pencil on paper, initialed/dtd 52/inscr, 9x12", SBY 2/16/89 UE ... 11,000

Rose et Compas, oil on canvas, sgn/dtd 25, 36x26", SBY 5/10/88 ... 687,500

Still Life of Bust (abstract), gouache/ink wash on paper, stamped signature, ca 1927-28, S-19x25", SBY 11/12/88 ... 88,000

Study for La Grand Parage, gouache/ink wash on paper, initialed/dtd 53, 22x27", SBY 11/12/88 OE ... 308,000

Tete de Femme, pen/brush/India ink over pencil on paper, initialed, 12x9", C-NY 11/15/88 ... 24,200

Un Vase Bleu, un Tapis Rouge; oil on canvas, sgn/dtd 52 twice, 21x26", SBY 5/11/88 ... 170,500

Untitled, pen/ink on brown paper backed w/another sheet, sgn/dtd 43, 9x12", SBY 11/16/89 ... 41,250

Untitled (abstract), gouache/watercolor/brush/India ink on paper, initialed/dtd 29, S-8x12", C-NY 5/11/89 ... 12,100

Untitled (The Divers), gouache/ink wash on paper, initialed/dtd 40, 12x16", SBY 11/16/89 OE ... 115,500

GER, Fernand; after (French, 1881-1955)

Composition Jaune, No 9; wool tapestry, artist's name stitched in margin, 90x45", C-E 11/17/88 ... 4,400

GER, H.

Theo (Maltese terrier-type dog on oriental rug w/walking stick nearby), oil on canvas, 22x25", DM 10/14/88 ... 1,000

GER, L.

Musical Gathering, oil on panel, sgn, 17x13", C-E 2/23/88 ... 880

GERE, Jon S. (20th C)

Slight Haze, tempera on masonite, sgn, 28x17", SBY 9/23/88 ... 1,100

GOUT-GERARD, Fernand Marie Eugene (French, 1856-1924)

Breton Fisherwomen, pastel on brown paper laid on stretched canvas, sgn, 8x10", C-NY 5/24/89 ... 2,860

Coin de Marches a Concarneau (busy marketplace), oil on canvas, sgn, 18x15", C-NY 2/23/89 ... 11,000

GRAND, Pierre Nicolas (Swiss, 1758-1829)

Portrait of Joseph Cange, Commissionnaire of Saint Lazare Rrison, half-length; oil on canvas, 28x22", C-M 12/3/88 ... 46,453

GRAND, Rene (French, 1923-)

Playing in the Shallows (children), oil on canvas, sgn, 24x30", WD 11/16/88 UE ... 3,000

GROS, Alphonse (British, 1837-1911)

Death Triumph, pen/black ink/brown & green wash heightened w/white, 11x17", C-NY 5/25/88 ... 770

Pair: Harvest; Returning Home; watercolor/charcoal/colored chalks on paper, 1 inscr, 12x19", C-E 5/23/88 ... 660

Portrait of a Young Woman, right profile; metal point, sgn/dtd 1888, 11x8", C-NY 2/25/88 OE ... 5,280

GUAY, Charles Etienne; att (French, 1762-1846)

Stag Hunt, gouache on paper, 14x18", WD 10/19/88 OE ... 7,000

HMANN, Henri (European, 19th C)

Female Nude, her arms upraised; pencil heightened w/white on gray laid paper, 7x6", C-NY 10/26/88 ... 715

Figure Studies of a Man in Oriental Costume, pencil/black & white chalk on tan paper, inscr, 15x9", C-E 5/23/88 ... 495

HMANN, Rudolph Wilhelm (German, 1819-1905)

Sisters (three figures on steps near doorway), oil on canvas, painted in circle, 32x32", PHL 10/28/88 UE ... 1,000

Washing Day, oil on canvas, sgn, 29x21", WAD 6/6/88 ... 5,500

HR, Adam (American, 1853-)

Floral Still Life, oil on board, sgn, 25x33", SBY 1/24/89 ... 990

HY, Paul (19th C)

Landscape with Sheep, oil on canvas, sgn, 20x30", WG 4/23/88 ... 275

ICKERT, Charles (Belgian, 1818-1907)

Marketplace in Winter, oil on panel, sgn, 15x13", C-NY 2/23/89 ... 9,900

IGH, William Robinson (American, 1866-1955)

Bronco Buster, oil on canvas, 12x14", B/B 6/9/88 ... 2,475

Mountain Man, oil on circular concave board, sgn, 12" dia, MG 11/19/88 UE ... 150

Rustler, oil on canvas, sgn/dtd 1912, 16x25", RWS 11/10/89 OE ... 64,000

Study of a Horse in a Stable Interior, oil on board, 9x10", PHL 6/16/88 ... 1,600

Sunset, Phoenix Valley (landscape); oil on canvas, sgn/dtd 1948, 13x17", SBY 5/24/89 ... 11,550

LEIGHTON, Frederick (British, 1830-1896)
Crenaia (Nymph of the Dargle), oil on canvas, 1880, 30x11", SBY 6/1/89 UE ... 165,00
Rendezvous, oil on canvas, initialed/dtd 1874, 27x20", C-E 10/25/88 OE ... 4,40

LEIGHTON, Kathryn Woodman (American, 1876-1952)
Archer, oil on canvas, sgn/inscr, 44x36", C-E 11/30/88 ... 3,08
Chippawa Indian, oil on canvas, sgn, 24x18", SBY 6/24/88 ... 2,42
Lake Louise, oil on canvas, sgn, 28x36", B/B 8/10/88 ... 1,10
Sierra Lake, oil on canvas, sgn, 18x24", B/B 10/6/88 ... 66

LEIGHTON, Scott (American, 1849-1898)
Charles in a Stable, oil on canvas, sgn, 12x20", SBY 6/24/88 ... 1,32
Chestnut Horse by a Barn, oil on canvas, sgn, 10x14", SBY 6/24/88 ... 1,21
Chestnut Horse in a Landscape, oil on canvas, sgn, 13x19", SBY 6/24/88 ... 1,10
Trotter on the Track, oil on canvas, sgn, 22x33", SBY 6/24/88 ... 6,05

LEIMANIS, Andris (Canadian, 1938-)
Late Fall (view of Dominion Square, Montreal), oil on board, sgn/dtd 1978, 16x20", FB 10/17/88 ... 55
Montreal Skyline From Mount Royal, oil on board, sgn/dtd 1977, 20x24", FB 4/25/88 ... 60
Waiting for Customers, oil on canvas, sgn/dtd 1981, 12x16", FB 4/25/88 ... 60

LEIS, Malle (Russian, 1940-)
Falling (eight red roses on white background), oil on canvas, sgn twice/dtd 70, 39x39", SBY 7/7/88 ... 5,00
Windy Day: N 3 (tiny white floating flowers on blue background); oil on canvas, sgn twice, dtd 72/85, 39x39", SBY 7/7/88 ... 5,60

LEISENRING, L.M.
Italian Architectural Scene, gouache, unfr, 20x13", LH 5/15/88 ... 16

LEITCH, William Leighton (British, 1804-1883)
Buildings in Cologne, pencil/blue & brown wash/white heightening on gray paper, sgn, unfr, 6x8", C-NY 10/31/89 UE ... 11
Stone Bridge Over a Village Canal, watercolor, 6x9", C-E 1/21/89 ... 66

LEITH-ROSS, Harry (American, 1886-)
Canal at Point Pleasant, oil on canvas mounted on masonite, sgn, 20x26", SBY 6/24/88 ... 3,30
March Sky, oil on board, sgn, 8x10", WD 4/13/88 ... 1,00
Rocks & Sea, Annisquam; oil on panel, sgn, 8x11", C-NY 9/30/88 ... 3,19
Stallion in a Storm, oil on board, sgn, 8x11", C-E 9/15/88 UE ... 27

LELAND, Henry (American, 1850-1877)
Barnyard Scene, oil on canvas, sgn/dtd 1877, 13x17", C-E 2/1/89 ... 93

LELEU, Alexandre Felix (French, 1871-)
On the Grand Canal, Venice; oil on canvas, sgn, 16x22", B/B 8/10/88 OE ... 3,85

LELIENBERGH, Cornelis; see Van Lelienbergh

LELOIR, Alexandre Louis (French, 1843-1884)
Chariot of Swallows, oil on canvas, sgn, 42x29", SBY 2/22/89 ... 18,70
Temptation of Saint Anthony, oil on canvas, sgn/dtd 1871, 29x40", SBY 2/22/89 ... 19,80

LELOIR, Maurice (French, 1853-1940)
Narrow Escape, oil on panel, sgn, 18x12", C-E 2/21/89 OE ... 6,38

LELONG, Rene (French, 19th C)
Deux Femmes, oil on cardboard, sgn, 21x16", SBY 5/23/89 OE ... 14,30
Grand Hotel, oil on canvas, sgn, 16x26", SBY 2/22/89 OE ... 34,10
Tennis Party, oil on canvas, sgn, 10x24", SBY 2/22/89 ... 9,90

LELSIE, Charles Robert; style of (British, 1794-1859)
Scene From the Merry Wives of Windsor, oil on canvas, 25x30", B/B 6/15/89 ... 3,57

LELY, Peter (British, 1618-1680)
Portrait of a Gentleman Said To Be the Duke of Monmouth; brown costume, by column, oil on canvas, 50x41", C-NY 4/8/88 ... 8,80
Portrait of the Duchess of Richmond as Diana, oil on canvas, 30x25", SBY 12/9/88 UE ... 1,98
Portrait of the Hon Elisabeth Finch, Mrs Grimston; in a landscape, oil on canvas, inscr, 50x42", C-NY 6/2/88 UE ... 11,00
Portrait of the Hon Samuel Crewe (half-length, wearing black coat & white ruff), oil on canvas, 29x24", SBY 4/29/88 ... 2,97
Portrait of Thomas, 2nd Baron Crewe of Stone (half-length wearing black coat); oil on canvas, 29x24", SBY 4/29/88 ... 5,22

LELY, Peter; & Studio (British, 1618-1680)
Portrait of a Lady Said To Be Anne of Austria, Regent of France (in a landscape); oil on canvas, 50x41", C-NY 1/15/88 ... 4,40

LELY, Peter; after (British, 1618-1680)
Portrait of a Lady Wearing Classical Attire, a stormy landscape in the distance; oil on canvas, 48x39", SBY 10/21/88 OE ... 9,35

LELY, Peter; att (British, 1618-1680)
Miss Pelham, Portrait of a Girl with Roses; oil on canvas, 29x24", RWS 6/17/89 ... 90

LELY, Peter; circle of (British, 1618-1680)
Portrait of a Lady, Seated Three-Quarter Length, in a Brown Dress & Blue Shawl; oil on canvas, 50x41", C-NY 10/12/89 ... 3,08

LELY, Peter; follower of (British, 1618-1680)
Portrait of a Gentleman, half-length, a landscape in the distance; oil on canvas, oval, 40x34", SBY 10/21/88 ... 4,40
Portrait of a Woman Said To Be Queen Catherine of Braganza, oil on canvas, 50x40", SBY 6/8/88 ... 2,75

LELY, Peter; school of (British, 1618-1680)
Duchess of Portsmouth, oil on canvas, 25x21", B/B 5/17/89 OE ... 1,32
Portrait of a Lady Wearing a Brown Cape, holding a red flower; oil on canvas, 35x29", C-E 6/1/88 ... 1,04
Portrait of Lady Hertford (three-quarter length), oil on canvas, 56x41", WG 4/23/88 UE ... 3,80

LELY, Peter; studio of (British, 1618-1680)
Portrait of Elizabeth Capell, Countess of Carnarvon (three-quarter length, seated); oil on canvas, 62x54", SBY 6/1/89 OE ... 18,70
Portrait of Louise Renee de Kerouaille, Duchess of Portsmouth; oil on canvas, 45x34", SBY 4/7/88 OE ... 4,67

MAIRE, Madeleine (French, 1845-1928)
Bunch of Carnations, watercolor on paper, sgn, 17x23", SBY 12/9/88 ... 1,100
Bunch of Roses, watercolor, sgn, 20x29", C-NY 5/25/88 ... 2,860
Bunches of Violets by a Basket, watercolor on paper, sgn, 12x20", SBY 12/9/88 ... 1,100
Reclining Nude in an Elegant Interior, oil on canvas, sgn, 38x51", C-NY 2/23/89 ... 28,600
Yellow Roses in a Vase (still life), watercolor, sgn, 21x16", C-NY 2/23/89 OE ... 4,180
MAIRE, Marie Therese
Splendid Bouquet of Assorted Flowers, oil on canvas, sgn, 26x32", C-NY 5/25/88 ... 6,050
MASSON, Paul
Village sous la Neige, oil on masonite, sgn/dtd 70, 11x9", C-E 5/13/88 ... 935
MBECK, Jack (American, 20th C)
Blue Noose (abstract composition), acrylic on canvas, sgn/dtd 1975 & Nov 1976, unfr, 64x49", C-E 11/17/88 ... 6,600
Loose Ends (abstract), acrylic on shaped canvas, sgn/dtd 1979, unfr, 79x104", C-NY 2/14/89 ... 15,400
Spring Street Echo, acrylic on canvas, sgn/inscr/dtd 1978, unfr, 42x36", C-E 5/13/88 OE ... 5,500
MBERT, P. (Continental, 19th/20th C)
Curious Kittens, oil on canvas, sgn, 18x26", C-E 2/21/89 OE ... 3,520
MEUNIER, Alfred Leon
Cavern: Design for an Opera Set; watercolor/gouache over black chalk, stamped signature, 17x23", C-NY 10/26/88 ... 770
MEUNIER, Basile (French, 1852-)
Paying the Harvester, oil on canvas, sgn, 30x38", C-NY 2/23/89 OE ... 10,450
MIEUX, Jean Paul (Canadian, 1904-)
Head of a Nun, oil on canvas, sgn/dtd 1982, 16x12", FB 10/17/88 ... 21,000
Sunday Outing (winter landscape w/horse pulling figures on sled), oil on board, sgn, 20x26", FB 10/30/89 ... 1,760
MMEN, Georges (Belgian, 1865-1916)
Bateaux a Collioures, ink on paper, stamped w/monogram/dtd ler Juin 93, 9x12", SBY 10/5/88 ... 2,420
Garconnet au Manteau Rouge (seated boy wearing red coat), oil on board, monogramed/dtd 1909, 24x20", C-NY 5/12/88 ... 20,900
Nu Assis (seated nude), oil on board, monogramed/dtd 1903, 10x7", SBY 2/16/89 ... 15,400
MMENS, E. (French, 19th C)
By the Hen House, oil on board, sgn, 7x11", WD 1/11/89 ... 1,000
MOINE, Elisabeth (French, fl 1783-)
Brothers of Joseph Selling Him into Slavery, oil on canvas, sgn/dtd 1783, unfr, 35x46", SBY 10/13/89 ... 14,300
Lady Wearing Elaborate Flowered Hat, Tying a Nosegay; oil on canvas, sgn/dtd 1783, 32x25", SBY 10/13/89 ... 9,900
MOINE, Francois; circle of (French, 1688-1737)
Reclining Male Nude, black chalk, bears inscription in graphite, 15x19", SBY 7/12/89 OE ... 5,775
MOINE, Marie Victoire (French, 18th C)
Lady Wearing an Elaborate Flowered Hat, Tying a Nosegay; oil on canvas, sgn/dtd 1783, oval, 32x25", SBY 1/12/89 ... 16,500
MORDANT, Jean Julien (French, 1878-)
Study of a Man, charcoal on brown paper, sgn, 17x14", C-E 5/23/88 UE ... 385
MPICKA, L. (Continental, 19th C)
Impressionistic Landscape of a Field of Poppies Along the Banks of a Stream, oil on canvas, sgn, 56x32", SLK 9/28/88 ... 2,750
MPICKA, Tamara; see De Lempicka
NOIR, Marcel (French, 1872-1931)
Le Pont de Brie, oil on canvas, sgn, 13x16", C-NY 2/25/88 ... 4,950
NTULOV, Aristarkh (Russian, 1882-1943)
Composition with Roses (abstract), oil on canvas, ca 1914-16, 23x26", C-L 10/8/88 OE ... 17,660
OCAT
Untitled (contemporary), tempera/colored chalks on paper laid down on paper, sgn/dtd 84, unfr, 59x126", C-E 5/9/89 ... 990
ON, Amanda; see De Leon
ON Y ESCOSURA, Ignacio; see De Leon Y Escosura
ONARD, A. (Continental School, 19th C)
Little Wood Gatherers, mother/two children huddle in architectural niche; oil on canvas, sgn, 26x21", RWS 8/20/88 UE ... 300
ONARD, John Henry
Artist by a College Bridge, watercolor, sgn/dtd 1881, 7x11", C-NY 5/25/88 UE ... 440
Extensive Lakeview, oil on panel, sgn, 22x34", C-E 10/25/88 ... 3,520
ONARD, Michael (British, 20th C)
Stooping Bather, acrylic on paper mounted on canvas, sgn/dtd 1980, 22x21", C-E 6/28/88 ... 660
ONARDI, A. (Italian, 19th C)
Beatrice Cenci in Her Cell, oil on canvas, sgn/dtd 17, 95x132", B/B 4/20/88 ... 1,320
ONE, John (20th C)
Hired Guns, oil on board, sgn/copyrighted/titled, 30x40", SBY 9/23/88 ... 3,025
Rounding Up Cattle, sgn/copyrighted, 30x40", SBY 9/23/88 ... 2,310
ONE, Ludovico; att (Padovanino)(Italian, 1542-1612)
Madonna & Child with a Male Saint, oil on canvas, unfr, 30x24", SBY 4/7/88 OE ... 2,200
ONEL (Continental, 19th C)
Market Place, Seville; oil on panel, sgn/dtd 1875, 9x15", SBY 7/12/89 ... 2,860
ONHARDT, J.
Malibu Canyon, oil on board, sgn/dtd 1929, 11x14", C-SK 11/10/88 ... 1,020
PAGE, J. (French, 19th C)
Musketeers Life, oil on canvas, sgn, 11x14", SBY 6/8/88 ... 2,750
PEINTRE, Charles (French, 1735-1803)
L'Enfant au Tambor (lady & child in interior), oil on panel, 14x11", C-E 2/21/89 ... 3,080

Portrait of a Lady, oil on canvas, 32x26", SBY 7/12/89 OE 2,475

LEPICIE, Nicolas Bernard (French, 1735-1784)
Allegory of Louis XV as Apollo, oil on canvas, sgn/dtd 1772, 51x35", SBY 10/13/89 16,500

LEPICIE, Nicolas Bernard; circle of (French, 1735-1784)
Interior with Family Seated Around a Table, oil on canvas, 41x67", SBY 4/7/89 5,225

LEPINAY, Paul Charles Emmanuel Gallard (French, 1842-1903)
Grand Canal with the Piazza San Marco in the Distance, oil on canvas, sgn, 60x44", C-E 10/25/88 OE 6,600

LEPINE, Stanislas Victor Edouard (French, 1835-1892)
Canal de la Villette, oil on canvas, sgn, 14x20", B/B 6/9/88 7,150
View of the Seine From the Pont Neuf, oil on canvas, 13x22", C-NY 5/25/88 4,180

LEPOITTEVIN, Louis (French, 1847-1909)
Mimicking the Call of the Wild Turkey (woman & turkeys in rural scene), oil on canvas, sgn, 20x26", C-E 5/22/89 2,860

LEPRIN, Marcel (French, 1891-)
Eglise a Caen, oil on canvas, sgn/inscr/dtd 1930, 18x22", C-E 5/13/88 OE........ 9,900
Paris Street Scene, oil on canvas, sgn, 16x13", B/B 3/22/89 2,090
Scene de Paris, oil on board, sgn, 13x16", C-E 5/13/88 OE 4,400

LEPRINCE, Jean Baptiste (French, 1734-1781)
Wooded River Landscape with Figure & a Dovecote, grisaille, sgn, 35x58", WD 1/25/89 OE 8,750

LEPRINCE, Jean Baptiste; att (French, 1734-1781)
Fete Champetre, oil on canvas, 46x36", SBY 10/13/89 15,400

LEPRINCE, Jean Baptiste; manner of (French, 1734-1781)
Scene en Chinoiserie, oil on canvas, 25x38", C-E 2/16/88........ 880

LEQUESNE, Eugene Louis
Young Lady, Half-Length, Holding a Red Flower; oil on canvas, sgn, unfr, 31x24", C-E 10/25/88 1,650

LERAY, Prudent Louis (French, 1820-1879)
Fetching Water From the Well, oil on panel, sgn, 16x13", C-E 5/22/89........ 1,980

LEROLLE, Henry (French, 1848-1929)
Mother Walking with Her Child Along the Banks of a River, oil on canvas, sgn, 24x30", C-E 5/22/89 UE 1,100

LEROUX, Jacques (French, 20th C)
Femme au Chapeau (woman in hat), oil on canvas, 11x9", C-E 5/3/88 495
Group of 8: Abstract Figure Studies; mixed media, sgn, 1 dtd 66, 23x98" to 6x7", SBY 2/14/89........ 825

LEROY, Jules (French, 1833-1865)
Mischief Makers (cats & dogs cavorting in interior), oil on canvas, sgn/dtd 1920, 22x18", C-NY 5/24/89........ 6,600
Mother Cat & Her Two Kittens, oil on panel, sgn/dtd 1921, 14x11", C-E 2/21/89 4,180
Playful Kittens, oil on canvas, sgn, 22x19", C-NY 5/25/88 4,400
Playful Kittens, oil on panel, sgn, unfr, 22x18", C-E 7/26/88 990

LEROY, Paul Alexandre Alfred (French, 1860-1942)
Les Filles d'Atlas (five huntresses w/bows & dogs in a landscape), oil on canvas, sgn/dtd 1896, 83x103", SBY6/1/89 UE 71,500

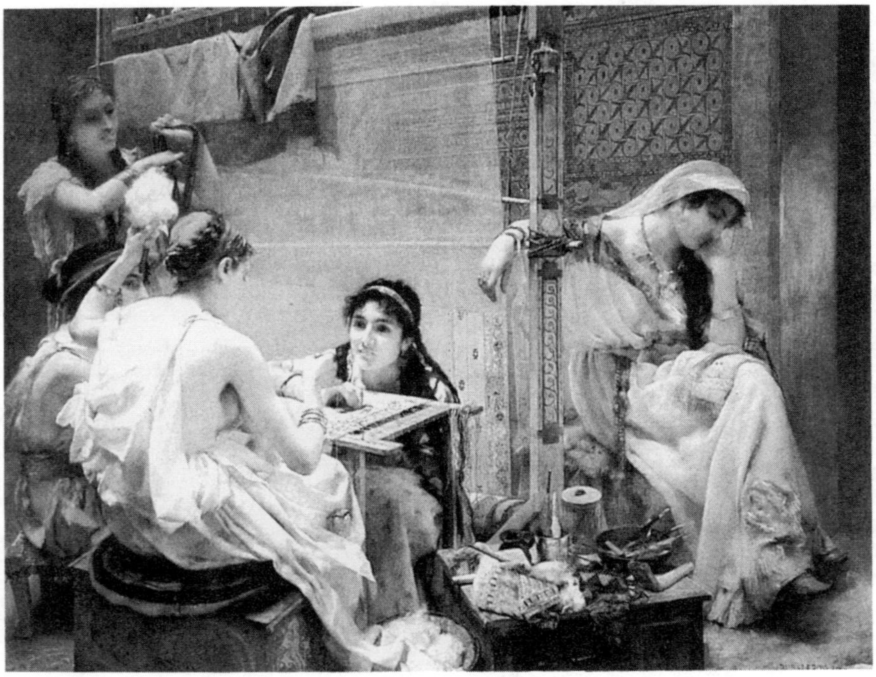

Penelope, oil on canvas, sgn/dtd 1894, 63x79", C-NY 5/24/89 OE; $115,500

LESIEUR, Pierre (French, 1920-)
Autobus a Londres, oil on canvas, sgn/dtd 63, 32x33", SBY 10/7/89 7,97
Nature Morte a la Table Jaune, oil on canvas, sgn/dtd 63, 33x32", SBY 10/7/89 5,22
Nu et Feuilles, oil on canvas, sgn/dtd 65, 55x55", SBY 10/7/89........ 4,95

aysage des Indes, oil on canvas, sgn/dtd twice 60, 58x55", SBY 10/5/88 OE ... **3,300**
SIO, A.; see De Lesio
SLIE, Alfred (American, 1927-)
Jeannette (seated pregnant nude), charcoal on paper, sgn/dtd 1972/titled, 40x30", SBY 11/11/88 ... **4,125**
ichard Miller & Floriano Vecchi (portrait), oil on canvas, sgn/dtd 1970-71, 108x72", C-NY 5/3/89 ... **44,000**
ntitled (abstract), oil on paper mounted on board, sgn/dtd 59, 18x20", SBY 10/5/89 OE ... **13,200**
ntitled (abstract), oil/paper collage on board, sgn twice/dtd 59 twice, 6x7", SBY 2/19/88 ... **1,650**
SLIE, Charles (British, 1840-)
ighland Loch & Fisherman, oil on canvas, sgn/dtd 1879, 18x35", WAD 6/6/88 ... **1,800**
ooded Lake Scene, oil on canvas, sgn/dtd 1880, 12x24", C-E 2/23/88 ... **935**
SLIE, Charles Robert (British, 1794-1859)
reamer (portrait of a woman), oil on canvas, initialed, 16x12", SBY 2/22/89 ... **11,000**
cene From Henry VIII, oil on canvas, 44x56", SBY 5/23/89 ... **6,600**
SLIE, George Dunlop (British, 1835-1921)
hree Marys (three ladies, men changing wheel on carriage), oil on canvas, sgn/dtd 1858, 39x53", SBY 12/9/88 UE ... **1,650**
SREL, Adolphe Alexandre (French, 1839-)
usical Gathering, oil on panel, sgn/dtd 1902, 23x19", C-NY 5/24/89 OE ... **13,200**
SSI, Giovanni (Italian, 1852-1922)
legant Ladies in the Park, pen/ink/watercolor on paper, sgn, 12x8", C-E 10/25/88 ... **825**
SUR, Henry Victor (French, 1863-)
eturning From the Flower Market, oil on panel, sgn, 18x21", C-NY 10/25/89 ... **6,600**
TCHWORTH, William (20th C)
amp, acrylic on canvas, sgn/dtd 1976, unfr, 28x38", C-E 5/13/88 UE ... **176**
THIERE, Guillon (French, 1760-1832)
hadow Painting, pen/black ink/brown wash/gold paint heightened w/white, sgn, unfr, 8x11", C-NY 10/31/89 ... **275**
TO, Antonio; called Leto De Capri (Italian, 1844-1913)
t the Well, oil on canvas, sgn/inscr, unfr, 14x21", C-NY 2/25/88 ... **8,250**
U, August Wilhelm (German, 1819-1897)
ountain Lake, oil on canvas, sgn/dtd 1869, unfr, 35x49", SBY 12/9/88 OE ... **9,075**
U, Oscar (German, 1864-)
ill Beside a River, oil on canvas, sgn, 28x38", C-E 2/21/89 ... **1,760**
URS, J.K. (Dutch)
olden September (cattle in landscape), oil on canvas, sgn, 18x24", FB 4/25/88 ... **2,100**
URS, Johannes Karel (Dutch, 1865-1938)
arm Scene (cattle in landscape, buildings beyond), oil on canvas, sgn, 18x24", FB 5/89 UE ... **1,100**
UTZE, Emmanuel Gottlieb (American, 1816-1868)
waiting Her Lover, oil on canvas, sgn/inscr/dtd 1840, 25x30", C-NY 12/2/88 ... **8,250**
ood Nymph (draped nude seated in forest landscape), oil on canvas, sgn/dtd 1855, 57x42" UE ... **7,000**
UUS, Jesus Mariano (Mexican, 20th C)
ombre Comiendo Sandia (abstract figure), oil on masonite, sgn/dtd Mex 1960, 17x13", C-NY 11/21/89 ... **1,650**
ombre Comiendo Sandia (abstract man eating watermelon), oil on masonite, sgn/dtd 1960, 17x13", C-NY 11/21/88 OE ... **4,180**
ujer y Nina (woman & child, contemporary), oil on masonite, sgn/dtd 62, 21x13", C-NY 11/21/89 ... **2,860**
air: Campesinos (contemporary); acrylic on masonite, sgn/dtd Mexico 66 & Mexico 67, 24x25", 20x24", SBY 11/21/88 ... **3,025**
VEBRE, Jules Joseph; att (19th C)
oung Girl in a Boat, oil on canvas, bears signature/dtd 1879, 43x33", SBY 12/9/88 ... **2,750**
VER, H. (Continental, 19th C)
ottage by a Lake at Sunset, oil on canvas, sgn, 9x11", FAP 4/15/89 ... **250**
VER, Henry
icnic, watercolor, sgn, 8x10", FB 10/30/89 ... **550**
VER, Richard Hayley (American, 1876-1958)
athing Machines, St Ives, Cornwall; oil on canvas, sgn, ca 1910, 18x24", SBY 9/14/89 ... **7,150**
attersea Bridge, Thames, London; watercolor/pencil, sgn/titled, 10x14", SWN 12/1/88 ... **660**
eachcroft Beach, Gloucester (figures on beach, sailboats beyond); mixed media, sgn, 11x15", C-NY 9/28/89 ... **4,400**
eached Boats, Late Afternoon; oil on canvasboard, sgn, 6x9", RWS 11/10/89 ... **1,500**
ellville, oil on canvas, sgn/inscr, 16x20", C-NY 5/26/88 ... **6,600**
oathouse, watercolor, sgn, 16x18", DM 5/13/88 ... **700**
oating on a Lake, oil on board, sgn, 8x11", SBY 4/14/89 ... **660**
oats, Cornwall (port scene); watercolor/black crayon on paper, sgn/inscr Cornwall England, 15x19", SBY 4/14/89 ... **2,310**
oats at Dock, watercolor on paper, initialed, 18x22", SBY 1/24/89 ... **1,320**
oats in Harbor, watercolor, sgn, 8x11", DM 1/15/88 ... **900**
reezy (group of sailboats in water), oil on canvas laid down on masonite, sgn, 10x12", C-E 6/1/89 OE ... **7,700**
rittany Harbor Scene, Fishing Boats Docking; oil on canvas laid down on board, sgn, 8x10", SBY 9/14/89 ... **1,320**
usy Harbor Scene, watercolor on paper, sgn, 15x19", C-E 6/1/88 ... **1,540**
harenton Near Paris, oil on canvas, sgn/dtd 02, 18x24", C-E 10/18/89 ... **4,400**
ity Island Yacht Yard, oil on panel, sgn/inscr/dtd 1946, 8x10", C-E 6/1/88 ... **880**
oastal Landscape, oil on canvas, sgn, 9x13", C-SK 11/10/88 OE ... **2,420**
rawbridge, Westchester, New York; oil on board, sgn, 10x12", SBY 9/23/88 ... **1,320**
ntrance to City Island, oil on canvasboard, sgn twice, 24x18", C-E 6/1/88 ... **1,320**
vening in the Harbour (St Ives, Cornwall), oil on canvas, sgn/#d 11, 18x24", C-SK 5/25/89 OE ... **12,860**
xmouth, England; black crayon on paper, initialed, 8x9", C-E 2/16/88 UE ... **55**
loral Still Life, oil on canvas, sgn, 20x16", SBY 6/24/88 ... **4,400**

Gloucester, oil on canvas, sgn, 40x50", C-NY 9/30/88 28,600
Gloucester (cityscape), oil on canvas laid down on board, sgn, 13x16", C-NY 9/28/89 4,400
Gloucester Harbor at Sunset, oil on canvasboard, sgn, 6x9", SBY 1/24/89 1,210
Hamburg Cove, oil on canvas, sgn, 18x22", C-E 11/30/88 3,300
Harbor Scene, watercolor on paper, sgn, 14x16", C-E 9/15/88 1,210
Harbor Scene at Menemsha, watercolor/India ink on paper, sgn/inscr/dtd 1931, 17x21", SBY 6/24/88 1,210
Haystacks-England; oil on canvas, sgn, 11x14", C-E 6/1/88 1,320
High Bridge, oil on canvas, sgn, 16x20", SBY 5/25/88 UE 9,900
Irises (floral still life), oil on canvasboard, sgn, 12x31", C-E 2/1/89 1,320
Landscape with Barn, oil on canvas, sgn, 26x24", SBY 9/14/89 3,300
Landscape with Stone Wall, oil on canvas, sgn, 16x20", C-E 11/30/88 2,420
Marblehead, oil on board, sgn/inscr, 18x24", C-NY 9/30/88 OE 24,000
Monhegan Island, oil on canvasboard, sgn, 25x30", C-NY 5/26/88 9,350
Monhegen Island, Maine; oil on panel, 1941, 8x10", C-NY 9/28/89 3,300
Nantucket, oil on canvas, sgn twice/inscr/dtd 1929, 18x24", C-NY 9/30/88 4,400
Nantucket Scallop Boats, oil on board, sgn, 8x10", SBY 4/14/89 605
New England House, oil on canvas, 20x24", C-NY 9/30/88 5,500
New Rochelle, oil on canvasboard, sgn twice, 14x16", C-E 6/1/88 1,100
New York Harbor, oil on canvasboard, sgn, 12x16", C-E 6/1/88 UE 1,870
Path Through the Woods, Caldwell, New Jersey; oil on board, sgn twice/inscr, 8x11", SBY 1/24/89 715
Pittsburgh, Pennsylvania 1916; oil on board, sgn/titled, 19x23", SBY 1/24/89 8,250
Racetrack (race in progress), oil on canvas, sgn, 10x12", RAB 8/9/88 UE 1,600
Reaching the Boat, St Ives; oil on masonite, sgn/dtd 1911, 13x16", SBY 6/24/88 2,530
Reflecting Stream, oil on canvas, sgn twice/inscr/dtd 1929, 14x18", C-E 6/1/88 1,320
Safe Harbor, oil on canvas, sgn, 24x36", C-NY 5/26/88 OE 28,600
Sailboats, oil on canvas, sgn, 7x10", C-E 11/30/88 1,100
Sailboats at the Dock, watercolor on paper, sgn, 8x11", C-E 11/8/88 462
Sailboats in a Cove, watercolor on paper, sgn/dtd 1926, 9x19", SBY 3/17/88 1,045
Say It with Flowers, oil on board, sgn/dtd 1934, 18x14", C-E 11/30/88 2,200
Sea Mist, Gloucester, Massachusetts (view of docks & ships in the mist); oil on canvas, sgn, 24x30", SBY 1/24/89 UE 4,950
Ship Building, Gloucester, Massachusetts; watercolor on paper, sgn, 17x20", SBY 3/17/88 1,100
Sky & Water, Cornwall; oil on canvas, sgn, ca 1908, 12x16", C-NY 3/11/88 6,600
Spring Blossoms (landscape), oil on board, 22x30", C-NY 5/26/88 6,600
Still Life (fruit), watercolor/pencil on paper, sgn, 16x21", RWS 11/3/88 750
Still Life of Cantaloupes & Pears, oil on canvas, sgn, 14x28", C-E 11/30/88 2,090
Still Life of Fruit, watercolor on paper, sgn, 14x20", FAP 4/15/89 770
Summer Flowers in a Glass, oil on canvas, sgn, 14x11", SBY 9/23/88 UE 550
Sunset, New Jersey; oil on canvasboard, sgn/indistinctly dtd, 5x6", C-E 11/8/88 UE 330
Surf, oil on canvas, sgn/dtd 1934, 24x36", SBY 6/28/89 OE 11,550
View of New York Harbor, oil on board, sgn/inscr/dtd 1928, 12x16", C-NY 3/11/88 7,150
Washington Square, pencil on paper, sgn, 4x6", C-E 2/16/88 UE 66
Washington Square Park (sketch), pencil on paper, sgn/initialed, no size given, C-E 6/1/89 880
Yacht Race, Nantucket; watercolor/brush/black ink/pencil on paper, sgn/dtd 1929, 14x21", C-E 11/30/88 3,850
Yachts Leaving Marblehead, oil on canvas, sgn, 24x36", C-NY 9/28/89 18,700
Zinnias, oil on canvas, sgn/dtd 1956, 20x24", C-NY 9/30/88 2,750

LEVI, Julian E. (American, 1900-)

Still Life with Flowers in a Vase, watercolor on paper, sgn/dtd 1929, 16x13", SBY 1/24/89 1,760

LEVICK, Milnes (American, 1887-)

Carnival, oil on canvas, sgn, 23x26", B/B 9/15/88 412
Fruit Stalls Under the El, oil on canvas, initialed, 12x17", B/B 9/15/88 440

LEVIER, Charles (American, 1920-)

Fleur sur la Plage (floral still life with boat on beach beyond), oil on canvas, sgn, 30x24", B/B 5/17/89 495
Fleurs et Feuilles, oil on canvas, sgn twice/inscr, 30x16", C-E 5/13/88 OE 660
Floral Still Life with Harbor, watercolor on paper, sgn, 20x15", B/B 5/17/89 UE 385
La Chaise Rouge, oil on canvas, sgn, 30x24", FB 5/28/89 900
Nature Morte aux Oignons (still life w/onions), oil on canvas, sgn, 30x40", SBY 10/7/89 2,200
Port, oil on canvas, sgn twice, 30x40", SBY 10/5/88 2,200
Village Corse (modernistic depiction), oil on canvas, sgn, 30x40", SBY 2/14/89 OE 3,300

LEVIEUX, Reynier (Reynaud)(French, 1613-1694)

Saint Catherine Before the Virgin & Child, oil on canvas, arched top, 48x35", C-NY 1/15/88 7,700

LEVIKOVA, Bela (Russian, 1939-)

Struggle (abstract), oil on canvas, initialed/dtd 77, 50x45", SBY 7/7/88 4,000
Three Dimensions (abstract), oil on canvas, initialed/dtd 78-80, 45x52", SBY 7/7/88 5,000
4th of May, 1978 (abstract); oil on canvas, initialed/dtd 78, 45x37", SBY 7/7/88 4,800

LEVINE, David (American, 1926-)

Birthday Greetings, watercolor/pen/black ink on paper, sgn, 7x8", C-NY 6/17/89 OE 605
Brighton Beach, watercolor on paper, initialed, 5x10", C-NY 6/17/89 OE 1,870
Connecticut Scene, sepia ink/wash, sgn/dtd 1959, 7x13", PHL 10/28/88 UE 100
Cuban Literature, pen/ink, sgn/dtd 1968, 10x7", SWN 12/1/88 358
Kneeling, charcoal on paper, sgn/dtd 63, 11x8", C-NY 6/17/89 OE 605
Noel Coward, pen/black ink on paper, sgn/dtd 68, 14x11", C-NY 3/11/88 550

'air: Bukharin; John Dean; pen/ink on paper, both sgn, 1 dtd 74, 15x12" & smaller, C-E 11/30/88 UE	**660**
'air: Man with Cat; Portrait of a Dog; oil on board, initialed, 10x8", 3x3", C-NY 6/17/89 OE	**11,000**
Jnder the Pier, oil on panel, sgn, 5x8", C-NY 6/17/89 OE	**4,620**
VINE, Jack (American, 1915-)	
Adam & Eve, oil on panel, sgn/dtd 51, 12x8", SBY 6/24/88 OE	**18,150**
Chief, wht pastel on gray paper, sgn, 19x25", SBY 6/28/89 OE	**2,090**
Expulsion (abstract), oil on canvas, sgn, 1951, 20x28", SBY 1/24/89 OE	**15,400**
Girl in Blue (portrait), oil on canvas, sgn, 20x16", SBY 3/17/88	**9,900**
Girl with Red Hair, oil on canvas, sgn, 32x26", C-NY 3/11/88OE	**6,050**
Great Society, oil on canvas, sgn, 1967, 56x64", SBY 5/25/88 OE	**93,500**
n the Valley of Kidron, oil on panel, sgn, ca 1982-83, 10x8", SBY 9/23/88	**7,700**
acob Wrestling with the Angel, oil on canvas, sgn, 1975, 40x35", SBY 9/23/88	**11,550**
King Saul, oil on panel, sgn, 1952, 12x9", SBY 9/23/88 OE	**15,400**
Portrait of Joan, (half-length nude), oil on canvas, sgn, 32x26", C-E 2/3/88	**9,020**
Rabbi in Discussion, brown wash on buff paper, sgn, 12x13", SBY 9/23/88	**935**
Reception in Miami: A Study; sepia ink on paper, sgn, 14x18", SBY 3/17/88	**1,650**
Three Graces, oil on canvas, sgn, ca 1959, 21x24", C-NY 3/11/88 OE	**33,000**
Titian Misremembered, oil on canvas, sgn, 21x24", C-NY 3/11/88 OE	**15,400**
Tombstone Cutter, oil on canvas, sgn, 1947, 36x30", SBY 9/23/88 OE	**11,550**
Two Black Crows (caricatures of Leverett Saltonstall & Paul A Deven), ink on paper, sgn, 8x10", RWS 9/29/88 UE	**100**
Volpone (a study), brush/brown ink on paper, sgn, 11x17", C-NY 6/17/89 OE	**2,200**
Volpone at San Marco (depicts three characters from play, Volpone), oil on canvas, sgn, 1977, 40x35", SBY 5/24/89	**46,750**
Young Girl, ink on paper, sgn, 8x5", RWS 3/16/89 UE	**300**
Young Justinian (half-length portrait), oil/gold paint on board, sgn, 1948, 20x8", SBY 6/28/89	**6,875**
VINE, Les (American, 1935-)	
Diamond Mine (bird print w/inscription), lead/wood/velvet/enamel, sgn/dtd 1978, 43x31", C-NY 5/4/89	**3,300**
VINE, Sherrie (20th C)	
After Willem de Kooning, charcoal on paper, sgn/dtd 1981, 14x11", SBY 2/15/89 OE	**7,700**
White Knot #2, casein on plywood, 1986, 30x24", C-NY 11/10/88 OE	**14,300**
VIS, Maurice (French, 1860-1902)	
Debarkation at Dinard, France; oil on canvas, sgn, 22x15", C-NY 5/25/88	**9,900**
Leloir a Roche-Marie (landscape), oil on panel, sgn/dtd 95, 9x14", C-NY 2/23/89	**4,400**
Les Ruines d'Herisson (landscape), oil on canvas, sgn, 13x16", C-NY 2/23/89	**5,500**
Sacred Pond, Trichinopoly, Southern India (figures in water, dwellings on shore); oil, sgn/inscr, 20x29", C-SK 5/25/89	**3,310**
Un Mare a Gournay (landscape), oil on canvas, sgn, 12x16", C-NY 2/23/89	**6,050**
Young Fisherman By a Woodland Stream, oil on canvas, sgn, 12x17", WAD 6/6/88	**1,900**
VITAN, Isaak Il'ich (Russian, 1860-1900)	
Sunlit Wood in Autumn, oil on canvas, inscr in Russian, 19x14", C-L 10/8/88 OE	**16,730**
VRAC-TOURNIERES, Robert (French, 1667-1752)	
Portrait of an Elegant Gentleman (three-quarter length), oil on canvas, 32x25", SBY 4/7/89	**7,700**
VRAC-TOURNIERES, Robert; att (French, 1667-1752)	
Portrait of a Gentleman in Armor, oil on canvas, oval, 27x20", SBY 10/21/88	**6,600**
VRAC-TOURNIERES, Robert; school of (French, 1667-1752)	
Portrait of a Gentleman, half-length, wearing an embroidered yellow jacket; oil on canvas, 32x25", C-NY 4/6/89	**1,980**
VY, Alexander O. (American, 1881-1947)	
Farm Stand (figures in roadside stand), oil on canvas, sgn, 40x41", SBY 3/17/88 UE	**1,430**
Two Women Bathing in a Stream (in an extensive landscape), oil on canvas, sgn/dtd 1914, 19x16", WG 4/23/88	**850**
Watching Fulton's Folly, oil on canvas, sgn, 36x26", SBY 9/23/88 UE	**990**
VY, Henry L. (French, 1840-1904)	
Kitchen Table, oil on canvas, sgn, 36x28", C-E 6/1/89 UE	**550**
VY, Jule Benoit	
Distractions, oil on canvas, sgn, 29x37", C-E 5/23/88	**2,750**
VY, Nat (American, 1896-1984)	
Gossipers, watercolor on paper, sgn, 17x23", B/B 10/6/88	**2,475**
Old Blacksmith Shop, watercolor on paper, sgn, 21x29", B/B 10/6/88	**1,870**
VY-DHURMER, Lucien (French, 1865-1953)	
Fantasmagorie (depiction of Tchaikovsky's Swan Lake), oil on canvas, sgn, ca 1900-05, 62x94", SBY 10/24/89 OE	**264,000**
Painting the Odalisque, pastel on paper, sgn, 18x24", SBY 5/23/89	**13,200**
Veiled Women: North Africa (impressionistic); pastel on paper, 22x33", SBY 2/22/89	**33,000**
WANDOWSKI, Edmund D. (American, 1914-)	
Grain Elevators (rural structures in landscape), oil on board, sgn/dtd 1940, 19x24", RWS 9/29/88 OE	**4,250**
WG, James (American, 19th C)	
Fruit Basket, oil on canvas, sgn/dtd 1891, 12x18", LH 9/10/89 OE	**275**
WIN, Stephen (British, 20th C)	
Sailboats at the Shore, watercolor on paper, sgn, unfr, 7x10", WL 5/20/88 UE	**75**
WIS, Charles James (British, 1830-1892)	
Ferry Crossing on an English River, oil on canvas, sgn, 16x31", B/B 12/8/88	**770**
WIS, Edmund Darch (American, 1835-1910)	
Approaching Shore, watercolor on paper, sgn, 16x28", FAP 12/8/89	**775**
Atlantic City, New Jersey; watercolor/gouache on paper, sgn/dtd 1879, 9x7", SBY 3/17/88	**1,760**
Atlantic City, watercolor/pencil on paper laid down on board, sgn/dtd 1909, 15x30", C-E 10/18/89	**3,520**

Cascade, oil on canvas, sgn/dtd 1905, 24x49", C-NY 9/30/88 UE 2,200
Coastal Inlet, New England Scene; oil on canvas, sgn/dtd 1877, unfr, 14x22", RWS 11/10/89 OE 3,000
Coastal Landscape, oil on canvas, sgn/dtd 1894, unfr, 25x71", SBY 9/23/88 2,200
Coastal View, watercolor/gouache on paper, sgn/dtd 1887, 9x19", SBY 3/17/88 715
Connecticut Valley, oil on canvas, sgn/dtd 1881, 18x32", C-E 6/1/88 5,280
Conversation (two figures by a fence in river landscape), oil on canvas, sgn/dtd 79, 18x25", C-E 2/1/89 3,300
Eastern Coastline, watercolor/gouache on paper, sgn/dtd 1894, 9x19", B/B 6/9/88 605
Evening on Lake Como, oil on canvas, sgn/dtd 1875, 33x60", WD 10/5/88 9,000
Fishing on the River, oil on canvas, sgn/dtd 1871, 11x19", B/B 10/9/88 3,300
Haystack in an Open Field, watercolor on paper, sgn/dtd 1874, 8x12", FAP 11/4/88 260
Indian Rock, Narrangansett (waves crashing on rocks); watercolor/gouache/pencil on board, sgn/dtd 1880, C-E 6/1/89 OE 2,090
Lazy Sunday (landscape), oil on canvas, sgn/dtd 1874, 30x50", C-NY 9/30/88 10,450
Moonlight Walk, watercolor/gouache on board, sgn/dtd 1887, 12x25", SBY 2/3/88 660
Mountainous Landscape, oil on canvas laid down on board, sgn/dtd 1888, 40x55", WD 4/13/88 5,000
Mountainous Landscape with Cattle Herder, oil on canvas, sgn/dtd 1867, 28x44", SBY 3/17/88 5,500
Mountainous Landscape with Men Fishing by Mill, oil on canvas laid down on panel, sgn, 30x50", FAP 4/15/89 3,630
Off Coast Sailing, watercolor on board, sgn/dtd 1882, 20x29", C-E 6/1/88 1,980
Pair: Mill in the Andirondacks & Sunset in Berkshires; oil on canvas, sgn/dtd 1875, 20x30", SBY 4/14/89 3,300
Pair: Views Across Mountain Lakes; watercolor/gouache on tan paper, sgn/dtd 1886 & 1884, 16x12", RWS 5/19/88 UE 1,500
Rising Moon, watercolor/gouache on paper, sgn/dtd 1881, 10x19", C-E 2/3/88 770
River Landscape, oil on canvas, sgn/dtd 1881, no size given, FAP 4/15/89 1,595
Rocky Coast with Sailing Ships at Sunset, oil on canvas, sgn, 12x19", FAP 12/8/89 1,850
Rowing on a River, watercolor/gouache on paper, sgn/dtd 1888, 13x26", C-E 6/1/88 UE 550
Sailing Off the Rocky Coast (sailboats & cliffs), watercolor on paper, sgn/dtd 1905), RAB 8/9/88 UE 650
Serene, watercolor on paper, sgn/dtd 1894, 27x35", C-E 4/7/88 UE 880
Ships in the Harbor, watercolor/gouache on paper, sgn/dtd 1887, 12x25", B/B 1/11/89 UE 550
Statue of Liberty, watercolor heightened w/gouache on paper, sgn/dtd 1890, 9x10", C-E 6/1/88 715
Stream Fishing, oil on canvas, sgn/dtd 1871, 30x50", C-E 11/30/88 3,520
Summer Landscape with Cows, watercolor on paper, sgn/dtd 1893, 9x21", SBY 9/14/89 935
Summer View of Valley with Distant River, watercolor on paper, sgn/dtd 1891, 9x20", SBY 9/14/89 1,320
Travelers by a Mountain Stream, watercolor heightened w/gouache, indistinctly sgn/dtd 1888, 23x12", C-E 2/3/88 UE 220
Waterfalls, watercolor on board, sgn/dtd 1888, 20x10", FAP 4/15/89 550
Wave, frothy ocean waves w/rocky coast in distance; watercolor/gouache on paper, sgn/dtd 1902, 22x34", RAB 3/27/89 UE 300
Windjammers Along the Coast, watercolor/gouache on paper, sgn/dtd 1881, 16x27", RAB 3/27/89 950
Yacht Races Newport, Rhode Island; watercolor on paper, sgn, 9x20", RAB 11/24/89 2,500
Young Boy Fishing, oil on canvas, sgn/dtd 1873, 30x20", C-E 6/1/88 3,740

LEWIS, Edmund Darch; manner of (American, 1835-1910)
Lake View, oil on canvas, bears signature, 22x35", FAP 4/15/89 1,155

LEWIS, Harry Emerson (American, 1892-1958)
Avila Adobe, watercolor/pencil on paper, sgn/dtd 33, 8x10", B/B 10/6/88 468
Shrimp Boilers, oil on canvas, sgn, 20x24", B/B 10/6/88 715

LEWIS, J. (British, 19th C)
Mickelham, Surrey (road w/figures & dwellings on a hillside), oil on canvas, sgn twice, 19x30", SBY 12/9/88 1,320

LEWIS, John Frederick (British, 1805-1876)
Frank Encampment in the Desert of Mount Sinai, oil on panel, sgn/dtd 1862, 16x32", SBY 5/23/89 UE 550,000
Kibab Shop, Scutari, Asia Minor; oil on panel, sgn/dtd 1858, inscr label on verso, 21x31", SBY 2/22/88 1,100,000
Landscape with Man Crossing Stream, oil on canvas, sgn, 14x18", FAP 11/4/88 400

LEWISHOHN, Rafael (German, 1863-1923)
Church Prayer, oil on canvas, sgn/dtd 91, 39x45", LH 9/10/89 UE 375

LEWITT, Sol (American, 1928-)
Arcs From Four Sides & Grid, pen/black ink on paper, sgn/inscr/dtd 1972, 13x13", C-NY 5/4/88 3,850
Blue, Red, Yellow, Black Arcs From Opposite Corners; pen/colored inks on paper, sgn/dtd 12-28-71, 11x11", C-NY 2/20/88 3,850
Forms Derived From a Cube (geometric composition), gouache/pencil on paper, sgn/dtd 1982, 22x22", SBY 5/3/89 5,500
Four-Color Line Drawing w/Progressively Wider Spaces Between, colored pencil on paper, sgn/dtd 72, 11x8", C-NY 2/14/89 1,650
Plans for Wall-Drawing, Apartment of Francoise Essellier...; ink on paper on linen, sgn/1970, 14x14", C-NY 2/14/89 OE 24,200
Untitled (contemporary design), India ink wash on paper, sgn/dtd 1986, 2-sided 5-panel screen, 72x150", C-NY 5/4/89 OE 57,200
Untitled (four geometric shapes), ink wash on paper, sgn, dtd 10/82, 22x22", SBY 11/11/88 OE 10,450
Untitled (working drawing, Come & Go), ink on paper, sgn/dtd 1969, 16x22", SBY 2/15/89 OE 2,750
Untitled (working drawing), ink on paper, sgn/dtd April 1969, 16x22", SBY 10/5/89 OE 3,850

LEYENDECKER, Frank Xavier (American, 1877-1924)
Greek Athlete, oil on canvas, 36x26", SBY 6/28/89 OE 4,125
Juggler, gouache on board, indistinctly sgn, 13x9", C-E 6/1/88 990
Kiss (couple w/in scrolled framework), gouache on paper, 20x14", SBY 6/28/89 OE 7,975
Letter (two men & lady by floor screen), gouache on paper, 21x15", SBY 6/28/89 OE 7,700
Mirror (maid dresses lady's hair), gouache on paper, sgn, 21x14", SBY 6/28/89 OE 7,975

LEYENDECKER, Joseph Christian (American, 1874-1951)
At Your Service, oil on canvas, initialed, 22x20", C-NY 9/28/89 OE 28,600
Flowers for the Lady, oil on canvas laid down on board, 27x20", C-NY 9/30/88 13,200
Gentleman (in profile, half-length, w/cane under arm), oil on canvas, 34x21", C-E 2/1/89 UE 770
In the Forest, gouache/black ink/charcoal on paper, sgn, C-E 6/1/88 1,760
Kuppenheimer Good Clothes, 1876; oil on canvas, 26x20", C-NY 9/30/88 6,600

Kuppenheimer Good Clothes, 1926; oil on canvas laid down on board, 27x20", C-NY 9/30/88 OE **12,100**
Start of a Race (boy shooting gun in air, little girl holding her ears), oil on canvas, sgn, 26x21", SBY 9/14/89 ..... **16,500**
Sunday Job, oil on canvas, sgn, 26x22", C-NY 9/30/88 ..... **9,350**

LEYENDECKER, Mathias (German, 1822-1871)
Hanging Game, oil on canvas, sgn/dtd 1870, unfr, 34x22", SBY 6/8/88 UE **1,045**

LEYSTER, Judith (Dutch, 1600-1660)
Concert (two gentlemen playing instruments, lady seated in middle), oil on canvas, ca 1633, 24x34", SBY 6/1/89 ..... **143,000**
Laughing Children with a Cat, oil on canvas, sgn w/monogram, dtd 1629(?), 24x21", C-NY 1/11/89 OE **528,000**

LHERMITTE, Leon Augustin (French, 1844-1925)
Au Bord de la Riviere (At the Edge of the River), pastel on paper, sgn, 28x36", SBY 5/23/89 ..... **82,500**
Cottage by a River, pastel on paper, sgn, 10x13", SBY 5/23/89 ..... **12,100**
Enfants a la Grotte (children by a cave tending sheep), pastel, sgn, 9x12", C-NY 10/26/88 OE **26,400**
Gleaners, oil on canvas, sgn, 20x30", C-NY 2/3/88 OE **71,500**
Gleaners, pastel, 16x25", C-NY 5/25/88 OE **35,200**
Harvesters (couple resting in field, river, hill beyond), pastel on paper, sgn, 22x17", SBY 10/24/89 ..... **27,500**
Harvesting in Late Afternoon, oil on canvas, sgn, 26x33", SBY 5/23/89 ..... **88,000**
In From the Fields, pastel on paper, sgn, 1905, 16x20", SBY 10/24/89 ..... **27,500**
Laveuses des Bords de la Marne, pastel on paper, sgn, 19x26", SBY 2/22/89 ..... **60,500**
Le Temps des Moissons, pastel on paper, sgn, 10x13", SBY 10/24/89 ..... **8,800**
Le Troupeau au Bord de l'Eau (cows watering), pastel on paper laid down on canvas, 36x48", C-NY 10/26/88 OE **59,400**
Manoir dans le Berry, pastel on paper, sgn, 10x12", SBY 2/22/89 ..... **7,700**
Paysans Bouvant (men drinking at table), black chalk on laid paper, sgn, 10x15", C-NY 2/23/89 ..... **4,180**
Pres de la Fontaine, oil on canvas, sgn, 35x44", SBY 2/22/89 ..... **55,000**
Puiseuses d'Eau (landscape w/two women getting water from a stream), oil on canvas, sgn, 21x16", C-NY 10/25/89 ..... **66,000**
Reaper (landscape w/figure), pastel on paper, sgn, 16x22", SBY 5/23/89 ..... **28,600**
Road to the Cathedral, pastel on paper, sgn, 13x10", SBY 2/22/89 ..... **6,600**
Shepherd & Flock at Rest on a Riverbank, pastel on paper on stretched canvas, sgn, 18x21", C-NY 10/26/88 ..... **31,900**
Une Vachere Pres d'une Village (village landscape w/cows & figure), pastel on paper, sgn, 28x36", SBY 5/23/89 ..... **55,000**
Washerwoman (in a landscape w/village beyond), oil on canvas, sgn, 21x30", C-NY 2/3/88 ..... **46,200**

LHOTE, Andre (French, 1885-1962)
Colloque des Muses (woman in a landscape), oil on paper laid down on canvas, sgn, 1909, 25x32", C-NY 5/11/89 ..... **77,000**
Femme dans un Interieur (woman seated in an interior), pastel on paper, sgn, 15x11", C-NY 10/6/88 ..... **3,850**
Femme Endormie (sleeping woman), pastel on gray paper, stamped, 1925, 19x25", C-NY 10/5/89 OE **19,800**
Femme Nue (female nude), oil on canvas, sgn, ca 1929, 16x21", C-NY 10/6/88 ..... **7,150**
Femme Nue Allongee, oil on paper, sgn, 23x27", C-NY 10/6/88 ..... **17,600**
Femme Nue Allongee (reclining female nude), oil on canvas, sgn, 14x18", C-NY 10/6/88 OE **14,300**
Femme Nue Assise (seated nude), oil on burlap, sgn, 36x29", C-NY 2/16/89 OE **22,000**
Femme Nue en Buste (portrait), oil on paper laid down on canvas, sgn, ca 1925, 30x24", SBY 10/7/88 ..... **13,200**
Femme Nue se Coiffant (abstract nude), oil on canvas, sgn, 29x20", SBY 10/7/88 ..... **15,400**
Figures in an Interior, pastel on paper, sgn twice, 20x26", SBY 10/5/88 ..... **9,350**
L'Architecture, oil/gouache on paper laid down on canvas, sgn, 33x47", C-NY 5/12/88 ..... **35,200**
L'Homme Nu (cubistic male nude), oil on paper laid down on canvas, sgn, 1929, 46x35", SBY 10/6/89 ..... **55,000**
L'Interieur (contemporary depiction of kitchen interior), gouache on paper, sgn, 15x11", SBY 10/7/89 ..... **4,400**
La Cuisine (contemporary view of artist's kitchen), oil on canvas, sgn, ca 1945, 24x20", C-NY 2/18/88 ..... **13,200**
Landscape, pastel on blue paper, sgn/inscr CA, 9x11", SBY 10/5/88 ..... **1,650**
Le Nile, gouache over pencil on paper, sgn, ca 1952, 15x23", C-NY 10/6/88 ..... **4,400**
Maison dans un Paysage (house in a landscape), gouache over pencil on paper, sgn, 12x16", C-NY 10/5/89 ..... **11,000**
Nature Morte (abstract still life), oil on burlap, sgn, ca 1958, 22x18", C-NY 5/12/88 ..... **18,700**
Nu Allonge (reclining nude), oil on canvas, sgn, 26x32", C-NY 5/12/88 ..... **38,500**
Nu Couche (reclining nude), oil on canvas, sgn, 1935, 20x29", C-NY 2/18/88 ..... **17,600**
Nu Rythme (abstract nude), oil on canvas, sgn, 1946, C-NY 2/16/89 ..... **26,400**
Nue Deploye (abstract figure), oil on canvas, sgn/dtd 53, 29x36", SBY 2/18/88 ..... **15,400**
Paris Etude Directe (oil study of Paris), oil on canvas, sgn, ca 1930, 32x24", P 11/15/88 ..... **11,000**
Paysage (abstract landscape), gouache on paper laid down on canvas, sgn, 26x20", SBY 10/7/88 ..... **13,200**
Paysage a Cliouselat (landscape), gouache/watercolor/pen/black ink over pencil on paper, sgn, 1930, 8x12", C-NY 10/5/89 ..... **7,700**
Paysage Parisien (modernistic Parisian landscape), oil on paper laid down on canvas, sgn/dtd 1909, 26x21", SBY 10/6/89 ..... **44,000**
Plage: Deux Figures Etendues; charcoal on paper laid down on board, sgn, ca 1928, 14x19", SBY 2/16/89 ..... **6,050**
Port de Bordeaux (14 Juillet), oil on canvas, sgn, 1913-14, 26x32", C-NY 5/11/89 ..... **165,000**
Portrait de Femme au Piano, oil on paper laid down on canvas, sgn, 1930, 47x29", C-NY 2/18/88 ..... **33,000**
Portrait de Jeune Femme, oil on canvas, sgn/dtd 1924, 37x29", C-NY 5/11/89 ..... **44,000**
Portrait of a Woman, pastel on paper, sgn, 25x18", SBY 10/5/88 OE **4,675**
Reclining Nude, pencil on paper, sgn, 9x12", SBY 10/7/89 ..... **1,540**
Sailing Vessels & Dolphins, oil on canvas, in painted oval, 17x27", C-NY 12/2/88 ..... **12,100**
Scene de Village, watercolor on paper laid down on board, sgn, 15x22", SBY 2/16/89 ..... **7,700**
St Tropez (modernistic port scene), watercolor over pencil on paper, sgn, ca 1936, 15x22", SBY 10/6/89 ..... **11,000**
Terrasse du Cafe Crouchard a Toulon, watercolor/gouache over pencil on paper, sgn, ca 1931, 9x12", SBY 10/6/89 OE **19,800**
Toulon (monderistic port scene), watercolor on paper, sgn, 1920, 15x23", SBY 10/6/89 ..... **11,000**
Two Bathers, watercolor/gouache/graphite on paper, sgn/dtd -25, 8x7", B/B 12/8/88 ..... **1,430**
View of Mirmonde, watercolor/pen/ink on paper laid down on board, 10x17", SBY 10/7/89 ..... **6,600**
Vue de Village (Gironde), watercolor/pencil on paper backed with paper, sgn, 14x21", SBY 10/7/88 ..... **11,000**

LIBBEY, Walter
Self-Portrait, oil on canvas, dtd June 1847, 21x17", C-NY 5/26/88 5,50
LIBERI, Marco (1640-1725)
Allegory with a Woman & Two Putti, oil on canvas, unfr, 34x25", SBY 10/21/88 OE 2,75
LIBERI, Pietro (Italian, 1614-1687)
Mercury & Venus, oil on canvas, 63x94", SBY 6/1/89 OE 33,00
LIBERI, Pietro; att (Italian, 1614-1687)
Berenice Cutting Her Hair, oil on canvas, 40x32", SBY 10/21/88 OE 11,00
Seated Female Nude Seen From Back, Her Head in Profile; black/white chalk on gray paper, inscr, 16x11", C-NY 1/12/88 6,05
LIBERI, Pietro; circle of (Italian, 1614-1687)
Venus & Cupid (portrait), oil on canvas, unfr, 21x26", SBY 7/12/89 1,87
LIBERMAN, Alexander (American, 1912-)
Erg XVI, acrylic on canvas, sgn/inscr/dtd 77, 60x96", C-E 5/13/88 OE 7,48
Gate XVI (abstract), paper collage/acrylic/charcoal on canvas, sgn/dtd 81, 84x60", C-E 11/14/89 OE 9,35
Untitled (abstract, two sheets on one mount), acrylic/watercolor/charcoal, 1 sgn/dtd 81, 40x26", C-E 11/14/89 OE 4,62
Version (abstract), acrylic on canvas, sgn/dtd 76, unfr, 84x36", C-E 11/14/89 OE 4,95
LIBERT, Georg Emil (Danish, 1820-1908)
Cattle Watering, oil on canvas, sgn, 21x29", C-E 10/26/89 1,98
LICHTENHELD, Wilhelm (German, 1817-1891)
After the Schlosserhog Im Mondlicht, oil on canvas, monogramed/dtd 1879, 36x32", WD 5/5/88 4,00
LICHTENSTEIN, Roy (American, 1923-)
Apple (abstract, two paintings on same side of canvas), oil/magna on canvas, sgn/dtd 83, 36x50", C-NY 5/3/89 495,00
Apple & Grapefruit (composition), acrylic on canvas, sgn/dtd 80, 20x24", SBY 11/8/89 467,50
Ball of Twine, graphite on paper, sgn/dtd 63, 19x15", C-NY 2/20/88 18,70
Crying Girl, graphite/colored pencil on paper, initialed/dtd 64, 5x6", C-NY 2/23/89 242,00
Cup of Coffee (contemporary), oil on canvas, initialed/dtd 1961, 20x16", SBY 5/2/88 176,00
Diptych: Double Mirror (abstract); oil/magna on canvas, sgn/dtd 70, 66x36", C-NY 11/9/88 286,00
Duridium, magna on canvas, sgn/dtd 64, 26x36", SBY 5/2/89 OE 506,00
Entablature #7 (contemporary), oil/magna on canvas, sgn/dtd 71, 18x96", SBY 11/10/88 148,50
Haystack (contemporary), oil/magna on canvas, sgn/dtd 69, 16x24", SBY 5/2/88 99,00
Haystack (contemporary), oil/magna on canvas, sgn/dtd 69, 18x24", SBY 5/2/88 82,50
Hotdog, enamel on steel, sgn/dtd 1964/#d 4/10, 24x48", SBY 5/2/89 121,00

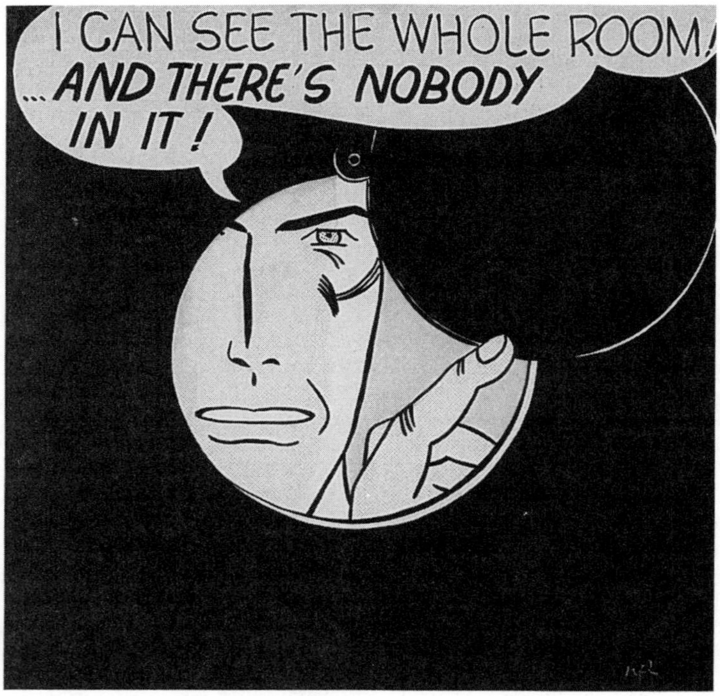

I Can See the Whole Room . . . & There's Nobody in It!, oil/graphite on canvas, initialed, 48x48", C-NY 11/9/88 OE; $2,090,000

Imperfect Painting (geometric composition), oil/magna on canvas, 1986, 83x79", SBY 5/2/89 OE 440,00
Laughing Cat (contemporary), oil on canvas, sgn/dtd 61, 32" dia, SBY 5/2/88 319,00
Leda & the Swan (contemporary), pencil/crayon on paper, initialed, 1968, 8x23", SBY 11/9/89 OE 231,00
Lion Skin, acrylic on canvas, sgn/dtd 67, 16x24", SBY 10/5/89 OE 242,00
Mirror (abstract), oil/magna on canvas, sgn/dtd 72, unfr, 36" dia, C-NY 5/3/88 154,00
Mirror (contemporary w/dots), oil/magna on canvas, sgn/dtd 70, 48" dia, SBY 5/2/88 OE 143,00
Mirror (contemporary), gouache/collage, 1970, 40x30", SBY 11/11/88 OE 110,00
Mirror (contemporary), oil/magna on canvas, sgn/dtd 71/inscr To Andy, 60x48", SBY 5/2/88 OE 286,00
On (light switch in yellow), oil on canvas, sgn/dtd 62, 28x18", SBY 5/2/89 OE 374,00

- Pink Sky (contemporary), plastic/magna on board, 1965, 27x15", C-NY 5/4/89 OE ... 44,000
- Sailboats (contemporary), oil/magna on canvas, sgn/dtd 74, 64x90", SBY 5/2/88 OE ... 605,000
- Sailboats III (abstract), oil/magna on canvas, sgn/dtd 74, 70x80", SBY 11/10/88 OE ... 1,320,000
- Seascape (abstract), rowlux/vinyl/paper collage, sgn, 1965, 6x8", SBY 2/19/88 ... 8,800
- Seductive Girl, graphite/colored pencils on paper, initialed, 1964, 6x6", C-NY 5/4/89 ... 154,000
- Setting Sun & Sea, enamel on steel, sgn/dtd 1964, 36x72", SBY 10/5/89 ... 132,000
- Setting Sun & Sea (contemporary), ed of 5, enamel on steel, sgn/dtd 1964, 36x72", SBY 5/2/88 OE ... 126,500
- Sponge II (hand w/yellow sponge making a swipe), oil on canvas, sgn/dtd 62, 36x36", SBY 5/2/89 OE ... 687,500
- Study for Abstract Painting (Morris Louis), colored pencil/graphite on paper, sgn/dtd 73, 6x5", C-NY 11/10/88 ... 16,500
- Study for Landscape, pencil/colored pencil on paper, initialed, 1964, 5x5", SBY 2/19/88 ... 8,250
- Study for Modern Painting with Ionic Column, graphite on paper, sgn/dtd 67, 27x34", SBY 11/19/89 OE ... 115,500
- Study for Still Life of Pitcher & Flowers, pencil/colored pencil on paper, 1973, S-7x9", SBY 5/3/88 ... 27,500
- Sunrise, enamel on steel, sgn/dtd 65, 23x36", SBY 10/8/88 ... 71,500
- Things on the Wall (contemporary), oil/magna on canvas, sgn/dtd 73, 60x74", C-NY 5/3/89 ... 1,012,000
- Those Two (contemporary), oil/magna on canvas, sgn/dtd 78, 50x60", SBY 5/2/88 ... 330,000
- Torpedo...Los (caricature drawing); oil on canvas, sgn/dtd 63, 68x80", C-NY 11/7/89 OE ... 5,500,000
- Untitled (yellow trash can w/woman's legs in red & white dress), oil on canvas, initialed, 1961, 18x16", SBY 10/5/89 OE ... 473,000

LIDDERDALE, Charles Sillem (British, 1831-1895)

- Girl Wearing a Bonnet, oil on canvas, initialed/dtd 79, 13x11", DM 2/19/88 ... 2,300
- Young Huntress (three-quarter length portrait), oil on canvas, monogramed/dtd 82, 36x27", C-NY 2/23/89 OE ... 8,250
- Young Maiden with a Dog in a Landscape, oil on canvas, sgn/dtd 80, C-E 10/25/88 UE ... 1,650

LIDSTONE, Arthur (Canadian, 1903-)

- Crashing Surf, oil on canvas, sgn, 12x15", WAD 6/12/89 UE ... 140

LIE, Jonas (American, 1880-1940)

- After the Snowfall (snow-laden tree), oil on canvas, sgn/dtd 08, 36x42", SBY 5/24/89 ... 19,800
- Birches (autumn river landscape), oil on canvas, sgn, 39x45", C-NY 5/25/89 OE ... 30,800
- Buy Liberty Bonds To Build Our Ships...: Study for War Bond Poster; oil, sgn/titled, ca 1936, 40x30", SBY 3/17/88 ... 3,300
- Figures on a Sailboat, oil on canvas, sgn, 35x42", C-NY 5/26/88 OE ... 37,400
- Gay Head (seascape with boats & shoreline), oil on canvas, sgn, 30x45", C-NY 12/2/88 ... 22,000
- Gray Dawn (harbor scene), oil on canvas, sgn, 21x32", WD 4/13/88 ... 4,800
- Maidens of the Forest, oil on canvas, sgn, 60x50", SBY 5/25/88 ... 17,600
- Sailboats Along the Coast, oil on canvas, sgn/dtd 24, 30x40", SBY 1/24/89 OE ... 25,300
- Southward, Idyll; oil on canvas, sgn/bears artist's estate stamp, 30x45", C-NY 9/30/88 ... 16,500
- Summer Landscape, oil on canvas, sgn, 26x35", SBY 3/17/88 ... 2,200
- Three Sailboats, oil on canvasboard, sgn, 10x14", C-E 10/18/89 ... 2,420
- View From Banner Hill, East Gloucester (port scene); oil on canvas laid down, sgn, 20x24", C-NY 5/25/89 OE ... 28,600
- Yellow Train (in landscape w/mountains in distance), oil on canvas, sgn, 30x40", SBY 5/24/89 ... 10,450

IE, Robert (20th C)

- Flying Cloud, oil on canvas, sgn/dtd NY 1970, 18x24", C-E 11/8/88 UE ... 550
- Ship on Rough Seas, oil on canvas, sgn/dtd 1951, 18x22", C-E 6/1/88 UE ... 1,100

IEBER, Tom (American, 1949-)

- Untitled (abstract), oil on canvas, sgn/dtd 1982, 72x66", SBY 10/8/88 ... 6,050

IEBERMANN, Max (German, 1847-1935)

- Boys Swimming, black chalk, sgn, 5x8", C-NY 3/25/88 OE ... 3,080
- Dutch Market, black chalk, sgn, 5x7", C-NY 2/25/88 OE ... 4,730
- Figures in a Park, black chalk on paper, sgn, 5x8", SBY 7/12/89 OE ... 3,300

IEBSCHER, Karl (Polish, 1851-1906)

- High Mountain Village, oil on panel, sgn/dtd 1896, 10x14", B/B 4/20/88 ... 880

IECK, Joseph (German, 1848-)

- The Toast, oil on canvas, sgn, 11x9", C-E 10/26/89 ... 1,320

IEGEOIS, Paul; att (French, 17th C)

- Still Life of Basket of Fruits, an Elaborate Gilt & Enamel Ewer...; oil on canvas, 33x44", SBY 1/12/89 ... 39,600

IES, Jozef Hendrik Hubert (Belgian, 1821-1865)

- Young Lady Reading, oil on panel, sgn, 17x14", C-E 5/23/88 ... 2,860

IESGANG, Helmuth (German, 1858-)

- Dorfweg, oil on canvas, sgn, unfr, 18x22", C-E 5/23/88 ... 3,520

IEVENS, Jan (Dutch, 1607-1674)

- Susannah & the Elders, oil on panel, 18x17", C-NY 6/2/88 ... 28,600

IGORIO, Pirro (Italian, ca 1500-1583)

- Diana & Apollo Killing the Children of Niobe, red chalk lightly squared in black chalk, 14x26", SBY 1/13/89 ... 15,400

IGORIO, Pirro; att (Italian, ca 1500-1583)

- Studies of Heads of Ladies, Warriors, & Gargoyles; pen/brown ink/brown wash, 12x9", C-NY 1/11/89 ... 7,150

GORIO, Pirro; circle of (Italian, ca 1500-1583)

- Woman with an Axe Attended by Putti, One with a Vase & Vine, the Other with Wheat; pen/ink/wash, 9x8", C-NY 1/11/89 ... 660

GOZZI, Jacopo (Italian, 1543-1627)

- Jael & Sisera, oil on canvas, 49x40", C-NY 1/15/88 ... 22,000

gurian School (16th C)

- Saint Catherine, oil on panel, 30x20", C-NY 10/12/89 ... 5,500

LJEFORS, Bruno (Swedish, 1860-1939)

- Fox in a Meadow, oil on canvas, sgn/dtd 1929, 27x39", LH 10/16/88 ... 2,600
- On the Prowl, oil on panel, sgn/dtd 84, 9x6", B/B 6/9/88 OE ... 33,000

LILLE, see De Lille
LILO, F. Coco (South American, 20th C)
Rio de Janeiro (coastal scene), oil on board, sgn, 16x13", C-SK 5/25/89 .... **510**
LILY, Peter; after
Portrait of the Duchess of Cleveland, oil on canvas, 30x25", B/B 1/11/89 OE **3,850**
LILY, Peter; style of
Portrait of a Young Woman in Blue Satin, oil on canvas, 46x36", B/B 1/11/89 OE **3,025**
LINDBERG, Harald (Swedish, 1901-1976)
Sailboat Off the Coast, oil on canvas, sgn, 20x26", B/B 4/20/88 OE **2,475**
LINDE, Ossip L. (American, 19th/20th C)
By the Canal, oil on canvas, sgn, 15x18", C-E 6/1/88 .... **1,100**
Steps in Venice, oil on panel, sgn, 11x14", C-E 2/3/88 .... **1,320**
LINDENMUTH, Tod (American, 1885-1976)
Bearskin Neck, Rockport, Massachusetts-Fishing Boats in Morning Fog; oil on panel, sgn, 9x11", RWS 3/16/89 OE **600**
Fishing by Moonlight, oil on board, sgn, 18x24", RAB 11/25/88 .... **500**
Lobster Bouys (contemporary), acrylic on masonite, sgn/inscr Rockport Mass/titled, 25x30", RWS 3/16/89 OE **2,400**
LINDER, Henry (Americna, 1854-1910)
Tasting the Fruits of Her Labor (lady w/basket of fruit), oil on board, sgn, 10x7", RAB 8/9/88 .... **1,200**
LINDERUM, Richard (German, 1851-)
Bishop's Move, oil on canvas, sgn/inscr, 16x20", C-NY 5/25/88 .... **5,280**
LINDIN, Carl Olaf Eric (American, 1869-)
Portrait of a Lady in a Lavender Dress (full-length), oil on canvas, sgn/dtd 1894, 64x28", C-NY 2/23/89 .... **3,300**
LINDNER, Richard (American/German, 1901-1978)
And Eve (man, woman, & serpent, contemporary), pencil on vellum, sgn/dtd NY 1970, 10x9", C-E 11/14/89 OE **5,500**
Angel in Me (expressionist figure), oil on canvas, sgn/dtd 1966, 70x60", C-NY 11/7/89 .... **220,000**
Couple 2 (contemporary abstract), colored pencil/crayon/ink/watercolor, sgn/dtd 1961, SBY 11/9/89 OE **66,000**
Girl (contemporary drawing), pencil/watercolor on paper, sgn/dtd 1955, 29x23", SBY 5/3/89 .... **35,750**
Hit (contemporary juke box), watercolor on paper/mylar, 24x20", SBY 2/15/89 .... **22,000**
Hommage a Brecht, watercolor/graphite on paper, sgn/dtd 1968, 20x14", SBY 5/3/89 .... **46,750**
Jacques, colored pencil/watercolor/paper collage/graphite on board, sgn/dtd 1965, 17x13", C-NY 11/10/88 OE **28,600**
L'As de Trefle (The Ace of Clubs, abstract figures), oil on canvas, sgn/dtd 1973, 79x71", SBY 11/10/88 .... **418,000**
Night Actor (abstract), oil on canvas, sgn/dtd twice, 1960 & 1959, 40x30", C-NY 5/3/88 OE **121,000**
One Way, pencil on vellum, sgn/dtd 1964, inscr Sketch for Painting One Way, 13x10", C-E 11/14/89 .... **3,520**
Two Women, watercolor/graphite/marker on paper, sgn/dtd 1977, 43x34", SBY 10/5/89 .... **49,500**
Untitled (abstract w/a woman's breast, man, & purse), watercolor/crayon on paper, sgn/inscr, 22x22", SBY 2/15/89 OE **30,250**
Untitled (abstract w/three figures & a ball), crayon/pastel/watercolor on paper, sgn/dtd 1962, 23x20", SBY 2/15/89 OE **17,600**
Untitled (contemporary, man & woman), watercolor, marker/paper collage on paper, sgn/dtd 1977, 22x17", SBY 2/15/89 OE **31,900**
We Are All One, crayons/graphite on paper, sgn/dtd 1967, 24x19", SBY 11/9/89 .... **27,500**
LINDSAY, Robert Henry (Canadian, 1868-1938)
Oat Harvest, oil on board, sgn, 10x14", WAD 11/30/89 .... **300**
Thousand Islands, Brockville, Ontario; oil on canvas, sgn, 21x29", FB 4/25/88 .... **280**
LINDSFORS
Bridge Over an Extensive Mountainous Stream, oil on canvas, sgn, 25x34", C-E 10/25/88 .... **2,860**
LINFORD, Charles (American, 1846-1947)
September Landscape, oil on canvas, sgn, 12x17", FAP 12/8/89 .... **800**
LINGELBACH, Johannes (Dutch, 1623-1674)
Hawking Party Assembled at a Country Mansion, oil on canvas, sgn, 19x25", SBY 1/12/89 .... **38,500**
LINNELL, James Thomas (British, 1826-1905)
Elijah Running Before Ahab, oil on canvas, sgn/dtd 1856, 40x55", S/A 2/18/89 .... **8,000**
LINNELL, John (British, 1792-1882)
Cows Watering, oil on canvas, bears signature, dtd 1857, 25x39", C-E 2/21/89 .... **1,870**
LINNIG, Egidius (Belgian, 1821-1860)
Pair: Hagemeister Off Antwerp; Sailing Off Geona; no media given, sgn/dtd, unfr, 20x29", WD 11/16/88 .... **5,500**
LINNIG, Willem the younger (Belgian, 1842-1890)
Interior with Lady & Dog, oil on panel, 20x16", RWS 11/3/88 .... **1,900**
LINS, Adolf (German, 1856-1927)
Pigs, oil on panel, sgn, 12x16", C-NY 5/25/88 .... **4,400**
Pigs, Roosters, & Cattle in the Fields (rural building beyond); oil on canvas, sgn, 28x22", C-E 5/22/89 .... **6,600**
LINSON, Corwin Knapp (American, 1864-1959)
Boulevard Montparnasse (street scene), oil on panel, sgn/dtd Paris 1894, unfr, 14x11", SBY 3/17/88 OE **42,900**
Circus, oil on board, initialed/dtd 1924, 7x10", C-E 2/3/88 .... **1,320**
Confidential (floral still life w/two figurines), oil on board, sgn, 14x14", WD 4/13/88 .... **2,100**
LINTON, William Evans (British, 1878-)
Cows at Noonday (in landscape), watercolor, sgn, 10x14", C-E 5/22/89 .... **660**
LINTON, William; att (British, 1791-1876)
Figures Above a Mediterranean Town, oil on paper laid down on board, 11x15", PHL 6/16/88 .... **800**
LINTOTT, Edward Barnard (American, 1875-1951)
Tuberose Begonia, oil on canvas, sgn, 30x25", RAB 8/9/88 UE **500**
LION, Flora (British, 19th/20th C)
Portrait of a Young Girl, oil on canvas, sgn, 14x12", B/B 1/11/89 .... **825**
LIONE, see Di Lione

LIOZU, Charles
Le Pont Bodin, Tam Aveyron; oil on canvas, sgn, 32x40", C-E 3/22/88 UE ... 352

LIPCHITZ, Jacques (French, 1891-1973)
Deux Figures avec Flute (Two Figures with Flute), brown ink transfer on paper, ca 1923, 8x11", C-NY 5/11/89 ... 7,000
Etude pour une Sculpture, colored wax crayons/pen/black ink on paper, sgn, ca 1914, C-NY 11/15/88 OE ... 12,100
Figure, watercolor/pencil/black ink on paper, sgn/dtd 48, 6x9", WD 5/5/88 ... 2,200
Le Cavalier, pen/ink wash on paper, sgn, 13x10", B/B 3/22/89 UE ... 1,760
Nature Morte aux Instruments de Musique (still life), pen/black ink on paper, ca 1923, 11x8", C-NY 5/11/89 ... 17,600
Sculpture Studies, ink/pencil on paper, sgn, unfr, 10x6", WD 5/5/88 UE ... 750
Sculpture Study, gouache on paper, sgn, 24x22", SBY 10/7/89 ... 6,050
Sculpture Study, watercolor/ink on paper, sgn, 12x9", SBY 10/7/89 ... 2,860
Studies for Blossoming, brush/black ink on buff paper, sgn, 14x11", C-E 5/13/88 ... 1,980
Study for Rape of Europa, ink/watercolor heightened w/white on buff paper, sgn, 11x9", PHL 11/15/88 ... 3,000

LIPCHITZ, Lippy (Isaac Israels)(1907-1980)
Portrait of a Young Girl, oil on canvas, 13x12", C-SK 5/25/88 ... 550

LIPPI, Fillipino; after (Italian, 1457-1504)
Florentine Madonna, oil on canvas, 16x22", LH 10/16/88 ... 400

LIPPI, Fillipino; manner of (Italian, 1457-1504)
Madonna & Child, oil on gold ground on panel, 23x15", C-E 6/1/88 ... 2,200

LIPPINCOTT, William Henry (American, 1849-1920)
Etretat (coastal view of men working on beached boat), oil on canvas, sgn/dtd 1890, 11x14", C-NY 5/25/89 OE ... 18,700
Feeding Chickens, oil on canvas, sgn/inscr, 21x25", C-E 2/3/88 OE ... 11,000
Lady with Fan, oil on panel, sgn/dtd 1885, 14x10", C-NY 5/26/88 ... 10,450

LISMER, Arthur (Canadian, 1885-1969)
Forest Interior, ink, sgn/dtd 1968, 17x12", FB 10/17/88 ... 625
Fred Taylor at the National War Effort Petition Committee Meeting, pencil, initialed, 8x10", FB 10/30/89 OE ... 484
Georgian Bay, oil on masonite, sgn/dtd 28, 8x10", RWS 11/3/88 OE ... 3,700
Moving Day, pencil on paper, initialed, 5x5", WAD 11/30/89 ... 850
Net Floats, ink, sgn, 8x10", WAD 11/30/89 ... 225
Nocturne, Ingonsia, Cape Breton; oil on board, sgn/dtd 1946, 12x16", FB 10/17/88 ... 5,200
Portrait, oil on board, sgn, 16x13", FB 10/17/88 UE ... 475
Star Fish, Vancouver, 1952; oil on board, sgn, 12x16", WAD 6/12/89 ... 5,000

LISSER, Onrico (Continental, 19th C)
Holiday-Makers at the Beach, oil on panel, indistinctly sgn, 18x24", SBY 2/22/89 OE ... 8,800

LISSITZKY, El (Lazar Lisitskii)(Russian, 1890-1941)
Wedge with Red Square (abstract), watercolor/gouache/pencil on paper, 1924, 17x16", C-L 10/8/88 ... 55,770

LISTER, T. (Scottish, 20th C)
Cattle in a Highland Landscape, oil on board, sgn/dtd 1911, 12x16", SLK 5/12/88 ... 425

LITSCHAUR, Karl Joseph (Austrian, 1830-1871)
Alchemist, oil on canvas, sgn, 26x33", C-NY 2/25/88 ... 5,500

LITTLE, Almaire (American, 20th C)
Southern Mansion & Mossy Trees, no media given, sgn, 17x21", MG 1/14/89 ... 300

LITTLE, John C. (Canadian, 1928-)
Epicerie Rue St Emile, St Henri; oil on canvas, sgn/dtd 1970, 10x12", FB 10/17/88 ... 2,300
Grocery Store, Milton Street at Durocher; oil on board, sgn/dtd 1959, 16x12", FB 10/17/88 OE ... 7,500
New Summer Hat, oil on board, sgn, 10x14", FB 4/25/88 ... 3,600
Patinore, Rues Gareau et Champlain (snow scene w/figures), oil on canvas, sgn/dtd 1979, 12x16", FB 4/25/88 ... 2,800
Rue Fleurie, Quebec; oil on board, sgn/dtd 1966, 16x20", FB 5/28/89 ... 5,200
Rue Laval, d'Autrefois (snowy street scene); oil on canvas, sgn/dtd 1987, 12x16", FB 10/17/88 ... 3,200
Rue Wolfe d'Autrefois, oil on canvas, sgn/dtd 1985, 12x16", FB 10/17/88 ... 3,800
View From Mt Royal, oil on board, sgn/dtd 1966, 12x16", FB 10/30/89 ... 4,180

LITTLE, Philip (American, 1857-1942)
Cliffs, conte crayon on paper, sgn, 15x18", C-E 2/3/88 UE ... 330
Wood & Rocks, Autumn; oil on canvas, sgn/dtd 1909, 25x30", RWS 11/10/89 UE ... 500

LITZINGER, Dorothea M. (American, 1889-1925)
Blue Still Life (wildflowers in a blue ceramic vase), oil on canvas, sgn, ca 1925, 40x30", RWS 9/29/88 OE ... 3,200
Floral Decoration, oil on canvas, sgn, 40x50", RWS 11/10/89 ... 2,200
Flowers in Front of Window, oil on canvas, sgn, 45x35", RWS 3/16/89 OE ... 2,800
Lake & Mountains Through Evergreens, oil on canvas, 40x42", RWS 9/8/89 ... 1,200
Landscape through Rhododendron Blossoms, oil on canvas, 40x42", RWS 9/8/89 OE ... 4,800
Landscape: Pines with Water & Clouds in the Background; oil on canvas, inscr, 40x42", RWS 3/16/89 ... 1,200
Mountain Pass, Early Fall (view of mountain through birch trees); oil on canvas, 40x42", RWS 3/31/88 UE ... 800
Still Life of Flowers, oil on canvas, 34x61", RWS 11/3/88 OE ... 3,100
Still Life of Flowers (arranged before an arched window), oil on canvas, sgn, 41x31", RWS 3/31/88 OE ... 2,900
Still Life of Peonies, oil on canvas, 40x50", RWS 11/3/88 OE ... 3,600
Still Life of Wildflowers, oil on canvas, 50x40", RWS 5/12/89 ... 1,700
Still Life of Zinnias & Wildflowers, oil on canvas, sgn, 60x50", RWS 5/19/88 OE ... 4,000
Wildflowers in Blue Vase, oil on canvas, sgn, 36x42", RWS 11/10/89 UE ... 1,100

LIUPENG, Su (Chinese, fl 1821-1861)
Contemplating Beneath the Pines (hanging scroll), ink/color on paper, sgn, 46x12", SBY 5/31/89 ... 770

LIVEMONT, Privat (Belgian, 1861-1936)
Proposal, pastel on paper, sgn/dtd 93, 12x20", WD 3/23/88 OE 1,200

LIVINGSTON, Nan C. (Scottish, 19th C)
Snow on the Pentlands, oil on board, sgn, 20x24", C-E 11/8/88 UE 300

LIZ, Domingo (Latin American, 20th C)
Rollers (fantasy abstract), oil on canvas, sgn/titled, 39x43", SBY 11/21/88 3,300
Space, oil on canvas, sgn twice/dtd 88, 32x40", SBY 5/17/88 OE 5,500
Untitled (fantasy abstract), oil on canvas, sgn, ca 1985, 30x40", SBY 5/16/89 OE 5,500

LIZCANO Y ESTEBAN, Angel (Spanish, 1846-)
Pair: Frightened Children; oil on panel, sgn, 7x11", C-E 5/23/88 660

LJUBA (European, 20th C)
Anabella ou la Soif du Mal, oil on canvas, sgn/dtd 1968-69, 59x79", C-NY 2/13/89 9,900
L'Hommage a JH Fussli, oil on canvas, sgn/dtd 1981, 58x40", C-E 11/17/88 7,150
La Plongee en Bleu, oil on canvas, sgn/dtd Paris 1981, 64x51", C-E 11/17/88 7,150

LKIMT, Gustav (Austrian, 1868-1918)
Sketch of Nude (study for the oil, Danal), brown crayon on paper, Nachlass stamp, 1903, 18x12", SBY 5/10/89 33,000

LLOYD, Thomas James (British, 1849-1910)
On the Dunes, watercolor/gouache w/scraping out, sgn, 24x19", C-NY 10/25/89 2,860

LOATES, Glen (Canadian, 1946-)
Elf Owl, pencil, sgn/dtd March 22nd, 1952, 15x13", WAD 6/12/89 600

LOBOS, Alfredo (Chilean, 1890-1917)
Pair: Paisaje, Los Andes, Chile; Fundo Los Alamos, San Felipe, Chile; oil on canvas, sgn/dtd 1938, 11x14", SBY 5/25/89 550
Set of 4: Chilean Scenes; oil on canvas, sgn, 17x21" & smaller, C-SK 11/10/88 1,210

LOBRICHON, Timoleon Marie (French, 1831-1914)
Portrait of a Young Girl, oil on canvas, sgn, 22x13", RWS 11/10/89 1,300

LOCATELLI, Andrea (Italian, 1693-1741)
Arcadian Landscapes with Shepherds & Travelers, oil on canvas, unfr, 20x25", C-NY 1/15/88 46,200
Southern Mediterranean River Landscape with Figures by Ruins...; oil on canvas, unfr, 24x38", SBY 4/7/88 OE 25,300

LOCATELLI, Andrea; att (Italian, 1693-1741)
Figures in a Landscape, a Ruined Keep Beyond; oil on canvas, unfr, 13x16", SBY 7/12/89 OE 5,775

LOCATELLI, Andrea; school of (Italian, 1693-1741)
Figures on a Path Under a Cliff in a Mountainous River Landscape, oil on canvas, 13x17", C-E 6/1/88 OE 2,200

LOCKERBY, Mabel I (Canadian, 1887-)
Cactus & Fruit (still life), oil on board, sgn, 20x16", FB 4/25/88 OE 2,900

LODENKAMP
Untitled, oil on canvas, sgn/dtd 9-19-10-74, unfr, 78x79", C-NY 2/13/89 OE 4,400

LODER, James (of Bath)(British, fl 1820-1860)
Bay Racehorse in a Loosebox, oil on canvas, sgn/dtd 1844, 23x30", SBY 6/10/88 4,950
Deception, Winner of the Oaks, 1839, with Jockey Up; oil on canvas, sgn/dtd 1839, 23x30", SBY 6/9/89 8,800
Gentleman on a Bay Hunter, oil on canvas, sgn/dtd 1851, 25x30", B/B 6/9/88 6,050

LODI, G. (Italian, 19th C)
Two Street Urchins Smoking Cigarettes, oil, sgn, 16x20", DM 2/19/88 UE 275

LODONE, Eusebio (Italian, 19th C)
Pair: Still Life of Flowers in a Basket; Fruit; no media given, sgn/dtd 1857, unfr, 21x26", PHL 10/28/88 3,300

LOEB, Louis (American, 1866-1909)
Dawn (nymphs in landscape), oil on canvas, sgn/copyright 1903, 38x55", WD 10/5/88 PE 12,000

LOEDING, Harmen (1637-1673)
Still Life of Plums, Lemons, Shrimp, Berries, an Apple, Glass of Wine...; oil on panel, sgn, 19x15", SBY 1/12/89 154,000

LOEDING, Harmen; att (1637-1673)
Still Life of a Banquet, oil on panel, 25x35", C-NY 1/11/89 28,600

LOEMANS, Arnold
Mountain Scene with Indian Camp, oil on canvas, sgn, 22x36", C-E 11/30/88 OE 6,050

LOFFLER, August (German, 1822-1866)
Pair: Landscape with Trees & Palms by a River; pen/ink on paper, initialed/1 dtd 1853, 7x9", 7x10", C-E 10/25/88 352

LOFTHUS, Arne Walhem (Norwegian, 1881-)
Man in Wheatfield, oil on canvas, sgn/dtd 1926, no size given, FAP 11/4/88 500

LOGAN, Robert Fulton (American, 1899-)
Pond in Summer, Sun & Shade; oil on canvas, sgn/dtd 17, 15x20", SBY 4/14/89 OE 5,500

LOGAN, Robert Henry (American, 1874-1942)
Autumn Winds, oil on board, artist's estate stamp, 8x9", RWS 11/10/89 UE 450
Rocky Coast, oil on panel, sgn, 8x10", RWS 9/8/89 UE 300
Ship Off Shore, oil on panel, sgn/artist's estate stamp, 7x9", RWS 11/10/89 UE 200

LOGCROFT, Thomas (British, fl 1783-1811)
Benares, pencil/watercolor, 8x14", C-SK 5/25/89 275

LOHR, August (German, 19th C)
Castillo de Chapultepec (castle of Chapultepec), oil on canvas, sgn/dtd 1915, 29x21", C-NY 5/18/88 3,850
Hut by a Mountain Lake, watercolor, sgn/dtd 1893, unfr, 8x10", C-E 2/21/89 220
Mexican Landscape, oil on canvas, sgn, 12x22", C-SK 11/10/88 4,090
Mexican Landscape, oil on canvas, sgn/dtd 1918, 24x40", C-SK 5/25/89 OE 15,610
Pair: Mexican Landscapes (w/figures); watercolor on paper, sgn/dtd Mexico 1911, 14x21", C-NY 11/21/89 OE 8,800
Pair: Paisaje con Iglesia; Arroyo (landscape/seascape); oil on canvas, sgn/dtd 1891, 10x13", C-NY 11/21/88 7,150

Paisaje Mexicano (Mexican landscape), crayon/watercolor on paper, sgn/dtd 1898, 10x16", C-NY 5/18/88 UE 1,650

LOHR, Otto

Scenes From the Life of General Stubin, watercolor/gouache on paper, sgn, shaped as a triptych, 5x11", C-E 2/23/88 550

LOIR, Luigi (French, 1845-1916)

Crepuscule-Place de la Republique, oil on board, sgn, 10x7", C-NY 5/25/88 8,250
La Seine, Environs de Suresnes; oil on canvas, sgn/dtd 79, 19x28", C-NY 2/23/89 OE 55,000
Restaurant Scene, watercolor, sgn, 9x7", FB 5/28/89 1,000
Souvenir de La Havre, oil on canvas, sgn, 11x18", C-NY 2/25/88 4,400

LOISEAU, Gustave (French, 1865-1935)

Bord de l'Eure (river landscape), oil on canvas, stamped signature, ca 1901, 26x32", C-NY 5/11/89 OE 176,000
Bords de l'Eure (shores of a river), oil on canvas, sgn/dtd 1913, 26x32", C-NY 5/12/88 OE 154,000
Bords de l'Oise (Le Quai du Pothuis a Pontoise, landscape), oil on canvas, sgn, ca 1920, 21x26", SBY 11/12/88 44,000
Bords de Riviere en Automne (autumn river landscape), oil on canvas, sgn/dtd 1912, 26x32", C-NY 5/11/89 165,000
Dieppe (harbor scene), oil on canvas, sgn/dtd 1929/titled, 24x29", C-NY 5/11/89 82,500
Harengs et Soupiere (still life of fish), oil on board, ca 1925, 15x18", C-NY 5/12/88 18,700
L'Allee des Peupliers (landscape w/poplars), oil on canvas, sgn/dtd 1905, 32x26", SBY 11/12/88 OE 165,000
L'Avant Port de Dieppe, oil on canvas, sgn, ca 1929, 21x29", SBY 2/18/88 29,700
L'Avant Port de Dieppe, oil on canvas, sgn/dtd 1926, 20x24", C-NY 10/5/89 60,500
L'Eglise Saint, Medard et la Rue Mouffetard, Paris (street scene w/church); oil, sgn, ca 1903, 18x22", C-NY 2/18/88 OE 121,000
La Maison au Pignon Rouge, oil on canvas, sgn/dtd 1910, 20x24", SBY 5/11/88 82,500
La Maison Rouge a Port Marly (landscape w/house), oil on canvas, sgn, 22x26", SBY 5/10/89 OE 154,000
La Place de la Basse Vielle Tour et le Marche de la Place, Rue de l'Epicerie; oil on canvas, sgn, 29x21", SBY 5/10/89 176,000
La Pointe de l'Ile Submergee, oil on canvas, sgn/dtd 1910, 24x32", SBY 10/6/89 77,000
La Porte d'Aval, Mer Basse, Etretat; oil on canvas, sgn/dtd 1902, 27x32", SBY 2/16/89 77,000
Le Moulin Simounou a Pont Aven, oil on canvas, sgn, 1927, 24x29", SBY 10/6/89 88,000
Les Meules, oil on canvas, sgn/dtd 1902, 22x29", SBY 2/16/89 UE 60,500
Les Rives de l'Eure, oil on canvas, sgn, 32x24", SBY 10/6/89 77,000
Les Rives de l'Eure a Louviers, oil on canvas, sgn, 1902, 21x26, SBY 10/7/88 OE 132,000
Maisons a Pont Aven (landscape w/houses), oil on canvas, sgn, ca 1926, 26x22", C-NY 2/18/88 46,200
Moret-sur-Loing (impressionistic landscape), oil on canvas, sgn/mk Atelier Loiseau, 21x29", C-NY 5/12/88 77,000
Paysage a la Maison (rural landscape with figures & buildings), oil on canvas, sgn/dtd 1910, 15x18", C-NY 11/16/88 51,700
Paysage de Seine-et-Oise (landscape), oil on canvas, sgn/dtd 1906/titled, 20x24", C-NY 11/16/88 OE 154,000
Petite Ferme au Bord de l'Eure (river landscape w/view of farm), oil on canvas, sgn, 15x19", SBY 11/12/88 93,500
Place de la Bastille (busy town square), oil on canvas, sgn, ca 1927, 20x24", SBY 5/10/89 UE 132,000
Pluie a Pont-Aven (view of roof tops in a landscape), oil on canvas, sgn, 25x20", C-NY 2/16/89 OE 148,500
Riviere en Normandie (St Cyr du Vaudreuil), oil on canvas, sgn, 1927, 20x24", SBY 5/11/88 88,000
Rochers de Saint-Lunaire, oil on canvas, sgn/dtd 1904, 24x32", SBY 5/11/88 60,500
Route du Village, oil on canvas, sgn, 20x24", SBY 2/18/88 41,800
Rue de L'Hopital le Vaudreuil, oil on canvas, sgn/dtd 1913, 22x18", SBY 2/18/88 66,000

LOMBAS, Arthur

Still Life with Peacock, Flowers, Parrot & Snail; oil on canvas, 39x52", LH 10/16/88 500

LOMBOS, Philip; see De Laszlo De Lombos

LOMI, Aurelio (Italian, 1556-1622)

Adoration of the Shepherds, oil on canvas, 69x53", C-NY 5/31/89 28,600

LOMMEN, Wilhelm (German, 1838-1895)

Friendly Exchange on an Open Road (rural panoramic landscape), oil on canvas, sgn, 26x41", C-E 5/22/89 7,700

LONDONER, Amy (American, 1878-)

Baby Playing with Dog, watercolor on paper, sgn, 9x12", C-E 9/15/88 385

LONG, Edwin (British, 1829-1891)

Going to the Market, oil on canvas, monogramed/dtd 1867, 36x29", SBY 10/24/89 5,225

LONGHI, Alessandro; circle of (Italian, 1733-1813)

Portrait of a Lady Holding a Mask & Fan, oil on canvas, 29x21", C-NY 10/20/88 OE 4,620
Portrait of an Artist, standing, half-length, wearing red jacket, holding a pencil; oil on canvas, 34x27", C-NY 4/8/88 4,620

LONGHI, Pietro; att (Italian, 1702-1785)

Woman & Boy, oil on canvas, 34x26", LH 10/16/88 UE 800

LONGHI, Pietro; style of (Italian, 1702-1785)

Dancing Lesson, oil on canvas, 28x21", B/B 9/15/88 660

LONGMAID, William (British, fl 1886-1909)

Dance of the Virgins, oil on canvas, sgn/dtd 1902, 44x56", C-E 10/26/89 3,300

LONGO, Robert (European, 20th C)

Study for Friends, acrylic/oil stick/colored dyes/graphite on paper, sgn/dtd 84, 27x29", C-NY 5/4/89 12,100
Untitled (man from behind), charcoal/white chalk on board, 1979, 30x40", C-NY 5/4/88 17,600
Untitled (man pulling on woman's arm), tempera on paper, sgn/dtd 82, 30x44", SBY 10/8/88 OE 34,100
Voice (The Golden Children), graphite/charcoal/ink/watercolor on paper, 1982-83, 96x48", SBY 5/3/88 OE 44,000

LONGOBARDI, Nino (20th C)

Untitled (abstract figure), graphite/brush/black ink on board, sgn/dtd 16/3/84, 29x20", C-NY 10/31/89 OE 3,300
Untitled (abstract), acrylic/plaster/charcoal/graphite on 2 sheets of paper, sgn/dtd 1983, 46x30", C-NY 5/4/89 2,640
Untitled (abstract), charcoal/oil/gouache on tan paper, 1983, 19x14", SBY 10/8/88 1,320

LONGPRE, see De Longpre

LONGSTAFF, Will (Australian, 1879-1953)

Summer Pasture, oil on canvas, sgn, 15x19", C-SK 6/9/88 2,600

LONGSTAFFE, Edgar (British, 1849-1912)
Pair: Untitled, cottages in landscapes w/figures; oil on canvas, monogramed/dtd, 10x14", SLK 4/7/89 1,000
LOO, see Van Loo
LOODGE, William (French, 19th/20th C)
Courtship (couple by gate in landscape), oil on canvas, sgn/dtd 1895, 37x26", B/B 5/17/89 605
LOOMIS, Andrew (American, 1892-1959)
Good Book, oil on canvas, sgn, 14x20", C-NY 9/30/88 2,090
Ouch (boy sucking thumb he has hit with a hammer, dog consoling him), oil on canvas, sgn, 28x36", DM 5/19/89 1,600
Portrait of a Young Girl (bust-length), crayon on paper, sgn/1913, 11x8", RAB 8/9/88 250
Wings of Progress (three-engine plane, 1934 Ford sedan with passengers), 24x34", DM 5/89 OE 2,750
LOOMIS, Charles Russell (American, 1857-1936)
On Ogunquit River (landscape beyond), watercolor on paper, initialed/dtd 94, 4x6", RWS 9/8/89 375
LOOMIS, Steve (American, 1943-)
Blackface, oil on canvas, sgn, 48x36", SLK 2/12/88 190
LOOSE, Basile; see De Loose
LOOTEN, Jan; att (Dutch, 1618-1681)
Forest Landscape with a Pair of Travelers on Horseback, oil on canvas, 34x45", C-NY 10/20/88 UE 4,400
LOPER, Edward (American, 20th C)
Cold Evening, oil on canvas, sgn/dtd, 27x33", FAP 4/15/89 1,870
LOPEZ, Gasparo (dei Fiori)(Italian, 1650-1732)
Still Life of an Urn Filled with Flowers in a Landscape, Surrounded by Other Flowers; oil on canvas, 39x29", SBY 4/7/88 7,700
LOPEZ, Gasparo (dei Fiori); circle of (Italian, 1650-1732)
Hydrangeas, Morning-Glory, & Other Flowers in an Urn, on a Ledge in a Landscape; oil on canvas, 16x29", C-NY 4/8/88 5,500
LOPEZ, Gasparo (dei Fiori); manner of (Italian, 1650-1732)
Still Life of Flowers & Fruit in a Parkland Setting, oil on canvas laid down on cardboard, 28x38", SBY 6/8/88 1,980
LOPEZ, Gasparo (dei Fiori); school of (Italian, 1650-1732)
Pair: Still Life of Fruit; Still Life of Flowers in an Urn by a Fountain; oil on panel, 10x13", C-E 6/1/88 990
Still Life of Fruit & Flowers on a Ledge, oil on canvas, 26x39", C-E 4/7/88 990
LOPEZ, Roman
Mexican Village (folk art scenes), oil on masonite, sgn/dtd 87, 16x20", GAI 9/1/89 45
LOPEZ DE AYALA, Manuel
The Toast, oil on canvas, sgn/dtd 1891, 37x42", C-NY 5/25/88 71,500
LOPEZ Y PORTANA, Vincente (Spanish, 1772-1850)
Portrait of Queen Isabella II of Spain, oil on canvas, 38x31", SBY 1/12/89 22,000
LOPP, Harry Leonard (American, 1888-)
Kintla Lake Near Ranger Station Glacier National Park, oil on canvas, sgn, 26x36", RWS 11/10/89 UE 550
LORAIN, Dolia
Sky, Smoke & City (abstract); oil on canvas, sgn/#d 6, 48x42", SBY 2/14/89 OE 2,970
LORAINE, see Gellee
LORENZ, Gottfried (German, 19th C)
Landscape, oil on canvas, 19x23", LH 10/16/88 180
LORENZ, Richard (American, 1858-1915)
Chinatown Balcony, oil on academy board, sgn, 14x11", S/A 2/18/89 2,000
Milwaukee Court House From His Rooming House Window, oil on academy board, initialed, 8x6", S/A 2/18/89 475
Mongolian Family, oil on masonite, sgn, 42x26", C-E 2/23/88 OE 5,280
Round Up, oil on canvas, sgn, 22x30", S/A 3/12/88 11,500
Shoreline View, oil on panel, sgn, 7x10", MAG 6/22/88 900
Street in Chinatown, oil on academy board, sgn, 14x11", S/A 2/18/89 950
Study of a Saddle Horse, oil on paper, sgn/dtd 1954, 12x14", S/A 2/18/89 525
Western Plains, oil on academy board, initialed, 8x12", S/A 2/18/89 1,060
LORENZO, see Di Lornezo
LORIA, Vincenzo (Italian, 1850-)
Fishermen in the Bay of Naples, watercolor on paper on board heightened w/white gouache, sgn/inscr, 15x23", C-E 5/23/88 715
Fishermen in the Bay of Naples, watercolor/gouache, sgn, 16x31", C-E 10/26/89 1,870
Pescatores, watercolor on paper, sgn, 12x22", B/B 9/15/88 605
LORING, W.H. (American, 19th C)
Hanging Quail, oil on canvas, sgn/dtd 1865, 21x17", SBY 6/28/89 660
LORJOU, Bernard (French, 1908-)
Adieu Colombus, acrylic on canvas, sgn, 22x18", C-E 5/13/88 OE 2,860
Fleurs dans un Pichet, acrylic on board mounted on canvas, sgn, 27x19", C-E 5/13/88 3,740
Fleurs dans un Vase Vert, acrylic on board mounted on canvas, sgn, 26x20", C-E 5/13/88 OE 3,960
Fleurs dans un Vase Vert (flowers in green vase), acrylic on paper laid down on board, sgn, 27x19", C-E 11/17/88 OE 4,950
Le Rois des Gitans (King of the Gypsies, portrait), acrylic on canvas, sgn/dtd 1964, 40x26", SBY 2/14/89 OE 6,160
Les Roses Blanches (still life of white roses), oil on canvas, sgn, 40x27", C-E 11/17/88 OE 13,200
Nature Morte au Poisson (still life w/fish), oil on canvas, sgn, 36x26", SBY 10/7/89 7,425
Ole, acrylic on canvas, sgn, 22x15", C-E 5/13/88 OE 2,860
Riri, gouache on paper laid down on canvas, sgn, 22x18", SBY 10/5/88 1,210
Still Life of Pineapple, oil on canvas, sgn, 24x29", SBY 10/7/89 10,450
Vase de Fleurs, acrylic on board mounted on canvas, sgn, 26x20", C-E 5/9/89 OE 5,500
Vase de Fleurs (still life), acrylic on board mounted on canvas, sgn, 27x19", C-E 5/9/89 OE 5,500
Vase de Fleurs Blanches, acrylic on board mounted on canvas, sgn, 26x20", C-E 5/13/88 OE 4,400

Vase de Roses (still life), oil on canvas, sgn/dtd 1953, 26x21", C-E 11/17/88 4,400
Vase of Flowers, oil on canvas, sgn, 22x18", SBY 10/7/89 8,250
Winter Landscape, oil on canvas, sgn, 32x40", SBY 10/7/89 8,525

LORNE, see De Lorne

LORRAIN, Claude; follower of
Set of 4: Pastoral Landscapes & Port Scenes; pen/brown ink/wash over black chalk, average 8x11", SBY 7/12/89 880

LORRAIN, Claude; school of
Classical Landscape with a Shepherd & His Flock Crossing a Bridge, oil on canvas, unfr, 15x19", C-E 6/1/88 OE 1,870
Shepherds with Their Flock Beside a Fountain in Mountainous River Landscape, oil on canvas, unfr, 14x18", C-E 6/1/88 OE 2,420

LOS, Waldemar (Polish, 1849-1888)
Preparing for the Departure, oil on canvas, sgn, 24x47", C-NY 10/25/89 9,350

LOSSOW, Heninrich (German, 1843-1897)
Proposal, oil on canvas, sgn/indistinctly dtd, 17x13", WD 3/23/88 UE 500

LOTH, Johann Karl (German, 1632-1698)
Apollo & Marsyas, oil on canvas, 48x51", C-NY 1/15/88 14,300
Double-Sided: Mythological Scene; Allegory of Time & Beauty; pen/ink heightened w/white, 10x7", SBY 1/13/89 1,650
Drunken Silenus, oil on canvas, 40x31", SBY 4/7/88 3,025
Drunken Silenus (three-quarter length portrait of man w/wine jug), oil on canvas, 45x38", SBY 4/7/89 20,900
Saint Mary Magdalene with the Instruments of the Passion, oil on canvas, unfr, 46x58", C-NY 4/8/88 5,280

LOTH, Johann Karl; att (German, 1632-1698)
Job, oil on canvas, 38x50", C-NY 6/2/88 3,300

LOTH, Johann Karl; follower of (German, 1632-1698)
Diana & Endymion, oil on canvas, 30x26", SBY 12/9/88 1,210

LOTTI, A.
Teatime, watercolor on paper, sgn, 11x8", C-E 5/23/88 OE 1,320

LOTTO, Lorenzo (Italian, 1480-1556)
Saint Onuphrius of Egypt, oil on canvas, 34x17", SBY 1/12/89 110,000

LOTZ, Matilda B. (American, 1858-1923)
Dog Waiting by the Gate, oil on canvas, sgn, unfr, 26x32", SBY 9/14/89 9,900
White Stallion in a Stable, oil on canvas, sgn, 19x25", B/B 6/9/88 6,050

LOUBON, Emile Charles (French, 1809-1863)
Return From the Field (oxen w/hay wagon & figures), oil on canvas, sgn, 15x18", C-NY 2/23/89 3,850

LOUDERBACK, Walt S. (American, 1877-1941)
Conversing Around the Campfire, oil on canvas, sgn/indistinctly dtd, 28x40", SBY 6/24/88 1,980
Morning Concert, oil on canvas, sgn, 32x35", NA 2/6/88 3,500
Set of 3: Defendent; Judge; Solister; oil on canvas, sgn, 12x19", C-E 2/3/88 825
Woman in Yellow (three-quarter length portrait of woman seated in profile), oil on canvas, sgn, 20x16", C-E 2/1/89 UE 660

LOUGHEED, Robert Elmer (American, 1910-)
Milk House, oil on board, sgn 3 times/titled/dtd 1981, 9x12", SBY 9/23/88 1,870
Passing Through Nambe, oil on masonite, sgn twice/monogramed/inscr/titled, 16x20", SBY 9/23/88 6,050
Retour on Village Near Fort Janvier, P Que (The Sleigh Ride); oil on canvasboard, sgn, 12x16", RWS 5/12/89 2,500
Winter Landscape with Horses, oil on board, sgn, 8x10", C-E 11/30/88 990

LOUIS, Morris (American, 1912-1962)

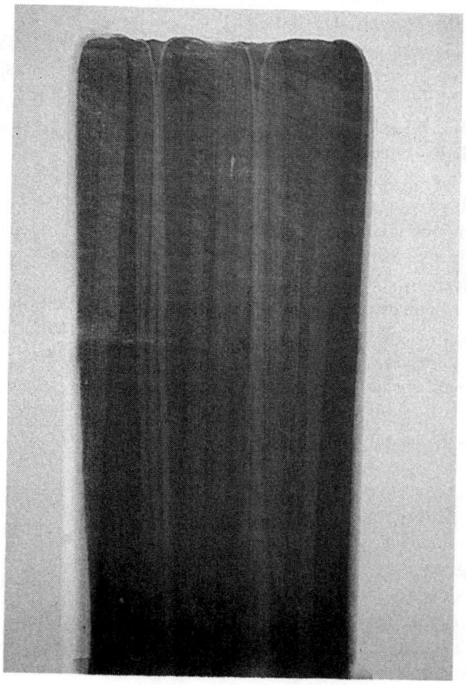

Gamma, acrylic on canvas, sgn/dtd 60, 81x54", C-NY 5/3/89; $440,000

Antares (abstract), acrylic on canvas, sgn/#d 132, 1961-62, 83x41", C-NY 5/3/88 ... 176,000
Beth Beth (abstract), acrylic on canvas, sgn/#d 113, 1958, 90x144", SBY 11/10/88 ... 198,000
Beth Zayin (abstract), acrylic on canvas, 1959, 100x142", SBY 5/2/88 ... 275,000
Gamma Nu (abstract), acrylic on canvas, sgn/#d 336, 1960, 104x140", SBY 11/10/88 OE ... 286,000
Gamma Tau (abstract), acrylic on canvas, 1960, 103x167", SBY 5/2/88 ... 286,000
Kuf (abstract), acrylic on canvas, 1958, 90x138", SBY 2/15/89 OE ... 159,500
Narrow Gauge (lineation), acrylic on canvas, 1962, 89x14", SBY 11/11/88 OE ... 88,000
Number-2-00 (vertical lineation), acrylic on canvas, 1962, 80x36", SBY 5/2/88 ... 198,000
Pillar of Fire (vertical lineation), magna on canvas, 1961, 93x48", SBY 5/2/89 OE ... 632,500
Spreading (abstract), acrylic on canvas, initialed/dtd 54, 79x97", C-NY 5/3/89 ... 385,000
Untitled (abstract), magna on canvas, 1959-60, 98x141", SBY 11/10/88 OE ... 1,017,000
Untitled (abstract), oil on canvas, sgn/dtd 55, 79x52", SBY 11/9/89 ... 165,000

LOURENS, B. (Belgian, 20th C)
Amsterdam (depicts buildings by a canal), oil on canvas, 24x48", DM 2/19/88 ... 120

LOUTHERBOURG, see De Loutherbourg

LOUYOT, Edmond (German, 1861-ca 1909)
House & Chapel in a Mountainous Landscape, oil on board, sgn, 19x24", WD 11/16/88 UE ... 1,000
Taste of Wine, oil on panel, sgn/indistinctly dtd, 15x18", C-E 10/26/89 ... 1,760

LOVATT, A.
Choppy Seas by a Harbour, oil on canvas, sgn/dtd 1904, 16x21", C-E 1/12/88 UE ... 418

LOVELL
Untitled (Indian encampment under a full moon), pastel on paper, 14x34", RAB 1/10/89 UE ... 100

LOVELL, Katherine (American, 19th/20th C)
Path Along the Cliff, oil on canvas, 18x22", C-NY 9/28/89 ... 1,100
Summer Afternoon (children in landscape), oil on canvas, sgn, 18x22", C-NY 9/28/89 ... 3,850

LOVELL, Tom (American, 1909-)
Cabeza de Vaca, charcoal on paper en grisaille, sgn, 31x42", SBY 9/23/88 OE ... 2,750
Spring Water Vendor, oil on board, sgn, 22x34", C-E 2/1/89 OE ... 4,400
Survey Party at Horsehead Crossing, charcoal/white chalk/on paper en grisaille, 29x57", SBY 9/23/88 OE ... 7,700

LOVEN, Frank W. (American, 1869-1941)
House in a Snowy Landscape, oil on board, sgn, 8x10", C-E 2/1/89 ... 770
Snow Scene, oil on canvas, sgn, 18x24", C-E 2/3/88 ... 1,980
Summer Forest Interior, oil on canvas, sgn/dtd 1915, 18x24", C-E 11/30/88 UE ... 935
Sunrise in the Forest, sgn twice/inscr, dtd 1912, 14x18", C-E 2/3/88 ... 1,540
Winter Stream, oil on canvas, sgn/dtd 1915, 30x40", C-NY 9/28/89 ... 5,720

LOVERIDGE, Clinton (American/British, 1824-1902)
Afternoon of Skating (figures on frozen pond), oil on board, sgn, 6x12", RWS 9/8/89 OE ... 2,100
Boating on Schroon Lake, oil on canvas, sgn, 30x25", SBY 4/14/89 ... 4,400
Cows Crossing a Stream, oil on canvas, sgn, 22x36", C-E 5/23/88 ... 1,320
Going Out to Pasture, watercolor on paper, sgn, 9x14", B/B 12/8/88 ... 550
Pair: Mount Washington; Cow in Landscape; oil on board/oil on canvas, sgn, 1 dtd 1867, 6x13", 12x10", C-E 6/1/89 OE ... 3,080
Pair: Spring & Fall by the Stream; oil on board, sgn, 7x13", WD 10/5/88 ... 5,500

LOVING, Richard (American, 1924-)
Pond Series, oil on birch panel, sgn/dtd 1975, 24x30", LH 9/10/89 ... 425

LOVMAND, Christine Marie (Danish, 1803-1872)
Still Life of Potted Spring Flowers, oil on canvas, initialed/dtd 1870, 17x15", SBY 10/24/89 OE ... 29,700
Still Life of Tulips, Crocuses, Primroses, Snowdrops, & Hyacinth; oil on canvas, sgn/dtd 1858, 15x13", SBY 5/23/89 ... 22,000

LOVYOX, E.
Dutch Girl with Spilled Milk, oil on canvas, sgn, 25x19", C-E 7/26/88 OE ... 1,430

LOW, Will Hicock (American, 1853-1932)
Early Morning at Gloucester, oil on canvas, sgn/inscr/dtd 1919, 8x10", C-NY 12/2/88 OE ... 18,700
Souvenir of Nantucket, oil on canvas, sgn/dtd 1878, 24x13", SBY 5/25/88 ... 45,100

LOWCOCK, Charles Frederick (British, fl 1878-1922)
Elegant Lady by a Veranda at Sunset, oil on panel, sgn, 20x8", C-E 5/23/88 ... 1,870

LOWELL, Milton H. (American, 1848-1927)
Early Autumn Landscape, oil on canvas, sgn/dtd 72, 10x12", RAB 3/27/89 UE ... 150
Landscape Scene with Figures, oil on canvas, sgn, 28x20", RWS 11/10/89 ... 1,600
Punt on a River, Berkshire Meadow; oil on canvas, sgn, 16x24", B/B 12/8/88 ... 385
Wooded River Landscape, oil on canvas, sgn, 16x24", PHL 12/1/88 ... 850

LOWELL, N.H.
New England Landscape, oil on canvas, sgn, 16x25", C-E 5/3/88 ... 330

LOYALFIELD
Farm in Distance, oil on canvas, sgn, 20x30", C-E 9/15/88 ... 1,210

LOZA, Luis Lopez (Latin American, 20th C)
Dream of an Historic Mountain, acrylic on canvas, 1979, 70x79", SBY 5/17/88 UE ... 2,200

LOZANO, Manuel Rodriguez
El Robozo Blanco (portrait of a woman), oil on canvas, sgn/dtd 43, 38x28", C-NY 5/18/88 ... 4,400

LOZOWICK, Louis (American, 1892-)
Airport Scene, charcoal, sgn, ca 1929, 8x10", SWN 6/15/89 OE ... 4,180
Tower, pen/brush/black ink on paper, sgn, 18x12", C-NY 5/26/88 ... 12,100

LU, Shi (Chinese, 1919-1982)

Lotus (hanging scroll), ink/color on paper, sgn, 35x19", SBY 5/31/89 ... 13,200

LUBIN, Arieh (Israeli, 20th C)

Jordan Valley, oil on canvas, sgn/dtd 47, 21x29", SBY 10/5/88 ... 1,650
Village Scene, oil on canvas, sgn, 24x29", SBY 5/30/89 ... 8,250

LUBITCH, Ossip (French, 20th C)

Nature Morte (still life of chair w/flowers & pitcher), oil on canvas, sgn/dtd 1930, 13x18", SBY 5/30/89 ... 2,200

LUBOVSKY, M.

Still Life, oil on canvas, sgn, 36x30", LH 5/15/88 ... 140

LUCAS, Albert Pike (American, 1862-1945)

Crescent Moon (moon over trees & water), oil on artist board, sgn, 16x12", RWS 5/19/88 ... 450
Miss Madelaine Kimball, Boston (bust-length portrait); oil on canvas, sgn/dtd 1922, 30x25", RWS 3/31/88 UE ... 1,600
Moonlit Pond (calm water with wooded landscape beyond), oil on canvasboard, sgn, 16x12", B/B 9/14/89 ... 990

LUCAS, G.A.

Bridge Over a Shallow River, oil on canvas, sgn, 30x12", C-E 2/16/88 UE ... 220

LUCAS Y PADILLA, Eugenio (Spanish, 1824-1870)

Bullfight, oil on canvas, 16x13", C-NY 10/25/89 ... 20,900

LUCAS Y PADILLA, Eugenio; att (Spanish, 1824-1870)

Maja (portrait of Spanish belle), oil on canvas, sgn, 18x10", SBY 12/9/88 OE ... 3,300

LUCAS Y VILLAAMIL, Eugenio (Spanish, 1858-1918)

Family Outing, oil on canvas, sgn, 14x21", C-NY 10/25/89 ... 17,600

LUCAS-LUCAS, Henry Frederick (British, -1943)

Baby Cooke on Beauty at Chester Place, Crewe; oil on canvas, sgn/dtd 1915, 14x18", C-E 10/26/89 ... 990
Pair: Bay Horses in Stalls; oil on canvas, sgn/dtd 1890, 20x26", SBY 6/10/88 ... 6,325

LUCAS-ROBIQUET, Marie Aimee Eliane (French, 1864-)

Jeune Femme se Tirant les Cartes, oil on canvas, sgn/dtd 90, 67x87", SBY 10/24/89 ... 44,000
Le Chapeau Rose (portrait of girl in hat), oil on canvas, sgn/dtd 1910, 36x29", SBY 10/24/89 ... 13,200

LUCE, L.W. (American, 19th C)

Cart Path, cart path cutting through grassy field & down to river; watercolor on paper, sgn, 9x13", RWS 8/20/88 ... 225

LUCE, Maximilien (French, 1858-1941)

Arcy-sur-Cure (landscape w/river), oil on panel, sgn/dtd 1906/titled, ca 1906, 9x13", C-NY 5/12/88 ... 14,300
Baignade a Moulineux (bathers in a landscape), oil on panel, stamped, 13x8", C-NY 2/18/88 ... 16,500
Baignade su les Berges de la Seine a Mericourt, charcoal/pen/brown ink/brush/brown wash, sgn, 11x16", C-NY 10/6/88 ... 3,520
Baignades de la Famille (family of nude bathers by a pond), oil on panel, sgn, 8x17", C-NY 2/18/88 OE ... 22,000
Bessy-Sur-Cure, dans l'Yonne; oil on board, sgn, 10x14", WD 5/5/88 ... 11,500
Bord de la Marne a Lagny (waterfront scene), oil on canvas, sgn/dtd 1905, 17x24", C-NY 11/16/88 OE ... 143,000
Bouquet de Fleurs dans un Pot, Tulipes et Dahlias; oil on paper laid down on canvas, sgn/dtd 30, 22x18", C-NY 5/11/89 ... 33,000
Carriere pres de Clamart, oil on paper laid down on canvas, sgn/dtd 1927, 12x20", C-NY 10/5/89 ... 19,800
Cour de Ferme, oil on canvas, sgn twice, 14x20", SBY 2/18/88 ... 20,900
Embouchure du Trieux (coastal view), oil on paper, sgn, 11x14", C-NY 2/18/88 ... 8,250
Femme Lisant, oil on paper laid down on board, sgn/dtd 1904, 18x25", SBY 5/11/88 ... 22,000
La Baignade a Mericourt (beach scene), oil on paper laid down on canvas, sgn, 1935, 16x21", C-NY 5/12/88 ... 33,000
La Rue des Abbesses (street scene), oil on cradled panel, sgn, ca 1895, 20x14", C-NY 2/18/88 ... 165,000
Le Bassin du Port, oil on canvas, sgn, ca 1935, 13x20", SBY 2/18/88 ... 17,600
Le Port de Rotterdam (port scene w/shipping), oil on canvas, sgn/dtd 1907, 21x26", SBY 5/10/89 ... 49,500
Le Port de Rouen (port scene), oil on canvas laid down on board, sgn twice, 13x16", C-NY 5/12/88 ... 20,900
Le Quai aux Marchandises (warf scene), oil on paper laid down on canvas, sgn, 1935-37, 16x22", C-NY 5/12/88 ... 22,000
Le Reveur (The Dreamer), brown wash over pencil on China Paper, cut/mounted on cardboard, unfr, 5x4", RWS 11/3/88 UE ... 175
Le Semaphore a Honfleur (seascape w/boats), oil on board, stamped, 1828, 10x12", C-NY 2/18/88 ... 8,800
Le Treport, Les Falaises (seascape w/coastline); oil on paper mounted on canvas, sgn/dtd 37, 12x19", SBY 5/11/89 UE ... 5,500
Le Treport, Pecheurs sur le Quai (fisherman on warf); oil on paper laid down on canvas, sgn twice, 10x16", C-NY 10/6/88 ... 15,400
Mericourt, l'Attente au Passage de l'Ecluse; oil on paper laid down on canvas, sgn, ca 1935, 13x21", SBY 10/6/89 ... 27,500
Moulineux, l'Etang; oil on board, sgn, 10x14", SBY 10/6/89 ... 23,100
Moulineux, la Moisson (harvest scene); oil on paper laid down on canvas, sgn/dtd 1929, 13x20", C-NY 10/5/89 ... 19,800
Paris, la Rue Saint-Honore (crowded street scene); oil on paper laid down, stamped signature, 14x18", SBY 10/6/89 ... 49,500
Paris, la Rue Saint-Honore; oil on canvas, sgn, 1905, 10x30", SBY 10/7/88 ... 24,200
Paris, le Percement de la Rue Reaumur (Paris street scene); oil on board, sgn twice/dtd 95, 18x14", C-NY 5/12/88 ... 60,500
Paris, les Egoutiers (street scene w/workers); oil on paper laid down on canvas, sgn, 12x17", C-NY 2/18/88 ... 16,500
Paysage, oil on board, sgn, 10x14", SBY 10/7/89 ... 14,300
Paysage a Mereville, oil on board, sgn, ca 1905, 12x15", SBY 10/7/88 ... 25,300
Paysage de Hollande (waterfront scene), oil on canvas, sgn/dtd 1907, 14x22", C-NY 11/16/88 OE ... 52,800
Paysage de Saint-Tropez (landscape of St-Tropez), oil on canvas, sgn, 1893, 18x22", C-NY 11/16/88 ... 121,000
Peniches Amarees Devant Bouquet d'Arbres et Pont, oil on canvas, sgn/stamped, 13x19", SBY 2/18/88 ... 28,600
River Landscape, oil on canvas laid down on board, sgn/dtd 1901, 10x14", SBY 10/7/89 OE ... 15,400
Rolleboise, Arbres au Bord de la Riviere (trees along a river); oil on canvas, sgn, ca 1935, 10x14", C-NY 5/12/88 ... 8,800
Rolleboise, Baignade; oil on canvas, sgn, ca 1920, 18x32", C-NY 11/16/88 ... 44,000
Rolleboise, la Cour; oil on canvas, sgn, 18x22", SBY 2/18/88 ... 23,100
Saint-Tropez, Baigneurs sous la Pinede; oil on cradled panel, sgn/dtd 1901, 34x21", SBY 5/11/88 ... 71,500
Scene de Rue a Paris (Paris street scene), oil on paper on canvas, stamped signature, 1935-37, 12x31", SBY 5/12/88 ... 38,500
Watertoren, Delftshaven; oil on canvas, sgn/dtd 1908, 18x26", SBY 2/18/88 ... 35,200

LUCE, Molly (American, 1896-1986)	
New Barn (erecting new barn), oil on canvas, sgn twice/dtd 38/titled, 22x28", SBY 3/17/88	**3,300**
LUCEBERT, Jean (Dutch, 1924-)	
Sweet Snow (abstract), gouache/watercolor/ballpoint pen/stamp/paper collage, sgn/dtd 66, 28x40", C-E 11/14/89 OE	**7,700**
Untitled (abstract figures), oil on canvas, sgn/dtd 67, 36x47", C-E 11/14/89 OE	**15,400**
Untitled (abstract figures), oil on canvas, sgn/dtd 68, 35x47", C-E 11/14/89 OE	**17,600**
LUCERNE, E.	
Portrait of a Young Girl at a Desk with a Cat & Books, oil on canvas, bears signature, 25x30", C-E 6/28/88 UE	**462**
LUCIONI, Luigi (Italian, 1900-)	
Barns in the Summer (well-kept buildings in a landscape), oil on canvasboard, sgn/dtd 36, 8x12", B/B 10/9/88	**3,850**
Elm & the Shadow (with barn in a landscape), oil on canvas, sgn/dtd 48, 7x11", SBY 1/24/89 OE	**7,150**
Harvest Epilogue (farm buildings in a rolling landscape), oil on board, sgn/dtd 51, 6x8", B/B 10/9/88	**3,300**
October Mood (farm buildings in a rolling landscape), oil on board, sgn/dtd 50, 6x8", B/B 10/9/88	**2,475**
LUCKENBACH, Reuben O.	
Autumn's Bounty (still life w/fruit & glass of wine), oil on canvas, 22x26", C-NY 9/28/89	**4,400**
LUDBY, Max (British, 1858-1943)	
An Extensive Landscape, watercolor, sgn, 20x28", PHL 6/16/88 UE	**350**
LUDOVICI, Julius (Italian, 19th C)	
Greek Woman at the Acropolis, oil on canvas, 45x32", B/B 4/20/88	**1,760**
LUINI, Bernardino (Italian, 1475-1532)	
Madonna & Child, oil on canvas, 18x18", C-NY 1/11/89	**44,000**
Saint Veronica (portrait), oil on panel, unfr, 25x21", C-M 6/16/89	**40,748**
LUKER, William Sr. (British, fl 1851-1889)	
Cows & Sheep Near a River, oil on canvas, sgn/dtd 1868, unfr, 24x36", WL 5/20/88 UE	**350**
LUKS, George Benjamin (American, 1867-1933)	
Bathers, pencil on paper, sgn/dtd 33, 10x8", C-E 6/1/89 OE	**990**
Double-Sided: Priests; charcoal on paper, 6x4", C-NY 6/17/89	**660**
Ducks, oil on canvas, sgn, 25x31", WD 4/13/88 OE	**18,000**
Farm in Autumn, watercolor on board, sgn, 14x20", C-NY 12/2/88 OE	**17,600**
Group of 3: Judge Davis; Man with Shovel; Theatre Audience; pencil on paper, ea 6x4", SBY 3/17/88 UE	**990**
In the Corner, oil on panel, sgn, 1920-21, 48x37", SBY 5/25/88	**385,000**
Men on the Beach, charcoal on paper, sgn, 9x7", RWS 11/3/88 UE	**475**
Miners, watercolor on paper, sgn, unfr, 16x22", SBY 1/24/89 OE	**16,500**
Mountain Landscape, watercolor/gouache on paper laid down, sgn, 14x20", C-NY 5/25/89 OE	**18,700**
My House (exterior view), watercolor on paper, sgn/inscr, 14x20", C-NY 12/2/88 OE	**24,200**
Pair: Polo Player; Nude Fighter; 1 pencil/1 charcoal, 1 sgn, 8x5", 10x7", SBY 6/24/88	**1,210**
Portrait of Mildred Morse, oil on canvas, sgn, 20x25", RWS 3/16/89	**4,750**
Portrait of Miss Ruth Breslin (young girl), oil on canvas, sgn/dtd 1925, 30x25", C-NY 5/25/89	**52,800**
Reclining Nude, oil on board, sgn, 16x20", SBY 6/24/88 OE	**10,450**
Seascape, oil on panel, sgn, 9x16", SBY 9/23/88 OE	**3,575**
Set of 3: Elephant; Gorilla: Ostrich; charcoal on paper, sgn, 8x10", C-E 2/3/88 OE	**1,210**
Set of 3: Hippos; Standing Lion; Resting Lion; charcoal on paper, 2 sgn/1 sgn/inscr, 8x10", C-E 2/3/88	**1,430**
Set of 4: Camels; Giraffe Drinking Water; Giraffe; Swing Monkey; charcoal on paper, sgn, 10x8", C-E 2/3/88 OE	**3,850**
Sick Doll (boy & girl w/doll in an interior), oil on canvas laid down on board, sgn, 11x9", C-NY 5/26/88	**13,200**
The Drummer (portrait of man), oil on panel, 31x23", SBY 4/14/89	**7,150**
Thompson & Bleeker Streets, New York City; oil on canvas, stamped twice, 20x30", SBY 5/25/88	**74,250**
Upstream (impressionistic), watercolor on paper, sgn, 14x20", C-NY 12/2/88	**19,800**
Young Girl Sitting, pencil on paper, sgn, 9x7", C-E 6/1/88	**605**
LUKS, George Benjamin; att (American, 1867-1933)	
Parke Scene, oil on panel, sgn, 10x14", SBY 1/24/89 OE	**13,200**
LUM, Bertha Boynton (American, 1879-1954)	
Balinese Dancer with Flower, watercolor/gouache/pen/ink on embossed paper, sgn, 19x12", B/B 10/6/88	**550**
Funeral Lanterns, gouache/gold leaf on built paper, sgn/titled, 13x8", RWS 4/22/89 OE	**1,100**
LUMLEY, Augustus Savile (British, fl 1856-1880)	
Jewel Casket, oil on panel, inscr, 24x18", SBY 12/9/88	**1,760**
LUNAMARK (American, 20th C)	
Seascape (sailboat in distance), oil on canvas, sgn, 20x24", RAB 3/27/89 UE	**200**
LUND, Carl Ove (Danish, 1857-1936)	
Kitchen Garden, oil on canvas, sgn/dtd 1884, 62x41", SBY 5/23/89	**8,250**
LUNGLOIS, M.V.	
The Cobbler, oil on canvas, sgn, 21x17", C-E 11/8/88	**1,100**
LUNGREN, Fernand Harvey (American, 1859-1932)	
Bastions of the Painted Desert, oil on canvas, sgn, 20x40", SBY 3/17/88 OE	**5,500**
Mustang Stampede, oil on canvas, sgn, 15x29", B/B 3/17/88	**3,300**
Tranquil Waters, oil on canvas, sgn, 18x36", B/B 10/6/88	**6,050**
LUNKS, George; att	
Figures Walking Along a Country Lane, watercolor on paper, sgn, 6x8", SBY 6/28/89	**1,100**
LUNY, Thomas (British, 1759-1937)	
Warren Shipwrecked on a Rocky Coast, oil on panel, sgn/dtd 1829, 12x16", C-NY 10/12/89	**3,300**
LUNY, Thomas; circle of (British, 1759-1937)	
Two Frigates in Heavy Seas, oil on canvas, 14x20", PHL 10/28/88 UE	**800**

LUPERTZ, Markus (European, 20th C)
MA, Dithyrambisch; oil on canvas, 97x69", C-NY 11/10/88 OE ... 44,000
LUPI, A.
Peasants by the Well, watercolor on paper, sgn/dtd Roma 83, 20x14", C-E 11/8/88 ... 600
LURCAT, Jean (French, 1892-)
Bateau sur la Plage (Boat on the Beach), oil on canvas, sgn/dtd 30, 36x26", C-E 11/17/88 ... 10,450
Bather in a Landscape, oil on canvas, sgn/dtd 31, 11x14", SBY 10/7/89 ... 4,675
Figure in Mountainous Landscape, gouache on paper, sgn, 12x15", SBY 10/7/89 ... 2,200
Sailors, pen/ink on paper, sgn/dtd 1930, 22x17", SBY 10/5/88 ... 935
LUTERO, see De Lutero
LUTEURGERT
Cavalry by a Village Entrance, oil on canvas, sgn/dtd 18(?)9, 14x11", C-E 2/23/88 ... 1,100
LUTI, Benedetto (Italian, 1666-1724)
Rebecca at the Well, oil on canvas, 38x53", SBY 6/2/89 OE ... 88,000
LUTI, Benedetto; att (Italian, 1666-1724)
Head of a Youth, red chalk, inscr, 12x9", C-NY 1/11/88 ... 1,320
LUTI, Benedetto; studio of (Italian, 1666-1724)
Head of a Woman in Profile, pastel on paper, 10x13", SBY 7/12/89 ... 1,540
LUTKEN, Mathias (Danish, 1841-1905)
Along the Coast, no media given, sgn/indistinctly dtd, unfr, 32x50", C-E 2/16/88 ... 352
LUTTER, Aino (Canadian)
Still Life of a Melon & Fruit, pastel, sgn, 18x23", WAD 11/30/89 OE ... 1,150
Two Tulips, pastel, sgn, 30x22", WAD 6/12/89 ... 850
LUTYENS, Charles Augustus Henry (British, 19th C)
Preparing for the Hunt, oil on canvas, 24x36", B/B 6/9/88 ... 7,150
Putti on a Cloud, oil on canvas, sgn, 10x14", FB 10/17/88 UE ... 475
LUTZ, A.A. (American, 20th C)
Child at Rest with Apple, oil on board, sgn, 6x10", FAP 4/15/89 ... 165
LUYCKX, Christiaan (Flemish, 1623-1653)
Floral Still Life in a Marble Niche with Butterflies & Caterpillars, oil on panel, monogramed, 26x20", C-NY 6/2/88 ... 28,600
LYALL, J. (British, 19th C)
River Landscape, oil on canvas, sgn, 25x30", SLK 5/12/88 ... 350
LYDSTON, William Jr. (Boston, fl 1835-1860)
Miniature Portrait of a Young Boy Wearing a Plaid Dress Holding a Whip, oil on ivory, sgn, 3x3", RWS 10/27/89 OE ... 1,300
LYFORD, Philip (American, 1887-1950)
Portrait of Ella Lyford, oil on canvas, sgn, 24x17", RWS 5/19/88 ... 3,800
Stubborn Child (lady holding child's hand at street crossing), oil on canvas, sgn, 27x21", C-NY 9/28/89 ... 3,300
LYMAN, Harry (American/British, 19th/20th C)
Autumn Leaf in a Loosebox (horse in an interior), oil on canvas laid down, sgn/dtd 1889, 22x27", SBY 6/9/89 ... 1,760
Stallion in a Stall, oil on masonite, sgn/dtd 1889, 22x28", C-E 5/23/88 OE ... 2,640
LYMAN, John (Canadian, 1886-1967)
Still Life of Fruits, oil on board, sgn, 10x14", FB 10/30/89 ... 3,080
LYNCH, Albert (Peruvian, 1851-)
At the Bullfight (posterior view of two ladies at bullfight), oil on panel, sgn, 18x13", C-NY 5/24/89 ... 16,500
La Tasse de The (woman seated at tea table), oil on canvas laid down on panel, sgn, 32x22", C-NY 2/23/89 ... 14,300
On Your Knees & Swear It (bedridden woman, grief-stricken man), watercolor/gouache/pencil on board, 9x11", RWS 3/31/88 ... 325
Pair: Standing Female Nude; Study of a Seated Girl; chalk on gray/tan paper, sgn, unfr, 22x19", C-E 2/21/89 UE ... 440
Picking Flowers, oil on canvas, sgn, 40x26", C-NY 2/25/88 ... 9,900
Woman Seated in a Park, oil on panel, sgn, 6x9", SBY 12/9/88 OE ... 3,300
LYNDE, Raymonde (British, 19th/20th C)
Portrait of a Young Beauty, oil on canvas, sgn, 24x20", C-E 10/26/89 ... 3,300
LYNE, Michael (British, 1912-)
Ascot, 1961 (racing scene); oil on canvas, sgn, 28x36", SBY 6/9/89 ... 15,400
Cub Hunting, Dawn (huntsmen on horses w/dogs in a landscape); oil on canvas, sgn, 20x31", C-E 5/22/89 ... 5,280
Neck & Neck, oil on canvas, sgn, 24x36", SBY 6/9/89 ... 4,500
LYNGBYE, Lauritz B.
American Frigate Under Sail, watercolor/pen/black ink on laid paper, sgn/inscr/dtd 1832 twice, 8x11", C-NY 5/25/88 ... 2,420
LYON, Corneille; see De Lyon
M.E. (19th C)
California Street, San Francisco; pencil/pen/ink/watercolor, #d 363/dtd 1877, unfr, 8x10", C-SK 5/25/89 OE ... 7,720
San Francisco From Telegraph Hill, pen/ink/watercolor, #d 368/dtd 1878, unfr, 6x10", C-SK 5/25/89 OE ... 5,880
MAAS, Dirck (Dutch, 1659-1717)
Pair: Extensive Landscapes with Travelers; oil on canvas, sgn, 22x27", SBY 6/2/89 OE ... 44,000
MAAS, Eugene Remy (Belgian, 1849-1931)
Chickens in a Landscape, oil on panel, sgn/dtd 1886(?), 9x14", SBY 7/12/89 ... 4,400
MAASS, David (20th C)
Open Water at the Point-Broadbills; oil on masonite, sgn, 18x24", SBY 9/14/89 ... 3,960
MABE, Manabu (Brazilian, 1924-)
Abstracto, oil on canvas, sgn/dtd 1977, 20x20", C-NY 5/18/88 ... 4,950
March (abstract), oil on canvas, sgn/dtd 68/titled, 48x61", SBY 11/21/88 OE ... 18,700
Sin Titulo (abstract), oil on canvas, sgn/dtd NY 1970, 22x28", C-NY 5/17/89 ... 5,500

Untitled (abstract), mixed media on canvas, sgn/dtd 66 twice, SBY 11/21/88 2,475
Vente de Inverno, oil on canvas, sgn/dtd Brasil 1966, 30x30", C-NY 11/21/89 5,500

MAC CAULEY, Lorna Lormer (Canadian, 1881-)
Returning Home, pastel, sgn, 13x16", FB 10/17/88 275

MAC CLELLAN, Charles Archibald (American, 1887-)
Quilters (two elderly ladies working on bright patchwork quilt), oil on board, sgn, 22x18", RAB 8/9/88 1,600

MAC CONNEL, Kim (American, 20th C)
Bronco Buster, gouache on folded paper, initialed/sgn/dtd 9/80, 15x22", C-E 11/14/89 1,980

MAC DONALD, James Edward Hervy (Canadian, 1873-1932)
Lake O'Hara From the North Shore, oil on board, sgn/dtd 29, 9x11", WAD 11/30/89 18,000
Wheatfield, Thornhill; oil on board, sgn/dtd 1931, 9x11", FB 5/28/89 9,500

MAC DONALD, Manly Edward (Canadian, 1889-1971)
Autumn Lake, oil on board, sgn, 10x13", WAD 11/30/89 1,150
Haytime, oil on board, sgn, 8x10", WAD 11/30/89 1,600
Riverside Mill, oil on canvas, sgn, 14x16", WAD 11/30/89 4,200
Winter Stream, oil on canvasboard, sgn, 12x16", WAD 6/12/89 2,800

MAC DONALD, Thomas Reid (Canadian, 1908-1978)
Full-Length Standing Nude, oil on canvas, sgn, 28x16", FB 10/30/89 275
Full-Length Standing Nude, oil on canvas, sgn, 28x16", FB 5/28/89 550
Seated by the Easel, oil on canvas, sgn, 16x12", WAD 6/12/89 325
Seated Nude, oil on canvas, sgn, 29x22", FB 10/17/88 800

MAC DONALD, Thomas; att (fl 1825-1837)
Portrait of Miss Ann Nichol (seated in an interior), watercolor/ink on paper, 1825, 9x7", RWS 10/27/89 4,750

MAC DONALD, W. Alister (British, 20th C)
Landing on a Caribbean Beach, watercolor on paper, indistinctly dtd, 10x15", B/B 1/11/89 715

MAC DONALD-WRIGHT, Stanton (American, 1890-1974)
Double-Sided: La Roce Degli Angeli (abstract); watercolor/gouache/pencil on paper, sgn/dtd 69, 26x19", C-NY 5/25/89 6,600
Firenze (abstract), watercolor/pencil on paper, sgn/dtd 70, 13x10", C-NY 9/28/89 4,950
Hawaiian Fantasy, oil on canvas laid down on panel, sgn, 9x8", C-NY 3/11/88 3,520

MAC DOUGAL HART, James (American, 1828-1901)
Cattle Watering, oil on canvas, sgn/dtd 1862, 16x26", C-SK 5/25/89 OE 17,450

MAC ENTYRE, Eduardo (Argentinian, 1929-)
On Green (circular composition), oil on canvas, sgn/dtd 73/titled Sobre verde, 39x39", SBY 11/21/88 OE 5,500

MAC GEORGE, William Stewart (British, 1861-1931)
Children in an Orchard, oil on canvas, sgn, 25x22", C-NY 5/25/88 OE 42,900
Sheep by a Brook, oil on canvas, sgn, 12x14", B/B 3/22/89 2,750

MAC GINNIS, Henry Ryan (American, 1875-1962)
Double Sided: Mountain Twilight (landacape); Floral Still Life; oil on particle board, sgn, 12x16", RWS 9/29/88 UE 150
West Field House (winter view of farmhouse), oil on canvas, sgn/dtd 1935, 25x30", RWS 9/29/88 UE 200

MAC INTOSH, Marian T. (American, 1871-1936)
Gray of Dusk-A Harbor View; oil on canvas, sgn, 25x30", RWS 3/16/89 UE 600
Summer Noon, oil on canvas, sgn, 28x30", RWS 3/16/89 2,300

MAC KAY, Edwin Murray (American, 1869-1926)
In the Garden, oil on canvas, bears artist's estate stamp, 25x30", C-NY 3/11/88 OE 7,150
Summers in the Garden, oil on canvas, bears artist's estate stamp, 25x31", C-NY 3/11/88 1,650

MAC KAY, J. (British, 19th C)
Highland Cattle By a Loch, oil on board, sgn, 19x28", WAD 6/6/88 900

MAC KAY, William Andrew (American, 1878-)
Winter Landscape, oil on canvasboard, sgn, 22x30", C-E 6/1/88 1,760

MAC KNIGHT, see Macknight

MAC MONNIES, Frederick William (American, 1863-1937)
Marjorie & Berthe Feed Their Pet Rooster, Coco; oil on canvas, 21x23", C-NY 5/26/88 28,600

MAC MONNIES, Mary Fairchild (American, 1859-1946)
Betty MacMonnies Preparing the Dolls` Dinner, oil on canvas, 18x15", WL 5/20/88 4,000

MAC NALL, E. (American, 20th C)
Still Life of Peaches & Pineapple, oil on canvas, sgn, 14x22", WL 5/20/88 450

MAC NEIL, Ambrose (Scottish, 1852-)
Sunset on a Mountain Stream, oil on canvas, sgn/dtd 1909, 12x10", WL 5/20/88 775

MAC RAE, Elmer Livingston (American, 1875-1953)
Bush-Holley House in Winter (Old House South End), oil on canvas, sgn twice, ca 1910, 25x25", C-NY 12/2/88 OE 31,900
Chickens, black ink/gouache on canvas, sgn, 14x19", SBY 1/24/89 880
In the Garden, watercolor/pen/ink on board, sgn/dtd 1900, unfr, 20x25", C-E 6/1/88 605
Looking Out the Window, watercolor/pencil on paper laid down on board, unfr, 19x12", C-E 6/1/88 352
Schooner in the Ice, View From the Bush-Holley House; oil on canvas, sgn/dtd 1909, 25x30", C-NY 12/2/88 46,200
View From the Porch, watercolor/ink on board, unfr, 19x13", C-E 6/1/88 UE 220

MACAULIFFE, James J. (American, 1848-1921)
Shipping Off a Coastline, oil on canvas, sgn/dtd 87, 22x36", PHL 12/1/88 2,600

MACCARI, Cesare (Italian, 1840-1919)
Arab Men at Leisure, watercolor over pencil, sgn/#d 53 B/Roma, 22x15", C-NY 10/25/89 3,080

MACCHIATI, Serafino (Italian, 1861-1916)
Lady with a Bouquet of Flowers, pastel, sgn, 19x8", C-E 10/26/89 880

MACCIO, Romulo (Argentinian, 1931-)
- Pintor Modelo, acrylic on canvas, sgn/dtd 1973, 51x53", SBY 5/17/88 16,500
- Vivir a Todo Trapo (abstract), oil on canvas, sgn/dtd 60, 32x32", C-NY 11/21/88 UE 1,320

MACGREGOR, Jessie (American, 20th C)
- Floral Still Life, oil on canvasboard, sgn, 15x11", B/B 1/11/89 330

MACHETANZ, Fred (American, 1908-)
- Big Mountain, oil on board, sgn/dtd 1961, 17x21", B/B 8/10/88 7,150
- Boy in a Parka, oil on board, sgn/dtd 1961, 18x16", B/B 8/10/88 OE 10,450
- Favorite Dog (portrait of a Huskie), oil on board, sgn/dtd 1959, 16x18", B/B 8/10/88 OE 7,700
- Frenchie (portrait of a man), oil on board, sgn/dtd 1959, 18x16", B/B 8/10/88 4,400
- Good Mushing, oil on board, sgn/dtd 1960, 26x32", B/B 8/10/88 17,600
- Land of the Totems, oil on board, sgn/dtd 1967, 16x20", B/B 8/10/88 3,300
- Moment of Truth, oil on board, sgn/dtd 1967, 16x20", B/B 8/10/88 OE 9,350
- Seal in His Heights, oil on board, sgn/dtd 1967, 16x20", B/B 8/10/88 7,150
- Search by Night (growling polar bear), oil on board, sgn/dtd 1969, 16x20", B/B 8/10/88 6,050

MACKE, Auguste (German, 1887-1914)
- Kleine Farbige Formenkomposition II (abstract), crayons/watercolor, Nachlass stamp/#d FSt64, 1913, 3x6", SBY 10/6/89 3,300

MACKELLAR, Duncan (British, 1849-1908)
- Man Reading, oil on canvas, sgn/dtd 1884, 12x20", WL 5/20/88 500

MACKENZIE, Alexander (British, 1848-)
- Countryside with Grazing Cattle, oil on canvas, sgn/dtd 1884, 15x27", B/B 12/8/88 770

MACKENZIE, Frank J. (American, 1867-1939)
- Portrait of a Gentleman, oil on canvas, sgn/dtd 1932, 31x25", B/B 4/20/88 522

MACKENZIE, Frederick (British, 1787-1854)
- Procession Entering the Northwest Door of Lincoln Cathedral, watercolor heightened w/gouache, 41x30", C-E 10/26/89 2,750

MACKENZIE, Roderick D. (American, 1865-)
- Set of 3: Benares, India; oil on canvas, ea sgn/1 dtd 1898, unfr, 20x26", C-SK 11/10/88 190
- Set of 3: Indian Festivities; Interior Study; oil on canvas, 1 sgn/dtd 1896, unfr, 21x27" & smaller, C-SK 11/10/88 260

MACKNIGHT, Dodge (American, 1860-1950)
- Autumn Grazing, shepherd/flock on steep hillside; watercolor on paper, sgn, 14x22", RAB 8/8/89 UE 600
- Blue Cliffs (seascape), watercolor on paper, sgn, 15x21", RAB 8/9/88 OE 5,100
- Canoeing on a Mountain Lake (landscape), watercolor on paper, sgn, 17x24", RWS 3/16/89 2,750
- Coastal View, watercolor on paper, sgn, 17x24", RWS 11/3/88 OE 4,000
- Le Puy 1895, watercolor on paper, sgn/inscr, 15x22", RWS 11/3/88 UE 1,600
- Mountain Lake, watercolor on paper laid down on board, sgn, 17x24", SBY 1/24/89 OE 2,090
- Tending the Flocks in Autumn Pastures, watercolor on paper, sgn, 16x22", RWS 11/10/89 2,000
- Western Landscape (canyon view), watercolor on paper, sgn, 17x21", SBY 9/14/89 1,540
- Woman on the Riverbanks, watercolor on paper, sgn, 16x23", RWS 3/16/89 1,200

MACLET, Elisee (French, 1881-1962)
- Barques dans un Port, oil on panel laid down on masonite, sgn, 18x21", C-NY 2/13/89 4,180
- Eglise de Banieu (view of church & figures on sidewalk), oil on board, sgn, 22x18", SBY 2/14/89 OE 9,900
- Eglise de Village, oil on board, sgn, 14x11", C-E 5/9/89 4,620
- Eglise du Breuil (view of a church), oil on board, sgn, 20x24", C-NY 2/18/88 5,500
- Eglise St Medard (church of St Medard), oil on canvas, sgn, 18x22", C-E 11/17/88 7,150
- L'Ile de Sieck, oil on canvas, sgn, 20x29", SBY 10/5/88 5,500
- La Lapin Agile au Temps d'Adele, oil on canvas, sgn, 18x22", C-NY 10/6/88 OE 11,000
- La rue Ravignam (street scene), oil on canvas, sgn/titled, 18x22", C-E 5/9/89 OE 37,400
- Le Lapin Agile au Temps d'Adele, oil on canvas, sgn, 18x22", C-NY 2/13/89 OE 17,600
- Le Maquis, oil on canvas, sgn, 18x22", SBY 10/7/89 OE 30,800
- Le Moulin, oil on canvas, sgn, 18x22", SBY 10/5/88 OE 12,100
- Le Port de La Rochelle (boats by shore w/figures & house), watercolor/pen/black ink, sgn, 12x15", C-E 11/17/88 OE 1,540
- Le Sacre Coeur, oil on canvas, sgn, 13x16", SBY 10/7/89 OE 18,700
- Le Theatre de l'Atelier a Montmartre (street scene), oil on board laid down on cradled panel, sgn, 16x19", C-E 5/9/89 OE 15,400
- Le Theatre l'Atelier, oil on board, sgn, 1917, 20x26", SBY 10/7/89 OE 18,700
- Maison de Berlioz, oil on canvas, sgn/inscr, 18x22", C-E 5/13/88 6,820
- Maison de Mimi-Pincon, Montmartre; oil on canvas, sgn, 18x22", C-NY 10/6/88 OE 13,200
- Montmartre, oil on canvas, sgn, unfr, 17x22", SBY 2/14/89 6,050
- Montmartre, oil on board, sgn, 24x18", C-NY 2/18/88 8,250
- Montreuil, oil on canvas, sgn, 13x16", SBY 10/7/89 OE 19,800
- Moulin de la Galette, oil on canvas, sgn, 18x22", SBY 10/7/89 OE 27,500
- Paris Street Scene, oil on canvas, sgn, 13x17", SBY 10/7/89 OE 18,700
- Paysage (impasto style landscape), oil on canvas, sgn, 20x26", PHL 6/16/88 9,500
- Rue de Saules Sous la Neige, oil on canvas, sgn, 11x14", C-E 5/13/88 4,620
- Rue de Village, oil on board, sgn, 11x17", C-NY 2/13/89 5,500
- Rue et Mont Cenis a Montmartre (winter street scene), oil on canvas, sgn, 11x14", C-NY 2/18/88 4,400
- Rue Lepic Montmartre (quiet street scene), oil on wood panel, sgn, 1919, 17x23", DM 9/16/88 9,000
- Sacre-Coeur vu de Loin (Sacred-Heart viewed from distance), oil on canvas, sgn/dtd 1960, 16x20", C-E 11/17/88 3,080
- Snowy Street Scene, oil on canvas, sgn, 11x14", SBY 2/14/89 OE 8,250
- Street Scene, Paris; oil on canvas, sgn, 18x22", SBY 10/5/88 OE 11,000
- Vaison-La Romaine (modernistic village scene); oil on canvas, sgn, 1926, 20x26", SBY 10/7/89 OE 24,200
- Village de Provence (impressionistic village scene), oil on panel, sgn, ca 1920, 11x9", C-E 11/17/88 3,080

Vue de Sacre-Coeur (view of Sacre-Coeur), oil on canvas, sgn, 18x22", C-E 11/17/88 OE 12,100

MACLISE, Daniel (British, 1806-1870)
Hamlet, Act III, Scene I; oil on panel, sgn, 11x19", B/B 5/17/89 UE 1,650

MACOMBER, Mary Lizzie (American, 1861-1916)
Faith, Hope, & Love; oil on canvas, sgn/inscr/dtd 1894, 33x24", SBY 5/25/88 13,200
Music Stand Central Park, New York City; oil on canvas, sgn, 8x10", RWS 5/12/89 OE 1,600
The Pearl (profile of girl holding pearl), oil on canvas, sgn/dtd 1907, 12x8", SBY 6/28/89 2,750
View of the Common, oil on canvas, sgn/dtd 1912, 12x20", C-NY 9/28/89 4,400

MACRAE, Elmer Livingston (American, 1875-1952)
Portrait of a Young Child (profile), pastel on gray paper, sgn/dtd 1911, 11x14", RWS 9/29/88 UE 325
Rocky Coastline, oil on canvas, sgn/dtd 1909, 14x18", C-NY 3/11/88 2,200

MACWHIRTER, John (English, 1839-1911)
Birchwood, Evening, Isle of Swan (sheep in wooded pasture); oil on canvas, sgn, 39x18", C-E 2/21/89 UE 1,100

MADDEN, Jan (American, 20th C)
Harbor Scene, oil on canvas, sgn, 25x30", RWS 5/12/89 8,000
View of Gloucester Harbor, oil on canvas, sgn, 25x30", RWS 5/12/89 1,800

MADDERSTEEG, Michiel (Dutch, 1659-1709)
Harbor at Amsterdam with a Man-O-War & Other Shipping in a Choppy Sea, oil on canvas, monogramed, 24x33", C-NY 5/31/89 28,600

MADELAIN, Gustave (French, 1867-1944)
Le Place St Augustin, Paris (busy street scene); oil on canvas, sgn, 29x36", WD 11/16/88 UE 6,000
Le 14 Juillet, Place de la Bastille, Paris; oil on canvas, sgn, 27x38", WD 5/5/88 OE 22,000
View of St Augustine, oil on canvas, sgn, 29x37", B/B 3/17/88 2,200

MADELINE, Paul (French, 1863-1920)
Mediterranean Landscape, oil on canvas, studio stamp, 32x40", LH 12/4/88 5,000

MADJEN, Oho
First Snow, oil on board, sgn, 11x14", C-E 9/15/88 UE 110

MADLENER, A. Joseph (German, 1881-)
Winter Landscape with Figures, oil on panel, sgn, 10x13", B/B 10/9/88 2,475

MADOU, Jean Baptiste (Belgian, 1796-1877)
Entertaining the Baby, oil on canvas, sgn twice, 17x20", C-NY 2/25/88 OE 18,700
Shipwrights Taking a Rest, watercolor, sgn/dtd 1846, 12x17", C-NY 5/25/88 4,620

MADRAZO Y GARRETA, see De Madrazo Y Garreta

MAECKER, Franz Wilhelm (German, 1855-1913)
Sandanen in der Heide, oil on canvas, sgn, 20x27", C-E 10/26/89 1,320

MAENTEL, Jacob (American, 1763-1863)
Portrait of a Man, watercolor on paper, 12x8", C-NY 10/1/88 UE 770
Portrait of a Woman Holding a Book, watercolor on paper, inscr, 11x8", C-NY 10/1/88 UE 1,540
Portrait of Johann & Susannah Beard, watercolor on paper, inscr, 11x17", C-NY 10/1/88 13,200

MAES, Eugene Remy (Belgian, 1849-1931)
Chickens, oil on canvas, sgn, 24x20", B/B 3/22/89 OE 8,800
Chickens in a Barnyard, oil on canvas, sgn twice/inscr, 16x12", SBY 6/8/88 OE 5,225
Fowl in a Barnyard, oil on panel, sgn, 13x17", B/B 3/22/89 2,750
Poultry in a Barnyard, oil on canvas, sgn/dtd 1878, 24x36", SBY 7/12/89 3,025
Poultry in a Farmyard, oil on canvas, sgn, 46x36", C-NY 10/25/89 OE 20,900

MAES, H. (British, 19th C)
Near Dort, oil on canvas, sgn twice/inscr/dtd 1885, 10x18", SBY 6/8/88 2,090

MAES, Hendrik (Dutch, 1793-1873)
Port Scene, oil on canvas, sgn, 14x25", WL 5/20/88 6,000

MAES, Nicolaes (Dutch, 1632-1693)
Pair: Portraits of Joost Van Hoogenhouck & His Wife, Anthonia des Quiens; oil on canvas, ea 17x13", SBY 6/2/89 22,000
Portrait of a Young Boy Holding a Bird, & Seated in a Landscape with a Dog; oil on canvas, sgn, 22x19", SBY 1/12/89 27,500

MAES, Nicolaes; att (Dutch, 1632-1693)
Milkmaid Ringing a Door Bell Beside a Group of Children, oil on canvas, sgn, 33x24", SBY 1/12/89 7,700

MAESTOSI, F. (Italian, 19th C)
Interior of the Pitti Palace, oil on canvas, sgn, 40x60", SBY 7/12/89 8,250

MAESTRI, Michelangelo (Italian, -1812)
Cupid with Swans, gouache on black paper, 91x126", C-M 6/16/89 1,141
Pair: Ora Prima di Giorno; Ora Quarta di Giorno; bodycolor over engraved bases, sgn/inscr, 17x13", C-NY 1/11/89 4,620
Pair: Ora Quarta di Notte; Ora Sesta di Notte; bodycolor over engraved bases, sgn/inscr, 17x13", C-NY 1/11/89 4,620

MAGAFAN, Ethel (American, 1916-)
Before the Mountain, oil on board, sgn, 9x22", C-E 10/18/89 1,320

MAGANZA, Alessandro (Italian, 1556-1630)
Deposition, with the Three Marys; black chalk/pen/brown ink/brown wash, wm, 10x7", C-NY 1/12/88 3,300

MAGARY (19th C)
Farmyard & Stables, oil on board, sgn, 12x16", WG 4/23/88 UE 200

MAGAUD, Dominique Antoine Jean Baptiste (French, 1817-1899)
Portrait of a Young Girl, oil on canvas, sgn, 41x34", C-NY 10/25/89 OE 12,100

MAGEE, James C. (American, 1846-1924)
Up for Repair (figure & boat in a landscape), oil on canvas, sgn, 16x20", C-E 6/1/88 990

MAGGIOTTO, school of (Italian, 18th C)
Young Girl Singing From Sheet Music, oil on canvas, 27x19", C-NY, 4/8/88 UE 1,100

MAGGS, John Charles (British, 1819-1896)
Christmas Coach, oil on canvas, sgn/dtd 1876, 14x26", SBY 6/10/88 3,300
Coach Outside an Inn in Winter, oil on canvas laid down on board, sgn/dtd 1876, 14x28", C-NY 10/25/89 5,500
Country Racecourse in the 18th Century, Starting; oil on canvas, sgn/dtd 1884, 14x27", SBY 6/9/89 14,300

MAGIDEY, W. (Continental, 19th/20th C)
Sunday Afternoon, oil on panel, sgn, 8x10", B/B 9/15/88 550

MAGNASCO, Alessandro (Italian, 1667-1749)
Christ on the Cross, oil on canvas, 22x10", C-M 12/3/88 9,360
Pentinent Monks in a Mountainous Landscape, oil on canvas, 38x21", C-NY 5/31/89 35,200

MAGNASCO, Alessandro; att (Italian, 1667-1749)
Death of Pulcinella, oil on canvas, unfr, 28x37", C-NY 1/15/88 OE 16,500

MAGNASCO, Alessandro; circle of (Italian, 1667-1749)
Saint Bruno & a Follower Praying in the Wilderness, oil on canvas, 28x24", C-NY 10/25/88 OE 19,800

MAGNASCO, Alessandro; follower of (Italian, 1667-1749)
Monks Meditating in a Landscape, oil on canvas, 13x19", SBY 10/13/89 3,300

MAGNASCO, Alessandro; school of (Italian, 1667-1749)
Mountainous River Landscape with Children, oil on canvas, 36x50", C-NY 4/8/88 OE 26,400
Saint Jerome in Landscape, oil on canvas, 38x52", C-NY 4/6/89 OE 9,900
Saint Mary Magdalene in the Wilderness, oil on canvas, unfr, 27x23", C-NY 4/6/89 1,320
Wooded Landscape with Figures, oil on canvas, 35x29", C-NY 1/15/88 OE 11,000

MAGNI, Giuseppe (Italian, 1869-)
After the Bath, oil on canvas, sgn/dtd 1929, 24x30", SBY 12/9/88 5,775
Angelo Custode (woman beside baby in basket), oil on canvas, sgn, 56x71", B/B 10/9/88 11,000
First Toast, oil on canvas, sgn/dtd 1902, 28x41", SBY 5/23/89 OE 47,300
Playful Kitten, oil on canvas, sgn, 26x36", SBY 2/22/89 OE 38,500
Testing the Vintage, oil on canvas, sgn, 28x41", C-NY 10/25/89 OE 71,500

MAGNUS, Camille (French, 1850-)
Femme dans une Clairiere (woman in a clearing), oil on canvas, sgn/dtd 75, 24x29", SBY 2/22/89 UE 4,400
Returning Home, oil on board, indistinctly sgn, 7x12", B/B 8/10/88 330

MAGRATH, Georges; see De Magrath

MAGRITTE, Rene (Belgian, 1898-1967)
Chant de la Violette (two male stone-like figures dressed in suits), oil on canvas, sgn/dtd 1951, SBY 11/11/88 OE 1,320,000
Double-Sided: Eagle & Floating Rock (enlargement on verso); pencil, ca 1957, 11x14", SWN 12/1/88 1,210
L'Age des Merveilles (surrealistic), oil on canvas, sgn, 1926, 48x32", SBY 5/10/88 473,000
L'Aimant (standing nude), pen/sepia/black ink on paper, sgn, ca 1940, 11x9", SBY 5/10/89 OE 24,200
L'Esprit du Voyager, oil on canvas, sgn, 1926, 26x30", SBY 5/11/88 OE 198,000
L'Etat de Veille (surrealistic view of windows in sky/building), gouache, sgn/dtd 1958, 8x10", SBY 5/11/88 OE 57,750
La Malediction (clouds in sky), oil on panel, indistinctly sgn, 6x5", C-NY 10/6/88 24,200
La Marche Triomphale, oil on canvas, sgn/dtd 1947/titled, 25x21", SBY 11/12/88 110,000
La Retour a la Nature, gouache on paper, sgn, ca 1938-39, 10x15", C-NY 10/6/88 OE 83,600
La Tempete, oil on canvas laid down on board, sgn, ca 1944, 18x22", C-NY 11/16/88 275,000
La Vocation, colored crayon on paper, sgn/dtd 1964/titled, 9x12", SBY 11/12/88 46,750
La Voix du Sang, gouache on paper, sgn/dtd 1948, 18x15", SBY 5/10/89 OE 253,000
La Voix du Sang (surrealistic), gouache on paper laid down on board, sgn, 9x7", SBY 5/11/88 OE 60,500
Le Carnaval du Sage, sanguine on paper, sgn twice/titled, ca 1948, 18x14", SBY 11/12/88 88,000
Le Coup au Coeur, oil on canvas, sgn/dtd 1956, 8x6", SBY 5/11/88 OE 176,000
Le Domaine d'Arnheim, oil on canvas, sgn, 1938, 29x39", C-NY 11/15/88 825,000
Le Lecon de Musique (The Music Lesson, ear drawn on top of bell), pen/ink on paper, sgn, 1964, 12x8", SBY 5/10/89 22,000
Le Maitre d'Ecole (The School Master), gouache on paper, sgn, 1954, 13x10", SBY 5/11/88 OE 308,000
Le Monde Poetique (surrealistic), oil on canvas, sgn, 1926, 39x29", SBY 11/15/89 605,000
Le Palais de Rideaux, gouache on paper, sgn, 1964, 14x22", SBY 4/29/88 OE 143,000
Les Promenades d'Euclide, gouache on paper laid down on board, sgn, ca 1955-56, 6x8", SBY 5/11/88 OE 93,500
Les Promenades d'Euclide, oil on canvas, sgn/dtd, 1956, 6x8", SBY 5/11/88 OE 264,000
Nude Among Pawns, watercolor on paper, ca 1930, 20x14", C-NY 10/6/88 OE 41,800
Souvenir de Voyage (surrealistic view of feather against leaning tower), gouache, sgn, 1955, 15x12", SBY 5/11/88 OE 275,000
Untitled (surrealistic composition), watercolor/gouache/charcoal/collage on paper, sgn, 1926, 22x16", SBY 4/29/88 OE 110,000
View-New York (for cover of View Magazine); watercolor/crayon/white gouache on paper, sgn, 1946, 12x9", SBY 5/11/88 44,000

MAGUILIES, Joseph
Beach Scene, watercolor & pencil on paper, sgn, 14x20", C-E 2/1/89 3,080

MAIER, Claus (German School, 19th/20th C)
Dice Game, oil on canvas, sgn/dtd 1895, 31x38", MG 11/19/88 800

MAIER, Emil
Arabs Near Steps, oil on canvas, sgn, 25x17", C-E 10/25/88 1,650

MAILLOL, Aristide Joseph Bonaventure (French, 1861-)
Assise de Dos (posterior view of seated nude), black crayon on paper, monogramed, ca 1907-08, 12x8", SBY 2/16/89 OE 7,700
Dina Debout de Dos (nude viewed from behind), red/black chalks on paper, monogramed, 1941, 14x10", C-NY 10/5/89 OE 23,100
Dos de Marie a la Draperie (posterior view of semi-nude figure), sanguine/chalk on paper, 1930, 15x12", SBY 2/16/88 11,550
Femme Nue Couchee (reclining nude, posterior view), charcoal on tan paper, monogramed, ca 1928, 10x15", C-NY 2/16/89 4,950
Femme Nue Debout (standing nude), pencil on paper, stamped w/monogram, 17x10", C-NY 5/11/89 OE 24,200
Jeune Fille Debout Devant l'Amandier (nude beside tree), sanguine/pastel on paper, monogramed, 15x10", SBY 5/10/89 OE 20,900
Nu de Dos (nude viewed from behind), pencil on paper, monogramed/inscr, 15x9", SBY 5/10/89 OE 30,800

Nu Debout, pencil on paper laid down on board, initialed, 11x8", SBY 10/27/89 OE **17,600**
Nu Debout: Vue de Dos (standing nude viewed from behind); sanguine on paper, monogramed, 14x5", SBY 10/6/89 ..... **8,800**

MAINE, Harry; see De Maine

MAINELLA, Raffaele (Italian, 1858-)
Arab Caravan, watercolor/pen on paper, sgn, 10x19", C-E 2/23/88 UE **242**
Fisherfolk in a Bay, watercolor on paper, sgn/inscr, 16x10", C-E 5/23/88 UE **495**

MAINERI, see De Maineri

MAISON, Mary Edith (American, 1886-1954)
Desert Dunes, oil on board, sgn, 16x20", B/B 1/11/89 ..... **440**
Desert Flowers, oil on board, sgn, 16x20", B/B 1/11/89 ..... **330**

MAJO, see De Majo

MAJOR, Ernest (American, 1864-)
Landscape Scene at Sunset, oil on canvas, sgn, 24x32", RWS 4/7/89 UE **375**

MAKART, Hans (Austrian, 1840-1884)
Lorelei (seated nude), oil on canvas, 29x18", C-E 5/22/89 ..... **4,400**

MAKOVSKII, Aleksandr Vladimirovich (Russian, 1869-1924)
Two Peasant Women of South Russia Drinking Tea on Steps of an Izba, oil on canvas, sgn/dtd 1916, 33x26", C-L 10/8/88 OE **13,000**
Village Market, oil on canvas, sgn/dtd 1919, 12x16", C-L 10/8/88 OE **8,920**

MAKOVSKII, Konstantin Egorovich (Russian, 1839-1915)
Lady at Her Easel in a Wooded Landscape, oil on canvas, sgn twice/dtd 1876, 29x19", C-L 10/8/88 ..... **13,000**
Lethe, oil on canvas, sgn, 44x35", SBY 7/12/89 ..... **3,575**
Pleased Fisherman (three-quarter length fisherman w/catch in landscape), oil on canvas, sgn, 38x27", C-L 10/8/88 ..... **15,800**
Summer Afternoon (landscape w/house & figures), oil on canvas, sgn, 29x47", SBY 10/24/89 ..... **18,700**
Three Generations (group portrait), pencil/watercolor on paper, sgn, 6x7", C-L 10/8/88 OE **2,790**

MAKOZERIALAN (Austrian, 20th C)
Reclining Female Nude on a Divan Draped with an Oriental Rug, oil on board, sgn/dtd 1917, 32x42", SLK 2/12/88 ..... **575**

MALAMPRE, Leo (British/French, 19th C)
Flower Market, oil on canvas, sgn, 24x16", C-E 2/23/88 ..... **3,080**
Portrait of a Young Girl with Daffodils, oil on canvas, sgn/dtd 1895, 26x20", B/B 3/17/88 ..... **6,600**

MALBET, Aurelie Leontine (French, fl 1868-1906)
Still Life of Spring Flowers & Peaches, oil on canvas, sgn, 32x26", SBY 2/22/89 ..... **7,150**

MALESPINA, Louis Ferdinand (French, 1874-)
Race, colored chalks/charcoal on brown paper, sgn, 15x22", C-E 5/23/88 C-E 5/23/88 ..... **825**

MALET, Albert (French, 1902-)
La Seine Pres d'Henouville, oil on masonite, sgn/titled, 18x22", C-E 5/9/89 ..... **2,970**

MALEVICH, Kasimir (Russian, 1878-1935)
Composition, pencil on paper, 10x6", C-NY 5/12/88 ..... **7,700**
Composition, pencil on paper, 9x5", C-NY 5/12/88 ..... **8,800**
Suprematist Compostion, pencil on buff paper, ca 1914-15, 7x4", SBY 11/12/88 OE **19,800**

MALFROY, Charles (French, 1862-)
Barques sur la Plage, oil on canvas, sgn, 18x26", C-NY 2/13/89 ..... **3,080**
Pointe de Bresson a Martiques, oil on canvas, sgn, 13x18", WAD 6/6/88 ..... **2,400**

MALFROY, Henry (French, 1895-)
Boats Along a Canal, oil on canvas, sgn, 20x26", C-E 5/22/89 ..... **3,850**
Fishing Village, oil on canvas, sgn, 24x37", C-E 2/23/88 ..... **3,300**
Les Martigues, oil on canvas, sgn, 17x25", WAD 6/6/88 ..... **2,200**
Southern Harbor, oil on canvas, sgn, 15x22", WD 5/5/88 OE **4,000**
Southern Port in the Late Afternoon, oil on canvas, sgn, 15x22", WD 5/5/88 ..... **3,200**

MALHAUPT, Frederick John (American, 1871-1938)
Harbor View, Gloucester; oil on canvas, sgn/dtd 07, 22x28", RWS 11/3/88 ..... **8,000**

MALHERBE, William (French, 1854-1951)
Bath, oil on canvas, sgn, 30x33", C-NY 9/30/88 ..... **4,180**
Femme au Chapeau de Paille, oil on canvas, sgn/dtd 28, 27x22", C-E 5/13/88 UE **1,100**
La Catherdrale de Rouen, oil on canvas, sgn/dtd 29, 29x24", SBY 10/5/88 ..... **2,310**
Women Carrying Platters of Fruit, oil on panel, 14x20", B/B 12/8/88 ..... **2,200**

MALIAVINE, Philippe Andreevich (Russian, 1869-1940)
Portrait of Woman, pencil/colored crayon on paper, sgn, 1933, 15x10", C-L 10/8/88 OE **930**
Young Woman Fastening Her Shawl (waist-length portrait), oil on canvas, sgn, 26x32", SBY 2/14/89 ..... **13,200**

MALIUTIN, Ivan (Russian, 1889-1932)
Costume Design, watercolor/brush/pen/ink on paper, sgn/dtd 1917, 12x9", C-L 10/8/88 OE **1,490**

MALLET, Gabrielle (American, 19th C)
Village Street, oil on canvas, sgn, 13x19", FAP 12/8/89 ..... **275**

MALLINA, Erich (1873-1954)
Throne Figure, pencil/watercolor heightened w/white & gold on paper, 1909, 9x9", C-L 6/27/88 ..... **4,162**

MALLO, Maruja
Blond Youth (head in profile), oil on canvas, sgn, 19x16", SBY 11/21/88 ..... **8,800**
Self-Portrait, oil on board, sgn, ca 1942, 19x30", SBY 5/17/88 ..... **11,000**

MALLOUEL, Jean; follower of
Deposition, tempera on panel, 8x9", SBY 7/12/89 ..... **3,300**

MALO, Vincent (Flemish, 1600-1650)
Cavalry Battle, oil on panel, initialed, 20x28", C-NY 4/8/88OE **4,400**

MALONEY, Louise B. (American, 20th C)
A Still Life of Flowers in a Vase, oil on canvas, sgn, 29x21", PHL 6/16/88 1,000

MALTESE, school of
Still Life of Green & Purple Grapes on a Cushion, & Berries in a Dish...; oil on canvas, unfr, 26x35", C-E 6/1/88 OE 5,500

MALTMAN, William (Canadian, 1901-1971)
Stop Sixteen, Markham Ontario, April 9th, 1960; watercolor, sgn/dtd 60, 14x16", WAD 6/12/89 750
Toronto Harbour, watercolor, sgn/dtd 34, 11x9", WAD 6/12/89 700

MALY, L. (Continental School, ca 1890)
Middle Eastern Street Scene, oil on canvas, sgn, 17x21", MG 6/25/88 UE 250

MAMMEN, Jeane
Pair: Pagen-Madchen; Heimfahrt; chalk over pencil on paper laid down, 1 initialed/1 sgn, 19x13" & smaller, C-E 11/17/88 2,090

MAN-RAY (Emmanuel Radinski)(American, 1890-1976)
Cactus (abstract), oil on canvas, sgn/dtd 45, 18x24", C-NY 11/16/88 38,500
Ciseaux-Lunettes, oil on board, sgn/dtd 1938, 9x6", SBY 4/29/88 OE 19,800
Composition (abstract), oil on panel, sgn/dtd 1929, 10x7", SBY 10/6/89 22,000
Composition (figure), oil on canvas, sgn twice/dtd 1940 & 1945, 20x16", C-NY 5/12/88 49,500
Composition Abstraite, watercolor/brush/India ink on paper, initialed/dtd MR-53, 21x15", C-NY 10/5/89 18,700
Composition II (abstract), oil on artist board, sgn, 8x10", SBY 2/16/89 OE 7,700
Composition VI (abstract), oil on masonite, sgn, 10x8", SBY 2/16/89 7,150
L'Age de Colle, collage of black construction paper/red cellophane on newspaper, dtd 18-7-59, 24x33", SBY 4/29/88 OE 13,200
La Maree (The Tide), oil on panel, sgn/dtd 49/titled, 15x19", C-NY 5/12/88 60,500
La Rose, oil on panel, sgn/dtd 1949, 14x10", C-NY 5/12/88 30,800
Landscape with Mountains, watercolor on thin board, sgn/dtd 1913, 6x7", SBY 2/18/88 OE 7,700
Mime-57 (abstract), gouache/ink wash on board, sgn twice/dtd 57 twice/titled, 14x11", SBY 2/16/88 9,900
Natural Painting, oil on masonite, sgn/dtd 63, 24x18", SBY 4/29/88 13,200
Peinture Feminine (abstract), oil on canvas, sgn/dtd 54, 50x44", SBY 4/29/88 OE 148,500
Peinture Naturelle, oil on masonite, sgn, 8x11", SBY 10/5/88 4,400
Pittura Naturale (abstract), acrylic on board, sgn, 1971, 20x14", C-E 5/9/89 OE 9,900
Rope Dancer (abstract), oil on canvas, sgn/dtd 1948, 17x14", SBY 11/12/88 OE 46,750
Sailboats at Sunset, pastel on paper, sgn/dtd 1969, 4x5", SBY 10/7/89 1,870
Untitled (abstract), oil on panel, sgn/dtd 58, 7x6", SBY 10/7/89 6,050
Untitled: Fortress & Eggs; pen/brown ink on paper, initialed/dtd 43, 4x6", SBY 4/29/88 OE 7,700

MANAIGO, Silvester; school of (Italian, 1670-1734)
Esther Before Ahasuerus, oil on canvas, 34x47", C-E 6/1/88 850

MANCINI, Antonio (Italian, 1852-1930)
Portrait of a Young Lady (bust-length), oil on wood panel, sgn, 7x6", RAB 8/8/89 800
Young Man with a Wine Bottle, oil on canvas, sgn, unfr, 39x24", SBY 5/23/89 18,700

MANCINI (Italian, 19th C)
Washerwomen Crossing the Stone Bridge, watercolor heightened w/gouache, sgn/dtd 1885, 22x15", C-E 10/26/89 3,080

MANDEL, John (American, 1941-)
Sins of Acquiescence (male nude), pencil/pastel on paper, sgn/dtd 1973/titled, 44x29", SBY 11/11/88 OE 1,210

MANDER, William Henry (British, fl 1880-1922)
Bend in the Road, oil on canvas, sgn, 30x25", C-E 10/26/89 1,980
Rapids, oil on canvas, sgn, 12x18", LH 10/16/88 2,600

MANE-KATZ (French, 1894-1962)
Beach with Breakwater, gouache on green paper, sgn/dtd 61, 18x24", C-E 5/13/88 OE 3,080
Bride & Groom, brush/black ink/gray wash on paper, sgn, 17x14", C-NY 2/13/89 1,430
Drummer, gouache on brown paper, initialed, 20x26", C-E 5/13/88 OE 4,400
Fiancee, varnished gouache on board, sgn, 28x22", C-E 5/13/88 4,400
Figure Studies, brown ink on buff paper, sgn, 11x17", PHL 11/15/88 900
Fishing Boats at Low Tide, gouache on paper, sgn/dtd 38, 18x24", B/B 3/22/89 2,750
Hasidim at School, oil on canvas, sgn, 25x30", SBY 5/30/89 41,800
Horn Player, oil on canvas, sgn, 10x8", SBY 10/5/88 UE 3,025
Jeune Juif (man in long coat), India ink/watercolor on paper, sgn, 12x9", SBY 2/14/89 OE 4,400
L'Orchestre (expressionistic depiction), oil on canvas, sgn, 30x25", SBY 10/7/89 OE 35,200
Landscape, oil on board, sgn/dtd 1959, 20x24", PHL 11/15/88 4,500
Landscape, varnished gouache on blue paper laid down on board, sgn, 20x26", C-NY 2/13/89 OE 3,850
Landscape with Cows, gouache on board, sgn/dtd 32, 19x25", WG 4/23/88 950
Landscape with Lake, varnished gouache on paper laid down on board, sgn, 20x25", C-E 5/13/88 1,210
Landscape with Trees, gouache on paper laid down on canvas, sgn, 20x24", C-E 5/9/89 2,090
Landscape with Windmill, gouache on board, sgn, 28x22", C-E 11/17/88 OE 4,180
Le Port de Saint Giles Croix en Vendee (port scene w/figures), oil on canvas, sgn/dtd 28, 45x58", C-NY 2/18/88 15,400
Les Jeunes Talmudistes (portrait of two young girls), oil on canvas, sgn/#d, 11x9", WD 11/16/88 OE 13,500
Les Marquerites Blanches (The White Daisies), oil on canvas, sgn, 13x16", C-E 11/17/88 770
Matador & Bull, India ink/ink wash/gouache on paper, sgn, 23x17", SBY 10/7/89 2,530
Mother & Child, brush/black ink on paper, sgn, 24x19", C-E 5/13/88 OE 1,045
Mother & Child, oil on board, initialed, 10x8", WD 11/16/88 4,750
Mother with Child, brush/black ink wash on paper, sgn, 24x18", C-E 11/17/88 605
Mountain Hut, gouache on blue paper, sgn, 20x26", C-E 5/13/88 2,860
Mountain Village, varnished gouache on green paper laid down on canvas, sgn, 20x23", C-E 11/17/88 OE 4,180
Musicians (contemporary), oil on canvas, sgn, 1958, 36x47", C-NY 2/18/88 33,000

Musiciens Juifs, gouache on board, sgn, 20x26", SBY 10/5/88 5,500
Nude (half-length), brush/black ink wash on paper, sgn, 24x18", C-E 11/17/88 OE 1,430
Palm Trees, gouache on gray paper, sgn, 20x15", C-E 11/17/88 1,760
Portrait of the Poet Shalom, pastels, sgn/dtd 59, 27x19", PHL 11/15/88 700
Prayer, gouache/watercolor over pencil on paper, sgn, 14x20", C-E 11/17/88 OE 5,280
Rabbi, oil on canvas, sgn, 13x10", C-NY 10/6/88 OE 7,700
Rabbi & Student, oil on canvas, sgn/dtd 60, 25x21", C-NY 2/18/88 OE 27,500
Rabbi Praying, brush/black ink on paper, sgn, 24x19", C-E 5/13/88 OE 1,870
Rabbi with Boy, brush/black ink/gray wash on paper, sgn, 24x19", C-NY 2/13/89 OE 3,850
Rabbi with Torah, oil on canvas, sgn/dtd 59, 13x9", SBY 5/30/89 24,200
Road to Jerusalem, gouache, sgn, 18x24", SBY 5/30/89 6,820
Rue de Paris (Paris street scene), oil on canvas, sgn, 9x12", C-NY 2/13/89 1,210
Seated Boy, gouache on paper laid down on board, sgn, 26x20", C-E 5/9/89 OE 7,480
Seated Nude, oil on canvas, sgn, 23x15", C-NY 10/6/88 4,400
Shepherd with Sheep, brush/black ink on paper, sgn, 24x19", C-E 5/13/88 OE 2,090
Shofar, brush/black ink wash on paper, sgn, 24x19", C-E 11/17/88 OE 5,500
Simha Torah (Jewish Celebration), oil on canvas, sgn, ca 1950, 45x58", C-NY 2/18/88 OE 77,000
Three Rabbis Reading the Torah, brush/black ink/gray wash on paper, sgn, 24x19", C-NY 2/13/89 3,520
Trombone Player, varnished gouache on paper laid down on board, sgn, 26x20", C-E 5/13/88 OE 9,020
Two African Women, varnished gouache on paper laid down on board, sgn, 25x19", C-E 5/13/88 2,860
Two Rabbi with Boys, varnished gouache on paper laid down on panel, sgn/dtd 62, 44x30", C-NY 2/18/88 OE 31,900
Vase de Fleurs (abstract floral still life), gouache on paper w/board laid down on canvas, sgn, 22x18", C-NY 10/5/89 OE 15,400
Vase of Flowers, gouache on yellow paper, sgn, 26x20", C-E 11/17/88 OE 6,050
Vase of Flowers, oil on canvas laid down on board, sgn, 12x8", C-NY 10/6/88 3,300
View From the Window, gouache on brown paper laid down on canvas, sgn, 18x22", C-E 5/9/89 OE 6,380
Wild Horse, oil on canvas, sgn, ca 1950, 20x26", C-NY 2/18/88 OE 15,400
Wild Horse (expressionistic depiction), oil on canvas, sgn, 18x22", SBY 10/7/89 7,700
Young Man with Hat, oil on canvas, sgn, 22x18", SBY 5/30/89 OE 17,600
Young Woman, oil on canvas, sgn, ca 1930, 19x12", C-NY 10/6/88 3,850

MANESSIER, Alfred (French, 1911-)

Alleluia Pascal (abstract), oil on canvas, sgn twice/dtd 64 twice/titled, 45x45", C-NY 5/12/88 OE 57,200
Clown, oil on canvas, sgn/dtd 1944, 18x13", C-NY 10/6/88 35,000
Composition (abstract), oil on canvas, sgn/dtd 57, 15x18", C-NY 10/5/89 OE 41,800
Hiver (abstract), oil on canvas, sgn/dtd 54/titled, 59x79", SBY 6/30/88 66,000
La Durance (abstract), oil on canvas, sgn/dtd 59/titled, 51x38", C-NY 5/12/88 OE 55,000
Le Port (abstract), oil on panel, sgn/dtd 52, 10x13", C-NY 10/6/88 OE 17,600
Nocturne (abstract), oil on canvas, sgn/dtd 1948, 57x35", C-NY 5/12/88 OE 68,200

MANET, Edouard (French, 1832-1883)

La Femme a l'Ombrelle (impressionistic portrait of lady w/umbrella), oil on canvas, ca 1875, 19x16", C-NY 11/14/88 1,760,000
Portrait de Monsieur Pagans, oil on parchment laid down on panel, 1879, 4x3", C-NY 2/18/88 24,200

MANETTI, Rutilio (Italian, 1571-1637)

Sleeping Cupid with Attributes of the Liberal Arts, oil on canvas laid down on board, 29x48", C-NY 1/15/88 22,000

MANFREDI, Bartolommeo; circle of (Italian, 1580-1620)

Portrait of a Young Woman Holding a Tambourine, oil on canvas, 21x16", C-NY 1/11/89 UE 8,800

MANFREDI, Bartolommeo; follower of (Italian, 1580-1620)

Mocking of Christ, no media given, 48x66", SBY 6/1/89 OE 55,000

MANGER, L.

Tyrolian Peasant, oil on panel, sgn/dtd 85, 8x6", C-E 2/23/88 UE 440

MANGLARD, Adriaen; att (French, 1695-1760)

Harbor Scene, oil on canvas, 15x18", C-NY 6/2/88 2,860

MANGOLD, Robert (American, 1937-)

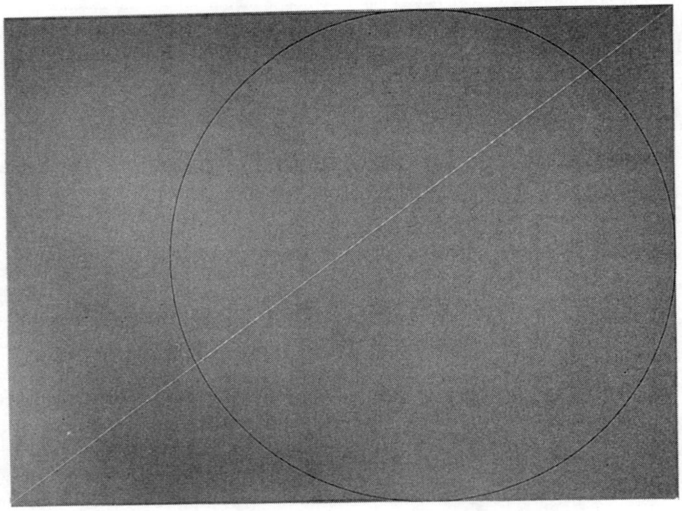

Triangle & Circle Within a Rectangle, acrylic/graphite/white pencil on canvas, sgn/inscr/dtd 1975, 72x96", C-NY 5/3/88; $176,000

Curved Line Within Two Distorted Rectangles, acrylic/graphite on masonite, 18x25", C-NY 2/20/88	13,200
Diagonal & Curved Line Within Two Rectangles, acrylic/pencil on canvas in 2 parts, sgn/dtd 1978, 70x91", SBY 5/2/89	154,000
Distorted Square Within a Square, acrylic/crayon on canvas, sgn/inscr/dtd 1974, 66x66", C-NY 11/9/88	88,000
Drawing for Silk Screenprint; Square Within Two Triangles; crayon on paper, sgn/dtd 1977, 16x23", C-NY 11/10/88	5,500
Elipse Within a Rectangle #1, acrylic/black pencil on canvas, sgn/dtd 1972, 48x72", SBY 5/3/89	93,500
Imperfect Circle #3, graphite on paper, sgn/dtd 1973/titled, 11x11", C-NY 11/10/88 OE	3,520
Painting for 3 Walls #1, Sketch, 1st Version; acrylic/graphite on paper, 1979, 39x55", SBY 2/15/89 OE	19,800
Rectangle Within a Circle, colored pencil/pencil on paper, sgn/dtd 1975, 31x23", SBY 11/9/89 OE	24,200
Red October (abstract composition), acrylic on canvas, sgn/dtd 1962, 76x50", C-E 11/17/88	2,860
4 Triangles Within a Square #1, graphite on paper, sgn/dtd 1974/titled, 22x22", C-NY 11/10/88	3,520
ANGOLD, Sylvia Plimack (French, 20th C)	
January 24th, 1986; ink/gouache/egg tempera on paper, sgn/dtd Jan 24-1986, 18x19", SBY 10/7/89	1,760
Study for Floor, Floor Mirror, Wall; acrylic on paper, sgn/dtd 1973/titled, 29x23", SBY 11/11/88 OE	1,870
Untitled (rectangular composition), oil on canvas, sgn/dtd Jan 1980, unfr, 20x30", C-NY 2/20/88	2,090
ANGUIN, Henri (French, 1874-1949)	
Fleurs et Fruits, oil on canvas, stamped signature, 1937, 26x20", C-NY 5/11/89	55,000
La Tasse a la Rose (still life), oil on canvas, sgn, 1942, 9x11", C-NY 5/12/88	17,600
Le Jardin de l'Oustalet (garden scene), oil on canvas, sgn, 1921, 36x29", C-NY 11/16/88	55,000
Still Life of Flowers, oil on canvas, sgn, 30x24", SBY 2/14/89	14,300
Tulipes a la Fenetre (vase of tulips in the window), oil on canvas, sgn, 32x26", C-NY 11/16/88	77,000
ANHU (20th C)	
Untitled (abstract figure), acrylic on canvas, sgn, 1984, 97x72", C-NY 5/4/89	825
Untitled (abstract figure), acrylic/spray enamel on canvas, sgn, 1984, 97x71", C-E 11/14/89	880
ANIGAULT, Edward Middleton (American, 1887-1922)	
Allegorical Scene (abstract male & female nudes in landscape), oil on canvas, dtd 1922, 32x50", RWS 9/29/88 OE	5,500
ANINI, Francesco; manner of (Italian, 1694-1758)	
Virgin & Child with Saint Anne & an Attendant Angel, oil on canvas, 46x62", C-NY 10/20/88 OE	5,500
ANLEY, Thomas R. (American, -1853)	
Farm (w/figure in landscape), oil on panel, 10x13", WG 4/23/88	700
ANLY, Charles MacDonald (Canadian, 1855-1924)	
Thundering Water, watercolor, sgn, 14x21", WAD 6/12/89	450
Towering Cliffs, oil on canvas, sgn, 15x12", WAD 6/12/89 UE	250
Working on the River Bank, watercolor, sgn, 15x11", WAD 11/30/89	400
ANN, Edith	
Summer Afternoon, oil on canvas, 18x14", C-E 10/18/89 OE	2,420
ANNHEIM, Jean (American, 1863-1945)	
Artist's Companion, oil on canvas, sgn, 20x16", B/B 10/6/88	4,125
Five Laborers in Brentford, London; oil on canvas, sgn, 16x20", B/B 10/6/88	3,575
Orange Flowers in a Blue Vase, oil on panel, sgn, 20x24", B/B 10/6/88	3,025
Sons of the Melting Pot (workers in foundry), oil on canvas, sgn, 24x36", PHL 12/1/88	4,250
Starry Night, oil on canvas, 36x24", B/B 10/6/88	1,650
ANNING, Douglas (Canadian, 1921-)	
Surprise, Surprise (fox creeping up on small prey); pastel, sgn, ca 1986, 13x29", FB 10/17/88	1,000
ANNING, W.W. (British, 1868-1954)	
Winter at Rawan Pond, New Jersey; oil on canvas, 26x38", C-E 11/30/88	2,640
ANQUIN, Henri (French, 1874-1949)	
Sailboats at Dock, crayon on paper, sgn/dtd 1904, 10x13", B/B 10/9/88	2,750
ANSFIELD, Shirley (American, 20th C)	
This Old House, oil on board, 19x15", LH 10/16/88 UE	70
ANTELET-MARTEL, Andre (French, 1876-)	
New Orleans Street Scene, oil on canvas, sgn, 12x20", SBY 1/24/89	7,425
ANUEL, Victor (Latin American, 19th/20th C)	
Gitana con Amante, oil on canvas, sgn, 24x20", C-NY 5/18/88	3,080
Untitled (landscape w/figures, houses & trees), oil on canvas, sgn, 27x21", SBY 5/17/88	2,420
ANZANA-PISSARRO, Georges (French, 1871-1961)	
Portrait de Madame John Wolf, oil on panel, sgn/dtd 1932, 42x32", C-NY 2/18/88	7,150
Scene de Port, oil on canvas, sgn, unfr, 14x20", C-E 5/13/88 OE	5,060
ANZONI, Piero (Italian, 1933-1963)	
Achrome (abstract), polyester soaked in cobalt chloride/flourescent paint, sgn/dtd 1961, 10x16", SBY 6/30/88	28,000
Petit Sujet (contemporary), oil/plaster on canvas on 4 panels, sgn/dtd 58, 10x7", C-NY 11/9/88 OE	220,000
ANZUOLI, Tommaso d'Antonio (Italian, 1536-1571)	
Nativity, black chalk on blue paper, 10x9", SBY 1/13/89	16,500
ANZUR, David (Colombian, 1929-)	
Elementos para un Angel (abstract), oil on canvas, sgn/dtd, 53x34", C-NY 5/17/89	4,400
Football Player, pastel on paper, 1988, 39x28", SBY 5/16/89	15,400
Pair: Figure Sentada; Dos Caras de Perfil (abstract); oil on panel, sgn/dtd 60, 15x9", 8x15", C-NY 11/21/88	2,200
Pajaros Miticos de las Americas (study for mural), gouache/watercolor/pencil, sgn/dtd 82, 17x21", C-NY 11/21/89	5,500
AR, see De La Mar	
ARA, Antonio; called Lo Scarpetta (Italian, 1680-1750)	
Pair: Globe, Guitar, & Other Items on a Console Table; oil on canvas, sgn w/monogram, C-NY 10/20/88 OE	77,000

MARAIS, Adolphe Charles (French, 1856-)
Cattle in a Landscape, oil on canvas, sgn, 26x32", SBY 6/8/88 2,75
Cows Grazing, oil on panel, sgn, 11x17", C-E 2/16/88 66
MARAIS, Adolphe Charles; after (French, 1856-)
Cows in a Landscape, oil on canvas, bears signature, unfr, 26x32", C-E 2/16/88 OE 93
MARAIS-MILTON, Victor (French, 1872-)
Cardinal's Lunch, oil on panel, sgn, 18x15", SBY 10/24/89 7,70
MARASCO, Antonio (Italian, 1886-)
Abstract Landscape with Figures, oil on canvas, sgn, 1917, 23x20", SBY 10/7/89 15,40
MARATTA, Carlo (Italian 1625-1713)
Head of a Girl, red/white chalk on light gray paper, inscr, 12x8", C-NY 1/11/89 7,70
Sheet of Studies of Putti & Drapery, red/white chalk on blue paper, 11x16", SBY 1/13/89 3,30
Study of Legs, pencil on paper, 14x10", LH 10/16/88 OE 70
MARATTA, Carlo; circle of (Italian 1625-1713)
Holy Family (shown before a blue curtain, two cherubs looking to the left), no medium given, 30x45", SBY 4/7/89 27,50
Portrait of a Cardinal, seated, three-quarter length, holding a scroll; oil on canvas, 51x43", C-NY 5/31/89 OE........ 77,00
Portrait of a Lady (as Flora), oil on canvas, 46x35", C-NY 6/2/88 UE........ 4,40
MARATTA, Carlo; follower of (Italian 1625-1713)
Adoration of the Magi, oil on canvas, unfr, 19x26", SBY 6/8/88 1,21
Double-Sided: Studies of Putti; black/red/white chalk, 16x10", SBY 1/13/89 OE 99
MARC, Franz (German, 1880-1916)
Abstracte Formen, watercolor/gouache/pencil/tempera on paper, #d 5, ca 1913-14, 7x9", SBY 11/12/88 OE 66,00
MARCA-RELLI, Conrad (American, 1913-)
Reclining Figure, painted canvas collage, sgn twice, 57x70", SBY 10/5/88 OE 7,15
Redemption (abstract composition) oil/canvas collage on canvas, sgn/dtd 2-9-56, 49x61", SBY 5/3/89 OE 46,75
Untitled, canvas collage with oil/black ink on canvas, sgn, unfr, 18x20", C-E 5/13/88 OE 2,42
Untitled (abstract), acrylic/collage on canvas, sgn twice/inscr, 36x36", SBY 10/5/88........ 4,67
Untitled (abstract), collage w/canvas & oil on canvas, sgn/dtd 5-1-58, 20x28", C-NY 5/4/89........ 9,90
Untitled (abstract), oil/canvas collage on canvas, sgn twice/dtd 5-1-58, 20x28", SBY 2/19/88 5,50
MARCEL-CLEMENT, Amedee Julien (French, 1873-)
Boats in a Harbor at Sunset, oil on canvas, sgn/dtd 1930, 24x32", SBY 12/9/88 OE 9,07
MARCH Y MARCO, Vicente (Spanish, 1859-1914)
Roman Courtyard in Summer, oil on panel, sgn, 17x11", SBY 2/22/89 OE........ 49,50
MARCHAND, Andre (French, 1907-)
Les Branches de Printemps (floral still life), oil on canvas, sgn, 18x22", SLK 9/28/88........ 1,80
Les Branches de Printemps (still life w/spring foliage), oil on canvas, sgn, 18x22", SLK 11/25/88 1,20
Looking Out the Window, oil on canvas, sgn, 20x16", B/B 8/10/88 71
Looking Out the Window, oil on canvas, sgn, 51x41", B/B 4/20/88 93
Village in Winter, oil on canvas, sgn, 16x20", B/B 4/20/88........ 77
MARCHAND, John Norval (American, 1875-1921)
Daydreaming, gouache/watercolor on board, sgn, 30x23", C-NY 9/30/88 1,10
Together They Sought the Trail & Followed It Westward, oil on canvas, sgn/dtd 1914, 33x23", SBY 6/28/89 OE........ 7,76
MARCHAND, Phillipe (French, 20th C)
First Snow, oil on canvas, sgn, 36x48", B/B 6/9/88........ 3,30
MARCHE, see De La Marche
MARCHETTI, Ludovico (Italian, 1853-1909)
Departure From the Hotel Royal, Venice; oil on canvas, sgn/dtd 1881, 24x20", C-NY 5/25/88 38,50
Preparing for the Hunt, watercolor over pencil heightened w/white, sgn, 13x21", C-NY 10/25/89 7,15
The Rose (portrait of a young woman, seated), oil on board, sgn/dtd 1879, 12x9", WG 9/16/88 3,00
Venice in the Time of the Dogs, oil on panel, sgn/indisinctly dtd, 17x24", C-NY 2/25/88 27,50
MARCHI, Vincenzo (Italian, 1818-1894)
Interior of the Vatican Library, watercolor/pen/brown ink over traces of pencil, sgn, 19x26", C-NY 2/25/88 OE 6,60
MARCHIONI, Elisabetta; manner of (Italian, 19th C)
Tulips, Roses, Morning-Glory, & Other Flowers in a Vase; oil on canvas, 27x39", SBY 10/13/89........ 3,85
MARCKS, Gerhard (German, 1864-1909)
Sitzender Akt, pencil on paper laid down on board, sgn, 15x11", C-E 11/17/88 UE 2,70
MARCO, see De Marco
MARCOLA, Giovanni Battista; circle of
Jacob Blessing the Sons of Joseph, black chalk/pen/brown ink/brown & gray wash, inscr, 11x16", C-NY 1/11/89 OE 1,54
MARCON, Charles
La Ville Rose (abstract), mixed media on board, initialed, 24x18", SBY 10/5/88 OE 11,00
Vase de Fleurs (floral still life), mixed media on canvas, sgn/dtd 1962, 30x22", SBY 10/7/89 OE 11,00
MARDEN, Brice (American, 1938-)
Card Drawing (Counting) #13, ink/gouache on paper, 1982, 6x6", SBY 5/3/89 OE........ 33,00
Flesh (Back Series), oil on canvas, sgn/dtd 1967-68/titled, 69x45", SBY 5/2/88 104,50
Untitled (abstract), ink/wash on paper, initialed/dtd 73, 12x8", SBY 10/5/88........ 3,85
Untitled (geometric composition), oil on paper mounted on canvas, sgn/dtd 1965-66, 21x28", SBY 5/3/89 OE........ 132,00
Untitled (horizontal/vertical lineation), ink/graphite on paper, sgn/dtd 79-80, 15x18", SBY 11/11/88 OE 33,00
Untitled (horizontal/vertical lineation), pen/ink on paper, sgn/dtd 78-79, 9x21", SBY 11/11/88 OE 38,50
Untitled (lineation), ink on paper, sgn/dtd 79, 10x11", SBY 2/15/89 OE 27,50
Untitled (sketch of open book), ink on paper, initialed/dtd 73, 12x15", SBY 2/15/89 5,50

Untitled (Suicide Note), ink on paper, initialed/dtd 72, 12x8", SBY 10/5/89 OE 23,100
Untitled (Suicide Note), ink on paper, sgn/dtd 72, 12x8", SBY 10/5/89 12,100
Untitled #19 (lineation w/spatters of ink), pen/ink on paper, sgn/dtd 73/titled, 17x14", SBY 11/11/88 OE 20,900

AREC, Victor (French, 1862-1920)
Man with Dog & Sheep, oil on canvas, sgn, 22x18", FAP 12/8/89 UE 600

AREVNA (Maria Vorobieff)(Russian, 1892-)
White Roses (contemporary still life), oil on canvas, sgn/dtd 63, 43x24", SBY 5/30/89 17,600

ARGULIES, Joseph (American, 1896-)
Fisherman Smoking a Pipe, watercolor/pencil on paper, sgn, 29x35", C-E 6/1/88 UE 286
Gloucester Harbor, oil on canvas, sgn, 24x30", RWS 5/12/89 1,800
Gloucester Harbor Scene (boats at dock, Gloucester hills beyond), oil on board, sgn, 19x25", RWS 3/31/88 800

ARIA, see De Maria

ARIANA, Carlo Maria (Italian, 1931-)
Immortale Nodo (nude woman w/child seated under tree), watercolor/pencil/charcoal on paper, 1985, 28x40", SBY 2/19/88 4,950
Untitled (two heads in hats), watercolor/pastel/pencil on paper, sgn/dtd 83, 28x39", SBY 10/5/89 5,500

ARIANI, Pompeo (Italian, 1857-1927)
Three Women, pastel on paper, 13x20", SBY 2/22/89 12,100

ARICH, Gordon (Canadian, 1913-1975)
Autumn Landscape, oil on canvas, sgn, 24x36", FB 4/25/88 375
Portrait, oil on canvas, sgn, 36x24", FB 10/17/88 325

ARIESCHI, Jacopo; circle of (Italian, 1711-1791)
Apotheosis of a Male Saint, oil on canvas, unfr, 28x18", C-NY 4/6/89 3,300

ARIESCHI, Michele (Italian, 1696-1743)
Pair: Capriccio View with Ruins; View of a Palace Near a Lake; oil on canvas, 28x37", SBY 6/3/88 110,000

ARIESCHI, Michele; att (Italian, 1696-1743)
Piazza San Marco, Venice; oil on canvas, 26x39", C-NY 1/15/88 OE 41,800

ARIESCHI, Michele; circle of (Italian, 1696-1743)
Pair: Christ & the Woman of Samaria; Architectural Capriccio with Flight into Egypt; oil on canvas, 22x31", C-NY 1/15/88 8,800

ARIESCHI, Michele; follower of (Italian, 1696-1743)
View of a Venetian Church Beside a Canal, oil on canvas, 13x20", SBY 10/13/89 5,500

ARIESCHI, Michele; school of (Italian, 1696-1743)
Grand Canal with the Rialto Bridge, oil on canvas, 31x43", RWS 11/10/89 UE 10,000
Pair: Capriccio of Ruins with Figures Resting in an Italianate Landscape; oil on canvas, 27x37", C-NY 10/12/89 9,350

ARIESCHI, Michele; studio of (Italian, 1696-1743)
View of Santa Maria Della Salute, Venice; oil on canvas, 24x38", SBY 1/12/89 36,300

ARIJNISSEN, A.
Sailboats on High Seas, oil on panel, sgn, 24x32", C-E 2/23 /88 1,045

ARIN, John (American, 1870-1953)
Autumn on the Road to Deblois, Maine No 1; watercolor/gouache/pencil on paper, sgn/dtd 52, 11x14", SBY 1/24/89 OE 13,200
Boat at Sea, charcoal/gray wash laid down on board, sgn/dtd 40, 6x7", SBY 3/17/88 3,410
Boat Fantasy, Deer Island, Maine #30 (abstract); watercolor on paper, sgn/dtd 28, 18x23", C-NY 5/26/88 41,800
Broadway, New York City (abstract); pencil on paper, sgn/dtd 10x12", WD 4/13/88 2,100
Brooklyn Bridge & River Movement, watercolor/pencil on paper, sgn/dtd 10, 15x17", C-NY 5/25/89 19,800
Brooklyn Bridge From Brooklyn, charcoal/blue crayon on paper affixed to mount, sgn, 1931, 6x9", SBY 3/17/88 5,500
Coach (& horses), pencil/pastel on green paper, sgn/dtd 05, 8x1", SBY 6/28/89 990
Deer Isle, Maine; watercolor/charcoal on paper, sgn/dtd 28, 27x22", C-NY 5/25/89 52,800
Deer Isle, Stonington, No 10, Maine; watercolor/charcoal on paper, sgn/dtd 24, 15x18", C-NY 12/2/88 55,000
Double-Sided: New York City with Tugboat; watercolor/pencil on paper, sgn, 1925, 10x8", 8x7", SBY 6/24/88 OE 11,000
East River (cityscape w/river), watercolor/pencil on paper, sgn/dtd 10, 14x16", SBY 5/24/89 11,550
Maine, Jordan's Delight Island; watercolor/gouache/pen/black ink on paper laid down, sgn/dtd 35, 16x22", C-NY 5/25/89 OE 60,500
New York, watercolor/charcoal on paper, inscr 1923, 25x22", C-NY 12/2/88 OE 165,000
Off the French Coast, watercolor on paper, 7x8", WD 4/13/88 UE 1,600
Seascape, Maine; oil on canvas, sgn/dtd 31, 21x28", SBY 5/25/88 40,700
Seascape with Mountains, watercolor/charcoal on paper laid down on board, sgn/dtd 21, 5x8", C-NY 9/28/89 6,050

ARINARI, Onorio; att (Italian, 1627-1715)
Saint Cecilia, oil on canvas, 43x35", SBY 4/7/88 4,950

ARINELLI, Vincenzo (Italian, 1820-1892)
Royal Procession, Northern Africa; oil on board, sgn, 17x41", C-E 2/21/89 4,180

ARINI, Antonio; att
Cavalry Skirmish, oil on canvas, 28x51", C-NY 10/12/89 OE 13,200

ARINI, Leonardo (Italian, 1730-1797)
Pair: Cavalleria Macedone; Cavalleria Armena; chalk/pen/ink/wash/watercolor, inscr, 13x9", C-NY 1/11/89 2,750

ARINI, Marino (Italian, 1901-1980)
Bagliori Nella Foresta (abstract), oil on canvas, sgn/initialed, 1958, 79x73", SBY 5/10/88 132,000
Cavaliere su un Cavallo Bianco (rider on white horse), gouache/watercolor on paper, sgn, 16x13", C-NY 5/12/88 44,000
Cavallo, gouache/India ink/pastel on paper, sgn/dtd 1955, 17x25", SBY 11/16/89 OE 49,500
Cavallo Cavaliere (abstract), gouache, sgn/dtd 1970, 20x16", FB 5/89 34,000
Cavallo e Cavaliere, gouache/pen/ink on buff paper, sgn, 10x13", SBY 11/16/89 30,250
Cavallo e Cavaliere (abstract), gouache/India ink on paper, sgn/dtd 1952, 18x14", C-NY 10/5/89 15,400
Cavallo e Giocoliere (horse & juggler at the circus), oil on canvas, sgn/dtd 1959-80, 59x45", C-NY 5/11/88 143,000
Cavallo e Tres Cavalieri su Sfondo Verde, gouache/pen/India ink on paper, sgn/dtd 1953, 25x17", C-NY 5/11/89 OE 57,200

Cheval (abstract), gouache/ink wash/gesso on paper mounted on canvas, sgn, 19x13", SBY 10/7/88 OE 25,30
Circus Horse, tempera on board, sgn/dtd 1953, 18x25", SBY 2/18/88 OE 23,10
Composizione, oil/gouache on paper, sgn/dtd 1957, 26x20", SBY 11/16/89 60,50
Composizione Cavalieri Rossi, tempera/collage on paper laid down on canvas, sgn/dtd 1970, 15x20", C-NY 5/11/89 OE 57,20
Figure of a Man, oil on panel, sgn, 10x7", SBY 10/7/89 13,75
Horse & Rider, gouache/pen/ink on buff paper, ca 1944-49, 20x14", SBY 11/12/88 18,70
Horse & Rider (abstract), pen/brush/ink/gouache on paper, sgn/dtd 1964, 14x10", SBY 10/6/89 12,10
Il Miracolo (abstract), oil/gouache on paper laid down on canvas, sgn/dtd 1958, 53x32", C-NY 10/5/89 55,00
La Promessa (abstract), oil on canvas, initialed, 1955, 61x61, SBY 5/10/88 198,00
Nude Study, pen/ink on paper, sgn, 15x11", SBY 10/5/88 1,32
Progetto Per Il Libro Idea e Spazio (abstract), oil on paper, sgn, 1962, 20x15", C-NY 2/18/88 15,40
Studio per Idea e Spazio (abstract), India ink/gouache/collage over lithograph, sgn, 1963, 20x16", SBY 10/6/89 17,60
Three Dancers & a Horse, brush/ink on buff paper, sgn, 20x14", SBY 2/16/89 OE 11,00

MARINUS, Ferdinand Joseph Bernard (Belgian, 1808-1890)
Reluctant Bull, oil on canvas, sgn/dtd 1858, 14x25", SBY 6/8/88 3,30

MARIOTTI (Italian, 19th C)
Peasant Boy, watercolor on paper, sgn/dtd, 25x20", C-E 5/23/88 UE 55

MARIS, Jacob (Dutch, 1837-1899)
Collecting Shellfish, oil on canvas, sgn, ca 1878-79, 50x37", C-NY 5/24/89 OE 88,00
Peasant on Horseback in Stormy Weather, oil on panel, sgn, 7x9", C-E 10/25/88 2,64
View of a Harbor Town, oil on canvas, sgn, 27x50", C-NY 10/25/89 41,80

MARIS, Willem (Dutch, 1844-1910)
Ducks by a Stream, oil on canvas, sgn, 12x11", SBY 12/9/88 UE 1,43

MARIS, Willem; att (Dutch, 1844-1910)
Boats in an Estuary, watercolor on paper, initialed, 20x17", C-E 2/23/88 77

MARK, George Washington (American, 1795-1879)
Chasing the Squirrel, oil on canvas laid down on panel, 33x37", C-NY 6/3/89 OE 38,50

MARKHAM, Kyra (American, 1891-1967)
Backstage (figures in an interior), oil on canvas mounted on masonite, sgn, 30x24", RWS 9/8/89 1,70

MARKO, Andreas (Austrian, 1824-1895)
Mountain Path to the Sea, oil on canvas, sgn/dtd 1869, 30x41", C-E 10/26/89 4,62

MARKO, Andreas; style of (Austrian, 1824-1895)
Pack Train Bound for a Distant Castle, oil on canvas, unfr, 31x45", B/B 4/20/88 49

MARKO, J.
Pair: Little Boy; Little Girl; oil on canvas, sgn, 8x6", C-E 4/7/88 99

MARKO, Karl (Hungarian, 1822-1891)
After the Storm (rocky landscape w/stream & figure), oil on canvas, sgn/dtd 1870, 16x22", B/B 3/22/89 3,57

MARKOS, Lajos (American, 1917-)
Blacksmith Apprentice (interior of blacksmith shop), oil on canvas, sgn twice/titled/inscr, 24x30", SBY 3/17/88 4,29

MARKS, Henry Stacey (German, 1829-1898)
Our Lady's Page in Disgrace (figures on walkway), oil on canvas, sgn/dtd 1866, 30x43", C-E 2/21/89 2,64
Success & Failure, oil on canvas, sgn, 26x36", C-E 4/7/88 1,98

MARLE, see Del Marle

MARLOW, William (British, 1740-1813)
River Landscape with Fishermen in a Boat & Cattle, chalk/pen/ink/watercolor, J Villedary wm, sgn, 10x17", C-NY 1/11/89 3,96

MARLOW, William; circle of (British, 1740-1813)
Mountainous River Landscape, a Satyr & Nymphs by a Waterfall; oil on canvas laid down on cardboard, 9x11", C-NY 10/20/88 1,32

MARNY, Paul (French, 1829-1914)
Activity by the Canal, watercolor heightened w/white, sgn, 24x17", FAP 4/15/89 46
Continental Town Square, watercolor on paper, sgn, 24x39", C-E 2/23/88 55

MARONIEZ, Georges Philibert Charles (French, 1865-)
Coastal Scene at Dusk with a Woman Walking to a Cottage Overlooking the Sea, oil on panel, sgn, 13x16", SLK 9/26/88 1,00
Landscape with Windmill & Haystacks, oil on canvas, sgn, 24x29", SBY 6/8/88 3,85

MARPLE, William L. (American, 1827-1910)
Coming in a Sunset, oil on panel, sgn/dtd 78, 6x12", C-E 11/30/88 1,54
Landscape, oil on canvas laid down on masonite, 32x40", SLK 2/12/88 30
Landscape (figure/cattle along river), oil on canvas, sgn, 12x20", SLK 11/25/88 57
Untitled, marshy river landscape w/middle distant mountain; oil on canvas, sgn/dtd 80, 32x22", SLK 11/25/88 62

MARQUET, Albert (French, 1875-1974)
Algerian Scene: Villa; watercolor/pencil on paper laid down on board, sgn/dtd 1930/inscr, 7x10", SBY 11/12/88 OE 20,90
Atelier de l'Artiste a Alger (exterior view of artist's studio), oil on canvas, sgn, 14x11", SBY 11/12/88 71,50
Bords de Seine, Herblay en Ete (view of Seine, loosely painted); oil on canvas, sgn, 13x16", C-NY 11/16/88 OE 121,00
Double-Sided: Strollers; Little Girl; ink on paper, initialed, 12x8", B/B 12/8/88 OE 1,43
Effet de Nauges, Herblay (landscape); oil on canvas, sgn twice/titled, 21x26", C-NY 11/16/88 OE 165,00
Femmes au Balcon (Ladies on a Balcony), black ink wash on paper, initialed, 7x11", SBY 2/14/89 OE 1,43
L'Arbre (waterfront scene), oil on masonite, sgn, 1938, 13x16", C-NY 11/16/88 110,00
La Route a Bougie (landscape w/figure & body of water beyond), oil on canvas, sgn, 1925, 20x24", SBY 11/12/88 396,00
La Seine a Triel, watercolor over pencil on paper laid down on board, sgn/dtd 1931, 8x11", SBY 10/27/89 13,20
Laghouat, watercolor/pencil on paper laid down on board, sgn/dtd 1929/titled, 9x11", SBY 11/12/88 15,40
Le Marche a Saint-Tropez, oil on canvas, sgn, 1905, 24x20", SBY 5/11/88 242,00
Le Port d'Alger (port scene), oil on canvas, sgn, 18x24", C-NY 5/12/88 143,00

Maison sur la Colline, oil on panel, sgn, 1944, 15x18", SBY 5/11/88 ... 66,000
Pont St Michel, Paris (river landscape); brown ink/pen on frontispiece of a book, sgn, 5x6", SBY 2/14/89 ... 990
Studies of Horses, black ink on paper, stamped w/signature, 7x8", SBY 10/5/88 ... 715
Vernet-les-Bains, watercolor over pencil on paper laid down on paper, initialed, 1940, 4x5", C-NY 10/5/89 ... 3,080
Vervet-les-Bains (landscape), watercolor on paper, sgn, ca 1940, 7x10", SBY 10/7/88 ... 6,325
Voiliers sur la Greve, watercolor/pencil on paper laid down on board, sgn, 10x14", C-NY 10/6/88 ... 8,800
Vue d'Hendaye, watercolor/pencil on paper laid down on thin board, sgn/dtd 26, 7x9", SBY 10/7/88 ... 8,800

MARREL, Jacob; att (Dutch, 1614-1681)
Still Life of Tulips, Peonies, & Other Flowers in a Glass Vase; oil on canvas, 17x13", SBY 1/12/89 ... 12,100

MARSANS, Luis (20th C)
Library III (abstract), oil on panel, sgn/dtd 1984, 14x14", SBY 10/7/89 OE ... 16,500

MARSCHNER, Arthur (American, 1884-)
Landscape with Family, oil on canvas, 28x36", DM 3/14/88 ... 350

MARSDEN (20th)
Gaslight & Jack, oil on cradled masonite, sgn/dtd 77, 25x31", C-E 10/25/88 UE ... 1,540

MARSH, J.P. (American, 20th C)
Early Spring on the River, oil on canvas, sgn, 28x38", WG 4/23/88 OE ... 400

MARSH, Reginald (American, 1898-1954)
Boat at Dock, watercolor on paper, sgn/dtd 1938, 13x20", SBY 3/17/88 ... 2,200
Carousel, watercolor/brush/ink on paper laid down on board, sgn/dtd 1947, 22x30", C-NY 3/11/88 OE ... 23,100
Church in Provincetown, watercolor on paper, 20x14", WL 5/20/88 ... 650
Circus Ride, watercolor on paper, 9x12", C-E 6/1/89 UE ... 2,090
City Stroller with Red Skirt (figure in street), oil on masonite, sgn/dtd 52, 5x4", SBY 1/24/89 ... 3,300
City Stroller with Yellow Dress (girl in street), oil on masonite, sgn, 5x4", SBY 1/24/89 ... 3,575
Discussion (seated/lounging men on street corner), tempera on panel, sgn/dtd 34, 18x24", SBY 5/24/89 ... 74,250
Double-Sided: Beneath the El; egg tempera on paper, sgn/dtd 1939, 29x22", C-NY 5/26/88 ... 28,600
Double-Sided: City Strollers; oil on board, sgn/dtd 50, initialed/dtd 1950 on reverse, 12x9", SBY 3/17/88 ... 7,150
Double-Sided: City Strollers; tempera on board, sgn/dtd 1949, 10x8", SBY 9/14/89 ... 6,600
Double-Sided: Lady Strolling; pencil/oil wash on panel, sgn/dtd 1951, 16x12", C-NY 5/26/88 ... 9,350
Double-Sided: Streetwalkers; oil on board, sgn/dtd 56, 16x12", SBY 3/17/88 ... 7,150
Double-Sided: Study of Six Women; Josiah Macy; wash/pencil on paper, sgn/dtd 1944.5, 15x22", SBY 6/28/89 OE ... 16,500
Double-Sided: Two Girls on the Promenade; brush/ink/ink wash/charcoal on paper, sgn/dtd 47, unfr, 16x22", C-NY 3/11/88 ... 4,950
Erie Basin, watercolor on paper, sgn/dtd 1927, unfr, 14x20", SBY 6/24/88 ... 3,410
Figure Studies, pen/ink on paper, inscr Marsh (FM)/#d DIII 42, 9x12", SBY 9/14/89 ... 1,540
Flying Concellos, tempera on panel, 10x11", C-NY 9/28/89 OE ... 22,000
Frolicking on the Beach, tempera on board, sgn/dtd 52/sketch on verso, 24x30", SBY 5/24/89 ... 19,800
Girl in a Red Skirt, ink/watercolor on paper, 8x6", B/B 1/11/89 ... 825
Girl on Boardwalk (standing, viewed from behind, head in profile), tempera on board, sgn, 6x3", SBY 9/14/89 ... 2,860
Girl Reading, pen/black ink/wash on paper, sgn/dtd Dec 24 1948, 7x6", C-E 10/18/89 ... 1,100
Girl Walking, oil on panel, sgn, 10x8", RWS 11/3/88 ... 2,100
Girl Walking (on city sidewalk), oil on watercolor on paper mounted on board, sgn/dtd 46, 28x22", SBY 4/14/89 OE ... 14,300
Lehigh Valley, watercolor on paper, sgn/inscr/dtd 38, 14x20", C-NY 12/2/88 OE ... 14,300
Manhattan Skyline, watercolor on paper, sgn, 14x20", SBY 6/28/89 ... 2,310
Merry-Go-Round, watercolor/pencil on paper, sgn/inscr DIV-8/#d 28 & 30, 10x14", SBY 4/14/89 ... 6,050
Muscle Beach, oil on masonite, sgn, 7x6", C-E 10/18/89 ... 3,520
New York Harbor, watercolor on paper, sgn/dtd 36, 14x20", C-NY 12/2/88 OE ... 9,900
Nude Studies, pen/ink on paper, sgn, 9x12", SBY 9/23/88 OE ... 2,860
Off To Battle, brush/black ink on paper, sgn, 11x10", C-NY 6/17/89 ... 715
On the Docks, brush/black ink/watercolor on paper, sgn/dtd 1944, 22x30", C-NY 12/2/88 ... 19,800
Pair: Two Versions of a Woman Walking; watercolor on paper, brush/pen/ink on paper, 8x5" & smaller, C-E 11/30/88 ... 1,210
Portrait of a Woman, oil on masonite, sgn/dtd 1943, 20x16", SBY 9/14/89 ... 2,750
Portrait of a Young Girl, oil on board, 8x7", C-E 11/30/88 UE ... 990
Reclining Figure, watercolor on paper, initialed, 12x18", C-E 2/3/88 ... 990
Seated Woman, watercolor/pencil on paper, sgn/dtd 1951, 5x5", B/B 3/22/89 ... 1,100
Set of 4: Figure Studies; charcoal/pencil on paper, unfr, 14x18" & smaller, C-E 11/30/88 ... 660
Shipping (view of ships near port), watercolor on paper, sgn/dtd 28, 14x20", SBY 4/14/89 ... 4,400
Street Scene with El Track, watercolor on paper, sgn/dtd 1929, 13x19", SBY 4/14/89 ... 4,125
The Tombs, New York; watercolor on paper, sgn/dtd 1922, 14x20", SBY 3/17/88 ... 2,090
Tug Boat, Grace Moran (w/figures on dock); black ink/gray wash on paper, dtd 1951, 22x31", SBY 3/17/88 ... 7,700
Two City Strollers (ladies), oil on canvasboard, sgn, 16x12", SBY 4/14/89 ... 4,675
Woman Walking, watercolor, sgn, ca 1946, 14x10", LH 10/16/88 ... 5,800

MARSHALL, Ben (British, 1767-1835)
Grey Hunter, Property of Lord Lonsdale, in a Landscape; oil on canvas, sgn/dtd 1799, 25x30", SBY 6/10/88 ... 27,500

MARSHALL, Ben; follower of (British, 1767-1835)
Francis Duckett Ashley on a Light Bay Hunter with His Hounds, oil on canvas, 28x36", SBY 6/9/89 ... 13,200

MARSHALL, Ben; manner of (British, 1767-1835)
Mr Denny of Egmore & Francis Astley, Esquire; oil on canvas, 27x34", C-E 5/22/89 ... 2,200

MARSHALL, Frank Warren (American, 1866-1930)
October Landscape (shocks in field, trees beyond), oil on canvas, sgn/dtd 1916, 36x50", RWS 5/19/88 ... 650

MARSHALL, Herbert (British, 1841-1913)
Coach & Four with a Hunt Beyond, oil on board, sgn, 14x20", C-E 2/23/88 ... 2,090

Pair: York to Leeds Coach with a Hunt; Coach Haulted by a Hunt; oil on canvas, sgn, 13x16", 10x18", C-E 2/23/88 ... 2,640
Set of 4: Setting Out; Over the Ditch; Over the Stream; The Kill; oil on canvas, sgn, 16x24", C-E 2/23/88 OE ... 9,680

MARSHALL, Thomas William (American, 1850-1874)
Blue Mountain Lake, oil on canvas, sgn/dtd 74, 16x24", WD 4/13/88 ... 4,250

MARSTON, Richard (American, 1842-1917)
Highland Loch, 1891 (figures on stony path); oil on paper, sgn, 17x23", RAB 8/9/88 UE ... 125

MARTEL, Paul Jean (American/Belgian, 1879-1942)
Flemish Farmhouse, 1920; oil on board, sgn/#d 494, 9x12", B/B 9/14/89 UE ... 715

MARTENS, Conrad (British, 1801-1878)
From Norton's Crossing, watercolor/bodycolor heightened w/gum arabic, 6x10", C-SK 5/25/89 ... 3,310

MARTENS, Ernest Edouard (French, 1865-)
Woman Seated in a Rocking Chair, oil on board, sgn, 11x9", B/B 3/22/89 ... 2,750

MARTENS, W.T. (French, 19th C)
Buying Roses From a Sleeping Woman, oil on board, sgn, 25x30", FAP 4/15/89 ... 385

MARTENS, Willem Johannes (Dutch, 1838-1895)
Devotion (woman lighting candle at alter w/kneeling figure), oil on panel, sgn/inscr, 22x16", C-NY 5/24/89 ... 7,700

MARTHE, H.
Batavia (now Djakarta), pencil/watercolor heightened w/white, sgn/dtd 1860, C-SK 10/10/88 OE ... 13,940

MARTIN, Agnes (American/Canadian, 1912-)
Buds (rows of faint circles), oil on canvas, sgn, 1959, 50x50", SBY 10/5/89 OE ... 99,000
David (two rectangles), oil on canvas, sgn/dtd 58, unfr, 25x25", C-E 11/14/89 OE ... 26,400
Drift of Summer (abstract in shades of yellow), oil on canvas, sgn/dtd 1957, unfr, 50x36", C-E 11/14/89 OE ... 24,200
Stone (horizontal lineation), graphite/gouache on paper, sgn twice/dtd 66 twice/titled, 9x9", SBY 11/11/88 OE ... 17,600
Untitled #13 (horizontal lineation), acrylic/liquitex/gesso/graphite on canvas, sgn/dtd 1980, 72x72", SBY 5/2/89 OE ... 176,000
Untitled #5 (horizontal lineation), gesso/acrylic/graphite on canvas, sgn/dtd 1981, 72x72", C-NY 5/3/89 OE ... 264,000

MARTIN, Benito Quinquela (Argentinian, 20th C)
Barco Iluminado (Illuminated Boat, impressionistic), oil on panel, sgn/dtd 1960, 24x28", C-NY 5/18/88 OE ... 18,700
Barcos de la Boca (impressionistic port scene), oil on board, sgn, 17x28", C-NY 11/21/88 ... 5,500
Impression (port scene), oil on board, sgn/dtd 1918, 14x22", C-NY 11/21/88 ... 11,000
In Full Sunlight (river w/skyline & boats), oil on canvas, sgn/titled, 1960, 36x39", SBY 11/21/88 ... 15,400
Tareas Portuarias (port scene), oil on masonite, sgn, 1949, 20x24", C-NY 11/21/89 ... 11,000
Unloading Wood, oil on board, sgn/dtd 1920/inscr, 20x28", SBY 5/17/88 ... 11,550

MARTIN, C.; see San Martin

MARTIN, David (British, 1736-1798)
Portrait of David Hume, the Philosopher, seated, half-length; oil on canvas, 30x25", C-NY 1/11/89 OE ... 24,200

MARTIN, E. (Spanish, 19th C)
Italian Village, oil on canvas, sgn, 31x19", C-E 2/21/89 ... 2,860

MARTIN, Eduardo; see De Martin

MARTIN, Fletcher (American, 1904-1979)
Fleet Fighter (boxer in ring corner), oil on canvas, sgn/indistinctly dtd, 44x26", SBY 5/24/89 ... 60,500
Out at Home (baseball scene w/umpire calling an out), oil on canvas, sgn/dtd 1940, 23x44", SBY 5/24/89 ... 41,250
Still Life, oil on canvas, sgn, 16x20", SBY 6/28/89 ... 2,750
Still Life, oil on masonite, sgn, 20x26", SBY 9/14/89 ... 3,025
Still Life of Fruit & Chair, oil on canvas, sgn, 16x20", B/B 8/10/88 ... 2,750

MARTIN, Franc A.
Nymphs Dancing by a River, oil on canvas, sgn, 50x41", C-E 2/23/88 ... 4,620

MARTIN, Fritz (German, 1859-1889)
Game of Chess (elegant couple), oil on canvas, sgn, 50x32", C-E 2/21/89 UE ... 2,200

MARTIN, Henri (French, 1860-1943)

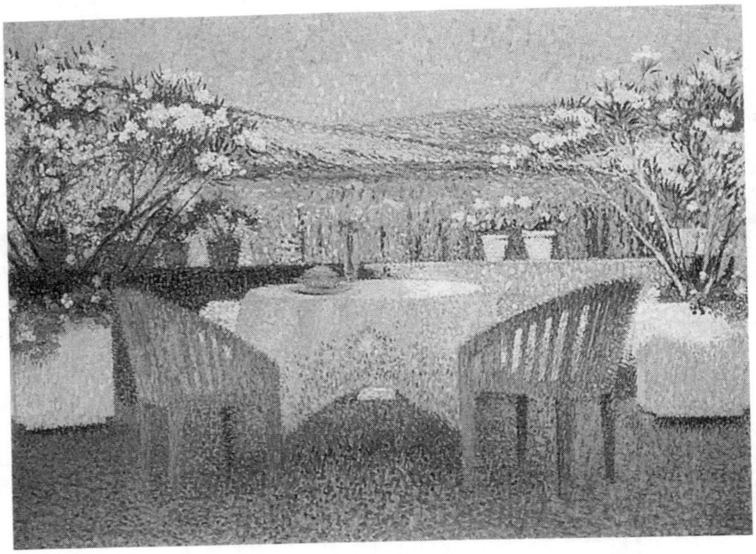

La Terrasse de Marquayrol, oil on canvas, sgn,1920, 31x42", C-NY 11/16/88 OE; $308,000

Au Bord de la Mer (impressionistic seascape w/coastline), oil on board, sgn, 13x10", C-NY 10/6/88 10,450
Auto-Portrait, oil on canvas, sgn, 20x24", SBY 10/7/88 OE 27,500
Bouquet de Dahlias (floral still life), oil on panel, sgn, 21x18", C-NY 10/5/89 45,000
Femme au Fleurs (three-quarter length portrait of woman w/flowers), oil on canvas, sgn, ca 1903, 30x22", C-NY 2/16/89 OE 52,800
Garcon avec Bateau (boy w/boat), oil on canvas, sgn, 29x21", C-NY 10/6/88 22,000
Girl with Garland, oil on canvas, sgn, ca 1890-1900, 20x22", C-L 6/27/88 37,840
L'Eglise de la Bastide du Vert (view of a church), sgn, 51x32", C-NY 11/16/88 OE 198,000
L'Entree de la Propriete de Marquayrol (view of entrance to a house), oil on canvas, sgn, 33x43", SBY 5/10/89 242,000
La Bastide du Vert, oil on canvas, sgn, 42x32", SBY 5/11/88 99,000
La Campagne (The Countryside), oil on canvas, sgn, ca 1935, 24x24", C-NY 11/16/88 99,000
La Cour du Jardin, oil on canvas, sgn, 33x26", SBY 5/11/88 OE 253,000
La Porte d'Entree a Marquayrol (view of open door w/pots of flowers), oil on canvas, sgn, 36x46", SBY 11/12/88 OE 473,000
Le Bassin de Marquayrol (garden scene), oil on canvas, sgn/dtd 1919, 22x38", C-NY 11/16/88 OE 275,000
Le Bastide du Vert (landscape w/house on hillside, stream in foreground), oil on canvas, sgn, 32x26", C-NY 11/16/88 132,000
Le Bouquet dans le Jardin (floral still life in garden), oil on canvas, sgn, 45x36", SBY 11/12/88 275,000
Le Pont de la Bastide (landscape w/bridge over water), oil on canvas, indistinctly sgn, 26x41", C-NY 11/16/88 93,500
Le Tailleur de Pierres (two impressionistic figures), oil on canvas, sgn, 24x18", C-NY 5/11/89 OE 71,500
Meditation (lady seated in landscape), oil on canvas, sgn/dtd 96, 22x27", C-NY 5/12/88 77,000
Mere et Enfant dans le Jardin (Mother & Baby in the Garden), oil on canvas, sgn, 33x29", SBY 11/12/88 OE 275,000
Paysanne, oil on canvas, sgn, 32x14", SBY 2/16/89 42,900
Portrait de Femme, oil on canvas, sgn, 38x22", C-NY 10/6/88 27,500
Riviere aux Peupliers d'Autome (River w/Autumn Poplars), oil on canvas, sgn, 32x21", C-NY 10/5/89 99,000
Saint-Cirq-Lapopie (landscape w/village on a hillside), oil on canvas, sgn, 43x35", SBY 11/12/88 137,500
Saint-Cirque (landscape w/houses on hillside), oil on canvas, sgn, 1920, 29x36", C-NY 5/11/89 121,000
Theiere Bleue sous la Pergola, oil on canvas, sgn, ca 1910-11, 32x26", SBY 5/11/88 OE 176,000

MARTIN, Homer Dodge (American, 1836-1897)
Along the Lake, oil on board, sgn, 7x12", C-E 2/1/89 4,400
Autumn at Mount Tarn, oil on canvas, 6x10", C-NY 9/30/88 OE 2,640
Autumn in the Adirondacks (wooded landscape w/stream & waterfall), oil on canvas, sgn, 29x19", DM 5/13/88 6,500
Cascading Falls, White Mountains; oil on canvas, 24x18", SBY 6/28/89 8,250
Criqueboeuf Church, Normandy (rural landscape); oil on canvas, sgn/dtd 1893, 26x38", C-E 6/1/89 OE 6,600
Dead River Pond, Near Berlin Falls, New Hampshire; oil on canvas, sgn/dtd 1865, 12x20", C-NY 3/11/88 4,620
Hudson River Landscape, oil on canvas, oval, 18x24", B/B 6/9/88 3,575
Mountain Scene, oil on canvas, sgn, 18x28", C-NY 3/11/88 7,700
Sunset Over the Valley, oil on canvas, sgn/dtd 1871, 12x19", C-E 10/18/89 2,860

MARTIN, J. Edward B. (American, 20th C)
Potomac Park, Washington, DC (racehorses & riders racing at track); oil on board, sgn, 21x29", SBY 6/10/88 2,200

MARTIN, Knox (20th C)
Woman Looking at Plant (abstract), paper collage/acrylic/enamel/pencil on paper, sgn/dtd 1986, 13x10", C-E 11/14/89 440

MARTIN, Scott (20th C)
Personal Victories (face on iron looking in mirror), oil on canvas, sgn, 20x24", SBY 10/7/89 2,970

MARTIN, Sylvester (British, fl 1856-1906)
Bromsgrove, oil on canvas, sgn/dtd 1870, 13x22", SBY 6/9/89 2,750
Set of 4: The Meet; Full Cry; Breaking Cover; The Death; ea oil on paper, ea sgn/dtd 1884, ea 6x12", C-E 5/22/89 OE 9,900
There's a Fox in the Spinney They Say (Spring Coppice, Umberslade), oil on canvas, sgn/dtd 1894, 18x51", SBY 6/10/88 6,050
Two Hounds in a Landscape, oil on canvas, sgn/inscr/dtd 1882, 21x16", SBY 6/10/88 4,400

MARTIN, Thomas Mower (Canadian, 1838-1934)
Coastal Scene, oil on board, sgn, 10x24", WAD 11/30/89 500
Fishing Boats-Venice; oil on board, sgn, 6x9", RAB 3/27/89 UE 300
Hay Wagon Crossing the Bridge, watercolor, sgn, 20x12", FB 5/28/89 UE 380
Long Island Coast, oil on canvas, sgn, 12x16", FB 5/28/89 900
Mountain & River Scene, watercolor, sgn, 7x11", FB 10/30/89 440
Oxen on a Forest Path, oil on canvas, sgn, 16x28", FB 5/28/89 900
Portaging Canoe, watercolor, sgn, 12x21", FB 10/30/89 770
River & Mountain Landscape, watercolor, sgn, 15x22", FB 5/28/89 900
Rocky Mountains, watercolor, sgn, 12x19", FB 10/30/89 UE 440
Rosedale Creek, oil on board, ca 1900, 7x10", FB 10/17/88 700
Sea Gulls on a Beach, oil on canvas, sgn, 18x26", FB 5/28/89 UE 400
Summer Landscape, watercolor, sgn, 20x13", WAD 6/12/89 375
Tending the Flock (lady/flock in landscape), oil on board, sgn/dtd 1915, 6x9", RAB 3/27/89 1,100
Woodland Scene, watercolor, sgn, 18x24", WAD 11/30/89 600

MARTIN-DELESTRE, Adolphe Alexandre (French, 1823-1858)
An Intimate Conversation, oil on canvas, sgn/dtd 1857, 26x21", SBY 12/9/88 3,025

MARTIN-FERRIERES, Jac (French, 1893-1974)
Automne au Jardin (abstract), oil on canvas, sgn, 26x20", SBY 2/14/89 4,400
Bateaux de Peche dans le Port (fishing boats going to port), oil on canvas, sgn/dtd 28, 20x36", C-NY 2/16/89 OE 22,000
Dahlias in a Vase, oil on canvas, sgn, 29x20", SBY 10/5/88 3,300
Le Village (village scene), oil on canvas, sgn/dtd 24, 39x23", C-NY 2/18/89 OE 14,300
Nature Morte (floral still life), oil on canvas, sgn, 26x20", C-NY 2/16/89 4,180
Pommier in Fleurs (blossoming tree in an extensive landscape), oil on canvas, sgn/dtd 27, 28x21", B/B 10/9/88 4,400
Port de Bordeaux, oil on canvas, sgn/dtd 21, 26x32", C-NY 10/6/88 15,400

Port de Pecheurs (port scene w/fisherman), oil on canvas, sgn, 21x29", C-NY 2/16/89 ... 12,10
Retour des Pecheurs, oil on canvas, sgn, 20x29", C-NY 10/6/88 OE ... 33,00
Retour des Pecheurs (port scene w/fishermen), oil on canvas, sgn, 20x29", C-NY 2/16/89 OE ... 25,30
Scene de Port, oil on canvas, sgn/dtd 1919, 20x29", C-NY 10/5/89 OE ... 26,40
Scene de Port, oil on panel, sgn, 15x18", C-NY 10/6/88 ... 3,85
Scene de Venise (canal scene), oil on canvas, sgn, 22x29", C-NY 10/5/89 ... 24,20
Sur la Plage (beach scene), oil on canvas, sgn, 18x26", C-NY 2/16/89 ... 15,40
Vase de Fleurs (floral still life), oil on canvas, sgn, 26x21", C-NY 2/18/88 ... 4,18
Vase de Fleurs et Sucrier (still life of flowers & sugar bowl), oil on canvas, sgn, 26x22", C-NY 10/6/88 ... 5,28
Ville (view of town w/water & hills, in pointilistic style), sgn/dtd 1919, 16x20", C-NY 10/6/88 ... 7,15

MARTIN-FERRIERRES, Jac
Pecheurs a Concarneau (port scene w/fisherman), oil on paper laid down on masonite, sgn/inscr, 18x15", C-NY 2/16/89 ... 6,60

MARTIN-KAVEL, Francois (French, 19th/20th C)
Femme au Tigre, oil on canvas, sgn, 18x36", SBY 5/23/89 ... 7,70

MARTINELLI, Giovanni (Italian, 1610-1659)
Polyhymnia, oil on canvas, 29x22", C-NY 10/20/88 ... 2,86
Vanitas: Double Portrait of Man & Wife; oil on canvas, 40x35", C-NY 4/6/89 ... 7,15

MARTINELLI, Giovanni; manner of (Italian, 1610-1659)
Allegory of Painting, oil on canvas, unfr, 29x23", SBY 6/8/88 ... 3,19

MARTINETTI, Maria (Italian, 1864-)
Armourer's Dealer, oil on canvas, sgn, 30x21", SBY 2/22/89 ... 19,80
Italian Peasant Woman with a Water Jug, watercolor, sgn/inscr Roma, 27x20", C-NY 2/23/89 ... 3,30

MARTINEZ, Alfredo Ramos (Mexican, 1872-1946)
Casamiento Indio (Indian wedding couple, contemporary), oil on canvas, sgn, 30x35", C-NY 11/21/89 OE ... 46,20
Dos Campesinos (Two Companions), gouache/crayon on newsprint, sgn, 1932, 23x17", C-NY 5/18/88 OE ... 3,08
La Malinche (portrait of woman's head), oil on canvas, sgn, 46x38", C-NY 5/17/89 OE ... 46,20
Rosas (floral still life), gouache/pastel on board, sgn, 22x28", C-NY 5/17/89 UE ... 4,40
Vendadores Frutas, pastel/gouache on newsprint, sgn, 21x16", B/B 6/9/88 ... 4,12

MARTINEZ, F.F. (Continental School, 19th/20th C)
Standing Nude in Gym, oil on canvas, sgn, 47x31", SBY 12/9/88 ... 1,32

MARTINEZ, Pedro Luis (Cuban, 20th C)
Don Panchito (portrait), oil on canvas, sgn, ca 1925, 23x18", SBY 5/16/89 ... 4,67

MARTINEZ, Ricardo (Mexican, 1918-)
El Sueno, watercolor/gouache/pencil on paper, sgn/dtd 44-4, 1944, 14x12", C-NY 5/18/88 OE ... 6,05
Mujer de Rodillas (woman kneeling), oil on canvas, sgn/dtd 84, 16x20", C-NY 5/17/89 OE ... 7,15
Mujer en el Rio (woman in the river, contemporary), oil on canvas, sgn/dtd 60, 41x31", C-NY 11/31/89 ... 15,40
Mujer en Repose (Woman in Repose), oil on canvas, sgn/dtd 84, 18x22", C-NY 5/17/89 OE ... 6,60
Untitled (squatting figure), oil on burlap, sgn/dtd 72, 63x51", SBY 11/21/88 OE ... 17,60
Woman, oil on canvas, sgn/dtd 61, 20x16", SBY 5/17/88 OE ... 7,70
Woman with Water Jug, oil on canvas, sgn/dtd 59, 22x16", SBY 5/17/88 ... 5,50

MARTINEZ, Xavier (American, 1869-1943)
On the King's Highway, Santa Ynez Mission; watercolor/white highlight, monogramed/dtd 1913, 7x9", B/B 1/11/89 ... 93
Paris Street Scene, oil on canvas laid down, monogramed, 9x12", B/B 10/6/88 ... 2,75

MARTINO, Antonio P. (American, 1902-1988)
Boats, Gloucester, Massachusetts; oil on panel, sgn, 13x20", FAP 12/8/89 ... 70
Land's End, Long Island; oil on panel, sgn, 13x20", FAP 12/8/89 ... 72
Street Scene in Manyunk, oil on canvas, sgn, 27x45", FAP 12/8/89 ... 1,55

MARTINO, Eduardo; see De Martino

MARTINO, Giovanni (American, 1908-)
January Snow, oil/tempera on panel, sgn, 12x16", FAP 12/8/89 OE ... 1,10
Ridge Avenue, oil on panel, sgn, 5x13", FAP 12/8/89 ... 52

MARTINO, Giovanni; att (American, 1908-)
Manyunk #6, oil on paper, 13x22", FAP 12/8/89 ... 25

MARUCCI, Lucio
Peasants by a Roman Arch, watercolor on paper, sgn/inscr, 20x14", C-E 10/25/88 OE ... 2,20

MARUSSIG, Anton (Austrian, 1868-1925)
Allegory of the Battlefield, WWI; oil on canvas, sgn/dtd 1923, unfr, 41x29", C-E 2/21/89 UE ... 1,10

MARX, Roberto Burle (Brazilian, 1909-1982)
Sin Titulo (abstract), acrylic on canvas, sgn/dtd 1986, 39x31", C-NY 5/18/88 ... 5,50

MARYAN (Burstein Pinchas)(Polish/French, 1927-1977)
Group of 12: Esctatic Figures; ink/watercolor on paper, sgn/dtd 66, 10x7", SBY 2/14/89 ... 10,45
Seated Woman (abstract), oil on canvas, sgn/dtd 55, 39x32", SBY 5/30/89 ... 8,25
Untitled (abstract head), acrylic on canvas in artist-decorated frame, sgn/dtd 75, 27x22", C-E 11/14/89 OE ... 8,80

MARYINSSEN
Skaters on a Frozen Pond, oil on panel, sgn, 7x10", C-E 9/15/88 UE ... 63

MARZELLE, Jean (French, 1916-)
Cubist Landscape, oil on canvas, sgn, 26x36", SBY 10/7/89 ... 1,76

MAS Y FONDEVILLA, Arturo (Spanish, 1850-)
Beauty & a Kitten, oil on canvas, sgn, 16x38", WAD 6/6/88 OE ... 16,50

MASCART, Gustave (French, 19th C)
Pair: Parisian Street Views; oil on panel, sgn, 9x11", C-E 5/22/89 OE ... 8,80

MASEREEL, Frans (Belgian, 1889-1972)
Le Parvenu, India Ink on paper, inscr/dtd 1922, 11x8", SBY 10/5/88 990
MASON, George Heming (British, 1818-1872)
Evening Matlock, the Harvest Moon; oil on canvas, 1867, 18x29", C-L 6/27/88 17,971
Study for the Evening Hymn, oil on canvas, ca 1868, 9x21", C-L 6/27/88 7,568
MASON, Maud M. (American, 1867-1956)
Still Life of Flowers & Fruit, oil on canvas, sgn, 30x25", C-E 6/1/89 OE 2,310
MASQUERIER, John James (British, 1778-1855)
Portrait of Lady Pollington, Later the Countess of Mexborough; oil on canvas, 30x25", SBY 6/8/88 UE 1,100
MASSANI, Pompeo (Italian, 1850-1920)
Artist's Studio, oil on canvas, sgn/inscr, 10x16", C-NY 5/25/88 5,500
Christening, oil on canvas, sgn, 28x37", FAP 4/15/89 468
Gamblers, oil on canvas, sgn/dtd 1880, 18x27", C-NY 2/25/88 7,700
Interior Tavern Scene with Two Cavaliers & Two Bar Maids, oil on canvas, sgn, 17x25", MAG 3/27/88 7,000
Old Woman Spinning Wool, oil on canvas, sgn, 12x16", C-E 10/26/89 4,180
Pair: Money Counter; Wine Merchant; oil on canvas, sgn, 12x10", C-NY 5/24/89 7,150
MASSON, Andre (French, 1896-)
Amoureux (abstract), pastel on canvas, sgn, 1950, 26x20", C-NY 5/12/88 OE 24,200
Combat d'Animaux, pastel on gray paper, sgn, ca 1929, 20x25", SBY 11/12/88 OE 38,500
Eclosion 3 (abstract), oil/sand on board, sgn, 36x28", WD 5/5/88 OE 27,000
Etude Pour la Metamorphose, pastel on paper, 1929, 30x39", SBY 11/16/89 OE 88,000
Genese I, oil on canvas, sgn twice/dtd 1958, 63x51", SBY 5/11/88 OE 99,000
L'Homme Solaire, oil on canvas, sgn, 1935, 35x46", SBY 4/29/88 OE 93,500
La Famille en Metamorphose (abstract), oil on canvas, sgn/dtd 1929, 59x177", SBY 11/11/88 605,000
La Rencontre (the meeting), oil on canvas, sgn, 1929, 23x14", SBY 4/29/88 OE 49,500
Labyrinthe Animal, oil on canvas, sgn/dtd 1956, 36x45", SBY 5/11/88 OE 154,000
Tete D'Or (abstract), pastel/gouache on gray paper, sgn, 1965, 26x20", C-NY 10/5/89 38,500
MASSON, Henri Leopold (Canadian, 1907-)
Autumn Landscape, oil on canvas, sgn, 12x16", FB 5/28/89 2,500
Covered Bridge, charcoal, sgn/dtd 1977, 18x24", FB 10/17/88 575
Forest in Autumn, oil on board, sgn, 20x16", FB 5/28/89 OE 2,500
Forest in Winter, oil on board, sgn, 10x12", FB 10/30/89 1,210
Gaspesie, oil on panel, sgn, 10x12", FB 4/25/88 2,400
Hiver a Maskour, oil on canvas, sgn, 18x24", FB 5/28/89 3,800
Musicians, oil on canvas, sgn, 12x16", FB 10/30/89 3,740
Portrait of a Young Boy, charcoal, sgn/dtd 1956, 20x14", FB 5/28/89 375
Reading, pencil/chalk, sgn, 12x17", WAD 11/30/89 425
MASSON, Paul; see Le Masson
MASSON (French, 19th C)
Elaborate Floral Still Life in a Cream-Colored Vase, oil on canvas, sgn/dtd 1844, 21x18", C-E 5/22/89 3,520
MASSYS, see Metsys
MASTELLETTA, see Donducci
MASTENBROEK, see Van Mastenbroek
Master of Hoogstraaten, manner of
Madonna & Child with Two Donors in a Landscape, oil on panel, 24x19", C-NY 10/12/89 OE 12,100
Master of Panzano
Triptich: Annunciation; tempera on panel, shaped top, 38x48", C-NY 5/31/89 OE 176,000
Master of Saint Giles, circle of
Mass of Saint Gregory (religious figures in an interior), oil on panel, 13x11", C-NY 5/31/89 UE 3,850
Master of the Female Half-Lengths
Lamentation with the Three Marys, oil on panel, unfr, 11x10", C-NY 10/20/88 OE 55,000
Master of the Fiesole Epiphany, att (15th C)
Madonna & Child w/St Francis &...St James the Younger; tempera/gilt on rounded panel, tabernacle fr, 27x17", SBY 4/7/89 26,400
Master of the Kress Landscapes, att
Madonna & Child with the Infant St John the Baptist in a Landscape, oil on panel, 18x14", C-NY 6/2/88 OE 18,700
Master of the Mansi Magdalene, att
Saint Mary Magdalene Holding an Ointment Jar, oil on panel, 22x18", C-NY 1/11/89 12,000
Saint Mary Magdalene Holding an Ointment Jar Before a Window, Landscape Beyond; oil on panel, 22x15", C-NY 10/12/89 16,500
Master of the Miller Tondo (fl 15th C)
Pair: Annunciation; tempera on panel, with a large, bipartite frame, 52x32", SBY 6/1/89 OE 275,000
Master of the Parrot (Flemish, 16th C)
Madonna & Child, oil on panel, 16x12", C-NY 1/15/88 12,100
MATHER, John (British, 1848-1916)
Purple Hills, watercolor on board, sgn/dtd 18, 19x33", C-E 5/23/88 550
MATHEWS, John Chester (British, 1884-1912)
Major Brown's Racehorse, The Primate, with Jockey Up; oil on canvas, sgn/dtd 1895, 22x30", SBY 6/9/89 5,225
MATHEWSON, Frank Convers (American, 1862-1941)
Landscape, oil on canvas, sgn/dtd 1902, 22x30", SBY 6/28/89 2,200
Oranges & Raisins, oil on board, sgn/dtd 83, 9x12", C-NY 3/11/88 3,300
San Antonio River (impressionistic view of houses at river's edge), watercolor on paper, sgn/dtd 27, 9x12", RWS 3/31/88 275

MATHIEU, Georges (French, 1921-)
Chouzy (abstract), oil on canvas, sgn/dtd 71, 26x36", SBY 5/3/88 ... 15,400
Composition, gouache/black ink on paper, sgn/dtd 58, 21x29", SBY 10/7/89 OE ... 11,000
Diogene, oil on canvas, sgn/dtd 58/titled, 35x57", SBY 2/19/88 OE ... 31,900
Nuite de Sang (abstract w/red on black ground), oil on canvas, sgn/dtd 52, 51x77", SBY 5/3/89 OE ... 132,000
Tombes Prematurees, oil on canvas, sgn/dtd 84/titled, 32x51", C-NY 11/10/88 ... 28,600
Untitled (abstract), ink on brown-toned paper, sgn/dtd 54, 20x26", SBY 2/15/89 ... 7,700
Untitled (abstract), oil on canvas, sgn/dtd 58, 32x51", SBY 10/8/88 ... 48,400
MATILLA, Segundo (Spanish, 19th C)
Workers Outside a Village, oil on canvas laid down on board, sgn, 14x26", C-E 2/21/89 ... 5,500
MATISSE, Auguste (French, 1866-1931)
Mer Orageux (seascape), oil on canvas, sgn, 13x22", B/B 9/14/89 UE ... 550
MATISSE, Camille (French, 19th/20th C)
Floral Still Life, oil on canvas, sgn, 24x16", B/B 6/9/88 ... 880
MATISSE, Henri (French, 1869-1954)
Auto-Portrait (line drawing), India ink on paper, sgn/dtd 11 Juin 45, 21x16", SBY 11/16/89 OE ... 440,000
Bord de la Mer Collioure (impressionistic shoreline view), watercolor on paper, initialed, 1905, 10x8", PHL 11/15/88 ... 31,000
Buste de Femme, charcoal on paper mounted at edges on board, sgn/dtd 46, 23x16", C-NY 11/15/88 OE ... 418,000
Buste de Femme, pencil on laid paper, sgn/dtd 15 Dec 46, 20x13", SBY 11/16/89 ... 66,000
Double-Drawing: Femme Nue Assise (seated nudes); pencil on paper, sgn/dtd 1901 & 1905, 14x8", SLK 2/12/88 ... 26,400
Double-Sided: Nu Etendu; pencil on paper, sgn/dtd Mai 44, 15x20", SBY 11/16/89 ... 132,000
Femme Accoudee, India ink on paper, sgn, 1919, 15x11", SBY 11/16/89 ... 132,000
Femme Assise, Bras Croises (line drawing); India ink on paper, sgn/dtd 37, 11x15", SBY 11/16/89 ... 88,000
Femme Assise (sketch of a seated lady), charcoal on paper, sgn/dtd 46, 21x16", C-NY 5/11/89 ... 187,000
Femme aux Roses (portrait of woman w/roses), oil on canvas, sgn, ca 1917-19, 16x13", C-NY 11/15/88 ... 852,500
Femme Debout avec les Bras Croises, brush/ink on paper, sgn, 20x16", SBY 11/12/88 OE ... 231,000
Femme en Maillot se Reposant (reclining woman), charcoal on laid paper, sgn/dtd Sept 44, 19x12", SBY 5/10/89 OE ... 330,000
Femme Etendu (close-up of a woman), pencil on heavy wove paper, sgn/dtd 44, 17x33", SBY 5/10/89 ... 110,000
Femme Lisant (seated lady at table w/book & vase of flowers), oil on canvas, sgn, 1920, 19x16", SBY 5/9/89 OE ... 2,035,000
Femme Nue Allongee sur une Chase (Reclining Nude in Chaise), pencil on paper, sgn, 1927, 12x9", SBY 5/10/89 ... 93,500
Jeune Femme Accoudee, charcoal on paper, sgn/dtd 6/41, 19x13", SBY 11/16/89 OE ... 231,000
Jeune Femme Lisant (Young Woman Reading), charcoal on paper, sgn, ca 1923, 15x10", SBY 5/10/89 ... 154,000
Jeune Hindoue, pencil on paper, sgn/dtd 29, 22x15", SBY 11/12/88 OE ... 220,000
La Blouse Rose (portrait), oil on canvas, sgn, ca 1922-23, 22x18", SBY 5/10/88 OE ... 3,080,000
La Danse I (study for a mural), gouache/pen/black ink/pencil on paper, 1932, 11x30", C-NY 5/11/89 OE ... 1,650,000
Le Pont de Sevres a St-Cloud (river landscape), oil on canvas, sgn, 1917, 18x22", C-NY 5/11/88 OE ... 440,000
Modele et Fougere, India ink on paper, sgn/dtd 44, 15x20", SBY 11/12/88 OE ... 82,500
Nature Morte (line drawing of still life), India ink on paper, sgn/dtd 41/#d G1, 16x21", SBY 11/16/89 OE ... 137,500
Nature Morte aux Citrons sur Fond Fleurdelise (still life), oil on canvas, sgn/dtd 43, 29x24", SBY 5/10/88 OE ... 5,720,000
Nu Allonge, pencil on paper, initialed, 9x12", C-NY 11/15/88 ... 44,000
Nu Assis (seated nude), pen/India ink on paper, initialed, 1926-27, 11x15", C-NY 5/12/88 ... 39,600
Nu au Collier Couche sur un Duvet Fleuri, India ink on paper, sgn/dtd 1935, 18x22", SBY 11/16/89 OE ... 308,000
Nu Debout (standing nude), charcoal/pencil on paper, sgn/dtd 50, 20x14", SBY 5/11/88 ... 66,000
Paysage, watercolor on paper laid down on board, initialed, ca 1905, 9x12", C-NY 11/15/88 OE ... 82,500
Port de Collioure, watercolor/crayon/pencil on paper, sgn, 1905, 13x19", SBY 11/16/89 OE ... 176,000
Port de Collioure (port scene), watercolor on paper, initialed, ca 1905, 9x10", SBY 5/11/88 OE ... 41,800
Portrait d'une Jeune Fille, India ink on paper laid down on board, sgn, 1930, 13x10", SBY 11/12/88 ... 49,500
Portrait de Femme (portrait of a lady), oil on panel, sgn, ca 1917, 14x11", SBY 5/10/89 OE ... 522,500
Reclining Nude, pen/ink on paper, stamped initials, 1928, 9x12", SBY 11/12/88 ... 99,000
Seated Model with a Guitar, charcoal/estompe on paper, sgn, ca 1921-23, 19x12", SBY 5/11/88 OE ... 253,000
Still Life, India ink on paper, stamped initials, 1947, 15x11", SBY 5/11/88 ... 71,500
Study for Model, stamped signature, ca 1930, 9x12", SBY 11/12/88 ... 44,000
Tete (head), charcoal on paper, sgn, 10x8", LH 10/16/88 ... 9,000
Tete de Femme, charcoal on paper, sgn/dtd 50, 21x16", C-NY 11/15/88 ... 60,500
Tete de Femme (line drawing, head of lady), pencil on page from sketchbook, sgn/dtd 40, 18x13", SBY 5/11/88 OE ... 71,500
Torso de Face (female nude torso), black crayon on paper, sgn/initialed, 20x13", SBY 5/10/89 ... 44,000
MATTA (Chilean, 1911-)
Bud Sucker (surrealistic), oil on canvas, sgn/dtd 54/titled, 81x83", SBY 11/21/88 OE ... 170,500
Candran d'Incendies (surrealistic), oil on canvas, sgn, 70x82", C-NY 11/21/88 ... 46,200
Composition (surrealistic composition), wax crayon on paper, #d 21, 18x30", C-NY 6820 ... 4,620
Composition I (surrealistic), oil on canvas, sgn, 1959, 24x29", SBY 11/21/88 ... 35,200
Demonstration (abstract), oil on canvas, sgn, 1957, 24x29", SBY 4/29/88 ... 27,500
Etre La, oil on canvas, sgn, 1950s, 24x29", SBY 4/29/88 ... 29,700
Figura (abstract), pastel on paper, sgn, 26x20", C-NY 5/18/88 ... 7,150
Fuse Fixione (surrealistic), pencil/crayon on paper, titled/inscr, 14x20", C-NY 11/21/88 OE ... 7,150
Group of 3: Untitled (surrealistic); gouache & crayon/pencil, 1 sgn, 1 13x20", 2 14x26", ca 1965, SBY 11/21/88 OE ... 7,150
L'Aile du Sexe (three female figures), crayon on paper, sgn/dtd 63, C-NY 5/18/88 OE ... 8,250
L'Aurora (surrealistic), oil on canvas, ca 1953, 32x39", SBY 11/21/88 OE ... 42,900
L'Eternite du Fini (surrealistic), oil on canvas, dtd Taxco 1941/titled, 22x29", SBY 5/16/89 ... 209,000
L'Ombre de l'Instant (surrealistic), oil on canvas, sgn twice/dtd 1966/titled, 55x60", C-NY 11/21/88 ... 30,800
La Montana Infinita (surrealistic), oil on canvas, sgn/dtd 57/titled, 20x28", SBY 5/16/89 ... 35,750

La Sang du Reve (surrealistic composition), oil on canvas, sgn, 35x41", C-NY 5/17/89 OE 39,600
Les Chants de la Retine (Le Honni Aveuglant), oil on canvas, sgn/dtd 1966, 76x80", C-NY 5/18/88 49,500
Les Fureurs de l'Espirit (abstract), oil on canvas, sgn/dtd 1957, 50x80", SBY 5/17/88 121,000
Liberte Provisoire (surrealistic), oil on canvas, sgn, 1969, 51x53", SBY 5/16/89 OE 39,600

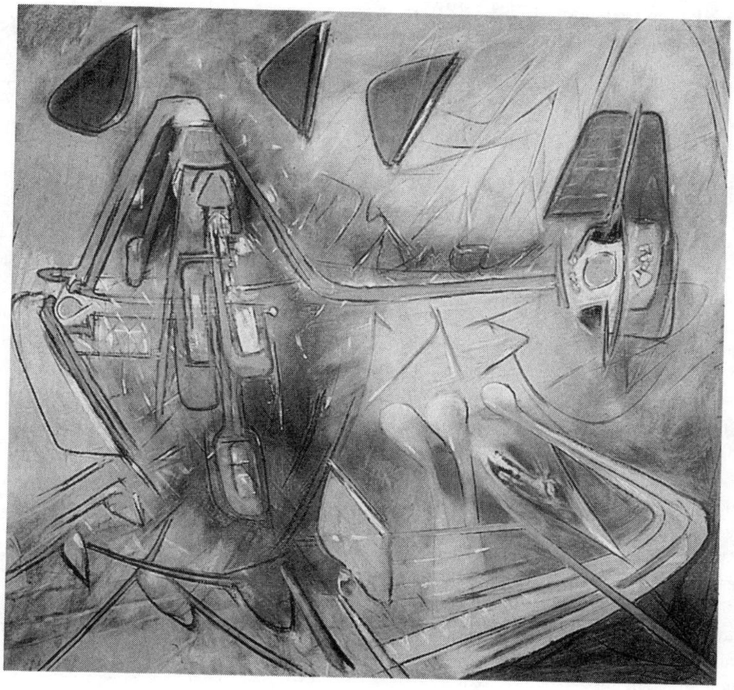

Snamers, oil on canvas, 1956, 56x58", C-NY 11/21/89 OE; $264,000

Orchestra Pit (abstract), oil on canvas, sgn, 50x38", SBY 5/17/88 46,750
Overture (Verdi), pastel on paper laid down on canvas, sgn, 1980, 31x30", C-NY 11/21/89 8,800
Par Implosion: Aspirinette (surrealistic); pencil/crayon on paper, sgn/titled, 20x26", SBY 5/16/89 OE 6,050
Par Implosion: L'Abame (surrealistic); crayon/pencil on paper, sgn/titled, 1967, 20x26", SBY 5/16/89 4,400
Personage, Girimbi; oil on canvas, 1953, 27x20", C-NY 11/21/89 OE 49,500
Prophet (surrealistic), oil on canvas, sgn/dtd 48/indistinctly inscr, 40x33", C-NY 11/21/88 93,500
Realite Nouvelle (surrealistic), pencil/crayon on paper, sgn/titled, 20x26", C-NY 11/21/88 OE 8,800
Sin Titulo (abstract), oil on canvas, sgn, 28x27", C-NY 5/18/88 11,000
Sin Titulo (surrealistic composition), crayon/gouache on paper, 20x26", C-NY 5/17/89 OE 6,050
Sin Titulo (surrealistic composition), oil on canvas, sgn/indistinctly inscr, 60x45", C-NY 5/17/89 OE 41,800
Sin Titulo (surrealistic), oil on canvas, sgn, 1952, 28x42", C-NY 11/21/88........ 44,000
Sin Titulo (surrealistic), pastel on paper, sgn, 40x28", C-NY 11/21/88........ 5,500
Springs of the Apple, oil on canvas, sgn, 25x23", C-NY 11/21/89 OE........ 30,800
Surprise at You! (surrealistic), pencil/crayon on paper, 14x20", C-NY 5/17/89 13,200
Surrealistique, pencil/crayon on paper, indistinctly inscr, 10x38", C-NY 5/17/89 OE 7,700
Tendre Mie, oil on canvas, sgn/dtd 55, 51x38", SBY 4/29/88........ 66,000
Tendre Mie (surrealistic), oil on canvas, sgn/dtd 55/titled, 50x37", C-NY 5/17/89 110,000
Un Giornambulo (abstract composition), oil on canvas, sgn, 1977, 42x38", C-NY 11/21/89 OE 52,800
Unititled (surrealistic), oil on canvas, sgn/dtd 55, 48x69", SBY 5/16/89........ 77,000
Universo (surrealistic), pencil/crayon on paper, sgn/dtd 51/indistinctly inscr, 20x26", C-NY 11/21/88 9,900
Untitled (abstract), oil on canvas, ca 1944-55, 45x58", SBY 4/29/88 UE........ 29,700
Untitled (abstract), oil on canvas, sgn, ca early 1960s, 40x33", SBY 5/17/88........ 26,400
Untitled (abstract), oil on canvas, 1958, 40x32", SBY 5/17/88 34,100
Untitled (surrealistic), colored crayon/lithography, sgn, #d 1/1, 12x16", SBY 5/16/89 OE 15,400
Untitled (surrealistic), oil on canvas, sgn, ca 1960s, 32x39", SBY 11/21/88 30,800
Untitled (surrealistic), oil on canvas, sgn, 45x57", SBY 11/21/88 OE........ 52,250
Untitled (surrealistic), oil on canvas, sgn/dtd 1967/inscr Lima 1968, 23x24", SBY 11/21/88 12,100
Untitled (surrealistic), pencil/crayon on paper, ca 1943, 18x22", SBY 5/16/89 OE 53,900
Untitled (surrealistic), pencil/crayon on paper, sgn, ca 1965, 14x26", SBY 11/21/88 3,575
Vivant l'Homme (abstract), oil on canvas, sgn/dtd 1976, 30x26", C-NY 5/18/88........ 19,800

ATTEIS, Paolo; see De Matteis

ATTHEWS, George (20th C)

Cottages in a Snowy Landscape, oil on canvas, sgn, 24x30", SBY 9/23/88 UE 275

ATTHEWS, Marmaduke (Canadian, 1837-1913)

Lake & Mountain Scene in Summer, watercolor, sgn, 20x30", FB 4/25/88........ 850
River Landscape, Dusk; watercolor, sgn, 15x10", WAD 6/12/89 UE........ 275

ATULKA, Jan (American, 1890-1972)

Brook, oil on board, sgn, 12x16", C-E 11/30/88........ 3,300
Houses in a Landscape, watercolor on paper, sgn, 12x19", SBY 3/17/88........ 1,760

Indians, oil on canvas, 1920s, 20x16", SBY 4/14/89 ... 7,700
Still Life of Basket of Fruit (guitar & other objects), oil on canvas, sgn, 24x30", SBY 9/14/89 ... 9,350
Still Life of Guitar, oil on canvas, sgn, 33x27", B/B 6/15/89 OE ... 46,750
Waterfall, oil on canvas, sgn/dtd 16, 26x20", SBY 9/14/89 ... 3,630

MATVEEV, Fedor Mikhailovich (Russian, 1758-1826)
Lake Maggiore & the Isola Bella (landscape), oil on canvas, sgn/dtd 1912/inscr Roma, 44x62", C-L 10/8/88 ... 33,462

MATZON, T.
Fall Landscape with Stream, oil on canvas, sgn, 18x24", C-E 4/7/88 UE ... 198

MAUBERT, James; att (British, 1666-1746)
Portrait of a Boy & Girl, Possibly the Children of a Naval Officer; oil on canvas, 55x50", SBY 10/13/89 ... 11,000

MAUFRA, Maxime (French, 1861-1918)
Cotes Rocheuses en Bretagne (coastal scene), oil on canvas, sgn, 28x36", C-NY 11/16/88 ... 33,000
Dernier Rayons du soir a Port Kerel, Belle Isle en Mer (coastal view); oil on canvas, sgn/dtd 1900, 26x32", C-NY 5/12/88 ... 39,600
L'Embarquer des Pecheurs (fisherman rowing to sea), oil on canvas, sgn, 22x26", C-NY 5/12/88 ... 41,800
La Vallee de Glencoe-Ecosse, oil on canvas, sgn/dtd 1895, 29x36", SBY 10/6/89 ... 38,500
Le Port de Gourney sur Marne (river landscape), oil on canvas, sgn/dtd 1906, 24x29", B/B 3/22/89 OE ... 60,500
Port Bara (presquile de quiberon), oil on canvas, sgn/dtd 1904, 26x32", SBY 10/6/89 ... 27,500
Tempete a Quiberon (stormy coastline), oil on canvas, sgn/dtd 1903/titled, 24x29", C-NY 5/12/88 ... 19,800

MAUNY, Jacques
Bridge Over a River, oil on canvas, sgn, 23x28", C-E 2/16/88 ... 264

MAURER, Alfred Henry (American, 1868-1932)
Cafe Scene, oil on board, sgn, 9x8", C-NY 5/26/88 ... 12,100
Head of a Woman, gouache/charcoal on paper, sgn, ca 1924, 21x17", SBY 9/14/89 OE ... 19,800
Landscape with Houses (impressionistic), oil on panel laid down, 11x11", C-NY 5/25/89 ... 11,000
Paris Nocturne (lady walking dog), oil on canvas, sgn, 27x29", WD 10/5/88 UE ... 7,000
Still Life of Breton Pottery, oil on board, sgn, 22x18", C-NY 5/25/89 OE ... 46,200
Strolling, watercolor/gouache/pencil on paper laid down on board, sgn, 22x14", C-E 11/30/88 UE ... 462
Woman in a Garden (impressionistic), oil on board, sgn, ca 1907, C-NY 5/25/89 OE ... 79,200
Yellow Screen (posterior view of seated nude, reading), oil on board, sgn, 36x26", C-NY 12/2/88 ... 49,500

MAURER, M. (American, 20th C)
Narberth Train Station, gouache on paper, sgn, 16x22", FAP 12/8/89 UE ... 125

MAURO, Mario (Canadian, 1920-1984)
Cabane a Sucre, Charlevoix; oil on board, sgn/dtd 1979, 24x30", FB 4/25/88 ... 600
Cabin in Winter Landscape, oil on board, sgn, 12x14", FB 5/28/89 ... 280

MAURY, Francois; att (French, 1861-1933)
Orchard in Bloom, oil on canvas, sgn, 15x18", RWS 11/3/88 ... 1,400

MAUVE, Anton (Dutch, 1838-1888)
Cows in a Meadow, Expansive Landscape Beyond; oil on canvas, sgn, 20x32", B/B 6/9/88 ... 6,050
Figure on a Beach, graphite on paper, sgn, 8x5", RWS 5/12/89 UE ... 150
Hauling Timber Beside a Canal, oil on panel, sgn, 14x22", SBY 2/22/89 OE ... 13,200
Mare & a Terrier in a Landscape, oil on canvas, sgn, 18x27", C-E 5/23/88 OE ... 5,500
Tending the Flock, oil on canvas, sgn, 13x18", C-NY 2/23/89 ... 4,180
Woman Sewing Outside Cottage, watercolor, sgn, 19x16", C-E 10/26/89 ... 3,850
Woodcutters, oil on canvas laid down on board, sgn, 13x17", C-NY 5/25/88 ... 3,520

MAUZEY, Merritt (American, 1895-1975)
Set of 6: Illustrations; graphite on paper, sgn, various sizes, WG 10/19/88 UE ... 50

MAX, Peter (American/German, 1937-)
Mystical Man, acrylic on canvas, sgn/dtd 72, 39x29", C-E 11/17/88 OE ... 4,180

MAXENCE, Edgard (French, 1871-1954)
Pensees Lointaines, oil on panel, sgn, 36x29", SBY 6/8/88 OE ... 5,775
Reading (portrait of a woman reading), pencil/watercolor/gouache on paper, sgn, 29x21", SBY 2/22/89 ... 7,150

MAXFIELD, J. Emery
Splinter, oil on canvas, sgn, 20x16", C-NY 11/30/88 ... 2,200

MAXWEYL (19th C)
Woodland Scene, oil on canvas, sgn, 46x36", DM 2/19/88 ... 1,400

MAYER, Frank Blackwell (American, 1827-1899)
Violinist, oil on panel, sgn/dtd 1860, 11x9", C-NY 9/30/88 UE ... 1,760

MAYER, Peter Bela (American, 1888-)
Artist's Cabin in Maine, oil on canvasboard, sgn, 24x20", C-NY 3/11/88 ... 4,400
Clock Tower, Roslyn, Long Island; oil on canvasboard, sgn, 18x24", SBY 9/23/88 UE ... 1,320
Farm Buildings on a Country Road, oil on canvasboard, sgn, 18x24", SBY 9/23/88 UE ... 1,045
Oyster Bay, oil on canvasboard, sgn, 12x16", C-E 2/3/88 OE ... 2,090
Summer Landscape with Village, oil on canvasboard, sgn, 20x24", SBY 9/14/89 ... 3,300

MAYER, William C. (20th C)
Dinner at Luigi's, oil on canvas, sgn, 40x32", SBY 9/14/89 OE ... 7,700

MAYET, Leon (French, 1858-)
Still Life of Flowers on a Table, oil on canvas, sgn, 22x26", B/B 4/20/88 OE ... 1,650

MAYHEW, Thomas (American, 19th C)
Portrait of Ruth Hulda Nichols of Cape Cod, oil on canvas relined on beaverboard, 27x22", RAB 9/8/88 UE ... 700

MAYNARD, George Willoughby (American, 1843-1923)
Bather in a Fountain, watercolor on paper, sgn/dtd 85, 10x5", SBY 6/24/88 ... 1,100

MAYNARD, Richard Field (American, 1875-)
Girl Reading, oil on canvas laid down on panel, sgn, 24x20", C-E 9/15/88 ... **880**
MAZE, Paul (French, 1887-1979)
Le Pont Neuf et l'Lle de la Cite, pastel on paper, sgn, 15x22", C-E 11/17/88 ... **880**
MAZEROLLE, Alexis Joseph (French, 1826-1899)
Classical Scene with Figures by a Pool, oil on canvas, sgn, 16x36", C-NY 2/25/88 ... **4,400**
Orestes & the Furies, oil on canvas, 11x8", SBY 10/24/89 ... **3,300**
MAZZANOVICH, Lawrence (American, 1872-1946)
Cloud Shadows, Tamworth, New Hampshire; oil on canvas, sgn, 22x26", SBY 6/24/88 ... **3,520**
Moonlight at Dawn, oil on canvas, sgn/inscr/titled, 22x26", SBY 1/24/89 ... **7,000**
Poplars Along the Canal, oil on canvas, sgn, 21x26", C-NY 5/25/89 ... **11,000**
Poplars in Twilight, oil on canvas, sgn, 26x32", LH 10/16/88 OE ... **9,500**
Violet Dusk (landscape), oil on canvas, sgn, 25x25", C-NY 12/2/88 ... **9,900**
MAZZANTE, Lodovico (Italian, 1679-1775)
Assumption of the Virgin, oil on canvas, 39x30", C-NY 4/6/89 OE ... **7,150**
MAZZOLA, Filippo
Madonna & Child with Saint Clare, oil on panel, indistinctly sgn, 26x17", C-NY 5/31/89 OE ... **44,000**
MAZZOLA, Filippo; att
Christ as Salvator Mundi, oil on panel, 19x14", C-NY 1/11/89 ... **22,000**
MAZZOLA, Francesco Maria (Italian, 1503-1540)
Reclining Nude Figures, black chalk, 6x7", SBY 1/13/89 ... **6,600**
MAZZOLINI, Giuseppe (Italian, 1748-1838)
Mother Watching Over Her Sleeping Child, oil on canvas, sgn, unfr, 25x19", C-E 10/26/89 ... **5,500**
Mother Watching Over Her Sleeping Child, oil on canvas, sgn/dtd 1872, 25x20", C-E 2/21/89 ... **4,950**
MAZZOLINI, Joseph (Italian, 19th C)
Ruth (portrait in a landscape), oil on canvas, sgn/inscr/dtd 1872, 50x34", C-E 5/22/89 ... **7,700**
MC ADAM, Walter (Scottish, 1866-1935)
Cherry Orchard, oil on academy board, 10x14", S/A 2/18/89 ... **50**
MC ALPINE, William; (British, 19th C)
Battle of Trafalgar, oil on canvas, sgn/indistinctly dtd, 40x50", SBY 6/8/88 ... **3,575**
MC ALPINE, William; att (British, 19th C)
Racing Off the Coast of Dover, watercolor on paper on board, 14x20", WG 9/16/88 UE ... **450**
MC AULIFFE, James J. (American, 1848-1921)
Pair Driving, 1895 (trotters on racecourse); oil on canvas, sgn/dtd 1895, 22x34", SBY 6/9/89 ... **11,550**
Trotter on a Racecourse, oil on canvas, sgn, 22x36", SBY 6/9/89 OE ... **12,650**
Trotting (trotting horse w/driver in landscape), oil on canvas, sgn/dtd 1866, 24x32", SBY 3/17/88 OE ... **12,100**
MC CARTHY, Doris Jean (Canadian, 1910-)
Cleaning the Catch, oil on board, sgn, 11x14", WAD 6/12/89 ... **800**
Pair: Snow Patterns at St-Adele; St-Boyd; oil on board, sgn/dtd 1946, 12x14", FB 10/30/89 ... **1,980**
MC CARTHY, Frank C. (American, 1924-)
Crooked Trail, Arizona, 1885; oil on masonite, sgn/dtd 78/# d 448, 24x48", SBY 9/23/88 OE ... **35,200**
Hunting Party (three figures on horses in snowy landscape), oil on canvasboard, sgn/dtd 78/#d 416, 15x30", SBY 9/14/89 ... **10,450**
Midstream, oil on masonite, sgn/inscr/copyrighted/dtd 1979, 26x48", SBY 9/23/88 OE ... **40,700**
Parting, oil on masonite, sgn twice/dtd 71/#d 54, 18x24", SBY 9/23/88 OE ... **8,250**
Patrol (riders in mountainous western landscape), oil on board, sgn/copyrighted 78, 18x24", SBY 6/28/89 ... **9,900**
Posse, oil on board, sgn, 27x17", SBY 6/24/88 ... **6,600**
Renegades (Indians on horseback), oil on masonite, sgn/copyrighted 1979, 15x30", SBY 6/28/89 ... **16,500**
Running Off the Horses, oil on board, sgn/dtd 1979/#d 508, 18x14", SBY 9/23/88 OE ... **11,000**
MC CARTHY, Helen K. (American, 1884-)
Landscape with Houses, oil on canvasboard, sgn, 12x15", C-E 2/16/89 UE ... **352**
MC CLEOD, John (British, 1872-)
Huddle (four small dogs huddled in a landscape), oil on canvas, sgn, 25x30", WD 3/23/88 ... **7,000**
In the Kennel, oil on canvas, sgn, 29x33", WD 3/23/88 ... **3,500**
MC CLINTOCK, Lucy
Puppy, oil on canvas, sgn, 24x18", C-E 11/30/88 ... **2,420**
MC CLOSKEY, William J. (American, 1859-1941)
Peaches Spilling From a Basket, oil on canvas, sgn, dtd NY 1888, 11x24", SBY 5/25/88 ... **82,500**
MC COLVIN, John (British, 19th C)
By the Light of the New Moon, lady in ruffled hat/maroon dress near gate; oil on canvas, sgn, 14x10", RAB 3/27/89 UE ... **225**
Two Women in a Rural Landscape, oil on canvas, 18x14", DM 10/14/88 UE ... **350**
MC COMAS, Francis John (American, 1875-1938)
Cliff Dwellings, watercolor on paper, sgn/dtd 1913, 10x11", B/B 10/6/88 ... **3,300**
MC CONNELL, George (American, 1852-1929)
Diamond Cove, Portland Harbor (seascape); oil on artist board, sgn/dtd 895, 13x38", RWS 8/20/88 ... **425**
MC CORD, George H. (American, 1848-1909)
Autumn on the Hudson, oil on canvas, sgn, 24x40", SBY 9/14/89 ... **5,500**
Barnyard Scene, oil on board, sgn, 15x19", WL 5/20/88 ... **750**
Breaking Waves, oil on canvas, sgn/dtd 1887-88, 24x40", C-E 4/7/88 ... **880**
Figures in a Coastal Inlet at Sunset, oil on canvas, sgn, 24x20", PHL 10/28/88 UE ... **500**
Fishing on a Bridge, oil on canvas, sgn/dtd 75, 10x8", C-E 6/1/89 ... **880**
Forest Lake, oil on canvas, sgn, 22x37", C-E 6/1/89 ... **2,860**

Lake Placid Mountain (landscape), oil on canvas, sgn/dtd 1876, 18x30", SBY 3/17/88 OE 5,225
Moonlight Row, oil on canvas, sgn, 10x14", C-E 11/30/88 1,430
Storm in the Shawanbank Mountains, oil on canvas, sgn/dtd 1873, 12x21", C-NY 9/30/88..... 4,950
Unloading the Days Catch, oil on canvas, sgn/dtd 1908, 30x25", C-E 6/1/88 1,650

MC CORD, Mary Nicholena
Street Steps, Annency France; watercolor on paper laid down on board, sgn, 15x11", C-E 6/1/89 UE 605

MC CORMACK J.
Cutty Sark, oil on canvas, sgn, 20x30", FB 4/25/88..... 450

MC CORMICK, Arthur David (British, 1860-1893)
Consulting the Oracle (four men in an interior, one w/drum), oil on canvas, sgn, 22x30", SBY 12/9/88 3,575

MC CRACKEN, John (American, 1934-)
Mandala IV (circles within circles), acrylic on canvas, sgn/dtd 1972, 72x72", C-E 11/17/88 OE 4,620

MC CREA, Samuel Harkness (American, 1867-)
Autumn Meadows & Woods, oil on canvas, sgn/dtd 1901, 20x24", RWS 3/16/89..... 600

Mc CULLOCH, Horatio (British, 1805-1867)
Castle on the Loch, oil on canvas, sgn, unfr, 10x14", C-E 2/16/88 UE 99

MC DERMITT, William (American, 1884-)
California Landscape, watercolor on paper, sgn/dtd 45, 16x20", B/B 12/8/88..... 550
California Stream with a Waterfall, watercolor on paper, sgn/dtd 44, 15x17", B/B 12/8/88..... 467

MC DERMOTT, David; & MC GOUGH, Peter (20th C)
Possession (man playing violin), oil on linen, sgn/dtd, 108x36", C-NY 5/4/89..... 8,800
Writing on the Wall (contemporary), acrylic on canvas, 59x44", SBY 1/15/89..... 17,600

MC DONALD, Manly Edward (Canadian, 1889-1971)
Laurentian Landscape, oil on canvas, sgn, 20x26", WAD 6/12/89 OE..... 7,000
Sunny Winter's Day, oil on canvas, sgn, 12x16", WAD 6/12/89 2,200

MC DOWELL-EAKINS, Susan Hannah (American, 1851-1938)
Lady Leaning on Her Arm, oil on board, 9x8", WL 5/20/88 UE 1,200

MC EHANEY, Laurence (19th C)
Portrait of Child with His Dog, oil on canvas, sgn/dtd 1899, 40x24", MG 5/28/88 700

MC ENTEE, Jervis (American, 1828-1891)
Brookside Autumn (landscape), oil on canvas, bears artist's stamp, dtd 57, 11x16", C-E 2/1/89 2,090
Danger Signal, oil on board, sgn/dtd 1871, artist's estate stamp, 16x24", C-NY 9/30/88 OE 35,200
Dead Tree (in winter landscape), pencil on paper, inscr/dtd 1869, 9x12", WL 5/20/88 475
Fire of Leaves, oil on canvas, initialed/dtd 1863, 11x18", C-NY 9/30/88 2,200
Forest Brook (landscape), oil on canvas, sgn/indistinctly dtd, unfr, 12x17", RAB 8/8/89 UE..... 1,100
Pair: Split Trees Sept, 1850; Snow Scene; pencil/gray wash/Chinese white on paper, 17x12", 6x5", RWS 3/31/88..... 275
Pond at the Door, pencil on paper, dtd 1869, 9x13", WL 5/20/88..... 525
Pond with Trees, pencil on paper, sgn/dtd 1871, 14x10", C-NY 12/2/88..... 1,650
Rustic Interior, pencil on paper, 10x15", WL 5/20/88 UE 225
Stream at the Corner, pencil on paper, dtd 69, 7x10", WL 5/20/88 OE 850
Summer's End, oil on canvas, 11x16", C-NY 9/30/88 OE..... 15,400
View of a Shrine at Ceppo Morelli (drawing from artist's sketchbook), pencil, dtd Sept 11-1868, 7x9", NA 2/6/88 200
Western Landscape, oil on canvas, monogramed/dtd 1882, 18x35", SBY 6/24/88 UE 7,700
Western Landscape, oil on canvas, sgn/dtd 1882, 18x35", SBY 1/24/89 9,350
Winter Sunset with Figure & Dog, oil on shaped board, sgn, 10x8", SBY 1/24/89 3,300

MC ENTEE, Jervis; att (American, 1828-1891)
Autumn Landscape, oil on canvas, 14x12", WD 4/13/88 2,300
Evening Train, oil on canvas, 22x36", C-NY 9/30/88 OE 16,500

MC EVOY, Henry Nesbitt (Canadian, fl 1865-1880)
Goshen Pass, Virginia; oil on board, sgn/dtd 1876, 13x9", WAD 6/12/89 UE..... 375
Moonlit Beach, oil on board, sgn, 12x18", WAD 6/12/89 650

MC EWAN, Thomas (British, 1846-1949)
Lullaby (man, woman & baby in interior), oil on canvas, sgn/dtd 81, 12x10", B/B 9/14/89 1,980

MC EWAN, William (American, 19th/20th C)
Foraging, oil on canvas, sgn/inscr, 14x12", B/B 6/15/89 3,300

MC EWEN, Jean Albert (Canadian, 1923-)
Blason du Chevalier Rouge, oil on canvas, sgn/dtd 1962, 40x40", FB 10/17/88 OE..... 10,000
Le Blason du Chevalier Jaune (abstract), oil on canvas, sgn/dtd 1962, 72x50", FB 10/30/89 29,700
Traversant le Jaune, Verticale; oil on canvas, sgn/dtd 1960, 24x21", FB 4/25/88 OE..... 2,600

MC EWEN, Walter (American, 1860-1943)
Ghost Story, oil on canvas, sgn/dtd 91, 32x40", SBY 5/25/88 14,300
Tavern Scene, New Amsterdam (many figures in an interior); oil on canvas, 30x43", WL 5/20/88..... 3,300

MC EWEN, Walter; att (American, 1860-1943)
Study for Hearth (interior scene), oil on canvas, unfr, 22x16", B/B 5/17/89 770

MC FEE, Henry Lee (American, 1886-1953)
Still Life of Roses in a Vase, oil on canvas, sgn, 24x20", SBY 6/24/88 OE 3,575

MC GEEHAN, Jessie M. (British, fl 1892-1913)
Surprised Catch, oil on canvas, sgn, 41x50", WD 5/5/88..... 11,500

MC GHIE, John M. (British, 1867-1941)
Fishing Off a Rocky Coast, oil on canvas, sgn, 29x37", C-E 2/21/89..... 5,500

: GILLIVRAY, Florence H. (Canadian, 1864-1938)
Seascape, watercolor, sgn, 15x11", FB 10/11/88 275
: GLYNN, Thomas (American, 1878-1966)
Eucalyptus Grove, oil on canvas, sgn, 21x19", B/B 6/15/89 7,700
: GRATH, Clarence (American, 1938-)
Wife of Ihi Baya, oil on board, sgn, 36x48", SBY 9/23/88 UE 5,225
: GREGOR, Robert (British, 1848-1922)
Break for Lunch in the Fields, oil on canvas, sgn, 23x16", C-E 10/25/88 3,080
: GREW, Ralph Brownell (American, 1916-)
Navajo Badhnii, oil on board, sgn, 20x16", SBY 9/23/88 OE 6,050
: ILHENNY, Charles Morgan (American, 1858-1908)
Lighthouse at Execution Rock, Long Island Sound; oil on canvas, sgn, 35x26", RWS 5/19/88.......... 850
: INNES, William Beckwith (Australian, 1889-1939)
Cottage Interior with an Elderly Lady Sewing by a Hearth, oil on canvas laid down on board, sgn, 17x23", C-SK 6/9/88.......... 2,230
: INTOSH, Pleasant Ray (American, 1897-)
Mural Study, oil/tempera on canvas, sgn/dtd 44, 25x36", SBY 1/24/89 2,200
Mural Study (woman holding child, male figures), oil/tempera on canvas, sgn/dtd 44, 25x36", SBY 9/14/89 1,540
Outa Work (two men in an interior), watercolor on paper, sgn, 20x25", B/B 9/14/89 UE 495
Pleasant Landscape, oil on canvas laid down, sgn/dtd 1928, 28x31", B/B 9/14/89.......... 935
: INTYRE, May
View of Tarrytown, watercolor/pencil on paper, sgn, 12x16", C-E 6/1/89 UE 110
: INTYRE, Robert
Village Lane, oil on canvas, 29x50", C-E 6/1/88 1,210
: KENNA, Stephen (20th C)
Et Ego in Arcadia (landscape), oil on linen, sgn/dtd 1985, 32x24", C-E 5/9/89 1,540
Et Ego in Argadia (eggs in basket, fish in bowl of water), oil on linen, initialed/sgn/dtd 1985, 32x24", C-E 11/14/89 990
: KENZIE, Mary Beth
Pink Shawl, oil on canvas, sgn, 14x18", C-E 2/16/88 UE 99
: KEWAN, David Hall (British, 1816-1873)
Stormy Weather, watercolor, sgn/dtd 1862, 21x30", LH 3/20/88 375
: KICKARD, James P.
Landscape with Sailboats on a Lake, oil on canvas, sgn/dtd 1917, 9x10", C-E 9/15/88 UE.......... 352
: KINLEY, J.
Highland Cattle, oil on canvas, sgn, 12x16", C-E 1/12/88.......... 352
: KNIGHT, Thomas
Atlantis (sinking into the sea), oil on canvas, sgn, 36x40", C-E 2/3/88 OE.......... 6,380
: LANE, Murtle Jean (American, 1878-)
Hilltop (mother & her three children blowing bubbles), oil on canvas, sgn/dtd 1907, 59x59", C-E 10/18/89 OE 19,800
: LAUGHLIN, John (American, 1898-1976)
#14 (horizontal lineation), oil on canvas, sgn, 1970, 48x60", C-NY 5/4/89 18,700
#19, 1960 (black rectangle w/red line in center); oil on canvas, sgn/dtd 1960, 36x48", SBY 11/9/89 OE 60,500
: LEAN, Bruce (European, 20th C)
Shoe & the Scone (abstract), acrylic/wax crayon on photographic paper, titled, 1981, 66x52", SBY 5/3/88 5,225
: LEAN, Howard (American, 20th C)
Peonies, oil on canvas, bears estate stamp, C-E 6/1/88 UE 880
: LEAN, Richard (American, 1934-)
Mackey Marie, oil on canvas, sgn/dtd 1971/titled, 56x71", C-NY 11/10/88 38,500
: LELLAN, Ralph (American, 1884-)
Indian Merchant (seated women w/Indian showing pottery & beads), oil on canvas, sgn/dtd 1921, 33x47", C-NY 12/2/88.......... 12,100
: LEOD, John (British, 19th C)
Going to the Market, oil on canvas, sgn, 16x22", FB 5/28/89 750
: MANUS, James Goodwin (American, 1882-1958)
Old Lyme Landscape, oil on canvas, sgn/dtd 44, initialed/inscr, 25x30", SBY 9/23/88 1,320
: MULLIN, Jeannette W. (American 19th/20th C)
Summer Sailing, oil on masonite, sgn/dtd 1920, 17x17", SBY 6/28/89 OE 2,970
: NAUGHT, Euphemia (Canadian)
Rider Leading Pack Horses, oil on board, sgn, 8x15", WAD 6/12/89.......... 225
: NEIL, George (American, 1908-)
Transitive (abstract), oil on masonite, sgn/dtd 52, unfr, 20x16", C-E 11/14/89.......... 1,760
Why #2 (abstract figures), oil on canvas, sgn/dtd 82, 48x44", C-NY 5/4/88 15,400
: PHEE, Olive (American, 20th C)
Middle Fork of the Saint Urania, oil on board, sgn, 17x21", FAP 12/8/89 UE 125
: RICKARD, James P. (American, 1872-)
Mountain Landscape with Houses & Barns, oil on canvas, sgn, 22x28", SBY 3/17/88 OE 2,640
CAULIFF, James J. (American, 1848-1921)
Tall Ship, oil on canvas, sgn, 16x24", MG 10/28/88 650
EACCHI, Ricciardo (Italian, 1856-)
Cortile, watercolor on paper, sgn, 15x10", SBY 7/12/89.......... 990
EADOWS, Arthur Joseph Sr. (British, 1843-1907)
Oyster Dredgers Near Shoreman, oil on canvas, sgn/dtd 1883-86, 10x14", PHL 10/28/88 3,250

Schoenberg on the Rhine, oil on canvas, sgn/dtd 1894, 36x28", C-NY 10/25/89 .... **7,700**
Smack Running into Ramsgate Harbor, oil on canvas, sgn/inscr, 12x22", C-E 2/23/88 .... **1,870**

MEADOWS, Gordon Arthur (British, 1868-)
Santa Maria Della Salute, Venice; oil on canvasboard, sgn, 6x9", B/B 1/11/89 .... **660**

MEADOWS, James Edwin (British, 1828-1888)
Camping by the Roadside, oil on canvas, sgn/dtd 1858, 30x48", B/B 3/17/88 .... **4,950**
Country Scene, oil on canvas, sgn, unfr, 38x53", WL 5/20/88 .... **2,600**
Storm Rolling In (seascape w/boats), oil on canvas, sgn/dtd 1857, 30x50", C-E 2/21/89 .... **3,740**

MEADOWS, William (British, 19th C)
Flock of Sheep in an Expansive Landscape, oil on canvas, sgn/dtd 1877, 30x50", B/B 3/22/89 .... **5,500**
Pair: Grand Canal, Venice; oil on canvas, sgn, 8x16", C-E 2/21/89 .... **1,980**
Venetian Scene, oil on board, sgn, 16x24", SBY 12/9/88 OE **1,870**

MEAKIN, Lewis Henry (American, 1853-1917)
Arrow Lake, British Columbia; oil on board, sgn, 12x20", B/B 12/8/88 .... **880**
Bow River, British Columbia (mountainous landscape); oil on canvas, sgn, unfr, 41x54", PHL 12/1/88 .... **4,250**
Chioggia From the Lagune, Venice; oil on canvas, sgn twice/inscr, 14x24", C-SK 6/9/88 OE **930**
Coming Storm, oil on board, sgn, 18x20", C-E 2/3/88 .... **1,760**
Purple Spotted Landscape, oil on canvas, sgn, 24x35", B/B 6/15/89 .... **1,430**

MEANEIMI, A.
Family Scene, oil on canvas, sgn/inscr, unfr, 30x40", C-E 5/23/88 .... **3,080**

MEAUX, J. (Continental, 18th/19th C)
Still Life of Flowers, oil on canvas on board, sgn, 25x29", WG 9/16/88 UE **300**

MEDCALF (American, 20th C)
Blacksmith's Shop Comes of Age (interior scene), oil on board, sgn, 31x30", B/B 3/22/89 .... **2,200**

MEDINA, John; att (British, 1721-1796)
Portrait of Lord John Hay, oil on canvas, oval, 30x25", B/B 5/17/89 OE **1,210**

MEDULLA, see Schiavone

MEEKER, Edwin J. (American, 19th C)
Army of Cumberland in Front of Chattanooga (Civil War), pen/ink on paper laid down, inscr, unfr, 12x16", C-E 11/30/88 OE **880**
Barbette Battery, Sumter (Civil War); pen/ink on paper laid down on board, sgn/inscr, unfr, 11x14", C-E 11/30/88 OE **715**
Battery No 4, Yorktown (Civil War); pen/ink on paper, initialed/inscr, 7x11", C-E 5/27/88 .... **880**
Bentonville, Morning After Battle (Civil War); pen/ink on paper, initialed/inscr, unfr, 12x19", C-E 11/30/88 .... **990**
Building Breastwork, Corinth (Civil War); pen/ink on paper, initialed/inscr, unfr, 12x19", C-E 11/30/88 .... **770**
Bulletin Board: Kearsarge Wrecked (Civil War); pen/ink on paper, initialed/inscr, 12x9", C-E 5/27/88 .... **385**
Camp Cooking & Washing Scene (Civil War), pen/ink on paper, sgn/inscr/dtd 85, 13x17", C-E 5/27/88 .... **550**
Camp of the 40th New York (Civil War), pen/ink on paper, initialed/inscr, 7x10", C-E 5/27/88 OE **2,860**
Confederate Battle Flag (Civil War), pen/ink on paper, inscr, unfr, 13x10", C-E 11/30/88 OE **715**
Crossing Fishing Creek (Civil War), pen/ink on paper, inscr, 8x14", C-E 5/27/88 .... **825**
Cumberland Gap (Civil War), pen/ink on paper, inscr/unfr, 13x16", C-E 11/30/88 OE **770**
First Confederate Monument (Civil War), pen/ink on paper, initialed/inscr, unfr, 9x12", C-E 11/30/88 .... **154**
Headquarters, Army of the Potomac, Brandy Station, Virginia (Civil War); pen/ink, initialed/inscr, 10x16", C-E 5/27/88 .... **330**
Headquarters of General Sedgwick (Civil War), pen/ink on paper, initialed/inscr, unfr, 13x15", C-E 11/30/88 OE **660**
Hovey's Division, Siege of Vicksburg (Civil War); pen/ink on paper, initialed, unfr, 13x19", C-E 11/30/88 OE **1,320**
Military RR Bridge Over Potomac Creek (Civil War), pen/ink on paper, sgn/inscr, unfr, 12x16", C-E 11/30/88 .... **330**
Pair: Commissary Depot, Cedar Level; 50th NY Engineers Depot (Civil War); pen/ink, sgn, unfr, 16x14", C-E 11/30/88 .... **308**
Panorama of the Chattanooga Area From Lookout Mountain (Civil War), pen/ink on paper, inscr, 9x18", C-E 5/27/88 OE **880**
Position of 7th Division, Siege of Vicksburg (Civil War); pen/ink, initialed/inscr, unfr, 13x19", C-E 11/30/88 OE **1,210**
Preaching at Camp Dick Robinson, Kentucky (Civil War); pen/ink on paper, inscr, 6x11", C-E 5/27/88 OE **1,210**
Rebel Works, Munson's Hill (Civil War); pen/ink on paper, inscr, unfr, 9x16", C-E 11/30/88 .... **308**
Ruins of Hampton, Virginia (Civil War); pen/ink on paper, inscr, 8x11", C-E 5/27/88 OE **1,430**
Secession Hall, Charleston (Civil War); pen/ink on board, initialed/inscr, unfr, 17x13", C-E 11/30/88 OE **825**
Swamp Angel Battery (Civil War), pen/ink on board, inscr, unfr, 6x12", C-E 11/30/88 .... **280**
Union Troops Entering Yorktown (Civil War), pen/ink on paper, initialed/inscr, 10x14", C-E 5/27/88 OE **2,420**
Union Wagon Train Entering Petersburg (Civil War), pen/ink on paper, initialed/inscr, unfr, 13x16", C-E 11/30/88 .... **660**
Waterhouse's Battery, Pittsburgh Landing; pen/ink on paper, inscr, unfr, 11x13", C-E 11/30/88 .... **660**

MEEKER, Joseph Rusling (American, 1827-1889)
Along the Yazoo River, oil on canvas, sgn/dtd 1878 on verso, 20x12", SBY 6/28/89 OE **23,100**
Country Bridge Spanning a Small River, oil on canvas, sgn, 18x24", WG 9/16/88 .... **2,100**
Lake Peppin on the Upper Mississippi, oil on canvas, sgn/dtd 1887, 18x30", SBY 9/14/89 .... **11,000**
Minnesota Bluffs, river landscape; oil on canvas, sgn/dtd 79/titled, 10x12", SLK 4/7/89 .... **3,000**
Near Pointe Brilliant, St James Parish, Louisiana; oil on canvas, sgn/dtd 1874, 12x10", NA 11/5/88 .... **5,200**
Near Yazoo Pass, Mississippi; oil on canvas, sgn/dtd 1873, 7x16", NA 5/13/89 .... **5,000**
River Landscape, oil on canvas, sgn/dtd 1870, 12x18", SBY 9/14/89 .... **4,400**
Untitled, river landscape w/middle distant town; oil on canvas, indistinctly sgn, 13x5", SLK 4/7/89 .... **250**

MEEKS, Eugene (American, 1843-)
View of Nuremberg, sgn/inscr/dtd 1875, 22x30", C-E 10/25/88 .... **1,650**

MEERTS, Frans (Belgian, 1836-1896)
Man Gauging the Sharpness of His Quill, oil on canvas, sgn, 16x12", FAP 4/15/89 .... **525**

MEESTERS, Dirk (British, 1899-1950)
Winter Wood (w/man, horse, & wagon), oil on canvas, sgn, 20x28", FB 10/30/89 .... **3,960**

MEGE, Lydia Marie (French, 19th C)
Floral Still Life, watercolor on paper, inscr/dtd 1839, 28x22", SBY 12/9/88 UE ... 1,320
MEHNER, Walter (19th/20th C)
Impressionist Landscape, oil on canvas, sgn, 18x24", MG 5/28/88 ... 650
MEI, Paolo (Italian, 19th C)
Italian Lady Seated on Open Veranda, oil on panel, sgn, 13x6", DM 9/16/88 ... 800
MEIDNER, Ludwig (German, 1884-1966)
Praying Jews, oil on board, initialed/dtd 47, 9x19", SBY 5/30/89 OE ... 5,500
MEIFREN Y ROIG, Eliseo (Spanish, 1857-)
Mediterranean Harbor, oil on canvas laid down on board, sgn, 10x14", C-NY 2/23/89 OE ... 18,700
MEIJER (British, 20th C)
Village Scene, oil on panel, sgn, 11x15", LH 9/10/89 ... 300
MEINDL, Albert (Austrian, 1891-1967)
Cabin in the Alps, oil on canvas, sgn, 12x16", B/B 11/9/88 UE ... 1,320
House on the Lake, oil on canvas, LH 10/16/88 UE ... 225
MEIRA, Monica (20th C)
Bathers (semi-nude figures), oil on canvas, sgn/dtd 1988, 54x46", SBY 11/21/88 UE ... 2,750
MEISELS, Marvin (American, 20th C)
Slaughter House, acrylic on canvas, initialed, 48x36", MG 5/28/88 ... 225
MEISSEL, Ernst (German, 1838-1895)
Flirtation, oil on canvas, sgn, 30x26", C-NY 10/25/89 ... 12,100
MEISSNER, Adolf Ernst (German, 1837-1902)
Madchen & Gansen, oil on canvas, sgn/inscr, 12x24", C-NY 5/25/88 ... 17,600
Newborn (man showing child new lamb in landscape), oil on canvas, sgn/inscr, 25x47", C-NY 5/24/89 ... 26,400
Shepherd & Flock on a Path in Winter, oil on canvas, sgn/inscr, 32x51", C-NY 2/25/88 UE ... 15,400
MEISSNER, Leo
Jugtown Road, North Carolina; oil on canvasboard, sgn, 22x28", C-E 6/1/88 UE ... 990
MEISSONIER, Jean Louis Ernest (French, 1815-1891)
Les Invirons de Poissy (landscape), oil on panel, monogramed, 5x8", PHL 1/28/88 ... 3,000
Mandolin Player in 18th-C Attire, oil on panel, sgn/dtd 1869, 10x6", WG 4/23/88 ... 2,100
Napoleonic Officer (portrait), oil on panel, monogramed, 6x4", C-NY 2/23/89 OE ... 10,450
Rembrandt in His Studio, oil on cradled panel, initialed, 9x7", B/B 10/9/88 OE ... 12,100
Serenade, watercolor, sgn, 18x11", C-NY 2/25/88 ... 1,980
Un Brigadier de Cuirassiers, oil on panel, sgn, 10x7", SBY 10/24/89 ... 8,250
MEISSONIER, Jean Louis Ernest; att (French, 1815-1891)
Cavalier in a Landscape, oil on canvas, sgn/dtd 1865, 9x7", C-E 10/25/88 ... 2,090
Courtship, oil on canvas, sgn, 16x12", C-E 2/23/88 ... 1,760
French Resistance (couple in interior), oil on panel, 7x5", C-E 2/21/89 ... 1,650
MEKELIN
Children's Haywagon Ride, oil on canvas, sgn, 42x34", C-E 10/25/88 ... 4,400
MELBYE, Fritz Sigfried Georg
Stormy Rocky Coast, oil on canvas, sgn/inscr/dtd 67, 14x26", C-E 10/25/88 ... 1,760
MELCARTH, Edward (American)
Street Scene, oil on canvas, sgn, 73x25", C-E 2/1/89 UE ... 1,100
MELCHER, George Henry (American, 1881-1975)
Lengthening Shadows, Topanga; oil on canvas, sgn, 24x30", B/B 10/6/88 ... 3,850
MELCHERS, Julius Gari (American, 1860-1932)
The Wedding (couple in profile), watercolor on board, sgn, 19x12", C-NY 9/28/89 ... 3,850
Vespers (two figures in a landscape), oil on canvas, sgn, 22x16", SBY 5/25/88 ... 25,300
Yugoslavian Village, watercolor on paper, sgn, 14x18", WD 4/13/88 ... 1,200
MELDOLLA, Andrea; see Shiavone
MELENDEZ, Luis; after (Italian, 1716-1780)
Still Life of Jug, Bread, & a Basket; oil on canvas, bears monogram on napkin, 19x13", SBY 6/3/88 UE ... 11,000
MELIN, Joseph (French, 1814-1886)
Chase, watercolor on paper laid down on board, sgn/dtd 1871, unfr, 6x9", C-E 5/23/88 UE ... 660
MELLON, Campbell A. (British, 1876-1955)
Stream of Sunlight, oil on board, sgn, 9x12", C-E 2/16/89 ... 220
MELLOR, William (British, 1851-1931)
Illswater From the Hills, Westmoreland; oil on canvas, sgn/inscr, 24x37", C-E 5/23/88 ... 3,300
Pair: Bridge Over Duck Pond; Old Mill on the Nidd Knaresbro Yorkshire; oil on canvas, sgn/1 inscr, 12x19", C-E 5/23/88 ... 3,520
Winding Stream, Derbyshire (hilly landscape); oil on canvas, inscr, 24x18", C-E 5/22/89 ... 3,960
Yorkshire Landscape with Sheep, oil on board, sgn, 12x18", SBY 6/8/88 OE ... 1,320
MELOHS, Charles (American, 20th C)
Floral Still Life, acrylic on canvas, sgn, 28x36", FAP 4/15/89 UE ... 165
MELROSE, Andrew W. (American, 1836-1901)
Encampment at the Base of Mt Shasta, oil on canvas, sgn, unfr, 40x30", SBY 3/17/88 OE ... 4,675
Fishermen in Boats (w/house at water's edge), oil on canvas, monogramed, 11x18", C-NY 9/28/89 ... 4,180
Mount Ascutney, Vermont; oil on canvas, sgn/inscr, 30x40", C-NY 3/11/88 ... 7,700
Southern Cabin on the River, oil on canvas, sgn, 14x20", NA 11/5/88 ... 12,000
Summer in the Lehigh Valley, Pennsylvania (man on wagon); oil on canvas, monogramed/dtd 79, 22x14", C-NY 9/28/89 ... 5,500

MELROSE, Andrew W.; after (American, 1836-1901)
Hudson River (w/figures seated on rocky ledge), oil on board, sgn/titled, 12x9", RAB 3/27/89 ... 3,000

MELROSE, Andrew W.; att (American, 1836-1901)
Fishing at the River (landscape), oil on board, bears signature, 17x26", SBY 3/17/88 UE ... 935

MELTSNER, Paul (American, 1905-)
Nude Woman with Child & Dog, oil on canvas, sgn, 30x24", SBY 1/24/89 UE ... 660

MELTZER, Anna Elkan (American, 1896-)
Pigtails, oil on canvas, sgn/dtd 40, unfr, 43x35", C-E 6/1/88 ... 1,320
WPA Project, oil on canvas, sgn/dtd 1938, 26x34", SBY 9/14/89 ... 3,575

MELTZER, Arthur (American, 1893-)
Beach at Cape May, oil on masonite, sgn, 22x30", SBY 6/28/89 ... 7,150
Green Forest, oil on canvas, sgn/dtd 23, 25x20", C-E 6/1/89 ... 1,650
Leaning Silo, oil on canvas, sgn/inscr/dtd 44, 32x36", C-NY 3/11/88 OE ... 8,800
Portrait of a Man with White Beard, oil on masonite, sgn, 10x8", FAP 11/4/88 ... 500

MELVILLE, Alex
Portrait of King Albert, oil on canvas, sgn/dtd 1844, 52x39", C-E 5/23/88 OE ... 8,800
Portrait of Queen Victoria, oil on canvas, sgn/dtd 1844, 52x39", C-E 5/23/88 OE ... 7,700

MELVILLE, R. (British, 19th C)
Untitled, landscape w/cottage & figures along road; oil on canvas, sgn, 24x36", SLK 4/7/89 ... 1,000

MEMEGAZZI, Carlo (Italian, 19th C)
Doge's Palace & Entrance to Piazza San Marco, Venice; watercolor/pen/ink, sgn, 7x12", C-E 5/22/89 ... 550

MEMENDEZ, J. (Cuban, 20th C)
Gathering Seaweed, oil on canvas, sgn/dtd 1939, 24x36", SLK 2/12/88 ... 375

MENARD, Marie Auguste Emile Rene (French, 1862-1930)
Baigneuse, oil on board, sgn, 15x19", SBY 6/8/88 ... 2,420
Rocky Bay at Sunset, oil on canvas, sgn, 19x28", LH 10/16/88 OE ... 1,100

MENASCO, Milton T. (American, 19th/20th C)
California Vista, oil on canvas, sgn, 18x40", B/B 1/11/89 ... 495
Jockeys (competition among five horses), oil on masonite, sgn, 20x24", RAB 8/9/88 UE ... 1,200

MENDENHALL, Jack (American, 1937-)
Man & Woman in Dining Room, oil on canvas, 1973, 82x72", SBY 2/19/88 ... 10,450

MENDOZA, Jose; see De Salazar Y Mendoza MENESCARDI, Giustino; att (Italian, 18th C)
Christ & the Woman of Samaria, oil on canvas, 28x37", C-NY 10/12/89 OE ... 14,300

MENGFU, Zhao (Chinese, 1254-1322)
Qian Zi Wen (Thousand Character Poem, hand scroll), ink on paper, sgn/dtd 1320, 9x395", SBY 5/31/89 OE ... 539,000

MENGS, Anton Raphael (German, 1728-1779)
Portrait of a Gentleman Said To Be Francois, Baron De Halleberg; oil on canvas, 39x31", SBY 6/3/88 ... 66,000

MENGS, Anton Raphael; att (German, 1728-1779)
Portrait of a Young Lady Said To Be the Daughter of Philip V, oil on canvas, 30x24", WD 10/19/88 ... 3,000

MENGS, Anton Raphael; circle of (German, 1728-1779)
Belusarius, black/white chalk on gray preparation, wm, 25x19", C-NY 1/12/88 OE ... 1,540
Portrait of Catherine the Great of Russia in State Robes, oil on canvas, 30x26", SBY 4/7/89 OE ... 3,300
Portrait of Ludwig VIII of Hesse-Darmstadt, half-length...; oil on canvas, inscr, 31x26", C-NY 1/11/89 UE ... 4,400

MENGS, Anton Raphael; studio of (German, 1728-1779)
Portrait of Pope Clement XIII (three-quarter length, seated), oil on canvas, 39x31", SBY 6/1/89 UE ... 7,700

MENKES, Sigmund Joseph (American, 1896-)
Boy with Harmonica, oil on canvas, sgn, 30x22", C-E 6/1/89 OE ... 2,200
Bride (contemporary depiction), oil on canvas, sgn, 30x24", C-E 6/1/89 ... 1,320
Cohanim Blessing, oil on canvas, sgn, 1964, 52x40", SBY 10/5/88 OE ... 4,125
Dancer (abstract composition), oil on canvas, sgn, 29x22", SBY 2/14/89 ... 2,200
Fleurs de Mimosas, oil on canvas, sgn, 22x18", SBY 10/7/89 ... 4,125
Girl with Mask, oil on canvas, indistinctly sgn, 26x18", SBY 10/7/89 OE ... 7,150
Still Life, oil on canvas, sgn, 30x20", RWS 11/10/89 ... 3,750
Sunflowers, oil on canvas, sgn, 31x23", SBY 10/5/88 ... 1,760

MENSES, Jan (Canadian, 1933-)
Friendly Gathering, sanguine on paper, sgn/dtd 1960, 13x25", FB 10/30/89 ... 468

MENTE, Charles (American, 19th/20th C)
Gaggle (figures & ducks in a landscape), watercolor/gouache on paper, sgn, 18x26", RWS 11/10/89 ... 500

MENTOR, Will (20th C)
One of the Eight Spheres of Yoga, oil on canvas, 1985, 80x57", C-NY 5/4/89 ... 8,800
Picasso's Microscope (abstract), oil on panel, sgn/dtd 1985, 23x18", C-NY 5/4/89 ... 6,600
When We Are Honest (abstract composition), oil on canvas, sgn/dtd 1985, 72x48", C-NY 2/20/88 ... 12,100

MENZLER-PEYTON, Bertha (American, 1871-1950)
Down Essex Way (landscape), oil on canvas, sgn, 30x32", SBY 4/14/89 ... 2,860

MERCIER, Charles; see Le Mercier

MERCIER, Monique (Canadian, 1934-)
Au Jardin, oil on canvas, sgn/dtd 1988, 20x16", FB 10/30/89 ... 660
Jeune Fille, oil on canvas, sgn, 39x29", FB 10/30/89 ... 660
L'Hiver sur le Village, oil on canvas, sgn/dtd 1989, 16x20", FB 10/30/89 ... 770
Reclining Nude, oil on canvas, sgn, 30x36", FB 10/30/89 ... 550

MERCIER, Philippe (French, 1689-1760)
Fete Champetre, oil on canvas, 32x26", C-NY 1/11/89 ... 16,500
MERCIER, Philippe; att (French, 1689-1760)
Elegant Company in a Grove with a Swing, oil on canvas, 36x40", SBY 10/21/88 ... 9,900
Musical Concert with Figures Playing the Lute, the Flute, & the Viol; oil on canvas, 45x35", SBY 4/7/89 ... 18,700
MERCIER, Philippe; manner of (1689-1760)
Pair: Fetes Champetres; oil on canvas, oval fr, 23x33", SBY 10/21/88 ... 7,150
MERIDA, Carlos (Mexican, 1891-)
Courtship of the Newlywed (abstract), politec on masonite, sgn/dtd 1960, 28x36", SBY 11/21/88 OE ... 12,100
Creacion (abstract), gouache/pen/black ink on linen laid down on board, sgn/dtd 1939, 20x24", C-NY 11/21/88 ... 8,250
Discussion (two abstract figures), petroplastic on panel, sgn/dtd 1960, 25x19", SBY 5/16/89 OE ... 23,100
Dos Figuras (abstract composition), gouache/pen/black ink on amate paper, sgn, 1949, 16x10", C-NY 11/21/89 ... 9,350
Eighth Heaven (abstract), oil on canvas, sgn/dtd 1961, 32x40", SBY 11/21/88 OE ... 24,200
El Pajaro y la Serpiente, oil/pen/black ink on amate paper laid down, sgn/dtd 1965, 31x24", C-NY 11/21/89 ... 16,500
Los Gemelos (abstract), gouache/pencil on paper, sgn/dtd 1969, 11x9", C-NY 11/21/88 OE ... 6,050
Los Hermanos y la Flauta (abstract), pen/black ink/watercolor on paper, sgn/dtd 1974, 26x20", C-NY 5/17/89 ... 4,950
Los Patriarcas (abstract), oil on board, sgn twice/dtd 1977, 30x18", C-NY 11/21/88 ... 22,000

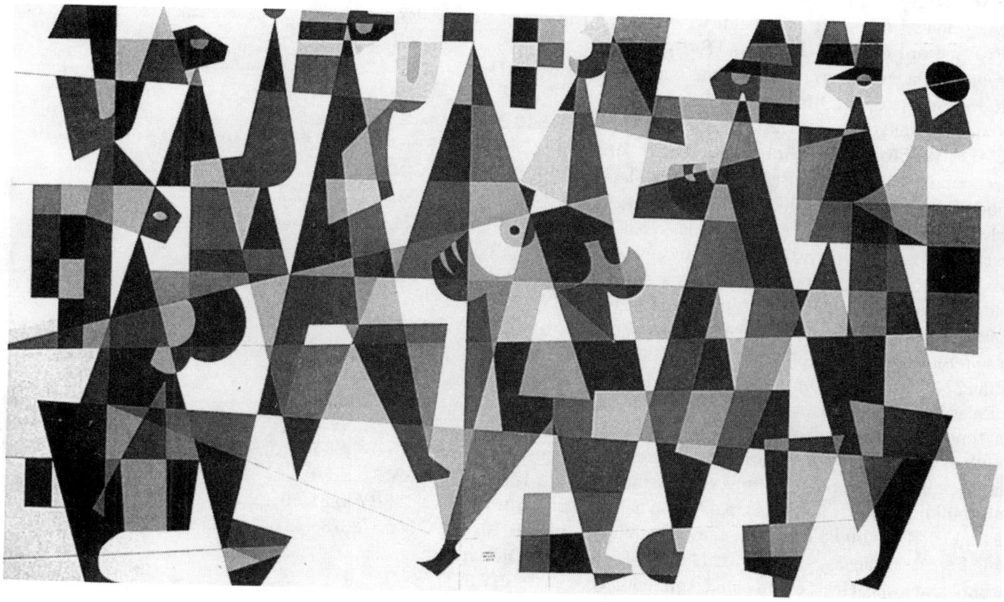

Los Tres Reyes (The Three Kings, abstract), politec on masonite, sgn/dtd 1958, 28x43", C-NY 11/21/89 OE; $82,500

Muchacha Frente a la Ventana (abstract portrait of a girl), oil on canvas, sgn/dtd 1926, 24x20", C-NY 5/18/88 OE ... 15,400
Pair: Boceto; Composicion (abstract); mixed media on paper, sgn, 3x5", 10x9", C-NY 11/21/88 OE ... 4,400
Paolo e Francesca (abstract composition), oil on canvas, sgn/dtd 1949, 16x18", C-NY 11/21/89 ... 9,350
Planes (abstract), oil on canvas, sgn/dtd 1960, 28x20", SBY 5/16/89 OE ... 13,200
Proyecto Para el Mural del Banco de Guatemala, watercolor/gold/silver/pencil, sgn/dtd 1964-65, 20x23", C-NY 11/21/89 OE ... 7,700
Proyecto para Murales-Banco de Guatemala-Credito Hipotecario Nacional; mixed media, sgn, 1963, 20x26", C-NY 11/21/88 OE ... 9,900
Puc el Majo (abstract), oil on masonite, sgn/dtd 1977, 18x13", C-NY 5/17/89 OE ... 14,300
Red Bird (abstract), petroplastic on panel, sgn/dtd 1961, 28x23", SBY 5/16/89 OE ... 19,800
Stele (abstract), petroplastic on panel, sgn/dtd 1960/titled, 55x18", SBY 11/21/88 UE ... 1,980
Submarine Landscape (abstract), mixed media on paper, sgn twice/dtd 1973/titled, 30x23", SBY 5/16/89 OE ... 22,000
Time in Amaranto (abstract), petroplastic on masonite, sgn/dtd 1966/titled, 23x27", SBY 11/21/88 ... 17,600
Tres Figuras (abstract), gouache/pen/black ink on incised Arches paper, sgn/dtd 1971, 30x22", C-NY 5/18/88 ... 12,100
Untitled (abstract figures), oil on canvas, sgn/dtd 1944, 20x25", SBY 5/16/89 UE ... 16,500
Untitled (abstract), gouache on paper, sgn, 18x8", SBY 5/17/88 OE ... 6,050
Xulu, El Adivino (abstract); politec on parchment laid down on panel, sgn/dtd 1975/titled, 31x24", C-NY 5/18/88 ... 26,400
IERK, Edward (Bavarian, 1816-1888)
Conversation (figures in an elegant interior), oil on panel, sgn, 16x20", B/B 5/17/89 UE ... 825
Discussion Between Two Cavaliers & a Lady, oil on panel, sgn, 16x20", B/B 5/17/89 UE ... 825
Serving of the Roast Pig, oil on canvas, sgn/dtd 02, unfr, 15x19", C-E 10/25/88 ... 1,650
IERLE, Georges (French, 19th C)
Coutier & a Lady in a Wooded Landscape, oil on canvas, sgn/dtd 1886, 30x20", SBY 6/8/88 ... 5,500
Fisherman with Woman & Child, oil on canvas, sgn/dtd 1880, 30x24", LH 5/15/88 ... 2,400
IERLE, Hugues (French, 1823-1881)
Afternoon Dreaming, oil on canvas, sgn/dtd 1859, 31x38", SBY 2/22/89 ... 20,900
Silent Persuasion, oil on canvas, sgn, 26x17", SBY 5/23/89 ... 16,500
IERLIN, Daniel (French, 1861-1933)
Two Kittens with Blue & White Vase, oil on canvas, sgn, 15x18", SBY 7/12/89 ... 8,525
IERLOT, Emile Justin (French, 1839-1900)
Cattle Grazing, oil on canvas, sgn, 22x29", SBY 6/8/88 ... 1,320

MERRIAM, J. (American, 1880-1951)
Dessert Landscape, oil on board, sgn, 16x20", NA 11/5/88 ... 300

MERRILL, Frank Thayer (American, 1848-)
Winning Circle, jockey on horseback parading before a crowd in winner's circle; watercolor, sgn, 17x11", RAB 11/24/89 ... 850

MERRILL, Robert S. (American, 1842-1924)
Hillside Village, oil on canvas, unfr, 12x18", RAB 8/8/89 UE ... 125
Ocean at Dusk (seascape), oil on cardboard, sgn, 9x16", RAB 8/8/89 UE ... 800

MERRITT, Warren Chase (American, 1897-1968)
Monterey Lone Pine, watercolor on paper, sgn, 8x7", B/B 1/11/89 ... 302

MERSFELDER, Jules (American, 1865-1937)
Cows Grazing in the Shadow of Mount Tamalpais, oil on canvas, sgn, 12x18", B/B 1/11/89 ... 660
Venetian Boats Off the Lido, watercolor on paper, sgn, 10x16", B/B 5/17/89 ... 330

MERSON, Luc Olivier (French, 1846-1920)
Etude pour la Figure de la Source a l'Opera Comique de Paris (reclining nude), oil on canvas, sgn, 18x24", SBY 10/24/89 ... 12,100
Heads on Pikes, pen/black ink/gray & white wash, initialed/sgn/inscr, 11x7", C-NY 5/25/88 ... 605

MESDAG, Hendrick Willem (Dutch, 1831-1915)
Sailboats at Anchor, watercolor, sgn/dtd 1895, 24x20", C-NY 5/25/88 OE ... 6,050

MESDAG, Hendrick Willem; att (Dutch, 1831-1915)
Fishing Boats Under Sail, watercolor w/whiting on paper, sgn, 15x20", RWS 5/12/89 UE ... 200

MESPLES, Paul Eugene (French, 1849-)
Souvenir de la Salpetriere, oil on canvas, sgn, unfr, 32x40", WD 5/5/88 UE ... 600

MESROS (American, 19th C)
Sailboat Docked, oil on canvas, sgn/dtd 1897, 10x8", DM 10/14/88 ... 275

METCALF, Willard Leroy (American, 1858-1925)
Afternoon in the Streets in Biskra, oil on panel, sgn/dtd 1887, 10x16", C-NY 9/30/88 OE ... 82,500
Cloudy Day, York Beach, Maine; oil on panel, sgn, 7x10", SBY 9/23/88 ... 6,600
Early October (landscape), oil on canvas, sgn/dtd 1906, 29x26", SBY 5/24/89 ... 101,750
First Thaw (landscape w/stream), oil on canvas, sgn, 26x29", WD 10/5/88 OE ... 140,000
Flying Shadows (landscape), oil on canvas, sgn/dtd 05, 26x29", SBY 5/24/89 ... 198,000
Golden Hour, oil on canvas, sgn/dtd 1907, 39x36", B/B 6/15/89 ... 253,000
Kennebunkport, Maine; oil on board, initialed/dtd 1920, 9x7", SBY 6/24/88 ... 7,150
Kiss on the Hand, watercolor/gouache on board, sgn/inscr/dtd 90, 19x14", SBY 9/23/88 ... 1,430
L'Etang Normandie (autumn landscape), oil on board, sgn, 9x12", C-NY 5/25/89 OE7 ... 30,800
Le Ruisseau, oil on canvas, sgn, 12x15", SBY 6/24/88 OE ... 25,300
Maytime (landscape), oil on canvas, sgn/dtd 1919, 36x39", SBY 5/25/88 ... 638,000
Mouth of the River at Walberswick, oil on canvas, sgn/inscr/dtd 1885, 13x16", SBY 5/25/88 ... 14,850
Pair: Meadow Study; Sunset Study; oil on panel, sgn/dtd 1911, 6x8", C-NY 5/25/89 ... 30,800
Path (building/figures in landscape), oil on canvas, sgn, ca 1915, 29x33", SBY 5/24/89 ... 308,000
Portrait of a Preston Baker, oil on canvas, sgn/inscr/dtd 89, 19x11", C-NY 5/26/88 ... 33,000
Santa Fe, oil on canvas, sgn/dtd 81, 14x17", SBY 6/24/88 OE ... 16,500
Spring Landscape, Grez; oil on panel, sgn/initialed, 9x13", SBY 3/17/88 OE ... 23,100
Trout Pool, November (hillside w/rocky creek bed); oil on canvas, sgn/dtd 1910, 29x26", C-NY 5/25/89 ... 99,000

METSU, Gabriel (Dutch, 1629-1667)
Portrait of a Man Said To Be the Artist, oil on panel, sgn, 7x5", SBY 6/3/88 ... 16,500

METSU, Gabriel; after (Dutch, 1629-1667)
Hunter's Gift, oil on canvas, unfr, 21x17", SBY 7/12/89 ... 275
Interior with Hunter Presenting the Kill to a Lady, oil on panel, unfr, 23x17", SBY 12/9/88 ... 1,870

METSU, Gabriel; circle of (Dutch, 1629-1667)
Woman Writing a Letter by a Window with a Cavalier Looking On, oil on panel, 16x18", C-NY 4/6/89 OE ... 10,450

METSU, Gabriel; manner of (Dutch, 1629-1667)
Sportsman Holding a Glass of Wine at a Window, oil on panel , 12x10", C-NY 1/15/88 ... 4,180

METSU, Gabriel; school of (Dutch, 1629-1667)
Vegetable Market, oil on canvas, 24x29", C-E 1/12/88 ... 1,650

METSYS, Cornelis; circle of (Flemish, 1510-1580)
Flight into Egypt, oil on panel, 22x19", C-NY 4/8/88 ... 5,500

METSYS, Jan; circle of (Flemish, 1509-1575)
Mother & Child, oil on panel, on gold ground, 40x12", C-NY 4/8/88 OE ... 10,450

METSYS, Quentin; circle of (Flemish, 1466-1530)
Money Changers, oil on canvas, 43x33", C-NY 1/15/88 ... 11,000
Portrait of a Gentleman with the Crown of Thorns, Another Figure Beyond; oil on panel, oval, 14x10", SBY 4/7/89 UE ... 4,400

METSYS, school of
Woman Pulling Her Hair, oil on panel, 31x45", C-E 1/12/88 UE ... 198

METZ, see De Metz

METZINGER, Jean (French, 1883-1956)
Cubist Female Nude, pencil on paper, sgn/dtd 1912, 13x9", B/B 3/22/89 OE ... 7,700
Deesse aux Instruments de Navigation, pen/black ink/white chalk over pencil, sgn, ca 1926, 14x11", C-NY 2/16/89 ... 7,700
Femme au Miroir, oil on canvas, sgn, 32x24", SBY 2/16/89 ... 55,000
Femme Avec Panier, oil on canvas, sgn twice/dtd 1912, 25x18", SBY 2/18/88 ... 44,000
Femme Cubiste (abstract), black/white/yellow chalk on paper, bears signature/dtd 1920, 14x10", SBY 10/7/88 OE ... 17,600
Fleurs, oil on canvas, sgn, 16x13", SBY 2/16/89 ... 23,100
L'Ecuyere (The Horsewoman), oil on canvas, sgn, ca 1926, 35x51", C-NY 11/16/88 OE ... 209,000

ɑ Village sur la Route (village scene), oil on canvas, sgn, 18x24", C-NY 5/12/88 OE	51,700
Nature Morte, oil on canvas, sgn, 19x22", SBY 2/18/88	37,400
Nature Morte, oil on canvas, sgn/dtd 24, 24x32", C-NY 5/11/89	88,000
Nature Morte (abstract still life), oil on canvas, sgn, ca 1927, 22x15", SBY 10/7/88 OE	27,500
Nature Morte (abstract still life), oil on canvas, sgn, 1920, 20x20", SBY 5/10/89 OE	203,500
Nature Morte (still life), oil on canvas, sgn, 13x18", C-NY 5/12/88	35,200
Nature Morte a la Cafetiere, oil on canvas, sgn, 1917, 24x36", SBY 5/11/88 OE	154,000
Nature Morte a la Guitare, oil on canvas, sgn, 1919, 37x29", SBY 5/11/88 OE	165,000
Nature Morte aux Fruits (abstract still life), oil on canvas, sgn, 1920, 20x26", C-NY 11/16/88	104,500
Nu Au Bateau (abstract), oil on canvas, sgn, 14x11", SBY 10/7/88 OE	25,300
Parc Monceau, oil on canvas, sgn, ca 1906, 21x29", SBY 10/6/89	55,000
Parc Montsouris (landscape), oil on canvas, sgn, ca 1906, 20x26", SBY 11/12/88	44,000
Paysage, oil on canvas, ca 1906, 26x36", SBY 5/11/88 OE	77,000
Portrait d'une Femme, oil on canvas, sgn, ca 1904-06, 18x15", SBY 10/7/88 OE	13,200
Portrait de Femme (abstract), oil on canvas, sgn, 26x22", SBY 11/12/88	104,500
Self-Portrait, seated, holding a drawing tablet; black chalk, sgn/dtd 1853, inscr twice, 14x12", C-NY 10/26/88	3,520
TZMACHER, Emile Pierre (French, 19th C)	
Songbird (woman with bird in an interior), oil on panel, sgn/dtd 1877, 24x16", C-NY 10/25/89	22,000
Young Beauty Crossing a Brook with a Hunter Beyond, oil on panel, sgn, 24x20", C-NY 10/25/89	28,600
UCCI, Michelangelo (Italian, 19th C)	
Pair: Ducks by a Pond; Chickens Feeding; oil on board, sgn, oval, 12x13", C-E 5/23/88	3,520
Pair: Game in an Interior; oil on board, sgn, inscr Firenze, oval, 9x7", WD 3/23/88 UE	1,000
Pair: Still Life of Dead Game & Fruit; oil on panel, sgn/dtd 1871, ovals, 3x11", C-E 2/23/88	1,100
Pair: Still Lifes (fruit, dead game); oil on canvasboard, sgn/dtd 1873 & 1872, 13x10" & smaller, C-E 2/21/89 UE	770
ULEN, Franz Pieter Ter (Dutch, 1843-1927)	
Boy with Cows, oil on canvas, 28x30", LH 10/16/88 OE	4,400
Sheep Outside the Barn, oil on canvas, sgn, 26x37", C-E 2/23/88	1,430
Shepherdess with Her Flock in a Woodland Clearing, oil on canvas, sgn, SBY 12/9/88	3,080
ULENER, Pieter (1602-1654)	
Battle w/Cannon, Arquebusier, & Pikemen Behind Palisade in Foreground; oil on panel, monogramed, 10x15", C-M 6/16/89 OE	9,779
ULENER, Pieter; circle of (1602-1654)	
Town Under Siege, oil on panel, 22x36", C-NY 10/12/89	6,600
UNIER, Georgette (Belgian, 1859-1951)	
Tranquil Waterway, oil on canvas, 18x27", NA 2/24/89	700
URER, Charles Alfred (American, 1865-1955)	
Lyon, France; oil on canvas, sgn/inscr/dtd 1893, sgn/dtd 1892 on verso, 14x24", C-E 6/1/88	935
Portrait of a Little Boy (in landscape), oil on canvas, sgn/dtd 88, 46x34", NA 5/13/89	1,000
Still Life of Currency & Pipe, oil on canvas, initialed, 10x10", RWS 6/10/89 OE	8,500
xican School (19th C)	
Bull Fight, oil on canvas, 22x26", C-SK 11/10/88	1,860
YER, Adolf; see De Meyer	
YER, Claus (German, 1856-1919)	
Playing Dice, oil on panel, sgn, 10x8", C-E 10/25/88	2,420
YER, Dennis (American, 20th C)	
Color Direction #1, 1973 (abstract); oil on canvas, sgn/dtd, 30x40", WG 4/23/88	210
YER, Emile (French, 19th C)	
Unveiling (group of three religious figures in an interior), oil on panel, sgn, 25x32", C-NY 5/24/89	16,500
YER, Ernest Frederick (American, 1863-1952)	
Summer Landscape, Connecticut; oil on canvasboard, sgn, 20x16", WD 4/13/88 UE	1,000
View of Essex, Connecticut; oil on artist board, estate stamp, 8x12", RAB 8/8/89	400
YER, Felicia (Mrs. Reginald Marsh)(American, 1913-)	
Cascades, oil on board, sgn, 23x19", C-NY 6/17/89	660
Eggs & Wedgewood, oil on board, sgn, 10x12", C-NY 6/17/89	605
Interior, oil on canvasboard, sgn, 16x12", C-NY 6/17/89	528
Landing, oil on canvas, sgn/dtd, 14x9", NA 5/13/89	225
YER, Georges	
Feeding Chickens, oil on canvas, sgn, 18x22", C-E 10/25/88	1,980
YER, Hendrik; see De Meyer	
YER, Johann Georg (German, 1813-1886)	
Feeding the Nanny Goat, oil on board, sgn/dtd 1875, 15x12", WD 5/5/88	10,500
YERHEIM, Friedrich Edouard; att (German, 1808-1879)	
Children's Outing, oil on canvas, 42x34", SBY 12/9/88	4,400
YERHEIM, Hermann (German, 1840-1880)	
A Busy Port, oil on canvas, sgn, 27x38", SBY 10/24/89	16,500
YERHEIN, Wilhelm Alexander (German 1815-1882)	
Street in Misdroy, oil on canvas, sgn, 27x37", LH 10/16/88	11,000
Village Snowman, oil on canvas, sgn/dtd 1853, 16x21", C-NY 5/25/88	10,450
YERHOFF	
Toast, watercolor on board, 15x22", C-E 5/23/88 UE	385
YERING, Albert; att (Dutch, 1645-1714)	
Classical Landscape w/Maidens Bearing Cinerary Urns Near Tombs in Foreground, no media given, unfr, 102x69", C-M 6/16/89	13,854

Classical Landscape with Fortune teller Near River in the Foreground, no media given, unfr, 102x69", C-M 6/16/89 .... **13,854**
Nymphs in a Grove Gathering Flowers by a Pedestal with Relief Bust of Diana, no media given, unfr, 103x72", C-M 6/16/89 .... **9,779**
Wooded Landscape with a Nymph Playing a Tambourine Near a Fountain, no media given, unfr, 102x68", C-M 6/16/89 .... **10,594**

MEYEROWITZ, William (American, 1898-1981)
Blue Cloud (abstract horses), oil on canvasboard, sgn, 12x71", C-E 10/18/89 .... **1,650**
Clarinetist (abstract), oil on canvas, sgn, 28x14", RWS 3/16/89 UE **500**
Village Life, Harborside; oil on canvas, sgn, 27x35", RWS 11/3/88 .... **4,000**
Violinist (abstract), oil on canvas, sgn/dtd 57, 34x17", RWS 3/16/89 .... **800**

MEYERS, Frank H. (American)
Good Sailing (hilly coastal view w/trees & sailboats in distance), oil on masonite, sgn, 18x24", C-E 2/1/89 .... **990**

MEYERSAHM, Exene Reed (American, 19th/20th C)
Still Life of Apples, oil on canvas, sgn, 12x18", RWS 10/27/89 .... **550**

MEZA, Guillermo (Mexican, 1917-)
El Cargador, gouache on paper, sgn, 15x18", C-NY 11/21/89 OE **5,500**
Trees (contemporary stormy landscape w/figures), gouache on paper, sgn, 18x22", SBY 11/21/88 OE **3,025**
Untitled (cloaked figure in fog w/full moon), gouache on paper, sgn/dtd 1950, 22x18", SBY 11/21/88 .... **1,650**

MEZZERA, Roas (Italian, 1791-1826)
Cadmus Slaying the Dragon in an Extensive Landscape, oil on canvas, sgn, 20x23", C-NY 4/6/89 .... **14,300**

MICHAELIS, Gerard Jan
Wooded Landscape with a Windmill & Two Figures, black chalk/gray wash, sgn/inscr, 10x15", C-NY 1/12/88 OE **2,420**

MICHAELS, J.
Wooded Landscape with River, oil on canvas, sgn/dtd 77, 22x36", DM 2/19/88 OE **5,000**

MICHAELS, S.
Skaters on a Frozen Lake at Sunset, oil on canvas, sgn, 22x36", C-E 10/25/88 UE **495**

MICHALLON, Achille Etna; att (1796-1822)
Landscape with a Hunter Standing in a Clearing & Firing His Gun, oil on canvas, 17x22", SBY 4/7/89 .... **3,025**

MICHAU, Theobald (Flemish, 1676-1765)
Grape Harvesters Making Wine by a Cottage on a River, oil on panel, sgn, 6x10", C-NY 1/11/89 OE **8,800**

MICHAU, Theobald; circle of (Flemish, 1676-1765)
Figures on a Path by a Pond in a Wooded Landscape, oil on panel, indistinctly inscr, 7x10", C-NY 10/20/88 OE **5,280**
Pair: Peasants on a Path by an Inn; Villagers by an Estuary Near a Town; oil on panel, 6x8", C-NY 10/20/88 .... **5,500**

MICHAUD, Leonie (French, 1873-)
Grieving Widow (group in interior), oil on canvas, 98x110", C-E 2/21/89 OE **7,700**

MICHAUX (French, 19th/20th C)
Velacypede, oil on panel, sgn/titled, 19x16", SBY 6/8/88 .... **1,210**

MICHEL, C. (Belgian, 1874-1940)
Afternoon Stroll (elegant lady walking dog), pastel, sgn/dtd 1909, 35x20", C-NY 2/23/89 .... **2,420**

MICHEL, Georges (French, 1763-1843)
Extensive Landscape with a Stormy Sky, oil on canvas laid down on board, 15x24", C-NY 10/25/89 .... **12,100**
Extensive Landscape with Windmills, oil on panel, 38x50", C-NY 10/25/89 .... **11,000**
Landscape with Windmills, oil on canvas, 24x34", SBY 2/22/89 UE **16,500**
Un Vieux Moulin, oil on canvas, 19x26", WD 11/16/88 OE **9,250**

MICHEL, Georges; att (French, 1763-1843)
Travellers on a Country Road, oil on canvas, 10x13", RWS 8/20/88 UE **150**

MICHEL, Henri (French, 1928-)
Les Bords de la Rievre, oil on canvas, sgn, 22x18", C-E 11/17/88 .... **4,620**
Paysage aux Fleurs, oil on canvas, sgn, 25x33", B/B 9/15/88 .... **1,210**
Yellow Cathedral, oil on canvas, sgn, 36x32", FAP 12/8/89 .... **400**

MICHETTI, Francesco Paolo (Italian, 1851-1929)
Young Girl with Chickens, oil on panel, sgn/dtd 73, 11x5", C-NY 10/25/89 OE **24,200**

MICHIELI, Andrea (Italian, 16th C)
Semiramis Hearing the News of a Revolt in Babylon, pen/ink/wash over black chalk, 8x11", SBY 1/13/89 OE **8,250**

MIDDENDORF, Helmut (German, 20th C)
Fruh am Morgen, Self-Portrait; watercolor/pencil on paper, sgn/dtd 82/titled, 16x12", SBY 2/19/88 .... **2,310**
Hand unt Pistole (man w/gun), watercolor/India ink on paper, sgn/dtd 83, 24x34", SBY 2/14/89 .... **2,750**
Street, oil on canvas, 1984, 78x117", SBY 10/8/88 OE **22,000**
Study for the Street, watercolor on paper, sgn/dtd 83/titled, 19x14", SBY 2/19/88 .... **2,310**
The Jump (male nude diving), acrylic on canvas, sgn/dtd 84/titled, 117x78", SBY 5/3/88 .... **16,500**
Untitled (contemporary figure w/yellow glow, town beyond), acrylic on canvas, sgn/dtd 1985, 84x70", SBY 10/5/89 .... **14,300**
Young Man & Bottle, oil on canvas, sgn/dtd Berlin 1983, 92x72", SBY 11/9/89 .... **18,700**
Young Man in the City, watercolor on paper, sgn/dtd 83/titled, 19x14", SBY 2/19/88 OE **3,850**

MIDDLETON, Stanley Grant (American, 1852-)
Hearth, oil on canvas, sgn, 25x21", C-E 3/22/88 .... **352**
Seaward Farewell (two ladies & child on shore waving to man in boat), oil on canvas, sgn, 17x22", C-E 2/1/89 .... **935**
Telling Her Fortune (lady in profile pouring tea leaves on saucer), oil on canvas, sgn/dtd 1932, 16x12", RWS 4/7/89 UE **175**

MIEL, Jan (Flemish, 1599-1663)
Peasants Outside a Fortress, oil on canvas, 33x43", SBY 6/2/89 .... **33,000**

MIEL, Jan; att (Flemish, 1599-1663)
Italian Peasants Playing Cards in a Courtyard, oil on canvas, inscr, 28x34", SBY 1/12/89 OE **10,450**
Peasants Carousing by a Tavern, oil on canvas, bears signature/dtd 1661, 28x38", C-NY 4/8/88 .... **7,150**

MIELICH, Leopold Alphons (Austrian, 1863-1929)
Orange Sellers, oil on panel, sgn, 4x6", C-NY 2/23/89 5,500
MIEMANN, Edmund John
Walking Through a Corridor, watercolor on board heightened w/white gouache, sgn, 16x12", C-E 2/23/88 UE 110
MIESLER, Ernst (German, 1879-)
Autumnal Lights, pastel, sgn, 20x16", C-E 10/26/89 330
MIGNARD, Pierre (French, 1612-1695)
Portrait of Princesse Marguerite Armande de Lorraine, Duchesse de Cadaval; oil on canvas, inscr, 35x29", SBY 1/12/89 77,000
MIGNARD, Pierre; after (French, 1612-1695)
Portrait of a Lady, oil on canvas mounted on board, oval, 27x22", C-E 2/16/88 2,090
MIGNARD, Pierre; att (French, 1612-1695)
Portrait of a Lady as Diana, oil on canvas, oval, 28x22", B/B 3/22/89 4,125
Portrait of a Lady in Allegorical Guise, Perhaps As Nereid; oil on canvas, 33x27", SBY 4/7/89 OE 6,050
Portrait of la Marquise de Sevigne, oil on canvas, sgn, 25x19", WD 10/19/88 4,750
MIGNARD, Pierre; circle of (French, 1612-1695)
Portrait of a Woman As Diana, oil on canvas, oval, 24x21", C-E 4/7/88 UE 462
Young General Leading a Horse, oil on canvas, 48x38", C-NY 4/6/89 8,800
MIGNARD, Pierre; follower of (French, 1612-1695)
Pair: Portrait of Lady in Elegant Dress, One Possibly Madame de Montespan; oil on canvas, oval, 29x23", SBY 4/7/89 OE 11,000
Portrait of a Lady, oil on canvas, 36x29", SBY 7/12/89 OE 2,750
Portrait of a Lady Said To Be Maria Mancini, oil on canvas, oval, 28x23", SBY 6/8/88 935
Portrait of Miss Charlotte Devitt, oil on canvas, in a painted oval, 29x23", SBY 12/9/88 2,200
MIGNARD, Pierre; school of (French, 1612-1695)
Portrait of a Lady (bust-length), oil on canvas, 17x13", C-E 6/1/88 UE 242
MIGNARD, Pierre; studio of (French, 1612-1695)
Portrait of Francois Angelique de Motte Houdancourt, Duchesse d'Aumont...; oil on canvas, oval, 38x31", C-NY 5/31/89 UE 4,950
MIGNON, Abraham (German, 1640-1679)
Basket of Fruit with Fishing Gear & Fish, oil on panel, 37x29", SBY 1/12/89 451,000
Floral Still Life in Glass Vase with Nectarines, Butterflies, & Other Insects; oil on canvas, 33x30", C-M 12/3/88 OE 26,000
Still Life of Grapes, Peaches, Blackberries, Acorns, Prickly Fruit...; oil on panel, monogramed, 16x13", SBY 1/12/89 341,000
MIGNON, Abraham; after (German, 1640-1679)
Still Life of Fruit, Roemer, Flute Glass, & Bread on a Folding Serving Panel; oil on board, 19x25", SBY 10/21/88 3,300
MIGNON, Abraham; manner of (German, 1640-1679)
Still Life of Fruit, with a Lizard, Butterfly, & a Nest of Eggs; oil on panel, shaped top, 14x14", SBY 6/8/88 770
MIGNOT, Louis Remy (American, 1831-1870)
Autumn Landscape, oil on canvas, sgn/dtd 1857, 30x21", SBY 5/25/88 UE 22,000
On the Orinoco, Venezuela; oil on board, sgn/dtd 1857, 12x18", C-NY 5/26/88 33,000
MIHAILESEN, D. (Romanian)
Village Outside the City, oil on canvas, sgn, 26x25", WG 9/16/88 UE 100
MIKKER, Jean Christiansz; att
Crossing of the Red Sea, oil on panel, 17x28", C-NY 4/6/89 UE 1,100
Milanese School (17th C)
Madonna & Child, oil on canvas, 24x21", WD 10/19/88 OE 2,000
Milanese School (18th C)
Studies of the Head & Hands of Christ, red/white chalk, inscr, ca 1700, 11x7", C-NY 1/12/88 330
Milanese School (19th C)
Design for a Throne: Front Side View; watercolor heightened w/white/yellow/gold, 12x15", SBY 1/13/89 880
Pair: Liberation of Saint Peter; black chalk/pen/brown ink/brown wash, ca 1800, 5x4", C-NY 1/12/88 UE 165
MILDER, Jay (American, 1934-)
Dreamscape #30, Le Mistral (abstract); oil on canvas, sgn, 1977, 58x52", SBY 2/15/89 4,125
Space Lion, acrylic/graphite on canvas, sgn/dtd 1976, 47x53", C-NY 2/13/89 1,650
MILES, Bernice (American, 20th C)
Cactus in Bloom, watercolor on paper, sgn, 19x15", WG 4/23/88 95
Parrot Tulips, laser on paper, sgn, 16x13", WG 4/23/88 UE 60
MILES, George F. (British, 1852-1891)
Two Figures by the River Bank (in an extensive landscape), oil on canvas, 23x29", WG 4/23/88 550
MILES, Jeanne Patterson (American, 20th C)
Chord, oil on canvas, sgn/dtd 1956-64, 48x58", LH 10/16/88 UE 70
MILES, Samuel S. (American, 19th C)
Near Freetown, Massachusetts (summer scene); oil on board, sgn, 6x9", RAB 8/9/88 350
Pair: Twin Mountain & Lake; Country Road & Summer Shower; oil on cardboard, sgn/dtd 1868, 6x7", RWS 3/31/88 UE 42,500
MILIONE, A. (Italian, 19th C)
Returning Home, oil on canvas, sgn, 25x37", C-E 2/23/88 1,760
MILLAIS, H. Raoul (British, 1901-)
After the Race (jockeys & mounts in a landscape), oil on canvas, sgn, 8x10", SBY 6/9/89 2,750
MILLAIS, John Everett (British, 1829-1896)
Christmas Eve, 1887 (landscape w/Murthley Castle beyond); oil on canvas, sgn w/monogram, dtd 1887, 61x52", C-NY 5/24/89 88,000
Yes (one of two sequels to artist's Yes or No?), oil on canvas, monogramed/dtd 77, 59x46", SBY 10/24/89 OE 407,000
MILLAIS, John Everett; att (British, 1829-1896)
Temporary Discord, oil on canvas, monogramed/dtd 1861, 37x24", WD 3/23/88 OE 1,800

MILLAR, Addison Thomas (American, 1850-1913)
Blue Fountain, Rue Bab Azoun, Algier; oil on canvas, sgn/initialed, unfr, 16x12", C-SK 11/10/88 ... 1,580
Harbor Alger, oil on board, sgn/inscr, 7x9", C-E 2/3/88 ... 1,430
Rug Market, oil on canvas, sgn, 16x13", C-E 2/3/88 ... 1,760
Rug Merchant, oil on canvas, sgn, 22x28", SBY 10/24/89 ... 33,000
Spanish Village (figures amid stucco & tile-roofed buildings), oil on panel, sgn, 5x4", RWS 3/31/88 UE ... 200
Tavern Scene, oil on board, sgn, 11x9", C-E 10/18/89 ... 2,860
Woman in White Dress (seated, viewed from behind), oil on canvas, sgn, 13x8", C-NY 12/2/88 ... 6,600

MILLARES, Manolo (Spanish, 1926-)
Cuadro (abstract), oil on canvas, sgn twice/dtd 1960/titled, 39x32", SBY 6/30/88 ... 104,000
Untitled (abstract), black ink/ink wash/gouache/ballpoint pen on board, sgn/dtd 66, 20x28", SBY 2/14/89 OE ... 55,000
Untitled (abstract), brush/black ink on paper mounted at corners on board, sgn, unfr, 19x15", C-E 11/17/88 OE ... 22,000
Untitled (abstract), gouache on cardbord, sgn/dtd 1962, 26x20", SBY 11/9/89 OE ... 104,500
Untitled (composition), gouache on paper, sgn/dtd 1961, 19x28", SBY 11/9/89 ... 60,500

MILLE, Jan Baptiste
Italianate Landscape with Figures on a Path, oil on canvas, sgn, 26x31", C-NY 10/12/89 ... 9,350

MILLER, Alfred Jacob; manner of (American, 1810-1874)
Pair: Indians Hunting on the Prairie; Indian Encampment by a River; oil on canvas, 20x24", 21x17", SBY 9/23/88 ... 1,760

MILLER, Barse (American, 1904-1973)
Christmas at the Firehouse, Auburn, California, 1947; oil on canvas, sgn, 28x20", B/B 6/15/89 ... 2,475
Ivory Bones with Heavenly Dots, oil on canvas, sgn/dtd 31, 22x25", B/B 6/15/89 ... 3,300

MILLER, Charles Henry (American, 1842-1922)
Haystacks in a Landscape, oil on canvas, sgn, 15x24", C-E 11/30/88 UE ... 550
Long Island Landscape, 1880s; oil on canvas, sgn, 16x24", WD 4/13/88 ... 2,200
New Moon-Long Island Meadows; no media given, sgn twice/inscr Queens NY/titled, 18x24", SBY 1/24/89 ... 1,100
Raining Summer Day, oil on board, sgn, 16x24", C-E 9/15/88 ... 715
River Landscape, Evening; oil on canvas, sgn, 22x30", PHL 12/1/88 UE ... 750
Shipping Off Gibraltar, oil on canvas, sgn/dtd 1877, 30x44", C-NY 10/25/89 ... 9,350
White-Capped Waves & Green-Capped Dunes, oil on canvas, sgn, 30x40", WG 4/23/88 ... 1,200

MILLER, Charles K. (British, 19th C)
Shipping Off the Coast, oil on board, initialed/dtd 1900, 13x28", C-E 11/8/88 UE ... 550

MILLER, Edith (American, 20th C)
Floral Still Life, oil on canvas, sgn, 9x12", FAP 12/8/89 ... 225

MILLER, Francis (American, 1885-1930)
Grapes & Pears, oil on canvas, sgn, 15x12", C-NY 9/30/88 ... 1,650

MILLER, Herbert McRae (Canadian, 1896-)
Winter Shadows, oil on canvas, sgn/dtd 1967, 20x26", FB 10/17/88 ... 225

MILLER, John Paul (American, 20th C)
After Many a Summer (old house on hill), watercolor on paper, sgn, 14x20", WG 4/23/88 ... 425

MILLER, Joseph (German, 19th C)
Lighting the Pipe (child lighting man's pipe in an interior), oil on canvas, sgn/indistinctly dtd, 25x22", SBY 12/9/88 ... 8,525

MILLER, Kenneth Hayes (American, 1876-1952)
Figure Composition, oil on canvas, sgn/dtd 26, 34x29", C-NY 9/30/88 ... 7,700
Mirror (seated nude viewed from behind), oil on board, 14x8", B/B 5/17/89 ... 935
Still Life of Glass, oil on canvas, sgn/dtd 1922, 17x14", C-NY 3/11/88 ... 2,640

MILLER, Lewis (1796-1882)
Set of 5: European Scenes; watercolor on paper, 4 sgn, 4x6", C-NY 10/1/88 ... 1,980

MILLER, Marim
Woman with Pedestal (allegorical or literary theme), watercolor, sgn, ca 1900, 14x9", DM 2/19/88 ... 100

MILLER, Ralph Davidson (American, 1859-1946)
Landscape, oil on canvas, sgn, 30x40", B/B 9/14/89 ... 990
Midwestern Farmlands, oil on canvas, sgn, 20x38", C-NY 9/28/89 ... 2,200
Western Landscape, oil on canvas, sgn, 30x40", B/B 12/8/88 ... 1,980

MILLER, Richard Emil (American, 1875-1943)
Black Mantilla (portrait of a woman), oil on canvas, sgn, 36x34", C-NY 5/26/88 ... 28,600
Harbor, oil on canvas, sgn, 24x29", SBY 6/24/88 ... 7,150
La Crinoline (portrait of seated lady in full crinoline skirt), oil on canvas, sgn, 46x32", SBY 5/24/89 ... 55,000
Portrait of a Young Man (wearing a blue jacket), oil on canvas, sgn/dtd 1935, 24x20", SLK 5/11/88 ... 3,400
Self-Portrait of the Artist As a Young Man, oil on canvas, 24x18", LH 5/15/88 ... 1,500
Sewing by Lamplight, oil on canvas, sgn, ca 1904, 24x24", SBY 5/25/88 OE ... 352,000
Tea Pot & Bowl, oil on canvas, sgn, 22x26", C-NY 5/26/88 ... 16,500
The Artist's Wife, oil on panel, sgn, ca 1913, 14x10", C-NY 9/28/89 OE ... 18,700

MILLER, William (fl 1830s)
View of the Fort at Ahmednagar, pen/black ink/watercolor, 11x20", C-SK 5/25/89 ... 275

MILLER, William Rickarby (American, 1850-1923)
Blooming Oak Shanty, oil on board, sgn/dtd 1880, 8x6", SBY 3/17/88 ... 1,650
Canal Scene, Susquehanna River; oil on canvas, sgn/dtd 1881, 12x20", C-E 6/1/89 ... 3,520
Feeding Time, oil on board, sgn/inscr, 8x6", C-E 11/30/88 ... 2,090
Four Bananas on a Table, oil on canvas, sgn/dtd 1885, 8x12", C-E 2/3/88 OE ... 2,750
On the Erie Canal, Little Falls, New York; watercolor/white gouache on paper, sgn/dtd 1852, 14x20", SBY 3/17/88 ... 2,530
River Walk Under Castle Point, Hoboken (figures in landscape), oil on canvas, sgn/dtd 18(?), 13x21", C-E 6/1/89 UE ... 990

Still Life of Grapes, oil on canvas, sgn/dtd 1863, 17x14", WD 4/13/88 2,700
Study of a Pineapple From Nature, oil on canvas, sgn/dtd 1885, 8x12", SBY 6/28/89 4,400

MILLESON, Royal Hill (American, 1849-)
Elk Mountain, New Mexico; oil on canvas, sgn, 10x14", B/B 1/11/89 302
Mountain Peak in an Evening Sunset, oil on canvas, sgn, 18x24", B/B 12/8/88 880
Stream in a Landscape, oil on canvas, sgn, 18x24", C-NY 3/11/88 1,980

MILLET, Clarence (American, 1897-1959)
Autumn, oil on canvas, sgn, 10x13", B/B 8/10/88 1,650
Cabin Scene, oil on board, 15x18", MG 5/28/88 275
French Landscape, oil on canvas, sgn, 12x18", MG 3/26/88 UE 450
French Quarter Courtyard, a Study; oil on artist board, sgn, 23x17", NA 5/13/89 750
French Quarter Street Scene, oil on academy board, sgn, 14x17', NA 2/24/89 OE 3,500
Harbor Scene, oil on board, sgn/dtd 21, 10x13", NA 11/5/88 1,500
Market Day, oil on canvas, sgn, 25x30", NA 2/6/88 6,000
St Louis Cathedral, oil on board, sgn, 20x11", NA 1/6/88 5,500

MILLET, Francis Davis (American, 1846-1912)
Newport Harbor, oil on canvas, sgn/titled, 10x16", RAB 3/27/89 3,500
Young Woman with an Urn, oil on canvas, sgn, 14x11", RWS 5/12/89 3,100

MILLET, Jean Francois (French, 1814-1875)
Classical Landscape w/Figures Walking on a Road & Buildings & Mountains in Distance, oil on canvas, 18x23", SBY 4/7/88 7,700

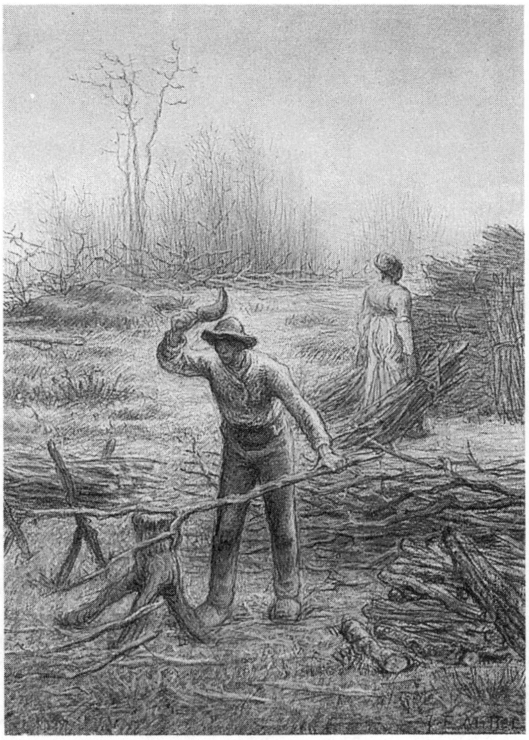

Bucheron Preparant des Fagots, pastel, sgn, 19x14", C-NY 10/25/89 OE; $825,000

Double-Sided: Study of Sheep; pencil, stamped initials, unfr, 2x4", C-NY 2/23/89 990
La Fin de la Moisson, black chalk/pen/brown ink heightened w/white, initialed, 6x9", C-NY 2/25/88 OE 187,000
Le Moulin a Eau, pen/ink on paper, stamped initials, ca 1866-67, 5x8", SBY 2/22/89 14,300
Pair: Study of a Child with an Infant; Study of a Mug; black chalk, stamp initialed, unfr, ca 2x4", C-NY 2/23/89 1,320
Study for the Reading Lesson, pencil on paper, stamped signature, ca 1860, 9x6", SBY 10/24/89 17,600
Study of a Hay Wagon with Figures in a Landscape, black chalk on laid paper, initialed, unfr, 4x9", C-NY 5/24/89 3,850
Study of a Shepherd, black chalk on gray laid paper, stamped initials, 9x6", C-NY 2/23/89 OE 7,700
Study of Hands, black chalk on lt tan laid paper, stamped w/initials, 9x6", C-NY 5/24/89 OE 2,860

MILLIERE, Maurice (French, 1871-)
Elegant Lady in the Famous Paris Restaurant, Vatel; oil on board, sgn/dtd 1905, 20x10", C-NY 10/25/89 12,100
Motoring (lady in early auto, terrier beside her), oil on canvas, sgn/dtd 03, 32x25", RWS 9/29/88 UE 2,500

MILNE, George R. (Australian)
Leadbeater's Cockatoo & Frilled Lizard (Australia), oil on board, sgn/dtd 45, 24x29", C-SK 11/10/88 OE 2,230

MILNE, Joseph (British, 1861-1911)
Figures on a Rocky Shore, oil on canvas, sgn, 12x18", WAD 6/6/88 1,900

MILNE, William Watt (British, 19th C)
Shepherdess & Sheep By a River, oil on canvas, sgn, 26x32", WAD 6/6/88 OE 10,500

MILNER, D. (British, 19th C)
Milton in an Interior with Daughter, Writing Paradise Lost; oil on canvas, sgn, 29x39", FAP 4/15/89 550

MILONE, A. (Italian, 19th C)
Center of Attention, oil on canvas, sgn, 24x41", FB 10/30/89 .... **1,650**
Cows Watering, oil on canvas, sgn/dtd 1872, 21x32", C-E 5/23/88 .... **3,300**

MILONE, G. (Italian, 19th C)
Shepherdess Tending Her Flock, no media given, sgn/dtd 1903, 19x32", C-E 2/21/89 .... **2,420**

MINAUX, Andre (French, 1923-)
La Modele dans l'Atelier (nude model in a studio), oil on canvas, sgn, 36x28", C-E 5/13/88 OE **2,090**

MINIFIE, C. (American, 19th C)
Whaleships in the Ice, oil on academy board, sgn/dtd 73, 9x14", RAB 8/1/89 UE **850**

MINNIG, Karl (American, 1890-1987)
Set of 3: Rural Scenes (folk art); on masonite or plywood, 16x36", 15x20", 24x55", GAI 9/1/89 .... **95**

MINOR, Robert Crannell (American, 1839-1904)
Landscape, oil on canvas, sgn, unfr, 14x20", C-E 4/7/88 UE **385**
Silver Birch Trees, oil on panel, sgn, 12x16", NA 2/24/89 .... **1,600**
Summer Walk in the Catskills, oil on canvas, sgn, 17x22", C-E 2/3/88 OE **3,080**
Sunset (landscape), oil on canvas, sgn, 16x20", C-E 6/1/89 UE **1,430**

MINTCHINE, Abraham (Russian, 1898-1931)
Paris Scene, oil on canvas, sgn, 26x32", SBY 5/30/89 OE **24,200**
Portrait of Joseph Duveen (famous art dealer), oil on canvas, sgn, ca 1925, 36x24", SBY 5/30/89 OE **15,400**

MIRALLES, Francisco (Spanish, 1850-1901)
Artist Sketching on a Beach, oil on panel, sgn/dtd 1880, 7x10", SBY 2/22/89 .... **99,000**
Avenue Foch with a View of the Arc de Triomphe, oil on canvas, sgn, 13x16", C-NY 10/25/89 .... **110,000**
Boating Party, oil on canvas, sgn, 29x36", SBY 2/22/89 OE **242,000**
Bringing in the Catch, oil on canvas, sgn, 29x37", SBY 2/22/89 OE **143,000**
Nosegay (full-length portrait of lady holding nosegay), oil on canvas laid down, sgn, 43x29", SBY 10/24/89 .... **14,300**
Trois Parisiennes dans le Bois de Boulogne, oil on canvas laid down, sgn, 24x20", B/B 3/17/88 OE **66,000**

MIRALLES-DARMANIN, Jose (Spanish, 1850-1900)
Courtyard Dancing Lesson (women & children in courtyard), watercolor on paper, sgn, 9x12", B/B 10/9/88 .... **3,300**
Eating Oysters, oil on canvas, sgn, 18x6", C-E 10/26/89 .... **2,090**

MIRANDA, see De Miranda

MIRMONT, Nora (20th C)
Hellas, oil on canvas, sgn/dtd 1959, 48x36", C-E 10/18/89 UE **110**

MIRO, Joachim (Spanish, 19th/20th C)
Bustling French Boulevard, oil on canvas, sgn, 15x22", C-NY 2/23/89 .... **7,150**
L'Opera Paris, oil on board, sgn, 10x14", C-E 2/23/88 .... **2,860**
Pair: Les Champs-Elysees, dans la Perspective de l'Arc de Triomphe; La Porte Saint-Denis; oil, sgn, 20x26", SBY 2/22/88 .... **17,600**
Pair: Pantheon, Paris; Tour St Jacques From Quai Megisserie, Paris; oil on board, sgn, 1 dtd 1905, 9x6", B/B 10/9/88 .... **6,600**
Pair: Paris Street Scenes; oil on panel, sgn, 9x15", C-NY 10/25/89 .... **13,200**
River Seine with Notre Dame in the Distance, oil on panel, indistinctly sgn, 9x13", C-E 2/23/88 .... **2,860**

MIRO, Joan (Spanish, 1893-1983)
Abstraction, mixed media, 38x28", LH 10/16/88 OE **2,400**
Composition, gouache/watercolor over etched elements on paper, sgn, ca 1965-67, 22x18", SBY 11/16/89 .... **49,500**
Composition, pencil on gessoed panel, sgn/dtd 27, 6x9", C-NY 11/15/88 OE **52,800**
Composition (abstract), conte crayon/collage on paper laid down on board, 1933-34, 25x19", C-NY 5/11/89 OE **330,000**
Composition (abstract), gouache over monotype on paper mounted on board, sgn, 19x23", C-NY 10/6/88 .... **60,500**
Composition (abstract), oil on board, sgn, dtd 16/6/34, 11x8", SBY 5/10/89 OE **495,000**
Composition (abstract), oil on fibro cement, sgn, 1953, 11x11", C-NY 5/12/88 OE **286,000**
Composition (on copy of Derriere le Miroir), crayon on paper, sgn, 15x11", C-NY 10/5/89 .... **19,800**
Composition pour Madame Zadock, ink wash/watercolor on paper, sgn/dtd 1962/inscr, 17x25", SBY 10/7/88 OE **34,100**
Danseuses (Dancers, abstract composition), watercolor/gouache on paper, sgn, dtd 21/3/63, 28x39", SBY 5/10/89 .... **352,000**
Deux Personnages (two abstract figures), India ink/pastel on laid paper, sgn, dtd 27/3/34, 25x18", SBY 5/10/89 OE **132,000**
Dog Attacking a Bird, oil/ink wash/crayon/pencil on paper laid down on canvas, sgn, 1980, 14x20", SBY 5/11/88 .... **60,500**
Elle et Lui (She & He, imaginary figures), oil on canvas, sgn/dtd 1925, 20x26", C-NY 11/15/88 .... **715,000**
Femme, oil/gouache/crayons on cardboard, sgn, dtd 4/VII/76, 24x20", SBY 11/16/89 .... **286,000**
Femme, Oiseau, Serpent, Etoiles; pastel/charcoal on paper, sgn/dtd 7-1-1942, 25x19", SBY 11/16/89 OE **550,000**
Femme, Oiseaux (woman, bird); gouache/ink wash/crayon/oil on wove paper, sgn/dtd 13.V.80, 26x21", SBY 5/10/89 OE **231,000**
Femme (abstract), oil/colored crayon/pencil on brown paper, sgn/inscr 27 IX 80, 12x9", SBY 11/12/88 .... **57,750**
Femme Assise (seated woman, expressionistic), gouache/watercolor/India ink on paper, sgn/dtd 35, 15x12", SBY 5/11/89 OE **209,000**
Femme et Oiseau Devant le Soleil, gouache/pen/brush/India ink on paper on board, sgn, 1942, 13x16", SBY 11/12/88 OE **275,000**
Femme Etoile, gouache/watercolor/ink wash on paper, sgn/titled, inscr 11/V/65, 29x12", SBY 11/12/88 .... **110,000**
Femmes, Oiseau; gouache/pastel/pencil on paper, sgn twice/dtd 77, 17x18", C-NY 11/15/88 .... **99,000**
Femmes dans la Nuit (Ladies of the Night), oil/tempera on canvas laid down on board, 1944, 7x8", C-NY 11/15/88 OE **550,000**
Femmes et Oiseau Devant le Soleil, oil on canvas, sgn/dtd 1944, 18x14", SBY 11/15/89 OE **1,375,00**
Fete, Oiseau (abstract); oil/black chalk/pencil on paper, sgn/dtd 1973, 14x20", C-NY 5/11/89 OE **110,000**
Figure (imaginative), oil on board, sgn/dtd 1950, 25x17", SBY 5/10/89 .... **385,000**
Figures of Birds in the Night (fantasy drawing), colored crayon/gray wash on paper, sgn, 21x26", SBY 5/11/88 .... **60,500**
Head (abstract self-portrait), gouache/watercolor/ink wash on paper, sgn, 1974, 39x28", SBY 5/11/88 OE **154,000**
Hommage a Miguel Hernandez, crayons/ink wash on paper w/printed text, sgn, 25x18", SBY 11/16/89 OE **104,500**
L'Enfance d'Ubu (abstract figures), black crayon/watercolor on paper, sgn, 13x20", SBY 10/6/89 OE **31,900**
L'Issue Derobee, gouache over monotype, sgn, ca 1976, 13x20", SBY 11/12/88 .... **110,000**
L'Issue Derobee (abstract composition), gouache over monotype, sgn, 1976, 13x20", SBY 5/10/89 .... **110,000**

L'Oiseau au Plumage Deploye Vole vers l'Arbre Argente, oil on canvas, sgn, dtd 12/11/53, 35x46", SBY 11/15/89 OE 9,350,000
L'Oiseau Lunaire (abstract), watercolor/brush/black ink, sgn twice/dtd, #d 2/VII/64/III, 1964, 11x14", C-NY 5/12/88 OE 52,800
L'Oiseau Messager (The Messenger Bird), gouache on paper, sgn/dtd 39, 13x16", C-NY 5/11/89 OE 506,000
La Lune (fantasy composition), oil on canvas, sgn/dtd 1948, 28x24", SBY 5/10/88 852,500
Les Amoureux (abstract), oil on canvas, sgn/dtd 1925, 29x36", SBY 11/11/88 605,000
Les Chants de Maldoror (abstract), brush/India ink on paper, sgn, 9x6", C-NY 10/5/89 9,350
Letter to Mr Charles Zadok: Three Two-Sided Sheets of Drawings; colored wax crayon on stationery, 11x9", SBY 10/7/88 10,450
Metamorphose, India ink on paper, sgn/dtd 2-36, 17x13", SBY 11/16/89 71,500
Oiseau (Bird, symbolistic), ink wash/watercolor on paper, sgn twice/dtd 75/titled, 15x11", SBY 5/11/88 OE 46,750
Peinture (abstract), oil on burlap, sgn/dtd 26.4.33, 39x51", SBY 11/11/88 OE 2,420,000
Peinture (abstract), oil/pencil on panel, sgn/dtd 14.8.24, 11x14", SBY 11/12/88 165,000
Personnage, oil/gouache over monotype on paper, sgn, ca 1976, 23x19", SBY 11/16/89 143,000
Personnage (abstract figure) gouache/watercolor/India ink on paper, sgn, dtd 25/9/35, 15x12", SBY 5/10/89 OE 495,000
Personnages, Oiseaux (abstract); pencil/gouache on paper, sgn/titled, dtd 29/V/76, 11x15", C-NY 5/12/88 65,800
Personnages, Oiseaux; gouache/watercolor/pencil on paper, sgn, dtd 29/X/76, 11x15", SBY 11/16/89 66,000
Personnages, Oiseaux; pen/black ink/brush/gray wash on paper, sgn, 34x56", C-NY 11/15/88 132,000
Personnages et Oiseau (abstract figures of birds), gouache on paper, sgn/dtd 23.10.1942, 20x25", SBY 5/10/89 352,000
Personnages Imaginaires (imaginary figures), crayons/watercolor on paper, sgn, ca 1950-51, 15x10", SBY 11/16/89 44,000
Pour Rene Bore (abstract), colored crayon/pencil on inside cover of Derriere le Miroir, sgn/inscr, 15x11", SBY 10/7/88 7,150
Scene Erotique, pencil on paper, sgn/dtd 1937, 9x12", SBY 5/11/88 OE 20,900
Scene Erotique (line drawing), pencil on paper, sgn/dtd 1937, 9x12", SBY 11/16/89 27,500
Signes et Figurations, watercolor/pen/India ink on paper, sgn twice/dtd, 14x18", C-NY 10/6/88 OE 52,800
Tete, Oiseaux (abstract); oil on canvas, sgn, dtd 18/II/76, 36x26", SBY 11/11/88 467,500
Tete (abstract), oil/gouache/monotype, sgn, ca 1976, 23x19", SBY 2/16/89 OE 143,000
Un Homme (imaginative figure of a man), oil on board, sgn/dtd 4/10/89 OE 522,500
Untitled, pen/ink/gouache on paper mounted on a section of cotton insulation, initialed/sgn/dtd 60, 13x8", SBY 2/18/88 28,600
Untitled (abstract), colored wax crayons on paper laid down on board, sgn/inscr, dtd VI/58, 13x20", SBY 2/18/88 11,550
Untitled (abstract), gouache/ink on buff paper backed with cardboard, initialed, dtd 1/6/60, 13x8", SBY 4/29/88 OE 26,400
Untitled (abstract), India ink/gouache/pencil on gray board, sgn, dtd 11/XI/73.II, 15x20", SBY 4/29/88 OE 38,500
Untitled (abstract), India ink/pastel on paper, sgn/dtd 34, 19x25", SBY 11/12/88 OE 99,000
Untitled (abstract), watercolor/pen/ink on blotter paper on construction paper, sgn/dtd 34, 19x26", SBY 11/12/88 OE 63,250
Untitled (two fantasy figures), colored crayons/charcoal/pencil on paper, sgn, 1924, 18x24", C-NY 5/11/89 OE 253,000
Woman, Bird, Star (abstract); India ink/pastel on canvas, sgn/dtd 1944, 14x11", SBY 5/10/89 OE 165,000
Young Girl Jumping a Rope (abstract), gouache/watercolor/India ink on paper, sgn, dtd 9/9/35, 15x12", SBY 5/10/89 OE 550,000

MIRO, Joan; after (Spanish, 1893-1983)
Untitled, figure next to red sun on blue ground; wool tapestry, 109x81", lot 268, LH 5/15/88 1,800

MISSAKIAN, Berge A. (Canadian, 1933-)
Autumn, oil on canvas, sgn, 24x20", FB 10/30/89 352
North Hatley, oil on canvas, sgn, 16x20", FB 5/28/89 450

MITCHELL, Colin S. (American, 20th C)
Summer Cottage by the Shore, oil on canvas, sgn, 18x24", C-E 6/1/89 UE 440

MITCHELL, George Bertrand (American, 1872-1966)
Country Auction, watercolor/pen/ink/pencil on paper, sgn, 23x20", C-E 6/1/89 1,045

MITCHELL, Glen (American, 1894-1972)
Lake Superior, oil on canvas, sgn or artist's stamp, 20x26", SBY 9/23/88 OE 3,300

MITCHELL, Hutton (Canadian, 1872-1939)
Winter Landscape, oil on canvas, sgn, 10x14", FB 10/30/89 412

MITCHELL, James A. (American, 20th C)
Beach Roses, oil on board, sgn, 12x18", RAB 8/8/89 UE 375
Cape, Outer Beach, North View (coastal seascape); oil on board, sgn/dtd 1987, 20x28", RAB 3/27/89 UE 300
Coastal Schooners Off the Cape, watercolor on paper, sgn/dtd 1988, 18x28", RAB 3/14/89 UE 400
Cow Bay/Vineyard (coastal seascape); oil on board, sgn/dtd 1988/titled, 20x36", RAB 8/8/89 UE 1,050
Ghost Dory, empty dory tossed by waves; watercolor on paper, sgn/dtd 1985, 14x24", RAB 3/14/89 450
Menemsha, Inner Harbor; oil on wood panel, sgn/titled, 24x36", RAB 3/27/89 UE 800

MITCHELL, Joan (American, 1936-)
Before, Again I (abstract); oil on linen, sgn, 1985, unfr, 110x79", C-NY 5/4/89 OE 165,000
Cythere (abstract), oil on canvas, sgn, ca 1960, 51x64", SBY 10/8/88 OE 126,000
Diptych: An Island (abstract); oil on canvas, 1977, 77x90", SBY 10/8/88 77,000
Diptych: Canada IV (abstract); oil on canvas, sgn right panel, 1975, 51x77" overall, SBY 11/11/88 82,500
Gentian Violet (abstract), oil on canvas, 1961, 88x80", SBY 11/10/88 OE 198,000
King of Spades (abstract), oil on canvas, sgn, 92x79", C-NY 5/3/89 OE 462,000
Mandres (abstract), oil on canvas, sgn/dtd 1961-62, 88x79", SBY 5/2/88 OE 137,500
My Landscape (abstract), oil on canvas, sgn, 1967, 77x51", C-NY 2/20/88 OE 143,000
Petit Matin (contemporary abstract), oil on canvas, sgn, 1982, 32x26", SBY 11/9/89 93,500
Rhubarb (abstract), oil on canvas, sgn/dtd 62/titled, 77x51", SBY 11/11/88 99,000
River II (abstract), oil on canvas, ca 1967, 105x77", C-NY 2/20/88 93,500
Thunderstorm, oil on canvas, sgn, 1957, 43x55", C-NY 11/9/88 79,200
Triptych: Parasol (abstract); oil on canvas, 1977, 40x96", SBY 5/5/89 OE 165,000
Triptych: Untitled (abstract); oil on canvas, 1971, 39x77", C-NY 2/20/88 OE 63,800
Untitled (abstract), oil on canvas, ca 1960, 36x35", SBY 10/5/89 OE 82,500
Untitled (abstract), oil on canvas, sgn, ca 1958, 74x71", SBY 11/8/89 506,000

Untitled (abstract), oil on canvas, sgn, ca 1960, 20x14", SBY 11/11/88 19,800
Untitled (abstract), oil on canvas, sgn, ca 1965, 77x51", SBY 11/9/89 247,500
Untitled (abstract), oil on canvas, sgn, ca 1975-80, 16x13", SBY 5/3/80 OE 35,750
Untitled (abstract), oil on canvas, sgn, 1960, 22x24", SBY 10/8/88 29,700
Untitled (abstract), oil on canvas, sgn, 1960, 44x45", SBY 2/19/88 OE 48,400
Untitled (abstract), oil on canvas, sgn, 20x17", C-NY 2/14/89 OE 28,600
Untitled (abstract), oil on canvas, sgn twice, 1960, 12x20", SBY 2/19/88 9,900
Untitled (abstract), pastel on paper, sgn, 1983, 23x16", SBY 5/3/89 OE 20,900

MITCHELL, John Campbell (American, 1862-1922)
Hazy Morning, oil on canvas, sgn/dtd 98, 18x29", WAD 6/6/88 1,600

MITCHELL, Philip (British, 1814-1896)
Waterfall & Landscape, watercolor, sgn, 14x20", FB 5/28/89 750

MITCHELL, Wallace MacMahon (American, 1911-)
Ducks & Wild Turkeys, oil on panel, initialed, 8x13", C-NY 11/30/88 UE 825

MITCHELL, William B. (British, 19th C)
Fishing Boat Becalmed Off Whitby Sunrise, oil on board, sgn, 11x10", FAP 11/4/88 260

MITCHILL, Neil (American, 20th C)
Nocturnal Marine Scene with Sails Visible in the Horizon & the Moonlight, oil on canvas, sgn, 8x15", SLK 5/12/88 130

MODIGLIANI, Amedeo (Italian, 1884-1920)
Angele, pencil on thin tan paper, sgn/titled, ca 1916, 17x10", SBY 11/12/88 44,000
Auto-Portrait, pencil on paper, sgn/inscr, 17x10", C-NY 11/15/88 22,000
Buste de Femme, blue crayon on thin paper, backed w/sheet of rice paper, sgn/dtd 1914, 22x18", SBY 2/18/88 OE 30,800
Caryatide Bleue II (sketch of nude caryatid), crayon on paper, sgn, ca 1912, 22x18", SBY 5/10/89 OE 357,500
Danseuse, brown wash on thin paper backed with a sheet of Japan paper, ca 1908, 14x11", SBY 2/18/88 7,700
Deux Figures, pencil on paper, sgn, 17x10", C-NY 11/15/88 31569 19,800
Donna Seduta, pencil on buff paper, unfr, 14x10", C-E 5/13/88 2,200
Femme Assise, pencil on paper laid down on board, sgn, 17x10", SBY 10/5/88 UE 6,600
Femme Assise, pencil on paper laid down on board, sgn, 17x10", SBY 2/16/89 9,900
Femme Nue, pencil on paper laid down on paper, sgn, 17x10", C-NY 10/6/88 11,000
Garcon a L'echarpe, brown wash/blue crayon on page from sketchbook, backed w/Japan paper, ca 1909, 14x11", SBY 2/18/88 6,600
Grande Nue Assise (large nude, seated), brush/purple-gray watercolor on paper, sgn, ca 1916, 21x17", SBY 5/10/89 110,000
Jeune Garcon Nu, watercolor/pencil on paper laid down on board, sgn, 1914, 17x10", C-NY 11/15/88 OE 121,000
Lunia Czechowska (la main gauche sur la joue), oil on board laid down on cradled panel, sgn, 1918, 22x18", C-NY 11/14/88 4,180,000
Nu Accroupi, black crayon on page from sketchbook backed with another sheet, sgn, ca 1910-11, 17x10", SBY 5/11/88 OE 104,500
Paesaggio nel Midi (Italian landscape), oil on canvas, sgn, 1919, 24x18", SBY 5/9/89 1,870,000
Portrait d'Une Jeune Femme (La Concierge), oil on canvas, sgn, ca 1916, 22x18", C-NY 11/15/88 1,540,000
Portrait de Gabrielle Soene, pencil on paper laid down on board, sgn, 11x8", SBY 11/16/89 OE 50,600
Portrait de Madame Zborowska, oil on canvas, sgn, 1918, 22x18", SBY 5/9/89 OE 3,080
Portrait de Ortis de Zarate, pencil on paper backed w/another sheet, sgn/1918, 19x12", SBY 11/16/89 26,400
Portrait of a Woman with Rosy Cheeks, oil on cradled panel, sgn, 14x11", C-NY 5/11/88 495,000
Portrait of the Painter Donato Frisia, pencil on paper, inscr/dtd 1919, 17x10", SBY 2/18/88 12,100
Ritratto di Oscar Miestchaninoff, oil on canvas, sgn/dtd 1917/inscr, 18x13", SBY 11/11/88 1,430,000

MODIGLIANI, Corinna (Italian, 19th/20th C)
New Bonnet, oil, sgn, 23x17", WD 1/11/89 OE 2,200

MOELLER, Gustav; att (American, 20th C)
Farm Landscape, Winter; oil on board, 8x10", S/A 2/18/89 100

MOELLER, Louis Charles (American, 1855-1930)
Billet-Doux (couple in interior), oil on canvas, sgn, 10x8", SBY 3/17/88 8,250
Inquisitive (maid reading w/books strewn about), oil on canvas, sgn/dtd 1893, 10x12", C-NY 5/25/89 15,400
Interested (two ladies sitting in parlor reading book), oil on canvas, sgn, 10x8", RAB 8/9/88 UE 5,500
Repairing the Shoe, oil on canvas, sgn, 18x24", C-NY 5/26/88 16,500
Talking About Old Times (older couple in an interior), oil on canvas, sgn, 18x24", WD 4/13/88 OE 15,000
Tea & Conversation (old couple in an interior), oil on paper laid down on canvas, sgn, 15x20", C-NY 5/25/89 16,500
Two Musicians, oil on canvas, sgn, 8x10", SBY 5/25/88 9,350

MOESELAGEN, Johannes (German, 19th C)
Kitchen Maid's Mirror, oil on canvas, sgn/dtd 1867, 26x23", C-NY 2/25/88 14,300

MOEYAERT, Nicolaes (Dutch, 1592-1655)
Adoration of the Golden Calf, oil on canvas, sgn/dtd 1641, 39x49", C-NY 1/11/89 35,200

MOFFETT, Ross E. (American, 1888-)
Abstract Composition, oil on board, sgn, 14x20", C-NY 9/28/89 1,870

MOGFORD, John (British, 1821-1885)
Caught in the Act, a boy with a Newfoundland dog & a cat; oil on canvas, 48x40", C-NY 10/12/89 9,900
Ferry (river landscape w/figures on a boat), oil on canvas, sgn, 22x36", WD 5/5/88 3,800
Old Lizard Head, Cornwall; watercolor over pencil, sgn/dtd 1875, 13x19", C-NY 5/25/88 825

MOHALY, Yolanda (20th C)
Abstract, oil on canvas, sgn/dtd 70, 44x30", SBY 11/21/88 3,410

MOHOLY-NAGY, Laszlo (American, 1895-1946)
Composition, colored wax crayons/pencil on paper, initialed/dtd 40, 21x10", C-NY 10/6/88 4,400
Truncated Pyramids (abstract), gouache/watercolor on paper, sgn/dtd 46, 18x14", SBY 10/7/88 OE 11,000
Untitled (abstract), tempera on celluloid, sgn twice/dtd 37, #d GLV, 20x16", SBY 10/7/88 23,100
Untitled (abstract), tempera on celluloid, sgn/dtd 1934/#d G11, 13x19", SBY 10/7/88 24,200

Untitled (geometric composition), watercolor/ink wash/flocked paper collage on paper, sgn, 1926, 16x12", SBY 5/10/89 OE

MOHRMANN, Henry (American, 19th/20th C) 60,500

Portrait of the British Steamship Tampican, oil on canvas, sgn/dtd 1903, 24x40", RAB 8/1/89 OE

MOISSET, Maurice (French, 1860-1946) 7,500

Spring Landscape, oil on canvas, sgn, 13x16", C-E 2/16/88

MOLA, Pier Francesco (Italian, 1612-1666) 550

Saint John the Baptist (in a landscape w/a sheep), oil on canvas, 17x13", SBY 1/12/89

MOLA, Pier Francesco; circle of (Italian, 1612-1666) 26,400

Allegorical Figure, Possibly Erato, Muse of Lyric Poetry; oil on canvas, 39x28", SBY 11/10/88

Amelia & the Shepherds, oil on canvas, unfr, 15x19", C-E 6/1/88 20,900

Moses, pen/brown ink, inscr, 7x5", C-NY 1/12/88 935

Portrait Head of a Young Boy, Bust-Length, Wearing a Brown Costume & White Ruff; oil on canvas, 21x17", C-NY 10/12/89 OE 550

MOLARSKY, Maurice (American, 1885-1950) 24,200

Yellow Shawl, oil on canvas, sgn, 52x38", FAP 4/15/89

MOLENAER, Claes (Flemish, 1540-1589) 4,400

Landscape of Houses by a River with Figures Along the Bank & in a Boat; oil on panel, sgn, 15x12", SBY 4/7/88

Landscape with Figures in Boats on a Canal by a Town, oil on panel, 24x33", SBY 10/21/88 UE 7,700

Travelers Before an Inn by a Cascade in a Mountainous Landscape, oil on canvas, sgn, 30x43", C-NY 4/6/89 4,400

MOLENAER, Jan Miense (Dutch, 1610-1668) 14,300

Pair: Dog's Sick Bed; Canine Funeral Cortege; oil on panel, sgn, 11x17", SBY 10/13/89

Peasants Drinking & Smoking in a Tavern, oil on panel, sgn, 19x20", C-NY 1/11/89 33,000

Tavern Interior, oil on panel, sgn, 12x15", lot 84, SBY 1/12/89 39,600

Tavern Interior, oil on panel, 16x15", lot 87, SBY 1/12/89 15,400

Two Children with a Cat, oil on panel, 20x15", C-NY 1/11/89 10,450

MOLENAER, Jan Miense; att (Dutch, 1610-1668) 8,800

Pair: Scenes of Unequal Love; Young Couple Standing By a Miser; oil on panel, bears signature, 10x10", C-NY 10/12/89

MOLES, E. (Continental, 19th C) 6,600

Merrymaking (festive group), oil on panel, sgn/dtd 94, 10x15", C-E 2/21/89

MOLET, Salvador (1773-1836) 4,400

Still Life of Flowers in an Elaborate Silver Urn on a Draped Ledge, oil on canvas, initialed, 48x34", SBY 6/2/89 OE

MOLINARI, Antonio (Italian, 1655-1727) 99,000

Adam & Eve, oil on canvas, 48x59", C-NY 1/11/89

MOLL, Carl (Austrian, 1861-1945) 37,400

Sunset Over the Snow-Covered Valley, oil on canvas, sgn, 17x34", B/B 6/9/88

MOLL, Evert (Dutch, 1878-1955) 5,500

Amsterdam-An Extensive View of the Port; oil on canvas, sgn/dtd, 36x48", SBY 5/23/89

Morgenstemming, oil on canvas, sgn, 10x11", SBY 10/5/88 12,100

MOLL, William John 880

Landscape in Connecticut, oil on artist board, sgn/dtd 25, 26x34", GAI 6/17/89

MOLNAR, Janos Z. (Czechoslovakian, 1880-) 85

Three Sisters (three young women in a landscape), oil on canvas, sgn, 32x24", WG 4/23/88 OE

Vase of Flowers on a Table, oil on board, sgn, 13x10", DM 3/14/88 1,500

MOLS, Robert Charles Gustave (Belgian, 1848-1903) 130

Amsterdam Harbor, oil on canvas, sgn, 34x54", SBY 6/8/88

MOLYN, Pieter (Dutch, 1595-1661) 3,850

Ambush, oil on panel, sgn, 15x22", C-NY 1/11/89

MOMA (Italian, 20th C) 28,600

Venetian Canal Scene, watercolor, sgn, 8x4", SLK 5/12/88

MOMPER, see De Momper 60

MONALDI, Paolo (Italian, fl ca 1760)

Group of Peasants Making Merry (figures in a landscape), oil on canvas, oval, 19x15", SBY 4/7/89 OE

Peasants in a Courtyard, oil on canvas, 35x42", C-NY 10/12/89 13,750

MONALDI, Paolo; circle of (Italian, fl ca 1760) 9,900

Pastoral Figures & Piper on Path in Mountainous River Landscape, oil on canvas, 19x41", C-NY 4/6/89

MONAMY, Peter (British, 1689-1749) 5,500

Katherine & the Royal Caroline in a Choppy Sea, oil on canvas, 28x39", C-NY 10/12/89

Ships at Sea, oil on canvas, 24x29", WG 4/23/88 UE 6,600

MONAMY, Peter; circle of (British, 1689-1749) 900

Naval Battle, oil on canvas, 28x46", C-NY 10/12/89 OE

Two Three-Deckers in a Gale, oil on canvas laid down on plastic laminate, 39x34", C-E 6/1/88 15,400

MONCHABLON, Jean Ferdinand (French, 1855-1904) 1,760

Bords de la Saone (river landscape), oil on panel, sgn/#d 212, 10x14", SBY 7/12/89 OE

Champs pres Fresnes (Ste Marne), oil on canvas, sgn/inscr twice, 21x29", C-NY 2/25/88 OE 9,900

Le Printemps, Amiens; oil on canvas, sgn, 15x22", SBY 10/24/89 35,200

Vieux Pont a Monthureux, Vosges (landscape w/waterway, village beyond); oil, sgn/#d 217, 13x18", C-NY 10/25/89 30,800

Wheat Fields, oil on canvas, sgn/dtd 1887, 22x29", B/B 3/17/88 OE 11,000

MONDRIAN, Piet (Dutch, 1872-1944) 20,900

A Rose (a single flower), watercolor/pencil on paper, sgn, ca 1910, 10x8", SBY 11/12/88

Blue Facade, Composition 9; oil on canvas laid down on masonite, sgn, ca 1913-14, 38x27", SBY 11/15/89 27,500

Composition (Classical Drawing No 2), charcoal on lined paper, 1935-36, 11x8", SBY 5/11/88 2,420,000

Composition in a Square, oil on canvas, initialed/dtd 26, 20x20", SBY 11/15/89 13,200

3,520,000

Flower Study: Chrysanthemum; charcoal on buff paper, sgn, ca 1908, 26x17", SBY 5/10/89 ..... **29,700**
French Windmill Along the Gein, charcoal on paper laid down on board, ca 1907-08, 18x32", SBY 11/12/88 OE **159,500**
House on the Gein, watercolor/gouache on paper, sgn/dtd 1900, 18x23", SBY 11/16/89 ..... **220,000**
Kantklossende Boerin (Lace-Maker), gouache/watercolor/black chalk on paper, sgn, ca 1895-1900, 21x16", SBY 5/10/89 ..... **35,750**
Portrait of Sibbetje (bust-length in blue dress, turban), oil on canvas, sgn, ca 1930, 26x20", SBY 10/6/89 ..... **35,750**
Study of a Rose, pencil on buff paper, sgn, ca 1910, 10x7", SBY 11/12/88 OE **41,250**

MONET, Claude (French, 1840-1926)

Alice Hoschede au Jardin (lady in garden landscape), oil on canvas, sgn/dtd 81, 32x26", SBY 5/9/89 ..... **8,800,00**
Bateau Echoue (view of beached sailing vessel, buildings beyond), oil on canvas, sgn, 1881, 32x24", C-NY 11/15/88 ..... **1,078,00**
Bois d'Oliviers au Jardin Moreno (impressionistic olive grove), oil on canvas, sgn/dtd 84, 26x32", C-NY 11/15/88 ..... **1,210,00**
Eglise de Vernon, Temps Gris (church in landscape); oil on canvas, sgn/dtd 94, 26x36", SBY 11/15/89 ..... **3,300,00**
Etretat, La Plage et la Falaise d'Aval (coastal seascape); oil on canvas, sgn/dtd 1884, 24x29", C-NY 11/15/88 ..... **1,045,00**
Fleurs a Vetheuil (close-up garden view w/village peering through), oil on canvas, sgn/dtd 1880, 24x30", C-NY 11/15/88 ..... **4,730,00**
Grotte de Port-Domois, oil on canvas, sgn/dtd 86, 26x33", SBY 5/10/88 ..... **1,815,00**
La Seine a Argenteuil (landscape w/water & sailboats), oil on canvas, sgn/dtd 74, 22x26", SBY 11/11/88 ..... **2,640,00**
La Seine pres de Giverny (impressionistic river landscape), oil on canvas, 1894, 21x32", C-NY 5/11/88 OE **605,00**
Le Port du Havre, Effet du Nuit (harbor night scene); oil on canvas, sgn, 1873, 24x32", C-NY 11/15/88 ..... **2,090,00**

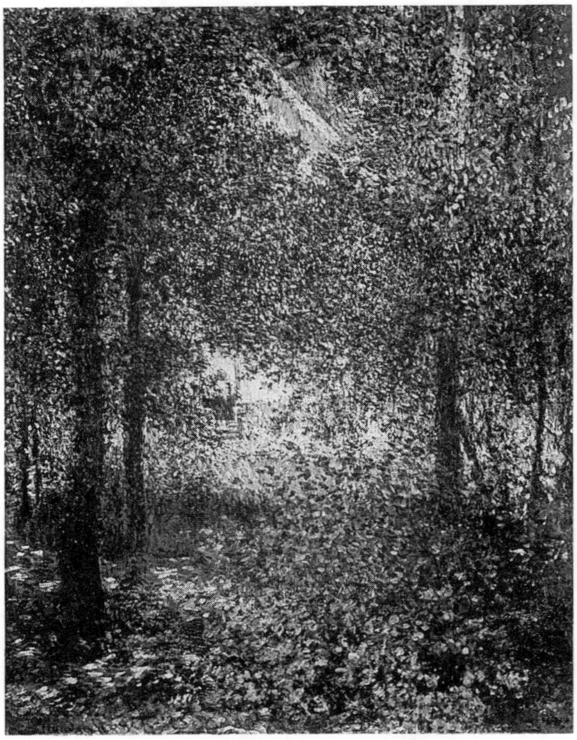

Les Broussailles, la Maison d'Argenteuil; oil on canvas, sgn, 1876, 31x24", C-NY 5/11/88 OE; $3,3000,000

Les Coteaux de Vetheuil, oil on canvas, sgn/dtd 1880, 24x40", SBY 5/10/88 OE **3,025,00**
Les Falaises a Sante Adresse (coastal view), pastel on tan paper, sgn/dtd 1861, 11x18", SBY 5/10/89 OE **297,00**
Les Meules, Giverny, Effet du Matin (haystack); oil on canvas, sgn/dtd 89, 26x36", SBY 11/15/89 ..... **6,710,00**
Nympheas (water lilies & irises on water), oil on canvas, stamped signature, ca 1914-17, 78x78", SBY 11/15/89 ..... **7,700,00**
Un Verger au Printemps (artist's wife seated in spring landscape), oil on canvas, sgn/dtd 86, 26x32", SBY 5/9/89 ..... **4,510,00**
Waterloo Bridge (impressionistic drawing), pastel on gray paper laid down, stamped, 1899, 15x21", C-NY 5/12/88 ..... **121,00**

MONFALLET, Adolphe Francois (French, 1816-1900)

Courtyard Performers, oil on panel, sgn, 19x25", SBY 10/24/89 OE **36,30**
Gazing Out the Window, oil on panel, 11x9", C-E 2/23/88 ..... **82**
Street Musician, oil on panel, sgn, 24x19", SBY 7/12/89 UE **2,75**

MONFORT, see De Monfort

MONFREID, see De Monfreid

MONGE, Luis

Amazon Jungle (landscape), oil on canvas, sgn/dtd 77, 50x68", SBY 5/16/89 ..... **18,70**

MONGINOT, Charles (French, 1825-1900)

Monkey & the Cat, oil on canvas, sgn, 22x18", RWS 5/19/88 ..... **2,40**
Still Life of a Basket of Fruit...on a Ledge; oil on canvas, initialed, 26x32", C-E 2/21/89 UE **2,20**

MONIEN, Julius (German, 1842-1897)

On a Wooded Lake, oil on board, sgn/dtd 76, 15x21", C-E 5/23/88 OE **2,42**

MONKS, John Austin Sands (American, 1850-1917)

Rocky Path, sheep meander winding trail in landscape; oil on canvas, sgn, 16x20", RAB 8/8/89 ..... **50**
Shelter From the Storm, oil on canvas, sgn/dtd 86, 30x45", RWS 11/3/88 UE **65**

MONLEON, Raphael (Spanish, 1847-1900)
Ships at Harbor, oil on board, sgn, 11x17", FAP 11/4/88 OE 575
MONNICKENDAM, J. (Dutch, 19th C)
Kitchen Interior, oil on board, sgn, 12x8", LH 10/16/88 OE 900
MONNOT, Maurice Louis (French, 1869-)
Still Life of Radishes & Brass Pot, oil on canvas, sgn, 16x11", SBY 6/8/88 1,320
MONNOYER, Antoine; att (French, 1670-1747)
Pair: Tulips, Carnations, & Other Flowers in a Glass Vase on a Ledge; oil on canvas, 17x12", C-NY 1/15/88 OE 17,600
MONNOYER, Jean Baptiste (French, 1636-1669)
Flowers in a Bronze Urn with Honeysuckle on a Ledge, oil on canvas, 35x28", C-NY 1/15/88 38,500
Pair: Sprig of Lilac; Spray of Variegated Roses; oil on canvas, sgn, 12x10", SBY 6/2/89 99,000
Still Life of Flowers in a Sculpted Vase on a Ledge, oil on canvas laid down on panel, 20x16", C-NY 1/11/89 33,000
Still Life of Peonies, Carnations, Daffodils, & Other Flowers in a Basket...; oil on canvas, 29x42", SBY 6/2/89 OE 55,000
MONNOYER, Jean Baptiste; att (French, 1636-1669)
Flowers, Basket of Strawberries, Fruit, English Salver...on a Ledge...; oil on canvas, 25x47", C-NY 5/31/89 24,200
Roses, Poppy, Tulip, Honeysuckle, Orange Blossom, & Other Flowers in Glass Urn; oil on canvas, 31x25", C-M 12/3/88 OE 78,040
Still Life of Peaches & Flowers, oil on canvas, 9x11", SBY 4/7/89 5,500
Still Life of Tulips, Peonies, Morning-Glories, Carnations, Narcissus...; oil on canvas, sgn, 35x27", SBY 1/12/89 OE 132,000
Still Life of Variegated Carnations & Other Flowers on a Ledge, oil on canvas, 13x16", SBY 4/7/89 UE 5,500
Tulips, Peonies, & Lilies by a Tree with Parrot & Squirrel; oil on canvas, 41x52", C-M 12/3/88 OE 18,581
MONNOYER, Jean Baptiste; circle of (French, 1636-1669)
Tulips, Morning-Glory & Carnations in a Sculpted Urn on a Pedestal; oil on canvas, 29x40", C-NY 10/12/89 4,400
Tulips, Narcissi, Roses, Lilacs, Morning-Glory, & Peonies, in Sculpted Urn; oil on canvas, 36x29", C-NY 6/2/88 OE 28,600
MONNOYER, Jean Baptiste; school of (French, 1636-1669)
Crown Imperial, Roses, Morning-Glory, Tulips, & Lilacs in a Sculpted Vase, oil on canvas, 31x37", C-NY 10/12/89 7,700
MONSTED, Peder Mork (Danish, 1859-1941)
Cottage on the Shore, oil on canvas, sgn/dtd 1904, 28x40", SBY 5/23/89 14,300
Sketching by the River Bank, oil on canvas, sgn/dtd 1888, 12x16", SBY 2/22/89 20,900
Summer Idyll, oil on canvas, sgn/dtd 1897, 18x18", SBY 5/23/89 OE 154,000
Woodland River in Summer, oil on canvas, sgn/dtd 1899, 19x37", SBY 2/22/89 17,600
Young Peasant Girl, oil on canvas, sgn/dtd 1883, 21x16", C-E 5/23/88 UE 1,430
MONTAGNY, L. (19th C)
Faggot Gatherer, oil on canvas, sgn, 20x29", C-E 2/23/88 990
MONTAGUE, A. (British, 19th C)
Man O'War & Fishermen Offshore, oil on canvas, sgn, 26x42", WAD 6/6/88 4,000
MONTAGUE, Frederich Leonard (British, 19th C)
Dock on a Lake, oil on canvas, sgn/dtd 1899, 9x12", C-E 7/26/88 UE 380
MONTALLIER, Pierre (French, 20th C)
Le Traghetto, oil on canvas, sgn, 38x58", C-E 5/13/88 OE 1,760
Standing Peasant Pouring Water From a Jug into a Plate Held by a Seated Woman, oil on canvas, 14x11", C-NY 5/31/89 8,800
MONTANE, Roger (French, 20th C)
Les Bouees a Palais, oil on canvas, sgn/dtd 57, 20x24", C-E 5/13/88 385
MONTE, see De Monte
MONTEFOSCOLI, Master of (fl ca 1415)
Madonna & Child, St Peter, John the Baptist, Anthony Abbot, & Two Angels; gold ground/tempera, 35x20", SBY 4/7/88 OE 28,600
MONTELATICI, Francesco (Cecco Bravo)(Italian, 1600-1661)
Cimon & Pero, Called Roman Charity; oil on canvas, 45x59", C-NY 1/11/89 33,000
MONTEMEZZANO, Francesco; cirlce of
Portrait of a Young Woman, Half-Length, with Down-cast Eyes; oil on canvas, 15x12", C-NY 10/12/89 3,850
MONTEMEZZO, Antonio (German, 1841-1898)
Feeding the Geese, oil on panel, sgn/dtd 79, 19x13", C-E 10/26/89 6,600
Woman Tending Animals, oil on canvas, sgn/inscr/dtd 82, 30x53", LH 3/20/88 10,000
MONTENEGRO, Julio (Ecuadorian, 1867-1932)
Moorish Courtyard, oil on canvas, sgn/initialed/dtd 86, 14x12", WD 5/5/88 UE 1,000
MONTENEGRO, Roberto (Mexican, 1885-1968)
Bodegon con Calabazas (Still Life of Pumpkins), oil on canvas, sgn/dtd 43, 44x51", C-NY 5/17/89 13,200
Nino con Caballos (contemporary depiction of boy w/horses), oil on canvas, sgn/dtd 1941, 29x26", C-NY 11/21/89 20,900
Retrato del Fotografo Hoyningen-Huene, oil on canvas, sgn, ca 1940, 26x22", C-NY 11/21/89 OE 22,000
MONTEZIN, Pierre Eugene (French, 1874-1946)
Au Bord de Riviere (river landscape), gouache on paper, sgn, 16x25", C-NY 5/12/88 16,500
Bords de l'Eure, oil on canvas, sgn/#d 19, 20x26", WD 5/5/88 17,000
Dans la Campagne, oil on canvas, sgn, 24x29", C-NY 5/11/89 24,200
La Croesette, Cannes; oil on canvas, sgn, 24x29", SBY 10/6/89 60,500
La Maison au Bord de Riviere (river landscape w/house), gouache on paper laid down on board, sgn, 13x16", C-NY 5/12/88 20,900
La Seine a St Monace (river landscape), oil on canvas, sgn, 12x27", SBY 2/14/89 OE 13,200
La Seine a St Montezin, oil on canvas, sgn, 13x28", WD 5/5/88 8,750
Les Halles, le Marcher aux Legumes (a busy vegetable market); oil on canvas, sgn, 23x29", C-NY 2/18/88 35,200
Paysage (landscape), oil on canvas, sgn, 24x29", SBY 10/6/89 22,000
Paysage en Ete (figures in landscape), oil on canvas, sgn, 24x29", SBY 10/7/88 28,600
Prairie aux Meules (field w/haystacks), oil on canvas, sgn, 20x26", C-NY 10/5/89 18,700
Promenade sous le Arbres (Walking Under the Trees), oil on masonite, sgn, 22x18", C-NY 11/16/88 OE 44,000

Rue de Village Anime (village scene), gouache over charcoal on paper, sgn, 14x16", C-NY 10/5/89 10,450

MONTFORT, Antoine Alphonse (French, 1802-1884)

At the Well, oil on canvas, sgn/dtd 1845, 27x36", SBY 10/24/89 8,800

MONTFORT, Octavius; att

Pair: Fruit in a Blue & White Porcelain Bowl on a Ledge; watercolor on vellum, 10x15", C-NY 5/31/89 OE 20,900

MONTGOMERY, Hugh J. (American, 20th C)

Bit of Cape Cod (Orleans, Massachusetts), oil on board, sgn/titled, 14x18", RAB 8/8/89 250

MONTI, Francesco (Italian, 1646-1712)

Ecstasy of Saint Benedict, oil on paper laid down on canvas, within a painted arch, 17x11", SBY 10/13/89 3,300
Martydom of a Saint, oil en grisaille on canvas, unfr, 16x12", SBY 4/7/88 3,025

MONTICELLI, Adolphe (French, 1824-1886)

L'Homme a la Cravate en X (portrait of a man), oil on canvas laid down on panel, ca 1872, 26x21", SBY 10/24/89 OE 27,500
Man in a Doorway, oil on panel, 15x12", C-NY 5/25/88 5,280
Portrait of Mademoiselle Milhau, oil on canvas, ca 1872, 29x24", SBY 10/24/89 11,000

MONTICELLI, Adolphe; manner of (French, 1824-1886)

Young Ladies in a Wooded Clearing, oil on panel, bears signature, 11x17", C-E 11/8/88 UE 350

MONTILLO, E. (19th C)

Peasants with Donkey by the Sea, oil on canvas, sgn/dtd 1874, unfr, 9x12", C-E 5/23/88 990

MONTINI, Giovanni (19th C)

Pair: Architectural Designs for a Theatre; Facade & Interior; pen/ink/wash, 1 sgn, 13x23", SBY 1/13/89 2,750

MONTOYA, Gustavo (Mexican, 1905-)

Nina Con Juguette, oil on canvas, sgn, 22x18", C-NY 11/21/89 5,500
Nina en Rosa, oil on canvas, sgn/dtd 1962, 22x18", C-NY 5/18/88 4,950
Nina Oaxaquena, oil on canvas, sgn/dtd 1968, 24x18", C-NY 11/21/89 5,500
Ninas Musicas, oil on canvas, sgn/dtd Mexico Agosto 66, 20x24", C-NY 11/21/89 6,050
Nino con Tambor, oil on canvas, sgn, 22x18", C-NY 5/18/88 OE 3,850
Nino Mexicano (Mexican Boy), oil on canvas, sgn twice/dtd Mexico 67/titled, 24x18", C-NY 5/17/89 OE 7,150
Nino Mexicano (portrait of a child), oil on canvas, sgn twice/dtd Mexico 1967, 24x18", C-NY 11/21/88 3,520
Pair: Companion Portraits of a Boy & Girl in Blue with Flowers; oil on canvas, sgn, 1959, ea 22x18", SBY 5/17/88 6,325
Portrait of a Girl (in landscape w/cacti & hills beyond), oil on canvas, sgn, ca 1970, 18x15", SBY 11/21/88 OE 4,950

MONTPETIT, Richard (Canadian, 20th C)

Le Vital, oil on canvas, sgn/dtd 1982, 16x20", FB 5/28/89 450
Solitaire, oil on board, sgn/dtd 1987, 6x8", FB 10/30/89 248
St-Esprit, Quebec; oil on canvas, sgn/dtd 1971, 12x16", FB 5/28/89 440

MONTZAIGLE, Edgar (French, 1867-)

Elegante Devant l'Opera de Paris, watercolor/gouche on paper, sgn/dtd 90, 22x14", SBY 5/23/89 8,800

MONVEL, see De Monvel

MOOR, see De Moor

MOORE, Albert Joseph (1841-1893)

Head of a Young Woman in Profile: Summer; black/white chalk on yellow paper, 17x14", C-NY 10/26/88 22,000

MOORE, Benson Bond (American, 1882-)

Spring Thaw (river in extensive landscape), oil on canvas, sgn, 20x24", NA 2/24/89 1,400

MOORE, Brett F. (American, 20th C)

Mountain Orchard, oil on canvasboard, sgn, 18x24", B/B 8/10/88 OE 4,125

MOORE, Harry Humphrey (American, 1844-1926)

Glimpse into the Yoshiwara (Pleasure Quarters), oil on canvas, sgn/dtd 87, 25x36", B/B 3/17/88 12,100
Listening to the Moonlight, oil on canvas, sgn/dtd 1918, 21x16", C-E 6/1/88 UE 385
Moorish Courtyard (two figures in landscape, buildings beyond), oil on board, sgn, 10x7", RWS 5/19/88 1,100

MOORE, Henry (O.M.)(British, 1898-1986)

Double-Sided: Drawing for Sculpture; pencil/conte crayon on paper, sgn/dtd 38, 7x11", SBY 11/12/88 OE 15,400
Double-Sided: Sculptor Carving a Colossal Figure; Draped Standing Figures; pen/ink, sgn/dtd 42/inscr, 9x7", SBY 11/12/88 16,500
Draped Reclining Figures, watercolor/pen/ink/charcoal/crayons over pencil, sgn/#d 65, 1942, 9x8", SBY 11/16/89 55,000
Ideas for Metal Sculpture: Reclining Figures; black crayon/wash on paper, sgn/dtd 35, 15x22", SBY 5/11/88 28,600
Ideas for Sculpture: Draped Standing Figures; watercolor/crayon/pen/ink/chalk on paper, sgn/dtd 42, 23x18", C-NY 5/11/89 154,000
Ideas for Sculpture: Studies of Reclining Figures; crayon/watercolor/pen/ink/pencil, sgn/dtd 34, 10x7", SBY 11/12/88 44,000
Reclining Figure: Idea for Sculpture; watercolor/crayon/pencil/chalk over photocopy, sgn, 1982, 8x12", C-NY 5/11/89 20,900
Reclining Figures, black chalk on paper, sgn/dtd 28, 10x10", C-NY 10/6/88 4,400
Reclining Nude, watercolor/crayon/charcoal/chinagraph over photocopy, sgn/#d 80/118, 1980, 8x9", C-NY 5/11/89 OE 29,700
Seated Family Group, watercolor/white & black crayon/pencil on paper, sgn/dtd 44, 5x7", SBY 11/12/88 44,000
Studies (for sculptures), crayon/brown wash/pen/ink/pencil on paper, sgn/dtd 42, 7x10", SBY 5/10/89 OE 37,400
Two Draped Figures, watercolor/crayons/charcoal/pen/white chalk on paper, sgn/dtd 42, 15x22", C-NY 5/11/89 110,000
Two Figures (seated on bench against a wall), pen/ink/charcoak/watercolor on paper, sgn/dtd 23/#d 23, 8x7", SBY 11/12/88 27,500
Two Seated Women II, watercolor/brush/black ink/black chinagraph/chalk over photocopy, sgn, 1982, 10x13", C-NY 5/11/89 22,000
Young Girl Seated at School Desk (From Notebook 5), India ink/charcoal/wash on paper, sgn, 1969, 10x7", SBY 5/11/88 22,000

MOORE, Henry (R.A.)(British, 1831-1895)

Rocky Shore, Afternoon Mist; oil on canvas, sgn/dtd 1884, RWS 9/8/89 OE 1,200

MOORE, John (British, 1820-1902)

Still Life with Spotlight (nude floating on back in water), oil on canvas, sgn/dtd 1969, 72x60", SBY 10/7/89 4,400
Untitled (still life), watercolor on paper, sgn/dtd 1974, 15x22", SBY 2/14/89 825

MOORE, Thomas Manning

Peaceful Landscape Scene with a Cottage in the Background, Pond in Foreground; oil on canvas, 24x36", DM 3/14/88 UE 325

)ORE, W.J. (American, 19th C)

Heading Out to Sea, oil on academy board, sgn, 19x30", RAB 3/14/89 ... 1,000

)ORE-PARK, Carlton (American, 1877-)

Fashionable Woman with Her Wolfhound, oil on canvas laid down on board, sgn, 45x30", SBY 6/24/88 ... 2,860

)RA, Francis Luis (American, 1874-1960)

At the Helm, study of young man at wheel of small boat; pencil on paper, titled, 8x6", RAB 8/8/89 UE ... 225
El Tango, oil on canvas, sgn, 22x18", SBY 9/23/88 ... 5,500
Girls Dancing in a Landscape, watercolor on paper, sgn, 13x17", SBY 9/23/88 ... 880
Out Sailing, man/woman in cockpit of sailboat; pencil on paper, titled, 8x5", RAB 8/8/89 UE ... 300
Portrait of a Gentleman (sketch), charcoal, sgn, 10x8", NA 2/6/88 UE ... 300
Portrait of a Seated Lady (full-length, period attire), pencil on paper, 8x11", RWS 3/31/88 UE ... 200
Reflecting Fountain, watercolor on paper, sgn, 13x19", C-E 11/8/88 ... 330
Set of 3: Indian Faces; Man Walking with Cane; Young Boy; pencil on paper, 2 sgn, 8x7", C-E 6/1/88 ... 770
Spanish Fair in the Time of Goya, watercolor/gouache/pencil on board, sgn/dtd 1906, 25x32", C-NY 9/28/89 ... 5,500
Spring Romp (artist's wife & daughter), oil on canvas, sgn, 12x25", LH 12/4/88 ... 2,800
The White Mantilla (full-length portrait of Spanish girl, standing), oil on canvas, sgn, 24x18", PHL 12/1/88 ... 2,250
Trapeze Artists (performing in circus tent), oil on canvas, sgn, 47x35", C-NY 9/28/89 OE ... 30,800
Waiting, pencil on paper, sgn, 10x7", C-E 2/1/89 UE ... 220
Woodland Cistern (landscape), watercolor on paper, sgn, 13x19", RWS 3/16/89 OE ... 1,000

)RAGAS Y TORRES, Tomas (Spanish, 1837-1906)

Beautiful Connoisseur, watercolor/gouache on paper, sgn/dtd 1874, 20x14", C-NY 5/24/89 ... 8,800

)RALES, Armando (Nicaraguan, 1927-)

Circus I (nude figure in the moonlight), oil/wax on canvas, sgn/dtd 82, 40x50", C-NY 5/18/88 OE ... 30,800
Desnudo con Fruta (Seated Nude with Fruit), oil on canvas, sgn/dtd 81, 40x32", C-NY 5/17/89 OE ... 60,500
Desnudo Junto a un Bote (nude reclining near beached boat, contemporary), oil, sgn/dtd 78, 32x26", C-NY 11/21/89 ... 19,800
Dry Season (abstract depiction of trees), oil on canvas, sgn/dtd 78, 26x16", C-NY 11/21/89 ... 22,000
Edge of the Jungle (contemporary), oil on canvas backed w/heavy card, sgn/dtd 77, 40x32", SBY 5/16/89 ... 27,500
Empty Can & Fruits, watercolor on paper, sgn/dtd 85, 7x10", SBY 11/21/88 UE ... 1,980
Empty Can & Pear, watercolor on paper, sgn/dtd 85, 8x10", SBY 11/21/88 UE ... 1,980
Escena Lacustre IV, oil on canvas, sgn/dtd 1978, 32x40", C-NY 11/21/89 OE ... 66,000
Estudio Lacustre, I (two nudes in water); oil on canvas, sgn/dtd 78, 19x22", C-NY 5/17/89 OE ... 30,800
Figuras, gouache/collage on paper, sgn/dtd 68/#d 211/inscr PRZCR, 50x62", C-NY 5/18/88 ... 9,900
Mangoes (contemporary still life), oil on canvas, sgn/dtd 80, 24x20", C-NY 11/21/89 OE ... 28,600
Naturaleza Muerta (still life), gouache on paper laid down on paper, sgn/dtd 81, 6x11", C-NY 5/18/88 OE ... 2,860
Nude, oil on canvas, sgn/dtd 73, 50x40", SBY 5/17/88 ... 25,300
Nude with Circus Animals (contemporary), pastel on paper, sgn/dtd 83, 19x24", SBY 5/16/89 ... 13,200
Two Figures & an Astronomical Observatory (contemporary), oil on canvas, sgn/dtd 81, 40x32", SBY 11/21/88 OE ... 41,800
Untitled (abstract), mixed media on canvas, sgn/dtd 66 twice, 32x26", SBY 5/16/89 OE ... 2,750
Untitled (abstract), oil on canvas, sgn/dtd 71, 64x51", SBY 5/16/89 OE ... 34,100
Untitled (abstract), oil w/applied burlap on canvas, sgn/dtd 57, 11x16", SBY 5/16/89 OE ... 2,200

)RALES, Dario (Columbian, 1944-)

Female Nude, pastel on paper, sgn twice/dtd 82, 59x39", SBY 5/16/89 UE ... 33,000

)RALES, Luis; see De Morales

)RAN, Edward (American, 1829-1901)

After the Wreck (seascape), oil on canvas, sgn/dtd 1856, 20x30", SBY 1/24/89 ... 2,475
Clipper Ship, watercolor on board, sgn, 20x26", C-E 6/1/88 ... 1,540
Early Morning (ships at sea), oil on canvas, sgn/dtd 1873, 18x29", C-NY 9/28/89 OE ... 35,200
Feeding the Geese, oil on canvas, sgn, 18x24", SBY 1/24/89 OE ... 11,000
Fisherman to the Rescue, oil on canvas, sgn/dtd 1859, 30x45", SBY 6/24/88 OE ... 10,450
Fishermen at Dawn (seascape w/figures), oil on canvas, sgn, 10x18", SBY 1/24/89 ... 2,750
Marketplace, oil on cradled panel, sgn, 13x19", C-E 10/25/88 OE ... 2,860
Moonlight on the Water, oil on canvas, sgn, 18x30", SBY 9/23/88 OE ... 9,900
Moonlight Sailing, oil on canvas, sgn, 12x18", C-E 6/1/88 UE ... 605
Off Portsmouth, oil on board, sgn, 10x17", SBY 6/24/88 ... 2,200
Sailing Vessels in Choppy Seas Under a Setting Sun, oil on canvas, sgn, 20x30", WD 4/13/88 ... 16,000
Seascape, oil & gouache on paper, 15x21", LH 10/16/88 ... 600
Ship at Sea, oil on canvas, sgn, 36x27", LH 10/16/88 OE ... 1,000
Ships at Sea, oil on canvas, sgn/dtd 1901, 13x11", SBY 3/17/88 OE ... 2,310
Ships in a Harbor, oil on canvas, sgn, 22x36", SBY 5/24/89 OE ... 31,900
Signaling the Ship, oil on canvas, sgn, 27x22", C-NY 3/11/88UE ... 4,950

)RAN, Edward Percy (American, 1862-1935)

Afternoon Tea (three ladies in interior), oil on canvas laid down on masonite, sgn, 19x30", C-E 2/1/89 OE ... 7,700
Battle of Bennington, oil on canvas, 21x30", C-E 10/18/89 ... 2,420
Blossom (woman w/baby & girl on garden path), oil on canvas, sgn, 20x16", C-E 6/1/89 ... 1,760
Courting Couple, watercolor, sgn, 12x9", PHL 10/28/88 UE ... 425
New Dress, watercolor, 18x12", PHL 10/28/88 UE ... 400
Spring Walk (elegant woman holding flowers in a landscape), oil on canvas, sgn, 18x14", SBY 1/24/89 ... 1,760
Waiting in the Garden, oil on canvas, sgn, 30x21", C-E 2/1/89 ... 1,980
Woman with Her Pet, watercolor on paper, sgn, 8x4", C-E 6/1/88 ... 528

)RAN, John Leon (American, 1864-1941)

Crossing the Bridge, watercolor on paper, sgn, 18x25", WD 1/11/89 ... 650

Girl in a Field, watercolor/pencil on board, sgn/dtd 1881, unfr, 12x18", C-NY 9/30/88 2,200
Moonlit Landscape, oil on canvas, sgn, 22x36", WG 4/23/88 325
Mother with Baby in Cradle, oil on canvas, sgn, 26x20", C-E 2/3/88 2,750

MORAN, Peter (American, 1841-1914)
Hay Wagon, oil on canvas, sgn, 16x32", C-NY 5/26/88 13,200
Herding the Sheep, oil on canvas, sgn/dtd 1869, 24x36", C-E 6/1/89, C-E 6/1/89 1,100
Western Scene (of building), charcoal/gouache on brown paper, sgn, 8x12", C-E 6/1/89 UE 440

MORAN, Thomas (American, 1837-1926)
Beside the Stream (figure in landscape), oil on canvas, sgn/artist's thumbprint, 8x10", SBY 3/17/88 OE 17,600
Canoeing on the Lake, watercolor/pencil on paper, signed, 9x18" OE 11,000
Cyclone Cove, pen/brush/black ink on paper, sgn/dtd 1893, 8x12", C-E 11/30/88 2,200
Entrance to the Grand Canal, oil on canvas, sgn/dtd 1900, 21x32", C-NY 5/25/89 110,000
Grand Canyon, oil on canvas, sgn/dtd 1921, 16x20", C-NY 5/25/88 OE 143,000
Landscape with Distant Castle, gouache on paper, sgn/dtd 1863, 12x18", SBY 5/25/88 17,600
Pair: On the Road to Manitou Canyon (landscapes); watercolor/pencil on paper, sgn/dtd/inscr 1901, 4x5", C-NY 5/26/88 OE 17,600
Pair: River Views; oil on canvas, 6x8", FAP 4/15/89 825
Showery Weather, East Hampton; oil on canvas, sgn/dtd twice, 1901, 20x30", SBY 5/25/88 OE 148,500
Summer Morning Coast, oil on paper laid down on board, 12x18", C-NY 9/28/89 17,600
Summer Squall (landscape), oil on canvas, monogramed/dtd 1889, 24x36", SBY 5/24/89 104,500
Sunset in Mid-Ocean, oil on canvas, sgn/dtd 1904, 30x40", SBY 5/24/89 148,500
Valley of Golden Dreams (wooded landscape with small creek), oil on canvas, sgn/dtd 1920, 28x38", B/B 10/9/88 UE 110,000
Venetian Scene, watercolor on paper, monogramed/dtd 1889, 16x23", SBY 5/24/89 19,800
Venice, oil on canvas, sgn/dtd 1898, 21x30", C-NY 12/2/88 OE 165,000

MORAN, Thomas; after (American, 1837-1926)
Landscape, oil on canvas, 28x26", LH 10/16/88 500

MORANDI, Giorgio (Italian, 1890-1964)
Grizzana (loose drawing of a building & tree), pencil on paper, sgn, 9x12", C-NY 10/6/88 9,900
Natura Morta, pencil on paper, sgn/dtd 1954, 7x9", C-NY 10/6/88 12,100
Natura Morta, pencil on paper, sgn/dtd 1956, 7x10", C-NY 11/15/88 11,000
Natura Morta (still life, simple sketch), pencil on paper, sgn/dtd 1961, 12x9", C-NY 10/5/89 18,700

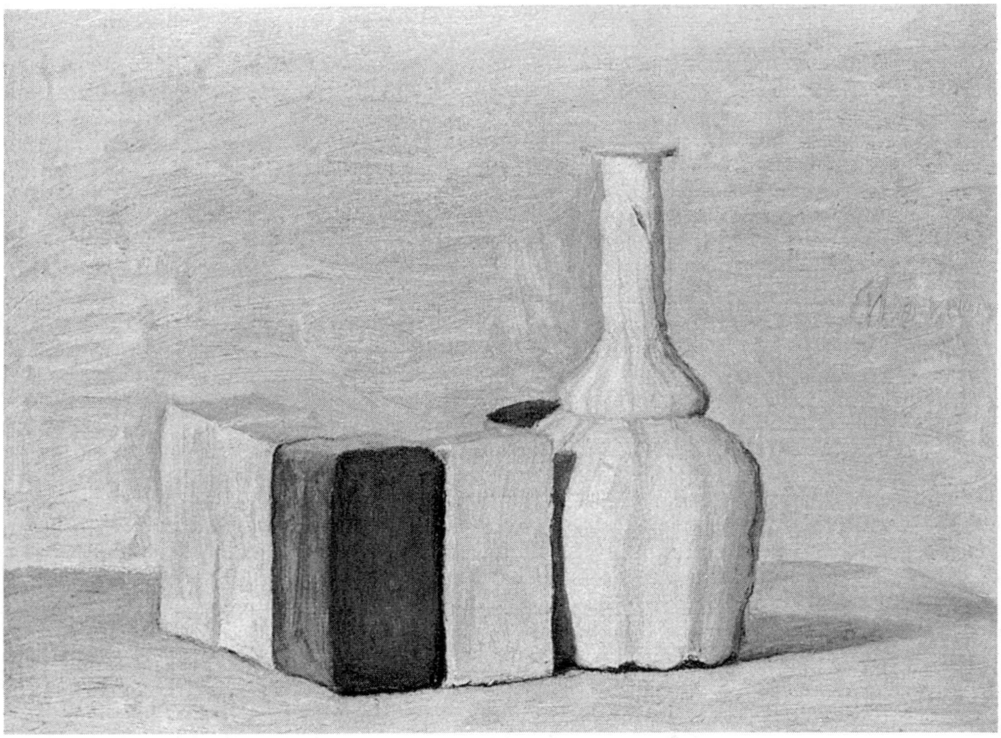

Natura Morta, oil on canvas, sgn, 1954, 12x16", C-NY 5/11/89 OE; $528,000

Natura Morta (still life), oil on canvas, sgn, 12x18", C-NY 5/11/88 OE 308,000
Natura Morta (still life), oil on canvas, sgn, 1957, 16x19", SBY 11/11/88 495,000
Natura Morta (still life), pencil on paper, sgn/dtd 1961, 9x13", C-NY 5/11/89 11,000

MORAS, Walter (German, 1856-1925)
Coastal Landscape with Houses, oil on canvas, sgn, 20x39", SBY 6/8/88 3,300
Cottages by a Lake at Sunset, oil on canvas, sgn, 26x36", C-E 2/21/89 2,860
Water Mill in an Autumn River Landscape, oil on canvas, sgn, 27x36", C-E 2/23/88 OE 3,520

MORATTI, P.
Young Peasant Girl Beneath a Grapevine, watercolor on paper, sgn, 18x11", C-E 2/23/88 660

RCHAIN, Paul Bernard (French, 1876-)
)isembarking on the Charente River, oil on canvas, sgn, 61x71", SBY 6/8/88 5,775
RE, Herman (American, 1887-1968)
'lowers in a Vase, oil on canvas, sgn, 22x20", SBY 9/23/88 UE 440
REAU, Adrien (French, 1843-1906)
long the Seine, oil on panel, sgn, 8x11", B/B 3/17/88 2,090
)utdoor Gathering, oil on canvas, sgn, 32x40", C-NY 2/23/89 28,600
REAU, Charles (French, 1830-)
lass of Wine (tipsy character seated in an interior), oil on canvas, sgn, 22x18", C-E 5/22/89 4,400
REAU, Chocarne (French, 19th C)
hildren's Games, oil on canvas, sgn, 21x19", C-E 2/23/88 OE 3,080
oung Romance (four lads showing off to a young girl), oil on canvas, sgn, 34x44", B/B 6/15/89 OE 9,350
REAU, Gustave (French, 1826-1898)
a Fiancee de la Duit ou, Le Cantique des Cantiques; oil on panel, sgn, ca 1892, 14x11", SBY 2/22/89 OE 726,000
e Poete la Sirene, Symbolic Struggle Between Man & Nature; oil on canvas, sgn, 1892-93, 38x25", SBY 10/24/89 2,750,000
REAU, Hippolyte (European, 20th C)
air: Tree on a Mountain; Haystacks by Cottages; oil on canvas, sgn, unfr, 19x13", 13x18", C-E 5/23/88 UE 1,980
REAU, Louis Gabriel (French, 1740-1806)
legant Figures in a Garden with a Temple by a Pool, oil on canvas, 13x16", C-NY 6/2/88 4,180
legant Figures Making Music in a Wild Garden, gouache on vellum laid down, sgn/dtd LM 1775, 11x8", SBY 1/13/89 46,200
REAU, Louis Gabriel; att (French, 1740-1806)
ishermen in a River Landscape with a Cottage, gouache on vellum, 11x15", SBY 1/13/89 3,850
iver Landscape with Cargo Boats & Fishermen, View of the Invalides Beyond; gouache on vellum, 11x15", SBY 1/13/89 OE 9,350
REAU, Louis Gabriel; follower of (French, 1740-1806)
air: Elegant Figures in Extensive River Landscapes; watercolor/gouache, monogramed/dtd 1782, 12x9", SBY 1/13/89 3,300
REELSE, Paulus (Dutch, 1571-1638)
llegory, Lady with a Pair of Doves; oil on canvas, sgn/dtd 1628, unfr, 32x26", SBY 6/3/88 OE 49,500
REL, Jan Evert II (Dutch, 1835-1905)
ogs Sleeping in the Square at Vitre, oil on panel, sgn/dtd 84, 13x8", B/B 9/14/89 935
inter Landscape, oil on board, sgn, 11x16", LH 10/16/88 OE 2,400
RELAND, George; after (British, 1763-1804)
oor of the Village Inn, oil on canvas, sgn, 20x25", LH 51/5/88 1,100
RELLI, Domenico (Italian, 1826-1901)
hrist in the Desert, oil on canvas, sgn, 22x25", SBY 6/8/88 UE 880
RET, Henry (French, 1856-1913)
alaise a Ouessant (seascape, coastline w/horse & figure), oil on canvas, sgn/dtd 95, 24x29", SBY 2/18/88 60,500
alaise de Moellan, Finistere; oil on canvas, sgn/dtd 1901, 24x29", SBY 5/11/88 66,000
ur de Brume a Dielette (Manche, coastal scene w/sailboats), oil on canvas, sgn/dtd 1912, 20x24", C-NY 2/16/89 46,200
a Baie de Hespant, oil on canvas, sgn/dtd 1902, 24x36", SBY 10/6/89 OE 85,250
a Cote Bretonne, oil on canvas, sgn, 1898, 22x26", SBY 5/11/88 71,500
e Port de Dielette, oil on canvas, sgn/dtd 1912, 21x29", SBY 2/16/89 44,000
latinee d'ete en Bretagne (coastal seascape w/sailboat), oil on canvas, sgn/dtd 1900, 24x32", C-NY 5/11/89 OE 126,500
RETTI, R. (Italian, 19th C)
roken String (figures in interior), watercolor heightened w/white over pencil, sgn/inscr Roma, 21x30", C-NY 2/23/89 1,100
he Tutorial, watercolor, sgn, 21x14", C-E 10/26/89 660
RGAN, Alexander Converse (American, 1849-1933)
irds on a Tree, watercolor on paper, sgn, 20x15", C-E 6/28/88 UE 50
RGAN, E. Percy (American, 1862-1935)
inging Cavalier, oil, sgn, 12x10", WD 1/11/89 1,000
RGAN, Frederick (British, 1856-1927)
arland (woman w/two children in a landscape), oil on canvas, sgn, 36x24", C-NY 10/25/89 26,400
ypsies, oil on canvas, sgn/dtd 82, 21x30", SBY 2/22/89 UE 6,600
elp Me Too (girl helping child across creek), oil on canvas, sgn, 31x24", C-NY 5/25/88 15,400
lidday Rest (figures along stream), oil on canvas, sgn/dtd 1878, 43x73", C-NY 2/23/89 28,600
aymates, oil on canvas, sgn, 25x36", C-NY 2/25/88 38,500
ortrait of a Young girl (resting on a bed), oil on canvas, sgn/dtd 1873), 20x24", RWS 5/19/88 OE 2,800
ustic Courtship, oil on canvas, sgn, 26x44", C-NY 5/25/88 12,100
chool Belles (young people on bridge in rural landscape), oil on canvas, sgn/dtd 1877, 47x70", C-NY 5/24/89 55,000
RGAN, John (British, 1823-1885)
arty Game, oil on canvas, sgn, 36x24", C-NY 2/25/88 OE 12,100
RGAN, L. Louisa (British, fl 1883-1905)
calasoig, Colonsay; oil on canvas mounted on panel, sgn, 12x18", WL 5/20/88 UE 175
RGAN, Mary; see De Neale Morgan
RGAN, William (American, 1826-1900)
eeding the Chicks, oil on canvas, sgn, 18x24", C-E 10/18/89 2,200
eeding the Chicks (young girl in barn), oil on board, sgn, 10x7", SBY 9/14/89 1,485
RGENSTJERNE-MUNTHE, Gerhard Arij Ludvig (Dutch, 1875-)
ishing Boats by the Beach, oil on panel, sgn, 14x10", C-E 2/21/89 UE 440
RGHEN, L. (19th C)
eeking Shelter From a Storm, oil on canvas, sgn, 27x36", FAP 11/4/88 850

MORIANY
Gentleman Reading, oil on canvas, sgn/dtd 1895, 39x27", C-E 2/23/88 ... 1,540
MORIER, David (Swiss, 1705-)
Portrait of William Augustus, Duke of Cumberland, on Horseback; oil on canvas, 50x41", C-NY 10/20/88 ... 15,400
MORISOT, Berthe (French, 1841-1895)
Fillette au Volant, pastel on gray paper, sgn, 1888, 21x16", SBY 10/27/89 ... 308,000
La Meule de Foin (The Haystack), oil on canvas, stamped signature, 1883, 22x18", C-NY 11/16/88 ... 143,000
Portrait de Alice Gamby, la Niece de la Niece de l'Artist; red chalk on paper, sgn, 1890, 20x13", C-NY 5/12/88 ... 41,800
Study for Fillette a la Chevre, sanguine on Arches laid paper, stamped signature, 1891, 21x17", SBY 11/16/89 ... 41,250
MORISSET, Francois Henri (French, 1870-)
Ladies at the Beach (in elegant costumes), oil on canvas mounted on board, sgn, 5x11", WG 4/23/88 ... 2,600
On the Beach (elegant figures in landscape), oil on canvas mounted on board, sgn, 5x11", WG 4/23/88 ... 2,600
MORLAND, George (British, 1763-1804)
Barnyard with Pigs, Two Farmers, & a Carthorse; oil on canvas, sgn, 35x27", C-NY 4/8/88 OE ... 6,600
Cat Drinking, oil on canvas, sgn/dtd 1792, 12x15", SBY 6/10/88 ... 9,625
Nursemaid & a Child Resting in the Woods, oil on canvas, initialed, 15x12", C-NY 4/8/88 ... 880
River Landscape with a Stone Bridge, oil on canvas, bears signature, 18x24", SBY 6/3/88 ... 9,900
Sorting the Catch, oil on canvas, sgn, 28x36", RWS 5/12/89 UE ... 5,000
Warrener (man coming home from rabbit hunt), oil on canvas, sgn/indistinctly dtd, 34x44", SBY 1/12/89 ... 22,000
MORLAND, George; after (British, 1763-1804)
Faggot Gatherer, oil on canvas, bears signature, 24x18", SBY 7/12/89 ... 715
MORLAND, George; att (British, 1763-1804)
Black Lion Inn, oil on oak panel, 8x12", S/A 2/18/89 ... 1,500
Dune Landscape with a Man by a Barn, oil on canvas, 10x12", C-NY 10/12/89 ... 1,980
Portrait of a Collector, seated, holding a painting by Morland; oil on canvas, bears signature, 30x25", C-NY 4/8/88 ... 1,760
The Smugglers, oil on canvas, initialed, 17x13", B/B 4/20/88 ... 1,210
MORLAND, George; circle of (British, 1763-1804)
Travelers at an Inn Within a Wooded Landscape, oil on canvas, 18x25", SBY 4/7/88 ... 1,870
MORLAND, George; manner of (British, 1763-1804)
Girl Carrying a Bucket, oil on canvas, 17x12", SBY 7/12/89 ... 330
MORLAND, George; school of (British, 1763-1804)
Father & Daughter with Animals in a Farmyard, oil on canvas, 19x24", C-E 4/7/88 ... 495
Figures by Cottages Near a Quarry, oil on canvas, 25x30", C-E 4/7/88 ... 1,100
Stable with a Milkmaid Conversing with a Farmhand, oil on canvas, 20x25", C-E 4/7/88 ... 880
MORLEY, Malcolm (American, 1931-)
Aix en Provence (woman standing w/child), watercolor/pencil on paper, sgn/titled, 1978, 31x22", SBY 2/19/88 ... 4,400
HMS Hood (ship w/figures), acrylic/silkscreen on canvas, sgn/dtd 1964, 9x12", SBY 11/9/89 ... 17,600
Indian Family (contemporary family portrait), watercolor on paper, 1986, 22x30", SBY 2/19/88 ... 29,700
Knitting Machine (abstract), oil on canvas, sgn/inscr w/title/dtd 71, 24x24", C-NY 5/4/89 ... 14,300
Lifeguard, watercolor on paper, sgn, 22x31", C-NY 5/4/88 ... 18,700
Mayor Rosebud's Garden (abstract), oil on canvas, ca 1963, 24x24", C-E 11/14/89 ... 4,950
Palm Beach, watercolor on paper, sgn, 31x23", SBY 11/9/89 ... 27,500
Parrots (contemporary), oil on canvas, 1978, 47x59", SBY 11/10/88 OE ... 506,000
Plymouth, watercolor on paper, sgn 3 times/inscr/dtd, 20x31", C-NY 5/4/88 ... 7,700
Study for Camel & Goats (abstract), watercolor on paper, sgn/dtd 1980, 22x26", SBY 5/3/88 ... 19,800
Untitled, oil on canvas, sgn, 1985, 5x14", SBY 2/15/89 ... 4,125
Untitled (abstract leopards in landscape), watercolor on paper, sgn, 15x23", C-NY 11/10/88 ... 5,280
Untitled (abstract nude), watercolor on paper, sgn, 1983, 18x14", C-NY 11/10/88 ... 8,250
Untitled (abstract portrait), watercolor on paper, sgn, 1983, 25x19", C-NY 11/10/88 ... 4,180
Untitled (abstract), watercolor on paper, sgn, 23x30", C-NY 2/14/89 ... 6,600
Untitled (Bearded Turk), watercolor/charcoal on paper, sgn, 1982, 18x15", C-NY 2/20/88 ... 6,600
Untitled (contemporary beach scene w/palm trees), watercolor on paper, sgn, 16x18", C-NY 10/4/89 ... 13,200
Untitled (cow), watercolor on paper, sgn, 10x13", SBY 2/15/89 ... 3,575
Untitled (Duck Pond), oil pastel/pencil on paper, sgn/dtd 79, 22x30", SBY 11/11/88 ... 7,700
Untitled (elephant), watercolor on paper, sgn, 13x17", SBY 2/15/89 ... 4,950
Untitled (loosely painted palm trees/foilage/figures), watercolor on paper, 1977, 12x17", SBY 2/19/88 ... 7,700
Untitled (two figures), watercolor on paper, sgn, 20x25", C-NY 5/4/89 ... 3,850
Untitled (woman), watercolor on paper, sgn, 11x15", SBY 2/15/89 ... 4,950
MORO, see Del Moro
MORONI, J. (Continental, 18th C)
Rinaldo e Armida (figures in landscape with dogs), oil on copper, sgn, 16x21", PHL 10/28/88 ... 1,500
MORRELL, Wayne (American, 1923-)
Cobblestone Beach, Rockport; oil on masonite, sgn, 11x14", RWS 11/10/89 ... 600
Essex Woods, felled tree in dark forest; oil on board, sgn/dtd Sept 1969 & 1975/titled, 7x10", RAB 3/27/89 UE ... 100
Indian Summer Reflections (landscape), oil on canvas, sgn/dtd 1965, 24x36", SBY 3/17/88 ... 1,540
Rockport Hills, March 1985 (landscape); oil on masonite, sgn/titled, 8x10", RAB 3/27/89 ... 250
MORRICE, James Wilson (Canadian, 1865-1924)
Cafe Tangiers at Night (three men at table by tree), oil on panel, 5x6", FB 10/17/88 ... 24,000
Dawn on the Seine (dock scene w/city beyond), oil on canvas, sgn/dtd 06, 25x21", C-NY 5/25/89 ... 44,000
MORRIS, Charles (British, 19th C)
Rural Landscape with Watermill, oil on panel, sgn/dtd 1864, 16x20", B/B 3/22/89 ... 1,100

ORRIS, Charles; att (British, 19th C)
Crossroads, oil on panel, bears signature, 12x10", SBY 7/12/89 ... 3,520
ORRIS, George L.K. (American, 1905-1975)
Baroque (abstraction), oil on canvas, sgn/dtd 1938, 18x25", C-NY 9/28/89 ... 19,800
Floating Figures (abstract), oil on canvas, sgn/dtd 1935, 12x10", C-NY 9/28/89 ... 14,300
Shipyard Composition (abstract), fresco inlaid with vitrolite & glass, sgn/dtd 1944, 22x18", C-NY 9/28/89 OE ... 33,000
Spring Sun (abstract), oil on canvas, sgn, 42x51", C-NY 5/25/89 OE ... 22,000
ORRIS, John (British, 19th C)
Goats & Sheep in a Landscape, oil on board, 26x34", WAD 6/6/88 ... 3,000
ORRIS, John Floyd (American, 20th C)
Desert Landscape with Tortoise, gouache on gray paper, sgn, 20x26", C-NY 10/6/88 OE ... 935
Green Mountain, watercolor on paper, sgn/dtd 44, green velvet cord frame, 15x23", C-NY 10/6/88 OE ... 1,430
Grotesque Pillar, gouache on paper, 25x19", C-NY 10/6/88 ... 550
Milne Bay, New Guinea; watercolor on paper, sgn/dtd 44, black velvet frame, 15x22", C-NY 10/6/88 OE ... 1,210
Oriental Figure Studies, pen/ink/gray wash on paper, sgn/dtd 1950, 14x10", C-NY 10/6/88 ... 220
Portrait of a Young Man, pen/orange ink on paper, sgn, 14x10", C-NY 10/6/88 ... 132
Set of 3: Imaginary Landscape; Marsyas; Doryphore; 2: pen/ink on paper, 1: watercolor, unfr, 14x10", C-NY 10/6/88 OE ... 352
Strange Parkland, oil on canvas, sgn, unfr, 21x67", C-NY 10/6/88 OE ... 8,800
ORRIS, Kyle (American, 1918-)
Floater, oil on canvas, sgn/dtd twice 61, 48x72", SBY 10/5/88 ... 880
20 January 1960 (abstract), oil on canvas, sgn/dtd 1960, 62x62", SBY 2/14/89 OE ... 7,425
ORRIS, Louis (20th C)
Gamma Iota (abstract composition), acrylic on canvas, sgn, 1960, 102x157", SBY 5/2/89 ... 253,000
Untitled B (abstract), magna on canvas, initialed/dtd 54, 103x79", SBY 5/2/89 ... 660,000
ORRIS, Philip Richard (British, 1836-1902)
Portrait of Lilly Langtry, oil on canvas, sgn, 30x20", SBY 7/12/89 ... 1,430
Young Girl Watching a Robin in the Trees, oil on canvas, sgn, 30x20", C-E 5/22/89 ... 3,850
ORRIS, Robert (American, 1931-)
Labyrinth, ink on paper, sgn/dtd 73, 42x60", SBY 10/8/88 ... 8,250
Labyrinth (circular maze composition), black ink on paper, sgn/dtd 73, 42x60", C-NY 5/4/89 OE ... 19,800
Studies of Water After Leonardo, lead mounted on wood w/nails, sgn, 6x11", C-NY 10/31/89 OE ... 9,900
Untitled (abstract), graphite on paper, sgn/dtd 73, 40x26", SBY 10/5/89 OE ... 15,400
37 Minutes, 3,879 Strokes; graphite on paper, sgn/inscr w/titled/dtd 2-18-61, 24x20", C-NY 10/31/89 OE ... 16,500
ORRIS, William H. (British, 1834-1896)
Falconer, oil on canvas, sgn/dtd 1856, 28x36", C-E 5/22/89 ... 4,950
ORRIS, William Walker; att (British, fl 1850-1867)
Highland Shooting, oil on canvas, 26x35", SBY 6/10/88 ... 4,950
ORRISON, K.M. (British, 20th C)
Bay at Cansand, 1931 (extensive view of bay & village from hilltop); oil on canvas, sgn, 17x21", B/B 9/14/89 UE ... 770
ORSE, Samuel Finley Breese (American, 1791-1872)
Portrait of Louisa Walter Bishop Hughes, oil on board, oval, 9x7", RWS 5/19/88 ... 3,800
Portrait of Nancy Babcock White, oil on canvas, 36x28", RWS 8/20/88 OE ... 2,400
Rachel Pomeroy Campbell (portrait), oil on canvas, 30x25", C-NY 12/2/88 OE ... 57,200
ORTELMANS, Frans (Belgian, 1865-)
At the Forge (interior of blacksmith's shop), oil on canvas, sgn/dtd 1887, 22x18", C-NY 5/24/89 ... 3,520
Cherry Blossoms in a Meiping Vase, with a Porcelain Figure & a Teacup on Tray; oil on canvas, sgn, 32x19", C-NY 2/23/89 ... 14,300
Still Life of Apple Blossoms & White Porcelain on a Table, oil on canvas, sgn, 40x21", C-NY 5/24/89 ... 9,900
ORTON, Edward (20th C)
Elephants, pencil & chalk, sgn/dtd 1936, 10x16", LH 10/16/88 OE ... 350
ORTON, Thomas Corsan (British, 19th C)
Rowing on a Stream, oil, sgn, 16x20", WD 1/11/89 ... 800
ORVILLER, Joseph (American, 1855-1870)
Beached, oil on canvas, in a painted oval, sgn/dtd 1851, 10x14", C-NY 3/11/88 ... 3,080
Winter in Malden, Massachusetts (skaters on pond); oil on canvas, sgn/dtd 1864, 16x26", C-NY 5/25/89 UE ... 8,800
ORZENTI
Mother Holding a Child, pastel on canvas, sgn, 41x41", C-E 11/8/88 UE ... 650
OSAR, Michelle
Around the Piano, oil on panel, sgn, 13x15", MAG 9/18/88 ... 300
OSELEY, Alice Latimer (American, 20th C)
Winter Farmyard Scene, oil on canvas, sgn, unfr, 24x24", LH 5/15/88 ... 90
OSER, James Henry (American, 1954-1913)
October Woods, Shenandoah (autumn landscape); watercolor on paper, sgn, 11x13", WL 5/20/88 ... 450
OSES, Anna Mary Robertson (Grandma)(American, 1860-1961)
Alan House (primitive landscape), oil on masonite, sgn/dtd 1948/#d 1346, 7x8", C-NY 5/25/89 ... 7,700
Arlington Green (primitive landscape), tempera on masonite, sgn/dtd Oct 18 1945/titled, 16x24", SBY 5/24/89 OE ... 55,000
Covered Bridge, oil on canvasboard, sgn/inscr, ca 1940, 11x16", C-NY 3/11/88 ... 7,700
Double-Sided: Cottage Road; oil on board, sgn, 10x12", RAB 8/8/89 OE ... 13,500
Empty Barn (primitive landscape), oil on panel, sgn/dtd July 2 1957/titled/#d 1775, 12x16", SBY 5/24/89 ... 27,500
Haying in Vermont (primitive landscape), oil on board, sgn/dtd October 5 1948/#d 1294, 16x24", SBY 5/24/89 OE ... 66,000
Hills of New England (primitive w/covered bridge), oil on board, sgn/dtd ca 1939, 14x17", C-NY 9/28/89 OE ... 63,800
Imagination (winter town scene), tempera on masonite, sgn/inscr/dtd 1951, 16x22", C-NY 9/30/88 OE ... 27,500

In the Andirondacks (primitive of cabin in a landscape), oil on masonite, sgn/copyrighted/#d 1043, 16x20", SBY 1/24/89 6,600
It Will Snow (primitive landscape), oil on masonite, sgn/dtd Oct 11th 1943/titled/#d 455, 19x25", SBY 5/24/89 60,500
Out in the Moonlight, tempera on masonite, sgn/inscr/dtd 1944, unfr, 7x10", C-NY 12/2/88 9,900
Quack Quack, tempera on masonite, sgn/inscr dtd 1954, 12x18", C-NY 12/2/88 15,400
Schoolhouse (folk art landscape w/figures), tempera on masonite, sgn, 21x25", SBY 5/25/88 82,500

MOSES, Bernard (American, fl 1860-1870)
Portrait of a New Orleans Gentleman, oil on canvas, oval, 28x25", MG 5/28/88 750

MOSES, Ed (American, 1926-)
Untitled (black square), black ink/masking tape on board, 17x14", C-E 11/14/89 880
Untitled (criss-crossed lineation in orange tones), pigment/polyester resin on canvas, 1973, 95x86", SBY 11/11/88 27,500

MOSES, Walter Farrington (American, 1874-)
Desert Foliage, oil on canvas, sgn, 25x30", B/B 10/6/88 1,430

MOSKOWITZ, Robert (American, 1935-)
Black Mill, oil on canvas, sgn/dtd 1981, 108x63", C-NY 11/7/89 OE 286,000
Untitled (row of airmail envelopes on blue-gray background), mixed media, sgn/dtd 1962, 24x24", SBY 2/15/89 OE 20,900

MOSLER, Gustave Henry (American, 1875-1906)
Clouds & Landscape, oil on canvas, sgn, 20x24", C-E 2/3/88 UE 440
Port CT Meyers Resting Place in Switzerland, oil on panel, indistinctly sgn, 6x10", C-E 2/3/88 550
Sheep, oil on canvas, sgn, 25x30", C-E 2/3/88 UE 550

MOSLER, Henry (American, 1841-1920)
Pair: View of Doge's Palace; Venetian Canal Scene; oil on panel, sgn/dtd 92, 7x11", 11x7", B/B 6/15/89 2,200
Portrait of a Steer, oil on canvas, sgn, 36x29", B/B 5/17/89 1,760
Portrait of an Old Woman, oil on panel, sgn/dtd Paris 1901, 9x13", MG 5/28/88 1,600
Woman in a Bonnet (bust-length), oil on canvas, sgn/dtd 1892, 13x9", C-NY 9/28/89 4,180

MOSLER, Henry; att (American, 1841-1920)
Pair: Men in Eastern European Costumes (portraits); oil on panel, 6x8", MG 5/28/88 400

MOSS, Charles E. (American, 1860-1901)
Mother & Child, oil on canvas, sgn, 44x38", B/B 6/9/88 OE 41,250

MOSS, Kevin (20th C)
La Quebrada (shaded path in landscape), oil on canvas, 1988, 54x70", SBY 2/15/89 4,400

MOSTYN, Thomas E. (British, 1864-1930)
Pool in the Wood (three bathers in woodland pool in autumn), oil on canvas, sgn, 30x38", RWS 3/31/88 550

MOTHERWELL, Robert (American, 1915-)
Beside the Sea with Sand Wave (abstract), acrylic/gouache on paper, initialed, dtd 68, 31x22", SBY 5/3/89 OE 121,000
Bete Noire (contemporary composition), acrylic on canvas, sgn/dtd 1973, 80x50", SBY 11/9/89 OE 209,000
Bird Study, oil on palette paper, initialed/dtd 54, 12x15", SBY 10/5/88 4,950
Bull #2 (abstract), oil on paper laid down on board, initialed/dtd 1958/titled, 14x23", SBY 5/3/88 55,000
Collage with German Music, mixed media on canvasboard, sgn/dtd 20 May 74, 73x36", SBY 11/9/89 137,500
Elegy (abstract), oil/pencil on paper, initialed, ca 1965, 7x9", SBY 11/11/88 34,100
Elegy for Spanish Republic #125, oil on canvas, sgn/dtd 72, 86x120", SBY 11/8/89 1,100,000
Elegy to the Spanish Republic #134 (abstract), acrylic on canvas, sgn/#d 134/dtd 74, unfr, 96x120", C-NY 5/3/89 880,000
Euclid's Sand (abstract), acrylic on canvasboard, sgn/dtd twice 1975, 18x14", SBY 10/8/88 OE 52,250
Figure Study III (abstract), ink on paper, initialed/dtd 50, 14x11", SBY 10/8/88 4,400
Galoise with Scarlett #19 (abstract), acrylic/paper collage on board, initialed/dtd 72, 20x16", C-NY 5/4/89 52,800
Gauloises on Scarlet & Yellow #1 (abstract), acrylic/paper collage on canvasboard, sgn/dtd 72, 24x10", SBY 2/19/88 18,700
German Line #5 (abstract), acrylic/collage on canvasboard, initialed/dtd 72, 30x12", SBY 5/3/88 OE 38,500
Gordon's, acrylic/paper collage on canvasboard, initialed/dtd 67/73, 24x18", SBY 10/8/88 24,200
Havana (abstract), collage/acrylic on board, initialed/dtd 77, 36x24", SBY 11/11/88 71,500
In Beige with Charcoal #1 (abstract), oil on canvasboard, sgn/dtd 3 Feb 73, 36x48", SBY 11/11/88 OE 66,000
Open #47 (abstract), oil/charcoal on canvas, sgn/dtd 1968, 25x30", SBY 5/5/89 35,750
Open #81 (abstract), acrylic on canvas, sgn/initialed/dtd 69, 72x42", C-NY 2/20/88 49,500
Open No 148 (White on Black), acrylic on canvas, sgn, 14x18", C-NY 11/10/88 OE 33,000
Open 22 (abstract), acrylic/charcoal on canvas, initialed/dtd 68, unfr, 90x129", C-NY 11/9/88 82,500
POE #3 (abstract), oil/collage on canvas, sgn/dtd 73, 36x48", SBY 2/15/89 OE 66,000
Red Head (abstract composition), oil on masonite, sgn/dtd 1946, 18x14", SBY 5/3/89 OE 19,800
Souvenir de Californie (abstract), paper collage/casein/pencil on cardboard, sgn/dtd 1953-55, 16x12", SBY 5/2/88 15,400
Summer Sea (abstract), acrylic on canvas mounted on board, sgn twice/inscr/dtd 1970, 15x30", C-NY 11/9/88 OE 50,600
Summer Studio (abstract), oil on canvas, initialed/dtd 77, 43x52", SBY 11/11/88 104,500
Tapestry Study #2 (black abstract on white), gouache on paper, initialed/dtd 72, 22x14", SBY 10/5/89 30,800
Tibor de Nagy Collage (abstract), oil on board w/paper collage/wax/string, sgn/dtd 73, 36x47", SBY 2/15/89 UE 27,500
Torino (abstract), acrylic/paper collage on canvasboard, sgn/dtd 75, 48x36", SBY 10/5/89 OE 148,000
Untitled (abstract), hand-painted acrylic over black inked lithograph, sgn, 1972, 22x17", SBY 10/5/89 35,700

MOTLEY, D. (British, 19th C)
A Pushing Family (farmyard scene with animals), oil on canvas, sgn, 20x30", SLK 5/11/88 1,700

MOTTET, Jeanie Gallup (American, 1884-1934)
Purple Hat, oil on canvas, sgn, 32x26", C-E 11/30/88 1,320

MOTZ, Peter
Reading on a Riverbank, oil on canvas, sgn, 20x28", C-E 2/23/88 495

MOUCHERON, see De Moucheron

MOUCHOT, Louis Claude (French, 1830-1891)
Flirtation, oil on panel, sgn, 18x15", C-E 10/26/89 3,300

Interior Scene, oil on panel, sgn, 16x12", FB 10/30/89 ... 605

MOULY, Marcel (French, 1920-)

Venetian Canal Scene, oil on canvas, sgn/dtd 58, 32x40", SBY 10/5/88 ... 715

MOUNT, Rita (Canadian, 1888-1967)

Glace Bay, New Brunswick; oil on board, sgn, 6x8", FB 4/25/88 ... 525

MOUNT, Shepard Alonzo (American, 1804-1868)

Portrait of Mrs John D Jones, oil on canvas, sgn/dtd 1853, oval, 27x22", SBY 6/28/89 ... 1,320
Songbird (portrait of a young girl w/a canary), oil on canvas, sgn/dtd 1850, orig gilt gesso frame, 27x22", RWS 9/8/89 ... 4,500
The Day's Catch (fish in lanscape), oil on canvas, sgn/dtd 1862, 18x24", SBY 4/14/89 ... 4,070

MOUNT, William Sidney (American, 1807-1868)

Mount Kitchen, Stony Brook; oil on canvas laid down on panel, sgn, 7x14", C-NY 5/26/88 ... 41,800
Spring Bouquet (floral still life), oil on paper, initialed/dtd May 28 57, 8x7", SBY 5/24/89 ... 33,000
Thomas Strong's House at Setauket, oil on paper laid down on panel, initialed/dtd 1864, 11x17", C-NY 5/26/88 OE ... 30,800

MOUSSET, Pierre (French, -1894)

Harem Favorite (half-length portrait of woman), oil on canvas, sgn, 26x21", B/B 10/9/88 ... 3,025

MOWBRAY, Henry Siddons (American, 1858-1928)

Glass of Wine, oil on panel, sgn, 13x10", C-E 2/1/89 ... 2,200
Man of Letters (man seated at table), oil on panel, sgn/dtd 81, 8x9", SBY 6/28/89 ... 4,400
Rose Festival (From Lalla Roohk), oil on canvas, sgn/dtd 87, 14x20", SBY 5/25/88 OE ... 41,250

MOWER, Martin (1870-)

Floral Still Life, oil on canvas, initialed, 27x20", SBY 1/24/89 ... 3,575

MOYAERT, see Moeyaert

MOYLAN, Lloyd (American, 1893-)

Mexican Travelers, oil on canvas, sgn, 30x40", SBY 3/17/88 ... 2,475

MOZART, Anton; circle of

Head of a Giant in the Form of a Landscape, oil on canvas, unfr, 16x13", C-NY 10x20/88 ... 2,200

MOZZANTI, Lodovico (1649-1775)

Christ Raising Lazarus From the Dead, oil on canvas, 17x28" , SBY 4/7/89 ... 4,950

MU, Luo (Chinese, 1622-1706)

Landscape (hanging scroll), ink on satin, sgn, 66x19", SBY 5/31/89 OE ... 9,350

MUCHA, Alphonse Maria (Czechoslovakian, 1860-1939)

Polytych: Four Precious Stones...; oil on canvas laid down, sgn/dtd 1902, 40x17, SBY 11/17/88 UE ... 57,750
Portrait of Milada Cerny (seated at piano), oil on canvas, sgn/dtd 1906, 50x36", SBY 10/24/89 ... 77,000
Study of a Peasant Girl, blue/brown chalk heightened w/white, sgn, arched top, 20x15", SBY 6/8/88 ... 3,300
Young Girl in a Moravian Costume, oil on canvas, sgn, 22x21", SBY 10/24/89 ... 44,000

MUCKE, Carl (German, 1847-1923)

Winters Greeting, oil on canvas, sgn/dtd 72, 28x23", C-E 10/25/88 ... 1,540

MUCKLEY, William Jabez (British, 1837-1905)

Adolescence (girl looking into mirror), watercolor/gouache, sgn/dtd 1874, 13x10", C-NY 2/23/89 ... 4,950
Rainy Afternoon's Amusement (children in interior), watercolor/gouache, sgn/dtd 1872, 12x10", C-NY 2/23/89 ... 2,860

MUDIE, Arthur

Auckland Harbor (harbor scene), pencil/watercolor, sgn twice/titled, 10x14", C-SK 6/9/88 ... 560

MUELLER, M. (19th C)

Mother's Prayers (young woman kneeling), oil on canvas, sgn, 34x24", WG 4/23/88 UE ... 550

MUELLER, Otto (German, 1874-1930)

Paar am Strand (two figures), distemper on linen, 1914, 39x72", SBY 5/10/88 ... 308,000
Sitzendes und Liegendes Madchen im Gras, brush/ink/watercolor/pastel on paper, ca 1920-25, 20x13", SBY 5/11/88 OE ... 93,500
Stehender Frauenakt, charcoal on paper laid down on paper, estate stamp, 22x18", C-NY 10/6/88 OE ... 7,150
Zwei Frauen (two women in a landscape, one nude), crayons/black ink mounted on board, 4x6", C-NY 5/12/88 OE ... 17,600

MUELLER, Stephen (European, 20th C)

Kuvasz 2 (abstract), acrylic on canvas, sgn/dtd 2.79, unfr, 59x64", C-NY 2/20/88 UE ... 935
Texas Gay, oil on paper, 36x26", SBY 2/14/89 ... 605
You Are Coming Too, acrylic/oil on canvas, sgn/dtd 1984, 70x74", SBY 2/15/89 ... 5,500

MUENIER, Jules Alexis (French, 1863-1942)

Afternoon Rest, oil on canvas, sgn/dtd 1909, unfr, 19x25", SBY 10/24/89 ... 7,700

MUHL, Roger (French, 1929-)

Le Bateau Blanc, oil on canvas, sgn, 13x10", SLK 4/7/89 ... 125
Les Arbres en Fleurs en Alsace, oil on canvas, sgn, 58x38", SBY 10/7/89 ... 3,850
Les Arbres en Fleurs en Alsace (abstract), oil on canvas, sgn, 58x38", SBY 2/14/89 OE ... 4,150
Pont d'Etna, oil on canvas, sgn, 21x32", SBY 10/5/88 OE ... 2,750
Porte Ouvert, oil on canvas, sgn, 48x44", SBY 10/7/89 ... 7,150
Printemps, la Prairie (spring landscape); oil on canvas, sgn, 32x40", SBY 2/14/89 ... 2,090
Saint Tropez, Vue du Port des Pecheurs; oil on canvas, sgn, 39x32", SBY 10/5/88 OE ... 2,530

MUHLENFELD, Otto (American, 1871-1907)

Portrait of the Ocean-Going Tug Onida, oil on canvas, indistinctly sgn, 18x24", RAB 3/14/89 ... 6,500
Portrait of the Ocean-Going Tug Onida, oil on canvas, 18x24", RAB 8/1/89 ... 4,000

MUHLIG, Meno (German, 1823-1873)

Peasants Outside a Cottage, oil on canvas, sgn, unfr, 24x31", C-E 5/23/88 OE ... 3,960

MUHLSTOCK, Louis (Canadian, 1904-)

Laurentian Landscape, oil on board, sgn, 6x8", FB 5/28/89 ... 300
Nude, pastel, sgn, 20x16", FB 4/25/88 OE ... 1,300

Old & Unemployed, charcoal, sgn/dtd 1932, 16x12", FB 5/28/89 475

MUHLSTOCK, Rachael (Canadian, 20th C)

Winter Landscape, oil on board, sgn/dtd 1981, 18x24", FB 4/25/88 220

MUHS, Frederick (American, 20th C)

Pair: Nudes; pencil heightened with watercolor, 1 sgn, 5x9", S/A 2/18/89 125

Rolling River Ozark Ark 1327, oil on academy board, sgn/Edition 1327, 9x11", S/A 2/18/89 60

MULDER, Anna (Dutch, 1935-)

Mother & Daughter at Household, oil on canvas, sgn, 12x16", B/B 12/8/88 275

MULERTT, Carel Eugene (American, 1869-1915)

Family the the Hearth, oil on canvas, sgn, 24x33", C-E 1/12/88 528

Getting Dressed (mother buttoning daughter's dress), oil on canvas, sgn, 63x81", C-E 2/1/89 1,540

Lady Sewing, gouache on paper, sgn, 15x18", FAP 4/15/89 935

Tying the Sash, oil on canvas, sgn, 22x18", C-E 2/1/89 880

MULHAUPT, Frederick John (American, 1871-1938)

An Afternoon in Port (Gloucester), oil on canvas, sgn, 18x24", SBY 5/25/88 17,600

Audiernes Bretagne, France; oil on board, sgn/titled, 10x14", SBY 6/24/88 1,210

Autumn, Ipswich; oil on canvas, sgn, 25x30", SBY 5/25/88 OE 24,200

Autumn Landscape, oil on canvas laid down, sgn/dtd 1912, 10x12", B/B 6/9/88 1,100

Autumn Reflections (landscape w/stream), oil on canvas, sgn, 30x25", C-NY 5/25/89 14,300

Autumn Trees, oil on canvas, sgn, 18x24", C-NY 9/28/89 6,600

Boats at Dock, oil on canvasboard, sgn, 8x10", C-NY 3/11/88 3,960

Boats in Rockport Harbor, oil on canvas, sgn, 18x24", B/B 10/9/88 OE 17,600

Dawn on the Seine (dock scene w/city beyond), oil on canvas, sgn/dtd 06, 25x21", C-NY 5/25/89 14,300

Gathering Apples in the Backyard, oil on canvas, sgn, 19x24", SBY 9/14/89 OE 12,100

Harbor View, Gloucester; oil on canvas, sgn/dtd 07, 22x28", RWS 11/10/89 7,000

New England Harbor View, oil on board, sgn, 12x16", SBY 1/24/89 8,250

Stilling Winds (autumn landscape), oil on canvas, sgn, 50x60", RWS 5/12/89 20,000

Sunlight & Shadows, oil on canvas, sgn, 30x25", SBY 5/25/88 13,200

Vermont Farmhouse in Winter, oil on canvas, sgn, 36x36", SBY 5/25/88 25,300

Winter Stream, oil on canvas, sgn/dtd 1910, 18x24", C-NY 12/2/88 4,400

MULHOLLAND, Sydney A. (British, 19th C)

Coastal Scene, watercolor on paper, sgn, 11x23", FAP 4/15/89 UE 165

Untitled, marine scene w/figures in rowboat in harbor at sunset; oil on canvas, sgn, 12x16", SLK 2/11/89 350

MULIER, Pieter the elder (Dutch, 1615-1670)

Shipping in a Choppy Sea, oil on panel, 14x20", C-NY 6/2/88 16,500

MULIER, Pieter the elder; circle of (Dutch, 1615-1670)

Landscape with Figures on a Road & Castle in the Distance, oil on canvas, 26x35", SBY 10/21/88 OE 4,950

Seascape with Sunset, pastel on paper, sgn, 18x23", SBY 4/14/89 3,410

MULIER, Pieter the younger (Dutch, 1637-1701)

Landscape with Figures Tending Livestock & Fortifications Beyond, oil on canvas, 35x48", SBY 4/7/89 OE 27,500

MULL, Evert (Dutch, 19th/20th C)

Cathedral by the Canal, oil on panel, sgn, 10x12", B/B 1/11/89 660

MULLER, Anton (German, 1865-1949)

Little Girl with Cello, oil on canvas, sgn, 20x18", C-E 5/23/88 UE 1,540

MULLER, August (German, 1836-1885

Portrait of an Artist, oil on canvas, sgn/inscr Munchen/dtd 84, 14x10", WD 3/23/88 UE 550

MULLER, Carl Friedrich Moritz (German, 1807-1865)

Letter (woman writing letter by candlelight), oil on panel, sgn/dtd 1838, 16x13", C-NY 2/23/89 OE 10,450

MULLER, Charles (French, 1815-1892)

Artist in His Studio, oil on canvas, sgn, 16x26", B/B 6/9/88 6,050

MULLER, E. (German, 19th C)

Tyrolean Peasant After the Shoot, oil on board, sgn/inscr, 16x9", C-E 2/23/88 1,210

MULLER, Fritz (German, 1913-)

Man with a Pipe, oil on masonite, sgn, 12x9", C-E 2/16/88 440

Pair: Tyrolean Peasant Smoking a Pipe; Tyrolean Peasant Drinking; oil on board, sgn/inscr, 9x7", C-E 5/23/88 1,210

Portrait of a Bearded Old Man with Pipe, oil on board, sgn, 12x10", DM 2/19/88 700

MULLER, Jan (American, 1922-1958)

Bacchanale, gouache on board, 15x22", C-NY 3/11/88 2,090

Double-Sided: Landscapes; watercolor on paper, 12x9", SBY 10/7/89 935

Double-Sided: Rider in the Forest; Portrait of a Woman; red chalk, 17x14", C-E 11/14/89 4,400

Mosaic Circle Abstraction (contemporary), oil on canvas, sgn/dtd 52/titled, 24x24", C-E 5/9/89 OE 19,800

Pair: Riders; Landscape; pastel on paper, 10x12", 8x12", SBY 10/5/88 OE 7,150

MULLER, Moritz (German, 1841-1899)

Captured Prey, oil on panel, sgn/dtd 96, unfr, 11x8", SBY 6/8/88 1,100

Deer in a Mountainous Landscape, oil on canvas, sgn, 22x30", C-NY 5/24/89 8,800

MULLER, Richard (Austrian, 1874-1930)

Pastoral Scene (extensive landscape), oil on board, sgn, 6x9", B/B 5/17/89 660

MULLER, William (British, 1812-1845)

Surrey Scene, oil on canvas, 17x21", B/B 5/17/89 1,540

MULLER-GRANTZOW, Ad (German 19th/20th C)

Midday Meal (man seated at table in interior), oil on canvas, sgn, 22x31", C-E 2/21/89 2,750

JLLER-LINGKE, Albert (German, 1844-)
Winter Landscape with Figures, oil on canvas, sgn/inscr, 11x20", SBY 7/12/89 3,300
JLLEY, Oskar (Austrian, 1891-)
Chalet in the Austrian Alps, oil on canvas, sgn, 32x51", C-NY 2/13/89 OE 11,000
JLLICAN, Matt (20th C)
Untitled (Black & White City), oil on canvas on 4 panels, 72x192", SBY 11/9/89 OE 33,000
Untitled (Green Elements), acrylic/oil on canvas, 96x48", SBY 11/9/89 23,100
JLREADY, Augustus E. (British, fl 1863-1905)
Happy While Sleeping, oil on canvas, sgn/dtd 1883, 6x8", WAD 6/6/88 3,800
JLREADY, William (British, 1786-1863)
Caught in the Act, oil, sgn, 21x28", WD 1/11/89 1,800
Family's Blessing, watercolor/gouache, sgn, 9x13", C-NY 5/25/88 UE 660
Love & Devotion, oil on panel, sgn, 19x16", WAD 6/6/88 3,200
JLREADY, William; after (British, 1786-1863)
Quarrel, oil on canvas, 27x20", LH 9/10/89 1,000
JLVAD, Emma (Danish, 1838-)
Still Life of Tulips, Hyancinth..., oil on canvas, initialed, 12x9", B/B 10/9/88 2,750
JNAKATA, Shiko (American, 19th C)
Bijin (woman's head, bare breasts), brush/ink/watercolor on rice paper, sgn/inscr, 13x14", SBY 5/10/89 OE 57,750
JNARI, Cristoforo (Italian, 1667-1720)
Girl Playing Mandolin, w/lute, viol, books & blue & white porcelain bowl on table; oil on canvas, 47x36", C-NY 5/31/89 66,000
Still Life of a Watermelon, Biscotti, Porcelain Cups...; oil on canvas laid down on board, 34x45", C-NY 6/2/89 OE 148,500
JNARI, Cristoforo; circle of (Italian, 1667-1720)
Pastries, Fruit, Nuts, a Bowl, Flask, & Glass of Wine on a Ledge; oil on canvas, 26x21", C-NY 4/8/88 16,500
JNCH, Edvard (Norwegian, 1863-1944)
Girls on the Jetty, oil on canvas, sgn, 1903, 36x31", SBY 11/11/88 3,300,000
JNCHAUSEN, see Von Munchausen
JNGER, Gilbert Davis (American, 1837-1903)
Near Ablon (cattle watering in landscape), oil on canvas, sgn, 24x29", C-SK 5/25/89 1,750
Yosemite, Halfdome; oil on canvas laid down on board, sgn, 18x32", SBY 6/24/88 OE 9,350
unich School (19th C)
Druids Preparing To Sacrifice to Their Gods...; oil on canvas, sgn, 29x54", S/A 2/18/89 6,000
JNIER, Emile (French, 1810-)
Special Moment, oil on panel, sgn/dtd 1874, 45x33", SBY 5/23/89 93,500
Young Girl with a Basket of Oranges, oil on canvas, sgn, unfr, 20x17", C-NY 2/25/88 OE 13,200
JNKINS, Cornelius
Still Life of Onions, oil on panel, sgn, 9x14", NA 10/1/88 1,300
JNNINGS, Alfred (British, 1878-1959)
Barrowby Hill Point-to-Point (fox hunt scene), oil on canvas, sgn, 24x30", SBY 6/10/88 93,500
Colonel Guy Blewitt's Show Dress, a Suffolk Punch Mare, with Her Foal; oil on panel, sgn, 16x28", SBY 6/9/89 110,000
Dartmoor Ponies, oil on panel, sgn, 7x10", SBY 6/9/89 8,250
Eleven O'Clock (fox hunt scene), oil on canvas, sgn, ca 1932, 38x42", SBY 6/10/88 220,000
Exmoor Ponies-Study No 11; oil on panel, sgn, unfr, 7x10", SBY 6/10/88 OE 16,500
Galatea II, oil on board, sgn/inscr w/horse's name/dtd 1940, 20x24", SBY 6/10/88 121,000
Going Out (hunt scene), watercolor/gouache on paper, sgn, 14x21", SBY 6/9/89 18,181
Going Out at Epsom (racehorse & riders jumping at track), oil on panel, 20x24", SBY 6/10/88 UE 110,000
His Old Demesne (fox hunt scene), oil on canvas, sgn, 28x34", SBY 6/10/88 286,000
Leader, a Bay Hunter in a Wooded Landscape; oil on canvas, sgn/dtd 1905, 20x25", SBY 6/10/88 18,700
Mayfly, a Chestnut Hunter in a Meadow; oil on canvas, sgn/dtd 1907, 20x24", SBY 6/10/88 24,200
Millhouse Lane, Mendham (landscape); oil on canvas, sgn/dtd 1909, 12x14", SBY 6/9/89 11,000
On the Beach, oil on canvas, sgn/dtd 01, 12x10", SBY 5/23/89 7,700
River at Dedham, oil on canvas, sgn/dtd 1911, 20x24", SBY 6/10/88 57,750
Saddled Hunter in a Landscape, oil on canvas, sgn, 19x24", C-NY 5/24/89 17,600
Silks & Satins of the Turf (racehorses & riders), oil on board, sgn, 20x24", SBY 6/10/88 352,000
Studies for Picture-Our Mutual Friend the Horse; pencil, inscr Begun 1928/Not Yet Finished, 8x6", SBY 6/9/89 3,575
Study of the Artist's Favorite Gray Hunter Isaac, oil on canvas, sgn, 26x32", SBY 6/10/88 143,000
Study: Jockeys at the Start, Newmarket; oil on canvasboard, sgn, 20x24", SBY 6/9/89 341,000
Willows Near Langham Pool, oil on canvas laid down on panel, sgn, 20x24", SBY 10/24/89 30,800
Young Herdsman at Mendham, oil on canvas, sgn/dtd 1910, 28x36", SBY 6/9/89 49,500
JNOZ, Domingo (Spanish, 1850-1912)
Old Soldier Posturing in the Snow, oil on board, sgn, 7x9", WG 4/23/88 900
JNOZ, M. (Spanish, 19th C)
Two Women in an Elegant Interior, watercolor, sgn, 21x31", C-NY 10/25/89 2,420
JNOZ, Oscar (Colombian, 1951-)
Still Life (interior scene), charcoal on paper, sgn/dtd 77, 39x27", SBY 5/16/89 2,310
JNOZ Y CUESTRA, Domingo (Spanish, 1850-1912)
Pair: Arab Caravan; Monk Outside a Church Gate; oil on panel, sgn, 5x7", C-E 10/25/88 OE 9,350
JNOZ Y LUCENA, Tomas (Spanish, 1860-1942)
In the Garden (lady in bentwood rocker, other figures beyond), oil on canvas, sgn, 12x26", SBY 10/24/89 11,000

MUNOZ-VERA, Guillermo (Latin American, 20th C)
Kitchen Interior, oil on canvas, initialed/dtd 87, 51x38", SBY 5/16/89 OE **9,900**
Still Life (bread loaf/pottery/wine & glass/Coca-Cola can on table), oil on canvas, sgn/dtd 89, 32x40", SBY 5/16/89 OE **9,900**
MUNTER, David H. (German, 1916-1879)
River Landscape with Figures & Sheep, oil on panel, sgn, 8x13", NA 2/6/88 ..... **325**
Rural Landscape with Buildings, Figures & Cattle; oil on canvas mounted on panel, sgn, 8x13", NA 2/6/88 ..... **450**
MUNTER, Gabriele (German, 1877-1962)
Blumen (abstract floral still life), oil on canvas, monogramed/dtd 47/stamped signature, 22x15", SBY 10/7/88 ..... **40,700**
Blumenstrauss (floral still life), oil on canvas, sgn/dtd 1919, 14x11", SBY 2/14/89 OE **18,700**
Blumentisch (abstract still life), oil on canvas, sgn/dtd 1934/titled, 15x22", C-NY 11/16/88 OE **46,200**
Hauser am Meer, Vaxholm; oil on canvasboard, monogramed, ca 1916-17, 7x12", SBY 2/16/89 ..... **33,000**
Landschaft (abstract), oil on board, sgn twice/dtd 1931, #d 68/31 on verso, 17x13", SBY 2/16/89 OE **44,000**
Landschaft mit Rotem Haus, oil on canvas laid down on board, stamped, ca 1908, 9x7", C-NY 10/6/88 OE **26,400**

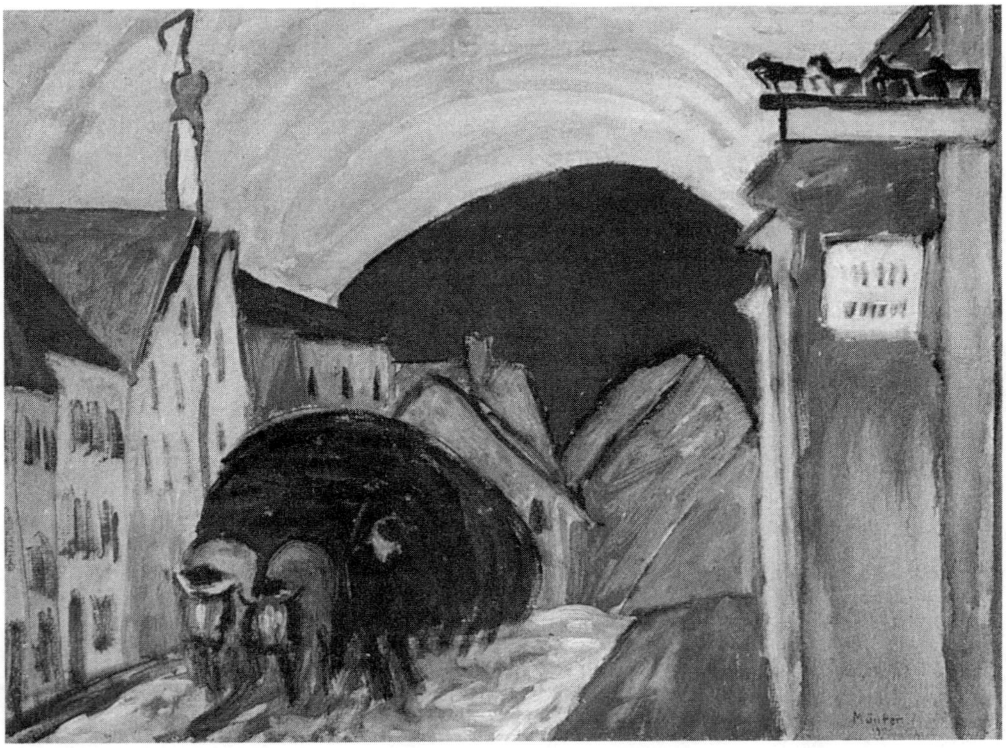

Murnauer Strasse mit Ochesengespann, oil on board laid down on masonite, sgn, 1911, 20x26", C-NY 2/16/89; $66,000

Ranunkel und Mimosen (floral still life), oil on buff paper laid down on board, 17x14", C-NY 2/16/89 OE **11,000**
Rote Hauser (road to house), oil on canvas laid down on board, monogramed, 7x10", SBY 2/14/89 OE **16,500**
Rotkappchen (hilly landscape w/buildings & figure on a road), oil on canvas, stamped, 1912, 13x16", C-NY 10/6/88 ..... **77,000**
Tunis: Der Letze Sonnenstrahl (landscape); oil on canvas laid down on board, sgn/dtd 05, 9x13", SBY 2/14/89 OE **18,700**
MURA, see De Mura
MURATON, Euphemie (French, 1840-)
Chien dans sa Niche, oil on canvas, sgn, 22x18", SBY 6/9/88 UE **3,025**
MURDAY, J.
View of the Ship Dryade on Her Passage From Sydney, New South Wales to London...; oil, sgn, 25x42", C-SK 6/9/88 ..... **7,065**
MURILLO, Bartolome Esteban; att (Spanish, 1618-1682)
Ecce Homo, oil on canvas, 26x20", SBY 10/21/88 UE **14,300**
Ecce Homo (portrait of Christ w/crown of thorns), oil on canvas, 27x19", C-NY 5/31/89 ..... **60,500**
Mater Dolorosa, oil on canvas, 26x20", SBY 10/21/88 UE **14,300**
Saint Judas Thaedo, Apostle (half-length); oil on canvas, 25x20", RAB 8/9/88 ..... **4,000**
MURILLO, Bartolome Esteban; circle of (Spanish, 1618-1682)
Boy Holding a Bottle & Glass, oil on canvas, 34x26", C-NY 4/8/88 ..... **2,420**
Christ Appearing to St Ignatius of Loyola at the Outskirts of Rome, oil on canvas, 60x80", SBY 4/7/89 OE **8,250**
MURPHY, Catherine (American, 1946-)
Elena, Harry & Alan in the Backyard (w/cityscape beyond); oil on canvas, 1978, 40x46", SBY 5/3/89 ..... **27,500**
Self-Portrait (artist seated at her easel), oil on canvas, sgn/dtd 73, 42x35", C-NY 5/4/89 OE **17,600**
MURPHY, Hermann Dudley (American, 1867-1945)
Basket of Flowers, oil on canvas, sgn, unfr, 22x16", C-E 6/1/89 ..... **880**
MURPHY, John Francis (American, 1853-1921)
Autumn Landscape, oil on canvas, sgn, 14x19", SBY 1/24/89 OE **5,225**
Autumn Landscape, oil on panel, sgn/dtd 1921, 7x10", SBY 4/14/89 ..... **3,080**
Canyon, oil on canvas, sgn, 17x12", C-E 4/7/88 UE **550**
Early Evening (figure sitting on ground by building), oil on canvas, sgn/dtd 1881, 8x10", C-NY 6/17/89 OE **8,800**

Farms in an Autumn Sunset, oil on canvas, sgn, 18x24", B/B 10/9/88 OE 4,125
In a Plowed Field, watercolor/pen/black ink on paper laid down on board, sgn, 14x20", C-NY 9/30/88 2,750
Indian Summer, oil on canvas, sgn, 18x24", C-NY 9/28/89 5,500
Indian Summer (impressionistic landscape), oil on canvas, sgn/dtd 1908, 24x33", C-NY 5/26/88 OE 16,500
Landscape with House, oil on panel, sgn, 9x11", C-E 10/18/89 4,950
Landscape with Trees, oil on canvas, sgn, 8x14", SBY 6/24/88 2,750
Late Afternoon (landscape), oil on canvas, sgn/dtd 1911, 16x22", B/B 3/22/89 3,300
Man Walking in Woods, pencil on paper, sgn, 7x10", C-E 6/1/88 OE 3,520
Meadow Landscape (Early Autumn), oil on canvas, sgn, 8x12", RWS 3/31/88 UE 1,300
October Clearing (landscape), oil on canvas laid down on board, sgn/dtd 1911, 7x9", WD 4/13/88 2,400
Old Mill (landscape scene w/mill on a hilltop), oil on canvas, sgn, 12x16", DM 3/14/88 UE 350
Pool (pool of water in a landscape), oil on canvas, sgn/dtd 97, 14x19", SBY 1/24/89 4,125
Spring Landscape, oil on board, sgn/dtd 1906, 14x10", SBY 6/24/88 2,640
Spring's First Light (landscape), oil on canvas, initialed/dtd 1912, 15x19", WD 10/5/88 6,000
Summer landscape, watercolor/pencil on paper laid down on board, sgn/dtd 89, 10x15", C-E 2/1/89 OE 4,950
Summer Morning, oil on canvas, sgn/dtd 1916, 24x36", C-NY 5/26/88 11,000
Summertime, oil on canvas, sgn/dtd 1916, 24x36", C-NY 12/2/88 8,250
Sunset (landscape), oil on canvas, sgn/dtd 98, 8x13", C-SK 5/25/89 2,570
Sycamores, oil on canvas, sgn, 27x41", C-NY 9/28/89 8,800
Tranquility, watercolor/pen/ink heightened w/gouache & pencil on paper, sgn/dtd 90, 10x14", C-E 11/30/88 1,430
Trees in a Summer Meadow, oil on canvas, sgn/dtd 1916, 16x20", SBY 4/14/89 OE 12,650
Winter Sunset, oil on canvas, sgn, 11x15", SBY 9/14/89 9,350

MURPHY, P.W. (American, 20th C)
Still Life of Flowers (carnations in a bowl), oil on canvas, sgn/dtd 19(?), 18x20", RAB 8/9/88 250

MURRAY, Elizabeth (American, 1940-)
Benjamin's Moving Derby (abstract), oil on canvas, sgn/dtd 71, 68x46", C-E 11/14/89 7,150
Birds of Vermont, oil on canvas, sgn/inscr/dtd 72, unfr, 42x48", C-E 5/13/88 3,080
Black & White Front Steps, oil on canvas, sgn/dtd 73, 66x14", C-E 11/14/89 OE 7,700
Car (composition), pastel on paper, sgn/dtd 1982, 33x48", SBY 11/9/89 24,750
Md Cezanne Falling Out of Chair, oil on canvas, sgn/inscr/dtd 72, 35x36", C-E 5/13/88 5,280

MURRAY, F. Richardson (American, 20th C)
At Pokey Paynes, Moving Day, 1932 (interior scene); watercolor on paper, sgn/dtd 1935, 13x9", RWS 5/12/89 OE 5,700
The Table-Central Park West (still life); watercolor on paper, sgn, 10x14", RWS 3/16/89 OE 3,500

MURRAY, H. (British, 19th/20th C)
Pair: Coaching Scenes; watercolor on paper, 1 heightened w/white, sgn, 8x11", C-E 5/22/89 1,100
Pair: Through the Gate; Over the Creek; watercolor on paper, sgn, 7x10", SBY 6/9/89 750
Set of 4: Coaching Scenes; watercolor/gouache on paper, sgn, 11x17", C-NY 5/24/89 OE 5,280
Set of 4: The Meet; Going Out; Full Cry; The Kill; watercolor/gouache on paper, sgn, about 7x10", C-NY 5/24/89 OE 3,850

MURRAY, Thomas; att (British, 1663-1734)
Portrait of a Young Woman, oil on canvas, oval, 30x25", SBY 6/8/88 880

MUSCHAMP, F. Sydney (British, -1929)
Landscape with Fisherman, oil on canvas laid down on board, sgn, 16x25", LH 12/4/88 500

MUSCHAMP, Francis (British, fl 1865-1881)
Picnicking Along the River, oil on canvas, sgn/dtd 1869, 22x18", WD 5/5/88 2,300

MUSGROVE, Alexander Johnston (Canadian, 1890-1952)
Evening (party in boats), watercolor, sgn, 7x10", WAD 6/12/89 160
Rushing River Falls, watercolor, sgn/dtd 1930, 10x14", WAD 6/12/89 140
Rushing Water, watercolor, sgn, 10x14", WAD 6/12/89 160

MUSIC, Antonio Zoran (Italian, 1909-1952)
Donne che Vanno al Mercato, oil on canvas, sgn/dtd 1948, 16x19", SBY 2/18/88 46,200
Horse & Rider, pastel/gouache on paper, sgn/dtd 1955, 11x9", SBY 10/5/88 1,100
Horses, pastel on paper, sgn/dtd 1953, 12x16", SBY 10/5/88 OE 12,100
Il Traghetto (contemporary), oil on canvas, sgn twice/dtd 1954 twice/titled, 21x26", SBY 10/7/88 OE 45,100
Motivo Dalmata, gouache on tan paper, sgn/dtd 1950, 15x21", C-E 5/13/88 OE 17,600
Motivo Dalmata, oil on canvas, sgn/inscr/dtd twice, 1952, 13x16", C-NY 10/6/88 OE 60,500

MUSIN, Francois Etienne (Belgian, 1820-1888)
Fishing Boats Moored Off the Coast, oil on panel, sgn, 7x14", SBY 6/8/88 2,420
Fishing Boats Returning at Sunset, oil on canvas, sgn, 22x36", C-NY 2/25/88 11,000

MUSMEEI, G. (Italian, 20th C)
Monk Reading by River, watercolor on paper, sgn, 14x20", FAP 4/15/89 155

MUTH, A.
Mexican Scene (woman on burro, man on horseback), oil on canvas, sgn, 22x33", C-E 6/1/89 1,320

MUTTER, Karl
Birches in a Storm, oil on canvas, sgn, 28x22", C-E 2/23/88 550

MUTTONI, see De Muttoni

MUYDEN, Evert Louis (Swiss, 1853-1922)
Man Holding a Gray Percheron, watercolor over pencil, sgn/inscr, 14x16", C-NY 5/25/88 2,860

MYERS, Bob (20th C)
Long Shadows-High Rims; oil on canvas, sgn twice, 18x24", SBY 9/23/88 OE 3,300

MYERS, Ethel H. Klink (American, 1881-1960)
Greenwich Village Block Party, pencil/watercolor on paper, 4x8", SBY 9/14/89 990

MYERS, Frank Harmon (American, 1899-1956)
Steamship (river landscape w/city view along shore), oil on canvas, sgn, 22x28", C-E 2/3/88 OE 3,850
MYERS, Jack F. (20th C)
Midwestern Town with Church, oil on masonite, sgn, 22x32", UE 150
MYERS, Jerome (American, 1867-1940)
Children Playing, Lake Gilead, New York; oil on board, sgn/dtd 192(?), 15x21", C-NY 9/28/89 7,700
Five Little Girls Playing (sketch), pencil on paper, 5x7", WG 10/19/88 300
In a Crosstown Car, pencil on paper, sgn/dtd 06/#d 237, 10x6", C-E 2/1/89 OE 935
Lake Gilead, New York; oil on board, sgn, 14x20", SBY 1/24/89 5,500
Self-Portrait, pen on paper, sgn, 6x5", C-E 2/1/89 715
Watching the Race (lady viewed from behind, man in profile), pen/pastel on paper, sgn/dtd 1908, 7x4", C-E 2/1/89 OE 990
MYLES, J. (fl early 19th C)
Portrait of a Guardsman Standing Outside the City Chambers, London; oil on board, sgn, 19x15", SBY 10/13/89 OE 6,050
MYRBACH-RHEINFELD, see De Myrbach-Rheinfeld
MYTENS, Jan; att (Dutch, 1614-1670)
Portrait of Gentleman As Actaeon & His Wife As Diana in a Landscape, oil on canvas, inscr, 72x76", C-NY 10/20/88 OE 33,000
MYTENS, Jan; circle of (Dutch, 1614-1670)
Portrait of a Lady, Possibly Henrietta Maria, standing, three-quarter length...; oil on canvas, 50x37", C-NY 5/31/89 OE 15,400
MYTENS, Martin (Swedish, 1648-1736)
Portrait Head of a Daughter of the Empress Maria Teresa, lead/pen/gray ink on varnished paper, wm, 9x7", C-NY 1/12/88 935
Portrait Head of the Archduke Ferdinand, pencil/pen/black ink on varnished paper, 12x7", C-NY 1/12/88 OE 4,400
NABERT, Wilhelm Julius August (German, 1830-1904)
Travelers in a Mediterranean Landscape, oil on canvas, sgn, 27x50", SBY 7/12/89 4,950
NADELMAN, Elie (American, 1882-1946)
Pair; Standing Man; Woman in Profile; pencil on lined paper, 9x5", C-E 2/1/89 4,620
Pair: Standing Woman; Studies of a Woman's Head; no media given, 6x3", 5x3", SBY 9/23/88 OE 2,090
NAEGELE, Charles Frederick (American, 1857-1944)
Reflecting Pool (Titianesque nude by pool, landscape beyond), oil on panel, sgn, 22x27", RWS 3/31/88 OE 1,800
NAGANO, Shozo (American/Japanese, 20th C)
Cube with Drape #2, acrylic on canvas laid down on panel, sgn/dtd 1980, 72x29", C-E 11/17/88 OE 2,420
Redemption #2, acrylic/white chalk on canvas laid down on panel, sgn/dtd 1980, 40x78", C-E 5/13/88 OE 2,640
NAGY, see De Nagy
NAHL, Perham Wilhelm (American, 1869-1935)
Silhouette (woman seated, reading by a window), oil on canvas, sgn/dtd 1921, 20x26", C-NY 12/2/88 OE 15,400
NAIVEU, Matthys; att (Dutch, 1647-1721)
Vanitas: Child Blowing Bubbles at a Window (w/a skull on the ledge); oil on canvas, 31x25", C-NY 5/31/89 8,800
NAKAGAWA, Hachiro (Japanese, 1877-1922)
Children at Play, oil on panel, sgn/dtd 1899, 20x16", SBY 7/12/89 3,850
NAKAMURA, Kazuo (Japanese, 1928-)
Landscape, Autumn 58; pen/ink, sgn/dtd 58, 15x21", WAD 11/30/89 450
Landscape, watercolor, sgn/dtd 62, 12x18", WAD 11/30/89 650
Landscape with Farm, watercolor, sgn, 18x13", WAD 6/12/89 500
NAKHOVA, Ira (Russian, 1955-)
Alphabet (opening doors in window-like frames), oil/tempera on 4 boards, sgn/dtd 1981, overall: 91x91", SBY 7/7/88 OE 9,600
Dyptich: Visual Boundaries (composition); oil on canvas, sgn/dtd 1980, overall: 39x79", SBY 7/7/88 5,000
Wall (composition), oil on canvas, sgn twice/dtd 78/titled/inscr, 59x79", SBY 7/7/88 OE 9,600
NAKIAN, Reuben (American, 1897-)
Europa & the Bull, watercolor on paper, sgn/dtd 77, 12x18", SBY 10/5/88 1,210
NAKKEN, Willem Carel (Dutch, 1835-1926)
Awaiting Carriage, oil on canvas, sgn/dtd 1867, 20x28", SBY 6/10/88 OE 9,075
Haying, oil on canvas, sgn, 21x30", WD 5/5/88 4,600
NAMATJIRA, Ewald (Australian, 1930-)
Central Australian Landscape, watercolor, sgn, 9x12", C-SK 6/9/88 316
NAN, Wen (Chinese, 1596-1667)
Figures in a Landscape (hand scroll), ink/color on silk, sgn/dtd 1637, 9x83", SBY 5/31/89 4,675
NANKIVELL, Fred (American, 1876-1950)
Fishermen (two men in dory), oil on canvas, sgn, 30x40", RAB 8/9/88 UE 1,600
NANTEUIL, Pierre; att (French, 1623-1678)
Portrait of a Nobleman, Presumably Jean Baptiste Budes, Compte de Guebriant; oil on canvas, 49x38", SBY 6/1/89 27,500
NANTEUIL, Pierre; circle of (French, 1623-1678)
Portrait of Louis XIV, bust-length, wearing embroidered coat with a lace collar; oil on canvas, 20x15", C-NY 4/6/89 UE 1,210
NAPOLETANO, Filippo (Italian, ca 1600-1640)
Boats Docking in a Harbor in a Mountainous Landscape, oil on canvas, 25x40", C-NY 10/12/89 7,700
NAPOLETANO, Filippo; circle of (ca 1600-1640)
Harbor Scene with Ships, Ruins, & Figures by an Archway; oil on panel, 16x22", SBY 4/7/88 7,150
NARDI, E. (Italian, 19th C)
Rug Sellers, watercolor/pencil heightened w/white on paper, sgn, 19x26", SBY 12/9/88 OE 7,700
NASH, Joanna (Canadian, 1949-)
California Lily (still life), oil on canvas, sgn, 54x29", FB 5/28/89 650
Summer Landscape, watercolor, sgn/dtd 1985, 21x29", FB 5/28/89 UE 260
Wrapped Iris, oil on canvas, sgn, 55x29", FB 10/17/88 900

NASH, Joseph (British, 1808-1878)
Drawing Room, Chastleton, Oxfordshire; watercolor/pencil/India ink on paper, sgn/dtd 1870, 13x19", SBY 7/12/89 ... 2,090

NASH, Manley Kerchaval
Park Scene, oil on board, sgn, 10x8", C-E 2/1/89 ... 2,640

NASI, G. (Italian, 19th C)
Messenger (figure in an interior), watercolor, sgn/dtd 1881, 20x14", C-E 5/22/89 ... 935

NASMYTH, Charlotte (British, 1804-)
On the Border of the New Forest Near Lymington Hampshire, oil on canvas, sgn, 15x19", DM 10/14/88 ... 2,000

NASMYTH, Patrick (British, 1787-1831)
View of Edinburgh Castle, oil on panel, sgn/dtd 1813, 12x16", C-E 5/23/88 OE ... 3,850

NASON, Pieter
Portrait of a Lady, Seated, in a Black Dress with White Collar & Cuffs; oil on canvas, 44x37", C-NY 10/12/89 ... 5,500

NATHAN, see De Nathan

NATKIN, Robert (American, 1930-)
Apollo Series (abstract), acrylic on paper, sgn, 1974, 23x30", C-NY 2/14/89 ... 1,870
Apollo Series (untitled), acrylic on canvas, sgn, 1973, 68x116", C-NY 5/4/88 OE ... 29,700
Apollo XI (abstract), acrylic on canvas, sgn, ca 1974, 1116x88", C-NY 11/10/88 ... 17,600
Bath, Apollo Series (abstract); acrylic on canvas, sgn, 1977, 19x22", SBY 10/5/88 ... 1,210
Bath Apollo (abstract), acrylic on canvas, ca 1974, 78x84", C-NY 10/4/89 ... 12,100
Bern Series (abstract), acrylic on canvas, sgn, 1980, 48x60", C-NY 2/14/89 ... 14,300
Bern Series (abstract), acrylic on canvas, sgn, 1980, 52x69", C-NY 5/4/88 ... 11,000
Bern Series (abstract), gouache on paper, sgn, 30x39", C-E 11/17/88 ... 2,420
Bern Series: Faust Laughter (abstract); acrylic on board, sgn, 1980, 40x60", C-E 11/17/88 OE ... 10,450
Faust Laughter (abstract), oil on canvas, sgn, 24x36", SBY 2/14/89 ... 4,675
Fieldmouse (abstract), oil on canvas, sgn, 60x72", C-NY 2/20/88 OE ... 16,500
Fieldmouse (abstract), oil on canvas, sgn/dtd 1969, 38x46", SBY 10/7/89 ... 8,800
Fieldmouse III (abstract), acrylic on paper mounted on board, sgn, 30x22", C-E 11/14/89 ... 2,200
Head of a Child, red chalk, inscr, 6x7", SBY 7/12/89 ... 1,650
Homage to FL Wright, oil on canvas, twice sgn/dtd 1966/titled, 72x60", C-NY 11/10/88 ... 12,100
Homage to Louis Sullivan & Frank Lloyd Wright, acrylic on canvas, sgn, 89x79", C-NY 2/14/89 ... 11,000
Intimate Lighting (abstract), acrylic on canvas, sgn/dtd 1972, 78x54", SBY 2/15/89 OE ... 15,400
Intimate Lighting Series (abstract), acrylic on canvas, sgn, 36x115", SBY 10/5/89 ... 16,500
Intimate Lighting Series #3 (abstract), acrylic/lithography on paper, sgn/dtd 1972, 30x22", C-E 11/14/89 ... 1,650
Intimate Lighting Suite #2 (abstract), acrylic on paper, sgn/dtd 1972, 30x22", C-E 11/17/88 ... 1,870
Lover's Tryst, Intimate Lighting (abstract); acrylic on canvas, sgn/dtd 1973, 18x40", SBY 2/15/89 ... 4,400
November Eve (abstract composition), acrylic on canvas, sgn/dtd 1971, 42x68", SBY 10/7/89 OE ... 14,300
Praise God (geometric composition), acrylic on canvas, sgn/dtd 1968, 88x78", SBY 2/15/89 UE ... 3,300
Redding View (abstract), acrylic on canvas, sgn, 33x55", C-E 11/14/89 ... 9,350
Redding View (abstract), oil on canvas, 34x55", C-NY 5/4/88 ... 8,250
Redding View #1 (abstract), acrylic on canvas, dtd 1972, 70x90", C-NY 10/4/89 ... 16,500
Scatting-For Louis Armstrong & Betty Carter; acrylic on canvas, sgn, 88x132", C-NY 11/10/88 OE ... 26,400
Untitled (abstract), acrylic on canvas, sgn, 1979, 72x96", SBY 10/8/88 ... 8,800
Untitled (abstract), acrylic on canvas, sgn, 1980, 35x48", C-NY 10/4/89 ... 4,950
Untitled (abstract), acrylic on canvas, sgn/dtd 1973, 43x52", SBY 10/5/89 ... 12,100
Untitled (abstract), acrylic on canvas, sgn/dtd 61, 90x61", C-E 11/17/88 ... 8,800
Untitled (abstract), acrylic on canvas, sgn/stamped signature/dtd 1980, 72x96", SBY 2/19/88 ... 11,000
Untitled (abstract), acrylic on paper, sgn/dtd 1979, 28x34", C-NY 2/14/89 ... 1,320
Untitled (abstract), acrylic on paper, 22x30", SBY 2/14/89 ... 1,540
Untitled (abstract), acrylic/watercolor on paper, sgn, 29x39", SBY 10/5/88 ... 1,760
Untitled (geometric composition), acrylic on canvas, sgn/dtd 1976, 42x22", C-E 11/14/89 ... 2,420

NATOIRE, Charles Joseph (French, 1700-1777)
Figures & Animals in the Colosseum, red & black chalk/pen/brown ink/gray wash, sgn/dtd 1758, 11x16", C-NY 1/11/89 OE ... 29,200
Figures on the Terrace of a Villa, chalk/pen/brown ink/watercolor/bodycolor on brown paper, sgn, 12x18", C-NY 1/11/89 OE ... 37,400
Youth Playing the Triangle, sanguine/white chalk on beige paper, 179x111", C-M 6/16/89 ... 16,300

ATOIRE, Charles Joseph; follower of (French, 1700-1777)
Reclining Female Figure, Possibly a River Goddess; black chalk/gray wash on blue paper, 10x15", SBY 1/13/89 OE ... 1,320

ATOIRE, Charles Joseph; manner of (French, 1700-1777)
Europa & the Bull, oil on canvas, 39x52", C-E 4/7/88 OE ... 7,480

ATTIER, Jean Marc (French, 1685-1766)
Portrait of Lady Said To Be Marquise de Boufflers...as a River Goddess...; oil on canvas, oval, 32x26", C-NY 5/31/89 OE ... 52,800
Portrait of Madame de Roissy, oil on canvas, sgn/dtd 1754, 31x25", SBY 1/12/89 OE ... 50,600

ATTIER, Jean Marc; follower of (French, 1685-1766)
Portrait of a Lady, oil on canvas, 26x20", SBY 7/12/89 ... 2,200
Portrait of a Lady Said To Be the Marquise de Marigny...As a River Goddess, oil on canvas, 38x31", SBY 4/7/89 OE ... 17,600
Woman Veiled in Black with Her Attendant Preparing To Depart, oil on canvas, unfr, 30x43", SBY 6/8/88 ... 1,045

ATTIER, Jean Marc; manner of (French, 1685-1766)
Portrait of a Lady, oil on canvas, 40x35", SBY 6/8/88 ... 1,760

ATTIER, Jean Marc; school of (French, 1685-1766)
Portrait of a Lady, standing on a balcony in a park; oil on canvas, 33x29", C-E 6/1/88 OE ... 4,180

NATTIER, Jean Marc; studio of (French, 1685-1766) 44,000
Portrait of Marquise d'Antin, Nee Francoise-Renee de Canisy, Later...; oil on canvas, unfr, 52x39", SBY 6/1/89 OE

NAUEZ, Joseph Francois (Belgian, 1787-1869) 1,500
Pair: Lady & Gentleman (portraits); oil on canvas, 43x30", FAP 11/4/88

NAUMAN, Bruce (American, 1941-)
Untitled (study of lips), ink/wash on paper, initialed/dtd 1967, 17x27", SBY 2/15/89 OE 27,500
White Anger, Red Danger, Yellow Peril, Black Death (abstract); acrylic/pencil, sgn/dtd 84, 50x38", SBY 2/15/89 OE 148,500

NAUMANN, Carl Georg (German, 1827-1902) 6,325
Freeing the Bird, oil on panel, sgn/dtd 1875, 11x7", SBY 2/22/89

NAUMER, Helmuth (American, 1907-) 1,430
Spring in Cerillos, New Mexico; pastel on board, sgn, 30x40", B/B 6/15/89

NAVARRA, Pietro (Italian, 17th/18th C) 24,200
Grapes, Figs, Pomegranates, & a Watermelon in a Landscape; oil on canvas, 24x33", C-NY 10/20/88

NAVARRO, Enrique (Spanish, 20th C) 358
Hansom Cab in the Snow, oil on canvas, sgn, 26x22", B/B 1/11/89

NAVEZ, Francois Joseph (Belgian, 1767-1869) 11,000
Portrait of a Lady with a Letter, oil on canvas, sgn/dtd 1827, 28x24", SBY 10/24/89

NAVLET, Joseph (French, 1821-1889) 7,150
Arrival of the Infantry, oil on canvas, sgn, 20x35", C-NY 10/25/89

NAVRATIL, Joseph (Czechoslovakian, 1798-1865) 440
Figures in a Boat on a Lake, gouache on paper, sgn, 9x11", B/B 12/8/88

NAVROS, David 2,200
Untitled (geometric composition), acrylic on paper, initialed/dtd 70, 12x16", SBY 2/15/89

NAZARENKO, Tatiana (Russian, 1944-) 8,400
Dyptich: The Town at Night (surrealistic); oil on canvas, sgn/1 dtd 1988/inscr, ea 36x36", SBY 7/7/88

NEALE, M. Hall (British, fl 1910-1960) 770
Casino Garden, oil on panel, 8x11", C-E 6/1/88

Neapolitan School (17th C)
Ascension, oil on canvas, 26x19", SBY 7/12/89 1,650
Christ & the Three Marys, oil on canvas, 25x19", SBY 4/7/88 3,300
Flowers in a Vase, Fruit in a Basket & Vegetables on a Ledge; oil on canvas, 27x34", C-NY 10/12/89 OE 17,600
Man on a Horse Riding Across a Battlefield, pen/brown ink/wash heightened w/white, 15x12", SBY 12/9/88 880
Pair: Mercury & Argus; Zephyr & Flora; oil on canvas, irregular shape, 36x58", SBY 4/7/88 OE 9,900
Torment of Christ, oil on canvas, unfr, 15x18", SBY 12/9/88 UE 1,100
Woman Preparing To Bathe by Candlelight, oil on canvas, 36x52", SBY 1/12/89 OE 30,800

Neapolitan School (18th C)
Architectural Capriccio with Figures, oil on canvas, 35x49", SBY 10/13/89 OE 13,200
Pair: Still Lifes of Melons & Fruits; oil on canvas, 28x40", SBY 10/21/88 OE 55,000
Pair: Views of a Harbor Town, Possibly Naples or Messina; oil on canvas, 17x38", SBY 4/7/88 OE 36,300
Portrait of a Gentleman in an Elaborately Embroidered Coat, oil on canvas, 48x38", SBY 10/13/89 7,150
Seleucus Presenting His Wife, Stratonike, to His Son, Antiochus, for Marriage; oil on canvas, 22x15", SBY 4/7/89 2,750
The Pentecost, oil on canvas, 39x29", C-NY 10/12/89 2,420
Vision of Saint Anthony, oil on canvas, 36x28", SBY 10/21/88 1,650

Neapolitan School (19th C)
Barque Aberdeen in Open Seas (ship), gouache on paper, 15x25", RWS 6/10/89 OE 1,800
Bay of Naples, gouache, 9x13", C-E 10/25/88 1,045
Brig Nancy Ann & Mount Vernon of Salem in the Bay of Naples, gouache/pen/black ink, inscr, 20x28", C-NY 5/25/88 1,540
Margelliina-The Bay of Naples; gouache on board, 12x18", C-E 2/23/88 825
Napoli da Carmine (coastline view of city/boats), gouache, titled, 21x28", C-NY 2/23/89 OE 4,180
Napoli da Mare: View of Naples Surrounded by Views of Environs; gouache, 17 framed together, 20x27", C-NY 2/23/89 OE 7,700
Set of 3: Casa di Diomeda; Palata de Scari d'Excolano; Ferni a Molino; watercolor, unfr, 5x8", C-NY 10/31/89 UE 121

NEBBIA, Cesare (Italian, ca 1536-1614) 4,400
Holy Ghost Descending on Soldiers Outside a Town, pen/brown ink/wash, squared in black chalk, 7x7", SBY 1/13/89

NEBEL, Otto (German, 1892-)
Noch Vow Ostern (abstract composition), gouache/ink on paper, sgn/inscr/#d U 2.222, 1947, 20x14", PHL 11/15/88 3,500
Violette Konfiguration, gouache/pen/black ink on paper laid down on paper, sgn/dtd 1940, 10x5", C-E 5/9/89 OE 2,420

NEEDHAM, Charles Austin (American, 1844-1922) 550
Boats in a Harbor, watercolor/gouache on paper, sgn, 10x14", B/B 4/20/88

NEEFFS, Pieter the elder (Flemish, 1578-1658) 66,000
Cathedral Interior with Figures, oil on panel, 18x27", C-NY 1/11/89

NEEFFS, Pieter the elder; circle of (1578-1658) 4,675
Interior of a Church with Elegant Figures, oil on panel, 13x17", SBY 10/21/88

NEER, see Van Der Neer

NEHER, Caspar (German, 1897-1962) 605
IRA-Study for Mahogonny; yellow/gray wash on paper, 14x10", C-NY 10/6/88

NEILSON, Raymond Perry Rodgers (American, 1881-1964) 1,760
Young Madonna, oil on canvas, 30x24", C-E 11/30/88

NEIMAN, Leroy (American, 1926-)
Jockey (standing in profile), acrylic on board, sgn/dtd 69, 28x16", C-E 2/3/88 OE 7,150
Pair: B Hull, Madison Square Garden November 26.66; Linebacker Waskiewicz; pen/ink on paper, sgn, 15x12", WG 10/19/88 UE 1,500

NEIMANN, Edmund John Sr. (British, 1813-1876)
On the Severn (coastal view), oil on canvas, 14x37", B/B 5/17/89 UE 770

NEIMEYER, John Henry (American, 1839-1932)
Apple Blossom Time (blooming trees), watercolor on paper, sgn, 11x8", RAB 8/9/88 UE 200

NEL-DUMOUCHEL, Jules (French, 19th C)
Celestial Choir, oil on canvas, sgn/dtd 85, shaped, unfr, no size given, WD 3/23/88 900

NELLIUS, Martinus (Dutch, 1670-1706)
Raspberries & Strawberries in Porcelain Bowls on a Table Covered with a White Cloth, oil, 18x16", C-NY 10/12/89 12,100

NELSON, George Laurence (American, 1887-1978)
Cataracts, Connecticut (waterfall in landscape); oil on canvas, sgn/dtd 1908, 25x30", RWS 3/16/89 OE 1,200

NELSON, Joan (20th C)
Untitled, charcoal on paper, sgn/dtd 1984, 23x30", SBY 2/15/89 3,850
Untitled (building w/no roof, uphill path, fence posts), egg tempera on masonite, sgn/dtd 1984, 24x18", SBY 5/3/89 11,000

NELSON, John McKerdy
Sunset at Williams Town, oil on canvas, sgn twice/titled, 8x12", C-SK 6/9/88 280

NEME, Clarel (Latin American, 20th C)
Cocktail (cocktail hour gathering of doll-like figures), oil on canvas, sgn, 1988, 69x55", SBY 5/16/89 8,250
Dolls Running, oil on canvas, sgn, 1978, 38x51", SBY 5/17/88 4,950
Figures (doll-like figures, motorcycle in interior), oil on canvas, sgn, 1978, 51x38", SBY 11/21/88 5,500

NEMETH, Frank (Canadian, 1919-)
Begonia with Book, oil on board, sgn/dtd 1983, 18x14", FB 10/17/88 650

NEMUKHIN, Vladimir (Russian, 1925-)
Playing Cards Table: Version N 2 (abstract); acrylic/collage on canvas, sgn twice/dtd 86 twice, 47x39", SBY 7/7/88 8,000
Still Life with Cards (abstract), acrylic/collage on canvas, sgn twice/dtd 1986-88 twice, 47x39", SBY 7/7/88 8,000

NEOGRADY, Antal (Hungarian, 1861-1942)
Cows Grazing, oil on canvas, sgn, 28x20", B/B 5/17/89 UE 275

NEOGRADY, Laszlo (Hungarian, 1900-)
Autumn River, oil on masonite, sgn, 13x24", RAB 8/9/88 UE 650
Depicting Two Girls Tending Flock of Geese, oil on canvas, sgn, 24x30", MAG 9/18/88 UE 1,800
Feeding the Ducks, oil on canvas, sgn, 25x30", C-E 10/26/89 1,650
Feeding the Geese, oil on canvas, sgn, 24x30", B/B 3/17/88 3,300
Garden Bench, oil on canvasboard, sgn, 10x14", B/B 5/17/89 OE 1,540
Maidens with Geese, oil on canvas, sgn, 23x31", B/B 3/17/88 3,300
Pair: Artist's Garden; oil on board, sgn, 10x14", B/B 6/9/88 1,760
Pair: Scenes with Peasant Woman & Geese; oil on board, sgn, 8x13", B/B 10/9/88 2,200
Pair: Woman on a Country Lane; Woman by a Farmhouse; watercolor/gouache on paper, sgn, 11x16"; 12x17", B/B 12/8/88 715
Peasant Girl with a Flock of Ducks, oil on canvas, sgn, 24x30", B/B 10/9/88 2,750
Peasants with Their Ducks by a Stream, oil on canvas, sgn, 24x30", SBY 12/9/88 2,200
Quiet Courtyard, oil on canvas, sgn, 13x17", WG 4/23/89 OE 1,600
Snow Mountains, oil on canvas, sgn, 24x30", C-E 5/23/88 1,100
Snow-Covered Forest in the Mountains, oil on canvas, sgn, 24x30", SBY 7/12/89 1,320
Sunlit Flower Garden, oil on canvas, sgn, 23x31", C-NY 2/23/89 6,050
Torchure (nude figures tied to stake), oil on canvas, sgn/dtd 924 (sic), 48x28", C-E 2/21/89 UE 220
Two Girls Resting by a Flowing Stream, oil on canvas, sgn, 24x32", C-E 5/22/89 UE 1,100
Village Stream, oil on canvas, sgn, 24x36", SBY 7/12/89 2,750
Wooded Landscape with Foreground Stream & Waterfall, oil on canvas, sgn, 24x32", SLK 2/12/88 350

NEOH, Anna T. (Canadian, 1926-)
Seal Hunters on Baffin Island, acrylic, sgn/dtd 1970, 12x16", FB 4/25/88 800

NEPOTE, Alexander (American, 1913-)
Fog Over Half Moon Bay, watercolor on paper, sgn, 15x22", B/B 10/6/88 1,540

NERI, F.
Putti Drawing with an Arrow, watercolor, sgn, 10x13", C-NY 2/25/88 1,650

NERI, Manuel (American, 20th C)
Pisano #55 1985, mixed media on paper, 27x22", B/B 12/8/88 3,025

NESBITT, Lowell (American, 1933-)
Antenna (one of a series based on space program), oil on canvas, sgn/dtd 70, 46x36", C-E 11/14/89 1,210
Dark Red Rose, oil on canvas, sgn/inscr/dtd 79, 24x24", C-E 5/13/88 1,045
Female Nude in Profile (Homage to Jack Mitchell), oil on canvas, sgn/dtd 70, 75x50", SBY 2/14/89 1,760
From the Garden (assorted fruits & vegetables), oil on canvas, sgn/dtd 79, 36x36", SBY 2/14/89 OE 4,125
IBM Magnetic Storage Drum (detailed rendering), oil on canvas, sgn/dtd 66, 60x48", SBY 2/14/89 UE 2,750
Iris on Gray, acrylic on canvas, sgn/dtd 69, 24x24", SBY 2/14/89 1,320
Joseph Raffael's Studio (view of drawing table), oil on canvas, sgn/dtd 67, 59x72", C-E 11/17/88 2,420
Lillium Candidum, oil on canvas, sgn/dtd 77, 50x36", C-E 11/14/89 OE 5,500
Rose Tulip, oil on canvas, sgn/dtd 72, 36x28", C-E 11/17/88 1,430
Studio Window with Palm, oil on canvas, sgn/dtd 75, 40x40", WL 5/20/88 OE 1,600
Three Yellow Iris, acrylic on canvas, sgn/dtd 1986, 30x22", C-E 11/14/89 1,760
White Iris, oil on canvas, sgn/dtd 65, 77x77", SBY 10/7/89 7,100
White Iris on Ivory, oil on canvas, sgn/inscr/dtd 78, 20x20", C-E 5/13/88 1,210
1930s Room (interior), oil on canvas, sgn/dtd 69/titled, 24x14", C-E 5/9/89 OE 990

ESTEROVA, Natalia (Russian, 1944-)
Carrousel in the Sand (contemporary), oil on canvas, sgn/dtd 1987, 51x67", SBY 7/7/88 13,000

Game of People: Cards (surrealistic); oil on canvas, sgn/dtd 1987, 47x59", SBY 7/7/88 .... **14,000**
NETER, see De Neter
Netherlandish School (16th C)
Madonna & Child in a Landscape, oil on panel, 21x15", SBY 4/7/89 OE **44,000**
Pair: Saint John the Baptist; Saint John the Evangelist; oil on panel, 17x7", SBY 7/12/89 OE **6,600**
Traveler on a Path in a Wooded Bluff, black chalk/pen/brown ink, inscr/eagle wm, 7x8", C-NY 1/12/88 .... **2,420**
NETSCHER, Caspar (1639-1684)
Portrait of a Lady, standing, three-quarter length...; oil on panel, unfr, 12x10", C-NY 1/11/89 .... **8,250**
NETSCHER, Caspar; att (1639-1684)
Allegorical Portrait of Hortense Mancini, Duchesse De Mazarin; oil on canvas, inscr, 48x34", SBY 10/21/88 OE **24,200**
NETSCHER, Constantyn (Dutch, 1668-1723)
Portrait of a Gentleman & His Wife Seated Beside Him Between Their Two Daughters; oil on canvas, 32x25", C-NY 10/20/88 .... **4,400**
NETSCHER, Constantyn; att (Dutch, 1668-1723)
Portrait of a Gentleman Said To Be the Dramatist & Architect Sir John Vanbrugh; oil on canvas, 20x17", C-NY 4/8/88 .... **2,420**
NETSCHER, Constantyn; circle of (Dutch, 1668-1723)
Portrait of a Gentleman, wearing brocaded costume, holding a letter; oil on canvas, inscr, 30x25", C-NY 10/20/88 .... **1,980**
NETSCHER, Constantyn; school of (Dutch, 1668-1723)
Set of 4: Portraits of Man, Woman, Girl, & Young Child; oil on canvas, oval, 23x19", C-NY 4/6/89 .... **1,950**
NETTLETON, Walter (American, 1867-1936)
Birch Tree (in snowy landscape), oil on board, sgn/dtd 26, 11x14", SBY 9/14/89 .... **2,750**
Snow in the Pines, oil on canvas, sgn/dtd 1921, 32x40", RWS 5/19/88 .... **1,000**
NEUBERT, Ludwig (German, 1846-1892)
Bavarian Farmhouse in an Extensive Landscape, oil on canvas, sgn, 13x21", C-E 2/21/89 OE **2,860**
NEUHUYS, Albert (Dutch, 1844-1914)
La Famille, oil on canvas, 48x38", C-NY 5/25/88 .... **4,620**
NEUHUYS, Joseph Hendrikus (Dutch, 1841-1889)
Woman at the Spinning Wheel, oil on panel, sgn/dtd 1877, 20x16", C-E 10/25/88 .... **3,080**
NEUMAN, Ernest (Canadian, 1907-1955)
Seminary of Philosophy, oil on board, sgn/dtd 1953, 20x26", FB 10/30/89 .... **880**
Street Scene, oil on board, sgn/dtd 1955, 20x26", FB 4/25/88 .... **950**
Un Moment de Tranquilite, oil on board, sgn, 18x24", FB 10/30/89 .... **605**
NEUMANN, Alexander
Figures at the Well, oil on canvas, sgn/dtd 02, 38x46", C-E 2/23/88 .... **1,980**
NEUMANN, Johan Jens (Danish, 1860-1940)
Danish Ship, Prins Christian Frederik, Engaged in Battle...; oil on canvas, sgn/dtd 1901, 34x53", SBY 7/12/89 .... **3,850**
NEUQUELMAN, Lucien (French, 1909-)
Ile de Brehat, Baie de la Corderio; oil on canvas, sgn twice, 18x24", SBY 10/5/88 .... **3,575**
NEUSTATTER, Ludwig (German, 1829-1899)
Chasing a Mouse (children in an interior), oil on panel, sgn, 14x10", SBY 7/12/89 .... **7,150**
NEUVILLE, see De Neuville
NEVELSON, Louise (American, 1900-)
Head of a Woman, watercolor on paper, sgn, 19x13", SBY 10/5/88 .... **1,650**
Pair: Figure Sketches; 1 pen/ink, 1 pencil on paper; sgn, 5x4" & smaller, C-E 6/1/88 .... **715**
Set of 7: Untitled, 3 pen/black ink on paper, 4 pencil on paper, ea sgn/1 dtd 1956, unfr, 22x15" & smaller, C-E 11/17/88 .... **5,500**
Two Nudes, pen/ink on paper, sgn, 12x8", SBY 10/5/88 .... **1,540**
Two Standing Nudes, pen/ink on paper, sgn, 18x8", SBY 10/5/88 .... **1,540**
Untitled (abstract horses), ink on paper, sgn/inscr/dtd 1930, 11x15", SBY 10/5/88 UE **990**
NEVIL, E.W. (British, 19th C)
17th-Century Street Scene with the Cathedral in the Background, watercolor, sgn/titled, 30x20", SLK 5/9/88 .... **325**
NEVILL, Eunice M. (British, 19th/20th C)
Pair: Antwerp; Brussels; watercolor, sgn, 11x8", C-E 10/26/89 .... **880**
Summer Garden (cottage scene), watercolor/gouache, 11x14", C-E 2/21/89 .... **1,100**
New Zealand School (19th C)
Capel Valley, Lake Wakatipu From Von's Gorge; pencil/watercolor, monogramed/dtd 1875, 12x28", C-SK 5/25/89 .... **1,840**
Maori Pa (view of native village), oil on canvas, 12x14", C-SK 6/9/88 OE **2,045**
Uncle William's New Store, Wellington (street scene); watercolor, titled/inscr 1876, 9x14", C-SK 5/25/89 OE **8,270**
NEWELL, George Glenn (American, 1870-1947)
Country Landscape, oil on canvas, sgn, 12x16", LH 5/15/88 UE **50**
Heading for the High Pasture, oil on canvas, sgn, 42x35", B/B 12/8/88 .... **1,980**
Loading Wood, oil on canvas, sgn/dtd 1920, 20x24", C-E 10/18/89 .... **2,750**
NEWELL, Hugh (American, 1830-1915)
Barnyard Scene, oil on canvas, 16x20", C-E 10/18/89 .... **1,430**
Conversation in an Interior, oil on canvas, sgn, unfr, 16x20", C-E 10/25/88 .... **1,100**
NEWMAN, Barnett (American, 1905-1970)
Euclidian Abyss, oil/gouache on canvasboard, sgn, 1946-47, 28x22", SBY 11/8/89 .... **704,000**
Moment II (abstract w/two vertical yellow lines), acrylic on canvas, initialed/dtd 69, 84x72", C-NY 2/23/89 .... **990,000**
Promise (black canvas w/two lines running vertical), oil on canvas, sgn/dtd twice 1949, 51x68", SBY 11/10/88 .... **1,650,000**
Untitled (two lines within a square), oil on canvas, 1949, 30x39", SBY 11/8/89 .... **770,000**
NEWMAN, Henry Roderick (American, 1833-1918)
Among the Ruins, watercolor on paper laid down, sgn/dtd Philae 19 Jan 1893, 26x17", C-NY 9/28/89 .... **13,200**
Ruins at Philae, watercolor on paper laid down on board, sgn/dtd 1894, 27x17", WD 1/11/89 .... **4,000**

Ruins at Philae, watercolor on paper mounted on panel, sgn/dtd Philae 1905/inscr, 26x17", SBY 3/17/88 OE 9,350
Statue of Justice, watercolor/pencil on paper, sgn/dtd 1880, 25x14", C-NY 12/2/88 6,600
View of Florence, watercolor/gouache/pencil on paper, 16x12", SBY 3/17/88 2,860

EWMAN, Robert Lofton (American, 1827-1912)
Fortune Teller, oil on canvas, sgn, 10x14", C-NY 9/30/88 5,720
Fortune Teller, oil on canvas, 12x18", C-NY 9/30/88 2,640

EWTON, Gilbert Stuart (American, 1794-1835)
Impatient Suitor, 25x20", WD 3/23/88 1,800
Lover's Quarrel, oil on panel, 11x9", SBY 7/12/89 660

EWTON, Herbert H. (British, 1881-)
Summer Landscape, oil on canvas, sgn/dtd 1952, 21x28", B/B 8/10/88 770

EWTON, Richard Jr.
Portrait of Mimi P Stillman, oil on canvas, sgn, unfr, 36x29", C-E 6/28/88 UE 200

EYLAND, Harry (American, 1877-1958)
Breakfast Time (chickens feeding in village street), oil on canvas, sgn/dtd 1904, 20x14", SBY 9/14/89 3,575
Etalage de Livres (people in a landscape), oil on board, sgn/dtd 1928, 10x6", C-E 6/1/89 3,520

EYMARK, Gustave Mardoche (French, 1850-)
Mounted Officer, oil on panel, sgn, 16x13", SBY 12/9/88 880
Pair: Mares & Foals in a Pasture; oil on canvas, sgn, 20x26", SBY 6/10/88 3,850

EYTS, Gillis (Flemish, 1623-1687)
Extensive Landscape with a Castle & a Distant View of a Town, oil on panel, sgn, 11x15", SBY 6/3/88 12,100
Mountainous Landscape with House & Tower by a Road, pen/brown ink/brown wash, sgn in monogram, 8x12", C-NY 1/12/88 4,950

IBBS, Richard Henry (British, 1816-1893)
Figures in an Interior, oil on canvas, sgn, 16x24", B/B 12/8/88 1,045

IBLETT, Gary (American, 1943-)
After the Rain, oil on canvas, sgn/inscr/copyrighted/dtd 79, 16x20", SBY 9/23/88 2,640
Alta Vista, oil on canvas, sgn/copyrighted/dtd 74, 24x30", SBY 9/23/88 OE 4,950
Branding, oil on canvas, sgn twice/copyrighted, 20x30", SBY 9/23/88 2,860
Extra Mounts, oil on canvas, sgn twice/copyrighted/indistinctly dtd, 22x28", SBY 9/23/88 4,125
Taos Man, oil on canvas, sgn twice/copyrighted/titled, 22x28", SBY 9/23/88 7,150
Trance (portrait of an Indian), watercolor/gouache, sgn/inscr/copyrighted/dtd 81, 19x25", SBY 9/23/88 1,430

ICCOLO, see Di Niccolo

ICE, Don (American, 1932-)
Alaska Totem: Walker Cove; oil on linen/watercolor on paper in 3 parts, sgn/dtd 82, 108x72", SBY 10/5/89 8,800
Camels, (cigarette package), watercolor on paper, sgn/dtd 75, 38x24", SBY 2/15/89 OE 6,050
Cape Cod Farm Lamb Study, pencil/watercolor on paper, sgn/dtd 1969/titled, 18x26", SBY 11/11/88 OE 2,475
Radishes, acrylic on canvas, sgn/inscr/dtd 66, 60x50", C-E 5/13/88 1,430

ICHOLAS, David (American, 20th C)
Still Life of Oranges, oil on canvas, sgn, 16x21", FAP 12/8/89 UE 100

ICHOLAS, Thomas (American, 1934-)
Autumn Birches, watercolor/graphite on paper, sgn, 8x10", RWS 9/8/89 UE 200

ICHOLL, Charles Wynn (Irish, 1831-1903)
Hopes & Fears (man & woman on a bridge in a landscape), oil on canvas, sgn, 36x44", SBY 7/12/89 UE 3,850

ICHOLL, T.J. (American, 19th C)
Mahoning Welcome, oil on canvas, sgn/dtd 1879, 20x30", WG 9/16/88 700

ICHOLLS, Bertram (British, 1883-)
Shand, St Clements Danes; oil on canvas, sgn, 27x30", FAP 11/4/88 OE 3,100

ICHOLLS, Burr H. (American, 1848-1915)
All He Surveys (hens & rooster in barnyard scene), oil on canvas, sgn, 13x18", RWS 3/31/88 800
An Old New England Bridge, oil on canvas, sgn/dtd 1887, 28x44", SBY 5/25/88 17,600
Feeding the Chickens (small girl before stone building), oil on canvas, sgn, 20x24", RAB 8/9/88 2,500
Forest Road (summer landscape), oil on academy board, sgn, 9x6", RAB 11/25/88 375
Glimpse of a Garden: Venice (foreground canal reflects enclosed garden); oil on artist board, sgn, 12x9", RWS 9/29/88 450
Red Door, Venice (arched doorway along canal, partial view of a gondola); oil on canvas, sgn, 20x14", RAB 8/9/88 OE 2,500
Red Door, Venice; oil on canvas, sgn, 20x14", RAB 8/9/88 OE 2,500
Road Near East Hampton, New Hampshire (with small cottage), oil on canvas, sgn, 24x20", RAB 8/9/88 1,000
Road Near Lockport (landscape), oil on academy board, sgn/titled, 9x12", RAB 11/25/88 850
Summer Landscape with Pond, oil on canvas, sgn, 24x36", SBY 4/14/89 5,500

ICHOLLS, George F. (British, 1885-1937)
Conversation (village scene w/ladies conversing), watercolor, sgn, 10x14", C-E 2/21/89 1,430
Women Stopping To Talk on a Village Road, watercolor, sgn, 11x9", C-E 2/21/89 770

ICHOLLS, Rhoda Holmes (American, 1854-1930)
Woman Sewing by Open Window, watercolor on paper, sgn, 13x10", SBY 9/14/89 2,750

ICHOLS, Abel (American, 19th C)
River Landscape with Figures, oil on canvas, sgn/dtd 1846(?), 11x14", SBY 1/24/89 1,100

ICHOLS, Dale William (American, 1904-)
Evening Before the Witches Ride (figures carrying pumpkins to barn), oil on canvas, sgn, 24x30", C-NY 9/28/89 9,350
Heading Home in the Snow (figure in winter landscape w/buildings), oil on canvas, sgn/dtd 1962, 24x30", SBY 3/17/88 5,940
Horse & Sleigh #11 (snow-covered farmstead w/figures in sleigh), oil on canvas, 30x40", RAB 8/8/89 8,000
WPA, Planting Young Trees (men & tree, farm landscape beyond); watercolor/gouache on paper, sgn, RWS 3/31/88 OE 2,000

NICHOLS, Dale William; att (American, 1904-)
American Farm Scene, Winter Evening; oil on canvas, 18x25", S/A 3/12/88 ... 200
Farmhouse & Barn, oil on canvas, sgn/dtd 34, 20x24", SBY 6/28/89 OE ... 6,600
NICHOLS, H.D. (American, 1859-)
California Mission-Style Building with Garden in the Foreground, oil on canvas, sgn/dtd 1930, 18x24", MAG 6/22/89 ... 200
NICHOLS, Henry Hobart (American, 1869-1962)
Indian Summer (forest scene w/woman picking foliage), oil on canvas, 31x25", DM 9/16/88 ... 2,000
New England Winter (landscape w/stone bridge, house & hills), oil on masonite, sgn, 22x18", RWS 9/8/89 OE ... 2,800
New Hampshire Winter (hilly landscape), oil on canvas, sgn, 39x43", C-NY 5/25/89 ... 11,000
Rising Storm (autumn landscape), oil on canvas, sgn/dtd 97, 20x16", RWS 11/10/89 ... 1,600
Seaside, oil on canvas, sgn, 14x18", C-NY 9/30/88 ... 6,600
Snow Fall, oil on canvas, titled, 25x30", C-NY 9/28/89 ... 14,300
Snowbound (farmstead w/mountains in distance), oil on canvas, sgn, 25x30", C-NY 9/28/89 ... 4,950
Springtime on the Marshes, oil on canvas, sgn, 16x20", B/B 6/15/89 ... 2,475
NICHOLS, William (20th C)
July Morning (landscape), acrylic on canvas, sgn/inscr/dtd 1978, 60x80", SBY 2/15/89 ... 22,000
NICHOLSON, Ben (British, 1894-1982)
August 1960 (Burnt Umber & Venetian Red), oil/pencil on masonite relief, 20x21", SBY 10/7/88 ... 46,750
Bishop's Glass (abstract drawing), watercolor/pencil on paper, sgn/dtd 72, 11x15", SBY 10/6/89 OE ... 16,500
Goblet & Vase, oil/graphite on panel, sgn/dtd 1955, 11x10", SBY 11/9/89 OE ... 60,500
Goblets (cigar box), oil on panel laid down on masonite, sgn/dtd/titled, 1951, 7x9", C-NY 11/16/88 ... 38,500
Holkham Sands (abstract composition), pencil/wash on paper, sgn/dtd 73, 15x15", SBY 5/3/89 ... 18,700
Jug & Oval (abstract drawing), watercolor/pencil on paper, sgn/dtd 73, 16x11", SBY 10/6/89 OE ... 13,200
March 14, 1952 (WBG) (abstract); oil on canvas, sgn/dtd 1952/titled, 23x39", SBY 11/12/88 ... 286,000
November 1960 (Winter Stone abstract), oil on carved pavatex board, sgn/dtd 60, 16x20", SBY 2/15/89 OE ... 96,250
Untitled (abstract), pencil/wash on paper, 14x14", SBY 11/12/88 ... 17,600
Urbino (abstract), gouache/ink wash/pen/black ink on paper, sgn/dtd 1965, 8x7", C-NY 5/12/88 OE ... 15,400
NICHOLSON, E.F. (American, 19th C)
Schooner in a Storm, oil on canvas, sgn, 15x20", RAB 8/1/89 UE ... 300
NICHOLSON, George W. (American, 1832-1912)
Arab Market, oil on panel, sgn, 24x20", FAP 11/4/88 ... 1,100
Arab Market Scene, oil on canvas, sgn, 40x30", SBY 1/24/89 ... 3,850
Awaiting the Ships, oil on canvas, sgn, 28x50", C-NY 9/30/88 ... 4,620
Cabin by the Falls, oil on panel, sgn, 16x11", WL 5/20/88 UE ... 275
Cows on Path, oil on panel, sgn, 20x30", C-E 2/3/88 ... 1,540
Dutch Landscape with Figures, oil on canvas, sgn, 12x22", SBY 6/24/88 OE ... 2,530
Fisherfolk by the Sea, gouache on paper, sgn, 10x14", B/B 9/15/88 ... 715
Morning on the Lake, oil on panel, sgn, 12x19", SBY 6/24/88 ... 2,200
Out To Do Chores, oil on unstretched canvas, sgn, 11x15", B/B 9/15/88 ... 605
River Landscape, oil on canvas, sgn, 12x16", SBY 6/24/88 OE ... 2,860
Village Marketplace, watercolor on paper, sgn, 15x11", B/B 9/15/88 ... 358
Village on the Shore, watercolor on paper, sgn, 11x16", B/B 9/15/88 ... 605
NICHOLSON, John (British, 1832-1915)
View of Gibraltar, with...Shipping, Customs House at Left; watercolor/crayon/oil on paper, 1870s, 23x42", SBY 1/28/88 OE ... 16,500
NICKELSEN, Ralf Edgar (American, 1903-)
Still Life of Lemons & Blue Glass, oil on canvas, sgn/inscr WPA 727, 20x24", RWS 3/16/89 ... 350
NICKLE, Lawrence (Canadian, 1931-)
Baldhead River, Algoma; oil on board, sgn/dtd 68, 10x12", WAD 11/30/89 ... 250
NICOLIE, Paul Emile (Belgian, 1828-1894)
Leisurely Afternoon, oil on cradled panel, sgn/dtd 1860, unfr, 16x23", SBY 6/8/88 ... 2,420
NICOLL, James Craig (American, 1846-1918)
Pond at Dusk, watercolor on paper, sgn/dtd 1890, 24x33", C-E 3/22/88 OE ... 715
NICOLLE, Victor Jean (French, 1754-1770)
Pair: View of Interior of Church of Selle-en-Harmois; View of Porch of a Church; oil, sgn, 69x47", C-M 6/16/89 ... 2,607
Shepherd Reading an Antique Inscription, watercolor over pen/reddish-brown ink, 6x9", SBY 1/13/89 ... 1,430
NICZKY, Eduard (German, 1850-1919)
Gathering Spring Blossoms (woman in landscape), oil on canvas, sgn, 17x10", SBY 2/22/89 OE ... 8,800
Portrait of a Young Woman, oil on panel, sgn/dtd 78, 8x6", RWS 5/19/88 ... 500
NIELSEN, Carl (Norwegian, 1848-1908)
Boaters on a Norwegian Fjord, oil on canvas, sgn/dtd 1889, 12x10", B/B 4/20/88 ... 1,650
NIEMAN, Leroy (20th C)
Longchamp, felt-tip pen on paper, sgn/dtd 1960, 12x8", SBY 10/5/88 OE ... 715
NIEMANN, Edmund John Jr. (British, 19th C)
View in Yorkshire, oil on canvas laid down on board, sgn, 20x30", SBY 6/8/88 ... 1,760
NIEMANN, Edmund John Jr.; att (British, 19th C)
View of the River Swall, oil on canvas, sgn, 20x30", FAP 11/4/88 ... 1,700
NIEMANN, Edmund John Sr. (British, 1813-1876)
Country Path with a Village in the Distance, oil on canvas, sgn, 20x30", C-E 5/23/88 ... 3,520
Landscape with a Castle in the Distance, oil on canvas, sgn, 24x42", C-NY 5/25/88 ... 5,500
Richmond Castle, Yorkshire; oil on canvas, sgn, 20x36", SBY 2/22/89 ... 9,900
View of Richmond, Yorkshire; oil on canvas, sgn/inscr, 30x50", WD 11/16/88 OE ... 3,500

NIEMANN, Edmund John Sr.; att (British, 1813-1876)
Figures on a Road Outside a Town, oil on canvas, 24x36", SBY 12/9/88 OE 3,850
NIEMANN, Edward H. (British, 19th C)
On the Wharf (figure in a landscape), oil on canvas, indistinctly sgn, 24x42", SBY 12/9/88 4,125
Pair: Riverscapes; oil on canvas, sgn, 12x23", MG 10/28/88 550
NIEMEYER, John Henry (American, 1839-1932)
Apple Blossom Time (trees in bloom), watercolor on paper, sgn, 11x8", RAB 8/9/88 UE 200
Lakeside Village, oil on canvas, sgn/dtd 1905, 20x26", B/B 10/9/88 6,050
NIERMAN, Leonardo (Mexican, 20th C)
Bird Fury, acrylic on board, sgn/dtd 66, 18x48", B/B 12/8/88 1,650
The Firebird, oil on canvas, sgn/dtd 64, 24x16", DM 10/14/88 500
NIETO, Rudolfo (Latin American, 20th C)
Composicion en Azul, oil on canvas, sgn/dtd Julio 1965, 29x24", C-NY 11/21/89 3,520
Composicion en Rojo, oil on canvas, sgn, 1965, 29x24", C-NY 11/21/89 3,520
Composition Abstraite, oil on canvas, sgn twice/dtd 62, 39x29", C-E 5/13/88 990
El Astronomo (abstract), gouache/watercolor on paper, sgn, 28x39", C-NY 11/21/88 4,950
Flautista (abstract flutist), gouache/watercolor on paper, sgn, 39x28", C-NY 11/21/88 OE 6,600
Untitled (abstract), oil on canvas, sgn, 1963, 49x47", SBY 11/21/88 11,000
NIEULANDT, see Van Nieulandt
NIJLAND, Gesina Christina (Dutch, 1937-)
Village in Winter, oil on canvas, 16x20", B/B 1/11/89 660
NIKEL, Lea (Russian, 1918-)
Still Life (abstract), oil on canvas, sgn/dtd 1950, 20x26", SBY 5/30/89 OE 8,800
Untitled Composition (abstract), oil on canvas, sgn/dtd 1973, 29x24", SBY 5/30/89 OE 4,620
NINO, Carmelo (Latin American, 20th C)
Sin Titulo (man/two seated ladies in an interior by window), oil on canvas, sgn, 1983, 55x43", C-NY 11/21/88 OE 6,600
NIRTI (Italian, 19th/20th C)
Study of a Boy Holding a Violin & Smoking a Cigarette, oil on canvas, 24x12", SLK 2/12/88 450
NISBET, Robert H. (American, 1879-1961)
Macedonia Brook, oil on canvas, sgn, 25x30", RWS 11/10/89 800
Moonrise at Sunset, oil on canvas, sgn, 24x30", SBY 9/14/89 5,225
NISSL, Rudolf (Austrian, 1870-1955)
Artist's Model (nude), oil on canvas, sgn, 29x23", C-E 5/22/89 3,850
NITTIS, see De Nittis
NIVOLA, Constantino (Sardinian, 1911-)
Study for Sculpture, black felt-tip pen on paper, sgn/dtd 1957, 17x14", C-E 11/17/88 UE 55
NIXON, W.R. (British, 19th C)
Steamer Flying the Union Jack Under Sail, oil on canvas, sgn/dtd 1875, 60x89", SBY 7/12/89 1,320
NOBLE, John (American, 1874-1935)
Red Begonia, oil on canvas, sgn, 14x10", RAB 8/9/88 UE 300
NOBLE, John Sargeant (British, 1848-1896)
Hillside Garden, oil on board, sgn, 12x16", DM 3/14/88 1,200
NOEH, Anna T. (Canadian, 1903-)
Arctic Family by the Shore, mixed media, sgn, 12x16", FB 4/25/88 850
Davidee with Catch, mixed media, sgn/dtd 1972, 12x16", FB 10/30/89 1,320
Eskimo Mothers with Their Children, mixed media, sgn/dtd 1972, 12x17", FB 5/28/89 1,000
Family in Pangnirtung Fjord, mixed media, sgn/dtd 1977, 16x20", FB 10/17/88 1,800
Harpooning Seals, Cumberland Sound; oil on board, sgn/dtd 1976, 12x16", FB 10/17/88 1,700
Mother & Child, mixed media, sgn/dtd 1971, 12x16", FB 5/28/89 750
Mother & Child, mixed media, sgn/dtd 1982, 6x8", FB 10/17/88 700
Ready for the Seal Hunt (Eskimo family in winter landscape), mixed media, sgn/dtd 1984, 24x30", FB 5/28/89 3,000
NOEL, Alexandre Jean (French, 1752-1834)
Figures & Boats on an Estuary, gouache, 7x11", SBY 1/13/89 2,750
Pair: Coastal Landscape with Figures; Peasants Watering Their Animals; gouache, 1 sgn, oval, 6x7", SBY 1/13/89 5,225
NOEL, I.
Arab Caravan, oil on panel, sgn, 9x16", C-E 2/23/88 UE 418
NOEL, J.R. (French)
Figures in a Landscape, oil on panel, sgn, 8x11", FB 5/28/89 UE 475
NOEL, Jules (French, 1815-1881)
Britanny Coast, oil on canvas, sgn, 15x22", SBY 2/22/89 11,000
Dockyard, oil on board, sgn, 12x15", C-E 10/25/88 UE 1,980
Eastern Port, oil on canvas, sgn, 22x29", C-NY 2/23/89 18,700
View of a Middle-Eastern Harbor, oil on canvas, sgn/dtd 1861, 27x38", C-NY 2/23/89 24,200
View of the Coastal Town, Treport; oil on canvas, sgn/dtd 1849, 15x22", C-NY 5/25/88 8,800
NOELSMITH, Thomas (British, 19th C)
Cottage in a Landscape, watercolor on paper, sgn, 11x15", FAP 4/15/89 1,320
Cottage Near Shepton Somerset, watercolor, sgn, 14x21", PHL 10/28/88 425
NOKIFOR (Polish, 1893-1968)
Cityscape Vista (contemporary), crayon/pencil on paper, 6x8", RWS 9/29/88 475
NOLAN, Sidney Robert (Australian, 1917-)
Leda & the Swan, ripolin on paper, sgn/dtd twice 1960/inscr, unfr, 12x10", C-SK 6/9/88 2,600

NOLAND, Kenneth (American, 1924-)
Adjoin (abstract), acrylic on canvas, sgn/dtd 1980, 90x179", C-NY 5/4/89 52,800
Aforethought (lineation), acrylic on canvas, sgn/dtd 1977, 63x105", C-NY 5/4/89 30,800
Alleluja (contemporary composition), acrylic on canvas, sgn/dtd 1967, 24x96", SBY 11/9/89 OE 88,000
Autumn Spirit (abstract), acrylic on canvas, sgn/inscr/dtd 1965, 85x85", C-NY 5/3/88 60,500
Brass Sound (composition), acrylic on canvas, 1962, 72x72", SBY 11/8/89 OE 451,000
Bridge (composition of V shapes), acrylic on canvas, 1964, 89x98", SBY 5/2/88 308,000
Cite (right-angle lineation), acrylic on canvas, sgn/dtd 1964, 64x63", C-NY 2/20/88 OE 25,300
Curious Course (abstract), acrylic on canvas, sgn/dtd 1975, 98x98", SBY 10/8/88 OE 28,600
Empyrean (composition), oil on canvas, titled/dtd 1960, 82x82", SBY 11/8/89 OE 2,035,000
Fetch (horizontal lineation), acrylic on canvas, sgn/titled, 1969, 45x102", SBY 5/3/88 44,000
Half-Day (horizontal lineation), acrylic on canvas, 1967, 43x108", SBY 5/3/89 OE 82,500
Half-Long (abstract), acrylic on canvas, sgn/inscr/dtd 1976, 71x113", C-NY 5/4/88 19,800
Her Irish (vertical lineation), acrylic on canvas, sgn/dtd 1969, 6x102", C-NY 5/4/89 26,400
Herein (abstracts in pinks w/blue vertical line), acrylic on canvas, sgn/dtd 1975, 98x98", SBY 10/5/89 44,000
Level (abstract), acrylic on canvas, sgn/dtd 1967/titled, 24x204", SBY 5/3/88 35,750
Mute (distorted diamond shape w/red, gold, & blue), acrylic on canvas, sgn, 1967, 24x96", C-NY 2/20/88 16,500
Off (right-angle composition), acrylic on canvas, 1965, 60x60", C-NY 5/4/89 OE 85,800
Passage (geometric abstract), acrylic on canvas, sgn/dtd 1963, 69x139", SBY 10/5/89 44,000
Pitch (geometric composition), acrylic on canvas, sgn/dtd 1966, 96x24", SBY 2/15/89 OE 66,000
Red, White, & Gray (contemporary); acrylic on canvas, sgn/dtd 1978, 66x66", SBY 11/9/89 71,500
Regal Gray, acrylic on canvas, 1970, 65x115", SBY 10/8/88 17,600
Resect (geometric abstract), acrylic on canvas, sgn/dtd 1979/titled, 29x120", SBY 2/19/88 10,450
Shift (horizontal lines), acrylic on canvas, sgn/dtd 1967/titled, 78x197", SBY 2/19/88 OE 41,800
Streak (horizontal lineation), acrylic on canvas, sgn, 1968, 32x148", SBY 2/15/89 OE 66,000
Stria (horizontal lineation), acrylic on canvas, sgn/dtd 1967, 78x195", C-NY 10/4/89 OE 88,000
Summer's Gold (abstract composition), acrylic on canvas, 1983, 82x69", SBY 5/3/89 OE 71,500
Teton Noir (various colored circles within circles), acrylic on canvas, 1961, 81x81", SBY 5/2/89 495,000
Thaw (geometric abstract), acrylic on canvas, sgn, ca 1967, 19x102", SBY 5/3/89 OE 49,500
Treble (abstract), acrylic on canvas, 1980, 96x178", SBY 10/5/89 46,750
Tut (horizontal lineation), acrylic on canvas, sgn/dtd 1968, 17x185", SBY 2/15/89 20,900
Twenty Times (lineation), acrylic on canvas, sgn/dtd 1969, 6x96", SBY 10/5/89 OE 46,750
Untitled (dark colors), handmade colored paper, sgn/dtd 78, 50x33", SBY 10/5/89 18,700
Upright (contemporary), acrylic on canvas, sgn/dtd 1981, 93x20", SBY 11/9/89 35,750
Voyager (abstract w/two vertical lines), acrylic on canvas, sgn/dtd 1975/titled, 98x98", SBY 2/19/88 19,800

NOLDE, Emil (German, 1867-1956)
Am Strand, watercolor on buff paper, sgn, 10x12", SBY 2/16/89 OE 38,500
Blumen (floral painting), watercolor on paper, sgn, 19x14", SBY 11/12/88 88,000
Exotishe Blumen, watercolor on Japan paper, sgn, ca 1913-14, 14x19", C-NY 11/15/88 46,200
Kopf Eines Sudsee-Madchens (girl's head in profile), watercolor on buff paper, sgn, ca 1913, 16x13", SBY 5/11/88 OE 28,600
Mann und Junge Tochter (portrait of man & woman), oil on canvas, sgn/inscr, 1926, 33x25", SBY 11/11/88 825,000
Meuhlen (landscape w/two windmills), watercolor on paper mounted at edges on board, sgn, 1914-20, 14x19", C-NY 5/12/88 132,000
Still Life of Statuette, watercolor on paper, sgn, 11x18", SBY 11/16/89 46,750
Tanzende Madchen (two female nudes), oil on canvas, sgn twice, dtd 1925, 42x32", SBY 11/11/88 935,000
Woman with Red Hair (profile), watercolor on paper, sgn, 9x6", SBY 11/16/89 OE 71,500

NOLLEKENS, Josef Frans; att (Flemish, 18th C)
Pair: Children Disporting Themselves in Interiors; oil on canvas, 14x12", C-NY 4/8/88 3,300

NOLPE, Pieter (Dutch, 1613-1652)
Dune Landscape with Two Figures Drawing From a Well, oil on panel, sgn/dtd 1631, 14x20", SBY 4/7/88 UE 7,700

NOME, see De Nome

NONNOTTE, Donat (1708-1785)
Portrait of the Marquise de Gast, oil on canvas, sgn, 39x32", SBY 1/12/89 27,500

NOORT, see Van Noort

NORBERT, Fridrich (19th C)
Musical Party Under the Trees, oil on canvas, sgn/dtd 1876, 27x43", WD 3/23/88 1,300

NORDALM, Federico (South American, 19th/20th C)
Basket of Fruit (viewed from above), oil on canvas, sgn/dtd 86, 35x36", SBY 5/16/89 6,050
Box (still life), oil on canvas, sgn/dtd 1988, 36x39", C-NY 11/21/89 9,900
Naturaleza Muerta con Calabaza (still life), oil on canvas, sgn/dtd 1985, 25x39", C-NY 5/18/88 OE 8,800
Naturaleza Muerta con Cebollas (still life, onions & peppers), oil on canvas, sgn/dtd 1987, 35x39", C-NY 11/21/88 5,500
Naturaleza Muerta con Naranjas y Ciruelas (still life of fruit), oil on canvas, sgn/dtd 88, 42x57", C-NY 5/17/89 OE 10,450
Still Life (package, oranges, & garlic), oil on canvas, sgn/dtd 88, 40x48", SBY 11/21/88 6,875

NORDELL, Carl J. (American, 1885-)
Fall Landscape, oil on canvas, sgn, 30x25", PHL 12/1/88 1,700

NORDEN, Gerald (British, 20th C)
Still Life of Fruit & Nuts, oil on masonite, sgn/dtd 82, 9x12", SBY 7/12/89 660

NORDENBERG, Bengt (Swedish, 1822-1902)
First Steps, oil on canvas, sgn/dtd 1868, 16x22", SBY 5/23/89 OE 17,600

NORDFELDT, Bror Julius Olsson (American, 1878-1955)
Country Road, pastel/charcoal on paper, sgn, 12x16", C-NY 9/30/88 2,090
Fort Bragg, California; watercolor/pencil on paper, sgn/dtd 1953, 8x11", SBY 9/14/89 715

Indian Dance (w/landscape on reverse), oil on canvas, sgn/dtd 1919, 29x36", C-NY 5/25/89 ... 33,000
Set of 12: Figure Drawings & Farmers; 10 charcoal on paper, 3 pastel on paper, 9 sgn, unfr, 24x19", C-E 11/30/88 ... 1,870
Summer Dusk, oil on canvas, sgn/inscr, unfr, 30x36", C-NY 3/11/88 ... 20,900
Tiger Lilies in a Clay Pot, oil on canvas, sgn, 38x24", B/B 3/17/88 ... 22,000

NORDFELT, B.J.O. (American, 1897-1955)
Abstract, watercolor on paper, sgn/dtd 51, 15x23", WD 11/16/88 UE ... 3,400

NORDSTROM, Carl Harold (American, 1876-1934)
Dock Workers, oil on masonite, sgn, 16x20", RWS 5/12/89 OE ... 2,100
Pair: Portrait of a Young Lady; Portrait of a Lady; charcoal on laid paper, sgn/dtd 08, 25x19", RWS 3/16/89 ... 225
Pair: Woman in White Gown; Woman Holding a Wrap; charcoal on paper, sgn/dtd 1910 & 06, unfr, S-25x19", RWS 3/16/89 UE ... 125
Sailboats in a Harbor, oil on canvas, unfr, 24x30", C-E 6/1/89 OE ... 2,310

NORMANN, Adelsteen (Norwegian, 1848-1918)
Norwegian Loch Village, oil on canvas attached to board, sgn, 19x24", MG 10/28/88 UE ... 1,000

NORRIS, Walter (American, 1868-)
Blue Mountains Said To Be the Rockies, oil on canvas, sgn, 26x24", C-E 6/1/89 ... 1,320

NORTHCOTE, James (British, 1746-1831)
Figures by a River in a Wooded Landscape, oil on paper, sgn, 10x20", C-E 2/21/89 ... 1,650
Milkmaid & Her Dog Kneeling by a Bucket in a Landscape, oil on canvas, sgn/dtd 1783, 48x40", C-NY 1/11/89 OE ... 14,300
Portrait of Admiral Bridgeport, three-quarter length, standing in uniform; oil on canvas, 51x40", SBY 4/7/88 ... 5,500
Portrait of Joshua Pym, three-quarter length, seated in black coat...; oil, sgn/dtd 1809, unfr, 40x33", C-SK 5/25/89 OE ... 5,510
Portrait of a Lady Said To Be Lady Burton, half-length; oil on canvas, in painted oval, unfr, 28x23", C-NY 4/8/88 ... 5,500

NORTHCOTE, Joseph (19th C)
Gathering Berries, oil on canvas, sgn/dtd 1880, 8x12", C-E 2/3/88 ... 2,090

Northern European School (19th C)
Shepherd & Shepherdess with Flock in Alpine Landscape, oil on canvas, unfr, 19x24", C-E 6/28/88 UE ... 55

Northern Italian School (15th C)
San Bernardio of Siena, bust-length, in profile, holding a book; oil on panel on gold ground, 19x13", C-NY 5/31/89 ... 16,500

Northern Italian School (16th C)
Double-Sided: Saint Dominic; Skull in a Niche; oil on panel, inscr, 13x9", SBY 10/21/88 ... 2,475
Nativity, oil on panel, 40x34", SBY 4/7/88 OE ... 13,200
Portrait of a Lawyer, oil on panel, inscr, 40x33", SBY 4/7/88 OE ... 15,400
Saint Jerome Doing Penance Before a Cross, tempera on panel, 15x11", SBY 10/21/88 ... 5,500
Seated Boy Playing a Pipe, black chalk, 10x6", SBY 1/13/89 ... 11,000

Northern Italian School (17th C)
Adoration of the Magi, oil on copper, 5x4", SBY 12/9/88 UE ... 1,650
Allegory of Mortality, oil on canvas, 18x24", SBY 7/12/89 UE ... 660
Christ Healing the Lame Man, oil on canvas, unfr, 24x30", SBY 6/8/88 UE ... 770
Crucifixion, oil on canvas, 28x19", C-NY 4/8/88 ... 1,980
Judgement of King Solomon, oil on canvas, unfr, 16x25", SBY 10/13/89 ... 2,200
King Solomon Making Burnt Offerings in the Temple, oil on canvas, 31x45", SBY 4/7/89 ... 3,300
Madonna & Child with Saint Joseph, oil on canvas, 60x48", SBY 6/8/88 ... 880
Madonna & Sleeping Christ Child, oil on canvas, 38x28", C-E 4/7/88 UE ... 550
Portrait of a Young Girl Said To Be the Infanta Isabel, oil on canvas, 28x22", C-NY 10/20/88 OE ... 4,400
Portrait of Phillip Chetwynd, three-quarter length; oil on canvas, 48x39", SBY 10/21/88 ... 9,900
Portrait of the Blessed Tesauro de Beccaria, oil on canvas, inscr, 31x25", SBY 7/12/89 ... 4,125
Rinaldo & Armida, oil on canvas, 24x28", SBY 10/21/88 ... 3,850
St John the Baptist As an Infant, oil on canvas, 37x29", WD 10/19/88 ... 1,500
Saint Joseph Holding the Christ Child, oil on canvas, 30x23", SBY 6/8/88 UE ... 550

Northern Italian School (18th C)
Flaying of Marsyas, oil/gold leaf on panel, 46x44", SBY 12/9/88 UE ... 1,320
Illustration of a Proverb, oil on canvas, 12x14", SBY 7/12/89 ... 330
Interior of a Palatial Building, oil on canvas, unfr, 14x21", SBY 10/13/89 ... 3,300
Pair: Landscapes with Classical Ruins by the Shore; Galleys & Ships in Distance; oil on panel, 21x28", SBY 4/7/89 OE ... 11,000
Pair: Landscapes with Coach & Figures; oil on canvas, 17x24", SBY 10/21/88 OE ... 16,500
Peasants in an Interior Including a Mother, Child, & Smokers; oil on canvas, 22x18", SBY 6/8/88 OE ... 3,410
Portrait of a Lady, wearing blue & white dress, & red shawl; oil on canvas, in oval, unfr, 31x24", C-NY 10/20/88 OE ... 4,620
Presentation of the Virgin in the Temple, oil on canvas, 28x19", SBY 10/21/88 ... 3,850
Rest on the Flight into Egypt, oil on canvas, unfr, 26x37", SBY 7/12/89 ... 2,200
Sacrifice of Isaac (angel above figures in landscape), oil on canvas, 41x30", C-NY 4/6/89 ... 3,850
Travelers on a Path, oil on canvas, 13x21", WD 1/25/89 ... 4,000
Two Boys with Their Dog & the Results of a Hunt, oil on canvas, 26x36", SBY 7/12/89 ... 2,750

NORTON, Benjamin Cam (British, 1835-1900)
Bay Racehorse in a Loosebox, oil on canvas, sgn/dtd 1874, 21x28", SBY 6/9/89 ... 2,860

NORTON, Lewis Doyle (American, 1867-)
Along the Village Path, oil on canvasboard, sgn/inscr, 10x13", RWS 11/3/88 ... 550
Paris, Along the Seine; oil on canvas, sgn/titled, 15x13", RWS 7/13/89 OE ... 650

NORTON, William Edward (American, 1843-1916)
Bay (coastal view w/fishing shack & boats), oil on panel, sgn, 12x16", C-E 2/1/89 UE ... 1,100
Brittany Scene, watercolor on board, sgn, 12x16", C-NY 9/30/88 ... 1,100
Cattle Grazing in a Wooded Landscape, oil on panel, sgn, 12x16", C-SK 11/10/88 ... 1,300

Corner of a Meadow (woman & child), oil on canvas laid down, sgn, unfr, 18x14", C-SK 5/25/89 ... 1,190
Distant Windmills, oil on canvasboard, sgn, 12x16", C-E 2/1/89 ... 880
Drying the Nets, oil on canvas, sgn, 11x16", C-E 2/1/89 ... 1,100
Heading Out, view of a large two-masted schooner sailing briskly past a lighthouse; oil on canvas, 16x27", RAB 11/24/89 ... 6,000
Marine Scene (ship Ann Boston at sea), oil on metal, sgn, 12x21", RWS 9/8/89 OE ... 3,000
Mill Place House, oil on panel, sgn, 12x16", C-E 2/1/89 ... 1,650
Pair: Staten Island Ferry; Stapleton, Staten Island; oil on panel, sgn, 6x8", SBY 6/28/89 ... 2,420
Sailing Off Boston Harbor, oil on canvas, sgn, 20x30", SBY 6/24/88 ... 7,150
Ship Betsy Jane of Nantucket, oil on canvas, sgn, 20x16", DM 1/15/88 OE ... 3,500
Steamships & Sailboats in Boston Harbor, oil on panel, intialed, 8x10", RWS 3/16/89 OE ... 1,700

NORWELL, Graham N. (Canadian, 1901-1967)
Laurentian Summer Landscape, oil on board, sgn, 4x6", FB 10/30/89 ... 198
Laurentian Winter, watercolor, sgn, 22x26", WAD 11/30/89 ... 400
Laurentian Winter Landscape, oil on board, initialed, 4x6", FB 10/30/89 OE ... 330
Scene d'Hiver, Laurentides (Laurentian winter scene); watercolor, sgn, 19x25", FB 4/25/88 ... 650
Sunset in the Laurentians, watercolor, sgn, 12x16", FB 10/30/89 ... 412
Winter Landscape, oil on board, sgn, 12x16", FB 10/17/88 ... 500
Winter Landscape, oil on board, sgn, 16x20", FB 4/25/88 ... 550
Winter Landscape, oil on canvas, sgn, 20x24", FB 4/25/88 ... 1,400
Winter Landscape, watercolor, sgn, 12x18", FB 4/25/88 ... 360
Winter Landscape with Homestead, oil on board, 12x15", FB 5/28/89 ... 700
Winter Landscape with Houses, oil on board, sgn, 12x16", FB 5/28/89 ... 350

NOTER, David; see De Norter

NOTERMAN, Emanuel (Flemish, 1808-1863)
Reading the News, oil on canvas, sgn/dtd 1836, 17x14", FB 10/30/89 ... 2,200

NOTERMAN, Zacharias (German, 1829-1890)
Dog & Bird's Nest with a Cage, oil on panel, sgn/dtd 18(?), 10x12", C-E 5/23/88 ... 2,090
In the Barn (sheep dog & other objects in an interior), oil on panel, sgn, 10x12", SBY 6/9/89 OE ... 5,500
Man's Best Friends (two dogs w/monkey in an interior), oil on canvas, sgn, 26x32", B/B 3/22/89 ... 4,950
The Cartographers, oil on panel, sgn, 12x16", B/B 6/9/88 ... 2,750

NOURSE, Elizabeth (American, 1859-1938)
Blue Irises in a Crockery Vase, watercolor/gouache on brown paper, sgn, 48x40", B/B 3/22/89 ... 7,150
Le Soulier Nuef (mother putting shoe on child), oil on canvas, sgn, ca 1910, 25x20", SBY 5/24/89 ... 35,200

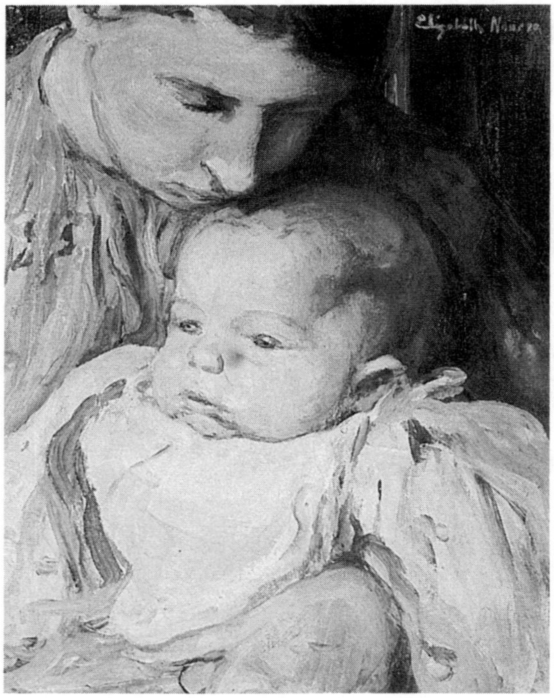

Mere et Bebe, oil on canvas, sgn, ca 1912, 14x11", C-NY 3/11/88 OE; $28,600

NOVELLI, Gastone (Italian, 1925-1968)
Paura Clandestina (abstract), sand/oil on canvas, sgn/dtd 59, 51x38", C-E 11/17/88 OE ... 7,150

NOVELLI, Jane
Sunlit Venetian View, oil on canvas, sgn/dtd 1937, 24x32", SLK 5/12/88 ... 110

NOVELLI, Pietro Antonio III (Italian, 1729-1804)
Judith with the Head of Holofernes, oil on canvas, unfr, 25x35", SBY 12/9/88 ... 3,300

NOVELLI, Pietro; att (Italian)
Saint Elizabeth of Hungary with Putti, oil on canvas, unfr, 49x40", C-NY 10/20/88 OE ... 4,400

OVELLI, Pietro; manner of (Italian, 1603-1647)
Saint Thomas, oil on canvas, 34x26", SBY 10/21/88 OE **85,800**
OVO, Stefano (Italian, 1862-)
Vegetable Vendor, oil on canvas, sgn, 19x30", C-E 2/23/88 .... **3,300**
OVOTNY, E.L. (American, 1909-)
Symbols of the Southwest (shuttered window, steer's skull on adobe wall), oil on board, sgn, 32x47", WG 4/23/88 UE **4,700**
OVROS, David (American, 1941-)
Three panels: Untitled (composition of rectangles in colors); oil on canvas, sgn/dtd 70-71, SBY 5/3/89 OE **25,300**
Untitled #6 (geometric composition), oil, initialed/dtd 72, 3 panels: 76x37", 76x75", 84x54", SBY 2/15/89 .... **24,750**
OWAK, Franz (Austrian, 20th C)
Pair: Still Life of Fruit & Teapot; Fruit; oil on panel, sgn, 8x10", FAP 4/15/89 OE **908**
Pair: Still Lifes with Fruit; oil on panel, sgn, 7x10", 8x10", B/B 9/15/88 OE **935**
OWEY, Adolf D. (Continental, 19th C)
Sheepfold (three sheep in a dark stone barn), oil on wood panel, sgn, 6x8", RAB 8/9/88 UE **175**
OYER, Denis Paul (French, 20th C)
Town Street, oil on canvas, sgn/dtd 1969, 24x30", MG 5/28/88 UE **375**
OYER, Philippe (French, 1917-)
Arlequin, watercolor on paper, sgn/dtd 1965, 25x20", B/B 4/20/88 .... **605**
Arlequin et Oiseau, oil on panel, sgn/dtd 45, 29x24", C-E 11/17/88 .... **1,760**
Au Bord de la Mer (fantasy composition), oil on canvas, sgn/dtd 65, 11x14", C-E 5/9/89 OE **1,100**
Children of Count de Reiset, oil on panel, sgn/dtd 45, 28x23", SBY 10/7/89 .... **2,750**
Children with Pets, oil on canvas, sgn/dtd 46, 29x24", SBY 10/7/89 .... **2,860**
Girl by a Fountain, acrylic on canvas, sgn/dtd 1961, 39x20", SBY 10/5/88 .... **2,750**
Group of 3: Girl w/Dachsunds; Girl w/Parrot; Girl by River; marker/watercolor, sgn/dtd 1964, 28x22", SBY 2/14/89 OE **4,125**
Le Petit Matin, acrylic on canvas, sgn/dtd 1964, 39x25", SBY 10/7/89 .... **5,500**
Petite Musique pour la Famille, oil on canvas, sgn/dtd 69, 40x32", SBY 10/7/89 .... **2,970**
Portrait de Femme, oil on canvas, sgn/dtd 59, 29x24", B/B 6/15/89 .... **3,300**
Portrait of a Reclining Woman on a Green Sofa, oil on canvas, sgn/dtd 64, 24x29", B/B 9/15/88 .... **1,650**
OYES, George Loftus (Canadian, 1864-1951)
Autumn Landscape, oil on canvas mounted on board, sgn, 12x16", SBY 4/14/89 .... **2,310**
Dock Side, Gloucester Harbor; oil on canvasboard, sgn, 15x14", RWS 5/12/89 .... **6,000**
Fishing Boats, oil on canvas, sgn, 20x24", C-NY 9/30/88 .... **7,700**
Green Valley (landscape), watercolor on paper, sgn, 5x9", RAB 3/27/89 UE **250**
House of the Four Winds, Monterey Peninsula; oil on canvas, sgn, 21x24", RWS 3/16/89 .... **3,750**
Landscape with Mountains & Trees, oil on board, sgn, 16x12", SBY 6/28/89 OE **3,300**
Midwinter, oil on canvasboard, sgn, 16x20", C-NY 9/30/88 .... **4,400**
Pennsylvania Landscape, oil on canvas mounted on board, sgn, 13x15", SBY 3/17/88 .... **23,100**
S Giorgio Maggiore at Sunset, oil on canvasboard, sgn, 6x6", RWS 11/3/88 .... **1,000**
Spirit of the Woods, oil on canvas, sgn/dtd 1919, 20x16", RWS 5/19/88 UE **1,500**
Springtime at Venice (landscape), oil on canvas laid down on board, sgn, 15x16", SBY 3/17/88 .... **2,860**
View of the Scene with Tugboat, oil on masonite, sgn, 14x16", SBY 9/14/89 OE **11,550**
Washday: Sunlight & Shadow; oil on canvas, sgn, 13x10", SBY 9/14/89 .... **1,980**
Water Lilies, watercolor on paper, sgn, 14x17", RAB 8/9/88 OE **1,000**
UDERSCHER, Frank B. (American, 1880-1959)
Call of Autumn (autumnal landscape, Ozark hill country), oil on canvas, sgn, 25x30", SLK 9/27/88 .... **1,600**
Carr Park, winter street scene; oil on canvas, sgn/titled, 16x19", SLK 11/25/88 .... **2,700**
Farmyard in Spring, oil on board, sgn, 16x20", SLK 9/26/88 .... **800**
Pair: Creek in the Ozark Valley; Spring in the Ozarks; oil on canvasboard, sgn, 1944, 19x19", 7x9", SLK 5/9/88 .... **650**
Sappington House, Crestwood, Missouri; watercolor, sgn/dtd 1915, 15x18", SLK 9/26/88 .... **500**
Untitled, street scene of construction crews in St Louis; oil on canvas, sgn/dtd 17, 30x40", SLK 11/25/88 .... **8,000**
Untitled (rural town street scene), oil on board, ca 1890, 23x17", SLK 11/25/88 .... **950**
Wharf, New England scene w/boats around pier; oil on artist board, sgn, 12x14", SLK 11/25/88 .... **900**
Workers Harvesting Hay in an Extensive Landscape, oil on canvas, sgn, 25x30", SLK 9/27/88 .... **2,200**
UMMERS, Frederick Adolph; att
Country Scene, black chalk on paper, unfr, 8x13", WD 1/25/89 UE **600**
UNEZ, Armando Garcia (Latin American, 19th/20th C)
El Penon (landscape), pastel/pencil on paper, sgn/dtd 1917/titled, 11x18", C-NY 5/17/89 OE **4,400**
Group of 4: Scenes in Mexico; oil on board, sgn, 9x16" & smaller, C-SK 6/9/88 OE **2,230**
Paisaje Rural (rural landscape), oil on canvas, sgn, ca 1898, 20x29", C-NY 11/21/88 OE **8,800**
uremberg School (16th C)
Triptych: Coronation of a Pope; Martyrdom of Two Saints; oil on panel, center: 41x27", wings: 16x43", C-NY 1/15/88 .... **22,000**
UTT, Jim (American, 1938-)
A Trifle Fastidious (caricature figures), crayon/pencil on paper, sgn/dtd 1981, 11x16", SBY 10/7/89 .... **2,475**
Pink Encounter (surrealistic), acrylic on metal, 1970-71, 23x18", SBY 11/11/88 .... **14,300**
Running Wild (surrealistic), acrylic on metal, 1970, 46x44", SBY 11/11/88 .... **23,100**
Tight Lips & Dreams (surrealistic), oil on board, 1972, 16x16", SBY 11/11/88 .... **7,700**
You're Giving Me Trouble (nude fantasy figures), acrylic on canvas, 1974, 87x74", C-NY 5/4/89 .... **38,500**
UTTING, Wallace (American, 1861-)
Path Through the Orchard, oil on canvas, sgn, unfr, 12x15", RWS 9/8/89 .... **400**
YE, Edgar H. (American, 1879-1943)
Gloucester Schooners, oil on canvas, sgn, 18x22", RWS 11/3/88 OE **3,600**

NYROP, Borge (Danish, 1881-1948)
Kelp Gatherer, oil on canvas, sgn, 21x27", NA 5/12/89 800

NYS, Carl (Belgian, 1858-)
Ny au Bras Leve, oil on canvas, sgn, 29x24", C-E 2/23/88 880
Young Woman of the Casbah (portrait), oil on canvas, sgn, 48x32", B/B 6/15/89 4,950

NYSSEN, L.
Gathering by a Village Doorway, oil on canvas, sgn, 22x29", C-E 5/23/88 UE 550

O'BOURKE, Terina (American, 20th C)
Contemplation (nude draped with robe reclines against stool), oil on canvas, sgn, 21x27", RAB 8/9/88 UE 750

O'BRIEN, Lucius R. (Canadian, 1832-1899)
Abandoned Boat, watercolor, sgn/dtd 1882, 12x19", FB 10/30/89 1,045
Figures on a City Street, watercolor, initialed, 9x11", WAD 11/30/89 850
Marine Scene, watercolor, sgn/dtd 1883, 8x18", FB 10/17/88 850
Meadow, watercolor, sgn, 18x24", WAD 11/30/89 2,400
Orchard Grove with Stream, watercolor, sgn, 9x6", FB 10/30/89 330
River Stroll, watercolor, sgn/dtd 1898, 13x17", WAD 11/30/89 2,800

O'DONOGHUE, Hughie (British, 20th C)
Boxer (abstract), acrylic on canvas, unfr, 48x40", C-NY 5/4/89 5,170
Run to Earth (abstract), wood construction/oil on canvas, sgn/dtd 85, 107x89", C-NY 5/4/89 OE 14,300

O'GORMAN, Juan (Mexican, 1905-1982)
Anarchy-Study for a Mural; pencil on tracing paper laid down on linen, sgn, 1939, 16x14", C-NY 11/21/89 16,500
Autoretrato (self-portrait), tempera on canvas laid down on masonite, sgn/dtd 1957, 18x11", C-NY 5/17/89 44,000
Beceto (woman & child, study for mural), pencil/crayon on paper, sgn/dtd 1964, 11x7", C-NY 11/21/88 2,090
Boceto para Gentes de Tehuantepec, charcoal/pencil on tracing paper laid on linen, 1955, 28x24", C-NY 11/21/88 11,000
El Credito Transforma a Mexico, pencil on paper laid down on canvas, sgn/titled, ca 1963-64, 17x94", C-NY 5/18/88 24,200
El Estanque de Walden (Walden Pond), tempera on gessoed panel, sgn twice/titled, ca 1955, 17x13", C-NY 11/21/88 44,000
La Conquista del Aire por el Hombre, pencil on paper laid down on linen, sgn/titled, 1937, 21x72", C-NY 11/21/88 8,800
Los Mitos (The Myths, surrealistic), tempera on panel, sgn/dtd 1944, 48x36", C-NY 5/17/89 385,000
Los Mitos Paganos (derogatory depiction of German Facist leaders), tempera on panel, sgn, 1947, 43x49", C-NY 11/21/89 550,000
Monument to the Metaphysical: Homage to G Arcimboldo 1530-1593; oil on panel, sgn/inscr, ca 1978, 17x13", SBY 5/16/89 60,500

O'HARA, Eliot (American, 1890-1969)
Monhegan Looks East (landscape), watercolor on paper, sgn/dtd, 22x17", RWS 3/16/89 OE 450

O'HIGGINS, Pablo (Mexican, 1905-)
Foreman (seated man in thought), oil on canvas, sgn/dtd 1942, 23x17", SBY 5/16/89 OE 7,700
Nocturnal Landscape (contemporary), oil on canvas, sgn, 31x41", SBY 5/16/89 OE 12,100

O'KEEFFE, Georgia (American, 1887-1986)
Abstraction, Red & Black Night; oil on board, sgn/dtd NYC 1929, 13x10", C-NY 5/25/89 264,000
Apple Blossoms, oil on canvas, sgn/dtd 1930, 32x20", SBY 5/25/88 660,000
Autumn Oak Leaves, oil on canvas, sgn/inscr, 1923, 12x9", SBY 5/25/88 126,000
Dark Iris, No 2 (contemporary); oil on canvas, initialed/dtd 1927/artist's star/titled, 32x21", SBY 5/24/89 OE 1,650,000
Road Past the View, oil on canvas, sgn/bears artist's label on the backing, 1964, 24x30", C-NY 5/25/89 748,000
Winter Cottonfield Trees, East III: oil on canvas, dtd 53, 22x26", C-NY 5/25/89 275,000
Yellow Cactus Flowers, oil on canvas, sgn/dtd 1929/titled, 30x42", SBY 5/24/89 1,320,000

O'KELLY, Aloysius (British, 1853-)
Market Place, Tangier, Morocco; oil on canvas, sgn, 13x15", WD 11/16/88 OE 9,000

O'MALLEY, Power (American, 1870-1946)
Pair: Venice in Winter; oil on canvas, sgn, 8x11", C-E 9/15/88 495

O'NEIL, Rose (American, 1875-1944)
First Love, watercolor/gouache on paper laid down on board, sgn, 25x18", B/B 3/17/88 6,600

O'SULLIVAN, Daniel
Near the Causeway, oil on canvas, sgn/dtd 19, 18x24", C-NY 6/17/89 220

O'SULLIVAN, M.L. (American, 20th C)
Almond Orchard, Costa Blanca; oil on canvas, sgn, 24x36", B/B 1/11/89 UE 248

OAKES, John Wright (British, 1820-1887)
Rushing Brook, oil on canvas, sgn, 12x18", C-E 5/23/88 825
Rustic Farm in a Landscape, oil on canvas, sgn, 14x22", SBY 6/8/88 1,320

OAKES, Wilbur L. (American, 1876-1934)
Early Autumn, oil on canvas, sgn/dtd 26, 25x30", C-E 6/1/88 990
Edge of the Woods, oil on canvas, sgn/indistinctly dtd 13, 18x22", SBY 9/14/89 2,970

OAKLEY, Octavius (British, 1800-1867)
Farmerette (portrait in landscape), watercolor/gouache, sgn/dtd 1860, 19x13", C-E 2/21/89 990

OAKLEY, Thorton (American, 1881-1953)
Isle of Robinson Crusoe, watercolor on paper, sgn, 22x29", FAP 4/15/89 550

OAKMAN, Arthur (American, 1910-)
Bird's-Eye View of a New England Harbor, oil on board, sgn/dtd 1940, 24x20", RWS 9/8/89 UE 400

OATTINGER, Joseph (American, 20th C)
Mountain Lake Landscape, oil on canvas, sgn/dtd 1938, 22x30", WL 5/20/88 UE 175

OBERTEUFFER, George (American, 1878-1940)
Booth Bay Harbor, oil on canvas, sgn, 25x30", C-NY 5/26/88 OE 16,500
Moret Mora River, oil on canvas, bears signature/inscr/dtd 1923, 21x26", C-E 11/30/88 3,300
Stream in Autumn Landscape, oil on canvas, sgn/dtd 1910, unfr, 25x32", C-E 6/1/88 OE 5,280

OBERTS, Goodridge (Canadian, 1904-1974)
River Landscape, oil on board, sgn, 20x24", FB 4/25/88 ..... **3,600**
OBIN, Seneque (Haitian, 1893-1977)
Black Mountain (figures in landscape), oil on masonite, inscr Cap Haitien Haiti Montagne-Noir, 21x24", SBY 11/21/88 ..... **2,750**
Mademoiselle X (woman reclining under grape arbor in landscape), oil on masonite, sgn/dtd 1960, 24x30", SBY 5/16/89 OE **9,900**
Still Life of Fruit & Flowers, oil on masonite, sgn/inscr Cap Haitien Haiti, 20x24", SBY 5/16/89 ..... **4,125**
OBIT, L. (European, 19th C)
Pair: Untitled, horse-drawn sledge in winter landscape; oil on panel, sgn, 6x9", SLK 4/7/89 ..... **700**
OBREGON, Alejandro (Colombian, 1920-)
Composicion con Pajaro (abstract composition of bird), oil on canvas, sgn, ca 1959, 31x39", C-NY 11/21/89 ..... **20,900**
Fall in the Desert No 1, oil on panel, sgn, 1971, 15x19", SBY 5/17/88 OE **8,250**
Music (abstract), oil on canvas, sgn/titled, ca 1955, 12x16", SBY 5/16/89 ..... **2,750**
Pair: Barracuda; Insect & Flower; gouche on paper & gouache on thin card, 20x28"/7x7", SBY 11/21/88 ..... **5,225**
OCHTERVELT, Jacob; school of (Dutch, 1635-1708)
A Reading, oil on canvas, 16x13", FAP 12/8/89 ..... **1,100**
OCHTMAN, Leonard (American, 1854-1934)
Approach at Evening, oil on canvas, sgn/dtd 1919, 16x22", SBY 9/14/89 ..... **2,970**
Autumn Landscape, oil on board, sgn, 16x20", B/B 3/22/89 ..... **4,675**
Early Sunrise (landscape), oil on canvas, sgn, 30x40", C-NY 5/25/89 UE **3,850**
Moonlight Harbor, oil on canvas, 30x40", DM 5/13/88 ..... **2,200**
Pool at Greyledge, oil on canvas, sgn/dtd 1925, 24x30", WD 4/13/88 ..... **4,000**
Snowy Landscape, oil on canvas, sgn/dtd 1907, 36x52", C-NY 9/28/89 ..... **23,100**
Summer Landscape, oil on canvas, sgn/dtd 1890, 12x16", B/B 6/15/89 ..... **4,950**
Woodland Brook (landscape), oil on canvas, sgn/titled, 12x16", SBY 1/24/89 ..... **2,420**
OCHTMAN, Mina Fonda (American, 1862-1924)
Autumn, oil on panel, sgn, 12x16", C-E 10/18/89 ..... **1,100**
Russet Oak, oil on panel, sgn/inscr, 12x16", SBY 9/23/88 ..... **880**
ODDIE, Walter M. (American, 1808-1865)
Connecticut River Scene, oil on canvas, sgn/dtd 1856, 18x24", SBY 6/24/88 ..... **3,630**
Country Road, oil on canvas, sgn/dtd 1855, 35x50", NA 10/1/88 OE **1,500**
OEDER, George (German, 1846-1931)
Forest Scene, oil on canvas, sgn, 29x47", LH 10/16/88 ..... **3,200**
Mushroom Pickers in a Forest, oil on canvas, sgn, 31x47", C-E 2/21/89 ..... **3,300**
OERDER, Frans (Dutch, 1866-1944)
Bountiful Harvest, oil on canvas, sgn, 31x24", C-SK 11/10/88 ..... **7,060**
OERTEL, Johannes Adam Simon (American, 1823-)
Shipwrecked Maiden (figure clinging to stone cross above waves), oil on canvas, sgn/dtd 1867, 49x28", SBY 3/17/88 OE **3,080**
OERTEL, Wilhelm (German, 1870-)
Bringing the Cows Home, oil on panel, sgn, 18x24", B/B 8/10/88 ..... **825**
Ships in Harbor, oil on canvas, sgn, 17x13", B/B 3/17/88 ..... **2,090**
OETS, Pieter (1721-1790)
Pair: Portraits of a Man & Woman; pastel on paper, sgn/dtd 1749 & 1750, 16x13", SBY 10/13/89 ..... **3,850**
OGDEN, Frederick D. (American, 19th/20th C)
Western Landscape with Stream, oil on canvas, sgn, 24x35", LH 9/10/89 ..... **600**
OGDEN, Henry A. (American, 1856-1936)
Ambulance Camp (Civil War), pen/ink on paper, sgn/inscr, 11x16", C-E 5/27/88 ..... **220**
Hornet's Nest: Battle of Shiloh (Civil War); pen/ink/charcoal on board, sgn/inscr, 13x18", C-E 5/27/88 OE **1,760**
Set of 3: Union Troops Uniforms (Civil War); pen/ink on paper, titled, 8x6" & smaller, C-E 5/27/88 ..... **220**
Set of 4: Confederate Soldiers (Civil War); pen/ink on paper, inscr, 8x6" & smaller, C-E 5/27/88 OE **550**
Set of 4: Union Troops Uniforms (Civil War); pen/ink on paper, inscr, 8x6" & smaller, C-E 5/27/88 OE **385**
Set of 4: Union Troops Uniforms (Civil War); pen/ink on paper, inscr, 8x6" & smaller, C-E 5/27/88 ..... **330**
OGILVIE, J. Clinton (American, 1838-1900)
Woodland Scene, oil on canvas, sgn/dtd 1877, 15x10", NA 11/5/88 ..... **600**
OGILVY, William Abernathy (Canadian, 1901-)
Open Fields, oil on canvasboard, sgn/dtd 75, 12x16", WAD 6/12/89 ..... **400**
OHTAKE, Tomie (Brazilian, 1917-)
Sin Titulo (composition in dark red), oil on canvas, sgn, 59x59", C-NY 11/21/88 ..... **7,700**
OKADA, Kenzo (American, 1902-)
Flight No 1 (abstract), oil on canvas, sgn, 1955, SBY 10/5/89 OE **66,000**
Lemon Yellow, oil on canvas, sgn, 56x43", C-NY 11/10/88 ..... **26,400**
Often (abstract), oil on canvas, sgn, 1956, 63x43", SBY 5/3/88 OE **46,200**
Untitled (abstract), Japan paper collage on canvas, sgn, 54x62", SBY 2/15/89 ..... **28,600**
Untitled (abstract), oil on canvas, sgn, ca 1955, 28x39", SBY 10/5/89 OE **49,500**
OKAMURA, Arthur (American, 1932-)
Fabric of Nature, oil on canvas, sgn/dtd 61, 53x38", SBY 10/5/88 ..... **330**
Knife with Lemon Wedges, oil on canvas, sgn/dtd 39, 23x20", SBY 10/5/88 ..... **770**
Past Tense for a Square, oil on canvas, sgn/dtd 60, 40x40", SBY 10/5/88 UE **495**
Primevals, oil on canvas, sgn/dtd 61, unfr, 40x48", SBY 10/5/88 UE **495**
OKAWIE, Thomas F. (American, 1935-)
Santa Maria del Fiore, acrylic on masonite, 1966, 72x48", LH 10/16/88 OE **3,600**

OLDAL (German, 20th C)
Genre Subject with Three Figures Outside a Stone Cottage, oil on canvas, sgn/dtd 1910, 33x25", SLK 5/12/88 500
OLDENBURG, Claes (American/Swedish, 1929-)
Baked Potato, watercolor/crayon on paper, initialed/inscr/dtd 72, 9x12", SBY 10/8/88 22,000
Base of Colossal Drainpipe Monument, Toronto; ink/watercolor on paper, 11x9", SBY 10/5/89 OE 15,400
Beach House for East Hampton in the Form of a Door Handle, pencil on paper, initialed/dtd 67, 22x30", SBY 11/11/88 29,700
Coltello Ship From Above, crayons/graphite on paper, sgn/dtd 85, 30x20", C-NY 10/31/89 22,000
Design for a Bowling Alley in the Form of a Cigarette & Smoke, crayon/watercolor/pencil, sgn/dtd 68, 22x30", SBY 5/2/88 19,800
Hanging Three-Way Plug, pastel on paper, initialed/dtd 1973, 14x11", SBY 5/3/89 19,800
Poached Egg (contemporary), watercolor/crayon on paper, initialed/dtd 65/titled, 14x17", SBY 5/2/88 OE 28,600
Pool Ball Breasts-Instructions for a Multiple (Not Realized); collage/crayons/pencil/watercolor, 22x30", C-NY 5/4/88 30,800
Proposed Colossal Monument To Enliven a Quiet Street London: Gorilla; watercolor/chalk, 1966, 15x22", C-NY 11/10/88 OE 35,200
Sailboat Thinking of Q (contemporary), crayon/watercolor on paper, initialed/dtd 73, 8x6", SBY 10/5/89 13,200
Shirt, watercolor/crayon on paper, initialed/dtd 73, 9x6", SBY 5/5/89 9,900
Sketch of Toilet From Overhead, crayon/tempera on paper, initialed/dtd 63, 17x14", SBY 5/2/89 OE 71,500
Smog Mask, watercolor/crayon/masking tape/paper collage on paper, sgn/dtd 66, 15x13", SBY 10/5/89 OE 17,600
Street Figure (Using Movie Section, with Manhole), ink/newspaper collage, initialed/dtd 61, 14x10", SBY 10/5/89 OE 55,000

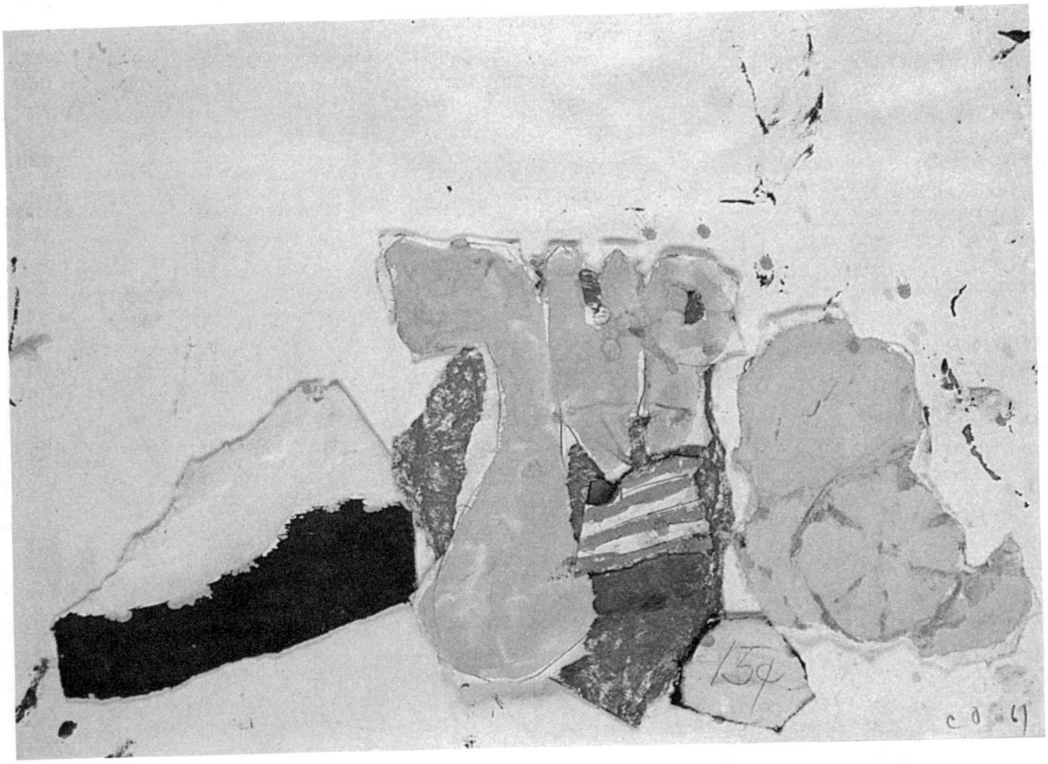

Studies for Store Objects-Pie, 7-Up, Flag, Oranges, Fifteen Cents; mixed media, sgn/dtd 61, 15x20", C-NY 11/9/88 OE; $88,000

Study for Chicago Stuffed with Numbers, watercolor/crayon on paper, initialed/dtd 75, 17x13", SBY 5/3/88 25,300
Study for Double Nose Punching Bag, Purse, & Ashtray; crayon/watercolor, initialed/dtd 1969, 10x10", SBY 10/5/89 27,500
Three Hats (drawn on abstract background), charcoal/pastel on paper, initialed/dtd 72, 38x25", SBY 5/2/88 OE 66,000
Untitled (pants), watercolor/crayon on paper, initialed/dtd 1962, 10x8", SBY 10/5/89 22,000
OLDFIELD, Otis (American/Swedish, 1890-1969)
Artist & His Wife, oil on canvas, sgn, 27x22", C-NY 9/28/89 OE 27,500
On the Dock (view of part of auto, building & ship's bow), oil on board, sgn/dtd 1926, 13x16", C-NY 9/28/89 4,400
OLINSKY, Tosca (American, 1909-)
Spring Petunias, oil on canvas, sgn, 24x18", C-E 6/1/89 UE 1,430
OLITSKI, Jules (Russian, 1922-)
Absalom Passage 19, acrylic on canvas, sgn/dtd 1973/titled, 88x43", SBY 2/19/88 6,050
Absalom Passage 6, acrylic on canvas, sgn/dtd 1973, 78x56", SBY 10/8/88 UE 1,650
Areteas Replies 4 (abstract), acrylic on canvas, sgn/inscr/dtd 1974, 109x78", C-NY 5/4/88 7,150
Catari Imagined, acrylic on canvas, sgn/dtd twice 1977, 48x66", SBY 10/8/88 5,500
First Love II (abstract), acrylic on canvas, sgn/dtd 1972/titled, 87x79", SBY 5/3/88 OE 18,700
Habakkuk Radiance 28, acrylic on canvas, sgn/dtd 1973, 66x66", SBY 2/19/88 7,975
Ishtar Descent #2 (abstract), acrylic on canvas, sgn/dtd 1980, 13x51", SBY 10/8/88 2,750
Jevel's Rapture 1 (abstract), acrylic on canvas, sgn/dtd 1981, 26x47", SBY 10/5/89 OE 24,200
Jevel's Rapture 3 (abstract), acrylic on canvas, sgn/dtd 81, 28x90", C-NY 2/20/88 5,500
Key of Solomon (abstract), acrylic on canvas, 90x38", SBY 2/15/89 OE 13,200
Lament of Absalom 20 (abstract), acrylic on canvas, sgn/dtd 1973, 85x56", SBY 2/19/88 5,500
Mother of Night (abstract), acrylic on canvas, sgn/dtd 1973/titled, 85x58", SBY 5/3/88 9,350

Nude Lying, Head on Arm; black/red pencil on paper, 14x17", C-E 5/13/88 660
Pink Shush, acrylic on canvas, 1965, 79x66", SBY 11/8/89 OE 159,500
Plan de la Tour Motif, acrylic on canvas, sgn/inscr/dtd 1971, 84x18", C-NY 5/4/88 OE 7,700
Portrait of a Woman, oil on canvas, indistinctly sgn, 20x13", C-E 2/3/88 UE 550
Radical Correspondence (abstract), acrylic on canvas, sgn/dtd 82, 67x33", C-NY 2/20/88 9,350
Salome's Breath (abstract), acrylic on canvas, sgn/dtd 65/titled, 70x66", SBY 2/19/88 18,700
Suspension (abstract), acrylic on canvas, sgn/dtd 1967, 105x33", SBY 10/5/89 OE 104,500
Untitled (abstract), acrylic on paper mounted on canvas, sgn/dtd 1967-69, 30x22", C-E 11/17/88 OE 6,600
Zeno's Half (abstract), acrylic on canvas, sgn/inscr/dtd 1971, 93x135", C-NY 5/4/88 OE 35,200

OLIVER, Emma (British, 1819-1885)
Landscape in the Lake District, oil on canvas, sgn, 12x21", C-E 1/12/88 825

OLIVER, Frederick W. (American, 1876-1963)
Rockport Harbor Scene (boats docked, warehouses beyond), oil on canvas, dtd 1928, 16x20", RWS 9/29/88 OE 1,600

OLIVER, J. (British, 19th C)
Two Sheep in a Landscape, oil on canvas, sgn/dtd 1880, 20x30", SBY 7/12/89 2,090

OLIVER, T. Clark (American, 19th/20th C)
Stopping To Help (large ship near smaller ship), oil on canvas, sgn/dtd 79, 13x20", RAB 8/1/89 OE 10,000

OLIVER, William (British, fl 1867-1882)
Rest From Her Labors (young woman seated in a landscape), oil on canvas, sgn/dtd 1865, 20x16", RWS 11/10/89 1,200

OLIVER, William (British, 1805-1853)
Letter (seated lady w/letter in landscape), oil on canvas, sgn, 21x17", C-NY 2/23/89 4,400
Portrait of a Lady, oil on canvas, sgn/dtd 1885, 13x11", C-E 2/23/88 1,760
Portrait of an Elegant Lady (seated in landscape), oil on canvas, sgn, 54x35", C-E 2/21/89 3,300
The Letter, oil on canvas, sgn, 37x24", C-E 10/26/89 2,860

OLIVETTI, Luigi (Italian, 19th/20th C)
Beauteous Sight, watercolor, sgn/dtd MCMXIII, 21x14", C-E 10/26/89 1,980
Helping the Grape Gatherer into a Boat, watercolor on paper, sgn, 30x21", B/B 3/22/89 2,475
Italian Peasant Girl Under an Arch, watercolor, sgn/dtd MCMIII, 22x14", C-E 10/26/89 1,650
Picking Fruit, watercolor, sgn/dtd 1907, 20x13", LH 12/4/88 750
Song of Love, watercolor over pencil, sgn/dtd 1923, 21x15", C-E 2/21/89 990
Spinning Wood, watercolor/gouache, sgn/dtd MCMXII, 21x14", C-E 10/26/89 990

OLIVIER MERSON, Luc (French, 1846-1920)
The Chimera, oil on board, sgn/dtd MCCNCX, 14x26", WD 1/11/89 OE 4,000

OLLER, Francisco
Plantains & Bananas, oil on board, sgn, ca 1893, 19x36", SBY 5/17/88 OE 132,000
Still Life with Coconuts, oil on panel, sgn, ca 1893, 19x36", SBY 5/17/88 OE 132,000

OLSEN, Chr Benjamin (Danish, 1873-1935)
Old Norwegian Ship Being Towed From a Harbor, oil on canvas, sgn, 16x24", B/B 9/15/88 1,870
Sailboats, oil on canvas, sgn/dtd 1918, 12x12", SBY 7/12/89 3,410

OLSEN, Herb (American, 1905-1973)
At the Zoo, watercolor on paper, sgn, 17x28", WG 4/23/88 OE 160
Furling a Sail, watercolor, sgn, 22x31", WG 9/16/88 200
Shortening Sail (man working in ship's rigging), watercolor on paper, sgn, 22x29", WG 4/23/88 OE 285
Stopping for a Chat, watercolor, sgn, 22x29", WG 9/16/88 OE 325
Watching the Waves, watercolor, sgn, 22x26", WG 9/16/88 OE 325

OLSEN, Joseph Olaf (American, 1894-1979)
Double-Sided: On the Beach; Rockport Fishing Shacks; watercolor on paper, sgn/dtd 62, 18x24", RAB 8/8/89 UE 300
Double-Sided: Pete Miner's House; Drydocked; watercolor on paper, sgn/dtd 63, 18x24", RAB 8/8/89 UE 350
Harbor View (animated scene w/numerous vessels), watercolor on paper, sgn/dtd 31, 16x22", C-E 2/21/89 350
Mexican Village, watercolor on paper, sgn, 15x22", C-E 2/3/88 UE 330
Palma de Majorca Spanish Fishing Boats, oil on canvas, sgn/dtd 26, unfr, 24x30", C-E 10/18/89 3,850
Portrait of a Young Girl (three-quarter length), oil on canvas, sgn/dtd 30, 36x25", PHL 10/28/88 UE 325
Repairing the Net, oil on panel, sgn, 24x30", C-NY 3/11/88 4,400
Spring Thaw, watercolor on paper, sgn/dtd Mar 20 69, 18x24", RAB 8/8/89 UE 650

OLYPHANT, Donald (American, 20th C)
Rowboats on the Beach, oil on canvas, sgn/dtd 1923, 17x23", FAP 12/8/89 350

OMWAKE, William (20th C)
Bugreey Koncur, acrylic/glitter on canvas, sgn/dtd 8-71, unfr, 48x52", C-E 11/14/89 UE 110

ONDERDONK, Julian (American, 1882-1922)
At Evening (landscape), oil on panel, sgn/dtd 1909, 10x15", B/B 3/22/89 1,430
Autumn Forest, oil on panel, sgn/dtd 1908, 9x12", C-NY 3/11/88 2,640
In Indian Summer, oil on panel, sgn, 6x9", SBY 4/14/89 3,080
Landscape, oil on canvas, sgn, 12x16", NA 2/24/89 UE 1,200
Landscape with Dogwoods & House, oil on canvas, sgn, 12x16", C-E 6/1/88 OE 3,300
Landscape with Town in Distance, oil on canvas, sgn, 12x16", C-E 4/7/88 990
Morning Sunlight, San Antonio, Texas; oil on canvas, sgn/dtd 1911, 20x31", B/B 10/9/88 OE 22,000
October Day, oil on board, sgn/dtd 1908, 5x7", SBY 9/14/89 1,320
Pair: Glowing Twilight; Autumn River Landscape; oil on panel, sgn/dtd 1909, 6x9", SBY 6/28/89 UE 2,200
Summer Landscape, oil on panel, sgn, 5x7", SBY 1/24/89 1,650

ONDERDONK, Robert Jenkins (American, 1853-1917)
Faggot Gatherer, oil on board, sgn, 6x10", B/B 12/8/88 OE 2,750

ONGANIA, Umberto (Italian, 19th/20th C)
Santa Maria Della Salute, watercolor, sgn, 5x11", LH 12/4/88 UE **50**
Venetian Canal Scene, watercolor on paper, sgn, 4x8", B/B 5/17/89 .... **550**

ONLEY, Toni (Canadian, 1928-)
Farmhouse From Via Di Leonardo, Florence; pencil, sgn/dtd May 13, 1972, 6x8", WAD 11/30/89 .... **180**

ONTHANK, Nahum Ball (American, 1823-1888)
Portrait of a Young Girl Seated in a Loggia, oil on canvas, sgn/dtd 65, 46x36", RWS 4/7/89 .... **1,800**

OPDENHOFF, George Willem (Dutch, 1807-1873)
Boats on a Stormy Sea, oil on panel, sgn, 16x33", SBY 7/12/89 UE **2,750**

OPERTI, Albert J. (Italian, 1852-)
Cutting the Blanket Piece, oil on canvas backed on beaverboard, sgn/dtd 1915, 40x32", RAB 3/14/89 UE **600**

OPIE, John (British, 1761-1807)
Portrait of a Gentleman Said To Be Samuel Tayler Coleridge, bust-length...; oil on canvas, 20x16", C-NY 5/31/89 .... **4,400**
Portrait of a Gentleman with His Three Children, three-quarter length; oil on canvas, 50x40", SBY 4/7/89 .... **8,350**
Portrait of a Lady, wearing a white dress & turban, in a landscape; oil on canvas, 30x26", C-NY 6/2/88 .... **1,760**

OPIE, John; att (British, 1761-1807)
Portrait of Amelia Opie As the Gleaner, oil on canvas, 37x30", SBY 4/29/88 .... **3,575**

OPIE, John; school of (British, 1761-1807)
Portrait of a Family, oil on canvas, 28x32", C-E 1/12/88 .... **1,650**

OPIE, Julian (20th C)
Legend of Europe (contemporary), oil on metal, 1984, 60x42x15", SBY 11/11/88 OE **9,900**

OPPENHEIM, Dennis (American, 1928-)
Project for the Ago Toronto, pencil/colored pencil/oil wash/pastel on paper, sgn/dtd 1982, 50x75", SBY 2/15/89 .... **4,400**
Second Sight for a Staircase, 2 sheets in 1 mount, mixed media, sgn/dtd 1980, 77x50", C-E 11/17/88 .... **3,850**
Station for Detaining & Blinding Radioactive Horses, colored pencils on paper, sgn/dtd 1979, 38x50", C-E 11/17/88 .... **2,200**
Study for Accelerator for Evil Thoughts, gouache/colored chalks on paper, sgn/inscr/dtd 1983, 50x38", C-E 5/13/88 .... **4,950**
Study for Caged Vacuum Projectiles, pencil/colored pencil/oil wash/oil pastel, sgn/dtd 1979, 70x50", SBY 10/7/89 .... **2,750**
Study for Final Stroke-Project for a Glass Factory; 2 sheets on 1 mount, mixed media, sgn/dtd 1980, 50x77", C-E 11/17/88 .... **5,830**
Study for Object with a Memory, pencils/oil wash/oil pastel/pastel/glitter, sgn/dtd 1984, 50x77", SBY 2/15/89 .... **3,850**
Study for Roots in Cubism, Hearts in the Stars, Berlin Project; oil/pastel/charcoal, sgn/dtd 1983, 74x50", SBY 10/8/88 .... **3,300**
Study for the Radiator Project, pen/black ink/acrylic/oil/colored chalk, sgn/dtd 1983, 50x38", C-E 11/14/89 OE **4,950**

ORDONEZ, Sylvia (20th C)
Table with Fruit (contemporary), oil on canvas, sgn/dtd 88, 36x43", SBY 11/21/88 .... **3,575**
Untitled (open door to interior view), oil on canvas, sgn/dtd 88, 60x41", SBY 11/21/88 .... **1,650**

ORGAN, Margorie (Mrs. Robert Henri)(American, 1866-)
William Butler Yeats Reading to His Friends, pen/ink on paper, unfr, 20x24", WL 5/20/88 .... **400**

ORLOVSKII, Aleksandr Osipovich (Polish/Russian, 1777-1838)
Caricature of a Young Waiter Holding a Coffeepot, pencil on paper, sgn/dtd AD 1822/inscr, 20x13", C-L 10/8/88 .... **2,790**
Two Peasants with Horses, watercolor/pencil on paper, monogramed/dtd 1802, 10x14", C-L 10/8/88 OE **3,530**

OROZCO, Jose Clemente (Mexican, 1883-1949)
Caballos (horses, impressionistic), oil on board, sgn, 17x13", C-NY 5/18/88 .... **26,400**
Desnudo (seated nude w/elbow resting on knee), pencil on paper, sgn, 1942, 9x18", C-NY 5/17/89 .... **1,760**
Desnudo (sketch of nude, three-quarter length), gouache on paper, sgn, 19x14", C-NY 11/21/88 .... **4,400**
Desnudo de Mujer (nude), black ink/brush on paper, 19x25", C-NY 5/17/89 UE **4,620**
Escena Revolucionaria, brush/black ink on paper, sgn, 9x12", C-NY 11/21/89 .... **3,300**
Guerreros Aztecas (Aztec warriors), gouache on paper, sgn, 15x18", C-NY 11/21/89 .... **16,500**
Prostitutes, tempera on board, sgn, 17x22", SBY 5/17/88 OE **31,900**
Strike, brush/India ink on paper, sgn, 12x17", C-NY 5/17/89 OE **26,400**
Trotsky en Exilio, crayon on brown paper, sgn, 11x9", C-NY 11/21/89 .... **5,280**
Unemployed (view of three men in hats & coats), oil on canvas, sgn, ca 1928-30, 26x20", C-NY 5/17/89 OE **93,500**

ORR, C.S. (American, 19th C)
Swamp Scene, watercolor, sgn, 6x12", MG 10/28/88 .... **1,000**

ORSELLI, Arturo (Italian, 19th C)
Couple Sharing a Bottle of Wine, watercolor on paper, sgn, 13x17", B/B 4/20/88 .... **2,090**

ORSI, school of (Italian, 16th C)
Christ & the Three Marys, oil on copper, 7x7", C-E 6/1/88 UE **550**

ORTIZ, Emilio (Mexican, 1936-)
Double-Sided Screen: (abstract); oil on panel, sgn, 1979, 75x106", SBY 5/17/88 .... **11,000**

ORTLIEB, Friedrich (German, 1839-1909)
Moment of Prayer, oil on canvas, sgn, 30x25", B/B 3/22/89 .... **4,400**
The Wayfarer, oil on canvas, sgn/inscr Munchen, 20x24", SBY 10/24/89 .... **12,100**

ORTOLANI, Giovanni Battista D. (Russian, ca 1750-after 1810)
Portrait of Princess Ekaterina Aleksandrovna Dolgurukaia, oil on canvas, no size given, C-L 10/8/88 .... **33,460**

OSEN, Erwin
Stehende Akt (standing, draped nude), watercolor/pencil on paper, sgn, 17x12", SBY 10/6/89 OE **8,800**

OSGOOD, Edward; att (American, 1849-1928)
City of Haverhill (ship) Passing Beneath the Newburyport Chain Bridge, oil on canvas, 26x35", RAB 11/25/88 .... **2,800**

OSHIVER, Harry James (20th C)
Peonies, oil on canvas, sgn/dtd 1930, 30x25", C-E 4/7/88 UE **198**

OSNAGHI, J. (European, ca 1900)
Still Life of Cherries & Crystal, oil on canvas, sgn, 14x24", DM 5/13/88 OE **3,250**

)SNIS, Benedict A.; att (American, 1872-)
Hercules & Omphale, oil on panel, 11x8", FAP 12/8/89 .... **200**
)SSO, A. (German, 20th C)
Heidelberg, watercolor on paper, sgn, 9x12", FAP 4/15/89 .... **358**
)SSORIO, Alfonso (Italian, 20th C)
Abstract, charcoal/watercolor, dtd 26.1x.79, 20x16", PHL 6/16/88 .... **900**
)STADE, see Van Ostade
)STERLIND, Anders (French, 1887-1960)
Cottage by a Road, oil on canvas, sgn/dtd 28, 23x29", C-E 5/23/88 .... **1,650**
Equestrian Statue in a Park, oil on canvas, sgn/dtd 1926, 24x29", C-E 5/13/88 .... **660**
Les Mesnuls, oil on canvas, sgn/dtd 1947, 24x36", C-E 11/17/88 OE **1,430**
)STERMAN, Karl Emil (Swedish, 1870-)
Two Girls by a Chinese Lantern, oil on canvas, sgn, 29x22", B/B 1/11/89 .... **1,980**
)STHAUS, Edmund Henry (American/German, 1858-1928)
A Shipperke, watercolor on board, sgn, 23x27", C-E 2/1/89 UE **770**
Afield (two setters in a landscape), oil on canvas, sgn, 24x36", SBY 6/9/89 .... **39,600**
Black & White Spaniel, watercolor, sgn, 11x15", DM 10/14/88 .... **2,750**
Collies in a Formal Garden, oil on canvas, sgn, unfr, 53x45", SBY 6/9/89 UE **5,000**
English Setter, watercolor on board, sgn/dtd 92, 6x8", DM 2/19/88 .... **1,700**
Family of Puppies, oil on canvas, sgn, 33x30", SBY 6/9/89 .... **38,500**
Puppies (in a landscape), oil on canvas, sgn, 24x31", C-NY 9/28/89 .... **11,000**
Setter in a Landscape, watercolor, sgn, 16x23", DM 10/14/88 .... **6,000**
Setter in Autumn Landscape, watercolor, sgn, 28x48", DM 10/14/88 .... **16,000**
Three Pointers, oil on canvas, sgn, 7x28", SBY 6/10/88 .... **3,850**
Three Setters Afield, oil on canvas, sgn, 24x36", SBY 6/9/89 .... **36,300**
Two Jack Russell Terriers in a Yard, watercolor on board, 18x25", WD 10/5/88 UE **4,000**
Two Pointers in a Landscape, watercolor heightened w/white on paper, sgn/dtd 94, unfr, 16x24", SBY 6/10/88 .... **4,400**
)SWALD, J.H. (British, 19th/20th C)
Paris, a Gray Day; oil on canvas, sgn, 20x34", PHL 6/16/88 UE **300**
)TIS, Bass (American, 1784-1861)
Portrait of a Man Said To Be Gilpin Bennett of West Chester, Pennsylvania; oil on canvas, 36x28", SBY 3/17/88 OE **8,800**
)TIS, Bass; att (American, 1784-1861)
Pair: Portraits of Mr & Mrs Holmes Hinkley; oil on canvas, 34x27", SBY 4/14/89 .... **2,200**
Self-Portrait, oil on canvas, 30x25", FAP 11/4/88 UE **600**
)TIS, George Demont (American, 1877-1962)
In the Canyon (shack in mountainous landscape), oil on canvas, sgn, 22x28", C-E 2/1/89 UE **1,650**
)TT, Jerry (20th C)
Nude (with 1971 Painting As a Backdrop), acrylic on canvas, sgn/inscr/dtd 1972, unfr, 80x96", C-E 5/13/88 .... **1,650**
)TTESEN, Otto Didrik (Danish, 1816-1892)
Still Life of Strawberries, oil on panel, sgn/dtd 1857, unfr, 8x10", SBY 7/12/89 .... **2,640**
Still Life of Strawberries on a Marble Ledge, oil on panel, sgn/dtd 1852, 8x10", SBY 10/24/89 .... **7,700**
Still Life of Tulips & Roses & a Bird's Nest in a Marble Niche, oil on panel, sgn/dtd 1866, 12x9", SBY 5/23/89 .... **8,800**
)TTOMANN, Henri (French, 1877-1927)
Girl with a Blue Hat, pastel, sgn, 10x8", MG 5/28/88 OE **450**
Woman with a Bird Cage, pen/ink/watercolor/crayon, sgn, 9x7", MG 5/28/88 .... **275**
)UDERAA, see Van Der Ouderaa
)UDINOT, Achille Francois; att (French, 1820-1891)
Landscape Scene with Figure Fording River, oil on panel, inscr, 22x18", RWS 11/3/88 .... **1,200**
)UDOT, Roland (French, 1897-)
Fete Champetre, oil on canvas, sgn, ca 1942, 11x18", C-NY 10/6/88 .... **2,310**
Flowers in a Glass Vase on a Table, oil on canvas, sgn, 32x26", WD 5/5/88 .... **4,750**
Montfort l'Amaury (rural landscape w/buildings), oil on canvas, sgn, 25x36", C-NY 2/18/88 OE **8,250**
Paysage d'Automne, oil on canvas, sgn, 1945, 10x13", C-NY 10/6/88 .... **3,300**
Paysage de Printemps (springtime landscape, folk-art style), oil on canvas, sgn, 24x32", C-NY 10/6/88 .... **3,960**
Paysannes, oil on board, sgn, 19x6", C-E 11/17/88 .... **1,320**
Wheatfield, oil on canvas, sgn, 11x16", B/B 1/11/89 .... **1,650**
)UDRY, Jacques Charles; circle of (French, 1720-1778)
Hawk Threatens a Duck's Nest, oil on canvas, 37x38", SBY 10/13/89 .... **6,600**
)UDRY, Jean Baptiste (French, 1686-1755)
Cathedral Seen Through a Grove of Trees, black/white chalk on blue paper, 24x20", SBY 1/13/89 .... **28,600**
Head of a Woman with Flowers in Her Hair, red/black/white chalk on blue paper, sgn, 10x6", C-NY 1/12/88 .... **11,000**
L'Homme e la Puce, black chalk/brush/ink/gray heightened w/white on blue paper, sgn/dtd 1732, 9x8", C-NY 1/12/88 .... **7,700**
La Cerf Malade, black chalk/brush/ink/gray wash heightened w/white on blue paper, sgn/dtd 1733, 10x8", C-NY 1/12/88 .... **10,450**
La Cour du Lion, black chalk/brush/ink/gray wash heightened w/white on blue, sgn/dtd 1731, 10x8", C-NY 1/12/88 .... **10,450**
Ostrich, black/white chalk on faded blue paper, 12x13", SBY 1/13/89 OE **18,700**
Pheasant, black/white chalk on blue paper, 11x15", SBY 1/13/89 .... **4,400**
Royal Black Cat, Le General; oil on canvas, sgn/inscr/dtd 1728, unfr, 47x64", C-NY 10/20/88 OE **46,200**
Study of a Chamois, black/white on blue paper, 11x13", SBY 1/13/89 .... **3,300**
Study of a Civet, black/white on blue paper, 11x14", SBY 1/13/89 OE **8,250**
Study of a Parrot, black/white chalk on blue paper, 8x14", SBY 1/13/89 .... **3,300**
Two Studies of a Crane, black/white chalk on faded blue paper, 12x13", SBY 1/13/89 .... **5,500**

OUDRY, Jean Baptiste; circle of (French, 1686-1755)
Portrait of a Gentleman Holding a Small Dog, oil on canvas, 36x29", SBY 4/7/89 ..... **4,125**
OUELLET, Robert
La Grange (the barn), oil on canvas, sgn, 16x20", FB 4/25/88 ..... **150**
OUREN, Karl (American, 1882-1934)
Mountain Field, Norway; oil on canvas, sgn, 18x24", PHL 12/1/88 ..... **900**
OVIEDO, Ramon (Latin American, 20th C)
Atavico Corredor, oil on canvas, sgn, 40x30", C-NY 11/21/89 ..... **7,150**
Children Behind the Masks, mixed media on canvas, sgn twice/titled, 30x40", SBY 11/21/88 OE **5,225**
Consultorio Infantil (abstract figures), oil on canvas, sgn, 24x36", C-NY 5/18/88 OE **7,150**
Design for the Future (abstract), oil on canvas, sgn, 30x40", SBY 5/17/88 OE **6,050**
Diaphanous Figures (abstract), oil on canvas, sgn/titled, 1982, 40x50", SBY 5/16/89 ..... **12,100**
OWEN, Robert Emmett (American, 1878-1957)
Autumn Forest, oil on canvas, 18x24", WG 4/23/88 UE **1,200**
Field in the Early Autumn Sunlight, oil on canvas, sgn, 31x41", B/B 1/11/89 ..... **4,400**
Houses in the Snow, oil on canvas, sgn, 30x40", WD 4/13/88 ..... **4,250**
October Afternoon (farm scene), oil on canvasboard, sgn, 12x16", C-E 6/1/89 UE **1,100**
October Afternoon (road meandering through the woods), oil on canvas, sgn, 34x36", C-NY 9/28/89 ..... **2,750**
Silver Mine, oil on canvas, sgn, 30x37", C-E 10/18/89 ..... **1,760**
Twilight (winter scene), oil on canvas, sgn, 20x24", C-E 2/1/89 OE **1,760**
Winter Road (landscape), oil on canvas, sgn, 30x40", RAB 8/8/89 ..... **2,750**
OWEN, William (British, 1769-1825)
Child & Her Doll, oil on canvas, 31x25", S/A 2/18/89 ..... **7,500**
Portrait of Lady Fornsque, oil on canvasboard, inscr w/title, 32x26", LH 5/15/88 ..... **900**
OWEN, William; att (British, 1769-1825)
Portrait of Master George Palmer, bust-length, wearing a black jacket; oil on canvas, 21x17", C-NY 1/15/88 ..... **7,700**
OZIER, Kenneth
Indian Chief, oil on canvas, sgn, 40x36", C-E 10/18/89 ..... **2,640**
Paaduan School (17th C)
Baptism of Saint Justina of Padua by Saint Prosdocimus, oil on canvas, 47x36", SBY 4/7/89 UE **1,320**
PACHECO, Maria Luisa (Bolivian, 1919-)
El Angel de lo Chocante (abstract composition), oil on canvas mounted on board, sgn/dtd 73, 59x28", WL 5/20/88 ..... **1,400**
Espacial (abstract), oil on canvas, sgn twice/dtd 61 twice/titled, 39x47", SBY 5/16/89 ..... **1,925**
PACHER, Ferdinand (German, 1852-1911)
Training the Dog, oil on canvas, sgn/dtd 1882, 17x13", C-E 10/26/89 ..... **4,180**
PACZKA, Cornelia Wagner
Extensive View From the Veranda, oil on canvas, sgn, 36x30", C-E 7/26/88 UE **750**
PADDOCK, Ethel Louise (American, 1887-)
Rowing in a Harbor, pastel on paper, sgn, no size given, C-E 9/15/88 ..... **330**
PADDOCK, Josephine (American, 1885-)
Red Bow (girl seated in wicker chair), oil on canvas, sgn, 30x25", RAB 8/9/88 UE **275**
PADWICK, Philip Hugh (British, 1876-1936)
Quiet Harbor (several ships in a small harbor), oil on canvas, sgn, 24x36", RAB 8/9/88 UE **250**
PAEZ, see De Paez
PAGANI, Gregorio (Italian, 1558-1605)
Madonna & Child with Symbols of the Immaculate Conception, oil on canvas, 26x21", SBY 10/21/88 ..... **3,850**
PAGANI, Paolo (Italian, 1661-1716)
Saint Anthony of Padua Holding the Infant Christ, oil on canvas, unfr, 39x29", C-NY 4/8/88 ..... **1,980**
PAGANI, Vincenzo; att (Italian)
Madonna & Child with the Infant Saint John the Baptist & an Angel, oil on panel, unfr, 24x15", C-NY 4/8/88 ..... **5,500**
PAGE, Henry Maurice (British, 19th C)
Moonrise Abinger Surrey, oil on canvas, sgn/inscr/dtd 1882, 33x23", C-E 5/23/88 ..... **1,430**
PAGE, Walter Gilman (American, 1862-1934)
Portrait of a Lady, oil on board, sgn/dtd 1919, 15x11", C-E 9/15/88 UE **495**
PAGE, William (American, 1811-1885)
Portrait of a Mother & Child (seated in an interior), oil canvas mounted on board, 46x35", SBY 1/28/88 OE **6,325**
PAGES, Irene (American, 20th C)
Sur la Plage a Monte Carlo (beach scene at Monte Carlo), oil on canvas, sgn, 13x19", C-E 11/17/88 ..... **1,210**
PAGES, Jules (American, 1867-1946)
Seascape, oil on canvas, sgn, 21x25", B/B 4/20/88 ..... **1,650**
View of Notre Dame, Spring; oil on canvas, sgn, 32x26", B/B 6/9/88 ..... **12,100**
PAGLIACCI, Aldo (Italian, 20th C)
View of the Capitoline Hill, oil on cradled panel, sgn/dtd 1951, 23x29", B/B 1/11/89 ..... **715**
PAGON, Katherine Dunn (American, 1892-)
Little Green House, Nantucket; oil on canvas, 16x18", C-E 10/18/89 UE **660**
Nantucket Moors, oil on paper, sgn/dtd 1930, 8x10", WG 9/16/88 ..... **375**
PAICE, George (British, 19th C)
Portrait of a Bulldog, oil on canvas, sgn/dtd 1881, 21x17", C-E 2/21/89 ..... **1,320**
PAIL, Edouard (French, 1851-)
Summer Landscape, oil on canvas, sgn, 34x45", C-NY 10/25/89 OE **20,900**
PAIRPOINT, Nellie M. (American, 19th/20th C)
In the Blacksmith's Shop, oil on canvas, sgn/dtd 1896, 25x38", RWS 12/10/88 ..... **425**

AJETTA, Pietro (Italian, 1845-1911)
Wooded River Landscape, oil on canvas laid down on masonite, sgn, 26x38", C-E 2/23/88 1,430
AL, Fried (Hungarian, 1914-)
Annabelle, oil on canvas, sgn/inscr, 24x30", PHL 11/15/88 UE 400
Ballet Dancers, oil on canvas, sgn/inscr Paris, 26x20", PHL 6/16/88 800
Nude, oil on canvasboard, sgn, 20x16", SBY 10/5/88 1,320
Sleeping Beauty, oil on canvas, sgn, 24x30", PHL 11/15/88 900
ALACI, Fran (20th C)
Untitled (contemporary), acrylic on sheet metal, sgn/dtd 1983, 14x34", C-NY 2/14/89 OE 1,045
Untitled (Jamaican travel tax receipt), acrylic on sheet metal, sgn/dtd 1983, 34x36", C-NY 2/14/89 880
ALACIOS, Alirio (Cuban, 1897-1968)
Hela Entre el Taller y el Paisaje (abstract), charcoal/sanguine/collage on canvas, 1980, 56x61", C-NY 5/17/89 11,000
Images in Landscape No 3, oil/mixed media on paper, sgn/titled/inscr, 1987-88, 59x67", SBY 5/16/89 12,100
Jai Street, mixed media on paper, sgn/dtd 86-87/inscr Drawing 3, stamped, 68x58", SBY 5/17/88 13,200
ALADINO, Mimmo (Italian, 1948-)
Bosforo (contemporary), watercolor on paper, 1982, 23x31", SBY 2/15/89 9,900
Il Battesimo del Leoni, oil on paper mounted on canvas, sgn/dtd 1982, 53x81", SBY 10/8/88 38,500
Ore Chi Guidera i Miei Passi, crayons/chalks/gouache/graphite/paper collage, sgn/inscr/dtd 1980, 19x27", C-NY 5/4/88 3,300
Sonno al Tiempo (Sleep at the Shrine, contemporary composition), oil/wood/collage on canvas, 1984, 79x59", SBY 5/3/89 OE 181,500
Triptych: Poeta All'Ombra (abstract); acrylic/plaster/papier-mache on canvas, sgn/dtd 1980, unfr, 87x165x4", C-NY 5/4/89 99,000
Untitled (abstract figures), charcoal/ink/pen/collage on paper, sgn/dtd 1982, 31x22", SBY 10/8/88 6,600
Untitled (abstract w/masks), oil/pastel on paper, 1983, 36x24", SBY 5/3/88 OE 30,250
Untitled (composition in blue & yellow), oil on paper laid down on canvas, sgn/dtd 1986, 56x45", SBY 10/5/89 OE 88,000
Untitled (contemporary), brush & black ink/graphite on paper, initialed/dtd 85, unfr, 12x16", C-NY 2/20/88 1,760
Untitled (contemporary), gouache/colored crayons/graphite on paper, sgn/dtd 1985, unfr, 12x16", C-NY 2/20/88 2,420
Untitled (contemporary), oil/acrylic/leather glove on jute, 1984, 41x55", C-NY 5/4/89 OE 35,200
ALAMEDES, Anthonie (Dutch, 1601-1673)
Cavaliers in a Guardroom Interior, oil on copper, sgn, 11x14", C-NY 10/12/89 8,250
Cavaliers Preparing To Ride, oil on panel, sgn, 20x28", NA 10/1/88 3,000
ALAMEDES, Palamedesz I (Dutch, 1607-1638)
Military Encampment, oil on panel, sgn/dtd 1634, 17x12", SBY 6/3/88 25,300
ALARDY, Jean (Canadian, 1905-)
La Petite Route (village scene), oil on board, sgn/dtd 1936, 10x12", FB 5/28/89 OE 900
ALIZZI, Filippo (Italian, 1818-1899)
In the Stable, oil on canvas, sgn/dtd 1858, 30x41", C-NY 2/23/89 28,600
ALLARES Y ALLUSTANTE, Joaquin (Spanish, 19th C)
La Madeleine, oil on canvas, sgn, 11x16", SBY 6/8/88 3,025
Portrait of a Young Girl with Her Doll, oil on canvas, sgn, 15x12", C-E 10/26/89 4,950
ALLIERE, Armand Julien (19th C)
Portrait of a Young Boy Holding a Toy Soldier, oil on canvas, sgn/dtd 1810, in painted oval, 18x14", C-NY 4/8/88 7,700
ALLYA, Celesztin (Hungarian, 1864-1948)
Mermaids (nudes floating in waves in seascape), oil on canvasboard, sgn, 10x14", B/B 5/17/89 357
ALM, Anna (Norwegian, 1854-1924)
Italian Fishing Boats, watercolor/gouache over traces of pencil, sgn, 7x10", C-NY 5/25/88 1,760
ALMA, Jacopo (Italian, 16th/17th C)
Crucifixion, oil on canvas, 41x35", C-NY 6/2/88 UE 7,700
Studies of Statue of Bacchus, Seated Woman, & Half-Length Portrait of Seated Woman; pen/brown ink, 10x8", SBY 1/13/89 3,025
ALMA, Jacopo; att (Italian, 16th/17th C)
Madonna, Child, & St Catherine; oil on canvas, 37x27", repaired, RAB 8/9/88 OE 21,000
ALMA, Jacopo; circle of (Italian, 16th/17th C)
Torment of Christ, oil on canvas, 19x15", C-NY 6/2/88 2,860
ALMA, Jacopo; school of (Italian, 16th/17th C)
Madonna & Child with Angels, oil on panel, 23x29", WD 1/25/89 UE 800
ALMAROLI Y GONZALEZ, Vicente (Spanish, 1834-1896)
At the Beach (elegant lady w/parasol, man in distance), oil on panel, sgn, 12x16", SBY 10/24/89 36,300
Letter, oil on panel, sgn, 11x10", SBY 5/23/89 15,400
ALMER, Cecil
Nancy Hanks, the World Champion Trotter; oil on canvas, sgn, 30x40", C-E 2/16/88 880
ALMER, Fanny Frances (American, 1812-1876)
Figures by a Cottage, watercolor on paper, sgn/inscr, 12x15", B/B 12/8/88 440
ALMER, Fanny Frances; att (American, 1812-1876)
View of West Point, oil on canvas laid down, 24x32", B/B 10/9/88 3,025
ALMER, Harry Sutton (British, 1854-1933)
Old Mill at Brill, Buckinghamshire, England; watercolor, sgn, 10x14", C-E 5/22/89 990
Sheep Grazing on the Moors, watercolor, sgn/dtd 1872, 11x17", C-E 7/26/88 UE 462
Wooded Landscape with a Stone-Covered Path, watercolor, sgn, unfr, 14x10", C-NY 2/23/89 UE 165
ALMER, Herbert Sidney (Canadian, 1881-1971)
April Skies, oil on panel, sgn, 8x11", WAD 6/12/89 1,400
Gnarled Maple (Belfontaine, Ontario), oil on board, sgn, 14x17", WAD 11/30/89 850
On the Gull River, Haliburton; oil on board, sgn, 11x14", WAD 11/30/89 950

Summer Sunset, Saskatchewan; oil on board, sgn, 16x20", WAD 6/12/89 1,800
Sunshine & Shadow, oil on canvas, sgn, 24x30", WAD 11/30/89 2,500

PALMER, Pauline (American, 1869-1938)
Landscape, oil on canvas, sgn/dtd 1911, 25x32", LH 10/16/88 4,000
Theatrical Performer, oil on canvas, sgn, 45x38", RWS 5/12/89 UE 1,800

PALMER, Samuel (British, 1805-1881)
Hilly Landscape with Farmers Ploughing, watercolor/pencil on paper laid down, 4x6", WD 5/5/88 OE 21,000

PALMER, Walter Launt (American, 1854-1932)
Farm in Winter Twilight, Albany, New York; watercolor/gouache on blue board, sgn/dtd 1890, 13x17", RWS 5/12/89 4,200
Fishing Boat, Venice; oil on canvas, sgn, 17x12", SBY 1/24/89 2,200
Forest Shelter in Winter, watercolor/gouache on paper, sgn, 18x23", B/B 6/9/88 OE 13,200
In the Glen (snowy landscape), watercolor/gouache on paper mounted on board, sgn, 18x24", SBY 4/14/89 OE 9,350
Jewelled Pines (winter landscape), no media given, sgn twice/titled, 24x32", SBY 5/24/89 26,400
November Snow, oil on canvas, sgn, 21x28", SBY 9/23/88 OE 22,000
Snow-Covered Stream at Sunset, oil on canvas, sgn, 24x18", C-NY 5/25/89 16,500
Snowy Pines, watercolor/gouache/pencil on board, sgn, 18x24", C-NY 9/28/89 3,300
State Building, Albany; oil on canvas, sgn/dtd 1907, 23x30", C-NY 9/28/89 OE 27,500
Venetian Boats, oil on canvas, sgn, 16x24", SBY 9/23/88 OE 7,700
Winter Sun (landscape), watercolor/gouache on board, sgn, 20x15", C-NY 5/26/88 8,250
Winter Sundown (snowy landscape), oil on canvas, 24x21", C-NY 12/2/88 OE 12,100

PALUMBO, Alphonse
Brooklyn Bridge & Tug Boats, oil on canvas, sgn, 25x30", C-NY 9/30/88 2,420

PANABAKER, Frank Shirley (Canadian, 1904-)
Georgian Bay, oil on board, sgn, 20x26", WAD 6/12/89 1,900
Georgian Bay Pines & Rocks, oil on board, sgn, 16x20", WAD 11/30/89 OE 1,400

PANCOAST, Morris Hall (American, 1877-)
Harbor Vista, oil on canvas, sgn, unfr, 32x40", SBY 1/24/89 3,850
Rockport Sunrise, oil on canvas, sgn, 12x16", RWS 5/12/89 350
Texas Landscape, oil on board, sgn, 16x16", B/B 12/8/88 1,045
Wet Day, oil on canvas, sgn/inscr/titled, 22x26", SBY 9/23/88 2,750

PANFILI, Pio (Italian, 1723-1812)
Monumental Square with an Obelisk, chalk/pen/ink wash, Strasburg bend above V wm, 11x13", C-NY 1/11/89 1,650

PANINI, Giovanni Paolo (Italian, 1692-1765)
Capriccio of Classical Ruins with Soldiers, oil on canvas, 38x54", C-NY 5/31/89 OE 126,500
Pair: Architectural Capriccio with Roman Monuments; oil on canvas, 27x31", SBY 6/3/88 187,000

PANINI, Giovanni Paolo; & Studio (Italian, 1692-1765)
Figures in an Architectural Capriccio with the Three Columns of the Dioscuri...; oil on canvas, 31x45", SBY 6/2/89 44,000

PANINI, Giovanni Paolo; att (Italian, 1692-1765)
Classical Figure with Figures, oil on canvas, 26x21", WD 10/19/88 7,000
Classical Scene, pen/ink/wash on paper, 8x11", WG 10/19/88 OE 700

PANINI, Giovanni Paolo; circle of (Italian, 1692-1765)
Pair: Colosseum; Palazzo del Quirianale; oil on canvas, 28x39", C-NY 4/6/89 OE 66,000

PANINI, Giovanni Paolo; follower of (Italian, 1692-1765)
Architectural Fantasy with an Oracle Making a Prediction, oil on canvas, 61x30", SBY 10/13/89 11,000

PANINI, Giovanni Paolo; manner of (Italian, 1692-1765)
Architectural Capriccio, oil on canvas, unfr, 38x50", WD 1/25/89 OE 9,000
Figures Among Classical Ruins, oil on canvas, 38x29", WD 1/25/89 4,000
Figures Conversing Among Architectural Ruins, oil on canvas, 29x39", SBY 12/9/88 OE 4,675

PANINI, Giovanni Paolo; school of (Italian, 1692-1765)
Pair: Classical Buildings with Figures; oil on canvas, 23x28", WD 10/19/88 OE 6,750

PANINI, Giovanni Paolo; studio of (Italian, 1692-1765)
Alexander the Great Discovering the Tomb of Achilles, oil on canvas, 30x39", C-NY 10/20/88 OE 24,200
Capriccio of the Monuments of Rome with a Beggar & Other Figures, oil on canvas, sgn, 43x53", SBY 10/21/88 OE 25,300

PANNETT, R.
La Toilette, gouache, sgn, unfr, 21x15", C-NY 5/25/88 4,950

PANORIOS, K. (Greek, 19th/20th C)
Daydream, oil on canvas, sgn, 32x25", FAP 12/8/89 3,200

PANSING, Fred (American, fl 1885-1905)
On Block Island, oil on canvas, sgn/inscr/dtd 1895, 12x16", C-E 6/1/88 OE 1,045
Schooner Entering Harbor at Sunset, oil on canvas, sgn, 12x18", RAB 8/1/88 5,000

PANTON, Lawrence Arthur Colley (Canadian, 1894-1954)
Sunlight in the Forest, oil on board, sgn, 20x24", WAD 6/12/89 1,500

PANUNZI, Sebastiano (American/Italian, 1845-)
Horses at Rest, watercolor heightened w/gouache, sgn, 8x10", FAP 12/8/89 150

PANZA, Giovanni (Italian, 19th C)
Young Vegetable Vendor, oil on canvas, sgn, 28x35", C-E 2/21/89 2,750

PAOLETTI, Antonio Ermolao (Italian, 1834-1912)
Venetian Girls Spinning Wool, oil on panel, sgn, 10x15", C-E 2/2/189 OE 7,150

PAOLINI, Pietro (Italian, 1490-1547)
Bagpiper, oil on canvas, initialed, inscr, 48x37", C-NY 1/11/89 46,200
Portrait of a Young Man Wearing a Feathered Cap, oil on panel, 15x14", C-NY 6/2/88 8,250

OLINI, Pietro; circle of (Italian, 1490-1547)
Allegory of Fate: Young Woman & Old Woman with a Spindle; oil on canvas, 25x33", C-NY 4/6/89 ... 3,300
PALUCA, L. (Italian, 19th/20th C)
Sailing Ship, oil on panel, sgn, 24x31", LH 3/20/88 ... 250
PART, Max (French, 1911-)
Dynamique Florale, oil on canvas, sgn/#d 48B OZ, 33x26", WD 5/5/88 ... 1,800
Le Rire de Gilda (abstract), oil on canvas, sgn/#d 42B OX, 32x26", WD 5/5/88 ... 1,800
Vase of Flowers, oil on canvas, sgn, 22x18", SBY 10/7/89 ... 4,125
PE, Eric (American, 1870-1938)
Courtyard of the Sadat, Cairo; oil on canvas, sgn/dtd 91, unfr, 36x28", RWS 11/10/89 ... 3,700
Early Morning-Annisquam, New England Fishing Village; oil on canvas, sgn/dtd 1900, 46x31", RWS 11/10/89 ... 9,000
Mermaids & Sea Nymphs, oil on canvas, sgn, 58x37", SBY 6/28/89 ... 12,100
The Guest, 1860 (portrait of a young woman holding umbrella in a landscape); pastel, sgn, 38x26", RWS 11/10/89 ... 5,000
PE, Friedrich Edouard (German, 1817-1905)
Landscape with Goats, oil on canvas, sgn/dtd 60, 45x37", B/B 6/15/89 ... 6,600
PI, see Dell'Altissimo
QUET, Guy (Canadian, 19th C)
Le Temps d'une Pause, oil on canvas, sgn, 10x12", FB 5/28/89 UE ... 180
QUIN, Pauline (Canadian, 20th C)
Snow Man's Nearly Ready, oil on canvas, sgn, 16x20", WAD 6/12/89 ... 500
RAPARNT, T.
Sheep Grazing, oil on canvas, sgn, 24x29", C-E 2/23/88 UE ... 990
REDES, see De Paredes
RENTINO, Bernardo (Italian, 1437-1531)
Christ at the Column, black chalk/pen/brown ink, paper rubbed in red chalk, 9x6", C-NY 1/12/88 ... 74,800
REROULTJA, Otto (Australian, 20th C)
Central Australian Landscape, pencil/watercolor, sgn, 11x14", C-SK 6/9/88 ... 148
RET Y ALCAZAR, Luis; circle of (Spanish, 1747-1799)
Allegory with an American Native Kneeling Before a Regal Figure, oil on canvas, 12x27", SBY 1/12/89 ... 5,500
Pair: Portrait of King George III; Portrait of Queen Charlotte; oil on panel, 16x12", C-NY 4/6/89 OE ... 6,050
RINI (Italian, 19th/20th C)
Village Square, watercolor on paper, sgn, 8x12", RAB 8/8/89 UE ... 350
RIS, Alfred Jean Marie (French, 1846-1908)
Watering the Horses, watercolor heightened w/white over pencil, sgn/dtd 1895, 18x24", C-NY 10/25/89 OE ... 4,620
RIS, Pierre Adrien (1745-1819)
Landscape with a House, black chalk, 10x8", SBY 7/12/89 ... 770
RK, David (American, 1911-1960)
Two Figures, graphite on paper, sgn/dtd 66, 17x14", C-NY 5/4/88 ... 3,080
Untitled (two half-length figures w/abstract landscape background), oil on canvas, sgn/dtd 57, 25x27", SBY 10/5/89 OE ... 88,000
RKER, E.A. (American, 1876-)
Fishermen on the River, oil on board, sgn, 9x12", WG 9/16/88 ... 225
RKER, H.E. (British, 19th C)
Preparing for a Ride, oil on canvas, initialed/sgn on verso, 8x11", SBY 12/9/88 ... 935
RKER, Henry H. (British, 1858-1930)
Cows Grazing, oil on canvas, sgn, 31x22", C-E 10/25/88 ... 4,620
Loading the Haywagon, oil on canvas, 18x24", C-E 2/23/88 ... 1,540
Where the Peaceful Waters Glide (landscape with stream & cows), oil on canvas, sgn twice, 24x36", SBY 12/9/88 ... 8,525
RKER, Lawton S. (American, 1868-1954)
Cottage Beyond a Grove of Trees, oil on board, sgn, 11x14", B/B 12/8/88 ... 3,025
Secret Garden, oil on canvas, sgn, 30x24", C-NY 9/28/89 ... 11,000
Woman in a Boat, oil on canvas, sgn, 30x24", SBY 5/25/88 ... 198,000
RKER, Paul (American, 1905-)
Still Life of Fruit & Wine, oil on canvas, sgn/dtd 1977, 20x24", B/B 8/10/88 ... 412
RKER, Ray (American, 1922-)
Untitled (abstract), acrylic on canvas, sgn twice/dtd 1965 & 1966, unfr, 56x70", C-E 5/9/89 OE ... 2,860
Untitled (abstract), acrylic on canvas, sgn/dtd 1963, 39x45", SBY 10/7/89 ... 2,860
Untitled (abstract), oil on canvas, sgn, 68x60", SBY 10/7/89 ... 4,125
Untitled (abstract), oil on canvas, sgn twice/dtd 1960, 68x70", C-E 5/13/88 ... 5,060
RKHURST, Thomas (American, 1853-1923)
Surf, oil on board, sgn, 12x16", B/B 12/8/88 ... 1,320
ROLARI, G.
Gondolier on a Venetian Canal, watercolor over pencil, sgn, 27x16", C-E 11/8/88 ... 2,090
RRA, Jose Felipe (Spanish, 19th C)
Goldfish Bowl, oil on canvas, bears signature, unfr, 22x17", SBY 2/22/89 ... 4,400
RRASIO, Micheli (Italian, 1516-1578)
Saint Cecilia, oil on panel, 39x32", WD 10/19/88 ... 3,000
RRISH, David (American, 1939-)
Motorcycle, oil on canvas, sgn/dtd 1971, 40x40", SBY 10/7/89 OE ... 14,300
RRISH, Maxfield (American, 1870-1966)
Architectural Design for Radnor House, graphite on tracing paper, initialed, 10x7", B/B 1/11/89 ... 550
Cadmus Sowing the Dragon's Teeth, oil on canvas laid down, sgn/dtd 1907, 41x32", B/B 3/22/89 ... 110,000

Head of a Woman, oil on canvas, initialed, 6x6", SBY 4/29/88 ... 8,25
Hill Top (two girls lying under tree), sgn/dtd, 1926, 36x22", C-NY 12/2/88 OE ... 198,00
Knave of Hearts, oil on panel, initialed/sgn/inscr 1924, 20x16", C-NY 9/30/88 OE ... 104,50
Morning, oil on panel, initialed/sgn/inscr, dtd 1922 twice, 20x15", C-NY 9/30/88 OE ... 77,00
Old Mill, oil on masonite, sgn/dtd 1942, inscr/#d 1348, 22x19", C-NY 12/2/88 OE ... 66,00

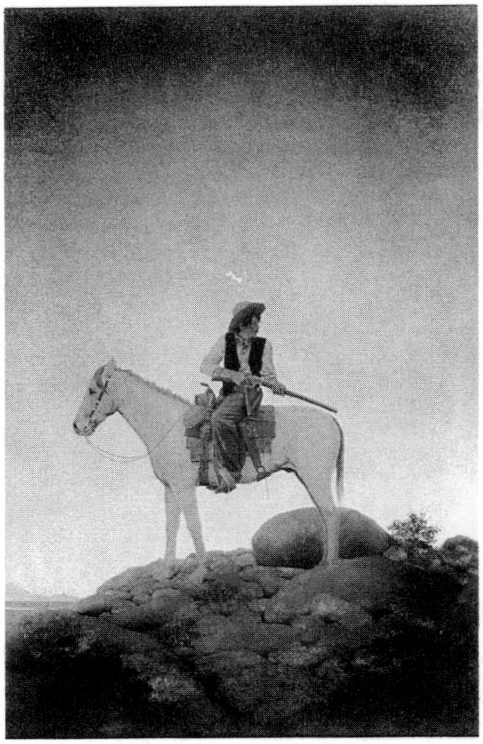

Outlaw, tempera/oil on board, initialed, 17x12", RWS 11/3/88 OE; $75,000

Prometheus (commissioned for GE Calendar in 1920), oil on board, sgn, 32x21", C-NY 5/25/89 ... 74,80
Set of 4: Comic Cop; Pencil Study for Page; Two Mask Studies; mixed media, no sizes given, B/B 10/9/88 UE ... 2,20
Study for Scenery for the Tempest, oil on panel, sgn/initialed/dtd 09, 16x16", SBY 4/29/88 ... 27,50
The Glen (landscape), oil on masonite, sgn/dtd 1936/inscr MP #58, 33x28", SBY 4/29/88 ... 71,50
The Knight, colored marker on paper, initialed, 16x12", B/B 10/9/88 ... 4,95
Young King of the Black Isles, oil on paper, sgn/initialed/dtd 1906, 20x16", SBY 4/29/89 OE ... 96,25

PARRISH, Stephen (American, 1846-1938)
Rocky Landscape, oil on canvas, sgn/dtd 1915, 25x35", SBY 9/23/88 OE ... 4,67

PARROCEL, Charles (French, 1688-1752)
Portrait of Louis XV of France on Horseback, oil on canvas, 35x37", SBY 10/21/88 UE ... 9,90

PARROCEL, Charles; att (French, 1685-1752)
Road to Calvary, oil on canvas, unfr, 29x23", SBY 4/7/88 ... 2,47

PARROTT, William Samuel (American, 1844-1915)
Distant Peak (landscape), oil on canvas, sgn, 20x15", SBY 3/17/88 OE ... 4,12
Mount Hood, oil on canvas, sgn, 15x20", SBY 4/14/89 ... 3,30
Mount Hood From Bull Run Lake, oil on board, sgn, 10x12", SBY 1/24/89 ... 3,30

PARSONS, Alfred William (British, 1847-1920)
Garden Path, watercolor on paper, sgn/dtd 1906, 10x14", SBY 7/12/89 ... 1,98
Woodland Garden, watercolor, sgn, 13x20", C-NY 10/25/89 ... 2,42

PARSONS, Beatrice (British, 1870-1955)
Garden Path, watercolor on paper, sgn, 15x10", WD 5/5/88 ... 3,40

PARSONS, J.W. (American, 19th/20th C)
Autumnal River Landscape, oil on canvas, sgn/dtd 1900, 25x30", SLK 5/11/88 ... 90

PARSONS, L.A. (American, 20th C)
Still Life Flower Box with Pitcher, oil on canvas stretched on board, sgn, 12x18", WG 4/23/88 UE ... 17

PARSONS, Max (British)
Harbor Scene, oil on panel, sgn, 16x20", FB 10/30/89 ... 30
Pair: Le Havre; Boulogne; oil on panel, sgn, 20x30", 21x27", FB 10/17/88 ... 67

PARSONS, Orrin Sheldon (American, 1866-1943)
Arroyo, Santa Fe; oil on board, sgn, 20x24", C-SK 11/10/88 OE ... 2,79

PARTON, Arthur (American, 1842-1914)
Camp at Van Cortland Park, oil on canvas, sgn, unfr, 13x22", C-E 2/3/88 ... 1,43
Cows Crossing a Stream, oil on canvas, sgn, 16x24", C-E 6/1/89 ... 1,98
Cows Wading (mountains & mist beyond), oil on canvas, sgn, 24x34", C-E 6/1/89 ... 1,65
Fishing by Moonlight (moonlit scene w/two fishermen in a rowboat), oil on canvas, sgn/dtd 75, 12x20", RWS 3/31/88 UE ... 1,30

.andscape Scene with Cows (cows fording stream in summer), oil on canvas, sgn, 19x25", RWS 3/31/88 OE	1,600
.ogs & Rapids, oil on canvas, sgn, 11x18", C-E 6/1/89	1,100
Mountain Landscape, oil on canvas, monogramed, 7x9", C-E 6/1/89	825
Mountainous River Landscape, Cattle Watering; oil on canvas, sgn, 26x40", WD 10/5/88 UE	2,900
)ut Fishing-Hudson River; oil on canvas, sgn, 18x24", RAB 8/8/89 UE	1,900
'assing Shower (river landscape), oil on canvas, sgn, 19x30", WD 10/5/88	8,000
River Landscape, oil on canvas, sgn/dtd 1881, 35x26", SBY 6/28/89 UE	1,320
Rushing Water, oil on canvas, sgn, 36x60", C-E 11/30/88	1,980
Spring in the Catskills (cows at water's edge, figure on bridge), oil on canvas, sgn/dtd 1867, 10x16", C-NY 9/28/89	8,800
Summer Trees Along a Stream, oil on canvas, sgn, 18x24", MAG 4/24/88	2,000
RTON, Ernest (American, 1845-1933)	
Mountain River, oil on canvas, sgn, unfr, 26x18", C-SK 11/10/88	1,490
'air: English River Scenes; oil on canvas, sgn, 17x26", WAD 6/6/88	2,800
Springtime on the Thames, England; oil on canvas, sgn, unfr, 16x24", SBY 9/23/88 OE	6,050
Virginia Waters, oil on canvas, sgn, 36x28", C-E 10/18/89 OE	4,400
Walk Along the River (figure with fishing pole on bank of calm river), oil on canvas, sgn, 36x48", RAB 8/9/88	3,500
RTON, Professor B. (British, 19th/20th C)	
The Plea, oil on panel, sgn/dtd 06, 14x17", B/B 9/15/88 OE	2,750
SCAL, Paul (French, 1832-1903)	
Moonlit Harbor View, watercolor heightened w/gouache on paper, sgn/dtd 1885, 3x5", FAP 4/15/89	468
'enetian Canal, watercolor, sgn, 14x21", NA 11/5/88	425
Walking Along the Bluffs, gouache, sgn/dtd 187(?), 4x3", C-E 10/26/89	550
SCAL, Paul B. (French, 1867-)	
Algerian Encampment, watercolor on gouache, sgn, 9x26", C-E 5/22/89	770
Arab Shepherds, gouache, 11x16", LH 12/4/88	750
Arabs Resting, watercolor/gouache, sgn/dtd 1880, 6x10", C-E 5/22/89	660
Evening at the Oasis (figures & camel at water, palms beyond), watercolor on paper, sgn/dtd 1896, 18x13", WG 4/23/88	750
.andscape with Shepherd & Flock, gouache on paper, sgn/dtd 1901, 12x9", WL 5/20/88 UE	400
SCHKE, Ed (American, 20th C)	
Brand-X, oil on canvas, sgn/dtd 80, 32x72", SBY 2/15/89	19,800
El Baggio, oil on canvas, sgn/dtd 81, 36x32", C-NY 5/4/88	9,900
Trio (contemporary), oil on canvas, sgn/dtd 70, 50x42", C-E 11/14/89 OE	11,000
SCIN, Jules (American/French, 1885-1930)	
Au Balcon (figures on balcony), gouache/watercolor/pen/India ink on paper, sgn, 10x10", C-E 5/9/89	2,310
Baptism, ink/wash on paper, stamped signature, 8x8", SBY 10/7/89	2,860
Beach Scene, watercolor on paper, stamped signature/inscr Bayonne 1928, 5x8", SBY 10/5/88 UE	1,320
Bobette Allongee (nude), oil/pencil on board laid down on panel, stamped signature, 1927, 29x24", C-NY 5/11/89 OE	165,000
Brothel Scene, pen/ink/wash on paper, ca 1906, 7x11", SBY 10/6/89	14,300
Card Players, India ink on paper, stamped signature/atelier stamp/dtd 1915, 7x7", SBY 10/7/89	3,300
Central Park, New York; colored crayons/pencil on paper, stamped, ca 1918, 9x12", SBY 2/18/88	4,400
Composition aux Femmes, oil on canvas, sgn, 1911, 10x11", SBY 10/7/88	33,000
Cuba, pencil on paper, stamped signature/atelier stamp, 6x7", SBY 10/5/88 OE	935
Cuban Street Scene, watercolor/gouache, stamped signature/atelier stamp, 7x7", SBY 5/30/89	5,500
Deux Femmes Nues Allongees (two reclining female nudes), pencil on paper, stamped signature, 20x15", C-NY 10/5/89	8,580
Deux Jeunes Filles dans le Bois, watercolor/pen/black ink on paper mounted at edges on board, 9x5", C-E 5/13/88 UE	550
Double-Sided: Femme au Chapeau; verso: watercolor on paper, recto: pencil on paper, stamped, 1906, 7x5", C-NY 10/6/88	715
Double-Sided: Portrait of Peter Lorre; pencil on buff paper, atelier stamp/estate stamp, 17x12", SBY 4/29/88 OE	12,650
Double-Sided: Trois Personnages; Trois Etudes; verso: pencil/watercolor, recto: pencil, stamped, 5x7", C-NY 10/6/88	1,320
En Floride (figures in a Florida scene), watercolor/pen/India ink on buff paper, sgn, 8x11", C-NY 10/6/88	8,250
Femme Assisse sur un Divan (woman seated on divan), charcoal on buff paper, sgn, 15x11", PHL 11/15/88	1,100
Femme au Chaise (nude reclining on chaise), pencil on paper, stamped signature, 12x9", SBY 10/7/89	4,400
Femme au Chapeau (seated female wearing hat), watercolor/pen/ink on paper, atelier & estate stamps, 8x6", SBY 10/7/88	3,850
Femme Couchante (sleeping lady), oil on panel, sgn, 14x17", SBY 5/10/89 OE	132,000
Femme Nue Assise (seated nude), pencil on paper, stamped signature/atelier stamp, 1920, 11x9", SBY 10/6/89	2,200
Femme sur un Divan et Homme Debout (sketch of woman on sofa, man standing), charcoal on buff, sgn, 11x15", PHL 11/15/88	1,100
Figures in a Cuban Landscape, ink/watercolor on paper, sgn, studio stamp, 7x11", PHL 6/16/88 UE	500
Fin de Seance (reclining nude), pen/black ink in paper, stamped signature, 1928, 25x19", C-NY 10/5/89	7,700
Flute Player with Mother & Child, watercolor/ink on paper, sgn, 26x20", SBY 10/7/89	4,950
Group of Women, pencil on paper, Wood Gaylor estate stamp/#d 362, 17x22", SBY 10/7/89	2,750
Groupe de Jeunes Filles de Charleston, watercolor/pen/ink on paper, sgn/dtd Charleston 1919, 11x11", C-E 5/9/89	5,720
Hermine David, Nu Devant la Table; pen/black ink/charcoal on paper, sgn/stamped, 19x25", C-NY 10/6/88	16,500
Hermine David Reading, oil on board, atelier/succession stamp, ca 1908, 18x14", SBY 5/30/89 OE	26,400
Hermine Reveuse (modernistic bust-length portrait), oil on canvas, sgn, 1919, 18x15", SBY 10/6/89	44,000
Homme et Femme dans un Intereur (man & woman in an interior), charcoal on buff paper, sgn, 11x15", PHL 11/15/88	1,200
Hommes a New York, watercolor/pen/ink/pencil on paper mounted on board, sgn/dtd 1918, 7x9", C-E 5/9/89	2,420
Jeune Adolescente, oil on canvas, bears signature, 1929, 36x26", SBY 5/11/88	66,000
Jeune Fille Assise, crayon/pencil on paper, stamped signature, 9x6", C-E 5/9/89	1,650
Jeune Fille Assise (portrait of a seated girl), oil on board laid down on panel, sgn/dtd 1921, 26x21", C-NY 5/11/89 OE	187,000
Jeune Fille Etendue (reclining nude), watercolor/pen/ink on paper, sgn, 11x15", C-NY 2/18/88	4,620
Jeune Fille Nue Assise, watercolor/pen/black ink on paper, stamped/signature, atelier stamp, 7x8", C-NY 10/6/88	2,640
Jeune Garcon Posant (seated male nude), charcoal/pencil on paper, stamped signature, ca 1924-25, 20x13", SBY 5/11/88 OE	7,700

L'Homme au Chien (Portrait d'un Peintre Allemand), oil on canvas, stamped signature, 1912, 27x22", C-NY 5/11/89 .... **99,00**
La Brodeuse au Mexique (portrait), oil on canvas, dtd 1919/indistinctly inscr, 17x25", SBY 11/12/88 .... **77,00**
La Cabaret (woman seated on bench, one standing viewed from behind), charcoal on buff paper, sgn, 11x15", PHL 11/15/88 .... **1,10**
La Dame au Turban (portrait), oil on canvas, atelier/succession stamp, 1907, 16x13", SBY 5/30/89 .... **41,80**
La Gaiete Montparnasse (figures in profile), pencil heightened w/colored wash, studio stamp, 1910-12, 7x5", PHL 11/15/88.......... **70**
La Limousine (reclining woman), oil on canvas, sgn, 21x26", C-NY 2/18/88 OE **71,50**
La Modele (seated woman), oil/pencil on canvas, sgn, 1928, 32x26", C-NY 5/12/88 .... **220,00**
La Petite Marianne (girl seated in a chair), pencil on paper, sgn, 1929, 22x16", C-NY 2/18/88 .... **6,05**
Le Client, ink transfer on paper, ca 1920-25, 12x16", SBY 10/7/88 .... **3,30**
Le Petite Bretonne (seated nude), oil over pencil on canvas, stamped signature, 1912, 29x24", C-NY 11/16/88 .... **132,00**
Les Amies (The Friends), charcoal/pencil on paper, sgn, 25x19", SBY 11/16/89 OE **137,50**
Les Arabes (in landscape), pencil on paper, stamped signature, 9x7", C-E 5/9/89 .... **1,10**
Les Deux Modeles (two nude girls), pencil on paper, sgn, ca 1924, 19x17", C-NY 10/5/89 .... **7,70**
Les Deux Soeurs, pencil on laid paper, sgn, ca 1928, 25x19", SBY 2/18/88 OE **7,15**
Les Trois Modeles (The Three Models), oil on board, sgn, 1916, 18x22", SBY 5/10/89.......... **60,50**
Nu Allonge (reclining nude), pencil on paper, stamped, 11x9", C-NY 10/6/88.......... **1,65**
Nu Assis, watercolor/crayon on paper, stamped signature, ca 1910, no size given, C-E 5/9/89 OE **2,31**
Nude in an Interior, pen/ink, stamped signature/atelier stamp, 6x6", SBY 5/30/89 OE **2,75**
Nue Debout (standing nude), pencil/brown & gray wash on paper laid down on board, sgn, 13x19", PHL 11/15/88 .... **3,50**
Offrande a Venus (Offerings to Venus), pencil/charcoal on paper, sgn, 18x22", C-NY 2/18/88.......... **2,20**
Plage Americaine (figures on beach), watercolor/black wax crayon/pencil/pen/India ink on buff paper, 9x11", C-NY 10/6/88.......... **8,25**
Reclining Woman, pencil on paper, sgn, 16x14", SBY 2/14/89.......... **4,95**
Scene de Cuba, watercolor/pen/black ink/pencil on paper, sgn, 5x9", C-NY 10/6/88.......... **3,30**
Set of 3: Femme Nue; La Famille; L'Attelage; pencil on paper, sgn, 12x10" & smaller, C-NY 2/18/88 .... **2,42**
Set of 6: Cafe du Dome Personalities; 5 pen/ink/pencil & pen/ink, ca 1906, ea 7x9", SBY 2/16/89 .... **13,20**
Society Talk, India ink/watercolor on paper, stamped signature/atelier stamp, 5x8", SBY 10/7/88 .... **2,75**
St Martin, pen/ink/oil on board laid down on canvas, sgn, 1921, 20x25", SBY 10/7/88 .... **23,10**
Standing Nude, gouache, stamped signature, 9x7", SBY 5/30/89 OE **5,50**
Trois Amis sur un Divan, brown carbon paper drawing on paper laid down on board, sgn, ca 1930, 17x22", SBY 2/18/88 .... **3,57**
Trois Femmes Nues (three nudes), watercolor over pen/India ink on paper, stamped signature, 9x11", C-NY 10/5/89 .... **2,86**
Trois Jeunes Femmes, pen/ink/watercolor on paper laid down on stiff card, ca 1918, S-10x9", SBY 10/7/88 .... **3,57**
Tunisian Leading a Donkey, pen/brown ink/watercolor on paper, sgn, ca 1924-26, 10x12", SBY 10/7/89.......... **2,09**
Two Seated Women, watercolor/pencil, stamped signature/atelier stamp, 7x7", SBY 5/30/89 OE **3,85**
Une Nuit d'Arabie, pen/ink/watercolor/charcoal on paper, sgn, ca 1922, 8x10", SBY 10/6/89 .... **4,40**
Young Woman, Seated (legs crossed, cigarette in hand); pen/ink/watercolor on paper, sgn, 16x12", SBY 10/6/89.......... **16,50**

PASCOE, William (British, 19th C)
Connamara, A McCarthy Up (jockey/horse in landscape); oil on canvas, sgn/dtd 1886/titled, 20x30", RAB 3/27/89 .... **90**

PASINELLI, Lorenzo; circle of (1629-1700)
Saint Cecilia with Two Angels Playing a Horn & an Organ, oil on canvas laid down on board, 39x29", SBY 10/21/88 OE.......... **11,00**

PASINI, Alberto (Italian, 1826-1899)
Arab Street Scene, watercolor on paper, sgn, 11x13", SBY 6/8/88 OE **3,30**
Arabs Camped at an Oasis, oil on panel, sgn/dtd 1869, unfr, 9x16", B/B 6/9/88 .... **7,15**
Encampment, oil on canvas, sgn/dtd 1869, 9x16", SBY 2/22/89 OE.......... **23,10**
Going to the Pasture, Early Morning; oil on canvas, sgn/dtd 53, 19x27", SBY 2/22/89 .... **13,20**
Porte de Leoni Spagua Alambra, oil on canvas, sgn/inscr/dtd 1879, 14x11", C-E 10/25/88.......... **3,30**
Standing Guard, oil on canvas, sgn, 14x11", C-NY 10/25/89 OE **26,40**
Street Scene in Damascus, oil on canvas, sgn/dtd 1861, 24x20", C-NY 2/23/89 .... **19,80**
Turks Overlooking the Bosphore, oil on canvas, sgn, 23x32", C-NY 5/24/89.......... **16,50**
View From a Veranda, oil on canvasboard, sgn, 12x16", C-E 5/23/88 UE **66**
View of the Mediterranean, oil on canvas, sgn, 20x28", B/B 3/17/88 .... **3,30**

PASKELL, William Frederick (American, 1866-1951)
Harbor Village, stone buildings on wooded pier by blue harbor; watercolor on paper, sgn, 9x13", RAB 8/8/89 UE **35**
Haystacks on the Marsh, watercolor on paper, sgn, 9x16", RAB 8/9/88 OE.......... **90**
Running Stream, oil on canvas, sgn, 20x14", C-E 6/1/88 UE **52**

PASSAROTTI, Bartolomeo (Italian, 1529-1592)
Study of a Seated Pope (study after a bronze by Alessandro Mengante), pen/brown ink, 15x10", SBY 1/13/89.......... **5,50**
Study of Hands, pen/brown ink over black chalk on buff paper, 16x11", SBY 1/13/89 OE **13,20**

PASSAROTTI, Bartolomeo; att (Italian, 1529-1592)
Annunciation, oil on panel, inscr, 26x20", SBY 4/7/88 OE.......... **12,65**

PASSET, Gerard (French, 20th C)
Automne en Ile de France, oil on canvas, sgn, 32x31", WD 5/5/88 .... **2,30**

PASSEY, Charles H. (British, fl 1883-1885)
Fishing on the Dee, oil on canvas, sgn, 30x49", WAD 6/6/88.......... **3,40**

PASSINI, Ludwig (Austrian, 1832-1903)
Latin Class, watercolor over traces of pencil, sgn/dtd 1869, 19x27", C-NY 10/26/88 UE **8,25**
Laundress, watercolor on paper, sgn/inscr/dtd 1873, 9x11", SBY 6/8/88 .... **2,86**
Mass in a Church at Chiogga, watercolor, sgn/dtd Vendig 1879, unfr, 21x41", C-NY 2/23/89 OE **20,90**

PASTEGA, Luigi (Italian, 1858-1927)
At the Market, oil on canvas, sgn, 24x32", B/B 6/9/88 .... **4,67**
Visit to the Vegetable Stall, oil on canvas, sgn, 24x32", SBY 2/22/89 .... **7,70**
Water Carrier, oil on canvas, sgn, 24x12", SBY 12/9/88 OE **4,67**

TEL, Antoine Pierre (French, 1648-1707)
Harbor Landscape with Ships Coming to Shore, oil on canvas, sgn/dtd 1701, 26x32", C-NY 10/20/88 OE **24,200**
TEL, Antoine Pierre; att (French, 1648-1707)
Landscape with Classical Figures Among the Ruins of a City, oil on canvas, 32x46", SBY 4/7/89 OE **18,700**
TEL, Antoine Pierre; circle of (French, 1648-1707)
Archimedes of Syracuse Thinking in a Ruined Graveyard, oil on canvas, 14x20", SBY 12/9/88 OE **2,640**
Southern Harbor with Figures, oil on copper, unfr, 5x6", SBY 4/19/88 .... **1,980**
TEL, Antoine Pierre; follower of (French, 1648-1707)
Classical Landscape with Ruins, oil on canvas, 25x32", SBY 6/8/88 OE **4,070**
TER, Jean Baptiste; follower of (French, 1695-1736)
Fete Champetre, oil on canvas, 26x32", SBY 6/3/88 OE **14,300**
TER, Jean Baptiste; school of (French, 1695-1736)
Lady with a Man Playing a Bagpipe in a Landscape, oil on panel, 6x9", C-NY 6/17/89 .... **1,870**
TERS, Charles Rollo (American, 1862-1928)
Sutter's Fort, Nocturne; oil on canvas, sgn/dtd 1922, 16x24", B/B 10/6/88 .... **3,300**
TERSON, Mary Viola (American, 1899-1982)
Figure on the Beach with Sun Umbrella, oil on panel, sgn, 11x14", RWS 8/12/89 OE **2,300**
TON, Frank (British, 1856-1909)
Pair: Rabbits; watercolor on paper, sgn/dtd 1896, 17x20", SBY 6/10/88 UE **4,400**
TON, Joseph Noel (British, 1821-1900)
Man with the Muck Rake, oil on canvas, monogramed/dtd 1871, in painted oval, 17x11", SBY 12/9/88 .... **440**
TON, Walter Hugh (British, 1828-1895)
Ascog Bay, watercolor heightened w/gouache over traces of pencil, sgn/dtd 1849, 5x9", C-E 10/26/89 .... **550**
TRIX, Michel (French, 1917-1973)
Portrait of a Man, oil on canvas, sgn/dtd 29, 37x28", C-E 10/18/89 UE **462**
TTEIN, Cesar (French, fl 1882-1914)
Afternoon Rest, oil on canvas, sgn/dtd 1892, 20x29", SBY 10/24/89 .... **9,075**
Harvesters, oil on canvas, sgn/dtd 1926, 32x46", C-NY 5/24/89 .... **7,150**
TTERSON, Charles Robert (American, 1878-1950)
Calcutta in the Days of Sail, View From Below Princeps Ghat; oil on canvas, sgn, 29x42", SBY 3/17/88 .... **6,600**
Novia Scotia Ship, oil on canvas, sgn/inscr, 24x20", C-E 2/3/88 OE **4,180**
TTERSON, Margaret Jordan (American, 1867-1950)
Bruges, pastel on board, sgn, 15x11", RWS 11/10/89 .... **1,000**
Grande Marina, Capri (coastal inlet scene w/trees); watercolor on paper, sgn/dtd 1943, 15x18", RWS 3/31/88 UE **700**
Pink House, Torcello; watercolor/gouache/graphite on board, sgn, 15x18", RWS 9/8/89 .... **1,100**
Three Trees (in foreground by dirt road, open fields beyond), oil on canvas, 20x24", RWS 3/31/88 .... **500**
TTERSON, Russell (American, 1896-1977)
Summer Day, oil on canvas, sgn, ca 1922, 20x26", C-NY 9/28/89 .... **4,400**
TTON, Katherine (American, 20th C)
Wood Interior, oil on canvas, sgn, 18x24", C-E 10/18/89 .... **880**
TTY, William A. (American, 1889-)
Still Life with Vase, oil on canvas, sgn, 21x23", LH 10/16/88 .... **160**
UL, Davis
Architectural Design for an Altar, watercolor/charcoal/pencil on paper, sgn, 34x30", C-E 2/16/88 .... **385**
UL, Gen (20th C)
Cavaliers au Bois, gouache on paper, sgn, 20x26", C-E 5/13/88 .... **2,860**
Clown a la Guitare (contemporary), oil on panel, sgn, 14x9", C-E 5/9/89 OE **6,600**
Course de Chevaux a Auteuil, pastel/gouache/brush/black ink on paper, sgn/inscr, 19x25", C-E 5/13/88 .... **2,200**
Crucifixion (contemporary), watercolor/pen/ink on paper, sgn, 16x13", C-E 5/9/89 .... **462**
Horse & Rider, oil on board, 16x11", SBY 10/7/89 .... **6,050**
Le Violoniste, pencil/charcoal on paper, sgn/dtd 52, 26x19", C-E 11/17/88 .... **770**
Man Driving a Carriage, watercolor/black chalk on paper laid down on board, sgn, 19x25", C-E 11/17/88 .... **1,320**
Musicians, charcoal/colored crayons on paper, sgn/inscr, 16x12", SBY 10/5/88 .... **825**
Vase de Fleurs, colored wax crayons on paper, sgn, 17x12", C-NY 2/13/89 .... **880**
Vue de Montmartre (contemporary), chalk/crayon/pen/ink on paper laid down on board, sgn, 18x15", C-E 5/9/89 .... **2,090**
UL, John (British, 1775-1852)
Old Northumberland House, Charing Cross, London; oil on canvas, 30x50", C-NY 6/2/88 .... **18,700**
View of Westminster Hall, London; oil on canvas, 18x24", SBY 10/21/88 .... **2,750**
ULA FERG, see De Paula Ferg
ULEY, H.
New England River Scene, oil on canvas, sgn, 22x36", C-E 6/28/88 .... **330**
ULIS (20th C)
Impressionistic Landscape, oil on canvas, sgn, 20x29", MG 7/30/88 UE **100**
ULSEN, N. Chr (Danish, 19th C)
Ships Entering Copenhagen Harbor, oil on canvas, sgn, 29x41", B/B 10/9/88 .... **2,750**
ULUS, Francis Petraus (American, 1862-1933)
Portrait of Mrs Francis Petraus, oil on canvas, sgn/dtd 1912, 55x45", LH 10/16/88 .... **700**
ULY, Erik Bogdanffy (Hungarian, 1869-)
Draped Nude, oil on canvas, sgn, 27x20", B/B 1/11/89 OE **825**
UWELS, H.J. (Belgian, 20th C)
Belgian Village Street Scene, oil on canvas, sgn, 36x27", B/B 12/8/88 .... **935**

PAVESI, Pietro (Italian, 19th C)
Pool Game (three religious figures playing pool), watercolor, sgn, 20x30", DM 5/13/88 2,00
Roman Senator Studying His Scrolls, watercolor on paper, sgn/dtd 1895, 21x14", B/B 12/8/88 2,20
Two Women & Scribe, gouache on board, sgn/dtd 1895, 25x19", lot 418A, SBY 12/9/88 2,75
Two Women & Scribe, gouache on board, sgn/dtd 1895, 25x19", lot 562, SBY 7/12/89 1,43

PAVESI, Pietro; att (Italian, 19th C)
Barmaid's Serenade, watercolor on paper, 15x21", B/B 5/17/89 UE 55

PAVIA, Philip (20th C)
Abstract Composition, watercolor/ballpoint pen on paper, sgn/dtd 64, 16x18", SBY 2/14/89 60

PAVIL, Elie Anatole (French, 1873-1948)
A Vue de la Ville (view of city from across the river), oil on canvas, sgn, 18x24", PHL 11/15/88 2,10

PAVLOA (Portugese, 20th C)
Untitled, harbor scene w/fishermen; oil on board, sgn, 11x14", SLK 2/11/89 40

PAVY, Eugene (French, fl 1878-1890)
Arab Bazaar, oil on canvas, sgn/dtd 1886, 38x31", C-NY 10/25/89 OE 19,80
Street Musicians, oil on panel, sgn/dtd 1883, 16x12", SBY 6/8/88 UE 2,86

PAVY, Philippe (French, fl 1877-1887)
Orange-Sellers, oil on panel, sgn/dtd 1887, 8x4", SBY 6/8/88 2,20
Oriental Scene (woman & boy in an interior), oil on canvas, sgn/dtd 1877, 21x24", C-E 2/21/89 3,08

PAWLIKOWSKI, Andre (American/Polish, 1940-)
Nu aux Buildings (modernistic, seated & draped nude with buildings beyond), oil on canvas, sgn, 40x30", B/B 9/14/89 82

PAXSON, Edgar Samuel (American, 1852-1919)
Chief Little Bear, oil on canvas, sgn/dtd 1897, 18x12", SBY 5/25/88 6,60
Indian Chief, watercolor heightened w/white gouache on board, sgn/dtd 1902, 11x8", C-NY 9/30/88 3,52
Indian Girl Reclining (after an oil, Keeoma, by Charles M Russell), gouache/watercolor, sgn/dtd 1917, 6x8", SBY 9/14/89 1,32
Messenger, oil on canvas, sgn/dtd 1901, 22x16", SBY 9/23/88 OE 8,25
Officer, oil on canvas, sgn/dtd 1897, 18x12", SBY 5/25/88 6,60
Pursuit (Indians on horseback being pursued), oil on canvas, 20x24", C-NY 12/2/88 15,40

PAXSON, Ethel (American, 1885-1982)
Irises, oil on cardboard, sgn/dtd 1929, 24x18", RWS 5/19/88 OE 2,40
Phlox & Butterflies, Kew Gardens, New York; oil on masonite, sgn/dtd 1940, 22x21", RWS 9/29/88 50
Pink Fields, oil on board, sgn/inscr, 12x16", RWS 11/3/88 UE 45
Summer Haze (landscape w/running fence & trees), oil on board, sgn/dtd 1936, 16x16", RWS 3/31/88 37
Village Rooftops, Morning (landscape); oil on masonite, sgn, 24x26", RWS 3/16/89 40
Windham, Vermont; oil on board, sgn, 22x22", RWS 3/16/89 47

PAXTON, Elizabeth V.O. (American, 1877-1971)
Silver Coffeepot (detailed still life of coffee service & fruit), oil on canvas, sgn, 9x12", RWS 9/29/88 OE 7,50

PAXTON, William McGregor (American, 1869-1941)
Hollyhocks (flowers against house), pastel on paper, sgn, 27x22", SBY 5/24/89 38,50
Interior of the Paris Studio, oil on panel, 1890, 14x10", C-NY 5/25/89 22,00
Spring Bouquet (in green vase, white background), oil on canvas, sgn, 20x16", C-NY 9/28/89 16,50
Study of a Standing Female Nude, pencil on paper, 13x8", RWS 5/19/88 65
Woman Knitting, pencil on paper, sgn, 10x9", C-E 4/7/88 66

PAYNE, Charlie Johnson (British, 1884-1967)
Soldiers (thirteen jockey studies on one sheet), watercolor on paper, sgn/inscr, 18x25", SBY 6/9/89 27,50

PAYNE, David (British, 19th C)
Gypsy Encampment, oil on canvas, sgn twice/inscr, 15x26", SBY 12/9/88 OE 4,12
View in Metchbey Park, oil on canvas, sgn/inscr/dtd 1885, 30x51", C-E 5/23/88 UE 1,98

PAYNE, Edgar (American, 1882-1947)
Breton Fishing Boats, oil on canvas, sgn, 20x24", B/B 10/6/88 15,40
Breton Tuna Boats, oil on canvas, sgn, 20x24", B/B 10/6/88 9,35
Brittany Harbor, oil on canvas, sgn, 22x26", B/B 6/15/89 19,80
Canyon de Chelly, Arizona; oil on canvas, 18x24", SBY 6/24/88 OE 9,90
Coming of Spring (spring scene with snow on the mountains), oil on canvas, sgn, 36x40", DM 5/19/89 OE 10,00
Desert Study, oil on board, sgn, 16x22", SBY 9/23/88 6,60
French Tuna Boats, oil on canvas, sgn, 20x24", B/B 10/6/88 9,35
High Places (mountainous landscape), oil on canvas, sgn, 34x34", SBY 1/24/89 OE 35,20
High Sierras, oil on board, sgn, 12x13", B/B 6/15/89 3,85
Laguna Seascape, oil on masonite, sgn, 16x20", C-E 10/18/89 3,85
Landscape, oil on canvas laid down on board, sgn, 15x47", SBY 6/24/88 8,80
Late Afternoon, Alta Dena; oil on canvas, sgn, 20x23", B/B 6/9/88 8,80
Low Tide in a French Harbor, no media given, sgn, 29x29", B/B 10/6/88 38,50
Riders on Horseback, oil on canvas laid down, sgn, unfr, 8x10", B/B 10/6/88 1,98
Sierra Landscape, oil on canvas, sgn, 20x24", B/B 10/6/88 OE 18,70
South Lake, California Sierra; oil on board, sgn, 12x14", B/B 10/6/88 3,85
Study for Fishing Boats at Anchor, oil on board, sgn, 4x5", B/B 10/6/88 1,21
Two Indians in a Western Landscape, oil on board, sgn, 12x16", SBY 6/24/88 OE 9,35
Untitled (deer in mountainous winter landscape), oil on canvas, sgn, 20x24", SLK 4/7/89 6,00
View of the Swiss Alps, oil on masonite, sgn, 16x20", RWS 5/12/89 UE 2,50

PAYNE, George Forest (American, 20th C)
Sand Dunes, watercolor on paper, sgn, 16x22", B/B 5/17/89 49

YNE, George S. (American, 1860-1938)
Still Life of Trailing Arbutus, watercolor/gouache on paper, sgn, 8x10", RWS 3/16/89 OE ... 600
YNE, William (British, 1760-1830)
Fishermen Returning From the Day, watercolor on paper, sgn, 6x8", B/B 8/10/88 ... 550
YSANT, Claude Louis (American, 20th C)
Alone, cresting waves, gathering storm clouds; oil on canvas, sgn/titled, 24x40", RAB 8/8/89 UE ... 100
Hauling in the Nets, yellow-slickered fishermen; oil on canvas, sgn, 30x36", RAB 8/8/89 ... 700
HEL'NIKOVA, Ol'ga (Russian, fl 1925)
Abstract Composition, watercolor/pen/ink on thick brown paper, 12x8", C-L 10/8/88 ... 1,860
ACOCK, George Edward (Australian, 19th/20th C)
Port Jackson Overlooking the Heads, From the South Head; oil, initialed/dtd 1844, unfr, 5x6", C-SK 11/10/88 ... 5,210
Sydney & Port Jackson From the South Head, oil, initialed/dtd 1844, unfr, 5x6", C-SK 11/10/88 ... 5,210
ALE, Margaretta Angelica (19th C)
Still Life of Peaches, a Pear, & Grapes; oil on canvas, sgn/dtd 1864, 13x18", C-NY 9/28/89 OE ... 12,100
ALE, Rembrandt (American, 1778-1860)
George Washington, oil on canvas, sgn, ca 1795, 36x29", SBY 5/24/89 OE ... 115,500
George Washington (portrait), pencil on paper laid down on paper, sgn/dtd 1855/inscr, 10x8", C-NY 5/26/88 OE ... 24,200
Olive Foote Lay (portrait), oil on canvas laid down on masonite, 31x27", C-NY 5/26/88 ... 17,600
ALE, Sarah Miriam (American, 1800-1885)
Still Life of Watermelon, oil on panel, sgn/dtd 1822/inscr Mrs Rockhill, 14x20", SBY 5/24/89 OE ... 42,900
ALLZOR, Estelle (American, 20th C)
Wooded Spring Landscape, oil on canvas, sgn, 20x15", SLK 9/29/88 ... 225
AN, Louis Rene (French, 1875-)
Pierette et Arlequin, oil on canvas, sgn, 51x35", SBY 2/22/89 UE ... 4,675
ARCE, Charles Sprague (American, 1851-1914)
Fresh Gleanings (woman w/sickle standing in harvested field), oil on canvas, sgn/inscr, 28x22", C-NY 12/2/88 ... 16,500
Girl in the Fields, oil on canvas, sgn/inscr, 29x24", SBY 5/25/88 ... 14,300
ARLMUTTER, Stella
Iris #2, oil on canvas, sgn, 37x37", SLK 9/27/88 ... 800
Red Poppies, oil on canvas, sgn, 61x36", SLK 9/27/88 ... 1,000
Young Girl Dressed in Black Leotards, oil on masonite, sgn/dtd 60, 13x41", SLK 9/26/88 ... 500
ARLSTEIN, Philip (American, 1924-)
Female Model by Ladder (nude), sepia on paper, sgn/dtd 76, 30x22", C-NY 2/14/89 OE ... 5,500
Female Model Reclining on Empire Sofa (nude), oil on canvas, sgn, 1973, unfr, 48x72", C-NY 5/4/89 ... 24,200
Male & Female Models Reclining (nude), oil on canvas, 1966, 54x72", SBY 11/9/89 ... 33,000
Male & Female Models Seated on Indian Rug (nudes), sepia ink on paper, sgn, dtd 4/1973, 22x30", SBY 11/11/88 ... 4,400
Male Nude (resting, viewed from behind), brush/sepia ink on paper, sgn/dtd 2-3-62, 16x14", C-NY 6/17/89 OE ... 3,520
Mary, Seated on Green Cushion; oil on canvas, sgn/dtd 63, unfr, 26x22", C-NY 5/4/88 ... 8,800
Model Seated in Rocking Rattan Lounge, oil on canvas, sgn/dtd 1984, 72x60", SBY 5/3/88 ... 38,500
Nude, Female Model, Seated; pencil on paper, sgn/dtd 69, 24x19", SBY 10/8/88 ... 3,850
Reclining Female Model on Blanket (nude), graphite on paper, sgn/dtd 1972, 19x24", SBY 11/11/88 ... 3,850
Seated Nude, pencil on paper, sgn/dtd 67, unfr, 14x22", C-E 11/14/89 ... 2,200
Seated Nude (on a stool), brown conte crayon on paper, sgn/dtd 1984, 29x23", C-E 11/14/89 ... 5,500
Standing Male Model & Mirror (nude), sepia ink on paper, sgn, dtd 5/1972, 22x30", SBY 11/11/88 ... 1,980
Two Female Models on a Stool & Rocker, sepia on paper, sgn/inscr/dtd 1974, 21x30", SBY 10/5/88 ... 3,575
Two Female Nudes, sepia on paper, sgn/dtd 1965, 19x24", DM 1/15/88 ... 1,400
Two Nudes, brush/brown ink on paper, sgn/dtd 62, 17x14", C-E 5/9/89 OE ... 2,640
Two Nudes, oil on canvas, sgn/dtd 67, 22x30", C-NY 10/4/89 ... 9,900
Two Nudes, pencil on paper, sgn, ca 1961, 14x17", C-NY 2/13/89 ... 1,980
ARS, Charles (British, 1873-1958)
Clipper Ship & Attendant Tug, oil on canvas, sgn, 23x35", WAD 6/6/88 ... 3,000
ARSON, Marguerite Stuber (American, 1898-1978)
Along the Village Road (lady w/umbrella on path, houses beyond), oil on canvas mounted on board, 16x15", RWS 3/31/88 UE ... 550
At the Piano (lady in an interior scene), oil on canvas, sgn, 30x36", B/B 3/22/89 ... 17,600
Bather by a Lily Pond, oil on canvasboard, sgn/estate stamp, 20x16", RWS 3/16/89 ... 1,000
Blue Danube (lady in blue dress playing piano), oil on canvas, sgn, 30x36", C-NY 5/25/89 ... 17,600
Clouds, Rockport-View Out to Sea (seascape); oil on canvasboard, sgn/estate stamp/titled, 14x16", RWS 3/16/89 UE ... 750
Daffodils (still life), oil on canvasboard, sgn, 20x24", SBY 3/17/88 ... 2,310
Fall Street Scene, oil on canvasboard, sgn, 12x16", RWS 5/12/89 ... 1,200
Floral Still Life, oil on canvasboard, artist's estate stamp, 8x10", RWS 5/12/89 ... 1,800
November Day (quiet neighborhood street scene), oil on canvas, sgn/inscr, 30x36", C-E 2/3/88 OE ... 880
Rockport Cottage, oil on board, sgn, 10x8", C-E 6/1/88 ... 715
Sailboats & Seagulls, oil on canvasboard, sgn, 20x24", C-E 10/18/89 ... 2,200
Sailing in a Twilight, oil on canvas, sgn/dtd 1925, 22x32", C-E 10/18/89 UE ... 880
Tulips & Scotch Broom (still life), oil on canvas, sgn, 30x25", RAB 8/9/88 ... 4,100
Winter Afternoon (lady in red dress seated at picture window), oil on canvas, sgn, 31x36", C-NY 5/25/89 ... 16,500
CHAUBES, Eugene (French, 1890-1967)
Horserace, oil on canvas, sgn, 17x21", WG 4/23/88 ... 2,050
Neck & Neck (racing scene), oil on canvas, sgn, 18x22", SBY 6/9/89 ... 3,000
Pair: Races at Longchamp & St Cloud, 1928; oil on canvas, sgn/inscr/dtd 1928, 13x37", SBY 6/10/88 ... 18,700

PECHE, Dale (American, 20th C)
Fisherman's Wharf, oil on board, sgn, 12x16", WG 9/16/88 UE 90
PECHSTEIN, Max (German, 1881-1955)
Anna Gartner und Frank (pair of nudes), pen/ink/watercolor on paper, inscr/dtd Nidden 25 August 1919, 13x8", SBY 6/16/88..... 8,80
Fischerhaus, oil on canvas, sgn twice/dtd 09, 18x25", SBY 11/11/88..... 440,00

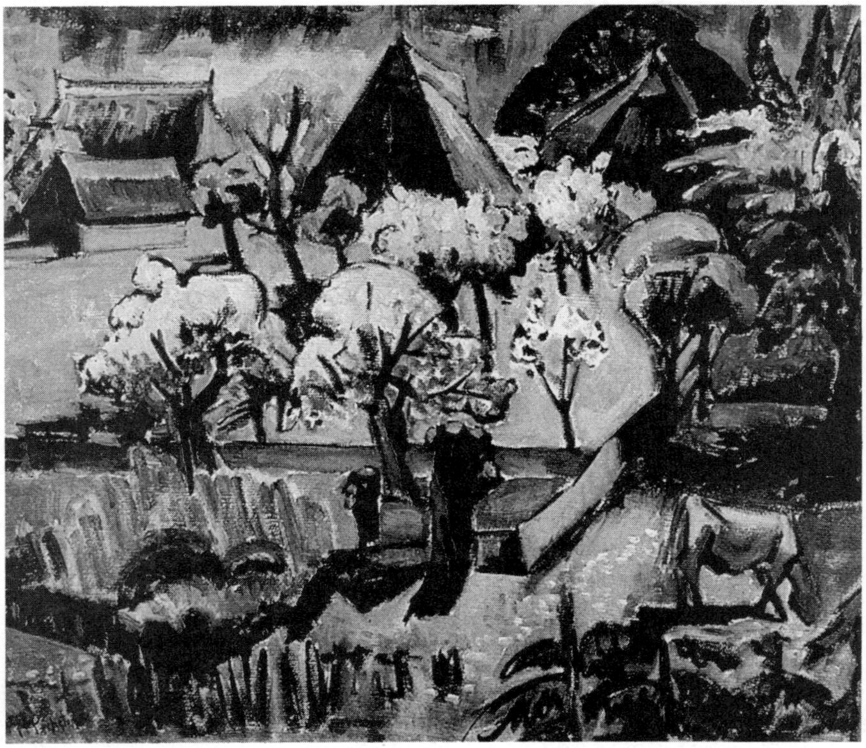

Fruhling, oil on canvas, sgn, 1918, 27x31", C-NY 5/11/89 OE; $209,000

Grosses Netz, gouache/watercolor on paper mounted at edges on board, sgn/dtd 1930, 25x20", C-NY 10/6/88 OE 28,60
Interior with Figure, ink/wax crayons on paper affixed to another sheet, indistinctly inscr, unfr, 6x8", SBY 10/5/88 UE 88
Kartoffelernte, ink wash/gray wash on paper laid down on board, sgn/dtd 1924, 16x22", SBY 2/18/88 OE..... 6,87
Landschaft (landscape w/church, horse, & rider), brush/black ink on paper, sgn/dtd 1917, 15x19", C-NY 5/11/89 11,00
Liegender Akt (reclining nude), watercolor over charcoal on buff paper, initialed/dtd 1912, 13x17", C-NY 5/11/89..... 11,00
Liegender Akt (reclining nude), watercolor/pencil on paper, initialed/dtd 1917, 14x20", SBY 10/6/89 9,90
Madchen mit Kopfuch (portrait of a girl), oil on canvas, indistinctly sgn/dtd 09, 18x15", SBY 11/12/88 220,00
Malven (floral still life), watercolor over pencil on tan board, initialed/dtd 1918, 23x18", SBY 5/11/88 28,60
Murmel Spielende Knaben (two lads), gouache/watercolor/brush/black ink/pencil, initialed, 1910, 11x9", C-NY 5/12/88 9,90
Rekonvalescentin (contemporary portrait), oil on canvas, initialed/dtd 1920, 40x31", C-NY 5/11/89 82,50
Sonnen Aufgang am Meer, watercolor on paper, sgn/dtd 1944, 24x30", SBY 2/18/88 OE 20,90
Stillben (still life), gouache on board, initialed/dtd 32, 23x28", SBY 11/12/88 OE 57,75
Zwei Liegende Frauen, watercolor/gouache/ink wash, initialed/sgn/inscr/dtd 08, 9x11", SBY 2/18/88 OE..... 18,70
PECK, E.M. (American, 20th C)
Young Fisherman (boy in boat), oil on board, 12x20", RAB 8/9/88 UE..... 17
PECK, Henry Jarvis (American, 1880-1964)
Country Schoolroom (classroom in turmoil), pencil on paper, sgn, 28x38", RAB 8/9/88 60
Snowy Winter Scene in New England with a Man Plowing Snow with a Draft Horse, oil on canvas, sgn, 19x21", SLK 2/12/88 27
Spouter Inn, Nantucket, Massachusetts; pencil on paper, titled, 3x4", RAB 11/25/88 UE 10
PECK, Sheldon (1797-1869)
Gentleman in Forest-Green Coat...; oil on cardboard mounted on wood, ca 1845, 6x5", SBY 1/28/88 OE..... 11,55
PECRUS, Camille (French, 1826-1907)
The Victor (gentleman sheathing his sword), oil on wood panel, sgn, 13x9", DM 5/13/88 85
PEDERSEN, Carl Henning (Danish, 1913-)
Untitled (abstract), gouache on paper mounted on board, initialed/dtd 50, 8x11", C-NY 2/20/88 2,20
PEDERSEN, Finn (Danish, 20th C)
Untitled, oil on canvas, sgn/dtd 86, 24x20", lot 112, PHL 11/15/88 90
Untitled, oil on canvas, sgn/dtd 86, 32x39", lot 108, PHL 11/15/88 1,50
Untitled, oil on canvas, sgn/dtd 86, 39x52", lot 107, PHL 11/15/88 2,00
Untitled (abstract), oil on canvas, sgn/dtd Copenhagen-86, 40x53", lot 6904, C-NY 10/4/89 4,40
Untitled (abstract), oil on canvas, sgn/dtd 8-88, 51x40", C-NY 5/4/89 6,38
Untitled (abstract), oil on canvas, sgn/dtd 88, 51x38", lot 6904, C-NY 10/4/89..... 4,40
PEEL, James (British, 1811-1906)
Cattle Wading on a Hilly River, oil on canvas, sgn, 18x30", C-E 10/25/88..... 2,20
Shepherd with His Flock, oil on canvas, sgn/indistinctly dtd, 24x40", SBY 2/22/89 UE..... 3,02

ΞL, S. (19th C)
'lea Market, watercolor on paper, sgn/dtd 1857, 14x10", C-E 11/8/88 UE ... 110
ΞLE, John Thomas; after (19th C)
oung Girl Holding a Black Cat, oil on canvas, sgn/dtd 1853, 34x26", C-E 5/23/88 ... 3,960
ΞRLESS, Thomas (American, 1822-1897)
outh Island Landscape, pencil/watercolor, sgn/dtd 1887, 17x25", C-SK 5/25/89 OE ... 735
ΞRS, Gordon Franklin (American, 1909-)
ooking From Pilgrim Heights Toward Provincetown...; oil on canvas, sgn/dtd 39/titled, 20x30", RAB 11/25/88 UE ... 200
ΞRS, Tom (American, 20th C)
'isherman, man wearing red shirt fishes off gray rocks in blue water; oil on board, sgn/dtd 59, 28x20", RAB 8/8/89 UE ... 50
RCE, H. Winthrop (American, 1850-)
'nder the Chancel Window (two young girls seated in pew), watercolor on canvasboard, sgn, 15x12", C-E 2/1/89 ... 1,540
RCE, Waldo (American, 1884-1970)
Vebber Meredith's House, oil on canvas, sgn twice/dtd Dec 42 & 21 Dec 43/inscr Pomona NY, 25x30", SBY 1/24/89 ... 3,025
SLEY, John W.
'isherman, oil on canvas laid down on masonite, indistinctly sgn, 16x20", C-E 6/1/88 UE ... 770
AEZ, Amelia (Cuban, 1897-1968)
iseno (abstract), gouache on paper, sgn/dtd 59, 22x30", C-NY 5/17/89 ... 2,200
rutero (abstract fruit dish w/apple), oil on canvas, sgn/dtd 1932, 23x20", C-NY 5/17/89 OE ... 15,400
aturaleza Muerta (abstract still life), gouache/watercolor on paper, sgn/dtd 1942, 30x28", C-NY 11/21/89 ... 14,300
till Life (abstract), gouache/India ink on paper laid down on canvas, sgn/dtd 1949, 38x26", SBY 11/21/88 OE ... 15,400
HAM, Thomas Kent (British, 19th C)
Vaterbearer, oil on canvas, sgn, 30x18", C-E 5/23/88 ... 2,200
IKAN, Alfred G. (American, 20th C)
ptimist, acrylic on illustration board, sgn, 6x4", S/A 2/18/89 ... 30
LAGALE, W.E. (American, 19th C)
andscape Scene with Figure of Lady in Foreground, oil on canvas, sgn/dtd 1882, 16x22", DM 10/14/88 ... 300
LAN, Alfred (Canadian, 1906-1988)
)ie de l'Aube, oil on board, sgn, no size given, WAD 11/30/89 OE ... 23,000
Ille Genevieve Tirot (portrait), oil on canvas, sgn, 16x13", FB 10/30/89 OE ... 28,600
LEGRINI, Giovanni Antonio (Italian, 1675-1741)
llegory of Age & Prudence (old man & young girl), oil on canvas, 28x22", C-NY 6/2/88 ... 5,500
t Catherine of Alexandria, oil on canvas, 39x30", SBY 6/3/88 ... 66,000
LEGRINI, Giovanni Antonio; circle of (Italian, 1675-1741)
air: Two Scenes From Roman History; oil on canvas, 14x18", SBY 4/7/88 ... 3,025
LEGRINI, Riccardo (Italian, 1863-1934)
harpening the Sword, oil on canvas, sgn/dtd 1894, 27x20", C-E 2/23/88 ... 2,200
LEGRINI, Vincenzo (Italian, 1575-1612)
inding of Moses, oil on canvas laid down on board, 17x22", WD 10/19/88 OE ... 12,500
LETIER, Pierre Jacques (French, 1869-1931)
es Bords au Riviere avec Pecheurs, oil on canvas, sgn, 25x36", WAD 6/6/88 ... 3,600
'he Riverside Hamlet, oil on canvas, sgn, 9x13", WAD 6/6/88 ... 800
LUS, Michel (Canadian)
andscape with Castle, oil on canvas, sgn, 10x12", FB 10/30/89 UE ... 302
MMAN, J.A.
alian Peasant, oil on board, sgn, 12x8", C-E 5/23/88 UE ... 550
OUSE, Leon Germain (French, 1838-1891)
aysage, oil on canvas, sgn, 15x22", RWS 8/12/89 OE ... 1,400
S, Albert (American, 1910-)
xpress Train to New York, oil on canvas, sgn, 12x16", C-E 10/18/89 OE ... 2,200
ady in Red Hat, oil on masonite, sgn, 13x15", C-E 9/15/88 ... 1,210
ortrait of Jo Davidson, oil on canvas, sgn, 30x24", WG 9/1688 UE ... 200
TON, Agnes (American, 1881-1961)
ld Smoke Tree, oil on canvas, sgn, 16x20", C-E 10/18/89 ... 1,320
Vater Mill, Long Island; oil on canvas, sgn/dtd 1927, 32x36", SBY 5/25/88 OE ... 27,500
USO, Francesco (Italian, 1863-)
appy Company, oil on canvas, sgn, 18x24", LH 10/16/88 ... 2,600
terior Scene (man standing by sitting woman), oil on canvas, sgn, 15x11", WL 5/20/88 ... 2,200
and Storm (Arabs & camels on a desert), oil on canvas, sgn, 26x56", C-E 5/22/89 ... 3,300
erenade, oil on canvas, sgn, 24x17", SBY 12/9/88 ... 4,400
'he Serenade, oil on canvas, sgn, 16x13", C-E 10/26/89 ... 3,080
Vine & Song, oil on panel, sgn, 18x24", C-E 10/26/89 ... 3,520
VA, Angel (South American, 20th C)
ovia con Perro, acrylic on canvas, sgn/inscr, 59x47", C-NY 5/18/88 ... 3,520
ffering (figure in contemporary landscape), acrylic on canvas, sgn/titled, 1985, 59x47", SBY 11/21/88 ... 4,400
areja con Paisaje (Couple in Landscape), acrylic on canvas, sgn, 59x71", C-NY 5/17/89 OE ... 15,400
VA, Narcisse Virgile; see Diaz de la Pena
VALOSA Y SANOVAL, see De Penalosa y Sanoval
VCE, Authur L. (American, 20th C)
Vinter Landscape, oil on canvas, sgn/dtd 1974, 23x17", S/A 3/12/88 ... 450

PENCK, A.R. (German, 1939-)
Dummkopf N 1, acrylic on canvas, sgn/inscr, unfr, 1978, 59x59", C-NY 5/4/88 ... **7,150**
Figure with a Gun (abstract), tempera on paper, sgn/dtd 83, 22x30", SBY 2/15/89 OE ... **29,700**
Fur Jochen Hiltmann (contemporary), oil on canvas, 1979, 51x69", SBY 11/11/88 OE ... **88,000**
Geheime Wege (abstract), oil on canvas, sgn, 1985, 28x32", SBY 10/5/89 OE ... **66,000**
O A TE MI 2, graphic elements around a human figure; dispersion on canvas, sgn, 1981, unfr, 99x131", C-NY 11/7/89 ... **242,000**
Que Peut-Il Resulter de ce Qui Est Systeme I (abstract composition); acrylic on canvas, sgn/dtd 81, 39x59", SBY 10/5/89 ... **33,000**
Sketchbook: Untitled (150 pages); watercolor on paper, sgn/dtd 1970, 12x8", C-NY 10/4/89 ... **38,500**
Untitled (abstract composition, black on white), ink on paper, sgn, 55x60", SBY 10/5/89 ... **22,000**
Untitled (abstract composition), gouache on paper, initialed/dtd 81, 24x17", SBY 5/3/89 OE ... **12,650**
Untitled (abstract composition), oil on canvas, monogramed twice, 1968-69, 59x55", SBY 11/11/88 OE ... **143,000**
Untitled (abstract figures), oil on cardboard, sgn, 1981, 59x78", SBY 10/8/88 OE ... **17,600**
Untitled (abstract stick figures), ink on paper, sgn, 21x33", SBY 10/8/88 ... **7,425**
Untitled (abstract), black gouache on cardboard, sgn, 59x79", C-NY 5/8/88 ... **15,400**
Untitled (abstract), gouache on paper, sgn Ralf, 17x23", SBY 2/15/89 ... **7,700**
Untitled (abstract), gouache on paper board, sgn/dtd 82, 22x30", SBY 5/3/88 ... **5,500**
Vulkan von Oben (abstract), oil on masonite, 1966, 70x47", SBY 2/15/89 UE ... **26,400**
Welt des Adlers IV (contemporary), acrylic on canvas, 1981, 71x111", SBY 2/19/88 OE ... **60,500**

PENDERGAST, Maurice B. (American, 1859-1924)
Sunset (festive gathering in a cove), oil on canvas, sgn, ca 1917, 21x32", SBY 5/24/89 OE ... **1,815,000**

PENFIELD, Edward (American, 1866-1925)
Steeplechase, watercolor on paper, monogramed, 14x12", SBY 6/9/89 ... **3,575**

PENLEY, Aaron Edwin (British, 1807-1870)
The Convict Returned, watercolor heightened w/gouache, sgn, 21x28", C-E 10/26/89 ... **660**

PENNADES, J. Dias
Lady Wearing a Mantilla on a Balcony, oil on canvas, sgn/dtd 1902, 51x35", C-E 5/23/88 ... **2,860**

PENNE, see De Penne

PENNELL, Joseph (American, 1860-1926)
Gathering Leaves, black ink on paper, sgn/dtd 1884, 13x21", SBY 9/23/88 UE ... **715**
Mont St Michel, pen/ink on paper, sgn/dtd 1902, 26x20", B/B 5/17/89 ... **700**
Near the Market Place, Stuttgart; India ink on paper, sgn/titled, 14x10", SBY 9/23/88 UE ... **550**
New York Harbor, watercolor/gouache/pencil on paper, sgn/inscr, 7x9", C-NY 9/30/88 ... **3,850**
Pair: Pall Mall, East London; Charing Cross Station, London; watercolor on paper, sgn, 7x10", 10x14", C-NY 5/26/88 OE ... **7,700**
Street, Indian Exhibition; ink on paper, sgn/inscr, 7x8", SBY 6/24/88 UE ... **715**
Train Yard, brush/black ink/gouache/pencil on tan paper, sgn, 5x8", C-NY 9/28/89 ... **1,320**
West Front of St Paul's From Ludgate Hill (busy street scene), gouache en grisaille on paper, 20x14", C-NY 9/28/89 OE ... **14,300**

PENNINGTON, Harper (American, 1854-1920)
Why He Was Not Killed No One Knows (Civil War), pen/ink on paper, sgn/inscr, 15x12", C-E 5/27/88 OE ... **550**

PENNOYER, Albert Sheldon (American, 1888-1957)
Alfa Farm, oil on canvas, sgn twice/titled, 30x40", C-E 9/15/88 UE ... **550**
Mount Davidson, Virginia City at the Divide (buildings in extensive landscape); oil on canvas, sgn, 24x30", B/B 10/9/88 ... **2,200**
Royal Blue Limited, oil on canvas, sgn/inscr, 30x25", C-E 6/1/88 ... **1,980**
Starting Point (snow-covered mountains w/figures), oil on canvas, sgn/unfr, 25x30", C-E 10/18/89 ... **1,650**

PENNY, James
Old House, Queens; oil on canvas, sgn, 18x14", C-NY 9/30/88 ... **3,300**

PENNY, William Daniel (British, 1834-1924)
Harbor at Bridlington, oil on canvas, sgn/dtd 1890, 22x36", SBY 7/12/89 ... **2,970**

PENOT, Albert Joseph (French, 20th C)
Cardinal After a Good Meal, oil on canvas, sgn, 19x13", FAP 4/15/89 OE ... **3,300**

PEPPER, George Douglas (Canadian)
St Lawrence River, oil on board, sgn, 13x15", C-SK 11/10/88 UE ... **280**

PERAIRE, Paul Emmanuel (French, 1829-1893)
Bords de la Seine, oil on canvas, sgn, 33x46", SBY 2/22/89 OE ... **20,900**

PERBOYRE, Paul Emile Leon (French, 1826-)
Cavalry Patrol, oil on canvas, sgn, 29x40", WD 3/23/88 ... **4,500**
French Artillery Train, oil on canvas, sgn, 18x22", SBY 12/9/88 UE ... **3,575**
Rendez-Vous de Chasse, oil on panel, sgn, 15x18", SBY 6/10/88 ... **10,450**

PERCHEM, Nicolaes Pietersz; manner of (1620-1683)
Italian Landscape with Peasants & Animals, oil on canvas, 36x45", SBY 4/7/89 OE ... **5,225**

PERCY, Sidney Richard (British, 1821-1886)
Cattle Fording a River, oil on canvas, sgn/dtd 1883, 24x38", SBY 2/22/89 OE ... **39,600**
Faggot Gatherers Along a Country Path, oil on canvas, sgn/dtd 1851, 16x23", SBY 5/23/89 ... **6,600**
Figures Beside a Path with Cattle Watering Beyond, oil on canvas, sgn/dtd 1875, 24x38", C-NY 2/25/88 OE ... **28,600**
Highland Stream, oil on canvas, sgn, 12x21", SBY 10/24/89 ... **8,800**
Killen, Perthshire; oil on canvas, sgn, 24x36", SBY 10/24/89 ... **9,350**
On the Causeway, North Wales; oil on canvas, sgn/dtd 1858, 26x42", C-NY 2/23/89 ... **17,600**
Paysage, Bords de Riviere (river landscape with cows watering); oil on canvas, sgn/dtd 1876, 23x30", FB 5/28/89 ... **6,000**

PEREDA, see De Pereda

PEREIRA, Irene Rice (American, 1907-1971)
Alone to the Alone, oil on canvas, sgn/inscr, 30x42", C-E 5/13/88 ... **1,760**
Dancing Figures, gouache, sgn, dtd 5/18/52, 17x24", PHL 6/16/88 ... **700**

Mercuricus, gouache/watercolor on paper, sgn/dtd 7-16-61, 24x18", C-NY 2/13/89 ... 605
Soul of Space, acrylic on canvas, sgn/titled twice, 44x36", C-E 5/9/89 OE ... 4,620
The Diagonal (abstract composition), oil on canvas, sgn/dtd 38, 34x28", PHL 12/1/88 ... 9,500
The Light of Spring (abstract composition), oil on canvas, sgn, 1959, 42x32", PHL 12/1/88 ... 2,500
Transforming Night (abstract composition), oil on canvas, sgn/dtd 1952, 40x30", PHL 12/1/88 OE ... 7,000
Traveler From the East (contemporary figure), gouache w/charcoal on paper laid down, sgn/dtd 8-59, 36x24", PHL 12/1/88 ... 1,300
Two Women, gouache/pen/black ink on paper, sgn/dtd 1968, 38x28", C-E 11/14/89 ... 660
Untitled, oil on canvas, sgn, unfr, 32x43", lot 203, C-E 5/13/88 ... 1,980
Untitled, pen/brown/black ink on paper, sgn/dtd twice, 1934, inscr, 12x9", lot 183, C-E 5/13/88 ... 352
Untitled (abstract composition w/figure), watercolor/gouache on paper, sgn, dtd 1950 & 7/28/52, 22x29", C-E 11/14/89 ... 605

PERELLI, Achille (Italian, 1927-)
Near the Rigolets, oil on board, sgn, 9x12", NA 2/6/88 OE ... 2,500

PEREZ, Alonzo (Spanish, 1858-1914)
Dancing in the Forest, watercolor on paper, sgn/dtd Paris 91, 24x18", FAP 4/15/89 ... 2,145
Elegant Company in the Park, oil on panel, sgn, 18x15", C-NY 2/23/89 ... 6,600
Elegant Gathering in an Outdoor Cafe, oil on panel, sgn, 20x24", C-NY 2/23/89 ... 10,450
Flirtation, oil on canvas, sgn, 22x15", C-NY 2/25/88 ... 6,600
Marche aux Fleurs (flower market), oil on canvas, sgn, 18x15", SBY 2/22/89 ... 5,500
New Bonnets (man holding umbrella over ladies), oil on panel, sgn, 18x15", C-NY 2/23/89 ... 5,500
Pink Cloak (portrait of a girl), oil on canvas, sgn/dtd 1890, 26x20", SBY 12/9/88 ... 2,750

PEREZ, Alonzo; style of (Spanish, 1858-1914)
Flower Vendor (gentleman buying flowers for lady), oil on panel, 14x19", B/B 3/22/89 ... 2,475

PERIGNON, Fernand
Satyr, oil on canvas, sgn/dtd 1895, 39x32", C-E 5/23/88 UE ... 550

PERIGNY, Monique (Canadian, 20th C)
Children in a Forest, oil on canvas, sgn/dtd 1979, 20x26", FB 10/17/88 ... 225

PERILLO, Gregory (American, 1929-)
Black Foot, oil on canvas, sgn, 20x16", SBY 1/24/89 OE ... 1,320

PERKINS, Granville (American, 1830-1895)
Bargaining on the Beach, watercolor on paper, sgn/dtd 1892, 15x21", SBY 3/17/88 OE ... 1,980
Boats on Hudson (river scene), watercolor on paper, sgn, 14x22", SBY 3/17/88 ... 1,430
Caribbean Market, oil on canvas, sgn/dtd 1889, 10x14", C-NY 9/30/88 ... 2,860
Low Tide (beached boat near salt marsh haystack), oil on canvas, sgn/dtd 1888, 10x16", RAB 3/27/89 ... 2,500
New York Harbor (boats in rough water), oil on canvas, sgn/dtd 1889, 10x14", C-NY 9/28/89 ... 6,600
Off Long Island, oil on canvas, sgn/dtd 186(?), 10x18", C-NY 9/28/89 ... 2,200
Reflections on a River, watercolor on paper laid down on board, sgn/dtd 1893, 16x22", C-E 2/1/89 UE ... 550
Rough Seas, oil on canvas, initialed/dtd 1895, unfr, 30x48", SBY 9/14/89 ... 6,875
Sails & Stream, oil on canvas, sgn/dtd 1891, 14x24", C-E 11/30/88 OE ... 11,000
Summer on the Lake, oil on canvas, sgn, 10x14", RAB 3/27/89 ... 1,100
Sunset Over the Palisades, oil on canvas, sgn/dtd 1869, 12x18", C-NY 5/25/89 ... 14,300
Tropical Landscape, oil on canvas, sgn, 30x41", C-E 2/3/88 ... 3,080
Wilderness Stream, oil on canvas, sgn, 10x14", RAB 3/27/89 UE ... 600

PERKINS, M.S. (American, 19th/20th C)
Market Place, oil on canvas, sgn, 20x16", FAP 4/15/89 OE ... 962

PERKINS, Parker S. (American, 1862-)
East Wind (rough coastal scene), oil on canvas, sgn, 36x48", RWS 5/12/89 ... 800
Fisherman at Sea, oil on canvas w/graphite, 27x22", RWS 5/12/89 ... 400
Kittens at Play, oil on canvas, sgn/dtd 1899, 14x18", RWS 5/12/89 ... 800
Rough Seas, oil on board, 25x30", RAB 8/9/88 UE ... 300
Rough Seas (waves crashing against shore), oil on board, sgn, 25x30", RAB 8/9/88 UE ... 300
Ship Yard, oil on canvas, sgn, 18x22", RWS 5/12/89 ... 650
When the Tide Turns (New England coastal scene), oil on particle board, sgn, ca 1931, 20x22", RWS 9/29/88 OE ... 750

PERKINS, Sarah; att (American, 1771-1831)
Major Andrew Billings, oil on canvas laid on board, ca 1785, 30x25", C-NY 1/20/89 ... 20,900

ERKINS, W. Thompson (American, 20th C)
Ship at Sea, oil on canvas, sgn, 16x26", LH 10/16/88 ... 200

ERLBERG, Friedrich (German, 1848-1921)
Marina Grande in Capri, pen/brown ink/watercolor/gouache, sgn/inscr, 18x27", C-NY 5/25/88 ... 880
Pair: Nuremburg Street Scenes; watercolor on paper, sgn, 15x11", DM 9/16/88 OE ... 4,000

ERLIS, Donald (American, 20th C)
Mary Jane Reclining on a Fur Coat (nude), oil on canvasboard, sgn/dtd 1971, 16x12", C-NY 6/17/89 ... 550

ERMEKE, Constant (Belgian, 1866-1952)
Pair: Woman Standing; Woman with Broom; charcoal on paper, sgn, 11x7", 10x8", SBY 10/7/89 ... 2,530

ERNET, Jean Henri Alexandre (French, 1763-)
Pair: Italian Garden with an Obelisk; Italian Garden with Ruins & Fountain; pen/ink/watercolor, 6 " dia, C-NY 1/12/88 OE ... 3,520

ERNET, Jean Henri Alexandre; att (French, 1763-)
Italian Terraced Garden, pen/black ink/watercolor heightened w/white, necklace wm, oval, 10x8", C-NY 1/12/88 OE ... 880

EROT, Anna Lovering (American, 1854-)
Spring Landscape, oil on canvas, sgn, 30x25", FAP 12/8/89 UE ... 150

ERRACHON, Andre (French, 1827-1909)
Floral Still Life, oil on canvas, sgn, 18x15", C-E 2/21/89 ... 3,080

PERRACHON, Andre; att (French, 1827-1909) 3,080
Pair: Floral & Fruit Still Lifes; gouache on paper, 13x15", SBY 12/9/88 ....
PERRAULT, Henry (French, 1867-1932) 11,000
Shepherdess, oil on canvas, sgn, 54x38", C-NY 5/25/88 ....
PERRAULT, Leon Jean Basile (French, 1832-1908) 11,000
Flower Vendor, oil on canvas, 51x33", SBY 7/12/89 55,000
Le Miroir de la Nature, oil on canvas, indistinctly sgn/bears signature, 50x33", SBY 10/24/89 OE........ 38,500
Vanitas (partially nude woman looking into mirror), oil on canvas, sgn/dtd 1886, 43x51", SBY 2/22/89 13,200
Young Girl with Orange, oil on canvas, sgn/dtd 68, 16x13", SBY 10/24/89 1,980
Young Peasant Girl with a Violin, oil on canvas, sgn/dtd, 14x9", C-E 10/25/88 UE ....
PERRE, Henri (Canadian, 1828-1890) 450
Figure on a Country Road, watercolor, sgn, 6x9", WAD 6/12/89 ....
PERRET, Aime (French, 1847-1927) 12,100
La Bergere, oil on canvas, sgn, 29x24", C-E 10/26/89 OE ....
PERRET, Aime; att (French, 1847-1927) 2,200
Shepherdess with Her Flock, oil on canvas, bears signature, 32x26", C-E 2/21/89 13,200
Still Life of Wildflowers in a Vase, oil on canvas, sgn, 34x21", C-NY 10/25/89........
PERREY, Julien Auguste 1,650
Woman with a Bird Cage, oil on canvas, sgn, 30x22", C-E 2/23/88 ....
PERRIGARD, Hal Ross (Canadian, 1891-1960) 605
An August Day, oil on board, sgn/dtd 1928, 9x7", FB 10/30/89 2,000
Eastern Townships Farm, oil on board, sgn, 11x14", WAD 11/30/89 900
Sherbrooke Summer, oil on board, sgn/dtd 1916, 9x7", FB 10/17/88 OE 1,000
Street in Old Quebec, oil on panel, sgn/dtd 1921, 9x7", FB 4/25/88........ 1,100
Winding Stream-Winter; oil on board, sgn, 10x12", FB 4/25/88........
PERRIN, C. Robert (American, 1915-) 300
The Old Howard, Winter Morning (pigeons & vagrants on early morning streets); watercolor on paper, 30x13", RWS 3/31/88........
PERRIN, Gabriel (French, 19th C) 440
Along the River Tourgeville, oil on panel, sgn, 8x14", C-E 1/12/88........
PERRINE, Robert (American, 20th C) 550
Ghost Town, oil on masonite, sgn, 21x17", FAP 4/15/89 ....
PERRON, Charles Clement Francis (French, 1893-1958) 4,950
Cat by a Doorway, oil on panel, sgn, 9x6", SBY 7/12/89 OE 4,675
Escalier aux Geraniums, oil on canvas, sgn, 29x22", SBY 7/12/89 OE........ 6,875
Interior with Open Door, oil on panel, 14x17", SBY 7/12/89 OE 2,310
Sunlit Doorway, oil on panel, sgn, 11x9", SBY 7/12/89 OE........ 5,775
The Doorway, oil on panel, sgn, 14x22", SBY 7/12/89 OE........
PERRON, Louis Paul (Canadian, 1919-) 700
Le Pere Laporte, oil on board, sgn, 7x6", FB 5/28/89........ 1,650
Mon Oncle Arthur, oil on canvas, sgn, 20x16", FB 10/30/89 1,800
Winter Scene with Horses & Sleighs, pastel, sgn, 19x26", FB 5/28/89 ....
PERRONEAU, Jean Baptiste (French, 1715-1783) 6,600
Portrait of a Gentleman, half-length, wearing a red jacket & an order; oil on canvas, oval, 28x22", C-NY 5/31/89 UE ....
PERRONEAU, Jean Baptiste; att (French, 1715-1783) 13,200
Portrait of Miss Elizabeth Van Neck, seated, three-quarter length; pastel, 25x21", C-NY 1/15/88 ....
PERRONEAU, Jean Baptiste; school of (French, 1715-1783) 4,180
Portrait of Gentleman Said To Be Marquis Daubail, standing half-length...; oil on canvas, 32x25", C-NY 4/6/89 ....
PERRY, Clara Greenleaf (American, 1871-1960) 1,320
Walking on the Rocks (figures by a lake), oil on canvas, sgn/dtd 1908, 22x26", C-E 6/1/89 ....
PERRY, Enoch Wood (American, 1831-1915) 30,800
Fruit Seller (oriental lady seated under parasol, selling fruit), oil on canvas, sgn/dtd 62, 12x14", C-NY 5/25/89 OE........ 495
Knitting, oil on board, sgn/dtd 1908, 16x12", SBY 3/17/88 UE........ 1,760
Stairs in Venice, oil on canvas, sgn/dtd Venice 1865, 12x16", C-E 2/1/89 1,800
Young Girl with a Water Jug, oil on canvas, sgn/dtd 92, 20x16", RWS 5/12/89 ....
PERRY, J. (19th C) 1,200
Vista del Valle del Rimac en la Ciudad de Lima (landscape), watercolor/pencil on paper, sgn, ca 1820, 6x9", C-NY 5/17/89........
PERRY, Lilla Cabot (American, 1848-1933) 1,600
Child in a Blue Dress (sketch), oil on canvas, 14x10", WL 5/20/88 OE 12,100
Cup of Tea (portrait of lady seated at a table drinking tea), oil on canvas, 32x26", C-NY 5/25/89 9,900
Lady in Black (portrait), pastel on paper, sgn, 33x26", C-NY 5/26/88........ 3,250
Meeting Street, Charleston, South Carolina; oil on academy board, sgn/dtd 1925, 12x14", DM 9/16/88........ 1,100
Profile of a Young Girl, oil on canvas, sgn, 16x14", C-E 2/1/89 UE 1,900
Sheltie Dog, oil on canvas, sgn/dtd 1931, unfr, 25x30", WL 5/20/88 OE 600
Sheltie Dog, Profile (seated on a chair); oil on canvas, sgn/dtd 1931, unfr, 25x30", WL 5/20/88 UE ....
PERUGINO, after (Italian, 1446-1523) 500
Madonna of the Sack (kneeling w/an angel, the Christ Child, & the infant St John), oil on canvas, 22x22", SLK 5/11/88 ....
PERUGINO, school of (Italian, 1446-1523) 77,000
Madonna & Child, oil on panel, 31x23", C-NY 10/12/89 OE ....
Peruvian School (19th C) 7,700
Archangel, oil on canvas, 45x29", SBY 5/17/88 5,775
Archangel Sariel, oil on canvas, inscr Sealtiel, 45x29", SBY 5/17/88 ....

ELLINO, att (Italian, 15th C)
ladonna & Child, oil on panel, 27x18", C-NY 4/8/88 OE 82,500
KE, Jean (French, 1880-1949)
laternite aux Trois Enfants (mother & three children), oil on board, sgn, 22x18", C-E 11/17/88 2,420
NE, Antoine (French, 1683-1757)
egetable Seller, oil on canvas, 21x19", C-NY 1/11/89 OE 33,000
NE, Antoine; att (French, 1683-1757)
ortrait of a Flutist, oil on canvas, 29x23", SBY 4/7/89 3,575
ortrait of a Young Girl, bust-length, in profile; oil on canvas, 24x20", C-NY 4/6/89 4,620
NE, Antoine; circle of (French, 1683-1757)
ortrait of a Lady, oil on canvas, 32x25", SBY 6/8/88 UE 495
ER, Emmanuel
ortrait of a Young Woman Wearing a Flowered Hat, watercolor/gouache, sgn, 5x4", C-E 11/8/88 280
ER, George (American, 19th/20th C)
oat Load of Plants & Flowers, oil on academy board, sgn, 27x20", S/A 3/12/88 850
uffalo Hunt, oil on panel, sgn, 10x20", S/A 2/8/89 500
andscape with Cattle & Geese, oil on panel, sgn, 6x10", S/A 3/12/88 350
illage Pond (landscape), oil on panel, initialed, 6x10", S/A 3/12/88 400
ER, Nori (Canadian, 19th C)
lother & Sleeping Child, oil on board, sgn, 20x24", WAD 11/30/89 450
ERS, Carl William (American, 1897-1980)
larbor-Side Shack (figure by rowboat), oil on canvas, 20x24", RAB 8/9/88 UE 900
ockport (harbor scene), oil on canvas, sgn, 20x24", WD 4/13/88 1,800
inter Landscape, oil on canvas, estate stamp, 20x24", SBY 1/24/89 1,760
inter Landscape with River, oil on canvas, estate stamp, 25x30", SBY 1/24/89 OE 4,950
ERS, Charles Rollo (American, 1862-1928)
abin at Midnight, oil on canvas, sgn, 16x24", B/B 10/6/88 3,300
louse of the Four Winds (house in landscape), oil on canvas, sgn/dtd 1920/titled, 16x24", RWS 3/16/89 OE 2,250
lonterey Moonlight, oil on canvas, sgn, 13x16", B/B 10/6/88 4,125
lonterey Nocturne, oil on canvas, 13x19", B/B 1/11/89 OE 3,300
loonlight, Monterey Bay; oil on panel, sgn, 6x9", B/B 10/6/88 1,650
octurnal Landscape, Monterey; oil on canvas, sgn, 16x24", SBY 9/23/88 3,300
locturnal Sketch, oil on canvas, sgn, 24x16", B/B 1/11/89 495
nettisham Church, oil on canvas, sgn, 21x15", B/B 10/6/88 2,750
ERS, Matthew William; att (British, 1742-1814)
enus Disarming Cupid, oil on canvas, 32x28", SBY 4/7/89 UE 3,850
ERS, Pietronella (Dutch, 1848-1924)
uppet Show, oil on canvas, sgn, 15x20", C-E 10/26/89 OE 14,300
ERSEN, Edvard Frederik (Danish, 1841-1911)
alk in the Woods, oil on canvas, sgn/dtd 1902, 18x24", SBY 2/22/89 13,200
ERSEN, John Eric Christian (American, 1839-1874)
rant Rock Nahant (coastal scene w/figures in boat), oil on canvas, initialed, 13x19", RWS 9/8/89 OE 2,700
ERSON, H. (American, 20th C)
all Landscape, oil on board, 14x16", LH 9/10/89 200
ERSON, H. (German, 19th C)
hip Centurion, Daniel P Caulhins, Master, Passing Heligoland; oil on canvas, sgn/dtd 1859, 18x26", RAB 3/14/89 OE 7,000
ERSON, Jane (American, 1876-1965)
y the Barn, barn w/fresh hay in foreground; oil on board, sgn, 11x14", RAB 3/27/89 2,200
hattering Macaws, watercolor on paper, sgn, 20x27", B/B 8/10/88 935
ogwood Blossoms in a Vase, oil on canvas, sgn, 32x32", C-NY 5/26/88 14,300
estival, oil on canvas, sgn, 18x24", C-NY 5/26/88 OE 12,100
ishing Boats, Venice; gouache on paper laid down on board, sgn, 18x18", PHL 12/1/88 9,000
lorida Beach (w/palm trees & figures), watercolor/pen/black ink/pencil on buff paper, sgn, 14x20", C-NY 9/28/89 3,300
ountain of the Lions (fountain in landscape), oil on canvas, sgn, 18x24", SBY 3/17/88 2,970
ossips (three colorful parrots on branch), watercolor on paper mounted on cardboard, sgn, 20x26", RWS 3/31/88 UE 425
roup of 3: White House, Florida; Two Tropical Scenes; watercolor on paper, sgn, 11x14", 5x7", 6x9", RWS 3/31/88 650
louse in a Tropical Landscape, watercolor/pencil on paper, sgn, 11x15", C-E 11/30/88 528
n the Grand Canal, Venice; gouache on paper laid down on board, sgn, 18x18", PHL 12/1/88 3,250
air: Lily Pads; Bean Plants; watercolor/gouache on paper, sgn, 21x15", 20x21", SBY 6/28/89 1,760
alm Trees on the Beach, gouache on paper, sgn, 15x21", B/B 8/10/88 1,650
iazza, Venice; oil/pencil on academy board, sgn, 16x12", RWS 9/29/88 OE 1,400
ink Hollyhocks Amidst Yellow Flowers, oil on canvas, sgn, 18x18", SBY 6/28/89 2,090
ed Cannas, oil on canvas, sgn/inscr, unfr, 32x32", C-NY 3/11/88 OE 12,100
ed Cross Fete Evening, watercolor/gouache, sgn 1918, 18x24", PHL 6/16/88 OE 9,500
hododendrons, oil on canvas, sgn, 40x30", SBY 5/25/88 UE 5,500
even Hollyhocks (profuse plants), oil on canvas, sgn/titled, 30x25", RAB 8/8/89 6,000
till Life of Pink & White Cosmos, oil on canvas, sgn, 30x24", SBY 6/28/89 3,080
till Life with Ceramic Animals, gouache/India ink over pencil on paper, sgn, 23x29", SBY 3/17/88 1,650
till Life with Roses (multicolored flowers in aquamarine vase), watercolor on paper, sgn, 11x8", RWS 3/31/88 UE 550
unset, Gloucester, Massachusetts; oil on canvasboard, sgn, 11x14", RWS 5/12/89 3,100
hree Yellow Calla Lilies (still life), oil on canvas, sgn, 24x20", SBY 1/24/89 5,500

Tiger Lilies, oil on canvas, sgn, 24x24", SBY 6/28/89 3,41
Tomatoes, oil on board, sgn/inscr/dtd 1940, 18x18", RWS 11/3/88 2,40
Toucans, oil on board, sgn, 42x34", WD 4/13/88 3,60
Tropical Beach Scene (palm trees, sailboats beyond), watercolor/India ink on paper, sgn, 11x17", SBY 9/14/89 2,09
Tropical Scene with Palms & Flamingos, watercolor/gouache/graphite on paper, sgn, 21x29", RWS 11/10/89 1,20
Two Ducks, watercolor/gouache/graphite on paper, sgn, 18x23", RWS 11/10/89 1,10
Venetian Canal Scene, gouache on paper laid down on board, sgn, 12x16", SBY 1/24/89 3,57

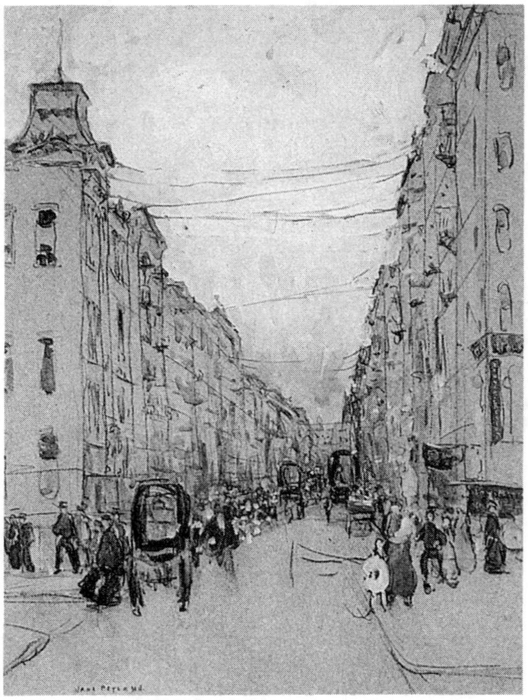

A Street-New York; watercolor/gouache/charcoal on brown paper, sgn, 24x18", C-NY 5/25/89; $16,500

Venetian Scene with Figures, gouache on paper, sgn, 12x16", SBY 4/14/89 OE 4,12
Venice, oil on board, 18x18", C-NY 9/28/89 6,05
Venice Twilight, oil on canvas, sgn/inscr, 6x9", RWS 3/16/89 OE 1,60
View of Gloucester (port scene), oil on board, sgn, 16x18", SBY 3/17/88 4,67
View of San Giorgio Maggiore, Venice; oil on board, sgn, 11x14", SBY 9/14/89 6,05
White Blossoms (still life), oil on canvas, sgn, 32x32", SBY 1/24/89 4,67
White Lilies, oil on board, sgn, 24x18", RWS 11/10/89 OE 6,00
White Lilies (still life), oil on artist board, sgn, 24x18", RWS 5/19/88 2,70
Wild Zinnias (bright garden still life), watercolor on paper, sgn, 15x11", RWS 3/31/88 1,00
Woman at the Beach, oil on canvasboard, sgn, 20x24", C-E 11/30/88 1,98
Zinnias, oil on board, sgn, 18x18", C-NY 9/30/88 3,85
Zinnias, oil on canvas, sgn, 30x24", SBY 3/17/88 4,95
Zinnias, oil on canvas, sgn, 30x24", SBY 6/28/89 OE 6,05

PETERSON, Jane; att (American, 1876-1965)
Portrait of a Lady Said To Be the Artist's Aunt, oil on canvas, 53x36", WD 3/23/88 OE 2,10

PETERSON, Johann Erik Christian (19th C)
Provisioning the Ship, oil on canvas, sgn/dtd 1869, 28x50", C-NY 5/26/88 8,80

PETHER, Henry; att (British, 1828-1865)
Doge's Palace & the Grand Canal by Moonlight, oil on canvas, dtd 1853, 21x17", C-NY 2/25/88 5,50

PETHER, Sebastian (British, 1790-1844)
Pair: Fortress Overlooking a River; Full Moon Over a Lake; oil on canvas, oil on panel, 14x8", C-E 2/21/89 3,30

PETIT, E. (French, 1839-1886)
Hunting Dogs, oil on canvas, sgn, 20x24", DM 10/14/88 1,30
Pointers in a Hilly Landscape, oil on canvas, sgn, 15x19", C-E 5/23/88 UE 1,54

PETIT-GERARD, Pierre (French, 1852-)
Hunt Master with His Hounds, oil on board, sgn, 16x13", WD 1/25/89 1,40
L'Entree des Militaires, oil on canvas, sgn/dtd 1891, 36x48", SBY 10/24/89 8,80

PETITJEAN, Edmond Marie (French, 1844-1925)
Along the Canal, oil on canvas, sgn, 11x14", SBY 7/12/89 OE 5,77
French Village on a River, oil on canvas, sgn, 19x27", C-NY 10/25/89 7,70
Going to Market, oil on canvas, sgn, 26x19", C-E 10/26/89 3,85

PETITJEAN, Hippolyte (French, 1854-1929)
Eglise du Maconais (Church of Maconais), watercolor on paper laid down on board, sgn, 16x13", C-NY 5/11/89 OE 24,20
Les Toits de la Ville, watercolor/gouache on paper, initialed, 12x10", C-E 5/9/89 1,21

aysage (landscape w/buildings & hills beyond), oil on canvas, sgn, ca 1920, 15x22", C-NY 10/5/89	15,400
'O, John Frederick (American, 1854-1907)	
opper Kettle, oil on board, 6x9", C-NY 5/25/89 OE	18,700
antern, Books, & Corncob Pipe (still life on draped table), oil on board, 19x14", C-NY 5/25/89	110,000
till Life of Mug, Pipe & Biscuits; oil on panel, sgn, 7x10", B/B 6/9/88	16,500
till Life of Mugs, Bottle, & Pipe; oil on canvas, sgn/dtd, 12x16", C-NY 5/26/88	176,000
'RASSI, L.	
ucks on a Garden Pond, oil on board, sgn, 17x23", C-E 10/25/88 UE	660
'ROCELLI, Arturo (Italian, 1856-)	
oung Couple, oil on canvas, sgn, 26x17", SBY 12/9/88 OE	2,200
'RONI, Andrea (Italian, 1863-)	
'iew of Naples From Virgils Tomb, gouache/watercolor on paper, sgn, 13x18", B/B 5/17/89 UE	330
'ROV, Arkadi (Russian, 1940-)	
rchestra Plays (couple on park bench w/title in corner), oil on canvas, sgn/dtd 1980, 62x79", SBY 7/7/88	6,000
'wo Portraits (folk art style, seated figures in peasant landscape), oil on canvas, sgn/dtd 1982, 56x42", SBY 7/7/88 OE	8,000
'RUOLO, Salvatore (Italian, 1857-)	
alais Generalifa, watercolor/pen/brown ink over pencil, sgn, 12x21", C-NY 10/25/89	1,430
'TER, Franz Xaver (Austrian, 1791-1866)	
'air: Floral Still Lifes; oil on canvas, sgn, 16x12", SBY 5/23/89 OE	28,600
'TITT, Charles (British, 19th C)	
laramara Mountain & Borrowdale From Near Bowder, oil on canvas, sgn/dtd 1866, 18x30", SBY 2/22/89	11,000
'anorama of the English Countryside, watercolor on paper, sgn, 7x9", B/B 1/11/89	440
'TITT, Joseph Paul (British, -1882)	
xtensive Mountainous Landscape, oil on canvas, sgn, 15x24", C-E 10/25/88	1,210
'TORUTI, Emilio (Argentinian, 1895-1971)	
osques de Auronsc (abstract), oil on canvas, sgn/dtd 1917, 20x12", C-NY 5/18/88	24,200
hianti (still life of bottle of wine w/glass), oil on canvas, sgn/dtd 1948/titled, 39x29", C-NY 5/17/89	99,000
repuscule Marin (abstract), oil on canvas, sgn twice/dtd 54 twice/titled, 58x43", C-NY 11/21/88	132,000
l Jardin (The Garden), watercolor/pencil on board, sgn, 9x8", C-NY 5/17/89	4,400
a Resistencia (contemporary harlequin), oil on canvas, sgn/dtd 1950/titled, 21x18", C-NY 11/21/88 OE	126,500
a Voce (a periodical), collage on board, sgn/dtd 1916, 19x15", SBY 5/17/88 OE	115,500
Iaria (abstract portrait), oil on board, sgn twice/dtd Roma 1917 twice, 20x16", C-NY 11/21/88	25,300
'aturaleza Muerta (abstract), pen/brush/India ink on paper, sgn/dtd 920/inscr, 8x10", C-NY 11/21/88	4,620
ranges (contemporary still life), oil on canvas, sgn/dtd 944, 24x32", SBY 11/21/88	60,500
erenata Romantica (full-length abstract figure), oil on canvas, sgn/dtd 1938, 71x28", C-NY 5/18/88	242,000
heet of Music (contemporary still life), oil on canvas, sgn/dtd 950 twice/titled/inscr, 15x22", SBY 5/16/89	49,500
warthy Rogue (last in Harlequin series), oil on canvas, sgn twice/dtd 53 twice/titled, 24x20", SBY 5/16/89	115,500
'ino Rubi (contemporary still life), oil on canvas, sgn, 1945, 20x26", C-NY 11/21/89	66,000
'UA, Leon Jean (French, 1846-1921)	
usanna & the Elders (nude in garden), oil on canvas, sgn twice/dtd 1880, 69x47", C-NY 2/23/89	24,200
IOTTO, Ernest Clifford	
tatue in the Park, oil on canvas, sgn, 26x20", C-E 11/30/88 UE	880
'RAT, Louis (French, 20th C)	
'lace de Theatre, oil on canvas, sgn/#d, 20x24", B/B 1/11/89	550
acre Coeur, Montmartre; oil on canvas, sgn/dtd 1964, 18x22", B/B 1/11/89	550
'RAUD, Frank Charles (American, 1858-)	
ucks on a Path (weathered buildings beyond), oil on canvas, sgn/dtd 01, 14x18", RWS 9/29/88 OE	1,100
'ROL-BONHEUR, Juliette (French, 1830-1891)	
Valk Through the Woods (woman w/cow), oil on canvas, sgn, 54x41", C-NY 2/23/89 UE	2,860
'TON, Bertha Menzler (American, 1871-1950)	
nto the Night (nymph w/flute dancing under trees, two leopards following), oil on canvas, sgn, 27x40", RWS 3/31/88 OE	3,000
Iisty Morning Valley, oil on canvas, sgn, 18x20", RWS 5/12/89 OE	2,100
AFF, Judy (American, 1946-)	
Jntitled (abstract), mixed adhesive plastics on mylar graph paper, sgn, 31x46", C-NY 5/4/89 OE	49,500
AHL, Charles (American, 1946-)	
Jew Chandelier, 1984; oil on canvas, sgn, 36x30", RWS 11/10/89	3,750
EIFFER, Fritz (American, 1875-1960)	
bstract Composition, oil on paper, sgn/inscr/dtd 1928, 13x11", SBY 6/24/88	3,630
and Dunes of Provincetown, oil on canvasboard, sgn/dtd 1931, 10x13", RWS 3/16/89 OE	600
EIFFER, Gordon (Canadian, 1899-1983)	
bandoned Farm, oil on board, sgn, 8x10", FB 10/30/89	358
eauport Road, oil on board, sgn/dtd 1970, 12x16", FB 5/28/89	750
ape Diamond, Quebec; oil on panel, sgn/dtd 1945, 11x13", FB 4/25/88	600
Iountains, River, & Trees; oil on board, sgn, 8x10", FB 4/25/88	240
ff to Market, oil on canvas laid down on board, sgn, 9x11", FB 10/30/89	605
load to Notre Dame de Monts, Murray Bay; oil on canvas, sgn, 18x24", FB 10/30/89	880
olitude in October, oil on board, sgn, 30x40", FB 4/25/88	1,700
EIFFER, Wilhelm (German, 1822-1891)	
Vorkmates to the Haying Fields, oil on canvas, sgn/Munchen stamp on reverse, 27x23", RWS 11/10/89	3,500
JLLER, Minna (German, 1824-1907)	
listorical Scene, oil on canvas, sgn/inscr/dtd 1856, unfr, 60x70", SBY 6/8/88 OE	2,420

PHELAN, H. (American, 1881-)
Tree-Lined Drive Beside a Stream, oil on canvas, sgn, 18x16", C-E 6/28/88 352
PHELPS, Edith Catlin (American, 1871-1961)
Nude by a Vanity, oil on canvas laid down, sgn, 36x30", B/B 12/8/88 1,430
PHELPS, William Preston (American, 1848-1923)
View of Charles River, Autumn; oil on canvasboard, initialed, 8x13", RWS 11/10/89 550
PHILIP, James George (British, 1816-1885)
Rocky Coastal Scene with Fisherman, watercolor on paper, sgn, 18x25", WL 5/20/88 UE 350
PHILIPP, Robert (American, 1895-1981)
Amsterdam, Holland (outdoor cafe scene); oil on canvas, sgn/dtd 1972, 18x22", WD 11/16/88 4,500
Apres the Bain (After the Bath, nude woman viewed from behind), pastel on paper, sgn, 30x19", C-E 6/1/89 1,045
At the Beach, oil on canvas, sgn twice/dtd 79, unfr, 30x40", C-E 6/1/88 1,650
Cafe Scene, oil on board, sgn, 12x16", SBY 6/24/88 660
Day Dreaming, oil on canvas, sgn, 14x12", C-E 6/1/89 UE 770
Daydreams (portrait of a young girl at table), gouache on board, sgn, 28x24", WD 4/13/88 2,400
Dreamer (portait of a woman), oil on canvas, sgn, 30x25", SBY 6/28/89 1,980
Girl in Red, oil on canvas, sgn, 9x8", C-E 6/1/88 OE 1,430
Girl in Sweater (three-quarter length portrait), oil on masonite, sgn, 18x10", C-E 6/1/89 2,420
In Central Park: Young Janis with Book; oil on canvas, sgn/dtd 1977, 24x48", WD 10/5/88 6,250
In Love Again (man & woman having drinks), gouache on heavy paper laid down, sgn/dtd 1980, 35x29", WD 4/13/88 3,000
La Liseuse (girl reading at table), oil on board laid down on pressed wood, sgn/dtd 72, 22x30", WD 11/16/88 4,500
My Mona Lisa (three-quarter length portrait), pastel/watercolor on heavy paper, sgn/dtd 76, 29x21", WD 10/5/88 OE 1,500
My Mona Lisa (woman seated next to vase of flowers), pastel on paper, sgn/dtd 76, 29x21", PHL 12/1/88 UE 1,500
Nude with Raised Arms, pastel on buff paper, sgn, 25x17", SBY 3/17/88 880
Of Myself, oil on canvas, sgn/inscr/dtd 1960, 12x8", C-E 6/1/88 UE 1,540
Red Roses in Vases, oil on canvas, sgn, 15x5", C-E 4/7/88 UE 715
Robert & Rochelle Philipp on the Terrace at Tarrytown, oil on canvas, sgn/dtd 1971, 30x46", WD 4/13/88 6,250
Rochelle at Gloucester (girl reading at table by open door), oil on canvas, sgn/dtd 81, 25x25", WD 11/16/88 5,000
Rochelle in Blue (portrait of woman, leaning on elbows, reflecting), oil on canvas, sgn, 23x31", C-E 2/1/89 OE 4,400
Rochelle Sewing #2, The Red Room at Gloucester; oil on board, sgn, 29x35", WD 10/5/88 5,500
Spring in Paris (woman at table, waterscape beyond), oil on canvas, sgn/dtd 1976, 18x24", C-E 6/1/89 1,045
Still Life of Flowers in a Vase, oil on canvas, sgn, 20x12", C-E 6/1/89 2,090
Still Life of Fruit, pastel on paper, 11x12", C-E 4/7/88 440
Study of a Young Girl with Blond Hair, oil on canvas, sgn/dtd 1969, 22x18", SBY 9/14/89 3,025
Tavern on the Green, oil on canvas, sgn/inscr, 30x36", C-NY 3/11/88 OE 16,500
Young Woman, oil on canvas, sgn twice, 1956, 9x8", SBY 3/17/88 OE 1,100
PHILIPPE, Pierre (Canadian)
L'Heure de The (Teatime), oil on board, sgn, 24x18", FB 5/28/89 400
PHILLIP, John (British, 1817-1887)
El Aqua Benedita, oil on canvas, sgn/inscr/dtd 1862 twice, 38x32", C-E 10/25/88 2,750
Hero of the Hour, oil on canvas, sgn/indistinctly dtd, 24x18", SBY 6/8/88 UE 935
PHILLIPS, Ammi (American, 1788-1865)
Pair: Philo & Abigail Reynolds Reed (portraits); oil on canvas, unfr, 31x25", RWS 10/27/89 UE 25,000
Pair: Portraits of James Ketcham & Lois Belding Ketcham; oil on canvas, 32x27", SBY 1/28/88 OE 115,500
Portrait of a Gentleman with a White Clay Pipe, oil on canvas, ca 1825, 30x24", SBY 1/28/88 OE 33,000
Portrait of a Lady in a White Lace Bonnet, oil on canvas, ca 1830, 32x23", SBY 1/28/88 OE 14,300
Portrait of a Woman in a Black Dress with White Lace Collar & Cuffs, oil on canvas, ca 1840, 31x24", SBY 1/28/88 3,850
Portrait of Gentleman in...Frock Coat...Holding a Newspaper Entitled Flag; oil on canvas, 1850s, 32x43", SBY 1/28/88 UE 7,700
PHILLIPS, Bert Greer (American, 1868-1956)
Aspen Forest & Mountain Peak, oil on canvas, sgn/inscr, 24x20", SBY 5/25/88 13,200
Indian Fishing, oil on board, sgn, 10x8", SBY 9/23/88 5,500
Road to Taos, oil on board, sgn, 10x8", SBY 6/24/88 2,090
Taos Canyon, oil on canvas, sgn, 24x18", SBY 6/28/89 9,900
Taos Mountain, oil on board, sgn, 10x8", SBY 6/24/88 1,980
PHILLIPS, Charles
Portrait of a Gentleman, His Wife & Three Children Standing on a Terrace; oil on canvas, 29x29", C-NY 10/20/88 3,300
PHILLIPS, G. Whitehead (American, 20th C)
Calm Autumn Day, oil on board, sgn, 20x16", FAP 12/8/89 150
PHILLIPS, Gordon (American, 1927-)
One the Game Trail (hunter on horse near forest), oil on canvas, sgn, 24x36", SBY 4/14/89 6,050
PHILLIPS, Henry Wyndham (British, 1820-1868)
Leopard Skin, oil on canvas, sgn, 12x25", SBY 6/8/88 3,575
PHILLIPS, James (American, 1913-)
Portrait of Martha in a Green Hat, oil on masonite, sgn/inscr/dtd 56, 13x9", C-NY 3/11/88 1,100
Rain & Shine, watercolor on paper laid down, sgn, 16x23", B/B 10/6/88 495
Robert Manserrat (portrait), oil on canvas, sgn/dtd 56, 11x13", C-NY 3/11/88 UE 770
PHILLIPS, S. George (American, 20th C)
Autumn Landscape, oil on canvas, sgn, 18x16", FAP 4/15/89 880
PHILLIPS, Thomas; att (British, 1770-1845)
Portrait of a Lady, oil on canvas, 29x25", SBY 6/8/88 UE 275
Portrait of Jane & Mary Huntley, oil on canvas, 37x30", C-E 1/12/88 1,210

PHILPOT, Glyn Warren (British, 1884-1937)

Man & the Fates, oil on canvas, initialed, 1933, 86x72", C-L 6/27/88 ... 64,328

PHIPPEN, George (American, 1916-1966)

Brush with the Hostiles, oil on canvas, sgn, 30x40", SBY 9/23/88 OE ... 9,900

PHIZ (American, 19th/20th C)

Set of 3: Domestic Scenes; watercolor/pen/ink/pencil on paper, 2 sgn, 7x5", B/B 1/11/89 ... 825

PHO, see Le Pho

PIAZZETTA, Giovanni Battista (Italian, 1682-1754)

Double-Sided: Standing Nude; David with Head of Goliath; black chalk heightened w/white on gray, 23x18", C-NY 1/12/88 ... 22,000

PIAZZETTA, Giovanni Battista; att (Italian, 1682-1754)

Head of Saint Simenon in Profile to the Right, black/white chalk on buff paper, 15x11", C-NY 1/11/89 OE ... 2,860

PIAZZONI, Gottardo (American, 1872-1945)

Haystacks, Carmel; oil on canvas laid down, ca 1916, 10x13", B/B 10/6/88 ... 1,870

Ranch, oil on board, sgn/dtd 28, 6x9", B/B 10/6/88 ... 1,100

PICABIA, Francis (French, 1878-1953)

Au Bord de Fleuve (landscape w/river & houses), oil on canvas, sgn/dtd 1902, 12x16", C-NY 5/12/88 OE ... 22,000

Bord de Loing, oil on canvas, sgn/dtd 1905, 13x18", SBY 5/11/88 OE ... 52,250

Deux Chiens (two dogs, abstract), oil on board, sgn/dtd 1949, 21x26", C-NY 10/6/88 ... 30,800

Deux Chines (two dogs, abstract), oil on board, sgn/dtd 1949, 21x26", C-NY 5/11/89 ... 38,500

Deux Tetes de Femmes (two women's heads overlapped), watercolor/pencil on paper, sgn, 14x11", C-NY 2/16/89 ... 11,000

Homme Assis, watercolor over pencil on paper, sgn, 10x7", C-NY 10/6/88 ... 3,080

Ior (allegory), oil on canvas, sgn/titled, 1931, 34x29", SBY 11/12/88 OE ... 176,000

L'Eglise de Montigny-Soleil de Septembre (landscape); oil on canvas, sgn/dtd 1905/titled, 36x29", C-NY 11/16/88 OE ... 198,000

L'Espagnole a la Fleur (portrait of Spanish woman), watercolor/black chalk/pencil, sgn, 26x20", C-NY 2/16/89 OE ... 17,600

L'Espagnole aux Perles (portrait, Spanish woman w/pearls), watercolor/black chalk, sgn, 26x20", C-NY 2/16/89 OE ... 16,500

Nu Debout (nude standing), oil on paper laid down on board), sgn, 12x7", C-NY 10/6/88 OE ... 7,480

Oeil Poche (abstract), oil on canvas, sgn/dtd 1948/titled, 64x51", C-NY 5/12/88 ... 143,000

Portrait de Femme, oil on canvas, sgn, 18x15", C-NY 10/6/88 ... 17,600

Portrait de Femme (portrait of a woman), mixed media on board, sgn, 1942, 18x15", SBY 10/6/89 ... 38,500

Tabarin, oil on paper laid down on panel, sgn/titled, ca 1946-47, 41x30", SBY 2/16/89 OE ... 71,500

Untitled (Called Monster), oil on masonite, sgn/dtd 1946, 42x30", SBY 4/29/88 ... 60,500

Untitled (contemporary portrait of a woman), oil on canvas, sgn, ca 1934, 36x28", SBY 4/29/88 ... 99,000

Villeneuve-sur-Yonne sous la Neige; oil on canvas, sgn/dtd 1906, 29x36", SBY 10/7/88 OE ... 55,000

PICASSO, Pablo (Spanish, 1881-1973)

Arles: Les Arenes Devant le Rhone (abstract view of arena); oil on canvas, sgn/dtd 8.4.60/#d II, 24x29", SBY 5/9/89 ... 1,210,000

Bull's Head, purple wash on thin paper, ca 1940s, 11x14", SBY 2/16/89 ... 6,600

Bust d'Homme aux Mains Croisees, colored pen on paper, sgn/dtd 26 5 69/#d VII, 12x9", SBY 11/16/89 ... 49,500

Bust of a Woman (Dora Maar), black pencil on paper, dtd 23.4.42, 15x12", SBY 11/12/88 OE ... 242,000

Buste d'Homme Barbu, oil on canvas, sgn/dtd 17.3.65, 24x20", SBY 11/15/89 ... 742,000

Buste de Femme (abstract portrait of a woman), oil on canvas, sgn/dtd 28A.38, 22x15", C-NY 11/15/88 ... 902,000

Buste de Femme (abstract), oil on canvas, sgn/dtd 40, 29x22", SBY 11/11/88 OE ... 1,485,000

Buste de Femme Souriante (portrait), oil on board laid down on panel, sgn, 1901, 30x23", SBY 5/10/88 OE ... 4,400,000

Buste de Matador (abstract), oil on canvas, dtd 27.9.70/#d IV 51x38", SBY 11/11/88 ... 880,000

Chevaux (two horses in a barn), pencil/yellow watercolor on paper, ca 1940, 7x9", SBY 5/11/88 OE ... 15,400

Clown et Acrobate, colored crayon on paper, sgn/dtd 30.1.54/#d I, 10x13", SBY 5/11/88 ... 49,500

Clown et Ecuyere, colored crayon on paper, sgn/dtd 30.1.54.III, 10x13", SBY 2/16/89 ... 34,100

Clown et Ecuyere, colored crayon on paper, sgn/dtd 30.1.54.III, 10x13", C-NY 10/7/89 OE ... 82,500

Composition, crayons on paper laid down on paper, indistinctly sgn/dtd 7.11.56, 12x9", C-NY 10/5/89 ... 8,800

Coupe, Cruche et Boite a Lait; watercolor on paper, sgn, 1905, 14x11", C-NY 11/15/88 ... 209,000

Curt, blue ballpoint pen on paper, sgn, 8x5", SBY 10/7/89 ... 3,850

Deux Femmes Nues (two nudes), brown crayon on paper, sgn/dtd 22.12.66/#d II, 20x24", C-NY 5/11/89 OE ... 143,000

Deux Tetes (two heads, abstract), oil on canvas, 1929, 9x6", C-NY 5/11/89 OE ... 159,500

Double-Sided: Artist's Family; Artist's Daughter; pencil on paper, ca 1940, 8x11", SBY 5/10/89 OE ... 39,700

Double-Sided: Dessin pour la Couverture de Ragtime de Strawinsky; Study for Ragtime; pen/ink, sgn, 10x8", SBY 5/11/88 ... 77,000

Double-Sided: Femme Nue Allongee; Nue et Etudes de Lits; watercolor/pen/ink & wash/watercolor, sgn, 12x16", SBY 5/11/88 ... 154,000

Double-Sided: Head & Bust of a Man; colored inks on paper, dgn/dtd 16.12.70, 11x8", SBY 5/10/89 ... 79,750

Double-Sided: Head; Head; recto: crayon, verso: brush/ink/wash on paper, sgn/dtd 67, 15x11", C-NY 5/11/89 ... 176,000

Double-Sided: La Famille de l'Artiste; La Fille de l'Artiste; pencil on paper, ca 1940, 8x11", SBY 5/11/88 OE ... 29,700

Double-Sided: Maya; La Fille de l'Artiste; colored crayon on cut-out paper, ca 1940s, 7x3", SBY 11/12/88 OE ... 27,500

Espana (done for a cover of a pamplet), colored pencil on paper laid down on board, sgn, 1952, 11x8", C-NY 2/18/88 OE ... 28,600

Etude pour le Dejeuner sur L'Herbe, pencil on paper, sgn/dtd 30 7 60/#d III, 16x12", SBY 11/16/89 ... 46,750

Etude pour Nu a la Draperie, pen/ink on fragment from newspaper Le Vieux Marcheur, sgn, ca 1907, 6x4", SBY 11/12/88 OE ... 38,500

Etudes (Studies), pencil on paper, 1952, 8x11", C-NY 5/11/89 ... 18,700

Faunes et Flore, colored wax crayons on buff paper, sgn/titled/dtd 30.9.59, 25x19", C-NY 5/12/88 OE ... 19,800

Femme a la Cithare, pencil on paper, sgn, ca 1913, 25x19", SBY 11/12/88 OE ... 77,000

Femme Assise (abstract), oil on canvas, sgn/dtd 20.11.62/#d 11.12.13, 51x38", SBY 5/10/88 OE ... 1,155,000

Femme Assise (abstract), oil on canvas, 1918-19, 51x35", SBY 5/10/88 ... 3,190,000

Femme Assise (Francoise), oil on canvas, sgn, 1946, 51x35", SBY 11/10/88 OE ... 2,530,000

Femme Assise (Woman in a Red Hat), oil on canvas, sgn/dtd September XXXIV, 64x51", SBY 11/10/88 ... 4,400,000

Femme Assise (woman seated, full-length), gouache over pencil on paper, sgn, 1920, 11x8", C-NY 5/11/89 ... 385,000

Femme Assise sur une Terrasse, watercolor/pen/India ink on paper, sgn/inscr/dtd, 13x18", C-NY 11/15/88 OE ... 132,000

Femme au Corsage Bleu (abstract portrait), oil on canvas, sgn/dtd 8 Juin 41, 36x24", SBY 5/9/89	1,815,000
Femme au Miroir et Enfant, brown crayon on paper, sgn/dtd 21 67/#d II, 20x24", SBY 11/16/89 OE	126,500
Femme Couchee, oil on canvas, sgn, 1910, 9x18", SBY 11/15/89	3,410,000
Femme Couronee de Fleurs (portrait of woman w/crown of flowers), oil on canvas, dtd 24.6.37, 18x13", C-NY 5/11/88	715,000
Femme et Homme a la Coupe, crayons/pencil on paper, sgn, dtd 14.15.16.17.18./10.67, 11x18", SBY 11/15/89	660,000
Femme et Nain (nude woman & nude dwarf), India ink on paper, sgn/dtd 18.12.53, 14x11", SBY 5/10/89	66,000
Femme Fleur (fantasy drawing of lady w/flower), pencil on paper, sgn/dtd 48/#d II, 26x20", C-NY 5/11/89 OE	99,000
Femme Nue Assise, oil on canvas, sgn, dtd 14.2.59/10.2.59/12.22/2.-9.-3.59, 57x45", SBY 11/10/88 OE	6,050,000
Fleurs (floral still life), oil on canvas, sgn, 20x16", SBY 5/9/89 OE	2,420,000
Guitare et Verre sur Une Table, pencil on paper, sgn, 1912, 19x12", SBY 4/29/88 OE	104,500
Head of a Woman, black/brown wash on paper, dtd 29.4.45, 26x20", SBY 11/12/88	110,000
Homme a la Pipe (abstract of man w/a pipe), oil on canvas, sgn/dtd 5.10.68, 65x38", C-NY 11/15/88	1,870,000
Homme avec Agneau, ink/wash on paper, 13x9", C-NY 11/15/88 OE	46,200
Homme et Femme Nus (male & female nudes), ink on cardboard, sgn/dtd/#d 30.4.69.V., 9x11", SBY 10/6/89	38,500
Homme Portant un Enfant, oil on canvas, sgn/dtd 24.2.65.III, 36x29", SBY 5/11/88	462,000
Horse & Rider: Verve, Picasso a Vallauris Cover Design; collage/pen/ink/crayon on paper, ca 1950, 11x8", SBY 11/12/88 OE	39,600
Interieur (drawing), colored wax crayons on paper, sgn/dtd/#d 15.11.55. II, 1955, 10x12", C-NY 5/12/88	38,500
L'Amour Masque (The Love Mask, kneeling nude, Cupid), brush/ink on paper, sgn/dtd 5.1.54, 12x9", SBY 5/10/89	93,500
L'Arlequin (Harlequin), pencil on paper, sgn, ca 1918, 5x4", C-NY 10/5/89 OE	26,400
L'Atelier, oil on canvas, sgn/dtd 1er Avril 56 Cannes, 35x46", SBY 11/10/88 OE	2,860,000
La Coiffure (woman combing her hair), soft pencil/charcoal on laid paper laid down on card, 1906, 12x9", SBY 11/12/88	330,000
La Conversation (Le Couple), conte crayon heightened w/white on paper, sgn twice, ca 1901, 9x13", SBY 11/12/88	52,250
La Femme a Resille (Femme aux Cheveux Verts), ink wash/scratched highlights on zinc plate, 1956, 28x22", SBY 5/10/89 OE	363,000
La Presenation (abstract), ink wash/gray wash on paper, sgn/dtd Dimanche 12.1.58, 11x15", SBY 2/16/89 OE	61,600
Le Clown au Singe (clown w/monkey), oil on canvas, sgn, 1901, 13x8", SBY 11/15/89	2,420,000
Le Dejeuner, pencil on paper, sgn/dtd 14 6 64/#d V, 11x17", SBY 11/16/89	66,000
Le Gueridon, gouache/watercolor on paper, sgn, 1920, 11x9", SBY 11/12/88 OE	187,000
Le Gueridon (The Pedestal Table, abstract), gouache on paper laid down on stiff card, sgn, ca 1920, 11x8", SBY 5/10/89	170,500
Le Peintre et Son Modele, wool tapestry, sgn/dtd 17.7.70/#d I & EA1, Atelier de Saint Cyr label, 71x93", SBY 10/7/88	55,000
Le Petit Pierrot aux Fleurs (portrait of artist's son), oil on canvas, sgn/dtd 29, 26x29", C-NY 11/14/88	5,170,000
Le Verre (abstract), black crayon over collage, 1945, 6x5", C-NY 5/12/88	10,450
Les Amoureux IV (The Lovers), ink wash/blue pencil on paper, sgn/dtd/#d 23.7.67.IV, 1967, 22x29", C-NY 5/12/88 OE	99,000
Les Dejeuners, pencil on paper laid down on paper, sgn/dtd/#d 6.6.61.VII, 13x20", SBY 11/12/88 OE	79,750
Les Femmes d'Alger (Version C), oil on canvas, sgn/dtd 28 Dec 54, 21x26", SBY 11/10/88	962,500
Les Joutes (port scene), mosaic, sgn/dtd 6.7.57, 28x37", SBY 10/7/88 OE	126,500
Les Trois Baigneuses (the three bathers), oil on canvas, sgn/dtd Boisegeloup 15 Septembre XXXII, 11x16", SBY 5/9/89	440,000
Maison a Juan-Les-Pins, oil on canvas, 1931, 9x14", SBY 5/10/88	209,000
Man's Head Smoking a Cigarette, crayon on paper, sgn/dtd 16.5.64/#d VI, 26x20", SBY 5/10/89 OE	286,000
Mandoline, pencil on paper, sgn/dtd Novembre 1925, 5x4", SBY 11/12/88	22,000
Marie-Therese et Maya, pencil on lined paper, ca 1940, 9x7", SBY 11/16/89	17,600
Mendiant Aveugle (a blind begger), pen/black ink on paper laid down on board, sgn, 1905, 7x4", C-NY 10/5/89 OE	26,400

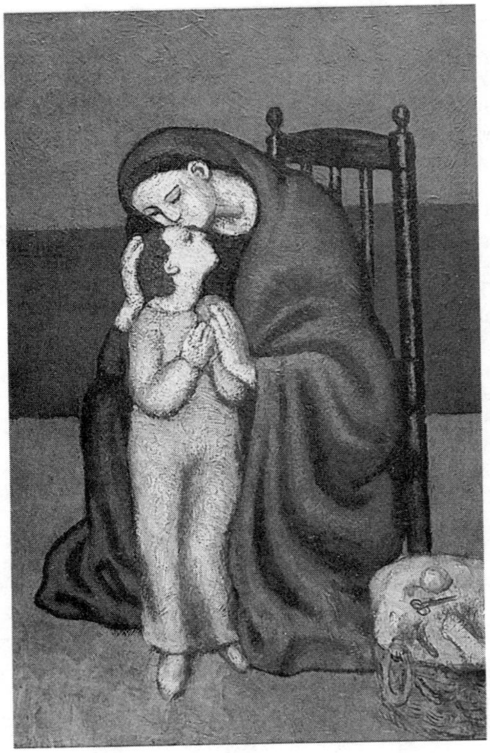

Maternite, oil on canvas, sgn, 1901, 36x24", C-NY 11/14/88; $24,750,000

Mercure: La Danse; pencil on paper, sgn, ca 1924, 8x10", SBY 11/16/89 30,800
Mere et Enfant (abstract of mother & child), oil on canvas, sgn/dtd/#d 27.10.65.II, 51x38", C-NY 5/11/88 770,000
Mere et Enfant (nude seated in profile w/child), conte crayon on buff paper, sgn/dtd 1902, 10x8", SBY 11/16/89 OE 104,500
Mousquetaire, oil/colored crayon/pencil on paper, dtd 23.7.69, 26x20", SBY 11/12/88 OE 176,000
Mousquetaire, pen/brush/black ink/gray wash on paper, sgn/dtd twice 67, 25x19", C-NY 11/15/88 143,000
Musicien et Femme Nue I (abstract), green felt-tip pen on board, sgn/dtd/#d 16.6.70.I, 1970, 8x11", C-NY 5/12/88 55,000
Nature Morte (abstract still life), oil on canvas, sgn, 1934, 29x36", C-NY 5/11/88 1,045,000
Nature Morte a la Palette (abstract still life w/palette), pencil on paper, bears signature, 1925, 5x9", C-NY 5/12/88 14,300
Nature Morte aux Oursins, colored crayons on paper, sgn/dtd 3.10.48/#d VIII, 20x26", WD 5/5/88 55,000
Nature Morte Devant une Fenetre (still life), watercolor/pen/ink over pencil on paper, sgn, 8x4", SBY 5/11/88 297,000
Nature Morte: Pommes (abstract still life of apples); collage/black crayon on paper, dtd 1945, 3x13", SBY 5/11/88 OE 29,700
Nu Couche, ballpoint pen/black felt-tip pen on paper, sgn/dtd 72, 7x14", C-NY 11/15/88 28,600
Nu Couche (abstract nude), colored crayons/ink on paper, sgn/dtd 11 Aout 1972, 14x19", SBY 11/16/89 176,000
Nu Couche (abstract nude), pencil on paper, sgn/dtd 14.7.72/#d VI, 5x8", SBY 2/16/89 OE 27,500
Nu Debout et Deux Hommes, ink wash on Ingres paper, sgn/dtd /#d 19.12.68 III, 12x17", SBY 2/18/88 OE 46,750
Nude Woman, Man Seated, & Veiled Woman in an Interior; pencil on paper, sgn/dtd 17.1.69/#d III, 23x31", SBY 5/10/89 OE 148,500
Oiseau (Bird), oil on canvas, dtd 39, 6x7", C-NY 5/11/89 OE 132,000
Pair: Picador et Cheval; Serenade; brush/ink on paper (1st on 2 joined sheets), 1957, 14x3", SBY 2/16/89 15,400
Pair: Verve, Picasso a Vallauris (title page & back cover); crayon/ink wash on paper, sgn, 10x8", SBY 10/7/88 11,000
Paysage a Juan-Les-Pins (fantasy landscape), oil on canvas, sgn/dtd 24, 8x13", SBY 5/10/89 OE 341,000
Personnage sur un Char (person on a chariot), pencil on paper laid down on paper, sgn/dtd 9.5.65, 12x11", C-NY 2/18/88 22,000
Portrait de Dora Maar (abstract view), oil on canvas, sgn/dtd 39 twice, 24x18", SBY 5/9/89 2,090,000
Portrait de Famille (Picasso & family), purple ballpoint pen on paper, 1951, 11x8", C-NY 5/11/89 19,800
Portrait de Fernande Olivier (bust-length nude), pencil on paper, sgn, ca 1902-03, 11x8", SBY 11/16/89 115,500
Portrait de Francoise, oil on canvas, sgn/dtd 21.3.49/#d II, 24x15", SBY 11/11/88 OE 2,200,000
Portrait de Maria Dalbaicin, pencil on the inside cover of a menu, sgn, 1921, 13x9", SBY 11/16/89 99,000
Portrait Feerique, crayon on title page of Le Petit Monde de Pablo Picasso, sgn, 1960, 11x8", C-NY 5/11/89 26,400
Pot et Compotier avec Fruits (still life), pencil on paper, sgn, 1919, 14x10", SBY 5/11/89 OE 121,000
Poupee (sketch of a baby), colored pencil/graphite on paper, dtd twice 13.3.40, 11x8", C-NY 5/12/88 14,300
Scene Gaillarde (ball scene), black crayon on paper, sgn/dtd 67/#d I, 30x22", C-NY 5/11/89 OE 198,000
Standing Nude with Three Men's Heads, crayon on gray sketchbook paper, sgn/dtd 4.2.69 & 5.2.69, 17x12", SBY 5/10/89 OE 137,500
Studio in a Painted Frame, oil on canvas, sgn, 1956, 35x46", SBY 11/15/89 2,970,000
Tauromachie, colored wax crayons on board, sgn/dtd 1957, 11x20", C-NY 10/6/88 29,700
Tete (abstract head), colored pens on Arches paper, sgn/dtd 9.2.71, 13x10", SBY 5/10/89 38,500
Tete d'Homme, ink on paper, sgn/dtd 15 6 69/#d IX, 16x13", SBY 11/16/89 41,250
Tete d'Homme (abstract of man's head), oil on canvas, sgn/dtd 2.4.65./#d III, 16x13", SBY 5/10/89 OE 385,000
Tete d'Homme (abstract portrait of head), oil on canvas, sgn/dtd 2.4.64/#d III, 16x13", SBY 11/12/88 OE 297,000
Tete d'Homme (abstract), ink wash on paper, sgn, dtd 15/4/64, 25x20", SBY 5/10/89 OE 77,000
Tete d'Homme (man's head), pen/brown ink/brush/brown wash on paper, sgn/dtd 19.8.65, 9x3", C-NY 10/5/89 13,200
Tete d'Homme (poster for painter's exposition, 1956), brush/black ink/crayons over poster, sgn, 26x20", C-NY 2/18/88 OE 19,800
Tete d'Homme a la Moustache (Portait du Professeur Calmette), gouache on paper, sgn, 1939, 25x18", C-NY 5/11/89 OE 605,000
Tete d'Homme Barbu a la Cigarette, colored wax crayons on paper, sgn/dtd 18 5 64/#d IV, 26x20", SBY 11/16/89 192,500
Tete d'Homme de Profil (man's head in profile), oil on panel, dtd 64, 7x7", C-NY 5/1/89 OE 88,000
Tete de Dora Maar (Head of Dora Maar, abstract), pen/ink on ruled paper, sgn/inscr, 1939, 9x7", SBY 5/11/88 33,000
Tete de Femme, India ink on board, sgn/dtd 26 4 72, 11x8", SBY 11/16/89 44,000
Tete de Femme, oil on canvas, dtd 1.6.65/#d I, 24x20", SBY 4/29/88 OE 286,000
Tete de Femme (Dora Maar, abstract), pen/ink on ruled paper, sgn, 1939, 8x7", SBY 5/11/88 27,500
Tete de Femme (woman's head), pen/black ink on paper, sgn/dtd 1946, 13x10", C-NY 2/18/88 OE 13,200
Tete de Garcon (head of boy, abstract), oil on canvas, dtd 1964, 14x11", C-NY 11/16/88 154,000
Tete de Mousquetaire (Head of Musketeer), gray wash/pastel on paper, sgn/dtd 12.2.67, 26x20", SBY 5/11/88 OE 209,000
Tete de Singe (two head studies of monkeys), blue ballpoint pen on paper, 1951, 11x8", C-NY 10/5/89 4,950
Tete Surrealiste (surrealistic head), pen/ink on ruled paper, sgn, 1939, 9x7", SBY 11/12/88 16,500
Toros y Toreros, red & black felt-tip pens/white gouache on paper, sgn/dtd 18.12.62, 15x11", C-NY 10/5/89 OE 24,200
Torse de Femme (woman's torso), gouache on paper, sgn, 1908, 24x19", SBY 11/12/88 522,500
Trois Personnages, colored crayon/pencil on paper, sgn/dtd 4.11.66. & 5.11.66., 24x20", SBY 11/12/88 71,500
Vigne (line drawing of grapevine), charcoal on paper laid down on stretched paper, sgn, 1921, 25x19", C-NY 5/11/89 OE 198,000

PICCINI, Gaetano (fl 1724-1744)

Pair: Grotesque Heads; pen/brown ink, 1 sgn, 5" dia, SBY 1/13/89 825

PICCOLI, Jaunita Pereval (American, 1915-)

Itinerary of Life, oil on canvas, sgn/dtd 61, 39x53", LH 10/16/88 UE 200
Lights of Tivoli, acrylic on canvas, sgn, dtd 75, 20x25", LH 10/16/88 UE 100

PICHLER, Rudolf (German, 1863-)

Peonies & Tulips in a Vase on a Ledge, oil on canvas, sgn, unfr, 23x50", C-E 2/21/89 UE 935

PICHOT, Emile Jules (French, 19th/20th C)

Jeane Fille Lisant, oil on canvas, sgn, 32x26", C-E 10/26/89 4,180
Male Nude, seated in profile; black chalk on laid paper, sgn, D&C in a cartouch wm, 18x17", C-NY 10/26/88 880

PICHOT, Marie Louise

La Fete sur la Plage (Holiday on the Beach), oil on board, sgn, 20x30", C-E 5/13/88 OE 4,840

PICIBIA, Francis (French, 1878-1953)

Tete de Jeune Femme (portrait of a woman), pencil/ink/watercolor on paper, sgn, 1922, 25x19", PHL 11/15/88 11,000

PICINICH, C.E. (20th C)

Sunset Over a City (harbor view w/skyscrapers beyond), oil on canvas, sgn/dtd 1932, 24x30", C-E 2/1/89 935

PICKERSGILL, Henry William (British, 1782-1875)
Portrait of Maria Liddell, oil on canvas, 30x25", SBY 6/8/88 UE 440
PICKETT, Joseph (American, 1848-1918)
Red Brick House in the Wintertime, oil on canvas, sgn/inscr ART, 13x10", SBY 1/24/89 UE 2,200
PICKNELL, William Lamb (American, 1854-1897)
At End of Day (man among haystacks in landscape), oil on canvas, sgn, 30x36", C-NY 12/2/88 9,900
House on a Lake, oil on canvas, sgn, 16x24", C-E 6/1/88 OE 9,020
In the Olive Grove, oil on canvas, 22x27", C-NY 5/25/89 UE 8,250
Landscape with Man Carrying a Scythe, black ink/wash w/white highlights, sgn, 5x7", FAP 4/15/89 220
Midwinter in Florida (realistic landscape w/figure on path), oil on canvas, sgn/titled, 24x36", SBY 5/24/89 37,400
View From a Meadow, oil on canvas, sgn, 30x40", C-NY 12/2/88 OE 49,500
PICOT, Francois Eduoard (French, 1786-1868)
L'Amour et Psyche, oil on canvas, sgn, 16x19", SBY 6/1/89 OE 154,000
PICOT, Jean (French, 20th C)
Still Life with Coffeepot, oil on canvas, sgn, 24x20", B/B 12/8/88 440
PIECHOWSKI, Martha (20th C)
Three Women by the Road, oil on canvas, sgn/dtd 1939, 36x30", LH 5/15/88 OE 550
PIELER, Franz Xavier (Austrian, 1879-1952)
Elaborate Still Life with Vase, oil on canvas, sgn, 20x15", C-E 2/23/88 2,420
Floral Still Life, oil on canvas, sgn, 30x25", B/B 10/9/88 6,050
Still Life of a Pocket Watch on a Marble Ledge, oil on canvas, sgn, 38x30", SBY 10/24/89 20,900
PIERCE, Charles Franklin (American, 1844-1920)
Shepherd & His Flock of Sheep, oil on canvas, sgn, 12x16", B/B 3/22/89 1,650
PIERCE, H. Winthrop (19th C)
Hayfields, oil on canvas, sgn/dtd Paris 1883, 17x21", C-E 10/18/89 3,080
PIERCE, Waldo (American, 1884-1970)
Still Life of Wildflowers, oil on canvas, inscr, 24x18", RWS 11/3/88 1,300
Susanna & the Elders, oil on canvas, sgn, 15x22", C-E 10/18/89 UE 715
PIERRY
Floral Still Life, oil on canvas, sgn, 12x9", LH 3/20/89 225
PIERSON, G. (19th C)
Battle Scene, Amelia, Virginia, 1781; oil on canvas, sgn, 29x32", SBY 1/28/88 OE 8,800
PIETERE, Edmond; see De Pietere
PIETERS, Evert (Dutch, 1856-1932)
Afternoon Pastimes, oil on canvas, sgn/dtd 1917, 35x42", C-NY 5/25/88 16,500
Doll's Supper, oil on canvas, sgn, 25x20", C-NY 10/25/89 11,000
Dutch Interior with Young Mother & Children, oil on canvas, sgn, 24x20", WAD 6/6/88 11,000
Minding the Baby, oil on canvas, sgn, 20x24", C-E 5/23/88 3,300
Mother & Children, oil on canvas, sgn, 24x20", C-NY 2/25/88 7,700
Mussel Gatherers at Seashore, oil on canvas, sgn, 24x20", S/A 3/12/88 2,000
On the Beach (figure w/horse-drawn wagon on beach), oil on canvas, sgn, 37x31", SBY 10/24/89 11,000
Sisters (children in interior), oil on canvas, sgn, 24x20", C-NY 2/23/89 OE 24,200
Still Life of Apples & a Knife on a Platter, oil on canvas, sgn, 20x24", B/B 10/9/88 2,200
Twilight by the Dock, oil on canvas, sgn, 30x40", SBY 5/23/89 11,000
PIETRO, Alvaro di; see Portoghese
PIETRO, Sano; see Di Pietro
PIETRONI, Antonio
Sailboats by a Dock, oil on board, sgn, 25x21", C-E 2/23/88 1,760
PIETTE, Ludovic (French, 1826-1877)
View of Antoise, oil on canvas, sgn/dtd 1877, 33x51", B/B 6/15/89 27,500
PIFFARD, Harold Hume (British, fl 1895-1899)
Recital in a Japanese Garden, oil on canvas, sgn, 25x20", C-NY 2/25/88 5,500
Saragossa: 10 February, 1809 (French & Spanish fighting in a Spanish church); oil on canvas, sgn, 54x36", SBY 2/22/89 33,000
Sleeping Harem Girl, oil on canvas, sgn, 36x66", C-E 5/22/89 3,960
Speak for It! (young girl feeding dog at a table in a landscape), oil on canvas, sgn, 28x36", SBY 2/22/89 22,000
PIGMA, A. (Italian, 19th C)
When Claudius Is Away, Messalina Will Play (interior scene); oil on canvas, sgn/dtd 1911, 22x42", SBY 2/23/89 8,250
PIGNON, Edouard (French, 1905-)
Combat de Coqs, oil on canvas, sgn/dtd 59-61, 55x77", C-E 5/13/88 OE 13,200
Composition (abstract), oil/ink wash on canvas, sgn/dtd 63, 18x24", SBY 2/14/89 OE 4,675
Composition Abstraite, oil on canvas, sgn/dtd 60, 51x38", C-E 5/13/88 OE 8,250
Ile de Bandol, oil on canvas, sgn/dtd 57, 45x58", C-E 5/13/88 OE 14,850
Landscape with Thresher, oil on canvas, sgn/dtd 1959, 24x32", LH 10/16/88 UE 1,600
Les Repiqueurs, oil on canvas, sgn/dtd twice, 57, inscr, 29x36", C-E 5/13/88 10,780
Paysage, oil on canvas, sgn/dtd 59, 26x32", C-E 5/13/88 OE 7,700
PIGNONI, Simone; att (Italian, 1614-1698)
Venus & Mars Attended by a Putto, oil on canvas, 47x39", C-NY 4/8/88 4,400
PIGNONI, Simone; circle of (Italian, 1614-1698)
Pero As Roman Charity, oil on canvas, unfr, 28x22", C-NY 4/6/89 OE 1,870
PIJNACKER, Adam (1622-1673)
Sheer Rocky Coastline with Oriental Figures Near Barges & a Fort on a Cliff, oil on canvas, sgn, 26x40", SBY 6/3/88 OE 264,000

IKE, William Henry (British, 1846-1908)
Cornwall Landscape with Figures, oil on board, sgn/dtd 1888, 11x17", FAP 4/15/89 880
ILLEMENT, Jean (French, 1728-1808)
Coastal Scene with Fishermen by Ruins & Shipping in Choppy Seas, black chalk, sgn, 14x18", SBY 7/12/89 990
Night Scene, black conte pencil w/traces of ink, sgn, ca 1762, 11x16", SWN 6/15/89 1,100
Pair: Mountainous Landscapes w/Travelers on Path & Travelers at Rest; pencil on paper, sgn/1803, 6" dia, WD 10/19/88 OE 1,500
Southern Landscape with Herdsmen & Travelers, oil on canvas, sgn/dtd 1785, 21x31", SBY 6/3/88 33,000
Waterfall, oil on canvas, sgn/dtd 1789, 28x40", C-NY 6/2/88 33,000
Winter Landscape with Cottage Under Snow, Peasants Gathering Faggots in Forground; pastel, sgn, 19x24", C-M 12/3/88 9,290
ILLEMENT, Jean; circle of (French, 1728-1808)
Oriental Sitting Under an Arch & Another Kneeling on a Footbridge, a Pelican Below; chalk, inscr, 11x9", C-NY 1/11/89 990
Pastoral Landscape with Fisherman, blue en grisaille/oil on canvas, 30x28", C-NY 6/2/88 3,300
ILOT, Robert Wakeham (Canadian, 1898-1968)
Champs de Mars, Montreal; ink, sgn, ca 1922, 5x8", FB 4/25/88 950
House at Senneville, Quebec; oil on panel, sgn, 14x17", FB 10/17/88 9,000
Les Eboulements, Quebec; oil on panel, sgn/dtd 1962, 8x11", FB 10/17/88 OE 4,200
Middle-Eastern Street Scene, watercolor, sgn, 11x9", FB 5/28/89 500
Mountain Winter Landscape, oil on canvas, sgn/dtd 1936, 28x36", FB 10/17/88 UE 19,500
North Beach, Gaspe; oil on canvas, sgn, 18x24", FB 10/17/88 21,000
Spring Ice: Montreal From St Helen's Island (impressionistic landscape); oil on panel, sgn/dtd 50, RWS 9/29/88 12,000
Wolfe's Cove, Quebec; oil on board, sgn/dtd 1951, 10x12", C-SK 5/25/89 OE 7,720
ILS, Isidore Alexandre Augustin (French, 1813-1875)
Esquisse pour le Voyage de l'Empereur et de l'Imperatrice en Algerie, 1860; oil on canvas, sgn, 31x40", C-NY 5/25/88 OE 18,700
Shepherd Boy, oil on canvas, sgn/dtd 1874, 22x18", C-NY 5/24/89 6,600
IMENTEL, Rodrigo Ramirez (Latin American, 20th C)
Guerrero (contemporary depiction of warrior), oil on canvas, sgn/dtd 1972, 32x40", C-NY 11/21/89 13,200
Quetzales (contemporary birds), oil on canvas, sgn, 28x36", C-NY 5/17/89 4,620
INAL, Ferdinand (French, 1881-)
Flowering Trees Overlooking a River Valley, oil on canvas, sgn, 18x22", C-NY 2/23/89 3,520
INCHON, Joseph Porphyre (French, 1871-)
Pair: La Course & La Chasse; Rallye Sapinette au Comte d'Andigne; oil on canvas, sgn, 12x25", SBY 6/10/88 11,550
INCHON, Robert (French, 1886-1943)
Bord de la Riviere (river landscape), oil on canvas, sgn, 29x36", SBY 10/7/88 OE 40,700
INEL, Gustave Nicolas (French, 1842-1896)
Pair: Elegant Ladies; oil on canvas, sgn, unfr, 21x11", C-NY 5/24/89 11,000
INELLI, Bartolomeo; att (Italian, 1781-1835)
Villagers Conversing & Drinking Outside a Tavern, black chalk/pen/gray & brown ink, 12x17", C-NY 1/11/89 1,980
INELLO, Jose (Spanish, 19th/20th C)
Mother & Child by an Orange Grove, sgn/dtd 93, 24x14", C-E 10/25/88 OE 4,950
INGGERA, H. (Italian, 19th C)
Chess Game, oil on canvas, sgn, 30x40", FB 4/25/88 1,300
INGRET, Edouard (French, 1788-1875)
At the Dentist's, oil on canvas, sgn, 20x24", SBY 7/12/89 3,200
Portrait of His Excellency Amedee Gaillard de Ferry, French Ambassador to Cuba; oil, sgn/dtd 1855, 29x24", SBY 5/25/89 1,470
INO, Marco; att (Italian, 1525-1588)
Portrait of a Man, oil on canvas, 21x15", SBY 12/9/88 OE 935
INTO, Alberto (Portuguese, 19th C)
Deux Femmes de Bretagnes, oil on canvas, sgn, 24x20", C-E 5/23/88 1,980
INTO, Blagio (American, 20th C)
Mardi Gras, oil on masonite, sgn, 10x13", FAP 12/8/89 2,000
INTO, Jody (American, 1942-)
Tongues of Fire in a Landscape (abstract), watercolor/ink/colored chalks/graphite, sgn, 30x40", C-E 11/14/89 1,210
IOLA, Domenico (Italian, 1627-1703)
Nymphs Giving the Infant Achilles to Chiron, black chalk/brown wash, 17x12", C-NY 1/11/89 UE 1,650
IOLA, Domenico; circle of (Italian, 1627-1703)
Charity, oil on canvas, 10x8", C-NY 10/20/88 1,980
IOMBO, see Del Piombo
IOT, Adolphe (French, 1850-1910)
Italian Girl with a Bird's Nest, oil on canvas, sgn, 35x26", C-E 10/25/88 4,400
IOTROWSKI, Antoni (Polish, 1853-1924)
Hunting Party, oil on panel, sgn/dtd 1883, 13x16", SBY 6/10/88 3,850
Two Soldiers Riding Through a Forest, oil on canvas, sgn/dtd Paris 1880, 26x40", SBY 12/9/88 6,325
IPER, John (British, 1903-)
Port in War Time, gouache on paper, sgn, 22x28", SBY 2/14/89 OE 15,400
Teifi Valley Near Carmarthen (landscape), gouache/watercolor/crayon on paper laid down on board, sgn, 15x22", C-E 5/9/89 5,720
IPPI, Giulio; see Romano, Giulio
IPPIN, Horace (American, 1888-1946)
Friends Meeting House, oil on canvas, sgn/dtd 1940, 22x36", C-NY 5/25/89 OE 165,000
IRATSKII, Konstantin A. (Russian, fl 1840-1870)
Le Regiment de Grenadiers-a-Cheval (Garde Tenue) 18, watercolor on paper, 13x9", C-L 10/8/88 480

Pisan School (15th C)
Madonna & Child, oil on panel on gold ground, arched top, ca 1400, 24x18", C-NY 4/6/89 OE **14,300**
PISSARRO, Camille (French, 1830-1903)
Bore de Seine, Pres de Rouen; watercolor on paper, initialed, 7x10", C-NY 10/6/88 .... **26,400**
Chateau de la Roche Guyon, pen/black ink over pencil laid down on canvas, stamped initials, 12x19", C-NY 2/16/89 OE **23,100**
Conversation (two women conversing), pencil on paper, initialed, 7x5", B/B 10/9/88.......... **3,575**
Double-Sided: Chemin au Bois; Femme Assis dans le Paysage; pencil on paper, initialed, 8x5", SBY 2/18/88.......... **2,750**
Double-Sided: Paysanne de Dos; Paysanne Allongee, recto: charcoal, verso: pastel, initialed, 19x12", C-NY 11/15/88 OE **148,500**
Etang de Montfoucault (landscape), pastel on gray paper on board, indistinctly sgn, ca 1874-75, 10x15", SBY 5/10/89 OE.......... **99,000**
Etude pour un Eventail: La Vachere (cowherd study for a fan); black chalk, initialed, 13x19", C-NY 2/18/88 .... **5,280**
Femme a la Barriere (woman at a gate), pen/ink on paper, stamped initials, ca 1886-89, 7x5", SBY 5/11/88 OE **18,700**
Femme en Profile (woman in profile), pencil on brown paper, stamped initials, ca 1890, 7x5", C-E 11/17/88 .... **715**

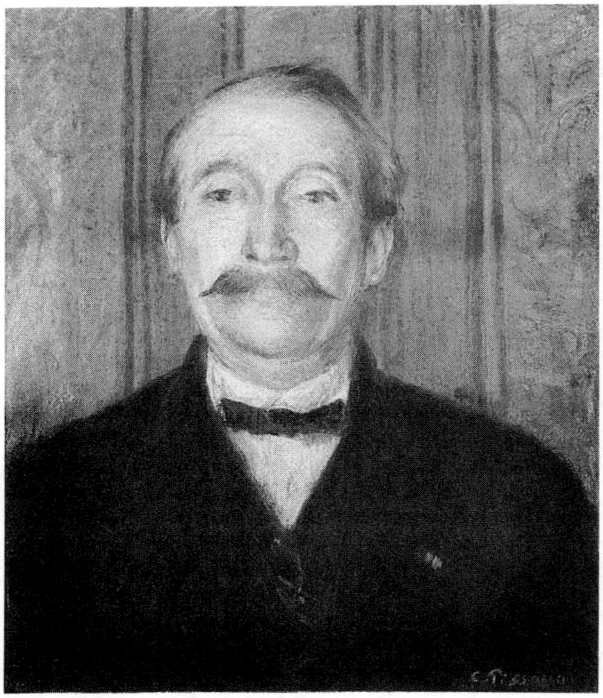

Portrait de Pere Papeille, Pontoisse, pastel on paper laid down on canvas, sgn, ca 1890-95, 22x18", C-NY 11/15/88 OE; $187,000

Gardeuse d'Oies, charcoal on fan-shaped laid paper, sgn, ca 1886, 8x17", SBY 2/16/89 .... **23,100**
Group of 3: Peasant Women...; Women at the Market; Digger; mixed media on paper, 7x4" & smaller, SBY 2/24/89 OE **6,325**
Hampton Court Green (landscape), watercolor over pencil on paper laid down on board, sgn/dtd 90, 7x10", SBY 5/10/89 OE.......... **104,500**
Haymaking, Eragny (landscape w/figure & hay wagon); pencil/ink/wash on paper, 4x8", SBY 2/14/89 OE **4,125**
L'Eglise Saint-Jacques a Dieppe Matin, Soleil (church in sun); oil on canvas, sgn/dtd 1901, 29x36", C-NY 11/15/88 OE.......... **3,190,000**
La Cuisiniere, charcoal/white chalk on blue paper, stamped initials/#d Lugt #613a, 16x9", SBY 5/10/89 OE.......... **34,100**
La Fenaison a Montfoucault (landscape with figures), oil on canvas, sgn/dtd 1876, 22x36", SBY 5/10/88 OE.......... **935,000**
La Prairie de Bazincourt (figure among trees in landscape), oil on canvas, sgn/dtd 1885, 18x22", SBY 5/9/89 OE.......... **1,375,000**
Le Louvre, Matin, Effet de Neige; oil on canvas, sgn/dtd 1903, 19x22", SBY 11/11/88 .... **577,500**
Les Pommiers, Soleil Couchant, Eragny (landscape); oil on canvas, sgn/dtd 1896, 32x26", SBY 5/10/88 .... **907,500**
Marche a la Volaille a Gisors, charcoal/wash heightened w/gouache on paper, sgn, ca 1894-95, 12x9", SBY 11/16/89 OE **82,500**
Marche a Pontoise, charcoal/gray wash on paper, initialed/inscr, 5x8", SBY 2/18/88.......... **3,575**
Matin, Ponniers en Fleurs a Eragny (figures in morning landscape); oil on canvas, sgn/dtd 98, 24x29", SBY 5/9/89 OE **1,650,000**
Pair: Paysanne a la Faux; pencil on buff paper, stamped, 10x8", C-NY 2/18/88.......... **2,640**
Pair: Trois Etudes de Travailleur et d'une Femme; pen/brown ink/pencil on paper, stamped initials, 13x10", C-E 5/13/88.......... **1,980**
Paysage a Louveciennes (village landscape w/figures), oil on canvas, sgn/dtd 1870, 19x22", C-NY 11/15/88 .... **792,000**
Paysage avec une Vachere (landscape w/cow & figure), oil on canvas, sgn, ca 1872, SBY 11/11/88.......... **632,500**
Paysanne Assise (peasant woman seated in profile), pen/ink/pencil/gray wash on paper, initialed, 8x5", SBY 10/6/89.......... **13,200**
Paysanne Assise (seated peasant girl in landscape), oil on canvas, initialed, 24x30", 1883, SBY 5/9/89 OE **1,705,000**
Paysanne et sa Fillette, Eragny; gouache on linen laid down on board, sgn, ca 1903, 10x9", C-NY 11/15/88 OE **352,000**
Portrait du Fils de l'Artiste: Ludovic-Rodolphe; watercolor/pencil, stamped signature, ca 1885-88, 12x10", SBY 11/12/88 .... **60,500**
Route de Versailles a Saint Germain a Louveciennes, oil on canvas, sgn/dtd 1872, 13x18", SBY 11/15/89 .... **1,265,000**
Scene de Rue (street scene), watercolor/pencil laid down on paper, stamped initials, 13x24", C-NY 5/11/89 .... **33,000**
Seated Breton Woman, watercolor/pencil on paper, initialed, 6x7", SBY 10/5/88 OE.......... **2,750**
September Festival in Pontoise, oil on canvas, sgn/dtd 1872, 18x22", SBY 5/9/89 .... **1,980,000**
Set of 3: Pencil Sketches; pencil on paper, initialed, 5x8", or 8x5", B/B 10/9/88 .... **14,300**
Set of 3: Pencil Sketches; pencil on paper, initialed, 7x5", B/B 10/9/88 .... **3,575**
Soliel Couchant et Brouillard a Eragny (misty morning landscape), oil on canvas, sgn/dtd 1891, 22x26", SBY 5/9/89 OE.......... **1,045,000**

Sortie de Bois (landscape), pencil on laid paper, initialed, 8x5", SBY 2/18/88 OE **5,500**
St Thomas, pencil on paper, initialed, 9x12", SBY 2/18/88 .... **3,300**
Temps Gris, Matin avec Figures, Eragny (figures in landscape); oil on canvas, sgn/dtd 99, 24x29", SBY 5/9/89 OE **1,485,000**
Une Paysanne Broie de Pommes, charcoal on paper, stamped initials, 5x7", SBY 10/7/88 .... **1,375**
Vachere sur le Chemin (herder & child in landscape), pen/brown ink/wash on paper, stamped initials, 9x7", SBY 5/10/89 OE **29,700**
Village, pencil/wash on paper, stamped initials, 7x9", SBY 10/5/88 .... **1,760**
Village Scene, Charigny; pencil on paper, stamped initials, 4x6", SBY 10/5/88 OE **2,860**
Village with Windmill, watercolor over pencil on paper, initialed, 4x3", SBY 2/18/88 .... **3,300**
Woman in an Interior, watercolor/pen/ink on paper, sgn, 3x4", B/B 6/9/88 .... **2,750**

ISSARRO, Claude
La Ruelle Capt a Themericourt (village street), oil on canvas, sgn twice/titled, 18x22", C-E 5/9/89 OE **10,450**

ISSARRO, Lucien (French, 1863-1944)
L'Apres-Midi a Brough, Effet de Braume; oil on canvas, monogramed/dtd 1914, 24x29", SBY 10/7/88 .... **55,000**
Les Olivers du Cabanon, Toulon (landscape); oil on canvas, monogramed/dtd 1931, 21x26", C-NY 5/11/89 .... **38,500**
Swindale, Brough (mountainous landscape); oil on canvas, monogramed/dtd 1914, 23x28", WD 5/5/88 .... **27,500**
The Sycamore, Fishpond; oil on canvas, monogramed/dtd 1940, 21x18", SBY 10/6/89 .... **24,200**

ISSARRO, Paul Emile (French, 1884-)
Cabane en Hiver (interior scene), oil on canvas, sgn, unfr, 18x24", C-E 5/9/89 .... **1,100**
Costal View, pastel on paper, sgn, 9x13", WD 11/16/88 .... **2,500**
Fishing Off a Bridge, oil on canvas, sgn, 16x13", SBY 10/5/88 .... **2,310**
Homme sur un Pont, oil on canvas, sgn, unfr, 18x24", C-NY 2/13/89 OE **2,750**
House Along a Road, oil on canvas, sgn, 17x13", SBY 10/5/88 .... **3,850**
L'Arbre Blanc, Clecy; oil on canvas, sgn, unfr, 18x22", C-E 11/17/88 .... **1,650**
L'Etang in River (winter landscape w/pond), oil on canvas, sgn, unfr, 24x18", C-E 11/17/88 .... **1,320**
L'Hermitage, colored/black chalks on paper, sgn, 8x11", C-E 11/17/88 .... **1,430**
La Ferme (farm in landscape), watercolor/chalk on paper, sgn, 10x13", C-E 5/9/89 .... **770**
La Mare aux Saules, oil on canvas, sgn, 22x26", SBY 10/7/89 .... **7,700**
La Riviere en Hiver, colored chalks on paper, sgn, 10x13", C-NY 2/13/89 .... **825**
Le Chasseur et Son Chien, oil on canvas, sgn/inscr, unfr, 22x18", C-E 5/13/88 .... **1,210**
Le Chemin de la Chaise, Neige; oil on canvas, sgn, unfr, 22x18", C-NY 2/13/89 .... **1,870**
Le Jardin de Paulemile en Hiver, watercolor/charcoal/black chalk, stamped signature/inscr, 10x13", C-E 5/13/88 .... **1,100**
Le Lac (The Lake, landscape), oil on canvas, sgn, 20x24", C-E 5/13/88 .... **2,640**
Le Lac en Automne, colored crayons/black chalk/gouache on paper, sgn, 10x13", C-NY 2/13/89 .... **880**
Le Mont-Aigu, Soleil Couchant; oil on canvas, sgn, unfr, 13x16", C-NY 2/13/89 .... **1,210**
Le Pecheur a la Ligne (landscape), oil on canvas, sgn, unfr, 18x22", C-E 5/9/89 .... **880**
Le Pere Fouque, oil on canvas, sgn, 13x16", C-E 5/13/88 .... **1,650**
Le Sentier du Mont-Aigu-Neige (figure on path in snowy landscape), oil on canvas, sgn, unfr, 22x18", C-E 11/17/88 .... **1,980**
Le Viaduc (landscape), watercolor/chalk on paper, sgn/titled, 10x13", C-E 5/9/89 .... **660**
Les Bouleaux (landscape w/birch trees), oil on canvas, sgn, unfr, 22x18", C-E 11/17/88 .... **1,210**
Les Fermiers, watercolor/colored felt-tip pens on paper, sgn, 10x13", C-NY 2/13/89 .... **528**
Les Joncs Jaunes, oil on canvas, sgn, unfr, 15x18", C-NY 2/13/89 .... **2,090**
Maison sous la Neige, oil on canvas, sgn, unfr, 24x18", C-E 5/13/88 .... **1,430**
Meules d'Avoine, watercolor/black chalk on paper, sgn, 10x13", C-NY 2/13/89 .... **715**
Nature Morte (still life of flagon, vase, pipe & book), oil on canvas, 18x22", WD 11/16/ 22 .... **2,600**
Neige, oil on canvas, sgn, unfr, 18x24", C-E 5/13/88 .... **1,320**
Pair: Orchard; Tree-Lined Path; charcoal/watercolor on paper, 10x13", 13x10", SBY 10/5/88 .... **1,650**
River Landscape, India ink/ink wash/watercolor on paper, 10x12", SBY 10/5/88 .... **880**
Snowy Path, watercolor on paper, sgn, 10x12", WD 5/5/88 .... **2,000**
Winter Landscape, oil on masonite, sgn, 18x22", SBY 10/5/88 .... **3,080**

ISTOLETTO, Michelangelo (Italian, 1933-)
Conversation (two young men), silkscreened paper collage on stainless steel, sgn/dtd 1962-79, 91x47", SBY 5/3/89 .... **27,500**

ITALL, Rhoda Hahma
Woman Sewing in a Rocking Chair by a Window, watercolor on paper, 14x11", C-E 2/1/89 .... **715**

ITARD, Ferdinand
Avant la Seance dans l'Atelier de Carpeaux, oil on canvas, sgn/dtd 1888, 46x36", C-NY 2/25/88 OE **12,100**

ITERS, Evert (Dutch, 1856-fl 1932)
Hay Wagons, oil on canvas, sgn, 24x20", LH 5/15/88 .... **2,800**

ITTMAN, Hobson (American, 1898-1972)
Orange Blossoms, watercolor on paper, sgn/dtd 68, unfr, no size given, C-E 6/1/89 UE **495**
Peonies & Roses, oil on canvas, sgn, 36x48", C-E 11/30/88 .... **2,860**
The Model (vacant chair on studio platform), oil on masonite, sgn, 17x26", SBY 6/28/89 OE **4,950**

ITTONI, Giovanni Battista (Italian, 1687-1767)
Holy Family, oil on copper, 10x8", C-NY 10/12/89 .... **11,000**
Madonna & Child with Saints Rosa, Dominic, Bonaventure, & Carlo Barromeo; oil on canvas, unfr, 20x12", SBY 6/3/88 .... **45,100**

ITTONI, Giovanni Battista; after (Italian, 1687-1767)
Adoration of the Magi, oil on canvas, 22x28", WD 1/25/89 OE **3,250**

ITTONI, Giovanni Battista; att (Italian, 1687-1767)
St Carlo Borromeo Interceeding with Virgin & Child on Behalf of Plague Victims, pen/ink/wash, 16x9", SBY 1/13/89 .... **2,200**

ITTONI, Giovanni Battista; circle of (Italian, 1687-1767)
Lot & His Daughters, oil on canvas, 15x20", C-NY 10/12/89 .... **4,950**

PITZNER, Max Joseph (German, 1855-1912)
Afternoon Break in the Fields, oil on panel, sgn/inscr, 9x13", C-E 10/25/88 6,050
PIVOT, Louis
Still Life of Peonies & Anemones in a Glass Vase, oil on canvas, sgn, 22x18", C-E 10/25/88 1,650
PIZZI, P. (20th C)
Canal Scene, oil on canvas, sgn, 20x14", WG 4/23/88 UE 200
PLANQUETTE, Felix (French, 1873-)
Bringing Home the Herd, oil on canvas, sgn/dtd 1904, 32x46", B/B 1/11/89 1,760
PLANSON, Andre (French, 1898-1981)
Reclining Woman, oil on canvas, sgn, 10x16", SBY 10/5/88 1,540
PLASKETT, Joseph Francis (Canadian, 1918-)
Fisherman's Whey, Victoria, British Columbia; pastel, sgn/dtd 53, 13x20", WAD 11/30/89 450
Fungi on Table, oil on canvas, sgn/dtd 1963, 24x24", WAD 11/30/89 700
PLASSAN, Antoine Emile (French, 1817-1903)
Interior Genre, oil on panel, sgn/dtd 67, 4x6", NA 2/24/89 2,200
PLATZER, Johann Georg (Austrian, 1704-1761)
Allegory of the Five Senses: Elegant Figures on a Portico; oil on copper, inscr/dtd 1731, 15x22", C-NY 6/2/88 44,000
PLAVINSKY, Dimitri (Russian, 1937-)
Vertical Son et Lumiere (abstract), oil/mixed media on canvas, sgn/dtd 1987, 98x22", SBY 7/7/88 OE 15,600
PLEISSNER, Ogden Minton (American, 1905-1983)
Afternoon in Summer, Chartres; oil on canvas, sgn, 24x40", C-NY 5/26/88 41,800
Big One Hooked, watercolor on paper, sgn, 18x28", SBY 5/25/88 OE 37,400
Causeway (extensive landscape w/distant mountains & buildings), oil on canvas, 14x25", WD 10/5/88 9,750
Courtyard Fountainebleau, watercolor/pencil on paper, sgn, 20x29", C-NY 3/11/88 OE 10,450
Fighting Salmon, watercolor on paper, sgn, 1936, 16x26", SBY 5/25/88 30,800
Fisherman on a River (landscape), watercolor on paper, sgn, 19x29", SBY 5/24/89 20,350
Nova Scotia, oil on canvasboard, sgn twice/inscr, 12x16", C-NY 9/30/88 9,900
Pink House, Portugal (domestic landscape); oil on canvas, sgn/titled, 24x30", SBY 5/24/89 23,100
Repairs (boat in dry dock), watercolor on paper, sgn, 15x22", SBY 6/28/89 4,400
Salmon Fishing, watercolor on paper, sgn, 17x24", SBY 5/25/88 23,100
Salmon Fishing on Cains River, New Brunswick; watercolor on paper, sgn, 17x26", SBY 5/25/88 24,200
St Georges, Bermuda; watercolor on paper, sgn, 18x28", SBY 5/25/88 38,500
Summit of Montmartre, watercolor on paper, sgn, 18x30", SBY 5/25/88 9,350
Sunlight on Clapboards, watercolor/gouache/graphite on paper, sgn, 16x22", RWS 11/10/89 15,000
US Air Force Outpost, Adak, Aleutian Islands; watercolor on paper, sgn, 15x25", SBY 6/28/89 3,850
Vietre sul Mare, watercolor on paper, sgn, 19x29", SBY 5/25/88 7,150
PLEISSNER, Ogden Minton; att (American, 1905-1983)
Fisherman's Table (docked boat w/figures), watercolor heightened w/gouache on paper, bears signature, 12x16", C-E 6/1/89 495
PLEPP, Hans Jacob (Swiss, 1560-1595)
Design for a Stained Glass Window, pen/gray ink/gray wash, 17x12", SBY 1/13/89 7,150
PLESNER, R. (French, 20th C)
Paris Street Scene at Night, oil on canvas, sgn, 19x27", C-E 4/7/88 715
Winter Day in Paris (street scene), oil on cardboard, sgn/titled, 26x36", RAB 8/8/89 1,550
PLIMPTON, William E. (British, 19th C)
Sleeping Fisherman, oil on canvas, sgn, 19x27", C-E 6/1/89 1,045
PLOQUIN, Gaston (French, 20th C)
Roses et Faiences, oil on panel, sgn, 29x21", SBY 7/12/89 5,500
PLOWDEN, Trevor John (1784-1836)
Natives Outside an Indian Temple, pencil/watercolor, unfr, 6x8", C-SK 5/25/89 220
PLUMMER, William H. (American, 19th/20th C)
Stone Wall (landscape w/pond & barn, a house in the distance), oil on board, sgn/dtd 1884, 7x17", C-E 10/18/89 1,650
The Race (ship in full sail), oil on canvas, sgn/dtd 1868, 30x40", B/B 10/9/88 9,350
POCCETTI, Bernardino (Italian, 1548-1612)
Study of a Boy Walking & of a Girl's Head & Shoulders, black chalk heightened w/white chalk, 9x7", SBY 1/13/89 880
PODCHERNIKOFF, Alexis M. (American, 1912-)
Cows Wading, oil on canvas, sgn, 28x36", C-E 10/18/89 1,100
Rural Landscape with Grazing Cattle, oil on panel, 10x14", WG 4/23/88 UE 350
The Golden Hour, Santa Barbara; oil on canvas, sgn/dtd 1929, 36x42", B/B 10/6/88 1,760
PODRYSKI, Misha (American, 20th C)
Girl in Black, oil on canvas, sgn/dtd 1936, 30x42", SBY 6/24/88 OE 3,850
POERSON, Charles (1653-1725)
Servant Pouring Wine for a Queen, oil on canvas, unfr, 55x50", SBY 1/12/89 28,600
POGANY, Willy (American, 1882-1955)
Entwining Roses Embracing a Violin in a Surrealistic Manner, pencil on rag illustration board, sgn, 8x6", SWN 12/1/88 358
Nude Woman Startled by a Bird in Flight, pencil/India ink on board, sgn, 9x6", SWN 12/1/88 145
POGEDAIEFF, see De Pogedaieff
POHLE, Leon (German, 1841-1908)
Woman Gazing Out Her Window, oil on canvas, sgn/inscr, 38x25", B/B 6/15/89 UE 2,750
POINCY, Paul (American, 1833-1909)
Portrait of a Young Boy, oil on canvas, sgn/dtd 1875, 18x22", MG 10/28/88 1,200

POINT, Armand (French, 1860-1932)
Horses Grazing with Arab Attendants, oil on panel, sgn/dtd 1879, 14x20", B/B 3/17/88 .... **6,600**
La Sirene, oil on canvas, monogramed/dtd 1897, frame made after a design by the artist, 36x29", C-L 6/28/88 OE **245,960**
POIRIER, Denise (Canadian)
Jeune Femme au Bouquet Rose (young woman seated at a table staring at a rose), oil on canvas, sgn, 24x30", FB 10/30/89 .... **1,650**
POIRIER, Narcisse (Canadian, 1883-1983)
Bridge Crossing, Winter; oil on canvas, sgn/dtd 1930, 18x24", FB 10/30/89 .... **825**
Cabane a Sucre a St Canut, oil on board, sgn, 12x16", FB 5/28/89 .... **500**
Moulin Ancienne Lorette, oil on canvas, sgn, 16x20", FB 10/17/88 .... **400**
Moulin de l'Ete aux Coudres, oil on canvas, sgn/dtd 1928, 24x30", FB 10/30/89 .... **990**
Paysage a Piedmont (landscape), oil on board, sgn, 12x16", FB 4/25/88 .... **900**
Still Life of Fruit, oil on canvas, sgn, 18x22", FB 5/28/89 .... **850**
Vieille Maison, Rue Vincent, Vieux Montreal; oil on canvas, sgn/dtd 1928, 18x30", FB 10/30/89 .... **1,045**
POISSON, Louverature (Haitian, 1914-1985)
Attente (figure in bedroom standing at open window), oil on canvas, sgn, 18x22", C-NY 11/21/89 UE **2,200**
Fete Native, oil on linen, sgn, 18x23", C-NY 5/18/88 UE **1,870**
Le Femme Contagieuse (nude seated in interior), oil on board, sgn, dtd 18/10/44, 18x25", C-NY 11/21/88 .... **6,600**
Maison de Campagne, oil on masonite, sgn/dtd 48/titled, 24x30", C-NY 5/18/88 OE **12,100**
POITEVIN, Auguste Flavien (French, 19th C)
Figure Resting in a Clearing, oil on canvas, sgn/dtd 87, 51x64", C-NY 5/24/89 .... **15,400**
POKITONOW, Ivan (Russian, 1851-1924)
Boar Hunt in Winter, oil on panel, sgn/inscr/dtd 1886, 4x6", SBY 6/8/88 OE **2,310**
POLEO, Hector (Venezuelan, 1918-)
Cabeza de Mujer (scarf-wrapped head of a woman), oil on canvas, sgn/dtd Paris 59, 14x11", C-NY 11/21/89 .... **26,400**
Campesinos (contemporary village scene w/peasants), oil on gessoed burlap, ca 1942, 20x16", C-NY 11/21/89 .... **49,500**
De la Tierra a la Tierra (man/woman among ruins), oil on panel, sgn/dtd NY 47, 27x23", C-NY 11/21/88 OE **88,000**
La Espera, oil on canvas, sgn/dtd 48, 18x16", C-NY 5/18/88 OE **79,200**
La Rose (abstract portraits of man & woman), oil on canvas, sgn twice/dtd Paris 62, 13x18", SBY 11/21/88 .... **11,000**
Le Chapeau Rose (abstract), oil on canvas, sgn/dtd Paris 69, 21x26", C-NY 11/21/89 .... **33,000**
Trabajadores (laborers in a landscape), oil on canvas laid down on canvas, sgn/dtd 1942, 27x24", C-NY 5/17/89 OE **110,000**
POLESELLO, Rogelio (South American, 1939-)
Sur (abstract), acrylic on canvas, sgn/dtd 1988/titled, 51x51", SBY 11/21/88 .... **5,500**
POLGARY, Geza (Hungarian, 1862-)
Hunter & the Hunted, oil on canvas, sgn/dtd 1914, 84x48", C-E 10/18/89 .... **2,860**
POLIAKOFF, Serge (French, 1906-1969)
Composition (abstract), oil on canvas, sgn, 1966, 32x39", SBY 6/30/88 .... **132,100**
Composition (abstract), oil on canvas, sgn/dtd 54, 35x46", SBY 6/30/88 .... **260,200**
Composition Abstraite, Bleu et Grenat; oil on paper mounted on canvas, sgn, 1965, 29x36", C-NY 11/9/88 .... **57,200**
Compostion (abstract), oil on canvas, sgn, ca 1957-58, SBY 6/30/88 .... **180,200**
Untitled (abstract), gouache on paper, sgn, 20x26", SBY 2/19/88 OE **15,400**
POLIDORO DA CARAVAGGIO, after (Italian, 1495-1543)
Confrontation of Camillus & Brennus Weighing the Indemnity of the Romans(?), chalk/wash on paper, 13x9", C-NY 1/11/89 .... **550**
Urns, Drapery & a Roman with a Sabine, After the Palazzo Milesi Frieze; chalk/pen/ink/wash on paper, 8x14", C-NY 1/11/89 .... **1,540**
POLIDORO DA CARAVAGGIO, follower of (Italian, 1495-1543)
Roman Warriors, pen/black ink/gray wash on blue paper, 5x8", C-NY 1/111/89 .... **385**
Polish School (19th/20th C)
Gentlemen Negotiating a Contract, oil on canvas, indistinctly sgn, 19x40", B/B 9/14/89 OE **1,540**
Stanislau Square in the Snow, oil on canvas, indistinctly sgn, 14x10", B/B 1/11/89 .... **880**
POLKE, Sigmar (European, 1941-)
Arcimi Boldi (abstract), mixed media on fabric, initialed/dtd 84, 59x71", SBY 5/2/89 OE **253,000**
Fules+Rusel=Frusel (abstract), gouache on paper, sgn, 28x39", SBY 5/3/89 OE **33,000**
Golda Meier, acrylic on cotton, sgn/dtd 83, 28x35", SBY 5/3/89 .... **49,500**
Untitled (abstract composition), gouache on paper, sgn/dtd 84, 39x27", SBY 5/3/89 OE **19,800**
Untitled (abstract), acrylic on canvas, sgn/dtd 69, unfr, 59x49", C-NY 11/9/88 OE **286,000**
Untitled (family under palm tree), copper-colored paint on paper, sgn/dtd 76, 20x28", SBY 11/11/88 OE **15,400**
Was Machen Die Russen in Mexico, dispersion on burlap/wool blanket, sgn, 79x71", SBY 10/8/88 OE **170,500**
POLLACK, Mark (American, 20th C)
Still Life with Bowl of Fruit & Statue, oil on canvas, sgn, 19x29", LH 10/16/88 .... **500**
POLLARD, James (British, 1792-1867)
Leeds Royal Mail Coach, oil on canvas, sgn/dtd 1828, 9x12", SBY 6/10/88 UE **5,500**
Tandem: Stanhope on a Country Road; oil on panel, sgn, 12x16", SBY 6/10/88 .... **8,800**
POLLARD, James; att (British, 1792-1867)
Royal Mail Coach, oil on canvas, bears signature/dtd 1831, 10x12", SBY 6/9/89 OE **7,150**
Royal Mails at the Angel, Islington on the Night of His Majesty George IV's Birthday, 1828; oil, 20x30", SBY 6/9/89 UE **3,850**
POLLARD, James; circle of (British, 1792-1867)
Pair: Out of the Kennel; Full Cry; oil on canvas, 12x24", SBY 6/10/88 .... **11,000**
POLLARD, James; manner of (British, 1792-1867)
Chester Royal Mail Coach, oil on canvas, 20x24", SBY 6/10/88 .... **2,750**
POLLET, Joseph (American, 1879-)
Overlook Mountain, oil on canvas, sgn, 20x30", C-E 1/12/88 UE **220**

POLLINI, Cesare (Italian, 1560-1630)
Studies of Madonna & Child & of Man in Prayer, pen/brown ink/brown wash, wm, 8x10", C-NY 1/12/88 .... **1,430**
POLLOCK, Jackson (American, 1912-1956)
Composition with Oval Forms, oil on masonite, sgn, ca 1934-38, 11x17", SBY 5/2/88 OE **99,000**
Frieze (abstract), oil/enamel/aluminum paint on canvas, sgn/dtd 53-55, 26x86", C-NY 11/9/88 .... **5,720,000**
Man with Hand Plow, oil on canvas, sgn, 22x28", C-NY 11/10/88 OE **66,000**
Number 19, 1949 (abstract); enamel on parchment mounted on board, sgn/dtd 49, 31x23", SBY 5/2/89 .... **3,960,000**
Number 20, 1949 (abstract); enamel on paper mounted on masonite, sgn/dtd 49, 28x19", SBY 5/2/88 .... **1,760,000**
Number 31, 1949; oil/enamel/aluminum paint on gesso ground on paper, mounted on panel, sgn/dtd 49, 31x22", C-NY 5/3/88 .... **3,520,000**
Red Painting I (abstract), oil on canvas, ca 1950, 21x13", C-NY 11/9/88 OE **187,000**
Search (abstract), oil/enamel on canvas, sgn/dtd 55, 58x90", SBY 5/2/88 OE **4,840,000**
Triptich: No 24, 1949; No 25, 1949; No 29, 1949; oil on canvas on masonite, sgn/dtd 49, 28x12" & smaller, C-NY 5/3/89 .... **2,200,000**
Untitled (abstract), black & colored ink/gouache on mulberry paper, sgn/dtd 1951, 25x39", SBY 11/10/88 OE **451,000**
Untitled (abstract), brush/spatter/ink on paper, sgn, ca 1946, 19x25", SBY 5/2/88OE **418,000**
Untitled (abstract), colored pencil on paper, 12x18", SBY 10/8/88 .... **25,300**
Untitled (abstract), enamel on paper, ca 1951, 18x22", SBY 11/10/88 .... **242,000**
Untitled (abstract), gouache/brush/pen/ink/wash on paper, sgn/dtd 44, 23x31", SBY 11/8/89 OE **880,000**
Untitled (abstract), India ink on paper, sgn, 1942, 5x6", SBY 11/9/89 .... **25,300**
POLLOG, Robert Karl (German, 1882-)
Still Life of Roses, oil on panel, sgn, 15x13", B/B 6/15/89 .... **1,980**
POLSE
Cityscape, oil on canvas, sgn, 28x36", C-E 6/28/88 UE **50**
PONCE DE LEON, Fidelio (Cuban, 1895-1949)
Hermanas (portrait of two sisters), pastel on paper, sgn, ca 1940, 19x19", C-NY 5/17/89 .... **4,180**
Mujer de Cuello Alto, oil on gessoed canvas, sgn, ca 1940, 20x16", C-NY 11/21/89 .... **4,400**
Peces, oil on canvas, sgn, 1945, 24x20", C-NY 11/21/89 .... **8,800**
POND, Clayton (American, 1941-)
Untitled, acrylic on canvas, 84x120", SBY 10/5/88 OE **1,210**
PONSEN, Tunis (American, 20th C)
Harbor Scene, watercolor on paper, sgn, 16x20", WG 4/23/88 .... **200**
PONSOT, C. (American, 20th C)
Head of a Young Woman, charcoal on paper, sgn/dtd 50, 20x16", FAP 4/15/89 UE **55**
PONTE, Francesco; see Da Ponte
PONTE, Gerolamo; see De Ponte
PONTE, Jacapo; see Bassano
PONTORMO, see Carucci, Jacapo
PONTOY, Henry Jean (French, 1885?)
Tree-Lined Street (with figure standing by horse & cart), oil on canvas, sgn, 9x12", WG 4/23/88 OE **500**
POOLE, Abraham (American, 1883-)
Portrait of Carlota Montery (Mrs Eugene O'Neill), oil on canvas, 74x45", C-E 6/1/88 .... **4,620**
POOLE, Frederick Victor (American, -1936)
Seated Lady, pencil on paper, 12x10", LH 10/16/88 UE **70**
Woman with Fan, pencil, sgn/dtd 1908, 11x8", LH 10/16/88 UE **70**
POOLE, Paul Falconer (British, 1807-1879)
Imogen & Pisanio (taken from Cymbeline, Act 3, Scene 4), oil on canvas, 30x25", C-E 5/22/89 .... **1,760**
POONS, Larry (American, 1937-)
Angela D (abstract), acrylic on canvas, sgn/dtd 1981, 82x26", C-NY 10/4/89 .... **13,200**
Bear Marys Painting (abstract), acrylic on canvas, sgn/dtd 1975, 71x21", C-NY 2/14/89 OE **11,000**
Cherry Smash (light blue dots on red background), oil on canvas, sgn/dtd 1963, 56x56", SBY 10/5/89 OE **77,000**
Jessica's Hartford, oil on canvas, 1965, 80x128", SBY 11/9/89 .... **176,000**
Night Journey (abstract), acrylic on canvas, 1968, 108x124", SBY 11/11/88 OE **56,100**
Southern Loss (abstract), acrylic on canvas, sgn/dtd 1978, 79x43", C-NY 2/14/89 .... **11,000**
Tony (abstract), acrylic on canvas, sgn/dtd 1981, 75x21", C-NY 5/4/89 OE **15,400**
Untitled, acrylic on canvas, sgn/dtd 1978, 77x30", C-NY 2/13/89 .... **5,280**
Untitled, acrylic on canvas, sgn/dtd 1978, 80x38", C-NY 2/13/89 .... **8,250**
Untitled (abstract), acrylic on canvas, dtd 78G-7, 80x40", C-NY 2/14/89 .... **7,700**
Untitled (abstract), acrylic on canvas, initialed/dtd 78, 75x26", C-NY 5/4/88 .... **7,150**
Untitled (abstract), acrylic on canvas, sgn/dtd 1971, 65x40", SBY 10/5/88 .... **3,025**
Untitled (abstract), acrylic on canvas, sgn/dtd 1972, 106x42", C-NY 5/4/88 OE **15,400**
Untitled (abstract), acrylic on canvas, sgn/dtd 1973, 72x10", SBY 10/5/89 OE **10,450**
Untitled (abstract), acrylic on canvas, sgn/dtd 1976, 69x13", C-E 11/14/89 .... **9,900**
Untitled (abstract), acrylic on canvas, sgn/dtd 1977, 106x51", SBY 2/15/89 OE **12,100**
Untitled (abstract), acrylic on canvas, sgn/dtd 78, 100x32", SBY 2/15/89 .... **6,600**
Untitled (abstract), acrylic on canvas, sgn/dtd 78, 82x59", C-NY 2/14/89 .... **14,300**
Untitled (abstract), acrylic on canvas, 112x47", SBY 10/8/88 OE **10,450**
Untitled (abstract), acrylic on canvas, 17x55", SBY 10/5/88 .... **3,025**
Untitled (abstract), acrylic on canvas, 1976-77, 78x28", SBY 10/8/88 .... **4,675**
Untitled (abstract), acrylic on canvas, 74x70", C-NY 5/4/88 .... **5,500**
Untitled (abstract), encaustic on canvas, 12x80", SBY 10/5/88 .... **3,025**
Untitled (abstract), oil on canvas, 84x134", SBY 10/5/89 .... **9,350**
Wild Cat Arrival (abstract), acrylic on canvas, sgn/dtd 1966, 110x190", SBY 5/3/89 OE **99,000**

POOR, Henry Varnum (American, 1888-1970)
Landscape, oil on canvas, sgn, 37x46", SBY 1/24/89 ... 3,300
POORE, Henry Rankin (American, 1859-1940)
After the Hunt, oil on canvas, initialed/dtd 95, 20x30", SBY 6/28/89 OE ... 6,600
POORTER, see De Poorter
POOTER, see De Pooter
POPE, Alexander (American, 1849-1924)
Afternoon Nap (sleeping puppy on cushion), pastel on canvas, sgn, 14x18", RAB 8/8/89 UE ... 600
Don, an Irish Setter; oil on canvas, sgn/inscr/dtd 96, 20x15", C-E 11/30/88 ... 1,760
Good Dog!, oil on canvas, sgn/dtd 95, 23x21", RWS 11/3/88 UE ... 900
On the Mend, No Hunting!; oil on canvas, sgn, 18x24", RWS 11/3/88 ... 10,000
Pointer with Pheasant, oil on canvas, sgn, 20x26", C-NY 5/25/89 OE ... 19,800
Rooster, oil on canvas, sgn, 20x16", C-E 2/3/88 OE ... 3,850
Shore & Game Birds (Trompe l'Oeil), oil on canvas, sgn/dtd 1871, 20x16", RWS 12/10/88 ... 1,400
POPE, Henry Martin (British, 1843-1908)
Shepherd with His Flock, watercolor on paper, 27x18", FAP 4/15/89 UE ... 302
POPP (19th C)
Ship at Sea, oil on canvas, sgn, 12x9", FAP 4/15/89 ... 302
POPPE, Fedor (German, 1850-)
18th-Century Style Outdoor Party Scene, oil on bevelled wood panel, 12x14", DM 3/14/88 ... 2,250
PORCELLIS, Jan (Dutch, 1584-1632)
Shipping in a Rough Sea, oil on panel, indistinctly sgn, unfr, 12x16", SBY 1/12/89 ... 13,200
PORCELLIS, Jan; circle of (Dutch, 1584-1632)
Skiff & Ships on a Stormy Sea, oil on panel, 8x10", SBY 7/12/89 ... 1,540
PORCHERON, Lucien Emile (French, 1876-1957)
Ruines d'Etableau, oil on canvas, sgn, 26x32", B/B 6/9/88 ... 22,000
PORCIA, see Di Porcia
PORIRIER, Denise (Canadian, fl 1935)
La Lettre (portait of seated woman), oil on canvas, sgn, 24x12", FB 10/17/88 OE ... 1,300
PORPORA, Paolo; circle of (Italian, -1673)
Pair: Tulips, Carnations, Morning-Glory, Roses, & a Butterfly; oil on canvas, 15x19", C-NY 10/20/88 ... 3,850
PORTA, Baccio della; see Bartolommeo, Fra
PORTER, Charles Ethan (American, 1847-1923)
Still Life of Apples, oil on canvas, 12x16", SBY 9/14/89 ... 2,860
PORTER, Fairfield (American, 1907-1975)
Autumn, 1 (contemporary suburban scene); oil on canvas, sgn twice/dtd 67/titled, 19x18", SBY 5/24/89 OE ... 38,500
Driveway (suburban landscape), oil on canvas, sgn twice/dtd 1967 twice/titled, 20x15", SBY 5/24/89 ... 24,750
Elizabeth on the Porch, pencil on paper, sgn, 10x14", SBY 6/28/89 ... 3,575
John Ashberry (portrait of a man seated in front of window), oil on canvas, sgn/dtd 70, 32x20", C-NY 5/25/89 ... 5,500
Study of a Seated Woman, marker on paper, sgn/dtd 65, 16x14"", SBY 6/28/89 UE ... 1,100
Wheat (wheat field w/white farmhouse & barn), oil on canvas, sgn/dtd 1960, 34x34", C-NY 5/25/89 ... 110,000
PORTER, Frederick J.
Interior with Flowers & Fruit on a Table, oil on canvas, sgn, 25x19", C-SK 6/9/88 ... 1,200
PORTER, Katherine (American, 20th C)
Evening of the Day (abstract), acrylic on canvas, 1970, 72x132", SBY 10/5/89 ... 11,000
Father's Letter (abstract), oil on canvas, 1980, unfr, 88x65", C-NY 5/4/89 ... 33,000
Postcard From North Antrim, oil on canvas, 1982, 91x114", SBY 2/15/89 ... 27,500
Sear of Every Metamorphosis, oil on canvas, 1983, 91x77", SBY 2/19/88 UE ... 16,500
Whirlwind (abstract), oil on masonite, 19x17", C-NY 2/14/89 ... 3,300
Wind Tunnel (contemporary), oil on panel, sgn/dtd 1979, C-NY 5/4/89 OE ... 4,950
PORTER, Rufus; att (American, fl 1814-1845)
Miniature Portrait in Two Views of a Young Gentleman, watercolor/ink on paper, 4x3", RWS 10/27/89 ... 8,000
Miniature Portrait of a Little Girl, watercolor on paper, 3x3", RWS 10/27/89 ... 1,400
Miniature Portrait of a Young Gentleman, watercolor on paper, 4x3", RWS 10/27/89 ... 1,200
PORTER, Tom (American, 20th C)
Lift Bridge, oil on masonite, sgn, 1978, 64x48", LH 12/4/88 UE ... 200
PORTER, V.F. (American, 20th C)
Clipper Ship at Sea, oil on canvas, sgn, 24x32", RAB 8/1/89 UE ... 700
PORTIELJE, Edward Antoon (Belgian, 1861-1949)
Visit (two seated women in interior reading a letter), oil on panel, sgn, 19x15", C-NY 2/23/89 ... 9,350
PORTIELJE, Gerard (Belgian, 1856-1929)
Jewelry Box, oil on canvas, sgn, 43x33", C-NY 2/23/89 ... 16,500
Minor Calamity, oil on canvas, sgn twice/dtd 1887 twice, inscr, 15x11", C-NY 5/25/88 ... 6,050
PORTIELJE, Jan Frederik Pieter (Dutch, 1829-1895)
Admiring Her Jewels (portrait of a seated woman in profile), oil on canvas, sgn/inscr/dtd 1887, 44x34", C-NY 5/24/89 ... 19,800
Butterfly (girl in profile gazing at butterfly), oil on panel, sgn/inscr Anvers, 30x24", SBY 10/24/89 ... 11,000
Butterfly (three-quarter length portrait of a girl), oil on panel, sgn, 30x24", SBY 5/23/89 ... 13,200
PORTINARI, Candido (Brazilian, 1903-1962)
Cabeza de Homen (head of a man), pen/ink on paper, sgn/dtd 1947, 9x8", C-NY 11/21/88 OE ... 1,430
Danca com os Guardachuvas (contemporary dancers), oil on panel, sgn/dtd 58, 64x44", C-NY 11/21/88 ... 275,000
Galo (large rooster w/figure flying kite beyond), oil on canvas, 18x22", C-NY 11/21/89 ... 35,000

Natureza Morta con Limoes (still life of lemons), oil/sand on linen, sgn/dtd 1939, 15x18", C-NY 5/18/88 ... 26,400
Sacrifice of Abraham, oil on canvas, sgn/dtd 1939, 18x15", SBY 5/17/88 ... 44,000
Ultimo Baluarte (surrealistic), pen/brush/India ink on paper laid down on board, sgn/titled, 11x14", C-NY 11/21/88 ... 6,050

PORTOCARRERO, Rene (Cuban, 1912-)
Cathedral (contemporary), oil on canvas, sgn/dtd 77, 28x20", SBY 11/21/88 ... 8,800
Cathedral (contemporary), oil on paper, sgn/dtd 62, 22x15", C-NY 5/17/89 OE ... 7,700
Figura en Azul (figure in blue), oil on canvas, sgn/dtd 1951, 30x23", LH 10/16/88 ... 3,400
Landscape (figures among palm trees w/houses & mountains in distance), oil on board, sgn, 25x32", SBY 5/17/88 ... 30,800
Nude (contemporary), oil on canvas, sgn/dtd 59, 29x21", SBY 11/21/88 UE ... 4,950
Rhythm (abstract), oil on board, sgn/dtd 1946, 21x27", SBY 11/21/88 ... 5,500

PORTOGHESE, Alvaro (European, 18th C)
Saints Catherine of Alexander & Mary Magdalene, oil on gold ground on arched panel, 56x28", C-NY 1/11/89 ... 85,000

PORUBSZKY, Istvan (Hungarian, 20th C)
Winter Landscape, oil on canvas, sgn, 24x36", B/B 1/11/89 UE ... 440

POSCHEWSKY, H.
Pair: Cattle in a Stream; Cattle in a Landscape; watercolor on paper, sgn/inscr, 7x9", C-E 10/25/88 ... 220

POSEN, Stephen (American, 1939-)
Untitled (abstract), oil/acrylic/pencil on canvas, sgn, 1973, 40x32", C-E 11/14/89 OE ... 3,850

POSSIN, Rudolf (German, 1861-)
Storytelling Hour (interior scene), oil on canvas, sgn, 30x39", SBY 7/12/89 ... 1,540

POSSNER, Hugo A. (American, 19th/20th C)
Apples in a Straw Hat, oil on canvas, sgn, 14x19", C-E 10/18/89 ... 2,420
Pair: Flowering Meadow; Foggy Morning Desert; oil on board, sgn, 1 dtd 28, 7x10", 8x12", B/B 5/17/89 ... 412

POST, William Merritt (American, 1856-1935)
Autumn Landscape, oil on board, sgn, 8x10", WG 4/23/88 ... 200
Autumn Landscape, oil on canvas, sgn, 13x19", LH 10/16/88 ... 850
Autumn Landscape, oil on canvas, sgn, 25x30", C-E 6/1/89 ... 3,520
Autumn Landscape with Stream, oil on canvas, sgn, 10x8", WG 9/16/88 ... 350
Autumn Landscape with Stream, oil on canvas, sgn, 16x24", SBY 4/14/89 OE ... 3,575
Birch Trees Along Stream, watercolor/gouache on paper, sgn, 17x27", C-E 11/30/88 ... 935
Hay Field with Farm Buildings, oil on canvas, sgn, 10x14", SBY 3/17/88 OE ... 4,400
Landscape at Twilight (w/stream), oil on canvas, sgn, 12x16", C-E 2/1/89 ... 2,750
Shady Path (cows grazing), oil on canvas, sgn, 14x20", C-NY 9/28/89 ... 7,150
Spring (landscape w/pond), oil on canvas, sgn, 12x16", SBY 6/24/88 OE ... 2,475
Summer Landscape, oil on canvas, sgn, 16x26", SBY 9/23/88 ... 2,090
Trees & Pond, oil on panel, sgn, 4x6", C-E 6/1/88 UE ... 110
Woodland Stream, oil on canvas, sgn, 18x25", B/B 8/10/88 ... 1,980

POSTIGLIONE, Luca (Italian, 1876-1936)
Roman Ticisano, oil on panel, sgn, 20x16", WL 5/20/88 ... 1,100

POSTIGLIONE, Salvatore (Italian, 1861-1906)
Two Young Shepherdesses, oil on canvas, sgn, 25x41", S/A 2/18/89 ... 17,000

POT, Hendrick Gerritsz (Dutch, 1585-1657)
Portrait of a Woman, in a black dress with white ruff & cuff; oil on panel, in painted oval, 7x5", SBY 6/3/88 ... 4,400

POTHAST, Bernard (Dutch, 1882-1966)
Baby's Mealtime, oil on canvas, sgn, 20x24", C-NY 10/25/89 ... 12,100
Center of Attention (baby in cradle w/mother & sibblings watching), oil on canvas, sgn, 31x39", C-NY 5/24/89 ... 16,500

POTT, Laslett John (British, 1837-1898)
Napoleon's Farewell to Josephine, My Destiny & France Demand It; oil on canvas, sgn, 53x37", SBY 2/22/89 OE ... 60,500

POTTER, William J. (American, 1883-1964)
Gordes Provence, sgn/inscr/dtd 1925, 33x26", C-E 11/30/88 ... 825
St Ives, fishing boats harbored near village; oil on board, sgn, 16x13", RAB 8/8/89 OE ... 925

POTTHAST, Edward Henry (American, 1857-1927)
At the Beach (impressionistic figures in surf), oil on board, sgn, 9x12", SBY 5/24/89 ... 44,000
Bathing in a Cove (inpressionistic), oil on panel, sgn, 9x12", C-NY 12/2/88 OE ... 26,400
Beach (impressionistic beach scene), oil on canvas, sgn, 12x14", C-NY 5/25/89 ... 66,000
Blacksmith (working in his shop), oil on canvas, sgn, 20x16", C-NY 5/25/89 ... 18,700
By the Water, oil on canvas, sgn, 24x30", C-NY 5/26/88 OE ... 110,000
In the Garden (mother & small children in garden), watercolor/gouache on paper, sgn, 30x39", SBY 5/24/89 ... 22,000
In the Surf (figures playing in ocean), oil on canvasboard, sgn/titled/#d 14, 12x16", SBY 5/24/89 ... 110,000
Ironing, oil on canvas, sgn, 10x14", C-NY 9/30/88 OE ... 15,400
Moonlight (seascape), oil on board, sgn, 16x20", C-NY 5/26/88 ... 16,500
On the Beach (mother/two daughters walking on beach), oil on board, sgn, 16x12", SBY 5/24/89 ... 77,000
Playtime (portrait of baby), oil on panel, sgn/dtd 1914, 13x16", SBY 5/24/89 OE ... 25,300
Sunday Afternoon, oil on panel, sgn, 12x16", SBY 5/25/88 ... 79,750
Surf Bathing (figures along shore), oil on panel, sgn, 12x16", B/B 10/9/88 ... 55,000
Surf in Moonlight, oil on canvas, sgn, 41x51", C-NY 5/28/88 ... 46,200
Three of a Kind (three figures in water), oil on canvas laid down on board, sgn twice/inscr, 12x16", C-NY 12/2/88 ... 77,000

POUGIALIS, Constantin (American/Greek, 1894-)
Dancer, oil on canvas, no size given, LH 9/10/89 ... 350
Girl in Red Dress, oil on canvas, sgn, 23x29", S/A 3/12/88 ... 600

POULIN, Chantel (Canadian, 20th C)
Douce Moitee, oil on canvas, sgn/dtd 1986, 20x24", FB 10/17/88 475
Ne Pars Pas, oil on canvas, sgn/dtd 1986, 16x20", FB 10/30/89 506
POURBUS, Frans the elder; att (Flemish, 1545-1581)
Abraham & Lot Leaving Egypt for Canaan, oil on panel, 28x35", C-NY 10/12/89 8,800
POURBUS, Frans the younger; att (Flemish, 1570-1622)
Portrait of the Archduke Albert & the Infanta Isabella of Spain, oil on canvas, 27x22", C-NY 1/15/88 OE 33,000
POURIER, Denise (Canadian, 20th C)
Scene d'Hiver (winter scene with mother & child), oil on canvas, sgn/dtd 1979, 18x14", FB 5/28/89 OE 2,200
POUSETTE-DART, Richard (American, 1916-)
Earth & Sky (abstract), watercolor/gold paint on paper, sgn, 7x10", SBY 10/5/88 OE 2,200
Untitled (abstract), gouache/watercolor/colored inks on paper, sgn, 6x10", C-NY 10/4/89 5,500
Untitled (abstract), titanium white oil/pencil on paper, 1977, 23x30", SBY 2/15/89 OE 10,450
Untitled (abstract), watercolor/ink on paper, ca 1948, 6x9", SBY 11/9/89 OE 27,500
White Composition, oil/graphite/gesso on canvas, 1952, 24x20", SBY 10/8/88 OE 7,700
White Gothic #4 (abstract), oil on canvas, sgn, 1959, 72x58", SBY 11/11/88 OE 99,000
POUSSIN, Gaspard; see Dughet, Gaspard
POUSSIN, Nicolas; circle of (French, 1594-1665)
Narcissus at the Pool in an Arcadian Landscape, oil on canvas, unfr, 36x46", C-NY 10/12/89 3,300
POUSSIN, Nicolas; school of (French, 1594-1665)
Tobias & the Angel, oil on canvas, 30x40", C-E 4/7/88 1,760
POUWELSEN, Willem (Dutch, 19th C)
Children Picking Flowers at the Edge of the Forest, oil on canvas, sgn, 20x24", B/B 6/9/88 1,540
POVEDA, Carlos (Latin American, 20th C)
Straits (contemporary coastal seascape), mixed media on canvas, sgn/titled Estrechos, 1988, 36x48", SBY 5/16/89 5,225
Tepuy (landscape), mixed media on canvas, sgn/titled, 1985, 36x48", SBY 11/21/88 3,300
POWELL, Arthur James Emery (American, 1864-1956)
Broken Dam (water rushing in landscape), oil on masonite, sgn, 16x20", C-E 6/1/89 770
Sun Camp, oil on canvas, sgn, 32x40", C-E 2/1/89 1,540
Winter, Central Park; oil on canvasboard, sgn, 8x10", SBY 9/14/89 550
POWELL, Charles Martin (British, -1824)
Becalmed (sailing vessels & figures in small boats), oil on canvas laid down, sgn, 24x36", B/B 10/9/88 OE 13,200
POWELL, Lucien Whiting (American, 1846-1930)
Farm Scene, watercolor, sgn, 15x27", DM 10/14/88 300
Grand Canyon (extensive landscape), oil on canvas, sgn, 24x36", WG 4/23/88 2,600
Winding Road Through a Forest, watercolor on paper, sgn, 24x29", WL 5/20/88 700
POWERS, Richard Gorman
Fields, Dorset Hollow, Vermont; oil on masonite, sgn/dtd 58, 24x30", C-E 6/1/89 UE 220
POYNTER, Edward John (British, 1836-1919)
Set of 3: Drapery Studies; black chalk on tan/brown paper, artist's Vente stamp, unfr, 15x12", C-NY 10/31/89 385
POYNTER, Edward John; att (British, 1836-1919)
Samson & Delilah, oil on canvas, bears signature, FAP 11/4/88 OE 3,700
POZZI, Stefano; att (Italian, ca 1707-1768)
Portrait of a Cleric Holding a Crucifix, oil on canvas, unfr, 46x39", SBY 4/7/88 OE 4,675
PRADEL (Continental, 19th C)
Moored Boats, oil on canvas, sgn/inscr/dtd 77, unfr, 20x30", SBY 6/8/88 1,045
PRADES, see Da Prades
PRAMPOLINI, Enrico (Italian, 1894-1956)
Nudo All'Aperto, gouache/oil on board, sgn, 1946, 17x10", SBY 10/5/88 OE 6,050
PRATELLA, Attilio (Italian, 1856-1949)
Busy Mediterranean Port, oil on panel, sgn, 8x14", SBY 2/22/89 14,300
Fishing Boats in the Bay of Naples, oil on panel, sgn, 9x14", C-NY 2/23/89 OE 26,400
Pair: Fishing Boats in the Bay of Naples; oil on panel, sgn, 8x14", SBY 2/22/89 OE 38,500
Seaside Village, gouache on paper, sgn, 11x17", SBY 7/12/89 UE 1,980
Water Carrier, watercolor/gouache on cardboard, sgn, 20x12", C-NY 10/25/89 OE 4,620
PRATELLA, Attilio; att (Italian, 1856-1949)
Paris Street, oil on canvas, bears signature D Nittis, 14x10", SBY 2/22/89 18,700
PRATT, Sam
Rural Landscape with Buildings, oil on board, sgn, 1953, 19x24", DM 5/89 250
PRELL, Hermann (German, 1854-1922)
Die Wasserfrau, oil on canvas board, sgn, 36x29", SBY 2/22/89 OE 15,400
PRELLWITZ, Henry (American, 1865-)
Along the Coast, oil on board, sgn, 13x18", C-E 11/30/88 UE 880
PRENDERGAST, Charles (American, 1868-)
Autumn Sampler, pastel on paper, 9x12", C-NY 5/26/88 4,950
Offering, oil/gouache/watercolor/gold leaf/pencil on carved gessoed panel, sgn, 13x19", C-NY 5/25/89 OE 52,800
PRENDERGAST, Maurice Brazil (American, 1861-1924)
Balloon, oil on wood panel, sgn, 12x14", C-NY 5/26/88 154,000
Bathers & Strollers at Marblehead, watercolor/pastel/gouache/pencil on paper, sgn, 16x22", C-NY 5/25/89 253,000
Boat Landing, Nahant, Massachusetts; watercolor/pastel on paper, sgn, 14x20", C-NY 12/2/88 385,000
Capri, watercolor/pencil on paper, sgn/inscr/dtd 1899, 14x20", C-NY 12/2/88 220,000

Crescent Beach, watercolor/pencil on paper laid down, sgn/dtd 1896, 14x10", C-NY 5/25/89 OE **198,000**
Fantasy (exotic landscape w/people & animals), tempera on paper laid down on board, sgn, 15x19", WD 10/5/88 .... **45,000**
Low Tide, Afternoon, Treport; watercolor/pencil on paper, sgn/dtd 92, 13x9", C-NY 12/2/88 .... **55,000**
New England Village, watercolor/pastel/gouache/pencil on paper, sgn, 14x20", C-NY 5/25/89 .... **110,000**
Promenade (strollers in Luxembourg Gardens, Paris), oil on board, sgn, 11x14", C-NY 5/25/89 OE **330,000**
Romantic Couple (sketch), pencil on paper laid down on board, sgn/initialed, 5x8", C-E 6/1/89 OE **4,400**
Shady Trees on the Shore, watercolor on paper, sgn, 15x22", C-NY 12/2/88 OE **88,000**
Still Life of Flowers, oil on board, sgn, ca 1910-13, 19x15", SBY 5/24/89 OE **187,000**
Telegraph Hill (figures in landscape), watercolor/pencil on paper, sgn/titled/#d 48, 14x21", SBY 5/24/89 OE **1,870,000**
The Park (w/figures), sepia ink on paper, sgn, 12x9", C-NY 12/2/88 .... **49,500**
Watching the Regatta, watercolor/pencil on paper, dtd 1907, 11x15", WD 4/13/88 .... **125,000**
Woman (sketch), pencil on paper, initialed, 7x3", C-E 6/1/89 .... **1,650**
Woman in Red Dress, watercolor/pencil on paper, 7x10", SBY 4/29/88 UE **577**

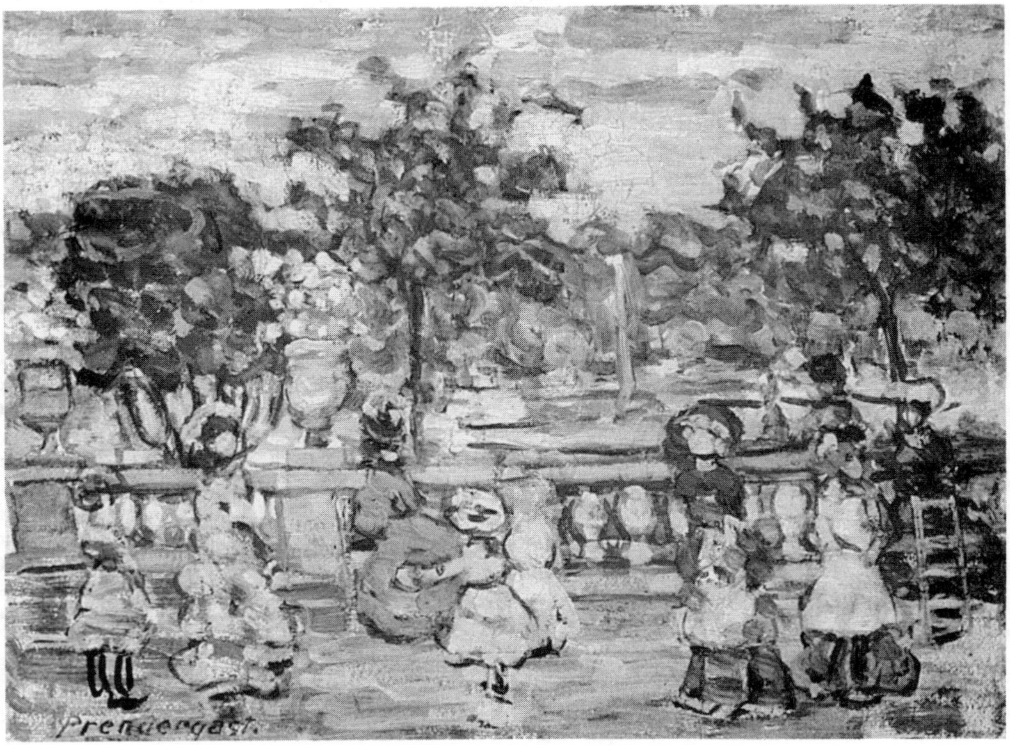

Promenade, oil on board, sgn, 11x14", C-NY 5/25/89 OE; $330,000

PRENTICE, Levi Wells (American, 1851-1935)
Adirondacks, oil on canvas, sgn/dtd 1873, 18x32", C-NY 12/2/88 .... **26,400**
Apples in a Hat, oil on canvas, sgn, 12x18", C-NY 5/26/88 .... **22,000**
Basket of Plums (still life), oil on canvas, sgn, 12x10", SBY 5/24/89 .... **8,800**
Baskets of Strawberries, oil on canvas, sgn, 10x15", SBY 5/25/88 .... **12,100**
Floating Screw, watercolor/black crayon on paper, initialed/dtd 72, 12x9", C-NY 11/10/88 OE **19,800**
Melons, Peaches, & Pineapple; oil on canvas, sgn, 12x19", C-NY 12/2/88 .... **11,000**
Niagara River at La Salle, oil on canvas, sgn/dtd 188(?), 12x18", C-NY 12/2/88 .... **38,500**
Pines at the Crossroads, oil on canvas, sgn, 12x18", C-NY 3/11/88 .... **2,200**
Pirates by Moonlight (seascape), oil on wood panel, sgn, 15x33", RAB 8/8/89 UE **2,250**
Raspberries in a Tin Bowl: Temptation; oil on canvas, sgn, 12x9", WD 4/13/88 .... **14,500**
Still Life of Red Currants, oil on canvas, sgn, 6x9", SBY 3/17/88 .... **7,700**

PRENTICE, Levi Wells; circle of (American, 1851-1935)
Study of Apples on a Branch, oil on canvas, 14x22", PHL 6/16/88 .... **550**

PRENTZEL, Hans (German, 1880-1956)
Summer Splendor, Blossoming Flower Garden with Victorian Lady Walking Down Path; oil on canvas, 20x24", DM 3/14/88 OE **2,600**

PRESSER, Joseph (American/Russian, 1907-1967)
Three Girls (heads), watercolor/gouache/pastel/charcoal, sgn, 24x17", RWS 9/8/89 OE **5,500**

PRESSMANE, Joseph (French, 1904-1967)
Picnic in the Park (village & hills beyond), oil on board, sgn, 39x59", SBY 5/30/89 .... **24,200**
Woman with Birds, oil on panel, sgn, 15x15", SBY 5/30/89 .... **4,400**

PRESTON, May Wilson (American, 1873-1945)
Fruit & Vegetable Market (20s couple at market), watercolor/pencil on board, sgn/dtd 29, unfr, 16x15", WL 5/20/88 OE **700**
Head of a Woman in a Dutch Cap, oil on board, sgn/#d 324, 16x13", WL 5/20/88 UE **200**
Mother & Daughter Sewing, oil on board, sgn/#d 27/dtd 32, 20x16", WL 5/20/88 .... **900**
Pair: Portrait of Woman Wearing Hat; Seated Nude; oil on canvas/oil on board, 1 sgn, unfr, 16x13, 13x16", WL 5/20/88 UE **200**
Sailboats on the Beach, oil on board, sgn/#d 346, 13x16", WL 5/20/88 .... **375**

PRESTOPINO, Gregario (American, 1907-)
Church on a Hill, oil on canvas, sgn, 24x20", C-E 11/30/88 ... 1,650
Green Tug, oil on canvas, sgn, 24x36", B/B 6/15/89 UE ... 5,500
PRETI, Mattia (Italian, 1613-1699)
Erminia, Princess of Antioch; oil on canvas, inscr, 38x29", SBY 6/2/89 UE ... 46,750
Samuel Anointing David, oil on canvas, 84x120", SBY 1/12/89 OE ... 1,155,000
PRETI, Mattia; circle of (Italian, 1613-1699)
Card Players, oil on canvas, 33x40", SBY 10/21/88 ... 3,740
PREUSHER (Continental, 19th C)
Portrait of a Woman (in red & white), oil on canvas, 39x28", SLK 9/29/88 ... 175
PREUX, Henri (French, 19th C)
Elevation of Notre Dame de Paris, pen/ink/watercolor, sgn, 24x17", SBY 6/8/88 ... 660
PREVAL, see De Preval
PREYER, Emilie (German, 1849-1930)
Still Life of a Bowl of Fruit on a Marble Table, oil on canvas, sgn/dtd 1870, 16x14", SBY 2/22/89 ... 36,300
Still Life of Peaches, Grapes, Plums, Cherries, & Glass of Champagne; oil on canvas, sgn/dtd 1876, 14x20", C-NY 2/25/88 ... 57,200
PRICE, Alan (British, 20th C)
March Thaw, tempera on masonite, sgn/dtd 1963, 24x48", C-NY 3/11/88 ... 4,180
PRICE, William Lake (British, 1810-1891)
Doge's Palace, Venice; watercolor/gouache, initialed/dtd 1843, 13x19", C-E 10/26/89 ... 1,320
PRICE, Winchell Addison (Canadian, 1907-)
Awakening, oil on canvasboard, sgn, 24x30", WAD 6/12/89 ... 800
September Day, oil on canvas, sgn, 28x36", WAD 6/12/89 ... 900
Springtime, oil on canvas, sgn, 24x30", WAD 11/30/89 ... 1,500
PRIECHENFRIED, Alois (German, 1867-1953)
Glass of Sherry, oil on panel, sgn, 5x4", DM 3/14/88 ... 500
The Inventory, oil on panel, sgn, 18x13", WAD 6/6/88 ... 3,000
PRIESTLEY, Edward (British, 19th C)
At the Bull's Head Inn, oil on canvas, sgn/dtd 79, 18x32", WAD 6/6/88 ... 1,300
Cascade, oil on canvas, sgn, 24x16", C-E 5/23/88 ... 1,320
Landscape with Waterfall, oil on canvas, 24x18", SLK 9/29/88 ... 700
PRIKING, Frantz (German, 1927-)
Still Life of Fruit & Flowers, oil on canvas, sgn/dtd 57, 30x36", RWS 12/10/88 OE ... 900
PRINCE, P. (American, 19th/20th C)
Coastal Scene, oil on canvas, sgn/dtd 94, 11x27", FAP 12/8/89 UE ... 250
PRINCETEAU, Rene (French, 1844-1914)
Full Cry (fox hunt scene), oil on panel, sgn, 11x9", C-NY 5/24/89 OE ... 33,000
PRINGLE, William J. (British, fl 1834-1858)
Huntsman on a Bay Hunter, oil on canvas, sgn, 21x26", SBY 6/9/89 UE ... 3,000
PRINS, Benjamin (Dutch, 1860-1934)
Moorish Guard, oil on panel, sgn/dtd 1886, 14x11", C-E 20/25/88 ... 2,090
PRINSEP, Valentine Cameron (British, 1836-1904)
Il Barbagianni, oil on canvas, sgn, 31x21", C-NY 10/25/89 ... 41,800
PRIOR, M. Elizabeth (American, 20th C)
Southern Magnolia (white blossoms with green leaves on blue ground), oil on canvas, sgn, 40x36", RAB 8/9/88 ... 700
PRIOR, William Matthew (American, 1806-1873)
Group of 3: Boy Holding Whip; Infant with Cherries & Bouquet; Girl Holding Wildflowers; oil, 14x10", RWS 10/27/89 ... 49,000
Lake Scene with Mountains & Stone Cottage, oil on canvas, 26x36", SBY 1/28/88 UE ... 3,850
Mount Vernon at Night, oil on canvas, artist's stamp, 19x25", SBY 1/24/89 ... 1,870
Portrait of a Baby, oil on board, ca 1840, 14x10", C-NY 1/20/89 ... 6,050
Portrait of a Gentleman, oil on board, 14x10", RWS 10/27/89 ... 3,500
Portrait of Dr Leonard Hanna of Columbiana County, Ohio; oil on canvas, 26x22", GAI 9/1/89 ... 8,500
Prior-Hamblen School (19th C)
Pair: Gentleman with Plaid Neck Tie; Woman with White Lace Collar; oil on paper laid down on board, 24x19", SBY 1/28/88 ... 13,200
Portrait of a Lady, oil on board, 14x9", C-E 4/26/88 ... 770
Portrait of Octavia Poor Emerson, oil on board, ca 1940, C-NY 1/20/89 ... 3,520
PRIOU, Louis (French, 1845-)
Le Serment, oil on canvas, sgn/dtd 1880, 53x34", SBY 6/8/88 UE ... 3,300
PRITCHARD, Edward F.D. (British, 1809-1905)
Skaters on a River in a Winter Landscape, oil on canvas laid down on masonite, sgn/dtd 1846, 23x32", WD 1/11/89 ... 1,800
PRITCHARD, George Thompson (American, 1878-1962)
Clipper in Full Sail, oil on canvas, sgn, 25x30", WAD 6/6/88 ... 700
London Harbor, oil on canvas, sgn, unfr, 25x30", B/B 10/6/88 ... 1,650
Sunset Landscape, oil on canvas, sgn, unfr, 25x30", B/B 10/6/88 ... 2,090
Winding Forest Stream, oil on canvas, sgn/dtd 1933, unfr, 25x30", B/B 12/8/88 ... 880
Winter Landscape, oil on canvas, unfr, 25x30", B/B 10/6/88 ... 1,210
PRITCHARD, H. (American, 19th C)
Old Salt, bearded sailor holds shell to his ear; oil on canvas, sgn/dtd 1886, 32x24", RAB 3/27/89 UE ... 500
PRITCHARD, J. Ambrose (American, 1858-1905)
La Coquette, oil on canvas, sgn/dtd Paris 1887, 32x26", C-E 10/18/89 UE ... 825

PRITCHETT, Robert Taylor (British, 1823-1907)
Figures Outside a Country Manor, watercolor/gouache, sgn/dt 1875, 10x18", C-E 2/21/89 UE 440
PROCACCINI, Camillo (Italian, 1546-1629)
Sacrifice of Isaac, oil on canvas, 72x47", SBY 6/3/88 68,750
PROCACCINI, Carlantonio (Italian, 1571-1630)
Garden of Eden, oil on panel, sgn, 13x18", SBY 6/3/88 19,800
PROCACCINI, Giulio Cesare (Italian, 1570-1625)
Apollo & Minerva, oil on canvas, 80x47", C-NY 4/8/88 18,700
PROCHAZKA, Karl
Cigarette (portrait of a woman, full-length, seated on arm of chair), pastel, sgn, 47x32", C-NY 10/26/88 7,150
PROCTOR, Burt (American, 1901-1980)
At the Spring, oil on canvas, sgn, 29x23", SBY 6/24/88 2,420
PROL, Rick (20th C)
Untitled, acrylic on canvas, sgn/dtd 1984, 40x30", C-NY 2/13/89 550
PROLSS, Frederich Anton Otto (German, 1855-)
Bavarian Girl (portrait), oil on panel, sgn/dtd 96, 13x9", C-E 5/22/89 OE 6,380
Die Herzoglich Nassauische Jagerei zu Mittenwald...; oil on canvas, sgn/dtd 1886, 34x46", SBY 2/22/89 33,000
PRONK, Cornelis (Dutch, 1691-1759)
Portrait of a Young Girl, Possibly of the Cardinaal Family...; oil on canvas, sgn, 28x22", C-NY 1/11/89 OE 41,800
PROSDOCINI, Alberto (Italian, 1852-)
Moored Fishing Boats, watercolor/gouache on paper, sgn, 8x13", C-E 5/23/88 550
Palazzos on the Grand Canal, Venice; watercolor on paper, sgn, 14x22", B/B 12/8/88 OE 1,430
Venetian Canal, watercolor, sgn, 33x19", C-E 2/21/89 OE 1,870
Venetian Lagoon Scene, watercolor on paper, sgn, 26x65", SBY 7/12/89 UE 770
PROUST, S.; att
View of Cologne City Hall, watercolor, 13x10", C-E 2/16/89 UE 44
PROUT, John Skinner (British, 1806-1876)
Fort Macquarie & Government House From Mrs Macquarie's Chair, pencil/watercolor, sgn, 6x10", C-SK 11/10/88 4,830
PROUT, Samuel (British, 1783-1852)
At Mass in a Cathedral in Northern France, watercolor/pen/brown ink heightened w/white, sgn, 17x12", C-NY 10/26/88 1,980
Doge's Palace & the Bacino, Venice; watercolor/gouache, 29x44", C-NY 10/26/88 OE 17,600
PROUT, Samuel; att (British, 1783-1852)
First Sun on a Sleeping Town, oil on canvas, bears signature, 13x18", C-E 5/22/89 UE 330
PROVISOR, Janis (American, 20th C)
Second Impressions (abstract compositions), oil/acrylic on canvas, sgn/dtd 1980, unfr, 23x23", C-E 11/14/89 UE 110
Sherman (abstract composition), acrylic/oil on canvas, sgn/dtd 1979, unfr, 22x23", C-E 11/14/89 UE 220
PROVOST, Jan; circle of (Flemish, ca 1465-1529)
Adoration of the Shepherds, oil on panel, arched top, 30x21", SBY 10/13/89 8,800
PRUCHA, Gustav (Austrian, 1875-)
Sleighing Party, oil on canvas mounted on masonite, sgn, 29x41", SBY 6/8/88 3,850
PRUD'HON, Pierre Paul (French, 1758-1823)
Kneeling Child Wearing a Bonnet, black/white chalk on cream paper, 13x10", C-NY 1/11/89 15,400
PRUD'HON, Pierre Paul; att (French, 1758-1823)
Head of a Man, white/brown/gray wash w/pencil on paper, bears signature, 10x8", WD 10/19/88 UE 275
PRUD'HON, Pierre Paul; follower of (French, 1758-1823)
Amour with Doves (in a landscape), oil on canvas, 52x30", SBY 6/1/89 UE 9,900
PRUD'HON, Pierre Paul; style of (French, 1758-1823)
Muse in a Classical Landscape, oil on panel, oval, 14x12", B/B 9/14/89 1,650
PRUEY, F.W.
Barnyard, oil on canvas, sgn, 16x26", C-E 5/23/88 1,760
PRUNA, Pedro (Spanish, 1904-)
David Lichine in the Ballet Protee, oil on board, sgn, 19x12", SBY 10/7/89 OE 7,700
PRUSHECK, Harvey Gregory
Slovenian Village, oil on masonite, sgn, ca 1930, 28x30", C-E 10/18/89 OE 2,640
PUJOL DE GUASTAVINO, Clement (French, 19th C)
Artist's Model (reclining, reading a book), oil on canvas, sgn, 21x14", C-NY 2/23/89 17,600
PULIGO, Domenico (Italian, 1492-1527)
Lucretia (portrait), oil on panel, 23x17", SBY 4/7/88 7,975
Madonna & Child with the Infant Saint John the Baptist, oil on panel, 39x30", C-NY 1/11/89 110,000
PULIGO, Domenico; att (Italian, 1492-1527)
Portrait of a Lady, bust-length, wearing a turban; oil on panel, 25x19", C-NY 1/11/89 OE 19,800
PULIGO, Domenico; follower of (Italian, 1492-1527)
Mary Magdelen (portrait), oil on canvas, 24x19, SBY 4/7/89 OE 4,400
PULIGO, Domenico; school of (Italian, 1492-1527)
Holy Family with the Infant Saint John the Baptist, oil on panel, 30x23", C-NY 4/8/88 14,300
Madonna & Child with Infant Saint John the Baptist, oil on panel, 28x19", C-NY 4/6/89 3,300
PULLER, John Anthony (British, 19th C)
The Gleaners, oil on canvas, sgn, 13x15", C-E 10/26/89 3,300
PULZONE, school of (Italian, 16th C)
Portrait of a Pope, seated, three-quarter length; oil on canvas, 51x38", C-NY 4/6/89 2,200

MMIL, Robert (American, 1936-)
Last of Them (cowboy rounding up steers), oil on masonite, sgn/dtd 80, 20x30", SBY 9/23/88 OE ... 5,500
Matter of Right of Way, oil on canvas, sgn/copyrighted/dtd 81, 40x60", SBY 9/23/88 OE ... 9,900
Plows & Calico, oil on masonite, sgn/copyrighted/dtd 80, 30x45", SBY 9/23/88 ... 3,575
Spittin' Mud, oil on canvas, sgn/copyrighted/dtd 83, 24x30", SBY 9/23/88 OE ... 6,050
NI, Ivan (Russian, 1894-1956)
Cafe at Vitebsk (abstract), brush/ink on blue paper, ca 1919, 13x10", C-L 10/8/88 OE ... 13,940
Horse-Drawn Sleigh, gouache on paper, Pougny studio stamp, 1926, 19x25", C-L 10/8/89 ... 3,350
Theatre for Itself (abstract), collage/watercolor/pencil on paper, titled, ca 1915-16, 8x5", C-L 10/8/88 ... 20,450
OSSIN, Nicolas; after
Choice of Hercules, oil on canvas, unfr, 37x30", SBY 7/12/89 ... 1,540
PINI, Biagio (Dalle Lame)(Dutch, 1511-1575)
Birth of the Virgin, brush/brown wash heightened w/white over black chalk, 13x8", SBY 1/13/89 ... 6,050
Scene From Ancient History: Woman Brought by Soldiers in Front of a General; pen/ink/wash, 11x8", SBY 1/13/89 ... 5,500
RDY, Albert J. (American, 1835-1909)
Toy Sail Boat, oil on canvas, sgn/dtd 1899, 42x32", C-E 6/1/88 ... 6,380
RLIN, Paul (American, 1886-1969)
Taos Pueblo (buildings in barren landscape), oil on board, 16x20", B/B 10/9/88 ... 1,980
RY, see De Pury
RYGIN, Leonid (Russian, fl 1969-)
Moluk (surrealistic), oil on composite panel w/hinges, sgn/dtd 1988, 31x38", SBY 7/7/88 OE ... 7,000
Pipa (surrealistic), oil on canvas w/text by artist in artist-made frame, sgn/dtd 1985, 41x35", SBY 7/7/88 ... 10,000
SHMAN, Hovsep (American, 1877-1966)
Dancing Girl (still life), oil on panel, sgn, 18x15", SBY 3/17/88 ... 6,325
Fruit Seller, oil on canvas, sgn, 44x29", SBY 9/23/88 ... 13,200
Memento of Old Madrid (portrait of a woman), oil on panel, sgn, 31x23", C-NY 5/25/89 ... 10,450
THUFF, Hanson Duvall (American, 1875-1972)
Empurpled Summits, oil on board, sgn, 12x16", B/B 6/9/88 ... 5,225
Sequestered Valley, oil on canvas, sgn, 24x30", B/B 10/6/88 OE ... 17,600
TMAN, Donald (Putt)(American, 1927-)
Bordello, gouache on board, sgn Putt, 20x22", SBY 3/17/88 UE ... 495
TNAM, Marlene Evans (American, 20th C)
Summer Sea (waves crashing over rocks), oil on canvas, sgn, 18x24", RWS 3/31/88 ... 550
TTNER, Josef Carl Berthold (Austrian, 1821-1881)
Off the Coast of Malta, oil on canvas, sgn/dtd 1847, 28x38", C-NY 2/25/88 ... 3,300
YROCHE-WAGNER, Elise (German, 1828-1895)
Floral Still Life by the Edge of a Stream, oil on canvas, sgn/dtd 1866, 35x40", SBY 10/24/89 ... 9,900
LE, Howard (American, 1853-1911)
George Washington Conferring with His Generals at Newburgh, gouache en grisaille on paper, sgn, 9x12", SBY 3/17/88 OE ... 4,125
Washington Refusing the Crown, watercolor/gouache en grisaille on paper, sgn, 12x9", SBY 3/17/88 OE ... 4,125
NE, James Baker (British, 1800-1870)
Extensive Landscape with Oxen on a Path & a Castle Beyond, oil on canvas, 30x50", C-NY 5/25/88 ... 8,250
Old Mill, figures in rocky grounds near abandoned mill; watercolor/wash on paper, sgn/dtd 1868, 13x19", RAB 3/27/89 UE ... 375
View of Windsor Castle & Eton College, oil on canvas, 37x60", B/B 6/15/89 ... 3,850
NE, Robert Lorrdine (American, 19th C)
Bronx River, New York; oil on canvas, sgn/dtd 1871, 22x16", RWS 8/20/88 UE ... 250
NE, Thomas; att (British, 1843-1935)
River Landscape with Thatched Cottages, oil on board, 10x14", C-E 2/23/88 ... 1,430
GXIA, Wu (Chinese, 1910-)
Nine Fish (Jiu Yu Tu, hanging scroll), ink/color on paper, sgn/dtd 1941, 40x17", SBY 5/31/89 ... 1,210
EI, Gao (Chinese, 1672?-1734)
Guan Gong (hanging scroll), ink/color on paper, sgn/dtd 1714, 78x33", SBY 5/31/89 OE ... 8,800
HAN, Zhu (Chinese, 1892-)
Wisteria (hanging scroll), ink/color on paper, sgn/dtd 1980, 35x19", SBY 5/31/89 OE ... 9,350
A, Sun (Chinese, ca 1860-1870)
Ship Roscius Approaching Hong Kong, oil on canvas, sgn twice, orig frame, 18x24", RAB 11/25/88 OE ... 20,000
Ship Roscius in a Storm, oil on canvas, orig Chippendale frame, 18x24", RAB 11/25/88 ... 8,000
ADAL, Martin Ferdinand (German, 1736-1811)
Pair: Portrait of John Mathews, Esq; Portrait of Anna Mathews; oil on canvas, sgn/dtd 1776, 24x20", C-E 4/7/88 ... 1,210
ARTLEY, Arthur (American, 1839-1886)
Landscape with Cows, oil on board, sgn/dtd 1877, 10x8", RWS 5/19/88 ... 1,400
Marshlands in Moonlight, oil on canvas, sgn, 8x10", RWS 5/19/88 ... 1,400
View of Naragansett Pier, oil on canvas, sgn/dtd 1877, 13x24", C-E 10/18/89 OE ... 3,850
AST, Pieter; att (Dutch, 1606-1647)
Alchemist (man with book at table in detailed interior), oil on panel, indistinctly initialed, unfr, 15x11", C-NY 4/6/89 ... 11,000
Merry Company, oil on panel, 17x24", C-NY 10/12/89 OE ... 23,100
ELLINUS, Erasmus II (Flemish, 1607-1678)
Triumph of Love & Hope, oil on panel, ca 1636-37, 29x29", SBY 6/1/89 OE ... 46,750
ENCE, Raymond
Printemps a Honfleur, oil on canvas, sgn, 29x36", PHL 11/15/88 ... 700

QUIMBEY, Fred G. (American, 1863-1923)
Winter Landscape, New Hampshire; oil on canvas, sgn, 43x54", RWS 5/19/88 ... 4,50

QUINSA, Giovanni (17th C)
Slices of Watermelon, Peaches, Quinces, Pears, Plums, & Bird; oil on canvas, sgn/dtd 1641, unfr, 23x42", C-NY 4/8/88 OE ... 68,20

QUINSAC, Paul Francois (French, 1858-)
Young Lady Seated in Profile, oil on canvas, sgn/dtd 1890, 22x17", C-E 5/23/88 ... 2,86

QUINTERO, Daniel (European, 20th C)
Yellow Door, oil on canvas stretched over panel, sgn, 1979-80, 16x13", C-E 11/14/89 ... 1,54

QUINTIN, H.J. (British, 19th C)
Fancy Leominster, Bred by J Taylor, Stretford Court; oil on canvas, sgn/dtd 1860, 25x30", SBY 6/10/88 OE ... 9,90

QUINTON, J. (British, 19th C)
Benedict in a Stall (racehorse), oil on canvas, sgn/dtd 1879, 25x30", SBY 6/9/89 UE ... 2,75

QUIROLO, A.E.
Landscape in the Andes, oil on canvas, sgn/inscr, 24x28", C-SK 11/10/88 ... 56

QUIROS, see De Quiros

QUIRT, Walter (American, 1902-1968)
Untitled (abstract composition), oil on canvas, sgn, 30x40", PHL 12/1/88 ... 2,50

QUISTGAARD, Johan Valdemar (Danish, 1877-)
Portrait of a Woman, oil on canvas, sgn/dtd 1929/unidentified wax stamp, 41x30", RWS 3/16/89 ... 50

QUIZET, Leon Alphonse (French, 1888-1955)
Automne Dans un Village (autumn village scene), oil on canvas, sgn, unfr, 27x35", C-E 11/17/88 OE ... 13,20
Le Moulin de la Galette, oil on masonite, sgn, 15x18", C-E 11/17/88 OE ... 9,90
Rue de Village (quiet street scene), oil on masonite, sgn, unfr, 32x39", C-E 11/17/88 OE ... 17,60
Rue de Village (landscape), oil on masonite, sgn/dtd 1946, 15x18", C-E 5/13/88 OE ... 6,0

R.W. (American, 19th/20th C)
River Landscape with Birch Trees Alongside a Country Road, indistinctly sgn, 12x24", SLK 2/12/88 ... 30

RAAB, George (American, 1866-1943)
Summer Landscape, oil on canvas, sgn, 10x12", S/A 2/18/89 ... 30

RAAPHORST, Cornelis (Dutch, 1875-1954)
Playful Kittens, oil on canvas, sgn, 16x20", SBY 12/9/88 ... 4,9
Three Kittens on a Cushion, oil on canvas laid down on board, sgn, 8x10", C-E 2/21/89 ... 3,52

RACE, G. (American, 20th C)
Steamship, oil on board, sgn/dtd 1902, 10x18", LH 9/10/89 OE ... 35

RACHMIEL, A. (French, 19th/20th C)
Pastoral Lake Scene, oil on canvas, 26x32", B/B 1/11/89 ... 1,21

RACKHAM, Arthur (British, 1867-1939)
Balloon Seller, pen/ink/watercolor heightened with white on paper, sgn/dtd 06, 12x7", SBY 2/22/89 OE ... 22,00
Bob Cratchet, From A Christmas Carol; ink/watercolor on paper laid down on board, sgn, unfr, 11x8", B/B 6/9/88 ... 8,80
Evil Spell, watercolor/pen/India ink on paper, sgn/dtd 1900, 6x7", SBY 2/22/89 ... 13,20
Illustration of Catskin in English Fairy Tale, watercolor on paper, sgn, 10x7", B/B 3/22/89 ... 11,00
Song of the Lark (young lady seated in landscape), watercolor on paper, sgn, 14x20", WD 11/16/88 ... 7,25
The Ingoldsby Legends: Frontispiece; pen/black ink/watercolor, sgn/dtd 07/inscr, 13x9", C-NY 2/23/89 OE ... 39,60

RADEMAKER, Abraham (Dutch, 1675-1735)
Extensive River Landscape with Figures by Ruins & an Elegant House, gouache on paper, sgn, 5x7", SBY 1/13/89 OE ... 7,15
View of Velsen, black chalk/pen/brown ink/brown/gray wash, inscr, 5x11", C-NY 1/12/88 ... 60

RADEMAKER, Abraham; att (Dutch, 1675-1735)
Town on a River with Wagon & Sailing Boats, black chalk/pen/brown ink/gray wash, inscr/wm, 8x13", C-NY 1/12/88 ... 1,98

RADULOVICH, Savo (American, 20th C)
Portrait of a Woman, oil on board, 20x16", SLK 9/29/88 ... 30

RAEBURN, Henry (British, 1756-1823)
Pair: Portrait of John Smellie, of Torbanhill; Portrait of Mrs John Smellie; oil on canvas, 30x25", C-NY 1/15/88 OE ... 11,00
Portrait of a Gentleman, half-length, wearing jacket, yellow waistcoat & white jabot; oil on canvas, 30x25", C-NY 4/6/89 ... 1,54
Portrait of a Lady of Rank, oil on canvas, 27x22", WG 9/16/88 UE ... 25
Portrait of a Mrs Hunter, Margaret Douglas of Brigton, Seated in a Landscape; oil on canvas, 36x28", C-NY 6/2/88 ... 38,50
Portrait of Colonel Kelso (half-length, in red regimental uniform), oil on canvas, 30x25", SBY 10/13/89 OE ... 12,10
Portrait of Dr Welsh Tennant of Tennant House, Fife, Holding a Medical Book; oil on canvas, 50x40", C-NY 1/15/88 ... 5,50
Portrait of Dr Welsh Tennant of Tennant House, Fife, Holding a Medical Book; oil on canvas, 50x40", C-NY 10/20/88 ... 4,40
Portrait of Mrs Elizabeth Stewart Richardson, Seated, Wearing a Red Dress & Turban; oil on canvas, 40x50", C-NY 6/2/88 ... 13,20
Portrait of Professor Andrew Dalzel in Academic Robes, by a Table; oil on canvas, 50x40", C-NY 1/15/88 ... 11,00
Portrait of Sir Francis Horner, bust-length; oil on canvas laid down, 31x26", C-NY 10/20/88 OE ... 8,80
Portrait of William Hunt of Pittencrieff, Dunfermline (full-length, dog at side); oil on canvas, 79x53", SBY 6/1/89 UE ... 110,00

RAEBURN, Henry; att (British, 1756-1823)
Portrait of a Boy, oil on canvas, 24x20", LH 12/4/88 ... 90

RAEBURN, Henry; school of (British, 1756-1823)
Portrait of a Lady, seated half-length in peach dress & coral necklace in landscape; no media given, 30x25", C-E 6/1/88 ... 55

RAFFAELE, Joseph (American, 1933-)
Couples, oil/paper collage on canvas, sgn/dtd 66, 45x37", C-E 11/17/88 ... 1,21
Untitled (abstract), oil on canvas, sgn/dtd 1974, unfr, 15x27", C-NY 5/4/89 ... 6,60
Watercolor G (abstract), watercolor on cardboard, sgn, 1973, 30x49", SBY 11/11/88 ... 1,98

RAFFAELLI, Jean Francois (French, 1850-1924)
Afternoon Tea (couple having tea w/cat on window sill), oil on canvas, sgn, 14x12", C-NY 2/23/89 ... 22,00

Afternoon's Walk Near the Village Church, oil on cradled panel, sgn, 28x21", SBY 2/22/89 ... 33,000
Banlieue de Paris, oil on canvas, sgn, 15x30", SBY 5/23/89 ... 11,000
Cavalier in White, oil on canvas, sgn/dtd 1876, 37x28", B/B 3/17/88 ... 6,600
French Country Farm, oil on canvas, sgn, 15x18", C-NY 10/25/89 ... 6,600
Infanzia (portrait of a girl), oil on canvas, sgn/titled, 18" dia, SBY 2/22/89 ... 6,600
Le Geolier, black chalk/gray wash, initialed, 8x14", C-NY 2/25/88 UE ... 990
Le Grandpere, oil on panel, sgn, 29x24", C-NY 2/25/88 ... 28,600
Le Petit Rentier Francais (old man sitting on bench by pond), oil on board, sgn, 19x13", SBY 10/24/89 OE ... 57,750
Les Petits Metiers de Paris: Le Crieur Public; oil on cradled panel, sgn, 25x20", SBY 2/22/89 ... 49,500
Maire et Conseiller Municipal, oil on canvas, sgn, 21x29", C-NY 5/25/88 ... 28,600
Nature Morte, oil on canvas, sgn, 22x28", SBY 2/22/89 ... 33,000
Portrait of a Young Woman, mixed media on linen, sgn, 32x26", SBY 2/22/89 OE ... 11,000
St Etienne-du-Mont, Paris; oil on canvas, sgn, 26x23", SBY 5/23/89 ... 29,700
Un Clochard (tramp looking at road signs in a landscape), oil on canvas, sgn, 14x10", C-NY 5/24/89 OE ... 12,100
Vagabond, oil on paper laid down on panel, sgn/dtd 79, 22x15", C-NY 5/25/88 ... 6,600
Vase of Chrysanthemums, oil on panel, sgn, 29x22", C-NY 10/25/89 ... 10,450

FFAELLI, Jean Francois; att (French, 1850-1924)
Newsboy, black chalk w/colored highlights on gray paper, bears signature, 18x12", MG 5/28/88 OE ... 950

FFALT, Ignaz (Austrian, 1800-1857)
Figures Outside a Tavern, oil on panel, sgn/dtd 1840, 13x17", C-NY 5/25/88 ... 5,500

FFET, Auguste (French, 1804-1860)
Set of Three: Prussian Officers Uniforms; pencil/watercolor on paper, 2 stamped/1 sgn, ea 8x6", SBY 2/22/89 UE ... 1,100

GGI, E. (Italian, 19th C)
Arab Merchant, watercolor on paper, sgn, 20x14", B/B 8/10/88 ... 829
Harem Girl with a Tambourine, watercolor, sgn, 21x15", C-E 2/21/89 ... 880

GGIO, G. (Italian, 19th C)
Herding the Cattle, oil on canvas laid down on board, sgn/inscr, 14x25", SBY 6/8/88 OE ... 3,575

GINOE, Raffaele (Italian, 1851-1925)
Children Playing (in landscape), oil on panel, sgn, 12x18", C-E 2/21/89 OE ... 6,050

GOT, Jules Felix (French, 19th C)
Still Life of Roses & Grapes, oil on canvas, sgn, 17x24", B/B 1/11/89 ... 990

IBOLINI, Francesco di Marco di Diacomo (1450-1517)
Madonna & Child with an Angel & Saint John, oil on panel, 24x20", ca 1495, SBY 6/1/89 ... 407,000

INER, Arnulf (Austrian, 1929-)
Le Lattre de Passion, oil on photograph, sgn, 9x8", C-NY 10/4/89 ... 3,960

LL, G. (German, 19th C)
Busy Harbor, oil on canvas, sgn, 25x33", WAD 6/6/88 ... 1,800

LLI, Theodore Jacques (Greek, 1852-1909)
Eastern Guard, oil on canvas laid down on masonite, sgn/dtd 79, 26x18", SBY 2/22/89 OE ... 44,000
Home From the Fields (woman on path), oil on canvas, sgn, 22x15", RWS 5/19/88 OE ... 2,300

MBERT, Rene
Notre-Dame vue de Ioin, Paris; oil on canvas, sgn/inscr, 16x24", C-E 10/25/88 ... 2,200

MIREZ, Saturnino (European, 1946-)
Billiard Parlor, oil on canvas, sgn/dtd 81, 29x24", SBY 5/17/88 ... 2,640

MM, John Henry (American, 1879-1948)
Autumn Afternoon, oil on canvas, sgn, 30x40", B/B 1/11/89 ... 1,045

MONO, Giulio (Italian, 1499-1546)
Study of a Ewer (characteristic design for tableware), pen/brown ink/wash, 10x6", SBY 1/13/89 ... 4,950

MOS, Mel (American, 1935-)
Barbara (portrait), oil on canvas, sgn/dtd 1966, 18x14", SBY 2/15/89 OE ... 20,900
Lucky Lulu (nude on a package of Lucky Strikes), oil on canvas, 1965, 48x40", SBY 5/5/89 OE ... 110,000
Miss Lions International (nude in logo), oil on canvas, sgn/dtd 1964, inscr w/title, 50x50", C-NY 2/20/88 OE ... 104,500
Peek-a-Boo, Brunette #2 (view of nude through keyhole); acrylic on canvas, sgn/dtd 1964, 44x32", C-NY 5/4/89 OE ... 99,000
Peek-a-Boo, Brunette #3 (contemporary); acrylic on canvas, sgn/inscr, 1964, 60x44", C-NY 11/9/88 ... 49,500
Pha-White Goddess (Jane Russell), oil on canvas, sgn/dtd 1963, 49x43", SBY 11/9/89 OE ... 143,000
Phantom #2, oil on canvas, 1963, 30x19", SBY 30x19", SBY 5/3/88 ... 28,600
Portrait of Beatrice Lillie, oil on canvas, 16x20", SBY 10/7/89 ... 6,325
Red Coat (lady in red coat w/breast exposed), oil on canvas/masonite, sgn/dtd 1966, 47x30x3", SBY 10/5/89 ... 41,250
Tiger Girl (contemporary), oil on canvas, 1963, 40x36", C-NY 11/9/88 ... 60,500
Untitled (nude on Hershey candy bar), graphite on paper, sgn/dtd 67, 17x24", C- NY 5/4/89 OE ... 18,700
Untitled (nude standing before AC monogram), graphite on paper, sgn/dtd 67, 28x28", C-NY 11/10/88 OE ... 5,280
Untitled (reclining nude w/leopard), graphite on paper, sgn/dtd 67, 17x24", C-NY 5/4/89 OE ... 15,400
Untitled (reclining nude), watercolor on paper, sgn/dtd 76, 22x30", C-NY 5/4/89 OE ... 28,600
Woman with Colgate Tube, gouache on board, sgn/dtd 1965, 24x20", C-NY 11/10/88 OE ... 44,000

MOS, Tod (British, 20th C)
Open Ditch-Cheltenham (Gold Cup 1985); oil on canvas, sgn, 36x48", SBY 6/10/88 ... 11,000

MSAY, Allan; after (British, 1713-1784)
Portrait of Jean Jacques Rousseau, oil on panel, oval 12x9", RWS 8/12/89 ... 325

MSAY, Allan; studio of (British, 1713-1784)
Pair: King George III & Queen Charlotte Sophia of Mecklenburg-Strelitz; oil on canvas, 90x57", SBY 4/29/88 OE ... 40,700

RAMSDELL, Frederick Winthrop (American, 1865-1915)
Harvested Corn in an Autumn Sunset, oil on canvas, sgn, 20x24", B/B 9/15/88 OE 1,54
Outposts, Island of Monhegan, Maine; oil on canvas, sgn, 25x30", B/B 5/17/89 88
RAMSEY, Charles Frederick
Cloud, oil on canvas, ca 1919, 22x18", C-NY 3/11/88 6,05
RAMSEY, Milne (American, 1847-1915)
Landscape of Cottage by Lake, watercolor on paper, sgn, 14x8", FAP 11/4/88 OE 90
Still Life with Chrysanthemums in an Oriental Vase, oil on canvas, sgn/dtd 11.89, 30x24", SBY 3/17/88 4,95
RAND, Henry Asbury (American, 1886-)
Sunlit Slope (landscape), oil on canvas, sgn/indistinctly dtd, 16x20", SBY 3/17/88 1,32
RANFT, Richard (Swiss, 1862-)
Punting & Fishing on the Lake, oil on board, sgn, 21x27", SBY 2/14/89 UE 2,75
RANGER, Henry Ward (American, 1858-1916)
Autumn Glow (landscape), oil on canvas, sgn/dtd 97, 18x26", C-E 2/1/89 OE 6,60
Autumn Landscape, oil on artist board, sgn/dtd 97, 12x16", RAB 8/9/88 OE 4,25
Autumn Landscape, oil on panel, sgn, 13x16", FAP 12/8/89 UE 1,05
Autumn Landscape (forest scene with calm water), oil on artist board, sgn/dtd 97, 12x16", RAB 8/9/88 4,25
Barge on the River, watercolor on paper, sgn, 20x28", SBY 9/14/89 1,43
Boat on a Beach, Bahamas; oil on board, estate stamp/titled, 12x16", RAB 3/27/89 UE 60
Boats in a Harbor, Holland; oil on board, initialed/sgn/dtd 1888, 12x14", SBY 6/24/88 OE 2,31
Cityscape, oil on board, sgn/dtd 1915, 12x16", B/B 9/15/88 1,04
Forest Interior, oil on board, sgn, 12x16", C-E 6/1/88 OE 2,64
Holland Village, oil on board, bears estate stamp, #d B424, 12x16", C-E 2/1/89 OE 2,42
Interior of Forest, oil on board, sgn, 12x16", C-E 2/1/89 1,32
Landscape Scene, oil on canvas, sgn, 24x30", RWS 11/3/88 1,30
Landscape with Cloudy Sky, oil on canvas, sgn/stamped/dtd 92, estate stamp/#d E-22, 28x36", SBY 9/23/88 3,85
On the Barge at Dusk, watercolor/gouache on board, estate stamp/#d W 60, 13x17", SBY 6/24/88 1,87
Pair: Autumn Trees by a Path; House Near Road; oil on board, sgn/estate stamp, dtd 1902 & 1905, 12x15", C-NY 3/11/88 2,42
Seascape, oil on canvas, sgn, 11x14", LH 10/16/88 2,80
Ships in a Harbor, oil on canvas, sgn/dtd 1906, 18x26", SBY 6/24/88 7,15
Wedding-Old Lyme, Connecticut (wedding party in tree-lined avenue w/church); oil on canvas, sgn, 6x8", RAB 8/8/89 3,00
RANKEN, William Bruce Ellis (British, 1881-)
Lady on a Terrace, in Profile; oil on canvas, indistinctly sgn/dtd 1915, 18x18", C-E 10/26/89 2,20
RANSOM, Fletcher C.
Chasing the Pig, oil on canvas, sgn, 22x31", C-NY 9/30/88 OE 7,15
RANSON, Paul (French, 1864-1909)
Baigneuse, oil on canvas, 24x20", C-NY 10/6/88 30,80
Pair: Poissons et Crustaces (fish & other crustaceans); oil on canvas, monogramed, ca 1902, 34x21", C-NY 5/12/88 77,00
Pommier aux Fruits Rouges (landscape w/apple tree), oil on canvas, sgn, ca 1902, 34x47", C-NY 5/12/88 OE 159,50
Vignes (vineyard in landscape), oil on canvas, initialed, ca 1902, 34x67", C-NY 5/12/88 88,00
RANSWYK, J. (Dutch, 19th/20th C)
Cornish Coast After the Rain, oil on canvas, sgn, 16x30", B/B 8/10/88 85
RANZONI, Hans the elder (Austrian, 1868-)
Street in an Austrian Town, oil on board, sgn, 10x14", C-E 2/21/89 1,32
Vienna in the Spring, oil on board, sgn/dtd 921, 21x18", WD 3/23/88 OE 1,80
RAOUX, Jean (French, 1677-1734)
Offering in the Temple of Vesta, oil on canvas, shaped top, inscr, 88x66", C-NY 6/2/88 20,90
RAOUX, Jean; circle of (French, 1677-1734)
Portrait of a Woman in Sixteenth-Century Costume, oil on canvas, oval, 26x22", SBY 10/21/88 OE 4,67
RAPHAEL, after (Italian, 1483-1520)
La Perle: Madonna, Infant Christ, St Anne, & John the Baptist; oil on canvas, 17x14", RWS 12/10/88 60
Madonna & the Goldfinch, oil on canvas, 41x30", SBY 12/9/88 OE 3,57
Madonna of Divine Love, oil on canvas, 39x31", SBY 7/12/89 OE 2,20
Madonna with Christ & Saint John, oil on panel, 16x13", SBY 12/9/88 OE 2,31
RAPHAEL, Joseph (American, 1869-1950)
A View of Zoute, Holland; pen/ink on paper, sgn, 15x24", B/B 10/6/88 77
Old Tower, Amsterdam; oil on panel, sgn, 9x11", B/B 10/6/88 1,54
Passing Band, Marche St Caterien, France; pencil/chalk/brush/pen/black ink, oil, sgn, 20x27", C-SK 11/10/88 1,39
Portrait of a Dutch Woman, oil on canvas laid down, sgn, 19x15", B/B 10/6/88 4,95
Winter, Linkebeck Village, Belgium; pen/ink/wash on paper, sgn/dtd 1911, 19x23", B/B 10/6/88 1,54
RAPIN, Alexander (French, 1839-1889)
Scene d'Hospital, oil on canvas, sgn, 45x34", WAD 6/6/88 6,00
RAPP, J.H.T. (American, 19th/20th C)
Pointers in a Landscape, oil on canvas, sgn, 10x14", SBY 6/10/88 OE 4,40
RAPPINI, Vittorio
Arab Merchant, watercolor/gouache over pencil, sgn, 20x15", C-NY 2/25/88 OE 4,40
RARASYN, Edgard (Belgian, 1858-1938)
Broken Wheel (man w/broken down wagon on cobbled road), oil on canvas, sgn, 28x43", C-E 5/22/89 1,76
RASCHEN, Henry (American, 1854-1937)
Campfire Stories (figures in landscape), oil on canvas, sgn, 26x46", SBY 6/28/89 UE 5,50
Campfire Stories (three Indians around a campfire), oil on canvas, sgn, 30x60", C-NY 2/3/88 17,60

Canyon Sunrise (Indian on horse in a landscape), oil on canvas, sgn, 30x40", B/B 3/22/89 6,600
ndian Scouts (in hilly landscape by a stream), oil on canvas, sgn, 26x46", C-NY 2/3/88 19,800
ndian Storyteller (three Indians around a campfire), oil on on canvas, sgn, 30x40", C-NY 2/3/88 13,200
Portrait of a Bearded Trapper, oil on canvas, sgn, 12x10", B/B 1/11/89 715
Sunset, Colorado River (Indian resting on rock viewing sunset); oil on canvas, sgn, 36x60", C-NY 2/3/88 11,000
Trail into the Mountains (two horses/riders in hilly landscape), oil on canvas, sgn, 26x46", SBY 5/24/89 9,900

SINELLI, Roberto (Italian, 19th C)

Reading in the Garden, oil on board, sgn, 22x14", C-E 10/26/89 2,750

SKIN, Joseph (American, 1897-1981)

Dancers, oil on canvas, sgn, 30x40", SBY 9/14/89 6,050
Edith Darning (seated at table w/vase of flowers), oil on canvas, sgn, 30x40", SBY 4/14/89 1,650

SMUSSEN, Georg Anton (Norwegian, 1842-1914)

Fjord Scene in Summer, oil on canvas, sgn/dtd DF 78, 25x37", C-NY 2/25/88 8,250
Gathering Along the Fjord, oil on canvas, sgn/dtd 67, 21x30", SBY 7/12/89 2,750

THBONE, John (British, 1750-1807)

River Landscape with Anglers, oil on canvas, initialed/dtd 1767, 24x35", C-NY 4/8/88 1,980

TLIFF, Blanche Cooley (American, 1896-)

Floral Still Life, oil on board, sgn, 12x13", WG 9/16/88 UE 180

TTI, Eduard (German, 1816-)

Linda of Chamouni, oil, 55x40", WD 1/11/89 3,000

TTNER, Abraham (American, 1895-1978)

Costume Figure with Mask, oil on canvas lined with cork, sgn/indistinctly inscr, 1950, 26x20", SBY 9/23/88 3,190
Masks Composition #4, oil on canvas, sgn twice/inscr/dtd 1948, 24x29", SBY 6/24/88 UE 2,860
Moses (abstract), oil on canvas, sgn twice, 1956, 29x24", SBY 1/24/89 3,025
Moses (abstract), watercolor/gouache on paper, sgn/dtd 58, 19x12", SBY 6/24/88 1,100
Shapes in Summer, oil on canvas, sgn, 18x24", C-E 2/3/88 990
Three Heads, oil on canvas, sgn/inscr/dtd 1948, 13x18", SBY 9/23/88 1,210
Up From the Wilderness #1 (abstract), oil on canvas, sgn/dtd 63, titled/dtd, 38x51", SBY 9/23/88 3,300

U, Emil Karl (German, 1858-1940)

Genre Scene (courting couple at table before window), oil on canvas, sgn, 25x20", DM 10/14/88 11,000
Girl Reading Beside a Window, oil on canvas, sgn, 29x23", SBY 12/9/88 OE 13,200

UCHINGER, Heinrich (1858-1942)

Backyard, oil on board, sgn, 18x14", C-E 5/23/88 UE 880
Gathering of Peasant Women, oil on canvas, sgn, 22x15", C-E 5/23/88 UE 550
Spring Landscape, oil on board, sgn, 23x19", C-E 2/23/88 1,430
Still Life of Cyclamens, Glass, Napkin, & Tea Cup on a Table; oil on canvas, sgn, 24x20", C-E 5/23/88 825

UFER, Aloys (German, 1794-1856)

Interesting Move, Cardinals Playing Chess; oil on board, sgn, 16x21", RAB 3/27/89 2,900

ULAND, Orland

Sailboats Coming into Harbor, oil on canvas, sgn, 25x30", C-E 2/3/88 OE 4,180

UPP, Karl (German, 1837-1871)

Midday Rest (peasants resting in a rural landscape), oil on canvas, sgn, 41x60", B/B 6/15/89 UE 15,400

USCHENBERG, Robert (American, 1925-)

April's Fool V (abstract), solvent transfer on paper, sgn/dtd 1986, 13x10", SBY 5/3/89 OE 18,700
Ash-Gate (composition), solvent transfer/acrylic/fabric collage/oil on paper, sgn/dtd 79, 84x37", SBY 5/2/88 OE 39,600
Beaker (Hoarfrost), solvent transfer on silk/cotton collage, sgn/dtd 75, 64x36", SBY 2/15/89 OE 60,500
Black Mail (abstract), oil/fabric collage/photo transfer/mirror on canvas, sgn/dtd 58, 16x24", SBY 11/10/88 198,000
Claptrap (abstract), solvent transfer/acrylic/fabric collage on paper, sgn/dtd 80, 31x23", SBY 2/15/89 OE 35,750
Compass (abstract), solvent transfer on fabric collage laid down on panel, sgn/dtd 78, 36x36", SBY 10/5/89 OE 46,750
Crane, mixed media on panel, sgn/dtd 78, 84x36", C-NY 5/4/89 OE 93,500
Crib (composition), solvent transfer/fabric collage/acrylic on paper, sgn/dtd 80, 32x24", SBY 5/2/88 OE 23,100
Cup (abstract), solvent transfer/graphite/watercolor on paper, sgn/dtd 1958, 23x29", C-NY 11/9/88 OE 143,000
Diehard (abstract), oil on canvas w/silkscreen on 3 panels, sgn/dtd 1963, 72x144", SBY 5/2/89 1,760,000
Drawing for American Chess Foundation, paper/transfer/gouache/string/tape/soil/graphite, 1965, 20x30", C-NY 11/10/88 OE 29,700
Epcot (abstract), solvent transfer/pencil on paper, sgn/dtd 81, 24x36", SBY 10/5/89 33,000
Grip (abstract), solvent transfer/gouache on paper, sgn/dtd 66, 29x23", SBY 5/3/89 41,250
Gully (composition), solvent transfer/acrylic/fabric collage on paper, 30x22", SBY 5/2/88 OE 23,100
Headline (abstract), pencil/solvent transfer/tempera/watercolor on paper, sgn/dtd Oct 1962/titled, 37x45", SBY 5/2/88 OE 66,000
Ladle (contemporary), solvent transfer/acrylic/fabric collage on paper, sgn/dtd 80, 32x24", SBY 5/2/88 OE 23,100
Lots (abstract), colored pencil/solvent transfer/tempera/watercolor on paper, sgn/dtd 1961, 23x29", SBY 2/15/89 99,000
Monument, solvent transfer/colored crayons/watercolor/graphite on paper, sgn/inscr/dtd 58, 23x29", C-NY 11/9/88 OE 132,000
Poop Deck (contemporary), solvent transfer/collage on paper, sgn/dtd 80, 32x24", SBY 5/2/88 OE 19,800
Rebus, oil/pencil/fabric/paper collage on canvas, 1955, 96x131", SBY 11/10/88 OE 6,325,000
Ringer State (composition), collage w/solvent transfer on silk linen, sgn/#d 5-15/dtd 74, 68x35", C-NY 5/4/89 OE 30,800
Rusa 18 (Cloister Series), mixed media on board, 1980, 96x72", SBY 2/19/88 OE 63,250
Shovel (Signal), solvent transfer/oil/colored ink on fabric mounted on panel, sgn/dtd 80, 32x32", C-NY 11/10/88 OE 41,800
Snowflake Crime IX (abstract), solvent transfer on paper, 1981, 7x8", SBY 5/3/89 8,800
Trap (abstract), oil/silkscreen on canvas, sgn/dtd 1964/titled, 40x30", SBY 11/10/88 OE 418,000
Untitled (abstract), acrylic on fabric laminated on paper, sgn/dtd 85, 32x29", SBY 5/3/88 OE 27,500
Untitled (abstract), acrylic/corrosives/polishes on copper sheet, 1986, 79x40", SBY 5/2/88 OE 104,500
Untitled (abstract), collage w/paper/oil/metal on canvas, 1960, 9x9", C-NY 5/4/89 165,000

Untitled (abstract), colored pencil/solvent transfer/tempera/watercolor, sgn/dtd 69, 30x42", SBY 10/8/88 OE **115,50**
Untitled (abstract), pencil/solvent transfer/watercolor/tempera on paper, sgn/dtd 68, 22x30", SBY 5/2/88 OE **71,50**
Untitled (abstract), solvent transfer on fabric w/plastic ruler/metal zipper on paper, sgn/79, 9x15", C-NY 2/14/89 OE **26,40**
Untitled (abstract), solvent transfer on paper, sgn/dtd 82, 42x37", SBY 5/3/89 OE **44,00**
Untitled (abstract), solvent transfer on paper with fabric/oil/paper collage, 31x23", C-NY 2/14/89 .... **34,10**
Untitled (abstract), solvent transfer/pencil on paper, sgn/dtd 73, 30x22", SBY 5/3/89 OE.......... **26,40**
Untitled (abstract), solvent transfer/pencil/mylar collage on paper, sgn/dtd 66, 15x20", SBY 2/15/89 OE **46,75**
Untitled (abstract), tempera/watercolor/solvent transfer on paper, sgn/dtd 68, 22x30", SBY 5/2/88 OE.......... **24,20**
Untitled (composition), mixed media on paper, sgn/dtd 1958, 23x29", SBY 11/8/89 OE **275,00**
Untitled (composition), solvent transfer/gauze on lithographic proof (Tampa 12), sgn/dtd 74, 66x40", SBY 5/2/88 OE **31,90**
Untitled Drawing in Two Parts (abstract), solvent transfer/pencil on 2 sheets of paper, 46x30", SBY 5/2/88 OE **20,90**
Winter Pool, oil/paper/fabric/metal/handkerchief/tape/button/wood on canvas with ladder, 1959, 90x60", SBY 11/10/88 OE **3,740,0**

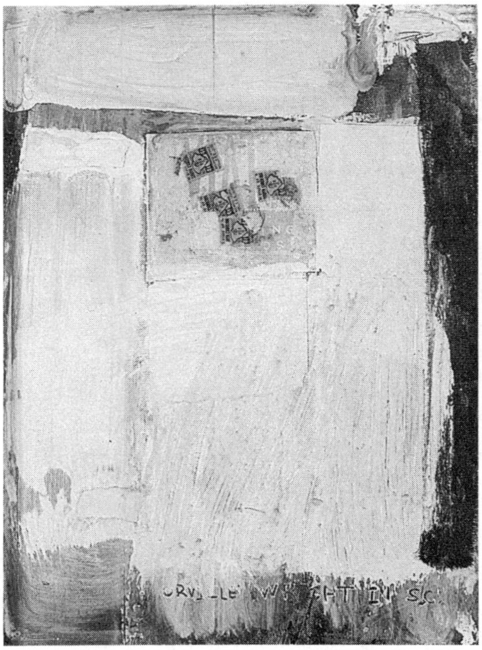

Orville Wright in South Carolina, oil/paper/fabric on panel, sgn/dtd 1954, 10x7", C-NY 2/14/89 OE; $253,000

RAV, F. (German, 19th C)
Young Girl with Basket of Fruit, oil on canvas, sgn, 42x35", FAP 12/8/89 UE **95**
RAVEN, Samuel (British, 1775-1847)
Pair: Pointer; Vixen with Cubs; oil on panel, initialed, 7x9", SBY 6/10/88.......... **3,02**
The Kill (dog attacking a fox), oil on panel, 7x9", C-E 2/23/88 .... **1,32**
RAVENSTEYN, H.
Portrait of a Woman Wearing a Broad Lace Collar & Pearl Jewelry, oil on panel, sgn/dtd 1638, 25x19", SBY 10/21/88 .... **2,20**
RAVESTEYN, Jan A.; follower of (Dutch, 1570-1657)
Portrait of a Woman with Lace Collar, oil on canvas, 27x23", SBY 7/12/89 UE **16**
RAWORTH, William Henry (New Zealander, 1820-1905)
Wooded Estuary with a Quayside, Possibly Dunedin; watercolor, sgn, 12x19", C-SK 11/10/88.......... **52**
RAWSON, Carl W. (American, 1884-1970)
Early Fall, oil on canvas, sgn/dtd 48, 32x25", C-E 11/8/88 UE **55**
Falls Beyond the Mills, oil on board, sgn/dtd, 10x12", RWS 11/3/88.......... **80**
RAWSON, Carl W.; att (American, 1884-1970)
Clipper Ship, oil on canvas, bears signature, 22x32", LH 9/10/89 UE **22**
RAY, Ruth (American, 20th C)
Navajo Landscape (surrealistic depiction), oil on canvas, sgn/dtd 1948, 10x12", C-NY 9/28/89.......... **1,87**
RAYO, Omar (Colombian, 1928-)
Mandaladman II (abstract), acrylic on canvas, sgn/dtd 1986, 40x40", C-NY 5/18/88 .... **7,70**
READ, Ralph (American, 20th C)
Market Port au Prince Haiti (market scene), oil on canvas, sgn/dtd 1940, 30x31", RWS 3/31/88.......... **30**
READ, Thomas (British, 19th C)
Pair: Huntsman with His Hounds; oil on canvas, 1 sgn, 29x21", B/B 3/22/89 .... **4,40**
READ, Thomas Buchanan (American, 1822-1872)
Alice & Andrew McCormick, portrait, oil on canvas, 54x41", C-NY 3/11/88 .... **1,65**
REAM, Carducius Plantagenet (American, 1837-1917)
Claret & Fruit, oil on canvas, sgn, 15x20", C-NY 5/26/88.......... **7,15**
Lion, oil on canvas, sgn, 24x18", C-E 2/1/89 .... **2,86**
Orange, Pear, & Grapes; oil on board laid down on panel, sgn, 10x14", C-NY 9/30/88 .... **4,40**
Pair: Still Lifes of Fruit on a Ledge; oil on canvas, sgn, 1 unfr, 12x10", SBY 5/25/88 .... **11,55**

Peaches, oil on canvas, sgn, 14x18", SBY 6/24/88 3,520
Peaches in a Basket, oil on canvas, sgn, 30x25", WD 4/13/88 6,000
Raspberries (still life), oil on canvas, sgn, 12x14", C-NY 9/30/88 4,400
Still Life of Apples (three apples in grass), oil on board, sgn/titled, 9x12", RAB 8/8/89 2,700
Still Life of Apples & Grapes, oil on board, sgn, 10x12", SBY 9/14/89 3,960
Still Life of Apples in a Bowl, oil on canvas, sgn, 15x20", B/B 3/22/89 4,400
Still Life of Fruit, oil on panel, sgn, 8x12", S/A 2/18/89 1,500
Still Life of Melon, Grapes, & Orange; oil on canvas, sgn, 14x18", C-NY 3/11/88 3,300
Still Life of Plums on the Grass, oil on canvas, 18x26", MAG 4/24/88 2,200
Tray of Grapes, oil on canvas, sgn, 14x18", C-NY 5/25/89 5,500

AM, Morston Constantin (American, 1840-1898)

Still Life of Spilled Cherries, oil on canvas, sgn, 12x10", FAP 11/4/88 3,200

ASER, Wilbur Aaron (American, 1860-1942)

Italian Coastal Town, oil on canvas, sgn, 25x56", B/B 1/11/89 1,870

BAY, Hilla (American, 1890-1967)

Crosses, 1944 (abstract composition); oil on canvas, sgn, 59x79", PHL 11/15/88 5,000
Gracioso, oil on canvas, sgn twice/dtd 1943-45/#d 10, 49x80", C-E 5/9/89 OE 14,300
Improvisation, watercolor/gouache/colored chalks on paper laid down on board, initialed, 9x12", C-E 5/9/89 990
Red & Green, watercolor/gouache/crayon, initialed/dtd 1947, 10x7", SBY 2/14/89 OE 1,540
White Cross (abstract composition), pencil/ink/watercolor/gouache on paper, sgn, 11x13", PHL 11/15/88 1,300

BRY, Gaston (Canadian, 1933-)

Tournant des Saisons, oil on canvas, sgn/dtd 1988, 16x20", FB 10/30/89 OE 1,210

DDIE, Mac Ivor (American, 20th C)

Harvest (cornstalks, distant farmhouse), watercolor on paper, sgn, 21x28", RAB 8/9/88 1,200
Turbulent Sea, oil on masonite, sgn, 26x38", RAB 8/9/88 UE 900
Turbulent Sea (heavy surf against gray rocks), oil on masonite, 26x38", RAB 8/9/88 UE 900

DEIN, Alexander (American, 1912-1965)

Downtown New York, oil on canvas, sgn, 24x30", C-E 6/1/89 770

DFIELD, Edward Willis (American, 1869-1965)

Autumn Haystacks, oil on canvas, sgn, 23x32", C-E 2/1/89 4,400
Barnyard (sunny impressionistic landscape), oil on canvas, sgn/dtd 45, 26x32", C-NY 5/25/89 55,000
Bridge Over the Seine, oil on canvas, sgn/dtd 98, 25x32", C-NY 12/2/88 OE 26,400
Bridges & Barges on the River, oil on canvas, sgn, 28x36", C-NY 9/30/88 11,000
Burning of Center Bridge, oil on canvas, sgn, 30x50", C-NY 12/2/88 93,500
Coastal Town, oil on canvas, sgn, 19x22", C-NY 3/11/88 OE 16,500
Easter Morning, oil on canvas, sgn, 26x32", SBY 5/25/88 37,400
Harbor Decoration (coastal scene), oil on canvas, sgn/dtd 1925/titled, 26x32", SBY 5/24/89 OE 55,000
Monhegan Harbor, oil on canvas, sgn, 1928, 26x32", C-NY 12/2/88 33,000
Two Boats, oil on canvas laid down on masonite, 24x29", C-NY 12/2/88 28,600
Winter Landscape, oil on board, sgn, 14x12", SBY 4/14/89 OE 12,100
Winter Landscape (w/stream), oil on canvas, sgn, 26x32", C-NY 12/2/88 55,000

DMOND, Granville (American, 1871-1935)

Alameda Marshes, oil on canvas, sgn, 20x30", B/B 10/6/88 7,150
Marin Marshes, oil on canvas, sgn/dtd 1913, 20x30", B/B 10/6/88 OE 19,800
Moonlit Seascape, oil on canvas, sgn, 25x30", B/B 10/6/88 OE 30,250
Sailboats Off the Coast, oil on canvas, sgn, 14x18", B/B 10/6/88 7,700
San Pedro Harbor, 1904; oil on canvas, sgn/inscr, unfr, 14x24", B/B 6/15/89 5,500
Spring Landscape, oil on canvas, sgn, 25x30", SBY 1/24/89 OE 23,100

DMORE, Henry (British, 1820-1887)

Marine Scene, oil on canvas, sgn, 8x12", C-E 2/21/89 2,200
Pair: Seascapes; oil on board, sgn/dtd 1887, 13x21", SBY 6/8/88 6,875
Rescue in Stormy Seas, oil on canvas, sgn/dtd 1872, 24x38", SBY 10/24/89 3,850

DON, Odilon (French, 1840-1916)

Birth of Venus (Venus descending from shell), oil on canvas, sgn, 1912, 57x25", SBY 5/9/89 1,650,000
Bouquet de Fleurs, oil on canvas laid down on panel, sgn, 9x6", SBY 11/12/88 OE 99,000
Child in a Sphere of Light, pastel on gray brown paper, sgn, ca 1900, 25x19", SBY 11/16/89 OE 1,155,000
Le Centaure (mythological), oil on panel, sgn, ca 1910, 12x11", C-NY 5/11/88 220,000
Le Christ Couronne (Christ wearing crown of thorns), pencil on paper, initialed, 8x5", SBY 2/18/88 3,300
Le Puits, charcoal on tan paper, sgn, 14x9", C-NY 11/15/88 104,500
Le Reve (The Dream, abstract), oil on pale gray paper, 20x15", SBY 5/11/88 165,000
Le Vase Bleu (The Blue Vase), watercolor/pencil on paper, sgn, ca 1910-12, 8x6", C-NY 5/11/89 57,200
Phaeton's Downfall, charcoal on tan paper, sgn, 21x15", SBY 11/12/88 OE 363,000
Saint Sebastien, pastel on paper, sgn, ca 1910, 26x21", SBY 11/16/89 OE 907,500
Study of Heads: Two Saints; pencil on tan paper, initialed, ca 1870, SBY 2/16/89 OE 12,100
Tete Mystique (Mystical Head), oil on paper laid down on cradled panel, 21x15", SBY 5/10/89 253,000
Trois Vases de Fleurs, pastel on brown paper laid down on stretched paper, sgn, 28x21", SBY 5/10/88 330,000
Vase de Fleurs, pastel on paper mounted on board, sgn on vase, ca 1905, 32x26", SBY 11/15/89 OE 2,310,000

DOUTE, Pierre Joseph (French, 1759-1840)

Albuca Minor Albuca Jaunatre, pencil/watercolor on vellum, sgn, 19x14", C-NY 2/23/89 20,900
Camellia, black chalk/watercolor on vellum, sgn, 10x8", C-NY 1/11/89 6,050
Gladiolus Carneous Glayeul Couleur de Chair, watercolor/pencil on vellum, sgn, 19x13", C-NY 10/26/88 19,800

Iris Martinicensis Iris de la Martinique, pencil/watercolor on vellum, sgn, 19x14", C-NY 2/23/89 13,20
Ixia Miniata Ixia Minium, pencil/watercolor on vellum, sgn, 19x13", C-NY 2/23/89 28,60
Lachenalia Tricolor: Cape Cowslip; watercolor/gouache/pen/gray ink on vellum, sgn, 18x14", C-NY 2/25/88 OE 24,20
Tritoma Media Triotoma Intermediaire, watercolor over traces of pencil on vellum, sgn, 18x13", C-NY 2/23/89 24,20

REDOUTE, Pierre Joseph; circle of (French, 1759-1840)
Pair: Pink Rose with Butterfly; Pale Bluish-Pink Rose; chalk/watercolor, 1 monogramed/dtd 1809, 13x9", C-NY 1/12/88 OE 5,50

REDWOOD, Allen C. (American, 1834-1922)
Battle of Shiloh, Attack on Camp (Civil War); pen/ink on paper, sgn/dtd 84, 10x14", C-E 5/27/88 OE 3,08
Captured by Stonewall Jackson (Civil War), pen/ink on paper, sgn/inscr, 18x12", C-E 5/27/88 OE 1,87
Confederate Sharpshooters, Fredericksburg (Civil War); pen/ink on paper, sgn/dtd 1886, 13x10", C-E 5/27/88 OE 4,95
Confederate Sharpshooters in a Swamp, New Orleans (Civil War); pen/ink, initialed/inscr, 13x11", C-E 5/27/88 OE 2,64
Confederate Trenches, Chesterfield Bridge (Civil War); pen/ink on paper, inscr, 11x15", C-E 5/27/88 OE 1,21
Confederate Troops Preparing To Ford the River (Civil War), tempera on paper, initialed, 11x13", C-E 5/27/88 OE 1,04
Confederate Types (Civil War), pen/ink on paper, inscr, 10x11", C-E 5/27/88 OE 1,87
Dead Confederate Soldier (Civil War), pen/ink on paper, sgn/inscr, unfr, 14x13", C-E 11/30/88 OE 82
In the Trenches (Civil War), watercolor on paper, initialed, 19x14", C-E 5/27/88 44
Steuart's Brigade at Culp's Hill, Gettysburg (Civil War); watercolor on board, initialed/dtd 86, 12x16", C-E 5/27/88 OE 3,85
Talking to an Orderly (Civil War), watercolor on board, initialed/inscr, 17x13", C-E 5/27/88 OE 66

REED, Charles (American, 19th C)
Terrible Decision (Civil War), watercolor on paper laid down on board, sgn/inscr, 10x15", C-E 5/27/88 OE 44

REED, Marjorie (American, 1915-)
Heading for the High Country, oil on canvasboard, sgn, 16x20", B/B 8/10/88 77
Thunderbird (Indians riding at night w/monoplane overhead), oil on artist board, sgn/titled, unfr, 8x10", RAB 1/10/89 UE 15

REED, Scott (American, 20th C)
Untitled, acrylic/wax crayon/mixed media on paper, 48x60", B/B 12/8/88 1,10

REED, W.T. (British, 19th C)
Pair: Fishing Off a Lake; oil on canvas, sgn, 12x18", C-E 10/25/88 1,65

REEDY, Leonard Howard (American, 1899-1956)
Coach Ride, watercolor on paper, sgn, 8x10", C-E 2/3/88 41
Indian Guide, watercolor, sgn, 8x11", PHL 10/28/88 45
Pair: Cheyenne Warriors; Mexican Rides; watercolor/pencil on paper, sgn, 8x11", C-E 6/1/88 71
Pair: Indian Making Smoke Signals; Making Get Away; watercolor/pencil on paper, sgn, 8x11", C-E 6/1/88 88
Pair: Stagecoaches; watercolor on paper, sgn, 9x12", C-E 9/ 15/88 UE 77
Prairie Fire, watercolor, sgn, 8x11", PHL 10/28/88 UE 40
Range, watercolor, sgn, 8x11", LH 10/16/88 32
Rescue, watercolor on paper, sgn, 8x11", C-E 2/3/88 38
Stagecoach, oil on canvas, sgn, 25x30", B/B 5/17/89 UE 1,47

REEVS, George M. (American, 20th C)
Bit of Long Island, watercolor on paper, sgn/dtd 1904, 13x17", C-E 11/30/88 71

REGGIANINI, Vittorio (Italian, 1858-)
Afternoon Concert-Out of Tune; oil on canvas, sgn, 27x36", C-NY 5/24/89 55,00
Green Satin Dress (full-length portrait of woman seated in an interior), oil on canvas, sgn, 22x14", SBY 2/22/89 14,30
Poetry Reading, oil on canvas, sgn, 28x38", C-NY OE 93,50

REGNAULT, Henri Alexandre Georges (French, 1843-1871)
L'Aigle (Eagle), watercolor on paper, sgn/dtd 1857, 9x8", SBY 2/22/89 22,00
Nude Study, oil on cradled panel, sgn, 11x8", SBY 12/9/88 2,31

REGNAULT, Jean Baptiste (French, 1754-1829)
Fortune, pen/gray ink/wash w/touches of brown ink, sgn, 7x5", SBY 1/13/89 60
La Toilette de Venus, oil on canvas, sgn/dtd 1815, 97x81", SBY 6/1/89 OE 825,00

REGNIER, Nicolas (Flemish, 1590-1667)
Bravo Carrying a Musket (portrait), oil on canvas, 25x20", C-NY 1/11/89 14,30

REGNIER, Nicolas; att (Flemish, 1590-1667)
Penitent Saint Mary Magdalene, oil on canvas, unfr, 42x36", C-NY 10/12/89 OE 18,70

REGNIER, Nicolas; circle of (Flemish, 1590-1667)
Saint John the Baptist As a Boy, oil on canvas, 22x17", SBY 4/7/88 3,85

REHDER, Julius Christian (German, 1861-1945)
Self-Portrait (bearded man, bust-length), oil on canvas, sgn/dtd 94, 22x18", B/B 10/9/88 UE 1,10

REHN, Frank Knox Morton (American, 1848-1914)
Breaking Wave, oil on canvas, sgn, 16x28", SBY 9/23/88 1,32
Fruit Still Life, oil on canvas, sgn/dtd 187(?), 11x14", C-NY 9/30/88 2,86
Giant Surge (rocky coast w/crashing waves), oil on canvas, sgn, 25x30", SBY 3/17/88 1,37
Giant Surge (surf crashing on rocks), oil on canvas, sgn, 25x30", SBY 4/14/89 2,20
Pair: Landscape Near the Sea; Sunset Landscape; oil on canvas, sgn/1 dtd 95, unfr, 16x28", SBY 6/24/88 OE 2,09
Pair: Landscape with Tied Boats; Seascape; oil on canvas, 16x23", SBY 3/17/88 2,42
Sailboat at Sunset, oil on canvas, sgn, 16x28", SBY 9/23/88 1,54
Sailing in Rough Seas, oil on canvas, sgn/inscr, 22x36", C-NY 9/30/88 4,18
Seascape with Distant Ships, watercolor gouache on paper, sgn, 14x20", SBY 9/23/88 UE 44
Summer Landscape III, oil on canvas, sgn, 16x25", C-NY 3/11/88 2,42
Sunset Sail (seascape w/ship), oil on canvas, sgn, 16x24", SBY 3/17/88 93
Twilight at Venice, oil on canvas, sgn/dtd 92, unfr, 16x24", SBY 6/24/88 OE 1,98
Venetian Canal, oil on canvas, sgn, unfr, 25x30", SBY 9/23/88 UE 71

'enetian Canal at Night, oil on canvas, sgn, 16x24", SBY 3/17/88 1,100
ICH, Albert (German, 1881-)
The Dandy, oil on panel, sgn/indistinctly dtd, 9x12", B/B 3/17/88 2,200
ICHARDT, Ferdinand (American, 1819-1895)
Harlem River, oil on canvas, sgn/dtd 24 April 1858/titled, 12x18", SBY 3/17/88 3,850
ICHERT, Carl (Austrian, 1836-1918)
Barnyard Friends, oil on panel, sgn, 12x8", B/B 12/8/88 OE 4,125
'our Kittens Toying with Beetles, oil on panel, sgn, 24x18", FAP 4/15/89 OE 8,800
St Bernard, oil on panel, sgn, 8x10", C-E 2/21/89 OE 7,150
The Cynic & the Philosopher, oil on panel, sgn, 6x10", SBY 10/24/89 6,600
ID, Flora M. (British, 19th/20th C)
)oubtful Bargain (figures in market scene), oil on canvas, sgn/dtd, 11x15", PHL 10/28/88 6,500
ID, George Agnew (Canadian, 1860-1947)
'orest Stream with Waterfall, oil on board, sgn/dtd 1892, 14x18", WAD 6/12/89 3,000
.ullaby (mother w/cradled baby), oil on canvas, sgn/dtd 92, 12x16", C-SK 6/9/88 OE 4,090
ID, George Ogilvy (British, 1851-1928)
)n the Coast of Kingsham, oil on canvas, sgn/inscr, 14x21" ,C-E 5/21/88 UE 440
ID, John Robertson (British, 1851-1926)
Surf Casting Off the Rocks, oil on canvas, sgn, 20x15", C-E 2/23/88 1,100
ID, Robert Louis (American, 1862-1929)
Autumn Landscape, oil on canvas, sgn, 25x30", C-NY 5/25/89 66,000
Breezy Day (girl, three-quarter length profile in a landscape), oil on canvas, sgn, 37x34", C-NY 5/25/89 .... '198,000
Iouse on a Lake (Cos Cob), oil on canvas, sgn, 7x14", C-NY 5/25/89 OE 13,200
)ut of My Window (landscape), oil on canvas, sgn, 26x29", SBY 5/24/89 30,800
'lains, oil on panel, sgn, 12x16", C-E 6/1/88 OE 3,300
'ortrait of a Lady with a Cat, pastel on paper, sgn, 26x20", WD 4/13/88 5,500
Quiet Brook in Summer, oil on canvas, 12x16", C-NY 12/2/88 7,150
Ruth (portrait), oil on canvas, 20x16", C-NY 12/2/88 8,800
Silvie (woman seated at a table), oil on board, sgn, 12x16", C-NY 5/26/88 15,400
Willow Castle, Stockbridge, Massachusetts; Home of S Russell (outer door), oil on board, sgn/dtd 1916, 11x8", RAB 8/9/88 1,100
ID, Robert Payton (British, 1859-1945)
Barker (abstract of announcer at side-show act), oil on canvas, sgn twice/dtd 1968/titled, 40x50", SBY 3/17/88 7,150
'eeding the Doves, oil on canvas, sgn/dtd 1897, 25x20", C-E 10/25/88 2,200
Grand Canal, Venice; oil on panel, sgn, 8x11", WAD 6/6/88 600
ID, Stephen (British, 19th C)
.ady in an Interior, oil on canvas, sgn/dtd 1930, 24x18", B/B 12/8/88 2,475
Rehearsal, oil on canvas, sgn/dtd 1934, 31x41", C-E 10/25/88 UE 1,650
IDER, Marcel (French, 1852-)
Reverie in Blue, oil on canvas, sgn, 18x15", SBY 6/8/88 2,530
IFFEL, Charles (American, 1862-1942)
'ebruary Thaw, Silvermine, Connecticut; oil on canvas, sgn/inscr, 34x38", C-NY 3/11/88 OE 13,200
.ate Afternoon Glow, oil on board, sgn twice/inscr/dtd 1933, 20x24", C-NY 9/30/88 6,600
Rainbow After the Storm, oil on canvas, sgn, 20x24", B/B 3/17/88 7,700
Spring in the Mountains, oil on canvas, sgn/dtd 1940, unfr, 34x37", SBY 6/28/89 16,500
Summer in North Wilton, oil on canvas, sgn, 24x28", B/B 3/17/88 7,700
White Horse, oil on board, sgn twice/inscr, 10x10", C-E 11/30/88 1,100
IN, Johan Eimerich (Norwegian, 1827-1900)
Coastal Scene, oil on canvas mounted & cradled on masonite, sgn, 29x64", RWS 5/19/88 2,200
INAGLE, Phillip (British, 1749-1833)
'ointer in a Wooded Landscape, oil on canvas, unfr, 25x28", C-E 5/23/88 3,850
INAGLE, Phillip; manner of (British, 1749-1833)
Coursing, oil on canvas, 21x17", C-E 9/15/88 1,100
INDEL, William George (American, 1871-1948)
.ate Autumn Landscape, no media given, sgn/dtd 1910, 14x16", WG 9/16/88 UE 100
Winter Landscape with Barn in Distance, oil on canvas, sgn/dtd 1913, 14x18", C-E 6/1/88 935
INERT, A.
Boating on a Lake, oil on canvas laid down on masonite, sgn, 22x36", C-E 5/23/88 1,650
INHARDT, Ad (American, 1913-1967)
'16-1955 (solid dark blue canvas), oil on canvas, 1955, 80x42", SBY 10/8/88 60,500
Abstract, oil on canvas, sgn/dtd 1956, 80x50", C-NY 5/3/89 UE 176,000
Abstract Painting, Blue, 1952; oil/acrylic on canvas, sgn/dtd, 24x24", SBY 5/3/89 OE 231,000
Abstract Painting, Blue, 1953; oil on canvas, cardboard backing, sgn/dtd 1953, 20x10", C-NY 2/20/88 OE 49,500
Abstract Painting, 1956 (Diptych); oil on canvas, sgn/dtd 1956, 20x14", SBY 11/9/89 88,000
Abstract Painting, 1962; oil on canvas in artist-made frame, sgn, 24x24", SBY 5/2/89 297,000
Gathering Clouds, oil on canvas, sgn/dtd 81, 9x12", C-E 10/18/89 1,650
ris Mystique (contemporary), oil on canvas, inscr signature/dtd 1957, 44x23", SBY 11/9/89 OE 148,500
'ainting, 1960 (contemporary); oil on canvas, sgn/dtd 1960/titled, 17x15", SBY 11/11/88 OE 115,500
'ainting (solid blue-gray canvas), oil on canvas, sgn/dtd 1960/titled, 30x30", SBY 11/11/88 34,100
Timeless Painting (solid color), oil on canvas with artist's frame, sgn/dtd 1960-65, 60x60", SBY 5/2/89 275,000
Untitled (abstract), oil on canvas, sgn/dtd 48, 16x20", SBY 5/3/89 OE 44,000
Untitled (abstract), oil on canvas, 1947, 40x32", SBY 5/3/88 OE 77,000

Untitled (abstract), watercolor/pen/black ink on paper, sgn/dtd 49, 22x31", C-NY 5/4/88 OE **24,200**

REINHARDT, Louis (Ludwig)(German, -1870)

Cattle & Ducks by a Watering Spot, oil on canvas, sgn, 26x34", C-E 10/26/89 ..... **2,090**
Shepherdess & Her Flock, oil on canvas, sgn, 18x30", C-NY 2/25/88 ..... **4,400**

REINHOLD, Franz (Austrian, 1816-1893)

Outside the Blacksmith's, oil on canvas, sgn, 18x22", C-NY 2/25/88 ..... **7,700**

REINI, Guido; after

Adoration of the Shepherds, oil on canvas, unfr, octagonal, 39x39", SBY 7/12/89 ..... **2,200**

REINIGER, Otto (German, 1863-1909)

Ponds on the Edge of the Woods, oil on board, bears artist's label, 11x16", B/B 6/15/89 ..... **1,045**

REISMAN, Philip (American, 1904-)

The Shoe Peddler, oil on masonite, sgn/dtd 38, 18x14", C-NY 9/28/89 ..... **4,950**

REISS, Lionel S. (American, 1894-)

Winter, Washington Square; oil on canvas, sgn twice/inscr, 17x21", C-NY 9/30/88 UE **1,980**

REISS, Winold (American, 1888-1953)

Walking Bear, Cree Indian; watercolor on paper, sgn, 30x21", SBY 6/28/89 OE **5,775**

REISZ, Frank

Bronx River (snowscape), oil on masonite, sgn, 12x16", C-E 6/1/89 ..... **880**

REMBRANDT, Harmensz (Dutch, 1606-1669)

Adam & Eve, pen/brown ink/dry brush, inscr, 5x5", C-NY 1/12/88 ..... **79,200**
Buildings by the Diemerdijk, pen/brown ink/wash w/corrections in white bodycolor, 4x7", SBY 1/13/89 ..... **610,000**

REMBRANDT, Harmensz; after (Dutch, 1606-1669)

Syndics of the Cloth Hall, oil on canvas, 30x40", C-E 6/1/88 ..... **1,870**

REMBRANDT, Harmensz; att (Dutch, 1606-1669)

King Saul (portrait), oil on panel, 9x8", C-NY 5/31/89 OE **41,800**

REMBRANDT, Harmensz; circle of (Dutch, 1606-1669)

Samson & His Father-in-Law, oil on canvas, 62x52", SBY 6/1/89 ..... **28,600**

REMBRANDT, Harmensz; follower of (Dutch, 1606-1669)

Portrait of a Man Believed To Be Nicolaes Van Bambeek (bust-length), oil on canvas, 23x19", SBY 7/12/89 ..... **3,300**
Samson & Delilah, oil on canvas, 24x19", SBY 10/21/88 ..... **5,500**

REMBRANDT, Harmensz; manner of (Dutch, 1606-1669)

Old Man, Wearing Fur-Lined Coat with Gold Chain; oil on panel, unfr, 9x8", C-NY 1/15/88 OE **1,210**
Portrait of a Man, oil on panel, 11x9", C-E 4/7/88 ..... **1,210**
Portrait of a Man in a Hat & Collar, oil on canvas, 19x15", C-E 6/1/88 ..... **880**
Portrait of Lady, bust-length, wearing cap with pearls & feather; oil on canvas, unfr, 23x18", C-E 6/1/88 ..... **880**

REMBRANDT, Harmensz; school of (Dutch, 1606-1669)

Head of a Woman, oil on canvas laid down, 18x16", FAP 12/8/89 ..... **525**
Portrait of a Man, half-length, wearing black costume with white collar; oil on canvas, 28x22", C-NY 4/8/88 ..... **4,950**

REMINGTON, Frederic (American, 1861-1909)

Candido Ramos, Wolf of the West; India ink/wash on paper, sgn, 16x9", SBY 9/23/88 ..... **15,400**
Cheyenne Warchief, India ink/wash heightened w/white on paper, sgn/inscr Copyright 1899, 21x21", SBY 5/25/88 ..... **60,500**
Mexican Gendarmes Asking the Way, pen/brush/black ink on paper laid down, sgn/dtd 90, 14x23", C-NY 5/25/89 ..... **22,000**
Miners Prospecting for Gold, oil en grisaille on board, sgn/inscr/stamped, 1887, 18x24", SBY 5/25/88 ..... **38,500**
Tumble From the Trail, oil en grisaille on canvas, sgn, 28x18", SBY 5/25/88 ..... **66,000**
Vacquero, oil on panel, sgn, 28x18", SBY 5/25/88 ..... **99,000**
Waneepah (US calvary attack Indians), gouache en grisaille on paper mounted on board, sgn/titled, 15x12", SBY 5/24/89 ..... **9,900**

REMISOFF, Nicolai (American/Russian, 1894-1975)

Group of 6: Ballet Costume Sketches; gouache on paper, initialed, 13x10", B/B 1/11/89 ..... **990**
Russian Picnic, gouache on board, sgn, 20x15", B/B 1/11/89 ..... **935**

RENARD, Emile (French, 1850-1930)

Reclining Nude by a Stream, oil on panel, sgn, 11x15", C-E 5/23/88 UE **880**

RENARD, Paul (French, 19th/20th C)

Left Bank Book Stalls, oil on canvas, sgn, 16x14", B/B 1/11/89 ..... **880**
Pair: Parisian Street Scenes; watercolor on paper, sgn, 7x11", B/B 3/22/89 ..... **4,675**

RENAUDIN, Alfred (French, 1866-)

Luneville, oil on canvas, sgn/dtd Luneville 1922, 28x24", SBY 5/23/89 ..... **18,700**

RENAULT, Charles (French, 1829-1905)

Airplane Over Metz, oil on canvas, sgn, 19x25", WG 9/16/88 UE **300**

RENAULT, Gaston

There Is No Joy in Mudville (draped nude), oil on canvas, sgn/dtd 1880, 86x64", C-E 5/23/88 ..... **3,520**

RENDEUSE, Renier (1684-1754)

Christ on the Cross, red/white chalks, 20x11", SBY 7/12/89 ..... **1,870**

RENDON, Manuel (South American, 20th C)

Abstract, oil on board, sgn, 1957, 24x32", SBY 11/21/88 UE2750 ..... **2,750**

RENE, Jean Jacques (French, 1943-)

En Plein Air (man painting in a landscape), oil on panel, sgn/dtd 76, 12x9", SBY 2/22/89 ..... **3,300**
Italian Village Scene, oil on canvas, sgn, 24x36", LH 10/16/88 ..... **1,800**

RENEN (17th C)

Extensive Landscape with Figures on Horseback & Cattle by a Cottage, oil on canvas, sgn/dtd 1655, 28x39", SBY 4/7/88 OE **18,700**

RENESSE, Constantine; circle of (Dutch, 1626-1680)

Man Holding a Basket of Fish Beside a Still Life of Fish & Peppers on a Table, oil on canvas, 40x34", SBY 10/21/88 ..... **5,225**

NI, Guido (Italian, 1575-1642)
Iead of Christ, black/red/white chalk on gray-blue paper, 15x10", C-NY 1/11/89 OE 17,600
'entitent Saint Peter, oil on canvas, 30x23", SBY 6/3/88 88,000
ibyl Writing, with a Putto; red/black chalk/pen/brown ink, #d 54, 9x8", C-NY 1/12/88 7,700
NI, Guido; after (Italian, 1575-1642)
Iadonna & Child, oil on canvas, 69x49", B/B 4/20/88 3,850
Iary Magdalene (reclining in landscape), oil on canvas, 34x59", B/B 5/17/89 OE 2,475
ibyl (Woman in Turban), oil on canvas, 19x15", C-E 6/1/88 UE 495
NI, Guido; follower of (Italian, 1575-1642)
'leopatra, oil on canvas, 30x24", SBY 10/13/89 2,200
Ioly Family, oil on canvas, 30x25", WD 1/25/89 OE 15,000
NI, Guido; manner of (Italian, 1575-1642)
'hrist Child Asleep on a Cross, oil on canvas, 26x30", C-E 4/7/88 UE 440
nmaculate Conception, oil on canvas laid down on masonite, 54x39", C-E 6/1/88 UE 950
NNER, O.
Vasherwoman by a Village, watercolor heightened w/white, sgn/dtd 1894, 13x9", C-E 10/25/88 UE 550
NOIR, Pierre Auguste (French, 1841-1919)
.nemomes (floral still life), oil on canvas, sgn, 1909, 19x16", SBY 11/11/88 1,210,000
aigneuse (Femme en Jupe Rouge s'Essuyant les Pieds), oil on canvas, sgn, ca 1888, 26x20", SBY 11/11/88 8,525,000
aigneuse Debout (nude bather), charcoal on paper, initialed, 31x13", SBY 5/11/88 OE 66,000
uste de Femme en Corsage Rouge et Chapeau Garni de Fleurs, oil on canvas, sgn, 1914, 18x15", SBY 11/11/88 1,540,000
uste de Jeune Femme de Profil, oil on canvas, stamped initials, 1916, 5x6", SBY 2/16/89 104,500
uste de Jeune Fille (portrait of a young girl), oil on canvas, initialed, ca 1895, 10x7", C-NY 5/11/89 198,000
'laude Renoir Peintre (Renoir's younger son), oil on canvas, stamped signature, 1907, 22x18", SBY 5/10/88 OE 3,190,000
'oco Holding an Orange, pastel, sgn, 1904, 23x18", SBY 5/10/88 OE 962,500
'ouche de Soleil a Douarnenez (sun setting over water at Douarneneg), oil on canvas, sgn, ca 1883, 21x26", C-NY 11/15/88 825,000
eux Jeunes Filles Lisant (portrait of two young girls), pencil on paper, sgn, 17x21", SBY 11/12/88 82,500
eux Roses, oil on canvas, 4x7", C-NY 2/16/89 OE 17,600
nvirons de Paris, Pres de Louveciennes (impressionistic landscape); oil on canvas, initialed, 10x14", C-NY 2/16/89 OE 165,000
'squisse de Fleurs, oil on canvas, stamped, 1913, 9x9", SBY 5/11/88 93,500
'tude de Femme (full-length lady in landscape), oil on canvas, sgn, ca 1890, 50x16", SBY 5/9/89 1,485,000
tude pour Enfants Jouant a la Balle (drawing of girl bent over), black chalk/pastel, initialed, 12x18", C-NY 2/18/88 OE 11,000
'emme au Corsage Bleu (woman in blue dress & hat), pastel on paper, sgn, 1882-83, 24x18", SBY 11/15/89 1,100,000
'emme au Corsage Rose (seated woman in red blouse), oil on canvas, sgn, 1914, 13x10", C-NY 11/15/88 OE 682,000
emme Nue Allongee (reclining nude), oil on canvas, sgn, 6x8", C-NY 5/12/88 OE 181,500
emme Nue Assise et Pommes (seated nude w/apples in foreground), oil on canvas, sgn, ca 1908, 15x11", C-NY 11/15/88 440,000
'emme Nue Couchee (reclining nude), stamped signature, 1915, 11x20", SBY 11/12/88 330,000
euille d'Etudes-Couple Assis, Femme au Chapeau et Petit Garcon; India ink/charcoal/chalk, sgn, 16x12", SBY 11/12/88 OE 60,500
illette au Chien (portrait of young girl & dog), oil on canvas, sgn, ca 1875, 12x9", C-NY 5/11/88 OE 550,000
leure dans un Vase Bleue (flowers in a blue vase), oil on canvas, sgn, 16x14", C-NY 11/15/88 OE 770,000
laieuls au Vase Bleu (still life of gladiolus in blue vase), oil on canvas, sgn, 1884, 26x21", C-NY 5/11/88 1,100,000
eune Femme a l'Ombrelle Japonaise, oil on canvas, sgn, ca 1876, 20x24", SBY 5/10/88 OE 4,840,000
eune Femme d'Essuyant, oil on canvas, 4x8", SBY 5/11/88 38,500
eune Femme dans un Jardin (seated lady in garden), oil on canvas, stamped signature, ca 1916, 16x20", C-NY 11/14/88 OE 1,265,000
eune Femme Decorant Une Poterie (seated nude viewed from behind), oil on canvas, sgn, 1918, 11x10", SBY 11/15/89 1,430,000
eune Fille Arrangeant son Chapeau, pencil on paper laid down on board, initialed, ca 1885, 26x20", C-NY 11/15/88 OE 770,000
'Ombrelle (portrait of woman w/parasol in sunny landscape), oil on canvas, sgn, 1878, 24x20", C-NY 5/11/88 OE 6,600,000
a Cabane aux Aloes (landscape w/shed), oil on canvas, sgn, 9x11", C-NY 5/11/89 242,000
a Femme au Panier de Fleur (lady w/basket of flowers in landscape), oil on canvas, sgn, 50x16", SBY 5/9/89 2,970,000
a Ferme (artist's farm w/figures), oil on canvas, sgn, 1914, 22x26", SBY 5/9/89 OE 1,595,000
a Modiste, sanguine/white chalk on grayish-green paper, ca 1885, 11x19", SBY 10/27/89 522,500
a Petite Maison (The Small House), oil on board, initialed, 5x8", SBY 10/7/88 33,000
andscape with White House, oil on canvas, sgn, 8x16", SBY 5/10/89 OE 187,000
e Jardin ou dans le Parc (figures in a garden), oil on canvas, ca 1875, sgn, 22x26", SBY 5/10/88 OE 6,600,000
e Pichet (impressionistic still life), oil on canvas, stamped signature, ca 1914-19, 10x9", SBY 11/12/88 66,000
e Printemps ou la Conversation (two figures in Renoir's garden), oil on canvas, sgn, 1876, 24x20", SBY 11/11/88 4,840,000
es Alpilles (landscape), oil on canvas, stamped signature, 1902, 8x11", C-NY 11/16/88 88,000
es Amoureux, sanguine heightened w/white on paper laid down on canvas, sgn, 1885, 27x22", SBY 11/16/89 OE 550,000
es Canotieres, black chalk on paper, 12x15", C-NY 11/15/88 49,500
Iaternite (portrait), red crayon/white chalk on paper laid down on canvas, sgn, ca 1885-85, 28x21", SBY 5/10/89 OE 495,000
Iaternite ou Femme Allaitant Son Infant (woman nursing baby), oil on canvas, sgn/dtd 86, 29x21", SBY 5/10/88 8,800,000
Iature Morte aux Fraises (still life of strawberries), oil on canvas, sgn, 10x18", SBY 5/10/89 473,000
Iature Morte aux Peches (still life of peaches), oil on canvas, sgn, ca 1902-04, 8x18", C-NY 11/16/88 176,000
Iature Morte aux Pommes et Grenades, oil on canvas, sgn, 1901, 7x13", SBY 10/27/89 198,000
'aysage, oil on canvas, initialed, 4x7", SBY 2/16/89 60,500
'aysage aux Environs de Cagnes (landscape w/trees), oil on canvas, sgn, 8x11", SBY 5/10/89 OE 154,000
aysage avec Pont (impressionistic landscape), oil on canvas, sgn, ca 1900, 18x22", C-NY 5/11/88 UE 600,000
etite Riviere, oil on canvas, sgn, 12x17", SBY 5/11/88 OE 181,500
'ortrait a la Robe Rose (portrait of lady in red dress), pastel on paper, sgn, ca 1880, 25x20", C-NY 5/11/89 550,000
ortrait d'Enfant, pastel on paper mounted at the edges on board, sgn, ca 1879, 17x12", C-NY 11/15/88 341,000
ortrait de Coco (artist's son), oil on canvas, initialed, ca 1904-05, 7x5", SBY 5/10/89 231,000

Portrait de Femme, oil on canvas, sgn, 1911, 19x15", SBY 11/12/88 OE ... 429,0
Portrait de Femmes, oil on canvas, sgn, 1882, 9x7", C-NY 11/16/88 ... 71,5
Portrait de Madeleine Adam, pastel/pencil on paper, sgn/dtd 87, 24x29", SBY 5/9/89 OE ... 2,860,0
Portrait de Mademoiselle Amelie Dieterle au Chapeau, charcoal on paper, initialed, ca 1896, 20x16", C-NY 5/11/89 ... 495,0
Portrait of Gabrielle (young woman with flowers), oil on canvas, sgn, 18x22", SBY 11/15/89 ... 4,620,0
Roses avec un Petit Paysage, oil on canvas, ca 1912, 5x10", SBY 10/7/88 OE ... 29,7
Seated Couple, oil on canvas, sgn, 13x10", SBY 5/9/89 ... 3,080,0
Spring Landscape, oil on canvas, initialed, 5x7", B/B 6/9/88 ... 13,2
Study of Children's Heads, black chalk on paper laid down on board, initialed, 1888, 12x17", C-NY 5/11/89 OE ... 26,4
Tete de Jeune Fille (head of young girl in profile), oil on canvas, sgn, 1878, 10x9", SBY 5/10/89 OE ... 880,0
Tete de Jeune Fille (portrait of young woman, bust-length), oil on canvas, sgn, 13x12", C-NY 5/11/88 OE ... 715,0
Tete de Jeune Fille (portrait of young woman, bust-length), oil on canvas, sgn, 1888, 16x13", C-NY 5/11/88 ... 792,0
Torse Nu de Femme (nude torso of a woman), oil on canvas, sgn, 9x7", SBY 11/12/88 OE ... 264,0
Trois Jeunes Filles au Jardin, pastel on laid paper, sgn w/initial R, ca 1895, 9x12", SBY 1/12/88 ... 88,0

RENOUARD, George (American, 19th/20th C)
Cleaves St Rockport, oil on canvas, sgn, 20x24", RWS 5/12/89 ... 1,1
Summer Scene, oil on canvas, sgn, 18x22", RWS 11/10/89 ... 4

RENOUF, Edda (American/Mexican, 1943-)
Manhattan Dawn No 1 (abstract), oil stick/red felt-tip pen on paper, sgn/dtd 1984, 42x30", C-NY 2/14/89 ... 3,3

RENSHAN, Su (Chinese, 1814-1849?)
Figures in Landscape (hanging scroll), ink/lt color on paper, 41x16", SBY 5/31/89 ... 1,3
Tao Yuanming Beneath a Pine (hanging scroll), ink on paper, sgn, 40x23", SBY 5/31/89 ... 3,3

REPIN, Ilya Efimovich (Russian, 1844-1930)
Family Portrait: The Artist's Daughter, Tatyana, & Her Family; oil on canvas, sgn in cyrillic, 1905, 35x71", SBY 5/23/89 ... 1,100,0
Peasant with a Staff-The Wanderer; oil on canvas, sgn, 14x11", C-NY 5/25/88 ... 3,0
Portrait of a Lady in a Yellow & Black Gown Adorned with Lilies...; oil on canvas, sgn/dtd 1901, 46x25", C-L 10/8/88 OE ... 83,6
Portrait of a Man, oil on canvas, sgn, 14x12", WD 5/5/88 ... 4,6
Portrait of a Peasant, oil on canvas laid down on board, sgn in cyrillic, 26x19", SBY 10/24/89 ... 8,8
Study of a Lady for Painting, a Parisian Cafe; no media given, sgn/dtd 1875, 14x10", C-L 10/8/88 ... 29,7

REPIN, Ilya Efimovich; after (Russian, 1844-1930)
Mongal Warriers, oil on canvas, 38x49", C-E 2/23/88 ... 1,7

RESCHI, Pandolfo (Polish, 1643-1699)
Landscape with Horseman Talking & Peasants by a Road, oil on canvas, 40x55", SBY 4/7/89 OE ... 25,3
Saint Bruno in the Wilderness, oil on canvas, 28x22", SBY 4/7/88 ... 16,5

RESIKA, Paul (American, 1928-)
Early Evening, oil on canvas, sgn/dtd 1967, 13x13", C-NY 6/17/89 ... 7
Figure Studying, pastel on gray paper, sgn, 12x9", C-NY 3/11/88 ... 5
Van Campers From the Delaware, pastel on paper, sgn, 10x13", C-NY 3/11/88 ... 7

RESNICK, Milton (American, 1917-)
Emil (abstract), oil on canvas, sgn/dtd 1960, 71x50", SBY 2/19/88 ... 34,1
Hawkeye #13 (abstract), acrylic on paper mounted on board, ca 1973, 50x38", C-NY 2/20/88 ... 3,8
Newspaper (abstract), oil on paper laid down on board, sgn/dtd 1959, 31x23", SBY 5/3/89 ... 13,2
Prospect (abstract), oil on canvas, sgn/dtd 1959, 50x40", SBY 2/15/89 OE ... 28,6
Queens, oil on paper mounted on board, sgn, 21x27", SBY 11/9/89 OE ... 23,1
Red, Green, & Black (abstract); oil on paper laid down on composition board, sgn/dtd 1959, 27x20", SBY 5/3/89 ... 13,2
Return (abstract), oil on canvas, sgn, 1960, 84x53", SBY 10/8/88 OE ... 58,3
Straws, oil on cardboard, sgn/dtd 1982, 40x30", C-E 11/17/88 ... 2,2
Unicorn (abstract), oil on canvas, sgn/dtd 1959, 50x40", SBY 2/15/89 OE ... 33,0
Untitled (abstract), oil on board, sgn twice/dtd 1958, 18x18", C-E 5/9/89 OE ... 6,6
Untitled (abstract), oil on canvas, sgn/dtd 1983, unfr, 60x80", C-NY 5/4/88 ... 22,0
Untitled (abstract), oil on canvas, sgn/dtd 56, 37x41", SBY 10/8/88 OE ... 26,4
Untitled (abstract), oil on canvas, sgn/dtd 59, 35x23", SBY 10/5/89 ... 11,0
Untitled (abstract), oil on canvas, sgn/dtd 67, 63x37", C-NY 2/20/88 ... 12,1
Untitled (abstract), oil on paper, sgn/dtd 1975, 30x22", SBY 10/5/88 ... 2,2
Untitled (abstract), oil on paper, 1966, 30x22", C-NY 10/4/89 ... 4,4
Untitled (abstract), oil on paper laid down on board, sgn/dtd 57, 19x19", SBY 10/7/89 ... 7,1
Untitled (abstract), oil on paper mounted on board, sgn/dtd 55, 16x20", SBY 10/5/89 ... 13,2

RESTOUT, Jean the younger (French, 1692-1768)
Diana & Endymion, oil on canvas, oval, 37x31", C-NY 6/2/88 OE ... 9,9
Saint Paul Healing the Sick at Ephesus, oil on canvas, 32x26", C-NY 4/8/88 ... 3,8

RESTOUT, Jean the younger; att (French, 1692-1768)
Saint Jerome, oil on canvas, 24x20", C-NY 10/12/89 OE ... 26,4

RETBERG, Ralf Leopold
Set of 6: Portrait Studies; pencil on paper, 3 sgn/4 dtd, 10x8", C-E 10/25/88 UE ... 2

RETH, Alfred (French, 1884-1966)
Restaurant Terrace at Antibes, oil on canvas, sgn/dtd 92, 32x26", WD 5/5/88 ... 10,0
Two Figures, pencil on paper laid down on board, sgn/dtd 46, 23x15", C-E 5/9/89 OE ... 4,4

RETTIG, John (American, 1860-1932)
Dutch Woman in an Interior, oil on canvas, sgn/dtd 25, 18x15", SBY 9/23/88 ... 9

RETTIG, Martin (American, 20th C)
Peonies (in tall white vase), oil on board, sgn, 14x12", RAB 8/9/88 ... 6

Zinnias (in tall green vase), oil on board, sgn, 15x12", RAB 8/9/88 700
TZ, Eudes; see De Retz
UTERDAHL, Henry (American, 1871-1925)
Battle at Sea, watercolor/gouche on board, sgn/inscr Copyright 1898, C-E 2/23/88 880
Off Key West, watercolor on paper, sgn, copyright 1898 by Truth Co, 14x29", WL 5/20/88 800
VELL, William (Canadian, 1830-1902)
On the Humber River, North of Baby Point; watercolor, sgn/dtd 1896, 24x40", WAD 6/12/89 1,100
Pair: On the Sisters Islands; sgn/dtd 1898, 9x3", WAD 11/30/89 160
VERON, Armando (Venezuelan, 1890-1954)
Juanita Sentada (impressionistic portrait), gouache on paper laid down, sgn/dtd 37, 35x23", C-NY 11/21/89 26,400
La Mujer del Rio (seated nude), oil on canvas, sgn/dtd 39, 52x57", C-NY 5/17/89 OE 143,000
Mujer Sentada (La Maja), oil/charcoal/sanguine on burlap laid down, sgn, ca 1948, 34x34", C-NY 11/21/89 26,400
Playa de Naiguata (contemporary depiction of beach & palm trees), oil on canvas, sgn, 1924, 20x29", C-NY 11/21/89 OE 154,000
Vista del Litoral (view of the coast), oil on burlap, sgn, 27x41", C-NY 5/18/88 42,900
YES, Jesus (Mexican, 20th C)
Floral Still Life, oil on paper, 28x19", B/B 1/11/89 660
YMANN, J.
Pair: Arabs by a Campsite; Arabs Outside a Village Wall; oil on canvas, sgn, 8x20", C-E 10/25/88 1,650
YNA, Antonio (Spanish, 1862-1937)
Church of the Frairi, Venice; oil on canvas, sgn, 13x29", NA 2/24/89 5,500
Grand Canal, oil on canvas, sgn, 13x30", lot 41, WD 11/16/88 OE 30,000
Grand Canal, oil on canvas, sgn/inscr Venezia, 13x30", lot 153, SBY 10/24/89 44,000
Grand Canal, Venice; oil on canvas, sgn, 12x20", lot 91, WD 5/5/88 OE 9,750
Persian Market, oil on canvas, sgn/inscr Roma, 10x20", C-NY 2/23/89 OE 26,400
Venetian Canal, oil on canvas, sgn/inscr, 14x30", C-E 5/23/88 OE 20,900
Venetian Canal & Palazza, oil on panel, sgn, 11x7", WAD 6/6/88 2,000
Venetian Canal Scene, oil on panel, sgn, 13x8", C-E 2/21/89 OE 8,250
YNAUD, Marius (French, 19th C)
Sailboats at Sea, oil on canvas, sgn, 22x15", C-E 2/23/88 1,320
YNOLDS, Alan (British, 1926-)
Little Drawing, watercolor/brush/black ink on paper, sgn/dtd 53/#37, 6x8", C-E 11/17/88 OE 1,760
YNOLDS, Charles H. (American, 20th C)
Approaching Storm (wooded mountain landscape), oil on canvas, sgn, 30x26", SLK 9/26/88 150
Southwest American Indian Pueblo Scene, watercolor, sgn, 16x20", SLK 9/29/88 200
YNOLDS, James E. (American, 1926-)
Diamond-A Cowboy, oil on masonite, sgn twice/copyrighted/dtd 1984, 24x36", SBY 9/23/88 OE 27,500
Old Way, oil on masonite, sgn twice/copyrighted/titled/dtd 84, 30x48", SBY 9/23/88 OE 33,000
Working on the Gray, oil on masonite, sgn twice/dtd 1985, titled, 30x43", SBY 9/23/88 OE 16,500
YNOLDS, Joshua (British, 1723-1792)
Portrait of a Lady in Pink Said To Be Mrs Elizabeth Sheridan, oil on canvas, in a painted oval, 29x24", SBY 1/12/89 24,200
Portrait of Anne, Countess Winterton, holding a fan, in a landscape; oil on canvas, 50x40", C-NY 10/20/88 OE 39,600
Portrait of Captain Sir Robert Salusbury Cotton, half-length; oil on canvas, in painted oval, 30x25", SBY 4/7/88 16,500
Portrait of Miss Anne Mead, oil on canvas, 30x24", SBY 10/21/88 8,800
YNOLDS, Joshua; after (British, 1723-1792)
Portrait of a Gentleman Said To Be the Archbishop Robinson, half-length; oil on canvas, 50x40", C-E 4/7/88 UE 1,100
Portrait of a Lady of Rank, oil on canvas, 36x28", WG 9/16/88 UE 400
Portrait of Miss Barbara Montgomery, oil on canvas, ca 1757-88, 30x25", SBY 6/1/89 7,150
YNOLDS, Joshua; att (British, 1723-1792)
Portrait of a Gentleman in Red, oil on canvas, 30x25", B/B 5/17/89 1,210
YNOLDS, Joshua; circle of (British, 1723-1792)
Portrait of a Boy, half-length, wearing a pink Van Dyke costume; oil on canvas, 24x20", SBY 4/7/88 OE 5,775
Portrait of John Manners, Marquis of Granby, stormy landscape in the distance; oil on canvas, 89x44", SBY 10/21/88 UE 4,400
Portrait of Samuel Foote, wearing gray coat & gold brocaded waistcoat; oil on canvas, 48x39", SBY 10/21/88 3,300
YNOLDS, Joshua; follower of (British, 1723-1792)
Portrait of a Gentleman Believed To Be Admiral Barrington (half-length), oil on canvas, 30x25", SBY 7/12/89 990
Portrait of a Lady, oil on canvas, 30x25", SBY 6/8/88 1,100
YNOLDS, Joshua; manner of (British, 1723-1792)
Portrait of a Man in Pinks (half-length), oil on canvas, 30x25", C-E 2/16/89 715
YNOLDS, Joshua; school of (British, 1723-1792)
Evangelist, oil on canvas, 30x25", C-NY 4/8/88 4,180
Portrait of a Lady Said To Be the Honorable Mrs Stanhope, oil on canvas, 25x31", C-NY 4/6/89 1,320
YNOLDS, Joshua; studio of (British, 1723-1792)
Portrait of the Hon Leicester, standing three-quarter length, wearing white dress...; oil on canvas, 30x25", C-NY 4/6/89 7,150
YNOLDS, Thomas (American, 1927-)
Old Salt (man in weathered cap & overalls stands by old white dory), watercolor on paper, sgn, 12x18", RAB 8/9/88 600
YNOLDS, Wellington Jarrard (American, 1866-)
Dutchmaid Among the FLowers, oil on board, sgn, 20x30", B/B 9/15/88 1,100
YNTJENS, Henrich Engelbert (Dutch, 1817-1859)
Discussion, oil on panel, sgn, 16x13", C-E 5/23/88 3,300
Entertaining Evening, oil on panel, sgn/dtd 1861, 14x19", C-E 2/23/88 1,760
Interesting Story (gathering of ladies & gentlemen), oil on panel, sgn, 11x15", C-E 2/21/89 3,850

Letter (group around table in elaborate interior), oil on board, sgn/dtd 1892, 16x13", RAB 8/9/88 2,000
Une Lecture Moderne, oil on panel, sgn/inscr, 4x5", C-E 10/25/88 UE 550
18th-Century Salon with Ladies & Gentleman Around a Table Enjoying a Game of Chess, oil on canvas, sgn, SLK 2/12/88 1,700

REZIA, Felice A. (French, 19th/20th C)
Church Interior, oil on panel, sgn, 10x14", B/B 1/11/89 825

REZNIKOFF, M.
Head of a Clown, watercolor on paper, sgn, unfr, 18x13", C-E 2/16/88 22

RHEAME, Jeanne (Canadian, 1915-)
Still Life with Mask, Fruit & Flowers; watercolor, sgn/dtd 1956, 33x27", FB 5/28/89 1,000

Rhenish School (17th C)
Judith with the Head of Holofernes, oil on canvas, 29x21", WD 10/19/88 OE 7,000

RHODES, George M. (American, 20th C)
Untitled, figure in winter landscape; watercolor, sgn/dtd 1893, 27x14", SLK 2/11/89 275

RHOMBERG, Hanno (German, 1820-1869)
Portrait of a Young Lady in White, oil on canvas, sgn/dtd 1845, 34x27", RWS 12/10/88 700

RHYS, Oliver (British, fl 1876-1893)
Daydreaming, oil on canvas, sgn, 43x34", C-E 11/30/88 OE 12,100
Interesting Story, oil on canvas, 22x30", WAD 6/6/88 2,600
On a Grecian Balcony, oil on canvas, sgn, 24x12", SBY 6/8/88 2,750

RIBAK, Louis (American, 1902-)
Taos Encampment at Night, oil on canvas, sgn, 12x18", SBY 9/14/89 1,650
Taos View, oil on canvas, sgn, 14x21", SBY 9/14/89 1,650

RIBALTA, after
Saint Francis Being Crowned by Christ Upon the Cross, oil on canvas, unfr, 34x23", C-NY 4/6/89 1,980

RIBCOWSKY, see De Ribcowsky

RIBERA, Jusepe; see De Ribera

RIBOT, Germain Theodore (French, 1830-1893)
Still Life of Delft Bowl with Fruit & Orange Peel, oil on canvas, sgn, 12x22", RWS 8/12/89 OE 85,200
Still Life of Vase of Flowers & Fruit, oil on panel, sgn, 17x15", C-NY 10/25/89 OE 49,500
Vase de Fleurs, oil on canvas, sgn, 24x20", RWS 8/12/89 OE 6,250

RIBOT, Theodule Augustin (French, 1823-1891)
Christ Breaking Bread, black chalk on brown paper, sgn/partial wm, 9x7", C-NY 10/25/89 1,100
Deposition, oil on canvas, sgn, 14x18", SBY 2/22/89 5,500
Nature Morte, oil on canvas, sgn, 21x37", SBY 10/24/89 OE 17,600

RICCI, Alfredo (Italian, 1864-1889)
Pair: Fishermen (w/baskets & barefoot helper w/water jug & pail); oil on wood panel, sgn, unfr, 12x7", DM 3/14/88 UE 1,000

RICCI, Danti (Italian, 1879-)
Interior View of Cathedral, watercolor on paper laid down on canvas, 28x33", FAP 4/15/89 248

RICCI, E.
Musician, oil on canvas, sgn, 12x16", C-E 5/23/88 880

RICCI, M.
Off to Market, oil on panel, 13x7", DM 1/15/88 1,750

RICCI, Marco; circle of (Italian, 1676-1729)
Hebrew Doctors in the Temple, oil on canvas, unfr, 24x33", C-NY 10/12/89 OE 12,650

RICCI, Marco; manner of (Italian, 1676-1729)
Pair: Landscapes with Figures by Streams; oil on canvas, 35x13", SBY 10/13/89 5,500

RICCI, Marco; school of (Italian, 1676-1729)
Figures Below a Monastery in a Mountainous River Landscape, oil on canvas, 11x27", C-NY 10/20/88 2,860
Hearders & Their Flocks Resting on a Mountainous Path, oil on canvas, 13x11", C-E 6/1/88 2,200

RICCI, Pio (Italian, -1919)
Bouquet, oil on canvas, sgn, 26x18", C-NY 5/25/88 11,000
Proposition, oil on canvas, sgn, 18x14", C-NY 5/25/88 OE 11,000
The Suitor, oil on canvas, sgn, 18x15", LH 5/15/88 4,200

RICCI, Pio; att (Italian, -1919)
Recital (musicians in elegant attire), oil on canvas, bears signature, 29x42", C-E 2/21/89 2,860

RICCI, Sebastiano (Italian, 1659-1734)
Cinncinatus, oil on canvas, unfr, 21x23", C-NY 1/11/89 46,200
Last Supper, oil on canvas, 29x50", C-NY 1/11/89 OE 209,000
Martydom of a Female Saint (Design for a Ceiling), black chalk/pen/brown ink/brown wash, shaped, 21x15", C-NY 1/11/89 2,860

RICCI, Sebastiano; att (Italian, 1659-1734)
Madonna & Child in Glory with a Guardian Angel Rescuing a Child From the Devil, oil on canvas, 36x24", C-NY 10/20/88 5,500

RICCI, Sebastiano; school of (Italian, 1659-1734)
Discovery of Antiope by Jupiter, oil on canvas, 30x25", C-NY 4/8/88 3,300

RICCIARDI, Caesare (American, 1892-)
Autumn Landscape, oil on canvas, sgn/dtd 54, 34x27", FAP 12/8/89 UE 200
Old Grist Mill, oil on canvas, sgn/dtd 54, 24x36", FAP 12/8/89 275
Summer Landscape Roxborough, oil on canvas, sgn/dtd 57, 28x36", FAP 4/15/89 330

RICCIARDI, Oscar (Italian, 1864-)
Venetian Canal Scene, oil on panel, sgn, 16x11", B/B 12/8/88 990

RICE, Henry W. (American, 1853-1934)
Pair: Across Highlands to Distant Sea; Summer House by the Sea (landscape); watercolor on paper, sgn, 8x12", RWS 3/16/89 325

HARD, N.L.

andscape with Trees, oil on canvas, sgn, 14x18", C-E 6/28/88 UE 50

HARD, Rene (Canadian, 1895-1982)

aie St Paul, oil on board, sgn, 16x20", FB 5/28/89 2,100

aie St Paul, oil on board, sgn, 16x20", FB 5/28/89 3,400

aie St Paul, oil on board, sgn, 20x26", FB 10/17/88 5,000

aie St Paul, oil on board, sgn/dtd 1971, 16x20", FB 5/28/89 4,600

aie St Paul (coastal scene), oil on board, sgn, 9x12", FB 5/28/89 1,600

ap aux Corbeaux, oil on board, sgn, 16x18", FB 10/17/88 2,800

ncampment, ink drawing, sgn, 13x14", FB 4/25/88 900

ncampment by the River, oil on board, sgn, 18x24", FB 10/30/89 4,620

ncampment by the River with View of Mountains, oil on board, sgn, 24x30", FB 5/28/89 11,500

xpedition de l'Ungava, Mission Avec Jacques Rousseau; oil on board, sgn/dtd 1957, 16x20", FB 10/30/89 4,840

andscape with Trees, oil on board, sgn, 10x12", FB 5/28/89 1,300

Iountain Majesty, oil on board, sgn, 32x34", FB 10/30/89 9,350

ointe du Lac, oil on board, sgn, 41x48", FB 10/30/89 8,250

uebec Village Scene, oil on board, sgn, 20x24", FB 10/30/89 OE 12,100

cene de Nord du Quebec, oil on board, sgn, 34x72", FB 10/30/89 7,700

te-Rosa sur le Saguenay, oil on board, sgn, 12x16", FB 4/25/88 2,000

iew of Farm in Winter, oil on board, sgn, 18x24", FB 5/28/89 2,600

ue Des Hauteurs de Bagotville, sur le Saguenay; oil on board, sgn/dtd 1945, 10x14", FB 10/30/89 OE 3,960

Vinter Encampment Scene (man, dog & sled), oil on board, sgn, ca 1970, 47x40", FB 10/17/88 17,000

HARDS, Anna Marie (American, 1870-1952)

oung Woman Daydreaming, watercolor, sgn/dtd 97, 12x10", LH 5/15/88 OE 1,150

HARDS, Frederick; see De Berg Richards

HARDS, George Mather (American, 1880-)

ocky Shore, Newport (waves crashing on rocky shore); oil on canvas, sgn/dtd 05, 18x28", RWS 9/29/88 UE 500

HARDS, W. (British, 19th C)

ishing by a Lake in the Late Afternoon, oil on canvas, sgn, 20x30", FAP 4/15/89 1,045

HARDS, William Trost (American, 1833-1905)

Snow-covered Trees, oil on canvas laid down on board, sgn/dtd 1866, 18x14", C-NY 9/28/89 OE; $176,000

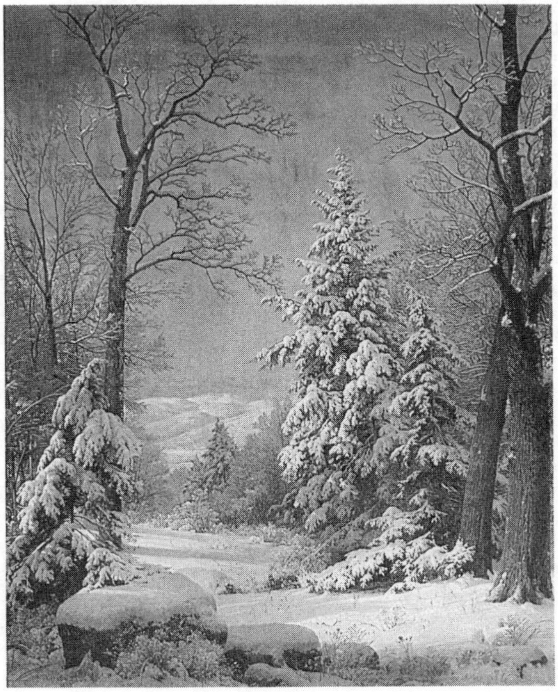

n Apple, watercolor on paper, sgn, 6x6", SBY 6/24/88 3,850

eyond the Breakers (seascape), oil on board, sgn, 10x19", SBY 9/14/89 4,400

reaking Waves, oil on canvas, sgn, 8x14", WD 4/13/88 5,000

rigantine Beach, oil on canvas, sgn/dtd 1900, 30x52", SBY 6/24/88 OE 25,300

oastal Landscape, watercolor on paper, sgn/dtd 1872, 15x28", RWS 5/12/89 OE 17,000

oastal Scene, oil on canvas laid down on board, sgn, 9x16", C-E 10/18/89 3,850

ows by the Seashore, watercolor on paper, sgn, 5x9", SBY 3/17/88 OE 4,400

rashing Surf (seascape), oil on canvas, sgn/dtd 03, 25x20", SBY 3/17/88 7,700

uck Pond, watercolor/gouache on paper laid down on board, ca 1865, 5x10", C-NY 3/11/88 4,400

aston Point, Newport (waves crashing on rocks); watercolor/gouache on board, sgn/dtd 90, 20x15", C-E 2/1/89 3,300

uropean Coastal Scene, pencil on paper, sgn, 5x8", RAB 3/27/89 750

ventide, oil on board, bears inscription/titled, 6x9", SBY 6/24/88 1,650

Homage to the Sea, watercolor/pencil on paper laid down on board, sgn/dtd 1882, 10x15", C-NY 3/11/88 OE 12,100
Kettle Bottom Rock, Narragansett Bay; watercolor on board, sgn/dtd 90, 12x24", C-NY 9/30/88 3,850
Landscape in Chester County, Pennsylvania; oil on board, 10x20", SBY 1/24/89 1,870
Moonlight Reflections, oil on paper laid down on canvas, sgn, 11x23", C-NY 9/30/88 11,000
Morntide, oil on board, sgn/titled, 6x9", SBY 6/24/88 2,750
Near Rough Point, Newport, Rhode Island; watercolor/gouache on paper, sgn/inscr/dtd 1876, 9x15", SBY 5/25/88 OE 16,500
New Jersey Coast, oil on canvas, sgn/inscr/dtd 1874, 20x39", SBY 5/25/88 71,500
Newport (coastal scene), oil on canvas, sgn/dtd 1874, 14x20", WD 10/5/88 UE 3,500
Noontide, oil on panel, sgn/bears inscription, 5x9", SBY 6/24/88 4,125
Passing Clouds (stormy seascape), watercolor on paper laid down on board, sgn, 35x25", C-NY 9/28/89 8,250
Path in the Forest, oil on panel, sgn/dtd Phil, 1865, 18x14", C-NY 9/28/89 OE 121,000
Rocky Coast, watercolor/pencil/Chinese white on paper laid down on board, sgn/dtd 91, 26x20", C-E 2/3/88 2,090
Seascape, oil on canvas, sgn, 20x30", SBY 1/24/89 OE 20,900
Seascape, oil on canvas, sgn/dtd 1889, 48x36", SBY 5/24/89 29,700
Seascape, oil on canvas, sgn/dtd 91, 20x30", RAB 8/8/89 4,500
Seascape, oil on panel, sgn/dtd 99, 6x10", SBY 9/23/88 3,300
Seascape, watercolor on paper, sgn/dtd 90, 18x32", C-E 6/1/88 3,850
Seascape with Distant Ship, watercolor on paper, initialed/sgn/dtd 91, 12x24", SBY 6/24/88 4,125
Stormy Seas, watercolor heightened w/white, sgn, 34x25", C-SK 5/25/89 3,630
Summer Landscape with Figures Boating on a Pond, oil on canvas, sgn, 11x8", SBY 4/14/89 6,600
Sunlit Clouds & Sea, oil on canvas, sgn/dtd 97, 34x60", C-NY 5/26/88 44,000
Waves Breaking on the Rocks, oil on canvas, sgn/dtd 93, 23x44", B/B 6/9/88 18,700
Yellow Carn of Cornwall (seascape w/shoreline), oil on canvas, sgn/dtd 1879, 25x45", C-NY 12/2/88 46,200

RICHARDS, William Trost; att (American, 1833-1905)
Coastal Scene, oil on canvas, sgn/dtd 1902, 22x36", SBY 6/24/88 5,225

RICHARDSON, Francis Henry (American, 1859-1934)
Return to the Fold (shepherd & sheep), pastel on brown paper mounted on board, sgn/dtd 1885, 16x20", RWS 3/31/88 500

RICHARDSON, Jonathan (British, 1665-1745)
Portrait of a Lady Said To Be Lady Mary Wortley Montague, oil on canvas, 49x39", SBY 12/9/88 2,860

RICHARDSON, Louis H. (American, 1853-1923)
Landscape with Birches & Marsh, oil on canvas, sgn/dtd 1917, 25x30", RWS 11/3/88 OE 3,800
New Moon (landscape), oil on canvas, sgn, 13x24", RAB 8/8/89 UE 500

RICHARDSON, Mary Curtis (American, 1848-1931)
Portrait of a Child with a Pacifier, oil on canvas, sgn/dtd 1915, B/B 1/11/89 UE 660

RICHARDSON, Thomas Miles Jr. (British, 1813-1890)
Above Lake Maggiorre, watercolor, initialed, ca 1843, 13x9", SWN 6/15/89 825
Day's Catch, watercolor heightened w/white on paper, sgn, 15x10", SBY 12/9/88 OE 1,980
Figure With a Cart on a Track, pencil/watercolor heightened with bodycolor, initialed, 13x9", PHL 6/16/88 UE 275

RICHARDSON, Thomas Miles Jr.; manner of (British, 1813-1890)
Alpine Lake, watercolor on paper, initialed/dtd 1851, 9x13", FAP 4/15/89 UE 385

RICHARDT, Ferdinand (American, 1819-1895)
Landscape with Distant Train (possibly San Francisco, Oakland Bay area ca 1875), oil on canvas, sgn, 13x22", SBY 9/14/89 8,800

RICHE, Adele (French, 1791-)
Chinese Primrose in a Pot, watercolor heightened w/white, sgn, 12x10", C-NY 2/25/88 440

RICHER, Wilhelm (19th C)
Armor, oil on board, sgn/dtd 1852, unfr, 10x14", C-E 6/28/88 264

RICHERT, Charles Henry (American, 1880-)
Autumn Trees, oil on canvasboard, sgn, 14x11", RWS 9/8/89 UE 125
Country Cabin, Sunset; oil on canvasboard, sgn, 8x10", RWS 9/8/89 375
Dunes of West Barnstable, oil on cardboard, sgn, 8x10", RAB 3/27/89 UE 125
Farm Scene (pastoral scene w/farm in mid-ground), watercolor on paper, sgn, 15x20", RWS 9/29/88 UE 125
House by the Sea, watercolor on paper, sgn, 15x20", RAB 8/9/88 UE 250
House by the Sea (old house, dock exposed by low tide, wooded bank), watercolor on paper, sgn, 15x20", RAB 8/9/88 UE 250
In the Country (weathered house in a field near a stand of trees), watercolor on paper, sgn, 15x20", RAB 8/9/88 300
Landscape-Farmhouse in Spring; oil on canvasboard, sgn, 14x18", RWS 3/16/89 UE 300
Mountain Reflection, watercolor on paper, sgn, 15x20", RWS 3/16/89 275
Overlooking the Charles River (bare trees by river, village beyond), watercolor on paper, sgn, 15x20", RWS 3/31/88 425
Red Cottages, Harbor Side; watercolor on paper, sgn, 15x20", RWS 5/19/88 UE 375
Still Life with Pumpkin Squash (vegetables & cooking pot on table), oil on canvas, sgn, 20x24", RWS 9/29/88 450

RICHET, Leon (French, 1847-1907)
Au Bords de la Riviere (river landscape w/figures), oil on canvas, sgn, 12x18", C-E 2/21/89 2,640
Faggot Gatherer in a Landscape, oil on canvas laid down on board, sgn, 17x16", C-NY 10/25/89 9,350
Faggot Gatherer in a Windswept Landscape, oil on canvas, sgn, 33x53", SBY 2/22/89 8,800
French Landscape, oil on canvas, sgn, 13x22", DM 1/15/88 3,750
Paysage de Riviere au Crepuscule, oil on canvas, sgn, 23x32", SBY 10/24/89 8,800
Return with the Harvest, oil on canvas, sgn/indistinctly dtd 1881, 40x30", B/B 5/17/89 UE 1,870
River Landscape at Sunset, oil on canvas, sgn, 17x26", SBY 6/8/88 1,980

RICHET, Leon; att (French, 1847-1907)
Landscape with Figures, oil on panel, 15x22", SBY 7/12/89 1,320

RICHEY, Rik (American, 20th C)
Untitled 1988, oil on paper, 60x8", B/B 12/8/88 330

ICHIR, Herman (Belgian, 1866-)
Elegie, oil on canvas, sgn twice/inscr, 54x43", C-NY 2/25/88 ... 9,900
ICHMOND, Agnes M. (American, 1870-1964)
Children Shucking Corn, oil on canvas, sgn, 24x30", SBY 5/24/89 ... 13,200
Fawn at the Water's Edge, oil on canvas, sgn, 18x24", WD 10/5/88 UE ... 2,400
ICHMOND, Leonard (British, 1965-)
Brentford Bridge, pastel on gray paper, sgn/dtd 1914, 9x14", B/B 4/20/88 ... 935
ICHTER, A. (German, 19th C)
Untitled, ships in high seas passing near marker; pastel, sgn/indisctinctly dtd Paris, 24x39", SLK 4/7/89 ... 650
ICHTER, Edouard Frederic Wilhelm (French, 1844-1913)
Harem Dancer, oil on canvas, sgn, 19x12", WAD 6/6/88 ... 9,000
ICHTER, Gerhard (German, 1932-)
Fingermatereien (abstract), oil on paper mounted on canvas, 1971, 16x16", SBY 10/5/89 OE ... 17,600
Grau (contemporary), oil on canvas, sgn/dtd 1976, 79x79", SBY 11/9/89 ... 165,000
Untitled (abstract), oil on canvas, sgn/dtd 73, 10x21", SBY 5/3/89 ... 15,400
ICHTER, H. Davis (British, 1874-1955)
Little Room in the Country, oil on canvas, sgn, 24x21", C-E 10/25/88 ... 1,760
ICHTER, Karl Ludwig Gustave (German, 1803-1884)
Commander, oil on panel, sgn/dtd 1848, oval, 9x8", C-E 4/7/88 UE ... 550
RICHTER, Leopoldo
La Conversation, oil on canvas, sgn, 39x29", C-NY 11/21/89 ... 4,400
Madre y Nina, gouache/watercolor on paper, initialed/dtd 57, 22x14", C-NY 11/21/89 ... 2,200
ICHTER-REICH, F.M. (German, 1896-)
Flower Sellers by a Canal, oil on canvas, sgn, 24x36", B/B 9/15/88 UE ... 550
ICKS, Don (20th C)
Bathed in Sunlight, oil on canvas, sgn/copyrighted, 30x40", SBY 9/23/88 UE ... 770
ICKS, J. (British, 19th/20th C)
Attentive Dog, oil on canvas, sgn/dtd 1907, 14x12", SBY 6/10/88 OE ... 3,575
ICO Y ORTEGA, Martin (Spanish, 1833-1908)
Garden of the Doge in the Lagoon, oil on canvas, sgn, 28x21", SBY 10/24/89 OE ... 40,700
Grand Canal, Venice; oil on canvas, sgn, 18x29", C-NY 2/23/89 OE ... 165,000
Grand Canal at the Vendramin Palace, oil on canvas, 18x30", WD 11/16/88 OE ... 50,000
Santa Marie Della Salute, oil on canvas, sgn, 20x21", WD 11/16/88 OE ... 90,000
Spring Day in Venice, oil on canvas, sgn, 19x14", FAP 12/8/89 OE ... 34,000
Summer Day (landscape), oil on canvas, sgn, 16x30", C-NY 2/23/89 ... 60,500
Venetian Canal Scene, oil on canvas, bears signature, 10x8", C-E 2/21/89 ... 1,320
Venetian Canal Scene, oil on canvas, sgn, 20x28", C-NY 5/25/88 OE ... 71,500
Venetian Terrace, oil on panel, sgn, 14x9", C-NY 2/23/89 ... 41,800
Village of Chartres, oil on canvas, sgn, 17x28", C-NY 5/24/89 ... 55,000
RIDDEL, James (British, 1858-1928)
Cows Watering, oil on canvas, sgn, 12x16", C-E 11/8/88 UE ... 650
RIDEOUT, Phillip H. (British, fl 1897-1912)
Pair: Coaching Scenes; oil on canvas, sgn/dtd 1907, 8x15", LH 10/16/88 OE ... 1,600
Pair: Summer & Winter (Coaching Paintings); oil on board, sgn/dtd 1910, 6x10", SBY 6/9/89 ... 990
RIDER, Arthur Grover (American, 1886-1975)
Through the Doorway, San Juan, Capistrano; oil on panel, sgn, unfr, 22x22", B/B 10/6/88 OE ... 7,150
RIDER, Henry Orne (American, 1860-)
In the Franconia Valley, New Hampshire (landscape); oil on canvas, sgn/dtd 1936, 30x40", RWS 9/29/88 UE ... 550
RIDGEWOOD, Lester (American, 19th/20th C)
Clam Diggers, oil on canvas, sgn/dtd 1904, 11x17", FAP 12/8/89 ... 525
RIECK, Ernst (German, 19th C)
North African City on the Coast, oil on canvas, sgn, 20x32", C-E 5/22/89 ... 2,750
RIECKE, George (American, 1848-1924)
Asking the Way (man in wagon asking a herdsman the way), oil on canvas, sgn, 30x36", WD 4/13/88 ... 2,900
Sheep by a Barn, oil, sgn, 10x14", WD 1/11/89 ... 850
RIECKE, Johann Georg Lodewyck (Dutch, 1817-1898)
Sheep in an Extensive Landscape, oil on canvas, sgn, 22x36", SLK 2/12/88 ... 2,600
RIEDMAYER, Francesco Marie (18th C)
Holy Family with the Father & Holy Ghost in Glory Above, oil on canvas, sgn/dtd 1798, 16x14", SBY 10/13/89 ... 3,300
RIEGER, Albert (Austrian, 1834-)
Alpine Landscape, oil on canvas, sgn, 29x40", SBY 7/12/89 ... 1,760
View of Trieste, oil on canvas, sgn, 34x50", C-NY 5/25/88 OE ... 15,400
RIELLE, Rainer Zstvanffy Gabinelle
Dog Sleeping by a Pillow, colored chalks/charcoal on paper, sgn, 6x8", C-E 2/23/88 OE ... 1,045
RIELLY, Henry (Australian, 19th/20th C)
River Landscape, oil on canvas, sgn/dtd 1897, 32x50", C-SK 11/10/88 UE ... 1,490
RIESENBERG, Sidney (American, 1885-)
View of the River, oil on canvas, sgn, 12x16", B/B 9/15/88 ... 248
RIESENER, Henri Francois (French, 1767-1828)
Portrait of an Elegant Lady, oil on canvas, 40x32", C-E 10/26/89 ... 5,500

RIETSCHOOF, Jan Claes (Dutch, 1652-1719)
Wijdschip, Yachet & Man-of-War Off Jetty; oil, 20x31, WD 1/25/89 8,500
RIFKA, Judy (20th C)
Amazonomachy III, oil/wool/fabric on canvas, sgn/dtd 83, 62x50", SBY 10/8/88 5,500
Two Panels: Wall of Nudes I (two nudes, three-quarter length); oil on linen, 1985, 85x96", C-NY 5/4/89 3,300
Untitled (abstract), oil on canvas, sgn, 47x35", SBY 2/19/88 1,540
RIGAUD, Hyacinthe; follower of (French, 1659-1743)
Portrait of a Gentleman Said To Be the Comte de Bruyere, oil on canvas, oval, 28x23", SBY 12/9/88 UE 990
RIGAUD, John Francis (British, 1742-1810)
Captain Vincenzo Lunardi the Balloonist, Giving a Display; oil on canvas, 38x29", SBY 6/1/89 34,100
RIGAUD, Pierre Gaston (French, 1874-)
St Gervais Paris, oil on canvas, sgn/inscr, 18x13", C-E 5/23/88 UE 440
Stained Glass Window of the Apse, Chartres; oil on canvas, sgn/dtd 1926, C-E 2/21/89 1,980
RIGAUD, Pierre Gaston; school of (French, 1874-)
Portrait of a Man, in a Wig, Wearing White Jabot & Brown Coat; oil on canvas, unfr, 35x28", C-E 4/7/88 440
RIGGS, Robert (American, 1896-1970)
Catcher on the Line (trying to catch ball, fans & players watching), oil on panel, sgn, 23x30", C-NY 9/28/89 OE 24,200
RIGNANO, Vittorio (Italian, 1860-1916)
Picking Grapes From a Vine, oil on canvas, sgn, 40x20", C-E 2/21/89 2,860
Piggy-Back Ride (two children), oil on canvas, sgn, 37x15", C-E 2/21/89 2,420
RIGOLOT, Albert Gabriel (French, 1862-1932)
La Partie de Campagne (two ladies in landscape), oil on canvas, sgn, 29x39", SBY 10/24/89 OE 39,600
Soleil Eauchant, Vallee de la Somme (lake scene); oil on canvas, sgn, 20x40", FB 10/17/88 3,800
RIJ-ROUSSEAU, Jeanne (French, 1870-1956)
Still Life of Fish, pastel on paper, studio stamp, 15x21", WL 5/20/88 1,200
RIKELME, Claudio (Latin American, 20th C)
Amanecer del Solitario (landscape w/tree), acrylic on canvas, sgn, 1988, 32x39", C-NY 5/17/89 4,620
En Medio de la Pampa (stand of trees across open field), acrylic on canvas, sgn, 35x51", C-NY 11/21/89 OE 9,350
RILEY, Bridget (British, 1931-)
Shiver (geometric composition), emulsion on board, sgn/dtd 64, 27x27", SBY 10/5/89 OE 26,400
Turn, emulsion on panel, sgn twice/dtd 64/titled, unfr, 20x20", C-NY 11/10/88 OE 30,800
RILEY, John (British, 1646-1691)
Portrait of Sir William Elliot, oil on canvas, 49x37", SBY 12/9/88 3,575
RIMSA, Juan (Lithuanian, 1903-)
Dance, oil on canvas, sgn, ca late 1940s, 24x24", SBY 5/17/88 3,300
RINALDI, Claudio (Italian, 19th C)
Song of Praise, oil on canvas, sgn, 30x43", C-E 10/26/89 2,750
RINALDI, F. (Italian, 19th C)
Game of Bacci (three men playing, woman watching from doorway), oil on panel, sgn, 20x14", C-E 5/22/89 2,200
RINCON, Agapito
Ixtaccihuatl (extensive landscape), pastel/charcoal on paper, sgn/dtd 1924, 12x18", C-NY 5/17/89 3,080
RINES, Frank M. (American, 1892-)
Sunlight & Shadow, Rockport (trees in foreground, house beyond); oil on canvasboard, sgn, 12x16", RWS 9/8/89 350
RING, Ole (Danish, 1902-1972)
Country Path, oil on canvas, sgn, 18x26", C-E 5/23/88 UE 1,980
Rear View of a Street, oil on canvas, sgn, 17x12", C-E 5/23/88 UE 1,210
RING, Pieter; see De Ring
RIO, see Del Rio
RIOLO, T. (Italian, 19th C)
Bay of Naples, gouache, sgn, 8x13", C-E 10/26/89 1,320
RIOLO, Tommaso
View From a Monastery, gouache on paper, sgn/dtd 1898, 10x14", C-E 5/23/88 UE 275
RIOPELLE, Jean Paul (Canadian, 1923-)
Abstract, watercolor, sgn/dtd 1948, 9x12", FB 10/30/89 27,500
Abstract Composition, oil on canvas, sgn/dtd 1955, 80x120", SBY 11/8/89 852,500
Composition, oil on canvas, sgn/dtd 1955, 35x46", FB 5/28/89 290,000
Composition, oil on canvas, sgn/dtd 1959, 20x26", WAD 11/30/89 30,000
Filets Frontiere (abstract), oil on canvas, sgn twice/dtd 51 twice/titled, 41x48", SBY 6/30/88 OE 440,400
Le Roi de Thule (abstract), acrylic/charcoal/pastel on paper, sgn/dtd 1973, 23x19", SBY 10/5/88 OE 6,875
Leaves (abstract), watercolor/India ink on paper, sgn/dtd 54, 20x25", SBY 10/5/88 OE 23,100
Pays (abstract), oil on canvas, sgn twice/dtd 54 twice/titled/#d 15, 10x14", SBY 5/3/88 OE 20,900
Peinture (abstract), oil on canvas, sgn/dtd 1960, 24x32", C-NY 2/20/88 26,400
Untitled (abstract, oil on canvas, sgn, ca 1955, 78x138", SBY 5/3/89 OE 1,540,000
Untitled (abstract), oil on canvas, sgn, ca 1965, 24x29", SBY 11/9/89 OE 110,000
Untitled (abstract), oil on canvas, sgn, 1955, 45x77", C-NY 5/3/88 143,000
Untitled (abstract), oil on canvas, sgn, 1958, 21x26", SBY 10/5/89 OE 74,250
Untitled (abstract), oil on canvas, sgn, 20x26", WAD 11/30/89 OE 115,000
RIORDON, Eric (Canadian, 1906-1949)
March, St Jovite Country; oil on board, sgn, 20x24", FB 10/30/89 3,520
March Morning on the Mulet River, oil on canvas, sgn, 15x18", FB 4/25/88 2,500

RIP, Willem Cornelio (Dutch, 1856-)
October in the Land Van Kyuk, oil on canvas, sgn, 18x22", S/A 2/18/89 ... 2,000
RIPARI, Virgilio (Italian, 1843-1902)
Gondola on a Canal, oil on canvas, sgn, 12x18", C-E 10/25/88... 2,200
RIPATRANSONE, see Da Ripatransone
RIPLEY, Aiden Lassell (American, 1896-1969)
Ducks at Hyde Park (mallards in pond), watercolor on paper, dtd 1924, 11x15", RWS 9/29/88 UE ... 550
Group of 2: Woodcock in Flight; He Would Watch the Ducks Flying...; ink on paper, sgn, 12x8", 15x10", RWS 3/16/89 ... 450
Harvest Time, watercolor on paper, 5x7", RAB 8/8/89 ... 400
Landscape (dog flushing out pheasants, farm scene beyond), pencil/charcoal on board, 9x14", RWS 3/31/88 ... 450
Much Ado Along the River (river scene w/figures, bridge, & train), gouache on paper, sgn, 13x20", SBY 3/17/88 ... 3,300
Pair: Hunters, Southern Hunting Party; Prey, Grouse on Branch; pencil on paper, 4x5", RWS 9/29/88 UE ... 175
Pair: Quail Hunting; pencil on paper, 6x8", RWS 9/29/88 UE ... 150
Pair: Trout; Stream of Consciousness (trout & fishing gear); ink on paper, 8x13", RWS 3/31/88 ... 450
Quail Shooting, watercolor/gouache/graphite on paperboard, 12x19", RWS 9/8/89 ... 3,100
Village Farm Plot, Spring; watercolor/gouache on paper, sgn/dtd 49, 14x21", RWS 5/12/89 ... 2,700
Woodbury Church (panoramic valley view, village in mid-ground), watercolor on board, sgn, 10x14", RWS 3/31/88 UE ... 475
Woodcock Shooting (hunters in a landscape), oil on canvas, sgn/dtd 1944, 27x40", SBY 5/25/88 OE ... 38,500
RIPLEY, Hob
Fisherman, watercolor/pencil on paper, sgn, 9x12", C-E 6/1/88 ... 660
RISTOLETTO, Michelangelo (20th C)
Man on the Telephone, silkscreen paper collage on stainless steel, 1981, 91x49", SBY 11/11/88 OE... 35,750
RITCHIE, Duncan S. (British, 19th C)
Portrait of a Young Girl, oil on canvas, sgn, 26x18", C-E 5/22/89 ... 2,530
RITCHIE, John (British, 19th C)
Picnic in the Woods, oil on canvas, sgn, 20x24", C-NY 2/25/88 ... 9,350
RITMAN, Louis (American, 1889-1963)
At Eventide (rural landscape w/house), oil on canvas, sgn, 20x26", SBY 4/14/89... 5,500
Country Lane, oil on canvas, sgn, 22x26", SBY 4/14/89 ... 8,800
Early Morning Sunshine (woman seated in window looking out), oil on canvas, sgn, 36x29", C-NY 12/2/88 OE ... 242,000
Freshly-Picked Flowers (lady standing by a window arranging flowers), oil on canvas, sgn, ca 1914, 31x32", C-NY 5/25/89 ... 132,000
Garden at Giverny, oil on canvas, ca 1912-13, 36x28", SBY 5/25/88 ... 88,000
Improvised Flower Basket (woman picking flowers in garden), oil on canvas, sgn, 36x36", C-NY 12/2/88 ... 418,000
Lady with Flower Basket, Giverny (lady in landscape); oil on canvas, 32x32", SBY 5/24/89... 110,000
Nude in Chair, oil on canvas, 32x32", C-NY 12/2/88 ... 13,200
Nude Seated in an Interior, oil on canvas, sgn, 26x32", SBY 4/14/89 UE... 6,875
Sunlight (lady at window in interior), oil on canvas, sgn, 40x40", SBY 5/24/89 OE ... 451,000
Woman Dressing (by open window), oil on canvas, sgn twice/dtd Dec 3-25, 37x29", SBY 5/24/89 OE... 132,000
Woman Sewing in a Garden, oil on canvas, sgn, 32x32", SBY 5/24/89 OE... 52,250
RITSCHEL, William P. (American, 1864-1949)
Carmel Oncoming Tide, oil on board, sgn, 15x19", B/B 10/6/88... 2,200
Dunes, oil on canvas, sgn/dtd 1912, 48x58", C-NY 3/11/88 OE ... 66,000
Glimpse of Monterey's Shores, oil on canvas laid down on board, sgn, 10x12", SBY 9/14/89... 4,125
Harbor Scene, oil on board, sgn, 12x16", B/B 10/6/88... 5,225
Monterey Coastline, oil on canvas, sgn, 20x24", B/B 10/6/88 ... 13,200
Monterey Cypress, oil on canvas, sgn, 40x45", B/B 10/6/88 OE... 38,500
Monterey Tide Pool, oil on canvas, sgn, 20x24", B/B 10/6/88 ... 13,200
Moon Path, oil on canvas, sgn/dtd 1924, 30x40", B/B 10/6/88 OE... 66,000
Morning on the Pacific Coast, oil on canvas, sgn twice/inscr, 30x40", C-NY 9/30/88 OE ... 55,000
RITSCHL, Otto (German, 20th C)
Still Life (fruit & objects on a table), oil on canvas, sgn/dtd 23, 21x33", SBY 10/5/88 ... 3,850
RITT, Augustin
Allegory of Military Honor Celebrating Count Alexander Loumorow, gouache on ivory, sgn, oval, 8x6", C-NY 10/12/89 ... 1,320
RITTENBERG, Henry R. (American, 1879-1969)
Study of an Interior (Living Room at Mill Stones), oil on canvasboard, 12x16", RWS 5/12/89... 950
RITTER, Paul (American, 1829-1907)
Mill by a Stream, oil on canvas, sgn, 37x29", C-E 2/21/89 UE... 1,980
Waterfall in a Fantastic South American Landscape, oil on canvas, sgn, 29x46", WD 4/13/88 ... 3,500
RIVAS, Antonio (Italian, 19th/20th C)
Floral Still Life of Fruit & Parrot, oil on canvas, sgn, 24x32", SBY 7/12/89 ... 4,675
Still Life of Flowers & Fruits, oil on panel, sgn, 20x16", SBY 12/9/88 OE ... 6,050
Virgin & Child, oil on panel, sgn, 15x11", SBY 7/12/89... 1,320
RIVERA, Diego (Mexican, 1886-1957)
Bather (nude from behind), brush/ink on paper, sgn, ca 1925, 25x19", SBY 5/16/89... 13,200
Boy with Dog & Firecracker, oil on canvas laid down on masonite, sgn twice/dtd 55 twice/titled, 47x32", SBY 5/16/89 ... 308,000
Cabeza de Mujer (head of a woman), pencil on tracing paper, sgn/dtd 40, 14x11", C-NY 11/21/88 ... 4,400
Campesina en e Portal, watercolor/black pencil on rice paper, sgn/dtd 28, 6x8", C-NY 11/21/89 ... 9,900
Campesino (peasant in profile), watercolor/pencil on paper, sgn/dtd 36, 24x19", C-NY 11/21/89 ... 22,000
Dance in Tehuantepec, oil on canvas, sgn/dtd 26, 22x18", SBY 5/17/88... 198,000
Desnudo de Espaldas (posterior view of seated nude), watercolor on rice paper, sgn/dtd 44, 16x11", C-NY 11/21/88 ... 17,600
Dos Tehuanas Sentadas (two seated women), watercolor on rice paper, sgn/dtd 1936, 11x15", C-NY 5/17/89 OE ... 30,800

El Mercado (the market), brush/black ink on paper, 8x12", C-NY 5/18/88 .... **6,600**
Estudio para Mural (study for mural), pencil on paper laid down on board, sgn/dtd 26, 15x11", C-NY 11/21/88 UE **1,100**
Figura Asteca (abstract), pencil on paper, sgn, 26x17", C-NY 5/18/88 OE **1,980**
Hombre Cargando Huacales (man carrying bundles), pen/ink on rice paper, sgn, 15x11", C-NY 5/17/89 .... **7,700**
Hombre con Sombrero (portrait of man w/hat), watercolor/charcoal on paper, sgn/dtd 28, 25x19", C-NY 11/21/88 .... **16,500**
India con Sombrero (Indian w/sombrero in profile), watercolor on rice paper, sgn, 15x11", C-NY 11/21/88 .... **30,800**
La Venus de la Quebrada, Acapulco; oil on canvas, sgn/dtd 1956, 43x52", C-NY 11/21/88 OE **209,000**
Landscape, charcoal on paper, sgn, ca 1937, 11x15", SBY 5/16/89 OE **8,800**
Landscape, oil on canvas, sgn/dtd 39, 24x32", SBY 5/17/88 .... **32,400**
Man with Pickax, ink on Japan paper, sgn/dtd 1944/inscr Para Chucho Marin, 11x15", SBY 11/21/88 OE **12,100**
Market (seated woman before laid-out piglets), India ink/watercolor on rice paper, sgn, 8x11", SBY 5/16/89 OE **12,100**
Market Woman, watercolor/gouache on paper, sgn, 15x11", B/B 6/9/88 .... **13,200**
Mujer Recolectando Limas (woman picking limes), watercolor/black pencil on paper, sgn/dtd 28, 16x13", C-NY 11/21/89 OE **30,800**

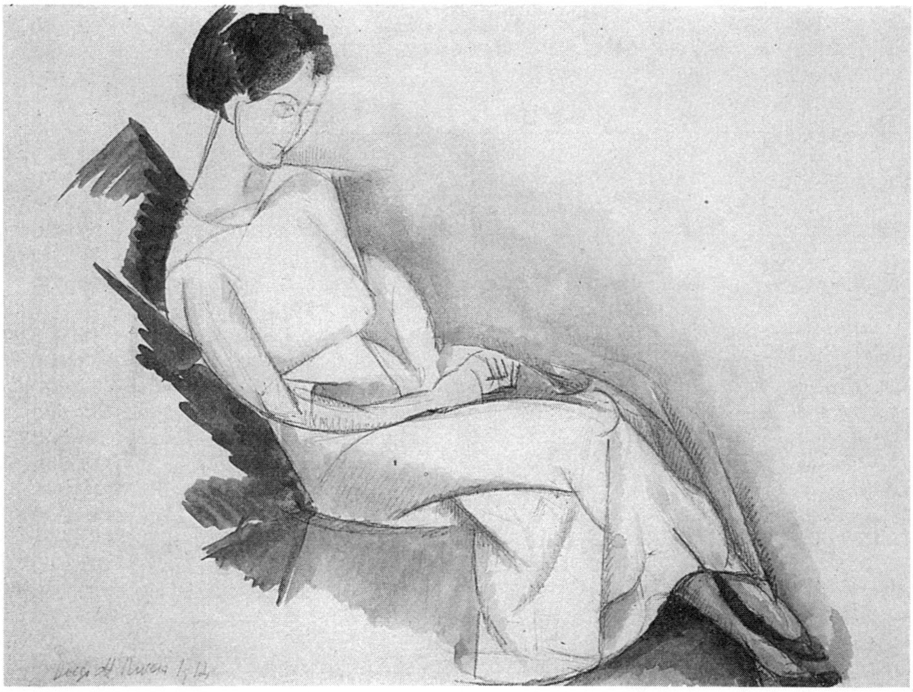

Mujer Sentada, watercolor/pencil on paper, sgn/dtd 1914/inscr Arcueil, 32x26", C-NY 5/17/89 OE; $181,500

Naturaleza Muerta con Pipa y Fosforos (pipe & matches), oil on canvas, sgn/dtd 1915, 13x19", C-NY 5/18/88 OE **170,500**
Nina, oil on canvas possibly with encaustic, sgn, ca 1975, 28x24", SBY 5/17/88 OE **79,750**
Nina, watercolor on rice paper, sgn, 11x15", SBY 5/17/88 OE **16,500**
Nina (portrait in profile), pastel on paper, sgn, ca 1950s, 15x11", SBY 5/16/89 OE **25,300**
Nina Cargando un Balde (girl w/bucket), watercolor on rice paper, sgn, 15x10", C-NY 5/18/88 .... **20,900**
Nina con Canasta (woman w/large basket), crayon on paper, sgn, 10x8", C-NY 11/21/88 .... **4,400**
Nina Endomingada, oil on canvas, sgn/dtd 1930, 22x14", SBY 5/17/88 OE **104,500**
Ninas Junto al Rio, watercolor on rice paper laid down on board, sgn/dtd 34/inscr, 11x15", C-NY 5/18/88 OE **8,250**
Nino, watercolor on rice paper, sgn, 15x11", SBY 5/17/88 .... **17,600**
Nino Vestido de Azul (portrait), pastel/charcoal/watercolor on paper, sgn, 52x27", C-NY 5/18/88 UE **19,800**
Nude with Flowers (1 of series for Ciro's nightclub), oil on canvas mounted on panel, sgn/dtd 44, 62x47", SBY 5/16/89 .... **440,000**
Nude with Flowers (1 of series for Ciro's nightclub), oil on canvas mounted on board, sgn, ca 1944, 61x48", SBY 5/16/88 .... **440,000**
Paisaje con Cactus (cacti in landscape), watercolor/pencil on paper, sgn, 10x13", C-NY 11/21/88 OE **12,100**
Paisaje de Rusia, watercolor/pencil on paper, sgn/dtd 56, 8x12", B/B 6/9/88 .... **3,300**
Paisaje de Toscana, pencil on tan paper, sgn/dtd 1921, 9x11", C-NY 11/21/89 .... **2,860**
Pareja Indigena (angry couple), watercolor on rice paper, sgn, 8x12", C-NY 11/21/88 OE **15,400**
Paysage d'Arcueil (landscape), oil on canvas, sgn twice/dtd 18 twice/inscr Arcueil, 32x26", C-NY 5/17/89 .... **242,000**
Paysage des Iles Baleres (abstract), oil on canvas, sgn/dtd 1915, 26x32", C-NY 5/18/88 OE **198,000**
Peasant Carrying a Bundle, pencil on paper, sgn/dtd 41, 12x9", B/B 10/9/88 .... **6,050**
Peasant with Bundle, watercolor on paper, sgn/dtd 43, 16x11", B/B 6/9/88 .... **16,500**
Peasants Working, watercolor on Japan paper, sgn/dtd 1941, 11x15", SBY 5/16/89 OE **24,200**
Portrait of a Man (in profile), charcoal/pastel on paper, sgn/dtd 47, 16x12", SBY 11/21/88 OE **27,500**
Portrait of Alice Leone, charcoal on paper, sgn/dtd 1938/inscr to sitter, 24x19", SBY 5/16/89 .... **7,425**
Portrait of Eva Frejaville, oil on canvas, sgn/dtd 20, 25x21", SBY 5/16/89 .... **46,750**
Portrait of Ignacio Sanchez (young boy), oil on canvas, sgn/dtd Mexico 1927, 33x25", C-NY 11/21/89 .... **264,000**
Portrait of Jacques Levy, oil on canvas, sgn/dtd 20, 16x10", SBY 5/17/88 .... **52,800**
Portrait of Senorita Matilda Palou (singer/actress), oil on canvas, sgn/dtd 1951, 81x48", SBY 11/21/88 OE **203,500**
Retrato de Nina (portrait), pencil/paper laid down on paper, sgn/dtd 29, 11x8", C-NY 11/21/88 OE **12,100**

Retrato de Nino (seated boy holding hat), oil on canvas, sgn/dtd 1954, 30x24", C-NY 11/21/89 242,000
Retrato de Teresa (three-quarter length portrait), tempera on canvas, sgn/dtd 1951, 37x28", C-NY 5/17/89 44,000
Scharmel Iris (portrait), oil on artist board, sgn, 17x22", MAG 6/22/88 UE 9,000
Seated Woman (nude), oil on canvas, sgn/dtd 42, 40x30", SBY 11/21/88 330,000
Set of 4: Escenas Campesinas (rough sketches); pencil on paper, sgn, 14x5", C-NY 5/18/88 OE 3,300
Suite of 7: Dancers; watercolor on paper, sgn, ca 1951, about 11x15", SBY 5/17/88 38,500
Tejedora (weaver, contemporary depiction), black ink/watercolor on rice paper, sgn/dtd 37, 23x21", C-NY 11/21/89 26,400
Trabajador (worker), pencil/colored wash on paper, sgn, 11x15", C-NY 5/18/88 2,860
Tres Pordioseras (three beggars), crayon on paper, sgn, 10x8", C-NY 11/21/88 2,860
Two Women (meeting before wall), watercolor on paper, sgn/dtd 36, 15x11", SBY 5/16/89 19,800
Untitled (man carrying bundles on back), watercolor on paper, sgn/dtd 44, 15x11", SBY 5/16/89 OE 28,600
Vendedora de Flores (flower seller), watercolor on rice paper, sgn, 12x18", C-NY 5/18/88 26,400
Vendedora de Palmas (girl selling palms), watercolor on rice paper laid down on board, 1938, 16x11", C-NY 11/21/88 17,600
Woman Bathing, watercolor on paper, sgn, 16x11", B/B 6/9/88 17,600
Woman with Fruit (full-length w/basket of fruit on her head), gouache on paper, sgn/dtd 31, 16x12", SBY 5/16/89 OE 20,900
Young Girl, watercolor/pencil on paper, sgn/inscr Para Chapo, 15x11", SBY 5/16/89 OE 6,050

RIVERS, Larry (American, 1923-)

Carbon Copy of Francois de Menil, transfer drawing on 2 joined sheets of paper, 1976, 26x55", SBY 5/3/88 7,150
Downtown Lion, graphite on paper, sgn/dtd 67/#d Trial Proof 1 of 4, 14x22", C-NY 5/4/89 9,350
Drug Store (abstract w/figures), oil/charcoal on canvas mounted on panel, sgn/dtd 1960, 17x17", C-NY 10/4/89 44,000
East Coast, Tareyton (abstract); oil on canvas, sgn/dtd 61, 20x16", C-NY 5/4/89 OE 55,000
Final Veteran: The Last Civil War Veteran in the Coffin (abstract); oil on canvas, sgn/dtd 61, 80x51", SBY 5/2/89 OE 286,000
Infanta (girl), cardboard/paper/colored cellophane/tape/acrylic/pencil collage on board, sgn, 28x26", SBY 2/19/88 5,280
Last Civil War Veteran, pencil/oil on canvas, sgn, 12x9", SBY 5/3/88 OE 35,750
Last Civil War Veteran (contemporary), gouache/pencil/tape/paper/foil collage on paper, sgn, 1961, 17x14", SBY 5/5/89 OE 60,500
Lisa Stroud (nude), pencil/colored colored crayons on paper, sgn, 14x17", SBY 10/7/89 8,800
Parts of the Body: French Vocabulary Lesson III; oil on canvas, 1962, 73x48", SBY 11/10/88 231,000
Queen of Clubs, oil on canvas, sgn, 1960, 28x22", SBY 11/9/89 77,000
Seated Figures (contemporary), oil/black crayon on canvas, sgn/dtd 57, 14x16", C-NY 2/20/88 OE 13,200
Untitled (Dreyfus Fund), pencil/crayon/scotch tape on graph paper, sgn/inscr/dtd 64, 20x14", SBY 2/15/89 6,050
1st Day, collage/graphite/colored pencils/cellophane tape on paper, sgn, 14x14", C-E 11/17/88 OE 5,500
2nd Avenue With The (abstract composition), oil on canvas, sgn/dtd 58, 80x76", SBY 5/3/89 104,500

RIVERS, Leopold (British, 1852-1905)

Hampshire Cottage, watercolor, sgn, 10x14", FB 5/28/89 550
Worcester Landscape, oil on canvas, sgn/indistinctly titled, 20x30", SBY 7/12/89 660

RIVIERE, Briton (British, 1840-1920)

Confederates (dog returning game to hunter), oil on canvas, sgn, 31x45", C-E 2/21/89 3,300

RIVOIRE, Francois (French, 1842-1919)

Still Life of Roses & Other Flowers in a Blue & White Vase...; gouache on paper, sgn/dtd 1876, 29x21", C-NY 5/24/89 11,000

RIX, Julian (American, 1850-1903)

Autumn, River Mist; watercolor/gouache on paper, sgn, 15x23", RWS 11/10/89 425
Autumn Landscape, oil on board, sgn, 23x10", B/B 9/14/89 UE 1,100
Bend in the River, oil on canvas, indistinctly sgn, 18x26", B/B 10/6/88 3,300
Fall Sunlight, oil on canvas, indistinctly sgn, 18x26", C-E 6/1/88 2,200
Mt Tamalpais, oil on canvas, sgn, unfr, 20x36", B/B 10/6/88 7,700
Winter Sun, oil on canvas, sgn, unfr, 24x42", SBY 9/23/88 OE 7,150
Yosemite Valley, mixed media on paper, sgn, 16x23", B/B 10/6/88 2,200

RIZZO, E. (Italian, 19th/20th C)

Conversation, oil on canvas, sgn, 20x24", B/B 4/20/88 1,650

ROACH, J.W.

On an Old Warburton Track, watercolor, sgn, 16x11", C-SK 11/10/88 190

ROBBE, Henri (Belgian, 1807-1899)

Still Life of Roses, Peonies & Other Flowers in an Oriental Vase; oil on panel, sgn, 36x29", SBY 10/24/89 55,000

ROBBE, Louis (Belgian, 1806-1887)

Noonday, oil on panel, sgn, 35x26", C-E 10/26/89 6,600
Pastoral Scene, oil on canvas, sgn, 20x27", C-E 2/21/89 2,640
Rocky Torrent, oil on canvas, sgn/inscr, 18x16", C-E 2/23/88 2,750

ROBBINS, Bruce (American, 1948-)

Cardinal (abstract), encaustic/oil/aluminum/plaster/wire mesh on wood, sgn/dtd 1985/titled, 90x36", SBY 5/3/88 18,700
Untitled (abstract), acrylic/aluminum/charcoal/cardboard strips on paper, 1981, 45x36", C-NY 5/4/88 2,750
Untitled (abstract), charcoal/oil/gold leaf on paper, sgn/dtd 1984, 42x29", SBY 2/14/89 OE 3,300

ROBBINS, Ellen (American, 1828-1905)

Floral Still Life, oil on artist board, initialed/dtd 1885, 18x8", lot 52, RAB 3/27/89 UE 400
Floral Still Life, oil on artist board, initialed/dtd 1885, 18x8", RAB 3/27/89 UE 300

ROBERT, Anton

The Smoker, oil on canvas, sgn/dtd 1911, 18x22", WD 3/23/88 1,100

ROBERT, Hubert (French, 1733-1808)

Banditti by a Fountain with a Statue of Abundance, two pyramids beyond; oil on canvas, 36x26", C-NY 5/31/89 OE 132,000
Figures Standing on a Staircase in a Palace, pen/ink/red chalk w/touches of gray-brown wash, 9x25", SBY 1/13/89 OE 25,300
Pair: Villa Madama; Sheep Fold; brown ink/red chalk on paper, 1 inscribed Villa Madama Robert 56, 19x14", WD 1/25/89 OE 26,000
View of the Campidoglio, Rome; red chalk, dtd 1762, 12x18", SBY 1/13/89 OE 25,300

ROBERT, Hubert; att (French, 1733-1808)
Washerwoman on a Stone Embankment, oil on canvas, 12x15", C-NY 10/20/88 UE ... 8,800

ROBERT, Hubert; circle of (French, 1733-1808)
Colosseum, Rome; black chalk, twice encircled fleur-de-lys, wm, 14x18", C-NY 1/11/89 OE ... 3,850
Figures Resting by Classical Ruins in a Mountainous Landscape, oil on canvas, 40x61", C-NY 10/12/89 OE ... 28,600

ROBERT, Hubert; manner of (French, 1733-1808)
Architectural Ruins with Figures, oil on canvas, unfr, 29x23", C-E 4/7/88 OE ... 1,760
Italianate Landscape with Figures Boating, oil on shaped canvas, 45x30", C-E 6/1/88 ... 440
Pair: Figures in a Classical Ruin by a Villa; Mother & Child by a Canal; oil on canvas, unfr, 76x46", C-NY 10/12/89 OE ... 22,000
Peasants Under a Ruined Archway, oil on canvas, shaped top, 54x48", C-E 4/7/88 ... 3,520

ROBERT, Hubert; school of (French, 1733-1808)
Old Red Mill, oil on board, sgn/inscr, 10x14", C-NY 9/30/88 OE ... 8,800
Pair: Landscape with Trees & Figures; oil on canvas, 68x33", C-E 6/1/88 OE ... 15,400
Pair: Washerwoman by a Fountain; Washerwoman Approaching an Arch; oil on panel, unfr, 13x17", C-NY 10/20/88 OE ... 2,860

ROBERT-FLEURY, Joseph Nicholas (French, 1797-1890)
Portrait of Victor-Felix-Marie Masse, black chalk heightened w/red chalk, initialed, oval, 14x12", C-NY 10/26/88 ... 880

ROBERTO, Luigi; att (Italian, 19th C)
SY Albion (steam yacht in calm seas), gouache on paper, titled, 15x25", RAB 3/14/89 ... 900

ROBERTS, David (British, 1796-1864)
Couple in a Rustic Landscape, oil on canvas, sgn, 12x16", B/B 12/8/88 ... 605
Tower of Comares, Alhambra, Granada; oil on panel, sgn/dtd 1838, 20x16", SBY 5/23/89 ... 41,800

ROBERTS, Edwin (British, 1840-1917)
More Jam, oil on canvas, sgn, 14x12", FB 4/25/88 OE ... 1,700
Pair: Jolly Angler, a Nibble; Complete Angler; oil on canvas, twice sgn, unfr, ea 24x18", SBY 2/22/89 OE ... 26,400
Picnicking, oil on canvas, sgn, 14x18", B/B 3/17/88 ... 6,050

ROBERTS, Elizabeth W. (American, 1871-1927)
Still Life of Orange Chrysanthemums, pastel on tan paper, 10x8", RWS 5/12/89 ... 600
Still Life of Pansies, pastel on tan paper, 11x6", RWS 5/12/89 ... 800

ROBERTS, Goodridge (Canadian, 1904-1974)
Boat (small boat by seashore), oil on panel, sgn, 8x10", FB 10/17/88 ... 5,800
Forest Interior, oil on board, sgn, 8x10", FB 10/17/88 ... 1,800
Georgian Bay, oil on board, sgn/dtd 1969, 25x32", FB 4/25/88 UE ... 6,200
Georgian Bay, watercolor, sgn, 10x14", FB 10/30/89 ... 2,200
Lakeroad in Summer, watercolor, sgn, 14x21", WAD 11/30/89 UE ... 750
Pines on Lower St Lawrence, oil on masonite, sgn, 32x48", WD 10/5/88 OE ... 13,000
Rockcliff Park, Ottawa (Early 1930s); watercolor, sgn, 8x12", WAD 6/12/89 ... 2,200
Still Life of Pottery, Pots, & Flowers; oil on board, sgn, 12x16", FB 10/30/89 ... 2,420
Wheat Fields, oil on board, sgn, 26x32", FB 5/28/89 ... 1,500

ROBERTS, Helen
Service Flag, pastel on paper, sgn, 24x28", C-E 10/18/89 UE ... 330

ROBERTS, Henry Benjamin (British, 1831-1915)
Still Life with Fruit, oil on canvas, sgn/dtd 1862, 21x17", B/B 5/17/89 ... 1,760

ROBERTS, I. (American, 19th C)
Battle of Lexington, oil on canvas, 21x31", C-E 6/22/88 ... 1,760

ROBERTS, Joseph L. (American, 19th C)
Still Life with Fruit, oil on canvas, sgn, 11x15", C-E 2/1/89 ... 3,300

ROBERTS, Priscilla (American, 1918-)
Canary, oil on panel, 17x24", LH 10/16/88 ... 800

ROBERTS, Thomas the elder (18th C)
Wooded Landscape with Stags & a Doe, oil on canvas, sgn/inscr/dtd 1774, 44x60", C-NY 1/15/88 OE ... 253,000

ROBERTS, Tom (Canadian, 1909-)
Centre Island, Toronto; oil on board, sgn/dtd 1935, 12x15", WAD 11/30/89 ... 350
Changing Weather, Lake Superior, Quebec; oil on board, sgn, 18x24", WAD 11/30/89 ... 600
Cheticamp Harbor, Cape Breton Island; oil on board, sgn, 14x20", WAD 11/30/89 ... 850
Luskville in the Laurentians, oil on board, sgn, 18x24", WAD 11/30/89 OE ... 3,200
March, Halton Country; oil on board, sgn, 12x22", WAD 11/30/89 ... 1,100
North Shore, Ille d'Orleans; oil on board, sgn, 12x22", WAD 11/30/89 ... 1,350
Pair: Le Trou; Cape Trinity; oil on board, sgn, 8x12", WAD 11/30/89 OE ... 1,000
Parrsboro Store, oil on board, sgn, 12x16", WAD 6/12/89 ... 475
Red Fish House, Cheticamp, Cape Breton Island; oil on board, sgn, 14x24", WAD 11/30/89 ... 700
St Maurice de l'Echourie, oil on board, sgn, 12x20", FB 5/28/89 OE ... 2,200
St Simeon, North Shore; oil on board, sgn, 12x22", WAD 11/30/89 ... 1,400

ROBERTSON, Charles (British, 1844-1891)
Flower Market, Damascus; watercolor/gouache on paper, sgn, 21x14", C-NY 5/24/89 ... 7,700

ROBICHON, Jules Paul Victor (French, 19th C)
Peasant Working in a Field, oil, initialed, 13x18", WD 1/11/89 ... 1,000

ROBIE, Jean Baptiste (Belgian, 1821-1910)
Portrait of Jeanne, oil on panel, sgn/inscr/dtd 1874, 25x20", C-E 2/23/88 ... 1,320
Still Life of Flowers on a Table, oil on canvas, sgn, 44x34", B/B 3/22/89 OE ... 14,300
Still Life of Fruit, oil on canvas, sgn, 18x14", DM 10/14/88 ... 2,300
Still Life of Roses, oil on canvas, sgn, 16x28", C-NY 2/23/89 ... 6,600

Still Life of Roses, oil on panel, sgn/dtd 1884, 17x13", C-NY 10/25/89 ... 6,600
ROBIN, Jean Baptiste Claude (1734-1818)
Portrait of Trophime Gerard, Marquise de Lallytollendal, Vindicating Honor...; oil on canvas, 57x45", SBY 6/1/89 OE ... 115,500
ROBINSON, Albert Henry (Canadian, 1881-1956)
Winter Landscapes with Cabins, oil on canvasboard, sgn, 6x8", WAD 11/30/89 ... 1,000
ROBINSON, Alexander (American, 1867-1940)
Italian Fountain, watercolor, sgn/dtd 1916, 19x24", NA 2/24/89 ... 900
Sketch of Cathedral at Toledo, May 1910; gouache on brown paper, sgn, 24x18", RWS 5/19/88 UE ... 500
Street in Provence, watercolor, sgn/dtd 1912, 30x20", NA 11/5/88 ... 750
ROBINSON, Charles Dorman (American, 1847-1933)
Lake Lagunitas, Marin County; oil on canvas, sgn, 20x26", B/B 10/6/88 ... 3,850
Marin Wildflowers, oil on canvas, sgn, 16x26", B/B 10/6/88 ... 4,071
Rocky Inlet Near Monterey, oil on canvas, sgn/dtd 1908, 16x24", B/B 10/6/88 ... 1,100
Sunset Landscape, oil on canvas, sgn/dtd 1886, 19x15", C-E 6/1/88 ... 1,100
Three Sisters, Yosemite; pastel on paper, sgn, 10x13", B/B 12/8/88 ... 467
White Hills Canyon, Marin County; sgn/dtd 1907, 28x36", B/B 10/6/88 ... 5,225
Wildflowers Amongst Sand Dunes, oil on canvas, sgn, 16x22", B/B 10/6/88 ... 3,850
ROBINSON, Florence Vincent (American, 1874-1937)
Lady Fencer, watercolor on paper, sgn, 10x15", C-E 5/23/88 UE ... 110
Pair: Italian Landscape with Hill Town; Italian Garden Wall; watercolor on paper, 2nd sgn, 15x10", SBY 3/17/88 UE ... 660
Sunday Afternoon in Paris, watercolor on paper laid down on cardboard, sgn, 14x19", WD 4/13/88 ... 1,400
Wandering Thoughts (woman in garden on an autumn day), watercolor/pencil on paper, sgn, 18x13", RWS 9/29/88 UE ... 250
Woman with Urn, watercolor/pencil on paper, sgn/estate stamp on verso, 17x13", RWS 12/10/88 UE ... 250
ROBINSON, Gladys Lloyd (American, 20th C)
Parisian Landscape, oil on canvas, sgn/dtd 48, 11x16", B/B 9/15/88 ... 440
ROBINSON, H. (American, 19th/20th C)
Near Granby, Connecticut; oil on canvas, 30x43", FAP 11/4/88 ... 700
ROBINSON, Hal (American, 20th C)
Autumn Landscape, oil on canvas, sgn, 16x20", SBY 3/17/88 ... 1,100
Snow-Covered Road, oil on canvas, sgn, 24x26", MG 5/28/88 ... 750
Winter Landscape with Pond, oil on canvas, sgn/dtd 09, 24x30", SBY 3/17/88 ... 1,650
ROBINSON, Margaret Frances (American, 1908-)
French Quarter Balcony, oil on board, sgn, 14x10", NA 5/13/89 UE ... 225
ROBINSON, Matthias (British, fl 1856-1884)
Family in an Interior, oil on canvas, sgn, 17x26", SBY 7/12/89 ... 3,025
ROBINSON, Mrs. E.D. (American, 20th C)
Lost Rock, oil on artist board, sgn, 18x24", SLK 2/12/88 ... 100
ROBINSON, Theodore (American, 1852-1896)
Country Road, oil on canvas, sgn, 1890, 14x10", C-NY 12/2/88 ... 33,000
Farm House in Brittany, oil on canvas, 23x40", C-NY 12/2/88 ... 33,000
Farmhouse at Grez (landscape w/farm), oil on canvas, 15x22", SBY 5/24/89 ... 176,000
On the Seine, pencil/watercolor heightened w/white, sgn, 13x8", C-SK 11/10/88 ... 40,900
Springtime, oil on canvas, sgn/dtd 92, 18x22", C-NY 5/26/88 ... 110,000
Sweet Girl Graduate, watercolor on paper mounted on canvas, sgn/dtd 1893, 17x11", SBY 5/25/88 ... 77,000
Virginia Woods, oil on canvas, sgn/dtd 93, 18x22", C-NY 12/2/88 ... 77,000
ROBINSON, Thomas (American, 1835-1888)
Grazing Cows & Sheep, oil on canvas, sgn, 21x26", RWS 8/20/88 ... 900
ROBINSON, William S. (American, 1861-1945)
Borderland (landscape w/buildings in foreground, mountains beyond), oil on canvas, sgn, 39x49", NA 11/5/88 ... 5,500
Gloucester, 1897 (seascape w/stormy sky & land beyond); oil on canvas mounted on board, sgn, 12x16", RWS 5/19/88 ... 1,100
Gloucester Harbor, 1931; oil on board, sgn/monogramed, dtd 1931, 12x16", WL 5/20/88 OE ... 2,800
Street Spotlight, oil on board, sgn, 12x14", C-E 6/1/88 UE ... 550
Tintwhistle (landscape), watercolor on paper, sgn/dtd 1892, 13x21", RAB 3/27/89 UE ... 550
ROBINSON, William S.; att (American, 1861-1945)
Spring Wetlands (landscape), oil on canvas, 8x10", RWS 3/16/89 ... 650
ROBINSON, William T. (American, 1852-)
Secret Cove, oil on canvas, sgn, 10x14", RWS 9/8/89 ... 450
Venetian Scene (gondolas & sailboats in water), oil on board, sgn, 8x12", B/B 5/17/89 ... 385
ROBLEY, Horatio Gordon (New Zealander, 19th C)
Leader of the War Dance, watercolor heightened w/white, initialed/dtd 1864/titled, 10x7", C-SK 6/9/88 OE ... 1,766
Leader of the War Dance, watercolor heightened w/white, initialed/dtd 1864, 10x7", C-SK 11/10/88 ... 710
Maori Chief, Thames River, New Zealand (portrait); pencil/watercolor, initialed/dtd 1964/inscr, 8x6", C-SK 6/9/88 OE ... 1,580
ROBUS, Hugo (American, 1885-1964)
Group of 3: Study for Mother Uplifting Child; Figure in Grief; Nude Woman; pencil on paper, 21x16" & smaller, C-E 6/1/89 ... 2,090
ROBUSTI, Jacopo (Tintoretto)(Italian, 1518-1594)
Portrait of a Man Said To Be Andreas Vesalius the Anatomist, oil on canvas, 46x38", C-NY 1/15/88 ... 17,600
Portrait of Marco Grimani, standing, three-quarter length, wearing a red robe...; oil on canvas, 47x38", C-NY 5/31/89 OE ... 99,000
Standing Figure of a Man, black chalk heightened w/white on blue paper, 17x10", SBY 1/13/89 ... 25,300
ROBUSTI, Jacopo (Tintoretto); follower of (Italian, 1518-1594)
Adoration of the Golden Calf, oil on canvas, 29x16", SBY 4/7/89 ... 2,750
Portrait of Vincenzo Capellus, Admiral of the Sea; oil on canvas, inscr, unfr, 31x34", SBY 12/9/88 ... 2,200

Visitation, oil on canvas laid down on board, unfr, 34x27", SBY 12/9/88 ... 825

ROCCA, Giovanni; see Della Rocca, Giovanni

ROCCA, Michele; circle of (Italian, 1670-1751)

David with the Head of Goliath, oil on canvas, 39x30", C-NY 4/8/88 ... 1,760
Jupiter Visiting Danae As a Shower of Gold, oil on canvas, unfr, 25x19", SBY 6/8/88 UE ... 660

ROCHUSSEN, Charles (Dutch, 1824-1894)

Republique Batane, watercolor/pencil on paper, initialed/dtd CR 74, 8x14", B/B 3/17/88 ... 1,980

ROCKBURNE, Dorothea (American/Canadian, 20th C)

Combination Series #15 (geometric composition), vellum/colored pencil/varnish/glue on ragboard, 1978, 43x33", SBY 5/3/89 ... 20,900
Copol C (abstract), mixed media on paper board, sgn/dtd 77, 39x29", SBY 2/15/89 ... 10,450
F.P. 1.17 (lineation), pen/black ink on folded paper, sgn/dtd 73, titled, 30x40", C-NY 11/10/88 ... 2,200
Indication of Installation Separate, carbon paper/graphite on paper, sgn/dtd 73/titled, 38x50", C-NY 11/10/88 ... 3,300
Rubbing Piece #6, charcoal on folded paper mounted on board, initialed/dtd 73, 30x39", C-NY 11/10/88 ... 2,860
Untitled (lineation), pen/black ink on folded paper, sgn/dtd 72, 30x40", C-NY 11/10/88 ... 2,200

ROCKENSCHAUB, Gerwald

Pair: Untitled (abstracts); oil on canvas, initialed/dtd 86, 12x10", SBY 2/15/89 ... 3,190
Untitled (abstract), oil on canvas, initialed/dtd 84, unfr, 16x16", C-NY 5/4/89 ... 1,650

ROCKMORE, Noel (American, 20th C)

Encounter No 2 (contemporary), oil on canvas, sgn/dtd 71, 24x18", MG 3/26/88 UE ... 250
Jury I (contemporary), oil on canvas, sgn/dtd 1981, 31x25", MG 10/28/88 ... 2,100
Last Supper (contemporary), oil on panel, sgn/dtd 77, 20x14", MG 3/26/88 ... 575
Louisiana Purchase (contemporary), mixed media on canvas, sgn/dtd 74, 50x40", MG 3/26/88 ... 1,800
Major General Stan Blair & Staff, gouache on paper, sgn, 14x11", MG 5/28/88 ... 140
Old Man with Riva & Model, watercolor, sgn/dtd December 19, 1970, 13x19", MG 5/28/88 UE ... 140
Portrait of the Artist's Mother, oil on board, sgn/dtd 55, 12x16", MG 10/28/88 UE ... 425
Study of a Man on Sofa (contemporary), watercolor on paper, sgn/dtd Feb 71, 13x11", MG 3/26/88 ... 175

ROCKWELL, Cleveland (American, 1837-1907)

Columbia River Gorge, oil on canvas, sgn/dtd 1881, 28x48", B/B 6/9/88 OE ... 41,250
Mount Hood (extensive landscape), oil on canvasboard, sgn/dtd 1884, 12x20", B/B 3/22/89 ... 1,320

ROCKWELL, Norman (American, 1894-1978)

Abraham Lincoln (reproduced for cover illustration), oil on canvas, sgn, 49x36", SBY 5/24/89 ... 77,000
And Every Lad May Be Aladdin (Crackers in Bed), oil on canvas, sgn, 49x28", C-NY 5/26/88 OE ... 242,000
Braced for a Feud, oil on illustration board, sgn/inscr dedication, 18x15", SBY 3/17/88 OE ... 14,300
Countdown to Takeoff (drawing for ad), charcoal/colored pencil on board, sgn, unfr, 11x12", C-NY 9/28/89 OE ... 11,000
Don't Say I Said It (two women gossiping), oil on canvas, sgn, 1922, 30x26", C-NY 5/25/89 ... 66,000
Fall (from the Four Seasons: Man & Boy, preliminary), graphite on paper, sgn/dtd 1948, 25x21", WG 10/19/88 OE ... 31,000
Magician, oil on canvas, sgn, 29x20", SBY 5/25/88 OE ... 63,250
New York Central Diner (study for cover illustration), oil on paper, sgn, 11x10", SBY 5/24/89 ... 44,000
Pair: Have You Lips That Make Good Resolutions; Hot Toddy; charcoal on board, sgn, unfr, 10x9", 15x13", C-NY 9/28/89 ... 5,720
Pair: Mr Harold Arlen; Boy in the Shower; charcoal/pencil on board, sgn, unfr, 11x13", 16x10", C-NY 9/28/89 ... 6,600
Portrait of Arthur Godfrey, pencil/charcoal, sgn, unfr, 17x13", DM 1/15/88 OE ... 3,500
Portrait of Jackie Kennedy, oil on canvasboard, sgn, 1963, 14x11", SBY 4/29/88 OE ... 28,600
Russian Schoolroom, oil on canvas, sgn, 15x37", MG 10/28/88 ... 64,000
Study for Picasso vs Sargent (figures in an art gallery), oil on paper laid down on board, sgn, 14x11", C-E 6/1/89 UE ... 495
Traveling Salesman & the Milkmaid, watercolor/pencil on paper, sgn, 16x16", SBY 5/25/88 OE ... 44,000
While the Audience Waits (circus performer bandaging dog's paw), oil on canvas, sgn, 1922, 23x20", C-NY 5/25/89 ... 60,500
Wishbone, oil on canvas, sgn, 18x17", C-NY 9/28/89 OE ... 88,000

ROCQUEPLAN, Camille

Lesson, oil on panel, sgn, 18x15", C-E 2/25/88 ... 2,200

RODCHENKO, Alexander (Russian, 1891-1956)

Clown, Circus Scene (contemporary); oil on canvas, sgn/stamped signature on verso, 1935, 32x23", SBY 7/7/88 ... 56,000
Composition (abstract), gouache on heavy paper, sgn/dtd 16, 11x8", SBY 7/7/88 OE ... 360,000
Composition (abstract), oil on prepared panel, sgn/dtd 18, 20x16", C-L 10/8/88 ... 260,260
Line (lineation), oil on canvas, sgn/dtd 1920/#d 125, 23x20", SBY 7/7/88 OE ... 600,000
Photomontage, collage on paper, ca 1922, 12x9", C-L 10/8/88 OE ... 33,460

RODDE

Untitled, Mediterranean harbor scene w/figures; oil on canvas, sgn, 24x19", SLK 11/25/88 ... 350

RODGRIGUE, George (American, 20th C)

Louisiana Landscape, oil on canvas, sgn, 11x21", NA 5/13/89 ... 1,500

RODIN, Auguste (French, 1840-1917)

Crouching Nude, watercolor/pencil on paper, sgn, 12x10", B/B 3/17/88 ... 9,350
Danseuse (sketch of a dancer), watercolor/pencil on paper, sgn, 13x10", SBY 10/6/89 ... 13,200
Deux Ecorches, pencil/pen/ink on paper affixed to board, initialed, 7x4", SBY 11/16/89 ... 24,200
Femme Assise, watercolor/pencil on paper, inscr, 13x10", SBY 2/16/88 OE ... 22,000
Femme et Sirene (nude & mermaid), watercolor over pencil on buff paper, sgn, 13x10", C-NY 5/12/88 OE ... 35,200
Figural Group, watercolor/ink wash/pastel/pencil on paper, sgn, 15x10", B/B 10/9/88 ... 11,000
Man & Serpent, pen/ink/brown wash over pencil on paper, irregular, 6x4", SBY 11/16/89 ... 24,200
Medea, watercolor/pen/ink wash heightened/collage on paper, 9x7", SBY 11/16/89 OE ... 104,500

RODIN, Auguste; att (French, 1840-1917)

Inner Voice, black chalk/watercolor/wash, ca 1900, 22x17", SWN 6/15/89 ... 715
Set of 3: Studies of Female Nudes; pencil/pen/ink, 9x6", MG 5/28/88 ... 750

RODON, Francisco (20th C)
Portrait of a President, oil on canvas, sgn twice/dtd 79-83, 83x56", SBY 5/17/88 OE 49,500
Portrait of Vaslav Nijinsky (contemporary), oil on canvas, sgn/dtd 1983, 57x77", SBY 11/21/88 OE 104,500

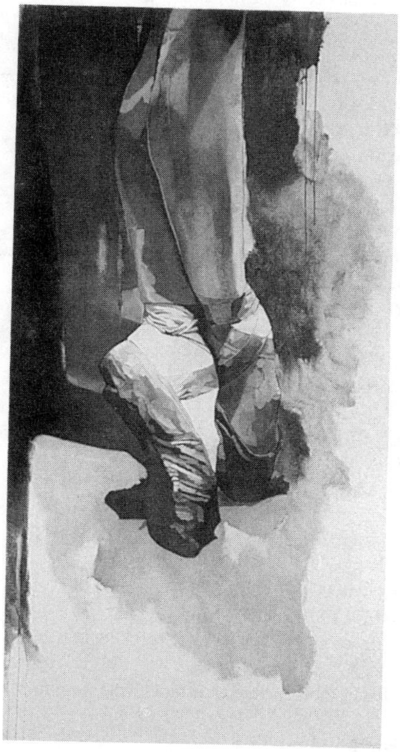

Homenaje a Alicia Alonso, oil on canvas, sgn/dtd 82, 98x51", C-NY 5/18/88 OE; $71,500

RODRIGUEZ, Alirio (Venezuelan, 1934-)
Pair: Before the Abyss; New Humanity Tensions; gouache, 1987, 22x15", SBY 11/21/88 2,750
RODRIGUEZ, E.J. (20th C)
Clipper Ship, oil on canvas, sgn/dtd 1940, 23x34", MG 5/28/88 OE 1,325
RODRIGUEZ, Mariano (Latin American, 20th C)
Figura Abstracta (abstract figure), oil on masonite, sgn, ca 1948-50, 43x31", C-NY 5/17/89 OE 15,400
Mujer y Gallo (woman & rooster), gouache on paper laid down on masonite, sgn, ca 1940, 27x32", C-NY 11/21/89 9,900
ROE, Clarence (British, -1909)
After the Storm (figures gather wreckage along rocky shore), oil on canvas, sgn, 24x42", RWS 9/29/88 950
Peasant Girl by a Stream, oil on canvas, sgn, 24x37", C-E 2/21/89 UE 1,210
Seascape, oil on canvas, sgn, 20x30", C-E 11/8/88 UE 440
ROE, Colin Graeme (British, fl 1858-1913)
Farmyard in Late Afternoon, oil on canvas, sgn/dtd 84, 20x30", SBY 6/10/88 7,150
Sheep in a Landscape, oil on canvas, sgn/inscr/dtd 99, 20x30", SBY 6/10/88 4,400
ROE, Frederick Rushing (American, 1887-1947)
Autumnal Landscape, oil on canvas, sgn, 17x23", SLK 2/12/88 130
ROE, Willem (Dutch, 1822-1897)
Milking Cows by the River, watercolor on paper, sgn, 12x19", RAB 3/27/89 UE 200
River Scene in Holland, oil on canvas, sgn, 18x31", WD 11/16/88 OE 13,000
Untitled, landscape w/figure & windmill beside water; watercolor, sgn, 20x28", SLK 4/7/89 8,250
ROEHN, Jean Alphonse (French, 1799-1864)
La Toilette de Mannequin (women dressing a mannequin), oil on canvas, sgn/dtd 1835, 22x18", C-NY 2/23/89 7,150
ROELOFS, Willem (Dutch, 1822-1897)
Angler in a Wooded Landscape at Twilight, oil on panel, sgn/dtd 1849, 22x30", SBY 5/23/89 25,300
Approaching Storm (Dutch Romantic landscape), oil on canvas, sgn/dtd 1850, 36x56", C-NY 5/24/89 OE 20,900
Dutch River Landscape with Figures, watercolor, sgn/dtd 44, 11x14", SLK 2/12/88 500
Fran Utrecht (port scene), oil on canvas, sgn/indistinctly dtd 18-9, 26x32", SBY 5/23/89 18,700
River View, watercolor on paper, sgn, 14x21", RWS 11/3/88 2,600
ROELOFS, Willem Elisa (Dutch, 1874-1940)
Chrysanthemums, oil on canvas, sgn, 24x28", SBY 10/24/89 7,150
ROEPEL, Coenraet (Dutch, 1678-1748)
Still Life of Fruit on a Ledge & in a Blue & White Porcelain Bowl, oil on canvas, sgn, 20x17", SBY 6/3/88 OE 88,000
ROERICH, Nikolai Konstantinovich (Russian, 1874-1947)
Karelia, Eternal Expectation (figures meditating in landscape); oil on canvas, 19x30", C-L 10/8/88 OE 24,170
ROESEN, Severin (American/German, 1815-1872)
Floral Still Life, oil on canvas, 36x29", SBY 5/24/89 OE 104,500
Flowers & Nest, oil on panel, sgn, 11x15", C-NY 5/26/88 OE 38,500

Peaches & Grapes in a Basket, oil on canvas, sgn, 10x12", SBY 9/23/88 ... **7,700**
Still Life of Flowers, oil on canvas laid down on masonite, 19x16", C-E 6/1/89 ... **1,980**
Still Life of Fruit, oil on panel, sgn, 14x18", C-NY 12/2/88 OE ... **33,000**
Still Life of Fruit & Bird's Nest, oil on canvas, sgn, oval, 20x16", C-NY 9/30/88 OE ... **15,400**
Still Life of Fruit & Champagne Glass, oil on canvas, ca 1855-60, 20x36", SBY 5/25/88 ... **22,000**
Still Life of Fruits, oil on canvas, sgn, 25x35", SBY 9/23/88 OE ... **16,500**
Tabletop Still Life, oil on panel, sgn, 14x18", C-NY 9/28/89 OE ... **28,600**
Vase of Flowers in Footed Glass Bowl with Bird's Nest, oil on canvas mounted on panel, sgn/dtd 1852, 40x30", SBY 5/25/88 ... **104,500**

ROESEN, Severin; att (American/German, 1815-1872)
Still Life of Fruit & Glass of Lemonade, oil on canvas, 25x30", SBY 6/28/89 ... **6,600**

ROESLER, Ettore Franz (Italian, 1845-1907)
Italian Garden with Ruins, watercolor, sgn/inscr, 17x24", C-NY 10/26/88 OE ... **3,520**

ROESSLER, George (German, 1861-1925)
Tyrolean Man with Red Scarf, oil on canvas, sgn, 13x10", LH 5/15/88 ... **850**

ROESSLER, Walter (Russian, 19th/20th C)
Card Player, oil on panel, sgn, 10x7", PHL 10/28/88 UE ... **150**
Pair: Tyrolean Peasant Smoking a Pipe; Tyrolean Peasant; oil on panel, 8x6", C-E 5/23/88 ... **1,210**

ROFFIAEN, Jean Francois Xavier (Belgian, 1820-1898)
View Across an Alpine Lake, Switzerland; oil on canvas, sgn/dtd 1870, 19x32", C-NY 2/25/88 ... **4,180**

ROGER, Augustin (French, 19th C)
Afternoon Calm, oil on panel, sgn, 5x7", FAP 12/8/89 ... **325**

ROGER, Guillaume (Dutch, 1867-1943)
Harbor at Dusk, oil on canvas, sgn, 22x18", FAP 12/8/89 UE ... **250**

ROGERS, D (American, 19th C)
Portrait of a Little Girl, oil on canvas, sgn/dtd 1856, 45x30", SBY 4/14/89 OE ... **3,575**

ROGERS, L. (20th C)
Afternoon, Boston; oil on masonite, sgn, 22x28", SBY 9/23/88 ... **82**

ROGERS, Phillip Hutchins (British, 1789-1853)
View of Nove Lake, oil on board, sgn, ca 1813, 25x33", LH 10/16/88 ... **3,000**

ROGERS, T. (20th C)
Beach Comber (couple seated on beach house steps), oil on canvas, sgn, unfr, 17x25", SBY 4/14/89 ... **2,200**

ROGGE, Wilhelm
Tavern Discourse, oil on board, sgn, 18x15", C-NY 5/25/88 ... **3,080**

ROGHMAN, Roeland (Dutch, 1597-1686)
Rocky Wooded River Landscape with Peasants on a Path & Herdsmen by a Footbridge, oil on canvas, 36x47", C-NY 4/8/88 OE ... **11,550**

ROGHMAN, Roeland; att (Dutch, 1597-1686)
Castle Surrounded by Trees, black chalk/gray wash/black chalk framing lines, inscr, 5x7", C-NY 1/11/89 ... **2,090**

ROGISONZKY, Joseph (Austrian, 1821-)
View of Entrance to Country House, oil on canvas, sgn, 35x39", WG 4/23/88 ... **1,000**

ROHL, Karl Peter (German, 1890-1975)
Untitled (abstract), gouache/pen/ink on paper, sgn/dtd 1923, 20x13", C-NY 10/6/88 ... **3,520**

ROIG, Jose (Spanish, 19th/20th C)
Leading Oxen Along the Seashore, oil on canvas, sgn, unstretched/unfr, 11x15", C-E 2/21/89 ... **1,650**
Oxen Plowing a Field (man behind team, woman along side), oil on canvas, sgn, unstretched/unfr, 10x14", C-E 2/21/89 ... **2,090**

ROINA
Cliffs by the Sea, oil on panel, sgn, 6x7", C-E 9/15/88 ... **880**

ROJAS, Elmar (Guatemalan, 1938-)
Espantapajaros Pescadores en Taboga, oil on canvas, sgn/dtd 87, 53x40", C-NY 11/21/89 OE ... **19,800**

ROLDAN, Enrique (Spanish, 19th C)
Puerto de Postigo (ancient gateway at Seville), oil on canvas, sgn/dtd 1876, 14x10", DM 5/19/89 ... **1,400**

ROLF, R.
Chickens, oil on board, 8x10", DM 10/14/88 UE ... **300**

ROLFE, A.F.
Pair: Panorama of a South American Inland Harbor; One-Decker Passing a Colonial Fort; oil, 1 sgn, 16x24", C-SK 6/9/88 ... **2,790**

ROLLIN, Claude (Canadian, 1950-)
St Irenee, Charlevoix (coastal scene with farms); oil on canvas, sgn, 24x30", FB 5/28/89 ... **380**
St Placide, Village de Charlevois; oil on board, sgn, 26x32", FB 10/30/89 ... **385**

ROLLINS, Tim (20th C)
Chun Doo-Huan (contemporary), acrylic/graphite/collage, sgn/dtd 1986-87, unfr, 26x20", C-NY 5/4/89 ... **6,600**

ROLLINS, Warren E. (American, 1862-1962)
Arizona Adobe, oil on canvas laid down, sgn, unfr, 9x14", B/B 10/6/88 ... **770**
California Landscape, oil on canvas laid down, sgn, unfr, 9x14", B/B 10/6/88 ... **770**
Desert Mesa, oil on canvas laid down, sgn, unfr, 9x14", B/B 10/6/88 ... **522**
Desert Mood, oil on board, sgn, unfr, 9x12", B/B 10/6/88 ... **330**
Hopi Burden Carrier, oil on canvas laid down, sgn, unfr, 10x14", B/B 10/6/88 ... **770**
Indian Home, oil on canvas laid down, sgn, unfr, 8x16", B/B 10/6/88 ... **770**
Indian Playing Flute, oil on canvas, sgn, 30x20", SBY 9/23/88 OE ... **10,450**
Land of Mesas, oil on canvas laid down, sgn, unfr, 9x17", B/B 10/6/88 ... **715**
Mt Rainier, Sunset (landscape); oil on canvas, sgn twice/dtd 89/titled, 42x61", SBY 5/24/89 ... **27,500**
Pair: Sunset on the Mesa; Evening Desert; oil on unstretched canvas, sgn, 6x14", 6x12", B/B 10/6/88 ... **550**

ROLPH, Joseph Thomas (Canadian, 1831-1916)
Landscape with Cattle, watercolor, sgn/dtd 1900, 10x14", WAD 11/30/89 UE 150
Trees in a Landscape, watercolor, sgn, 6x9", WAD 11/30/89 UE 80

ROLSHOVEN, Julius (American, 1858-1930)
Coming of the Spanish (Indians on steps, soldiers behind), gouache on paper, sgn, 37x28", C-NY 9/28/89 6,050
Continental Riverside Town, oil on board, sgn/dtd Feb 4, 1914, 13x19", NA 2/6/88 UE 1,400
Continental Riverside Town, oil on canvas, sgn/dtd Feb 4, 1917, 13x19", NA 11/5/88 UE 500

ROLT, Charles (Italian, 19th C)
Cupid, tempera on paper, sgn/dtd 1855, 7x4", LH 10/16/88 OE 190

ROMAIN, Filippo
Vue Generale du Forum Romanum, pen/black ink/watercolor/gouache on laid paper, sgn/inscr twice, 21x29", C-NY 10/26/88 OE 4,400

ROMAN, R.
Village Street Scene, oil on board, 15x10", C-E 6/28/88 150

Roman School (15th C)
Double-Sided: Presentation of the Virgin; Circumcision; chalk/pen/ink/wash & black chalk, ca 1600, 13x11", C-NY 1/11/89 1,100
Vision of Saint Francis, oil on canvas, ca 1610, 64x46", SBY 6/3/88 OE 605,000

Roman School (16th C)
Madonna, oil on canvas, ca 1700, 22x18", SBY 4/7/88 2,350
Madonna Blessing a Saint, black chalk, inscr arch on blue-gray paper, ca 1730, 13x9", C-NY 1/12/88 440
Mystic Marriage of Saint Catherine, oil on canvas, ca 1700, 53x39", SBY 6/1/89 31,900
Pair: Apollo & Coronis; pen/brown ink/wash over traces of black chalk, 8x12", SBY 1/13/89 880
Tarquin & Lucretia, pen/brown ink/wash on paper, 6x7", SBY 1/13/89 OE 12,100

Roman School (17th C)
Female Nude, half-length; oil on canvas, unfr, 31x26", PHL 6/16/88 600
Group of Figures After Raphael, pen/brown ink/brown wash, wm, 5x6", C-NY 1/11/89 880
Landscape with Figures Beside an Arched Pavilion by a Harbor, oil on canvas, 38x69", SBY 4/7/89 OE 29,700
Madonna & Child, oil on canvas, 28x22", SBY 10/13/89 2,750
Pentinent Magdalene, oil on canvas, 29x22", C-NY 4/8/88 2,200
Portrait of a Seated Gentleman, Possibly Matteo Neroni; oil on canvas, ca 1635, 79x60", SBY 6/1/89 UE 110,000
Saint Paul, oil on canvas, 34x27", C-NY 10/12/89 4,950

Roman School (18th C)
Allegory of Peace & Justice, oil on canvas, 19x25", SBY 4/7/89 UE 2,750
Italianate Harbor with Galleys & Other Shipping, oil on canvas, 61x82", SBY 10/13/89 OE 23,100
Last Supper, oil on canvas, 22x31", SBY 12/9/88 880
Pair: Personifications of Spring & Summer; oil on canvas, 24x19", SBY 4/7/88 OE 10,450

ROMANACH, Leopoldo (Chilean, 1862-1936)
Paisaje (Landscape), oil on canvas laid down on board, sgn, 12x15", C-NY 11/21/88 1,980

ROMANELLI, Giovanni Francesco (Italian, 1610-1662)
Achilles Among the Daughters of Lycomedes, oil on canvas, 78x82", SBY 6/2/89 165,000
Angel Appearing to Hagar & Ishmael in the Desert, oil on canvas, unfr, 27x32", FAP 11/4/88 1,100

ROMANI, Juana (Italian, 1869-1924)
Little Hyrdedreng (full-length portrait in a landscape), oil on canvas, sgn, 19x15", C-E 5/22/89 2,420

ROMANO, Antoniazzo; studio of (Italian, 1435-1511)
Madonna & Child, The Holy Ghost Above; tempera on gold ground on panel, engaged tabernacle frame, 16x12", SBY 6/2/89 OE 57,750

ROMANO, Giulio; follower of (Italian, 1499-1546)
Cavalry Battle, black chalk/pen/brown ink/brown wash, 11x15", C-NY 1/11/89 495
Polyphemus, pen/brown ink/brown wash, inscr, 13x10", C-NY 1/11/89 OE 1,540

ROMANO, Giulio; school of (Italian, 1499-1546)
Portrait of an Emperor, oil on canvas, 54x43", C-NY 10/12/89 8,250

ROMANOVSKY, Dimitri (American, 20th C)
Portrait of a Young Girl, oil on canvas, sgn/inscr 1914, 34x25", SBY 9/23/88 2,475

ROMBOUTS, Salomon (Dutch, 1652-1702)
Toll House by a Canal, View of Haarlem Beyond; oil on canvas, indistinctly sgn, unfr, 53x72", C-NY 10/12/89 9,350

ROMBOUTS, Theodor; follower of (Flemish, 1597-1637)
Four Men Singing, oil on canvas, 32x50", SBY 4/7/88 2,475

ROMBOUTS, Theodore; school of (Flemish, 1597-1637)
Return of the Prodigal Son, oil on canvas, 41x60", C-NY 4/8/88 OE 26,400

ROMEK, Arpad (Hungarian, 1883-)
Still Life of Glass Vessels, oil on canvas, sgn, 26x21", WG 9/16/88 UE 500

ROMERO, Carlos Orozco (Mexican, 1898-)
Untitled (village street scene), oil on board, sgn/dtd 1919, 22x18", SBY 5/16/89 OE 6,600

ROMES, A. (Italian, 19th C)
Flower Girl, oil on canvas, sgn, 20x12", LH 9/10/89 700

ROMNEY, George (British, 1734-1802)
Head of a Sleeping Child, oil on canvas, 14x14", SBY 1/12/89 OE 25,300
Portrait of a Gentleman, in a red coat, seated; oil on canvas, 49x39", SBY 6/8/88 OE 7,975
Portrait of a Gentleman (half-length wearing powdered wig & red suit), oil on canvas, 30x25", SBY 10/13/89 OE 7,700
Portrait of a Lady Said To Be Elizabeth, Mrs Montagu Burgoyne (half-length); oil on canvas, 30x24", SBY 4/7/89 OE 8,800
Portrait of Diana, Lady Milner, half-length; oil on canvas, 29x24", SBY 10/21/88 OE 13,200
Portrait of Edward Wilbraham Bootle & His Brother Randle, oil on canvas, 96x60", SBY 6/2/89 660,000
Portrait of Emma, Lady Hamilton, bust-length, wearing a white scarf; oil on paper, 12x9", C-NY 5/31/89 OE 26,400

Portrait of George Capel Coningsby, 5th Earl of Essex, half-length; oil on canvas, 29x24", SBY 10/13/89 OE **25,300**
Portrait of Mrs James Lowther, oil on canvas, 30x25", SBY 6/2/89 ..... **82,500**
Portrait of Mrs Maria Howard, half-length, wearing a blue dress with ermine trim; oil on canvas, 30x25", C-NY 1/15/88 ..... **6,050**

ROMNEY, George; after (British, 1734-1802)
Portrait of Lady Hamilton, oil on canvas, 23x19", WG 9/16/88 UE **225**

ROMNEY, George; att (British, 1734-1802)
Portrait of a Gentleman in Black (bust-length), oil on canvas, 30x25", B/B 9/14/89 ..... **825**

ROMULO, Teodulo (Mexican, 1943-)
Fantastic Landscape with Cow, oil on unstretched canvas, sgn/dtd 1986, 23x31", SBY 5/17/88 OE **8,800**
Girl with Parrot & Pliers, oil on canvas, sgn/dtd 1981, 22x30", SBY 11/21/88 ..... **5,500**
Ride Through Life (surrealistic), oil on unstretched canvas, sgn/dtd MEX 1987, 23x32", SBY 11/21/88 ..... **4,950**
Sin Titulo (abstract), acrylic/plaster on canvas, sgn/dtd 1986, 23x31", C-NY 11/21/88 ..... **3,300**

RONAI, Jozsef Rippl
Interieur sous le Directoire (interior scene), oil on canvas, sgn/dtd 89, 11x16", SBY 10/7/89 ..... **3,080**

RONALD, William (Canadian, 1926-)
Triptych: Takashi; oil on canvas, sgn, ea panel 48x50", SBY 2/14/89 ..... **880**

RONDEL, Frederic (American, 1826-1892)
Manor House on the Hudson (landscape), oil on canvas, sgn/dtd 1855, 18x24", SBY 1/24/89 ..... **9,075**

RONDEL, Henri (French, 1857-1919)
Portrait of a Red-Headed Beauty, oil on canvas, sgn, 26x20", C-E 5/22/89 ..... **4,400**

RONER, F.
Waterfall in the Woods, oil on board, sgn, 10x9", WD 3/23/88 ..... **325**

RONNER, Alice (Belgian, 1857-)
Still Life of Roses, oil on canvas, sgn/dtd 01, 9x32", B/B 6/9/88 ..... **2,200**

RONNER-KNIP, Henriette (Dutch, 1821-1909)
After the Hunt (dogs laying on a path in the woods), watercolor on paper, sgn, 10x8", SBY 6/9/89 UE **1,430**
Best Friends, watercolor on paper, sgn, 12x10", SBY 12/9/88 ..... **5,500**
Best Friends (dog & cat in an interior), oil on canvas, sgn, 25x18", C-NY 10/25/89 ..... **8,800**
Cat and Canary, oil on canvas, sgn, 27x21", LH 5/15/88 ..... **6,400**
Puppies in a Basket, oil on canvas, sgn, 16x20", B/B 6/9/88 ..... **4,400**
Study of Cats, charcoal on paper, sgn, 17x24", B/B 3/17/88 ..... **2,750**
Two Kittens, oil on panel, sgn/dtd 95, 10x13", B/B 6/9/88 ..... **8,250**

ROODENBURG, Hendrikus Elias (Dutch, 1895-1983)
Amsterdam Canal Scene, oil on canvas, sgn, 24x36", B/B 3/22/89 ..... **2,200**

ROOS, Johann Heinrich (German, 1631-1685)
Extensive Landscape with Shepherds & Their Flock, oil on canvas, sgn/dtd 1656, 37x31", SBY 10/13/89 OE **16,500**

ROOS, Johann Heinrich; circle of (German, 1631-1685)
Encounter Between a Rooster & a Ferret, oil on canvas, unfr, 25x31", SBY 4/29/88 OE **14,300**

ROOS, Joseph (Austrian, 1726-1805)
Herder with Cows by a Cascade in an Extensive Landscape, oil on canvas, sgn/dtd 1785, 23x30", C-NY 5/31/89 OE **9,900**
Herders Resting with Their Flock on Path in Rocky River Landscape...; oil on canvas, unfr, 33x47", C-NY 5/31/89 ..... **11,000**

ROOS, Philipp Peter (German, 1657-1706)
Pair: Herdsmen with Their Animals in Southern Landscapes with Ruins; oil on canvas, 29x53", SBY 10/13/89 OE **28,600**
Pair: Landscape with Animals by a Stream; Italianate Town; oil on canvas, 37x52", SBY 10/13/89 ..... **3,300**

ROOS, Philipp Peter; circle of (German, 1657-1706)
Bull Attacked by Dogs, oil on canvas, 27x38", SBY 6/8/88 OE **1,540**
Herdsman with Goats, Sheep & a Dog in a Landscape; oil on canvas, 38x52", SBY 4/7/89 ..... **4,400**

ROOSENBOOM, Albert (Belgian, 1845-1875)
Bouquet, oil on canvas, sgn, 10x8", SBY 12/9/88 OE **4,400**
Grandmother's Pets, oil on canvas, sgn, 19x14", C-NY 5/25/88 ..... **12,100**
In the Conservatory, oil on canvas, sgn, 10x8", SBY 12/9/88 OE **4,125**
Pair: Children Picking Flowers; The Swing; oil on canvas, sgn, 12x9", SBY 6/8/88 ..... **2,200**

ROOSENBOOM, Margarete (Dutch, 1843-1896)
Still Life of Hollyhocks, Morning-Glories & Grapes on a Marble Ledge; oil on canvas, sgn, 27x23", SBY 10/24/89 OE **23,100**

ROOSKENS, Anton (Dutch, 1906-)
Composition (abstract), oil on canvas, sgn, ca 1950-51, 39x31", SBY 6/30/88 ..... **48,000**
Telle Sortant du Puits (abstract), acrylic on canvas, sgn twice/dtd 74, 45x61", SBY 6/30/88 ..... **60,000**
Untitled, acrylic on sand canvas, sgn/dtd twice 65, inscr, 79x55", C-E 5/13/88 OE **22,000**
Untitled (abstract), gouache on paper, sgn/dtd 68, 15x20", SBY 10/7/89 ..... **3,740**

ROOY, see De Rooy

ROPE, George Thomas (British, 1846-1929)
Gone to Earth, oil on canvas, initialed, 40x60", WAD 6/6/88 ..... **7,500**

ROPER, Edward (Canadian, 1857-1891)
Sugar! Sugar! Sugar! Have Sugar Got?, Gathered at Camp for Dinner; oil en grisaille, sgn, 6x9", C-SK 5/25/89 ..... **640**

ROSA, Herve; see Di Rosa

ROSA, Louis
Les Bois Domaniaux, oil on panel, sgn, arched top, 21x35", C-E 2/16/88 ..... **495**

ROSA, Salvator (Italian, 1615-1673)
Mercury & Argos by a Pool in a Forest Landscape, oil on canvas, 49x74", C-NY 1/11/89 OE **71,500**
Studies of Two Figures on Rearing Horses, pen/brown ink/wash over black chalk, 11x7", SBY 1/13/89 OE **23,100**

ROSA, Salvator; after (Italian, 1615-1673)
Harbor Scene with Sailing Ships, by AS Falardeau, oil on canvas, sgn/dtd 1867, 45x64", FB 5/28/89 ... 1,500
Marine Scene, oil on canvas, 42x70", B/B 4/20/88 ... 1,870
Penitent Magdalene, oil on canvas, 34x31", C-E 6/1/88 ... 1,870

ROSA, Salvator; circle of (Italian, 1615-1673)
Italianate Landscape with Figures & a Ruined Temple on a Cliff, oil on copper, 12x16", SBY 4/7/89 OE ... 9,900
Wooded River Landscape with Figures Conversing on a Hill, oil on canvas, 25x29", SBY 4/7/88 ... 3,575

ROSA, Salvator; manner of (Italian, 1615-1673)
Pair: Battle by a Fort; Battle by a Castle; oil on canvas, 13x39", WD 1/25/89 ... 16,000

ROSA, Salvator; school of (Italian, 1615-1673)
Cavalry Skirmish, oil on canvas, unfr, 14x20", C-E 6571 OE ... 2,090
Italianate Harbor Scene with Figures, oil on canvas, 30x45", C-NY 10/12/89 ... 3,300
Rocky Landscape with Fishermen, oil on canvas, 25x19", C-NY 10/12/89 ... 3,300

ROSA, Salvator; style of (Italian, 1615-1673)
St Martin of Tours Splitting His Cape, oil on canvas, 37x28", B/B 6/9/88 ... 3,025

ROSA, school of
Gamblers Dicing in a Landscape, oil on canvas, 18x14", C-NY 10/20/88 ... 6,600
Sunset Landscape, oil on canvas, unfr, 24x36", C-NY 10/20/88 OE ... 3,080

ROSAI, Ottone (Italian, 1895-1957)
Pair: Red Table; Two Farmers; oil on panel/oil on board, sgn, 7x8", 4x4", SBY 10/5/88 ... 3,300

ROSAIRE, Arthur Dominque (Canadian, 1879-1932)
Eastern Township Farm, oil on board, sgn, 10x14", WAD 11/30/89 ... 260

ROSANO (Italian, 19th C)
Lady with Tamborine & Wine, watercolor on paper, sgn, 20x14", WG 4/23/88 ... 550

ROSATI, Giulio (Italian, 1858-1917)
Arab Bazaar, oil on canvas, sgn, 9x16", C-NY 2/23/89 OE ... 13,200
Arab Caravan Outside City, watercolor on paper, sgn, 14x21", WL 5/20/88 ... 6,000
Escape, oil on canvas, sgn, 20x40", C-NY 10/25/89 OE ... 26,400
In the Harem, watercolor on paper laid down on card, sgn, 12x18", SBY 6/8/88 ... 8,525
Visitor for Tea, oil on canvas, sgn/dtd 83, 22x32", SBY 2/22/89 ... 22,000

ROSE, Guy (American, 1867-1925)
The End of the Day (La Fin de la Journee), oil on canvas, sgn/dtd 1891, 40x98", B/B 10/6/88 ... 110,000

ROSE, Herman (American, 1909-)
New York City Skyline, oil on canvas, sgn/dtd 56, 24x27", RWS 11/10/89 UE ... 1,800
Still Life & Self-Portrait, oil on canvasboard, sgn, 16x20", SBY 6/28/89 ... 1,210
Wildflowers in White Pitcher, oil on canvas, sgn/dtd 56, 31x27", RWS 11/10/89 UE ... 1,800

ROSE, Iver (American, 1899-1972)
Flower Vendor, oil on board, sgn/dtd 43, 10x8", SBY 1/24/89 ... 440
Green Stones, oil on paper, sgn, 19x25", C-E 6/1/89 ... 550
Outdoor Fruit Seller, gouache/pencil on paper, sgn, 16x16", C-E 6/1/89 ... 880

ROSE, Jack Manley (American, 20th C)
Portsmouth, watercolor on paper, sgn/titled, 14x9", RAB 8/8/89 UE ... 50

ROSE, William (British, 1810-1875)
Gossip at the Well, oil on canvas, sgn/dtd 1871, 48x30", C-E 11/8/88 ... 880

ROSEBEE (American, 20th C)
New England Village, oil on board, sgn, 14x18", RAB 8/8/89 ... 500
Our Worldly Possessions, Some Great, Some Small...; oil on board, sgn/titled on frame, 12x16", RAB 8/8/89 ... 400
Valentine, portrait of ship set off by sailors, flags, & designs; oil on board, sgn, 20x24", RAB 8/8/89 ... 250

ROSELAND, Harry (American, 1868-1950)
Bottomless Pit (Black girl seated, eating from bowl), oil on canvasboard, sgn/dtd Dec 24, 45, 11x9", PHL 12/1/88 ... 3,750
Breaking Waves, oil on board, sgn, 5x8", C-E 2/3/88 OE ... 1,650
Budding Scholar (man, woman & child reading in an interior), oil on canvas, sgn, 18x26", C-NY 5/26/88 ... 35,200
Composing (young girl sitting at desk), oil on canvas, sgn/dtd 1892, 24x18", C-E 10/18/89 ... 2,200
Fortune Teller, oil on canvas, sgn, 12x16", SBY 1/24/89 OE ... 3,300
Good Night to Baby, oil on canvas, sgn, 10x14", SBY 9/23/88 ... 3,025
Happy Mother & Baby, oil on board, sgn, 8x10", C-E 10/18/89 ... 2,200
He Loves Me...; oil on canvas, sgn/inscr, 18x14", SBY 9/23/88 ... 4,400
It's All in the Cards (lady having her cards read), oil on canvas, sgn/dtd 98, 20x30", C-NY 5/25/89 ... 13,200
Palm Reader (interior scene w/two figures), oil on canvas, sgn/dtd 98, 20x30", C-NY 5/25/89 UE ... 8,800
Reading the Magic Waters (two women by a hearth), oil on canvas, sgn, 24x30", PHL 10/28/88 OE ... 2,000

ROSEN, Charles (American, 1878-1950)
Autumn Landscape, oil on canvasboard, sgn, 12x16", C-E 2/1/89 UE ... 880
Bouquet (floral still life), oil on canvas, sgn, 20x16", C-E 2/1/89 ... 3,850
Landscape, oil on board, bears signature/initialed, 16x12", C-E 11/30/88 ... 3,300

ROSEN, Charles; att (American, 1878-1950)
River Scene, Pennsylvania; oil on canvas, sgn, 40x42", LH 12/4/88 ... 5,000

ROSEN, Jane
After Nature, brown/black charcoal on paper, sgn/dtd 86, 62x42", SBY 10/5/88 ... 880
Mt Hurricane, a View of the Adirondacks; oil on board, monogramed/dtd 60, RWS 9/8/89 ... 1,000

ROSENBOOM, Albert (Belgian, 19th C)
Woman Gazing Out a Window, oil on panel, sgn, 17x14", B/B 10/9/88 ... 4,400

ROSENFELD, Eugen
Oriental Butler, oil on canvas, sgn, 27x31", C-E 10/25/88 ... **2,640**
ROSENKRANZ, Clarence C. (American, 19th/20th C)
Landscape with Haystacks, oil on canvas, sgn/dtd 1916, 12x16", WG 9/16/88 ... **300**
Landscape with Pond, oil on canvas laid down on board, sgn/dtd 05, unfr, 16x12", C-E 2/16/88 ... **110**
ROSENQUIST, James (American, 1933-)
Big Bo, oil on canvas, sgn/dtd 1966, 92x67", SBY 5/2/89 ... **110,000**
Black Star with Pointer (abstract), ink/chalk/paper collage/paper mobile wheel insert, sgn, 1977, 22x44", SBY 5/2/88 OE ... **23,100**
Drawing #6 for Time Flowers, dry pigment stenciled on paper, sgn/dtd 1980, 20x28", SBY 10/5/89 ... **9,900**
Elbow Lake (abstract), acrylic/charcoal/pencil/fabric & string collage on paper, sgn/dtd 75, 36x74", SBY 11/11/88 OE ... **44,000**
Head on Another Shape: Study for Big Bo; oil on canvas, sgn/dtd 1966, 35x25", SBY 5/2/89 ... **55,000**
Hoarfrost (Keeper), collage/solvent transfer on cloth, 1974, 88x43", SBY 11/11/88 OE ... **66,000**
Kabuki Blushes (contemporary composition), acrylic on canvas, 1984, 39x42", SBY 11/9/89 OE ... **143,000**
Leaky Neck (contemporary), acrylic on canvas, sgn/dtd 1978/titled, 20x36", SBY 5/2/88 OE ... **35,750**
Mask (Come Play with Me/Hey, Let's Go For a Ride), oil on canvas, sgn/dtd 1961/titled, 34x36", C-NY 11/9/88 OE ... **440,000**
More Points on a Bachelor's Tie (abstract), mixed media collage on paper, sgn/dtd 1977, 22x24", SBY 2/15/89 OE ... **27,500**
Plateau (abstract), oil on canvas, 1980, 78x66", SBY 11/10/88 ... **110,000**
Sketch for Artist Rights, mixed media on paper, sgn/dtd 1975, 30x23", WD 5/5/88 ... **3,000**
Sketch for Circle of Confusion GE, oil on canvas, sgn/inscr/dtd 1966, unfr, 14" dia, C-NY 5/3/88 ... **35,200**
Telephone Explosion (illustration), oil on canvas, sgn/dtd 1983/titled, 78x66", SBY 11/11/88 OE ... **143,000**
Towel Wipes the Paint Off Later, acrylic/graphite/paper collage on paper, sgn/dtd 1977/titled, 22x44", SBY 11/11/88 OE ... **24,750**
Two New Clear Women, colored chalks/graphite on paper, sgn/dtd 1983, 37x92", C-NY 10/4/89 ... **88,000**
Untitled (abstract composition w/pair of eyes), oil on canvas, sgn/dtd 1987, 30x30", SBY 11/9/89 OE ... **110,000**
Untitled (contemporary), oil on canvas, sgn/dtd 1969, 12x18", SBY 11/11/88 ... **49,500**
Untitled (contemporary), oil on canvas, sgn/dtd 1969, 24x30", SBY 5/2/88 OE ... **93,500**
White Tunnel (abstract), watercolor/gouache/paper collage/colored pencils, sgn/dtd 1977, 22x44", SBY 10/5/89 ... **28,600**
ROSENTHAL, Ben
Farm Workers in an Open Landscape, oil on cardboard, sgn, 24x35", C-E 6/28/88 ... **550**
ROSENTHAL, Lillian (American, 20th C)
Woman in Red Dress, oil on canvas, sgn, 20x16", FAP 4/15/89 OE ... **908**
ROSENTHAL, Max (American/Polish, 1833-1918)
Portrait of a Boy in a Sailor Suit, oil on canvas, sgn/dtd 1891, 30x25", SLK 9/26/88 ... **350**
ROSLIN, Alexandre (Swedish, 1718-1793)
Portrait of Ninon Lenclos, oil on canvas, 23x19", SBY 6/3/88 ... **37,400**
Presentation Scene with a Nobleman Surrounded by His Entourage, oil on canvas, indistinctly sgn, 15x18", C-NY 1/15/88 ... **17,600**
ROSLIN, Alexandre; manner of (Swedish, 1718-1793)
Portrait of a Lady, oil on canvas, 30x25", SBY 7/12/89 ... **2,200**
ROSS, Alvin
Fishing on the Arno, no media given, sgn/dtd 80, 24x34", C-NY 6/17/89 OE ... **1,430**
Reclining Nude, watercolor on paper, sgn, 7x11", C-NY 6/17/89 ... **352**
ROSS, Chandler R. (European, 19th C)
Still (flowers & objects on a table), oil on canvas, sgn, 28x36", C-E 2/3/88 ... **2,310**
ROSS, Fred (Canadian, 1927-)
Girl with White Shawl, pastel/ink, sgn, 25x20", FB 4/25/88 ... **650**
ROSS, Harry Leith
Fall Landscape with Fence, oil on canvas, sgn/dtd 1920, 25x30", DM 3/14/88 UE ... **500**
ROSS, T.
Travelers Departing From a Terrace, oil on canvas, sgn, 25x30", C-NY 4/6/89 ... **6,600**
ROSSEAU, M. (French, 19th/20th C)
A la Plage (at the beach), oil on panel, sgn, 15x22", SBY 7/12/89 ... **4,125**
ROSSEAU, Marguarita (Belgian, 1888-1948)
Mother & Child, oil on canvas, sgn, 15x18", B/B 6/15/89 ... **7,700**
ROSSEAU, Percival Leonard (American, 1859-1937)
On Point (two pointers in morning landscape), oil on canvas, sgn/dtd 1909, 32x40", C-NY 2/3/88 OE ... **34,100**
Pointers with Their Kill, oil on canvas, sgn, 22x63", SBY 6/9/89 ... **27,500**
Setter & a Spaniel Pointing, oil on canvas, sgn/dtd 1921, 12x19", SBY 6/10/88 OE ... **14,300**
Setter Retrieving a Duck, oil on canvas, sgn/dtd 1905, 24x32", SBY 6/10/88 ... **19,800**
Two Pointers (in a landscape), oil on canvas laid down on masonite, sgn/dtd 1909, 26x32", SBY 5/25/89 ... **30,800**
ROSSELLI, Bernardo
Madonna & Child Enthroned with St John the Baptist in the Distance, tempera on panel, arched top, 29x16", SBY 4/7/88 OE ... **17,600**
ROSSELLI, Cosimo (Italian, 1439-1507)
Saint Ansanus & Saint Anthony of Padua, oil on panel, inscr, 36x20", C-NY 1/11/89 UE ... **44,000**
ROSSELLI, Cosimo; circle of (Italian, 1439-1507)
A Tondo: Madonna & Child with Two Angels in a Landscape; oil on panel laid down, 42" dia, C-NY 10/12/89 ... **24,200**
ROSSELLI, Matteo; att (Italian, 1578-1650)
Portrait of a Young Man Holding a Broken Staff, oil on canvas, 36x28", SBY 1/12/89 ... **15,950**
ROSSER, C. (American, 20th C)
At the Beach (woman/three children along beach), oil on board, sgn, 13x17", RAB 3/27/89 ... **325**
ROSSERT, Paul (French, 1851-1918)
Lady Seated by the Seashore, oil on canvas, sgn, 13x19", C-E 5/22/89 OE ... **7,150**

ROSSETTI, Dante Gabriel (British, 1828-1882)
Madonna Pietra (nude, bust-length, holding crystal globe), pastel on paper, monogramed/dtd 1874, 35x22", SBY 6/1/89 .... **165,000**
ROSSI, Alexander M. (British, 19th C)
Young Woman Resting by a Stream, oil on canvas, sgn/dtd 77, 25x36", C-NY 2/23/89 .... **14,300**
ROSSI, Lucio (Lucius)(French, 1846-1913)
Distinguished Guest (elegant gathering in interior), watercolor/gouache/pencil, sgn, 14x20", C-NY 2/23/89 .... **4,180**
Gallantry (gentleman helping ladies over stone wall), oil on panel, sgn/dtd 75, 14x11", SBY 10/24/89 OE **31,900**
Tiresome Story (young woman asleep with open book on lap), oil on panel, sgn/dtd 1868, 14x17", B/B 10/9/88 OE **35,750**
ROSSI, Luigi (Italian, 1853-1923)
Elegant Couple on a Terrace, oil on canvas, sgn, 18x28", C-NY 10/25/89 .... **26,400**
In the Park (mothers w/babes on park bench), oil on canvas, sgn, 18x30", SBY 10/24/89 OE **60,500**
ROSSI, Marlo
Sailboats at Sunset, oil on canvas, sgn, unfr, 24x36", C-E 6/28/88 UE **50**
ROSZAK, Theodore (American, 1907-)
Study for Sea Quarry, pen/black ink/wash on paper, sgn/dtd 49, 15x11", SBY 10/7/89 .... **2,200**
ROTH, Andreas (Swiss, 20th C)
Glacier Above an Alpine Lake, oil on canvas laid down, sgn, 23x28", B/B 4/20/88 .... **110**
ROTH, Ernest David (American, 1879-)
Sketch in Segovia, oil on board, sgn, 9x10", C-E 11/30/88 .... **1,210**
ROTHAUG, Leopold (Austrian, 1868-1959)
Elegant Figures Before a House in a Park, watercolor heightened with bodycolor, sgn/dtd 1901, 16x23", PHL 10/28/88 .... **950**
ROTHBORT, Laurence (American, 20th C)
Remains of New Amsterdam, oil on canvas laid down, sgn/dtd 1949, 25x30", B/B 9/14/89 UE **1,100**
ROTHBORT, Samuel (American, 1882-1971)
Floral Still Life, oil on board, 26x18", B/B 3/22/89 .... **7,150**
Garden, oil on canvas, sgn, 30x36", C-E 10/18/89 .... **1,980**
George Washington Bridge & the Cloisters, oil on canvas, sgn, 21x25", SBY 9/14/89 .... **2,420**
My Garden in Brooklyn, oil on board, 15x18", B/B 3/17/88 .... **4,400**
Sunday in Prospect Park, oil on canvas, sgn, 22x30", C-E 10/18/89 UE **1,650**
View of a Bridge, oil on board, estate stamp, 24x30", B/B 6/15/89 UE **1,650**
ROTHENBERG, Susan (American, 1945-)
Head & Circle #3 (abstract), acrylic/flashe on canvas, sgn/dtd 1980, 48x42", SBY 5/2/88 .... **121,000**
Hector Protector (contemporary), acrylic/tempera on canvas, 1976, 67x112", SBY 11/8/89 .... **550,000**
Horse (abstract), oil/lithograph on paper, sgn/dtd 1977, #d 2/18, 12x16", SBY 5/3/88 OE **31,900**
Little Spook (abstract), oil on canvas, sgn/dtd 1982, 33x24", SBY 5/3/89 .... **71,500**
Untitled (abstract), acrylic on paper, 1979, 15x14", SBY 11/11/88 OE **38,500**
Untitled (abstract), acrylic/gouache on paper, sgn/dtd 1978, 38x50", C-NY 5/4/89 .... **46,200**
Untitled (contemporary), charcoal on paper, sgn/dtd 1986, 30x21", SBY 11/11/88 .... **25,300**
Untitled (sketch of two horses), oil/crayon/lithograph on paper, sgn/dtd 1977/#d, 12x16", SBY 5/3/89 .... **38,500**
ROTHENSTEIN, William (British, 1872-1945)
Group Portrait (full-length portrait of artist's friends), oil on canvas, ca 1892-94, 44x34", SBY 2/22/89 .... **66,000**
ROTHKO, Mark (American, 1903-1970)

Number 8, oil on canvas, sgn/dtd 1952/#d 8, unfr, 81x69", C-NY 11/9/88 OE; $2,750,000

Black, Red-Brown on Violet (abstract); tempera on paper mounted on board, 1969, 39x26", SBY 11/11/88 OE **231,000**
Black Area in Reds, oil on canvas, sgn/dtd 1958, 70x92", SBY 11/8/89 OE **3,630,000**
Double-Sided: Dining Room; Girl Reading; watercolor on paper, 13x20", SBY 2/14/89 ..... **3,025**
Four Reds (abstract), oil on canvas, sgn/dtd 1957, 81x51", SBY 5/2/89 ..... **1,870,000**
Green Divided by Blue, acrylic on paper mounted on canvas, sgn, 1968, 24x18", C-NY 5/3/88 OE **187,000**
Olive Over Red (abstract), oil on canvas, sgn/dtd 1956, 93x58", SBY 11/10/88 ..... **1,045,000**
Orange on Red (abstract), oil on canvas, 1956, 69x39", SBY 5/2/88 ..... **605,000**
Red Painting, oil on canvas, sgn/dtd 1957, 62x57", SBY 11/8/89 OE **3,410,000**
Untitled (abstract in dark blue), oil on paper laid down on canvas, 1969, SBY 5/3/89 OE **451,000**
Untitled (abstract), acrylic on paper mounted on board, 1968, 24x19", SBY 5/2/88 ..... **187,000**
Untitled (abstract), acrylic on paper mounted on canvas, 1969, 49x41", SBY 5/2/88 ..... **308,000**
Untitled (abstract), oil on canvas, sgn/dtd 1960, 92x69", SBY 11/10/88 OE **1,540,000**
Untitled (abstract), oil on paper laid down on canvas, sgn/dtd 1967, 24x18", SBY 2/15/89 OE **198,000**
Untitled (seated woman), oil on plasterboard, sgn, ca 1930s, sgn, 7x5", SBY 10/5/89 OE **16,500**
White, Yellow, Red on Yellow (abstract); oil on canvas, sgn, 1953, 91x71", SBY 11/10/88 ..... **198,000**

ROTINI, Valerio (Italian, 1911-)
Two Figures in an Extensive Landscape, oil on canvas, sgn, 28x38", WG 9/16/88 UE **95**

ROTTENHAMMER, Hans (German, 1564-1625)
Judgement of Midas, oil on copper, 10x14", C-NY 4/8/88 ..... **19,800**

ROTTENHAMMER, Hans; follower of (German, 1564-1625)
Diana & Her Nymphs Discovering the Pregnancy of Callisto, oil on canvas, 17x34", SBY 10/21/88 ..... **2,200**

ROTTMANN, Mozart (Hungarian, 1874-)
Art Critic, oil on canvas, sgn, 32x24", C-E 10/25/88 ..... **3,300**
Family Gathered Together (interior), oil on canvas, sgn, unfr, 54x38", C-E 2/21/89 ..... **6,050**

ROTTONARA, Franz Angelo (Austrian, 1848-)
Room Interior, gouache on paper, sgn/dtd 1904, 24x34", B/B 10/9/88 UE **1,100**

ROUAULT, Georges (French, 1871-1958)
Acrobate, oil/gouache/brush/India ink on paper laid down on board, sgn, ca 1929-39, 8x8", C-NY 5/11/89 OE **93,500**
Apparition (Christ Sortant du Tombeau), oil on canvas, ca 1935-36, 15x11", SBY 5/10/89 ..... **286,000**
Au Theatre (I), gouache/brush/India ink/pastel on board, sgn, ca 1925-29, 18x10", C-NY 11/16/88 ..... **220,000**
Christ (contemporary portrait), oil on paper laid down on canvas, sgn, 1937-38, 12x11", C-NY 5/11/89 ..... **407,000**
Christ en Banlieu (Christ at the edge of town), oil on paper laid down on canvas, sgn, 1934, 13x10", SBY 11/12/88 OE **137,500**
Clown a la Parade, oil on paper laid down on canvas, sgn, 1939, 22x16", C-NY 5/11/89 OE **462,000**
Discorde I, watercolor/crayon on paper backed w/another sheet, sgn, ca 1913-15, 12x8", SBY 11/16/89 ..... **44,000**
Double-Sided: Fille de Cirque; gouache/watercolor/pastel on paper, sgn/dtd 1903 or 1905, 8x6", SBY 11/12/88 OE **187,000**
Femme a la Rose (portrait of lady w/rose in her hair), oil on canvas, sgn, 28x24", SBY 5/10/89 OE **1,210,000**
Fille (nude sitting on bed), watercolor/pastel on paper, ca 1905, 9x8", SBY 11/12/88 OE **143,000**
Fleurs Decoratives (floral still life), oil on paper laid down on canvas, sgn, ca 1933-39, 24x20", SBY 5/10/89 OE **605,000**
Grock (two heads, one in profile), gouache on paper, sgn/dtd 1931, 6x12", WD 11/16/89 ..... **32,000**
Juanita, gouache/India ink on paper w/printed text, sgn/dtd 1932, 8x9", SBY 11/16/89 ..... **176,000**
Juge (portrait of a judge), watercolor on paper, 1907, 8x5", C-NY 5/11/89 OE **93,500**
Juges, gouache/watercolor on paper, 1907, 8x8", SBY 11/16/89 ..... **55,000**
L'Aristocrate (portrait), oil on paper laid down on canvas, sgn, ca 1945-46, 16x13", SBY 11/11/88 ..... **550,000**
Le Clown Pale, oil on paper, sgn/Cachet de l'atelier stamp, ca 1920-29, 28x16", SBY 11/12/88 ..... **308,000**
Nu Assis (seated nude), watercolor/ink wash on thin paper laid down on board, sgn/dtd 1907, 10x8", SBY 5/11/88 ..... **16,500**
O Vase de Tristesse, O Grande Taciturne?, ink wash on paper, ca 1925, 5x4", SBY 10/6/89 OE **17,600**
Passion (portrait), oil on paper laid down on canvas, sgn, 1937, 26x18", SBY 11/11/88 OE **605,000**
Paysage Africain (abstract), gouache on paper laid down on canvas, ca 1919, 11x16", lot 55, C-NY 10/5/89 ..... **20,000**
Paysage Africain (abstract), gouache on paper laid down on canvas, ca 1919, 11x16", lot 56, C-NY 10/5/89 ..... **26,400**
Paysage Biblique, oil on board, sgn, ca 1940-48, 16x13", SBY 11/12/88 OE **308,000**
Pierette (portrait of a woman's head), oil on metal foil, sgn, 1939, 14x11", SBY 5/10/89 OE **440,000**
Pierrot Bleu (portrait of woman's head), oil on canvas, sgn, ca 1937-38, 25x20", SBY 5/10/89 OE **1,017,000**
Profil de Christ, oil on paper laid down on canvas, 12x9", SBY 5/11/88 ..... **110,000**
Satan, oil on paper laid down on canvas, sgn, 1938, 8x7", SBY 2/16/89 OE **107,250**
Satan I, ink wash on paper, ca 1925, 5x4", SBY 10/6/89 OE **13,200**
Still Life of Vase of Flowers, watercolor, sgn, 20x12", WG 9/16/88 UE **11,000**
Vieux Faubourg, oil on canvas, sgn, 18x24", SBY 5/11/88 OE **462,000**

ROUBAUD, Franz (Russian, 1856-1928)
Cherkesses Crossing a River, oil on canvas, sgn, 23x33", C-L 10/8/88 ..... **13,000**
Cossacks Crossing the Plains, oil on panel, sgn, 12x20", C-NY 2/23/89 ..... **3,850**

ROUCY TRIOSON, Anne; see De Roucy Trioson

ROUGET, Georges (French, 1784-1869)
Portrait of a Gentleman, bust-length, wearing gray jacket; oil on canvas, sgn/dtd 1817, 26x21", C-M 12/3/88 ..... **8,370**

ROULAND, Orlando (American, 1871-1945)
Marblehead, Massachusetts, Harbor View; oil on canvas, sgn, 18x20", RWS 5/12/89 OE **6,600**
St Etienne, Pas de Calais (shepherd w/sheep in landscape); oil on canvas, sgn, 20x30", C-E 6/1/89 UE **770**

ROUSSEAU, Albert (Canadian, 1908-1982)
Abstract Composition, oil on canvas, sgn, 1966, 24x30", FB 5/28/89 ..... **750**
Automne, oil on board, sgn/dtd 1977, 8x10", FB 10/30/89 ..... **990**
Bernard, Baie des Francais; oil on board, sgn/dtd 1960, 30x48", FB 10/17/88 ..... **1,900**
Boat at Dock, oil on board, sgn, 12x16", FB 4/25/88 ..... **700**

Buildings in a Landscape, oil on canvas, sgn, 18x24", FB 10/17/88 1,500
Houses & Trees, oil on board, sgn, 12x16", FB 10/17/88.......... 1,100
Landscape, oil on board, 16x20", FB 4/25/88 750
Maison de Baie St Paul, oil on board, sgn/dtd 1969, 12x16", FB 5/28/89 950
Peggy's Cove, oil on board, sgn, 16x20", FB 5/28/89 900
Row of Houses (village scene with mountains beyond), oil on canvas, sgn/dtd 1970, 16x20", FB 5/28/89 850
St Simeon (village scene), oil on canvas, sgn, 18x24", FB 5/28/89 1,900
Street Scene, oil on canvas, sgn/dtd 1964, 24x30", FB 10/30/89.......... 1,430
Sur le Saguenay, oil on canvas, sgn, 20x24", FB 4/25/88 1,500

OUSSEAU, Charles (Belgian, 1862-1916)
Brush Factory, oil on canvas, sgn/inscr/dtd 1892, 21x25", C-NY 2/25/88.......... 3,850
In the Studio, oil on canvas, sgn/dtd 1888, C-NY 2/25/88.......... 4,400

OUSSEAU, Etienne Pierre Theodore (French, 1812-1867)
Faggot Gatherer in a Landscape, oil on panel, sgn, 6x9", C-NY 2/23/89 OE.......... 20,900
Figure on a Path in a Wooded Landscape, oil on panel, sgn, 24x29", C-NY 10/25/89 88,000
Figure Walking Along a Tree-Lined Path, oil on panel, sgn, 8x6", C-E 10/26/89 4,620
Figures by a Tree on Woodland Path, oil on paper laid down on canvas, sgn, 10x9", SBY 2/22/89 OE 12,100
Marshy Landscape, black chalk heightened w/white on blue paper, sgn, 7x16", C-NY 10/25/89 OE.......... 8,800
Study of a Cottage in a Landscape, pen/ink on paper, stamped THR/wm in shield, 8x11", C-NY 10/25/89.......... 1,650
Sunset at Barbizon, oil on panel, sgn, 17x26", C-NY 2/3/88 OE 99,000

OUSSEAU, Henri; att (French, 1844-1910)
Still Life of Tropical Fruits, oil on canvas, inscr/dtd 1908, 26x32", SBY 5/11/88 OE.......... 209,000

OUSSEAU, Jean Jacques (1861-1911)
Canton (figures in boats, city beyond), oil on canvas, sgn, 11x18", C-SK 5/25/89.......... 1,285

OUSSEAU, Marguerite (Belgian, 1888-1948)
Bathers (beach scene), oil on board, sgn/dtd 19, 18x21", C-NY 5/24/89 7,700
Elegant Lady Entering a Coach, oil on board, sgn/dtd 19, 13x18", C-NY 5/24/89 6,600
Les Falaises d'Etretat, Normandie (beach scene); oil on panel, sgn/dtd 18, 18x25", C-NY 2/23/89 5,500

OUSSEAUX, see De Rousseaux

OUSSEL, Ker Xavier (French, 1867-1944)
Les Amoureux au Bord de la Riviere, pastel over peinture a la calle on board, indistinctly sgn, 26x32", C-NY 2/18/88 OE 28,600
Les Baigneuses (bathers in a landscape), pastel on paper laid down on canvas, 18x18", C-NY 2/18/88 OE 17,600
Maisons dans la Campagne, pastel on tan paper, sgn, ca 1910, 13x13", SBY 10/7/88.......... 3,300

OUSSEL, Pierre (French, 1927-)
Chez la Couturiere (at the dressmakers), oil on canvas, sgn, 26x32", C-E 5/9/89 OE.......... 3,960
Girls Sitting at a Table, oil on canvas, sgn, 26x21", SBY 10/7/89 OE.......... 8,525
Lady in Her Garden, oil on canvas, sgn, 26x40", SBY 10/7/89 OE.......... 10,725
Le Salon, gouache/watercolor/chalk on brown board, sgn, 25x32", C-E 5/9/89 OE 3,300

OUWETTE, Paul
Lady with a Blue Hat, oil on canvas, sgn, 22x32", C-E 2/23/88 1,760

OUX, Guillermo (Argentinian, 1929-)
Placita de Arraial, watercolor on paper, sgn/dtd 71, 21x26", SBY 5/17/88 UE 2,750

OVERE, see Della Rovere

OWAN, Marion Ellis (Austrailian, 1858-1922)
Spring Landscape, pencil/watercolor heightened with bodycolor, sgn, 20x33", C-SK 6/9/88 4,090

OWBOTHAM, Charles (British, 1877-)
Alpine Lake with Figures by a Jetty (landscape), watercolor/gouache, sgn, 5x7", C-NY 2/23/89 UE 770
Figures on an Alpine Lake Shore, watercolor/gouache, sgn, 5x7", C-NY 2/23/89 UE 550

OWBOTHAM, Claude H. (British, fl ca 1910-)
Bray Church, watercolor, sgn/dtd 1890, 9x14", C-E 2/16/88 275

OWE, Sydney Grant (British, 19th/20th C)
Bridge Over a Stream, watercolor on paper, sgn, 14x20", C-E 5/23/88 550

OWLANDSON, George Derville (British, 1861-)
Over the Fence, oil on canvas, sgn, 16x24", lot 461, C-E 10/25/88 4,180
Over the Fence, oil on canvas, sgn, 24x16", lot 477, C-E 10/25/88 2,200
Over the Hedge, oil on canvas, sgn, 20x30", SBY 6/10/88 2,750

OWLANDSON, Thomas (British, 1756-1827)
Apollo & Daphne, pen/brown ink/brown wash, sgn twice, 6x4", C-NY 2/23/89.......... 1,980
Black Man & Two Lions, watercolor/pen/brown ink over pencil, sgn, 6x6", C-NY 2/25/88.......... 660
Brawl, watercolor, sgn/dtd 1798, 5x8", FB 5/28/89 850
Dr Syntax, a Rural Scene; ink/watercolor on laid paper, sgn, 6x9", SBY 6/8/88 1,540
How Much the Old Farmer Looks Like His Hogs, pen/brown ink/watercolor, sgn/dtd 1779, 5x4", C-NY 2/25/88 660
Leda & the Swan, pen/brown ink/watercolor, sgn/dtd 1797, 5x7", C-NY 2/25/88 1,430
Prize Fight, watercolor on paper, sgn, 6x9", WG 4/23/88 UE.......... 1,100
Repairing the Sidewalk, brown ink/ink wash/watercolor on paper laid down, 6x9", SBY 7/12/89 OE.......... 2,475
Rivals (figures in an interior), watercolor/pencil on paper, sgn, 9x12", B/B 10/9/88.......... 3,850
Set of 3: Helping Hand; Carried Away; Looking at the Globe; watercolor/pencil on paper, sgn, 7x6", 6x5", B/B 10/9/88.......... 3,850
Stag Hunting, watercolor/pencil on paper, sgn, 8x10", B/B 10/9/88 3,300

OWLANDSON, Thomas; att (British, 1756-1827)
View of the Entrance to Fishguard From Goodwych Sands, watercolor/pen/ink in bistre, ca 1800, 7x9", SWN 12/1/88 440

Y, Harold; see Le Roy

ROY, Pierre (French, 1880-1950)
Amusing Physique, oil on canvas, sgn, 1929, 36x26", C-NY 5/12/88 OE **143,000**
Pair: Noeud Rose et Coquillage au Bord Mer; Noeud Bleu et Epis de Ble Pres du Chateau; oil, sgn, 21x6", C-NY 2/18/88 OE **30,800**
Prognostication, oil on canvas, sgn, 14x11", SBY 2/16/89 OE **44,000**
Trees on a Hillside, watercolor on paper, sgn/dtd 1912, 14x18", B/B 12/8/88 ..... **1,045**
ROYBET, Ferdinand (French, 1840-1920)
Cavalier (full-length portrait), oil on panel, sgn, 16x11", C-E 5/22/89 ..... **2,750**
L'Homme a la Fraise, oil on panel, sgn, 24x18", C-NY 2/25/88 ..... **3,520**
Un Gentilhomme de Louis XVIII (portrait), oil on panel, sgn, 32x27", C-NY 2/23/89 ..... **5,500**
ROYER, Lionel Noel (French, 1852-1926)
The Fisherman, oil on canvas, sgn, 33x20", C-E 10/26/89 ..... **3,850**
RUBEN, Franz Leo (Austrian, 1842-1920)
Fan Seller, oil on canvas laid down on board, sgn/dtd 1882, 34x34", C-NY 5/25/88 ..... **8,800**
Sunny Day on the Beach, Venice; watercolor on paper, sgn/dtd 1871, 7x11", WD 1/11/89 ..... **1,800**
RUBENS, Peter Paul (Flemish, 1577-1640)
Early Morning, oil on canvas, sgn/dtd 1864, 14x18", B/B 12/8/88 ..... **880**
Head of Cyrus Brought to Queen Tamyris, oil on canvas, 47x54", RWS 6/17/89 ..... **750**
Hunt of Diana (oil sketch produced as part of a commission), oil on panel, 10x21", SBY 6/2/89 ..... **462,000**
Portrait of a Bearded Man, bust-length; oil on panel, 28x21", C-NY 1/11/89 OE **528,000**
Portrait of Sir Theodore Turquet de Mayerne, oil on canvas, 45x35", C-NY 1/11/89 UE **77,000**
Two Saints, oil on panel, 26x20", C-NY 1/11/89 UE **33,000**
RUBENS, Peter Paul; after (Flemish, 1577-1640)
Allegory, oil on canvas, 52x38", C-E 4/7/88 ..... **3,080**
Garden of Love, oil on canvas, 50x72", SBY 4/7/88 OE **12,100**
Lot & His Family Escaping Sodom, oil on board, 16x20", SBY 12/9/88 OE **2,750**
Self-Portrait, oil on canvas laid down, 31x26", B/B 4/20/88 ..... **550**
RUBENS, Peter Paul; att (Flemish, 1577-1640)
Madonna & Child, oil on panel, unfr, 38x29", C-NY 1/15/88 ..... **33,000**
RUBENS, Peter Paul; circle of (Flemish, 1577-1640)
Abraham & Melchizedek, oil on canvas, 13x21", C-NY 10/20/88 ..... **2,200**
Achilles Among the Daughters of Lycomedes, oil on canvas, 44x67", SBY 10/21/88 OE **17,050**
Christ & the Woman Taken in Adultery, oil on panel, 41x53", C-NY 10/12/89 OE **82,500**
Portrait of a Gentleman, bust-length, wearing a black costume with a white ruff; oil on panel, 12x10", C-NY 4/6/89 ..... **1,650**
Portrait of Paracelsus, wearing a fur hat, holding a book, a landscape beyond; oil on panel, 31x25", C-NY 6/2/88 OE **11,000**
Rape of Persephone, oil on panel, 31x42", SBY 6/1/89 OE **63,250**
RUBENS, Peter Paul; follower of (Flemish, 1577-1640)
Portrait of Charles the Bold (three-quarter length), oil on canvas, 48x37", SBY 6/1/89 ..... **10,450**
Reconciliation of Jacob & Esau, oil on panel, 18x16", SBY 4/7/88 ..... **11,000**
RUBENS, Peter Paul; manner of (Flemish, 1577-1640)
Portrait of the Artist, oil on canvas, 31x24", C-NY 3/22/89 ..... **2,750**
Queen of Sheba Presenting Solomon with Gifts, oil on canvas, 22x17", C-E 6/1/88 ..... **935**
RUBENS, Peter Paul; school of (Flemish, 1577-1640)
Allegory of Earth & Water, oil on canvas, 66x89", C-NY 10/20/88 ..... **13,200**
Drunken Silenus, oil on panel, 10x15", C-NY 10/20/88 UE **1,100**
Sleeping Nymphs Watched by Satyrs in a Landscape, oil on copper, unfr, 19x28", C-NY 10/20/88 OE **8,250**
Susanna & the Elders, oil on canvas, unfr, 45x66", C-NY 4/6/89 ..... **4,950**
Visitation, oil on copper, 29x22", C-E 4/7/88 OE **1,980**
RUBENS, Peter Paul; studio of (Flemish, 1577-1640)
Atalanta & Meleager, oil on canvas, 49x38", SBY 4/7/89 ..... **7,150**
Madonna & Child Surrounded by Bonaventura, George, & Gerome with Angels & Figures; oil on canvas, 89x78", SBY 1/12/89 ..... **22,000**
RUBENS, Peter Paul; style of (Flemish, 1577-1640)
Study of Four Warriors, sepia ink on paper, bears signature, 8x9", B/B 4/20/88 ..... **550**
RUBENS & BRUEGHEL, school of (Flemish, 16th/17th C)
Sleeping Nymphs Watched by Satyrs, with Dogs, in a Landscape; oil on panel, unfr, 24x42", C-NY 6/2/88 ..... **16,500**
RUBIN, Reuven (Israeli, 1893-1974)
Anemonies (still life), oil on canvas, sgn twice/dtd 1945, 13x11", C-E 5/9/89 ..... **13,750**
Fisherman (turbaned figure holding fish in each hand), oil on canvas, sgn, 14x10", SBY 10/7/89 ..... **17,600**
Flute Player, pen/brush/ink/wash, sgn, 29x21", SBY 5/30/89 ..... **6,600**
Galilean Landscape, sgn, 26x32", C-NY 5/12/88 ..... **38,500**
La Peche Miraculeuse, pen/brown & black ink/brown wash on paper, sgn/dtd 1935, 22x15", C-NY 2/18/88 ..... **2,420**
Milk Man (man on burrow spilling milk while gawking at maiden), oil on canvas, sgn/dtd 28, 36x29", SBY 5/30/89 OE **74,800**
Mimosas & Irises (still life), oil on canvas, sgn/dtd 1964-65, 36x29", SBY 5/30/89 OE **71,500**
New Settlement in Galilee, oil on canvas, sgn, 22x26", SBY 2/14/89 OE **27,500**
Olive Grove (w/pickers & village on hilltop), oil on canvas, sgn, 21x26", SBY 5/30/89 ..... **38,500**
Pomegranates (still life), oil on canvas, sgn twice, 18x22", SBY 5/30/89 ..... **28,600**
Poppies in the Field, oil on canvas, sgn/dtd 1965, 24x36", SBY 5/30/89 OE **44,000**
Reclining Nude, pencil/ink/graphite on paper, sgn/dtd 29, 10x14", C-E 5/9/89 ..... **1,540**
Road to Safed, oil on canvas, sgn, 13x16", C-NY 10/6/88 ..... **22,000**
Road to Safed (landscape w/figures & village on hilltop), oil on canvas, sgn, ca 1960, 21x29", C-NY 2/16/89 OE **44,000**
Silent Prayer (impressionistic portrait), oil on canvas, sgn, ca 1940, 22x18", C-NY 2/16/89 ..... **18,700**
Simchath Torah (three men w/torahs), oil on canvas, sgn, 18x15", SBY 5/30/89 ..... **31,900**

Springtime in the Galilee (pickers in an olive grove), oil on canvas, sgn/dtd 1964, 29x36", SBY 5/30/89 OE ... **55,000**
Three Musicians, brush/ink/wash on buff paper, sgn, 21x15", SBY 5/30/89 ... **4,400**
Vase of Chrysanthemums, oil on canvas, sgn twice/dtd 1945, 26x32", C-NY 5/12/88 OE ... **41,800**
View of the Old Port, Jaffa; oil on canvas, sgn, ca 1923, 20x26", SBY 5/30/88 OE ... **74,800**
Woman in Oriental Dress, watercolor over pencil, sgn, 17x13", SBY 5/30/89 OE ... **7,920**

JCKER, Robert (American, 20th C)
Courtyard Scene, watercolor on board, sgn, 10x40", MG 6/25/88 UE ... **315**

JCKMAN, Grace Merrill
Mixed Flowers in a Pitcher, oil on canvas, sgn, 22x20", C-E 6/1/89 UE ... **550**

JDD, N. (American, 19th C)
Swampscott & Nahant From Revere Beach, Massachusetts; oil on canvas, sgn/dtd 1884/titled, 15x25", RAB 8/8/89 UE ... **2,500**

JDE, Sophie (French, 1797-1867)
Portrait of Madeleine Allart-Dumont & Children, oil on canvas, sgn/dtd 1840, 40x32", LH 12/4/88 OE ... **1,900**

JDISUHLI, Hermann (Swiss, 1864-1945)
Ancient Ruins by a Lake, oil on board, sgn/inscr, 21x33", C-E 5/22/89 ... **3,080**

JDOLPH, Harold (American, 1850-1884)
Cabin in the Mountains, oil on canvas, sgn, 11x14", NA 2/6/88 ... **1,500**
Fisherman Hauling Nets, oil on canvas, sgn, 10x16", NA 5/13/89 OE ... **900**
Louisiana Log Cabin, oil on canvas, sgn, 15x10", MG 5/28/88 ... **4,000**

JE, see De La Rue

JETER, Georg (Dutch, 1875-)
Artist with Model in a Studio, oil on canvas, sgn/dtd 37, 39x27", B/B 9/14/89 ... **1,210**

FFIERE, Noel
Ships in a Harbor, oil on panel, sgn/dtd 94, 7x40", C-E 11/8/88 UE ... **300**

GENDAS, Johann Moritz (German, 1802-1858)
Caca de Jacare, watercolor on paper, 6x8", C-NY 11/21/89 OE ... **15,400**
El Paraje (courtyard scene), watercolor on paper, initialed, ca 1838, 10x12", C-NY 5/18/88 ... **8,800**
Mexican Landscape, oil on paper laid down on board, 10x16", C-SK 6/9/88 ... **27,880**
Peruvian Landscape, oil on canvas, sgn/dtd Lima 1843, 14x18", SBY 11/21/88 ... **41,250**
Procesion de Nuestra Senora del Rosario (street scene), pencil/wash on esecum paper, 9x13", C-NY 11/21/88 ... **5,500**

GENDAS, Johann Moritz; att (German, 1802-1858)
Valley of Mexico, oil on paper laid down on canvas, 13x18", C-SK 5/25/89 ... **3,670**

GENDAS, Johann Moritz; circle of (German, 1802-1858)
Shipping Off a Coast in a Storm, oil on canvas, bears signature, 17x22", PHL 10/28/88 ... **700**

GER, H. Otto (German, 19th C)
Two Pack Horses Drinking From a Well, oil on canvas, sgn/inscr, 16x9", SBY 7/12/89 ... **2,200**

IQING, Li (Chinese, 1867-1920)
Couplet in Kai Shu (regular script, hanging scrolls), ink on paper, sgn, 51x13", SBY 5/31/89 ... **660**

ISDAEL, Jacob; att (Dutch, 1625-1682)
Northern Wooded River Landscape with a Waterfall, oil on canvas, 19x24", SBY 4/7/88 ... **6,050**

ISDAEL, Jacob; see Van Ruisdael

ITI, Zhang (Chinese, -1644)
Prose-Poem in Xing-Cao Shu Running Cursive Script (hand scroll); ink on satin, sgn/dtd 1626, 11x204", SBY 5/31/89 ... **27,500**

MMELHOFF, John (American, 20th C)
Evel Knievel, acrylic on canvas, sgn/dtd 74, 60x60", C-E 5/13/88 ... **2,420**

NGALDIER, Ignaz
Study of Two Children, watercolor, sgn, 5x9", C-NY 10/26/88 ... **1,980**

NGE, J.F.
Libby Prison Escape, Sectional View (Civil War); pen/ink on paper, inscr, unfr, 10x11", C-E 11/30/88 ... **176**

NGE, Phillip Otto; circle of (German, 19th C)
Three Children with Roses, oil on canvas, 22x28", WAD 6/6/88 ... **2,800**

NGIUS, Carl (American, 1869-1959)
King of the Mountain (moose in mountainous landscape), oil on canvas, sgn, 30x34", WD 10/5/88 ... **57,000**
Moose in a Landscape, oil on canvas, sgn, 16x24", SBY 5/25/88 ... **22,000**

OPPOLO, Giuseppe; manner of (Italian, 1639-1710)
Still Life of Melon, Grapes, a Pomegranate & Other Fruit; oil on canvas, 29x36", SBY 4/7/89 OE ... **31,900**

SCHA, Ed (American, 1937-)
A Heavy Shower of Screws (white letters on black background), gunpowder on paper, sgn/dtd 1976, 23x29", C-NY 5/4/89 OE ... **20,900**
Atlas, dry pigment on paper, sgn/dtd 1983, 22x30", SBY 11/9/89 OE ... **52,250**
Bamboo Pole (contemporary), oil on canvas, sgn/dtd 1980, 20x159", SBY 11/9/89 ... **220,000**
Face Shield, watercolor on paper, sgn/dtd 1974, 11x29", SBY 11/9/89 OE ... **35,200**
Falling Cameras, Rising Binoculars (contemporary); dry pigment on paper, 1983, 45x65", SBY 11/9/89 ... **71,500**
Falling Chiclets (abstract), oil on canvas, sgn/dtd 1963-64, 67x50", C-NY 11/9/88 OE ... **176,000**
Fear Smeared From Here to Here (title printed on dark background), dry pigment, sgn/dtd 1982, 40x60", SBY 10/5/89 ... **41,250**
Flood, gunpowder on paper, sgn/dtd 1967, 15x23", SBY 11/9/89 OE ... **82,500**
Forgotten Landing Zone, dry pigment on paper, sgn/dtd 1982, 23x29", SBY 5/3/89 OE ... **28,600**
Funnelling of You-Know-What (contemporary), acrylic/dry pigment on paper, sgn/dtd 1985, 40x60", SBY 5/3/89 OE ... **49,500**
Future (printing on blue horizon w/blue-green background), oil on canvas, sgn/dtd 1981, 22x80", SBY 5/2/89 OE ... **209,000**
Hawaiian Music, egg yolk on taffeta, sgn/inscr/dtd 1974, unfr, 36x40", C-NY 5/4/88 ... **15,400**
Honey I Twisted Through More...; oil on canvas, sgn/dtd 1984, 72x72", SBY 11/9/89 ... **297,000**
Hourglass, dry pigment/acrylic on paper, sgn/dtd 1988, 60x40", SBY 11/9/89 OE ... **187,000**

It's OK, Everything's OK (contemporary); acrylic on canvas, 1979, 22x80", C-NY 5/4/89 OE ... 132,000
Jr (title printed on dark ground w/white sprayed-on letters), dry pigment/acrylic, sgn/dtd 1988, 60x40", SBY 10/5/89 OE ... 60,500
Lisp (contemporary), oil on canvas, sgn/dtd 1968, 59x55", SBY 11/10/88 OE ... 192,500
Miniature Nightmares, Micro; dry pigment/acrylic on paper, sgn/dtd 1985, 40x60", SBY 11/9/89 OE ... 132,000
Nerve Increasing Activity (contemporary), dry pigment on paper, 1984, 23x29", SBY 11/9/89 OE ... 77,000
Nerves (printed on blue background), dry pigment on paper, sgn/dtd 1985, 38x58", SBY 2/15/89 OE ... 46,750
Policy, gunpowder on paper, sgn, 1970, 10x27", SBY 11/9/89 OE ... 68,750
Polynesian Sickness (in printed letters), dry pigment on paper, sgn/dtd 1984, 21x29", SBY 5/3/89 OE ... 30,800
Protein (white letters on pastel background), pastel on paper, sgn/dtd 1970, 22x27", SBY 11/11/88 OE ... 23,100
Royal (curving white letters on green background), gunpowder/pastel on paper, sgn/dtd 1971, 22x28", SBY 11/11/88 OE ... 35,750
Stage Fright (small figure on long horizontal line), ink on paper, sgn/dtd 1979, 15x40", C-NY 2/20/88 ... 3,300
Strength, gunpowder/colored chalk on paper, sgn/dtd 83, 60x40", C-NY 11/10/88 OE ... 33,000
Sugar, watercolor on paper, sgn/dtd 1971, 12x29", SBY 11/9/89 OE ... 68,750
Surgical (contemporary), oil on canvas, sgn/dtd 1967, 20x24", SBY 11/9/89 ... 93,500
Twelve Priests, gunpowder on paper, sgn/dtd 1974, 14x23", C-NY 11/10/88 OE ... 8,800
U (gathering of bubbles shaped like a U), oil on canvas, sgn/dtd 1968, 20x24", SBY 5/3/88 ... 29,700
Various Miracles (title printed on yellow & violet background), gunpowder/watercolor, 1975, 22x29", SBY 10/5/89 OE ... 55,000
We're This & We're That Aren't We? (in printed letters), dry pigment on paper, sgn/dtd 84, 23x29", SBY 5/3/89 OE ... 52,250
Wen Out for Cigrets, oil/enamel on canvas, sgn/dtd 1985, 64x64", SBY 10/8/88 OE ... 77,000
Zero (contemporary), dry pigment on paper, sgn/dtd 1982, 60x40", SBY 11/9/89 ... 63,250

RUSINOL, Santiago (Spanish, 1861-1931)
Mercado en Valencia, oil on canvas, sgn, 32x40", SBY 10/24/89 ... 352,000

RUSK, L.S. (20th C)
Impressionistic Landscape, oil on canvas, 8x10", WG 4/23/88 UE ... 100

RUSS, Harry (American, 19th/20th C)
Hay Wagon, oil on canvas, sgn, 30x40", SBY 6/28/89 OE ... 5,500

RUSSELL, Benjamin (American, 1804-1885)
Schooner DM Antony James McLane Master (ship), watercolor on paper, sgn/dtd 1874/titled, 21x34", RAB 8/1/88 ... 4,500

RUSSELL, Charles Marion (American, 1864-1926)
Assiniboine Chief, India ink/gray wash heightened w/white, sgn/dtd 1900, 12x10", SBY 5/25/88 OE ... 18,700
Blackfoot Scout, watercolor/pencil on paper, initialed, 6x5", SBY 5/25/88 ... 19,800
Here's to the Days of the Open Range (drawing w/letter), ink on paper, ea sgn, framed together, 2x3", 6x5", SBY 1/24/89 ... 1,430
Indian Rider, watercolor on paper, sgn/dtd 94, 17x22", SBY 5/25/88 ... 19,800
New Year's Greeting, India ink/watercolor/gouache on paper, initialed/dtd 1923, 4x12", SBY 9/23/88 OE ... 17,600
Pack Train, ink/wash on paper, initialed, 13x21", C-NY 12/2/88 ... 14,300
Pigeon Hunting Party, watercolor on paper, sgn twice/dtd 94, 16x20, SBY 5/25/88 ... 66,000
Pointing Out the Trail, watercolor on paper, sgn, 20x27", SBY 5/25/88 ... 99,000

RUSSELL, George Horne (Canadian, 1861-1933)
Light Houses at Dusk, oil on board, sgn, 9x13", FB 4/25/88 ... 650
Morning Fog, St Andrews, New Brunswick; oil on board, sgn, 13x18", FB 10/30/89 ... 715
Schooner by a Wharf, New Brunswick; watercolor, sgn/dtd 1909, 10x14", FB 4/25/88 ... 400

RUSSELL, Gyrth (Canadian, 1892-1970)
Clovelly, oil on board, sgn, 10x15", WAD 6/12/89 ... 475
Ipsham, Quay, Devon; oil on board, sgn, 13x12", WAD 6/12/89 UE ... 275
Road Stand, oil on paper, sgn, no size given, FAP 12/8/89 ... 350

RUSSELL, John (British, 1745-1806)
Portrait of a Man, oil on canvas, sgn/dtd 1767, 29x25", SBY 10/13/89 ... 7,150
Portrait of Anthony Aufree As a Boy, pastel on paper, 23x18", SBY 4/7/88 OE ... 9,900
Portrait of Artist's Daughter in a Landscape, pastel on paper laid down on canvas, sgn/dtd 1778, 24x20", SBY 10/21/88 OE ... 10,450

RUSSELL, John Wentworth (Canadian, 1879-1959)
Honfleur Harbor (France), oil on board, sgn, 13x16", WAD 6/12/89 ... 3,600

RUSSELL, Morgan (American, 1886-1953)
Bather (posterior view of nude), oil on canvas, sgn, 37x24", C-E 6/1/89 UE ... 2,200
Male Bather, oil on canvas, sgn, 39x32", C-E 6/1/89 ... 2,200
Still Life of Marble Bust, pencils on paper, sgn, 6x5", WG 4/23/88 UE ... 2,100

RUSSELL, W.S. (American, 20th C)
Garden Gate (shingled structure in a flower garden), oil on cardboard, sgn/dtd 1927, 9x8", RAB 8/9/88 UE ... 300

Russian School (19th C)
Charge of the Cossacks, oil on canvas/panel, 12x19", B/B 12/8/88 OE ... 3,025
Kitchen Flirtation, oil on panel, indistinctly sgn, 22x18", SBY 7/12/89 ... 1,760
Mending Nets, oil on canvas, bears signature/indistinctly inscr, 23x37", C-E 2/23/88 ... 1,100
Portrait of Countess Anna Baranova (born Vasil'chikov), watercolor on paper, inscr Fricero 1842, 7x4", C-L 10/8/88 OE ... 4,090
Sailboats Off a Rocky Cliff, oil on canvas, sgn/dtd 1896, 24x35", C-E 10/25/88 ... 990
Serving the Wine, oil on canvas, indistinctly sgn, 28x33", WD 3/23/88 OE ... 2,200
Sleigh Ride Home, gouache on board, indistinctly sgn, 13x19", RWS 11/10/89 ... 850
Two Horse-Drawn Sleighs, oil on canvas, 13x16", C-L 10/8/88 ... 1,580

Russian School (20th C)
Windblown Fields, oil on canvas, initialed, 25x30", B/B 12/8/88 ... 715

RUTHART, Karl Andreas; circle of (German, 1630-1703)
Leopard Attacking a Mandrill Baboon in a Tropical Landscape, oil on canvas, unfr, 69x60", C-NY 6/2/88 OE ... 63,800

RUTLEGE, William (British, 19th C)
London Bridge, oil on canvas, sgn, 32x40", FB 5/28/89 850
Sheet of Studies of Five Stems of Auriculas & a Flower, watercolor/gouache, sgn/dtd 1869, 12x14", SBY 1/13/89 1,760
RUYSCH, Rachel (Dutch, 1664-1750)
Floral Still Life, with a Snail on a Carved Stone Plinth; oil on canvas, sgn, 25x20", C-NY 6/2/88 82,500
Still Life of Peaches, Grapes, Plums, Melons, an Orange...; oil on canvas, sgn/dtd 1712(?), 25x21", C-NY 1/11/89 OE 165,000
RUYSCH, Rachel; after (Dutch, 1664-1750)
Still Life of Fruit, Flowers, & Insects; oil on canvas, sgn/dtd 1716, 35x28", SBY 7/12/89 5,775
Still Life of Various Fruits & Vegetables with Insects & Reptiles, oil on canvas, 34x26", SBY 10/21/88 UE 8,800
Still Life of Various Fruits & Vegetables with Insects & Reptiles, oil on canvas, bears monogram, 36x28", SBY 4/7/88 OE 23,100
RUYSCH, Rachel; manner of (Dutch, 1664-1750)
Still Life of Assorted Fruits, Insects, Lizard, & a Nest; oil on canvas laid down on board, 18x21", SBY 10/21/88 7,700
RUYSCH, Rachel; style of (Dutch, 1664-1750)
Floral Still Life, oil on canvas, 30x25", B/B 6/9/88 6,050
RUYSDAEL, Jacob; see Van Ruisdael
RUYTIN, Alfred (Belgian, 1871-)
Elaborate Floral Still Life on a Ledge, oil on panel, sgn, 12x10", C-E 10/26/89 3,520
Vase of Chrysanthemums, oil on canvas, sgn, 49x32", C-NY 10/25/89 8,800
RYAN, Anne (American, 1889-1954)
Pineapple Still Life, mixed media on mounted paper, 12x8", RWS 11/10/89 UE 325
RYAN, L.S. (American, 19th C)
Low Tide (sailboat on marsh grass near stream), oil on canvas, sgn, 10x20", RAB 8/9/88 625
RYAN, Tom (American, 1922-)
Bucking Horse, oil on canvas, sgn, 24x30", SBY 9/23/88 5,500
RYBACK, Issachar (Russian, 1897-)
Bride, oil on canvas, sgn, 26x22", SBY 5/30/89 13,200
Die Schweigermutter (caricature portrait), brown chalk on buff paper, sgn in Yiddish, 1915, 25x20", SBY 5/30/89 3,850
Fisherman at Sea, oil/gouache over pencil on paper laid down on board, sgn, 23x36", SBY 5/30/89 OE 6,820
La Soupe du Pauvre, oil on canvas, sgn, ca 1930s, 39x32", SBY 5/30/89 13,200
Sailing Boats, watercolor/brush/ink, sgn, 25x19", SBY 5/30/89 OE 4,400
Snow Scene in Russia (couple in horse-drawn sleigh), oil on canvas, sgn, 26x36", SBY 5/30/89 OE 24,200
RYCKAERT, David III; att (Flemish, 1612-1661)
Card Players, oil on panel, unfr, 12x15", SBY 12/9/88 1,650
RYCKAERT, David the younger; att (Flemish, 1596-1642)
Gates of Hell, oil on panel, 23x33", C-NY 6/2/88 7,700
RYCKAERT, Marten; follower of (Flemish, 1587-1631)
Pair: River Scenes; oil on copper, 5x8", SBY 10/21/88 OE 11,000
RYDAY, J.S.
Meeting Vessels, oil on canvas, sgn, 22x29", C-E 7/26/88 462
RYDER, Chauncey Foster (American, 1868-1949)
Across the Valley (landscape), oil on canvas, sgn, 20x24", C-NY 5/25/89 8,800
Autumn Landscape, oil on canvas, sgn, 12x16", SBY 6/28/89 4,400
Cabin at Bear Creek Gap, oil on canvas, sgn, titled/inscr on label, 25x30", SBY 6/24/88 OE 12,100
Creek Through the Meadow, oil on canvas, sgn, 16x20", SBY 9/23/88 4,125
Double-Sided: Fall Landscapes; oil on panel, sgn, 6x9", SBY 9/23/88 2,090
Haystack, oil on panel, sgn, 14x11", C-E 11/30/88 1,650
In the White Mountains, oil on panel, sgn, 6x9", RWS 9/8/89 900
Moonlight (moon peering through trees in a landscape), oil on canvas, sgn, 16x20, SBY 1/24/89 OE 7,700
Promenade at Menton Fence, watercolor on paper laid down on board, sgn, 17x21", C-NY 3/11/88 2,640
Roman Amphitheater, Fiesole; oil on panel, sgn, unfr, 9x11", RWS 11/10/89 850
Squaw Mountain (landscape), oil on canvas, sgn, 32x40", C-NY 5/25/89 13,200
Summer, oil on panel, sgn, 6x9", C-E 11/30/88 1,870
Valley at Copake, oil on canvas stretched over panel, sgn/inscr, 25x30", C-NY 3/11/88 8,800
YDER, J.S. (American, 19th C)
Off Highland, Provincetown, 1877; oil on canvas, sgn/titled, 20x28", RAB 8/1/89 OE 2,500
YDER, Platt Powell (American, 1821-1896)
Knitting by a Window (interior scene), watercolor/gouache on paper, sgn, 8x12", SBY 3/17/88 OE 2,530
Portrait of a Lady in a Winter Coat & Hat, oil on canvas, sgn/dtd 73, 14x10", C-E 6/1/89 1,760
YLAND, Robert Knight (American, 1873-1951)
Striped Dress (woman on sofa), oil on board, sgn/dtd 1940, 25x20", C-NY 9/30/88 2,090
YMAN, Robert (American, 1930-)
Eagle Turquoise 7H #2 (faint squared lines in white circle), graphite on paper, sgn/dtd 66, 12" dia, SBY 10/5/89 OE 41,250
Mars Lunograph 8H #1, graphite on paper in plasctic frame, sgn twice/dtd 66/titled, 13" dia, C-NY 11/10/88 OE 27,500
Untitled (abstract), oil on canvas, sgn twice/dtd 61, 49x49", SBY 11/10/88 OE 550,000
Untitled (abstract), oil on fiberglas, sgn/dtd 69, 20x20", SBY 10/5/89 OE 143,000
Untitled (abstract), oil on mylar, sgn/dtd 69, 18x18", SBY 5/3/89 OE 121,000
Untitled (lineation), oil on linen, sgn/dtd 65, 11x11", SBY 10/8/88 OE 148,500
YSBRACK, John Michael (1693-1770)
Pluto & Persephone, pen/brown ink/wash over black chalk, inscr/#d 29 & 1076, 6x5", SBY 7/12/89 OE 1,430
YSBRACK, Peter (Dutch, fl ca 1670)
Holy Family, ink/brown wash/red chalk on paper, unfr, 6x7", WD 1/25/89 UE 450

SAAR, Betye (American, 20th C)
Nothing Remains the Same, mixed media collage, 11x12", B/B 12/8/88 ..... **330**
SAARNIIT, John (Canadian, 1909-)
Algonquin Park, oil on board, sgn/dtd 1958, 20x24", WAD 11/30/89 ..... **225**
SABATINI, I. (Continental, 19th/20th C)
Marriage Proposal, oil on canvas, sgn, 28x20", C-E 10/26/89 ..... **4,620**
SACKS, Joseph (American, 1887-)
Chinatown, oil on board, sgn, 13x16", B/B 5/17/89 ..... **1,650**
City Neighborhood, oil on board, sgn, 166x20", C-E 2/1/89 ..... **2,690**
Portrait of a Woman (half-length), oil on canvas, sgn, bears estate stamp, 30x25", RAB 8/9/88 UE **1,200**
Still Life of Vase & Figurine, oil on canvas, sgn, 30x25", RAB 8/9/88 UE **1,500**
SACKS, Walter T. (American, 1895-)
Prelude to Evening (atmospheric landscape), oil on canvas, sgn, 28x33", RWS 9/29/88 ..... **550**
SADEE, Philippe Lodowyck Jacob Frederik (Dutch, 1837-1904)
Ankerligten, oil on canvas, sgn/inscr #II, 29x45", SBY 2/22/89 ..... **16,500**
SADLER, Walter Dendy (British, 1854-1923)
Study of Two Boys, oil on canvas, sgn, 18x14", SBY 12/9/88 OE **1,320**
SAEGER, Edward (American, 1809-1886)
Bacharach on the Rhine, pencil, sgn/dtd 1847, 9x13", NA 2/24/89 UE **175**
Stone Bridge, view from a riverbed; pencil on paper, sgn/titled, 9x11", RAB 8/8/89 UE **75**
SAFTLEVEN, Cornelis (Dutch, 1607-1681)
Kneeling Monk, black chalk, sgn/monogramed/dtd 1633, 10x7", SBY 1/13/89 ..... **3,575**
SAFTLEVEN, Herman (Dutch, ca 1609-1685)
De Bok Tower with the Eastern Gateway of the Weert...; chalk/wash, wm, inscr, 18x12", C-NY 1/11/89 OE **39,600**
Heath Landscape Seen From the Margin of a Wood, black chalk/brown wash, 8x12", SBY 1/13/89 ..... **7,700**
SAFTLEVEN, Herman; att (Dutch, ca 1609-1685)
Figures on a Ruined Bridge, black chalk/gray wash, 11x8", SBY 1/13/89 ..... **990**
Peasants Resting by a Tree in a Landscape, black chalk, monogramed(?), 4x5", C-NY 1/11/89 UE **220**
SAGE, Kay (American, 1898-1963)
Untitled, pencil on paper laid down on paper, sgn/dtd 43, 10x6", C-E 11/17/88 OE **1,760**
SAGRESTANI, Giovanni Camillo (Italian, 1660-1731)
A Franciscan, Possibly Saint Bonaventura, in Glory; oil on canvas, 21x28", SBY 6/3/88 UE **1,760**
Sleeping Woman with a Servant Approaching, oil on canvas, unfr, 20x29", SBY 6/3/88 ..... **4,400**
SAIMAON, L.
Ducks Over Water, oil on canvas, sgn, 24x36" **330**
SAINT-ANDRE, see De Saint-Andre
SAINT-AUBIN, see De Saint-Aubin
SAINT-EVRE, Gillot (French, 1791-1858)
Portrait of a Seated Lady, oil on canvas, sgn/dtd 1827, 37x29", SBY 12/9/88 ..... **1,100**
SAINT-OURS, Jean Pierre Paul; att (Swiss, 1752-1809)
Scene From Roman History, pen/brown ink/wash, indistinctly sgn, 21x32", SBY 1/13/89 ..... **660**
SAINT-PHALLE, see De Saint-Phalle
SAKAI, Kazuya
Little Theater (abstract), acrylic/mixed media on canvas, sgn twice/dtd 64 twice/titled, 50x50", C-NY 5/17/89 ..... **3,300**
SALA, Paolo (Italian, 1859-1924)
Gondolas & Fisherman, watercolor on board, sgn, 9x13", FAP 4/15/89 ..... **798**
Gondolas on a Canal, watercolor on board, sgn, unfr, 14x21", B/B 10/9/88 ..... **3,300**
SALA Y FRANCES, Emilio (Spanish, 1850-1910)
Tea Time, oil on canvas, sgn, 15x22", SBY 2/22/89 ..... **33,000**
SALABET, Jean (French, 20th C)
Montmartre, oil on canvas, sgn/dtd 1951, 9x13", MG 10/28/88 UE **175**
Montmartre, oil on canvas, sgn/dtd 1951, 9x13", MG 5/28/88 ..... **150**
SALANSON, Eugenie Marie (French, fl 1864-1892)
Day's Catch (three-quarter length portrait of a girl w/a basket of fish), oil on canvas, sgn, 50x32", SBY 2/22/89 ..... **20,900**
SALANSON, G.
Stopping for Flowers, oil on panel, sgn, 18x22", C-NY 2/25/88 ..... **3,850**
SALAZAR, Carlos (Colombian, 1956-)
Tanagra Tantrica (clothed figure seated on bed), oil on canvas, sgn twice/dtd 88 twice/titled, 67x59", SBY 5/16/89 ..... **4,675**
SALAZAR, Ignacio (Mexican, 1947-)
Dolphin II (abstract hinged four-panel screen), oil/acrylic on linen, 1986-87, 95x95", SBY 11/21/88 UE **5,500**
SALAZAR Y MENDOZA, see De Salazar y Mendoza
SALDANA, Mateo (20th C)
Valle de Mexico (landscape), oil on board, sgn, 9x11", C-NY 5/18/88 OE **2,860**
SALEMME, Attilio (American, 1911-1958)
Love & Nemesis on a Street Corner (geometric figures), oil on canvas, sgn/dtd 48, 34x22", SBY 10/7/89 ..... **4,675**
Morning in Infinity (geometric figures), oil on canvas, sgn/dtd 48, 20x34", SBY 10/7/89 ..... **3,850**
Pair: Anniversary; Here We Are; pen/ink/watercolor on paper, sgn, dtd 2/24/49 & 47, 6x9", 7x10", SBY 10/7/89 ..... **1,650**
Pair: Happy Occasion; Holy Ones; pen/ink/watercolor, sgn/dtd 50, sgn/dtd 43, 9x11", SBY 10/7/89 ..... **2,640**
SALENTIN, Hubert (German, 1822-1910)
Preparing a Meal, oil on canvas, sgn/dtd 57, 15x11", B/B 6/9/88 ..... **6,050**

LIGO, Charles Louis
Still Life of Mixed Flowers, Fruit, & a Dead Gamebird on a Stone Ledge; oil on canvas, sgn/dtd 1854, 25x20", C-E 2/23/88 ... **3,850**
LINAS, Pablo (Spanish, 1871-1946)
La Carta (interior scene of cardinal writing letter), oil on canvas, sgn, 10x9", C-NY 2/23/89 ... **11,000**
Welcome for the Cardinal, oil on panel, sgn, 5x9", SBY 2/22/89 ... **27,500**
LINAS Y TERUEL, Augustin (Spanish, 1871-)
Surprise Present, oil on canvas, sgn/dtd 83, 16x10", C-E 2/23/88 ... **3,520**
LING, Paul E. (American, 1876-1936)
Old Lyme, Connecticut, ca 1920 (autumn landscape); oil on canvas, sgn/dtd, 25x30", RWS 9/29/88 ... **750**
Shad Fisherman at Home, oil on canvas, sgn, 34x40", C-E 11/30/88 ... **1,210**
LISBURY, J. Elmer (American, 20th C)
Portrait of William Howard Taft, oil on canvas, sgn/dtd 1908/inscr, 60x40", LH 10/16/88 UE ... **300**
LLA, Salvatore
Winter Landscape, oil on canvasboard, indistinctly sgn, 16x20", C-E 2/3/88 ... **770**
LLAI (Continental, 19th C)
Pair: Ladies in Spring Landscapes; oil on canvas, sgn, 32x14", B/B 9/14/89 ... **2,200**
LLE, David (American, 1952-)
Bones (abstract), acrylic on canvas, 1983, 102x84", SBY 11/10/88 ... **143,000**
Diptych: In the Documentary Mode (abstract); acrylic/flannel/charcoal on canvas, 1981, 86x100", C-NY 11/9/88 ... **60,500**
In the Documentary Mode (abstract), acrylic/flannel collage/charcoal on canvas, 1981, 86x100", SBY 10/5/89 ... **77,000**
Normal Sentences (abstract), oil on canvas, 1982, 96x56", SBY 10/8/88 ... **66,000**
Proust or Canada (two scenes on one canvas), acrylic on canvas, 1982, 60x84", SBY 5/3/88 ... **71,500**
Shirts (abstract composition), oil on canvas w/fabric collage, 1984, 52x72", SBY 5/3/89 ... **66,000**
Untitled, pastel on paper, sgn/dtd 1978, 28x40", SBY 2/15/89 ... **7,700**
Untitled (abstract figures), brush/black ink on paper, sgn/dtd 82, 22x30", C-NY 5/4/88 OE ... **9,900**
Untitled (abstract), brush/black ink on paper, sgn/dtd 1982, 28x39", C-NY 11/10/88 ... **9,350**
Untitled (abstract), brush/black ink on paper, sgn/dtd 82 twice, 30x42", C-NY 11/10/88 ... **6,714**
Untitled (contemporary), acrylic on paper, sgn/dtd 1981, 40x26", SBY 5/3/89 OE ... **14,300**
Untitled (nude, a profile, & abstract), brush/black ink/acrylic on paper, sgn/dtd 1982, 22x30", C-NY 11/10/88 ... **5,500**
Untitled (woman in red dress), watercolor on paper, sgn/dtd 1985, 18x24", SBY 5/3/88 ... **15,400**
Untitled #9 (abstract), watercolor on paper, sgn/dtd 84, 18x24", SBY 11/9/89 ... **15,400**
LMON, John Cuthbert (British, 1844-1917)
Landscape, watercolor, sgn, 30x50", FB 4/25/88 UE ... **450**
LMON, Robert (American, 1775-1842)
A Fishing Boat & Shipping Off a Lighthouse, oil on panel, initialed/dtd 1836/#d 860, 16x20", PHL 12/1/88 OE ... **29,000**
Boston Harbor, oil on panel, initialed/inscr/dtd 1843, 10x14", C-NY 5/26/88 OE ... **88,000**
British Ships Off the English Coast, oil on canvas, initialed/dtd 1822, 17x25", B/B 3/22/89 OE ... **60,500**
Off a Rocky Cliff (anchored ships), oil on canvas, initialed/dtd 1822, 16x25", C-NY 5/25/89 OE ... **60,500**
Sailing in the Summer, oil on canvas, 13x16", C-E 6/1/89 UE ... **715**
Storm Scene (distressed ships w/sailors in dingy), oil on panel, sgn/dtd 1838/#d 648, 17x24", C-NY 5/25/89 OE ... **115,500**
View of Greenock on the Clyde (large ship in harbor, figures an shore), oil on panel, sgn/dtd 1812, 12x15", WL 5/20/88 ... **29,000**
LOMON, Gabriel
Sin Titulo (abstract), mixed media on board laid down on masonite, sgn/dtd 85, 40x40", C-NY 11/21/88 ... **2,200**
LVI, Ensel (Italian, 20th C)
Sailing Along the Coast, oil on canvas, sgn/inscr No 950, 24x36", C-E 11/8/88 ... **990**
LVI, Giovanni Battista (Italian, 1609-1685)
Madonna & Child, oil on canvas, 23x28", SBY 6/1/89 OE ... **37,400**
Madonna & Child in Glory with Cherubs, oil on canvas, 30x40", C-NY 6/2/88 UE ... **7,700**
Madonna with the Infant Christ Holding a Goldfinch, oil on canvas, 39x32", C-NY 1/11/89 OE ... **24,200**
Virgin Annunciate, oil on canvas, 33x26", SBY 4/7/88 ... **20,900**
Virgin in Prayer, oil on canvas, 20x16", C-NY 1/11/89 ... **11,000**
LVI, Giovanni Battista; school of (Italian, 1609-1685)
Madonna & Sleeping Child, oil on canvas, 33x37", C-E 4/7/88 ... **605**
LVIATI, Giuseppe; att
Pieta, oil on panel, 23x18", C-NY 1/15/88 ... **19,800**
LVO (Italian, 1947-)
Untitled (cemetery), oil on canvas, sgn/dtd 84, 24x12", C-E 5/9/89 OE ... **4,620**
Untitled (contemporary landscape w/buildings), oil on paperboard, sgn/dtd 85, 14x10", SBY 5/3/89 OE ... **3,575**
M, Joe (American, 20th C)
India, oil/mixed media, 60x60", B/B 12/8/88 ... **1,760**
MARAS, Lucas (American, 1936-)
Chair Transformation, graphite on paper, initialed/dtd Dec 14-69, 13x9", C-NY 10/4/89 ... **1,540**
Reconstruction #93 (abstract), sewn on fabric, 1979, 66x68", SBY 2/15/89 ... **9,350**
Untitled, pastel/silver paint on paper, initialed/dtd June 21, 1958, 9x12", SBY 10/7/89 ... **4,675**
Untitled (abstract), colored chalks on paper, 13x10", C-NY 5/4/88 ... **3,080**
Untitled #2 (man sleeping), pastel on paper, 1961, 12x9", SBY 10/8/88 ... **4,400**
MMANN, Detlef (American, 20th C)
Birch Trees, landscape scene; oil on canvas, sgn, 22x17", DM 1/15/88 OE ... **800**
Pair: The History of the West; oil on canvas, sgn/dtd 1910, 28x40", C-NY 2/3/88 ... **5,500**
MMONS, Carl (American, 1886-1968)
Sierra Landscape, oil on canvas, sgn, 24x30", B/B 10/6/88 ... **1,980**

SAMOKISH, Nikolai Semenovich (Russian, 1860-1944)
Under the Silver Birches (landscape), oil on canvas, sgn/dtd 84, 9x16", C-L 10/8/88 ... 14,870
SAMPLE, Paul Starrett (American, 1896-1974)
Back Roads (landscape), watercolor on paper, sgn, 11x14", SBY 9/23/88 OE ... 2,750
Barnyard with Fowl, Autumn (carriage & red buildings in foreground); watercolor on paper, sgn, 11x15", RWS 3/31/88 OE ... 2,700
Farm Near Willoughby, watercolor on paper, 11x17", B/B 8/10/88 ... 1,320
From the Lower Pasture, watercolor on paper, sgn, 16x19", C-E 6/1/89 ... 1,045
Iceland Fisherman, oil on canvas, sgn, 20x40", C-E 6/1/88 OE ... 2,640
Jumping at the Fair, oil on masonite, sgn, 15x20", SBY 9/23/88 OE ... 9,350
New England Village in the Snow, oil on board, sgn, 18x24", WD 4/13/88 ... 4,750
New Hampshire Landscape (buildings & rolling hills), watercolor on paper laid down on board, sgn, 11x15", C-E 6/1/89 OE ... 1,870
Paisaje Espanol 2 (figures & cattle in landscape w/town in distance), oil on board, sgn, 24x40", RWS 3/16/89 UE ... 1,800
Snow-Covered Village, oil on canvas, sgn, 30x36", C-E 6/1/88 ... 5,280
Still Life with Shells, oil on canvas, sgn twice/titled, 16x20", SBY 3/17/88 ... 3,575
Village in Vermont (in extensive landscape), oil on canvas, sgn, 30x36", B/B 10/9/88 ... 12,100
Winter Landscape with Bridge, watercolor on paper, sgn, 13x22", SBY 3/17/88 ... 1,540
SAMSON, Jeanne (French, 19th C)
Afternoon Tea, oil on canvas, sgn/dtd 1879, 23x33", SBY 6/8/88 ... 6,050
SAN CLEMENT, Francisco Rodriguez (Spanish, 1861-1956)
Elegant Woman Watching a Bull Fight, oil on canvas, sgn, 31x51", C-NY 10/25/89 OE ... 16,500
SAN FRIANO, see Da San Friano
SAN MARTIN, C. (Continental, 19th C)
Ready for the Dance, oil on canvas, sgn, 14x11", SBY 6/8/88 ... 1,540
SANBORN, Percy (1849-1929)
Ship Ivanhoe (in full sail), oil on canvas, sgn/dtd 1864, 26x40", SBY 1/28/88 ... 4,675
SANCHES, Harriet; see De Sanches
SANCHES-PESCADOZ, J.L. (19th C)
Projecto de una Nueva Entrada para Vista-Allegre, watercolor, sgn/dtd 1864, 25x38", C-E 1/12/88 ... 528
SANCHEZ, Edgar (Venezuelan, 1940-)
Skin Gestations 1913 (abstract), acrylic on canvas, sgn, 1987, 45x58", SBY 5/17/88 ... 6,050
SANCHEZ, Emilio (Cuban, 1921-)
Group of 4: Houses (contemporary); watercolor, initialed, 22x30", SBY 11/21/88 ... 2,200
House (contemporary), oil on canvas, sgn, 79x79", SBY 11/21/88 ... 6,600
Untitled (architecture graphics), oil on canvas, initialed, 48x48", SBY 5/17/88 ... 6,600
SANCHEZ, Enrique (Mexican, 1940-)
En el Valle de Mexico-26 de Junio, 1986 (extensive landscape); acrylic on canvas, sgn, 1986, 18x33", C-NY 5/17/89 ... 4,400
Valle de Mexico (extensive landscape), acrylic on canvas, sgn/dtd 1986, 26x42", C-NY 11/21/89 ... 8,800
SANCHEZ, Tomas (Cuban, 1948-)
Lagoon & Sea, oil on canvas, sgn twice/dtd 88, 44x59", SBY 5/17/88 ... 7,150
Triptico de las Lluvias: La Sequia; El Aguacero; Reverdecer; acrylic on canvas, sgn/dtd 87, ea 51x37", C-NY 5/18/88 ... 12,100
SANCHEZ-COELLO, Alonso; follower of (Spanish, 1531-1588)
Portrait of a Boy in Elegant Dress Standing by a Table, oil on canvas, 40x32", SBY 10/13/89 OE ... 12,100
SANCHEZ-COTAN, Fray Juan; att (Spanish, 1560-1627)
Still Life of Fruit in a Bowl with Two Artichokes, oil on canvas, 27x44", SBY 6/3/88 OE ... 286,000
SANCHEZ-PERRIER, Emilio (Spanish, 1855-1907)
Boating at the Edge of the Town, oil on panel, sgn, 17x10", SBY 5/23/89 ... 19,800
Bord d'une Riviere, Seville; oil on panel, sgn, 15x18", SBY 5/23/89 ... 26,400
Fishing on the River's Edge, oil on panel, sgn, 15x20", C-NY 5/24/89 ... 15,400
L'Oise sur Auvers, oil on panel, sgn, 17x13", C-NY 10/25/89 ... 35,200
SANDBY, Paul; att (British, 1730-1809)
Landscape with Castle, watercolor, sgn/dtd 1795, 6x9", LH 12/4/88 ... 250
SANDERS, Walter, G. (British, fl 1884-1901)
Still Life of Hollyhocks (in an ornate vase), oil on canvas, sgn/dtd 1889, 36x21", B/B 10/9/88 ... 3,025
SANDERSON-WELLS, John (British, 1872-1955)
Over the Fall, oil on canvas, sgn, 16x22", FB 10/30/89 ... 7,150
The London Coach, oil on canvas, sgn, 28x48", WAD 6/6/88 ... 10,000
SANDHAM, Henry (American, 1842-1910)
Bedouin's Charge, gouache on paper laid down on board/en grisaille, 12x8", C-E 5/23/88 ... 605
Falaise, watercolor, 90x14", MAG 11/30/89 ... 500
Idle & Industrious Apprentice, watercolor, sgn, 14x9", WAD 6/12/89 ... 600
Sunrise, Lake Fishing; watercolor w/graphite/gouache on paper, sgn/dtd 1887, 12x25", RWS 11/10/89 ... 550
SANDOLO, Gio (20th C)
Italian Rocky Coastline with House, oil on canvas, sgn, 32x48", DM 5/13/88 ... 250
SANDOVAL, see De Penalosa Y Sandoval
SANDRUCCI, Giovanni (Italian, 19th C)
Playful Temptation (man teasing child, family watching), oil on canvas, sgn/inscr Firenze, 27x40", SBY 10/24/89 ... 15,400
Sewing the Torn Umbrella (interior scene), oil on canvas, sgn, 24x32", C-E 5/22/89 ... 4,180
SANDZEN, Sven Birger (American, 1871-1954)
Sunrise by the Coast, oil on canvas, sgn/dtd 1913, 16x24", C-NY 9/30/88 OE ... 6,600
SANI, Alessandro (Italian, 19th/20th C)
Checking the Vintage, oil on canvas, sgn, 25x19", C-NY 2/25/88 OE ... 8,800

Good Vintage (three-quarter length of man with wine glass & pitcher), oil on canvas laid down, sgn, 16x13", B/B 9/14/89 — **1,210**
Wayfarer (interior scene), oil on canvas, sgn, 28x38", C-E 2/21/89 — **3,300**
What? A Boy Trying To Sew?; oil on canvas, sgn, 14x19", SBY 12/9/88 OE — **6,050**

SANQUIRICO, Alessandro; att (Italian, 1777-1849)
Design for a Ceiling Decoration, pen/brown ink/wash/watercolor, 10x13", SBY 1/13/89 — **1,320**
Stage Design: Abandoned Country Church w/Elaborate Porch w/Moorish Decoration; watercolor/chalk, 10x10", SBY 1/13/89 — **1,650**

SANT, James (British, 1820-1916)
Distant Memories, oil on canvas, 29x25", C-E 11/8/88 UE — **1,100**
Portrait of a Young Girl, oil on canvas, monogramed, 24x20", C-E 10/26/89 — **3,300**

SANTACROCE, see Da Santacroce

SANTERRE, Jean Baptiste; att (French, 1651-1717)
Portrait of a la Comtesse de Perigny, oil on canvas, oval, 31x25", SBY 10/21/88 — **4,950**

SANTERRE, Jean Baptiste; manner of (French, 1651-1717)
Portrait of a Lady Holding a Mask, oil on canvas, 39x30", SBY 10/13/89 — **2,200**

SANTINI, Giuseppe (European, fl 1663-)
Landscape with a Birdhouse, pen/brown ink, #d 37, 8x8", SBY 1/13/89 — **715**
Pair: Landscapes with Groups of Figures in the Foreground; pen/brown ink/wash, #d 24 & 27, 8x8", SBY 1/13/89 — **880**

SANTOMASSO, Giuseppe (Italian, 1907-)
Rosso e Nero (abstract), acrylic/sand/white chalk/pencil on canvas, sgn/dtd 1981, 55x48", C-E 11/17/88 OE — **16,500**

SANTORO, Joseph L. (American, 20th C)
Woodland Waterfall, watercolor on paper, sgn, 21x29", RAB 8/9/88 — **500**

SANTORO, Rubens (Italian, 1859-1942)
Grand Canal, oil on panel, sgn, 13x16", C-NY 2/23/89 OE — **35,200**
Venetian Canal Scene, oil on canvas, sgn, 15x8", lot 148, C-NY 5/25/88 — **14,300**
Venetian Canal Scene, oil on canvas, sgn, 25x20", lot 150, C-NY 5/25/88 — **14,300**
Venetian Sunset, oil on canvasboard, sgn, unfr, 8x11", SBY 12/9/88 — **4,400**
Venice-The End of the Day; oil on panel, sgn, 9x15", C-NY 5/25/88 OE — **11,000**

SANTRY, Daniel (American, 1867-1951)
Autumn Sunset, oil on canvas, 16x20", RWS 8/20/88 — **550**
Village Wall, oil on canvas, sgn, 18x24", C-E 6573 — **1,320**

SANTVOORT, see Van Santvoort

SANZIO, Raffaello; see Raphael

SAPHIER, Louis
New York City in Snow, oil on masonite, sgn, 18x14", C-E 4/7/88 UE — **385**

SAPORETTI, Adolpho
Standing Man with Sun Crown, oil on canvas, sgn, unfr, 28x18", SBY 2/14/89 UE — **520**

SAPP, Allen (Canadian, 1929-)
Baby Going to Man, acrylic on canvas, sgn/dtd 1969, 16x20", FB 10/17/88 — **1,200**
Drying Deer Meat at Stoney Reserve, oil on canvas, sgn/dtd 1974, 30x48", FB 4/25/88 — **2,800**

SARGEANT, Geneve Rixford (American, 1868-1957)
Flowers in Brass, oil on canvas, sgn/dtd 1890, 16x14", B/B 10/6/88 OE — **1,320**
Portrait of a Woman, oil on canvas, sgn, 24x18", B/B 10/6/88 — **1,430**
The Sacred Heart, oil/gold leaf on canvasboard, sgn, 16x12", B/B 10/6/88 — **550**

SARGENT, John Singer (American, 1856-1925)
Double-Sided: Head of a Man; Head of a Woman; pencil on paper, dtd 1877, 7x5", SBY 6/24/88 OE — **3,300**
Fellah Woman (portrait), oil on canvas, sgn, 22x18", C-NY 12/2/88 — **264,000**
Il Gesuati, Venice; watercolor/pencil on paper, sgn, 18x12", SBY 5/25/88 OE — **154,000**
Ilex Wood, Majorca (landscape); oil on canvas, artist estate stamp, 23x29", SBY 5/24/89 — **55,000**
Lake Louise, Canadian Rockies; watercolor/pencil on paper laid down, sgn, 1916, 15x21", C-NY 5/25/89 — **38,500**
Landscape with Trees, oil on canvas, ca 1888-89, 20x26", SBY 5/24/89 — **16,500**
Mrs Charles Stewart Carstairs (portrait), charcoal on paper, sgn/dtd 1914, 24x19", C-NY 5/26/88 OE — **26,400**
Portrait of Eugene Juillerat, Artist; oil on canvas, sgn/inscr, ca 1880, 16x13", SBY 5/25/88 OE — **231,000**
Portrait of Miss Sally Fairchild, oil on canvas, ca 1887, 20x25", SBY 5/25/88 — **60,500**
Portrait of Mrs Charles Hunter in a Gondola, watercolor/pencil on paper, initialed/dtd 1902, 18x12", SBY 5/25/88 — **99,000**
Portrait of WS Gilbert, pencil on paper, sgn, 11x8", SBY 1/24/89 — **2,200**
Simplon, watercolor on paper, sgn, ca 1910, 14x20", SBY 5/25/88 — **26,400**
The Simplon (mountainous landscape), watercolor/pencil on paper, sgn, 14x20", C-NY 5/25/89 — **28,600**

ARGENT, John Singer; att (American, 1856-1925)
Portrait of a Lady, Madame X; oil on canvas, 29x21", DM 3/14/88 — **2,250**

ARKISIAN, Paul (American, 1928-)
Untitled #12 (abstract), acrylic on linen, 1980, 46x48", C-NY 5/4/89 OE — **19,800**

ARKISIAN, Sarkis (American, 1909-1977)
Still Life of a Jar with Fruit, oil on canvas, sgn/dtd 31, 30x20", DM 2/19/88 — **400**

ARTAIN, Emily (American, 1927-)
Mrs Beach of Hartford, oil on canvas, sgn/dtd 1888, unfr, 84x55", B/B 12/8/88 — **2,200**

ARTAIN, William (American, 1843-1924)
Middle-Eastern Teacher & Students, oil on canvas, sgn, unfr, 26x36", FAP 11/4/88 — **525**

ARTORELLI, Francesco (Italian, 1856-1939)
Venetian Canal Scene, oil on canvas, sgn, 32x51", WL 5/20/88 — **7,000**

ARTORIO, Giulio Aristide (Italian, 1861-1932)
Messico Santagelo le Cupole del Carmine (street scene), oil on canvas laid down on board, sgn, 31x23", C-NY 2/23/89 — **9,350**

Vicino al Mare (nude on beach viewed from behind), oil on panel, sgn, C-E 5/22/89 OE 7,700

SARTORIO, Giulio Aristide; att (Italian, 1861-1932)

His First Verses, oil on canvas, indistinctly sgn, 24x34", C-E 10/26/89 4,620

SARTORIUS, Francis (British, 1734-1804)

Charlton Hunt Drawing a Covert, oil on canvas, sgn/dtd, 15x23", SBY 6/9/89 OE 16,500

SARTORIUS, Francis; style of (British, 1734-1804)

Gentleman with His Steed & Two Greyhounds, oil on canvas, 24x32", B/B 10/9/88 6,600
Groom on a Stud, oil on canvas, 25x30", B/B 10/9/88 OE 7,150

SARTORIUS, John Francis; att (British, 1775-1831)

Bay Hunter in a Landscape, oil on canvas, bears signature, 14x17", SBY 6/9/89 2,475

SARTORIUS, John Nost (British, 1759-1828)

Chestnut Hunter Tethered to a Fence, oil on canvas, sgn/dtd 79, 13x18", C-NY 5/24/89 5,500
Full Cry (hunt scene in a panoramic landscape), oil on canvas, 31x56", SBY 6/9/89 55,000
Heavyweight Hunter (horse in a landscape), oil on canvas, sgn/dtd 1798, 28x36", SBY 6/9/89 20,900
Pair: Smelensco & Eclipse with Jockeys Up; oil on canvas, 1 sgn, unfr, 14x17", SBY 6/9/89 OE 15,400
Phenomina with Jockey Up, oil on canvas, sgn, 12x15", SBY 6/9/89 3,850
Setting Out, oil on canvas, sgn/dtd 1817, 14x18", C-NY 10/25/89 8,250
The Kill (hunters & dog w/fox), oil on canvas, sgn/dtd 1808, 28x36", C-NY 5/24/89 OE 20,900
Three Racehorses with Two Riders Up at a Starting Post, oil on canvas, 25x30", SBY 6/9/89 UE 4,500

SARTORIUS, John Nost; att (British, 1759-1828)

Gray Hunter Tethered to a Gate with a Hound in a Landscape, oil on canvas, 20x24", SBY 6/9/89 2,750

SARTORIUS, John Nost; follower of (British, 1759-1828)

Bay Hunter, Property of John Ives of Sasburgh, Norfolk, in a Landscape; oil on canvas, 25x33", SBY 6/9/89 6,875

SASHOGYE, Kalman (Hungarian, 1887-)

Shepherd Herding Sheep Along Country Lane with Background of an Orange Sunset, oil on canvas, sgn, 24x32", SLK 5/12/88 350
Shepherd Herding Sheep Along Country Lane with Background of an Orange Sunset, oil on canvas, sgn, 24x32", SLK 2/12/88 275

SASSOFERRATO, Giovanni; see Salvi, Giovanni Battista

SATTERLEE, Walter (American, 1844-1908)

Young Bookworm, oil on canvas, oil on canvas, sgn, 20x14", C-E 6/1/89 1,650

SATTLER, Hubert (Austrian, 1817-1904)

Cows Grazing, oil on canvas, sgn/dtd 18(?)3, 24x32", C-E 5/23/88 UE 1,100

SATURNIN, Felix (French, 1818-1892)

Brissot de Warville, Berger Donduisant son Troupeau; oil on panel, indistinctly sgn, 6x12", B/B 5/17/89 440

SAUL, Peter (American, 1934-)

Combat Happy Joe (fantasy composition), crayons/felt-tip pens/ballpoint pen, sgn/dtd 65, 54x40", C-E 11/14/89 OE 9,900
Study for Picasso's Guernica, acrylic/crayon/graphite on board, sgn/dtd 76, 20x44", lot 250, C-NY 5/4/89 OE 12,100
Study for Picasso's Guernica, acrylic/crayon/graphite on paper, sgn/dtd 76, 20x44", lot 249, C-NY 5/4/89 OE 8,250
Untitled (abstract), pastel/gouache on paper, sgn/dtd 61, 26x30", SBY 10/7/89 1,320

SAULACROY, F.

Cavalry Man, oil on canvas, sgn, 20x16", WG 4/23/88 1,100

SAUNDERS, H. Wenderoth (American, 20th C)

South Station Complex (train yard), oil on paper, sgn/titled, 20x27", RAB 8/8/89 UE 350

SAUNIER, Noel (French, 1847-1890)

Pair: Reading in the Forest; The Picnic; oil on canvas, both sgn/1 dtd 1871, ea 16x22", SBY 5/23/89 29,700

SAURA, Domingo Texdury

Presentation in the Temple, oil on copper, sgn, 25x19", C-E 1/12/88 OE 2,420

SAURFELT, Leonard (French, 19th C)

L'Arrivee a l'Hotel de l'Ecu de France, oil on canvas, sgn/dtd 89, 19x31", SBY 10/24/89 7,150
Proclamation, oil on canvas, sgn/dtd 1873, 19x15", C-E 4/7/88 990

SAUSSY, Hattie

View From a Window, oil on board, sgn/dtd 1928, 14x10", C-NY 9/28/89 2,970

SAUTEUR, see Le Sauteur

SAUVAGE, Arsene Symphorien

Playing with a Hoop, oil on canvas, sgn, unfr, 29x21", C-E 5/23/88 1,650

SAUVAGE, Pieter Joseph (Piat)(Flemish, 1744-1818)

Putti Playing with a Goat, oil en grisaille on canvas, irregular shape, 37x44", SBY 4/7/89 OE 12,100

SAUVAGE, Pieter Joseph (Piat); att (Flemish, 1744-1818)

Tromp l'Oeil Portrait of Napoleon, en grisaille/oil on canvas, 29x24", C-NY 6/2/88 2,200

SAVAGE, Anne Douglas (Canadian, 1897-1971)

Cottage at Mont St Hilaire, oil on board, sgn, 12x14", WAD 6/12/89 OE 1,050
Landscape with Flowers, oil on board, sgn, 17x16", WAD 6/12/89 OE 1,100
The Poppy, oil on canvas, sgn, 24x20", WAD 6/12/89 1,900

SAVIN, Maurice (French, 1894-1973)

Market Scene, oil on canvas, sgn, 24x29", LH 9/10/89 UE 3,600

SAVINIO, Alberto (Italian, 1891-1952)

Design for the Drop Cloth for the Tales of Hoffman, pencil on paper, sgn/dtd 49, 12x14", SBY 10/7/89 7,700

SAWFORD-DYE, Ernest (Canadian, 1873-1965)

East Coast Shore Scene, watercolor, sgn, 11x15", WAD 11/30/89 240

SAWYER, Helen Alton (American, 1900-)

Old Salt (fisherman in dory), oil on cardboard, sgn/dtd 1941(?), 16x14", RAB 8/8/89 UE 600

SAWYER, Wells M. (American, 1863-1961)
November, oil on canvas, sgn, 20x16", C-E 10/18/89 880
SAWYIER, Paul (American, 1865-1917)
Barge on the Kentucky River, watercolor on paper, sgn, 14x20", SBY 6/28/89 11,000
Cottage in a Summer Landscape, watercolor on paper, sgn, 6x12", SBY 6/28/89 5,500
Pair: Street Scene; River Scene; watercolor on paper, sgn, 13x20", SBY 1/24/89 OE 23,100
SAXILD, Karl (American, 19th/20th C)
Azure Mountains, oil on canvas, sgn, 7x9", FAP 12/8/89 400
Castle on the River, oil on canvas, sgn, 10x12", FAP 12/8/89 UE 100
Farm in Early Autumn, oil on board, sgn, 12x16", FAP 12/8/89 UE 125
SAXON, Lulu King (American, -1927)
Uptown Street, New Orleans (may be Magazine Street); oil on canvas, sgn/dtd 90, 90x68", NA 3/26/88 2,500
SAYRE, F. Grayson (American, 1879-1939)
Coachella Valley in Bloom, oil on canvas, sgn, 20x24", B/B 10/6/88 4,950
SCACCIATI, Andrea; att (Italian, 1642-1710)
Still Life of Flowers in an Elaborate Urn on a Ledge with Butterflies, oil on canvas, oval, 29x24", SBY 10/21/88 OE 6,600
SCALBERT, Jules (French, 1851-)
Bathers, oil on canvas, sgn, 18x15", C-NY 2/25/88 7,700
Bathing Beauty, oil on panel, sgn, 22x18", SBY 6/8/88 4,950
Dance of the Three Graces, oil on canvas, sgn, 26x32", SBY 2/22/89 7,700
Pair: Elegant Figures by the Sea; Elegant Figures by a Lake; watercolor on paper, sgn, 13x20", C-E 10/25/88 UE 550
Swing (woman & cherubs swinging in a landscape), oil on canvas, sgn, 40x30", SBY 2/22/89 9,900
SCALINI, F. (Italian, 19th/20th C)
Mother & Child in a Rustic Interior, oil on canvas, sgn/inscr, 17x19", SBY 12/9/88 7,425
SCAMPERLE, Livio (20th C)
Ciclista de la Belle Epoque (man on high-wheeled bicycle), oil on canvas, sgn/dtd 1987, 36x29", C-NY 11/21/88 3,520
Primavera en Rojo, oil on canvas, sgn/dtd 87, 40x30", C-NY 5/17/89 3,300
Scandinavian School (19th C)
Young Boy Sleeping, oil on canvas, indistinctly sgn, unfr, 13x13", C-E 10/25/88 OE 4,400
Scandinavian School (19th/20th C)
Fjord, oil on canvas, indistinctly sgn, 44x63", SBY 6/8/88 1,540
SCANES, Ernest William
Grand Morrais, oil on masonite, 20x34", C-E 10/18/89 UE 440
SCANGA, Italo (American, 1932-)
Hubert Humphrey Lecturing to the Brisley, charcoal on paper, initialed/dtd 1981, 34x26", C-NY 11/10/88 1,100
Nude with Two Skulls (contemporary), charcoal on paper in painted wood frame, sgn/dtd 1984, 47x37", C-NY 2/14/89 1,760
Untitled (abstract), charcoal on paper, sgn/dtd 82, painted wood frame, 49x38", C-NY 5/4/88 2,090
SCARLETT, Rolph (American, 19th/20th C)
Geometric Abstraction, oil on canvas, sgn, ca 1937-38, 34x50", C-NY 9/28/89 22,000
SCARSELLA, see Scarsellino
SCARSELLINO, Ippolito (Italian, 1551-1620)
Holy Family with Saint John the Baptist, oil on copper, unfr, 9x11", SBY 4/7/88 OE 17,600
SCARSELLINO, Ippolito; school of (Italian, 1551-1620)
Putti Fishing & Picking Fruit, oil on canvas, 47x62", C-NY 6/2/88 7,700
SCHABELITZ, Rudolph Frederick (American, 1884-)
Woman Seated in an Exotic Interior, oil on canvas, sgn, 20x24", SBY 3/17/88 1,925
SCHAD-ROSSA, Paul (German, 1862-1916)
Bathers, oil on canvas, 39x25", SBY 12/9/88 1,210
SCHAEFFER, Henri (French, 1900-1975)
Paris Street Scene, The Grand Hotel; oil on canvas, sgn, 18x22", B/B 6/9/88 6,050
SCHAEFFER, John Simon
Raspberries & Fruit (still life), oil on canvas, sgn, 16x14", C-E 6/1/89 1,980
SCHAEFFER, Meade (American, 1898-1979)
As High As My Heart (lady dancing with soldier), oil on canvas, sgn, 35x24", WL 5/20/88 1,600
Pair: Coral Beach, Bermuda; watercolor on paper, 15x22", WL 5/20/88 UE 400
Tropical Adventure (two figures in exotic landscape), oil on canvas, 39x29", WL 5/20/88 1,100
SCHAFER, Dirch (Dutch, 1864-1941)
Still Life of Zinnias, oil on canvas, sgn, 16x20", B/B 3/22/89 1,870
SCHAFER, Frederick (American, 1839-1927)
Bridal Veil Falls, Yosemite; oil on canvas, sgn/dtd 1890, unfr, 30x50", B/B 10/6/88 1,540
Cattle Along a River, Marin County; oil on canvas, sgn, 20x36", B/B 8/10/88 1,650
Glacier in Alaska, oil on canvas, sgn/dtd 1889, unfr, 30x50", B/B 10/6/88 2,090
Going to Pow-Wow, Montana (Indians riding in single file across plain); oil on canvas, sgn, 12x24", RWS 8/20/88 1,000
North Heads on the Pacific Coast, California; oil on canvas, sgn/titled, 30x50", SBY 3/17/88 1,320
Scott Creek in Lake Tahoe, oil on canvas, sgn, 14x10", B/B 1/11/89 220
Sunset on the Willamette, Oregon; oil on canvas, sgn, 20x36", B/B 8/10/88 715
CHAFER, Henry (British/French, 19th C)
Antwerp, oil on canvas, monogramed, 16x12", C-E 10/26/89 3,080
Cathedral of St Martin, Ypres, Belgium; watercolor, sgn, 18x14", C-E 10/26/89 550
Cathedral Scene, oil on canvas mounted on board, sgn, 26x20", DM 9/16/88 1,400
Morlaix, oil on canvas, monogramed, 16x12", C-E 10/26/89 2,860

Pair: Notre Dame, Rouen, Normandy; Freiburg, Baden; pencil on paper, sgn/inscr, 10x9", C-E 10/25/88 1,100
Pair: Street Scene in Normandy; Cathedral Interior; watercolor on paper, sgn/inscr, 24x18", SBY 12/9/88 1,540
Pair: View of Normandy & Cathedral Interior; watercolor on paper, sgn/inscr, 24x18", 18x13", SBY 12/9/88 1,210
Pair: Views of Strasbourg & Normandy; watercolor on paper, sgn/inscr, 18x14", 17x12", SBY 12/9/88 1,540
Square in Antwerp, watercolor/gouache over pencil, sgn/inscr, 25x18", C-NY 5/25/88 1,320
St Madeleine-Truyes, France; oil on canvas, sgn/inscr, 12x10", C-E 2/23/88 UE 605
St Stephen's Cathedral, Vienna; oil on canvas, sgn, 27x20", PHL 6/16/88 700
Street Scene, oil on canvas, sgn, 18x24", SBY 12/9/88 2,475

SCHAFER, Henry Thomas (British, fl 1872-1915)
Classical Maiden, oil on canvas, sgn/dtd 1881, 36x11", SBY 6/8/88 1,320
Feeding the Doves, oil on canvas, sgn/dtd 1887, 23x14", SBY 4/29/88 OE 8,250
Fragrant Bouquet, oil on canvas, sgn/indistinctly dtd, 24x14", SBY 12/9/88 OE 7,150
Lilies, oil on canvas, sgn, 23x11", WAD 6/6/88 4,200
Toledo Cathedral, North Transept; watercolor/pen/brown ink/gouache/pencil, sgn/titled, 40x29", C-NY 2/23/89 2,420
Young Girl with Her Slate, oil on canvas laid down on board, sgn/dtd 1875, 22x18", WD 11/16/88 3,250

SCHAFER, Hermann (German, 1880-)
Town Square, oil on canvas, sgn, 13x9", B/B 5/17/89 UE 770

SCHAFF, Gordon
Grecian Village, oil on canvas, 20x24", C-E 10/18/89 UE 330

SCHALCKEN, Godfried (Dutch, 1643-1706)
Man Writing by Candlelight, oil on canvas, sgn, 33x26", C-NY 1/11/89 16,500

SCHALCKEN, Godfried; school of (Dutch, 1643-1706)
Young Woman & Man Illuminated by Candle, oil on canvas, 23x19", C-E 1/12/88 605

SCHALCKEN, Godried; after (Dutch, 1643-1706)
Boy Blowing Charcoal To Light a Candle, oil on panel, 13x10", SBY 6/8/88 1,100

SCHALDAGH, William (American, 1896-)
Speckled Trout (trout leaping from stream), oil on canvas, sgn, 25x20", SBY 3/17/88 1,100

SCHALL, Jean Frederic (French, 1752-1825)
Portrait of a Young Lady, seated full-length, in green dress, holding a letter; oil on panel, 18x15", C-M 6/16/89 14,670
Portrait of a Young Lady in Provencal Costume (full-length, in a landscape), oil on panel, 13x9", SBY 4/7/89 9,350

SCHALL, Jean Frederic; manner of (French, 1752-1825)
Young Woman Reclining on a Bed Playing with a Rose, oil on canvas, oval, 13x16", C-M 12/3/88 1,300

SCHAMBERG, Morton Livingston (American, 1881-1918)
Composition 1916 (abstract), pastel/pencil on paper, sgn, ca 1916, 8x6", C-NY 5/25/89 8,800
Seascape (w/coastal view), pastel on board, ca 1910-11, 5x7", C-NY 5/25/89 2,750

SCHANKER, Louis (American, 1903-)
Mardi Gras, watercolor/pen/black ink on paper, 20x25", C-E 10/18/89 1,980
Seated Figure, watercolor/pen/ink on paper, sgn twice, 23x17", C-E 11/8/88 UE 550

SCHAPHERDERS, Jaak (Dutch, 19th/20th C)
Fisherman in Storm, oil on panel, sgn, 7x10", LH 12/4/88 850

SCHARF, Kenny (American, 1958-)
Untitled-Elroys; acrylic on plastic, sgn, ca 1981, 58x60", C-NY 11/10/88 5,720
Cat (abstract), spray paint/acrylic on masonite, sgn/dtd 82, 38x26", SBY 10/8/88 6,050
Diptych: Cinquinta/Cinguinta-50/50; acrylic/enamel on canvas, sgn/dtd 85, unfr, 48x36", C-NY 5/4/88 11,000
Idea Falls into Place in Space (fantasy composition), acrylic/spray paint, sgn/dtd 84, unfr, 96x108", C-NY 5/5/89 OE 49,500
Untitled (imaginative characters), ink/gouache/watercolor on paper, 19x24", SBY 2/14/89 UE 990
Whoa Nellie (George Jetson in space city), acrylic on canvasboard, 1981, 20x16", SBY 2/14/89 OE 7,150

SCHARL, Josef (German, 1896-1954)
Lesender Mann (man seated at table w/open book), oil on canvas, sgn/dtd 1933, 39x32", C-NY 10/5/89 OE 20,900
Portrat (seated man wearing striped scarf & hat), oil on canvas, sgn/dtd 1930, 32x26", C-NY 10/5/89 10,450

SCHATTENSTEIN, Nicol (American/Russian, 1877-1954)
Portrait of a Woman, oil on canvas, sgn, 79x49", SBY 4/29/88 11,550

SCHAUDOLPH, Johann (German, 1808-1917)
Caught in the Act, altar boys drinking from pewter mug; oil on board, monogramed/dtd 72/titled, 14x10", RAB 3/27/89 UE 550

SCHEERES, Hendricus Johannes (Dutch, 1829-1864)
Pair: Drink of Water; Visit with the Blacksmith; oil on panel, sgn/dtd 59, 8x6", C-E 10/26/89 1,650

SCHEIBER, Hugo (Hungarian, 1873-1950)
Cafe Scene, chalk on tan paper, sgn, 19x14", C-E 5/9/89 2,420
Composition (abstract), gouache/pastel on paper, sgn, unfr, 22x20", SBY 10/7/89 2,860
Femme Lisant (seated woman in blue dress), gouache on paper, sgn, 1926, 34x26", C-NY 2/18/88 5,280
Horse & Carriage at Night (contemporary), gouache over pencil, sgn, 13x9", SBY 5/30/89 OE 3,960
Man Reading a Newspaper, gouache/black chalk on paper laid down on board, sgn, 26x24", C-E 11/17/88 2,200
Portrait of a Woman, gouache/black chalk on buff paper, sgn, 19x14", C-E 5/13/88 935
Primitiv Tanz (abstract), charcoal/crayon on paper, sgn, unfr, 17x12", SBY 10/7/89 1,430
Self-Portrait, gouache/pastel/black chalk on orange paper laid down on board, sgn, 27x19", C-E 11/17/88 1,210
Tanzerin (abstract), gouache/colored chalk on paper, sgn, 26x20", SBY 10/7/89 4,125

SCHEIBL, Hubert (20th C)
Tired Warrior (abstract), oil on canvas, sgn/dtd 1983, unfr, 79x99", C-NY 2/20/88 UE 1,320

SCHEICH, Eduard the younger; follower of (German, 1853-1893)
Untitled, peasants harvesting crop in river landscape under threatening sky; oil on canvas, sgn, 30x47", SLK 4/7/89 1,300

HELFHOUT, Andreas (Dutch, 1787-1870)

Winter Dutch Coastal Village at Sunset, oil on panel, sgn/dtd 1855, 16x20", RWS 5/12/89 ... 6,000

HELFHOUT, Andreas; att (Dutch, 1787-1870)

Winter Genre Scene, oil on cradled panel, sgn, 21x26", RWS 11/3/88 OE ... 4,000

HELL, Frank H. (American, 1830-1909)

Confederate Gunboat Cotton, Bayou Teche (Civil War); pen/ink on paper, sgn/inscr/dtd 1862, 13x9", C-E 5/27/88 OE ... 2,860

Incident on the Antietam Battlefield, NS Angle of East Wood (Civil War); pen/ink, sgn, unfr, 15x16", C-E 11/30/88 OE ... 770

March of the Federal 19th Corps to Port Hudson (Civil War), pen/ink, sgn/inscr/dtd 1883, 11x14", C-E 5/27/88 OE ... 1,980

HELL, Frank H.; & HOGAN, Thomas (American, 19th C)

Attacking Confederate Batteries at Watson's Landing (Civil War), watercolor, initialed/inscr, 12x19", C-E 5/27/88 ... 1,045

Battle of Belmont: Re-embarkation of Grant's Troops (Civil War); pen/ink on board, initialed, 10x14", C-E 5/27/88 ... 550

Ironclads at Fort Pillow (Civil War), pen/ink on board, sgn/inscr, unfr, 12x18", C-E 11/30/88 OE ... 1,650

Rebel Ramo: Arkansas vs Carondolet (Civil War); pen/ink on board, initialed/inscr, unfr, 11x15", C-E 11/30/88 OE ... 1,210

HELLINK, Hendrik (Dutch, 1795-1848)

River Landscape with Cattle & Herdsman, oil on canvas, sgn/dtd 1827, 13x15", WD 11/16/88 ... 4,500

HENCK, August Friedrich Albrecht (Danish, 1828-1901)

Battling a Winter Storm, oil on canvas, sgn, 52x44", C-E 10/25/88 ... 3,520

Sheep in a Winter Landscape, oil on canvas, sgn, 15x20", C-E 2/23/88 ... 1,540

HENDEL, see Van Schendel

HENK, Pieter I (1660-ca 1718)

Trompe l'Oeil Still Life of a Board with a Print, Almanac, & a Comb; oil on canvas, sgn/inscr, 26x23", SBY 4/7/88 ... 3,300

HEPERS, Maria (18th C)

Pair: Still Lifes of Flowers in a Glass Vase; oil on canvas, sgn/dtd 1791, 17x13", SBY 6/3/88 ... 33,000

HERMAN, Tony

Margaret Posing As Liberty, encaustic on canvas, sgn/dtd 82, 72x48", SBY 10/5/88 OE ... 3,850

HERREWITZ, Johan (Dutch, 1868-1951)

Carting Sand, North Holland; oil on canvas, sgn, 12x16", FB 4/25/88 ... 5,400

Clamming (figure w/horse-drawn wagon on beach), oil on canvas, sgn, 36x32", SBY 10/24/89 ... 7,700

Fisherfolk by the Sea, oil on canvas, sgn, 16x23", C-E 5/23/88 OE ... 8,250

Fisherman & His Wagon by the Sea, oil on panel, sgn, 18x19", C-E 10/25/88 UE ... 770

Milking Time, oil on panel, sgn, 11x14", C-E 10/25/88 ... 2,420

Milking Time, oil on panel, sgn, 11x18", C-E 10/25/88 ... 1,870

Unloading the Catch (coastal scene with fishermen & horses), oil on canvas, sgn, 34x28", PHL 10/28/88 OE ... 22,000

Unloading the Fishing Boat, oil on panel, sgn, 16x13", B/B 3/17/88 ... 4,400

HEUERER, Julius (German, 1859-1913)

Chickens, oil on panel, sgn, 9x6", LH 10/16/88 UE ... 300

Ducks, oil on panel, sgn, 9x6", LH 10/16/88 ... 2,800

Farmyard Scene with Exotic Fowl, oil on panel, sgn/inscr, 5x14", SBY 6/8/88 OE ... 5,500

Turkeys in a Forest Glade, oil on canvas laid down on panel, sgn, 9x7", SBY 6/8/88 UE ... 550

HEURSTEEN, Thomas (American, 19th C)

Still Life of Fruit & a Glass of Wine, oil on canvas mounted on board, sgn/dtd 1895(?), 8x10", SBY 6/28/89 ... 1,045

HIAVONE, Andrea; att (Italian, 1522-1563)

Annunciation, oil on panel, 7x10", SBY 10/21/88 ... 2,750

HIAVONI, Natale (Italian, 1777-1858)

Hebe Holding a Flask & Giving Drink to an Eagle, oil on canvas, sgn/dtd 1851, 42x33", C-E 11/8/88 OE ... 2,310

HIDONE, Bartolomeo; school of (Italian, 1570-1615)

Cupid Musing, oil on canvas, 16x13", C-NY 10/20/88 ... 1,760

Cupid with a Vase, oil on canvas, 16x13", C-NY 10/20/88 ... 1,760

HIELE, Egon (German, 1890-1918)

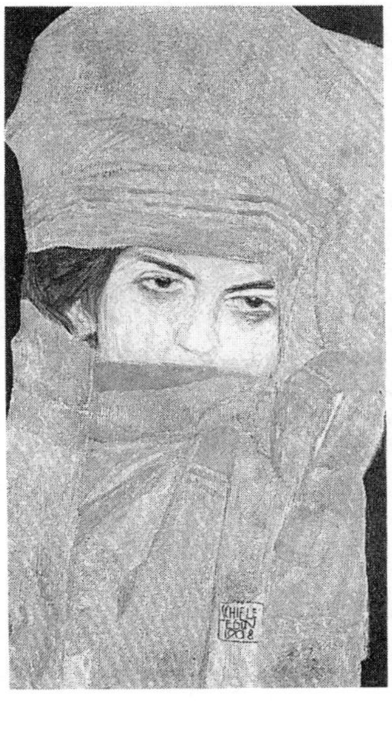

Die Schwester des Kunstlers, Melanie; oil on canvas, sgn/dtd 1908, 20x12", C-NY 11/14/89; $1,210,000

Blondes Madchen im Unterhemd, gouache/pencil on paper, sgn/dtd 1913, 12x18", SBY 11/12/88 OE **220,000**
Blumengarten (view of the garden in bloom), oil on board, sgn/dtd 07, 14x10", C-NY 5/11/89 ..... **82,500**
Liegender Akt, watercolor/pencil on paper, sgn/dtd 1913, 13x19", SBY 11/12/88 ..... **88,000**
Liegender Akt (reclining nude), watercolor/gouache over pencil on buff paper, initialed/dtd 10, 22x15", SBY 5/10/89 OE **308,000**
Liegender Weiblicher Akt (nude), charcoal on paper, sgn/dtd 1918, 12x18", SBY 11/16/89 ..... **99,000**
Liegendes Madchen mit Schwarzen Strumpen, gouache/watercolor/pencil on paper, sgn/dtd 1913, 12x19", SBY 11/12/88 OE **126,500**
Madchen, Rock Ausziehend (nude); pencil on buff paper, initialed/dtd 1911, 22x15", SBY 11/16/89 ..... **49,500**
Portrait of a Lady (Serena Lederer), soft lead pencil on paper, sgn/dtd 1917, 18x12", SBY 11/12/88 OE **165,000**
Pregnant Woman in Gold Dress (portrait), watercolor/gold paint/pencil on buff paper, sgn/dtd 08, 12x9", SBY 5/10/89 ..... **110,000**
Sitzende Frau (seated woman), black crayon on paper, sgn/dtd 1914, 19x13", SBY 5/10/89 ..... **66,000**
Sitzende Frau mit Grunen Strumpfen, watercolor/gouache/pencil on buff paper, sgn/dtd 1918, 18x12", SBY 11/16/89 OE **330,000**
Sonnenblumen, gouache/black crayon on paper, sgn/dtd 1918, 18x12", SBY 11/12/88 OE **341,000**
Stehende Ake (nude from behind), black crayon on buff paper, sgn/dtd 1918, 18x12", SBY 5/10/89 ..... **44,000**
Zwei Akte (two nudes), gouache/pencil on paper, initialed/dtd 1911, 21x14", SBY 11/12/88 ..... **308,000**

SCHIERL, Josef (German, fl 1835-)
Feline Chorus (singing cats, mice musicians), oil on board, sgn/dtd 1832, 10x13", C-E 2/21/89 ..... **3,300**

SCHIFANO, Mario (Italian, 1934-)
Orto Botanico (abstract), enamel on canvas, sgn/dtd 82/Aug 5, unfr, 80x119", C-E 11/14/89 ..... **13,200**

SCHIFFER, Ethel B. (American, 1879-)
Red Rubber Boots (women & children trudge through snow, houses beyond), oil on canvas, sgn, 22x20", RWS 3/31/88 ..... **550**

SCHILDER, Andrei Nicolajevitch (Russian, 1861-)
Thatched Cottages Along a Stream, oil on canvas, sgn, 29x42", C-NY 5/24/89 ..... **6,050**

SCHILLE, Alice (American, -1955)
Figures on a Beach, watercolor on paper, sgn, 7x6", RWS 5/12/89 OE **5,500**

SCHIND, R.
Peasant Girls by a Fountain, oil on panel, sgn, unfr, 16x9", C-E 11/8/88 UE **600**

SCHINDLER, Emil Jacob (Austrian, 1842-1892)
Sunlight Through Pine Trees, watercolor/gouache, 9x14", C-NY 10/26/88 ..... **4,400**

SCHINDLER, Thomas (German, 20th C)
Das Idol un Seine Leidenschaft (contemporary), oil on canvas, 1983, 87x71", SBY 2/15/89 ..... **2,750**
Ein Historisches Ratsel u Sein Losung II (contemporary), oil on canvas, sgn/dtd 1983, 87x98", C-NY 2/14/89 ..... **6,600**
Fisch I, oil on canvas, sgn/dtd 1982/titled, 87x75", C-NY 11/10/88 UE **3,860**

SCHINOLLE, J. (19th C)
Austrian Soldiers Riding Through a Village, watercolor/pencil on paper, sgn, 6x9", WG 4/23/88 UE **125**

SCHIODTE, Harald Valdemar Immanuel (Danish, 1852-1924)
Suitors, oil on canvas, sgn/dtd 1882, 27x30", SBY 5/23/89 ..... **7,700**

SCHIRMER, Johann Wilhelm (German, 1807-1863)
In the Roman Campagna (landscape), watercolor/gouache/pencil, sgn, 9x16", C-NY 2/23/89 OE **2,420**

SCHLEICHER, Carl (Austrian, fl 1859-1871)
Threading a Needle, oil on canvas, sgn, 8x7", C-E 5/23/88 ..... **1,650**

SCHLEISCH, Anton (19th C)
Pair: Landscape with Cattle Grazing by a Chalet; Man with Dog by a Chalet; pencil, sgn/dtd 1849, 5x6", C-E 10/25/88 ..... **154**

SCHLESINGER, Felix (German, 1833-1910)
Mushroom Gatherers (woman & two children in an interior), oil on panel, sgn, 20x24", SBY 2/22/89 ..... **26,400**
Two Children Playing with Rabbits, oil on panel, sgn, 14x16", C-NY 10/25/89 ..... **28,600**
Young Girl Snuggling with Rabbits, oil on canvas, sgn, 12x9", FAP 12/8/89 ..... **15,500**

SCHLESINGER, Henri Guillaume (French, 1814-1893)
Blowing Bubbles (two children laying on pillow/blowing bubbles), oil on canvas, sgn, 30x35", SBY 2/22/89 ..... **12,100**

SCHLOESSER, Carl Bernhard (German, 1832-1914)
New Pupil, oil on canvas, sgn/dtd 1862, 29x24", C-NY 2/25/88 ..... **11,000**

SCHMALIX, Hubert (Austrian, 1952-)
Krischna, oil on linen, unfr, 79x79", C-E 5/13/88 ..... **4,620**

SCHMID, David Alois (Swiss, 1791-1861)
Vue de la Ville et des Environs de Lucerne, pen/ink/watercolor on paper, sgn/inscr, 13x20", SBY 6/8/88 OE **4,400**

SCHMIDT, Albert H. (American, 1885-1957)
Village Blacksmith (man working at anvil in a detailed interior), oil on canvas, ca 1918, 30x38", WL 5/20/88 ..... **2,600**

SCHMIDT, Franz (German, 1917-)
Bavarian Village, gouache/watercolor on paper, sgn, 16x12", B/B 1/11/89 ..... **550**
European Courtyard, gouache on paper, 16x13", B/B 9/14/89 ..... **1,100**

SCHMIDT, Frederic Albert (French, 1846-1916)
Cloudy Skies, oil on canvas laid down on board, sgn, 18x33", WD 5/5/88 ..... **1,500**

SCHMIDT, Hans (German, 1859-)
Near Chester Springs, oil on board, sgn/titled, 16x18", C-E 10/18/89 ..... **880**

SCHMIDT, Johann Georg (Wienerschmidt)(German, 1694-1767)
Martyrdom of a Saint, possibly the Sainted Pope Stephen I; oil on canvas, 12x8", SBY 6/3/88 ..... **6,600**

SCHMIDT, Karl (American, 1890-1962)
Foot of Burnthead, Maine; oil on board, sgn/dtd 1914, 8x10", B/B 10/6/88 ..... **825**

SCHMIDT, Kaspar
The Arrest, oil on canvas, sgn, 20x40", WD 3/23/88 ..... **1,100**

SCHMIDT, Katherine (American, 1898-)
Country Lane, oil on canvas, sgn/dtd 29, unfr, 25x30", C-E 4/7/88 UE **440**

Portrait of a Young Man, oil/pencil on canvasboard, sgn, 14x10", C-NY 6/17/89
SCHMIDT, Maggie (Canadian) 440
Party Girl in Red, oil on paper, sgn, 30x22", FB 10/11/88
SCHMITT, D. 700
Pair: Travelers Resting Along the Road; oil on canvas, 1 sgn, 18x15", SBY 10/21/88
SCHMITT, Georg Philipp (German, 1808-1873) 4,950
Wedding Picture, oil on canvas, sgn, unfr, 15x12", B/B 8/10/88 OE
SCHMITT, Nathaniel (German, 1847-1918) 1,210
Generous Lady, oil on canvas, sgn/dtd Roma 1874, 31x23", C-NY 10/25/89 UE
SCHMITT, Paul Leon Felix (French, 1856-1902) 2,420
Village aux Printemps (springtime scene), oil on canvas, sgn, 20x29", C-E 2/21/89
SCHMUTZER, Jakob Mathias (Austrian, 1733-1811) 2,750
Head of a Hooded Woman, brown chalk, crowned coat of arms & PB wm, sgn, 19x16", C-NY 1/11/89 UE
Head of a Man with a Moustache, reddish-brown chalk, sgn, 21x17", C-NY 1/11/89 220
Head of a Turbanned Man with Moustache Looking Upwards...; red chalk, jester & FTW wm, sgn, 18x16", C-NY 1/11/89 UE 1,650
Head of a Woman with Pearls in Her Hair...; brown chalk, jester & FTW wm, sgn, 16x13", C-NY 1/11/89 440
Head of a Young Man Looking to the Left, chalk, crowned coat of arms & PB wm, sgn/dtd 777, 19x15", C-NY 1/11/89 OE 1,650
Head of a Youth Looking Over His Left Shoulder, red chalk, SW wm, sgn, 23x17", C-NY 1/11/89 OE 6,050
Resting Youth with His Legs Raised Against a Wall, chalk, jester & FTW wm, sgn/dtd 1764, 21x16", C-NY 1/11/89 UE 4,400
Sleeping Youth Seated on a Rock, red chalk, jester & FTW wm, sgn, 17x22", C-NY 1/11/89 OE 1,100
SCHMUTZLER, Leopold (German, 1864-1941) 4,400
Liberty (three-quarter length portrait), oil on board, sgn, 38x30", C-NY 5/25/88
Lovely Duet, oil on panel, sgn, oval, 30x30", C-E 10/26/89 4,950
SCHNABEL, Julian (American, 1951-) 4,400
Draw a Man & a Woman, pencil/gouache on paper, sgn/inscr, 15x22", C-E 5/13/88
Drawing of a Baby (abstract), tempera on paper map, sgn/dtd 1982 Dec/titled, 38x28", SBY 2/19/88 2,750
The Act (abstract, light blue on red background), oil on panel, 1982, 95x72", C-NY 11/7/89 OE 6,325
Untitled (abstract), graphite on paper, sgn, 1975, 12x9", C-NY 11/10/88 OE 220,000
Untitled (abstract), graphite/oil on paper, sgn/dtd 79, 28x39", C-NY 11/10/88 OE 3,960
Untitled (abstract), ink/colored ink wash on paper, sgn/dtd 81, 38x50", SBY 5/3/88 7,150
Untitled (abstract), oil stick/pencil on 2 sheets paper, sgn, dtd 5/8/79, 56x40", SBY 2/19/88 5,500
Untitled (abstract), oil/oil stick on paper, sgn/dtd 1975, 15x22", SBY 10/5/89 OE 5,775
Untitled (contemporary), ink on paper, sgn/dtd 1978, 28x60", SBY 5/5/89 11,000
You Must Be Intimate with a Token Few (abstract), encaustic on canvas, sgn/inscr/dtd 1979, 102x60", C-NY 11/9/88 16,500
SCHNEIDER, Bernhard (American, 19th C) 154,000
Landscape with Water, Building, & Figures; oil on panel, sgn, 5x8", S/A 2/18/89
SCHNEIDER, George (20th C) 225
Composition (abstract), oil on canvas, sgn/dtd 50, 25x21", SBY 10/8/88 OE
SCHNEIDER, Mary (Canadian, 1900-) 19,800
Backyard, watercolor, sgn, 14x11", WAD 11/30/89
SCHNEIDER, Otto Henry (American, 1865-1950) 100
Normandy, oil on canvas laid down on plywood, sgn/inscr, 25x36", C-NY 9/30/88 OE
SCHNEIDER (German, 19th C) 22,000
Castle on the Rhine, oil on canvas, sgn, 12x21", B/B 9/14/89
SCHODL, Max (Austrian, 1834-1921) 1,650
Still Life of Globe, oil on panel, sgn/dtd 1902, 9x7", SBY 12/9/88
SCHOEFFT, August Theodore (Hungarian, 1809-1888) 3,300
View of the Benares, oil on canvas, ca 1840, 38x52", C-SK 5/25/89
SCHOENBERG, Violeta (American, 20th C) 1,380
River Landscape, oil on canvas, sgn/dtd 1934, 18x23", SLK 9/29/88
SCHOEVAERTS, Mathyas; circle of (Flemish, 1665-1694) 130
Village Pageant, oil on panel, 11x14", SBY 6/8/88 OE
SCHOFIELD, J.W. (American, 20th C) 6,050
Young Woman Picking Flowers, oil on board, sgn/dtd 1902, 18x18", B/B 12/8/88
SCHOFIELD, Walter Elmer (American, 1867-1944) 715
August Afternoon (rocky coastal scene), oil on canvas, sgn/dtd 22, 26x30", C-NY 5/25/89
Boat Basin at Santa Barbara, oil on panel, sgn, 24x30", C-NY 5/25/89 13,200
Early Landscape, oil on canvas, sgn twice, 24x30", SBY 1/24/89 13,200
Morning Light, the Coast; oil on canvas, sgn, 30x37", SBY 6/28/89 5,500
Pennsylvania Barn in Snow, oil on canvas, ca 1930, 20x24", C-NY 5/25/89 9,350
Reflections (on a wooded stream), oil on canvas, sgn, ca 1925, 20x24", C-NY 9/28/89 20,900
Rose Point, oil on canvas, initialed/inscr/dtd 24, 16x18", C-NY 3/11/88 OE 7,150
Village Bridge (leading to hillside village), oil on canvas, sgn, 16x20", C-NY 5/25/89 7,150
Wooded Landscape, oil on woodboard, sgn, 30x36", PHL 12/1/88 UE 9,350
SCHOLDER, Fritz (American, 1937-) 2,300
American Portrait with Earth Vibration, acrylic on canvas, sgn/dtd 1975/titled, 80x68", C-NY 11/10/88 OE
Cowboy Indian, oil on canvas, sgn twice/dtd 1974/titled, 80x68", C-NY 11/10/88 OE 33,000
Eagle Dancer, acrylic on canvas, sgn/inscr/dtd 1977, unfr, 68x54", C-NY 5/4/88 34,100
Indian Cowboy with High School Jacket, oil on canvas, sgn/dtd 1980/titled, SBY 5/2/88 OE 24,200
Indian in Hollywood with Woman, acrylic on canvas, sgn/dtd 1973/titled, unfr, 68x52", C-NY 11/10/88 33,000
19,800

SCHOLZ, Max (German, 1855-)
Discussion Between Two Monks (interior scene), oil on canvas, sgn/inscr, 14x17", B/B 6/15/89 3,850
Monk with Snuff Box, oil on panel, sgn/inscr, 14x10", C-E 5/23/88 2,860
SCHOMMER, Francois (French, 1850-1935)
The Artist's Model, oil on canvas, sgn, 20x12", C-E 10/26/89 1,210
SCHONBERG, Harold (20th C)
John Koch, pen/brush/black ink on paper, sgn/dtd 1946, 17x14", C-NY 6/17/89 220
SCHONFELD, Johann Heinrich; att (German, 1609-1682)
Martyrdom of Saint Lawrence, oil on canvas, 29x24", SBY 6/3/88 4,400
Saint John the Baptist Preaching to the Multitude in the Moonlight, oil on canvas, unfr, 37x49", SBY 10/13/89 OE 5,775
SCHONFELD, Johann Heinrich; circle of (German, 1609-1682)
Landscape with Cattle by a Footbridge, oil on canvas, 27x40", C-NY 1/11/89 UE 4,400
Salome with the Head of St John the Baptist, oil on canvas, 37x29", C-E 1/12/88 242
SCHONFELD, Johann Heinrich; school of (German, 1609-1682)
Figures by Classical Ruins, oil on canvas, 34x46", WD 10/19/88 3,000
SCHONIAN, Alfred (German, 1856-)
Pair: Shepherd Returning Home with His Flock; Woman Feeding Geese; oil on canvas, sgn, 20x15", C-E 2/21/89 3,520
SCHONLEBER, Gustave (German, 1851-1917)
Bridge in Bruges, Belgium; oil on canvas laid down, sgn/dtd 1910, 29x35", B/B 3/17/88 7,150
SCHOOL, Max (Austrian, 1834-1921)
Still Life of Books, Shawl, & Delft Jar with Cover; oil on panel, sgn/dtd 1919, 13x10", SBY 12/9/88 UE 1,650
School of the Veneto (18th C)
Landscape with a Rider & a Herdsman Tending His Flock, oil on canvas, 22x28", SBY 10/21/88 3,300
SCHOONLINGEN, J.H. (Dutch, 20th)
Canal Scene, Amsterdam; oil on canvas, sgn, 24x32", B/B 5/17/89 990
SCHOONOVER, Frank Earle (American, 1877-1972)
Autumn Landscape, oil on canvas, sgn/dtd 36, 28x36", SBY 9/23/88 1,980
Green Jacket, Red Cap & White Owl's Feather! (pixies); ink/watercolor/gouache on board, monogramed, 14x9", RWS 3/31/88 425
Haystacks with Church Steeple in the Distance, oil on canvas, sgn, 16x48", C-E 6/1/89 2,420
Man From the North, oil on canvas, sgn/dtd 20, 28x36", SBY 6/24/88 7,700
Prairie Girl (woman in profile in landscape), oil on canvasboard, sgn, 13x11", C-E 2/1/89 UE 880
SCHOPIN, Frederic Henri (French, 1804-1880)
Judgement of Solomon, oil on canvas, sgn/dtd 1842, unfr, 135x110", SBY 10/24/89 66,000
Slave Market, oil on canvas, sgn, 24x20", SBY 10/24/89 OE 126,500
SCHORDER, Paul (Continental, 19th C)
Harvesters (resting in a landscape), oil on canvas, sgn, 28x39", C-E 5/22/89 2,860
SCHOUMAN, Aert (Dutch, 1710-1792)
Magnificent Pheasant Pigeon, watercolor, sgn/dtd 1756, 14x10", SBY 1/13/89 6,325
Parrots & Other Exotic Birds in a Landscape, oil on canvas, sgn, 53x56", SBY 6/2/89 OE 77,000
SCHOUMANN, Martinus (Dutch, 1770-1848)
Shipping in Rough Waters, oil on canvas, sgn, 28x38", SBY 10/21/88 11,000
SCHOUTEN, Henry (Belgian, 1864-1927)
Les Savetier, oil on canvas, sgn/dtd 1895, 26x22", C-E 10/26/89 7,150
Out Shooting (hunter shooting at fowl, retrievers waiting), oil on canvas, indistinctly sgn, 32x24", SBY 6/9/89 4,400
Pasture by the Sea, oil on canvas, sgn, 30x40", RWS 6/17/89 UE 300
Setters Rabbiting, oil on canvas, indistinctly sgn, 32x47", SBY 6/9/89 5,500
SCHOYERER, Josef (German, 1844-1923)
Hauling in the Nets, oil on canvas, sgn/indistinctly dtd, 17x26", C-E 10/26/89 2,860
Two Figures Looking Towards a Distant Village, oil on canvas, sgn, unfr, 7x14", B/B 5/17/89 OE 1,100
SCHRADER, Theodore (Continental, 19th C)
Pair: Floral Still Life with Parakeet; Floral Still Life with Butterfly; oil on canvas, 1 sgn, 20x16", C-E 2/21/89 7,700
SCHRAEGLE, G. (American, 20th C)
Mountain Landscape, oil on canvas, sgn/dtd, 20x24", WG 9/16/88 UE 75
SCHRAG, Karl (German, 1912-)
Beach Grasses & Cloud, pen on paper, sgn, 16x12", WG 10/19/88 UE 225
SCHRAM, Alois Hans (Austrian, 1864-1919)
Kid Gloves, oil on canvas, sgn/dtd 1906, 32x24", RWS 5/12/89 4,500
SCHRANZ, Joseph; att (German, 1803-)
Shipping Off a Harbor on Stormy Seas, oil on canvas, 18x29", C-E 2/23/88 1,650
SCHREIBER, George (American, 1904-1977)
Bomb Shelter, oil on canvas, sgn/dtd 42, 28x33", C-NY 9/30/88 6,600
Brooklyn Bridge, black crayon/watercolor on paper, sgn/dtd 45, 22x30", SBY 4/14/89 OE 2,200
Carousel Horses, watercolor on paper, sgn/dtd 45, 21x27", SBY 9/14/89 2,860
Peasants by a Waterfall, gouache on board, sgn, 24x19", C-E 2/1/89 550
Train Station, oil on canvas, indistinctly sgn, 15x17", C-E 11/30/88 OE 2,420
SCHREYER, Adolf (German, 1828-1899)
Arab Cavalry Approaching an Oasis, oil on canvas, sgn, 28x40", C-NY 5/24/89 49,500
Arab Chieftain & His Entourage, oil on canvas, sgn, 18x26", C-NY 5/24/89 33,000
Arab Horsemen with a Village Beyond, oil on canvas, sgn, 13x24", C-NY 2/23/89 22,000
Arab Warrior Leading a Charge, oil on canvas, sgn, 33x27", SBY 2/22/89 OE 41,250
Arab Warriors Descending a Mountain, oil on canvas, sgn, 20x33", B/B 6/15/89 35,750

Arabian Horsemen, oil on canvas, sgn, 34x47", SBY 2/22/89 148,500
Arabian Horsemen, oil on canvas, sgn, 34x48", C-NY 5/24/89..... 104,500
Arabian Horsemen Descending From the Hills, oil on canvas, sgn, 20x33", SBY 10/24/89..... 66,000
Arabian Patrol, oil on canvas, sgn, 28x40", C-NY 5/24/89 OE 115,500
At the Watering Place (Arabs watering horses), oil on canvas, sgn, 34x51", C-NY 5/24/89 49,500
Bullock Cart, oil on canvas, sgn, 9x7", C-NY 2/23/89..... 4,400
Homewards, oil on wood panel, sgn, 12x16", S/A 2/18/89..... 13,000
Patrol (Arabs on horses overlooking Mediterranean), oil on cradled panel, sgn, 21x27", S/A 2/18/89..... 18,000
Troika on a Snowy Evening, oil on canvas, sgn, 29x39", C-NY 2/23/89 28,600

:HREYER, C.W.

Still Life of Peaches on a Table, oil on canvas, sgn/dtd 96, 12x18", C-E 2/23/88..... 935

:HREYVOGEL, Charles (American, 1861-1912)

Stormy Night Landscape, oil on canvas, sgn, 12x18", C-E 9/15/88 UE..... 352
Teepee on a Plain, oil on board, sgn, 10x8", SBY 3/17/88..... 7,150

:HRIJVER, A. (Dutch, 20th C)

Rotterdam, oil on canvas, sgn, 24x31", SLK 9/29/88..... 550

:HRODER, Povl (Danish, 1894-1957)

Room Interior, oil on canvas, 33x39", B/B 9/14/89 UE 770

:HROETER, Paul K. (German, 1866-)

Mother with Her Children in an Interior, oil on canvas, sgn, 24x32", B/B 4/20/88 1,100

:HROFF, Alfred Hermann (American, 1863-1939)

Pastoral Landscape (cow grazing, forest & farm in distance), watercolor on paper, sgn, 13x20", RAB 8/9/88 UE..... 150
Summer Afternoon, oil on canvas, sgn, 15x18", C-E 6/1/88..... 880

:HROTER, G. (German)

Travelers & Animals Near a River, oil on panel, sgn, 16x12", FB 4/25/88 UE 475

:HRYVER, see De Schryver

:HUBERT, Orlando Vincent (American, 1844-1928)

Afternoon Thunderstorm, watercolor, sgn, 9x12", NA 5/13/89..... 175
Cuban Landscape, watercolor, sgn/dtd 1891, 9x12", NA 11/5/88 175
Long Pier, Cleveland Harbor; oil on panel, sgn, 10x13", NA 2/24/89..... 240
Marshlands, watercolor, sgn, 5x8", NA 5/13/89 110
Small Inlet, watercolor, sgn, 6x9", NA 2/6/88 UE..... 80
View Across the Sound, watercolor, sgn, 8x10", NA 3/26/88 175

:HUERER, S. (German, 19th C)

Two Children Seated in a Glade, oil on canvas, sgn, 32x23", SBY 6/8/88 1,650

:HUFFENECKER, Claude Emile (French, 1851-1934)

Au Bord de la Mer (seascape/coastline), pastel on paper mounted at edges to mat, stamped w/cipher, 10x12", C-NY 10/6/88 6,600
Children Playing Marbles, black chalk, sgn twice, 11x14", C-NY 10/26/88 OE..... 4,180
Les Meules de Foin (landscapes w/stacks of hay), oil on canvas, monogramed/dtd 1886, 18x22", C-NY 5/11/89 30,800
Pair: Girl Holding a Cat; Sketch of a Small Dog; pencil on laid paper, estate stamp, unfr, ca 1888, 6x5", RWS 11/3/88 275
Pair: Point d'Aval; Point de Hoche; pastel on paper, stamped monogramed, 9x11", SBY 10/6/89 8,800

:HULMAN, Lion (Dutch, 1851-1942)

City of Edam, Holland; oil on canvas, 18x29", DM 2/19/88..... 1,200

:HULTZ, George F. (American, 1869-)

Boat House, oil on canvas, sgn, 20x30", C-E 10/18/89 UE 990
Forest Interior, oil on canvas, sgn, 26x45", C-E 2/16/88 UE 264
Green & Gold, oil on canvas, sgn, 24x32", LH 12/4/88..... 1,500
Harbor at Sunset, oil on canvas, sgn, 26x32", LH 10/16/88 1,800
Monhegan Island, oil on canvas, sgn, 19x28", S/A 2/18/89..... 900
Off the Coast of Maine, oil on canvas, sgn, 20x30", S/A 2/18/89 550
On the Way From the Market, oil on canvas, sgn, 16x22", C-E 11/30/88 UE 660
Path Through the Woods, pastel on board, sgn, 19x28", C-E 11/30/88 UE 660
Sunset Along the Courtyard, pastel on paper, sgn, 16x21", C-E 2/1/89 UE 660

:HULTZE, Bernard (German, 1915-)

Gelachter (abstract), paper construction/mixed media in wooden & glass frame, sgn/dtd 64, 27x35", C-E 11/17/88 OE 6,820
Menschenfrichs Gemenge (abstract), paper construction/printed paper/mixed media, sgn/dtd 1964, 30x37", C-E 11/17/88 OE..... 8,250

:HULTZE, Robert (German, 1828-)

Tyrolean Village Near a River, oil on canvas, sgn, 12x16", B/B 10/9/88 OE 6,600

:HUMACHER, Emil (German, 1912-)

Kalimbi IV (abstract), oil/mixed media on canvas, sgn/dtd 59, 39x31", SBY 6/30/88 OE..... 52,000

:HUSTER, Donna (American, 1883-1953)

Double-Sided: Construction Work; Exposition Facade; watercolor/pencil on paper, 1 sgn, unfr, 17x18", B/B 10/6/88..... 1,045
Morning Silver, oil on board, sgn, 16x20", B/B 10/6/88 2,475

:HUT, Cornelis; att (Flemish, 1597-1655)

Madonna & Child, oil on copper, 14x10", C-NY 10/12/89 17,600

:HUT, Cornelis; circle of (Flemish, 1597-1655)

Christ Before Pilate, oil on copper, 24x32", C-NY 10/12/89 1,650

:HUTZ, Christian Georg I (German, 1718-1791)

Extensive River Landscape, oil on canvas, 9x14", SBY 1/12/89..... 9,350
Extensive River Landscape, oil on panel, 10x14", SBY 4/7/89 3,575
Herder with Cows by a Pool in a Wooded Clearing, oil on copper, sgn/dtd 1785, 17x21", C-NY 1/15/88 6,600

SCHUTZE, August (German, 1805-1847)
Pair: Pet Rabbits; Pet Squirrel; oil on canvas, sgn/dtd 37, 10x8", SBY 7/12/89 OE 12,
SCHUTZENBERGER, Paul Rene (French, 1860-1916)
Nu a la Toilette, oil on canvas, sgn, 59x39", SBY 6/8/88 OE 5,
SCHUYFF, Peter (20th C)
Untitled (abstract composition), acrylic on canvas, sgn/dtd 1984, 66x46", SBY 10/5/89 23,
Untitled (abstract composition), acrylic on canvas, 1985, 72x100", C-NY 5/4/89 17,
Untitled (abstract composition), acrylic on linen, sgn/dtd 85, unfr, 90x66", C-NY 5/4/89 OE 33,
Untitled (abstract), acrylic on canvas, sgn twice, 1984, unfr, 90x66", C-NY 11/10/88 OE 15,
Untitled (abstract), acrylic on canvas, sgn/dtd 84, 74x90", SBY 11/11/88 9,
Untitled (abstract), acrylic on linen, sgn/dtd 85, 75x75", SBY 5/3/88 11,
Untitled (abstract), acrylic on linen, 1984, 90x66", SBY 2/15/89 11,
Untitled (abstract), acrylic on linen, 1988, 75x75", SBY 2/15/89 6,
Untitled (canal scene w/abstract superimposed), oil on canvas, sgn/dtd 84, 45x65", SBY 5/3/89 8,
Untitled (lineation, circles & shapes in red, yellow & green), acrylic on canvas, sgn/dtd 84, 67x46", C-NY 2/14/89 8,
Untitled (vertical lineation), watercolor on paper, initialed, 1987, 16x12", C-NY 2/14/89 1,
SCHUYLER, Remington (American, 1884-1955)
The Ceremony, oil on canvas, ca 1925, 36x24", B/B 3/17/88 1,
The Dance, oil on canvas, sgn, 36x24", B/B 3/17/88 1,
The Meeting, oil on canvas, sgn, 36x24", B/B 3/17/88 2,
SCHUZ, Christian Georg the elder (German, 1718-1791)
Christ Healing the Paralytic at the Pool of Bethesda, oil on panel, sgn, 12x18", SBY 10/21/88 2,
SCHWACKA, George
In the Valley (nocturnal view), oil on canvasboard, sgn, 25x30", C-E 2/1/89 UE 1,
SCHWAR, Wilhelm (German, 1860-)
Two Cats, oil on canvas, sgn, 16x20", SBY 7/12/89 2,
SCHWARTZ, Albert Gustav (German, 1833-)
Mother & Child Under Canopy of Greenery, oil on canvas, sgn/dtd 1878, 55x41", SBY 12/9/88 5,
SCHWARTZ, Andrew Thomas (American, 1867-1942)
Catskills, New York; oil on canvas, sgn, 24x30", RWS 9/8/89 ....
October, oil on canvas, sgn, 25x30", SBY 6/28/89 UE 1,
Pine Trees (extensive landscape), oil on canvas, sgn, 20x24", C-E 6/1/89 1,
SCHWARTZ, Chaija (Israeli, 20th C)
Seated Woman in a Blue Slip, oil on canvas, sgn/dtd 57, 30x19", RWS 3/16/89 UE ....
SCHWARTZ, Davis Francis (American, 1879-1969)
Lakeside Path in the Moonlight, oil on board, sgn, 9x12", B/B 1/11/89 ....
SCHWARTZ, William S. (American, 1896-1977)
Fishing for Crabs, gouache on board, sgn twice/inscr, 18x22", C-NY 9/30/88 2,
My Model, oil on canvas, sgn twice/inscr/dtd 1928, 30x36", C-NY 9/30/88 7,
Summer Resort in Michigan, oil on canvas, sgn, 27x44", C-NY 9/30/88 4,
SCHWARZSCHILD, Alfred (German, 1874-)
After the Climb (tavern interior w/figures), oil on canvas, sgn/dtd 1913, 40x30", SLK 9/28/88 3,
SCHWEICKHARDT, Hendrick Willem (German, 1746-1797)
Pair: Figures in a Boat by a Gazebo & Cottage; Landscape with a Ferryboat; oil on canvas, unfr, 93x73", C-NY 6/2/88 OE 66,
SCHWENINGER, Carl the elder (Austrian, 1818-1887)
Recital (elegant interior scene w/gentlemen playing instruments), oil on panel, sgn, 16x12", C-NY 2/23/89 8,
Serenade (two women, man, & monkey in an interior), oil on canvas, sgn, 21x18", SBY 2/22/89 11,
Sylvia, oil on canvas, sgn, 19x24", SBY 5/23/89 OE 30,
SCHWENINGER, Carl the younger (Austrian, 1854-1903)
Interior Parlor Scene with Two Ladies, oil on canvas, sgn, 18x23", MAG 4/24/88 OE 5,
SCHWENINGER, Rosa (Austrian, 1849-)
Young Girl with Rabbits, oil on board, sgn, 17x21", C-NY 2/23/89 17,
SCHWIND, Edouard (French, 19th C)
Portrait of an Elegant Lady in a Black Evening Dress, oil on canvas, sgn/dtd 1841, 40x32", C-E 10/26/89 2,
SCHWITTERS, Kurt (German, 1887-1948)
Asbestos Mat (abstract), oil on wood/asbestos, ca 1943-45, 20x16", SBY 5/10/89 115,
Exponiert, collage on board mounted on board, sgn/dtd 1929/#d 32, overall 18x13", SBY 5/11/88 OE 71,
In (abstract), collage on paper, sgn/dtd 1926, 10x7", C-NY 11/15/88 39,
Land, collage, sgn/dtd 1947, 6x5", C-NY 11/15/88 22,
Napoleon, collage on paper mounted on board, sgn/dtd 1929, 14x10", SBY 11/16/89 OE 71,
Ntwurf: Kurt Schwitters; collage of photographic elements/pencil/ink/wash on paper, sgn/dtd 1931, 13x10", SBY 5/11/88 44,
Senior Service (abstract composition), collage on board mounted on thin stiff card, sgn/dtd 1947, 11x9", SBY 5/11/88 44,
Two Yellow Spots, collage on paper mounted on board, sgn/dtd 1947/#d 16a, 7x5", SBY 11/16/89 44,
Untitled (abstract), collage of colored papers/tickets/corrugated card over photograph, sgn/dtd, 9x7", SBY 11/12/88 38,
SCHWURLES, Theodore (Dutch, 19th/20th C)
Portrait of a Woman in a White Blouse, oil on board, sgn, 18x12", B/B 5/17/89 ....
SCIALOJA, Toti (Italian, 1914-)
Gray Sleep, oil on canvas, sgn/dtd 56, 57x45", C-E 5/13/88 OE 4,
SCOGNAMIGLIO (Italian, 18th/19th C)
Music with Tambourine Player, oil on canvas, sgn, 30x20", WG 9/16/88 2,

COPPETTA, Pietro (Italian, 1863-1920)
Courting on a Country Lane, oil on canvas, sgn, 11x14", C-E 10/26/89 ... 3,080
Figures Walking Along a Country Road, oil on board, sgn, 6x8", C-E 2/21/89 ... 3,520
COTT, Adam Sherriff (Canadian, 1887-1980)
Bacchanal, oil on board, sgn, 7x9", FB 5/28/89 OE ... 360
Homecoming (Eskimo family by igloo), oil on canvas, sgn, 24x30", FB 10/11/88 ... 5,200
Lambert's Pond, oil on panel, sgn, 20x24", FB 10/17/88 UE ... 1,800
Mother (portrait), oil on canvas, sgn, 32x24", FB 10/17/88 ... 2,200
Native Indian Portrait, oil on canvas, sgn, 20x16", FB 10/30/89 OE ... 3,300
Portrait, charcoal on canvas, sgn/dtd 1960, 24x20", FB 4/25/88 ... 500
Portrait of an Eskimo, oil on canvas, sgn, 24x18", FB 4/25/88 ... 2,800
Portrait of an Indian Chief, oil on canvas, sgn, 24x18", FB 10/30/89 ... 2,860
River & Landscape, oil on canvas, sgn, 20x24", FB 4/25/88 ... 2,700
Sunrise on a Winter Landscape, oil on board, sgn, 13x16", WAD 11/30/89 ... 1,000
COTT, Alexander (British, 19th/20th C)
In the Himalayas, oil on canvas, sgn, 19x24", C-SK 6/9/88 ... 1,200
View of Mt Everest & the Pumori Ridge, oil on canvas, sgn, 14x10", SBY 7/12/89 ... 1,210
Yosemite Valley, California; oil on board, 6x10", C-SK 6/9/88 ... 595
COTT, Campbell (Scottish, 19th/20th C)
Scottish Lake, oil on canvas, sgn, 24x36", DM 2/19/88 UE ... 700
Sunset on a Lake, oil on canvas, sgn, 24x37", C-E 11/8/88 UE ... 350
COTT, Frank Edwin (American, 1862-1929)
Church, Santa Maria Della Salute, Venice; oil on canvas, sgn/inscr, 22x18", C-NY 5/26/88 ... 3,520
Flower Market, oil on panel, sgn, 12x13", PHL 10/28/88 UE ... 400
St German-Des-Pres, oil on canvas, sgn, 33x36", SBY 9/14/89 ... 3,850
COTT, Henry Edward (American, 1900-)
Blowing Fresh, Mid-Atlantic (view across ship deck to clipper in high waves); oil on canvas, sgn, 28x42", SBY 3/17/88 OE ... 8,250
Outward Bound-American Clipper, Sovereign of the Seas; oil on canvas, sgn, 28x42", SBY 3/17/88 OE ... 7,975
COTT, James Fraser (Australian, 1878-1932)
Sydney (coastal view), watercolor heightened w/white, sgn/dtd 1916/inscr, 9x11", C-SK 6/9/88 ... 980
COTT, James Powell (American, 1909-)
Arizona Twilight (landscape), oil on canvas, sgn, 15x21", RWS 5/12/89 ... 750
New England Landscape, oil on masonite, sgn, 20x40", C-E 11/8/88 ... 550
COTT, John White Allen (American, 1815-1907)
Indian Encampment by the Lake, oil on canvas laid down on board, sgn/dtd 83, 24x36", SBY 9/23/88 ... 4,510
Landscape Scene with Fishermen, oil on canvas, sgn/dtd 1863, 37x29", RWS 3/31/88 ... 800
COTT, Julian (American, 1846-1901)
Battle Scene Near Seven Pines, Fair Oaks (Civil War); pen/ink on paper, initialed/inscr, 10x15", C-E 5/27/88 OE ... 1,540
Kiowa Woman, oil on board, sgn/dtd 90, 13x10", SBY 9/23/88 ... 3,300
COTT, Lloyd (Canadian, 1911-1968)
Carriage & Castles, watercolor, sgn/dtd 1938, 14x11", WAD 11/30/89 ... 180
COTT, Robert Bagge (British, -1896)
Ships at Sea, oil on canvas, sgn, 19x29", FAP 4/15/89 ... 880
COTT, Samuel (British, 1703-1772)
Battle of Porto Bello, oil on canvas, 53x78", C-NY 10/20/88 OE ... 26,400
COTT, W.J. (British, 19th C)
Raven Crag Burn, Haltwhistle (landscape); oil on panel, sgn/dtd 1886, 14x19", SLK 9/29/88 ... 750
COTT, William (British, 1913-)
Reclining Nude (abstract), silver paint/tempera/black chalk on paper, sgn, 30x41", C-E 11/17/88 OE ... 18,150
cottish School (19th C)
Portrait of a Seated Gentleman (half-length), oil on canvas, 14x12", WL 5/20/88 ... 500
CROTH, L.D. (American, 20th C)
Summer Landscape (path along shore, arched bridge & buildings), oil on canvas, sgn/dtd 1926, 30x42", WL 5/20/88 ... 1,300
CULLY, Sean (British, 1946-)
Small Brown Painting #2 (vertical lineation), acrylic on canvas, sgn/dtd 1978, unfr, 15x15", C-NY 5/4/89 OE ... 22,000
Untitled, oil crayon on paper, sgn/dtd 2.14.83, 30x22", SBY 2/15/89 ... 4,400
Untitled (abstract), pastel on paper, sgn/dtd 1-29-84, 30x22", SBY 5/3/89 ... 4,950
Untitled (dark rectangle), acrylic on paper, sgn/dtd 77, 24x24", C-NY 10/4/89 ... 3,850
CUTENAIRE, Jean
Clouds Over the Metropolis, collage, sgn, 20x13", C-NY 10/6/88 OE ... 2,200
EAGER, Edward (American, 1809-1886)
Half-Timbered Houses, pencil on paper, sgn/titled, 11x7", RAB 8/8/89 UE ... 200
Outside the Church, pencil on paper, sgn/titled, 7x10", RAB 8/8/89 UE ... 150
Roxburry Near Boston, Residence of General Warren; pencil/wash on paper, titled, 6x9", RAB 8/8/89 UE ... 150
EAGO, Edward (British, 1910-1974)
Barrage at Amfreville, oil on canvas, sgn, 20x26", WAD 6/6/88 ... 23,000
Queen's Carriage, watercolor on paper, sgn, 8x11", WD 5/5/88 ... 850
Windsor Castle by the River, watercolor on paper, sgn, 14x21", WD 5/5/88 ... 2,100
EAGO, Edward; att (British, 1910-1974)
Coastal Village, oil on board, 16x20", B/B 4/20/88 ... 550

SEARLE, Ronald (British, 1920-)
Kiki de Montparnasse, ink on paper, sgn/inscr, unfr, 9x10", RWS 11/3/88 UE 100
SEARS, Benjamin Willard (American, 1846-1905)
By the Campfire, oil on canvas, sgn, 14x18", B/B 10/6/88 1,650
SEARS, Francis (British, 19th/20th C)
Set of 3: Marine Scenes; oil on panel, sgn/dtd 12, 13, & 19, 10x12", 12x16", SBY 12/9/88 OE 4,675
SEARS, Taber (American, 1870-1950)
Fleet at Evening, oil on canvas, sgn, 24x20", SBY 6/28/89 UE 990
Painting the Dory, oil on canvasboard, sgn, 16x20", SBY 6/28/89 UE 935
SEAVEY, George W. (American, 1841-1916)
Still Life of Pansies, oil on canvas, sgn, 8x16", RWS 11/10/89 UE 450
Still Life of Red & White Geraniums, oil on canvas, sgn, 14x10", RWS 11/10/89 500
Still Life of Violets, oil on canvas, sgn, 7x10", RWS 3/31/88 700
SEBES, Pieter Willem (Dutch, 1830-1906)
Family Scene, oil on panel, sgn/dtd 1876, 15x11", C-E 10/26/89 3,080
Quiet Evening at Home, oil on canvas, sgn, 32x26", B/B 10/9/88 8,800
SEBILLE, A. (French, 19th C)
Still Life of Fruit & Wine, oil on canvas, sgn, 8x3", LH 10/16/88 300
SEBIRE, Gaston (French, 1920-)
Au Havre, oil on canvas, sgn, 10x20", SBY 10/7/89 2,420
Figures in a Landscape, oil on canvas, sgn, 47x60", SBY 10/5/88 2,475
La Nature Morte Bleu (The Blue Still Life), oil on canvas, sgn, 45x57", LH 3/20/88 OE 3,800
Sur la Plage (figures on beach with boats in distance), oil on canvas, sgn, 12x16", NA 5/13/89 1,700
SEBOTH, Josef (Austrian, 1814-1883)
Still Life of Song Bird & Fruit in a Crystal Tazza, oil on canvas, sgn, 24x32", SBY 10/24/89 34,100
SEBREE, Charles (American, 1912-)
Head of Woman, oil on masonite, sgn, 16x12", C-E 10/18/89 1,320
SECUNDA, Arturo (Italian, 20th C)
Large Head of a Man, pencil/ink wash on paper, sgn, 23x17", B/B 4/20/88 275
SEDGLEY, Peter (British, 1930-)
Mirage, acrylic on canvas, sgn/dtd 1966, 60x60", C-E 11/14/89 2,200
Red + Blue Modulations, gouache on paper, sgn/dtd twice, 64, inscr, 11x10", C-E 5/13/88 UE 110
SEDLACEK, Stephan (European, 19th/20th C)
Elegant Repast, oil on canvas, sgn, 26x37", SBY 6/8/88 UE 605
SEEL, Adolf (German, 1829-1907)
Nubian Guard, oil on canvas laid down on masonite, sgn, 37x23", SBY 2/22/89 16,500
Slave Auction in Cairo, oil on canvas, sgn, 39x50", SBY 2/23/89 46,200
SEERY, John (American, 1941-)
Master Eckhart (abstract), acrylic on canvas, sgn, 1971, 100x50", SBY 2/14/89 OE 2,860
Voyage (abstract), acrylic on canvas, sgn/dtd 1976, 62x55", C-E 11/17/88 2,640
SEEVAGEN, Lucien (French, 1887-1959)
Boboli Gardens in Florence, oil on canvas, sgn/dtd 1930, 16x11", B/B 9/14/89 UE 550
Riviere en Morvan, oil on canvas, sgn, 18x22", C-E 2/23/88 UE 440
SEFAN, Ross (American, 20th C)
Heading for Shonto (rider on horseback seen from behind), no media given, sgn/titled, 20x24", SBY 1/24/89 2,475
SEGAL, George (American, 1924-)
Nude Female Torso, chalks on paper, sgn/dtd 64, 18x12", C-E 11/14/88 OE 6,600
Seated Nude, pastel on colored paper, sgn/dtd 65, 18x12", SBY 10/7/89 3,575
Untitled (abstract), chalk on paper, sgn/dtd 62, 12x18", C-NY 2/14/89 3,850
SEGALL, Julius (American, ca 1858-)
Summer Landscape with Water, oil on canvas, sgn, 9x17", S/A 2/18/89 125
SEGALL, Lasar (Russian, 1890-1957)
Mae e Filho (mother & child), pen/brush/black ink on paper, sgn/dtd 1945, 19x13", C-NY 11/21/88 2,860
SEGAR, William (British, 16th/17th C)
Portrait of Elizabeth Stafford, Lady Drury; oil on panel in painted oval, 27x21", C-NY 1/11/89 38,500
SEGHERS, Hendrik (Flemish, 19th C)
Poultry & Figures in a Village Landscape, watercolor on paper, sgn, 12x18", FAP 11/4/88 260
SEGONZAC, Andre; see Dunoyer De Segonzac
SEGOROV, A. (Scandanavian, 20th C)
Winter Sleigh, gouache/tempera on board, sgn, 13x19", B/B 8/10/88 495
SEGOVIA, Andres (Argentinian, 1921-)
Still Life with Blue Vase, oil on canvas, sgn/dtd 50, 29x24", SBY 10/7/89 2,420
Vase de Fleurs sur Fond Rouge, oil on masonite, sgn, 26x10", C-E 5/13/88 UE 330
SEGUI, Antonio (Argentinian, 1934-)
Beronja Encastilado, mixed media on paper, sgn/dtd 1962, 19x25", SLK 4/7/89 400
Bucolico Serrando (surrealistic figures/landscape), mixed media on paper on canvas, sgn/dtd 1982, 39x39", C-NY 11/21/88 19,800
Cara Blanca, bust-length portrait of a man; mixed media on paper, sgn/dtd 1966, 19x25", SLK 4/7/89 650
De un Verano No 1, oil on canvas, sgn/dtd March 1967/titled, 20x24", SLK 4/7/89 500
De un Verano No 4, oil on canvas, sgn/dtd 67, 20x24", SLK 4/7/89 250
Distancia de la Mirada No 6 (man looking out over brick wall), oil on canvas, sgn, 1976, 59x59", C-NY 11/21/89 13,200
Ena Morado, bust-length portrait of a man wearing bright tie; gouache/pastel on paper, sgn/dtd 1963, 19x25", SLK 4/7/89 900

- Escapulario, portrait of seated woman; oil on panel, sgn/dtd 1961, unfr, 10x12", SLK 4/7/89 — 90
- Figura Contre Biomb, standing female figure; oil on panel, sgn/dtd 1961/titled, 10x12", SLK 4/7/89 — 200
- Homme avec Souliers, mixed media on paper, sgn/dtd 1967, 19x25", SLK 4/7/89 — 150
- Kijkend Naar Links, bust-length portrait of man w/hat; gouache/pastel on paper, sgn, 19x25", SLK 4/7/89 — 650
- Paisaje con Hombre y Casa, oil on canvas, sgn/dtd 62, 13x16", C-NY 11/21/89 — 7,700
- Personaje con Flores (seated lady w/bouquet), oil on board, sgn/dtd 62, 10x12", SLK 4/7/89 — 325
- Saco Sport, mixed media on paper, sgn/dtd, 25x19", SLK 4/7/89 — 130
- Untitled (contemporary), mixed media/collage on triangular panel in shadowbox frame, sgn/dtd 1967, 28", SLK 4/7/89 — 450
- Zitten de Man, mixed media on paper, sgn/dtd 1969, 25x19", SLK 4/7/89 — 300

SEGUIN, Armand

- Nature Morte au Pommes (still life of apples), oil on canvas, sgn/dtd Avril 1896, 18x22", C-NY 5/12/88 OE — 143,000

SEIFERT, Alfred (Czechoslovakian/German, 1850-1901)

- Bride, oil on panel, sgn, 15x11", FAP 4/15/89 — 990
- Portrait of a Young Girl (shoulder-length), oil on panel, 8x6", WG 4/23/88 — 800
- Resting Beauty, oil on canvas, sgn, 17x14", B/B 3/17/88 — 3,300

SEIGNAC, Guillaume (French, 19th/20th C)

- Anemone (portrait), oil on canvas, sgn, 13x10", SBY 12/9/88 — 3,300
- Confidence, oil on canvas, sgn, 69x38", SBY 10/24/89 — 82,500
- L'Innocence (nymph & two cherubs), oil on canvas, sgn, 40x32", SBY 10/24/89 — 99,000
- Nymph with Cherubs, oil on canvas, sgn, 26x21", SBY 10/24/89 — 35,200

SEIGNAC, Paul (French, 1826-1904)

- Artist in Her Studio, oil on canvas, sgn, 14x11", RWS 11/3/88 — 3,300
- Dressing, oil on panel, sgn, 11x9", C-E 2/23/88 — 1,430
- Feeding the Baby Birds, oil on canvas, sgn, 14x11", C-NY 10/25/89 OE — 13,200
- L'Artiste Peintre, oil on canvas, sgn, ca 1880, unfr, 14x11", SBY 6/8/88 — 2,200

SEILER, Carl Wilhelm Anton (German, 1846-1921)

- Portfolio, oil on panel, sgn/dtd 1884, 7x6", C-NY 2/25/88 — 5,500

SEITER, Daniel (Italian, 1649-1705)

- Martyrdom of Saint Lawrence, oil on canvas, 68x53", C-NY 4/8/88 — 8,800

SEITZ, Johann Georg (German, 1810-1870)

- Still Life of Basket of Grapes & Mixed Fruit on a Stone Ledge, oil on canvas, sgn, 29x40", C-NY 5/25/88 OE — 11,000
- Still Life of Grapes, Peaches, & Walnuts in a Basket; oil on canvas, 20x24", C-E 2/23/88 — 4,950

SELDON, Richard (American, 20th C)

- Sprat, Piper & Swine; oil on masonite, framed by artist, 25x31", WD 4/23/88 — 1,100

SELIGMANN, Kurt (Swiss, 1900-1962)

- Indian Myth, oil on canvas, sgn/dtd 46, 27x29", SBY 4/29/88 — 20,900
- Le Menuet (surrealistic figures), oil on canvas, dtd 46-7 on stretcher, 14x17", SBY 10/7/88 — 12,100
- Surrealistic Figure, pen/ink on paper, ca 1940, 24x19", SBY 10/7/88 OE — 3,575

SELINGER, Emily H. McGary (American, 19th/20th C)

- Still Life of Roses (many roses in glass bowl, one in slim vase), oil on canvas, sgn/dtd 1886, 20x24", RWS 9/8/89 OE — 1,500

SELL, Christian (German, 1831-1883)

- Pair: Cavalry Charge; Mountainous Climb; oil on canvas, sgn, 16x20", C-E 2/23/88 — 3,300
- Spying From Behind a Wall, oil on canvas, sgn, 8x11", WG 9/16/88 UE — 550
- Winter March, oil on canvas, sgn, 9x11", WG 9/16/88 UE — 600

SELMERSHEIM-DESGRANGE, Jean (French, 20th C)

- Dans le Jardin (in the garden), oil on canvas, sgn/dtd 1909, 24x29", C-NY 10/5/89 OE — 38,500

SELTZER, Olaf Carl (American, 1877-1957)

- Escorting the Herd of Horses, watercolor/gouache on paper, sgn, 15x20", SBY 9/23/88 OE — 19,800
- Lone Wolf (in snowy landscape), oil on canvas, sgn, 24x36", C-NY 9/28/89 — 8,800
- Medicine Man, gouache/watercolor/pencil on paper, sgn, 12x9", SBY 5/25/88 — 9,900
- Portrait of an Indian, watercolor on board, sgn, 13x10", C-E 10/18/89 — 3,300
- Wreck of the Chippena, oil on canvas, sgn, 20x30", LH 12/4/88 OE — 22,000

SELTZER, William S.

- Moving Camp, gouache on board, sgn, 17x23", C-NY 9/30/88 — 4,400

SELYHR, Conrad (Scandinavian, 19th/20th C)

- Near Ostend, Belgium (fleet of sailboats); oil on canvas, sgn/dtd 12/titled, 14x20", RAB 11/25/88 — 775

SEMENOWSKY, Eisman (French, 19th C)

- Beauty in a Feathered Hat, oil on panel, sgn, 14x10", WAD 6/6/88 — 4,500
- Beauty on the Veranda, oil on panel, sgn, 34x11", RWS 11/10/89 — 6,500
- Le Chapeau (portrait of young girl in hat), oil on canvas, sgn/inscr Paris, 13x10", C-NY 2/23/89 OE — 24,200
- Portrait of a Young Woman, oil on panel, sgn, 14x11", C-NY 2/25/88 — 2,860
- Ripe Fruit, oil on panel, sgn, 18x7", C-E 10/26/89 — 3,300
- Roman Beauties with a Garland of Roses, oil on canvas, sgn/inscr Primaevo Flore Juventus, 22x37", C-NY 2/23/89 — 11,000
- Young Beauty, oil on panel, sgn, 23x12", C-E 10/26/89 — 4,620

SEMINO, Andrea; att (Italian, ca 1525-1594)

- Mars, Venus, & Cupid; pen/brown ink/wash over traces of black chalk, 6x5", SBY 1/13/89 OE — 3,025

SEMINO, Ottavio (Italian, 1520-1604)

- Cambyses Learning of the Insurrection of Gaumata, chalk/pen/ink/wash on blue paper, inscr, 10x14", C-NY 1/11/89 — 5,280

SENAT, Prosper L. (American, 1852-1925)

- Coastal Landscape, oil on canvas, sgn/dtd 90, 20x36", SBY 4/14/89 — 1,870
- In the Adirondacks, oil on canvas, sgn, 24x18", SBY 9/23/88 — 1,760

Landscape, watercolor/pencil on paper laid down on board, sgn/dtd 96, 12x9", C-E 11/8/88 UE 132
Old Dock, oil on board, sgn/inscr Study From Nature, 14x23", C-E 9/15/88 UE 462

SENDAK, Maurice (American, 1928-)
Seven Monsters, hand-painted film celluloid, 8x10", FAP 12/8/89 150

SENECOURT, see De Senecourt

SENET, Rafael (Spanish, 1856-)
Day's Catch, oil on panel, sgn, 8x13", C-NY 10/25/89 12,100
Pair: Venetian Canal; Doge's Palace; watercolor, sgn, 15x8", C-NY 10/26/88 1,980

SENNHAUSER, John (American, 1907-)
Black Lines No 18 (abstract), watercolor on paper, sgn/dtd 44, 11x9", C-E 2/1/89 660

SENNO, Pietro (Italian, 1831-1904)
Island View, oil on canvas, sgn/indistinctly inscr, unfr, 21x32", C-E 5/23/88 1,980
Mountain Home, oil on canvas, sgn, 41x55", RWS 11/3/88 UE 1,700

SENSE, J.
Landscape with Stream, oil on canvas, sgn, 18x22", LH 10/16/88 550

SENTIS, Juan Alfonso Camo (Spanish, 1920-)
El Arroyo (men on horseback w/hunting dogs near a stream), oil on canvas, sgn, 32x39", DM 3/14/88 550

SERBIE, Gaston
L'Ambassade des Etates-Unis a Paris; oil on canvas, sgn, 29x36", PHL 11/15/88 1,900

SERENI, G. (19th C)
Reluctant Goat, watercolor heightened w/white, sgn/dtd 1854, 12x16", C-NY 10/26/88 1,980

SERGEANT, Edgar (American, 1877-)
Fishing Boats in Menemsha, oil on canvas, sgn, 20x24", C-E 2/1/89 UE 1,100

SERGENT, Lucien Pierre (French, 1849-1904)
Study of a Soldier, oil on paper laid down on board, sgn, 8x8", C-E 10/26/89 880

SERNA, see De La Serna

SERPAN, Jaroslav (European, 1922-)
Duhaudi (abstract), oil on canvas, sgn/dtd 14.7 1957, 39x32", C-E 11/14/89 OE 3,520

SERRA, Richard (American, 1939-)
Study for the Harlem Installation (circle drawing), black oil stick on paper, initialed, 1970, 41x30", C-NY 5/4/89 OE 20,900
TWU #11 (abstract), paint stick on paper, 1980, 53x41", SBY 5/3/89 30,250
Untitled (abstract), paint stick on paper, 1987, 72x37", SBY 2/15/89 OE 46,750
Untitled (circular abstract), charcoal on paper, sgn/dtd 71, 27x40", SBY 11/11/88 OE 25,300

SERRA Y AUGUE, Enrique (Spanish, 1859-1918)
Marshy Stream, oil on canvas, sgn/inscr, 17x32", C-E 2/23/88 3,520
River Landscape, oil on canvas, sgn/dtd 1909, 23x48", C-E 5/23/88 5,280
Washerwomen at the River's Edge, oil on canvas, sgn, 8x16", SBY 2/22/89 OE 20,900

SERRANO, Manuel Gonzalez (Latin American, 20th C)
Frutas en al Ventana, oil on masonite, sgn, 15x16", C-NY 11/21/89 5,500
La Chirimoya (still life), oil on board, sgn, 16x19", C-NY 11/21/88 OE 5,500
Mi Mujer, oil on canvas, sgn, 40x59", C-NY 5/18/88 6,600
Naturaleza Muerta con Ventano y Candado, oil on board, sgn, 12x16", C-NY 11/21/89 OE 6,600
Neptuno (male nude wearing hat seated on ocean bottom), oil on board, sgn, 19x27", C-NY 5/17/89 OE 6,600

SERRET, Alan
Untitled Abstraction, pastel on paper, 22x30", SBY 2/14/89 OE 1,210

SERRI, Alfredo (Italian, 1897-1972)
Trompe l'Oeil Still Life with Self-Portrait, oil on canvas, sgn, 16x20", LH 9/10/89 OE 1,800

SERRURE, Auguste (Belgian, 1825-1903)
Outdoor Gathering, oil on panel, sgn/dtd 1878, 23x34", C-NY 10/25/89 13,200
Toasting the Winner, oil on panel, sgn/dtd 1870, 23x34", C-NY 5/24/89 16,500

SERUSIER, Paul (French, 1863-1927)
Bretonnes a la Fontaine de Chateaueuf du Faou, oil on canvas, indistinctly sgn, 1893, 23x28", SBY 11/12/88 99,000
Paysage d'Automme (autumn landscape), oil on board laid down on cradled panel, sgn, ca 1915, 10x13", C-NY 2/16/89 9,350
Seated Female Nude, pencil on paper, estate stamp/vente stamp, 8x10", B/B 3/22/89 1,100
Study of Thatch-Roofed Houses, pastel on paper, initialed, 12x19", SBY 10/7/89 OE 4,675

SERVEAU, Clement (French, 1886-)
Le Jardin des Hesperides, oil on paper laid down on canvas, sgn/dtd 1928, 37x88", SBY 6/10/88 OE 4,400

SESSIONS, James Milton (American, 1882-1962)
After a Day of Sailing, watercolor/pencil on paper, sgn, 18x23", C-E 11/30/88 3,080
Children Fishing, watercolor on paper, sgn, 15x22", C-NY 3/11/88 OE 3,520
Drying Sails (ships in port), watercolor on board, sgn, 22x30", C-E 2/1/89 1,210
Fishing Wharf, watercolor/pencil on board, sgn, 15x22", C-NY 3/11/88 2,420
Harbor Scene, watercolor on paper, sgn/dtd 31, 16x20", C-E 6/1/88 1,870
Jamaican Women Carrying Fruit Baskets, watercolor on paper, sgn/dtd 1940, 14x18", SBY 3/17/88 UE 660
Joe's Diner, watercolor, sgn, 7x9", LH 12/4/88 170
Pair: Jeep & Plain; Handshake; gouache/watercolor/pencil on board, sgn, 18x22", 27x37", C-E 6/1/89 UE 825

SETHER, Gulbrand (Norwegian, fl 1890-1910)
Wintry Road, oil on canvas, sgn, 13x19", LH 3/20/88 325

SETHER, Gunther (American, 20th C)
Shovelling Snow, oil on canvas, sgn, 20x30", B/B 8/10/88 UE 440

ETON, John Thomas; att (fl 1758-1806)
Portrait of a Family in an Adam Room, oil on canvas, 45x39", SBY 10/21/88 ... 20,900
ETTLE, William Frederick (British, 1821-1897)
Seeking Shelter From the Storm, watercolor, sgn/dtd 67, 7x14", C-E 2/21/89 ... 1,045
EURAT, Georges (French, 1859-1891)
Femme au Parapluie (woman in profile w/umbrella), conte crayon on paper, ca 1883, 12x9", C-NY 5/11/89 ... 407,000

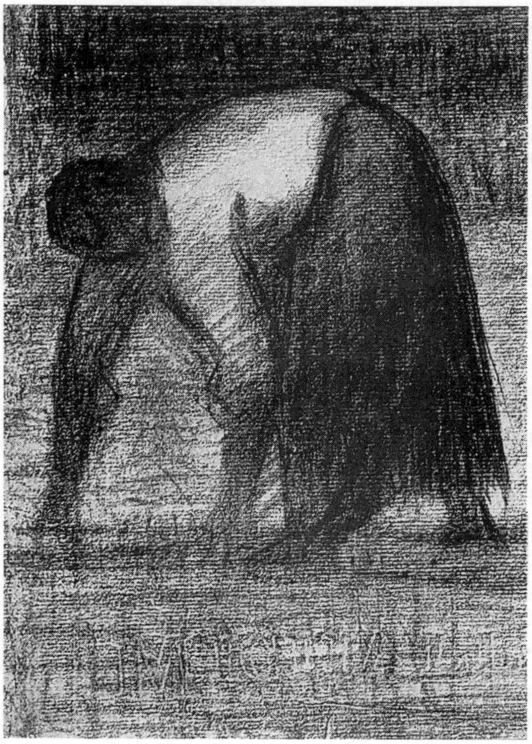

Paysanne les Mains au Sol, conte crayon on paper, ca 1882, 9x7", C-NY 11/14/89; $407,000

Standing Male Nude in Profile, pencil on paper, ca 1877-79, 13x9", SBY 11/16/89 ... 19,800
EVERINI, Gini (Italian, 1883-1966)
Natura Morta (still life of flowers, fish, & fruit), oil on panel, sgn, 19x14", C-NY 2/16/89 ... 42,900
Natura Morta con Uva Pere (still life), oil on panel, sgn, 9x12", SBY 10/7/88 OE ... 37,400
Nature Morte, pencil on paper, sgn, 9x12", SBY 10/5/88 ... 4,125
Nord-Sud (Le Metro), charcoal/white & yellow chalk on paper laid down on board, ca 1915, 12x19", SBY 5/10/89 OE ... 137,500
Still Life of Nude & Guitar, gouache on brown paper, sgn, 26x20", SBY 2/18/88 OE ... 37,400
EVERN, Arthur (British, 1842-1931)
Interior of Church Chapel, watercolor, sgn/dtd 1888, 13x21", MG 3/26/88 UE ... 175
EVILLE, school of (17th C)
Dominican Saint Preaching, oil on canvas, inscr, 46x35", C-NY 4/8/88 ... 1,320
Immaculate Conception, oil on canvas, unfr, 61x38", C-E 1/12/88 OE ... 825
EWELL, Robert Van Vorst (American, 1860-1924)
Windswept (flowing-robed lady clasping tree branch in landscape), oil on canvas, sgn, 37x16", RAB 8/8/89 ... 600
EXTON, Frederick Lester (American, 1889-)
Creek at Branford Point, Connecticut; oil on canvas, sgn/dtd 30, 16x20", B/B 3/17/88 ... 3,575
EYFERT (19th C)
Mountainous Landscape, oil on panel, sgn/dtd 1816, 11x13", C-E 5/23/88 ... 1,430
EYMOUR, George L. (British, 19th C)
Portrait of a Woman with Fur Collar, oil on panel, sgn, 16x12", C-E 2/21/89 ... 2,640
Portrait of a Young Woman, oil on panel, sgn, 16x10", RWS 11/3/88 UE ... 2,100
EYMOUR, James; after (British, 1702-1752)
Chaise Match Run on Newmarket Heath on Wednesday the 29th of August, 1750; oil on canvas, 19x32", SBY 6/9/89 ... 9,900
EYMOUR, M. (American, 19th/20th C)
Cattle in a River, watercolor on paper, sgn, 14x21", FAP 12/8/89 UE ... 175
EYMOUR, Tom (British, 19th C)
Cascade, oil on canvas, sgn, 31x20", WD 3/23/88 ... 950
Shepherd Closing the Gate, oil on canvas, sgn, 10x8", SBY 6/8/88 ... 1,100
HADBOLT, Jack Leonard (Canadian, 1909-)
Fallen Branch, ink/gouache, sgn/dtd 1958, 22x30", WAD 11/30/89 OE ... 4,400
Muskes Country (sketch), oil on board, sgn/dtd 63, 15x20", WAD 6/12/89 OE ... 1,750
Sketch, Muskes Country; oil on board, sgn/dtd 1963, 15x20", FB 10/17/88 ... 750
Winter Presences (fantasy composition), mixed media, sgn/dtd 1951, 27x20", FB 10/17/88 ... 1,400
HAFER, S.P.
Red & Black Raspberries, oil on canvas, sgn/indistinctly dtd, 12x10", C-E 2/3/88 ... 990

SHAHN, Ben (American, 1898-1969)
Apothesosis, watercolor/gouache/India ink on paper, sgn/inscr w/text, 8x48", SBY 6/24/88 OE 19,800
From the Marriage of Heaven & Hell, watercolor/ink on paper, sgn/inscr, 35x25", SBY 9/23/88 OE 18,700
Glyph for Charles (abstract), black ink/watercolor on paper, sgn, 39x25", SBY 4/14/89 4,125
Head of a Rabbi (Boy From Prague), ink/wash on paper, sgn, 13x10", SBY 9/23/88 1,760
Ice Cream Cone (abstract figure w/three scoops), gouache/watercolor/ink on paper, sgn, 18x13", SBY 9/14/89 8,800
Jazz, black ink/tissue collage on board, sgn, 11x9", C-NY 5/26/88 4,400
Jeremiah 9:1 (clinched fists, Hebrew inscription); watercolor/gouache on paper laid down, sgn, 30x27", SBY 6/28/89 OE 13,750
Laborer, gouache on board, sgn, 8x6", C-E 10/18/89 2,200
Owl, pen/ink on paper, sgn/dtd 24, 10x6", C-E 10/18/89 550
Pair: Slap; Sorrowing Man; pen/ink on paper, sgn, 6x9" & smaller, C-E 11/30/88 2,200
Ram's Horn & Menorah, tempera/gold leaf on board, sgn/inscr w/Hebrew text, 17x28", SBY 6/24/88 OE 22,000
Study for Ecclesiastes, watercolor w/white heightening ink on artist board, sgn/inscr, 20x10", SBY 6/24/88 3,850
Sweatshop, gouache/watercolor/ink on paper laid down on board, sgn, 17x11", SBY 9/14/89 7,150
The Phoenix (bird), gouache/India ink on board, sgn, 19x19", SBY 6/24/88 OE 12,100

SHAN, Li (Chinese, 1686-)
Autumn Colors (hanging scroll), ink/color on paper, sgn/dtd 1750, 67x35", SBY 5/31/89 11,000

SHANKS, Alec (French, 19th/20th C)
Chair et Metal, Paris (costume design for Folies Bergere); gouache on paper, sgn/dtd/titled, 1931, 15x12", C-E 6/16/88 330
L'Orchidee Exotique, gouache on paper, sgn/dtd/titled, ca 1930, 14x10", C-E 6/16/88 330
Les Orchidees...1931; watercolor/gouache/pencil on paper, sgn/inscr, 14x10", RWS 11/3/88 300

SHANNON, Charles Haslewood (British, 1863-1937)
Mermaid, oil on canvas, 21x24", C-L 6/27/88 OE 30,272
Mermaid, pencil/charcoal heightened w/white chalk on paper, initialed/inscr/dtd 1917, 10x9", C-L 6/27/88 OE 4,162

SHANNON, James Jebusa (British, 1862-1923)
Dirkja: Portrait of a Dutch Girl; oil on canvas, sgn, ca 1891-96, 16x12", SBY 5/23/89 13,200
Woman in White (portrait), oil on canvas, sgn/dtd 1891, 60x45", C-NY 5/26/88 UE 6,600

SHAPIRO, Babe (20th C)
Vessa, acrylic on canvas, sgn/dtd 1969, unfr, 50x60", C-NY 2/13/89 550

SHAPLAND, John (Britisn, 1901-1929)
Orpheus & Euridyce, oil on canvas, sgn, 72x42", LH 5/15/88 OE 2,000

SHAPLEIGH, Frank Henry (American, 1842-1906)
Crawford Valley From Mount Willard, oil on canvas, sgn twice/dtd 1877/titled, 21x36", SBY 1/24/89 4,675
Ellis River Meadows at Jackson, New Hampshire; oil on canvas, sgn/dtd 1881, 10x16", RWS 11/10/89 2,900
Franconia Mountains From North Woodstock, New Hampshire; oil on canvas, sgn/dtd 1875, 20x30", RWS 5/12/89 UE 2,750
In Hospital St, St Augustine, Florida (street scene); oil on board, 8x13", RWS 5/19/88 1,800
Jackson Falls (panoramic landscape), oil on landscape, sgn/dtd 1877, 10x16", RWS 5/19/88 2,300
Matterhorn & Village of Zermatt, Switzerland; oil on canvas, sgn/dtd 1873, 43x30", RWS 11/3/88 UE 1,700
Mt Washington & Ammonoosuc River (narrow river, mountains beyond), oil on canvas, sgn/dtd 1890, 14x20", RWS 9/29/88 UE 1,100
Mt Washington & Walker's Pond From Old Barn in Conway, New Hampshire; oil on canvas, sgn, 1879, 10x16", RWS 6/10/89 OE 3,600
Mt Washington From Jackson, oil on canvas, sgn/dtd 1882, 22x36", RWS 11/10/89 UE 5,000
Old Settler (giant tree in forest), watercolor/charcoal on paper, initialed/dtd 77, 25x15", SBY 3/17/88 2,310
Presidential Range From Old Logging Camp Near Crawford House, oil on canvas, sgn/dtd 1885, 22x36", RWS 11/10/89 6,500

SHARP, Joseph Henry (American, 1859-1953)
At a Pueblo Window, oil on canvas, sgn, 14x10", SBY 5/25/88 14,300
At a Pueblo Window-Firelight & Daylight (Indian by window); oil on canvas, sgn, 16x12", SBY 5/24/89 OE 24,200
Bawling Deer, Firelight & Twilight (Indian inside teepee); oil on canvas, sgn/titled, 14x17", SBY 5/24/89 OE 24,200
Beat of the Drum (portrait of an Indian, seated), oil on canvas, sgn, 14x10", C-NY 5/25/89 13,200
Council (three Indians in teepee interior), oil on canvas, sgn, 25x31", SBY 5/24/89 39,600
Hunting Son, Taos Indian; oil on canvas, sgn, 16x20", B/B 6/15/89 33,000
Indian Encampment, oil on board, sgn, 7x10", SBY 9/14/89 7,150
Indian Smoking a Pipe in a Teepee, oil on canvas, sgn, 20x24", WD 10/5/88 OE 20,000
Lightly Falling Snow, oil on canvas, sgn/titled/inscr Foot of Custer Battlefield, unfr, 20x30", SBY 3/17/88 OE 8,800
Low Tide, La Jolla, California; oil on panel, sgn/inscr, 6x9", SBY 9/23/88 2,090
Mt Wheeler, New Mexico; oil on canvas, sgn, 16x20", B/B 6/15/89 8,800
Shepherd, oil on canvas, sgn/inscr, 32x50", C-NY 3/11/88 OE 8,250
Site of Old Fort Custer, Big Horn River, Montana; oil on board, sgn, 10x14", SBY 9/14/89 6,050
Taos Valley in the Fall, oil on canvas, sgn, 16x24", SBY 5/24/89 23,100

SHARP, Joseph Henry; att (American, 1859-1953)
Teepee, oil on canvas, 10x14", SBY 6/28/89 1,870

SHARP, Louis Hovey (American, 1875-1946)
Castle in the Tirol, oil on canvas, sgn, 26x36", B/B 10/6/88 990
Smoke Tree (tree in an extensive landscape), oil on canvas, sgn/dtd 1930, 20x26", B/B 9/14/89 1,650

SHATTUCK, Aaron Draper (American, 1832-1928)
Cattle in a Landscape, Granby, Connecticut; oil on board, sgn, 11x16", SBY 1/24/89 4,125
Early Summer, oil on canvas, sgn/dtd 1860, 26x42", SBY 6/24/88 OE 10,450
Farmington River, ink wash on paper, inscr/dtd 1867, 11x18", C-E 2/3/88 1,430
Meadow Near Granby, Connecticut; oil on canvas, sgn, 12x22", C-NY 9/3/88 3,300
Mount Washington & the Presidential Range, oil on artist board, 10x18", RWS 9/29/88 2,000
September (landscape), oil on board, sgn, 10x14", SBY 3/17/88 1,540
Sheep Grazing in a Mountainous Landscape, oil on canvas, sgn/indistinctly dtd 18(?), 26x36", WD 4/13/88 OE 4,000

Sunset Over Lake George, oil on canvas laid down on board, sgn, 1870, 9x12", C-E 10/18/89 ..... **2,200**

HAW, Alan Winter (American, 1894-)

Bringing Home the Cows, watercolor on paper, sgn, 16x22", B/B 1/11/89 ..... **825**

HAW, Charles Green (American, 1892-1974)

Cityscape (modernistic depiction), oil on board, sgn, ca 1932, 30x22", C-NY 5/25/89 OE **17,600**
Event 2 (abstract), oil on canvasboard, sgn, 16x12", C-NY 9/28/89 ..... **1,540**
Geometric Abstract, oil on canvas, sgn, ca 1937, 30x18" ,C-NY 5/25/89 ..... **16,500**
Harbor (abstract), oil on masonite, sgn twice/dtd 1954 twice, 24x36", SBY 3/17/88 ..... **3,025**
Lagoon, oil on panel, sgn, 1959, 8x10", PHL 12/1/88 UE **250**
Marine Abstract, oil on canvasboard, sgn/dtd 1941, 20x16", C-NY 5/25/89 OE **16,500**
Opening (five cubistic heads), oil on masonite, sgn/dtd 1949, 36x24", C-NY 5/25/89 ..... **4,400**

HAW, John Byam Liston (British, 1872-1919)

Truth, oil on canvas laid down on panel, sgn/dtd 1898, 54x62", WD 5/5/88 OE **95,000**

HAW, Sydney Dale (American, 1879-1946)

Picnic, oil on board laid down on fiberglass, sgn, 20x16", C-E 11/30/88 UE **1,100**

HAW, William (British, -1773)

Dutchess, Bay Racehorse with Grooms by Rubbing Down House; oil on canvas, sgn/inscr/dtd 1757, 40x50", SBY 6/10/88 OE **68,750**

HAYER, Charles Waller (British, 19th C)

Peasants by a Campsite, oil on panel, bears signature, 9x12", C-E 5/23/88 ..... **1,760**

HAYER, William Jr. (British, 1811-1892)

After the Hunt, oil on canvas, 30x25", SBY 6/10/88 ..... **9,350**
Figures on Horses in a Landscape, oil on canvas, 28x36", SBY 6/8/88 ..... **3,300**
Hunting Vignettes, oil on board, 12x12", SBY 6/10/88 ..... **5,775**
Red Lion Inn, oil on canvas, indistinctly sgn/dtd 1838, 20x27", SBY 10/24/89 ..... **4,950**

HAYER, William Sr. (British, 1788-1879)

Cottage Girl, oil on canvas, sgn, 24x21", C-E 10/26/89 ..... **5,280**
Farm, East Hampton; oil on canvas, 29x40", DM 5/13/88 ..... **8,000**
Fisherfolk on the Shore, oil on canvas, sgn, 28x35", WAD 6/6/88 ..... **6,500**
Fisherman's Return, oil on canvas, 30x37", NA 5/13/89 ..... **900**
Fisherwoman, oil on canvas, sgn, 14x12", SBY 7/12/89 UE **1,980**
Helping Daddy, oil on canvas, 40x33", S/A 2/18/89 ..... **5,500**
Homestead, oil on canvas, sgn, 25x21", C-E 10/26/89 ..... **1,650**
Supper Break (landscape with figures & plow horses), oil on canvas, sgn, 28x36", RWS 5/12/89 ..... **5,500**

HAYER, William Sr.; att (British, 1788-1879)

Surrey Farmstead, oil on canvas, sgn, 19x24", RWS 5/12/89 ..... **1,800**

HAYER, William; att (British, 19th C)

Milking Cows, oil on canvas, bears signature, 21x28", C-E 2/23/88 ..... **1,430**
Milking Time, oil on canvas, bears signature, 40x33", C-E 10/25/88 ..... **2,970**
Vieja Luna (abstract), acrylic on canvas, sgn/dtd NYC 1982, 57x73", SBY 5/3/88 UE **4,400**
Young Maiden with a Donkey on a Path, oil on canvas, 24x20", C-E 5/23/88 ..... **1,650**
Young Maiden with a Donkey on a Path, oil on canvas, 24x20", C-E 7/26/88 ..... **715**

HEAN, Charles M. (American, -1925)

Springtime, gouache on paper laid down on canvas, sgn/dtd 19(?)4, 30x25", C-E 6/1/89 ..... **880**

HEARBON, Andrew (British, 19th C)

Attempt on the Queen's Life, oil on canvas laid down on board, sgn/dtd 1868, 24x20", C-E 10/26/89 ..... **3,850**

HEARER, Christopher H. (American, 1840-1926)

Blue Landscape, oil on canvas, sgn/dtd 1921, 27x34", C-E 2/3/88 ..... **1,760**
Cattle by a Forest Stream, oil on canvas, sgn/dtd 1900, 29x49", FAP 4/15/89 ..... **1,100**
Country Landscape with House in the Distance, oil on canvas, sgn/dtd 1907, 14x24", C-E 11/30/88 ..... **1,100**
Forest View, oil on canvas, sgn, 30x40", FAP 12/8/89 ..... **700**
Scene in the White Mountains, oil on canvas, sgn/dtd 1876, 36x29", RWS 11/3/88 ..... **4,100**
Walk in the Country, oil on canvas, sgn/dtd 1883, 30x50", C-E 6/1/88 ..... **3,960**
Wooded Landscape, oil on canvas, sgn, 24x21", FAP 4/15/89 ..... **880**
Woodland Landscape, oil on canvas laid down on board, sgn/dtd 1894, 22x36", SBY 1/24/89 ..... **1,320**

HEE, Martin Archer (British, 1769-1850)

Portrait of Gentleman, oil on canvas, 30x25", DM 5/19/89 ..... **2,500**
Portrait of Mrs Williamson As Diana the Huntress, oil on canvas, 94x58", B/B 10/9/88 ..... **22,000**
Portrait of Sir John Paul, the Artist's Son; oil on canvas, 48x38", SBY 6/1/89 UE **5,500**

HEE, Martin Archer; att (British, 1769-1850)

Portrait of a Child Holding a Pet Rabbit Said To Be Mrs Edward Halsall As a Girl, oil on canvas, 36x28", SBY 4/7/89 OE **18,700**
Portrait of the Chester Bagot Children in a Landscape, oil on canvas, 50x40", SBY 10/21/88 ..... **16,500**

HEE, Martin Archer; circle of (British, 1769-1850)

Portrait of a Boy & Girl with Their Pet Dog (seated in landscape), oil on canvas, 44x34", SBY 10/13/89 OE **8,525**
Portrait of Miss Bailey, seated, in a landscape, holding a hat; oil on canvas, 30x25", SBY 10/21/88 UE **2,475**

HEELER, Charles (American, 1883-1965)

Birdsnest (view of house), oil on canvas, sgn/dtd 44, 24x30", C-NY 5/26/88 ..... **198,000**
Gray Barns, tempera on board, sgn/dtd 1946, 14x21", C-NY 5/26/88 ..... **165,000**
Nice/Promenade Along the Beach; oil on panel, sgn/inscr, 5x9", RWS 11/3/88 OE **14,000**
Study for Classic Landscape, watercolor/pencil on paper, sgn/#d 2245, ca 1931, 4x5", SBY 5/24/89 ..... **27,500**

HEERBOOM, Andreas (Andrew)(Dutch, 1832-1880)

Canterbury Tales, oil on canvas, sgn, 22x32", FB 10/30/89 ..... **2,090**

SHEETS, Millard (American, 1907-)

- Field Patterns, Patzcuaro; watercolor on paper, sgn, 25x30", B/B 6/9/88 ... 8,800
- Horses by the River, watercolor on paper, sgn/dtd 1972, 22x30", B/B 3/22/89 OE ... 27,500
- Loire River, France; oil on canvas, sgn/dtd 1929, 18x21", B/B 3/22/89 ... 6,050

SHEFFER, Glen C. (American, 1881-1948)

- Day at the Beach, oil on canvas, sgn/dtd 26, 12x16", SBY 4/14/89 ... 2,750

SHELTON, William H. (American, 19th C)

- Arrival at Headen's (Civil War), oil on paper, sgn/inscr, 15x20", C-E 5/27/88 ... 550
- Attack of the Prisoners (Civil War), oil on board, initialed, 25x19", C-E 5/27/88 ... 495
- Escape of Headen (Civil War), tempera on board, inscr, 25x19", C-E 5/27/88 ... 440
- General Duke Searching for Tracks (Civil War), oil on board, sgn/inscr, 19x25", C-E 5/27/88 ... 660
- Get Those Mules Out of the Road, Union Teamsters Blocking a Road (Civil War); pen/ink, sgn, unfr, 14x19", C-E 11/30/88 ... 330
- John Hunt Morgan Passing Over the Outer Wall To Escape (Civil War), oil on board, sgn/inscr, 19x25", C-E 5/27/88 ... 495
- Loading a Musket Behind a Stump (Civil War), pen/ink on paper, sgn/inscr, 13x16", C-E 5/27/88 OE ... 660
- Morgan Recruit, Farmer From Calf's Run (Civil War); oil on board, sgn/inscr, 25x19", C-E 5/27/88 OE ... 495
- Old Citizen at Dicherts (Civil War), oil on board, sgn/inscr, 19x25", C-E 5/27/88 ... 385
- Prisoners Admitted to Campfire (Civil War), oil on canvas, sgn/inscr, 19x25", C-E 5/27/88 ... 495
- Quartermaster's Battery (Civil War), watercolor on paper, inscr, unfr, 13x17", C-E 11/30/88 ... 660
- Selling Bread, POWs (Civil War); oil on board, sgn/inscr, 19x25", C-E 5/27/88 OE ... 440
- Soldiers Around a Fireplace (Civil War), oil on board, inscr, 19x25", C-E 5/27/88 ... 165
- Transports at Wharf (Civil War), pen/ink on paper, sgn/inscr, unfr, 12x17", C-E 11/30/88 ... 770
- Troopers at a Well (Civil War), oil on board, sgn/inscr, 19x25", C-E 5/27/88 ... 550

SHEN, Huang (Chinese, 1687-after 1768)

- Figure with Bat (horizontal scroll), ink/color on paper, sgn, 36x47", SBY 5/31/89 ... 17,600

SHENK, G. (American, 20th C)

- Equestrian Huntsman in a Wooded Landscape, oil on canvas, sgn, 35x53", SLK 9/26/88 ... 225
- Racing Scene, oil on canvas, sgn, 38x29", SLK 9/29/88 ... 250

SHEPARD, Ernest Howard (British, 1879-1976)

- Christopher Robin in the Top of His Tree, pen/black ink heightened with white on card, sgn twice, 10x9", C-NY 5/24/89 OE ... 14,300

SHEPPARD, Joseph Sherly (American, 1930-)

- Sunday Morning, tropical island street near church; oil on masonite, sgn/titled, 26x18", RAB 8/8/89 UE ... 125

SHEPPARD, Warren (American, 1859-1937)

- Around the Lighthouse (sailing ships, moonlit night), oil on canvas, sgn, 40x32", C-E 6/1/89 ... 1,650
- Dusk (sailboats at sea), watercolor on paper laid down on board, sgn, 8x12", C-E 6/1/89 ... 2,200
- Pulling Traps (two figures working from dory in calm water), watercolor on paper, sgn, 9x14", RAB 8/9/88 ... 800
- Seascape, oil on canvas, sgn, 20x30", SBY 6/28/89 ... 1,870
- Seashore at Sunset, oil on canvas, sgn, 20x30", SBY 9/23/88 UE ... 1,870
- Ship at Sail, oil on canvas, sgn, 28x22", SBY 1/24/89 ... 1,430
- Ships at Sea, oil on canvas, sgn, 16x28", WL 5/20/88 UE ... 1,150
- Ships in Moonlight, oil on canvas, sgn, 24x36", C-E 10/18/89 ... 2,860
- Spring in Venice (Venetian canal scene), oil on canvas, sgn, 14x20", C-NY 5/25/89 UE ... 5,500
- Sunlight & Sails, oil on canvas, sgn/dtd 1912, 12x18", C-NY 9/30/88 ... 3,300
- Sunset Seascape, oil on canvas, sgn, 16x24", WL 5/20/88 ... 1,400
- Venetian Canal, oil on canvas, sgn, 20x30", B/B 10/9/88 ... 3,300
- Venetian Canal Scene, oil on canvas, unfr, sgn, 24x14", C-E 9/8/89 UE ... 935
- Venice (harbor scene), oil on canvas, sgn, 20x30", C-E 10/18/89 ... 3,850
- View of a Canal in Venice, oil on canvas, sgn, 15x8", C-E 9/15/88 UE ... 440
- Yacht Cornelia, oil on canvas, sgn/dtd 75, 20x30", C-NY 3/11/88 ... 16,500

SHEPPARD, William Ludwell (American, 1833-1912)

- Confederate Soldiers at a Well (Civil War), pen/ink on paper, initialed/inscr, 13x16", C-E 5/27/88 OE ... 2,420
- Confederate Soldiers Grinding Corn (Civil War), pen/ink on paper, initialed/inscr, 12x11", C-E 5/27/88 OE ... 2,860
- Crater, Petersburg After the Explosion (Civil War); pen/ink on paper, initialed/inscr, 6x10", C-E 5/27/88 OE ... 715
- Cutting Down Guns at Appomattox (Civil War), watercolor on paper, sgn/inscr, 8x11", C-E 5/27/88 OE ... 5,280
- Day After Their First Fight (Civil War), pen/ink on paper, initialed/inscr, unfr, 10x8", C-E 11/30/88 OE ... 880
- Detachment, Floyd's Command, Gauley Bridge, West Virginia (Civil War); pen/ink, initialed, unfr, 13x11", C-E 11/30/88 OE ... 2,420
- Exterior Line, Richmond Defenses (Civil War); watercolor on paper, sgn/inscr, unfr, 11x14", C-E 11/30/88 ... 495
- Incident in the Peninsula Campaign (Civil War), pen/ink on board, sgn/inscr, 16x21", C-E 5/27/88 OE ... 1,650
- Nature Morte aux Pommes (still life w/apples), oil on panel, ca 1942, sgn, 16x20", FB 4/25/88 ... 2,400
- Pair: Clifton House, Richmond; New Cold Harbor Tavern (Civil War); pen/ink, initialed/inscr, 14x10", C-E 5/27/88 ... 550
- Rabbit in Camp (Civil War), pen/ink on paper, initialed/inscr, 8x13", C-E 5/27/88 OE ... 2,420
- Reinforcing Culps Hill, an Incident at Gettysburg (Civil War); pen/ink on paper, sgn/inscr, 14x18", C-E 5/27/88 OE ... 3,850
- Siege of Petersburg Shell Behind Confederate Works (Civil War), watercolor on paper, sgn/dtd 86, 9x12", C-E 5/27/88 OE ... 2,420
- Slaves Digging Entrenchments (Civil War), ink wash on board, sgn/inscr, 14x18", C-E 5/27/88 OE ... 1,045
- Under Fire at Chancellorsville (Civil War), watercolor on paper, sgn/inscr, 8x13", C-E 5/27/88 OE ... 2,090

SHERMAN, G. (American, 20th C)

- Fairground, oil on canvas, sgn, 24x20", SBY 6/28/89 OE ... 4,675

SHERRIN, Daniel (British, 20th C)

- Barque Under Full Sail, oil on canvas, sgn, 19x29", WAD 6/6/88 ... 1,600
- Cottage by a Waterfall, oil on canvas, sgn, 20x30", DM 2/19/88 ... 800
- Day's End (seascape), oil on canvas, sgn, 20x30", RAB 8/9/88 ... 3,250
- English Landscape, oil on canvas, sgn, 20x30", WAD 6/6/88 ... 1,400

English River Scene, oil on canvas, sgn, unfr, 24x36", C-E 5/22/89	**2,420**
Figures by a Pool in a Landscape, oil on canvas laid down on board, sgn, 36x24", PHL 10/28/88 UE	**1,200**
Highland Sheep in Winter, oil on canvas, 24x43", C-E 9/15/88	**880**
Landscape with Figures, oil on canvas, sgn, 20x30", FB 4/25/88	**1,800**
Pair: Untitled (landscape w/cattle); oil on canvas, sgn, 20x30", SLK 11/25/88	**1,450**
Purple Sunset Over a Church in the Distance, oil on canvas, sgn, 20x30", B/B 9/14/89	**1,320**
Ship at Sea, oil on canvas, sgn, 24x36", SLK 9/27/88	**900**
Surrey Landscape, oil on canvas, sgn, 30x20", WAD 6/6/88	**2,200**
Untitled (ship at sea), oil on canvas, 24x36", SLK 11 25/88	**300**
HERRY, William Grant	
Apparition, watercolor on paper, sgn on mount, 8x8", C-NY 10/6/88 OE	**330**
HERWOOD, Vladimir Osipovich (Russian, 1832-1897)	
Extensive River Landscape, oil on canvas, sgn in cyrillic, unfr, 28x42", SBY 2/22/89	**6,600**
HERWOOD, W.S. (American, 20th C)	
Concert in the Barn, boy sings/plays banjo to three girls; oil on board, sgn, 17x14", RAB 3/27/89 UE	**350**
HERWOOD, William Albert (American/Canadian, 1875-1951)	
Au Portes de Place, Dubrounik; oil on canvas, sgn, 24x28", FAP 11/4/88 OE	**1,250**
Bord du Camp, oil on canvas, sgn, 22x19", FAP 4/15/89	**1,705**
Les Naqures Dubrovink, oil on canvas, sgn, 26x30", FAP 12/8/89	**1,500**
Marche aux Legumes-Dubrounik; oil on canvas, sgn, 39x39", FAP 11/4/88 OE	**1,700**
Variation en Gris, oil on canvas, sgn, 35x25", FAP 11/4/88 OE	**2,600**
HI, Su; att (Chinese 1036-1101)	
Kunyang Cheng Prose-Poem in Xing Shu Running Script (hand scroll); ink on paper, sgn, 14x39", SBY 5/31/89 OE	**209,000**
HIAVONE, Andrea (Italian, 1522-1563)	
Christ in the House of Jairus, oil on canvas, ca 1549-50, 42x69", SBY 6/1/89 UE	**55,000**
Samaritan Woman at the Well, oil, 56x40", WD 1/25/89	**7,250**
HIAVONE, Andrea; att (Italian, 1522-1563)	
Presentation in the Temple, black chalk/gray/brown/white oil on lt brown preparation, 9x13", C-NY 1/12/88	**3,300**
HIBIAO, Zha (Chinese, 1615-1698)	
Calligraphy in Xing Shu Running Script (hanging scroll), ink on paper, sgn, 62x18", SBY 5/31/89	**1,320**
Landscape After Dong Yuan (hanging scroll), ink on silk, sgn, 74x24", SBY 5/31/89 UE	**6,600**
HIELDS, Alan (American, 1944-)	
Untitled (abstract), acrylic on cotton belt thread, 60x60", SBY 2/14/89	**2,420**
Well My Dear Set #6 (Heavy Dome), watercolor on paper, sgn/dtd 74/titled, unfr, 16x12", C-E 5/9/89	**308**
HIELDS, Thomas W. (American, 1849-1920)	
Private Concert (interior scene), oil on panel, sgn/dtd 1887 (?), 9x12", SBY 1/24/89 UE	**990**
HIFA, Cheng (Chinese, 1921-)	
Faust (hanging scroll), ink/color on paper, sgn, 18x26", SBY 5/31/89	**1,980**
HIFFNER, Barbara (British, 1896-)	
Pair: At the Hunt; Horses Grazing; oil on canvasboard/oil on panel, sgn/dtd 1923, 7x10", 10x13", WL 5/20/88 OE	**450**
HIKLER, Aaron (American, 1922-)	
Children Playing (with string in an interior), pastel on paper, sgn/dtd 62, 10x12", C-NY 6/17/89	**3,520**
Meditation (woman seated at table), oil on canvas, sgn/dtd 60, 35x29", SBY 5/25/88	**9,350**
Mother & Child, oil on panel, sgn, 7x5", C-NY 6/17/89	**715**
Student (a study), gouache on paper, initialed/dtd 77, 8x10", C-NY 6/17/89 OE	**2,420**
Waiting for Tea Service, oil on board, sgn/dtd 55, 10x12", C-NY 6/17/89	**2,090**
HILLING, Alexander (American, 1859-)	
Moonlit Landscape, oil on panel, sgn, 13x15", C-E 6/1/89 UE	**770**
HILLING, Arthur (Canadian, 1941-)	
Figure in a Forest, oil on canvas, sgn, 33x23", WAD 6/12/89	**4,400**
HINDLE, Evelyn K. (American?, 20th C)	
Still Life of Vase of Flowers, pastel on paper, sgn, 16x13", RAB 8/21/89	**150**
HINN, Everett (American, 1876-1953)	
After the Brawl (two figures on floor, others watching), red chalk on tan paper, sgn/dtd 1904, 16x22", SBY 9/14/89	**2,750**
George Sand's Son Calls Chopin a Sponge, watercolor/pencil on paper, sgn/dtd 1942, 13x9", SBY 9/23/88	**1,045**
Goddess Among Trees, pencil/brush/ink/collage on board, sgn/dtd 1943, 17x14", C-NY 3/11/88	**935**
Golden Lancet, pencil/ink/watercolor on paper, inscr/titled, 8x7", SBY 9/23/88 UE	**440**
Lady at Doorway, pastel, sgn, 35x21", WL 5/20/88	**4,800**
Lady at the Door, red conte on paper, sgn, 12x17", SBY 3/17/88	**1,430**
Mural Study, watercolor on tan paper, 4x3", C-NY 6/17/89	**605**
Prophecy, watercolor on paper, sgn/dtd 1945, 16x15", SBY 1/24/89	**990**
Snow Storm, Madison Square, New York; pastel/pencil on gray paper laid down, sgn/dtd 98, 23x26", C-NY 5/25/89	**55,000**
Street in Paris, pastel on canvas, sgn, 36x25", SBY 5/25/88	**23,100**
Trapeze Artist, pastel on paper, sgn/dtd 1949, 22x18", SBY 6/24/88 UE	**8,250**
Windswept Street, New York (windblown figures); red conte crayon, sgn/dtd 1907, 12x39", C-NY 5/25/89	**11,000**
Winter Street Scene, Paris, 1910; pastel on canvas, sgn/dtd 1910, 22x26", C-NY 5/26/88 OE	**308,000**
Woman on a Veranda, pencil/watercolor wash on board, 19x7", C-E 6/1/89	**1,210**
Woman Tying Her Slippers, sanguine on paper, 18x12", SBY 9/14/89	**825**
Young King From Happy Prince, watercolor on paper, sgn/dtd 1940, 18x14", SBY 6/24/88	**8,250**
Young Woman & Her Maid, pastel on paper, sgn/dtd 1949, 16x12", SBY 5/25/88	**25,300**

SHINN, Everett; att (American, 1876-1953) **200**
Theatrical Subject, mixed media on board, sgn, 17x17", SLK 9/27/88

SHIRLAW, Walter (American, 1838-1910) **2,200**
Lost Stitch (girl knitting), oil on panel, sgn, 15x13", C-E 6/1/89 ..... **275**
On the Edge, pencil/watercolor on paper, sgn, 12x8", WL 5/20/88 ..... **220**
Trees, watercolor/pencil on paper, sgn, 13x9", C-E 9/15/88 UE

SHIRLEY, Henry (British, 19th C) **413**
Highland Cattle, oil on canvas, sgn, 24x36", B/B 4/20/88

SHONBORN, John Lewis (British, 19th C) **700**
Arab Warriors on Horseback, oil on canvas, sgn, unfr, 24x36", WL 5/20/88 UE

SHORES, J.W. (British, 19th C) **600**
Wooded Snowy Winter Landscape with Stone Bridge, oil on canvas, sgn, 24x20", SLK 9/29/88

SHORTT, James W. (Canadian, 20th C) **200**
Spring Break-Up, Old Woman Bay, Lake Superior; oil on canvasboard, sgn/dtd April 1972, 10x12", WAD 6/12/89

SHOTWELL, Helen Harvey (American, 1808-) **412**
Canal View, oil on panel, sgn, 19x24", FAP 4/15/89

SHOUMATOFF, Elizabeth (American, 20th C) **150**
Portrait of a Society Beauty, watercolor on paper, sgn/dtd 1934, 12x9", WD 3/23/88 UE

SHOUMIN, Bian (Chinese, fl 1725-1747) **2,750**
Wild Geese (hanging scroll), ink/color on paper, sgn, 79x37", SBY 5/31/89

SHOUQI, Wan (Chinese, 1603-1652) **880**
Sitting Alone in Landscape (hanging scroll), ink/color on silk, sgn, 48x22", SBY 5/31/89 UE

SHOUTIE, Qian (Chinese, 1896-1967) **880**
Peonies (hanging scroll), ink/color on paper, sgn, 28x12", SBY 5/31/89

SHOWELL, Ken (American, 1939-) **330**
Spillway (abstract), acrylic on canvas, sgn/dtd 1969, 80x90", C-E 11/14/89 UE **825**
Untitled (contemporary), acrylic on canvas, sgn/dtd 1970/#d 124, 39x48", C-E 5/9/89

SHOWELL, William (Canadian, 1903-1984) **1,210**
Avenue in Winter, oil on canvas, sgn/dtd 1973, 24x20", FB 10/30/89 ..... **500**
Avenue in Winter, oil on canvas, sgn/dtd 1973, 24x20", WAD 6/12/89 UE **935**
Kite, oil on canvas, sgn/dtd 1976, 16x20", FB 10/30/89 ..... **275**
Reclining Figure, pastel, sgn, 12x20", FB 4/25/88

SHU, Gang (Chinese, 19th/20th C) **1,320**
Cats (hanging scroll), ink on paper, sgn/dtd 1908, 58x18", SBY 5/31/89

SHU, Xianyu (Chinese, 1257-1302) **49,500**
Travels in Jie'wu, in Xing Shu Running Script (hand scroll); ink on silk, sgn/dtd 1298, 9x37", SBY 5/31/89

SHULZ, Ada M. (American, 20th C) **8,250**
In the Garden, oil on canvas, sgn, 16x20", MG 5/28/88 OE

SHULZ, Adolph Robert (American, 1869-1963) **1,320**
Blue Skies, oil on board, sgn/dtd 6.10.19, 12x16", C-E 10/18/89 ..... **125**
Country Road Landscape, oil on board, sgn, 11x13", MG 10/28/88 UE **770**
Horse & Carriage in an Autumn Landscape, oil on board, sgn, 11x14", B/B 4/20/88 ..... **750**
Impressionistic Landscape, oil on board, sgn, 12x16", MG 5/28/88 OE **1,500**
Pair: Landscapes; no media given, 8x14", MG 5/28/88 OE

SHUN, Chen (Chinese, 1483-1544) **7,700**
Flowers (hand scroll), ink on paper, sgn/dtd 1537, 13x83", SBY 5/31/89

SHURTLEFF, Roswell Morse (American, 1838-1915) **825**
Autumn in Kreen Valley, oil on canvas, sgn, 12x16", B/B 12/8/88 ..... **715**
Deer in Wooded Landscape, oil on canvas, sgn, 20x25", B/B 12/8/88 ..... **2,640**
Fall Landscape, oil on canvas, sgn, 18x25", C-E 2/3/88 ..... **1,300**
Forest Stream, oil on canvas, sgn, 16x20", RWS 11/3/88

SHUTOV, Serguei (Russian/East German, 1955-) **6,000**
Aunts & Nephews (abstract), oil/collage on canvas, sgn/dtd 87, 79x118", SBY 7/7/88 ..... **7,600**
Death to the Assassins (abstract composition), oil/mixed media on canvas, sgn/dtd 1987, 51x61", SBY 7/7/88 OE **12,000**
Tryptich: New & Savage Private Life (fantasy figures); oil on 3 canvases, sgn/dtd 87, 59x79", SBY 7/7/88

SHUTTLEWORTH, Claire (American, -1930) **2,200**
Shiner Alley, San Antonio, Texas; oil on canvas, sgn, 10x14", C-E 11/30/88

SIBERECHTS, Jan (Flemish, 1627-) **18,000**
Mountain Landscape with Goats & Herders, oil on canvas, sgn/dtd 1669, 29x43", RWS 11/10/89 ..... **110,000**
Pastoral Landscape with a Shepherdess on a Donkey...; oil on canvas, sgn/dtd 1683, 54x49", C-NY 1/11/89 UE

SICHEL, Nathaniel (German, 1843-1907) **200**
Roman Maiden, watercolor, sgn/dtd 1883, 20x11", PHL 6/16/88 UE

SICILIA, Jose Maria (20th C) **33,000**
Bastilla 2 (abstract), oil on canvas, sgn/inscr/dtd 1984, 116x78", C-NY 5/4/88 OE **35,200**
Flor Verde (abstract), acrylic/sand on canvas, sgn/dtd Paris 87, unfr, 40x16", C-E 11/14/89 OE **33,000**
Flor 47, acrylic on canvas in 3 panels, sgn/dtd 85, overall: 40x119", SBY 2/15/89 ..... **15,400**
Four Panels: Flor (abstract); acrylic on canvas, sgn/dtd NY 186/inscr, unfr, 65x65", C-NY 2/20/88 ..... **19,800**
Frame White Flower II (abstract), acrylic on canvas, 2 panels, sgn/dtd NY 5.86, 89x96", SBY 10/8/88 ..... **52,250**
Red Flower XIII (compostion), acrylic on canvas, 1986, 119x119", SBY 11/11/88 OE **20,900**
Tulip II (abstract), acrylic on canvas, sgn/inscr/dtd 6.85, 74x51", C-NY 2/20/88 OE **41,800**
Tulip 1, acrylic on canvas, sgn/dtd 5.85.NY/titled, unfr, 102x99", C-NY 11/10/88 OE

Tulip 7, acrylic on canvas, sgn/dtd 5-8 XIX, 1985, 103x99", SBY 11/9/89 .... **71,500**
Tulip 8 (abstract), oil on canvas, sgn/dtd NYC 5-85/titled, 103x99", SBY 11/11/88 OE **60,500**
Tulip 9 (abstract), acrylic on canvas, sgn/dtd 5.85 NY, 99x103", SBY 10/5/89 .... **55,000**
Two Panels: Red Flower (abstract); acrylic on linen, sgn/dtd 86, 95x32", C-NY 5/4/89 OE **60,500**
Ventilateur, oil on canvas, sgn/dtd 83, 77x52", C-NY 11/10/88 OE **28,600**

CKERT, Walter Richard (British, 1860-1942)
Courtship, oil on canvas, sgn, 20x30", B/B 6/9/88 .... **3,300**
Study for Suspense (woman seated by hearth), pen/ink on paper, sgn, 15x10", B/B 5/17/89 .... **1,430**

DANER, see Le Sidaner

EBERT, Edward Selmar (American, 1856-1938)
Cart Path Through the Field, oil on cardboard mounted on panel, sgn, 8x12", RWS 5/12/89 UE **325**
Harbor Scene, oil on canvas, sgn, 24x36", RWS 9/8/89 UE **325**
Still Life of Fruit, oil on canvas, sgn/dtd 1913, 20x30", RWS 5/19/88 OE **1,800**
Street Scene, Rochester; oil on cardboard mounted on panel, inscr, 8x12", RWS 5/12/89 UE **325**
Summer Afternoon at Chesapeake Bay, oil on canvas, sgn/dtd 1927, 27x33", RWS 5/12/89 .... **18,000**

EFERT, August Friedrich (German, 1820-1883)
Homeward Bound, oil on canvas, sgn/dtd 1878, 19x26", C-E 10/26/89 .... **1,430**

EGEN, August (German, 19th C)
Port of Montevideo, oil on canvas, sgn, 20x33", B/B 6/15/89 .... **4,400**

GNAC, Paul (French, 1863-1935)
Antibes, watercolor/pencil on paper laid down on board, sgn/dtd 1913/titled, 9x12", SBY 2/16/89 OE **14,300**
Audierne, gouache/watercolor over black chalk on paper laid down, sgn/inser/dtd 1927, 8x11", C-NY 11/15/88 OE **35,200**
Avignon, watercolor/charcoal on paper, sgn/inscr Avignon 18 Mai 26, 11x18", SBY 11/12/88 .... **28,600**
Bateaux a Barfleur, watercolor/black chalk on paper, inscr/dtd 31, 9x12", C-NY 11/15/88 OE **14,300**
Bateaux a l'Entree du Port, watercolor/charcoal on ruled paper, initialed/dtd 11 Nov 30/inscr, 4x7", SBY 10/7/88 .... **5,775**
Cap d'Antibes, watercolor/charcoal on paper, sgn/inscr Pour Mireille Pegurier, 10x7", SBY 2/16/89 OE **19,800**
Constantinople (port scene), watercolor/charcoal on paper, sgn, 7x10", SBY 11/16/89 OE **26,400**
Cote d'Emeraude (ships/sea), watercolor/charcoal on ruled paper laid down on card, sgn/dtd 14 Oct, 4x7", SBY 10/7/88 OE **6,875**
Croix de Vie, charcoal/watercolor on paper, sgn/dtd 11 Sept 20, 11x16", B/B 6/9/88 .... **16,500**
Islands Off the Coast of St Tropez, oil on panel, sgn, 7x11", B/B 6/9/88 .... **13,200**
La Cote d'Or, la Suleimanie, Constantinople (pointillistic landscape); oil on canvas, sgn/dtd 1907, 18x22", SBY 5/9/89 .... **715,000**
La Jetee, watercolor/charcoal on ruled paper, initialed/inscr 15 Oct, ca 1930, 4x7", SBY 5/11/88 .... **7,150**
La Passerelle du Pont des Arts, watercolor/charcoal on paper, sgn/dtd 1925, 11x17", SBY 2/16/89 OE **20,900**
La Rochelle (port scene), watercolor/charcoal on paper laid down on board, sgn/dtd 1911, 11x17", SBY 5/11/88 OE **42,900**

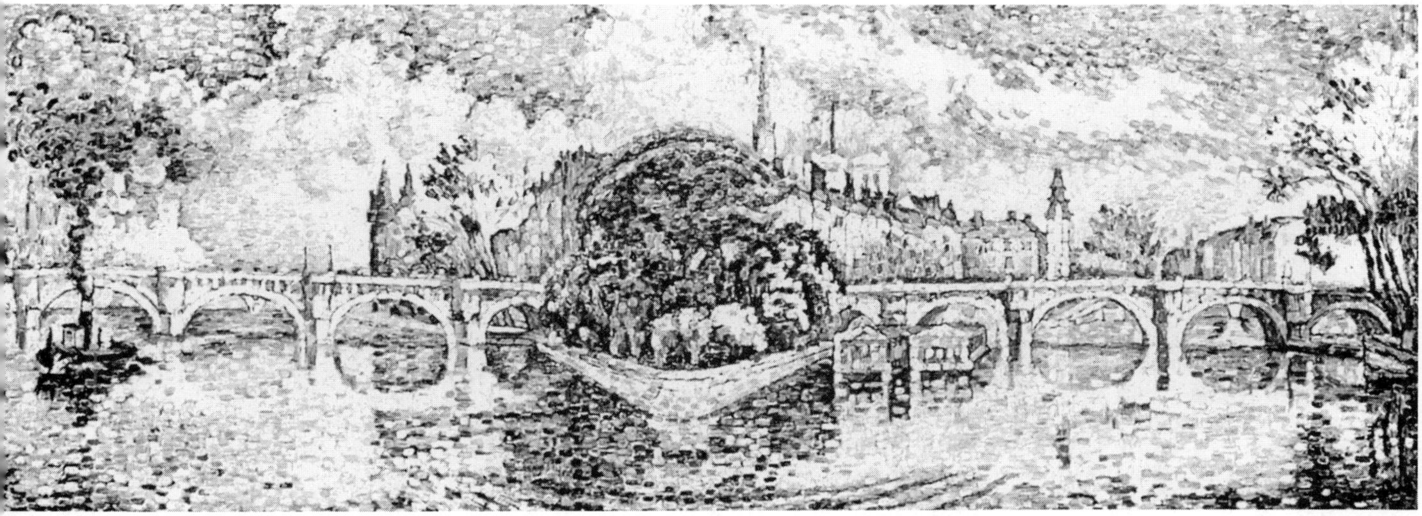

Paris, La Pont-Neuf; oil on canvas, ca 1928, 18x46", C-NY 11/15/88; $792,000

Le Pont (The Bridge), watercolor/black chalk on paper laid down on paper laid down on board, sgn, 10x16", C-NY 5/11/89 .... **19,800**
Le Pont de Viviers (river landscape w/bridge), gouache/watercolor/black chalk, sgn/dtd 1923, 11x17", C-NY 5/12/88 .... **18,700**
Le Pont des Saint Peres, watercolor/charcoal on paper, sgn/dtd 1925/inscr, 11x17", SBY 11/12/88 OE **31,900**
Le Port (port scene), watercolor/charcoal on paper laid down on board, sgn/dtd 1927, 12x16", C-NY 5/12/88 OE **33,000**
Le Port de Marsielle, oil on canvas laid down on board, sgn/incorrectly dtd 1903, ca 1906, 10x14", SBY 5/11/88 .... **93,500**
Le Trieux (landscape), gouache/watercolor/black chalk on paper laid down on board, ca 1925, 7x18", C-NY 5/11/89 .... **15,400**
Les Thoniers, Soleil Couchant, Groix (seascape at sunset w/two boats); oil on canvas, sgn, 1922, 18x22", SBY 5/10/89 OE **660,000**
Longuivy Bretagne (port scene), watercolor/charcoal/gouache on paper laid down, sgn/11 Oct 29, 12x18", SBY 5/10/89 OE **37,400**
Marsaille (port scene), watercolor on paper laid down on paper, sgn/inscr, 7x10", SBY 5/10/89 OE **20,900**
Neuville sur Saone, watercolor/charcoal on paper laid down on board, sgn/inscr, 11x17", SBY 2/18/88 OE **19,800**
Notre Dame, watercolor/charcoal/pencil on paper, sgn/dtd 1923, 7x5", SBY 2/16/89 OE **7,965**
Paysage de Montagnes (landscape), watercolor/charcoal on paper, stamped signature, 6x9", SBY 5/11/88 OE **14,850**

Petit Andely, gouache/watercolor/black chalk/pencil on paper laid down on board, sgn/dtd 25, 11x15", C-NY 5/11/89 **19,800**
Pont d'Austerlitz (river landscape), watercolor/charcoal on paper laid down on board, sgn/dtd 1910, 10x16", SBY 5/10/89 **20,900**
Port, Sables; watercolor/pencil on paper laid down on board, sgn/inscr/dtd 29, 12x17", C-NY 11/15/88 OE **48,400**
Port Louis, watercolor/black chalk on paper laid down on board, sgn, 17x10", C-NY 2/16/89 OE **28,600**
Quai du Louvre, gouache/watercolor/black chalk on paper mounted at edges on board, sgn/dtd 1925, 12x17", C-NY 5/11/89 **29,400**
Quai Suffren, Saint Tropez; watercolor/pencil on paper, stamped signature, 7x10", SBY 10/6/89 **15,400**
Saint Tropez, le Sentier de Douane (pointillistic landscape); oil on canvas, sgn/dtd 1902, 27x29", SBY 5/9/89 OE **1,100,000**
St Malo, gouache/watercolor/black chalk on paper laid down on paper, sgn/dtd 28, 11x17", C-NY 5/11/89 **35,200**
St Tropez, watercolor/charcoal on paper laid down on paper, sgn/dtd 98/titled, 7x10", SBY 2/16/89 **13,750**
Viviers (hilly landscape w/river & village), watercolor/charcoal on paper, inscr/dtd 26, 11x17", SBY 5/10/89 OE **38,500**
Vue de la Seine, watercolor/pencil on paper, sgn, 12x18", SBY 2/16/89 OE **18,700**
Vue de Paris (View of Paris), watercolor/charcoal on paper, sgn, 11x16", SBY 5/10/89 OE **28,600**

SIGNAC, Paul; att (French, 1863-1935)
Scene de Port, watercolor/pencil on paper, sgn, ca 1910, 10x14", RWS 11/3/88 UE **1,000**

SIGNORELLI, Luca; & Studio (Italian, 1441-1523)
Pair: Scenes From the Life of Saints Cecilia, Valerian & Tibertius; oil on panel, 11x42", 11x41", SBY 6/1/89 OE **93,500**

SIGNORINI, Giovanni (Italian, 1808-1858)
Concert, oil on canvas, sgn/dtd 77, 30x42", C-E 10/25/88 OE **7,150**

SIGNORINI, Giuseppe (Italian, 1857-1932)
Cardinal's Dream, watercolor, sgn/inscr, 17x23", C-NY 5/25/88 **3,080**
Man on a Donkey, watercolor/pencil/gum arabic, sgn/inscr Roma, 20x15", C-NY 2/23/89 **2,420**

SIGRISTE, Guido (Swiss, 1864-1915)
Rehearsal, oil on panel, sgn/dtd 99, 11x14", C-E 5/23/88 **2,860**

SIGWORTH, Martha P. (American, 20th C)
Snowbound Stream, oil on canvas laid down on board, sgn, 9x12", FAP 12/8/89 UE **125**

SILBERT, Max (French, 1871-)
Family Supper, oil on canvas, sgn, 24x29", C-E 5/23/88 **3,300**
Marketplace, oil on canvas, sgn, 21x26", RWS 3/16/89 **3,500**
Storytime, oil on canvas, sgn, 24x29", PHL 6/16/88 **2,100**
Woman Sewing, oil on canvas, sgn, 32x25", C-NY 5/25/88 **4,950**
Workhorses Being Driven Along the Banks of a River, oil on canvas, sgn/dtd 1925, 20x29", C-E 5/22/89 **2,200**

SILLEN, Herman (Swedish, 1857-1908)
French Ironclads, oil on canvas, sgn/dtd 1893, 54x42", C-NY 2/25/88 OE **17,600**

SILLETT, James (British, 1764-1840)
Still Life of Flowers, oil on canvas, sgn, 17x14", SBY 10/21/88 **12,100**

SILVA, Benjamin (20th C)
Quarta Feira de Cinzas (abstract), oil on masonite, sgn twice/dtd 1987 twice/titled, 24x23", C-NY 5/17/89 OE **5,280**

SILVA, Francis Augustus (American, 1835-1886)
Coast of Maine (view of cliffs w/sailboat in distance), oil on canvas, sgn/dtd 71, 10x18", SBY 9/14/89 **4,840**
Coastal Scene (w/sailing vessels), oil on canvas, sgn, 14x24", C-NY 9/28/89 **8,800**
Dunes, oil on canvas, sgn/dtd 1875, 11x30", C-NY 9/30/88 **9,350**
Sailboats at Dusk, gouache on paper, sgn, 9x20", B/B 4/20/88 **1,430**
Seascape at Sunset, oil on canvas, sgn/dtd 74, 14x26", SBY 5/25/88 OE **46,200**
September Day on the Coast (Pont Judith, Rhode Island), oil on canvas, sgn/dtd 79, 20x38", RAB 8/8/89 **24,000**
Sunset Off City Island, oil on canvas, sgn, 14x24", C-NY 12/2/88 OE **38,500**
Sunset on the Coast, oil on canvas, sgn, 9x18", RAB 11/25/88 **13,000**

SILVA, Jose; see Da Silva

SILVA, Marie; see Da Silva

SILVA, William Posey (American, 1859-1948)
California Springtime (landscape), oil on canvas, sgn, 25x30", NA 5/13/89 OE **1,750**
Carmel Dunes, oil on board, sgn, 16x20", B/B 10/6/88 **1,430**
Fog Over the Carmel Dunes, oil on board, sgn/dtd 1920, 11x14", B/B 10/6/88 **2,750**
In the Cypress Grove, Point Lobos, California; oil on canvas mounted on panel, sgn, 11x14", RWS 5/12/89 **600**
Magnolia Gardens, Charleston, North Carolina; oil on canvas, sgn, 30x35", B/B 1/11/89 OE **4,675**
Sandy Hill, Seaside; oil on board, sgn, 8x10", B/B 1/11/89 **605**

SILVESTRE, Israel; circle of (French, 1621-1691)
View of the Chateau & Gardens at Versailles, pen/black ink/bodycolor heightened w/gold on vellum, 11x15", C-NY 1/12/88 **2,860**

SILVESTRE, Louis; see De Silvestre

SIMARD, Claude A. (Canadian, 1943-)
Spring, acrylic, sgn/dtd 1983, 12x6", FB 5/28/89 **300**
Still Life of Flowers, oil on canvas, sgn/dtd 1987, 14x18", FB 5/28/89 **550**

SIMBARI, Nicola (Italian, 1927-)
Artist's Wife Reading, oil on canvas, sgn/dtd 57, 28x16", SBY 10/5/88 **2,200**
Beach in Yellow & Blue, oil on canvas, sgn/dtd 63, 20x40", SBY 2/14/89 OE **3,850**
Blugiallo, oil on canvas, sgn/dtd 54, 12x20", RWS 9/8/89 UE **600**
Boy on a Bicycle (in contemporary landscape), oil on canvas, sgn/dtd 66, 30x40", SBY 2/14/89 **7,150**
Carrozze in Verde, oil on canvas, sgn, 16x20", SBY 10/5/88 UE **660**
Femme sur la Plage (woman on the beach), oil on canvas, sgn/dtd 64, 26x20", PHL 11/15/88 UE **2,000**
Flowers in a Vase, oil on canvas, sgn/dtd 63, 16x14", WD 5/5/88 **2,500**
Girl by the Sea, oil on canvas, sgn, 20x24", C-E 11/17/88 **3,850**
Girl Walking in a Tropical Landscape, oil on canvas, sgn/dtd 66, 36x40", SBY 2/14/89 **6,600**

Green & Yellow in Pozzuoli, oil on canvas, sgn/dtd 63, 36x40", SBY 10/5/88 ... 5,500
Ischitana (contemporary beach scene), oil on canvas, 36x40", SBY 2/14/89 ... 14,300
La Promenade, oil on canvas, sgn, 36x40", C-E 5/9/89 OE ... 9,350
Little Harbor, oil on canvas, sgn, 24x28", RWS 5/12/89 ... 5,500
Marina of Scilla, oil on canvas, sgn/titled, 8x16", C-E 5/9/89 ... 1,430
Nu Assis dans un Interieur (posterior view of nude seated on bed); oil on canvas, sgn, 51x64", PHL 6/16/88 ... 11,500
Old Carriages, oil on canvas, sgn/dtd 57, 12x16", SBY 2/14/89 ... 3,575
On the Laguna, oil on canvas, sgn, 31x23", SBY 10/7/89 ... 11,000
Pizza Vendor, oil on canvas, sgn/dtd 57, 24x28", SBY 2/14/89 ... 2,750
Rooftops & Sea View, oil on canvas, sgn, 28x32", SBY 10/5/88 ... 5,500
Sardinian Green, oil on canvas, sgn, 23x32", SBY 10/7/89 ... 8,800
Strollers, oil on canvas, sgn, 24x31", SBY 10/7/89 ... 9,625
Window Shopping (lady looking in shop window), oil on canvas, sgn, 25x33", WG 4/23/88 UE ... 5,700
Yellow in St Tropez, oil on canvas, sgn, 36x40", SBY 10/7/89 ... 9,350
Young Girl on a Windy Beach, oil on canvas, sgn, 27x39", WG 4/23/88 ... 8,700
Young Girl on the Beach, oil on canvas, sgn, 22x30", SBY 2/14/89 OE ... 11,000

SIMKINS, Ron (Canadian, 1942-)
Autumn, North Hatley; oil on board, sgn/dtd 1974, 16x20", FB 5/28/89 ... 375

SIMKOVITCH, Simkha (American, 1893-)
Naomi Seated, oil on canvas, sgn/dtd 40, 20x24", C-E 10/18/89 ... 1,980

SIMM, Franz Xaver (Austrian, 1853-1918)
Young Beauty in a White Hat, oil on panel, sgn, 13x9", C-NY 5/25/88 OE ... 9,900

SIMMONS, Edward Emerson (American, 1852-1932)
Landscape, oil on panel, sgn, 5x9", C-E 10/18/89 UE ... 220
Landscape with Clouds in the Distance, watercolor/gouache on paper, sgn, 21x16", C-E 2/1/89 ... 1,650
Mediterranean Courtyard, watercolor/pencil on watercolor board, sgn/dtd 1882, 9x11", RWS 12/10/88 UE ... 100

SIMMONS, Eyres (British, 20th C)
Farm Scene, watercolor, sgn, 10x14", FB 5/28/89 ... 400

SIMON, Hermann Gustav (19th C)
Elfin Gorge Dingman's Ferry, Berks County, Pennsylvania; oil on canvas, sgn/dtd 1892, 45x30", SBY 9/14/89 ... 3,300

SIMON, Lucien (French, 1861-1945)
Nasturtiums, oil on canvas, sgn, 31x19", C-E 2/23/88 ... 880
Paris Street Scene in Winter, oil on canvas, sgn, 13x18", C-NY 10/25/89 ... 9,900

SIMON, Tavik Franktisek (Czechoslovakian, 1877-1942)
Seated Nude, oil on canvas, sgn/dtd twice 1920, 24x24", SBY 6/8/88 ... 2,750

SIMONAU, Gustave Adolphe (Belgian, 1810-1870)
Figures on a Street in a Continental Town, watercolor, sgn/dtd 1865, 26x20", C-E 10/26/89 ... 1,100

SIMONE, see De Simone

SIMONET, Augustin (French, 19th C)
Celebration Over Bosphorus, oil on canvas, sgn/indistinctly dtd, 18x24", C-NY 10/25/89 ... 5,500

SIMONETTI, Attilio (Italian, 1843-1925)
Mediterranean Street Scene, oil on panel, sgn/dtd Ischia 1876, 7x11", SBY 12/9/88 OE ... 2,475
Rag Merchant, watercolor, sgn/inscr Roma, 17x11", WG 9/16/88 ... 750

SIMONETTI, C.A. (Italian, 19th C)
Attracting Attention, oil on panel, sgn, 19x14", SBY 6/8/88 ... 4,675

SIMONETTI, C.G. (Italian, 19th C)
Last Melody, watercolor over pencil, sgn, 15x21", C-E 2/21/89 UE ... 770

IMONETTI, Ettore (Italian, 19th C)
Christening, oil on canvas, sgn, 40x30", C-NY 5/25/88 OE ... 33,000
Jewelry Merchant, watercolor/gouache over pencil, sgn/inscr, 29x21", C-NY 10/26/88 OE ... 26,400

IMONETTI (Italian, 19th C)
Peasant Playing a Flute, oil on canvas, sgn/inscr Roma, 20x16", C-E 7/26/88 UE ... 440

IMONI, A.; see De Simoni

IMONI, Gustavo (Italian, 1846-)
Street in Biskra, Algeria; oil on canvas, sgn, 35x24", SBY 10/24/89 UE ... 16,500

IMONI, Scipione (Italian, 19th C)
Italian Women at Their Daily Tasks, watercolor, sgn/dtd 1898, 30x20", C-NY 2/25/88 ... 1,650

IMONINI, Francesco (Italian, 1686-1753)
Cavalry Skirmish (battle scene), oil on canvas, 12x9", C-NY 4/6/89 OE ... 4,950
Cavalry Skirmish Between European & Eastern Armies (battle scene), oil on canvas, 9x13", SBY 4/7/89 ... 2,750
Pair: Military Skirmishes Near Towers; Walled Town; oil on canvas, 13x17", SBY 10/21/88 OE ... 10,450

MONINI, Francesco; att (Italian, 1686-1753)
Cavalry Skirmish, oil on canvas, 8x13", C-NY 10/12/89 ... 3,080

MONS, George Gardner (American, 1863-1910)
Mt San Antonio (Old Baldy) & San Gabriel Valley, oil on canvas, sgn, 32x51", LH 3/20/88 ... 17,000

MONS, Michel (Dutch, -1673)
Still Life of Basket, Porcelain Dish, & Tazza Filled w/Various Fruits...; oil on canvas, initialed, 30x40", SBY 1/12/89 ... 63,250

MONSEN, Niels (Danish, 1807-1885)
Arabs in a Hilltop Fort, oil on canvas, sgn, 24x33", SBY 2/22/89 ... 28,600
Meeting of Generals, oil on canvas, sgn/dtd 1870, 19x25", SBY 2/22/89 ... 17,600
Pirates' Attack, oil on canvas, sgn/dtd 1853, 39x56", SBY 2/22/89 ... 12,100

SIMONSEN, Soren (Danish, 1843-1900)
Winter Landscape with Figure, oil on canvas, sgn, 30x37", SBY 6/8/88 UE ... **1,650**
SIMONSON, David (German, 1831-1896)
Portrait of a Man, oil on canvas, sgn/dtd 1886, 24x21", C-NY 5/24/89 OE ... **11,000**
SIMPKINS, Z. (American, 20th C)
Woman Reclining on a Seashore Gazing at the Sea with a Parasol Behind Her, watercolor, sgn, 7x10", SLK 2/12/88 ... **250**
SIMPSON, Charles Walter (Canadian, 1878-1942)
First Snow, Montreal River; oil on board, sgn/dtd 1935, 13x16", FB 10/30/89 ... **660**
Houseboat on Frozen River, oil on canvas, sgn/dtd 1938, 30x40", WAD 11/30/89 ... **2,200**
SIMPSON, Lavinia Scholes (1826-1880)
Portrait of Lavinia & Ella Simpson, oil on canvas, ca 1854, 42x36", C-NY 6/3/89 ... **5,500**
SIMPSON, William (British, 1823-1899)
Nagasaki, Japan; pencil/pen/brown ink/gray wash, sgn/dtd 1873, 8x10", C-SK 5/25/89 ... **200**
SIMS, Charles (British, 1873-1926)
Infantry on Monoeuvres, pencil/oil on canvas laid down on board, sgn, 28x36", C-E 10/25/88 ... **3,080**
SIMS, J.W. (British, 19th C)
Set of 4: Coursing; oil on paper laid down on panel, 1 sgn/1 initialed, 5x7", SBY 6/10/88 ... **3,300**
SIMSON, J.A.
Pair: Still Lifes of Flowers; bodycolor on vellum laid down on board, sgn/dtd 1747, 24x18", C-NY 1/12/88 ... **20,900**
SINCLAIR, Gerrit V. (American, 1890-1955)
English Move Down From Assiago to Paive, oil on masonite, sgn/1942, 20x15", S/A 2/18/89 ... **200**
Professors at Ann Arbor, watercolor, sgn/dtd 47, 14x21", S/A 3/12/88 ... **275**
Scene in Italy, 1920; pen/ink/pencil, initialed, 7x5", S/A 2/18/89 ... **75**
SINCLAIR, M. (British, 19th C)
Worms Cathedral & Market Place on a Wednesday, oil on canvas, sgn/initialed, 41x30", WD 3/23/88 ... **4,800**
SINCLAIR, Olga
Nostalgie du Dernier Rendez-vous, oil on canvas, sgn/dtd 88, 48x60", C-NY 11/21/89 ... **6,600**
SINGER, Clyde (American, 1908-)
Flower Sellers on a City Street, oil on board, sgn/dtd 47, 10x20", SBY 4/14/89 ... **1,540**
Fulton Fish (woman w/umbrella in street scene), oil on panel, sgn/dtd, 18x21", WG 4/23/88 ... **1,450**
Girl Walking, oil on canvas on board, sgn, 15x6", WG 4/23/88 ... **425**
Group at McSorley's (figures at bar), casein on paper, sgn twice/dtd 1-63/titled, 19x15", SBY 1/24/89 ... **1,760**
Hotel Back Door (street scene), oil on canvas, sgn twice/dtd 1953 twice/titled, 18x40", SBY 1/24/89 OE ... **9,900**
Landscape with Two Figures, oil on board, sgn, 8x13", WG 4/23/88 UE ... **200**
Masterpiece at the MET, 1964; oil on canvas, sgn, 18x18", WG 4/23/88 ... **900**
Rendezvous on 84th (seated couple & waitress in interior), oil on masonite, sgn twice/dtd 1970, 18x28", SBY 1/24/89 ... **2,750**
Side Yard, watercolor on paper, sgn/dtd 41, 11x13", WG 4/23/88 UE ... **300**
Steakhouse Exit (street scene), oil on masonite, sgn twice/dtd 1971 twice/titled, 16x20", SBY 1/24/89 UE ... **825**
Strolling Woman Seen From the Back, oil on board, sgn/dtd 1982, 14x8", WG 4/23/88 UE ... **350**
The Search (man looking through garbage), oil on panel, sgn, 9x7", WG 4/23/88 ... **500**
Urban Scene, oil on board, sgn/dtd 1978, 9x6", WG 4/23/88 UE ... **250**
Village Vendor, oil on board, sgn, 10x7", WG 4/23/88 UE ... **225**
Washington Square, pen/ink wash on paper, sgn/dtd 12-1933, 11x13", WG 4/23/88 ... **800**
Woman in Landscape, oil on canvas, sgn/dtd 46, 18x24", WG 4/23/88 ... **500**
Youngstown Backyard (large house viewed from backyard), watercolor on paper, sgn/dtd 41, 11x13", WG 4/23/88 UE ... **325**
57th & 7th (street scene), casein on masonite, sgn twice/dtd 1967/titled, 36x39", SBY 1/24/89 OE ... **7,700**
SINGER, William H. (American, 1868-1943)
The Sentinel, oil on canvas, sgn, 34x32", B/B 12/8/88 ... **3,300**
SINGIER, Gustave (French, 1909-)
Aqua-Theme Nereides de Juillet; oil on canvas, sgn/dtd twice, 68, inscr, 36x29", C-E 5/13/88 OE ... **16,500**
Le Reveil, oil on canvas, sgn/dtd 49, 29x24", C-E 5/13/88 OE ... **19,800**
SINGLETON, Henry (British, 1766-1839)
Young Couple Dancing by a Tavern, oil on canvas, 14x12", C-NY 6/2/88 ... **3,300**
SINIBALDI, Jean Paul (French, 1857-1909)
Nude Woman Washing Her Hair, oil on canvas, sgn, 23x13", C-E 5/23/88 ... **3,520**
SIQUEIROS, David Alfaro (Mexican, 1896-1974)
Abstracto, oil on masonite, sgn/dtd 52, 35x48", C-NY 5/17/89 ... **17,600**
Campesino Orando (kneeling peasant), oil on gesso on burlap, indistinctly sgn, ca 1928, 16x12", C-NY 11/21/88 ... **13,200**
Campesinos Mexicanos (portrait of Mexican peasants), oil on masonite, sgn/dtd 59, 33x28", C-NY 11/21/88 OE ... **71,500**
Embrace (abstract), acrylic on panel, sgn/dtd 69, 26x20", SBY 5/17/88 ... **9,900**
Exodus (abstract landscape), pyroxylin on panel, sgn twice/dtd Marzo de 1963/titled/inscr, 18x24", SBY 5/16/89 OE ... **27,500**
La Marcha de la Humanidad (abstract), acrylic on masonite, sgn/dtd 59, 31x24", C-NY 5/18/88 ... **22,000**
Landscape (abstract), pyroxylin on board, sgn twice/dtd Mexico 4-1971/titled, 23x47", SBY 5/16/89 UE ... **22,000**
Movement (two abstract figures), acrylic on paper mounted on panel, sgn/dtd 12-68, 25x20", SBY 5/16/89 ... **15,400**
Nina Madre (young girl w/baby strapped to back), encaustic on panel, sgn/dtd Mex 1936, 30x24", C-NY 11/21/89 OE ... **363,000**
Oaxaca Dancer (contemporary), vinylite on masonite, sgn/dtd 54, 30x24", C-NY 11/21/89 ... **25,300**
Paisaje (abstract landscape), oil on paper laid down on panel, sgn/dtd 61, 16x14", C-NY 5/18/88 ... **7,700**
Retrato Estructural los Dos Davides (portrait), pyroxylin on panel, sgn/dtd 63, 24x18", C-NY 5/18/88 ... **28,600**
Sin Titulo (abstract), acrylic/composite board, sgn/dtd 9-47, 32x36", C-NY 11/21/88 OE ... **5,500**
Untitled (abstract), oil on board mounted on canvas, sgn, 16x20", SBY 5/16/89 OE ... **5,225**
Women in a World of Hunger & Terror (contemporary), politec on panel, sgn/dtd 64, 22x15", C-NY 5/17/89 ... **19,800**

Women of Lorca (portrait of three heads), pyroxylin on panel, ca 1938, 20x29", SBY 11/21/88 ... 66,000

IRANI, Giovanni Andrea (Italian, 1610-1670)

Infant Christ Reclining Before a Red Curtain with Two Angels, oil on canvas, 30x38", C-NY 4/8/88 ... 3,300

IRONI, Mario (Italian, 1885-1961)

Composition, gouache on paper, 8x15", SBY 2/14/89 OE ... 4,675

Composizione, gouache/watercolor/pen/black ink/pencil on board, sgn/dtd 1950, 14x20", C-NY 10/6/88 ... 6,820

Composizione (abstract), oil/gouache on buff paper, sgn/17x13", SBY 10/7/88 ... 3,025

ISLEY, Alfred (French, 1839-1899)

Bords du Loing (shoreline view of boats/house), oil on canvas, sgn/dtd 90, 18x22", SBY 5/9/89 ... 715,000

Bords du Loing a Saint-Mammes (canal scene at St Mammes); oil on canvas, sgn/dtd 85, 22x29", C-NY 11/14/88 OE ... 3,630,000

La Meulle de Paille (impressionistic landscape), oil on canvas, sgn/dtd 77, 15x22", C-NY 11/15/88 ... 286,000

La Seine a Saint-Cloud (impressionistic river landscape), oil on canvas, sgn, 1877, 15x22", C-NY 5/11/88 ... 528,000

Le Pont de Moret au Soleil, oil on canvas, sgn/dtd 92, 26x32", SBY 5/10/88 OE ... 1,375,000

Moret sur Loing (river landscape, Moret beyond), pastel on gray paper on board, sgn, ca 1888, 13x17", SBY 5/10/89 OE ... 192,500

Route a Lentree du Village (village street scene), oil on canvas, sgn, 13x18", SBY 11/15/89 ... 907,500

Route de Veneux a Moret, Jour de Printemps (landscape w/figures); oil on canvas, sgn/dtd 86, 24x29", C-NY 11/15/88 OE ... 1,870,000

Saint Mammes, le Soir; oil on canvas, sgn/dtd 85, 15x22", SBY 11/15/89 ... 1,100,000

Un Verger, pastel on paper, initialed, 1885, 7x10", SBY 11/16/89 OE ... 29,700

SLEY, Alfred; school of (French, 1839-1899)

Country Road in Autumn, oil on canvas, bears signature, 14x20", B/B 1/11/89 ... 770

SSON, Frederick Rhodes (American, 1893-1962)

Night Walk (street scene), oil on canvas, sgn, 20x24", SBY 3/17/88 OE ... 1,320

SSON, Laurence P. (American, 1928-)

Coastal Landscape, oil on beaverboard, sgn, 24x36", RAB 11/24/89 ... 2,000

Maine Fog, Burning Off-Boothbay Harbor, Maine; watercolor on paper, sgn/dtd 1968, 22x30", RWS 3/16/89 ... 850

Maine Tidal Pools, oil on masonite, sgn, 40x60", RWS 5/12/89 ... 4,250

Ode to Grieg, Winter Harbor; oil on masonite, 10x14", RWS 5/12/89 UE ... 1,500

Where Time Begins, oil on masonite, initialed/dtd 73, 10x22", RWS 5/12/89 UE ... 1,500

STI (American, 19th C)

Early Spring Landscape, oil on canvas, sgn, 24x29", WG 4/23/88 UE ... 250

TNIKOV, Alexander (Russian, 1945-)

Black Bull (abstract composition), oil/mixed media on canvas, sgn/dtd 86/titled, 59x55", SBY 7/7/88 OE ... 15,000

Butterfly (abstract composition), oil/papier-mache/collage on canvas, sgn/dtd 1987, 170x140", SBY 7/7/88 ... 7,600

KEAPING, John Rattenbury (British, 1901-1980)

Saratoga (racing scene), gouache on paper, sgn/dtd 72, 20x27", SBY 6/9/89 ... 3,300

KELTON, Red (American, 20th C)

Portrait of a Clown, oil on canvas, sgn, 20x17", B/B 5/17/89 OE ... 1,760

Portrait of a Juggling Clown, oil on canvas, sgn, 20x16", B/B 5/17/89 OE ... 1,760

KILLING, William (American/British, 20th C)

Two Running Dogs, oil, sgn, 48x61", WD 1/11/89 ... 4,750

KINNER, Charlotte B. (American, 1879-)

Fern Creek Canyon (extensive landscape), oil on canvas, sgn/dtd 1933, 24x28", B/B 5/17/89 ... 495

KIPWORTH, Frank Markham (British, 1854-1929)

Indolence (girl relaxing in chair, playing w/kitten), oil on canvas, sgn/dtd 84, 24x35", SBY 10/24/89 OE ... 88,000

KOTNES, Cecil

Death of Shaka, oil on panel, sgn, unfr, 48x48", C-SK 11/10/88 UE ... 260

KOU, Sigurd (American/Norwegian, 1878-1929)

Coastal Scene, watercolor on paper, sgn/dtd 1922, 10x11", LH 9/10/88 UE ... 100

Gypsies at Sea, oil on panel, sgn, 25x30", C-E 6/1/88 ... 3,300

Lady of the Sea, oil on canvas laid down on panel, sgn, 17x17", SBY 1/24/89 ... 990

KOV, Christian (American, 1856-1942)

Mission Delores, oil on canvas, sgn, 7x10", B/B 1/11/89 ... 330

KRAINKA (American, 20th C)

Aviary Beside a Table with Large Jardiniere Filled with Ferns, oil on panel, sgn, 18x12", SLK 2/12/88 ... 150

KUTEZKY, Dominic (Hungarian, 1850-1921)

Workers Bailing Hay in the Field, oil on panel, sgn, 8x11", C-E 10/26/89 ... 1,980

ADE, Caleb Arnold (American, 1882-1961)

Cottages Through a Wood (landscape), oil on canvas, sgn, 22x25", SBY 3/17/88 ... 1,980

Portrait of a Man (bust-length portrait), oil on board, sgn/dtd 1911, 17x13", RAB 3/27/89 UE ... 150

APLEIGH, Frank Henry (American, 1842-1906)

New Hampshire Mountain Stream, oil on canvas, 24x14", RWS 5/12/89 ... 350

ATER, John Falconer (British, 1857-1937)

Along the River (landscape), oil on canvas laid down on masonite, sgn, 25x38", RAB 3/27/89 UE ... 250

Country Road with Horse-Drawn Cart, oil on canvas, sgn, 24x36", SBY 7/12/89 ... 1,320

EPYSHEV, Anatoli (Russian, 1932-)

Misty Morning (impressionistic figures in landscape, a six-part work), oil on canvas, sgn/dtd 1986, 79x95", SBY 7/7/88 ... 18,000

Street-The Crowd (impressionistic); oil on canvas, sgn/dtd 1982, 32x39", SBY 7/7/88 OE ... 7,000

Suburb (impressionistic), oil on canvas, sgn/dtd 1980, 32x39", SBY 7/7/88 ... 5,200

OAN, Jeanette Pasin (American, 1946-)

Boca Raton Tondo (still life of apple & silver), acrylic/pencil on paper, circular format, sgn, 24" dia, RWS 9/8/89 UE ... 200

SLOAN, John (American, 1871-1951)
Big Bow (half-length portrait of girl w/bow in hair), oil on canvas, sgn, 1916, 24x20", C-E 2/1/89 UE 5,50
Cats Paws (coastal view w/shipping), oil on canvas, sgn, ca 1914, 20x24", C-NY 5/25/89 38,50
Factory Landscape, oil on canvas, sgn, 6x8", MG 5/28/88 35
Fog Bank, Rocky Neck (coastal scene), oil on canvas, sgn/inscr Orange Rock-Neck 1916 #202, 20x24", SBY 5/24/89 UE 19,80
Girl Dressing, brown chalk on paper, sgn, 16x10", C-NY 6/17/89 OE 1,76
Gloucester Inlet (landscape), oil on canvas, sgn, ca 1914, 20x24", SBY 5/24/89 16,50
Landscape with Two Figures, oil on canvas, sgn/indistinctly inscr, 9x11", SBY 6/24/88 7,97
Little Tesuque Canyon (stormy canyon scene w/two rainbows), oil on canvas, sgn, 20x24", C-NY 12/22/88 24,20
Lone Pine (in mountainous landscape), oil on canvas, sgn, 1925, 24x20", C-NY 9/28/89 10,45
Nude & Copper Cat, Fireplace; oil on board, sgn, 1942, 14x18", SBY 6/28/89 8,80
On a Night Boat (lady hitting man's chin w/elbow, other figures), gray wash/charcoal on paper, sgn, 14x19", SBY 9/14/89 7,70
Pancoast Sketching (artist at easel in landscape), oil on board, sgn/dtd 1907, 9x11", C-NY 5/25/89 16,50
Reclining Female Nude, pencil on paper, initialed/dtd 38, 7x10", B/B 6/15/89 2,20
Recumbent Nude, charcoal on paper, sgn, 24x29", C-E 11/30/88 1,43
Reddy at the Pool (boy perched on rock), oil on canvas, sgn, 20x24", C-NY 9/28/89 26,40
Road Barnyard, oil on canvas, sgn/dtd 07, 9x11", SBY 9/23/88 OE 16,50
Standing Nude, ink on paper, bears signature/initialed/dtd 1942, 14x9", C-E 2/3/88 77
Tailored Hat (portrait), oil on board, sgn twice/inscr/dtd 35, 22x18", C-NY 9/30/88 OE 19,80
Three Nudes Arranging Flowers (in an interior), charcoal on paper, sgn, 10x11", C-NY 6/17/89 1,21
Walpi Mesa (rocky outcrop), pencil on paper, sgn, 7x9", RAB 8/9/88 1,60
Yosene Ker, Girl in Reverie; oil on panel, sgn/inscr, 16x22", C-NY 5/26/88 12,10

SLOAN, John; att (American, 1871-1951)
Set of 6: Nudes; ink on paper, 18x12", WG 4/23/88 UE 80

SLOANE, Eric (American, 1910-1985)
Airplane Above the Clouds, oil on canvas, sgn, 34x41", B/B 3/17/88 3,57
Autumn Gold (extensive landscape w/wheat field, farm, & hills beyond), oil on masonite, sgn, 17x45", SBY 1/24/89 7,15
Clouds, acrylic on masonite, sgn/inscr/dtd 1975, 48x48", C-E 2/3/88 OE 3,85
Clouds & Thunderstorms, oil on canvas, sgn, 36x48", C-E 6/1/89 4,62
Cottage in a Winter Landscape, oil on canvas, sgn, 16x20", SBY 3/17/88 2,31
Cumulo Nimbus at Eleven-Thousand Feet, oil on board, sgn/titled, 26x18", SBY 6/24/88 2,31
Curtis P40's (small planes flying above clouds), oil on masonite, sgn twice, 20x23", SBY 9/23/88 2,09
Die Jungfrau, oil on canvas, sgn, 36x48", SBY 6/24/88 4,67
Flying Above the Clouds, oil on masonite, sgn twice/dtd 1939, 19x28", SBY 6/24/88 1,87
Geese in Flight Over a Lake, oil on canvasboard, sgn, 16x20", SBY 3/17/88 2,97
New Milford, Connecticut (landscape); oil on masonite, sgn/inscr, 28x36", C-NY 5/26/88 OE 12,10
Night Riders, oil on masonite, sgn twice/titled, 20x16", SBY 6/24/88 2,42
Single Plane on the Edge of a Storm, oil on canvas, sgn, 45x50", SBY 9/23/88 OE 7,15
Skiing (figures on slope), oil on panel, sgn, 36x48", C-NY 9/28/89 9,35
Sunlight & Surf, oil on masonite, sgn, 18x24", C-E 2/1/89 2,20
Thunderhead, oil on masonite, sgn/inscr description, 35x42", SBY 6/28/89 1,87
West Arlington, Vermont (view of covered bridge in summer); oil on masonite, sgn, 20x24", RWS 9/29/88 5,00

SLOANE, Marian P. (American, 19th/20th C)
Eagle Lake, Maine; oil on canvas, sgn, 20x25", RWS 9/8/89 UE 55
Rapids in the Forest, oil on canvas, sgn, 24x30", C-E 2/1/89 UE 1,32
The Farm, oil on canvasboard, sgn, 8x10", RWS 5/12/89 70

SLOCOMBE, Frederick Albert (British, 1847-)
Picking Berries (woman & two children in a landscape), oil on canvas, sgn/dtd 1879, 30x56", C-NY 5/24/89 OE 12,10

SMALL, Arthur (American, 20th C)
Ship Gathpool Off Rio Janeiro, oil on canvas, sgn/dtd 1929, orig frame, 33x44", RAB 11/10/88 UE 1,10

SMALL, H.
Mother & Daughter Embracing, oil on canvas, sgn/dtd 1902, 36x28", C-E 10/25/88 2,20

SMEDLEY, William Thomas (American, 1858-1920)
Ennui (elegant couple in opulent drawing room); watercolor on paper, sgn/dtd 1913, 12x16", RWS 3/31/89 OE 2,20
Her Merry Conceit Being To Serve the Beverage: Episodes of the Marquis de Valueflores; watercolor/gouache, RWS 8/20/88 10
Yacht Race, en grisaille heightened w/gouache on paper laid down on panel, sgn/indistinctly dtd, 14x22", C-E 6/1/88 UE 55

SMEE, Esther (American, 20th C)
California Sycamores, oil on canvas, sgn/dtd 1936, 30x36", B/B 10/6/88 52

SMEERS, Frans (Belgian, 1873-1960)
Woman Serving Tea, oil on board, sgn, 14x11", C-E 2/21/89 OE 2,42

SMET, F. (Belgian, 19th C)
Figures Near a Watermill in an Extensive Landscape, oil on canvas, sgn, 20x27", C-NY 2/23/89 3,52

SMETS, A. (Continental, 19th/20th Century)
Sheep in a Barn, oil on board, sgn/dtd 1875, 15x21", WD 11/16/88 5,00

SMETS, Louis (Dutch, 1918-)
Winter Scene with Skaters, oil on canvas, sgn, 25x35", SBY 7/12/89 OE 8,25

SMILLIE, George Henry (American, 1840-1921)
Apple Blossoms, oil on canvas, sgn, unfr, 16x24", C-E 6/1/88 OE 3,52
Bronxville Woods, oil on canvas, sgn, 20x30", SBY 1/24/89 2,75
Bronxville Woods (figure in landscape), oil on canvas, 20x31", WD 10/5/88 UE 2,80
Evening Among the Cedars (landscape w/figures by pond), oil on canvas, sgn/dtd 1883, 9x15", RWS 9/8/89 2,90

Farmyard, watercolor/pencil on paper laid down on board, sgn/dtd 1884, 15x21", C-NY 3/11/88 1,980
Harvest Time (men in hay field beside sea), oil on canvas, sgn, 20x30", C-E 6/1/89 OE 7,700
Katerskill Falls on Giant Mountain in the Adirondacks, oil on canvas, sgn/dtd 67-, 21x36", SBY 9/14/89 9,900
Landscape Viewed at Sunset, oil on canvas, sgn, 20x31", WD 4/13/88 1,900
View From His Favorite Tree, oil on arched canvas, sgn, 9x7", SBY 1/24/89 OE 3,850

MILLIE, James David (American, 1833-1909)
Cliffs Along the Sea, oil on canvas, sgn/dtd July 18 84, 15x23", RAB 3/27/89 UE 700
Keene Valley, New York; oil on canvas, initialed/dtd 1870, 11x15", WD 4/13/88 3,400
Madison Square Garden, oil on canvas, ca 1898-1900, 40x24", C-NY 9/28/89 20,900

MIT, Jan Borritsz (Dutch, fl 1721-1768)
Dutch Shipping in an Estuary with Figures on a Jetty, oil on panel, sgn on flag, 16x27", SBY 6/3/88 49,500

MITH, Albert Delmont (American, 1886-1962)
Church by the Sea, oil on canvas, sgn/inscr, 16x20", RWS 11/3/88 800

MITH, Andre (American, 20th C)
Florida Cabin Scene, watercolor, sgn, 12x17", NA 11/5/88 400

MITH, Archibald Cary (American, 1837-1911)
Artist at the Shore, oil on canvas, sgn, 10x16", SBY 4/14/89 OE 6,050
Ship, oil on canvas, sgn, 16x25", C-E 2/3/88 OE 7,700
Ships Off the Coast at Sunset, oil on canvas, sgn, 10x18", SBY 4/14/89 3,300

MITH, Carlton Alfred (British, 1853-1946)
Artist's Daughter, watercolor/gouache over traces of pencil, sgn/dtd 1909, 15x10", C-NY 5/25/88 OE 9,350

MITH, Charles L.A. (American, 1871-1937)
Rocky Coastal Scene, oil on canvas, sgn/dtd 1918, 30x45", B/B 9/14/89 1,760
Tranquil Bay View, oil on board, sgn/dtd 1915, 12x16", B/B 10/6/88 1,430

MITH, Charles Lorraine (British, 1751-1835)
Belvoir Hunt, 1805; oil on canvas, 25x35", C-E 5/22/89 1,650

MITH, David (American, 1906-1965)
Sentinal I (abstract), ink/gouache on paper, titled/dtd 10-20-1956, 8x11", SBY 10/5/89 OE 13,200
Untitled, sprayed enamel on paper, sgn/dtd 1959, 18x12", C-NY 5/4/88 6,050
Untitled (abstract), brush/black ink on paper, initialed, dtd 9/5/4/53, 16x21", C-NY 2/20/88 7,150
Untitled (abstract), ink/egg tempera on paper, sgn/dtd 59, 26x40", SBY 10/8/88 OE 13,200
Untitled (abstract), oil on paper, sgn, dtd 12/29/57, 17x22", SBY 2/19/88 4,400
Untitled (studies for personnages), pen/black ink on paper, 1954, 11x8", C-NY 10/4/89 7,700
Untitled (two-length relationships), ink/ballpoint on paper, dtd 9/1/56, 11x8", SBY 5/3/89 6,500

MITH, Elmer Boyd (American, 1860-1943)
Late Afternoon, Summer; oil on canvas, sgn, 15x22", SBY 6/24/88 OE 16,500
Robinson Crusoe, watercolor/gouache on paper, sgn, 13x8", B/B 12/8/88 660

MITH, Ernest Browning (American, 1866-1952)
California Foothills, oil on canvas, sgn, 20x24", B/B 1/11/89 440

MITH, Francis Hopkinson (American, 1838-1915)

Luncheon at the Inn, gouache/charcoal on board, sgn/dtd 81, 18x25", C-NY 5/25/89; $46,200

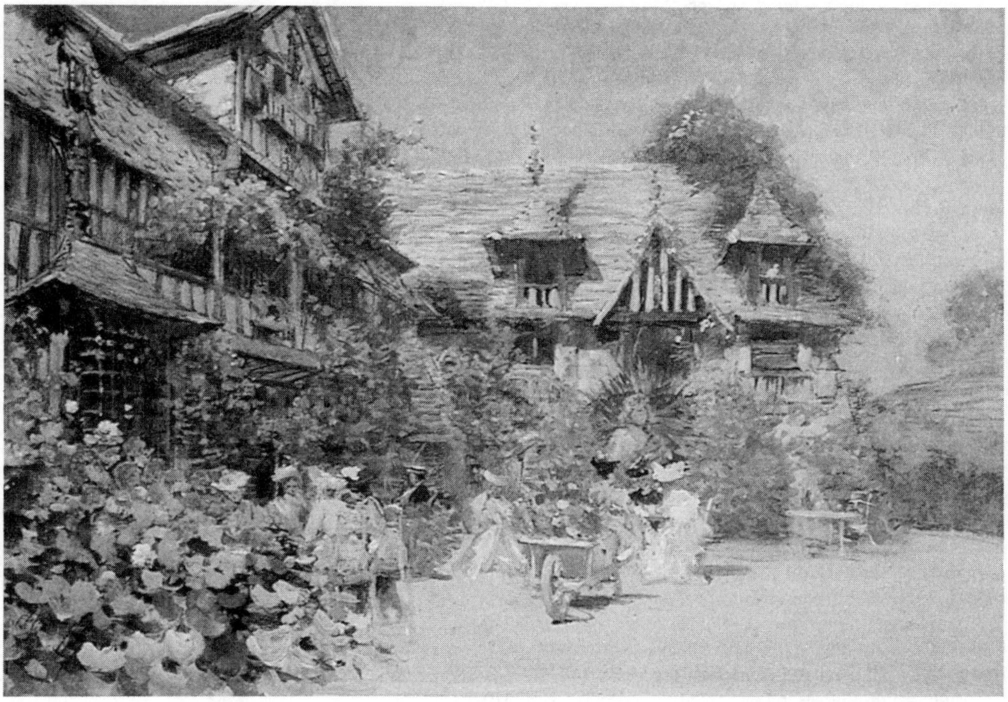

Afternoon in Venice, watercolor/gouache/charcoal on board, sgn, ca 1880, 14x34", C-NY 3/11/88 OE 9,350
Canal Scene, watercolor/gouache/pencil on gray paper, sgn, 25x15", C-NY 5/26/88 8,800

Dordrecht, black crayon/watercolor/gouache on paper, sgn, 20x27", SBY 4/14/89 OE **9,350**
Dutch Canal Scene, gouache/watercolor/pencil on board, sgn, 14x25", C-NY 5/25/89........ **11,000**
Greenhouse (figure), watercolor/pencil on paper, 22x16", C-NY 5/26/88 .... **7,700**
Inside Westminster Abbey, charcoal/white chalk on paper laid down on board, sgn, 31x23", C-E 11/30/88 UE........ **385**
Market Day, watercolor/gouache/pencil/pen/ink on paper laid down on board, sgn, 14x25", C-NY 9/30/88 .... **3,300**
Out in the Pasture (cattle in landscape), watercolor/gouache on board, 19x32", WD 10/5/88 UE........ **3,000**
Ponte Olio, Venice (canal scene); gouache/charcoal/watercolor on paper, 28x19", SBY 5/24/89 .... **11,000**
Summer Day (figures walking by quay, buildings beyond), watercolor/gouache/pencil on paper, sgn, 13x24", RWS/3/31/88 OE **2,250**
Sunny Day, Italy (street scene); gouache/charcoal on paper, sgn, 22x14", SBY 5/24/89........ **14,300**
Venetian View, watercolor/gouache/pencil on paper, sgn, 14x24", SBY 3/17/88 .... **5,500**
Venice, watercolor/charcoal/gouache/pencil on paper laid down on board, sgn, 15x25", C-NY 12/2/88 .... **6,050**
Venice Harbor with Fisherman Docking, watercolor/gouache/pencil on paper, sgn, 15x25", C-NY 9/30/88 .... **8,250**

SMITH, Frank Vining (American, 1879-1967)
Before the Gale-Flying Cloud; oil on canvas laid down on masonite, sgn, 41x40", C-E 11/30/88........ **4,180**
Surf, Cohasset (rocky coastal scene); oil on masonite, sgn, 18x24", RWS 5/12/89 .... **900**

SMITH, Frederick Carl (American, 1868-1955)
Canal Scene in Venice, oil on canvas, 20x28", WL 5/20/88........ **750**

SMITH, Frederick W. (American, 1885-)
Old Corner Bookstore (horse-drawn carriages & figures on busy street), oil on board, sgn, 1828, 9x12", RWS 9/29/88 .... **1,300**

SMITH, George (British, fl 1802-1838)
Rival in Possession, oil on panel, sgn, 12x16", FB 10/30/89 .... **3,190**

SMITH, George of Chinchester (British, 1714-1776)
Wooded River Landscape with Figures by a Cottage, a Castle in the Distance; oil on canvas, 17x24", C-NY 6/2/88........ **9,900**

SMITH, Grace (Australian, 1892-)
Portrait of Christian Gorden, oil on canvas, 24x18", DM 5/13/88 .... **275**

SMITH, Hassel (American, 1915-)
No Deposit No Return II (table w/still life in corner of room), oil on canvas, sgn/dtd 1961, 68x48", SBY 10/7/89 OE **12,100**
Untitled (abstract), oil on canvas, sgn/dtd twice 1961, 68x48", C-NY 5/4/88 .... **5,280**

SMITH, Hely Augustus Morton (British, 1862-1934)
Soldiers at Sailors Monument, watercolor on paper, sgn, 7x5", WL 5/20/88 .... **525**
Third Avenue, El Train (cityscape); watercolor on paper, sgn, 7x5", WL 5/20/88........ **550**
View of New York Harbor, watercolor on paper, sgn, 7x10", C-E 10/25/88 UE **770**

SMITH, Henry Pember (American, 1854-1907)
Apple Blossoms by a Country Cottage, oil on canvas, sgn, 20x28", WD 10/5/88 .... **5,000**
Boat on High Seas, oil on canvas, sgn/dtd 81, 12x18", C-E 2/1/89 .... **1,045**
Canal Scene, oil on canvas, sgn, 20x28", C-NY 12/2/88 .... **5,500**
Gray Morning (mountainous landscape), oil on canvas, sgn/dtd 1883, 18x28", C-NY 9/28/89 .... **8,250**
Home in Connecticut, oil on canvas, sgn, 20x28", C-NY 3/11/88 .... **6,050**
House by a Stream (landscape), oil on canvas, sgn, 14x20", SBY 3/17/88........ **6,050**
Landscape with Figure, oil on panel, sgn, 10x14", SBY 1/24/89 .... **3,025**
Moonlight on the Sea, oil on canvas, sgn, 12x17", C-E 6/1/88........ **1,540**
Morning on Lake Como, oil on canvas, sgn, 20x28", SBY 1/24/89 .... **4,400**
Oaks (landscape), oil on canvas, sgn, 25x38", WD 10/5/88 .... **5,500**
Old Homestead (landscape), oil on canvas, sgn, 12x15", B/B 5/17/89........ **1,760**
Old Oak by the Lily Pond, oil on canvas, sgn, 22x27", WD 4/13/88........ **7,750**
Old Oak Tree (large tree beside road in landscape), oil on canvas, sgn, 14x20", RWS 5/19/88 .... **2,300**
Quiet Canal in Venice, oil on canvas, sgn, 28x20", SBY, 6/28/89 .... **4,675**
Serenity (landscape w/figure in boat, ducks on pond), oil on panel, sgn/dtd 84, 8x6", C-E 6/1/89........ **2,090**
Ship Sailing Along the Storm Front, oil on panel, sgn/dtd 85, 10x16", RWS 11/10/89........ **1,300**
Spanish Villa, oil on canvas, sgn, 20x29", C-NY 9/30/88 .... **2,200**
Springtime (river landscape w/cottage), oil on canvas, 20x28", WD 10/5/88 OE **6,000**
Summer Landscape with Farmhouse & Fisherman, oil on canvas, sgn, 20x28", SBY 1/24/89........ **5,775**
Summer Morning Along the Lake (figure in boat, cottage by shore), oil on canvas, sgn, 13x8", WD 4/13/88 .... **5,500**
Sunny Afternoon in Venice (large villa on canal), oil on canvas, sgn, 20x28", WD 10/5/88 .... **5,250**
Venetian Scene, oil on canvas, sgn, 12x16", SBY 9/14/89 .... **5,500**

SMITH, Hobbe (Dutch, 1862-1942)
Sailing Barges at Sea, oil on panel, sgn, 12x8", PHL 10/28/88 UE........ **700**

SMITH, Howard E. (American, 1885-1970)
Two Sisters, oil on canvas, sgn, unfr, 50x40", B/B 6/15/89........ **8,250**

SMITH, J. (American, 19th/20th C)
On the Trail, oil on canvas, sgn, unfr, 16x22", C-SK 5/25/89........ **1,190**

SMITH, J.S. (American, 19th C)
Landscape at Sunset, oil on canvas, sgn, 14x22", LH 12/4/88 UE **50**

SMITH, Jack Wilkinson (American, 1874-1949)
Autumn Trees, oil on canvas, sgn, 16x20", B/B 8/10/88 OE........ **2,475**
Land of the Sky Blue Water, oil on canvas, sgn, 28x34", B/B 6/9/88........ **13,200**
Lofty Mountain Peak, oil on canvas, sgn, 46x50", B/B 6/9/88 .... **49,500**
Morning, High Sierras; oil on canvas, sgn, 28x34", B/B 6/9/88 .... **17,60**
Sierra Lake, oil on canvas, sgn, 30x40", B/B 6/9/88 .... **17,600**
Woodland Stream, oil on canvas, sgn, 24x28", PHL 6/16/88........ **3,500**

MITH, James Burrell (British, 1822-1897)
Falls of the River Alm, at Alnwick, Northumberland; oil on canvas laid down, sgn/dtd 189(?), 19x25", B/B 3/17/88 1,980
MITH, Jessie Wilcox (American, 1863-1935)
Rebecca of Sunny Brook Farm, oil/charcoal on board, sgn, 18x16", C-NY 9/28/89 OE 16,500
MITH, John (British, 18th C)
On the Island of Capria, watercolor on paper, 4x7", FAP 4/15/89 412
MITH, John Brandon (British, 1848-1884)
Cascade in the Moors, oil on canvas, sgn/dtd 1896, 36x28", B/B 3/22/89 OE 11,000
Falls at Hespe, Wales; oil on canvas, sgn/dtd 1871, 14x18", B/B 6/15/89 4,950
Figures Along the Hespe, Wales (river landscape); oil on canvas, sgn/dtd 1876, 14x18", B/B 6/15/89 3,300
Misty Falls in Autumn, oil on canvas, sgn/dtd 1895, 26x36", B/B 3/22/89 OE 14,300
Pastoral River Scene, oil on canvas, sgn/dtd 1896, 21x17", B/B 3/22/89 2,090
Waterfall in the Gorge, oil on canvas, sgn/dtd 1875, 36x28", B/B 3/22/89 OE 9,350
MITH, John Henry; att (British, 19th C)
Pair: Interior Scenes; oil on canvas, bears signature, 1 dtd 1852, 20x24", C-E 2/21/89 2,200
MITH, Jori (Canadian, 1907-)
Paris Canal Scene, gouache, sgn/dtd Paris France 1951, 8x10", FB 10/30/89 358
Portrait (Gabriel Roy, Quebec writer), oil on canvas, sgn/dtd 1945, 20x16", FB 10/17/88 1,100
MITH, Juanita
French Window, oil on canvas, 23x20", C-E 10/18/89 1,760
MITH, Leon Polk (American, 1906-)
Correspondence Blue & Yellow, oil on canvas, sgn/dtd 1963, 36x30", SBY 5/2/89 OE 13,200
MITH, Letta Crapo (American, 1862-1921)
Girls at the Beach, pastel/charcoal on paper, sgn/dtd 1900, 21x14", C-NY 12/2/88 OE 16,500
MITH, Mary (American, 1842-1878)
Three Chicks, oil on canvas, sgn/dtd 1866, 9x12", SBY 9/14/89 3,300
MITH, Miriam T. (American, 20th C)
Self-Portrait, oil on masonite, sgn, 42x50", FAP 12/8/89 450
Self-Portrait with Model, oil on canvas, sgn/dtd 39, 45x36", C-E 10/18/89 3,300
MITH, Patti
Death of Spanish Animal, graphite/crayons on paper, inscr w/title, 11x9", C-NY 10/31/89 OE 770
MITH, Richard (British, 1931-)
Composition, watercolor/black crayon on paper, sgn/dtd 60, 19x25", SBY 10/7/89 1,650
Untitled Drawing (abstract), pastel on cut paper, sgn/dtd 69, 15x22", SBY 10/7/89 770
IITH, Rufus Way (American, 1900-)
Market Scene, oil on canvas, sgn/dtd, 16x12", WG 4/23/88 775
MITH, Russell (American, 1812-1896)
Along the Shore (two figures at shoreline in landscape), oil on canvas, sgn/dtd 1890, 13x18", RAB 8/8/89 UE 650
Backyard of RS House, oil on board, sgn/dtd 1895, 12x16", FAP 4/15/89 1,375
Cave in Chelton Hills, oil on canvas, initialed/dtd 76, 20x16", C-E 2/1/89 OE 6,380
Landscape with Haystacks, oil on canvas, initialed/dtd 1896, 18x12", FAP 4/15/89 1,815
Portrait of Xanthus Russell Smith, oil on board, 4x5", lot 657, FAP 4/15/89 220
Portrait of Xanthus Smith, oil on canvas, 20x16", lot 700, FAP 4/15/89 825
Rocks Near the Juniatta Crossing, oil on paperboard, inscr w/signature/dtd 1840, 8x11", RWS 11/10/89 UE 350
Storm Cloud Rising in the West, oil on paper, sgn/dtd 1850, 8x11", RWS 5/12/89 2,700
West Coast of Mull, oil on canvas, sgn/dtd 1882, 36x54", FAP 4/15/89 2,970
MITH, Russell; att (American, 1812-1896)
Hudson Valley View, oil on canvas, sgn/inscr, 24x36", SBY 6/24/88 3,575
Isles of Heiere Mediterranean, oil on canvas, 25x38", FAP 11/4/88 UE 750
MITH, Steve
Untitled (landscape), oil on canvas, sgn, 22x26", lot 347, GAI 6/17/89 555
MITH, Thomas Henry (American, 19th C)
Girl Seated by a Stove, oil on canvas, sgn/dtd 1864, 33x28", SBY 9/23/88 660
Reflection, oil on canvas, sgn/dtd 1864, 22x18", FAP 12/8/89 1,250
MITH, Thomas Lochlan (American, 1835-1884)
Winter Landscape with Peasant on Path, oil canvas, sgn/dtd 1865,OE 2,420
IITH, Tony (American, 1912-)
Louisenberg, No 5 (two circles); oil on canvas, 20x40", C-NY 10/31/89 OE 16,500
MITH, Walter Granville (American, 1870-1938)
Country Landscape, oil on canvas, sgn/dtd 1936, 25x30", C-E 2/1/89 2,420
Phelps Homestead, Old Saybrook, Connecticut; oil on board, sgn/dtd 1936, 12x16", RAB 8/9/88 UE 2,250
Prussian Officers (two men at table being served by barmaid), watercolor on paper, sgn/dtd 1891, 15x13", C-E 2/1/89 3,300
Trout Stream, oil on canvas, sgn/dtd 1921, 24x32", SBY 4/14/89 OE 6,050
Two Men in a General Store, pencil on paper, sgn, 28x18", C-E 6/1/89 880
MITH, William Russell (American, 1812-1896)
Painters House on Edge Hill From the Tacoy, 1884; oil on canvas, initialed/inscr, 12x18", RWS 11/3/88 UE 1,000
IITH, William Thomas (Canadian, 1862-1947)
Cottage by Rocky Stream, watercolor, sgn, 12x18", WAD 11/30/89 700
Fisherman's Wife, watercolor, sgn, 13x10", WAD 6/12/89 450
Fleet Setting Out, watercolor, sgn, 18x12", WAD 6/12/89 1,100

SMITH, William Thompson Russell (American, 1812-1896)
Chocurua Peak, New Hampshire; oil on canvas, sgn, 31x51", C-E 10/18/89 10,450
Tomb of Cicilier Aletella (figures in an extensive landscape), oil on canvas, sgn/dtd 1877, 24x36", RWS 9/8/89 UE 3,850

SMITH, Xanthus Russell (American, 1839-1929)
Fort Paluski, Georgia, After Its Surrender (Civil War); pen/ink on paper, sgn/inscr, 6x13", C-E 5/27/88 OE 2,200
Hilton Head, South Carolina (Civil War); pen/ink on paper, initialed/inscr, 5x15", C-E 5/27/88 OE 3,300
Hove To for the Pilot (classic marine scene), oil on canvas, sgn/dtd 1881/titled, 20x30", RAB 11/25/88 8,750
Storm Near Port Royal, watercolor on paper, sgn/titled, 7x9", RAB 3/14/89 900
USS Galena (Civil War), pen/ink on paper, initialed/inscr, 9x15", C-E 5/27/88 OE 1,210
View of the (?) Wire Bridge Across the Merrimac(?), oil on board, sgn/dtd, 7x10", RAB 3/27/89 2,500

SMITH, Xanthus Russell; att (American, 1839-1929)
Cabin Scene Near Beaufort, South Carolina; oil on canvas, 6x9", SBY 6/28/89 9,350

SMITHSON, Robert (American, 1938-1973)
Museum of the Void, pencil on paper, ca 1970, 18x24", SBY 10/8/88 4,400
Pierced Spirals, pencil on paper, sgn/dtd 1971, 19x14", SBY 10/8/88 3,300
Spirals, pencil on paper, sgn/dtd 71, 12x15", SBY 10/8/88 3,575

SMYTHE, Edward Robert (British, 1810-1899)
Conversation (man, woman, & horse in a landscape), oil on canvas, sgn, 10x12", B/B 1/11/89 OE 3,575
Two Girls in a Winter Landscape, oil on canvas, sgn/dtd 1846, 18x14", B/B 1/11/89 OE 6,600

SMYTHE, F. (American, 19th C)
House by the Water, oil on canvas, sgn, 24x36", LH 10/16/88 OE 800

SMYTHE, Minnie (British, fl 1896-1939)
Showery Weather, watercolor/gouache, sgn twice/inscr, 13x21", C-NY 5/25/88 OE 26,400

SMYTHE, Thomas (British, 1825-1906)
Gypsy Camp, oil on canvas, sgn, 20x30", C-E 2/21/89 4,620

SNELL, Henry Bayley (American, 1858-1943)
Cargo Boat, oil on canvas, sgn, 25x30", C-E 10/18/89 2,200
Gloucester Harbor, oil on canvas, sgn, 22x28", RWS 11/10/89 3,600
Rocky Harbor (sailboat near rocky shore), oil on artist board, sgn, 12x14", RWS 5/19/88 1,200

SNODGRASS, James (American, 20th C)
Daisy, pastel/gouache, sgn, 60x40", LH 12/4/88 UE 60

SNOECK, Jacques (Dutch, 1881-1921)
Filling the Kettle, woman pours water from pot to kettle; oil on canvas, sgn, 14x16", RAB 3/27/89 OE 1,800

SNYDER, Clarence W. (American, 1883-)
Tiered Waterfall, watercolor on paper, sgn/dtd 1911, 28x22", FAP 4/15/89 330

SNYDER, Joan (American, 1940-)
Poems Past (abstract), oil on canvas, sgn/dtd March-May 71, 31x66", SBY 10/5/89 13,200
Symphony IV (abstract), acrylic/fabric/linoleum/plastic/graphite on canvas, 1977, unfr, 60x123", C-NY 5/4/89 18,700
Triptych: Small Symphony for Women II; mixed media on mounted canvas, 1976, 24x24", C-NY 5/4/89 OE 24,200
Untitled (abstract), acrylic/flocking material on canvas, sgn/dtd 1969, 71x71", C-E 11/17/88 3,850
Victory, acrylic/oil/wallpaper flocking/felt-tip pen/ink/graphite on canvas, unfr, 48x96", C-NY 11/10/88 OE 20,900
We Really Didn't Cuddle Today (abstract), oil/acrylic on canvas, sgn/dtd Sept 27, 1971, 48x96", SBY 5/3/89 OE 15,400

SNYDER, W. Mek (Danish, 19th C)
Road Through Sunlit Woods, oil on canvas, sgn/dtd 1912, 23x38", WG 9/16/88 OE 1,500

SNYDERS, Frans (Dutch, 1579-1657)
Wolf Hunt, oil on canvas, 63x118", C-NY 1/15/88 33,000

SNYDERS, Frans; att (Dutch, 1579-1657)
Vegetables, Game, Tazza with Grapes...on a Table with a Red Cloth; oil on canvas, 25x42", C-NY 5/31/89 OE 19,800

SNYDERS, Frans; follower of (Dutch, 1579-1657)
Young Hunter with a Still Life (dead game), oil on canvas, monogramed/dtd 1630, 64x83", SBY 6/1/89 OE 33,000

SNYDERS, Frans; manner of (Dutch, 1579-1657)
Still Life of Fruits, with a Parrot, Monkey, & Woman; oil on panel, bears signature, 24x34", SBY 12/9/88 OE 3,080

SNYDERS, Frans; studio of (Dutch, 1579-1657)
Dogs & Cats Fighting in an Interior with Still Lifes of Fruit & Vegetables, oil on canvas, 54x90", SBY 4/7/88 23,100

SNYERS, Peter (Flemish, 1681-1752)
Savoyard Playing with a Marmot, oil on canvas, 17x13", C-NY 10/12/89 4,950

SOARES, Pablo (Latin American, 20th C)
Contra Luz (still life by a window), oil on canvas, sgn/dtd 1977/titled, 39x32", C-NY 5/17/89 3,300

SOCHER, Richard (Continental, 19th C)
Arab Street Scene, watercolor on paper, sgn/dtd 1895, 11x7", B/B 1/11/89 825
Two Seated Arab Figures, gouache on paper, sgn, 16x23", B/B 1/11/89 1,430

SOCHER, Richard; att (Continental, 19th C)
Gentlemen in an Interior, watercolor on paper, 25x38", B/B 1/11/89 990

SOENS, Jan (Dutch, 1547-1611)
Rest on the Flight into Egypt, oil on canvas, 36x50", C-NY 6/2/88 OE 60,500

SOHIER, Alice Ruggles (American, 1880-)
Rehearsal (lady in diaphanous gown dancing in a studio), oil on canvas, sgn/dtd 1915, 25x30", RWS 9/29/88 OE 9,000

SOHN, E. (American, 20th C)
Untitled, hunter/dog in landscape; oil on canvas, sgn, 20x26", SLK 2/11/89 225

SOKOLOFF, Stanley N. (American, 20th C)
Volcano, oil on canvas, sgn/dtd 1965, 20x16", FAP 12/8/89 UE 100

LANA, Nicolas; att
Angel (painted decoration with Eucharist on reverse), tempera on panel, on gold ground, arched top, 22x15", C-NY 4/6/89 .... **6,050**
LARI, Achille (Italian, 1835-)
Figures in an Italian Landscape, oil on canvas, sgn, 16x24", B/B 1/11/89 .... **412**
LE, see Dal Sole
LFAROLA, Carlos Antonio (Italian, 1668-1738)
Saint John the Baptist Filling His Cup at a Waterfall, an Extensive Landscape Beyond; oil on canvas, 28x24", SBY 6/2/89 .... **10,450**
LFAROLA, Carlos Antonio; circle of (Italian, 1668-1738)
Landscape with Figures Traveling Along a Wooded Road, oil on canvas, 16x24", SBY 7/12/89 .... **1,760**
LIMENA, Francesco (Italian, 1657-1747)
Adam Accepting the Fruit From Eve While Observed by the Serpent, oil on panel, octagonal, 34x20", C-NY 6/2/88 .... **22,000**
Faith, Hope, & Charity; chalk/pen/ink/wash, inscr, 10x16", C-NY 1/11/89 .... **605**
Miracolo di San Giovanni di Dio, oil on canvas, unfr, 37x30", SBY 4/7/88 .... **4,675**
Pair: Humility; Faith; oil on canvas, 19x15", C-NY 6/2/88 .... **38,500**
Portrait of a Nobleman (three-quarter length, standing, hand on hip), oil on canvas, ca 1730-31, 50x40", SBY 6/1/89 UE **42,900**
LIMENA, Francesco; att (Italian, 1657-1747)
Saint Villebaldo Receiving the Blessing of Gregory III, oil on canvas, 20x28", SBY 4/7/88 .... **1,925**
Vision of Saint Theresa of Avila, oil on canvas, 30x25", C-NY 10/20/88 OE **12,100**
LIMENA, Francesco; follower of (Italian, 1657-1747)
Holy Family, oil on canvas, octagonal, 25x20", SBY 12/9/88 OE **1,870**
Madonna & Child with an Adoring Saint, oil on canvas, 26x18", SBY 12/9/88 .... **605**
LIMENA, Francesco; school of (Italian, 1657-1747)
Saint Joseph & the Infant Christ, oil on canvas, oval, 22x35", C-NY 4/8/88 .... **1,980**
LMAN, Joseph (American, 1909-)
Adele (portrait), oil on board, sgn/initialed/dtd 1968, 24x16", SBY 6/24/88 .... **1,100**
Girl Resting, oil on board, initialed, 20x24", SBY 4/14/89 OE **2,750**
Group of 3: Subway Riders; mixed media, about 15x10", SBY 3/17/88 OE **2,310**
Reclining Nude, oil on board, initialed/dtd 1968/titled, 18x24", SBY 3/17/88 OE **3,300**
Seated Figure, watercolor/gouache/pencil on newsprint, sgn/dtd 1960, 12x6", RWS 3/16/89 UE **175**
Seated Woman in Red Blouse, oil on canvas, sgn, 48x24", SBY 9/14/89 .... **1,100**
LOMON, Abraham (British, 1824-1862)
Young Lady, half-length; oil on board, sgn/dtd 1854, 12x10", C-E 10/25/88 .... **1,540**
LOMON, Joseph (British, 1860-1927)
Lucille, oil on canvas, sgn w/monogram, dtd 90/inscr, 24x20", SBY 5/23/89 .... **9,900**
LOTAREFF, Boris (American/Russian, 1889-1966)
Femme a sa Toilette, oil on canvas, sgn, 25x19", WG 4/23/88 UE **200**
Plaza New York, watercolor/graphite on paper, sgn/titled, 5x8", RWS 6/17/89 .... **200**
LY, Albric (Canadian)
Morin Heights, oil on board, sgn, 10x12", FB 10/30/89 .... **275**
MERSCALES, Thomas Jacques (British, 1842-1927)
Battle of Punta Gruesa-The Independencia Abandoning Ship with Covadonga Beyond; oil, sgn/dtd 96, 10x15", C-SK 11/10/88 .... **8,370**
Brigantine & Two Dorys Off a Coastline, oil on canvas, sgn/dtd 05, 12x18", C-SK 5/25/89 .... **6,430**
Homeward Bound, oil on canvas, sgn/dtd 1913, 16x22", C-E 10/26/89 .... **7,150**
MM, Henry (French, 1844-1907)
Woman with Fur Stole, pastel on tan paper, sgn, 12x8", RWS 5/12/89 UE **200**
MMER, William (American, 1867-1949)
African Female Figure, watercolor, sgn, 12x9", WG 9/16/88 .... **275**
Decorative Cows, watercolor on paper, sgn, 12x19", WG 4/23/88 UE **350**
Farmhouse at Sunset, watercolor/ink on paper, sgn, 12x17", WG 4/23/88 .... **375**
Horses, pen/ink on paper, sgn, 8x10", WG 10/19/88 .... **200**
New Mexican Landscape with Church, oil on board, sgn, 12x8", DM 10/14/88 OE **500**
Nude of a Young Woman, ink on paper, sgn, 17x11", WG 4/23/88 .... **375**
Portrait of Artist's Son Seated on a Chair, pen/ink on paper, sgn, 19x12", WG 4/23/88 UE **300**
Seated Female Figure & a Cresent Moon, watercolor/chalk, sgn/dtd 1921, 9x12", WG 9/16/88 UE **275**
Standing Nude Female, chalk/ink, 22x17", WG 9/16/88 UE **200**
Three Graces (female nudes), ink/watercolor, sgn, 8x10", WG 9/16/88 .... **325**
MMERS, Otto
View of Lake George, oil on canvas, sgn, 24x36", C-NY 5/25/89 OE **39,400**
NDERBORG, Kurt (German, 1923-)
Untitled, oil on vinyl sheet laid down on panel, sgn/dtd 61, 43x28", C-E 11/17/88 OE **20,900**
NJE, Jan Gabrielsz (Dutch, 1625-1707)
Travelers on a Path, oil on panel, monogramed, 11x15", C-NY 1/11/89 OE **9,900**
NN, Albert H. (American, 1869-)
On Guard, watercolor w/traces of pencil, sgn, ca 1897, 13x9", SWN 6/15/89 .... **523**
NNENSTERN, Friedrich Schroder (German, 1892-)
Der Mondschwanenpuppentanz, colored pencils/pastel on board, sgn/dtd twice 1956, 20x29", SBY 2/18/88 OE **6,050**
NNEVELD, Carl (American, 19th/20th C)
Mount Torence, Washington; oil on panel, sgn, 10x12", B/B 12/8/88 .... **550**
NNIER, Keith
Runic Diptych (abstract), marker on paper, 84x50", SBY 2/15/89 .... **6,050**

SONNTAG, William Louis Jr. (American, 1870-)
Finery in Peril (figure in a landscape), watercolor on paper laid down on board, sgn, 14x21", C-NY 5/26/88 — 13,200
Hillside Farm, watercolor/gouache on paper laid down on paper, sgn, 14x21", C-NY 12/2/88 — 4,400
Lead Mine Bridge, watercolor on paper laid down on canvas, sgn, 20x24", C-NY 3/11/88 — 3,850
Old Mill, watercolor/gouache on paper laid down on board, sgn, 14x21", C-NY 12/2/88 — 7,700

SONNTAG, William Louis Sr. (American, 1822-1900)
Androscoggin, New Hampshire (scenic river view w/mountains beyond); oil on canvas, sgn, 18x31", C-NY 9/28/89 OE — 26,400
Edge of a Pond, New Hampshire; oil on masonite, sgn, 20x36", B/B 10/9/88 — 22,000
Figure by a Mountain Lake (landscape), oil on canvas, sgn, 16x24", SBY 3/17/88 OE — 9,625
Front Lake, oil on canvas, sgn, 9x11", SBY 6/28/89 — 4,950
Hudson River View, watercolor on paper, sgn/dtd 91, 10x13", SBY 9/14/89 — 1,320
Misty Mountain View, oil on canvas, sgn, 17x26", C-NY 12/8/88 OE — 24,200
Morning in the White Mountains, New Hampshire (figures by a lake); oil on canvas, sgn/dtd 1881, 36x56", PHL 12/1/88 — 34,000
Mountain Haze, oil on canvas, sgn, 30x50", C-NY 3/11/88 — 17,600
Mountain River in Morning Mist (landscape), oil on canvas, sgn, 16x24", RWS 3/16/89 OE — 5,500
On the Shenandoah, oil on canvas, sgn, 30x54", C-NY 5/26/88 — 24,200
Pair: Woodland Scenes; ink/wash on paper, 1 heightened w/gouache, sgn, 6x5", SBY 6/28/89 — 1,760
Placid Afternoon, oil on canvas, sgn, 36x50", C-NY 12/2/88 OE — 55,000
River Scene, oil on canvas, sgn/inscr Brooklyn, 15x22", C-SK 6/9/88 — 5,020
Road Leading to Glen House, New Hampshire; oil on canvas, sgn/inscr, 18x30", C-NY 3/11/88 — 13,200
Scene Near Grafton, West Virginia; oil on canvas, sgn/dtd 1864, 30x50", C-NY 5/26/88 — 27,500
Sunrise, oil on canvas, sgn, 12x20", C-NY 9/30/88 — 7,700
Wooded River Landscape, oil on canvas, sgn, 32x54", PHL 12/1/88 — 17,000
Woodland Pond, oil on canvas, sgn, 10x12", C-NY 9/30/88 — 4,400

SONNTAG, William Louis; & TAIT, Arthur Fitzwilliam
Early Morning with Mountains, oil on canvas laid down on masonite, sgn, 32x47", C-NY 12/2/88 — 13,200

SOOLMAKER, Jan Frans; att (Flemish, 1635-1666)
Italianate Landscape with Ruins & Shepherds, Washerwoman, & Livestock by a Stream; oil on canvas, 29x35", SBY 4/7/88 — 8,250

SORBINI, A. (Italian, 19th C)
Exotic Coastal Town, oil on canvas, sgn, 27x41", C-NY 2/23/89 OE — 16,500

SOREN, Albert (Canadian)
Approaching Storm, oil on board, sgn, 18x24", WAD 6/12/89 — 250
Bruce Trail, oil on board, sgn, 9x12", WAD 11/30/89 — 400
Deadwood, oil on board, sgn, 9x12", WAD 11/30/89 OE — 500

SORENSEN, Carl Frederick (Danish, 1818-1879)
Twilight Over the Fishing Village, oil on canvas, sgn/dtd 1852, 16x22", C-E 10/26/89 — 3,850

SORGH, Hendrick Martensz Rokes (Dutch, 1611-1670)
Kitchen Interior, oil on panel, 8x9", SBY 6/3/88 — 6,050

SORGH, Hendrick Martensz Rokes; circle of (Dutch, 1611-1670)
Peasants in an Interior Preparing a Feast of Mussels, Vegetables, Game, Fruits...; oil on panel, 14x20", SBY 10/13/89 — 3,575

SORIANO, Juan (Mexican, 1920-)
El Toro Echado (the lazy bull), oil/tempera on canvas, 1978, 45x59", C-NY 5/17/89 OE — 35,200
La Nina de la Sabana (lady on balcony in landscape), 1947, 20x43", C-NY 11/21/88 — 35,200
Las Vegas, oil on canvas, sgn, 1958, 38x38", C-NY 11/21/89 — 8,800
Pair: Portraits; pencil on paper/charcoal on paper, sgn/dtd 42 & 49, 18x13", 23x19", SBY 11/21/88 OE — 1,650
Pajaro en Vuelo, oil on canvas, sgn/dtd 81, 38x77", C-NY 11/21/89 — 13,200
Romantic Figures in a Landscape, gouache on paper, sgn/dtd 50, 20x26", SBY 11/21/88 OE — 4,675

SORMAN, Steven (American, 1948-)
Our Lady of the Pines, mixed media, 1975, 52x103", C-E 11/14/89 — 880
Our Lady of the Pines, mixed media, 1975, 52x103", C-E 5/13/88 UE — 550

SORMANI, Gian Luciano
Village Scene, oil on board, sgn, 8x10", C-E 2/16/88 UE — 330

SOROLLA Y BASTIDA, Joaquin (Spanish, 1863-1923)
El Beso de Fausto, oil on canvas, sgn/dtd 87, 21x31", SBY 10/24/89 OE — 352,000
Elaboracion de Pasas, Javea; oil on canvas, sgn/dtd/inscr #109, 23x35", SBY 2/22/89 — 385,000
Familia Segoviana (interior genre scene), oil on canvas, sgn/dtd 1894, 22x31", SBY 10/24/89 OE — 770,000
Figures on a Beach, oil on canvas, sgn/dtd 10, 6x8", C-NY 5/25/88 OE — 44,000
L'Inondation, Effets de Soleil Bords de l'Yonne; oil on canvas, sgn/dtd 1906/indistinctly titled, 18x22", SBY 2/16/89 — 44,000
Mercado del Berbes (Vigo), oil on board, sgn/inscr No 262, 4x6", SBY 5/23/89 — 27,500
Ninos en el Mar (sketch of children playing in the sea), oil on board laid down on panel, sgn, 6x9", C-NY 5/24/89 — 66,000
Pair: Man & Two Women at a Table; Portrait Head Studies, pencil, 1 sgn/dtd 1910, 1 sgn/inscr, 8x6", C-NY 2/25/88 — 2,420
Playa de Valencia, oil on canvas, sgn/dtd 1908/#d 330, 20x25", SBY 10/24/89 OE — 682,000
Playa de Valencia (beach scene w/figures in water), oil on canvas, sgn, 6x10", C-NY 2/23/89 OE — 88,000
Portrait of a Child, oil on panel, sgn, 16x13", C-NY 2/23/89 — 44,000
Sandy Bank, oil on board, sgn, 7x10", C-NY 5/25/88 OE — 49,500
Three Boats by a Shore, oil on board, sgn/dtd 1899, 7x11", C-NY 5/24/89 — 38,500
Washerwoman, oil on canvas, sgn, 8x11", B/B 3/17/88 — 60,500

SOTO, Jesus Rafael (Venezuelan, 1923-)
Dos Grandes Barras (composition), mixed media on panel, sgn/dtd 1971/titled, 49x41", C-NY 11/21/88 OE — 22,000
Escultura con Circulo Negro, oil on wood w/nylon cord & painted wire, sgn/dtd 1976, 45x45", C-NY 5/18/88 OE — 17,600
Grand Rond Jaune, oil on wood/painted metal/nylon cord, titled, 60x60", C-NY 5/18/88 OE — 27,500

Relations Jaune et Argente (composition w/squares), mixed media on panel, sgn/dtd 65, 63x42", C-NY 11/21/88 OE 28,600
TER, George William (American, 1879-)
Red Barn in Spring, oil on canvas, sgn, 18x24", FAP 12/8/89 UE 8,100
TOCORNOLA, Giovanni (Italian, 1855-1917)
Young Fruit Seller, oil on canvas, sgn/dtd 93, 51x29", SBY 10/24/89 35,200
UDEIKINE, Sergi (Russian, 1883-1940)
Clown, oil on board, sgn, 18x22", C-NY 2/13/89 935
Dime a Dance, pastel/gouache on paper, sgn, 11x15", SBY 10/5/88 1,650
Night Club in Harlem, tempera on board, sgn, ca 1924, 11x16", SBY 10/5/88 UE 990
Six Russian Dancers, gouache/ink on paper, sgn, 9x10", SBY 10/7/89 1,430
ULACROIX, Charles Joseph Frederic (French, 1825-1879)
Audience with the Cardinal, oil on panel, sgn/inscr, 24x15", C-E 5/23/88 3,300
Between Friends, oil on canvas, sgn, 34x27", SBY 10/24/89 OE 79,750
Elegant Connoisseur (woman seated in an interior), 22x14", C-NY 5/24/89 OE 28,600
Intimate Moment, oil on canvas, sgn, 33x26", SBY 5/23/89 22,000
Le Coiffret aux Bijoux, oil on canvas, bears signature, 21x15", C-NY 10/25/89 14,300
Pearl Necklace (man & woman seated in an interior), oil on canvas, sgn, 33x26", SBY 2/22/89 35,750
Recital, oil on canvas, sgn, 23x32", C-NY 2/25/88 6,050
Satin Rose, oil on canvas, sgn/inscr, 24x14", LH 10/16/88 OE 15,000
ULAGES, Pierre (French, 1919-)
Composition Abstraite (abstract), oil on paper laid down on canvas, sgn/dtd 49/inscr, 26x18", SBY 11/11/88 OE 20,900
Three Questions (contemporary), acrylic on canvas, sgn/ca 1969, 64x51", C-NY 2/20/88 OE 79,200
' Septembre 1966 (abstract), oil on canvas, sgn twice/dtd 2-9-66, 36x29", SBY 11/11/88 OE 77,000
ULIKIAS, Paul (Canadian, 1926-)
Maisons Vues de la Fenetre, oil on canvas, sgn/dtd 1980, 20x24", FB 4/25/88 1,100
St Jovite, oil on board, sgn/dtd 1965, 16x20", FB 5/89 500
th American School (17th C)
Blessed Roch Gonzales, Alphonsus Rodriguez, & John del Castillo, Priests & Martyrs; oil on canvas, 11x8", C-SK 6/9/88 650
th American School (19th C)
Tropical Landscape, oil on canvas, 34x52", C-E 2/23/88 OE 4,400
th German School (15th C)
Annunciation, oil on panel, ca 1470, 20x10", SBY 6/1/89 UE 30,250
Christ Among the Doctors, oil on panel, 27x20", SBY 4/7/88 4,400
th German School (17th C)
Mars & Venus, pen/black ink/blue-gray wash heightened w/white, dtd 1615, 13" dia, SBY 1/13/89 UE 550
UTHWICK, Jeanie Epa (American, 20th C)
Shiun-ku Tokio, watercolor on paper, sgn/inscr/dtd 1916, 14x20", C-E 2/3/88 220
UTINE, Chaim (Russian, 1894-1943)
Cite Falguiere (exterior view of artist's studio), oil on canvas, sgn, 1917, 32x21", SBY 5/30/89 OE 214,500
Glaieuls (floral still life), oil on canvas, sgn, ca 1919, 22x15", C-NY 11/16/88 143,000

elle Demeure aux Environs de artres (Leves), oil on canvas, sgn, 33-34, 19x25", C-NY 5/11/89 ; $330,000

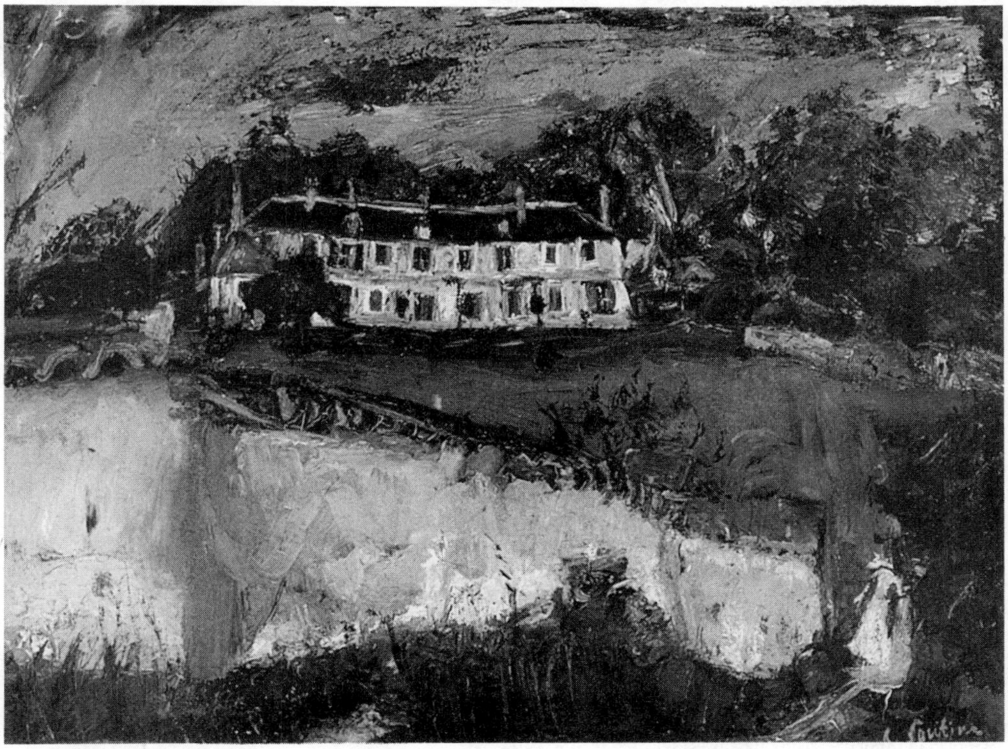

La Route Folle a Cagnes (La Gaude), oil on canvas, sgn, 1924, 32x26", C-NY 11/15/88 ... 440,000
Le Chasseur (portrait of a young man), oil on canvas, sgn, 1926, 26x20", C-NY 11/14/88 OE ... 715,000
Maisons aux Toits Rouges Derriere les Arbres, oil on canvas, sgn, 1918, 21x26", SBY 5/11/88 ... 148,000
Man in a Blue Suit (caricature portrait), oil on canvas, sgn, ca 1923-24, 32x24", SBY 5/10/89 OE ... 770,000
Nature Morte (still life of three pitchers), oil on canvas, sgn, 24x20", SBY 5/10/89 OE ... 181,500
Portrait de Femme sur Fond Bleu, oil on paper laid down on canvas, sgn, 1927-28, 26x22", C-NY 5/11/89 OE ... 418,000
Portrait of a Girl, oil on canvas, sgn, 1927, 22x18", C-NY 5/11/88 OE ... 253,000
Portrait of Lady in Red Dress Standing by an Armchair, oil on canvas, sgn, 1918, 36x28", SBY 5/10/89 ... 407,000
Portrait Rose, oil on canvas, sgn, ca 1916, 17x20", SBY 11/12/88 ... 209,000

SOUTMAN, Pieter; circle of (Dutch, 1580-1657)
Portrait of a Young Lady, half-length; oil on panel, 18x12", C-NY 4/6/89 OE ... 7,700

SOUVERBIE, Jean (French, 1891-)
Femme Nue Allongee (reclining nude), oil on canvas, sgn, 20x26", C-NY 2/18/88 OE ... 6,600

SOUZA-PINTO, see De Souza-Pinto

SOYER, Avron
Angels with Heads, gouache/pastel on board, sgn, 14x11", C-E 11/30/88 UE ... 220

SOYER, Isaac (American, 1907-)
After the Bath (three-quarter length portrait of woman, nude from waist-up), oil on canvas, sgn, 30x24", C-E 6/1/89 ... 1,430
Defense Plant Worker, Buffalo; oil on canvas, sgn, 30x25", C-NY 5/25/89 ... 8,800
Looking into a Mirror, oil on canvas, sgn, 24x14", C-E 10/18/89 OE ... 4,620
Red Stockings (full-length portrait of lady in underwear), oil on canvas, sgn, 28x15", C-NY 9/28/89 ... 4,400
Where Next?, oil on canvas, sgn/dtd 38, 50x46", C-NY 12/2/88 OE ... 26,400

SOYER, Moses (American, 1899-1974)
Artist & Model (in the mirror), oil on canvas, sgn, 22x18", SBY 9/14/89 ... 9,350
Dancer in Blue Leotard, oil on canvas, sgn, 20x10", SBY 4/14/89 OE ... 4,675
Dancer Resting, oil on canvas, bears signature, 22x19", SBY 9/14/89 ... 2,640
Dancer Resting, oil on canvas, sgn, 20x16", C-NY 3/11/88 UE ... 1,980
Dancers in Rehearsal, oil on canvas, sgn/dtd 51, 30x36", C-NY 9/28/89 ... 16,500
Dancers in Yellow, oil on canvas, sgn/dtd 53, 24x18", C-E 10/18/89 ... 5,280
Female Nude, pencil, sgn, 16x9", WG 9/16/88 UE ... 400
Group of 4: Studies of Women; 3 pastel on paper/2 charcoal, sgn, 17x12" to 15x19", SBY 6/28/89 ... 1,430
Head of a Girl, oil on canvas, sgn, unfr, 10x10", WL 5/20/88 ... 950
In the Dance Studio, oil on canvas, sgn/dtd 1944, 26x18", SBY 4/14/89 OE ... 7,150
Man & Reclining Woman, pastel/watercolor on paper, sgn twice, 18x24", SBY 9/23/88 ... 1,320
Mother & Child, oil on canvas, sgn/dtd 32, 30x24", SBY 9/23/88 ... 3,300
Nude, oil on canvas, sgn, 24x20", C-E 10/18/89 ... 1,760
Nude Looking in the Mirror, oil on canvas, sgn, 24x15", SBY 9/23/88 ... 2,860
Odalisque, oil on canvas, sgn, 12x16", C-E 6/1/88 OE ... 2,090
Pair: Reclining Nudes; pastel/pencil on paper, sgn, 13x21", C-E 9/15/88 ... 715
Pair: Sleeping Nudes; Standing Nude; charcoal on paper, sgn, 15x22", 21x15", C-E 6/1/89 ... 880
Portrait of a Young Dancer (bust-length), oil on canvas, sgn, 25x18", SBY 4/14/89 ... 2,750
Portrait of a Young Woman Seated at a Table, oil on canvas, sgn, 15x13", MAG 9/18/88 ... 1,500
Reclining Nude, conte crayon/orange wash on paper, sgn, 17x18", C-NY 3/11/88 ... 825
Rehearsal Break, oil on canvas, sgn, 36x22", C-E 10/18/89 ... 4,400
Seated Nude, oil on canvas, sgn, 18x24", SBY 9/23/88 ... 2,200
Seated Woman, watercolor/pencil on paper, sgn, 12x9", C-NY 6/17/89 ... 660
Seated Woman in an Interior (nude putting on hosiery), oil on canvas, sgn, 20x16", SBY 9/14/89 ... 3,025
Self-Portrait (half-length), oil on canvas, sgn/dtd 1926, 30x24", C-E 6/1/89 ... 2,640
Sketch of Two Women, charcoal on paper, sgn, 10x16", B/B 5/17/89 ... 522
Standing Nude, pen/ink on paper, sgn, 16x9", C-E 2/1/89 UE ... 440
Three Dancers, oil on canvas, sgn, 30x16", SBY 9/14/89 ... 6,325
Two Female Nudes, watercolor/black ink wash on paper, sgn, 14x18", SBY 4/14/89 OE ... 2,640
White Slip (woman in profile holding slip to breasts), oil on canvas, sgn/dtd 46, 16x12", C-E 6/1/89 ... 1,760
Young Girl (half-length portrait of girl, seated), oil on canvas, sgn/dtd 29, 14x11", C-E 2/1/89 ... 1,980

SOYER, Moses; manner of (American, 1899-1974)
Reclining Nude, graphite on paper, bears signature, 16x18", FAP 11/4/88 ... 150

SOYER, Raphael (American, 1899-1987)
Actress (portrait of lady in red), oil on canvas, sgn, 20x24", C-NY 5/25/89 ... 16,500
Artist & His Wife, oil on canvas, sgn, 15x14", C-NY 12/2/88 ... 9,900
At the Sink, oil on masonite, sgn, 14x10", SBY 6/24/88 OE ... 16,500
Blond in a Blue Skirt, pastel on paper, sgn, ca 1962, 21x16", SBY 3/17/88 ... 2,420
Charcoal Sketch of Two Women, charcoal on paper, sgn, 16x22", B/B 8/10/88 ... 1,650
Cynthia (portrait), watercolor/gouache/pencil on paper, sgn, 14x12", B/B 3/22/89 ... 1,430
Dressing, pen/ink/ink wash on paper, sgn, 11x8", C-E 2/1/89 ... 715
Embracing Couple, pastel on paper, sgn, 24x15", SBY 9/23/88 ... 1,760
Female Nude, red marker/pencil on paper, sgn, 12x9", SBY 4/14/89 ... 660
Female Nude Studies, watercolor/pencil on paper, sgn, 15x21", SBY 9/23/88 ... 1,650
Flowered Skirt (portrait of a lady seated in profile w/hand on head), oil on canvas, sgn, 26x22", C-NY 5/25/89 ... 28,600
Front & Back View of a Nude, pencil on paper, 11x8", C-E 11/30/88 ... 825
Georgiana (portrait), oil on canvas, sgn, 18x14", SBY 6/24/8 ... 7,700
Girl Before a Mirror, ink/wash on paper, sgn, 13x9", SBY 4/14/89 ... 1,430

Girl in Slip, oil on canvas, sgn, 16x12", C-E 2/1/89	5,500
In My Studio, oil on canvas, sgn, 26x32", SBY 3/17/88 OE	14,300
Jackson Park, oil on canvas, sgn, 11x26", C-NY 12/2/88	7,700
Joan in Green, oil on canvas, sgn, 8x10", C-E 2/3/88 OE	4,400
Kate (portrait), oil on canvas, sgn, 12x31", C-E 2/3/88 OE	5,280
Looking Left, pastel on paper, sgn, 18x15" C-E 2/1/89	1,100
Model in the Studio, oil on canvas, sgn, 20x16", SBY 9/14/89	8,250
Model with Folded Arms, oil on canvas, sgn, 20x16", C-NY 9/28/89	11,000
Model with Folded Arms (nude from waist up), oil on canvas, sgn, 24x21", C-NY 12/2/88	13,200
Mother To Be, pencil on paper, sgn, unfr, 18x16", SBY 6/24/88	660
Nude Bathing (sketch), charcoal on paper, sgn, unfr, 20x15", SBY 9/14/89	1,320
Nude Reclining, pencil, sgn, 18x13", PHL 6/16/88	500
Nude Rising, pencil/watercolor on paper, sgn, 19x15", C-NY 3/11/88	2,310
Nude Standing by a Door, charcoal on paper, sgn twice, 19x12", SBY 1/24/89	935
Nude Studies, watercolor/pencil on paper, sgn, 15x11", SBY 9/23/88	1,210
Nude with Arms Behind Her Head, pen/ink on paper, sgn, 12x9", C-E 11/30/88	825
Nude Woman From the Back, charcoal on paper, sgn twice, 20x13", SBY 1/24/89	715
Pair: Artist Model; pen/ink on paper, sgn, unfr, 14x9", C-E 6/1/88	935
Pair: Figure Drawings; pen/ink on paper, sgn, unfr, 12x18" & smaller, C-E 6/1/88	935
Pair: School Girls; pen/ink on paper, sgn, unfr, 11x8", C-E 6/1/88	825
Pair: Standing Female Nude; Two Seated Female Nudes; watercolor/crayon/pencil/wash, sgn, SBY 3/17/88 UE	1,100
Pensive, pen & brown ink on paper, sgn, 8x10", C-E 2/1/89	715
Portrait of a Girl with Her Arms Folded, oil on cradled panel, sgn/dtd 1939, 19x15", SBY 9/23/88	11,000
Portrait of Emil J Arnold, oil on canvas, sgn, 32x26", SBY 9/23/88	7,425
Portrait of Nell (shoulder-length, wearing hat), oil on canvas, sgn/dtd 1943, 12x9", SBY 9/14/89	3,575
Reclining Nude, oil on canvas, sgn, 12x16", C-E 11/30/88	2,860
Reclining Nude, oil on canvas mounted on board, sgn, ca 1950, 8x16", SBY 3/17/88	2,310
Reclining Woman, oil on canvas, sgn, 12x24", SBY 6/28/89	8,800
Red Grooms with Mimi Gross, watercolor/pencil on paper, sgn, 11x13", SBY 3/17/88 OE	2,200
Repose, pen/ink on paper, sgn, 9x14", C-E 11/30/88 UE	550
Repose Duet (portrait), oil on canvas, sgn/inscr Duet, 1961, 12x9", SBY 3/17/88	1,870
Resting, pen/brown ink/ink wash on paper, 9x13", C-E 2/1/89	605
Seated Figure, pen/ink wash on paper, sgn, 11x7", C-E 6/1/88	605
Seated Girl with Red Beret, pastel/pencil on paper, sgn, 12x10", SBY 4/14/89	870
Seated Model, oil on canvas, sgn, 24x20", SBY 6/24/88	8,800
Seated Nude, oil on canvas, sgn, 10x14", SBY 6/28/89	2,860
Seated Nude, oil on canvas, sgn, 24x20", SBY 6/28/89	11,500
Seated Nude, pencil, signed, 13x12", LH 10/16/88	900
Seated Nudes, oil on canvas, sgn, 24x21", SBY 6/28/89	6,600
Seated Woman with Long Hair, watercolor/pencil on paper, sgn, 22x16", SBY 3/17/88	17,600
Self-Portrait with Models, oil on paper laid down on canvas, sgn, 16x20", C-E 2/1/89	4,180
Sleeping Nude, pen/brown ink on paper, sgn/dtd Dec 23 1960, 7x10", C-NY 6/17/89	770
Sleeping Nude, pencil on paper, sgn, 17x24", C-E 11/30/88	770
Something Evil, watercolor/pencil on paper, sgn, 22x16", C-E11/30/88	2,090
Standing Nude, pen/brown ink/ink wash on paper, sgn, 8x11", C-E 2/1/89	770
Standing Nude, pencil on paper, sgn, 17x10", SBY 9/14/89	825
Standing Nude, watercolor/gouache/pencil on paper, sgn, 17x12", SBY 6/28/89	1,760
Standing Woman, watercolor/charcoal on paper, sgn, 22x12", SBY 6/24/88	1,650
Still Life of Mandolin, oil on canvas, sgn, 1929, 25x28", SBY 9/23/88	4,675
Street in Gloucester, watercolor on paper, sgn, 11x15", SBY 9/23/88 OE	3,575
Street Scene with Moses Soyer, oil on canvas, sgn, 30x22", C-NY 5/26/88	35,200
Study of a Female Nude, pencil, sgn, 19x14", PHL 6/16/88	475
Study of a Woman (standing nude), pencil on gray paper, sgn, 19x12", SBY 6/28/89	1,320
Study of a Young Girl, bust portrait of young girl w/short brown hair; oil on canvas, sgn, 11x8", RAB 3/27/89 OE	1,000
Study of Five Female Nudes, ink/ink wash/white chalk on paper, sgn, 18x23", SBY 6/28/89	1,760
Study of Nude Holding a Basket, charcoal on green-oatmeal paper, sgn, ca 1970, 18x12", SWN 12/1/88	220
Study of Nudes, pencil on paper, sgn, 16x23", SBY 1/24/89	1,870
Thoughtful (portrait of a girl), oil on canvas, sgn, 10x8", C-NY 3/11/88	3,080
Two Dancers (in interior), oil on canvas, sgn, 1957, 25x26", SBY 3/17/88	14,300
Two Nudes, oil on canvasboard, sgn, 12x9", SBY 4/14/89	2,640
Woman Dressing, pen/ink on paper, sgn, 14x10", C-E 11/30/88	770
Woman in a Red Sweater, oil on canvas, sgn, 21x10", SBY 4/14/89	6,600
Woman in Purple, oil on canvas, sgn, 20x24", C-E 2/1/89	1,650
Woman on a Subway (portrait), watercolor/pencil on paper, sgn/dtd 1928, 24x19", C-NY 5/25/89 OE	16,500
Young Girl Seated, watercolor over black crayon, sgn, 17x13", SBY 4/14/89	2,200
ADINO, Giovanni Paolo (Italian, 17th C)	
Pomegranates, Grapes & Fowl on a Ledge; oil on canvas, 12x17", C-NY 4/6/89	3,500
Vase of Flowers, Peaches, & Artichokes on a Ledge; oil on canvas, 29x39", C-NY 10/20/88	29,700
ANG, Frederick (American, 1831-1909)	
Portrait of a Clergyman, oil on canvas, 30x25", FAP 4/15/89	1,650

Spanish School (14th C)
Crucifixion with Saints Mary & John in a Landscape, oil on panel, on gold ground, shaped top, 39x34", C-NY 4/8/88 .... **4,400**
Monk, standing, oil on panel, on gold ground, shaped top, 33x21", ca 1500, C-NY 4/8/88 .... **2,200**
Spanish School (15th C)
Pair: Prophets of the Old Testament; tempera on panel on gold ground, 37x15", 37x12", SBY 10/13/89 .... **12,100**
Pair: St Catherine of Alexandria; Saint Barbara, tempera on panel, gold ground, arched top, 30x10", SBY 6/3/88 .... **11,550**
Spanish School (16th C)
Last Supper, oil on canvas, 20x46", SBY 4/7/88 .... **2,750**
Martyrdom of Saint Barbara, oil on panel, unfr, 38x28", SBY 7/12/89 .... **2,475**
Portrait of a Man Said To Be the Duke of Alba, half-length, oil on canvas, 28x24", C-E 4/7/88 UE **550**
Portrait of a Woman Said To Be Infanta Clara Isabella, oil on panel, 15x11", C-E 4/7/88 .... **1,320**
Saint James in His Study, oil on canvas, 39x29", C-NY 4/8/88 .... **770**
Saints John the Baptist, James the Greater, & Bernardino of Siena; oil on panel, 57x39", SBY 10/13/89 .... **23,100**
Spanish School (17th C)
Holy Family, pen/brown ink/gray wash over traces of black chalk, 9x8", SBY 1/13/89 .... **1,100**
Holy Family with God the Father in a Landscape, oil on canvas, 24x15", C-E 6/1/88 UE **440**
Monk in Contemplation, oil on canvas laid down on panel, oval, 26x22", C-E 4/7/88 UE **242**
Portrait of a Gentleman, standing, three-quarter length...before a curtain; oil on canvas, 59x44", C-NY 4/6/89 .... **4,400**
Portrait of a Man, half-length, in armor, oil on canvas, 26x20", C-E 4/7/88 .... **352**
Portrait of a Man, three-quarter length, holds portrait medallion; oil on canvas, 43x36", C-E 1/12/88 .... **1,650**
Portrait of Diane de Poitier, oil on panel, 15x12", SBY 6/8/88 .... **1,320**
Still Life of Flowers in a Glass Vase in a Niche, a Tazza in the Foreground; oil on canvas, 36x29", SBY 4/7/88 OE **8,800**
Spanish School (18th C)
Arrival of the Ship into Port, oil on canvas, 45x75", C-E 4/7/88 .... **1,650**
Head of a Woman, oil on canvas, octagonal, 19x13", SBY 7/12/89 OE **1,760**
Holy Family, oil on canvas, 21x17", WD 1/25/89 .... **650**
Pair: Venetian Gentleman, three-quarter length; Venetian Lady, full-length; oil on copper, inscr, 7x5", C-NY 10/20/88 .... **1,210**
Portrait of a Nobleman, oil on canvas, 23x18", SBY 7/12/89 .... **1,980**
Portrait of Carlos II (1661-1700), oil on canvas, 38x29", LH 10/16/88 UE **600**
Preaching in the Indies, oil on canvas, octagonal frame, 32x41", NA 2/24/89 .... **1,800**
Romantic Landscape with Castles in the Background, oil on canvas, 30x39", C-E 1/12/88 .... **1,320**
Saint Francis (full-length portrait), oil on canvas, 42x29", B/B 9/14/89 .... **2,200**
Young Girl Giving a Coin to a Beggar, oil on canvas, 36x50", C-NY 10/12/89 .... **5,500**
Young Jesuit in Prayer, oil on canvas, 41x29", SBY 6/8/88 .... **1,760**
Spanish School (19th C)
Bullfighter, oil on panel, initialed, 13x12", C-E 9/15/88 UE **440**
Bust-Length Portrait of a Girl, oil on board, 10x8", SLK 2/11/89 .... **200**
Immaculate Conception, oil on copper, 17x11", WD 1/25/89 .... **800**
Mother & Child in a Garden, oil on canvas, indistinctly sgn, 27x20", C-E 5/23/88 .... **3,300**
Pair: Floral Still Lifes; oil on canvas, 17x14", SBY 7/12/89 UE **1,650**
Peasant Woman Holding Geraniums, oil on canvas, indistinctly sgn, 17x13", C-E 10/25/88 .... **1,650**
Portrait of a Gentleman, oil on canvas, 21x18", SBY 12/9/88 .... **1,210**
Portrait of an Officer, oil on canvas, 21x16", C-E 4/7/88 .... **990**
St Thomas Adoring the Crucifix, oil on canvas, 31x23", C-E 1/12/88 .... **330**
Still Life of Flowers in an Urn, oil on canvas, 57x80", SBY 7/12/89 OE **52,800**
Tarde en el Jardin (Afternoon in a Garden), oil on canvas, indistinctly sgn, 10x18", B/B 5/17/89 .... **550**
Two Clerics Walking on a Path with a Church Beyond, oil on canvas, 29x26", C-E 6/1/88 UE **550**
Spanish School (20th C)
Horses in a Landscape, oil on canvas, 28x28", FAP 4/15/89 UE **132**
Pair: Plowhorses & Horses in a Village; oil on board, 13x19", FAP 4/15/89 .... **220**
Pair: Still Life in a Glass Vase on a Ledge; Portrait of a Girl; oil on canvas, 9x7", C-E 4/7/88 .... **550**
SPANZOTTI, Giovanni Martino; follower of (Italian, ca 1500)
Nativity, tempera on arched panel, 37x16", SBY 4/7/89 .... **35,200**
SPARE, Austin Osman (British, 1888-1956)
Female Nude, half-length; pencil, initialed, 10x6", PHL 6/16/88 .... **425**
Female Nude (standing w/arms hehind head), pencil/watercolor, 12x8", PHL 6/16/88 UE **600**
SPARKS, Norma R.
Wooded Landscape, pencil/pen/watercolor, sgn, 14x21", C-SK 11/10/88 UE **70**
SPARKS, Will (American, 1862-1937)
Adobe at the Edge of Town, oil on panel, sgn, 8x10", B/B 12/8/88 .... **935**
Old Gate, Monterey (figure in a landscape); oil on canvas, sgn, 10x13", B/B 9/14/89 OE **1,980**
On the Santa Cruz River, oil on canvas, sgn, 8x11", B/B 10/6/88 .... **1,760**
SPAT, Gabriel (American, 1890-1967)
At the Beach, oil on board, sgn, 8x10", C-E 2/3/88 .... **1,650**
At the Races, oil on canvas, sgn, 22x28", C-NY 3/11/88 OE **12,100**
Automne au Bois de Boulogne, Paris; oil on canvas, sgn, 22x28", C-NY 3/11/88 .... **5,500**
Avant la Course (lady on shoulders of man in water at the beach), oil on board, sgn, 6x11", C-E 2/3/88 .... **1,320**
Ballet Maquillage, oil on masonite, sgn, 18x16", C-NY 9/30/88 .... **3,300**
Ballet Rehearsal, oil on canvasboard, sgn, 10x16", C-E 6/1/88 .... **1,980**
Bois de Boulogne (landscape), oil on canvasboard, sgn, 5x6", WL 5/20/88 .... **800**
By the Beach, oil on canvas, sgn, 7x10", WL 5/20/88 UE **150**

:ourses a Chantilly, oil on canvasboard, sgn, 6x9", C-E 2/1/89 1,100
:n Bretagne (in Brittany), oil on board, sgn, 5x13", PHL 11/15/88 2,500
:vening in the Park, oil on canvas, sgn, 22x28", C-NY 9/30/88 7,150
ardin de Luxembourg Autrefois, oil on board, sgn, 5x6", FAP 4/15/89 798
ardin des Tuileries, oil on board, sgn, 9x12", C-E 11/30/88 1,100
.a Conciergerie, oil on board, sgn, 9x13", C-E 6/1/88 UE 770
'orte Dauphine, Paris; oil on board, sgn, 8x11", C-E 9/15/88 UE 319
:endevous, oil on board, sgn, 8x6", C-E 11/30/88 660
:ue de Rivoli, oil on board, sgn, 9x10", C-E 6/1/88 UE 770

AULDING, Henry Plympton (American, 1868-)
/leadow with Grazing Cattle, watercolor/gouache on paper, sgn/dtd 1900, 12x15", RWS 9/8/89 OE 475

:EAR, Arthur Prince (American, 1879-1959)
Iymph, pastel on gray paper laid down on board, sgn, 20x24", C-NY 3/11/88 UE 385
'wilight Reverie, oil on canvas, sgn, 31x26", RWS 5/12/89 OE 2,200

:EAR, Ruskin (British, 1911-)
Vinter Landscape (vase of jasmine on piano w/sheet music), oil on board, 17x21", SBY 10/7/89 6,600

:EICHER, Eugene (American, 1883-1962)
:ouquet, oil on canvas, sgn, 16x20", B/B 12/8/88 2,200
:ood Book (nude leaning on chair w/book), oil on canvas, sgn, 40x51", C-NY 5/25/89 UE 8,250
etty (coastal landscape), oil on canvas, sgn, 17x22", C-E 6/1/89 UE 1,100
Iude Leaning on a Chair, pencil/charcoal on paper, sgn/inscr, 9x10", C-E 6/1/88 770
)ctober Meadows, Saugerties, New York; oil on canvas, sgn, 16x20", C-NY 9/28/89 1,650
'assing Storm, oil on canvas, sgn/dtd 1907, 21x36", C-NY 5/26/88 10,450
/ase of Peonies, oil on canvas, sgn, 22x18", RWS 5/19/88 UE 1,000
Voman in White Shawl, oil on canvas, sgn, 22x19", C-E 10/18/89 3,080

ENCE, Thomas Ralph (British, fl 1876-1903)
'igures in a Classical Garden, oil/gouache on board, initialed, 18x29", SBY 12/9/88 UE 660

ENCELAYH, Charles (British, 1865-1958)
:ourtship, oil on canvas, sgn, 28x40", SBY 12/9/88 3,300

ENCER, Jean (American, 20th C)
:till Life with Marigold, oil on panel, sgn, 23x20", LH 9/10/89 170

ENCER, John C. (American, 19th/20th C)
'layful Kittens, oil on canvas, sgn/dtd 1903, 14x22", RWS 11/3/88 1,900

ENCER, Lilly Martin (American, 1822-1902)
:eauty Barberized, pencil on paper, 12x10", WL 5/20/88 525
:hild with a Dandelion, charcoal, 12x17", NA 2/16/88 250
)ead Warrior & His Widow, pencil/charcoal/chalk, 15x20", NA 10/1/88 200
Iamlet & Ophelia, pencil on bluish-gray paper, inscr Hamlet-Hie Thee to a Nunnery, 12x14", WL 5/20/88 400
nsanity, study of young woman clutching her legs; pencil on buff paper, titled, 8x11", RAB 8/8/89 500
sabella & Angelo, pencil/ink/sepia wash on paper, 15x19", WL 5/20/88 UE 250
ane Eleanor Sherman Lacey & Her Son Edward, oil on canvas, ca 1858, 49x36", SBY 6/24/88 4,400
:neeling Warrior with Female, pencil, 8x12", NA 2/24/89 175
.ife Without Hope, pencil on blue tinted paper, inscr, 15x20", RWS 11/3/88 500
/lischief (kitten lapping milk from teacup), oil on board, sgn, 11x9", C-E 6/1/89 5,500
/lother with Sleeping Child, pencil on paper, 15x20", WL 5/20/88 650
'icnic, oil on canvas, sgn/dtd 1856, 12x16", C-NY 9/28/89 12,100
'ortrait of a Boy, pencil on paper, sgn, 13x10", WL 5/20/88 UE 200
Voman & Child with a Parrot, pencil on paper, 15x20", WL 5/20/88 250
'outh & Age (man & three children in landscape), oil on canvas, sgn/dtd 1948, 45x34", WD 10/5/88 UE 5,000

ENCER, Meade Ashley (American, 20th C)
:oys at Play, oil on board, initialed, 18x24", WG 4/23/88 250

ENCER, R.B. (British, 19th C)
\bandoning the Flagship, oil on canvas, sgn, 24x36", B/B 1/11/89 OE 3,025
:roadsiding the French Flagship, oil on canvas, initialed, 24x36", B/B 1/11/89 OE 3,300
:ngaging the French Fleet, oil on canvas, sgn, 24x36", B/B 1/11/89 OE 3,025
:unning the Broadside, oil on canvas, sgn, 24x36", B/B 1/11/89 OE 3,300

ENCER, Robert (American, 1879-1931)
'ohicken Valley, Point Pleasant, Pennsylvania; oil on canvas, sgn/dtd 1920, 25x30", C-NY 9/30/88 23,100

ENCER, Stanley (British, 1891-1959)
'ortrait of the Artist's Wife Hilda, pencil on paper, sgn/dtd 1931, 14x10", SBY 10/5/88 2,090

ERLICH, Sophie (German, 19th C)
'layful Kittens, oil on panel, sgn, 10x13", PHL 10/28/88 2,300

ERLING, Heinrich (German, 1844-1924)
/laltese Terrier, oil on canvas, sgn/dtd 84, 29x22", SBY 6/9/89 13,200

EYER, J.
.andscape with Figure by a Stream, oil on canvas, sgn, 34x14", C-E 7/26/88 UE 220

ICUZZA, Francesco (American, 1883-1962)
:athers at Bradford Beach, oil on academy board, sgn, 10x14", S/A 3/12/88 250
:each Scene with Eight Figures, oil on board, sgn, unfr, 8x10", MAG 6/22/88 380
'loral Still Life, oil on academy board, sgn, 24x18", S/A 3/12/88 425
'loral Still Life, oil on canvas, sgn, 30x25", B/B 8/10/88 550

Floral Still Life, oil on panel, sgn, 30x20", MAG 6/22/89 .... **200**
Hollycocks, oil on canvas, 24x30", MAG 4/24/88 .... **150**
Lake Michigan Water Scene, pastel, sgn, 25x29", MAG 9/18/88 .... **300**
Lake Scene, pastel, sgn, 23x29", MAG 3/27/88 .... **600**
Pair: Floral Studies; oil on board, sgn, 14x10", MAG 4/24/88 .... **75**
Pair: Floral Studies; pastel, 19x13", MAG 4/24/88 .... **350**
Sailing Ships & Lake Steamer on Lake Michigan, pastel, sgn, 14x13", S/A 2/18/89 .... **400**
Spring Orchard, oil on board, sgn, unfr, 22x28", MAG 6/22/88UE **60**
Stormy Scene, oil on canvas, sgn/dtd 1907, unfr, 20x23", MAG 3/27/88 UE **125**
Summer Landscape, pastel, 16x19", MAG 4/24/88 .... **175**
Wisconsin Farm Scene, oil on panel, sgn, 24x29", MAG 6/22/89 .... **325**

SPIELTER, Carl Johann (German, 1851-1922)
In the Carpenter's Workshop, oil on canvas, sgn/dtd 1902, 40x50", SBY 2/22/89 .... **5,500**

SPILIMBERGO, Lino Eneas (Argentinian, 1896-1964)
Estudio de Cabeza de Mujer (study of woman's head), sanguine on wallpaper, sgn, 29x22", C-NY 11/21/88 .... **3,080**

SPINETTI, Mario (Italian, 19th/20th C)
Pair: Arrival of a Lovely Lady; Game of Shuttlecock; watercolor on paper, sgn/inscr, 21x30", 19x29", SBY 12/9/88 .... **4,400**

SPINKS, Thomas (British, 19th/20th C)
Overlooking Wharfdale, oil on canvas, sgn, 14x21", SBY 7/12/89 UE **990**

SPIRIDON, Ignace (Italian, 20th C)
Interrupted Picnic, oil on panel, sgn/inscr, 21x25", LH 10/16/88 UE **9,000**

SPIRO, George (French, 1909-1948)
Paysage Fantastique avec Oiseaux (fantasy landscape w/bird), oil on canvas, sgn, 11x14", C-E 11/17/88 .... **1,210**
Rue de Village avec Marrons et Journal, oil on canvas, sgn, 11x14", C-E 11/17/88 OE **2,090**

SPISANELLI, Vincenzo Spisano
Descent From the Cross, oil on slate, arched top, 18x10", C-NY 4/6/89 .... **3,300**

SPITZER, Walter (German, 1927-)
Adam et Eve, oil on canvas, sgn/dtd 25.1.67, 8x24", C-E 11/17/88 OE **825**
Toledo, oil on canvas, sgn/dtd 65, 13x18", C-E 11/17/88 .... **990**

SPODE, Samuel (British, fl 1825-1858)
Harnessed Carriage Horse in a Stall, oil on canvas, sgn, 20x24", SBY 6/9/89 OE **2,090**

SPOEL, Jacob (Dutch, 1830-1868)
Mother & Baby at a Spinning Wheel, oil on canvas, sgn/dtd 1892, 18x16", C-E 10/25/88 .... **2,420**

SPOHLER, Jan Jacob (Dutch, 1811-1879)
Dutch Street Scene, oil on panel, sgn, 11x8", C-NY 5/24/89 .... **6,600**
Figures in a Frozen Landscape, oil on canvas, 28x32", RWS 11/3/88 .... **8,000**
Winter Landscape, oil on canvas, sgn, 27x38", SBY 2/22/89 .... **49,500**

SPOHLER, Jan Jacob Coenraad (Dutch, 1837-1923)
Figures Skating On a Frozen River, oil on canvas, sgn, 17x26", PHL 6/16/88 .... **3,500**
Summer Landscape with Windmill, oil on canvas, sgn, unfr, 25x37", WL 5/20/88 .... **3,000**

SPOHLER, Johannes Franciscus (Dutch, 1853-1894)
Drawbridge Over a Canal, oil on panel, sgn, 8x6", C-E 10/26/89 .... **9,350**
Dutch Canal Scene (figures on bridge, buildings beyond); oil on panel, sgn, 8x6", PHL 10/28/88 .... **4,000**
Dutch Street Scene, oil on panel, sgn, 10x8", C-NY 5/25/88 .... **4,400**
Dutch Street Scene, oil on panel, sgn, 13x11", C-NY 5/25/88 .... **6,600**
Dutch Street Scene in Winter, oil on panel, sgn, 8x6", C-NY 2/24/89 .... **4,400**
Dutch Town Scene by a Canal, oil on panel, sgn, 18x6", C-NY 5/25/88 .... **4,180**
Rowing on a Canal, oil on panel, sgn, 8x6", C-E 10/26/89 .... **9,350**
Village Street, oil on panel, sgn, 8x6", DM 2/19/88 .... **550**

SPOHN, Clay Edgar (American, 1898-)
Untitled (abstract), oil on canvas, sgn/dtd 1963, 36x45", C-E 11/14/89 .... **1,870**

SPRANGER, Bartolomeus; circle of (Flemish, 1546-1627)
Venus & Cupid with Attendants Offering Fruits & Flowers, oil on slate, 10x8", SBY 4/7/88 .... **4,675**

SPRING, Alfons (German, 1843-1908)
In the Wine Cellar (four men around a keg), oil on paper laid down, sgn, 9x12", SBY 7/12/89 .... **5,225**

SPRINGCHORN, Carl (American, 1887-1971)
Central Park, oil on canvas, sgn, 24x32", C-NY 9/30/88 .... **2,200**
River & Woods, oil on canvasboard, sgn, 13x17", C-E 6/1/89 .... **1,210**
Sailor (caricature drawings), pen/black ink/watercolor on paper laid down on board, sgn, 13x12", C-E 6/1/89 .... **935**
Two Sailors (leaning against barn), watercolor/crayon on paper laid down on board, 16x12", C-E 6/1/89 .... **495**

SPRINGER, Charles Henry (American, 1857-1920)
Fisherman, oil on canvas, sgn/dtd 1888, 16x20", NA 2/24/89 .... **650**

SPRINGETT, Louis C.
Somenos Lake, Vancouver Island; oil on panel, inscr, unfr, 12x27", C-SK 6/9/88 .... **278**

SPRUYT, Johannes (Jan); att (1627-1671)
Fancy Hen & Her Chicks, oil on canvas, bears signature, 25x18", SBY 10/21/88 .... **3,300**

STACEY, Anna Lee (American, 1871-1943)
Matilija Poppies, oil on canvas, sgn, 36x34", LH 3/20/88 OE **3,000**
Picking Flowers, oil on canvas, sgn/dtd 19(?), 16x20", C-NY 3/11/88 .... **6,050**
Still Life of Bouquet, oil on masonite, sgn/dtd 42, 34x36", LH 12/4/88 UE **500**
Still Life of Daffodils, oil on canvas, sgn, 24x20", B/B 12/8/88 .... **440**

ACKHOUSE, Robert (20th C)
Shiphall at Walker Art Center, gouache/watercolor/charcoal on paper, sgn/inscr/dtd 12-19-77, 29x41", SBY 10/5/88 .... **2,475**
ACQUET, Henry (Belgian, 1838-1907)
Elderly Peasant Seated by the Hearth, watercolor on paper, sgn, 14x15", C-E 10/25/88 .... **990**
ADEMANN, Adolf (German, 1824-1895)
River Landscape, oil on canvas, sgn, 11x14", C-E 5/23/88 .... **3,520**
AEL, Nicholas; see De Stael
AHL, Friedrich (1863-1940)
Adam & Eve, oil on canvas, sgn/dtd Florenz 1909-10, lot 725, 43x44", C-L 6/27/88 .... **47,300**
Adam & Eve, oil on canvas, sgn/inscr, ca 1910, 28x28", lot 726, C-L 6/27/88 .... **17,028**
Judgement of Paris, oil on canvas, sgn/dtd Florenz 1909-10, 42x58", C-L 6/27/88 .... **66,220**
AINFORTH, Martin; att (Australian, 20th C)
Horse in a Landscape, oil on canvas, 14x18", FAP 4/15/89 .... **798**
ALSER, Hans
Wooded Lake, oil on panel, sgn, 14x12", C-E 5/23/88 .... **715**
AMOS, Theodoros (American, 1922-)
Abstraction, watercolor on paper, sgn/dtd 48, 15x22", SBY 10/8/88 .... **6,600**

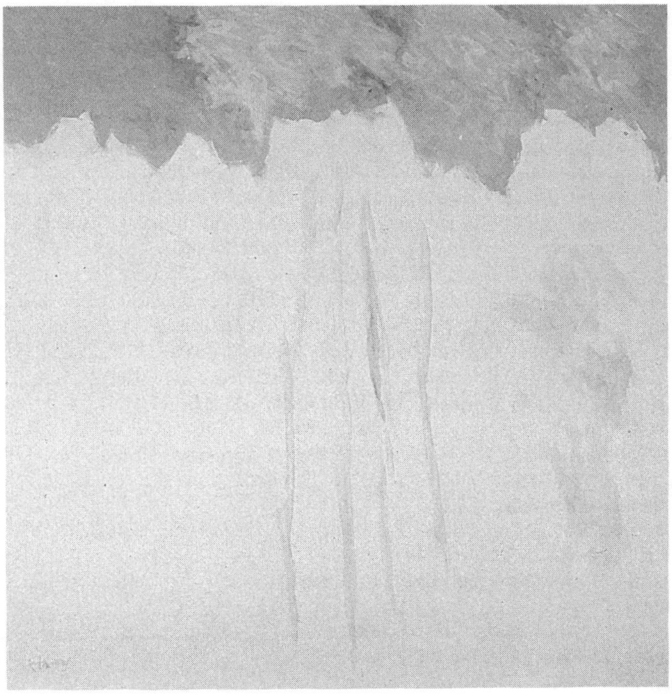

Sun Games, acrylic/oil on canvas, sgn/dtd 1956-79, unfr, 71x66, C-NY 5/3/89; $110,000

Adriatic Souvenir (abstract), oil on masonite, sgn/dtd NYC 45/titled, 30x24", SBY 11/11/88 OE **39,600**
After Edna (abstract), oil on canvas, sgn/dtd 54, unfr, 70x35", C-NY 5/4/89 .... **17,600**
Albatross (abstract), oil on canvas, sgn twice/dtd 60/titled, 70x70", SBY 2/19/88 .... **55,000**
Altar, oil on masonite, twice sgn/dtd 48/titled, 48x36", C-NY 11/10/88 OE **77,000**
Byzantium III, oil on canvas, twice sgn/dtd 1958/titled, 72x69", C-NY 11/10/88 .... **66,000**
Cataclysm (abstract), oil on canvas, 1946, 30x24", SBY 11/11/88 .... **39,600**
Day the Phoenix Rose (abstract), oil on canvas, sgn/dtd 1956, 71x49", SBY 11/9/89 .... **46,750**
Delphic Sun Box (abstract), oil on canvas, sgn/dtd 1968, unfr, 56x32", C-NY 5/4/89 .... **7,150**
Drift Fishing the Weed Line, oil on board, sgn/dtd 1984, 20x24", WAD 6/12/89 .... **900**
Edge of Burning Bush (abstract), acrylic on canvas, sgn/dtd 1980, unfr, 34x30", C-NY 5/4/89 .... **13,200**
Edge of Day (abstract), oil on canvas, sgn twice/dtd 1961, 60x25", SBY 5/3/88 OE **49,500**
Flowering Rock (abstract), gouache on cardboard, sgn twice/titled, ca 1945-50, 17x13", SBY 2/19/88 .... **6,875**
High Snow, Low Sun (abstract); oil on canvas, sgn, 1957, 57x57", SBY 5/3/88 OE **115,500**
Infinity Field, Delphi Series (abstract); acrylic on paper, sgn/dtd 1983, 31x23", SBY 2/15/89 .... **6,050**
Infinity Field, Jerusalem Series #16; acrylic on paper, sgn/dtd 1984, 30x22", C-NY 5/4/89 .... **5,500**
Infinity Field, Jerusalem Series; acrylic on canvas, sgn/dtd 1984/titled, 62x54", lot 199, SBY 2/19/88 .... **19,800**
Infinity Field, Jerusalem Series; acrylic on canvas, sgn/dtd 1983, 46x36", SBY 10/8/88 OE **14,300**
Infinity Field, Lefkada Series (abstract); acrylic on canvas, sgn/dtd 1980/titled, 38x28", SBY 2/19/88 .... **6,600**
Infinity Field, Lefkada Series (abstract); acrylic on canvas, sgn/dtd 1978, 68x42", SBY 10/5/89 .... **14,300**
Infinity Field, Lefkada Series (abstract); acrylic on canvas, sgn/dtd 1972, 68x18", SBY 10/5/88 UE **3,300**
Infinity Field, Lefkada Series (abstract); acrylic on canvas, sgn/dtd 1972, 24x18", SBY 10/5/88 UE **2,200**
Infinity Field, Lefkada Series (abstract); acrylic on canvas, 1970, 24x18", SBY 10/5/88 UE **2,200**
Infinity Field, Lefkada Series (abstract); acrylic on canvas, sgn/inscr/dtd 1980, unfr, 43x26", C-NY 5/4/88 .... **10,450**
Infinity Field, Lefkada Series (abstract); acrylic on canvas, 1982, 72x55", SBY 2/15/89 .... **4,950**
Infinity Field, Lefkada Series (abstract); acrylic on canvas, sgn/dtd 1980, unfr, 58x70", C-NY 5/4/89 .... **35,200**

Infinity Field, Lefkada Series (abstract); acrylic on canvas, sgn/dtd 1980, 72x60", C-NY 5/4/89 ... 16,500
Infinity Field, Lefkada Series (abstract); acrylic on paper, sgn/dtd 1980/titled, 30x23", SBY 2/19/88 ... 4,400
Infinity Field, Lefkada Series (abstract); acrylic on paper, sgn/dtd 1980-81/titled, 30x22", SBY 11/11/88 ... 6,600
Infinity Field, Lefkada Series (abstract); acrylic on paper, sgn/dtd 1975, 30x22", SBY 10/5/89 ... 4,400
Infinity Field, Lefkada Series (abstract); acrylic on paper, 30x22", SBY 10/5/88 ... 1,540
Infinity Field, Lefkada Series (abstract); acrylic on paper, sgn/dtd 1980, 23x30", SBY 5/3/89 ... 6,050
Infinity Field, Lefkada Series (abstract); pastel/watercolor/gouache on paper, sgn/dtd 1969, 31x22", SBY 10/5/88 ... 2,310
Infinity Field, Lefkada Series (abstract); watercolor/gouache on paper, 30x22", SBY 10/5/88 ... 2,200
Infinity Field, Lefkada Series #1; acrylic on canvas, sgn/dtd 1977/titled, unfr, 72x56", C-NY 11/10/88 ... 33,000
Infinity Field, Lefkada Series #2 (abstract); acrylic on paper, sgn/dtd 1975, 30x22", C-NY 5/4/89 ... 3,850
Infinity Field, Lefkada Series for CD Friedrich (abstract); acrylic on paper, sgn/dtd 1980, 20x23", SBY 2/19/88 ... 6,875
Infinity Field, Lefkada Series for CD Friedrich (abstract); acrylic on canvas, sgn/dtd 1980, unfr, 68x46", C-NY 5/4/88 ... 20,900
Infinity Field, Lefkada Series for CD Friedrich (abstract); oil on canvas, sgn/dtd 1980, 66x40", SBY 2/15/89 ... 14,300
Infinity Field, Lefkada Series III (abstract); acrylic on canvas, sgn/dtd 1978, 56x52", SBY 10/8/88 ... 16,500
Infinity Field, Lefkada Series IX (abstract); acrylic on canvas, sgn/dtd 1978, 77x68", SBY 10/5/89 ... 9,900
Infinity Field, Olympia (abstract); acrylic on canvas, sgn/dtd 1970, 56x79", SBY 2/15/89 ... 13,200
Infinity Field, Olympia III; acrylic on paper, sgn/dtd 1971/titled, 30x22", C-E 5/9/89 OE ... 3,080
Infinity Field, Series #2 (abstract); acrylic on canvas, sgn/dtd twice 1975, 30x48", SBY 5/3/88 ... 17,600
Jewel of Memory, oil on masonite, twice sgn/dtd 47, 24x30", C-NY 11/10/88 OE ... 35,200
Levant #1 (abstract), oil on canvas, sgn twice/dtd 1960, 42x58", SBY 10/8/88 ... 49,500
Low White Sun (abstract), oil on canvas, sgn/dtd 1962, 56x52", SBY 2/15/89 ... 35,200
Oriental Beggar (abstract), oil on masonite, sgn, ca 1948, 30x24", SBY 10/5/89 ... 22,000
Sentinel (abstract), acrylic on canvas, sgn/inscr/dtd 1962, 68x60", C-NY 11/9/88 ... 143,000
Soundings #4 (abstract), oil on canvas, sgn twice/dtd 1964, 48x36", SBY 10/8/88 OE ... 110,000
Southold (abstract), oil on masonite, sgn/dtd 1948, 6x24", SBY 2/19/88 UE ... 3,575
Sun Games (abstract), acrylic/oil on canvas, sgn/dtd 1956-79, unfr, 71x66", C-NY 5/3/89 ... 110,000
Sun in the Vine, oil on canvas laid down on masonite, sgn/initialed/dtd 1950, 24x8", C-E 11/14/88 ... 4,620
Tundra Light, oil on canvas, sgn twice/dtd 1966, 48x72", SBY 10/8/88 ... 15,400
Untitled, oil on canvas, sgn/dtd March 24, 1959, 8x12", SBY 10/7/89 ... 3,300
Untitled (abstract), mixed media on board, sgn/dtd 49, 13x8", PHL 11/15/88 ... 3,500
Untitled (abstract), oil on masonite, sgn/dtd NYC 47, 24x11", SBY 10/5/89 ... 12,100
Untitled (abstract), oil on masonite, sgn/dtd 1947, 11x18", SBY 10/5/89 OE ... 12,100
Untitled (abstract), watercolor/ink/oil on linen, sgn/dtd 47, 8x11", SBY 2/14/89 OE ... 2,200
Untitled (contemporary), acrylic on paper, sgn/dtd 1972, 30x22", C-E 5/9/89 OE ... 2,640
Untitled (contemporary), gouache on paper, sgn/dtd Christmas 1980, 8x7", C-E 5/9/89 ... 1,210
White Spring #1 (abstract), oil on canvas, sgn twice/dtd 1936-4/titled, 60x44", SBY 2/19/88 OE ... 192,500
Yord (abstract), oil on canvas, sgn, 1955, 68x60", SBY 11/11/88 ... 60,500

STAMPER, James William (British, 1873-)
Still Life of Fruit & Wine Bottle, oil on canvas, sgn, 18x24", LH 12/4/88 ... 1,200

STANDISH, Frank B. (American, 1860-1944)
Summer Village Scene, oil on canvas, sgn, 16x20", B/B 10/6/88 ... 2,090

STANE, S. (American, 20th C)
Abstract Composition, oil on canvas, sgn/dtd 59, 32x29", FAP 4/15/89 ... 165

STANFIELD, Clarkson; att (British, 19th C)
Mist Off the Coast, oil on panel, 12x16", C-E 11/8/88 UE ... 520

STANFIELD, Clarkson; circle of (British, 19th C)
Shipping Off a Harbor (sailing ships near a harbor in rough seas), oil on canvas, 20x30", PHL 10/28/88 ... 1,600

STANFIELD, George Clarkson (British, 1828-1878)
Fishermen Launching Their Boat Out Into Bay, oil on canvas, sgn/dtd, 34x48", DM 2/19/88 ... 4,250

STANFIELD, William Clarkson (British, 1793-1867)
Ship Amid Active Sea, oil on board, sgn, 7x10", FAP 4/15/89 ... 550
Ship in High Sea, oil on board, sgn, 7x10", FAP 4/15/89 ... 742

STANFIELD, William Clarkson; att (British, 1793-1867)
Ben Lomond, oil on board, inscr, 6x9", C-E 5/23/88 ... 880

STANI, G. (Italian, 20th C)
Venice, watercolor, sgn, 7x5", FAP 12/8/89 ... 150

STANIFORD, Lydia S. (American, ca 1830-)
Full Bowl: Theorem Painting Still Life with Sheaves of Wheat; watercolor/mica on paper, 17x15", SBY 1/28/88 OE ... 11,550

STANLEY, Dorothy Tennant (British, 1855-1926)
Seated Nude, oil on panel, sgn/dtd 1885, 8x6", FB 10/30/89 ... 1,100

STANNARD, George Henry; circle of
Still Life of Grapes, Pineapple, & Peaches; oil on panel, 17x17", C-E 6/28/88 ... 1,540

STANNARD, Henry (British, 1844-1920)
Old Homestead, watercolor, sgn twice/inscr, 10x14", C-NY 5/25/88 ... 4,620
Shepherd with His Flock in a Field, watercolor, sgn, 13x19", PHL 10/28/88 ... 850

STANNARD, Henry Sylvester (British, 1870-1951)
Evening at the Old Mill, watercolor/gouache, sgn, 10x14", C-E 10/26/89 ... 3,300
Figures in an Extensive English Landscape, watercolor/gouache, sgn/dtd 08, 13x19", C-NY 2/23/89 ... 1,870
Old England in May, watercolor, sgn, 10x14", FB 10/30/89 OE ... 3,850
Shepherd & His Flock, watercolor on paper, sgn, 14x20", C-E 5/23/88 ... 660
Woodland Pond, watercolor, sgn, 11x15", FB 10/30/89 ... 1,980

ANNARD, Lillian (British, 1844-)
Brick-Walled Garden in Summer, watercolor, sgn, 20x14", C-NY 5/25/88 880
ANNARD, Sylvester Theresa (British, 1898-1947)
In Granny's Garden, watercolor/gouache, sgn/inscr/dtd 07, 15x10", C-NY 2/25/88 1,870
Pussy's Teatime, watercolor heightened w/gouache, sgn/inscr, 15x11", C-NY 2/25/88 1,870
Road Through an English Village in Summer, watercolor heightened w/white, sgn, 11x15", C-NY 10/26/88 1,100
ANNUS, Anthony (British, 19th C)
Castle of San Juan de Uloa-Reinforcements Entering Varacruz; watercolor/pencil on JW, ca 1838, 10x14", C-NY 11/12/88 2,420
ANTON, Gideon T. (American, 1885-)
Pasteur, oil on board, sgn, 12x16", MG 5/28/88 275
Teche River Packet, oil on canvas, sgn, 28x34", NA 10/1/88 900
ANTON, John Aloysius (American, 1857-1929)
Lower Reaches of the Thames, oil on canvas, sgn, 14x22", B/B 10/6/88 990
ANZIONE, Massimo; circle of (Italian, 1585-1656)
Cleopatra (portrait), oil on canvas, 46x35", SBY 12/9/88 2,200
ANZIONE, Massimo; manner of (Italian, 1585-1656)
Poultry Seller, oil on canvas, 41x54", C-NY 10/12/89 8,800
APLES, William L. (American, 19th/20th C)
Heavy Traffic (four large ships), oil on canvas, sgn/dtd 1908, 22x36", RAB 3/14/89 UE 400
APPERS, Julien (Belgian, 19th C)
Mimosa & Violets in Vases on a Lace Tablecloth, oil on canvas, sgn, 24x30", C-E 10/26/89 2,750
Oriental Still Life, oil on canvas, sgn, 40x32", C-E 10/26/89 4,400
APRANS, Raimonds (American, 1926-)
Abstract Composition, oil on canvas, sgn/dtd 67, 22x25", B/B 5/17/89 UE 467
ARACE, Girolamo
Miracle at Foggia: Assumption & Coronation of Saint Luke's Portrait of the Virgin, oil on canvas, 40x30", C-NY 10/12/89 5,500
ARK, Jack Gage (American, 1882-1950)
Malaga, oil on panel, 7x9", B/B 10/6/88 358
ARK, James (British, 1794-1859)
Fishing Lake, oil on panel, 7x9", FB 4/25/88 750
ARK, James; att (British, 1794-1859)
On the River Yare, oil on panel, 23x35", SBY 10/13/89 8,250
ARK, Larry (American, 20th C)
Official Government Photography Area, acrylic on canvas, 46x66", SBY 2/14/89 550
ARK, Otto (American, 1859-1926)
Cabbage Planter (full-length), oil on canvas, sgn, 24x18", SBY 6/28/89 OE 17,600
ARKEY, George (19th C)
Fishing Off a Stream, oil on canvas, sgn/dtd 1883, 25x20", C-E 5/23/88 1,320
ARKWEATHER, William Howard Bloomfield (1879-1969)
Pair: Calm & Rough Seascapes; oil on board, sgn, 12x16", C-E 11/30/88 1,540
Pair: Hills at Oneonta; Orchard Shadows; oil on canvas, sgn twice/dtd 1933, 18x24", SBY 9/23/88 1,540
ARRETT, Paul (American, 1896-1974)
Cottages in a Winter Landscape, watercolor on paper, sgn, 14x17", SBY 3/17/88 1,650
ASCHUS, Daniel
Boats at Dock, oil on canvas, sgn, 25x30", C-NY 5/25/88 UE 770
AUDER, Karl (18th C)
Portrait of Young Man, half-length, wearing orange coat w/embroidery; oil on canvas, sgn/dtd 1726, 33x24", C-NY 4/6/89 3,300
AUNTON, Phineas Jr. (American, 1817-1867)
Pair: Portraits; oil on canvas, 1 sgn, 30x25", SBY 9/14/89 1,100
AVROWSKY, Oleg (American, 20th C)
Battle for the Harem, acrylic on canvas, sgn/dtd 72, 48x34", B/B 9/15/88 1,100
EARNS, Junius Brutus (American, 1810-1885)
Picker (two men in interior, one studying a portrait), oil on board, initialed, 10x8", C-NY 9/30/88 2,200
EBBINGS, H. (British, 19th C)
Shipwreck (English coastal scene), oil on canvas, sgn, 27x42", RAB 6/27/89 400
EELE, Edwin (British, 19th C)
Still Life, Tazza of Fruit, Apples, Grapes, & Pears; oil on canvas, sgn, 16x10", NA 2/6/88 550
Still Life of Flowers on a Ledge, oil on canvas, sgn/dtd 1893, 22x17", MAG 4/24/88 500
Still Life of Fruit, oil on panel, sgn, 10x18", LH 5/15/88 800
Still Life of Tulips, Lilies, & Fruit; oil on canvas, sgn/dtd 1894, 24x20", RWS 5/12/89 1,200
Thames at Marlowe, oil on canvas, sgn, 13x24", WAD 6/6/88 2,200
EELE, Theodore Clement (American, 1847-1926)
Autumn in the Woods, oil on canvas, sgn/dtd 1914, 22x27", SBY 9/14/89 3,850
Autumn Landscape, oil on canvas, sgn/dtd 1914, 40x58", SBY 3/17/88 OE 18,700
Early Spring, oil on canvas, sgn/dtd 1916, 30x40", C-E 10/18/89 OE 12,100
From the Hillside, oil on canvas, sgn/dtd 1914, 30x40", C-NY 9/30/88 7,150
EELINK, Willem (Dutch, 1826-1913)
Sheep Grazing, watercolor w/gouache, sgn, 12x21", C-E 2/21/89 1,320
Sheep Grazing in a Meadow, watercolor heightened w/white, sgn/dtd 862, 15x25", C-NY 2/25/88 880
EELL, Gourlay (British, 1819-94)
Lord Strathnairm's Arab, Charger; oil on board, sgn, 40x45", SBY 6/10/88 OE 33,000

STEEN, Jan (Dutch, 1623-1679)
Family Saying Grace in an Interior, oil on panel, sgn/inscr, unfr, 19x17", C-NY 1/15/88 OE **330,000**
Figures in an Interior with a Man & Woman Seated at Table Playing Cards, oil on panel, sgn, 19x24", SBY 6/2/89 OE **2,970,000**
Satyr & the Family, oil on canvas, sgn, 18x21", C-NY 1/15/88 .... **74,800**

STEEN, Jan; after (Dutch, 1623-1679)
Dutch Cavalier at His Desk, oil on canvas, 24x18", B/B 1/11/89 OE **825**

STEEN, Jan; att (Dutch, 1623-1679)
Children Teasing a Cat & Dog, oil on canvas, indistinctly sgn, 22x18", C-NY 1/15/88 OE **18,150**
Marriage of Tobias & Sarah, oil on canvas, bears monogram, 46x69", SBY 1/11/89 .... **16,500**

STEEN, Jan; manner of (Dutch, 1623-1679)
Profession of Affection, oil on panel, 11x9", SBY 12/9/88 .... **1,100**

STEENS, D.
Pair: Four Elements; oil on canvas, 1 sgn, unfr, 35x49", C-NY 4/6/89 .... **4,400**

STEER, Philip Wilson (British, 1860-1942)
Ocean View (seascape), watercolor, sgn/dtd 1929, 7x10", C-E 2/21/89 .... **660**
Stranded Barges, Maldon; watercolor, sgn/dtd 1933, 9x12", C-E 10/25/88 .... **660**

STEFAN, Ross (American, 1934-)
Awaiting the Dummers, Taos (group of Indians); acrylic on cavas, sgn, 29x36", SBY 6/28/89 .... **4,675**
I Wonder As I Wander (figure on horse leading a pack horse), oil on canvas, sgn/#d 37-B, 28x36", SBY 9/14/89 .... **2,750**
Lunch Time (figures around a campfire w/wagon & horses), oil on canvas, sgn, 34x34", SBY 1/24/89 .... **2,475**
Morning Sunlight-San Ildefonso; oil on canvas, sgn/#d 44, 36x28", SBY 9/14/89 .... **3,080**
San Ysidro Fiesta, Taos (Indians); acrylic on canvas, sgn/titled, 30x24", SBY 6/28/89 .... **2,310**
Whispers of the Past, acrylic on canvas, sgn, 12x16", SBY 6/28/89 UE **1,320**

STEFANOFF, Christof (Canadian, 1898-1966)
Cabins in Winter, oil on board, sgn/dtd 54, 24x36", WAD 11/30/89 .... **600**
Tournesol (still life w/sunflowers, books, & brushes), oil on canvas, sgn/dated 1957, 30x24", FB 4/25/88 .... **1,900**

STEICHEN, Edward (American, 1879-1973)
Gibson Girl in a Rowboat, watercolor, sgn/dtd 98, S/A 3/12/88 .... **650**
Landscape with Water, watercolor, sgn, 5x6", S/A 3/12/88 .... **350**
Self-Portrait, oil on canvas, sgn/dtd 97, 30x21", S/A 3/12/88 .... **1,500**

STEIN, Georges (French, 1870-)
Evening on a Parisian Boulevard, gouache over black chalk on paper, sgn/inscr, 15x20", C-NY 5/24/89 .... **9,900**
Figures on a Parisian Boulevard, Arc de Triomphe in the Distance; watercolor, sgn/indistinctly dtd, 9x13", C-NY 10/25/89 .... **2,860**
Flower Market Along the Seine, oil on canvas, sgn, unfr, 18x22", C-NY 10/25/89 .... **13,200**
La Place de la Madelaine, oil on canvas, sgn, 15x22", SBY 7/12/89 .... **8,800**
On the Boulevard, watercolor over pencil on paper, sgn/inscr, 12x9", C-NY 5/24/89 .... **1,650**

STEIN, Janos (Hungarian, 1874-1944)
Reclining Nude, oil on canvasboard, sgn, 8x10", B/B 5/17/89 UE **330**

STEINBERG, Edward (Russian, 1937-)
Composition II: October (abstract); oil on canvas, initialed/dtd 1987, 47x47", SBY 7/7/88 OE **14,000**
Composition III: October (abstract); oil on canvas, initialed/dtd 1987, 47x47", SBY 7/7/88 OE **13,000**
Composition: November (abstract); oil on canvas, sgn twice/dtd 1987/inscr, 47x47", SBY 7/7/88 OE **17,000**
Composition: October-November (abstract); oil on canvas, initialed/dtd 1987, 47x47", SBY 7/7/88 OE **44,000**

STEINBERG, Saul (American, 1914-)
Album, pen/ink/watercolor/rubber stamps/graphite/altered photo on board, sgn/dtd 1953 & 1958, 19x23", C-NY 2/14/89 .... **22,000**
Artist & Invented Landscape #49, pen/black ink/crayon/paper collage on paper, sgn/dtd 1965-66, 23x29", C-NY 5/4/89 .... **24,200**
Bicyclist/Gendarme, ink/crayon/watercolor on paper, sgn, ca 1948-50, 15x23", SBY 2/15/89 OE **15,400**
Bridge, pen/black ink on paper, sgn/dtd 1953, 23x29", C-NY 5/4/88 .... **9,350**
Camp I, pen/rubber stamps w/black ink/colored chalks on paper mounted on panel, sgn/dtd 1969, 41x28", C-NY 5/4/89 .... **11,000**
Chess Game, ink/pencil/crayon/watercolor on paper, sgn/dtd 1968, 29x23", SBY 10/8/88 .... **16,500**
Classical Study, pen/black ink/crayon on paper, sgn/dtd 68, 22x30", C-NY 2/14/89 .... **11,000**
Computers at MIT (abstract), pen/ink on paper, sgn, 14x22", SBY 5/3/88 .... **7,150**
Diploma, ink/watercolor/rubber stamp/paper collage, sgn, 15x23", SBY 10/5/89 .... **15,400**
Diploma, pen/ink/watercolor/crayon/postage stamps/paper seal on paper, sgn/dtd 1950, unfr, 15x23", C-NY 11/10/88 OE **18,700**
Double-Sided: Three Heads; Three Men Standing; pen/black ink/pencil on paper, sgn, 11x14", C-E 5/13/88 .... **1,210**
Double-Sided: Untitled (men composing music); pen/ink/stamp on sheet music, sgn/dtd 67, unfr, 19x13", C-NY 11/10/88 OE **9,900**
Explorer Table, mixed media, sgn/dtd 1981/titled, 28x23", SBY 11/11/88 OE **33,000**
False Front Culture, paper collage/watercolor/chalks/crayons/pen/ink on board, sgn/dtd 67, 22x28", C-NY 5/4/88 OE **13,200**
Group of 4: First Class; Second Class; Third Class; Fourth Class; colored pencil/pencil on paper, S-15x23", SBY 11/11/88 .... **49,500**
Happy Birthday to Moncha, rubber stamps/pen/black ink on paper, sgn/inscr/dtd 1951, 11x14", C-E 5/13/88 .... **825**
Hard-Edge Artist, ink/pastel/oil/rubber stamp on paper, 20x29", SBY 5/3/88 .... **13,200**
Illustration of the Lamp, pen/black ink on paper, 11x8", C-E 2/16/88 UE **33**
Indians & Bicycle (contemporary), ink/rubber stamp on paper, sgn/dtd 1968, 23x29", SBY 2/15/89 .... **11,000**
Interior (menu drawing), ink on paper, sgn, 8x16", NA 11/5/88 .... **450**
I1 Gabinetto del Proprio Niente, mixed media, sgn/dtd 1966, 29x23", C-NY 10/4/89 .... **26,400**
Kampala, oil/watercolor on paper, sgn/dtd 1972, 30x20", C-NY 5/4/88 OE **19,800**
Ladies on Horses (caricature drawing), ink on paper, sgn, ca 1965, 15x23", SBY 11/11/88 .... **9,900**
Landscape with Document, watercolor/ink/rubber stamp/label on paper, sgn/dtd 1976, 30x20", SBY 11/9/89 .... **19,800**
Man Writing, pen/brown ink on paper, sgn/dtd 64, 14x21", SBY 10/7/89 .... **8,250**
Manassas, Virginia, Main Street; colored pencil/pencil on paper, sgn/dtd 1978, 29x23", SBY 11/11/88 .... **24,200**
March-April V, watercolor/gouache/crayon/pen/ink/graphite on paper, sgn/dtd 1965, 23x15", C-NY 11/10/88 OE **17,600**

March-April VI (contemporary), colored crayons/pencil on paper, initialed/sgn/inscr/dtd twice 1965, 23x14", SBY 10/8/88 4,950
Mason (figure w/Masonic symbols), crayon/graphite/ink on paper, sgn, ca 1955, 14x17", SBY 5/2/88 OE 14,300
Mestre #45, ink/gouache/rubber stamp on paper, sgn/dtd 1969, 23x29", SBY 2/15/89 UE 17,600
Milano Table, painted wood/foil/rubber stamp on wood, sgn/dtd 1973, 23x28", SBY 5/3/89 44,000
Monte Carlo (fantasy depiction), gouache/pencil/collage on paper, sgn/dtd 1951, 12x15", SBY 5/3/89 17,600
Napeague, the Fish Factory; watercolor/black ink/rubber stamp on paper, sgn/dtd 1969, 18x24", SBY 2/15/89 UE 16,000
New Yorker Air Mail, ink/crayon/pencil/paper collage/rubber stamp on paper, sgn, 23x29", SBY 11/9/89 30,800
Nice (contemporary view), black ink/watercolor on paper, sgn/dtd 1952/titled, 15x22", SBY 11/11/88 19,800
Nose Still Life (contemporary), watercolor/colored pencil/ink/rubber stamp on paper, sgn/dtd 78, 20x29", SBY 11/11/88 OE 41,250
Paper Palette Table, painted wood/pencils/rubber stamp/ink/acrylic/paper collage on wood, sgn, 1973, 23x28", SBY 5/3/89 33,000
Politecnico Table, watercolor/ink/rubber stamps/painted objects on wood/metal collage, sgn/dtd 1974, 28x23", SBY 10/5/89 38,500
Red Lining Table, mixed media, sgn/dtd 1980, 24x18", C-NY 10/4/89 27,500
Self-Portrait (abstract), ink on paper, sgn/dtd 1946, 12x10", SBY 2/15/89 OE 8,250
Table Series: Diary; mixed media, sgn/dtd 1972, 20x26", SBY 10/5/89 27,500
Tree Nine Variations No 6, lithograph/watercolor/crayon/ink/collage/rubber stamps, 22x29", C-NY 2/14/89 7,150
Two Eastern Sunsets, watercolor/rubber stamp on paper, sgn/dtd 1973, 30x20", SBY 5/3/89 22,000
Untitled, paper collage/crayons/gouache/oil/silver paint/pen/inks on board, sgn/dtd 1967, 30x24", lot 139, C-NY 5/4/88 24,200
Untitled (abstract), ink/rubber stamp/crayon on paper, sgn/dtd 68, 23x29", SBY 11/11/88 11,000
Untitled (man & woman seated in interior reading paper w/their dogs beside them), pen/ink, sgn, 1949, 10x8", SBY 11/9/89 3,850
Untitled (nude in interior w/cat & dog), pen/black ink on sheet music, sgn/dtd 48, unfr, 12x9", C-NY 11/10/88 OE 7,700
Upper Volta, oil/ink/rubber stamp/collage of wood & metal on wood, sgn/dtd 78, 21x16", SBY 5/3/88 18,700
View From 9th Avenue (contemporary depiction), colored pencil/crayon/watercolor, sgn/dtd 1976, 27x20", SBY 10/5/89 OE 110,000
Watercolor Pyramid (contemporary), watercolor/graphite/rubber stamp on paper, sgn/dtd 1972, 20x30", SBY 5/3/89 15,400

TEINER, Agnes (German, 1845-1925)
Floral Still Life, oil on canvas, sgn, 30x24", SBY 12/9/88 1,210

TEINER-PRAG, Hugo
Der Tannenbaum, pen/brush/black ink heightened w/white on light tan paper, sgn/inscr/dtd 1905, unfr, 6x5", C-NY 2/25/88 660

TEINLEN, Theophile (Swiss, 1859-1933)
Etudes de Femme Debout (two women standing), charcoal on paper, atelier stamp, 26x20", C-NY 10/6/88 2,310
Figure Study of Two Female Nudes, charcoal, estate stamp, 15x10", NA 2/6/88 500
Le Peintre a Son Chevalet (the painter at his easel), oil on canvas laid down on board, sgn, 12x7", C-E 11/17/88 3,080
Pair: Jeune Fille Ecrivant; L'Arbre; pen/ink/pencil on paper, 1 initialed, 6x7", 11x9", C-E 11/17/88 660
Seated Nude, watercolor heightened w/white chalk on board, sgn/dtd Paris 1921, 27x21", C-E 11/17/88 2,090
Set of 3: Mother & Baby; Young Girl; Portrait of a Woman; pen/brown ink, initialed, 11x8" & smaller, C-E 11/17/88 880
Three Studies of a Seated Woman, pencil on paper, bears signature, 21x13", C-E 7/26/88 UE 320

TEIR, Pat (American, 1940-)
Black Drawing, gouache/colored crayons/black & white chalks on paper, dtd 1977, 26x40", C-E 11/17/88 2,750
Moon & the Wave: Courbet's Moon; oil on canvas, 1986-87, 86" dia, SBY 2/15/89 33,000

TELLA, Frank (American, 1935-)
#17 Janow Sokolski (contemporary), mixed media on wood, sgn/titled, 1972, 84x108", SBY 11/9/89 148,500
Bermuda Petrel (abstract), silkscreen/acrylic/colored oil stick on Tycore panel, 1980, 60x84", SBY 5/2/88 OE 44,000
Corona del Mar, marker on graph paper, sgn/dtd 69, 21x30", SBY 10/8/88 9,900
Damascus Gate Variation II (geometric composition), polymer/fluorescent polymer on canvas, 1969, 60x240", C-NY 11/7/89 605,000
Hiraqla III, flourescent acrylic on canvas, 1968, 120x240", SBY 11/10/88 OE 467,500
Kufa Gate 111-B (abstract), fluorescent acrylic on canvas, sgn/dtd 68, 60x60", SBY 10/8/88 110,000
Mitered Squares (geometric composition), alkyd on canvas, 1968, unfr, 69x138", C-NY 11/7/89 OE 660,000
Narowla (sketch), acrylic/fabric collage on printed paperboard, sgn/dtd 73, 33x30", SBY 2/15/89 OE 34,100
Narowla (sketch), felt/fabric collage with paint on board, sgn/dtd 72/titled, 33x30", SBY 5/3/88 OE 26,400
Nasielk (sketch), acrylic/oil stick/fabric/paper collage on printed paperboard, sgn/dtd 73, 32x27", SBY 2/15/89 OE 30,250
Newport Beach (abstract), acrylic/colored felt-tip pens/collage/graphite on paper, sgn/dtd 67, 24x39", C-NY 5/4/89 OE 50,600
Parzeczew (contemporary), fabric collage/gouache on paperboard, sgn/dtd 1972, 36x30", SBY 11/9/89 44,000
Polar Co-Ordinates, screenprint/offset lithograph/acrylic/oil stick/paint on paper, sgn/dtd 80, 38x38", SBY 5/3/89 OE 46,750
Polar Co-Ordinates, screenprint/offset litho/acrylic/oil stick on paper, sgn/dtd 1980, 38x38", SBY 11/11/88 OE 38,500
Protractor Variation (contemporary), acrylic on canvas, 1969, 120x120", SBY 11/10/88 OE 352,000
Protractor Variation X (abstract), fluorescent polymer on canvas, sgn/dtd 68/titled, 60x120", SBY 11/10/88 OE 308,000
Quathlamba (from Notched V series), metallic powder in polymer emulsion on canvas, 1964, 78x179", SBY 5/2/89 1,320,000
Sacramento Mall Proposal #2 (square composition), acrylic on canvas, 1978, 105x105", SBY 5/2/88 OE 264,000
Sinjerli III (composition), polymer/flourescent polymer on canvas, 1967, 120" dia, SBY 11/8/89 418,000
Tahk-I-Sulayman III (geometric composition), fluorescent alkyd on canvas, 1967, 120x240", SBY 5/2/89 330,000
Tomlinson Court Park, Second Version (rectangles within rectangles); black enamel on canvas, 84x109", SBY 11/8/89 OE 5,060,000
Untitled (contemporary composition), acrylic on canvas, sgn/dtd 68, 60x60", SBY 11/9/89 154,000
Untitled (contemporary lineation), aluminum paint on canvas, 1962, 9x9", SBY 11/9/89 154,000
Untitled (geometric abstract), mixed media on graph paper, initialed/dtd 66, 17x22", SBY 2/19/88 7,150
Untitled (geometric composition), acrylic on canvas, sgn/dtd 68, unfr, 85x85", C-NY 5/3/89 OE 187,000
Untitled (geometric composition), crayon on graph paper, sgn, ca 1971, 17x22", SBY 5/3/89 OE 60,500
Wake Island Rail (contemporary), acrylic/pastel/glitter on tycore, 1977, 18x23x4", SBY 11/9/89 OE 154,000

TELLA, Frank; after (American, 1935-)
Sinjerli II (wool tapestry), sgn on label, 119" dia, C-E 11/14/89 OE 12,100

TELLA, Ignaz; see Stern, Ignaz

TELLA, Jacques; see De Stella

TELLA, Joseph (American, 1877-1946)
Abstract Green Form, oil on canvas, sgn/inscr, 13x13", C-NY 5/26/88 9,350

Abstraction, crayon/pencil/silverpoint on paper, 13x10", C-NY 9/28/89 2,200
Amazon (woman's head in profile, landscape beyond), oil on canvas, sgn, 1924, 27x22", SBY 4/29/88 OE 23,100
Arrangement with Gladiolas & Birds, crayon/pencil on paper, sgn/dtd 1944, C-NY 3/11/88 8,800
In the Forest, charcoal/pastel on paper, sgn/dtd 1944, 18x24", SBY 6/28/89 3,300
Italian Immigrant (incomplete portrait), pencil/red chalk on paper, sgn/dtd 1898, 9x8", SBY 3/17/88 OE 4,675
Landscape (contemporary), oil on canvas, ca 1928-30, 16x25", SBY 5/24/89 OE 63,250
Landscape III, 1937; pastel on paper, sgn, 18x25", C-NY 5/26/88 3,300
Lettuce & Lemons (still life), pencil/colored pencils on paper, sgn/dtd 1944, 12x17", SBY 1/24/89 OE 17,600
Man Wearing a Black Hat, black/colored crayon on paper, sgn, 7x5", C-E 3/22/88 UE 132
Nocturne (village at night, mountain beyond), oil on canvas, sgn, 15x19", SBY 4/14/89 OE 12,100
Pink Rose, pencil/colored pencil on paper, 19x12", C-NY 5/26/88 6,600
Recollections (seated man wearing a cloak, holding a hat), oil on canvas, sgn/titled, 17x13", SBY 3/17/88 OE 5,775
Rose, Dogwood, & Dandelion; silverpoint/colored pencil on prepared paper, sgn, 15x13", C-NY 5/26/88 OE 14,300
Sleeping Dogs, pencil/crayon/watercolor on paper, sgn, 12x14", C-E 2/1/89 OE 4,180
Sleeping Woman, pencil on brown paper, sgn, 9x6", C-E 2/1/89 1,210
Sparrows, colored pencil/charcoal on paper, sgn/dtd 1919, 14x10", SBY 5/25/88 12,100
Still Life of Bird (w/other objects), oil on canvas, sgn, 16x12", SBY 16x12", SBY 6/28/89 OE 7,425
Still Life of Chrysanthemums & Goldfish, oil on canvas, sgn, 24x20", C-NY 9/28/89 2,750
Still Life of Fruit, colored pencil on paper, sgn/dtd 1944, 14x11", C-NY 9/30/88 1,870
Study of a Man, charcoal on paper, sgn/dtd 1920, 24x19", SBY 9/14/89 4,125
Study of a Man in Fedora, colored pencil on brown paper, sgn, ca 1914, 7x4", C-E 2/16/88 308

STENBERRY, Algot (American, 1902-)

Midsummer, Central Park; oil on canvas, sgn/dtd 1935, 24x30", SBY 9/23/88 2,090

STEPANOVA, Varvara (Russian, 1894-1958)

Fabric Design (contemporary), gouache on paper, atelier mark, ca 1924, 11x7", SBY 7/7/88 OE 13,000
Fabric Design (contemporary), gouache on 3 sheets of paper, stamped signature/atelier mark, ca 1924, 8x11", SBY 7/7/88 9,000
Landscape (naturalistic), oil on board, sgn/dtd 40/atelier mark, 22x28", SBY 7/7/88 OE 16,000
Photomontage, collage on paper, ca 1930, 14x11", C-L 10/8/88 OE 20,450
Photomontage 26, collage on paper, ca 1930, 13x8", C-L 10/8/88 OE 24,170
Two Figures (abstract), oil on canvas, sgn/dtd 1921/#d 27, 28x22", SBY 7/7/88 OE 150,000

STEPHAN, A. (Dutch, 19th/20th C)

Untitled, interior w/figures gathered in front of hearth; oil on canvas, sgn, 29x38", SLK 4/7/89 1,750

STEPHAN, Gary (American, 20th C)

He Was Transfigured (abstract), oil on canvas, sgn/dtd 1977, 80x60", SBY 10/8/88 11,000
Le Balcon, acrylic on jute, initialed/dtd 74, unfr, 63x52", C-NY 5/4/89 4,180
Pink (abstract), acrylic on shaped burlap, unfr, 69x98", C-NY 2/20/88 1,100
Schools (abstract), acrylic on canvas, sgn/dtd 1981, unfr, 96x64", C-NY 10/4/89 8,800
Untitled (abstract composition), acrylic on canvas, sgn/dtd 1985, unfr, 32x20", C-E 11/14/89 OE 4,950

STEPHAN, John (20th C)

Disc No 3, acrylic on canvas, sgn/dtd 1972, 54x52", LH 10/16/88 UE 50

STEPHEN, Laurence Lowry; after

Figures on the Steps of a House, watercolor on paper, bears signature, 9x6", C-E 2/16/88 44

STEPPE, Romain (Belgian, 1859-1927)

Boats Along a Canal, oil on canvas, sgn, 40x47", B/B 6/15/89 2,200
Sailing Ships on Choppy Seas, oil on canvas, sgn, 24x33", WD 3/23/88 800

STERN, Bernard (American, 20th C)

Fruit Crates, oil on canvas, 1972, 72x72", SBY 10/8/88 OE 26,400
Summer in Washington Square, New York City (abstract); oil on canvas, sgn/dtd 1981, 72x72", SBY 10/8/88 16,500
Sunday in Central Park (contemporary), oil on canvas, 1979-80, 72x72", SBY 2/19/88 OE 25,300
Tourism in Japan (contemporary), oil on canvas, sgn/dtd 82, 64x51", SBY 2/15/89 14,300

STERN, Ignaz (Stella)(German, 1680-1748)

Allegory of Spring, oil on canvas, indistinctly sgn, 59x41", C-NY 1/11/89 44,000
Triumph of Venus: Venus on Chariot Drawn by Putti & Young Satyrs, oil on copper, 10x14", C-M 12/3/88 14,856

STERN, Max (German, 1872-1943)

Fishermen Pulling in the Net, oil on canvas, sgn, 21x19", SBY 10/7/89 3,300

STERNE, Hedda (Romanian, 1916-)

On the Beach, tempera on board, sgn/dtd 1941, 20x24", SBY 10/5/88 880

STERNE, Maurice (American, 1877-1957)

Bali Woman (seated semi-nude), pastel/pencil on paper, sgn, 18x14", SBY 6/28/89 OE 1,870
Balinese Landscape, oil on canvas laid down on masonite, estate stamp, 13x17", SBY 3/17/88 1,320
Eggs, oil on paper, bears estate stamp, 14x18", C-E 11/30/88 UE 550
Nude, ink on paper, sgn, 10x8", C-E 2/16/88 187
Portrait of a Woman, oil on canvas, sgn, 18x14", C-E 10/18/89 1,320
Seascape (waves washing over rocky coast), oil on masonite, sgn, 16x20", RAB 8/9/88 OE 1,600
Seated Nude, ink on paper, sgn, 10x8", lot 83, C-E 2/16/88 154
Seated Nude, ink on paper, sgn, 10x8", lot 84, C-E 2/16/88 176
Two Women, Benares (interior scene); oil on paper, sgn/dtd Benares 1912, 12x17", SBY 3/17/88 1,650

STERNER, Albert Edward (American, 1863-1946)

Accusation, pen/ink/ink wash/Chinese white on paper, sgn, 12x10", C-E 11/30/88 UE 330
Artist's Table (still life), oil on canvas, sgn/dtd 1934, 30x25", C-NY 9/28/89 2,750

Goldfish Bowl, oil on canvas, sgn/dtd 1919, 34x29", C-E 11/30/88 1,650
Portrait of a Woman (half-length, seated, wearing plaid dress), watercolor on paper, 14x12", RAB 8/9/88 UE 150
Portrait of a Woman (half-length), watercolor on paper, 14x12", RAB 8/9/88 UE 150
Portrait of Miss V Tilton in Evening Dress, oil, 87x45", WD 1/11/89 3,000
Removing Wounded From the Field (Civil War), pen/ink on paper, sgn/inscr, 16x21", C-E 5/27/88 495
Secrets, pastel/Chinese white/pencil on paper, 16x19", C-E 11/30/88 528
Woman in Red, pastel/pencil on paper, sgn/dtd 1925, 15x10", C-E 11/30/88 UE 308

TETSON, Charles Walter (American, 1858-1911)

Female Nude in an Arcadian Setting, watercolor on board, sgn/dtd 1910, 9x5", B/B 12/8/88 550
From My Window After Rain, Pasadena; oil on canvas, sgn/inscr twice, 20x24", C-NY 9/30/88 4,950
Portrait of a Young Woman (profile), oil on panel, monogramed, 11x8", RWS 9/29/88 500

TEVENS, Aime (Belgian, 1879-)

Au Cafe (man & woman seated at an outdoor cafe), oil on canvas, sgn, 39x48", SBY 2/22/89 41,250

TEVENS, Alfred (Belgian, 1823-1906)

Boating, oil on panel, sgn, 14x11", C-E 10/26/89 3,850

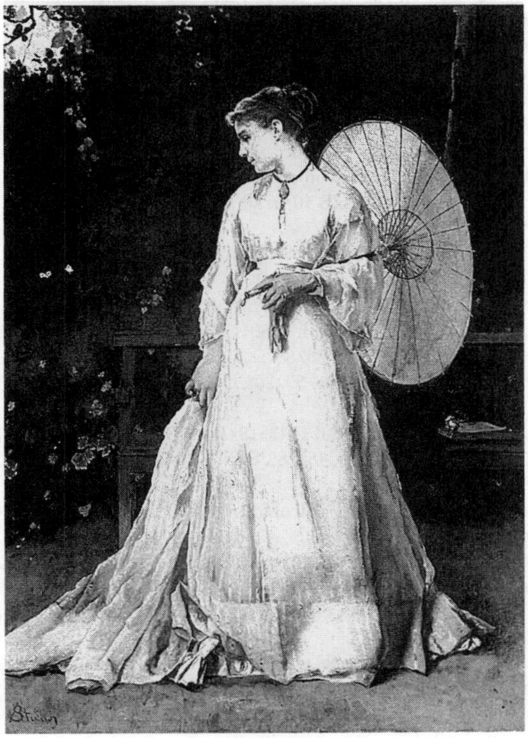

In the Country, oil on canvas, sgn, ca 1867, 31x22", C-NY 2/23/89 OE; $462,000

L'Amour et l'Hymenee, oil on panel, sgn, 42x24", SBY 10/24/89 28,600
La Boule de Verre, woman in garden glancing at convex mirror; oil on canvas, sgn, ca 1875, 37x26", SBY 10/24/89 286,000
La Femme au Bracelet (portrait), oil on panel, sgn w/monogram, 9x7", SBY 2/22/89 OE 38,500
Miser, charcoal, sgn/dtd 1871, 15x11", LH 10/16/88 200
Sailboats & Steamship, oil on panel, sgn, 14x11", RWS 5/12/89 OE 2,900

TEVENS, William Lester (American, 1888-1969)

Autumn Hills (farmhouse nestled in rolling hills), oil on masonite, sgn, 24x30", RWS 9/29/88 UE 750
Autumnal Landscape, New England; oil on canvas, sgn, 20x24", RWS 11/10/89 800
Barn in Distance, watercolor on paper, sgn, 16x22", C-E 6/1/88 660
Bay at North Head Grand Manan, oil on masonite, sgn, 34x38", RWS 11/10/89 1,400
Boats in a Harbor, oil on canvas, sgn, 25x30", SBY 9/23/88 2,200
By the Sea, oil on canvas, sgn, 25x30", WD 4/13/88 1,500
Farmhouse in Shade, Autumn; oil on canvas, sgn, 20x24", RWS 9/8/89 800
Hayfield (autumn landscape), oil on canvas, sgn, 24x30", RWS 9/8/89 2,800
Hilltops, Gloucester; oil on canvas, sgn, 36x32", SBY 9/23/88 7,700
Moore's Corner, N Leverett, Massachusetts (landscape); oil on board, sgn, 16x20", RWS 3/31/88 1,600
Ognuquit Harbor, oil on canvas laid down on masonite, sgn, 24x30", SBY 6/28/89 3,300
Old Mill, oil on canvas, sgn, 42x48", C-E 6/1/88 5,500
Path Through the Field, oil on canvas mounted on masonite, sgn, 12x14", RWS 9/8/89 425
Red Silo, oil on canvas, sgn, 30x36", RWS 11/3/88 2,500
Road into the Valley (landscape), watercolor on paper, sgn, 15x21", RWS 3/16/89 UE 375
Road to the Farm Valley, watercolor on paper, sgn, 18x22", RWS 5/12/89 500
Rockport Boatyard, watercolor on paper, sgn, 17x22", RWS 3/16/89 UE 350
Sailboats on a Woodland Lake, oil on canvas mounted on masonite, sgn, 24x30", RWS 5/12/89 2,300

White House with Chickens, oil on canvas, sgn, 18x22", RWS 5/19/88 2,400
Winter in New England (snowscape), oil on canvas, sgn/dtd 1921, 25x30", RWS 9/8/89 3,000
Winter in Vermont, oil on canvas, sgn, orig frame, 25x30", RAB 11/25/88 3,200
Winter Scene, Making Maple Syrup; oil on canvas, sgn, 30x36", RWS 5/19/88 UE 3,500
Woodland Clearing, Spring; oil on canvas, sgn, 33x39", RWS 5/19/88 7,000

STEWART, A.M. (British, 19th C)
French City on Market Day with Gothic Cathedral Tower in the Background, oil on canvas, sgn, 14x10", SLK 9/29/88 600

STEWART, B.P.
Making a Garland of Flowers, oil on panel, sgn, 20x16", C-E 10/25/88 1,650

STEWART, Charles Edward (British, fl 1890-1930)
Warm Day Out, oil on canvas, sgn, 15x21", C-E 2/23/88 2,750

STEWART, E. (British, 19th C)
Highland Reverie, oil on canvas, sgn, 42x56", SBY 7/12/89 3,300

STEWART, Elsie D. (20th C)
Sydney Skyline From Vaucluse, watercolor/pencil, sgn/dtd 1961/inscr, 11x15", C-SK 6/9/88 110

STEWART, Frank Algernon (British, 1877-1945)
Set of 4: Hunt Scenes; pencil/watercolor on paper, sgn, 9x28", SBY 6/9/89 17,600

STEWART, Julius (American, 1855-1919)
Casual Confidence (full-length portrait of lady seated), oil on canvas, 43x29", C-NY 5/25/89 UE 7,975
Lady on a Pink Divan, oil on canvas, sgn/dtd 1877, 20x25", SBY 5/25/88 23,100
Pink Sheet (full-length nude), oil on canvas, sgn/dtd 1907, 12x8", SBY 6/28/89 2,750
Portrait of a Young Woman (in profile), oil on panel, sgn, 24x18", SBY 1/24/89 OE 4,675

STICK, Frank (American, 1884-1966)
Big Catch (two men pulling large fish into boat), oil on canvas, sgn, 32x24", B/B 10/9/88 3,300
Stopping for a Drink, oil on canvas, sgn, 30x32", B/B 10/9/88 3,300

STICKS, George Blackie (British, 1843-1938)
Rocky Sea Coast, oil on canvas, sgn/dtd 1896, 25x50", NA 2/24/89 OE 2,200

STIEPEVICH, Vincent G. (Russian, 19th C)
Feeding the Pigeons, oil on canvas, sgn, 26x17", C-E 10/26/89 OE 19,800
Music in the Harem, oil on canvas, sgn, 20x30", RWS 4/7/89 3,900
Rooftop Repose, oil on canvas, sgn, 18x24", C-NY 2/25/88 2,860
Two Harem Beauties on a Rooftop, oil on canvas, sgn, 30x20", C-E 10/26/89 OE 18,700

STILL, Clyfford (American, 1904-)
Untitled (abstract composition), oil on paper, sgn/dtd 1943, 18x12", SBY 11/9/89 OE 82,500
Untitled (abstract nudes), oil on canvas, ca 1937-38, 48x38", SBY 11/9/89 OE 104,500

STILLMAN-MYERS, Joyce (American, 20th C)
Breakout (egg containers opened in box w/flowers), oil on canvas, sgn/dtd 1980, 53x72", C-E 11/14/89 OE 4,180

STILSON, William W. (American, 19th C)
Pair: Scenes From the Civil War; gouache on paper, sgn, 9x11, 11x9", B/B 4/20/88 770

STIMSON, John Ward (American, 1850-1930)
Male Nude, left hand on hip, right fist raised; black chalk on laid paper, sgn twice/inscr, 24x15", C-NY 5/25/88 550

STINSKI, Gerald (American, 1929-)
Apples & Glass, oil on board, sgn, 4x9", B/B 9/15/88 OE 2,200
Lemon with Knife, oil on panel, sgn, 7x13", B/B 9/15/88 OE 4,125
Tangerines, oil on canvasboard, sgn, 8x20", B/B 9/15/88 2,475

STOBWASSER, Gustav (German, 19th C)
Portrait of a Young Lady Holding Flowers, oil on canvas, sgn/dtd 1884, framed as oval, 24x25", WD 1/25/89 3,500

STOCK, Joseph Whiting (American, 1815-1855)
Portrait of Henry David Whitcomb (full-length), oil on canvas, dtd 1843, 50x38", RAB 7/12/88 31,000
Two Little Girls with Red Dresses & White Pantaloons, oil on canvas, 42x35", SBY 4/29/88 OE 85,250

STOCK, Joseph Whiting; att (American, 1815-1855)
Miniature Portrait of a Child with Toy Horse in a Landscape, watercolor on ivory, 4x3", RWS 10/27/89 OE 5,500

STODDARD, Alice Kent (American, 1893-1967)
Garden Path, oil on canvas, sgn, 30x36", SBY 6/28/89 17,600

STOILOFF, Constantin (Russian, 1850-1924)
Cossack Riding a Sleigh on a Snowy Path, oil on canvas, sgn, 20x33", C-E 10/25/88 1,760
Cossacks on the Charge, oil on panel, sgn, 12x19", C-E 10/25/88 2,750
Pair: Cossacks Charging; oil on board, sgn, 12x19", C-E 2/21/98 4,180

STOILOFF, Constantin; manner of (Russian, 1850-1924)
Pair: Cossacks in the Snow; oil on panel, bears signature, 6x13", C-E 6/28/88 UE 1,000

STOITZNER, Rudolph (Austrian, 1873-1933)
Still Life of Fruit, Flowers & a Nautilus Cup; oil on canvas, sgn, 39x28", WAD 6/6/88 2,400

STOJANOW, Constantine (Russian, 19th C)
Troika, oil on canvas, sgn, 13x21", C-E 10/25/88 1,210

STOJNOV, Joseph; att
Pair: Still Life of Tulips, Narcissi, Morning-Glory, Other Flowers on a Ledge; oil on panel, sgn, 15x15", C-NY 1/11/89 18,700

STOKES, Frank Wilbert (American, 1858-)
Tucker's Landing, Marblehead, Massachusetts; oil on academy board, initialed, 9x12", RWS 11/10/89 900

STOLL, J. (19th C)
Harvest Time, oil on canvas, sgn, 17x21", S/A 2/18/89 1,500

STOMER, Matthias; att (Flemish, 17th C)
Saint Jerome in His Study, oil on canvas, 36x52", C-NY 6/2/88 OE 30,800
Saint Paul (man writing at table), oil on canvas, 31x36", C-NY 4/6/89 OE 5,500
Young Man Holding a Fiddle, oil, unfr, 32x25", WD 1/25/89 OE 65,000

STOMER, Matthias; follower of (Flemish, 17th C)
Old Woman Saying Her Rosary by Lamplight with Skull & Book, oil on canvas, 36x28", SBY 4/7/89 UE 1,650

STONE, Don (American, 20th C)
Linda (young woman sitting on rocky bluff looking out to sea), watercolor on paper, sgn, 14x21", RAB 8/9/88 OE 1,100

STONE, Marcus (British, 1840-1921)
Le Roi Est Mort! Vie le Roi!; oil on canvas, sgn/dtd 1873, 14x21", SBY 6/8/88 3,300
Pair: Wild Flowers; Garden Flowers (portraits); oil on canvas, sgn, 1890, 37x12", SBY 5/23/89 UE 33,000

STONE, Robert (Australian, 20th C)
Set of 4 Hunt Scenes: Meet; Full Cry; Into the Lane; Over the Fence; oil on panel, sgn, 6x12", lot 188, SBY 6/10/88 OE 14,850
Set of 4 Hunt Scenes: Meet; Out of the Brush; Full Cry; The Kill; oil on panel, sgn, 6x12", lot 186, SBY 6/10/88 OE 12,100
Set of 4 Hunt Scenes: Meet; Taking a Fence; Full Cry; The Kill; oil on panel, sgn, unfr, 7x13", lot 20, C-E 10/25/88 4,620
Set of 4: Hunting Scenes; oil on panel, sgn, 6x12", lot 110, SBY 6/9/89 17,600
Set of 4: Hunting Scenes; oil on panel, sgn, 6x12", lot 127, SBY 6/9/89 16,500

STONE, Thomas Albert (Canadian, 1897-1978)
Pair: Clam Lake, Near Kearney; Peters Lake, Near Kearney; oil on board, sgn, 14x18", WAD 6/12/89 525

STOOPS, Herbert Morton (American, 1888-1948)
Posse, oil on canvas, 26x36", C-E 6/1/88 880

STORCK, Abraham Jansz (Dutch, 1635-1710)
Pair: Shipping in a Choppy Sea; Shipping in a Calm; oil on panel, initialed, 6x7", C-NY 4/8/88 OE 44,000
Ships & Fishing Boats Near a Mediterranean Port, oil on canvas, sgn, 21x25", SBY 10/21/88 24,750

STORCK, Abraham Jansz; follower of (Dutch, 1635-1710)
Mediterranean Harbor Scene, oil on canvas, 26x36", FB 4/25/88 750

STORCK, Jacobus; circle of (Dutch, 17th C)
Three-Decker at Anchor & Other Ships Off a Harbor Town, oil on canvas, 31x38", C-NY 6/2/88 10,450

STORM, H.
At Church, oil on canvas, 27x36", C-E 4/7/88 UE 110

STORY, George Henry (British, 1834-1919)
New England Professor of Psalmody, oil on board, sgn/dtd 75, 16x12", SBY 5/25/88 12,650
Portrait of Hallie Hutchinson, no media given, sgn/dtd 1869, oval, 24x19", C-E 2/16/89 UE 198

STOTHARD, Thomas (British, 1775-1834)
Poseidon, oil on canvas, 50x53", SBY 12/9/88 OE 2,090

STOTT, William R.S. (American, 20th C)
Naval Encounter, oil on canvas, sgn/dtd 35, 24x18", WAD 6/6/88 2,000

STOUT, Myron (American, 1908-)
Untitled (abstract), charcoal on paper, 25x19", lot 133, C-NY 11/10/88 OE 44,000

STRACHAN, Claude (British, 1865-1929)
Cottage Garden in June, watercolor/gouache, sgn, 13x10", C-NY 10/26/88 OE 4,400
Devon Cottage, watercolor/gouache on paper, sgn, 15x21", C-NY 5/24/89 6,600
Moment in the Garden (peasant holding cat on steps of cottage), watercolor on paper, sgn, 15x11", B/B 3/22/89 OE 5,225
Streatly Mill, watercolor/gouache, sgn/#d 120, 12x18", C-NY 10/25/89 3,520
Worcestershire Cottage, watercolor/gouache, sgn, 12x19", C-NY 10/25/89 6,600

STRADA, Vespasiano; att (ca 1582-1622)
Franciscan Exorcising a Demon in a Church Interior, pen/ink/wash heightened w/white, 8x16", SBY 1/13/89 2,750

STRAHALM, Franz (Frank)(American, 1879-1935)
Landscape, oil on board, sgn, 8x11", NA 11/5/88 450

STRAIN, Daniel; att (American, fl 1865-1890)
Boys Fishing (seated on footbridge in landscape), oil on canvas, sgn, 18x15", RWS 3/16/89 OE 2,100

STRANG, Ray (American, 1893-1975)
Prairie Fire (illustration for Harpers & a book), oil on canvas, sgn, 36x22", B/B 3/22/89 4,400

STRANOVER, Tobias (Czechoslovakian, 1684-1724)
Cluster of Grapes on a Nail, oil on canvas, sgn, 15x12", C-NY 10/12/89 4,400
Peacock, Merganser, Hummingbird, Parakeets, & Other Birds by a Pond; oil on canvas, 39x54", C-NY 6/2/88 OE 44,000
Rooster, Hen, Peasant, & Other Birds in an Extensive Landscape; oil on canvas, sgn, 39x50", SBY 10/13/89 39,600

STRANOVER, Tobias; att (Czechoslovakian, 1684-1724)
Still Life of Various Fruits & Nuts in a Landscape, oil on canvas, 26x24", C-E 4/7/88 4,400

STRANOVER, Tobias; manner of (Czechoslovakian, 1684-1724)
Peaches, Grapes, Cherries, Currants, Melon & Bird on a Ledge; oil on canvas, 17x23", C-NY 4/6/89 2,090

STRAOUTEN, B.V. (Belgian, 19th C)
Figures Outside the Wall of a Town, oil on panel, sgn/dtd 1824, 16x20", B/B 3/22/89 4,125

STRAUS, Meyer (American, 1831-1905)
Pinto Lake, Santa Cruz; watercolor on paper, sgn/dtd 1897, 7x14", B/B 1/11/89 UE 220
Siskiyou County Forest, oil on canvas, sgn/dtd June 26.9?, 13x10", B/B 10/6/88 715

STRAWBRIDGE, Edward Richie (American, 1903-)
Nantucket Wharf, watercolor on paper, sgn/dtd 50, 9x12", RAB 8/8/89 UE 175

STREATFIELD, W.S.
Town of Port Louis, Mauritus; pencil/watercolor, dtd 1817, unfr, 5x8", C-SK 6/9/88 670

STREET, Frank (American, 1893-1944)
Mrs Wickey in Her Garden, oil on masonite, sgn, 17x24", SBY 6/28/89 1,540
STREET, Robert (American, 1796-1865)
Portrait of a Gentleman, oil on canvas, sgn/dtd 1833, 30x25", WD 4/13/88 2,100
Portrait of a Small Child with Black & White Kitten, oil on canvas, sgn/dtd 1829, SBY 1/28/88 OE 10,175
Portrait of Man Holding a book, oil on canvas, sgn/dtd 1832, 30x25", B/B 9/14/89 OE 2,475
Two Boys & a Dog, oil on canvas, sgn/dtd 1839, 60x41", B/B 3/22/89 16,500
Two Boys & a Dog, oil on canvas, sgn/dtd 1839, 60x41", C-NY 5/26/88 OE 12,100
Young Boy & His Hobby Horse, oil on canvas, sgn, 46x32", FAP 11/4/88 OE 9,000
STREET, Robert; att (American, 1796-1865)
Portrait of Young Boy in White Pleated Shirt & Brown Jacket, oil on canvas, 27x21", SBY 1/28/88 2,860
STREETS, Guillaume; att (16th C)
Portrait of a Man Said To Be Lord Sheffield; oil on panel, bears inscription/dtd 1547, unfr, 18x14", C-NY 1/15/88 OE 48,400
STREICHMAN, Yehzkel (Israeli, 1906-)
Landscape (abstract), oil on canvas, sgn/dtd 55, 32x28", SBY 5/30/89 OE 17,600
STRETTON, Phillip Eustace (British, fl 1884-1919)
Happy Family (portrait of four dogs), oil on canvas, sgn/dtd 1908, oval, 21x32", PHL 10/28/88 1,700
Washerman by a River with a Palatial Estate in the Background, oil on canvas, sgn, unfr, 28x36", C-E 11/8/88 1,100
STRICKLAND, Charlotte (British, 1759-1833)
Black Briony: Tamus Communis (floral); watercolor, intialed/#d 50-51, no size given, C-E 2/21/89 UE 350
Tutsan: Hypericum Andriscemum (floral); watercolor, initialed/#d 43, 14x9", C-E 2/21/89 UE 350
STRICKLAND, Juliana Sabina (European, 19th C)
Purple-Spiked Loosestrife: Lythrum Salicaria; watercolor, initialed/inscr/#d 24, 14x9", C-NY 2/25/88 OE 1,100
Round-Leaved Bell Flower: Campanula Rotundifolio; watercolor, initialed/inscr/#d 6, 14x9", C-NY 2/25/88 440
Virgins Bower: Clematis Vitalba; watercolor, initialed/inscr/#d 34, 14x9", C-NY 2/25/88 660
STRINGER, Francis (British, fl 1760-1772)
Earl of Stamford's Tinker Held by a Groom in the Grounds of Dunham Massey, oil on canvas, 24x30", SBY 6/9/89 OE 15,400
STRISIK, Paul (American, 1918-)
Babson Place, oil on canvas, sgn, 24x30", C-E 6/28/88 UE 110
STROBEL, see De Strobel
STROEBEL, Johann Antoine Balthasar (Dutch, 1821-1905)
Mother & Child, oil on panel, sgn/indistinctly dtd, 10x7", SBY 12/9/88 605
STROHLING, Peter Eduard (Russian, 1768-1826)
Russian Soldier, oil on copper, 24x19", C-NY 10/25/89 14,300
STRONG, Elizabeth (American, 1855-)
Cottage on a Pond, oil on canvas laid down on board, sgn/dtd 1921, 10x12", C-E 11/8/88 440
Red Setter & a Kuvaz, oil on canvas, sgn, 13x16", C-SK 5/25/89 880
STRONG, J.D.; att (19th C)
Island Princess, Fiji; oil on canvasboard, titled, 10x14", C-SK 5/25/89 515
STRONG, Ray Stanford (American, 1905-)
Tuolumne Lake, oil on canvasboard, sgn, 10x12", B/B 5/17/89 495
STROUD, Ida Wells (American, 1869-)
Down by the River, gouache on tan paper, sgn, 10x9", RWS 11/10/89 900
STROZZI, Bernardo; circle of (Italian, 1581-1644)
Madonna & Child, oil on canvas, 63x36", SBY 4/7/88 OE 28,600
Virgin in Adoration, oil on canvas, 30x24", SBY 4/7/88 UE 1,925
STRROBANT, Francois (Belgian, 1819-1916)
Le Pont du Roi a Prague (bridge w/city beyond), oil on canvas, sgn/dtd 1866, 59x43", SBY 7/12/89 3,300
STRUCK, Herman (American, 1887-1954)
Fisherman in a Rough Sea, oil on canvas laid down, sgn, 14x21", B/B 10/6/88 1,210
Lone House Along the Coast, oil on canvasboard, sgn, 16x20", B/B 10/6/88 1,100
STRUTT, William (British, 1826-1915)
David's First Victory, oil on canvas, sgn, 38x22", B/B 12/8/88 OE 5,500
STRY, see Van Stry
STUART, Gilbert (American, 1755-1828)
Portrait of Humphrey Devereux of Salem, Massachusetts, Aged 38; oil on canvas mounted on panel, 27x22", WD 10/5/88 UE 3,750
Portrait of Mrs Robert Morris, oil on canvas, 23x19", FAP 12/8/89 1,050
Steigerwalt-Parker-Hart Portrait of George Washington, oil on canvas, 30x25", C-NY 5/25/89 242,000
STUART, Gilbert; after (American, 1755-1828)
Portrait of George Washington, bust-length in black coat; oil on canvas laid down on board, 21x18", C-SK 6/9/88 2,790
Portrait of George Washington, oil on canvas, 38x27", LH 10/16/88 650
Portrait of George Washington (bust-length), oil on canvas, 26x22", C-E 6/1/89 935
Portrait of George Washington (full-length), oil on wood panel, 27x18", RAB 5/23/89 OE 2,300
Portrait of Mrs James (Dolly) Madison, oil on canvas, unfr, 30x25", LH 10/16/88 450
STUART, Gilbert; att (American, 1755-1828)
Portrait of Tom Payne, oil on canvas, 27x22", WD 4/13/88 UE 1,600
STUART, James (Athenian); att (British, 1713-1788)
Design for the Friezes of Two Mantelpieces...; black chalk/pen/gray ink/gray wash, 15x16", C-NY 1/11/89 1,100
STUART, James Everett (American, 1852-1941)
Bay Trees, Sausalito; oil on canvas, sgn/dtd July 8.1916, 12x18", B/B 8/10/88 440
Near Camp Taylor, California; oil on board, sgn/dtd 1921, 10x14", DM 3/14/88 400

Near Carmel, oil on panel, sgn/dtd 1928, unfr, 15x20", B/B 1/11/89 550
Near Monterey, oil on panel, sgn/dtd 1924, unfr, 15x20", B/B 1/11/89 440
Near Stockton, oil on canvasboard, sgn/dtd 1906/#d 1512, 9x12", C-E 2/1/89 1,210
Portrait of Grace Lanetta Bagwell, oil on canvas, sgn/#d 1502/dtd 1909, 24x20", B/B 5/17/89 605
Red Roof Adobe, oil on canvas, sgn/dtd March 14 1892, 14x22", B/B 8/10/88 660
Showers Near Cottonwood, oil on canvas, sgn/dtd 1933, 10x15", B/B 12/8/88 385
Sunset Glow at Mount Hood, oil on canvas, sgn/dtd 1917, unfr, 20x24", B/B 1/11/89 OE 990
Sunset Near Monterey, oil on canvas, sgn/dtd Dec 19, 1913, 14x22", B/B 10/6/88 1,100
Sunshine & Shadow Near Livermore, oil on canvas, sgn/dtd 1915, 12x18", B/B 12/8/88 385

STUART, Jane (American, 1812-1888)
Pair: George & Martha Washington; oil on canvas, in painted oval, 17x15", C-NY 9/28/89 OE 12,100
Portrait of George Washington, oil on canvas, sgn/inscr/dtd 1856, 30x25", C-E 11/30/88 OE 3,850

STUART, William (British, 19th C)
Battle of Trafalgar, oil on canvas, sgn, 71x115", B/B 3/17/88 OE 15,400

STUBBS, George (British, 1724-1806)
Rt Hon Lord Grosvenor's Bandy Held by a Groom, the River Dee Beyond; oil on canvas, sgn, 39x49", SBY 6/10/88 OE 1,072,500

STUBBS, George; after (British, 1724-1806)
William Anderson with Two Saddled Horses, oil on canvas, 20x28", SBY 6/9/89 UE 3,300

STUBBS, William P. (American, 1842-1909)
Bark in a Storm, ship under shortened sail on heavy seas; oil on canvas, 14x22", lot 174, RAB 8/1/88 UE 1,700
Bark in a Storm (ship in rough sea), oil on canvas, 14x22", lot 142, RAB 3/14/89 UE 1,000
Bark in a Storm (ship under shortened sail on heavy seas), oil on canvas, 14x22", lot 173, RAB 8/1/88 UE 1,250
Brig in a Storm (masted ship in rough sea), oil on canvas, 14x22", lot 143, RAB 3/14/89 UE 900
Brig Mary Gibbs, Capt SO Moore, Off Cape Hattiras March 17, 1882; oil on canvas, sgn/dtd 83, 22x36", RAB 8/1/88 3,600
Sailing Ship in a Storm, oil on canvas mounted on board, sgn/dtd 1891, 25x60", SBY 6/24/88 3,575

STUBER, Dedrick Brandes (American, 1878-1954)
Tuunga Hills, oil on panel, sgn, 16x20", SBY 9/14/89 1,980
Whispering Trees, oil on board, sgn, 16x20", B/B 10/6/88 4,400

STUCK, Carl (German, 19th/20th C)
Nina (half-length portrait), oil on canvas, sgn/dtd 1897, 19x16", B/B 10/9/88 UE 1,210

STUEMPFIG, Walter (American, 1914-1970)
Portrait of a Woman, oil on canvas, sgn, 28x15", C-E 6/1/89 935
Strathmere (beach scene w/figure & dog), oil on canvas, 36x48", SBY 3/17/88 OE 10,450
Under the Boardwalk, oil on canvas, sgn twice, 26x20", C-NY 9/30/88 7,150
Waterworks (village w/church steeple in background), oil on canvas, sgn, 28x36", SBY 4/14/89 OE 18,700

STUHLMULLER, Karl (German, 1858-1930)
Cattle Market in Dachau, oil on board, sgn/inscr, 14x22", C-NY 5/24/89 8,800

STULL, Henry (American, 1852-1913)
August Belmont II's Margrave, Winner of Belmont Stakes, 1896, by a Stream; oil on canvas, sgn/dtd 96, 25x30", SBY 6/9/89 5,500
Jockey on Mount (in landscape), oil on canvas, sgn/dtd 1904, 24x29", B/B 3/22/89 6,600
Moving Mount (jockey up, in a landscape), oil on canvas, sgn/dtd 1908, 24x29", B/B 3/22/89 7,150
Municipal Handicap, 1900; oil on canvas, sgn/dtd 1901, 22x26", SBY 6/10/88 11,000
Pair: Foxhall; Iroquois (horses); oil on panel, 1 sgn/dtd 88, 1 sgn/indistinctly dtd, 6x4", SBY 6/9/89 1,430
Racehorse, Sensation, in a Stall; oil on canvas, sgn/dtd 1879, 12x16", SBY 6/10/88 4,400

STURGIS, Katherine
Getting Ready for the Circus, oil on canvas, sgn, 20x24", C-E 2/3/88 825

STURTEVANT, Helena (American, 1872-1946)
Early Spring Landscape with Tower, pastel on gray-brown paper, sgn/dtd 1927, 15x12", RWS 11/10/89 250

STUVEN, Ernst (German, 1660-1712)
Still Life of Peonies, Tulips, an Iris, & Other Flowers...; oil on canvas, sgn, unfr, 30x24", SBY 1/12/89 OE 93,500

STVROWSKY, Oleg (American, 20th C)
Unexpected Meeting, oil/acrylic on canvas, 36x24", B/B 9/15/88 770

STYKA, Adam (French, 1890-)
At the Watering Hole, oil on canvas, sgn, 29x36", C-E 10/26/89 5,500
Les Enchantes Maroc, oil on canvas, sgn, 25x32", FB 10/30/89 5,720

STYKA, Jan (French, 1858-1925)
Captives, oil on canvas, sgn, 24x20", FB 10/30/89 880

STYKA, Tade (French, 1883-)
Tigers, oil on board, sgn, 18x22", C-E 10/26/89 2,200

SUBLEYRAS, Pierre; after (French, 1699-1749)
La Courtisane Amoureuse, oil on canvas, 13x11", SBY 4/7/88 OE 2,750

SUCHODOLSKI, January; att
Soldier on Horseback, oil on canvas, 28x23", FB 10/30/89 1,100

SUCHY, Adalbert (European, 1783-1849)
Portrait of an Elegant Gentleman, waist-length; watercolor/gouache, sgn/dtd 824, oval, 8x6", C-NY 10/26/88 UE 770

SUDKOVSKY, Rufin
Storm Off a Jetty, oil on canvas, sgn, 22x30", C-E 10/25/88 2,420

SUES, Jean Jacques; att
Portrait of a Man Said To Be Jean Henry Weynman, oil on canvas, inscr, 29x25", SBY 7/12/89 660

SUETIN, Nikolai (Russian, 1897-1954)
Woman with Walking Stick (design for a plate), gouache on paper, sgn/dtd 1929, 15x9", C-L 10/8/88 OE 5,210

SUEUR, Eustache; see Le Sueur

SUGAI, Kumi (Japanese, 1919-)

Kou (abstract), oil on canvas, sgn/dtd 1957, 29x24", SBY 2/15/89 OE **20,900**
Oki (abstract), oil on canvas, sgn/dtd 60, 64x51", SBY 10/5/89 OE **132,000**
Paysage de Nuit (abstract nocturnal landscape), oil on canvas, sgn/dtd 1955, 35x77", C-NY 2/14/89 OE **71,500**
Red Skeleton, gouache/charcoal on flocked paper, sgn, 7x25", C-E 5/13/88 OE **3,300**
Tsuki (abstract), oil on canvas, sgn twice/dtd 1956/#d 174, 45x39", SBY 6/30/88 ..... **56,000**
Untitled (abstract), oil on canvas, sgn/dtd 55, 8x32", C-NY 2/14/89 ..... **25,300**
Yorokobi (abstract), oil on canvas, sgn twice/dtd 1959 twice/titled, 50x40", SBY 11/11/88 OE **88,000**

SUGARMAN, George (American, 1912-)

Untitled (abstract), paper collage on paper mounted on board, sgn, 18x11", C-E 11/14/89 ..... **1,100**

SULLIVAN, Bill (American, 1946-)

Irises, pastel on paper, sgn/dtd 79, 30x23", RWS 9/8/89 UE **200**

SULLIVAN, William Holmes (British, -1908)

Bivouac-The British Lines, the Night Before the Battle of Waterloo...; oil on canvas, sgn twice, 24x36", SBY 2/22/89 UE **18,700**

SULLY, Thomas (American, 1783-1872)

Contemplation (portrait of a woman), oil on canvas, 24x20", C-NY 9/30/88 ..... **6,050**
Ganymede (portrait of a woman), oil on canvas, initialed/inscr, 18x15", C-NY 3/11/88 ..... **3,080**
Lady & Fan (bust-length portrait), oil on canvas, 21x17", RAB 8/9/88 ..... **2,250**
Portrait of Andrew Jackson, oil on canvas laid down on panel, 34x27", C-NY 12/2/88 ..... **41,800**
Portrait of Blanche Sully, oil on canvas, monogramed, 25x20", WG 9/16/88 UE **10,000**
Portrait of Louise Melizet Koecker, oil on canvas, sgn, 20x17", SBY 9/14/89 ..... **1,980**
Portrait of Sarah Cresson Emlen, oil on canvas, initialed/dtd 1826, 18x15", SBY 3/17/88 ..... **3,740**
Thomas Jefferson (portrait), oil on canvas, 35x28", C-NY 12/2/88 OE **143,000**

SULLY, Thomas; after (American, 1783-1872)

Portrait of a Lady Said To Be Mrs Benjamin (Martha Maxwell) Bullock, oil on canvas, 30x25", LH 10/16/88 ..... **500**

SULLY, Thomas; att (American, 1783-1872)

Portrait of a Young Girl with Her Dog, oil on canvas, monogramed, 27x22", SBY 3/17/88 UE **2,420**
Portrait of a Young Woman in Blue Dress, oil on canvas, 30x25", RAB 11/24/89 UE **500**

SULLY, Thomas; style of (American, 1783-1872)

Portrait of a Gentleman, oil on panel, 30x25", B/B 3/22/89 UE **1,870**

SULTAN, Altoon (American, 20th C)

Red Farm & Maple (farm scene), oil on canvas, sgn/dtd 83, 20x38", C-E 11/14/89 OE **3,300**

SULTAN, Donald (American, 1951-)

April 1, 1979 (abstract); brush/black ink on paper, initialed, 12x12", C-NY 5/4/89 ..... **4,400**
April 19, 1979 (abstract); oil/graphite on vinyl tile mounted on panel, initialed/dtd 1979, unfr, 13x13", C-NY 5/3/88 ..... **18,700**

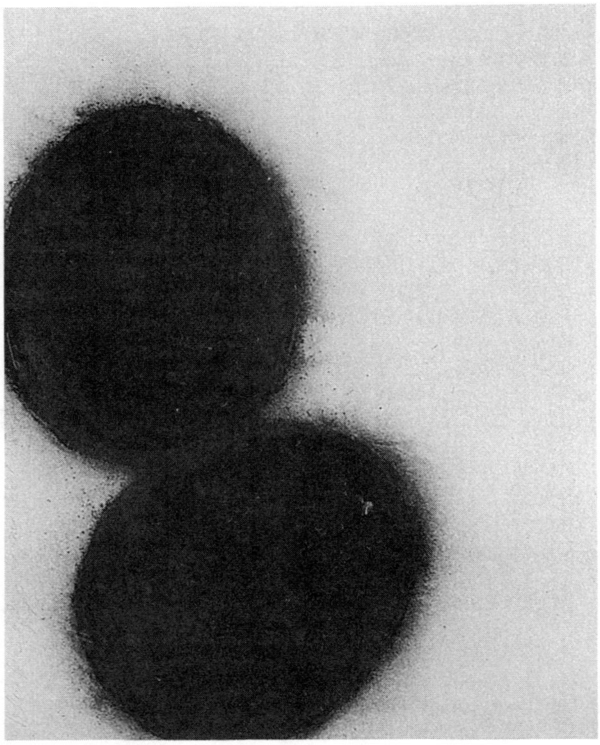

Black Eggs, April 20, 1988; charcoal on paper, initialed/titled/dtd April 20, 1988, 60x48", C-NY 11/8/89; $52,800

Black Flowers (contemporary), India ink on paper, initialed/dtd April 18th, 1987, 16x18", SBY 11/9/89 OE **30,250**
Black Tulip, February 15, 1983; charcoal on paper, initialed/dtd, 50x38", SBY 5/3/89 OE **77,000**
Black Tulip, May 16, 1983; charcoal on paper, initialed/dtd, 50x38", SBY 5/3/89 OE **60,500**
Black Tulip, May 18, 1983; charcoal on paper, initialed/dtd May 18, 1983, 50x36", SBY 11/9/89 OE **115,000**

Blue Iris, June 24, 1981; watercolor/graphite on paper, initialed/inscr/dtd 1981, 50x38", C-NY 5/4/88 OE **27,500**
Building Canyon July 25, 1980 (contemporary); oil on tile over masonite, 1980, 48x48", SBY 11/8/89 ..... **198,000**
February 8, 1979; tile/pencil/oil on masonite, 1979, 60x48", SBY 5/3/88 ..... **27,500**
June 12, 1978 (abstract); crayon/tar/pencil on paper with wood frame, 55x43", SBY 5/3/89 OE **23,100**
Lemons, Aug 26, 1984 (abstract); oil/tar/spackle on vinyl tile, initialed/inscr/dtd 1984, unfr, 13x13", C-NY 5/3/88 OE **55,000**
Pears, April 2, 1984 (contemporary); oil/spackle/tar on vinyl tile, initialed/dtd, 12x12", SBY 5/3/89 OE **93,500**
Streetlight, March 11, 1982 (contemporary); oil/graphite/spackle on tiles over masonite, 1982, 97x48", SBY 11/8/89 OE **231,000**
Three Lemons, April 1985; ink on paper, initialed/dtd April 5, 1985, 15x15", SBY 11/9/89 ..... **19,800**
Three Lemons, June 29, 1984; oil/tar/spackle on vinyl tile mounted on wood panel, 13x13", SBY 11/11/88 OE **71,500**
Two Half Hats & a Square, graphite/vinyl on masonite & wood construction, initialed, sgn/dtd 1980, 48x48", SBY 5/3/89 ..... **27,500**
Umbrella, October 20, 1980; black lacquer/blue watercolor/graphite on paper, initialed/inscr, 18x18", C-NY 5/4/88 OE **20,900**
Untitled (contemporary), oil pastel/charcoal on paper, initialed/dtd June 15, 1977, 38x50", SBY 5/3/89 ..... **8,250**
Untitled (July 30, 1979), watercolor on paper, initialed/dtd July 30, 1979, 12x12", SBY 2/15/89 ..... **4,950**
Yellow Iris (contemporary), oil/tar/spackle on tile over masonite, 1981, 12x12", SBY 11/9/89 OE **143,000**
Yellow Tulip, January 16, 1982; acrylic/graphite on paper, initialed/dtd Jan 16, 1982, 50x38", SBY 2/15/89 ..... **27,500**

UMMA, Emily B. (American, 1875-)
Autumnal Landscape, two children having picnic; oil on canvas, sgn, 16x20", SLK 11/25/88 ..... **350**
Spring Garden Scene, oil on canvas, sgn, 30x40", SLK 9/27/88 ..... **1,600**
Untitled, impressionistic scene of children in garden; oil on canvas, sgn, 11x15", SLK 11/25/88 ..... **950**

UMMER, Elsa (American, 20th C)
Blimp Over Akron (extensive landscape w/blimp overhead), oil on canvasboard, 24x20", WG 4/23/88 UE **525**
Doll & Green Vase, watercolor, sgn, 16x13", WG 9/16/88 UE **40**

UMMERS, Ivan (American, -1964)
Group of 3: Farmhouse; Autumn Charm; Afternoon Light Snow; oil on board, sgn, 10x12", C-E 2/1/89 UE **880**
Pair: St Louis Cathedral; Meeting Street; oil on board, sgn, 10x12", C-E 11/30/88 ..... **1,045**

UMMERS, Robert (1940-)
Cooling Off (three cowboys on horseback riding in stream), oil on masonite, sgn/dtd 1981, 30x48", SBY 9/23/88 ..... **6,050**
Heading West, oil on masonite, sgn/copyrighted, 24x36", SBY 9/23/88 ..... **4,950**
Moonlighters (stagecoach being robbed), oil on masonite, sgn/copyrighted/dtd 1984, 36x60", SBY 9/23/88 ..... **17,600**
Six Cowboys in Autumn Golden Morn, oil on masonite, sgn/copyrighted/dtd 1982, 36x60", SBY 9/23/88 ..... **14,300**
Stepping in the Sunshine, oil on masonite, sgn/copyrighted/dtd 1982, 24x36", SBY 9/23/88 OE **4,510**

UMNER, Maud Eyston (1902-1985)
Gaas Baai Near Hermanns, Cape Province (coastal landscape); oil on canvas, sgn, 20x24", C-SK 5/25/89 ..... **1,470**
Kirstenbosch Botanic Garden, oil on canvas, sgn, 18x22", C-SK 5/25/89 ..... **2,390**

UNDBLOM, Haddon Hubbard (American, 1899-1976)
Proposal, oil on canvas, sgn, 28x22", C-E 10/18/89 ..... **3,300**

URENDORF, Charles (American, 1906-1979)
Mother Lode, watercolor on paper, sgn, 15x22", B/B 10/6/88 ..... **550**

URREY, Philip (Canadian, 1910-)
St Jacques, Coin St Remi (windy street scene); oil on board, sgn, ca 1976, 12x20", FB 10/14/88 ..... **8,500**

URTEES, John (British, 1817-)
Summer Landscape with Pond & Cows, oil on canvas, sgn, 24x42", SBY 7/12/89 ..... **2,750**

URVAGE, Leopold (French, 1879-1968)
Composition (abstract), brush/black ink on paper, sgn/dtd 13, atelier stamp, 19x18", C-NY 10/6/88 ..... **3,520**
Feuille et Main, No 3 (contemporary); oil on canvas, sgn/dtd 30, 22x26", C-NY 2/18/88 OE **10,450**
Les Baigneuses (three nude bathers, contemporary); oil on canvas, sgn/dtd 1912, 39x32", PHL 11/15/88 ..... **65,000**

USENIER, Abraham (Dutch, 1620-1664)
Carp, Pike, & Other Fish, with a Sieve & Brass Bucket...; oil on canvas, sgn/dtd 1661, unfr, 28x40", C-NY 4/8/88 OE **37,400**
Still Life of Fruit in Bowl, Roemers, Silver Pitcher, Crab, & Bread Roll; oil on canvas, sgn/dtd 1640, SBY 6/3/88 OE **81,400**

USS, Johann (Austrian, 1857-)
Flower Girl, oil on canvas, sgn, 39x20", B/B 9/15/88 ..... **1,980**

USTERMANS, Justus (Flemish, 1597-1681)
Woman Holding a Cupid, with a Bacchanalian Figure; oil on canvas, oval, 29x22", C-NY 1/15/88 OE **19,800**

USTERMANS, Justus; circle of (Flemish, 1597-1681)
Portrait of a Gentleman, bust-length, wearing embroidered costume w/white collar; oil on canvas, 18x15", C-NY 4/8/88 ..... **3,300**

USTERMANS, Justus; school of (Flemish, 1597-1681)
Portrait of Galileo, wearing a black costume with white collar & cuff; oil on canvas, inscr, 26x21", C-NY 10/20/88 OE **4,180**

USTRIS, Lambert; att (Dutch, 1540-1599)
Portrait of a Man, Aged Twenty-Five, three-quarter length; oil on panel, dtd 1550, inscr, 46x35", C-NY 1/11/89 ..... **41,800**

UTIL, Francisca (Chilean, 1952-)
Forces No 17 (abstract), handmade paper painting, sgn/dtd 1984-85, 72x42", SBY 5/17/88 ..... **3,850**

UTTON, Harry Jr. (American, 1897-1984)
Still Life, flowers & sculptural pieces; oil on canvasboard, Guild of Boston Artists label, 20x16", RWS 3/16/89 ..... **400**
Still Life of Sculpture & Screen, oil on canvasboard, 24x20", RWS 9/8/89 UE **275**

UVEE, Joseph Benoit; att (Flemish, 1743-1807)
Italian Landscape, black chalk, 18x13", SBY 1/13/89 ..... **2,530**

UVERO, see Di Suvero

UZOR-COTE, Marc Aurele de Foy (Canadian, 1869-1937)
Forest Landscape, oil on canvas, sgn/dtd 1894, 27x14", FB 5/28/89 ..... **10,000**
Paysage d'Automne (autumn landscape), oil on board, sgn/dtd 1916, 2x3", FB 10/17/88 ..... **1,100**
Reclining Nude, pencil, sgn, 18x24", FB 4/25/88 ..... **1,900**

Study of an Indian, pencil, sgn/dtd 1913, 9x5", FB 10/17/88	450
Tete de Vieillard, charcoal, sgn, 21x17", FB 10/17/88	1,100
SVENDSON, Svend (American/Norweigan, 1864-1915)	
Blue Cottages (in a snowy landscape), oil on canvas, sgn, 24x18", C-E 10/18/89	1,100
Footsteps in the Snow, oil on canvas, sgn, 24x30", LH 5/15/88	600
Forest Glow, oil on canvas, sgn, 24x18", B/B 1/11/89	550
Lake Geneva, watercolor on paper, sgn, 10x16", WL 5/20/88 UE	100
Landscape, oil on canvas, sgn, 21x28", LH 10/16/88	1,300
Pink Birches (snowy path & fields, mountains beyond), oil on canvas, sgn, 30x25", RWS 9/29/88 UE	300
Snowbound, oil on canvas, sgn, 24x18", B/B 4/20/88	880
Sunset in Winter, oil on canvas, sgn, 12x18", C-E 11/30/88	2,090
Untitled, coastal scene; oil on canvas, sgn, 20x28", SLK 4/7/89	150
Untitled, snowy winter landscape w/birch trees; oil on canvas laid down on masonite, sgn, 31x23", SLK 11/25/88	350
Winter Landscape with River, oil on canvas, sgn, 30x40", SBY 7/12/89 UE	1,650
Winter Twilight, oil on canvas, sgn, 20x16", C-E 2/3/88 UE	770
SVENSSON, Charles W. (Swedish)	
Woodland Interior, oil on board, 17x16", FAP 4/15/89 UE	83
SVERCHKOV, Nikolai Egorovich (Russian, 1817-1898)	
Mounted Huntsman, pencil/watercolor, sgn/dtd 1862, 11x15", C-L 10/8/88	1,670
Mounted Huntsman with a Fallen Wolf, oil on canvas, sgn, 37x51", C-L 10/8/88 OE	8,365
SVERTSCHKOFF, Nicolas Gregorovitch (Russian, 1817-1898)	
Hauling Hay Through a Snowy Winter Landscape, oil on canvas, sgn, 16x27", C-E 10/25/88	2,420
SWAINE, Francis (British, 1740-1782)	
British Frigates in Choppy Coastal Waters, oil on copper, sgn, 6x8", SBY 10/21/88 OE	10,450
Man-O-War in a Storm Off a Coast, oil on canvas, indistinctly sgn, 26x54", C-NY 4/6/89 OE	9,900
SWAN, Cuthbert Edmund (British, 1870-1931)	
Puma & Cubs, oil on canvas, sgn/dtd 1905, 25x50", SBY 6/10/88	4,400
SWANN, S.S.	
Still Life of Grapes in a Basket, oil on canvas, sgn/dtd 1893, 12x16", C-E 7/26/88	605
SWANSON, Mark (20th C)	
Heel Catch, oil on masonite, sgn/dtd 82, 24x35", SBY 9/23/88 OE	3,300
SWEBACH, Edouard (French, 1800-1870)	
Polish Lancers on Campaign in Spain 1808, oil on canvas, 15x18", SBY 7/12/89	3,300
SWEBACH-DESFONTAINES, Jacques Francois (French, 1769-1823)	
Officer Conversing with a Gentleman on a Road, oil on canvas, indistinctly initialed, unfr, 10x13", C-NY 10/12/89	8,800
SWEERTS, Michiel; circle of (Dutch, 1624-1664)	
Backgammon Players in an Interior, in the style of David Teniers II; oil on panel, 23x28", C-NY 5/31/89	4,400
SWEERTS, Michiel; manner of (Dutch, 1624-1664)	
Study of a Boy in Green, oil on canvas, 18x13", SBY 7/12/89	2,200
SWIFT, C.A. (American, 20th C)	
Billboards (several/large, advertising in factory district), watercolor/gouache on paper, sgn, 9x6", RAB 8/8/89 UE	75
Ferris Wheel, Back Bay, Fens, Boston; watercolor/gouache on paper, sgn/titled, 9x7", RAB 8/8/89 UE	175
SWIFT, Clemment Nye (American, 1846-1918)	
Kitchen Interior, oil on canvas laid down on cardboard, sgn, 16x24", RAB 8/8/89 UE	550
SWINNERTON, James G. (American, 1875-1974)	
Bank of the Colorado River Near St George, oil on canvas, sgn, 30x40", B/B 10/6/88	3,575
Early Morning, Grand Canyon; oil on board, sgn, 17x14", B/B 10/6/88	1,100
In Southern Utah, oil on canvas, sgn/inscr, 30x30", C-NY 3/11/88	2,860
Sacred Cave, oil on canvas, sgn, unfr, 36x30", B/B 6/15/89	2,475
SWINNEY (20th C)	
French Quarter Street Scene, oil on card, sgn/dtd 1934, 20x10", NA 2/6/88	525
SWINNY, S. (19th C)	
Mauritius, watercolor, sgn/dtd 1847, 3x11", C-SK 11/10/88	520
SWINTON, Marion	
Sharing the Gingerbread (toddler sharing w/chickens), oil on canvas, sgn, unstretched, 10x8", C-E 6/1/89	1,045
Swiss School (19th C)	
Alpine Landscape, oil on canvas, 29x40", WD 3/23/88	1,400
Extensive View of the Alps, oil on canvas, indistinctly monogramed/dtd 1898, 31x38", C-E 10/25/88	1,650
SWOPE, H. Vance (American, 1879-1926)	
Along the Hudson, oil on canvasboard, sgn, 23x25", SBY 6/24/88 UE	990
SWOPE, Kate (American, 19th/20th C)	
Homage to Van Gogh, oil on canvas, sgn, 24x14", FAP 12/8/89	150
SWORD, James Brade (American, 1839-1915)	
Angler's Glen, Lake Dunmore, Vermont; watercolor on paper, sgn/dtd 74, 14x11", SBY 6/28/89	880
Coastal Scene, stone fort on rocky peak along quiet shore; oil on canvas, sgn, 16x26", RAB 8/8/89 UE	300
Fishing in Autumn, oil on canvas, sgn/dtd 73, 12x9", SBY 9/23/88	3,520
Gypsy Encampment, oil on canvas, sgn, 20x36", SBY 3/17/88 OE	6,325
House at Narrangensett Bay, oil on canvas, sgn, 22x36", RWS 5/19/88 UE	3,400
Long Pond, Martha's Vineyard; oil on canvas, sgn, 18x30", SBY 1/24/89	7,150
Rural Landscape with Stream, oil on canvas, sgn, 14x22", SBY 3/17/88	880

SYBORCK, R.
Horse-Drawn Carriages at Night, oil on canvas, sgn, 27x19", C-E 10/25/88 1,980

SYCHKOV, Fedor Vasil'evich (Russian, 1870-1958)
Frolicking in the Snow, oil on canvas, sgn/dtd 1932, 21x27", C-L 10/8/88 OE 10,780

SYER, John (British, 1815-1885)
Farmyard Scene with Figures & Grazing Sheep, oil on canvas, sgn/dtd 73, 30x40", RWS 12/10/88 1,700
Mountain Stream, oil on canvas, sgn/dtd 82, 27x36", C-E 5/23/88 3,520
Old Mill, oil on canvas, sgn/dtd 18(?), 26x36", WD 3/23/88 2,800
Trout Fishing, oil on canvas, sgn/dtd 18(?)4, 27x37", C-E 10/25/88 OE 4,620

SYKES, Charles Henry (American, 1882-)
Golfer Eating Sundae, oil on canvas, unfr, 30x25", FAP 4/15/89 578

SYKES, W. (British, 18th C)
Half-Length Portrait of a Man, oil on canvas, sgn, 29x25", RWS 12/10/88 325

SYLVESTER, Frederick Oakes (American, 1869-1915)
Landscape Scene, oil on board, sgn/dtd 10, 12x10", LH 10/16/88 500
Pair: Autumn Landscapes Overlooking Valleys; oil on board, sgn/dtd 1913, 10x8", WG 9/16/88 UE 300

SYMES, John (American, -1888)
Suspension Bridge, New York; oil on canvas, sgn/titled/dtd 1880, 25x45", B/B 9/15/88 1,650

SYMONS, George Gardner (American, 1863-1930)
Autumn Morning, watercolor on paper, sgn, 9x14", RWS 9/8/89 UE 300
Barn in a Landscape, oil on canvas, sgn, 13x15", C-E 2/1/89 2,860
Breaking Ice in the River, oil on panel, sgn, 10x14", SBY 9/14/89 2,200
Cottage, watercolor on paper, sgn, 7x10", C-E 2/1/89 OE 1,045
Creek in Winter, oil on canvas, sgn, 20x25", C-NY 9/28/89 8,800
Deep Valley, Cornwall; oil on canvas, sgn, 30x41", WD 4/13/88 13,500
European Village & Aquaduct, oil on panel, sgn/initialed, 7x9", RWS 11/3/88 600
Hillside Road (snowy landscape, yellow sky), oil on canvas, sgn, 25x30", C-NY 9/28/89 OE 20,900
House Beside a Road, oil on canvas laid down on board, sgn, 10x12", C-E 11/30/88 2,420
House in the Country (small white house in green landscape), oil on board, sgn, bears estate stamp, 8x10", RAB 8/9/88 UE 850
In the Winter Woods, oil on canvas, sgn, 12x16", C-E 11/30/88 OE 7,150
Landscape with Mountains, oil on board, initialed, 7x9", SBY 6/28/89 990
Lone Tree in Autumn, oil on canvasboard, initialed, 8x10", B/B 3/22/89 3,025
Near Shelbourne Falls, Massachusetts (river landscape); oil on canvas, sgn, 26x31", B/B 3/22/89 35,750
On a Country Path, oil on canvas, sgn, 14x24", C-E 11/30/88 UE 1,100
River Boulders, Shelbourne Falls, New York; oil on canvasboard, sgn, 15x18", C-NY 9/28/89 4,180
Rural Landscape, oil on board, sgn, 10x14", B/B 10/6/88 2,750
Southern Residence, oil on canvas, sgn, 15x18", C-E 6/1/89 1,980
Stone Wall (in wooded landscape), oil on canvasboard, sgn, 15x18", C-NY 9/28/89 3,960
Stream in Snow-Covered Hills, oil on canvas, sgn, 20x25", B/B 6/15/89 33,000
Summer Landscape with Pond, oil on board, sgn, 6x9", RWS 11/3/88 650
Sunshine (stand of trees in shadow, sunny hill beyond), oil on canvasboard, sgn, 15x18", C-NY 9/28/89 3,850
Valley Stream in Winter, oil on canvas, sgn, 25x30", B/B 10/9/88 OE 52,250
Winding Through the Hills to the Valley (river landscape), oil on canvas, sgn twice, 48x40", C-NY 12/2/88 OE 46,200
Winter Forest, oil on canvasboard, sgn, 15x18", C-NY 9/30/88 UE 2,750
Winter Landscape, oil on board, initialed, 7x9", SBY 6/28/89 OE 1,980
Winter Landscape (with red brick building), oil on board, sgn, 5x6", RAB 8/9/88 UE 600
Wooded River Scene, oil on board, sgn, 11x14", B/B 3/22/89 3,025

SZYK, Arthur (Polish, 1894-)
Hitler Making Speech: Ranting Berlin Sportpalast (caricature drawing); pen/ink, sgn/dtd 42, no size given, SWN 12/1/88 220
Never Mind, He Will Be Alright Soon; pen/ink/watercolor wash on paper, sgn/dtd Ottawa 1940, 14x11", SWN 12/1/88 660

SZYKIER, Fiekierz (Polish, 19th C)
Return Home (two lads in horse-drawn sleigh in winter), oil on canvas laid down on board, sgn/inscr, 24x16", SBY 2/23/89 7,150

SZYSZLO, see De Szyszlo

TAAFFE, Philip (20th C)
Forest Lantern, oil on masonite & tape, sgn/titled/dtd 1981-82, 53x48", C-NY 10/31/89 OE 49,500
Untitled (abstract), acrylic on paper, sgn/dtd 1986, 22x34", C-NY 11/10/88 OE 3,520
Untitled (abstract), graphite on paper, sgn/dtd 1986, 19x24", SBY 11/9/89 6,600

TABACHNICK, Anne (20th C)
Floral Still Life, acrylic on canvas, sgn/dtd 1970, 36x20", SBY 10/5/88 UE 385

TABENKIN, Ilya (Russian, 1914-)
Composition 1982, oil on canvas, sgn/dtd 1982/titled/inscr, 21x29", SBY 7/7/88 OE 7,600
Composition 1987, oil on canvas, sgn/dtd 1987/titled/inscr, 26x34", SBY 7/7/88 4,000
Gilles or the Paper Boat, oil on canvas, sgn/dtd 1984/titled/inscr, 24x32", SBY 7/7/88 4,000

TABENKIN, Lev (Russian, 1952-)
Choice (figures in gallery-type interior w/pictures of birds), oil on canvas, sgn/dtd 1987, 55x49", SBY 7/7/88 OE 15,000
Old Men (posterior view of two men, half-length), oil on canvas, sgn/dtd 1987, 37x48", SBY 7/7/88 OE 11,000
Salesman (posterior view of seated man by pigeons in cage), oil on canvas, sgn/dtd 1986, 43x47", SBY 7/7/88 OE 10,400

TABER, I. Walton (American, 19th C)
Alabama Crewman: An Object of Curiosity (Civil War); pen/ink on board, inscr, unfr, 12x9", C-E 11/30/88 OE 1,320
Andersonville, Visitors in Guard Tower (Civil War); pen/ink on board, inscr, unfr, 14x11", C-E 11/30/88 132
Andersonville, Weary Hours (Civil War); pen/ink on paper, sgn/inscr, 11x17", C-E 5/27/88 OE 935

Andersonville Prison: Escape (Civil War); pen/ink/wash on paper laid down on board, inscr, 17x13", C-E 5/27/88	165
Andrews Raid: Abandoning the General (Civil War); pen/ink on paper, sgn/inscr, 14x19", C-E 5/27/88 OE	935
Andrews Raid: Confederates in Pursuit (Civil War); pen/ink on paper, sgn/inscr, 13x21", C-E 5/27/88 OE	1,210
Army Forge (Civil War), pen/ink on paper, sgn/inscr, unfr, 12x13", C-E 11/30/88	418
Awkward Squad (Civil War), pen/ink on paper, sgn/inscr, 7x13", C-E 5/27/88 OE	1,540
Bird's-Eye View of North End of Andersonville (Civil War), pen/ink on board, sgn/inscr, 14x22", C-E 5/27/88	330
Burying the Dead, Antietam (Civil War); pen/ink on paper, sgn/dtd 85, 11x15", C-E 5/27/88 OE	935
Calvary Orderly (Civil War), pen/ink on paper, sgn/inscr, unfr, 8x13", C-E 11/30/88 OE	440
Camp Cooking (Civil War), pen/ink on paper, sgn/inscr, unfr, 9x10", C-E 11/30/88 UE	66
Commissary Tent (Civil War), pen/ink on paper, sgn/inscr, unfr, 13x15", C-E 11/30/88 OE	308
Confederate Water Battery (Civil War), pen/ink on paper, sgn/inscr, unfr, 15x18", C-E 11/30/88 OE	880
Confederate Wounded After Antietam (Civil War), ink/crayon on paper, sgn/inscr, 13x18", C-E 5/27/88 OE	1,100
Cox's Brigade at Cincinnati (Civil War), pen/ink on paper, inscr, unfr, 10x13", C-E 11/30/88	154
Crew at Quarters, Kearsarge (Civil War); pen/ink on paper, sgn/inscr, unfr, 12x13", C-E 11/30/88 OE	495
Custer Battlefield (Civil War), pen/ink on paper, inscr, unfr, 13x16", C-E 11/30/88	220
Cutting the Canal at Island No 10 (Civil War), pen/ink on paper, inscr, 9x14", C-E 11/30/88	176
Deadline, Johnson's Island (Civil War); pen/ink on paper, sgn/inscr, 9x8", C-E 5/27/88 OE	660
Deserted Camp, Federal Winter Quarters, Falmouth, Virginia; pen/ink, sgn/inscr, unfr, 10x13", C-E 11/30/88 OE	418
Drummer Boys (Civil War), ink/crayon on paper, sgn/inscr/dtd 87, 6x15", C-E 5/27/88 OE	2,420
Federal Right, Murfreesboro, Battle of Stone River (Civil War); pen/ink on paper, sgn/inscr, 12x20", C-E 5/27/88	715
Federal Wounded on the Grounds of the Marye House, Fredericksburg (Civil War); pen/ink, sgn, 9x13", C-E 5/27/88 OE	1,760
Fort Sumter, Casemates in Ruin (Civil War); pen/ink on paper, sgn/inscr, 7x7", C-E 5/27/88 OE	1,100
Fort Sumter, Southwest Face (Civil War); pen/ink on paper, inscr, unfr, 11x18", C-E 11/30/88 OE	605
Fort Sumter Interior, Showing Sally Port & Flag Staff (Civil War); pen/ink, sgn/inscr, unfr, 7x7", C-E 11/30/88	242
Fortress Monroe (Civil War), pen/ink on paper, inscr, unfr, 13x17", C-E 11/30/88	165
Four Views of Confederate Batteries (Civil War), pen/ink on paper, sgn/inscr, unfr, 14x13", C-E 11/30/88	330
Fugitive Negroes Fording Rappahannook River (Civil War), pen/ink on paper, sgn/inscr, unfr, 10x11", C-E 11/30/88 OE	385
General Beauregarde Headquarters, Manassas (Civil War); pen/ink on paper, sgn/inscr, unfr, 8x10", C-E 11/30/88	132
General Hooker & Staff (Civil War), pen/ink on paper, sgn/inscr, 13x17", C-E 5/27/88 OE	660
Going into Action Under Fire (Civil War), pen/ink/charcoal on paper, inscr, 13x17", C-E 5/27/88	385
Going to the Front (Civil War), pen/ink on paper, sgn/inscr, 12x17", C-E 5/27/88 OE	1,100
Gun Monument in National Cemetery (Civil War), pen/ink on paper, sgn/inscr, unfr, 8x13", C-E 11/30/88	110
Hoffman Battalion, Johnson's Island (Civil War); pen/ink on board, sgn/inscr, unfr, 11x14", C-E 11/30/88	352
Hospital at Fair Oaks (Civil War), pen/ink on paper, sgn/inscr, 11x15", C-E 11/30/88	198
Howitzer (Civil War), pen/ink on paper, sgn/inscr, unfr, 13x11", C-E 11/30/88 OE	605
Interior of Fort Sumter After the Surrender (Civil War), pen/ink on paper, sgn/inscr, 7x10", C-E 5/27/89 OE	1,100
Looking for a Friend (Civil War), pen/ink on paper, sgn/inscr, 5x7", C-E 5/27/88 OE	2,420
Louisiana (Civil War), pen/ink on paper, sgn/inscr, unfr, 9x14", C-E 11/30/88 OE	770
Military Telegraph Pole Being Hit by a Shell (Civil War), pen/ink on board, sgn/inscr, 22x14", C-E 5/27/88	165
Morning Reveille (Civil War), ink/crayon on paper, sgn/inscr, 7x14", C-E 5/27/88	165
Navy Department, Washington (Civil War); pen/ink on paper, sgn/inscr, unfr, 10x13", C-E 11/30/88	88
Old Cold Harbor Tavern (Civil War), pen/ink on paper, sgn/inscr, unfr, 13x17", C-E 11/30/88	165
Old Wooden Canteen (Civil War), pen/ink on paper, sgn/inscr, unfr, 11x8", C-E 11/30/88	176
On the Road to Richmond (Civil War), pen/ink on paper, sgn/inscr, unfr, 9x13", C-E 11/30/88	154
Pair: Ditch on Right Wing, Antietam; Camp Gossip (Civil War); pen/ink, sgn/dtd 85, about 13x17", C-E 5/27/88	550
Pair: USS Mississippi; USS Winona (Civil War); pen/ink on paper, sgn/inscr, unfr, 13x17", C-E 11/30/88	198
Parade of the 110th Pennsylvania Infantry at Falmouth (Civil War), pen/ink on paper, sgn/inscr, 13x18", C-E 5/27/88 OE	935
Phillips House (Civil War), pen/ink on paper, sgn/inscr, unfr, 11x13", C-E 11/30/88	154
Prisoner Near Florence, South Carolina (Civil War); pen/ink on board, inscr, unfr, 8x13", C-E 11/30/88	176
Quaker Gun, 1st Bull Run (Civil War); pen/ink on paper, sgn/inscr, unfr, 8x8", C-E 11/30/88	88
Rowlett Mill (Civil War), pen/ink/wash on paper, sgn/inscr, unfr, 16x13", C-E 11/30/88	88
Ruins of Gaine's Mill (Civil War), pen/ink on paper, sgn/inscr, unfr, 13x15", C-E 11/30/88	176
Salem Church (Civil War), pen/ink on paper, sgn/inscr, unfr, 13x16", C-E 11/30/88 OE	352
Self-Portrait of the Artist As a Young Man, oil on canvas, 24x18", LH 5/15/88	1,500
Set of 3: VMI Cadet, Dress Uniform; Umbrella Rock; Army Wagon (Civil War); pen/ink, 11x8" & smaller, C-E 5/27/88 OE	605
Sherman's Soldiers Tearing Up the Railroads, Atlanta (Civil War); pen/ink on paper, sgn/inscr, 6x10", C-E 5/27/88 OE	1,870
Siege Battery: Last Line at Pittsburgh (Civil War); pen/ink on paper, sgn/inscr, 11x14", C-E 11/30/88 OE	825
Soldiers at Pontoon Bridge, Second Bull Run; pen/ink on paper, sgn/inscr, unfr, 13x16", C-E 11/30/88	330
South Gate Entrance, Andersonville Prison (Civil War); pen/ink on board, inscr, unfr, 8x15", C-E 11/30/88 OE	352
State Capitol, Nashville (Civil War); pen/ink on board, sgn/inscr, 14x18", C-E 5/27/88 OE	550
Telegraphing in the Field (Civil War), pen/ink on paper, sgn/inscr, 12x19", C-E 5/27/88 OE	3,300
Tent Lodgings of Andersonville (Civil War), pen/ink/wash on paper, sgn/inscr, 12x7", C-E 5/27/88 OE	1,100
Third Pennsylvania Artillery on Parade (Civil War), pen/ink on paper, sgn/inscr, unfr, 14x20", C-E 11/30/88 OE	605
Union Battery, Petersburg (Civil War); pen/ink on paper, sgn/inscr, 8x15", C-E 5/27/88 OE	935
Union Charge Through the Corn Field (Civil War), pen/ink on paper, inscr, 14x19", C-E 5/27/88 OE	3,300
US Military Bridge at Chattanooga (Civil War), pen/ink on paper, sgn/inscr, 14x24", C-E 5/27/88	440
View Looking Down Potomac From Harper's Ferry (Civil War), pen/ink on paper, sgn/inscr, unfr, 11x14", C-E 11/30/88	352
VMI Cadet-Field Uniform (Civil War); pen/ink on paper, inscr, unfr, 11x8", C-E 11/30/88	132
114th Pennsylvania Infantry, Provost Guard, Petersburg (Civil War); pen/ink on paper, sgn/inscr, 14x18", C-E 5/27/88 OE	880
14th New York Volunteer (Civil War), pen/ink on paper, sgn/inscr/dtd 84, 17x12", C-E 5/27/88 OE	1,540

TACK, Augustus Vincent (American, 1870-1949)

Untitled (abstract), oil on canvas laid down on gessoed masonite, sgn, 37x32", C-NY 12/2/88 .... **49,500**

TACK, Augustus Vincent; att (American, 1870-1949)

Portrait of Two Sons of Thomas Fortune Ryan, oil on canvas, unfr, 25x30", SBY 9/14/89 .... **2,310**

TADEMA, Lawrence Alma

Portrait of a Woman, Possibly Mrs HG Marquand; pencil, sgn/inscr/dtd 90, 9x6", C-NY 10/26/88 OE **13,200**

TAFURI, Clemente (Italian, 1903-1971)

Broken Net (boy mending net), oil on canvas, sgn, 57x36", WD 11/16/88 .... **5,250**

TAGE (20th C)

Swiss Village & Mountains, oil on canvas, sgn/dtd 1939, 40x52", FAP 4/15/89 UE **550**

TAHITOTH, Nandor (Hungarian, 20th C)

Under the Sea, oil on canvas, sgn, unfr, 20x24", RWS 12/10/88 UE **150**

TAIT, Arthur Fitzwilliam (American, 1819-1905)

Chicks, oil on panel, in painted tondo, sgn/dtd 63, 11x11", C-NY 5/26/88 .... **14,300**
Ducks & Little Blue Heron in a Landscape, oil on canvas, sgn/dtd 67, RWS 5/19/88 .... **21,000**
Expectation (horse & sheep in pen, dog & feed bag on stone fence), oil canvas, sgn/dtd 99, 19x27", B/B 10/9/88 .... **16,500**
Little Pets (close-up of baby chicks), oil on panel, sgn/dtd 99, 10x14", C-NY 5/25/89 .... **19,800**
Quail & Young, oil on canvas, sgn/dtd 1863, 18x24", B/B 6/15/89 .... **38,500**
Reality (seated hunter reflecting, dead buck lying beside), oil on canvas, sgn/dtd NY 1850, 18x24", SBY 9/14/89 UE **4,125**
Tecumseh, oil on artist board, sgn/inscr/dtd 1856, 10x14", SBY 6/10/88 .... **3,575**
Woodcock Nesting, oil on canvas, sgn/dtd NY 1856, 25x20", C-SK 6/9/88 .... **7,440**

TAIT, Arthur Fitzwilliam; after (American, 1819-1905)

Last War Whoop, oil on canvas, 22x27", B/B 1/11/89 .... **770**

TAKAMATSU

Oriental Market Scene, watercolor on paper, sgn, 19x13", RAB 11/24/89 .... **450**

TALBOT, Jesse (American, 1806-1879)

Erastus in the Happy Valley, oil on canvas, 49x73", SBY 6/24/88 .... **6,600**

TAMAYO, Rufino (Mexican, 1900-)

Astronomer (abstract), oil on canvas, sgn/dtd 0-54, 24x30", SBY 11/21/88 .... **253,000**
Bather (posterior view of nude), gouache on paper, sgn/dtd 27, 9x7", SBY 11/21/88 .... **7,700**
Bathing Women (viewed from behind), gouache on paper, sgn/dtd 41, 17x13", SBY 5/16/89 OE **44,000**

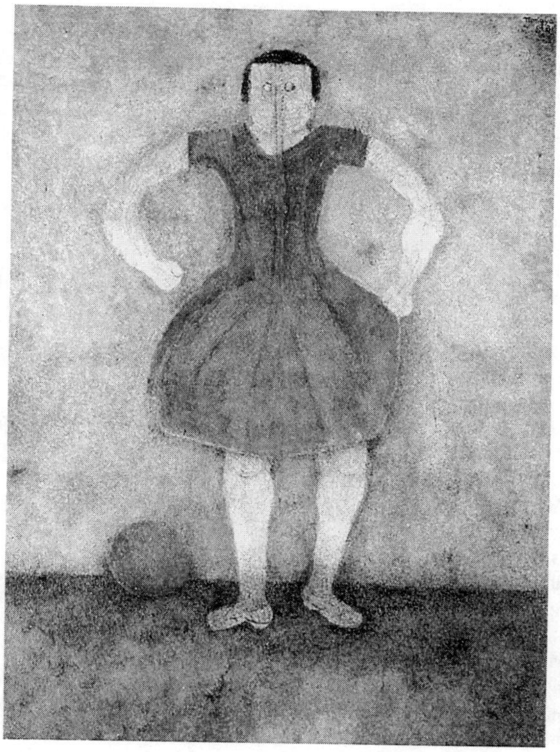

La Nina Atleta, oil on canvas, sgn/dtd 0-81, 51x37", C-NY 11/21/89; $385,000

Bathing Women of Tehuantepec, watercolor on paper, sgn/dtd 37, 17x14", SBY 5/17/88 .... **27,500**
Buscador de Estrellas (abstract), oil on canvas, sgn/dtd 0-56, 39x32", C-NY 5/18/88 .... **308,000**
Children at Play, gouache on paper, sgn/dtd 34, 13x20", SBY 5/17/88 .... **17,600**
Day & Night (abstract), oil on canvas, sgn/dtd 0-53, 33x40", SBY 5/16/89 .... **264,000**
Desnudo, gouache/pencil on paper, sgn/dtd 27, 18x12", C-NY 11/21/89 OE **26,400**
Dos Mujeres (two women), gouache/pencil on paper, sgn/dtd 37, 11x7", C-NY 11/21/88 .... **19,800**
Double-Sided: Portrait of a Man; charcoal, sgn, 14x10", SBY 11/21/88 .... **3,025**
Figure, oil/sand on canvas, sgn/dtd 1960, 21x18", SBY 5/17/88 .... **82,500**
Head (contemporary), oil on canvas, sgn/dtd 0-70, 13x18", SBY 5/16/89 OE **115,500**

Hombre (abstract of a man), pencil/colored pencil on heavy paper, sgn/dtd 67, 12x9", C-NY 5/17/89 **8,800**
Hombre Asombrado de la Aviacon (man w/fear of airplanes), oil/sand on canvas, sgn/dtd 0-46, 42x34", C-NY 5/17/89 **385,000**
Hombre con Fondo Verde (man on green background), oil/sand on canvas, sgn/dtd 0-87, 15x20", C-NY 11/21/88 **93,500**
Interior with an Alarm Clock, oil on canvas, sgn, 1928, 21x21", SBY 5/16/89 OE **148,500**
Las Sembradoras, watercolor/gouache on board, sgn/dtd 40, 16x13", C-NY 5/18/88 OE **24,200**
Muchacha Llevando un Fuente de Frutas (woman carrying dish of fruit), oil on canvas, sgn/dtd 1926, 35x27", C-NY 5/17/89 **77,000**
Mujer Apoyada Contra la Pared (woman leaning against wall), watercolor/pencil on paper, sgn, 24x18", C-NY 11/21/88 **17,600**
Mujer con Canasta (kneeling woman w/basket), watercolor/pencil on paper, sgn, 8x6", C-NY 5/17/89 OE **16,500**
Mujer con Cantaro (woman with bowl on head), gouache on paper, sgn, ca 1940, 17x13", C-NY 11/21/89 **33,000**
Mujer de Espaldas (posterior view of woman), watercolor on paper, sgn, 9x8", C-NY 5/17/89 OE **19,800**
Naturaleza Muerta (still life), oil/sand on canvas, sgn/dtd twice 76, 32x40", C-NY 5/17/89 **209,000**
New York (contemporary scene w/figures), gouache on paper, sgn/dtd 34, 12x15", SBY 11/21/88 OE **52,800**
Paisaje Arido (barren landscape), oil/sand on canvas, sgn/dtd 0-73/titled, 38x51", C-NY 11/21/88 **165,000**
Pareja en Rojo (two abstract figures), oil on canvas, sgn/dtd 0-62, 51x38", C-NY 5/18/88 **253,000**
Pearl (fantasy figures, study for oil painting), pencil on paper, sgn/dtd 1950, 18x12", SBY 11/21/88 OE **26,400**
Portrait of a Woman, gouache on paper, sgn/dtd 40, 12x9", SBY 5/16/89 OE **28,600**
Project for a Mural, pencil on paper, sgn/dtd 0-51, 16x35", SBY 11/21/88 OE **20,900**
Project for a Mural, pencil on paper, 14x36", lot 19, C-NY 5/17/89 **13,200**
Proyecto para el Mural America at the University of Puerto Rico, pencil on paper, 20x37", C-NY 5/17/89 **15,400**
Retrato de Olga (portrait), oil on masonite, sgn/dtd 0-48, 48x36", C-NY 11/21/88 **330,000**
Three Women (standing, posterior view), gouache on paper, sgn/dtd 39, 12x9", SBY 5/16/89 **22,000**
Two Women, ink on paper, sgn, ca 1920s, 9x7", SBY 11/21/88 OE **12,100**
Untitled (contemporary nocturnal landscape w/full moon), oil on canvas, sgn/dtd 32, 22x30", SBY 5/16/89 **126,500**
Woman Chasing Butterflies, oil on canvas, sgn/dtd 0-44, 37x45", SBY 5/17/88 **192,500**
Woman in Red by Moonlight, crayon, sgn, 11x8", S/A 3/12/88 **1,700**
Woman Smoothing Her Hair, gouache on paper, sgn/dtd 0-44, 29x23", SBY 5/17/88 **77,000**

TAMBA (Italian, 19th C)
Woman Reading, watercolor, sgn/inscr, 21x14", LH 10/16/88 **250**

TAMBURINI, Arnaldo (Italian, 1843-)
Fine Glass of Wine (man seated at table), oil on panel, sgn, unfr, 12x10", B/B 9/14/89 **1,100**
Monk Carrying Basket of Wine Bottles, oil on canvas, sgn/inscr, 12x10", SBY 12/9/88 **4,400**
Monks Tasting the Wine, oil on canvas, sgn, 18x22", C-E 2/21/89 **3,520**
Reminiscing, oil on canvas, sgn/inscr, 12x10", C-E 2/23/88 **3,960**

TANGUY, Yves (American/French, 1900-1955)
Abstract Composition, India ink on paper, 12x8", SBY 10/7/89 **3,300**
Avec le Noir (surrealistic composition), gouache on board, sgn/dtd 51, 19x13", C-NY 5/11/89 **198,000**
Composition (abstract), pencil on paper, sgn/dtd 35, 10x7", SBY 2/16/89 **14,300**
Composition sur Fond Noir (black background), gouache/India ink on black paper, sgn/dtd 47, 11x14", C-NY 5/12/88 **60,500**
Compostion (surrealistic), gouache/watercolor on black paper, sgn/dtd 47, 14x11", SBY 11/12/88 OE **74,250**
Le Bon Jour Dore (abstract), oil on canvas, sgn, 1929, 26x36", SBY 11/11/88 **495,000**
Untitled (abstract composition), pen/ink, sgn/dtd 33, 11x9", PHL 11/15/88 **4,500**
Ver d'Anciens Appels, oil on canvas, sgn/dtd 1946, 28x23", C-NY 5/11/88 OE **506,000**

TANNER, Henry Ossawa (American, 1859-1937)
Christ's Tomb, oil on canvas, sgn, 20x26", SBY 9/14/89 OE **17,050**
Figures in a Landscape, oil on board, sgn, 9x10", SBY 1/24/89 OE **4,125**
Good Shepherd (landscape), oil on canvas, sgn, 26x32", C-NY 5/26/88 **15,400**

TANNING, Dorothea (American, 1910-)
Fatal (surrealistic composition), oil on canvas, sgn, 1949, 10x7", SBY 10/7/89 OE **22,000**
Truth About Comets & Little Girls, oil on canvas, sgn/dtd 45, 24x24", C-NY 10/6/88 OE **33,000**

TANOBE, Miyuki (Canadian, 1937-)
Restaurant du Coin (corner restaurant), sgn/dtd 1979, 16x12", FB 4/25/88 **2,100**

TANOUX, Adrien Henri (French, 1865-1923)
Sowers, oil on canvas, sgn/dtd 1910, 24x29", SBY 10/24/89 **7,150**

TANZI, Leon Louis (French, 1846-1913)
La Baigeneuse, oil on canvas, sgn, 18x24", SBY 12/9/88 **4,730**

TAPIES, Antoni (Spanish, 1923-)
Collage No 8-B, oil/paper collage on canvas, twice sgn/dtd 1960, 26x32", C-NY 11/10/88 OE **82,500**
Composition, fabric/twine/oil on canvas, sgn, 64x39", C-NY 11/9/88 OE **176,000**
Grisamb Impressions en Forma de Ferradura (abstract), oil/sand on canvas, sgn/dtd 1963, 11x19", SBY 11/11/88 OE **77,000**
Grisamb Impressions en Forma de Ferradura (abstract), oil/sand on canvas, sgn/dtd 1963, 11x19", SBY 5/3/89 OE **143,000**
Pittura Negra (abstract), plaster/oil/sand on canvas, 1956, 45x57", SBY 6/30/88 **104,000**
Verticals in Carmine (abstract), oil/sand on canvas, sgn/dtd 1959, 32x24", SBY 5/3/88 OE **88,000**

TAPORO Y BARO, Jose (Spanish, 1830-1913)
Harem Spinner, watercolor, sgn, 27x19", C-NY 5/25/88 **9,350**

TAPPERT, Georg (German, 1880-1957)
Double-Sided: Zwei Akte in Landscaft; Szei Tanzerinnen auf der Guhne; oil on canvas, 1911 & 1920, 57x48", SBY 11/11/88 **495,000**

TARBELL, Edmund Charles (American, 1862-1938)
Girl in the Pines, oil on canvas, sgn, 29x22", SBY 5/25/88 **55,000**
Girl Sewing in an Orchard, oil on canvas, sgn/dtd 1892, 20x24", SBY 5/25/88 **198,000**
Portrait of a Seated Woman, watercolor over pencil w/scratching out on paper, sgn, 21x14", SBY 9/14/89 **3,300**
Rosemary (portrait), oil on canvas, sgn/dtd 97, 27x20", C-NY 5/26/88 OE **28,600**

RDIF, Marie (Canadian, 20th C)
La Rue en Fete, oil on canvas, sgn/dtd 1987, 24x30", FB 4/25/88 600
RENGHI, Enrico (Italian, 1848-)
Arab & His Camel in the Desert, a Caravan Beyond; watercolor, sgn, 24x33", C-NY 2/23/89 2,200
Arab Coffee Shop, watercolor over traces of pencil, sgn, 21x14", C-NY 2/25/88 2,860
Arab Scene, oil on canvas, indistinctly sgn, 27x20", B/B 8/10/88 1,650
Distraction au Chateau, oil on canvas, sgn, 16x20", C-NY 2/25/88 3,300
Garden of the Convent, oil on canvas, sgn, 16x28", C-NY 5/25/88 UE 2,200
Pottery Merchant, watercolor, sgn, 21x15", C-NY 2/25/88 4,180
Travelers at the Sphynx & Great Pyramid, watercolor/pencil on paper, sgn, 15x21", SBY 12/9/88 1,100
RENNE, Roger
Country Home (landscape), oil on panel, sgn, 10x16", NA 5/13/89 325
St Andrews Cathedral, Bordeaux, France; oil on canvas, sgn/dtd 1933, 24x17", NA 5/13/89 650
RTAR, Eve (American, 20th C)
Sargasso Sea, cut paper on board, sgn, 21x17", B/B 5/17/89 UE 165
SCA, Luigi; att
Courtyard of a Castle with an Equestrian Monument, black chalk/pen/black ink/gray wash, #d 41, 8x8", C-NY 1/11/89 1,045
SSAERT, Octave (French, 1800-1874)
Blind Woman, oil on canvas, sgn, 16x12", C-E 2/23/88 UE 605
SSI, Agostino (Italian, 1565-1644)
Southern Port Scene with Boats & Figures Along the Shore, oil on canvas, unfr, 16x25", SBY 10/21/88 4,400
SSI, Agostino; att (Italian, 1565-1644)
Mediterranean Harbor with Shipping Below a Fortress, oil on canvas, 15x19", C-NY 4/6/89 OE 5,500
TKA, L. (19th/20th C)
Indians on Horseback, the War Party; oil on canvas, sgn/dtd 1761, 22x31", WG 9/16/88 UE 100
TOSSIAN, Armand (Canadian, 1948-)
Arbres pres de la Riviere, oil on canvas, sgn, 24x20", FB 10/30/89 770
La Cargaison (the cargo), oil on canvas, sgn, 12x16", FB 4/25/88 500
Port de Montreal, oil on canvas, sgn/dtd 1976, 16x20", FB 4/25/88 500
UBES, Frederic (American, 1900-1981)
Allegorical Figures in a Landscape, oil on canvas, sgn, 14x20", SBY 1/24/89 1,760
Untitled, floral still life w/bird; oil on canvas, sgn, 14x18", SLK 4/7/89 150
UNAY, Nicolas Antoine (French, 1755-1830)
Monks Giving Alms in a City Square, oil on panel, 21x32", C-NY 5/31/89 22,000
UNAY, Nicolas Antoine; school of (French, 1755-1830)
Promenade with Figures in a Park, oil on canvas, 22x26", C-NY 10/20/88 1,650
UPENOT, Madamoiselle (French, 19th/20th C)
Innocents in Paradise, oil on canvas, sgn, 74x101", B/B 6/9/88 3,300
VAR, Ivan
Sadness of Altazor, oil on canvas, sgn twice/dtd Santo Domingo 82/titled, 29x24", SBY 5/16/89 OE 7,150
VELLA, Carlo Antonio; see Solfarola
VERNIER, Jules (American, 1844-1889)
Indian Encampment, oil on canvas, sgn, 18x31", SBY 5/24/89 OE 57,750
VERNIER, Paul (French, 1852-)
Equipage de Bonnelles-Rambouillet a Madame la Duchesse d'Uzes; oil on canvas, sgn, 38x51", SBY 6/10/88 11,550
Fox Hunt, oil on canvas, sgn, 20x25", C-E 9/15/88 990
YLER, Albert Chevallier (British, 1862-1925)
Gray Drawing Room (interior scene w/seated man reading), oil on canvas, sgn/dtd 1917, 54x41", RAB 8/21/89 5,250
YLOR, C.B. (American, 20th C)
Sunlit View of a Harbor with Multiple Sailboats, oil on canvas, sgn, 24x30", SLK 2/12/88 2,500
YLOR, Frederick B. (Canadian, 1906-1987)
Asters in a Silver Mug, oil on board, sgn/dtd 1974, 6x8", FB 10/30/89 209
Back Galleries (rear of an apartment w/woman on balcony, children in snow), oil on canvas, sgn/1946, 28x35", FB 4/25/88 2,600
Beached Fishing Boat, watercolor, sgn, 10x14", FB 10/17/88 325
Bottles & Mug, oil on board, sgn, 12x16", WAD 11/30/89 650
Les Eboulements, China ink, initialed/dtd 1958, 10x14", FB 4/25/88 UE 300
Limestone Quarry, Montreal; pencil, sgn/dtd 1935, 9x13", FB 5/89 220
Marguerites in a White Jug, oil on canvas, sgn, 20x16", FB 10/30/89 302
Still Life (fruit, vegetables, green bottle, white jug), oil on canvas, sgn/dtd 1979, 18x24", FB 5/89 1,000
Three Apples, oil on board, sgn/dtd 1976, 7x8", FB 10/30/89 165
YLOR, H.W.
Rapids with Mountains in Distance, oil on canvas, sgn, 8x13", C-E 9/15/88 UE 110
YLOR, James E. (American, 1839-1901)
Sherman's 17th Corps Crossing the Saluda River (Civil War), watercolor on paper, sgn/inscr, 6x16", C-E 5/27/88 OE 1,760
YLOR, John (American, 1735-1806)
Pair: Travelers in a Covered Wagon; Timber Haulers Resting by a Tree; oil on canvas, sgn, 6x8", SBY 10/13/89 OE 5,500
YLOR, Loretta (20th C)
Homeplace, watercolor on paper, sgn, 22x30", SBY 9/23/88 UE 275
YLOR, Ralph
Mother & Child, oil on board, sgn, 10x8", C-E 6/1/89 OE 880

TAYLOR, Sydney (British, 1952-)
Cape Town, gouache, sgn, 16x20", C-SK 11/10/88 370
TAYLOR, Walter (American, 20th C)
Nude, pastel on paper, sgn, 17x12", C-E 6/1/89 286
TAYLOR, William H. (Canadian, 1891-)
St Anne's Church, oil on panel, sgn/dtd 1933, 7x9", FB 4/25/88 400
TCHELITCHEW, Pavel (American/Russian, 1898-1957)
Allegorical Composition, oil & tempera on canvas, 31x26", C-NY 10/6/88 9,900
At the Cafe (three figures at a table), pen/black ink on paper, sgn/dtd 1924, 13x9", C-E 11/17/88 880
Bearded Lady, silverpoint, sgn, 18x12", C-NY 10/6/88 1,430
Boating Party, brush/pen/India ink on paper, sgn/dtd 36, 10x14", C-NY 10/6/88 OE 1,100
Bullfight, gouache on board laid down on wood, sgn/dtd 34, 42x30", SBY 5/11/88 22,000
Churchyard (figures in clouds above church), pen/sepia ink/wash on paper, sgn/dtd 32, 13x19", C-E 5/9/89 1,210
Costume Design for Ondine, India ink/watercolor on paper, sgn/dtd 1939, 11x8", SBY 10/7/89 2,750
Costume Design for Savanarola, gouache/gold paint on paper, sgn, 1922, 20x14", C-L 10/8/88 9,300
Danseuse Espagnole (still-life figure of hands/feet/hammock), oil on canvas, sgn, 1930, 39x29", C-NY 5/12/88 19,800
Decor Design for Concerto, First Movement; gouache on paper, inscr, unfr, 20x29", SBY 10/7/89 3,575
Decor Design for Concerto, Second Movement; gouache on paper, inscr, unfr, 20x29", SBY 10/7/89 3,575
Decor Design for Concerto, Third Movement; gouache on paper, inscr, unfr, 17x26", SBY 10/7/89 6,600
Figure by a Tree, pen/ink on blotting paper, 11x15", C-NY 10/6/88 550
Figure in a Mythological Landscape, pen/brown ink/wash on paper, sgn/dtd 32, 12x16", SBY 10/7/89 1,540
Figures in a Geometric Landscape, gouache/pen/black ink on paper, sgn/dtd 36, 9x14", C-NY 10/6/88 4,950
Five Figures, ink sketch, sgn/dtd 35, 7x13", LH 5/15/88 450
Flower of Sight, gouache on 3 pieces of paper, sgn, 17x13", C-NY 10/6/88 4,950
Head, Interior Landscape; colored chalks on paper, sgn/dtd 46, 14x10", C-NY 10/6/88 4,620
Indian Dance, watercolor on black paper, sgn/dtd 1938, 13x16", C-NY 10/6/88 OE 1,540
Mad Woman, silverpoint, sgn/dtd 37, 19x13", C-NY 10/6/88 1,320
Man Leaning Against a Drafting Table, pen/black ink on paper, sgn/dtd 29, 7x4", C-E 11/17/88 OE 1,320
Metamorphosis (abstract), watercolor/pen/black ink on paper, sgn/dtd 1941-42, 11x14", C-NY 2/18/88 2,750
Pair: Veiled Woman; Woman Reclining: brown wash on paper, 1 sgn/dtd 33, 10x8", 8x10", SBY 10/7/89 1,650
Portrait of a Woman, gouache on paper, sgn/dtd 25, 25x19", SBY 2/14/89 OE 5,225
Portrait of a Young Man, brush/gray ink wash on paper, sgn/dtd 49, 20x15", C-E 5/9/89 990
Portrait of Charles Henri Ford Standing, brown ink on paper, sgn/dtd 35, 13x8", SBY 10/7/89 1,540
Portrait of Monroe Wheeler, pen/ink/wash on paper laid down on paper, 13x10", C-E 5/9/89 1,320
Set of 4: Studies of Vertebrae-Interior Landscapes; colored crayons on paper, 3 sgn/dtd 49, 12x9", C-NY 10/6/88 OE 6,050
Shepherd, oil on canvas, sgn/dtd 30, 39x29", C-NY 10/6/88 17,600
Skull, Interior Landscape; colored chalks w/pen/black ink on paper, sgn/dtd 46, 14x10", C-NY 10/6/88 4,400
Still Life of Apples, oil on canvas, sgn, 26x21", C-NY 10/6/88 4,950
Studies of a Boy, silverpoint, sgn/dtd 36, 20x12", C-NY 10/6/88 OE 3,300
Studies of a Male Nude, silverpoint, sgn/dtd 36, 20x12", C-NY 10/6/88 OE 3,850
Studies of Two Figures, brush/pen/India ink on paper, 8x12", C-NY 10/6/88 990
Study for Hide & Seek, brush/India ink on paper, sgn/dtd 1941, 9x11", C-NY 10/6/88 OE 2,860
Study for Phenomena, brown wash on paper, sgn/dtd 1934, 10x13", SBY 10/7/89 1,650
Study for Phenomena, ink wash heightened with white on paper, sgn/dtd 36, unfr, 15x20", SBY 10/7/89 1,430
Study for the Cover of View Magazine, brown ink/collage on paper, unfr, 9x11", SBY 10/7/89 2,640
Study for Theatre Francais (figures in balcony), pen & ink/wash on paper, sgn/dtd 31, 8x10", SBY 2/14/89 2,200
Study of the Head, pen/ink on paper, sgn/dtd 1930, unfr, 18x11", B/B 4/20/88 880
Three Sitting Together, oil on board, sgn/dtd 33, 29x41", C-NY 10/6/88 14,300
Three Women (depicting woman's misery), pen/sepia/black inks on brown paper, sgn/dtd 37, 14x10", C-NY 10/6/88 1,100
TCHERIKOVA, Ludmilla
La Suite Bizarre, Eleven Costume Designs; watercolor/pencil on paper, sgn, unfr, 16x11" & smaller, SBY 2/14/89 UE 1,100
TEAGUE, Donald (American, 1897-)
Barges on the Seine, watercolor on paper, sgn, 4x7", B/B 1/11/89 OE 2,475
Wedding Party, watercolor/gouache on paper, sgn/inscr/copyrighted, 20x29", SBY 9/23/88 OE 27,500
TEARLE, John H. (American, 20th C)
View of Boston Harbor, watercolor on paper, sgn/dtd 1921, orig fr, 18x22", RAB 8/1/88 650
TEBARIN, A.
Courtship, oil on canvas, sgn, 22x19", C-E 2/23/88 1,430
TEDESCHI (Italian, 1923-)
River Landscape, oil on canvas, sgn, 24x36", LH 5/15/88 UE 100
TEED, Douglas Arthur (American, 1864-1929)
By the Fishbowl, oil on canvas, sgn/dtd 1919, 30x36", SBY 9/23/88 2,090
Figure & Cattle in a Sunset Landscape, oil on canvas, sgn, 15x30", SBY 1/24/89 1,540
Interior Mosque Scene, oil on canvas, sgn, 20x24", DM 10/14/88 UE 900
Interior of a Mosque, oil on canvas laid down on board, sgn, 42x33", DM 5/13/88 1,500
Landscape Scene (small river & cows grazing), oil on canvas, sgn/dtd 1925, 24x36", DM 3/14/88 1,700
Middle-Eastern Scene (seated Arab w/pots), oil on canvas, sgn/dtd 1925, 24x30", DM 5/19/89 1,200
Moorish Courtyard, oil on canvas, sgn/dtd 1920, 20x30", DM 3/14/88 2,500
Rug Bazaar Scene, oil on canvas, sgn/dtd 1925, 33x40", DM 1/15/88 3,000
Rug Merchants at the Bazaar, oil on canvas, sgn, 11x15", WG 4/23/88 UE 600

EL, Lewis Woods (American, 1883-)
Spring in Sacramento, oil on board, sgn, 12x18", B/B 12/8/88 935
IDEMANS, Jean (Canadian)
Portrait of a Woman, oil on canvas, sgn, 24x18", FB 10/17/88..... 175
LINGATER, Solomon (Russian, 1903-1969)
Photomontage, collage on paper, 13x10", C-L 10/8/88 OE..... 7,440
Photomontage, collage on paper, 15x11", C-L 10/8/88 3,720
Photomontage with Watch, collage on paper, 16x12", C-L 10/8/88 OE 11,150
LSER, A. (Continental, 19th/20th C)
Fashioning a Garland on a Pleasant Spring Day, oil on canvas, sgn, 13x16", SBY 6/8/88 1,430
MPESTA, Antonio; att (Italian, 1555-1667)
Washerwomen in a Mountainous River Landscape, oil on canvas, 53x52", WD 10/19/88 OE 7,750
MPESTA, Antonio; circle of (Italian, 1555-1667)
Conversion of St Paul, pen/brown ink/brown wash heightened w/white on gray paper, inscr, 7x8", C-E 4/7/88 UE 220
St George & the Dragon (preparatory study for an engraving), pen/ink/wash over black chalk, 9x7", SBY 1/13/89 2,640
N CATE, Hendrik Gerrit (Dutch, 1803-1856)
Faggot Gatherer in a Winter Landscape, watercolor over traces of pencil, sgn/dtd 1838, 9x12", C-E 2/21/89 990
N KATE, Herman Frederick Carel (Dutch, 1822-1891)
Card Game, oil on panel, sgn/dtd 1862, 16x20", RWS 11/3/88..... 4,500
Dispatch, oil on panel, sgn, 6x8", SBY 12/9/88..... 1,980
Guard Room, oil on panel, sgn/dtd 1864, 13x17", C-NY 10/25/89 7,150
Surrender (figures in an interior), oil on panel, sgn, 24x36", B/B 10/9/88..... 17,600
Tavern Interior, watercolor on paper, sgn/dtd 1864, 11x18", B/B 3/17/88 2,750
N KATE, Johan Mari (Dutch, 1831-1910)
Children's Picnic, watercolor on paper laid down on board, sgn, 14x19", SBY 12/9/88 OE..... 9,350
Figures on a Beach, watercolor heightened w/white, sgn, 13x20", C-NY 10/26/88 3,520
Fisherfolk Returning Home, oil on canvas, sgn, 31x43", C-NY 10/25/89 36,300
On the Scent (dog in a landscape), oil on canvas, sgn, unfr, 21x14", C-E 5/22/89..... 3,300
NCY, Jean Baptiste
Men Building a Boat & Ship Being Careened, oil on panel, sgn, 20x29", C-NY 1/15/88..... 9,350
NGNAGEL, see De Tengnagel
NIERS, David the elder; follower of (Flemish, 1582-1649)
Figures in an Extensive Landscape, oil on canvas, 25x31", SBY 7/12/89 2,200
Travelers in a Landscape, oil on canvas, 37x47", SBY 7/12/89 5,225
NIERS, David the younger (Flemish, 1610-1690)
Figures, Some Gathered Talking, on the Outskirts of a Town; oil on panel, monogramed, 7x12", SBY 1/12/89..... 49,500
Peasants Smoking & Drinking in a Tavern, oil on panel, sgn, 15x22", C-NY 1/11/89..... 110,000
Traveler Encountering a Gypsy Fortuneteller, oil on panel, monogramed, 7x10", C-NY 1/11/89 OE 49,500
Vanitas: Lady...at Table Surrounded by Objects & Children Blowing Bubbles...; oil on panel, sgn, 18x28", C-NY 5/31/89 126,500
NIERS, David the younger; att (Flemish, 1610-1690)
Animals Drinking at the Cask (cat-like people in cellar), oil on tin, 14x10", RAB 3/27/89 UE..... 300
Travelers Along a Mountain Path, oil on canvas, 10x13", SBY 7/12/89 2,750
NIERS, David the younger; circle of (Flemish, 1610-1690)
Gaurdroom Interior with the Captain of the Guard & His Page, oil copper, dtd 1646, 23x31", C-NY 6/2/88 19,800
Landscape with Archers Practicing Marksmanship, oil on panel, bears signature/dtd 1665, 16x21", SBY 4/7/89 OE 7,700
Man Drawing at a Table with an Elderly Man Beside Him, oil on panel, 10x8", SBY 4/7/88..... 1,650
Tavern Interior with Figures Smoking & Playing Cards, oil on canvas, 18x28", SBY 4/7/89 7,150
Woman Peeling Apples in a Cottage Interior, oil on panel, 14x19", C-NY 5/31/89..... 8,250
NIERS, David the younger; follower of (Flemish, 1610-1690)
Interior of a Guardroom with Soldiers Playing Cards & a Still Life of Arms & Armor, oil on canvas, 23x34", SBY 10/21/88 7,700
NIERS, David the younger; manner of (Flemish, 1610-1690)
Card Players (interior scene), watercolor on vellum, 16x24", C-E 1/12/88 OE 2,640
Figures & Boats by a Cove, oil on panel, 9x12", SBY 7/12/89 550
Figures in an Extensive Landscape, oil on canvas, 25x31", SBY 7/12/89 2,200
Tavern Scene, oil on panel, 16x23", SBY 7/12/89 660
Village Feast, oil on panel, 28x36", SBY 12/9/88 OE 4,675
NIERS, David the younger; school of (Flemish, 1610-1690)
Rustic Interior, oil on panel, 9x12", FAP 12/8/89 UE 900
Village Festival, oil on panel, 14x19", C-NY 1/15/88 OE 14,300
NIERS, David; after (Flemish, 17th C)
Festival Scene (figures making merry), oil on laminated canvas, 25x31", DM 3/14/88..... 1,000
NIERS, David; att (Flemish, 17th C)
Charles V Leaving the Town of Dort, oil, bears initials, 23x39", WD 1/25/89 6,000
Couple Eating at a Table in an Interior, oil on copper, bears signature, 7x9", C-NY 4/8/88 6,600
NIERS, David; manner of (Flemish, 17th C)
Six Figures in an Interior, oil on canvas laid down on board, 17x22", C-E 2/16/88 374
Village Landscape, oil on canvas, 25x39", C-E 6/1/88..... 990
NIERS, David; school of (Flemish, 17th C)
Archery Contest by an Inn, oil on panel, 11x15", C-E 4/7/88 OE..... 2,090
Peasant Merrymaking Outside a Tavern, oil on canvas, 17x24", C-E 4/7/88 OE..... 4,400
Peasants Merrymaking Before a Tavern, oil on canvas, 32x40", C-NY 4/6/89 OE 8,800

Peasants Merrymaking in a Tavern (many figures in an interior), oil on copper, 8x10", C-NY 4/6/89 OE ... 4,180
Portrait of a Man with a Pipe, oil on panel, 3x2", C-E 4/7/88 ... 462
Tavern Scene, oil on panel, 10x13", DM 9/16/88 ... 1,000
Temptation of Saint Anthony, oil on canvas, 16x23", C-NY 4/8/88 ... 4,400

TENRE, Charles Henry (French, 1864-1926)
Blossoming Friendship Between a Soldier & a Lady, oil on canvas, sgn, 29x36", FAP 4/15/89 OE ... 9,460
French Interior, watercolor on paper, sgn, 17x15", WD 3/23/88 ... 950

TEPPER, Saul (American, 1899-)
Factory Interior Scene, oil on canvas, sgn/dtd 29, 27x40", RWS 9/8/89 ... 4,700
Sand Hogs (laborers), oil on canvas, sgn, 22x32", SBY 6/24/88 ... 2,750
Wrestling Match-Gorgeous George; oil on canvas mounted on masonite, sgn, 36x40", RWS 3/16/89 OE ... 3,500

TER MEULEN, Frans Pieter (Dutch, 1843-1927)
Sheep Grazing, oil on canvas, sgn, 22x32", FB 4/25/88 ... 1,300

TERBORCH, Gerard (Dutch, 1617-1681)
Lady at Her Toilet Attended by a Maid, oil on canvas, 26x21", C-NY 1/15/88 ... 13,200
Portrait of Johanna Quadacker Bannier, oil on canvas, 28x20", SBY 6/3/88 ... 478,500

TERBORCH, Gerard; after (Dutch, 1617-1681)
Boy Grooming Horse, oil on panel, 7x9", LH 3/20/88 OE ... 550

TERBORCH, Gerard; circle of (Dutch, 1617-1681)
Elegant Lady Seated at a Table Playing the Lute, oil on canvas, bears signature/dtd 1669, unfr, 20x16", SBY 10/21/88 ... 5,500

TERBRUGGHEN, Hendrick; follower of (Dutch, 1588-1629)
Roman Charity or Cimon & Pero, oil on canvas, unfr, 53x60", SBY 10/13/89 ... 4,960

TERECHKOVITCH, Constantin (Russian/French, 1902-1978)
Femme Assise au Chapeau (seated woman in striped caftan & hat), oil on canvas, sgn/dtd 66, 36x26", C-NY 10/5/89 OE ... 79,200

TERPNING, Howard A. (American, 1927-)
Rocky Mountain Shootin' Match, oil on masonite, sgn twice/inscr/copyrighted/dtd 1981, 20x28", SBY 9/23/88 OE ... 33,000
Twas the Night Before Christmas, oil on canvas, sgn, 37x29", C-NY 9/30/88 ... 17,600

TERUZ, Orlando (Brazil, 1902-1984)
Cabra Cega, oil on canvas, sgn/dtd Rio 1982, 36x29", C-NY 11/21/89 ... 26,400

TESSIER, Louis Adolphe (French, 19th C)
Testing the Vintage (woman opening wine bottle), oil on canvas, sgn, 44x30", C-NY 2/23/89 ... 6,600

TESSIER, Louis; att (French, 1719-1781)
Flowers & Butterflies in a Porcelain Vase on a Ledge, oil on canvas, unfr, 33x25", C-NY 1/15/88 ... 20,900

TESSON, Louis (French, fl 1841-1867)
An Egyptian Street, oil on canvas, 18x24", SBY 12/9/88 ... 4,950

TESTA, Pietro (Italian, 1611-1650)
Arcadian Landscape with St Jerome in the Foreground, pen/brown ink, 7x9", SBY 1/13/89 ... 8,800
Landscape with Two Figures Mourning Over the Body of a Man, pen/brown ink/wash over red chalk, 7x7", SBY 1/13/89 OE ... 29,700

TESTA, Pietro; att (Italian, 1611-1650)
Sheet of Figure Studies for a Scene of Violence, pen/brown ink/wash, 7x9", SBY 1/13/89 ... 11,000

TESTU, Paul (German, 1900-)
Breaking for Lunch, oil on canvas, sgn, 26x36", C-E 10/25/88 OE ... 4,180
Fisherfolk with the Day's Catch, oil on canvas, sgn, 14x17", PHL 10/28/88 ... 425

THALINGER, E. Oscar (American, 1885-1965)
Interior of a Barn, oil on masonite, bears inscription, 23x19", SLK 9/29/88 ... 275
Missouri River, oil on masonite, sgn/dtd 47, 27x35", SLK 9/26/88 ... 125

THAULOW, Frits (Norwegian, 1847-1906)
Bridge, oil on canvas, sgn, 29x37", SBY 5/23/89 ... 63,250
Les Bords de l'Hautie, Effet de Lune; oil on canvas, sgn, unfr, 22x18", C-NY 5/25/88 UE ... 15,400
Morning River Scene, oil on canvas laid down on aluminium, sgn, 26x32", SBY 10/24/89 ... 42,900
Orchard on the Banks of a River, oil on canvas, sgn, 26x37", SBY 2/22/89 ... 35,750
River in Winter, oil on canvas, sgn/dtd 91, 29x36", SBY 10/24/89 ... 77,000
Twilight Along the River, oil on canvas, sgn, 22x28", RAB 3/27/89 UE ... 4,000
Untitled, nocturnal scene in a village square; oil on canvas, ca 1894, 25x33", SLK 11/25/88 ... 15,000
Venetian Canal Scene, oil on canvas, sgn, 26x32", C-NY 5/25/88 UE ... 19,800
Winter Landscape with a Winding Stream, oil on canvas, sgn, 20x24", C-NY 10/25/89 ... 66,000
Winter on the Mesna River Near Lillehammer, oil on canvas, sgn, ca 1905-06, 26x32", C-NY 2/23/89 OE ... 101,200
Winter Stream, oil on panel, sgn, 16x13", B/B 6/9/88 ... 15,400

THAYER, Abbott Handerson (American, 1849-1921)
Garden with House, watercolor/gouache/pencil on paper, sgn/dtd 1893, 7x12", C-NY 5/26/88 ... 2,200
Mary Thayer Asleep (portrait of a child), oil on canvas laid down on panel, sgn/dtd 1877/inscr, 11x13", C-SK 6/9/88 OE ... 9,295
Portrait of a Golden Retriever, oil on canvas, sgn/dtd 1874, 20x16", RWS 5/19/88 ... 1,700
Portrait of Eleanor Fischer, oil on panel, sgn/dtd 1908, 36x28", SBY 5/25/88 ... 9,900
Woman Reading, oil on canvas, 14x10", C-E 6/1/88 ... 1,540

THAYER, Albert R. (American, 19th/20th C)
Annesquam River, oil on cardboard, sgn, 10x13", RAB 8/8/89 ... 1,100

THEIL, E. Dre
River Landscape at Dusk, oil on board, sgn, 20x30", C-E 4/7/88 UE ... 220

THEMMEN, C. (German, 19th C)
Sunset in the Mountains, oil on canvas, sgn/dtd 1889, 48x30", RAB 8/9/88 ... 1,750
Wild Turkeys, oil on canvas, sgn/dtd 1892, 40x32", RAB 8/9/88 ... 3,000

EMMEN, Charles (American, 19th C)
n the Woods (landscape w/stream), oil on canvas, sgn/dtd 1889, 48x30", C-E 2/1/89 UE **550**
Sunset in the Berkshires (landscape), oil on canvas, sgn/dtd 1889, 48x30", RAB 8/8/89 .... **1,500**
EOPOKOPOULS, Domenikos; see Greco
ERKILDSEN, Michael (Danish, 1850-1925)
Cow on a Path, oil on canvas, initialed/dtd 94, 18x25", C-NY 5/24/89 .... **6,600**
ERRIEN, Robert (20th C)
Bird, tempera/graphite on paper, 1979, 10x11", C-NY 10/31/89 OE **7,700**
Untitled (Red Corner Painting), oil on canvas mounted on wood, 84x64", C-NY 10/31/89 .... **30,800**
IEBAUD, Wayne (American, 1920-)
Box Rows, oil on linen, sgn/dtd 1963, 16x26", SBY 10/5/89 OE **418,000**
Boxes, oil on canvas, sgn/dtd 1963, 12x10", SBY 10/5/89 .... **121,000**
Cake, India ink on paper, 1965, 10x10", SBY 5/3/89 .... **14,300**
Cliffs (contempory), acrylic on canvas, sgn/dtd 1968, 100x87", C-NY 5/3/89 .... **495,000**
Cracker Rows (contemporary), oil on canvas, sgn/dtd 1963, 6x10", C-NY 11/9/88 OE **82,500**
Crown Tart (still life), watercolor/ink on paper, sgn, 1964, 9x11", SBY 11/11/88 .... **44,000**

ink Syrups, oil on canvas, sgn/dtd 61, 24x36", C-NY 11/7/89; $330,000

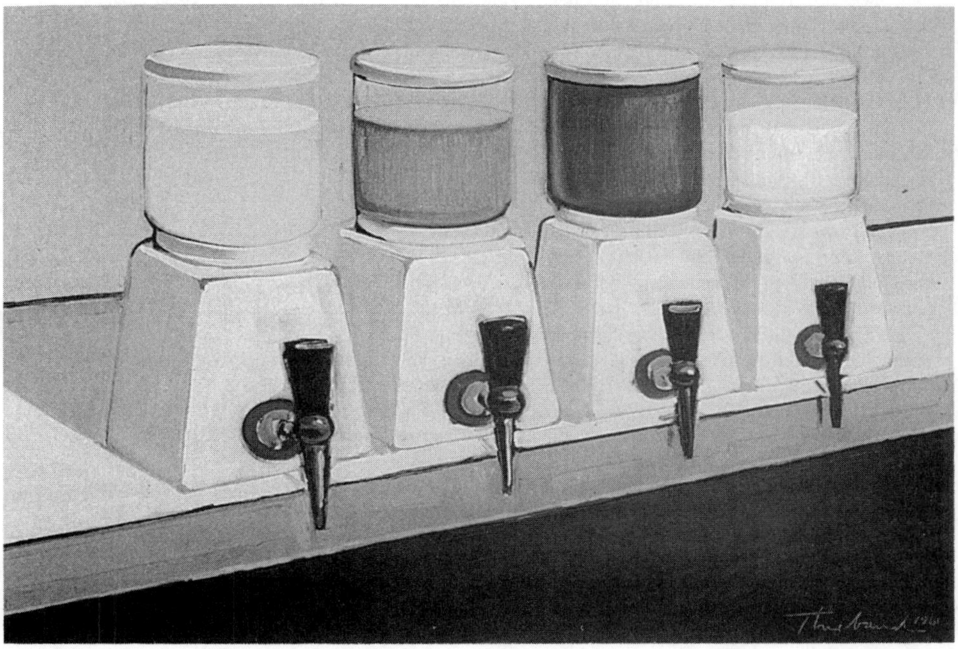

Heart Cakes (Valentine Cakes, Four Valentine Cakes), oil on canvas, sgn, 1975, 36x48", C-NY 5/3/88 .... **605,000**
Knife (still life), charcoal on paper, sgn/dtd 1972, 20x16", SBY 11/11/88 .... **19,800**
Ocean Hill, graphite/pastel on paper, ca 1965, 7x13", SBY 5/3/89 .... **14,300**
Out Box, oil on canvas, sgn, 1972-73, 14x16", SBY 2/19/88 OE **159,500**
Portrait of a Woman, conte crayon on vellum, sgn/dtd 53, 5x8", SBY 10/7/89 .... **2,420**
Power Drill, graphite on paper, sgn/dtd 1971, 30x22", SBY 11/11/88 .... **22,000**
River Sunset (contemporary landscape), oil on canvas, 1969, 20x29", SBY 11/11/88 .... **88,000**
Seven Jelly Apples, ink on paper, sgn/dtd 1964, 12x12", SBY 5/3/88 .... **13,200**
Shelf Pies (pieces of pie on four shelves), oil on canvas, sgn/dtd 1961, 24x18", SBY 5/2/89 .... **330,000**
Telephone Directory, Ruler & Letter Addressed to Allan Stone; pastel on paper, sgn/dtd 1972, 22x30", SBY 11/11/88 .... **38,500**
Toy Counter Study, oil on canvas, sgn/dtd 1962, 10x12", C-NY 11/9/88 .... **121,000**
Untitled (alphabet block RST), pastel on paper laid down on board, sgn/dtd 1964, 7x9", SBY 5/3/89 .... **55,000**
EBLIN, Reine Josephine (French, 19th/20th C)
till Life of Vase of Flowers on a Marble Table, oil on panel, sgn/inscr, 16x12", SBY 12/9/88 .... **3,575**
ELEMANN, A. (Continental, 19th C)
till Life of Fruit & Wine, oil on canvas, sgn, 23x27", SBY 6/8/88 .... **1,760**
EME, Anthony (American, 1888-1954)
After the Storm in a Dutch Harbor, oil on board, sgn, 14x17", B/B 8/10/88 .... **1,430**
Autumn (house/trees in landscape), oil on board, sgn/artist stamp/titled, 9x8", RAB 3/27/89 .... **1,000**
Bass Rocks, Gloucester; oil on canvas, sgn, 30x36", RAB 8/9/88 UE **2,000**
Blue Water, oil on canvas, sgn, 30x36", C-E 6/1/88 .... **7,700**
Bright Morning, oil on canvas, sgn/inscr/titled, unfr, 30x36", SBY 6/24/88 OE **12,100**
Buggy Ride on the River Road, Autumn; oil on canvas, sgn, 30x36", RWS 5/12/89 .... **5,000**
Cove Hill (shaded autumn street scene w/figures), oil on canvas, sgn, 30x36", C-NY 9/28/89 OE **36,300**
Dutch Farm (on a sunny day), oil on canvas, sgn, 25x30", SBY 1/24/89 .... **2,750**
Early Morning, oil on canvas, sgn, 20x24", C-NY 9/30/88 OE **9,350**
First Snow: Winter in Rockport; oil on canvas, sgn, 25x30", WD 4/13/88 .... **5,600**

Gloucester, oil on canvas, sgn, 30x36", C-NY 9/30/88 ... 13,200
Gloucester (sailboats coming into harbor), oil on canvas, sgn, 25x31", WD 4/13/88 OE ... 8,000
Gloucester Harbor, oil on canvas, sgn, 26x31", C-E 6/1/88 ... 3,740
Gloucester Harbor, oil on canvasboard, sgn, 18x20", B/B 3/17/88 ... 3,300
Harbor at Night, oil on canvas, sgn/copyrighted/titled, 30x36", SBY 1/24/89 ... 11,000
Harbor Scene, oil on canvas, sgn, 20x30", C-E 2/3/88 OE ... 2,420
Harbor Scene, oil on canvas, sgn, 25x30", SBY 1/24/89 ... 3,025
Harborside, Gloucester (docked sailboats); oil on canvas, sgn, 32x36", C-NY 9/28/89 OE ... 17,600
In the Harbor, oil on canvas, sgn/artist stamp, 20x25", SBY 6/28/89 ... 7,425
Le Pont Marie (bridge & water, street & trees along side), oil on canvasboard, sgn/dtd 1950, 20x24", C-E 6/1/89 ... 3,300
Louisville Shore, oil on canvas, sgn, 25x30", WD 4/13/88 OE ... 16,000
Mexican Village Scene, oil on canvas, sgn, 30x36", SBY 4/14/89 OE ... 7,700
Morning Breeze (ship at full sail), oil on canvas, sgn, 30x25", C-SK 5/25/89 OE ... 4,590
Mountain Stream, oil on canvas, sgn, 25x30", SBY 6/28/89 ... 3,300
Old Gloucester, oil on canvasboard, sgn, 16x20", C-E 11/30/88 ... 3,300
Old Houses, oil on canvas, sgn, 30x36", WD 4/13/88 ... 5,750
Pair: Awibeare; Temple; watercolor on paper, ea sgn/1 inscr, 22x29" & smaller, C-E 2/3/88 ... 825
Pair: Castle; St Augustine Florida; watercolor on paper, ea sgn/1 inscr, 15x21" & smaller, C-E 2/3/88 OE ... 1,210
Peaceful Street (w/view of church), oil on canvas, sgn, 25x30", C-NY 9/28/89 ... 5,500
Pigeon Cove, oil on canvas, sgn, 36x30", NA 2/24/89 ... 5,250
Plaza Capuchinos, oil on canvas, sgn, 20x24", WD 4/13/88 ... 2,400
Reflection Series: Brown Fish Houses & Boats; oil on board, sgn/titled, 12x16", SBY 6/24/88 OE ... 2,090
Rockport Afternoon, oil on canvas, sgn/inscr, 25x30", RWS 11/3/88 ... 3,900
Rockport Harbor, oil on canvas, sgn, 25x31", WD 4/13/88 ... 5,500
Rockport Harbor, oil on canvas, sgn, 8x10", B/B 6/15/89 ... 2,200
Sailboat Leaving the Pier, no media given, sgn, unfr, 25x30", C-E 2/16/88 UE ... 220
Sailing, oil on canvas, sgn/titled, 20x24", SBY 9/23/88 ... 3,300
Sea Gulls (birds at pier, man in boat beyond), oil on canvas, sgn, 30x36", RWS 5/19/88 OE ... 2,000
Seaweed Gathers, oil on board, sgn, 8x18", C-E 11/30/88 ... 1,760
Sound Through the Fog, oil on board, sgn/inscr, 8x10", SBY 9/23/88 OE ... 2,970
Spring in the Rain(cottages & trees glisten in rain), oil on canvas mounted on cardboard, sgn, 8x10", RWS 9/29/88 ... 950
Summertime, oil on canvas, sgn/inscr, 30x36", C-E 2/3/88 OE ... 7,480
Village House (sunny landscape w/two figures), oil on canvas, sgn, 30x36", SBY 1/24/89 OE ... 8,800
Wet Day (docked boat w/figures on pier), oil on canvas, sgn/titled, 10x24", SBY 9/23/88 ... 6,600

THIEME, Carl (German, 1816-1884)
Merry Village, oil on canvas, sgn/dtd 1875, 16x23", C-E 10/26/89 ... 1,320

THIERRENS, see De Thierrens THIERRIAT, Augustin ALexandre (1789-1870)
Bouquet of Flowers, watercolor over pencil, sgn/dtd 1829, 10x7", SBY 1/13/89 ... 1,760

THINSEN, C.
Mother & Baby (mother sewing, baby in cradle), oil on canvas, sgn, 18x21", DM 9/16/88 ... 1,400

THIRION, Victor Charles (French, 1833-1878)
Reprimand (woman scolding lad), oil on canvas, sgn, 14x11", C-NY 2/23/89 ... 5,500

THOM, James Crawford (American, 1835-1898)
Courtship (peasant couple at barn door), oil on panel, sgn, 23x16", C-E 6/1/89 UE ... 1,430
Fisherman Before His Shack, oil on canvas, sgn, 6x10", RWS 9/8/89 ... 600
Protected (children in barn, woman at doorway), oil on panel, sgn, 23x16", C-E 6/1/89 UE ... 1,320
Sailing Off the Coast, oil on panel, sgn, inscr, 5x11", C-E 2/1/89 OE ... 2,420
Shopping List (gentleman & two children in an interior), oil on canvas, sgn, 20x30", C-SK 11/10/88 ... 2,040
Trees, watercolor on paper, sgn, 11x7", C-E 6/1/88 UE ... 275
Woodsman, oil on canvas, sgn, 27x6", C-NY 11/30/88 UE ... 462

THOMAS, Pat (American, 20th C)
Firewood, oil on canvas, sgn/dtd 1977, 18x24", MAG 9/18/88 ... 900

THOMAS, Reynolds (American, 1927-)
Old Salt (man stands by old dory), watercolor on paper, sgn, 13x18", RAB 8/9/88 ... 600

THOMAS, Stephen Seymour (American, 1868-1956)
Sunset on River Wall, Rijsoord, Holland; oil on canvas, sgn, 10x17", NA 10/1/88 ... 475

THOMASSE, Adolphe (French, 1850-1930)
Frehja, Goddess of Carnal Love (portrait); oil on canvas, sgn, 26x20", B/B 3/22/89 ... 1,980

THOMASSIN, Desire (Austrian, 1858-1933)
Hunter in the Snow, oil on canvas, sgn, 22x18", B/B 3/17/88 ... 4,675
Young Shepherdess with Her Flock & Donkeys, oil, in a painted oval, 14x18", WD 1/11/89 ... 600

THOMPSON, Albert (American, 1853-)
Cowherd in a Stormy Landscape, oil on canvas, sgn/dtd 1878, 34x54", B/B 3/17/88 ... 2,200

THOMPSON, Alfred Wordsworth (American, 1840-1896)
At the Ford, oil on canvas, sgn/dtd 76, 10x18", SBY 9/23/88 OE ... 5,775
In the Deep South (farm scene w/man loading wagon), oil on canvas, sgn/dtd 1879, 17x21", SBY 5/24/89 ... 24,200
In the Fields (landscape), oil on canvas, sgn, 11x19", SBY 1/24/89 OE ... 7,425
Lesson by the Sea, oil on canvas, sgn, 10x18", C-E 11/30/88 OE ... 6,050
Port of Algiers, oil on canvas, sgn/titled, 22x36", SBY 2/22/89 ... 44,000

THOMPSON, Bob (American, 1937-1966)
Christ (contemporary), oil on canvas, sgn/dtd Paris 61, 5x7", C-NY 5/4/89 ... 5,280

lub (contemporary group of figures, one w/club), oil on panel, sgn, ca 1960, C-NY 2/20/88	6,600
he Trek (abstract), oil on wood, sgn/dtd 60, 5x55", C-E 11/14/89 OE	3,520
rying (contemporary landscape w/figures & horse), oil on panel, sgn/dtd 1960, unfr, 5x16", C-NY 2/20/88	4,180
ntitled (abstract landscape w/figures), oil on canvas, twice sgn/dtd 61, 25x21", C-NY 11/10/88 OE	17,600
OMPSON, C.L. (American, 19th C)	
till Life of Game, oil on canvas, sgn/dtd 1888, 21x15", SBY 1/24/89 UE	660
OMPSON, Frederick Louis (American, 1868-)	
Veirs Off Horseneck Beach (coastal landscape), oil on canvas, sgn, 18x30", RAB 8/8/89 UE	1,000
OMPSON, G. (British, 19th C)	
iew of Westwater, oil on canvas, sgn, 10x18", PHL 10/28/88	250
OMPSON, George Albert (American, 1868-1938)	
udding Oaks, oil on panel, sgn/dtd 1913, 12x16", C-E 6/1/88	1,100
ouse in the Woods, oil on board, sgn, 8x10", RAB 8/9/88 UE	150
OMPSON, H.J.	
ishing at Sunset, oil on canvas, sgn, 33x48", C-E 5/23/88 UE	330
OMPSON, J. Leslie (Continental, 19th/20th C)	
t the Foot of the Mountains (herd in a landscape), oil on canvas, sgn, unfr, 30x50", C-E 5/22/89	2,200
OMPSON, Jerome (American, 1814-1886)	
y the Stream; or, Indian Maiden's Toilet; oil on canvas, sgn/dtd 1865, 34x30", SBY 9/14/89	18,700
OMPSON, John S. (British, 19th/20th C)	
ee Valley, oil on canvas, sgn, 10x18", B/B 9/15/88	880
OMPSON, William John (British, 1771-1845)	
ortrait of Grecian Williams, oil on ivory, sgn, 5x4", RAB 3/27/89 UE	225
OMSON, Chandler (British, 20th C)	
Vindmill Near Kent, watercolor on paper, sgn, 11x15", B/B 1/11/89	412
OMSON, George (Canadian, 1868-1965)	
alley Farm, oil on board, sgn, 15x18", WAD 11/30/89	175
OMSON, Henry	
irst Step (mother & daughter in landscape), oil on canvas, 52x87", SBY 6/1/89	14,300
OMSON, John Murray (British, 19th/20th C)	
oxhounds & a Terrier in a Kennel, oil on canvas, sgn, 16x30", SBY 6/10/88	6,600
ONY, Eduard (German, 1866-1950)	
air: Indian on Horseback; Cowboy on Horseback; watercolor heightened w/gouache, sgn, 11x9", C-E 2/3/88	1,430
ORBURN, Archibald (British, 1860-1935)	
hore Bird, watercolor heightened w/white, sgn/dtd 1898, 16x23", C-NY 10/25/89 OE	30,800
tudy of a Bird, gouache/en grisaille, sgn, unfr, 14x10", C-NY 10/25/89	1,650
OREN, see Von Thoren	
ORNAM, Emmy Marie Caroline (Danish, 1852-1935)	
tudy of Pink Primroses, oil on canvas, sgn, 13x18", SBY 7/12/89	1,430
ORNE, Joan (American, 20th C)	
vur (abstract), acrylic on canvas, sgn/dtd 1980, unfr, 75x103", C-NY 2/20/88 OE	3,300
ORNENFELD, Anton Erik Christian (Danish, 1839-1907)	
n Stille Sommerdag: Hellebok mod Kronborg; oil on canvas, twice sgn/dtd 1887, 39x62", SBY 5/23/89	17,600
ORNLEY, L. (German, 17th C)	
isherman at Sea, oil on canvas, sgn, 9x16", WG 4/23/88 UE	800
ORNLEY, William (British, 19th/20th C)	
air: Queensborough on the Medway; Steamships & Sails; oil on panel, sgn, 10x8", SBY 6/8/88 OE	4,125
air: Shipping Off the Coast; oil on canvas, sgn, 21x16", C-E 2/23/88	1,650
hipping Off the Coast, oil on canvas, sgn/inscr, 16x24", C-E 2/23/88	2,750
ORS, Joseph (British, fl 1863-1900)	
ritish Country House, oil on canvas, sgn, 17x23", B/B 12/8/88	3,850
hildren by a Duck Pond Near Cottages, oil on canvas, sgn, 9x13", FAP 11/4/88 OE	1,350
andscape with Ponds & Ducks, oil on board, sgn, 9x12", SBY 6/8/88 OE	1,045
ear Frattan in Hampshire, oil on canvas, sgn, 30x40", C-E 10/26/89	3,850
Valk Through a Wooded Path, oil on canvas, sgn/inscr, 24x36", C-E 5/23/88	3,080
ULSTRUP, see De Thulstrup	
VAITES, Charles (American, 20th C)	
omposition, Bathers (three nudes in landscape); oil on board, sgn, 8x14", B/B 9/14/89 UE	550
SEN, Carolus Johannes (Dutch, 1867-1917)	
lealtime (woman & two children in interior), oil on canvas, sgn, 16x19", NA 2/6/88	1,200
reparing the Midday Meal (woman at hearth), oil on panel, sgn, unfr, 15x11", C-E 5/22/89	1,980
N, Ni (Chinese, 1855-1919)	
hongkui (hanging scroll), ink/color on paper, sgn/dtd 1913, 53x26", SBY 5/31/89	2,090
HO, Anna (Israeli, 20th C)	
ortrait of a Woman, watercolor/pen/India ink, sgn, 13x10", SBY 5/30/89	3,850
LENS, Alexandre (Belgian, 1868-)	
ill Life of Lilacs & Roses, oil on canvas, sgn, 39x32", B/B 6/9/88	3,850
POLO, Giovanni Battista (Italian, 1696-1770)	
aricature of a Man Holding a Muff, in Profile to the Left; pen/black ink/gray wash, 8x6", C-NY 1/11/89	8,250
i Sotto in Study of a Woman Holding a Bowl & a Spindle, chalk/pen/ink/wash, inscr 113, 13x8", C-NY 1/11/89	12,100
roup of Women & Other Figures Around an Urn, pen/brown ink, shield with kneeling pilgrim wm, 13x10", C-NY 1/11/89 OE	31,900

Madonna & Child Adored by Sts Anthony of Padua, Jerome, Mark, & Female St; pen/ink/wash over chalk, 16x10", SBY 1/13/89 37,400
Queen Esther Introducing Mordecai to Ahasuerus, oil on canvas, 21x28", C-NY 1/11/89 71,500
Standing Figure of an Oriental, pen/brown ink/wash, 8x6", SBY 1/13/89 45,100
Three Studies of Heads of Cherubs & Study of a Staff, red chalk heightened w/white, 15x9", SBY 1/13/89 OE 35,200

TIEPOLO, Giovanni Battista; circle of (Italian, 1696-1770)
Virgin & Child, black chalk, 9x6", SBY 1/13/89 3,025

TIEPOLO, Giovanni Domenico (Italian, 1727-1804)
Assumption of the Virgin, pen/brown/gray ink/gray-brown washes, sgn/GF wm, 10x8", C-NY 1/12/88 8,800
Cupid & Putti with a Dove & Wreaths on Clouds...; pen/ink/wash, sgn/#d 58, corners cut, 7x11", C-NY 1/11/89 9,900
Cupid & Putti with Doves in Clouds, pen/ink/wash, sgn, 7x11", C-NY 1/11/89 7,700
Head of a Man in Profile to the Left, black/white chalk on blue paper, 12x8", C-NY 1/12/88.... 4,620
Hercules & Antaeus, a Lion at Their Side; chalk/pen/ink/wash, wm, sgn, 9x6", C-NY 1/11/89 17,600
Putti in the Clouds, black chalk/pen/brown ink/brown wash, sgn, 16x9", C-NY 1/12/88 4,400
Woman Standing, wearing long dress & veil...; black/white chalk on blue paper, 10x7", C-NY 1/12/88.... 4,400
Woman Standing by a Cypress in a Landscape, black chalk/pen/brown ink/brown wash, sgn/JI wm, 11x7", C-NY 1/12/88 8,800

TIEPOLO, Giovanni Domenico; follower of (Italian, 1727-1804)
Allegory of Time Revealing Truth, oil on canvas, 15x9", SBY 6/3/88.... 3,850

TIEPOLO, Lorenzo (Italian, 1736-1776)
Head of a Man in an Ermine-Trimmed Hat, black/red/white chalk on blue-gray paper, M wm, corners cut, 13x8", C-NY 1/12/88.... 6,050

TIFFANY, Louis Comfort (American, 1848-1933)
Algerian Figures, pastel on paper, sgn/dtd 1876-77/inscr The Pallace Le Paghe, 16x11", SBY 3/17/88.... 2,530
Arab Street Scene, watercolor on paper laid down on board, sgn/inscr Noel, 11x8", SBY 9/14/89 4,675
Arabic Figures on an Inclined Street, watercolor on paper, sgn, 11x7", SBY 9/14/89.... 2,090
Harbor Scene with Moored Ships & Distant Mountains, oil on canvas, sgn, 8x14", SBY 9/14/89 1,650
Hillside Town, oil on canvas, initialed, 14x17", SBY 6/24/88 OE 5,500
North African Street Scene, oil on canvasboard, initialed, 10x14", SBY 3/17/88.... 3,080
Storyteller, oil on board laid down on board, sgn, 12x9", C-NY 3/11/88.... 3,300
Yellowstone Canyon (landscape), watercolor/chalk on paper, sgn/dtd 1917, 11x8", SBY 3/17/88 1,980

TIGLIO, M. (Argentinian, 20th C)
Abstract Still Life, oil on paper, sgn/dtd 53, 14x20", B/B 8/10/88.... 495

TILBORCH, see Van Tilborch

TILLEMANS, P.J. (19th C)
Peasants in an Interior, sgn/dtd 1846, 22x29", C-E 10/25/88 1,980

TILOT, H. (French, 19th/20th C)
Horses at a Well, oil on panel, sgn, 5x6", B/B 5/17/89 495

TILSA (TSUCHIYA)(Latin American, 20th C)
Pair: Animales Alados (imaginary animals); pen/India ink/crayon on paper, sgn, 1971, about 13x6", C-NY 5/17/89.... 1,100
Pair: Mujer y Reptiles; Figuras Morfologicas; mixed media on paper, 13x10", C-NY 5/18/88 OE 4,180
Sin Titulo (abstract), watercolor/India ink/pencil on paper, 26x20", C-NY 5/18/88 3,520

TIMMERMANS, Louis (French, 1846-1910)
Bridge Over a Wooded Stream, oil on canvas, sgn, 21x37", C-E 2/23/88 1,650

TIMMONS, Edward J. Finley (American, 1882-1960)
Children Playing Along a River, oil on canvas, sgn, 18x25", B/B 5/17/89 880

TINDALE, Edward H. (American, 1879-)
Valley Farm, Winter; pastel on artist board, sgn, 19x26", RWS 5/19/88 UE.... 325

TING, Nam (Chinese, 19th C)
Chinese Junk, oil on canvas, sgn, orig frame, RAB 11/25/88.... 1,000

TING, Walasse (American/Chinese, 1929-)
Pillow Talk (two nudes), acrylic on canvas, sgn/dtd 74, 40x59", C-E 11/17/88 OE 10,120
Untitled (contemporary nude in erotic pose), acrylic/crayons on paper, sgn/dtd 79, 28x39", C-E 11/14/89 3,520

TINGQUA, att
At the Opera (ladies in box seat), oil on canvas, 28x36", C-SK 6/9/88 3,718

TINTORETTO, Domenico (Italian, 1562-1637)
Portrait of Joannes Gritti, oil on canvas, inscr, 38x36", SBY 6/3/88 OE 13,200

TINTORETTO, Jacopo R.; see Robusti

TIRATELLI, Aurelio (Italian, 1842-1900)
Return From Spring Pastures, oil on canvas, sgn/inscr, 19x36", C-NY 2/25/88 13,200

TIRONI, Francesco (Italian, -1800)
View of Saint Peter's, Rome; oil on canvas, 35x58", SBY 6/3/88.... 33,000

TIRONI, Francesco; circle of (Italian, -1800)
View of the Grand Canal with the Rialto Bridge, Venice; oil on canvas, 13x22", SBY 10/13/89 11,000

TIRONI, Francesco; follower of (Italian, -1800)
Grand Canal From Santa Maria Della Carita to the Bacino di San Marco, Venice; oil on canvas, 11x18", SBY 10/13/89 OE.... 5,500

TISCHBEIN, circle of (German, 18th/19th C)
Portrait of a Lady, Seated, Half-Length, in a Blue Dress with Lace & Fur Trim; oil on panel, 39x28", C-NY 10/12/89.... 1,100

TISSOT, James Jacques Joseph (French, 1836-1902)
Jeunes Femmes Regardant des Objets Japonais, oil on canvas, sgn, ca 1869-70, 25x19", SBY 2/22/89.... 302,500
Kathleen Newton at the Piano, oil on canvas, sgn, ca 1881, 44x31", SBY 2/22/89.... 440,000
Lady in a Black & White Dress, gouache/watercolor over traces of black chalk on blue paper, sgn, 16x10", C-NY 5/24/89 198,000
Marguerite au Rempart, oil on canvas, sgn/dtd 1861, 44x34", SBY 5/23/89 OE.... 231,000
Princesse de Broglie (seated on table wearing green cape), pastel on linen, sgn, ca 1895, 66x38", SBY 10/24/89....1,100,00

Reading the News, oil on canvas, sgn, ca 1874, 34x21", SBY 5/23/89 ..... **1,375,000**
Soiree d'Ete, watercolor on paper, sgn, ca 1881, 9x16", SBY 5/23/89 ..... **187,000**
Tryst at a Riverside Cafe, oil on canvas, sgn, ca 1869, 16x21", SBY 5/23/89 ..... **495,000**
Type of Beauty, Kathleen Newton (portrait); oil on canvas, sgn, 1880, 24x18", SBY 2/22/89 ..... **742,500**
I, Tiberio; att (1573-1627)
Portrait of a Nobleman (standing, full-length); oil on canvas, ca early 1920s, unfr, 80x44", SBY 6/1/89 ..... **18,700**
IAN, after (Italian, 1477-1576)
Danae & the Shower of Gold (reclining nude & cupid), oil on canvas, 49x70", SBY 4/7/89 OE **9,900**
Portrait of Caterina Cornaro, Queen of Cyprus; oil on canvas, 40x30", B/B 5/17/89 ..... **825**
Saint Nicholas of Bari, oil on canvas, 59x37", C-NY 4/6/89 ..... **3,520**
St Mary Magdalene in Penitence, oil on canvas, 47x36", SBY 7/12/89 OE **6,050**
IAN, circle of (Italian, 1477-1576)
Portrait of a Bearded Man, bust-length, in a fur-lined cape & white collar; oil on canvas, 29x24", C-NY 5/31/89 OE **82,500**
IAN, follower of (Italian, 1477-1576)
Madonna & Child, oil on canvas, 32x35", SBY 7/12/89 ..... **3,575**
IAN, manner of (Italian, 1477-1576)
Portrait of a Gentleman, half-length, in profile & wearing armor; oil on panel, 36x31", C-E 4/7/88 UE **385**
IAN, studio of (Italian, 1477-1576)
Entombment, oil on canvas, 44x67", SBY 10/21/88 OE **9,350**
IAN (Italian, 1477-1576)
Penitent Magdalene (portrait), oil on canvas, 44x31", SBY 6/2/89 ..... **2,640,000**
O, see Di Tito
JTRIUMOV, Nikanor Leont'evich (Russian, 1821-1877)
Portrait of a Bemedalled Officer, watercolor, cyrillic sgn, oval, 8x7", C-L 10/8/88 ..... **700**
View of the Hermitage, St Petersburg; pencil/pen/ink/watercolor on paper, 10x15", C-L 10/8/88 OE **3,350**
View of the St Nicholas Bridge Across the Neva, St Petersburg; pencil/pen/ink/watercolor, 1852, 10x15", C-L 10/8/88 OE **3,720**
OLI, see Da Tivoli
BEY, Mark (American, 1890-1976)
Composition (abstract), brush/black ink on board mounted on canvas, sgn/dtd 57, 34x25", C-NY 2/20/88 ..... **4,400**
Composition Fond Vieux Rose, gouache on paper, sgn/dtd 1970, 39x28", C-NY 11/10/88 ..... **6,600**
Dance Memories (abstract), tempera on paperboard, sgn/dtd 48, 17x31", SBY 10/5/89 OE **17,600**
Delta (abstract), oil/tempera on cardboard, sgn/dtd 52, 44x28", SBY 5/3/88 OE **35,200**
Double-Sided: Untitled (abstracts); tempera/gouache on cardboard, sgn, 15x11", WD 5/5/88 ..... **8,250**
Garden (abstract), tempera on paper laid down on fiberboard, sgn/dtd 56, 24x36", SBY 11/11/88 OE **46,200**
Ikonostas (contemporary composition), tempera on board, sgn/dtd 49, 11x16", SBY 10/5/89 OE **29,700**
Inner City (abstract), gouache/tempera/watercolor on paper, sgn/dtd 45, 20x15", SBY 2/19/88 ..... **7,700**
Intervals (abstract), gouache/watercolor on board, sgn, 1943, SBY 2/19/88 OE **28,600**
Landscape (abstract), tempera on paper, sgn/inscr/dtd 56, 18x24", SBY 10/5/88 ..... **2,750**
Light of Spring (abstract), watercolor on paper, sgn/dtd 69, 40x28", SBY 2/15/89 OE **55,000**
Lights III (abstract), tempera on paper laid down on board, sgn/dtd 54, 18x12", SBY 10/8/88 OE **12,100**
Misty Pastures (abstract), tempera on paper mounted on paperboard, sgn/dtd 55, 18x23", SBY 11/11/88 ..... **13,200**
Night (abstract), tempera on paper laid down on paperboard, sgn/dtd 54, 18x12", SBY 5/3/88 OE **38,500**
Orb, tempera on paper mounted on painted cardboard, sgn/dtd 57, 9x13", SBY 10/8/88 OE **16,500**
Orpheus (abstract), tempera on paper, sgn/dtd 54, 6x10", SBY 10/8/88 OE **9,350**
Paysage Imaginaire (abstract), tempera on paper mounted on masonite, sgn/dtd 55, 24x35", C-NY 10/4/89 ..... **28,600**
Sky World (abstract), tempera on cardboard, sgn/dtd 45, 13x6", SBY 10/8/88 ..... **6,600**
Space Ritual #14 (abstract), Sumi ink on paper, sgn/dtd 57, 23x35", C-NY 5/4/88 OE **9,350**
Space Ritual #16, brush/Sumi ink on rice paper, 21x29", C-NY 11/10/88 ..... **6,380**
Transcendence (abstract), watercolor on paper, sgn/dtd 66, 8x6", C-NY 2/20/88 ..... **4,950**
Untitled (abstract), gouache on paper, sgn/dtd 64, 6x4", WD 5/5/88 ..... **1,500**
Untitled (abstract), tempera on paper, sgn/dtd 65, 12x8", SBY 5/2/88 OE **7,700**
Untitled (abstract), watercolor on paper, sgn/dtd 66, 12x10", C-NY 2/14/89 ..... **4,400**
Untitled (abstract), watercolor on paper mounted on board, sgn/dtd 59, 27x20", C-NY 2/14/89 OE **41,800**
Untitled (abstract), watercolor/gouache/graphite on paper mounted on board, sgn/dtd 67, 7x8", C-NY 10/4/89 ..... **6,600**
Untitled (contemporary), tempera on black paper, sgn/dtd 59, 18x12", C-NY 2/14/89 OE **18,700**
Watchers, tempera on panel, sgn/dtd 54, 12x16", SBY 10/5/88 ..... **2,200**
Yellow Structure (abstract), gouache/pen on paper, sgn/dtd 54, 13x6", SBY 11/11/88 UE **4,950**
BIASSE, Theo (French, 1927-)
Je Danse avec Ma Princesse-Fiancee, oil on canvas, sgn/dtd 70, 29x36", SBY 10/8/88 OE **20,900**
La Bouilloire Rouge, oil on canvas, sgn/dtd 68, 10x8", B/B 6/15/89 ..... **2,090**
Un Gros Chat Lezard (cat & girl), oil on canvas, sgn/dtd 63, 21x26", SBY 2/15/89 ..... **16,500**
Un Oiseau ne des Rumeurs de la Fete, gouache on paper, sgn/dtd 74, 26x20", SBY 10/7/89 ..... **9,350**
DAHL, John O. (American, 1884-)
Dockside Reflections, oil on cardboard, sgn, RAB 3/27/89 UE **250**
Fishing Boat at Dock, oil on cardboard, sgn, 11x9", RAB 3/27/89 ..... **275**
DD, Marie (American, 20th C)
Portrait of a Woman, oil on canvas, sgn, 18x24", LH 12/4/88 UE **30**
ECHE, Carl Johann Friedrich (German, 1814-1890)
Preparing the Family Meal (interior scene), oil on canvas, sgn/dtd 1852, 13x16", C-E 5/22/89 ..... **2,420**
EPUT, Lodewijk; att (Flemish, 1550-1603)
Mountainous River Landscape at Sunset, pen/brown ink/brown wash, 7x9", C-NY 1/11/89 ..... **1,760**

TOFANO, Edouardo (Italian, 1838-1920)
Woman Sleeping, watercolor on paper, sgn, 8x5", WL 5/20/88 ... 450
Young Woman in a Red Cap & Scarf, watercolor, sgn, 11x8", C-NY 2/25/88 ... 770

TOFT, Alfonso
Paper Mills, Grand Falls, Newfoundland; watercolor, sgn, 7x10", FB 10/17/88 ... 90

TOFT, Peter Petersen (Danish, 1925-1901)
View of Hastings, watercolor highlighted w/white on paper, sgn/dtd 80, 14x21", WL 5/20/88 ... 450

TOJETTI, Domenico (American/Italian, 1806-1892)
Battle of the Centaurs, oil on canvas, sgn/dtd 1875, 69x124", B/B 10/9/88 ... 6,600
Exotic Dancer with Tambourine, oil on canvas, indistinctly sgn, 50x30", B/B 9/15/89 ... 770

TOJETTI, Virgilio (Italian, 1851-1901)
Masquerade (elegant woman seated w/mask & flowers on floor), oil on canvas, sgn/dtd 90, 35x20", C-NY 5/24/89 ... 14,300
Sleeping Child, oil on canvas, sgn/dtd 95, 20x28", SBY 12/9/88 OE ... 5,775
Spanish Beauty, oil on canvas, sgn/inscr Paris, 21x18", WD 3/23/88 UE ... 600

TOLEDO, Francisco (Mexican, 1940-)
Bridge (abstract), gouache on paper, 1987, 11x15", SBY 5/16/89 ... 8,800
Buho y Conejo (abstract), oil/sand on canvas, sgn, 26x36", C-NY 5/17/89 OE ... 26,400
Circus (abstract), oil/sand on burlap, sgn/dtd 61, 38x51", SBY 5/17/88 ... 27,500
Clinch III (wrestlers in ring), mixed media on amate paper, sgn, 1987, 22x30", C-NY 11/21/89 ... 30,800
Conos y Alacranes (rows of cones w/scorpions), India ink/watercolor on heavy paper, sgn, 26x20", C-NY 11/21/88 ... 11,000
Corral en Juchitan (abstract), gouache/sand/pen/black ink on paper, 19x25", C-NY 5/18/88 ... 17,600
Cow (contemporary), watercolor on paper, 1968, 25x19", SBY 11/21/88 OE ... 9,350
Coyotes Looking at a Woman, gouache on paper, sgn, 9x14", SBY 11/21/88 ... 7,700
Don't Get Tied Up (abstract), watercolor/pencil on paper, sgn/titled, 10x12", SBY 11/21/88 ... 5,500
Donde Termina el Arco Iris (abstract composition), watercolor/pen/black ink, sgn, 16x13", C-NY 11/21/89 ... 3,300
Double-Sided: Untitled Gouache (abstract); gouache on paper, sgn 1 side, 12x10", SBY 5/16/89 ... 4,125
El Perro Ocioso, oil/sand on canvas, sgn/titled/dtd 1972, 26x33", C-NY 5/17/89 ... 33,000
Figura (abstract composition), pen/India ink/watercolor/gouache, sgn, ca 1965, 15x25", C-NY 11/21/89 ... 6,600
Figura a Caballo Atacada por una Serpiente (composition), watercolor/pen/ink on paper, sgn, 16x21", C-NY 11/21/89 OE ... 8,250
Figura Asteca (abstract Aztec figure), watercolor/gouache on paper, sgn, 20x23", C-NY 5/17/89 ... 3,520
Figura Verde (abstract), gouache/watercolor on paper, sgn, 18x18", C-NY 5/17/89 OE ... 8,250
Figuras con Fondo Azul (abstract), watercolor/pen/ink on paper, sgn, 12x12", C-NY 5/18/88 ... 3,520
Hombre con Animales, watercolor/pencil on paper, sgn, 15x18", C-NY 5/18/88 ... 2,090
Hombre con Cara Redonda (abstract), gouache/blue ink on paper, sgn, 10x8", C-NY 5/18/88 ... 4,950
Lizard & Turtle (contemporary), gouache on paper, 25x39", SBY 11/21/88 ... 23,100
Mujer, Cerdo y Serpiente (abstract); watercolor/pencil on paper, sgn, 23x15", C-NY 5/18/88 OE ... 6,600
Mujer con Pescado (abstract of woman/fish), oil on canvas laid down on masonite, sgn/dtd 1971, 21x21", C-NY 11/21/88 OE ... 20,900
Mujer Rubia (abstract of blonde woman), gouache/pencil on paper, sgn, ca 1965-68, 11x8", C-NY 5/18/88 ... 3,850
Mujer y Perros (seated woman w/three dogs), watercolor/pen/ink on paper, sgn/inscr, 1975, 10x14", C-NY 11/21/88 ... 8,250
Pair: Sin Titulo (abstract); watercolor/gouache/pen/black ink on paper, sgn, 8x12", C-NY 5/17/89 ... 6,600
Pair: Untitled (contemporary); watercolor on paper, sgn/dtd Paris 63, 9x12", SBY 11/21/88 ... 6,600
Pair: Untitled Watercolors (abstract); watercolor/ink on paper, sgn, 9x12", SBY 5/16/89 ... 2,750
Pajaros Guerreros, gouache/pen/ink on paper, sgn/dtd Paris 63, 10x13", C-NY 11/21/89 ... 4,400
Pajaros Verdes (abstract), gouache/watercolor/pen/black ink on paper, sgn, 8x9", C-NY 5/18/88 ... 3,520
Pez (abstract), watercolor/pen/black ink on paper, sgn, 18x25", C-NY 5/17/89 ... 7,700
Rana (abstract frog), gouache on paper, sgn, 19x24", C-NY 5/17/89 ... 3,520
Retrato de Hombre (portrait of a man), watercolor/pen on paper, sgn, 11x8", C-NY 11/21/88 ... 4,400
Sin Titulo, watercolor/pen/brown ink on paper, sgn, 12x16", C-NY 11/21/89 ... 3,300
Sin Titulo (abstract), gouache/watercolor/pen/ink on paper, sgn, 21x16", C-NY 11/21/88 OE ... 16,500
Sin Titulo (abstract), oil/sand on canvas laid down on panel, 32x22", C-NY 5/18/88 ... 16,500
Sin Titulo (abstract), watercolor/pen/ink on paper, sgn, 11x13", C-NY 11/21/89 ... 1,320
Sueno (abstract composition), oil/sand on canvas laid down on masonite, 1969, 24x31", C-NY 11/21/89 ... 22,000
Untitled (abstract figure), gouache on paper, sgn, 12x10", SBY 5/16/89 ... 4,675
Untitled (abstract), gouache on paper, sgn/dtd 64, 10x12", SBY 5/17/88 ... 3,300
Untitled (abstract), sgn, 1964, 23x28", SBY 5/17/88 ... 19,800
Untitled (abstract), watercolor/ink on paper, sgn, 19x24", SBY 5/16/89 ... 4,675
Untitled (contemporary view of cows, crocodile, & duck), gouache/sand on paper, 9x12", SBY 5/16/89 ... 17,600
Untitled (contemporary view of tree & two goats), watercolor on paper, sgn, 1974, 22x30", SBY 5/16/89 OE ... 55,000
Untitled (fantasy figures w/donkey tied to post), pen/ink/watercolor/gouache on paper, sgn, 19x26", SBY 5/16/89 OE ... 20,900
Woman Floating (abstract), gouache on paper, 1965, 30x22", SBY 5/17/88 ... 19,800
Wooden Cart (abstract), oil on burlap, sgn/dtd 60, 39x32", SBY 5/17/88 ... 15,400

TOLMAN, Ruel Pardee
In the Garden, oil on canvas, sgn, 30x26", C-E 6/1/88 ... 1,430

TOMALTY, Terry (Canadian, 19th C)
Berthierville, oil on board, sgn/dtd 1978, 12x16", FB 10/30/89 ... 715
Coach, oil on board, sgn/dtd 77, 12x16", WAD 6/12/89 ... 675
Quebec Farm, oil on board, sgn/dtd 77, 8x10", WAD 6/12/89 ... 280
Rue Acquin, St Henri; oil on board, sgn/dtd 1980, 10x12", FB 10/30/89 ... 495
St Basile, Quebec; oil on board, sgn/dtd 1971, 18x24", FB 4/25/88 ... 600
St Patin, oil on board, sgn/dtd 1978, 8x10", FB 10/30/89 ... 522

MANEK, Joseph (American/Czechoslovakian, 1899-)
Nude Portrait in Summer Wooded Scene, oil on panel, sgn, 14x10", MAG 6/22/88 ... 1,200
MBA, Casimiro (Italian, 1857-1929)
Life Drawing, watercolor heightened w/white over pencil, sgn/inscr, 24x19", C-NY 10/26/88 ... 2,200
MINETTI, A.
Shepherdess & Her Flock Near a Mountainside, oil on canvas, sgn, 14x24", C-E 2/16/88 ... 1,045
MINZ, Alfredo (Italian, 1854-1936)
Carriage Ride, oil on canvas, sgn/dtd 99, 23x15", C-NY 2/23/89 ... 8,800
MLIN, Bradley Walker (American, 1899-1959)
All Souls Night (abstract), oil on canvas, sgn, 1948, 43x64", SBY 11/9/89 ... 165,000
MMASO (Maso da San Friano), att (1532-1571)
Birth of Saint John the Baptist, oil on panel, unfr, 35x48", C-M 6/16/89 ... 24,449
MPKINS, Frank Hector (American, 1847-1922)
Neponset River, Mattapan; oil on canvasboard, sgn/dtd May 1 1905, 12x16", SBY 9/14/89 ... 605
Portrait of Jonathan Griffin, oil on canvas, 34x27", SBY 4/14/89 ... 660
MSEN, Carl Christian Frederik Jacob (Danish, 1847-1912)
Afternoon at the Lake, oil on canvas, sgn/dtd 1898, 22x18", SBY 2/22/89 ... 15,400
NGHE, Weng (Chinese, 1830-1904)
Calligraphy In Xing Shu Running Script (horizontal scroll), ink on paper, sgn, 13x34", SBY 5/31/89 OE ... 3,575
Set of 4: Calligraphy in Xing Shu Running Script (hanging scrolls); ink on paper, 1 sgn/dtd 1901, 28x14", SBY 5/31/89 ... 1,430
NGIANI, V. (American/Continental, 19th/20th C)
Innocents, four mischevious kittens in formal parlor; oil on canvas, sgn, 24x36", RAB 8/8/89 ... 2,000
NNY, Kristian
Pair: Composition with Horses; pen/white ink on black paper, sgn, 20x25", C-E 4/7/88 ... 220
Set of 3: Compositions with Nudes; pen/brown ink on paper, sgn, 21x27", C-E 4/7/88 ... 330
ORENVLIET, Jacob (Dutch, 1641-1719)
Old Serving Woman Reading Document to Old Man & Young Woman, oil on copper, sgn, 13x10", C-M 12/3/88 ... 13,936
PANELIAN, Fanny N. (American, 20th C)
Summer on Cape Cod (children on beach, cottage beyond), watercolor on paper, 6x9", RAB 8/9/88 ... 250
PHAM, Francis William Warwick (British, 1838-1924)
David (in leopard skin w/slingshot), oil on canvas, sgn/dtd1910, 42x30", SBY 10/24/89 ... 5,500
PHAM, Thurston W. (Canadian, 1886-1967)
Interior of Mr Deacon's House, Waterloo; oil on board, sgn/dtd 1936, 16x12", FB 5/28/89 UE ... 180
Old Quebec in Moonlight, oil on board, sgn, 12x16", FB 4/25/88 OE ... 1,200
POR, Roland (European, 1938-)
Au Claire de la Terre, watercolor/pen/black ink on paper, sgn/dtd 1977, 13x10", C-E 11/17/88 OE ... 990
PPING, James (American, 1879-1949)
Fox River Valley, oil on canvas, sgn, 25x30", LH 5/15/88 ... 1,200
RBIDO, Francesco; att (Italian, 1482-1562)
Madonna & Child & St John the Baptist, black chalk, 14x10", SBY 1/13/89 UE ... 15,400
RDI, Sinibaldo (Italian, 1876-1955)
Kiss on the Hand, oil on canvas, sgn/inscr, 15x10", SBY 12/9/88 ... 3,300
Waltz, oil on canvas, sgn, 14x23", C-E 10/26/89 ... 2,860
RI, Guiseppe (Italian, 19th C)
Pope Clement XIII, oil on canvas, sgn, 43x36", C-E 10/26/89 ... 1,650
RLAKSON, James (American, 1951-)
Last Night (fun house), gouache/watercolor on paper, sgn twice/inscr/dtd 1983, 15x9", C-E 5/13/88 ... 880
Table Rock II, watercolor/pencil on paper, sgn/dtd 1980/titled, 36x50", C-E 5/9/89 ... 1,760
RO, A.
Lady Seated Holding a Pink Flower, oil on canvas, sgn, 32x25", C-E 10/25/88 ... 2,420
RRE, see Del Torre
RRES, Antonio (Spanish, 1851-)
By the Waterfall, oil on canvas laid down on board, sgn, 31x26", WD 3/23/88 ... 1,500
Water Girl, oil on canvas laid down on board, sgn, 31x26", C-E 1/12/88 ... 880
RRES-GARCIA, Joaquin (Uruguayan, 1874-1949)
Arte Constructivo, oil on board, initialed/dtd 47, 22x28", C-NY 11/21/89 OE ... 165,000
Composicion Constructiva (Constructive Composition), oil on canvas, sgn/dtd 32, 22x18", C-NY 11/21/88 OE ... 88,000
Dibujo Constructivo, pen/ink on paper, sgn/dtd 1932, 7x5", C-NY 5/17/89 OE ... 6,600
Dibujo Constructivo, pen/ink/pencil on paper laid down, initialed/dtd 36, 7x5", C-NY 11/21/89 ... 9,350
Dibujo Constructivo (abstract), pen/ink/pencil on paper laid down on paper, initialed/dtd 36, 7x5", C-NY 11/21/88 OE ... 7,150
Estructura con Objectos Esquematicos, oil on board laid down on canvas, initialed/dtd 43, 20x24", C-NY 5/18/88 ... 68,200
Forma Ocre con Formas Rojas, watercolor/pen/ink/pencil on paper laid down, initialed/dtd 39, 5x5", C-NY 11/21/89 OE ... 22,000
Grafismo Indo-Americano, oil on board, initialed/dtd 1942, 21x32", C-NY 11/21/89 ... 121,000
Interior, oil on board, initialed/dtd 23, 12x15", C-NY 5/18/88 ... 20,900
Pareja (contemporary portrait of couple), oil on canvas, sgn/dtd 30, 16x20", C-NY 11/21/88 OE ... 44,000
Puerto de Villefranche (port scene), oil on canvas, sgn/dtd 41, 19x25", C-NY 5/18/88 OE ... 41,800
Puerto de Villefranche-sur-Mer (port scene w/buildings), oil on canvas, sgn/dtd 41, 21x30", C-NY 5/17/89 ... 49,500
Secando la Ropa (abstract), oil on canvas, sgn/dtd 27, 13x18", C-NY 5/18/88 ... 17,600
Serrure avec Clef (lock w/key, contemporary), oil on canvas, sgn/dtd 28, 14x18", C-NY 11/21/89 OE ... 55,000
Tragic Dinner, oil on board, initialed/dtd 1922, 13x19", C-NY 11/21/89 OE ... 44,000

TORRESCASSANA, Francisco (Spanish, 1865-1918)
Marine Scene, oil on board, sgn, 23x34", MG 6/25/88 500
TORREY, Charles (American, 1859-1921)
Portrait of an American Sailing Ship, oil on canvas, sgn, 18x24", RAB 8/1/88 1,350
TORREY, Elliot (American, 1867-1949)
Still Life of Pears & Apples, oil on board, sgn, 16x17", B/B 1/11/89 OE 2,475
Waves Crashing on Rocks, oil on canvas, sgn, 25x30", B/B 9/14/89 UE 880
TORRIGLIA, Giovanni Battista (Italian, 1858-)
Divine Inspiration, oil on canvas, sgn, 24x36", C-NY 10/25/89 16,500
Il Manaco Scultore, oil on canvas, sgn, 23x29", SBY 10/24/89 7,150
TORRINI, E. (Italian, 19th C)
Old Man Reading the Paper, oil on canvas, sgn, 12x9", SBY 6/8/88 1,430
Priest in a Church Interior, watercolor on paper, sgn, 24x30", SBY 6/8/88 990
TORRINI, Pietro (Italian, 1852-)
Grandparent's Joy, oil on canvas, sgn, 32x30", SBY 2/22/89 OE 12,100
TOSINI, Michele; follower of (Italian, 1503-1577)
Madonna & Child with Infant Saint John the Baptist & Two Angels, oil on panel, unfr, 40x29", SBY 10/13/89 OE 8,800
TOSINI, Michele; school of (Italian, 1503-1577)
Saint Mary Magdalene, oil on panel, 24x27", C-NY 10/20/88 UE 2,200
TOTH, Jean (Hungarian, 19th C)
Les Heures, watercolor, sgn, 9x10", FB 5/28/89 UE 120
TOTI, Lewis C (American, 20th C)
Woods in June, oil on board, sgn, 18x22", B/B 12/8/88 110
TOTOSSIAN, Armand (Canadian, 1948-)
Deux d'Enfants au Parc Westmount, oil on board, sgn/dtd 1972, 11x14", FB 10/17/88 350
TOUCHE, see De Latouche
TOULMOUCHE, Auguste (French, 1829-1890)
Desillusions (full-length portrait of a woman), oil on canvas, sgn/dtd 1880, 26x19", SBY 5/23/89 OE 19,800
Exotic Beauty in an Interior, oil on canvas, sgn/dtd 1883, 20x15", C-NY 5/24/89 11,000
Lady with a Letter, oil on canvas, sgn/dtd 1870, 25x18", C-NY 2/23/89 41,800
Love Letter (woman in an interior), oil on canvas, sgn/dtd 1883, 25x17", C-NY 10/25/89 17,600
TOULOUSE-LAUTREC, Henri de (French, 1864-1901)

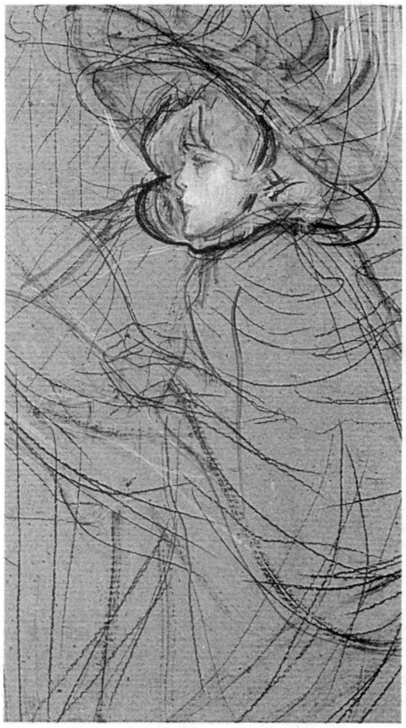

Profil de Femme; Jane Avril; oil on board, 1893, 22x14", C-NY 5/11/88; $1,650,000

Allegorie: Le Printemps de la Vie (mythological scene); oil on canvas, monogramed, 1883, 22x17", C-NY 11/15/88 220,000
Amazone et Divers, pen/India ink on paper, stamped w/monogram, ca 1883, 8x13", C-NY 11/15/88 OE 35,200
Au Cirque: Ecuyere (circus performer); oil on vellum, sgn, 1888, 10" dia, C-NY 5/11/88 165,000
Double-Sided: Hommes et Tete de Cheval; Chevaux; recto: watercolor over pencil, verso: pencil, 6x10", C-NY 2/16/89 OE 17,600
Double-Sided: Pecheur Nicoise (standing male nude & two head studies); pencil/watercolor, 8x5", PHL 11/15/88 19,500
Double-Sided: Portrait d'Homme; Paysage; pencil on paper, monogramed, 1881, 11x7", SBY 10/6/89 OE 19,800
Homme Qui Fume, pencil/pen/brown ink on paper, 10x7", SBY 10/6/89 3,850
Jockeys, left half of larger sheet of studies which have been split; pen/ink on paper, 1895, 6x8", SBY 10/6/89 OE 29,700
Le Peintre Rachou (artist seated at easel in a landscape), oil on canvas, initialed, ca 1882, 20x24", SBY 5/10/89 OE 660,000
Les Fetes Parisiennes Nouveaux Confettis, gouache/blue chalk on cardboard, monogramed, ca 1892, 17x21", SBY 11/12/88 OE 101,750

M Caudieux, Acteur de Cafe Concert; gouache/pencil on paper, monogramed, 1893, 27x19", SBY 11/15/89 OE 3,080,000
Partie de Campagne (figures relaxing on the hay), oil on canvas, monogramed, ca 1882, 18x15", C-NY 5/11/89 308,000
Portrait de Femme de la Maison de la Rue d'Ambroise, oil on paper laid down on canvas, 1892, 11x9", SBY 5/10/89 165,000
Set of 3: Tetes de Marins; Marin de Face; Marins de Profil; pencil on paper, 1875-80, 6x3", C-NY 10/5/89 11,000
Study of Three Figures, pencil on paper, stamped monogram, 7x11", B/B 10/9/88 2,475
Tetes de Soldats, Cavaliers; pen/brown ink on paper, ca 1880, 9x6", SBY 10/6/89 12,100

UPIN, Fernand (Canadian, 1930-)
Abstract, oil on board, sgn/dtd 1979, 8x6", FB 5/28/89 180
Ile au Bleu de Cobalt, acrylic on board, sgn/dtd 1981, 36x29", FB 10/30/89 1,540
Iris de Givre, acrylic on canvas, sgn/dtd 1981, 26x21", FB 10/30/89 935

URNACHON, Gaspard Felix; called Nadar
Parisian in the Bois de Boulogne (three-quarter length portrait), pastel, sgn, 51x32", C-NY 10/26/88 5,500

URNIER, Nicholas (French, 1590-1660)
Joseph & Potiphar's Wife, oil on canvas, 78x58", C-NY 1/15/88 39,600

USSAINT, Fernand (Belgian, 1873-1955)
Hopeful Suitor (elegant couple in landscape), oil on panel, sgn, 20x28", SBY 7/12/89 5,500

USSAINT, Louis (German, 1826-)
Old Woman Reading, oil on panel, sgn/dtd 92, 21x16", SBY 12/9/88 990

USSAINT, Pierre Joseph (Belgian, 1822-1888)
Studio Assistant, oil on panel, sgn/dtd 1857, 18x13", C-E 2/23/88 OE 4,400

UTENEL, Lodewak Jan Petrus (Belgian, 1819-1883)
Burgermeister Inspecting Six Paintings in Rembrandt's Studio, oil on canvas, sgn, 32x25", C-E 2/21/89 3,300

VAR, Ivan (Dominican Republic, 1942-)
Hatred (surrealistic), oil on canvas, sgn/dtd 73, 26x32", SBY 11/21/88 OE 9,350
One of the Many Secrets of Love, oil on canvas, twice sgn/titled/dtd 1982, 29x24", SBY 5/17/88 2,200

WN, Harold Barling (Canadian, 1924-)
Sign As Tumult (abstract), lucite/oil on board, sgn/dtd 1960, 12x12", WAD 11/30/89 OE 5,500

WNE, Charles (British, 1736-1840)
Chestnut Racehorse with Jocky Up at a Meet, oil on canvas, sgn/dtd 1793, 35x48", WD 10/19/88 OE 35,000
Dapple Gray Hunter with a Spaniel in a Wooded River Landscape, oil on canvas, sgn/dtd 1827, 10x12", SBY 6/9/89 10,450
Dog Spotting a Partridge, oil on panel, 14x16", C-NY 4/6/89 11,000
Travelers Stopped by a Sandy Bank, oil on canvas, sgn/dtd 1830, unfr, 20x25", C-NY 2/25/88 OE 35,200

WNSEND, Diane
Blueberries & Apple, pastel on paper, 1982, 29x42", SBY 11/9/89 5,500

WNSHEND, James (British, 19th/20th C)
Shakespeare's Country, Welford in Avon; watercolor on paper, 10x9", FAP 4/15/89 385

ZER, Henry Spernon (British, 20th C)
Pair: Morning Pipe; Evening of Life; oil on canvas, sgn/dtd 1888, 9x12", FB 4/25/88 3,600

ACY, John M. (American, 1844-)
Count Howard & Princess Beatrice III (hunter w/setters on point), oil on canvas, sgn, 24x36", SBY 6/9/89 27,500

ASH, D.
Contemplating, pen/ink wash on paper, sgn, 5x4", C-E 1/12/88 UE 33
Two Women by Street Sign, watercolor/pencil on paper, sgn, 13x11", C-E 1/12/88 UE 242

AULLWEILLER (Continental, 20th C)
Messy Room, oil on canvas, sgn, 24x32", C-E 10/26/89 4,180

AUTMANN, Johann George (German, 1713-1769)
Nocturnal Encampment with Thieves Counting Their Loot, oil on canvas, sgn, 14x18", C-NY 10/12/89 3,300

AVER, George A. (American, 1864-1928)
Spring (landscape), oil on board, sgn, 18x25", WD 4/13/88 1,800

AYER, Jean Baptiste Jules (French, 1824-1908)
La Priere, oil on canvas, sgn/dtd 1861, 54x38", SBY 5/23/89 11,000
Woman Sewing by an Open Window, oil on panel, sgn, 16x13", C-NY 2/23/89 7,700

AYNER, John C. (American, 20th C)
Irish Landscape, oil on canvas, sgn, 24x26", LH 12/4/88 1,300

EADWELL, Charles A. (American, 1827-1890)
Pair: Portraits of Hulda Hood Peacock & Jacob Treadwell; oil on canvas laid down on board, 28x24", C-E 6/20/89 UE 330
Pair: Portraits of Melinda Leavitt Treadwell & Relative; sgn/dtd 1856, 29x26", C-E 6/20/89 UE 440
Portrait of a Boy in the Woods, oil on canvas laid down on board, 34x24", C-E 6/20/89 880
Portrait of a Boy with a Hat, oil on canvas, sgn, 30x25", C-NY 6/3/89 3,080
Portrait of Frank Treadwell, 1849; oil on canvas, 25x30", C-NY 6/3/89 3,960

EBILCOCK, Paul (American, 1902-)
Amaylia in Capri (portrait of artist's wife), oil on canvas, unfr, ca late 1920s, 43x34", C-E 6/1/89 1,540
Seated Nude, oil on aluminum, sgn, 26x20", C-E 6/1/88 1,045

EDUPP, Charles Friederich Albert Jr. (American, 1864-1936)
Moonlit Dutch Landscape, oil on canvas, sgn/dtd 1901, 20x30", B/B 4/20/88 825
Moonlit Harbor Scene, oil on panel, sgn, 10x7", S/A 2/18/89 275
Moonlit Landscape with Deer at Water's Edge, oil on academy board, sgn/dtd 1913, 9x12", S/A 2/18/89 250

EIMAN, Joyce (American, 1922-)
Study for Big Lautrec: Self-Portrait; oil on canvas, sgn, 20x16", C-E 11/17/88 935

EMBLAY, Louis (Canadian, 1949-)
Grand Fond, colored pencil, sgn, 8x10", FB 10/30/89 275

Quebec Village Scene, oil on board, sgn, 12x14", FB 10/30/89 ... 308
Ste Rose du Nord, oil on board, sgn, 10x12", FB 10/30/89 ... 385

TREMBLE, Leo (Canadian, 1923-)
Entree de Baie St Paul, oil on board, sgn, 12x16", FB 10/17/88 OE ... 375

TRENHOLM, William Carpenter (American, 1856-1931)
Down East Schooner, oil on canvas, sgn/artist's symbol, 22x37", WD 10/5/88 ... 10,000

TREVISAN, A. (20th C)
Pair: Venetian Scenes; watercolor, sgn, 16x27", WG 12/10/88 UE ... 275

TREVISANI, Francesco (Italian, 1656-1746)
Adoration of the Shepherds, oil on canvas, 76x47", C-NY 6/2/88 ... 28,600
Mystic Marriage of Saint Catherine, oil on canvas, 42x33", C-NY 4/8/88 ... 8,800
Putti Holding a Cornucopia in a Landscape, black chalk/gray wash, 8x7", C-NY 1/11/89 OE ... 1,430
Saint Sylvester Baptizing Constantine, oil on canvas, 28x20", SBY 1/12/89 ... 18,700

TREVISANI, Francesco; follower of (Italian, 1656-1746)
Hagar & the Angel, oil on canvas, 51x37", SBY 4/7/88 OE ... 6,600
Madonna, oil on canvas, 29x24", SBY 6/8/88 UE ... 302
Madonna & Child with a Male Saint, oil on canvas, in painted oval, 29x24", SBY 10/21/88 ... 3,850

TREVOR, Helen Mabel (British, fl 1881-1897)
Mediterranean Coastal Scene, oil on canvas, sgn, 24x36", WL 5/20/88 ... 400

TRINQUESSE, Louis Rolland; att (French, 1746-1800)
Secret Voice, oil on canvas, bears signature/dtd 1787, 17x12", WD 10/19/88 OE ... 1,700
Young Lady Discovering Her Pet Dog Beneath Her Coverlet, oil on canvas, 29x34", SBY 10/13/89 ... 22,000

TRINXET, Joaquin Mir; att
Young Lady at Her Boudoir, oil on canvas, unfr, 12x10", C-E 5/23/88 OE ... 3,850

TRIOSON, Anne; see De Roucy Trioson

TRIPET, Alfred (French, fl 1861-82)
Apparition de Vinvela a Shilric-le Chasseur, oil on canvas, sgn/dtd 1870, 35x53", SBY 10/24/89 ... 16,500

TRIPPEL, Albert Ludwig (German, 1813-1854)
Italianate Landscape, oil on canvas laid down on board, sgn, 8x10", WD 1/11/89 ... 2,400

TRIVILINO, Vincent (American, 20th C)
Cityscape, oil on artist board, sgn, 8x10", RWS 5/19/88 ... 300

TROMP, Jan Zoetelief (Dutch, 1872-)
Pet Lamb, oil on canvas, sgn, 26x39", SBY 2/22/89 ... 52,250

TROMPIZ, Virgilio (Venezuelan, 20th C)
Dama en el Sofa (woman reclining on sofa), oil/sand on canvas, sgn, ca 1985, 45x58", C-NY 11/21/89 OE ... 13,200

TROPININ, Vassili Andreevich (Russian, 1776-1857)
Peasant Woman, charcoal on paper, sgn/dtd 1839, 13x8", C-E 5/23/88 ... 550
Portrait of a Gentleman in a Fur Coat, oil on canvas, sgn/dtd 1846, 29x24", C-L 10/8/88 ... 8,920

TROTTER, Newbold Hough (American, 1827-1898)
Inlet House From Barnegat, oil on panel, sgn, 5x14", FAP 12/8/89 OE ... 950
Last Glow (birds in an extensive landscape at sunset), oil on canvas, sgn/dtd 1889, 16x26", WD 4/13/88 ... 6,000
Man Coming Home From Fishing, oil on board, sgn, 10x13", C-E 2/3/88 ... 770
Surprised (retreivers in landscape), oil on canvas, sgn twice/dtd 1893/inscr #CXRR/titled, 14x20", SBY 1/24/89 ... 2,475
Visit, oil on board, sgn, 9x13", C-E 2/3/88 ... 1,320

TROTTI, Giovanni Battista; circle of (Italian, 1555-1619)
Double-Sided: Four Apostles; Studies of the Crucifixion; pen/brown ink, recto: brown wash, wm, 12x12", C-NY 1/12/88 OE ... 1,045

TROUBETZKOY, Paul (Russian, 1866-1938)
Lady in a Red Dress, oil on canvas, sgn/dtd 1918, 36x20", WG 9/16/88 ... 1,900

TROUILLEBERT, Paul Desire (French, 1829-1900)
Early Autumn on a Lake, oil on canvas, sgn, 18x22", SBY 5/23/89 ... 14,300
Femme sur un Chemin, oil on canvas, sgn, 22x18", SBY 2/22/89 OE ... 23,100
Paysage au Pont, oil on canvas, sgn, 16x22", SBY 5/23/89 ... 12,100
Pont sur l'Oise, oil on canvas, sgn, 15x22", SBY 2/22/89 ... 22,000
Reclining Nude, oil on panel, sgn, 9x16", C-NY 2/25/88 ... 4,950
River Landscape with a Fisherman, oil on canvas, sgn, 16x13", C-NY 10/25/89 ... 10,450
Village Paysans, oil on canvas, sgn, 21x32", SBY 2/22/89 ... 29,700
Washerwoman in a River Landscape, oil on panel, sgn, 12x16", C-NY 2/25/88 ... 9,900
Wooded River Landscape with a Cow & a Peasant Woman, oil on canvas, sgn, 14x19", C-NY 2/23/89 OE ... 12,100

TROVA, Ernest (American, 1929-)
FM Study, acrylic/canvas collage on canvas, sgn/dtd 66AD, 40x40", C-E 11/14/89 ... 4,620
Study for Falling Man, acrylic over pencil on canvas, 1963, 24x24", C-E 11/14/89 ... 3,520
Untitled (contemporary), casein/latex on paper, sgn/dtd 1959, 28x44", C-E 5/9/89 UE ... 990

TROY, see De Troy

TROYA, Rafael (19th C)
Paisaje Ecuatoriano con Volcanes (extensive landscape), oil on canvas, ca 1871-74, 22x29", C-NY 5/17/89 ... 4,400

TROYE, Edward (American, 1808-1874)
Gray Fanny (racehorse by stall), oil on canvas, 22x27", NA 11/5/88 ... 30,000

TROYEN, Michel (French, 1875-1915)
Parisian Boulevard, oil on canvas, sgn, 26x30", SBY 6/8/88 ... 3,080

TROYON, Constant (French, 1810-1865)
Approaching Storm, oil on canvas, estate stamp, 37x51", FAP 12/8/89 ... 28,000

Country Carnival, oil on canvas, sgn/dtd 1849, 18x15", B/B 3/22/89 OE ... 7,150
Frolicking Goats, oil on canvas, sgn, 10x8", C-NY 5/25/88 ... 5,500
Three Prize Cows, oil on canvas, initialed, 32x46", RWS 5/12/89 UE ... 2,500

UCHET, Abel (French, 1857-1918)
Beach Scene, oil on panel, sgn, 11x15", SBY 10/7/89 ... 3,190
Bouvelard in Paris, watercolor/chalk/crayon on paper, sgn/dtd 1890, 16x28", C-E 2/23/88 ... 990
Paris Street Scene, watercolor/pencil, sgn/dtd 1890, 17x28", C-E 10/26/89 ... 2,640
Place Pigalle, oil on board, sgn/inscr/dtd 1905, 13x18", SBY 10/5/88 ... 3,575
Plade de le Republique, pastel on paper, sgn, 20x26", WD 3/23/88 OE ... 4,000

UE, David (20th C)
Untitled (abstract animal figure), oil/graphite on canvas, sgn/dtd 81, 48x36", C-NY 10/4/89 ... 5,500

UESDELL, Gaylord Sangston (American, 1850-1899)
Man Caning a Chair (in interior), oil on canvas, sgn/dtd Paris 1885, 20x24", C-NY 2/23/89 ... 3,520

UFFAUT, Georges
Contemplating in a Hilly Landscape, oil on panel, initialed, 14x20", C-E 5/23/88 ... 660

UIJEN, Johannes Paulus Franciscus (Dutch, 1928-)
Family of Mallards, oil on canvas, sgn, 15x20", B/B 8/10/88 ... 850

UJILLO, Guillermo (Panamanian, 1927-)
Aquelarre in Cricamola (contemporary), oil on canvas, sgn, 1974, 24x30", SBY 5/16/89 ... 1,760

UMBULL, Edward (American, 19th/20th C)
Bridge Builders (landscape w/bridge), pencil/watercolor on paper, sgn/dtd 48, 14x24", SBY 3/17/88 ... 1,320
Landscape with Figures, oil on board, sgn/dtd 31, 34x21", SBY 4/14/89 ... 825

UMBULL, John; att (American, 1756-1843)
Portrait of a Lady, half-length, wearing lace collar; oil on canvas, 30x25", C-E 11/8/88 UE ... 300

UMP, Petronella (Dutch, 19th/20th C)
Still Life of Roses, oil on canvas, sgn, 12x36", B/B 9/14/89 ... 1,870

YON, Dwight William (American, 1849-1925)
Autumn (landscape), pastel on gray paper, sgn/dtd 1913, 8x12", C-NY 2/3/88 OE ... 6,050
Autumn Morning (landscape), oil on panel, sgn/dtd 1913, 11x16", C-NY 2/3/88 OE ... 18,700
Autumn Twilight, oil on canvas, sgn/dtd 1913, 22x32", B/B 6/15/89 OE ... 55,000
Dawn: Early Spring (landscape); oil on panel, sgn/dtd 1913-14, 20x30", C-NY 2/3/88 OE ... 71,500
Evening-Autumn (landscape); oil on panel, sgn/dtd 1914, 16x24", C-NY 2/3/88 OE ... 17,600
Fall Landscape, oil on panel, sgn, 14x20", B/B 10/9/88 ... 16,500
Gathering Seaweed, Block Island; oil on paper laid down on canvas, initialed, ca 1875, C-NY 12/2/88 OE ... 11,000
Newburyport, Haystacks in the Moonlight; oil on canvas, sgn, 25x30", C-NY 5/25/89 ... 13,200
Night (landscape w/house), oil on panel, sgn/dtd 1913, 16x24", C-NY 2/3/88 ... 7,700
October (landscape), oil on panel, sgn twice/dtd 1920 twice/titled, 7x11", SBY 1/24/89 OE ... 15,400
October Morning (landscape), pastel on gray paper, sgn/dtd 1913, 8x12", C-NY 2/3/88 ... 5,500
Pair: Calm Sunset; Stormy Clouds; pastel on gray paper laid down on board, sgn/dtd 1906, 8x12", C-NY 9/28/89 ... 7,150
Sunshine & Shadow (rural scene w/barn & haystack), oil on canvas, sgn, 20x30", C-NY 5/25/89 ... 11,000

CHACBASOV, Nahum (American, 1899-)
Fruit Tree, oil on masonite, sgn/dtd 45, 24x19", C-E 11/17/88 ... 825

CHAGGENY, Charles Philogene (Belgian, 1815-1894)
Journeyman with Covered Wagon, oil on panel, sgn/dtd twice 1858, inscr, 16x21", SBY 6/8/88 ... 770

CHAGGENY, Edmond (Belgian, 1818-1873)
Shepherdess, oil on canvas, sgn, 23x30", SBY 6/8/88 ... 5,225

ENG, Yu-Ho (American, 1923-)
Somewhere, watercolor mounted on 4 panels, sgn, ea panel: 15x24", LH 10/16/88 UE ... 50

EREGOTY, N.G. (Russian, 19th C)
White Night at St Petersburg, oil on board, sgn, 20x41", SBY 7/12/89 ... 3,300

JCKER, Ada (British, 19th C)
Kitten & Company, oil on canvas, sgn, 12x16", C-NY 5/25/88 ... 3,300

JCKER, Allen (American, 1866-1939)
Spindle (landscape), oil on canvas, sgn/inscr, 25x34", C-SK 6/9/88 OE ... 5,575

JCKER, Arthur (British, 1864-1929)
Waves Breaking on Cliffs, watercolor on paper, sgn, 35x21", B/B 6/15/89 UE ... 1,650

JCKER, William (20th C)
Law, charcoal on paper, sgn/dtd 1980, 28x40", C-NY 5/4/89 OE ... 2,860

JDGAY, J. (British, 19th C)
Clipper Ship Centurion Off the Eddystone Lighthouse, oil on canvas, sgn/dtd 1892, 20x30", C-NY 10/25/89 ... 8,800
Clipper Ship Off the Coast, oil on canvas, sgn/dtd 1863, 26x36", C-NY 10/25/89 ... 9,350
Untitled (double portrait of ship entering/leaving port), oil on canvas, sgn/dtd 1847, 24x36", RAB 8/1/88 ... 6,750

JER, Herbert (17th C)
Portrait of a Gentleman, three-quarter length, in armor; oil on canvas, sgn/dtd 1680, 46x37", C-NY 10/20/88 ... 2,420

JKE, Henry Scott (British, 1858-1928)
Boy on a Beach, oil on board, sgn/dtd 1912, 10x14", C-NY 5/25/88 ... 6,600
Harbor Scene, watercolor, sgn, 7x10", FB 5/28/89 ... 1,100
Sun Bathers, oil on canvas, sgn/dtd 1927, 36x48", C-NY 5/25/88 ... 66,000

JLLIDGE, J. (American, 19th/20th C)
Icebound Alaskan Passage, oil on canvas, sgn/dtd 1882, 15x29", B/B 5/17/89 ... 715

TUPMAN, George Lionel (19th C)
Rio de Janeiro, pencil/watercolor heightened w/white, sgn/dtd 1862, oval, 6x9", C-SK 6/9/88 OE **890**
TURCATO, Giulio (Italian, 1912-)
Paesaggio Archeologico, oil on canvas, sgn, 20x29", SBY 10/5/88 .... **5,500**
TURCHI, Alessandro (called L'Orbetto)(Italian, 1578-1649)
Hercules & Omphale, grisaille on paper, 25x11", SBY 1/13/89 OE **29,700**
TURGOT, F. (French, 19th C)
In the Garden (full-length portrait of elegant lady), oil on cradled panel, sgn, 25x10", B/B 6/15/89 .... **2,750**
TURNER, C.E. (20th C)
Plaza Miramar, Vina de Mare, Chile; pencil/gouache, sgn, 14x13", C-SK 5/25/89 .... **1,290**
TURNER, Charles Yardley (American, 1850-1919)
Turning a Phrase, oil on canvas, sgn/inscr/dtd 1916, 30x36", C-NY 3/11/88 .... **2,420**
Water Carrier (portrait of woman in landscape), gouache on board, sgn/dtd 1882, 40x25", SBY 3/17/88 .... **3,190**
TURNER, Charles Yardley; att (American, 1850-1919)
Coastal View, oil on canvas mounted on masonite, bears signature, 14x20", SBY 1/24/89 UE **550**
TURNER, E.
South Carolina Coastal Island, oil on canvas laid down on board, sgn, 24x35", NA 11/5/88 .... **1,900**
TURNER, Francis Calcraft (British, 1782-1846)
The Meet (two horses w/riders in a landscape), oil on board, sgn/dtd 1834, 9x12", SBY 6/9/89 .... **5,225**
TURNER, Francis Calcraft; att (British, 1782-1846)
Jumping the Ditch, oil on canvas, 12x20", SBY 6/9/89 .... **4,400**
Lady & Her Son Out Riding, oil on canvas, 18x24", WD 10/19/88 OE **7,750**
TURNER, Frank (British, 19th C)
Young Fisherman (in boat in a landscape), oil on canvas, sgn/dtd 79, 20x27", B/B 6/15/89 .... **1,100**
TURNER, George (British, 1843-1910)
Camping on the Road to Nottingham, oil on canvas, sgn/dtd 73, 24x40", LH 12/4/88 .... **1,900**
Ducks on a Pond with Cottages, oil on canvas, sgn, 20x30", C-E 11/8/88 .... **1,870**
Hillside at Ingleby, Derbyshire; oil on board, sgn/dtd, 10x15", B/B 9/15/88 .... **1,430**
Near Stanton by Bridge, Derbyshire; oil on canvas, sgn, 10x14", B/B 9/15/88 .... **1,760**
Panoramic Landscape, oil on canvas, sgn/dtd 83, 14x21", B/B 4/20/88 .... **660**
Scene Near Knowle Hill, Derbyshire; no media given, sgn/dtd 1883, 16x26", C-E 5/22/89 OE **4,400**
TURNER, Helen Mary (American, 1858-1943)
Mountain Valley in the Spring, oil on canvas, sgn, 22x28", B/B 10/9/88 .... **5,500**
Winter Panes (view through window, floral still life, icy mountains beyond), oil on canvas, 28x22", RWS 3/31/88 OE **2,400**
TURNER, J.A. (British, 19th C)
Haystack in a Field, oil on panel, sgn/dtd 1891, 12x10", B/B 5/17/89 .... **1,320**
TURNER, Joseph Mallord Williams (British, 1775-1851)
Iron Bridge at Coalbrookdale, blue/gray wash over pencil, 11x15", C-NY 5/25/88 OE **17,600**
Lake of Perugia, watercolor over pencil, bears Turner signature, 10x16", C-NY 2/25/88 OE **4,400**
Strid Bolton Abbey, Yorkshire (river landscape w/angler casting); watercolor on paper, 11x15", SBY 10/24/89 .... **77,000**
TURNER, Joseph Mallord Williams; after (British, 1775-1851)
Deal Beach, oil on canvas, 8x13", LH 10/16/88 UE **400**
Early Morning on the Coast, the Mist on the Waters; oil on canvas, 10x14", LH 10/16/88 OE **1,800**
TURNER, Joseph Mallord Williams; att (British, 1775-1851)
Rhine with Aquaduct, watercolor, 9x12", FB 10/17/88 .... **400**
Temple of Minerva, oil on canvas, 20x23", FB 10/17/88 .... **1,900**
TURNER, Ross Sterling (American, 1847-1915)
Bell Tower (figures in plaza, stucco building beyond), watercolor/pencil on paper, sgn/dtd 1910, 22x16", RWS 3/31/88 .... **1,100**
TUTTLE, Richard (American, 1941-)
#3 Paris, 1974; graphite on paper on masonite mounted in wooden frame, sgn/dtd 1974, 6x4", C-NY 11/10/88 OE **2,860**
Mist (abstract), oil on panel, sgn/dtd 1965/titled, unfr, 23x52", C-NY 11/9/88 .... **44,000**
Untitled (abstract), ink on paper, 12x10", SBY 2/15/89 OE **3,850**
Untitled (abstract), watercolor on paper in painted wooden frame, sgn/dtd 1981, 10x14", C-NY 2x14/89 .... **2,860**
TWACHTMAN, John Henry (American, 1853-1902)
Autumn in Greenwich, oil on board, sgn, 12x18", RAB 8/9/88 UE **6,250**
Horseneck Falls, Greenwich, Connecticut; oil on canvas, ca 1890-1900, 25x25", C-NY 5/25/89 .... **104,500**
River Scene at Cos Cob, oil on canvas, 25x25", C-NY 12/2/88 .... **132,000**
Winter in Cincinnati, oil on panel, sgn, 13x16", C-NY 12/2/88 .... **46,200**
TWACHTMAN, John Henry; att (American, 1853-1902)
Farm Landscape with House Among Trees, pastel on paper, sgn, 8x10", LH 9/10/89 .... **2,200**
TWARDOWICZ, Stanley (American 1917-)
#32-1962 Polish Delight, magna & oil on canvas, sgn, 1962, 71x48", LH 10/16/88 UE **400**
TWINING, Yvonne (American, 1907-)
Park in Spring, oil on canvas, sgn twice/dtd 1937 twice, 27x40", SBY 1/24/89 OE **9,350**
Side Street (city street scene), oil on canvas, sgn/dtd 39/titled, 20x24", RAB 3/27/89 .... **4,700**
TWOMBLY, Cy (American, 1929-)
Capitoli (abstract), oil/crayon/pencil on canvas, sgn twice/dtd Roma 1962/titled twice, 52x59", SBY 6/30/88 .... **360,000**
Composition (abstract), oil/pencil on canvas, sgn/dtd Roma 1962, 32x40", SBY 5/3/89 OE **374,000**
Formian Dreams & Actuality (abstract composition), oil/oil stick on paper, sgn/dtd Aug 15 83, 39x28", SBY 11/8/89 OE **577,500**
How Long You Must Go (abstract composition), pencil/oil/crayon on canvas, sgn/dtd Sept 1964, 78x102", SBY 11/8/89 .... **1,705,000**
Landscape (abstract), oil/paper collage on wood panel, sgn/dtd 1952, 11x21", SBY 5/3/89 .... **110,000**

Naxos (abstract), gouache/crayon/graphite on 3 sheets, initialed/dtd Mar-12-82, overall: 69x134", SBY 2/15/89 OE 561,000
Untitled (abstract composition), oil/sand on canvas, ca 1952, 16x20", SBY 11/9/89 OE 374,000
Untitled (abstract), acrylic/colored crayons/graphite on canvas, sgn/dtd 1961, 40x58", C-NY 11/9/88 OE 638,000
Untitled (abstract), oil on paper, 1967, 21x23", SBY 11/10/88 OE 286,000
Untitled (abstract), oil/crayon on canvas, 1967, 79x104", SBY 5/2/88 OE 990,000
Untitled (abstract), oil/crayon/pencil on canvas, sgn, 1962, 39x22", SBY 5/2/88 OE 209,000
Untitled (abstract), oil/graphite on canvas, sgn/dtd 1967, 59x49", SBY 5/2/89 OE 462,000
Untitled (abstract), oil/pencil/colored crayon on canvas, sgn twice/dtd 61/inscr, 16x20", SBY 6/30/88 OE 172,000
Untitled (abstract), oil/sand on canvas, ca 1952, 16x20", SBY 2/19/88 8,800
Untitled (abstract), pencil on paper, sgn/dtd 1960/inscr Galleria La Tartaruga, 12x14", SBY 5/2/88 OE 35,750
Untitled (abstract), pencil/crayon on paper, sgn/dtd 1964, 28x39", SBY 2/15/89 OE 137,500
Untitled (abstract), pencil/crayon/ballpoint pen on paper, sgn/dtd Roma 1963, 20x28", SBY 2/19/88 OE 60,500
Untitled (abstract), pencil/crayon/red ballpoint pen on paper, inscr See Napels & Die, 20x28", SBY 5/2/88 OE 93,500
Untitled (abstract), pencil/pen/ink/marker on paper, sgn/dtd 1968/inscr To Andy, 18x24", SBY 5/2/88 OE 77,000
Untitled (contemporary composition), pencil/pen/ink/marker on paper, sgn/dtd 1968, 18x24", SBY 11/9/89 OE 385,000
Untitled (irregular horizontal lineation), gouache/crayon/graphite on paper, sgn/dtd 1971, 26x20", C-NY 2/14/89 OE 88,000
Untitled (linear abstract), gouache/crayon on paper, dtd 7-16-78, 26x20", SBY 2/19/88 OE 38,500
Untitled (Roman Note No 10), oil/crayons on paper, sgn/dtd Mar 1970, 27x34", SBY 11/9/89 OE 231,000
Untitled (Roman Note No 21), oil/colored crayon on paper, ca 1970, 27x34", SBY 5/2/88 OE 71,500

TWORKOV, Jack (American, 1900-1982)

Bloomfield (abstract), oil on canvas, sgn/dtd 1969, 80x70", SBY 10/8/88 22,000
Choir (abstract), oil on canvas, sgn/dtd 51, 45x42", C-NY 2/20/88 46,200
Indian Red Series #4, oil on canvas, sgn/dtd 79/titled, unfr, 72x72", C-NY 11/10/88 28,500
Male Figure (contemporary), oil on board, sgn/dtd 54, 26x20", C-NY 5/4/89 19,800
Queen III (abstract), oil on canvas, sgn/dtd 57-8, 69x41", SBY 5/2/88 63,250
RA on P#3 (abstract), acrylic on paper, sgn/dtd 72, 22x30", SBY 10/8/88 2,200
SS-68-1 (abstract), oil on canvas, sgn/dtd 68, 40x36", SBY 10/5/89 16,500
Still Life, oil on canvas, sgn, 18x32", C-E 5/13/88 1,320
Untitled (abstract), oil on canvas, sgn/dtd 61, 20x14", SBY 10/5/89 11,000
Untitled (abstract), oil on canvas, sgn/dtd 61, 21x19", SBY 2/15/89 OE 10,450
Untitled (Sun Series), oil on canvas, sgn, painted ca 1953, 14x12", C-NY 5/4/88 3,300

TYLER, Bayard Henry (American, 1855-1931)

Clouds & Sunshine, oil on canvas, sgn/dtd 1911, 12x16", C-E 6/1/88 660
Mountain Path, oil on canvas, sgn/dtd 1918, 16x20", RWS 3/31/88 1,200
On the Lake (calm waters & wooded shore), oil on canvas, sgn, 12x16", RWS 3/31/88 1,800
Palisades (landscape), oil on canvas, sgn, 25x30", SBY 3/17/88 OE 3,410
Sailing on the Hudson, oil on canvas, sgn/dtd 1906, 18x24", C-NY 9/28/89 4,620

TYLER, George Washington (American, 1803-1833)

Portrait of Mrs Sarah Louisa Taylor, oil on canvas, 29x24", LH 10/16/88 UE 750

TYLER, James Gale (American, 1851-1931)

At Quarantine, oil on canvas, sgn/dtd 1919, 16x26", SBY 3/17/88 1,320
Before the Winds, oil on canvas, sgn, 23x32", C-E 2/1/89 OE 4,620
Coming Home From Fishing, oil on board, sgn, 9x12", C-E 2/3/88 1,870
Crashing Through the Waves, oil on canvas, sgn, 16x22", RWS 5/12/89 1,900
Full Moon (marine scene), oil on canvas, sgn/dtd 1905, 8x12", RWS 3/16/89 600
In the Heat of the Battle (ships firing cannon), oil on canvas, 32x37", SBY 3/17/88 3,300
Moonlight Fishing, oil on canvas, sgn/inscr, 26x32", C-NY 3/11/88 UE 3,080
Moonlight Sail (schooner seen in moonlight), oil on canvas, sgn/titled, 20x16", RAB 11/10/88 UE 900
Moonlight Sailing, oil on canvas, sgn, 20x16", DM 5/13/88 1,100
Night at Sea (ship), oil on canvas, sgn/dtd 1903, 20x30", SBY 1/24/89 2,750
On a Reach (sailing ship on high seas), oil on canvas, sgn, 12x18", RWS 9/29/88 1,300
Rounding the Point, oil on canvas, sgn, 12x18", C-E 6/1/88 1,540
Sailboat in Choppy Waters, oil on canvas, sgn, 14x20", SBY 9/23/88 1,870
Sailing at Dawn, oil on canvas, indistinctly sgn, 20x16", C-E 6/1/89 UE 770
Sailing at Moonlight, oil on canvas, sgn, 20x15", C-E 2/3/88 2,090
Sailing on Rough Seas, oil on canvasboard, sgn, 8x10", C-E 6/1/88 1,650
Sanding the Hull (ship at coastline), oil on canvas mounted on masonite, sgn/dtd 1908, 25x30", SBY 3/17/88 3,080
Ship at Sea, oil on canvas, sgn, 18x24", SBY 9/14/89 3,520
Ship on the Moonlit Sea, oil on canvas, sgn, 24x20", SBY 3/17/88 UE 1,320
Sloop Running at Night, oil on canvas, sgn, 20x16", SBY 4/14/89 990
Stormy Day (ship in heavy sea), oil on canvas, sgn/indistinctly dtd, 20x26", RAB 3/27/89 1,600
Stranger From Afar (ship under sail), oil on canvas, sgn, 24x33", SBY 3/17/88 UE 1,980
The Yacht Vigilant Wins the 1893 America's Cup Race, oil on canvas, sgn, 40x32", RWS 5/19/88 UE 14,000
Untitled (waves breaking on huge rocks w/lighthouse), oil on canvas, sgn, 20x30", SLK 4/7/89 3,250
Waiting for the Wind (coastal scene), oil on canvas, sgn, 18x30", RAB 8/8/89 UE 4,500

YLER, William Richardson (American, 1825-1896)

Fishing Off Martha's Vineyard, 1886; oil on canvas, sgn/dtd 1886, 22x38", RAB 8/9/88 5,600

YSON, Carroll S. (American, 1877-1956)

House on Cliff, oil on canvas, sgn/dtd 1907, 25x30", SBY 6/24/88 3,025
John Murphy's Place, oil on canvas laid down on board, sgn/dtd 1984, 30x36", C-E 10/18/89 3,300
Johns Island, Bass Harbor, Maine (boats & buildings, harbor beyond); oil on canvas, sgn/dtd 1946, WL 5/20/88 2,000

Lake View with Sailboats, oil on canvas, 34x29", WL 5/20/88	900
Path, oil on canvas, unfr, 24x16", SBY 6/24/88 UE	330
Seascape (impressionistic marine scene w/ships & lighthouse), oil on canvas, 25x30", RWS 3/31/88	2,750
View of the Lake, oil on canvas, 20x24", NA 2/6/88 UE	500
Western Mountain, Mount Desert; no media given, sgn/dtd 1944, 25x30", SBY 6/24/88	2,200
Yacht Noma, Nassau; oil on board, sgn/dtd 1915, 16x21", WL 5/20/88 UE	2,000
TYTGAT, Edgard (Belgian, 1879-1957)	
Au Temple de l'Inspiration, watercolor/gouache on paper, sgn/dtd 1930, 16x14", SBY 10/7/89 OE	7,150
UBEDA, Augustin (Spanish, 1925-)	
Cubist Composition with Figures, oil on canvas, sgn/inscr 25 Mai 59 on verso, 29x36", RWS 12/10/88	700
UDALTSOVA, Nadezhda (Russian, 1886-1961)	
Composition (abstract), gouache over pencil on paper, 9x8", SBY 7/7/88	20,000
Composition (abstract), watercolor w/gold on paper, 1916, 8x8", C-NY 7/7/88	32,000
Composition: N 26 (abstract); gouache over pencil on paper, 10x9", SBY 7/7/88	20,000
Still Life with Bottle (abstract, study for large oil), pencil on paper, 1914, 10x8", SBY 7/7/88 OE	24,000
UDVARY, Paul	
Cypress Trees on a Path, oil on board, sgn/inscr Budapest, 13x16", C-E 11/8/88 UE	300
UFER, Walter (American, 1876-1936)	
Companions (landscape w/Indians), oil on canvas, sgn/inscr, 25x30", C-NY 5/26/88 UE	77,000
Indian Family (portrait), oil on canvas, sgn, 25x30", SBY 5/24/89	30,800
Indian Woman, Isleta, New Mexico; oil on canvas, sgn/inscr, 30x25", SBY 5/25/88	121,000
Nude in an Interior, oil on canvas, sgn, 30x30", SBY 5/24/89	29,700
Taos Indian (three-quarter figure on village street), oil on canvas, sgn/titled, 30x25", SBY 5/24/89	82,500
UHL, S. Jerome (American, 1842-1916)	
Midget (seated girl w/bouquet), oil on canvas, sgn/dtd 19(?), 12x10", RWS 5/12/89 UE	325
Portrait of Charles A Uhl, oil on canvas, sgn, 23x20", WG 4/23/88	500
UHRIG, Albert E.	
After Hunting, oil on canvas, sgn, 35x22", NA 3/26/88	600
ULBRICHT, Elsa (American, 1885-)	
Summer Landscape, oil on canvas, sgn, 12x16", MAG 6/22/89	175
ULLMAN, Eugene Paul (American, 1897-1953)	
A la Toilette (bust-length portrait of nude), oil on canvas, sgn, 18x22", RWS 5/19/88 UE	500
Umbrian School (16th C)	
Holy Family with the Infant Saint John the Baptist, oil on panel, 30x22", C-NY 4/8/88	26,400
Portrait of a Young Man, Bust-Length, in a Blue Vest...in Landscape; oil on panel, 16x13", C-NY 10/12/89	11,000
UNGER, Hans, (German, 1872-1936)	
Still Life of Flowers in an Urn with a Parrot, oil on canvas, sgn, 36x30", PHL 10/28/88 UE	1,000
UNSWORTH, Edna Ganzhorn (American, 1890-)	
He Dealt His Last Hand (confrontation w/man drawing gun), oil on board, oval, 23x17", B/B 3/22/89	2,200
UNTERBERGER, Franz Richard (Belgian, 1838-1902)	
Alpine Landscape with Cottage & Farm Animals, oil on canvas, sgn, 22x34", SBY 7/12/89	3,300
Amalfi-Golf de Salerne; oil on canvas, sgn/titled, 24x40", SBY 2/22/89 OE	57,750
Motio du Lac du Garda, oil on panel, sgn/initialed/titled, 21x32", SBY 5/23/89	15,400
Neapolitian Market with a View of Vesuvius, oil on canvas, sgn, 23x44", C-NY 2/23/89	13,200
Pair: Gondola Ride; Fishing Boats Near the Salute; oil on panel, sgn, 22x14", SBY 10/24/89	41,250
Two Figures on a Terrace with an Extensive View of Naples Beyond, oil on canvas, sgn, 20x27", C-NY 2/23/89	7,700
UNTERBERGER, Franz Richard; manner of (Belgian, 1838-1902)	
Fishing Nets by the Bay of Naples, oil on canvas, 17x29", C-E 10/25/88	3,850
UNTERBUSCH, W. (British, 19th C)	
Tavern Interior, oil on canvas, sgn, 27x39", SLK 9/27/88	350
UPDYKE, Jonathan (Canadian)	
Olympics, Strait of Juan de Fuca; oil on board, sgn, 8x10", WAD 6/12/89	170
UPELNECKS, Arthur (American, 20th C)	
Seascape, oil on canvas, sgn, 20x16", LH 5/15/88 UE	120
Ship at Sea, oil on canvas, sgn, 9x12", LH 5/15/88 OE	300
URBAN, Humberto (Mexican, 1936-)	
Orchard with Arch, oil on canvas, sgn/dtd 86, 39x32", SBY 5/16/89 OE	3,575
Walls (adobe walls w/two doorways), oil on canvas, sgn/dtd 87, 47x59", SBY 11/21/88	3,300
UREN, John Clarkson (British, 1885-1898)	
Lizard Bay (coastal scene w/fisherman in boat), watercolor, sgn, 10x20", C-E 2/21/89	825
URLAUB, Georg Anton Abraham (1744-1788)	
Portrait of a Young Woman in Hunting Dress, oil on canvas, sgn/dtd 1768, 16x12", SBY 4/7/89 OE	23,100
URQUHART, Anthony Morse (Canadian, 1934-)	
Evocation of Summer, oil on canvas, sgn/dtd 56, 40x30", WAD 11/30/89 OE	3,000
URUETA, Cordelia (Mexican, 1908-)	
Oxido (composition w/cylindrical shapes), oil/sand on canvas, sgn twice/dtd 77 twice/titled, 51x67", C-NY 5/17/89 OE	26,400
Ship, oil on canvas, sgn/dtd 87, 48x59", SBY 5/17/88 OE	23,600
URY, Lesser (German, 1861-1931)	
Landscape with Lake, pastel on board, sgn/dtd 1898, 14x20", B/B 6/15/89	12,100
Nachtbeleuchtung (street scene at night w/two women in foreground), pastel on board, sgn, 1889, 20x14", C-NY 5/11/89	79,200
Nollendorf Platz, Berlin (street scene at night); oil on canvas, sgn/dtd 1922, 28x40", C-NY 10/6/88 OE	79,200

Strassenszene (street scene), pastel on board, sgn, 14x20", C-NY 5/11/89

USSI, Stefano (1822-1901) **60,500**

The Angel, oil on panel, 12x7", C-L 6/27/88

UTRILLO, Maurice (French, 1883-1955) **3,784**

Au Foyer, Montmartre; oil on canvas laid down on board, sgn, 1934-35, 22x18", C-NY 11/16/88

Carrefour du Val de Beaute et la Rue de Moulin a Nogent sur Marne, oil on board, sgn, 21x30", C-NY 11/16/88 **308,000**

Eglise de Campagne (view of church in a landscape), oil on canvas, sgn, ca 1912, 22x27", SBY 5/10/89 **242,000**

Eglise de Fareins Ain (street scene w/church), oil on canvas, sgn/dtd 1934, 20x24", C-NY 5/11/89 **363,000**

Eglise de Groslay, oil on board laid down on cradled panel, sgn, ca 1914, 22x29", SBY 2/16/89 OE **198,000**

Eglise de Saint Leonard des Bois, Sarthe; gouache on paper, sgn/dtd 1933, 15x20", SBY 11/16/89 **280,500**

Eglise de St Pierre (church glimpsed over a rooftop), oil on canvas, sgn/dtd 1935, 22x15", SBY 5/10/89 **99,000**

Eglise Saint-Andre de Bage (Ain); gouache on paper, sgn/dtd 1930/titled, 20x13", SBY 11/12/88 **143,000**

Eglise Saint-Severin a Paris (St Severin Church in Paris); oil on canvas, sgn, ca 1936, 19x22", C-NY 2/18/88 OE **49,500**

Eglise Sainte-Colonne a Andorre; gouache on paper, sgn/dtd 1933, 19x12", C-NY 11/15/88 **198,000**

La Chapelle d'Ardon a Chatillon-de-Michaille (Ain), oil on canvas, sgn/dtd 1933, 25x19", C-NY 11/16/88 OE **33,000**

La Maison (the house), oil/gouache on paper, laid down on board, sgn/dtd Avril, 10x13", SBY 10/6/89 **176,000**

La Maison de Mimi Pinson a Montmartre, oil on canvas, sgn/inscr, ca 1940, 15x24", C-NY 11/16/88 **44,000**

La Place Jean Baptiste Clement a Montmartre (street scene), oil on canvas, sgn, 1945, 18x24", SBY 11/12/88 **154,000**

La Promenade (street scene), oil on board laid down on cradled panel, sgn/dtd 1922, 14x16", SBY 11/12/88 OE **132,000**

La Rue Hautefeuille (quiet street scene w/tall buildings), oil on canvas, sgn, ca 1912, 32x24", SBY 5/10/89 OE **159,500**

La Rue Lepic (street scene), oil on canvas, sgn, ca 1935, 14x21", B/B 10/9/88 OE **506,000**

Le Chateau aux Poivreres (view of estate), oil on canvas, sgn, ca 1923, 16x26", C-NY 11/16/88 **55,000**

Le Chateaux des Mesnuls sous la Neige (snowy village scene), oil on board, sgn twice/inscr, 1940, 18x22", C-NY 5/12/88 **187,000**

Le Lapin Agile (landscape w/buildings), oil on board laid down, sgn, ca 1910, 20x26", C-NY 5/11/88 OE **187,000**

Le Lapin Agile sous la Neige, gouache/pencil on thin board, sgn/inscr Montmartre, ca 1937-39, 29x25", SBY 11/12/88 OE **605,000**

Le Maquis de Montmartre (street scene w/figures), oil on canvas, sgn, 15x18", SBY 5/10/89 **148,500**

Le Moulin de la Galette, gouache on paper, sgn, ca 1954, 15x13", SBY 10/6/89 **253,000**

Le Moulin de la Galette, watercolor/gouache/pencil/black crayon on paper, sgn/dtd 1923, 12x20", SBY 5/11/88 OE **57,750**

Le Moulin de la Galette (landscape w/mill & figures), gouache on board, sgn/dtd 1923, 13x21", C-NY 2/18/88 **74,250**

Le Moulin de la Reine a Trianon (house of the queen of Trianon), oil on board, sgn, ca 1919, 15x20", C-NY 2/16/89 **22,000**

Le Moulin de Sannois, oil on canvas, sgn/inscr Sannois (Seine-et-Oise), ca 1938, 13x22", SBY 10/27/89 **154,000**

154,000

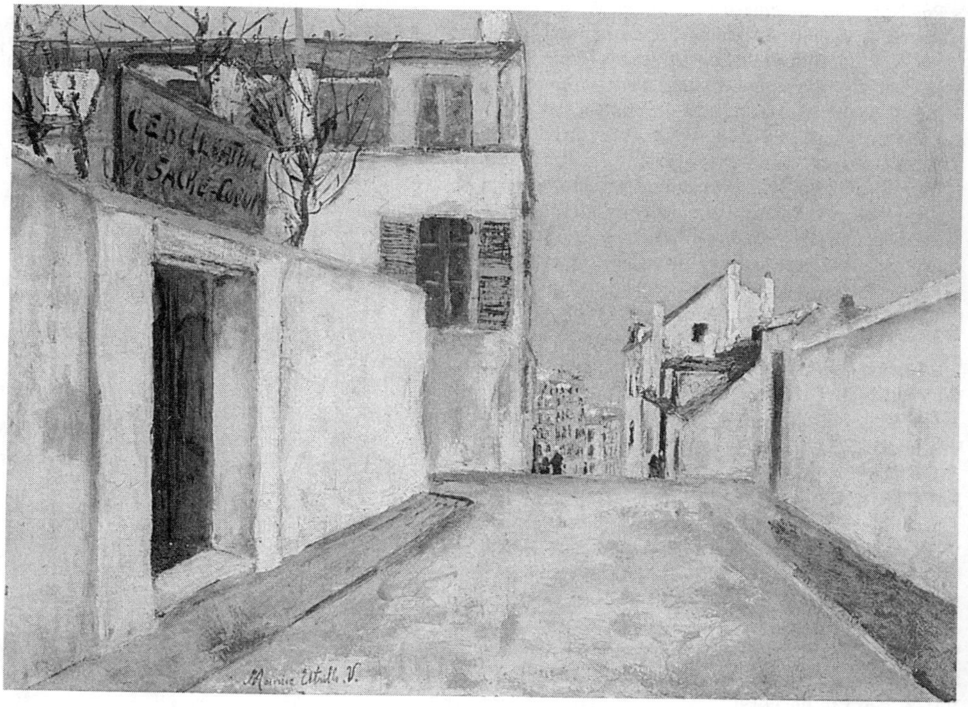

Rue du Mont-Cenis, oil on canvas, sgn, ca 1910, 21x29", C-NY 11/14/89; $825,000

Le Moulin de Sannois (the mill at Sannois), oil on board laid down on cradled panel, sgn, 14x18", C-NY 5/11/89

Le Moulin de Sannois sous la Neige, oil on canvas, sgn, ca 1954, 18x22", SBY 10/6/89 **110,000**

Le Parc de M et Mme Utrillo au Vesinet (park scene w/figures), oil on canvas, sgn, ca 1940, 38x51", SBY 11/12/88 **176,000**

Le Pont de l'Avenue de Saint Ouen, oil on canvas, sgn, 19x22", SBY 10/6/89 **528,000**

Le Restaurant de Pre Catelan, oil on board, sgn twice/titled, ca 1917-18, 21x29", C-NY 11/16/88 **159,500**

Le Sacre Coeur a Montmartre et le Square Saint Pierre, gouache on paper, sgn/dtd 1928, 11x14", C-NY 5/11/89 **220,000**

Le Village, oil on canvas, sgn, 24x32", SBY 11/12/88 **132,000**

Les Remparts (city wall in landscape), oil on paper laid down on panel, sgn/dtd 1922, 9x11", C-NY 5/12/88 **286,000**

Maison de Mimi Pinson, pencil on paper, sgn, 17x22", C-NY 11/15/88 **44,000**

Montmarte, gouache on paper laid down on board, sgn/dtd 1926, 13x17", C-NY 11/15/88 **22,000**

70,400

Montmarte, Sacre Coeur (street scene); oil on canvas, sgn, 11x9", C-NY 5/12/88 OE ... 110,000
Montmartre, Scene de Marche (street scene); oil on board, sgn/dtd 1924, 15x20", C-NY 5/12/88 OE ... 176,000
Montmartre (cityscape w/figures), oil on canvas, sgn, 17x21", SBY 10/6/89 ... 143,000
Montmartre (street scene), oil on canvas, sgn, 18x15", C-NY 2/16/89 ... 165,000
Montmartre (street scene), oil on canvas, sgn/titled, 18x22", SBY 11/12/88 ... 165,000
Montmartre: Cabaret du Lapin Agile; gouache on board, sgn/inscr, 12x19", C-NY 11/15/88 OE ... 132,000
Moulin de la Galette (landscape w/buildings & windmill), oil on board, sgn/dtd 1922, 7x11", SBY 10/7/88 ... 63,250
Paysage a Montmagny (landscape), oil on board laid down on cradled panel, sgn, ca 1907, 14x19", C-NY 5/12/88 OE ... 143,000
Paysage en Beaujolais, oil on canvas, sgn/dtd 1933/titled, 13x21", SBY 2/16/89 ... 137,500
Place du Tertre a Montmartre (last painting executed by Utrillo), oil on canvas, 1955, 18x22", C-NY 2/18/88 ... 33,000
Place Saint Pierre et le Sacre-Coeur sous la Neige, oil on canvas, sgn/inscr, 1940-42, C-NY 11/16/88 ... 308,000
Plante dans un Pot de Tercuite (still life of potted plant), oil on board, sgn, 14x11", C-NY 11/16/88 ... 28,600
Pont Aven (Finistere) la Chapelle Tremolo au Bois d'Amour, oil on canvas, sgn twice/dtd 1931, 29x37", SBY 2/16/89 OE ... 231,000
Roses, oil on paper laid down on canvas, sgn/dtd Septembre 1920, 13x10", SBY 10/6/89 ... 55,000
Rue a Corte (Corse), gouache on board, sgn/dtd 1937, 19x25", C-NY 11/15/88 ... 99,000
Rue a Montmartre, oil on board laid down on masonite, sgn, ca 1919-20, 30x20", SBY 5/11/88 OE ... 242,000
Rue a Montmartre (quiet street scene), oil on board, sgn, ca 1914, 22x30", SBY 5/10/89 ... 253,000
Rue a Montmartre (street scene), gouache/watercolor on paper, sgn/dtd 1926, 19x23", SBY 5/10/89 OE ... 181,500
Rue a Pre-Saint-Gervais (quiet street scene), oil on board, sgn, ca 1921, 18x23", SBY 11/12/88 ... 203,500
Rue Corte a Montmartre, oil on canvas, sgn, ca 1938, 19x22", C-NY 5/11/89 ... 154,000
Rue Cortot a Montmartre (quiet street scene), oil on canvas, sgn, ca 1904-06, 22x15", C-NY 2/18/88 ... 49,500
Rue de l'Abreuvoir, gouache on paper laid down on board, sgn, 11x15", SBY 10/6/89 ... 55,000
Rue de l'Abreuvoir (quiet street scene), oil on cradled panel, sgn, 21x29", SBY 10/6/89 ... 159,500
Rue de l'Abreuvoir a Montmartre, crayons on paper, sgn/dtd 1933, 14x21", SBY 11/16/89 ... 38,500
Rue de l'Abreuvoir a Montmartre, gouache on paper laid down on thin board, sgn/dtd 1933/titled, 12x18", SBY 11/12/88 ... 104,500
Rue de l'Abreuvoir a Montmartre, oil on canvas, sgn, ca 1937, 18x22", SBY 2/18/88 OE ... 137,000
Rue de l'Abreuvoir a Montmartre, oil on canvas, sgn, ca 1939-40, 22x19", SBY 11/12/88 OE ... 275,000
Rue de l'Abreuvoir a Montmartre (street scene w/figures), oil on canvas, sgn, ca 1937, 20x24", C-NY 11/16/88 ... 176,000
Rue de l'Arbreuvoir a Montmartre (quiet street scene w/figures), oil on board, sgn, 1934, 22x30", SBY 5/10/89 ... 264,000
Rue de Paris (Paris street scene), gouache on paper, sgn/dtd 1917, 15x20", C-NY 5/12/88 ... 110,000
Rue du Mont-Cenis a Montmartre, oil on canvas, sgn/inscr, ca 1935-36, 22x18", SBY 5/11/88 OE ... 209,000
Rue du Mont-Cenis a Montmartre (quiet street scene), oil on board laid down on cradled panel, sgn, 29x23", SBY 11/12/88 ... 187,000
Rue Norvins a Montmartre, oil on canvas, sgn, ca 1915-16, 22x18", SBY 2/16/89 OE ... 203,500
Rue Saint Rustique a Montmartre (street scene w/figures), oil on board, sgn/inscr, 1933, 24x20", C-NY 11/16/88 ... 308,000
Rue Saint-Vincent a Montmartre sous la Neige (street scene), oil on canvas, sgn, ca 1940-42, 18x24", SBY 11/12/88 ... 192,500
Rue Sarrette a Paris (quiet street scene w/figures), oil on canvas, sgn, 18x22", SBY 5/10/89 ... 198,000
Rue St Rustique a Montmartre (quiet steet scene w/figures), oil on canvas, sgn, 15x18", SBY 5/10/89 ... 242,000
Sacre Coeur, colored crayons over pencil on paper laid down on board, sgn, 10x11", SBY 10/6/89 ... 15,400
Sacre Coeur de Montmartre et Rue Norvins, gouache on paper laid down on board, sgn, 12x18", C-NY 11/15/88 OE ... 99,000
Sacre Coeur de Montmartre et Rue Norvins, oil on canvas, sgn, 18x13", SBY 2/18/88 ... 143,000
Sacre Coeur de Montmartre, et Rue de l'Abreuvoir; gouache on paper laid down on board, sgn, 20x25", SBY 5/10/89 ... 132,000
Saint-Seine l'Abbaye-(Cote-d'Or), oil on canvas, sgn/dtd 1932, 19x26", SBY 11/12/88 ... 154,000
Scene de Rue, colored wax crayons/pencil heightened w/white gouache on thin board, sgn, 10x9", SBY 2/18/88 OE ... 17,600
Scene de Rue, gouache on paper laid down on board, sgn, 13x19", C-NY 11/15/88 ... 110,000

UTTER, Andre (French, 1886-1948)
No 9 Composition (landscape), oil on canvas, sgn, 15x18", SBY 2/14/89 OE ... 4,950

VA, Barry; see Le Va

VA VALENTINI (Italian, 19th C)
Old Man with a Young Girl, oil on canvas, sgn/inscr Firenze, 35x20", LH 9/10/89 OE ... 2,600

VACCAREZZA, Andrew Victor
Cartoon (cover illus for the St Louis Globe Democrat), watercolor heightened w/gouache, sgn, 17x14", SLK 5/12/88 ... 300

VACCARO, Andrea (Italian, 1598-1670)
Saint Mary Magdalene, oil on canvas, initialed, 30x25", C-NY 4/6/89 ... 3,520

VACCARO, Domenico Antonio (Italian, 1680-1750)
Prudence with Putto on a Cloud, Cupid to the Right; pen/gray ink/gray wash, inscr, 9x7", C-NY 1/12/88 ... 385

VACCARO, Nicola (Italian, 1634-1709)
Angel Appearing to Jochim & Anna, oil on canvas, initialed, 69x89", C-NY 4/6/89 ... 20,900

VACHET, G.A. (Canadian)
Vieux Coin, oil on canvas, sgn, 30x24", FB 5/28/89 ... 160

VAGA, see Buonaccorsi

VAGO, Sandor (American/Hungarian, 1887-)
Artist & His Wife, oil on board, 16x20", WG 9/16/88 ... 500
Portrait of Mrs Vago, oil on canvas, sgn, 26x19", WG 9/16/88 ... 550
Self-Portrait, graphite on paper, sgn, 18x14", WG 4/23/88 UE ... 200

VAIL, Eugene Laurent (American, 1857-1934)
Dutch Girl, oil on canvas, sgn, 12x16", C-NY 5/26/88 ... 6,600
Madone, Still Life with Orange & Figure; oil on canvasboard, sgn/titled, 11x9", RWS 3/16/89 ... 550
View From the Wharf (woman & child look out, boats in water), oil on canvas, sgn, 43x53", RWS 5/19/88 OE ... 9,500

VALADE, Gabrielle Marie Marguerite (French, 19th C)
Bonnet Filled with Wildflowers, oil on canvas, sgn, 24x29", SBY 10/24/89 ... 12,100

VALADON, Suzanne (French, 1865-1938)
Adam et Eve, oil on canvas, sgn/dtd 1910, 47x51", SBY 11/12/88 ... 79,750
Nu Allonge sur un Canape (nude lying on sofa), oil on canvas, sgn/dtd 1928, 28x63", C-NY 5/12/88 ... 62,700
Nu Debout se Drapant (standing nude), oil on canvas, sgn/dtd 1919, 32x24", C-NY 11/16/88 OE ... 104,500
Rue Cortot, oil on paper laid down on canvas, bears signature, ca 1914, 20x24", SBY 2/18/88 ... 8,250
Vase de Fleurs sur un Fauteuil (floral still life on armchair), oil on canvas, sgn/dtd 1924, 24x20", C-NY 10/5/89 OE ... 55,000

VALBUENA, Ricardo
Untitled (jockey on horse in mid-stride), charcoal/pastel on paper, sgn/dtd 87, 56x59", SBY 5/16/89 OE ... 13,200

VALDES NICA LEAL, see De Valdes Nica Leal

VALE, R. (European, 19th C)
British Three-Decker of the Squadron with Other Vessels Off the Coast, oil on canvas, 39x49", C-NY 10/20/88 OE ... 15,400

VALENCIA, F. (Continental, 19th/20th C)
Winter Scene, no media given, sgn, 12x18", MG 12/10/88 UE ... 100

VALENCIA, Manuel (American, 1856-1935)
Cathedral on a Bank, watercolor on paper, sgn, 24x15", B/B 1/11/89 ... 330
Marine Landscape, oil on canvas, sgn, 20x30", B/B 10/6/88 ... 1,320
Mission Delores, oil on canvas, sgn, 24x16", B/B 12/8/88 ... 1,760
Panoramic Marine Landscape, oil on canvas, sgn, 30x50", B/B 10/6/88 ... 6,050

VALENKAMPH, Theodore V.C. (American, 1868-1924)
Full Sail (ship in churning water), oil on canvas, sgn/dtd 1908, 16x20", RWS 5/19/88 ... 1,700
Harbor in Winter, oil on canvas, sgn, 18x24", RWS 9/8/89 OE ... 3,800
Marine Scene (vessels sailing at edge of a storm front), oil on canvas, sgn, 28x36", RWS 9/29/88 UE ... 850
Off a Rocky Coast, oil on canvas, sgn/dtd 1908, 18x24", RWS 11/3/88 ... 1,200
Sailing Vessel, Morning; oil on canvas, sgn/dtd 98, 20x24", RWS 3/16/89 OE ... 1,900
Three-Mast Ship Underway, oil on canvas, sgn, 24x30", RWS 9/8/89 OE ... 2,000

VALERIO, Theodore (French, 1819-1879)
Head of a Bearded Man, pencil, artist's vente stamp, 9x7", C-NY 5/25/88 ... 1,100
Head of a Young Girl, pencil on laid paper, crown wm, stamped Vente Valerio, 13x10", C-NY 2/23/89 UE ... 660

VALETTE, Rene (French, 19th C)
Two Hunting Dogs (in a landscape), watercolor on paper, sgn, 6x9", WG 4/23/88 UE ... 350

VALKENBORCH, see Van Valkenborch

VALKENBURG, Dirk; att (Dutch, 1675-1727)
Game with Hunting Implements on a Ledge in a Landscape, oil on canvas, 50x40", C-NY 10/20/88 OE ... 11,000

VALLET (French, 19th C)
Still Life of Grapes, Cherries, & Porcelain Vase; oil on canvas, sgn, 22x18", B/B 8/10/88 ... 412

VALLIANCE, R.B.
In the Cotton Fields, oil on canvas, sgn, 18x28", NA 3/26/88 ... 950

VALLIN, Jacques Antoine (French, 1760-1831)
Young Nude Woman Reclining in a Landscape, oil on panel, 7x9", C-M 6/16/89 ... 4,564

VALLOTTON, Felix (Swiss, 1865-1925)
L'Arno a Florence, oil on panel, sgn/dtd 12, 6x10", SBY 10/7/89 OE ... 12,100

VALMONT, Guy (Canadian, 1925-)
Shawbridge, Laurentians; oil on canvas, sgn/dtd 1972, 20x26", FB 5/28/89 UE ... 325

VALTAT, Louis (French, 1869-1952)
Anemones et Tulipes dans un Vase Bleu (floral still life), oil on canvas, sgn, ca 1912, 26x21", C-NY 5/12/88 ... 60,500
Au Bal (the ball), oil on canvas, initialed, ca 1897, 26x32", C-NY 5/12/88 ... 49,500
Barque au Bois de Boulogne, oil on canvas, sgn, 11x14", SBY 10/7/89 ... 26,400
Boules de Neige (floral still life), oil on canvas, sgn, 26x18", C-NY 10/5/89 OE ... 28,600
Bouquet Anemones, Tulipes Cruche Marron (floral still life); oil on canvas, sgn, 1926, 24x20", C-NY 5/12/88 ... 41,800
Bouquet de Fleurs au Pot Bleu (floral still life), oil on canvas, initialed, 9x7", DM 9/16/88 ... 7,500
Composition, Femme a la Tunique Rose; oil on canvas, atelier stamp, 11x9", C-NY 10/6/88 ... 15,400
Composition de Fleurs, oil on canvas, initialed, 1916, 19x29", SBY 10/7/88 ... 17,600
Cruche Beige, Dahlias (floral still life); oil on canvas, sgn, 1937, 29x24", SBY 10/7/88 ... 68,750
Deux Vases de Roses (floral still life), oil on board, initialed, 1907, 17x16", C-NY 2/18/88 ... 19,800
Femme a la Petite Table (woman standing at small table), oil on canvas, stamped, 1922, 11x7", C-NY 2/18/88 ... 5,500
Femme Assise (woman seated, full-length, in profile), oil on canvas, 1925-30, 32x26", C-NY 10/5/89 ... 17,600
Femme au Fauteuil, oil on canvas, stamped, 1918, 29x36", SBY 5/11/88 ... 52,250
Feuillages d'Automne (still life of autumn foliage), oil on canvas, sgn, 1926, 32x39", C-NY 5/12/88 ... 77,000
Fleurs, Cruche Verte (flowers in green vase); oil on panel, sgn, 10x8", C-NY 10/5/89 ... 11,000
Fleurs Blanches, Vase Rond; oil on canvas laid down on panel, initials, 1940, 12x11", SBY 10/7/89 ... 14,300
Fleurs dans un Vase a Deux Anses (floral still life), oil on canvas, initialed, 14x19", DM 9/16/88 ... 27,500
Fleurs et Fruits (floral still life w/fruit), oil on canvas, sgn, 1899, 24x29", SBY 5/10/89 ... 242,000
Houx et Gui (holly & mistletoe), oil on canvas, initialed, 20x16", WD 11/16/88 OE ... 14,000
In the Park, oil on canvas laid down on board, sgn, 8x10", SBY 10/7/89 ... 12,100
Jetee de Fleurs, oil on canvas, sgn, 29x36", SBY 5/11/88 ... 82,500
Jetee de Fleurs (floral composition), oil on canvas, sgn, 1918, 32x40", SBY 10/6/89 OE ... 99,000
Jeune Femme Assise dans un Fauteuil (seated young lady), oil on canvas, sgn, 51x35", C-NY 5/12/88 ... 29,150
L'Ancien Trocadero, Vu des Quais (wharf scene w/city beyond); oil on canvas, sgn, ca 1902, 18x22", SBY 5/10/89 OE ... 159,500
La Barriere et les Peupliers a Choisel (landscape), oil on canvas, sgn, 1927, 15x22", C-NY 5/11/89 ... 38,500
La Couturiere, oil on panel, 5x7", SBY 10/7/89 ... 3,575
La Fillette a la Couronne de Lauriers, oil on canvas, initialed, 1927, 16x11", SBY 5/11/88 ... 22,000

La Loseraie Bagatelle, oil on canvas, sgn, 15x22", DM 9/16/88 ... 25,000
La Maison et le Trois-Mats (landscape), oil on canvas, initialed, 1893, 18x22", C-NY 5/12/88 OE ... 35,200
La Tireuse de Cartes, oil on board laid down on panel, stamped, 1922, 13x13", SBY 2/18/88 ... 19,800
Le Bebe (portrait of a baby), oil on board, initialed, 1909, 14x13", C-NY 2/18/88 OE ... 17,600
Le Jardin de l'Artiste a Choisel (artist's garden), oil on canvas, sgn, ca 1935, 26x32", C-NY 5/11/89 ... 46,200
Les Barques au Bois de Boulogne (river landscape w/boats), oil on canvas, sgn, 1939, 11x14", C-NY 10/5/89 ... 28,600
Les Deux Vases, oil on canvas, sgn, 1901, 29x37", SBY 5/11/88 OE ... 148,500
Les Grenades (still life), oil on canvas, initialed, 9x11", SBY 10/7/88 ... 13,200
Les Roches Rouges (coastal view w/red rocks & trees), oil on canvas, sgn, 1901, 26x32", SBY 5/10/89 ... 132,000
Maison au Bord de l'Eau (house on the banks of a river), oil on canvas, initialed, 1907, 13x16", C-NY 5/12/88 ... 24,200
Marguerites (floral still life), oil on canvas, sgn, 1921, 22x17", SBY 10/7/88 ... 35,750
Marguerites Jaunes, Cruche Verte (floral still life); oil on panel, sgn, 1943, 10x8", C-NY 10/5/89 ... 11,000
Mere et Enfant (mother & child), oil on paper laid down on canvas, initialed, 10x8", C-NY 2/16/89 ... 16,500
Nature Morte, oil on canvasboard, stamped initials, 9x13", SBY 10/7/89 ... 16,500
Nature Morte aux Fruits, oil on canvas, sgn, 1935-40, 18x21", C-NY 11/16/88 ... 22,000
Nature Morte aux Pommes (still life of apples), oil on canvas, sgn, 11x16", C-NY 10/5/89 OE ... 35,200
Panneau de Fleurs (floral painting), oil on canvas, stamped initials, 16x9", SBY 10/6/89 ... 11,550
Panneau de Roses, oil on canvas, sgn, 17x40", SBY 5/10/89 ... 99,000
Paysage, watercolor/pencil on paper laid down on board, stamped initials, 10x13", SBY 2/16/89 ... 9,350
Paysage avec Phare, watercolor/charcoal on paper, stamped initials, 10x13", SBY 2/16/89 ... 8,800
Physallies et Fleurs Jaunes (floral still life), oil on canvas, sgn, 1942, 22x18", C-NY 5/11/89 ... 24,200
Pichet aux Fleurs (floral still life), oil on canvas, sgn/atelier stamp, 24x18", C-NY 5/12/88 ... 15,400
Poires et Pommes, oil on panel, stamped w/initials, 6x9", C-E 5/13/88 ... 7,700
Pommes et Poire (still life of apples & pear), oil on board, initialed, 6x7", PHL 11/15/88 ... 7,500
Portrait de Femme, oil on canvas, initialed/atelier stamp, 1925-30, 29x21", C-NY 5/12/88 ... 35,200
Portrait de Madame Valtat, oil on board laid down on panel, stamped initials, 21x18", SBY 5/10/89 ... 49,500
River Landscape, oil on canvas, sgn/dtd 69, 12x20", SBY 6/24/88 OE ... 14,850
Vase Bleu aux Oeillets (floral still life), oil on panel, sgn, 1942, 9x7", C-NY 2/18/88 ... 9,350
Vase Blue, Anemones; oil on canvas, sgn, 1919, 16x11", SBY 2/16/89 ... 24,200
Vase Cristal, Anemones et Mimosas (flowers in crystal vase); oil on canvas, stamped initials, 1940, 16x13", SBY 10/6/89 ... 30,800
Vase de Chrysanthemes (still life), oil on canvas, sgn, 18x15", SBY 10/7/88 ... 19,800
Vase de Fleurs, oil on canvas, sgn, 1941, 13x16", C-NY 11/16/88 OE ... 77,000
Vase de Fleurs, oil on canvas, stamped initials, 1943, 18x15", C-NY 2/18/88 ... 19,800
Vase de Fleurs (floral still life), oil on canvas, sgn, 1935-40, 30x22", C-NY 5/12/88 ... 41,800
Vase de Fleurs (floral still life), oil on canvas, sgn, 29x22", C-NY 11/16/88 ... 60,500
Vase de Fleurs et Feuillage d'Automne (floral still life), oil on canvas, sgn, 1936, 32x26", C-NY 5/11/89 ... 71,500
Vase de Fleurs Verte (floral still life in green vase), oil on canvas, initialed, 14x11", PHL 11/15/88 ... 17,000
Vase de Tulipes (still life), oil on canvas, sgn, 1928, 32x26", SBY 2/16/89 OE ... 159,500
Vue d'Alber (street scene w/figures), oil on canvas, sgn, 1906, 26x32", SBY 2/16/89 OE ... 88,000

VAN AELST, Pieter Coecke (Flemish, 1502-1550)
Madonna & Child Seated Below a Painting Depicting the Annunciation in an Interior, oil on panel, 39x31", C-NY 5/31/89 ... 104,500
Saint Jerome in His Study, tempera/oil on wood, unfr, 32x25", C-NY 1/11/89 OE ... 60,500

VAN AELST, Pieter Coecke; att (Flemish, 1502-1550)
Last Supper, oil on panel, 24x32", C-NY 5/31/89 ... 8,800

VAN AELST, Pieter Coecke; circle of (Flemish, 1502-1550)
Crucifixion with the Three Marys, oil on panel, 26x8", SBY 10/13/89 ... 2,750

VAN AELST, Pieter Coecke; school of (Flemish, 1502-1550)
Madonna & Child, oil on canvas, unfr, 25x19", C-E 6/1/88 ... 880

VAN AELST, Pieter Coecke; studio of (Flemish, 1502-1550)
Madonna & Child Before a Ledge with Fruit Under a Canopy, a Landscape Beyond; oil on canvas, 18x13", C-NY 1/11/89 ... 11,000
Virgin with the Veil, a Landscape Beyond; oil on panel, 29x21", C-NY 5/31/89 OE ... 48,400

VAN AENVANCK, Theodor (Flemish, 1663-1690)
Pair: Still Life w/Fruit, Kraak Porcelain Bowls, Silver Tazza, Roemer, Shrimp & Crab; oil on canvas, 19x22", SBY 4/7/89 ... 44,000

VAN APSHOVEN, Thomas (Flemish, 1622-1664)
Tavern Interior with Peasants Dancing & Making Merry, oil on canvas, 22x31", SBY 4/7/89 OE ... 12,100

VAN AVONT, Pieter; & VAN OOSTEN, Isaac (Flemish, 17th C)
Allegory of the Four Elements, oil on panel, 25x37", C-NY 10/12/89 ... 52,800
Pair: Allegories of the Elements, Fire & Air; Water & Earth; oil on panel, 25x22", C-NY 6/2/88 ... 24,200

VAN AVONT, Pieter; circle of (Flemish, 1600-1632)
Garden of a Chateau, with Madonna & Child with Putti; oil on canvas, 38x45", C-NY 4/8/88 ... 3,850

VAN BABUREN, Dirck (Dutch, 1590-1624)
Christ Among the Doctors, oil on canvas, 66x80", SBY 6/3/88 ... 220,000
Narcissus Gazing at His Reflections, oil on canvas, 36x44", SBY 1/12/89 ... 44,000

VAN BABUREN, Dirck; circle of (Dutch, 1590-1624)
Saint Bartholomew (portrait in profile), in painted oval, 25x31", C-NY 4/6/89 ... 2,090

VAN BADEN, Hans Jurrianensz (Dutch, 1604-1663)
Church Interior with Figures, oil on panel, sgn, 13x11", SBY 4/7/88 ... 2,970

VAN BALEN, Hendrik the elder (Dutch, 1575-1632)
Battle of Hercules & the Amazons, oil on panel, 52x59", SBY 10/21/88 UE ... 24,750
Triumph of Love, oil on canvas, octagonal, 33x31", SBY 10/13/89 ... 16,500

VAN BALEN, Hendrik the elder; school of (Dutch, 1575-1632)
Cepahlus & Procris, oil on panel, bears signature/dtd 1610, 9x13", C-E 1/12/88 UE 440
VAN BALLARN, Frans
Twilight Landscape with Ducks on a Pond, oil on board, sgn/dtd 1878, 27x22", C-E 11/8/88 990
VAN BEERS, Jan (Belgian, 1852-1927)
Flight of Birds at Dusk, the Marshes of Holland; oil on board, sgn/dtd 1875, 11x25", C-L 6/27/88 OE 15,136
Portrait of a Young Woman, oil on panel, sgn/dtd Paris 1881, 13x10", B/B 3/17/88 1,870
VAN BEEST, Albert (American/Dutch, 1820-1860)
Meeting the Pilot (pilot boat heading out to meet vessel in rough seas), oil on canvas, sgn/dtd 1851, 18x28", RAB 8/9/88 8,000
VAN BERGEN, Dirck (Dutch, 1645-1690)
Pastoral Landscape with Mother & Child Surrounded by Cattle, oil on canvas, indistinctly sgn, 17x22", C-NY 1/15/88 8,250
Peasant Riding in a Cart Drawn by Oxen, chalk/pen/ink/wash, Arms of Nassau(?) & VE wm, inscr, 6x7", C-NY 1/11/89 UE 550
VAN BERGEN, Dirck; att (Dutch, 1645-1690)
Nativity Scene, oil on canvas, 13x16", SBY 12/9/88 UE 660
VAN BEVERLOO, Cornelius Guillaume; see Corneille
VAN BLARENBERGHE, Henri Joseph (French, 1741-1826)
Figures in a Landscape Amidst Roman Ruins, gouache on paper, sgn, 9x14", B/B 3/22/89 9,900
VAN BLARENBERGHE, Louis Nicholas; att (French, 1716-1794)
Pair: Military Camps; gouache on board, 7x9", C-NY 6/2/88 4,950
VAN BLOEMEN, Jan Frans (Flemish, 1662-1749)
Classical Landscape with Figures, oil on canvas, sgn w/monogram, 10x14", C-NY 10/20/88 3,520
Figures in a Classical Landscape, oil on canvas, oval frame, 18x14", SBY 10/21/88 14,300
Roman Landscape with the Arch of Giano & San Giorgio Al Velabro w/Figures & Animals, oil on canvas, 18x24", SBY 10/21/88 4,125
VAN BLOEMEN, Jan Frans; circle of (Flemish, 1662-1749)
Landscape with Classical Figures by a River & a Building, oil on canvas laid down on board, 33x33", SBY 4/7/89 3,300
Pair: Landscapes with Figures Fishing in Rivers; oil on panel, 8x7", SBY 10/21/88 4,675
VAN BLOEMEN, Pieter (Flemish, 1657-1720)
Cavalry Skirmish, oil on canvas, sgn/dtd 1709, 13x18", C-NY 10/20/88 OE 12,100
VAN BLOEMEN, Pieter; circle of (Flemish, 1657-1720)
Peasants Eating & Drinking by a Tavern, oil on canvas, 32x42", C-NY 10/20/88 UE 2,200
VAN BLOEMEN, school of (Flemish, 17th/18th C)
Death of Orpheus, oil on canvas, 28x36", C-NY 4/8/88 2,860
VAN BOECKHORST, Jan (German, 1605-1668)
Cupid Holding Scales & a Banner, oil on canvas, 45x28", C-NY 4/6/89 4,400
VAN BOECKHORST, Jan; circle of (German, 1605-1668)
Saint Catherine, oil on canvas, 32x22", C-NY 10/12/89 2,860
VAN BOMMEL, Elias Pieter (Dutch, 1819-1890)
Busy Harbor, oil on canvas, sgn/dtd 32, 37x49", SBY 5/23/89 44,000
Market Day in a Riverside Town, oil on canvas, sgn/dtd 42, 24x31", B/B 3/17/88 4,125
VAN BOSKERCK, Robert Ward (American, 1855-1932)
Peacedale, Rhode Island; oil on canvas, sgn twice/titled, 32x40", SBY 9/23/88 OE 4,125
Rhode Island Landscape with Pond, oil on canvas, sgn, 20x30", SBY 9/23/88 1,430
Summer (birch trees surround a lake, path in foreground), oil on canvas, sgn, 20x25", RWS 9/29/88 1,600
Washerwoman, oil on canvas, sgn, 23x31", C-E 6/1/88 1,540
VAN BRAEDAEL, Alexander (1663-1720)
Landscape with Ruins & Peasants by a Fountain, oil on canvas, sgn, 18x23", SBY 6/3/88 16,500
VAN BREDAEL, Jan Peter II (Flemish, 1683-1735)
Taking of Belgrade by Prince Eugene of Savoy From the Turks in 1717, no media given, 23x28", C-M 12/3/88 14,865
VAN BREDAEL, Joseph; school of (Flemish, 1688-1739)
Horse Fair, oil on canvas, 34x47", C-NY 4/8/88 7,700
VAN BREDAEL, Pieter (Flemish, 1629-1719)
Coastal Storm with Shipwreck, oil on canvas laid down on board, sgn/indistinctly dtd 17(?), 11x17", SBY 6/8/88 1,760
VAN BREDAEL, Pieter; circle of (Flemish, 1629-1719)
Soldiers Attacking a Village, oil on panel, 9x13", SBY 4/7/88 6,600
VAN BREE, Joseph (Dutch 19th/20th C)
Dutch Kitchen, oil on canvas, 22x24", LH 10/16/88 2,600
VAN BREKELENKAM, Quiryn Gerritsz (Dutch, 1620-1668)
Kitchen Maid, oil on panel, initialed, 18x15", C-NY 1/11/89 28,600
VAN BREKELENKAM, Quiryn Gerritsz; att (Dutch, 1620-1668)
Cobbler Working at His Bench, oil on panel, sgn, 15x12", SBY 12/9/88 OE 5,775
VAN BRONCKHORST, Jan; follower of (Dutch, ca 1603-1677)
King Drinks, oil on canvas, unfr, 41x50", SBY 4/7/88 OE 4,675
VAN BRUSSEL, Anneke
Child's Dress, watercolor on paper, sgn/dtd 1988, 24x18", SBY 11/11/88 OE 7,700
VAN BUNNIK, Jan
Biblical Scene in a Rocky Landscape, oil on canvas, sgn w/monogram, 25x22", C-NY 10/20/88 5,500
VAN BYLANDT, Alfred Edouard (Dutch, 1929-1990)
Alpine Lake View, oil on canvas mounted on board, sgn, 21x32", SBY 6/8/88 UE 1,100
VAN BYLERT, Jan; att (Dutch, 1603-1673)
Concert, oil on canvas, 45x62", SBY 1/12/89 31,900
VAN CALRAET, Abraham (Dutch, 1642-1722)
Still Life of Peaches on Red Cloth, oil on canvas, 11x14", SBY 10/13/89 22,000

VAN CAMPEN, Susan Headley (American, 20th C)
Day Lilies, watercolor on paper, sgn/dtd 1980, 23x30", SBY 6/28/89 ..... **440**
VAN CAULAERT, J.D.
Portrait of Alice Roberte, oil on canvas, sgn/inscr/dtd XXX, 75x43", SBY 10/5/88 ..... **4,675**
VAN CEULEN, see Jonson, Cornelis
VAN CHELMINSKI, Jan (Polish, 1851-1925)
Afternoon Ride (lady riding side saddle), oil on canvas, sgn, 32x22", C-NY 2/23/89 ..... **5,280**
Napoleon & His Escort, oil on canvas, sgn, 16x26", C-NY 2/23/89 ..... **6,050**
VAN CLEVE, Cornelis (Flemish, 1520-1567)
Madonna & Child in a Landscape, oil on panel, 26x21", C-NY 5/31/89 ..... **35,200**
VAN CLEVE, Joos; circle of (Dutch, 1485-1540)
Madonna in Prayer, oil on canvas, 19x15", C-NY 10/12/89 ..... **4,400**
VAN CLEVE, Joos; manner of (Dutch, 1485-1540)
Holy Family, oil on panel, 20x17", C-E 6571 OE **1,760**
VAN CLEVE, Martin; follower of (Flemish, 1527-1581)
Peasants Drinking, Dancing, & Making Pancakes in an Interior; oil on panel, 32x34", SBY 6/2/89 ..... **17,600**
VAN CONINXLOO, Gillis; att (Flemish, 1544-1607)
Extensive River Landscape with Hunters & a Village in the Distance, oil on canvas, 41x61", SBY 4/7/88 ..... **24,200**
VAN COUVER, Jan (Dutch, 1836-1909)
Marken, Holland (dock scene); oil on canvas, sgn, 20x30", DM 5/13/88 ..... **1,800**
Rivertown, watercolor on paper, sgn, 15x21", FAP 4/15/89 UE **192**
VAN COUWENBERGH, Christian
Death of Croesus, oil on panel, initialed/dtd 1644, 22x26", C-NY 6/2/88 OE **14,300**
Laughing Boy Holding a Jug & a Glass of Wine, oil on canvas, 27x24", C-NY 1/11/89 ..... **44,000**
VAN CRAESBEECK, Joos (Flemish, 1606-1654)
Ecce Homo, oil on panel, sgn w/monogram, 46x36", C-NY 1/11/89 UE **29,700**
Two Peasants Drinking & Smoking in a Tavern Interior, oil on panel, sgn, 7x6", SBY 10/13/89 UE **660**
VAN DAMME-SYLVA, Emile (Belgian, 1853-1935)
Cows (scattered herd in an open landscape), oil on canvas, sgn, 21x30", WL 5/20/88 ..... **1,400**
VAN DE BECK
Farm Scene with Farmers Wife Near the Well, oil on board, sgn, 16x23", DM 2/19/88 ..... **400**
VAN DE KERCKHOVEN, Jacob (Flemish, 1667-1724)
Fish, Turnips, Scallops, & Celery on a Table; oil on canvas, 18x23", C-NY 1/15/88 OE **17,600**
VAN DE LAAR, Jan Hendrik; att (Dutch, 1807-1874)
Delivering the Letter, oil on canvas, 29x23", C-E 10/25/88 UE **880**
VAN DE SANDE BAKHUYZEN, Julius Jacobus (Dutch, 1835-1925)
Cows & Figures in a Landscape, watercolor on paper, sgn, 9x14", SBY 7/12/89 ..... **1,100**
VAN DE VELDE, Cornelis (fl 1699-1729)
Dutch Shipping in a Battle, oil on canvas, monogramed, unfr, 16x22", SBY 4/7/88 ..... **5,500**
VAN DE VELDE, Esaias (Dutch, 1590-1630)
Cavalry Skirmish, brush/black ink/gray wash on vellum, sgn/dtd 1624, 6x8", SBY 1/13/89 OE **15,400**
VAN DE VELDE, Henri (Belgian, 1863-1957)
Still Life of Flowers (contemporary), oil on canvas, sgn/dtd 1928, 28x24", DM 3/14/88 ..... **325**
VAN DE VELDE, Willem II (Dutch, 1633-1707)
Small Dutch Vessel at Sea in a Gale, Head to Wind, with Mainsail Being Lowered; chalk/stumping, sgn, 7x11", SBY 1/13/89 ..... **1,210**
VAN DE VELDE, Willem II; circle of (Dutch, 1633-1707)
Shipping in a Choppy Sea, pen/brown ink/gray wash, inscr/crowned coat of arms wm, 7x12", C-NY 1/12/88 OE **1,100**
VAN DE VELDE, Willem II; studio of (Dutch, 1633-1707)
Ships in a Calm Preparing To Sail, oil on canvas, 26x31", SBY 6/3/88 ..... **17,600**
VAN DE VELDE, Willem the elder (Dutch, 1611-1693)

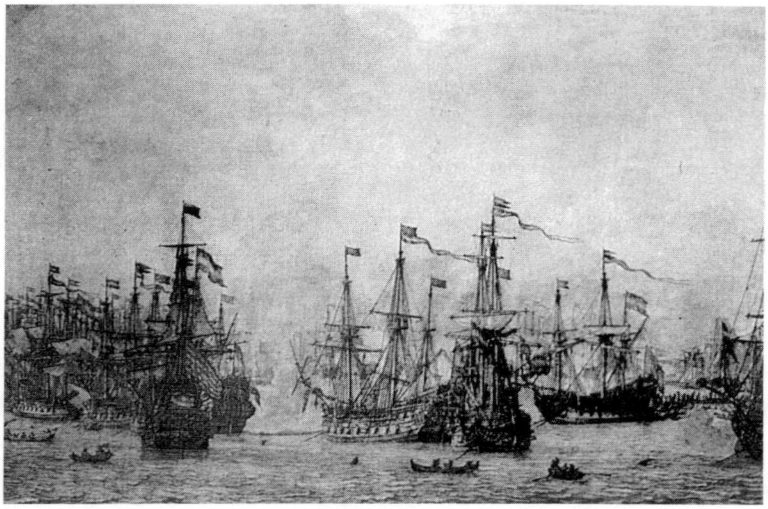

Action at Bergen, Norway, August 12th, 1665; grisaille on canvas, sgn/dtd 1668, 40x58", C-NY 5/31/89 OE; $462,000

Dutch Warships at Anchor in a Calm, pen/brown ink over black chalk/gray wash, 8x12", SBY 1/13/89 OE **11,000**
'AN DE VELDE, Willem; manner of (Dutch, 17th/18th C)
Calm Sea with Fishing Boats Near a Quai, oil on canvas laid down on board, 19x16", SBY 6/8/88 .... **3,630**
'AN DE VENNE, Adriaen (Dutch, 1589-1662)
Dutch Proverb (only strong legs can carry wealth), oil on panel, inscr, 24x19", C-NY 1/11/89 .... **9,900**
'AN DEN BERGHE, Charles Auguste (Belgian, 1798-1853)
Egisthe, Croyant Decouvrir le Corps d'Oreste Mort; oil on canvas, 1823, 45x58", SBY 10/24/89.......... **27,500**
'AN DEN BOS, Georges (Belgian, 1835-1911)
Letter (two women in a landscape), oil on canvas, sgn, 37x24", C-NY 2/25/88 .... **3,300**
Portrait of a Young Beauty (seated, three-quarter length), oil on canvas, sgn, 24x35", C-E 5/22/89.......... **4,950**
Untitled (three-quarter length portrait of harem girl w/peacock fan), oil on canvas, sgn, 31x23", SLK 11/25/88.......... **3,000**
'AN DEN BOSCH, Pieter (Dutch, 17th C)
Woman in a Kitchen Interior, oil on canvas, bears initials GD, 23x18", C-NY 6/2/88.......... **22,000**
'AN DEN BOSSCHE, Balthasar (Flemish, 1681-1715)
Artist in His Studio, oil on canvas, bears signature, unfr, 17x34", C-NY 4/6/89 OE.......... **12,100**
Pair: Elegant Company Having a Picnic in a Park; Rest From the Hunt; oil on canvas, 18x22", SBY 4/7/89.......... **11,550**
'AN DEN BOSSCHE, Balthasar; att (Flemish, 1681-1715)
Twelfth Night, oil on canvas, 27x34", C-NY 10/12/89 .... **7,150**
'AN DEN BROECK, Elias (Dutch, 1650-1708)
Flowers with a Salamander & Butterflies in a Landscape, oil on canvas, 19x24", C-NY 5/31/89 .... **33,000**
Mushrooms, Thistles, Cornflowers...in a Landscape; oil on panel, unfr, 11x9", C-NY 5/31/89 OE **33,000**
Still Life of Roses, Morning-Glory, & Other Flowers with Insects & Snails; oil on canvas, 27x22", SBY 6/2/89 OE **82,500**
'AN DEN BUSCH, S. (Belgian, 19th/20th C)
Germaine Garlanded for Spring, pastel on paper, sgn, 20x27", B/B 3/22/89 UE **1,650**
'AN DEN EECKHOUT, Gerbrand (Dutch, 1621-1674)
Ruth & Boaz (harvesters in a landscape), oil on canvas, sgn/dtd 1672, 58x66", SBY 6/2/89 OE **88,000**
'AN DEN EYCKEN, Charles (Belgian, 1859-1923)
L'Evade (dogs watching lobsters in a basket), oil on canvas, sgn/dtd twice 1889, 14x18", SBY 6/10/88.......... **4,950**
Milk Cart, oil on panel, sgn/dtd 1888, 11x14", C-NY 2/25/88 .... **3,300**
Surprise! (two dogs watching snail), oil on canvas, sgn/dtd 1892, 20x30", SBY 10/24/89 .... **22,000**
Two Against One, oil on canvas, sgn, 26x22", C-NY 10/25/89 .... **9,900**
Visitor, oil on canvas, sgn/inscr/dtd 1885, 16x12", C-E 10/25/88 .... **3,850**
'AN DEN TEMPEL, Abraham; att (Dutch, 1622-1672)
Portrait of Anna Maria Van Schurman, oil on canvas, 48x40", SBY 1/12/89 .... **45,100**
'AN DEN TEMPEL, Abraham; circle of (Dutch, 1622-1672)
Portrait of a Yound Girl, Half-Length, Wearing a Red Dress, w/Vase of Flowers; oil on canvas, 31x26", C-NY 10/12/89 OE.......... **37,400**
'AN DER BILT, Cornelis (fl 1670)
Parrot Out of Its Cage, oil on canvas, sgn, 24x33", SBY 6/3/88 OE **68,750**
'AN DER BROECK, Pieter; att
Peacock with Roosters & Other Birds in a Park, oil on canvas, bears signature, 37x52", C-E 1/12/88.......... **2,420**
'AN DER BURGH, Hendrik (Dutch, 1769-1858)
Family by a Window in an Interior, oil on canvas, 23x25", C-NY 1/15/88 OE **198,000**
'AN DER CROOS, Anthony Jansz (Dutch, 1606-1662)
View of Rijswyck Castle, oil on panel, indistinctly sgn & dtd, 19x25", SBY 4/7/89 .... **13,200**
'AN DER CROOS, Jacob; circle of
Men Fishing on the Banks of a River, oil on panel, bears indistinct signature, 12x11", C-NY 1/15/88 OE.......... **13,200**
'AN DER CROOS, Pieter (Dutch, 1610-1701)
Shipping Scene, oil on panel, sgn, 10x14", SBY 1/12/89.......... **9,350**
'AN DER EYCKEN, Charles (Belgian, 1809-)
Figures in a Winter Landscape, oil on panel, sgn, 21x28", SBY 2/22/89 .... **11,000**
'AN DER HAZEL, C. (Belgian, 1876-1942)
Return of the Flock, oil on canvas, sgn, 24x16", LH 12/4/88 .... **1,000**
'AN DER HELST, school of (Dutch, 1613-1670)
Portrait of a Sculptor, half-length, wearing a black costume...; oil on canvas, 51x39", C-NY 4/6/89 OE.......... **35,200**
'AN DER HEYDEN, Gerard (Belgium, 19th C)
Amerspoort Moat, tempera/wash on paper laid down, sgn, 19x24", FAP 4/15/89.......... **578**
'AN DER HEYDEN, Jan (Dutch, 1637-1712)
Extensive Mountainous Landscape, oil on glass (reverse painted), monogramed, 7x11", SBY 6/2/89.......... **77,000**
The Park of the Old Palace, Brussels (landscape, buildings beyond); oil on canvas laid down, 14x17", C-NY 5/31/89 .... **16,500**
'AN DER HEYDEN, Jan; after (Dutch, 1637-1712)
Baroque Palace in a Square with Church, oil on panel, bears monogram/dtd 1675, 7x10", SBY 7/12/89 .... **770**
'AN DER HEYDEN, Jan; att (Dutch, 1637-1712)
Figures in a Pastoral Landscape, oil on panel, monogramed, 10x12", B/B 6/9/88 .... **5,500**
'AN DER HEYDEN, Jan; follower of (Dutch, 1637-1712)
Church on a Square, oil on canvas, bears signature/dtd 1663, 19x23", SBY 7/12/89 .... **3,300**
'AN DER HOEF, Abraham (Dutch, 1542-1659)
Cavalry Battle, oil on panel, bears initials, 20x26", C-NY 1/15/88 .... **4,950**
Cavalry Skirmish with a Bridge in the Distance, oil on panel, indistinctly monogramed/dtd 164(?), 21x33", SBY 10/13/89.......... **8,525**
'AN DER HULST, J. (Belgian, 19th C)
Shipwreck, oil, sgn/dtd 1886, 24x36", WD 1/11/89 .... **600**

VAN DER JACOBSZ, Christoffel Jacobsz
Merry Company, oil on panel, bears Francken signature, 20x23", C-NY 1/11/89 .... **28,600**
VAN DER KUYL, Gysbrecht (Dutch, 1604-1673)
Musical Party (group seated at a table), oil on canvas, 49x71", SBY 6/1/89 OE **115,500**
VAN DER LAECK, Renier; att (Dutch, -1658)
Triton & Amphitrite, oil on panel, 7x9", C-E 1/12/88 OE **1,320**
VAN DER LANEN, Jaspar; circle of (Flemish, 1592-1626)
Allegory of Spring, oil on panel, 24x42", C-NY 10/12/89 OE **14,300**
VAN DER LISSE: Dirck; att (Dutch, -1669)
Discovery of Callisto (draped nudes in a landscape), oil on panel, 9x15", C-NY 4/6/89 .... **6,600**
VAN DER MEER, Barend (Dutch, 1659-1702)
Still Life of Grapes, Peaches, Berries in a Bowl & Basket, Together...; oil on canvas, 28x25", SBY 1/12/89........ **11,000**
Still Life of Grapes, Peaches, Melon, & Strawberries with a Parrot...; oil on canvas, sgn, 24x50", SBY 6/2/89 OE **68,500**
VAN DER MEULEN, Adam Franz; att (Flemish, 1632-1690)
Cavalry Skirmish, oil on canvas, 22x30", C-NY 10/12/89 .... **11,000**
VAN DER MY, Hieronymus (Dutch, 1687-1761)
Portrait of a Lady in a Dark Velvet Dress with Lace Collar & Headdress, oil on canvas, sgn/dtd 1735, 32x26", SBY 7/12/89........ **2,200**
VAN DER MYN, Frances (Dutch, 1719-1783)
Portrait of Mrs Crowther, oil on canvas, 30x28", RWS 8/12/89........ **2,300**
VAN DER MYN, Herman; circle of (Dutch, 1684-1741)
Portrait of a Lady Said To Be Francoise Marie de Bourbon, Duchess d'Orleans; oil on canvas, 39x34", SBY 10/21/88 .... **4,950**
VAN DER NEER, Aert (Dutch, 1603-1677)
Skaters & Golf Players on a Frozen Canal Near a Village, oil on panel, inscr, 33x29", SBY 6/3/88 .... **34,100**
VAN DER NEER, Aert; att (Dutch, 1603-1677)
Villagers Skating After the Freeze, oil on canvas, monogramed, 19x26", SBY 1/12/89........ **18,700**
VAN DER NEER, Aert; school of (Dutch, 1603-1677)
Moonlit River Landscape with Fishermen Collecting Their Nets, oil on panel, bears monogram, 15x22", C-NY 10/12/89 .... **3,300**
VAN DER NEER, Eglon Hendrik (Dutch, 1634-1703)
Portrait of a Lady, in white satin dress, by a fountain in a park; oil on canvas, sgn/dtd 1671, 46x37", C-NY 10/20/88 .... **8,800**
VAN DER OUDERAA, Pierre Jan (Flemish, 1841-1915)
Mediterranean Beauty, oil on panel, sgn/dtd 72, 40x29", C-NY 2/25/88........ **3,520**
VAN DER PLUYM, Carel; follower of (Dutch, 1625-1672)
Scholar in an Interior, oil on canvas, 40x37", SBY 10/21/88 OE........ **7,150**
VAN DER POEL, Egbert (Dutch, 1621-1664)
Townspeople Scrambling To Extinguish a Burning Building by a River, oil on panel, 11x9", SBY 10/13/89 .... **3,300**
VAN DER POEL, Theo (Dutch, 20th C)
Floral Still Life, oil on canvas, sgn, 31x24", B/B 5/17/89 UE **330**
VAN DER POL, Louis (Dutch, 1896-1982)
Carriages on a Parisian Side Street, oil on panel, sgn, 12x16", B/B 1/11/89 .... **715**
Mother & Her Children on Sandy Cliff, oil on panel, sgn, 12x16", C-E 5/23/88........ **440**
Seated on a Beach, oil on panel, sgn, 8x11", C-E 9/15/88 UE **200**
VAN DER POLL, Herbert (Dutch, 1877-)
Afrikaanscher Reuzenreiger, oil on canvas, sgn twice, unfr, 67x51", C-SK 6/9/88 .... **930**
VAN DER STOCK, Ignatius (Dutch, 17th C)
Angel Appearing to Hagar & Ishmael in the Wilderness, oil on panel, 31x21", SBY 10/13/89 UE **15,400**
VAN DER STOFFE, Jan Jacobsz (Dutch, 1611-1682)
Cavalry Action by a River (battle scene), oil on panel, sgn, 19x25", C-NY 4/6/89........ **6,600**
Cavalry Skirmish, oil on panel, sgn, 16x22", SBY 10/21/88 .... **4,400**
Cavalry Skirmish, oil on panel, 18x25", C-NY 1/11/89........ **6,600**
VAN DER STOK, Jacobus (Dutch, 1795-1864)
Peasants Ice Skating, oil on canvas, sgn/dtd 18(?), 15x19", C-E 5/23/88 .... **2,090**
VAN DER STRAATEN, Hendrick (Dutch, 1665-1722)
Family in an Interior, oil on canvas, sgn, 16x24", C-E 9/15/88 UE **550**
VAN DER STRAET, Jan (Stradanus)(Flemish, 1523-1605)
Two Hunters Using the Stalking Cow To Shoot Deer, pen/brown ink over black chalk, 8x11", SBY 1/13/89........ **19,800**
VAN DER TONGEN, Louis (Lammert)(Dutch, 1871-1937)
Feeding the Baby (mother & children in an interior), oil on canvas, sgn, 18x22", PHL 10/28/88 .... **2,200**
Mother & Sleeping Child (in an interior), oil on canvas, sgn, 23x29", PHL 10/28/88........ **4,250**
Spilt Milk, watercolor on paper, sgn, 22x15", SBY 6/8/88 .... **770**
VAN DER ULFT, Jacob (Dutch, 1627-1689)
Dido Showing Aeneas the Construction of the City of Carthage, oil on canvas, 32x53", SBY 10/21/88 OE........ **50,600**
VAN DER VAART, W. (Dutch, 19th/20th C)
Woman by Window with Children, oil on canvas, sgn, 16x20", B/B 5/17 89........ **660**
VAN DER VELDEN, Petrus (Dutch, 1837-1915)
Gathering Twigs in a Snowstorm, watercolor/gouache on board, sgn, 23x18", C-E 5/23/88 .... **1,430**
VAN DER VENNE, Adolf (Austrian, 1828-1911)
Farmer Playing the Violin (standing by hut w/horses in a landscape), sgn/dtd 1873, 24x36", B/B 6/15/89........ **1,430**
VAN DER VENNE, Fritz (German, 1900-)
Homeward Bound, oil on canvas, sgn/inscr, 16x24", C-E 5/23/88 .... **2,860**
Winter Sleigh Ride, oil on canvas, sgn, 28x39", B/B 3/17/88 .... **6,050**

VAN DER VLIET, Willem (Dutch, 1584-1642)

Portrait of a Nobleman (half-length, seated), oil on panel, sgn/dtd 1624, 32x26", SBY 6/1/89

VAN DER VOORT, Cornelis (Flemish, 1576-1624) ... 18,700

Pair: Portrait of a Lady, Aged 45; Portrait of a Man, Aged 63; oil on canvas, inscr/dtd 1617, 38x27", C-NY 6/2/88 OE

VAN DER WEELE, Herman Johannes (Dutch, 1852-1930) ... 52,800

Shepherdess with Flock in a Landscape, oil on canvas, no size given, DM 1/15/88

VAN DER WERFF, Adriaen (Dutch, 1659-1722) ... 2,750

Hagar & Isamael Banished by Abraham, gouache, sgn/indistinctly dtd, 6x8", SBY 7/12/89

VAN DER WERFF, Adriaen; after (Dutch, 1659-1722) ... 880

Expulsion of Hagar, oil on canvas, 34x27", C-NY 4/6/89

VAN DER WERFF, Adriaen; school of (Dutch, 1659-1722) ... 7,150

Mary Magdalene, oil on panel, 26x19", WD 1/25/89 UE

VAN DER WEYDEN, Harry (American, 1868-) ... 450

Pair: Wooded Landscape; Beached Boats at Dusk; oil on board, sgn, 7x9" & smaller, C-SK 6/9/88

Tranquil Waters, oil, sgn, 20x29", C-SK 6/9/88 ... 1,392

Winter Bouquet (portrait of a lady w/bouquet in snowy landscape), oil on canvas, 20x14", C-NY 5/25/89 ... 2,230

VAN DEVENTER, Willem Antonie (Dutch, 1824-1893) ... 8,800

Bringing Down the Sails, oil on panel, sgn, 9x7", C-E 2/23/88 UE

VAN DIEGHAM (European, 19th C) ... 935

Sheep on a Mountain Side, oil on panel, sgn/dtd 1866, 7x9", NA 11/5/88

VAN DIEPENBECK, Abraham (Flemish, 1596-1675) ... 1,000

Portrait of a Long-Maned Gray Horse, oil on canvas, 61x71", SBY 6/3/88

VAN DONGEN, Dionys (Dutch, 1748-1819) ... 77,000

Pair: Landscapes with Travelers & Livestock Along a Road; oil on panel, 1 sgn/dtd 1778, 8x9", SBY 12/9/88

VAN DONGEN, Kees (Dutch, 1877-1968) ... 4,400

Cannes, la Plage (beach scene at Cannes); oil on canvas, sgn, 1925, 21x26", C-NY 11/16/88

Chateau l'Eveque (Dordogne), oil on canvas, sgn, ca 1925, 21x26", SBY 10/6/89 OE ... 187,000

Cheval Pie, Normandie; oil on canvas, sgn, ca 1947-49, 18x22", SBY 5/11/88 ... 121,000

Dans Mon Atelier, oil on canvas, sgn, 1922-23, 36x29", C-NY 11/15/88 ... 71,500

Danseuse se Maquillant, gouache/black chalk on buff paper, ca 1897, 8x11", C-NY 11/15/88 OE ... 748,000

Diner Chez la Duchesse de Guermantes, watercolor/gouache over pencil, stamped signature, ca 1946-47, 12x8", SBY 11/16/89 ... 38,500

Femme au Collier (portrait of a woman), oil on canvas, sgn, ca 1908, 22x18", C-NY 5/11/88 ... 82,500

La Chimise d'Argent, oil on canvas, sgn twice, ca 1917, 58x46", SBY 11/11/88 ... 253,000

Le Moulin, watercolor on paper, sgn, 2x3", WD 5/5/88 ... 1,100,000

Le Petit Chien (abstract), oil on canvas, sgn twice/dtd 1905, 6x9", SBY 10/7/88 ... 1,500

Les Deux Clowns, gouache/watercolor on paper, sgn/inscr, 23x15", C-NY 11/15/88 OE ... 17,600

Moi et la Femme (two figures), oil on canvas, 1917, 51x76", SBY 11/11/88 ... 49,500

Nu Debout (standing nude), watercolor/pen/black ink/brush/gray wash on paper laid down, sgn, 17x11", C-NY 2/16/89 ... 522,500

Portrait de Jeune Fille, oil on canvas, sgn, ca 1932-35, 22x15", C-NY 11/16/88 ... 7,150

Rue de la Paix, Paris (modernistic figures & dogs); oil on canvas, sgn, ca 1922-23, 39x32", SBY 5/9/89 ... 198,000

Standing Woman with Hat, watercolor/ink wash on brown paper, initialed, ca 1901, 18x11", SBY 10/7/88 ... 770,000

Une Dame (sketch of woman in hat), pencil/gouache on buff paper, sgn, ca 1902, 18x11", SBY 10/6/89 OE ... 9,900

VAN DOORN, Jan (Dutch, 1916-) ... 22,000

Fishing Boat at Low Tide, oil on panel, sgn, 9x6", B/B 12/8/88

Kittens, oil on panel, sgn, 10x12", B/B 12/8/88 OE ... 660

Mother & Child, oil on panel, sgn, 16x20", B/B 12/8/88 OE ... 1,980

VAN DOORN, Janine (Dutch, 1944-) ... 1,210

Children Playing with a Boat on the Beach, oil on canvas, sgn, 16x20", B/B 1/11/89

Kittens & Flowers, oil on canvas, sgn, 16x20", B/B 5/17/89 ... 1,100

Three Kittens, oil on panel, sgn, 8x10", B/B 1/11/89 ... 935

VAN DOREN, Emile (Belgian, 1865-) ... 440

Automne a Bruges, oil on canvas, sgn, 16x20", C-E 2/23/88

VAN DRIELST, Egbert (Dutch, 1746-1818) ... 935

Set of 5: Wooded Landscapes with Peasants; oil on canvas, 1 sgn/dtd 1788, 4 139x55", 1 139x107", SBY 10/21/88

VAN DROUET, Jan ... 44,000

Still Life of Wildflowers in an Urn on a Ledge, oil on canvas, sgn, 20x30", C-E 7/26/88

VAN DUYVEN, Steven ... 715

Portrait of a Scholar Seated in a Library, oil on canvas, sgn, 27x22", SBY 6/8/88

VAN DYCK, Anthony (Flemish, 1599-1641) ... 2,860

Portrait of a Cavalier, oil on panel, dtd 1634/inscr AET.s 57, 29x22", SBY 6/2/89 OE

Portrait of Nicholox, Aged 76, bust-length, wearing black costume...; oil en grisaille on panel, 6" dia, C-NY 5/31/89 OE ... 374,000

VAN DYCK, Anthony; & Studio (Flemish, 1599-1641) ... 231,000

Portrait of Charles, Marquis de la Vieuville (full-length, standing); oil on canvas, ca 1634-35, 84x47", SBY 6/1/89 OE

VAN DYCK, Anthony; after (Flemish, 1599-1641) ... 242,000

Portrait of an Elegant Lady, oil on canvas, sgn, 52x37", RWS 7/13/89 UE

Portrait of Cardinal Guido Bentivoglio, oil on canvas, 79x58", C-NY 4/6/89 ... 750

Portrait of Charles I, oil on canvas, 48x39", SBY 12/9/88 ... 3,850

Portrait of T Howard, oil on canvas, 29x26", B/B 1/11/89 OE ... 2,420

Self-Portrait, oil on canvas, 24x20", C-E 6/1/88 UE ... 2,750

VAN DYCK, Anthony; att (Flemish, 1599-1641) ... 550

Count Williams (portrait of William Hocuet), oil on canvas, 27x22", S/A 2/18/89 ... 15,000

Portrait of a Man, Possibly Marchese Cattaneo, Half-Length; oil on canvas, 30x24", C-NY 1/15/88 OE ... **28,600**
Portrait of Francois Langlois, Called Ciartres; oil on canvas, 41x33", SBY 1/12/89 ... **60,500**

VAN DYCK, Anthony; circle of (Flemish, 1599-1641)
Madonna & Child with Donor, oil on canvas, 55x64", SBY 7/12/89 UE ... **1,100**
Penitent Magdalene, oil on panel, 26x20", SBY 4/7/89 ... **3,575**
Portrait of a Boy Said To Be the Son of Charles II, oil on canvas, 15x12", SBY 4/7/88 ... **6,050**

VAN DYCK, Anthony; follower of (Flemish, 1599-1641)
Portrait of Queen Henrietta Maria, oil on canvas, 42x30", SBY 10/13/89 ... **5,775**

VAN DYCK, Anthony; manner of (Flemish, 1599-1641)
Charity, oil on canvas, 57x45", C-E 4/7/88 OE ... **3,080**
Head of a Bearded Man, oil on canvas, 19x15", SBY 6/8/88 ... **990**
Portrait of a Man, oil on canvas, oval frame, 29x24", SBY 6/8/88 ... **1,760**
Portrait of Charles I, oil on canvas, 46x28", SBY 6/8/88 UE ... **990**
Portrait of Charles II, oil on canvas, 50x32", WD 1/25/89 OE ... **3,000**
St Catherine & Child (flanked by St Bartholomew), oil on canvas, 58x45", C-E 1/12/88 ... **2,200**

VAN DYCK, Anthony; school of (Flemish, 1599-1641)
Madonna & Child, oil on canvas, 53x40", C-NY 4/6/89 OE ... **18,700**
Portrait of a Gentleman in Armor, oil on canvas, unfr, 29x24", B/B 5/17/89 ... **1,760**
Portrait of a Young Man (half-length), oil on board, WG 4/23/88 ... **5,200**
Portrait of King Charles I on Horseback, oil on canvas, 39x30", C-NY 4/6/89 ... **12,100**

VAN DYCK, Anthony; studio of (Flemish, 1599-1641)
Portrait of a Gentleman, oil on canvas, unfr, 42x33", SBY 10/13/89 ... **9,350**
Portrait of Robert Bertier, 1st Earl of Lindsey, in Armor; oil on canvas, inscr, 84x51", C-NY 6/2/88 OE ... **15,400**

VAN EERTVELT, Andries
Naval Battle, oil on canvas, sgn, unfr, 19x25", C-NY 6/2/88 ... **7,700**

VAN EIJBERGEN, Johanna Gerarda Theodora (Dutch, 1865-1950)
Sewing by Lamplight, oil on board, sgn, 19x15", WAD 6/6/88 ... **1,300**

VAN ELTEN, Hendrik Dirk Kruseman (American, 1829-1904)
Figures Boating in a River Landscape, oil on canvas, sgn, 10x15", SBY 1/24/89 ... **2,310**
Figures in a Landscape, oil on canvas, sgn, 15x23", SBY 9/23/88 ... **3,300**
Landscape with Windmill, oil on canvas, sgn, 13x21", SBY 7/12/89 ... **770**
Summer Landscape, Long Island; oil on canvas, sgn, 15x22", WD 4/13/88 ... **3,000**
Thatched Cottage in a Landscape, oil on board, sgn, 13x20", SBY 1/24/89 ... **2,740**

VAN ES, Jacob (Dutch, 1596-1666)
Still Life of Lobster, Shrimp, Grapes, & Other Fruit; oil on panel, 21x39", SBY 10/21/88 ... **66,000**

VAN ESSEN, Johanne Cornelis (Dutch, 1854-1936)
Adjutant-Birds From the Zoological Garden Amsterdam; watercolor w/whiting on paper, sgn/dtd 1886, 13x10", RWS 5/12/89 ... **950**

VAN EVERDINGEN, Allart (Dutch, 1621-1675)
Mountainous Landscape in the Tyrol(?)...; chalk/pen/ink/watercolor, initialed/inscr L82, 4x6", C-NY 1/11/89 OE ... **5,720**

VAN EVERDINGEN, Allart; att (Dutch, 1621-1675)
Extensive River Landscape with a Waterfall & Goats, oil on canvas, 39x47", SBY 6/8/88 ... **1,100**

VAN EVERDINGEN, Cesar Boetius (Dutch, ca 1617-1678)
Rape of Europa (women wave good-by as Europa rides off on white bull), oil on canvas, 60x47", SBY 6/1/89 ... **286,000**
Young Boy Blowing Bubbles, oil on canvas, 28x22", C-NY 1/11/89 ... **8,800**

VAN EVEREN, Jay
Abstract, watercolor/gouache on paper, 6x6", C-E 2/1/89 OE ... **2,090**

VAN EYCK, Gaspard (Flemish, 1613-1673)
Landscape with a Blacksmith Shoeing a Horse & Other Figures Outside a Cottage, oil on canvas, 16x18", SBY 4/7/89 ... **7,150**

VAN GILDER, A
Fishing Fleet Entering Port, oil on canvas, sgn, 26x20", NA 3/26/88 ... **500**

VAN GILST, Aarnout (Dutch, 1898-)
Homeward in the Snow, oil on canvas, sgn, 18x15", WAD 6/6/88 ... **1,700**

VAN GOGH, Vincent (Dutch, 1853-1890)
Backyard with Two Figures (sketch), charcoal on ivory laid paper, 1882, 10x14", SBY 5/10/89 ... **330,000**
Double-Sided: Study of People; Study of a Woman; pencil on paper, 1890, 17x11", C-NY 5/11/89 ... **110,000**
Le Garcon Forgeron (blacksmith), black chalk/pencil on paper mounted at edges to board, 1882, 18x10", C-NY 5/12/88 ... **110,000**
Le Moissonneur (D'Apres Millet), oil on canvas, 1889, 17x10", SBY 11/11/88 ... **3,410,000**
Nature Morte: Scabiosa et Ranuculus (floral still life); oil on canvas, 1886, 10x8", SBY 11/12/88 OE ... **407,000**

VAN GORDER, Luther Emerson (American, 1861-)
Paris Flower Seller Near l'Arc de Triomphe, oil on canvas, sgn, 24x18", B/B 10/9/88 ... **4,400**
Tree-Lined Lake, oil on board, sgn, 10x8", C-E 2/3/88 UE ... **550**

VAN GOYEN, Jan (Dutch, 1596-1656)
Chapel on the Bank of an Estuary, oil on panel, sgn w/monogram, 14x12", C-NY 1/11/89 ... **28,600**
Figures on the Beach at Scheveningen, oil on panel, sgn/dtd 1642, 13x22", SBY 10/27/89 OE ... **132,000**
Figures Resting by a Grove of Trees Near a Road, oil on canvas, sgn/dtd 1633, 26x30", SBY 6/3/88 ... **37,400**
Landscape with Figures on Dunes, Large Church in the Distance; oil on panel, monogramed/dtd 164(?), 16x23", SBY 1/12/89 ... **68,750**
Landscape with Fishermen on Boats & Windmills & Other Buildings Beyond, oil on panel, 13x21", SBY 4/7/89 OE ... **63,250**
Scene with Fishing Boats & Warships in an Estuary, oil on panel, initialed/dtd 1655, 11x13", SBY 6/3/88 ... **104,500**
Travelers Congregating on a Path by a Cottage, oil on panel, sgn/dtd 1628, 13x22", C-NY 1/11/89 ... **55,000**
Travelers Conversing on a Footbridge, oil on panel, sgn w/monogram, 13x17", lot 70, C-NY 1/11/89 ... **55,000**

VAN GOYEN, Jan; att (Dutch, 1596-1656)
Boats Near Moerdyck, oil on canvas, indistinctly sgn in monogram/dtd 1654, 15x24", SBY 1/12/89 OE 16,500
VAN GOYEN, Jan; circle of (Dutch, 1596-1656)
Three Sailing Craft & a Rowboat in Windy Seas with a Town in the Distance, oil on panel, dtd 1643, 16x24", SBY 4/7/88 7,975
VAN GOYEN, Jan; follower of (Dutch, 1596-1656)
View of the Rhine with Men in Boats, Town of Rhenen Beyond; oil on panel, bears monogram, 8x10", SBY 10/27/89 27,500
VAN GOYEN, Jan; manner of (Dutch, 1596-1656)
Figures by a Farm in a Landscape, oil on canvas, 16x22", C-E 4/7/88 OE 1,210
River Landscape, oil on panel, 31x45", C-E 1/12/88 UE 609
VAN GOYEN, Jan; school of (Dutch, 1596-1656)
Beach at Rhenen, oil on panel, bears signature/dtd 16(?), 15x22", C-NY 10/12/89 OE 22,000
VAN GROENEWEGEN, Adrianus Johannes (Dutch, 1874-1963)
Children Playing, watercolor on paper, sgn/inscr, 6x10", C-E 2/23/88 990
Windmill by a River, watercolor on paper, sgn, 8x6", C-E 4/7/88 220
VAN GRONINGEN, Jan Swart (Flemish, ca 1520-1558)
King Denouncing a Monk at a Banquet, pen/black ink/gray wash, 10x7", SBY 1/13/89 UE 660
Moses with the Ten Commandments, pen/black ink/brown wash, 10x8", SBY 1/13/89 OE 14,300
VAN GROOTVELT, Jan Hendrich (Dutch, 1808-1865)
Rocking the Baby Asleep by Candlelight, oil on panel, sgn, 16x13", C-E 5/23/88 3,080
VAN HAALEN, Arnout
Portrait of an Artist Supported by Music & Painting, chalk/pen/brown wash, inscr, oval frame, 8x6", C-NY 1/12/88 UE 275
VAN HAANEN, Cecil (Dutch, 1844-1914)
Wading in the Canal, oil on canvas, sgn, 27x18", SBY 5/23/89 7,700
VAN HAANEN, Remigius Adrianus (Dutch, 1812-1894)
Windmill in Moonlight, oil on canvas, sgn, 12x20", SBY 6/8/88 4,950
VAN HAARLEM, Cornelis (Dutch, 1562-1638)
Ruler Holding an Olive Branch, Possibly King David; oil on panel, initialed/dtd 1620, 24x18", SBY 4/7/89 9,350
VAN HAARLEM, Jan Vermeer; the younger (Dutch, 1628-1691)
Extensive River Landscape with Figures, oil on canvas, 14x18", C-NY 6/2/88 16,500
VAN HAELSZAEL, Johann Baptist; att
Pair: Floral Still Life with Insects in a Blue Vase; bodycolor on vellum, hexagonal, 15x13", C-NY 1/12/88 17,600
VAN HAENSBERGEN, Jan (Dutch, 17th C)
Rest on the Flight into Egypt, oil on panel, 9x12", C-NY 1/11/89 13,200
VAN HAMME, Alexis (Belgian, 1818-1875)
Lacemaker, oil on panel, sgn/dtd 1856, 20x15", C-NY 5/24/89 OE 8,800
Maidservant by a Window with Dead Game, oil on canvas, sgn/dtd 1875, 23x20", C-NY 2/23/89 4,180
Wafflemaker, oil on panel, sgn/dtd 1857, 26x22", B/B 3/17/88 7,700
VAN HEEMSKERK, Egbert (Dutch, 1634-1704)
Boors Playing Cards in a Tavern, oil on panel, 8x6", C-NY 10/12/89 5,500
Peasants Having a Meal in a Kitchen Interior, oil on canvas, 19x22", C-NY 10/12/89 3,300
VAN HEEMSKERK, Egbert; att (Dutch, 1634-1704)
Old Man & Old Woman, oil on canvas laid down on panel, oval, 5x4", SBY 7/12/89 1,210
Peasants Merrymaking in a Tavern, oil on canvas, 25x30", C-NY 10/12/89 OE 9,350
VAN HEIL, Daniel; att (Flemish, 1604-1662)
Escape From Troy (city ablaze, people fleeing, Trojan horse in silhouette), oil on canvas, 33x43", C-NY 6/17/89 4,400
VAN HELMONT, Zeger Jacob (1683-1726)
Guardroom Interior (figures w/swords & pieces of armor in an interior), oil on panel, sgn, 32x23", SBY 4/7/89 7,700
VAN HEMESSEN, Catharina; att
Triptych (wings): The Resurrection; Christ on the Road to Calvary; oil on panel, 35x29", C-NY 1/11/89 OE 26,400
VAN HEMESSEN, Jan; follower of (Flemish, 1504-1566)
Christ Carrying the Cross, oil on panel, 48x38", SBY 6/1/89 9,900
VAN HERP, Willem (Flemish, 1614-1677)
Adoration of the Shepherds, oil on copper, 27x34", C-NY 4/6/89 9,900
Angels Preparing the Virgin for Presentation in the Temple, oil on copper, 27x34", C-NY 4/6/89 6,600
Birth of the Virgin, oil on copper, 38x47", C-NY 10/20/88 15,400
Judgement of King Solomon, oil on copper, 24x33", SBY 10/13/89 13,200
Woman with Two Children Preparing Food in an Interior of a Cottage, oil on canvas laid down, 23x31", C-NY 5/31/89 OE 24,200
VAN HERP, Willem; circle of (Flemish, 1614-1677)
Parable of the Foolish Virgins, oil on copper, 22x29", C-NY 4/8/88 6,050
VAN HIER, A. (Dutch, 19th/20th C)
Venice at Sunset From the Lido, oil on canvas, sgn/dtd 1897, 18x32", B/B 12/8/88 OE 1,650
VAN HOEY, Joseph Ignace (19th C)
Un Ecole en Belge, oil on canvas, sgn/dtd 1872, 38x47", C-NY 2/25/88 3,850
VAN HONTHORST, Gerrit (Dutch, 1590-1656)
Death of Seneca (figures in an interior), oil on canvas, 77x97", SBY 6/1/89 286,000
Denial of Peter, ink/brown wash on paper, unfr, 8x12", WD 1/25/89 UE 700
VAN HONTHORST, Gerrit; studio of (Dutch, 1590-1656)
Portrait of Frederick V Von Der Pfalz, Elector of the Palatina; oil on panel, 17x14", SBY 1/12/89 7,700
VAN HONTHORST, Willem (Dutch, 1594-1666)
Portrait of a Man, half-length, in armor; oil on panel, sgn/dtd 1643, 29x23", C-NY 4/8/88 OE 4,620

VAN HOOGSTRAATEN, Samuel (Flemish, 1627-1678)
White Cock (still life of dead rooster with cat beyond), oil on canvas, monogramed/dtd 1669, 30x26", C-NY 5/31/89 ..... **33,000**

VAN HORSSEN, Winand Bastien (Dutch, 1863-)
Still Life of Flowers in a Vase on a Table, oil on canvas, sgn/dtd 1901, 29x22", C-E 10/26/89 ..... **2,420**

VAN HORT, J. (Dutch, 20th C)
Venetian Scene, oil on panel, sgn, 11x9", SLK 5/12/88 ..... **300**

VAN HOUTEN, Gerard (Dutch, -1706)
Sculptor in His Studio, red chalk/pen/brown ink/gray wash, indistinct wm, sgn, 6x4", C-NY 1/11/89 ..... **880**

VAN HOVE, Bartholomeus (Dutch, 1790-1880)
Dutch Canal Scene, watercolor over pencil, sgn, 7x11", C-NY 10/25/89 ..... **1,760**

VAN HOVE, Hubertus (Dutch, 1814-1865)
Interruption (interior genre scene), oil on canvas, sgn/indistinctly inscr, 28x25", RWS 5/12/88 ..... **2,200**

VAN HUCHTENBURGH, Jan (Dutch, 1647-1733)
Cavalry Skirmish with Artillery & Infantry in the Distance, oil on canvas, sgn, unfr, 26x35", SBY 10/13/89 OE **9,900**
Military Skirmish in an Extensive Wooded River Landscape, oil on canvas, initialed, 36x47", SBY 4/7/89 ..... **17,600**

VAN HUYSUM, Jan (Dutch, 1682-1749)
Figures in a Classical Landscape, pen/black ink, sgn/bears signature, 7x8", SBY 7/12/89 OE **2,475**
Rocky River Landscape with Classical Buildings & Figures, chalk/pen/ink/wash, sgn/dtd 1726, 11x16", C-NY 1/11/89 OE **10,450**
Sheet of Studies of Poppies, graphite/pink/red/green watercolor, 14x9", SBY 1/13/89 ..... **2,475**

VAN HUYSUM, Jan; after (Dutch, 1682-1749)
Floral Still Life, oil on canvas, 17x14", C-E 2/21/89 ..... **1,320**

VAN HUYSUM, Jan; circle of (Dutch, 1682-1749)
Italianate Landscape with Figures by a River, oil on canvas, 25x38", SBY 10/21/88 OE **6,600**

VAN HUYSUM, Jan; manner of (Dutch, 1682-1749)
Field Flowers in Vase & Fruit on a Table, oil on canvas, 35x24", SBY 7/12/89 OE **4,125**

VAN HUYSUM, Jan; school of (Dutch, 1682-1749)
Figures in a Classical Landscape, oil on canvas, 14x18", SBY 7/12/89 ..... **2,200**
Zwei Bluten (abstract), pen/ink/pencil on paper mounted on board, sgn/dtd 1927/titled/#d 315, 12x10", SBY 2/16/89 ..... **20,900**

VAN HUYSUM, Justus (Dutch, 17th/18th C)
Still Life of Flowers in a Glass Vase on a Ledge, oil on canvas, sgn, 33x26", C-NY 1/15/88 ..... **13,200**

VAN INGEN, Henry (Hendrik)(American/Dutch, 1833-1898)
Farmyard Scene with Horses, Boys & Dog, Woman...; oil on canvas mounted on masonite, sgn/dtd 55, 20x25", S/A 2/18/89 ..... **5,000**

VAN ISENDYCK, Anton (Belgian, 1801-1875)
Portrait of Mimi Kesterloot, the Artist's Fiancee; oil on panel, framed as oval, 29x22", B/B 12/8/88 ..... **1,430**

VAN KALRAET, Abraham
Peaches, Grapes & Flacon de Venice with Butterflies on a Ledge; oil on panel, sgn, 17x15", C-NY 5/31/89 OE **36,300**

VAN KESSEL, Jan (Flemish, 1626-1679)
Collecting the Tithes (satirical, monkeys in interior); oil on panel, sgn/dtd 1643, 15x20", C-M 6/16/89 OE **35,859**
Garden of a Palace with Vertumnus & Pomona, oil on panel, 31x38", C-NY 1/15/88 ..... **52,800**

VAN KESSEL, Jan; att (Flemish, 1626-1679)
Flight into Egypt, Surrounded by a Floral Wreath; oil on panel, inscr, 28x21", C-NY 1/15/88 OE **10,450**
Venus & Mars Amongst Ruins, with Vulcan at His Forge, a Fantastical Town Beyond; oil on copper, 20x29", C-NY 4/6/89 ..... **10,450**

VAN KESSEL, Jan; circle of (Flemish, 1626-1679)
Creation of the Birds & Fishes, oil on copper, 10x7", C-NY 10/12/89 ..... **7,150**
Tulips, Roses & Other Flowers in a Glass Vase; oil on panel, unfr, 7x5", C-NY 10/12/89 OE **16,500**

VAN KESSEL, Jan; follower of (Flemish, 1626-1679)
Orpheus Charming the Beasts, oil on canvas, 16x22", SBY 10/21/88 OE **8,250**

VAN KESSEL, Jan; manner of (Flemish, 1626-1679)
Bird Choir, oil on panel, inscr with artist's name, 7x8", WD 1/25/89 OE **26,000**

VAN KESSEL, Peter (-1668)
Still Life with a Violin, Skull...& Dice on a Draped Ledge, a Vanitas; oil on canvas, sgn/dtd 1664, SBY 4/7/89 ..... **22,000**

VAN LAER, Alexander Theobald (American, 1857-1920)
Winter Landscape, oil on canvas, 12x18", C-E 9/15/88 UE **880**

VAN LAER, Pieter; circle of (Dutch, 1592-1642)
Peasants with Donkeys & Barrow by an Archway, oil on canvas, 22x18", SBY 12/9/88 ..... **2,200**

VAN LEEMPUTTEN, Cornelis (Belgian, 1841-1902)
Driving Home the Flock, oil on canvas, sgn, 16x22", SBY 6/8/88 UE **2,640**
Sheep & Poultry in a Barn, oil on canvas, sgn, 22x36", RAB 8/8/89 ..... **3,100**
Shepherdess & Her Flock, oil on canvas, sgn, 23x31", C-E 5/23/88 ..... **4,950**
Shepherdess with Flock by a River, oil on canvas, sgn, 24x31", C-E 2/23/88 ..... **2,750**
Watching Over the Flock, oil on panel, sgn, 15x20", B/B 4/20/88 ..... **1,320**
Young Shepherd with His Flock, oil on panel, sgn, 7x10", B/B 1/11/89 ..... **1,760**

VAN LEEMPUTTEN, Frans (Belgian, 1850-1914)
Changing Pasture, oil on board, sgn, 20x28", C-E 10/26/89 ..... **3,300**

VAN LEEMPUTTEN, J.L. (Belgian, 19th C)
Pair: Roosters in Landscapes; oil on panel, ea sgn, 1 dtd 1869, 13x19", SBY 12/9/88 ..... **4,400**

VAN LELIENBERGH, Cornelis (Dutch, 1626-1676)
Still Life of a Mallard & Vegetables in a Basket with Hares...; oil on panel, sgn/dtd 1664, 28x22", C-NY 1/11/89 OE **10,450**

VAN LINT, Hendrik Frans (Flemish, 1684-1763)
View of the Baths of Diocletian, oil on canvas laid down on panel, sgn, 13x23", C-NY 4/6/89 OE **38,500**
View of Valmontone, oil on canvas, sgn/dtd 1750, 19x29", SBY 6/3/88 OE **36,300**

VAN LINT, Hendrik Frans; circle of (Flemish, 1684-1763)
View of the Castle Sant'Angelo, Rome; oil on canvas, 18x28", SBY 10/13/89 25,300
VAN LINT, Hendrik Frans; follower of (Flemish, 1684-1763)
Pair: Ponte Rotto, Rome; View of an Italian Town; oil on canvas, 16x25", SBY 4/7/89 8,800
VAN LINT, Pieter (Flemish, 1609-1690)
Christ & St Mary Magdalene Surrounded by Old & New Testament Figures...; oil on canvas, sgn, unfr, 26x21", C-NY 4/6/89 8,250
Saint Jerome in the Wilderness, oil on canvas, 72x47", C-NY 6/2/88 OE 33,000
VAN LINT, Pieter; att (Flemish, 1609-1690)
Abraham & the Three Angels, oil on canvas, 48x65", C-NY 4/6/89 11,000
VAN LOO, Carle (French, 1705-1765)
Portrait of a Lady, oil on canvas, sgn/dtd 1760, 35x28", SBY 6/3/88 15,200
Susanna & the Elders (three figures by fountain), oil on canvas, C-NY 5/31/89 OE 46,200
Trompe l'Oeil of a Soft-Ground Etching Under Broken Glass, oil on canvas, inscr, 14x11", C-NY 10/20/88 2,640
VAN LOO, Carle; att (French, 1705-1765)
Standing Figure in Oriental Costume Holding a Sword, red chalk, 22x12", SBY 1/13/89 11,000
VAN LOO, Carle; circle of (French, 1705-1765)
Portrait of the Actor Bellecourt, Standing Half-Length...Holding a Sword; oil on canvas, 39x32", C-NY 4/6/89 UE 2,200
VAN LOO, Jean Baptiste (French, 1684-1745)
Portrait of a Lady, Standing, Holding a Mask, Being Crowned by Putti; oil on canvas, unfr, 51x41", C-NY 10/12/89 OE 35,700
VAN LOO, Jean Baptiste; att (French, 1684-1745)
Head of a Girl, black/brown/red/white chalk on buff paper, 16x13", C-NY 1/11/89 OE 20,900
Portrait of James Fitzgerald, Earl of Kildare & 1st Duke of Leinster; oil on canvas, 30x25", SBY 10/13/89 7,700
VAN LOO, Jean Baptiste; studio of (French, 1684-1745)
Portrait of King Louis XV, Standing Half-Length...; oil on canvas, 39x30", C-NY 1/11/89 6,600
VAN LOO, Louis Michel (French, 1707-1771)
Portrait of Countess Beaurepaire (seated in a landscape), oil on canvas, sgn/dtd 1766, 58x45", SBY 6/1/89 132,000
Portrait of Princess Catherine Galitzin, Half-Length; oil on canvas, sgn/dtd 1764, 23x19", C-NY 1/15/88 30,800
VAN LOO, Pieter (Dutch, 1731-1784)
Arrowhead, black chalk/watercolor, fragmentary Strasburg Lily wm, 15x10", C-NY 1/12/88 495
Branch of a Tulip Tree, black chalk/watercolor, inscr/fragmentary Strasburg Lily wm, 15x10", C-NY 1/12/88 495
Kniphofia?, black chalk/watercolor, fragmentary LVG wm, 15x11", C-NY 1/12/88 880
Set of 4: Wild Pansy; Marigold; Montebretia; Daisy; black chalk/watercolor, inscr/wm, 15x10", C-NY 1/12/88 1,870
VAN LOO, Pieter; school of (Dutch, 1731-1784)
Diana & Her Maidens Bathing by a Pond, oil on canvas, indistinctly sgn, 25x30", C-NY 4/6/89 2,420
VAN MAASDIJK, Alexander Henri Robert (Dutch, 1856-1931)
Flirtation (man & woman seated in an interior reading), oil on canvas, sgn, 18x15", B/B 1/11/89 825
VAN MARCKE, Emile (Belgian, 1797-1839)
Cow Wading in a Stream, oil on canvas, sgn, 10x14", C-E 10/26/89 1,650
VAN MARCKE DE LUMMEN, Emile (French, 1827-1890)
Cattle by a Pond, oil on canvas, sgn, 25x40", WD 5/5/88 6,250
Herder & Her Flock, oil on canvas, sgn, 36x26", RWS 11/3/88 1,500
VAN MASTENBROEK, Johan Hendrik (Dutch, 1875-1945)
Bridge Over a Canal, watercolor, sgn/dtd 1893, 12x18", C-E 10/25/88 1,210
Harbor Scene with Barges, charcoal/watercolor on paper, sgn, 13x18", B/B 5/17/89 OE 1,320
Winter on a Dutch Canal, watercolor on paper heightened w/white gouache, sgn/dtd twice 1905/inscr, 8x10", C-E 2/23/88 OE 2,640
VAN MIEREVELT, Michiel (Dutch, 1567-1641)
Portrait of a Lady, wearing embroidered costume & lace headdress; oil on panel, inscr/dtd 1612, 28x23", C-NY 6/2/88 15,400
Portrait of a Man Said To Be the Duke of Buckingham, oil on panel, inscr w/monogram/dtd 1605, 19x15", SBY 12/9/88 OE 3,300
VAN MIERIS, Frans; after (Dutch, 1635-1681)
Smoker, oil on panel, sgn, 10x8", WD 10/19/88 900
VAN MIERIS, Frans; att (Dutch, 1635-1681)
Lady Playing a Lute by Candlelight, oil on panel, bears signature, 7x6", C-NY 1/15/88 4,620
VAN MIERIS, Frans; school of (Dutch, 1635-1681)
Pan & Syrinx, oil on board, 14x13", C-E 6/1/88 1,540
VAN MIERIS, Willem (Dutch, 1662-1747)
Diana & Callisto, black chalk on vellum, sgn/dtd 1706, 14x16", SBY 1/13/89 OE 7,150
Soldier Smoking a Pipe (possibly a self-portrait), oil on panel, 6x5", C-NY 6/2/88 38,500
VAN MIERIS, Willem; school of (Dutch, 1662-1747)
Susannah & the Elders, oil on panel, 13x11", C-NY 4/8/88 2,860
VAN MIERVELT, Michiel (Dutch, 1567-1641)
Portrait of a Gentleman Said To Be Pieter de Schilder, Counselor of Brabant; oil on panel, 49x35", SBY 4/7/89 11,000
VAN MOER, Jean Baptiste (Belgian, 1819-1884)
By the Church, oil on panel, sgn/dtd 1846, 12x10", C-E 2/23/88 1,430
VAN MORRISON (Continental, 19th/20th C)
Floral Still Life in a Vase, oil on canvas, sgn, 36x25", C-E 2/21/89 2,640
VAN MORTEL, Jan; att (Dutch, 1650-1719)
Garland of Flowers with Butterflies Before a Niche, oil on canvas, initialed, 27x22", C-NY 4/6/89 11,000
VAN NAGLER, Edith Kroger (American, 1895-1978)
At the Pasture Bars, oil on canvas, sgn, 16x24", RWS 9/8/89 UE 425
Hillside with Brush Cutter, oil on masonite, sgn, 24x30", RWS 11/3/88 1,500

VAN NECK, Jan (Dutch, 1634-1714)
Child in Classical Dress Tying a Bow Around a Fawn's Neck, oil on canvas, 41x31", SBY 4/7/88 .... **3,850**
Portrait of a Boy, oil on canvas, sgn/dtd 1693, 41x33", SBY 4/7/88 OE **5,500**
Portrait of an Ecclesiastic, oil on canvas, 37x30", SBY 10/21/88 .... **2,750**
VAN NEICKELE, Isaac
Interior of Saint Bavo, Haarlem, Looking East; oil on canvas, 51x61", C-NY 5/31/89 UE **11,000**
VAN NIEULANDT, Willem II (Flemish, 1584-1635)
Israelites Fleeing From Egypt in a Rocky-River Landscape, oil on panel, 22x30", C-NY 6/2/88 .... **28,600**
Old Testament Scene, oil on panel, 29x42", SBY 4/7/88 .... **13,200**
VAN NOORDT, Jan (Dutch, 1620-1676)
Hagar & the Angel (in a landscape), oil on canvas, 36x45", SBY 6/1/89 .... **16,500**
VAN NOORDT, Jan; att (Dutch, 1620-1676)
Portrait of a Young Girl, seated three-quarter length, wearing a white dress...; oil on canvas, 31x24", C-NY 1/11/89 OE **41,800**
VAN NOORT, Adrianus Cornelis (Dutch, 1914-)
Beach, oil on panel, sgn, 12x16", WG 4/23/88 .... **900**
Beach Scene, oil on panel, sgn, 12x18", C-E 10/25/88 OE **2,090**
Beach Scene, oil on panel, sgn, 18x24", SBY 7/12/89 .... **2,750**
Children at the Beach, oil on panel, sgn, unfr, 23x35", C-E 10/25/88 .... **4,950**
Children at the Beach, oil on panel, sgn, 12x16", C-E 10/25/88 .... **1,430**
Children Playing at the Beach, oil on canvas, sgn, 16x20", C-E 5/3/88 OE **1,650**
Children Wading, oil on panel, sgn, 18x22", SBY 7/12/89 .... **2,200**
Playing in the Snow, oil on panel, sgn, 13x16", C-E 5/3/88 .... **880**
VAN NUYSSEN, Abraham Janssens; studio of
Allegory of Winter, oil on canvas, 43x35", C-NY 10/12/89 .... **12,100**
VAN OOSTEN, Isaac (Flemish, 1613-1661)
Tinkers by the Entrance to a Cave Beside a Pond, oil on panel, 11x15", C-NY 10/20/88 OE **31,900**
VAN OOSTEN, Isaac; circle of (Flemish, 1613-1661)
Village with Figures in a Wooded Landscape, oil on panel, unfr, 20x26", C-NY 10/20/88 .... **13,200**
VAN ORLEY, Barent (Flemish, 1493-1542)
Madonna & Child with St Ann, Surrounded by Angels & Donors; oil on shaped panel, 40x33", SBY 6/2/89 .... **77,000**
VAN OS, Jan; circle of (Dutch, 1744-1808)
Dutch Shipping on Choppy Waters Beside a Jetty, oil on canvas, 20x30", SBY 10/21/88 OE **4,950**
VAN OS, Pieter Frederick (Dutch, 1808-1860)
Animals & Figures Along a Country Road, oil on canvas, sgn, 26x31", SBY 12/9/88 OE **2,200**
VAN OS-DELHEZ, Henri (Dutch, 1880-1976)
Still Life of Apple Blossoms, oil on canvas, sgn, 32x28", B/B 10/9/88 UE **1,540**
Still Life of Chrysanthemums in a Conservatory, oil on canvas, sgn, 40x30", B/B 9/15/88 .... **1,430**
VAN OSTADE, Adriaen (Dutch, 1610-1684)
Kermess, oil on canvas, bears signature/indistinctly dtd 1664, unfr, 17x22", C-NY 1/15/88 .... **28,600**
Man with Clay Pipe, Serving Woman & Other Peasants in a Country Tavern Courtyard; oil on panel, 17x15", C-NY 1/11/89 .... **93,500**
Peasant Family Outside a Cottage, oil on vellum laid down, sgn/dtd 1668, 9x11", SBY 1/12/89 .... **110,000**
Rustic Interior with Peasants Smoking & a Child Eating, oil on panel, sgn, 16x14", C-NY 1/15/88 .... **30,800**
Three Peasants Drinking & Smoking in an Interior, oil on panel, indistinctly sgn, 6x6", SBY 4/7/89 .... **12,100**
VAN OSTADE, Adriaen; att (Dutch, 1610-1684)
Peasant Smoking in an Interior with Another Figure...; oil on panel, bears signature, 12x10", C-NY 1/11/89 OE **33,000**
VAN OSTADE, Adriaen; circle of (Dutch, 1610-1684)
Drinker, oil on panel, 9x11", SBY 6/8/88 .... **1,980**
Family Gathered Outside a Cottage, pen/ink/wash/brown ink framing lines, 6x6", C-NY 1/11/89 UE **550**
Peasant Filling a Pipe in an Interior, oil on panel, 9x7", C-NY 4/8/88 .... **3,520**
Peasant with Plumed Hat, oil on panel, 11x9", SBY 6/8/88 UE **990**
VAN OSTADE, after (Dutch, 17th C)
Peasants at a Country Tavern, oil on panel, 16x23", LH 12/4/88 OE **2,800**
VAN OSTADE, Isaac; circle of (Dutch, 1610-1684)
Peasants Making Merry in a Barn, oil on panel, 20x16", SBY 4/7/89 .... **8,800**
VAN OUST, Jan; manner of
Boats in an Estuary, oil on canvas, bears signature, 16x21", C-E 7/26/88 .... **440**
VAN PATTAN HALL, Sadie (American, 20th C)
Shanty by the Dock, oil on board, sgn, 14x18", B/B 8/10/88 .... **770**
VAN PLAS, Pieter (Dutch, 1810-1853)
Still Life of Shank of Mutton on Pewter Plate, a Knife, & a Porcelain Dish...; oil on canvas, 28x24", C-NY 1/11/89 .... **8,800**
VAN PLATTENBERG, Matthieu; follower of (Flemish, 1608-1660)
Pair: Shipping in Choppy Seas Near Shore; Figures Disembarking; oil on canvas, 38x57", SBY 4/7/88 OE **10,450**
VAN POELENBURGH, Cornelis (Dutch, 1586-1667)
Rest on the Flight into Egypt, oil on panel, unfr, 12x15", SBY 4/7/88 .... **8,800**
VAN POELENBURGH, Cornelis; circle of (Dutch, 1586-1667)
Extensive Italianate Landscape with Herders, oil on panel, bears initials, 15x22", C-NY 10/12/89 .... **2,200**
VAN POL, Christian (Dutch, 1752-1813)
Still Life of Crown Imperial, Roses, Hydrangeas, Tulips, Delphiniums...; oil on canvas, sgn, 37x29", C-NY 1/11/89 OE **187,000**
VAN RAVESTEYN, Dirck de Quade (Dutch, fl 1576-1612)
Allegory of Fecundity (woman surrounded by many children), oil on canvas, monogramed/dtd 1593, 67x54", SBY 6/1/89 OE **176,000**

N RAVESTEYN, Jan Anthonisz (Dutch, 1570-1657)

Portrait of a Lady, oil on panel, sgn in monogram/inscr, 27x23", SBY 10/21/88 OE	13,200
Portrait of a Lady (wearing wide ruff collar & elaborate cap, holding book), oil on panel, 41x31", SBY 6/2/89	15,400

N RAVESTEYN, Jan Anthonisz; studio of (Dutch, 1570-1657)

Portrait of an Officer, standing, three-quarter length, wearing suit of armor...; oil on canvas, 50x40", C-NY 5/31/89 OE	15,400

N REYMERSWAELE, Marinus; att (Dutch, 1493-1567)

Christ As Salvator Mundi, oil on panel, 18x12", C-NY 10/12/89	3,300

N RIJIN, Rembrandt; see Rembrandt

N RIJSWIJK, Johanna (Dutch, 1893-1956)

Landscape with View of Windmill & Farmhouse by River, oil on panel, sgn, 10x12", FAP 11/4/88 OE	950

N ROEKENS, Paulette

Side Show, oil on canvas, sgn, 12x4", C-E 1/12/88	462

N ROSSUM DU CHATTEL, Fredericus Jacobus (Dutch, 1856-1917)

Along a Dutch Canal, watercolor/gouache, sgn, 13x19", C-NY 10/26/88	1,980

N RUISDAEL, Jacob (Dutch, 1625-1682)

Bentheim Castle with Figures on a Path, oil on canvas, sgn, 17x20", C-NY 6/2/88	88,000
Forest Landscape with a Stream, oil on panel, initialed, 9x8", C-NY 1/11/89 OE	35,200
Horseman on a Path by a River & Women Laying Out Laundry...; oil on panel, sgn, 21x27", C-NY 1/11/89 OE	44,000
Landscape with Waterfall, oil on canvas, 26x21", SBY 6/3/88	77,000
Waterfall in a Wooded Landscape, oil on canvas, indistinctly sgn, 28x22", C-NY 5/31/89	165,000
Waterfall in a Wooded Landscape, oil on canvas, sgn, 26x21", C-NY 1/11/89	110,000
Winter Landscape with Figures Along a Road, oil on canvas, sgn, 15x13", SBY 1/12/89	143,000
Wooded Landscape with a Stream, oil on panel, sgn in monogram, 14x18", SBY 10/21/88 OE	319,000
Wooded Mountainous Landscape, oil on canvas, monogramed, ca 1650, 39x50", SBY 6/2/89	297,000

N RUISDAEL, Jacob; att (Dutch, 1625-1682)

Light & Shadow on the City, watercolor heightened w/gouache on paper, 11x15", C-E 2/3/88	1,540

N RUISDAEL, Jacob; circle of (Dutch, 1625-1682)

Landscape with Family Resting by a Road with Building & Bridge Beyond, oil on canvas, 21x27", SBY 10/13/89 OE	14,300

N RUISDAEL, Jacob; school of (Dutch, 1625-1682)

Waterfall with Travelers in the Distance, oil on panel, 17x17", C-NY 10/12/89	4,180

N RUISDAEL, Salomon (Dutch, 1600-1670)

Coastal Scene with Boats on the Sand & Fishermen Unloading Their Catch, oil on canvas, sgn/dtd 1636, 29x43", SBY 4/7/88	33,000
Dune Landscape with Horse & Rider on a Road & Two Figures on a Rock, oil on panel, sgn/dtd 1628, 11x16", SBY 6/3/88	88,000
Landscape with Cattle Resting in a Clearing Beside a Country Road, oil on panel, 20x27", SBY 10/13/89	16,500
Landscape with the Ruins of Egmond Abbey in the Distance, oil on panel, sgn/dtd 1644, 27x39", SBY 6/2/89	330,000
Shipping in a Choppy Sea, oil on panel, monogramed, 13" dia, SBY 1/12/89 OE	407,000
Travelers on a Path in a Wooded River Landscape, oil on panel, 15x26", C-NY 1/11/89	49,500

N RUISDAEL, Salomon; att (Dutch, 1600-1670)

Wooded Landscape with a Waterfall, oil, unfr, 20x28", WD 1/25/89	1,600

N RYDER, Jack (American, 1898-1968)

Morning on the Mesa, oil on canvasboard, sgn/dtd 1928, 12x16", B/B 9/15/88	1,045

N RYSEWYK, Johanna Bastiana (Dutch, 1873-1956)

Winter Canal Scene, oil on panel, sgn, 18x24", B/B 8/10/88	495

N RYSSELBERGHE, Theo (Belgian, 1862-1926)

Etude pour la Femme Couchee, red chalk on paper, monogramed/dtd 09, 13x18", C-NY 2/13/89	1,430
Femme au Violin (portrait of daughter of Galerie Druet), oil on canvas, monogramed/dtd 1910, 38x28", C-NY 2/18/88	46,200
Femme Nue Allongee, watercolor on tan paper laid down on board, initialed, 15x20", C-E 5/9/89	1,760
Les Falaises de Douvres (coastal seascape), oil on canvas, sgn/dtd 81, 39x78", SBY 10/7/88	11,000
Veere sous un Ciel Brumeux (study for oil), gouache/oil/black chalk on board, stamped monogram, 1906, 10x9", SBY 5/10/89	27,500

N SANTVOORT, Dirck (Dutch, 1610-1680)

Portrait of a Yound Girl, oil on panel, 28x23", SBY 1/12/89 OE	20,900

N SCHAGEN, Gerbrand Ferderick (Dutch, 1880-1968)

Warmeer, Warga; oil on canvas, sgn/dtd 1933, 16x20", LH 9/10/89 OE	1,100

N SCHENDEL, Petrus (Belgian, 1806-1870)

Candlelit Market, oil on canvas, sgn, 31x39", SBY 2/22/89	60,500
Letter (two women in an interior), oil on canvas, sgn/dtd 1870, 15x11", C-NY 5/24/89	17,600
Market by Candlelight, oil on wood panel, sgn, 9x7", DM 9/16/88	2,750
Moonlit Market Scene, oil on panel, sgn/indistinctly dtd, 26x20", C-NY 5/25/88 OE	41,800

N SCHENDEL, Petrus; after (Dutch, 1806-1870)

Vegetable Vendor by Candlelight, oil on canvas, 21x17", C-E 5/23/88	3,080

N SCHOOTEN, Floris Gerritsz (fl 1590-1655)

Still Life of Fruit with Porcelain Bowls, oil on panel, 15x18", SBY 6/3/88	66,000
Still Life of Grapes, Apples, & Other Fruit in a Bowl on a Wooden Table; oil on panel, 20x28", SBY 10/13/89	33,000
Still Life of Meat Pies, Bread, Butter, Cheese, & Olives with Glassware; oil on panel, sgn, 20x33", SBY 6/3/88	34,100

N SCHRIECK, Otto Marseus (Dutch, 1619-1678)

Still Life of Wildflowers Including Cyclamen, Crocus, Delphinium, with a Snake...; oil on canvas, 28x21", SBY 6/2/89 OE	104,500

N SCOREL, Jan; after (Dutch, 1495-1562)

St Mary Magdalene, oil on canvas, inscr Bol/dtd 1646, 25x19", C-E 6/1/88	1,210

N SCOREL, Jan; att (Dutch, 1495-1562)

Adam & Eve in Paradise, oil on arched panel, 19x13", C-NY 1/11/89	33,000

VAN SCOREL, Jan; circle of (Dutch, 1495-1562)

Portrait of a Young Man in a Black Costume, oil on panel, inscr/dtd 1533, arched top, 11x8", C-NY 1/15/88 OE ... **18,700**

Saint Sebastian, oil on panel, 16x12", SBY 10/21/88 OE ... **14,300**

VAN SEVERDONCK, Franz (Belgian, 1809-1889)

Chickens Feeding, oil on panel, sgn, 7x10", C-E 10/25/88 ... **2,640**

Sheep, Fowl, & a Goat in a Barn; oil on panel, sgn/inscr/dtd 1886, 7x10", SBY 12/9/88 ... **1,320**

Sheep & Ducks on a Grassy Hill, oil on panel, sgn/dtd 1876, unfr, 9x13", C-E 10/26/89 ... **2,420**

Sheep & Fowl (figures & animals in a landscape), sgn/dtd 1863, 7x9", RAB 8/8/89 ... **2,700**

Sheep in a Landscape, oil on panel, sgn twice/inscr/dtd 1883, unfr, 7x10", SBY 12/9/88 ... **1,650**

Sheep in Meadow, oil on canvas, sgn/dtd 186(?), 22x27", SBY 12/8/88 UE ... **3,300**

VAN SEVERDONCK, Joseph (Belgian, 1819-1905)

Return From the Campaign, oil on canvas, sgn, 20x36", B/B 6/9/88 ... **2,750**

VAN SHELDON

Having Tea, oil on panel, sgn, 27x20", C-E 5/23/88 ... **2,200**

VAN SLOUN, Frank (American, 1879-1938)

Elk Club Mural Study, oil on board, 16x8", B/B 9/15/88 ... **330**

Exodus From Palestine, oil on board, sgn/dtd 1935, 8x10", B/B 1/11/89 ... **412**

Set of 3: Nude Studies; watercolor/sanguine/ink on paper, sgn, various sizes, B/B 1/11/89 UE ... **385**

Set of 4: Figural Studies; ink/graphite on paper, sgn, various sizes, B/B 1/11/89 ... **660**

VAN SLUYS, Theo (Belgian, 19th C)

Hay Manger with Sheep & Hens, oil on canvas, sgn, 16x23", RWS 5/12/89 OE ... **3,500**

Sheep, Roosters, & Chickens in a Barn; oil on canvas, sgn, 24x32", C-E 5/23/88 ... **3,850**

VAN SOMER, Hendrick (Dutch, 17th C)

Saint Jerome (portrait, holding a skull), oil on canvas, monogramed/dtd 1654, 51x40", C-NY 5/31/89 ... **71,500**

VAN SON, Joris (Flemish, 1623-1667)

Red & White Grapes & Peaches in Silver Tazza with Shrimp & Lobster on Ledge...; oil on panel, sgn, 13x10", C-NY 5/31/89 ... **22,000**

VAN SON, Joris; circle of (Flemish, 1623-1667)

Lobster on a Pewter Plate, Glass of Wine, Grapes, Lemon, Pomegranate & Objects; oil on canvas, 37x49", C-NY 4/8/88 OE ... **12,100**

VAN SPAENDONCK, Cornelis (French, 1756-1840)

Een Boeket in een Hoge Mand (floral still life), oil on canvas, sgn/dtd 1821, 20x16", SBY 5/23/89 ... **110,000**

Roses in a Glass Vase on a Ledge, oil on panel, sgn, 13x11", C-NY 6/2/88 OE ... **68,200**

Still Life of Cockscomb, Roses, Tulips, Daffodils, Morning-Glory...; oil on canvas, sgn/dtd 1817, 32x26", C-NY 1/11/89 ... **28,600**

VAN SPAENDONCK, Gerard (French, 1746-1822)

Still Life of Flowers in a Stone Vase with a Basket of Flowers & a Nest, oil on canvas, sgn, 31x25", SBY 6/3/88 OE ... **797,500**

VAN SPAENDONCK, Gerard; follower of (French, 1746-1822)

Still Life of Spring Flowers, oil on canvas, 15x11", SBY 12/9/88 UE ... **1,980**

VAN STARKENBORGH, Jacobus Tjarda (Dutch, 1822-1895)

Hay Wagon (man w/horses & wagon in field), oil on canvas, sgn, 13x16", RWS 5/19/88 OE ... **1,600**

VAN STARKENBORGH, Jacobus Tjarda; att (Dutch, 1822-1895)

Cowherd with Cows (man driving cattle in an extensive landscape), oil on panel, sgn, 14x18", WL 5/20/88 UE ... **1,500**

VAN STEENWYCK, Harmen (Dutch, 1612-1656)

Fruit in a Blue & White Bowl, a Roll, a Jug & Knife on a Table; oil on panel, indistinctly sgn, 12x13", C-NY 1/15/88 OE ... **17,600**

VAN STEENWYCK, Hendrick (Dutch, 1550-1603)

Gothic Interior with Figures Conversing, oil on canvas, sgn/dtd 1624, C-NY 6/2/88 ... **22,000**

VAN STEENWYCK, Hendrick II; att (Dutch, 1580-1649)

Cathedral Interior with Figures, oil on panel, 6x8", C-NY 10/20/88 ... **6,600**

VAN STEENWYCK, Hendrick II; circle of (Dutch, 1580-1649)

Interior of a Church with Elegant Figures & Beggars, oil on canvas, 33x40", SBY 12/9/88 OE ... **6,325**

VAN STRAVEREN, Jan Adrianensz; circle of (1625-after 1668)

Saint Jerome in the Wilderness, oil on panel, 17x13", SBY 6/8/88 ... **935**

VAN STRIJ, Abraham; manner of (German, 1753-1826)

Cattle, Sheep, & Goat by a Stream; oil on canvas, 32x25", SBY 6/8/88 OE ... **770**

VAN STRY, Abraham (Dutch, 1790-1840)

Preparing the Meal, oil on canvas, sgn/dtd 18(?), 25x21", C-NY 10/25/89 UE ... **1,100**

VAN STRY, Abraham; school of (Dutch, 1790-1840)

Muleteers Under a Cliff, oil on panel, 16x20", C-NY 6/2/88 ... **2,860**

VAN STRYDONCK, Guillaume (Belgian, 1861-1937)

Elegant Lady in Pink, oil on canvas, sgn/dtd 1883, unfr, 49x40", C-NY 5/24/89 OE ... **24,200**

VAN THIELEN, Jan Philips (Flemish, 1618-1669)

Still Life of Flowers in a Glass Vase, oil on panel, sgn, 25x17", SBY 6/3/88 ... **110,000**

VAN THULDEN, Theodor (Flemish, 1606-1669)

Allegory of Peace & Plenty, oil on canvas, 80x87", SBY 6/1/89 OE ... **49,500**

VAN TILBORCH, Gillis (Flemish, 1625-1678)

Kermesse (village fair), oil on canvas, unfr, 48x69", SBY 6/1/89 OE ... **110,000**

VAN TILBORCH, Gillis; circle of (Flemish, 1625-1678)

Peasants Beside a Cottage in a Landscape, oil on canvas, 35x46", SBY 4/7/88 ... **4,950**

VAN TILBORCH, Gillis; manner of (Flemish, 1625-1678)

Peasant Family Around a Table, oil on canvas, 44x69", SBY 12/9/88 OE ... **8,250**

VAN TROYEN, Rombout; circle of (Dutch, 1605-1650)

Lot & His Daughters, oil on copper, 20x25", SBY 4/7/88 ... **1,650**

VAN VALCKENBORCH, Frederik; att (ca 1570-1623)

Battle Scene in a Extensive Landscape, oil on panel, 13x20", SBY 4/7/88 OE ... **5,225**

N VALCKENBORCH, Lucas; circle of (Flemish, 1530-1625)	
Triumphal Entry of Francois, Duc d'Anjou, into Antwerp or Ghent, 1582; oil on panel, inscr, 25x33", C-NY 1/11/89 OE	71,500
N VALCKENBORCH, Lucas; school of (Flemish, 1530-1625)	
Fish Vendors, oil on canvas, unstretched/unfr, 51x36", C-NY 10/20/88	6,050
N VALCKENBORCH, Lucas; studio of (Flemish, 1530-1625)	
Meat & Fish Market in Winter, oil on canvas, 42x72", SBY 6/2/89	13,200
N VEEN, Otto (Flemish, 1556-1629)	
Fortuna, oil on panel, 42x30", C-NY 4/8/88 OE	17,600
N VEEN, Otto; circle of (Flemish, 1556-1629)	
Danae, oil on canvas, unfr, 32x46", C-NY 10/20/88 OE	2,640
Portraits of the Twelve Caesars, oil on panel, 9" dia, C-NY 4/8/88	14,300
N VEERENDAEL, Nicolaes (Belgian, 1640-1691)	
Still Life of Flowers in a Glass Vase, oil on panel, 15x11", SBY 6/2/89	165,000
N VELDE, Bram (Dutch, 1910-)	
Floral Still Life (contemporary), oil on canvas, sgn, ca 1925, 26x18", SBY 5/3/89 OE	19,800
Nature Morte (abstract still life), oil on canvas, sgn, ca 1927-29, 29x36", SBY 6/30/88	60,000
N VENNE, Fritz (German, 1900-)	
Traveling Performers, oil on panel, sgn/inscr, 10x13", C-NY 5/25/88	5,280
N VLIET, Don (20th C)	
Menthola Together Sit Put (abstract), oil on masonite, sgn/dtd 72, 24x24", C-E 11/14/89	1,760
N VREELAND, F. (Dutch, 19th C)	
Dutch Canal Scene, watercolor, sgn, 13x21", FAP 11/4/88	280
Sheep Heading into a Barn, watercolor/gouache, sgn, 20x26", C-E 6/28/88 UE	198
N VRIES, Roelof (Dutch, 1631-1681)	
Fishermen Along a Canal, oil on canvas, sgn, 35x51", WD 10/19/88 OE	11,000
Wooded Landscape with Cottages by a Path, oil on canvas, unfr, 32x40", C-NY 1/15/88	14,300
N VRIES, Roelof; att (Dutch, 1631-1681)	
Fishermen Along a Canal, oil on canvas, bears signature, unfr, 52x45", WD 1/25/89	4,500
N WALSCAPELLE, Jacob (Dutch, 1644-1727)	
Still Life of Peonies, Roses, Irises, & Poppies, Butterflies & Insects on a Ledge; oil on panel, 24x18", SBY 1/12/89 OE	181,500
N WIERINGEN, Cornelis Claesz (Dutch, ca 1580-1633)	
Dutch Vessels in a Harbor, pen/brown ink, 5x7", SBY 1/13/89	6,600
N WITTEL, Gaspar (Dutch, 1653-1736)	
Landscape at Dusk with a Villa Above the River & Distant Hills...; watercolor/bodycolor, inscr, 11x17", C-NY 1/11/89	22,000
Landscape with Figures by Classical Buildings Near a Bridge...; chalk/pen/ink/watercolor, inscr, 11x17", C-NY 1/11/89	18,700
Pair: Arch of Constantine; The Colosseum; oil on canvas, sgn, ca 1703, 18x29", C-NY 1/11/89 OE	242,000
River Landscape with a Waterfall & Cliffs, a Bay Beyond; chalk/pen/ink/watercolor/bodycolor, wm, 11x17", C-NY 1/11/89	13,200
Town on a River, black chalk/pen/brown ink/watercolor/bodycolor, initialed/inscr N.12, 11x17", C-NY 1/11/89 OE	37,400
N WITTEL, Gaspar; circle of (Dutch, 1653-1736)	
View of the Piazza Santi Apostoli, Rome; oil on canvas, 20x30", SBY 10/13/89	4,400
N WYK, Henri (Dutch, 1833-)	
Caravan Leaving the City, oil on canvas, sgn, unfr, 14x25", C-E 2/21/89 OE	4,180
N WYNGAERDT, Anthonie Jacobus (Dutch, 1808-1887)	
Cottages Flanking a River, oil on panel, sgn, 11x17", FAP 4/15/89	385
N ZEVENBERGHEN, Georges Antoine (Belgian, 1877-1968)	
Fruit Sellers (two ladies w/produce gathered on table), oil on canvas, sgn/dtd 04, 48x56", C-E 5/22/89	7,150
Nocturne (woman in an interior), oil on board, sgn/dtd 32, 14x11", WL 5/20/88 UE	500
NBRABANT, Victor	
Extensive Spring Landscape with Houses, oil on canvas, sgn, 24x31", C-E 2/25/88	825
NDERBANK, John (British, 1694-1739)	
Portrait of Elizabeth Affleck, oil on canvas, indistinctly sgn/dtd, bears inscription, 30x25", SBY 6/8/88	2,310
NDERBANK, John; school of (British, 1694-1739)	
Portrait of George II, wearing robes of state, Order of St George, & ermine robe; oil on canvas, 56x48", C-NY 10/20/88	6,050
NDERHOOF, Charles A. (American, -1918)	
Allatoona Pass, Georgia (Civil War); pen/ink on paper, sgn/inscr, unfr, 17x21", C-E 11/30/88	440
Chancellorsville, Hooker's Headquarters (Civil War); pen/ink on paper, initialed/inscr, unfr, 8x11", C-E 11/30/88	242
Confederate Works, Bank of Chattahoochie (Civil War); pen/ink on paper, sgn/inscr, unfr, 17x21", C-E 11/30/88 OE	1,100
Fort Sanders, Knoxville (Civil War); pen/ink on paper, inscr, unfr, 12x15", C-E 11/30/88	220
Front of Kennesaw (Civil War), pen/ink on paper, inscr, unfr, 17x21", C-E 11/30/88 OE	660
Helena, Arkansas (Civil War); pen/ink on paper, sgn/inscr, unfr, 13x15", C-E 11/30/88	220
Mill, pencil, sgn, unfr, 9x13", C-NY 10/31/89 UE	55
Set of 3: Views of Fort Pulaski (Civil War); pen/ink on paper, initialed/inscr, unfr, 15x13", C-E 11/30/88	242
Turkey Creek Bridge, Penninsula Campaign (Civil War); pen/ink on paper, inscr, 6x13", C-E 11/30/88	352
Valley Pike, Cedar Creek (Civil War); pen/ink on paper, sgn/inscr, unfr, 17x21", C-E 11/30/88	286
Vicksburg Courthouse (Civil War), pen/ink on paper, initialed/inscr, unfr, 15x18", C-E 11/30/88 OE	715
Warrenton Junction, Virginia (Civil War); pen/ink on paper, inscr, 7x11", C-E 5/27/88	165
Wreck of the Star of West-Tullahatchie River (Civil War), pen/ink on paper, inscr, unfr, 13x20", C-E 11/30/88 UE	154
NDERLYN, John; att (American, 1775-1852)	
Interior with Mother & Child Surrounded by Trompe l'Oeil Marble Cartouch, pen/ink/washes, sgn, 12x14", SBY 1/13/89 OE	5,500
Pair: Portraits of a Man & Woman Said To Be Mr & Mrs Ruben Rowley; oil on canvas, oval, unfr, 30x25", SBY 9/23/88 UE	880

Portrait of Queen Mary II, three quarter-length, orb & crown behind; oil on canvas, 49x39", SBY 10/21/88 OE ... 6,05
VANNI, Guido
St Peters, Rome; oil on canvas, sgn/dtd 1790, 10x8", WD 3/23/88 OE ... 2,00
VANNINI, Ottavio (Italian, 1585-1643)
Gathering of Manna, oil on canvas, unfr, 80x100", C-NY 1/15/88 ... 55,00
VANNUCCI, see Perugino
VARA, Guttierrez Augustin; att
Two Saints Tied to a Pole, Being Stoned; black chalk/pen/brown ink/gray wash, inscr, 7x9", C-NY 1/12/88 ... 22
VARLEY, Frederick Horsman (Canadian, 1891-1969)
Kootenay Valley, charcoal, sgn, 8x12", WAD 6/12/89 ... 2,80
Landed Supplies, Arctic; pencil/wash, sgn, 8x12", WAD 11/30/89 ... 2,60
VARLEY, John (British, 1778-1842)
Figures by Road in an Italianate Landscape, watercolor heightened w/gum arabic paper, sgn/dtd 1840, 8x15", C-NY 5/25/88 ... 2,20
River & Landscape, watercolor, sgn/dtd 1827, 7x11", FB 10/30/89 ... 1,04
VARLSON, John F. (American, 1875-1945)
Village Center, pencil/watercolor, sgn, 15x22", PHL 12/1/88 ... 95
VARO, Remedios (Spanish, 1900-1963)
Armonia (Harmony), oil on masonite, sgn, 1966, 30x37", C-NY 5/18/88 ... 385,00
Center of the Universe (surrealistic portrait of artist's husband), gouache on paper, sgn, 1961, 27x21", SBY 11/21/88 ... 46,75
El Encuentro (surrealistic), oil on masonite, sgn, 1962, 25x18", C-NY 5/18/88 OE ... 187,00
El Minotauro (surrealistic figure), oil on masonite, sgn, 24x12", C-NY 11/21/89 ... 198,00
Forest (abstract landscape), oil on masonite, 12x13", SBY 11/21/88 ... 37,40
Jardin d'Amour (surrealistic), gouache on board, ca 1951, 14x12", C-NY 5/18/88 OE ... 71,50
La Batalla, advertisement created for pharmaceutical products; gouache on board, sgn, 15x11", C-NY 11/21/89 ... 28,60
La Contaminacion del Agua (surrealistic market place w/cloaked skeleton), gouache on paper, sgn, 10x8", C-NY 11/21/88 OE ... 28,60

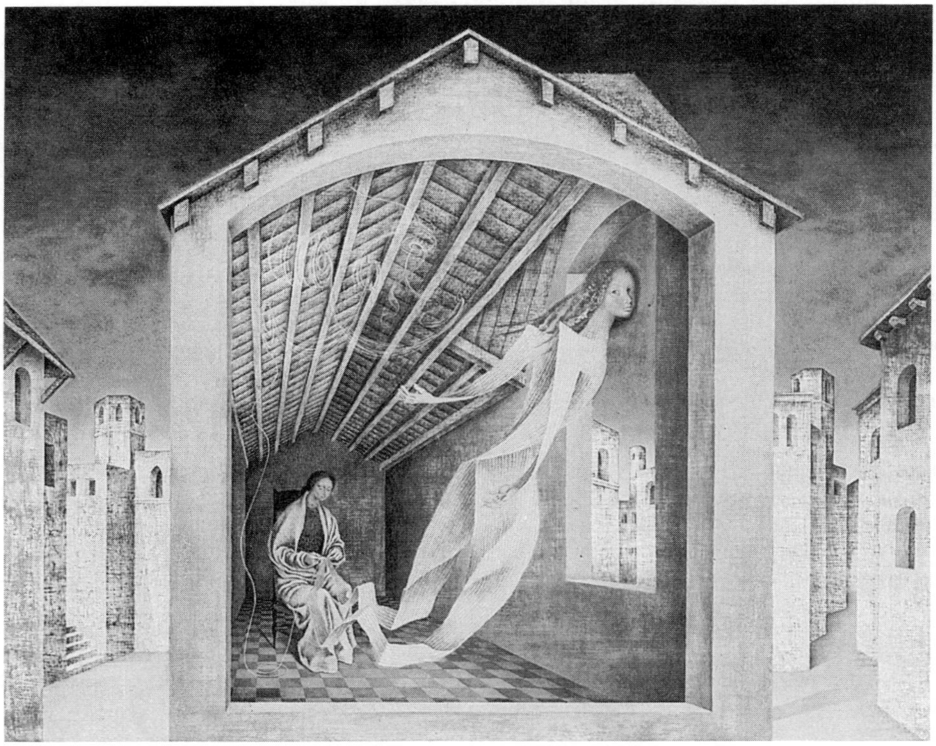

La Tejedora de Verona, oil on masonite, sgn, 34x41", C-NY 11/21/89; $484,000

Libeluls, advertisement created for pharmaceutical products; gouache on paper, sgn, 10x9", C-NY 11/21/89 ... 20,90
Tailleur Pour Dames, pencil on paper, 1957, 9x7", SBY 11/21/88 UE ... 4,40
Tiforal (surrealistic garden/figure), gouache on paper, sgn Uranga/titled, ca 1947-49, 10x13", C-NY 11/21/88 OE ... 33,00
Vuelo Magico o La Zamfonia (surrealistic), oil on masonite w/mother-of-pearl, sgn/dtd 1956, 34x41", C-NY 5/17/88 ... 385,00
VASARELY, Victor (Hungarian, 1908-)
Akos (geometric composition), oil on canvas, sgn/dtd 1974, 79x79", C-NY 10/4/89 ... 41,80
Beta (abstract), oil on cardboard mounted on panel, sgn twice/dtd 1948-50, 18x12", SBY 10/8/88 OE ... 18,70
BIA (geometric pattern of circles, diamonds & squares), acrylic on pressed wood, sgn, 1964, 24x24", RWS 9/29/88 OE ... 4,00
Bika-Zett (geometric composition), oil on canvas, sgn/dtd 1976, 83x83", C-NY 10/4/89 OE ... 88,00
Cephei (black & white composition), oil on canvas, sgn/dtd 1959, 77x51", SBY 11/9/89 ... 77,00
Deuton GG (abstract), tempera on board w/painted wood frame, sgn twice/dtd 1967, 25x24", SBY 10/8/88 ... 8,25
Elche (abstract), oil on board, sgn twice/dtd 1950/titled, 20x19", SBY 2/19/88 ... 13,20
Horn (abstract), oil on paper mounted on board, sgn twice/dtd 1956/titled, 12x9", SBY 11/11/88 ... 11,00
Malew-Ess, tempera on board, sgn twice/dtd 1956-76, 22x19", SBY 10/8/88 ... 12,10
Oltar-Zoeld (geometric composition), acrylic on canvas, sgn/dtd 1981, 27x14", C-NY 10/4/89 ... 11,00

Onix 3 (composition), oil on masonite, sgn twice/dtd 1966/#d 0666, 33x33", SBY 5/2/88 OE ... 17,600
OP (geometric composition), oil on panel, sgn, 1955, 13x9", C-NY 5/4/89 OE ... 24,200
Pair: Untitled (lineation); ink/paper collage on paper, sgn/dtd 52, 9x8", SBY 2/15/89 ... 4,125
Sikkaso (geometric composition), casein on paperboard, sgn/dtd 1957-62, 17x16", SBY 2/15/89 ... 13,200
Six (geometric composition in red, purple, & blue), acrylic on canvas, sgn/dtd 1972-74, 43x37", C-E 11/14/89 OE ... 41,800
Trio-2 (geometric composition), acrylic on panel, sgn/dtd 1976/#d 2915, 19x15", C-E 11/14/89 OE ... 9,020
Untitled (geometric composition), colored paper collage on paper, sgn, 9x7", C-E 11/14/89 OE ... 2,530
Yellan (abstract), oil on wood panel, sgn/dtd 1949-55, 11x14", SBY 2/15/89 OE ... 26,400

SARI, Giorgio (Italian, 1511-1574)
Madonna & Child with the Infant Saint John the Baptist, oil on panel, 29x22", C-NY 6/2/88 OE ... 132,000

SARI, Giorgio; att (Italian, 1511-1574)
Holy Family with the Infant Saint John the Baptist, oil on panel, 43x32", SBY 6/1/89 OE ... 77,000

SSILIEFF, Nicholai Ivanovich (American, 1892-1970)
Harbor (sailboats & village), oil on canvas, sgn, 20x39", RAB 8/9/88 ... 2,200
Harbor (sailing vessels lining a waterfront, buildings beyond), oil on canvas, sgn, 30x39", RAB 8/9/88 ... 2,200
Seated Woman, oil on canvas, sgn/dtd 31, 34x26", SBY 1/24/89 ... 1,650
Still Life of Fish & Melon, oil on canvas, sgn, unfr, 28x36", SBY 1/24/89 ... 1,540

SSOS, John
Elegant Arrival, gouache on board, unfr, 29x22", SBY 4/23/88 OE ... 6,050
Skiers, gouache on paper, sgn, 20x16", SBY 4/23/88 OE ... 3,960

STAGH, Geza (Hungarian, 1866-1919)
Coronation of a Young King (young man kneeling at altar), oil on board, sgn, 16x13", C-E 2/21/89 UE ... 550

BER, Anthon (German, 1833-1909)
Artist's Fantasy, watercolor on paper, initialed/dtd 1865, 19x14", B/B 5/17/89 OE ... 1,870

CCHIA, Pietro; see De Muttoni

CCHIO, Palma; school of
St Catherine of Alexandria, oil on canvas, 29x25", C-E 6/1/88 ... 1,430

CELLIO, Tiziano see Titian

DDER, Elihu (American, 1836-1923)
Cypress Trees on San Miniato, Florence; oil on paper laid down on canvas, initialed/sgn/inscr, 10x7", C-NY 9/30/88 ... 3,850
Etruscan Girl, oil on paper laid down on canvas, initialed/dtd 1868, 9x8", C-NY 5/26/88 ... 9,900
Gloomy Path, oil on board, monogramed/dtd 1865, 10x6", SBY 9/14/89 ... 6,875
Grand Canal, Venice; oil on canvas, initialed, 7x11", C-NY 3/11/88 ... 2,420
Love & Cupid, oil on canvas, sgn/inscr/titled, 8x13", SBY 9/23/88 ... 2,750
Mediterranean Coastal Scene, oil on canvas, initialed/dtd 1866, 10x16", C-NY 5/26/88 OE ... 26,400
Old Tree on the Way to Tel el Armarna...; oil on canvas, sgn, 1890-91, 12x17", RWS 11/10/89 ... 8,500
Pair: Wildflowers; Greek Pottery; oil on board mounted on panel, initialed/dtd 1880, 17x3", SBY 1/24/89 ... 6,600
Tinker, oil on panel, 12x16", C-NY 5/26/88 OE ... 18,700
View of the Tiber Near Orte, oil on canvas, sgn/dtd 1902, 15x20", SBY 6/24/88 ... 2,310

GA, Jose; see De La Vega

GA Y MUNOZ, Pedro (Spanish, 19th C)
Pair: Toledo; Seville; oil on panel, sgn, 10x13", B/B 10/9/88 OE ... 4,675
Spanish Courtyard, oil on panel, sgn/inscr, 10x13", C-NY 5/24/89 ... 4,950
Spanish Square, oil on canvas, sgn/inscr, 10x13", C-NY 5/24/89 ... 4,950

JARANO, Gustavo (Santiago)(Colombian, 1952-)
Fire (abstract), oil on canvas, sgn/dtd Paris 87, 57x44", SBY 11/21/88 ... 1,650

LASCO, Jose Maria (Mexican, 1840-1912)
Orizaba Morning (mountainous landscape), oil on canvas, sgn/dtd Mexico 1892, 40x63", SBY 5/16/89 OE ... 341,000
Valle de Mexico (landscape), charcoal/white chalk on tan paper, sgn, 8x12", C-NY 5/18/88 ... 11,000
Valle de Mexico con Volcanes (landscape), red & white chalk on tan paper, sgn, 8x11", C-NY 5/18/88 ... 7,700

LASQUEZ, Diego; after (Spanish, 1599-1660)
Infanta (three-quarter length portrait of young girl), oil on canvas, 32x24", B/B 9/14/89 UE ... 770

LASQUEZ, Jose Antonio (Honduran, 1906-1985)
Domingo de Ramos (village scene on Palm Sunday), oil on canvas, sgn/dtd Honduras CA 1965, 19x25", C-NY 11/21/89 ... 7,150
San Antonio Oriente (village scene), oil on canvas, sgn/dtd Honduras CA 1968, 20x14", lot 256, C-NY 11/21/89 ... 4,180
San Antonio Oriente (village scene), oil on canvas, sgn/dtd Honduras CA 1968, 20x14", lot 257, C-NY 11/21/89 ... 3,300
Untitled (church/figures in landscape), oil on canvas, sgn/dtd Honduras CA 78, 21x18", SBY 11/21/88 ... 3,300
View of San Antonio de Oriente, oil on canvas, sgn/dtd 1953, 29x21", SBY 5/17/88 ... 4,675
View of San Antonio de Oriente, oil on canvas, sgn/dtd 1958, 46x59", SBY 5/17/88 OE ... 46,200
View of San Antonio de Oriente, oil on canvas mounted on board, sgn/dtd Honduras CA 1955, 18x21", SBY 11/21/88 ... 3,300

LASQUEZ, Juan Ramon (Puerto Rican, 1950-)
Funeral (abstract), pencil on paper, sgn/dtd 12-74, 42x39", SBY 5/17/88 ... 660

LASQUEZ, Luis A. (South American, 19th C)
Portrait of a Boy, standing full-length, in a dark blue suit, by a chair...; stamped signature, 43x32", C-SK 5/25/89 ... 480

LASQUEZ, school of
Portrait of a Young Boy, wearing yellow costume with pink bows; oil on canvas, unfr, 17x14", C-NY 1/15/88 OE ... 24,200

LDUIJZEN, Johannes Hendrik (Dutch, 1831-1910)
Secret Admirer (figures in a landscape), oil on canvas, sgn, 34x28", B/B 10/9/88 ... 4,400

LTEN, Wilhelm (Russian, 1847-1929)
Fording the River on a Winter's Day, oil on panel, sgn, 8x11", C-E 10/26/89 ... 5,500
Pair: Travelers on Country Roads; oil on panel, sgn, unfr, 6x9", SBY 7/12/89 ... 5,775

Riders Before a Castle, oil on panel, sgn, 10x7", SBY 7/12/89 UE ... 1,100

VELY, Anatole (French, 1839-1882)

Choosing His Weapon, oil on board, sgn/dtd 1896, 29x23", LH 5/15/88 ... 2,500

Paolo & Francesca, oil on canvas, sgn, 40x30", C-E 5/23/88 ... 3,300

VENARD, Claude (French, 1913-)

La Cafeteria (abstract study in red, white & black), oil on canvas, sgn, 10x8", RAB 8/9/88 UE ... 450

La Tour Eiffel vue de Loin, oil on canvas, sgn, 51x38", C-E 5/13/88 ... 1,540

Landscape, oil on masonite, sgn, 35x51", FB 10/17/88 ... 4,000

Le Quai (a wharf), oil on canvas, sgn, unfr, 14x18", C-E 11/17/88 ... 605

Nature Morte (still life), oil on canvas, sgn, 16x13", SBY 10/5/88 ... 880

Nature Morte (still life), oil on canvas, sgn, 18x22", C-E 5/9/89 OE ... 2,090

Nature Morte avec Bouteilles (still life with bottles), oil on canvas, sgn, 18x22", C-E 11/17/88 ... 835

Nature Morte Fauve, oil on canvas, sgn, 30x30", FB 10/30/89 ... 3,960

Nature Morte Fauve, oil on canvas, sgn, 30x30", SBY 10/5/88 ... 1,430

Pair: Lumiere d'Automne; La Cafetiere; oil on canvas, sgn, 30x29", 18x22", SBY 10/7/89 OE ... 8,250

Piano in an Interior, oil on canvas, sgn, 39x39", B/B 12/8/88 ... 1,320

Still Life, oil on canvas, sgn, 15x18", B/B 1/11/89 OE ... 825

Still Life (abstract), oil on canvas, sgn, 30x30", SBY 10/5/88 ... 880

Still Life of Sunflowers, Pears & a Pitcher; oil & sand on canvas, sgn/#d 1675, 40x40", SBY 10/7/89 ... 4,950

Still Life with Coffeepot & Goblet (abstract), oil on canvas, sgn/#d, 24x24", SBY 2/14/89 OE ... 2,200

Table Top Still Life, oil on canvas, sgn, 30x30", SBY 10/7/89 ... 3,300

Voiles et Nuages, oil on canvas, sgn, 40x39", SBY 10/7/89 ... 3,575

Venetian School (16th C)

Circumcision, oil on canvas, 39x37", C-E 4/7/88 UE ... 550

Venetian School (17th C)

Adoration of the Magi, oil on canvas, 19x15", SBY 6/2/89 ... 13,200

Double-Sided: Christ Carrying the Cross; Study of the Head & Hands of a Youth; chalk, wm, 13x9", C-NY 1/11/89 ... 1,320

Portrait of Astronomer...Beside Table with Globe of Constellations; oil on canvas, unfr, 57x59", C-NY 4/6/89 ... 11,000

Venetian School (18th C)

Adoration of the Magi in an Elaborate Architectural Caprice, oil on canvas, 40x53", SBY 10/13/89 OE ... 16,500

Architectural Capriccio of Figures Within Ruins & a Landscape Beyond, oil on canvas, 41x33", SBY 4/7/88 OE ... 7,150

Capriccio of a Seaport with Classical Ruins, oil on canvas laid down, indistinctly sgn/dtd 1746, 31x50", C-NY 10/12/89 ... 13,200

Courtesan, oil on canvas, 22x17", SBY 12/9/88 ... 770

Gideon & the Angel, pen/brown ink, 7x8", SBY 1/13/89 ... 440

Lady Holding a Mask in a Plumed Hat with a Dog, oil on canvas, 21x16", SBY 10/21/88 ... 3,575

Lady with a Song Bird, oil on canvas, 29x22", WD 1/25/89 OE ... 6,250

Lady with Red Roses in Her Hair, oil on canvas, 29x22", WD 1/25/89 OE ... 4,750

Madonna & Child, red chalk, 4x3", ca 1700, SBY 1/13/89 OE ... 935

Pair: Roman Sacrificial Scenes; oil on canvas, 35x58", SBY 10/21/88 ... 3,300

Pair: Two Noblemen; pastel on paper laid down on canvas, 15x10", SBY 6/8/88 UE ... 1,540

Portrait of a Young Nobleman, seated, full-length, with sword & tricorn hat; oil on canvas, 44x31", C-NY 4/8/88 ... 6,050

Portrait of a Young Nobleman, seated full-length, with sword & tricorn hat; oil on canvas, 44x31", C-NY 4/6/89 ... 5,500

Preaching of Saint John the Baptist, pen/brown ink/wash, 19x13", SBY 7/12/89 ... 1,650

Sacrifice of Alexander, oil on canvas, 39x56", C-NY 4/6/89 OE ... 7,700

Venetian School (19th C)

Gondolas on the Lagoon, oil on canvas, 12x16", WD 10/19/88 OE ... 38,000

Madonna & Child with the Infant Saint John the Baptist & an Angel, oil on canvas, unfr, 39x30", SBY 7/12/89 ... 1,100

View of the Grand Canal, oil on canvas, 9x21", WD 1/25/89 OE ... 1,900

View of the Rialto Bridge From the North, Venice; oil on canvas, 37x42", ca 1800, SBY 4/7/88 OE ... 20,900

Venetian-Byzantine School (16th C)

Crucifixion, oil on panel, 16x13", C-NY 4/6/89 ... 1,760

VENETO, school of (18th C)

Extensive Landscape with Figures by a Waterfall, oil on canvas, 28x35", SBY 6/8/88 ... 4,125

VENIG, Bogdan Bagdanovich (Russian, 1830-1908)

Boyars' Departure After the Feast (exterior winter scene), oil on canvas, sgn/dtd 1889, 21x28", C-L 10/8/88 OE ... 12,000

VENNE, see Van Venne

VENNEMAN, Charles (Flemish, 1802-1875)

Flower Seller, oil on panel, sgn, 14x10", SLK 9/28/88 ... 1,400

Kitchen Suitor, oil on panel, sgn/dtd 1851, 22x19", SBY 5/23/89 ... 10,450

VENNER, W.H.T.

Peasant Drinking, oil on canvas, sgn, 36x29", C-E 2/23/88 ... 1,210

VENTNER, D. (American, 19th C)

River Landscape with Fisherman, oil on canvas, 21x36", FAP 4/15/89 ... 578

VERAY, Joe

Cows Resting, oil on canvas, sgn, 14x17", DM 1/15/88 ... 800

VERBERGHEN, P.

Landscape Scene (man loading firewood on horse-drawn cart), oil on canvas, sgn, 20x28", DM 5/13/88 ... 600

VERBOECKHOVEN, B.; att (Dutch, 1799-1881)

Sheep, oil on canvas, sgn/dtd 1870, 12x16", LH 9/10/89 OE ... 700

VERBOECKHOVEN, Charles Louis (Belgian, 1802-1889)

Bringing in the Catch, oil on canvas, indistinctly sgn, 23x30", SBY 10/24/89 ... 8,800

:RBOECKHOVEN, Eugene Joseph (Belgian, 1799-1881)
Barnyard Scene, oil on panel, sgn/dtd 1876, 7x10", SBY 12/9/88 ... 2,750
Bull in a Landscape, oil on canvas, sgn, 22x27", SBY 2/23/89 ... 5,500
Bull in Expansive Landscape with Ducks in Foreground, a Distant Village Beyond; oil on canvas, sgn, 22x27", SLK 5/11/88 ... 7,500
Horse, Sheep, & Goat in a Landscape; oil on canvas, 27x35", C-NY 10/25/89 ... 11,000
Sheep & Chicken in a Landscape, oil on canvas, sgn/dtd 1873, 29x44", C-NY 2/25/88 ... 14,300
Sheep & Rooster in a Landscape, oil on panel, sgn/dtd 1874, 6x8", C-E 10/25/88 ... 3,520
Sheep with Chickens & a Goat in a Barn, oil on canvas, sgn/dtd 1877, 32x40", SBY 2/22/89 ... 11,000
Shepherd Leading His Flock into the Barn, oil on panel, twice sgn/dtd 1878, 15x22", SBY 5/23/89 ... 13,200

'RBOOM, Adriaen (Dutch, 1628-1670)
Landscape with a Lone Traveler on a Road Beside a Wood, oil on panel, sgn, 12x11", SBY 4/7/89 ... 4,400

RBRUGGEN, Gaspar Pieter the elder (Flemish, 1635-1687)
Still Life of Flowers in a Sculpted Urn on a Ledge, oil on canvas, sgn in monogram, unfr, 48x39", SBY 10/21/88 OE ... 13,200

'RBRUGGEN, Gaspar Pieter the younger (Flemish, 1664-1730)
Christ & Woman of Samaria within a Cartouch, oil on canvas, sgn/dtd 1688, 47x34", C-NY 4/6/89 UE ... 11,000
Portrait of a Woman As Flora with an Urn of Flowers, oil on canvas, 72x52", SBY 4/7/88 ... 12,100
Still Life of Roses, Tulips, Chrysanthemum, Morning-Glory...; oil on canvas, sgn/dtd 1696, 53x45", C-NY 1/11/89 OE ... 71,500

RBRUGGEN, Gaspar Pieter; school of (Flemish, 17th/18th C)
Carnations...Flowers in a Sculpted Urn with an Overturned Pitcher on a Draped Table; oil on canvas, 32x26", C-NY 4/6/89 ... 7,150
Flower Market in a French Town, watercolor/gouache on paper, sgn w/monogram, dtd 1899, 24x36", C-NY 5/24/89 OE ... 14,300
Pair: Floral Still Lifes; oil on canvas, unfr, 16x11", C-NY 4/6/89 OE ... 19,800
Tulips, Roses, & Other Flowers in a Glass Vase, on a Ledge; oil on canvas, 17x14", C-NY 4/8/88 ... 9,350

RBURGH, Dioniys (Dutch, 1655-1722)
View of a Walled Town on a River with a Dutch Packet & Other Shipping, oil on panel, 35x61", SBY 10/21/88 OE ... 12,100

RBURGH, Rutger (Belgian, 1678-)
Peasants Merrymaking Before an Inn, oil on canvas, indistinctly sgn, 24x31", C-NY 1/15/88 OE ... 8,800

RDIANA, Santa; master of
Madonna & Child, Enthroned, with St Catherine, Christ Blessing Above; oil on panel, shaped top, 47x19", C-NY 1/15/88 OE ... 66,000

RDIER, Francois (French, 1631-1730)
Antique Scene of Divination, red chalk on paper, unfr, 12x10", WD 1/25/89 UE ... 400
Deluge, black & white chalk/gray wash on 4 attached sheets, inscr, 10x17", C-NY 1/12/88 ... 660
Old Man Approaching Hercules & Other Gods, black chalk/gray wash, 10x19", SBY 1/13/89 ... 990

RDIER, Jules Victor (French, 1862-)
Reflection (nude woman looking at reflection), oil on canvas, 41x35", C-E 5/23/88 ... 1,980

RDILHAN, Louis Mathieu (French, 1876-1929)
Les Jardins a Versailles, oil on canvas, sgn, 30x40", C-E 5/13/88 OE ... 6,600

RDUSSEN, Jan Peeter (Flemish, 1700-1763)
Cavalry Commander with His Officers, a Battle Beyond; oil on canvas, 32x51", C-NY 4/8/88 ... 8,250

RDUSSEN, Jan Peeter; school of (Flemish, 1700-1763)
Cavalry Battle, oil on canvas, 16x24", C-NY 4/6/89 ... 3,300

RELST, William (Belgian, fl 1734-ca 1756)
Portrait of a Young Boy with His Dog (full-length, in a landscape), oil on canvas, sgn/dtd 1739, 49x39", SBY 4/7/89 ... 12,100

RESMITH, Daniel Albert (American, 1861-1932)
Doll Shop, oil on canvas laid down on panel, sgn/dtd 1917, 24x29", SBY 6/24/88 ... 1,430

RESS, T. Zoltan (Hungarian, 1868-1935)
Two Children with a Watermelon, oil on canvas, sgn/dtd 1919, 18x16", C-E 10/25/88 ... 935

REY, Arthur (British, 19th C)
Hop Gatherers, oil on canvas, sgn/dtd 1882, unfr, 33x55", SBY 7/12/89 ... 1,650

RGNE, John Louis
River Landscape (contemporary), oil on canvas, sgn, 31x45", MG 5/28/88 ... 475

RHAECHT, Tobias (Flemish, 1561-1631)
Landscape with the Ten Soldiers of David Saluting the Miser Nabal, oil on canvas, 59x43", SBY 1/12/89 ... 38,500

RHAERT, Piet (Dutch, 1852-1903)
River Landscape in Summer, oil on panel, sgn, 22x27", LH 9/10/89 UE ... 1,000

RHAS, Frans (Belgian, 1827-1897)
Out of Reach (mother/child in interior), oil on panel, sgn/dtd 1874, 40x23", C-NY 2/23/89 ... 19,800

RHEY, Johanna Louise Antoinette (Dutch, 1886-1966)
Children Riding Donkeys on the Beach, oil on canvas laid down, sgn, 20x28", B/B 8/10/88 ... 1,320

RHEYDEN, Francois (Belgian, 1806-1889)
Country Cottage & Garden, oil on canvas, sgn, 11x14", B/B 3/22/89 ... 2,750
Gypsy & Clown Playing with a Dog, oil on panel, sgn/inscr, 3x4", C-E 2/23/88 ... 1,760
Landscape, oil on canvas, sgn, 23x25", WG 4/23/88 ... 900

RHEYDEN, Isidore (Belgian, 1846-1905)
Landscape with Forground Meandering Stream & Middle Distant Buildings, oil on panel, sgn, 13x20", SLK 5/11/88 ... 1,600

RHOESEN, Albertus (Dutch, 1806-1881)
Barnyard Fowl at Waters Edge, oil on panel, sgn/dtd 1870, 5x7", NA 2/6/88 OE ... 2,000
Cows in a Landscape, oil on panel, sgn/dtd 1873, 5x7", NA 2/6/88 OE ... 1,900
Peacocks & Poultry, oil on canvas, sgn/dtd 1867, 16x20", C-NY 2/25/88 ... 3,850
Poultry Yard, oil on panel, sgn, 16x20", C-E 10/26/89 ... 4,950
Scene Before a Hen House, oil on panel, sgn/indistinctly dtd, 7x9", RWS 11/10/89 UE ... 700
Social Session (rooster & hens by a hen house), oil on panel, sgn/dtd 1868, 6x7", C-E 5/22/89 ... 2,200

Tax Collectors, oil on canvas, sgn/dtd 1847, 32x25", SBY 7/12/89 ... 4,950

VERHOEVEN-BALL, Adrien Joseph (Belgian, 1824-1882)

Game Market at Antwerp, oil on canvas, sgn/dtd 1872, 19x24", C-NY 2/25/88 ... 5,500
Vegetable Seller, oil on panel, sgn/dtd 1863, unfr, 20x15", C-E 2/23/88 ... 1,045

VERKOLJE, Jan (Dutch, 1650-1693)

Portrait of a Young Lady, seated on a terrace with a dog; oil on canvas, sgn/dtd 1686, 26x21", SBY 4/7/88 OE ... 20,900

VERKOLJE, Jan; circle of (Dutch, 1650-1693)

Venus Begging Adonis Not To Hunt, oil on canvas, 29x34", SBY 4/7/89 ... 4,400

VERLAT, Charles Michel Maria (Belgian, 1824-1890)

Chien et Perdix (dog & partridge), oil on panel, sgn, 26x21", SBY 6/9/89 ... 5,775

VERMEHREN, Johan Frederick Nicolai (Danish, 1823-1910)

Zouave (full-length portrait), oil on canvas, sgn/dtd 1855, 24x15", SBY 5/23/89 ... 15,400

VERMEULEN, Andries; manner of (Dutch, 1763-1814)

Cowherd Tending Cattle in Extensive Mountainous Landscape, oil on copper, bears signature, oval, 10x14", C-NY 4/6/89 UE ... 1,100

VERMEULEN, J.

Heading Home by Moonlight, oil on canvas, sgn, 32x25", S/A 2/18/89 ... 450

VERNER, Elizabeth O'Neill (American, 1883-)

Flower Seller (woman w/flowers smoking a pipe), pastel on silk mounted on board, 9x9", SBY 6/24/88 OE ... 2,640
Man with a Pipe, pastel on silk mounted on board, sgn, 9x9", SBY 3/17/88 OE ... 2,750

VERNER, Frederick Arthur (Canadian, 1836-1928)

Buffalo in the Evening, watercolor, sgn/dtd 1902, 12x24", WAD 11/30/89 ... 4,400
Indian Camp, West Coast; watercolor, sgn/dtd 1899, 12x24", WAD 11/30/89 UE ... 5,500
Indian Standing in a Canoe, watercolor, sgn/dtd 1904, 12x22", C-SK 6/9/88 OE ... 3,718
Landscape with Buffalo Grazing at Sunset, watercolor on paper, sgn/dtd 1906, 9x13", RWS 5/19/88 OE ... 3,600
Landscape with Grazing Sheep, watercolor, sgn/dtd 1899, no size given, WAD 11/30/89 ... 750
Pair: Indian Cemetery; Leader of the Herd; gray wash/black chalk, 1 sgn/dtd 1899/1 initialed, 13x9", 8x13", C-SK 5/25/89 ... 1,100

VERNET, Carle Antoine Charles Horace (French, 1758-1836)

Cheval de Chasse Anglais, black chalk heightened w/white, sgn/dtd, 17x24", C-NY 2/25/88 ... 7,150

VERNET, Claude Joseph (French, 1714-1789)

Pair: Morning Fog; Sunset in Italianate Ports; oil on canvas, sgn/dtd 1745, gilded wooden frame, 32x55", SBY 1/12/89 OE ... 880,000
Ship Thrown Upon the Rocks by a Stormy Sea, oil on canvas, sgn, 35x66", SBY 6/2/89 ... 132,000
Shipping on a Estuary, oil on canvas, bears signature/dtd 86, 31x27", SBY 10/13/89 OE ... 9,900

VERNET, Claude Joseph; circle of (French, 1714-1789)

Bather with Attendants Withdrawing From Lake, Ruins on Hill & Waterfall Beyond; oil on copper, unfr, 17x23", C-NY 4/6/89 ... 12,100
Coastal Scene with a Ship Floundering on Rocks, oil on canvas, 23x39", SBY 6/3/88 ... 8,800

VERNET, Claude Joseph; follower of (French, 1714-1789)

Coastal Scene with Figures, oil on canvas, 24x18", SBY 6/8/88 ... 2,090
Figures in a Gorge, a Town & Fortress on a Mountain Beyond; oil on canvas, 20x31", SBY 4/7/88 OE ... 4,125

VERNET, Claude Joseph; manner of (French, 1714-1789)

Italianate Harbor Scene with Figures on a Pier & a House on a Cliff, oil on canvas mounted on board, 16x22", SBY 6/8/88 ... 1,540
Pair: Waterfalls at Tivoli with Figures Resting in the Foreground, oil on canvas, 10x13", C-NY 10/12/89 ... 2,860
Set of 8: Italianate Lake Scenes; oil on canvas, unstretched, unfr, 77x114" & smaller, C-NY 4/6/89 OE ... 49,500

VERNIER, Emile Louis (French, 1829-1887)

Scene de Plage, oil on panel, sgn, 10x16", RWS 8/12/89 ... 1,800

VERNIER, Fortune

Dead Hare, oil on canvas, sgn, unfr, 31x26", C-E 2/23/88 ... 825

VERNIER, J. (French, 19th C)

Fishing Village, oil on canvas, 25x13", FAP 4/15/89 ... 495

VERNILE (Italian, 19th C)

Reading the News (two children in artist's studio), oil on canvas, sgn, 27x19", B/B 3/22/89 ... 4,400

VERNON, Arthur Langley (British, 19th C)

English Country House, oil on canvas, sgn/dtd 1901, 24x38", LH 3/20/88 ... 1,300

VERNON, Emile (French, 19th/20th C)

Among the Blossoms (seated nude), oil on canvas, sgn/dtd 1904, 36x24", SBY 10/24/89 OE ... 68,750
Fancy Bonnet (portrait of an elegant lady in bonnet holding a bouquet), oil on canvas, sgn, 24x20", C-NY 5/24/89 ... 7,700
Well at Springtime, oil on canvas, sgn/dtd 1917, 16x49", SBY 10/24/89 ... 12,100
Woodland Beauty (portrait), oil on canvas, sgn, 24x20", SBY 5/23/89 OE ... 22,000

VERNON, Emile; att (French, 19th/20th C)

Profile of a Young Girl, oil on canvas, bears signature, 20x16", C-E 2/21/89 ... 1,650

VERNON, Paul (French, 1796-1875)

Autumn River Landscape, oil on panel, sgn, 9x14", C-E 5/23/88 ... 1,320

VERON, Alexandre Rene (French, 1826-1897)

Rafting on a River, oil on canvas, sgn/dtd 1872, unfr, 24x36", SBY 7/12/89 ... 4,180

VERON-FARE, Jules Henri (French, 19th C)

Village Marketplace, oil on canvas, sgn, 14x30", C-E 10/25/88 ... 1,045

VERONA, Juan; see De Arellano, Juan

VERONESE, after (Italian, 15th/16th C)

Dead Christ Supported by Angels, oil on canvas, unfr, 52x37", C-E 4/7/88 UE ... 110
Mercury & Herse, oil on canvas, 89x65", C-NY 10/20/88 ... 16,500

VERONESE, Bonifazio; school of (Italian, 1487-1553)

Holy Family, oil on canvas, 32x28", C-NY 4/6/89 OE ... 12,100

RONESE, circle of (Italian, 15th/16th C)
Portait of a Man Said To Be Johannes de Medici, in profile, oil on canvas, inscr, 24x19", C-NY 4/8/88 ... 2,750
RONESE, school of (Italian, 15th/16th C)
Feast of St Gregory the Greater, oil on canvas, 29x53", C-NY 10/20/88 UE ... 3,850
Rape of Europa, oil on canvas, 73x66", C-E 6/1/88 OE ... 4,400
Woman with Baskets of Flowers Before a Priapic Statue in a Basilica, chalk/pen/ink/wash, 14x10", C-NY 1/11/89 ... 7,700
RPOEKEN, Hendrik (Dutch, 1791-1869)
Wooded Landscape, oil on canvas, sgn, 34x39", SBY 5/23/89 ... 7,700
RREAUX, Louis Leon Nicolas (French, 19th C)
Fifth Madras Light Cavalry, oil on canvas, 14x18", C-E 5/3/88 ... 1,100
RSCHUUR, Wouter (Dutch, 1812-1874)
At the Well (exterior scene w/figures & animals), oil on panel, sgn, 6x8", C-NY 2/23/89 ... 6,600
Country Folk in a Frozen Winter Landscape, oil on canvas, sgn, 30x40", C-NY 5/24/89 OE ... 88,000
RSCHUUR, Wouter; after (Dutch, 1812-1874)
The Wayside, oil on canvas, 24x29", C-E 11/8/88 ... 1,980
RTANGEN, Daniel (Dutch, 1598-1684)
Finding of Moses, oil on panel, 16x20", C-NY 10/20/88 ... 11,000
Landscape with a Hunting Party, oil on canvas, sgn, 26x34", SBY 6/3/88 UE ... 12,100
RTES, Marcel (French, 1895-1961)
Deux Enfants (two children), oil on canvas, sgn, 40x30", C-E 11/17/88 OE ... 6,600
Esquisse (sketch), pen/black ink on paper, sgn/stamped Atelier Vertes, 16x21", C-E 11/17/88 ... 330
Joueuse de Mandoline (playing the mandolin), oil on canvas, sgn, ca 1948, 38x59", C-E 5/9/89 ... 4,180
Nature Morte d'Apres Chardin (still life), oil on canvas, sgn, unfr, 36x48", C-E 5/9/89 OE ... 4,400
Pair: Cerf; Le Chien Fluffy; oil on canvas/gouache over black chalk, sgn, 1 unfr, 23x19", C-E 11/17/88 ... 825
Pair: Le Taureau; Jeune Fille (contemporary); pen/ink on brown paper, pen on paper, sgn, 19x23", 11x8", C-E 5/9/89 OE ... 1,650
Pont de l'Ama, oil on canvas, stamped w/signature, ca 1952, unfr, 29x36", SBY 10/5/88 UE ... 770
Set of 4: Scenes From Helen of Troy; black ballpoint pen on paper, stamped signature, 8x10", 8x11", C-E 11/17/88 ... 440
Sketch of Circus Performer with Horses, pastel on paper, sgn, 17x23", B/B 4/20/88 ... 248
RUTTI, A.
Venice at Sunset, watercolor, sgn, 10x15", WG 9/16/88 ... 200
RVEER, Salomon Leonardus (Dutch, 1813-1876)
Washerwomen by a Seaport, sepia/watercolor on paper w/traces of pencil, sgn/dtd 49, 5x8", C-E 5/23/88 ... 440
RWEE, Louis Pierre (Belgian, 1807-1877)
Shepherd with His Flock, oil on panel, sgn, 19x25", C-E 5/22/89 ... 2,200
RWEST, Jules (Belgian, 1883-1957)
Flowers Arranged in a Bowl of Water, oil on canvas, sgn, 16x21", C-E 10/26/89 ... 3,850
RY, Marjorie (American, 20th C)
Benjamin River, Maine; pastel on brown paper, sgn, 20x26", RWS 9/8/89 UE ... 225
Penobscot Bay, pastel on brown paper, sgn, 18x25", RWS 9/8/89 ... 550
SIN, Jaroslav Fr Julius (Bulgarian, 1859-1915)
Horse Training, oil on canvas, sgn/dtd 1898, 32x55", SBY 12/9/88 ... 7,150
SSELY, Boris Theo (French, 19th/20th C)
At the Temple of Sweet Waters, oil on canvas, sgn/dtd 1911, 26x16", C-NY 5/24/89 ... 6,600
STER, Willem (Dutch, 1824-1871)
Skaters in a Frozen Landscape, oil on canvas, sgn/dtd 1867, 26x38", C-NY 5/24/89 ... 33,000
STIER, Antoine; att (French, 1740-1824)
Portrait of a Lady, oil on canvas, oval, 28x22", SBY 10/13/89 ... 6,325
Portrait of a Lady (seated, hands crossed, flowers in vase on table at side), oil on canvas, oval, 42x35", SBY 6/1/89 UE ... 16,500
STIER, Antoine; circle of (French, 1740-1824)
Portrait of an Elegant Lady in a Fur-Trimmed Cloak & Plumed Headdress, oil on canvas, oval, 28x22", SBY 10/13/89 ... 2,200
STIER, Antoine; manner of (French, 1740-1824)
Portrait of a Lady, oil on canvas, 30x25", SBY 6/8/88 OE ... 8,800
TRAIO, see Bembo
YRASSAT, Jules Jacques (French, 1828-1893)
Chevaux s'Abreuvant dans la Seine Derriere Notre Dame, oil on canvas, 15x20", C-NY 5/24/89 ... 11,000
Hay Harvest (figures working in hay field, houses beyond), oil on panel, sgn, 9x18", B/B 10/9/88 ... 6,050
Wooded River Landscape with Town Beyond, black/white/red chalk on gray paper, dtd 73, unfr, 8x12", C-NY 5/25/88 ... 550
ALOV, Konstantin (Russian, 1900-1976)
Le Patronage Rouge (men w/farm machinery), oil on canvas, sgn, 50x39", C-L 10/8/88 ... 27,890
Suprematistic Composition (abstract), oil on prepared board, ca 1919, 7x5", C-L 10/8/88 ... 3,346
ANA, Raul Santos (20th C)
Pair: Toledo; Cadiz; oil on canvas, sgn/dtd 69, 10x23", C-E 11/17/88 ... 286
ANDEN, Heinrich (American, 1814-1899)
Traveler in a Stormy Landscape, oil on canvas, sgn, 22x27", B/B 1/11/89 ... 2,475
ANELLO, Cesare (Italian, 19th C)
Procession in a Cathedral, oil on panel, sgn, 12x10", C-E 2/21/89 OE ... 3,520
AVANT, George Louis (American, 1872-1925)
Nature Morte, Songbird; watercolor, sgn/dtd 1912, 14x10", NA 2/6/88 ... 650
Nature Morte (still life of fish hanging from a nail), watercolor, sgn/dtd New Orleans 1921, 20x11", NA 11/5/88 ... 1,000
BERT, Jean Georges (French, 1840-1902)
Cardinal at a Window, oil on panel, sgn, unfr, 18x15", C-NY 2/25/88 ... 12,100

Convent Choir (rehearsing in an interior), oil on panel, sgn/dtd 1865, 15x18", C-NY 5/24/89 6,050
Le Petit-Neveu, oil on canvas, sgn, 18x22", SBY 12/9/88 UE 2,750
Seated Cardinal (in landscape), gouache on paper, sgn, 10x7", B/B 3/22/89 3,300
Serenade, oil on cradled panel, sgn, 18x15", SBY 2/22/89 44,000

VICENTE, Esteban (Spanish, 1904-)
Black & Blue (abstract), paper/linen collage on panel, sgn, 1961, 24x27", SBY 2/14/89 OE 5,500
Hosta (abstract), acrylic on canvas, sgn/dtd 1979, 64x52", SBY 10/5/88 7,700
Untitled #18 (abstract), charcoal on paper, sgn/dtd 1958, 40x51", SBY 2/14/89 OE 3,850

VICENTINO, Andrea (Italian, 16th C)
David Victorious Over Goliath, Fighting Armies of the Israelites & Philistines Beyond; oil, 60x86", SBY 10/13/89 13,200

VICKERS, Alfred H. (British, 19th C)
Pair: Along the Conway Shore Wales; Near Bettway Castle; oil on canvas, sgn, 14x10", B/B 9/14/89 1,650

VICKERS, C. (British, 19th C)
Landscape with Mill House & Figures, oil on canvas, sgn, 16x24", SLK 9/26/88 950

VICKERS, Henry Harold (British, 1851-1919)
Ont the Gatineau, oil on board, sgn/dtd 1892, 10x14", WAD 11/30/89 525
Pair: Cattle & Sheep in Barns; oil on board, sgn/dtd, 7x10", WAD 6/6/88 2,200
Sheep & Cattle by a River, oil on board, sgn/dtd 1898, 13x12", WAD 6/6/88 1,450

VICKERY, Robert (American, 1926-)
Bird in Flight (boy making a bird w/hand shadows), oil on masonite, sgn, 31x45", WD 11/16/88 11,000
Catcher, pen/sepia ink on paper, sgn, 23x29", C-NY 3/11/88 1,650

VICTORS, Jacobus (Dutch, 1640-1705)
Fighting Cocks with Pigeons & Duck by Stone Wall in Landscape with Sunflowers, oil on canvas, 45x51", C-NY 4/6/89 UE 7,150

VIDAL, Gustave (Canadian, 19th C)
Bord de Mer, Ile Ste Marguerite; oil on canvas, sgn, 18x35", FB 10/30/89 880

VIEIRA DA SILVA, Maria Elena (French, 1908-)
Composition, Ville; gouache on canvas, sgn/dtd 49, 11x9", C-NY 11/16/88 99,000
Entre la Nuit et le Chemin (abstract), oil on canvas, sgn/dtd 61, 38x51", SBY 6/30/88 164,000
Hill-Side (abstract), tempera on paper, sgn/dtd 62, 26x20", SBY 5/3/88 OE 44,000
Les Cent Pas (abstract), oil on canvas, sgn/dtd 65/titled, 26x32", SBY 2/19/88 OE 44,000

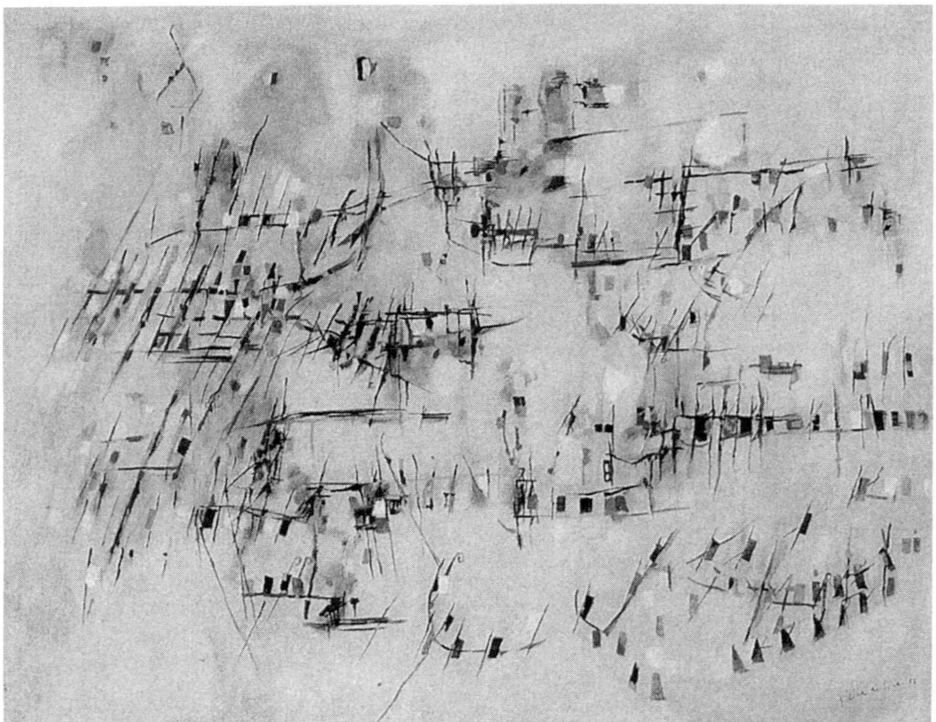

Les Oiseaux, oil on canvas, sgn/dtd 52 23x29", C-NY 11/16/88 OE; $132,000

Untitled (abstract), oil on canvas, sgn/dtd 57, 21x26", SBY 6/30/88 OE 136,100

VIEN, Joseph Marie the younger (French, 1762-1848)
Trompe l'Oeil of Framed Bronze Medallions Hanging on Wooden Wall, oil on panel, sgn/dtd 1817, 16x14", C-NY 10/20/88 OE 9,900

VIENA, F.
The Kiss, oil on canvas, sgn, 29x33", DM 3/14/88 2,200

VIERIN, Emmanuel (Belgian, 1869-)
Belgian Village Street Scene, oil on canvas, 24x32", B/B 8/10/88 1,100

VIGEE-LEBRUN, Marie Louise E. (French, 1755-1842)
Portrait of Anna, Comtesse Potocka; oil on canvas, sgn/dtd 1791, 55x49", SBY 6/2/89 UE 300,000
Portrait of Emilie de Coutances, la Presidente de Becdelievre; oil on canvas, sgn/dtd 1778, 39x31", SBY 10/13/89 16,500

GEE-LEBRUN, Marie Louise E.; after (French, 1755-1842)
Portrait of Marie Antoinette, oil on canvas, 37x28", C-E 2/16/88 OE ... **1,045**
Portrait of Marie-Gabrielle de Sinety, Duchess de Gramont-Caderousse; oil on canvas, SBY 4/7/89 OE ... **6,050**
GEE-LEBRUN, Marie Louise E.; circle of (French, 1755-1842)
Portrait of a Young Girl, bust-length, wearing a veil decorated with flowers; oil on canvas, 18x15", C-NY 5/31/89 ... **13,200**
GEE-LEBRUN, Marie Louise E.; follower of
Young Prince Lubomirski As Amour, oil on canvas, 42x34", SBY 6/1/89 UE ... **38,500**
GEE-LEBRUN, Marie Louise E.; manner of (French, 1755-1842)
Portrait of a Boy, oil on canvas, in a painted oval, 24x20", SBY 12/9/88 UE ... **440**
GEE-LEBRUN, Marie Louise E.; school of (French, 1755-1842)
Portrait of Madame LeBrun, half-length; oil on canvas, unfr, 23x16", C-NY 1/11/89 ... **17,600**
GNAUD, Jean (French, 1775-1826)
Group Portrait of Lady Seated with Son & Daughter, oil on canvas, sgn/dtd 1813, 39x32", C-M 12/3/88 ... **11,149**
GNAUD (Continental, 19th C)
Winter Landscape, oil on canvas, sgn, 9x12", MG 10/28/88 UE ... **1,400**
GNERON, Pierre Roch (French, 1789-1872)
Open Window (woman seated, reading by window), oil on canvas, sgn, 12x10", SBY 10/24/89 ... **12,100**
GNET, Henri (French, 20th C)
Vue de Rouen (extensive landscape), oil on canvas, sgn, 26x32", C-E 11/17/88 ... **3,850**
GNOLES, Andre (French, 20th C)
Landscape, oil on canvas, sgn/dtd 59, 25x32", SBY 10/7/89 ... **2,640**
Still Life of Fruits & Vegetables, oil on canvas, sgn/dtd 67, 38x51", SBY 10/7/89 ... **3,575**
GNON, Claude (French, 1593-1670)
St Paul, pen/brown ink/wash over red chalk, 15x9", SBY 1/13/89 OE ... **41,250**
Youth, Half-Length, Wearing Plumed Hat, Making a Toast As He Sings; oil on canvas, 43x34", C-M 12/3/88 ... **111,486**
GNON, Claude; att (French, 1593-1670)
Sacrifice of Melchizedek, oil on canvas, 48x60", C-NY 5/31/89 ... **10,450**
Study of an Elegant Lady, red chalk, 11x6", SBY 1/13/89 OE ... **3,575**
GNON, Victor (French, 1847-1909)
Bateaux sur la Riviere (landscape w/river view), oil on canvas, sgn, 13x18", C-NY 2/16/89 ... **14,300**
Hameau sous la Neige (landscape), oil on canvas, sgn, 16x23", RWS 8/12/89 OE ... **6,500**
Le Chemin de Lavoir a Drocourt (landscape w/house & figure on path), oil on canvas, sgn, 15x18", C-NY 2/16/89 OE ... **14,300**
Nature Morte aux Fraises (still life), oil on canvas, sgn, 7x11", RWS 8/12/89 ... **5,500**
Paysanne dans les Champs (peasant in a field), oil on canvas, sgn/dtd 1887, 18x22", C-NY 10/5/89 ... **17,600**
Paysans Conduisant des Vaches dans un Sous-Bois, oil on canvas, sgn/dtd 1907, 35x41", C-NY 2/16/89 OE ... **20,900**
GNY, Sylvain (French, 1902-1970)
Street Scene, gouache on masonite, sgn, 18x22", SBY 10/7/89 ... **660**
GON, Louis Jacques (French, 20th C)
Old Street in Rouen, France (wood & stucco buildings on cobblestone street); oil on canvas, sgn, 24x36", RAB 8/9/88 UE ... **250**
LALLONGA, see De Vilallonga
LLA, A.
Contemplating on the Beach, oil on panel, sgn, 12x20", C-E 2/16/88 UE ... **462**
LLA, Hernando Gonzalla (American, 1881-1952)
Indian Chief, mixed media on board, sgn, 22x15", B/B 9/15/88 ... **550**
Maria Estacion & the Crippled Don Miguel, oil on board, sgn/dtd Oct 7 1926, 18x13", B/B 8/10/88 ... **302**
Portrait of a Mounted Cowboy, watercolor on paper, sgn/dtd 38, 24x18", B/B 10/6/88 ... **1,980**
Portrait of an Indian, oil on board, sgn, 30x24", B/B 10/6/88 ... **1,430**
Riders in a Western Landscape, oil on canvas, sgn/dtd 23, 20x28", B/B 10/6/88 ... **2,475**
LLA Y PRADES, Julio (Spanish, 19th/20th C)
Portrait of Dona Maria Cantrellas, oil on canvas, sgn, 34x25", B/B 6/9/88 ... **4,950**
LLACRES, Cesar A. (Ecuadorian, 1880-)
Pair: Place du Tertre; Basilique du Sacre Coeur, Montmartre; oil on canvas, sgn, 12x10", WD 11/16/88 UE ... **3,250**
Parisian Street Scene, oil on canvas, sgn, 25x30", WD 5/5/88 ... **5,000**
LLANUEVA, Juan P.
Catholic Mass, oil on panel, sgn/dtd, 10x7", C-E 2/23/88 ... **1,210**
LLANUEVA, Leoncio (Peruvian, 1936-)
Fragments of an Inventory (contemporary), acrylic on canvas, sgn/titled, 1984, 45x57", SBY 5/16/89 ... **12,100**
LLEGAS Y CORDERO, Jose (Spanish, 1848-1922)
Antiquarian (figure in interior), oil on panel, sgn, 13x10", C-NY 2/23/89 OE ... **16,500**
In the Garden (two young girls), oil on panel, sgn/dtd MDCCCXXXXII, 14x9", C-NY 5/24/89 ... **19,800**
Siesta, oil on canvas, sgn/dtd 1907, 27x39", SBY 5/23/89 OE ... **770,000**
LLENEUVE, Arthur (Canadian, 1910-)
Abstract, oil on board, sgn/dtd 1966, 15x18", FB 10/17/88 ... **800**
L'Iindustrie de Baie Comeau (contemporary industrial cityscape), oil on canvas, sgn/dtd 61, 25x30", FB 4/25/88 ... **2,300**
Passing the Ball, oil on board, sgn, 6x9", FB 10/30/89 ... **440**
Still Life, mixed media, sgn/dtd 1971, 5x4", FB 10/17/88 ... **200**
Sugar Shack, oil on board, sgn/dtd 1975, 8x10", FB 10/30/89 ... **660**
LLON, Eugene (French, 1879-)
Pair: St Marks Square on Rainy Day; Basin of St Marks...; watercolor, sgn/dtd 1926, 11x15", B/B 9/14/89 OE ... **1,540**
LLON, Jacques (French, 1875-1963)
Jeune Fille Assise avec Son Chat Noir, ink wash/watercolor on paper, sgn twice/dtd 95, 38x25", SBY 2/18/88 ... **13,200**

L'Arbre Rouge (abstract), oil on canvas, sgn twice/dtd 48/titled, 11x16", SBY 10/7/88 OE ... 35,200
La Cirque, oil on canvas, sgn/dtd 33, 32x46", SBY 5/11/88 OE ... 132,000
Le Globe de Mariee (abstract), watercolor on paper, sgn/dtd 1950, 14x10", WD 11/16/88 ... 7,000
Les Fonds de St Paul, oil on canvas, sgn twice/dtd, 1945, 24x36", 24x36", SBY 5/11/88 OE ... 115,000
North African, watercolor/colored wax crayons/ink on paper, sgn twice/inscr/dtd 1903, 18x12", SBY 10/5/88 ... 2,860
Pair: Etude pour l'Agneau Pascal; pen/ink on paper, sgn/dtd 56, 10x10", 10x8", SBY 2/14/89 OE ... 3,850
Puteaux: Les Fumees et les Arbres en Fleur (abstract); oil on canvas, sgn, 1912, 45x58", SBY 10/7/88 OE ... 363,000
Tete de Femme Vue de Dos, watercolor over black chalk/pencil on light green paper, sgn, 8x5", C-NY 2/13/89 ... 3,080
Torse (abstract), oil on canvas, sgn twice/dtd 1919/titled, 29x23", SBY 11/12/88 ... 63,250

VINAY, Jean (French, 1907-1978)
L'Albenc, Isere; oil on canvas, sgn twice/inscr, 10x13", C-E 5/13/88 ... 440

VINCELETTE, Romeo (Canadian, 1902-1979)
Quebec Village in Winter, pastel, sgn, 20x26", FB 4/25/88 ... 1,000
Returning Home (landscape w/figure, houses, & snow-covered mountains), pastel, sgn, 19x25", FB 10/30/89 ... 880
Sur le Mont Royal, oil on panel, sgn, 12x16", FB 4/25/88 ... 300

VINCENT, Francois Andre (French, 1746-1816)
Woman From Santa Lucia in Naples, oil on canvas, sgn/indistinctly dtd, 32x20", SBY 6/3/88 ... 462,000

VINCENT, George (British, 1796-1830)
Landscape with Thatched Huts, oil on canvas, 30x19", SBY 12/9/88 ... 1,650

VINCENT, H.
Still Life of Peonies & Fruit in an Urn, oil on board, sgn, 30x21", C-E 2/23/88 ... 1,320

VINCENT, Harry Aiken (American, 1864-1931)
Across the Harbor, Provincetown (sailing ships docked in harbor); oil on board, sgn, 8x10", RWS 5/19/88 ... 1,400
Autumn Coast, Rockport (view across fields to distant shoreline); oil on panel, sgn/dtd 05, 12x16", RWS 9/29/88 UE ... 200
Boats at Rockport, oil on canvas, sgn, 24x30", C-E 6/1/89 OE ... 8,250
Gloucester Harbor Scene, oil on canvasboard, sgn, 11x14", RWS 11/3/88 ... 1,800
In the Harbor, oil on canvas, sgn, 25x31", C-E 10/18/89 OE ... 8,800
Rockport, Massachusetts (village scene); oil on canvas, sgn, 30x25", RWS 5/19/88 OE ... 11,000
Rocky Inlet, Gloucester; oil on board, sgn, 11x14", RWS 11/3/88 ... 1,300

VINCENZINO, Giuseppe; att (Italian, 18th C)
Game & Fruit on a Ledge, oil on canvas, 29x38", C-NY 1/15/88 OE ... 36,300

VINCI, see Da Vinci

VINCKEBOONS, David; school of (Flemish, 1576-1629)
A Kermess (church festival), oil on canvas, 39x53", C-NY 5/31/89 ... 38,500

VINE, J. (British, 19th C)
Red Bull in a Landscape, oil on canvas, sgn, 18x24", C-E 10/25/88 ... 2,750
White Shorthorn Cow in a Landscape, oil on canvas, sgn, 20x24", C-E 5/22/89 ... 2,200

VINEA, Francesco (Italian, 1845-1902)
Peasant Guard, oil on panel, sgn, 10x7", C-E 4/7/88 ... 1,320
Pinch of Snuff, oil on panel, sgn/dtd 1871, 5x7", WAD 6/6/88 ... 2,600

VINIEGRA Y LASSO, Salvador (Spanish, 1862-1915)
La Faraona (portrait of a woman), oil on canvas, sgn, 32x26", SBY 12/9/88 ... 4,400

VINTER, John Alfred (British, 1828-1905)
Mother & Children Repairing a Toy Boat, oil on canvas, sgn/dtd 1862, 25x19", C-E 5/23/88 ... 2,420

VINTON, Frederick Porter (American, 1846-1911)
Riverscape, green trees line placid river; oil on artist board, sgn, RAB 8/8/89 OE ... 2,200

VIPOND, Frederick Charles (Canadian, 1865-1907)
Cows Grazing by a River, oil on canvas, sgn, 15x22", FB 5/28/89 ... 850

VISCONTI, Alphonse Adolfo Ferraguti (French, 1850-1924)
Still Life of a Gold Chalice, Bowl & Yellow Roses; oil on panel, sgn/dtd 81, 26x18", SBY 10/24/89 ... 7,700

VISENTINI, circle of (Italian, 17th/18th C)
Capriccio of Classical Architecture with Figures, oil on canvas, unfr, 29x42", C-NY 4/8/88 ... 7,150

VISKI, Janos (Hungarian, 1891-)
Rounding Up the Horses, oil on canvas, sgn, 23x32", WG 9/16/88 ... 300
Wild Horses, oil on canvas, unfr, 24x33", MAG 9/18/88 ... 525

VISO, Nicola (Italian, 18th C)
Mountainous River Landscape with Herdsmen, oil on canvas, sgn, 17x52", C-NY 6/2/88 OE ... 12,100

VISPRE, Francois Xavier; att (British/French, 1730-1790)
Portrait of a Young Girl Wearing a Pink Satin Dress, oil on canvas, 18x15", SBY 4/7/88 OE ... 6,050

VISSO, see Da Visso

VITALI, E. (Italian, 19th C)
Franciscan at Work, watercolor on paper, sgn, 13x6", FAP 11/4/88 ... 375
Pair: Elderly Man with a Pipe; Elderly Woman (w/scarf over head); oil on canvas, sgn, 10x7", WG 4/23/88 UE ... 300

VITIELLO, Pasquale (Italian, 1912-1962)
Red Castle, oil on cardboard, sgn, 1960, 19x19", LH 10/16/88 OE ... 110

VITRINGA, Wigerus; att (Flemish, 1657-1721)
Dutch Shipping in a Storm Off a Quay, oil on canvas, 17x23", SBY 4/7/88 OE ... 15,400

VIVARINI, Alvise; manner of (Italian, 15th/16th C)
Portrait of a Gentleman, wearing a black & white costume & black hat; oil on canvas, 19x14", C-NY 10/20/88 OE ... 3,520

VIVARINI, Alvise; school of (Italian, 15th/16th C)
Pair: Saint Sebastian; Saint Francis (full-length portraits); oil on panel, on gold ground, 49x21", C-NY 5/31/89 ... 46,200

IAN, Calthea (American, 1857-1943)	
·easant Girl Collecting Flowers, oil on canvas laid down, sgn, 30x19", B/B 10/6/88	**1,045**
IAN, G.	
'enetian Canal, oil on canvas, sgn, 18x30", C-E 10/25/88	**1,760**
IAN, John (British, 19th C)	
;rand Canal, Venice; oil on canvas, sgn, 35x21", C-E 10/25/88	**2,420**
IN, Louis (French, 1861-1936)	
'ue de Langres, oil on canvas, sgn, 20x24", C-E 11/17/88 OE	**16,500**
O, Pio	
'isherfolk by the Coast with Vesuvius in the Distance, oil on canvas, sgn/inscr, 17x31", C-E 5/23/88 OE	**2,420**
REL, Andre Leon (French, 1896-1976)	
ւu Printemps les Arbres en Fleurs, oil on canvas, sgn/dtd 07, 15x22", WD 5/5/88 UE	**800**
·ersonnages au Bord du Lac, oil on canvas, sgn/dtd 1931, 18x22", WD 5/5/88 UE	**700**
'illage aux Arbres Fleuries, oil on canvas, sgn/dtd 1903, 18x22", WD 5/5/88 UE	**650**
ZOTTO, Alberti Guiseppe (Italian, 1862-1931)	
₹eturning Fishermen, watercolor on paper, sgn, 6x9", B/B 10/9/88	**2,200**
AMINCK, see De Vlaminck	
EGELE, A. (German, 19th C)	
:legant Gentleman in Smoking Attire, oil on canvas, sgn/dtd 1861, 15x11", SBY 6/8/88	**1,210**
GEL, Cornelis Jan; see De Vogel	
GEL, Valentine (American, -1965)	
Jntitled, standing nude figure silhouetted on balcony; oil on canvas, sgn, 24x16", SLK 2/11/89	**575**
GEL (German, 19th/20th C)	
nterior of a Cathedral, oil on canvas, sgn, 24x20", WG 9/16/88 UE	**300**
GELSANG, Christian Rudolph	
:leonora Christine Ulfeld in Prison, oil on canvas, sgn/dtd 1861, 38x32", C-E 10/25/88	**1,650**
GT, Louis Charles (American, 1864-)	
'arm in Summer, oil on canvas, sgn, 16x21", RWS 5/19/88 OE	**1,900**
₹ainy Day in Norwalk, oil on canvas, indistinctly sgn, 18x15", C-E 10/18/89	**1,320**
ILLEMONT, Charles (French, 1823-1893)	
'enus, oil on canvas laid down, sgn/dtd 1857, 18x12", B/B 9/14/89	**1,320**
IRIN, Leon Joseph (French, 1833-1887)	
.a Terrasse du Cafe du Glacier, Place Stanislas a Nancy; oil on canvas, sgn/dtd 1882, 28x36", SBY 10/24/89 OE	**148,500**
IRIOT, Guillaume	
·ortrait of Monsieur Aublet, seated three-quarter length...; oil on canvas, initialed, 51x38", C-NY 1/11/89	**52,800**
LCK, Adalbert John	
)ead Ducks, oil on canvas, initialed, 21x18", C-NY 5/26/88	**2,860**
LGER, Paul (French, 1852-1904)	
/illage Scene, oil on canvas, sgn, 24x30", FB 10/17/88	**1,400**
LKERS, Emil (German, 1831-1905)	
·ortrait of a Dappled-Gray Horse, oil on panel, sgn/dtd 1901, 13x17", RWS 11/10/89	**1,500**
₹omanian Country Folk on the Way to Market, oil on canvas, sgn/dtd 1869/inscr Ddf, 30x50", C-NY 2/23/89	**8,800**
LKERT, Edward Charles (American, 1871-1935)	
:ows in a Summer Landscape, oil on canvas, sgn, 33x29", SBY 4/14/89	**4,950**
Aorning in Lyme, oil on board, sgn/inscr, 12x16", SBY 6/24/88	**5,500**
LKHART, Max (German, 1848-1924)	
:legant Outing, oil on canvas, sgn/inscr, 27x39", C-NY 2/25/88 OE	**41,800**
LKOV, Serguei (Russian, 1956-)	
)oves (contemporary), oil on 2 canvases, sgn/dtd 1987, overall: 43x71", SBY 7/7/88 OE	**18,000**
:mblem: Knowledge (contemporary); oil on canvas, sgn/dtd 1987, 79x55", SBY 7/7/88	**11,000**
:mblem: Laurel Wreath (contemporary); oil on canvas, sgn/dtd 1987, 79x55", SBY 7/7/88	**8,400**
:mblem: Medicine (contemporary); oil on canvas, sgn/dtd 1988, 48x39", SBY 7/7/88 OE	**9,600**
Iares (contemporary), oil on canvas, sgn/dtd 1987, 59x79", SBY 7/7/88 OE	**17,000**
LL, see De Voll	
LLERDT, Johann Christian (German, 1708-1769)	
₹hine River Landscape with a Castle & a Covered Bridge, oil on canvas, 24x30", C-NY 10/20/88	**11,000**
LLMAR, Ludwig (German, 1842-1884)	
\dmonition, oil on canvas, sgn/inscr, 29x23", C-NY 2/25/88 OE	**15,400**
LLMER, Grace Libby (American, 1884-1977)	
\dobe Village, oil on board, sgn, unfr, 24x28", B/B 8/10/88	**880**
LLMERING, Joseph (American, 1810-1887)	
['ally Ho Coach in the Glen Near Newport, oil on canvas, indistinctly initialed, 22x29", SBY 9/23/88 UE	**3,300**
LLON, Alexis (French, 1865-)	
.e Quai du Louvre, Paris; oil on canvas, sgn, 11x14", C-NY 2/25/88	**4,950**
LLON, Antoine (French, 1833-1900)	
·ortrait of a Man, oil on canvas, sgn, 24x20", C-NY 5/24/89	**5,500**
3hipyard, oil on canvas, sgn, 9x21", SBY 10/24/89	**7,150**
3till Life of Ewer & Roses, oil on panel, sgn, 10x7", SBY 7/12/89 UE	**3,300**
3till Life of Fruit & an 18th-Century Marseilles Faience Soup Tureen, oil on canvas, sgn, 21x26", C-NY 5/24/89 OE	**44,000**
3till Life of Lilacs, Copper Pot, & Vessels; oil on canvas, sgn, 16x13", C-NY 5/25/88	**7,700**
3till Life of Silver Pitcher (w/tipped container & fruit on tray), oil on board, sgn, 9x7", RAB 8/9/88 UE	**500**

VOLMAR, E. (Swiss, 19th C)
Man & Young Woman Beside a Garden Gate with Sunlit Landscape & Village Beyond, oil on canvas, sgn, 27x18", SLK 2/12/88 ... 350
VOLPE, Vincenzo (Italian, 1855-1929)
In the Studio, oil on canvas, sgn, 13x10", SBY 2/22/89 OE ... 10,450
Wine & Song, oil on panel, sgn/dtd, 7x10", B/B 1/11/89 ... 770
VOLTAT, Louis (20th C)
Nature Morte aux Fleurs (floral still life), oil on canvas, initialed, ca 1940, 15x18", C-NY 2/16/89 OE ... 26,400
Vase de Fleurs (floral still life), oil on canvas, initialed, 1910, 16x14", C-NY 2/16/89 ... 16,500
VOLTZ, Friedrich Johann (German, 1817-1886)
Bringing the Herd To Drink, oil on panel, sgn/dtd 1878, 17x41", SBY 10/24/89 ... 37,400
Bulls Stopping for a Drink, oil on cradled panel, sgn, 17x11", B/B 10/9/88 OE ... 20,900
Herdsman & Cattle in a Pasture Near a Village, pencil/gray wash on gray paper, sgn/dtd 56, unfr, 6x9", C-NY 2/23/89 ... 1,210
Refreshing Water, oil on canvas, sgn/dtd 1856, unfr, 24x37", C-E 10/26/89 OE ... 24,200
VON AACHEN, Hans; att (German, 1552-1615)
Contest of Apollo & Marsyas, pen/brown ink/wash, 10x9", SBY 1/13/89 ... 4,400
VON AACHEN, Hans; circle of (German, 1552-1615)
Bathsheba at Her Toilette, oil on canvas, 54x37", C-NY 10/20/88 ... 5,500
VON AACHEN, Hans; studio of (German, 1552-1615)
Allegory of the Three Fates, oil on copper, 11" dia, SBY 4/7/88 ... 3,300
VON AHRENS, Carl Henry (Canadian, 1863-1936)
Woodland Scene, oil on canvas, sgn/dtd 14, 12x10", WAD 6/12/89 ... 300
VON AJDUKIEWICZ, Thaddeus (Polish, 1852-)
View of a Moroccan Basbah with Orange Vender, oil on canvas, sgn/dtd 1879, 26x21", B/B 9/14/89 OE ... 2,475
VON ALT, Rudolf (Austrian, 1812-1905)
Statthalterie und Thomaskirche, Brunn; watercolor heightened w/gouache over pencil, sgn, 6x7", C-NY 10/26/88 OE ... 20,900
VON AMBROS, Raphael (Czechoslovakian, 1855-1895)
Still Life of a Hookah, Tambourine, & Other Oriental Objects, oil on panel, sgn/dtd 86, 18x14", C-NY 2/25/88 ... 8,250
VON BEMMEL, Karl Sebastian; att (German, 1743-1796)
Pair: River Landscapes; gouache/vellum, 6x8", SBY 7/12/89 ... 1,870
VON BLAAS, Eugene (Austrian, 1843-1931)
At the Laundry Steps (woman standing on steps), oil on canvas, sgn/dtd, 57x29", FB 4/25/88 UE ... 18,000
Selecting the Trousseau, oil on canvas, sgn, 40x53", C-NY 5/25/88 ... 60,500
VON BREMEN, Johann Georg Meyer (German, 1813-1886)
At the Cradle, oil on canvas, sgn/dtd 1872, 22x17", C-NY 2/25/88 OE ... 37,400
At the Well (young man courting young lady), oil on canvas, sgn/dtd 1872, 27x21", C-NY 5/24/89 OE ... 44,000
Das Lesende Madchen (girl reading book in an interior), oil on canvas, ca 1848-52, 18x48", SBY 2/22/89 UE ... 8,800
Early Riser, oil on canvas, sgn, 24x20", C-NY 2/25/88 ... 16,500
First Aid, young mother seated by flax wheel bandages daughter's finger; oil on panel, sgn/dtd 1860, 11x8", RAB 11/25/88 ... 10,000
Paying the Toll, oil on panel, sgn, 6x5", C-NY 5/25/88 OE ... 9,900
Returning From the Woods, oil on canvas, sgn/dtd 1865, 20x16", C-NY 2/25/88 OE ... 33,000
Schlafendes Kind im Bett (two children watching baby sleep), oil on canvas, sgn/dtd 1851, 16x13", SBY 2/22/89 ... 15,400
VON BREMEN, Johann Georg Meyer; circle of
Feeding the Baby, oil on panel, bears signature, unfr, 24x18", C-E 5/23/88 ... 2,420
VON CALCAR, Jan Stephan (Italian, 1499-1546)
Portrait of a Man, standing three-quarter length, wearing a black costume...; oil on canvas, 38x30", C-NY 1/11/89 ... 6,050
VON DEFREGGER, Franz (German, 1835-1921)
Buberl mit Hut, oil on canvas laid down on panel, sgn, 17x13", SBY 5/23/89 ... 7,700
VON DIEPOLD, Maximilian Klein (German, 1873-)
Cows Grazing, oil on canvas, sgn, unfr, 50x60", C-E 5/23/88 ... 1,320
Fox in a Winter Landscape, oil on panel, sgn, unfr, 10x13", SBY 7/12/89 ... 880
VON ELTEN, Hendrik Dirk Kruseman (Dutch, 1829-1904)
Anglers by a Wooded Stream, oil on panel, monogramed, 15x12", PHL 10/28/88 UE ... 1,000
VON ESCHKE, Wilhelm Benjamin Hermann
Stormy Seas by Cliffs, oil on canvas, sgn/dtd 1859, 30x44", C-E 10/25/88 ... 1,640
VON FABER DU FAUR, Otto (German, 1828-1901)
Arabian Horses Drinking at Trough, oil on canvas, unfr, 53x66", SBY 2/22/89 OE ... 13,200
VON GEGERFELT, Wilhelm (Swedish, 1844-1920)
Along a Venetian Canal, watercolor over pencil, sgn, 11x7", C-NY 5/25/88 ... 825
VON GELDER, Lucia Mathilde (German, 1865-1899)
Three Generations (interior scene w/mother & children), oil on canvas, sgn, 31x26", SBY 7/12/89 UE ... 2,420
VON GLEHN, Oswald (1858-)
Lovers, Boreas & Orithyia; oil on canvas, sgn w/monogram, 1879, 25x63", C-L 6/27/88 ... 28,380
VON GRUTZNER, Eduard (German, 1846-1925)
Gentleman Filling His Pipe, oil on panel, sgn/dtd 89, 15x12", C-NY 2/23/89 ... 24,200
VON HAGEN, Eduard (German, 1934-1909)
Antique Dealer, oil on canvas, sgn, 8x6", B/B 5/17/89 ... 880
VON HERKOMER, Hubert (British, 1849-1914)
Memories, watercolor on paper, sgn/dtd 1876, 16x22", SBY 6/8/88 ... 2,420
Pair: Italian Peasant Girl; Girl with a Tambourine; watercolor, sgn/dtd 77 & 73, 8x6", FB 4/25/88 ... 380
Portrait of a Dutch Gentleman, oil on panel, monogramed/dtd 75, 12x9", B/B 1/11/89 ... 248

VON HOERMANN, Theodor (Austrian, 1840-1895)
Marche aux Fleurs a la Madeleine, oil on canvas, sgn, 18x24", SBY 10/24/89 OE ... 63,250
Marche aux Fleurs a la Madeleine avec Plantes Potageres, oil on canvas, sgn, 18x24", SBY 10/24/89 OE ... 41,800

VON JAWLENSKY, Alexej (Russian, 1864-1941)
Frauenakt (seated nude), pencil/watercolor on paper, sgn/dtd 3.2.29, 12x8", C-NY 5/12/88 ... 9,350
Frauenkopf (abstract portrait), oil on board laid down on canvas, sgn, ca 1910, 26x21", SBY 11/12/88 ... 220,000
Fruhlingsstimmung (abstract head), oil on canvas laid down on board, initialed/dtd 34, 7x4", C-NY 5/11/89 OE ... 137,500
Gesenkter Kopf, oil on board, sgn/dtd 1909/#d 25, 26x21", SBY 5/10/88 OE ... 550,000
Grosse Variation: Roter Weg; oil on canvas laid down on board, dtd 1916/#d 18, 22x14", C-NY 5/11/89 OE ... 187,000
Kopf in Gruen Farben (abstract portrait), oil on board, sgn twice/dtd 1915/titled, 15x11", SBY 11/12/88 OE ... 154,000
Kopf mit Geschlossenen Augen, watercolor/brush/ink on paper, initialed/#d 11, ca 1920-22, 10x7", SBY 5/11/88 OE ... 52,250
Liegender Akt (reclining nude), pencil on paper, 1912, 12x19", C-NY 2/16/89 OE ... 13,200
Mysticher Kopf (abstract portrait of a head), oil on board, sgn/titled, ca 1918, 20x16", SBY 11/12/88 OE ... 286,000

VON KAULBACH, Friedrich August (Geman, 1822-1903)
Portrait of Max Beckmann's Mother-in-Law, oil on canvas, sgn/dtd 1916, 43x35" oval, C-NY 2/23/89 ... 8,800

VON KLECZYNSKI, Bodhan (Polish, -1850)
Troika in the Snow, oil on canvas, sgn/dtd 1887, 32x52", C-NY 10/25/89 ... 18,700

VON KLEVER, Julius Sergius (Russian, 1850-1924)
Along the River, oil, sgn/dtd 1912, 32x27", WD 1/11/89 ... 1,300
Snow-Covered Forest at Moonlight, oil on canvas, sgn/dtd 1880, 59x41", C-NY 2/23/89 OE ... 22,000

VON KOSSAK, Woiciech (Polish, 1857-1942)
Afternoon Horse Ride, oil on canvas, sgn/dtd 1922, 41x53", C-E 10/25/88 OE ... 5,500
Bloody Sunday in St Petersburg, oil on canvas, sgn/dtd 1905, 36x63", C-L 10/8/88 ... 33,460
On Maneuvers (woman by fence, soldier w/horses, building beyond), oil on board, sgn/dtd 1928, 16x20", RWS 3/31/88 UE ... 1,200
Soldier & Nun, oil on canvas, sgn/dtd 1911, 30x23", FB 10/30/89 OE ... 3,740
Young Woman with Horse & Dog, oil on canvas, 36x30", RAB 8/9/88 ... 2,400

VON KREUZNACH, Konrad Faber (16th C)
Portrait of Dorothea von Stralenburg, Aged 26; oil on panel, inscr/dtd 1533, 20x14", C-NY 1/11/89 ... 82,500

VON LENBACH, Franz Seraph (German, 1836-1904)
Bounteous Feast, oil on canvas, sgn, 35x30", LH 10/16/88 ... 5,500
Pair: Portraits of a Man & a Woman; oil on board, in a painted oval, sgn/dtd 1894, 28x25", SBY 7/12/89 ... 12,100
Portrait of the Singer Lola Betz, oil on canvas, sgn/dtd 1898, 51x41", SBY 10/24/89 UE ... 4,950

VON MENZEL, Adolf (German, 1815-1905)
Departure, pencil on paper, sgn/dtd 92, 5x8", SBY 2/22/89 OE ... 27,500
Man in a Rocking Chair, pencil on paper, sgn/dtd 92, 5x8", SBY 2/22/89 ... 16,500

VON MUNCHAUSEN, A.
Polo, a Goalmouth Incident; colored chalk on paper, sgn/dtd 35, 25x19", C-E 10/25/88 ... 1,045

VON PAUSINGER, Clemens (German, 1855-1936)
Geisha Girl, pastel on paper laid down on canvas, sgn/dtd Munchen 88, 50x32", SBY 12/9/88 UE ... 1,980

VON PERBANDT, Carl (American, 1832-1911)
Cattle Along a River, oil on canvas, sgn, 20x36", B/B 10/6/88 ... 5,225
Figures by a House, oil on canvas, sgn/dtd 73, 15x29", B/B 6/15/89 ... 2,475

VON PERSOGLIA, Franz (Austrian, 1852-?)
Ladies Fishing in a Stream, oil on panel, sgn, 16x12", C-E 10/26/89 ... 4,950

VON PETTENKOFEN, August Xaver Carl (Austrian, 1822-1898)
Horses Fording a Stream, oil on panel, monogramed, 12x18", SBY 7/12/89 ... 4,950

VON PUTEANI, Friedrich (German, 1849-1917)
Pair: Man Carrying Water Jug; Man Warming Himself by the Fire; oil on panel, sgn/dtd 1900, 8x5", C-E 2/21/89 ... 3,850

VON SCHEIDEL, Franz Anton (1731-1801)
Anteater, watercolor over black chalk, 13x18", SBY 1/13/89 ... 1,760
Lemur, watercolor over black chalk, 13x18", SBY 1/13/89 ... 2,200
Monkey, watercolor over black chalk, 18x13", SBY 1/13/89 ... 2,200
Sheet of Studies of Conch Shells, watercolor over black chalk, #d 15, 19x13", SBY 1/13/89 ... 3,025
Sheet of Studies of Seashells, watercolor over black chalk, #d 30, 20x13", SBY 1/13/89 ... 3,025
Sheet of Studies of Shells, watercolor over black chalk, #d 71, 19x13", SBY 1/13/89 ... 1,650
Water Buffalo, watercolor over black chalk, 13x18", SBY 1/13/89 ... 1,650

VON SCHMIDT, Harold (American, 1893-)
In the Heat of the Battle (Indians rushing to fight the cavalry), oil on canvas, sgn/dtd 1951, 27x42", C-NY 5/25/89 ... 14,300
Riders in the Woods (men driving horses in wooded landscape), gouache on paper, sgn/dtd 1949, 18x25", B/B 10/9/88 ... 2,200
Shepherd of Guadaloupe (lady on veranda), no media given, sgn/dtd 1928, 34x30", SBY 6/28/89 UE ... 3,300

VON SCHNEIDAU, Christian (American, 1893-1976)
Path into the Valley, oil on canvas, sgn/dtd 1922, 18x24", B/B 10/6/88 ... 4,125
Southern California Landscape, oil on canvas, sgn/dtd 1922, 20x24", B/B 10/6/88 ... 2,750

VON SCHWEINITZ, H.
Beer Stein, oil on panel, sgn, 10x7", C-E 9/15/88 UE ... 330

VON SEVERDONCK, Franz (Belgian, 1809-1889)
Pair: Sheeps, Ducks, Rooster, & Chickens in a Landscape; oil on panel, sgn/dtd 1866, 7x10", C-E 5/23/88 OE ... 4,840

VON SIKIERS, A. (Continental, 19th C)
Homeward Bound, oil on canvas, sgn/unfr, 20x30", SBY 12/9/88 ... 990

VON STUCK, Franz (German, 1863-1928)
Dancing Nymphs (in a landscape), oil on panel, sgn, 34x36", C-NY 2/23/89 ... 24,200

Quellnymphe von Faunen Belauscht, oil on panel, sgn/dtd 1911, orig frame, 43x37", SBY 2/22/89 27,500
Tristan & Isolde, pen/ink on paper, sgn/inscr, 17x11", C-L 6/27/88 OE 4,540

VON THOREN, Karl Kasimir Otto (Austrian, 1828-1889)
Two Lost Dogs, oil on canvas, sgn, 30x24", C-E 2/23/88 UE 550

VON TROSCH, Ferdinand (Austrian, 1839-1896)
Courtesan with a Fur, oil on canvas, 39x25", WAD 6/6/88 1,200

VON WAGNER, Alexander (Hungarian, 1838-1919)
Spanish Mail Coach in Toledo, oil on canvas, sgn, 48x95", C-NY 2/25/88 OE 35,200

VON WATZDORF, M.
Guarding His Domain, oil on canvas, sgn, 32x42", C-NY 2/25/88 4,400

VON WEBER, Anton; att
Curious Elves: The Artist Looks On; watercolor/pen/gray ink, initialed/dtd 1885, 18x14", C-NY 2/25/88 UE.......... 462

VON WIEGAND, Charmion (American, 1899-)
Sarcophagus (geometric abstract), oil on canvas, sgn/inscr/dtd 1951-52, 28x12", C-NY 12/2/88 OE 17,600

VON WIERUSZ-KOWALSKI, Alfred (Polish, 1849-1915)
Der Gutsherr (hunt scene in landscape w/farmers beyond), oil on canvas, sgn, 30x41", C-NY 5/24/89 28,600
Mare & Her Foal in a Landscape, oil on canvas, sgn, 18x24", C-NY 10/25/89 9,350

VON ZUGEL, Heinrich (German, 1850-1941)
Between Gardens, oil on panel, sgn/inscr, 23x16", C-NY 2/25/88 OE 143,000
Cowherd (man leading two cows in landscape), oil on canvas, sgn/dtd 1908, 15x24", SBY 2/22/89 33,000

VONNOH, Robert (American, 1858-1933)
Baby's Bottle (portrait of grandmother feeding baby), oil on canvas, sgn, 18x22", C-NY 5/25/89.......... 24,200
Spring's Early Days (landscape), oil on panel, 6x11", C-NY 5/25/89 OE 11,000

VOOGD, Hendrick (Dutch, 1768-1839)
Landscape with Figures by a River & Mountains in the Distance, oil on canvas, sgn/dtd 1794, 19x25", SBY 1/12/89 33,000

VOORABES, J. (Continental, 19th C)
Still Life w/Peaches, Plums, Grapes, & Ewer on Table; oil on panel, sgn, 9x6", C-E 2/21/89.......... 2,200

VOORHEES, Clark Greenwood (American, 1871-1933)
Noonday Sun (view of lake), oil on canvas, 28x36", C-NY 12/2/88 12,100
Wooded Summer Landscape, oil on canvas, sgn, 12x18", NA 2/6/88.......... 650

VOORTMAN, Clara (German, 19th C)
Rhododendron in a Basket, oil on canvas, sgn/dtd 1884, 21x32", C-E 10/26/89 1,540

VOROB'EV, Maksim Nikiforovich (Russian, 1787-1855)
View of the Imperial Winter Palace, pen/ink/watercolor on paper, sgn twice/dtd 1818, 13x20", C-L 10/8/88 OE 12,080
View of the Ivan Velikii Church, Moscow; pen/ink/watercolor on paper, sgn/dtd 1818, 13x21", C-L 10/8/88 OE.......... 13,000
View of the Neva, St Petersburg; pen/ink/watercolor on paper, ca 1820, 13x23", C-L 10/8/88 OE 8,920

VOS, Hubert (American, 1855-1935)
Portrait of a Young Woman, pastel, sgn/dtd 93, 20x16", PHL 6/16/88 800

VOS, Maerten; see De Vos

VOSMAER, Jan Woutersz (1584-1641)
Study of Three Beetles, oil on panel, 3x6", SBY 1/12/89 8,800

VOSS, Carl Leopold (German, 1856-1921)
Raucous Merriment (tavern interior), oil on canvas, sgn, 27x35", C-E 2/21/89 OE 8,250
Sewing by the Window (Dutch Interior), oil on canvas, 20x16", S/A 2/18/89 4,600

VOSS, F.
Canal Scene, Holland; oil on panel, sgn, 12x16", C-E 6/28/88.......... 330

VOSS, Franklin Brooke (American, 1880-1953)
Horse in a Pasture, oil on canvas, sgn/dtd 1913, 16x22", SBY 6/10/88 2,310
Set of 3: Lapwing; Miss Hobbs; Glimmer (horses in their stables); oil on canvas, sgn/dtd 1919, 16x22", SBY 6/9/89 3,850
St James in a Landscape (horse), oil on canvas, sgn/dtd 1924, 17x24", SBY 6/9/89.......... 4,950

VOUET, Simon (French, 1590-1649)
Madonna & Child, oil on canvas, 37" dia, C-NY 1/15/88 110,000
Madonna & Child, Seated at the Foot of a Tree, a Curtain Draped Above; oil on canvas, 20x15", C-NY 5/31/89 104,500

VOUET, Simon; circle of (French, 1590-1649)
Madonna & Child, oil on canvas, 34x28", C-NY 4/6/89 UE.......... 2,200

VRANCX, Sebastian (Flemish, 1573-1647)
Elegant Company on a Terrace with a Cavalier on a Rearing Horse, oil on panel, sgn w/monogram, 13x19", SBY 6/3/88 UE.......... 34,100
Peasant Leading a Wagon Towards a House & Travelers on a Path...; oil on panel, 27x40", C-NY 1/11/89 UE 31,900

VRANCX, Sebastian; att (Flemish, 1573-1647)
Largo di Palazzo, Naples; oil on canvas, 37x58", C-NY 10/12/89 OE 46,200

VRANCX, Sebastian; circle of (Flemish, 1573-1647)
Extensive Landscape with Figures & Cottages, a Castle in the Distance; oil on canvas, 28x44", SBY 4/7/88 OE 20,900
Pair: Town in Winter & Spring; oil on canvas, 30x45", SBY 10/21/88 OE 99,000
Turkish Army Attacking an Encampment, oil on canvas, 48x70", C-NY 10/12/89 OE 46,200

VREEDENBURGH, Cornelius (Dutch, 1880-1946)
Calm Cove, oil on canvas laid down on board, sgn, 23x35", C-E 5/22/89 6,820
Peaceful Canal & Farm, oil on canvas, sgn, 16x24", B/B 3/22/89.......... 3,850
Washerwoman at a River, oil on canvas, sgn, 19x30", PHL 10/28/88 OE 4,750

VREELAND, Francis William (American, 1879-1954)
Shepherdess, watercolor on paper, sgn, unfr, 26x20", B/B 9/15/88.......... 385

VREL, Jacobus; circle of (fl 1654-1662)
View of a Small Street in a Dutch Town, oil on panel, 15x13", SBY 10/13/89 OE ... **31,900**
View of a Small Street in a Dutch Town, oil on panel, 15x13", SBY 6/3/88 ... **17,600**
VRIENDT, see De Vriendt
VRIES, see De Vries
VUILLARD, Edouard (French, 1868-1940)
Auto-Portrait, charcoal on paper, stamped initials, ca 1888-89, 11x7", SBY 10/6/89 OE ... **18,700**
Dans le Jardin, pastel on bluish-green paper, stamped initials, ca 1926, 10x13", SBY 11/12/88 OE ... **46,750**
Deux Femmes au Fauteuil, pencil on sketchbook paper, stamped w/initials, ca 1930, 7x4", SBY 10/7/88 ... **2,475**
Double-Sided: Nature Morte; Homme; recto: pastel, verso: charcoal, stamped signature, ca 1889, 13x16", C-NY 11/15/88 ... **55,000**
Femme avec un Chapeau (portrait), oil on board mounted to stretcher, stamped signature, 1901, 18x15", C-NY 11/14/88 OE ... **242,000**
Femme Lisant (La Lettre), oil on board, stamped signature, ca 1893, 8x10", C-NY 11/14/88 OE ... **319,000**
Interieur, oil/pastel on canvas-backed paper laid down on masonite, stamped signature, ca 1905, 25x22", SBY 11/12/88 OE ... **126,500**
Interieur Mystere (mysterious interior), oil on board, stamped signature, ca 1895, 14x15", C-NY 5/11/89 ... **286,000**

Jeu de Cartes, pastel on paper laid down on canvas, sgn, 1932, 13x10", C-NY 11/15/89 OE; $143,000

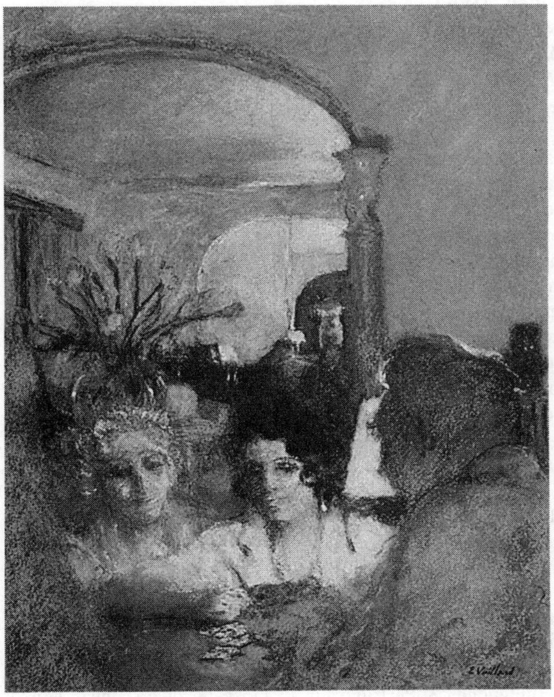

Joueurs de Cartes, peinture a la calle on paper laid down on canvas, stamped, 1909, 17x22", C-NY 11/15/88 OE ... **209,000**
La Goule et Valentin le Deposse, pastel on tan paper, stamped signature, #d Lugt #2497b, 1895, 10x6", SBY 5/10/89 OE ... **79,200**
La Robe Rose (robed figure on mount), oil on board, stamped signature, ca 1890, 8x11", C-NY 11/14/88 OE ... **121,000**
La Route Ensoleilee l'Etang-la-Ville, oil on canvas, sgn, 1899, 9x14", SBY 5/11/88 ... **82,500**
La Table de Salle a Manger (still life in interior), oil on canvas, stamped signature, 18x15", SBY 10/7/88 OE ... **37,400**
Le Metro a Paris, Wagon Premiere Classe; peinture a la colle on brown paper on canvas, stamped, 22x21", C-NY 5/12/88 OE ... **93,500**
Le Petit Jardinier (the little gardener), oil on board, stamped signature, 10x10", C-NY 5/11/89 ... **77,000**
Le Salon, portrait of Mme Lilita Henraux in her salon; oil on canvas, sgn, ca 1935-36, 35x37", SBY 11/15/89 OE ... **1,650,000**
Le Tennis (seated lady by tennis court), oil/pencil on board laid down on canvas, initialed, 1907, 8x5", C-NY 11/14/88 ... **82,500**
Les Communs aux Clayes (landscape), pastel on brown paper laid down on board, stamped initials, 9x10", C-NY 2/18/88 OE ... **13,200**
Ma Grand-Mere (portrait), oil on board laid down on cradled panel, stamped signature, 1890, 8x7", C-NY 11/14/88 OE ... **308,000**
Ma Mere (profile view of artist's seated mother), oil on board, sgn, ca 1895, 10x8", C-NY 11/14/88 ... **198,000**
Madame Hessel dans le Jardin, pastel on reddish-brown paper affixed to board, sgn, ca 1920, 10x14", SBY 5/11/88 OE ... **110,000**
Madame Hessel dans son Salon, Rue de Rivoli (interior scene); oil on cradled panel, sgn, ca 1900, 22x19", SBY 5/9/89 ... **742,500**
Madame Hessel Lisant, peinture l'essence on paper laid down on canvas, stamped signature, ca 1917, 43x24", SBY 11/12/88 ... **49,500**
Madame Roussel at Dresser, oil on board, stamped signature, ca 1893, 12x9", SBY 5/10/89 ... **137,000**
Pair: Femme Assise dans un Fauteuil; Femme se Reposant sur un Canape; pencil on sketchbook paper, ca 1918, SBY 2/16/89 ... **6,600**
Pair: Floral Still Life; Studies of a Young Girl; pencil on paper, stamped initials, 5x5", 6x4", SBY 2/14/89 ... **5,500**
Portrait de Femme, colored chalk on buff paper laid down on board, initialed/dtd 93, 9x5" irregular shape, SBY 10/7/88 ... **7,150**
Portrait de Jane Renouart, First Version; oil on canvas, sgn, 1926, 40x32", SBY 5/10/89 ... **308,000**
Portrait of a Seated Lady (Annette Salomon), pastel on gray paper, stamped signature, ca 1928, 24x19", SBY 5/11/88 OE ... **93,500**
Pot de Roses, oil on board, stamped w/initials, 12x11", SBY 5/11/88 ... **41,250**
Sacha Guitry dans sa Loge (interior scene of dressing room), pastel on paper, sgn, ca 1911-12, 30x38", C-NY 5/12/88 OE ... **418,000**
Scene Interieur: Madame Vuillard dans sa Salle a Manger; pencil on paper, stamp initialed, ca 1900, 4x7", SBY 2/16/89 ... **4,400**
Vase de Fleurs, oil on canvas, sgn, 12x10", SBY 11/12/88 ... **93,500**
Visage de Profil (woman's face in profile), oil on board, stamped signature, 6x4", C-NY 5/11/89 OE ... **79,200**
14 Juillet (night scene), oil on canvas, initialed, 10x4", SBY 10/6/89 OE ... **46,750**

VULLIAMY, Gerard (French, 1909-)
Composition 132, oil on canvas, sgn/dtd 60, 31x51", LH 10/16/88 OE 1,100
VYTLACIL, Vaclav (American, 1892-)
Abstraction, casein/tempera on board, sgn/dtd 1938, 24x18", SBY 6/24/88 OE 4,675
Composition, oil on masonite, sgn twice/titled/inscr Sparkill NY Price $400, 21x25", SBY 1/24/89 2,200
Still Life with Melons (contemporary), gouache on board, sgn twice/dtd 1931/titled, 17x24", SBY 1/24/89 2,475
Two Girls, casein/tempera on board, sgn/dtd 1947, 20x16", SBY 9/23/88 UE 880
WACHTEL, Elmer (American, 1864-1929)
California Ranch, oil on canvasboard, sgn, 14x18", B/B 10/6/88 6,050
WACHTEL, Marion Kavanaugh (American, 1876-1954)
California Landscape, watercolor on paper, sgn/inscr artist insignia, 20x30", SBY 5/24/89 34,100
Distant Sea, watercolor on paper, sgn, 24x32", C-NY 12/2/88 OE 66,000
Eucalyptus at Sunset, watercolor on paper, sgn, 20x16", SBY 6/24/88 OE 22,000
Mazatlan, Mexico; oil on board, sgn, 10x12", B/B 10/6/88 2,090
Valley, watercolor on paper laid down on board, sgn, 18x24", C-NY 9/30/88 OE 25,300
WADHAM, B.B. (British, 19th C)
Rivers Landscape with Fishermen, oil on canvas, sgn, 20x30", WG 4/23/88 325
WAEL, see De Wael
WAGEMAEKERS, Victor (Flemish, 1876-)
Wooded Landscape with Streams, oil on canvas, sgn, 24x20", SLK 5/11/88 850
WAGNER, F.
Landscape with Boats, oil on canvas, sgn, 29x40", LH 5/15/88 OE 800
WAGNER, Ferdinand (German, 1819-1891)
Vegetable Market, oil on canvas, sgn, 62x96", SBY 10/24/89 49,500
WAGNER, Fritz (German, 1896-1939)
Fine Vintage, oil on canvas, sgn, 9x7", DM 1/15/88 1,600
Happy Monk, oil on canvas, sgn, 9x7", DM 1/15/88 1,400
Listening to the Lute Player, oil on canvas, sgn/inscr, 28x34", SBY 12/9/88 4,950
Peasants Carousing in a Tavern, oil on canvas, sgn/inscr, 24x20", C-E 2/23/88 OE 4,180
WAGNER, Helene (German, 19th C)
Scene in Wiesenthal (extensive landscape), oil on canvas, sgn, 27x39", B/B 10/9/88 3,300
WAGNER, Karl (German/Austrian, 19th/20th C)
Garden View Along the Capri Coast, oil on canvas, sgn, 29x39", B/B 5/17/89 4,950
WAGSTAFF, Samuel (British, 19th C)
On the River Nidd, Knaresboro; oil on canvas, sgn/dtd 1881, 18x22", C-E 1/12/88 UE 385
WAHLBERG, Alfred (Swedish, 1834-1906)
Moonlit River Landscape with a Figure, oil on panel, sgn, 20x29", C-NY 10/25/89 7,150
WAIN, Louis William (British, 1860-1939)
Champagne Breakfast (satirical, dogs drinking champagne at table), oil on canvas, 27x46", SBY 6/10/88 11,000
WAINEWRIGHT, Thomas Francis (British, 19th C)
Richmond Hill, Surrey; oil on canvas, sgn, 36x48", C-NY 5/25/88 4,400
WAINWRIGHT, John (British, 19th C)
Dead Rabbit, Snipe, Bullfinches, & Partridges in a Landscape; oil on canvas, sgn/dtd 1855, 19x23", C-E 2/23/88 1,650
WAIT, Blanche E. (American, 1895-1934)
Child in a Woodland Setting, oil on canvas, sgn, 30x26", B/B 8/10/88 522
WAITE, Harold; att (British, 1870-1939)
Footbridge (children picking flowers beside footbridge), oi l on canvas, 24x18", RWS 3/31/88 425
Waite, M.C. (American, 20th C)
Rough Surf, oil on canvas, sgn, 22x28", RAB 8/9/88 UE 125
WALBOURN, Ernest (British, fl 1897-1904)
Garden Gate, three figures in landscape w/farm building; oil on canvas, sgn, 20x30", SLK 4/7/89 2,500
On the River, oil on canvas, sgn, 23x36", SBY 5/23/89 11,000
Primrose Time, Surrey; oil on canvas, sgn, 26x32", WAD 6/6/88 OE 11,500
WALCOTT, Harry Mills (American, 1870-1944)
School's Out, oil on canvas, sgn/dtd Copyright 1904, 23x35", SBY 5/25/88 OE 159,000
WALD, Paul Johann
Marshy Stream, oil on canvas, sgn/dtd Munchen, 23x46", C-E 2/16/88 UE 440
WALDE, Alfons (Austrian, 1891-1958)
Einsame Hausung, oil on board, sgn, ca 1934-35, 28x20", SBY 10/6/89 41,250
Tiroler Dorf (Aurach), oil on board, sgn, ca 1925, 18x12", SBY 10/6/89 29,700
WALDEN, Lionel (American, 1861-1933)
Gondola, watercolor on paper, sgn, 11x16", C-E 4/7/88 UE 220
Venice Harbor, watercolor on paper, sgn, 11x16", C-E 4/7/88 UE 275
WALDMULLER, Ferdinand Georg; circle of (Austrian, 1793-1865)
Son's Gift, oil on canvas, 17x14", C-E 10/26/89 2,420
WALDO, Samuel Lovett (American, 1783-1861)
Marie Underhill Van Zandt (portrait), oil on canvas, 30x25", C-NY 5/25/89 4,400
WALDO, Samuel Lovett; & JEWETT, Wm. (American, 17th/18th C)
Pair: Dr FL & Mrs Margaret Chirvis Wilsey; oil on canvas, sgn/dtd New York 1852, 29x36", SBY 3/17/88 2,200
WALKER, Charles Alvah (American, 1848-1920)
Road in Winter (woman on snowy path), watercolor/gouache on paper, sgn, 13x19", RWS 9/29/88 275

WALKER, Ethel (British, 1861-1951)
Three Graces, watercolor on paper, sgn/dtd 1928, 27x33", C-L 6/27/88 OE 4,919
WALKER, Frank H. (British, fl 1878-1893)
Quiet Moment by the River, watercolor on paper, sgn/dtd 92, 14x21", SBY 12/9/88 1,540
WALKER, Frederick (British, 1840-1875)
Woman Picking Flowers, watercolor on paper, initialed, no size given, FAP 11/4/88 UE 225
WALKER, Frederick; after (British, 1840-1875)
Destitute Family, oil on canvas, 33x50", SBY 6/8/88 605
WALKER, Harold E. (American, 1890-)
Fishing Boats at Port, oil on canvas, sgn, 20x34", RWS 3/16/89 475
WALKER, Henry Oliver (American, 1843-1929)
Ambition, oil on board, sgn/dtd on label on verso, 17x14", SBY 3/17/88 1,100
Mother & Child, pastel on paper, sgn/dtd 1886, 29x24", WL 5/20/88 750
Still Life of Roses (in a green glass vase), oil on canvas, sgn, 13x16", RWS 9/29/88 OE 1,600
WALKER, Horatio (Canadian, 1858-1838)
Loading the Sleigh at Dusk (barn, man & oxen), oil on canvas, sgn/dtd 1918, 18x24", FB 10/17/88 39,000
WALKER, James Alexander (British, 1841-1898)
Mounted Arabs, oil on canvas, sgn, 36x29", SBY 12/9/88 2,750
Napoleon Watching the Battle of Friedland, 1807; oil on canvas, sgn/dtd 1885, 39x60", SBY 2/22/89 OE 132,000
Napoleon's Dragoons of the Guard Lost in the Snow, oil on canvas, sgn/dtd 1882, 23x36", SBY 5/23/89 18,700
WALKER, John (20th C)
Form & Image (abstract composition), oil on canvas, sgn/dtd 83, 85x67", SBY 11/9/89 30,250
Lesson One (contemporary), oil on canvas, 1984, 96x78", SBY 11/11/88 30,800
Oceania III (abstract), oil on canvas, 1982, 96x120", SBY 11/9/89 35,750
Shape & Ornament Clam (abstract), oil on canvas, 1985, 84x66", SBY 2/15/89 22,000
Study for Martyr, oil on canvas, sgn/dtd 1981, 24x20", SBY 2/15/89 4,950
Two Cultures I (contemporary), oil on canvas, sgn, 1983, 85x67", SBY 5/3/89 24,200
Untitled (abstract composition), charcoal on paper, sgn/dtd 82, 50x38", lot 322, SBY 2/15/89 1,980
Untitled (abstract composition), charcoal on paper, sgn/dtd 82, 50x38", lot 321, SBY 2/15/89 2,200
Untitled (abstract sketch), colored chalks on paper, sgn/dtd 1982, 43x30", C-NY 10/4/89 1,980
Untitled (abstract), charcoal/conte crayon on paper, sgn/dtd 82, 50x38", C-NY 11/10/88 2,860
Untitled (abstract), oil on canvas, sgn/dtd 1982, 16x12", C-NY 11/10/88 4,950
Untitled (Alba with Skull), oil on canvas, 81x56", C-NY 11/10/88 OE 35,200
WALKER, M. (British, 19th C)
Highlands Lake with Sailboats, oil on canvas, sgn, 11x14", SLK 9/29/88 130
Pair: Highland Landscapes at Sunset with Foreground Water; oil on canvas, 10x14", SLK 5/12/88 175
WALKER, Robert; school of
Portrait of Oliver Cromwell, wearing suit of armor, with an attendant; oil on canvas, inscr, 81x49", C-NY 10/20/88 OE 8,800
WALKER, William Aiken (American, 1838-1921)
At the Levee, oil on panel, sgn, 6x12", C-NY 5/26/88 9,350
Boy with Torn Jacket (portrait), oil on canvas, sgn/dtd 1890, 8x7", C-NY 5/26/88 5,500
Cabin, oil on board, sgn, 9x12", SBY 9/23/88 6,600
Cabin (landscape w/cotton pickers & cabin), oil on board, sgn, 6x12", C-NY 12/2/88 6,600
Cabin Chores (landscape w/cabin & cotton pickers), oil on board, sgn, 6x12", C-NY 12/2/88 8,800
Cabin Porch, oil on board, sgn, 9x12", SBY 9/23/88 9,350
Cabin Scene, oil on board, sgn, 6x12", SBY 6/28/89 7,700
Cabin Scene, oil on panel, sgn, 6x12", NA 2/24/89 5,000
Cotton Picker (full-length portrait), oil on board, initialed, 12x16", C-NY 9/28/89 4,400
Cotton Pickers, oil on board, sgn, 9x12", NA 3/26/88 9,000
Cotton Pickers Returning From the Fields, oil on board, sgn, 7x13", SBY 9/14/89 11,000
Cuban Man, oil on canvas, 10x8", C-E 6/1/88 OE 3,520
Family Outside the Cabin, oil on board, sgn, 6x12", SBY 9/23/88 8,250
Female Cotton Picker, oil on board, sgn, 12x6", LH 10/16/88 OE 5,500
Figures on a Cabin Porch, oil on board, sgn, 6x12", B/B 3/17/88 5,500
Flower Girl (standing full-length in landscape), oil on card, sgn, 13x10", PHL 12/1/88 11,000
Good Crop (two cotton pickers in landscape), oil on panel, sgn, 6x12", C-NY 12/2/88 7,150
Making a Point (two figures by cotton field, cotton picker & house beyond), oil on panel, sgn, 10x5", NA 2/6/88 1,600
Male Cotton Picker, oil on board, sgn, 12x6", LH 10/16/88 OE 5,500
Man's Labor & a Man's Pleasure, oil on board, 9x12", C-NY 9/30/88 2,420
Opossum Hunter (man holds opossom, cotton field beyond), oil on board, sgn, 14x6", NA 5/13/89 7,500
Pair: Cotton Pickers (full-length portraits); oil on board, ea sgn, ea 13x7", SBY 6/28/89 9,350
Pair: Cotton Pickers; oil on board, sgn, 10x6", C-SK 6/9/88 14,870
Pair: Cotton Pickers; oil on board, sgn, 12x6", C-NY 3/11/88 7,700
Ruins of South Carolina Home, oil on board, sgn/dtd Oct 16, 1918, 12x6", NA 3/26/88 4,250
Sharecroppers, oil on board, sgn, 6x13", SBY 9/23/88 6,050
Sharecroppers' Cabins, oil on board, sgn, 6x12", SBY 1/24/89 7,700
South Carolina Cabin with Figures & Cotton Field, oil on board, sgn, unfr, 6x12", SBY 9/23/88 7,700
Study of a Sea Trout, oil on canvas, sgn/dtd 1903, unfr, 16x31", RAB 11/25/88 OE 4,750
Summer Meadows, oil on canvas, sgn/dtd 1909, 8x14", B/B 9/14/89 UE 550
Taking Cotton to Market, oil on panel, sgn, 6x12", C-NY 5/26/88 8,250
Two Plantation Workers in Cotton Field, oil on board, sgn, unfr, 6x12", SBY 9/23/88 7,150

Whoa Mule, oil on board, sgn, 12x9", C-NY 5/26/88 6,600

WALKER, William Aiken; att (American, 1838-1921)
Rabbit Hunter, oil on canvas, 9x8", NA 5/13/89 UE 2,000

WALKLEY, David Birdsey (American, 1849-1934)
Coastal Scene, oil on canvas, sgn, 12x16", C-E 9/15/88 OE 2,090

WALKOWITZ, Abraham (American, 1880-1965)
Abstract Design, watercolor/pencil/India ink on paper, sgn/dtd 1912, 18x12", SBY 4/14/89..... 1,650
At the Beach (figures in water & on shore), oil on canvas, sgn, 8x11", C-E 6/1/89 1,540
Bather (seated, posterior view), oil on canvasboard, sgn, 16x12", C-NY 9/28/89..... 6,600
Carnival (figures before/inside House of Clowns), oil on canvas, sgn, 25x40", SBY 5/24/89 22,000
Dancing Figure, pen/ink/watercolor, sgn, 13x8", PHL 10/28/88..... 500
Fishermen, watercolor/pencil on paper, sgn, 22x31", C-E 6/1/88..... 2,420
Group of 5: Isadora Duncan Dancing; black ink/pencil/watercolor on paper, sgn, unfr, 7x3", lot 271, SBY 6/28/89 1,320
Group of 5: Isadora Duncan Dancing; black ink/pencil/watercolor on paper, unfr, 11x8" to 14x9", lot 272, SBY 6/28/89 2,420
Head of a Rabbi, watercolor, sgn/dtd 1910, 10x8", PHL 10/28/88 UE 200
Isadora Duncan Dancing, watercolor/pencil on paper, sgn/dtd 1939, 14x8", SBY 4/14/89..... 880
Nude Bathers, oil on canvas, sgn, 25x30", C-NY 5/26/88..... 9,350
Trees on a Hillside, watercolor on paper, sgn/dtd 1912, 14x18", B/B 12/8/88 1,045
Untitled (human abstract), pencil/charcoal on paper, sgn, 21x16", SBY 6/24/88 OE..... 1,540
Woman Bathing (in bathtub), oil on canvas laid down on board, sgn, 18x24", SBY 4/14/89 4,400

WALL, J.
Pair: Reading to Grandmother; Playing with Dolls; oil on canvas, sgn, 13x8", C-E 5/23/88 UE 220

WALL, W. (American, 19th C)
Beached, oil on canvas, sgn, 12x25", C-E 2/23/88..... 1,210

WALL, William Allen (American, 1801-1885)
Monument (Battle Monument at Condord, Massachusetts), watercolor/gouache on paper, sgn, 13x19", RAB 8/8/89 UE 1,600

WALL, William Guy (American, 1792-1862)
Rowers on a Lake, oil on canvas, sgn, 15x25", C-NY 5/26/88..... 9,900
Stroll Along the Lake, oil on board, sgn, 8x11", C-NY 5/26/88 3,300
West Point on the Hudson, oil on panel, in painted oval, sgn, 8x10", C-NY 5/26/88 OE..... 8,800
West Point on the Hudson (panoramic view), oil on panel, sgn, in a painted oval, 8x10", C-NY 9/28/89..... 6,600

WALLACE, David (American, 20th C)
Plowing, watercolor, sgn/dtd, 20x24", FAP 11/4/88 OE..... 800

WALLACE, Donald (British, 20th C)
Tiger, Tiger; oil on canvas, sgn, 24x36", FAP 4/15/89 495

WALLACE, James (British, -1911)
Landscape with Figures & Cottages by a Stream, oil on canvas, sgn, 20x30", C-E 6/28/88 UE 440

WALLACE, Raymond L. (American, 20th C)
International String Quartette, four tuxedoed men playing in concert; oil on masonite, sgn/dtd 67, 34x45", RAB 8/8/89 UE..... 350

WALLER, Frank (American, 1842-1923)
Shady New York Road, oil on canvasboard, sgn/dtd 22, 7x11", B/B 5/17/89 UE..... 302
Tomb of Mameluke, oil on canvas, sgn/dtd 75, 12x28", C-E 10/18/89 2,860
Walk in the Country (man walking along road beside woods), oil on canvas, sgn, 13x20", RWS 9/29/88..... 800

WALLER, Samuel Edmond (British, 1850-1903)
Horsemen Outside the Traveler's Joy Inn, oil on canvas, sgn, 19x29", WAD 6/6/88 2,200

WALRAVEN, Jan (Dutch, 1827-1874)
Schoolgirl, oil on panel, sgn, 16x13", C-E 5/23/88..... 2,860

WALSH, A.A. (American, 19th/20th C)
Hamilton's Flight Between Philadelphia & New York, oil on canvas, sgn/dtd 1910/titled, 30x24", SBY 1/24/89..... 935

WALTENSPERGER, Charles E. (American, 1871-1931)
Dutch Interior with Mother & Child, oil on canvas, sgn, 16x20", DM 10/14/88 1,000
Meeting at the Dock, oil on board, sgn/titled, 11x14", RAB 8/8/89 UE..... 1,000
Small Bouquet of Daisies (side view of seated lady), oil on canvas, sgn, 20x16", C-NY 9/28/89 1,980

WALTER, Christian J. (American, 1872-1938)
Impressionistic View of the Allegheny, the Hogger-Weimer Homestead; oil on canvas, sgn, 31x40", RWS 3/31/88 3,200

WALTER, Martha (American, 1875-1976)
At the Beach (close-up of figures on beach), oil on gessoed board, 14x18", C-NY 5/25/89 OE..... 44,000
Beach Scene (impressionistic), oil on canvasboard, sgn, 13x18", C-NY 5/25/89 OE 19,800
Breton Fishermen (four fishermen talking), oil on canvas, sgn, 16x20", WD 10/5/88 2,000
Czechoslovakian Immigrants, Ellis Island; oil on board artist estate stamp/sgn, 14x18", C-NY 5/25/89..... 7,700
Little Miss Echman (portrait), oil on canvasboard, ca 1913-14, 16x13", C-NY 3/11/88 3,850
Red-Haired Child (portrait), oil on board, sgn/bears estate stamp, 18x14", C-NY 12/2/88 6,050
Spanish Gypsies Dancing in a Cave Where They Lived, oil on artist board, sgn, 16x20", WD 10/5/88 2,200
Two Children & Their Pets (in an interior), oil on canvas, sgn, 40x35", C-E 6/1/89..... 6,820

WALTERS, Emile (American, 1893-)
House, oil on canvas, sgn, 20x32", C-E 2/1/89 1,100

WALTERS, George Stanfield (British, 1838-1924)
Elegant Lady with Flowers & Pearls Said To Be Madame de Chaumette, oil on canvas, sgn, 20x24", C-E 5/23/88 1,650
Sailboats, watercolor on paper, sgn/dtd 1872, 8x15", B/B 1/11/89 OE 1,210
Southwold Boats Going Out, watercolor heightened w/white, sgn, 7x10", C-E 2/21/89 770
Thames Barges in an Estuary, watercolor, sgn, 7x10", PHL 10/28/88 550

Wreck Off the Welsh Coast, watercolor, bears signature, 9x18", FAP 12/8/89 275

WALTON, Frank (British, 1840-1928)

Garden View, oil on canvas, sgn/dtd 1914, 22x36", C-E 5/22/89 3,520

WANKIE, Wladyslaw (19th C)

Halt by the Way, oil on canvas, sgn/dtd 1881, 27x22", C-E 10/25/88 4,400

WARD, Edgar Melville Jr. (American, 1887-)

In the Kitchen (lady sits at open window peeling apples), oil on canvas mounted on board, sgn, 27x19", RWS 3/31/88 550

WARD, Edward Matthew (British, 1816-1879)

Autolycus, Perdita & Florizet-the Winters Tale; oil on panel, sgn, 14x18", C-E 11/8/88 1,000

WARD, James (British, 1769-1859)

Death of Phaethon, oil on canvas, initialed/dtd 1806, 18x15", WD 5/5/88 10,500
Discussing the Catch, oil on canvas, sgn/dtd 1797, 12x14", C-NY 2/25/88 3,520
Marquess of Londonderry's Arabian Stallion in a Landscape, oil on canvas, monogramed/dtd 1831, 37x49", SBY 6/9/89 297,000
Pair: Disobedience in Danger; Disobedience Detected; oil on canvas, 1 sgn/dtd 1797, 28x36", SBY 6/3/88 40,700
Shepherd Tending His Flock, oil on canvas, sgn/dtd 1796, 18x23", SBY 4/7/89 OE 7,150
Studies of Feet & Hands, From the Elgin Marbles; black/white chalk on paper, initialed, unfr, 12x9", C-NY 10/31/89 UE 110

WARD, S. (British, 19th C)

Constitution & Guerriere (ships at sea), watercolor on paper, sgn/dtd 1812, 6x9", RAB 3/14/89 UE 400

WARDLE, Arthur (British, 1864-1949)

Among Friends (woman reading by garden steps, dogs resting about feet), oil on canvas, sgn, 31x20", SBY 10/24/89 23,100
Champion Bulldogs, oil on canvas, sgn/dtd 1903, 30x48", SBY 6/10/88 OE 44,000
Fox Terrier with Hare, oil on canvas, sgn, 30x25", SBY 6/9/89 3,960
I Only Want To Play (cat & dog in an interior), oil on canvas, sgn/dtd 1890, 30x25", SBY 6/10/88 5,775
Japanese Chin (portrait of a dog's head), oil on canvas, sgn, 22x14", C-NY 2/23/89 OE 14,300
Rabbiting, oil on canvas, sgn/dtd 1907, 17x22", SBY 6/9/89 11,000
Reluctant Playmates (girl w/puppies), oil on canvas, sgn, 26x36", C-NY 5/25/88 20,900
Terriers on the Scent, oil on canvas, sgn, 24x18", C-NY 5/24/89 11,000
Two Scotties in a Landscape, oil on canvas laid down on panel, sgn, 23x17", C-NY 5/24/89 15,400
Woman Reading in the Garden with Her Collies, oil on canvas, sgn, 31x20", B/B 6/15/89 OE 13,200

WARDLEWORTH, J.L. (British, 19th C)

Courtship (couple in interior), oil on canvas, sgn/dtd 92, 37x38", C-E 2/21/89 330

WARE, G.S. (American, 19th C)

Wading Through a River, oil on canvas, sgn/dtd 1892, 19x31", FAP 4/15/89 220

WARHOL, Andy (American, 1928-1987)

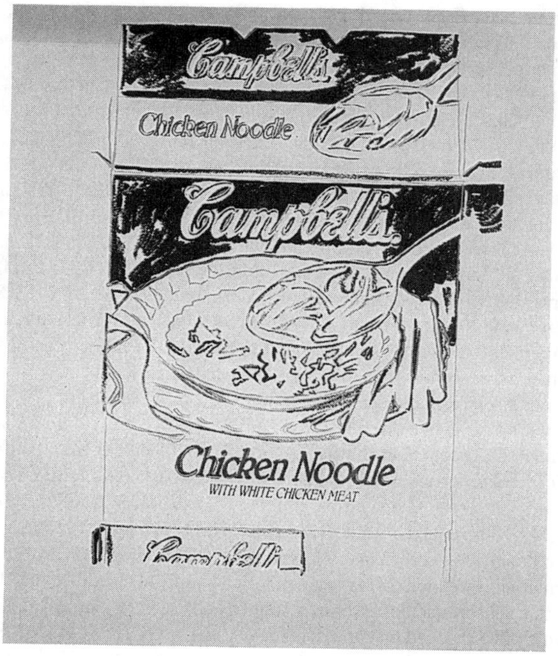

Campbell's Soup Box: Chicken Noodle; synthetic polymer silkscreen on canvas, sgn/dtd 85, 72x60" C-NY 11/8/89; $220,000

$, synthetic polymer silkscreened on canvas, sgn, ca 1982, 10x8", SBY 5/3/88 OE 24,200
$, synthetic polymer silkscreened on canvas, sgn/dtd 1982, 10x8", lot 255, C-NY 5/4/88 OE 27,500
$, synthetic polymer silkscreened on canvas, sgn/dtd 81, lot 36, SBY 11/11/88 35,750
$, synthetic polymer silkscreened on canvas, sgn/dtd 81, 10x8", lot 213, SBY 10/5/89 27,500
$, synthetic polymer silkscreened on canvas, sgn/dtd 81, 20x16", lot 192, SBY 10/8/88 41,250
$, synthetic polymer silkscreened on canvas, sgn/dtd 81, 90x70", SBY 2/15/89 OE 203,500
$, synthetic polymer silkscreened on canvas, sgn/dtd 82, 10x8", lot 322A, SBY 5/3/89 OE 35,750
$, synthetic polymer silkscreened on canvas, sgn/dtd 82, 10x8", lot 308, SBY 5/3/89 18,700
$, synthetic polymer silkscreened on canvas, sgn/dtd 82, 20x16", lot 325, SBY 5/3/89 OE 49,500

$, synthetic polymer silkscreened on canvas, sgn/inscr, 16x20", SBY 2/15/89	25,300
$, synthetic polymer silkscreened on canvas, sgn/inscr/dtd 81, 10x8", lot 327, SBY 10/8/88	20,900
$, synthetic polymer silkscreened on canvas, stamped signature/dtd 1982, 10x8", lot 209, SBY 10/5/89 OE	30,250
$, synthetic polymer silkscreened on canvas, 1981, 90x70", lot 337, SBY 11/11/88	165,000
A&P Surprise, gold leaf/pen/black ink/varnished paper cutouts on paper, sgn, 22x28", C-NY 2/20/88	9,900
Air Mail, acrylic silkscreened on canvas, sgn/dtd 1962, 8x10", SBY 5/3/88	13,200
Album of a Mat Queen (female wrestler), synthetic polymer silkscreened on canvas, inscr, 1963, 10x20", SBY 2/15/89	19,800
Andy Warhol's Mother (cat caricature), pen/black ink on paper, sgn, ca 1957, 23x14", C-NY 2/14/89 OE	7,700
Angel (line drawing), pen/ink on paper, 11x8", SBY 10/7/89	2,310
Anne Willaumez` Dog, gold leaf/brush/black ink on paper, sgn, 19x10", C-NY 11/10/88 OE	41,800
Be a Somebody with a Body, synthetic polymer on canvas, sgn/dtd 85, unfr, 8x10", C-NY 5/4/89 OE	12,100
Be a Somebody with a Body, synthetic polymer silkscreened on canvas, inscr/dtd 1986, 11x14", SBY 5/3/89	19,800
Be a Somebody with a Body, synthetic polymer silkscreened on canvas, sgn/dtd 85, unfr, 8x10", C-NY 10/4/89	14,300
Blue Lobster, synthetic polymer silkscreened on canvas, sgn, unfr, 20x16", C-NY 2/14/89 OE	37,400
Campbell's Noodle Soup Box, synthetic polymer silkscreened on canvas, sgn/dtd 86, 20x20", C-NY 5/4/89 OE	51,700
Campbell's Onion Soup Box, synthetic polymer silkscreened on canvas, sgn/dtd 86, unfr, 14x14", C-NY 2/14/89 OE	35,200
Campbell's Soup Box: Chicken Rice; synthetic polymer silkscreened on canvas, sgn/dtd 86, 20x20", SBY 5/3/89 OE	49,500
Campbell's Soup Box: Onion Mushroom; synthetic polymer silkscreened on canvas, sgn/dtd 86, 20x20", SBY 5/3/89	44,000
Campbell's Soup Can, synthetic polymer silkscreened on canvas, sgn/dtd 85, 20x16", C-NY 2/14/89	31,900
Candy Box, diamond dust/synthetic polymer paint silkscreened on canvas, 14x11", SBY 2/15/89 OE	22,000
Chris Evert (portrait), synthetic polymer silkscreened on canvas, 1977, 40x40", SBY 5/3/89 OE	88,000
Colored Campbell's Soup Can, synthetic polymer silkscreened on canvas, 1965, 36x24", SBY 11/9/89 OE	528,000
Dog, acrylic & synthetic polymer silkscreened on canvas, sgn/dtd 1976, 50x40", C-NY 5/3/89	88,000
Donald Judd, synthetic polymer silkscreened on canvas, sgn/dtd 1967, 5x6", C-NY 5/4/88 OE	24,200
Double Dollar Sign, graphite on handmade paper, sgn/inscr/dtd 81, 32x24", SBY 10/8/88	9,900
Double Lavender Disaster, synthetic polymer silkscreened on canvas, 1963, 38x67", SBY 11/10/88	451,000
Drag Queen, graphite on paper, sgn, 40x27", C-NY 11/10/88 OE	15,400
Drag Queen, synthetic polymer silkscreened on canvas, sgn/dtd 1975, unfr, 50x40", C-NY 2/14/89 OE	176,000
Drag Queen (portrait in profile), synthetic polymer silkscreened on canvas, sgn/dtd 77, unfr, 14x11", C-NY 5/4/89	24,200
Eighteen One Dollar Bills, synthetic polymer/stencil on canvas, sgn/dtd 62, 24x30", SBY 5/2/89 OE	264,000
Electric Chair, synthetic polymer silkscreened on canvas, sgn/dtd 64, 22x28", SBY 11/9/89 OE	220,000
Elvis IV, silver paint/synthetic polymer silkscreened on canvas, unfr, 1964, 82x52", C-NY 5/3/88 OE	880,000
Fifteen One Dollar Bills, woodblock/black ink on paper, sgn/dtd 1962, 21x29", C-NY 11/10/88 OE	93,500
Five Deaths Twice I, synthetic polymer silkscreened on canvas, 1963, 30x60", SBY 5/2/89	522,500
Floating Dollar Bills, synthetic polymer/stencil on canvas, stamped/inscr, 1962, 16x20", SBY 2/15/89	209,000
Flowers, acrylic silkscreened on canvas, sgn/dtd 64, 5x5", SBY 11/11/88	16,500
Flowers, synthetic polymer silkscreened on canvas, initialed/dtd 64, 8x8", lot 285, SBY 5/5/89 OE	55,000
Flowers, synthetic polymer silkscreened on canvas, initialed/dtd 64, 8x8", lot 178, SBY 10/5/89	35,750
Flowers, synthetic polymer silkscreened on canvas, sgn, ca 1964, 8x8", lot 154, C-NY 5/4/88 OE	66,000
Flowers, synthetic polymer silkscreened on canvas, sgn, unfr, 8x8", lot 141, C-NY 11/10/88 OE	24,200
Flowers, synthetic polymer silkscreened on canvas, sgn, 5x5", lot 148, C-NY 5/4/88 OE	11,000
Flowers, synthetic polymer silkscreened on canvas, sgn/dtd 1964, 8x8", lot 86, SBY 2/19/88 OE	23,100
Flowers, synthetic polymer silkscreened on canvas, sgn/dtd 1964, 8x8", lot 195, SBY 5/3/88 OE	22,000
Flowers, synthetic polymer silkscreened on canvas, sgn/dtd 1964, 8x8", lot 86, SBY 2/19/88	23,100
Flowers, synthetic polymer silkscreened on canvas, sgn/dtd 64, 8x8", SBY 5/3/88 OE	22,000
Flowers, synthetic polymer silkscreened on canvas, sgn/dtd 64, unfr, 24x24", C-NY 2/14/89	154,000
Flowers, synthetic polymer silkscreened on canvas, sgn/dtd 64, unfr, 8x8", lot 44, C-NY 2/14/89	17,600
Flowers, synthetic polymer silkscreened on canvas, sgn/dtd 64, 24x24", C-NY 5/4/89	165,000
Flowers, synthetic polymer silkscreened on canvas, sgn/dtd 64, 8x8", lot 159, C-NY 5/4/89 OE	38,500
Flowers, synthetic polymer silkscreened on canvas, sgn/dtd 64, 24x24", lot 165, C-NY 5/4/89	165,000
Flowers, synthetic polymer silkscreened on canvas, sgn/dtd 64, 14x14", lot 137, C-NY 5/4/89	52,800
Flowers, synthetic polymer silkscreened on canvas, sgn/dtd 64, 24x24", lot 182, SBY 10/8/88	77,000
Flowers, synthetic polymer silkscreened on canvas, sgn/dtd 64, 8x8", lot 209, SBY 10/8/88	16,500
Flowers, synthetic polymer silkscreened on canvas, sgn/dtd 64, 20x20", lot 341, SBY 11/9/89 OE	165,000
Flowers, synthetic polymer silkscreened on canvas, sgn/dtd 64, 5x5", lot 342, SBY 11/9/89	22,000
Flowers, synthetic polymer silkscreened on canvas, sgn/dtd 64, 14x14", lot 334, SBY 11/9/89 OE	115,500
Flowers, synthetic polymer silkscreened on canvas, sgn/dtd 67, 8x8", SBY 2/19/88	15,400
Flowers, synthetic polymer silkscreened on canvas, sgn/dtd 64, unfr, 14x14", C-NY 11/10/88	41,800
Flowers, synthetic polymer silkscreened on canvas, sgn/inscr, unfr, 24x24", lot 219, C-NY 5/4/88 OE	143,000
Flowers, synthetic polymer silkscreened on canvas, stamped/inscr, 1965, 8x8", lot 188, SBY 10/8/88 OE	38,500
Flowers, synthetic polymer silkscreened on canvas, 1964, 80x160", lot 58, SBY 11/8/89 OE	1,100,000
Flowers, synthetic polymer silkscreened on canvas, 1964, 82x162", lot 48, SBY 5/2/89	1,540,000
Flowers, synthetic polymer silkscreened on canvas, 1964, 82x82", SBY 5/2/89 OE	797,500
Flowers, synthetic polymer silkscreened on canvas, 24x24", lot 71, C-NY 11/9/88 OE	165,000
Flowers (in red/black/white), synthetic polymer silkscreened on canvas, sgn/dtd 64, unfr, 14x14", lot 169, C-NY 11/10/88	60,500
Ford Car, graphite on paper, sgn, ca 1983-84, unfr, 12x16", C-NY 2/14/89	5,500
Four Electric Chairs, synthetic polymer silkscreened on canvas in 4 panels, sgn/dtd 64, 44x56", SBY 11/8/89	1,650,000
Four Marilyns, synthetic polymer silkscreened on canvas, ca 1962, 30x24", C-NY 5/3/88 OE	484,000
Four Multicolored Marilyns, acrylic silkscreened on canvas, sgn/dtd 79-86, 36x28", SBY 10/5/89 OE	467,500
Four-Foot Flowers, synthetic polymer silkscreened on canvas, sgn/dtd 64, 48x48", SBY 11/9/89 OE	687,500
Four-Foot Flowers, synthetic polymer silkscreened on canvas, sgn/dtd 64, 48x48", SBY 11/9/89 OE	539,000

Four-Foot Flowers, synthetic polymer silkscreened on canvas, sgn/dtd 64, 48x48", C-NY 11/7/89 OE	605,000
Frank Stella, acrylic silkscreened on canvas, sgn/dtd 1967, 8x8", lot 200A, SBY 5/3/88	13,200
Frank Stella, acrylic silkscreened on canvas, sgn/dtd 1967, 8x8", SBY 5/3/88	13,200
Frank Stella, synthetic polymer silkscreened on canvas, sgn, 8x8", C-NY 2/14/89	11,000
Gold Jackie, synthetic polymer silkscreened on canvas, artist's stamp, 1964, 20x16", SBY 10/5/89 OE	82,500
Gold Rose, gold leaf/blotted ink on violet paper, sgn, 1957, 18x7", SBY 10/8/88 OE	15,400
Group of Five Campbell's Soup Cans, acrylic/graphite on canvas, sgn/dtd 62, 20x16", C-NY 5/3/88	264,000
Hamburger, synthetic polymer silkscreened on canvas, sgn/dtd 86/inscr Richard, 10x12", SBY 11/11/88	8,800
Hammer & Sickle, synthetic polymer silkscreened on canvas, sgn/dtd 1977, 72x86", SBY 5/3/89 OE	231,000
Hammer & Sickle, synthetic polymer silkscreened on canvas, sgn/dtd 76, 14x19", SBY 5/3/88 OE	24,750
Happy (portrait of Happy Rockefeller 100 times), synthetic polymer silkscreened on canvas, 1968, 72x59", SBY 11/10/88	187,000
Head of a Young Man (line drawing), pen/ink on paper, unfr, 17x14", lot 249, SBY 2/14/89 OE	3,575
Iced Lemon Dessert, watercolor on paper, sgn/inscr, 1958-59, 40x22", SBY 10/8/88	7,150
Jack (line drawing), pen/ink on paper, unfr, 18x14", SBY 2/14/89 OE	7,975
Jack Wearing a Yellow Ring, pen/ink on paper, 17x14", SBY 2/14/89 OE	4,070
Jackie, synthetic polymer silkscreened on canvas, sgn, ca 1964, 20x16", lot 211, SBY 10/8/88	38,500
Jackie, synthetic polymer silkscreened on canvas, sgn, 1964, 20x16", C-NY 10/4/89 OE	55,000
Jackie, synthetic polymer silkscreened on canvas, sgn, 20x16", C-NY 11/10/88	71,500
Jackie, synthetic polymer silkscreened on canvas, sgn twice/dtd 64 twice/inscr To Marie, 20x16", lot 197, SBY 5/3/88 OE	52,250
Jackie, synthetic polymer silkscreened on canvas, sgn twice/inscr/dtd 1964, 20x16", lot 197, SBY 5/3/88 OE	52,250
Jackie, synthetic polymer silkscreened on canvas, sgn/dtd 64, 20x16", SBY 5/3/89	71,500
Jackie, synthetic polymer silkscreened on canvas, 1964, 20x16", lot 321, SBY 11/11/88	66,000
Johnnie Krug/Me (head in profile line drawing), pen/ink on paper, 16x14", SBY 10/7/89	2,310
Jon (head in profile w/out features), graphite on paper, sgn/dtd 82, 32x24", C-NY 5/4/89	8,250
Judge Blasts Lynch, synthetic polymer silkscreened on canvas, sgn/dtd 83, 11x14", SBY 10/5/89	17,600
Kareem Abdul Jabar, synthetic polymer silkscreened on canvas, ca 1977, 40x40", SBY 11/9/89 OE	104,500
Kiss Painting (line drawing), pen/ink on paper, unfr, 17x13", SBY 2/14/89 OE	4,675
Knives, synthetic polymer silkscreened on canvas, sgn/dtd 81, 20x16", SBY 5/3/89 OE	30,250
Ladies & Gentleman, synthetic polymer silkscreened on canvas, artist's stamp, 50x40", SBY 11/9/89	121,000
Ladies & Gentleman (portrait), synthetic polymer silkscreened on canvas, sgn/dtd 1975, 50x40", SBY 10/5/89	126,000
Larry Poons (portrait), synthetic polymer silkscreened on canvas, sgn/dtd 1969, 8x5", C-NY 2/14/89	11,000
Last Supper, synthetic polymer silkscreened on canvas, stamped signature, 1986, 78x306", SBY 5/2/89	682,000
Last Supper, synthetic polymer silkscreened on canvas, stamped signature/dtd 1986, 78x400", SBY 11/8/89 OE	1,760,000
Liz As Cleopatra, synthetic polymer silkscreened on canvas, sgn, 1962, 31x18", SBY 11/8/89 OE	605,000
Man with a Bird, pen/black ink on paper, sgn, 1953, 18x13", C-E 11/14/89 OE	7,700
Mao, acrylic silkscreened on canvas, sgn, 1973, 12x10", lot 320, SBY 11/11/88 OE	115,500
Mao, acrylic/silkscreen on canvas, sgn/dtd 73, 26x22", lot 291, SBY 5/3/89	192,500
Mao, synthetic polymer silkscreened on canvas, sgn, ca 1973, 12x10", lot 81, C-NY 2/20/88	24,200
Mao (portrait), synthetic polymer silkscreened on canvas, 1973, 51x42", SBY 5/2/89 OE	484,000
Marilyn Monroe (Twenty Times), synthetic polymer/silkscreened on canvas, sgn/dtd 62, 77x45", SBY 11/10/88 OE	3,960,000
Men in Her Life (Mike Todd & Eddie Fisher), synthetic polymer silkscreened on canvas, sgn, 13x80", lot 21, C-NY 5/3/89	286,000
Men in Her Life (Mike Todd & Eddie Fisher), synthetic polymer silkscreened on canvas, sgn/dtd 1962, 17x27", C-NY 11/9/88	77,000
Nine Multicolored Marilyns, acrylic silkscreened on canvas, sgn/dtd 79-86, 55x42", SBY 5/2/89 OE	632,500
Nose & Speaking Lips, pen/ink on paper, unfr, 17x14", SBY 2/14/89	1,870
Open This End, acrylic silkscreened on canvas, sgn/dtd 1962, unfr, 8x11", C-NY 5/4/88	15,400
Pair: Little Race Riots; synthetic polymer silkscreened on canvas, sgn/dtd 64, 30x33", SBY 11/10/88 OE	522,500
Pair: Martha Graham; graphite on paper, sgn/dtd 83, 32x24", lot 348, SBY 11/9/89	33,000
Pair: Shoes; diamond dust/synthetic polymer silkscreened on canvas, sgn/inscr To Carol, 1980, 18x14", SBY 11/11/88 OE	38,500
Peekabo (line drawing, young man in profile), pen/ink on paper, unfr, 17x14", SBY 2/14/89 OE	5,225
Perfume Bottles, synthetic polymer silkscreened on canvas, sgn, 22x30", SBY 11/9/89 OE	82,500
Poinsettia, acrylic silkscreened on canvas, sgn/dtd 82/inscr, 10x10", SBY 11/11/88	11,000
Poinsettia, synthetic polymer silkscreened on canvas, sgn/inscr/dtd 82, 8x8", SBY 10/8/88	11,000
Poinsettia, synthetic polymer silkscreened on canvas, stamped signature, 11x14", SBY 10/5/89	20,900
Portrait of Diana Vreeland (three profiles), graphite on paper, sgn/dtd 84, 32x24", C-NY 2/14/89	4,620
Portrait of Golda Meir, no media given, stamped signature/inscr, 1975, 40x40", SBY 2/19/88	49,500
Portrait of Halston, synthetic polymer silkscreened on canvas, artist's stamp/dtd 1974, 40x40", SBY 11/9/89 OE	88,000
Portrait of Joseph Beuys, synthetic polymer/diamond dust silk-creened on canvas, sgn/dtd 1980, 40x40", SBY 10/5/89	231,000
Portrait of Joseph Beuys (head done twenty times), synthetic polymer/diamond dust on canvas, sgn/dtd 1980, C-NY 5/3/89	308,000
Portrait of Lowell Jones, charcoal on paper, sgn/dtd 81, 40x30", SBY 2/15/89	8,800
Portrait of Madame Smith, synthetic polymer silkscreened on canvas, 40x40", SBY 2/15/89 OE	63,250
Portrait of Martha Graham, synthetic polymer/diamond dust on canvas, sgn/inscr/dtd 1980, 40x40", lot 189, SBY 2/15/89 OE	49,500
Portrait of Robert Mapplethorpe, synthetic polymer silkscreened on canvas, sgn/dtd 83, unfr, 40x40", C-NY 10/31/89	88,000
Portrait of Troy Donahue, acrylic on canvas, twice sgn/dtd 1962, 14x10", C-NY 11/10/88	38,500
Profile of a Young Man Looking Up, pen/ink on paper, unfr, 17x14", SBY 2/14/89 OE	4,125
Profile of a Young Man with Long Lashes, pen/ink on paper, unfr, 17x14", SBY 2/14/89 OE	7,975
Putto Boy & Putto Girl, gouache/brush/black ink on paper, sgn, 13x16", RWS 11/10/89 UE	2,000
Queen Elizabeth, silkscreen/paper collage w/overlaid mylar sheets, sgn, 41x31", SBY 11/9/89	38,500
Rainbow Jackson, 1984; synthetic polymer/acrylic on canvas, sgn/dtd 84, 30x20", B/B 6/19/87	220,000
Red Airmail Stamps, synthetic polymer silkscreened on canvas, unfr, 20x16", C-NY 11/9/88	242,000
Red Jackie, synthetic polymer silkscreened on canvas, 1963, 40x40", SBY 5/2/89 OE	825,000
Red Lobster, synthetic polymer silkscreened on canvas, sgn, unfr, 20x16", C-NY 2/14/89	17,600

Robert Rauschenberg, acrylic silkscreened on canvas, sgn/dtd 67 on verso, 11x11", SBY 5/3/88 19,800
Robert Rauschenberg, acrylic silkscreened on canvas, sgn/dtd 67, 11x11", lot 199A, SBY 5/3/88 OE 19,800
Round Marilyn, gold synthetic polymer silkscreened on canvas, sgn/dtd 62/inscr Christmas Marilyn, 18" dia, C-NY 11/9/88 385,000
Roy Lichtenstein (portrait), synthetic polymer silkscreened on canvas, sgn/dtd 1967, 7x5", C-NY 2/14/89 15,400
San Francisco Silverspot, acrycil/enamel silkscreened on canvas, sgn/dtd 83, unfr, 60x60", C-NY 5/3/88 OE 110,000
Self-Portrait, acrylic silkscreened on canvas, sgn/dtd 86, 10x10", SBY 5/3/89 OE 44,000
Self-Portrait, synthetic polymer paint silkscreened on canvas, sgn/dtd 65, 20x16", SBY 11/11/88 OE 154,000
Self-Portrait with Skull, acrylic silkscreened on canvas, sgn/dtd 1978, 16x13", SBY 5/3/88 22,000
Self-Portrait: Skeleton Arm & Madonna After Edvard Munch; acrylic silkscreen, sgn/dtd 84, 71x51", lot 192, SBY 2/15/89 165,000
Self-Portrait: Skeleton Arm & Madonna After Edvard Munch; acrylic silkscreen, sgn/dtd 84, 71x51", lot 170, SBY 2/15/89 110,000
Shadow, synthetic polymer/diamond dust silkscreened on canvas, sgn/dtd 1979, 14x11", SBY 11/9/89 25,300
Shadows, diamond dust/synthetic polymer silkscreened on canvas, sgn/dtd 1980, 78x50", SBY 5/3/89 OE 154,000
Shadows, synthetic polymer silkscreened on canvas, sgn/dtd 1978, 11x14", SBY 2/15/89 OE 20,900
Shoe (Santa Claus), tempera on wood, 1958, 5x9x3", SBY 11/9/89 OE 30,250
Shoes, diamond dust/synthetic polymer silkscreened on canvas, sgn/dtd 82, unfr, 50x42", C-NY 2/14/89 OE 132,000
Shot Red Marilyn, synthetic polymer silkscreened on canvas, sgn/dtd 64, 40x40", C-NY 5/3/89 OE 4,070,000
Soup Can Drawing (wording reversed on can), graphite on paper, sgn/dtd 64, 18x13", C-NY 2/14/89 38,500
Statue of Liberty, acrylic silkscreen on canvas, sgn/dtd 86, 72x72", SBY 11/11/88 231,000
Steaks 99¢, synthetic polymer silkscreened on canvas, sgn/dtd 84, unfr, 20x16", C-NY 2/14/89 17,600
Still Life, synthetic polymer silkscreened on canvas, sgn, 1976, 15x19", C-NY 11/10/88 OE 38,500
Three-Panel Screen, stamped black ink design on white ground, inscr To Fritzie Miller, 1959-60, 65x17", PHL 11/15/88 18,000
To Shoe or Not To Shoe, watercolor/pen/black ink on paper, sgn, 1955, 10x14", C-NY 5/4/89 OE 6,050
Tomato Soup, synthetic polymer silkscreened on canvas, sgn/dtd 85, 20x16", SBY 5/3/89 OE 38,500
Triple Elvis, synthetic polymer silkscreened on canvas, 1964, 82x48", SBY 11/8/89 2,200,000
True Love, synthetic polymer silkscreened on canvas, sgn/inscr, 10x8", SBY 2/15/89 9,900
True Love (decorated heart on red backbround), synthetic polymer silkscreened on canvas, sgn, 84, 10x10", SBY 11/11/88 17,600
Two Dollar Bill, acrylic silkscreened on canvas, sgn/dtd 62, 9x14", SBY 5/3/88 OE 16,500
Two Dollar Bill, synthetic polymer silkscreened on canvas, sgn/dtd 62, 6x10", C-NY 11/10/88 30,800
Untitled (abstract composition), gold leaf/pen/black ink on paper, sgn, ca 1957, 9x10", C-NY 10/4/89 OE 13,200
Untitled (abstract figure), synthetic polymer silkscreened on canvas, estate stamp, ca 1985, 32x24", SBY 11/9/89 OE 49,500
Untitled (abstract), acrylic on canvas, sgn, 11x11", lot 174, C-NY 2/14/89 OE 7,150
Untitled (abstract), oxidized/bronze-coated canvas, sgn/dtd 86, unfr, 14x10", lot 175, C-NY 2/14/89 17,600
Untitled (abstract), oxidized/bronze-coated canvas, sgn/dtd 79, unfr, 16x12", C-NY 5/4/89 OE 18,700
Untitled (abstract), oxidized/bronze-coated canvas strips, sgn/inscr, ca 1978, 12x12", lot 190, SBY 10/8/88 16,500
Untitled (abstract), synthetic polymer silkscreened on canvas, sgn/dtd 1977, unfr, 15x19", C-NY 5/4/89 OE 20,900
Untitled (alligator), watercolor/brush/black ink on paper, sgn, 1955, 23x29", C-NY 5/4/89 OE 12,100
Untitled (cat & gifts), watercolor over blotted ink line on paper, sgn, 13x16", SBY 10/8/88 7,700
Untitled (four girls, ad for Harper's Bazaar), watercolor/blotted ink/collage, 1958, 20x16", SBY 10/8/88 5,500
Untitled (From Wild Raspberries), watercolor/black ink on paper, sgn, 1959, 28x22", C-NY 5/4/89 14,300
Untitled (head w/orange, blue, pink & red), gouache/graphite on paper, sgn/dtd 62, 24x18", C-NY 2/14/89 OE 24,200
Untitled (hyacinths), watercolor/blotted ink, 1958, 11x15", SBY 10/8/88 5,500
Untitled (lady kneeling by chair), pen/black ink on paper, inscr Meow, 1957, unfr, 9x11", lot 266, C-E 5/9/89 OE 4,400
Untitled (lobster), synthetic polymer silkscreened on canvas, sgn/dtd 84, 20x16", SBY 5/3/89 OE 30,250
Untitled (Martha Graham Series), graphite on paper, sgn/dtd 86, 32x24", SBY 11/9/89 18,700
Untitled (Martha Graham Series), graphite on paper, sgn/dtd 86, 32x24", SBY 11/9/89 16,500
Untitled (Martha Graham Series), graphite on paper, sgn/dtd 86, 31x24", SBY 11/9/89 18,700
Untitled (Martha Graham Series), synthetic polymer on paper, sgn/dtd 86, 32x24", lot 393, SBY 11/9/89 20,900
Untitled (Martha Graham Series), synthetic polymer on paper, sgn/dtd 86, 32x24", lot 395, SBY 11/9/89 18,700
Untitled (Martha Graham Series), synthetic polymer on paper, sgn/dtd 86, 32x24", SBY 11/9/89 23,100
Untitled (Mickey Mouse), black crayon on paper, sgn, 16x11", SBY 10/5/89 OE 24,200
Untitled (Oscar Mayer wiener on bun), graphite on paper, sgn/dtd 62, 14x16", C-NY 5/4/89 OE 10,450
Untitled (pear w/leaves), gold leaf, collage/pen/black ink on paper, sgn, ca 1957, 10x8", C-NY 5/4/89 OE 16,500
Untitled (portraits of man & cat), black ink on paper, ca 1956, unfr, 14x12", C-E 5/9/89 OE 2,860
Untitled (reclining cat), watercolor/brush/black ink on paper, sgn, 8x26", C-NY 10/4/89 OE 22,000
Untitled (twelve painted objects), synthetic polymer silkscreened on canvas, ca 1960, 30x32, SBY 10/5/89 OE 93,500
Untitled (two heads on abstract background), oil/ink on canvas, sgn, 1958, 40x48", SBY 10/5/89 OE 49,500
Victor Hugo, graphite on paper, sgn/dtd 79, 32x24", SBY 11/9/89 17,600
White on White Mona Lisa (Reversal Series), synthetic polymer silkscreened on canvas, sgn, 79, 25x20", C-NY 10/31/89 OE 165,000
Women Over 40, synthetic polymer silkscreened on canvas, sgn/dtd 84, 20x16", C-NY 2/14/89 OE 28,600
40 Two Dollar Bills in Green, synthetic polymer & stencil on canvas, sgn/dtd 62, 83x19", SBY 5/2/89 330,000
40 Two Dollar Bills in Red, acrylic/stencil on canvas, sgn/dtd 62, 83x19", SBY 11/10/88 OE 319,000
70 S&H Green Stamps, rubber stamp/acrylic on canvas with metal staples, sgn/dtd 62, 16x20", C-NY 11/9/88 OE 143,000

WARNER, Everett Longley (American, 1877-1963)

Burg Tor, Rothenburg OT; oil on canvas, sgn, 32x23", SBY 6/28/89 5,500

WARNER, Nell Walker (American, 1891-1970)

Back From Deep Waters, oil on canvas, sgn, 24x20", C-E 2/3/88 1,430
Floral Still Life, oil on canvasboard, sgn, 16x12", B/B 10/6/88 825
Think It Will Rain (figures before a house), oil on canvas, sgn, 20x24", C-E 2/3/88 2,310

WARREN, Edmund George

Harvesters Rest, watercolor/gouache over pencil, sgn, 21x27", C-NY 5/25/88 OE 5,280

WARREN, Elisabeth Boardman (American, 1886-)

Boys Playing Amid Boats, watercolor on paper, sgn, 12x16", FAP 11/4/88 ... 250

Sunlight, watercolor on paper, 20x16", C-E 6/1/88 UE ... 385

WARREN, Emily Mary Bibbens (Canadian, 1869-1956)

Church Interior with Streams of Sunlight, watercolor on paper w/traces of pencil, sgn, 21x16", C-E 5/23/88 UE ... 124

Gothic Church Interior, watercolor on paper w/traces of pencil, sgn/dtd 1900, 21x18", C-E 5/23/88 ... 550

WARREN, Harold Broadfield (American, 1859-1934)

Village Gate (figures in shade of stone arch, mountain view beyond), watercolor on paper, sgn/dtd 88, 14x11", RAB 8/9/88 ... 400

WARREN, Melvin C. (American, 1920-)

Adobe at Santa Clara, oil on canvas, sgn/inscr/copyrighted/dtd 1977, 20x30", SBY 9/23/88 OE ... 25,300

Going to the Wedding, oil on canvas, sgn/inscr/copyrighted/dtd 1980, 24x36", SBY 9/23/88 OE ... 17,600

Headin` for the Roundup, oil on canvas, sgn/copyrighted/dtd 1976, 36x60", SBY 9/23/88 OE ... 45,100

Selling of the White Stallion, oil on canvas, sgn/inscr/copyrighted/dtd 1972, 24x36", SBY 9/23/88 OE ... 41,800

WARREN, Russ

Self-Portrait with Burro (contemporary), acrylic on canvas, sgn/dtd 3/81, 44x37", C-E 11/14/89 ... 715

WARREN, W. (British, 19th C)

Terriers Rabbiting, oil on canvas, sgn, 16x22", SBY 6/10/88 ... 2,200

WARSHAW, Howard (American, 1920-)

Sacks, oil on canvas, sgn/dtd 47, 5x8", C-NY 10/6/88 OE ... 1,430

Strange Tree with Rose, oil on canvas, sgn/dtd 44, 12x8", C-NY 10/6/88 OE ... 2,090

Untitled (abstract head), oil on canvas, sgn/dtd 61, 12x16", B/B 6/15/89 UE ... 2,200

WARSHAW, Howard; att (American, 1920-)

Figure Study, pen/ink wash on paper, 9x5", B/B 5/17/89 ... 440

WARSHAWSKY, Abel G. (American, 1883-1962)

Autumn, oil on panel, sgn, 16x13", WG 4/23/88 ... 1,500

French Coastal Village, oil on canvas, sgn, 26x32", WG 9/16/88 UE ... 2,000

Overlooking Antibes, oil on canvas, 26x32", WG 4/23/88 ... 7,500

Portrait of a Peasant Girl, oil on board, sgn/dtd 1934, 16x13", B/B 1/11/89 ... 440

Sailing in the Harbor, oil on board, 9x11", WG 9/16/88 UE ... 550

Woman with the Colorful Hat, oil on paper, initialed, 6x3", WG 9/16/88 ... 200

WARSHAWSKY, Alexander (American, 1887-1962)

Still Life Bouquet, oil on board, sgn, 20x16", WG 4/23/88 ... 500

WARVILLE, see De Warville

WASHINGTON, Georges (French, 1827-1910)

Cavaliers Arabes a l'Abreuvoir, oil on canvas, sgn, 24x30", SBY 2/22/89 ... 14,300

Restive Place in the Desert, oil on canvas, sgn, 30x24", B/ B 6/15/89 OE ... 15,400

WATELET, Charles Joseph (Belgian, 1867-)

The Proud Owner, oil on canvas, sgn, 41x33", B/B 3/17/88 ... 6,600

WATELIN, Louis (French, 1838-1905)

Cattle Watering by a Pond, oil on canvas, sgn, 19x22", C-E 10/26/89 ... 1,210

WATERLOO, Anthonie (Flemish, 1609-1690)

View in a Wooded Gully with Steps Ascending, black chalk/gray wash on blue paper, 10x11", SBY 1/13/89 ... 2,200

WATERLOW, Ernest Albert (British, 1850-1919)

Feeding Time, watercolor on paper, sgn, 11x7", WL 5/20/88 OE ... 750

Forest Interior with Figures, oil on canvas, sgn, 26x41", FB 10/30/89 ... 4,840

WATERMAN, Marcus A. (American, 1834-1914)

Gathering Seaweed on Cape Cod, oil on canvas, sgn, 20x30", RWS 11/3/88 ... 1,600

Gypsies in the Desert, oil on canvas, sgn/dtd 1886, 36x46", C-E 11/8/88 UE ... 850

Summer Landscape, oil on canvas, sgn, 16x20", C-SK 6/9/88 ... 835

WATERS, George W. (American, 1832-1912)

Old Pasture Bridge, watercolor on paper laid on board, sgn, 14x21", C-E 2/1/89 UE ... 550

Path in the Woods, oil on canvas, sgn/dtd 87, 21x31", WD 4/13/88 ... 1,800

WATERS, Susan (American, 1823-1900)

Barnyard Scene, oil on canvas, sgn/inscr, 36x42", C-E 2/3/88 ... 5,720

Cache of Raspberries (squirrels eating, cat watching), oil on canvas, sgn, 20x16", C-NY 9/30/88 ... 15,400

Mountain Lake Scene, oil on canvas, sgn/dtd 87, 20x32", LH 5/15/88 ... 3,400

Portrait of Catherine Quackenbush Slade, oil on canvas, ca 1944, 30x25", C-NY 1/20/89 ... 4,180

Sheep Resting in Landscape, oil on canvas, sgn/dtd 1886, 24x37", C-E 6/1/88 ... 6,380

Winter Landscape at Sunset, oil on canvas, sgn, 20x32", LH 5/15/88 ... 3,600

WATKINS, Franklin C. (American, 1894-)

Cat on Chair Next to Pitcher, Still Life on Desk; oil on canvas, sgn, 34x18", DM 5/13/88 OE ... 1,500

Death in the Orchard (angels hovering over body), oil on canvas, initialed, 34x28", DM 5/13/88 OE ... 2,750

My Son, My Son; oil on canvas, sgn/dtd 1946, 28x36", DM 5/13/88 OE ... 1,500

Portrait of Mrs Steinman, oil on canvas, initialed, 40x36", DM 5/13/88 OE ... 1,300

Reclining Nude, oil on canvas, initialed, 14x24", DM 5/13/88 OE ... 1,100

Still Life of Flowers, oil on canvas, sgn, 30x25", DM 5/13/88 OE ... 2,000

Study for Ressurection, oil on canvas, initialed, 17x28", DM 5/13/88 OE ... 1,400

WATKINS, W.H.

Peasant Girl, oil on canvas, sgn, 23x19", C-E 5/23/88 UE ... 605

WATROUS, Harry Willson (American, 1857-1940)

Lake Scene, oil on canvas, sgn, 25x30", C-E 6/1/88 ... 1,180

Matador (full-length portrait), oil on canvas, sgn, 21x11", RWS 5/19/88 UE 300
Nude in Forest, watercolor/gouache on paper, sgn, 15x10", C-E 6/1/88 1,320
Still Life of Oriental Vases & Bowl, oil on canvas, sgn, 21x16", C-NY 3/11/88 3,850

WATSON, Albermale (British, fl 1884-1899)
Critic, oil on canvas, sgn/dtd 89, 17x22", FB 4/25/88 475

WATSON, Amelia Montague (American, 1856-1934)
Dennis, Massachusetts Marshes; watercolor on paper, sgn, 13x19", RAB 8/8/89 400

WATSON, C.E. (British, 19th/20th C)
Highland Calves by the Loch-Side, oil on canvas, sgn/dtd 1925, 13x19", B/B 4/20/88 1,320

WATSON, Dawson (American, 1864-1939)
Landscape Near Giverny, oil on canvas, sgn/dtd 1892, 17x33", RWS 5/12/89 7,500

WATSON, Edgar Melville (American, 1877-1956)
After the Snow (large house/trees in winter landscape), oil on masonite, sgn, 24x30", RAB 8/8/89 300

WATSON, George; att (British, 1767-1837)
Portrait of Joseph Hume, Esquire, Half-Length; oil on canvas, dedicatory frame,29x25", SBY 10/21/88 OE 9,900

WATSON, Harry S. (British, 1822-1911)
Moontide Rescue, oil on canvas, bears monogram/sgn, 12x18", FAP 12/8/89 225

WATSON, Homer Ransford (Canadian, 1855-1936)
Approaching Storm, oil on canvas, sgn, 13x17", WAD 6/12/89 3,000
Sunlit Farm, oil on board, sgn, 12x16", WAD 11/30/89 2,800

WATSON, J. (19th C)
Still Life of Fruit & a Vase on a Tabletop, oil on canvas, sgn/dtd 1848, 18x24", SBY 5/25/88 OE 26,400

WATSON, Jessie N. (American, 1870-1963)
Rocky Landscape, watercolor on paper, sgn, 10x13", B/B 1/11/89 302

WATSON, Robert (American, 1923-)
Encounter, oil on canvas, sgn, 1971, 15x19", LH 10/16/88 UE 120
Surrealistic Landscape, oil on canvas, sgn, no size given, FAP 11/4/88 260

WATSON, Robert (British, 1877-1915)
Bringing in the Herd, oil on canvas, sgn, 24x30", DM 5/13/88 1,300
Highland Cattle by a Misty Loch, oil on canvas, sgn/dtd 1904, 20x30", WAD 6/6/88 2,400

WATSON, Walter J. (British, 1879-)
Highland Cattle, Inverness Shire; oil on canvas, sgn, 20x30", B/B 4/20/88 2,475
Landscape, North Wales; oil on canvas, sgn/dtd 1925, 13x19", FB 5/28/89 3,400
On the Lugwy, North Wales; oil on canvas, sgn/dtd 1930, 13x19", LH 10/16/88 OE 1,900

WATSON, William (British, -1921)
Bull in Scottish Highlands, oil on canvas, sgn/dtd 1895, 24x42", MG 8/27/88 350
Morning in the Glen, Highland Cattle; oil on canvas, sgn/dtd 1913, 33x48", C-NY 2/3/88 OE 8,250
Pair: Glen Lean, Argyleshire; Loch Earn Head, Perth; no media given, sgn/dtd 1900 & 1904, 24x36", SBY 10/24/89 OE 19,250

WATTEAU, Jean Antoine (French, 1684-1721)
Double-Sided: Studies of Two Elegant Ladies, Seated; Studies of Peasant Figures; red chalk, 1711, 7x8", SBY 10/27/89 55,000
Portrait of a Girl with Her Head Turned Right, red/black chalk/gray wash on buff paper, ca 1720, 8x6", SBY 10/27/89 OE 385,000

WATTEAU, Jean Antoine; after (French, 1684-1721)
Head Studies, charcoal/red chalk/sepia on paper, 7x10", C-E 1/12/88 OE 286

WATTEAU, Jean Antoine; follower of (French, 1684-1721)
Pair: Fetes Champetres; oil on panel, unfr, 9x6", SBY 12/9/88 OE 3,300

WATTEAU, Jean Antoine; manner of (French, 1684-1721)
Figures From the Commedia Dell'Arte Standing in a Landscape, oil on canvas, 41x47", SBY 10/13/89 OE 46,750
L'Heureux Age, oil on canvas, 11" dia, SBY 6/8/88 OE 5,500
Pair: Fetes Champetres; oil on panel, 9x13", SBY 6/8/88 OE 2,420

WATTEAU, Jean Antoine; school of (French, 1684-1721)
Pair: Fete Champetres; oil on canvas, 19x25", lot 249, C-NY 4/6/89 8,800

WATTS, A. (British, 19th C)
Pair: Lowland Landscapes; oil on canvas, sgn, 20x30", WAD 6/6/88 1,600

WATTS, Frederick William (British, 1800-1862)
Lake in Summer, oil on canvas, 34x40", SBY 10/24/89 11,000

WATTS, George Frederick (British, 1817-1904)
Portrait of Alexander Cassavetti, Son of Demetrius & Euphrosyne Cassavetti; oil on canvas, sgn, 25x20", C-NY 5/25/88 UE 4,400
Study for a Portrait of Mrs Charles Coltman Rogers of Stanage Park, chalk on paper, sgn, 1894, 21x17", SBY 5/23/89 7,700

WATTS, Sidney (British, 19th/20th C)
Untitled, Welsh landscape w/figure in front of cottage; oil on canvas, sgn, 16x24", SLK 4/7/89 625

WATTS, William Clothier (American, 1869-1961)
California Coastal Trees, watercolor on paper, sgn, 22x26", B/B 1/11/89 770

WATZELHAN, Carl (German, 1867-1942)
Reading Lesson (woman & young girl seated at a table), oil on canvas, sgn, 25x29", C-E 5/22/89 6,820

WAUCH, S.B. (19th C)
Portrait of a Woman (half-length), oil on canvas, sgn/dtd 1873, 24x20", C-E 2/16/88 UE 264

WAUD, Alfred R. (American, 1828-1891)
Attack of Smith's Corps, Cold Harbor (Civil War); pen/ink on paper, initialed/inscr, 7x13", C-E 5/27/88 825
Battle of Cedar Creek (Civil War), pen/ink on paper, initialed/inscr, 10x13", C-E 2/27/88 935
Battle of the Crater (Civil War), pen/ink on paper, initialed/inscr, 12x15", C-E 5/27/88 OE 2,420
Confederate Retreat Through Mechanicsville (Civil War), pen/ink on paper, initialed/inscr, 13x15", C-E 5/27/88 1,760

Crossing North Edisto (Civil War), pen/ink on paper, inscr, 5x9", C-E 5/27/88 OE ... 1,320
Explosion of the Petersburg Mine (Civil War), pen/ink on paper, initialed/inscr, 10x13", C-E 5/27/88 OE ... 5,720
Fate of the Rail Fence (Civil War), pen/ink on paper, sgn/inscr, 9x8", C-E 5/27/88 ... 770

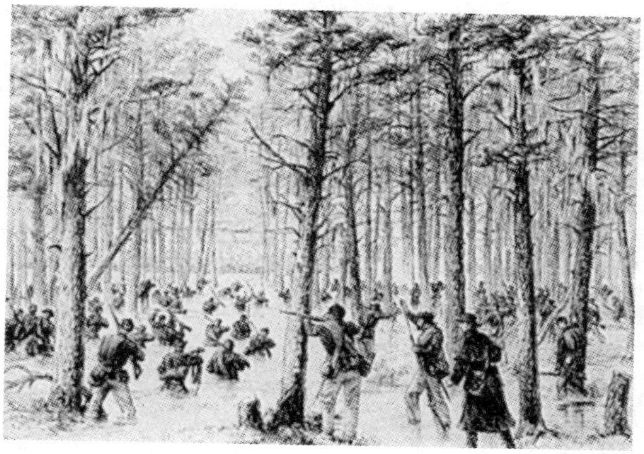

Forcing a Crossing of the Little Salkehatchie, pen/ink on paper, sgn, 9x12", C-E 5/27/88 OE; $1,980

Fortified Battery, Petersburg, Casemated Field Work (Civil War); pen/ink on paper, sgn/inscr, 11x14", C-E 5/27/88 OE ... 1,430
Hancock's Front, Entrenching at Cold Harbor (Civil War); pen/ink on paper, initialed/inscr, 13x15", C-E 5/27/88 ... 825
Harrison House (Civil War), pen/ink on paper, initialed/inscr, 11x13", C-E 5/27/88 OE ... 1,320
On Picket Duty in Front of Fort Hell (Civil War), pen/ink on paper, initialed/inscr, unfr, 13x15", C-E 11/30/88 OE ... 770
Pair: Sharpshooters in the Federal Lines at Petersburg (Civil War); pen/ink on paper, initialed, 10x14", C-E 5/27/88 OE ... 1,210
Vincent's Brigade, Devil's Den, Gettysburg (Civil War); pen/ink, initialed/inscr, 7x9", C-E 5/27/88 OE ... 5,720
White House Before & After the Fire, Pamunkey River (Civil War); pen/ink on paper, sgn/inscr, 10x13", C-E 5/27/88 OE ... 1,650

WAUGH, Frederick Judd (American, 1861-1940)

After the Storm (coastal seascape), oil on canvas, sgn, 25x30", RAB 8/8/89 UE ... 3,750
At the Base of the Cliff (waves crashing over rocks), oil on canvas, sgn, 1908, 40x50", C-NY 5/25/89 OE ... 28,600
Before the Fog, oil on board, sgn twice/titled, 30x40", SBY 6/24/88 ... 6,600
Breaking Day (coastal view w/cliffs), oil on canvas, sgn, 25x30", C-NY 9/28/89 ... 6,600
By Seas at High Water, oil on canvasboard, sgn/titled/#d R 2325, 25x30", SBY 9/23/88 ... 4,125
Coast of Maine, oil on canvas, sgn, 25x30", C-NY 9/30/88 OE ... 8,250
Crashing Surf with Rocks, oil on board, sgn, 12x16", SBY 6/24/88 ... 2,860
Crashing Surf with Rocks, oil on masonite, sgn, 30x36", SBY 9/23/88 ... 5,500
Crashing Waves, oil on board, sgn, 12x18", WD 4/13/88 ... 4,000
Evening, Charing Cross Road; oil on board, sgn/bears inscription, 7x6", SBY 6/24/88 OE ... 7,700
Farmhouse at Sunset, oil on canvas, sgn/dtd twice, 1886, 16x30", SBY 9/23/88 UE ... 3,300
Fog Signals, oil on board, sgn/inscr, 30x40", C-NY 9/30/88 ... 4,180
London Snowfall Near St Paul's Cathedral, oil on board, sgn, 7x6", SBY 6/24/88 OE ... 6,050
Looking From Desolation Sound, oil on board, sgn/titled, 30x38", SBY 6/24/88 ... 4,400
Marine Scene, oil on canvasboard, sgn, 25x30", RWS 11/10/89 ... 4,000
Mill Pond, oil on board, sgn, 11x14", C-E 6/1/89 OE ... 6,050
Orange Sunset, oil on masonite, sgn/titled, 36x48", SBY 6/24/88 UE ... 4,950
Rain Clouds & Sea, oil on masonite, sgn, 30x40", C-NY 3/11/88 ... 7,700
Risen Moon (coastal seascape), oil on canvasboard, sgn, 25x30", SBY 3/17/88 ... 3,850
Silver Light (seascape), oil on canvasboard, sgn/inscr, 25x30", C-NY 3/11/88 ... 7,480
Study for Invading Surf, oil on masonite, sgn, 11x14", C-E 11/30/88 ... 2,200
Unknown Seas (coastal seascape), oil on masonite, sgn/titled, 14x18", SBY 3/17/88 ... 2,750
Village by the Sea, oil on canvasboard, sgn, 15x12", C-E 2/3/88 ... 880

WAUGH, Henry W. (American, 19th C)

Old Stone Bridge, Ohio; pen/sepia ink on paper, titled, 5x9", RAB 8/8/89 UE ... 125
View of an Iowa Farm, wash on paper, titled, 5x8", RAB 8/8/89 UE ... 125

WAY, Andrew John Henry (American, 1826-1888)

An Abundance of Fruit (still life), oil on canvas, sgn, 22x30", SBY 6/24/88 ... 3,575
Beer & Oysters (still life), oil on canvas, sgn/dtd 78, 12x10", C-NY 5/25/89 OE ... 18,700
Ripe Peaches, oil on board, sgn, 9x12", C-NY 9/30/88 ... 3,300

WAY, Andrew John Henry; att (American, 1826-1888)

Still Life of Fruit, oil on canvas, 8x10", S/A 2/18/89 ... 275
Still Life of Peaches, oil on canvas, initialed, 8x10", S/A 2/18/89 ... 250

WAY, Andrew John Henry; manner of (American, 1826-1888)

Still Life of Grapes, oil on artist board, 14x10", RWS 8/20/88 UE ... 80

WAY, Charles Jones (Canadian, 1835-1919)

Fishing Boats on a Stormy Beach, watercolor, sgn/dtd 73, 10x16", WAD 6/12/89 OE ... 1,000
Rushing Mountain Stream, watercolor, sgn, 19x15", FB 10/30/89 ... 1,650

WAY, Tom Robert

Margaret Way at Deal, pastel on light gray paper, inscr, 5x7", C-NY 10/26/88 ... 990

WAYNE, June Claire (American, 1918-)
Moving Symbols, oil on canvas, sgn/dtd 1948, unfr, 36x30", C-E 6/1/89 .... **770**
Witching Hour (abstract composition), oil on canvas, sgn/dtd 1948, unfr, 36x30", C-E 6/1/89 UE **715**
WEARE, Shane (American, 20th C)
Untitled, pastel on handmade paper, 22x30", lot 4051, B/B 12/8/88 .... **330**
WEATHERBEE, George Faulkner (American, 1851-1920)
Summer Sea, nude walking along beach; oil on canvas, sgn, 20x30", SLK 11/25/88 .... **4,500**
WEATHERHEAD, William Harris (British, 1843-1903)
Churning Butter, oil on canvas, sgn, 48x31", SBY 7/12/89 .... **3,850**
WEAVER, Thomas (British, 1774-1843)
Prize Cattle in a Landscape, oil on canvas, sgn/dtd 1833, 28x36", SBY 6/9/89 .... **14,300**
WEAVER, Thomas; att (British, 1774-1843)
Prize Bull in a Landscape, oil on canvas, 20x24", SBY 6/9/89 .... **6,875**
WEBB, A.C. (American, 1888-)
Lower Manhattan, charcoal heightened w/white chalk on paper, sgn/inscr/dtd 1930, 25x15", C-E 4/7/88 UE **352**
WEBB, Charles Meer (British, 1830-1895)
Alchemist (man seated in an interior), oil on canvas, sgn/dtd 1864, 18x15", B/B 3/22/89 .... **2,475**
Rolling Dice, oil on canvas, sgn/dtd 1891, 25x20", NA 10/1/88 .... **5,250**
WEBB, Charles T. (American, 1825-1911)
Homestead, oil on canvas, 16x24", LH 10/16/88 .... **650**
Three Children, oil on canvas, sgn, 24x21", WG 4/23/88 .... **1,200**
WEBB, J. (British, 20th C)
Young Girl on a Swing (in grassy landscape), oil on board, sgn, 16x12", WG 4/23/88 UE **500**
WEBB, James (British, 1825-1895)
Beached, oil on canvas, sgn/dtd 1888, 44x65", FAP 11/4/88 .... **8,000**
Boats Moored at a Quai Side, oil on canvas, sgn, 10x14", FB 10/17/88 .... **500**
Castillo de la Conception at Cartegena, oil on canvas, sgn, 31x51", B/B 6/15/89 .... **14,300**
Constantinople (port scene), oil on canvas, sgn/dtd 1875, 14x24", FB 5/28/89 OE **8,500**
Fisherfolk on a Shore, oil on canvas, sgn, 30x44", C-NY 2/25/88 .... **4,400**
Fisherfolk on the Shore, oil on canvas, sgn, 30x45", FB 10/30/89 .... **6,600**
Loading Limestone (on a ship), oil on canvas, sgn/dtd 1875, 9x15", C-E 2/21/89 .... **2,530**
Sailboats Off Dover, oil on panel, sgn, 10x14", SBY 7/12/89 .... **3,850**
Shipwreck Off a Rocky Isle, oil on canvas, sgn/dtd 78, 24x36", C-NY 10/25/89 .... **6,600**
WEBB, Robert (Canadian)
Blue Bird, oil on board, sgn, 8x10", FB 10/30/89 .... **248**
Lark I, oil on board, sgn, 8x10", FB 10/30/89 .... **248**
WEBB, William (British, 1819-1850)
Bay Hunter in a Landscape, oil on canvas, sgn/dtd 1850, 33x42", SBY 6/9/89 .... **18,700**
WEBBER, W.O.
Cows Grazing by a Riverbank, oil on canvas, sgn, 18x26", C-E 1/12/88 .... **495**
WEBBER, Wesley (American, 1839-1914)
Crashing Waves, oil on canvas, sgn, 22x36", C-E 9/15/88 UE **660**
Harpoon Hunters Off Nantucket, oil on canvas, sgn, 14x24", SBY 9/23/88 .... **2,090**
Maine Landscape Scene with Hunters, oil on canvas, sgn/dtd 1870, 20x36", RWS 11/3/88 .... **2,100**
Marine Scene of Women with Parasols on a Rocky Outcropping, oil on academy board, sgn, unfr, 8x10", RWS 3/16/89 OE **1,900**
Moonlight Sail, oil on canvas, sgn, 28x22", C-E 2/3/88 UE **825**
Moonlight Sail (marine scene), oil on canvas, sgn, 20x16", RWS 3/16/89 .... **650**
New England Coastal Scene, oil on canvas, sgn/dtd 1881, 16x28", RWS 3/31/88 OE **2,500**
Sailboats by Moonlight, oil on canvas, sgn, 20x16", DM 5/13/88 .... **1,000**
Sailing Ship Off a Dramatic Shoreline with Icebergs, oil on canvas, sgn/dtd 1879, 12x20", RWS 5/12/89 .... **1,700**
Sunset, oil on canvas, sgn, 13x18", C-E 6/1/88 .... **770**
USS Constitution Victorious Over HMS Gurriere, oil on canvas, sgn, 18x24", RWS 9/8/89 UE **2,700**
WEBER, Alfred (Swiss, 1859-)
A False Note, oil on panel, sgn, 22x18", C-E 10/26/89 .... **2,200**
Tea on the Terrace, oil on canvas, sgn, 19x26", WD 3/23/88 UE **1,100**
WEBER, Alfred Charles (French, 1862-1922)
Spill on the Road, watercolor on paper, sgn, 18x12", WD 1/11/89 .... **700**
WEBER, Anton; see Von Weber
WEBER, Carl (American, 1850-1921)
Cattle Grazing, oil on canvas, sgn, 18x14", FAP 12/8/89 UE **400**
Country Landscape with Two Figures & Pond, watercolor on paper, sgn, 12x24", FAP 11/4/88 .... **625**
Country Road Leading Toward White House, watercolor on paper, sgn, 12x24", FAP 11/4/88 .... **600**
Grazing Sheep, oil on canvas, sgn, 14x23", C-E 2/1/89 .... **1,320**
Meadow Near Philadelphia, oil on canvas, sgn, 17x26", FAP 4/15/89 .... **1,045**
Old Farm in Spring, watercolor on paper, sgn, unfr, 18x28", B/B 9/15/88 .... **1,100**
Resting Sheep (pastoral landscape), watercolor/gouache/pencil on paper laid down on board, sgn, 14x37", C-E 6/1/89 OE **1,100**
Rural Landscape with Sheep & Water, watercolor, sgn, 14x27", S/A 2/18/89 .... **500**
Sheep Grazing, watercolor on paper laid down on board, 30x20", C-E 5/3/88 UE **440**
Sheep Grazing Under Flowering Magnolias, watercolor on paper laid down on board, sgn, 24x35", C-E 5/3/88 .... **770**
Sheep in a Spring Landscape, oil on canvas, sgn, 24x36", SBY 1/24/89 .... **2,750**
Sunset on a River, watercolor/gouache on paper, sgn, 14x26", C-E 6/1/88 .... **990**

View of the Hudson River, oil on canvas, sgn/dtd 1879, 20x34", SBY 9/23/88 OE 4,125

WEBER, Charles Philip (American, 1849-)

Mountain Lakeside Village, oil on canvas, sgn/dtd 1882, 22x30", B/B 4/20/88 2,090
Mountain River Landscape, oil on canvas, sgn, 41x61", B/B 4/20/88 2,475
Outing on the River, oil on canvas, sgn, 20x36", SBY 6/24/88 2,750
Waterfall in the Rocky Mountains, oil on canvas, sgn/dtd 1879, 75x32", SBY 6/24/88 OE 4,950

WEBER, Frederick (American, 1883-1956)

Mother & Daughter, watercolor/pastel on paper, sgn, 22x30", C-E 2/3/88 1,100

WEBER, Gottlieb Daniel Paul (German, 1823-1916)

Near Obersdorf Bavaria (children & dog tending sheep in a landscape), oil on canvas, sgn, 28x48", C-NY 5/24/89 OE 38,500

WEBER, Heinrich (German, 1843-1913)

Pretty Maiden with Vegetables, oil on canvas, sgn, 37x29", SBY 12/9/88 4,125
Startled, lady walking dog surprised upon finding sleeping laborers; oil on canvas, sgn, 23x31", RAB 3/27/89 UE 700
Watching Their Goldfish (three children in interior), no media given, sgn, 18x15", C-E 2/21/89 1,430

WEBER, M. (Maria?)(German, 19th C)

Music Lesson, oil on canvas, sgn, 44x27", SBY 5/23/89 11,000

WEBER, Max (American, 1881-1961)

Among the Trees, oil on canvas, sgn/dtd 1911, 18x16", C-NY 5/26/88 38,500
Balcony, oil on canvas, sgn, 1939, 23x29", SBY 9/23/88 14,300
Chrysanthemums, oil on board/paper laid down on board, 17x8", SBY 6/28/89 3,850
Contemplation, pastel on brown paper, sgn/dtd 1946-47, 18x13", SBY 1/24/89 OE 4,125
Discourse (abstract figures), oil on canvas, sgn/dtd 1950, 25x30", SBY 6/24/88 OE 19,250
Figure in Blue, gouache/pastel on paper, sgn, 5x4", SBY 9/14/89 2,200
Meeting (abstract), pastel on brown paper, sgn/dtd 17, 15x8", SBY 6/24/88 OE 18,700
Rabbi, gouache on paper, sgn/dtd 56, 17x13", SBY 6/24/88 OE 8,800
Still Life of Flowers, oil on canvas, sgn/dtd 46, 36x18", C-NY 12/2/88 UE 5,500
Walking Figures, gouache/pencil on paper, sgn/dtd 49, 5x9", C-E 6/1/89 1,210

WEBER, Otis (American, 19th C)

Schooners at Sea, oil on canvas, sgn/dtd 79, 24x36", C-E 10/18/89 OE 3,850
Sloop Passing a Lighthouse, oil on academy board, sgn, 19x12", RAB 3/14/89 170

WEBER, Paul (American, 1823-1916)

Churchyard in Winter, Sunrise; oil on canvas, 15x21", RAB 8/9/88 3,000
Delaware Water Gap, oil on canvas, sgn/dtd 1853, 21x30", C-NY 5/26/88 19,800
Heading Out To Graze, oil on canvas, sgn, 16x25", C-E 10/26/89 7,700
Mountain Landscape with Waterfall, oil on canvas, sgn/dtd 1855, 40x34", C-NY 9/30/88 UE 4,400
Pair: Cottage on Cliff; Sailboat Ashore; oil on canvas, 10x8", C-E 10/18/89 UE 1,320

WEBER, Rudolf (Austrian, 1872-)

Relaxing by the Lake (figures/beached dory by water), oil on canvas, sgn, 20x30", RAB 3/27/89 UE 1,800
Rowboat on a Wooded River, oil on canvas, sgn, 29x40", C-E 10/25/88 1,320

WEBER, Theodore Alexander (French, 1838-1907)

Coming Ashore (boats), oil on canvas, sgn, 13x22", C-E 2/21/89 OE 4,180
In From the Storm, oil on canvas, sgn, unfr, 30x24", SBY 2/22/89 4,675
Leaving Harbor in a Squall, oil on canvas, sgn, 22x31", SBY 2/22/89 7,700
Salvaging a Shipwreck Off St Michael's Mount, oil on canvas, sgn, 43x75", C-NY 2/23/89 16,500

WEBER, W. (British, 19th C)

Moment of Reflection, oil on canvas, sgn, 35x18", B/B 6/9/88 1,980

WEBSTER, George (British, 19th C)

Extensive Coastal Landscape with Fishermen on a Beach, oil on canvas, sgn, 27x37", C-NY 5/25/88 4,950

WEBSTER, Thomas (British, 1800-1886)

Minding Baby (interior w/child knitting by sleeping baby), oil on panel, sgn/dtd 1856, 16x12", C-E 2/21/89 4,180

WEBSTER, Thomas; att (British, 1800-1886)

Morning Panel, oil on panel, bears signature/dtd 1819, 24x19", B/B 5/17/89 UE 495

WEEKES, Henry Jr. (British, fl 1849-1888)

Hunter's Repast, oil on canvas, sgn/dtd 1860, 28x36", SBY 6/9/89 UE 5,500

WEEKES, Herbert William (British, fl 1864-1904)

Backyard Gossip (two dogs meeting at garden wall), oil on panel, sgn, 11x8", SBY 10/24/89 11,000

WEEKS, Edwin Lord (American, 1849-1903)

Along the Nile, oil on canvas, sgn, 23x36", SBY 2/22/89 35,750
Caravan at a River Crossing, oil on canvas, sgn/dtd 1880, 35x60", C-NY 2/25/88 55,000
Caravanseray at Shiraz, Persia; oil en grisaille on canvas laid down on board, sgn, ca 1894, 15x18", C-NY 3/11/88 3,300
Departure of a Caravan From the Gate of Shelah, Morocco; oil on canvas, sgn/dtd 1880, 36x61", SBY 2/22/89 OE 242,000
Indian Hunting Party, oil on canvas laid down on board, sgn, 18x22", SBY 2/22/89 OE 52,250
Market in Ahmadabad, India; oil on canvas, sgn, 18x22", SBY 5/23/89 27,500
Marketplace in Ispahan, oil on canvas, sgn, 19x23", C-NY 10/25/89 22,000
Moorish Cafe, Tetuan, Morocco; oil on canvas, sgn/inscr/dtd 1878, 27x42", SBY 5/25/88 14,300
Return From Bombay, oil on canvas, sgn, 20x24", RWS 11/3/88 9,000
Standing Arab Woman, oil on board, 16x12", C-E 10/25/88 UE 1,760
Two Nautch Girls, oil on canvas, stamped signature & dates of a sale, 26x21", SBY 1/24/89 5,225
Wedding Feast-Ajmere; oil on canvas, sgn, unfr, 40x32", SBY 5/23/89 OE 34,100

WEEKS, Edwin Lord; att (American, 1849-1903)

North African Street Scene, oil on canvas, initialed/inscr/dtd 81, unfr, 20x13", C-E 5/23/88 OE 4,180

WEENIX, Jan Baptist the elder (Dutch, 1621-1663)
Hound with a Joint of Meat, a Cat Looking On; oil on canvas, sgn, 45x51", SBY 1/12/89 38,500
Portrait of a Man Holding a Wine Glass in a Landscape, oil on canvas, sgn, 31x25", C-NY 6/2/88 OE 41,800

WEENIX, Jan Baptist the younger (Dutch, 1640-1719)
Sportsman & His Dog Resting by a Statue of Minerva in a Plain, no media given, 20x24", C-M 6/16/89 5,704

WEENIX, Jan Baptist; circle of (Dutch, 17th/18th C)
Game, a Hare & Hunting Implements on a Ledge in a Park; oil on canvas, 32x39", C-NY 10/12/89 11,000
Seaport with a Gentleman & Two Courtesans, Rape of the Sabine's Beyond; oil on canvas, 34x29", C-NY 1/15/88 12,100

WEENIX, Jan Baptist; manner of (Dutch, 17th/18th C)
White Peacock, Hare & Other Wild Game Before a Palace Garden with a Pond; oil on canvas, SBY 4/7/89 28,600

WEGUELIN, John Reinhard (British, 1849-1927)
Lament of El Mulock, From a Poem by Thos Bailey Aldrich; gray wash over pencil, sgn twice/inscr, 16x13", C-NY 2/25/88 UE 330

WEHRSCHMIDT, Daniel Albert; see Veresmith

WEICHBERGER, Eduard (German, 1843-1913)
Wooded Landscape, gouache, sgn, 21x17", C-E 4/7/88 1,045

WEICHBERGER, Philip (European, 1936-)
Untitled, oil on canvas, sgn/dtd 62, unfr, 40x32", lot 194, SBY 2/14/89 440

WEIDENBACH, Augustus (American, fl 1853-1869)
Pair: View of West Point; The Hudson River From West Point; watercolor/gouache on paper, 11x14", SBY 3/17/88 OE 5,775

WEIGHORST, Olaf Carl (American/Danish, 1899-1975)
At Home, oil on canvas, sgn/dtd 26, unfr, 16x20", C-E 11/30/88 1,430
Beaver Trail, oil on canvas, sgn/inscr w/artist's brand, 28x24", SBY 5/25/88 OE 57,750
Bronco Buster, watercolor/pen/ink on paper, sgn, 11x9", B/B 6/9/88 4,675
Bucking Horse, oil on canvasboard, sgn, 10x14", C-E 11/30/88 2,420
Cowboy on Black Bucking Bronco, oil on canvasboard, sgn, 10x14", C-E 11/30/88 2,200
Cowboy on Bucking Bronco, oil on board, sgn, 16x12", C-E 11/30/88 2,200
Cowboy on Horseback at Sunset, oil on burlap, sgn, 20x24", SBY 6/24/88 13,200
Crossing the Stream, oil on canvas, sgn, 30x36", SBY 5/25/88 OE 36,300
Indian on Horseback, watercolor/pen/ink on paper, sgn, 11x9", B/B 6/9/88 5,225
Indians on a Cliff, oil on canvas, sgn, 28x38", C-NY 5/26/88 OE 41,800
Lonesome Brave (Indian w/horse looking out over valley), oil on canvas, 46x46", B/B 3/22/89 7,700
Mexican Bandito, India ink/gouache/watercolor on paper, sgn w/insignia, 12x10", SBY 9/23/88 OE 3,080
Nightwatch, oil on canvas, sgn, 26x20", SBY 5/25/88 OE 17,600
Only One Chance (man on bucking horse, wounded man watching), oil on canvas, sgn, unfr, 28x38", C-NY 9/28/89 8,800
Plains Indian on Horse, India ink/watercolor on board, sgn twice w/insignia, 10x8", SBY 9/23/88 5,170
Portrait of an Indian, watercolor/gouache on paper, sgn w/insignia, 10x8", SBY 9/23/88 OE 2,420
Roundup, oil on canvas, sgn/inscr w/artist's brand, ca early 1950s, 30x40", SBY 5/25/88 38,500
Set of 12: Sketches of Cowboys; India ink/watercolor/gouache on paper, sgn w/monogram, 12x11", SBY 9/23/88 OE 40,700
Snow-Covered Cabin in the Moonlight, oil on canvas, initialed, unfr, 9x12", B/B 9/15/88 1,760
Train Robbers (men dropping boulder in front of train), gouache on board, sgn, 16x13", B/B 3/22/89 2,750
Wood Gathers (landscape w/horse-drawn wagon & mounted rider), oil on canvas, sgn, 24x30", SBY 3/17/88 OE 35,200

WEIL, Harrison (19th C)
Rabbits, watercolor/gouache/pen/black & brown ink, sgn/dtd 1871, 7x10", C-NY 5/25/88 2,640

WEILER, Casper (American, 19th/20th C)
Shooting Oil Well, oil on canvas, indistinctly signed, 24x20", SBY 4/14/89 440

WEINGARTNER, Hans (20th C)
Rough Seas, oil on board, sgn/dtd 1938, 19x28", C-E 9/15/88 880

WEINGOTT, Victor Marcus (British, 1887-)
Dawn, oil on canvas, sgn/dtd 1935, 34x29", WAD 6/6/88 6,800

WEINRICH, Agnes (American, 20th C)
Houses, watercolor on paper, sgn, unfr, 12x19", C-E 6/1/88 UE 176

WEIR, Julian Alden (American, 1852-1919)
Branchville Brook, pastel on brown paper, sgn, ca 1905, 9x9", B/B 6/9/88 2,475
Church in a Landscape, watercolor on paper, sgn/inscr, 13x17", SBY 6/24/88 2,420
Cora (portrait), oil on canvas, sgn, 27x23", C-NY 12/2/88 22,000
Farmer's Lawn, oil on canvas, sgn, ca 1890, 21x29", SBY 5/25/88 110,000
Mills Along the River, watercolor on paper laid down on board, 12x16", C-E 2/3/88 2,200
Peonies (still life), oil on canvas, 36x32", C-NY 5/25/89 38,500
Roses in a Vase, watercolor/pencil on paper, sgn/dtd 84, 10x14", C-E 2/1/89 4,180
Rowboat on the Lakeshore, watercolor on paper, sgn, 10x14", B/B 3/17/88 1,870
Rushing River, oil on canvas, bears signature, 10x14", C-E 11/8/88 UE 220

WEIR, Robert Walter (American, 1803-1889)
Landing of Henry Hudson, 1608 at Verplanck Point, Near Peekskill, New York; oil on canvas, 33x48", C-NY 12/2/88 88,000
Playful Companions (dog & monkey), oil on canvas, 13x16", C-E-2/1/89 3,960

WEIROTTER, Franz; att (Austrian, 1730-1771)
Austrian Landscape, black chalk on gray paper, ca 1760, 8x12", SWN 12/1/88 358

WEIS, John Ellsworth (American, 1892-)
Summer Landscape, oil on board, sgn, 14x16", SBY 9/23/88 1,320

WEISBUCH, Claude (French, 1927-)
Harlequin (portrait), oil on canvas, sgn/dtd 67, 37x29", WD 11/16/88 OE 7,750

WEISHAUPT, Victor (German, 1848-1925)
Cows Watering, oil on canvas, sgn, 13x19", C-E 5/23/88 ... 1,980

WEISS, Emil Rudolf (German, 1875-1942)
Afternoon Pastimes (seated couple in interior), oil on canvas, sgn/dtd 1874, 24x18", C-NY 2/23/89 ... 3,080

WEISS, Georges (French, 1861-)
Flower Market, oil on canvas, sgn/dtd 1898, 29x24", C-NY 2/25/88 OE ... 22,000

WEISS, Johann Baptist (German, 1812-1879)
Fishing Ships on the Open Water, oil on canvas, sgn, 27x38", C-E 10/26/89 ... 4,400

WEISS, Jose (British, 1859-)
Corfe Castle, oil on canvas, sgn, 33x51", C-E 10/26/89 ... 4,400
June in the Country, oil on canvas, sgn, 16x24", FB 5/28/89 ... 1,100
Stone Bridge Over a River, oil on canvas, sgn, 16x24", C-E 2/23/88 ... 2,640
Summer Day, oil on canvas, sgn, 32x48", SBY 5/23/89 ... 11,000

WEISS, Samuel A. (American, -1918)
Swamp, oil on panel, sgn, 10x12", C-E 11/8/88 UE ... 280

WEISSE, Rudolph (Austrian, 1869-)
Le Garde du Harem, oil on panel, sgn/dtd 88, 18x12", SBY 10/24/89 ... 44,000
New Acquisition, oil on panel, sgn/dtd 86, 24x19", SBY 5/23/89 ... 71,500

WEISSMAN, W.H. (American, 19th/20th C)
Track in an Extensive Landscape, oil on canvas, sgn, 18x36", PHL 6/16/88 ... 800

WEISZ, Adolphe (French, 1868-)
Othello & Desdemona, oil on canvas, sgn, 53x79", SBY 2/22/89 OE ... 27,500

WEIZE (Chinese, 14th C)
Calligraphy in Xing Shu Running Script (hand scroll), ink on paper, sgn/dtd 1341, 13x452", SBY 5/31/89 OE ... 66,000

WELCH, E.M. (19th C)
Mountain Lake, oil on panel, sgn/dtd Feb 1894, 12x18", NA 10/1/88 UE ... 225

WELCH, Ludmilla Pilat (American, 1867-1925)
Double-Sided: Marine Landscape; oil on cigar box top, dtd 1904, 5x8", B/B 10/6/88 ... 440
Marin County Foothills with Lake, oil on board, sgn, 7x11", B/B 9/15/88 ... 330

WELCH, Thaddeus (American, 1844-1919)
Cattle Grazing Along a Riverbank, oil on canvas, sgn/dtd 1911, 20x36", B/B 10/6/88 ... 5,500
Cattle Grazing in a Meadow, oil on canvas laid down, 10x18", B/B 10/6/88 ... 825

WELDON, Charles Dater
Souvenir of Japan (portrait), pastel on paper laid down on board, initialed/dtd 86, 20x16", C-NY 3/11/88 ... 935

WELL, John Sanderson (British, fl 1872-1943)
Out Hunting, pencil/watercolor on paper, sgn, 16x24", SBY 6/9/89 ... 3,300

WELLIVER, Neil (American, 1929-)
Beaver House, oil on canvas, sgn, 1974, 96x96", SBY 10/8/88 ... 38,500
Mejunticook Mountain, oil on canvas, sgn, 1984, 24x36", C-E 11/14/89 ... 5,500
Sacred Bull (w/two nudes & young boy in landscape), oil/charcoal on canvas, sgn, 1964, 97x78", C-NY 2/14/89 ... 6,600
Untitled (abstract), acrylic on canvas, sgn, 38x42", SBY 10/7/89 ... 3,410
Untitled (contemporary depiction of wooded stream), oil on canvas, sgn/dtd 1979, 14x14", C-NY 10/4/89 ... 3,850
Vicky II (nude bather in wooded stream), oil on canvas, sgn/dtd 1973, 60x60", C-NY 10/4/89 ... 8,800
West Slope (wooded landscape), oil on canvas, 1978, 96x120", SBY 5/3/89 ... 33,000

WELLS, John Sanderson (British, 1872-)
Hunt Passing a Coach, oil on canvas, sgn, 16x24", C-NY 5/24/89 ... 7,150
Pair: Whodden Chase; Berkeley Hunt; oil on canvas, sgn, 16x12", WD 10/19/88 OE ... 5,250
Portrait of a Young Girl with Flowers (half-length), oil on canvas, sgn, 21x17", B/B 3/22/89 ... 1,870
Ruins, watercolor/pencil on paper, indistinctly sgn, 11x20", C-E 6/1/89 UE ... 143
Set of Three: The Meet; Well Over; The Kill; oil on canvas, sgn, 16x24", WD 10/19/88 OE ... 15,000

WELLS, Lynton (American, 1940-)
Untitled (abstract), oil on photosensitized linen laid down on canvas, sgn/dtd CE 72, unfr, 45x20", C-E 11/14/89 UE ... 385

WELLS, Mary (American, ca 1820-)
Map of New York with Parts of Pennsylvania, New Jersey, Etc; pen/ink/watercolor, sgn, 47x54", C-NY 6/3/89 ... 1,320

WELLS, T.
In the Forest, oil on canvas, sgn, 10x8", C-E 9/15/88 UE ... 143

WENBAN, Sion Longley (American, 1848-1897)
Landscape with Gray Sky, oil on canvas, sgn/dtd 1885(?), 6x14", SBY 6/24/88 ... 825

WENDEL, Theodore (American, 1859-1932)
In a Cove, pastel on board, sgn, 26x20", C-NY 9/30/88 ... 7,700
Moroccan Woman, oil on canvas, sgn/dtd 86, 24x18", C-NY 9/30/88 OE ... 5,500

WENDEROTH, August (German, ca 1817-)
Town Fair, oil on canvas, sgn/dtd New York 1850, 38x55", SBY 4/29/88 ... 41,250

WENDRICH, M.
Harbor Scene, oil on canvas, sgn/dtd 62, 15x19", LH 5/15/88 UE ... 100

WENDT, William (American, 1865-1946)
Afternoon Shadows, oil on canvas, sgn/dtd 1923, 25x30", B/B 10/6/88 OE ... 22,000
California Landscape, oil on canvas, sgn, unfr, 12x18", B/B 10/6/88 ... 2,750
Cornish Coast, oil on canvas, sgn, 18x22", C-NY 3/11/88 OE ... 15,400
Fountain at Santa Barbara, oil on canvas, sgn, 25x30", C-NY 9/30/88 ... 8,250
Gentle Evening Bendeth, oil on canvas, sgn/dtd 1938, 30x36", B/B 10/6/88 OE ... 35,750

Landscape, oil on canvas, sgn/dtd 1908, 23x35", LH 10/16/88 OE **22,000**
Midsummer, oil on canvas, sgn/dtd 1926, 25x30", B/B 10/6/88 ..... **22,000**
Mount Williamson, oil on canvas, sgn/dtd 1930, 25x30", B/B 10/6/88 ..... **22,000**
Old & New Near San Luis Obispo, oil on canvas, sgn/dtd 1928, 25x30", B/B 10/6/88 OE **46,750**
Pastoral Meadow, oil on canvas, sgn, 15x20", LH 10/16/88 OE **21,000**
River Valley in Autumn, oil on canvas, sgn/dtd 1908, 20x36", LH 10/16/88 OE **22,000**
Rocks & Trees, oil on canvas, sgn/dtd 1919, 16x20", C-NY 9/28/89 ..... **7,700**
Santa Clara, oil on canvas, sgn/inscr, dtd twice 1909, 28x36", C-NY 9/30/88 OE **27,500**
Soil-Near San Luis Obispo (landscape); oil on canvas, sgn/dtd 1926, 30x36", SBY 1/24/89 OE **49,500**
Southern California Landscape, oil on canvas, sgn/dtd 1941, 30x36", B/B 10/6/88 ..... **24,750**
When All the World Is Young, oil on canvas, sgn/dtd 1911, 40x55", LH 3/20/88 OE **64,000**
Wooded Hillside, oil on canvas, sgn/dtd 1906, 30x40", LH 10/16/88 OE **40,000**

WENFNER, Johann Conrad (German, 1728-1806)
Ceiling Sketch Depicting Miracle at Tomb of St Peter, watercolor/ink/pencil, sgn/#d 1026, 1774, 18x14", WD 1/25/89 OE **1,500**

WENGENROTH, Stow (American, 1906-1978)
Lighthouse, Eastern Point, East Gloucester; ink wash/graphite/crayon on board, bears signature, 19x25", RWS 9/8/89 OE **1,300**
Old Garden Beach, Rockport; ink wash/graphite/crayon on board, bears signature, 19x25", RWS 9/8/89 OE **900**

WENGER, John (American, 1887-)
Day of Prayer, watercolor on paper, sgn/dtd 62, unfr, 30x22", C-E 2/3/88 ..... **385**
Tryptich: Columbus Circle; watercolor on paper, 2 sgn, unfr, 15x10" & smaller, C-E 2/3/88 UE **440**
Tryptich: Elegy; gouache on paper/oil on board, sgn, unfr, 8x10" & smaller, C-E 2/3/88 UE **440**

WENGLEIN, Joseph (German, 1845-1919)
Spat Sommer im Moos Bei Munchen (landscape), oil on canvas, sgn/titled/inscr, 28x44", SBY 2/22/89 OE **46,750**
Woman Working in a Field, oil on board, sgn, 9x11", C-E 10/25/88 ..... **2,640**

WENTWORTH, S.D.
Interior Scene Depicting a Child Warming His Hands Before a Hearth, oil on panel, sgn/dtd 1884, 10x12", MAG 6/22/88 ..... **300**

WENXUE, Li (Chinese, 20th C)
One Hundred Insects (hanging scroll), ink/color on paper, sgn/dtd 1923, 17x26", SBY 5/31/89 OE **2,750**

WENZELL, Albert Beck (American, 1864-1917)
Evening Landscape, oil on canvas, sgn, 30x39", RWS 3/16/89 ..... **850**

WERETSHCHAGIN, Piotr Petrovitch (Russian, 1836-1886)
View of St Petersburg, oil on canvas, sgn, 16x35", C-NY 10/25/89 OE **24,200**

WERNER (German, 19th/20th C)
Before the Ride, oil on panel, initialed/dtd 1866, 14x17", C-NY 6544 OE **13,200**
New York Times (paper & other objects on a table), oil on canvas, sgn, 22x26", C-E 2/3/88 ..... **3,520**

WERNTZ, Carl N. (American, 1874-1944)
Outing at the Lake, oil on canvas, sgn, 38x30", SBY 6/24/88 OE **9,900**

WERTHEIMER, Gustav (Austrian, 1847-1904)
Beauty & the Beast, oil on canvas, sgn/dtd 1886, 45x69", SBY 5/23/89 UE **11,000**

WESCOTT, Paul (American, 1904-1970)
Barn Scene, oil on canvas, 30x37", C-E 10/18/89 ..... **2,420**
Collamores Cove, oil on canvasboard, sgn/inscr Mary Audobon Post Prize 1944, 18x30", C-E 10/18/89 UE **880**
Landscape with Farm in Distance, oil on canvas, sgn/dtd 1940, 25x36", C-E 6/1/88 UE **495**

WESSEL, Herman Henry (American, 1878-1969)
Coastal Scene, Brittany (figures in foreground, ships beyond); oil on canvas, initialed, 14x20", RWS 5/19/88 UE **2,100**
Gloucester Harbor, oil on canvas, sgn, 25x30", C-E 2/3/88 OE **2,970**

WESSELING, H. (American, 20th C)
Portrait of an Elderly Man in Light Green Tunic, oil on board, 15x11", WG 4/23/88 UE **110**

WESSELMANN, Tom (American, 1931-)
Bedroom Painting #38, oil on canvas, sgn/dtd 1977, 10x11", SBY 11/9/89 OE **71,500**
Big Brown Nude (contemporary), oil on canvas, sgn/dtd 71, 62x97", C-NY 5/3/89 OE **308,000**
California Nude #1, acrylic/graphite on board, sgn/#d #1/dtd 81, 6x8", C-NY 10/4/89 OE **26,400**
Claire's Valentine (Open-Ended Edition) #42, pencil/thinned liquitex on ragboard, sgn/dtd 74, 10x8", SBY 5/3/89 OE **15,400**
Diptych: Still Life #26; oil/acrylic polymer/paper/fabric collage on canvas, sgn/dtd 63 twice, 96x120", SBY 11/10/88 ..... **231,000**
Drawing for Great American Nude #17, charcoal on paper, sgn/dtd 61, 48x48", C-NY 2/20/88 OE **28,600**
Drawing for Most Beautiful Foot, pencil on Bristol board, sgn/dtd Cape Cod 68/inscr, 9x11", SBY 5/2/88 OE **24,200**
Embossed Nude VI, pencil on paper, sgn/dtd 65-66, 9x11", SBY 11/11/88 OE **11,000**
Feet (contemporary), gouache on paper, sgn/dtd 65, 18x23", C-NY 5/4/89 OE **15,400**
Fingertips with Cigarette, watercolor/charcoal on paper, sgn/dtd 78, 22x31", SBY 11/9/89 ..... **60,500**
Great American Nude #10, oil/paper collage on panel, sgn/dtd 61/inscr, unfr, 48" dia, C-NY 11/10/88 OE **132,000**
Great American Nude #4, mixed media on paper mounted on cardboard, initialed/dtd 60, 8x10", C-NY 5/4/89 OE **101,200**
Great American Nude #43, mixed media, sgn/dtd 63, 48x47", C-NY 11/7/89 ..... **495,000**
Great American Nude #58, collage with paper/liquitex/graphite on panel, sgn/dtd 1965, 48x42", C-NY 5/3/89 ..... **440,000**
Great American Nude VIII, mixed media on panel, sgn/dtd 1961/titled twice, unfr, 48" dia, C-NY 11/9/88 OE **462,000**
Little Great American Nude #25 (contemporary), liquitex on board, sgn/dtd 65, 13x12", SBY 11/9/89 OE **181,500**
Little Still Life #7, collage w/paper/acrylic/formed plastic on panel, sgn/dtd 63, 17x22", C- NY 5/4/89 OE **275,000**
Open Ended Nude #129, pencil/acrylic on paper, sgn/inscr #129/dtd 82, 4x9", SBY 10/5/88 OE **4,675**
Portrait Collage #2 (Pink Collar Lady), mixed media collage on panel, sgn/dtd 59, 13x10", SBY 10/5/89 ..... **44,000**
Portrait Collage #9 (Woman at Table-Three Trees), mixed media collage on panel, sgn/dtd 59, 10x14", SBY 10/5/89 ..... **49,500**
Still Life (beer can, sandwich, & cigarettes, contemporary), graphite on paper, sgn/dtd 63, 17x22", SBY 11/9/89 OE **93,500**
Still Life #56, oil on canvas, sgn/dtd 1967-69, 94x108", SBY 5/2/88 ..... **154,000**

Study for a Toothbrush, pencil/colored pencil on tracing paper, sgn/dtd 75, 7x16", SBY 5/3/89 OE **70,000**
Study for Bedroom Blonde, Black & Green Pillows; liquitex on bristol paper, sgn/dtd 86, 14x17", C-NY 5/4/89 OE **35,200**
Study for Bedroom Painting #19, oil on canvas, sgn/dtd 69, 8x10", SBY 11/9/89 ..... **38,500**
Study for Great American Nude, pencil on paper, sgn/dtd 65, 6x7", lot 296, SBY 5/3/89 OE **17,600**
Study for Great American Nude, pencil on paper, 1965, 27x34", lot 273, SBY 5/3/89 ..... **66,000**
Study for Great American Nude 1975, watercolor/pencil on paper, sgn/dtd 75, 15x22", SBY 10/5/89 OE **60,500**
Study for Marilyn's Mouth, oil on canvas, sgn/dtd 67/titled, 12x16", SBY 5/3/88 OE **33,000**
Study for Necklace for Still Life #60, liquitex/graphite on board, sgn twice/inscr/dtd 1973, 10x16", C-NY 5/4/88 ..... **3,080**
Study for Seascape Dropout, pencil/colored pencil on tracing paper, sgn/dtd 82, 14x17", SBY 5/3/89 OE **31,900**
Study for Shiny Nude (contemporary), pencil/colored pencil on tracing paper, sgn/dtd 76, 6x7", SBY 11/9/89 OE **27,500**
Study for Smoker #15 (abstract), liquitex/pencil on ragboard, sgn/dtd 73 twice/titled, 14x19", SBY 2/19/88 ..... **3,575**
Tiny Shoe & Tulip #23, liquitex on bristol board on formica base, sgn twice/dtd 1984, 5x6x3", C-NY 11/10/88 OE **11,000**
Untitled (mouth & bust of nude in rectangle), pencil on yellow paper, initialed/dtd 65, 7x5", C-E 11/14/89 OE **9,350**
Untitled (nude), graphite on paper, sgn/dtd 64, 10x11", C-NY 11/10/88 ..... **5,500**

Coca-Cola LSL #9, oil/paper collage on panel, sgn/titled twice/dtd 63, 9x11", C-NY 11/8/89 OE; $148,500

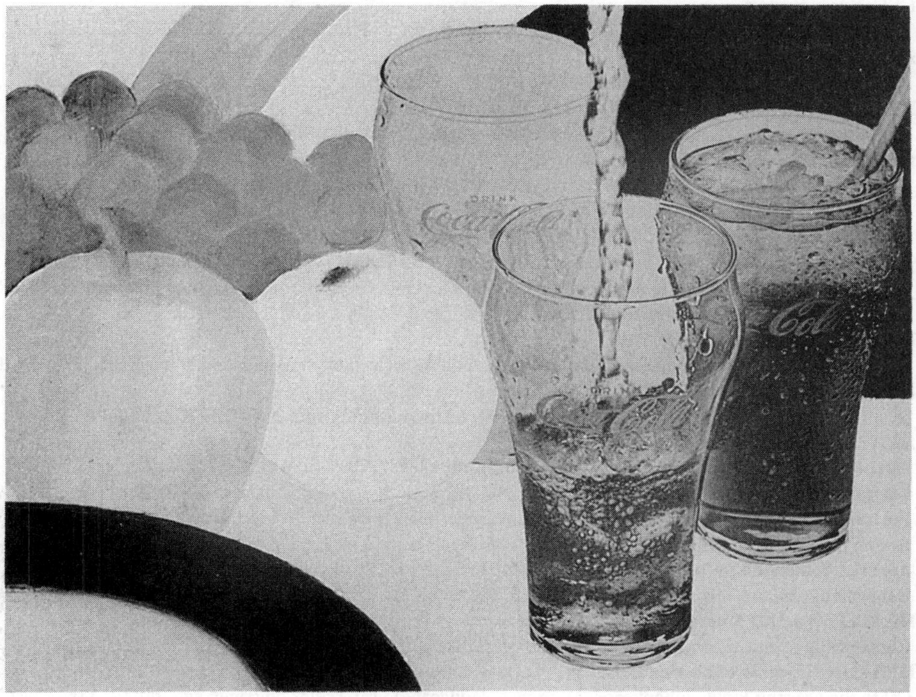

ESSELS, Albert (Dutch, 20th C)
Sunset on the Marsh, oil on canvas, sgn, 12x20", B/B 5/17/89 ..... **440**
ESSLEY, Anton (Austrian, 1848-)
Lady Riding Sidesaddle (w/dog at side, in a landscape), oil on canvas, sgn, 29x40", C-E 2/21/89 ..... **5,500**
EST, Benjamin; circle of (American, 1738-1820)
Portrait of a Man, half-length, in a white waistcoat & dark coat; oil on canvas, 30x25", C-E 4/7/88 UE **385**
Rest on the Flight into Egypt (after Correggio), oil on canvas, unfr, 29x24", SBY 12/9/88 UE **1,320**
EST, Francis
Ships at Sea, oil on canvasboard, sgn, 15x23", C-E 5/3/88 UE **190**
EST, Raphael Lamar (American, 1769-1850)
Fear, pen/brown ink, 7x9", C-NY 1/11/89 UE **550**
EST, W.J. (European, 19th C)
Valley Road (landscape), oil on canvas, sgn/dtd 1883, 21x30", RAB 11/25/88 UE **425**
ESTALL, William (British, 1781-1850)
Island of Timor, pencil/brush/India ink, initialed/inscr, unfr, 7x11", C-SK 6/9/88 ..... **557**
ESTCHILOFF, Constantin (American/Russian, 1880-1945)
Adriondack View, oil on canvas, sgn, 26x34", C-E 2/3/88 ..... **880**
Coastal View, oil on board, sgn, 6x9", NA 5/13/89 ..... **800**
Harbor Scene (impressionistic veiw of moored boats), oil on cardboard, sgn, 9x10", RWS 9/29/88 UE **300**
Maine Landscape, oil on canvas, sgn/inscr Maine, 34x41", SBY 1/24/89 ..... **1,980**
Ognuquit, Maine; oil on canvas, sgn, 23x29", SBY 6/28/89 ..... **1,210**
Pink Flowering Tree, oil on canvas, sgn/inscr, 36x44", SBY 12/9/88 ..... **1,375**
Snowy River Banks, oil on canvas, sgn, 26x32", C-E 11/8/88 ..... **500**
ESTERBURG, Gus Pieter, after; (Dutch, 1791-1873)
Country Scent, oil on canvas, 13x18", LH 10/16/88 ..... **450**
ESTERMANN, Horace Clifford (American, 1922-)
Kiss Me Good-Bye, ink/watercolor on paper, sgn/dtd 1969, 23x30", SBY 10/5/89 ..... **11,000**

Progresso (contemporary), ink/wash on paper, sgn/dtd 1971/inscr dedication, 15x22", SBY 2/19/88 OE	6,875
See America First, watercolor/pen/black ink/paper collage, sgn/dtd 68, 18x22", C-NY 10/31/89 OE	4,180
Untitled, watercolor/pen/black ink on paper, initialed/dtd 78, 12x9", lot 98, C-NY 10/4/89	7,150
WESTON, Harold (American, 1894-1972)	
Duck & Bath (duck, soap & tub of water on table), oil on canvas, sgn, 20x26", RWS 5/19/88	1,100
Group of 3: Cliffords Brooke; Landscape; Farm Scene; gouache/watercolor on paper, sgn, 12x19", C-E 6/1/89	660
WET, see De Wet	
WETHERBEE, George Faulkner (American, 1851-1920)	
Harvesting, oil on canvas, sgn/dtd 1885, 50x35", C-E 10/25/88	3,850
WETHERILL, Elisha Kent Kane (American, 1874-1925)	
Breton Peasant Woman with Rooster, oil on canvas, sgn/dtd 1905, 37x29", FAP 12/8/89 UE	1,000
Delicatessen, oil on canvas, 60x54", SBY 6/24/88	7,425
Sag Harbor (neighborhood view), oil on canvas, sgn/dtd 1916, 40x36", SBY 5/24/89	14,300
Upper Hudson, oil on canvas, 20x20", C-NY 3/11/88	3,850
Winter Symphony, oil on canvas, sgn, 21x22", C-NY 5/26/88	3,850
WETTERAU, Rudolf	
Early Snowfall, oil on canvas, sgn, 12x16", C-E 2/16/88 UE	99
WEX, Willibald (German, 1831-1892)	
Rowboat on Stormy Seas, oil on canvas, 45x34", C-E 5/23/88 OE	3,520
WEYGANDT, John H. (American, -1951)	
Clouding Over, oil on canvas laid down on board, sgn, 9x12", FAP 12/8/89	175
WEYL, Max (American, 1837-1914)	
Clearing in the Forest, oil on canvas, sgn, 24x20", B/B 1/11/89	880
Dancing Bathers, oil on board, sgn/dtd 1910, 15x21", C-E 10/18/89	1,430
Ducks, oil on canvas, sgn/dtd 1910, 24x20", C-E 10/18/89	1,320
Ducks Along Maryland River Bank, oil on canvas, sgn, 24x36", C-E 10/18/89	2,860
Lurline of Sunderland, Capt James Gooding Passing Flushing, 1863; oil reverse-painted on glass, 22x28", RAB 11/10/88	4,250
Morning, Venice; oil on canvas, sgn/inscr, 12x18", C-E 2/3/88 OE	4,180
WHATLEY, Ernest	
Venezuelan Landscapes, pencil/watercolor heightened w/bodycolor, sgn/indistinctly inscr, 32x22", C-SK 11/10/88 UE	150
WHEAT, John (American, 1920-)	
Summer Gold (rural landscape w/village & farms), oil on masonite, sgn, 20x30", SBY 3/17/88 OE	3,575
WHEATLEY, Francis (British, 1747-1801)	
Landscape with Cattle by a Waterfall, oil on canvas, initialed, 25x30", SBY 1/12/89	15,400
Portrait of an Officer, oil on canvas, sgn/dtd 1782, within a feigned oval, 29x24", SBY 10/13/89	11,000
Portrait of Ralph Winstanley Wood & His Son Warren, in a wooded landscape; oil on canvas, 28x35", C-NY 1/15/88 OE	66,000
Reconciliation, oil on canvas, 19x14", C-NY 10/12/89	6,600
WHEATLEY, Francis; after (British, 1747-1801)	
Benevolent Cottage, oil on canvas, 24x20", PHL 10/28/88	850
WHEATLEY, G.H. (American, 20th C)	
Clipper Ship at Sea, oil on canvas, sgn, 24x36", B/B 4/20/88	1,320
WHEATON, Francis (American, 1849-)	
Off to the Grazing Fields (shepherdess/lambs in landscape), watercolor on paper, sgn/dtd 91, 14x22", RAB 3/27/89 UE	350
WHEELER, (German, 20th C)	
Beaufort Hunt (gentleman on horse in extensive landscape), oil on canvas, sgn, 28x37", C-E 5/22/89	5,500
WHEELER, Clifton A. (American, 1883-)	
Double-Sided: Wooded Figure; Portrait of a Man; oil on masonite, 1 sgn/dtd 40, 1 sgn/dtd 41, 21x17", C-E 2/3/88 OE	2,090
WHEELER, J. (British, 19th C)	
Royal Mail Coach, oil on canvas, sgn, 25x36", WD 10/19/88	3,250
WHEELER, James Thomas (British, 1849-1888)	
Pony & Spaniels in a Landscape, oil on board, sgn, 19x21", SBY 6/9/89	2,420
WHEELER, John Alfred (British, 1821-1903)	
Chestnut Hunter in the Grounds of Badminton House, oil on canvas, sgn/inscr, 25x30", SBY 6/10/88	11,000
Lord Sherborne's Gray Arab in a Stable, oil on canvas, sgn/dtd 1865, 28x36", SBY 6/10/88 OE	17,600
Steeplechasing, oil on canvas, 18x30", SBY 6/10/88	7,425
WHEELER, John Arnold (British, 1821-1877)	
Jockey on a Racehorse, oil on canvas, sgn, 14x18", C-E 2/12/89	3,520
Ormonde, oil on canvas, sgn, 20x24", B/B 6/9/88	4,400
Over the Fence, oil on board, 9x12", C-E 10/25/88 UE	880
St Simon, oil on canvas, sgn, 20x24", B/B 6/9/88	3,850
WHEELER, W.R. (American, 1832-)	
Allegorical Landscape, oil on canvas, sgn/dtd 18(?), 36x54", C-E 11/30/88	4,180
Portrait of a Gentleman (three-quarter length, facing forward holding a paper), oil on canvas, sgn, 30x25", SLK 2/12/88	650
WHEELWRIGHT, W.H. (British, fl 1857-1897)	
Set of 12: Sporting Screen; oil on board, sgn/dtd 86-89-91, 8 12x20", 4 26x20", SBY 6/9/89	22,000
WHIPPLE, Charles Ayer (American, 1859-1928)	
Sisters (young woman holding small girl on her lap in wooded landscape), oil on canvas, sgn, 44x30", RAB 8/9/88	1,000
WHISTLER, James Abbott McNeill (American, 1834-1903)	
Gray & Pink, a Draped Model with Fan; pastel/watercolor on paper, sgn w/butterfly, #d 59, ca 1890s, 11x8", SBY 5/24/89	38,500
Nude Reclining, pastel on brown paper, sgn, ca 1900, 7x11", C-NY 12/2/88 OE	99,000
Portrait of a Lady, pencil on paper, unfr, 6x4", C-NY 9/30/88	4,950

HISTLER, Rex (British, 1905-1944)
Dungeon, First Sketch; watercolor/pen/black ink on paper, 6x8", C-NY 10/5/88 OE **1,760**
HITAKER, George William (American, 1841-1916)
At Seconet, 1898; oil on mounted canvas, sgn, 14x20", RWS 5/12/89 .... **450**
Barnyard Scene, oil on panel, sgn/dtd 1886, 15x26", RWS 9/8/89 OE **1,500**
Forest Road (two figures on shady road), oil on canvas, sgn/dtd 1908, 22x28", RAB 8/9/88 .... **525**
Mother & Child-A Walk Through the Woods; oil on canvas, sgn/dtd 94, 12x10", RWS 5/12/89 UE **300**
Path by the River, oil on canvas, sgn, 15x25", RWS 5/12/89 .... **1,000**
Pond in a Woodland Grove, oil on canvas, sgn, 14x24", B/B 12/8/88 .... **660**
Still Life of Fruit, oil on canvas, sgn/dtd 84, 31x49", SBY 4/14/89 .... **1,320**
HITAKER, William (American, 1943-)
Hudson Bay Blanket, oil on board, sgn/copyrighted/dtd 1977, 20x16", SBY 9/23/88 OE **1,210**
Portrait of Mia, pastel on paper, sgn/dtd 78, 28x34", SBY 9/23/88 OE **2,475**
Study for Sacajawea, pastel on paper, sgn/copyrighted/dtd 1975, 39x26", SBY 9/23/88 OE **2,200**
HITCOMBE, H. (British, 19th C)
Sailing Ship at Sea, oil on canvas, sgn, 20x30", SBY 12/9/88 .... **3,300**
HITE, Alvin A. (American, 20th C)
Bee Tree in the Woods (bear & cubs below bee tree), oil on canvas, sgn/titled, 11x10", RAB 8/8/89 .... **300**
Hoxie House, Sandwich, Massachusetts; oil on canvas, sgn/titled, 11x15", RAB 3/27/89 UE **150**
Sandy Neck, West Barnstable; oil on canvas, sgn/dtd 86, 10x14", RAB 8/9/88 .... **600**
HITE, Belle Cady (American, 1868-1945)
Chatham Center Church (in landscape), watercolor on paper, sgn/dtd 1933, 10x15", RAB 3/27/89 UE **80**
Connecticut Valley (landscape), watercolor on paper, sgn/titled, 14x20", RAB 3/27/89 UE **75**
HITE, Clarence Scott (American, 1872-)
Coastal Scene, oil on board, sgn, 9x11", RWS 9/8/89 .... **375**
Coastal Scene (pine & grasses on a rocky ledge, ocean beyond), oil on board, sgn, 9x11", RWS 3/31/88 UE **400**
Solitude (lone figure on rocky shore, rushing water below, pines beyond), oil on board, sgn, 7x6", RWS 3/31/88 .... **600**
Winter Lane (landscape), oil on board, sgn, 11x13", RAB 11/25/88 UE **450**
HITE, Edith (American, 1855-1946)
Pink Roses, oil on canvas, sgn, 15x19", B/B 10/6/88 .... **1,650**
Pink Roses (still life), oil on canvas, sgn/dtd 1897, 34x27", SBY 4/14/89 .... **5,225**
HITE, Edwin (American, 1817-1877)
Calvinists Embarking for America, oil on canvas, sgn/dtd Paris 1859, 42x59", C-E 6/1/89 UE **2,200**
HITE, George Harlow (Canadian, 1817-1888)
Creek with Mountains, watercolor, sgn/dtd 1877, 5x9", WAD 6/12/89 .... **375**
HITE, Newton H. (American, 19th C)
Untitled, two setters on point; oil on canvas, sgn/dtd 96, 29x59", SLK 11/25/88 .... **1,100**
HITE, Orrin A. (American, 1883-1969)
California Vista, oil on canvas, sgn, 22x28", B/B 10/6/88 .... **5,225**
Sierra Lake, oil on canvas, sgn, 20x24", B/B 10/6/88 .... **1,430**
HITE, Thomas Gilbert (American, 1877-1939)
Garden Walk, oil on canvas, sgn, 24x32", SBY 6/28/89 OE **5,500**
On the Lake, oil on canvas, sgn, 24x32", SBY 6/28/89 .... **2,200**
HITEHEAD, Frederick William Newton (British, 1853-1938)
Sligahm, Skye (horses on a beach w/mountain beyond); oil on canvas, sgn, 28x48", C-E 5/22/89 .... **4,400**
HITING, Henry W. (American, 20th C)
Seascape, oil on canvas, sgn, 14x24", C-E 4/7/88 .... **1,980**
HITLEY, G.
Gathering Twigs, oil on canvas laid down on board, sgn/dtd 99, 30x26", C-E 5/23/88 UE **1,320**
HITMORE, Coby (American, 1913-)
Lovers` Rendezvous (in landscape), oil on canvasboard, sgn, 16x24", B/B 3/22/89 .... **2,200**
HITMORE, R.H. (American, 20th C)
Home by Moonlight, oil on canvas, sgn/dtd 1925, 30x36", WG 9/16/88 UE **150**
HITMORE, William R. (American, 19th/20th C)
Old Wooden Bridge-Holyoke, Springfield, Massachusetts; oil on canvas, sgn/dtd 1911, 25x30", RAB 8/8/89 UE **400**
HITNEY, E.S. (American, 19th C)
Squantom, South Boston in Distance (landscape), oil on canvas, sgn/titled, 14x24", RAB 3/27/89 .... **600**
HITTAKER, James (British, 1828-1876)
Feeding Time (hounds feeding from trough), oil on canvas, sgn/indistinctly dtd, 16x24", C-E 5/22/89 OE **5,280**
HITTAKER, John Barnard (American, 1836-)
Portrait of a Young Girl, oil on canvas, sgn, 22x18", C-E 9/15/88 UE **154**
HITTEMORE, C. Helen Simpson (American, 19th/20th C)
Marion Davies (bust-length), watercolor on paper, sgn/dtd 1924, 15x10", WD 3/23/88 .... **1,000**
HITTEMORE, William John (American, 1860-1955)
Dragon & Chinese Figures, oil on canvas mounted on board, sgn/dtd 1923, 10x9", SBY 9/23/88 UE **550**
Field of Flowers, oil on panel, sgn/dtd 85, 14x10", C-E 11/30/88 .... **1,650**
Necklace, watercolor on board, sgn, 36x20", SBY 4/14/89 OE **6,600**
Portrait of a Lady in an Interior, pastel on paper mounted on canvas, sgn, 30x25", SBY 6/24/88 .... **1,540**
HITTLE, Thomas (British, 19th C)
Nature's Bounty, oil on canvas, sgn/dtd 1866, 18x25", C-E 10/26/89 .... **3,300**

WHITTREDGE, Thomas Worthington (American, 1820-1910)
Along the New England Coast, oil on canvas, sgn, 10x16", C-NY 5/26/88 ..... **6,600**
Brook, oil on canvas, sgn, 14x11", C-E 10/18/89 ..... **3,300**
Clearing in the Forest, oil on canvas, sgn, 27x20", C-NY 5/25/89 ..... **17,600**
Deer Along the Ohio, oil on panel, sgn/dtd 1847, 10x12", C-NY 5/26/88 ..... **16,500**
In the Mountains, oil on board, sgn, 13x10", RAB 8/8/89 UE **2,500**
Lake Village, oil on canvas, sgn/dtd 1860, C-NY 3/11/88 ..... **24,200**
Roman Campagna (landscape), oil on canvas, sgn/dtd Rome 1857, 26x40", SBY 1/24/89 ..... **9,350**
Second Beach, Newport (landscape); oil on canvas, sgn, ca 1878-80, 30x50", SBY 5/24/89 ..... **1,870,000**
Tree Study, oil on paper laid down on board, bears signature/inscr, 13x9", C-E 11/30/88 ..... **3,080**

WHORF, Harry C. (American, 20th C)
Cape Cod Sand Dunes, crayon on paper, sgn, 9x13", RAB 8/8/89 UE **70**

WHORF, John (American, 1903-1959)
African Street (figures by a whitewashed wall, glimpses of palms), watercolor on paper, sgn, 13x20", RAB 8/9/88 UE **500**
Artist's Backyard, Winthrop; oil on canvas, ca 1940, 30x30", RWS 11/10/89 ..... **2,400**
Circus Days #32 (clowns riding in wagon of Floto Circus), watercolor on paper, sgn/titled, 21x14", RAB 8/8/89 ..... **4,750**
Connecticut Farm (snowy landscape w/figures clearing driveway), watercolor on paper, sgn/titled, 15x21", RAB 8/8/89 ..... **4,000**
Crashing Waves, watercolor/gouache/pencil on paper, sgn/ 15x23", C-E 6/1/89 UE **550**
Double-Sided: Sea Gull; Alpine Village; watercolor on paper, sgn, 15x22", RAB 8/9/88 ..... **2,750**
End of Day (coastal town with figures & sailboats), watercolor on paper, sgn, 20x26", RAB 8/9/88 ..... **1,300**
Fleet's Return, oil on canvas, sgn, 20x28", RAB 8/9/88 OE **4,500**
Freight Yard Smoke (locomotive), watercolor on paper, sgn, 15x21", WD 10/5/88 ..... **3,250**
Gale (coastal seascape), watercolor on paper, sgn/titled, 15x21", RAB 8/8/89 ..... **2,250**
Gale (crashing waves), watercolor on paper, sgn, 15x22", WD 10/5/88 UE **950**
High Tide (waves crashing on rocky shore), watercolor/gouache on paper, sgn, 15x21", B/B 9/14/89 ..... **990**
Log Jam, watercolor on paper, sgn, 16x23", C-E 2/1/89 UE **1,540**
Mountain Farm, Twilight; oil on canvas, sgn, 29x36", RWS 5/19/88 UE **1,700**
Out of the Cove (two men in boat), watercolor on paper, sgn, 15x21", WD 10/5/88 ..... **2,800**
Scene in Provincetown, watercolor on paper, sgn, 16x22", RWS 11/3/88 ..... **2,200**
Snowy & Gray, watercolor/graphite on paper, sgn, 13x21", RWS 11/10/89 UE **950**
Sunbathers, watercolor on paper, sgn, 21x15", RAB 8/9/88 ..... **2,400**
Winter Day (landscape), watercolor/gouache on paper, sgn, 10x19", RAB 8/8/89 ..... **1,700**
Winter Landscape, watercolor on paper, sgn, 15x20", SBY 4/14/89 UE **528**

WICHERA, Raimund (Austrian, 1862-)
Elegant Ladies in a Garden, oil on canvas, sgn, 28x34", C-NY 2/23/89 ..... **7,150**
Portrait of a Lady with Her Pekingese, oil on canvas, sgn, 34x28", SBY 7/12/89 OE **7,150**

WICKENDEN, Robert J. (Canadian, 1861-1931)
Guitarist (woman sitting & strumming guitar), oil on panel, sgn/dtd 1884, 16x9", RWS 9/29/88 UE **325**
Riverside Mill, watercolor, sgn, 10x14", WAD 11/30/89 ..... **280**

WICKER, Mary H. (American, 20th C)
Sailboats, Brittany; oil on panel, 22x18", LH 12/4/88 ..... **250**

WIDDAS, Richard Dodd (British, 1826-1885)
Set of 4: The Meet; Full Cry; Cornering the Fox; The Kill (hunt scenes); oil, 2 sgn/1 dtd 1852, 18x27", SBY 6/9/89 ..... **34,100**

WIDER, Wilhelm (German, 1818-1884)
Carnival in Rome, oil on canvas, sgn/dtd 52, 25x19", SBY 2/22/88 ..... **16,500**

WIDFORSS, Gunnar Mauritz (American, 1879-1934)
Canyon Walls in the Sunlight (extensive rocky landscape), watercolor on paper, sgn/dtd 1922, 17x14", B/B 10/9/88 OE **9,900**
Goblet & Vase, oil/graphite on panel, sgn/dtd 1955, 11x10", SBY 11/9/89 OE **60,500**
Rock Formation in the Desert, watercolor on paper, sgn/dtd 1923, 18x14" OE **8,800**
Sierra Nevada Mountains, watercolor on paper, sgn, 23x20", B/B 6/9/88 ..... **6,600**
View of Mt Whitney, watercolor on paper, sgn, 9x15", B/B 10/6/88 ..... **3,850**

WIDFORSS, Gunnar Mauritz; att (American, 1879-1934)
View of the High Country, watercolor on paper, bears partial signature, 10x13", B/B 1/11/89 ..... **550**

WIDGERY, Frederick John (British, 1861-1942)
On the Moors (landscape near Dartmoor South Devonshire), oil on canvas, sgn, 43x27", SLK 9/27/88 ..... **475**

WIDGERY, William; att (British, 1822-1893)
Misty Glen, watercolor/gouache, bears signature, 18x23", LH 12/4/88 UE **800**

WIECK, Johann
Island Dock, oil on panel, sgn, 9x12", NA 11/5/88 ..... **750**

WIEGAND, Gustave Adolf (American, 1870-1957)
Barren Landscape, oil on canvas, sgn, 24x28", C-E 11/30/88 UE **880**
Clearing in the Woods, oil on canvas, sgn, 30x25", B/B 9/15/88 ..... **880**
Country Road, oil on canvas, sgn, 24x36", C-E 6/1/88 OE **2,420**
Fall Landscape, oil on canvas, sgn, 24x36", C-SK 5/25/89 ..... **2,760**
Fallen Tree, oil on canvas, sgn, 16x20", C-E 2/1/89 ..... **3,300**
Gold & Brown (autumn landscape), oil on cardboard, sgn twice/titled, unfr, 8x10", RAB 8/8/89 UE **500**
Lakeside Landscape, oil on canvas, sgn, 20x30", SBY 3/17/88 ..... **1,430**
Landscape at Dusk, oil on canvas, sgn, 13x20", WG 4/23/88 UE **400**
Landscape with Red Cottage, oil on board, sgn, 12x10", SBY 3/17/88 ..... **1,045**
Pair: A Red-Roofed Farmhouse; A Country House in Spring; oil on canvas, sgn/dtd 1901, 14x19", 10x14", SBY 4/14/89 ..... **2,200**
Pair: Spring Landscape; White Cottage (in a landscape); oil on canvas, sgn, unfr, 10x14", C-SK 11/10/88 ..... **1,490**

Road in Autumn (landscape), oil on cardboard, sgn/titled, 8x10", RAB 8/8/89 UE ... 750
Silver Melody (landscape), oil on canvas, sgn, 34x32", SBY 9/23/88 ... 5,500
Springtime (landscape), oil on canvas, sgn/dtd 1927, 16x21", C-E 2/1/89 OE ... 2,860
Summer Bouquet (still life of flowers), oil on artist board, sgn, 20x16", RWS 3/31/88 OE ... 1,600
Summer Day (boy fishing from boat on riverbank w/green trees near house), oil on canvas, sgn, 18x30", RAB 8/8/89 ... 2,400
Trees by a Lake, oil on canvas, sgn, 16x12", SBY 3/17/88 ... 660
Trees by a Lake, oil on panel, sgn, 30x23", C-E 10/18/89 ... 1,650
Winter Landscape, oil on canvas, sgn, 16x20", C-E 6/1/89 UE ... 385

WIEGANDT, Bernhard (German, 1851-1918)

Amazonas, pencil/brown wash heightened w/white & gum arabic, sgn, unfr, 10x15", C-SK 11/10/88 ... 370
Artist Overlooking the Bay of Rio de Janeiro, pencil/watercolor heightened w/white, sgn/dtd 79, 10x15", C-SK 11/10/88 OE ... 2,600
Brazilian Coastal Landscape, pencil/brown wash heightened w/white, sgn/dtd 1880, unfr, 9x25", C-SK 5/25/89 ... 3,310
Corner of a Garden, Rio; black chalk/watercolor heightened w/white & gum arabic, 12x17", C-SK 6/9/88 ... 740
Girl in a Hammock Painting a Bowl, gray wash, initialed/studio stamp, unfr, 8x13", C-SK 5/25/89 ... 480
Mountains of Rio, pencil/brown wash heightened w/white, sgn/dtd 1880/#d 164, 10x25", C-SK 5/25/89 ... 3,310
Para (Belem), pencil/brown wash heightened w/white & gum arabic, sgn/dtd 1877, unfr, 13x20", C-SK 5/25/89 ... 3,670
Rio de Janeiro, pencil/watercolor heightened w/white, unfr, 15x39", C-SK 11/10/88 OE ... 2,230
Rue St Clemente, Rio de Janeiro (quiet street scene); pencil/watercolor, sgn, unfr, 19x13", C-SK 5/25/89 OE ... 8,270
Trees, pencil/watercolor heightened w/white, sgn, unfr, 11x17", C-SK 11/10/88 ... 280
Water Carriers at Para de Belem, pencil/watercolor heightened w/white, sgn, unfr, 13x20", C-SK 11/10/88 ... 2,040
Woodcutter, Para (Belem); pencil/brown wash heightened w/white & gum arabic, sgn/dtd 1878, 14x20", SBY 5/25/89 ... 3,670

WIELAND, Hans Beat (Swiss, 1867-1945)

Blau & Weiss, oil on canvas, sgn/dtd 1907-08, 60x47", C-E 10/26/89 ... 8,250

WIERICX, Jan (Flemish, 1553-1619)

Bacchanal, pen/brown ink on vellum, 7x3", SBY 1/13/89 ... 4,400

WIESENTHAL, Franz (Austrian/Hungarian, 1856-)

Children's Game, oil on canvas, sgn/dtd 1896, 31x25", SBY 2/22/89 ... 7,700
Le Potage Renverse, oil on canvas, sgn, 21x28", C-E 5/23/88 UE ... 1,650
Overturned Milk (baby & dog in interior), oil on canvas, sgn, 21x28", SBY 7/12/89 ... 4,400

WIGGINS, Guy Carleton (American, 1883-1962)

At the Plaza, (snowy plaza), oil on canvasboard, sgn twice/inscr, 12x16", C-NY 12/2/88 ... 6,050
Autumn Days, oil on board, sgn, 9x12", C-E 11/30/88 ... 1,430
Autumn Sunset, oil on canvas, sgn/dtd 06, 12x16", RWS 11/3/88 ... 1,500
Blizzard in Manhattan (cityscape), oil on artist board, sgn, 12x9", RWS 5/19/88 ... 8,500
Broadway at Herald Square (winter street scene), oil on canvas, sgn, 1919, 20x24", SBY 5/24/89 ... 39,600
Carriage Trade at the Plaza, oil on canvas, sgn/inscr/dtd 1957, 20x30", C-NY 5/26/88 ... 17,600
Central Park in Winter, Near Bergdrof's; oil on board, sgn, 12x16", WD 10/5/88 ... 16,500
Chicago Blizzard (winter street scene), oil on canvas, sgn, 25x30", SBY 5/24/89 ... 18,700
Down the Avenue, oil on canvas, sgn twice/inscr/dtd 1927, 16x12", C-NY 9/30/88 ... 14,300
Fifth Avenue Storm (snowy street scene), oil on canvasboard, sgn, 18x24", C-NY 5/25/89 ... 14,300
Hill-Farm, Winter; oil on canvas, sgn/inscr, 20x24", C-NY 5/26/88 ... 7,150
Landscape with Cows, oil on academy board, sgn, 12x16", RWS 9/29/88 UE ... 550

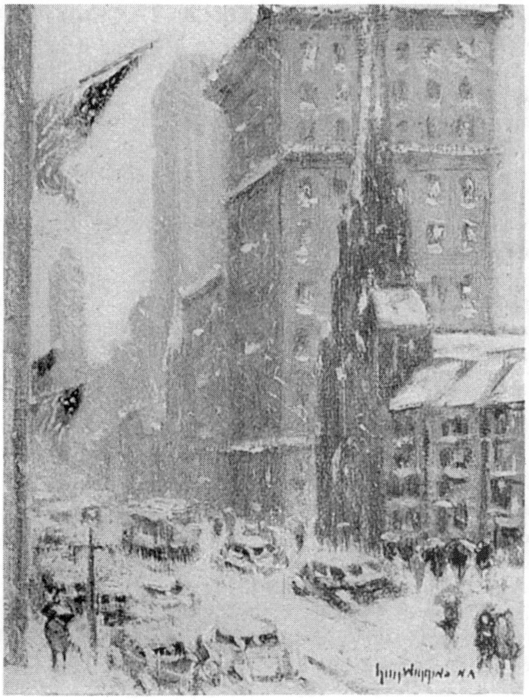

Fifth Avenue Winter, oil on canvasboard, sgn twice/titled, 16x12", C-NY 9/28/89; $8,800

Looking Down the Avenue (snowy street scene), oil on canvasboard, sgn twice/inscr, 16x12", C-NY 12/2/88 OE ... 28,600
Lower Broadway in Winter, oil on canvas, sgn/inscr/dtd 1961, 20x24", C-NY 5/26/88 ... 19,800
New England Lane, oil on canvas, sgn, 20x24", C-NY 3/11/88 ... 7,150
New York in Winter, oil on canvas, sgn, 10x8", C-NY 5/26/88 ... 6,050
New York in Winter, oil on canvas, sgn, 16x19", SBY 6/24/88 ... 5,500
New York Skyline (impressionistic cityscape), oil on canvas, sgn twice/dtd 1929 twice/titled, 25x30", SBY 5/24/89 ... 31,900
New York Winter, oil on canvas, sgn twice/dtd 1931/titled, 12x16", SBY 1/24/89 ... 8,250
New York Winter, oil on canvasboard, sgn, 5x7", C-NY 9/28/89 ... 5,720
Old & New New York From Washington Square, oil on artist board, sgn, 12x9", RWS 5/19/88 UE ... 4,250
Old Lyme Landscape, oil on canvas, sgn twice/titled, 12x16", SBY 3/17/88 ... 2,475
Old Wood Lot, oil on canvas, sgn/inscr/dtd 1924, 12x16", C-NY 3/11/88 ... 5,830
On Dorest Hills, Vermont Winter; oil on canvas, sgn/inscr, 20x24", C-NY 3/11/88 ... 6,600
Pair: Midtown-New York Winter; Washington's Arch; oil on canvasboard, sgn/inscr, 12x9", C-NY 5/26/88 ... 8,800
Pair: Wall Street; Library; oil on canvas, sgn, 9x12", SBY 6/28/89 ... 12,100
Red Barn, oil on canvas, sgn, 16x20", C-NY 9/30/88 ... 4,180
St Ives, Cornwall; oil on board laid down on masonite, sgn, 12x16", C-E 10/18/89 ... 4,400
Summer Bouquet, oil on canvas, sgn twice/inscr, 25x30", C-NY 9/30/88 ... 2,750
Victory in Winter (winter street scene w/statue), oil on canvas, sgn twice/titled, 25x30", SBY 5/24/89 ... 23,100
View Through the Park, Early Spring; oil on cardboard, sgn, 11x17", RWS 5/12/89 ... 2,100
Washington Square, oil on canvasboard, sgn, 9x12", C-NY 9/30/88 ... 4,400
Washington Square, Winter; oil on canvas, sgn/inscr/dtd 1934, 30x26", C-NY 5/26/88 ... 15,400
Winter at the Library (snowy street scene), oil on canvas, sgn, 25x30", WD 4/13/88 ... 23,000
86th Street & Broadway, oil on board, sgn, ca 1915, 12x16", C-E 2/1/89 OE ... 19,800

WIGGINS, John Carleton (American, 1848-1932)
Cows & Fence, watercolor on paper, sgn, 9x13", C-E 2/3/88 OE ... 1,045
Cows in a Landscape, oil on canvas, sgn/dtd 1885, 23x33", RWS 11/3/88 ... 2,600
Gray Day in October, oil on canvas, sgn, 25x30", C-E 9/15/88 ... 935
Lake Landscape at Sunset, oil on canvas, sgn/dtd 75, unfr, 20x36", SBY 3/17/88 OE ... 2,090
Landscape, watercolor on paper, sgn w/monogram, 8x10", C-E 2/3/88 ... 605
October Morning, oil on panel, sgn, 12x16", C-E 6/1/88 ... 1,045
Peasant & Cow, graphite/gouache/watercolor on tan paper, sgn, 5x9", RWS 11/10/89 ... 350
Scything (figures in wheat field), oil on canvas, sgn/dtd 95, 18x30", C-E 6/1/89 OE ... 6,050
Side Hill (landscape), oil on canvas, sgn twice/inscr 1151 Bway NY/titled, 25x30", SBY 1/24/89 ... 3,850
Two Cows Grazing in a Pasture by the Water, oil on board, sgn, 12x16", WG 4/23/88 UE ... 800

WIGHT, Moses (American, 1827-1895)
Washington Departing New York City, 1783; oil on canvas, 42x60", SBY 1/28/88 ... 13,200

WIKSTROM, Bror Anders (Swedish, 1840-1909)
On the Beach, Miami, Florida; oil on canvas, sgn/dtd 1902, 16x22", NA 3/26/88 ... 950

WILBUR, Isaac E. (19th C)
Landscape, oil on canvas, sgn/dtd 1875, 24x42", SBY 9/23/88 ... 1,650

WILBUR, Lawrence Nelson (American, 1897-)
Coca-Cola Girl (woman w/Coke seated on rock pulling on dog's leash), oil on canvas, sgn, unfr, 51x30", SBY 4/14/89 OE ... 4,125
Street in Rockport, watercolor on paper, sgn, 12x18", RWS 11/10/89 ... 425

WILCOX, W.H. (American, 1831-)
Open Gate (wooded landscape), oil on canvas, sgn/dtd 1869, 25x20", WD 10/5/88 UE ... 2,400

WILDE, John (American, 1919-)
Small Renaissance Murder (two figures), oil on masonite, inscr L JWA MW (?), ca 1948, 5x7", SBY 6/28/89 ... 1,980

WILDENS, Jan; circle of (Flemish, 1586-1653)
Landscape with Figures Along a Country Road, oil on canvas, 25x38", SBY 10/13/89 ... 8,250

WILDER, Arthur B. (American, 1857-1949)
Gray Day in Winter, oil on canvas, sgn/dtd 1928, 16x20", C-NY 3/11/88 ... 1,320
Spring Landscape, oil on canvas, sgn, 20x24", FAP 11/4/88 ... 475
Valley Panorama in Winter (winter landscape w/road, mountains beyond), oil on board, sgn/dtd 1940, RWS 3/31/88 UE ... 250

WILES, Irving Ramsey (American, 1861-1948)
Bathing by the Pier, oil on board, sgn, 10x14", WD 4/13/88 ... 2,000
Cuban Girl, oil on panel, sgn, 18x14", C-NY 9/28/89 ... 5,720
Doorway in Yarmouth, oil on panel, sgn/dtd Sept 1916, no size given, SBY 9/14/89 ... 8,525
Double-Sided: Garden Scene, Peconic, New York; Houses Along the Water; oil on panel, sgn, 13x9", SBY 4/14/89 UE ... 2,420
Head of a Lady in Exotic Dress (portrait), oil on canvas laid down on board, sgn, 11x8", SBY 1/24/89 ... 2,475
Portrait of a Lady, oil on canvas, sgn, 40x27", SBY 6/28/89 OE ... 18,700
Purple Clematis, watercolor on paper, sgn/dtd 85, 17x14", SBY 5/25/88 OE ... 46,750
Sailboats in Dock, oil on canvasboard, sgn, 10x14", WD 4/13/88 ... 2,000
Ship, pen/ink on paper, sgn/dtd Dec 1919, 8x6", SBY 9/14/89 ... 302
Summer Day, oil on panel, sgn, ca 1919, 9x14", SBY 5/24/89 OE ... 77,000
Yacht at Dock, oil on canvas, sgn, 9x16", SBY 6/28/89 ... 8,800
Yacht at Dock, oil on canvas, sgn, 9x16", SBY 9/23/88 OE ... 16,500

WILES, Lemuel Maynard (American, 1826-1905)
Coast of Santa Cruz, oil on canvas, sgn/inscr/dtd 1881, 24x40", C-NY 5/26/88 ... 11,000
Homeward Bound (stagecoach in snowy landscape), oil on canvas, sgn/dtd 1871, 18x30", SBY 4/14/89 ... 2,200
Seated Nude, red chalk, wm CAB with heart, inscr, 11x15", C-NY 1/11/89 ... 2,200
Silver Lake, oil on board, 4x8", C-NY 9/30/88 ... 2,750

Storm the Fort, oil on canvas, sgn/dtd 1878, 18x30", C-E 6/1/88 3,300

ILEY, William T. (American, 1931-)

Lode Star, oil on canvas, sgn twice/dtd 60, 68x73", C-NY 11/10/88 OE 35,200

ILHELMI, Heinrich (German, 1816-1912)

Grandmother's Green Thumb (woman watering plants while child watches), oil on canvas, sgn/dtd 1880, 24x19", C-NY 2/23/89 20,900

ILHEM, A. Wayne

Train Station, oil on canvas, sgn, 18x26", C-E 6/1/88 1,540

ILKE, David; school of (British, 1783-1841)

Blind Fiddler, oil on panel, bears signature, 8x10", B/B 1/11/89 770

ILKIE, Robert D. (American, 1828-1903)

Birds & Brambles (birds nesting in briars), oil on canvas laid down on board, sgn, 26x14" on 35x23" liner, RAB 8/9/88 7,000
Birds Bathing at the Creek, oil on canvas laid down on board, sgn, 39x34" on decorated 51x35" liner, RAB 8/9/88 OE 16,000
Cattle Fording a River, a Scene in the Adirondacks; oil on canvas, sgn/inscr, 28x54", RWS 11/3/88 OE 3,250
Disappointed Hopes (two birds viewing overturned nest), oil on canvas, sgn, 16x22", RAB 8/9/88 UE 2,000
Ellsworth Lake in New Hampshire, oil on wood panel, sgn, 15x30", RAB 11/24/89 2,750
Narrow Escape (bird flying from cat & dog in Victorian interior), oil on canvas, sgn, 48x22", RAB 8/9/88 5,000
Sunset in the Mountains (stag pausing in a stream in extensive landscape), oil on canvas, sgn, 48x22", RAB 8/9/88 1,700

ILKINSON, Norman (British, 1878-1934)

Airplane in Flight, watercolor/gouache on paper, sgn/dtd France 18, 10x13", C-E 11/8/88 OE 1,540
Portrait of SS Eagle (ship), watercolor on heavy cardboard, sgn/dtd 10/titled, unfr, 11x16", RAB 8/1/88 UE 150
Portrait of the Tug Hercules, watercolor on heavy pasteboard, sgn/dtd 10, unfr, 10z16", RAB 8/1/88 250

ILKINSON, Thomas Harrison (Canadian, 1847-1929)

Mountain Reflection, watercolor, sgn, 9x15", WAD 11/30/89 300
Rocky Coast, watercolor, sgn, 7x10", WAD 11/30/89 300

ILKS, Maurice C. (British, fl 1933-1940)

Boats at Rockport, Co Antrim; oil on board, sgn, 12x14", C-E 2/21/89 1,540
In Glencon, Co Antrim (hilly landscape); oil on board, sgn, 12x14", C-E 2/21/89 880
Whate-Para Bay, Co Antrim (gentle water along rocky shore); oil on board, sgn, 12x14", C-E 2/21/89 825

ILLAERT, Ferdinand (Belgian, 1861-1938)

Harbor Scene, oil on canvas, sgn, 43x58, SBY 6/8/88 6,325

ILLAERTS, Adam (Dutch, 1577-1664)

Dutch Men-of-War in an Estuary, One Firing Salute...; oil on panel, initialed/dtd 1632, 18x38", C-M 6/16/89 OE 143,436

ILLAERTS, Isaac (Dutch, ca 1620-1693)

Shipping Off a Rocky Shore, oil on canvas, sgn/dtd 1668, 25x40", SBY 10/21/88 OE 33,000

ILLARD, Archibald M. (American, 1836-1918)

Mountain Landscape, oil on canvas, 12x16", GAI 6/17/89 225

ILLE, O.

Dutch Harbor Scene, oil on canvas, sgn, 19x41", DM 3/14/88 UE 850

ILLEMS, Florent (Belgian, 1823-1905)

An Elegant Lady with Her Parrot (seated, full-length), oil on panel, sgn, 14x11", C-E 5/22/89 3,850

ILLGAN, H.

Cows Watering at a Stream, oil on canvas, sgn, 30x20", MAG 6/22/88 OE 750

ILLIAMS, A. (19th C)

Giles Loring (schooner), oil on canvas, sgn, 21x31", SBY 1/28/88 4,950
The Archer (sailing ship), oil on canvas, sgn, 21x20", SBY 1/28/88 3,300

ILLIAMS, Albert Henry (British, 1874-1929)

English Country Cottage, oil on panel, sgn, 12x16", LH 9/10/89 550

ILLIAMS, Charles H. (19th C)

Bridge of Badia-River Arno, Tuscany; oil on canvas, sgn/dtd 1870, 36x28", C-E 5/23/88 UE 2,640

ILLIAMS, Dwight; att (American, 1856-1932)

Mexican Indian Huts on Judge Henry D Bartos Ranch in Vera Cruse, watercolor, 1901, 10x14", SLK 2/12/88 110

ILLIAMS, Edward Charles (British, fl 1807-1881)

Figures by a Highland Lake, oil on canvas, sgn/dtd 1863, 20x30", SBY 12/9/88 3,575
Goring-on-Thames, oil on canvas, monogramed/dtd 1859, 24x42", C-NY 2/25/88 UE 7,700
Mountain Lake with Cattle, oil on canvas, sgn, 16x30", WAD, 6/6/88 1,400
Oncoming Storm, oil on canvas, sgn, 20x23", SBY 7/12/89 2,750
Pair: Coming Home; Playing in the Sand; oil on canvas, sgn, 18x14", WD 3/23/88 3,500

ILLIAMS, Edward K. (American, 1870-)

Edge of the Village (buildings & bare trees), oil on canvas, sgn, 24x28", RWS 9/8/89 1,900

ILLIAMS, Edward; att (19th C)

Watermill, oil on canvas, 26x34", WD 3/23/88 OE 1,700

ILLIAMS, Florence White (American, -1953)

Group of 3: Portrait of Woman; 1 ink/pencil on paper, 2 charcoal/chalk on paper, 13x6", 11x6", 5x4", RWS 3/31/88 200
View of Taos (flowering branch w/mountains beyond), oil on artist board, sgn, 16x20", RWS 3/31/88 UE 300

ILLIAMS, Frederick Ballard (American, 1871-1956)

Opening in the Forest, oil on board, sgn/dtd 99, 12x15", C-E 10/18/89 UE 770
Scottish Landscape, oil on canvas, sgn, 25x30", C-E 9/15/88 UE 715
Serenade in the Park, oil on canvas, sgn, 25x30", B/B 6/15/89 1,760
Trio 1909, oil on canvas, sgn/dtd 09, 10x9", C-E 6/1/89 UE 880
Two Mythological Figures, oil on canvas, sgn/dtd 03, 24x16", C-E 4/7/88 UE 440
Windy Day, oil on panel, sgn, 14x12", C-E 10/18/89 2,200

Woman in a Garden, oil on canvas, sgn/dtd 14, 24x16", B/B 6/15/89 .... **1,650**

WILLIAMS, Frederick Dickinson (American, 1829-1915)

Farm in Summer, oil on canvas, sgn/dtd 1876, 18x26", RWS 9/8/89 .... **1,800**

WILLIAMS, George Alfred (American, 1875-1932)

Battleship Texas Showing Damage (Spanish-American War), oil on board, sgn/dtd 99, 20x20", C-E 11/30/88 .... **550**

Moon Rise (full moon over calm seas), watercolor/ink on board, sgn/dtd 1910, 5x8", RWS 3/31/88 .... **1,000**

WILLIAMS, George Augustus (British, 1914-1901)

Ferry, Richmond Surrey (landscape with river, figures on bank); oil on canvas, monogramed, 1854, 19x29", DM 5/19/89 OE **4,500**

WILLIAMS, Graham (British, 19th C)

Scottish Highland Scene, oil on canvas laid down, sgn, 24x36", B/B 9/15/88 .... **770**

WILLIAMS, John Haynes (British, 19th C)

T'was in Trafalger's Bay (interior scene), oil on canvas, sgn/dtd 1892, 32x46", C-E 5/22/89 OE **11,000**

WILLIAMS, Paul (American, 1934-)

Boat Race, oil on canvas, sgn/dtd 87, 24x36", WD 4/13/88 .... **4,500**

Flower Girls (impressionistic depiction), oil on canvas, sgn, 20x24", PHL 6/16/88 UE **1,500**

Melanie (elegant lady seated in impressionistic landscape),oil on canvas, sgn, 30x24", PHL 6/16/88 UE **1,700**

Seashore (impressionistic view of mother & daughter at the seashore), oil on canvas, sgn, 24x20", PHL 10/28/88 UE **1,400**

WILLIAMS, Penry (British, 1798-1885)

Mother & Sleeping Child in a Landscape, oil on canvas, sgn/dtd 1848, 24x20", FAP 4/15/89 .... **1,210**

Spinning Wood Beside Her Sleeping Child, oil on canvas, sgn/dtd 1843, 25x20", C-E 10/26/89 .... **1,540**

WILLIAMS, Terrick (British, 1860-1937)

Brixham Harbor, oil on canvas, sgn, 20x30", C-NY 5/25/88 .... **12,650**

Lobster Fishermen, pastel on paper, sgn/dtd 98, 20x30", C-NY 5/24/89 .... **5,500**

Moonlight, Venice; oil on canavs, sgn twice, 10x16", SBY 12/9/88 OE **9,900**

Notre Dame, Paris; oil on canvas, sgn twice/inscr, 37x30", C-NY 5/25/88 OE **24,200**

Red & Gold Brixham (sailing boats in harbor), oil on canvas, sgn, 40x60", C-NY 5/24/89 .... **30,800**

WILLIAMS, Virgil (American, 1830-1886)

Children at Play (in an interior), watercolor on paper, initialed, 10x9", B/B 3/22/89 .... **1,650**

Italian Landscape with Figures, oil on canvas, sgn/dtd 1867, 34x58", SBY 6/24/88 .... **5,500**

WILLIAMS, Walter Heath (British, 1835-1906)

Figure by a Watermill, oil on canvas, 12x20", B/B 12/8/88 .... **2,200**

Figures by a Country Stream, oil on canvas, 12x20", B/B 12/8/88 .... **2,200**

Landscape at Evening with Two Houses, oil on canvas, 11x8", WG 4/23/88 UE **450**

South Devon Landscape (with figures), oil on canvas, indistinctly sgn, 18x26", B/B 3/22/89 .... **4,400**

Windmill in an Extensive River Landscape, oil on canvas, sgn, 19x24", C-E 5/23/88 .... **2,860**

Winter Stroll Past the Church (figures in landscape, building beyond), oil on canvas, sgn, 10x8", WG 4/23/88 UE **500**

WILLIAMSON, Arthur T. (American, 20th C)

Untitled (interior scene of man struck by baseball coming through window), oil on canvas, sgn, 26x20", SLK 2/11/89 .... **900**

WILLIAMSON, C. (British, 19th C)

Farm & Landscape, watercolor, sgn/dtd 1874, 13x20", FB 5/28/89 OE **850**

WILLIAMSON, E.E. (American, 19th C)

Stormy Landscape, oil on canvas, sgn/dtd 1882, 18x30", LH 9/10/89 OE **650**

WILLIAMSON, John (American, 1826-1885)

Sycamore, Catskill Cove Below Haines Falls; oil on canvas, 23x17", C-NY 9/28/89 .... **1,980**

WILLIAMSON, William Henry (British, 1820-1883)

Coastal Scene, oil on artist board, sgn, 7x20", RAB 3/27/89 UE **450**

Pair: Coastal Fishing; oil on canvas, sgn, 10x18", SBY 6/8/88 .... **1,650**

WILLIE, Robert D. (British, 19th C)

Still Life, oil on canvas mounted on mirror, sgn, 29x31", RWS 8/12/89 .... **1,600**

WILLIS, Charles (British, 20th C)

The Soloist, oil on canvas, 20x26", WAD 6/6/88 .... **1,900**

WILLIS, Edmund Aylburton (American, 1808-1899)

Peasants Working Near a Brook, oil on canvas, sgn/dtd 1888, 16x24", C-E 9/15/88 .... **1,100**

Travelers Encampment (figures in an extensive landscape), oil on canvas, sgn/dtd 1866, 35x55", C-E 6/1/89 .... **3,300**

WILLIS, Henry Brittan (British, 1810-1884)

Shepherds Driving Their Sheep & Oxen to Pasture, oil on canvas, sgn, 24x18", C-E 2/21/89 .... **2,420**

Shetlands & Cattle by the Shore, oil on canvas, sgn, 52x83", SBY 6/9/88 .... **27,500**

WILLIS, James (Australian, 19th C)

Montego Bay, Jamaica; watercolor, sgn/dtd 1890, 6x10", C-SK 11/10/88 .... **410**

WILLIS, Thomas H. (American, 1850-1912)

American Destroyer, silk threads/velvet on canvas, 13x21", C-E 4/26/88 .... **1,210**

American Schooner, silk/velvet/oil on silk, 27x34", C-E 4/26/88 .... **1,100**

GT Ray & Sutherland, Robert Coutts, Master (ships at sea); silk/velvet, Eastlake-style frame, 19x29", RAB 8/1/89 .... **1,900**

Schooner Yacht Saghaya, oil/fabric on canvas, sgn/titled, 20x36", RAB 11/10/88 .... **1,800**

SS Martha Washington, silk/velvet/oil on canvas, sgn, 24x41", C-E 4/26/88 .... **2,860**

Untitled (American steam yacht on sea), oil/silk/velvet on canvas, sgn, 16x32", RAB 8/1/89 .... **1,300**

WILLIS, W.

Along a French Canal, oil on board, sgn, 9x12", C-E 2/16/88 .... **550**

WILLIS, W.H. (Canadian)

Hauling Logs, oil on board, sgn, 18x24", WAD 11/30/89 .... **225**

LLMANN, Michael Lucas L.; circle of (German, 1630-1706)
Angel Appearing to Hagar (three figures in a landscape), oil on canvas, 22x31", SBY 4/7/89 6,600
LLMS, Albert (French, 19th/20th C)
Chasse au Lievre, Equipage du Sendat a Mr Vatin Perignon; oil on panel, sgn, 10x13", SBY 6/10/88 2,750
LLNIS, Albert (American, 19th/20th C)
Two Setters in a Landscape, oil on panel, sgn, 9x13", SBY 6/8/88 2,200
LLROIDER, Ludwig (German, 1845-1910)
Along the Dunes, oil on canvas, sgn, 12x17", RWS 11/3/88 OE 3,750
Cattle in a Landscape, oil on canvas laid down on board, sgn, 9x12", SBY 7/12/89 4,400
Figures in a Green Meadow, oil on canvas laid down on board, sgn, 10x14", SBY 7/12/89 4,950
Landscape with Shepherd & Sheep, oil on panel, sgn, unfr, 11x14", B/B 3/22/89 4,400
Stormy Skies, oil on canvas, sgn, 15x18", B/B 3/17/88 4,400
Wooded Stream with Cottages in the Distance, oil on board, sgn, 9x13", C-E 5/23/88 OE 4,180
LLS (British, 19th C)
Bay Racehorse in a Misty Landscape, oil on canvas, sgn/dtd 1856, 28x36", SBY 6/9/89 2,200
LMARTH, Lemuel Everett (American, 1835-1918)
Pause To View (hunter in landscape), oil on canvas, sgn, 12x16", RAB 8/8/89 1,600
LS, Jan (Dutch, ca 1600-1666)
Baptism of the Eunuch, oil on panel, 31x42", SBY 4/7/88 4,950
LSON, Bryan (American, 20th C)
Hawk & Pine Cone, oil on canvas, sgn/dtd 1961, 48x48", B/B 9/15/88 935
LSON, Charles Edward (British, 19th C)
Country Beauty (woman on a bridge), watercolor over traces of pencil heightened w/gouache, sgn, 30x20", C-NY 5/25/88 13,200
Feeding Chickens, watercolor on paper, sgn, 11x8", C-NY 5/24/89 3,850
LSON, David Forrester (British, 1873-1950)
Reverie, oil on canvas, sgn, 36x28", SBY 7/12/89 5,225
Wind (two women & billy goat in the woods), oil on canvas, sgn, unfr, 58x90", SBY 4/29/88 OE 110,000
LSON, Edward A. (American, 20th C)
Flag of Truce (Indians & troops on plains), watercolor on paper, initialed, 6x9", RAB 1/10/89 90
LSON, Frederick (American, 1858-)
Heaven's Glow, oil on canvas, initialed/dtd 1901, 30x18", C-E 2/1/89 880
LSON, H. (American, 20th C)
Summer on the River, oil on canvas, sgn, 12x14", B/B 1/11/89 385
LSON, J. (British, 19th C)
English Village Scene, oil on canvas, sgn, 33x41", B/B 6/15/89 3,850
LSON, J. Coggeshall (American, 19th C)
French Market Scene, oil on canvas, sgn, 35x35", B/B 5/17/89 UE 770
LSON, Jane (American, 1924-)
Drawing Table, oil on canvas, sgn/dtd 1973, 15x42", C-E 11/14/89 2,090
Mirrored Salmon (still life w/reflection), oil on canvas, initialed/sgn/dtd 1972, 30x21", C-E 11/14/89 1,870
North Sea Beach, oil on canvas, sgn, 1961, 14x13", SBY 2/14/89 715
Still Life of Blackboard & Eggs, oil on canvas, sgn, 14x21", C-NY 6/17/89 1,045
LSON, John (British, 19th C)
Marine Scene, oil on canvas, sgn/dtd 76, RWS 6/17/89 600
LSON, John James (American, 1818-1875)
Waiting for the Boat, oil on canvas, sgn, 25x43", C-E 5/23/88 4,620
LSON, Margaret E. (19th C)
94-110 Cheyne Walk Chelsea, oil on canvas, sgn, 28x37", C-E 2/23/88 1,540
ILSON, Ray (American, 1906-1972)
View of Alcatraz, watercolor on paper, sgn, 15x21", B/B 10/6/88 880
LSON, Richard (British, 1714-1782)
River Landscape with a Tower, black & white chalk on gray preparation, inscr, 8" dia, C-NY 1/11/89 660
White Monk, oil on canvas, 21x27", SBY 4/7/88 6,600
ILSON, Richard; att (British, 1714-1782)
Italianate Landscape, oil on canvas, sgn/dtd 1760, 28x36", B/B 6/15/89 3,850
Quayside of the Styx, oil on canvas, 30sx25", RWS 6/17/89 UE 200
ILSON, Richard; circle of (British, 1714-1782)
Moonlit Landscape with Figures in the Foreground, a Castle & City in Distance; oil on canvas, unfr, 31x49", SBY 7/12/89 1,540
ILSON, Richard; school of (British, 1714-1782)
Mountainous River Landscape, oil on panel, 14x17", C-E 1/12/88 UE 1,100
ILSON, Ronald York (Canadian, 1907-)
Laurentian Farm, oil on board, sgn, 12x16", WAD 11/30/89 450
Red Wall, Venice; oil on board, sgn, no size given, WAD 11/30/89 400
ILSON, Sol (American/Polish, 1896-1974)
Blessing the Fleet, oil on canvas, sgn, 12x16", C-E 11/8/88 UE 110
Men Working, pen/ink/crayon on paper, sgn, 7x9", C-E 6/28/88 UE 22
Still Life of Shells, oil on board, sgn, 24x18", C-E 11/30/88 UE 550
ILTON, Olive M. (British, 20th C)
New Number (woman in robe reading book at table), oil on canvas, sgn, 30x36", PHL 10/28/88 1,900
IMAR, Charles (American, 1828-1862)
Portrait Study of Iron Horn, oil on canvas, sgn, 7x4", SBY 5/25/88 13,200

WIMPERIS, Edmund M. (British, 1835-1900)
Figures in a Wagon Crossing a Marsh, watercolor, initialed/dtd 95, unfr, 22x35", C-E 2/21/89 ... 880
Murchison Falls, pencil/watercolor/bodycolor, inscr, unfr, 16x11", C-SK 6/9/88 ... 1,210
WINCK, Johann Amandus (German, 1748-1817)
Walnuts, Peaches, Bunches of Grapes, Cherries...on a Ledge; oil on panel, sgn, 13x16", C-NY 4/6/89 OE ... 16,500
WINCK, Johann Christian T. (German, 1738-1797)
Martydom of Saint Sebastian, oil on canvas, 18x13", C-NY 4/6/89 ... 2,420
WINCK, Johann Christian T.; circle of (German, 1738-1797)
Resurrection, oil on panel, shaped carved frame, 27x19", SBY 10/21/88 ... 3,850
WINDMAIER, Anton (German, 1840-1896)
Pair: Figures in a Winter Landscape; Figures Walking in Summer Rain; oil on canvas, sgn, unfr, 18x32", SBY 12/9/88 ... 6,050
WINEGAR, Samuel P. (American, 1845-)
Photographing the New Yacht (rocky inlet scene), oil on canvas, initialed, 16x26", RWS 3/11/89 ... 1,300
Whaler Adeline Gibbs Under Jury Rig After Being Dismasted, pastel on paper, sgn/dtd 1907, 16x23", RAB 11/10/88 UE ... 550
Yankee Whalers in Action, watercolor on paper, sgn/dtd 1907, orig frame, 17x23", RAB 11/10/88 ... 1,050
WINGANTS, manner of
Houses by a Lake, oil on panel, bears signature, 9x11", C-E 11/8/88 ... 550
WINN, Richard
Lapeer, oil on board, sgn, 24x28", LH 3/20/88 OE ... 180
WINT, see De Wint
WINTER, Andrew (American, 1892-1958)
Burnt Head, Monhegan; oil on masonite, sgn, 24x40", SBY 6/28/89 ... 880
Harbor View, oil on canvas laid down on board, sgn/dtd 27, 20x24", SBY 3/17/88 ... 2,420
Sailing Off Long Island, oil on canvas, sgn/dtd 28, 25x30", SBY 6/24/88 ... 3,850
Wharf in Winter, Monhegan Island; oil on canvas, sgn/inscr/dtd 1951, 24x36", C-NY 5/26/88 ... 11,000
WINTER, Charles Allan (American, 1869-1942)
Gloucester, Massachusetts (impressionistic landscape); oil on canvas mounted on masonite, sgn, 20x24", RWS 3/31/88 ... 2,900
Gloucester Scene, Dogtown (landscape); oil on canvas, sgn, 20x24", RWS 3/16/89 UE ... 1,100
Playing the Piano, oil on canvas, sgn/dtd 1901, 24x20", C-E 11/30/88 ... 3,080
Toy Sailboat, oil on canvas, 24x20", RWS 11/10/89 UE ... 400
WINTER, Fritz (German, 1905-1978)
Composition, oil on paper mounted on canvas, sgn/dtd 54, 29x39", SBY 11/9/89 OE ... 17,600
Untitled (abstract), oil on canvas, sgn/dtd 61, 32x35", SBY 6/30/88 ... 22,000
WINTER, Milo Kendall Jr. (American, 1913-1956)
Dark Wood (gnome in forest at night, creatures watching), ink/watercolor on tinted paper, sgn, 16x12", RWS 3/31/88 ... 425
WINTER, William Arthur (Canadian, 1909-)
Barrow Women, oil on canvasboard, sgn, 12x16", WAD 6/12/89 ... 750
Boy in Green Cap, oil on board, sgn, 10x8", WAD 11/30/89 ... 200
Brother & Sister, oil on board, sgn, 8x10", FB 4/25/88 ... 360
From a Train (children waving to train, old house beyond), oil on board, sgn, 16x19", WAD 11/30/89 ... 750
Yellow Shirt, oil on board, sgn, 10x8", WAD 6/12/89 ... 350
WINTERBERG (American, 20th C)
Mexican Village Scene, oil on canvas, sgn/dtd 37, 35x47", FAP 4/15/89 ... 165
WINTERHALTER, Franz Xaver (German, 1805-1873)
Portrait of a Girl, Half-Length, in Black Dress & Plumed Hat; oil on canvas, sgn/dtd 1850, oval, 32x26", C-M 12/3/88 ... 213,682
Young Girl with a Blue Shawl, oil on canvas, sgn, 18x15", C-E 2/23/88 ... 6,380
WINTERHALTER, Franz Xavier; att (German, 1805-1873)
Grinding the Coffee, oil on panel, indistinctly sgn, 16x11", SBY 6/8/88 ... 3,575
WINTERHALTER, Franz Xavier; school of (German, 1805-1873)
Queen Victoria (three-quarter length), oil on canvas, 53x40", C-E 5/22/89 ... 4,620
WINTERMOTE, Mamie Withers (American, 1885-1945)
Eucalyptus in the Mountain Shadows, oil on canvas, sgn, 24x30", B/B 1/11/89 ... 495
WINTERS, Robin (20th C)
Dualistis Self-Portrait, oil/plastic blocks/cloth on canvas, sgn/dtd 1980, 60x50", SBY 2/15/89 ... 4,950
Eighty Noses (contemporary), gouache on separate sheets of paper mounted on black paper, 1980, 56x53", SBY 2/19/88 OE ... 3,850
Untitled (abstract figure picking apple), watercolor/graphite/ink on paper, 22x30", C-E 11/14/89 ... 880
WINTERS, Terry (20th C)
Schema, oil sticks/charcoal on paper, initialed/dtd 1985-86, 12x9", C-NY 5/4/89 OE ... 28,600
Untitled (abstract), graphite on paper, initialed, 1985, 13x9", C-NY 11/10/88 ... 1,650
Untitled (abstract), graphite/charcoal on paper, initialed, 1985, 14x11", SBY 11/11/88 ... 6,050
Untitled (abstract), oil on linen, initialed/dtd 1983, 30x22", SBY 11/9/89 OE ... 60,500
Untitled (composition), graphite on paper, initialed/dtd 1985, 16x12", SBY 11/9/89 ... 6,600
Untitled (contemporary composition), crayon/charcoal/chalk on paper, initialed/dtd 1985, 30x22", SBY 5/3/89 UE ... 13,200
WINTHER, Frederick (Danish, 1853-1916)
Summer Pond Landscape, oil on canvas, sgn/dtd 1914, 34x54", LH 9/10/89 UE ... 950
WIRGMAN, Charles A. (British, 1832-1891)
Japanese Landscape, oil, sgn/dtd 98, 13x25", C-SK 5/25/89 ... 1,560
Mountain Village, oil on canvas, sgn, 9x14", C-SK 6/9/88 OE ... 2,788
WIRTH, Paul (fl 1571-1578)
King David & His Court Rejoicing As They Lead the Ark of Covenant to Jerusalem, oil, sgn/dtd 1571, 21x28", SBY 10/13/89 ... 7,700

RTS, Stephen (American, 19th/20th C)
City Gate, watercolor, sgn/dtd March 1897, 12x17", MG 5/28/88 275
SE, Jack (Canadian, 1928-)
Turkish Delight, mixed media, 11x16", FB 4/25/88 UE 180
SEMAN, Robert P. (American, 19th C)
Still Life of Fish in Basket, oil on canvas, sgn, 15x22", C-E 6/1/88 1,430
SSING, William (Willem)(Dutch, 1653-1687)
Portrait of a Young Lady, seated, holding flowers in a landscape; oil on canvas, 50x40", C-NY 6/2/88 3,080
SSING, William (Willem); att (Dutch, 1653-1687)
Portrait of Lady Said To Be Lady Chesterfield As Saint Agnes, Seated...; oil on canvas, 49x39", C-NY 5/31/89 OE 9,900
T, see De Wit
THEMS, J. (Continental, 19th/20th C)
Venetian Scene, oil on canvas, sgn, 15x22", SBY 7/12/89 1,540
THERINGTON, Frederick William (British, 1785-1865)
Figures Riding in a Cart, oil on canvas, sgn, 20x30", SBY 12/9/88 3,850
THERS, Walter (Australian, 1857-1914)
Moored Boats (in river landscape), oil on panel, sgn, 9x14", C-SK 6/9/88 7,800
THOOS, Alida (Dutch, 1659-1715)
Study of a Michaelmas Daisy, watercolor/gouache over traces of black chalk, sgn/#d 18, 15x10", SBY 1/13/89 1,320
THOOS, Franz
Plants & Flowering Vines with a Lizard Entering a Bird's Nest, oil on canvas, sgn, 31x26", C-NY 10/20/88 OE 14,300
ITHOOS, Matthias (Dutch, 1627-1703)
Still Life, a Landscape Beyond; oil on panel, sgn, 26x22", SBY 4/7/89 15,400
Still Life of Red Poppies, Morning-Glory, Honeysuckle, Plants, & Moths in a Landscape; oil, 34x24", SBY 10/13/89 7,150
Still Life of Sunflowers in a Broken Pot, oil on canvas, 35x28", SBY 10/21/88 OE 12,100
ITKOWSKI, Karl (American, 1860-1910)
April Showers, oil on canvas, sgn, 24x20", C-NY 9/30/88 7,150
Boy with Basket, oil on canvas, sgn, unfr, 18x22", B/B 3/17/88 5,225
Boys Fishing on Dock, oil on canvas, sgn, 24x30", C-E 6/1/88 1,650
Boys Wrestling, oil on canvas, sgn/dtd 1885, 22x27", DM 10/14/88 OE 4,250
Mending the Baseball (boy seated on threshold), oil on canvas, sgn, 24x18", C-NY 5/25/89 14,300
Pick a Hand (two boys seated, choosing which hand), oil on canvas, sgn/dtd 89, 26x20", C-NY 12/2/88 10,450
Tired Hunter (young boy seated under tree), oil on canvas laid down on board, sgn, 24x20", C-NY 9/30/88 4,400
ITMAN, C.F. (American, 19th C)
Very Cold (farm buildings, animals, & figure in winter), oil on canvas, sgn, 39x50", SBY 1/24/89 2,475
ITT, John Henry (Harrison)(American, 1840-1901)
Long Island Landscape, oil on canvas, sgn, 24x32", B/B 4/20/88 1,430
Ohio River, oil on canvas, sgn/dtd 1867, 12x20", C-NY 5/26/88 1,980
Portrait of a Woman, oil on canvas, sgn/dtd 1863, 27x22", B/B 4/20/88 1,045
Woman with a Fan (portrait), oil on canvas, sgn, 24x18", SBY 3/17/88 UE 1,210
ITTE, see De Witte
LERICK, Robert (French, 1882-1944)
Study of a Female Nude, sanguine/chalk, sgn, 10x16", PHL 6/16/88 UE 500
OELFLE, Arthur William (American, 1873-1936)
Lady of the Directoire, Portrait of the Artist's Wife; oil on canvas, sgn, 50x40", SBY 6/24/88 1,210
Portrait of Harold Putnam Browne (three-quarter length), oil on canvas, sgn, 40x30", RAB 8/9/88 UE 500
OEN, William (1769-1825)
Portrait of a Girl in a Straw Hat (full-length, seated in a glade), oil on canvas, 45x34", SBY 10/13/89 UE 5,500
OHL, Mildred (American, 20th C)
Abstract, oil on panel, sgn/dtd 77, 48x36", NA 2/24/89 1,800
Fly (abstract), oil on masonite, sgn, 48x36", NA 2/24/89 1,500
OICESKE, Ronau William (American, 1887-1953)
Snowy Landscape with Sheep Under a Shelter, oil on canvas, sgn, 24x30", SLK 5/9/88 175
OJNAROWICZ, David (American, 1954-)
Peter Hujar Dreaming, enamel/paper collage on masonite, unfr, 48x48", C-NY 11/10/88 UE 2,200
World View, enamel on masonite, 1983, 49x49", SBY 10/8/88 3,300
OKURKA, Doris (American, 20th C)
Floral Still Life, green vase with forsythia; watercolor, 28x20", MAG 4/24/88 UE 85
Pears in Yellow, oil on masonite, sgn, 7x8", S/A 2/18/89 65
OLCOTT, Harold C. (American, 20th C)
Bookshop, Rockport, Massachusetts; oil on canvas, sgn, 25x30", RWS 5/12/89 2,500
Winter in Vermont, oil on canvas, sgn, 26x32", WD 4/13/88 2,200
OLCOTT, J. (British, 19th C)
Extensive Landscape, oil on canvas, sgn/dtd 1837, 24x30", SBY 6/8/88 1,045
OLEVER, Adeleine (American, 1886-)
Ogunquit Beach (bathers cavort at water's edge), oil on canvas mounted on board, sgn, 8x10", RWS 3/31/88 900
OLF, A. (Continental, 19th C)
Musical Gathering, Venice (group on steps), oil on canvas, sgn, 41x59", C-E 2/21/89 2,640
OLFERT, C.H.
Arab Carpet Traders, oil on canvas, sgn, 23x31", NA 10/1/88 850

WOLFF, Gustaf (American, 1863-1935)
Dutch River Landscape, oil on canvas, sgn, 16x20", SLK 11/25/88 ... **450**
WOLFLE, Franz Xavier (Austrian, 1896-)
Pair: Tyrolean Peasant; oil on panel, sgn, 8x6", C-E 2/23/88 ... **1,430**
WOLINS, Joseph (American, 1901-)
At the Shore, oil on canvas, sgn, 32x34", C-E 6/1/89 ... **935**
Chicken Market (figures & hanging fowl in street scene), oil on canvas, sgn/dtd, 25x10", C-E 6/1/89 UE ... **605**
Hester Park, oil on canvas, sgn/dtd 1937, 24x30", C-E 6/1/89UE ... **605**
WOLKIE, D. (British, 19th C)
Man Reading the London News, oil on canvas, sgn, 27x27", DM 3/14/88 ... **1,500**
WOLKIN, F.L.H. (American, 19th C)
Hull, July 26, 1884 (sailboat, distant village); watercolor on paper, sgn/dtd 1890, 10x16", RAB 8/9/88 ... **500**
WOLMARK, Alfred Aaron (British, 1877-1961)
Holy Family (man, woman, & child reading the Bible), oil on canvas, sgn/dtd 1903, 42x42", SBY 12/9/88 UE ... **2,640**
WOLRUNG, F.
Dancing Lady in Purple, pastel on canvas, sgn/inscr/dtd 10, 36x36", C-E 10/25/88 ... **3,850**
WOLSKI, Stanislaw Politan (Polish, 1859-1894)
Tumble From the Troika, oil on canvas, sgn, 24x34", C-NY 2/25/88 ... **6,600**
WOLSTENHOLME, Dean Sr. (British, 1757-1837)
Creme O' Th' Chase, the Essex Hunt Near Epping; oil on canvas, 28x36", SBY 6/9/89 ... **49,500**
Pair: Crossing a Ditch; Treeing the Fox; oil on canvas, 25x34", SBY 6/10/88 ... **36,300**
WOLSTENHOLME, Dean Sr.; att (British, 1757-1837)
Driver Trotting Galloway, Under Fourteen Hands, Property of Duke of Gordon, 1833; oil on canvas, 19x26", C-E 2/21/89 ... **2,640**
WOLTZE, Berthold; att (German, 1829-1896)
Young Girl with a Bird, oil on canvas, bears signature, 21x17", C-E 5/23/88 ... **2,200**
WONG, Frederick (American/Chinese, 20th C)
Reflection, watercolor on paper, sgn/dtd 66, 17x17", SBY 4/15/89 UE ... **66**
WONNER, Paul (American, 1920-)
Dutch Still Life with Plants & Butterfly Book, acrylic on canvas, 1979, 70x70", SBY 2/19/88 ... **30,800**
WONTNER, William Clark (British, 19th/20th C)
Portrait of a Woman in a Yellow Shawl (bust-length), oil on canvas, sgn/dtd 1923, B/B 10/9/88 ... **22,000**
WOOD, Charles King (American, 19th/20th C)
Castle on the Sea, watercolor, bears signature/dtd 03, 14x22", FAP 12/8/89 ... **100**
WOOD, Grant (American, 1892-1942)
Arch at St Emilion (landscape), oil on board, sgn, 13x16", B/B 10/9/88 ... **4,400**
Hired Man, gouache/colored pencil on brown paper, sgn, 11x8", C-NY 9/28/89 ... **52,800**
Porte de l'English d'Moret, oil on panel, sgn/inscr, 16x13", C-NY 5/26/88 ... **3,520**
Study for American Gothic, pencil on paper, titled American Gothic twice, 1930, 5x4", SBY 5/24/89 ... **55,000**
Village, oil on board, 13x15", B/B 12/8/88 ... **2,750**
WOOD, John (British, 1801-1870)
Princess Sabrina & Her Nymphs, oil on canvas, sgn, 18x37", B/B 5/17/89 ... **1,650**
WOOD, Lewis John (British, 1831-1901)
Angsburg Normandy, 1861 (cityscape w/churches, bridge over river, figures); oil on canvas, sgn, 30x25", DM 10/14/88 ... **3,750**
WOOD, Ogden (American, 1851-1912)
Shepherdess Returning Home, oil on canvas, sgn, 38x27", C-E 11/30/88 UE ... **880**
WOOD, Robert E. (American, 1889-1979)
Arizona Desert (landscape), oil on canvas, sgn, 25x30", SBY 4/14/89 ... **2,750**
Arizona Sunset, oil on canvas, sgn, 24x30", SBY 1/24/89 ... **5,226**
Autumn Evening, oil on canvas, sgn/dtd 45, 24x30", WL 5/20/88 ... **1,800**
Autumn Landscape, oil on canvas, sgn, 12x19", C-NY 9/30/88 ... **2,860**
Autumn on the Guadalupe, oil on canvas, sgn/inscr, 36x48", SBY 9/23/88 OE ... **8,250**
California Mountains, oil on canvas, sgn/dtd 43, 25x30", C-E 6/1/88 ... **2,860**
Fall Landscape, oil on canvas, sgn, 24x29", WG 4/23/88 OE ... **2,700**
Late Afternoon Reflections, oil on canvas, sgn, 24x20", B/B 10/6/88 ... **2,200**
Monterey Coast, oil on canvas, sgn, 25x30", SBY 9/23/88 OE ... **7,150**
Mountain Landscape, oil on canvas, sgn, 20x24", C-E 2/1/89 ... **2,200**
Mountain Stream, oil on canvas, sgn, 25x31", C-E 6/1/88 ... **2,860**
Mountain View, oil on canvas, sgn, 30x36", C-E 6/1/88 ... **3,520**
Owen's River, Bishop, California; oil on canvas, sgn, 24x48", B/B 10/6/88 ... **4,675**
Pair: Carmel, Spring; California Mountains; oil on canvas/oil on board, 1 sgn, 1 dtd 47, 12x16", C-NY 3/11/88 ... **6,050**
Pink Mountain Range, oil on canvas, sgn, 30x36", C-E 6/1/88 ... **2,860**
Swimming Hole, oil on canvas, sgn/inscr/artist's stamp, 36x24", SBY 9/23/88 OE ... **7,150**
Wood's Cove, Laguna Beach; oil on canvas, sgn/dtd 54, 23x34", B/B 10/6/88 ... **1,980**
WOOD, Thomas Waterman (American, 1823-1903)
Arguing the Question, gouache/watercolor/pencil on paper laid down on canvas, sgn/dtd 1877, 20x28", C-NY 5/26/88 ... **93,500**
King Charles Spaniels, After Edwin Landseer; oil on canvas, dtd 1845, 29x36", SBY 6/9/89 ... **2,750**
Old Man with Pipe (leaning against post, dog at side), oil on canvas, sgn/dtd 1874, 10x7", SBY 9/14/89 ... **4,400**
Pickaback (girl on man's back descending from hayloft), oil on canvas, sgn/dtd 1875, 20x14", C-NY 5/25/89 ... **17,600**
Portrait of a Gentleman, oil on paper laid down on board, sgn/dtd 1859, in a painted oval, 11x9", C-E 10/18/89 ... **1,100**
Secret (girl standing on chair whispering in woman's ear), oil on canvas, sgn/dtd 1886, 24x18", C-NY 9/28/89 ... **11,000**
Shining Shoes, oil on canvas, sgn, 13x10", RWS 11/3/88 ... **8,000**

Spring Violets, oil on canvas, sgn/dtd 1868, 14x11", B/B 3/17/88 OE ... 14,300
Spring Violets (portrait of young girl), oil on canvas, sgn/dtd 1868, 14x11", C-NY 5/25/89 ... 18,700

OOD, W.T. (Canadian)
Shadow Lake, Rocky Mountains; watercolor, sgn, 14x20", WAD 6/12/89 ... 250

OOD, William Reuben Clark (American, 1875-1915)
Sunset Beyond the Hills, oil on canvas, sgn/dtd 1910, 18x24", RWS 9/8/89 ... 1,500

OODBURY, Charles Herbert (American, 1864-1940)
At Cliff's Edge, oil on board, sgn/stamped signature/estate stamp, 10x14", SBY 3/17/88 OE ... 2,750
Boats by the Shore, oil on canvas, sgn, unfr, 12x18", SBY 3/17/88 OE ... 4,510
Clowns on Outdoor Stage, oil on canvas, sgn/titled, 14x20", RWS 3/16/89 ... 1,700
Color Note (seascape), oil on canvasboard, 8x10", RWS 9/8/89 UE ... 550
Fishing Village, Summer; oil on canvas, inscr w/title, 20x28", WD 4/13/88 ... 1,800
Front of Fisherman's Village, Ogunquit, Maine; oil on canvas, sgn, 14x19", RWS 11/10/89 ... 1,900
Garden Party (night scene w/gathering & lighted lanterns), oil on canvas, 1905, 10x14", RWS 9/8/89 OE ... 1,900
Landscape with Distant Windmills, oil on canvas, sgn/dtd 91, 10x14", RWS 11/3/88 ... 1,100
Manadnoc (winter), oil on canvasboard, artist's estate stamp, 8x10", RWS 9/8/89 UE ... 750
Quarry Swimming (swimmer in mid-ground, rock formations beyond), oil on board, 12x17", RWS 3/31/88 OE ... 4,200
Sheep in a Coastal Landscape, oil on canvas, 28x36", SBY 9/14/89 ... 1,320
Smoke Screen (Charles River), oil on canvasboard, estate stamp/titled, 10x14", RWS 3/16/89 ... 1,200
Sunspots (swimmers in a rocky cove), oil on canvas, artist's estate stamp, 17x21", RWS 5/12/89 ... 4,600
Tanker & Tug (seascape), oil on board, estate stamp/titled, 10x14", RAB 8/8/89 ... 1,750
Victory Parade, Boston (crowd along parade route); oil on canvas, sgn/dtd Apr 25 1919/titled, 29x36", SBY 5/24/89 ... 82,500

OODCOCK, Hartwell L. (American, 1853-1929)
Bahamian Shipping Boats at Anchor, watercolor on paper, sgn/dtd 1908, 13x20", RAB 8/1/88 OE ... 1,600

OODFORD, Don (American, 20th C)
Still Life, oil on canvas, 48x54", LH 12/4/88 UE ... 30

OODHOUSE, William (British, 1857-1939)
Feeding Time, oil on canvas, sgn, 12x19", DM 2/19/88 ... 1,400

OODLEIGH, Alma (American, 19th/20th C)
Orphan Rock, Mersey River, Tasmania; oil on canvas, sgn/dtd 1878, 33x24", B/B 10/9/88 ... 2,090

OODSIDE, John Archibald Sr. (American, 1781-1852)
Still Life of Hunting Dog, oil on canvas, sgn/dtd 1833, 40x44", SBY 5/25/88 ... 41,800

OODVILLE, Richard Caton (British, 1856-1927)
Lifeguards Charging at the Battle of Waterloo, oil on canvas, sgn/dtd 1899, 35x23", SBY 2/22/89 ... 12,100

OODWARD, Ellsworth (American, 1861-1939)
European Village, Germany; watercolor, sgn/dtd 09, 14x20", NA 5/13/89 ... 1,600
Newcomb Chapel (landscape w/church), oil on artist board, sgn, 6x9", NA 11/5/88 ... 1,000
Pigs in the Chicken Yard, watercolor, sgn, 14x11", NA 10/1/88 ... 600
Wooded Landscape, oil on canvas, initialed, 16x24", NA 2/6/88 ... 800

OODWARD, Hildegard H. (American, 19th/20th C)
Nortre Dame de Paris (landscape), watercolor on paper, sgn/titled, 12x8", RAB 8/8/89 ... 400

OODWARD, J.D. (American, 19th C)
Crater Relics, Petersburg, Virginia (Civil War); pen/ink on paper, inscr, 14x11", C-E 5/27/88 ... 275
Grave of Colonel Jesse Rodgers, Corinth (Civil War); watercolor on paper, initialed/inscr, 6x11", C-E 5/27/88 OE ... 495
Post Office-Shebang (Civil War); pen/ink on paper, initialed, unfr, 13x15", C-E 11/30/88 ... 242
Robinson's House, 1st Bull (Civil War); pen/ink on paper, initialed/inscr, unfr, 8x13", C-E 11/30/88 ... 176

OODWARD, Laura (American, 19th C)
Tamaka Creek Near Brunswide Florida, oil on canvas, sgn, 18x27", NA 11/5/88 ... 1,700

OODWARD, Mabel May (American, 1877-1945)
Notre Dame de Paris (evening view of cathedral), watercolor on paper, sgn, 12x8", RAB 8/9/88 ... 700
Old Fountain of Sicily, oil on canvas laid down on board, sgn, 10x13", C-NY 9/30/88 ... 3,850
Peasant Woman, Brittany (woman w/baskets walking on road at dawn); oil on board, dtd 1919, 8x5", RWS 9/29/88 UE ... 300
Still Life of Dahlias & Honeysuckle, oil on artist board, sgn, 20x24", RWS 5/19/88 UE ... 1,500
Still Life of White Roses, oil on canvas, sgn, 17x24", RWS 5/19/99 UE ... 1,000

OODWARD, Robert Strong (American, 1885-1960)
Hale House, Buckland, Massachusetts (view of farmhouse through trees); oil on canvas, sgn, 25x30", RWS 9/29/88 UE ... 600
Passing New England (mountain cabin), oil on canvas, sgn, 30x36", RWS 5/12/89 ... 2,500

OODWARD, Stanley Wingate (American, 1890-1970)
Afternoon Surf, oil on artist board, sgn, 12x16", RWS 3/31/88 UE ... 600
Approaching Mist, oil on canvas, sgn, 25x30", SBY 4/14/89 ... 990
Beaching in a Rocky Cove, oil on canvas, sgn, 25x30", RWS 5/12/89 UE ... 1,300
Crashing Waves, watercolor on paper, sgn, 10x15", C-E 2/3/88 ... 330
Fall Reveries, oil on canvasboard, sgn/inscr, 16x12", RWS 11/3/88 ... 1,300
Gray Skies (waves along rocky shore, gray skies beyond), oil on canvas, sgn, 28x36", RWS 5/19/88 ... 1,600
Land's End Cape Hedge Rocks, Rockport; oil on canvasboard, sgn, 16x20", RWS 9/8/89 UE ... 275
Monhegan Island (waves breaking against rocky wall), watercolor on paper, sgn, 22x28", RAB 8/9/88 UE ... 200
Patrol Waters (distant steamer off rocky coast), oil on canvas, sgn, 28x36", RWS 5/12/89 ... 1,400
Threatening Storm (waves crashing on rocky shore, dark sky), oil on artist board, sgn, 18x24", RWS 5/19/88 UE ... 900

OODWARD, William (American, 1859-1934)
Alleyway with Laundry, oil on canvas, 10x14", B/B 1/11/89 UE ... 165
Cabildo, New Orleans (street scene); oil on canvas, sgn/inscr Cabildo NO, 19x15", SBY 3/17/88 OE ... 2,970

Entrance to Lovers Lane, Ocean Springs, Mississippi; oil on board, sgn, 14x20", NA 2/6/88 1,000
House in Kensington, oil on board, sgn/dtd 08, 9x13", NA 10/1/88 525
Portrait of George Ohr, watercolor, sgn, 12x10", NA 11/5/88 4,000
Still Life of Fruit, oil on canvas, sgn/dtd 99, 6x8", NA 11/5/88 325

WOODWORTH, Hiram Goodman (American, 19th C)
Portrait of a Bird, watercolor/ink on paper, 1843, 6x8", C-NY 1/20/89 OE 440

WOOG, Raymond (French, 1875-)
Boy with a Hobby Horse in a Landscape, monogramed/dtd 1922, 50x34", SBY 12/9/88 6,600

WOOLF, Samuel Johnson (American, 1880-1948)
Plotting the Battles, oil on panel, sgn/inscr, 27x21", C-NY 9/30/88 3,300

WOOLMER, Alfred Joseph (British, 1805-1895)
Sleeping Beauty, oil on canvas, 9x12", C-E 5/23/88 UE 605

WOOLRYCH, F. Humphrey W. (American, 1868-)
Verdant Sunlit Landscape, oil on canvas, sgn, 30x50", SLK 9/28/88 1,800

WOOSTER, Austin C. (American, 19th/20th C)
Apples Spilling From a Basket (still life), oil on canvas, sgn/dtd 1908, 14x18", SBY 4/14/89........ 4,125
Basket of Peaches, oil on canvas, sgn twice/dtd 1907, 10x14", SBY 9/23/88 1,210
Outdoor Country Kitchen Table with Fruit, oil on canvas, sgn/dtd 1891, 13x29", C-E 11/30/88 1,980
Still Life of Apples, Grapes & a Jar; oil on canvas, sgn/dtd 1910, 8x14", B/B 4/20/88 1,430

WOOTTON, Frank (British, 1914-)
Kennels, Badminton; oil on canvas, sgn, inscr w/artist's name, 15x18", SBY 6/9/89 2,530

WOOTTON, John (British, 1683-1764)
Duke of Somerset's Gray Wyndham Beating Duke of Bolton's Bay Bolton in a Match...; oil on canvas, 18x36", SBY 6/9/89........ 44,000
Earl of Plymouth's Chestnut Hunter Tethered to a Tree, a Hunting Party Beyond; oil on canvas, 40x50", SBY 6/9/89 30,250

WORES, Theodore (American, 1859-1939)
Boating Through the Lillypads, watercolor on paper, sgn, 12x19", SBY 9/14/89........ 1,100
Cherry Blossoms, oil on canvas, sgn/dtd 1927, 12x16", B/B 6/15/89 6,050
Coastal Scene, Carmel; oil on canvas, sgn, 12x16", B/B 10/6/88........ 7,150
Summer Landscape, oil on canvas, bears signature/dtd 1915, 16x20", B/B 10/6/88 3,850

WORF, John (American, 1903-1959)
Snowy New England Road, watercolor on paper, sgn, 15x21", SBY 3/17/88 UE........ 990

WORMS, Jules (French, 1832-1924)
Friendly Coachman, oil on panel, sgn, 14x11", LH 12/4/88 UE 900
Matador's New Clothes (matador & seamstress), oil on canvas, 19x22", WD 11/16/88 OE 11,500
Proposal of Marriage, oil on canvas, sgn, 28x40", C-NY 10/25/89 41,800
Urgent Appointment (lady helping man w/coat in an interior), watercolor on paper, sgn, 12x16", B/B 3/22/89 3,850

WORSEY, Thomas (British, 1829-1875)
Violets & Other Wildflowers by a Nest with Eggs, oil on canvas, sgn/dtd 1871, 16x13", C-E 10/26/89........ 3,850

WORSLEY, Charles Nathaniel (Australian, fl 1886-1923)
Waimea Estuary (Nelson), pencil/watercolor, sgn/inscr, 9x19", C-SK 5/25/89 OE 590

WORTH, Thomas (American, 1834-1917)
Licensed Vender, City Street Scene; watercolor on paper, sgn, 8x9", FAP 4/15/89 220

WORTHINGTON, Thomas Locke; att (British, 19th C)
Woman on a Country Lane Stopping To Play with a Kid, oil on canvas, sgn, 32x23", SLK 5/9/88 550

WOTRUBA, Fritz (Austrian, 1907-1975)
Double-Sided: Abstract Standing Female Nudes; Two Men; airbrush/pencil on paper, 19x19", RWS 9/29/88 650

WOU, Claes Claesz (Dutch, 1592-1665)
Men-O-War in a Choppy Sea with a Rainbow, oil on panel, sgn, 25x48", C-NY 5/31/89 20,900

WOU-KI, Zao (Chinese, 1921-)

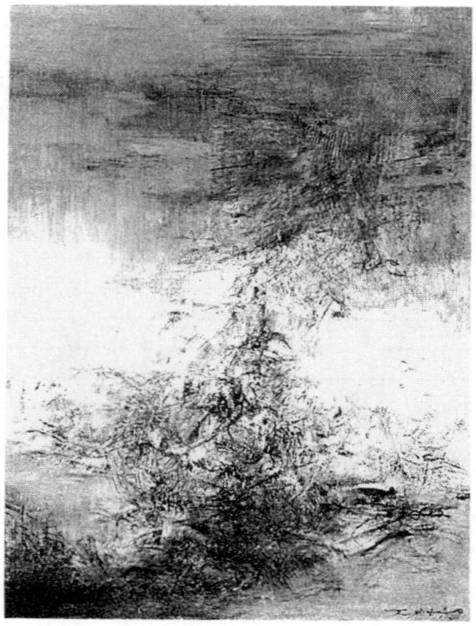

Untitled, oil on canvas, sgn twice/dtd 11.11.60, 46x35", C-NY 10/4/89; $52,800

Abstract Composition, oil on canvas, sgn/dtd 26.4.62, 38x75", SBY 11/9/89 OE ... 71,500
Entre Deux Villes (abstract), watercolor/pen/black ink on paper, sgn/dtd 55, 9x11", C-E 11/14/89 OE ... 9,350
Nature Moret et Fleurs (contemporary floral still life), oil on canvas, sgn/dtd 53, 24x32", C-NY 2/14/89 OE ... 38,500
Petit Jardin Abandonne, oil on canvas, sgn twice/dtd I-54, 13x16", SBY 10/8/88 ... 8,250
Still Life of Lemons, watercolor/pen/black ink on paper, initialed/sgn/dtd 52, 15x18", C-E 11/17/88 OE ... 3,850
Untitled (abstract landscape), oil on canvas, sgn/dtd 8 Mars 1966, 59x64", SBY 11/9/89 OE ... 99,000
Untitled (abstract), oil on canvas, sgn twice/dtd 58 twice, 26x36", SBY 2/19/88 OE ... 26,400
Untitled (abstract), oil on canvas, sgn twice/dtd 68, 32x46", C-NY 5/4/88 OE ... 24,200
Untitled (abstract), oil on canvas, sgn twice/dtd 72, 26x32", C-NY 5/4/88 OE ... 17,600
Untitled (abstract), oil on canvas, sgn/dtd 1966, 63x78", SBY 11/11/88 OE ... 93,500
Untitled (abstract), oil on canvas, sgn/dtd 2-4-60, 45x57", SBY 5/3/89 OE ... 82,500
Untitled (abstract), oil on canvas, sgn/dtd 20.3.64, 35x46", C-NY 2/20/88 OE ... 19,800
Untitled (abstract), oil on canvas, sgn/dtd 21-6-61, 24x29", SBY 2/15/89 OE ... 35,750
Untitled (abstract), oil on canvas, sgn/dtd 4-3-59, 46x35", SBY 2/15/89 OE ... 60,500
Untitled (abstract), oil on canvas, sgn/dtd 54, 18x24", SBY 2/15/89 OE ... 22,000

WOUTERS, Frans (Flemish, 1614-1659)
Extensive Wooded Landscape with Nymphs & Satyrs, a Hunter Approaching; oil on panel, initialed, 21x33", SBY 10/13/89 ... 17,600
Three Graces Holding a Basket of Flowers in a Landscape, oil on panel, initialed, 12x10", C-NY 10/12/89 OE ... 16,500

WOUTERS, Frans; att (Flemish, 1614-1659)
Rape of Europa, oil on copper, 28x33", SBY 10/13/89 ... 6,050

WOUTERS, Jan; circle of
Madonna & Child, with two angels holding a lamb in a landscape; oil on copper, 11x14", C-NY 4/6/89 OE ... 3,300

WOUWERMAN, circle of (Dutch, 17th C)
Hunters & Travelers Before an Inn, oil on canvas, 21x31", C-NY 4/6/89 ... 4,950

WOUWERMAN, Jan Pawelsz (Dutch, 1629-1666)
Dune Landscape with a Dog, oil on panel, 7x8", SBY 6/3/88 ... 13,200

WOUWERMAN, manner of (Dutch, 17th C)
Riders on a Bluff, oil on canvas, 17x21", C-E 4/7/88 ... 715

WOUWERMAN, Philips (Dutch, 1619-1668)
Cavalry Engagement with a Burning Windmill, oil on panel, sgn w/monogram, 22x33", C-NY 4/8/88 ... 26,400
Peasants Unloading a Cart Onto a Ferry by the Shore, oil on panel, unfr, 13x17", C-NY 6/2/88 OE ... 165,000
Stag Hunt (figures on horses & on foot w/dogs in a landscape), oil on copper, monogramed, 11x14", C-NY 5/31/89 OE ... 638,000

WOUWERMAN, Philips; circle of (Dutch, 1619-1668)
Campsite with Figures & a Horse, oil on panel, 8x10", SBY 7/12/89 ... 1,650
Cavaliers by a Pool with Children Playing with a Toy Boat, oil on panel, 19x14", C-NY 1/15/88 ... 4,400
Hunt Party Stopping To Rest, oil on panel, initialed, 18x24", SBY 10/21/88 ... 5,500

WOUWERMAN, Philips; manner of (Dutch, 1619-1668)
Departing for the Hunt, oil on canvas, unfr, 29x40", SBY 12/9/88 ... 605
Pair: Figures Setting Out To Hunt; Figures Resting in a Landscape; oil on canvas, 12x16", SBY 12/9/88 ... 2,750

WOUWERMAN, Pieter (Dutch, 1623-1682)
At the Farriers, oil, 21x27", WD 1/25/89 ... 7,250

WOUWERMAN, Pieter; follower of (Dutch, 1623-1682)
Travelers on Horseback Fording a River, 20x24", WD 1/25/89 ... 5,750

WRAY, Henry Russell (American, 1864-1927)
Mesa & Plains, oil on board, sgn, 12x16", C-E 2/3/88 ... 1,100

WRIGHT, Cory B. (American, 19th/20th C)
View Through the Redwoods, oil on canvas, sgn, 44x32", B/B 6/9/88 ... 1,320

WRIGHT, Emma R. (American, 20th C)
Pair: Coastal Scenes; oil on artist board, sgn, 8x10", RWS 3/16/89 ... 350

WRIGHT, Ethel
Faraway Thoughts, oil on canvas, sgn, 57x38", C-NY 2/25/88 ... 11,000

WRIGHT, George (British, 1860-1942)
Bull Inn, Dartford (coach arriving with passengers in courtyard), oil on canvas, sgn, 14x24", PHL 10/28/88 OE ... 18,000
Horse in a Stall, oil on canvas, sgn, 15x20", SBY 6/9/89 ... 2,200
Hunters Belvoir, Winsome, & Dandy at Grass; oil on canvas, sgn/inscr w/horse's names, 24x38", SBY 6/10/88 ... 6,600
Hunters Cautious, Maid O' the Mist, & Silver Coin at Grass; oil on canvas, sgn/inscr, 24x38", SBY 6/10/88 ... 7,150
Huntsman by a Gate, oil on canvas, sgn, 10x12", C-E 2/23/88 ... 2,750
Lookout (hunter on horse in a landscape), oil on canvas, sgn, 10x12", SBY 6/10/88 ... 5,775
Master of the Hounds (huntsmen on mount by stable), oil on canvas, sgn/dtd 88, unfr, 10x16", SBY 6/9/89 ... 2,310
Red-Polled Shorthorn, oil on canvas, sgn, 15x18", C-E 10/25/88 UE ... 1,540
Run of the Season (hounds distressing plow horses in a field), oil on canvas, sgn, 7x12", SBY 6/9/89 OE ... 9,350
Shooting-Setters, oil on canvas, sgn/dtd 26, 16x24", RWS 11/3/88 ... 4,000

WRIGHT, George Hand (British, 1873-1951)
Afternoon at the Beach, pastel on tan paper, sgn, 19x25", RWS 11/10/89 ... 2,000
Jockeys & Trainer, oil on canvas, sgn, 12x18", WG 4/23/88 OE ... 1,900

WRIGHT, James Henry (American, 1813-1883)
Capturing a Whale, oil on wood panel, sgn, 13x16", RAB 8/1/89 OE ... 2,200
Portrait of a Gentleman, oil on canvas, sgn/inscr/dtd 1869, unfr, 50x40", SBY 6/24/88 UE ... 660
Portrait of a Woman, oil on canvas, sgn/dtd 1869, unfr, 50x40", WL 5/20/88 UE ... 650

WRIGHT, Joseph of Derby (British, 1734-1797)
Portrait of Miss Bentley, Seated (full-length, in a landscape); oil on canvas, 51x40", C-NY 1/15/88 ... 44,000

Portrait of Miss Frances Warren (full-length, holding a lamb, a wooded park beyond), oil on canvas, 49x39", SBY 1/12/89 ... 71,500

WRIGHT, P.J. (British, 19th C)
Untitled, coaching scene, oil on canvas, sgn, 40x30", SLK 4/7/89 ... 4,000

WRIGHT, Redmond Stephens (American, 1903-)
Waves Breaking Along a Rocky Shoreline, oil on canvasboard, sgn, 24x30", B/B 10/6/88 ... 468

WRIGHT, Richard; att (British, 1735-1774)
Landscape with a Ship Foundering & Breaking on the Rocks by the Shore, oil on canvas, 24x35", SBY 10/13/89 ... 4,400

WRIGHT, Robert L. (Canadian)
Winters End, oil on board, sgn, 20x27", WAD 11/30/89 ... 950

WROBELS, Steven (French, 20th C)
Paris Dock Yard Scene, watercolor on paper, sgn, 10x12", B/B 1/11/89 ... 302

WTEWAEL, Joachim Anthonisz (Dutch, 1566-1638)
Holy Family w/Angel Offering Fruit to Infant St John, Elizabeth, & Simon Zelotes...; oil on copper, 4x6", C-M 6/16/89 OE ... 489,000
Venus & Cupid with Bacchus & Ceres, oil on copper, oval, unfr, 5x4", SBY 6/3/88 OE ... 33,000

WU JECT-KEY (American, 20th C)
Sunlit Interior, oil on canvasboard, sgn, 16x12", RWS 11/10/89 UE ... 275

WUERMER, Carl (American, 1900-1982)
Birches in Winter (w/village & hills beyond), oil on canvas, sgn, 25x31", C-NY 9/28/89 ... 4,400
Old Lyme, Connecticut; watercolor/gouache on paper, sgn, 21x28", C-E 6/1/88 ... 1,650
Wintry River, oil on canvas, sgn, 25x30", LH 5/15/88 ... 3,800
Wintry River, oil on canvas, sgn twice/inscr/#d 163, C-NY 12/2/88 ... 7,700

WUERPEL, Edmund Henry (American, 1866-1958)
River Landscape, oil on board, sgn, 10x8", SLK 9/29/88 ... 200

WUJIK, Theo (20th C)
Richard Anuskiewicz (portrait), silverpoint on paper, sgn/dtd 1973 twice, 22x26", SBY 11/11/88 ... 385

WUNDERLICH, Paul (German, 1927-)
At a Right Angle, gouache/graphite on paper, sgn/copyrighted/dtd 69, 35x28", WD 11/16/88 OE ... 2,300
I Bulldogge, I Spartakistin & I Berufsmodeil; oil on canvas, sgn/dtd 1972, 64x51", C-E 11/14/89 OE ... 18,700
Jabdpoesie (surrealistic), oil on canvas, sgn/dtd 74, 58x45", SBY 2/19/88 ... 19,800
Naturphanomene (surrealistic), gouache on plywood, sgn/dtd 75, 62x48", SBY 2/19/88 OE ... 13,200
Standing Female Nude (missing head & arm), gouache/graphite on paper, sgn/dtd 70, 34x27", WD 11/16/88 OE ... 2,600
Trapezistin (surrealistic), paper collage/gouache/chalk on paper, sgn/dtd 1971, 36x29", C-E 5/9/89 OE ... 5,280
Two German Spartakists Posing As Jupiter & Thetis (Hommage a Ingres), oil/pencil, sgn/dtd 73, 51x38", C-E 11/14/89 OE ... 16,500
Untitled (figure on a chair), watercolor/colored pencils/pencil on paper, sgn/dtd 72, 34x27", C-E 11/14/89 OE ... 5,500
Zauberer mit Roter Weste (surrealistic), gouache/pencil on cardboard, sgn/dtd 1976, 62x47", SBY 10/8/88 ... 8,250

WUNNENBERG, Carl (German, 1850-1929)
Shepherdess, oil on canvas, sgn, 38x23", C-NY 5/25/88 ... 11,000

WYANT, Alexander Helwig (American, 1836-1892)
Above the Lake, watercolor on paper, sgn, 14x10", C-NY 5/25/89 ... 6,000
Cows Grazing in an Extensive Landscape, oil on canvas, sgn, 15x22", SBY 9/14/89 OE ... 10,450
Early Shoot (figure in morning landscape), oil on canvas, sgn/dtd 79, 19x14", C-NY 9/28/89 ... 4,950
Evening, oil on canvas, sgn, 11x16", SBY 6/24/88 ... 2,750
Evening (landscape), oil on canvas, sgn, 10x14", B/B 3/22/89 ... 1,650
In the Adirondacks (figures on a path in a mountainous landscape), oil on canvas, sgn, 12x20", WD 4/13/88 ... 7,500
Landscape of Pastoral Lake, oil on board, sgn, 6x8", FAP 11/4/88 ... 475
Meadow at Sunset, oil on canvas, sgn/dtd 84, 16x20", LH 10/16/88 UE ... 2,000
Open Fields, oil on canvas, sgn, 14x20", C-E 2/16/88 ... 1,540
Pair: Spring; Fall; oil on board, 1 indistinctly sgn, 7x9", C-E 2/1/89 ... 1,100
River Tang, New Brunswick; oil on canvas laid down on board, sgn, 21x31", C-NY 5/25/89 ... 11,000
Storm Approaching, oil on panel, sgn, 16x22", C-NY 5/26/88 ... 4,400
Summer Landscape, oil on panel, sgn, 12x19", SBY 1/24/89 ... 5,500

WYANT, Alexander Helwig; att (American, 1836-1892)
In the Catskills, oil on canvas, 6x9", WL 5/20/88 ... 900

WYATT, Kenneth (American, 20th C)
Mapmaker, oil on canvas, sgn/dtd 1981, 30x40", SBY 6/28/89 UE ... 275
Talkin' Distance, oil on canvas, sgn twice/copyrighted/dtd 1982, titled/#d 1294, 18x24", SBY 9/23/88 ... 165
50-Yard Line, oil on canvas, sgn twice/copyrighted/dtd 1982, 30x40", SBY 9/23/88 UE ... 660

WYCK, Thomas; att (Dutch, 1616-1686)
Figures Unloading Barrels Under an Arch, red chalk, 6x5", C-NY 1/11/89 ... 715
Interior with Peasant Family Eating, oil on canvas, unfr, 18x15", SBY 10/21/88 UE ... 880

WYCK, Thomas; manner of (Dutch, 1616-1686)
Thatched Cottages, watercolor on paper, bears initials/dtd 1666, octagonal, 9x14", C-E 5/23/88 UE ... 242

WYDEVELD, Arnoud (American, fl 1855-1862)
Fine Catch, oil on canvas, sgn/inscr, 18x32", SBY 6/10/88 ... 3,575

WYETH, Andrew (American, 1917-)
Abandoned Boat, watercolor/gouache on paper, sgn, 1950, 17x27", SBY 5/25/88 OE ... 71,500
Blackberry Picker (landscape), tempera on panel, sgn, 29x48", C-NY 5/26/88 ... 385,000
Blackledge (coastal seascape), watercolor on paper, sgn, 1941, 21x29", SBY 5/24/89 ... 34,100
British General at Brandywine, watercolor on paper laid down on board, sgn, unfr, 18x26", C-NY 12/2/88 ... 13,200
Coon's House (house in landscape), watercolor/pencil on paper, sgn/inscr, 14x21", SBY 5/24/89 ... 18,700
Cross Country Skier, Mt Kearsage; watercolor on paper, sgn, 20x29", FAP 4/15/89 OE ... 39,600

Grist Mill (landscape of Chadds Ford, Pennsylvania), watercolor on paper laid down, sgn, 1968, 20x28", C-NY 5/25/89 OE 165,000
Headgate (landscape of Chadds Ford, Pennsylvania), watercolor on paper laid down, sgn/dtd 1966, 19x28", C-NY 5/25/89 121,000
Heavy Snow, dry brush on paper, sgn, 1967, 20x40", SBY 5/25/88 209,000
Ice Storm (figure looking out window), dry brush on paper laid down, sgn, 1971, 29x23", C-NY 5/25/89 OE 319,000
Inlet, watercolor/pencil on paper, sgn, 14x20", C-NY 5/26/88 77,000
Jack Be Nimble, watercolor/pencil on paper, sgn, 1976, 53x31", SBY 5/25/88 192,500
Sundown (pumpkin on post w/house beyond), watercolor on paper, sgn, 22x30", C-NY 5/25/89 165,000

WYETH, James (American, 1946-)
Bailing Twine (twine bundle hanging on building), watercolor on paper, sgn, 1968, 19x24", SBY 5/24/89 OE 23,100

WYETH, Newell Convers (American, 1882-1945)
Bucking Bronco, oil on canvas, sgn, 34x25", C-NY 12/2/88 OE 66,000
Chicken Coop, oil on canvas, 24x26", SBY 6/28/89 6,600
I Ain't Through with You Yet (Canadian Mounty & rider on horses), oil on canvas, sgn, 24x16", SBY 4/14/89 OE 20,350
Lindbergh Family, oil on canvas, sgn, 22x42", SBY 6/24/88 14,300
Moose Call (two men hunting moose in landscape), oil on canvas, sgn, 36x40", C-NY 12/2/88 OE 66,000
Pilgrim Thanksgiving, oil on canvas, sgn, 14x50", SBY 6/24/88 OE 15,400
Ships by Moonlight, oil on canvas, sgn, 52x76", SBY 6/8/88 UE 2,640
Supply Wagons, oil on canvas, sgn/dtd 1905, inscr 1907, 38x26", C-NY 5/26/88 37,400
Water Turtle, watercolor/drybrush on paper laid down on board, sgn, 1948, 23x30", C-NY 9/28/89 61,600

WYGRZYWALSKI, Felix K. (Polish, 1875-)
Nude & Sea, seated on rock listening to seashell; oil on canvas, sgn, 22x30", RAB 8/8/89 UE 200

WYLD, William (British, 1806-1889)
Mediterranean Landscape, oil on canvas, 10x16", B/B 4/20/88 1,760

WYLLIE, William Lionel (British, 1851-1931)
Ship on High Seas, oil on canvas, 10x8", C-E 4/7/88 UE 264

WYMAN, M.R. (American, 19th/20th C)
Still Life of Grapes, oil on canvas, sgn/dtd 1906, 18x25", LH 9/10/89 110

WYNANTS, Jan (Dutch, 1620-1682)
Landscape with Figures in a Formal Garden by a House, oil on canvas, sgn/dtd 1680, SBY 6/3/88 28,600
Travelers on a Path in an Extensive Mountainous River Landscape, oil on canvas, sgn, unfr, 60x66", C-NY 10/12/89 16,500

WYNANTS, Jan; circle of (Dutch, 1620-1682)
Peasants Begging Alms on a Road in a Dune Landscape, oil on panel, 19x27", WD 10/19/88 OE 7,250

WYNDHAM, Robert
Winter Landscape, oil on canvas, sgn, 24x37", LH 5/15/88 110

WYSMULLER, Jan Hillebrand (Dutch, 1855-1925)
Dutch Village, Autumn; oil on canvas, sgn, 26x34", C-E 2/21/89 1,980

WYTMANS, Mattheus; circle of
Old Man Reading a Book in a Cottage Interior, oil on panel, bears initials, 10x9", C-NY 10/12/89 4,950

WYWIORSKI, Michal G. (Polish, 1861-1926)
Rest Along the Way, oil on canvas, sgn/dtd 85, C-NY 5/25/88 UE 10,450

XAVERY, Jakob (Dutch, 1736-1769)
Travelers & Herdsmen on a Path in a Mountainous Landscape, oil on canvas, 58x40", WD 10/19/88 OE 13,000

XCERON, Jean (John)(American, 1890-1967)
Untitled Facade, pencil/ink/watercolor, sgn/dtd 60, unfr, 8x11", LH 12/4/88 450
White & Gray #256 (geometric composition), oil on canvas, sgn/dtd 1941/#d 256, 32x26", SBY 3/17/88 15,400

XI, Zeng (Chinese, 1861-1930)
Calligraphy In Li Shu Clerical Script (hanging scroll), ink on paper, sgn/dtd 1924, 41x21", SBY 5/31/89 1,100

XIA, Zhou (Chinese, 17th C)
Landscape (hanging scroll), ink/color on silk, sgn/dtd 1673, 88x41", SBY 5/31/89 6,050

XIANG, Yun (Chinese, 1586-1655)
Landscape (hanging scroll), ink on paper, sgn, 37x15", SBY 5/31/89 4,400

XIE, Zheng (Chinese, 1693-1765)
Orchids (hanging scroll), ink on paper, sgn, 25x16", SBY 5/31/89 6,050

XIE, Zheng; att (Chinese, 1693-1765)
Bamboo & Rock (hanging scroll), ink on paper, sgn/dtd 1764, 53x25", SBY 5/31/89 14,300

XIMENES, Ettore (Italian, 1855-1926)
Bacchanalian Revelry, watercolor, sgn/dtd 1898, oval, 17x17", C-E 10/26/89 1,100

XING, Chen (Chinese 18th C)
Gazing at the Moon (hanging scroll), ink/color on silk, sgn/dtd 1785(?), 52x23", SBY 5/31/89 990

XIONG, Zhang (Chinese, 1803-1884)
Flowers & Birds (hanging scroll), ink/color on paper, sgn/dtd 1878, 52x13", SBY 5/31/89 1,210
Landscape (hanging scroll), ink on paper, sgn/dtd 1866, 42x19", SBY 5/31/89 1,650
Mandarin Ducks & Wisteria (hanging scroll), ink/color on paper, sgn, 60x18", SBY 5/31/89 1,650

XUEHAO, Wang (Chinese, 1754-1832)
Landscape (hanging scroll), ink/color on gold-flecked paper, sgn, 53x16", SBY 5/31/89 2,200

XUL SOLAR, Alejandro (Argentinian, 1877-1963)
Axende Encurvas Miflama Hasta El Sol (abstract composition), mixed media, initialed/dtd 1922, 8x5", C-NY 11/21/89 22,000
Mansilla 2936 (abstract), watercolor on paper, dtd 1920, 5x7", SBY 5/16/89 24,200
Mask (abstract), watercolor on paper, sgn/dtd 1923, 8x9", SBY 5/16/89 20,900
Masks, watercolor on board, sgn/dtd 1924, 58x8", SBY 5/17/88 OE 20,900

XUN, Fang (Chinese, 1736-1799)
Landscape After Ni Zan (hanging scroll), ink on paper, sgn/dtd 1778, 47x14", SBY 5/31/89 OE 5,225
XUN, Ren (Chinese, 1835-1893)
Set of 4: Figures (hanging scrolls); ink/color on paper, sgn/dtd 1887, 94x23", SBY 5/31/89 OE 18,700
YAN, Hua (Chinese, 1682-1756)
Calligraphy in Xing Shu Running Script (hanging scroll), ink on paper, sgn, 59x11", SBY 5/31/89 OE..... 10,450
YANDONG, Zeng (Chinese, 18th/19th C)
Rock (hanging scroll), ink on paper, sgn/dtd 1843, 49x15", SBY 5/31/89..... 2,200
YANG-HUI, Huang (20th C)
Constructing Highways, charcoal on paper, sgn & inscribed in Chinese, ca 1940s, 15x23", RWS 9/29/88 UE..... 100
YANKILEVSKY, Vladimir (Russian, 1938-)
Tryptich N 13: Hommage to His Father (abstract); mixed media on 3 canvases, sgn/dtd 1985, overall: 47x197", SBY 7/7/88..... 24,000
YANYONG, Ding (Chinese, 1902-1978)
Figures (hanging scroll), ink/color on paper, sgn/dtd 1978, 27x18", SBY 5/31/89 2,200
Orchids & Bamboo (horizontal scroll); ink on paper, sgn/dtd 1975, 13x31", SBY 5/31/89 880
Set of 4: Landscapes; ink/color on paper, ea sgn/2 dtd 1975/2 dtd 1976, 27x19", SBY 5/31/89 4,675
YAO, Yuan (Chinese, fl 1746-1780)
Returning to the Cottage (hanging scroll), ink/color on silk, sgn/dtd 1756, 70x48", SBY 5/31/89 11,000
YARBER, Robert (20th C)
Beachside Bar, acrylic on canvas, unfr, 66x66", C-NY 11/10/88 11,000
Casino Drop (interior view of casino w/figure floating above), oil on canvas, 1985, 66x66", SBY 5/3/89 OE 16,500
Falling Couple, oil on canvas, 66x66", C-NY 5/4/88 12,100
Falling Figures Over City #39, colored chalk on black paper, sgn/dtd 83, 40x30", C-NY 5/4/89 OE 5,500
Fatal Passion, acrylic/oil on canvas, sgn/dtd 84, unfr, 84x84", C-NY 5/4/89 OE 16,500
Lapse, colored chalk on black paper, sgn/dtd 85, 40x30", C-NY 5/4/89 OE 6,050
Pool Drop (contemporary), pastel on paper, sgn/dtd 84, 40x28", SBY 2/15/89 3,575
Resort, oil/acrylic on canvas, sgn/dtd 1985, 72x132", SBY 11/9/89 23,100
Untitled (glow on woman, darkened background & building beyond), chalk on black paper, sgn/dtd 84, 41x28", C-NY 2/14/89 3,850
YARD, Sidney Janis (American, 1855-1909)
Californian Landscape, watercolor, sgn/dtd 99, 11x14", C-SK 11/10/88 840
YARNOLD, B. (British, 19th C)
Wooded Waterfall, oil on canvas, sgn, 21x17", PHL 10/28/88 OE 950
YARNOLD, M. (British, 19th C)
Marine Scene with Fleet of War Ships Leaving Harbor, oil on canvas, sgn/dtd 1838, 20x29", SLK 5/11/88 2,000
YATES, Cullen (American, 1866-1945)
Arrangement (floral still life), oil on panel, sgn, 30x25", RWS 11/10/89 OE 4,300
Blue & Gold, oil on canvas, sgn, 12x16", RWS 11/10/89 OE..... 6,500
Cove, oil on board, sgn, 12x16", C-E 11/30/88 UE 880
First Snow, Shawnee on Delaware, Pennsylvania; oil on masonite, sgn, 36x41", RWS 11/10/89 OE..... 17,000
Impressionistic Landscape, oil on canvas, sgn, 12x16", LH 9/10/89 OE..... 1,300
Opalescent Sea, Maine; oil on canvas, sgn twice/dtd 1X7X on verso, 12x16", C-E 9/15/88 1,045
Rural Landscape, oil on canvas, sgn/dtd, 8x9", WG 4/23/88 750
Teahouse, oil on canvas, sgn, 12x16", SBY 6/28/89 OE 2,750
Transformation (winter landscape), oil on canvas, sgn, 36x40", RWS 11/10/89 7,750
YATES, Thomas (British, -1796)
Set of 4: British Frigates Engaging French Ships on the Channel; oil, 2 sgn/dtd 1792 & 1793, 18x26", SBY 10/13/89 49,500
YATES, William Henry (American, 1848-1934)
Brook in the Woods, oil on canvas, sgn, 21x27", SBY 4/14/89 990
Study of a Pheasant, oil on board, sgn/dtd 1912, 35x17", LH 5/15/88 OE 250
YEAGER, Ira (American, 20th C)
Portrait of a Woman, oil on canvas, sgn/dtd 1965, 16x16", B/B 5/17/89 UE..... 412
YEAMES, William Frederick (British, 1835-1918)
Beggar Woman, oil on canvas, monogramed/inscr, 35x29", C-E 2/25/88 2,310
YEGOZOVZ (Russian)
Winter Scene, watercolor, sgn, 10x13", LH 5/15/88 450
YELLAND, Raymond Dab (American, 1848-1900)
River in a Fall Landscape, oil on panel, monogramed, 9x13", B/B 1/11/89 OE..... 1,210
YENS, Karl (American, 1868-1945)
America the Beautiful, oil on canvas, sgn, ca 1918, 40x52", SBY 5/25/88 14,300
Bluepurple's Charm, oil on canvas, sgn/dtd MCMXXXVI, 26x21", B/B 10/6/88 6,600
Dignity of the Tree, watercolor on paper, sgn/dtd 1929, 11x15", B/B 1/11/89 550
Edge of the Woods, oil on canvas laid down, sgn, 13x16", B/B 10/6/88..... 550
O Sacred Solitude, Divine Retreat; oil on canvas, sgn/dtd 1923, 50x60", B/B 10/6/88 2,750
Shack in the Desert, oil on board, sgn, 26x22", B/B 10/6/88 3,575
View of Half Dome From Yosemite Valley, oil on canvas laid down, sgn/dtd 1919, 33x42", B/B 6/15/89 5,225
YEPES, Tomas (Spanish, 1600-1674)
Girl Making Nosegays Surrounded by Elaborate Pots Growing Iris, Carnations...; oil on canvas, sgn, 40x61", SBY 6/2/89 OE.....1,017,500
YGAN, D. (American, 20th C)
Cape Cod Sand Dunes (landscape w/ocean beyond), oil on canvas, sgn, 16x22", RAB 11/25/88 UE 400
YI, Ren (Chinese, 1840-1896)
Figure in Landscape, After Hua Yan (hanging scroll); ink/color on paper, sgn/dtd 1883, 37x14", SBY 5/31/89 4,400

YIN, Tang (Chinese, 1470-1523)
Summer Gathering in a Mountain Pavilion (hanging scroll), ink/light color on silk, sgn, 74x42", SBY 5/31/89 24,200
YING, Qian (Chinese, 17th C)
Landscape (hanging scroll), ink/color on silk, sgn, 62x35", SBY 5/31/89 2,475
YING, Qiu (Chinese, 1494-1552)
Fording the Stream, After Liu Songnian (hanging scroll); ink/color on silk, sgn/dtd 1936, 46x25", SBY 5/31/89 OE 154,000
YINGJUN, Zhang (Chinese, 18th C)
West Lake (hand scroll), ink on paper, sgn/dtd 1791, 7x56", SBY 5/31/89 3,850
YONG, Joe; see De Yong
YONG, Liu (Chinese, 1720-1804)
Pair: Couplet in Xing Shu Running Script (hanging scrolls); ink on gold-flecked paper, sgn, 49x11", SBY 5/31/89 1,430
YORKE, William G. (British, 19th C)
The Benjamin Webster (sailing ship), oil on canvas, sgn, 26x36", SBY 1/28/88 20,900
YORKE, William Howard (British, 1858-1913)
Holme Force, oil on canvas, sgn/indistinctly dtd, 12x18", SBY 7/12/89 3,300
Montagnais at Sea, oil on canvas, sgn/dtd 1879, 24x36", C-NY 2/25/88 OE 13,200
YORKE, William Howard; att (British, 1858-1913)
Frigate at Sea, oil on canvas, 24x36", C-E 10/26/89 3,300
YOUENS, Clement T. (American, 19th/20th C)
Hillside Spring, Grimes Co, Texas; oil on paper mounted on canvas, 10x14", C-E 2/3/88 UE 605
Swamp Scene, Burlison Co, Texas; oil on paper mounted on canvas, sgn, 14x10", C-E 2/3/88 UE 605
Swamp Scene, Texas, USA; oil on canvas, 14x10", C-E 2/3/88 UE 550
YOUNG, August (American, 1839-1913)
In the Heat of the Battle, oil, sgn/dtd 1858, unfr, 30x38", WD 1/11/89 500
YOUNG, Charles Morris (American, 1869-1964)
Awakening Spring, oil on canvas, sgn, 12x16", SBY 12x16", SBY 1/24/89 1,100
YOUNG, Harry (American, 19th C)
Indian Encampment (tents, figures, approaching storm), oil on canvas, sgn, 27x45", RAB 8/9/88 2,100
YOUNG, J.P. (Continental, 19th C)
The Hunt, oil on canvas, sgn/indistinctly dtd, 29x48", C-E 5/22/89 3,300
YOUNG, Nancy J. (American, 20th C)
Group of 3: Canyons, dyed handmade paper collage, sgn/dtd 83 or 84, 23" dia, 22x36", SBY 6/28/89 440
YOUNG, William S. (American, 19th C)
Approaching Storm (rural landscape), oil on canvas, sgn/dtd 1874(?), 30x50", SBY 4/14/89 3,300
Hudson River Scene, oil on canvas, sgn/dtd 1874, 25x41", C-E 11/30/88 3,300
YOUNGERMAN, Jack (American, 1926-)
Black-White Tondo, acrylic on canvas, sgn/dtd December 1965, unfr, 42x34", C-E 11/17/88 2,310
Blue & Green (abstract), oil on canvas, 71x39", SBY 10/7/89 3,300
Untitled, cut paper/collage, initialed/dtd 72, 14x11", SBY 2/14/89 UE 520
Untitled, paper collage mounted at the corners on board, initialed/dtd 70, 8x8", C-E 11/17/88 605
YOUNIAN, Ye (Chinese, 1590-after 1669)
Figures in Landscape (hanging scroll), ink/light color on paper, sgn/dtd 1672, 51x25", SBY 5/31/89 3,025
YOUQUA (American, 19th C)
Chinese Ladies in a Garden, oil on canvas, 13x16", C-SK 11/10/88 2,600
YUAN, Ruan (Chinese, 1764-1849)
Pair: Couplet in Li Shu Clerical Script (hanging scrolls); ink on paper, sgn, 51x11", SBY 5/31/89 1,540
YUHUANG, Du (Chinese)
Harbor Scene (hanging scroll), ink/color on silk, sgn, 12x14", SBY 5/31/89 1,650
YUN, Wu (Chinese, 1811-1883)
Clearing at Xianxia Pass (hand scroll), ink on paper, sgn/dtd 1854, 12x50", SBY 5/31/89 5,500
YURCHENCO, B.
Pair: City Scape; Dee Jay; watercolor/gouache on paper, 1 sgn/dtd 1907, 12x15" & smaller, C-E 6/1/88 440
YVON, Adolphe; att (German, 1817-1893)
Battle Scene, oil on paper laid down, 12x18", SBY 7/12/89 770
ZABALETA, Vladimir (Venezuelan, 1944-)
Menina (surrealistic portrait), oil on canvas, sgn, 1988, 63x55", SBY 11/21/88 OE 9,350
Nocturnal Menina (surrealistic), oil on canvas, sgn/dtd 1989/titled, 57x71", SBY 5/16/89 OE 14,300
ZADKINE, Ossip (French, 1890-1967)
Les Saltimbanques, gouache/pen/ink on paper mounted at the edges, sgn/dtd 27, 26x18", C-NY 2/18/88 5,280
Paysage (landscape), gouache on paper, sgn/dtd 25, 20x27", C-NY 2/18/88 3,300
ZAFAUREK, Gustav (Austrian, 1841-1906)
Fronleichnam-Corpus Christi Day; watercolor over pencil, sgn, 7x10", C-NY 2/25/88 UE 330
ZAIS, Guiseppe (German, 1709-1784)
Pair: Italian Pastoral Landscapes; oil on canvas, 23x29", SBY 10/21/88 46,750
ZAK, Eugene (Polish, 1884-1926)
Maestro, pastel on paper, sgn, 12x9", SBY 2/14/89 2,750
ZAKANITCH, Robert (American, 1935-)
Angelman I (circular composition), acrylic on canvas, sgn/dtd 67, unfr, 84x84", C-E 11/17/88 1,760
Orange Lift (vertical rectangle composition), acrylic on canvas, sgn/dtd 68, unfr, 54x12", C-E 11/17/88 440
Rooster, acrylic on canvas, 1978, 84x165", SBY 2/15/89 11,000
Triptych: Raven; acrylic on canvas, sgn/titled, unfr, 54x68" overall, C-E 5/9/89 3,850

ZAKHAROV, Feodor (American/Russian, 1882-)
View Through Trees to the Sea, oil on canvas, sgn, 18x24", RWS 3/16/89 OE 900
ZAKHAROV, Vadim (Russian, 1959-)
A-4 (abstract figure), oil on canvas, sgn/dtd 1985, 79x59", SBY 7/7/88 9,000
AS-5 (abstract composition), oil/enamel on canvas, sgn/dtd 1987, 79x118", SBY 7/7/88 OE 12,000
B-4 (abstract composition), oil on canvas, sgn/dtd 1985, 63x83", SBY 7/7/88 OE 12,000
B-5 (abstract composition), oil on canvas, sgn/dtd 1986, 79x118", SBY 7/7/88 6,000
D-4 (abstract composition), oil/enamel on canvas, sgn/dtd 1986, SBY 7/7/88 7,600
G-5 (abstract composition), oil/enamel on canvas, sgn/dtd 197, 79x118", SBY 7/7/88 8,400
N-4 (abstract composition), oil/enamel on canvas, sgn/dtd 1986, 59x79", SBY 7/7/88 6,000
N-5 (abstract composition), oil/enamel on canvas, sgn/dtd 1986, 59x79", SBY 7/7/88 6,000
ZAMACOIS Y ZABALA, Eduardo (Spanish, 1842-1871)
Education of a Prince, oil on canvas, sgn/dtd 70, 25x40", C-NY 5/24/89 OE 104,500
Returning From Market, oil on canvas, sgn/dtd 68, 22x39", C-NY 10/25/89 OE 104,500
ZAMPIGHI, Eugenio (Italian, 1859-1944)
Amusing Story in the Paper, oil on canvas, sgn, 9x12", SBY 12/9/88 1,925
Country Dancing, oil on canvas, sgn, 29x41", SBY 2/22/89 23,100
Cows Watering at a Quiet Pool, oil on canvas, sgn, 26x34", C-NY 10/25/89 8,250
Friar's Visit, oil on canvas, sgn, 29x41", lot 491, SBY 2/22/89 OE 34,100
Friar's Visit, oil on canvas, sgn, 29x42", lot 485, SBY 2/22/89 22,000
Game of Cards, oil on canvas, sgn, 15x21", C-E 10/26/89 OE 13,200
Happy Family (interior scene), oil on canvas, sgn, 22x31", C-NY 2/23/89 18,700
Hunter's Tale, oil on canvas, sgn, 31x43", C-NY 10/25/89 16,500
Important Decision (interior w/man standing & two ladies seated at table), oil on canvas, sgn, 14x20", DM 9/16/88 3,750
Interior Scene with Visiting Grandparents Entering an Already Lively Farmhouse, oil on canvas, sgn, 30x50", SLK 9/28/88 19,500
Mealtime, oil on canvas, sgn, 22z31", C-NY 10/25/89 OE 20,900
Mother & Child in an Interior, watercolor, sgn, 22x15", C-NY 10/26/88 4,400
Needle & Thread, oil on canvas, sgn, 22x30", C-NY 2/25/88 OE 11,000
Old Friends (man & woman visiting in an interior), watercolor on paper, sgn, 22x15", SBY 6/8/88 OE 2,860
Pair: No More; The Card Game; oil on canvas, sgn, 14x21", SBY 10/24/89 OE 26,400
Reading the News, oil on canvas, sgn, 22x30", C-NY 10/25/89 OE 17,600
Salute (three figures at table saluting w/wine glasses), oil on canvas, sgn, 14x20", SBY 6/8/88 4,950
Song of Italy (man playing guitar & woman singing in an interior), oil on canvas, 24x20", MG 3/26/88 UE 5,750
Teatime (peasant couple in interior with hen & chicks under foot), oil on canvas, sgn, 24x18", PHL 10/28/88 5,500
Tender Moment (mother holding up child by window), oil on canvas, sgn, 24x18", C-NY 2/23/89 9,350
Work of Art (lady & gentleman playing cards w/lady holding jug of wine), oil on canvas, sgn, 14x20", DM 9/16/88 4,000
ZANAZIO, G. (Italian, 19th/20th C)
Romantic Portrait of a Young Woman, oil on canvas, sgn, 29x24", RWS 5/12/89 800
ZANCHI, Antonio; circle of (Italian, 1631-1722)
Joseph Interpreting Dreams While in Prison, oil on canvas, 49x39", C-NY 10/20/88 2,200
ZANDOMENEGHI, Federigo (Italian, 1841-1917)
Young Girl Reading, oil on canvas, sgn, 15x18", C-NY 10/25/89 OE 462,000
ZANETTI-ZILLA, Vettore (Italian, 1864-1945)
Along the Canal, Venice; watercolor on paper, sgn, 39x22", WD 1/11/89 750
Levantine Boat, watercolor on paper, sgn, 14x10", B/B 1/11/89 440
Venetian Canal Scene, watercolor over traces of pencil, sgn, 38x22", C-E 5/22/89 1,430
ZANG, John J. (American, 19th C)
Figures in a Winter Landscape, oil on canvas, bears signature, 32x44", SBY 1/24/89 1,650
Figures in a Winter Landscape, oil on canvas, sgn, 32x44", SBY 9/23/88 2,640
Winter Landscape with Figures & Horses Pulling Logs by Sleigh, oil on canvas, sgn, 30x40", SBY 6/28/89 2,530
ZANGSTZINGER, M.G. (American, 20th C)
Cranes, watercolor/gouache on paper, sgn, 22x21", FAP 4/15/89 440
ZATZKA, Hans (Austrian, 1859-1945)
Alpenzauber, oil on canvas, sgn, 25x31", SBY 10/24/89 11,000
Amorous Serenade, oil on canvas, sgn/copyrighted, 25x31", SBY 12/9/88 OE 5,225
At the Palace (two harem girls w/birds), oil on canvas, sgn, 32x20", C-NY 2/23/89 OE 14,300
Butterflies, oil on canvas, sgn, 31x22", SBY 10/24/89 17,600
Eintrett Verbeten (man trying to enter bedroom w/lady leaning against door), oil on canvas, sgn, 27x19", C-E 5/22/89 OE 8,250
Floral Still Life of a Vase on a Ledge with Butterflies & Cricket, oil on canvas, sgn, oval, 28x33", C-E 2/21/89 3,850
Floral Still Life of Vase & Lily of the Valley in Glass...; oil on canvas, sgn, 30x22", C-E 2/21/89 4,950
Floral Still Life with a Cockatiel, Butterflies, a Dragonfly...; oil on canvas, sgn, 30x25", C-NY 2/23/89 OE 7,700
Floral Still Life with Parrot, oil on canvas, sgn, 30x25", B/B 6/9/88 6,600
Goddess of Spring, oil on canvas, sgn, 32x20", SBY 2/22/89 16,500
Gossamer Ladies (w/cupid by a stream), oil on canvas, sgn, 31x22", B/B 3/22/89 OE 8,250
In the Harem, oil on canvas, sgn, 24x30", C-NY 2/23/89 OE 15,400
Pink Flamingoes, oil on canvas, sgn, 24x32", SBY 10/24/89 13,200
Set of 4: Allegory of Spring; oil on canvas, sgn, 24x20", C-NY 2/25/88 16,500
Still Lifes of Flowers, oil on canvas, sgn, 30x25", WG 9/16/88 UE 1,100
Venus & Her Attendants, oil on canvas, sgn, 27x42", C-NY 2/23/89 UE 9,900
ZDANEVICH, Kiril (Russian, 1882-1970)
Pair: Composition No 36 (abstract); Composition with Circles; wash & charcoal on paper, 7x5", 6x8", C-L 10/8/88 OE 2,970

ZEGEDY, Alice
Pair: El Penseroso; watercolor, sgn, 13x13", LH 3/20/88 OE ... 425
ZEIM, Felix (French, 1821-1911)
Venetian Harbor Scene, oil on panel, sgn, 10x16", FB 10/17/88 ... 1,400
ZELLINSKY, C.L. (American, 19th C)
Celebrated Winning Racehorses & Jockeys of the American Turf, oil on canvas, sgn/dtd 1888, 24x48", SBY 6/9/89 ... 9,350
ZENG, Fan (Chinese, 1938-)
Bird Perched on a Rock (hanging scroll), ink/color on paper, sgn/dtd 1975, 18x14", SBY 5/31/89 ... 990
ZENLAR, F.
Cattle in a Summer Landscape, oil on canvas, sgn/dtd 1904, 20x30", NA 3/26/88 ... 375
ZENO, Jorge (American, 1956-)
Hermes (surrealistic view w/seated figure), oil on canvas, sgn, 28x22", SBY 11/21/88 ... 3,850
Mission (surrealistic figure coming out of water), oil on canvas, 1988, 48x36", SBY 5/16/89 ... 5,225
ZERBE, Karl (American, 1903-1972)
Columbus Circle, gouache on paper, sgn, 1946, 22x31", SBY 6/24/88 ... 1,540
Gilded (man seated), gouache/gold paint on paper, sgn, 20x15", SBY 6/24/88 ... 1,540
ZERMATI, J. (Italian, 19th/20th C)
Dictation, oil on canvas, sgn, 18x24", C-E 2/23/88 ... 1,760
ZETSCHE, Edouard (Austrian, 1844-1927)
Horsemen Stopping for a Rest, oil on canvas, sgn, 20x16", B/B 5/17/89 UE ... 770
Traveler on a Winding Village Road, watercolor/pen, sgn/dtd 1900, 11x15", C-E 2/21/89 OE ... 1,870
ZETTEL, Josephine (American, 20th C)
Working Drawing for a Rookwood Pot, Cincinnati; pencil & colored pencil on paper, 17x12", LH 10/16/88 ... 375
ZEWY, Karl (Austrian, 1855-1929)
Portrait of a Young Girl Holding Flowers & Watching Butterflies, oil on cradled panel, sgn, 31x21", B/B 3/22/89 ... 4,400
ZHAO, Shen (Chinese, 1427-1509)
Hollyhock & Rocks (hand scroll), ink/color on paper, sgn w/3 artist's seals, 9x62", SBY 5/31/89 OE ... 242,000
ZHAO, Wang (Chinese, fl 1500)
Fishermen (hanging scroll), ink on paper, sgn/dtd 1583, 48x20", SBY 5/31/89 ... 4,675
ZHEN, Wang (Chinese, 1867-1938)
Bodhidharma (hanging scroll), ink/color on paper, sgn/dtd 1919, 32x12", SBY 5/31/89 ... 1,430
Chrysanthemums (hanging scroll), ink/color on paper, sgn/dtd 1933, 54x13", SBY 5/31/89 ... 1,430
Turtles Beneath the Pine (hanging scroll), ink/color on paper, sgn/dtd 1905, 39x13", SBY 5/13/89 ... 3,850
ZHENGKUI, Cheng (Chinese, 17th C)
River Landscape (hand scroll), ink/color on paper, sgn/dtd 1659, 11x277", SBY 5/31/89 OE ... 88,000
ZHENGMING, Wen (Chinese, 1470-1559)
Biography of Zhan Qianshan in Xing Shu Running Script (hand scroll), ink on sutra, sgn/dtd 1550, 11x80", SBY 5/31/89 ... 13,200
ZHENGMING, Wen; att (Chinese, 1470-1559)
Snowscape (hanging scroll), ink/color on paper, sgn, 46x11", SBY 5/31/89 ... 3,300
ZHEZUO, Wang (Chinese, 17th/18th C)
Traveling in the Autumn Mountains, After Fan Kuan (hanging scroll); ink/color, sgn/dtd 1716, 59x26", SBY 5/31/89 ... 6,600
ZHI, Lu (Chinese, Ming Dynasty)
Flowers (hand scroll), ink/color on paper, sgn, 17x304", SBY 5/31/89 OE ... 9,900
ZHIMIAN, Zhou (Chinese, fl 1542-1606)
Birds & Flowers (hanging scroll), ink/color on silk, sgn, 65x35", SBY 5/31/89 OE ... 3,850
ZIEGLER, Eustace Paul (American, 1881-1941)
Cache, oil on board, sgn, 10x8", B/B 8/10/88 OE ... 8,250
Crossing the Water (covered wagon w/figures), oil on board, sgn, 11x22", B/B 3/22/89 ... 7,700
Double-Sided: Boy on Top of Mountain with Two Horses; Mountain; oil on panel, unfr, 16x19", C-E 11/30/88 ... 1,980
Eskimo Portrait, oil on canvasboard, sgn, 12x10", B/B 3/22/89 ... 4,400
Fish Boat, oil on board, sgn, 8x10", B/B 8/10/88 OE ... 8,800
Fishermen (pulling in their nets), oil on canvas, sgn, 34x40", B/B 3/22/89 OE ... 41,250
Kobuk Native, Alaska, I; oil on canvas, sgn/monogramed, 12x10", B/B 3/17/88 ... 3,575
Lower Yukon Native, oil on canvasboard, sgn, 12x10", B/B 6/9/88 ... 6,050
Mountain Landscape, oil on panel, sgn/dtd 1919, 8x10", C-E 6/1/88 ... 2,090
Mountain Ranger, oil on panel, sgn, 8x10", C-E 10/18/89 ... 2,420
Moving the Target, oil on canvas laid down, sgn, 40x33", B/B 3/22/89 ... 13,200
Old Homestead, oil on board, sgn/indistinctly inscr, 13x16", B/B 3/22/89 ... 3,850
Old Woman, Tanana, Alaska; oil on canvas, sgn/monogramed, 12x10", B/B 3/17/88 ... 3,300
Pack Horse, oil on board, sgn, 16x20", B/B 8/10/88 OE ... 16,500
Picnic (figures in a landscape), oil on canvasboard, sgn, 7x11", B/B 3/22/89 ... 3,300
Portrait of an Eskimo, oil on canvas, sgn/monogramed, 12x10", B/B 3/17/88 ... 3,025
Prospector (mining scene w/figure & shack perched on a cliff), oil on canvas, sgn, unfr, 22x28", B/B 3/22/89 ... 4,950
Self-Portrait (artist standing at easel viewed from behind), oil on board, sgn, 16x12", B/B 3/22/89 ... 3,850
Skyline Trail (riders in landscape), oil on board, sgn, 8x10", B/B 3/22/89 ... 5,225
Star Is Born (man panning for gold), oil on canvas, sgn, 20x16", B/B 3/22/89 ... 13,200
Two Men in a Tavern, oil on canvasboard, sgn, 14x16", B/B 6/15/89 ... 5,500
Water Flume Gold Dredge, oil on canvas, sgn, 40x60", B/B 8/10/88 OE ... 30,250
ZIEGLER, Nellie Evelyn (American, 20th C)
Coastal Scene, California (sailboats between beach & sandbar); oil on canvas, sgn, 20x24", RWS 9/29/88 OE ... 1,400
Santa Anita Wash, oil on canvas, sgn, 18x22", B/B 10/6/88 ... 4,675

ZIEM, Felix (French, 1821-1911)
Campment (men with camels camping by some ruins), oil on canvas, sgn, 33x46", SBY 2/22/89 ... **40,700**
Constantinople, oil on panel, sgn, 22x32", SBY 2/22/89 ... **26,400**
Grand Canal, oil on canvas, sgn, 21x31", C-NY 2/23/89 ... **19,800**
Grand Canal, Venice; oil on canvas, sgn, 22x32", C-E 10/25/88 ... **6,600**
Harbor of St Mark's, Venice; oil on canvas, sgn, 20x25", WD 11/16/88 UE ... **5,000**
L'Excursion, oil on panel transferred to masonite, sgn, 30x44", SBY 5/23/89 ... **17,600**
Sailing into Venice, oil on canvas, initialed, unfr, 18x26", WD 5/5/88 ... **2,500**
Santa Maria Della Salute, Venice, by Moonlight; oil on panel, sgn, 15x20", SBY 10/24/89 ... **10,450**
Sur le Grand Canal, Venise; oil on canvas, sgn, 21x33", SBY 2/22/89 ... **19,800**
Venetian Scene, oil on panel, sgn, 11x18", C-E 5/22/89 ... **6,050**
Venice, the Entrance to the Grand Canal; oil on canvas, sgn, 33x53", C-NY 2/3/88 OE ... **24,200**
Venice, le Grand Canal; oil on canvas, sgn, 27x42", SBY 2/22/89 ... **17,600**
Venice Scene, oil on canvas, sgn, 17x23", B/B 10/9/88 OE ... **6,600**
View of Venice with the Doge's Palace, oil on canvas, sgn, 33x49", C-NY 5/25/88 ... **16,500**

ZIER, Edouard (French, 1856-1924)
Portrait of Young Lady in Ball Gown, oil on canvas, sgn/dtd 1906, 17x14", DM 5/13/88 ... **2,750**

ZIGLIARA, Eugene (French, 1873-1918)
Young Lady Holding Yellow & Pink Roses, oil on canvas, sgn, 32x24", C-E 2/23/88 ... **1,650**

ZIGPOLI, G. (Italian, 19th C)
In the Market Place, oil on canvas, sgn, 16x10", RWS 12/10/88 UE ... **300**

ZILLER (Continental, 19th/20th C)
View of Venice, oil on canvas, sgn, 21x32", SBY 12/9/88 OE ... **1,980**

ZIMMERMAN, Carl (American, 19th/20th C)
Berry Pickers, oil on canvas, sgn, 38x50", C-E 10/18/89 UE ... **1,650**
Mountainous Landscape, oil on canvas, sgn, 22x36", C-E 10/25/88 UE ... **1,100**
Trees Along a Valley, oil on canvas, sgn, 20x24", WG 9/16/88 UE ... **650**

ZIMMERMAN, Frederick Almond (American, 1886-1974)
Early Winter in the Sierras, oil on canvas, sgn/dtd 36, 36x42", B/B 10/6/88 ... **2,750**

ZIMMERMAN, Karl (German, 1796-1857)
Artist's Studio, oil on canvas, sgn/indistinctly dtd Wien 18, 16x24", C-NY 2/23/89 ... **17,600**

ZINGONI, Aurelio (Italian, 1857-1922)
Writing a Letter, oil on canvas, sgn/inscr, unfr, 34x24", C-E 5/23/88 ... **3,850**

ZINNOGGER, Leopold (Scandinavian, 1811-1872)
Still Life of Fruit, Nuts, & Insects; oil on canvas, sgn/dtd 1835, 21x26", C-NY 5/25/88 ... **8,800**

ZISHEN, Wu (Chinese, 1894-1972)
Bamboo & Pine (hanging scroll), ink on paper, sgn/dtd 1955, 57x30", SBY 5/31/89 ... **1,650**

ZLOWE, Florence (American, 20th C)
Panis de Fleurs, oil on canvas, 30x22", FAP 12/8/89 ... **375**

ZO, Henri A. (French, 1873-1933)
Boulevard in Paris, oil on panel, sgn, 8x10", C-E 5/23/88 ... **3,300**
Bullfight, oil on panel, sgn, 7x6", C-E 11/8/88 ... **380**

ZOBEL, B. (British, 18th/19th C)
Farmyard Scene with Horses & Pigs, oil on canvas, bears signature/dtd 1803, 22x29", SBY 6/9/89 OE ... **4,125**

ZOFFANY, Johann; att (British, 1733-1810)
Portrait of Elisabeth with Her Rabbit (three-quarter length portrait in a landscape), oil, 30x25", WD 1/25/89 OE ... **4,500**

ZOFFOLI, A. (Italian, 19th C)
Classical Figures in a Garden, oil on canvas, sgn, 18x25", SBY 2/22/89 ... **8,250**

ZOGBAUM, Rufus F. (American, 1849-1925)
Headquarters in the Battlefield (Civil War), pen/ink on paper, inscr, 10x15", C-E 5/27/88 OE ... **1,760**

ZOLAN, Donald James (American, 20th C)
Blowing the Shofar, acrylic on canvas, sgn, 21x17", B/B 9/15/88 ... **385**
Fog in the Morning, acrylic on canvas, sgn/dtd 74, 32x26", B/B 9/15/88 ... **522**
Old European Peasant, acrylic on canvas, sgn, 14x11", B/B 9/15/88 ... **165**
Old Sea Captain, acrylic on canvas, sgn, 14x11", B/B 9/15/88 UE ... **248**

ZOMPINI, Gaetano Gherardo; att (Italian, 1700-1778)
Pair: Commedia del Arte Characters; oil on canvas, 64x28", SBY 1/12/89 ... **2,750**
Set of 4: Commedia del Arte Characters; oil on canvas, 64x28", SBY 1/12/89 ... **26,400**

ZOPPI, Antonio (Italian, 1860-1926)
Musical Gathe ring (interior scene w/figures), oil on canvas, sgn, 21x27", C-NY 2/23/89 ... **6,600**

ZORACH, Marguerite (American, 1888-1968)
Fantasy Landscape, watercolor/pencil on buff paper laid down on board, sgn, C-NY 9/30/88 OE ... **8,800**
Male & Female Nude, oil on panel, sgn, 8x10", WL 5/20/88 OE ... **4,100**

ZORACH, William (American, 1887-1966)
Hill Top Looking Out to the Bay, watercolor/pencil on paper laid down on board, sgn/dtd 1957, 15x22", C-E 6/1/89 ... **3,300**
House on a Point in Maine, watercolor/pencil on paper, sgn, 16x22", C-E 6/1/89 ... **5,500**
Landscape with Cottage by the Sea, watercolor on paper, sgn/dtd 1916, 14x11", SBY 9/23/88 OE ... **7,425**
Mother & Child, pencil/watercolor/charcoal on paper, sgn/dtd 1920, 22x15", SBY 6/28/89 ... **4,675**
Rocky Coastline (trees beyond), watercolor on paper laid down on board, sgn/dtd 1930, 11x19", C-E 6/1/89 OE ... **2,640**
Still Life with Flowers in a Vase, watercolor on paper, sgn/dtd June 16, 1962, 20x14", B/B 12/8/88 ... **1,980**
Tree (large tree in landscape), watercolor/pencil on paper, sgn/dtd 1918, 9x11", SBY 3/17/88 ... **1,760**

ORKOCZY, Guyla (Hungarian, 1873-1932)
Fishing by a Brook, oil on canvas, sgn, 22x27", B/B 9/14/89 880
Vielles Maissons au Borde de l'Eure, oil on canvas, sgn, 29x21", B/B 9/14/89 1,650

ORN, Anders (Swedish, 1860-1920)
In the Woods, oil on composition board, sgn/dtd 93, 22x15", SBY 5/23/89 962,500
Portrait of Mr William B Ogden, oil on canvas mounted on masonite, sgn/dtd 1895, 31x23", SBY 10/24/89 154,000
Portrait of Mrs Eben Richards, oil on canvas, sgn/dtd 99, 60x42", SBY 10/24/89 495,000

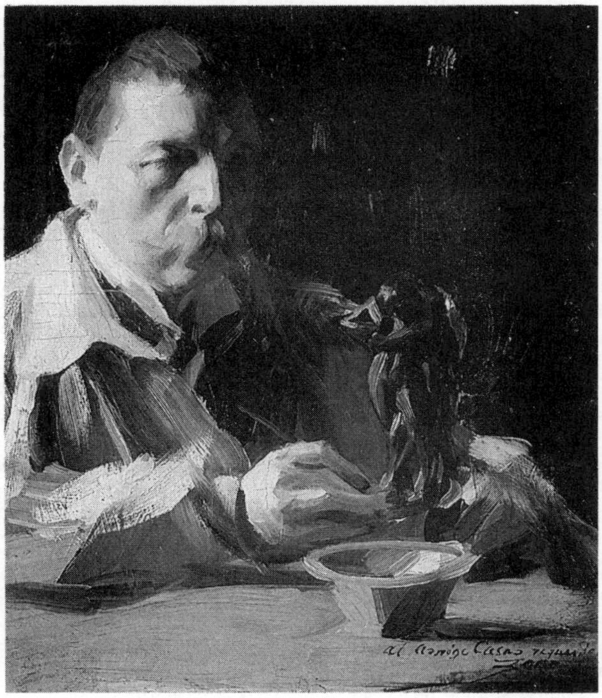

Self-Portrait with Faun & Nymph, oil on canvas, sgn, 1895, 19x16", C-NY 10/25/89; $462,000

ORRO, Andy (Canadian)
Pair: Birches, Charlevoix Shore; acrylic on board, sgn, 9x12", 8x10", FB 5/28/89 UE 100

OX, Larry (American, 1936-)
Argo (geometric composition), acrylic on canvas, 50x100", SBY 2/14/89 1,980
Napeaque A (abstract), acrylic on canvas, sgn, 54x86", C-E 11/14/89 3,300
Quinque (geometric composition), acrylic on canvas, sgn/dtd 1965, 40x44", C-E 11/14/89 825

UBER-BUHLER, Fritz (Swiss, 1822-1896)
Bath, oil on panel, sgn, 14x10", C-NY 2/25/88 6,600
La Parure de Cerises (girl holding her cat in a landscape), oil on canvas, sgn, 14x11", RWS 11/10/89 5,000
Portrait (depicts standing woman in a blue velvet dress), pastel, oval, 20x15", DM 9/16/88 UE 450
Woman Daydreaming, oil on canvas, 11x8", LH 10/16/88 3,200
Young Girl Holding a Doll, oil on canvas, sgn, 23x19", C-NY 5/24/89 OE 55,000

UBIAURRE, see De Zubiaurre

UCCARELLI, Francesco (Italian, 1702-1788)
Italianate Landscape with a Woman & Child, oil on canvas, 18x24", WD 1/25/89 24,000

UCCARELLI, Francesco; manner of (Italian, 1702-1788)
Extensive Country Landscape with Peasants & a Cottage by a Stream, oil on canvas, 8x19", SBY 7/12/89 OE 3,025
Woman Bathing in a Stream, Italianate Landscape Beyond; oil on canvas, 22x29", SBY 10/13/89 2,420

UCCARELLI, Frencesco; att (Italian, 1702-1788)
Macbeth & Banquo Hearing the Prophecies of the Three Weird Sisters, oil on canvas, 20x21", SBY 4/7/89 7,700

UCCARO, Federico; circle of (Italian, 1542-1609)
Battle Scene Outside the Walls of Rome, Retouched by Peter Paul Rubens; chalk/pen/ink/wash, 9x15", C-NY 1/11/89 15,400

UCKER, Joseph (Joe)(American, 1941-)
Ar, Ar (abstract); mixed media on canvas, sgn/dtd 78, 75x120", lot 420, SBY 11/9/89 17,600
North Dakota Windmill, mixed media on canvas, 1974, 48x24", lot 334, SBY 5/3/89 OE 11,000

UGNO, Francesco (Italian, 1709-1787)
Anthony & Cleopatra, oil on canvas, shaped top, 56x105", SBY 6/3/88 OE 70,400

UGNO, Francesco; circle of (Italian, 1709-1787)
Madonna & Child with Saints Francis of Assisi & Peter & Archangel Gabriel, oil on arched canvas, 24x15", SBY 4/7/89 OE 13,200

UILL, Abbie Luella (American, 1856-1924)
Mice & Walnut, oil on milk glass, sgn, 5x5", RAB 8/9/88 325

ULOAGA Y ZABALETA, Ignacio (Spanish, 1870-1945)
Elegant Lady Fanning Herself, oil on canvas, sgn, 38x27", C-NY 10/25/89 60,500
Extensive View of Toledo, oil on canvas, sgn, 38x55", SBY 10/24/89 341,000

ZUNIGA, Francisco (Costa Rican, 1913-)
Adolescente Sentada (seated nude), pastel on heavy paper, sgn/dtd 1972, 20x25", C-NY 5/17/89 OE ... 8,250
Boy with Hat, crayon on paper, sgn/dtd 1976, 28x20", SBY 5/17/88 ... 4,400
Desnudo (nude), crayon/charcoal on paper, sgn/dtd 1979, 25x19", lot 88, C-NY 5/18/88 ... 3,080
Desnudo (nude), crayon/charcoal on paper, sgn/dtd 62, 19x23", lot 89, C-NY 5/18/88 ... 2,860
Desnudo Acostado (reclining nude), pastel/charcoal on paper, sgn/dtd 1983, 20x28", C-NY 11/21/88 ... 4,950
Desnudo Durmiendo (nude in repose), charcoal on paper, sgn/dtd 1975, 20x28", C-NY 5/17/89 ... 4,400
Desnudo Setado (nude woman), brown wash/charcoal/crayon on paper, sgn/dtd 1979, 19x28", C-NY 5/18/88 ... 2,200
Dos Madres y sus Ninos (two mothers w/their children), charcoal/white chalk, sgn/dtd 1976, 21x28", C-NY 11/21/89 ... 3,080
Dos Mujeres Sentadas (two seated women), colored chalk/charcoal on paper, sgn/dtd 1974, 20x26", C-NY 11/21/88 OE ... 7,150
Dos Tehuanas con Naranjas (two women w/oranges), watercolor/pen/ink on paper, sgn/dtd 1965, 20x26", C-NY 5/17/89 ... 19,800
El Umbral (woman in doorway w/child in window), charcoal/chalk on paper, sgn/dtd 1974, 19x26", C-NY 11/21/88 ... 4,950
Estudio de Anciana, charcoal/white chalk on tan paper, sgn/dtd 1973, 26x20", C-NY 11/21/89 OE ... 8,250
Estudios de Desnudos, pen/ink/pencil on paper, sgn/dtd 1962, 11x17", C-NY 11/21/89 ... 4,180
Girl with Extended Legs, pastel on paper, sgn/dtd 1974, 19x26", SBY 5/17/88 ... 2,410
Grupo Familiar (four large women w/nude child), watercolor/charcoal on paper, sgn/dtd 1968, 20x26", C-NY 11/21/89 OE ... 13,200
La Falda Azul (seated woman), colored chalk/charcoal on gray paper, sgn/dtd 1981, 30x38", C-NY 5/18/88 ... 8,800
La Sopa (woman setting bowl on table), crayon/charcoal on paper, sgn/dtd 1963, 20x26", C-NY 11/21/88 ... 3,080
Madres y Nino en la Puerta (two mothers & child in doorway), charcoal/white chalk, sgn/dtd 74, 26x18", C-NY 11/21/89 OE ... 7,150
Mujer de Pie (standing woman), charcoal/white chalk/pastel on paper, sgn/dtd 1983, 20x28", C-NY 5/17/89 ... 4,400
Mujer Descansando (woman resting), charcoal/white chalk on paper, sgn/dtd 1978, 20x28", C-NY 5/18/88 ... 2,860
Mujer Desnuda Tendida de Espaldas (reclining nude), charcoal/pastel on paper, sgn/dtd 1979, 20x28", C-NY 11/21/88 OE ... 6,050
Mujer en una Silla (seated draped nude), charcoal/white chalk on paper, sgn/dtd 1979, 20x28", C-NY 11/21/88 ... 3,850
Mujer Sentada (seated nude), pencil/charcoal on paper, sgn/dtd 1980, 22x28", C-NY 5/17/89 OE ... 7,920
Mujeres con Espejo (two seated women w/mirror), charcoal/colored chalk on paper, sgn/dtd 1978, 19x28", C-NY 11/21/88 ... 3,850
Nude, charcoal on paper, sgn/dtd 1980, 20x28", SBY 5/17/88 ... 4,400
Nude (prone posterior view), pastel on paper, sgn/dtd 1973, 20x26", SBY 5/17/88 UE ... 1,980
Reclining Nude, charcoal on paper, sgn/dtd 1979, 20x28", SBY 5/16/89 ... 7,150
Seated Nude, charcoal on paper, sgn/dtd 66, 19x25", SBY 5/16/89 ... 5,225
Seated Woman (nude), pastel on paper, sgn/dtd 1965, 24x20", SBY 5/16/89 OE ... 9,350
Tres Mujeres Caminando, crayon/black/white chalk on buff paper, sgn/dtd 1979, 20x28", C-NY 5/18/88 OE ... 6,600
Two Seated Women, colored chalk on paper, sgn/dtd 1975, 19x26", SBY 5/17/88 OE ... 5,225
Two Women, colored chalk on paper, sgn/dtd 1974, 19x26", SBY 5/17/88 OE ... 5,225
Two Women & a Child, watercolor/pencil on paper, sgn/dtd 60, 18x25", SBY 5/17/88 OE ... 7,150

ZURBARAN, school of (Spanish, 17th C)
Virgin with St Joachim & St Anne, oil on canvas, 58x43", C-NY 10/20/88 ... 15,400

ZUYDERLAND, Siet (Dutch, 1942-)
Federal Detention Headquarters, West Street, New York City; oil on board, sgn/dtd 1975, 20x26", C-E 11/17/88 ... 770

ZUYIN, Pan (Chinese, 1830-1890)
Calligraphy in Xing Shu Running Script (hanging scroll), ink on gold-flecked paper, sgn, 50x13", SBY 5/31/89 ... 1,100

ZWAAN, Cornelisz C. (Dutch, 1882-1964)
Afternoon Story (interior scene w/mother & children), oil on canvas, sgn, 20x24", SBY 7/12/89 ... 3,300
Mother & Children in an Interior, oil on canvas, estate stamp, 30x36", SBY 7/12/89 UE ... 1,650
Woman Reading in an Interior, oil on board, 16x12", SBY 4/14/89 ... 1,100

ZWACK, Michael (American, 20th C)
History of the World Series, colored chalks on paper mounted on canvas, 32x21", C-NY 5/4/88 OE ... 2,200

ZWARA
Autumn Landscape, oil on canvas, sgn, 23x33", DM 1/15/88 ... 450

ZYGMUNTOWIEZ (Continental, 19th C)
Horse-Drawn Sleighs in a Winter Landscape, oil on board, sgn, 9x13", C-E 2/21/89 UE ... 450

Photographs

ABBOTT, Berenice (American, 1898-)
American Shops, 4/40, p/s on mount, portfolio stp on verso, 1930s/ca 1982, 18x23", Parasol, SBY 4/26/89 ... 1,980
Blossom Restaurant, p/s on mount, studio stp on verso, 1930s/later, 11x13", SBY 11/1/88 ... 770
Broadway to the Battery, From the Roof of Irving Trust Company Building, One Wall Street; slvr, 13x10", B/B 4/19/88 UE ... 358
Broome Street, #504-506; sgn/Gamma Picture Agency stp on verso, matted, 1930s, 8x10", SBY 4/26/89 OE ... 2,475
Centre Street, 10/40, p/s, portfolio stp on verso, 1930s/ca 1982, 18x23", Parasol, SBY 5/4/88 ... 1,430
Christopher Street Shop, p/s on mount, studio stp on verso, 1930s/later, 13x10", SBY 11/1/88 ... 770
City Arabesque, Berenice Abbott Retrospective; 10/40, p/s, portfolio stp on verso, 1930s/ca 1982, 23x17", SBY 5/4/88 ... 880
City Arabesque, 10/40, p/s, portfolio stp on verso, 1930s/ca 1982, 23x17", Parasol, SBY 5/4/88 ... 880
City Street Through a Rain-Covered Window, p/s on mount, sgn/studio stp on verso, 1930s/later, 13x10", SBY 11/1/88 OE ... 1,760
Edna St Vincent Millay, p/s on mount, inscr/dtd by sitter on img, 1931, matted, 7x9", SBY 5/4/88 ... 1,210
El, Berenice Abbott Retrospective; 10/40, p/s on mount, portfolio stp on verso, 1930s/ca 1982, 23x18", SBY 11/1/88 ... 880
El, 2nd & 3rd Avenue, Hanover Square & Pearl Street; slvr, Commerce St stp on verso, 1936, 10x8", SWN 10/30/88 ... 1,540
Eugene Atget, #22, total ed of 55, p/s, portfolio label on verso, 1930s/ca 1976, fr, 13x10", Witkin-Berley, SBY 5/4/88 ... 660

Exchange Place, #22, total ed of 55, p/s, portfolio label on verso, 1930s/ca 1976, 14x4", Witkin-Berley, SBY 5/4/88 OE	1,320
Factory Warehouse, Berenice Abbott Ten Photographs; #22, total ed of 55, p/s, 1930s/ca 1976, fr, 11x14", SBY 11/1/88	660
Fifth Avenue at 8th Street, #22, total ed of 55, p/s, 1930s/ca 1976, matted/fr, 11x14", Witkin-Berley, SBY 5/4/88 OE	1,320
Fifth Avenue at 8th Street, p/s on mount, Maine studio stp on verso, 1936/later, 23x18", SBY 11/1/88	2,475
Fifth Avenue Coach Company, 4/40, p/s on mount, portfolio stp on verso, 1930s/ca 1982, 15x19", SBY 4/26/89	1,980
Flatiron, 10/40, p/s, portfolio stp on verso, 1930s/ca 1982, 23x18", Parasol, SBY 5/4/88	1,045
From West Street, sgn/Gamma Picture Agency stp on verso, matted, 1930s, 8x10", SBY 4/26/89 OE	3,300
Fulton Street Dock, Manhattan Skyline; toned slvr, Federal Art Project stp/titled on verso, 1935, 8x10", SWN 10/30/88	880
George Washington Bridge, sgn/1 W 67th Street & Julien Levy Gallery stp on verso, ca 1931, 9x7", SBY 4/26/89 OE	4,125
Grand Street, #511-513, Manhattan; dtd/titled/studio & Federal Art Project stps, matted, 1937, 8x10", SBY 4/26/89	1,870
Grand Street #605-607-609, dtd/titled/studio & Federal Art Project stps on verso, matted, 1937, 8x10", SBY 4/26/89	880
Group of 3: Iron Girders; Shelter on the Water Front, Coenties Slip, Pier 5...; Changing New York; 1930s, SBY 5/4/88 OE	2,750
Group of 3: Trinity Churchyard; Soap Bubbles; Greenwich Village; sgn/titled on verso, 2 1940s & 1 1930s, SBY 11/1/88	1,210
Gunsmith, sgn/title label on mount, Commerce Street studio stp/Federal Art Project label, 1920s, 9x7", SBY 4/26/89 OE	3,850
Hannover Square, sgn/Gamma Picture Agency stp on verso, matted, 1930s, 8x10", SBY 4/26/89 OE	1,870
Hardware Store, 316-318 Bowery; slvr flush-mounted on board, 50 Commerce St stp on verso, 1938, 13x17", SWN 4/24/89	1,980
Hoboken Ferry Terminal, Barclay Street; slvr, p/s on mount recto, Abbott stp on verso, 1930s/later, 15x19", SWN 4/24/89	935
Interior of McSorley's Ale House, East 7th St Near 3rd Avenue; slvr, titled on verso, 1930s, 8x10", SWN 4/24/89	990
James Joyce, slvr, p/s, stp on verso, 1928/ca 1070s, 14x11", B/B 10/4/88	825
John Sloan, slvr, p/s, stp on verso, 10x9", B/B 10/4/88 UE	300
Looking Toward Brooklyn, sgn/50 Commerce Street studio stp on verso, matted, 1930s, 7x5", SBY 4/26/89 OE	11,000
Lyric Theatre, 10/40, p/s, portfolio stp on verso, 1930s/ca 1982, 18x23", Parasol, SBY 5/4/88	1,100
Madison Square, toned slvr, Federal Art Project Changing New York stp/titled/dtd on verso, 1936, 8x10", SWN 4/24/89 UE	715
Manhattan Skyline, slvr, Commerce St stp on verso, 10x8", B/B 4/19/88	660
Max Ernst, Peggy Guggenheim's Apartment, New York; slvr, p/s, Abbott Maine stp, 1941/later, 10x8", SWN 10/30/88 OE	1,100
New York at Night, Berenice Abbott Ten Photographs; 22/55, p/s on mount, matted, 1930s/ca 1976, fr, 13x10", SBY 11/1/88	1,100
New York at Night, p/s on mount, studio stp on verso, matted, 1934/later, fr, 23x18", SBY 4/26/89	3,740
New York at Night, p/s on mount, studio stp on verso, 1934/later, 23x18", SBY 11/1/88	3,300
New York at Night, p/s on mount, studio stp on verso, 1934/later, 14x11", SBY 5/4/88	1,045
New York at Night, slvr, p/s, Maine stp on verso, 1934/later, 14x11", B/B 10/4/88	1,320
New York at Night, slvr, p/s on mount, Maine stp on mount verso, 1934/1960s, 14x11", B/B 4/19/88	1,320
New York at Night, 51/60, p/s on mount, stp on verso, matted, 1934/ca 1979, fr, 23x18", Parasol, SBY 5/4/88	2,970
New York Stock Exchange, 10/40, p/s, portfolio stp on verso, 1930s/ca 1982, 23x18", Parasol, SBY 5/4/88	880
Oyster Houses Are Gone, slvr, p/s, titled/dtd/All Rights Reserved on verso, 1954, 6x5", SWN 4/24/89 OE	2,860
Pair: Edward Hopper; Reflection; #22, total ed of 55, p/s, label on verso, 1930s/ca 1976, fr, 13x10", SBY 11/1/88	550
Pair: Greyhound Bus Terminal; North River Savings Bank; 19/60, p/s, matted, 1930s/ca 1979, fr, 16x20", SBY 5/4/88	1,650
Pair: James Joyce; Princess Murat; #22, total ed of 55, p/s on mount, label on verso, 1930s/ca 1976, 14x10", SBY 11/1/88	836
Parafoti, 4/40, p/s on mount, portfolio stp on verso, 1930s/ca 1982, 19x23", Parasol, SBY 4/26/89	880
Pennsylvania Station, p/s on mount, Maine studio stp on verso, ca 1934/later, 19x15", SBY 11/1/88	1,760
Pennsylvania Station, 2/100, p/s on mount, stps on verso, 1930s/later, fr, 11x14", Bernice Abbott, SBY 5/4/88	935
Portfolio: Faces of the 20s; 38/60, total ed of 65, 12 photos, p/s, 1920s/ca 1981, 14x11", Parasol, SBY 5/4/88	2,970
Portrait of Atget, slvr, p/s, stp on verso, 1927/later, 13x10", B/B 10/4/88	770
Portrait of Djuna Barnes, slvr, p/s on mount recto, Abbott Maine stp on verso, 1926/later, 10x8", SWN 4/24/89	523
Portrait of Huddie Ledbetter (Leadbelly), slvr flush-mounted on board, sgn/Commerce St stp, 1930s, 13x10", SWN 4/24/89	990
Portrait of Marie Laurencin, slvr, 44 Rue du Bac Paris stp on verso, 1926, 9x7", SWN 4/24/89 OE	2,420
Portrait of Paul Cross, slvr, 1 West 67th St NYC stp/dtd on verso, 1925, 10x8", SWN 4/24/89	770
Princess Eugene Marat, slvr, p/s on mount, 1930/later, 10x8", SWN 4/24/89 UE	330
Railroad Yard, 10/40, p/s, portfolio stp on verso, 1930s/ca 1982, 18x23", Parasol, SBY 5/4/88	990

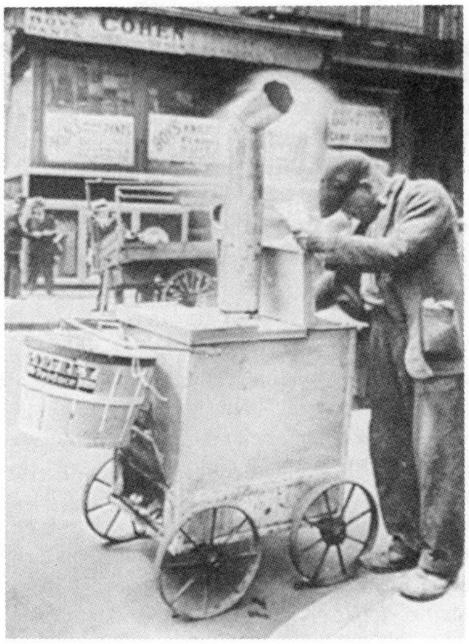

Roast Corn Man, Orchard & Hester Streets, Manhattan; slvr, Federal Art Project stp/dtd on verso, 10x8", SWN 4/24/88 OE; $3,080

Railroad Yard, 4/40, p/s on mount, artist portfolio stp on verso, 1930s/ca 1982, 18x23", SBY 4/26/89 OE **2,200**
Rhinelander Houses, 5th Avenue, Nos 4, 6, & 8; slvr, p/s on mount, Abbott Maine stp, 1936/later, 11x14", SWN 10/30/88 .... **523**
Rope Store, sgn/dtd/titled/Commerce Street studio stp on verso, matted, 1936, fr, 8x10", SBY 11/1/88 .... **1,210**
Row Houses, Washington Square North; slvr, red pencil inscr on verso, 1940s, 7x8", SWN 10/30/88 .... **385**
Saint Mark's Church with Skywriting, slvr, p/s on mount recto, 2 a/stp on verso, 1937/later, 10x8", SWN 10/30/88 UE **220**
Snuff Shop, dtd/inscr/Federal Art Project stp on verso, 1938, 9x8", SBY 11/1/88 .... **770**
Suits Topcoats, p/s on mount/mat, studio stp on verso, 1930s/later, 13x10", SBY 11/1/88 .... **880**
Treasury Building, p/s in mrg, Maine Studio stp on verso, 1930s/later, 19x15", SBY 11/1/88 .... **1,100**
Tri-Boro Barber Shop, 9/40, p/s on mount, portfolio stp on verso, 1930s/ca 1982, 19x24", SBY 11/1/88 .... **880**
Union Square West, Nos 31-41; slvr, sgn/titled/artist name stp on verso, 8x10", SWN 4/24/89 .... **1,100**
Untitled (Triple Bridge), sgn/Gamma Picture Agency stp on verso, matted, 1930s, 6x4", SBY 4/26/89 OE **3,300**
Vanderbilt Avenue, toned slvr, 56 West 53rd St NYC/WPA stps on verso, titled/dtd on verso, 1935, 9x7", SWN 4/24/89 .... **715**
West Street Row: V; Federal Art Project stp/NY Public Library stp on verso, matted, 1930s, 8x10", SBY 4/26/89 OE **2,750**
Whitehall Building, #17 Battery Place, Battery, Foot of West St; slvr, WPA/artist stp on verso, 1936, 10x8", SWN 4/24/89 .... **248**
Yuban Warehouse, Water & Dock Streets, Brooklyn, slvr, p/s on mount, Maine stp, 1936/1970s, 11x14", B/B 4/19/88 UE **495**

ABE, James

Anna Pavlova & Her Two Premier Danseurs, Volinine & Novikoff; slvr, titled in ink on verso, ca 1925, 8x6", SWN 10/30/88 .... **605**

ADAMS, Ansel (American, 1902-1984)

Aspens, New Mexico; ink sgn in mrg, Sierra Club This Is the Earth stp on verso, 1958/1959-63, 15x19", SBY 11/1/88 .... **8,800**
Aspens, Northern New Mexico (Horizontal); p/s on mount, Carmel studio stp on verso, 1958/later, 15x19", SBY 4/26/89 OE **10,450**
Aspens, Northern New Mexico; ink sgn on mount, titled/Carmel studio stp on verso, 1958/1959-63, 15x18", SBY 5/4/88 .... **6,875**
Aspens, Northern New Mexico; p/s on mount, Carmel studio stp on verso, 1958/1978, 20x16", SBY 5/4/88 .... **4,125**
Aspens, Northern New Mexico; 53/115, slvr, Portfolio 7 stp on mount verso, 1958/1976, fr, 18x23", B/B 4/19/88 .... **6,600**
At Zabriskie Point, Death Valley; artist stps/Art Institute of Chicago stp on verso, matted, 1950, 10x8", SBY 11/1/88 .... **880**
Barn, Sonoma County; p/s on verso, San Francisco studio label on verso, mounted/matted, 1930s, 11x14", SBY 4/26/89 .... **1,100**
Book: Ansel Adams, Images, 1923-1974; 67/1000, sgn, 1961/ca 1974, folio, blk cloth, New York Graphic Soc, SBY 5/4/88 OE **1,650**
Bridalveil Fall, #130, total ed of 258, sgn in mrg, portfolio stp on verso, ca 1952/ca 1959, 11x8", SBY 4/26/89 .... **1,980**
Buddhist Grave Markers, Maui, Hawaii; p/s on mount, Carmel studio stp on verso, ca 1956/1978, 16x20", SBY 5/4/88 .... **1,870**
Clearing Storm, Sonoma County Hills, California; #217, total ed of 260, 1951/ca 1963, 9x12", SBY 11/1/88 .... **1,760**
Clearing Winter Storm, Yosemite National Park; #9, slvr, ink sgn, stp on verso, 1944/1959, 8x9", B/B 10/4/88 .... **2,475**
Clearing Winter Storm, Yosemite National Park; artist name stp, matted, 1944/ca early 1950s, 10x13", SBY 4/26/89 OE **5,500**
Clearing Winter Storm, Yosemite National Park; p/s, Carmel studio stp on verso, 1944/later, 16x19", SBY 5/4/88 .... **7,150**
Clearing Winter Storm, Yosemite National Park; p/s, Carmel studio stp on verso, 1944/1977, 15x19", SBY 4/26/89 OE **10,450**
Clearing Winter Storm, Yosemite National Park; slvr, p/s on mount, Carmel stp on verso, 1944/later, 16x19", B/B 4/19/88 .... **4,950**
Coast & Surf, Timber Cove; ink sgn on mount, Timber Cove Inn stp on verso, 1960s, fr, 11x14", SBY 5/4/88 .... **1,320**
Cottage in Yosemite, slvr, p/s on mount, artist name label on mount verso, ca 1940, 10x14", B/B 4/19/88 .... **358**
Dawn, Autumn, Great Smoky Mountains National Park, Tennessee; p/s, Carmel studio stp, 1948/1974, 20x15", SBY 11/1/88 OE **4,400**
Dawn, Autumn, Great Smoky Mountains National Park, Tennessee; slvr, p/s, Carmel stp, 1948/ca 1976, 19x13", B/B 10/4/88 .... **2,200**
Dawn, Autumn Forest, Great Smoky Mountains National Park, Tennessee; p/s on mount, 1948/ca 1950, 12x9", SBY 4/26/89 OE **3,850**
Dead Tree, Sunset Crater National Monument, Arizona; #89, p/s, portfolio stp, 1947, 10x7", SBY 4/26/89 .... **880**
Dogwood Blossoms, #130, total ed of 258, sgn on mount, portfolio stp on verso, 1938/ca 1959, 9x6", SBY 4/26/89 OE **3,025**
Eagle Peak & Middle Brother, Yosemite National Park; slvr, p/s, Carmel stp, ca 1968/later, 10x13", B/B 10/4/88 .... **1,320**
Edward Weston, Carmel Highlands, California; slvr, p/s, Carmel stp on verso, 1945/ca 1970, 14x11", B/B 10/4/88 .... **8,250**
Edward Weston, sgn/artist stp/Art Institute of Chicago stp on verso, early 1950s, 7x6", SBY 11/1/88 .... **935**
El Capitan, Winter Sunrise, Yosemite National Park; sgn/Carmel studio stp, 1968/1968-70, 19x15", SBY 11/1/88 OE **6,600**
El Capitan Fall, Yosemite National Park; slvr, p/s, Carmel stp on verso, ca 1940/1970, 11x14", B/B 10/4/88 .... **1,320**
Face of Half Dome, Yosemite; backed w/card, San Francisco studio label on verso, ca 1926/pre-1962, 8x6", SBY 11/1/88 .... **1,650**
Fern Springs, Yosemite Valley; sgn on mount, Carmel studio stp on verso, 1961, 14x10", SBY 4/26/89 OE **3,025**
Forest Floor, Yosemite Valley, California; p/s on mount, Carmel studio stp on verso, ca 1950/ca 1978, 15x19", SBY 5/4/88 .... **3,190**
Fresh Snow, Yosemite Valley, California; p/s, sgn/dtd/inscr For Ted & Jeanette, ca 1947/1978, 15x19", SBY 4/26/88 .... **6,050**
Frozen Lake & Cliffs, Sierra Nevada, California; p/s on mount, Carmel studio stp, 1932/ca 1932, 10x13", SBY 5/4/88 OE **3,850**
Frozen Lake & Cliffs, Sierra Nevada, California; slvr, p/s on mount, Carmel stp, 1927/later, 10x13", B/B 4/19/88 .... **2,475**
Graduation Dress, 61/110, p/s in mrg, portfolio stp on verso, matted, 1948/ca 1974, fr, 20x15", SBY 4/26/89 .... **880**
Group of 3: Massachusetts Women's Defense Corps; artist stp on verso, ca 1947, various sizes, SBY 5/4/88 .... **880**
Half Dome, Blowing Snow, Yosemite National Park; p/s, Carmel studio stp on verso, ca 1955/later, fr, 15x19", SBY 5/4/88 .... **4,400**
Half Dome, Thundercloud, Yosemite National Park; sgn on mount, dtd/titled on verso, ca 1956/1959, 10x7", SBY 4/26/89 .... **2,200**
Half Dome From Washburn Point, Thunderstorm, Yosemite...; sgn on img, dtd on verso, ca 1947/ca 1959, 10x11", SBY 4/26/89 .... **1,925**
Juniper, Cliffs & River, Upper Merced River Canyon, Yosemite National Park; 46/50, 1936/ca 1979, 13x19", SBY 5/4/88 .... **1,540**
Lake Tenaya, Yosemite National Park, California; slvr, ink sgn, Carmel stp, ca 1946/ca 1960, 11x14", B/B 10/4/88 .... **1,100**
Leaves, Mt Rainier National Park, Washington; p/s on mount, Carmel stp on verso, 1942/1976, 19x14", SBY 5/4/88 .... **4,125**
Library at Saratoga, slvr, p/s on mount, artist San Francisco label/ET Spencer stp on verso, 1930s, 10x14", SWN 4/24/89 .... **550**
Lodgepole Pines, Lyell Fork of the Merced River, Yosemite National Park; p/s, ca 1923/1979, 10x13", SBY 11/1/88 .... **2,750**
Manly Beacon, Death Valley National Monument; slvr, p/s on mount, Carmel stp on verso, 1952/1977, 16x20", B/B 4/19/88 .... **3,025**
Martha Porter, Pioneer Woman, Orderville, Utah; slvr, p/s on mount, Carmel stp, ca 1960/1982, 12x11", SWN 4/24/89 UE **880**
Mattes Crest, Yosemite National Park; sgn on mount, titled/Carmel studio stp on verso, 1938/1962, 8x9", SBY 5/4/88 UE **3,190**
Mattes Crest, Yosemite National Park; sgn on mount, titled/Carmel stp on verso, 1938/ca 1962, 7x9", SBY 5/4/88 UE **1,100**
Mesa Verde Ruins, slvr, p/s & titled in mrg, 1920s, 6x8", SBY 5/4/88 .... **1,760**
Minarets, Storm; slvr, ink sgn on mount, titled/Carmel stp on verso, ca 1937/later, 8x10", B/B 10/4/88 .... **1,100**
Monolith, Face of Half Dome, Yosemite National Park, California; Carmel stp, 1926/later, 20x15", SBY 5/4/88 .... **4,950**
Monolith, Face of Half Dome, Yosemite National Park, California; p/s, ca 1926/later, 19x14", SBY 4/26/89 .... **7,150**
Monolith, Face of Half Dome; slvr, p/s on mount, dtd/inscr/stp on verso, 1927/1979, fr, 20x15", B/B 10/4/88 .... **4,400**

Monument Valley, Utah; p/s on mount, Carmel studio stp on verso, 1958/1975, 16x20", SBY 11/1/88 5,500
Moon & Half Dome, Yosemite National Park; p/s on mount, Carmel stp on verso, 1960/later, fr, 20x15", SBY 5/4/88 7,425

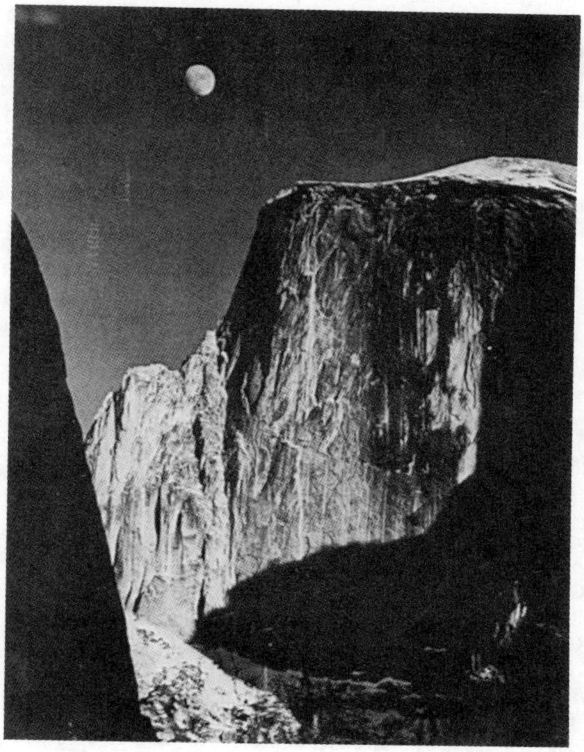

Moon & Half Dome, Yosemite National Park; slvr, p/s, Carmel stp on verso, 1960, 20x15", B/B 10/4/88; $7,700

Moonrise, Hernandez, New Mexico; ink sgn on mount, Carmel stp on verso, 1944/1959-63, 16x20", SBY 5/4/88 8,250
Moonrise, Hernandez, New Mexico; p/s, Carmel studio stp on verso, matted, ca 1941/later, fr, 15x19", SBY 11/1/88 OE 14,300
Moonrise, Hernandez, New Mexico; p/s, Carmel studio stp on verso, matted, ca 1941/later, 15x19", fr, SBY 4/26/89 OE 15,400
Moonrise, Hernandez, New Mexico; slvr, p/s on mount, Carmel stp on mount verso, 1941/1962-72, fr, 16x20", B/B 4/19/88 6,600
Moonrise, Hernandez, New Mexico; slvr, p/s on mount, Carmel stp on mount verso, 1941/1970s, fr, 16x20", B/B 4/19/88 7,150
Moonrise Over Hernandez, slvr, ink sgn on mount, titled/stp on verso, 1946/ca 1960s, fr, 15x20", B/B 10/4/88 8,250
Mount McKinley From Wonder Lake, p/s on mount, Carmel studio stp on verso, 1947/later, 16x19", SBY 4/26/89 OE 8,800
Mount Resplendent, sgn/titled in mrg, matted, 1928, 15x11", SBY 4/26/89 OE 14,300
Mount Williamson, Sierra Nevada, From the Owens Valley, California; Carmel studio stp, 1944/1978, 14x19", SBY 11/1/88 OE 4,400
Mount Williamson, Sierra Nevada From Manzanar, California; p/s, Carmel stp, 1944/later, 15x18", SBY 11/1/88 7,150
Mount Williamson From Manzanar, California; p/s on mount, studio stp on verso, 1944/pre-1962, 13x16", SBY 5/4/88 4,400
Mt Robson From Mt Resplendent, Mt Robson National Park, Canada; sgn/inscr To William E Colby, 1928, 8x6", SBY 5/4/88 6,600
Nevada Fall, Rainbow, Yosemite National Park; slvr, ink sgn, Carmel stp on verso, ca 1947/1959, 10x7", B/B 10/4/88 1,045
Oak Tree, Snowstorm, Yosemite National Park, California; p/s, Carmel studio stp, 1948/ca 1975, 14x11", SBY 4/26/89 OE 4,125
Oak Tree, Snowstorm, Yosemite National Park; p/s on mount, Carmel studio stp on verso, 1948/1980, 20x16", SBY 11/1/88 OE 9,350
Old Faithful Geyser, Late Evening, Yellowstone National Park, Wyoming; #42, p/s, 1942/ca 1950, 10x7", SBY 4/26/89 1,430
Old Faithful Geyser, Yellowstone National Park, Wyoming; p/s, Carmel studio stp, ca 1942/1976, 20x14", SBY 11/1/88 OE 4,675
Pair: Ranch House; p/s on mount, San Francisco name label on verso, matted, ca 1930s, 10x14", SBY 4/26/89 1,100
Pair: Surf, Timber Cove, N California Coast; N California Coast, Timber Cove; slvr, 1960s, 10x12"/10x11", SWN 10/30/88 990
Pine Branch in Snow, Yosemite Valley, California; sgn in mrg, Carmel studio stp, ca 1932/1959, 9x7", SBY 4/26/89 2,200
Poplars, Owen Valley, California; p/s on mount, Carmel stp on verso, 1936/later, 14x10", SBY 5/4/88 UE 715
Portfolio II, National Parks & Monuments; #97, total ed 105, 1941-49, various sizes, Grabhorn, SBY 5/4/88 14,300
Portfolio II: National Parks & Monuments; #13, total ed of 105, 15 photos, p/s on mount, 1941-49, 9x7", SBY 11/1/88 14,300
Portfolio II: National Parks & Monuments; #66, total ed of 105, 15 photos, p/s on mount, 1941-49/ca 1950, SBY 4/26/89 16,500
Portfolio III: Yosemite Valley; 48/250, 16 photos, sgn on mount, stp on verso, 1926-56/ca 1959, SBY 4/26/89 20,900
Portfolio VI, 63/110, 10 photos, p/s on mount, portfolio stp on verso, 1932-53/ca 1974, 16x20", SBY 11/1/88 13,200
Portfolio: Parmelian Prints of the High Sierras; 18 photos, sgn/titled in mrg, 1920s/ca 1927, 6x8", SBY 4/26/89 OE 22,000
Rails & Jet Trails, Roseville, California; slvr, p/s, artist/Hasselblad stp on verso, 1953/1960s, 14x10", SWN 4/24/89 UE 880
Redwoods, Bull Creek Flat, Northern California; p/s, Carmel stp on verso, ca 1960/1980, 15x19", SBY 5/4/88 OE 3,850
Redwoods, Bull Creek Flat, Northern California; p/s, Carmel studio stp on verso, ca 1960/ca 1974, 11x13", SBY 11/1/88 2,750
Refugio Beach, titled/inscr For Reproduction Only, portfolio/Pollack stps on verso, 1946/pre-1948, 7x9", SBY 4/26/89 OE 1,760
Rice Fields, Northern California; slvr, titled in ink/stps on verso, 1960s, 12x10", SWN 4/24/89 715
Roaring River Falls, parmelian print, p/s, 1927, 8x6", Jean Chambers Moore, w/separate laid paper folder, SBY 5/4/88 1,870
Sand Dunes, Sunrise, Death Valley National Monument; p/s, Carmel studio stp on verso, 1948/later, 18x14", SBY 11/1/88 5,500
Sand Dunes, Sunrise, Death Valley National Monument; p/s, Carmel stp on verso, 1948/1977, 20x15", SBY 5/4/88 OE 7,700
Sequoia Gigantea Roots, Yosemite National Park; p/s, Carmel stp on verso, ca 1950/later, 19x15", SBY 5/4/88 2,530
Storm Surf, Timber Cove, California; slvr, p/s, Carmel stp/titled/dtd on verso, ca 1960/1982, 11x14", SWN 4/24/89 1,760
Stream, Sea, Clouds, Rodeo Lagoon, Marin County, California; sgn/Carmel studio stp, 1962/1978, 20x15", SBY 11/1/88 2,090

Stream, Sea, Clouds, Rodeo Lagoon, Marin County, California; slvr, p/s, Carmel stp, 1962/1978, 19x15", B/B 10/4/88 **1,650**
Sundown, the Pacific; p/s on mount, Carmel studio stp on verso, matted, 1960s, 19x15", SBY 11/1/88 **2,310**
Sunrise, Mount Tom, Sierra Nevada, California; slvr, p/s on mount, Carmel stp, 1948/later, 10x13", B/B 4/19/88 OE **2,575**
Tenaya Creek, Spring Rain; slvr, ink sgn on mount, Portfolio 3 stp on verso, ca 1948/1959, 8x9", B/B 4/19/88 **1,100**
Teton Range & the Snake River, Grand Teton National Park, Wyoming; Carmel stp, 1942/later, 16x20", SBY 5/4/88 **6,050**
Teton Range & the Snake River, p/s on mount, Carmel studio stp on verso, matted, 1942/later, fr, 15x18", SBY 4/26/89 **7,150**
Teton Range & the Snake River, slvr, p/s on mount, Carmel stp on mount verso, 1942/later, 11x13", B/B 4/19/88 **2,750**
Tetons & Snake River, p/s, titled/dtd/Carmel stp on verso, 1942/1980, 19x23", SBY 5/4/88 **8,800**
Tony Lujan of Taos Pueblo, New Mexico; p/s on mount, Carmel studio stp on verso, ca 1930/ca 1976, 10x7", SBY 11/1/88 **1,760**
Trailer-Camp Children, Richmond, California; p/s, Carmel stp on verso, 1944/1977, 14x20", SBY 5/4/88 **2,750**
Tuolumne Meadows, Yosemite National Park, California; #129, total ed of 260, matted, 1941/ca 1963, 9x7", SBY 11/1/88 **1,100**
Upper Kern Canyon, Sierra Nevada; ink sgn on mount, titled/Carmel stp on verso, 1930/ca 1962, 10x13", SBY 5/4/88 **1,650**
Vernal Falls, Yosemite; #6, slvr, Carmel/Portfolio 4 stps on mount verso, 1948/1963, 11x8", B/B 4/19/88 **1,045**
Walbridge Ranch, Sonoma County; slvr, p/s, artist label on verso, ca 1935, 11x14", B/B 10/4/88 **935**
White Branches, Mono Lake, California; #19, total ed of 115, sgn/#d on mount, 1958/ca 1976, 15x10", SBY 11/1/88 **2,200**
White House Ruin, Morning, Canyon de Chelley National Monument, Arizona; slvr, p/s, 1949/1950, 10x7", B/B 4/19/88 **1,100**
Winter Sunrise, Sierra Nevada From Lone Pine; p/s, Carmel studio stp, mounted, 1944/later, 17x23", SBY 4/26/89 **11,000**
Winter Sunrise, Sierra Nevada From Lone Pine, California; p/s, studio stp on verso, 1944/1979, 17x23", SBY 5/4/88 **9,900**
Winter Sunrise, Sierra Nevada From Lone Pine; slvr, p/s, Carmel stp on verso, 1944/later, 15x19", B/B 10/4/88 **4,675**
Zabriskie Point, Death Valley National Monument, California; #65, p/s on mount, 1942/ca 1950, 10x8", SBY 4/26/89 **2,090**

ADAMS, Ansel (American, 1902-1984); & JONES, Pirkle
Vat Room, sgn/titled by Adams on mount & verso, artists stp on verso, matted, early 1960s, fr, 15x19", SBY 5/4/88 **990**

AGHA, M.F.
Doll's Face, slvr, 1930s, 10x8", SWN 4/24/89 **523**
Untitled, composition of mask/string/doilies; slvr, 1930s, 10x8", SWN 4/24/89 UE **300**

ALBERGAMO, Giuseppe
Rayons, ca 1939, matted, 3x5", SBY 5/4/88 **935**

ALBERS, Josef (American, 1888-1976)
Wand-Glasbild, Schwarz-Grau auf Weiss; slvr, sgn/titled on verso, 1920s, 5x7", SWN 10/30/88 OE **1,430**

ALBOK, John (American?, New York, -1982)
In the Store of Tailor Shop, slvr, sgn/dtd/titled on verso, 1935, 9x8", B/B 10/4/88 UE **138**
WPA Street Cleaners, slvr, p/s, sgn/stp on verso, 1936, 8x10", B/B 10/4/88 **330**

ALLEN, Albert Arthur
Group of 15: Nude Studies; slvr, 1920s, 7x10", B/B 4/19/88 **935**

ANDERSON, James (19th C)
Appian Way & the Aqueduct of Claudius, alb, a/bstp on mount, 1850s, 9x16", SWN 10/30/88 **660**
Arch of Septimius Severus, sltp or early alb, a/bstp on mount, #d 47 in negative, 1850s, 11x15", SWN 10/30/88 OE **1,870**
Church of Saint Peter, sltp or early alb, a/bstp on mount, 1850s, 11x15", SWN 10/30/88 **1,540**
Forum of Trajan with Trajan's Column & the Church of Santa Maria di Loreto, sltp or early alb, 1850s, SWN 10/30/88 OE **1,870**
Interior of the Basilica of Saint Paul, Facing Altar; #160, alb, a/bstp on mount, 1850s, 14x13", SWN 10/30/88 **825**
Pantheon, Rome; alb, mounted, 1850s, 11x15", SWN 4/24/89 **1,540**
Pantheon, sltp or early alb, a/bstp on mount, #77 in negative, 11x15", SWN 4/24/89 OE **1,760**

ANDERSON, James; att (19th C)
Forum, the Temple of Saturn in the Foreground; sltp or early alb, #51 in negative, mounted, 1850s, 12x15", SWN 10/30/88 **1,210**
View of Saint Peter's From Monte Pincio, alb, #d 87 in negative, mounted, 10x14", SWN 4/24/89 **715**

ANDERSON, Laurie (20th C)
Pair: Talking Papers; slvr, marker titled on img, 1977, mounted/matted together, 28x19", SBY 5/4/88 **935**

ANDERSON, Paul L.
Snowscape, pltn, tipped to paper mount, early 1900s, 10x8", SWN 10/30/88 **550**

ANDRE, Rogi
Exposition Picasso, titled/dtd/artist stp on verso, 1931, matted, 7x9", SBY 5/4/88 **660**

Anonymous (European, 19th C)
Three Children in Front of Curtain Backdrop, dag, 4th pl, contemporary paper mat/wood fr, 1840s, SWN 4/24/89 **825**

Anonymous (19th C)
Album: Hong Kong; 65 alb, 1887-89, 6x8" to 9x12", gilt titled/decor leather, folio-sized cover, B/B 10/4/88 **1,540**
Album: Pairs; 50 alb, titled/#d on mount, ex-library stp on flyleaf, ca 1890, 9x11", half leather folio, B/B 10/4/88 **330**
Armed Union Soldier Kneeling with His Rifle & Attached Bayonet, ambro, 6th pl, patriotic mat/plastic case, CEG 5/7/88 **250**
Blind Man Wearing Dark Glasses, Holds Cane Upright; tnty, 6th pl, cased, CEG 5/7/88 **20**
Brigadier General Henry Baxter & Staff, alb, mounted, irregular edges, ca 1863, 9x15", SWN 4/24/89 UE **300**
British Soldier, seated/holds riding crop/books on nearby table; tnty, bent corner, 7x4", CEG 5/7/88 **30**
Bugler in Confederate Kepi with Colt Revolver, seated/full-length; tnty, 6th pl, thermoplastic case, CEG 5/7/88 **205**
California Gold Miner Said To Be Edwards Crossing (seated in landscape), dag, 6th pl, full case, ca 1850s, CEG 5/7/88 **1,000**
Captain, 4th Vermont Infantry with Saber Across Chest (standing/3-quarter pose); tnty, half leather case, CEG 5/7/88 **205**
Castine, Maine, Area Panoramic View; hc ambro, 4th pl, CEG 5/7/88 **200**
Cavalry Soldier with Saber in His Hand, Kepi with Crossed Sword Insignia, full-figure; tnty in CDV holder, CEG 5/7/88 **85**
Civil War Company at Dress Rehersal, alb on orig card mount, lt stn on mount, ca 1860s, L-7x9", CEG 6/23/89 **85**
Civil War Company of Soldiers Lined Up, holding muskets w/attached bayonets; alb on orig mount, lt scr, 5x8", CEG 5/7/88 **140**
Colonel Burnside, Welcome Home; alb, mounted, early 1860s, 10x15", SWN 4/24/89 **660**
Fifth New York National Guard in Pre-War Uniform with White Cross Belts, ambro, 4th pl, full leather case, CEG 5/7/88 **600**
Five Confederate Generals in Mexico, alb mounted on card w/hand-drawn gilt border, 1865, 3x2", SWN 4/24/89 UE **275**
Fully Equipped Infantryman, full-length/standing; tnty, 6th pl, thermoplastic case w/patriotic design, CEG 5/7/88 **175**

Item	Price
Hall of Science Building, Century of Progress Exposition, Chicago; oro, titled, orig fr, 1933, 5x4", SWN 4/24/89 OE	495
Hard Pancut, 1888, Redwood River (western scene); alb, titled, 5x9", lot 253, CEG 6/23/89	30
Henri de Toulouse-Lautrec & Model in His Studio, alb, mounted, ca 1894, 5x7", SBY 4/26/89 OE	4,675
Horse-Drawn Peddler's Wagon, men standing near it; dag, 4th pl, leather case, 1840s, SWN 4/24/89	2,200
House with Classical Pediment & Columns, 6 boys standing at fence; dag, half pl, leather case, ca 1850, SWN 4/24/89	1,430
Indian, standing/full-figure/probably Apache; tnty, 6th pl, cased, lt spotting, CEG 5/7/88	165
Mother & Daughter, shawl-draped table between them; dag, full pl, felt board mat/contemporary fr, 1850s, SWN 4/24/89	2,200
Northern California Lumber Camp, dag, half pl, full case, ca 1850s, scr/scuff img, CEG 5/7/88	800
Occupational: Bandsmen, uniformed/holding drum & major's staff; tnty, half pl, CEG 5/7/88	60
Occupational: Explorer or Architect, seated man w/coat & peaked cap holds papers & map; dag, 9th pl, CEG 5/7/88	40
Occupational: Fireman (long coat/peaked cap/insignia); tnty, 6th pl, in CDV paper holder, lot 257, CEG 6/23/89	35
Occupational: Tobacco Salesman; tnty, full pl, 9x7", lot 254, CEG 6/23/89	250
Occupational: Violinist, playing his instrument; dag, 6th pl, full case, CEG 5/7/88	90
Occupational: Window Glazier, standing/working; tnty, metal mat/preserver, CEG 5/7/88	85
Outdoor View (houses/picket fence/woods beyond), dag, 4th pl, brass mat/preserver, 1840s, SWN 10/30/88 OE	1,650
Pair of Cavalry Soldiers, Both Holding Sabers, Both Holding Pistols Against Chests; tnty, 6th pl, half case, CEG 5/7/88	230
Pennsylvania Infantryman, standing/full-length; Union Forever motto on blk thermoplastic case, CEG 5/7/88	165
President William McKinley & Wife, cbnt, ca 1897, lot 275, CEG 6/23/89	15
Shaggy Dog on a Carpet, dag, 6th pl, sealed/cased, 1850s, SWN 4/24/89 OE	715
Street Scene in a New England Town (Possibly Connecticut), ambro, 4th pl, metal mat/half case, CEG 5/7/88	150
Street Scene in Machias, Maine; dag, 4th pl, full case, ca 1850, lt oxidation at mat opening, CEG 5/7/88	1,100
Tennis Player, tnty in paper holder, 6th pl, ca 1870s, CEG 1/13/89	35

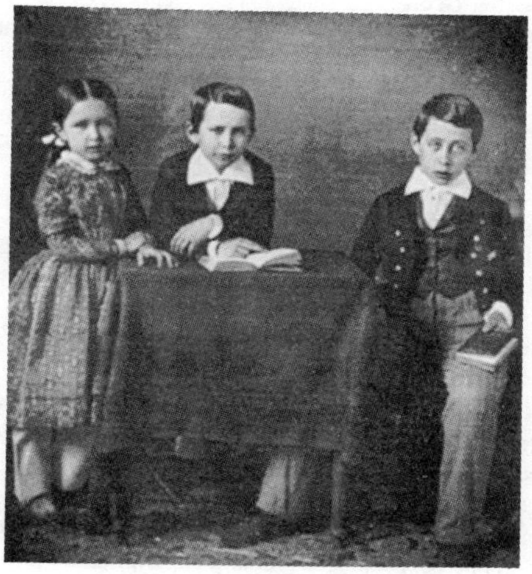

Three Children, Boy & Girl Standing Beside a Table with Boy Seated to One Side; dag, early 1840s, 5x5", SWN 10/30/88 OE; $1,760

Item	Price
Three Indian Women in Long Dresses (probably from Washington/NW Coast area), cbnt, CEG 5/7/88	70
Travel & Transport Building, Century of Progress Exposition, Chicago, 1933; oro, orig fr, 1933, 5x4", SWN 4/24/89 OE	660
Union Trooper with Rifle & Bayonet Wears Bowie Knife on Belt, 3-quarter pose; tnty, 6th pl, plastic case, CEG 5/7/88	165
Union Zouave Mascot or Drummer Boy Seated at Table, full-length pose; ambro, 9th pl, red thermoplastic case, CEG 5/7/88	275
US Marine in Frock Coat & Sheathed Sword, 3-quarter studio pose; ambro, 6th pl, metal mat/surround, CEG 1/13/89	150
Well-Armed Union Soldier, full-length; tnty, 6th pl, full case, CEG 5/7/88	85
Young Black Man, possibly a house slave; dag, fine leather case, RAB 7/12/88	200
Young Black Woman, seated in photographer's studio; dag, 9th pl, thermoplastic case, 1850s, SWN 4/24/89	523
Young Gentleman with Goatee Beard, ambro, half pl, full case, unbroken seals, CEG 5/7/88	50
Zouave of 14th Brooklyn ZouavesHolds Kep, seated/3-quarter pose; tnty, 6th pl, full thermoplastic case, CEG 5/7/88	350

Anonymous (20th C)

Item	Price
Hall of Science Building, Century of Progress Exposition, Chicgo, 1933; oro, titled, orig fr, 5x4", SWN 10/30/88	275

ANTHONY, E. (19th C)

Item	Price
Start, Camp Mohave; stereo on chrome mount, ca 1871, lt sl, CEG 5/7/88	80

ARBUS, Diane (American, 1923-1971)

Item	Price
Human Pincushion (Ronald C Harrison), backed w/card, sgn/titled/limitation stp on verso, 1962, 10x7", SBY 4/26/89	3,850
Identical Twins, Roselle, New Jersey; sgn/dtd/titled on verso, 1966/ca 1967, 2x2", SBY 4/26/89	9,350
Jayne Mansfield, p/s & titled on verso, ca 1965, matted, fr, 10x9", SBY 5/4/88	5,706
Series of 3: Chamberlain Twins; 1968, 11x11", Harper's Bazaar, SBY 5/4/88	3,300
Waitress, Nudist Camp, New Jersey; sgn/titled/inscr Dear Valentina; 1963/ca 1967, 3x3", SBY 5/4/88	3,300

ARBUS, Diane; & SELKIRK, Neil (20th C)

Item	Price
Portfolio: Box of Ten Photographs; 36/50, sgn by Doon Arbus, 1966-79/ca 1971, 15x15", plexiglas box, SBY 11/1/88	12,100

ARNOLD, C.D. (20th C)

Item	Price
Transportation Building, World's Columbian Exposition, Chicago; pltn, artist copyright stp, mounted, 18x21", SWN 4/24/89	880

ATGET, Eugene (French, 19th/20th C)

Item	Price
Atget's Studio, printing-out paper, ca 1900, 9x7", SBY 11/1/88	2,200
Conseil d'Etats, Palais Royal; printing-out paper, titled on verso, matted, early 1900s, 9x7", SBY 11/1/88 OE	3,025
Cour 12 Rue Pierre du Lard, #398, printing-out paper, titled/Rue Campagne Premiere stp, 1900s, 9x7", SBY 5/4/88 UE	550

Flowers, #804, printing-out paper, #d in negative/on verso, matted, early 1900s, 7x9", SBY 11/1/88 UE **770**
Frog Fountain, Saint Cloud; #1200, printing-out paper, sgn/titled on verso, ca 1923, 9x7", lot 168, SWN 4/24/89 OE **2,420**
Hotel de Clermont Connerre Rue du Cherche-Midi, printing-out paper, titled, mounted, ca 1900, 8x7", SBY 4/26/89 UE **880**
Le Cherche-Midi (Demoli) Rue du Cherche-Midi, printing-out paper, titled, mounted/matted, ca 1900, 8x7", SBY 4/26/89 ..... **1,210**
Magasin, Avenue des Gobelins; printing-out paper, archivally mounted, 1925, 9x7", SWN 10/30/88 ..... **4,620**
Montmartre, Rue Cortot; printing-out paper mounted on card, sgn/dtd/titled on mount, 1899, matted, 9x7", SBY 5/4/88 UE **1,430**
Parc de Sceaux, #27, alb, 1925, 7x9", SBY 4/26/89 OE **6,600**
Petit Hotel Montmareney Rue de Cherche-Midi, printing-out paper, titled, mounted, ca 1900, 8x7", SBY 4/26/89 UE **880**
Rue de la Barre a Montmartre (Sacre Coeur Under Construction), printing-out paper, matted, 1899, 8x7", SBY 4/26/89 UE **1,100**
Rue de la Barre a Montmartre (Sacre Coeur), printing-out paper, titled, mounted/matted, ca 1900, 8x7", SBY 4/26/89 ..... **1,980**
Vieulle Boutique Louis XVI Quai Bourdon 3, #3926, printing-out paper, titled on verso, 1900s, 9x7", SBY 5/4/88 ..... **880**
Vu Coin Du Quai D'Orleans, #1612, titled on verso, early 1900s, matted, fr, 7x8", SBY 5/4/88 ..... **770**
129 Rue de Grenelle, #5386, printing-out paper, Rue Campagne Premiere Paris stp on verso, 1900s, 9x7", SBY 5/4/88 UE **770**

ATGET, Eugene; & ABBOTT, Berenice
Pair: Street Walker; Organ Grinder; mounted/1 matted, ca 1898 & early 1900s/1950s, 9x7", SBY 11/1/88 ..... **990**

ATHIS, Alfred (Natanson)
Edouard Vuillard, pltn, mounted, 1890s, 7x4", SBY 4/26/89 ..... **1,650**
Pair: Pierre Auguste Renoir; mounted, 1890s, 5x7", SBY 4/26/89 ..... **2,200**

AUBRY, Charles (19th C)
Study of Roses, alb, sgn/#d 55 in negative, mounted to bl card, ca 1870, 11x15", SWN 4/24/89 ..... **1,320**

AUER, Alois (19th C)
Leaves, electrotype printed in gr, mounted/matted, 1850s, fr, 18x11", SBY 4/26/89 ..... **660**

AUERBACH, Ellen; & STERN, Grete
Still Life with Eggs, sgn by both artists, Ringl & Pit studio stps on verso, matted, ca 1930, 6x4", SBY 4/26/89 ..... **1,980**

Aurora Studios (20th C)
Nude, full-length frontal pose w/outstretched arms; slvr, copyright 1913, 8x5", CEG 6/23/89 ..... **60**

AVEDON, Richard (American, 1923-)
Anna Magnani, backed w/card, matted, early 1950s, 13x11", SBY 4/26/89 OE **1,980**
Cecil Beaton & Truman Capote, mounted on card, 1952, 9x9", SBY 4/26/89 OE **3,025**
Charlie Chaplin, 5/35, ink sgn in mrg, 1952, fr, 18x24", SBY 5/4/88 ..... **1,320**
Dovima with Elephants, 45/50, copyright/ed/title stps on verso, matted, 1955/ca 1980, 23x18", SBY 11/1/88 ..... **4,400**
Gertrude Lawrence & Her Dog in Pennsylvania Station, mounted on card, 1951, 11x11", Harper's Bazaar, SBY 4/26/89 ..... **2,200**
Gloria Swanson & Jose Ferrer at Pennsylvania Station, mounted on card, matted, 1951, 14x11", SBY 4/26/89 OE **4,675**
Isak Dineson, 5/35, sgn in mrg, 1958/later, 23x20", SBY 4/26/89 UE **990**
Jimmy Durante & Beatrice Lillie, matted, 1952, 10x11",SBY 4/26/89 OE **3,025**
John Szarkowski, Curator, New York City; 6/50, sgn, limitation/coypright stps on verso, 1975, 10x8", SBY 4/26/89 ..... **880**
Marlon Brando Shaving, mounted on card, early 1950s, 13x12", SBY 4/26/89 OE **3,300**
Montgomery Clift, matted, early 1950s, 11x11", lot 448, SBY 4/26/89 OE **3,300**
Montgomery Clift, matted, early 1950s, 11x11", lot 449, SBY 4/26/89 ..... **1,980**
Mr & Mrs Jean Renoir, backed w/card, matted, early 1950s, 13x10", SBY 4/26/89 ..... **1,980**
Nastassja Kinsky & the Serpent, 16/200, p/s on mount, copyright/ed/title stps on verso, 1981/1982, 28x43", SBY 5/4/88 ..... **3,300**
Rex Harrison, matted, 1956, 13x11", SBY 4/26/89 OE **1,980**
Teresa & Luisillo of the Ballets Espagnols, matted, 1955, 10x13", SBY 4/26/89 OE **2,090**

AVEDON, Richard; & DALI, Salvador
Salvador Dali & Dovima with Jewelry Designed by Dali, dye, 110 East 58th St stp on verso, 1963, 17x14", SBY 11/1/88 ..... **19,800**

BABBITT, Platt D. (fl 1853-1870)
Niagara Falls, from American side, men in foreground; dag, full pl, brass mat/leather case, ca 1855, SWN 4/24/89 UE **5,500**

BAILEY, DIX, & MEAD (Fort Randall, Dakota Territory)
Steps, Nez Perces Indian, without right hand or feet; cbnt, 1882, CEG 5/7/88 ..... **40**

BALDUS, Edouard Denis (19th C)
Hotel de Ville, alb, artist facsimile sgn stp on mount, ca 1855, 12x18", SWN 10/30/88 OE **2,420**
La Corniche, #95, alb, a/bstp on mount, sgn/titled/#d in negative, 1850s, 17x14", SWN 10/30/88 OE **3,080**
Notre Dame de Paris, alb, a/bstp on mount, ca 1855, 13x18", SWN 10/30/88 UE **550**
Pair: Place de la Concorde; Tour St Jacques; alb, artist facimile signature stp on mount, ca 1860, 11x7", SWN 4/24/89 UE **300**
Pavillon Richelieu, alb, a/bstp on mount, ca 1855, 17x14", SWN 10/30/88 ..... **935**
Roman Theatre at Arles, alb, artist fascimile sgn stp on mount, mounted, ca 1860, 8x11", SWN 4/24/89 UE **413**
Saint Clotilde, Paris; alb, #d 63 in negative, mounted, ca 1855, 14x18", SWN 10/30/88 ..... **1,045**

BALLMER, Theo
Group of 3: Bulb; Shere; House in Snow; 1 backed w/card, matted, 1920s-1930s, various sizes, SBY 11/1/88 ..... **880**
Helvetia, photocollage (5 panels w/1 blk paper panel) covered by netting/ink/paper, 1930s, 12x17", SBY 4/26/89 OE **2,475**
Pair: Untitled (cars parked in warehouse & stacks of industrial cans); slvr, 1920s-30s, 9x12"/8x12", SWN 4/24/89 UE **440**

BANGS, Frank C.
Pair: Bonnie Maud, in the Boys & Betty; Maud Madison & Bonnie Maud in the Boys & Betty; slvr, 1910, 7x4", B/B 4/19/88 ..... **192**

BARKER, George; att (19th C)
Niagara (cote Americain), alb, titled on verso, mounted, 1860s-70s, 13x17", SWN 4/24/89 OE **1,650**
Niagara Falls, Looking Toward Horseshoe Fall & the Canadian Side; alb, mounted, 1870s, 20x17", SWN 10/30/88 ..... **193**

BARNARD, George N. (American, 1819-1902)
City of Atlanta, Georgia No 1; alb, printed title/artist credit stp on mount, 1860s/1866, 10x14", SWN 4/24/89 ..... **2,200**
Hero (locomotive), alb, sgn/titled on verso, 1860s, 8x6", SWN 4/24/89 ..... **385**
Rebel Works in Front of Atlanta, Georgia No 3; Pl 41, alb on Sherman's Campaign mount, 1860s/1866, 10x14", SWN 4/24/89 ..... **715**
Rebel Works in Front of Atlanta, Georgia No 4; Pl 42, alb on Sherman's Campaign mount, 1860s/1866, 10x14", SWN 4/24/89 ..... **1,100**

BARNARD, George N.; att (American, 1819-1902)
Office AQ M-U-S M-R-R, Chattanooga, Tennessee; alb, titled on mount, ca 1864, 10x13", SWN 4/24/89 UE 358
BARNBAUM, Bruce (20th C)
Mud Flats, Paria Canyon; slvr, sgn/dtd on mount, titled/dtd/stp on mount verso, 1978, 14x11", B/B 4/19/88 UE 138
Wall Curves, Lower Antelope Canyon; slvr, sgn/dtd on mount, titled/stp on mount verso, 1983/1984, 20x16", B/B 4/19/88 412
BARRY, D.F. (19th C)
Chief Gall (bust-length portrait), sepia, a/bstp, fr, 10x7", CEG 1/13/89 350
Chief Low Dog, a/bstp, orig folder w/stp on verso, oval, 8x6", lot 250, CEG 6/23/89 275
BAYER, Herbert (20th C)
Metamorphosis, p/s & dtd on img, inscr Trial Proof on verso, 1936/later, matted, 10x14", SBY 5/4/88 2,750
Self-Portrait, p/s on img, sgn/artist name stp on verso, matted, 1932/later, 14x10", SBY 4/26/89 OE 8,250
BEALS, Jessie Tarbox
Chestnut Street, Boston; toned slvr, triple-mounted, titled/sgn on 1st mount, early 1900s, 9x7", SWN 4/24/89 UE 300
BEATO, Felice (19th C)
Secunder Bagh, Where 2000 Were Killed at the Relief of Lucknow by Lord Clyde; salt or early alb, 1858, SWN 10/30/88 OE 3,080
BEATON, Cecil (British, 1904-1980)
Andy Warhol & Candy Darling, artist name stp on verso, matted, 1969, fr, 13x8", SBY 11/1/88 UE 330
Edith Sitwell, p/s on mount, 1962/later, 17x13", SBY 11/1/88 1,100
Gary Cooper, p/s on mount, artist name stp on verso, 1931/later, 18x12", SBY 11/1/88 1,760
Gertrude Lawrence, p/s on mount, artist name stp on verso, 1930/later, 18x14", SBY 11/1/88 1,980
Irving Berlin, p/s on mount, artist stp on verso, early 1930s/later, 18x14", SBY 4/26/89 UE .... 330 Marion
Davies, p/s on mount, artist name stp on verso, 1930s/later, 18x14", SBY 11/1/88 605

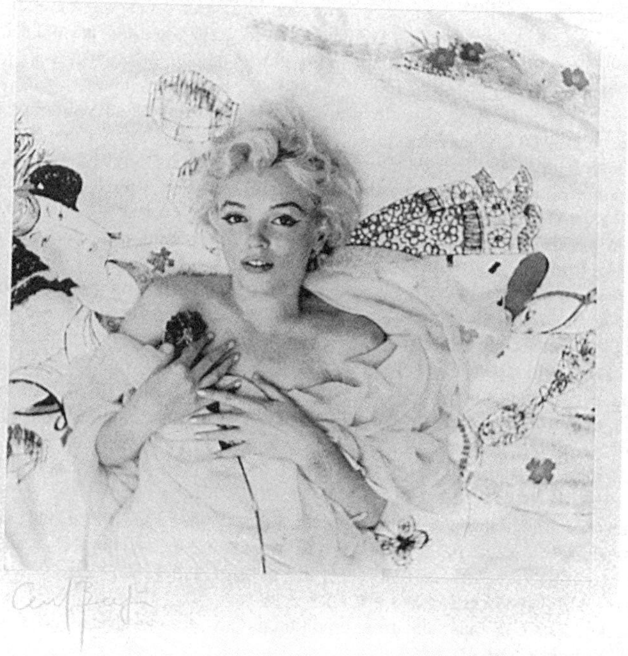

Marilyn Monroe, a Photographic Study; sgn, mounted on cardboard, ca 1956, 10x10", C-NY 6/11/88; $4,180

Mrs Winston Churchill in Virginia, slvr, 1940, 10x8", SWN 10/30/88 413
Pair: Bernard Berenson in Florence; artist name/Harper's Bazaar stps on verso, 1955, 10x9"/8x8", SBY 4/26/89 880
Pair: Rudolph Nureyev; In the Garden; sgn on mount, 1960s & 1920s/later, 17x13", SBY 4/26/89 1,210
Rex Harrison & Julie Andrews in My Fair Lady, Harper's Bazaar stp on verso, matted, 1956, 12x10", SBY 4/26/89 OE 3,025
Rudolf Nureyev, slvr, Camera Ltd stp on verso, 1960s, 10x10", SWN 10/30/88 495
Self-Portrait, ink sgn on img, matted, 1960, 5x4", SBY 11/1/88 605
Tallulah Bankhead, p/s on mount, artist name stp on verso, 1930s/later, 17x15", SBY 11/1/88 1,650
Three Hat-Check Girls, matted, 1930s, 8x10", SBY 4/26/89 1,210
ECHER, Arthur E.
Woman on Couch, sepia-toned pltn on tissue, mounted/matted, ca 1900, 7x5", SBY 11/1/88 UE 715
ECKMANN, Hannes (20th C)
Hand, slvr, sgn on mount, ca 1935, 9x7", SWN 10/30/88 605
ELL, C.M. (19th C)
Elias Cornelius Boudinot, standing; cbnt, sgn by sitter on mount recto, 1870s, SWN 4/24/89 275
ELL, William (19th C)
Colorado River, Mouth of Kanab Wash, Looking West; alb on Wheeler Survey mount, #d 5 in negative, 1872, SWN 4/24/89 1,100
Grand Canyon, Colorado River, Near Paria Creek, Looking West; alb on Wheeler Survey mount, 1872, 11x8", SWN 4/24/89 UE 600
Limestone Walls, Kanab Wash, Colorado River; Pl 31, #15, alb on Wheeler Survey mount, 1872, 11x8", SWN 4/24/89 UE 300
Looking South into the Grand Canyon, Colorado River, Sheavwitz Crossing; alb on Wheeler Survey mount, 1872, SBY 5/4/88 550

Recovery, Without Amputation, After Gunshot Fracture of the Right Patella; #64, alb, ca 1865, 9x7", SWN 10/30/88 ... 605
Resection of the Shaft of the Humerus for Gunshot Fracture, alb, letterpress titled, ca 1865, 8x6", SWN 10/30/88 ... 440
Successful Excision of the Head of the Right Humerus, #198, alb, letterpress titled, ca 1867-68, 8x6", SWN 10/30/88 ... 440

BELLMER, Hans (20th C)
Untitled, From Les Jeux de la Poupee; hc slvr, 1936-37/1949, 6x5", B/B 10/4/88 OE ... 935

BERNHARD, Ruth (American, 1905-)
Apple Tree, slvr, p/s on mount, sgn/titled/dtd on mount verso, 1973/later, 8x10", B/B 4/19/88 ... 550
Aura, slvr, p/s on mount, sgn/titled on mount verso, 1970s/later, 14x10", B/B 4/19/88 UE ... 248
Dollshead, p/s on mount, sgn/dtd/titled on verso, 1936/later, 7x9", SBY 4/26/89 ... 880
Garden Hose, slvr, 1969/later, 13x10", B/B 4/19/88 ... 522
In the Box, Horizontal; slvr, p/s on mount, titled on mount verso, 1962, 6x10", B/B 4/19/88 OE ... 1,210
In the Box, Horizontal; slvr, 1962/later, 7x14", lot 4680, B/B 4/19/88 OE ... 770
Nude in Box, ink sgn on mount, matted, 1962, 6x10", SBY 4/26/89 OE ... 4,675
Pair: Starshell; Shell & Driftwood; sgn/titled on verso, mounted, 1943/later, 11x14"/11x13", SBY 11/1/88 ... 660
Pair: Studies of Leaves; slvr, 1940s-50s, 13x10", SWN 10/30/88 ... 770
Rockport Nude, slvr, sgn in wht pencil on blk mount, ca 1945, 14x9", B/B 4/19/88 ... 715
Scull & Rosery (sic), p/s on mount, sgn/titled/artist stp on verso, 1940s/later, 14x8", SBY 4/26/89 ... 880
Silk, slvr, p/s, sgn/titled on verso, 1968/later, 7x14", B/B 10/4/88 ... 605
Sympiosis, slvr, p/s, sgn/titled/dtd on mount, 1971/later, 14x8", B/B 10/4/88 ... 440
Teapot, slvr, p/s, sgn/dtd/titled on verso, 1975/later, 11x13", B/B 10/4/88 ... 495
Three Dolls, slvr, p/s on mount, sgn/titled on mount verso, ca 1946/later, 10x14", B/B 4/19/88 ... 358
Torso with Hands, slvr, p/s, titled/label on verso, 1971, 14x 11", B/B 10/4/88 ... 605

BING, Ilse (20th C)
Beethoven Autograph: Ode to Joy; slvr, ink sgn/dtd on img, sgn/dtd/titled on verso, 1933-48, 6x4", B/B 10/4/88 UE ... 385
Brissago Garden Table & Chair, sgn/dtd on img, sgn/dtd/titled on verso, mounted/matted, 1934, 11x9", SBY 5/4/88 UE ... 550
NY Battery & Statue of Liberty, sgn/dtd on img & verso, 1936, mounted/matted, 7x11", SBY 5/4/88 ... 1,100
Paris Merry-Go-Round, slvr, sgn/dtd in ink on img, name stp/dtd on verso, 1932, 11x10", B/B 4/19/88 ... 715

BISSON-FRERES (19th C)
Le Calvaire a l'Eglise St Paul, Anvers; alb w/arched top, artist red ink stp on mount, ca 1855, 18x13", SWN 4/24/89 ... 358

BLANC, Theo; & DEMILLY, Antoine
Man in Hat with Pipe, toned slvr, sgn in red ink on verso, 9x7", SWN 4/24/89 UE ... 330
Still Life, 31 rue Grenette Lyon studio paper label on verso, 1920s, 10x15", SBY 5/4/88 ... 1,100

BLANQUART-EVRARD IMPRIMERIE (19th C)
Untitled, young man/horse; sltp on Etudes Photographiques mount, inscr Serie No 20 on mount, 1853, 6x9", SWN 4/24/89 ... 1,100

BLUMANN, Sigismund
Little Mandarin, slvr on gr paper, p/s on mount, titled in ink on label on mount verso, 1900, 9x7", B/B 4/19/88 UE ... 165

BLUMBERG, A.
Group of 4: San Francisco Earthquake Scenes; slvr, 1906, 5x6" to 8x10", B/B 10/4/88 ... 330

BLUMENFELD, Erwin (20th C)
Cecil Beaton, artist estate stp on verso, matted, 1930s/later, fr, 13x10", SBY 4/26/89 ... 1,320
Maillol Sculpture (Multiple Exposure), estate stp on verso, matted, ca 1938/later, 13x11", SBY 4/26/89 UE ... 550
Solarization, sgn/dtd/titled/artist estate stp on verso, matted, ca 1944, 13x10", SBY 4/26/89 OE ... 3,300
Solarized Torso, p/s on verso, inscr To Hans e Tuth on img, matted, 1936, 12x9", SBY 4/26/89 OE ... 3,850

BODINE, A. Aubrey (20th C)
Baltimore Harbor, Day; toned slvr, gilt ink sgn on verso, titled/estate stp, ca 1950, 12x18", SWN 10/30/88 ... 605
Pair: Baltimore Street Scene; Photogram; cbrn & slvr, ca 1920 & 1945, 14x11"/13x17", B/B 10/4/88 UE ... 385
Pair: Carroll County; Park Avenue, Baltimore; slvr, ink sgn in mrg, 805 Park Ave stp, 1940s-50s, 13x10", SWN 10/30/88 ... 468

BOGARDUS & BENDANN BROS. (19th C)
Horace Greeley, seated in chair; alb, artist credit on mount, letterpress label on verso, sitter sgn, 1872, SWN 4/24/89 ... 440

BOURDEAU, Robert (20th C)
Pair: County Wicklow, Ireland; Cumbria, England; 1/30, sgn/dtd on mount, 1975 & 1980, 8x10"/11x14", SBY 11/1/88 ... 660

BOURKE-WHITE, Margaret (American, 1904-1971)
Airship Akron, ink sgn on img, 1931, orig duralumin fr, 17x23", SBY 11/1/88 ... 5,225
Airship Akron, Winner Goodyear, Zeppelin Race; ink sgn on img, titled/dtd 1931 on duralumin fr, 17x23", SBY 5/4/88 OE ... 8,800
Bartender, p/s on mount, artist name stp on verso, ca 1930s, 10x14", SBY 4/26/89 ... 2,475
Bombay in Monsson Time, Stockbrokers & Stock Market Clerks Going to Work; slvr, ca 1946, 14x11", B/B 4/19/88 ... 1,045
Borscht, Georgia; sepia-toned slvr, p/s on mount, 1932, 5x7", SBY 11/1/88 OE ... 4,675
Famine in India: Old Man in Agali; slvr, Life Photo/dtd stps on verso, 1946, 14x10", SWN 4/24/89 ... 715
Farmers, Eastern Europe; artist name stp on verso, late 1930s, 7x9", SBY 4/26/89 ... 1,100
Fort Peck, Montana; sgn/dtd on verso, mounted/matted, 1930s, 10x13", SBY 11/1/88 ... 1,980
Gooseherdess, Ganders, & Geese, Poprad, Slovakia; slvr, 1930s, 3x4", SWN 10/30/88 ... 605
Group of 3: Dust Bowl-Taken Near LaMar, CO; Caterpillars; Hand Melon, Schuylerville, NY; 1940s, lot 203, SBY 5/4/88 ... 2,970
Iron Puddlers, Stalingrad; matted, 1930, 14x9", SBY 5/4/88 ... 1,980
Iron Puddlers, Stalingrad; sepia-toned slvr, matted, ca 1930, 11x8", SBY 11/1/88 ... 880
Kremlin, Moscow; sepia-toned slvr, p/s, mounted/matted, 13x20", SBY 11/1/88 ... 5,500
Making Caldrons, sepia-toned slvr, p/s, mounted/matted, ca 1930, fr, 13x9", SBY 11/1/88 ... 9,350
Man With Cooking Utensils, Czechoslovakia; name stp on verso, late 1930s, 7x9", SBY 5/4/88 ... 1,210
Pair: Fort Peck Construction Camp, Wheeler, Montana; Bar Scene; Life Photo stp, 1936/1956, 15x20"/10x13", SBY 4/26/89 OE ... 3,575
Portfolio: WWII, Army Forces, Italy, North Africa, & North America; 57 photos, p/s, #d, leather slipcase, SBY 5/4/88 OE ... 34,100
Portfolio: WWII, Army Service Forces, Italy, & North Africa; 55 photos, p/s, 1944, leather slipcase, SBY 5/4/88 UE ... 9,900
Russian Land, sepia-toned slvr, sgn/inscr To Bill Clyne, mounted/matted, ca 1930, 13x18", SBY 11/1/88 ... 3,300

Self-Portrait with Camera, artist name stp on verso, ca 1933, 13x9", SBY 4/26/89 OE 22,000
Tenant Farmer's Wife, Life Photo by Margaret Bourke-White stp on verso, matted, 1936/ca 1936, 14x10", SBY 11/1/88 990
Terminal Tower with the High Level Bridge, Cleveland; slvr, Archivally Reprocessed stp, 1928, 13x10", SBY 11/1/88 1,870

BOWERS, Harry (20th C)

Skirts I've Known, Jane, Chicago; 5/5, ektacolor, sgn/titled/dtd in mrg, 1978, 37x28", B/B 4/19/88 UE 412

BRADY, Mathew (American, 19th C)

Abraham Lincoln Seated in the Brady Chair, alb, titled/studio credit on mount, 1865, oval 8x6", SWN 4/24/89 OE 9,350
Confederate White House (Jefferson Davis Mansion), Richmond, Virginia; alb, titled, mounted, 1865, 6x8", SBY 4/26/89 1,650
James Longstreet Seated in a Chair, cbnt, sgn/inscr by Longstreet, ca 1880, SWN 10/30/88 100
Managers of the House of Representatives of the Impeachment of Andrew Johnson, CDV, copyright/stp, lot 311, CEG 1/13/89 185
Robert E Lee, alb, titled on verso, Brady backstamp, ca 1860s, 4x2", B/B 10/4/88 412
Robert E Lee in the Brady Chair, alb on gilt-bordered studio mount, copyright/credit, 1869, oval 8x6", SWN 4/24/89 OE 10,450
Robert E Lee on Front Porch of His Richmond, Virginia, Home; alb, trm mount, 1865, 9x5", SWN 4/24/89 330
Three Johnnie Reb Prisoners, War for the Union Series; #2288, Taylor & Huntinton orange mount, ca 1870s, CEG 6/23/89 100

BRANDT, Bill (20th C)

Brassai, ink sgn, 81 Faubourg St Jacques Paris studio stp on verso, matted, ca 1932/later, 12x9", SBY 11/1/88 1,650
Coal Miner's Bath, slvr, ink sgn on mount, ca 1930, 14x12", B/B 4/19/88 495
Connemara Peasants Looking Out of Their Cottage Door, titled/artist name stp, matted, ca 1946, 9x7", SBY 4/26/89 1,100
Costello Village, South Connemara, Co Galway; titled/artist name stp on verso, matted, ca 1946, 9x8", SBY 4/26/89 880
Domino Players in London, ink sgn in mrg, mounted, 1930s/later, 13x12", SBY 11/1/88 OE 1,320
Early Morning on the River, London Bridge; slvr, ink sgn on mount, ca 1930s/later, 14x12", B/B 10/4/88 935
East Sussex Coast, slvr, ink sgn on mount, 1958/later, 14x12", B/B 4/19/88 825
Group of 3: Miners Returning to Daylight, South Wales; Coal-Searcher Going Home to Jarrow; Nude with Mirror; SBY 5/4/88 1,430
Group of 3: Nude Studies; ink sgn, 2 mounted, 1950s/later, 14x12", SBY 11/1/88 1,320
Hardy's Wessex, titled/photographer stp on verso, 1940s, fr, 9x8", SBY 5/4/88 1,760
Hornton Street, Campden Hill, London; slvr, ink sgn on mount, 1930s/1970s, 13x12", SWN 4/24/89 413
In Chelsea, titled/studio stp on verso, matted, ca 1944, 9x8", SBY 4/26/89 1,320
John Piper, slvr, artist sgn/Piper in mrg, Hillfield Court stp on verso, 1948, 9x8", SWN 10/30/88 660
London Pub, artist name & Hillfield Court studio stps on verso, matted, 1945, 8x7", SBY 4/26/89 1,430
Lord McDonald's Forest, Isle of Skye; ink sgn on mount, 1947/later, 14x12", SBY 11/1/88 440
Lott's Cottage, Flatford Mill, Suffolk; 32/100, slvr, sgn on mount, 1976/later, 11x12", SWN 10/30/88 440
Nude, Hamstead, London; artist name & Museum of Modern art stps on verso, early 1950s, 9x7", SBY 4/26/89 1,320
Nude, ink sgn in mrg, 1952/later, fr, 20x16", SBY 5/4/88 1,540
Nude (Bent Elbow), ink sgn in mrg, 1952/later, 14x12", SBY 5/4/88 OE 2,090
Nude (Bent Elbow), sgn in mrg, matted, 1952/later, 14x12", SBY 4/26/89 OE 3,850
Nude Abstraction, ink sgn on mount, 1950s/later, 14x12", SBY 5/4/88 UE 440
Nude with Mirror, slvr, ink sgn on mount, 1953/later, 13x11", B/B 10/4/88 935
Pair: Coal-Miner's Bath, Chester-le-Street, Durham; East Durham Coal-Miner Just Home From the Pit; 1930s, SBY 11/1/88 UE 660
Pair: Customers at the Crooked Billet, Tower Hill; Coal Searcher Coming Home to Jarrow; 1930s/later, 14x11", SBY 11/1/88 825
Pair: Early Morning on the River, London Bridge; Evening in Kew Gardens; sgn, 1930s/later, 14x12", SBY 11/1/88 1,320
Pair: Skye Mountains; Stonehenge Under Snow; ink sgn on mount, 1947/later, 14x12", SBY 11/1/88 1,430
Pair: Snicket in Halifax; Northumbrian Miner at His Evening Meal; sgn on mount, 1930s/later, 14x12", SBY 4/26/89 OE 2,090
Rene Magritte with His Picture, Great War, Brussels; slvr, ink sgn on mount, 1966, 14x12" B/B 10/4/88 715
Sonntags im Bois de Boulogne, slvr, titled/credit label on verso, 1930s, 7x8", SWN 10/30/88 468
Stonehenge Under Snow, sgn on mount, 1947/later, 14x12", SBY 4/26/89 990
Summer Evening in Bradford-on-Avon, artist name stp/Harper's Bazaar stp on verso, matted, 1945, fr, 9x7", SBY 11/1/88 990
Young Girl, ink sgn in mrg, 1950s/later, fr, 11x15", SBY 5/4/88 OE 1,100

BRASSAI (Guyla Halasz)(European, 20th C)

Alberto Giacometti, Atelier, Il-Maindron a Paris; 10/30, slvr, sgn, dtd/stp on verso, 1948/later, 12x9", B/B 10/4/88 1,320
Group of 3: Transmutation; 81 Rue du Faub St Jacques studio stp on verso, 1934-35, 9x7", SBY 11/1/88 1,650
Henri Matisse Drawing From the Nude, slvr, ink sgn in mrg, copyright stp on verso, 1939/later, 14x11", B/B 4/19/88 OE 1,870
Juan-Les-Pins, Follies-Bergere; p/s, 81 Faubourg St Jacques` Paris stp on verso, ca 1932/later, fr, 12x9", SBY 5/4/88 1,760
Kiki & Her Friends, ink sgn in mrg, sgn/copyright stp on verso, 1930s/later, 8x11", SBY 5/4/88 1,980
L'Oiseau, sgn/copyright stp on verso, matted, ca 1928, 12x9", SBY 4/26/89 1,540
La Femme au Parapluie Rue de Rivoli, 22/30, ink sgn in mrg, titled/dtd/stps on verso, 1937/later, 12x9", SBY 5/4/88 OE 1,870
Lover's Quarrel, ink sgn in mrg, copyright/repro limitation stps on verso, matted, 1930s/later, 12x9", SBY 11/1/88 OE 1,430
Lovers, Place d'Italie; ink sgn in mrg, copyright stp on verso, mounted/matted, 1932/later, 10x8", SBY 11/1/88 OE 2,750
Maillol's Studio, studio/copyright stps, label/Rapho Pictures sticker on verso, matted, 1930s, 9x7", SBY 4/26/89 880
Mannequin, studio stp on verso, matted, ca 1950, 11x8", SBY 4/26/89 880
Marchande de Vin, Rue de L'Abbaye; sgn/studio & copyright stps on verso, matted, 1931, 11x9", SBY 5/4/88 880
Mon Premier Portrait de Dali, ink sgn in mrg, titled/dtd/stps on verso, matted, 1932/later, fr, 14x10", SBY 4/26/89 OE 1,980
Pair: Ballets de Paris; studio stp on verso, matted, ca 1948, 12x7"/12x8", SBY 4/26/89 1,320
Pair: Black Cat, Paris; studio stp on verso, matted, ca 1950, 12x10", SBY 4/26/89 1,430
Pair: Dog on Stone Steps; Three Breton Women; stps on verso, 1930s, 9x11", SBY 11/1/88 880
Pair: Poster Hanger, Paris; L'Horologer; studio stp on verso, matted, 1930s, 9x7", SBY 5/4/88 1,320
Plane Tree Along One of Quais, 81 Rue du Faub St-Jacques/Rapho Guillumette Pictures stps, 1930s, 12x9", SBY 11/1/88 825
Pont des Arts, 5/30, ink sgn in mrg, sgn/81 Faugourg St Jacques stp on verso, 1934/later, 13x10", SBY 5/4/88 1,430
Prostitute Playing Russian Billiards, sgn/dtd/titled/copyright stps on verso, matted, 1932/later, 12x9", SBY 4/26/89 OE 1,870
Quarreling Lovers, Paris; 11/30, sgn in mrg, studio/copyright stps on verso, ca 1932, 11x8", SBY 4/26/89 OE 1,980
Tabletop Still Life, studio stp on verso, matted, early 1950s, 9x11", SBY 4/26/89 1,320
Woman Drinking at Fountain, studio stp on verso, matted, ca 1949, 12x9", SBY 4/26/89 UE 990

BRAUN, Adolphe (19th C)
Gorge du Trient, alb, 1860s, 19x15", SBY 5/4/88 UE 770
Hofstetten (Near Thun), carbon, titled, mounted/matted, mid-1860s, 15x19", SBY 4/26/89 660

BRAUNTUCH, Troy (20th C)
Untitled (contemporary), photo on paper, 1979, 12x12", SBY 11/11/88 715

BRAVO, Manuel Alvarez (20th C)
Henri Bartier-Bresson, p/s on mount, titled on verso, matted, 1930s/later, fr, 10x8", SBY 4/26/89 990
Medical Corsets, 33/75, slvr, p/s on mount, ca 1930s/ca 1970s, 10x8", B/B 10/4/88 715
Nude, pldm, sgn/inscr Mexico in mrg, 1930s/later, 7x10", SBY 11/1/88 770
Nude, pltn, p/s in mrg, 1970s, 7x10", SWN 10/30/88 550
Pair: Good Reputation Sleeping; Skiff on the Shore; sgn/inscr Mexico, matted, 1930s/later, 7x9", SBY 4/26/89 990
Retracto de lo Externo (Girl Combing Hair), sgn/inscr Mexico on mount, 1930s/later, 9x8", SBY 5/4/88 550
Retrato de lo Eterno, pltn, p/s in mrg, titled on verso, matted, ca 1932/later, 9x7", SBY 4/26/89 1,210
Study of Child, Sprinkler System, & Rainbow; C-print, sgn/inscr Mexico on verso, 1960s/unknown, 10x7", SWN 10/30/88 220
Trabajadores de Fuego (Fire Fighters), pltn, sgn/inscr Mexico in mrg, 1935/later, 9x7", SBY 5/4/88 1,430
Untitled Nude Figure, slvr, sgn/inscr Mexico in pencil on verso, ca 1970s, 9x7", B/B 10/4/88 468

BREED, Charles
Group of 3: Elizabeth & Ann Breed; Henry Breed Jr; Princeton University; slvr, ca 1912, 10x12" to 13x11", B/B 10/4/88 358

BRIGMAN, Anne W.
Ballet de Mer, pltn, pencil sgn/dtd on img, 1913, 9x7", B/B 10/4/88 OE 3,575
Carl Seyffarth, pltn, tipped to paper mount, sgn by artist/Seyffarth, ca 1920, 7x5", SWN 10/30/88 440

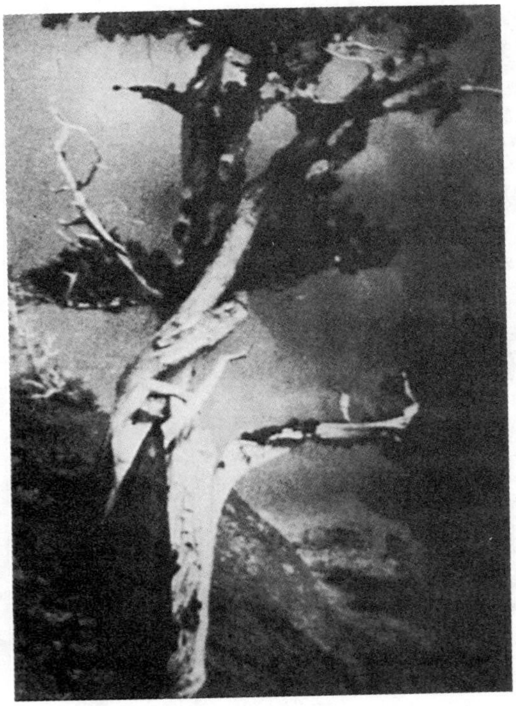

Dying Cedar, #4, slvr, p/s, titled/label on verso, ca 1909, 10x7", B/B 10/4/88; $4,125

Heart of the Storm, sgn/dtd on mount, titled on verso, matted, 1912, fr, 10x8", SBY 11/1/88 3,300
Heart of the Storm, slvr, p/s on mount, titled on mount verso, 1918, fr, 10x8", B/B 4/19/88 OE 4,125
Invictus, artist monogram on img, sgn on mount, studio stp/label on verso, ca 1908, 10x7", SBY 4/26/89 OE 3,300
Rhythm, slvr, sgn/dtd on mount, titled on verso, 1919, 7x10", B/B 10/4/88 2,750

BRISTOL, Horace
Bookbinder at Caxton Press, Idaho; p/s on mount, sgn/dtd on mat, 1939, 13x11", SBY 5/4/88 UE 330
Design of Tunnel Entrance, slvr, sgn/dtd on mount & mat, 1932, 9x7", B/B 4/19/88 OE 1,210
Golden Gate Bridge Under Construction, svr, sgn/titled/dtd on mount, 1936, 9x7", B/B 10/4/88 UE 550
Gunner of a PBY Rescue Plane, sgn/dtd on mat, 1944, 11x10", SBY 4/26/89 OE 7,150
Insulated Gas Scrubber, California Oil Fields; sgn/dtd on mount, mounted/matted, 1937, 10x8", SBY 5/4/88 UE 495
Pair: City Scene; Smoke Stacks; sgn/dtd on mount, matted, ca 1933, 9x7"/10x8", SBY 4/26/89 OE 3,025
Pair: Gas Scrubber, California Oil Fields; Gasoline Crackers, California Refinery; sgn/dtd, 1933 & 1937, SBY 11/1/88 990
Pair: Gasoline Scrubber in California; Wooden Derricks; sgn/dtd on mat, 1933, 13x10", SBY 11/1/88 825
Pattern in Tanks, slvr, p/s on mount & mat, 1933, 10x8", B/B 4/19/88 660
PB4Y Navy Bomber in Pacific, slvr, sgn/dtd on mount & mat, 1943, 11x14", B/B 4/19/88 715
Refinery Heat Converter, California Oil Fields; sgn/dtd on mount, 1934, 10x7", SBY 5/4/88 660
Telegraph Hill, sepia-toned slvr, p/s on verso, mounted/matted, 1934, 7x9", SBY 11/1/88 660
Telegraph Hill, slvr, sgn/dtd on overmat, 1935, 10x7", B/B 10/4/88 770
Three Men Working on Golden Gate Tower, slvr, sgn/dtd on mount & mat, 1935, 10x7", B/B 4/19/88 660
Tunnel Entrance, sepia-toned slvr, sgn/dtd, mounted/matted, 1933, 8x7", SBY 11/1/88 OE 1,430
Yehudi Munuhin Playing the Violin, sgn/dtd on mat, 1937, 13x10", SBY 5/4/88 UE 495

OWN, Nicolas; att (19th C)
Kit Carson, Members of the Union Army General Staff, New Mexico Territory...; alb, 1866, orig fr, 13x17", SBY 5/4/88 OE 4,400
UEHL, Anton
Night Landscape with Moon (Central Park?), pltn on tissue, tipped to mount, ca 1925, 6x8", SWN 10/30/88 715
Pair: Industrial Studies; sgn, 1930s & 1950s, 14x11", SBY 11/1/88 1,100
Rope Maker, slvr, stp on verso, ca 1930s, 14x11", B/B 10/4/88 412
UEHL, Martin
Black Fighter, slvr, stp twice on verso, ca 1930s, 13x11", B/B 10/4/88 UE 385
Industrial Study, slvr, p/s on overmat, mounted/matted, 1930s, 10x8", SWN 10/30/88 660
UGUIERE, Francis
Palace of Fine Arts, Panama Pacific Exposition; hc slvr, sgn/dtd on mount, 1916, fr, 14x11", B/B 10/4/88 UE 412
Palace of Fine Arts, Panama Pacific Exposition; slvr, p/s on img, 14x11", B/B 10/4/88 358
Rosalind Fuller & Sebastian Drost, The Way; photomontage, matted, 1920s, 10x8", SBY 11/1/88 UE 880
UNING, Walter P.
Vision, pltn, sgn/dtd/titled in mrg, double matted, 1919, 9x7", SBY 11/1/88 UE 550
LLOCK, Wynn (American, 1902-1975)
Child in Forest, p/s on mount, 1951/later, 8x10", SBY 4/26/89 OE 3,025
Child on Forest Road, sgn/dtd on mount, 1958/later, 10x8", SBY 4/26/89 OE 3,300
Floating Logs, p/s, mounted/matted, 1957/later, 6x10", SBY 5/4/88 UE 440
eanne on Bed, titled/155 Mar Vista Drive studio stp on verso, matted, late 1950s, 8x10", SBY 5/4/88 770
Leda & the Swan, p/s on mount, inscr To Jack With Affection on verso, ca 1968, 8x9", SBY 4/26/89 OE 1,540
Let There Be Light, ink sgn on mount, inscr Dear Bob & Marion Happy Christmas, 1954, 7x5", SBY 11/1/88 660
Lynne, Logs, & Doll; p/s on mount, titled/dtd on verso, matted, 1958/later, 8x10", SBY 5/4/88 1,100
Navigation Without Numbers, p/s on mount, inscr August 16-1980 for Jack & Jo, 1957/later, 7x9", SBY 4/26/89 1,760
Navigation Without Numbers, p/s on mount, matted, ca 1957/later, 7x9", SBY 11/1/88 1,210
Nude in Cobweb Window, p/s on mount, 1955/later, 9x7", SBY 4/26/89 1,760
Shore, p/s on mount, dtd/titled on verso, matted, 1966, 8x9", SBY 11/1/88 OE 3,025
Shore, sgn/dtd on mount, sgn/dtd/titled on verso, matted, 1966, 7x8", SBY 4/26/89 OE 2,200
Sleeping Girl, p/s on mount, inscr To Joan With Love on verso, mounted, 1968, 10x7", SBY 4/26/89 1,320
Stark Tree, p/s on mount, matted, 1956/later, 8x9", SBY 11/1/88 OE 1,540
Window, sgn/dtd on mount, dtd/titled/Monterey studio stp on verso, 1955/1959, 10x8", SBY 5/4/88 OE 1,650
Woman & Dog in Forest, p/s on mount, matted, 1953/later, 8x9", SBY 11/1/88 OE 2,090
Woman & Dog in Forest, p/s on mount, 1953/later, 8x10", SBY 4/26/89 OE 2,200
Woman's Hands, p/s on mount, dtd/titled on verso, mounted/matted, 1956/later, 8x9", SBY 5/4/88 660
Woman's Hands, p/s on mount, 1956/later, 7x9", SBY 4/26/89 880
Woman's Hands, slvr, p/s on mount, titled/dtd on mount verso, 1956/later, 8x10", B/B 4/19/88 UE 660
RCHARD, Jerry (20th C)
Nude Study, 14/25, ektacolor, ink sgn in mrg, ca 1980, 13x20", B/B 4/19/88 165
RNS, Marsh (20th C)
Figure Behind Curtain, slvr, ink sgn/stp on mount verso, ca 1979, 7x9", B/B 4/19/88 OE 412
Untitled Nude, slvr, ink sgn/stp on verso, ca 1970s, 9x6", B/B 10/4/88 605
ERS, Robert K.
Spotted Lake, Near Osoyoos, British Columbia, Canada; slvr, sgn on mount, typed label, 1982/1986, 20x16", B/B 4/19/88 275
LLAHAN, Harry (American, 1912-)
Aix-En-Provence, p/s in mrg, matted, 1957/later, fr, 9x12", SBY 5/4/88 UE 220
Cape Cod, slvr, p/s in mrg, 1972/later, 10x10", SWN 10/30/88 275
Chicago (Trees), p/s in mrg, matted, 1950/later, fr, 8x10", SBY 4/26/89 3,575
Eleanor, Chicago; slvr, sgn in mrg, 1947/later, fr, 5x3", B/B 10/4/88 OE 935
Eleanor, intl in mrg, matted, ca 1947/later, 5x3", SBY 11/1/88 825
Eleanor, intl in mrg, matted, ca 1947/later, 5x3", SBY 5/4/88 660
Eleanor, Port Huron; p/s in mrg, matted, 1954/later, fr, 7x7", SBY 5/4/88 550
Eleanor, Port Huron; slvr, p/s in mrg, ca 1954/later, 7x7", B/B 4/19/88 440
Eleanor in the Water, slvr, p/s in mrg, 1949/later, 10x9", SWN 10/30/88 550
Pair: Cape Cod; p/s in mrg, dtd/titled on verso, matted, 1972 & 1975, 7x7"/9x12", SBY 11/1/88 UE 440
Pair: Eleanor in the Water; Eleanor & Barbara, Lake Michigan; p/s in mrg, 1950s/later, 10x9"/8x10", SBY 11/1/88 770
Pair: Rome; Trees, Chicago; p/s in mrg, 1968 & ca 1950/later, 9x9"/8x10", SBY 11/1/88 990
Pair: Sun Bather; Volley Ball Net; p/s on img, 1960s-70s, 9x11"/10x13", SBY 4/26/89 825
Pair: Weed Against the Sky; Beach Houses; p/s in mrg, matted, late 1940s/later, 7x10", SBY 11/1/88 770
Portfolio: Landscapes; 11/25, 10 photos, p/s on mount, 1941-1971/ca 1972, various sizes, folder, cased, SBY 11/1/88 2,200
Weed Against the Sky, Chicago; p/s in mrg, matted, ca 1948/later, fr, 7x8", SBY 5/4/88 770
MERON, Julia Margaret (European, 19th C)
Group of 3: Maud by Moonlight; Woman Praying; Woman with Arms Crossed; alb, 1860s, various sizes, SBY 5/4/88 440
Hattie Campbell (The Echo), alb, titled/inscr For My Dear Nephew Conny, Colnaghi bstp, ca 1868, 11x9", SBY 11/1/88 1,100
King Arthur, alb, From Life Registered Photograph Copyright on mount, 1879, 14x11", B/B 4/19/88 660
King Arthur, Alfred Tennyson's Idylls of the King; alb, sgn/dtd/titled, mounted/matted, 1874, 14x11", SBY 5/4/88 770
Kiss of Peace, alb, sgn/titled/inscr From Life Registered Photograph Copyright, mounted, 1869, 14x11", SBY 11/1/88 OE 7,150
Madonna, alb, archivally mounted, titled, 1860s, 5x4", SWN 10/30/88 358
May Prinsep, alb, 1860s, 13x10", SBY 5/4/88 1,210
Miss Florence Anson, alb, sgn/dtd/titled/inscr From Life Registered Photographer on mount, 1870, 13x11", B/B 10/4/88 UE 495
Pair: Circe; Elaine Watching the Shield of Lancelot; alb, sgn/dtd, mounted, 1870s, 10x8"/10x11", SBY 11/1/88 OE 4,125
Pair: Paul & Virginia; La Madonna Riposata; alb mounted on album page, 1860s, 11x8", SBY 11/1/88 1,980

Parting of Sir Lancelot & Queen Guinevere, Idylls of the King; Pl 9, alb, sgn/titled, 1875, 14x11", SBY 4/26/89 OE 7,700
Resting in Hope, alb on Colnaghi mount, sgn/titled/inscr From Life on mount, 1865, 10x8", SWN 10/30/88.......... 605

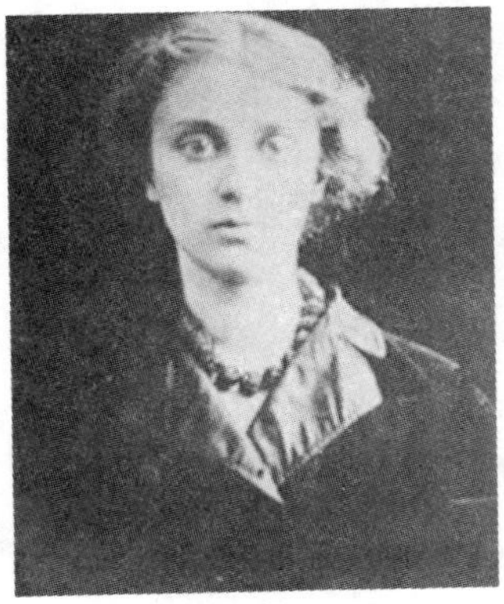

Egeria, Study of Miss Huth; alb, sgn/inscr From Life on mount, ca 1868, 12x10", B/B 10/4/88; $935

CANEVA, Giacomo (19th C)
Bauli, Golfe de Naples; alb sltp, titled on mount, ca 1855, 8x13", SWN 4/24/89 1,650

CAPA, Robert (20th C)
Grieving Mothers in Naples, artist name stp/repro limitation stp on verso, matted, 1944, 8x11", SBY 11/1/88 1,100

CAPONIGRO, Paul (American, 1932-)
County Wicklow, Ireland (White Running Deer); p/s on mount, matted, 1967/later, 7x19", SBY 11/1/88 OE 4,125
County Wicklow, Ireland (White Running Deer); p/s on mount, matted, 1967/later, fr, 7x19", SBY 4/26/89 OE 4,400
County Wicklow, Ireland (White Running Deer); sgn/dtd on mount, mounted/matted, 1967, fr, 7x19", SBY 5/4/88 OE.......... 4,125
Monument Valley, Utah; slvr, p/s on mount, 9x13", B/B 4/19/88 495
Pair: Hiei-San, Japan; Trees & Stream; p/s on mount, matted, 1976 & 1970s, 1 fr, 10x13", SBY 5/4/88 1,100
Pair: New York City; Cape Kiwanda, Oregon; p/s on mount, matted, 1964 & 1959/later, 6x7"/8x10", SBY 5/4/88 660
Pair: Winthrop, Massachusetts; Apples; p/s on mount, 1964/later, 7x10"/6x9", SBY 5/4/88 660
Portfolio I, 38/50, 12 photos, p/s on mount, 1958-60, 6 fr, various sizes, cased, SBY 4/26/89 4,125
Portfolio II, 54/100, 8 photos, p/s on mount, 1957-1970/ca 1973, various sizes, cased, SBY 5/4/88 3,025
Redding, Connecticut; sgn/dtd on mount, 1968, fr, 10x13", SBY 4/26/89 OE 3,575
Stonehenge, p/s on mount, mounted/matted, ca 1972, 14x19", SBY 5/4/88 OE 1,320

CARJAT, Etienne (19th C)
Gustave Courbet, alb, artist bstp on mount, mounted, early 1860s, 9x7", w/invitation to sitter's funeral, SBY 11/1/88 OE.......... 2,750

CARTIER-BRESSON, Henri (European, 20th C)
Academician on His Way to a Ceremony, Paris; ink sgn in mrg, 1953/later, 14x10", SBY 11/1/88.......... 990
Ahmedabad, India: Women Drying Saris; slvr, ink sgn/copyright stp in mrg, 1966/later, 10x14", SWN 10/30/88.......... 880
Allees du Prado, Marseilles; sgn/bstp in mrg, 1932/later, 14x9", SBY 5/4/88 1,210
At Curragh Racecourse, Near Dublin, Ireland; sgn in mrg, 1955/later, 10x14", SBY 4/26/89.......... 880
Bebe, sgn/dtd/titled on verso, matted, 1934, 9x6", SBY 4/26/89.......... 1,980
Bridal Couple on Horseback, France; artist credit/Harper's Bazaar stps on verso, 1954, 12x8", SBY 4/26/89 1,100
Brie, France; ink sgn/artist bstp in mrg, 1968/later, 10x15", SBY 11/1/88 2,090
Brie, France; sgn in mrg, 1968/later, 10x14", SBY 4/26/89 OE.......... 3,300
Brie, France; sgn/bstp in mrg, matted, 1968, no size given, SBY 5/4/88.......... 2,090
Brussels, ink sgn in mrg, 1932/later, 10x14", SBY 11/1/88 OE.......... 2,090
Brussels, sgn/bstp in mrg, matted, 1932/later, fr, 10x14", SBY 5/4/88 1,650
Brussels, sgn/bstp in mrg, matted, 1932/later, fr, 9x14", SBY 4/26/89 1,320
Canteen for Workers Constructing the Hotel Metropol, Moscow; ink sgn in mrg, matted, 1954/later, 12x18", SBY 5/4/88 1,870
China (workers), slvr, Magnum copyright stp on verso, 1950s, 12x8", SWN 10/30/88 358
Exra Pound, slvr, ink sgn in mrg, 1970/later, 20x13", SWN 4/24/89 770
France (housewives looking at dead game brought from market), slvr, Magnum copyright stp, ca 1950, 12x8", SWN 10/30/88.......... 495
Funeral of a Kabuki Actor, Japan; sgn in mrg, matted, 1965/later, 10x15", SBY 4/26/89 990
Henri Matisse, Vence, France; sgn in mrg, mounted/matted, 1944/later, fr, 9x14", SBY 4/26/89 OE 3,300
Hyeres, France; ink sgn in mrg, matted, 1932/later, 10x14", SBY 5/4/88 OE 2,750
Hyeres, France; ink sgn in mrg, 1932/later, 10x14", SBY 11/1/88 OE 2,750
Hyeres, France; sgn/bstp in mrg, 1932/later, 10x14", SBY 4/26/89 OE 2,475
Ile de la Cite, ink sgn in mrg, 1952/later, 10x14", SBY 11/1/88 1,980
Independence Celebrations, Djakarta; slvr, artist Life stp on verso, 9x14", SWN 4/24/89 UE 248
India (mother & children in field), slvr, Magnum copyright stp on verso, 1964, 8x12", SWN 10/30/88.......... 413
Liverpool, England; ink sgn in mrg, matted, 1962/later, 11x14", SBY 5/4/88.......... 1,100
New England, ink sgn in mrg, matted, 1947/later, 14x9", SBY 11/1/88 1,760
On the Banks of the Marne, ink sgn/copyright stp in mrg, matted, 1938/later, 8x14", SBY 5/4/88.......... 1,430
On the Banks of the Marne, sgn/bstp in mrg, matted, 1938/later, 12x18", SBY 5/4/88 2,310
Pair: Untitled, man under canvas sails & view of harbor; slvr, 1930s, 5x7"/10x8", SWN 4/24/89 UE.......... 660
Palais-Royal, Paris; sgn/bstp in mrg, 1960/later, 14x10", SBY 5/4/88.......... 1,210
Roman Amphitheater, Valencia, Spain; ink sgn in mrg, 1933/later, 10x14", SBY 11/1/88.......... 1,870
Rue Mouffetard, Paris; sgn/bstp in mrg, matted, 1954/later, 18x12", SBY 5/4/88 OE 3,850
Rue Mouffetard, Paris; sgn/bstp in mrg, 1954/later, 18x12", SBY 4/26/89 OE.......... 4,125

Seville, Spain; sgn in mrg, 1933/later, 10x14", SBY 4/26/89 1,430
Siphnos, Greece; sgn in mrg, matted, 1961/later, 9x14", SBY 4/26/89 OE 2,200
Sringagar, Kashmir; inscr Toute mon amitie Henri, artist name stp on verso, matted, 1948, 10x15", SBY 4/26/89 OE 7,150
Swiss Tourists on the Beach at Biarritz, artist credit/Harper's Bazaar stps on verso, matted, 1954, 7x10", SBY 4/26/89 1,980
Trieste, Italy; ink sgn in mrg, matted, 1933/later, 10x14", SBY 5/4/88 UE 660
Two Children in a Cemetery, ink sgn in mrg, title label on verso, mounted, 1950s/later, 12x21", SBY 11/1/88 1,100
William Faulkner, Oxford, Mississippi; slvr, ink sgn in mrg, 1947/1970s, 14x10", B/B 4/19/88 715

'ASTAGNERI, Mario
Four Men Posed with a Painting, bl-toned slvr, matted, 1930s, 12x9", SBY 11/1/88 1,430
Viva L'Italia (First Futurist Congress), sgn/titled on img, matted, 1924, 12x9", SBY 5/4/88 OE 3,080

'AVAEL, Rolf
Untitled, photogram, facsimile sgn on mount, matted, 1920s, 7x4", lot 243, SBY 4/26/89 2,475

'HAPPELL, Walter (20th C)
White Fence & Wall, slvr, sgn/dtd on mount, stp on mount verso, 1958, 10x13", B/B 4/19/88 220

'HARLESWORTH, Sarah (20th C)
Harness, Objects of Desire; laminated cbcr, ink intl within artist name stp on img, 1984, fr, 39x30", SBY 11/1/88 2,090

'HARNAY, Desire (19th C)
Palais du Cirque, a Chichen-Itza; Pl 34, alb, artist/editor credits, mounted/matted, ca 1860, 13x17", SBY 4/26/89 OE 4,125

'HISLETT, John
River at Dusk, pltn tip-mounted to blk paper, matted, ca 1910, 9x7", SBY 11/1/88 1,320

'HOCHOLA, Vaclav (20th C)
Lampa, slvr, sgn/titled/dtd on verso, 1947, 13x11", B/B 4/19/88 275
Maska, slvr, sgn/titled/dtd on verso, 1947, 13x11", B/B 4/19/88 UE 165
Zada, Kolaz (Back, Collage); slvr, sgn/titled/dtd on verso, 1960, 13x9", B/B 4/19/88 192

'HURCH, Albert Cook (19th C)
Untitled (whaleship at dock in New Bedford harbor), vintage, orig fr, 30x22", RAB 8/1/89 OE 900

'ITROEN, Paul (20th C)
Franz Osborn, Retrospektive Fotografie; Pl 50, slvr, sgn/titled/dtd on verso, 1934, 9x7", SWN 4/24/89 825
Woman (Helene), Amsterdam; slvr, p/s, dtd on verso, 1934, 10x7", SWN 10/30/88 715

'LERGUE, Lucien (20th C)
Coco du Grand Herbier, 23/30, fresson, p/s in mrg, sgn/dtd/titled/#d on verso, matted, 1975/1981, 17x12", SBY 5/4/88 770
Les Geantes, 9/20, ink sgn in mrg, sgn/dtd on verso, matted, 1978/1981, 10x15", SBY 11/1/88 880
Les Seidentes (nudes in surf), slvr, p/s, sgn/titled, stp on verso, 1978, 10x14", B/B 10/4/88 468
Nu de la Mer, #10, sgn/dtd/inscr To Creilly & Peter Pollack, studio/limitation stps on verso, 1964, 20x24", SBY 11/1/88 1,375
Pair: Nudes; #2 & #6, artist credit/copyright/studio stps on verso, matted, 1960s, 11x11", SBY 4/26/89 770
Portfolio: Urban Nude; VI/L, 12 photos, sgn in mrg, 1975-79/ca 1981, 14x10", cased, SBY 5/4/88 1,100

'LESS, See Mc Cless

'LIFFORD, Charles (19th C)
Detail of Entrance to Alcazar, Seville; alb, titled/bstp, 1850s, 13x15", B/B 10/4/88 358
Saddle, alb, titled/inscr Chinese 16th C on mount, matted, early 1860s, 13x10", SBY 4/26/89 OE 3,025

'OBURN, Alvin Landgon (American, 1882-1966)
Book: London; 28 photogr on gray paper, early 1900s/ca 1909, various sizes, gray boards/leather spine, SBY 4/26/89 3,300
Island of Machen, matted, early 1900s, 11x15", SBY 4/26/89 1,210
Island of Machen, Holland; hand-pulled photogr, ca 1908, 11x15", SWN 4/24/89 715
Singer Building, Noon; photogr, tipped to orig gray mount, 1909, 9x3", SWN 4/24/89 330

'OLE, Henry H. or Roderic M.; att (19th C)
Abraham Lincoln, alb or alb sltp, sgn by Lincoln on mount, ca 1858, fr, oval 7x5", SBY 4/26/89 OE 49,500

'ONTENT, Marjorie
Equivalent, sgn/dtd on verso, matted, ca 1933, 7x5", SBY 11/1/88 1,100
Marsden Hartley, sgn/dtd on verso, matted, 1929, 4x3", SBY 11/1/88 OE 2,090

'OPPOLA, Horacio
Zwei Strohblumen (Still Life), sgn/dtd/titled on verso, matted, 1932, 6x8", SBY 4/26/89 1,650

'ORDUAN, Joseph (American, fl 1839-1843)
Man (half-length/mid-aged), dag, 6th pl, pl stp Corduan NY, gold foil mat/leather case, ca 1839-40, SWN 4/24/89 OE 1,210

'ORNELL, Joseph (American, 1903-1972)
Penny Arcade Series (Valentina), photo collage on panel, sgn/dtd Spring 1962/inscr, 12x9", SBY 5/3/88 7,150

'ORPRON, Carlotta (20th C)
Fluid Light Design, p/s on mount, titled/artist name stp on verso, 1940s, 3x3", SBY 4/26/89 1,320

'ORY, Kate (20th C)
Portfolio: Hopi; #B, ed of 4, 41 slvr, 1905-1912/1978, 7x9", B/B 10/4/88 OE 935

'OSTER, Gordon (20th C)
Lucien Lelong Perfume Advertisement, sgn/dtd on img, sgn/dtd/inscr For Marshall Field, ca 1935, 13x10", SBY 4/26/89 770

'RAMER, Konrad (20th C)
Plant Study, sgn/inscr Woodstock on mount, matted, 1930s, 10x8", SBY 4/26/89 1,540

'RAWFORD, Ralston (20th C)
Lift Bridge (In Negative), estate stp on verso, matted, 1949, 7x10", SBY 4/26/89 1,980
Vent on the Deck of the Queen Mary, backed w/card, sgn/estate stp on verso, matted, 1951, 7x9", SBY 4/26/89 1,980

'RAWFORD, Winifred E. (20th C)
Group of 6: Fan Pattern; Easter; Wheels; Wind for the Threshing; Lone Ascent; Camouflage; slvr brom, 1945, B/B 10/4/88 248

CUCCIONI, Tommaso (19th C)

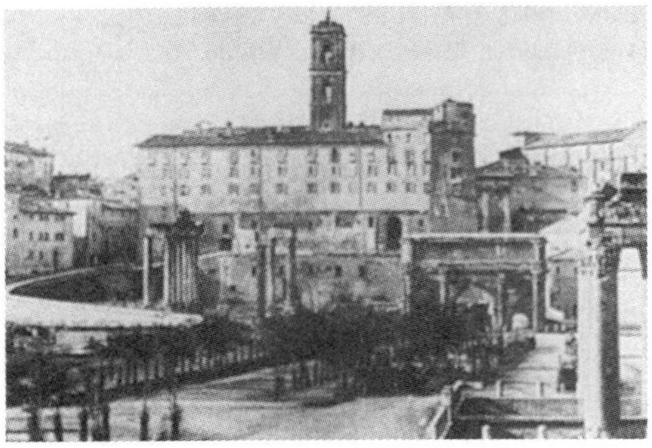

Forum & the Capitol, #19, alb, 1850s, 14x18", SWN 10/30/88 OE; $1,760

South Relief Inside the Arch of Titus, #24, alb, 1850s, 13x18", SWN 10/30/88 OE	**1,210**
CUNNINGHAM, Imogen (American, 1883-1976)	
Adolph Blom, 1331 Green Street San Francisco studio stp on verso, ca 1921, no size given, SBY 5/4/88	**1,100**
Alfred Stieglitz, p/s on mount, artist label on verso, 1934, fr, 10x8", SBY 5/4/88	**2,420**
Auragia, sgn/dtd on mount, Cunningham Trust paper label on verso, 1953/1974-76, 14x11", SBY 4/26/89	**825**
Banana Plant, p/s on mount, sgn/dtd/titled/inscr 4540 Harbor View Oakland on verso, late 1920s, 9x7", SBY 4/26/89 OE	**23,100**
Davidia Blossom, slvr, ca 1950s, 4x4", B/B 10/4/88 UE	**220**
Day in Arizona, No 5; brom, San Francisco Soc of Women Artist label on verso, mounted, 1939, 7x7", SWN 4/24/89	**600**
Frieda Kahlo Rivera, Painter & Wife of Diego Rivera; inscr on verso, matted, 1934/1960s, 13x10", SBY 4/26/89 OE	**3,850**
Frieda Kahlo Rivera, Painter & Wife of Diego Rivera; p/s on verso, matted, 1931/later, 12x10", SBY 5/4/88 OE	**2,200**
Hands of Composer, Henry Cowell; slvr, stp on verso, 1926, 8x8", B/B 10/4/88	**660**
Her & Her Shadow, matted, 1936, 5x4", SBY 5/4/88	**2,970**
John Masefield, brml, p/s on mount recto, 4540 Harbor View stp on verso, 1930s, 6x5", SWN 4/24/89 UE	**605**
Leaf Pattern, inscr on verso, matted, late 1920s/1960s, 12x10", SBY 4/26/89 OE	**3,247**
Magnolia Blossom (Tower of Jewels), p/s on verso, matted, 1925/1955-65, 10x7", SBY 5/4/88	**2,420**
Martha Graham, p/s on mount, matted, 1931, 6x8", SBY 11/1/88 OE	**3,025**
Northwest Native, sgn/dtd on mount, artist label on verso, mounted/matted, 1934/pre-1976, 14x11", SBY 5/4/88	**550**
Nude, sgn/dtd on mount, Green Street studio label on verso, matted, 1923, fr, 7x9", SBY 4/26/89 OE	**2,750**
Phoenix Recumbent, sgn/dtd on mount, 1331 Green Street San Francisco label on verso, 1968, 10x9", SBY 5/4/88 OE	**2,420**
Portia Hume, matted, 1930s, 4x5", SBY 5/4/88	**880**
Rufugio Beach, slvr, titled, stp on verso, ca 1920s, 4x5", B/B 10/4/88 UE	**220**
Sherwood Anderson, matted, 1920s, 4x3", SBY 5/4/88 OE	**1,320**
Snake (Negative), inscr on verso, matted, 1929/1960s, 12x10", SBY 4/26/89	**1,430**
Two Callas, sgn/dtd on mount, artist Trust title label on verso, matted, ca 1929/1975-76, 14x11", SBY 11/1/88 OE	**2,750**
Unmade Bed, sgn/dtd on mount, artist label on verso, 1957/pre-1976, 11x14", SBY 5/4/88 OE	**3,190**
CURTIS, Edward S. (American, 1868-1952)	
Canyon de Chelley, oro, ink sgn on img, 1904, fr, 11x14", B/B 4/19/88	**1,870**
Castle O'Dreams, bl-toned slvr, sgn in negative, titled/Los Angeles studio stp, 1900s, orig fr, 14x11", SBY 11/1/88	**1,045**
Chief of the Desert, oro, sgn/copyright stp in gold on img, ca 1900, 14x11", SBY 11/1/88 UE	**880**
Conyon del Muerto, pltn, sgn in negative, orig studio label on fr verso, ca 1900, 8x6", B/B 4/19/88	**358**
Cree Canoe on Lake Les Isles, North American Indian; Pl 621, photogr, 1926, lg folio, CEG 1/13/89	**100**
Flathead Indians in Ceremonial Dance Near Missoula, oro, pl/s, Art Nouveau fr, 11x14", lot 1059, CEG 5/7/88	**1,200**
Group of 4: Apache Reaper; Indian Chief on White Horse; Three Indian Braves on Horseback; Clam Digger; SBY 4/26/89 OE	**3,850**
Group of 49: North American Indian Portraits; slvr & pltn, 32 sgn, early 1900s, various sizes, SBY 11/1/88 OE	**17,600**
Hopi Maiden, pltn/slvr, copyright bstp on img, ca 1904, orig studio fr, 17x9", SBY 11/1/88	**1,870**
In the Lands of the Apsaroke, photogr on Japan paper, L-4x8", CEG 1/13/89	**25**
Indian Profile, pltn/slvr, ink sgn on img, artist bstp in mrg, mounted/matted, 1916, fr, 16x12", SBY 11/1/88 OE	**3,300**
Indian Woman, oro, sgn in gold on img, early 1900s, fr, 8x10", SBY 11/1/88	**605**
Indian Woman Weaving Baskets, pltn/slvr, sgn/copyright bstp on img, matted, early 1900s, 13x16", SBY 5/4/88	**660**
Medicine man, toned pltn, #d 513-07 in negative, sgn on recto, artist stp on verso, early 1900s, 16x12", SWN 4/24/89 OE	**1,320**
Oasis in the Badlands, hc slvr, sgn in red ink on img, ca 1905, fr, 10x13", B/B 4/19/88	**660**
Oasis in the Badlands, pltn, sgn on img, tipped on orig presentation folder, ca 1905, 6x8", B/B 10/4/88 OE	**880**
Old Well at Acoma, slvr, ink sgn in mrg, ca 1904, 6x8", B/B 4/19/88	**605**
Pair: Studies of Elderly Indian Women; slvr, artist studio sgn on recto, ca 1900, 8x6"/7x6", SWN 10/30/88 UE	**110**
Pair: Vanishing Race; Women at Well, Acoma; pltn/slvr, copyright bstp on img, early 1900s, orig fr, 6x8", SBY 5/4/88	**1,870**
Sioux Chief, pltn, ink sgn/bstp on img, dtd/#d in negative, sgn on mount, 1905, 6x8", B/B 4/19/88	**522**
Siwashes, Puget-Sound; pltn, ink sgn on mount, credit/dtd in negative, 1898, 6x7", B/B 4/19/88	**467**
Standing Brave, toned slvr, early 1900s, 7x5", SWN 10/30/88	**440**
Study of Indians on Horseback in a Canyon, pltn, #d in negative, studio sgn/copyright stp, 1905, 6x8", SWN 4/24/89 OE	**660**
Three Chiefs, sgn/artist copyright insignia in negative, studio label on verso, 1900s, orig fr, 8x9", SBY 4/26/89	**1,980**
Vanishing Race, oro, sgn in gold ink on img, studio label on orig fr verso, ca 1904, 11x14", B/B 4/19/88	**1,980**
Vanishing Race, pltn/slvr, sgn/Seattle bstp on img, backed w/brown paper, early 1900s, orig fr, 16x21", SBY 5/4/88 OE	**3,300**
Water Carriers, pltn/slvr, sgn/bstp on img, matted, early 1900s, 13x18", SBY 5/4/88	**660**
DAHL-WOLFE, Louise (20th C)	
Keep the Home Fires Burning (June Vincent), ink sgn on verso, matted, 1942, 12x10", SBY 11/1/88 OE	**2,475**

Model in Evening Wear, p/s on verso, matted, early 1950s, 14x11", SBY 4/26/89 .... **715**

ASSONVILLE, William E. (20th C)

Alcatraz Island, San Francisco Harbor; p/s in mrg, 1920s, 8x10", SBY 11/1/88 .... **825**
Boat at Dock, p/s in mrg, 1920s, 8x10", SBY 4/26/89 OE **1,540**
California Ranch, p/s in mrg, exhibition labels on verso, overmatted, early 1930s, 8x10", SBY 5/4/88 .... **1,100**
Carmel Dunes, slvr on tissue, ink sgn in mrg, matted, 1920s, 7x9", SBY 5/4/88 .... **660**
Deck of Ship, San Francisco Harbor; p/s in mrg, mounted/matted, 1920s, 8x10", lot 164, SBY 5/4/88 OE **2,750**
Deck of Ship, San Francisco Harbor; p/s in mrg, 1920s, 7x10", lot 176, SBY 11/1/88 .... **1,210**
Deck of Ship, San Francisco Harbor; p/s in mrg, 1920s, 8x10", lot 175, SBY 11/1/88 OE **1,980**
Eucalyptus Tree, San Francisco; p/s in mrg, mounted/matted, 1920s, 9x9", SBY 4/26/89 .... **660**
Flower Study, pltn, ink sgn on img, San Francisco studio bstp on cover, ca 1900, 8x6", SBY 5/4/88 .... **770**
Industrial Study, ink sgn on img, matted, 1920s, 11x8", SBY 5/4/88 .... **770**
Industrial Study, p/s in mrg, matted, 1920s, 12x9", SBY 5/4/88 .... **1,210**
Pair: People on the Beach; Moored Boat; 1 p/s in mrg, matted, 1920s, 8x10", SBY 5/4/88 OE **1,870**
Rolling Hills, California; p/s in mrg, mounted/matted, 1920s, 8x10", SBY 4/26/89 OE **1,320**
San Francisco Skyline, p/s in mrg, mounted/matted, 1920s, 8x10", SBY 11/1/88 .... **1,045**
Ships, San Francisco Bay; p/s in mrg, mounted/matted, 1920s, 10x8", SBY 5/4/88 OE **1,870**
Steam, p/s on mount, 1920s, 11x9", SBY 4/26/89 OE **1,760**
Yosemite, Cathedral Rocks; pltn, ink sgn on img, matted, ca 1907, 6x8", SBY 5/4/88 OE **1,210**

ATER, Judy (American, 1941-)

Imogen & Twinka, slvr, sgn/dtd/titled, 1974/later, 10x8", B/B 10/4/88 .... **1,100**
Imogen & Twinka at Yosemite, p/s on mount, titled/dtd/copyright stp on verso, 1974/later, 10x8", SBY 5/4/88 .... **880**
Kathleen Kelly, slvr, sgn/dtd on verso, 1972/later, no size given, B/B 10/4/88 .... **330**
Marc, slvr, sgn/dtd on verso, 1977, fr, 11x14", B/B 4/19/88 .... **468**
Summer Bath, slvr, p/s in mrg, titled/dtd on verso, 1975, fr, 12x16", B/B 4/19/88 .... **248**
Twinka, p/s on mount, titled/dtd on verso, mounted/matted, 1970, fr, 13x10", SBY 5/4/88 .... **660**

AVIDSON, Bruce (20th C)

Pair: Man in Restaurant; Man Walking the Moors with His Dog; p/s on verso, matted, 1960/later, 8x12", SBY 11/1/88 .... **715**
Subway, C-print, matted, ca 1980, fr, 28x37", SBY 5/4/88 .... **715**

AVIS, Dwight A.

Bird Fountain, gum bcro, titled, mounted/matted, ca 1910, 12x10", SBY 11/1/88 .... **660**
Old Settlers, pltn, titled in mat, mounted/double matted, ca 1908, 9x8", SBY 11/1/88 .... **715**
Snowy Path, pltn, double matted, ca 1910, 8x10", SBY 11/1/88 .... **605**

AVIS, Lynn (20th C)

Group of 3: Nude Studies; ed of 10 & 5, ink sgn on verso, matted, 1979, various sizes, SBY 11/1/88 UE **330**

AY, F. Holland

Nude in Forest, pltn, intl/dtd/titled on paper label on verso, matted, 1897, fr, 5x6", SBY 4/26/89 .... **3,025**
Portrait of Maynard P White, pltn, ca 1910, 9x7", B/B 10/4/88 .... **715**

E MEYER, Adolf

Eleonora Duse, pltn mounted on blk paper, matted, fr, 1922, 11x6", SBY 5/4/88 .... **880**
Jinny Alden Carpenter (Mrs Hill of Washington, DC), p/s, Eastman Kodak enlargement stp, late 1920s, SBY 4/26/89 .... **2,475**
Mrs Rita de Acosta Lydig, pltn, paper label on verso, 1913, 9x8", SBY 5/4/88 .... **1,210**
Pair: Vera Fokine; pltn, 1 w/Harper's Bazaar repro stp on verso, 1926, 8x9", SBY 5/4/88 .... **1,210**
Portrait of Ina Claire, slvr, p/s, ca 1920, fr, 10x7", B/B 10/4/88 UE **440**
Seated Woman, double-mounted on card/tissue, 1920s, 8x9", SBY 5/4/88 .... **1,100**

E MONVEL, Boutet; att

Paul Gauguin, sltp, inscr Vendredi 13 Fev 91 on verso, 1891, 3x5", SBY 4/26/89 .... **3,300**

ELACROIX, E. (American, 20th C)

Pair: Little Theatre Courtyard; Stairway; sgn, 4x6", lot 167, MG 5/28/88 .... **100**
Pair: Pirates Alley; View From a Balcony; sgn, 4x6", lot 166, MG 5/28/88 .... **160**
Pair: St Louis Cathedral; Spanish Court, sgn, 4x6", lot 165, MG 5/28/88 .... **160**

etroit Photographic Company

Delaware Water Gap, #59033, photochrome, artist credit stp in gilt on img, 1900, 17x21", SWN 4/24/89 OE **1,540**

IAMOND, Hugh (19th C)

Asylum Inmate in Striped Dress & Lace Cap, alb, matted, early 1850s, 8x5", SBY 11/1/88 .... **8,800**

ISRAELI, Robert (20th C)

Automat, artist name stp on verso, matted, 1940s, 6x8", SBY 4/26/89 .... **770**

OISNEAU, Robert (20th C)

Pair: Les Pains de Picasso; Sortie de la Messe a Sceaux; sgn in mrg, 1952 & 1944/1976, 13x11", SBY 11/1/88 OE **1,320**
Pair: Musique de Chambre; Les Freres; sgn in mrg, intl/titled on verso, matted, 1934 & 1957/1981, 10x12", SBY 11/1/88 .... **1,100**
Pair: Waiting in Line; Boxers; backed w/card or paper, matted, 1940s, 11x16", SBY 4/26/89 OE **1,870**
Portfolio: Robert Doisneau; 4/100, 15 photos, ink sgn on verso, matted, 1944-72/ca 1979, 10x12", case, SBY 5/4/88 .... **4,125**
Portfolio: Robert Doisneau; 5/100, 15 photos, sgn on verso, matted, 1944-72/ca 1979, 10x12, cased, SBY 4/26/89 OE **9,900**

ORNAC & CIE

Paul Verlaine, the Poet, in a Paris Cafe; alb, artist credit/titled on mount, ca 1895, 5x7", SBY 4/26/89 .... **1,100**

OVIZIELLI, Pietro

Cascate delle Ferriere, Tivoli; #122, alb, mounted, 12x15", SWN 4/24/89 OE **880**

RTIKOL, Frantisek

Bacchanalian Dancers, slvr, sgn/dtd on mount, credit/dtd bstp on img, 1920, 6x10", B/B 4/19/88 .... **1,045**
Dancer, sgn/dtd on img, matted, 1912, 9x7", SBY 11/1/88 OE **3,850**

Group of 3: Studio Portraits; slvr, bstp on img/mount, 1917/1926/1932, 6x4" to 9x7", B/B 10/4/88 UE ... 192
Nude, slvr, sgn/dtd on img, 1912, 9x7", B/B 4/19/88 ... 660
Nude Study, sgn in negative, matted, 1920s, 4x3", SBY 5/4/88 ... 1,100

DRTIKOL, Frantisek; & SKARDA, Augustin
Woman Sweeping Street, brml, sgn/dtd in mrg, matted, 7x8", SBY 11/1/88 ... 880

DU CAMP, Maxine (19th C)
Temple de Kardassy, #87, sltp, mounted/matted, 1849-1851, 7x9", SBY 5/4/88 ... 880

DURANDELLE, Edouard (19th C)
Le Nouvel Opera de Paris, No 7; alb, artist/publisher credit stps on mount, ca 1875, 15x11", SWN 4/24/89 ... 523

EAGLE, Arnold (20th C)
Pair: Under the El; 3rd Ave El; dtd on verso, matted, 1936, 5x4"/13x9", SBY 4/26/89 ... 880

EAKINS, Thomas (20th C)
Mary (Dolly) MacDowell, pltn mounted to thin card, 1880s, oval 7x5", SWN 4/24/89 ... 1,870

EAKINS, Thomas; att (20th C)
William H MacDowell in Hat & Coat, pltn mounted on bl card, ca 1884, 9x5", SWN 4/24/89 UE ... 1,100

EDGERTON, Harold (American, 1903-)
Pair: Football Kick; Golfer; p/s on verso, 1930s/later, 18x14"/10x10", SBY 5/4/88 UE ... 550
Portfolio: Seeing the Unseen; 54/60, 5 dye, p/s on verso, matted, 1934-36/ca 1977, various sizes, cased, SBY 5/4/88 ... 2,475

EDWARDS, John Paul
Untitled Landscape, chloride, p/s, 1918, 14x11", B/B 10/4/88 OE ... 605

EGGLESTON, William (20th C)
Greenwood, Mississippi; 6/7, dye, ink sgn, ed/copyright stps on verso, ca 1972/1986, 21x14", SBY 11/1/88 UE ... 770
Near Jackson, Mississippi; 4/5, dye, ink sgn, ed/copyright stps on verso, ca 1972/1986, 21x14", SBY 11/1/88 UE ... 770
Summer, Mississippi; 2/7, dye, ink sgn, ed/copyright stps on verso, matted, ca 1972/1986, 21x14", SBY 11/1/88 UE ... 770

EHM, Josef (20th C)
Nude Torso Study, slvr, sgn/dtd on verso, 1946, 10x12", B/B 4/19/88 ... 715

EICKEMEYER, Rudolf Jr.
November on the Dunes, #10, toned slvr, sgn/copyright, titled on verso, 1916, 11x14", SWN 10/30/88 ... 1,320

EISENSTAEDT, Alfred (20th C)
Dr Joseph Goebbels, Hitler's Minister of Propaganda, Geneva; Life Photo/date stps, 1933/pre-1954, 13x9", SBY 4/26/89 ... 14,300
Foot Soldier, Ethiopia; Life Photo stp on verso, matted, 1935/early 1950s, 13x10", SBY 4/26/89 OE ... 1,870
La Scala, Milan; Life Photo stp on verso, matted, 1934/early 1950s, 13x11", SBY 4/26/89 OE ... 1,045
Marlene Dietrich, Berlin; Life Photo/date stps on verso, matted, 1929/pre-1952, 13x10", SBY 4/26/89 OE ... 3,575
Pair: Ice Skating Waiter, St Moritz; Officer Embraced by Woman; Life Photo stp, pre-1954, 14x11", SBY 4/26/89 OE ... 2,640
V-J Day, Times Square, 1945; slvr, Life Magazine stp on verso, 1945/pre-1966, 10x8", SWN 10/30/88 OE ... 935
V-J Day, Times Square; Life Photo stp on verso, matted, 1945/early 1950s, 9x7", SBY 4/26/89 OE ... 4,125

ELISOFON, Eliot (20th C)
Running Zebras, dye, p/s in mrg, mounted, 1950s, 15x19", SBY 11/1/88 ... 715

ELLIS, William Shewell
Joseph Pennell At Work in His Studio, brom slvr on double mount, titled/studio label, early 1900s, 15x18", SWN 4/24/89 ... 495

EMERSON, Peter Henry (European, 20th C)
Cattle on the Marshes, Pl 30, ed of 200, pltn, mounted/matted, ca 1886, 8x11", SBY 5/4/88 UE ... 440
Coming Home From the Marshes, Pl 1, ed of 200, pltn, mounted/matted, ca 1886, 8x11", SBY 5/4/88 ... 1,870

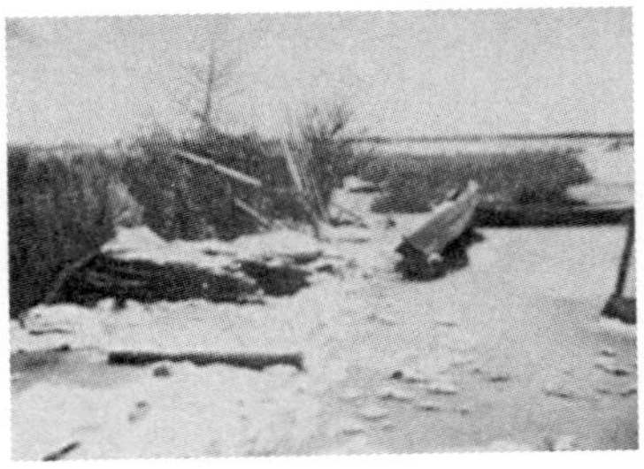

First Frost, XIV, pltn, titled, 1886, 8x11", orig tissue guard, B/B 10/4/88 OE; $880

Fowler's Return, Life & Landscape on the Norfolk Broads; ed of 200, pltn, mounted/matted, 1886, fr, 7x11", SBY 11/1/88 ... 1,320
Group of 3: Life & Landscape on the Norfolk Broads; Pl 5, Pl 23, Pl 38, pltn, ed of 200, 1885-86/1886, 9x11", SBY 5/4/88 ... 1,650
Marsh Farm, Life & Landscape on Norfolk Broads; Pl 29, pltn, orig mount, 9x11", SWN 4/24/89 ... 880
Marsh Farm, Life & Landscape on the Norfolk Broads; ed of 200, pltn, mounted/matted, ca 1886, 9x12", SBY 11/1/88 ... 990
Old Order & the New, Life & Landscape on the Norfolk Broads; pltn, mounted/matted, ca 1886, fr, 5x9", SBY 11/1/88 OE ... 4,950
Pair: Quanting the Gladdon; Evening; ed of 200, pltn, mounted, 1885-86/ca 1886, 9x12"/7x11", SBY 11/1/88 ... 1,650
Ricking the Reed, Life & Landscape on the Norfolk Broads; edof 200, pltn, mounted/matted, ca 1886, 9x11", SBY 11/1/88 ... 2,090
Ricking the Reed, Life & Landscape on the Norfolk Broads; ed of 200, pltn, mounted/matted, ca 1886, 9x11", SBY 4/26/89 ... 1,980
Ricking the Reed, Life & Landscape on the Norfolk Broads; Pl 27, pltn, orig tissue guard, 1886, 9x11", SWN 10/30/88 ... 1,540
Sailing Mathe at Horning, Life & Landscape on the Norfolk Broads; pltn, mounted/matted, ca 1886, 9x11", SBY 11/1/88 ... 1,540

ERNST, Max (American, 1891-1976)
Book: Mr Knife, Miss Fork; 24/50, 19 slvr of photograms on Holland paper, sgn, 1931, Black Sun, SBY 4/26/89 OE ... 11,000

ERWITT, Elliot (20th C)
Portfolio: Photographs Elliot Erwitt; 34/100, 15 photos, sgn/#d on verso, 1948-68/ca 1977, 7x10", cased, SBY 5/4/88 UE ... 990

EVANS, Frederick

Aubrey Beardsley, Profile Portrait; ca 1894, 5x4", SWN 10/30/88	660
Bourges Cathedral: Porch in West Front; pltn, titled/sgn on mount, early 1900s, 11x7", SWN 4/24/89	1,320
F Holland Day: Boston (In Arab Costume); pltn, sgn/titled on mount, matted, 1901, fr, 10x4", SBY 4/26/89 OE	7,150
Gloster, North Transept; pltn, sgn/titled on mount, matted, ca 1900, 5x3", SBY 4/26/89	880
Great Gable, From Westlake; slvr, sgn/titled, ex libras lable on verso, ca 1900s, 9x10", B/B 10/4/88	468
Group of 5: Grotesques at Lincoln Cathedral; pltn mounted together in window overmat, p/s, 1891, 8x20", SBY 11/1/88	1,320
In Sure & Certain Hope, photogr mounted on tissue tipped to paper, p/s, ca 1902, 8x6", SWN 4/24/89	1,430
La Maison, Bourgtheroulde; pltn, a/bstp, early 1900s, 10x8", SWN 10/30/88 UE	660
Life Mask of Beethoven, pltn, sgn/titled on mount, matted, 1900s, 8x6", SBY 5/4/88	1,980
Lincoln Cathedral, Part of Angel Choir; pltn, artist bstp, ex libras label on verso, ca 1900, 5x6", B/B 10/4/88 UE	385
Nantes Cathedral: Organ Staircase; pltn, sgn/titled on mount, matted, early 1900s, 11x5", SBY 4/26/89 OE	7,700
Pair: Durham Cathedral: The Font; Ely Cathedral: Galilee Porch into Nave; pltn & slvr, 1900s, 10x5"/9x7", SBY 1/11/88	1,430

EVANS, Walker (American, 1903-1975)

Architectural Abstraction, New York; artist name stp on verso, matted, ca 1929, 3x2", SBY 4/26/89	3,575
Architectural Photomontage, on post card stock, artist stp on verso, matted, ca 1929, fr, 3x3", SBY 5/4/88 UE	1,650
Bleecker Street (Street Photographer), sgn twice, dtd/titled/stp on verso, matted, ca 1933, fr, 6x8", SBY 5/4/88 OE	2,090
Cafe, on post card, matted, 1930s, 3x5", SBY 4/26/89	1,100
Canadian National Grain Silos, p/s, artist name stp on verso, matted, 1930s, 7x5", SBY 4/26/89	3,575
Columbia Heights, Brooklyn; slvr, artist estate stp on verso, ca 1938(?)/unknown, 6x8", SWN 4/24/89	413
Dock Workers, Havana; artist stp on verso, matted, 1932/later, fr, 6x8", SBY 5/4/88	935
Dock Workers, Havana; slvr, artist estate stp on verso, 1932, 5x5", SWN 4/24/89 OE	2,420
Dry Cleaning, outdoor advertising sgn near Baton Rouge; slvr, artist estate stp on verso, 1935/later, 8x10", SWN 4/24/89	660
Feed Store in a Small Town, Alabama; slvr, 1936/later, fr, 8x10", B/B 4/19/88 UE	330
Flood Refugees, Forrest City, Arkansas; slvr, artist estate stp on verso, 1937/later, 7x7", SWN 4/24/89	660
Frame Houses, on post card stock, matted, 1930s, 5x3", SBY 4/26/89 OE	2,475
Garage, Atlanta, Georgia; slvr, artist estate stp on verso, 1936/later, 14x10", SWN 4/24/89 OE	2,200
Grand Man, artist name/credit/Old Lyme CT studio stps on verso, matted, 1940s, 7x5", SBY 4/26/89	770
Group of 4: Joe's Auto Grayeyard (variant); Pennsylvania; Portrait of a Young Woman; Rope Shop; slvr, 1930s, B/B 10/4/88	440
Havana, a Courtyard; sgn/dtd on mount, sgn/dtd/titled/artist Rights Reserved stp on verso, 1931/later, 6x8", SBY 4/26/89	1,540
Home of William (Bud) Fields, a Cotton Sharecropper, Hale County, Alabama, Summer; slvr, 1936, 8x10", B/B 10/4/88 UE	385
Interior with Stove, slvr, 6x8", SWN 4/24/89	523
Juan-Les-Pins (Self-Portrait), dtd/titled on verso, matted, 1927, fr, 6x4", SBY 5/4/88 OE	6,600
Kitchen Interior, slvr, stp on verso, 1930s, 4x5", B/B 4/19/88	1,100
Louisiana Plantation House, slvr, titled/dtd/artist estate stp on verso, 1935/later, 8x10", SWN 4/24/89	770
Main Street, Ossining, New York; p/s on mat, 1932/later, 6x9", SBY 5/4/88	990
Minstrel Showbill, Alabama; inscr A/P, ps/ on mount, matted, 1936/later, 16x12", SBY 5/4/88 UE	770
Movie Poster, Louisville; slvr, p/s, stp twice/Robert Schoelkopf Gallery label on verso, 1935, 7x11", B/B 10/4/88	1,100
Negroes` Church, South Carolina; slvr, artist name stp on verso, 1936, 4x6", SWN 4/24/89	880
New York City From the Brooklyn Bridge, p/s on mount, artist name stp on verso, ca 1929/later, 11x6", SBY 11/1/88	2,475
New York Subway Portrait, matted, ca 1938-43, 5x8", SBY 5/4/88	990
Pair: Chicago Theatre, Burlesque Posters; Subway Snapshot; stp on verso, 1947 & 1938-41, 7x7"/5x7", SBY 5/4/88 UE	880
Pair: Trott's Sign; Pepsi Cola Sign; C-prints, early 1970s, 10x8", SBY 4/26/89	1,430
Portfolio: Walker Evans; 70/100, 14 photos, p/s on mount, 1931-36/ca 1971, various sizes, folder, cased, SBY 4/26/89 OE	9,350
Portfolio: Walker Evans; 73/100, 14 photos, sgn/dtd on mount, 1931-36/ca 1971, various sizes, folder, cased, SBY 11/1/88	7,700

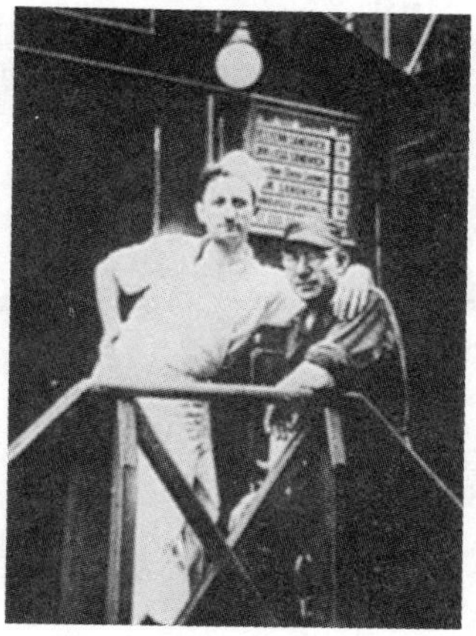

Posed Portraits, New York, American Photographs, Part I; Pl 40, slvr, p/s, estate stp, 1931/unknown, 8x6", SWN 4/24/89 OE; $4,180

Self-Portrait, Antibes; p/s, dtd/inscr Antibes on verso, matted, 1927, 5x3", SBY 4/26/89 OE	6,050
Self-Portrait, matted, ca 1930, fr, 2x4", SBY 11/1/88	2,200
Shoeshine Sign in a Southern Town, artist name stp on verso, 1936/later, 4x6", SBY 4/26/89 OE	2,750
Shoeshine Sign in a Southern Town, slvr, artist estate stp on verso, 1936/unknown, 8x10", SWN 4/24/89	935
Skyscraper, matted, ca 1929, 3x2", SBY 4/26/89	2,475
Skyscraper & Crane, matted, ca 1930, 2x2", SBY 4/26/89	2,475
South 3rd Street, Paducah, Kentucky; toned slvr, artist estate stp on verso, 1947, 10x9", SWN 4/24/89 OE	1,540

Study of a Victorian House, toned slvr, inscr on verso by Berenice Abbott, early 1930s, 6x5", SWN 10/30/88	385
Study of Dresses & Costumes on Hangers, slvr, p/s on mat, 1950s, 9x6", SWN 10/30/88	193
Study of Two-Headed African Sculpture, toned slvr, artist estate stp on verso, ca 1935, 10x8", SWN 10/30/88	358
Subway Portrait of Two Men, slvr, artist estate stp on verso, 1950s, 5x7", SWN 10/30/88	770
Tahiti (Self-Portrait), dtd/titled on verso, matted, 1932, 5x3", SBY 4/26/89	1,320
Unemployed Worker's Home, Morgantown, West Virginia; toned slvr print, artist estate stp, 1935/later, 9x7", SWN 4/24/89	1,650
Victorian House, artist stp on verso, mounted/matted, ca 1932, 5x7", SBY 5/4/88	1,210
Washroom in the Dog Run of Floyd Burroughs' Home, Hale County, Alabama; slvr, 1936/unknown, 6x7", SWN 4/24/89 OE	1,650
Waterloo Station Ramp, London; p/s on mount, artist stp on verso, mounted/matted, ca 1957, 9x10", SBY 5/4/88 UE	550
Westchester, New York; 51/100, p/s on mount, 1936/ca 1971, 5x7", SBY 4/26/89 OE	1,760
Worcester Square, inscr Photograph Given to Berenice Abbott on verso, mounted/matted, 1930s, 5x5", SBY 11/1/88	1,650
You Are Crazy To Be a Good Gril (sic), slvr, p/s on verso, 1940s, 6x9", SWN 10/30/88 UE	300
42nd Street (woman in cloche hat), slvr, artist estate stp on verso, 1929/later, 7x10", SWN 4/24/89 OE	2,200
FADDEN, M. (American, Boston, MA; 19th C)	
Western Cowboy with Lariat, full-length; cbnt, lot 287, CEG 1/13/89	165
FASSBENDER, Adolf (20th C)	
White Night, New York; artist name/copyright stps on verso, matted, 1934, 20x14", SBY 4/26/89 OE	4,125
FASSETT, Samuel M. (19th C)	
Abraham Lincoln, alb, mounted, 1859, oval 5x4", SWN 4/24/89	468
FEININGER, Andreas (American, 1906-)	
Brooklyn Bridge, sgn/dtd/artist name stp on verso, matted, 1940, 10x8", SBY 4/26/89 OE	3,300
Lilo, backed w/paper, matted, ca 1932, 8x9", SBY 4/26/89	1,210
Pair: Downtown From the Brooklyn Bridge; Battery Park; p/s on verso, matted, 1940s/later, 22x18", SBY 11/1/88 OE	1,870
FENTON, Roger (19th C)	
Group of Croat Chiefs, sltp on Agnew mount, artist/publisher credits, Agnew bstp, 1856, 8x6", SWN 4/24/89 OE	2,420
York: The West Porch; Pl 36, alb, orig wrappers/tissue guard, ca 1856/1864, 13x16", Francis Frith, SWN 4/24/89	1,100
FENWICK, George J. (19th C)	
View of Florence, sltp, intl/dtd May 55, orig manuscript caption label, 1855, 7x10", SWN 4/25/89	880
FENWICK, George J.; att (19th C)	
Coliseum, Rome; sltp, orig manuscript caption label, ca 1855, 8x10", SWN 4/24/89	825
FINK, Larry (20th C)	
Pair: Pat's Eighth Birthday Party; Hungarian Debutante Ball; slvr, 1977 & 1978/later, 15x15"/14x14", SWN 4/24/89	605
FINSLER, Hans (20th C)	
Ceramic Coffeepot, slvr, Werkstaetten der Stadt Halle stp on verso, 1920s, 9x6", SWN 4/24/89 UE	220
Study of Balls of Twine, slvr, ca 1940(?), 9x7", SWN 10/30/88	330
Study of Silverware, slvr, ca 1930, 6x8", SWN 10/30/88 UE	440
Untitled (Egg Abstraction), matted, ca 1925-26, 9x7", SBY 4/26/89	1,760
Untitled (Fabric Study), matted, ca 1929, 9x6", SBY 4/26/89	1,650
Verschiedene Blumenschalen (study of bowls), slvr, Werkstaetten Stadt Halle stp on verso, 1920s, 7x9", SWN 10/30/88 UE	330
FIRTH, Francis (19th C)	
Cairo, From the Citadel, First View; alb on letterpress mount, 1860s, 16x19", SWN 10/30/88	1,650
Rameseum of El-Kurneh, Thebes, First View; alb on letterpress mount, 1860s, 15x18", SWN 10/30/88 OE	3,960
FITZ, Grancel (20th C)	
Camel Cigarettes, artist name stp on verso, matted, 1930s, 11x14", SBY 11/1/88 OE	1,760
Canada Dry Ginger Ale, slvr, p/s on mount, 1930s, 8x9", B/B 4/19/88 UE	440
Card Players, slvr, stp on verso, 1930s, 5x7", B/B 10/4/88 UE	275
Hassim Seeks the Genie of the Rocks, gum on tissue, intl in mrg, titled on mount verso, pre-1919, 13x10", SWN 10/30/88	660
Percy Grainger's Hands on a Steinway Keyboard, slvr, double-mounted, Graybar Building stp, ca 1929, 5x7", SWN 10/30/88	935
Windsor Tower, slvr, stp on verso, 1938, 8x11", B/B 10/4/88 UE	275
Woman with Orchids, toned slvr on double mount, p/s on mount, ca 1930, 8x6", SWN 4/24/89 UE	248
FLACH, Hannes	
Berlin (Alexanderplatz railway tracks), slvr, titled/Koeln-Zollstock stp on verso, 1920s, 7x9", SWN 10/30/88 UE	385
FLAHERTY, Frances	
Group of 7: Scenes From Man of Aran; p/s on mount, Man of Aran copyright stp on verso, 1936, 19x15", SBY 11/1/88 UE	825
FLAHERTY, Robert (Revillon Freres)	
Portrait of an Inuit Mother & Child, photogr, a/bstp, 1913/1920, 7x8", B/B 10/4/88 UE	138
FLETCHER, Christine B. (20th C)	
Floral Study, slvr, ca 1920s, 10x12", B/B 4/19/88	248
Pair: Floral Arrangement; Still Life with Strawberries; pltn & chlorobrom, 1930s, 13x10/11x14", B/B 10/4/88	165
FOLBERG, Neil (20th C)	
Hassid Saying Afternoon Prayer, slvr, sgn/titled/dtd on verso, 1974/1975, 9x13", B/B 4/19/88 UE	110
FOUX, Egbert Guy (19th C)	
General Sedgwick & Staff, alb, titled/credit on mount, early 1860s, 6x8", SWN 10/30/88	660
FRANK, Robert (American, 1924-)	
Ann Arbor, Michigan; slvr, sgn/dtd/titled, 1955/later, 9x14", B/B 10/4/88	1,045
Belle Isle, Detroit; sgn/dtd 1977 in mrg, archive stp on verso, matted, 1955-56/later, 13x9", SBY 4/26/89	2,475
Belle Isle, Detroit; slvr, sgn/titled/dtd in mrg, 1955/1970s, 9x13", B/B 4/19/88 UE	605
Butte, sgn/dtd 1977/titled in mrg, archive stp on verso, matted, 1956/later, 8x12", SBY 4/26/89	1,870
Candy Store-New York City; sgn/dtd 1977 in mrg, archive stp on verso, matted, ca 1955/later, 9x12", SBY 4/26/89	2,475
Car Accident, sgn/dtd in mrg, archive stp on verso, matted, 1956/later, 8x13", SBY 4/26/89 OE	3,575
Car Accident, US 66, Between Winslow & Flagstaff, Arizona; slvr, sgn/archive stp, 1955-56/later, 8x13", B/B 4/19/88	770

Cemetery, sgn/dtd/titled in mrg, sgn/dtd/artist name & copyright stps on verso, matted, 1956/1978, 14x8", SBY 11/1/88 UE 770
Charleston, sgn/dtd/titled in mrg, titled/copyright stp on verso, matted, 1956/later, 13x9", SBY 5/4/88 2,860
Chicago (Political Rally), sgn/dtd 1976/titled in mrg, matted, 1956, 13x9", SBY 4/26/89 OE.......... 8,800
Daytona, sgn/dtd titled in mrg, matted, 1961/later, 9x13", SBY 5/4/88 1,100
Detroit, slvr, sgn/dtd/titled in mrg, 1955/later, 7x13", B/B 10/4/88 UE 660
Frogmore, South Carolina; slvr, sgn/titled/dtd in mrg, 1955/later, 9x13", B/B 4/19/88 UE 550
From Europe to US, sgn/dtd/titled in mrg, copyright stp on verso, matted, 1952/later, 9x13", SBY 4/26/89 1,540
Georgetown, South Carolina; sgn/dtd 1977 in mrg, archive stp on verso, matted, ca 1955/later, 12x8", SBY 4/26/89 1,980
Gretta Garbo & George Schee in the Auction Room, matted, early 1950s, 14x11", SBY 4/26/89 880
Horse & Wagon, Paris; sgn, artist credit/archive/copyright stps on verso, matted, 1952, 5x7", SBY 4/26/89 1,430
LA (Rooming House-Bunker Hill, Los Angeles), sgn/dtd 1977/titled in mrg, archive stp, 1956/later, 12x8", SBY 4/26/89 1,870
London, sgn/dtd/titled in img, mounted/matted, 1951, 13x7", SBY 4/26/89 OE 3,300
London, 1951; slvr, sgn/titled/dtd in ink in mrg, 1951, 9x13", SWN 10/30/88 OE.......... 6,600
NYC, slvr, sgn/dtd/titled in mrg, Robert Frank Archive/copyright stps on verso, 1964(?)/ca 1978, 13x9", B/B 10/4/88 990
Pair: Paris; London Bus; sgn/copyright stp on verso, matted, ca 1949, 9x13", SBY 5/4/88 1,210
Rooftops, ink sgn in mrg, sgn/dtd/copyright stp on verso, matted, 1950s, 14x10", SBY 5/4/88 1,980
St Helena (Funeral), sgn/dtd 1977/titled in mrg, archive stp on verso, matted, 1955/later, 13x8", SBY 4/26/89 1,870
Tatoo (sic) Parlor 8th Avenue, NYC; sgn/dtd/titled in mrg, archive/copyright stps, 1956/later, 13x9", SBY 4/26/89 1,540
Trolley, New Orleans; inscr Robert Frank Works Hard 1973 in mrg, 1955-56/1973, 11x16", SBY 11/1/88 OE 7,700
US 30 Between Ogallala & North Platte, Nebraska; sgn/titled, archive/copyright stps, 1955/later, 9x13", SBY 5/4/88 OE 1,650
Valencia, Spain, 1950; slvr, sgn/titled/dtd on recto, Museum of Modern Art label on verso, 1950, 9x13", SWN 4/24/89 OE.......... 2,420
Washington 1956, sgn/dtd/titled in mrg, archive stp on verso, matted, 1956/pre-1977, 9x13", SBY 5/4/88 OE 2,475
Welsh Miners, slvr, flush-mounted to masonite, sgn on verso, Museum of Modern Art label, ca 1950, 9x14", SWN 10/30/88 3,300

FRASER, William A.
Wet Night-Columbus Circle, pigment backed w/card, ink sgn on img, early 1900s, orig fr, 20x17", SBY 11/1/88 OE 4,950

FRENCH, J.A. (American, Keene, NH; 19th C)
Statue of Liberty, alb, lt fox, lot 271, CEG 6/23/89 50
Statue of Liberty, alb on card, lt fox, lot 304, CEG 1/13/89 35

FRIEDLANDER, Lee (20th C)
Dog & Fire Hydrant, sgn/copyright stp on verso, matted, 1970s, 8x11", SBY 4/26/89 OE 2,475
Pair: NYC; New Mexico; sgn/titled/copyright stp on verso, matted, 1978, 11x8", SBY 5/4/88 550

FRITH, Francis (19th C)
Hypaethral Temple, Philae; alb, titled on mount, matted, late 1850s, fr, 15x19", SBY 4/26/89.......... 4,125
Street View, Cairo; alb, sgn/dtd in negative, mounted, 1858, 19x15", SBY 4/26/89.......... 1,760

FUNKE, Jaromir (20th C)
Abstraction, backed w/card, matted, 1930s, fr, 5x8", SBY 5/4/88 OE 3,190
Nude Behind Glass, matted, early 1930s, 10x7", SBY 4/26/89 3,300
Nude Under Glass, artist name stp on verso, matted, early 1930s, 7x9", SBY 4/26/89.......... 3,025
Untitled (Light Abstraction), matted, ca 1927, 6x5", lot 205, SBY 4/26/89 OE 5,225
Untitled (Light Abstraction), matted, ca 1927, 6x5", lot 208, SBY 4/26/89 3,850

GAGLIANI, Oliver (20th C)
Untitled Landscape, slvr, sgn/dtd on mount, stp on verso, 1970s, fr, 7x9", B/B 10/4/88 412

GARDNER, Alexander (American, 19th C)
Abraham Lincoln Seated in Chair, CDV, dtd 24 February 1861, unmounted, SWN 4/24/89.......... 385
Castle Rock, alb, titled/Washington studio credit on mount, ca 1868, 6x8", SWN 4/24/89 UE 220
Members of a Masonic Lodge, alb, matted, ca 1890, 11x15", SBY 11/1/88 UE 605

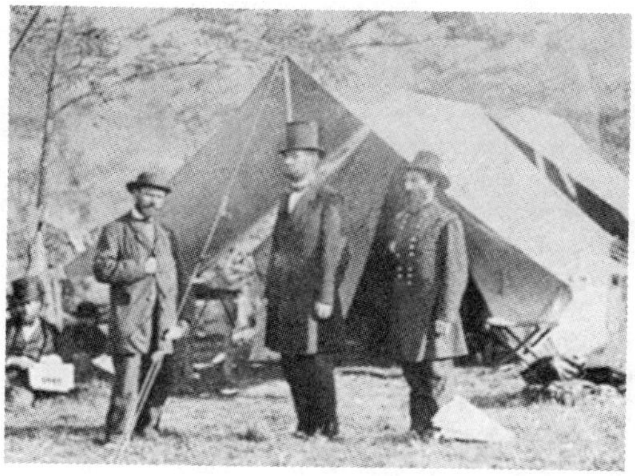

President Lincoln, Major Allan Pinkerton, & General McClernad, Antietam, October, 1862; #7949, alb, 1862/later, 6x8", SWN 4/24/89 OE; $2,860

Scouts & Guides to the Army of the Potomac, Pl 28, alb on letterpress mount, 1862/1866, 7x9", SWN 4/24/89 990
Sharpshooter's Last Sleep, Gettysburg, Pennsylvania; alb on Sketchbook mount, 1863, 7x9", SWN 10/30/88 UE 1,980
Soldiers & Children on the Porch of a Station, alb, Washington studio credit, ca 1867-68, 7x9", SWN 4/24/89 605
What Do I Want, John Henry?; Pl 27, alb on letterpress mount, 1962/1866, 7x9", SWN 4/24/89 1,045

GARDNER, James (19th C)
Breaking Camp, Brandy Station, May 1864; alb, 7x9", SWN 10/30/88 UE 303

GARDNER, studio of (19th C)
Cottage & Garden, Soldier & Two Men Seated to One Side; alb, 1860s, 7x9", SWN 10/30/88.......... 303

Two Photographers or Photographer's Assistants Outside Their Campsite Darkroom, alb, 1860s, 7x9", SWN 10/30/88 935

GARNETT, William (20th C)

Butte, Marble Canyon, Arizona; slvr, p/s, sgn/dtd/titled/copyright stp on verso, 1954/1979, 20x16", B/B 10/4/88 UE 440
Four-Sided Sand Dune, Death Valley, California; backed w/card, Altadena studio stp on verso, 1954, 13x10", SBY 11/1/88 1,320
Nude Dune, Death Valley, California; backed w/card, titled/Altadena studio stp on verso, 1954, 14x10", SBY 11/1/88 990
Sand Dune, Death Valley #1 California, p/s on mount, sgn/dtd/titled/studio stp on verso, 1954/later, 20x16", SBY 5/4/88 1,430

GENTHE, Arnold (American, 1869-1942)

Children Smoking in Chinatown, slvr, Library of Congress stp on verso, ca 1900, 11x9", B/B 10/4/88 OE 935
From the School of Isadora Duncan, slvr, ca 1915, 14x10", B/B 10/4/88 358
Group of 5: Dope Fiend; Street of the Gamblers; Busy Day; Chinese Family; Street Scene; sgn, ca 1895, SBY 11/1/88 4,125
Pair: Family Group; Pointed Arches; toned slvr on double mount, early 1920s, 9x7"/13x10", SWN 4/24/89 UE 550
Steps That Lead to Nowhere (After the Fire), slvr, mounted ca 1942 on AGFA paper package, 1906, 5x7", B/B 4/19/88 300
White House, Washington, DC; slvr, titled/#d on verso, typed artist credit, 7x9", SWN 4/24/89 UE 165

GIACOMELLI, Mario (20th C)

Dancing Priests, sgn/stp inscr on verso, 1968/later, 16x12", SBY 4/26/89 1,100
Landscape, slvr, ink sgn on verso, 1956/later, 12x16", SWN 10/30/88 440
Scanno, Italia del Sud; sgn/titled stp on verso, ca 1958/later, 12x16", SBY 4/26/89 1,430

GIBSON, Ralph (20th C)

Collarbone, 25/25, slvr, 1979, sgn/dtd, 1979, 12x18", B/B 10/4/88 UE 358
Group of 3: Glass of Water & Salt Shaker; Untitled; Man in a Pinstriped Suit; sgn/dtd/#d in mrg, 1974-75, SBY 5/4/88 UE 660
Pair: Man in Bowler Hat; Line on Pavement; sgn/dtd, 1972 & 1975/1975, 13x8", SBY 11/1/88 880
Pair: Nude on Sandy Beach; Nude Abstraction; 7/25 & 25/25, sgn/dtd, matted, 1972 & 1975, 12x18"/6x9", SBY 4/26/89 1,210
Pair: Open Door; Pen in Hand; sgn/dtd, 1975 & 1975, 13x9", SBY 11/1/88 OE 2,200
Pair: Portraits of Women; ink sgn/dtd in mrg, matted, 1974 & 1975, 13x8", SBY 11/1/88 880
Portfolio: Chiaroscuro; 56/100, 15 photos, bstp in mrg, sgn/dtd, matted, 1972-81, various sizes, cased, SBY 4/26/89 880
Untitled Nude Torso, 9/25, slvr, sgn/dtd in mrg, 1975, 12x18", B/B 4/19/88 UE 248

GILBERT & GEORGE (20th C)

Christian (contemporary), 15 photo mounted in fr, sgn/dtd 1982/titled, 71x99", SBY 11/11/88 52,250
Red Morning: Attack; 25 photos mounted in frs, sgn/titled on center panel, 1977, 119x99", SBY 5/2/88 OE 115,500
Red Morning: Killing; 16 photographs mounted in frs, sgn/titled, 1977, overall 95x79", SBY 6/30/88 OE 96,000
Red Youth (contemporary), 12 photos mounted in frs, sgn/dtd 1982/titled, 71x79", SBY 11/11/88 55,000
Wine God, 20 photos together in frs mounted in 1 lg fr, sgn/dtd 1982, 95x99", lot 243, SBY 2/15/89 57,750

GILPIN, Laura (20th C)

Ason Kinlichine, sgn/dtd on mat, studio titled label on verso, mounted/matted, 1963, 10x8", SBY 5/4/88 OE 1,320
From the DH Lawrence Ranch, New Mexico; sgn/dtd on mat, studio title label on verso, 1971, 11x14", SBY 5/4/88 UE 550
Old Mining Mill, Colorado; slvr, typed title label on mount verso, 1940s, 8x10", B/B 4/19/88 440
Ole Lady Long Salt, sgn/dtd on mount, studio label on verso, matted, 1954/later, 14x11", SBY 5/4/88 OE 1,430
Ranchos de Taos Church, p/s on mat, studio label on verso, 1930/later, 8x10", SBY 5/4/88 2,090

GLOEDEN, see Von Gloeden

GOLDBECK, E.O. (20th C)

Indoctrination Division, Air Training Command, Lackland Air Base, San Antonio, Texas; slvr, 1947, 16x14", SWN 4/24/89 550

GOOD, Frank Mason (19th C)

Rural Landscape with Lane & Trees, alb, 11x14", SWN 4/24/89 UE 120

GORNY, Hein

Modernes Portraet (Self-Portrait with a Woman), slvr, Kuemmelstrasse stp on verso, 1920s, 5x7", SWN 4/24/89 OE 605

GRAY, see La Gray

GREEN, John Bulkley (19th C)

Mortuary Temple, sltp, sgn in negative, ca 1854, 9x11", SBY 11/1/88 2,200
Temple de Zournak(?), Thebes; sltp from a waxed paper negative, sgn in negative, ca 1854, 9x12", SWN 4/24/89 1,045

GREENE, Milton (American, 20th C)

Group of 12: Marilyn Monroe; 101/250, 11 slvr/1 dye, sgn/copyright stps on verso, 1953/ca 1979, SBY 5/4/88 2,750
Group of 3: Marilyn Monroe; sgn/dtd/artist name & copyright stps on verso, 1953/1978, fr, 20x16", SBY 11/1/88 OE 1,760
Group of 3: Marilyn Monroe; sgn/dtd/copyright stp on verso, matted, 1953/1979, fr, various sizes, SBY 11/1/88 OE 1,760
Lauren Hutton, backed w/card, sgn/dtd/titled/New York Cultural Center label on verso, 1967, 16x20", SBY 4/26/89 OE 1,650
Marlene Dietrich, sgn/dtd/copyright & limitation stps on verso, matted, 1952/1978, fr, 14x15", SBY 11/1/88 OE 1,760
Pair: Marilyn Monroe; sgn/copyright stp on verso, 1953/1978 & 1979, 16x20", SBY 5/4/88 770
Pair: Marilyn Monroe; sgn/dtd, artist name/copyright stps on verso, 1953/1979, 16x20", SBY 4/26/89 OE 2,750
Pair: Marilyn Monroe; sgn/dtd/copyright stp on verso, 1953/1978, fr, 16x20", SBY 5/4/88 880

GROOVER, Jan (American, 1943-)

Still Life with Flatware & Bowl, 3/3, cbcr, sgn/dtd/#d in mrg, matted, 1979, fr, 15x19", SBY 5/4/88 OE 3,300
Untitled (still life of flatware/dishes), 1/3, C-print, sgn/dtd in mrg, matted, 1978, 15x19", lot 622, SBY 4/26/89 2,475
Untitled (still life of flatware/dishes), 1/3, C-print, sgn/dtd in mrg, matted, 1978, 15x19", lot 623, SBY 4/26/89 2,200
Untitled (still life of forks in glass bowl), 3/3, C-print, sgn/dtd in mrg, matted, 1979, fr, 19x15", SBY 4/26/89 2,475

GRUEN, John (American, 20th C)

Group of 3: Still Lifes; ed of 60, slvr, sgn, 1975-79/ca 1981, 15x19", B/B 10/4/88 UE 330
Portfolio: Still Lifes; 12/60, 8 photos, sgn/#d in mrg, 1975-78/ca 1981, 15x19", cased, Symbax Inc, SBY 11/1/88 1,980

GUIDALEVITCH, Victor

Anvers Night Scene, sgn/dtd on mount, Antwerp studio stp on verso, matted, 1939, 14x11", SBY 11/1/88 UE 330

GUTCH, John Wheeley Gough (19th C)

Pair: English Parish Churches; sltp, titled/#d on verso, mid-1850s, 7x9"/9x7", SWN 4/24/89 UE 248

GUTEKUNST (American, Philadelphia; 19th C)
Dodge City, Kansas Street Scene; CDV, artist backstp, CEG 5/7/88 30
GUTMANN, John
Omen, slvr, sgn/titled/dtd on verso, 1934/later, 9x7", B/B 4/19/88 440
HAAS, Ernst (20th C)
Portfolio: The Creation; 13/300, 10 dye, p/s on mount, copyright on verso, 1962-81/ca 1981, cased, SBY 11/1/88 OE 3,850
HAGEMEYER, Johan
Edward Weston, double-mounted on blk paper/cream card, sgn/dtd/titled on mount, 1925, 9x7", SBY 5/4/88..... 1,540
Robinson Jeffers, double-mounted on blk paper/cream card, sgn/titled on mount, early 1930s, 9x6", SBY 5/4/88 UE 1,540
Self-Portrait, mounted on cream card, sgn/dtd/titled on mount, 1923, 9x8", SBY 5/4/88 1,540
HAJEK, Karel (20th C)
Gymnastics Parade From the Window, slvr, titled/stp on verso, 1950s, 16x12", B/B 4/19/88 UE 165
Hands, slvr, stp on verso, 1940s, 8x6", B/B 4/19/88 UE..... 220
HAJEK-HALKE, Heinz; & HAUSMANN, Raoul
Pair: Schneesturm (Fotogramm); Photocollage; titled in ink, 1952 & 1930s, 10x7"/7x6", SBY 11/1/88 770
HALSMAN, Philippe (American, 1906-1979)
Albert Einstein, Abrams Limited Edition Series; sgn on img, 1954/ca 1972, 20x16", SBY 4/26/89 OE 5,500
Albert Einstein, Abrams Limited Edition; 56/99, sgn on img, matted, 1954/ca 1972, fr, 20x16", SBY 11/1/88 OE..... 2,090
Albert Einstein, slvr, artist copyright stp on verso, 1954/later, 13x10", SWN 4/24/89 OE..... 440
Andre Gide, ink sgn on img, mounted on card, sgn/artist name stp on verso, 1935, 16x12", SBY 4/26/89..... 660
Dali Atomicus, slvr, sgn/titled/dtd/stp on verso, 1948/ca 1969-70, 14x11", B/B 4/19/88..... 990
Dali's Skull, printing notations on mount, 1951/pre-1962, 14x11", SBY 11/1/88 1,210
HAMMERBECK, Wanda
Untitled Landscape, ektacolor, sgn/dtd in mrg, 1979, 18x26", B/B 4/19/88 UE 192
HANFSTAENGL, Franz (19th C)
Couple Under the Stars, Munchen studio bstp on mount, 1918, fr, 5x4", SBY 4/26/89 OE..... 1,650
Die Glyptothek in Muenchen, sltp, titled in negative, credit on mount, 1850s, 12x15", SWN 10/30/88 660
Die Ruhmeshalle und die Bavaria in Muenchen, sltp, titled in negative, credit on mount, 1850s, 12x15", SWN 10/30/88 OE..... 2,860
Gartenhaus, sltp, titled/artist & architect credits on mount, 10x12", SWN 10/30/88..... 935
Minister von der Pfordten, sltp, double-mounted, 1850s, 11x9", SWN 10/30/88 1,100
Saint Georg, sltp, titled/artist & sculptor credits on mount, 1850s, 10x8", SWN 10/30/88 UE 220
HARE, James
Williamsburg Bridge, p/s on verso, matted, early 1900s, 8x10", SBY 11/1/88..... 990
HARRIS, R. (19th C)
Album: South African Scenery, Port Elizabeth; 108 alb, print titled, ca 1885, 5x8" to 11x14", B/B 10/4/88 495
HARRISON (19th C)
Foret de Fontainebleau, carbon, a/bstp on img, titled/Asnieres studio credit on mount, 1860s, 7x7", SWN 4/24/89 330
HARTSOOK (American, California; 20th C)
Mary Pickford, full-figure/holds kitten; simulated autograph of sitter, 10x8", lot 279, CEG 6/23/89 25
Woodrow Wilson, seated w/pen in hand; 11x8", lot 281, CEG 6/23/89 75
HARVEY, Harold L.
Industrial Photomontage, matted, ca 1930s, 9x12", SBY 11/1/88 OE..... 2,530
New York, pigment, sgn/dtd/titled on verso, matted, 1930, 9x12", SBY 11/1/88 UE 605
Wheels, mounted/matted, ca 1928, 13x10", SBY 11/1/88 UE 605
HAUSMANN, Raoul (20th C)
Photogram A, slvr, sgn/titled/dtd/copyright on verso, 1953, 7x6", SWN 10/30/88..... 935
HAVILAND, Paul B.
New York at Night, Camera Work No 46; Pl 1, toned slvr, 1914, 6x8", SWN 10/30/88 990
HAVILAND, Paul E.
Lady in Shawl, pltn, matted, early 1900s, 7x5", SBY 11/1/88 OE..... 1,650
Miss GG, matted, ca 1908, 10x8", SBY 11/1/88 UE 605
HAVINDEN, John
Gretton Photographs, toned slvr, ca 1930, 8x10", SWN 4/24/89..... 385
Monte Carlo, slvr, copyright stp in mrg, 1930s, 9x7", SWN 4/24/89 385
Photomontage of Light Bulb with Stoplight, toned slvr, Grettonphoto Ltd/copyright stps, 1930, 9x6", SWN 10/30/88 OE 1,210
Smoker in a Tuxedo, slvr, mounted, 1930s, 11x8", SWN 10/30/88 660
IAYNES, Frank J.
Old Faithful Geyser, Yellowstone National Park; hc slvr, artist studio stp on img, early 1900s, 24x20", SBY 4/26/89 UE 1,100
IENLE, Fritz
Munich Central Station, sgn/titled on mount, repro limitation stp on verso, 1920s, 3x4", SBY 5/4/88 1,100
IENRI, Florence (20th C)
Jean Arp, 23/50, slvr, ink sgn on mount, ca 1929/1974, 9x7", SWN 4/24/89 770
Self-Portrait in Mirror, 13/50, sgn on mount, dtd 1974, matted, 1928/1974, 10x7", SBY 4/26/89 1,870
IESLER, Alexander; & AYRES, George B. (19th C)
Abraham Lincoln, alb, Ayres copyright bstp on recto/verso, 1860/1881, 10x7", SWN 4/24/89..... 1,100
HILL, David Octavius; & ADAMSON, Robert (19th C)
General John Munro of Teanich, calo, ca 1845, 8x6", SWN 4/24/89 UE 440
James Ballantine, David Octavius Hill, & Dr George Bell; calo tipped to gray album leaf, ca 1845, 5x8", SWN 4/24/89 OE..... 4,400
Royal Institution & Part of the Castle Edinburgh, #12, calo, sgn/dtd/titled, matted, 1844, 8x6", SBY 5/4/88 2,750
Sleeping Child, Miss Bell; calo, tipped at corners to album leaf, ca 1845, 6x8", SWN 10/30/88 1,760
Two Newhaven Fisherwomen, calo, tipped at corners to album leaf, ca 1845, 6x5", SWN 10/30/88..... 1,210

Woman, Full-Length, Standing; calo, tipped to album leaf, ca 1845, 8x6", SWN 10/30/88 UE 1,100

HILLERS, John K. (American, 1843-1925)
A-Sa-Wa-Ka-Red-I-Hewl, alb on gilt-ruled bl card mount, titled/credit on mount, 1870s, 9x8", SWN 10/30/88 385
Boulder Creek, Utah; alb on Smithsonian mount, ca 1870, 9x7", B/B 4/19/88 UE 192
Grand Canyon, Colorado River, Arizona; alb, artist credit/titled in negative, matted, 1871, fr, 13x10", SBY 5/4/88 1,210
Grand Canyon, Colorado; alb on gray Smithsonian mount, sgn/titled in negative, ca 1871, 13x10", SWN 10/30/88 1,430
Lemon's Peak, Utah; alb on gray Smithsonian mount, titled in negative, ca 1875, 10x13", SWN 4/24/89 880
Mary's Veil, Vuillion Canon, Utah; alb on gray Smithsonian mount, titled in negative, ca 1874, 13x10", SWN 4/24/89 825
Modisi, a Moki Girl; alb, sgn/titled in negative, mounted/matted, 9x7", SBY 11/1/88 770
Pillings Cascade, Bullion Canyon, Utah; alb on gray Smithsonian mount, titled/credited in negative, ca 1874, SWN 4/24/89 660
Zuni Transportation, alb on Smithsonian mount, credit/titled in negative, 1878, 7x9", B/B 10/4/88 468

HINE, Lewis W. (American, 1879-1940)
Coil Winding Room of the Westinghouse Electric & Manufacturing Company, late 1920s, orig fr, 15x19", SBY 11/1/88 2,420
Construction Worker, Empire State Building; slvr, Hastings-on-Hudson stp on verso, ca 1931, 8x10", SWN 10/30/88 UE 440
Girl at Loom, sgn/dtd/titled on verso, matted, ca 1910, 10x8", SBY 4/26/89 2,512
Joys & Sorrows of Ellis Island, #104, dtd/titled/#d on verso, mounted, 1905/1930s, 7x9", SBY 11/1/88 880
New York Is Such a Friendly Town, slvr on early exhibition mount, titled/credit on verso, 1915, 8x10", SWN 10/30/88 990
Pair: Cotton Mill Workers, Virginia; Young Factory Workers, Cincinnati; #d, matted, 1900s, 5x6", SBY 5/4/88 660
Red Cross Headquarters, Johnstown, New York; slvr, Hastings-on-Hudson stp on verso, early 1900s, 7x10", SWN 4/24/89 880
Track Walker on the Rails, slvr, Hastings-on-Hudson stp on verso, ca 1920, 5x7", SWN 10/30/88 413
Young Spinner in a Carolina Cotton Mill, slvr, titled/credit on verso, 1908/unknown, 8x10", SWN 10/30/88 OE 2,200

HOCKNEY, David (British, 1937-)
Portfolio: Twenty Photographic Pictures; 2/80, C-print, sgn/#d in mrg, 1970-1975/1976, 10x7", SBY 5/4/88 OE 12,650
Tulips in a Vase, Twenty Photographic Pictures; 22/80, intl in mrg, matted, early 1970s/ca 1975, 10x7", SBY 5/4/88 770
Walking in the Zen Garden at the Ryoanji Temple, Kyoto; 20/20, photocollage, sgn, 1983, fr, S-40x61", SBY 5/4/88 22,000

HOLLISTER (19th C)
Niagara Falls, couple in front of Horse Shoe Falls on Canadian side; ambro, half pl, cased, ca 1857, SWN 4/24/89 OE 413

HOPPE, Emil Otto
AA Milne with Pipe, #2615-L, slvr, tipped to board mount, 7 Crowell Pl S Kensington label, ca 1910-30, SWN 10/30/88 495
Aldous Huxley, #15811-C, toned slvr, tipped to board mount, 7 Cromwell Pl S Kensington label, ca 1910-30, SWN 10/30/88 330
George Bernard Shaw, #16076-D, toned slvr, tipped to board mount, 7 Cromwell Pl S Kensington label, 8x9", SWN 10/30/88 523
HG Wells, #1438, toned slvr, tipped to board mount, 7 Cromwell Pl S Kensington label, ca 1910-30, 9x7", SWN 10/30/88 UE 303
Industrial Study, toned slvr, flush-mounted to board, sgn/copyright stp on verso, 1920s, 6x9", SWN 10/30/88 UE 220
John Galsworthy, toned slvr, tipped to board mount, 7 Cromwell Pl S Kensington label, ca 1910-30, 37x8", SWN 10/30/88 UE 220
Martin Hardie, sgn on img, sgn/inscr To Sidney Woodward, South Kensington stp on verso, 1920s, fr, 10x7", C-NY 5/4/88 770
Vita Sackvill-West, #13074-Y, slvr, tipped to board mount, 7 Cromwell Pl S Kensington label, ca 1910-30, SWN 10/30/88 495
Walter de la Mare, #1841, slvr, tipped to board mount, 7 Crowell Pl S Kensington label, ca 1910-30, SWN 10/30/88 303

HORST, Horst P. (20th C)
Duchess of Windsor, Vogue Studio; p/s, copyright stp on verso, matted, 1940, 10x8", SBY 11/1/88 770
Gloria Vanderbilt, sgn/title label on verso, matted, 1940, 9x7", SBY 11/1/88 OE 3,025
Lisa (Fonssagrives-Penn), sgn/dtd/titled on verso, matted, ca 1940, 10x8", SBY 11/1/88 OE 2,750
Mainbocher Corset, 4/50, p/s, artist name stp on verso, matted, 1939/later, fr, 10x8", SBY 4/26/89 OE 2,475
Noel Coward, p/s on mount, sgn/titled/copyright stp on verso, matted, 1930s, 10x7", SBY 11/1/88 1,320
Nude (Lisa Fonssagrives Penn), p/s on verso, matted, early 1940s, 10x8", SBY 5/4/88 1,210
Portfolio: 12 Photographs; 20/75, p/s, copyright stp on verso, 1930s-40s/ca 1977, 19x16", slipcase, lot 416, SBY 4/26/89 3,575
Self-Portrait with Gertrude Stein, stp on verso, matted, 8x8", SBY 5/4/88 1,100

HOWE, G.M. (American, Portland, ME; fl 1853-1866)
Pair: Portraits of a Lady & Her Husband; dag, 6th pl, artist name stp on mat, full case, ca 1850s, CEG 5/7/88 60
Pair: Post Mortem of Girl with Roses in Hands Crossed at Chest; Her Mother; dag, 6th pl, sgn on mat, case, CEG 5/7/88 125

HOYNINGEN-HUENE, George (20th C)
Gertrude Lawrence & Noel Coward, Harper's Bazaar stp on verso, matted, ca 1947, 11x11", SBY 4/26/89 UE 550
Greece, hc slvr, sgn/dtd on img, matted, 1950, 15x20", SBY 5/4/88 1,760
Greta Garbo, mounted, late 1940s, 14x11", SBY 4/26/89 OE 2,475
Group of 3: Gertrude Lawrence; repro stps, ca 1928, 8x7", SBY 5/4/88 1,100

HUFFMAN, Laton Alton (American, Montana; -1931)
#300 Trailing Sheep, Powder River Badlands; deep sepia calo, copyright/dtd 1884, 8x10", CEG 1/13/89 35
BB Sheffield's Diamond W Ranch, Calabar, Montana; hc photo, sgn/titled on mat, 8x20", CEG 1/13/89 55
Hot Sheep, Powder River; hc photogr calo on linen weave card, copyright stp/titled on img, 8x10", CEG 1/13/89 25
Old Lu (Lu Bar) Cow Camp, North Montana, 1884; sepia calo, 9x18", CEG 1/13/89 80
Old Piper Dan Ranch, Tongue River; hc photo mounted on backing card, titled, 14x18", CEG 1/13/89 65
Sheep Grazing on Winter Bed Ground, sepia calo, 9x16", lot 275, CEG 1/13/89 45

HUGO, Leopold
Group of 5: California Coastal Landscapes; slvr, sgn, ca 1915, 9x7" to 13x10", B/B 10/4/88 OE 468

HURRELL, George (20th C)
Greta Garbo, slvr, sgn, 1930s/later, 10x9", B/B 10/4/88 UE 385
Jane Russell, 49/110, slvr, sgn, 1930s/ca 1980, fr, 10x14", B/B 10/4/88 715
Portfolio: Hurrell II; 85/110, 8 slvr, ink sgn in mrg, gray cloth case, 1920s-40s/ca 1980, B/B 4/19/88 990
Ramon Novarro, a/bstp in mrg, sgn/dtd on mat, inscr Sincerely Ramon Novarro on img, 1930, 13x10", SBY 11/1/88 1,100

INSLEY, Henry E. (American, fl 1840-1857)
Couple with Their Little Girl, child holds doll; dag, half pl, brass mat/leather case, 1840s, SWN 4/24/89 660

JACKSON, William Henry (American, 1843-1942)
Bee Hive Group of Geysers, Yellowstone Park; alb mounted to gilt-edged board, titled in negative, ca 1880, SWN 4/24/89 ... 1,210
Grand Canyon of the Yellowstone, alb on Hayden Geological Survey mount, titled in negative, 1870s, 13x10", SWN 4/24/89 ... 1,045
Joe Clark & Jose on Horseback, Bringing in Elk Meat, Teton Canyon; #302, alb, 1872, 7x9", SWN 10/30/88 ... 935
Rosemma Falls, Pike's Peak Trail; #320, alb mounted on heavy gilt-edged board, titled, 1880s, 10x14", SWN 4/24/89 ... 468

JACOBI, Lotte (20th C)
Kaethe Kollwitz, slvr, sgn twice/46 W 52nd St NYC stp on verso, 1930, 13x10", SWN 10/30/88 ... 935
Marc Chagall & Daughter, Ida, New York; p/s on img, 1945/later, 10x10", SBY 5/4/88 ... 770
Pair: Peter Lorre; Lotte Lenya; p/s on img, ca 1930/ca 1970s, 10x7"/8x9", SBY 4/26/89 ... 1,210
Paul Strand, slvr, p/s on recto, 1963/later, 10x8", SWN 10/30/88 UE ... 303
Photogenic, copyright stp on verso, matted, later 1940s/early 1950s, 10x8", SBY 11/1/88 ... 1,430
Photogenic, p/s on verso, matted, 1950s, 14x11", SBY 5/4/88 ... 990
Portfolio I, #11, total ed of 30, 10 photos, p/s on img, matted, 1928-1939, various sizes, cased, SBY 5/4/88 ... 5,500
Portrait of JD Salinger, p/s on img, studio stp on verso, matted, ca 1951, 10x8", SBY 5/4/88 ... 1,320

JAQUES, Ronny (20th C)
Marlon Brando As Stanley Kowalski in A Streetcar Named Desire, Harper's Bazaar stp, ca 1948, 12x10", SBY 4/26/89 OE ... 2,200

JENNINGS, Humphrey (20th C)
Wet Street of Paving Blocks, slvr, 1930s, 12x8", SWN 4/24/89 UE ... 550

JOB, Charles
Gypsy Camp, Ludfield; gum, sgn/titled in ink on verso, early 1900s, 6x8", SWN 10/30/88 UE ... 248

JOHNSTON, Alfred Cheney
Marilyn Miller, toned slvr, ink sgn on mount recto, a/bstp on img, 1920s, 13x9", SWN 10/30/88 ... 935
Marion Davies, slvr, ink sgn on mount recto, titled on mount verso, 1920s, 9x7", SWN 10/30/88 ... 935
Nude with Black Stockings, ink sgn, mounted/matted, ca 1922, 13x10", SBY 11/1/88 ... 3,630

JOHNSTON, Frances Benjamin
Organization of the 59th Congress New York Delegation Taking the Oath, pltn, sgn/dtd, matted, 1906, 8x10", SBY 4/26/89 ... 1,540

JOSEPHSON, Ken (20th C)
Portfolio: Ken Josephson; #8, total ed of 31, 10 photos, p/s on mount, 1961-73/ca 1975, 6x9", SBY 11/1/88 ... 1,980

KALLIN-FISCHER, Grit
Hilde Rantzsch, matted, ca 1927, 12x9", SBY 4/26/89 OE ... 5,500
Hilde Rantzsch (Negative Portrait), matted, ca 1927, 8x6", SBY 4/26/89 ... 2,475
Untitled Portrait, slvr w/ink & wht paint, sgn/inscr Knesebeckstrasse 96 Berlin Charl 2, ca 1927, 11x8", SBY 4/26/89 ... 4,675

KANAGA, Consuela
Pair: Girl in Straw Hat; Brooklyn Bridge; p/s on mount, 1940s & 1920s/later, matted, 13x9"/3x3", SBY 4/26/89 OE ... 3,575
Widow Watson (mother & son), slvr, p/s on mount, 1925, 4x3", SWN 10/30/88 OE ... 825

KARSH, Yousuf (American, 1908-)
Albert Einstein, ink sgn on mount, artist stp on verso, 1948/later, 17x16", SBY 5/4/88 OE ... 1,210
Albert Einstein, sgn in mrg, mounted/matted, 1948/1970s, 10x8", SBY 11/1/88 OE ... 2,200
Ernest Hemingway, sgn on mount, artist name stp on verso, 1957/later, 20x16", SBY 11/1/88 ... 990
Ernest Hemingway, sgn on mount, 1957/later, 20x16", SBY 4/26/89 OE ... 1,760
Ernest Hemingway, slvr, ink sgn on mount, stp on verso, 1957/1970s, 20x16", B/B 4/19/88 ... 715
George Bernard Shaw, p/s on img, copyright stp on verso, matted, 1943/1960s, fr, 9x7", SBY 11/1/88 ... 1,650
George Bernard Shaw, sgn/inscr Ottawa on img, sgn/inscr 130 Sparks St Ottawa on verso, 1943, fr, 20x16", SBY 4/26/89 ... 1,210

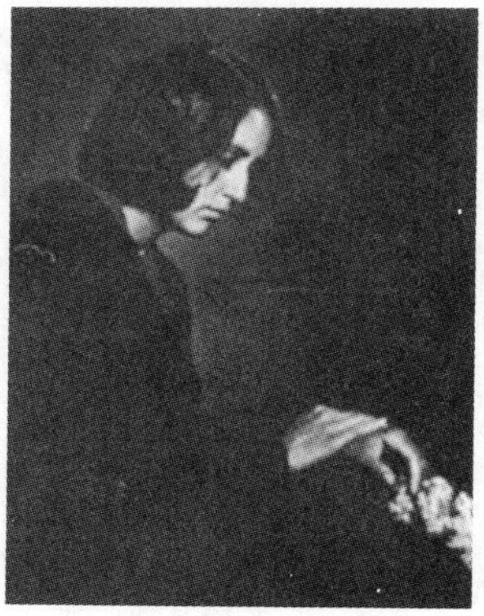

Joan Baez, slvr, sgn on mount, titled on verso, 1960s/later, 16x20", B/B 10/4/88; $715

Marc Chagall, slvr, ink sgn on mount, stp on mount verso, 1965/1970s, 16x18", B/B 4/19/88 ... 660
Pablo Casals, ink sgn on mount, artist stp on verso, 1954/later, 20x16", SBY 5/4/88 ... 880
Pair: Ernest Hemingway; George Bernard Shaw; sgn on mount, artist stp on verso, 1957 & 1943, 20x16", SBY 5/4/88 OE ... 1,540
Queen Elizabeth II & Prince Philip with Charles & Anne, p/s, sgn by sitters in mrg, 1951, 8x9", SBY 4/26/89 UE ... 880
Winston Churchill, artist name/copyright in negative, p/s in mrg, copyright stp on verso, 1941, fr, 9x7", SBY 4/26/89 OE ... 2,475
Winston Churchill, sgn in mrg, mounted, 1941/later, 20x16", SBY 11/1/88 OE ... 1,210
Winston Churchill, sgn on mount, stp on verso, 1941/later, 20x16", SBY 5/4/88 ... 990

KASEBIER, Gertrude (American, 1852-1934)
Boy with Dog, pltn, matted, early 1900s, 8x6", SBY 11/1/88 ... 3,575
Charlotte Paddock with Picnic Basket, pltn, inscr Paddock on verso, matted, early 1900s, 8x6", SBY 4/26/89 ... 1,980
Chief Kills-Close-to-the-Lodge, pltn, a/bstp on img, mk Copyright 1898 on mount, 1898, 8x6", SWN 4/24/89 ... 3,080

Frederick Evans, pltn, matted, early 1900s, 5x3", SBY 4/26/89 1,980
Misses Gerson, pltn, sgn on img, mounted/matted, ca 1900, 12x9", SBY 4/26/89 9,900
Nancy & Bubby (At Five Months) Autumn of 1900, pltn, titled on verso, double mounted/matted, 1900, 8x6", SBY 5/4/88 1,100
Pastoral, pltn on gray-gr paper, sgn/dtd on mount, matted, ca 1905, fr, 8x6", SBY 5/4/88.... 4,400

KEILEY, Joseph T.
Harbor Study, pltn, tipped to paper mount, ca 1901, 1x3", SWN 10/30/88 UE 275

KELLOGG, A.L.
Still Life of Dead Game, pltn, sgn/dtd on recto, artist copyright stp on verso, 1907, 14x11", SWN 4/24/89 413

KENNA, Michael (20th C)
Titled Poles, Rhyl, Wales; 5/45, slvr, sgn/dtd on mount, stp on mount verso, 1985, 6x10", B/B 4/19/88 468

KEPES, Gyorgy (20th C)
Chicago, sgn/dtd/titled on verso, matted, 1938, 14x11", SBY 5/4/88.... 550
Julia, ink sgn/dtd on img, p/s on verso, matted, 1939, 20x16", SBY 5/4/88 UE.... 1,320
Juliet's Shadow Caged, sgn/dtd on verso, matted, 1938, 12x9", SBY 4/26/89 2,200

KERTESZ, Andre (Hungarian, 1894-)
Accordionist, Esztergom; sgn/dtd/titled on verso, matted, 1916/later, fr, 16x18", SBY 4/26/89 1,210
Alexander Calder, sgn/dtd on verso, matted, 1929/later, fr, 8x10", SBY 5/4/88 1,430
Anne Marie Merkel, on post card, sgn/inscr Paris in mrg, matted, 1926, fr, 4x3", SBY 4/26/89 OE 18,700
At the Bistro, sgn/dtd/inscr Paris on verso, 1931/later, 11x13", SBY 11/1/88.... 990
Ballet, New York City; 67 W 44th Street studio stp on verso, matted, 1938, 8x9", SBY 4/26/89 3,300
Billboard, Paris; sgn/dtd/inscr Paris on verso, matted, 1931-33(?), fr, 2x2", SBY 4/26/89 OE.... 7,150
Boskay Ter, Budapest; p/s on verso, matted, 1914/later, 8x10", SBY 5/4/88 1,320
Brancusi with Giacometti; slvr, sgn/dtd on verso, 1929/1970s, sgn/dtd on verso, 10x8", B/B 4/19/88 UE 385
Brick Walls, sgn/dtd on verso, matted, 1962/later, fr, 10x7", SBY 4/26/89 1,210
Broken Plate, Paris; sgn/dtd on verso, matted, 1929/later, fr, 11x14", SBY 4/26/89 OE 2,750
Broken Plate, sgn/dtd/titled/inscr To Debby on verso, 1929/pre-1977, 16x20", SBY 5/4/88 1,980
Budapest, sgn/dtd/titled on verso, matted, 1915/later, fr, 11x14", SBY 5/4/88 1,210
Carrefour, sgn/dtd on verso, matted, 1930/later, 16x20", SBY 4/26/89 OE 3,300
Carrefour, sgn/dtd on verso, matted, 1930/later, 8x10", SBY 11/1/88 1,100
Chagall & His Family, sgn/dtd on verso, matted, 1933/later, 8x10", SBY 5/4/88 UE.... 550
Chez Mondrain, sgn/dtd/inscr Paris on verso, 1926/later, 10x7", SBY 11/1/88 OE.... 3,850
Chez Mondrian, p/s, dtd on verso, 1916/later, 14x10", SBY 4/26/89 OE.... 4,125
Chez Mondrian, sgn/dtd/titled on verso, matted, 1926/later, fr, 10x7", SBY 5/4/88 OE.... 2,420
Colette, Paris; sgn/dtd on verso, matted, 1930/later, fr, 8x10", SBY 4/26/89 OE 1,870
Disappearing Act, sgn/dtd/titled/copyright stp on verso, 1955/later, 10x8", SBY 11/1/88 OE.... 1,430
Distortion, dtd/#d 76/studio stp on verso, 1933/ca 1940s or 1950s, 8x9", SBY 5/4/88 880
Distortion 91 (Self-Portrait), sgn/inscr C'est Moi in mrg, sgn/dtd/inscr To Debbie on verso, 1933/pre-1977, SBY 5/4/88 1,430
Esztergom, dtd/titled on verso, matted, 1916, 2x2", SBY 4/26/89 2,475
Fork, sgn/dtd on verso, matted, 1928/later, fr, 8x9", SBY 11/1/88 OE.... 1,430
Fork, sgn/dtd/inscr Paris on verso, matted, 1928/later, 8x10", SBY 5/4/88 990
Goblet, sgn/dtd/inscr To Debbie on verso, 1943/pre-1977, 10x6", SBY 5/4/88.... 1,100
Hawaii, #4, sgn/dtd/#d on verso, 1974/later, 6x10", SBY 11/1/88 550
L'Hotel, inscr Eine Typhische Montmartre, artist name stp/label on verso, matted, ca 1927, fr, 9x7", SBY 11/1/88.... 1,980
La Loire, matted, ca 1934, 8x10", SBY 11/1/88 1,100
Landscape, p/s, Rue de Vanves Paris studio/repro stps on verso, matted, 1920s, 6x9", SBY 11/1/88.... 1,100
Lost Cloud, slvr, sgn/dtd/inscr New York on verso, 1937/later, 10x7", B/B 4/19/88 UE.... 1,540
Lovers, Budapest; sgn/dtd/titled on verso, matted, 1915/later, fr, 15x19", SBY 4/26/89.... 2,475
Mannequins, New York; dtd/artist name stp on verso, 1965, 10x7", SBY 11/1/88 880
Martinique, sgn/dtd/titled on verso, matted, 1972, 8x10", SBY 11/1/88 OE.... 1,760
Martinique, sgn/dtd/titled on verso, matted, 1972/later, 15x20", SBY 5/4/88 2,310
Martinique, sgn/dtd/titled on verso, 1972/later, 8x10", SBY 4/26/89 OE.... 3,300
Martinique, slvr, sgn/dtd on verso, 1972, 16x20", B/B 4/19/88 1,100

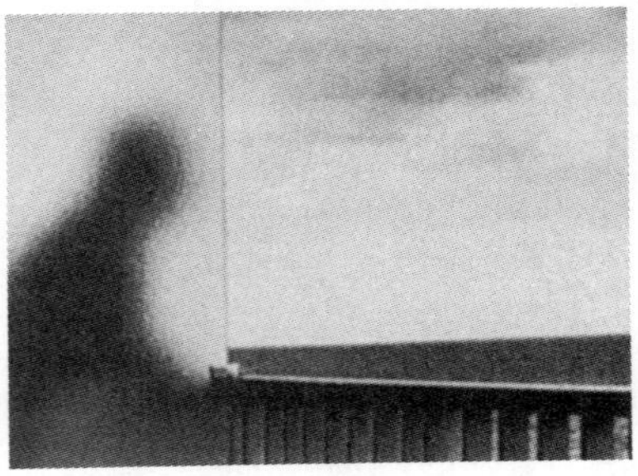

Martinique, slvr, sgn/dtd/titled, 1972, 11x14", B/B 10/4/88; $2,200

Meiji Shrine, Tokyo; sgn/dtd/titled on verso, matted, 1968/later, 7x10", SBY 5/4/88 770
Melancholic Tulip, sgn/dtd on verso, matted, 1939/later, fr, 14x10", SBY 4/26/89 OE 3,300
Melancholic Tulip, slvr, sgn/titled/dtd on verso, 1939/1976, 10x7", B/B 4/19/88 550
Metro, Paris; titled in German/studio stp on verso, matted, ca 1930, 6x8", SBY 4/26/89 UE 660
Monsieur Aguet, slvr on post card, sgn/inscr Paris on img, matted, 1927, fr, 4x2", SBY 11/1/88.... 9,900
New York, dtd/titled/artist name stp on verso, 1966, 10x8", SBY 4/26/89 1,320

New York, sgn/dtd 1960/inscr To Debbie Jan 10-1977, artist stp on verso, 1960/pre-1977, 14x11", SBY 5/4/88 ... 1,210
New York, slvr, sgn/dtd on mount, 1961/later, 10x7", SWN 10/30/88 ... 605
New York, 1961; slvr, sgn/dtd on mount, 1961/later, 10x7", SWN 10/30/88 ... 605
New York (Landing Pigeon), matted, 1960, 11x14", SBY 11/1/88 OE ... 2,200
Notre Dame, sgn/dtd/titled on verso, mounted/matted, 1925, fr, 3x3", SBY 4/26/89 OE ... 20,900
Ossip Zadkine in His Studio, on post card, sgn/inscr Paris in mrg, mounted/matted, 1926, 4x3", SBY 4/26/89 OE ... 9,350
Pair: Distortion 141; Distortion 6; sgn/dtd/titled/inscr To Debbie on verso, 1933/pre-1977, 8x9"/10x6", SBY 5/4/88 ... 1,100
Pair: Distortions 167; Distortion 96; sgn/titled/dtd/inscr To Debbie, 1933/pre-1977, 10x5"/10x6", SBY 5/4/88 ... 1,320
Portfolio: Photographs Volume I; 16/50, 10 photos, sgn/dtd on mount, 1913-1929/ca 1973, various sizes, SBY 11/1/88 ... 6,875
Portfolio: Photographs Volume II; 17/50, 10 photos, sgn/dtd on mount, 1930-72/ca 1973, various sizes, cased, SBY 11/1/88 ... 7,425
Promenade, New York, 17 October 1962; slvr, sgn/dtd on mount, 1962/later, 10x8", SWN 10/30/88 UE ... 413
Satiric Dancer, sgn/dtd on verso, matted, 1926/later, 10x8", SBY 11/1/88 OE ... 2,310
Satiric Dancer, sgn/dtd on verso, matted, 1926/later, 14x11", SBY 5/4/88 ... 2,090
Satiric Dancer, sgn/dtd/inscr Paris on verso, 1926/later, 10x8", SBY 4/26/89 OE ... 3,300
Satiric Dancer, slvr, sgn/dtd on verso, 1927/1970s, 19x15", lot 4802, B/B 4/19/88 ... 2,090
Satiric Dancer, slvr, sgn/dtd/inscr Paris on verso, 1926/1979, 10x8", B/B 4/19/88 ... 1,430
Shadows on the Sidewalk, sgn/dtd on verso, matted, 1931/later, 6x10", SBY 5/4/88 ... 1,210
Sidewalk, Paris; sgn/dtd on verso, 1929/later, 10x8", SBY 4/26/89 OE ... 1,430
St Jean du Doigt (finistere) Britany, dtd/titled/artist name stp on verso, 1931/later, 10x7", SBY 11/1/88 ... 880
Stairs of Montmartre, sgn/dtd on verso, matted, 1925/later, fr, 8x10", SBY 5/4/88 ... 1,100
Swimming, sgn/dtd on verso, 1919/later, 10x8", SBY 11/1/88 ... 880
Thornton Wilder, p/s, 67th W 44th Street studio stp on verso, matted, ca 1938, 9x8", SBY 4/26/89 ... 1,100
Tokyo, sgn/dtd/titled/artist name stp on verso, 1968, 10x8", SBY 4/26/89 OE ... 2,750
Torok-Balint, Hungary; sgn/dtd/titled on verso, matted, 1922/later, 7x10", SBY 5/4/88 UE ... 440
Washington Square, dtd/titled/copyright stps on verso, 1954/pre-1967, 10x7", SBY 11/1/88 OE ... 1,760
White Horse, New York; slvr, artist stp/dtd on verso, 1962, 14x10", SWN 4/24/89 ... 1,100
10th Street East, New York City; slvr, artist name stp/dtd on verso, 1960, 11x14", SWN 4/24/89 ... 825

KESTING, Edmund (20th C)
Bewegungstudie Einer Taenzerin (portrait of Dore Hoyer), slvr, titled/dtd on verso, 1946, 16x12", SWN 10/30/88 UE ... 385

KLEIN, William (20th C)
Hat with 3 Roses, sgn/dtd on verso, matted, 1956/later, 18x13", SBY 4/26/89 ... 2,200

KLOUB, Vaclav
Die Wendeltreppe des Turms auf der Burg Borozov in Maehren, slvr, Praque/Pawel Barchan stps, ca 1930s(?), SWN 4/24/89 ... 825

KOCH, R.
Study of Abstract Sculpture, toned slvr, credit on verso, 1920s, 7x4", SWN 10/30/88 ... 275

KOMARMELAMID (Russian, 20th C)
Portfolio: Catalogue of Superobjects Supercomfort for Superpeople; 36 photos, 1976, 8x10", boxed, SBY 4/26/89 ... 3,575

KOUDELKA, Josef (20th C)
Pair: Spain; Man with Pigeon; ink sgn in mrg, matted, 1960s/later, 9x14", SBY 11/1/88 OE ... 1,210

KRUGER, Barbara (20th C)
Now You See Us, photo on board, 1982, 74x48", lot 271, SBY 10/5/89 ... 38,500
We Have Received Orders Not To Move, 1/2, photo on board, 1982, 72x48", SBY 11/11/88 OE ... 35,750
What You See Is What You Get, photo, mounted on board, 1984, 54x50", lot 350, SBY 5/3/89 OE ... 44,000
You Are Giving Us the Evil Eye, photo, mounted on board, 1984, 48x76", lot 348, SBY 5/3/89 OE ... 49,500
Your Seeing Is Believing, photo on board, 1984, 45x98", lot 261, SBY 10/5/89 ... 24,750

KUEHN, Heinrich
Hans & Lotte on a Grassy Slope, pltn on tissue, matted, early 1900s, 8x11", SBY 5/4/88 OE ... 1,870
Hans in a Meadow, gum bcro, matted, ca 1905, fr, 14x18", SBY 4/26/89 ... 8,250
Mother & Child, photogr, early 1900s, 8x12", SBY 11/1/88 ... 1,650

LANGE, Dorothea
Fourth of July, Near Chapel Hill, North Carolina; slvr, FSA stp, typed caption on verso, 1930s, 8x8", SWN 4/24/89 ... 825

LARTIGUE, Jacques Henri
At the Beach, Etretat; ink sgn in mrg, early 1900s/later, 9x13", SBY 11/1/88 ... 715
Automobile Driver, ink sgn on img, matted, ca 1912/later, fr, 10x11", SBY 4/26/89 ... 660
Carriage Ride, sgn on img, copyright stp on verso, matted, early 1900s/later, 12x16", SBY 5/4/88 ... 880
Drag Racing Day at the Auteuil Races, sgn in mrg, matted, ca 1911/later, fr, 8x11", SBY 4/26/89 ... 1,100
Dudu, the Nanny, Tossing a Ball; toned slvr, ink sgn in mrg, early 1900s/later, 14x10", SWN 4/24/89 UE ... 440
First Prize of the ACF Dieppe Circuit, ink sgn/bstp in mrg, matted, 1912, 9x14", SBY 4/26/89 OE ... 2,750
Ma Cousine Simone Roussel, ink sgn on img, titled/dtd on verso, mounted/matted, 1913/later, fr, 12x16", SBY 4/26/89 ... 1,430
On the Beach, ink sgn in mrg, matted, early 1900s/later, 10x14", SBY 11/1/88 OE ... 2,475
Pair: Bibi in Marseilles; Woman Seated on a Pebble Beach; sgn in mrg, 1928 & 1900s/later, 8x12"/10x11", SBY 4/26/88 OE ... 3,300
Pair: Bichonnade; Tennis Player; sgn/bstp in mrg, matted, 1905 & early 1900s/later, fr, 10x12", 10x13", SBY 4/26/89 OE ... 3,850
Pair: Cousin Caro & Mr Plantevigne; Photographer's Parents at Pont de l'Arche; 1906 & 1902/later, SBY 4/26/89 OE ... 2,475
Pair: Early Flight, repro limitation/Rapho Guillumette Pictures stps on verso, early 1900s, 10x11"/10x12", SBY 11/1/88 ... 1,980
Pair: Storm, Biarritz; Zissou Takes Off in His ZYX 24, Rouzat; sgn, 1927 & 1910/later, fr, 7x14"/9x13", SBY 4/26/88 OE ... 3,025
Pair: Stormy Day; Two Children Astride a Log; ink sgn in mrg, matted, early 1900s/later, fr, 8x14"/10x13", SBY 4/26/89 ... 1,870
Zissou Playing Ball, toned slvr, ink sgn in mrg, early 1900s/later, 14x10", SWN 4/24/89 ... 550

LATIMER, Walter R. Sr.
Concourse, Jersey City, New Jersey Station; matted, 1915, 10x12", SBY 11/1/88 ... 880

LAUGHLIN, Clarence John (American, 1905-)
Around a Hole in Space: 1964; slvr, sgn/titled/dtd on recto, copyright stp on mount verso, 11x14", SWN 10/30/88 UE ... 413

Bird of the Death Dream, sgn/dtd/titled on mount, dtd/titled/studio stp on verso, matted, 1953, 11x12", SBY 4/26/89 1,100
Compressed, & Decompressed, Rectangles; sgn/dtd/titled on mount, copyright stp on verso, matted, 1952, 10x8", SBY 5/4/88 880
Enigma, sgn/dtd/titled in mrg, copyright stp/typed label on verso, mounted, 1941/1973, 14x11", SBY 11/1/88 1,430
Faceless Figure, dtd/typed label on verso, matted, early 1940s, 14x11", SBY 4/26/89 1,100
Grandeur & Ruin (No 1) (Belle Grove Plantation), sgn/dtd/titled/studio stp, 1948, fr, 11x14", SBY 4/26/89 660
Pair: Clock in Suspended Time; Poem for a Lost Time; 627 Decatur Street stp, 1950 & 1954, 13x11"/10x8", SBY 4/26/89 1,100
Passage to Never Land, sgn/dtd/titled/studio stp on verso, matted, 1958, fr, 11x13", SBY 4/26/89 OE 4,950
Repulsive Bed, sgn/dtd/titled on mount, matted, 1941, 16x20", SBY 4/26/89 1,650

LAVENSON, Alma
Tanks-Standard Oil Co; sgn on mount, Piedmont studio/exhibition labels on verso, matted, 1931, 10x7", SBY 4/26/89 OE 8,800

LE GRAY, Gustave (19th C)
Brig Upon the Water, alb, mounted, 1858-59, 13x16", SWN 10/30/88 UE 825

LEATHERDALE, Marcus (20th C)
Pair: Lisa Lyon I; Lisa Lyon II; sgn/dtd/titled/artist name & copyright stps, 1980/1984-85, SBY 4/26/89 1,210

LENORMAND, Charles (19th C)
Monaco Cathedrale, Terrasse Espanade Devant le Portail; alb, titled/artist stp on mount, ca 1870, 12x10", SWN 4/24/89 1,430

LEVITT, Helen (20th C)
Mexico, slvr, sgn/titled/dtd on verso, 1941/later, 7x9", B/B 4/19/88 330
Wall Drawing, matted, ca 1941, 9x7", SBY 4/26/89 1,650

LILIENTHAL, Theodore (American, New Orleans, LA; 19th C)
Album: Series of Views of New Orleans & Vicinity; 24 alb, mounted, ca 1880, 4x3", gilt brn leather cover, SBY 5/4/88 660
General Franklin Gardner, vignetted/bust-length; CDV, artist stp, lot 240, CEG 6/23/89 70

LINCOLN, Edwin Hale
Group of 3: Caraway; Swamp Milkweed; Fireweed, Great Willow Herb; pltn, titled/#d on mount, 1904, 9x7", B/B 10/4/88 275

LINK, O. Winston (20th C)
At the Drive-In, sgn/dtd/studio & copyright stps on verso, matted, 1950s/1986, 16x20", SBY 5/4/88 OE 2,970
Hot Shot Eastbound, Iaeger, West Virginia; sgn/dtd/studio & copyright stps on verso, 1956/1987, 16x20", SBY 11/1/88 OE 2,530
Hot Shot Eastbound, Iaeger, West Virginia; sgn/dtd/studio stp on verso, matted, 1956/1986, 16x20", SBY 4/26/89 OE 2,475
Maud Bows to the Virginia Creeper, Green Cove, Virginia; slvr, studio stp/sgn/dtd, 1956/1988, 16x19", SWN 4/24/89 770
Pair: Main Line on Main Street; No 17 at Rural Retreat; sgn/dtd/stps on verso, 1957-58/1987, 15x18", SBY 11/1/88 1,430
Swimming Pool, Welch, West Virginia; slvr, 381 Park Ave South/copyright stps, 1958/1986, 16x19", SWN 4/24/89 605

LIST, Herbert (20th C)
Am Strand, North Sea; artist name stp on verso, matted, ca 1933, 15x12", SBY 4/26/89 UE 880
Bicycle, Paris; Paris studio & gallery exhibition stps on verso, 1930s, 10x9", SBY 4/26/89 1,320
Chapel, artist name stp on verso, matted, 1930s, 14x11", SBY 11/1/88 1,650
Colette, copyright stp on verso, early 1950s, 11x8", SBY 11/1/88 660
Collage, photocollage, dtd/titled/artist name stp on verso, matted, 1936, 11x9", SBY 4/26/89 UE 1,100
Couple Embracing, artist name stp on verso, matted, 1950s, 11x9", SBY 4/26/89 2,475
Delos, slvr, titled/stp on verso, 1937, 9x11", B/B 4/19/88 OE 935
In the Shower, artist name stp on verso, matted, 1930s, 12x6", SBY 11/1/88 OE 2,530
Man in Cap, Denim Shorts, & Boots; slvr, artist name stp on verso, 1950s, 9x12", SWN 4/24/89 1,540
Steamer, matted, 1930s, 10x9", SBY 4/26/89 OE 7,700

LOOMIS, G.H. (American?, Boston, MA; fl ca 1860s)
General William M McArthur, fully uniformed; CDV, artist backstamp, lot 1035, CEG 5/7/88 60

LUMMIS, Charles (19th C)
Study of an Adobe Inerior with Seated Man, cyan, ca 1888, 5x7", SWN 4/24/89 OE 220

LYNES, George Platt (American, 1907-1955)
Boat Abstraction, artist name stp in mrg, mounted/matted, ca 1940s, 7x5", SBY 4/26/89 1,320
Burt Lancaster, crayon sgn on mount, fr, 1940s, 10x8", SBY 11/1/88 880
Gertrude Stein, slvr, titled/stp on verso, 1934, 9x7", B/B 4/19/88 UE 220
Group of 5: Yul Brynner; 4 artist name stp/1 studio stp/1 proof stp on verso, matted, 1942, various sizes, SBY 11/1/88 3,575
Machinery Abstraction, artist name stp on mat, mounted, 1930s, fr, 7x5", SBY 4/26/89 OE 3,025
Nude Study, studio stamp on verso, matted, 1950s, fr, 9x7", SBY 5/4/88 660
Pair: Nude Studies of Ted Starkowski; slvr, artist/collector stps on verso, ca 1953, 9x8", B/B 10/4/88 495
Pair: Nude Studies; artist name stp on verso, matted, 1940s, 9x8", SBY 4/26/89 OE 1,760

LYON, Danny (20th C)
Cottonpickers, Ferguson Unit TDC; sgn/dtd/titled on verso, mounted/matted, 1969, fr, 9x12", SBY 5/4/88 550
Inmate Outside Warden's Office About To Be Transferred by Local Authorities, slvr, 1968/1970s, 14x9", B/B 4/19/88 220
Pair: Cell Block Table; Weight Lifters; p/s on verso, matted, late 1960s/later, 8x12", SBY 4/26/89 OE 2,090
Pair: Shakedown; Shakedown Before Returning to the Building; p/s on verso, matted, 1960s/later, 8x12", SBY 4/26/89 UE 440
Track, McHenry, Illinois, From the Bikeriders; slvr, sgn/dtd/titled, 1965, no size given, B/B 10/4/88 275
Truck in the Desert, Yuma, California; slvr, sgn/titled/dtd on verso, 1962/later, 9x13", B/B 4/19/88 192

LYON, Nathan (20th C)
Wall Mural, slvr, sgn/dtd on mount, Photographic Studies Workshop label on verso, 1957, fr, 8x10", B/B 10/4/88 192

MAC PHERSON, Robert (19th C)
Group of 9: Italian Architectural Views; alb, titled/#d, 1860s, 12x16", B/B 10/4/88 OE 1,980

MACRAE, Wendell (20th C)
Rockefeller Center, Christmas, 1940; slvr, Rockefeller Center stp on verso, 1940, 8x10", SWN 10/30/88 UE 303

MAGRAS, J. (American, Boston, MA; fl ca 1850s)
Black Sailor in Full Uniform, tntp, 6th pl, loss of emulsion at top area beneath paper mat, CEG 5/7/88 110

MAN-RAY (Emmanuel Radinski)(American, 1890-1976)

Alexander Alekhine, Chess Champion; backed w/card, sgn/dtd/inscr Paris 1928, matted, 1928, fr, 9x6", SBY 5/4/88 ... 2,475
Au Chateau Tremblant, Paris; slvr, p/s on img, ca 1930, 7x9", B/B 4/19/88 ... 3,300
Danger/Dancer, sgn/titled/inscr on verso, matted, ca 1922, 8x5", SBY 5/4/88 ... 5,775
De Mode Signee, mounted on archival card, sgn on img, matted, 1930s, 9x7", SBY 4/26/89 OE ... 12,100
Group of 3: A Passing Buddy, Yacht on the Mediterranean; Portrait of a Mother & Child; Portrait of a Man; SBY 5/4/88 ... 1,430
Group of 3: Homage a Harpo et Atget!; mounted on fld card tomake booklet, 1920, 12x8", plexiglas box, SBY 4/26/89 ... 5,500
Henri Matisse, slvr, 31 Bis Rue Campagne Premiere stp on verso, p/s on mount, 1920s, 8x6", SWN 4/24/89 OE ... 7,700
Joan Miro, 81 bis Rue Campagne Premiere/atelier stps on verso, matted, late 1920s/early 1930s, fr, 9x7", SBY 5/4/88 ... 3,575
Kiki, slvr, p/s, 31 Bis Rue Campagne Premiere stp on verso, 1920s, 8x7", SWN 10/30/88 OE ... 2,750
Kiki, slvr, 1924, 9x7", SWN 10/30/88 OE ... 2,860
Kiki (female portrait), slvr, 31 Bis Rue Campagne Premiere stp on verso, ca 1925, 6x5", SWN 4/24/89 OE ... 4,620
Lamp of the Borgias, slvr, sgn/titled in red pencil on verso, 1930s, 7x5", SWN 4/24/89 ... 1,320
Mathematical Object, tip-mounted on blk card, studio/artist name stps on verso, 1936, fr, 12x9", SBY 11/1/88 ... 3,960
Portrait of Duchamp, artist name stp on verso, matted, ca 1930s/1960s, 11x9", SBY 4/26/89 OE ... 3,300
Scene on a Beach, slvr, 8 Rue du Val-de-Grace Paris 5/repro limitation stps on verso, ca 1925, 10x8", SWN 4/24/89 ... 2,200
Still Life, slvr, tipped to paper mount, sgn/dtd on mount recto, stp on verso, 1935, 9x7", SWN 10/30/88 ... 2,860
Study for Illustration of Louis Aragon's Poem, Aurelion; slvr, artist stp/titled, 1960s, 11x9", SWN 4/24/89 ... 1,430
Study of Legs in Stockings & Heels, slvr, 31 Bis Rue Campagne Premiere stp on verso, 1920s, 6x5", SWN 10/30/88 OE ... 6,600
Thistles, slvr, intl in corner, ca 1930/unknown, 11x9", SWN 4/24/89 ... 5,280
Untitled, orig rayograph, p/s on img, dtd/31 bis rue Campagne Premiere stp on verso, matted, 1926, 14x11", SBY 5/4/88 ... 37,400
Untitled (Crank), slvr of rayograph, sgn/dtd in negative, artist name stp on verso, 1923/1960s, 11x9", SBY 11/1/88 ... 2,475
Untitled (Self-Portrait), slvr of rayograph, sgn in negative, name stps on verso, 1920s/1960s, 12x9", SBY 11/1/88 ... 3,575
Untitled (sphere/cone/wooden figure), sgn/Rue du Val-de-Grace stp on verso, matted, ca 1926, 11x14", SBY 5/4/88 ... 6,600
Untitled (Spiral), slvr of rayograph, artist name/credit stps on verso, 1920s/1960s, 11x9", SBY 11/1/88 ... 1,760
Untitled Rayograph, slvr, sgn/dtd in negative, p/s on img, sgn on vero, 1920s/1960s, 11x9", lot 169, SBY 4/26/89 ... 2,750
Woman (portrait of Meret Oppenheim?), solarized slvr, sgn/dtd on recto, 1931, 7x4", SWN 10/30/88 OE ... 5,940

MANTZ, Werner

Koln (Architectural Montage), sgn/dtd/titled on verso, matted, 1928, 6x9", SBY 4/26/89 ... 1,980

MAPPLETHORPE, Robert (American, 1946-)

Ajitto, 8/15, sgn/dtd in mrg, sgn/dtd/copyright stp on verso, matted, 1981, fr, 18x18", SBY 4/26/89 OE ... 7,150
Bean Rundgren, sgn/dtd/inscr For Clarissa, backed w/card, matted, 1983, fr, 19x15", SBY 4/26/89 ... 3,300
Calla Lily, 5/7, dye clr, sgn/dtd in mrg, copyright stp on verso, 1987/1988, 19x19", SBY 4/26/89 OE ... 16,500
Contact, a/p, aside from ed of 10, sgn/dtd in mrg, sgn/dtd/copyright stp on verso, 1979, fr, 14x14", SBY 5/4/88 OE ... 2,640
Dennis Walsh, ed of 10, sgn/dtd in mrg, backed w/card, 1976, fr, 15x15", lot 628, SBY 4/26/89 OE ... 4,675
Dennis Walsh, ed of 10, sgn/dtd/inscr For Dennis on img, 1979, 19x15", lot 627, SBY 4/26/89 OE ... 6,050
Francois` Nose; slvr on wht/bl/yel or red paper, sgn/dtd 74 on verso, ca 1975, trapezoidal fr, 23x23", SBY 5/4/88 OE ... 6,875
George Bussey, 1/10, sgn/dtd/copyright stp on verso, backed w/card, 1979, 14x14", SBY 4/26/89 OE ... 4,675
Group of 3: Carnations & Striped Vase; 1/10, backed w/card & matted together, 1984, fr, 15x45" overall, SBY 4/26/89 OE ... 8,800
Group of 3: Floral Studies, Y Portfolio; 1/25, sgn/#d on mount, matted, 1978, fr, 8x8", SBY 11/1/88 OE ... 2,200
Ken Moody, ed of 60, clr photogr, sgn/inscr For Ken in mrg, 1984, 22x18", SBY 4/26/89 ... 3,025
Ken Moody & Robert Sherman, ed of 10, sgn/dtd/inscr For Ken, backed w/card, 1984, 15x19", SBY 4/26/89 OE ... 8,250
Man Seated on Chair, 3/15, sgn in mrg, sgn/dtd/copyright stp on verso, backed w/card, 1981, 14x14", SBY 4/26/89 OE ... 4,125
Nude (Ken Moody), ed of 10, sgn/dtd/inscr For Ken in mrg, backed w/card, 15x15", SBY 4/26/89 OE ... 8,250
Nude Torso, 4/15, sgn/dtd in mrg, sgn/dtd/copyright stp on verso, 1980, 14x14", SBY 4/26/89 OE ... 7,700
Orchid & Palmetto, backed w/card, sgn/dtd/inscr Artist Proof in mrg, copyright stp on verso, 1982, 15x15", SBY 11/1/88 ... 2,860
Orchids, 4/15, sgn/dtd in mrg, copyright stp on verso, matted, 1980, fr, 14x14", SBY 4/26/89 OE ... 7,150
Phillip, backed w/card, ink sgn in mrg, sgn/dtd/copyright stp on verso, silk mat, 1979, fr, 20x20", SBY 11/1/88 ... 3,850
Portfolio: Flowers; aside from ed of 40, 10 photogr, sgn/inscr PP in mrg, 1984, 22x18", boxed, SBY 11/1/88 OE ... 26,400
Portfolio: Flowers; 16/40, 10 photogr, sgn/#d in mrg, 1984, 22x18", boxed, Barbara Gladstone Gallery, SBY 4/26/89 OE ... 39,600
Portrait of a Tattooed Man, 3/15, sgn/dtd in mrg, copyright stp on verso, matted, 1980, fr, 14x14", SBY 5/4/88 OE ... 1,430
Robert Sherman, ed of 10, sgn/dtd/inscr For Robert in mrg, 1983, fr, 15x15", SBY 4/26/89 ... 4,400
Tattooed Man Standing, 2/10, sgn/dtd/copyright stps on verso, matted, 1982, fr, 19x15", SBY 5/4/88 OE ... 1,540

MARTIN, W.H.

Geronimo, Greatest Indian Chief, As a US Prisoner; on post card, 1909, CEG 5/7/88 ... 65

MARVILLE, Charles (19th C)

Chartes Cathedral, sltp, sgn/dtd in negative, 1854, 14x10", B/B 10/4/88 ... 468

MARVILLE, Charles; att (19th C)

Vue du Pont des Arts, Melanges Photographiques; Pl 33, sltp, titled/credits on mount, early 1850s, 6x8", SBY 11/1/88 ... 880

MATHER, Margrethe

Johan Hagemyer (sic) & Edward Weston, pltn mounted on cream card, sgn/dtd/titled on mount, 1921, 8x7", SBY 5/4/88 OE ... 30,800

MAYNARD, Florence; & MAYNARD, Karl

Mother & Children, p/s on img, intl on mount, matted, early 1900s, 13x7", SBY 11/1/88 ... 770

MC CLESS, J.E. (American, Philadelphia, PA; 19th C)

US Grant in Civil War General's Uniform, hand on hip/other hand on chair; lot 1085, CEG 5/7/88 ... 55

MEATYARD, Ralph Eugene (20th C)

Child with Doll, sgn by Madelyn Meatyard/Lexington studio stp on verso, mounted, 1960s, 7x8", SBY 11/1/88 OE ... 1,870
Portfolio 3: Work of Ralph Eugene Meatyard; #42, total ed of 130, 10 photos, 1959-71/ca 1974, 7x7", SBY 4/26/89 OE ... 2,475
Untitled, #2, sgn/dtd/addressed twice on verso, matted, 1958, 10x6", SBY 4/26/89 ... 1,100

METZNER, Sheila (20th C)

Eyvan, bstp in mrg, matted, 1978, fr, 18x13", SBY 5/4/88 UE ... 440

Pair: Flower Still Life; fresson, a/bstp in mrg, sgn/dtd on verso, matted, 1981, 16x11", SBY 11/1/88 ... 1,430

MEYER, see De Meyer

MEYEROWITZ, Joel (20th C)

Provincetown, ektacolor, sgn/titled/dtd on verso, 1977, 20x16", B/B 4/19/88 ... 385

MICHALS, Duane (20th C)

Bill Brandt, sgn/titled in mrg, 1974, 5x7", SBY 11/1/88 ... 550
Bound Woman, 1/25, sgn/titled/#d in mrg, matted, 1969, fr, 5x7", SBY 11/1/88 ... 495
Letter From My Father, 19/25, sgn/dtd/titled in mrg, mounted/matted, 1970s, 5x7", SBY 11/1/88 OE ... 1,760
Unfortunate Man, 4/25, sgn/titled in mrg, matted, 1976, fr, 5x7", SBY 4/26/89 OE ... 1,760

MILI, Gjon (20th C)

New York Horse Show, dtd/titled/studio & Romeo Martinez Collection stps on verso, 1948, 13x10", SBY 5/4/88 ... 550

MILLER, Milton (19th C)

Aristocratic Chinese Lady, possibly wife of Huang Tsan-t'ang; alb, ca 1862, 11x8", SWN 4/24/89 ... 358

MINICK, Roger (20th C)

Pair: Walnut Grove, California, 1967; Sacramento Delta, 1969; slvr, p/s on mount, 16x20", B/B 4/19/88 ... 220

MISRACH, Richard (20th C)

Landscape Near Lake Mead (#1), 1/25, dye, sgn/dtd/titled in mrg, matted, 1986, fr, 18x23", SBY 4/26/89 ... 990

MODEL, Lisette (20th C)

Banker, Wall Street; sgn on verso, matted, ca 1945, fr, 13x10", SBY 11/1/88 ... 3,025
Beggar, Paris; mounted on nspt backed w/card, matted, ca 1937, fr, 11x9", SBY 5/4/88 ... 1,870
Bridal Shop Window, sgn on verso, matted, 1940s, fr, 13x11", SBY 11/1/88 UE ... 1,100
Fifth Avenue, sgn/copyright stp on verso, matted, ca 1942, 14x11", SBY 5/4/88 OE ... 4,675
Portfolio: Twelve Photographs; 49/75, 10 photos (lacks 2 pls), sgn/copyright stp on verso, 1930s-40s/ca 1977, SBY 11/1/88 ... 3,300
Woman, San Francisco; 18/75, slvr, p/s & stp on verso, ca 1947/1977, 20x16", B/B 4/19/88 ... 330

MOHOLY, Lucia

Charlady, slvr, sgn/titled/Mecklenburg Square & copyright stps on verso, 1930s, 12x10", SWN 10/30/88 ... 550
Man's Hand (Blackett) Smoking Pipe, slvr, 39 Mecklenburg Squre studio stp on verso, 1930s, 9x7", SWN 4/24/89 ... 660
Self-Portrait, slvr, sgn in ink, dtd/copyright stp on verso, 1931, 3x4", SWN 4/24/89 ... 770

MOHOLY-NAGY, Laszlo (American/Hungarian, 1895-1946)

Arrival (Scandinavia), sgn/Fredericiastr 27 Berlin studio stp on verso, matted, ca 1930, 10x7", SBY 4/26/89 OE ... 25,300
Blumenphotogramm, photogram, sgn/titled/dtd on verso, matted, 1925, 9x7", lot 383, SBY 11/1/88 OE ... 16,500
Kameraloses (Without a Camera) Fotogramm, photogram, sgn/dtd/titled/name stp on verso, 1925, 9x7", SBY 11/1/88 OE ... 33,000
LK II, slvr of a painting by Moholy-Nagy, sgn/dtd/titled on verso, 1936, 5x5", SBY 5/4/88 OE ... 2,310
Lucia, artist name stp on verso, matted, 1920s, 4x3", SBY 11/1/88 ... 1,210
Lucia Moholy, slvr, 1920s, 3x2", SWN 10/30/88 ... 715
Marseille, titled/Fredericiastr 27 Berlin studio & Foto Moholy-Nagy stps on verso, ca 1929, 11x9", SBY 4/26/89 OE ... 10,450
Oscar Schlemmer, matted, 1926, 9x7", SBY 4/26/89 OE ... 18,700
Photogram, matted, ca 1925, 7x9", lot 386, SBY 11/1/88 OE ... 27,500
Photogram, matted, ca 1925, 9x7", lot 384, SBY 11/1/88 OE ... 18,700
Photogram, p/s on verso, matted, late 1920s/early 1930s, 10x8", lot 387, SBY 11/1/88 OE ... 34,100
Photogram, sepia-toned photogram, sgn Moholy-Nagy/intl on verso, matted, early 1920s, 5x7", SBY 11/1/88 OE ... 49,500
Photogram, sepia-toned photogram, sgn/inscr Photogramm Fur die Klischeeanstalt, Berlin stp, 1925, 9x7", SBY 11/1/88 OE ... 50,600
Photogram, sgn/dtd/inscr Photogram on verso, matted, 1939, 8x10", lot 382, SBY 11/1/88 OE ... 14,300
Photogram (Self-Portrait), matted, ca 1926, 10x7", lot 381, SBY 11/1/88 OE ... 27,500
Sailor, sgn/typed paper title label on verso, matted, ca 1927, 9x7", SBY 4/26/89 OE ... 12,100
Ship's Deck, Fredericiastr 27 Berlin studio stp/Foto Moholy-Nagy stps on verso, matted, ca 1930, 9x7", SBY 4/26/89 OE ... 7,150
Spreewald, sgn/titled on verso, matted, 1930s, 9x7", SBY 11/1/88 ... 1,650
Telegraphed Cinema, slvr of photogram mounted on card, matted, 1925, fr, 38x27", SBY 5/4/88 ... 16,500
Untitled, photogram, sgn/dtd on verso, matted, 1929, 12x9", lot 190, SBY 4/26/89 ... 33,000
Untitled, photogram, sgn/dtd on verso, matted, 1929, 12x9", lot 189, SBY 4/26/89 OE ... 71,500
Untitled, photogram, sgn/dtd on verso, matted, 1929, 9x12", lot 191, SBY 4/26/89 ... 30,250

MOLE, Arthur; & THOMAS, John D.

Human US Shield, 30,000 Officers & Men, Camp Custer...; slvr, titled, credit/copyright stps, 1918, 13x11", SWN 4/24/89 ... 825

MOLINIER, Pierre (20th C)

Festin de Manes, slvr, sgn/titled, 1967, 8x6", B/B 10/4/88 ... 990

MONVEL, see De Monvel

MOON, Karl

Indian Sampson, toned slvr, sgn/dtd in corner, Fred Harvey copyright stp, titled on mount, 1907, 8x9", SWN 10/30/88 UE ... 468
Pair: Black Jar; Corn Maiden; toned slvr, copyright bstp on img, titled on mount, 1914, 14x17", SWN 10/30/88 ... 770
Warrior's Return, brom, sgn/dtd 1930/titled/inscr Taos, 1900/later, 14x17", B/B 10/4/88 ... 935

MOORE, Henry (British, 1898-1986)

Figure (Sculpture of Bird's-Eye Marble), sgn/titled/Museum of Modern Art Library stps on verso, 1938, 11x8", SBY 4/26/89 ... 1,980

MOORE, Henry P. (19th C)

Nursery at Elliott's, Hilton Head, South Carolina; alb, credit label on mount, ca 1862, 5x8", SWN 4/24/89 UE ... 300

MOORHOUSE, Cultus George

Indian (seated) & His Wife (standing/wearing blanket & tradecloth dress), sepia toned, matted, 14x11", CEG 5/7/88 ... 80
Indian Girl in Bead & Bone Decorated Dress, Eagle Dollar Pendant, Bone Necklace; sepia toned, matted, 14x11", CEG 5/7/88 ... 85
Indian Squaw with Papoose in Cradleboard, standing/3-quarter pose; sepia toned, matted, 14x11", CEG 5/7/88 ... 70
Plains Chieftan Wearing Pipe-Bone Necklace Choker, Eagle Talon Necklace, & Full Headdress; matted, 14x11", CEG 5/7/88 ... 140
Plains Indian Warrior in Full Costume, standing/3-quarter side pose; sepia toned, pl/s, matted, 14x11", CEG 5/7/88 ... 160

MORGAN, Barbara (American, 1900-)

Letter to the World (Kick), slvr, sgn/dtd on mount & mount verso, 1938-72/1979, 10x13", B/B 4/19/88 UE 330

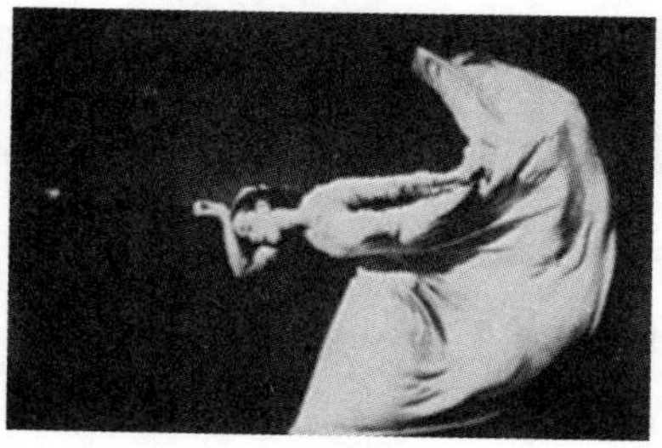

Martha Graham-Letter to the World (Kick); slvr, sgn/dtd/titled, 1940/1980, 13x18", B/B 10/4/88; $660

Martha Graham-Letter to the World; sgn/dtd/titled on mount, copyright/credit stps, 1940/1980, 15x19", SBY 4/26/89 OE 2,420
Pair: Martha Graham-Letter to the World (Kick); Martha Graham-Letter to the World (Swirl); 1940/1975-76, SBY 5/4/88 1,100
Pair: Spring on Madison Square; City Shell; sgn/dtd/titled, 1938/1970s, 15x18"/9x7", SBY 11/1/88 UE 660
Spring on Madison Square, slvr, sgn/dtd/titled in mrg, 1938/ca 1980, 14x17", B/B 10/4/88 522
Spring on Madison Square, slvr, sgn/titled/dtd on mount & vemount verso, 1938-72/1979, 10x13", B/B 4/19/88 UE 275

MORIN, Jacques L. (20th C)

Rosa Ponselle in the Music Room at Villa Pace, sgn on mat, ca 1955, 13x10", C-E 11/15/88 220

MORROW, S.J. (Dakota Studios at Yankton, 19th C)

Rain-In-Face, holds pipe/blanket; stereo on cream-yellow mount, ca 1870s, CEG 5/7/88 125

MORTENSEN, William (20th C)

George Dunham-In the Manner of El Greco; hc slvr, sgn/dtd/titled in mrg, 1957, 13x11", SBY 11/1/88 UE 660
Pair: Girl of Zaragoza; Asleep; sgn/titled in mrg, 1930s, 13x11"/11x12", SBY 4/26/89 OE 3,025

MOSES & PIFFET (American, New Orleans, LA; 19th C)

Confederate Officer, full uniform/sword at side/campaign hat on pedestal; CDV, a/bstp, lot 241, CEG 6/23/89 125

MOULIN, Gabriel (Spring Valley Water Co.)

Book: Typical Views of San Francisco's Water Supply & Surroundings; 50 slvr, 1910, 8x10", leather cover, B/B 10/4/88 OE 412

MUCHA, Alphonse (Czechoslovakian, 1860-1939)

Boy with a Basket, ink grid on img, mounted/matted, early 1900s, 5x4", SBY 5/4/88 660
Judith se Redresse, Fiere d'Aboir Sauve son Pueple; alb or slvr brml, studio stp on mount verso, 1890s, SWN 10/30/88 715

MULLINS, William J.

Evening, North(?) River; pltn, triple-mounted, p/s on mount recto, titled on verso, early 1900s, 1x4", SWN 10/30/88 UE 220
Landscape II, pltn, double mounted/matted, ca 1900, 3x4", SBY 11/1/88 UE 660

MULLOCK, Ben (19th C)

Pair: South American Studies of Bahia Passenger Station & S Anna do Catu; #308 & #204, alb, 1860, 7x10", SWN 4/24/89 UE 330

MUNKACSI, Martin

Group of 3: Kasetrager auf dem Market, Holland; Woman on Ladder Pulling On Silk Stocking; Dog Market; 1930s, SBY 5/4/88 880
Schatten, Berlin studio stp on verso, matted, 1928, 11x9", SBY 4/26/89 OE 8,250

MUYBRIDGE, Eadweard (American, 1830-1904)

Album: Panorama of San Francisco From California Street Hill; 11 alb, 1877, 7x8", gilt fabric cover, SBY 4/26/89 OE 8,800
Album: Panorama of San Francisco; 13 alb, copyright on img, mounted 1 on page, 1877, 23x16", SBY 4/26/89 OE 132,000
Animal Locomotion, Pl 396, collo, printed series titled/copyright stp, 1887, oblong folio, SWN 10/30/88 330
Confluence of the Merced & Yosemite Creek, Yosemite Valley; alb, ca 1869/1870s, 17x21", Bradley & Rulofson, SBY 11/1/88 990
Group of 18: Animal Locomotion; collo, artist credit/#d/copyright dtd in mrg, ca 1887, S-19x24", SBY 11/1/88 OE 2,970
Group of 29: Animal Locomotion; collo, artist credit/#d/copyright dtd in mrg, ca 1887, S-19x24", SBY 11/1/88 3,410
Group of 9: Animal Locomotion, #3, #53, #74, #97, #98, #99, #104, #105, #108, collo, dtd/#d in mrg, B/B 10/4/88 UE 275
Group of 9: Animal Locomotion; #137, #144, #146, #149, #170, #175, #177, #178, #182, collo, dtd/#d, B/B 10/4/88 UE 275
Group of 9: Animal Locomotion; #291, #298, #334, #402, #408, #409, #411, #436, #465, collo, dtd/#d, B/B 10/4/88 UE 275
Group of 9: Animal Locomotion: #183, #185, #190, #209, #214, #235, #238, #266, #290, collo, sgn/#d, B/B 10/4/88 UE 275
Yosemite Creek, Valley of the Yosemite, Summit of the Fall at Low Water; #44, alb, ca 1870, 17x21", SWN 4/24/89 1,210

NADAR, Gaspard Felix Tournachron (19th C)

Gioacchino Rossini, sltp, mounted, ca 1855, 6x4", SWN 10/30/88 UE 550
Group of 10: 1862 Japanese Embassy to France; 4 alb & 6 CDV, bstp on mount, 1862, various sizes, SBY 5/4/88 26,400
Marechal Canrobert, sltp, titled in ink on verso, ca 1855, 6x4", SWN 10/30/88 UE 605

NADAR, Gaspard Felix Tournachron; & NADAR, Paul (19th C)

Sarah Bernhardt in Le Baiser, slvr, sgn on img, 48 Rue Bassano stp on verso, 1870s/early 1900s, 12x9", SBY 5/4/88 2,200

NAMUTH, Hans (20th C)

Jackson Pollock, Harper's Bazaar stp on verso, matted, ca 1951, 14x11", SBY 4/26/89 2,475

NATANSON, Alfred; see Athis

NELSON, Lusha

Group of 15: Alfred Stieglitz at His Lake George Home; bstp, early 1935, various sizes, lot 301, SBY 4/26/89 OE 2,200

NEWMAN, Arnold (American, 1918-)

David Hockney, London; sgn/dtd/titled on mount, copyright stp on verso, matted, 1978, 10x8", SBY 4/26/89 880
Eero Saarinen in Plastic Shell Chair, sgn/dtd/titled/inscr For Life on img, mounted/matted, 1948, 13x11", SBY 4/26/89 1,100
Group of 4: Spanish Village, Spinner, 1951; Welsh Miners, 1950; Soldier Drinking, WWII, 1944; Okinawa, 1945; SBY 11/1/88 4,125
Igor Stravinsky, sgn/dtd/titled in mrg, copyright stp on verso, matted, 1946/later, 7x13", SBY 5/4/88 OE 1,430

Igor Stravinsky, sgn/dtd/titled in mrg, copyright stp on verso, matted, 1946/later, fr, 7x13", SBY 4/26/89 OE 2,750
Pawnbroker's Signs, sgn/inscr For Bernie Quint on mount, early 1950s, 8x10", SBY 4/26/89..... 550

NEWTON, Helmut (20th C)
Bergstrom, Paris; slvr, sgn/dtd on verso, 1976, fr, 17x12", B/B 10/4/88 UE..... 330
Diving Tower, Old Beach Hotel, Monte Carlo; 23/85, p/s, copyright stp on verso, 1981/ca 1984, 11x11", SBY 11/1/88 880
Pair: Rue Aubriot, Paris; Mannequins, Quai d'Orsay, Paris; sgn/dtd/titled, matted, 1975 & 1977, 12x8", SBY 4/26/89 OE 2,200
Paris, sgn/dtd/titled/copyright stp on verso, matted, 1978, 17x12", SBY 5/4/88 1,210

NIXON, Nicholas (20th C)
Boston Common, slvr, sgn/titled/dtd on verso, 1979, 8x10", B/B 4/19/88 330
View of Copley Square Boston, 1974, slvr, sgn/titled/dtd on verso, 1974, 8x10", B/B 4/19/88 275
View Toward Midtown From Wall Street, New York City; slvr, sgn/titled/dtd on verso, 1975, 8x10", B/B 4/19/88..... 275

NOBEL, Pierre
Study of Sculptural Form with Glass Globe, slvr brom, 1920s, 13x11", SWN 10/30/88 605

NORMAN, Dorothy (20th C)
Pair: Alfred Stieglitz; sgn/New York studio stp & Phil Museum Art collection stp on verso, 1932 & 1934, 3x2", SBY 5/4/88..... 770

O'SULLIVAN, Timothy H. (American, 1840-1882)
Aboriginal Life Among the Navajo Indians, Near Old Fort Defiance, New Mexico; alb on Wheeler Survey, 1873, SWN 4/24/89 3,520
American (Fork) Canyon, Wahsatch Mountains, Utah; #98, alb, mounted on card, 1869, 8x11", SWN 10/30/88 UE 770
Apache Lake, Sierra Blanca Range, Arizona; alb mounted on Wheeler Survey letterpress, 1873, fr, 8x11", SBY 11/1/88 OE 1,045
Astronomical Observatory, South Ruby Valley, Nevada; alb, 1868, 7x11", SWN 10/30/88 OE..... 5,720
Black Canyon, Colorado River, Looking Below Near Camp 7; Pl 7, alb on Wheeler Survey mount, 1871, 8x11", B/B 4/19/88..... 468
Bloody Canyon, Sierra Nevada Range, Near Mono Lake California; alb, 8x11", SWN 10/30/88 2,200
Bodies of Federal Soldiers, McPherson Woods, Gettysburg; alb, mounted/matted, 1863, 8x9", SBY 11/1/88 5,766
Body of Confederate Sharpshooter Among the Rocks of Little Round Top, Gettysburg, PA; alb, 1863, fr, 7x9", SBY 5/4/88 OE 2,860
East Humboldt Mountains, Nevada; alb, 1868, 11x8", SWN 10/30/88 1,760
Glacier Canyon, East Humboldt Range, Nevada; alb, 1868, 8x11", SWN 10/30/88 1,210
Group of Pah-Ute Indians, Nevada; #2, alb, titled/#d on Wheeler Survey mount, 1871, 8x11", B/B 10/4/88..... 522
Head of Bear River, Wyoming; alb, #d 111 in negative, 1869, 8x11", SWN 10/30/88 UE..... 660
Hot Sulphur Spring, Ruby Valley, Nevada; alb, 1868, 8x11", SWN 10/30/89 3,300
Lake Marian, Summits of East Humboldt Mountains, Nevada; alb, 1868, 8x11", SWN 10/30/88 1,100
Long Ravine Bridge on the Central Pacific Railroad, California; alb, 1867-68, 8x11", SWN 10/30/88 1,650
Montezuma Furnace, Smelting Works, Oreana, Nevada; alb, 1867, 8x11", SWN 10/30/88 2,860
Provo Canyon Falls, Utah; alb, 1869, 8x11", SWN 10/30/89..... 1,760
Rhyolite Hills, Pahute Range, Nevada; alb, 1867, 8x11", SWN 10/30/88 1,100
Saft Cage, Savage Silver Mining Works, Virginia City, Nevada; alb, 1867-68, 7x5", SWN 10/30/88 OE 2,420
Salt Lake City From a Distance, alb, ca 1867, 9x12", SWN 10/30/88 880
Savage Hoisting Works, Savage Silver Mining Works, Virginia City, Nevada; alb, 1867-68, 8x11", SWN 10/30/88 OE..... 5,280
Shoshone Falls, Snake River, Idaho, From the South Bank (another view); alb, 1868, 8x11", lot 399, SWN 10/30/88 3,520
Shoshone Falls, Snake River, Idaho, From the South Bank; alb, 1868, 8x11", lot 398, SWN 10/30/88 3,300

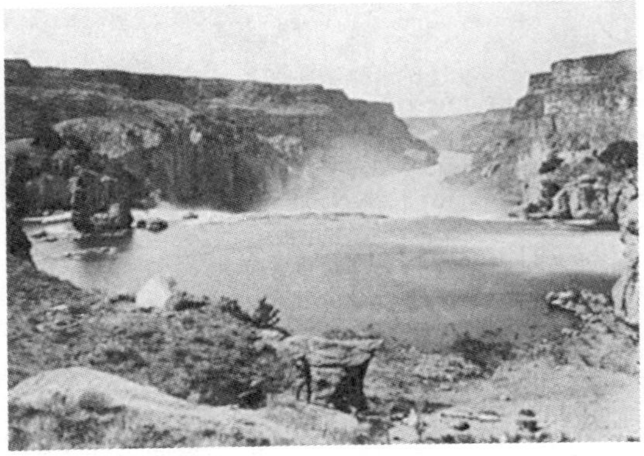

Shoshone Falls, Snake River, Idaho; alb, 1868, 8x11", lot 397, SWN 10/30/88 OE; $3,960

South From Lone Peak, Wahsatch Mountains, Utah; alb, #d 107 in negative, 1869, 8x11", SWN 10/30/88..... 935
Summit of Uintah Mountains, Lake Lal, Utah; alb, 1869, 11x9", SWN 10/30/88..... 1,100
Top of Anaho Island, Pyramid Lake, Nevada; alb, 1867, 7x9", SWN 10/30/88 OE 3,740
View on Apache Lake, Sierra Blanca Range, Arizona; #3, alb on Wheeler Survey mount, 1873, 11x8", B/B 4/19/88..... 440
Volcanic Hill, Near Mono Lake, California; alb, ca 1868, 8x11", SWN 10/30/88..... 1,760

O'SULLIVAN, Timothy H.; att (American, 1840-1882)
Building Stockade at Alexandria, Virginia; #524, alb, remounted to linen, titled on mount, 1860s, 9x13", SWN 10/30/88 OE..... 2,860

OFFICER, Robert A. (American, 20th C)
Innocence, slvr, p/s, titled on mount, 1932, 9x10", lot 166, WG 10/19/88 UE 110
Innocence, slvr, sgn/titled/stp on mount, exhibition labels on mount verso, ca 1932, 7x10", B/B 4/19/88 220
Kaminski, slvr, sgn/titled on mount, exhibition labels on mount verso, 1930s, 10x9", B/B 4/19/88..... 385
Oriental (Nautch Dancer), slvr, p/s, titled/exhibition label on verso, 1930s, 14x11", B/B 4/19/88 412

ORKIN, Ruth (20th C)
American Girl in Florence Italy, slvr, sgn/titled/dtd in mrg & on verso, 1951/1980, 8x12", B/B 4/19/88..... 770
American Girl in Italy (The Greeting), sgn/titled on verso, 1951, 4x9", SBY 4/26/89 OE 4,950

RLAND, Ted (20th C)
Jerry Uelsmann Receiving the Baptism of the Godphotographers of the West...; slvr, 1969/unknown, 7x6", SWN 10/30/88 220

UTERBRIDGE, Paul (American, 1896-1958)
Christmas Gifts, pltn, sgn/dtd on mount, Harper's Bazaar stp on verso, matted, 1924, fr, 4x3", SBY 4/26/89 8,800
Jewelry Still Life, artist estate stp on verso, mounted/matted, ca 1924, fr, 5x7", SBY 11/1/88 UE 550
Standing Nude, pltn, mounted/matted, ca 1922, fr, 10x7", SBY 11/1/88 5,500
Still Life (print/perfume bottles/ring box on table top), mounted/matted, ca 1926, fr, 4x8", SBY 4/26/89 1,210

ACH BROS. (American?, New York, NY; 19th C)
Album: New York City Parade, Union Square; alb, studio credit on mount, 1890s, 10x14", SBY 4/26/89 UE 550

ANAGGI, Ivo
Construction, sgn/inscr Futurista Hans Zampini in Esonatoglia Schlafzimmer on verso, matted, 1920s, 7x5", SBY 5/4/88 990

ARKER, Olivia (American, 1941-)
Bosc (pear), sgn/dtd/titled in mrg, matted, 1977/1980, 8x9", SBY 5/4/88 OE 770
Group of 4: Whelks; Saturday; Roses; Pods of Chance; sgn/dtd/titled in mrg, matted, ca 1977-81, SBY 5/4/88 1,540
Mask, #5, printing-out paper, sgn/titled/dtd in mrg, 1977, 7x5", B/B 4/19/88 275
Portfolio: Lost Objects; 12, total ed of 39, 10 photos, sgn/dtd/titled in mrg, matted, ca 1980, cased, SBY 5/4/88 2,420

ARKHURST, T. Harmon
Pair: Indian Maiden; Indian Grandmother; slvr, ink sgn on img, ca 1930, 10x8", B/B 4/19/88 358

ARRY, Roger
Handshake, sgn/dtd by Madeleine Parry on verso, matted, 1931, 10x7", SBY 11/1/88 2,200
Portrait Collage, 2 photos cropped/mounted together, p/s on paper affixed to mount, 1930s, 12x4", SBY 5/4/88 880
Solarization, sgn/dtd by Madeleine Parry on verso, matted, 1937, fr, 12x10", SBY 11/1/88 660

ENN, Irving (American, 1917-)
American Ballet Theatre, sgn/inscr For Hugh Laing on mount, name/copyright stps on verso, 1947, 14x19", SBY 11/1/88 OE 6,050
Black & White Vogue Cover, 32/34, pltn-pldm, sgn/dtd/copyright on verso, matted, 1950, fr, 18x15", SBY 11/1/88 OE 6,600
Camel Pack, 57/68, pltn-pldm, sgn/dtd/titled/ed & copyright stps on verso, matted, 1975, fr, 10x8", SBY 11/1/88 1,980
Cat Woman, New Guinea; 11/20, pltn-pldm mounted on aluminum, sgn/copyright stp on verso, 1971/1979, 21x19", SBY 5/4/88 2,640
Cat Woman, New Guinea; 5/20, pltn-pldm mounted on aluminum, sgn/dtd/copyright stp, 1971/1979, 21x19", SBY 11/1/88 OE 3,575
Colette, 12/50, pltn-pldm mounted on aluminum, sgn/dtd/titled/copyright stp on verso, 1951/1976, fr, 20x19", SBY 4/26/89 4,675
Cretan Landscape, 15/25, pltn/pldm/iridium/pigment mounted on aluminum, copyright stp, 1964/1968, 15x22", SBY 11/1/88 3,575
Cuzco Woman with Child, artist name/Conde Nast copyright stps on verso, mounted/matted, 1948, 8x7", SBY 4/26/89 4,125
Enga Warrior, 8/15, pltn-pldm mounted on aluminum, sgn/dtd/copyright stps on verso, 1970, 20x19", SBY 4/26/89 4,675
Five Okapa Warriors (New Guinea), 18/35, pltn-pldm mounted on aluminum, sgn/dtd/#d, 1970/1972, fr, 20x20", SBY 5/4/88 2,640
Girl Behind Bottle, 5/33, pltn-pldm mounted on aluminum, sgn/dtd/titled/copyright stp, 1949/1978, 19x18", SBY 11/1/88 3,300
Group of 3: Marchand de Concombres, Paris; Fishmonger, London; Butcher, London; 1950-51/1967 & 1974, SBY 11/1/88 3,025
Group of 3: Road Sweeper, London; Sewer Cleaner, London; Chimney Sweeper, London; pltn-pldm, 1950-51/1976, SBY 11/1/88 3,300
Hell's Angel: Doug; 23/40, hand-coated pltn-pldm, sgn/titled/dtd/stp on verso, 1967/1976, 19x21", B/B 4/19/88 4,125
John Marin, 20/40, pltn-pldm mounted on aluminum, sgn/titled/copyright stp on verso, 1948/1977, 21x16", SBY 5/4/88 UE 1,760
New York Still Life, 18/65, pltn-pldm mounted on aluminum, sgn/copyright stp on verso, 1947/1978, fr, 18x23", SBY 5/4/88 5,775
Nude, sgn/ed & copyright stps on verso, matted, 1949-50/ca 1980, 15x15", SBY 11/1/88 1,210
Nude (torso), sgn/copyright stp on verso, matted, 1949-50/1980, fr, 15x15", SBY 5/4/88 1,650
Pair: Pagoda; Soot Paper; 16/49 & 2/24, sgn/dtd/titled/copyright stp on verso, 1975/1975 & 1976, 10x8", SBY 5/4/88 1,650
Playing Card, 34/55, pltn-pldm, sgn/titled/dtd/copyright stp on verso, matted, 1975/1976, fr, 28x21", SBY 11/1/88 3,025
Playing Card, 50/55, pltn-pldm, sgn/dtd/titled/copyright stp on verso, 1975, fr,11x9", SBY 5/4/88 1,540
Rock Groups (San Francisco) (Big Brother & the Holding Company & the Grateful Dead), 22/50, 1967/1974, SBY 4/26/89 OE 6,600
Sculptor's Model, Paris; 28/35, pltn-pldm, sgn/dtd/titled, copyright stp on verso, 1951, 16x12", SBY 4/26/89 2,200
Sitting Girl (Nubile Beauty), 12/40, pltn-pldm mounted on aluminum, sgn/copyright stp, 1947/1978, 19x20", SBY 4/26/88 4,675
Sitting Man with Pink Face, 3/50, pltn-pldm mounted on aluminum, sgn/copyright stp, 1970/1979, 21x20", SBY 5/4/88 3,300
Two Cuzco Men, artist name/copyright stps on verso, mounted/matted, 1948, 10x8", SBY 4/26/88 2,200
Two Guedras, 30/40, pltn-pldm mounted on aluminum, sgn/dtd/titled/#d on verso, matted, 1974/1977, 20x17", SBY 5/4/88 5,775
Two New Guinea Men Holding Hands, 5/31, pltn-pldm mounted on aluminum, matted, 1970/1979, fr, 16x16", SBY 5/4/88 1,980
Woman with Roses (Lisa Fonssagrives Penn), 2/40, pltn-pldm mounted on aluminum, sgn/dtd, 1950/1977, 22x15", SBY 11/1/88 3,300
Young Enga Couple, 11/30, pltn-pldm mounted on aluminum, sgn/copyright stp on verso, 1970/1979, 20x20", SBY 4/26/89 3,300

ETERHANS, Walter
Still Life with Lemon, p/s in mrg, matted, ca 1929, 9x9", SBY 4/26/89 OE 16,500
Study of Cinderblocks, Pl 32, slvr, late 1920s, 8x6", SWN 4/24/89 UE 770
Toter Hase, sgn/titled in mrg, matted, ca 1929, 9x9", SBY 4/26/89 OE 29,700

ETSCHOW, Robert
Haeuschen an der Mulde bei Duben, slvr, Gerlin-Steglitz stp on verso, ca 1930, 4x5", SWN 4/24/89 523

HERSON, see Mac Pherson

OLIAKOV, Lev (20th C)
Group of 5: Russia; ink sgn/copyright stp on verso, mounted, 1960s-70s/later, 10x14", SBY 5/4/88 UE 440

ONTING, Herbert
Photographer's Darkroom, Antarctia; bstp in mrg, title label on verso, 1910-12, 13x18", SBY 4/26/89 UE 440

ORTERFIELD, W.H.
Maid of the West, pigment, titled/dtd on mount, Buffalo Fine Arts Academy Alright Art stp, 1910, 13x10", SBY 11/1/88 UE 605
Main Street, Ellicott Square, Buffalo; pigment, p/s, titled/dtd on mount recto, 1907, 10x12", SWN 10/30/88 1,100
Midwinter, pigment print, intl/dtd on img, titled on mount, Buffalo Fine Arts Gallery stp, 1910, fr, 9x13", SBY 5/4/88 1,320

OST, William B.
Landscape with Split Rail Fence, pltn, p/s on img, mounted/matted, early 1900s, 7x9", SBY 11/1/88 605
Study of Birch Trees, toned slvr tipped to thin card mount, p/s, ca 1900, 10x4", SWN 4/24/89 715

QUIGLEY, Edward
Phoenix, sgn/titled on mount, 1712 Walnut Street studio stp on verso, early 1930s, 14x11", SBY 4/26/89 OE ... 1,540

RABINOVITCH, Ben Magid
Calla Lily, sgn/inscr NY 32 on img, matted, 1932/fr, 10x8", SBY 11/1/88 OE ... 2,200
Pair: Nude Studies (variants of same negative); matted, early 1930s, 14x11", SBY 11/1/88 UE ... 550

RADINSKI, Emmanual; see Man-Ray

RADKAI, Karen (20th C)
Dejeuner sur l'Herbe, matted 1950, 13x14", SBY 4/26/89 ... 1,210

RANDALL, A.F.
Apache Squaw (Nal-Tzucwei-Oh), Spy, in Chiricahua Campaign; alb on cabinet card, CEG 1/13/89 ... 150
Cato, Chiricahua Apache Chief, full-length/studio pose; alb on cabinet card, CEG 1/13/89 ... 275
Chiricahua Apache, seated warrior in full dress/holds pipe, bow, & sheath; alb on cabinet card, CEG 1/13/89 ... 190
Chiricahua Apache Brave (standing w/bow & bow case) & Squaw (holds basket), alb on cabinet card, CEG 1/13/89 ... 135
Comanche John, holds fire rattle/quiver case nearby; alb on cabinet card, CEG 1/13/89 ... 175
Forty Horse & Sister, Apache woman standing or seated in full costume; alb on cabinet card, CEG 1/13/89 ... 90
Fox Lauier, Indian holds infant fox; alb on cabinet card, corner of mount chipped, CEG 1/13/89 ... 100
Se-Le (head wrapped/holds rifle) & Wife, Tzas-Tone, Apaches; alb on cabinet card, CEG 1/13/89 ... 175
Son of Mangas Colorado, Apache, full-length; alb on cabinet card, CEG 1/13/89 ... 275

RAU, William H.
Parallel Tracks, alb, artist credit in negative, mounted, ca 1900, 17x21", SBY 11/1/88 ... 1,100
Reversed Curve, Black Creek; alb, artist credit/titled in negative, mounted, ca 1900, 17x21", SBY 11/1/88 ... 1,100

RAWLINGS, John (20th C)
Pair: Nude Studies; p/s, mounted/matted, ca 1960s, 14x11", SBY 11/1/88 ... 990

RAYMOND, Lilo (20th C)
Group of 3: Pillows on the Dresser; Hanging Night Gown; Oysters; sgn in mrg, late 1970s, various sizes, SBY 5/4/88 ... 1,210
Pair: Vase on Mantel; Three Roses Against a Frosted Window; sgn/dtd in mrg, matted, 19x12", SBY 5/4/88 OE ... 1,100
Portfolio: Six Still-Lifes; 4/15, 6 photos, ink sgn in mrg, matted, ca 1971-6/ca 1976, 9x13", cased, SBY 5/4/88 ... 2,200

REED, Roland (American, 1864-1934)
Alone with the Past, 11/350, sepia, embossed seal on mount, orig tissue guard, 1890s, 20x16", CEG 1/13/89 ... 200
Ancient Dwelling #2, 11/350, sepia, embossed seal on mount, orig tissue guard, 1890s, 20x16", CEG 1/13/89 ... 300
Bread Maker (Hopi portrait), 11/350, sepia, embossed seal on mount, orig tissue guard, 1890s, 20x16", CEG 1/13/89 ... 300
Broken Arrow (Navajo portrait), 11/350, sepia, embossed seal on mount, orig tissue guard, 1890s, 20x16", CEG 1/13/89 ... 150
Brothers (Navajos wrapped in blankets), sepia, embossed seal on mount, orig tissue guard, 20x16", CEG 5/7/88 ... 175
Cheverra, 3-quarter Indian portrait; 11/250, sepia embossed seal on mount, orig tissue guard, 20x16", CEG 5/7/88 ... 140
Crossing de Chelly, 11/350, sepia, embossed seal on mount, orig tissue guard, 1890s, 20x16", lot 285, CEG 1/13/89 ... 200
Departure, Indians/horses in landscape; 11/350, sepia, embossed seal on mount, tissue guard, 20x16", CEG 5/7/88 ... 75
Evergreen Tree, Cochiti portrait; 11/350, sepia, embossed seal on mount, orig tissue guard, 1890s, 20x16", CEG 1/13/89 ... 250
Many Goats (Navajo portrait), 11/350, sepia, embossed seal on mount, orig tissue guard, 1890s, 20x16", CEG 1/13/89 ... 150
Meeting Place, Hopi/Navajo/horses in landscape; 11/350, sepia, seal on mount, orig guard, 20x16", CEG 5/7/88 ... 90
Night Runner (half-length Navajo), 11/350, sepia, embossed seal on mount, orig tissue guard, 20x16", CEG 5/7/88 ... 175
Reflections (Navajo Indians), 11/350, sepia, embossed seal on mat, orig tissue guard, 20x16", CEG 5/7/88 ... 175
Shepherd of the Hills, 11/350, sepia, embossed seal on mount, orig tissue guard, 1890s, 20x16", CEG 1/13/89 ... 200
Sighting the Arrow, Hopi in profile on hill; 11/350, sepia, embossed seal on mount, orig guard, 20x16", CEG 5/7/88 ... 60
Sons of Manuelito (Indians on cliff), 11/350, sepia, embossed seal on mount, orig tissue guard, 20x16", C-E 5/7/88 ... 60
Stringing the Bow (Navajo portrait), 11/350, embossed seal on mount, orig tissue guard, 1890s, 20x16", CEG 1/13/89 ... 200
Sun Chaser, Navajo Portrait; 11/350, sepia, embossed seal on mount, orig tissue guard, 1890s, 20x16", CEG 1/13/89 ... 300
Trading Post (Navajo street scene), 11/350, sepia, embossed seal on mount, orig tissue guard, 20x16", CEG 5/7/88 ... 65
Walpi Village, 11/350, sepia, embossed seal on mount, orig tissue guard, ca 1890s, 20x16", CEG 5/7/88 ... 75

REES & CO. (19th C)
Colonel William Martin, Confederate Army; ambro, half pl, sgn in negative, 1860s, thermoplastic fr, SBY 5/4/88 OE ... 6,050

REES & CO; att (19th C)
Private Charles Croxton, Richmond Howitzers, Army, CSA; ambro, half pl, gilt mat, ca 1862, 5x6", cased, SBY 4/26/89 ... 1,650

REICHMAN, Vilem (20th C)
Nude with Vines, sgn/dtd on verso, 1940, 9x6", SBY 11/1/88 ... 660

REJLANDER, Oscar Gustave (19th C)
John the Baptist, alb, 1860s, oval 5x6", B/B 10/4/88 OE ... 715
Nude Study (vignetted), alb, mounted, ca 1860, oval 6x5", SWN 10/30/88 ... 440
Poor Old Man, alb on double mount, titled on mount, 1850s, oval 5x4", SWN 4/24/89 ... 550
Self-Portrait, As Garibaldi; alb, sgn on mount, ca 1862, 8x6", SBY 11/1/88 ... 1,980

RENGER-PATZSCH, Albert
Buttons, Essen studio stp on verso, 1930s, 9x7", SBY 4/26/89 ... 2,200
Deck of Ship, Essen studio/repro limitation stps on verso, matted, ca 1946, 9x7", SBY 4/26/89 ... 1,980
Factory Study, artist studio stp on verso, matted, late 1940s, 9x7", SBY 4/26/89 ... 1,980
Junger Orang Utan, slvr, Bad-Harzburg/repro limitation stps on verso, ca 1925, 7x4", SWN 4/24/89 UE ... 300
Machinery, Essen studio stp on verso, matted, early 1930s, 9x7", SBY 11/1/88 ... 880
Study of Cactus, #12, slvr, titled/Auriga Verlag & repro limitation stps on verso, 1920s, 7x9", SWN 4/24/89 ... 358
Study of Cactus, #87, slvr, titled/Auriga Verlag & repro limitation stps on verso, 1920s, 6x7", SWN 4/24/89 UE ... 275
Tree in Landscape, Wamel-Dorf studio stp on verso, matted, ca 1929, 15x11", SBY 4/26/89 ... 4,400

REVESZ-BIRO, Emeri
Dreher Crackers Advertising Study, intl on img, intl/titled on mount, matted, 1920s, 17x13", SBY 4/26/89 ... 990

Schmoll Pasta Advertising Study, slvr w/ink, intl on mount, matted, 1920s, 12x9", SBY 4/26/89 1,760

BOUD, Marc (20th C)

Group of 3: Painter on the Eiffel; Photographers` Rally, Japan; China; sgn on verso, 1953/1958/1975, 14x10", SBY 5/4/88 1,540

Painter on the Eiffel, sgn/dtd/titled on verso, matted, 1953/later, 14x9", SBY 4/26/89 OE 2,475

CHARDS, Wynn

Fashion Study, p/s on mount, matted, 1930s, 10x8", SBY 4/26/89 880

CHEBOURG, A. (19th C)

Arsenal de Tsarkoe-Selo (study of swords), alb w/arched top, ca 1859, 13x9", SWN 4/24/89 413

EBICKE, Gerhard

Study of a Nude Couple with Beach Ball, slvr, Charlottenburg copyright stp on verso, 1920s, 7x8", SWN 10/30/88 OE 275

EFENSTAHL, Leni (20th C)

Group of 3: Olympics, Germany, 1936: Discus Thrower; Nude Athlete; Gymnast on the Parallel Bars; 11x9", SBY 4/26/89 3,300

NEHART, F.A.

Group of 20: Indian Portraits; pltn, sgn/dtd/#d/titled in negative, mounted, 1898, 9x7", SBY 11/1/88 3,575

OBERTSON, James (19th C)

Porch of the Caryatids, the Erechtheum, Athens; alb, sgn in negative, early 1850s/1860s, 12x10", SWN 4/24/89 OE 715

Scutari Cemetary, alb, sgn/titled in negative, mounted, late 1850s, 12x10", SBY 4/26/89 715

ODCHENKO, Alexander (Russian, 1891-1956)

Pole Vault, orig photogr, executed ca 1926, Atelier stp on verso, 11x16", SBY 7/7/88 OE 15,000

Red Square, Series: Dance; orig photogr, ca 1934, stp sgn/mk Rodchenko Stepanova Atelier, 11x15", SBY 7/7/88 OE 11,000

Vladimir Durov & the Sea Lion, orig photogr, 1940, sgn/mk Atelier, 16x11", SBY 7/7/88 OE 7,600

OH, Franz

Deck of Ship, artist name stp on verso, matted, 1920s, 5x9", SBY 4/26/89 1,540

Nude, matted, 1920s, 9x5", SBY 4/26/89 2,475

Street Cart, Muchen studio stp on verso, matted, ca 1927, 7x9", SBY 4/26/89 2,090

Woman on Bridge, artist stp on verso, matted, 1920s, 6x9", SBY 4/26/89 1,980

OHDE, Werner

Mannequin, sgn/dtd/Bremen studio stp on verso, matted, 1930, 9x6", SBY 4/26/89 OE 4,675

OSSLER, Jaroslav

Abstraction, sgn/dtd on verso, matted, 1923, fr, 10x9", SBY 5/4/88 OE 4,125

Beauty Cream, sgn/dtd/inscr Paris/Praha studio stp on verso, matted, 1934, 9x8", SBY 11/1/88 1,100

Ier Avec Mentor, sgn/dtd/titled on verso, matted, ca 1927, 10x9", lot 230, SBY 4/26/89 2,475

Ier Avec Mentor, sgn/dtd/titled on verso, matted, ca 1927, 10x9", lot 229, SBY 4/26/89 2,750

Montage Portrait of a Woman, sgn/dtd/inscr Paris/Praha studio stp on verso, matted, 1931, 7x7", SBY 5/4/88 OE 5,225

Radiomater, photocollage w/ink & pencil, titled on img, sgn on verso, matted, 1920s, 12x10", SBY 4/26/89 4,125

Untitled, photogram, sgn/dtd/inscr Paris on verso, matted, 1930, 8x6", SBY 4/26/89 3,850

OTAN, Thurman

Skyscrapers, photomontage, sgn/dtd/titled/bstp in mrg, artist stp on verso, matted, 1932/later, 10x19", SBY 4/26/89 OE 2,750

OTHSTEIN, Arthur (American, 1915-)

Farm Family, St Charles County, Wisconsin; slvr, p/s in mrg, titled/dtd on verso, 1939/1970s, 13x10", B/B 4/19/88 302

Pair: Dust Storm, Oklahoma; Unemployed Mineworker, Bush, Illinois; titled, 1936-39/later, 10x9"/10x13", SBY 11/1/88 OE 1,650

UBINCAM, Harry C.

Aritist's Son with a Toy Train, pltn, mounted to patterned paper, ca 1905, 7x9", SWN 10/30/88 OE 1,210

UDOLPH, Charlotte

Der Gruene Tisch: Pantomime der Folkwangbuehne, Essen...; slvr, titled, Dresden credit, 1930s, 4x5", SWN 10/30/88 413

UDOMINE, Albert

Etude de Nu, sgn in red ink in mrg, matted, ca 1930, 9x7", SBY 4/26/89 3,575

USSELL, E.L.

Joe Hess, Reformed Prizefighter; cbnt, CEG 5/7/88 15

UZICKA, D.J.

Few Drops of Rain, slvr, sgn/dtd/titled on verso, stp/exhibition labels on verso, 1932, 14x11", B/B 10/4/88 UE 330

ALOMON, Erich

Gustav Stresemann Addressing the League of Nations, slvr, ca 1927, 4x6", SWN 10/30/88 UE 358

ALZMANN, Auguste (19th C)

Arc de l'Ecce Homo, Details; sltp on orig mount, artist/publisher/printer credits, ca 1854, 13x9", SWN 4/24/89 1,430

Enciente du Temple, Face Sud de l'Angle Sud-Est; sltp, artist/publisher/printer credits, ca 1854, 13x9", SWN 4/24/89 OE 1,650

Vallee de Hinnom, Jerusalem; sltp, titled/editor & printer credits on mount, matted, ca 1852, 9x13", SBY 4/26/89 OE 7,700

AMARAS, Lucas (20th C)

Phototransformation, SX-70 Polaroid, dtd on verso, matted, 1973, fr, 3x3", SBY 11/1/88 OE 2,475

Phototransformation, SX-70 Polaroid, dtd on verso, matted, 1976, fr, 3x3", lot 430, SBY 5/4/88 OE 1,650

Portotransformation (Self-Portrait), SX-70 Polaroid, dtd on verso, matted, 1976, fr, 3x3", SBY 5/4/88 OE 1,650

ANDER, August (20th C)

Allianz Building, Cologne; slvr w/ink additions, Koln stp on verso, matted, ca 1932, 9x7", SBY 5/4/88 2,200

Coal Carrier, Berlin; sgn/Koln studio bstp on img, Koln studio stp on verso, matted, 1930s, 9x7", SBY 4/26/89 OE 8,250

Cretin, Westerwald; studio bstp on img, sgn/dtd/inscr Koln on mat, studio label on verso, 1926, 8x6", SBY 11/1/88 OE 4,400

German Couple (portrait), slvr on Duerenerstrasse 201 studio mount, 1920s, 6x4", SWN 10/30/88 UE 220

Group of 3: Courtyard; The Rhine; Rural Landscape; Koln stp, matted, 1930s, various sizes, SBY 11/1/88 UE 660

Hunter, Koln studio bstp on img, studio stp on verso, matted, 1920s/1950s, fr, 10x7", SBY 5/4/88 OE 3,300

Hunter with Dog, Koln bstp on img, studio stp on verso, matted, 1930s/1950s, 11x9", SBY 11/1/88 1,870

Jean Loosen (portrait), slvr, Lindenthal Koln bstp, 1928, 78x6", SWN 10/30/88 ... **1,430**
Man with Bowler Hat, hinge-mounted on card, 1920s/1950s, 12x9", SBY 5/4/88 UE ... **1,100**
Norary (Dr Quinke), Koln studio stp on verso, matted, ca 1925, fr, 9x7", SBY 5/4/88 ... **1,210**
Old Man with a Cane, Koln studio stp on verso, matted, 1912/1970s, 12x9", SBY 5/4/88 UE ... **440**
One-Legged Man, sgn/Koln bstp on img, Koln stp on verso, mounted/matted, 1930s, 9x7", SBY 4/26/89 OE ... **6,600**
Pair: Leutesdorf; Kreuzberg; slvr, 1940s, 7x9", SWN 10/30/88 ... **605**
Pair: Postal Inspector Doppler; Young Girl in Victorian Dress; mounted on wove paper, ca 1906 & ca 1910, SBY 5/4/88 UE ... **770**
Pair: Weinfelder Maar; Bend on the Rhine Near Boppard; slvr, Koln-Lindenthal stp, 1930s, 7x9", SWN 4/24/89 ... **715**
Portrait of a Woman, Koln studio bstp on img, inscr Baverin aus dem Westerwald, matted, 1920s, 12x9", SBY 4/26/89 ... **1,870**
Professor Korenski (bust-length), gum bichromate, sgn/dtd/titled on mount, 1906, 9x7", SWN 4/24/89 ... **1,430**
Rhine River, Koln bstp on img, studio/copyright stps on verso, matted, 1930s, 7x9", SBY 5/4/88 UE ... **550**
Riverscape, Koln bstp on img, Koln studio stp on verso, 1930s/1950s, 9x12", SBY 5/4/88 UE ... **660**
Steamships on the Rhine River, matted, 1930s, 7x9", SBY 5/4/88 UE ... **550**
Strassenarbeiter Kolonne, slvr, p/s on mat, Lindenthal Koln bstp, 1927, 7x9", SWN 10/30/88 ... **3,520**
Taxi Driver, sgn/Koln bstp on img, Koln studio stp on verso, matted, 1930s, 9x7", SBY 4/26/89 OE ... **7,700**

SAUDEK, Jan (20th C)
End of Orgy, #13, hc slvr, sgn/dtd/titled, 1970s/1987, 11x10", B/B 10/4/88 ... **825**
Father & Son (man & nude baby), slvr, ink sgn on recto, 1966/unknown, 10x8", SWN 10/30/88 OE ... **880**
Man with Child #35, sgn on img, matted, 1970s/1988, 15x11", SBY 11/1/88 ... **770**

SCAVULLO, Francesco (20th C)
Model in China, 11/15, sgn/dtd/repro & ed stps on verso, 1962, 19x14", SBY 4/26/89 OE ... **3,025**
Model in Crowd, 12/15, sgn/dtd/repro & ed stps on verso, 1962, 19x15", SBY 5/4/88 ... **1,210**

SCHATT, Roy (20th C)
Group of 3: James Dean; sgn/dtd on img, studio stp on verso, matted, 1954, 14x11", SBY 4/26/89 OE ... **3,575**

SCHIFF, Hans
Bookbinding Study, slvr, 1930s, 9x7", SWN 10/30/88 ... **330**

SCHMIDT, Joost
Flowers, sgn/titled on verso, matted, 1920s, 9x9", SBY 11/1/88 ... **1,210**
Untitled (Weimar Relief), backed w/paper, matted, ca 1925, 4x2", SBY 4/26/89 ... **1,980**

SCHOLTEN, John A. (American, St. Louis, MO; 19th C)
Civil War Soldier in a Greatcoat, alb, artist studio stp on img, 1860s, 7x6", SWN 4/24/89 UE ... **220**

SCOTT, Ethel Grant
Girl Frolicking with Bubble, slvr, p/s on img, late 1900, 12x10", B/B 4/19/88 UE ... **100**
Pair: Portrait of a Young Girl Playing in a Garden; Portrait of a Young Girl Resting; autochromes, 1910, B/B 10/4/88 UE ... **192**

SEELEY, George H.
Lake at Dusk, pltn, sgn/dtd on img, mounted/matted, 8x10", SBY 11/1/88 ... **1,100**
Landscape, Birches; pltn, sgn on img, sgn/titled/Japanese chop mk on verso, ca 1926, 10x8", B/B 10/4/88 UE ... **522**
Running White Ducks, gum backed w/card, sgn/dtd on img, matted, 1925, 14x17", SBY 5/4/88 ... **2,640**

SHAHN, Ben (American, 1898-1969)
Bowery, titled, mounted/matted, 1930s, 7x9", SBY 11/1/88 ... **1,650**
Ozark Landscape with Shacks, slvr, Resettlement Adm stp on verso, ca 1935, 8x10", SWN 10/30/88 ... **385**

SHAW & JOHNSON (American?, San Francisco, CA; 19th C)
Elderly Couple, 3-quarter pose; ambro, half pl, artist name stp, leather case (split), ca 1855, CEG 5/7/88 ... **155**
Occupational: Painter, large brush/holds coat or drop cloth, full-figured; tin, mat/preserver, CEG 5/7/88 ... **32**

SHEEHAN, Robert F. III
Construction, Cammadion Film/Generale Fuchsweise stps/address label on verso, mounted/matted, 11x11", SBY 11/1/88 OE ... **1,650**
Jaguar, Gammadion Film/paper address label on verso, mounted/matted, late 1930s, 8x8", SBY 11/1/88 ... **880**

SHEELER, Charles (American, 1883-1965)
Chartes Cathedral, exhibition stp/title label on verso, matted, 1929/ca 1939, 10x8", SBY 11/1/88 ... **8,800**
Savoy-Plaza Hotel, mounted/matted, mid-1920s, 10x7", SBY 4/26/89 ... **29,700**

SHERMAN, Cindy (American, 1954-)
Self-Portrait As Marilyn Monroe, 21/125, C-print, intl/dtd in mrg, 1982, 16x9", SBY 4/26/89 OE ... **4,400**
Untitled (Film Still Series), 1 of proposed ed of 3, matted, 1979, fr, 28x37", SBY 5/4/88 ... **2,310**
Untitled (portrait), 5/10, C-print, dtd on verso, mounted/matted, 1982, 45x30", SBY 4/26/89 ... **3,300**
Untitled #121, 2/18, C-print, sgn/dtd on verso, matted, 1983, 35x21", SBY 11/1/88 ... **1,650**
Untitled Self-Portrait, slvr, sgn/dtd on verso, 1975, 17x12", B/B 4/19/88 ... **300**

SHINDO, T.K.
Water & Oil, slvr, sgn/titled/Tokyo Salon label on verso, ca 1935, 13x11", B/B 10/4/88 ... **330**

SHUNK, Harry (Shonk-Kender)(20th C)
Christo: Wrapped Coast, One Million Square Feet, Little Bay, Australia; sgn by Christo, 1969, 32x49", SBY 4/26/89 OE ... **4,675**

SIEGEL, Arthur (20th C)
Chicago, photomontage, sgn/dtd/inscr Only Print on verso, mounted/matted, ca 1950, 3x4", SBY 4/26/89 ... **1,760**
Crowd Scene, sgn/dtd/inscr One of Two Prints on verso, matted, 1939, 5x4", SBY 5/4/88 ... **2,090**

SIMON, Stella
Overhead View, ink sgn on img, matted, ca 1930, 7x10", SBY 11/1/88 UE ... **605**

SINSABAUGH, Art (20th C)
Chi La #155; sgn/dtd/titled on mount, 1964, 11x19", SBY 4/26/89 OE ... **3,300**
Mark & Sherry, sgn/dtd/titled on mount, 1969, 12x20", SBY 4/26/89 ... **1,540**

SISKIND, Aaron (American, 1903-)
Group of 3: Pleasures & Terrors of Levitaion 37; Badlands; Durango; sgn, matted, various sizes, SBY 4/26/89 ... **1,320**
Group of 3: Woonsocket 9; Lima 80 (Homage to FK); Hudson 44; sgn/dtd, matted, early 1970s/later, SBY 5/4/88 ... **880**

Group of 4: Chicago, 1960; Gloucester, 1944; Terracotta, 1960; Gloucester, 1944; sgn, matted, SBY 11/1/88 825
Group of 4: Martha's Vineyard, 1954; Mexico, 1955; Terracotta, 1960; Mexico, 1955; matted, various sizes, SBY 5/4/88 880
Martha's Vineyard, sgn/dtd in mrg, matted, 1954/later, fr, 14x18", SBY 4/26/89 OE 2,090
Pair: Martha's Vineyard; Mexico; sgn/dtd/titled on verso, 1951 & 1955, 9x13"/11x14", SBY 5/4/88 1,320
Pari: Chicago; Tehuantepec; sgn/dtd/titled, 1949 & 1955/later, 12x16"/13x16", SBY 11/1/88 UE 605
Portfolio: 75th Anniversary; 6/50, 12 photos, sgn/titled in mrg, 1936-1976, various sizes, cased, SBY 5/4/88 UE 2,475
Rome 66, slvr, sgn/titled/dtd in mrg, 1963, 10x8", B/B 4/19/88 UE 440

SKOFF, Gail (American, 20th C)
Light Strip, hc slvr, sgn/titled/dtd in mrg & verso, 1979, 13x19", B/B 4/19/88 412

SKOGLAND, Sandra Louise (American, 1946-)
Hangers, 17/20, cbcr, sgn/dtd/titled on verso, matted, 1980, fr, 26x33", SBY 5/4/88 1,760
Radioactive Cats, 9/20, cbcr, sgn/dtd/titled on verso, matted, 1980, fr, 26x33", SBY 4/26/89 OE 13,200

SLOANE, Thomas O'Connor Jr.
Nude Study, orange-toned pigment, matted, ca 1900, 8x6", SBY 11/1/88 990
Profile Portrait, pigment, matted, ca 1900, 9x6", SBY 11/1/88 UE 990
Untitled (bust-length portrait of a woman), gum, tipped to mount, ca 1905-10, 7x6", SWN 10/30/88 770

SMITH, W. Eugene (American, 1918-1978)
Dance of the Flaming Coke, Pittsburgh; sgn/dtd/titled on mount, 1955/later, 8x13", SBY 5/4/88 3,300
Death of Gus Gus, sgn/titled in mrg, matted, 1955/later, 7x9", SBY 5/4/88 2,420
Death of Gus Gus, sgn/titled in mrg, matted, 1955/later, 7x9", SBY 4/26/89 1,100
Dr Schweitzer, Aspen; sgn w/stylus on img, sgn/titled on mount, matted, 1950s/later, 10x13", SBY 4/26/89 2,200
Group of 4: Jean Pearson; 1949, various sizes, SBY 5/4/88 1,320
Guardia Civil, Spanish Village; estate stp on verso, matted, 1951/later, 12x15", SBY 11/1/88 1,100
Haiti, Man of Mercy; matted, ca 1958/later, 9x13", SBY 5/4/88 660
House on Hill, Pittsburgh; sgn w/stylus on img, copyright/studio stps on verso, 1955-56, 8x13", SBY 11/1/88 990
Keep Off, copyright credit stp on verso, matted, 1950s, no size given, SBY 4/26/89 1,100
Ku Klux Klan Member, sgn w/stylus on img, p/s on img, mounted/matted, 1950s/later, 8x6", SBY 4/26/89 1,650
Mad Eyes, Haiti; mounted on black card, copyright stp on verso, 1958-59, 13x16", SBY 4/26/89 1,540
Pride Street, Pittsburgh; artist name/credit/copyright/New York studio stps, matted, ca 1955, 14x9", SBY 4/26/89 1,980
Saipan, slvr, estate stp on verso, 1944/pre-1978, 18x14", B/B 4/19/88 UE 550
Spanish Spinner, Spanish Village; mounted on card, estate stp on verso, matted, 1951/later, fr, 17x24", SBY 11/1/88 6,050
Spanish Spinner, Spanish Village; sgn w/stylus on img, sgn/titled on mount, 1951/later, 13x9", SBY 5/4/88 2,310

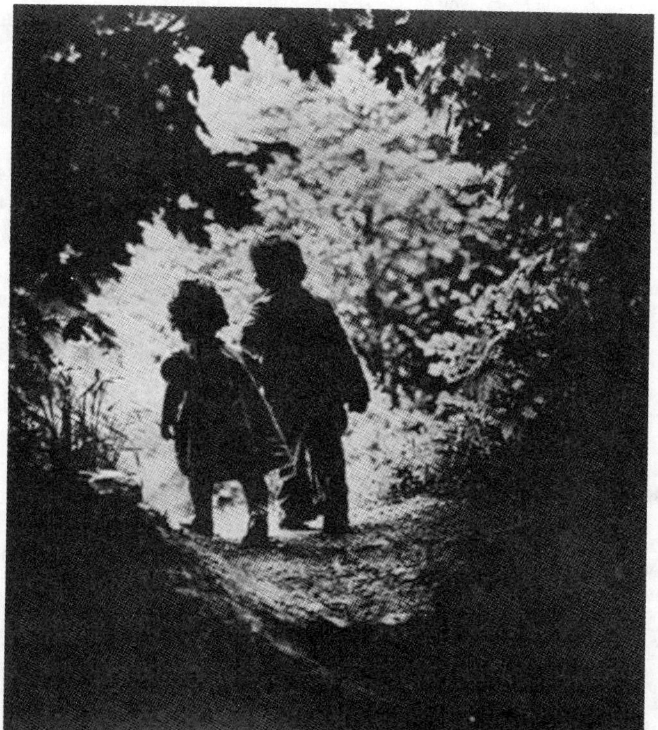

Walk Through Paradise Garden, slvr, sgn w/stylus on img, 1946/later, 15x13", B/B 10/4/88; $7,700

Walk to Paradise Garden, p/s on mount, estate stp on verso, matted, 1946/later, 12x10", SBY 5/4/88 OE 6,600
Walk to Paradise Garden, sgn/titled on mount, 1946/later, 12x10", SBY 11/1/88 OE 7,700
Welsh Miners, sgn w/stylus on img, artist estate stp on verso, matted, 1950/later, 10x13", SBY 4/26/89 1,980
Young Girl Drying Dishes, Migrant Workers; Croton-on-Hudson/repro limitation stps, 1953, 14x9", SBY 5/4/88 660

MITH & JAGARD (American, Philadelphia; 19th C)
Post Mortem of Young Girl Surrounded by Lit Candles Holds Doll, CDV, ca 1860s, lot 270, CEG 6/23/89 40

NELSON, Kenneth (20th C)
Isle de la Cite Panorama, 4/6, C-print, sgn/dtd on img, matted, 1984, 9x48", SBY 4/26/89 880

Times Square Panorama, 4/15, sgn/dtd on img, 1980, fr, 16x109", SBY 4/26/89 3,300

SOMMER, Frederick (American, 1905-)
Circumnavigation of the Blood, sgn/dtd/titled on verso, mounted/matted, 1950, fr, 4x6", SBY 5/4/88 7,700

SOMMER, Georgio (19th C)
Group of 5: Views in Italy; alb, 1870s, 8x10", B/B 10/4/88 UE 138

SOUGEZ, Emmanuel
Reclining Nude, artist name stp on verso, matted, 1930s, 5x11", SBY 11/1/88 1,210

SOULIER, Charles (19th C)
Arc de Septime Severe, Rome; #318, alb, double-mounted, titled/credit, ca 1865, 12x16", SWN 10/30/88 UE 121

SOUTHWORTH & HAWES (19th C)
Elderly Lady in a Ruffled Cap, bust-length; dag, half pl, leather case, ca 1850, SWN 4/24/89 468
Little Girl Sitting in a Chair, dag, 6th Scovill Extra pl, 1850s, SWN 4/24/89 OE 660

SPENCER, Ema
Pair: Elizabeth & Nanette Were Drawing; Her First Sled; pltn, titled on mount, 8x6"/8x3", B/B 10/4/88 358

STACKPOLE, Peter (20th C)
Beam Composition, slvr, sgn/dtd on mount, 1935/1970s, 9x13", B/B 4/19/88 275

STACKPOLE, Ralph (20th C)
Men in Action Atop Hammerhead Crane, slvr, p/s & dtd on mount, ca 1934/later, 10x14", B/B 10/4/88 248

STANKOWSKI, Anton (20th C)
Pair: Man Smoking; Park Chairs; sgn/dtd, 1 studio stp on verso, matted, 1934 & 1936, 7x9", SBY 11/1/88 660
Photogram of Keys, 4/5, slvr of photogram, sgn/dtd on mount, matted, 1929/1970s, 12x15", SBY 5/4/88 440

STARN, Mike; & STARN, Doug
Untitled (bust portrait w/brick wall background), sepia toned photo, sgn/dtd 84-85 on verso, 20x16", lot 349, SBY 5/3/89 8,800

STEGEMEYER, Elfriede
Hand (Photogram), photogram w/ink, sgn/dtd/inscr Fotogramm on verso, matted, 1933, 9x7", SBY 4/26/89 3,575

STEICHEN, Edward (American, 1879-1973)
Broadway Lights, photomontage, p/s on img, titled/inscr #4 North Wall on verso, matted, 1933, fr, 41x35", SBY 5/4/88 OE 40,700
Carmel Snow, sgn/dtd on mat, mounted, 1924, 10x8", SBY 4/26/89 1,980
Charlie Chaplin, slvr, artist name stp on mount verso, 1925/1950s-60s, 17x14", SWN 4/24/89 5,500
Ethel Barrymore in Dramatic Pose, toned slvr, 80 W 40th St NYC stp on verso, 1925, 10x8", SWN 10/30/88 660
Grasshopper, artist name stp on verso, matted, 1920s/1950s-60s, 14x11", SBY 11/1/88 990
Group of 3: Carl Sandburg with His Goats, Lake Michigan; 1935, 8x8", SBY 4/26/89 1,430
Group of 4: Lon & Nell; Mary, Nell & Kate; Nell & Joan; Nell; matted, late 1920s-early 1930s, various sizes, SBY 4/26/89 1,540
Lotus, inscr Lotus Cry Over This One on verso, matted, 1915, 10x8", SBY 4/26/89 OE 28,600
Lotus Flower, backed w/card, artist name stp on verso, 1915/1950s-60s, 14x11", SBY 11/1/88 8,250
Paul Robeson As Emperor Jones, artist stp on verso, matted, 1933/ca 1950s, fr, 10x8", SBY 5/4/88 1,320
Portrait of Mary, pltn on post card, postmk June 1 & 2 1906, addressed to Lilian Steichen, 5x3", B/B 10/4/88 UE 1,045
Rodin, Paris; sgn in negative, artist name stp on verso, matted, 1910/1950s, 14x11", SBY 11/1/88 1,870
Rodin-Le Penseur, carbon, sgn/dtd MDCCCCII in negative, 1902, 14x17", SBY 5/4/88 16,500
Spiral Shell, toned slvr, artist name stp/titled/dtd on verso, 1921/later, 14x11", SWN 4/24/89 3,300
Steichen & Wife Clara on Their Honeymoon, Lake George, New York; pltn, sgn in negative, ca 1904, 11x11", SBY 4/26/89 OE 17,600
Sunday Papers, West 86th St, New York; slvr, stp on verso, 1922, 9x7", B/B 4/19/88 495

STEINER, Ralph (American, 1899-)
American Rural Baroque (Rocking Chair), mounted on card, sgn/dtd on verso, matted, 1929/1980, 8x10", SBY 5/4/88 770
Cars Parked on a Street of Row Houses, slvr flush-mounted to board, 1920s, 10x8", SWN 4/24/89 OE 3,080
Group of 3: Ship in Harbor, 1922; Hanging Sheets, 1965; Tree, ca 1957; sgn on verso, matted, various sizes, SBY 5/4/88 660
Self-Portrait with Camera & Billboard, sgn/dtd on verso, matted, 1929/1979, 10x7", SBY 4/26/89 880

STERN, Bert (20th C)
Portfolio: The Last Sitting; 104/250, 10 C-prints, sgn, matted, 1962/1978, 19x19", folder, Shorewood Press, SBY 4/26/89 5,225

STERN, Phil (20th C)
Group of 3: James Dean; artist repro limitation/credit stps on verso, matted, early 1950s, 10x8", SBY 4/26/89 1,210

STETTNER, Louis (20th C)
Aubervilliers, a/p, p/s on mount, matted, 1947/later, fr, 17x14", SBY 5/4/88 550

STIEGLITZ, Alfred (American, 1864-1946)
Camera Work No 14, April 1906; photogr/haft, printed gray wrappers missing, B/B 10/4/88 935
Camera Work No 36, Dirigible; Pl 8, photogr on orig 4to leaf, 7x7", SWN 4/24/89 440
Camera Work No 4, October 1903; photogr/haft, printed gray wrappers missing, B/B 10/4/88 522
City of Ambition, Camera Work No 36; Pl 1, 1911, SWN 10/30/88 OE 358
Edward Steichen Picking Daisies with Elizabeth & Flora Stieglitz at Lake George, matted, ca 1904, 5x4", SBY 11/1/88 1,760
From an American Place, backed w/card, sgn/dtd, 1935, 10x8", SBY 11/1/88 16,500
Letterbox, pltn on card, sgn/dtd/titled/inscr Orig Platinum Print, mounted/matted, 1894, orig fr, 8x6", SBY 5/4/88 OE 26,400
Marie Rapp, pltn, matted, 1920s, 10x8", SBY 5/4/88 UE 4,950
New York Street, pltn, mounted/matted, ca 1900, 3x4", SBY 11/1/88 1,760
Pair: Winter Sky-Central Park, 1897; Two Towers-New York, Camera Work 65, 1913; photogr, 9x7"/8x6", SBY 5/4/88 OE 2,420
Portfolio: Picturesque Bits of New York & Other Studies; 12 photogr, 1894-1897, various sizes, SBY 11/1/88 9,900
Steerage, Camera Work No 36, October 1911; photogr, 1911, sm format, SBY 4/26/89 OE 2,750
Steerage, From #7-8 of 291; photogr on vellum, matted, 1911, large format, SBY 4/26/89 OE 6,600
Steerage, photogr on vellum, matted, 1911, fr, large format, SBY 11/1/88 OE 7,150
Steerage, photogr on vellum w/orig backing board, American Place Gallery stps on verso, 1911, SBY 5/4/88 OE 7,150
Yvonne Boursault at Lake George, mounted/matted, 1923, fr, 3x4", SBY 11/1/88 4,125

STONE, Cami
- Crossing the Street, Berlin studio repro limitation stp on verso, matted, ca 1925, 9x7", SBY 4/26/89 ..... **1,650**
- Street Scene, slvr, Berlin Atelier/Verlag Dr Hans Epstein stps on verso, 1920s, 4x6", SWN 10/30/88 ..... **330**

STOUMEN, Lou (American, 1917-)
- Black Cat Cafe, slvr, sgn/dtd on mount, 1942/1970s, 19x14", B/B 4/19/88 ..... **330**
- Times Square in Rain, ink sgn in mrg, dtd/titled on verso, matted, 1941/later, 18x13", SBY 11/1/88 OE **990**

STRAND, Paul (American, 1890-1976)
- Fish Houses, Corea, Maine; sgn/dtd/titled on verso, matted, 1945, 10x8", SBY 11/1/88 ..... **6,050**
- Lighthouse, New England; backed w/card, sgn, dtd/titled by Anne Kennedy on verso, matted, 1945, fr, 6x5", SBY 5/4/88 ..... **4,950**
- Man, Tenancingo, Mexico; pltn backed w/card, sgn/dtd/inscr Platinum Print on verso, matted, 1933, 6x5", SBY 5/4/88 ..... **9,350**
- New York, the Backyards; sgn/dtd/titled on verso, matted, 1915/later, 7x9", SBY 4/26/89 ..... **6,600**
- Portfolio: Mexican Portfolio; 512/1000, 20 photogr, sgn on justification page, 1930s/ca 1967, cased, SBY 5/4/88 ..... **880**
- San Antonio, Texas; pltn, matted, 1918, 7x9", SBY 5/4/88 ..... **7,700**
- Stockburgers Farm, East Jamaica, Vermont; slvr, sgn/titled/dtd in gr ink on verso, 1943, 10x8", SWN 4/24/89 ..... **4,620**
- Winter Landscape, pltn on card, ca 1910, 7x9", SBY 4/26/89 UE **9,900**

STRUSS, Karl
- Arverne, pltn, dtd on mount, sgn/dtd/titled on verso, matted, 1912, 4x4", SBY 11/1/88 ..... **1,320**
- Ducks, Lake Como; pltn, dtd on mount, artist name/Hollywood studio stp on verso, matted, 1909, 4x5", SBY 11/1/88 ..... **1,980**
- End of Board Walk (Arverne), pltn, sgn/dtd on img & verso, matted, 1909, 9x7", SBY 11/1/88 UE **880**
- Fifth Avenue, Twilight, New York; toned brom, sgn/dtd on img, matted, ca 1914, 12x9", SBY 5/4/88 ..... **8,250**
- Group of 3: Nude Studies; slvr, copyright mk in negative, #d/stp on verso, ca 1920, 7x9", B/B 10/4/88 ..... **440**
- Monterey Fields, pldm, sgn/dtd on mount, titled/dtd/Hollywood studio stp on verso, matted, 1921, fr, 4x5", SBY 5/4/88 ..... **1,320**
- Morning on the River (New York), sepia-toned gum pltn, sgn/dtd, Hollywood stp on verso, 1911, 8x6", SBY 11/1/88 ..... **2,475**
- New York Public Library, brom, artist stp on verso, matted, 1912, 5x4", SBY 5/4/88 UE **550**
- Pair: Water's Edge; Untitled Landscape; pltn & haft, p/s, 1911 & ca 1900, 4x5"/8x6", B/B 10/4/88 UE **550**
- Vaslav Nijinsky in Scene From L'Apres-Midi d'un Faune, mounted on advertisement card, ca 1912, 5x4", SBY 5/4/88 OE **1,760**
- Venice, pltn, dtd on mount, sgn/dtd on verso, matted, 1909, 4x3", SBY 11/1/88 ..... **605**

STRUWE, Carl (20th C)
- Formen des Mikrokosmos, slvr, sgn/stp on verso, 1950s, 15x11", B/B 10/4/88 ..... **412**

SUDEK, Josef (20th C)
- Blasted Trees, slvr, sgn w/stylus in lower mrg, 1950s, 5x6", SWN 4/24/89 ..... **605**
- Blossoming Tree, Springtime; sgn/dtd/inscr in mrg, sgn/inscr on verso, 1964, 9x12", SBY 4/26/89 ..... **1,980**
- Book: Praha Panoramaticka; oversize oblong 4to, fabric-covered boards, orig dust jacket, 1959, Prague, SBY 11/1/88 UE **440**
- Bridge Over River at Night, Prague; 5/12, sgn/inscr H-I on img, matted, 1960s, fr, 7x5", SBY 5/4/88 OE **2,530**
- Country Villa Panorama, p/s on img, matted, 1960s, fr, 4x12", SBY 5/4/88 ..... **1,320**
- Evening on Charles Bridge (Prague), p/s in mrg, 1940s, 5x7", SBY 4/26/89 OE **1,540**
- Garden, slvr, sgn/dtd/inscr in mrg, 1964, 11x15", SBY 4/26/89 ..... **1,760**
- Glass, brml on paper coated w/silver flakes, 1950s, 6x4", SBY 5/4/88 OE **2,310**
- Group of 3: Scenes in Prague; slvr, 1 sgn/dtd on verso, ca 1960, 3x3" to 9x6", B/B 10/4/88 UE **385**
- Group of 4: Woodland Sketches; sgn/titled, 1960s-1970s, various sizes, SBY 11/1/88 ..... **1,760**
- Group of 5: Street Lamp at Night; Light Reflection; Windows in Afternoon; Snowy Night; Open Gates; 1950-70s, SBY 5/4/88 ..... **2,090**
- Labyrinth on My Table, sgn/dtd/inscr in mrg, matted, 1967, 11x9", SBY 5/4/88 OE **3,575**
- Pair: Garden Chairs; Egg Study; titled, 1950s, 4x7"/3x4", SBY 4/26/89 OE **1,650**
- Pair: Window Display; Architectural Study; sgn w/stylus in img, 1970s, 12x9"/7x9", SBY 11/1/88 UE **440**
- Pair: Winter Street at Night; Small Panoramic View of Prague; slvr, titled, 1950s & 1968, 5x7"/2x6", SWN 10/30/88 UE **385**

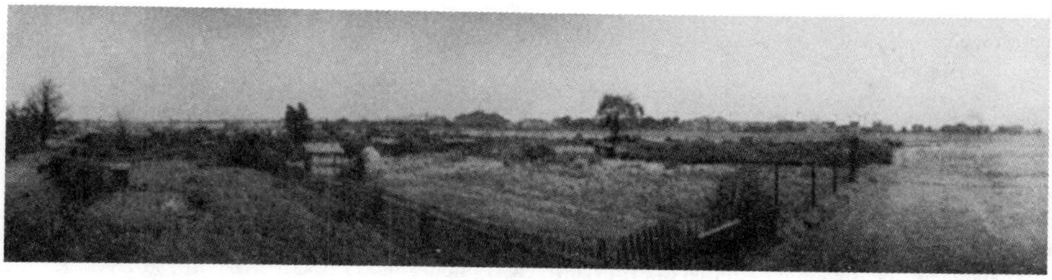

Panorama, slvr, sgn w/stylus in lower mrg, dtd 1959 on verso, 4x11", SWN 4/24/89; $660

- Rose, sgn/dtd/titled on img, 1967, 7x9", SBY 11/1/88 OE **1,540**
- Spring, gr-toned slvr, sgn/dtd/inscr in mrg, matted, 1968, fr, 9x11", SBY 5/4/88 ..... **990**
- Statue of Madonna & Child, slvr on lg paper, p/s in lower mrg, ca 1960, 6x4", SWN 4/24/89 ..... **440**
- Still Life, sgn/inscr/dtd in mrg, inscr on verso, matted, 1969, 9x7", SBY 5/4/88 ..... **1,650**
- Still Life (Glass with Egg), p/s on verso, matted, early 1950s, 5x7", SBY 4/26/89 ..... **4,125**
- Study of Bidding Branches, gr-toned slvr, titled in pencil on verso, ca 1960, 6x4", SWN 4/24/89 ..... **660**
- Study of Blossoms, toned slvr, sgn w/stylus in mrg, ca 1960, 6x4", SWN 10/30/88 ..... **495**
- Tree Study, slvr on lg paper, sgn w/stylus in mrg, dtd in pencil on verso, 1917/later, 2x2", SWN 4/24/89 ..... **413**
- View Through Window, slvr, ca 1966, 9x7", B/B 4/19/88 UE **358**
- Water Glass, p/s in mrg, matted, 1950s, 6x5", SBY 11/1/88 OE **1,540**
- Winter Sunset, brn-toned slvr mounted on vellum, p/s in mrg, matted, 1920s, 8x11", SBY 11/1/88 ..... **2,200**

SUTCLIFFE, Frank Meadow (19th C)
Pair: Whitby Harbor; Signpost; 1880s, orig studio fr, 9x11"/8x9", SBY 11/1/88 ... 990
SUTNAR, Ladislav
Toys, slvr on post card, sgn on verso, ca 1927, SWN 10/30/88 ... 715
TABARD, Maurice
Le Studio Abandon, titled/dtd/studio stps on verso, matted, 1926, 7x9", SBY 4/26/89 ... 3,025
Route du Mans, solarized slvr, flush-mounted to board, titled/Paris stp on verso, ca 1930, 9x7", SWN 10/30/88 ... 825
Solarization, p/s on mount, sgn in negative, matted, 1933, 10x7", SBY 4/26/89 ... 2,200
Solarized Portrait, sgn/dtd/Paris studio & artist name stps on verso, matted, 1930, fr, 9x7", SBY 4/26/89 ... 1,650
Untitled (portrait), photocollage, sgn/dtd on img, exhibition label on verso, matted, 1930, S-12x10", SBY 4/26/89 OE ... 31,900
TABER, Isaiah; & WATKINS, Carleton (19th C)
Seal Rock, Pacific Ocean; #561, alb, credit in negative, mounted, 1870s-80s, 16x21", SWN 4/24/89 OE ... 990
TALBOT, William Henry (19th C)
Pair: Highland Hut on the Banks of Loch Katrine; Scenery of Loch Katrine; #14 & #15, calo, 1945, 3x4", SWN 4/24/89 ... 605
Specimen of Talbotype (or Calotype) Photogenic Drawing, calo, 1843, 3x4", SWN 10/30/88 ... 440
TATO (Guglielmo Sansoni)
Self-Portrait, matted, 1923, 4x6", SBY 5/4/88 ... 1,540
THALEMANN, Elsa
Lokomotivendetail, slvr, typed label/artist credit mounted on verso, ca 1926, 7x9", SWN 4/24/89 ... 605
THOMPSON, Fred
Portland Head (view of lighthouse), tinted print on orig mount, sgn/titled below img, 5x9", CEG 6/23/89 ... 30
TICE, George A. (20th C)
Group of 3: Mount Desert Island; Snow; Water Lillies; 2 in ed of 100, sgn, 1970s, various sizes, SBY 5/4/88 ... 1,045
Oak Tree, Holmdel, New Jersey; toned slvr, p/s on mount, titled/dtd on mount verso, 1970/1980, 11x13", B/B 4/19/88 ... 300
Pitcher, p/s on mount, 1970s, 13x19", SBY 5/4/88 ... 880
Portfolio: Bodie; 45/55, 12 photos, artist bstp on mount, 1965/ca 1977, 5x5", cased, SBY 5/4/88 ... 1,980
Woods, Cushing, Maine; slvr, p/s on mount recto, sgn/titled/dtd on mount verso, 1970/unknown, 8x10", SWN 10/30/88 ... 220
TRESS, Arthur (20th C)
Girl with Goldfish, France; 39/50, slvr, sgn/titled in mrg, 1970s, 11x11", B/B 4/19/88 ... 192
TRUMP, Georg
Typewriter with Feldmuehle Stationery, slvr, Muenchen 2 Pranckhstrasse 2 stp on verso, 1920s, 10x7", SWN 4/24/89 ... 440
TURBEVILLE, Deborah (20th C)
Sonai Rykiel, Fashion Study; 1/5, sgn in mrg, matted, 1976, 8x11", SBY 4/26/89 OE ... 3,025
UELSMANN, Jerry (20th C)
All American Sunset, intl/dtd on mount, sgn/dtd/titled/studio label on verso, 1971, 7x8", SBY 11/1/88 ... 715
Man & Monkey, slvr, intl/dtd on mount, sgn/dtd/label on verso, 1976, 14x9", B/B 10/4/88 ... 440
Pair: Self-Portrait As Robinson & Rejlander; Boy Plays on Hearth; sgn/titled, matted, 1964 & 1972, 13x9", SBY 11/1/88 ... 660
Rock-Tree, slvr, intl/dtd on mount, sgn/dtd/titled/label on verso, 1969, 13x9", B/B 10/4/88 ... 522
ULMANN, Doris
Boy at Farmgate, pltn, p/s on mount, ca 1929, 8x6", B/B 10/4/88 ... 302
UMBO (Otto Umbehr)(20th C)
Portfolio: 10 Photographs 1927-1930; sgn on img, estate/portfolio stps on verso, 1927-30/ca 1980, SBY 11/1/88 ... 2,750
Untitled (Portrait of a Woman), sgn on img, dtd/inscr on verso, matted, 1927, 7x5", SBY 4/26/89 ... 3,300
UNDERWOOD (20th C)
Charles Lindbergh with Spirit of St Louis, slvr, mounted, 1927, fr, 12x16", CEG 5/7/88 ... 100
UNDERWOOD & UNDERWOOD
Marey Camera, artist/credit stps on verso, matted, early 1900s, 4x5", SBY 11/1/88 ... 660
VALLET, C. (20th C)
Illuminated Fountain, Paris; sgn/dtd on mount, matted, ca 1935, 9x7", SBY 11/1/88 ... 550
VAN DER ZEE, James (American, 1886-1980)
Couple in Racoon Coats, 18 Photographs; 72/90, sgn/dtd in negative, matted, 1932/later, 8x10", SBY 5/4/88 ... 1,320
Heiress, in evening dress/standing in living room; slvr, 1938, 7x9", SWN 4/24/89 ... 1,100
Heiress, slvr, sgn/dtd in negative, GGG Photo stp on verso, 1938, 8x10", SWN 10/30/88 OE ... 1,210
Mother Josephine Becton, slvr, GGG Photo Studio 2065 7th Ave stp on verso, 1934, 8x10", SWN 4/24/89 ... 330
Panoramic Group of the Congregation Outside the Refuge Church of Christ, slvr, GGG Photo studio stp, 4x9", SWN 10/30/88 ... 248
VISHNIAC, Roman Munkatch (20th C)
Beggars in Lublin, sgn/dtd/titled on mount, matted, 1937/later, 10x10", SBY 5/4/88 ... 990
But Mother Has Nothing at Home, sgn/dtd/titled in mrg, matted, 1938/later, 8x10", SBY 11/1/88 UE ... 440
Lodz 1938, the Result of Boycot (sic)-Ruin; sgn/dtd/titled on mount, matted, 1938, 15x11", SBY 5/4/88 ... 1,100
Man & Woman in Market, sgn in mrg, matted, late 1930s/later, 20x16", SBY 4/26/89 UE ... 1,100
Munkatch Rabbi Baruch Rabinovich, sgn/dtd/titled in mrg & on verso, matted, 1938/later, 10x13", SBY 11/1/88 ... 1,540
Oldest Synagogue in Cracow, sgn/titled in mrg, 1930s/later, 10x13", SBY 11/1/88 ... 1,980
Rabbi of Cracow, dtd/titled in mrg, matted, 1937/later, 8x10", SBY 4/26/89 OE ... 1,760
Trade But No Customers, Cracow; sgn/dtd/titled in mrg, matted, 1938/later, 8x10", SBY 4/26/89 OE ... 2,200
VON GLOEDEN, Wilhelm
Group of 10: Male Figure Studies; 4 sgn/2 dtd on img, 1916-26, various sizes, SBY 5/4/88 OE ... 13,750
Group of 10: Nude Studies; 4 sgn/2 dtd on img, 3 Taormina studio stp on verso, 1916-26, various sizes, SBY 11/1/88 OE ... 4,400
Pair: Young Boy; Young Girl; Taormina studio stp on verso, matted, early 1900s, fr, 9x6", SBY 11/1/88 ... 660
WARD, John (20th C)
Pair: Fin, Arches National Park, Utah; Betatakin Cave, Navajo National Monument, Arizona; slvr, ca 1974, B/B 4/19/88 ... 358
Pair: Mills Lake, Rocky Mountain National Park, Colorado; Hancock Brook, Vermont; slvr, 1969 & 1975, 16x20", B/B 4/19/88 ... 275

WARHOL, Andy (American, 1928-1987)
Milton Berle, 6 photos stitched together & mounted on card, sgn/dtd on verso, 1986, fr, 27x32", SBY 4/26/89 ... 11,000
Self-Portrait, Polaroid, Factory Fotos stp/inscr Feb 1971 Germany on verso, matted, 1971, fr, 4x3", SBY 11/1/88 UE ... 495
WARREN, Henry F. (19th C)
Abraham Lincoln, alb, dtd/titled in mrg, label on verso, 1860s, oval 7x5", B/B 10/4/88 UE ... 192
Latest Photograph of President Lincoln Taken on Balcony at White House, March 6, 1865; alb, 14x11", SWN 4/24/89 ... 550
WATKINS, Carleton E. (American, 1829-1916)
Bridal Veil 900 Ft, No 16; alb, titled on verso, 1860s, 21x15", SBY 5/4/88 ... 1,320
Seal Rocks at the Cliff House, alb, mounted, 1870s, 8x12", SWN 4/24/89 ... 550
WEBB, Todd (American, 1905-)
Nevada, slvr, sgn/titled/dtd on verso, 1955/later, 13x10", SWN 4/24/89 ... 192
Pair: Maisie, Queen of the Bowery; Coney Island; slvr, sgn/titled/dtd on verso, 1946/unknown, 12x9"/13x10", SWN 4/24/89 ... 385
Paris, slvr, sgn/titled/dtd on verso, 1949/later, 10x8", B/B 4/19/88 ... 300
WEED, C.L.; att (19th C)
Eadweard Muybridge Below the US Grant Sequoia, alb, mounted, ca 1865/early 1870s, 8x7", SWN 4/24/89 ... 550
WEEGEE (American, 1899-1968)
Book: Movie Theatre; 26 photos mounted 1 to page, titled, various stps, 1940s, various sizes, SBY 4/26/89 UE ... 19,800
Carousel, dtd in mrg, artist credit stp on verso, matted, 1940, 11x13", SBY 4/26/89 ... 880
Coney Island, artist credit/studio stps on verso, early 1940s, 10x13", SBY 4/26/89 OE ... 6,050
Critic, credit stp on verso, matted, early 1940s, 13x17", SBY 11/1/88 OE ... 4,400
Critic, printed on linen paper, artist credit stp on verso, matted, early 1940s, 11x14", SBY 4/26/89 OE ... 4,675

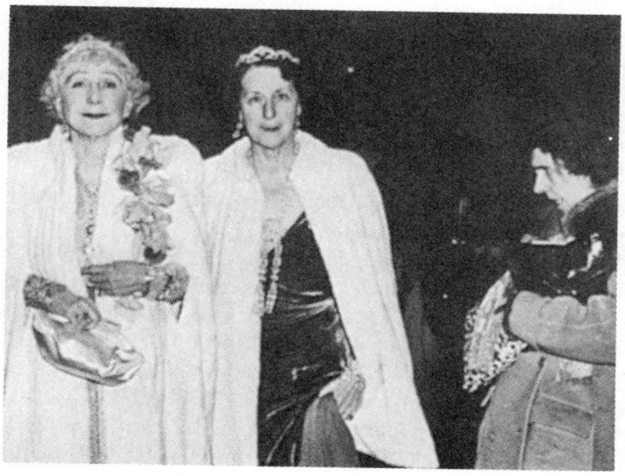

Critic, slvr, Arthur Fellig/Weegee the Famous stps on verso, 1943/probably 1940s, 11x13", lot 482, SWN 10/30/88; $2,640

Easter Sunday, artist credit/studio stps on verso, matted, 1940s, 13x11", SBY 4/26/89 ... 2,750
Embarrassing Moment, New York City; titled/artist name & studio stp on verso, early 1940s, 13x10", SBY 4/26/89 ... 660
Hollywood Double Feature (wedding distortion), slvr, Weegee the Famous/Photo-Representatives stps, 1959, SWN 4/24/89 UE ... 468
I Cried When I Took This Picture, studio stp on verso, matted, early 1940s, 11x14", SBY 4/26/89 ... 1,100
Marilyn Monroe Distortion, slvr, Weegee the Famous/Photo-Representatives stps on verso, 1960s, 14x11", SWN 4/24/89 ... 825
Merry-Go-Round, Coney Island; #22, slvr, stp on verso, ca 1940, 11x13", B/B 4/19/88 ... 385
Nude, slvr, sgn/dtd on mount, 1975/1978, 10x14", SWN 10/30/88 ... 1,100
Pair: Drunk in a Bottle; Street Sleepers; matted, 1940s, fr, 9x4"/5x7", SBY 11/1/88 UE ... 440
Pair: Self-Portraits; credit stp on verso, matted, 1950s, 9x5"/9x8", SBY 11/1/88 ... 880
Pair: Tenement Penthouse (fat man asleep on fire escape); Elephant Sleeping; slvr, mounted together, 9x8", SWN 4/24/89 ... 550
Pair: Times Square-5 in the Morning, Star Spangled Banner; Photomontage with Trapeze Artists; 1940s, SBY 4/26/89 OE ... 1,760
Puritan, slvr, Weegee the Famous/Photo-Representatives stps on verso, 1945, 14x11", SWN 4/24/89 ... 413
Sailor & His Girlfriend on a Bench, slvr, Arthur Fellig 5 Center Market Pl NYC stp on verso, 1940s, 14x11", SWN 4/24/89 ... 468
Self-Portrait, sgn 4 times on img, mounted on masonite, sgn/artist name & credit stps, 1950s, 24x20", SBY 4/26/89 ... 2,200
Self-Portrait Holding a Polaroid Camera, slvr, Photo-Representatives stp on verso, ca 1960, 8x7", SWN 10/30/88 ... 440
Self-Portrait with Camera, artist stp on verso, mounted/matted, 1940s, 11x4", SBY 5/4/88 OE ... 1,210
Ship Aground, New York Harbor; artist name/Market Place studio stps on verso, 1940s, 11x13", SBY 11/1/88 OE ... 1,650
Sleeper in a Bar, slvr, Weegee the Famous/451 W 47th St NYC stps on verso, 1939, 11x14", SWN 4/24/89 ... 523
Temenent Children, mounted on masonite, sgn exhibition label/credit stp on verso, 1940s, 21x25", lot 496, SBY 4/26/89 ... 7,150
Tenement Children, artist credit stp/inscr Printed by Weegee 2-24-81, matted, 1940s, 13x11", lot 497, SBY 4/26/89 OE ... 18,700
Tramp, slvr, Please Credit Photograph by Weegee stp on verso, 1930s, 14x11", SWN 4/24/89 UE ... 468
Winter Night's Fire, slvr, Photo-Representatives/451 W 47th St NYC/Eye Magazine stps on verso, 1947, 13x11", SWN 4/24/89 ... 1,100
Woman Smoking Cigarette, Harlem; slvr, Photo-Representatives stp on verso, 1930s-40s, 14x11", SWN 4/24/89 ... 770
EGMAN, William (American, 1943-)
Family Combinations, ed of 6, sequence of 6 photos, sgn/#d/title label, 1972, ea fr, ea 13x11", SBY 11/1/88 OE ... 16,500
Mailbox (& Man Ray), slvr w/ink, intl/dtd on verso, mounted/matted, 1977, fr, 10x13", SBY 5/4/88 ... 1,100
Rangeley, Maine; 32/75, C-print, sgn/dtd/titled on img, matted, 1981, 20x19", SBY 4/26/89 ... 1,650
Watching Skier, slvr w/ink, intl/dtd on verso, matted, 1975, fr, 11x11", SBY 5/4/88 ... 1,100
Watching Two TV's, slvr w/ink, intl/dtd on verso, mounted/matted, 1975, 8x7", SBY 5/4/88 ... 1,820
ENDEROTH, TAYLOR, & BROWN (19th C)
Ulysses S Grant, Imperial sltp, Phil studio label on mount, 1860s, oval 20x16", SWN 4/24/89 ... 4,400

WERNER, Mantz	
Study of a House, slvr, Koeln Hohenstaufenring 46/copyright stps on verso, 1928, 9x7", SWN 10/30/88 UE	358
WESTON, Brett (20th C)	
Abstraction, pltn mounted on cream card, sgn/dtd/inscr California on mount, 1937, 9x7", SBY 5/4/88 OE	2,860
Cactus, Baja, California; slvr, sgn/dtd on mount, 1967, 10x8", B/B 10/4/88	660
Dunes, White Sands; intl/dtd on mount, #d D1 on verso, matted, 1947/later, fr, 8x10", lot 512, SBY 5/4/88	990
Fern Fronds, sgn/dtd on mount, matted, 1978, 11x13", SBY 5/4/88	660
Forest, sgn/dtd on mount, matted, 1951/later, 10x14", SBY 11/1/88	660
Garapata Beach, sgn/dtd on mount, 1954/later, 11x13", SBY 5/4/88	1,100
Glen Canyon, sgn/dtd on mount, 1959/later, 14x11", SBY 5/4/88 OE	1,210
Headstone & Lichen, Japan; slvr, sgn/dtd on mount, 1970, 8x9", B/B 10/4/88	495
Horse Trailer, California; slvr, sgn/dtd on mount, 1972, 8x10", B/B 4/19/88 UE	248
Lake Patzcuaro, Mexico; slvr, sgn/dtd on mount, 1976/1978, 11x14", B/B 4/19/88	660
Leaves in Snow, sgn/dtd on overmat, mounted/matted, 1951, 10x14", SBY 4/26/89	1,100
Mendenhall Glacier, Alaska; #15, slvr, sgn/dtd on mount, 1973/1978, 10x13", B/B 4/19/88	1,320
Monterey Fog, sgn/dtd on mount, 1961, 10x8", SBY 11/1/88 OE	1,320
Monterey Pine & Fog, sgn/dtd, mounted/matted, 1963, 14x10", SBY 11/1/88	770
Pair: Country Landscape; Cardons & Bay, Baja, California; sgn/dtd on mount, 1964 & 1966, 15x19", SBY 4/26/89 OE	2,200
Pair: Fern; Abstraction; sgn/dtd on mount, sgn/dtd/Amon Carter Museum label on verso, 1946 & 1955, 8x10", SBY 4/26/89 OE	1,320
Pair: Ocean Views; sgn/dtd on mount, Amon Carter Museum label on verso, 1954 & 1960, 8x10", SBY 4/26/89 OE	1,650
Pair: Statues; Horses in Snowy Field; sgn/dtd on mount, Amon Carter Museum label, 1955 & 1960, 8x10", SBY 4/26/89	990
Reclining Nude, slvr, 1975/1978, p/s on mount, 11x14", B/B 4/19/88 UE	440
Rock Forms, Westgard Pass, California; slvr, sgn/dtd on mount, 1969, 10x8", B/B 4/19/88	550
Sand Dunes, intl/dtd on mount, #d DE 227 on verso, mounted/matted, 1954, fr, 8x10", lot 511, SBY 5/4/88 OE	1,430
Sand Dunes, sgn/dtd on mount, sgn/inscr 1325 Greenwich St/#d 345 on verso, 1936, 8x10", lot 510, SBY 5/4/88	1,210
Tidal Pool, Point Lobos, California; slvr, sgn/dtd on mount, 1975, 10x8", B/B 4/19/88	522
Tree Roots, 1973, slvr, sgn/dtd on mount, 1973, 10x8", B/B 4/19/88 UE	220
WESTON, Cole (20th C)	
Palo Corona Ranch, Carmel; dye, sgn/dtd on mount, stp on mount verso, 1962, 14x19", B/B 4/19/88	330
WESTON, Edward (American, 1886-1958)	
Back of Wrecked Ford, Mojave Desert; sgn/dtd on mount, titled/inscr MD-HSS-2G on verso, matted, 1937, 8x10", SBY 11/1/88	3,025
Boat Builder, 9/40, slvr, p/s on mount, titled on mount verso, 1935, 10x8", B/B 4/19/88	1,980
Bull From the Town of Santa Cruz Near Tonala, matted, 1926, 7x9", SBY 11/1/88	2,200
Carmen Maracci, sgn/dtd on mount, matted, 1937, 5x4", SBY 5/4/88 UE	660
Cloud, slvr, facsimile stp/sgn by Brett Weston on mount verso, 1936/1955, 8x10", B/B 4/19/88 UE	330
Cypress Root, sgn/dtd/titled on mount, matted, 1929, 9x8", SBY 11/1/88	3,575
Death Valley, sgn/dtd on mount, titled/inscr DV-39C-6G on verso, matted, 1938, 8x10", SBY 4/26/89	7,150
Death Valley (Zabriskie Point), sgn/dtd on mount, titled/#d DV-3-4S on verso, matted, 1937, 8x10", SBY 11/1/88	4,125
Dunes, Oceano; intl/dtd on mount, dtd/titled/#d 52SO/inscr For Dudley, matted, 1936, fr, 7x10", lot 543, SBY 11/1/88	16,500
Dunes, Oceano; intl/dtd on mount, sgn/dtd/titled on verso, matted, 1936, 8x10", lot 542, SBY 11/1/88	28,600
Dunes, Oceano; sgn/dtd on mount, #d 29SO on verso, matted, 1936, 8x10", lot 545, SBY 11/1/88	23,100
Dunes, Oceano; sgn/dtd/inscr Courtesy Federal Art Project on mount, exhibition label, 1936, 8x10", lot 544, SBY 11/1/88	6,600
Dunes, Oceano; sgn/dtd/titled/Art Institute of Chicago stp on verso, matted, 1936, 8x10", lot 221, SBY 11/1/88	4,125
Eel River Ranch, inscr Edward Loves Zohmah/exhibition stp/loan label on verso, mounted, 1938, 8x10", SBY 11/1/88	3,025
Eggs & Slicer, 7/50, sgn/intl/dtd/#d on mount, matted, 1930, 8x10", SBY 5/4/88 OE	26,400
Embarcadero, San Francisco; sgn/dtd on mount, inscr Neil Happy Birthday, matted, 1937, 7x9", SBY 5/4/88	2,750
Eroded Plank From Barley Sifter, 6/50, sgn/dtd on mount, inscr 53T 1931 on verso, matted, 1931, 10x8", SBY 11/1/88 OE	7,700
Eroded Rock, sgn/dtd/titled on mount, matted, 1929, 8x10", SBY 11/1/88	3,850
Figurine, Burned, Plantation House, New Orleans; intl on mount, titled/#d L41-PH-13 on verso, 1941, 10x8", SBY 5/4/88 UE	2,090
Fragment, Burned Piano, Louisiana; intl/dtd on mount, sgn/titled on verso, 1941, 10x8", SBY 5/4/88	4,950
Gourd, sgn/dtd 1927 on mount, sgn/dtd 1928/inscr To OG & May on verso, matted, 1927, 10x8", SBY 5/4/88	4,400
Glass & Lily, intl/dtd on mount, inscr C39-MI-5, matted, 1939, fr, 10x8", SBY 4/26/89 OE	12,100
Gourd & Pumpkin on Tray, sgn/dtd on mount, inscr To Cousin Sarah 1930, matted, 1927, 8x10", SBY 11/1/88	16,500
Group of 4: Lois Rasamond Edbrooke; sgn/inscr Carmel on mount, 1929, 9x7", SBY 4/26/89	2,750
Johan Hagemeyer, pltn mounted on cream card, sgn/dtd/titled on mount, 1921, 10x8", SBY 5/4/88	2,750
Kitty, John Weston in Panther Pose; slvr, sgn/titled on mount verso, 1944, fr, 8x10", B/B 4/19/88	1,980
Lincoln Steffens, sgn/dtd/titled/inscr To Zohmah Day Lincoln Steffens, matted, 1931, 10x8", SBY 11/1/88 OE	5,225
Louisiana Farm, mounted, ca 1941, 8x10", SBY 5/4/88	2,200
Margrethe Mather (nude on beach), matted, 1923, 7x10", SBY 5/4/88 UE	3,025
Melting Ice, intl/dtd on mount, sgn/dtd/titled on verso, 1938, 10x8", SBY 5/4/88	2,750
Metro Goldwyn Mayer, Hollywood; sgn/titled on verso, matted, 1939, fr, 10x8", SBY 5/4/88	1,210
New Mexico, sgn/dtd on mount, titled/inscr NM S7-11G on verso, matted, 1937, 8x10", SBY 11/1/88 OE	3,850
Nude, sgn/dtd on mount, matted, 1935, 4x3", SBY 11/1/88	22,000
Nude (Sonya Noskowiak), 1/50, dtd/#d 86N on verso, matted, 1933, 4x5", SBY 11/1/88 UE	5,500
Oceano, California; 10/52, sgn/dtd on mount, inscr To Frances on verso, 1934, fr, 8x10", SBY 11/1/88	19,800
Oregon Coast, intl/dtd on mount, sgn/dtd/titled on verso, 1939, 8x10", SBY 5/4/88	5,775
Pelican's Wing, 11/50, sgn/dtd on mount, matted, 1931, 9x10", SBY 11/1/88	4,400
Pepper, p/s on verso, mounted, 1930, 9x7", SBY 5/4/88	5,706
Pepper, sgn/dtd/titled/inscr 35P on verso, matted, 1930, 10x8", SBY 4/26/89	7,700
Point Lobos, sgn/dtd on mount, titled on verso, 1938, 8x10", SBY 11/1/88 OE	8,800
Portfolio: Edward Weston; #28, total ed of 55, 9 slvr & 1 dye, 1925-1948/ca 1971, various sizes, Cole Weston, SBY 5/4/88	2,970

Portrait of Cole, slvr, ca 1925, 4x3", B/B 10/4/88 UE 440
Pyramide Del Sol, Mexico; matted, 1923, 8x9", SBY 11/1/88 4,125
Rock Erosion, Point Lobos, California; sgn/dtd/#d 38-40 on mount, sgn/dtd on verso, matted, 1935, 10x8", SBY 11/1/88 3,025
Rock Erosion, Point Lobos; intl/dtd on mount, matted, 1942, fr, 10x8", SBY 4/26/89 2,750
Shack, Tomales Bay; intl/dtd on mount, matted, 1932, fr, 8x9", SBY 5/4/88 1,100
Self-Portrait, p/s on mount, matted, mid-1920s, 10x7", SBY 4/26/89 12,100
Shell, sgn/dtd on mount, matted, 1927, 10x7", SBY 4/26/89 OE 115,500
Starfish, 1/50, intl/#d on mount, matted, 1920s, 8x10", SBY 5/4/88 1,650
Stump Against Sky, sgn/dtd/inscr 6-40 on mount, titled on verso, matted, 1937, 10x8", SBY 11/1/88 2,200
Tide Pool, Point Lobos; intl/dtd on mount, sgn/dtd/titled/inscr PL-P-1G For Dody on verso, 1938, 8x10", SBY 11/1/88 2,750
Toilet, Death Valley; sgn/dtd on mount, inscr New Years Day Golden Circle Mine Death Valley, 1939, 10x8", SBY 11/1/88 OE 4,400
Twenty Mule Team Canyon, mounted/matted, 1938, 8x10", SBY 11/1/88 OE 5,500
Victoria, sgn/dtd in mrg, mounted/matted, 1926, 10x7", SBY 11/1/88 8,250
Water Stained Wall Board, sgn/dtd on mount, titled/inscr Y-Mc-1G No 390 on verso, matted, 1937, 7x9", SBY 11/1/88 1,980
Woman in Doorway, matted, ca 1921, 9x7", SBY 11/1/88 3,025
Woman Wearing a Pearl Necklace, ink sgn on img, matted ca 1910, 17x12", SBY 11/1/88 6,600
Wrecked Car, Crescent Beach; intl/dtd on mount, sgn/dtd/titled on verso, matted, 1939, 8x10", SBY 5/4/88 UE 770

WHALEY, Jo (American, 20th C)

Music Maker, slvr, sgn/dtd on mount & mount verso, 1979, 14x11", B/B 4/19/88 UE 55

WHITE, Clarence H. (American, 1871-1925)

Bride; or, Illustration to Beneath the Wrinkle; pltn, p/s on img, matted, early 1900s, 8x6", SBY 11/1/88 2,200
Nude Study, brn-toned gum bcro multi-mounted on vellum, p/s on img, ca 1900, 8x4", SBY 5/4/88 8,800
Nude Study (Mabel Cramer), waxed pltn, multi-mounted on vellum, intl on img/mount, 1907, 10x8", SBY 5/4/88 OE 7,975

WHITE, Clarence; & STIEGLITZ, Alfred

Miss Mabel C, Camera Work No 27; photogr, 1909, B/B 4/19/88 OE 358

WHITE, Minor (American, 1908-1976)

Autumn Solstice, sgn/dtd on mount, sgn/dtd/titled on verso, 1961, 10x13", SBY 4/26/89 OE 2,090
Beginnings-Rochester, New York; slvr, p/s in mrg, Princeton University stp on verso, 1962/later, 12x9", B/B 10/4/88 OE 1,650
Birdlime & Surf, Point Lobos, California; p/s in mrg, Princeton University copyright stp, 1951/later, 9x11", SBY 4/26/89 1,210
Book: Song Without Words; 23 slvr, p/s on text page, 1947, ea 4x5", spiral-bound, clear plastic cover, B/B 10/4/88 10,450
Cobblestone House, p/s in mrg, matted, 1958/later, fr, 12x15", SBY 5/4/88 OE 2,475
Feet, Tom Murphy, San Francisco; p/s on verso, matted, 1947, 4x5", SBY 11/1/88 770
Fog Bank, sgn/dtd on mount, matted, 1947, 4x5", SBY 5/4/88 OE 1,650
Ice Abstraction, sgn/dtd on mount, sgn/inscr to orig owner on verso, mounted, 1963, 9x6", SBY 5/4/88 880
Ivy, Portland, Oregon; p/s in mrg, mounted/matted, 1964/later, 12x9", SBY 4/26/89 OE 2,750
Ivy, Portland, Oregon; slvr, sgn/dtd on mount, 1964, fr, 13x9", B/B 10/4/88 1,320
Lobos (Twisted Tree), sgn/titled on mount, matted, 1951, fr, 9x7", SBY 5/4/88 1,760
Navigation Markers, Cape Breton, Nova Scotia; p/s in mrg, titled/dtd on mount, matted, 1970, 9x11", SBY 4/26/89 880
Portfolio: Jupiter Portfolio; 19/100, 12 photos, p/s in mrg, mounted/matted, 1947-71/ca 1975, 9x11", SBY 11/1/88 7,150
Rings & Roses, Cemetery, Ponce, Puerto Rico; p/s on verso, 1973, 9x12", SBY 11/1/88 3,025
Rock Disintegration, Cape Meares, Oregon; sgn/dtd on mount, 1960, 9x8", SBY 4/26/89 880
Truck Sign, China Basin, San Francisco; sgn/dtd/titled on verso, matted, 1973, 9x11", SBY 5/4/88 990

WILLIAMS, James W. (19th C)

Woman in a Cap, talbotype, Williams/Talbotype label on mount verso, ca 1850s, 8x6", SWN 10/30/88 OE 770

WIMBERLEY, John (20th C)

Portfolio: Presence; ed of 20, 12 slvr, 1971-80/1981, various sizes, B/B 4/19/88 880

WINOGRAND, Garry (20th C)

Group of 6: Beautiful, Woman Are Beautiful; p/s on verso, matted, 1969-80/ca 1980, 9x13", SBY 5/4/88 770
Portfolio: Fifteen Photographs; 59/75, sgn/#d on mount, ca 1974, 9x13", cased, Double Elephant Press, SBY 5/4/88 4,400
Portfolio: Women Are Beautiful; 11/75, 15 photos, p/s on verso, matted, 1969-80/ca 1980, 9x13", cased, SBY 11/1/88 OE 2,750
Staten Island Ferry, p/s on verso, matted, 1971, 9x13", SBY 4/26/89 1,320

WITKIN, Joel Peter (20th C)

Australian Drag Queen, inscr AP2, ed of 15, sgn/titled, 1982, 14x14", SBY 4/26/89 1,650
Bacchante, ed of 15, sgn/dtd/titled/inscr Gift Print on verso, matted, 1987, fr, 11x11", SBY 4/26/89 OE 1,540
Revenge of Guernica, a/p, aside from ed of 15, sgn/dtd/titled on verso, 1982, 15x15", SBY 5/4/88 990
Wife of Cain, 1/3, sgn/dtd/titled/#d on verso, matted, 1981/1984, fr, 28x28", SBY 11/1/88 4,400

WOLCOTT, Marion Post (20th C)

Pair: Wendell Drug Co; Belzoni, Mississippi; sgn/dtd on verso, ca 1940/1983, 10x12"/9x12", SBY 4/26/89 OE 1,760
Young Cotton Pickers Waiting in Plantation Store To Be Paid Off, Mileston, Mississippi; slvr, 1939/1978, B/B 4/19/88 UE 220

WOODWARD, Joseph Janvier (19th C)

Book: Toner Lectures, On Structure of Cancerous Tumors...; 74 alb on War Dept letterpress, 1873, 6x6", SBY 4/26/89 4,400
Test Podura Scale Showing Exclamation Marks, alb photomicrograph on War Dept mount, 1870s, 6x6", SWN 10/30/88 193
Trees, Snowbank, Badger Pass, Yosemite National Park; ink sgn/Carmel stp, ca 1955/ca 1962, 7x9", SBY 5/4/88 2,200

WOOLF, Paul

New York Skyscrapers at Night, 14 E 37th Street studio stp on verso, matted, 1930s, 6x4", SBY 4/26/89 OE 1,870

WORTH, Don (20th C)

Succulent (Echeveria Subrigida Hybrid), slvr, p/s on mount, sgn/titled/dtd on mount verso, 1968, 8x9", B/B 4/19/88 358

WULZ, Wanda

Still Life Composition (toiletry items), sgn/inscr Trieste on img, matted, 1930s, 9x11", SBY 4/26/89 5,500

YAVNO, Max (20th C)
Army Street, San Francisco; slvr, p/s on mount, 1947/later, 10x13", B/B 10/4/88 ... 880
Chinese Boy, slvr, p/s on mount, 1947/later, 14x11", B/B 4/19/88 UE ... 165
Lineup, sgn/printing notations on verso, matted, ca 1947, 7x10", SBY 11/1/88 OE ... 1,540
Muscle Beach, p/s on verso, matted, 1949, 12x20", SBY 5/4/88 OE ... 5,706
San Francisco Cityscape, slvr, p/s & stp on verso, ca 1947, 7x10", B/B 4/19/88 ... 880
Telgraph Hill, slvr, p/s & stp on verso, ca 1947/later, 10x7", B/B 4/19/88 ... 358
ZEE, see Van Der Zee
ZUCKERMAN, Bea Ullrich (20th C)
All-American Bubblers, slvr, ink sgn/typed label/stp on verso, 1954/1960, 14x10", B/B 4/19/88 ... 220
Girl Leaning Against Telephone Pole, slvr, p/s on verso, ca 1940, 8x7", B/B 4/19/88 ... 220
Observer, slvr, stp on verso/label attached to verso, 1962, 14x11", B/B 4/19/88 ... 248
ZWART, Piet
Library Interior, slvr, stp on verso, 1929-30, 5x7", B/B 4/19/88 ... 88
Shadow Composition (Self-Portrait?), Wassenaar Holland studio stp on verso, matted, 1930s, fr, 5x7", SBY 5/4/88 ... 1,760
Untitled (Lumberyard), slvr w/wht paint, Wassenaar Holland studio stp on verso, matted, 1930s, 5x7", SBY 4/26/89 OE ... 4,675

Prints

ABBE, William P. (American, 20th C)
City Monuments, 14/30, litho, p/s, 14x11", lot 303, WG 10/19/88 OE ... 150
ABBOT, L.F.; after (18th C)
To Society of Goffers at Blackheath, hc mezzo, 1790, stn/rpr tr/cr img, stn/sl mrgs, laid down, L-23x17", C-NY 1/22/88 ... 440
ABBOTT, William (American, 1892-)
Slipper, #53, clr etch/drypt, 1923, p/s, L'Estampe Moderne bstp, fox, 20x16", lot 278, SBY 12/12/88 ... 440
ACKERMANN, Arthur (19th C)
Preaching, Dr Syntax Series; hc litho, 1812, trm mrgs, 8x11", lot 15, GAI 8/12/88 ... 65
Set of 4: Preaching; Rural Sport; With My Lord; Entertaining at College; hc litho, 1812, 10x13", lot 96, GAI 9/22/89 ... 220
ADAMS, Kenneth Miller (American, 1897-1966)
Untitled, portrait of an Indian; litho/Rives, p/s, 11x7", SLK 9/26/88 ... 100
AFFLECK, Andrew (Scottish, 20th C)
Castle, etch/drypt, p/s, 11x19", lot 89, WG 10/19/88 ... 50
AGAM, Yaacov (Israeli, 1928-)
+-X9VI, 99/99, srgph, p/s, 27x7", lot 145, MG 5/28/88 ... 100
Set of 5: Vertical Spirals; 168/180, clr slksc, p/s, 49x8", lot 343, LH 5/15/88 ... 650
ALBERS, Anni (American, 1899-)
Pair: Triangulated Intaglio I; Triangulated Intaglio IV; etch, 1976, p/s, TGL bstp, P-13x12", lot 82, RWS 9/8/89 ... 650
Pair: Triangulated Intaglio II; Triangulated Intaglio II (abstracts); etch, 1976, p/s, 13x12", lot 84, RWS 9/8/89 ... 700
Pair: Triangulated Intaglio V; Triangulated Intaglio VI (abstracts); etch, 1976, p/s, TGL bstp, 13x13", RWS 9/8/89 ... 500
ALBERS, Josef (American, 1888-1976)
Book: Formulation: Articulation (2 vol set); 998/1000, 115 scrpt, 1972, Abrams bstp, orig wrappers, lot 566, C-NY 11/1/88 ... 2,200
Book: Formulation: Articulation (2 vol set); 555, 1972, Abrams/Ives-Sillman, lot 479, SBY 2/25/88 OE ... 3,850
Book: Formulation: Articulation (2 vol set); 770, 127 clr slksc, 1972, Abrams/Ives-Sillman, lot 601, SBY 2/23/89 ... 2,200
Book: Formulation: Articulation (2 vol set); 897/1000, clr slksc, 1972, orig wrappers, Abrams/Ives-Sillman, SBY 11/5/88 ... 2,200
Fenced, 11/30, linocut, 1944, p/s, titled/dtd, full mrgs, lt stn, 10x12", Biltmore, lot 701, SBY 11/5/88 ... 2,740
Gray Instrumentation, 20/36, clr slksc/wht wove paper, 1974, p/s, TGL bstp, lg mrgs, 11x11", lot 2996, B/B 4/19/88 ... 935
Homage to the Square, 83/125, blk/gray slksc, 1964, p/s, laid down, L-11x11", lot 79, RWS 9/8/89 ... 425
I-Sj, 66/100, clr scrpt/wove paper, 1973, intl/titled/dtd, lt sl, S-30x40", lot 567, C-NY 11/1/88 ... 935
I-5 Vac I, 36/150, clr slksc/cream wove paper, 1969, p/s, titled, 23x26", lot 2995, B/B 4/19/88 ... 440
Pair: I-Sj; I-Sk; 56/100, clr scrpt/wove paper, 1973, L-25x25", lot 391, C-NY 5/11/88 OE ... 2,420
Pair: I-Sj; I-Sk; 59/100, clr slksc, 1973, p/s, titled, Ives-Sillman bstp, full mrgs, 30x40", lot 602, SBY 2/23/89 OE ... 3,850
Pair: I-Sj; I-Sk; 73/100, clr slksc, 1973, p/s, pub bstp, full mrgs, unfr, S-30x40", Ives Sillman, SBY 5/14/88 OE ... 4,675
Pair: I-Sj; I-Sk; 77/100, clr slksc, 1973, p/s, Ives Sillman bstp, full mrgs, S-30x40", lot 902, SBY 5/13/89 ... 3,300
Pair: Josef Albers Honors the Hirshhorn Museum; Sculpture Garden; 91/144, scrpt, Ives-Sillman, lot 568, C-NY 11/1/88 ... 1,980
Pair: Josef Albers Honors the Hirshhorn Museum; Sculpture Gardens; 2 slksc, 1973, HKL Ltd/Parasol, lot 704, SBY 11/5/88 ... 1,925
Pair: Variant I; Variant VIII; 64/200, slksc, 1966, Ives-Sillman bstp, full mrgs, 9x13"/11x12", lot 600, SBY 2/23/89 OE ... 1,210
Pair: Josef Albers Honors the Hirshhorn Museum; Sculpture Garden; 53/144, slksc, 1973, S-25x35", SBY 2/23/89 UE ... 1,100
Portfolio: Midnight & Noon; 6/20, 8 clr litho, 1964, orig wrappers, S-19x21", Tamarind, lot 900, SBY 5/13/89 OE ... 9,900
Tlaloc (contemporary), 25/35, wc/Japan, 1944, p/s, titled, full mrgs, lt cr mrgs, L-12x12", lot 388, C-NY 5/11/88 OE ... 4,950
Untitled (contemporary), 94/125, clr scrpt/wove paper, 1964, intl/dtd, L-11x11", lot 389, C-NY 5/11/88 ... 330
White Line Square XII, 78/125, clr litho/Arches, 1966, p/s, titled, Gemini bstp, 16x16", lot 2994, B/B 4/19/88 ... 550
ALBRIGHT, Ivan Le Lorraine (American, 1897-1985)
Fleeting Time, Thou Hast Left Me Old; litho, p/s, full mrgs, L-14x10", lot 6, PHL 10/28/88 ... 1,700
Fleeting Time, Thou Hast Left Me Old; ed of 250, litho, 1945, p/s, trm/stn/sl, unfr, L-14x10", C-NY 1/22/88 ... 880
Hail to the Pure, 55/100, litho/wove paper, 1977, p/s, titled, L-18x13", lot 108, C-NY 1/19/89 ... 1,045
Pair: Fleeting Time, Thou Hast Left Me Old; Follow Me; ed of 250, litho, 1945 & 1948, 13x9"/13x10", lot 1, SBY 2/23/89 ... 1,650
Sail Lofts of Corea, Maine; ed of 10, litho/wove paper, 1947, p/s, lg mrgs, lt stn/sl, 11x19", lot 1A, SBY 2/23/89 ... 1,980

Self-Portrait at 55 East Division Street, ed of 250, litho, 1747, p/s, 2 cr mrg edge, L-14x10", C-NY 1/22/88 ... 880
Self-Portrait at 55 East Division Street, ed of 250, litho, p/s, full mrgs, 14x10", lot 1, SBY 2/25/88 UE ... 1,210

ALDEGREVER, Heinrich (German, 1502-)
Hercules, copper engr, 1560, intl, trm mrgs, 3x3", lot 1017, S/A 2/18/89 ... 475

ALKEN, Henry Jr. (British, 1810-1894)
Throwing Off (hunt scene), lt sl, no size given, lot 108, FAP 2/24/89 UE ... 75

ALKEN, Henry Sr. (British, 1785-1851)
Pair: Full Cry; The Death (hunt scenes); etch/aqua, 1824, Thomas McClean/T Sutherland, FAP 6/16/89 ... 250
Set of 4: Grouse; Snipe; Partridge; Bittern; clr litho, 6x9", lot 113, FAP 2/24/89 ... 275

ALKEN, Henry; after
Group of 3: Appointment; Getting Away; Death; by J Gleadah, aqua, 12x20", Treager, lot 852, WAD 11/28/88 UE ... 600
Pair: Bull Baiting; hc aqua, pl/s, 8x12", lot 806, LH 10/16/88 ... 180
Racing, clr engr, P-8x12", C-E 5/3/88 UE ... 154

ALKIN, S.; after (British, 18th or 18th/19th C)
Race Horses, Mounting; clr engr, P-4x7", C-E 5/3/88 UE ... 110

ALMA-TADEMA, Lawrence; after (British, 1836-1912)
Untitled, figures in classical setting; hc litho, 14x24", SLK 2/11/89 ... 1,900

ALTDORFER, Albrecht (German, 1480-1538)
Virgin with the Child in a Landscape, engr/wm Gothic P & Flower paper, ca 1515, lt stn, rpr tr, 6x5", lot 1, SBY 5/11/89 ... 3,960

ALVAR (Italian, 20th C)
Woman with Bird, V/LXXV, ed of 75 a/p, clr etch/aqua, 19x26", lot 336, LH 9/10/89 OE ... 400

AMAN-JEAN, Edmund Francois (French, 1860-1935)
Head of a Woman, clr litho, unfr, 14x11", lot 249, FAP 2/24/89 UE ... 120

AMEN, Irving (American, 1918-)
Chess Players, #2; clr wc, p/s, titled, 18x24", lot 421, WG 10/19/88 ... 85

AMENOFF, Gregory (20th C)
Chamber, 16/35, clr wc/Suzuki, 1985, p/s, full mrgs, lt rpl mrg, S-37x42", Diane Villani, lot 569, C-NY 11/1/88 ... 1,100

American School (19th C)
Gentleman with Document, hc print mounted on glass, indistinctly sgn, trm mrgs, oval 9x7", FAP 6/16/89 ... 175

American School (20th C)
Dartmouth Winter Carnival, clr litho/poster paper, 34x22", lot 227, FAP 2/24/89 OE ... 100
Procession of Automobiles, scrpt/fabric, 34x33", lot 278, FAP 2/24/89 UE ... 40
Snow Train, clr litho/poster paper, 42x28", lot 259, FAP 2/24/89 ... 110
Talkies, litho/poster paper, lt cr, linen backed, 64x42", lot 273, FAP 2/24/89 ... 60
Uncle Tom Says Only You Can Prevent Ghetto Fires, clr litho/poster, no size given, Sawyer, lot 234, FAP 2/24/89 OE ... 90

ANDERSON, Clarence W. (American, 1891-)
Early Speed, litho, p/s, titled, lt stn, 9x12", lot 273, WG 10/19/88 OE ... 170
Rodeo Sketches, litho, p/s, titled, 11x16", Assn Am Aritsts, lot 193, WG 10/19/88 ... 40

ANDRADE, Edna (American, 1917-)
Group of 3: Gray Dream; Space Game; Space Game; blk/gray litho, p/s, 24x24", lot 82, FAP 2/24/89 OE ... 250
Pair: Black, White Cross; Free & Last; 1/50 & a/p, litho, p/s, 23x23", lot 84, FAP 2/24/89 ... 110
Space Cage, litho/blk plexiglas, p/s, 12x12", lot 80, FAP 2/24/89 ... 60
Space Game, 9/20, clr litho, 24x24", lot 90, FAP 2/24/89 ... 90

ANDREWS, Benny (American, 1930-)
Julia, 25/100, clr litho, sgn, 16x22", lot 138, MG 5/28/88 ... 40

ANDREWS, Sybil (American, 1898-1870)
Bringing in the Boat, 31/60, clr linocut/tissue-thin Japan, 1933, p/s, tp in corners, S-14x12", lot 201, C-NY 11/1/88 ... 1,870

APPEL, Karl (Dutch, 1921-)
Composition, 1960; clr litho/wove paper, p/s, tr, no size given, lot 95, FAP 2/24/89 UE ... 75
Composition, 1970; 19/100, clr litho, p/s, 40x26", lot 98, FAP 2/24/89 ... 300
Dog, p/p, clr litho, p/s, 21x29", lot 13, SWN 6/15/89 ... 248
Face, a/p, litho, 21x13", lot 99, FAP 2/24/89 ... 225
Laughing Frog & All His Friends, EPI, clr srgph/wove paper, 1979, p/s, S-41x72", Ed Pr, lot 2998, B/B 4/19/88 ... 660
Miaow, 84/110, clr litho, p/s, 20x26", lot 377, WG 10/19/88 ... 325
Portfolio: Circus Volume III; 33/130, 10 clr wc, 1978, sgn on justification, ABCD Eds, lot 482, SBY 2/25/88 ... 4,125
Suite: Romantic; 74/100, 6 clr litho/Arches, sgn, lt tstn, S-25x38", C-E 5/13/88 OE ... 715
Toi et Moi, 113/200, clr litho/Arches, ca 1960s, sgn/titled, L-25x19", C-E 5/13/88 OE ... 550
Walking with My Bird, 100/160, clr litho, p/s, 21x30", lot 14, SWN 6/15/89 ... 385

APPLETON (18th/19th C)
City of Detroit, blk/wht engr, 14x17", lot 340, GAI 11/24/89 ... 25

ARAKAWA, Shusaku (Japanese, 1936-)
Degrees of Blank, 2/38, litho/slksc, 1981, p/s, titled, full mrgs, 34x62", Studio X, lot 904, SBY 5/13/89 OE ... 3,575
Distance of Forming, 19/48, clr litho, 1980, p/s, full mrgs, 34x63", Studio X, lot 903, SBY 5/13/88 OE ... 6,050
La Gioconda, 75/100, clr slksc, 1970-71, p/s, full mrgs, lt glue, 40x30", lot 483, SBY 2/25/88 OE ... 1,760
Look at It, 23/85, clr scrpt/golden foil, 1968, sgn in ink, lt scr/sl, S-36x48", lot 571, C-NY 11/1/88 UE ... 440
Point Blank I, 36/38, clr litho, 1979, p/s, S-31x59", Vermilion, lot 708, SBY 11/5/88 OE ... 4,950
Set of 7: Signified or If...#1-7; AP14/15, clr etch, 1975-76, p/s, full mrgs, lt cr, 24x36", lot 707, SBY 11/5/88 OE ... 12,100
Webster's New 20th-C Dictionary, 82/95, photo-offset litho, 1965, L-42x30", lot 570, C-NY 11/1/88 OE ... 1,980

ARCHIPENKO, Alexander (American, 1887-1964)
Rencontre, apart from ed of 50, litho/BFK Rives, 1963, St Gallen bstp, lt cr/mstn, S-35x20", lot 202, C-NY 11/1/88 ... 352

ARMAN, Fernandez (French/Spanish, 1928-)
Chessboard: Homage to Marcel Duchamp; 98/100, scrpt/beige & brn plastic chessboard, ca 1973, 17x17", C-NY 11/1/88 UE 165
Suite: Romantic Suite; 22/100, 6 clr litho, 1976, sgn/#d, lt tstn/sl, S-25x38", Prestige Art, lot 573, C-NY 11/1/88 605

ARMITAGE, Kenneth (British, 1916-)
Aspiration, La Madeleine, Verneuil-sur-Avre; V/XXV, etch/laid paper, 1939, p/s, full mrgs, P-16x10", lot 2, PHL 6/16/88 400

ARMS, John Taylor (American, 1887-1953)
American Cathedral, 10/75, dk brn etch, 1921, p/s, laid down, 17x7", lot 2, SBY 2/25/88 OE 1,980
Aspiration, total ed of 419, 5th/final state, etch, 1939, p/s, dtd/inscr V, lt cr/ink mrgs, unfr, P-16x10", C-NY 1/22/88 440
Battle Wagon USS Alabama Outfitting at Norfolk...; ed of 872, aqua/etch, 1943, lt stn, unfr, P-12x18", C-NY 1/22/88 495
Canale San Barnaba, Venezia; ed of 48, etch/laid paper, 1933, p/s, lt lstn/tstn, tp stn mrg, P-5x7", C-NY 1/22/88 UE 143
Cathedral, ed of unknown size, engr, p/s, 4x7", lot 116, FAP 2/24/89 UE 100
Colise Notre Dame, etch, 1946, 3x2", lot 118, FAP 2/24/89 UE 75
Destroyers in West Basin at Federal Shipbuilding & Drydock Co...; ed of 875, etch, 1942, p/s, P-10x17", C-NY 1/22/88 330
French Lace, ed of 306, 2nd state, etch/laid paper, p/s, full mrgs, P-8x5", lot 115, C-NY 1/19/89 198

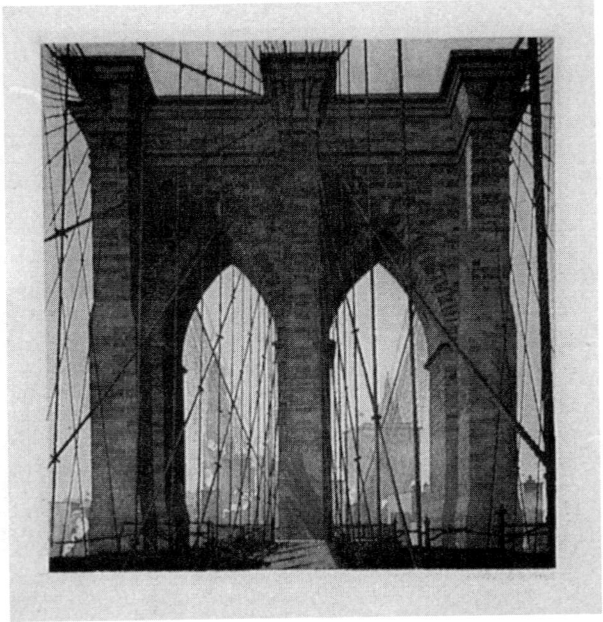

Gates of the City, 2nd state, clr etch/aqua/laid paper, 1922, full mrgs, lt stn/tr, P-9x8", lot 110, C-NY 1/19/89 OE; $8,800

Group of 3: Somewhere in Oxfordshire; Chartes Magnificent; Somewhere in Warwickshire; etch, C-NY 1/22/88 UE 110
In Memoriam, ed of 312, etch/laid paper, 1939, p/s, inscr To Helen From John, full mrgs, 15x12", lot 3, SBY 11/3/88 2,860
La Bella Venezia, Ed 70, etch, 1930, p/s, lt fox/stn, 7x17", lot 1, SBY 11/3/88 1,100
Le Penseur de Notre Dame, 1st state, etch/wove paper, 1923, p/s, lt stn/skinned, P-13x10", lot 111, C-NY 1/19/89 OE 4,400
Lescure, Une Tour des Ramparts; ed of 145, etch/laid paper, 1928, p/s, pl/s, lt stn, P-6x4", RWS 3/16/89 UE 70
Memoriam, ed of 312, 2nd state, etch/laid paper, 1939,p/s, dtd, stn mrgs/verso, P-15x12", C-NY 1/22/88 880
Pair: Cavendish Church; Castello, Umbria; ed of 155/51, etch/wove paper, ca 1940s, p/s, dtd, lt stn, C-NY 1/22/88 UE 132
Pair: Cavendish Common; Herbert Lowell Dillon Gymnasium...; ed of 150/356, etch, 1942/1947, lt sl, unfr, C-NY 1/22/88 330
Pair: Crystal & Jade; Cavendish Church; ed of 377 & 155, aqua/etch, 1940 & 1944, 8x7"/10x6", lot 18, SWN 6/15/89 UE 248
Pair: Rose Beauvais; Rodez; ed of 156 & 120, etch, 1925 & 1927, lt stn, 12x7"/12x5", lot 1B, SBY 2/23/89 880
Palazzo Dell'Angelo, Ed 100, ed of 131, 2nd state of 3, brn etch/laid paper, 1931, p/s, P-7x7", C-NY 1/22/88 UE 440
Sketch, Grolier Club Library; etch, 1941, p/s, titled, 4x6", lot 8, SWN 12/1/88 110
Spanish Profile, Palencia; ed of 308, 3rd state, etch/JW, 1948-50, p/s, dtd, lt cr/stn mrgs, unfr, P-14x7", C-NY 1/22/88 418
St Germain L'Auzerrois, ed of 362, etch/cream laid paper, 1928, Chicago Soc Etchers bstp, 10x5", lot 2927, B/B 4/19/88 330
Stanwick, ed of 150, 3rd state, etch/laid wm England, 1939, p/s, lt stn, unfr, P-7x3", RWS 3/16/89 UE 100
Stockholm, total ed of 395, 3rd/final state, aqua/etch/JW, 1940, p/s, dtd/inscr III, lt sl, unfr, P-8x14", C-NY 1/22/88 990
Study in Stone, Cathedral of Orense; ed of 162, etch/gr laid paper, 1933, inscr, sl mrgs, unfr, P-7x6", C-NY 1/22/88 385
USS Columbia Under Construction at New York Shipbuilding Corp...; 2nd state, etch/drypt, 1945, P-12x17", C-NY 1/22/88 605
Valley of the Savery, Wyoming; etch/bl-gr wove paper, 1934, p/s, full mrgs, lt stn, P-8x14", lot 114, C-NY 1/19/89 385
Venetian Filigree, ed of 100, 2nd state, etch/Dard Hunter, 1931, p/s, 3 full mrgs, P-11x11", lot 113, C-NY 1/19/89 OE 4,950
Venetian Filigree, Ed 100, etch, 1931, p/s, full mrgs, lt stn, 11x11", lot 3, SBY 2/25/88 3,520
Venetian Filigree, Ed 100, etch/thin laid paper, 1931, p/s, full mrgs, lt stn, 11x11", lot 2, SBY 11/3/88 4,070
Venetian Mirror, 1st ed of 146, 2nd state, etch, 1935, p/s, lt stn mrgs/verso, P-6x14", David Strang, C-NY 1/22/88 OE 2,750
Venetian Mirror; or, The Grand Canal, Venice; total ed of 169, wm David Strang, p/s, full mrgs, P-7x14", C-NY 5/11/88 2,750
Wilby Church, etch, 1940, p/s, ls in corner, 5x2", lot 324, WG 10/19/88 OE 70

ARNESON, Robert (American, 1930-)
Broken Brick, etch/aqua/cream wove paper, 1975, p/s, titled, Landfall bstp, lg mrgs, 10x11", lot 3004, B/B 4/19/88 UE 88
California Brick, p/p, etch/aqua/cream wove paper, 1975, p/s, titled, Landfall bstp, lg mrgs, 10x10", B/B 4/19/88 300

ARP, Jean Hans (French, 1887-1966)
Composition, 98/100, clr wc, p/s, no size given, lot 83, FAP 2/24/89 225

Composition mit Funf Formen, EA, clr litho/Rives, 1964, p/s, full sheet, S-20x14", lot 203, C-NY 11/1/88 UE 110
Presque Vase et Fleurs, 35/200, clr litho, p/s, full mrgs, L-20x17", lot 44, PHL 6/16/88 225
Suite: Vers Le Blanc Infini; 328/600, 8 etch w/text, 1960, p/s on justification, gray slipcase, lot 74, C-NY 5/11/88 770

ARTZYBASHEFF, Boris (American, 20th C)

Centaurs, wood engr/wove paper, 1940, p/s, titled, full mrgs, lt stn, tp to overmat, L-8x11", lot 117, C-NY 1/19/89 330

AUDUBON, John James (American, 1785-1851)

American Beaver, Pl 46, hc litho, ca 1845, lt mstn mrgs, lt fox, 16x24", Bowen, lot 795, SBY 1/28/88 880
American Flamingo, JW/1838, lt stn/fox/cr, lt tr edge, S-38x26", Havell, lot 23, C-NY 1/19/89 OE 7,700
American Goldfinch, Pl 33, JW Turkey Mill, stn, P-20x12", Havell, lot 469, FAP 4/15/88 900
American Redstart, Pl 40, JW/1833, lg mrgs, lt fox/cr/ls, S-39x27", Havell, lot 637, SBY 1/28/88 2,310
American White Pelican, Pl 311, JW/1838, cr corner, rpr ls/tr edge, stn/fox/sl, 38x25", Havell, lot 18, C-NY 1/19/89 OE 9,900
American Widgeon, Pl 345, JW/1836, lg mrgs, lt fox/stn, ls mrg corner, stn verso, S-25x38", Havell, SBY 1/28/88 2,200
Azure Warbler, Pl 48, JW/1831, lt sl mrgs, tstn mrg edges, unfr, S-38x25", Havell, lot 6, C-NY 1/22/88 UE 352
Azure Warbler, Pl 48, JW/1831, lt trm mrg, lt stn/fox, fox verso, P-19x12", Havell, lot 5, C-NY 1/22/88 UE 352
Baltimore Oriole, Pl 12, JW/1833, lt stn/fox, S-40x27", lot 627, SBY 1/28/88 6,600
Band-Tailed Pigeon, aqua/engr/JW, trm mrgs, lt fox/stn, laid down, S-32x24", Havell, lot 21, C-NY 1/19/89 OE 1,320
Barn Owl, Pl 171, hc aqua/engr/wove paper, fox/stn, tp at edges, S-38x26", Havell, lot 9, C-NY 1/19/89 OE 4,620
Barn Owl, Pl 171, JW Turkey Mill/1833, lt tr/ls/cr/stn, S-40x27", Havell, lot 681, SBY 1/28/88 7,150
Barn Swallow, Pl 173, JW/1836, lt stn/fox, S-38x25", Havell, lot 682, SBY 1/28/88 OE 2,200
Bemaculated Duck, Pl 338, JW/1836, lg mrgs, lt fox/stn mrgs, S-26x39", Havell, lot 744, SBY 1/28/88 2,750
Black Guillemont, Pl 219, JW Turkey Mill, lt trm/stn mrgs, lt scuff/fox img, unfr, S-25x38", Havell, C-NY 1/22/88 UE 418
Black or Surf Duck, Pl 317, JW/1836, lt fox bottom mrg, lt offprint, lt rpr nicks, S-27x40", Havell, SBY 1/28/88 1,870
Black Vulture or Carrion Crow, Pl 106, lt trm mrgs, tr/lt stn edges, unfr, S-25x38", Havell, lot 9, C-NY 1/22/88 UE 660
Black Vulture or Carrion Crow (Cathartes Atratus), Pl 106, JW/1831, lt rpr/sl, S-25x38", Havell, lot 6, C-NY 1/19/89 1,210
Black-Bellied Darter, Pl 316, hc engr/etch/aqua, 1836, lt fox/cr, lt tr edges, S-39x26", Havell, lot 733, SBY 1/28/88 4,950
Black-Bellied Darter, Pl 316, JW/1836, lt stn/fox, lt scr img, S-38x25", Havell, lot 19, C-NY 1/19/89 OE 3,850
Blue Jay, Pl 231, chromolitho, 27x40", lot 206, Bein, MG 11/19/88 UE 600
Blue-Winged Teal, Pl 313, JW/1836, lt fox/sl/stn, S-26x39", Havell, lot 729, SBY 1/28/88 3,850
Bonaparte's Flycatcher, Pl 5, JW/1830, lt trm/sl/cr mrgs, unfr, S-38x26", Havell, C-NY 1/22/88 UE 418
Bonaparte's Flycatcher, Pl 5, JW/1838, lt fox/cr mrg, S-38x26", Havell, lot 625, SBY 1/28/88 1,210
Bonapartian Gull, Pl 324, engr, fox, 21x16", Havell, lot 279, NA 10/1/88 325
Bonapartian Gull, Pl 324, JW/1836, lg mrgs, lt fox/stn, lt tr/ls corner & edges, S-39x25", Havell, lot 739, SBY 1/28/88 880
Bonapartian Gull, Pl 324, JW/1838, lt sl/fox, 2 sm tr mrg edge, S-38x26", Havell, lot 738, SBY 1/28/88 2,200
Brown Pelican, Pl 421, JW/1838, full mrgs, stn/lt fox, tp stn/tr mrg, P-23x35", Havell, C-NY 1/22/88 OE 3,080
Burrowing Owl, Pl 432, JW/1838, lt stn/sl/fox, S-27x39", Havell, lot 783, SBY 1/28/88 OE 880
Californian Vulture, Pl 426, JW/1838, trm mrgs, lt fox/stn/sl, S-38x25", Havell, lot 781, SBY 1/28/88 UE 1,650
Canada Goose, Pl 201, JW Turkey Mill/1834, lt rpr tr, lt sl/fox, S-38x25", Havell, lot 694, SBY 1/28/88 17,600
Cardinal Grosbeak, Pl 154, JW/1833, lstn/tstn, lt fox mrgs on recto/verso, P-19x12", Havell, C-NY 1/22/88 OE 3,850
Carolina Parrot, Pl 26, JW Turkey Mill/1827, lt stn/sl mrgs, lt fox/stn/tr mrgs, S-38x25", Havell, lot 631, SBY 1/28/88 12,100
Carolina Parrot, Pl 26, JW Turkey Mill/1827, lt trm mrgs, lt sl/rub/stn, S-37x25", Havell, lot 3, SBY 2/23/89 6,600
Cayenne Tern, Pl 273, JW/1835, lt stn/sl/fox, rpr tr/ls mrg, backed w/Japan, S-25x39", Havell, lot 716, SBY 1/28/88 1,540
Cinnamon Bear (Male & Female), Pl 127, hc litho, ca 1845, rpr tr/cr mrg, stn edge, 18x25", Bowen, lot 789, SBY 1/28/88 1,320
Cock of the Plains, Pl 371, JW/1837, lt fox/ls/stn, S-26x39", Havell, lot 757, SBY 1/28/88 2,475
Common American Swan, Pl 411, JW/1838, trm mrgs, rpr holes/scr in img, lt ls, S-26x38", Havell, lot 771, SBY 1/28/88 14,300
Common Buzzard, Pl 372, JW Turkey Mill/1837, lg mrgs, lt tr/cr/ls in edges, S-39x26", Havell, lot 758, SBY 1/28/88 1,210
Common Cormorant, Pl 266, JW/1835, lt sl mrgs, lt fox, lt offprint on verso, S-26x38", Havell, lot 715, SBY 1/28/88 2,750
Common Crossbill, Pl 198, JW/1838, lt fox/stn, S-38x26", Havell, lot 693, SBY 1/28/88 1,870
Crested Titmouse, Pl 39, JW Turkey Mill, lt ls/stn, S-36x24", Havell, lot 466, FAP 4/15/88 600
Double-Crested Cormorant, Pl 257, JW/1834, lt sl/fox, rpr ls/tr mrgs, S-39x25", Havell, lot 709, SBY 1/28/88 UE 1,100
Dusky Albatross, Pl 407, JW/1837, full mrgs, lt fox/rpr tr mrg, lt mstn/tstn, ink verso, P-20x28", Havell, C-NY 1/22/88 880
Dusky Duck, Pl 302, JW/1836, lt mstn/sl/fox, lt tr edges, S-27x39", Havell, lot 725, SBY 1/28/88 OE 8,800
Fish Hawk or Osprey, Pl 81, JW/1838, lstn/sl/lt fox, rpr tr/ls mrg edge, tp verso, P-37x22", Havell, C-NY 1/22/88 3,300
Flamingo, litho, ca 1972-73, P-25x39", Leipzig Ed, lot 208, MG 12/10/88 275
Fulmar Petrel, Pl 264, JW/1831, lt stn/sl/fox mrgs, rpr tr/ls edge, backed w/Japan, 25x39", Havell, lot 714, SBY 1/28/88 660
Gadwall Duck, Pl 348, #70, Amsterdam Ed, lot 10, MG 5/28/88 350
Gadwall Duck, Pl 348, JW/1837, 1836, lg mrgs, lt tr/cr/fox, sl, S-26x38", Havell, lot 746, SBY 1/28/88 3,300
Golden Eagle, Pl 181, JW/1833, sm mrgs, lt tr/sl/fox mrgs & verso, S-38x25", Havell, lot 687, SBY 1/28/88 5,500
Golden-Crested Wren, Pl 183, JW/1833, lt fox/stn, ls/lt sl/tstn mrg edges, lt sl verso, unfr, Havell, C-NY 1/22/88 UE 154
Gray Fox, Pl 21, hc litho, ca 1845, lt fox mrg/img, lt stn edge/verso, 18x24", Bowen, lot 792, SBY 1/28/88 2,090
Gray Fox, Pl 21, hc litho, 1843, lt stn mrg corner, lt mstn, 18x24", Bowen, lot 793, SBY 1/28/88 3,575
Great American Cock Male, Pl 1, JW/1826, trm mrgs, lt ls/tr edges, fox/sl, 38x25", Lizars/Havell, lot 623, SBY 1/28/88 19,800
Great American Hen & Young, Pl 6, JW/1827, lt tr/ls/stn, 2" tr mrg, S-26x38", Lizars/Havell, lot 626, SBY 1/28/88 17,600
Great American Shrike or Butcher Bird, Pl 192, JW/1834, lt cr img, lt sl/tr, S-38x25", Havell, lot 690, SBY 1/28/88 UE 880
Great Blue Heron, JW Turkey Mill/1834, lt fox/stn, rpr tr/ls edges, stn verso, 39x26", Havell, lot 12, C-NY 1/19/89 OE 27,500
Great Footed Hawk, Pl 20, chromolitho, 27x40", Bien, lot 203, MG 11/19/88 UE 400
Great Marbled Godwit, Pl 238, JW/1834, lt lstn/tstn, cr img, sl mrgs, stn/fox verso, P-12x21", Havell, C-NY 1/22/88 UE 660
Great White Heron, Pl 281, JW/1836, 1835, lt rpr scr img, lt stn/tr/ls edges, S-25x37", Havell, lot 721, SBY 1/28/88 OE 9,350
Ground Dove, Pl 182, JW Turkey Mill/1833, stn, P-26x21", Havell, lot 473, FAP 4/15/88 1,070
Hooded Merganser, Pl 232, JW Turkey Mill/1834, lt sl/fox, lt tr/ls mrg corner, S-25x38", Havell, lot 702, SBY 1/28/88 2,530
Hooded Merganser, Pl 232, lt ink stn, lt sl img, lt ls/rpr tr/sl mrgs, unfr, S-23x28", Havell, lot 17, C-NY 1/22/88 660
Hooping Crane, Pl 226, JW Turkey Mill/1834, lt fox/nick, lt stn/sl edges, S-39x26", Havell, lot 14, C-NY 1/19/89 16,500

Hunslows Bunting (Male), Pl 163, 6/9, chromolitho, 1860, full mrgs, lt cr/stn/tr, 18x11", Bien, lot 252, RWS 10/29/88 UE	275
Hutchin's Barnacle Goose, Pl 277, JW/1836, 1935, lt fox/stn/sl, rpr/ls, S-39x25", Havell, lot 719, SBY 1/28/88	1,650
Iceland or Jer Falcon, Pl 346, JW/1837, lt fox img, lt stn mrgs, S-38x25", Havell, lot 755, SBY 1/28/88 OE	22,000
Ivory-Billed Woodpecker (Picus Principalis), Pl 66, JW/1833, lt stn/fox/rub, S-38x25", Havell, lot 5, C-NY 1/19/89 OE	7,480
Key West Dove, Pl 167, JW Turkey Mill/1831, 1833, lt stn/fox, S-25x36", Havell, lot 680, SBY 1/28/88	2,310
Labrador Falcon, Pl 196, JW/1834, lt sl/stn/fox/cr, tp stn on verso, S-38x25", Havell, lot 691, SBY 1/28/88	1,650
Lesser Tern, Pl 319, JW/1838, lt stn/fox/tr mrg, fld mrg, stn verso, S-38x25", Havell, lot 20, C-NY 1/19/89	440
Long-Tailed Duck, Pl 312, JW/1836, lg mrgs, lt fox/sl/stn, rpr corner, S-26x38", Havell, lot 728, SBY 1/28/88	2,750
Long-Tailed or Dusky Grouse, Pl 341, JW/1837, lt cr center, lt fox/stn/sl mrgs, S-26x39", Havell, lot 752, SBY 1/28/88	1,925
Louisiana Heron, litho, ca 1872-73, P-22x34", Leipzig Ed, 22x34", lot 207, MG 12/10/88	250
Louisiana Heron, Pl 217, JW Turkey Mill/1831, lg mrgs, lt scuff/sl/cr, lt fox on verso, S-26x38", Havell, SBY 1/28/88	17,600
Mocking Bird, JW Turkey Mill/1827, lt stn/sl/fox, stn/nick mrg, S-38x25", Havell, SBY 1/28/88	4,950
Night Heron or Qua Bird, Pl 236, JW/1834(?), lt fox/stn, laid down on board, S-26x39", Havell, lot 15, C-NY 1/19/89	5,500
Night Heron or Qua Bird, Pl 236, JW/1835, lt stn/sl mrgs, lt fox/ls, S-27x39", Havell, lot 703, SBY 1/28/88	9,350
Nuttalls Lesser-Marsh Hen, Pl 125, JW Turkey Mill/1833, lg mrgs, lt fox/tr, S-39x25", Havell, lot 684, SBY 1/28/88	770
Ocelot or Leopard Cat (Male), Pl 86, litho, ca 1845, lt stn mrgs, sl mrg/verso, S-21x27", Bowen, lot 797, SBY 1/28/88 OE	2,750
Orchard Oriole, Pl 219, chromolitho, 1860, lt stn, S-36x36", Bien, lot 447, FAP 4/15/88	275
Pair: Children's Warbler; Kentucky Warbler; chromolitho, 27x40", Bien, lot 202, MG 11/19/88	105
Pair: Solitary Flycatcher; Children's Warbler; Pl 28 & Pl 35, JW/1831, lt fox, rpr tr, S-39x25", lot 633, SBY 1/28/88 UE	880
Passenger Pigeon, clr litho, 26x32", Amsterdam Ed, lot 125, MG 10/28/88	700
Passenger Pigeon, Pl 62, lt stn/tstn/fox img, lt tr/ls mrg edges, lt stn verso, P-26x21", Havell, lot 7, C-NY 1/22/88	3,080
Pileated Woodpecker, chromolitho, 1860, tr img/mrg, lt stn/sl, laid down, L-37x24", Bien, lot 786, SBY 1/28/88 UE	880
Pileated Woodpecker, Pl 111, JW/1831, lt fox/stn mrg edges, S-39x26", Havell, lot 663, SBY 1/28/88	6,600
Pin-Tailed Duck, Pl 227, JW Turkey Mill, stn/scr img, trm/rpr, lt fox/stn mrgs, unfr, S-22x27", Havell, C-NY 1/22/88	825
Pin-Tailed Duck, Pl 227, JW Turkey Mill/1834, lg mrgs, lt stn/fox, lt ls/tr, S-25x39", Havell, lot 699, SBY 1/28/88	4,400
Pine Grosbeak, Pl 358, JW/1837, full mrgs, lt fox, tp on verso, P-21x15", Havell, RWS 6/10/89 UE	325
Plumed Partridge, Thick-Legged Partidge; Pl 423, JW/1838, lg mrgs, lt sl/stn/fox, S-26x39", Havell, SBY 1/28/88	1,320
Prairie Starling, Pl 420, JW/1838, lt fox img, lt stn/sl mrgs, 2 rpr trs, unfr, S-38x25", Havell, C-NY 1/22/88 UE	385
Pulmar Petrel, Pl 264, JW/1835, lt sl/stn/fox mrgs & verso, S-27x40", Havell, lot 713, SBY 1/28/88	1,100
Red-Breasted Merganser, Pl 401, JW Turkey Mill/1836, lt stn/fox/tr/rpl, S-25x38", Havell, lot 22, C-NY 1/19/89	2,090
Red-Cockaded Woodpecker, Pl 389, JW/1837, lg mrgs, lt stn/fox, rpr corner, S-39x26", Havell, lot 762, SBY 1/28/88 UE	660
Red-Headed Woodpecker, Pl 27, JW/1836, S-38x26", Havell, lot 632, SBY 1/28/88	2,750

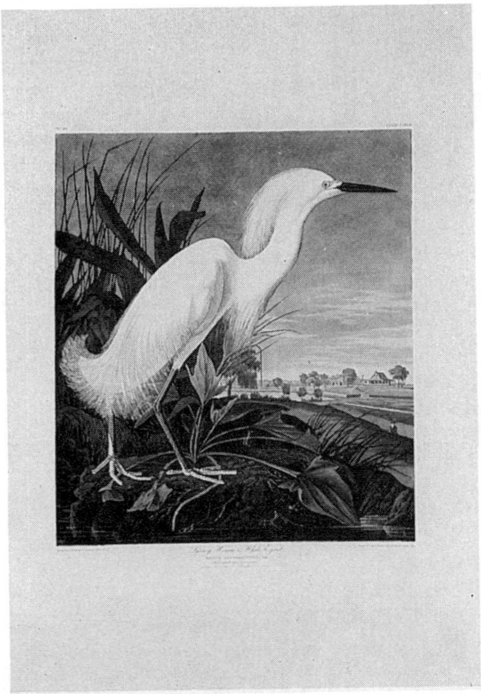

Snowy Heron, or White Egret . . . Rice Plantation, South Carolina (Ardea Candidissima); Pl 242, JW Turkey Mill/1835, S-39x26", Havell, lot 16, C-NY 1/19/89; $17,600

Red-Tailed Hawk, Pl 50, JW/1831, lt sl/fox, rpr tr mrg edges, S-39x25", Havell, lot 643, SBY 1/28/88	2,200
Roscoe's Yellow Throat, JW Turkey Mill/1827, lt fox, S-37x26", Havell, lot 630, SBY 1/28/88	440
Ruby-Crowned Wren, Pl 195, JW/1834, stn/fox, fld/stn mrg, other minor defects, S-37x25", Havell, lot 10, C-NY 1/19/89 UE	308
Ruddy Duck, Pl 343, #60, 39x26", Amsterdam Ed, lot 11, MG 5/28/88	350
Scolopaceus Courlan, Pl 377, JW/1838, full mrgs, lt fox/mstn/tstn, lt ls mrg, ink verso, 21x33", Havell, C-NY 1/22/88	1,650
Scoup Duck, Pl 229, #46, 39x26", Amsterdam Ed, lot 9, MG 5/28/88 UE	300
Sharp-Tailed Finch, Pl 149, JW/1832, lg mrgs, lt sl/fox/stn, rpr tr mrg/lt cr, S-38x25", Havell, lot 675, SBY 1/28/88 UE	880
Shoveller Duck, Pl 327, #66, 39x26", lot 8, Amsterdam Ed, MG 5/28/88	350
Snow Goose, Pl 381, JW/1837, lt scuff img, lt fox/stn/nick, tr/ls mrg, S-25x38", Havell, lot 760, SBY 1/28/88	2,640
Swallow-Tailed Hawk, Pl 72, hc engr/etch/aqua, 1829, lt stn/fox/tr, laid down, S-29x32", Havell, lot 646, SBY 1/28/88	990

Swallow-Tailed Hawk, Pl 72, JW/1831, lt stn/sl/fox, 2 rpr tr, S-25x37", Havell, lot 647, SBY 1/28/88 OE 5,500
Swift Fox (Male), Pl 52, hc litho, ca 1845, lt stn/sl mrgs & verso, fox/tr corner, 19x24", Bowen, lot 796, SBY 1/28/88 1,540
Tree Sparrow, Pl 188, JW Turkey Mill, lt fox mrgs, unfr, S-38x26", Havell, C-NY 1/22/88 UE 550
Tropic Bird, Pl 262, JW/1831, lt sl/fox mrgs, lt rpr tr/ls top mrg, lt stn, S-25x39", Havell, lot 712, SBY 1/28/88 3,300
Velvet Duck, Pl 247, JW Turkey Mill/1835, lt stn/fox/sl, ls in corner, S-25x38", Havell, lot 706, SBY 1/28/88 1,210
Vigor's Warbler, Pl 30, JW/1831, lt gray stn mrgs, 2" rpr tr/lt cr mrg, unfr, S-38x25", Havell, C-NY 1/22/88 UE 528
Virginia Partidge, chromolitho, 1850, lt scr/cr img, lt tr/cr mrg, lt stn, S-27x38", Bien, lot 787, SBY 1/28/88 1,540
Virginia Partridge, Pl 76, JW Turkey Mill/1830, 3" rpr tr, lt tr mrgs, lt ls/cr, S-26x39", Havell, lot 649, SBY 1/28/88 5,225
White Ibis, JW Turkey Mill/1834, lt stn/fox, 4 rpr tr in mrgs, S-39x26", Havell, lot 13, C-NY 1/19/89 1,540
White-Eyed Flycatcher or Vireo, Pl 63, hc etch, stn, laid down, S-29x18", Havell, lot 448, FAP 4/15/88 330
White-Headed Eagle, Pl 126, JW/1832, lt sl/stn/fox, lt offprint/fox on verso, S-38x25", Havell, lot 667, SBY 1/28/88 2,750
White-Headed Eagle, Pl 31, trm mrg, lt stn/scr img, lt tr/fox mrgs, P-25x38", Havell, lot 4, C-NY 1/22/88 OE 7,150
White-Headed Pigeon, #36, full mrgs, 1833, elephant folio, RAB 5/23/89 1,700
White-Winged Silvery Gull, Pl 282, hc aqua/engr/JW, ca 1830, lt sl/tr, laid down, S-26x33", Havell, lot 17, C-NY 1/19/89 1,540
Wild Turkey, proof imp(?), chromolitho, 1858, lt scuff img, lt ls mrg edges, S-39x27", Bien, lot 785, SBY 1/28/88 OE 6,600
Wild Turkey Male, Pl 1, JW Turkey Mill/1835, lt rpr tr/cr/stn/fox, S-38x26", Havell, lot 2, C-NY 1/19/89 OE 6,050
Wild Turkey Male, Pl 1, JW/1831, trm to img, rpr tr, ls in mrgs, lt stn/fox, unfr, S-36x23", Havell, C-NY 1/22/88 UE 2,750
Wooping Crane, Pl 226, JW Turkey Mill/1834, lt fox, lt nick/rpr tr mrg edges, S-39x27", Havell, lot 698, SBY 1/28/88 11,000
Yellow Shank, Pl 288, 1" mrgs, lt fox/mstn/tstn, unfr, S-17xx22", Havell, lot 19, C-NY 1/22/88 770
Yellow-Billed Cuckoo, Pl 275, chromolitho, 24x32", lot 207, MG 11/19/88 550
Yellow-Crowned Warbler, Pl 153, JW Turkey Mill, lt sl/cr img & mrgs, lt disclr, unfr, S-38x25, Havell, C-NY 1/22/88 UE 440
Yellow-Throated Viro, JW/1834, lt stn/fox/sl, fld mrg, S-37x25", Havell, lot 8, C-NY 1/19/89 440
Zenaida Dove, Pl 162, JW/1833, tstn, lt sl/rpl mrg edges, lt stn mrg recto/verso, P-26x21", Havell, C-NY 1/22/88 UE 1,100

AUSTIN, Robert Sargent (British, 1895-)
Group of 3: Scythes; Two Nuns; Woman of Sianno; ca 1920, various sizes, lot 19, SWN 6/15/89 220

AVATI, Mario (Italian, 1921-)
Two Balls of Twine, mezzo/heavy wove paper, pl/s, 8x9", lot 2829, B/B 2/16/88 300

AVERY, Milton (American, 1893-1965)
Birds and Sea, 11/20, dk bl wc/Japan, 1955, p/s, dtd, lt lstn, rub mrg, L-10x24", C-NY 1/22/88 OE 3,850
Fantail Pigeon, 27/30, bl & blk wc/thin Japan, 1953, p/s, dtd, cr img/mrgs, tr mrg, unfr, L-10x10", C-NY 1/22/88 1,100
Flight, ed of 100, brn & blk wc/thin Japan, 1953, p/s, lt stn, L-7x9", lot 121, C-NY 1/19/89 1,650
Gray Sea, 100/118, clr litho, 1963, p/s, full mrgs, lt cr mrgs, 21x26", lot 6, SBY 2/23/89 OE 1,540
Gray Sea, 83/118, clr litho, 1963, p/s, L-22x26", lot 420, C-NY 5/10/89 OE 2,090
Head, 16/25, bl wc/tissue-thin wove paper, 1955, p/s, lt stn/sl, L-12x10", lot 122, C-NY 1/19/89 1,870
Hen, 6/20, yel & blk wc/thin soft Japan, 1954, full mrgs, lt sl/cr in mrgs & verso, 12x10", lot 203, SBY 5/11/89 1,760
Lamb, 2/20, blk & yel wc/thin Japan, 1954, p/s, dtd, stn img/mrg, cr/fld mrg edges, unfr, 10x14", lot 152, C-N 1/22/88 550
My Wife, presumed ed of 100, drypt/wove paper, 1934, p/s, lt stn mrgs & verso, P-6x8", lot 118, C-NY 1/19/89 OE 1,320
Nude, 3/20, bl & blk wc/Japan, 1953, p/s, lt stn, 4x11", lot 4, C-NY 2/25/88 990
Nude Combing Hair, 31/90, drypt/thick wove paper, 1950, p/s, dtd, full mrgs, lt sl mrgs/verso, P-9x6", C-NY 1/22/88 OE 935
Nude with Long Torso (Reclining Nude), a/p, drypt, 1948, p/s, lt stn/sl/fld, P-6x15", lot 419, C-NY 5/10/89 6,600
Pair: My Wife Sally; Umbrella by the Sea; ed of 100, drypt, 1934/1948, p/s, unfr, 6x9"/5x7", SBY 5/12/88 OE 2,200
Reclining Nude, 27/100, drypt, 1941, p/s, lt scuff img, lt sl mrgs, 4x7", lot 204, SBY 5/11/89 2,420
Reclining Nude, 46/100, dk brn drypt/wove paper, 1941, p/s, lt stn/rub/sl, P-4x7", lot 120, C-NY 1/19/89 1,980
Sally with a Beret, 86/100, dk brn drypt/wove paper, 1939, p/s, dtd, full mrgs, P-8x6", C-NY 1/22/88 OE 1,760
Standing Nude, 13/60, 1941, p/s, full mrgs, lt stn/sl mrgs, 14x8", lot 202, SBY 5/11/89 2,420
Standing Nude, 44/60, drypt, 1941, sgn/dtd, lt rub/sl, P-14x8", lot 418, C-NY 5/10/89 OE 2,640
Three Birds, ed of 15, a/p, blk & bl wc/Japan, p/s, dtd, ink/tp verso mrgs, L-10x25", C-NY 1/22/88 OE 3,520
Twisted Tree, 57/60, drypt/heavy wove paper, 1943, p/s, lt cr, P-5x7", lot 119, C-NY 1/19/89 1,760
Young Girl Nude, S1/100, drypt, 1935, p/s, wide mrgs, P-10x10", lot 4, PHL 6/16/88 1,200

BACHER, Otto (American, 1856-1909)
Royal Garden Schleisshem, etch, p/s, 5x9", lot 116, WG 10/19/88 OE 300

BACHMAN, John (American, 19th C)
Baltimore in 1752, litho/wove paper, 1856, lstn, cr img, rpr/cr mrgs, tp overmat verso, L-20x29", Duval, C-NY 1/22/88 2,750
Bird's Eye View of Havana, hc litho, 1851, trm mrgs, lt scr/skinned/cr/tr, S-26x34", lot 516, SBY 1/28/88 1,760
Panorama of New York & Vicinity, hc litho, 1866, lt scuff/tr/cr/sl, L-22x35", Bien, lot 526, SBY 1/28/88 4,950

BACON, Francis (British, 1909-)
Group of 3: Three Studies for a Self-Portrait; 123/150, clr litho, 1979, p/s, Arts-Litho bstp, 19x41", SBY 11/5/88 4,400
La Mysticite Charnelle de Rene Crevel: Self-Portrait; 80/100, etch/aqua, 1976, p/s, lt cr, 11x9", SBY 11/5/88 OE 3,025
Man Writing Reflected in Mirror, 151/180, litho before letters, 1976, full mrgs, lt stn, 34x25", lot 711, SBY 11/5/88 OE 4,400
Man Writing Reflected in Mirror, 29/180, clr litho, 1976, full mrgs, stn/cr/sl, 34x25", Deschamps, lot 605, SBY 2/23/89 2,475
Metropolitan Triptych, 35/99, aqua/etch/1 sheet, 1981, p/s, full mrgs, lt cr/sl/stn, ea 15x12", Poligrafa, SBY 5/14/88 4,950
Metropolitan Triptych, 82/99, clr etch/aqua, 1981, p/s, full mrgs, lt stn, 15x12", lot 484, SBY 2/25/88 OE 5,775
Metropolitan Triptych, 82/99, etch/aqua, 1981, p/s, full mrgs, lt mstn, ea 15x12", Polifgrafa, lot 485, SBY 2/25/88 OE 4,125
Metropolitan Triptych: Center Panel; 64/99, clr etch/aqua, 1981, p/s, full mrgs, lt scuff/stn, 15x12", SBY 2/23/89 3,300
Metropolitan Triptych: 3 Panels; 68/90, aqua/etch, 1981, p/s, full mrgs, lt stn, ea 15x12", Poligrafa, SBY 5/14/88 OE 7,150
Metropolitan Tryptych, a/p, ed of 99, etch/aqua/1981, p/s, full mrgs, lt cr, P-15x12", Poligrafa, lot 3006, B/B 4/19/88 3,850
Oedipus & the Sphinx, HC, ed of 150, clr litho/wove paper, 1984, p/s, L-46x34", Maeght, lot 575, C-NY 11/1/88 5,500
Oedipus & the Sphinx After Ingres, HC, clr litho, 1984, Arts-Litho bstp, 46x34", lot 714, SBY 11/5/88 5,225
Oedipus & the Sphinx After Ingres, 141/150, litho, 1984, Arts-Litho bstp, full mrgs, lt sl, L-46x34", SBY 5/14/88 OE 8,525
Study for Bull Fight No 1, 145/150, clr litho, 1978, sgn, full mrgs, 40x45", lot 905, SBY 5/13/89 OE 11,550
Study for Self-Portrait, 155/180, clr litho before letters, 1973, full mrgs, lt cr, 34x25", Diamaiuto, SBY 11/5/88 4,400

Three Studies for a Self-Portrait, 50/150, clr litho, 1979/1981, S-19x41", Eds de la Difference, SBY 5/12/88 OE 7,425
Three Studies for a Self-Portrait, 62/150, 3 clr lithos/1 sheet Arches, 1980, 19x41", Maeght, lot 574, C-NY 11/1/88 OE 8,800
Triptych Inspired by Orestia of Aeschylus, 140/150, litho, 1979/1981, S-21x41", Eds de la Difference, SBY 5/14/88 4,950
Triptych Inspired by Orestia of Aeschylus; 64/150, clr litho, 1979, Arts-Litho bstp, 21x41", SBY 11/5/88 4,400
Triptyque l'Orestie D'Eschyle, XII/XXV, 3 litho/1 sheet, 1980, p/s, lt cr mrgs, 16x38", Maeght, lot 3005, B/B 4/19/88 3,025

BACON, Peggy (American, 1895-1987)
Happy Holiday, etch, 1930, p/s, titled, 12x17", lot 151, WG 10/19/88 OE 1,000
Mayor La Guardia, ed of about 35, litho, 1934, p/s, titled, 14x11", lot 20, SWN 6/15/89 660
Pair: Untilled Field; Contentment; drypt & litho/BFK Rives, 1936, p/s, titled, full mrgs, C-NY 1/22/88 605
Portrait of Girl, litho, sgn, 11x9", lot 365, WG 10/19/88 175
Untilled Field, ed of 250, drypt/wove France, 1937, p/s, titled, full mrgs, lt sl/tr, P-6x8", lot 123, C-NY 1/19/89 528

BAECHLER, Donald (20th C)
Portfolio: Increments; 16/17, 5 aqua/etch, 1987, full mrgs, S-35x28", lot 715, SBY 11/5/88 2,750

BAILEY, Owen (British, 19th C)
Road 1825, Commercial Traveler; aqua/engr, scr img, ca 1850, no size given, RAB 11/25/88 190

BAILLIE, J.
South Sea Whale Fishery, litho, lt trm mrgs, lt fox, sm folio, RAB 3/14/89 500

BARLACH, Ernst (German, 1870-1938)
Die Sterndeuter (Die Sterngucker) III, 25/30, litho, 1930, p/s, wide mrgs, lt fox, S-21x14", lot 3, C-NY 11/1/88 1,870
Set of 7: Die Wandlungen Gottes; ed of 110, wc/Japan, 1920-21, p/s, S-15x18", Cassirer/Pan-Presse, lot 2, C-NY 11/1/88 8,800

BARNET, Will (American, 1911-)
Madame Butterfly, 224/300, clr litho/wove paper, 1980, p/s, titled, lt fox, L-18x34", lot 76, RWS 9/8/89 650
Silent Seasons, Autumn; 5/110, litho, 1969, p/s, titled, 26x20", lot 457, FAP 4/15/88 550
Woman & White Cat, 13/200, clr slksc/cream wove paper, p/s, titled, lt stn, 23x20", lot 3007, B/B 4/19/88 600

BARRAUD, William Henry; after (British, 1811-1874)
Charles Davier on Traverser, by E Hacker, mezzo, 1849, 15x19", lot 854, WAD 11/28/88 UE 150
Pair: Traverse; Mr William Long on Bertha (equestrian); engr, 23x20", Backer, lot 1067, DM 2/19/88 450

BARTLETT, Charles (British, 1860-1940)
Udalpur 1910, clr wc, p/s, 9x12", lot 108, WG 10/19/89 250

BARTLETT, Jennifer (American, 1941-)
At Sea, Japan; clr slksc/wc/6 sheets handmade Kurotani Hosho, 1980, p/s, 22x101" overall, Simca, lot 910, SBY 5/13/89 OE 55,000
Day & Night I, 28/35, clr drypt, 1978, p/s, S-31x21", Multiples, lot 908, SBY 5/13/89 OE 5,500
Day & Night II, 28/35, clr drypt, 1978, p/s, S-31x21", Multiples, lot 909, SBY 5/13/89 OE 5,500
In the Garden #116, 76/100, clr slksc, 1983, p/s, Simca bstp, S-29x38", lot 718, SBY 11/5/88 9,900
In the Garden #118, p/p, clr slksc/Kozo Japanese paper, 1982, p/s, 29x38", Simca, lot 716, SBY 11/5/88 4,675
In the Garden #118, 40/50, clr scrpt/Kurotani Kozo handmade, 1982, p/s, S-29x38", Bartlett/Simca, lot 576, C-NY 11/1/88 3,850
In the Garden #118 A, 49/50, clr slksc/handmade Kurotani Kozo, 1982, p/s, full mrgs, S-29x38", lot 911, SBY 5/13/89 5,775
In the Garden #118 B, 18/30, blk/gray slksc/handmade Mino Kozo, 1982, p/s, 29x38", Bartlett/Simca, lot 912, SBY 5/13/89 2,200
In the Garden #190, 42/52, scrpt/wc/2 sheets Japanese Mino Hosho, 1982, p/s, Simca bstp, S-35x23", lot 577, C-NY 11/1/88 1,870
In the Garden #40, APX/XV, clr wc/slksc/4 sheets Japan Echizen Hosho, 1983, p/s, 46x60", Simca, SBY 5/14/88 6,600
In the Garden #40, 30/68, clr wc/scrpt/4 sheets Echizen Hasho, 1982, p/s, 23x30", Bartlett/Simca, lot 578, C-NY 11/1/88 5,500
In the Garden #40, 41/68, clr wc/slkcr/4 sheets Japanese Echizen Hosho, 1983, p/s, 45x60", Simca, lot 717, SBY 11/5/88 5,500

BASKETT, Charles Henry (British, 1872-1953)
Towpath, Heybridge; aqua, p/s, titled, 9x13", lot 93, WG 10/19/88 40

BASKIN, Leonard (American, 1922-)
Caffot, 46/50, engr/cream paper, 18x17", lot 87, FAP 2/24/89 140
Conrad, 26/90, wc, p/s, 5x4", lot 453, FAP 4/15/88 OE 120
Eakins, 29/50, etch, 1907, p/s, 9x7", lot 467, FAP 4/15/88 OE 265
Gerrault, 79/100, drypt, p/s, titled, full mrgs, lt stn, P-17x14", lot 12, PHL 10/28/88 275
Grape Tree, 23/50, drypt, p/s, lt stn, P-18x15", lot 13, PHL 10/28/88 300
Great Teasel, 17/125, etch/Arches, 1969, p/s, titled, lt stn, unfr, P-22x28", lot 96, RWS 9/8/89 350
Green Stem & Purple Flowers, 95/120, gr & purple etch/Arches, 1970, unfr, 18x12", CFA Graphics, lot 98, RWS 9/8/89 UE 275
Group of 3: Bird of Peace; Sage; Untitled (head); wc/Japan Hosho, ca 1950, no size given, lot 24, SWN 6/15/89 UE 195
Icarus, 97/100, blk/gr litho, p/s, titled, 32x22", lot 97, FAP 2/24/89 325
Iris for Lisa, 37/130, etch/aqua/Arches, 1970, p/s, unfr, S-18x12", CFA Graphics, lot 94, RWS 9/8/89 475
Le Tit, 5/50, etch, p/s, no size given, lot 452, FAP 4/15/88 165
Menzel, 46/50, etch, p/s, no size given, lot 470, FAP 4/15/88 UE 165
Pair: Ezekiel; View of Worcester; 23/50 & a/p, wc/Japan Hosho, p/s, no size given, lot 23, SWN 6/15/89 248
Pair: Portrait of Thomas Eakins; Portrait of Goltzius; wc & etch, p/s, titled, no size given, lot 2920, B/B 2/16/88 190
Pair: Walt Whitman; Leper; ed of unknown size, wc/Japan Hosho, 1955 & 1956, no size given, lot 22, SWN 6/15/89 UE 195
Portrait of a Man's Face, 17/100, clr wc, 1951, p/s, 33x24", lot 468, FAP 4/15/88 OE 265
Prodigal Son, 43/100, etch, p/s, 9x6", lot 456, FAP 4/15/88 120
Self-Portrait, 44/100, etch, p/s, 6x6", lot 476, FAP 4/15/88 132
Standing Man with Beard, wc, p/s, 16x8", lot 474, FAP 4/15/88 110
Suite: Laus Pictorum, Portraits of Fifteen 19th-C Artists; 126/175, 5 etch/10 engr, 1969, unfr, S-14x11", RWS 3/16/89 800
Tobias & the Angel, 91/300, wood engr/paper, 1958, p/s, lt stn/ls/old glue, L-14x15", lot 72, RWS 9/8/89 475
Twistle Ornament, 74/80, gr/blk woodblock, 23x32", lot 92, FAP 2/24/89 225

BASQUIAT, Jean Michel (European, 20th C)
Suite: Anatomy; 18 photoslksc, 1982, p/s, full mrgs, lt scr, 30x22", Annina Nosei Gallery, lot 486, SBY 2/25/88 4,400

BAUMANN, Gustave (American, 1881-1971)
Bound for Taos, 18/120, clr wc/laid wm Hand in Heart, ca 1927, p/s, titled, lt trm/stn mrg, unfr, L-10x11", C-NY 1/22/88 1,210

Cherry Bloom, 61/100, clr wc/lt tan wove paper, 1917, p/s, titled, full mrgs, L-10x11", lot 125, C-NY 1/19/89 OE ... 1,650
Landmark, 30/50, clr wc/wove paper, 1916, p/s, titled, tr mrg into img, lt stn/cr, L-11x10", lot 124, C-NY 1/19/89 OE ... 440
Leaves Red & Green, clr wc/tan laid paper, ca 1920, p/s, titled, lt stn, L-11x10", C-NY 5/11/88 ... 1,100
Night Ceremony, 6/125, clr wc/oatmeal Hand in Heart, 1948, p/s, full mrgs, lt cr/stn, L-8x8", lot 128, C-NY 1/19/89 OE ... 2,860
Pair: Morning in Mexico; El Velorio; 20/125 & 32/125, clr wc/wove paper, ca 1927, pencil inscr II, C-NY 1/22/88 ... 1,210
Pecos Valley, ed of 100, clr wc, 1921, p/s, artist chop mk, lt stn, laid down, 10x11", lot 5, SBY 2/25/88 ... 770
Summer Couds, 11/100, clr wc/fibrous oatmeal paper, 1926, p/s, titled, lt cr corner, 11x10", lot 2918, B/B 2/16/88 OE ... 1,540
Sycamores Salt Creek, 51/120, wc/thick tan wove paper, 1916(?), sgn/titled, lt stn mrgs, unfr, L-10x11", C-NY 1/22/88 ... 880
Tulips, 18/120, clr wc/slvr foil/tan laid wm Hand in Heart, ca 1930, lt stn, stn/glue mrgs, L-13x14", C-NY 1/22/88 ... 1,100
Windsor Trail, 4/100, clr wc/tan wove paper, ca 1921, p/s, titled, lt rub, L-11x10", lot 127, C-NY 1/19/89 OE ... 1,650
Winter Corral, clr wc/fibrous oatmeal paper, p/s, tp to mat, 13x13", lot 2919, B/B 2/16/88 OE ... 1,210
Woodland Meadows, 89/125, clr wc/lt tan laid paper, 1917, p/s, lt stn/old tp, L-10x11", lot 421, C-NY 5/10/88 OE ... 1,760

BAXTER, George; after (British, 1804-1867)
Pair: Gems of the Crystal Palace (interior/exterior views); clr litho, no size given, lot 72, FAP 2/24/89 ... 150

BAYNARD, Ed (American, 1940-)
Blue Tulips, 37/70, clr wc/Okawara handmade, 1980, p/s, Tyler Graphics bstp, lt cr, S-30x42", lot 393, C-NY 5/11/88 ... 1,650
Pair: Print Scarf; Blue Tulips; 22/70 & 17/70; clr wc/Okawara, 1980, S-30x42, Tyler Graphics, SBY 5/14/88 OE ... 2,750
Pair: Quarter Moon; Dark Pot with Roses; 21/70 & 17/70, clr wc/Okawara, 1980, S-42x30", Tyler Graphics, SBY 5/14/88 OE ... 2,475
Pair: Still Life with Orchid; Dragon Fly Vase; 28/70 & 21/70, clr wc/Okawara, S-30x42", Tyler Graphics, SBY 5/12/88 OE ... 3,300
Pair: Tulip Pitcher; China Pot; 21/70, clr wc/Okawara, p/s, TGL bstp, S-42x30", Tyler Graphics, SBY 5/14/88 ... 1,925
Print Scarf, a/p, 8/18, clr wc/Okawara, 1980, p/s, TGL bstp, lt scr/cr, S-30x42", lot 487, SBY 2/25/88 OE ... 880

BEAL, Reynolds (American, 1867-1950)
Bridgeport Oyster Boats, etch, sgn/titled, full mrgs, L-9x12", RAB 3/27/89 ... 225
Entering Port, etch, sgn/dtd 1928, full mrgs, L-9x13", RAB 3/27/89 UE ... 175
Racing Yachts-Marblehead; etch, sgn/dtd 1929/titled, L-8x12", RAB 3/27/89 UE ... 175
Under Sail, etch, sgn/dtd 1930, full mrgs, 9x13", RAB 3/27/89 ... 200

BEARDEN, Romare (American, 1914-)
Jazz Bass Player, PP5/5, clr litho, 34x24", lot 12, SWN 12/1/88 ... 415
Pair: Jazz Saxophonist & Drummer; Jazz Bass Player; p/p, clr litho, 34x24", lot 25, SWN 6/15/89 OE ... 3,300
Untitled (Figure with Three Small Boats & the Sea), clr monotype, ca 1970s, lt cr, S-41x30", lot 579, C-NY 11/1/88 ... 4,400

BEARDSLEY, Aubrey (British, 1872-1898)
Yellow Book, October 1894; clr litho, 15x11", lot 98, WG 10/19/88 ... 100

BEATRIZET, Nicolas (Italian, 1515-1560)
Pair: River Nile; River Tiber; 1st state, engr/wm ladder in circle, lt cr/sl, 14x22"/13x22", lot 579, SBY 2/25/88 ... 2,200

BEAUCHAMP, Robert (American, 1923-)
Apple Dream, AP18/25, aside from ed of 200, clr litho, 1980, sgn, 22x25", lot 26, SWN 6/15/89 ... 100

BEAUFOY, B.; after
View of Port Louis, Mauritius; by C Rosenberg, hc aqua, L-19x35", C-SK 6/9/88 ... 706

BECKMANN, Max (German, 1884-1950)
Abendegesellschaft, drypt/Butten, 1913, p/s, inscr 2 Zustand, lt stn/sl mrgs, P-6x8", lot 75, C-NY 5/11/88 ... 1,540
Album: Apokalypse, Bauersche Giesserei, Frankfurt am Main, 1943; 19/24, S-16x12", slipcase, lot 11, C-NY 11/1/88 OE ... 19,800
Bei der Toilett, 12/55, wc/cream laid paper, 1923, p/s, lt cr, C-27x19", lot 9, C-NY 11/1/88 OE ... 39,600
Der Raucher (Selbsbildnis), 6/20, drypt/van Gelder, 1916, p/s, lt fox/stn, S-17x10", Cassirer, lot 7, C-NY 11/1/88 OE ... 37,400
Gesellschaft, a/p, 1st state, drypt/simili Japan, 1915, p/s, full mrgs, lt cr/sl, P-10x12", lot 76, C-NY 5/11/88 OE ... 3,850
Gesellschaft, 2nd state, drypt/van Gelder, 1915, p/s, inscr II Zustand, S-13x18", Neumann, lot 8, C-NY 11/1/88 OE ... 6,050
Grosse Brucke (Der Eiserne Steg in Frankfurt/Main), drypt, 1922, p/s, lt fox/stn/sl, S-21x14", lot 6, C-NY 11/1/88 ... 41,800
Group of 3: Bildnis Friedel Battenberg; Bildnis Dr Heinrich Simon; Bildnis Einer Rumanin II; litho, SBY 5/12/88 UE ... 1,100
In der Trambahn, drypt/cream Japan, 1922, p/s, full mrgs, lt stn/fox/cr, 12x17", lot 96, SBY 2/25/88 OE ... 5,500
In der Trambahn, drypt/wove paper, 1922, p/s, full mrgs, lt sl/cr mrgs, P-11x17", lot 204, C-NY 11/1/88 OE ... 7,920
Kleines Selbstbildnis, drypt, 1912(?), p/s, lt sl/stn/fox, S-13x10", Neumann, lot 4, C-NY 11/1/88 OE ... 10,450
Liebespaar II, Gesichter; Pl 5, ed of 40, drypt/Japan, 1918, Marees-Gesellschaft bstp, P-9x10", lot 485, C-NY 5/10/89 OE ... 4,950
Lowenpaar, litho/cream wove paper, 1922, lt sl, 8x6", lot 281, B/B 4/19/88 ... 275
Mainlandschaft mit Regenbogen, 41/60, etch/simili Japan, 1923, p/s, lt stn/sl/cr, 10x8", Verlag, lot 97, SBY 2/25/88 OE ... 2,530
Selbstbildnis mit Steifem Hut, 2nd state, drypt/wm BSB laid paper, 1921, S-20x13", Neumann, lot 5, C-NY 11/1/88 OE ... 88,000
Set of 10: Der Jahrmarkt; 8/75, drypt/Japan, 1921, a/bstp, lt sl, S-22x17", Marees Gesellschaft, lot 10, C-NY 11/1/88 ... 22,000
Tamerlan, 7/60, etch/Butten, 1923, p/s, lg mrgs, lt fox/cr/sl/tr, no size given, lot 315, SBY 5/11/89 OE ... 16,500
Toilette, wc/handmade wove paper, 1923, p/s, full mrgs, lt sl/fox/cr, 9x6", Neumann, lot 101, SBY 2/23/89 ... 3,300
Wetterfahne, Day & Dream; Pl 2, 18/90 II, litho, 1946, p/s, full mrgs, lt stn, L-16x11", lot 77, C-NY 5/11/88 OE ... 1,320

BEHAM, Hans Sebald (German, 1500-1550)
Set of 7: Seven Planets with the Zodiacs; engr, ca 1540(?), trm/lt ls, 2x1", lot 580, SBY 2/25/88 OE ... 1,760

BELLA, Stefano Della (Italian, 1610-1664)
Set of 13: Paysages et Ruines de Rome; etch/wm Crowned T on Divided Shield, ca 1646, 5x5", lot 582, SBY 2/25/88 ... 1,540

BELLANGE, Jacques (French, 1576-1638)
Gardener with an Urn & Reticule, 2nd state of 2, etch, ca 1611(?), trm mrgs, lt cr/sl, S-13x7", lot 4, SBY 5/11/89 ... 2,860

BELLMER, Hans (German, 1902-1975)
Female Nude, red-brn aqua, 11x8", lot 251, FAP 2/24/89 ... 210
Scene Erotique, drypt, a/p, 8x8", lot 277, FAP 2/24/89 ... 200

BELLOTTO, Bernardo (Italian, 1724-1780)
Le Turc Genereux, etch/wm pine cone paper, 1759, lg mrgs, lt tr/stn/sl, 19x25", lot 5, SBY 5/11/89 ... 3,300

BELLOWS, George (American, 1882-1925)
Anne 1923, ed of 56, litho/wm Strathmore wove paper, 1923, p/s, inscr Bolton Brown imp, 10x8", lot 427, C-NY 5/10/89 OE ... 1,760

Arrangement, Emma in a Room; ed of 43, litho/Chine volant, 1921, p/s, inscr Bolton Brown imp, 9x7", lot 212, SBY 5/11/89	1,430
Artists Judging Works of Art, #30, ed of 52, litho/thin Japan, 1916, full mrgs, lt sl, 15x19", lot 6, SBY 11/3/88	3,025
Benediction in Georgia, a/p, ed of 80, litho/China paper, 1916, full mrgs, lt cr/sl, 16x20", lot 5, SBY 11/3/88 OE	3,300
Between Rounds, Small Second Stone; ed of 42, litho, 1923, p/s, inscr Bolton Brown, 18x15", lot 198, LH 10/16/88	6,500
Billy Sunday, ed of 60, litho/China paper, 1923, p/s, inscr Bolton Brown imp, lt rpr/rpl, 9x16", lot 10, SBY 2/25/88 OE	4,290
Billy Sunday, ed of 60, litho/thin wove paper, 1923, p/s, inscr Bolton Brown imp, lt cr, 9x16", lot 213, SBY 5/11/89 OE	7,150
Billy Sunday, hc litho/smooth wove paper, 1923, p/s, titled, lt nick img, lt sl mrgs, L-9x16", lot 133, C-NY 1/19/89	3,300
Businessmen's Class, 4/64, litho, 1916, p/s, titled, lt tr/rpr, 11x17", lot 203, LH 10/16/88 OE	4,800
Businessmen's Class (Businessmen's Class, YMCA), #35, ed of 64, litho, 1916, p/s, cr, 12x17", lot 8, SBY 2/23/89 OE	7,150
Dance in a Madouse, 27/69, litho/wove paper, 1917, inscr by artist's daughter, lt sl/stn, unfr, L-18x24", C-NY 1/22/88	3,300
Dempsey & Firpo, litho, 1923-24, p/s, titled/inscr Bolton Brown imp, full mrgs, 18x23", lot 12, C-NY 2/25/88	29,150
Dempsey & Firpo, litho/wove paper, 1923-24, p/s, inscr Bolton Brown imp, full mrgs, 18x23", lot 214, SBY 5/11/89 OE	63,250
Drunk, litho/Basingwerk Parchment, 1923-24, inscr Bolton Brown imp, full mrgs, lt stn/sl mrgs, L-16x13", C-NY 1/22/88 OE	1,210
Evening Snow, ed of 24, litho, 1921, p/s, titled/inscr Bolton Brown, 7x10", lot 201, LH 10/16/88 OE	9,000

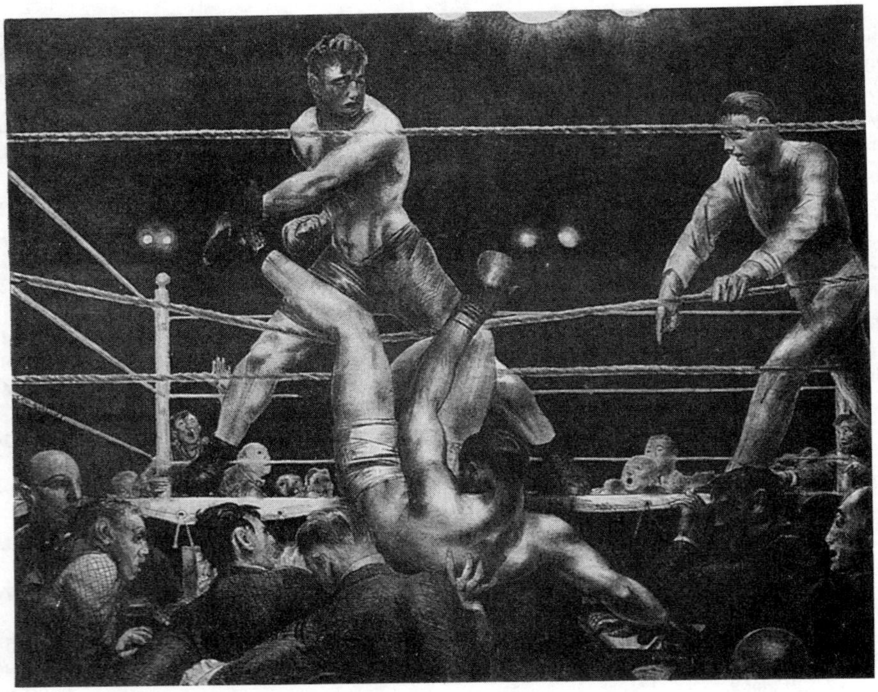

Dempsey & Firpo, ed of 103, litho/Basingwerk Parchment, 1923-24, inscr Bolton Brown Imp, full mrgs, lt stn, L-18x23", lot 12, C-NY 5/10/89 OE; $52,800

Hungry Dogs, 36/41, 1st state, litho, 1916, p/s, titled, 14x10", lot 200, LH 10/16/88	1,000
In the Park, Dark (In the Park, Second State); 50/81, litho, 1916, p/s, full mrgs, cr/sl, 17x21", lot 205A, SBY 5/11/89	3,300
In the Park, Light; 56/59, brn-blk litho/China, 1916, p/s, lt sl, 16x21", lot 205, SBY 5/11/89 OE	7,150
Initiation in the Frat, 2/16, litho/laid Japan, 1917, full mrgs, lt sl/cr mrg, L-10x13", lot 423, C-NY 5/10/88 OE	4,950
Introducing Georges Capentier, ed of about 50, litho, 1921, p/s, inscr Bolton Brown imp, 15x21", lot 211, SBY 5/11/89 OE	14,300
Introductions (Introducing the Champion No 2), ed of 57, litho, 1921, p/s, 9x7", lot 199, LH 10/16/88	5,500
Irish Fair, litho, 1923, p/s, titled/inscr Bolton Brown, lt cr, L-19x21", lot 5, PHL 6/16/88 OE	2,100
Jean in a Black Hat, ed of 48, 1st state, litho/Basingwerk Parchment, 1923, full mrgs, 11x9", lot 429, C-NY 5/10/88 OE	2,420
Law Is Too Slow, ed of 26, litho/Japan, 1923, p/s, titled, full mrgs, lt cr/sl/fox, 18x15", lot 11, SBY 2/23/89	1,210
Legs of the Sea, ed of 53, litho/thin laid paper, 1921, p/s, inscr Bolton Brown, L-9x11", lot 131, C-NY 1/19/89 OE	2,420
Mother & Children, 56/68, Myers & Ayres` 2nd state, litho/wove paper, 1916, p/s, lt stn/rpr, L-11x11", C-NY 1/19/89	1,650
Murder of Edith Cavell, #8, ed of 99, litho, 1918, p/s, lt sl/stn/rpr tr mrgs, sl on verso, L-19x25", C-NY 5/11/88	1,045
Murder of Edith Cavell, 71/99, litho, 1918, p/s, mstn, laid down, 19x25", lot 8, SBY 2/25/88	880
My Family, First Stone; ed of 32, litho/Chine volant, 1921, lt sl/stn, 10x8", lot 9, SBY 11/3/88	880
My Family, Second Stone; ed of 56, litho/Chine volant, p/s, inscr Bolton Brown imp, lt stn, 10x8", lot 10, SBY 11/3/88	1,430
Nude Study, Woman Lying on a Pillow; ed of 32, litho, 1923-24, p/s, inscr Bolton Brown imp, 6x10", lot 11, SBY 2/25/88	495
Old Billiard Player (Old Player), ed of 43, litho, 1921, p/s, inscr Bolton Brown imp, 9x8", lot 210, SBY 5/11/89 OE	6,875
Pair: Bathing Beach; Black Hat; ed of 22 & 55, litho, 1921, p/s, titled, laid down, 8x7"/13x9", lot 8, SBY 11/3/88	770
Pair: Portrait of Robert Aitken, First Stone; Portrait of Louis Bouche; ed of 32/42, litho, 1921, cr, C-NY 1/22/88 UE	550
Pair: Statuette; Nude Study, Girl Standing with Hand Raised to Mouth; litho, 1917/ca 1923, cr, C-NY 1/22/88	880
Plaid Shawl, ed of 31, litho/smooth wove paper, 1923, p/s, titled/inscr Bolton Brown, lt stn, L-13x10", C-NY 1/19/89 OE	3,850
Pool Player, ed of 43, litho/thin wove paper, 1921, p/s, inscr Bolton Brown imp, lt cr, 5x10", lot 209, SBY 5/11/89 OE	12,100
Portrait of J Carroll, litho/Chine volant, p/s, titled, lt cr/rpl, 11x9", Bolton Brown, lot 2930, B/B 4/19/88	880
Preliminaries (Preliminaries to the Big Bout), a/p, litho, 1916, p/s, lt fox/stn/rpr tr, 16x20", lot 9, SBY 2/23/89 OE	17,600
Preliminaries (Preliminaries to the Big Bout), 67/67, litho, 1916, p/s, ltstn/scr/stn, L-16x20", lot 422, C-NY 5/10/89	13,200
Punter, ed of 150, etch, 1927, p/s, full mrgs, lt cr img, lt lstn, 8x12", lot 214B, SBY 5/11/89	770
Sand Team, ed of 4, litho/wove applique, 1919, inscr by artist's widow, lt sl, L-17x24", lot 426, C-NY 5/10/89 OE	20,900

Sawdust Trail, 18/65, litho/thin wove paper, 1917, p/s, lt cr, 27x20", lot 207, SBY 5/11/89 3,025
Sawdust Trail, 62/65, Myers & Ayres` 2nd state, litho/Chine, 1917, p/s, lt stn mrg, L-26x20", lot 425, C-NY 5/10/89 OE 3,080
Shower Bath, ed of 36, 1st state, litho, 1917, sgn by artist's daughter, 16x24", lot 202, LH 10/16/88 2,600
Sixteen East Gay Street, ed of 72, litho/wove paper, 1923-24, p/s, inscr Bolton Brown imp, 10x12", lot 214A, SBY 5/11/89 5,500
Solitude, 59/60, litho/thin wove paper, 1917, p/s, lt stn/fox/cr, L-17x15", lot 130, C-NY 1/19/89 OE 5,280
Solitude, 6/20, litho/China, 1917, p/s, full mrgs, lt cr/tp hinges, 17x16", lot 205B, SBY 5/11/89 4,675
Splinter Beach, 31/70, litho/wove paper, 1916, p/s, titled, trm mrgs, lt sl mrg, laid down, L-15x20", C-NY 1/22/88 7,700
Stag at Sharkey's, 20/98, litho, 1917, p/s, titled, lt stn, 19x24", lot 197, LH 10/16/88 OE 75,000
Stag at Sharkey's, 27/98, litho/thick wove paper, 1947, p/s, lt stn/cr/tp in mrgs, L-19x24", lot 424, C-NY 5/10/89 66,000
Stag at Sharkey's, 82/98, brn-blk litho/China, 1917, lt cr/sl/stn, 19x24", lot 206, SBY 5/11/89 OE 85,250
Street, 49/54, litho/laid Japan, 1917, inscr by artist's daughter, full mrgs, lt stn/fox/sl, 19x15", lot 7, SBY 2/25/88 2,970
Tennis (Tennis Tournament), ed of about 63, litho/Chine volant, ca 1921, lt fox verso, 19x20", lot 7, SBY 11/3/88 6,050
Tournament (Tennis at Newport), #38, litho/China, ca 1921, p/s, inscr Bolton Brown imp, 15x18", lot 208, SBY 5/11/89 6,050

BENECKE, D.; after (19th C)

Sleighing in New York, by Thomas Benecke, chromolitho, 1855, lt cr/stn/rpr tr, L-22x31", Nigel/Lewis, C-NY 1/19/89 OE 770

BENEKER, Gerrit Albertus (American, 1882-)

Sure! We'll Finish the Job; clr litho/poster paper, ca 1918, laid down, 37x26", lot 171, FAP 2/24/89 40

BENNETT, William James (American, 1777-1844)

Baltimore From Federal Hill, hc aqua, 1831, trm mrgs, lt tr/ls, S-20x26", Megarey/Neale, lot 509, SBY 1/28/88 OE 9,075
Fulton Street & Market, hc aqua, ca 1834, trm mrgs, rpr ls, lt stn/sl, S-14x19", Megarey, lot 511, SBY 1/28/88 3,300
View of the Ruins After the Great Fire in New York...; hc aqua/wove paper, ca 1836, lt stn, L-20x27", C-NY 1/19/89 OE 1,045
West Point, From Above Washington Valley...; 1st state, aqua, 1833, trm/stn, S-20x26", Parker & Clover, C-NY 1/22/88 12,100
West Point, From Phillipstown; hc aqua/wove paper, 1830, lt stn img/mrg, tr mrg, Parker & Clover, C-NY 1/22/88 8,250
West Point, From Phillipstown; 1st state, hc aqua, 1831, trm mrgs, tr/cr, S-18x24", Parker & Clover, lot 510, SBY 1/28/88 2,420

BENSON, Frank Weston (American, 1862-1951)

Cloudy Dawn, ed of 150, etch/drypt laid England, 1922, p/s, lt stn/cr, L-10x12", lot 39, RWS 9/8/89 325
Dawn, ed of 271, etch/JW, 1924, p/s, full mrgs, lt lstn img/mrgs, sl mrgs, unfr, P-7x10", C-NY 1/22/88 UE 165
Duck Blind, ed of 150, etch/laid paper, 1925, p/s, lt rpl, unfr, P-8x11", RWS 3/16/89 OE 950
Ducks in Flight, etch/laid wm England, ca 1920, p/s, gstn/sl mrg, P-10x8", C-NY 1/22/88 605
Flying Brant, ed of 150, drypt/laid paper, 1925, p/s, lt stn, broken hinge, L-5x7", RWS 3/16/89 375
Geese Against the Sky, 14/50, ed of 50, etch/zinc/wm chrysanthemum Shogun, 1915, lt rpr/sl/rpl, unfr, 6x11", RWS 3/16/89 350
Group of 3: The Alarm; After Sunset; Marshes at Evening; ed, ca 1917-18, p/s, largest 9x11", lot 43, RWS 9/8/89 OE 650
Nightfall, 2; ed of 150, drypt/wm England Whatman, p/s, unfr, L-6x8", RWS 3/16/89 400
Over Currituck Marshes, ed of 150, drypt/laid JW, p/s, lt stn/sl, unfr, 7x12", RWS 3/16/89 375
Pair: Cloudy Dawn; Chickadee; etch & drypt on laid wm England/JW, 1922/1930, p/s, unfr, C-NY 1/22/88 352
Pair: Grouse in a Pine Bough; Mates, drypt, 1920/1918, p/s, lt lstn, fr/unfr, 3x2"/6x8", RWS 3/16/89 650
Pair: Sheldrake's Brood; Towering Widgeon; drypt & etch on laid paper, 1925, p/s, full mrgs, sl/fox, unfr, C-NY 1/22/88 715
Pair: Souvenir of Long Point; The Bridge; drypt/laid paper, 1918/ca 1920, p/s, full mrgs, lt stn, unfr, C-NY 1/22/88 462
Pair: Sunset; Swinging In; etch/laid paper, 1914 & 1927, full mrgs, stn/fox/tr, no size given, lot 134, C-NY 1/19/89 OE 462
Pair: Yellowlegs in Sunlight; Chickadees; drypt on laid wm England/wove paper, 1928/1919, sgn, unfr, C-NY 1/22/88 OE 1,210

BENTON, Thomas Hart (American, 1889-1975)

Aaron, aside from ed of 250, litho, 1941, p/s, full mrgs, L-13x10", lot 6, PHL 6/16/88 950
Aaron, litho, 1941, p/s, 10x13", lot 42, LH 10/16/88 850
Boy, litho, p/s, 10x13", Assn Am Artists, lot 219, WG 10/19/88 OE 800
Coming `Round the Mountain, ed of 75, litho/wove paper, 1931, p/s, inscr, lt cr/stn/sl, L-11x9", C-NY 1/22/88 OE 2,530
Coral, ed of 250, litho, 1948, p/s, 14x9", Assn Am Artists, lot 27, SWN 6/15/89 OE 1,100
Corral, ed of 250, litho/wove paper, 1948, p/s, lstn/mstn, tp overmat on verso mrgs, L-10x14", C-NY 1/22/88 352
Cradling Wheat, ed of 250, litho/Rives, 1939, p/s, lt stn mrgs, lt sl/rub verso, unfr, L-10x12", C-NY 1/22/88 1,320
Cradling Wheat, ed of 250, litho/wove paper, 1939, p/s, lt stn, tp to overmat, L-10x12", lot 140, C-NY 1/19/89 1,210
Cradling Wheat, ed of 250, litho/wove paper, 1939, p/s, trm mrgs, lt stn, L-10x12", lot 141, C-NY 1/19/89 1,100
Departure of the Joads, ed of 100, litho, 1939, p/s, full mrgs, lt cr/stn img, 13x19", lot 216, SBY 5/11/89 3,575
Departure of the Joads, ed of 100, litho, 1939, p/s, full mrgs, lt stn, 13x19", lot 12, SBY 11/3/88 OE 4,400
Down the River, ed of 250, litho/wove wm GCM, 1939, p/s, full mrgs, lt fox, 4 scr/stn verso, L-13x10", C-NY 1/22/88 330
Drink of Water, ed of 250, litho/cream wove paper, 1937, full mrgs, lt cr/sl, 15x10", Assn Am Artists, B/B 2/16/88 660
Edge of Town, ed of 250, litho/Rives, 1938, p/s, full mrgs, lt cr/tr/sl, L-9x11", lot 8, C-NY 5/11/88 OE 770
Farmer's Daughter, ed of 250, litho/USA Alexandra, 1944, p/s, lt stn/sl, L-10x13", lot 151, C-NY 1/19/89 1,430
Fence Mender, ed of 250, litho/wove paper, 1940, p/s, full mrgs, lt cr, L-10x14", lot 145, C-NY 1/19/89 OE 1,760
Fire in Barnyard, ed of 250, litho/wove paper, 1944, p/s, 2 trm mrgs, 1 brn stn in img, L-13x9", C-NY 1/22/88 OE 715
Flood, ed of 196, litho/wove paper, 1937, p/s, full mrgs, gstn mrg corner, unfr, L-9x12", C-NY 1/22/88 715
Frankie & Johnnie, ed of 100, litho, 1936, p/s, full mrgs, rpr tr/ls, 16x22", Assn Am Artists, lot 11, SBY 11/3/88 4,675
Goin` Home, ed of 250, litho/Rives, 1937, p/s, full mrgs, tp mrg corners, lt stn, L-9x12", lot 6, C-NY 5/11/88 OE 1,045
Group of 3: Drink of Water; Island Hay; Gateside Conversation; ed of 250, litho, Assn Am Artists, lot 13, C-NY 2/25/88 1,760
Group of 3: Lonesome Road; Sunday Morning; Night Firing; litho, ed of 250, 1938-43, p/s, Assn Am Artists, SBY 5/11/89 OE 3,850
Haystack, ed of 250, litho, 1938, p/s, full mrgs, lt stn, 10x13", Assn Am Artists, lot 15, SBY 2/25/88 990
Haystack, ed of 250, litho/Rives, 1938, p/s, full mrgs, lt stn, L-10x13", lot 431, C-NY 5/10/89 OE 1,980
Instruction, ed of 250, litho, 1940, p/s, lt mstn/fox/ls, glue verso, unfr, L-11x12", Assn Am Artists, SBY 5/12/88 OE 1,100
Instruction, ed of 250, litho/wove paper, 1940, p/s, lt fox/stn, L-10x12", lot 46, RWS 9/8/89 OE 1,900
Instruction, ed of 250, litho/wove paper, 1940, p/s, lt trm mrgs, lt fox/sl, L-10x12", lot 146, C-NY 1/19/89 1,430
Island Hay, ed of 250, litho/cream wove paper, 1945, lt trm mrgs, laid down, 10x13", Assn Am Artists, B/B 4/19/88 OE 825
Island Hay, ed of 250, litho/wove paper, 1945, p/s, lt tstn, L-10x13", lot 434, C-NY 5/10/88 OE 1,650
Julie Gordon, ed of 25, litho/wove paper, 1941, full mrgs, lt stn/cr, tp on verso, L-9x8", lot 150, C-NY 1/19/89 990

Loading Corn, ed of 250, litho/wove paper, p/s, lt stn/cr, L-10x13", lot 152, C-NY 1/19/89	1,210
Lonesome Road, ed of 250, litho, 1938, p/s, 10x13", lot 41, LH 10/16/88	1,200
Missouri Farmyard, ed of 250, litho, 1936, lt stn/sl/tp in mrgs, lt fox/tp on verso, L-10x16", lot 4, C-NY 5/11/88 OE	462
Missouri Farmyard, ed of 250, litho, 1936, p/s, lt sl, tp mrg corners, L-10x16", lot 5, C-NY 5/11/88 OE	660
Missouri Farmyard, ed of 250, litho/wove paper, 1936, p/s, fox mrgs/verso, lstn/sl, unfr, L-10x16", C-NY 1/22/88	352
Missouri Farmyard, ed of 250, litho/wove paper, 1936, p/s, lt stn/cr/ls, tp verso, unfr, L-10x16", C-NY 1/22/88 UE	330
Morning Train, ed of 250, litho/wove paper, 1943, p/s, trm mrgs, mtstn, tp verso, unfr, L-9x14", C-NY 1/22/88	605
Nebraska Evening, ed of 250, litho, 1941, p/s, 10x13", Assn Am Artists, lot 14, SWN 12/1/88	1,320
Pair: Flood; Homestead; ed of 196 & 250, litho/wove paper, 1937 & 1938, p/s, no size given, lot 136, C-NY 1/19/89	1,320
Pair: Frisky Day; Edge of Town; ed of 250, litho on Rives/wove paper, 1939/1938, p/s, C-NY 1/22/88	462
Pair: Homestead; Rainy Day; ed of 250, litho, 1938, p/s, lt stn, 10x13"/9x13", Assn Am Artists, lot 16, SBY 2/23/89	1,760
Pair: Instruction; Aaron; ed of 250, litho, 1940 & 1941, p/s, lt stn, 11x13"/13x10", lot 13, SBY 11/3/88	2,200
Pair: Island Hay; Letter From Overseas; ed of 250, litho, 1945/1943, full mrg, L-10x13", Assn Am Artists, SBY 5/12/88 OE	1,430
Pair: Loading Corn; Back From the Fields; ed of 250, litho/wove paper, 1945, p/s, full mrgs, lt fox, C-NY 1/19/89	2,090
Pair: Lonesome Road; Frisky Day; ed of 250, litho, 1939, p/s, 10x14"/8x13", Assn Am Artists, lot 15, SBY 2/23/89 OE	2,310
Pair: Missouri Farmyard; Goin' Home; ed of 250, litho/wove paper, 1936, lt rub/stn/fox, no size given, C-NY 1/19/89	1,430
Pair: Morning Train; The Corral; ed of 250, litho, 1943 & 1948, lt stn, 10x13", Assn Am Artists, lot 18, C-NY 2/25/88 OE	1,870
Pair: Nebraska Evening; Letter From Overseas; ed of 250, litho, 1941 & 1943, 10x13", Assn Am Artists, SBY 2/25/88	1,540
Pair: Old Man Reading; The Meeting; ed of 250, litho/wove paper, 1941, p/s, no size given, lot 147, C-NY 1/19/89 OE	1,650
Pair: Prodigal Son; The Woodpile; ed of 250, litho/wove paper, 1939, p/s, lt fox/stn, no size given, C-NY 1/19/89 OE	2,090
Pair: Rainy Day; Planting; ed of 250, litho/wove paper, 1938 & 1939, lt stn/cr, no size given, lot 138, C-NY 1/19/89 OE	1,650
Pair: Shallow Creek; Fence Mender; ed of 250, litho/wove paper, 1939 & 1940, p/s, trm mrgs, lot 143, C-NY 1/19/89	2,090
Photographing the Bull, 148/500, litho/wove paper, 1950, p/s, full mrgs, Twayne bstp, L-12x16", lot 154, C-NY 1/19/89	1,430
Photographing the Bull, 202/500, litho/wove paper, 1950, p/s, full mrgs, Twayne bstp, L-12x16", lot 435, C-NY 11/1/88 OE	1,760
Planting, ed of 250, litho/Rives, 1939, p/s, full mrgs, lt stn mrgs, L-10x13", lot 9, C-NY 5/11/88 OE	935
Planting, ed of 250, litho/wove paper, 1939, p/s, trm mrgs, lstn, mstn/tp mrg verso, L-10x13", C-NY 1/22/88 OE	506
Prayer Meeting, ed of 300, litho, 1949, p/s, lt stn/tp hinge, 9x12", lot 20, SBY 2/25/88	660
Preparing the Sloop, litho/wove paper, 1973, p/s, full mrgs, lt stn, L-14x18", lot 14, PHL 10/28/88	850
Prodigal Son, ed of 250, litho/wove paper, 1939, p/s, full mrgs, glue/paper in mrg, unfr, L-10x13", C-NY 1/22/88	660
Race, ed of 250, litho/wove paper, 1942, p/s, full mrgs, ltlstn, 2 pieces tp mrg edge, L-9x13", C-NY 1/22/88	4,180
Race, ed of 250, litho/wove paper, 1942, p/s, trm mrgs, mstn/old glue on mrg edges of verso, L-9x13", C-NY 1/22/88	1,320
Rainy Day, ed of 250, litho/Rives, p/s, lt sl/stn/rpr mrgs, rub verso, unfr, L-9x13", C-NY 1/22/88 UE	440
Slow Train Through Arkansas, ed of 250, litho, 1941, p/s, full mrgs, lt sl/cr mrgs, unfr, L-10x13", C-NY 1/22/88	1,430
Slow Train Through Arkansas, ed of 250, litho, 1941, p/s, lt stn/tr, 10x13", Assn Am Artists, lot 17, SBY 2/23/89 OE	1,540
Station, ed of 110, litho/wove paper, 1929, p/s, dtd/inscr, lt mstn mrgs, L-6x6", C-NY 1/22/88	1,980
Station, 10/110, litho/wove paper, 1929, p/s, full mrgs, lt cr/stn/tr, L-6x6", lot 430, C-NY 5/10/89	1,980

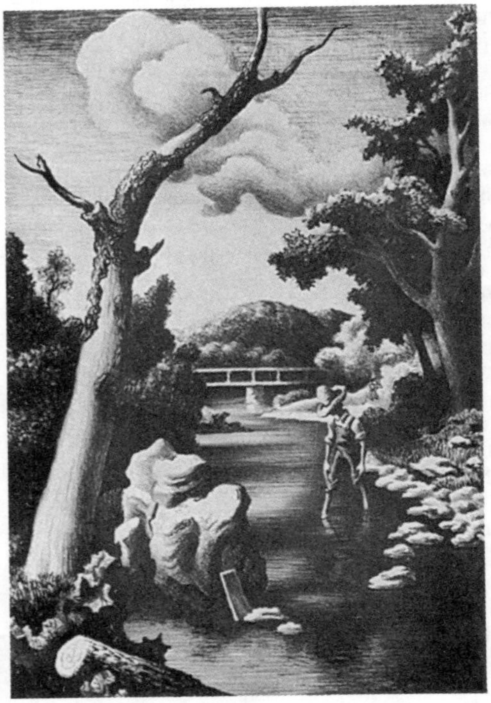

Shallow Creek, ed of 250,litho/cream wove paper, 1939, p/s, full mrgs, lt sl mrg, old hinge remains on upper corners, 14x10", Assn Am Artists, lot 2480, B/B 4/12/89 OE; $1,760

Sunday Morning, ed of 250, litho/Rives, 1939, p/s, full mrgs, lt rub in signature, sl mrg, unfr, L-10x13", C-NY 1/22/88	352
Sunday Morning, ed of 250, litho/wove paper, 1939, p/s, lt stn, tp to overmat, L-10x13", lot 139, C-NY 1/19/89 OE	1,100
Sunset, ed of 204, litho, 1941, p/s, lt stn, brn paper tp on verso mrg edges, L-10x13", lot 10, C-NY 5/11/88 OE	770
Swampland, ed of 100, litho, 1941, full mrgs, lt cr, L-18x13", lot 16, PHL 10/28/88	800
Swampland, ed of 100, litho/wove paper, 1941, tp to overmat, L-18x13", lot 148, C-NY 1/19/89	1,100

Ten-Pound Hammer, ed of 300, litho, 1967, p/s, full mrgs, lt mstn, 14x10", lot 217, SBY 5/11/89 ... 1,980
Threshing, ed of 250, litho/wove paper, 1941, p/s, full mrgs, unfr, L-9x14", C-NY 1/22/88 ... 2,200
White Calf, ed of 250, litho/wove paper, 1945, p/s, lt stn, L-10x13", lot 433, C-NY 5/10/89 OE ... 1,100
Woodpile, ed of 250, litho/wove paper, 1939, p/s, lt mstn, L-9x11", lot 432, C-NY 5/10/89 OE ... 1,430
Wreck of the Ol'97, ed of 250, litho, 1944, p/s, full mrgs, lt stn/fox, unfr, L-10x15", Assn Am Artists, SBY 5/12/88 OE ... 4,400
Wreck of the Ol'97, ed of 250, litho, 1944, p/s, full mrgs, lt stn/cr, L-10x15", lot 11, C-NY 5/11/88 ... 3,520
Wreck of the Ol'97, ed of 250, litho, 1944, p/s, lt stn/sl/ls mrgs, 10x15", Assn Am Artists, lot 18, SBY 2/23/89 ... 4,125
Wreck of the Ol'97, ed of 250, litho, 1944, p/s, lt tr, 10x15", lot 19, SBY 2/25/88 ... 1,540
Wreck of the Ol'97, ed of 250, litho on wove paper, p/s, 1944, L-10x15", C-SK 6/9/88 OE ... 3,345
Wreck of the Ol'97, ed of 250, litho/BFK Rives, 1944, p/s, full mrgs, rpr tr/stn mrgs, L-11/15", C-NY 1/22/88 ... 1,540
Wreck of the Ol'97, ed of 250, litho/cream wove paper, 1944, p/s, 10x15", Assn Am Artists, lot 2928, B/B 4/19/88 OE ... 3,850
Wreck of the Ol'97, ed of 250, litho/cream wove paper, 1944, p/s, tp mrgs, lt stn, 10x15", Assn Am Arists, B/B 2/16/88 ... 3,300

BERMAN, Alex (Continental, 20th C)
Final Judgement, engr, 1933, p/s, 10x8", lot 134, FAP 2/24/89 UE ... 35

BERNARD, Emile (French, 1868-1941)
Bretons dans une Barque, hc litho/cream wove paper, 1889, intl, full mrgs, laid down, L-12x10", lot 206, C-NY 11/1/88 OE ... 2,640
Cover for Les Bretonneries, hc litho/cream wove paper, 1889, intl, stn/ls, glue at edge, L-12x10", lot 205, C-NY 11/1/88 ... 5,280
Femmes au Porc, hc litho/cream wove paper, 1889, sgn in red watercolor, lt stn/scr, L-10x12", lot 207, C-NY 11/1/88 ... 6,600
Femmes Etendant du Linge, hc litho/cream wove paper, 1889, lt cr/rpl/ls/tr, L-10x12", lot 208, C-NY 11/1/88 ... 5,280
Femmes Faisant les Foins, hc litho/wove paper, 1889, lt stn, laid down, L-10x13", lot 209, C-NY 11/1/88 OE ... 9,900
Le Moissonneur, hc litho/cream wove paper, 1889, pl/s, lt stn/fox, laid down, L-9x12", lot 210, C-NY 11/1/88 OE ... 4,180

BERRY, Carroll Thayer (American, 1886-1978)
Old Coaster Before the Wind, linocut, p/s, titled, 14x9", lot 357, WG 10/19/88 ... 130

BERRY, Timothy
Still Life with Pencil, 10/30, etch/aqua/cream wove paper, p/s, titled, full mrgs, 6x15", lot 3008, B/B 4/19/88 ... 138

BERTHON, Paul (French, 1872-1909)
La Lyre, clr litho, ca 1901, pl/s, 20x24", lot 405, C-E 9/20/89 ... 550
Le Livre de Magda, clr litho, pl/s, 25x18", Chaix, C-E 3/24/88 ... 495
Les Boules de Niege, clr litho backed on linen, pl/s, 20x26", C-E 6/16/88 ... 462
Les Eglantines, clr litho, ca 1900, pl/s, 17x22", lot 404, C-E 9/20/89 UE ... 440
Les Eglantines, clr litho, 1900, pl/s, 20x26", C-E 6/16/88 ... 385
Les Fils de la Vierge, clr litho, pl/s, 25x19", C-E 3/24/88 UE ... 154
Portrait of Sarah Bernhardt, clr litho, 1901, pl/s, 26x20", C-E 6/16/88 UE ... 352
Queen, litho, 15x14", lot 222, LH 2/20/88 ... 325
Rose de Noel, clr litho/cream wove paper, 18x18", lot 286, FAP 2/24/89 UE ... 550
Sa Tres Gracieuse Majeste la Reine Wilhelmine, 2nd state B, clr litho/thick wove paper, 1901, L-16x14", PHL 10/28/88 ... 325
Sainte Marie des Fleurs, Roman par Rene Boylesue; clr litho poster, lt tr/cr, no size given, lot 312, FAP 2/24/89 ... 400

BERTON, Armand (French, 1854-1927)
Portrait of a Young Girl, litho/cream wove paper, pl/s, 14x11", lot 2819, B/B 4/19/88 ... 330

BEUYS, Joseph (French, 1921-1986)
Democracy Is Fun, 80/80, olive gr/blk scrpt, 1973, sgn, Edition Staeck stp, lt cr, S-29x45", lot 394, C-NY 5/11/88 ... 1,100
Quanten (to John Cage), 73/75, clr scrpt/2 sheets BFK Rives, 1982, p/s, full mrgs, S-14x10", lot 581, C-NY 11/1/88 OE ... 1,210
Untitled, Fondazione per la Rinascita dell'Agricoltura; a/p, X/X, scrpt, 1978, p/s, S-25x27", lot 580, C-NY 11/1/88 OE ... 935
Untitled, 3 Ton Edition; 240(?)/3t, scrpt/paint/polyvinylchloride, 1973, Edition Staeck, lot 395, C-NY 5/11/88 OE ... 2,530
Untitled, 3 Ton Edition; 314/3t, scrpt/polyvinylchloride, 1973, inscr Schafskof, Edition Staek, lot 396, C-NY 5/11/88 OE ... 1,980

BICKNELL, Albion Harris (American, 1837-1915)
Group of 3: Bit of Venice; Venetian Fishing Boats; Cottages Near Fontainebleau; 1887, 12x9", Dodd Mead, SWN 6/15/89 UE ... 120
Group of 3: Winter; River Pier; On the Marshes, Annisquam; etch, pl/s, 8x11" or 8x14", lot 30, SWN 6/15/89 UE ... 120

BICKNELL, William W. (American, 1860-)
Knoll, etch, 1921, p/s, 7x9", lot 113, WG 10/19/88 ... 30

BIDDLE, George (American, 1885-1973)
Adam & Eve, 53/100, litho, 1926, p/s, 14x9", lot 440, FAP 4/15/88 OE ... 110
Three Graces, etch, 1926, p/s, 13x10", lot 441, FAP 4/15/88 ... 100

BIEHLE, August F. (American, 1885-1979)
Cuyahoga River-The Flats; litho, p/s, dtd 1932, 8x12", lot 169, WG 10/19/88 ... 175

BIERSTADT, Albert; after (American, 1830-1902)
Sunset: California Scenery; chromolitho, 1868, trm to img, laid down, lt scuff, L-12x18", Prang, lot 530, SBY 1/28/88 ... 660

BILLMYER, John (American, 1912-)
Flowers, ed of 250, wood engr/handmade Goyu, 1935, 8x6", Cleveland Print Club, lot 213, WG 10/19/88 ... 25

BILLMYER, Mina & Joan (American, 20th C)
Pair: Rite of Spring; Flowers; wood engr, 1935, sgn, 6x8", Cleveland Print Club, lot 198, WG 10/19/88 ... 50

BINGHAM, George Caleb; after (American, 1811-1879)
Canvassing for a Vote, by Claude Regnier, litho, 1853, trm mrgs, lt stn/cr/fox, S-19x23", Knoedler, lot 539, SBY 1/28/88 ... 4,675
County Election, by John Sartain, engr/mezzo/rlt, 6th/final state, 1854, trm/rpr trs, unfr, S-24x32", C-NY 1/22/88 ... 1,870
In a Quandry, Mississippi Raftmen Playing Cards; litho, 1852, Goupil bstp, trm mrgs, lt stn/cr, S-19x22", SBY 1/28/88 OE ... 7,975
Jolly Flat Boat Men, by Thomas Doney, ed of 9666, 1st state, engr/wove paper, 1847, laid down, P-23x27", C-NY 1/22/88 OE ... 2,200
Marshall Law Order XI, by John Sartain, mezzo/engr, 22x31", SLK 2/11/89 ... 900
Pair: County Election; Martial Law; engr/mezzo, 1854 & 1872, lt stn/fox/sl, 22x31", Bingham, lot 541, SBY 1/28/88 OE ... 5,500
Stump Speaking, by Louis Adolphe Gautier, aqua/engr/rlt, 1856, L-22x30", Fishel/Adler/Schwartz, lot 26A, C-NY 1/19/89 ... 3,080

BIRCH, William Russell (American, 1755-1834)
High Street From the Country Marketplace, Phil, Procession of Death of George Washington; engr, 8x11", FAP 4/15/88 OE ... 176

Second St North From Market St West, Christ Church, Phil; etch/engr, 1800, stn/tr/ls, unfr, P-11x13", C-NY 1/22/88 550
Unfinished House, clr engr, 1880, 8x11", lot 977, FAP 12/8/88 UE 170

BISHOP, Isabel (American, 1902-)
Double Date Delayed, 20/50, etch/wove paper, 1948/1978, p/s, stn mrg, mtstn, P-5x3", Assn Am Artists, C-NY 1/22/88 OE 418
Strap Hangers, aside from ed of 50, etch/wove paper, 1940/1978, full mrgs, lt stn/sl, P-7x4", lot 27, C-NY 6/17/89 OE 715
Suite: Isabel Bishop; Eight Etchings 1930-1959; 20/50, etch/Rives, sgn, 14x11", buckram cover, lot 13, C-NY 5/11/88 1,540
Two Girls Chatting, etch, p/s, lt stn, P-7x5", lot 7, PHL 6/16/88 OE 950

BISHOP, Richard Evett (American, 1887-)
Group of 5: Into the Wind; Broad Bills; The Wise One; On the Eastern Shore; Up & On; engr, sgn, 8x13", FAP 6/16/89 OE 225
Pair: South Bound, 1926; Getting Out; engr, p/s, titled, 10x14", FAP 6/16/89 200

BLAKE, William (British, 1757-1827)
Set of 21: Illustrations of the Book of Job; engr/laid India on heavy wove paper, 1825/1874, S-18x14", SBY 5/11/89 OE 13,750

BLAMPIED, Edmund (British, 1886-1966)
Have Another Drink, litho, p/s, 10x14", FAP 6/16/89 OE 350
Pulling the Boat Ashore, etch, p/s, stn, 7x9", lot 123, WG 10/19/88 225
Wreck, litho, p/s, 10x16", lot 106, WG 10/19/88 300

BLECKNER, Ross (American, 1949-)
Untitled (Sphere & Moulding), 66/72, scrpt/wove paper, 1987, 40x32", Lincoln Center/List Art Posters, C-NY 11/1/88 OE 935

BLEKER, Gerrit Claesz (Dutch, 1610-1656)
Cowherd, 1st state, etch, 1638, trm, lt cr, 6x9", lot 584, SBY 2/25/88 2,200

BLINKS, Thomas; after (British, 1860-1912)
Pair: Finish; Found (hunt scenes); engr, 18x30", JB Pratt, FAP 6/16/89 UE 225

BOCHNER, Mel (American, 1940-)
Portfolio: Apices; 10/24, 3 aqua, 1974, p/s, full mrgs, orig wrappers, 26x46", Crown Point/Parasol, lot 914, SBY 5/13/89 1,650
Suite: QED; 4/25, 4 clr aqua/Chine colle & wove paper, 1974, full mrgs, orig portfolio, Parasol, lot 397, C-NY 5/11/88 880

BODMER, Karl; after (American, 1809-1893)
Steamer Yellowstone, clr aqua, 1840, lt stn/fox, 10x13", Ackermann, lot 123, FAP 2/24/89 200
View of the Stone Walls, clr aqua, lt fox/stn, 12x17", Ackermann, lot 125, FAP 2/24/89 225

BOLDRINI, Nicolo (Italian, 16th C)
Milo of Croton, wc, ca 1540, trm mrgs, 11x17", lot 16, SWN 12/1/88 468

BOLE, William; after
Set of 6: Russian Costume Dancers; clr engr, lt sl/stn, 11x9", lot 14, FAP 2/24/89 UE 80

BOND, W. (British?, 19th C)
Pair: Weary Sportsman; Shepherds Reposing; hc engr, 1803, 23x29", lot 631, GAI 12/9/88 150

BONE, David Muirhead (Scottish, 1876-1953)
Manhattan Excavation, etch/cream wove paper, p/s, full mrgs, lt sl mrgs, old tp on verso, 12x10", lot 2933, B/B 4/19/88 990
Pair: Trevi Fountain, Rome; Stockholm; 19th/5th state, drypt/fibrous Japan, 1913-28/1923-25, stn/cr, C-NY 1/22/88 OE 770
Piccadilly Circus, ed of 125, drypt, 1915, p/s, lt stn, laid down, L-12x15", RWS 3/16/89 UE 400

BONFILS, Robert (French, 1886-)
Exposition Internationale des Arts Decoratifs, lt stn/tr, linen backed, unfr, 24x15", lot 239, FAP 2/24/89 250

BONINGTON, Richard Parkes (British, 1801-1828)
Cathedral, litho, 1824, fox mrgs, 13x8", lot 131, FAP 2/24/89 UE 20

BONNARD, Pierre (French, 1867-1947)
Affiche de la Revue Blanche, clr litho, 1894, fld/cr/tr/ls, mounted on linen-backed paper, S-32x25", SBY 2/25/88 1,210
Boulevard, Pl 5, #45(?), ed of 100, clr litho/thin wove paper, 1899, p/s, lt stn, L-7x17", lot 82, C-NY 5/11/88 OE 17,600
Conversation, for L'Escarmouche; 6/100, dk brn litho/wove paper, 1893, lt sl/cr/tstn, unfr, S-15x11", C-NY 1/22/88 UE 385
Femme au Parapluie, rose/gray litho, 1894, p/s, full mrgs, lt stn/fox/cr, 9x5", lot 100, SBY 2/25/88 OE 6,875
Jeune Femme aux Bas Noirs, 23/100, brn-blk litho/smooth wove paper, 1893, p/s, full mrgs, 11x5", lot 317, SBY 5/11/89 2,640
L'Estampe et l'Affiche, clr litho/wove paper, 1897, full sheet, lt stn/tr/cr, laid down, S-32x24", lot 486, C-NY 5/10/89 2,750
La Coupe et le Compotier, ed of 100, litho, 1925, p/s, Galerie Graveuers bstp, full mrgs, 7x10", lot 102, SBY 2/25/88 OE 1,100
La Coupe et le Compotier, 36/100, 3rd state, litho, 1925, p/s, Galerie des Peintres bstp, lt fox, L-8x10", C-NY 5/11/88 1,210
La Revue Blanche, clr litho, 1894, lt ls mrgs, linen backed, S-31x24", Ancourt, lot 81, SBY 11/3/88 660
La Revue Blanche, clr litho, 1894, lt stn/tr/cr, linen backed, S-32x24", lot 102, SBY 2/23/89 2,200
La Revue Blanche, clr litho, 1894, trm/cr/stn, S-30x23", Ancourt, lot 318, SBY 5/11/89 OE 4,400
La Revue Blanche, clr litho/wove paper laid down on Japan, 1894, lt ls, L-30x23", lot 212, C-NY 11/1/88 OE 4,950
La Toilette Assise, 26/100, 3rd state, litho/wove paper, 1925, p/s, Frapier bstp, L-13x9", lot 213, C-NY 11/1/88 1,320
Le Menu, ed of 25, 3rd state, litho, ca 1925, p/s, Peintres Graveurs bstp, 14x11", Frapier, lot 31, SWN 6/15/89 OE 1,540
Marthe au Petit Chien, by Jacques Villon, 31/200, etch/aqua/cream wove paper, p/s, 20x10", lot 2924, B/B 4/19/88 OE 3,575
Paravent a Quatre Feuilles, ed of 110, clr litho/4 sheets wove paper on Japan, 1899, full mrgs, lot 487, C-NY 5/10/89 OE 462,000
Paysage du Midi, 42/100, 4th state, litho/wove paper, 1925, Peintres Graveurs bstp, L-9x12", lot 488, C-NY 5/10/89 880
Place Clichy, 35/100, clr litho, 1922, p/s, lt tr/rpr tr/cr/stn, L-15x25", Bernheim-Jeune, SBY 5/12/88 OE 6,600
Rue, Le Soir, Sous la Pluie; 64/100, clr litho, 1899, p/s, lt stn/fox, 10x14", Vollard, lot 82, SBY 11/3/88 11,550
Rue Vue d'en Haut, Pl 4, ed of 100, clr litho/thin wove paper, 1899, lt stn/cr/tp, L-15x9", lot 81, C-NY 5/11/88 1,320
Set of 19: Petites Scenes Familieres pour Piano; litho (illustrating complete songsheets), 1893, 14x11", SBY 2/25/88 1,980
Toilette, late imp, etch/cream wove paper, 9x6", lot 2820, B/B 4/19/88 275

BONNARD, Pierre; after (French, 1867-1947)
La Femme au Chine, by Jacques Villon, ed of 200, aqua/rlt, 1924-25, full mrgs, 20x10", Bernheim-Jeune, SBY 5/12/88 3,025

BONNET, Louis Marin (French, 1743-1793)
Pair: Provoking Fidelity; Pleasures of Education; etch/engr, 1775 & 1777, 13x10", lot 587, SBY 2/25/88 OE 5,940
Tete de Flore, etch/engr/Dupuy Auvergne, 1769, rpr tr, lt cr/rub, 16x13", lot 590, SBY 2/25/88 OE 9,900

BOREIN, Edward (American, 1872-1945)
Navajo Visitors at Oraibi, etch/drypt/Umbria Italia, p/s, full mrgs, lt cr, 8x13", lot 2927, B/B 2/16/88 OE 825
Riding High, etch/aqua/cream wove paper, p/s, lt trm mrgs, 4x3", lot 2931, B/B 4/19/88 600
Wooden Bridge at Taos, etch/drypt/heavy wove paper, p/s, lt stn/sl, 6x9", lot 2932, B/B 4/19/88 550
BORMANN, Emma (Austrian, 1887-)
Kaiserburg, Old Burse, clr wc/laid Japan, p/s, titled, 14x12", lot 64, WG 10/19/89 UE 140
BOROFSKY, Jonathan (American, 1942-)
Berlin Dream (Closeup) at No 29478, monotype/slksc, 1985, sgn, full mrgs, S-80x98", Gemini, lot 916, SBY 5/13/89 OE 10,450
BOSCH, Hieronymus; after (Dutch, 1450-1516)
Shrove Tuesday, Dutch Kitchen with Wafer Bakery; by Pieter van der Heyden, engr, 1567, 9x12", lot 8, SBY 5/11/89 OE 9,350
BOSMAN, Richard (American, 1944-)
Cat's Revenge, 3/40, etch/aqua, p/s, full mrgs, P-24x36", lot 114, PHL 10/28/88 350
Drowning Man I, 21/47, clr wc/Okawara, 1981, p/s, full mrgs, S-48x30", Brooke Alexander, lot 583, C-NY 11/1/88 1,980
Drowning Man I, 41/47, clr wc/Okawara, 1981, p/s, full mrgs, 40x24", Brooke Alexander, lot 719, SBY 11/5/88 2,750
Fall, 23/32, clr wc/Japan, 1983-84, p/s, full sheet, S-61x42", Experimental Workshop, lot 584, C-NY 11/1/88 OE 2,420
Full Moon, 5/35, clr wc/wove paper, 1986, p/s, full sheet, S-35x46", Experimental Workshop, lot 585, C-NY 11/1/88 990
BOTERO, Fernando (Colombian, 1932-)
Book: Botero; by Pierre Restany, 154/200, photolitho w/text, sgn, orig boards/slipcase, Abrams, lot 398, C-NY 5/11/88 OE 1,540
Book: Botero; by Pierre Restany, 50/200, photolitho w/text, sgn, orig wrappers, lot 586, C-NY 11/1/88 OE 1,870
Woman, total ed 226, clr litho, 1984, p/s, inscr D/z, full mrgs, L-16x13", Eds de la Difference, SBY 5/14/88 OE 2,750
Woman, XXXV/L, total ed of 226, clr litho, 1984, p/s, full mrgs, lt cr, 16x13", lot 611, SBY 2/23/89 1,925
Woman Dressing, total ed of 226, clr litho, 1984, p/s, inscr IV/L, L-16x13", Eds de la Difference, SBY 5/14/88 OE 2,530
Woman Dressing, total ed 226, clr litho, p/s, inscr E/z, full mrgs, L-16x13", Eds de la Difference, SBY 5/14/88 OE 2,750
Woman Dressing, XXXV/L, clr litho, 1984, p/s, full mrgs, 16x13", Ed de la Difference, lot 612, SBY 2/23/89 OE 3,300
BOWELS & CARVER (19th C)
Bowles's Moral Pictures; or, Poor Richard Illustrated...; hc engr, ca 1800, lt rpr tr/ls, S-19x24", C-NY 1/19/89 UE 110
BOWNE, T.
Pair: England; Scotland (maps); hc engr, 18x21", lot 302, GAI 6/17/89 90
BOYS, Thomas Shotter (British, 1803-1874)
Bank of London Looking Towards the Mansion House, clr litho, 17x13", lot 305, NA 10/1/88 120
Pair: Club Houses; Mansion House Cheepside; hc litho, 18x13", lot 918, LH 10/16/88 OE 600
BRADLEY, William H. (American, 1868-)
Chapbook, litho/poster paper, lt tr/fld, linen backed, lt fox mrgs, unfr, no size given, lot 290, FAP 2/24/89 500
Chapbook, clr litho, cr img, tr mrgs, 20x13", lot 284, FAP 2/24/89 700
Chapbook, clr litho, lt tr edges, 20x14", lot 311, FAP 2/24/89 825
Victor Bicycles, Les Maitres de L'Affiche; clr litho, pl/s, 8x12", C-E 6/16/88 220
Victor Bicycles, Les Maitres de L'Affiche; Pl 152, clr litho, pl/s, 16x11", lot 408, C-E 9/20/89 UE 110
When Hearts Are Trumps, Les Maitres de L'Affiche; Pl 52, clr litho, 16x11", lot 407, C-E 9/20/89 418
BRANGWYN, Frank William (British, 1867-1943)
Notre Dame, etch, p/s, 11x9", lot 21, FAP 2/24/89 UE 55
Old Houses Dixmuden, engr, p/s, 6x8", lot 26, FAP 2/24/89 35
BRAQUE, Georges (French, 1882-1963)
Astre et Oiseau I, 26/75, bl & blk litho/Arches, 1958-59, p/s, full mrgs, lt stn, L-11x13", lot 87, C-NY 5/11/88 UE 3,520
Astre et Oiseau I, 59/75, bl & blk litho/Arches, 1958-59, p/s, full mrgs, lt stn, L-11x13", lot 493, C-NY 5/10/89 OE 6,050
Astre et Oiseau II, 31/75, clr litho, 1958-59, sgn in blk ink, lt fox, 14x21", Maeght/Mourlot, lot 106, SBY 2/25/88 4,675
Char Blanc (Char IV), 35/75, etch, 1958, p/s, lt mstn/sl, tp hinge verso, P-10x11", Maeght, SBY 5/12/88 3,520
Ciel Gris, 112/275, gray/cream litho, p/s, full mrgs, lt stn, L-9x4", lot 45, PHL 6/16/88 750
Corbeille de Fleurs, 7/10, etch w/varnish, 1951, p/s, full mrgs, lt stn, 6x11", Maeght/Signovert, lot 324, SBY 5/11/89 4,400
Couple, Lettera Amorosa; 44/75, clr litho/Arches, 1963, p/s, full mrgs, lt stn/sl, L-12x8", lot 217, C-NY 11/1/88 OE 4,620
Etude de Nu, a/p, etch/drypt/Auvergne, 1907-08, p/s, lt stn, S-13x9", lot 320, SBY 5/11/89 OE 36,300
Feuilles, Couleur Lumiere; clr litho/wove paper, 1953-54, sgn in wht ink, S-39x24", lot 490, C-NY 5/10/89 OE 39,600
Feuilles, Couleur Lumiere; 51/75, clr litho, 1953-54, sgn in wht ink, lt ls/cr, S-38x24", lot 325, SBY 5/11/89 OE 41,800
Fleurs Devant la Fenetre, 25/75, clr litho/Arches, p/s, lt stn, 13x7", lot 2821, B/B 4/19/88 OE 880
Gelinotte, 5/75, clr litho, 1960, p/s, lt trm/cr/stn, 9x14", lot 88, SBY 11/3/88 OE 6,600
Helios II, 9/22, bl/blk litho, 1946, p/s, lt stn mrgs/verso, 13x10", Maeght/Mourlot, lot 322, SBY 5/11/89 6,600
Job, 17/100, drypt/Arches, 1911, p/s, lt stn/sl, S-18x24", Kahnweiler/Delatre, lot 13, C-NY 11/1/88 33,000
L'Essor I, 36/100, clr litho, 1961, p/s, full mrgs, lt stn/fox/sl, 10x14", lot 89, SBY 11/3/88 OE 4,400
L'Essor I, 57/100, clr litho/Arches, 1961, p/s, full mrgs, lt sl mrgs/verso, L-10x14", SBY 5/12/88 OE 4,675
L'Oiseau Blanc, 43/75, blk & bl litho/Arches, 1961, p/s, full mrgs, lt lstn, L-14x12", SBY 5/12/88 OE 6,875
L'Oiseau dans de Feuillage, 36/50, clr litho mounted on card as issued, 1961, p/s, lt cr, unfr, S-32x41", SBY 5/12/88 OE 38,500
L'Oiseau dans de Feuillage, 4/50, clr litho, 1961, p/s, lt scr/scr, 31x41", lot 90, SBY 11/3/88 38,500
L'Oiseau et Son Ombre I, 67/75, clr litho/wove paper, 1959, p/s, lt stn, laid down, L-23x33", lot 494, C-NY 5/10/89 15,400
L'Oiseau et Son Ombre I, 71/75, litho, 1959, p/s, full mrgs, sl/stn/cr, 23x33", Maeght/Mourlot, lot 87, SBY 11/3/88 OE 20,900
La Danse, ed of 250, etch, 1934, p/s, full mrgs, lt stn, 10x7", Chronique du Jour, lot 86, SBY 11/3/88 1,650
La Guitare, 20/95, brn/blk litho, 1953, sgn in wht ink, lt cr/scuff/fox, S-24x30", lot 106, SBY 2/23/89 OE 3,630
La Guitare, 28/95, brn & blk litho/Arches, 1953, sgn in wht ink, lt cr/scr/cr, S-24x30", lot 489, C-NY 5/10/89 2,750
Le Char II, 69/75, clr litho, 1953, p/s, lt trm, unfr, S-19x26", Maeght, SBY 5/12/88 7,700
Le Char II (Le Char), 63/75, clr litho, 1953, p/s, lt scuff/sl/stn, S-19x25", Mourlot/Maeght, SBY 5/12/88 OE 8,250
Le Char III (Char Verni), 10/75, clr litho w/varnish, 1955, p/s, full mrgs, lt stn, 13x17", Maeght, lot 327, SBY 5/11/89 11,000
Le Citrons, 87/100, clr litho, 1954, p/s, full mrgs, lt lstn/mstn, L-5x11", SBY 5/12/88 OE 2,200
Le Couple, Lettera Amorosa; 22/75, clr litho/Arches, 1963, p/s, lt stn, L-13x9", lot 496, C-NY 5/10/89 7,150

Le Nid (Oiseau IX), 17/25, etch/drypt/thin laid Japan, 1955, p/s, lt fox/stn, 9x13", Maeght, lot 329, SBY 5/11/89 2,200
Le Nid (Oiseau IX), 3/25, etch/drypt/Japan Imperial, 1955, p/s, full mrgs, lt cr/stn, P-9x13", SBY 5/12/88 880
Le Signe, 4/30, gold leaf/bronze litho, 1954, p/s, full mrgs, lt sl/stn/fox, 12x8", lot 326, SBY 5/11/89 1,540
Le Trefle, 26/75, clr litho/Arches, 1963, p/s, full mrgs, lt stn/tp in mrgs, L-8x8", lot 88, C-NY 5/11/88 1,870
Les Amaryllis, 61/75, clr aqua/wove paper, 1958, p/s, full mrgs, lt stn, laid down, P-22x18", lot 492, C-NY 5/10/89 27,500
Les Trois Oiseaux en Vol, 28/75, clr etch, 1961, p/s, lt fox/sl, S-29x23", Maeght, lot 107, SBY 2/25/88 7,975
Lettera Amorosa, 37/75, clr litho, 1963, p/s, full mrgs, lt stn, 12x9", Engelberts/Mourlot, lot 333, SBY 5/11/89 OE 7,700
Lettera Amorosa, 9/75, clr litho, 1963, p/s, full mrgs, lt stn, 10x9", Engelberts/Mourlot, lot 332, SBY 5/11/89 1,980

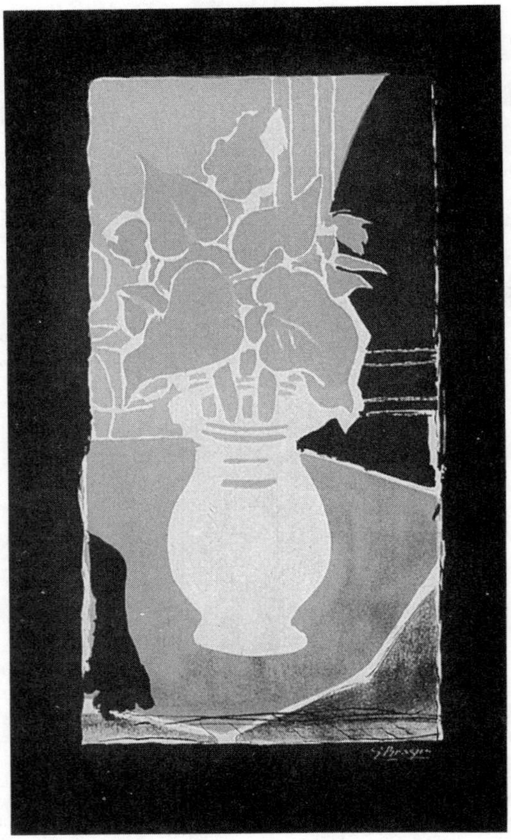

Feuilles, Couleur Lumiere; aside from #d ed of 75, clr litho/wove paper, 1953-54, sgn in wht ink, lt tr/skin/stn, S-39x24", lot 490, C-NY 5/10/89 OE; $39,600

Lettera Amorosa: Le Couple, 15/75, litho/Arches, 1963, p/s, full mrgs, stn, 12x8", Engelberts, lot 110, SBY 2/25/88 OE 5,225
Lettera Amorosa: Les Citrons, 58/75, clr litho/Arches, 1963, p/s, full mrgs, fox/stn, 10x9", Engelberts, SBY 2/25/88 OE 2,640
Leuilles, Couleur, Lumier; 6/75, clr litho, 1953-54, sgn, lt scuff/ls/cr/lstn, unfr, S-38x24", Maeght, SBY 5/12/88 27,500
Los Martinets, 229/275, clr litho/BFK Rives, ca 1956, p/s, Maeght bstp, lt lstn, L-4x8", RWS 3/16/89 OE 1,400
Metamorphose de la Fleur, Lettera Amorosa; 56/75, litho/Rives, p/s, trm mrgs, 10x7", lot 2833, B/B 2/16/88 1,540
Migration, 76/80, aqua/etch/canvas-textured wove paper, 1962, p/s, full mrgs, lt stn/sl, P-10x7", Maeght, SBY 5/12/88 OE 4,180
Nature Morte II, 32/50, clr etch/drypt/Arches, 1912/1953, tp in corners, P-13x18", lot 84, C-NY 5/11/88 OE 52,800
Nature Morte III (Verre et Fruits), ed of 120, litho/Chine volant, 1921, p/s, cr/tr/rpr mrgs, L-8x16", SBY 5/12/88 3,300
Nature Morte III (Verre et Fruits), 119/120, clr litho/Chine volant, 1921, lt cr/stn, 8x16", lot 84, SBY 11/3/88 OE 7,150
Nature Morte III (Verre et Fruits), 4/120, clr litho/Chine volant, 1921, p/s, full mrgs, lt cr/tr, 7x15", SBY 5/11/89 OE 4,620
Oiseau des Forets, 44/75, clr litho/Arches, 1958, p/s, L-15x9", lot 86, C-NY 5/11/88 4,950
Oiseau Noir sur Fond Bleu (Oiseau VIII), 9/75, clr etch, 1955, p/s, full mrgs, sl/fox/cr, 6x9", lot 108, SBY 2/23/89 OE 6,600
Oiseau sur Fond Carmin, 53/75, clr aqua/BFK Rives, 1958, p/s, lt stn/cr/scr, P-13x17", lot 85, C-NY 5/11/89 OE 7,150
Oiseau sur Fond Carmin (Oiseau XIV), 42/75, clr etch/BFK Rives, 1958, full mrgs, lt cr, P-13x17", SBY 5/12/88 OE 6,600
Oiseau sur Fond de X, 47/50, clr litho, 1958, p/s, full mrgs, lt scr/stn, 14x11", lot 105, SBY 2/25/88 OE 6,875
Pair: Aout; 62/70, gr-beige/blk aqua & bl aqua, 1958, p/s, 10x13", Crommelynck & Dutrou/Broder, lot 330, SBY 5/11/89 OE 8,250
Pair: Aout; 67/70, etch, 1958, p/s, full mrgs, 10x12", Crommelynck & Dutrou/Broder, lot 331, SBY 5/11/89 3,850
Persephone, 31/50, clr wood engr, 1948, sgn in blk crayon, full mrgs, lt stn/fox, 14x10", lot 323, SBY 5/11/89 OE 7,150
Pommes et Feuilles, 23/30, clr litho, 1958, p/s, full mrgs, lt stn/fox, 12x18", Mourlot, lot 104A, SBY 2/25/88 2,200
Si Je Mourais La-Bas: Fenetre: Poissons Bleus; 58/70, blk/bl wc, 1962, p/s, 13x23", Broder, lot 111, SBY 2/23/89 OE 3,850
Si Je Mourais La-Bas: Fenetre: Poissons Bleus; 58/70, blk/bl wc, 1962, p/s, unfr, L-13x23", Broder, SBY 5/12/88 OE 5,720
Si Je Mourais La-Bas: Les Pommes; 11/70, total ed of 230, wc/Auvergne, 1962, full mrgs, L-8x11", Broder, SBY 5/12/88 OE 3,080
Si Je Mourais La-Bas: Oiseau de Nuit Noire; V/X, blk & bl wc/vellum, 1962, p/s, lt cr/stn, 16x11", Broder, SBY 2/25/88 1,430
Tailpiece From Book, clr litho/thin laid paper, p/s, lt stn/cr, 10x12", lot 36, PHL 10/28/88 UE 100
Theire et Pommes, 37/75, clr litho/Arches, 1946, sgn in blk crayon, stn/sl, L-12x26", lot 214, C-NY 11/1/88 OE 24,200
Theire sur Fond Gris, 63/74, clr litho, 1946-47, sgn in blk crayon, 13x20", Mourlot/Kahnweiler, lot 104, SBY 2/25/88 3,850
Theogonie, 43/50, etch/wove van Gelder, 1932, brn crayon sgn, full mrgs, lt stn/fox, unfr, P-15x12", SBY 5/12/88 1,320
Theogonie, 7/50, etch/van Gelder, 1932, sgn in brn crayon, full mrgs, lt stn, 15x12", lot 85, SBY 11/3/88 1,980
Theogonie III, 59/75, litho, 1954, p/s, full mrgs, lt sl mrgs, 17x12", Maeght/Mourlot, lot 107, SBY 2/23/89 OE 3,025

Untitled, Descente aux Enfers; total ed of 220, clr litho/Japan nacre, 1961, L-10x9", Mourlot, lot 215, C-NY 11/1/88 1,870
Untitled, Si Je Mourais La-Bas; 68/70, clr wc/handmade wove paper, 1962, L-10x9", Broder, lot 216, C-NY 11/1/88 OE 1,210
Vol de Nuit (Oiseau XII), 62/75, clr litho/Arches, 1957, p/s, full mrgs, mstn/fox, L-15x27", Maeght, SBY 5/12/88 OE 27,500

RAQUE, Georges; after (French, 1882-1963)

Barques sur la Plage, 94/100, clr aqua/Arches, ca 1950s, p/s, full mrgs, P-12x18", lot 497, C-NY 5/10/89 OE 3,300
Bowl of Fruit, 88/300, clr litho, p/s, full mrgs, lt ls/stn/tr, L-10x14", lot 37, PHL 10/28/88 OE 900
Chair, 112/300, clr litho, p/s, trm mrgs, laid down, L-15x11", lot 44A, PHL 6/16/88 400
Espaces, ed of 300, clr litho/Richard de Bas, p/s, 19x16", Au Vent d'Arles, lot 34, SWN 6/15/89 385
Marine Noire, 199/400, clr litho/Rives, ca 1950, p/s, Maeght bstp, full mrgs, lt cr, S-26x36", lot 221, C-NY 11/1/88 OE 1,870
Oiseau Muliticolore, by Crommelynck, 139/200, etch/BFK Rives, ca 1950, p/s, P-10x20", Maeght, lot 220, C-NY 11/1/88 OE 2,640
Pichet Noir et Citrons, 192/200, etch/aqua, ca 1950, lt rpr, lt mstn/fox verso, P-15x18", Maeght, lot 219, C-NY 11/1/88 1,210
Vitrail de la Chapelle de Warengeville, 89/150, clr litho, ca 1940s, sgn in wht ink, S-30x18", lot 218, C-NY 11/1/88 550

RESDIN, Rodolphe (French, 1822-1885)

Le Bon Samaritain, Rodolphine ed, litho/Chine applique, 1861, lt tr/sl/stn, 22x17", lot 334, SBY 5/11/89 3,300
Le Bon Samaritain, total ed of 200, litho/Chine jaunatre applied to Chine applique, 1861, S-28x22", lot 14, C-NY 11/1/88 11,000
Le Repos en Egypt a l'Ane Bate, 2nd state, etch/bl-gr laid paper, 1871, S-16x13", lot 16, C-NY 11/1/88 4,950
Le Ruisseau des Gorges, transfer litho/imitation Chine applique, 1868-73, lt fox/sl, L-5x6", lot 15, C-NY 11/1/88 2,200

RIERLY, Oswald Walters (British, 1817-1894)

HMS Meander 44 Guns, Shortening Sail for Anchoring (ship); clr litho, 1852, L-10x14", Ackermann/Day, C-SK 6/9/88 560

RISCOE, Arthur (British, 1873-1934)

Abandoned, 39/75, etch/laid paper, 1930, sgn, lt sl, 9x16", lot 2823, B/B 4/19/88 300
Main Rigging, 32/75, etch, 1928, p/s, lt sl, 14x9", lot 2822, B/B 4/19/88 OE 600
Making Sail, 6/25, etch, 1928, sgn in ink, titled, 10x16", lot 144, SLK 2/12/88 170

ritish School (20th C)

Bachelor's Hall, Pl 4, 13x16", lot 114, FAP 2/24/89 175
Empress of Britain, litho/poster paper, 40x25", Sanders/Phillips/Bagnard, lot 230, FAP 2/24/89 OE 330
Protest Against the Rising Tide of Conformity, litho/poster paper, 44x30", lot 237, FAP 2/24/89 UE 30

ROCKHURST, Gerald Leslie (British, 1890-1978)

Adolescence, ed of 90, 5th/final state, etch/wove paper, 1932, p/s, lt sl mrgs, unfr, P-14x10", C-NY 1/22/88 OE 9,350
Adolescence (Kathleen Nancy Woodward), ed of 90, etch/cream wove paper, 1932, full mrgs, 15x10", lot 219, SBY 5/11/89 12,100
Adolescence (Kathleen Nancy Woodward), ed of 90, etch/wht wove paper, 1932, p/s, full mrgs, lt sl, P-14x10", SBY 5/12/88 7,150
Adolescence (Kathleen Nancy Woodward), ed of 90, etch/wht wove paper, 1932, p/s, full mrgs, 15x11", lot 14, SBY 11/3/88 15,400
Group of 3: By the Bidassoa; La Basquaise; Young Womanhood; etch/wove paper, 2 1920/1931, p/s, C-NY 1/22/88 715
In the Wood, or Around the Tree; ed of 110, 2nd state, etch/wove paper, 1920, p/s, unfr, P-5x6", C-NY 1/22/88 242
Pair: Black Silk Dress; Viba (Mrs Bobby Hazelton Ross); ed of 111, etch/wove paper, 1927/1929, p/s, C-NY 1/22/88 528
Pair: Mirror; Lassitude; ed of 55-76, etch/wove paper, 1920/1923-24, p/s, full mrgs, lt stn, tp verso, C-NY 1/22/88 605
Standing Nude, litho/wove paper, p/s, pl/s & dtd, inscr Model Proof, lt stn, unfr, L-15x15", RWS 3/16/89 300
Una, total ed of 111, etch/wove paper, 1929, p/s, lt stn, P-9x6", lot 325, C-NY 1/19/89 330
Young Womanhood, ed of 111, final state, etch, 1931, 9x7", lot 21, SWN 12/1/88 715

RODERS, Roger

Winter Sports in the Vosges (Alsace & Lorraine Railways), clr litho, pl/s, 39x24", C-E 3/24/88 330

ROGUE, David

Guilia Girse As Norma, engr, 1844, P-10x7", C-E 11/15/88 77

ROUET, August (Continental, 1872-1941)

Group of 3: Fishermen; Market; Ballerina Kneeling; ed of 75 or 100, etch, p/s, lt stn, no size given, SWN 6/15/89 415
Pair: Gypsy Encampment; Rag Merchant; 7/10 & #4, engr, p/s, 4x4"/4x7", lot 12, FAP 2/24/89 UE 50

ROWN, John George (American, 1831-1913)

Street Politician, engr, sgn, full mrgs, 1985, L-20x30", Charles Schlect, RAB 3/27/89 400

ROWN, Theophilus (American, 1919-)

Model Seated, Dark Background, Model Seated, White Background; 11/12, litho/Arches, 18x22", Ed Pr, B/B 4/19/88 UE 192

ROWN, William H. (American, 19th C)

Group of 10: Silhouettes of Statesmen; blk/wht litho, 1844, 13x17", Kellogg, lot 521, GAI 3/17/89 1,270
Pair: John Tyler; Henry Clay; hc litho, lt trm, 13x18", lot 76, GAI 5/13/88 250

RUEGHEL, Pieter the elder; after (Flemish, 1512-1569)

Christ in Hell, by Pieter van der Heyden, engr, ca 1560, trm mrgs, lt ls/scr/stn/cr, 9x11", lot 9, SBY 5/11/89 OE 2,310
Christ in Hell, by Pieter van der Heyden, engr/wm small high crown, ca 1965(?), lt fox, 9x12", lot 591, SBY 2/25/88 OE 3,410
Flight of the Money Bags, by Pieter van der Heyden, engr, ca 1560, trm mrgs, lt glue, 9x12", lot 10, SBY 5/11/89 OE 6,875
Nemo Non Everyman Looks for His Own Profit, 1st state, engr/wm Gothic lettered paper, ca 1563, lot 592, SBY 2/25/88 2,860

RUNIAS, Augustin (British, 1735-1810)

Pair: Negroes Dance in the Island of Dominica; Cudgelling Match Between English & French Negroes...; mezzo, C-SK 6/9/88 1,670
West India Flower Girl, from set of 6, mezzo laid down on sheet, 1810, trm mrgs, unfr, 9x7", Palser, C-SK 6/9/88 OE 520

UFFET, Bernard (French, 1928-)

Bread & Wine, 65/250, clr litho, 1964, p/s, full mrgs, lt cr/tr/skinned, 26x20", lot 116, SBY 2/23/89 OE 3,850
Bridge in Paris, 89/125, clr litho, ca 1970, p/s, full mrgs, lt stn/sl, 17x22", lot 98, SBY 11/3/88 OE 4,400
Cannes, 70/125, clr litho, 1960, p/s, full mrgs, lt stn recto/verso, L-26x20", SBY 5/12/88 OE 4,400
Chien Napoleon, 69/120, clr litho/wove paper, 1968, sgn in ink, lt cr, L-27x19", lot 507, C-NY 5/10/89 880
Cirque, 39/120, clr litho/wove paper, ca 1968, sgn in ink, lt cr/stn/sl, L-27x19", lot 508, C-NY 5/10/89 770
Clown on a Red Background, litho, 1968, sgn, trm, mounted on 2 layers heavy paper, L-12x9", RWS 3/16/89 UE 100
Galerie Charpentier Poster, 28/100, litho/Arches, 1958, p/s, lt stn/cr/stn, L-17x17", lot 499, C-NY 5/10/89 OE 2,860
Group of 13: From Mon Cirque; 8 #d 42/120, 1 #d 17/120, clr litho, 1968, 9 sgn, full mrgs, lot 345A, SBY 5/11/89 6,600
Group of 3: Mon Cirque: Le Clown Pointu; Bebert; Rearing Horse; 97/120, litho, 1968, 27x19", lot 345, SBY 5/11/89 2,200

Head of Clown, 31/250, clr litho, 1967, p/s, full mrgs, L-22x17", lot 46, PHL 6/16/88	800
Isle St Louis, clr litho, sgn/dtd 68, 23x19", lot 582, LH 5/15/88 OE	450
La Route, a/p, ed of 250, clr litho/Arches, 1962, p/s, full mrgs, ltstn/cr/stn, L-26x20", lot 503, C-NY 5/10/89	8,250
La Route (highway/landscape), ed of 220, clr litho, 1962, p/s, L-25x20", lot 58, RWS 9/29/88 OE	3,700
La Tour Solidor, 58/120, drypt/Arches, 1971, p/s, Lacouriere bstp, full mrgs, lt stn, P-28x41", lot 510, C-NY 5/10/89 OE	14,300
Le Sacre Coeur, 51/125, clr litho/Arches, 1965, p/s, full mrgs, lt stn, laid down, L-23x18", lot 506, C-NY 5/10/88 OE	8,800
Le Sacre Coeur, 8/125, clr litho, 1965, p/s, full mrgs, lt scr img, lt stn, 23x18", lot 119, SBY 2/23/89 OE	6,050
Mon Cirque: Le Dompteur; 45/120, clr litho, 1968, p/s, full mrgs, 27x19", Mourlot, lot 120, SBY 2/23/89	1,100
Musician, 119/150, clr litho/Arches, 1970s, p/s, full mrgs, L-27x20", lot 509, C-NY 5/10/89 UE	440
New York, a/p, total ed of 180, clr litho/Arches, 1965, p/s, full mrgs, lt stn/cr/sl, L-27x19", SBY 5/12/88 OE	6,325
New York I, 21/150, clr litho, 1965, p/s, laid down, 28x19", Mazo, lot 339, SBY 5/11/89 OE	10,450
New York III, 21/150, clr litho, 1965, p/s, laid down, 19x27", Mazo, lot 340, SBY 5/11/89 OE	10,450
New York IV, 83/150, clr litho, 1965, p/s, full mrgs, 27x19", lot 92, SBY 11/3/88 OE	11,000
New York IX, a/p, clr litho, 1965, p/s, full mrgs, lt tr/nick mrg, lt stn, 19x27", lot 117, SBY 2/23/89 OE	10,450
New York IX, 49/150, clr litho, 1965, p/s, full mrgs, lt stn, 19x27", Mazo, lot 343, SBY 5/11/89 OE	11,550
New York V, 53/150, clr litho, 1965, p/s, full mrgs, 25x20", lot 93, SBY 11/3/88 OE	14,300
New York V, 91/150, clr litho, 1965, p/s, full mrgs, lt stn, 25x20", Mazo, lot 341, SBY 5/11/89 OE	9,900
New York VI, 38/150, clr litho, 1965, p/s, full mrgs, 19x27", lot 94, SBY 11/3/88 OE	16,500
New York VII, 21/150, clr litho, 1965, p/s, full mrgs, lt stn/old tp hinges, 26x19", lot 95, SBY 11/3/88 OE	13,200
New York VIII, 16/150, clr litho, 1965, p/s, full mrgs, 25x19", lot 96, SBY 11/3/88 OE	15,400
New York VIII, 37/150, clr litho, 1965, p/s, full mrgs, lt scr/stn/cr, 25x20", Mazo, lot 342, SBY 5/11/89 OE	9,900
New York X, 21/150, clr litho, 1965, p/s, full mrgs, lt stn, 19x27", lot 97, SBY 11/3/88 OE	13,200
New York X, 21/150, clr litho, 1965, p/s, full mrgs, lt stn, 19x27", lot 97, SBY 11/3/88 OE	13,200
New York X, 49/150, clr litho/Arches, 1965, p/s, full mrgs, lt stn, L-22x27", lot 505, C-NY 5/10/89 OE	12,100
New York X, 64/150, clr litho, 1965, p/s, full mrgs, lt stn/fox, SBY 2/23/89 OE	9,900
Oil Lamp, 73/175, clr litho/BFK Rives, 1954, p/s, L'Oeuvre Grave bstp, full mrgs, stn, 16x22", lot 498, C-NY 5/10/89 OE	5,280
Pair: Clown; Head of a Woman; 44/120 & 156/220, clr litho/Arches, ca 1968, lt sl mrgs, lot 227, C-NY 11/1/88 OE	1,760
Pair: New York VI; New York VIII; 21/150, clr litho, 1965, p/s, full mrgs, lt lstn, L-19x17"/L-25x19", SBY 5/12/88 OE	13,200
Pair: Paris, La Porte Saint-Martin; Paris, The Eiffel Tower; 21/150 & 17/150, litho, 1962, L-21x27", SBY 5/12/88 OE	9,900
Pair: Wasp; Bee; HC, clr litho, 1964, p/s, full mrgs, lt sl/cr/stn, S-19x26", lot 115, SBY 2/23/89 OE	5,500
Paris, L'Arc de Triomphe; 12/150, clr litho/Rives, 1962, p/s, full mrgs, lt lstn, L-21x27", lot 224, C-NY 11/1/88 OE	10,450

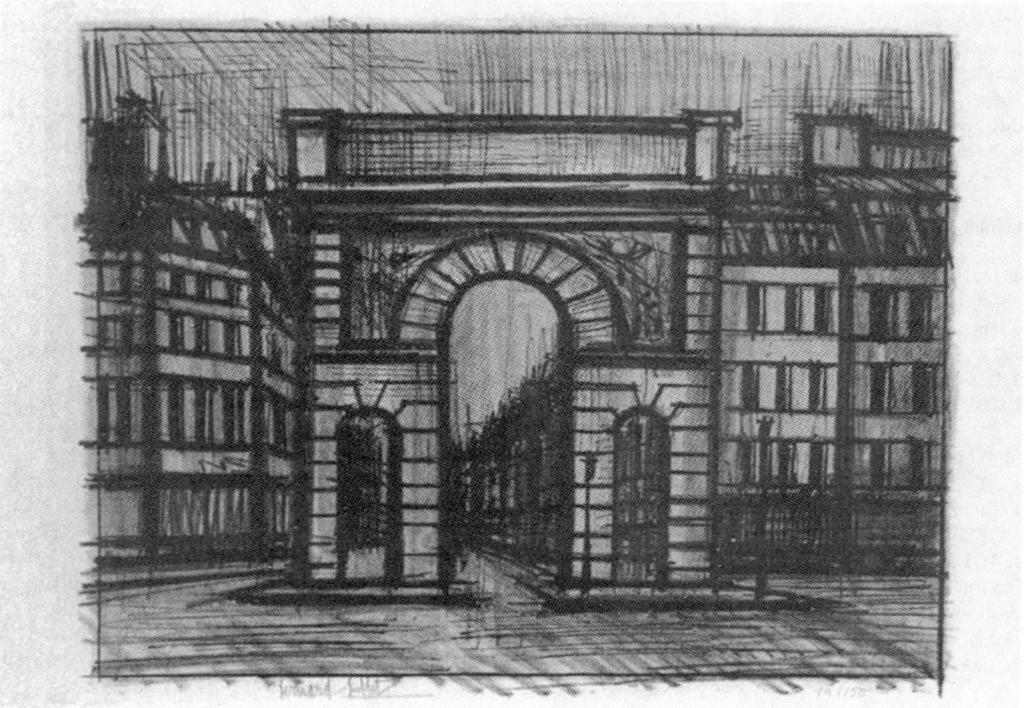

Paris, La Porte Saint-Martin litho/Rives, 1962, p/s, full mrgs, scr/stn, L-21x27", lot 504, C-N 5/10/89 OE; $12,100

Paris, Pont-du-Jour; 37/150, clr litho, 1962, p/s, lt stn, S-22x30", Mazo, lot 114, SBY 2/23/89 OE	9,350
Personnage dans l'Atelier (Self-Portrait), 15/200, drypt, 1948, p/s, full mrgs, lt cr, 12x9", lot 336, SBY 5/11/89 OE	2,200
Pont Neuf, 116/125, clr litho/Arches, ca 1960, p/s, full mrgs, lt sl/cr/scr, L-23x18", lot 225, C-NY 11/1/88 OE	3,520
Portfolio: Jeux de Dames; 238/250, 10 clr litho/Arches, 10 blk/wht litho, 1970, p/s, Les Ed Livre, SBY 5/12/88 OE	8,800
Portfolio: Mon Cirque; 52/120, 27 litho w/text, sgn, 27x19", lot 833, LH 10/16/88 OE	4,400
Red & Yellow Butterfly, EA, clr litho/Arches, 1964, p/s, lt sl verso, S-21x29", Mourlot, lot 90, C-NY 5/11/88 OE	1,760
Road, a/p, aside from #d ed of 250, clr litho, 1962, p/s, full mrgs, lt stn/old hinge, 26x20", lot 112, SBY 2/25/88 OE	2,200
Road, a/p, clr litho, 1962, p/s, full mrgs, 26x20", lot 338, SBY 5/11/89 OE	7,700
San Francisco, 97/150, clr litho/Arches, 1966, p/s, lt stn/cr mrgs, L-19x27", C-NY 11/1/88 OE	10,450

St Germain des Pres, 52/150, clr litho, 1965, p/s, full mrgs, lt scr/sl/stn, 23x18", lot 344, SBY 5/11/89 OE **7,150**
Statue of Liberty, 65/150, clr litho, ca 1975, p/s, full mrgs, 26x20", lot 346, SBY 5/11/89 .... **1,650**
Still Life with a Fried Egg, a/p, clr litho, 1955, p/s, full mrgs, 26x19", Beyeler Gallerie, lot 112, SBY 2/23/89 OE **4,950**
Sun Flowers & Melons, 24/125, clr litho/BFK Rives, 1955, p/s, full mrgs, lt scr/stn/tr, 25x19", lot 223, C-NY 11/1/88 OE **6,380**
Tents, 62/75, clr litho/BFK Rives, 1954, p/s, full mrgs, lt stn, L-17x24", Mourlot, lot 89, C-NY 5/11/88 OE **2,640**
Toreador, 37/150, clr litho/Arches, ca 1960, p/s, full mrgs, lt rpl, S-27x19", lot 500, C-NY 5/10/89 .... **1,100**
Toreadors, 105/150, clr litho/Arches, ca 1960, p/s, lt stn/sl, S-29x21", lot 501, C-NY 5/10/89 .... **1,430**
UNO, 86/200, drypt, 1959, p/s, full mrgs, lt stn, 21x27", lot 113, SBY 2/23/89 OE **3,575**
Vase of Anemones, 29/150, clr litho/Arches, ca 1960, p/s, full mrgs, lt stn, L-23x19", lot 502, C-NY 5/10/89 OE **6,050**
Windmills, 133/220, clr litho/wove paper, 1953, p/s, full mrgs, lt lstn, L-13x20", lot 222, C-NY 11/1/88 OE **11,000**
Windmills, a/p, XX/XX, clr litho, 1953, p/s, full mrgs, lt mstn, 13x20", lot 337, SBY 5/11/89 OE **9,350**
Woman in Bikini, clr litho, 12x10", lot 396, WG 10/19/88 .... **35**

UHOT, Felix (French, 1847-1898)

L'Hiver a Paris, ou la Neige a Paris; 3rd state, etch/aqua/Whatman, 1879, sgn, full mrgs, 10x14", lot 99, SBY 11/3/88 OE **3,300**
L'Hiver a Paris, ou la Neige a Paris; 5th state, etch/rlt/aqua/wove paper, 1879, lt stn/rpr, P-10x14", C-NY 1/19/89 .... **880**
L'Hiver de Paris, etch/laid paper, 1879, pl/s, lt stn, 10x14", lot 2834, B/B 2/16/88 .... **825**
L'Hiver de 1879 a Paris, etch/drypt/aqua, 1879, pl/s, 9x13", lot 65, WG 10/19/88 .... **575**
Les Gardiens du Logis ou les Amis du Saltimbanque, etch/rlt, pl/s, red stp, lt stn, laid down, 3x5", RWS 3/16/89 .... **120**
Les Voisins de Campagnes, 4th state, etch/aqua/drypt/simili Japan, 1879-80, a/bstp, P-5x7", lot 91, C-NY 5/11/88 OE **770**
Pair: L'Embarcadere; L'Hiver de 1879 a Paris; etch/aqua, 1877 & ca 1879, lt fox, 8x11"/10x14", lot 22, SWN 12/1/88 .... **715**
Pair: L'Orage; Le 20 Mars au Palais des Champs Elysees; 1877, 6x9", lot 23, SWN 12/1/88 OE **880**
Un Grain a Trouville, XVIII, 1st state, etch/Strasburg Lily, 1874, full mrgs, stn/sl, P-6x9", lot 326, C-NY 1/19/89 OE **935**
Une Jetee en Angleterre, Goodfriend's 2nd state, etch/aqua/drypt/rlt/laid Japan, 1879, P-12x8", lot 328, C-NY 1/19/89 .... **935**
Une Jetee en Angleterre, Goodfriend's 2nd state, etch/aqua/drypt/rlt/Japan, 1879, P-12x8", lot 329, C-NY 1/19/89 .... **1,045**
Westminster Bridge, Goodfriend's 7th state, etch/aqua/drypt/rlt, 1884, p/s, a/bstp, P-11x16", lot 331, C-NY 1/19/89 .... **1,980**
Westminster Bridge: Westminister Clock Tower; etch/aqua/drypt, 1884, a/bstp, 11x16", lot 771, LH 12/4/88 .... **800**
Westminster Palace, a/p, Goodfriend's 6th state, etch/Japan, 1884, p/s, lt stn, laid down, 12x16", lot 330, C-NY 1/19/89 .... **1,760**
Westminster Palace, final state, etch, 1884, a/bstp, lt stn/fox, rpr mrgs, stn verso, 11x16", lot 347, SBY 5/11/89 OE **1,760**
Westminster Palace, final state, etch/drypt, 1884, p/s, a/stp, lt stn/fox, 12x16", lot 101, SBY 11/3/88 .... **2,750**
Westminster Palace, intermediate state between Bourcard's 4th & 5th, etch/drypt, 1884, 12x16", lot 100, SBY 11/3/88 .... **3,025**

URCHFIELD, Charles (American, 1893-1967)

Autumn Wind, ed of 60, litho, 1951, p/s, lt stn, 8x14", lot 21, SBY 2/23/89 .... **8,800**
Crows in March, ed of 60, litho, 1951, lt stn/tr, 14x10", lot 22, SBY 2/23/89 .... **3,575**
Summer Benediction, ed of 260, litho, 1953, p/s, full mrgs, lt fox, 12x9", Cleveland Print Club, lot 220, SBY 5/11/89 OE **5,280**
Summer Benediction, total ed of 260, litho, 1953, p/s, full mrgs, Cleveland Print Club bstp, 12x9", SBY 2/25/88 OE **3,960**

URGDORFF, Ferdinand (American, 1883-1975)

Venus, etch, 1925, p/s, titled, 4x3", lot 126, WG 1/19/88 .... **30**

URKERT, Robert Randall (American, 1930-)

Burning City, 20/30, srgph, sgn/titled, L-30x20", lot 1367, S/A 3/12/88 .... **70**

URLIUK, David (American/Russian, 1882-1967)

Book: V Khlebnikov Riav (Riav); Perchatki (Gloves); 1908-1914, orig wrappers, 41 Degrees, lot 555, SBY 5/11/89 OE **3,300**

URR, George Elbert (American, 1859-1939)

Moraine Park, etch/laid paper, p/s, lt trm mrgs, lt stn mrgs/verso, 5x4", lot 2935, B/B 4/19/88 .... **300**
Soapweek, etch/aqua/laid paper, 1930, p/s, titled/dtd, tp on verso, lt stn, 10x7", lot 2930, B/B 2/16/88 .... **1,045**
Whirlwinds, Dead Mountains, Mojave Desert; etch/aqua/cream wove paper, 1929, p/s, lt stn/tr, 8x10", B/B 2/16/88 UE **440**

UTTERS, E. (German, 20th C)

Kermische Werkstaetten, clr litho, lt tr, 19x19", s/wrp, lot 215, FAP 2/24/89 .... **120**

ADDY, J.H.; after (19th C)

Group of 3: Scenery of the Windward & Leeward Islands; clr aqua, 1837, S-9x11", stn/tr/ls, Ackermann, C-SK 6/9/88 .... **220**

ADMUS, Paul (American, 1904-)

Arabesque, ed of 75, etch/laid paper, 1947, p/s, full mrgs, lt stn/fox/cr, 7x7", lot 24, SBY 2/25/88 .... **605**
Arabesque, ed of 75, etch/laid paper, 1947, p/s, mstn mrgs/verso, tp verso mrg edges, P-7x7", C-NY 1/22/88 OE **1,045**
Coney Island, 8/35, etch/wove paper, 1935/1979, p/s, full mrgs, P-9x10", Print Cabinet, lot 156, C-NY 1/19/89 .... **715**
Polo Spill, Aspects of Suburban Life; ed of about 75, etch/1938, p/s, lt stn mrg, P-7x10", lot 14, C-NY 5/11/88 .... **935**
Shore Leave, ed of 50, etch/drypt/laid paper, 1935, p/s, lt stn/fox, L-10x11", lot 26, RWS 9/8/89 OE **2,200**
Two Boys on a Beach, No 1; ed of 75, etch, 1938, p/s, full mrgs, lt sl mrgs, 5x7", lot 221, SBY 5/11/89 OE **1,320**
Two Boys on a Beach, No 2; a/p, apart from ed of 151, etch, 1939, p/s, inscr, lt fox/stn, P-5x3", C-NY 1/22/88 OE **1,430**
YMCA Locker Room, ed of 50, etch/BFK Rives, 1934, p/s, lt stn/ls, P-7x13", lot 155, C-NY 1/19/89 .... **1,980**
Youth with Kite, ed of 75, etch/laid Japan, 1941, p/s, lt sl mrg, mstn/tp verso, unfr, P-10x5", C-NY 1/22/88 .... **935**

ALDER, Alexander (American, 1898-1976)

Abstract Composition, 22/125, clr litho, p/s, 24x19", lot 89, FAP 2/24/89 .... **250**
Circles & Triangles, 73/90, clr litho, 18x13", lot 88, FAP 2/24/89 .... **200**
Circus, a/p, clr litho, p/s, floated on mat, S-26x38", lot 61, RWS 9/8/89 OE **1,400**
Crescent & Moon, 62/90, litho, p/s, 23x18", lot 444, FAP 4/15/88 .... **385**
Flower Images, 87/125, clr litho, p/s, 25x19", lot 861, WAD 11/28/88 UE **500**
Le Soleil Rouge, 59/90, litho, p/s, 22x32", lot 477, FAP 4/15/88 .... **385**
Little Balloons, clr litho, ca 1975, 14x11", lot 37, SWN 6/15/89 .... **195**
Pyramid, 32/90, clr litho, p/s, 19x13", lot 475, FAP 4/15/88 OE **300**
Red Nose, 59/75, clr litho, ca 1970, p/s, S-29x43", lot 613, SBY 2/23/89 .... **1,870**
Score for Ballet 0-100, ed of about 50, engr/Umbria Italia, 1942, full mrgs, lt fox/tr/cr. S-14x18", C-NY 1/19/89 OE **20,900**

Star & Moon, clr litho, p/s, 25x17", lot 395, WG 10/19/88 UE **225**
Three-Legged Figure with Raised Arms, ed of 75, clr litho, 15x11", lot 1235, LH 10/16/88 .... **90**
Tree with Red & Blue Fruit, 65/150, clr litho, p/s, wide mrgs, L-23x18", lot 38, PHL 10/28/88 .... **325**
Untitled, La Proue de la Table; 30/55, etch/wove paper, 1967, intl, S-15x11", lot 587, C-NY 11/1/88 OE **770**
Untitled (Circles & Stars), 47/100, clr litho, p/s, pub bstp, S-21x30", RWS 3/16/89 OE **1,100**
Untitled (Circles & Wave), 19/120, litho, p/s, S-35x24", RWS 3/16/89 OE **850**
Violin, 73/75, litho, p/s, 30x22", lot 463, FAP 4/15/88 .... **550**

CALLET, Antoine Francois (French, 1741-1823)
Pair: Courtship; clr engr, p/s, 10x12", lot 36, FAP 2/24/89 .... **85**

CALLOR, Louis (French, 19th C)
Country Landscape with Sheep, 15/300, aqua, p/s, 12x23", lot 640, LH 12/4/88 .... **200**

CALLOT, Jacques (French, 1592-1635)
Pair: Death of St Benoit; Pilate Washing His Hands; etch, trm mrgs, lt stn/sl/fox, no size given, lot 2801, B/B 4/19/88 .... **248**
Set of 18: Les Grandes Miseres de la Guerre; penultimate states, etch, 1633, lt sl/cr, 3x7", lot 594, SBY 2/25/88 OE **5,500**

CAMBELLOTTI, Duilio (Italian, 1876-1960)
Incandescenza Aver, clr litho, lt fox/tr mrgs, lt fld/tr, linen backed, unfr, 78x27", lot 304, FAP 2/24/89 .... **850**

CAMPENDONCK, Henrich (German, 1889-1957)
Begebenheit (Madchen mit Fisch und Vogeln), hc wc/thin Japan, 1920, p/s, lt stn, S-19x16", lot 18, C-NY 11/1/88 OE **9,900**
Halbakt mit Katze, 140/141, hc wc/thin Japan, 1912, p/s, lt ls/cr, S-12x17", lot 17, C-NY 11/1/88 OE **9,350**

CAMPIGLI, Massimo (Italian, 1895-1971)
Bathers, litho, 1955, sgn, glued to mat, 19x26", lot 29, SWN 12/1/88 .... **468**
Figures at the Beach, 77/200, litho/BFK Rives, 1954, p/s, L'Oeuvre Grave bstp, full mrgs, 19x13", lot 2836, B/B 2/16/88 .... **550**
Two Women, ed of 100, clr litho, 1959, p/s on img, lt stn on verso, lt cr mrgs, 21x26", lot 39, SWN 6/15/89 OE **1,540**

CANADE, Vincent (American/Italian, 1879-)
Double Self-Portrait, ed of 97, litho, 1927, 9x7", lot 30, SWN 12/1/88 .... **248**

Canadian School (20th C)
La Peninsule de Gaspe Peninsula, litho/poster paper, 36x24", lot 225, FAP 2/24/89 .... **60**

CANALETTO, Antonio (Italian, 1697-1768)
Bishop's Tomb, only state, etch/wm 3 crescents paper, before 1741(?), 12x12", lot 595, SBY 2/25/88 OE **8,360**
Imaginary View of S Giacomo di Rialto, 1st state, etch, pre-1741, thread mrgs, 6x8", lot 13, SBY 5/11/89 OE **4,400**
Landscape with Ruined Monuments, only state, etch, pre-1741, trm mrgs, lt stn, 6x9", lot 14, SBY 5/11/89 .... **4,125**
Market at Dolo, final state, etch, ca 1740, 6x8", lot 31, SWN 12/1/88 .... **1,045**
Padua, trm mrgs, 12x17", lot 33, FAP 2/24/89 UE **475**
Pair: Equestrian Monument; Landscape with the Pilgrim at Prayer; etch, 1741, lt cr, 6x8", lot 12, SBY 5/11/89 OE **2,310**

CANALLE, Antonio; see Canaletto

CARBONI, Erberto (Italian, 20th C)
Automobile Club Diparma, clr litho/poster paper, linen backed, 37x25", lot 274, FAP 2/24/89 OE **1,050**

CARDINAUX, Emile (Swiss, 1887-1936)
Palace Hotel, clr litho, 50x36", Wolfberg, C-E 3/24/88 OE **3,080**
Palace Hotel, St Moritz; 55/500, clr litho, 23x28", lot 154, FAP 2/24/89 UE **40**

CARLU, Jean Georges (French, 1900-)
Pair: Fly by Clipper to Australia & New Zealand; Scandanavia; litho/poster paper, 40x28", Pan Am, lot 156, FAP 2/24/89 .... **158**
Pepa Bonafe, clr litho, 1928, lt fld/stn, linen backed, unfr, 22x15", Picard, lot 240, FAP 2/24/89 .... **170**

CARNELISON, Maliz (South American, 20th C)
Native with Machete, wc, 1936, p/s, titled/dtd, 8x6", lot 232, WG 10/19/88 .... **30**

CAROT, Camille Jean Baptiste (French, 1796-1875)
Le Repos de Philosophes, ed of about 50, transfer litho, 1871-72, sgn, trm, L-9x6", lot 6, RWS 9/8/89 UE **750**

CARRIERE, Eugene (French, 1849-1906)
Auguste Rodin, #33, litho, p/s, laid down, 21x14", FAP 6/16/89 UE **425**
Mme Eugene Carriere, litho/Chine, 1893, unexamined out of fr, L-7x5", lot 333, C-NY 1/19/89 .... **385**
Portrait of a Man, litho/cream wove paper, p/s, 15x13", lot 2828, B/B 4/19/88 .... **825**

CARTER, Clarence Holbrook (American, 1904-)
Olive Trees, Capri; ed of 250, clr aqua, 1932, p/s, titled, full mrgs, P-6x7", Print-a-Month Club, lot 15, C-NY 5/11/88 .... **550**
Olive Trees, Capri; ed of 250, clr aqua/handmade paper, 1932, p/s, 7x8", Cleveland Print Club, lot 172, WG 10/19/88 .... **375**
Pair: Homestead; Factory; ed of 200, clr litho, 1979 & 1980, p/s, 22x28"/18x26", lot 41, SWN 6/15/89 UE **195**

CARWITHAM, John
Southwest View of the City of New York in North America, final state, etch/engr, S-14x19", Bowles/Carver, SBY 1/28/88 .... **8,800**

CASSANDRE, Adolphe M. (French, 1901-)
Bonal, clr litho, 1935, pl/s, 64x47", s/wrp, C-E 3/24/88 .... **440**
Etoile du Nord, clr litho, 1927, 41x29", lot 263, SBY 12/12/88 OE **3,025**
L'Oiseau Bleu, clr litho, 1929, S-39x24", lot 264, SBY 12/12/88 OE **2,420**
Normandie, New York Via le Havre et Southampton; clr litho, 1935, lt cr, linen backed, S-39x25", lot 286, SBY 3/10/89 .... **5,500**
Reglisse Florent, clr litho, 1925, pl/s, 60x39", C-E 3/24/88 OE **1,650**
Sourds Muets Aveugles, clr litho, 1927, lt cr, linen backed, S-40x24", Hachard & Cie, lot 285, SBY 3/10/89 OE **3,575**
Statendam, clr litho, 1928, 34x24", Nijgh en Van Ditmar, lot 360, SBY 6/8/88 .... **2,200**

CASSATT, Mary (American, 1855-1926)
After-Dinner Coffee, 1st state of 3, olive-gr sftgr etch, ca 1889, intl, lt cr/stn, P-8x6", SBY 5/12/88 .... **10,450**
Barefooted Child, ed of ca 50, aqua/drypt/laid paper, ca 1898, p/s, trm mrgs, lt cr/rpr ls, 10x13", SBY 5/12/88 OE **13,200**
Bonnet (portrait), drypt/cream laid paper, 1891, sgn, 7x6", C-SK 11/10/88 OE **12,080**
By the Pond, clr print/drypt/aqua/wm Adriaen Rogge laid paper, ca 1898, p/s, full mrgs, S-17x21", lot 222, SBY 5/11/89 .... **38,500**
Costume Study After Gavarni, 1st state, drypt/cream laid paper, ca 1879, intl, lt cr/stn, 8x5", lot 15, SBY 11/3/88 .... **4,400**

Looking into the Hand Mirror, No 2; drypt/pale bl paper, ca 1904/1928, lt stn, 8x6", Delatre, lot 43, SWN 6/15/89 715
Looking into the Hand Mirror, No 3; drypt/soft cream laid paper, ca 1905, hinged to mat, 9x5", lot 2932, B/B 2/16/88 495
Mandolin Player, 7th/final state, dk brn drypt/laid wm paper, ca 1889, p/s, bstp, full mrgs, lt mstn, 9x6", SBY 5/12/88 2,200
Map (The Lesson), ed of 25, 3rd state, drypt/Vanderley, 1890, p/s, full mrgs, lt sl/fox, P-6x9", lot 16, C-NY 5/11/88 19,800
Mlle Margot Wearing a Hat, brn-blk drypt/Japan, ca 1894, p/s, lt cr/stn, 10x7", lot 18, SBY 11/3/88 12,100
Reflection, unrecorded state, drypt/laid Verdatre, ca 1890, p/s, full mrgs, lt sl, S-16x10", lot 16, SBY 11/3/88 20,900
Sara Wearing a Large Bonnet & Coat, litho/Ingres d'Arches, ca 1904, full mrgs, lt stn/fox, L-20x17", C-NY 1/19/89 10,450
Sara Wearing Her Bonnet & Coat, litho/Ingres d'Arches, ca 1904, full mrgs, lt sl/stn/fox, unfr, L-20x17", SBY 5/12/88 13,200
Sara Wearing Her Bonnet & Coat, litho/Ingres d'Arches, ca 1904, full mrgs, lt stn, 20x17", lot 19, SBY 11/3/88 OE 17,600
Sara Wearing Her Bonnet & Coat, litho/wm MBM Ingres d'Arches, ca 1904, full mrgs, lt cr, L-20x17", lot 229, C-NY 11/1/88 12,100
Sarah Smiling, late imp, clr etch/drypt, full mrgs, lt stn, P-9x6", lot 17, PHL 10/28/88 OE 1,000

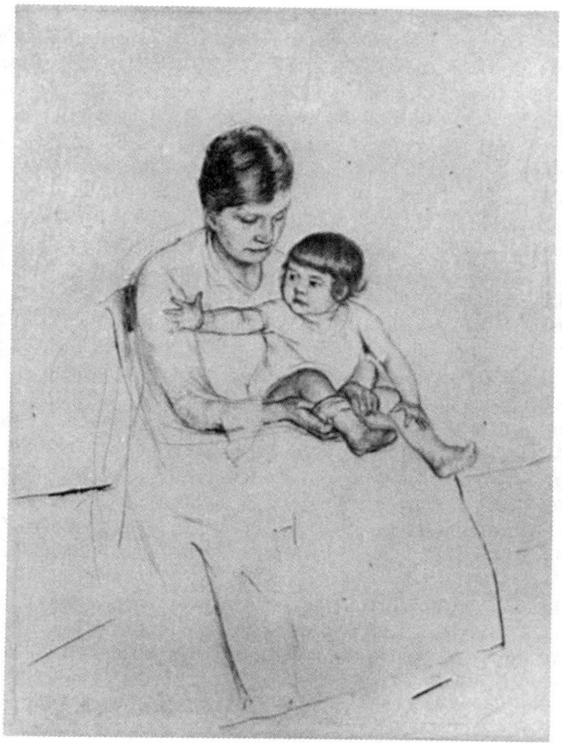

Seated Woman with Child, etch/drypt/laid paper, artist monogram stp, lt sl/fox, 10x7", lot 39, WD 12/8/88 OE; $10,500

CASSON, Joseph; after (Canadian, 1898-)
Pair: Wildflowers; White Pine; clr srgph, sgn, 10x13", lot 778, WAD 6/12/89 650
CASTELLON, Federico (American, 1914-1971)
Alchemist, #129, etch, ca 1965, p/s, P-19x15", lot 465, FAP 4/15/88 UE 110
Alchemist, etch/BFK Rives, ca 1965, p/s, full mrgs, lt cr, 19x15", lot 2933, B/B 2/16/88 137
Family, etch, 1947, p/s, 8x12", Assn Am Artists, lot 318, WG 10/19/88 150
Family (portrait), etch, p/s, lt stn, 8x12", Assn Am Artists, lot 297, WG 10/19/88 100
Gordan Knot, litho, 1936-37, no size given, Am Artist Group, lot 225, WG 10/19/88 UE 50
Pair: By the Arks; Road in Arizona; litho, p/s, full mrgs, lt stn, L-9x12"/L-10x14", lot 8, PHL 6/16/88 OE 350
CATESBY, Mark (British, 1679-1749)
Tulip Tree, Baltimore Bird; hc engr, 18x13", lot 1222, LH 10/16/88 300
CATLIN, George (American, 1794-1872)
Buffalo Hunt, On Snowshoes; 15, litho, lstn/fox img, stn/skinned verso/lacks support sheet, unfr, S-12x18", C-NY 1/22/88 375
Indians Playing Lacrosse, hc litho, 12x18", lot 1203, WAD 11/28/88 500
CAULFIELD, Patrick (British, 1936-)
Pair: Fern Pot; Plant Pot; 45/65 & 87/100, scpt, p/s, Waddington Graphics & Kelpra bstp, 1980/1979, 33x24", SLK 4/7/89 90
Pair: Signature Pots; Terra Cotta Vase; 63/70 & 56/70, scpt, p/s, 1975, 31x41", SLK 4/7/89 5
Picnic Set, 96/100, scpt, p/s, Waddington Graphics & Kelpra Studios bstp, ca 1970s, 38x36", SLK 4/7/89 35
CELMINS, Vija (20th C)
Untitled (contemporary), 17/65, gray litho, 1972, p/s, Cirrus bstp, full mrgs, lt sl, 29x46", lot 720, SBY 11/5/88 UE 440
CEZANNE, Paul (French, 1839-1906)
Las Baigneurs, Druick's 3rd state, litho/wm MBM laid paper, 1896-97, full mrgs, L-16x20", lot 230, C-NY 11/1/88 OE 46,200
Les Baigneurs, Johnson 1st state, Druick 2nd state, ed of 100, litho/wm MBM, 1896-8, L-16x21", lot 92, C-NY 5/11/88 OE 41,800
Les Baigneurs (Large Plate), Druick's 2nd state, litho/wm MBM laid paper, 1896-97, L-18x20", lot 514, C-NY 5/10/89 OE 41,800
Les Baigneurs (Large Plate), Druick's 3rd state, clr litho/MBM, 1896-97, full mrgs, S-19x25", lot 349, SBY 5/11/89 OE 57,750
Les Baigneurs (Small Plate), Druick's 1st state, litho/Chine volant, 1896-97, L-9x12", lot 513, C-NY 5/10/89 OE 7,150
Paysage a Auvers, Entree de Ferme rue Saint-Remy; etch/laid paper, 1873, trm mrgs, P-5x4", lot 39, PHL 10/28/88 650
Portrait de Cezanne, blk litho/wm MBM laid paper, 1896-97, lt fox/stn/tp, L-13x11", lot 231, C-NY 11/1/88 OE 1,045

Portrait de Cezanne par Lui-Meme, litho/Ingres d'Arches, ca 1896-97/1914, lt cr/tr, 13x11", lot 115, SBY 2/25/88 UE ... 550
Self-Portrait, ed of at least 200, litho/Vidalon, ca 1896-97, full mrgs, cr/rpr tr, 14x12", Vollard, lot 32, SWN 12/1/88 ... 550

CHAFFETZ, Asa (American, 1897-1965)

Clouds Over the Valley, wood engr, 1935, 15x8", Am Arists Group, lot 211, WG 10/19/88 ... 65

CHAGALL, Marc (Russian/French, 1887-1985)

Abdulah Discovering...Mountains of Water...; Pl 9, 80/90, p/s, rpr tr, sl mrgs, L-15x11", Mourlot, lot 242, C-NY 11/1/88 ... 19,800
Absalom Riding a Mule Is Caught by the Hair on the Branch of a Great Oak, 81/100, etch, 14x11", lot 45, LH 3/20/88 OE ... 2,000
Absolom Riding a Mule, Pl 72, 7/100, etch/Arches, 1930-55, p/s, full mrgs, P-12x10", Teriade, lot 242, C-NY 11/1/88 ... 2,200
Absolom Riding a Mule, 73/100, etch/Arches, 1930-55, p/s, full mrgs, lt stn, P-12x10", lot 524, C-NY 5/10/89 ... 1,760
Adam & Eve & the Forbidden Fruit, 36/50, clr litho/Arches, 1960, p/s, full mrgs, lt stn, L-14x11", lot 533, C-NY 5/10/89 ... 3,850
Adolescents, 1975, clr litho, p/s, full mrgs, L-26x20", SBY 5/12/88 OE ... 47,300
Adolescents, 38/50, clr litho, 1975, p/s, full mrgs, lt cr, 25x20", lot 187, SBY 2/23/89 ... 41,800
After Winter, ed of 5000, clr litho, 1972, 13x18", lot 489, LH 5/15/88 UE ... 190
Akt mit Facher, 2nd state, hc etch/drypt/laid paper, 1924, p/s, full mrgs, fox/stn/sl, P-8x11", lot 518, C-NY 5/10/89 OE ... 3,850
Ames Mortes, etch/wove paper, pl/s, lt sl verso, 11x9", lot 2841, B/B 2/16/88 ... 275
An der Staffelei, Pl 18, 80/110, etch/drypt, 1922, p/s, lg mrgs, lt stn, 10x8", Cassirer, lot 354, SBY 5/11/89 OE ... 9,350
An der Staffelei, Pl 18, 92/110, etch/drypt/laid paper, 1922, lt mstn/scr, laid down, P-11x8", lot 233, C-NY 11/1/88 OE ... 6,380
And You Wove for Your Tender Neck Seductive Garlands...; 35/75, clr litho, 1967, p/s, full mrgs, 15x13", SBY 11/3/88 ... 14,850
And You Wove for Your Tender Neck Seductive Garlands...; 65/75, litho, 1967, full mrgs, 15x13", lot 173, SBY 2/23/89 UE ... 6,600
Angel of Paradise, 63/75, clr litho, 1956, p/s, S-14x10", lot 137, SBY 2/23/89 OE ... 3,300
Appearance of King David, 11/50, clr litho, 1980, p/s, Mourlot bstp, full mrgs, lt mstn, L-16x13", SBY 5/12/88 ... 3,850
Arch de Triomphe, 35/50, clr litho/wove paper, 1976, p/s, full mrgs, lt stn, L-32x22", lot 562, C-NY 5/10/89 ... 13,200
Arrival of Dionysophanes, 20/60, clr litho, 1961, p/s, full mrgs, lt stn, 17x13", lot 385, SBY 5/11/89 OE ... 25,300
Artist & Biblical Themes, 35/40, clr litho, 1974, p/s, full mrgs, lt stn, 15x22", lot 183, SBY 2/23/89 ... 3,850
Artist & Biblical Themes, 46/50, clr litho, 1974, p/s, full mrgs, lt stn/cr, 15x23", lot 182, SBY 2/23/89 ... 4,400
Artist on a Black Background, 3/50, litho/Arches, 1972, p/s, lt stn, 22x15", lot 2831, B/B 4/19/88 ... 3,575
Artist's Bouquet, 16/75, clr litho/Arches, 1964, p/s, full mrgs, lt mstn, tp on verso, S-23x17", lot 110, C-NY 5/11/88 ... 4,950
Artist's Wife, 24/50, clr litho, 1971, p/s, full mrgs, lt stn, 25x20", lot 406, SBY 5/11/89 ... 44,000
At God's Command, Moses Throws Down His Rod...; Pl 30, 29/100, etch, 1930-55, P-12x9", Teriade, lot 239, C-NY 11/1/88 OE ... 2,860
Bacchante, AP3/4, clr litho, 1973, p/s, full mrgs, lt stn, 19x25", lot 154, SBY 11/3/88 ... 8,800
Baje des Anges, 4/50, clr litho, 1967, p/s, full mrgs, lt stn/cr, 15x17", lot 139, SBY 11/3/88 ... 13,200
Bastille, 23/75, clr litho, 1954, p/s, full mrgs, lt stn/sl, 20x26", lot 367, SBY 5/11/89 ... 66,000
Bay, 25/75, clr litho/Arches, 1962, p/s, lt tstn, lt stn verso, L-15x22", lot 256, C-NY 11/1/88 ... 10,450
Bay of Angels, ed of 5000, clr litho/poster paper, 1962, lt skinned/sl, 39x24", lot 165, SBY 2/23/89 ... 1,980
Bay of Angels, ed of 5000, clr litho/poster paper, 1962, S-39x24", lot 166, SBY 2/23/89 ... 2,310
Bay of Angels, 15/40, clr litho/Arches, 1960, p/s, mstn mrg edges/verso, L-14x11", lot 105, C-NY 5/11/88 ... 4,950
Bay of Angels, 5/40, clr litho, 1960, p/s, full mrgs, lt stn, 14x11", lot 369, SBY 5/11/89 OE ... 8,525
Behind the Mirror: Spring Day; 18/50, clr litho, 1972, p/s, full mrgs, lt stn/fox, unfr, L-15x11", SBY 5/12/88 OE ... 4,950
Bella, 19/100, etch/Arches, 1924, p/s, full mrgs, lt rub/stn, 9x5", Morance, lot 116, SBY 2/25/88 ... 3,740
Beside the Fountain, 33/60, clr litho, 1961, p/s, full mrgs, lt mstn/fox, skinned/cr mrgs, L-17x13", SBY 5/12/88 OE ... 34,100
Biblical Scene (Jacob), 17/50, litho, 1971, p/s, full mrgs, lt stn, 25x21", lot 178, SBY 2/23/89 OE ... 7,700
Big Peasant, 41/50, clr litho, 1968, p/s, full mrgs, lt stn, 24x18", lot 150, SBY 11/3/88 ... 7,700
Bird Chase, ed of 250, clr litho, 1961, S-17x25", lot 378, SBY 5/11/89 ... 9,900
Black & Blue Bouquet, 42/90, aside from ed of 6000, blk/bl litho, 1957, p/s, full mrgs, lt stn, L-9x7", SBY 5/12/88 ... 1,320
Blue Bouquet, 17/50, clr litho/Arches, 1974, p/s, full mrgs, lt stn/old glue, L-24x19", lot 557, C-NY 5/10/89 ... 17,600
Blue Studio, 26/50, clr litho/Arches, 1973, p/s, full mrgs, lt stn/cr/fox, L-16x15", Maeght, lot 40, PHL 10/28/88 ... 14,000
Book: Bible (2 vol set); 139/275, 105 etch w/text, 1930-55, sgn, cr/sl, orig wrappers, Teriade, lot 101, C-NY 5/11/88 OE ... 52,800
Book: Celui Qui Dit les Choses sans Rien Dire; 19/25, 25 aqua/etch, 25 etch, ea sgn artist/author, S-19x14", SBY 5/12/88 ... 110,000
Book: Chagall; by Jacques Lassaigne, ed of 6000, 1957, Maeght, lot 162, SBY 2/25/88 ... 1,430
Book: Cirque, Lithographies Originales de Marc Chagall; 38 litho w/text on Arches, 1967, Teriade, lot 115, C-NY 5/11/88 ... 198,000
Book: Dessins pour la Bible; French ed, 24 clr litho/96 blk & wht repro, 1960, Verve, SBY 5/12/88 ... 2,970
Book: Dessins pour la Bible; 25 clr litho/23 blk litho/96 repro, 1960, orig boards, lot 130, C-NY 5/11/88 ... 3,300
Book: Drawings for the Bible; English ed, 1960, orig dust jacket, Verve, lot 164, SBY 2/25/88 ... 3,190
Book: Drawings for the Bible; English ed, 1960, Verve, lot 219, SBY 2/23/89 ... 3,850
Book: Drawings for the Bible; English ed, 24 clr litho/96 blk & wht repro, 1960, Harcourt Brace/Verve, SBY 5/12/88 OE ... 3,850
Book: Drawings for the Bible; 37/38, English ed, 1960, Harcourt Brace/Verve, lot 179, SBY 11/3/88 ... 4,125
Book: Illustrations for the Bible; English ed, 1956, Harcourt Brace, lot 218, SBY 2/23/89 ... 3,960
Book: Illustrations for the Bible; English ed, 1956, Harcourt Brace/Verve, lot 178, SBY 11/3/88 OE ... 4,950
Book: Illustrations for the Bible; 16 clr litho/12 blk litho/105 repro etch, 1956, Verve/Harcourt Brace, SBY 5/12/88 OE ... 4,950
Book: Illustrations for the Bible; 18 clr litho/12 blk litho/105 repro, 1956, Verve, orig boards, lot 129, C-NY 5/11/88 ... 4,180
Book: Illustrations for the Bible; 1956, English ed, Harcourt Brace, lot 160, SBY 2/25/89 OE ... 4,125
Book: Les Sept Peches Capitaux; 57/300, 31 etch w/text, 1926, stn/broken binding, orig wrappers, lot 94, C-NY 5/11/88 OE ... 8,800
Book: Lettre a Marc Chagall; by Jersy Ficowski, XV, 1969, gray wrapper/slipcase, 11x8", Maeght, lot 177, SBY 2/23/89 OE ... 2,530
Book: Lithographs of Chagall, Vol I-IV; English ed, 1962, 1963, 1969, 1974, orig wrappers, Sauret, lot 221, SBY 2/23/89 ... 4,675
Book: Lithographs of Chagall, Vol I-IV; 1962, 1963, 1969, 1974, orig wrappers, Sauret, lot 170, SBY 2/25/88 ... 4,125
Book: Lithographs of Chagall, Vol II; 1963, Sauret, lot 172, SBY 2/25/88 OE ... 1,210
Book: Lithographs of Chagall Vol I & II; 17 clr litho/7 blk litho, 1960-63, Mourlot, lot 131, C-NY 5/11/88 OE ... 2,860
Book: Lithographs of Chagall Vol II; lithos w/text, 1963, German ed Mourlot, lot 577, C-NY 5/10/89 UE ... 880
Book: Marc Chagall: Life & Work; by Franz Meyer, 28/100, deluxe/English ed, 1961, red portfolio, Abrams, SBY 5/12/88 ... 2,200
Book: Psaumes de David; XV, 30 etch w/text, 1979, p/s, orig wrappers, S-11x9", Cramer, lot 415, SBY 5/11/89 OE ... 9,900
Book: Story of the Exodus; 159/250, litho/Arches, 1966, p/s, full mrgs, lt stn/cr, Amiel, lot 543, C-NY 5/10/89 ... 26,400

Book: The Bible (complete 2 vol set); 1931-39/1956, sgn on justification, S-17x13", Teriade, lot 358, SBY 5/11/89	52,250
Book: Troyer (Mourning); by David Hofstein, 8 line block w/text on glazed wove paper, 1922, lot 93, C-NY 5/11/88 OE	16,500
Bouquet Over the Town, 15/50, clr litho, 1983, p/s, full mrgs, lt sl/cr mrgs, 19x13", lot 426, SBY 5/11/89	3,850
Cain & Abel, 33/50, aside from ed Drawings for the Bible, clr litho, 1960, p/s, full mrgs, L-14x11", SBY 5/12/88	2,475
Captain Bryaxis's Dream, a/p, clr litho, 1961, p/s, inscr Pour Georges, lt sl/stn, 17x25", lot 376, SBY 5/11/89	11,000
Captain Bryaxis's Dream, from book ed of 250, clr litho, 1961, unfr, L-167x25", SBY 5/12/88 OE	3,575
Captain Bryaxis's Dream, 29/60, aside from book ed of 250, clr litho, 1961, p/s, full mrgs, unfr, L-17x25", SBY 5/12/88	9,900
Captain Bryaxis's Dream, 38/60, clr litho, 1961, p/s, full mrgs, lt stn, 13x25", lot 150, SBY 2/23/89 OE	7,700
Celebration, 11/50, clr litho, 1982, p/s, full mrgs, 12x21", lot 420, SBY 5/11/89 OE	6,050
Chagall Lithographs Vol III: Cover; 52/75, orange/blk litho, 1969, p/s, full mrgs, 13x10", lot 175, SBY 2/23/89	3,575
Chasing the Bluebird, 43/75, clr litho, 1969, p/s, full mrgs, 24x21", lot 138, SBY 2/25/88	30,800
Chasing the Bluebird, 53/75, clr litho, 1969, p/s, full mrgs, lt lstn/sl, 24x20", lot 176, SBY 2/23/89	34,100
Chloe, unsgn ed of 250, clr litho/wove paper, 1961, lt tstn, S-17x13", Verve, lot 255, C-NY 11/1/88 OE	10,450
Chloe, 20/60, clr litho, 1961, p/s, full mrgs, lt stn, 16x13", lot 383, SBY 5/11/89	30,800
Chloe, 29/60, clr litho/Arches, 1961, p/s, full mrgs, lt stn, lt scr verso, L-17x13", lot 109, C-NY 5/11/88	26,400
Chloe Is Carried Off by the Methymneans, 22/60, litho/Arches, 1961, p/s, full mrgs, lt stn, L-17x26", C-NY 5/11/88 OE	28,600
Chloe Is Carried Off by the Methymneans, 35/60, aside from book ed of 250, litho, 1961, unfr, L-17x25", SBY 5/12/88	27,500
Chloe Is Dressed & Braided by Cleariste, a/p, clr litho, 1961, full mrgs, 17x13", lot 160, SBY 2/23/89	28,600
Chloe Is Dressed & Braided by Cleariste, book ed of 250, clr litho, 1961, lt scr/stn, 17x13", lot 161, SBY 2/23/89 OE	6,600
Chloe Is Dressed & Braided by Cleariste, from book ed of 250, litho, 1961, unfr, S-17x13", SBY 5/12/88 OE	7,150
Chloe Is Dressed & Braided by Cleariste, 22/60, clr litho, 1961, p/s, full mrgs, lt stn, 17x13", lot 130, SBY 11/3/88	24,750
Chloe Is Dressed & Braided by Cleariste, 60/60, aside from book ed of 250, litho, 1961, unfr, L-17x13", SBY 5/12/88 OE	29,700
Chloe's Judgement, book ed of 250, clr litho, 1961, S-17x25", lot 372, SBY 5/11/89	9,900
Chloe's Kiss, book ed of 250, clr litho, 1961, lt stn, S-17x13", lot 142, SBY 2/23/89	6,600
Chloe's Kiss; book ed of 250, clr litho, 1961, S-17x13", lot 127, SBY 2/25/88	7,150
Circus, book ed of 250, clr litho, 1967, S-17x13", lot 394, SBY 5/11/89	2,750
Circus, book ed of 250, clr litho, 1967, S-17x13", lot 395, SBY 5/11/89	1,925
Circus, book ed of 250, clr litho, 1967, unfr, S-17x13", Verve, SBY 5/12/87	3,300
Circus, 10/24, clr litho, 1967, p/s, full mrgs, lt scr, 17x13", lot 398, SBY 5/11/89	35,750
Circus, 10/24, clr litho, 1967, p/s, full mrgs, 17x13", lot 140, SBY 11/3/88	46,750
Circus, 13/24, clr litho, 1967, p/s, full mrgs, 17x13", lot 399, SBY 5/11/89	41,250
Circus, 18/24, clr litho, 1967, p/s, full mrgs, lt lstn, 17x13", Verve, lot 393, SBY 5/11/89	34,100
Circus, 23/24, clr litho, 1967, p/s, full mrgs, 17x13", Verve, lot 141, SBY 11/3/88	44,000
Circus Girl (La Fille de Cirque), litho, 13x9", lot 304, FB 5/28/89	120
Circus Girl Rider, 10/50, clr litho, 1964, p/s, full mrgs, lt stn, 25x21", lot 137, SBY 11/3/88	18,150
Circus with the Angel, APXIV/XXV, clr litho, 1968, p/s, full mrgs, lt stn, 24x20", lot 148, SBY 11/3/88 OE	34,100
Circus with the Yellow Clown, 125/150, clr litho, 1967, p/s, full mrgs, lt lstn/cr/sl, unfr, L-27x20", SBY 5/12/88	7,150
Circus: Frontispiece; 12/24, aside from book ed of 250, litho, 1967, p/s, full mrgs, lt lstn, L-16x13", SBY 5/12/88 OE	57,750

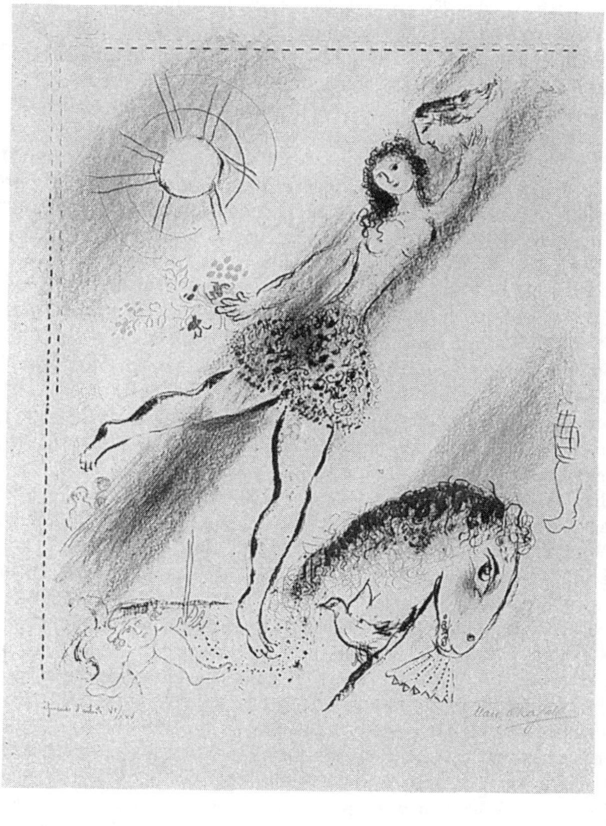

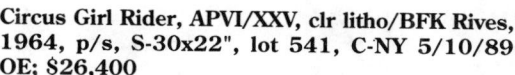

Circus Girl Rider, APVI/XXV, clr litho/BFK Rives, 1964, p/s, S-30x22", lot 541, C-NY 5/10/89 OE; $26,400

Clown in Love, 22/40, litho, 1963, p/s, large mrgs, lt stn/old hinges/fox, 13x10", lot 167, SBY 2/23/89	1,760
Come Muses, Sing This Rural Song...; 41/75, clr litho, 1967, p/s, full mrgs, lt stn, 18x14", lot 401, SBY 5/11/89	7,700
Come Muses, Sing This Rural Song...; 64/75, clr litho, 1967, p/s, full mrgs, lt stn/cr, unfr, L-8x14", SBY 5/12/88	7,150
Come Muses, Sing This...; Pl 7, 66/75, clr litho/Arches, p/s, lt stn/scr, L-18x15", Mazo, lot 549, C-NY 5/10/89	12,100
Conversation, 282/335, pl/s, 11x9", lot 348, LH 5/15/88	550
Coq et la Perle, Pl 11, ed of 100, etch/Verge de Montval, 1927-30, p/s, full mrgs, lt stn/scr, P-12x9", C-NY 5/10/89	1,100
Couple Against Black Background, 15/50, clr litho/Arches, 1973, p/s, lt stn, L-13x10", lot 123, C-NY 5/11/88	2,860
Couple in Ocher, 15/100, clr litho/Arches, 1959, p/s, lt scr/sl/stn, 25x20", lot 108, SBY 11/3/88	4,950
Couple in Ocher, 62/100, clr litho/Arches, 1952, p/s, lt stn/fox/cr mrgs, lt stn verso, L-25x20", lot 244, C-NY 11/1/88	5,500
Couple in Ochre, 15/100, clr litho/Arches, 1959, p/s, lt scr/sl/stn/cr, L-25x20", SBY 5/12/88	4,400
Creation, clr litho, 9x12", lot 140, MG 5/28/88	110
Daphnis & Chloe, Frontispiece; 12/60, clr litho/Arches, 1961, p/s, full mrgs, lt stn, L-17x13", lot 106, C-NY 5/11/88 OE	30,800
Daphnis & Chloe, 38/75, clr litho/Arches, 1959, p/s, full mrgs, lt stn, L-12x8", lot 248, C-NY 11/1/88	3,850
Daphnis & Chloe Beside the Fountain, book ed of 250, clr litho, S-17x13", lot 141, SBY 2/23/89	6,875
Daphnis & Chloe Beside the Fountain, book ed of 250, clr litho, 1961, lt stn, S-17x13", lot 371, SBY 5/11/89	5,500
Daphnis & Chloe Beside the Fountain, from book ed of 250, litho, 1961, S-17x13", SBY 5/12/88	6,050
Daphnis & Chloe Beside the Fountain; aside from book ed, clr litho, 1961, sgn, S-17x13", lot 115, SBY 11/3/88	6,600
Daphnis & Chloe: Daphnis Discovers Chloe; book ed of 250, clr litho, 1961, S-17x13", lot 126, SBY 2/25/88	4,950
Daphnis & Chloe: Frontispiece; from book ed of 250, clr litho, 1961, S-17x13", lot 124, SBY 2/25/88	8,250
Daphnis & Chloe: Lamon Discovers Daphnis; from book ed of 250, clr litho, 1961, S-17x13", lot 125, SBY 2/25/89 OE	8,800
Daphnis & Chloe: The Meal at Dryas's House; book ed of 250, clr litho, 1961, S-17x25", lot 130, SBY 2/25/88	7,150
Daphnis & Chloe: The Orchard; book ed of 250, clr litho, 1961, S-17x25", lot 132, SBY 2/25/88	13,200
Daphnis & Chloe: The Wolf Pit; a/p, clr litho, 1961, S-17x13", Teriade, lot 114, SBY 11/3/88	5,225
Daphnis & Chloe: The Wolf Pit; 55/60, clr litho, 1961, p/s, full mrgs, lt stn/old tp hinge, 17x13", lot 113, SBY 11/3/88	17,600
Daphnis & Chloe: The Wolf Pit; 55/60, clr litho, 1961, p/s, full mrgs, lt stn, 17x13", lot 129, SBY 2/25/88	25,300
Daphnis & Chloe: Winter; 55/60, clr litho, 1961, p/s, full mrgs, lt stn, 17x13", lot 129, SBY 11/3/88	19,800
Daphnis & Gnathon, a/p, clr litho, 1972, p/s, inscr Pour Georges, full mrgs, 17x13", lot 129, SBY 11/3/88	6,600
Daphnis & Gnathon, book ed of 250, clr litho, 1961, lt stn mrgs, S-17x13", lot 159, SBY 2/23/89 OE	6,600
Daphnis & Lycenion, from book ed of 250, clr litho, 1961, S-17x13", SBY 5/12/88	23,100
Daphnis & Lycenion, 29/60, clr litho, 1961, p/s, full mrgs, lt lstn/mstn mrgs, disclr verso, L-17x13", SBY 5/12/88	18,700
Daphnis Discovers Chloe, 20/60, aside from book ed, clr litho, 1961, full mrgs, lt stn, tp verso, L-17x13", SBY 5/12/87	23,100
Daphnis Discovers Chloe, 29/60, clr litho, 1961, p/s, full mrgs, lt mstn/cr/rub, disclr verso, L-17x13", SBY 5/12/88	6,050
Daphnis's Dream & the Nymphs, from book ed of 250, litho, 1961, S-17x13", SBY 5/12/88	30,800
Daphnis's Dream & the Nymphs, 20/60, aside from book ed of 250, litho, 1961, lt stn, L-17x13", SBY 5/12/88	24,200
Daphnis's Dream & the Nymphs, 29/60, clr litho, 1961, p/s, full mrgs, lt lstn/mstn, L-17x13", SBY 5/12/88	2,420
David (Verso of Pl 133), 66/75, litho, 1956, inscr To Tony Curtis, full mrgs, lt stn/fox, 14x9", lot 357, SBY 5/11/89 OE	4,180
David & Bathsheba, 42/50, clr litho/Japan nacre, 1979, p/s, full mrgs, Mourlot bstp, L-14x12", lot 566, C-NY 5/10/89	3,300
David & Bathsheba, 5/50, clr litho/Japan nacre, 1979, p/s, full mrgs, lt mstn, unfr, L-14x12", SBY 5/12/88	4,620
David Saved by Michal, 12/50, clr litho/Arches, 1960, p/s, full mrgs, lt stn/sl, L-14x11", lot 249, C-NY 11/1/88 OE	7,700
Death of Dorcon, a/p, clr litho, 1961, S-17x25", Teriade, lot 118, SBY 11/3/88	5,775
Death of Dorcon, book ed of 250, clr litho, 1961, lt skinned/stn, S-17x25", lot 144, SBY 2/23/89 OE	8,250
Death of Dorcon, from book ed of 250, clr litho, 1961, lt fox verso, S-17x25", SBY 5/12/88	22,000
Dedication, a/p, clr litho, 1968, p/s, full mrgs, lt fox mrgs, lt stn, 18x16", lot 172, SBY 2/23/89	20,900
Dedication, 44/50, clr litho, 1968, p/s, full mrgs, lt stn/fox, 18x16", lot 151, SBY 11/3/88 OE	3,850
Der Automobilist, Mein Legen; I/2, unrecorded proof before ed, etch/drypt, 1922, lt cr, P-8x7", lot 235, C-NY 11/1/88 OE	11,000
Der Esel Uber dem Dorf, ed of 40, etch/aqua/wove paper, 1951-52, p/s, rpr tr/stn, P-11x8", lot 525, C-NY 5/10/89	11,000
Der Esel Uber dem Dorf, ed of 40, hc etch/aqua, 1951-52, p/s, full mrgs, lt stn, 11x8", lot 103, SBY 11/3/88	4,950
Der Mann mit dem Regenschrim, 45/50, aqua/etch/Auvergne, 1926-27/1963, p/s, unfr, 14x12", Haasen, SBY 5/12/88	4,400
Der Mann mit dem Regenschirm, 20/50, etch/Richard de Bas, 1926-27/1963, full mrgs, lt stn, 15x12", lot 96, C-NY 5/11/88	7,150
Der Musiker, 9/110, etch/drypt/Japan, 1922, full mrgs, lt mstn/cr, P-11x9", lot 515, C-NY 5/10/89 OE	4,950
Der Rabbi, Pl 21, 37/110, etch/drypt/wm JW Zanders, 1922, full mrgs, tp to overmat, P-10x7", lot 234, C-NY 11/1/88 OE	6,325
Der Talmudlehrer, 68/110, etch/drypt, 1922, p/s, full mrgs, lt stn/fox, 10x7", Cassirer, lot 351, SBY 5/11/89 OE	12,100
Die Erscheinung, I; 14/100, hc etch/aqua/Arches, 1924-25, p/s, lt stn/fox, 15x11", lot 125, SBY 2/23/89 OE	31,900
Disrobing Her with His Own Hand, 4, 81/90, clr litho, 1949, lt faded/cr, L-15x11", Pantheon Books, SBY 5/12/88	17,600
Dorcon's Strategy, a/p, clr litho, 1961, sgn/inscr Pour Georges, full mrgs, 17x13", lot 116, SBY 11/3/88	4,180
Dorcon's Strategy, unsgn ed of 250, clr litho/wove paper, 1961, lt stn/tp, S-17x13", lot 252, C-NY 11/1/88	16,500
Dorcon's Strategy, 40/60, clr litho/Arches, 1961, p/s, full mrgs, lt stn, L-17x13", lot 535, C-NY 5/10/89	8,350
Double Portrait at the Easel, X/XV, clr litho/Japan nacre, 1976, p/s, full mrgs, scr/stn, 13x10", lot 159, SBY 11/3/88	7,700
Double Portrait at the Easel, 47/50, clr litho, 1976, p/s, full mrgs, L-13x11", SBY 5/12/88	11,550
Echo, Daphnis & Chloe; a/p, clr litho, 1961, lt scr, S-17x25", Teriade, lot 384, SBY 5/11/89 OE	9,900
Echo, from book ed of 250, clr litho, 1961, lt scuff img, unfr, S-17x25", SBY 5/12/88 OE	41,250
Echo, 52/60, clr litho, 1961, p/s, full mrgs, lt sl/cr/stn, 17x25", lot 127, SBY 11/3/88	1,870
Elie, du Haut du Mont Carmel...; Pl 86, 84/100, hc etch, 1931-39/1956, intl, 11x10", Teriade, lot 130, SBY 2/23/89 OE	7,700
Engagement at the Circus, 48/50, clr litho, 1983, p/s, full mrgs, 18x14", lot 168, SBY 11/3/88	5,775
Esther, 8/50, clr litho/Japan nacre, 1979, p/s, full mrgs, lt rub in mrg, 15x13", lot 413, SBY 5/11/89 OE	3,575
Eve Incurs God's Displeasure, 33/50, aside from ed Drawings for the Bible, litho, 1960, full mrgs, L-14x11", SBY 5/12/88	14,300
Exhibition Poster, 87/150, clr litho/Arches, 1967, p/s, tstn/cr mrg, stn verso, L-25x19", lot 261, C-NY 11/1/88 OE	2,200
Fable, 16/90, clr litho/heavy wove paper, p/s, trm mrgs, 10x9", lot 2833A, B/B 4/19/88 OE	7,150
Familiar Dream, 43/50, clr litho, 1969, p/s, full mrgs, lt sl/disclr/cr mrgs, L-15x20", SBY 5/12/88	7,700
Family with Cock, 41/50, clr litho, 1969, p/s, full mrgs, lt lstn, L-24x16", SBY 5/12/88	7,700
Fantastic Composition (Definitive Version), 34/50, litho/Arches, 1976, p/s, full mrgs, lt stn, L-25x19", C-NY 5/10/89 OE	7,700
Fantastic Village, 9/50, ochre/olive-gr/blk litho, 1965, p/s, full mrgs, lt stn/rub, 26x20", lot 170, SBY 2/23/89 OE	8,250

Flowers in Front of a Window, 28/50, clr litho, 1967, p/s, full mrgs, lt cr/stn, 18x17", lot 171, SBY 2/23/89 6,600
Flowers in Front of a Window, 6/50, clr litho, 1967, p/s, 1 trm mrg, L-18x17", SBY 5/12/88 8,250
Flute Player, book ed of 6000, clr litho, 9x15", lot 1160, LH 10/16/88 225
Flute Player, for Jacques Lassaigne; 24/90, litho/Arches, 1957, full mrgs, L-10x17", Maeght, lot 103, C-NY 5/11/88 OE 7,700
For a Woman, What Remains?...; Pl 6, 5/75, total ed of 120, litho/Arches, full mrgs, lt stn, L-18x15", C-NY 5/11/88 6,600
For Berggruen, 20/75, clr litho/wove paper, 1965, p/s, full mrgs, mstn/cr, L-12x8", C-NY 11/1/88 4,620
Four Seasons, ed of 5000, clr litho w/letters, 1974, inscr w/artist name, lt cr, 36x24", lot 158, SBY 11/3/88 2,200
Four Seasons, ed of 5000, clr litho/poster paper, 1974, full mrgs, S-37x25", lot 185, SBY 2/23/89 UE 1,430
Four Tales From the Arabian Nights Frontispiece; Pl 1, 35/90, litho, 1949, 15x11", Pantheon, lot 363, SBY 5/11/89 OE 55,000
Galerie Maeght Poster, a/p, clr litho before text, 1962, p/s, full mrgs, lt cr/sl, 27x20", lot 134, SBY 11/3/88 5,500
Garden of Eden, 50/50, clr litho/Japan nacre, 1974, p/s, full mrgs, lt scr/glue, 10x13", lot 141, SBY 2/25/88 OE 6,600
Golden Age, XXII/XXV, clr litho/Japan nacre, 1968, p/s, full mrgs, lt cr, 23x19", lot 402, SBY 5/11/89 40,700
Golden Age, 13/25, clr litho/Imperial Japan, 1968, p/s, full mrgs, lt stn/cr/tp, L-23x19", lot 120, C-NY 5/11/88 35,200
Granada, 38/50, clr etch/aqua/Auvergne, 1962, p/s, full mrgs, lt stn, 13x9", lot 389, SBY 5/11/89 OE 8,250
Green Acrobat, 31/50, clr litho/Arches, 1979, p/s, full mrgs, L-13x9", lot 126, C-NY 5/11/88 7,700
Green Branch, 7/50, clr litho/Arches, 1984, p/s, full mrgs, l-24x19", lot 575, C-NY 5/10/89 OE 9,900
Hagar in the Desert, 33/50, aside from ed Drawings for the Bible, litho, 1960, p/s, full mrgs, L-14x11", SBY 5/12/88 2,475
Half-Opened Window, 35/50, clr litho/Japan nacre, 1975, p/s, full mrgs, lt stn, 15x11", lot 143, SBY 2/25/88 OE 6,600
Happiness, 12/75, clr litho/Arches, 1969, p/s, full mrgs, lt disclr/stn, L-22x15", SBY 5/12/88 6,600
Happiness, 2/75, clr litho, 1969, p/s, full mrgs, 22x15", lot 174, SBY 2/23/89 OE 7,700
Happiness, 4/75, clr litho, 1969, p/s, full mrgs, lt stn/cr, 22x15", lot 136, SBY 2/25/88 7,700
Happiness, 57/75, clr litho, 1969, p/s, full mrgs, lt stn, 22x15", lot 152, SBY 11/3/88 5,500
Haus des Grossvaters, Pl 12, 102/110, etch/drypt, 1922, lg mrgs, lt fox, 8x6", Cassirer, lot 352, SBY 5/11/89 OE 6,875
He Went Up to the Couch & Found a Young Lady Asleep...; Pl 11, 28/90, 1949, p/s, 15x11", Pantheon, lot 107, SBY 11/3/88 30,250
Hymen, a/p, clr litho, 1961, S-17x25", Teriade, lot 388, SBY 5/11/89 7,700
Hymen, from book ed of 250, litho, unfr, S-17x25", SBY 5/12/88 8,800
Ile Saint-Louis, 28/75, clr litho, 1959, p/s, full mrgs, lt stn/cr/scr, unfr, L-20x26", SBY 5/12/88 UE 14,300
In Front of the Picture, 23/40, litho, 1963, p/s, lg mrgs, lt stn/tp hinges/fox, 12x9", lot 168, SBY 2/23/89 1,760
In the Sky of the Opera, 16/50, clr litho, 1980, p/s, full mrgs, lt cr/disclr mrgs, stn verso, L-38x24", SBY 5/12/88 23,100
Inspiration, 27/50, litho, 1976, p/s, lt cr, tp to mat, 29x21", Maeght, lot 145, SBY 2/25/88 OE 4,675
Interior, 41/50, clr litho, 1978, p/s, full mrgs, lt mstn, 13x10", lot 160, SBY 11/3/88 OE 8,250
Island of Poros, 20/50, clr litho, 1980, p/s, Mourlot bstp, full mrgs, 17x14", lot 416, SBY 5/11/89 OE 12,100
Island of Poros, 25/50, clr litho, 1980, p/s, Mourlot bstp, full mrgs, lt mstn, 18x14", lot 417, SBY 5/11/89 12,100
Jacob Wrestles with the Angel, 34/50, clr litho, 1972, p/s, full mrgs, lt stn/cr, 13x10", lot 180, SBY 2/23/89 OE 4,400
Jacob's Dream, 33/50, clr litho/Arches, 1977, p/s, lt stn mrgs, fld corner, L-17x13", lot 270, C-NY 11/1/88 OE 6,380
Jacob's Vision, 36/50, clr litho/Arches, 1971, full mrgs, lt stn, L-30x21", lot 556, C-NY 5/10/89 6,600
Jeremie Jete dans la Fosse, Pl 102, 58/100, etch, 1931-39/1956, intl, full mrgs, lt stn, 13x11", lot 119, SBY 2/25/88 OE 1,980
Job Praying, 13/50, clr litho/Arches, 1960, p/s, full mrgs, lt lstn/mstn/scratches, L-14x11", C-NY 1/22/88 OE 3,300
Jonah I, 34/50, clr litho, 1972, p/s, full mrgs, lt lstn/sl mrgs & verso, lt cr, L-14x10", SBY 5/12/88 3,300
Jonah II, 6/50, clr litho/Arches, 1972, p/s, lt lstn, fld mrg, L-13x10", lot 267, C-NY 11/1/88 1,870
Joshua Closes the Book of the Law, Pl 47, 53/100, etch, 1930-55, p/s, P-12x9", lot 523, C-NY 5/10/89 2,200
Joy of Life, 10/50, clr litho/Arches, 1967, p/s, lt stn/cr/fld/stn, L-15x22", lot 547, C-NY 5/10/89 OE 7,700
King David, 76/150, clr litho/Arches, 1973, p/s, full mrgs, lt stn, S-12x10", Musee Nationaux, lot 181, SBY 2/23/89 OE 2,970
King David with His Lyre, 44/50, clr litho/Japan nacre, 1979, p/s, full mrgs, lt cr, L-14x10", lot 564, C-NY 5/10/89 4,180
L'Echelle de Jacob, Pl 14, 79/100, hc etch, 1931-39/1956, intl, full mrgs, 12x10", Teriade, lot 127, SBY 2/23/89 1,870
La Bouquet a la Main, 50/90, blk/wht litho, 1957, p/s, titled, 20x24", lot 366, GAI 3/3/89 1,125
La Paix du Soir, Pl 6, 31/50, clr etch/wove paper, p/s, full mrgs, P-12x9", lot 569, C-NY 5/10/89 3,520
Lamon Discovers Daphnis, 44/60, clr litho/Arches, 1961, p/s, full mrgs, lt stn, L-17x13", lot 107, C-NY 5/11/88 28,600
Lamon's & Dryas's Dream, 34/60, aside from book ed, litho, 1961, p/s, full mrgs, lt stn, L-17x25", SBY 5/12/88 19,800
Landscape with Rooster, 26/100, clr litho/Arches, 1958, p/s, full mrgs, lt stn, L-15x22", lot 104, C-NY 5/11/88 8,250
Large Bouquet, 10/50, clr litho/BFK Rives, 1963, p/s, full mrgs, lt stn/cr, L-26x20", lot 257, C-NY 11/1/88 49,500
Large Bouquet, 48/50, clr litho, 1963, p/s, full mrgs, lt cr/stn/scr, 27x20", lot 133, SBY 2/25/88 46,750
Large Self-Portrait in Black, 28/50, litho/Arches, 1975, p/s, full mrgs, lt stn/cr/sl, L-25x19", lot 560, C-NY 5/10/89 2,750
Le Ciel des Amoreux, 1/40, clr litho, 1958, sgn, 13x10", lot 363, LH 10/16/88 950
Le Cordonnier, Pl 79, #79, ed of 100, etch, 1927-30, p/s, lt mstn, rpr tr in mrg, P-12x10", lot 98, C-NY 5/11/88 825
Le Geai Pare des Plumes du Paon, Pl 43, ed of 100, etch/Verge de Montval, 1927-30, p/s, P-12x9", lot 237, C-NY 11/1/88 550
Le Jeu des Arlequins, a/p, total ed of 50, clr litho/Arches, lt stn recto/verso, L-16x14", lot 60, RWS 9/8/89 1,100
Le Peintre, Pl 11, 31/50, clr etch/wove paper, 1981, p/s, full mrgs, P-12x9", lot 570, C-NY 5/10/89 3,300
Le Repas, Pl 4, 20/50, hc etch, 1981, p/s, full mrgs, 12x9", Cramer, lot 192, SBY 2/23/89 4,125
Le Retour de l'Enfant Prodigne, Pl 3, 31/50, hc etch, 1981, p/s, full mrgs, 12x10", Cramer, lot 427, SBY 5/11/89 3,850
Le Roi David a la Harpe, 18/30, clr etch/wove paper, 1978-81, p/s, full mrgs, P-13x10", lot 568, C-NY 5/10/89 1,980
Le Roi David a la Harpe, 30/30, clr etch/wove paper, 1978-81, p/s, full mrgs, P-13x10", lot 125, C-NY 5/11/88 2,420
Les Amoureux sous l'Arbre, 18/50, clr aqua/wm Hand & 2 Branches, 1968, p/s, full mrgs, P-17x24", lot 264, C-NY 11/1/88 9,900
Little Harlequins, 49/50, clr litho/Arches, 1962, p/s, lt stn, L-10x12", lot 538, C-NY 5/10/89 OE 5,500
Little Horse, 34/50, clr litho, 1972, p/s, full mrgs, lt lstn, lt sl mrgs, L-13x11", SBY 5/12/88 OE 6,050
Little Peasants I, 38/50, clr litho/Arches, 1968, p/s, full mrgs, lt stn, L-13x13", lot 552, C-NY 5/10/89 6,600
Little Swallow, from book ed of 250, clr litho, 1961, S-17x13", SBY 5/12/88 OE 9,350
Louanges, Pl 2, 35/50, hc etch, 1981, p/s, full mrgs, lt mstn, 12x10", Cramer, lot 191, SBY 2/23/89 3,080
Louanges, Pl 2, 40/50, clr etch/wove paper, 1981, p/s, full mrgs, P-12x9", lot 128, C-NY 5/11/88 4,180
Love Is a God, My Children; AP9/25, clr litho, 1967, p/s, full mrgs, lt stn, 17x13", lot 146, SBY 11/3/88 10,450
Lovers, 11/50, clr litho, 1982, p/s, full mrgs, 15x11", lot 419, lot 419, SBY 5/11/89 3,575

Lovers, 46/50, clr litho, 1982, p/s, full mrgs, 14x11", lot 166, SBY 11/3/88	3,850
Lovers, 8/50, clr litho, 1982, p/s, full mrgs, 14x11", lot 194, SBY 2/23/89 OE	6,710
Magic Flute III, 16/50, clr litho, 1972, p/s, full mrgs, lt lstn, L-17x13", SBY 5/12/88	7,700
Maison a Peskowatik, 55/110, etch/drypt laid paper, 1923, full mrgs, lt stn, 7x9", lot 2837, B/B 2/16/88 OE	2,475
Maternity au Centaur, 57/90, clr litho, 1957, sgn, 9x9", lot 364, LH 10/16/88	1,800
Maternity with Centaur, 84/90, clr litho, 1957, p/s, full mrgs, stn, tp stn verso, unfr, L-9x9", SBY 5/12/88	3,025
Maternity with Centaur, 84/90, clr litho, 1957, p/s, full mrgs, lt stn/cr, 9x9", lot 111, SBY 11/3/88 OE	3,850
Meal at Dryas's House, a/p, clr litho, 1961, S-17x25", Teriade, lot 124, SBY 11/3/88	8,800
Meal at Dryas's House, from book ed of 250, clr litho, 1961, laid down, unfr, L-17x25", SBY 5/12/88 OE	9,350
Meeting of Jacob & Rachael at the Well, Pl 15, 64/100, hc etch, 1956, lt stn, P-12x9", Teriade, lot 238, C-NY 11/1/88 OE	3,080
Megacles Recognizes His Daughter During the Feast, a/p, clr litho, 1961, S-17x25", Teriade, lot 132, SBY 11/3/88	8,800
Megacles Recognizes His Daughter During the Feast, book ed of 250, litho, 1961, stn, S-17x25", lot 163, SBY 2/23/89 OE	15,400
Megacles Recognizes His Daughter During the Feast, book ed of 250, litho, 1961, lt stn, S-17x25", lot 387, SBY 5/11/89	8,250
Megacles Recognizes His Daughter During the Feast, from book ed of 250, litho, 1961, unfr, S-17x25", SBY 5/12/88	9,900
Megacles Recognizes His Daughter During the Feast, 29/60, aside from book ed, litho, 1961, unfr, L-17x25", SBY 5/12/88	36,300
Midsummer Night's Dream, 18/75, yel & blk litho/Arches, 1975, p/s, full mrgs, lt stn, L-32x24", lot 561, C-NY 5/10/89	5,500
Mimosas, 34/50, clr litho/Arches, 1968, p/s, full mrgs, lt stn/cr, L-24x18", lot 551, C-NY 5/10/89	7,700
Mimosas, 4/50, clr litho, 1968, p/s, full mrgs, lt stn, 24x17", lot 149, SBY 11/3/88 OE	12,100
Moise et Aaron Devant Pharaon, Pl 30, 43/100, 1931-39/1956, intl, glued to mat/stn, 12x9", lot 128, SBY 2/23/89 OE	2,530
Monsters of Notre-Dame, HC, clr litho/wove paper, 1954, p/s, full mrgs, lt stn/mstn, L-14x11", lot 529, C-NY 5/10/89 OE	12,100
Moon in the Bouquet, AP3/4, clr litho, 1971, p/s, inscr Pour Georges, full mrgs, lt cr/fox, 21x26", lot 153, SBY 11/3/88	20,900
Moon in the Bouquet, 48/50, clr litho, 1971, p/s, full mrgs, lt stn, 20x26", lot 139, SBY 2/25/88 OE	16,500
Moses, 12/75, clr litho/Arches, 1956, p/s, full sheet, stn in mrg/verso, L-14x10", lot 102, C-NY 5/11/88 OE	3,300
Moses, 2/50, clr litho, 1956, p/s, lt skinned/fox, S-26x17 , lot 135, SBY 2/23/89 OE	4,400
Moses, 22/50, litho/Japan nacre, 1979, p/s, full mrgs, lt rub/old glue, L-21x15", lot 567, C-NY 5/10/89	3,850
Moses & Aaron, 29/50, clr litho/Japan nacre, 1979, p/s, full mrgs, lt cr, 14x12", lot 161, SBY 11/3/88	3,850
Moses & the Tables of the Law, 38/50, clr litho, 1962, p/s, full mrgs, L-26x20", SBY 5/12/88	4,125
Moses with Ten Commandments, 20/50, blk/wht/yel litho, ca 1979, p/s, 19x25", lot 442, GAI 3/3/89	1,700
Moses's Visions, 40/50, clr litho, 1973, p/s, full mrgs, lt lstn/mstn, L-31x25", SBY 5/12/88	6,050
Mother & Child Before Notre Dame, a/p, clr litho, 1952, sgn in pen, lt stn, S-14x11", lot 132, SBY 2/23/89 OE	7,150
Mounting the Ebony Horse He Took Her Up Behind Him, 12, 22/90, litho, 1948, unfr, L-15x11", Pantheon Books, SBY 5/12/88	22,000
Multicolored Bouquet, 1/50, clr litho/Arches, 1975, p/s, full mrgs, lt stn/cr, L-27x22", lot 559, C-NY 5/10/89	30,800
Multiflora, 5/50, clr litho, 1974, p/s, full mrgs, lt sl mrgs/verso, lt cr, 32x24", lot 409, SBY 5/11/89	16,500
Multiflora, 8/50, clr litho, 1974, p/s, full mrgs, lt cr/sl, 31x23", lot 157, SBY 11/3/88	23,100
Musical Clown, HC, clr litho/wove paper, 1957, p/s, full mrgs, lt stn/fox, 26x18", lot 109, SBY 11/3/88	4,180
Musical Clown, 88/150, yel/blk/gray litho, 1957, p/s, full mrgs, lt fox/sl, 26x18", lot 368, SBY 5/11/89	5,500
Musical Clowns, 23/50, clr litho, 1980, p/s, full mrgs, lt stn, 37x24", lot 189, SBY 2/23/89	17,600
Naomi & Her Daughters-in-Law, 13/50, clr litho, 1960, p/s, lt lstn/mstn, L-14x11", SBY 5/12/88 OE	3,850
Near St Jeannet, 5/50, clr litho, 1972, p/s, full mrgs, lt stn, 12x10", lot 179, SBY 2/23/89 OE	8,800
Noon in Summer; a/p, clr litho, 1961, S-17x13", Teriade, lot 117, SBY 11/3/88	6,600
Noon in Summer, from book ed of 250, clr litho, 1961, lt disclr verso, S-17x13", SBY 5/12/88 OE	9,350
Now the King Loved Science & Geometry...; Pl 10, 28/90, litho, 1949, p/s, lt cr, 15x12", Pantheon, lot 106, SBY 11/3/88	35,750
Nude with a Double Face, 10/50, clr litho/Arches, 1983, p/s, full mrgs, lt cr, lt sl, L-16x12", lot 573, C-NY 5/10/89	4,950
Nymphs` Cave, a/p, clr litho, 1961, S-17x25", Teriade, lot 118A, SBY 11/3/88	8,800
Nymphs` Cave, a/p, clr litho, 1961, S-17x25", Teriade, lot 374, SBY 5/11/89 OE	11,550
Nymphs` Cave, book ed of 250, clr litho, 1961, lt cr/stn, S-17x25", lot 145, SBY 2/23/89	9,900
Nymphs` Cave, from book ed of 250, clr litho, 1961, S-17x25", SBY 5/12/88 OE	13,750
Oh Happy Bridegroom, Thou Hast the Marriage Thou Desirest...; 30/75, litho, 1967, p/s, stn, unfr, L-18x14", SBY 5/12/88	20,900
Oh Happy Bridegroom...; Pl 10, a/p, 25/25, litho/Arches, 1967, p/s, full mrgs, lt stn, L-18x14", lot 119, C-NY 5/11/88	30,800
Opera, HC, clr litho/wove paper, 1954, p/s, full mrgs, lt stn, L-15x11", lot 530, C-NY 5/10/89	8,800
Opera, 21/50, clr litho, 1974, p/s, full mrgs, lt stn/cr, 32x24", lot 408, SBY 5/11/89 OE	44,000
Orchard, a/p, clr litho, 1961, lt scr, S-17x25", Teriade, lot 128, SBY 11/3/88 OE	25,400
Orchard, book ed of 250, clr litho, 1961, lt stn/old hinges, S-17x25", lot 157, SBY 2/23/89 OE	16,500
Orchard, unsgn ed of 250, clr litho/wove paper, 1961, full sheet, lt cr, S-17x25", lot 536, C-NY 5/10/89	18,700
Painted Bird, 14/50, clr litho, 1967, p/s, full mrgs, 13x11", SBY 2/25/88	4,125
Painter, 17/50, clr litho/Japan nacre, 1979, p/s, full mrgs, lt cr/stn, 17x12", lot 162, SBY 11/3/88	3,575
Painter at the Eiffel Tower, 40/50, clr litho/Japan nacre, 1979, p/s, full mrgs, 13x10", lot 188, SBY 2/23/89	2,750
Painter at the Eiffel Tower, 46/50, clr litho/Japan nacre, 1979, p/s, full mrgs, L-13x10", SBY 5/12/88	3,850
Painter with Palette, 8/70, clr litho, 1952, p/s, lt fox, L-23x20", SBY 5/12/88 OE	16,500
Painter with Three Bouquets, 11/50, clr litho, 1982, p/s, full mrgs, 13x18", lot 422, SBY 5/11/89	6,600
Painter with Three Bouquets, 15/50, clr litho, 1982, p/s, full mrgs, lt cr, 12x18", lot 196, SBY 2/23/89 OE	8,250
Painter with Three Bouquets, 46/50, clr litho, 1982, p/s, full mrgs, 13x18", lot 167, SBY 11/3/88	5,500
Painter's Bouquet, 56/75, clr litho, 1967, p/s, full mrgs, lt stn, 27x20", lot 392, SBY 5/11/89	20,900
Painter's Dream, 33/50, clr litho/Arches, 1967, p/s, full mrgs, lt cr/tstn, L-29x22", lot 114, C-NY 5/11/88 OE	6,600
Pair of Peasants, 33/50, clr litho/Arches, 1967, p/s, full mrgs, lt stn mrg/verso, L-26x20", lot 113, C-NY 5/11/88 OE	9,350
Pair with Basket of Fruit, 13/50, clr litho, 1967, p/s, full mrgs, lt cr, L-18x17", SBY 5/12/88	7,150
Pair: Abraham et les Trois Anges; Exhortation de Josue; Pl 7 & 50, etch, 1931-39, 12x10"/13x9", lot 359, SBY 5/11/89	3,575
Pair: Chapter Heading; End-piece; ed of 120, litho/Arches, unsgn, full mrgs, sl tstn, s/wrp, C-NY 1/22/88 UE	275
Pair: Ein Alter Jude; Der Mann Mit dem Korb; ed of 110, etch/drypt, 1922 & 1923, 4x4", Cassirer, lot 353, SBY 5/11/89 OE	5,225
Pair: Esther; Rahab & the Spies of Jericho; unsgn ed, clr litho, 1960, 14x10", Verve, lot 334, LH 5/15/88	375
Pair: Le Pot de Terre & Le Pot der Fer; Les Deux Pigeons; Pl 53 & 57, etch, 1952, Teriade, lot 118, SBY 2/25/88 OE	2,310

Pair: Le Repas de la Paque; David et le Lion; Pl 32 & 62, ed of 100, etch, 1931-39/1956, lot 361, SBY 5/11/89	3,575
Pair: Le Sacrifice d'Abraham; Vision d'Ezechiel; Pl 10 & 104, 1931-39, 12x10"/13x10", Teriade, lot 360, SBY 5/11/89	3,575
Pair: Le Soleil et les Grenouilles; Les Obseques de la Lionne; ed of 100, etch, p/s, P-12x10", lot 520, C-NY 5/10/89 OE	1,760
Pair: Sarah & Abimelech; Tamar, Daughter-in-Law of Judah; 33/50, litho, 1960, full mrgs, 14x11", lot 112, SBY 11/3/88 OE	4,950
Pan's Banquet, book ed of 250, clr litho, 1961, S-17x13", lot 153, SBY 2/23/89	6,050
Pan's Banquet, 19/60, clr litho, 1961, p/s, full mrgs, 17x13", lot 122, SBY 11/3/88	19,800
Paradise, 11/50, aside from ed Drawings for the Bible, litho, 1960, p/s, full mrgs, L-15x11", SBY 5/12/88 OE	8,800
Paravant, 57/100, 4 lithos/4-panel fld screen, 1963, sgn, orig oak fr, 58x75" overall, Cramer, lot 136, SBY 11/3/88	82,500
Paravant, 88/100, 4 litho varnished/mounted on 4-panel fld screen, lt stn, 57x75", Galerie Cramer, SBY 5/12/88	66,000
Paris on Holiday, 11/50, clr litho, 1982, p/s, full mrgs, 16x21", lot 421, SBY 5/11/89	4,125
Paris on Holiday, 8/50, clr litho, 1982, p/s, full mrgs, 15x21", lot 195, SBY 2/23/89	6,050
Paris Square, 14/75, clr litho, 1969, p/s, full mrgs, lt stn, 21x15", lot 405, SBY 5/11/89 OE	11,000
Pastoral, 46/50, clr litho, 1977, p/s, full mrgs, lt stn/tr, 16x23", lot 146, SBY 2/25/88 OE	17,600
Pastoral, 49/50, clr litho/Arches, 1971, p/s, lstn, old hinges on verso, S-17x19", lot 266, C-NY 11/1/88	3,850
Paysage aux Isbas for Jacques Lassaigne, 85/90, clr litho/Arches, 1957, lt stn, S-19x25", lot 246, C-NY 11/1/88	2,860
People of Israel Go Out of the Land of Egypt, Pl 33, 66/100, etch/Arches, 1930-55, P-10x13", lot 241, C-NY 11/1/88 OE	3,080
Philetas's Lesson, book ed of 250, clr litho, 1961, old hinge/stn verso, 17x13", lot 147, SBY 2/23/89 OE	7,700
Philetas's Lesson, book ed of 250, clr litho, 1961, S-17x13", lot 375, SBY 5/11/89	7,700
Philetas's Orchard, book ed of 250, clr litho, 1961, lt cr/old hinges, S-17x25", lot 149, SBY 2/23/89 OE	11,550
Philetas's Orchard, unsgn ed of 250, clr litho/wove paper, 1961, full sheet, S-17x25", Verve, lot 253, C-NY 11/1/88 OE	9,900
Philetas's Orchard, 38/60, clr litho, 1960, p/s, full mrgs, lt stn, 17x25", lot 120, SBY 11/3/88	38,500
Portfolio: Les Quinze Dernieres Lithographies de Marc Chagall; 32/50, 15 litho, 1984-84, S-25x19", lot 428, SBY 5/11/89	74,800
Portfolio: Shakespeare's The Tempest; 42/250, 50 litho, 1975, orig wrappers/box, S-17x13", Sauret, lot 412, SBY 5/11/89	5,500
Priere de Salomon, Pl 79, 40/100, hc etch, 1931-39, intl, full mrgs, lt stn/sl, 12x10", lot 102, SBY 11/3/88	2,200
Prophet & the Angel, 32/50, clr litho/Japan nacre, 1979, p/s, full mrgs, lt cr mrgs, 15x13", lot 163, SBY 11/3/88	3,850
Prophet Elijah, 2/30, litho/Japan nacre, 1970, p/s, full mrgs, L-13x10", lot 555, C-NY 5/10/89	2,090
Purple Bodice, a/p, clr litho, 1973, p/s, full mrgs, lt rub, 25x18", lot 407, SBY 5/11/89	22,000
Purple Bodice, AP4/4, clr litho, 1973, p/s, inscr Pour Georges, full mrgs, 25x18", lot 155, SBY 11/3/88	27,500
Quai de Bercy, a/p, apart from ed of 75, clr litho, 1954, p/s, full mrgs, lt stn/scr, S-15x18", lot 100, C-NY 5/11/88 OE	26,400
Quai de Bercy, a/p, clr litho, 1954, p/s, lt cr edge, lt skinned corners/verso, S-15x18", SBY 5/12/88	23,100
Quai des Celestins, 11/50, clr litho, 1975, p/s, full mrgs, 25x19", lot 186, SBY 2/23/89 OE	24,200

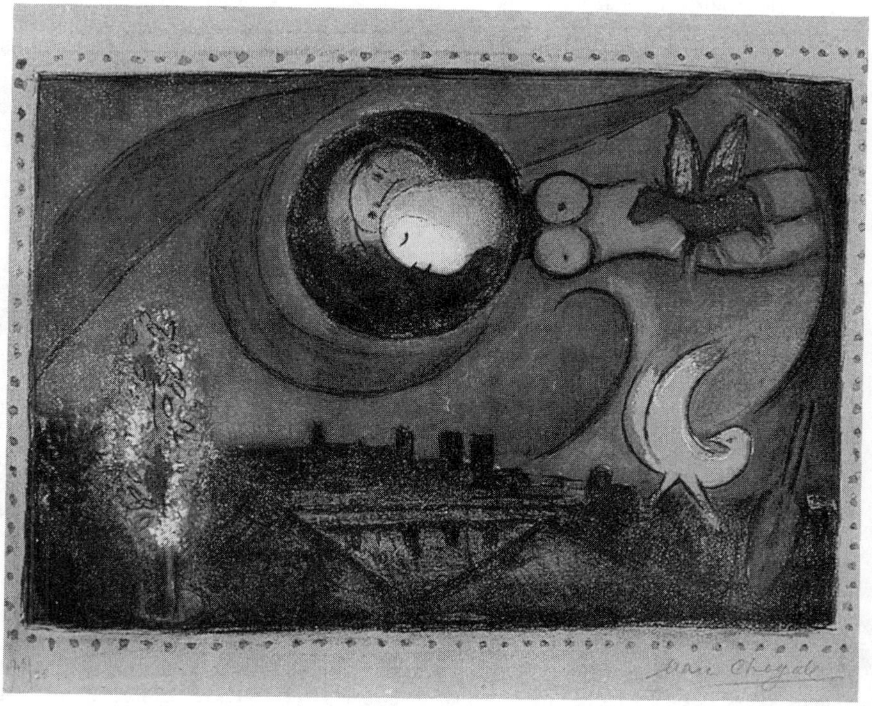

Quai de Bercy, 45/75, clr litho/wove paper, 1954, p/s, full sheet, lt stn/old tp, L-15x18", lot 527, C-NY 5/10/89 OE; $37,400

Rahab & the Spies of Jericho, 33/50, aside from ed Drawings for the Bible, litho, 1960, p/s, L-14x11", SBY 5/12/88	2,475
Rainbow, 23/75, clr litho, 1969, p/s, full mrgs, lt disclr mrgs/verso, lt sl/skinned verso, L-27x27", SBY 5/12/88 OE	35,200
Rebecca at the Well, 34/50, clr litho, 1972, p/s, full mrgs, lt lstn, lt sl verso, unfr, L-14x11", SBY 5/12/88 OE	4,400
Recontre de Moise et d'Aaron, 57/100, hc etch, intl, wide mrgs, P-11x9", lot 48, PHL 6/16/88	2,000
Red Acrobat, 21/50, clr litho, 1974, p/s, full mrgs, lt mstn/lstn, L-27x21", SBY 5/12/88	16,500
Red Circle, a/p, XIV/XXV, clr litho, 1966, p/s, old hinge, 20x25", lot 134, SBY 2/25/88 OE	19,800
Red Circle, 6/50, clr litho, 1966, p/s, full mrgs, lt cr/disclr mrgs, lt stn, unfr, L-19x25", SBY 5/12/88	24,200
Red Maternity, 46/50, clr litho, 1980, p/s, full mrgs, lt tr mrgs, 37x24", lot 190, SBY 2/23/89	23,100
Red Rooster, 2/200, clr litho, 1952, p/s, lt stn, S-15x22", lot 365, SBY 5/11/89	4,950
Rooster with Crescent, 49/90, clr litho, 1957, p/s, full mrgs, lt stn/sl, 8x5", lot 121, SBY 2/25/88	1,760

Sacrifices Made to the Nymphs, book ed of 250, clr litho, 1961, lt stn, S-17x13", lot 152, SBY 2/23/89	3,300
Sacrifices Made to the Nymphs, unsgn ed of 250, clr litho/wove paper, 1961, S-17x13", Verve, lot 254, C-NY 11/1/88	3,850
Samson & Delilah, 11/100, hc etch, 1956, intl, lt stn recto/verso, 11x10", Teriade, lot 47, SWN 6/15/89 OE	2,420
Sarah & Abimelech, 33/50, aside from ed Drawings for the Bible, litho, 1960, p/s, full mrgs, L-14x11", SBY 5/12/88 OE	4,400
Selbstildnis mit Grimasse, 89/100, 6th state b, etch/aqua/wove paper, 1924-25, p/s, full mrgs, P-15x11", lot 236, C-NY 11/1/88	17,600
Selbstportrait, Pl 17, 58/110, etch/drypt, 1922/1923, p/s, lg mrgs, fox/stn, 11x9", Cassirer, lot 355, SBY 5/11/89 OE	10,450
Self-Portrait at the Window, 10/20, litho, 1957, p/s, lt cr img, lt cr/sl mrgs, 22x15", lot 139, SBY 2/23/89 OE	4,950
Sequestered Garden, a/p, 16/25, clr litho/Arches, 1969, p/s, full mrgs, lstn, L-24x16", C-NY 11/1/88	8,250
Sequestered Garden, a/p, 8x25, clr litho/Arches, 1969, p/s, full mrgs, lt stn, L-24x16", lot 122, C-NY 5/11/88	8,800
Sequestered Garden, 41/50, clr litho, 1969, p/s, full mrgs, lt stn, 24x16", lot 137, SBY 2/25/88	8,800
Sequestered Garden, 48/50, clr litho, 1969, p/s, full mrgs, lt lstn, L-24x16", SBY 5/12/88	7,150
Set of 6: Les Ames Mortes; a/p, before ed of 368, etch/drypt/wm MBM, 1923-37, 15x11", Vollard/Fort, lot 19, C-NY 11/1/88	3,300
So I Came Forth of the Sea...; 5, 22/90, litho/laid paper, 1948, p/s, full mrg, unfr, L-15x11", Pantheon Books, SBY 5/12/88	14,300
So I Came Forth of the Sea...; Pl 5, a/p, clr litho, full mrgs, 15x11", lot 364, SBY 5/11/89	5,500
So I Came Forth of the Sea...; Pl 5, 21/90, clr litho, 1948, p/s, full mrgs, 15x11", Pantheon, lot 131, SBY 2/23/89 OE	22,000
Solomon, 63/75, aside from book ed, clr litho, 1956, p/s, lt stn, S-14x10", lot 138, SBY 2/23/89 OE	3,300
Solomon Greeting the Queen of Sheba, 64/100, hc etch/Arches, 1956, p/s, stn/old tp, 13x9", Teriade, lot 46, SWN 6/15/88	1,430
Songes: La Thora Rouge, Pl 19, 20/50, hc etch, 1981, p/s, full mrgs, 12x9", Cramer, lot 151, SBY 2/25/88	3,300
Songes: Le Couple; Pl 12, 20/50, hc etch, 1981, p/s, full mrgs, 12x10", Cramer, lot 149, SBY 2/25/88	3,575
Songes: Portrait au Bouquet, Pl 13, 20/50, hc etch, 1981, p/s, full mrgs, 12x9", Cramer, lot 150, SBY 2/25/88	4,400
Sorrel Horse, HC, ed of 200, clr litho/wove paper, 1952, p/s, lt stn/fox/cr, S-15x22", Mourlot, lot 99, C-NY 5/11/88	3,080
Sorrel Horse, 12/200, clr litho, 1952, p/s, full mrgs, lt stn/sl, S-15x22", lot 526, C-NY 5/10/89	3,300
Sorrel Horse, 186/200, clr litho, 1952, p/s, lt stn/fox, S-15x22", lot 366, SBY 5/11/89	4,950
Sorrel Horse, 74/200, clr litho, 1952, p/s, full sheet, lt stn/fox, S-15x22", lot 117, SBY 2/25/88 OE	4,675
Spring, 56/60, clr litho, 1961, p/s, full mrgs, 17x26", lot 125, SBY 11/3/88 OE	57,750
St Paul at Night, 37/50, clr litho, 1980, p/s, full mrgs, 20x15", lot 165, SBY 11/3/88	4,400
St-Germain-des-Pres, 27/75, clr litho, 1954, p/s, lt stn/old tp, S-16x11", lot 528, C-NY 5/10/89 OE	13,200
Studio at Night, 11/50, clr litho, 1980, p/s, full mrgs, lt cr, 20x15", lot 147, SBY 2/25/88 OE	4,400
Suite: Daphnis & Chloe; 206/250, 42 clr litho, 1961, ink sgn, text by Longus, L-17x25"/L-17x13", Verve, SBY 5/12/88	308,000
Suite: Story of Exodus; #83, 24 clr litho w/text, 1966, sgn on justification, orig wrappers, Amiel, lot 138, SBY 11/3/88	30,800
Suite: Story of Exodus; HC, ed of 15, 24 clr litho w/text on Arches, 1966, S-20x15", Amiel, lot 391, SBY 5/11/89	33,000
Suite: Story of Exodus; 149/285, 24 clr litho w/text, 1966, sgn, 20x15", Amiel, SBY 5/12/88	33,000
Summer Night, 40/50, clr litho/Arches, 1972, 22x15", lot 2833, B/B 4/19/88	2,750
Summer Season, book ed of 250, clr litho, 1961, S-16x13", lot 155, SBY 2/23/89	4,125
Summer Season, 29/60, clr litho, 1961, p/s, lt lstn/mstn mrgs, lt disclr verso, L-17x13", SBY 5/12/88	18,700
Summer Season, 35/60, clr litho, 1961, p/s, full mrgs, lt stn, 17x13", lot 381, SBY 5/11/89	27,500
Summer's Dream, 42/50, clr litho, 1983, p/s, full mrgs, 19x21", lot 425, SBY 5/11/89 OE	11,000
Summer's Night, 26/50, clr litho, 1973, p/s, full mrgs, lt sl/disclr/cr mrgs, L-22x15", SBY 5/12/88	3,025
Sunlit Studio, 29/50, clr litho/Arches, 1974, p/s, full mrgs, lt lstn, L-18x14", lot 268, C-NY 11/1/88	12,100
Sunlit Studio, 7/50, clr litho, 1974, p/s, full mrgs, lt stn, 18x15", lot 140, SBY 2/25/88 OE	15,400
Syrinx Fable, a/p, clr litho, 1961, S-17x13", Teriade, lot 123, SBY 11/3/88	7,150
Temple & History of Bacchus, a/p, clr litho, 1961, S-17x25", Teriade, lot 386, SBY 5/11/89	11,000
Temple & History of Bacchus, a/p, clr litho, 1961, sgn, S-17x25", Teriade, lot 131, SBY 11/3/88	11,000
Temple & History of Bacchus, book ed of 250, clr litho, 1961, S-17x25", lot 162, SBY 2/23/89 OE	13,200
Temple & History of Bacchus, from book ed of 250, litho, 1961, unfr, S-17x25", SBY 5/12/88	11,000
Temple & History of Bacchus, 47/60, clr litho/Arches, 1961, p/s, full mrgs, lt stn, L-17x26", lot 537, C-NY 5/10/89 OE	52,800
Tenderness, 32/50, clr litho, 1983, p/s, full mrgs, 19x13", lot 169, SBY 11/3/88 OE	7,700
The Bible (Title Page), 2/75, yel/blk litho, 1956, p/s, lt stn, S-15x11", lot 136, SBY 2/23/89	2,750
Then All Poured Libations...; Pl 9, 52/75, litho/Arches, 1967, trm mrgs, lt cr/stn, 18x12", Mazo, lot 263, C-NY 11/1/88	6,600
Then All Poured Libations...; Pl 9, 67/75, clr litho, 1967, p/s, full mrgs, lt stn/rub, L-18x12", lot 550, C-NY 5/10/89	8,800
Then He Spent the Night with Her Embracing & Clipping, 18/90, litho, 1949, L-15x11", Pantheon Books, SBY 5/12/88 OE	15,400
Then Moses Assembled All the Congregation...; Pl 19, ed of 285, litho/Arches, 1966, 18x13", Amiel, lot 112, C-NY 5/11/88	1,650
Then the Angel of the Lord Appeared...; Pl 3, clr litho/Arches, 1966, full mrgs, L-18x13", lot 544, C-NY 5/10/89	1,100
Then the Kink in Himself..., proof imp aside from ed of X, litho, unfr, L-15x11", Pantheon Books, SBY 5/12/88 OE	10,450
Then the Old Woman Mounted on the Ifrit's Back...; 30/90, litho/laid paper, 1948, 15x11", Pantheon, lot 104, SBY 11/3/88	41,250
Three Acrobats, a/p, clr litho/wove paper, 1956, p/s, full mrgs, lt stn/tr/stn, S-26x30", lot 531, C-NY 5/10/89	16,500
Throne of David, 11/50, clr litho, 1982, p/s, full mrgs, 19x13", lot 423, SBY 5/11/89 OE	4,400
Throne of David, 8/50, clr litho, 1982, p/s, full mrgs, 19x13", lot 197, SBY 2/23/89	3,575
Tomorrow My Fair One Shall Have a Dove..., 66/75, litho/Arches, 1967, full mrgs, unfr, L-17x15", SBY 5/12/88 OE	16,500
Trampled Flowers, book ed of 250, clr litho, 1961, lt stn/old tp hinge, S-17x12", lot 158, SBY 2/23/89 OE	7,150
Trapeze Acrobat with Bird, 21/75, clr litho, 1967, p/s, full mrgs, lt lstn/sl, L-11x9", SBY 5/12/88 OE	6,875
Tribute to the Eiffel Tower, a/p, clr litho/Arches, 1964, p/s, full mrgs, lt stn, L-25x19", lot 540, C-NY 5/10/89 OE	33,000
Trough, a/p, before sgn ed of 100, litho/Chine, 1924, lt cr mrgs, L-12x9", lot 517, C-NY 5/10/89 OE	3,080
Ville de Bruxelles, offset litho/poster paper, 1972, p/s, lt cr, 28x20", Mourlot, lot 48, SWN 6/15/89 UE	550
Violinist with Cock, 11/50, clr litho, 1982, p/s, full mrgs, 20x14", lot 424, SBY 5/11/89	6,600
Violinist with Cock, 8/50, clr litho, 1982, p/s, full mrgs, 19x14", lot 198, SBY 2/23/89 OE	7,150
Vision d'Esaie, Pl 91, 64/100, etch, 1931-39/1956, intl, full mrgs, lt stn/sl, 13x10", Teriade, lot 362, SBY 5/11/89	2,420
Vision d'Esaie, 91, 43/100, aside from ed of 250, etch, 1931-39/1956, trm mrgs, stn, P-12x10", Teriade, SBY 5/12/88	1,650
Vision of Moses, 53/75, clr litho, 1968, p/s, lt sl, S-23x30", SBY 5/12/88	4,950
We Live Among the Flowers of the Meadows...; AP2/25, clr litho, 1967, p/s, full mrgs, 18x14", lot 144, SBY 11/3/88	23,100

We Live Among the Flowers of the Meadows...; clr litho, 1967, p/s, inscr W, lt cr, 17x14", lot 145, SBY 11/3/88 17,600
We Live Among the Flowers...; Pl 3, 70/75, clr litho/Arches, 1967, p/s, full mrgs, L-18x14", lot 548, C-NY 5/10/89 19,800
Wedding Feast in the Nymphs' Grotto, a/p, clr litho, 1961, lt stn, S-17x25", Teriade, lot 164, SBY 2/23/89 OE 9,900
Wedding Feast in the Nymphs' Grotto, 41/60, clr litho, 1961, p/s, full mrgs, lt cr/stn, 17x25", lot 133, SBY 11/3/88 30,250
What Is Life, What Is Pleasure Without Golden Aphrodite?...; 30/75, litho, 1967, p/s, lt stn, L-20x16", SBY 5/12/88 OE 20,900
What Is Life, What Is Pleasure Without Golden Aphrodite?...; 21/75, litho/Arches, 1967, lt stn, L-20x16", SBY 5/12/88 15,400
What Is Life, What Is Pleasure...; 26/75, clr litho, 1967, p/s, full mrgs, lt stn, 20x16", lot 400, SBY 5/11/89 19,800
When Abdullah Got the Net Ashore, proof aside from sgn ed of 111, litho, 1949, L-15x11", Pantheon Books, SBY 5/12/88 4,950
While the Angel of Death Passes Over Egypt...; Pl 32, 62/100, etch, 1930-55, p/s, P-12x9", lot 240, C-NY 11/1/88 OE 2,860
Wine Harvest, book ed of 250, clr litho, 1961, lt cr/skinned, S-17x13", lot 146, SBY 2/23/89 OE 6,600
Winged Painter, 35/50/clr litho/Arches, 1984, stp/s, a/bstp, full mrgs, L-17x15", lot 576, C-NY 5/10/89 2,200
Winter, book ed of 250, clr litho, 1961, lt stn, S-17x12", lot 154, SBY 2/23/89 6,050
Winter, 29/60, aside from book ed of 250, clr litho, 1961, p/s, full mrgs, lt mstn, unfr, L-17x13", SBY 5/12/88 OE........ 23,100
Wolf Pit, book ed of 250, clr litho, 1961, lt stn, S-17x13", lot 140, SBY 2/23/89 OE........ 4,400
Wolf Pit, book ed of 250, clr litho, 1961, S-17x13", lot 370, SBY 5/11/89 4,290
Wolf Pit, unsgn ed of 250, clr litho/wove paper, 1961, lt stn verso, S-17x13", lot 251, C-NY 11/1/88 4,950
Wolf Pit, unsgn ed of 250, clr litho/wove paper, 1961, stn, S-17x13", Verve, lot 534, C-NY 5/10/89 7,150
Wolves & Laurels, etch/drypt/aqua/cream wove paper, 1952, p/s, 14x11", lot 2830, B/B 4/19/88........ 990
Woman Circus Rider, 96/100, clr litho/Rives, 1956, p/s, full sheet, lt cr, S-14x21", lot 245, C-NY 11/1/88 4,400
World of the Bible, 29/50, litho/Japan nacre, 1975, p/s, full mrgs, tp to mat, 18x26", lot 144, SBY 2/25/88 3,025
XXe Siecle, 2nd State; 29/75, clr litho/Arches, 1966, p/s, tp to overmat, L-12x18", lot 260, C-NY 11/1/88 OE........ 4,180
Young Girl with Bouquet, 47/50, clr litho, 1969, p/s, full mrgs, 13x10", lot 404, SBY 5/11/89 6,050
Young Methymneans, 27/60, clr litho, 1961, p/s, full mrgs, lt sl mrgs/verso, 17x13", lot 119, SBY 11/3/88 17,600
Young Methymneans, 29/60, clr litho, 1961, p/s, full mrgs, lt lstn/mstn, lt cr mrg, L-16x13", SBY 5/12/88 13,200
Youth Methymneans, book ed of 250, clr litho, 1961, S-17x13", lot 148, SBY 2/23/89 3,025

CHAGALL, Marc; after (Russian/French, 1887-1985)

Angel, by Charles Sorlier, offset litho, 1973, p/s, S-20x17", Mourlot, lot 51, SWN 6/15/89........ 770
Angel of Judgement, by Charles Sorlier, 177/200, clr litho/Arches, 1974, p/s, full mrgs, L-20x17", lot 152, C-NY 5/11/88 3,850
Avenue de la Victoire at Nice, by Charles Sorlier, Pl 6, 60/75, litho/Arches, 1967, 24x18", lot 287, C-NY 11/1/88 OE........ 8,800
Avenue de la Victorie at Nice, by Charles Sorlier, Pl 6, 69/75, litho/Arches, 1967, L-24x18", lot 149, C-NY 5/11/88 OE........ 9,350
Carmen, by Charles Sorlier, ed of 3000, clr litho w/text, 1966, lt rpr/cr, S-40x26", Mourlot, lot 49, PHL 6/16/88 3,750
Carmen, by Charles Sorlier, ed of 3000, clr litho w/text, 1966, S-39x25", Lincoln Center/Mourlot, lot 159, SBY 2/25/88........ 3,740
Carmen, by Charles Sorlier, ed of 3000, clr litho/poster paper, 1967, S-39x25", Metropolitan Opera, lot 174, SBY 11/3/88........ 4,950
Carmen, by Charles Sorlier, ed of 3000, litho, 1966, S-40x25", Mourlot/Metropolitan Opera House, SBY 5/12/88 OE 4,400
Carmen, by Charles Sorlier, ed of 3000, litho w/text, 1966, 39x25", Metropolitan Opera/Mourlot, lot 216, SBY 2/23/89........ 4,950
Carmen, by Charles Sorlier, ed of 3000, litho w/text, 1966, S-40x25", Metropolitan Opera/Mourlot, lot 217, SBY 2/23/89........ 3,300
Carmen, by Charles Sorlier, poster ed of 3000, litho w/text, 1966, S-40x26", Metropolitan Opera, lot 438, SBY 5/11/89 OE........ 5,225
Carmen, by Charles Sorlier, poster ed of 3000, litho w/text, 1967, S-39x25", Metropolitan Opera, lot 437, SBY 5/11/89 OE........ 5,500
Carmen, by Charles Sorlier, unsgn ed of 3000, clr litho w/text, 1966, L-40x26", lot 291, C-NY 11/1/88 4,950
Carmen, by Charles Sorlier, unsgn ed of 3000, clr litho w/text, 1966, rpr tr, S-40x25", s/wrp, lot 590, C-NY 5/10/89........ 4,620
Carmen, by Charles Sorlier, unsgn ed of 3000, litho, 1966, cr/ls in corner, scr verso, S-39x25", lot 148, C-NY 5/11/88........ 2,420
Carmen, by Charles Sorlier, 112/150, clr litho w/text on Arches, 1966, S-40x26", lot 292, C-NY 11/1/88 OE 12,100
Carmen, by Charles Sorlier, 162/200, clr litho/Arches, 1966, full mrgs, lt cr, 40x26", lot 176, SBY 11/3/88 33,000
Carmen, by Charles Sorlier, 51/150, clr litho w/text on Arches, 1967, lt stn on verso, S-40x26", lot 215, SBY 2/23/89 OE 10,450
Carmen, by Charles Sorlier, 73/150, litho/Arches, 1966, crayon sgn, full mrgs, sl verso, unfr, L-40x26", C-NY 1/22/88 OE........ 6,930
Carnival of Flowers, by Charles Sorlier, Pl 8, 41/75, litho/Arches, 1967, p/s, lt stn, 25x18", lot 288, C-NY 11/1/88 OE 8,800
Champs-Elysees, by Charles Sorlier, 11/200, clr litho, 1961, p/s, lg mrgs, lt stn, 24x17", SBY 2/23/89 OE 7,975
Couple in Mimosa, by Charles Sorlier, Pl 7, 41/75, litho/Arches, 1967, p/s, full mrgs, L-24x18", lot 150, C-NY 5/11/88........ 1,750
Die Zauberflote, by Charles Sorlier, clr litho w/text, 1967, lt ls/tr, L-40x26", Mourlot, lot 50, PHL 6/16/88 1,600
Gray Cock, by Charles Sorlier, clr litho before text, sgn by Chagall, lt cr, 30x21", Mourlot, lot 171, SBY 11/3/88 OE 4,950
L'Horloge, by George Visat, 188/300, clr etch, ca 1950, sgn by Chagall, full mrgs, 12x9", Maeght, lot 170, SBY 11/3/88 4,400
Magic Flute, by Charles Sorlier, poster ed of 3000, litho, S-43x26", Metropolitan Opera/Mourlot, lot 435, SBY 5/11/89 2,475
Magic Flute, by Charles Sorlier, poster ed of 3000, litho, 1967, S-40x26", Metropolitan Opera, lot 213, SBY 2/23/89 2,750
Magic Flute, by Charles Sorlier, unsgn ed of 3000, clr litho w/text, 1967, lt cr, S-40x26", lot 290, C-NY 11/1/88 2,420
Magic Flute, by Charles Sorlier, 11/200, clr litho before text, 1967, S-40x26", Metropolitan Opera, lot 433, SBY 5/11/89........ 6,380
Magic Flute, by Charles Sorlier, 112/200, clr litho, 1967, S-40x26", Metropolitan Opera/Mourlot, lot 434, SBY 5/11/89 18,700
Magic Flute, by Charles Sorlier, 42/200, clr litho, 1967, p/s, 40x26", Metropolitan Opera/Mourlot, lot 212, SBY 2/23/89 22,000
Magic Flute, by Charles Sorlier, 75/100, clr litho/Arches, 1967, sgn in blk crayon, S-40x26", lot 589, C-NY 5/10/89 4,950
Magic Flute, by Sorlier, a/p, litho w/text on Arches, 1967, sgn by Chagall, S-43x26", Mourlot, lot 157, SBY 2/25/88 6,600
Magic Flute, by Sorlier, ed of 3000, litho w/text on poster paper, 1967, S-43x26", Mourlot, lot 158, SBY 2/25/88 UE 1,980
Maternity, by Charles Sorlier, a/p, litho/Arches, 1954, sgn by Chagall, 21x27", Maeght, lot 152, SBY 2/25/88 OE 5,225
Nice & the Cote d'Azure, by Charles Sorlier, 36/150, litho, 1967, p/s by Chagall, 24x18", lot 155, SBY 2/25/88 OE........ 7,370
Nice & the Cote d'Azure: Sirene with Poet; by Charles Sorlier, LIV/LXXV, litho, 1967, 24x18", lot 172, SBY 11/3/88 OE 5,500
Nice & the Cote d'Azure: Sirene with Poet; LIV/LXXV, litho, 1967, p/s, full mrgs, fox, 24x18", lot 210, SBY 2/23/89 OE........ 8,800
Paris, by Charles Sorlier, clr litho, 1972, sgn in blk crayon, lt cr/stn, S-34x22", Mourlot, PHL 6/16/88........ 600
Paris en Fete, 21/50, clr litho, bears sgn, 16x20", lot 7, FAP 2/24/89 150
Paris Sun, by Charles Sorlier, 72/150, clr litho/Arches, 1977, p/s, full mrgs, lt stn, 22x18", lot 586, C-NY 5/10/89 OE 10,450
Revolution, by Charles Sorlier, 46/150, clr litho, 1963, p/s, full mrgs, lt stn, L-21x19", lot 134, C-NY 5/11/88 OE 3,080
Revolution, 133/150, clr litho/wove paper, p/s, full mrgs, lt cr, rpr splits, lt stn, L-21x19", lot 334, C-NY 1/19/89 OE........ 2,420
Romeo & Juliet, by Charles Sorlier, from poster ed of 5000, litho, 1964, with text, S-25x39", SBY 5/12/88 2,475
Romeo & Juliet, by Charles Sorlier, unsgn ed of 5000, clr litho w/text, 1964, S-25x39", lot 289, C-NY 11/1/88 1,760

Romeo & Juliet, by Charles Sorlier, unsgn ed of 5000, clr litho w/text, 1964, S-25x39", s/wrp, lot 587, C-NY 5/10/89 990
Romeo & Juliet, by Charles Sorlier, 144/200, clr litho, 1964, lt stn, S-26x40", Mourlot, lot 200, SBY 2/23/89 OE 31,900
Romeo & Juliet, by Charles Sorlier, 5/200, clr litho/Arches, 1964, p/s, S-26x40", lot 135, C-NY 5/11/88 19,800
Romeo & Juliet, by Sorlier, 158/200, litho (before text), 1964, p/s, 26x40", French Tourist Bureau, lot 153, SBY 2/25/88 24,200
Romeo & Juliet, poster ed of 5000, clr litho w/text, 1964, S-25x39", French Tourist Bureau/Mourlot, lot 430, SBY 5/11/89 1,100
Romeo & Juliet, poster ed of 5000, clr litho w/text, 1964, S-25x39", French Tourist Bureau/Mourlot, lot 429, SBY 5/11/89 990

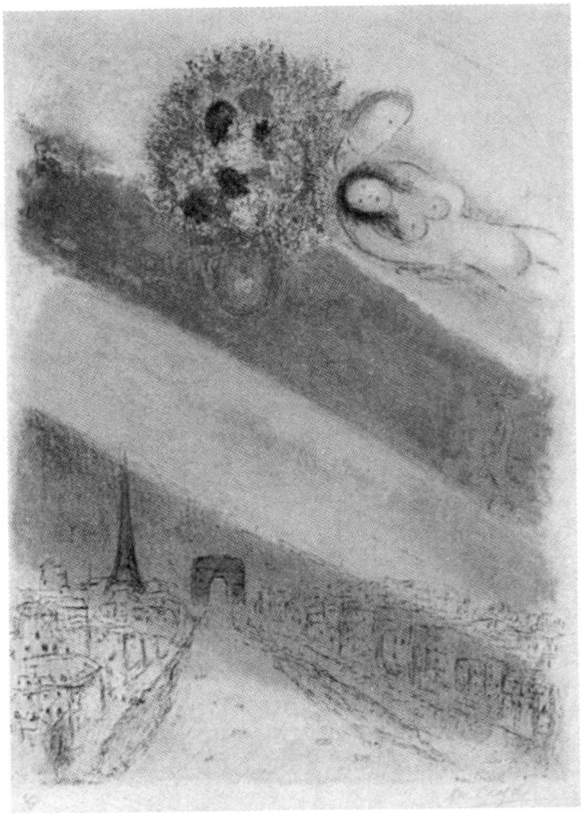

Champs-Elysees, by Charles Sorlier, 5/200, clr litho/Arches, 1954, p/s, full mrgs, lt stn/cr, L-24x17", lot 580, C-NY 5/10/89 OE; $13,200

Romeo & Juliet, unsgn ed of 5000, clr litho w/text, 1964, bears signature, S-25x39", lot 336, C-NY 1/19/89 1,320
Roses & Mimosa, by Charles Sorlier, Pl 4, 106/150, litho/Arches, 1967, p/s, full mrgs, 24x18", lot 286, C-NY 11/1/88 OE 9,350
Saint-Jean-Cap-Ferrat, by Charles Sorlier, a/p, litho/Marais, 1952, p/s, lt stn/cr, L-27x20", lot 579, C-NY 5/10/89 OE 12,100
Set of 16: Chagall; by Jacques Lassaigne, litho w/text, 1957, Maeght, w/sgn post card, lot 532, C-NY 5/10/89 1,430
Sirene with Pine, by Charles Sorlier, Pl 10, 68/75, litho/Arches, 1967, p/s, full mrgs, L-25x18", lot 151, C-NY 5/11/88 4,620
Tribe of Asher, by Charles Sorlier, Pl 9, HC, litho/Arches, 1961, p/s, full mrgs, L-24x18", lot 282, C-NY 11/1/88 OE 7,150
Tribe of Asher, by Charles Sorlier, Pl 9, 17/150, litho/Arches, 1961, p/s, full mrgs, 24x18", lot 144, C-NY 5/11/88 OE 6,600
Tribe of Benjamin, by Charles Sorlier, Pl 12, HC, litho/Arches, 1961, full mrgs, L-24x18", lot 285, C-NY 11/1/88 6,050
Tribe of Benjamin, by Charles Sorlier, Pl 12, 17/150, litho/Arches, 1961, full mrgs, L-24x18", lot 147, C-NY 5/11/88 OE 6,600
Tribe of Dan, by Charles Sorlier, Pl 7, 17/150, litho/Arches, 1961, full mrgs, lt stn, 24x18", lot 142, C-NY 5/11/88 OE 6,050
Tribe of Dan, Pl 7, 149/150, clr litho/Arches, 1964, p/s, full mrgs, lt mstn, L-24x18", lot 582, C-NY 5/10/89 OE 9,350
Tribe of Gad, by Charles Sorlier, Pl 8, HC, litho/Arches, 1961, full mrgs, lt stn, L-24x18", lot 281, C-NY 11/1/88 5,500
Tribe of Gad, by Charles Sorlier, Pl 8, 17/150, litho/Arches, 1961, p/s, full mrgs, L-24x18", lot 143, C-NY 5/11/88 OE 5,280
Tribe of Gad, by Charles Sorlier, 40/150, litho, 1964, p/s, full mrgs, lt disclr, L-25x18", Mourlot, SBY 5/12/88 4,675
Tribe of Gad, Pl 8, 120/150, litho/Arches, 1964, p/s, full mrgs, lt stn/cr, stn verso, L-24x18", lot 583, C-NY 5/10/89 4,950
Tribe of Issachar, by Charles Sorlier, Pl 6, HC, litho/Arches, 1961, lt stn/cr, L-24x18", lot 279, C-NY 11/1/88 OE 1,750
Tribe of Issachar, by Charles Sorlier, Pl 6, 17/150, litho/Arches, 1961, full mrgs, L-24x18", lot 141, C-NY 5/11/88 OE 6,050
Tribe of Issachar, by Charles Sorlier, 12/150, litho/Arches, 1964, p/s, full mrgs, lt stn, 24x18", lot 581, C-NY 5/10/89 7,150
Tribe of Joseph, by Charles Sorlier, Pl 11, 17/150, litho/Arches, 1961, full mrgs, L-24x18", lot 146, C-NY 5/11/88 OE 7,700
Tribe of Joseph, by Charles Sorlier, Pl 11, 63/150, litho/Arches, 1961, full mrgs, L-24x18", lot 284, C-NY 11/1/88 OE 6,600
Tribe of Judah, by Charles Sorlier, Pl 4, HC, litho/Arches, 1961, p/s, full mrgs, L-24x18", lot 277, C-NY 11/1/88 OE 6,600
Tribe of Judah, by Charles Sorlier, Pl 4, 17/150, litho/Arches, 1961, full mrgs, L-25x18", lot 138, C-NY 5/11/88 OE 5,280
Tribe of Levi, by Charles Sorlier, LXVIII/C, litho, 1964, p/s, full mrgs, 24x18", Mourlot, lot 205, SBY 2/23/89 OE 7,700
Tribe of Levi, by Charles Sorlier, LXXXI/C, clr litho, 1964, p/s, full mrgs, lt stn/sl, 24x18", lot 432, SBY 5/11/89 6,380
Tribe of Levi, by Charles Sorlier, Pl 3, HC, litho/Arches, 1961, full mrgs, lt mstn, L-24x18", lot 276, C-NY 11/1/88 OE 6,600
Tribe of Levi, by Charles Sorlier, Pl 3, 192/200, litho/Arches, 1961, p/s, full mrgs, L-24x18", lot 138, C-NY 5/11/88 6,050
Tribe of Levi, by Charles Sorlier, 21/200, litho, 1964, p/s, full mrgs, lt sl/fox/cr, L-24x18", Mourlot, SBY 5/12/88 5,775
Tribe of Naphtali, by Charles Sorlier, Pl 10, HC, litho/Arches, 1961, full mrgs, stn/cr, 24x18", lot 283, C-NY 11/1/88 6,050
Tribe of Naphtali, by Charles Sorlier, Pl 10, 17/150, litho/Arches, 1961, full mrgs, L-24x18", lot 145, C-NY 5/11/88 OE 7,150

Tribe of Naphtall, a/p, ed of 25, clr litho, 1964, p/s, full mrgs, lt stn, 24x18", lot 209, SBY 2/23/89 OE 6,600
Tribe of Ruben, by Charles Sorlier, Pl 1, 113/150, litho/Arches, 1961, p/s, full mrgs, 24x18", lot 274, C-NY 11/1/88 OE 7,150
Tribe of Ruben, by Charles Sorlier, Pl 1, 17/150, litho/Arches, 1961, p/s, lt stn, L-25x18", lot 136, C-NY 5/11/88 OE 6,600
Tribe of Ruben, by Charles Sorlier, 75/150, clr litho, 1964, p/s by Chagall, full mrgs, 25x18", Mourlot, SBY 2/25/88 OE 5,225
Tribe of Simeon, by Charles Sorlier, Pl 2, HC, litho/Arches, 1961, lt mstn/cr, L-24x18", lot 275, C-NY 11/1/88 OE 7,150
Tribe of Simeon, by Charles Sorlier, Pl 2, 17x150, litho/Arches, 1961, p/s, full mrgs, 24x18", lot 137, C-NY 5/11/88 OE 4,620
Tribe of Zebulon, by Charles Sorlier, a/p, ed of 25, litho, 1964, p/s, full mrgs, 25x18", lot 207, SBY 2/23/89 OE 6,600
Tribe of Zebulon, by Charles Sorlier, Pl 5, HC, litho/Arches, 1961, full mrgs, lt mstn, 24x18", lot 278, C-NY 11/1/88 OE 6,380
Tribe of Zebulon, by Charles Sorlier, Pl 5, 17/150, litho/Arches, 1961, p/s, full mrgs, 24x18", lot 140, C-NY 5/11/88 OE 5,500
Tribe of Zebulon, by Charles Sorlier, 138/150, litho, 1964, p/s, full mrgs, lt stn/cr, 25x18", lot 208, SBY 2/23/89 OE 6,600

IAHINE, Edgar (American/French, 1874-)

Gemma, 12/18, etch, p/s, 20x14", lot 241, LH 3/20/88 600
Jukiette, 18/40, 2nd/final state, drypt/S Regal MBM, 1903, p/s, trm mrgs, lt sl/mstn, tp verso, P-18x10", C-NY 1/22/88 880
Venise, Corte Colonna; 67/100, etch/drypt/Chine colle, 1922, p/s, titled, full mrgs, P-9x13", lot 337, C-NY 1/19/89 330

IALLE, after (French, 18th C)

Quand Hymen dort l'Amour Vielle, by Maucler, aqua, 14x19", C-E 11/15/88 OE 165

IAMBERLAIN, Richard (20th C)

Zrinka, clr monotype, 1986, sgn, full sheet, 30x42", Novak Graphics, lot 489, SBY 2/25/89 880

IAMBERLAIN, Samuel (American, 1895-1975)

Soaring Steel, 79/100, drypt/BFK Rives, 1929, p/s, full mrgs, lt tstn, unfr, P-13x10", C-NY 1/22/88 OE 770

IARLOT, Jean (American, 1898-1979)

Aztec Dancer, litho/cream wove paper, p/s, 14x10", lot 2939, B/B 4/19/88 165
Indian Family, litho/BFK Rives, 1957, p/s, full mrgs, lt cr, 10x14", lot 2935, B/B 2/16/88 357
Indian Snake Dance, litho/cream wove paper, p/s, full mrgs, lt stn, 14x10", lot 2936, B/B 2/16/88 357
Pair: El Volador; Indian Snake Dance; ed of 250, litho, 1949 & 1952, 14x10", Assn Am Artists, lot 52, SWN 6/15/89 248

IASE, Louisa L. (American, 1951-)

Cloudburst, 2/25, clr wc/Okawara, 1982, p/s, full mrgs, S-28x28", Diane Villani, lot 588, C-NY 11/1/88 880

IASE, Waldo S. (American, 20th C)

Silver Silence, a Mountain Landscape; clr woodblock, sgn/dtd 30/titled, L-8x14", RWS 4/22/89 225

IASE, William Merritt (American, 1849-1916)

Shore Scene, monotype/wove paper, ca 1885, lt rpr tr in mrgs, L-6x8", lot 159, C-NY 1/19/89 OE 4,950

IEFFETZ, Asa (American, 1897-1965)

Cold Chimneys, 13/40, wc/wove paper, p/s, lt stn, L-7x9", RWS 3/16/89 OE 800

IENEY, Philip (American, 20th C)

Estes Park, litho/BFK Rives, p/s, full mrgs, hinged to mat, 9x13", lot 2938, B/B 2/16/88 UE 88

IERET, Jules (French, 1836-1932)

Blanc de Noir, litho, tr, linen backed, 49x33", lot 294, FAP 2/24/89 UE 175
Cacao Lhara, clr litho/poster paper, lt tr edges, linen backed, 97x35", lot 307, FAP 2/24/89 UE 400

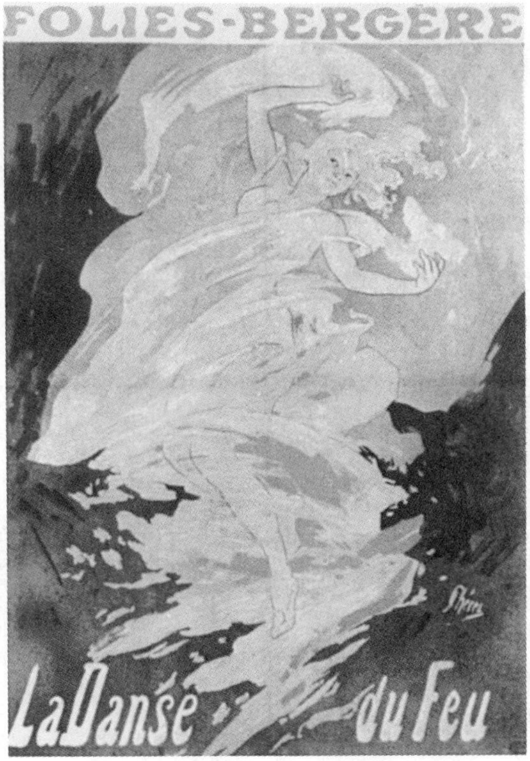

Pair: Folies Bergere; Musee Grevin, Les Dames Hongroises; clr litho/poster paper, lt sl/cr, 47x33", lot 51, WD 12/8/88 OE; $2,600; illustration of one

Folies Bergere, litho/poster paper, tr edges, fld imp, linen backed, 49x34", Chaix, lot 296, FAP 2/24/89 UE	500
Halle aux Chapeaux, clr litho poster, linen-backed, 34x47", Chaix, FAP 6/16/89	750
Jardin de Paris, clr litho, 1890, lt tr/center fld, 35x49", lot 75, WG 10/19/89	750
La Loie Fuller, clr litho, pl/s, cr/ls, 47x34", Chaix, C-E 7/12/88 UE	220
La Reine Indigo, clr litho poster, no size given, Cheret, FAP 6/16/89 UE	120
Lydia, litho/poster paper, 1895, 49x35", lot 1159, LH 10/16/88 OE	1,200
Musee Grevin, ed before letters, clr litho, 39x35", Chaix, C-E 3/24/88	1,430
Pair: Viviane; Les Turcs; clr litho, pl/s, 30x23", s/wrp, C-E 9/16/88	418
Palais de Glace, Champs-Elysees; clr litho, 1894, tax stp on img, lt cr/stn, L-23x13", Chaix, lot 49, PHL 10/28/88	350
Palais de Glace, clr litho, 1893, lt cr/tr img, linen backed, 49x38", Chaix, lot 295, FAP 2/24/89 UE	375
Viviane, clr litho, pl/s, 30x23", lot 412, C-E 9/20/89 UE	220
CHIA, Sandro (American/Italian, 1946-)	
Children's Holiday, 20/75, litho/6 panels, 1984, sgn, 71x77" overall, lot 918, SBY 5/13/89	7,700
In a Garden of Florence, a/p, etch/aqua/Chine colle, 1985, full mrgs, 1985, 22x15", Bonnier, lot 399, C-NY 5/11/88	1,430
Pair: Mechanical Figure I & II, ed of 15, etch/drypt, 1982, Schellman/Kluser bstp, S-30x23", lot 615, SBY 2/23/89	1,320
CHICAGO, Judy (American, 1930-)	
Peeling Back, 60/95, offset litho/cream wove paper, 1974, p/s, titled, 19x19", Periwinkle, lot 3014, B/B 4/19/88	275
CHIKANOBU (Japanese, 19th C)	
Warriors by the Sea, clr woodblock, sgn, lt stn/cr/scr, 14x9", RWS 8/20/88	150
CHILIDE, Eduardo	
Escarts, 42/50, etch, p/s, 13x14", lot 1199, LH 5/15/88 OE	225
CHRISTIANSEN, Kay (Danish, 1899-)	
Untitled, head of young girl; 16/20, litho, p/s, dtd Paris 1952, 14x19", SLK 4/7/89	60
CHRISTO (Javacheff)(Bulgarian, 1935-)	
Book: Modern Art; by Hunter & Jacobus, 7/120, sgn, 13x10x1", orig wrappers, Abrams Orig, lot 400, C-NY 5/11/88	1,430
Package on Handtruck, Project; 49/100, clr litho/collage, 1981, p/s, S-28x22", Abrams Orig, lot 722, SBY 11/5/88 OE	3,575
Puerto de Alcala, Wrapped Project for Madrid; HC, clr litho/collage, 1981, p/s, 28x22", Poligrafa, lot 919, SBY 5/13/89	4,675
Suite: (Some) Not Realized Projects; 6/100, 5 litho, 1971, p/s, S-28x22", Landfall, lot 721, SBY 11/5/88 OE	7,700
Suite: Wrapped Monument to Vittorio Emmanuele...; 46/75, 5 litho, 1975, lt cr, no box, S-28x22", Poligrafa, SBY 5/14/88	6,600
Wrapped, Project for Madrid, Puerta de Alcala; 24/99, clr litho/collage, 1981, p/s, 28x22", Poligrafa, SBY 11/5/88 OE	3,025
Wrapped, Project for Madrid, Puerta de Alcala; 76/99, litho/collage, 1981, lt sl, S-28x22", Poligrafa, SBY 5/14/88	2,420
Wrapped Building, Project for 1 Times Square, New York; AP 25/25, litho/collage, 1985, S-28x22", lot 920, SBY 5/13/89 OE	7,150
Wrapped Monument to Vittorio Emmanuel, Project for Piazza del Duomo, Milan; 38/75, litho, 1975, 28x22", SBY 2/25/88 OE	2,200
Wrapped Tree, Project; AP 1/10, clr litho, 1979, p/s, S-22x28", Poligrafa, lot 494, SBY 2/25/88	2,200
Wrapped Venus-Villa Borghese; 22/50, clr etch/litho, 1975, p/s, full mrgs, 24x18", Landfall, lot 492, SBY 2/25/88 OE	1,430
CHRISTY, Howard Chandler (American, 1873-1952)	
Americans All, clr litho/poster paper, 1919, laid down, 40x27", lot 163, FAP 2/24/89	100
Clear the Way, clr litho/poster paper, laid down, 30x20", lot 186, FAP 2/24/89	125
Fight, clr litho/poster paper, ca 1918, laid down, 41x27", lot 164, FAP 2/24/89	166
I Want You for the Navy, clr litho/poster paper, laid down, 41x27", lot 164, FAP 2/24/89 OE	300
CHRYSSA (Greek, 1933-)	
Suite: Gates to Time Square; 4/5, 20 clr scpt/wove paper, 1978, inscr HC, S-40x30", C-E 5/13/88	1,870
CIKOVSKY, Nicolai (American, 1894-1934)	
Unemployed, litho, ca 1932, p/s, titled, 7x9", lot 42, SWN 12/1/88	495
CLAGHORN, Joseph Conover (American, 1869-)	
From the South Portico of the White House, drypt, 1930, p/s, titled, 8x4", lot 157, WG 10/19/88 UE	20
CLARK, Rowland (American, 1874-1957)	
Geese, etch, p/s, lt stn/faded, 9x12", lot 200, WG 10/19/88 OE	75
CLAVE, Antoni (Spanish, 1913-)	
Composition, 22/80, etch, p/s, full mrgs, S-32x25", lot 51, PHL 10/28/88	180
CLEMENTE, Francesco (American/Italian, 1952-)	
Conversion to Her, 35/40, etch/aqua, 1986, p/s, full mrgs, lt cr, 37x44", Schellmann, lot 727, SBY 11/5/88	4,950
I (self-portrait), 34/100, clr wc/Japan, 1982, p/s, full mrgs, S-17x23", Crown Point, lot 593, C-NY 11/1/88	4,950
I (self-portrait), 11/100, clr wc/watercolor ink/Kozo, 1982, full mrgs, 14x20", Crown Point, lot 725, SBY 11/5/88	6,600
I (self-portrait), 33/100, clr wc/Kozo, 1982, p/s, full mrgs, lt cr/stn, 14x20", Crown Point, lot 923, SBY 5/13/89 OE	8,800
Morning, 23/100, clr wc/Kozo, 1982, p/s, full mrgs, 14x20", Crown Point, lot 724, SBY 11/5/88	4,950
Morning, 4/100, clr wc/Japan, 1982, p/s, full mrgs, lt rpl mrgs, S-17x23", Crown Point, lot 594, C-NY 11/1/88	3,300
Morning, 5/100, clr wc/Kozo, 1982, p/s, full mrgs, 14x20", Crown Point, lot 922, SBY 5/13/89	4,400
Pair: Faith; Hope; 34/40, clr aqua, 1986, p/s, full mrgs, lt cr, 18x24", Schellman, lot 617, SBY 2/23/89	1,925
Pair: Untitled (Face & Figure); Untitled (Two Figures); 6/25, litho, 1984, p/s, full mrgs, 20x16"/21x15", SBY 2/23/89 OE	3,575
Portfolio: Febbre Alta; 28/35, 10 wc/handmade paper, 1982, p/s, orig wrappers, S-27x21", Blum, lot 921, SBY 5/12/89 OE	5,500
Untitled, Brooklyn Academy of Music 1986-87 Artist's Portfolio; 18/75, sftgr etch, 1987, p/s, S-28x56", C-NY 11/1/88	660
Untitled (head), 75/200, clr wc/Japan, 1984, p/s, Crown Point bstp, S-16x23", lot 401, C-NY 5/11/88 OE	6,050
Untitled (portrait), 28/200, clr wc/Japan, 1984, p/s, Crown Point bstp, lt cr mrg, S-17x23", lot 596, C-NY 11/1/88	6,600
Untitled A, 52/100, litho/3 sheets wove paper, 1986, p/s, full sheets, lt cr, 27x40", Petersburg, lot 597, C-NY 11/1/88	3,520
Yes or No, 1/15, clr aqua/wove paper, 1982, p/s, full mrgs, lt scr/rub img, lt sl, S-30x44", Crown Point, C-NY 11/1/88	935
CLINKER, L.C. (American, 19th/20th C)	
Don't Waste Food While Others Starve!; clr litho/poster paper, 1916, 30x20", lot 184, FAP 2/24/89	50
CLOSE, Chuck (American, 1940-)	
Phil I, 3/15, handmade paper/cold pressed half-inch grid, 1982, p/s, S-69x54", Pace, lot 729, SBY 11/5/88 OE	14,300

Portfolio: Chuck Close Mezzotint Keith 1972; #20, 10 etch w/text, 1972, orig wrappers, 15x11", Crown Point, SBY 2/23/89 ... 770
Self-Portrait/White Ink; 13/35, wht etch/aqua on blk paper, 1978, titled, full mrgs, 44x35", Pace, lot 928, SBY 5/13/89 ... 10,450

COFFIN, W. Haskell (American, 1878-1941)
Pair: Share in the Victory; Joan of Arc Saved France; clr litho/poster paper, laid down, 30x20"/38x28", FAP 2/24/89 UE ... 30

COLE, Joseph Foxcroft (American, 1837-1892)
South Boston, 1859; litho, lt stn/fox/sl, rpr tr, L-19x29", JFA Cole of Boston, RWS 6/10/89 OE ... 400

COLE, Thomas (American, 1801-1848)
Good Shepherd, litho, 1849, lg mrgs, 11x17", John Ridner/Sarony & Major, lot 537A, SBY 1/28/88 ... 1,100

COLEMAN, Glenn O. (American, 1877-1932)
Still Life, 27/50, litho, p/s, lt stn, 15x12", lot 25, SBY 2/25/88 ... 3,080

COLEMAN, Samuel (American, 1832-1920)
European Landscape, etch, p/s, 11x15", lot 73, WG 10/19/88 ... 175

COLIN, Paul (French, 1892-)
Cie Gle Transatlantique, French Line; clr litho, ca 1937, S-23x15", Transatlantique, lot 250, FAP 2/24/89 UE ... 90
Cie Gle Transatlantique, French Line; litho/poster paper, ca 1937, 40x25", Transatlantique, lot 299, FAP 2/24/89 ... 325
Compagnie Transatlantique, clr litho backed in linen, pl/s, 23x15", C-E 6/16/88 ... 198
Compagnie Transatlantique, clr litho backed on linen, pl/s, 40x24", C-E 6/16/88 UE ... 154
Katherine Dunham, clr litho/poster paper, ca 1947, pl/s, 24x14", lot 415, C-E 9/20/89 UE ... 100
Paris 1937 Exposition Internationale, clr litho, pl/s, 23x15", Jules Simon, C-E 6/16/88 UE ... 160
Tabarin, clr litho/poster paper, 24x16", lot 235, FAP 2/24/89 OE ... 210
Tabarin, clr litho/poster paper, 24x16", lot 236, FAP 2/24/89 OE ... 200

CONDIT, W.J.; after (American, 19th C)
Government House, litho, 1847, lt fox/stn, laid down, 14x20", Currier, RWS 6/10/89 UE ... 200

Continental School (19th C)
Pair: Architecture; Music; hc etch applied to verso of glass, lt tr/stn, L-9x14", RWS 12/10/88 UE ... 300
Pair: View of Blackenwall Looking Toward Greenwich; Vue de la Ville de Cherbourg; engr, 8x15", lot 4, FAP 2/24/89 UE ... 30

Continental School (20th C)
Lady in a Park, clr litho, trm mrgs, 9x7", lot 28, FAP 2/24/89 UE ... 20

COOK, Howard (American, 1901-)
Edison Plant, #50, litho, 1930, p/s, titled in mrg, lt cr/stn, 14x10", lot 23, SBY 2/23/89 ... 2,530
Engine Room, #75, litho, 1930, p/s, full mrgs, lt stn, 10x12", lot 24, SBY 2/23/89 OE ... 2,090
Little Dolphin, litho, 12x8", Assn Am Artists, lot 188, WG 10/19/88 ... 160
Little Ranchero, 1st state, aqua, p/s, 12x9", lot 120, WG 1/19/89 UE ... 175
Pair: Self-Portrait, Paris; Self-Portrait; ed of 40/50, litho & wood engr, 1929/1931, unfr, C-NY 1/22/88 OE ... 715
Pedro, #37, sftgr etch/aqua/laid handmade paper, 1933, p/s, lt trm mrgs, lt sl, 12x7", lot 2940, B/B 4/19/88 ... 275
Rubber Center, ed of 50, wc/thin laid Japan, 1928, p/s, inscr To Dr E Eliot, lt sl/cr mrgs, 10x13", lot 224, SBY 5/11/89 ... 1,320

CORINTH, Lovis (German, 1858-1925)
Am Walchensee: Garten am Walchensee; a/p, drypt/van Gelder Zonen, 1920, p/s, full mrgs, lt tr, 10x7", SBY 2/25/88 ... 1,100
Wilhelmina (artist's daughter), ed of about 115, drypt, 1918, p/s, 7x5", lot 43, SWN 12/1/88 ... 330
Woman, wc/laid paper, ca 1920, p/s, lt stn img/mrg, L-10x9", lot 293, C-NY 11/1/88 UE ... 605

CORITA, Sister Mary
Market Basket, srgph, sgn, 29x39", lot 911, LH 3/20/88 ... 50

CORNEILLE, Cornelius (Willem)(French, 1922-)
Le Soleil Rouge, clr litho, p/s, 20x26", lot 144, FAP 2/24/89 UE ... 60

CORNELL, Joseph (American, 1903-1972)
Hotel du Nord, 115/125, clr scrpt, 1972, p/s, lt fox, S-20x16", Brooke Alexander, lot 600, C-NY 11/1/88 OE ... 1,760
Hotel du Nord, 55/125, clr litho, p/s, full mrgs, L-15x11", lot 115, PHL 10/28/88 ... 660

COROT, Jean Baptiste Camille (French, 1796-1875)
Environs de Rome, etch/laid paper, 1866, lt fox, 11x9", lot 179, SBY 2/25/89 ... 605
Portfolio: Douze Croquis & Dessins Originaux; litho, 1871, 23x16", orig wrappers, Lemercier/Robaut, lot 21, C-NY 11/1/88 ... 38,500
Sous Bois, litho/tan wove paper mounted on wove paper, 1871, full mrgs, rpr tr/fox, 9x7", lot 180, SBY 2/25/88 ... 1,100
Souvenir d'Italie, 1st state, etch/Japan, 1866, mrg corner missing, tp on verso, P-13x9", lot 592, C-NY 5/10/89 UE ... 550

CORREGIO, Antonio; after (Italian, 1494-1534)
Mystic Marriage of St Catherine, engr, ca 1630, 8x8", Capitelli, lot 44, SWN 12/1/88 UE ... 145

COSTIGAN, John (American, 1888-1972)
Family in the Fields, etch, p/s, no size given, WG 10/19/88 ... 100
Group of 3: Boy with Cows; Fishermen Three; Figures with Cow; etch/wove paper, 1939, p/s, lt stn, lot 2939, B/B 2/16/88 ... 220
Group of 3: Going Home; Workers of the Soil; Fall Plowing; etch, p/s, titled, P-9x14"/P-8x13", lot 9, PHL 6/16/88 UE ... 200

COTTINGHAM, Robert (American, 1935-)
Hot, 37/100, clr litho, 1973, p/s, L-21x21", lot 116, PHL 10/28/88 ... 275
Ice, 28/50, etch/aqua, 1975, p/s, Landfall bstp, full mrgs, lt cr, 11x11", lot 620, SBY 2/23/89 ... 440
Patte's, 8/10, aside from ed of 150, litho, 1980, p/s, 14x14", lot 62, SWN 6/15/89 ... 310

COVARRUBIAS, Miguel (Mexican, 1904-1957)
Rice Granary, Bali; ed of 250, litho, ca 1948, 13x10", Assn Am Artists, lot 63, SWN 6/15/89 UE ... 220

COZZENS, Frederick Shiller (American, 1856-1928)
International Yacht Race 1887 (Volunteer & Thistle), L-15x222", RAB 8/1/89 ... 1,200

COZZENS, Frederick Shiller; after (American, 1856-1928)
International Yacht Race 1887, litho, lt fox, 1888, lg folio, RAB 8/1/88 OE ... 700
Untitled (three American warships by the Statue of Liberty), litho, sm folio, RAB 3/14/89 ... 170
Untitled (yacht race between the America/Maria/Una/Ray), litho, L-14x21", RAB 3/14/89 OE ... 1,250

CRANACH, Lucas (German, 15th/16th C)
Penance of St John Chrysostom, 2nd state, etch/Arms of Saxony, 1509, trm, 6x8", lot 18, SBY 5/11/89 .... **17,050**
CRAWFORD, Ralston (American, 1906-1978)
Gray Street, clr scrpt/wove paper, 1940, p/s, titled, lt rpr, L-12x15", Cincinnati Modern Art Soc, lot 160, C-NY 1/19/89 .... **880**
Overseas Highway, ed of unrecorded size, clr scrpt, 1950, p/s, lt stn/sl, L-10x16", Jack Rich, lot 18, C-NY 5/11/88 OE **3,520**
Overseas Highway, 1/25, clr litho/wove paper, p/s, full mrgs, lt fox recto/verso, lt tr mrg, L-10x16", SBY 5/12/88 OE **24,200**
CRESPIN, Adolphe Louis Charles (Belgian, 1859-1944)
Exposition d'Art Ancien Bruxellois, clr litho/poster paper, lt fld img, unfr, 50x34", Couweloos, lot 293, FAP 2/24/89 UE **375**
Peinture Decorative et ce Batiment, clr litho/poster paper, linen backed 23x15", lot 244, FAP 2/24/89 UE **100**
CROSBY & CO. (19th C)
Hinkley Locomotive Works, Boston; chromolitho/gum arabic, 1860, lt stn/cr, S-20x30", lot 556, SBY 1/28/88 .... **1,100**
CROSS, Henri Edmond (French, 1856-1910)
In den Champs-Elysees, clr litho/Chine, 1898, lt cr/stn mrgs, lt scr verso, L-8x10", lot 594, C-NY 5/10/89 OE **935**
CUCCHI, Enzo (Italian, 1950-)
L'Elefante di Giotto, 33/45, brn & blk etch/aqua/drypt, 1986, p/s, S-54x100", Peter Blum, lot 601, C-NY 11/1/88 .... **6,050**
Triptych: La Lupa di Roma; 31/45, clr aqua/drypt/slksc, 1984-85, p/s, ea 77x38", Blum/Schellmann, lot 931, SBY 5/13/89 .... **13,200**
Triptych: La Lupa di Roma; 39/45, aqua/drypt/slksc, 1984-85, p/s, S-77x38", Blum/Schellmann, lot 731, SBY 11/5/88 .... **17,600**
Un Immagine Oscura, 22/30, aqua/slksc, 1982, p/s, full mrgs, 35x55", Blum, lot 930, SBY 5/13/89 .... **4,950**
CUEVAS, Jose Luis (Mexican, 1934-)
Portfolio: Recollections of Childhood; 13/200, 12 litho w/text, 1962, p/s, no size given, lot 25, SBY 2/23/89 OE **1,650**
Quevedo, V, etch/aqua/wht wove paper, p/s, Collector bstp, 22x16", lot 2940, B/B 2/16/88 .... **137**
CURRIER & IVES
Abraham Lincoln, hc litho, 1861, 11x14", lot 38, GAI 3/17/89 .... **275**
American Choice Fruits, hc litho/gum arabic, 1868, lt stn/scuff/tr, S-22x28", lot 562, SBY 1/28/88 OE **1,430**
American Country Life, October Afternoon; hc litho/wove paper, 1855, lt stn/sl mrgs, L-17x28", lot 37, C-NY 1/19/89 .... **1,045**
American Country Life, Pleasures of Winter; clr litho/wove paper, 1855, lt scr/stn, L-17x24", lot 38, C-NY 1/19/89 .... **660**
American Country Life, Pleasures of Winter; litho, lt fox, lg folio, RAB 5/23/89 UE **1,200**
American Express Train, clr litho/wove paper, 1855, lt fox/stn, L-16x26", lot 39, C-NY 1/19/89 OE **15,400**
American Farm Scenes No 1, hc litho/wove paper, 1853, lt fox img, lt sl/nick, stn verso, 17x24", lot 40, C-NY 1/19/89 .... **1,540**
American Farm Scenes No 2 (Summer), hc litho, 1853, lt cr img, lt tr/stn mrgs & verso, S-21x28", lot 577, SBY 1/28/88 .... **2,750**
American Farm Scenes No 2 (Summer), hc litho/gum arabic, 1853, lt stn/ls/sl, S-21x28", lot 573, SBY 1/28/88 .... **2,200**
American Farm Scenes No 3 (Autumn), hc litho/gum arabic, 1853, lt cr img, stn/sl/tr, S-22x29", lot 575, SBY 1/28/88 .... **2,200**
American Field Sports, Retrieving; hc litho, 1857, rpr tr mrg, lt scuff/stn/sl, S-23x30", lot 595, SBY 1/28/88 .... **2,860**
American Forest Scene, Maple Sugaring; litho, 1856, lt stn/fox, laid down, S-25x33", lot 576, SBY 1/28/88 OE **4,620**
American Frontier Life, On the War Path; hc litho/gum arabic/wove paper, 1863, lt scr/stn mrgs, L-18x27", C-NY 1/22/88 .... **2,200**
American Fruit Piece, hc litho, lt stn, 16x20", lot 307, GAI 5/13/88 .... **45**

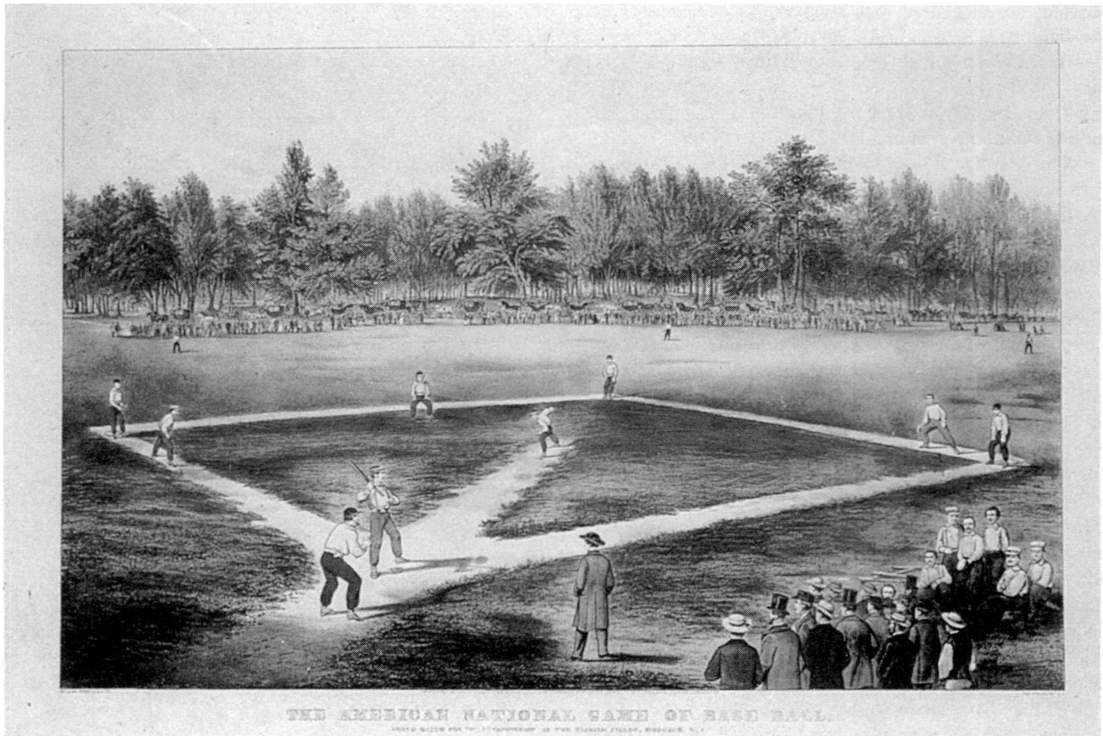

American National Game of Baseball, Grand Match of the Championship at the Elysian Fields, Hoboken, NJ; clr litho/wove paper, 1866, lt fox/stn/sl, L-20x30", lot 43, C-NY 1/19/89 OE; $30,800

American Homestead, Autumn; litho, lt fox, sm folio, RAB 9/8/88	350
American Homestead, Summer; litho, lt fox, sm folio, RAB 9/8/88	275
American Homestead, Winter; hc litho, trm mrgs, lt stn/faded, 10x14", lot 251, GAI 5/26/89	395
American Homestead, Winter; litho, sm folio, RAB 9/8/88 UE	700
American National Game of Baseball, hc litho/wove paper, 1866, rpr tr, cr corner, laid down, L-20x30", C-NY 1/22/88	11,000
American Railroad Scene, Lightning Express Trains Leaving the Junction; litho, 1874, 25x36", Parsons, SBY 1/28/88	19,800
American Railroad Scene, Lightning Express Trains...; litho, 1st state, 1874, fox/stn, unfr, L-19x32", C-NY 1/22/88 OE	22,000
American Steamboats on the Hudson, Passing the Highlands; chromolitho, 1874, S-24x38", Parsons, lot 566, SBY 1/28/88	2,200
American Winter Scenes, Morning; hc litho, 1854, titled, lt stn, L-17x24", lot 77, RWS 10/27/89 OE	5,500
American Winter Scenes, Morning; hc litho/gum arabic, 1854, lt fox/stn/scr, S-22x28", lot 579, SBY 1/28/88	5,500
American Winter Scenes, Morning; litho/wove paper, 1854, rpr tr/lt stn/sl/fox mrgs, unfr, L-17x24", C-NY 1/22/88 OE	4,180
Among the Pines, hc litho, 14x18", lot 636, GAI 9/22/89	100
Andrew Jackson, hc litho, 13x17", lot 39, GAI 3/17/89	325
Barefoot Boy, hc litho, 1873, lt stn, sm hole in title, 12x16", lot 96, GAI 7/8/88	75
Battle of Antietam, Maryland, September 17, 1862; hc litho, lt stn/tr mrg, 14x18", lot 408, GAI 3/17/89	225
Battle of Cerro Gordo April 18, 1847; hc litho, 1847, stn, 10x14", lot 573, GAI 3/17/89	115
Beauties of Billiards, Carom on the Dark Red; hc litho, 1869, lt stn/ls/tr mrgs, unfr, 16x25", RWS 8/20/88 OE	900
Black Duck Shooting, hc litho, 15x19", lot 276, GAI 4/7/89	150
Bombardment & Capture of Fort Henry, Tennessee, 1862; hc litho, lt stn/tr mrgs, 12x16", lot 407, GAI 3/17/89	250
Bouquet of Fruit, hc litho, 1875, 15x20", lot 586, GAI 11/24/89	65
Brook Trout, Just Caught; hc litho/gum arabic, ca 1838-72, lt scuff img, lt ls/cr/sl, S-15x20", lot 594, SBY 1/28/88	770
Brunn Castle, Valley of the Atmuhl, Bavaria; clr litho w/hc, lt sl/lstn mrgs, tstn, unfr, L-16x23", C-NY 1/22/88 UE	55
Camping Out, Some of the Right Sort; hc litho, 1856, lt ls mrg, lt sl/stn, S-22x30", lot 596, SBY 1/28/88 OE	6,325
Camping Out, Some of the Right Sort; hc litho/wove paper, 1856, lt stn/scuff, L-19x28", lot 47, C-NY 1/19/89	880
Camping Out, Some of the Right Sort; litho, lt trm mrgs, lg folio, RAB 9/8/88	1,400
Cares of a Family, hc litho/wove paper, 1856, trm mrgs, lt rpr/stn/sl, L-18x24", lot 48, C-NY 1/19/89 UE	220
Cass & Butler, hc litho, 1848, stn, 13x17", lot 150, GAI 3/17/89	225
Central Park, Bridge; hc litho/wove paper, titled, lt stn/sl/fox, L-8x13", lot 164, RWS 10/27/89 UE	250
Cherry Time, hc litho, 1866, lt stn/tr, L-10x16", lot 192, RWS 10/27/89	550
City of New York, chromolitho, 1870, lt stn/fox img, lt ls to edges, S-25x37", lot 608, SBY 1/28/88	4,400
City of New York, chromolitho, 1870, lt tr/stn img, lt sl/cr/tr mrgs, sl/scr verso, S-24x35", lot 609, SBY 1/28/88 OE	4,125
City of New York, From Jersey City; hc litho, 1849, lt stn/scuff img, lt ls/scr mrgs, S-11x15", lot 607, SBY 1/28/88	880
Clelland & Pendleton, hc litho, 1864, stn, 13x17", lot 145, GAI 3/17/89	275
Clipper Ship Cosmos, chromolitho, 1838-72, lt cr img, stn/fox verso, 10x14", lot 547, SBY 1/28/88	1,540
Clipper Ship Dreadnought...; hc litho/wove paper, 1856, lt cr img, rpr tr in mrgs, L-16x25", lot 49, C-NY 1/19/89 OE	1,540
Clipper Ship Racer, hc litho/gum arabic, ca 1855, trm mrgs, lt scuff, stn/sl/fox, 16x24", lot 553, SBY 1/28/88	4,180
Clipper Ship Sweepstakes, reprint litho, lg folio, RAB 3/14/89	225
Coming From the Trot, Sports on Home Stretch; hc litho/gum arabic, 1869, lt scuff/fox/stn, S-22x32", SBY 1/28/88	2,200
Cottage Door, Yard...Evening; hc litho, 1855, titled, lt stn/tr, L-10x15", lot 52, RWS 10/27/89	225
Danger Signal, chromolitho/thin wove paper, 1884, lt fox/sl, L-17x29", lot 51, C-NY 1/19/89 OE	2,860
Dark Town Trotter Ready for the Word...; 1892, lt fox, S-13x18", lot 219, FAP 2/24/89 UE	125
Daughter of the Regiment, hc litho, lt trm mrgs, lt cr/stn, 10x14", lot 196, GAI 3/17/89	125
Death of Andre 1780, hc litho, 1845, stn/faded, 10x14", lot 571, GAI 3/17/89	175
Death of General Zachary Taylor, hc litho, 1850, lt trm mrgs, lt tr, 10x14", lot 411, GAI 7/29/88	75
Death of General Zachary Taylor, hc litho, 1850, 10x14", lot 210, GAI 3/17/89	175
Death of Harrison, April 4, AD 1841; hc litho, 10x14", lot 209, GAI 3/17/89	480
Death of Major Ringgold, hc litho, 1846, stn, 12x16", lot 411, GAI 3/17/89	85
Death of Tecumseh, 10x14", lot 3, MG 5/28/88	110
Death of Warren, hc litho, lt stn, 10x14", lot 568, GAI 3/17/89	175
Eventide, October, The Village Inn; hc litho/wove paper, 1867, lt scr img, fox/stn, L-14x25", lot 52, C-NY 1/19/89 OE	1,650
Fall of Richmond, Virginia on the Night of April 2nd 1865; litho, lt fox, sm folio, RAB 9/8/88	225
Farmer's Home, Autumn; litho, 1864, lt stn img, lt tr mrgs, lt tr/cr/ls to edges, S-19x26", lot 581, SBY 1/28/88	2,475
Farmyard in Winter, hc litho/wove paper, 1861, lt stn, lt ls mrgs, old tp on verso, L-16x24", lot 53, C-NY 1/19/89	2,420
Finish Line, chromolitho, 1877, trm mrgs, lt scr/sl/stn/fox, 20x28", lot 600, SBY 1/28/88	770
Flowers & Fruit, hc litho, trm mrgs, title removed, stn, 10x13", lot 596, GAI 5/26/89	25
Four Seasons of Life: Middle Age, The Season of Strength; hc litho/wove paper, 1868, lt stn/sl, 15x23", C-NY 1/19/89 OE	1,210
Fremont & Cochrane, hc litho, 1864, 13x17", lot 144, GAI 3/17/89	350
Fremont & Dayton, hc litho, 1856, 13x17", lot 142, GAI 3/17/89	325
Fruit & Flowers, hc litho, stn/ls/tr, 16x19", lot 2, GAI 2/10/89	85
Fruit Piece, litho, full mrgs, orig fr, sm folio, RAB 5/17/88 UE	125
Fruits, Summer Varieties; hc litho, lt stn/ls mrgs, 16x20", lot 1, GAI 2/10/89	25
Fruits & Flowers of Summer, hc litho/gum arabic, 1866, lt stn/skinned, S-16x19", lot 565, SBY 1/28/88	660
General Franklin Pierce, hc litho, lt stn, 10x14", lot 41, GAI 3/17/89	175
General Israel Putnam, hc litho, 1845, lt trm mrgs, stn, 10x14", lot 417, GAI 7/29/88	95
General Lewis Cass, hc litho, 1846, lt stn, 10x14", lot 160, GAI 3/17/89	175
General Stoneman's Great Cavalry Raid May 1863, hc litho, lt stn, 10x13", lot 536, GAI 3/17/89	125
General William F Packer, Governor of Pennsylvania; hc litho, lt tr mrg, 12x16", lot 418, GAI 7/29/89	85
George M Dallas, hc litho, 1845, lt stn, 10x14", lot 558, GAI 3/17/89	65
Geroge Washington, hc litho, lt stn, 10x14", lot 37, GAI 3/17/89	275
Going Against the Stream, hc litho, tr/ls/rpr, 16x20", lot 67, GAI 9/22/89	35
Going to the Trot, Good Day & Good Track; hc litho/gum arabic, 1869, lt stn/fox/ls, S-22x32", lot 603, SBY 1/28/88	2,200

Grand National Democratic Banner, Cass & Butler; hc litho, lt stn, 12x16", lot 181, GAI 3/17/89	275
Grand National Democratic Banner, Pierce & King; hc litho, lt stn/ls, 12x16", lot 182, GAI 3/17/89	300
Grand National Democratic Banner, Polk & Dallas; hc litho, 1844, 10x14", lot 43, GAI 3/17/89	300
Grand National Whig Banner, Clay & Frelinghuysen; hc litho, 1844, lt stn, 10x14", lot 40, GAI 3/17/89	150
Grand National Whig Banner, Henry Clay; hc litho, 1844, lt stn, 10x14", lot 173, GAI 3/17/89	225
Great Bartholdi Statue, Liberty...; chromo, 1885, cr mrg, glued to overmat mrg, unfr, L-24x17", C-NY 1/22/88	1,760
Great Pacer Sorrel Dan, hc litho, 1880, lt stn/ls, 12x16", lot 21, GAI 4/21/89	225
Group of 3: Cross Matched Team; Point of the Joke; Trotting Queen Maud...; litho, 1878-81, lot 599, SBY 1/28/88	660
Group of 3: Glimpse of the Homestead; New England Home; Old Oaken Bucket; litho, ca 1870, lt stn/sl, SBY 1/28/88 OE	1,100
Group of 3: Infant Brood, Moosehead Lake, Trout Brook; hc litho/gum arabic, 1865/1862, stn, unfr, C-NY 1/22/88 OE	880
Group of 4: Home in the Wilderness; Meeting of the Waters; Jolly Young Ducks; Fruit Vase; litho, ca 1870, SBY 1/28/88	990
Harvesting, The Last Load; litho, lt fox, lt tr mrg/img, sm folio, RAB 5/23/89 UE	225
Haunted Castle, hc litho, lt trm mrgs, lt stn, 12x16", lot 147, GAI 2/10/89	75
Haying Time, The First Load; hc litho/wove paper, 1868, ltstn/fox/stn, L-16x24", lot 58, C-NY 1/19/89 OE	4,620
Haying Time, The First Load; hc litho/wove paper, 1868, trm to img, stn/cr, L-16x23", lot 57, C-NY 1/19/89 UE	220
Henry Clay Nominated for Eleventh President...; hc litho, lt stn/cr, 10x14", lot 175, GAI 3/17/89	140
Henry Clay of Kentucky, hc litho, 1844, lt stn, 10x14", lot 174, GAI 3/17/89	400
Heroine of the Monmouth, Molly Pitcher; hc litho, lt trm mrgs, 12x14", lot 3, GAI 3/17/89	225
Home of Washington, hc litho, stn, 22x26", lot 172, GAI 3/17/89	300
Home to Thanksgiving, hc litho/wove paper, 1867, 2 rpr tr img, lstn mrgs/verso, ls to mrg, L-15x21", C-NY 1/22/88 OE	8,250
Husking, hc litho/wove paper, 1861, full mrgs, lt fox/ls/tr, stn on verso, L-21x27", lot 59, C-NY 1/19/89	7,150
In the Northern Wilds, Trapping Beaver; hc litho/gum arabic, ca 1872-74, lt stn/sl, S-11x15", lot 597, SBY 1/28/88	495
Infant Brood, hc litho, lt stn/2 tr, 15x18", lot 231, GAI 4/21/89	150
Infant Savior, hc litho, lt trm mrgs, lt stn, 10x13", lot 203, GAI 2/10/89	45
James Buchanan, hc litho, lt cr, 10x14", lot 208, GAI 3/17/89	100
James K Polk, hc litho, 1846, full mrgs, lt stn, 14x19", lot 533, GAI 3/17/89	125
James K Polk, litho, orig fr, sm folio, RAB 5/17/88 UE	70
James Monroe, hc litho, 10x14", lot 205, GAI 3/17/89	275
John Adams, hc litho, lt stn, 10x14", lot 202, GAI 3/17/89	100
John C Breckinridge, hc litho, lt stn, 10x14", GAI 3/17/89	65
John C Fremont, hc litho, 1856, 10x14", lot 158, GAI 3/17/89	180
John C Fremont, Republican Candidate for 15th President...; hc litho, lt trm mrg, lt stn, unfr, 10x14", GAI 7/29/88	100
John Quincy Adams, hc litho, 10x14", lot 201, GAI 3/17/89	100
John Tyler, hc litho, 10x14", lot 42, GAI 3/17/89	225
Lafayette at the Tomb of Washington, hc litho, lt trm mrgs, lt stn, 10x14", lot 201, GAI 2/10/89	115
Lake George New York, litho, fox, orig fr, sm folio, RAB 5/17/88 UE	100
Landing of the Pilgrims, 10x14", lot 5, MG 5/28/88	115
Last War Whoop, litho/wove paper, 1st state of 2, 1856, lstn, rpr tr img, ls corners, tp verso, L-18x26", C-NY 1/22/88	1,760
Lexington of 1861, hc litho, lt trm mrgs, lt stn/rpr, 10x14", lot 416, GAI 7/29/88	175
Lieutenant-General Ulysses S Grant, hc litho, stn/tr, 10x14", lot 538, GAI 3/17/89	90
Life & Age of Woman, hc litho, lt trm mrgs, lt stn/ls, 10x14", lot 175, GAI 11/25/88	125
Life in the Woods, Returning to Camp; hc litho, 1860, titled, lt stn, L-19x28", lot 51, RWS 10/27/89	1,900
Life of a Fireman, hc litho, 17x26", lot 445, FAP 4/15/88 OE	1,430
Life of a Fireman, The Fire-Now Then with a Will-Shake Her Up Boys!; litho, 1854, L-17x26", lot 61, C-NY 1/19/89 OE	1,980
Life of a Fireman, The Ruins-Take Up-Man Your Rope; litho, 1854, lt stn/scuff, L-17x26", lot 62, C-NY 1/19/89	1,320
Life of a Sportsman, Going Out; hc litho/wove paper, 1872, lt stn/sl/fox, L-8x13", lot 63, C-NY 1/19/89	352
Life on the Prairie, The Buffalo Hunt; hc litho/gum arabic/wove paper, lt sl/fox, stn mrgs/verso, L-19x27", C-NY 1/22/88	3,300
Lightning Express Trains, Leaving the Junction; hc litho, 1863, lg mrgs, lt stn/tr, L-18x28", lot 64, C-NY 1/19/89 OE	19,800
Little Bear, clr litho, 12x10", lot 194, DM 10/14/88	65
Little Brother & Sister, hc litho, lt trm mrgs, 9x14", lot 470, GAI 4/7/89	100
Little Mamma, hc litho, lt trm mrgs, stn, 11x15", lot 202, GAI 2/10/89	75
Little More Grape, Captain Bragg; hc litho, 1847, stn/faded, 10x14", lot 548, GAI 3/17/89	100
Little Sisters, hc litho, lt trm mrgs, lt stn, 12x16", lot 98, GAI 7/8/88	60
Major-General Joseph Hooker, hc litho, 10x14", lot 410, GAI 3/17/89	150
Major-General Winfield Scott, hc litho, 1846, stn/sl, 10x14", lot 570, GAI 3/17/89	75
Major-General Winfield Scott, hc litho, 1847, stn/sl, lot 572, GAI 3/17/89	150
Martin Van Buren, hc litho, lt stn, 10x14", lot 206, GAI 3/17/89	250
Midnight Race on the Mississippi, hc litho/gum arabic, 1875, trm mrgs, rpr img, stn/fox, S-12x16", lot 567, SBY 1/28/88	440
Mink Trapping, Prime; hc litho/gum arabic/wove paper, lt trm mrgs, stn/sl mrgs/verso, rpr tr, L-19x28", C-NY 1/22/88	6,600
Moosehead Lake, hc litho, lt stn, 13x17", lot 236, GAI 4/21/89	125
Mountain Ramble, hc litho, 15x19", lot 637, GAI 5/26/89	200
Mountain Spring, hc litho, 1862, full mrgs, lt stn, 20x24", lot 2, GAI 9/23/88	350
Mrs James K Polk, hc litho, 1946, stn, 14x19", lot 534, GAI 3/17/89	125
My Boyhood's Home, litho, full mrgs, sm folio, RAB 9/8/88	325
Naval Heroes, hc litho, 1846, lt stn, 10x14", lot 44, GAI 3/17/89	400
New England Winter Scene, hc litho, 1861, lt cr img, lt tr/scr mrgs, backed w/wove paper, S-20x25", SBY 1/28/88	1,650
New England Winter Scene, hc litho/gum arabic/wove paper, 1861, tstn mrg edges/verso, L-16x24", C-NY 1/22/88 OE	7,150
New York Bay, From Bay Ridge; hc litho/wove paper, 1860, lt fox/stn, L-15x20", lot 65, C-NY 1/19/89 OE	2,420
Niagara Falls, hc litho, lt trm/tr mrgs, 12x15", lot 15, GAI 7/29/88	55
Noah's Ark, hc litho, ca 1845, lt trm mrgs, lt faded/rpr tr, 11x14", lot 419, GAI 7/29/88	135
Noah's Ark, hc litho, lt trm mrgs, 12x14", lot 2, GAI 7/29/88	235

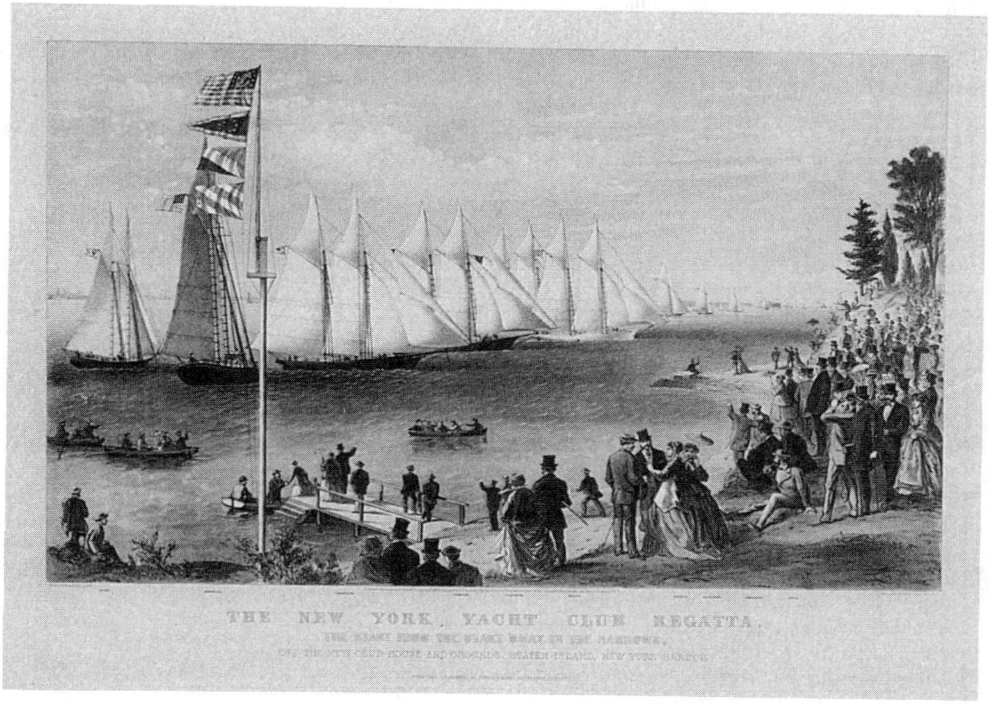

New York Yacht Club Regatta, by Parsons & Atwater, hc litho/gum arabic/wove paper, 1869, lt fox/stn/rub, L-17x28", lot 196, C-NY 6/3/89 OE; $12,100

Noah's Ark, litho, lt fox mrg, sm folio, RAB 5/23/89	250
Old Farm Gate, hc litho/wove paper, 1864, lt stn/sl mrgs, lt tr, stn on verso, L-16x23", lot 66, C-NY 1/19/89	825
Old Farm House, hc litho/gum arabic, 1872, lt stn/fox/ls, S-12x16", lot 585, SBY 1/28/88	770
Old Homestead in Winter, hc litho/gum arabic, 1864, lt fox img, lt sl/skinned/stn, S-24x31", lot 586, SBY 1/28/88	4,125
Old Homestead in Winter, hc litho/gum arabic/wove paper, 1864, lt fox/lstn/wstn, P-19x27", C-NY 1/22/88	8,250
Old Homestead in Winter, hc litho/gum arabic/wove paper, 1864, stn recto/verso, tstn mrgs, L-26x19", C-NY 1/22/88 OE	4,950
Old Homestead in Winter, 1864; hc litho, 1862, L-19x27", lot 50, RWS 10/27/89	5,500
Old Oaken Bucket, hc litho, 1872, stn/tr mrg, 11x15", lot 102, GAI 5/26/89	135
Old Oaken Bucket, hc litho, 1872, 16x20", lot 186, GAI 3/17/89	250
On a Point (dogs in landscape), litho, full mrgs, lt fox, sm folio, RAB 5/17/88 UE	550
Pair: American Homestead Winter; Central Park in Winter; hc litho, 1868 & ca 1872-74, S-11x15", SBY 1/28/88	1,980
Pair: Autumn Fruits; Summer Fruits; hc litho, 1861, lt faded/fox/stn, S-16x21", lot 563, SBY 1/28/88 OE	2,640
Pair: Celebrated Trotting Mares Maude S & Aldine...; Celebrated Trotting Team Edward & Swiveller; lot 604, SBY 1/28/88	2,750
Pair: Central Park, the Drive; Cozzen's Dock, West Point; hc litho, 1862, lt stn/fox, L-11x15", lot 163, RWS 10/27/89 OE	2,100
Pair: Custom House, New York; Capitol at Washington; hc litho/wove paper, w/mrgs, lt stn/fox, C-NY 1/22/88	770
Pair: Great Oyster Eating Match...The Start; The Finish; chromolitho, 1886, stn/tr, S-13x17", C-SK 6/9/88	740
Pair: Life of a Fireman; Jump Her Boys, Jump Her; hc litho, 1854, lt cr/rpr, lt cr img, L-17x26", lot 572, SBY 1/28/88	2,750
Pair: Maiden's Rock, Mississippi River; Off the Port; hc litho, ca 1850 & ca 1885, 8x13"/9x14", lot 606, SBY 1/28/88	770
Pair: Mountain Pass, Sierra Nevada; Pair of Nutcrackers; hc litho, 1867/undtd, unfr, C-NY 1/22/88 OE	1,980
Pair: On the Hudson; On the Mississippi; hc litho, 1869, lt sl/fox/stn mrgs, S-10x14", lot 569, SBY 1/28/88	1,100
Pair: Parole...Brown Gelding; Indianapolis; hc litho, 1879 & 1878, lt stn, L-18x23", lot 117, RWS 10/27/89	800
Pair: Pickerel; Strawberries; hc litho, 1870 & 1872, lt stn/fox, L-9x13", lot 194, RWS 10/27/89	450
Pair: Profit & Loss; Black Fish Nibble; hc litho, lt stn/tr mrgs, 9x13"/9x15", lot 213, FAP 2/24/89 OE	325
Pair: Pursuit; Last War-Whoop; hc litho, 1856, wstn, L-18x26", lot 79, RWS 10/27/89 UE	1,000
Pair: Rocky Mountains; Discovery of the Mississippi; litho, 10x13", SLK 9/26/88	225
Pair: Wild Duck Shooting, On the Wing; Morning in the Woods; hc litho, 1870 & 1852, 10x14"/17x21", SBY 1/28/88 UE	550
Pickerel, hc litho, 1872, lt stn, 16x20", lot 187, GAI 11/24/89	425
Pierce & King, hc litho, 1852, lt stn, 13x17", lot 141, GAI 3/17/89	250
Pigeon Shooting, Playing the Decoy; hc litho, 1862, stn/tr, L-19x28", lot 118, RWS 10/27/89 OE	1,500
Pocahontas Saving the Life of Captain John Smith, hc litho, stn/cr/tr, 12x16", lot 293, GAI 7/29/88	185
Portrait of Martin Van Buren, RAB 4/25/89	55
Prairie Hunter, One Rubbed Out!; hc litho/gum arabic/wove paper, 1852, rpr trs/lstn, L-14x21", C-NY 1/22/88	1,650
Presidents of the United States, hc litho, lt stn/faded, 10x14", lot 546, GAI 3/17/89	135
Presidents of the United States, Zachary Taylor (center medallion); hc litho, lt stn, tr mrg, 13x17", GAI 3/17/89	175
Presidents of the United States (Washington to President-Elect Polk); hc litho, sgn, 17x13", lot 69, GAI 9/22/89	75
RB Conkling's Bay Gelding Rarus, the King of Trotters, 1878; litho, sgn in stone, lt stn, L-17x26", RWS 8/20/88 OE	1,400
Rising Family, hc litho/gum arabic/wove paper, 1857, mstn, tp undermat at mrg edges, 18x24", C-NY 1/22/88	3,080
Rising Family, hc litho/wove paper, 1857, lt rpr img, tr/scr/ls, laid down, L-18x24", lot 67, C-NY 1/19/89	1,650
Roadside Mill, hc litho, 1870, lt stn, 13x17", lot 234, GAI 4/21/89	200
Sale of the Pet Lamb, hc litho, lt trm mrgs, stn, 18x22", lot 146, GAI 2/10/89	350
Scenery of the Catskills, hc litho, lt trm mrgs, lt stn, 10x14", lot 527, GAI 5/26/89	190
Scott & Graham, hc litho, 1852, lt stn, 13x17", lot 148, GAI 3/17/89	148

Seige of Charleston, August 1863; hc litho, stn, 10x14", lot 537, GAI 3/17/89 ... 275

Set of 4: American Homestead, Spring; Summer; Autumn; Winter; litho, 1868-69, lt stn, L-8x12", lot 193, RWS 10/27/89 ... 1,600

Set of 4: American Homestead, Spring; Summer; Autumn; Winter; litho, 1868-69, S-11x14", lot 577, SBY 1/28/88 OE ... 1,320

Set of 4: American Homestead, Spring; Summer;Autumn; Winter; hc litho/wove paper, 1868-69, L-8x13", lot 42, C-NY 1/19/89 ... 1,760

Sinking of the Cumberland by the Iron Clad Merrimac Off Newport News...; litho, fox/stn, sm folio, RAB 5/17/88 ... 250

Snowed Up, Ruffed Grouse in Winter; hc litho/wove paper, 1867, lt fox/mstn, sl mrg/verso, L-14x20", C-NY 1/22/88 OE ... 4,620

Snowy Morning, hc litho/wove paper, 1864, lt lstn, lt fox/sl mrg, fox/stn verso, unfr, L-12x16", C-NY 1/22/88 OE ... 5,280

Stages of Woman's Life From the Cradle to the Grave, hc litho, 1850, lt ls, 14x18", lot 1, GAI 5/26/89 ... 185

Stanch Pointer (dog), litho, lt fox, orig fr, sm folio, RAB 5/17/88 ... 450

Stanch Pointer (dog), hc litho, 1870, stn/fox, 15x19", lot 233, GAI 4/21/89 ... 175

Stanch Pointer (dog), hc litho, 1871, lt trm mrgs, 12x15", lot 271, GAI 7/8/88 ... 255

Steamer Penobscot, litho, full mrgs, lt fox/wstn/tr, 1883, lg folio, RAB 11/10/88 OE ... 2,300

Summer Fruits, hc litho, 1861, lt stn/ls, 19x23", lot 76, GAI 11/24/89 ... 300

Summer Fruits & Flowers, hc litho, stn, oval 11x14", lot 647, GAI 5/26/89 ... 195

Summer Shades, hc litho/wove paper, 1859, lt stn/sl mrgs, old glue/stn on verso, L-15x23", lot 68A, C-NY 1/19/89 OE ... 1,320

Sunny-Side on the Hudson, hc litho, lt trm mrgs, lt cr, 13x16", lot 36, GAI 2/10/89 ... 125

Surrender of Cornwallis, hc litho, 1846, lt stn/faded, 10x14", lot 569, GAI 3/17/89 ... 225

Taylor & Fillmore, hc litho, 1848, stn, 13x17", lot 145, GAI 3/17/89 ... 275

Taylor & Fillmore, hc litho, 1849, lt stn, 13x17", lot 149, GAI 3/17/89 ... 250

Theodore Frelinghuysen, hc litho, 1844, lt stn img/mrg, 10x14", lot 560, GAI 3/17/89 ... 65

Three Little White Kittens, Their First Mouse; hc litho, 1871, lt trm mrgs, stn, 10x14", lot 137, GAI 5/26/89 ... 110

Through to the Pacific, hc litho/gum arabic, 1870, lt stn/fox, 8x13", lot 559, SBY 1/28/88 ... 880

Trapper's Campfire, hc litho/gum arabic/wove paper, 1866, lt stn/sl mrgs/verso, mstn, L-17x26", C-NY 1/22/88 OE ... 3,520

Trapper's Last Shot, hc litho/wove paper, lstn, rpr tr img/mrg, cr mrgs, stn/tp to verso, L-11x16", C-NY 1/22/88 ... 550

Tree of Life, hc litho, 1892, lt trm mrgs, lt stn/ls, 23x33", lot 477, GAI 7/29/88 ... 75

Trolling for Blue Fish, hc litho/gum arabic, 1866, lt stn/ls, L-19x28", lot 116, RWS 10/27/89 OE ... 11,000

Trotting Cracks on the Snow, hc litho/wove paper, 1858, lt stn/tr, mstn on verso, L-17x28", lot 69, C-NY 1/19/89 UE ... 1,100

Untitled, memorial scene registering deaths; hc litho, 17x12", lot 566, GAI 9/22/89 ... 65

Upper & Lower Bay at New York From the Battery...; hc litho, stn, unfr, L-9x13", lot 161, RWS 10/27/89 ... 850

Vase of Flowers, hc litho, 1870, lt cr, 17x13", lot 77, GAI 11/24/89 ... 125

View of New York From Brooklyn Heights, chromolitho, ca 1849, 13x17", C-NY 1/20/89 ... 1,430

View on the Housatonic, hc litho/wove paper, 1861, rpr tr, other minor defects, L-14x21", lot 70, C-NY 1/19/89 ... 275

View on the St Lawrence, Indian Encampment; hc litho, 10x14", lot 11, GAI 5/26/89 ... 185

Village Blacksmith, hc litho, 1838-72, lt stn/skinned/sl, lt cr/stn mrgs, S-16x20", lot 587, SBY 1/28/88 ... 550

Washington (full-figure portrait), hc litho, lt trm/stn, 10x14", lot 288, GAI 3/17/89 ... 95

Washington at Mount Vernon, 10x14", lot 4, MG 5/28/88 ... 200

Washington's Reception by the Ladies...; hc litho, lt faded/stn, 13x17", lot 471, GAI 3/17/89 ... 125

Water Jump, chromolitho, 1884, lt stn mrgs, S-26x36", lot 605, SBY 1/28/88 ... 990

Why Don't He Come?; hc litho, stn, 15x18", lot 235, GAI 4/21/89 ... 45

Wild Duck Shooting, hc litho/gum arabic/wove paper, 1852, stn img/mrgs/verso, lt fox, L-13x20", C-NY 1/22/88 OE ... 4,400

William A Graham, Wig Candidate for Vice President; hc litho, 1852, lt stn, 10x14', lot 561, GAI 3/17/89 ... 65

William Bigler, hc litho, lt stn, 10x14", lot 161, GAI 3/17/89 ... 75

William Henry Harrison, hc litho, stn, 10x14", lot 207, GAI 3/17/89 ... 120

William Penn's Treaty with the Indians, 10x14", lot 2, MG 5/28/88 ... 70

Winter in the Country, Cold Morning; hc litho/gum arabic, 1864, trm mrgs, lt fox/scr/stn, S-22x30", SBY 1/28/88 ... 7,425

Winter in the Country, Getting Ice; hc litho, 1864, lt stn, L-19x27", lot 76, RWS 10/27/89 OE ... 11,000

Winter in the Country, the Old Grist Mill; hc litho, 1864, full mrgs, lt stn, L-19x27", lot 78, RWS 10/27/89 OE ... 12,000

Winter Morning, litho/gum arabic/wove paper, 1861, lt lstn, rpr tr/cr mrg/img, ls/stn mrgs, L-11x15", C-NY 1/22/88 OE ... 1,430

Winter Pastime, litho/wove paper, 1855, lstn/tstn, stn img/mrg, tp/glued to undermat verso, L-10x14", C-NY 1/22/88 OE ... 2,200

Wooding Up on the Mississippi; hc litho/wove paper, 1863, full mrgs, lt rpr/stn/sl, L-18x28", lot 72, C-NY 1/19/89 ... 7,700

Young Napoleon, hc litho, stn, 16x13", lot 45, GAI 9/22/89 ... 45

Zachary Taylor, hc litho, 1849, 10x14", lot 203, GAI 3/17/89 ... 250

CURRY, John Steuart (American, 1897-1946)

Coyotes Stealing a Pig, 12/16, litho, 1927, p/s, stone sgn, trm mrg, lt stn/fox, L-10x15", RWS 3/16/89 ... 275

John Brown, ed of 250, litho, 1939, p/s, full mrgs, lt scr img, tp/glue in mrg, L-15x11", lot 19, C-NY 5/11/88 ... 2,860

John Brown, ed of 250, litho/wht wove paper, 1939, p/s, full mrgs, tp/gstn mrg, unfr, L-15x11", C-NY 1/22/88 ... 1,980

Kansas Wheat Ranch, ed of 25, litho/wove wm France, 1930, p/s, stone sgn, lt fox/stn/tr, tp, L-10x14", RWS 3/16/89 OE ... 400

Missed Leap, ed of 150, litho/cream wove paper, 1932, p/s, lt stn, tp to mat, L-17x10", lot 10, PHL 6/16/88 ... 600

Missed Leap, 65/100, litho/wove paper, 1934, p/s, titled, lt rub/stn/fox, L-17x10", lot 161, C-NY 1/19/89 OE ... 825

Our Good Earth, ed of 250, litho, 1940-41, p/s, full mrgs, sl/scr/stn, 13x10", Assn Am Artists, lot 26, SBY 2/23/89 OE ... 2,860

Prize Stallions, ed of 250, litho, 1938, p/s, titled, full mrgs, lt stn, 13x9", Assn Am Artists, lot 22, SBY 11/3/88 ... 1,100

Prize Stallions, ed of 250, litho/cream wove paper, 1938, p/s, titled, full mrgs, 13x9", Assn Am Artists, B/B 4/19/88 ... 1,100

Prize Stallions, litho, p/s, titled, unfr, 13x9", Assn Am Artists, lot 19, LH 3/20/88 OE ... 1,100

Sanctuary, litho, 1944, p/s, full mrgs, lt stn, L-12x16", lot 11, PHL 6/16/88 ... 600

Self, litho/wove wm GCM, 1939, p/s, full mrgs, lt sl mrg, 2 pieces tp in mrg corners, unfr, L-11x9", C-NY 1/22/88 ... 2,750

Summer Afternoon, ed of 250, litho/BFK Rives, 1940, p/s, dtd 39, full mrgs, L-10x14", lot 162, C-NY 1/19/89 OE ... 770

To the Train, ed of 30, litho/Rives, 1932, p/s, full mrgs, tp mrg, lt mstn verso, unfr, L-10x14", C-NY 1/22/88 ... 1,045

Tornado, litho, 1932, p/s, titled/inscr 25 prints, full(?) mrgs, lt sl, 10x14", lot 21, SBY 11/3/88 OE ... 4,400

D'ARCANGELO, Allan (American, 1930-)

Bars, AP30/30, aside from ed of 175, clr srgph, 1979, p/s, 26x24", lot 15, SWN 6/15/89 ... 195

June Moon, APVII, slksc/heavy wove paper, 1969, p/s, trm mrgs, lt sl, L-24x26", Domberger, lot 102, RWS 9/8/89 800

DALI, Salvador (Spanish, 1904-1989)

Astarte, Pl 11, a/p, ed of 350, litho, p/s, 12x16", lot 435, MG 7/30/88 UE 175
Book: Alice's Adventures in Wonderland; #1327, 1979, orig wrappers, Maecenas/Random House, lot 183, SBY 2/25/88 990
Cervantes, etch, pl/s, 7x5", lot 1310, LH 10/16/88 60
Couple on Horseback, a/p, clr etch, sgn, 16x23", lot 305, MG 3/26/88 UE 400
God, Time, Space, & the Pope; AXX/XXXV, clr etch/drypt, 1974, S-16x12", Transworld/Ateliers Rial, lot 46, SWN 12/1/88 UE 330
Helen of Troy, 2/50, clr etch, p/s, 16x20", lot 159, MG 5/28/88 350
King David, SA 44/300, glitter & hc etch/Japan, ca 1973, p/s, full mrgs, L-22x16", lot 65, SWN 6/15/89 UE 220
Le Chants de Maldoror, blk etch, 1934, inscr Bon a tirer XS in mrg, lt sl/fox, 9x7", Skira, lot 182, SBY 2/25/89 OE 770
Le Jugement, litho, p/s, 29x21", lot 912, LH 5/15/88 140
Nymph on Horseback, 192/200, monotype/glitter/wove Arches, p/s, artist bstp, lt stn, P-16x10", RWS 3/16/89 600
Odalisque, a/p, etch, sgn, 15x23", lot 306, MG 3/26/88 UE 400
Pair: Battle of Tetuan; Two Women in a Landscape; clr engr, bears signature, 16x13", lot 11, FAP 2/24/89 200
Pair: Palais de Institute; Historical Origins; etch & mixed media etch, ca 1968 & ca 1975, 17x24"/21x16", SWN 6/15/89 300
Paradise 18, wc, p/s, 10x7", lot 781, LH 3/20/88 OE 325
Paradise 19, wc, sgn, 10x7", lot 963, LH 3/20/88 OE 350
Portfolio: Boccace, Decameron; #19, total ed of 150, 10 drypt, 1972, orig wrappers, Transworld, lot 239, SBY 2/23/89 OE 4,675
Portfolio: Our Historical Heritage; 251/400, 1975, orig wrappers/slipcase, S-26x20", lot 447, SBY 5/11/89 3,520
Portfolio: Ses Peintures, ses Objects, ses Tissus Simultanes, ses Modes; 20 pochoirs, ca 1930, lot 241, SBY 2/23/89 OE 4,675
Portfolio: Song of Songs of King Solomon; #105, 12 etch, 1971, orig wrappers, S-22x15", Amiel, lot 238A, SBY 2/23/89 OE 6,875
Reconstruction of Venice, 76/250, clr litho, p/s, unfr, 23x31", lot 750, LH 5/15/88 375
Rhinoceros, 22/75, drypt/etch, p/s, 5x7", lot 67, SWN 6/15/89 220
St George & the Dragon, ed of 250, etch, 1947, p/s, Cleveland Print bstp, full mrgs, lt stn, 18x11", SBY 2/23/89 OE 6,600
St George & the Dragon, ed of 250, etch, 1947, p/s, Cleveland Print Club bstp, 18x11", lot 185, SBY 11/3/88 3,850
St George & the Dragon, ed of 250, etch w/pl tone, 1947, p/s, Cleveland Print Club stp, lt stn, P-28x11", SBY 5/12/88 4,950
St George & the Dragon, ed of 250, etch, 1947, p/s, Cleveland Print Club bstp, lt stn, unfr, P-18x11", C-NY 1/22/88 3,300
Suite: After Fifty Years of Surrealism; A11/195, 12 drypt/aqua, 1973, S-27x21", Transworld, lot 186, SBY 11/3/88 3,025
Time in Space, 53/300, litho, 1975, p/s, 30x20", lot 1165, LH 10/16/88 190
Untitled (semi-abstract), 6/200, litho, sgn, full mrgs, 22x14", RAB 3/27/89 UE 150

DALI, Salvador; after (Spanish, 1904-1989)

Crucifixion, 95/250, clr etch, bears signature, 27x18", lot 6, FAP 2/24/89 85
Sacrament of the Last Supper, 94/250, clr etch, bears signature, 18x28", lot 9, FAP 2/24/89 225

DANBY, Kenneth Edison (1940-)

Awaiting Winter, 31/100, clr litho, 1972, p/s, 16x22", lot 971, WAD 6/12/89 1,000

DANE, J. (American, 19th C)

Sailing Vessels, etch, 1882, p/s, 7x10", lot 69, WG 10/19/88 40

DANFORTH, S. Chester (American, 20th C)

Chicago Board of Trade, ed of 250, etch, P-12x7", lot 348, S/A 3/12/88 95

DANIELL, Thomas & William (British, 19th C)

Gate of the Loll-Baug at Fyzabad, clr engr, 18x24", lot 17, FAP 2/24/89 OE 400

DAUBIGNY, Charles Francois (French, 1817-1878)

Trees with Crows, 2nd state, etch, 1867, pl/s, 9x12", lot 47, SWN 12/1/88 385

DAUMIER, Honore (French, 1808-1879)

Ah! Tu Veux Frotter a la Presse; Pl 319, litho, 1832, lt stn/sl, 9x8", lot 70, SWN 6/15/89 OE 880
Ce Qu'on Appelle, Aller Jouir a la Campagne...; Delteil's 1st state, litho, 1843, lt sl/ls/cr, 10x9", SBY 11/3/88 UE 880
En Chemin de Fer...un Voisin Agreable; final state, litho/Chine applique, 1862, lt sl/cr/ls/tr, L-8x10", SBY 5/12/88 2,200
Enfonce Lafayette...Attrappe mon Vieux; litho, 1834, lt fld/scr/fox/stn, 14x19", Aubert/Delaunois, lot 24, C-NY 11/1/88 4,400
Le Ventre Legislaif, litho, 1834, lt fld/fox/sl, S-14x21", Aubert, lot 22, C-NY 11/1/88 16,500
Ne Vous y Frottez Pas!; litho, 1834, lt fld/rpr tr/fox, S-14x21", Aubert/Delaunois, lot 23, C-NY 11/1/88 OE 3,850
Pair: Robert Macaire Negociant; Un Profession de Foi; litho, 1937 & ca 1938, 9x9"/8x9", lot 71, SWN 6/15/89 220
Rue Transonain, Le 15 Avril 1834; litho, 1934, lt fld/ls/tr/fox, S-14x20", Delaunois, lot 25, C-NY 11/1/88 OE 14,300
Set of 39: Les Gens de Justice; litho, 1845-48, lt sl/scr, L-11x7" or smaller, Aubert, lot 26, C-NY 11/1/88 66,000

DAVID, Gustave (French, 1824-1891)

Pair: Le Sport Nautique, Perissoire; Le Sport Nautique, As de Course; litho, lt fox, 12x19", lot 122, FAP 2/24/89 OE 675

DAVID, Jaques Louis (French, 1748-1825)

Passage Du Mont St Bernard, hc litho, lt fox/stn mrgs, 16x13", lot 74, FAP 2/24/89 UE 25

DAVIES, Arthur Bowen (American, 1862-1928)

Antique Mirror, ed of ca 16, sftgr etch/aqua/laid paper, 1919, lt fox, tp verso, 9x6", RWS 3/16/89 375
Greek Athletes, ed of 35, litho, 1920, p/s, 12x10", lot 72, SWN 6/15/89 UE 195
Group of 3: Fountain of Youth, Ruddy Summer, Pleidas; ed of 35/20/40, sftgr etch/aqua, 1919, unfr, C-NY 1/22/88 825
Group of 3: Guiding Spirit; Andante; Profile; ed of 20/10/40, drypt/rlt, drypt, sftgr etch/aqua, unfr, C-NY 1/22/88 OE 880
Group of 3: Resurrection; Iris; Cupid & Psyche; drypt/aqua/cream laid or wove paper, lt sl, lot 2942, B/B 2/16/88 412
Kingdom of the Sun, aqua/etch, ca 1920, 9x6", lot 73, SWN 6/15/89 523
Pair: Against Green; Day's Journey End; etch/aqua/cream wove paper, bears signature, lt sl/stn, lot 2944, B/B 2/16/88 385
Pair: Baptism; Bathos; drypt/thin wove paper, pl/s, lt trm mrgs, lt tr/stn, no size given, lot 2945, B/B 2/16/88 247
Pair: Moonlight on the Grassy Bank; Uprising; aqua & sftgr/aqua/etch, ca 1920, p/s, 8x12", lot 74, SWN 6/15/89 OE 715
Pair: Triad; Bathing Woman & Servant; etch/drypt/thin wove paper, pl/s, lt tr/sl mrgs, lot 2943, B/B 2/16/88 385
Untitled, Portrait of a Woman; 79/150, litho/cream paper, pl/s, lt stn, 15x12", lot 2943, B/B 4/19/88 275

DAVIES, Ronald (American, 1937-)

Brick, 21/40, clr litho/Arches, 1983, p/s, dtd, Gemini bstp, full mrgs, 35x26", lot 3015, B/B 4/19/88 880

DAVIS, Richard Barrett; after (British, 1782-1854)
Hunter Pilot, clr engr, lt fox, 14x18", lot 110, FAP 2/24/89 UE **150**

DAVIS, Ronald (American, 1937-)
Big Open Box, APIX, aqua/etch/drypt, 1975, p/s, TGL bstp, S-20x24", lot 86, RWS 9/8/89 OE **475**

DAVIS, Stark (American, 1885-)
Cats, 8/30, etch, p/s, titled, stn, 6x12", lot 111, WG 10/19/88 .... **110**

DAVIS, Stuart (American, 1894-1964)
Anchor, ed of 100, litho, 1936, sgn in stone, intl, 9x13", Am Artist School, lot 75, SWN 6/15/89 OE **1,430**
Arch No 1, 11/30, litho/India applique, 1929, p/s, lstn/scuff, trs/cr/stn mrgs, stn verso, unfr, L-9x13", C-NY 1/22/88 .... **1,100**
Arch No 1, 12/30, litho/Chine colle, 1929, p/s, lt stn, L-9x13", lot 436, C-NY 5/10/89 OE **8,800**
Bass Rocks, ed of 100, clr scrpt, 1941, p/s, lt stn/sl, L-9x12", lot 20, C-NY 5/11/88 OE **4,180**
Ivy League, clr slksc, 1953, sgn in img, lt stn/cr, tp on verso, L-5x8", lot 20, PHL 10/28/88 .... **425**
Place des Vosges, 8/100, litho/Chine colle, 1928, p/s, trm mrgs, lt stn/tr, laid down, L-9x13", lot 165, C-NY 1/19/89 OE **1,100**

DAWSON, Montague (British, 1895-1973)
Crescent Moon, chromolitho/wove paper, p/s, 24x30", lot 2946, B/B 2/16/88 .... **412**

DAWSON, Montague; after (British, 1895-1973)
Untitled, gaff-rigged yacht; trm mrgs, 20x30", RAB 3/14/89 UE **75**
Untitled, tall ships beating to windward; sgn, 1964, 26x32", Frost & Reed Ltd, RAB 3/14/89 .... **150**

DAY, Ward S. (American, 19th C)
Camp 5th New York Heavy Artillery, Camp Hill...; chromolitho, 1865, lt stn, 20x28", Sachs of Baltimore, RWS 8/20/88 .... **350**

DE BISSCHOP, Jan (Dutch, 1628-1671)
Joseph Distributing Grain in Egypt, 3rd state, etch, trm, lt cr/tr/scr, 19x26", lot 583, SBY 2/25/88 .... **660**
Joseph Distributing Grain in Egypt, 3rd state, etch, 17th C, trm/cr/tr, 19x26", lot 6, SBY 5/11/89 UE **385**

DE CALLATAY, Xavier
Trumpet Player, 19/50, linocut, sgn/titled, 13x10", lot 248, NA 3/26/88 .... **70**

DE CHAVANNES, Pierre Puvis (French, 1824-1898)
La Normandie, 53/100, brn litho/Chine applique, 1893, p/s, lt sl/stn, laid down, L-18x15", lot 329, C-NY 5/11/88 .... **385**

DE CHIRICO, Giorgio (Italian, 1888-1978)
Four Figures with Furniture, 65/80, litho, ca 1970, p/s, full mrgs, lt mstn/cr, lt ls mrg/verso, SBY 5/12/88 .... **1,760**
Il Trofeo, a/p, hc litho/Japan nacre, 1970, p/s, full mrgs, 24x18", lot 183, SBY 11/3/88 .... **1,650**
Pair: Glove in Triangle; Horse on Beach; ed of 99, clr litho, ca 1970, p/s, Caprini bstp, 25x18"/17x22", SBY 2/23/89 .... **1,980**
Pair: I Gladiatori; Il Trofeo; 20/90 & a/p, hc litho, 1970, p/s, full mrgs, 24x18", lot 445, SBY 5/11/89 .... **2,530**
Pair: Piazza d'Italia; Piazza; ed of 99, hc litho, 1973, p/s, Caprini bstp, full mrgs, 20x16"/14x20", SBY 5/11/89 OE **2,420**
Ricordo d'Autunno, 76/76, clr litho, 1969, p/s, full mrgs, lt sl/stn, 18x23", lot 173, SBY 2/25/88 .... **880**
Sole Spento, a/p, clr litho/Japan nacre, 1969, p/s, full mrgs, lt cr, 24x18", lot 174, SBY 2/25/88 .... **880**

DE GHEYN, Jacob (Dutch, 1565-1629)
Set of 12: Officers & Soldiers of the Bodyguard of Emperor Rudolph II; engr, 1587, 9x6", lot 44, SBY 5/11/89 .... **18,700**

DE GOYA Y LUCIENTES, Francisco Jose (Spanish, 1746-1828)
Book: Los Desastres de la Guerra; 4th ed, 80 plts, 1906, S-10x14", lot 66, SBY 5/11/89 OE **7,150**
Las Rinde el Sueno, etch/aqua, 9x7", lot 761, LH 5/15/88 .... **400**
Los Caprichos: Dios la Perdone, Y Era su Madre; etch/aqua/laid paper, 1799, full mrgs, 8x6", lot 56, SBY 5/11/89 OE **3,960**
Los Caprichos: El Sueno de la Razon Produce Monstruos; Pl 43, etch/aqua, 1799, fox/cr/sl, 8x6", lot 63, SBY 5/11/89 OE **6,600**
Los Caprichos: Franco Goya Y Lucientes, Pinter; ed of 300, etch/aqua, 1799, full mrgs, lt stn/sl, 9x6", SBY 2/25/88 OE **5,250**
Los Caprichos: La Descanona; Pl 35, etch/aqua/laid paper, 1799, full mrgs, lt fox/cr, 8x6", lot 61, SBY 5/11/89 .... **2,860**
Los Caprichos: Mala Noche; Pl 36, etch/aqua/laid paper, 1799, full mrgs, lt cr, 9x6", lot 62, SBY 5/11/89 OE **4,400**
Los Caprichos: Nohubo Remedio; Pl 24, etch/aqua/laid paper, 1799, full mrgs, lt fox/sl, 9x6", lot 58, SBY 5/11/89 .... **2,750**
Los Caprichos: Que se la Llevaron!; Pl 8, etch/aqua/laid paper, 1799, full mrgs, fox/cr/sl, 8x6", lot 55, SBY 5/11/89 OE **3,960**
Los Caprichos: Que Viene el Coco; Pl 3, etch/aqua, 1799, full mrgs, lt fox, 8x6", lot 52, SBY 5/11/89 .... **1,870**
Los Caprichos: Ya es Hora; Pl 80, etch/aqua/laid paper, 1799, lt stn, 8x6", lot 64, SBY 5/11/89 .... **1,320**
Los Caprichos: Ya Tienen Asiento; Pl 26, etch/aqua/laid paper, 1799, full mrgs, lt fox/cr, 8x6", lot 59, SBY 5/11/89 .... **2,640**
Los Caprichos: Ysele Quema la Casa; Pl 18, etch/aqua/laid paper, 1799, 9x6", lot 57, SBY 5/11/89 .... **1,540**
Los Caprichos: El de la Rollona; Pl 4, etch/aqua/laid paper, 1799, full mrgs, lt fox, 8x6", lot 53, SBY 5/11/89 .... **1,100**
Nadie se Conoce, Pl 6, etch/aqua/laid paper, 1799, full mrgs, lt fox/sl, 9x6", lot 54, SBY 5/11/89 .... **3,960**
Pair: Los Desastres de la Guerra, Por Que?; Grande Hazana con Muertos; Pl 32 & 39, S-10x13", lot 67, SBY 5/11/89 OE **2,860**
Pair: Ne se Puede Saber por Que; Estragos de la Guerre; etch, 5x7"/6x5", lot 237, LH 3/20/88 .... **350**
Por Temor no Pierdas Honor, Pl 2, aqua/etch/drypt/laid paper, laid down, 9x13", lot 2807, B/B 2/16/88 .... **330**
Que Sacrificio!; Pl 14, from 1st ed, etch/burnished aqua/drypt, 1799, lt stn/fox/sl, P-8x6", lot 624, C-NY 5/10/89 .... **935**
Que Sacrificio!; Pl 14, from 1st ed, etch/burnished aqua/drypt, 1799, lt tstn, P-8x6", lot 625, C-NY 5/10/89 .... **1,760**
Set of 80: Los Desastres de la Guerra; early part of 1st ed, 1863, various defects, S-10x13", lot 65, SBY 5/11/89 OE **88,000**
They Do Not Arrive in Time, Pl 52, posthumous ed, etch/aqua, ca 1828, 6x8", lot 100, SWN 6/15/89 .... **220**
Ya Tienen Asiento, Pl 26, from 1st ed, etch/burnished aqua, 1799, lt fox/tr mrgs, P-9x6", lot 626, C-NY 5/10/89 .... **1,100**

DE KOONING, Willem (American, 1904-)
Big (contemporary), 9/10, litho, 1970, p/s, Hollander bstp, full mrgs, lt cr/sl, 32x24", Knoedler, lot 1128, SBY 5/13/89 .... **6,600**
Clam Digger, 3/100, litho/wove paper, 1969, p/s, Hollander bstp, full mrgs, tp on verso, L-16x12", C-NY 1/19/89 OE **1,045**
Portfolio 9: Clam Digger; a/p, litho, 1966, p/s, lt cr/fox, S-17x22", Hollander, lot 697, SBY 2/23/89 OE **1,430**
Reflections: To Kermit for Our Trip to Japan; 12/28, litho/Akawara, 1971, p/s, Hollander bstp, 46x32", SBY 11/5/88 OE **3,850**
Revenge, 21 Etchings & Poems; a/p, ed of 50, etch/aqua, 1955-60, p/s, full mrgs, fox, 12x14", lot 699, C-NY 11/1/88 OE **3,520**
Revenge, 21 Etchings & Poems; a/p, etch/aqua/wove paper, 1955-60, lt sl, P-12x14", lot 443, C-NY 5/10/89 .... **4,620**

DE LATENAY, Gaston (Continental, 20th C)
Woman in the Woods, clr litho, p/s, unfr, 17x12", lot 211, FAP 2/24/89 .... **50**

DE LOSQUES, Daniel T. (French, 1890-1915)
Mistinguett, clr litho, 1908, 44x80", lot 100, WG 10/19/88 UE 800
DE MARTELLY, John S. (American, 1903-)
Economic Discussion, litho, 1936, p/s, 12x7", lot 223, WG 10/19/88.......... 250
Evangelist, 59/100, litho, p/s, titled, 13x10", lot 278, WG 10/19/88.......... 250
Give Us This Day, litho, 1937, p/s, 13x14", lot 224, WG 10/19/88.......... 300
DE PALEOLOGUE, Jean (French, 19th C)
Kola-Coca, litho/poster paper, linen backed, unfr, 63x45", Caby/Chardin, lot 300, FAP 2/24/89 UE.......... 350
DE RIBERA, Jiusepe (Spanish, 1588-1656)
St Jerome Hearing the Trumpet of the Last Judgment, etch, 1621, trm mrgs, lt rpr trs, 13x10", lot 696, SBY 2/25/88 OE 2,420
DE SAINT-AUBIN, Augustin (French, 1736-1807)
Pair: Au Moins Soyez Discret; Comptez sur Mes Sermens; 2nd state, engr/etch, 1789, cr, 14x10", lot 699, SBY 2/25/88 OE.......... 2,860
DE VLAMINCK, Maurice (French, 1876-1958)
Book: Tournant Dangereux; #20, 6 litho/Holland, 1930, slipcase, S-11x9", Librairie Stock, lot 522, SBY 2/23/89.......... 1,540
De l'Hotel de Ville, Pl 1, #57, etch/drypt/laid paper, 1927, p/s, lt stn, P-4x7", lot 359, C-NY 1/19/89 330
L'Eglise de Fessanvilliers, #12, etch/engr/wove paper, 1926, p/s, Guiot bspt, full mrgs, P-7x10", C-NY 1/19/89 UE 220
La Route a Valmondois, 9/50, clr litho/Arches, 1923, p/s, lt fox, S-22x25", Galerie Simon, lot 196, C-NY 11/1/88 OE 3,850
Le Moulin de la Naze, 7/35, state Ib, litho/Chine, 1924, p/s, lt fox, L-7x10", lot 562, C-NY 11/1/88 550
Le Pont a Chatou, 11/30, 2nd state, wc/van Gelder, 1914, full mrgs, lt stn/fox/scr, L-10x13", lot 384, C-NY 5/11/88 OE.......... 6,600
Maisons a Martiques, 19/30, wc/van Gelder, 1914, lt fox/stn, S-16x20", lot 195, C-NY 11/1/88 OE 3,850
Pair: L'Eglise de Beauche; L'Arbre Vert (II); ed of 100, etch/drypt & litho, 1926 & 1924, lot 468, SBY 2/25/89 OE 2,200
Rue Soufflot, ed of 250, litho, 1927, sgn in stone, 8x6", lot 1162, LH 10/16/88 UE.......... 80
Set of 48: Haute Folie; 15/260, clr litho w/text on Arches, 1964, sgn, unbound, slipcase, lot 855, C-NY 5/10/89 OE.......... 3,300
Street in a Village, 9/10(?), clr litho/BFK Rives, ca 1956, p/s, full mrgs, lt fox/stn/tp, L-12x15", C-NY 5/10/89 1,540
Tete de Femme, 17/30, blk & dk brn wc/Arches, 1922, p/s, lt ls/sl, S-22x18", Galerie Simon, lot 197, C-NY 11/1/88 OE.......... 9,900
Vallangoujard, 10/25, 2nd state e, litho/stiff wove paper, ca 1923, lt cr/mstn, L-10x13", lot 563, C-NY 11/1/88 550
DECKARD, John Silk
End of the World, 14/75, etch/drypt/aqua/wht wove paper, p/s, 13x37", lot 3016, B/B 4/19/88 OE.......... 468
DEGAS, Edgar (French, 1834-1917)
La Sortie du Baine (Grande Planche), 5th state, litho, 1891-92, French customs stp on verso, L-12x12", C-NY 5/11/88 OE.......... 52,800
Singer at a Cafe Concert, 1st state, litho, 1876-77, p/s, lt cr, 10x8", lot 449, SBY 5/11/89 OE 79,750
DEHN, Adolf Arthur (American, 1895-1968)
Group of 3: Deer in a Landscape; Golden Gate; Cranes; litho, 9x13", lot 70, FAP 2/24/89 OE 150
DEHNER, Dorothy (American, 1908-)
Pair: Man; River Landscape No 4 (abstracts); etch, 1958, p/s, lt stn/sl/fox, 8x2"/18x5", lot 81, RWS 9/8/89 OE.......... 425
DELACROIX, Ferdinand Victor Eugene (French, 1798-1863)
Muletiers de Tetuan, a/p prior to 1st state(?), litho/Chine volant, 1833, pl/s, cr img, 8x11", lot 49, SWN 12/1/88 OE 715
Rencontre de Cavaliers Maures, etch/Chine applique, 1834, trm, lt fox, 7x10", lot 189, SBY 11/3/88 OE 15,400
Tigre Couche a l'Entree de Son Antre, 5th state, etch/drypt/rlt, ca 1833, S-4x6", lot 188, SBY 11/3/88 4,950
Un Forgeron, 5th state, aqua/laid paper, 1833, lt stn img/mrgs, P-9x6", lot 595A, C-NY 5/10/89 UE 220
DELAUNAY, Robert (French, 1885-1941)

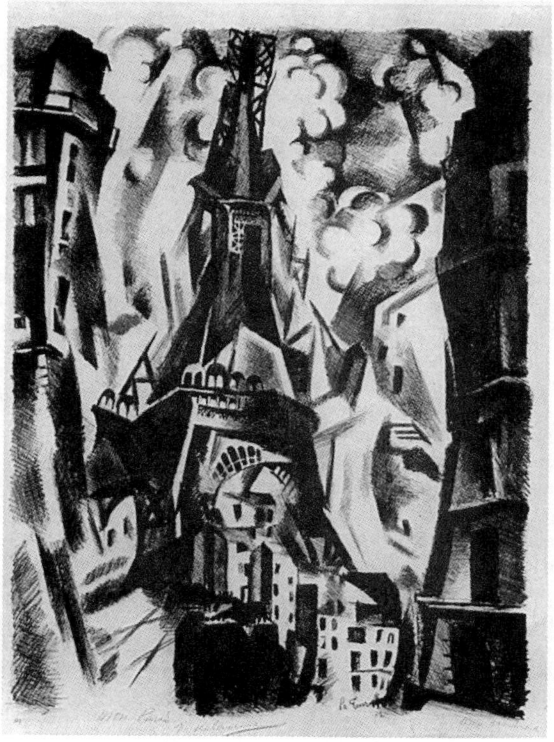

La Tour, #19, litho/thick soft wove paper, 1925, p/s, rpr trs, stn/cr, lt sl verso, L-24x18", lot 158, C-NY 5/11/88 OE; $57,200

Mon Paris, ed of 365, litho/laid paper, 1926, sgn, tr/rpl/lt sl, L-8x8", RWS 3/16/89 ..... **350**

DELAUNAY, Sonia (French, 1885-1979)

Composition with Blue, Red, & Green; 47/150, etch/aqua/Arches, 1970, p/s, full mrgs, lt cr, P-21x16", PHL 10/28/88 ..... **400**
Pair: Carreau Rouge; Olympia; clr litho, p/s, L-23x17"/L-23x18", lot 97, PHL 6/16/88 OE **1,000**
Portfolio: Les Illuminations; 34/90, 14 pochoirs, 1972, p/s, text by Arthur Rimbaud, S-21x15", SBY 5/12/88 OE **4,675**
Portfolio: Les Illuminations; 14 pochoirs w/text, by Arthur Rimbaud, 1973, S-21x15", lot 450, SBY 5/11/89 OE **6,875**
Suite: Suite IV; 57/75, 7 etch/aqua, 1974, p/s, full mrgs, lt stn, S-26x20", lot 451, SBY 5/11/89 OE **6,600**

DELINET, George Edwards (18th C)

American Water Rail (bird), etch/laid paper, 1757, 10x13", lot 283, GAI 4/21/89 ..... **175**

DELVAUX, Paul (Belgian, 1898-)

Beach, 46/75, clr litho, 1972, p/s, full mrgs, lt stn, 23x31", lot 455, SBY 5/11/89 OE **14,850**
Ends of the Earth, 48/75, clr litho, 1968, p/s, full mrgs, lt stn mrgs/verso, 21x30", lot 452, SBY 5/11/89 OE **25,950**
Garden, 58/75, clr litho, 1972, p/s, full mrgs, lt stn, 22x30", lot 453, SBY 5/11/89 OE **22,000**
La Gare, 14/75, litho/Arches, 1971, p/s, full mrgs, lt stn, L-23x31", lot 53, PHL 10/28/88 OE **2,600**
La Mere est Proche, 59/75, litho/Arches, 1966, p/s, full mrgs, L-26x20", lot 54, PHL 10/28/88 OE **1,300**
La Voute, 14/50, litho, 1973, p/s, full mrgs, L-23x31", lot 55, PHL 10/28/88 OE **3,300**
Lady with a Candle, 51/65, litho/Arches, 1966, p/s, full mrgs, lt stn, L-13x10", lot 294, C-NY 11/1/88 OE **2,200**
Lover, 20/75, blk/beige litho on Arches, 1971, p/s, full mrgs, lt sl/rub, 20x26", lot 245, SBY 2/23/89 OE **6,050**
Lover, 37/75, litho, 1971, p/s, full mrgs, lt stn, 20x26", lot 454, SBY 5/11/89 ..... **4,400**
Paiolive, 14/100, clr litho, 1975, p/s, full mrgs, lt cr, L-23x31", lot 56, PHL 10/28/88 OE **8,500**
Sleep, 39/75, clr litho, 1970, p/s, full mrgs, lt stn, 18x26", lot 244, SBY 2/23/89 OE **11,550**
Stained Glass Window, 15/50, etch/BFK Rives, 1969, p/s, full mrgs, lt scr mrg, P-15x11", lot 295, C-NY 11/1/88 OE **2,420**
Vichy, clr litho/poster paper, lt stn/tr mrgs, 39x24", Lucien Serre, lot 256, FAP 2/24/89 UE **50**

DENIS, Maurice (French, 1870-1943)

Les Attitudes Sont Faciles et Chastes, ed of 100, clr litho/thin wove paper, 1892-99, 15x11", lot 189A, SBY 11/3/88 OE **2,860**

DENNIS, Morgan (American, 1892-1960)

Provincetown Dunes, engr, p/s, 4x5", lot 152, WG 10/19/88 ..... **30**

DETMOLD, Edward Julius (British, 1883-1957)

Animated Indian Market Scene, etch/drypt/aqua, 1925, p/s, intl/dtd in pl, P-8x8", lot 49, RWS 9/29/88 ..... **125**
Captive, etch/JW, ca 1925, 14x12", lot 51, SWN 12/1/88 ..... **770**

DICKINSON, W.

Gardens of Carleton House, clr stpl engr, 18x25", lot 346, LH 3/20/88 ..... **190**

DIEBENKORN, Richard (American, 1922-)

#19, 23/25, etch/BFK Rives, 1963, p/s, dtd/titled, full mrgs, 8x7", lot 3017, B/B 4/19/88 ..... **1,760**
Black Club, 33/35, etch/drypt/aqua, 1981, intl/dtd, Crown Point bstp, full mrgs, 14x10", lot 935, SBY 5/13/89 OE **6,600**
Blue, 73/200, clr wc, 1985, intl, Crown Point bstp, full mrgs, 40x25", lot 742, SBY 11/5/88 ..... **24,200**
Blue, 82/100, clr wc/wove paper, 1984, intl, Crown Point bstp, full mrgs, lt cr, S-43x27", lot 606, C-NY 11/1/88 ..... **18,700**
Blue (contemporary), 127/200, clr wc, 1984, intl/dtd, Crown Point bstp, full mrgs, 40x25", lot 936, SBY 5/13/89 OE **34,100**
Blue Club, 33/35, sftgr etch/aqua/wove paper, 1981, p/s, Crown Point bstp, S-37x31", lot 402, C-NY 5/11/88 ..... **4,400**
Blue Softground, 28/35, sftgr etch, 1985, intl, full mrgs, lt cr, 14x24", Crown Point, lot 938, SBY 5/13/89 ..... **5,390**
Blue Surround, 30/35, spit-bite aqua/drypt, 1982, intl, full mrgs, lt cr mrgs, 22x19", Crown Point Press, SBY 5/14/88 OE **24,200**
Burnout, 50/60, clr litho, p/s, lt cr corners, lt ls verso, S-30x37", lot 100, PHL 6/16/88 ..... **650**
Center Square, 22/25, aqua/sftgr etch/drypt, 1985, intl, Crown Point bstp, full mrgs, 10x8", lot 624, SBY 2/23/89 OE **4,150**
Center Square, 7/25, bl & blk aqua/sftgr/drypt, 1985, intl, pub bstp, full mrgs, 10x8", Crown Point Press, SBY 5/14/88 ..... **1,430**
Clubs & Spades: Tri-Color; 16/35, etch/drypt/aqua, 1981, full mrgs, 14x10", Crown Point, lot 741, SBY 11/5/88 OE **7,700**
Combination, 33/40, clr drypt/aqua, 1981, intl/dtd, Crown Point bstp, full mrgs, 16x13", lot 934, SBY 5/13/89 ..... **11,000**
Construct (Drypoint), 5/35, drypt/etch/aqua/rlt, 1980, intl, full mrgs, 11x15", Crown Point, lot 738, SBY 11/5/88 ..... **3,025**
Construct (Grid), 5/35, etch/drypt/aqua, 1980, intl, full mrgs, 12x8", Crown Point, lot 737, SBY 11/5/88 OE **5,225**
Construct (Red), 19/35, spit-bite aqua/sftgr etch, 1980, intl, full mrgs, cr, 11x10", Crown Point, lot 739, SBY 11/5/88 ..... **3,025**
Folsom St Variations II (Gray), 11/35, etch/aqua/drypt, 1986, intl, full mrgs, lt cr, 20x30", lot 941, SBY 5/13/89 OE **10,450**
Folson St Variations III (Primaries), 9/60, etch/aqua, 1986, Crown Point bstp, 12x26", lot 743, SBY 11/5/88 ..... **9,350**
Grayland, 15/40, clr litho/Arches 88, 1985, intl/dtd 84, Gemini bstp, full mrgs, S-44x34", lot 409, C-NY 5/11/88 OE **3,850**
Green, AP1, clr aqua/etch/drypt, 1986, intl, full mrgs, 45x36", Crown Point, SBY 5/14/88 ..... **49,500**
Green (contemporary), 6/60, etch/aqua/drypt/Somerset, 1986, intl/dtd, full mrgs, S-53x41", Crown Point, C-NY 5/11/88 ..... **49,500**
Indigo Horizontal, 3/50, etch/aqua, 1985, p/s, full mrgs, S-36x49", Crown Point, lot 939, SBY 5/13/89 OE **42,900**
Large Bright Blue, 34/35, spit-bite aqua/sftgr etch, 1980, intl, full mrgs, 24x14", Crown Point, lot 735, SBY 11/5/88 OE **42,900**
M (contemporary), 7/60, clr litho/Arches, 1985, intl/dtd 84, Gemini bstp, full mrgs, S-30x22", lot 408, C-NY 5/11/88 ..... **1,430**
Ochre, 80/200, clr wc, 1983, intl, pub bstp, full mrgs, L-25x36", Crown Point Press, SBY 5/14/88 ..... **11,000**
Ochre (contemporary), 139/200, clr wc/Japan, 1983, intl/dtd, Crown Point bstp, S-27x38", lot 407, C-NY 5/11/88 OE **13,200**
Red-Yellow-Blue, 8/60, clr sftgr etch/aqua/drypt, 1986, intl, full mrgs, 16x30", Crown Point Press, SBY 5/14/88 ..... **8,800**
Red-Yellow-Blue (abstract), 47/60, clr etch/aqua, 1986, intl, full mrgs, 16x30", Crown Point, lot 940, SBY 5/13/89 OE **17,600**
Seated Woman Drinking From Cup, 24/100, litho, 1965, intl/dtd, lt cr, 28x21", Orig Pr, lot 733, SBY 11/5/88 OE **3,300**
Seated Woman in Armchair, 6/100, litho/BFK Rives, 1965, old hinge on verso, S-27x21", Orig Pr, lot 602, C-NY 11/1/88 OE **1,320**
Seated Woman with Crossed Hands, 61/100, litho/BFK Rives, 1965, intl, lt fox, 28x22", Orig Pr, lot 603, C-NY 11/1/88 OE **2,640**
Serge, 15/26, litho/Arches, 1985, intl/dtd, Gemini bstp, full mrgs, L-35x37", lot 410, C-NY 5/11/88 OE **1,540**
Six Softground Etchings: #5; #5, sftgr etch, 1978, intl, full mrgs, lt cr, 17x12", Crown Point, lot 622, SBY 2/23/89 OE **2,090**
Small Red, 5/35, spit-bite aqua/sftgr etch, 1980, intl, full mrgs, 12x8", Crown Point, lot 736, SBY 11/5/88 OE **12,100**
Softground Splay, 12/35, sftgr etch, 1982, intl/dtd on verso, Crown Point bstp, full mrgs, P-15x24", lot 99, PHL 6/16/88 ..... **850**
Spreading Spade, 1/35, clr aqua/drypt, 1981, intl, pub bstp, full mrgs, 18x19", Crown Point Press, SBY 5/14/88 ..... **8,800**
Spreading Spade, 33/35, clr drypt/aqua, 1981, intl/dtd, Crown Point bstp, full mrgs, 37x31", lot 404, C-NY 5/11/88 ..... **8,800**
Suite: Clubs & Spades; 23/35 or 25/40, 8 etch, 1981, intl, full mrgs, Crown Point, lot 932, SBY 5/13/88 OE **82,500**

Tri-Color, 33/35, etch/drypt/aqua/Arches, 1981, intl/dtd, full mrgs, S-30x23", Crown Point, lot 405, C-NY 5/11/88 4,400
Tri-Color II, 33/35, etch/aqua/wove paper, 1981, intl/dtd, full mrgs, S-38x31", Crown Point, lot 406, C-NY 5/11/88 5,500
Tri-Color Spade, 5/50, drypt/etch/aqua, 1982, intl, Crown Point bstp, full mrgs, lt sl, 10x9", lot 740, SBY 11/5/88 3,300
Tri-Color Spade, 9/50, etch/aqua/Rives, 1982, intl, Crown Point bstp, full mrgs, lt cr, S-26x20", C-NY 11/1/88 OE 3,080
Twelve, 27/50, clr litho/Arches 88, 1985, intl/dtd, Gemini bstp, full mrgs, 36x27", lot 937, SBY 5/13/89 OE 66,000
Two Way II, 5/40, clr aqua/drypt/ink transfer, 1982, pub bstp, full mrgs, lt cr, 24x15", Crown Point Press, SBY 5/14/88 4,950
Untitled (contemporary), 25/90, clr litho, 1969, intl, S-24x19", Collectors, lot 734, SBY 11/5/88 4,950
Untitled (Ocean Park), 63/90, clr litho, 1969, intl, Collector Pr bstp, full sheet, S-24x19", lot 604, C-NY 11/1/88 4,400
Woman Seated at Table, 20/75, litho, 1967, intl/dtd, lt cr, S-30x22", lot 933, SBY 5/13/89 9,350
Woman Seated at Table, 32/75, litho, 1967, intl, S-30x22", lot 621, SBY 2/23/89 OE 8,250
Woman Standing, No 28; 15/25, drypt, 1964-65, intl/dtd, full mrgs, L-13x7", lot 54, SWN 12/1/88 1,100

DINE, Jim (American, 1935-)

Atheism, 34/35, clr litho, 1986, p/s, lt cr, S-67x48", Pace, lot 757, SBY 11/5/88 13,200
Bathrobe, 143/150, red & blk litho/Green Penhurst, 1970, dtd 1970-76, S-32x23", Petersburg, lot 413, C-NY 5/11/88 1,540
Black & White Bathrobe, 6/60, litho, 1975, p/s, lt cr/old tp hinge, 36x24", Petersburg, lot 500, SBY 2/25/88 1,980
Black Venus in the Wood, 13/20, wc/Okawara, 1983, p/s, dtd, full sheet, S-60x37", Pace, lot 424, C-NY 5/11/88 1,980
Blue Haircut, 57/75, clr etch/offset litho/Green mould made, 1972, p/s, P-21x20", Petersburg, lot 417, C-NY 5/11/88 1,320
Bolt Cutters, a/p, 2nd state, etch/aqua/Handmade White Wove, 1973, lt cr, P-24x24", Petersburg, lot 416, C-NY 5/11/88 3,300
Cellist, a/p, total ed of 41, hc etch/German Etching, 1976, p/s, Pyramid Arts bstp, full mrgs, S-42x31", C-NY 11/1/88 1,650

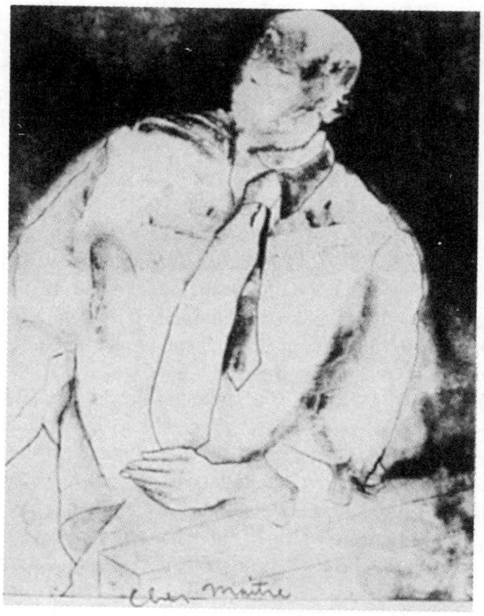

Cher Maitre, 1976; 4/30, hc etch/aqua/cream wove paper, p/s, Pyramid bstp, unfr, 26x20", lot 3530, B/B 4/12/89 OE; $1,540

Crash #3, 27/33, litho/Arches, p/s, full mrgs, lt stn, tp/ls on verso, L-20x17", lot 117, PHL 10/28/88 350
Diptych: Hammer (With Watercolor Marks); hc litho/2 sheets Arches Cover, 1982, S-45x62", Pace, lot 949, SBY 5/13/89 OE 9,900
Diptych: Two Very Strange Hearts, bl/blk wc/tan Japan & pk Oriental, 1983, S-35x40", Pace, lot 952, SBY 5/13/89 OE 23,100
Eight Sheets From an Undefined Novel: The Cellist; 28/30, hc etch, 1976, full mrgs, 24x20", Pyramid Arts, SBY 2/23/89 2,090
Etch, Self-Portrait (Primary Colors); 3 etch/cream Hodgkinson hand made, 1969-70, 12x28", Petersburg, SBY 5/14/88 2,750
Flower, 14/17, etch, 1978, p/s, full mrgs, lt stn/fox/tp hinge, 8x7", lot 628, SBY 2/23/89 OE 1,760
Fork, 4/100, litho, 1973, p/s, full mrgs, lt cr, S-28x22", Petersburg, lot 608, C-NY 11/1/88 825
Fourteen Color Woodcut Bathrobe, 56/75, clr wc, 1982, p/s, full mrgs, 66x36", Pace/Tullis, lot 751, SBY 11/5/88 13,750
Fourteen Color Woodcut Bathrobe, 63/75, clr wc, 1982, p/s, full mrgs, 66x36", Pace, lot 948, SBY 5/13/89 OE 23,100
Group of 3: Thirty Bones of My Body; 5/10, drypt/Crisbrook Waterleaf, 1972, full mrgs, S-31x22", lot 415, C-NY 5/11/88 1,540
Hammer (with Watercolor Marks), 41/46, hc litho/2 sheets Arches, 1982, lt sl, S-45x62", Pace, lot 617, C-NY 11/1/88 5,500
Hand Painting on the Mandala, 19/60, hc etch, 1986, p/s, full mrgs, 37x36", Pace, lot 960, SBY 5/13/89 OE 30,800
Hand-Painted Nancy, 12/12, clr wc/wove paper, 1983, full mrgs, lt tr/cr, S-51x39", Pace, lot 423, C-NY 5/11/88 880
Handmade Double Venus, 11/15, blk/wht litho, 1984, p/s, S-54x35", Pace, lot 754, SBY 11/5/88 2,200
Heart & the Wall, a/p, total ed of 34, sftgr etch/aqua/electric tooling, 1983, S-89x67", Pace, lot 618, C-NY 11/1/88 OE 14,300
Heart Called Paris Spring, 47/90, sftgr etch, 1982, p/s, full mrgs, 23x20", Crommelynck, lot 752, SBY 11/5/88 11,000
Heart Called Paris Spring, 79/90, sftgr etch/electric tooling/BFK Rives, S-36x25", Crommelynck, lot 420, C-NY 5/11/88 9,900
Heart Called Paris Spring, 90/90, clr sftgr etch, 1982, p/s, full mrgs, 23x20", Crommelynck, SBY 5/14/88 OE 9,900
Heart on the Rue de Grenelle, 16/36, etch/aqua, 1981, p/s, full mrgs, lt cr, 33x27", Pace, lot 947, SBY 5/13/89 OE 27,500
Heart on the Rue de Grenelle, 25/36, etch/sftgr etch/aqua/BFK Rives, 1981, S-42x30", Pace, lot 613, C-NY 11/1/88 OE 18,700
Heart on the Rue de Grenelle, 6/36, etch/aqua/BFK Rives, 1981, p/s, full mrgs, S-42x30", Pace, lot 419, C-NY 5/11/88 OE 15,400
Imogen II, clr litho/collage, p/s, S-9x9", lot 3020, B/B 4/19/88 825
Jerusalem Plant #1, 4/10, wht litho/blk Fabriano, 1982, p/s, ULAE bstp, S-41x26", lot 753, SBY 11/5/88 2,750
Jerusalem Plant #3, 4/11, blk wc/2 sheets Kozo, 1982, p/s, ULAE bstp, S-39x52", lot 755, SBY 11/5/88 2,475
Jerusalem Plant #6, 16/20, litho/buff Arches Cover, 1982, p/s, pub bstp, L-39x54", ULAE, SBY 5/14/88 1,320
Jerusalem Plant #6, 5/20, litho/Arches, 1982, p/s, ULAE bstp, full mrgs, S-40x60", s/wrp, lot 616, C-NY 11/1/88 1,540
Jerusalem Plant #8, 13/26, litho/drypt/etch/Canadian handmade, 1984, p/s, ULAE bstp, S-40x31", lot 619, C-NY 11/1/88 1,540

Kindergarten Robe, 18/75, clr wc/Lenox, 1983, p/s, full mrgs, S-60x74", Pace, lot 951, SBY 5/13/89 OE 15,400
Morning Glory, 46/47, etch/litho/scrpt/Hodgkinson mould made, 1972, p/s, L-12x16", Petersburg, lot 414, C-NY 5/11/88........ 1,980
Multi-Colored Robe, 3/10, offset litho/etch/drypt/Arches Cover, 1977, p/s, S-42x30", Pace, lot 943, SBY 5/13/89 OE........ 23,100
My Nights in Santa Monica, 6/20, etch/aqua/drypt, 1986, p/s, full mrgs, lt cr, 30x68", Pace, lot 961, SBY 5/13/89 OE 4,950
Nancy Outside in July III, 48/60, etch/sftgr etch/aqua/drypt/electric tooling/BFK Rives, 1978, S-42x29", C-NY 11/1/88 1,045
Nancy Outside in July VII, 10/25, hc etch/wax crayon, 1980, full mrgs, stn, 24x19", Crommelynck, lot 630, SBY 2/23/89 OE 4,400
Nancy Outside in July VII, 20/25, sftgr etch/drypt/watercolor/crayon, 1980, p/s, lt tr, 23x19", Crommelynck, SBY 5/14/88 3,025
Nancy Outside in July XX: Among French Plants; 23/26, aqua/electric tooling/photogravure, 1981, 36x25", C-NY 11/1/88........ 990
Night Venus & Sappho, 10/15, wht sftgr etch/blk Arches, 1985, p/s, full mrgs, S-38x30", Pace, lot 426, C-NY 5/11/88 OE 1,760
Nine Views of Winter, 4/24, ochre/red/gr wc on Arches, 1985, full sheet, S-53x37", Pace, lot 427, C-NY 5/11/88 OE 2,420
Nine Views of Winter (2), 7/24, red-orange/gr wc on buff Arches, 1985, full mrgs, S-53x37", Pace, lot 956, SBY 5/13/89........ 5,500
Nine Views of Winter (3), 9/35, gray/blk wc on buff Arches, 1985, p/s, lt scr img, 53x37", Pace, lot 957, SBY 5/13/89 OE........ 11,000
Nine Views of Winter (6), bl/yel/orange wc on Masa, 1985, p/s, lt cr, 52x37", Pace, lot 958, SBY 5/13/89 OE 6,600
Nine Views of Winter (9), 7/24, ochre/red/gr wc on buff Arches, 1985, S-52x37", Pace, lot 959, SBY 5/13/89........ 3,300
Nutcracker, 90/100, clr litho, 1973, p/s, full mrgs, 9x21", Petersburg/Dayton's Gallery 12, lot 499, SBY 2/25/88 660
Paintbrush, 58/75, etch/J Green Mould Made, 1971, p/s, full mrg, P-21x20", Petersburg, SBY 5/14/88 OE 2,090
Pink Chinese Scissors, 1/30, clr etch/French handmade paper, 1974-76, 28x24", Petersburg, lot 748, SBY 11/5/88 OE 6,050
Rancho Woodcut Heart, 13/75, clr wc, 1982, p/s, S-48x40", Pace, lot 756, SBY 11/5/88........ 7,700
Rancho Woodcut Heart, 48/75, clr wc, 1982, p/s, L-48x41", SBY 5/14/88 OE........ 7,975
Red, White, & Blue Venus for Mondale; 3/150, clr slksc, 1984, p/s, S-30x18", Dine/Pace, SBY 5/14/88 1,925
Red & Black Diptych Robe, 12/20, clr litho/2 sheets gray BFK Rives, 1980, p/s, S-38x59", Pace, lot 945, SBY 5/13/89 OE........ 7,700
Red Etching Robe, 19/36, red/blk etch, 1976, p/s, full mrgs, lt skinned/sl/disclr, P-36x24", Pace, SBY 5/14/88 OE 11,550
Red Robe, 1/5, red & blk offset litho/sftgr etch/drypt/Arches, 1977, p/s, S-42x29", Pace, lot 418, C-NY 5/11/88 OE........ 9,350
Robe Against the Desert Sky, 16/20, clr litho/slksc, 1979, p/s, full mrgs, lt cr, 36x24", Pace, lot 944, SBY 5/13/89 OE 5,225
Robe Goes to Town, 38/59, wht aqua/blk Arches hinged to clr scrpt on Arches, 1983, S-57x36", lot 421, C-NY 5/11/88 OE 1,210
Robe in France, 10/35, offset litho/sftgr etch/BFK Rives, 1985, p/s, full mrgs, 31x23", Pace, lot 955, SBY 5/13/89 OE 13,200
Robe in Los Angeles, 27/50, clr litho, 1984, p/s, S-54x35", Pace, SBY 5/14/88 OE........ 8,250
Robe in Los Angeles, 32/50, clr litho/buff Arches, 1984, p/s, S-54x35", Pace, lot 953, SBY 5/13/89 OE 13,200
Scissors & Rainbow, a/p, aside from #d ed of 75, litho, 1969, p/s, full mrgs, lt cr, 40x28", lot 498, SBY 2/25/88 660
Self-Portrait, 14/17, 12 clr stencil/collage/Hodgkinson mould made, 1970, p/s, S-60x40", Petersburg, SBY 5/14/88 OE 24,200
Self-Portrait (Stencil), 8/17, 12-clr stencil/Hodgkinson mould made, 1970, p/s, 60x40", Petersburg, lot 942, SBY 5/13/89 19,800
Self-Portrait on JD Paper, a/p, etch/aqua/drypt/handmade linen paper, 1978, p/s, full mrgs, 13x10", SBY 2/23/89 1,540
Self-Portrait: The Landscape; 40/75, clr litho/Hodgkinson mould made, 1969, S-53x38", lot 411, C-NY 5/11/88 OE 14,300
Set of 10: 10 Winter Tools; litho/Richard de Bas, 1973, full mrgs, lt stn, 26x20", Petersburg, lot 609, C-NY 11/1/88 UE 14,300
Set of 3: Sydney Close Woodcuts; 7/24, wc/Nonesuch, full sheets, S-46x32", Pace, lot 422, C-NY 5/11/88 1,650
Set of 6: Vegetables I; Vegetables II; Vegetables IV; Vegetables VI; Vegetables VII; Vegetables VIII; C-NY 11/1/88 OE 3,300
Side View of Florida, 7/15, hc etch, 1986, p/s, full mrgs, lt skinned/cr/sl, 42x39", Pace, lot 631, SBY 2/23/89 OE........ 3,300
Sky, 13/25, clr litho/wc/buff Arches, 1984, p/s, tp on verso, 54x35", Pace, lot 954, SBY 5/13/89 OE 6,600
Suite: Self-Portraits (1971); 9 brn-blk drypt/Hodgkinson Hand Made Tone-Weave, 1971, S-18x15", Petersburg, SBY 5/14/88........ 3,300
Sunny Woodcut, 25/42, clr wc/John Koller HMP, 1982, p/s, full mrgs, lt sl, 24x19", Pace, lot 950, SBY 5/13/89 OE 6,050
Temple of Flora: Anthurium; 21/30, hc etch, 1978, p/s, full mrgs, lt cr/sl mrgs & verso, P-24x18", Pace, SBY 5/14/88 OE 2,310
Toothbrushes #2, litho/Chatham British, 1962, p/s, inscr Proof, pub bstp, S-25x20", ULAE, SBY 5/14/88 770
Tree Painted in South Florida, 11/15, blk/lt yel-gr etch, 1981, p/s, full mrgs, 45x35", Pace, lot 946, SBY 5/13/89........ 4,400
Two Hearts for the Moment, 32/36, clr offset litho/etch, 1985, red crayon sgn, full mrgs, L-18x35", SBY 5/14/88 OE........ 8,525
Wall Chart IV, ed of 14, clr litho, 1974, p/s, dtd, full mrgs, lt cr, 43x30", Petersburg, lot 3019, B/B 4/19/88 1,650
Wallpaper in Paris, 15/30, sftgr etch/drypt/aqua/electric tooling/Dieu Donne, 1985, 34x44", Pace, lot 425, C-NY 5/11/88 1,320
White Robe on Black Paper, 30/100, offset litho/blk Fabriano, 1977, S-42x30", Am Friends of Israel Mus, SBY 2/23/89 OE........ 2,750
Wolfman, 47/120, etch/wc, 1967, p/s, no size given, lot 492, LH 5/15/88 375
Yellow Robe, 30/40, clr litho, 1980, p/s, Landfall bstp, S-50x35", lot 750, SBY 11/5/88 10,450

DIX, Otto (German, 1891-1969)

Artisten, IX/X, drypt/Butten, 1922, p/s, titled/dtd, lt lstn, 12x10", lot 187, SBY 2/25/88........ 7,150
Illusionsakt, Zirkus; 18/50, 2nd state, drypt/wove paper, 1922, p/s, lt stn, S-20x17", lot 30, C-NY 11/1/88 4,620
Kupplerin, 12/65, clr litho/laid paper, 1923, p/s, lt tr, S-24x18", Nierendorf, lot 28, C-NY 11/1/88 OE 71,500
Machen mit Katze I, total ed of 45 in 3 states, clr litho, 1956, trm mrgs, S-23x15", lot 188, SBY 2/25/88 OE 2,200
Matthaus Evangelium, ed of 2000, litho/wove paper, 1960, lt skinned, 7x9", lot 2842, B/B 2/16/88 UE 77
Mutter und Kind, clr litho, 1951, p/s, inscr IV Probe & Gut, full mrgs, lt cr/stn, L-22x18", SBY 5/12/88 OE 2,200
Schneeman (Karneval), 8/50, gray-gr litho/wove paper, 1948, p/s, lt sl/cr/stn, L-14x15", Heinrich Mock, SBY 5/12/88 UE........ 770
Selbstportrat, 50/60, litho/smooth wove paper, 1923, p/s, lt cr/ls/sl, S-26x19", Nierendorf, lot 29, C-NY 11/1/88 OE........ 5,280

DOBKIN, Alexander (American, 1908-1975)

Head of a Woman, 36/100, litho/cream paper, 18x20", lot 119, FAP 2/24/89 UE 50

DOHANOS, Steven (American, 1907-)

Homes, ed of 25, wood engr, p/s, titled, no size given, lot 368, WG 10/19/88 95
Man of the Soil, ed of 250, litho, 1935, p/s, L-12x10", Print-a-Month Club, lot 22, C-NY 5/11/88 286
State Fair, total ed of 235, wood engr/wove paper, 1949, p/s, full mrgs, L-13x9", C-NY 1/22/88........ 462

DOMERGUE, Jean Gabriel (French, 1889-1962)

Alice Soulie, clr litho, backed w/linen, 1926, pl/s, 63x46", C-E 6/16/88........ 550
Alice Soulie, clr litho, 1926, pl/s, 63x46", lot 418, C-E 9/20/89 440
Alice Soulie, clr litho, 1926, S-62x45", Chachoin, lot 266, SBY 12/12/88........ 385

DORO, Theo (French, 20th C)

La Syphilis, clr litho/poster paper, linen backed, unfr, 47x32", Legras, lot 303, FAP 2/24/89 UE 300

DOW, Arthur Wesley (American, 1857-1922)

Poster for the Magazine Modern Art, clr litho, 1895, pl/s, unfr, 16x21", Prang/Bowdes, RWS 4/22/89 OE ... 4,000

DOWD, J.H. (American, 20th C)

Smuggler's Cove, etch, p/s, 7x6", lot 74, WG 10/19/88 UE ... 30

DRABKIN, Stella (American, 1906-)

Mime, clr engr, p/s, 17x12", lot 79, FAP 2/24/89 ... 55

DREWES, Werner (American, 1899-1985)

Hungry-Birds Feeding; 14/XXX, blk & gr wc/Japan, 1958, p/s, full mrgs, lt stn/ls, L-9x24", lot 167A, C-NY 1/19/89 UE ... 55
It Can't Happen Here, Distorted Swastika; ed of 35, linocut/Japan, p/s, 3 full mrgs, lt sl, unfr, L-6x10", C-NY 1/22/88 ... 605

DROOCHSLOOT, Joost Cornelsz (Dutch, 1586-1666)

Three Beggars & a Woman Seated at a Table, 1st state, etch, 1610, lt stn/fox/rpr, 5x7", lot 598, SBY 2/25/88 ... 2,860

DRUMMOND, Anthony D.; after

Untitled (steam engine McKay of Little Hook/Fort Smith Line meeting Indians), litho, lg folio, RAB 1/10/89 UE ... 150

DUBUFFET, Jean (French, 1901-1985)

Affairements, APV/XIII, clr litho, 1964, p/s, full mrgs, lt scr, 22x16", lot 758, SBY 11/5/88 OE ... 8,250
Animation Contenue, Pl 16, 10/20, litho/cream Rives, 1959, p/s, titled, lt sl, L-21x15", lot 83, RWS 9/8/89 ... 550
Banque de L'Hourloupe-Cartes a Jourer et a Tirer (set of 52 playing cards), 160/350, clr slksc, boxed, SBY 5/14/88 OE ... 1,870
Book: Parade Funebre pour Charles Estienne; HC, 29 slksc, 1967, sgn, orig wrappers, S-11x9", Jeanne Bucher, SBY 2/23/89 ... 1,210
Fables: Course la Galope; 24/50, clr slksc, 1976, intl/dtd, full mrgs, 21x30", Pace, lot 967, SBY 5/13/89 ... 7,150
Fond der Mer, Pl 4, a/p, litho/Arches, p/s, lt stn/fox/scr, L-15x12", lot 598, C-NY 5/10/89 ... 880
Grand Palais, Festival d'Automne a Paris; 35/100, litho, 1973, lt cr/old hinge, 28x25", lot 502, SBY 2/25/88 ... 660
L'Enfle-Chique II; 16/20, clr litho/Arches, 1961, p/s, dtd 63, full mrgs, lt stn/cr, S-26x20", lot 159, C-NY 5/11/88 ... 9,350
L'Homme au Chapeau, 45/50, clr litho/Arches, 1961, p/s, full mrgs, lt stn, L-21x15", lot 599, C-NY 5/10/89 OE ... 11,000
Le Surintendant, 40/120, clr slksc, 1972, intl, S-20x12", Ed Jeanne Bucher/Pace, SBY 5/14/88 OE ... 3,410
Le Surintendant, 53/120, clr slksc, 1972, intl, S-20x12", Bucher/Pace, lot 760, SBY 11/5/88 ... 3,300
Le Surintendant, 95/120, clr slksc, 1972, intl/dtd, S-20x12", Ed Jeanne Bucher/Pace, lot 962, SBY 5/13/89 ... 3,575
Le Vizir, 18/50, clr scrpt/Arches, 1976, intl, full mrgs, S-35x28", Pace, lot 299, C-NY 11/1/88 ... 3,520
Les Herboristes, ochre/brn litho, 1953, p/s, titled, full mrgs, lt stn/cr, 11x20", lot 247, SBY 2/23/89 ... 2,970
Les Passants, 3/50, red & bl litho/wove paper, 1982, intl/dtd, full mrgs, L-27x40", Pace, lot 600, C-NY 5/10/89 OE ... 9,350
Loisirs, 37/40, clr litho, 1961, p/s, full mrgs, lt stn/sl/scr, 16x20", lot 191A, SBY 11/3/88 OE ... 5,500
Nez Carotte, 4/50, clr litho/Rives, 1961, p/s, dtd 62, full mrgs, lt scratch/rpr/stn, L-24x15", SBY 5/12/88 OE ... 31,900
Nez Carotte, 41/50, clr litho/Rives, 1961, p/s, titled, full mrgs, 24x15", lot 456, SBY 5/11/89 OE ... 88,000
Nez Carotte, 45/50, clr litho/BFK Rives, 1961, p/s, full mrgs, 24x15", lot 191, SBY 11/3/88 OE ... 57,750
Objectador, 37/100, clr scrpt/Dutch Etching, intl, full mrgs, L-20x13", Pace, lot 298, C-NY 11/1/88 ... 2,860
Organisme, a/p, clr slksc, 1974, intl, full mrgs, lt sl, 27x36", Ed Beyeler, lot 633, SBY 2/23/89 OE ... 3,575
Organisme, 19/50, clr slksc/Sirene Arjomari, 1974, p/s, full mrgs, lt cr, 26x35", Beyeler, lot 964, SBY 5/13/89 ... 7,150
Parcours, 60/80, blk slksc/silk backed with rag paper, 1981, intl, lt stn, 20x228", Pace, lot 764, SBY 11/5/88 ... 4,950
Paysage aux Fantasmes, 13/20, litho, 1953, p/s, dtd/titled, full mrgs, lt stn/scr, 18x21", lot 189, SBY 2/25/88 ... 1,650
Paysage aux Fantasmes, 18/20, litho/Arches, 1953, p/s, full mrgs, lt tstn/fox, L-18x21", lot 296, C-NY 11/1/88 UE ... 990
Paysage aux Papillons, a/p, litho/cream wove paper, titled, no size given, lot 2838, B/B 4/19/88 ... 715
Personnage au Chapeau, 35/50, clr litho/Arches, 1961, p/s, full mrgs, lt stn, 22x15", lot 251, SBY 2/23/89 ... 11,550
Personnage au Chapeau, 48/50, clr litho/Arches, 1961, p/s, dtd 62, full mrgs, lt cr/stn, L-22x15", SBY 5/12/88 OE ... 15,400
Personnage au Costume Rouge, 38/50, clr litho/Arches, 1961, p/s, lt scuff mrg/lstn/cr, L-21x15", SBY 5/12/88 ... 26,400
Personnage au Costume Rouge, 49/50, clr litho/Arches, 1961, p/s, full mrgs, lt scr, 21x15", lot 190, SBY 11/3/88 ... 30,800
Portfolio: Presences Fugaces; 25/100, 6 slksc, intl, lt cr/sl, S-30x22", Pace, lot 761, SBY 11/5/88 OE ... 17,600
Portfolio: Sols, Terres; XVIII/XXII, 18 litho, 1959, sgn on justification, S-25x17", lot 190, SBY 2/25/88 ... 495
Presences Fugaces: Protestator; 31/100, clr slksc, 1973, intl, full mrgs, lt stn, 20x13", Pace, lot 963, SBY 5/13/89 ... 3,025
Profil a Droit, 29/30, clr litho/Arches, 1962, p/s, dtd 62, full mrgs, lt cr/stn, L-21x15", SBY 5/12/88 ... 8,800
Profil a Droit, 23/30, clr litho, 1962, p/s, full mrgs, lt stn, 21x15", lot 192, SBY 11/3/88 ... 6,600
Protestator, 90/100, clr slksc, 1973, intl, full mrgs, 20x13", Pace, lot 762, SBY 11/5/88 ... 2,750
Quatre Personnages, 44/59, clr slksc, 1974, intl, lt scr/cr, 25x36", Beyeler, lot 763, SBY 11/5/88 ... 6,600
Samedi Tantot, a/p, aside from #d ed of 125, litho, 1964, p/s, full mrgs, lt stn, 22x16", lot 501, SBY 2/25/88 ... 4,620
Samedi Tantot, 108/125, clr litho, 1964, p/s, lt stn, 22x16", lot 252, SBY 2/23/89 ... 5,500
Samedi Tantot, 74/125, clr litho/Arches, 1964, p/s, lt stn/cr, L-22x16", Assn Friends of Phil Mus, lot 297, C-NY 11/1/88 ... 1,980
Scenario Bref, 24/50, clr litho, 1979, intl, Ed La Hume bstp, S-26x18", lot 634, SBY 2/23/89 OE ... 2,310
Serenite, 26/30, litho, 1959, sgn, 18x15", lot 96, FAP 2/24/89 OE ... 825
Set of 52: Banque de l'Hourloupe-Cartes a Jouer et a Tirer; slksc (playing cards), Eds Alecto, lot 759, SBY 11/5/88 OE ... 2,200
Sourire, 46/50, clr litho/Arches, 1961, p/s, dtd 62, full mrgs, lt mstn/cr, L-21x15", SBY 5/12/88 OE ... 12,100
Suite: Faits Memorables; 42/70, 3 clr slksc, 1978, intl/dtd, full mrgs, lt mstn, 26x39", Pace, lot 986, SBY 5/13/89 OE ... 26,400
Tourments, a/p, blk/wht litho, 1959, p/s, 21x15", lot 94, FAP 2/24/89 ... 525

UCHAMP, Marcel; after (American/French, 1887-1968)

La Mariee, by Jacques Villon, 61/200, clr aqua, 1934, sgn by Villon/Duchamp, full mrgs, 20x12", lot 467, SBY 2/25/88 OE ... 2,200

UFY, Jean (French, 1888-1964)

Circus, 214/250, clr litho, stp/s, L-18x25", lot 53, PHL 6/16/88 ... 160

UFY, Raoul (French, 1880-1953)

Gaigneuse, 20/40, clr litho, 1920, p/s, 22x29", lot 112, WG 10/19/88 ... 10,000
Seascape, 7/20, litho, ca 1930, p/s, lt stn mrgs, lt sl verso, 14x18", lot 457, SBY 5/11/89 ... 990
Untitled, Horse & Seashells; 72/150, litho/wove paper, p/s, full mrgs, lt stn, 11x14", lot 2844, B/B 2/16/88 ... 990
Untitled, Party; 3/10, litho/wove paper, lt stn/cr, 8x11", lot 2845, B/B 2/16/88 ... 660

UFY, Raoul; after (French, 1880-1953)

Le Havre, 71/150, clr litho/thin wove paper, ca 1945, p/s, lt nick, S-20x26", lot 253, SBY 2/23/89 ... 4,950

Le Havre, 83/150, clr ltiho, ca 1945, p/s, lt stn/cr, S-19x26", lot 254, SBY 2/23/89 .... **4,950**

DUNCAN, Frederick (American, 1881-)

Man May Be Down, But He's Never Out!; clr litho/poster paper, 1919, laid down, 40x30", lot 175, FAP 2/24/89 .... **80**

DUPAS, Jean Theodore (French, 1882-1964)

Bal des Etudiants, clr litho, 1927, S-77x50", Rousseau Freres, lot 216, SBY 4/23/88 OE **9,900**
Palais de la Mouveaute, clr litho, 1925, lt tr/cr, 35x46", Draeger, lot 220, SBY 4/23/88 OE **4,400**
Spring Fashions Are Here, clr litho, 1929, lt fox/stn/cr, 46x35", Tolmer, lot 219, SBY 4/23/88 OE **5,500**
Today in Comfort by Green Line Coach, clr litho, ca 1930, S-40x25", Johnson/Riddle, lot 218, SBY 4/23/88 OE **4,400**
XVME Salon des Artistes Decorateurs, clr litho, 45x29", Chachoin, lot 217, SBY 4/23/88 OE **7,150**

DUPAS, Jean Theodore; after (French, 1882-1964)

Le Taureau Noir, blk/hc etch, ca 1931, lg mrgs, 24x31", lot 221, SBY 4/23/88 .... **1,210**
Le Taureau Noir, 28/200, blk etch, 1931, p/s, 24x31", lot 287, SBY 3/10/89 .... **880**

DURAND, Asher Brown (American, 1796-1886)

Musidora, engr/thin China, 1825, lt stn/tr/fox, laid down, S-16x11", Burton/Valentine, lot 73, C-NY 1/19/89 OE **1,650**

DURER, Albrecht (German, 1471-1528)

Abduction of Proserpine, Meder I imp, etch on iron, 1516, trm/lt cr, 12x9", lot 600, SBY 2/25/88 .... **17,600**
Adam & Eve, Meder a (of d) imp, engr/wm bull's head, 1504, trm, rpr/stn, 10x7", lot 19, SBY 5/11/89 OE **19,250**
Apocalypse: Four Avenging Angels; wc w/Latin text, 1511, trm mrgs, rpr tr/ls, 16x11", lot 38, SBY 5/11/89 .... **1,540**
Apocalypse: Four Horsemen; a/p, wc/Imperial Orb, pre-1498, trm mrgs, rpr tr img, S-16x12", lot 34, SBY 5/11/89 .... **33,000**
Apocalypse: Four Horsemen; wc w/Latin text, 1511, trm mrgs, lt ls/tr/stn, 16x11", lot 35, SBY 5/11/89 .... **7,975**
Apocalypse: Four Horsemen; wc w/Latin text, 1511, trm/rpr tr, lt rub cr, 15x11", lot 610, SBY 2/25/88 .... **10,450**
Apocalypse: Opening of the Fifth & Sixth Seals; wc, pre-1498, trm, 16x11", lot 36, SBY 5/11/89 .... **3,025**
Apocalypse: St John Before God & the Elders; wc/Crowned Tower, 1511, lt tr/stn, 16x11", lot 33, SBY 5/11/89 .... **1,980**
Apocalypse: The Angel with the Key to the Bottomless Pit; wc, ca 1496-97, trm, lt stn, 16x11", lot 614, SBY 2/25/88 .... **3,410**
Apocalypse: The Angel with the Key to the Bottomless Pit; wc, ca 1496-97, trm, lt cr/sl, 15x11", lot 613, SBY 2/25/88 .... **3,850**
Apocalypse: The Four Angels Holding the Winds; wc w/Latin text, 1511, lt tr, 15x11", lot 612, SBY 2/25/88 OE **2,420**
Cardinal Albrecht of Brandenberg (The Small Cardinal), Meder Ib imp, engr, 1519, trm/rpr/cr, 5x4", lot 32, SBY 5/11/89 .... **2,530**
Christ Before Annas, late ed, etch, 5x4", lot 125, C-NY 1/19/89 UE **125**
Coat-of-Arms with a Lion & a Cock, engr, ca 1500, trm/stn/cr, 7x5", lot 29, SBY 5/11/89 .... **3,850**
Coat-of-Arms with the Skull, Meder Ib-c imp, engr, 1503, trm/rpr/cr, 8x6", lot 30, SBY 5/11/89 .... **3,025**
Cook & His Wife, Meder d imp, engr/wm L on shield paper, ca 1496, trm/stn/cr, 4x3", lot 28, SBY 5/11/89 .... **1,760**

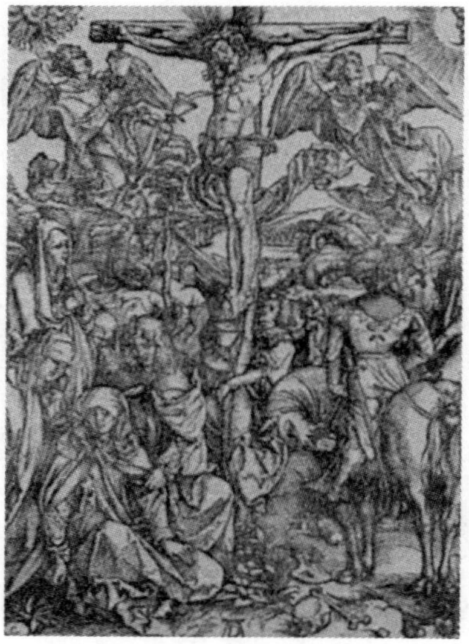

Crucifixion, Large Passion; P1 7, wc/laid paper, ca 1497-1500, intl block, trm img, lt fox/stn/cr, hinged top/bottom, S-15x11", lot 1, RWS 3/16/89 OE; $1,100

Desperate Man, Meder Ib (of c) imp, etch on iron, ca 1515, trm, lt cr, 7x5", lot 605, SBY 2/25/88 OE **17,600**
Ecce Homo, wc, ca 1510, 5x4", lot 405, LH 9/10/89 .... **300**
Hercules; or, The Effects of Jealousy; Meder IIb imp, engr, ca 1498, trm, lt tr,/cr/sl, lot 599, SBY 2/25/88 .... **4,950**
Hercules; or, The Effects of Jealousy; 2nd state, engr/High Crown, ca 1498, trm/rpr ls/fox, 13x9", lot 24, SBY 5/11/89 .... **3,190**
Holy Kinship with the Lute-Playing Angels, Meder a imp, wc, 1511, trm/cr/stn, 8x8", lot 41, SBY 5/11/89 .... **7,700**
Large Horse, engr/laid paper, trm mrgs, lt sl, 7x5", lot 2803, B/B 4/19/88 OE **3,300**
Large Passion: The Flagellation; wc w/Latin text, 1511, rpr tr, 15x11", lot 608, SBY 2/25/88 OE **2,420**
Life of the Virgin: Adoration of the Magi; wc w/Latin text on Crowned Tower, 1511, S-12x8", lot 40, SBY 5/11/89 OE **5,830**
Life of the Virgin: Death of the Virgin; Meder b imp, wc/wm bull's head, 1510, trm/fox, 11x8", lot 616, SBY 2/25/88 OE **2,640**
Little Fortune, Meder b-c (of d) imp, engr, ca 1497, trm, lt stn, 4x3", lot 601, SBY 2/25/88 .... **4,400**
Mass of St Gregory, Meder a (of h) imp, wc/wm High Crown paper, 1511, lt ls/sl/stn/cr, 12x8", lot 617, SBY 2/25/88 .... **2,310**
Melencolia I, Meder IIc(?) imp, engr, 1514, lt scr/ls, 9x7", lot 603, SBY 2/25/88 OE **19,800**
Nemesis (The Great Fortune), Meder IIa imp, engr/High Crown, ca 1501-02, lt cr/rpr nicks/fox, 13x9", lot 27, SBY 5/11/89 .... **4,400**
Pair: Hercules; or, The Effects of Jealousy; Nemesis, or, The Great Fortune; engr, 13x9", lot 25, SBY 5/11/89 OE **4,950**
Pair: Lamentaion for Christ; Christ in Limbo; late ed, etch, no size given, lot 24, WG 10/19/88 UE **150**
Pilate Washing His Hands, early imp, engr, 1512, pl sgn/dtd, 5x3", lot 284, LH 10/16/88 .... **2,800**
Scene From the Small Passion, wc, 1512, 5x3", lot 28, WG 10/19/88 OE **1,500**

Sea Monster, Meder c imp, engr/wm Gothic P paper, ca 1498, trm, rpr tr/cr, 10x8", lot 26, SBY 5/11/89 ... 24,200
Set of 36: Small Passion; wc, 1511, lt tr/fox/rub, S-7x5", lot 609, SBY 2/25/88 OE ... 42,900
St Eustance, engr, 1501/late 19th C, 14x10", lot 26, WG 10/19/89 ... 150
St George on Horseback, engr/laid paper, trm mrgs, lt sl, 4x4", lot 2802, B/B 4/19/88 OE ... 2,750
St Jerome in His Cell, Meder b(?) imp, wc, 1511, lt ls/cr, 9x6", lot 618, SBY 2/25/88 OE ... 3,630
St Jerome in His Study, engr, 1514, trm/rpr tr/lt stn, 10x8", lot 23, SBY 5/11/89 OE ... 20,900
Sudarium, posthumous ed, etch, 1516, trm mrgs, 7x5", lot 27, WG 10/18/89 UE ... 75
Three Genii, Meder b-c imp, engr, ca 1500-02, thread mrgs, lt stn, 5x3", lot 31, SBY 5/11/89 OE ... 4,950
Turkish Family, Meder c (of d) imp, engr, ca 1495-96, trm mrg, lt fox, 4x3", lot 604, SBY 2/25/88 ... 3,300
Virgin & Child with the Pear, Meder b (of c), engr/wm anchor in circle, 1511, rpr tr/lt cr, 6x4", lot 21, SBY 5/11/89 ... 2,090
Virgin with the Swaddled Child, Meder a-b (of e), engr, 1520, trm, 6x4", lot 22, SBY 5/11/89 ... 6,050

DUSART, Cornelis (Dutch, 1660-1704)
Large Village Fair, 2nd state, etch/Arms of Amsterdam, 1685, lt cr/sl, 11x14", lot 621, SBY 2/25/88 OE ... 3,960

DUTTON, T.G. (19th C)
Anglo-American Atlantic Yacht Race of 1870, hc litho/thick wove paper, 1870/1871, lt stn/tr/sl, L-15x25", C-NY 1/19/89 ... 1,980

DUVAL, P.S.; & SON. (19th C)
Washington's Triumphal Entry into New York...; chromo/wove paper, 1860, 3 tr to img/mrgs, L-35x47", C-NY 1/22/88 ... 825

DUVENECK, Frank (American, 1848-1919)
Riva Degli Schiavoni, No 1; ed of about 40, etch/wove paper, 1882, p/s, nick img, lt stn/sl, P-9x13", C-NY 1/22/88 ... 1,760
Riva Degli Schiavoni, No 2; ed of 15, etch/van Gelder, 1980, lt stn/sl/rpr tr, P-13x9", lot 168, C-NY 1/19/89 OE ... 990

DWIGHT, Mabel (20th C)
Pair: Staten Island Bathers; Tight Rope; ed of 25/30, litho, 1931/1930, p/s, lt sl, no size given, lot 23, C-NY 5/11/88 ... 880

EDELMANN, Yrjo (Finnish, 1941-)
Cut-Out Landscape, 46/175, beige & gray litho/wove paper, 1979, p/s, S-25x20", lot 97, RWS 9/8/89 ... 150

EDWARD, George (British, 18th C)
Pair: Squirrel; Little Owl; clr engr, 1749 & 1755, 9x7", lot 16, FAP 2/24/89 UE ... 70

EKSTER, see Exter

ELDRED, Lemuel D. (American, 1848-1921)
Fishing Village, etch, p/s, full mrgs, lt rpl, 4x7", lot 10, RAB 8/9/88 ... 375
Hauling Nets, etch, p/s, full mrgs, lt cr, 4x7", lot 9, RAB 8/9/88 ... 400
Ship Under Sail, etch, p/s, full mrgs, 7x12", lot 8, RAB 8/9/88 ... 550
Untitled (early whalers at dock w/city of Fairhaven in backbround), etch, sgn/dtd 1906, L-20x31", RAB 8/1/89 ... 800
Untitled (New Bedford waterfront with whaler departing), etch, sgn/dtd 1903, L-20x31", RAB 8/1/89 ... 1,200
Untitled (Venetian port scene), etch, no size given, RAB 11/25/88 UE ... 250
Untitled (view of Venice), etch, lt fox, 10x15", RAB 1/18/89 ... 175

ELMORE, Alfred; after
Origin of the Stocking Loom, engr, L-16x22", Francois Holl, lot 76, FAP 2/24/89 ... 25

ENDICOTT & CO.
Merchants & Miners Transportation Co Iron Steamer Benjamin Deford...; litho, fox/stn/4" tr, lg folio, RAB 11/10/88 OE ... 1,350
US Harbor & River Monitor, Manhattan; litho, ca 1853, lstn/tstn, lt tr mrg, stn/sl verso, P-12x26", C-NY 1/22/88 ... 550
US Schooner Flying-Fish, litho, L-23x32", RAB 8/1/89 ... 750

ENGLISH, Joseph Craig (American, 20th C)
Gaithersberg Train Station, 10/50, ed of 50, slksc/wove paper, 1976, p/s, unfr, L-16x23", RWS 3/16/89 UE ... 150

ENSOR, James Sidney (Belgian, 1860-1940)
Affiche pour le Carnival d'Ostende, clr litho, 1931, full mrgs, lt cr/stn, 16x12", lot 460, SBY 5/11/89 OE ... 3,410
Audo-da-fe, etch/simile Japan, 1893, p/s, dtd/titled, countersgn verso, full mrgs, lt cr, unfr, S-3x5", SBY 5/12/88 OE ... 2,420
Candelabra et Vase, etch/thick Japan, 1888, p/s, titled/dtd on verso, lt fox, P-5x3", lot 160, C-NY 5/11/88 ... 660
Carnaval d'Ostende, #216, clr litho, 1931, tax stp in corner, lt cr/scr, L-16x11", lot 57, PHL 10/28/88 ... 1,200
Flemish Farm, etch/Japan, 1888, p/s, 3 trm mrgs, lt fox/cr/sl, laid down, P-3x5", C-NY 1/22/88 UE ... 220
Iston, Pouffamatus, Cracozie et Transmouffe, Celebres Medecines Persans...; etch, 1886, 10x8", lot 193, SBY 11/3/88 OE ... 2,860
La Bataille des Eperons d'Or, aside from ed of 125, hc etch/simili Japan, 1895, S-11x16", lot 34, C-NY 11/1/88 OE ... 9,350
La Cathedrale (Premiere Planche), #2, 3rd state, etch/simili Japan, 1886, p/s, S-18x11", lot 31, C-NY 11/1/88 OE ... 12,100
La Kermesse au Moulin, etch/simili Japan, 1889, p/s, titled/dtd, sgn/lt cr on verso, P-6x7", lot 604, C-NY 5/10/89 ... 2,200
La Mort Poursuivant le Troupeau des Humains, Elesch's 3rd state, etch/drypt, 1896, S-18x14", lot 35, C-NY 11/1/88 ... 8,250
La Multiplication de Poissons, etch/drypt/simili Japan, 1891, p/s, titled, S-10x13", lot 33, C-NY 11/1/88 OE ... 3,300
La Multiplication de Poissons, etch/drypt/stiff cream simili Japan, 1891, p/s, lt mstn, 7x9", lot 197A, SBY 11/3/88 ... 2,530
La Musique rue de Flandres, 3rd state, etch/thick Japan, 1890, p/s, titled, lt scr, P-5x3", lot 164, C-NY 5/11/88 ... 1,430
La Reine Parysatis, etch/simile Japan, 1899, p/s, dtd 1900, lt cr, 7x5", lot 198, SBY 11/3/88 ... 2,750
La Tentation du Christ, etch/simili Japan, 1888, p/s, titled, full mrgs, 3x4", lot 459, SBY 5/11/89 ... 1,430
Le Fantome, etch/simile Japan, 1889, p/s, titled, lt fox, 3x5", lot 197, SBY 11/3/88 ... 1,540
Le Fantome, 4th state, etch/thick Japan, 1889, inscr Le genie des cataclysmes on verso, P-3x5", lot 163, C-NY 5/11/88 ... 1,650
Le Vidangeur, etch/Japan, 1896, p/s, sgn verso, rub/stn/lt sl mrgs, mstn, P-5x3", C-NY 1/22/88 UE ... 550
Les Cataclysmes, etch/simili Japan, 1888, p/s, dtd, counter sgn verso, lt stn/sl/cr, unfr, L-7x9", SBY 5/12/88 OE ... 2,530
Les Petites Barques, AP8, etch/Chine, 1894, p/s, lt fox/sl, P-4x6", C-NY 1/22/88 OE ... 990
Les Vieux...Polissons (La Visite Des Medecins); etch/China, 1895, p/s, lt cr/fox, P-4x6", SBY 5/12/88 OE ... 3,410
Mon Portrait en 1960, etch/simile Japan, 1888, p/s, titled, full mrgs, lt cr, 3x5", lot 196, SBY 11/3/88 ... 1,430
Ostend Carnival (poster), clr litho/wove paper, 1931, sgn/dtd in stone, full mrgs, cr, 16x11", lot 605, C-NY 5/10/89 OE ... 1,760
Pair: Hotel de Ville d'Audenaerde; Sou-Bois a Groenendael; etch/drypt & drypt, 1888, 6x5"/4x3", lot 194, SBY 11/3/88 ... 1,760
Pair: Menu pour Ernest Rousseau; Menu pour Charles Vos; etch/simile Japan or laid Japan, 1896, lot 199, SBY 11/3/88 ... 1,540
Peste Dessous Peste Dessus, Peste Partout; etch/Imperial Japan, 1904, p/s, French tax stp, 8x12", lot 300, C-NY 11/1/88 ... 3,850
Petites Figures Bizarres, 2nd state, etch/drypt/thick Japan, 1888, p/s, lt stn, P-5x4", lot 162, C-NY 5/11/88 ... 1,760

Prise d'une Ville Etrange, final state, etch, 1888, sgn in brn ink, lt sl, 7x10", lot 195, SBY 11/3/88 ... **4,950**
Triomphe Romain, 2nd state, etch/drypt/simili Japan, 1889, p/s, lt cr, S-11x15", lot 32, C-NY 11/1/88 OE ... **2,860**

ERNI, Hans (Swiss, 1909-)
Cats, 1/95, litho, p/s, 19x23", WG 10/19/88 ... **225**
Family of Three, ed of 100, litho, p/s, no size given, lot 352, WG 10/19/88 ... **155**
Female Nude, litho, 15x22", WG 10/19/88 ... **325**
Lovers, 6/50, litho, p/s, 24x35", lot 349, WG 10/19/88 ... **425**

ERNST, Max (American, 1891-1976)
Birds, II/XII, yel etch/Japan, p/s, full mrgs, P-11x8", lot 59, PHL 10/28/88 ... **400**
Book: La Femme 100 Tetes; 478/1003, 147 prints w/text, lt tr/sl/stn, Eds du Carrefour, lot 165, C-NY 5/11//88 ... **440**
Danseuses, a/p, aside from total ed of 287, litho/Arches, 1950, p/s, lt stn/fox, L-19x13", lot 166, C-NY 5/11/88 OE ... **1,650**
Etoile de Mer, XV/LX, clr litho, 1950, p/s, Guilde de la Gravure bstp, full mrgs, sl/fox, 22x15", lot 199B, SBY 11/3/88 ... **1,980**
Etoile de Mer, 50/200, clr litho/Arches, 1950, p/s, full mrgs, lt stn/sl/fox, L-17x11", lot 301, C-NY 11/1/88 ... **1,870**
Hibou, total ed of 255, clr litho, 1955, p/s, full mrgs, lt stn/sl, old tp on verso, L-19x14", lot 302, C-NY 11/1/88 OE ... **2,090**
La Ballade du Soldat, Pl 4, 32/79, clr litho/Japan nacre, 1972, p/s, full mrgs, 7x9", lot 462, SBY 5/11/89 ... **660**
La Cloche Rouge, 32/85, hc etch/Velin de Lana, 1970, p/s, full mrgs, lt cr/fox, P-10x7", lot 167, C-NY 5/11/88 ... **1,870**
Le Chateau Etoile, 48/50, clr frottage/thin laid paper, 1936, p/s, full mrgs, lt sl, 7x7", Skira, lot 461, SBY 5/11/89 ... **5,500**
Masques, ed of 312, clr litho/Arches, 1950, p/s, full mrgs, lt stn, 13x20", lot 2847, B/B 2/16/88 OE ... **1,980**
Ohne Titel, 29/30, total ed of 135, etch/aqua/BFK wove paper, 1950, p/s, tr/cr/fox, 5x7", Zerbib, lot 199A, SBY 11/3/88 ... **1,650**
Veilleuse au Seuil de nos Terrassements, 60/70, photolitho/Japan, 1969, L-19x15", Mourlot, lot 304, C-NY 11/1/88 OE ... **1,100**

ERTE, Romain de Tirtoff (Russian, 1892-1990)
A, From the Alphabet; 56/350, clr srgph, 1976, sgn, 16x11", Circle Fine Arts, C-E 3/24/88 ... **605**
Aces: Diamond, Heart, Spade, Club; #AP90, 4 litho, 1974, sgn, 26x20", Grosvenor Gallery/Bergruen et Cie, C-E 3/24/88 ... **6,533**
Adam & Eve, CVI/CXXV, clr srgph, 1982, sgn, 37x21", Chalk & Vermilion, C-E 3/24/88 ... **385**
After the Rain, 216/300, clr srgph, 1979, sgn, 31x23", Circle Fine Art, C-E 3/24/88 ... **660**
Aladdin & His Bride, APXXIII, clr srgph, 1984, sgn, 31x37", Sevenarts Ltd, C-E 3/24/88 ... **660**
Angel, AP 23/60, clr srgph, 1982, sgn, 27x38", Clark & Vermilion, C-E 3/24/88 ... **1,430**
Anger, 306/350, clr srgph, p/s, 9x14", lot 2047, DM 3/14/88 ... **425**
Arctic Sea, AP40/60, clr srgph w/foil stp, 1981, sgn, 19x25", Circle Fine Art, C-E 3/24/88 ... **3,300**
Autumn Song, From Twenties Remembered; 243/300, clr srgph, 1977, sgn, 25x22", Circle Fine Art, C-E 3/24/88 ... **660**
B, From the Alphabet; 56/350, clr srgph, 1976, sgn, 16x11", Circle Fine Art, C-E 3/24/88 ... **770**
Bagdad, 216/300, clr litho, 1979, sgn, 16x13", Circle Fine Art, C-E 3/24/88 ... **440**
Bird Cage, 167/300, clr srgph, 1981, sgn, 31x23", Circle Fine Art, C-E 3/24/88 ... **935**
Black Rose, clr srgph, 1975, sgn, 20x15", Circle Fine Art, 20x15", C-E 3/24/88 OE ... **770**
Broadway's in Fashion, 195/300, clr srgph w/foil stp, 1978, sgn, 24x17", Circle Fine Art, C-E 3/24/88 ... **660**
C, From the Alphabet; 56/350, clr srgph, sgn, 16x11", Circle Fine Art, C-E 3/24/88 ... **638**
Carnations, AP7, clr srgph w/foil stp, sgn, 22x24", Chalk & Vermilion, C-E 3/24/88 ... **990**
Charleston Couple, 204/300, blk/wht/cream srgph, 1980, sgn, 24x19", Circle Fine Art, C-E 3/24/88 ... **715**
Clasp, 292/300, clr srgph w/foil stp, 1982, sgn, 43x26", Chalk & Vermilion, C-E 3/24/88 ... **2,200**
Columbine, 73/200, clr srgph, 1983, sgn, 33x26", Chalk & Vermilion, C-E 3/24/88 ... **880**
Coming of Spring, AP36/60, clr srgph, 1981, sgn, 25x18", Circle Fine Art, C-E 3/24/88 OE ... **1,540**
Coming of Spring, 148/300, clr srgph, 1982, sgn, 30x24", Chalk & Vermilion, C-E 3/24/88 ... **825**
Compact Vanities, 81/260, clr srgph, 1974, sgn, 30x24", Circle Fine Art, C-E 3/24/88 ... **660**
Coquette, 260/300, clr srgph, 1981, sgn, 24x19", Circle Fine Art, C-E 3/24/88 ... **770**
D, From the Alphabet; 56/350, clr srgph, sgn, 16x11", Circle Fine Art, C-E 3/24/88 ... **825**
Dancer, From At the Theater; 264/300, clr srgph, 1982, sgn, 30x22", Kane Fine Art, C-E 3/24/88 ... **495**
E, From the Alphabet; 56/350, clr srgph, sgn, 16x11", C-E 3/24/88 ... **462**
Ebony & White, a/p, clr srgph, 1982, sgn, 22x30", Chalk & Vermilion, C-E 3/24/88 OE ... **1,210**
Enchanted Melody, HC4, clr srgph w/foil stp, 1983, sgn, 43x30", Chalk & Vermilion, C-E 3/24/88 ... **1,045**
End of the Romance, HC, clr srgph, 1981, sgn, 30x23", Circle Fine Art, C-E 3/24/88 ... **1,650**
Eyes of Jealousy, clr srgph, 1983, sgn, 25x40", Chalk & Vermilion, C-E 3/24/88 ... **880**
Eyes of Love, AP32, clr srgph, 1983, sgn, 25x40", Chalk & Vermilion, C-E 3/24/88 ... **990**
F, From the Alphabet; 56/350, clr srgph, sgn, 16x11", Circle Fine Art, C-E 3/24/88 ... **605**
Fall, 191/300, clr srgph, 1979, sgn, 30x24", Circle Fine Art, C-E 3/24/88 ... **1,100**
Fantasia, CXV/CXXV, clr srgph, 1982, sgn, 33x25", Chalk & Vermilion, C-E 3/24/88 ... **1,100**
Feather Gown, 202/300, clr srgph w/foil stp, 1985, sgn, 30x21", Chalk & Vermilion, C-E 3/24/88 ... **1,430**
First Dress, From Twenties Remembered Again; 122/300, clr srgph, sgn, 18x15", C-E 3/24/88 ... **605**
Fish Bowl, From Twenties Remembered; 156/300, clr srgph, 1977, sgn, 25x22", Circle Fine Art, C-E 3/24/88 ... **440**
Flames of Love, 91/300, clr srgph, 1978, sgn, 27x21", Circle Fine Art, C-E 3/24/88 ... **1,430**
French Rooster, 154/300, clr srgph, 1980, sgn, 31x23", Circle Fine Art, C-E 3/24/88 ... **3,190**
Furs, 69/260, clr srgph, 1974, sgn, 24x30", Circle Fine Art, C-E 3/24/88 OE ... **1,760**
G, From the Alphabet; 56/350, clr srgph, 1977, sgn, 16x11", Circle Fine Art, C-E 3/24/88 ... **495**
Giulietta, APXXVI, clr srgph, 1983, 30x22", Sevenarts Ltd, C-E 3/24/88 ... **715**
Golden Calf, From At the Theater; 264/300, clr srgph, 1982, sgn, 22x17", Kane Fine Art, C-E 3/24/88 ... **528**
Golden Cloak, 214/300, clr litho, 1979, sgn, 24x17", Circle Fine Art, C-E 3/24/88 ... **825**
H, From the Alphabet; 56/350, clr srgph, 1976, sgn, 16x11", Circle Fine Arts, C-E 3/24/88 ... **495**
Harlequin, CXI/CXXV, clr srgph, 1982, 31x24", Chalk & Vermilion, C-E 3/24/88 ... **605**
Heat, 25/300, clr srgph, 1980, sgn, 31x24", Circle Fine Art, 31x24", C-E 3/24/88 ... **1,650**
Helen of Troy, 3/300, clr srgph w/foil stp, 1985, sgn, 36x31", Chalk & Vermilion, C-E 3/24/88 ... **1,210**
I, From the Alphabet, 56/350, clr srgph, 1976, sgn, 16x11", Circle Fine Art, C-E 3/24/88 ... **385**
Indochina, 295/350, clr srgph, 1984, sgn, 26x22", Sevenarts Ltd, C-E 3/24/88 ... **440**

J, From the Alphabet; 56/350, clr srgph, 1976, sgn, 16x11", Circle Fine Art, C-E 3/24/88 605

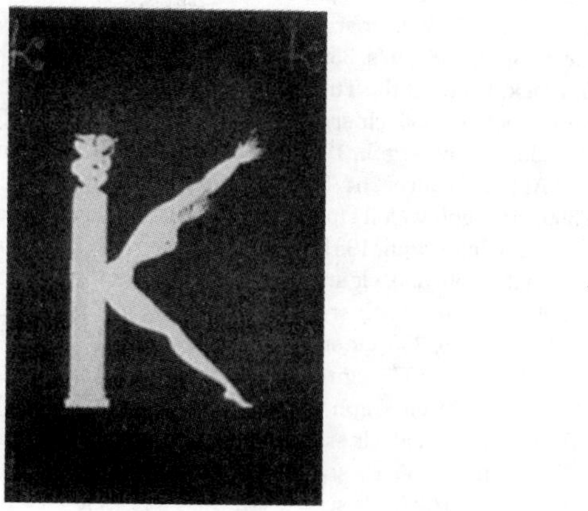

K, From the Alphabet; 56/350, clr srgph, 1977, sgn, 16x11", Circle Fine Art, lot 436, C-E 3/24/88; $1,210

King's Favorite, a/p, clr srgph, 1979, sgn, 25x20", Circle Fine Art, C-E 3/24/88 UE 440
L, From the Alphabet; 56/350, clr srgph, 1977, sgn, 16x11", Circle Fine Art, C-E 3/24/88 3,960
La Merveilleuse, 225/300, clr srgph, 1980, sgn, 31x23", Circle Fine Art, C-E 3/24/88 880
La Traviata, AP38, 1 of 64 a/p, clr srgph, 1982, sgn, 32x24", Chalk & Vermilion, C-E 3/24/88 418
Lafayette, 67/300, clr srgph, 1979, sgn, 32x24", Circle Fine Art, C-E 3/24/88 715
Legerte, From Twenties Remembered Again; 294/300, clr srgph, 1978, sgn, 24x20", Circle Fine Art, C-E 3/24/88 528
Les Bijoux de Perles, 206/300, clr srgph, sgn, 30x22", SBY 6/10/88 990
Loge de Theatre, XVI/CL, clr srgph w/foil stp, 1984, sgn, 33x27", Chalk & Vermilion, C-E 3/24/88 2,090
Love's Captive, 117/300, clr srgph, 1982, sgn, 32x28", Chalk & Vermilion, C-E 3/24/88 715
M, From the Alphabet; 56/350, clr srgph, 1977, sgn, 16x11", Circle Fine Art, C-E 3/24/88 2,200
Melisande, From At the Theatre; 264/300, clr srgph, sgn, 30x22", Kane Fine Art, C-E 3/24/88 825
Monte Carlo, 226/350, clr srgph, 1983, sgn, 25x18", Sevenarts Ltd, C-E 3/24/88 550
Mystique, 39/260, clr srgph, sgn, 1974, 40x26", Circle Fine Art, C-E 3/24/88 935
Mystique, 61/260, slksc, p/s, pub bstp, wide mrgs, L-32x20", lot 35, PHL 6/16/88 1,000
N, From the Alphabet; 56/350, clr srgph, sgn, 16x11", Circle Fine Art, C-E 3/24/88 495
O, From the Alphabet; 56/350, clr srgph, 1976, sgn, 16x11", Circle Fine Art, C-E 3/24/88 OE 374
Ondee, APXXV, clr srgph, 1983, sgn, 30x22", Sevenarts Ltd, C-E 3/24/88 528
P, From the Alphabet; 56/350, clr srgph, 1977, sgn, 16x11", Circle Fine Art, C-E 3/24/88 1,100
Pair: Circe; Diana; XIII/CL, clr srgph w/foil stp, 1985, sgn, 34x25", Chalk & Vermilion, C-E 3/24/88 3,850
Pair: Morning, Day; Evening, Night; HC4, clr srgph w/foil stp, 1985, sgn, 44x34", Chalk & Vermilion, C-E 3/24/88 UE 1,870
Pair: On the Avenue; Opening Night; XVIII/CL, clr srgph w/foil stp, 1985, sgn, 25x30", Chalk & Vermilion, C-E 3/24/88 4,620
Pair: Opium; Mah-Jongg; 4/300, clr srgph w/foil stp, 1985, sgn, 34x27", Chalk & Vermilion, C-E 3/24/88 2,860
Pair: Radiance; Wisdom; HC16, clr srgph w/foil stp, sgn, 34x27", Chalk & Vermilion, C-E 32/4/88 3,300
Pair: Sunrise; Moonlight; LXXXVIII/CXXV, clr srgph w/foil stp, 1984, sgn, 14x21"/20x20", Chalk & Vermilion, C-E 3/24/88 1,980
Perfume, XIX/CL, clr srgph w/foil stp, 1986, sgn, 40x24", Chalk & Vermilion, C-E 3/24/88 3,740
Phoenix Suite: Phoenix Reborn; Phoenix Triumphant; 32/300, clr srgph, 1983, 28x40", Chalk & Vermilion, C-E 3/24/88 1,650
Portfolio: Emotions Suite; 4 clr srgph, 1982, 23x18", C-E 3/24/88 3,850
Princess Lontaine, clr srgph, 1983, sgn, 22x16", Kane Fine Art, C-E 3/24/88 UE 440
Printemps, 32/260, clr srgph, 1975, sgn, 29x23", Circle Fine Art, C-E 3/24/88 495
Pursuit of Flore, 118/300, clr srgph, 1982, sgn, 33x26", Chalk & Vermilion, C-E 3/24/88 495
Q, From the Alphabet; 56/350, clr srgph, 1977, sgn, 16x11", Circle Fine Art, C-E 3/24/88 385
R, From the Alphabet; 56/350, clr srgph, 1977, sgn, 16x11", Circle Fine Art, C-E 3/24/88 990
Rain, 141/300, clr srgph w/foil stp, 1980, sgn, 10x20", Circle Fine Art, C-E 3/24/88 825
Rainbow in Blossom, From Twenties Remembered; 243/300, clr srgph, 1977, sgn, 24x20", Circle Fine Art, C-E 3/24/88 385
Rigoletto, XXII/CL, clr srgph w/foil stp, 1985, sgn, 38x31", Chalk & Vermilion, C-E 3/24/88 OE 3,300
Riviera, 206/300, clr srgph, 1980, sgn, 10x15", Circle Fine Art, C-E 3/24/88 660
Rose Dancer, LXVI/CXXV, clr srgph w/foil stp, 1984, sgn, 27x20", Chalk & Vermilion, C-E 3/24/88 OE 1,100
Russian Fairytale, From Twenties Remembered Again; 252/300, clr srgph, 1978, sgn, 24x19", Circle Fine Art, C-E 3/24/88 462
S, From the Alphabet; 56/350, clr srgph, 1977, sgn, 16x11", Circle Fine Art, C-E 3/24/88 990
Salome, 117/300, clr srgph w/foil stp, 1981, sgn, 17x23", Circle Fine Art, C-E 3/24/88 1,210
Samson & Delilah, XLVIII/XC, clr srgph w/foil stp, 1980, sgn, 15x21", Circle Fine Art, C-E 3/24/88 OE 2,310
Selection of a Heart, From Twenties Remembered; 16/300, clr srgph, 1978, sgn, Circle Fine Art, C-E 3/24/88 770
Slave, 255/300, clr srgph, 1983, sgn, 35x27", Chalk & Vermilion, 35x27", C-E 3/24/88 1,650
Sleeping Beauty, 170/300, clr srgph, 1983, sgn, 27x33", Chalk & Vermilion, C-E 3/24/88 605
Splendor, 89/260, clr srgph, 1974, sgn, 26x34", Circle Fine Art, C-E 3/24/88 3,300
Splendor, 64/260, clr slksc, p/s, pub bstp, wide mrgs, lt cr, L-27x21", lot 37, PHL 6/16/88 1,000
Spring Opening, From Twenties Remembered Again; 297/300, clr srgph, 1978, sgn, 24x19", Circle Fine Art, C-E 3/24/88 418
Stolen Kisses, 274/300, clr srgph, 1982, sgn, 29x24", Chalk & Vermilion, C-E 3/24/88 495
Stranded, 74/300, clr srgph, 1983, 33xx27", Chalk & Vermilion, C-E 3/24/88 605
Suite: Asian Princess; AP35, 3 clr srgph, sgn, 29x21", Chalk & Vermilion, C-E 3/24/88 1,980
Suite: Liberty, Day; Liberty, Night; XXI/CL, clr srgph w/foil stp, sgn, 35x26", Chalk & Vermilion, C-E 3/24/88 OE 2,310

Suite: Love & Passion; XV/CLXXV, 2 clr srgph w/foil stp, 1983-4, sgn, 29x34", Chalk & Vermilion, C-E 3/24/88 5,500
Suite: Numerals; 32/350, 10 clr srgph w/flocking, 1980, p/s, 23x17", Circle Fine Art, C-E 3/24/88 7,150
Summer Breeze, XVI/XVIII, clr srgph, 1978, sgn, 31x23", Circle Fine Art, C-E 3/24/88 1,650
Surprises of the Sea, 281/300, clr srgph, 1982, sgn, 33x25", Chalk & Vermilion, C-E 3/24/88 528
Swept Away, clr srgph, 1982, p/s, 33x24", Chalk & Vermilion, C-E 3/24/88 UE 550
Symphony in Black, From At the Theater; 264/300, clr srgph, 1982, sgn, 30x22", Kane Fine Art, C-E 3/24/88 OE 1,430
T, From the Alphabet, 56/350, clr srgph, 1977, sgn, 16x11", Circle Fine Art, C-E 3/24/88 935
Three Graces, 235/300, clr srgph, 1985, sgn, 33x25", Chalk & Vermilion, C-E 3/24/88 OE 2,310
Trapeze, From At the Theatre; 264/300, clr srgph, 1982, sgn, 30x22", Kane Fine Art, C-E 3/24/88 528
Tuxedo, 10/300, clr srgph w/foil stp, 1986, sgn, 31x22", Chalk & Vermilion, C-E 3/24/88 990
Twin Sisters, 76/350, clr srgph, 1981, sgn, 40x55", s/wrp, Circle Fine Art, C-E 3/24/88 3,080
U, From the Alphabet; 56/350, clr srgph, 1977, sgn, 16x11", Circle Fine Art, C-E 3/24/88 OE 440
V, From the Alphabet; 56/350, clr srgph, 1977, sgn, 16x11", Circle Fine Art, C-E 3/24/88 OE 495
W, From the Alphabet; 56/350, clr srgph, 1977, sgn, 16x11", Circle Fine Art, C-E 3/24/88 OE 660
Winter, 12/260, clr srgph, 1975, sgn, 20x14", Circle Fine Art, C-E 3/24/88 440
Winter's Arrival, 176/300, clr srgph w/foil stp, 1984, sgn, Chalk & Vermilion, C-E 3/24/88 660
X, From the Alphabet; 56/350, clr srgph, 1977, sgn, 16x11", Circle Fine Art, C-E 3/24/88 OE 385
Y, From the Alphabet; 56/350, clr srgph, 1977, sgn, 16x11", Circle Fine Art, C-E 3/24/88 OE 385
Z, From the Alphabet; 56/350, clr srgph, sgn, 16x11", Circle Fine Art, C-E 3/24/88 1,320

ESCHER, Maurits Cornelis (Dutch, 1898-)

Ascending & Decending, 34/52, litho/cream Holland paper, 1960, p/s, lt tr, 13x11", lot 204, SBY 11/3/88 6,050
Ascending & Descending, 91/108, litho/cream Holland, 1960, p/s, lt stn, 14x11", lot 2848, B/B 2/16/88 5,225
Bridge, 5/60, wc/cream Holland, 1930, p/s, full mrgs, lt stn/cr, 21x15", lot 464, SBY 5/11/89 OE 7,150
Bridge, 5/60, wc/Holland paper, 1930, p/s, full mrgs, lt stn/cr, 21x15", lot 201, SBY 11/3/88 3,850
Convex & Concave, 52/56 IV, litho/cream Holland, p/s, tp stn verso, L-11x13", SBY 5/12/88 4,675
Day & Night, blk & gr-gray wc/laid Japan, 1938, p/s, inscr Eigen druk, full mrgs, lt cr, 16x27", lot 202, SBY 11/3/88 9,350
Encounter, 157/200, litho/cream Holland, 1944, p/s, full mrgs, lt stn/fox, 13x18", lot 467, SBY 5/11/89 OE 4,400
Encounter, 77/200, litho/cream Holland, 1944, p/s, full mrgs, lt sl/cr, 14x18", lot 466, SBY 5/11/89 OE 4,400
Encounter, 77/200, litho/cream Holland paper, 1944, p/s, full mrgs, lt sl/cr, 14x18", lot 203, SBY 11/3/88 2,750
Illustration (page 19), From Scholastica; 91/300, wc/cream wove paper, 1932, pl/s, L-9x7", lot 168, C-NY 5/11/88 OE 330
Mummified Frog, 19/24, mezzo/laid van Gelder Zonen, 1946, p/s, full mrgs, lt stn/fox, 6x7", lot 469, SBY 5/11/89 1,925
Mummified Priests in Gangi, Sicily; 8/20, litho/heavy wht wove paper, 1932, p/s, lt fox, 8x11", lot 465, SBY 5/11/89 OE 2,475
Other World, ed of unknown size, wood engr/wc/thin Japan, 1947, p/s, inscr Eigen druk, lt stn, L-13x10", C-NY 5/10/89 OE 4,950
Print Gallery, 7/47II, litho/cream Holland, 1956, p/s, full mrgs, hinge stns, 13x13", lot 471, SBY 5/11/89 OE 9,350
Seashells, #5, mezzo/fine laid paper, 1949, p/s, inscr Eigen druk, full mrgs, lt stn/sl, 6x5", lot 305, C-NY 11/1/88 OE 2,310
Self-Portrait, 30/40, litho/heavy cream wove paper, 1929, p/s, full mrgs, lt stn/fox, 10x8", lot 463, SBY 5/11/89 4,125
Up & Down, litho/cream wove paper, 1947, p/s, lt rub/cr/stn, laid down on board, L-20x8", lot 610, C-NY 5/10/89 OE 3,300
Up & Down, 16/17II, litho, 1947, p/s, 20x18", lot 1337, WL 2/26/88 3,500
Up & Down, 3/36, litho/cream Holland, 1947, p/s, lt stn, 20x8", lot 193, SBY 2/25/88 3,300
Waterfall, 24/50V, litho/cream Holland, 1961, full mrgs, lt stn, 15x12", lot 2849, B/B 2/16/88 6,050
Waterfall, 33/57 II, litho/cream Hollland, 1961, p/s, full mrgs, lt stn, 16x11", lot 194, SBY 2/25/88 4,675

ESTES, Richard (American, 1936-)

Bus, 111/250, slkcr/Fabriano, 1981, p/s, Domberger bstp, unfr, L-14x20", lot 105, RWS 9/8/89 OE 1,500
Eiffel Tower, 111/250, slksc/Fabriano, 1981, p/s, unfr, L-14x20", lot 106, RWS 9/8/89 OE 1,900
Holland Hotel, 4/100, scrpt, 1984, sgn in golden ink, full mrgs, lt rpr/cr, S-48x72", Parasol, lot 622, C-NY 11/1/88 8,800
Manhattan, 111/250, slksc/Fabriano, 1981, p/s, Domberger bstp, unfr, L-14x20", lot 107, RWS 9/8/89 OE 1,800
New York Pressing, Urban Landscape II; 41/100, scrpt, 1979, p/s, Domberger bstp, 28x20", Parasol, lot 620, C-NY 11/1/88 1,430
Pair: Restaurant; Big Diamond; 27/100, clr slksc, 1979, p/s, full mrgs, S-28x20", Parasol, lot 971, SBY 5/13/89 3,575
Pair: Urban Landscapes II: Meat Department; Big Diamond; 15/100, slksc, 1979, p/s, full mrgs, S-28x20", SBY 5/14/88 OE 3,575
Pair: Urban Landscapes II: Venezia Murane; Escalator; 24/100, slksc, 1979, full mrgs, S-28x20", Parasol, SBY 5/14/88 OE 3,850
Pair: Urban Landscapes III: Roma; Sherman Shoes; 126/250, slksc, 1981, p/s, S-20x18", Parasol, SBY 5/14/88 OE 3,025
Qualicraft Shoes (The Chinese Lady), 8/100, clr slksc, 1974, p/s, full mrgs, 33x47", Parasol, lot 766, SBY 11/5/88 6,050
Restaurant Near Lincoln Center, 41/100, scrpt, 1979, p/s, Domberger bstp, lt scr, 28x20", Parasol, lot 621, C-NY 11/1/88 1,980
Roma, 111/250, slksc/Fabriano, 1981, p/s, Domberger bstp, unfr, L-14x20", lot 109, RWS 9/8/89 OE 2,600
Salzburg Cathedral, aside from #d ed of 250, clr slksc, 1982, p/s, Domberger bstp, 20x15", V&R Fine Arts, SBY 2/23/89 1,540
Salzburg Cathedral, 215/250, clr slksc, 1982, p/s, Domberger bstp, 20x15", V&R Fine Arts/Parasol, SBY 5/14/88 1,925
Salzburg Cathedral, 217/250, clr slksc, 1982, p/s, Domberger bstp, 20x15", V&R Fine Arts/Parasol, SBY 2/23/89 OE 6,600
Salzburg Cathedral, 229/250, clr slksc, 1982, p/s, Domberger bstp, 20x15", V&R Fine Arts/Parasol, lot 504, SBY 2/25/88 1,760
Shopping Center, 111/250, slksc/Fabriano, 1981, p/s, Domberger bstp, unfr, L-14x20", lot 108, RWS 9/8/89 OE 1,500
Subway Car, 111/250, slksc/Fabriano, 1981, p/s, Domberger bstp, unfr, L-14x20", lot 104, RWS 9/8/89 OE 1,600
Suite: Urban Landscapes I; 2/75, 8 clr slksc, 1972, p/s, full mrgs, orig wrappers, S-20x28", lot 636, SBY 2/23/89 13,200
Suite: Urban Landscapes I; 18/75, 8 clr slksc, 1972, p/s, full mrgs, orig wrappers, Parasol, lot 765, SBY 11/5/88 9,350
Suite: Urban Landscapes III; 155/250, 8 clr slksc, 1981, p/s, full mrgs, S-20x18", Parasol, lot 972, SBY 5/13/89 OE 18,700
Suite: Urban Lanscapes II; 6/100, 8 clr slksc, 1979, p/s, orig wrappers, S-28x20", Parasol, lot 969, SBY 5/13/89 OE 16,500
Urban Landscapes II: Escalator; 50/100, clr slkscr, 1979, p/s, full mrgs, 20x13", Parasol, lot 970, SBY 5/13/89 2,750
Urban Landscapes II: Meat Dept; 63/100, clr slksc, 1979, p/s, full mrgs, lt stn, 19x13", Parasol, lot 503, SBY 2/25/88 990

ETTINGER, Churchill (American, 20th C)

Group of 4: Pair of Pintails; Pintails; Lining Up; Surf Fisherman; etch, p/s, lt fox, Assn Am Artists, WG 10/19/88 160
Planning the Campaign, etch, p/s, titled, lt stn, 10x8", lot 275, WG 10/19/88 100

EVERGOOD, Philip (American, 1901-1973)

Three Figures, 2/25, litho, p/s, full mrgs, L-20x14", lot 21, PHL 10/28/88 275

EXTER, Alexandra (Russian, 1882-1949)
Decor for a Tragedy, gouache/pochoir, 1930, 11x12", lot 510, C-L 10/8/88 1,670
FANTIN-LATOUR, Ignace Henri Jean (French, 1836-1904)
Deposition de Croix, 2nd state, total ed of 44, litho/Chine, 1893, p/s, lt fox, L-13x18", lot 169, C-NY 5/11/88 462
Immortalite, litho/Chine applique, p/s, 9x6", lot 2850, B/B 2/16/88 OE 550
William Tell, litho/tissue paper, 1902, sgn/dtd in stone, lt cr, 15x15", lot 2841, B/B 4/19/88 385
FECHIN, Nicolai (American/Russian, 1881-1955)
Still Life with Flowers & Fruit, clr monotype/Japan, ca 1950, sgn, lt tr/cr/ls, S-20x17", lot 169, C-NY 1/19/89 OE 1,540
FEININGER, Lyonel (American, 1871-1956)
Anglers with Sun, wc/cream wove paper, 1921, lt cr img, 4x6", lot 2842, B/B 4/19/88 300
Die Grune Brucke, a/p, before eds of 175 & 100, hc etch, 1910-11, lt cr/tr/sl, S-18x14", lot 36, C-NY 11/1/88 OE 15,400
Die Grune Brucke (The Green Bridge), ed of 150, etch/JW Zanders, 1910-11, full mrgs, 10x8", lot 205, SBY 11/3/88 OE 7,425
Fishing Boats, posthumous ed of 252, wc/Japan, 1921, Cleveland Print Club bstp, unfr, L-12x15", C-NY 1/22/88 UE 121
Fishing Boats, posthumous ed of 50, wc, ca 1925/1971, 12x15", Cleveland Print Club, lot 84, SWN 6/15/89 OE 715
Gelbe Dorfkirche, 3; probably deluxe ed of 30, wc/thin Japan, 1931, lt stn/cr, L-8x9", Verlag, lot 41, C-NY 11/1/88 2,200
Gelmeroda, posthumous total ed of 300, wc/laid Sekishu, 1920/1958, 13x10", lot 386, WG 10/19/88 325
Gespenster (Ghosts), wc/thin soft laid Japan, 1915, full mrgs, lt stn/scr, 3x5", lot 195, SBY 2/25/88 880
Houses in Old Paris, posthumous ed of 50, 2nd state, wc/Japan Kozo, 1922/1971, 12x10", Hinzdovsky, lot 85, SWN 6/15/89 715
Manhattan, 1, Stone 1; 2/10, litho, 1951, p/s, full mrgs, lt stn/old hinges, 11x9", Miller, lot 196, SBY 2/25/88 3,080

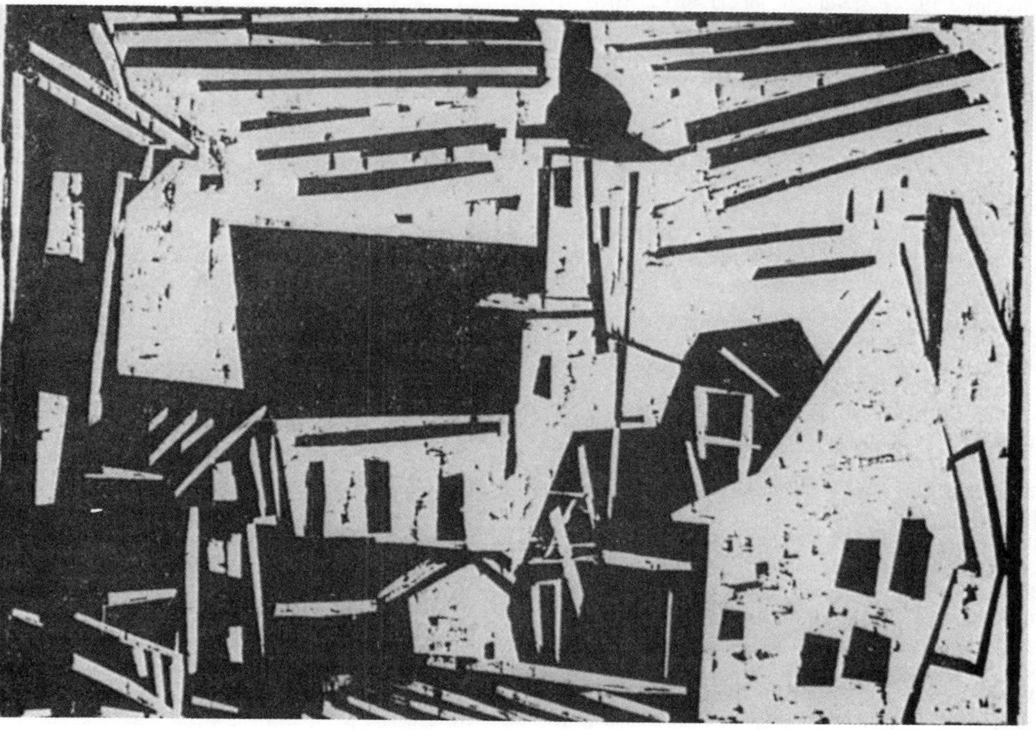

Mellingen Church, wc/laid Japan, p/s, estate stp, full mrgs, 5x7", lot 2343A, B/B 4/12/89 OE; $2,200

Night (Nacht), wc/violet tissue paper mounted on cream wove paper, 1918, p/s, lt cr, 5x7", lot 473, SBY 5/11/89 1,925
Off the Coast, Stone 3; 2nd state, litho/Rives, 1951, p/s, Cleveland Print Club bstp, unfr, L-9x14", C-NY 1/22/88 1,320
Off the Coast, Stone; ed of 250, litho, 1951, p/s, Cleveland Print Club bstp, full mrgs, unfr, L-9x14", SBY 5/12/88 1,320
Privateer, etch/drypt/Arches, 1911-12, p/s, full mrgs, lt fox/stn, ink stp on verso, P-5x9", lot 611, C-NY 5/10/89 OE 1,760
Privateer (Der Reeder), etch/wove paper, 1911-12, p/s, full mrgs, stn/sl, 6x9", Valentin/Molinie, lot 472, SBY 5/11/89 2,475
Promenaders (Spazierganger), ed of 10, wc/Kozo, 1921, p/s, full mrgs, lt cr/hinge stns, 15x12", lot 474, SBY 5/11/89 OE 9,350
Tahiti (Schiffe im Fjord), a/p, before ed of 50, wc/thin Japan, 1920, S-10x12", lot 40, C-NY 11/1/88 OE 3,300
Villa am Strande Four, a/p, before ed of 150, wc/thin Japan, 1920, p/s, S-12x15", lot 39, C-NY 11/1/88 OE 10,450
Villa am Strande Four (Villa on the Shore), total ed of 130, wc/Kozo, 1921, lt cr, L-11x14", Muller, SBY 5/12/88 OE 8,250
Village, with Square in Foreground (Dorf); wc/China paper, 1920, p/s, full mrgs, stn/cr, 9x13", lot 475, SBY 5/11/89 OE 3,850
Village Church, wc/tan laid paper, 1920, p/s, lt stn, L-6x7", lot 309, C-NY 11/1/88 1,760
Vollersroda (Kirche in Vollersoda), wc/yel Japan, 1919, p/s, full mrgs, lt stn/fox/cr, S-14x18", lot 38, C-NY 11/1/88 4,620
Windmuhle, a/p, before ed of 80, wc/thin Japan, 1919, p/s, titled, lt cr/fox, S-16x21", lot 37, C-NY 11/1/88 5,280
Windmuhle, ed of 80, wc/laid Japan, 1919, p/s, titled, L-10x12", lot 5/10/89 OE 8,800
FERNANDEZ, Armand; see Arman
FIENE, Ernest (American, 1894-1965)
City Lights, etch, p/s, 12x9", lot 201, WG 10/19/88 OE 775
Pair: New Snow; St Michael's in Brooklyn; litho, p/s, lt stn, L-9x13"/L-10x12", lot 13, PHL 6/16/88 225

Waterfront, Manhattan; 6/100, litho/BFK Rives, p/s, titled/dtd, full mrgs, unfr, L-11x18", C-NY 1/22/88 1,210

FIGURA, Hans (German, 20th C)

Street Scene with Cathedral in Background, clr etch, p/s, 11x9", ... 70

FISCHL, Eric (20th C)

Beach, 55/100, sftgr etch/burin/aqua/Hahnemuhl, 1987, Crommelynck bstp, full mrgs, 12x16", lot 773, SBY 11/5/88 3,300
Beach, 98/100, sftgr etch/burnishing/aqua/Hahnemuhl, 1987, Crommelynck bstp, 12x16", Parasol, lot 976, SBY 5/13/89 OE 3,300
Beach Balls, 28/40, sftgr etch/aqua/sugar-lift/spit-bite, 1982, p/s, Aeropress bstp, 48x35", Corinthian, SBY 11/5/88..... 6,050
Beach Balls, 38/40, sftgr etch/aqua/sugar-lift/spit-bite, 1982, p/s, Aeropress bstp, 48x34", Corinthian Ed, SBY 2/23/89 6,600
Puppet Tears, 35/50, clr aqua/drypt, 1985, p/s, full mrgs, 6x10", Blum, lot 769, SBY 11/5/88..... 1,925
Puppet Tears, 49/50, clr aqua/drypt, 1985, p/s, full mrgs, 6x10", Blum, lot 974, SBY 5/13/89 OE 2,750
Set of 5: Floating Island (Groningen Museum); aqua/sugar-lift/drypt/Zerkall, 1985, Peter Blum, lot 623, C-NY 11/1/88 7,920
Shower, 11/100, sftgr etch/burnishing/aqua/Hahnemuhl, 1987, p/s, Crommelynck bstp, 16x20", Parasol Press, SBY 5/14/88 3,025
Shower, 55/100, sftgr etch/burnishing/aqua/Hahnemuhl, 1987, Crommelynck bstp, full mrgs, 16x20", lot 975, SBY 5/13/89 1,925
Suite: Floating Islands; 42/45, aqua/drypt/scr, 1985, p/s, orig wrappers, Blum/Kneubuhler, lot 770, SBY 11/5/88 OE..... 8,800
Untitled (Shower), 63/100, sftgr etch/burnishing/aqua/Hahnemul, 1987, p/s, S-22x25", Parasol, lot 624, C-NY 11/1/88 2,420
Untitled 12.10.86 (figures in landscape), clr monotype, 1986, p/s, full mrgs, 11x16", lot 771, SBY 11/5/88..... 8,800
Year of the Drowned Dog (6 overlapping panels); 20/35, aqua/sftgr etch/drypt/scr, 1983, S-24x71", SBY 5/14/88 OE 41,250
Year of the Drowned Dog, 4/35, aqua/sftgr etch/drypt/scr, 1983, p/s, 24x71" overall, Kneubuhler, lot 973, SBY 5/13/89 OE..... 71,500

FISH, Janet (American, 1938-)

Mittens & Pears, 25/45, clr wc, 1985, p/s, S-20x28", lot 641, SBY 2/23/89 OE 1,540

FLAGG, James Montgomery (American, 1877-1960)

Pair: Together We Win; Our Regular Divisions; litho/poster paper, laid down, 39x29"/28x21", lot 170, FAP 2/24/89..... 175
Seeds of Victory Insure the Fruits of Peace, clr litho/poster paper, 1918, laid down, 33x22", lot 169, FAP 2/24/89 UE 40

FLINT, William Russell (British, 1880-1969)

Girls Admiring a Necklace, clr print, p/s, 22x29", lot 855, WAD 11/28/88 OE 2,200
Pair: Clatter & Whirl Granada; Prison Door; etch/drypt/laid paper, sgn in ink, lt fox, no size given, B/B 2/16/88 412
Resting Dancers, monotype, p/s, 12x23", WAD 11/28/88 OE 650
Spanish Dancers, clr print, 1963, p/s, 18x24", Frost & Reed, lot 856, WAD 11/28/88 1,000
Spanish Washergirl, clr print, 10x12", lot 859, WAD 11/28/88 OE 450
Three Spanish Girls, monotype, p/s, 19x27", lot 857, WAD 11/28/88 550
Woman in Interior, chromolitho, p/s, 18x24", Frost & Reed, lot 101, WG 10/19/88 UE..... 175

FOLON (20th C)

Face a Face, 23/300, clr slksc, 1971, p/s, lt scr, bl plastic fr, 18" dia, L'Atelier Marquet, lot 505, SBY 2/25/88 880
Set of 4: Over the Rainbow; total ed of 97, clr aqua, 1980-81, sgn, full mrgs, lt cr/stn, lot 506, SBY 2/25/88 OE 2,420

FORAIN, Jean Louis (French, 1852-1931)

L'Audience, litho/JL Forain, ca 1905, full mrgs, mstn/glue stn mrgs, ls in corner, L-10x14", lot 613, C-NY 5/10/89 UE 165
Le Jour des Rois, litho/JL Forain, ca 1905, p/s, full mrgs, lt cr/stn/fox, L-13x11", lot 340, C-NY 1/19/89 UE 198

FORES, S.W.

Randall, the Irish Lad & Belasco, the Jew Champion; clr engr, 11x14", lot 50, FAP 2/24/89 OE..... 350

FORINGER, Alonza Earl (American, 1878-)

Greatest Mother in the World, red/blk/gray litho on poster paper, 1918, laid down, 42x27", lot 174, FAP 2/24/89 UE 30

FORSYTHE, (Victor) Clyde (American, 1885-1962)

And They Said We Couldn't Fight, clr litho/poster paper, laid down, 30x20", lot 177, FAP 2/24/89..... 40

FORTUNY Y CARBO, Mariano (Spanish, 1838-1874)

Anachorete, etch/aqua/Japan, ca 1867, sgn pen/blk ink, S-16x22", lot 43, C-NY 11/1/88 OE 2,750
Kabyle Mort, etch/aqua/wm Huber laid paper, ca 1867, lt stn, S-18x24", Goupil/Delatre, lot 42, C-NY 11/1/88 OE..... 2,420

FOSTER, William Gilbert (British, 1855-1906)

Schooner Yacht Cambria, 199 Tons; litho, dtd October 21 1868, lg folio, RAB 8/1/188 OE 800

FOUJITA, Tsuguharu (Japanese, 1886-1968)

Bal de L'AAAA (Aide Amicale aux Artistes), clr litho, unfr, S-47x31", Agence Parisienne de Publicite, SBY 5/12/88 UE 1,210
Cat, clr wc, sgn in block, unfr, 13x18", lot 328, LH 12/4/88..... 750
Deux Femmes, 25/100, etch/rlt/Chine applique, ca 1930, p/s, lt stn/rub, P-23x16", lot 619, C-NY 5/10/89 OE 30,800
Deux Femmes, 55/100, clr etch/rlt/Chine applique, ca 1930, lt stn img, stn/tp verso, P-16x22", lot 311, C-NY 11/1/88 OE 14,300
Eve, 6/20, etch/fibrous Japan, 1959, sgn in ink, full mrgs, L-17x11", lot 61, PHL 10/28/88..... 700
Femme Nue Debout, 26/68, hc litho/Japan, ca 1930, p/s, lt stn/scr, S-22x17", lot 617, C-NY 5/10/89 OE 6,050
Friends, HC, hc litho, 1964, p/s, wide mrgs, lt cr img, L-22x18", lot 62, PHL 10/28/88..... 700
Furtive Blonde, clr woodblock, ca 1925, unfr, 15x10", lot 157, LH 5/15/88 1,700
Group of 4: Self-Portrait with Cat; Young Woman; Girl with Doll; White Cat; ed of 100, wc/Japan, lot 63, PHL 10/28/88 1,400
Jeune Fille a la Rose, late imp, etch/drypt/wht wove paper, full mrgs, 9x6", lot 2945, B/B 4/19/88 OE 440
Les Chats: Reclining Cat with Raised Head; 65/100, aqua/engr/rlt, 1930, p/s, full mrgs, 18x20", lot 210, SBY 11/3/88 OE 22,000
Les Chats: Sleeping Kitten; 71/100, aqua/engr/rlt/Chine colle, 1930, lt stn/rub, S-16x19", lot 209, SBY 11/3/88 OE..... 22,000
Les Deux Enfants, apart from ed of 100, etch/aqua/rlt/India applique, ca 1929, lt stn/cr, P-15x11", C-NY 5/10/89 OE 5,280
Les Enfants: Baby with Bows in Hair; HC2/5, etch/rlt/Chine applique, ca 1929, full mrgs, L-14x10", lot 482, SBY 5/11/89 11,000
Les Enfants: Jeune Fille; EA E/J, clr etch/rlt/Chine applique, ca 1929, lt cr/stn, P-15x11", lot 310, C-NY 11/1/88 OE 14,300
Les Enfants: Jeune Garcon; 13/100, clr etch/rlt/Chine applique, ca 1929, p/s, lt cr, P-15x11", lot 615, C-NY 5/10/89 4,400
Les Enfants: Jeune Garcon; 3/5 HC, clr etch/rlt/Chine applique, ca 1929, p/s, P-15x11", lot 171, C-NY 5/11/88 OE 4,400
Les Enfants: Little Boy with Scraggly Hair, Wrapped in a Green Blanket; HC2/5, etch/rlt, ca 1929, L-14x11", SBY 5/11/89 13,200
Les Enfants: Little Boy Wrapped in a Blanket; 9/100, clr etch/rlt, ca 1929, p/s, 14x11", Apollo Ed, lot 208, SBY 11/3/88..... 11,000
Les Enfants: Little Girl with Braid & Top Knot; 9/100, clr etch/rlt, ca 1929, p/s, 13x10", Apollo Ed, SBY 11/3/88 OE..... 15,400
Les Enfants: Little Girl with Top Knot, Holding a Bird; HC2/5, etch/rlt/Chine applique, ca 1929, L-14x10", SBY 5/11/89..... 20,900
Les Enfants: Sleeping Girl, Holding a Doll; HC2/5, etch/rlt/Chine applique, ca 1929, L-10x13", lot 484, SBY 5/11/89 OE..... 25,300

Les Enfants: Two Children; etch/rlt/Chine applique, 1929, lt scr/fox/stn/cr, 14x10", lot 198, SBY 2/25/88 2,475
Les Enfants: Two Little Boys, One with Hat & Muffler; HC2/5, etch/rlt/Chine applique, ca 1929, L-14x10", SBY 5/11/89 19,800
Les Enfants: Young Girl Holding a Kitten; HC2/5, clr etch/rlt/Chine applique, ca 1929, L-14x11", lot 477, SBY 5/11/89 OE 25,300
Pair: Self-Portrait; Young Girl; etch & litho, 1923 & 1964, sgn, 16x13"/16x11", lot 87, SWN 6/15/89 1,210
Portrait de l'Artiste, drypt/cream wove paper, pl/s, lt stn, 18x14", lot 2946, B/B 4/19/88 OE 1,320
Portrait de l'Artiste, X/XX, hc drypt, ca 1925, p/s, Chalcographie du Louvre bstp, full mrgs, 18x14", SBY 2/23/89 OE 7,150
Portrait of Claire & Ivan Goll, drypt/van Gelder, 1925, lt stn/tr, P-8x6", lot 341, C-NY 1/19/89 550
Reclining Woman, with Her Head on Her Elbow; 18/20, sftgr etch/cream Japan, ca 1930, p/s, 15x13", lot 484A, SBY 5/11/89 12,650
Reclining Woman with Cat, 65/100, etch, 1927, p/s, lt stn/fox/cr, 14x18", lot 197, SBY 2/25/88 4,125
Sleeping Kitten, proof aside from ed of 110, bl etch/rlt/Japan, ca 1930, cr/sl, SBY 5/12/88 OE 3,850
Standing Nude with Hand on Hip, 78/100, etch/rlt/Chine applique, 1930, p/s, full mrgs, L-22x15", lot 486, SBY 5/11/89 29,700
Tete de Femme, 77/100, sftgr etch/rlt/Parchemin Japan, ca 1930, lt stn, P-13x9", lot 618, C-NY 5/10/89 OE 7,700
Two Seated Nudes, 78/100, etch/rlt/Chine applique, 1930, p/s, full mrgs, lt rub, L-22x15", lot 487, SBY 5/11/89 OE 33,000
Two Seated Nudes, 77/100, etch/rlt/Chine applique, 1930, p/s, full mrgs, lt fox, L-22x15", Apollo, lot 485, SBY 5/11/89 30,800

Two Women in Contemplation, clr litho/cream wove paper, p/s, inscr EA, full mrgs, old tp/sl, 21x18", lot 2349, B/B 4/12/89 OE; $4,400

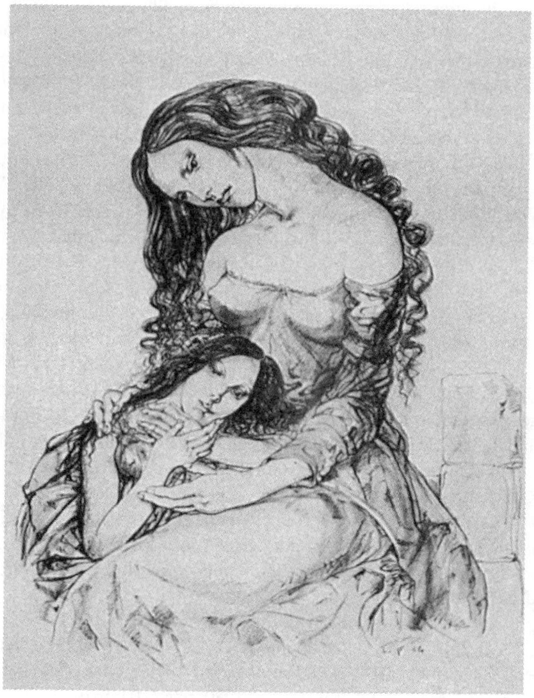

Untitled, Girl with Cat; 164/220, clr litho/BFK Rives, p/s, lt sl/fox/cr, 17x8", lot 2944, B/B 4/19/88 OE 1,045
Young Girl with Doll, clr woodblock, ca 1925, unfr, 16x9", lot 172, LH 5/15/88 1,700

FOUJITA, Tsuguharu; after (Japanese, 1886-1968)

Book: Book of Cats; by Michael Joseph, ed of 500, 1930, S-13x10", Covici Friede, lot 489, SBY 5/11/89 OE 2,420

FOUQUERAY, Dominique Charles (French, 19th/20th C)

VI Exposition Internationale de Locomotion Aerienne, litho/poster paper, 1919, laid down, 46x30", lot 168, FAP 2/24/89 100

FRANCIS, Sam (American, 1923-)

Affiche Kunsthalle Bern, 28/100, bl/dk gr litho, 1960, p/s, full mrgs, cr/tr, 34x25", Kornfeld, lot 979, SBY 5/13/89 OE 5,225
Affiche Moderna Museet Stockholm, 59/79, clr litho, 1960, p/s, lt stn, S-37x27", lot 980, SBY 5/13/89 OE 5,225
Ariel's Ring, 32/80, clr slksc, 1974, p/s, Gemini bstp, full mrgs, lt sl, 37x47", lot 649, SBY 2/23/89 OE 6,050
Bright Jade Gold Ghost, a/p, clr litho, p/s, lt cr, S-25x36", Kornfeld, lot 643, SBY 2/23/89 OE 7,150
Bright Jade Gold Ghost (Variant II), 35/125, clr litho, 1963, p/s, lt stn, S-25x36", Kornfeld, lot 775, SBY 11/5/88 OE 4,950
Composition Series, a/p, clr litho/wht wove paper, p/s, S-23x30", lot 3022, B/B 4/19/88 UE 660
Composition Series, 12/20, clr litho/wht wove paper, p/s, S-24x35", lot 3023, B/B 4/19/88 1,045
Concert Hall Set III, 11/75, clr litho, 1971, p/s, lt cr/old hinge, 26x35", Louisiana Mus, lot 983, SBY 5/13/89 6,600
Concert Hall Set III, 66/75, clr litho, 1977, p/s, lt cr/sl/rpr tr, ls in corner, 26x35", lot 650, SBY 2/23/89 OE 6,875
Demeter, clr litho, 1972, p/s, inscr CTPII, full sheet, S-18x24", lot 507, SBY 2/25/88 1,320
Demeter, 30/34, clr litho, 1972, p/s, S-22x24", lot 508, SBY 2/25/88 1,650
Deux Magots, 37/55, clr litho, 1960, p/s, lt cr/stn/rub, S-25x36", Kornfeld, lot 978, SBY 5/13/89 OE 5,775
Down Gyre (EXP-SF-51-03), clr wc monotype, 1983, p/s, S-31x25", Experimental Workshop, lot 778, SBY 11/5/88 17,600
For the Swiss Graphic Society, 25/125, clr litho/BFK Rives, 1975, p/s, inscr SF 194, L-22x17", lot 628, C-NY 11/1/88 OE 1,540
Four Stone Untitled, 19/25, clr litho/Japan, 1959-68, p/s, ULAE bstp, full mrgs, 18x14", lot 642, SBY 2/23/89 OE 3,520
Happy Death Stone, 30/90, clr litho, 1960, p/s, lt cr/stn, S-25x36", Kornfeld, lot 774, SBY 11/5/88 OE 6,600
Kayo Five Years Old, a/p, aside from ed of 10, bl/red/yel litho, 1963, p/s, 14x11", lot 644, SBY 2/23/89 OE 4,070
Of Vega, APVI, ed of 9 a/p, clr slksc, 1972, p/s, Gemini bstp, lt cr, S-38x26", lot 646, SBY 2/23/89 OE 1,650
Pair: Poemes dans le Ciel; 2/100, clr litho, 1986, p/s, S-30x22", Eds de la Difference, lot 509, SBY 2/25/88 3,300
Pasadena Box #6, 7/100, clr litho/BFK Rives, 1963, p/s, Japanese Art Assn bstp, S-20x15", lot 3021, B/B 4/19/88 990

Polar Red, 112/150, offset litho, 1973, p/s, titled/dtd, full mrgs, L-24x45", lot 119, PHL 10/28/88 900
Portrait de T 97/150, clr offset litho, 1958-59, p/s, full mrgs, L-31x23", lot 120, PHL 10/28/88........ 475
Set of 3: Poemes Dans le Ciel; 39/100, litho, 1986, p/s, S-30x22", Eds de la Difference, lot 780, SBY 11/5/88 3,575
Set of 8: Self-Portraits (SF-72 I, II, V, VI, VII, VIII, IX, X); etch, 1972-82, p/p, inscr BAT, 3EP Ltd, SBY 5/14/88........ 1,320
Silver Line, 32/57, clr litho/BFK Rives, 1971, p/s, full sheet, S-15x11", The Lithoshop, lot 627, C-NY 11/1/88 OE 7,700
Spleen (Red), 15/27, clr litho/Italia, 1971, p/s, Gemini bstp, full sheet, lt cr, S-35x79", lot 626, C-NY 11/1/88 6,600
Spun for James Kirsch, 53/100, clr slksc, 1972, p/s, Gemini bstp, S-29x23", SBY 5/14/88 OE 3,300
Ting, 40/75, clr slksc/Ariomari, 1972, p/s, Gemini bstp, S-24x30", lot 984, SBY 5/13/89 OE 7,150
Tokyo Mon Amour, a/p, clr litho/Japan, 1963, p/s, Joseph Pr bstp, full sheet, lt cr, S-32x19", lot 429, C-NY 5/11/88........ 2,200
Tokyo Mon Amour, a/p, clr litho/thin laid Japan, 1963, p/s, lt cr, S-32x19", Joseph Press, lot 981, SBY 5/13/89 OE........ 9,900
Towards Disappearance, APVIII, clr slksc/Arches #88, 1974, p/s, Gemini bstp, S-37x32", lot 985, SBY 5/13/89 OE........ 4,950
Untitled, #4, clr litho/wove paper, ca 1970s, p/s, inscr CTP, full sheet, S-18x24", lot 432, C-NY 5/11/88 550
Untitled, Pasadena Box; p/p, clr litho/Japan, 1966, p/s, 16x23", Art Alliance of Pasadena Museum, lot 625, C-NY 11/1/88 3,850
Untitled, Pasadena Box; 9/11, litho/wove paper, 1966, p/s, full sheet, S-16x23", Art Alliance, lot 430, C-NY 5/11/88 OE 3,080
Untitled, 70/100, clr litho/wove paper, 1976, p/s, full sheet, lt cr, S-22x39", lot 433, C-NY 5/11/88 OE........ 2,750
Untitled (abstract lineation), clr litho, 1978-79, p/s, S-29x42", SBY 5/14/88 OE 2,200
Untitled (abstract), 1 of 19 a/p, clr etch/aqua, 1982, p/s, full mrgs, lt cr/sl mrgs & verso, 24x18", SBY 5/14/88 770
Untitled (contemporary), 106/250, clr litho, 1982, p/s, S-48x34", Brooke Alexander, lot 776, SBY 11/5/88 OE 4,125
Untitled (EXP SF 54-#7-1982), clr wc monotype/Japan, 1982, S-43x78", Experimental Workshop, lot 777, SBY 11/5/88 24,200
Untitled (EXP-SF-0485-01), clr wc monotype, 1985, p/s, S-31x25", Experimental Workshop, SBY 5/14/88 18,700
Untitled (EXP-SF-49-2), clr monotype/handmade paper, 1982, p/s, S-25x30", Experimental Workshop, lot 986, SBY 5/13/89 OE........ 28,600
Untitled (EXP-SF-50-40), clr monotype, 1982, p/s, lt sl, S-30x26", Experimental Workshop, lot 629, C-NY 11/1/88 OE 16,500
Untitled (GTW-SF-03-B-1985), clr wc monotype, 1985, p/s, S-42x46", Tullis Workshop, lot 779, SBY 11/5/88 16,500
Untitled (GTW-SF-10-#3-1987), clr monotype/Japan, 1986-87, p/s, S-37x72", Garner Tullis Workshop, SBY 5/14/88 30,250
Untitled (Screen), Pasadena Box; 68/100, 3 litho/wove paper mounted on 3-panel screen (as issued), lot 431, C-NY 5/11/88........ 4,180
Untitled (SF 192), 90/100, clr litho, 1974, p/s, lt cr/skinned, S-22x39", Topanga Creek Graphics/Abrams, SBY 5/14/88 OE 2,860
Untitled (SF-319), AP, ed of 2 a/p, clr litho, 1987, p/s, S-45x28", Litho Shop, lot 781, SBY 11/5/88........ 5,500
Untitled (SFE 014), 20/29, clr aqua, 1984, p/s, full mrgs, 26x11", Litho Shop, lot 987, SBY 5/13/89 OE........ 9,900
Untitled (SFE 045), 8/20, etch/aqua, 1987, p/s, lt cr, S-57x33", Litho Shop, lot 988, SBY 5/13/89 OE 16,500
Untitled (SFE-014), 16/29, clr aqua, 1984, p/s, full mrgs, lt cr, S-26x11", Litho Shop, SBY 5/14/88 OE........ 5,775
Untitled (SMF-83-359), clr wc monotype/handmade paper, 1983, p/s, S-26x30", SBY 5/14/88 15,400
Vegetable Series: Vegetable I; 14/15, clr litho/BFK Rives, 1971, p/s, S-35x24", lot 982, SBY 5/13/89 OE 14,850
Very First Stone, 25/25, clr litho/British Crisbrook, 1959-68, ULAE bstp, full mrgs, S-31x23", lot 977, SBY 5/13/89 OE........ 3,850
Yunan-State I, 13/14, clr litho, 1971, p/s, Gemini bstp, lt cr, S-42x29", SBY 2/23/89 OE........ 2,200

FRANK, Mary (British, 1933-)

Amaryllis, 12/40, clr etch, 1979, p/s, Aeropress bstp, full mrgs, lt cr, 18x12", lot 651, SBY 2/23/89 1,320
Dancers, clr monotype, 1967, sgn/dtd in ink, 19x13", lot 510, SBY 2/25/88 440
Disappearance, clr monotype/3 sheets mounted between 2 sheets plexiglas, 1976, sgn, S-50x42", lot 782, SBY 11/5/88........ 2,475

FRANKENTHALER, Helen (American, 1928-)

Barcelona, 13/30, clr litho/John Collard 100% cotton handmade, 1977, TGL bstp, 32x24", lot 997, SBY 5/13/89 OE........ 11,550
Barcelona, 23/30, clr litho/John Collard handmade, 1977, p/s, S-41x32", Tyler Graphics, lot 636, C-NY 11/1/88 6,600
Bronze Smoke, 3/38, clr litho/JB Green Katusah, 1978, ULAE bstp, full mrgs, 25x19", lot 653, SBY 2/23/89 1,210
Cameo, 26/51, clr wc/gray-pk TGL handmade, 1980, p/s, TGL bstp, S-42x32", lot 998, SBY 5/13/89 OE 10,450
Cedar Hill, 42/75, clr wc/Japan, 1983, p/s, Crown Point bstp, S-20x25", lot 784, SBY 11/5/88 UE 4,400
Cedar Hill, 65/75, clr wc/Japan, 1983, p/s, Crown Point bstp, S-20x25", SBY 5/14/88 OE........ 8,800
Connected by Joy, 21/27, clr etch/aqua/brn handmade Jeff Goodman, 1969-73, ULAE bstp, 14x19", SBY 5/14/88 OE........ 4,400
Dream Walk, 34/47, clr litho/mauve HMP handmade, 1977, p/s, TGL bstp, full mrgs, 22x30", lot 996, SBY 5/13/89 OE........ 4,950
Essence Mulberry, 15/46, clr wc/Maniani Gampi handmade, 1977, TGL bstp, lt cr, S-39x19", lot 637, C-NY 11/1/88 UE 13,200
Essence Mulberry, 41/46, clr wc/Maniani Gampi handmade, 1977, p/s, Tyler Graphics bstp, S-39x19", lot 439, C-NY 5/11/88 27,500
First Stone, 11/12, clr litho, 1961, p/s, ULAE bstp, lt cr/sl, S-22x30", lot 989, SBY 5/13/89 OE........ 23,100
Ganymede, 15/49, clr etch/aqua/Arches Cover, 1978, Tyler Graphics bstp, full mrgs, S-22x17", lot 440, C-NY 5/11/88 OE 3,080
Harvest, 6/43, clr litho/cream HMP handmade, 1977, sgn/dtd 76, TGL bstp, S-26x22", lot 635, C-NY 11/1/88 2,200
In the Wings, 28/50, clr aqua/etch/litho/mauve HMP handmade, 1987, p/s, TGL bstp, 14x21", SBY 5/14/88 4,675
In the Wings, 28/50, etch/aqua/litho/mauve HMP, 1987, p/s, TGL bstp, S-14x21", lot 786, SBY 11/5/88 5,500
In the Wings, 31/50, etch/aqua/litho/mauve HMP handmade, 1987, p/s, TGL bstp, S-14x21", lot 999, SBY 5/13/89 OE 6,600
Message From Degas, 16/36, clr etch/aqua/JW 1956 English handmade, 1972-74, ULAE bstp, 7x10", lot 634, C-NY 11/1/88 2,860
Orange Hoop, a/p, clr litho/Auvergne a la Main, 1965, p/s, ULAE bstp, full mrgs, S-26x20", lot 435, C-NY 5/11/88........ 1,760
Orange Hoop, a/p, ed of 24, clr litho/Auvergne a la Main, 1965, p/s, ULAE bstp, full mrgs, 26x20", lot 632, C-NY 11/1/88........ 2,200
Orange Hoop, 23/34, clr litho, 1965, p/s, 26x20", lot 418, WG 10/19/88........ 1,200
Persian Garden, a/p, clr litho Auvergne, 1965-66, p/s, ULAE bstp, full mrgs, lt fox, 19x14", lot 990, SBY 5/13/89 2,750
Pompeii, 1/5, clr etch/drypt/liftgr/sftgr, 1976, p/s, a/p, full mrgs, 12x22", Don Steward, SBY 5/14/88 3,575
Pompeii, 9/42, etch/drypt/aqua, 1976, p/s, full mrgs, 22x12", Don Steward, lot 995, SBY 5/13/89 2,200
Ponti, 1/21, etch/aqua/Fabrino Rosapina, 1973, 2RC Editrice bstp, full mrgs, S-27x35", lot 438, C-NY 5/11/88........ 1,980
Red Sea, 26/58, clr litho/pk handmade paper, 1982, p/s, dtd, TGL bstp, full mrgs, 16x21", lot 3025, B/B 4/19/88 2,090
Red Sea, 50/58, clr litho/pk HMP handmade, 1982, p/s, Tyler Graphics bstp, full mrgs, L-16x21", lot 441, C-NY 5/11/88 OE 3,080
Sanguine Mood, 53/75, pochoir/scrpt/Green & Hayle Mill English, 1971, p/s, S-23x18", Chiron, lot 437, C-NY 5/11/88 2,200
Savage Breeze, a/p, clr wc/Nepalese handmade, 1974, p/s, inscr Glenn, ULAE bstp, L-30x25", lot 633, C-NY 11/1/88 OE 26,400
Savage Breeze, 29/31, clr wc/2 laminated sheets Nepalese, 1974, ULAE bstp, full mrgs, 30x25", lot 994, SBY 5/13/89 OE 44,000
Suite: What Red Lines Can Do; 68/75, 5 clr slksc, 1970, p/s, lt sl, S-39x26", Multiples, lot 991, SBY 5/13/89 OE........ 7,425
Sure Violet, 45/50, aqua/etch/drypt/TGL handmade, 1979, p/s, TGL bstp, full mrgs, 24x36", lot 658, SBY 5/14/88........ 7,700
Tribal Sign, 24/47, clr litho/wht TGL handmade, 1987, p/s, TGL bstp, S-24x19", lot 1000, SBY 5/13/89 OE 8,800

Variation II on Mauve Corner, 1/2, litho/Chatham British, 1969, ULAE bstp, full mrgs, S-20x25", lot 436, C-NY 5/11/88 ... 1,320
Vineyard Storm, 2/4, clr wc/2 sheets Nepalese handmade paper, 1974-76, p/s, ULAE bstp, full mrgs, 30x25", SBY 11/5/88 ... 14,300
Yellow Span, 36/75, clr aqua/Auvergne a la main, 1968, p/s, ULAE bstp, full mrgs, lt stn, 14x19", lot 652, SBY 2/23/89 ... 4,675

FRASCONI, Antonio (American, 1919-)
Day & Night, total ed of 300, wc/laid Kochi, 1952, p/s, 9x13", Cleveland Print Club, lot 353, WG 10/19/88 UE ... 30
Pair: Dog & the Crocodile; Day & Night; wc/Japan Hosho or Kochi, 1950 & 1952, 16x11"/10x13", lot 89, SWN 6/15/89 OE ... 468

FREEMAN, Don (American, 1908-)
Casting for Characters, litho/Rives, ca 1934, p/s, titled, full mrgs, unfr, L-10x12", C-NY 1/22/88 ... 528
Clown's Story, ed of 200, litho/cream wove paper, 1937, sgn in stone, lt trm mrgs, 9x12", Assn Am Artists, B/B 4/19/88 ... 275

FREEMAN, Mark (American, 1908-)
Brooklyn Bridge, Ed 50, clr litho/wove paper, 1952, p/s, titled/dtd, full mrgs, ink mrgs, unfr, L-21x11", C-NY 1/22/88 ... 330
Gas Tanks, brn & blk litho/wove paper, 1949, p/s, titled/dtd, full mrgs, ink mrgs, unfr, L-12x18", C-NY 1/22/88 ... 330
Giants, ed of 30, brn & blk litho/wove paper, ca 1950s, p/s, titled, full mrgs, stn mrgs, unfr, L-15x20", C-NY 1/22/88 ... 330
Manhattan Backdrop, ed of 90, litho/laid paper, 1933, p/s, titled, 14x8", lot 2947, B/B 4/19/88 ... 440
Manhattan Cliffs, ed of 30, transfer litho/wove paper, 1947, p/s, titled, full mrgs, lt stn, L-20x15", C-NY 1/19/89 ... 462
Manhattan Cliffs, Ed 30, brn & ochre transfer litho/wove paper, 1947, p/s, full mrgs, L-20x15", lot 440, C-NY 5/10/89 UE ... 220
Manhattan Parkways, Ed 90, litho, 1933, p/s, dtd/titled, full mrgs, unfr, L-14x9", SBY 5/12/88 UE ... 550
Pair: Gas Tanks; South Ferry El; a/p & ed of 30, transfer litho, 1947, full mrgs, lt cr, lot 170, C-NY 1/19/89 UE ... 220
Pair: Manhattan Backdrop; The City Sleeps; Ed 90 & a/p, litho, 1933/ca 1930, p/s, full mrgs, unfr, C-NY 1/22/88 OE ... 1,045
Pair: Shades & Shadows; The City Rests; a/p, litho/wove paper, 1933 & 1947, p/s, lt mstn, lot 439, C-NY 5/10/89 UE ... 550
Restless City, Ed 75, clr litho/wove paper, 1952, p/s, dtd, full mrgs, lt ink on mrgs, unfr, L-12x18", C-NY 1/22/88 ... 330
South Ferry El, ed of 30, transfer litho/wove paper, 1947, p/s, full mrgs, lt cr/stn, L-15x20", lot 172, C-NY 1/19/89 UE ... 330
2nd Avenue El, Ed 75, litho/wove paper, 1933, p/s, titled, full mrgs, tstn, L-10x14", lot 438, C-NY 5/10/88 ... 495
2nd Avenue El, ed of 75, litho, 1934, p/s, 10x14", lot 207, WG 10/19/88 UE ... 250
2nd Avenue El, 1/75, litho/thick wove paper, 1933, p/s, titled, full mrgs, stn/nick to mrg, unfr, L-10x14", C-NY 1/22/88 ... 825

French School (19th C)
Pair: L'Assemblee au Concert; L'Assemble au Salon; clr engr, 16x19", lot 38, FAP 2/24/89 ... 125

French School (20th C)
Movement for Peace 1960, litho poster, 46x32", Mourlot, FAP 6/16/89 ... 325
Pianos Daude, clr litho poster, unbacked, 62x46", FAP 6/16/89 ... 375
Pianos Daude, clr litho/poster paper, 62x46", lot 267, FAP 2/24/89 ... 450
Renault, clr litho/poster paper, lt tr img/mrg, linen backed, unfr, 36x45", lot 308, FAP 2/24/89 OE ... 950
Sports d'Hiver au Mont-Dore, litho/poster paper, 39x24", Chaix, lot 226, FAP 2/24/89 OE ... 227
Ville de nantes, Exposition des Arts Incoherents; clr litho/poster paper, lt stn/fox, 33x23", lot 257, FAP 2/24/89 UE ... 100

FREY, A. (American, 19th C)
Wissahickon Paper Mills, clr litho, lt sl/tr mrgs, 17x24", lot 51, FAP 2/24/89 OE ... 575

FRIEDLANDER, Johnny (French, 1912-)
Abstract Figures Reclining, 75/100, litho, p/s, 23x31", lot 443, FAP 4/15/88 ... 264
Chevaus, 88/240, aqua, p/s, 14x9", lot 880, LH 5/15/88 ... 250
Composition sur Fond Vert, 93/95, clr etch/aqua/wove paper, 1965, p/s, P-31x24", Touchstone, C-E 5/13/88 ... 495
Group of 3: Fish & Fly; Fish & Sphere; Petite Bestiaire; p/s, lt stn, various sizes, lot 92, SWN 6/15/89 ... 300
Le Mai, 8/95, clr etch/aqua/wove paper, 1965, p/s, 20x23", Touchstone, C-E 5/13/88 ... 418
Vers le Nord et Vers le Sud, 11/95, clr etch/aqua/wove paper, 1970, p/s, 29x22", Lubin Graphics, C-E 5/13/88 ... 418

GAIN, Charles W.
Kerind Persia, engr, sgn, 10x12", lot 328, WG 10/19/88 ... 40

GALE, George Albert (American, 1893-1951)
Nantucket Sleigh Ride, etch, p/s, titled, full mrgs, lt fox, L-12x9", RAB 11/25/88 UE ... 175

GALLAGHER, Sears (American, 1869-1955)
High Street Clovelly, litho, sgn/titled, 14x9", RAB 3/27/89 ... 60

GALLAND, A. (French, 20th C)
Engagez-Vous Dans, L'Aeronautique Maritime; clr litho, lt tr mrgs, 43x29", Lucien Serre, lot 254, FAP 2/24/89 OE ... 300

GANSO, Emil (American, 1895-1941)
Reverse Image of Fisher's Pond, litho, p/s, lt fox, 8x10", lot 206, WG 10/19/88 ... 115

GARDINER, Eliza Draper (American, 1871-1955)
Boy with Crab Net, 13/50, clr woodblock, sgn, 8x11", RWS 4/22/89 OE ... 1,100
Passaconaway (landscape), 29/40, clr woodblock, ca 1919, 8x10", RWS 4/22/89 ... 350

GARNERAY, Ambrose Louis (19th C)
Vue du Port de Baltimore, aqua, ca 1843, trm mrgs, tr/scr img, lstn/tr mrgs, tp/sl verso, L-11x27", C-NY 1/22/88 ... 1,210

GAUGUIN, Paul (French, 1848-1903)
Femmes, Animaux et Feuillages; #26, ed of 30, wc/Japan pelure, ca 1897, lt stn/cr, L-6x12", lot 313, C-NY 11/1/88 ... 13,200
Femmes Aux Fiques, late imp, etch/Arches, ca 1894, lg mrgs, lt cr, 11x17", lot 2844, B/B 4/19/88 ... 385
L'Univers est Cree, 30/100, wc/Chine volant, 1921, sgn/inscr by artist's son, lt cr/stn, L-8x14", Cato, SBY 5/12/88 ... 4,675
L'Univers est Cree, ed of 25-30, wc/buff Japan, 1893-94, lt cr img, lt cr/ls/tr mrgs, 8x14", lot 213, SBY 11/3/88 ... 16,500
Le Calvaire Breton (Souvenir de Bretagne), 7/25, brn-gray wc, sgn/inscr by artist's son, unfr, L-6x10", SBY 5/12/88 ... 2,200
Le Char a Boeufs-Souvenir de Bretagne; #1, ed of about 30, wc/tissue thin Japan, 1898-89, 9x12", lot 45, C-NY 11/1/88 ... 19,800
Mahna No Varua Ino, a/p, aside from ed of 100, wc/Chine volant, 1921, full mrgs, unfr, L-8x14", Cato, SBY 5/12/88 OE ... 2,640
Mahna No Varua Ino, #81, wc/Chine volant, 1921, sgn by artist's son, full mrgs, 8x14", Cato, lot 215, SBY 11/3/88 ... 5,225
Mahna No Varua Ino, 32/100, wc/Chine volant, 1921, sgn/inscr by artist's son, full mrgs, L-8x14", Cato, SBY 5/12/88 ... 5,500
Manao Tupapau, Guerin's 3rd state, wc/tissue-thin Japan, 1893-84, lt cr mrgs, L-14x8", lot 620, C-NY 5/10/89 ... 6,600
Manao Tupapau, 7/100, wc, 1921, sgn/inscr by artist's son, full mrgs, lt ls/cr/rpl, L-8x14", Cato, SBY 5/12/88 OE ... 6,600

Maruru, #33, ed of 100, wc/Chine volant, 1921, sgn, lt cr/rpr tr/scr, L-8x12", lot 314, C-NY 11/1/88 OE ... 1,750
Miseres Humaines, Pl 4, zinograph/simili Japan, 1894, lt stn, 12x9", lot 211, SBY 11/3/88 OE ... 3,300
Noa Noa, ed of 25-30, wc/buff Japan, 1893-94, 14x8", Louis Roy, lot 212, SBY 11/3/88 OE ... 49,500
Projet pour une Assiette-Leda, hc litho/yel wove paper, 1889, ink sgn, lt stn/sl, S-12x10", portfolio, C-NY 5/11/88 OE ... 63,800
Te Arii Vahine-Opoi; #3, ed of 30, wc/thin Japan, 1898, lt stn/cr/fox, S-7x12", lot 491, SBY 5/11/89 ... 35,200
Te Atua (Les Deux), ed of 25-30, blk & sienna wc/buff Japan, 1893-94, full mrgs, lt cr, 8x14", lot 214, SBY 11/3/88 ... 24,750
Te Po, #59, wc/Chine volant, 1921, sgn by artist's son, full mrgs, lt cr, 8x14", Cato, lot 214A, SBY 11/3/88 OE ... 8,525
Te Po, ed of 100, wc/Chine volant, sgn/inscr by artist's son, full mrgs, lt fox/sl/cr, L-8x14", Cato, SBY 5/12/88 ... 4,125

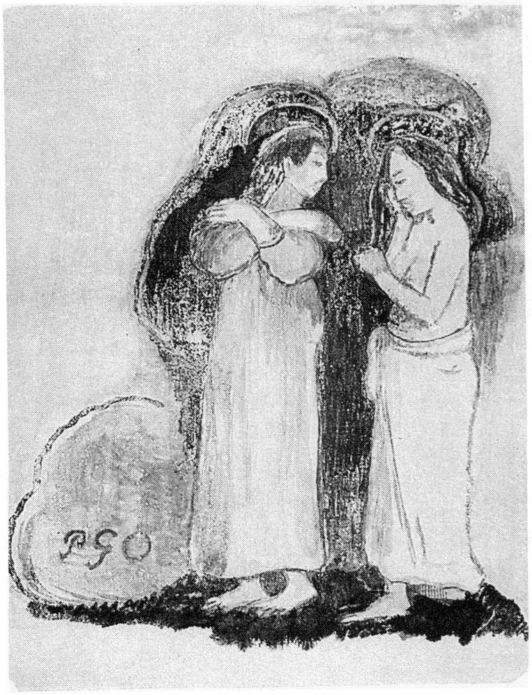

Two Standing Tahitian Women, clr monotype/Japan, 1894, intl, lt cr/rub, S-10x8", lot 173, C NY 5/11/88: $198,000

GAWTHORN, H.G.
Forth Bridge, On the London & North Eastern Railway of England & Scotland; litho, S-40x50", lot 317, C-NY 1/19/89 OE ... 2,640

GEARHART, Frances H. (American, 1869-1959)
Floral Still Life, clr woodblock, p/s, L-7x4", RWS 4/22/89 OE ... 550
Stark Country, clr woodblock/thin Japan, sgn/titled, lt sl/tp/stn, unfr, L-11x12", RWS 4/22/89 OE ... 750

GEISSLER, Paul (German, 1881-)
Blumenfrauen (Flower Ladies), clr etch, p/s, titled, P-12x11", lot 456, S/A 3/12/88 ... 60
Die Ersten Schneeglockchen, clr etch, 1951, p/s, titled, P-12x10", lot 1005, S/A 2/18/89 ... 185

GELLEE, Claude (French, 1600-1682)
La Danse sous les Arbres, Russell's 4th state of 5, etch, trm, lt skinned, 5x8", lot 624, SBY 2/25/88 ... 330
Pair: La Tempete; Danse Sous les Arbres; etch, 1630 & 1651, no mrgs, glued corners, 5x7"/6x8", lot 72, SWN 12/1/88 UE ... 195

GELLEE, Claude; after (French, 1600-1682)
Four Classical View, etch/rlt, 1774, lt fox/stn, laid down, P-8x10", John Boydell, lot 2, PHL 10/28/88 ... 250

GEMMELL, J.
In the Woods, hc litho, 13x17", lot 637, GAI 9/22/89 ... 35

GERICAULT, Jean Louise Andre Theodore (French, 1791-1824)
Album: La Serie Anglaise; #1, blk litho, 1821, S-20x15", Rodwell & Martin/Hullmandel, lot 46, C-NY 11/1/88 ... 110,000
Garcon Deonnant l'Avoine a un Cheval Detele, 2nd state, litho/wove paper, 1822, 17x13", lot 98, SWN 6/15/89 ... 125
Portrait de M Brunet, 2nd state, litho/cream wove paper, 1919, full mrgs, lt fox/stn, 7x6", lot 458, SBY 5/11/89 OE ... 1,650

GERITZ, Franz (American, 1895-1945)
Watchman (Zion National Park), clr wc, 1928, p/s, titled, 9x12", lot 135, WG 10/19/88 UE ... 250

German School (16th C)
St Jerome, engr, intl ISP/dtd 1520 in pl, 4x2", lot 850, WL 11/28/88 ... 200

German School (20th C)
Automobile Fabrik Perl, clr litho/poster paper, lt fld/tr mrgs, 37x25", lot 269, FAP 2/24/89 UE ... 500
General Motors, 1939; litho/poster paper, 34x24", lot 232, FAP 2/24/89 OE ... 350
Hamburg Sud, clr litho/poster paper, 33x24", lot 279, FAP 2/24/89 ... 375

GESMAR, Charles (European, 19th C)
Mistinguett, Casino de Paris, clr litho, 1922, S-62x46", lot 270, SBY 12/12/88 ... 1,760
Mistinguett, clr litho, 1925, lg mrgs, S-63x47", lot 269, SBY 12/12/89 ... 990
Mistinguett, Moulin Rouge; clr litho, ca 1926, sgn, 47x31", Chachion, C-E 6/16/88 ... 715
Mistinguett, Moulin Rouge; clr litho, 1926, S-49x33", Chachion, lot 272, SBY 12/12/88 ... 660

GEX, E. (French, 19th/20th C)
Supreme Pernot le Meilleur des Desserts Fins, clr litho/poster paper, lt fld/tr, linen backed, 48x34", FAP 2/24/89 UE 200
GHISI, Giorgio (16th C)
Judgment of Paris, 3rd state, engr, 1555, trm mrgs, lt rpr/cr/scuff/stn, 16x21", lot 45, SBY 5/11/89..... 4,125
GIACOMETTI, Alberto (Swiss, 1901-1966)
Album: Les Douze Portraits de Celebre Orbandale; 20/40, etch/Chine volant, 1962, S-14x7", lot 47, C-NY 11/1/88 OE 19,800
Artist's Mother at the Window, 4/75, litho/wht wove paper, 1964, p/s, full mrgs, L-22x15", SBY 5/12/88 OE 3,575
Artist's Mother Reading, aside from #d ed of 75, litho, 1964, p/s, full mrgs, lt sl/cr, 18x15", lot 494, SBY 5/11/89..... 3,300
Chair et Gueridon, aside from #d ed of 90, litho, 1960, p/s, full mrgs, lt fox, 15x11", Maeght, lot 493, SBY 5/11/89 3,300
Chaise et Gueridon, 9/90, gray litho, 1960, p/s, full mrgs, lt stn/tr, 15x10", Maeght, lot 261, SBY 2/23/89 OE..... 2,090
Dans L'Atelier, 14/15, etch/Japan, 1965, p/s, lt stn, P-10x8", lot 622, C-NY 5/10/89 OE 6,600
Giacometti's House in Maloja, HC, ed of 65, litho/wove paper, 1957, p/s, lt stn/cr, L-19x24", lot 621, C-NY 5/10/89 4,950
Giacometti's House in Maloja, 12/65, litho, 1957, p/s, lt sl/cr, S-20x26", Kornfeld/Klipstein, lor 492, SBY 5/11/89 OE..... 3,300
Head of a Young, 54/75, litho, 1964, p/s, full mrgs, lt cr img, 23x15", lot 205, SBY 2/25/88 OE 2,310
Head of Man, 62/100, litho, 1957, p/s, full mrgs, lt stn, S-16x11", Maeght, lot 206, SBY 2/26/88..... 1,430
Lamberto Vitali & Jean Leymarie, 16/100, litho w/text on Fabriano, sgn, orig box, lot 174, C-NY 5/11/88 OE 1,760
Pair: Bust a Nude; Nude; litho/wht paper, 1961, 15x11", lot 2847, B/B 4/19/88 110
Pair: Bust of a Seated Man; Head of a Man; litho/wht paper, 1961, 15x11", lot 2846, B/B 4/19/88 110
Pair: La magie Quotidienne; total #d ed of 74, etch, 1966, full mrgs, 17x11"/17x12", lot 208, SBY 2/25/88 990
Pair: Nude in Profile; Seated Nude, litho/white paper, 1961, 15x11", lot 2848, B/B 4/19/88..... 110
Reclining Woman, 53/90, litho, 1960, p/s, full mrgs, lt stn/fox, 15x11", Maeght, lot 202, SBY 2/25/88 3,080
Sculptures, 21/30, litho, 1954, p/s, full mrgs, lt stn/fox, 21x14", Maeght, lot 216, SBY 11/3/88 OE 6,050
Seated Nude, 63/75, litho, 1961, p/s, full mrgs, lt cr/mstn/cr, unfr, L-16x20", SBY 5/12/88 OE 4,950
Seated Nude (Nu Assis), 70/100, litho/BFK Rives, 1965, p/s, Gemini bstp, full mrgs, lt cr, 24x22", lot 2853, B/B 2/16/88..... 2,200
Studio with Two Pails, 16/50, etch/Arches, 1955, p/s, trm mrgs, lstn, stn/glue mrg/verso, unfr, P-11x8", C-NY 1/22/88 715
GIANAKOS, Steve (American, 1938-)
Set of 8: Missing Children; 23/41, clr litho, 1985, intl, S-16x13", orig wrappers, Solo/Rutgers, lot 442, C-NY 5/11/88..... 330
GIBSON, Charles Dana (American, 1867-1944)
Figures at a Table, etch, sgn, 10x13", lot 103, WG 10/19/88 50
GIFFORD, A.R.
Women's Edition (Buffalo) Courier, clr litho, ca 1895, pl/s, 24x15", lot 420, C-E 9/20/89 120
GIFFORD, Robert Swain (American, 1840-1905)
Blakesmoor, Hampshire, England; etch, sgn/dtd 1882, full mrgs, L-6x4", RAB 8/8/89 400
Captain Jackson's House on Bath Road, etch, sgn/dtd 1883, full mrgs, L-4x6", RAB 8/8/89 475
GILES, Jean
Bon Soir, young woman on stairs; clr etch, stp/s, 19x24", Morris & Bendien, lot 308, GAI 8/12/88..... 55
GILHOOLY, David (American, 1943-)
My Daily Bread, 1983, monotype/drypt/Arches, 1983, p/s, titled, 3EP Ltd bstp, 16x38", lot 3026, B/B 4/19/88 300
GINZBURG, Yankel (American, 1945-)
Black Jack, 103/250, clr slksc, p/s, 29x24", lot 1336F, WL 2/26/88 500
Candy Store (Maquette), AP51/75, clr slksc, p/s, 28x35", lot 1336H, WL 2/26/88..... 400
Royalty, 152/275, clr slksc, p/s, 29x24", lot 1336G, WL 2/26/88 UE..... 300
GLARNER, Fritz (Swiss, 1899-1972)
Color Drawing for Relational Painting 1963, 26/35, litho/British Crisbrook, 1963, p/s, ULAE bstp, 32x24", SBY 5/13/89 OE..... 5,225
Color Drawing for Tondo 1964, 2/30, clr litho/Angoumois, 1964, p/s, ULAE bstp, full mrgs, 26x20", lot 1002, SBY 5/13/89 3,300
GLEIZES, Albert (French, 1881-1953)
Cubist Composition, litho/wove paper, 1921, intl/Die Schaffenden bstp, full mrgs, lt cr/tp, L-14x11", C-NY 5/11/88..... 1,045
GOENEUTTE, Norbert (1854-1894)
Le Graveur dans l'Atelier, #3, 3rd state, drypt/laid paper, ca 1880, p/s, a/bstp, S-7x8", lot 48, C-NY 11/1/88..... 935
GOLAY, Mary
Brunette with Poppies, clr litho, pl/s, fr, 38x14", C-E 9/16/88 UE..... 132
GOLDTHWAITE, Anne (American, 1875-1944)
Group of 6: Columbia Library; Capitol; Hill Town in France; Little Oak; Landscape; View Through a Gate; C-NY 5/11/88..... 550
GOLINKEN, Joseph Webster (American, 1896-)
Joe Louis in Chicago, litho, p/s, 12s15", lot 1131, LH 12/4/88..... 375
Louis-Baer at Yankee Stadium, 37/50, litho/wove paper, 1935, p/s, full mrgs, lt sl mrgs, L-16x20", C-NY 1/22/88 462
1st Round Knockout, Louis-Schmeling; 28/50, litho/Rives, ca 1930, p/s, full mrgs, lt mstn/cr/fox, L-16x20", C-NY 5/10/89..... 440
GOLTZIUS, Hendrik (Dutch, 1558-1617)
Set of 6: Life of the Virgin; engr, 1593-94, small mrgs, lt fox/stn/cr, no size given, lot 49, SBY 5/11/89 OE 6,875
Set of 6: Life of the Virgin; 2nd or 3rd states of 5, engr, 1593-94, several minor defects, lot 625, SBY 2/25/88..... 6,875
GOLTZIUS, Hendrik; after (Dutch, 1558-1617)
Neptune & Amphitrite, by Jan Saenredam, engr, ca 1596, lt cr/tr, 13x9", lot 139A, SBY 5/11/89 OE..... 1,650
Pair: Athena Leaning on Her Shield; Juno Holding a Scepter; engr, 1596, trm/rpr tr, 14x10", lot 51, SBY 5/11/89 880
Perseus & Andromeda, by Jan Saenredam, 1st state, engr, 1601, thread mrgs, 10x7", lot 139B, SBY 5/11/89 OE..... 2,750
GORKY, Arshile (American, 1904-1948)
Mannikin, ed of 25, litho/wm France, ca 1931, p/s, inscr To Mr & Mrs Greacen, cr/stn, L-15x11", lot 25, C-NY 5/11/88 OE 27,500
GORNICK, April (American, 1953-)
Rain & Dust, 23/70, etch/sugar-lift/aqua, 1985, p/s, full mrgs, S-31x43", Hudson River Eds, lot 444, C-NY 5/11/88 OE 440
GOTTLIEB, Adolph (American, 1903-1974)
Chrome Green, 149/150, clr slksc, 1972, p/s, full mrgs, 24x18", lot 1005, SBY 5/13/89 OE 3,025
Crimson Ground, 50/150, slksc, 1972, p/s, full mrgs, lt rpl/stn, L-24x19", lot Marlborough, lot 90, RWS 9/8/89 OE 1,600

Flurry, 70/75, clr slksc, 1967, p/s, full mrgs, lt scuff/cr, S-22x30", lot 1004, SBY 5/13/89 OE **4,950**
Green Ground, Blue Disc; 45/50, clr slksc, 1966, p/s, lt cr/scuff, S-24x18", lot 1003, SBY 5/13/89 OE **4,400**
Night Glow, 25/65, clr etch/aqua, 1971, p/s, lg mrgs, lt stn/fox/sl, 24x18", lot 655, SBY 2/23/89 OE **3,850**
Pink Ground, 52/150, clr scrpt/Green, 1972, p/s, full mrgs, S-36x28", Marlborough, lot 445, C-NY 5/11/88 OE **770**

GOULD, John
Nester Productus (parrots), hc litho, lt trm/stn, 22x16", lot 342, GAI 11/24/89 ..... **105**
Palaeornis Derbianus (parrot), hc litho, trm mrgs, laid down, 15x21", lot 66, GAI 2/5/88 ..... **65**

GOULD & RICHTER
Purcrasia Castanea, Pl 27, chromolitho, 15x22", lot 205, MG 11/19/88 UE **300**

GRANT, Gordon Hope (American, 1875-1962)
Group of 3: Dockside; Deep Sea Larder; Harbor Traffic; litho, p/s, various sizes, Assn Am Artists, lot 294, WG 10/19/88 ..... **400**
Helmsman, 19/100, etch, p/s, no size given, lot 216, WG 10/19/88..... **80**
Old Coaster, litho, p/s, lt stn, 9x11", Assn Am Artists, lot 271, WG 10/19/88 UE **60**
Sand Dune, litho, p/s, full mrgs, 9x12", lot 5, RAB 8/9/88 UE **100**
School's Out (porpoise school in sea), litho, sgn/titled, L-9x12", Assn Am Artists, RAB 3/27/89 UE..... **50**
Sun & Shadow, litho, p/s, titled, full mrgs, 9x12", Assn Am Artists, lot 4, RAB 8/9/88 ..... **325**

GRASSET, Eugene Samuel (Swiss, 1845-1917)
La Grande Dame, clr engr, 11x7", lot 932, LH 10/16/88 ..... **160**
Young Woman & Irises, clr litho, lt tr, 29x20", Verdoux/Ducourtioux/Huillard, lot 288, FAP 2/24/88 UE **400**

GREATBACH, William
First Day of Oysters, hc engr, 18x20", lot 85, GAI 12/9/88..... **85**

GREFFET, Georges
Girl with a Parrot, clr etch/drypt, ca 1924, sgn/Estampe Moderne bstp, 16x12", C-E 9/16/88 UE **120**

GROMAIRE, Marcel (French, 1892-1971)
Nu Assis, 22/50, etch/Arches, 1925, p/s, lt sl/cr, S-21x17", Eds Jeanne Bucher, lot 50, C-NY 11/1/88 OE **1,100**
Providers, 43/70, etch, p/s, P-10x8", lot 55, PHL 6/16/88 ..... **200**

GROOMS, Charles Roger see Grooms, Red

GROOMS, Red (American, 1937-)
Coney Island 1976-1978, 16/34, clr etch/aqua, p/s, full mrgs, P-16x20", lot 103, PHL 6/16/88 OE **900**
Discount Store, 16/100, slksc/Arches, 1971, sgn/dtd, L-14x36", lot 62, RWS 9/29/88 ..... **550**
Gangster & Moll Dancing the Tango, clr srgph, 1973, p/s, 39x29", lot 75, SWN 12/1/88..... **825**
Manet, Romance; 15/40, etch/wht wove paper, 1976, p/s, titled, full mrgs, 19x18", lot 3030, B/B 4/19/88 ..... **330**
Museum 1978, 53/150, clr litho, 1978, p/s, full mrgs, lt stn, L-9x22", lot 104, PHL 6/16/88 OE..... **1,000**
Pierpont Morgan Library, AP16/40, total ed of 250, clr srgph, ca 1979, p/s, 11x34", lot 104, SWN 6/15/88 OE **1,320**
Rudy, 1/20, etch/wht wove paper, 1976, p/s, titled/dtd, full mrgs, 5x4", lot 3029, B/B 4/19/88..... **220**
Slushing, 38/75, clr litho/Arches, p/s, stp BSA, S-22x28", lot 63, RWS 9/29/88..... **750**
Van Gogh with Flowers, 14/75, clr litho, 1988, p/s, full mrgs, 16x22", Shark's Inc, lot 1010, SBY 5/13/89 ..... **4,400**

GROOMS, Reginald (American, 1900-)
Toe Hold, 16/40, litho, p/s, titled, 8x10", lot 168, WG 10/19/88..... **95**

GROPPER, William (American, 1897-1978)
Joe Magarac, litho, p/s, lt stn, 13x9", Assn Am Artists, lot 240, WG 10/19/88 ..... **175**
Pair: Orchestra; hc litho, trm mrgs, 12x14", lot 67, FAP 2/24/89 UE **50**
Red Cavalry, clr litho/wove paper, ca 1940, sgn in blk crayon, lt stn, L-14x18", lot 175, C-NY 1/19/89 UE **220**
Shtetl, 99/100, clr litho, ca 1969, p/s, 15x11", lot 103, SWN 6/15/89 ..... **360**
Unsettled Business, clr litho, p/s, 18x24", lot 961, FAP 12/8/88 ..... **350**
Wall Street, litho, ca 1941, p/s, titled, lt cr mrgs, 10x14", lot 76, SWN 12/1/88 OE..... **550**

GROSE, David T. (American, 20th C)
June, 43/200, p/s, 6x4", lot 63, FAP 2/24/89 UE **10**

GROSS, Chaim (American, 1904-)
Pair: Greetings; litho, 1963, p/s, 19x10", lot 23, FAP 2/24/89 ..... **160**
Purim, 112/200, clr litho/Rives, 1968, p/s, titled, L-15x21", lot 70, RWS 9/8/89 ..... **600**

GROSZ, George (American, 1893-1959)

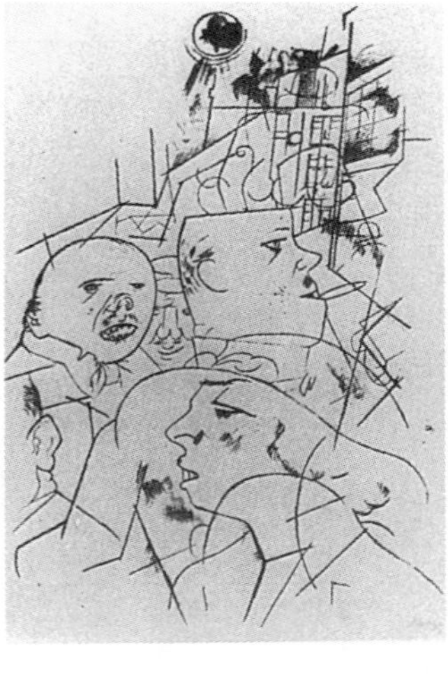

Strassensene, deluxe ed of 10, photo-litho/thin Japan, 1919-20, Bauhaus bstp, lt stn, S-20x14", lot 51, C-NY 11/1/88 OE; $2,860

Er Hat hindenburg Verspottet, litho/heavy wove paper, 1920, sgn/dtd, lt stn/fox, unfr, L-10x7", lot 25, RWS 9/8/89 250
Haifische, 19/30, photolitho/cream simili Japan, 1920-21, lt cr, S-20x26", Goltz, lot 52, C-NY 11/1/88 OE 1,650
Hall Bedroom, 149/150, clr colotype, 1933-34, p/s, lt stn, L-17x12", Ltd Ed Club, lot 44, RWS 9/29/88 325
Nachwuchs, 28/30, photolitho/laid paper, 1921-22, p/s, titled, lt sl/tr, S-26x20", Neumann, lot 53, C-NY 11/1/88 OE 1,100
Proletarier Haben Kein Ehrenwort!; Pl 8, litho/cream laid paper, 1923, p/s, lt ls/tr, L-12x10", lot 19, RWS 9/8/89 550
Self-Portrait with Dog in Front of the Easel, litho/tan wove paper, 1926, p/s, lt stn/cr, S-25x19", SBY 2/25/88 770
Set of 6: Bagdad-on-the-Subway; 40/150, orig tissues/wrapper/burlap-covered portfolio, Print Club, lot 315, C-NY 11/1/88 2,310
Storm Clouds, Cape Cod; total ed 242, litho/Italia, 1949, p/s, 9x13", Cleveland Print Club, lot 335, WG 10/19/88 250
Storm Clouds, litho/wht wove paper, 1949, p/s, rpr tr corner, 9x13", Cleveland Print Club, lot 2850, B/B 4/19/88 275

GRUM (French, 19th/20th C)
Enfin Seuls, clr litho, lt fox/tr, 32x24", lot 53, FAP 2/24/89 200

GUILBEAU, Honore (American, 1907-)
Market, litho/wove Sulgrave, 1935, p/s, titled, 14x11", Cleveland Print Club, lot 214, WG 10/14/88 35

GURO, E. (Russian, 20th C)
Book: E Guro, Sharmanka (Musical Box); prints w/text, 1909, lt cr/sl, St Petersburg, lot 556, SBY 5/11/89 1,320

GURR, Lena
Salome, ed of unrecorded size, clr scpt/blk wove paper, 1948-49, ink sgn, tp verso mrg edges, L-18x12", C-NY 1/22/88 330

GUSTON, Philip (American, 1913-)
August, Four on Plexi; 12/125, blk/ochre scrpt, 1966, 30x40", Multiples, lot 447, C-NY 5/11/88 UE 220

GUTZ, M. Richard (French, 20th C)
Banque Nationale de Credit, 1916, 32x47", Devambez, lot 276, FAP 2/24/89 110

GWATHMEY, Robert (American, 1903-)
Hitchhiker, clr slksc, ca 1952, ink sgn on img, 17x13", lot 106, SWN 6/15/89 OE 3,520
Non-Fiction, ed of about 25, clr slksc, ca 1941, ink sgn, lt scuff, 18x14", lot 107, SWN 6/15/89 1,320
Rural Home Front, clr slksc, ca 1945, ink sgn on img, lt ls, 10x18", lot 108, SWN 6/15/89 OE 1,540
Seated Woman, ed of 200, clr slksc/wove paper, 1954, p/s, lt scuff, tp to overmat, L-17x13", lot 176, C-NY 1/19/89 OE 440
Topping Tobacco, ed of 40, clr slksc, ca 1948, sgn, lt scuff img, 13x9", lot 109, SWN 6/15/89 OE 2,090

HABERMANN, Francois
Set of 4: Views of Quebec; hc etch, 10x16", lot 976, WAD 6/12/89 1,200

HADEN, Francis Seymour (British, 1818-1910)
Battersea Reach, 1st state, etch/laid paper, 1863, P-6x9", lot 343, C-NY 1/19/89 308
Brig at Anchor, etch/drypt/thin Japan, 1870, p/s, laid down, P-6x8", lot 56, PHL 6/16/88 UE 130
Sunset in Ireland, 6th state, etch/drypt, 1863, lt stn/fox, 5x8", lot 211, SBY 2/25/88 1,430
Thames Ditton (with a Sail), a/p, etch, 1864, 6x8", lot 44, WG 10/19/89 125
Wareham Bridge, a/p, etch/drypt, p/s, P-6x9", PHL 6/16/88 225
Water Meadow, 3rd state of 4, etch, 1859, p/s, 6x9", Goulding, lot 110, SWN 6/15/89 385

HAIG, Axel Herman (Spanish, 1835-1921)
Cathedral Interior, etch, p/s, 16x21", lot 860, WAD 11/28/88 UE 150

HAINES, Frederick Stanley (1879-1960)
Departure Day, aqua, p/s, 8x9", lot 782, WAD 6/12/89 150
Harvest Moon, aqua, p/s, titled, 10x9", lot 777, WAD 6/12/89 275

HALABY, Samia (Israel, 1936-)
Cleveland, 68/260, clr litho, 1974, p/s, titled, 14x14", Cleveland Print Club, lot 435, WG 10/19/88 85

HALL, Frederick G. (British, 1860-1948)
Englise de St Nicolas du Chardonnet, etch, p/s, 14x11", lot 102, WG 10/19/88 UE 20

HALLSWORTH, Joseph B. (American, 20th C)
Karmi, Most Startling Mystery of All Indies; litho/poster paper, 1914, rpr, 28x41", Nat'l Painting/Engr, FAP 2/24/89 UE 60
Karmi, Swallows on a Loaded Gun Barrel; litho/poster paper, 28x41", lot 263, FAP 2/24/89 UE 75

HAMAGUCHI, Yozo (Japanese, 1909-)
Ball of Yarn, aside from #d ed of 120, mezzo, 1981, inscr Bon a tirer 165XP, full mrgs, 3x5", lot 503, SBY 5/11/89 OE 8,250
Ball of Yarn, 102/120, clr mezzo, 1981, p/s, full mrgs, 3x5", lot 502, SBY 5/11/89 OE 8,800
Bit of Field, 39/150, mezzo, 1985, p/s, full mrgs, 10x22", lot 506, SBY 5/11/89 5,225
Blue Butterfly, 77/110, clr mezzo, 1982, p/s, full mrgs, lt yel stn, unfr, P-15x12", SBY 5/12/88 3,575
Blue Butterfly, 99/110, clr mezzo, 1982, p/s, full mrgs, S-15x12", lot 223A, SBY 11/3/88 OE 4,950
Blue Glass, 31/50, clr mezzo, 1957, p/s, lg mrgs, lt cr/stn, 5x5", lot 498, SBY 5/11/89 11,550
Blue Grapes, a/p, clr mezzo, 1956, p/s, full mrgs, lt cr/stn/ls, 6x8", lot 496, SBY 5/11/89 9,350
Book: Hamaguchi's Color Mezzotints; 41/222, sgn on justification, 1979, Nanteshi Gallery, lot 221, SBY 11/3/88 OE 4,125
Cloud, 22/50, mezzo, 1958, p/s, lt surface scuff, lt ls mrg, lt mstn/sl/cr, unfr, P-11x20", SBY 5/12/88 5,500
Face, 3/20, purple & blk drypt/aqua, 1954, p/s, full mrgs, 5x4", lot 495, SBY 5/11/89 OE 6,325
Fish & Cherries, 14/50, clr mezzo, 1956, p/s, lt stn, 6x8", lot 497, SBY 5/11/89 7,700
Fish & Cherries, 42/50, clr mezzo, 1956, p/s, full mrgs, lt stn/cr, 6x8", lot 219, SBY 11/3/88 11,000
Fish & Fruit, 11/50, mezzo, 1954, p/s, lt scr/cr, 12x16", lot 213, SBY 2/25/88 3,850
Fish & Fruit, 48/50, mezzo, 1954, p/s, lt trm mrgs, lt rub/sl/stn mrgs, unfr, P-12x16", SBY 5713 OE 7,150
Grapes & Lemon, a/p, aside from ed of 40, mezzo, 1962, p/s, full mrgs, lt stn/fox, 3x4", lot 500, SBY 5/11/89 OE 2,970
Knitting Needle, ed of 150, mezzo/BFK Rives, 1985, p/s, inscr PP & Bon Atirer, full mrgs, unfr, P-9x22", SBY 5/12/88 OE 4,950
Knitting Needle, 114/150, mezzo, 1985, p/s, full mrgs, lt sl, 9x22", lot 507, SBY 5/11/89 OE 4,400
Nine Shells, 70/75, mezzo, 1980, p/s, full mrgs, lt scuff/cr, 19x25", lot 501, SBY 5/11/89 OE 4,675
One Cherry, 2/50, clr mezzo, 1958, p/s, full mrgs, lt stn/cr, 4x6", lot 220, SBY 11/3/88 OE 8,800
Pair: Red Yarn; Spiral Shell; ed of 99, clr mezzo, 1979, full mrgs, 2x2", lot 222, SBY 11/3/88 3,300
Pair: Two Slices of Watermelon; Fish & Fruit; ed of 50, mezzo, 1954, full mrgs, 12x16", lot 217, SBY 11/3/88 3,740
Pair: Walnut; Greeting Card 3; mezzo/wht wove paper, 1960/1968, p/s, full mrgs, P-4x4"/P-2x2", SBY 5/12/88 OE 3,410

Papillon Rouge, ed of 250, mezzo/BFK Rives, 1972, p/s, Cleveland Print Club bstp, P-2x2", lot 176, C-NY 5/11/88 OE **2,860**
Papillon Rouge, ed of 260, mezzo/BFK Rives, 1973, p/s, full mrgs, 2x2", Cleveland Print Club, lot 111, SWN 6/15/89 OE **3,300**
Pomegranate, 1/250, mezzo, 1958, p/s, lt scuff img, unfr, P-12x14", SBY 5/12/88 OE **4,950**
Pomegranates & Grapes, aside from ed of 50, mezzo, 1957, p/s, full mrgs, lt stn/fox/sl, 12x18", lot 499, SBY 5/11/89 OE **12,650**
Red Butterfly, ed of 250, clr mezzo, 1972, p/s, trm mrgs, Cleveland Print Club, lot 215, SBY 2/25/88 .... **2,475**
Robina's Cherry, HC, aside from #d ed of 150, mezzo, 1981, p/s, full mrgs, lt stn/sl, 3x2", lot 505, SBY 5/11/89 OE **6,325**
Spanish Oil Bottle, 10/50, mezzo, 1954, p/s, full mrgs, lt scuff/fox/cr/rpr, 12x12", lot 264, SBY 2/23/89 OE **7,975**
Still Life with Pimentos, 2/50, clr mezzo, 1955, p/s, full mrgs, lt scr img, lt cr, 18x12", lot 218, SBY 11/3/88 OE **7,700**
Two Slices of Watermelon, 26/50, mezzo/wove paper, 1954, p/s, lt mstn, unfr, P-12x16", SBY 5/12/88 OE **5,500**
Watermelon, 10/150, clr mezzo/wht wove paper, 1981, p/s, full mrgs, 9x22", lot 223, SBY 11/3/88 OE **29,700**
Watermelon, 149/150, clr mezzo, 1981, p/s, full mrgs, 9x21", lot 504, SBY 5/11/89 .... **28,600**

HANCOCK, J. Carl (American, 20th C)
Pirates Alley, etch, p/s, 5x7", lot 233, MG 11/19/88 UE **35**

HAND, Thomas; after (British, 19th C)
Pair: Going Out; Drawing Covert; hc etch, P-13x16", lot 919, LH 10/16/88 UE **100**

HANKEY, William Lee (British, 1869-1952)
Contemplative Woman, engr, p/s, stp/s, 9x7", lot 29, FAP 2/24/89 UE **40**

HANKINS, Abraham P. (American, 1903-1963)
Mother & Child, etch, p/s, L-8x5", lot 431, FAP 4/15/88 .... **44**
Mummers, etch, p/s, L-8x6", lot 432, FAP 4/15/88 .... **44**

HANSEN, Armin Carl (American, 1886-1957)
Fishermen Walking, etch/laid paper, 1926, p/s, titled, lg mrgs, lt cr, 4x4", lot 2951, B/B 2/16/88 .... **358**

HANSEN, W.H. (American, 19th/20th C)
Pair: Western Scenes; hc litho, dtd 02, 19x14", lot 784, LH 10/16/88 .... **275**

HARDY, Jeremiah P. (American, 1880-1888)
Le Favore de Rosine, a/p, clr aqua/drypt, p/s, titled, laid down, P-16x21", lot 65, PHL 10/28/88 UE **70**

HARNETT, William Michael (American, 1848-1892)
Old Violin, chromolitho, 1887, lt stn/scr, laid down on card, S-35x25", Tuchfarber, lot 5A, PHL 10/28/88 .... **1,700**

HARRIS, Lawren Stewart (1885-1970)
Winter in the City, p/s, 5x7", Rous & Mann, lot 861A, WAD 6/12/89 OE **800**

HART, Charles (American, 1847-1918)
Farmer's Home, hc litho/wove paper, ca 1867, lt stn/fox img, lt stn verso, L-18x25", Farrel, lot 79, C-NY 1/19/89 UE **110**
Home in the Country, Summer; litho, full mrgs, lt stn/fox, lg folio, RAB 1/31/89 UE **150**

HART, George Overbury (Pop)(American, 1868-1933)
Excursion Boat, ed of unrecorded size, aqua/etch/simili Japan, 1926, p/s, stn/cr mrgs, unfr, P-10x14", C-NY 1/22/88 UE **165**
Haiti Market, litho/wove paper, 1924, p/s, 8x13", lot 78, SWN 12/1/88 .... **275**
Pair: Jersey Hills; Mammy; drypt & drypt/rlt on wove paper, 1923 & 1924, p/s, lt stn/cr, lot 177, C-NY 1/19/89 .... **418**
Pair: Landscape Santo Domingo; Moonlight in the Jungle; sftgr etch, 1925 & ca 1920, 7x11"/8x10", lot 79, SWN 12/1/88 .... **413**

HARTLEY, Marsden (American, 1877-1943)
Apples in a Basket, ed of 25, litho/fibrous tan paper, 1923, p/s, lt stn/tr/top, L-13x18", lot 26, C-NY 5/11/88 OE **1,760**
Grapes in Bowl, litho, 1923, p/s, full mrgs, lt stn/sl/cr/tr, 12x16", lot 23, SBY 11/3/88 OE **3,850**

HARTUNG, Hans (German, 1904-)
Black & Tan Abstraction, 88/100, etch/aqua/wove paper, p/s, wide mrgs, lt stn, P-9x12", lot 80, RWS 9/8/89 .... **250**
Composition 12, 17/50, litho, p/s, 26x20", lot 958, LH 5/15/88 .... **225**

HASEGAWA, Kiyoshi (Japanese, 1891-)
Anemones, 18/35, drypt, 1939, p/s, Jacquart bstp, full mrgs, lt sl/fox, 10x8", lot 265, SBY 2/23/89 OE **6,600**
Point d'Interrogation Sur Gratte-Ciels (New York), aside from #d ed of 20, mezzo, 1930, 8x12", lot 508, SBY 5/11/89 .... **6,600**
Vieil Acacia, 22/60, etch/Chine applique, 1954, p/s, a/bstp, full mrgs, lt lstn/sl, unfr, P-14x9", SBY 5/12/88 OE **5,775**

HASKELL & ALLEN
Leaving Brighton Hotel for Mill-Dam (Summer), litho w/varnish, 1871, stn, sl mrgs, laid down, L-18x25", C-NY 1/22/88 .... **605**
Pair: Leaving Brighton Hotel for the Mill-Dam: Winter & Summer; litho, 1871, lt fox, laid down, lot 80, C-NY 1/19/89 UE **165**
Trip Down the Harbor, litho, wstn img, lt tr mrg, lg folio, RAB 8/1/88 UE **100**
Yacht Fleetwing of New York 212 Tons, litho, fox, unfr, sm folio, RAB 5/17/88 .... **150**

HASSAM, Frederick Childe (American, 1859-1935)
Battery Park, 2nd state, etch/drypt, 1916, p/s, full mrgs, lt stn mrgs/verso, 13x7", lot 24, SBY 11/3/88 OE **12,650**
Big Cedar, etch/wove paper, 1927, p/s, cypher/inscr Imp, lstn, tp undermat mrg edges, L-10x12", C-NY 1/22/88 .... **880**
Chase House, Annapolis; etch/drypt, 1929, p/s, full mrgs, P-7x8", lot 22, PHL 10/28/88 .... **850**
Church at Old Lyme, a/p, etch/wove paper, 1924, p/s, lt stn, P-7x7", lot 180, C-NY 1/19/89 .... **1,320**
Church Doorway, Snow; etch/old laid Bible paper, 1916, p/s, inscr Imp, full mrgs, lt stn, 7x6", lot 29, SBY 2/23/89 OE **1,320**
Cos Cob, etch, p/s, 7x5", lot 156, WG 10/19/88 OE **700**
Diana's Pool Appledore, etch/wove paper, 1916, p/s, cypher/inscr Imp, trm mrgs, stn/sl, tp verso, L-11x7", C-NY 1/22/88 .... **825**
Easthampton, etch, 1917, p/s, inscr Imp, lt cr img, 8x11", lot 228, SBY 5/11/89 .... **2,475**
Easthampton Idyll, etch/wove paper, 1923, p/s, cypher/inscr Imp, lstn, tp undermat mrg edges, L-9x8", C-NY 1/22/88 .... **880**
Fifth Avenue, Noon; etch, 1916, p/s, inscr Imp, lt fox/stn, 10x7", lot 227, SBY 5/11/89 OE **6,600**
Floor of the Stock Exchange, etch/wove paper, 1927, p/s, cypher/inscr Imp, full mrgs, P-10x15", C-NY 1/22/88 OE **4,620**
Group of 3: Church Doorway, Snow; Church at Old Lime; Chase House; etch, 1916/1924/1929, p/s, lot 226, SBY 5/11/89 .... **3,080**
House on Main Street, Easthampton; etch, 1922, p/s, lt cr/stn, 6x12", lot 25, SBY 11/3/88 OE **4,400**
Lafayette Street, lithotint/glazed paper, 1918, p/s, inscr Imp/Trial, lt cr/stn, mstn verso, L-14x11", C-NY 1/22/88 OE **6,050**
Lion Gardiner House, Easthampton; etch/JW, 1920, p/s, full mrgs, lt stn/sl mrgs, P-10x14", lot 179, C-NY 1/19/89 OE **14,300**
Lion Gardiner House, etch, 1920, p/s, cypher/inscr Imp, lt mstn/lstn, sealed in mat, P-10x14", C-NY 1/22/88 OE **9,900**
Little Church Around the Corner, etch, 1923, p/s, inscr Imp, lt stn/old tp, 8x11", lot 230, SBY 5/11/89 .... **2,090**

Nyssa Sylvatica, etch, 1926, p/s, lt stn/fox/sl, tp hinges in corners, 9x11", lot 27, SBY 11/3/88 ... 825
Old Doorway, Easthampton; etch, 1920, p/s, inscr Imp, lt sl mrgs/verso, 10x12", lot 229, SBY 5/11/89 OE ... 6,325
Old Lace, etch, 1915, p/s, full mrgs, lt stn, 7x7", lot 29, SBY 2/25/88 OE ... 1,320
Pair: High Pool; Egeria, etch/wove paper, 1916/1924, p/s, cypher/inscr Imp, lt mstn/lstn, C-NY 1/22/88... 528
Pair: Vermont Village; Chase House, Annapolis; etch, 1923 & 2929, p/s, inscr Imp, 6x9"/7x8", lot 231, SBY 5/11/89 ... 2,420
Toby's, Cos Cob; a/p, etch/wove paper, 1915, p/s, lt stn mrgs, lt cr/fox, P-7x9", lot 178, C-NY 1/19/89 OE ... 3,520
Vermont Village, etch, 1923, p/s, inscr Imp, lt fox/stn, 6x9", lot 26, SBY 11/3/88 ... 1,320
Wayside Inn-Oaks in Spring, etch/wove paper, 1926, p/s, cypher/inscr Imp, lt lstn, lt sl mrg, P-10x8", C-NY 1/22/88 ... 462
Writing Desk, etch, 1915, p/s, inscr Imp, lt fox/stn, 10x7", lot 225, SBY 5/11/89 OE ... 15,400

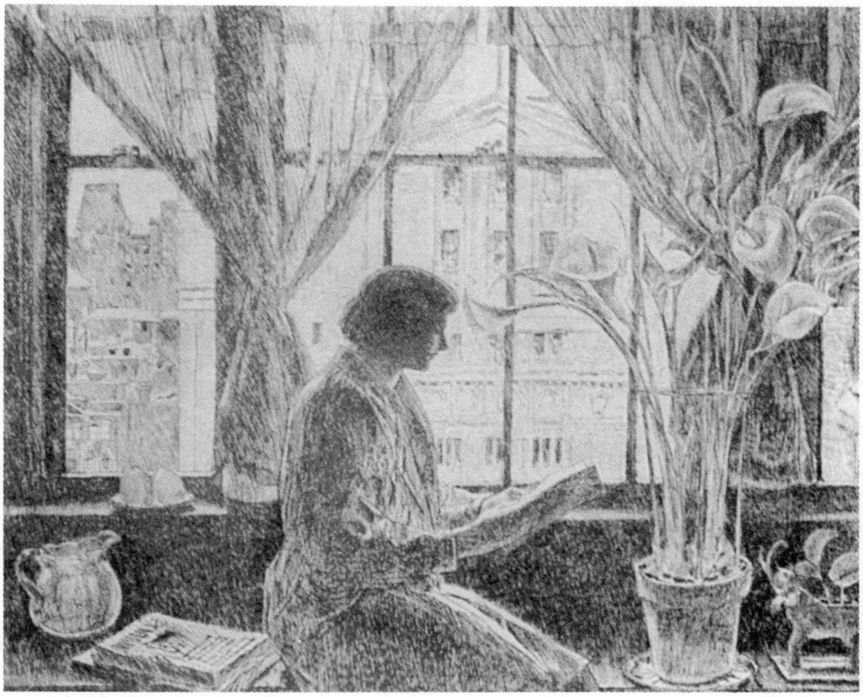

Virginia & a New York Winter Window, etch, 1934, artist monogram, inscr Imp, full mrgs, lt sl mrgs, 10x13", lot 76, WD 12/8/88 OE; $17,000

HAUGG, L. (19th C)
Pair: Freight Locomotive; Express Passenger Locomotive; chromolitho, 1856, stn/scuff, S-14x18", lot 557, SBY 1/28/88... 1,320
HAVELL, Robert (19th C)
Set of 4: Java & the Constitution (ships); Pl 1 through 4, hc print, 1814, P-24x27", Bardell, lot 171, GAI 11/25/88 ... 1,200
View of West Point, US Military Academy; hc aqua/gum arabic, 1848, lt tr/stn mrg, laid down, S-19x25", C-NY 1/22/88 OE... 8,800
HAYTER, Stanley William (British, 1901-1988)
Angels Wrestling, E3/5, engr/etch, 1930, p/s, titled, full mrgs, lt sl/cr/stn, 17x14", lot 509, SBY 5/11/89 ... 3,850
Angels Wrestling, 25/50, etch/engr/sftgr, 1950, p/s, lt stn/cr, 17x12", lot 114, SWN 6/15/89 OE ... 3,740
Book: Stanley William Hayter, 9 Engravings, 1933-1946; 24/100, on Barcham Green, orig wrappers, lot 316, C-NY 11/1/88 OE... 4,180
Cres, 30/50, etch/engr, 1948, p/s, titled, full mrgs, lt sl/cr mrgs, 24x16", lot 515, SBY 5/11/89 ... 4,125
Cronos, 44/50, engr/sftgr etch/relief/sturdy wove paper, 1944, p/s, full mrgs, lt sl/cr, 16x20", lot 513, SBY 5/11/89 OE... 8,800
Danae, 72/95, engr/etch/cream canvas-textured laid paper, 1954, p/s, full mrgs, lt sl, 16x12", lot 517, SBY 5/11/89 OE ... 5,500
Danae, 72/95, engr/sftgr etch/embossing/cream canvas-textured laid paper, 1954, p/s, 16x12", lot 223C, SBY 11/3/88 OE ... 4,400
Death by Water, 48/50, engr/relief, 1948, p/s, titled, full mrgs, lt cr/sl, 14x24", lot 223B, SBY 11/3/88 OE... 4,675
Fire Under Water, a/p, etch/engr, 1955, p/s, titled, glue on mat, 10x7", lot 267, SBY 2/23/89 UE... 770
Flight (?), 8/30, engr, 1944, p/s, full mrgs, lt sl, 15x10", lot 512, SBY 5/11/89 ... 2,640
Genoux, 5/30, etch/engr, 1950, p/s, titled, full mrgs, lt fox/stn, 10x6", lot 516, SBY 5/11/89... 2,200
La Noyee, 68/175, engr, 1955, p/s, L'Oeuvre Gravee bstp, full mrgs, lt rub/stn, 14x19", lot 518, SBY 5/11/89 OE ... 2,475
Paanes, 16/30, engr/etch/laid paper, 1936, p/s, full mrgs, lt sl/cr/ls, 12x7", lot 510, SBY 5/11/89 OE ... 4,400
Pair: Cheiromancy; Facile Proie; engr, 1935 & 1938, p/s, full mrgs, 8x6"/6x6", Assn Am Artists, lot 113, SWN 6/15/89 ... 220
Pillars, 4/50, engr/mixed media/wove paper, 1976, p/s, titled/dtd, full mrgs, lt sl mrg, unfr, P-23x17", C-NY 1/22/88 ... 418
Swimming Bird, 4/50, clr aqua/intg, 1969, p/s, titled, full mrgs, lt rpl, 17x22", lot 61, RWS 9/29/88 UE... 100
Tarantelle, 32/50, engr, 1943, p/s, titled, full mrgs, lt sl/cr/skinned/tr, 22x13", lot 511, SBY 5/11/89 OE ... 8,800
HEAP, George; att (18th C)
East Perspective of the City of Philadelphia...; etch/engr/cream laid paper, 1778, S-12x19", lot 500, SBY 1/28/88 ... 13,200
HEAPHY, Charles; after
View of Nelson Haven, in Tasman's Gulf, New Zealand...; by T Allom, hc litho, 15x21", Hullamandel, C-SK 6/9/88 ... 260
HEASLIP, William John (American, 1898-)
Propeller, engr, p/s, titled, 8x11", lot 69, FAP 2/24/89... 120
HECKEL, Erich (German, 1883-1970)
Am Strand, 3rd state, wc/wove paper, 1923, p/s, Marees-Gesellschaft bstp, lt stn, L-16x11", lot 629, C-NY 5/10/89 ... 2,090
Am Strand, 8/20, litho/laid Japan, 1923, p/s, titled, full mrgs, lt cr/sl, 15x13", lot 271, SBY 2/23/89 ... 880

Bildnis Dr M, ed of 30, drypt/Butten, 1915, p/s, dtd 16, rpr tr/lt cr/fox, 11x9", Verlag, lot 519, SBY 5/11/89 **990**
Frauenkopf, ed of 100, litho/buff wove paper, 1922, p/s, full mrgs, lt stn/fox/cr, 11x9", lot 270, SBY 2/23/89 UE **1,100**
Junges Madchen (Madchen Kopf), wc/wove paper, 1913/1920, sgn, lt stn/tr, L-10x7", Holzschnitt, lot 22, RWS 9/8/89 OE **550**
Jungling, ed of 100, wc/cream wove paper, 8x6", lot 2852, B/B 4/19/88 **358**
Kniende am Stein, unrecorded 1st state, wc/soft wove paper, 1913, lt ls/stn, S-26x17", lot 61, C-NY 11/1/88 **8,250**
Madchen Vorm Spiegel, 2nd state of 2, drypt/heavy wove paper, 1920, p/s, lt fox/sl mrgs, 13x8", SBY 5/12/88 OE **4,950**
Mannerbildnis (Self-Portrait), 1st state, wc/yel-gr laid paper, 1919, p/s, full mrgs, L-18x13", lot 318, C-NY 11/1/88 **18,700**
Mude, 2nd state, wc/Tower cream laid paper, 1913, p/s, inscr Holzsch Handdruck, S-27x20", lot 60, C-NY 11/1/88 OE **6,380**
Portrait of a Man, #15, wc/laid paper, p/s, lt trm mrgs, 2 sm tr mrgs, lt stn/cr, 14x11", lot 2855, B/B 2/16/88 **1,430**
Reckakt, ed of 30, drypt/handmade laid paper, 1919, p/s, full mrgs, lt tstn, P-9x10", lot 320, C-NY 11/1/88 **1,100**
Reiter in Berglandschaft, 4th state, wc/wove paper, 1960, p/s, full mrgs, lt sl, 25x19", lot 2851, B/B 4/19/88 OE **770**
Ruhende, 1st state, gray-blk & brn litho/firm cream wove paper, 1911, inscr Handdruck, S-21x14", lot 57, C-NY 11/1/88 OE **13,200**
Sitzende am Wasser, 1st state, wc/Drey Konige laid paper, 1913, p/s, lt cr/stn/sl, S-15x18", lot 59, C-NY 11/1/88 OE **9,350**
Sitzendes Madchen, 2nd state, litho/cream wove paper, 1907, p/s, lt fox/stn, S-19x15", lot 54, C-NY 11/1/88 **9,900**
Stehende, 10/13, litho/wove paper, 1947, p/s, trm mrgs, lt cr, 16x7", lot 2856, B/B 2/16/88 UE **300**
Strasse in Ostende, ed of 60, drypt, 1915, p/s, titled/dtd, lt stn/rpr, 9x6", Verlag, lot 216, SBY 2/25/88 **990**
Vorm Bad, 1st state, wc/wove paper, 1912, p/s, lt tr/cr/sl, S-14x18", lot 58, C-NY 11/1/88 **8,250**
Weibliches Gesicht, unrecorded 1st state, wc/firm laid paper, 1907, p/s, inscr Holzchn, L-8x6", lot 55, C-NY 11/1/88 OE **8,800**

HEDGES, W.S.; after
Colonial Scene with West Indies, hc litho, L-14x24", Day/Haghe, C-SK 6/9/88 **400**

HEEMSKERK, Marten J. (Dutch, 1498-1574)
Two Men Visit Mother & Child, etch, 1549/later, 10x8", lot 29, WG 10/19/89 UE **90**

HEINTZELMAN, Arthur William (American, 1890-1965)
Group of 3: Le Frandole; Man with Guitar; Group of Heads; ed of 100, etch, p/s, 10x12", lot 147, WG 10/19/88 OE **225**
Group of 3: Scene de Music Hall; Chanteur Populaire; Le Vigneron; etch, ed of 100 or 110, etch, p/s, lot 82, SWN 12/1/88 **300**
Group of 3: Woman in Mule Cart; Cow in Field; Portrait of a Man; etch, various sizes, lot 148, WG 10/19/88 OE **225**
Head of a Martyr, etch, 4x3", FAP 6/16/89 **70**
Pigeon, ed of 60, etch, 1933, p/s, 8x7", lot 55, WG 10/19/88 **55**

HELDNER, Knute (American, 1884-1952)
Ducks, Mallards; 1/20, etch, p/s, 7x8", lot 321, NA 2/6/88 **100**

HELLEU, Paul Cesar (French, 1859-1927)
Corsage a la Dentelle, drypt/wove paper, ca 1900, sgn, lt sl/mstn, laid down, P-16x12", lot 322, C-NY 11/1/88 **1,430**
Croquis, drypt/wove paper, ca 1900, p/s, full mrgs, lt mstn/sl mrgs & verso, 18x9", SBY 5/12/88 **1,100**
Femme au Chapeau Blue, clr drypt/heavy wove paper, ca 1900, lt cr img, lt fox/ls, P-23x18", lot 323, C-NY 11/1/88 **935**
Jeune Blonde, clr drypt/wove paper, ca 1900, p/s, lt fox, laid down, P-16x12", lot 324, C-NY 11/1/88 **2,090**
Jeune Blonde au Chapeau, clr drypt/wove paper, ca 1900, p/s, lt scr img, fox/stn mrgs, 22x14", lot 325, C-NY 11/1/88 OE **6,050**
Jeune Blonde au Chapeau Noir en Profile, clr drypt/wove paper, ca 1900, lt sl/stn, P-23x14", lot 177, C-NY 5/11/88 **2,530**
Jeune Blonde Coquette, clr drypt/wove paper, ca 1900, lt fox/stn/ls, laid down, P-22x13", lot 178, C-NY 5/11/88 **2,420**
Jeune Blonde en Profil, clr drypt/wove paper, ca 1900, p/s, lt stn, lt cr img, P-22x13", lot 630, C-NY 5/10/89 **880**
Jeune Femme, clr drypt/wove paper, ca 1900, p/s, lt scr/cr img, lt scr on verso,P-22x14", lot 179, C-NY 5/11/88 **2,200**
Le Visage Encadre, drypt/wove paper, ca 1902, p/s, lt stn, hing top, P-11x16", RWS 3/16/89 OE **2,300**
Les Cheveux Defaits, drypt/wove paper, ca 1900, p/s, trm mrgs, sgn/skinned mrgs, laid down, P-8x11", C-NY 1/22/88 **605**
Les Dessins de Watteau au Louvre, ed of unknown size, blk/sanguine drypt, ca 1910, 12x16", lot 520, SBY 5/11/89 OE **4,125**
Meditation, 65/100, drypt/laid van Gelder, 1894, p/s, pub bstp, full mrgs, lt stn/fox, 11x8", SBY 5/12/88 **990**
Mlle H, ed of 50, drypt/heavy wove paper, ca 1895, sgn in blk crayon, lt sl, 14x11", lot 272, SBY 2/23/89 OE **2,200**
Mme Helleu at Her Writing Desk, drypt/wove paper, ca 1898, sgn, lt sl/stn, 16x12", lot 276, SBY 2/23/89 OE **3,575**
Mme Helleu Leaning on a Gueridon, drypt/stiff wove paper, ca 1898, sgn, full mrgs, lt sl, 16x11", SBY 2/23/89 OE **3,575**
Mme Letellier, clr etch/drypt, ca 1900, p/s, lt sl mrgs/verso, 22x13", lot 217, SBY 2/25/88 **3,080**
Pair: Femme dans un Interieur avec Harpe; Jeune Femme, les Mains sur le Dossier d'un Siege; drypt, ca 1900, C-NY 1/22/88 **1,430**
Pair: Spanish Dancer; Woman Reading; drypt & litho, ca 1900, 16x12"/28x21", lot 277, SBY 2/23/89 **1,320**
Sagot, sepia litho/cream paper/backed on linen, pl/s, 41x17", C-E 6/16/88 **110**
Two Women with Fan Conversing, drypt/laid van Gelder Zonen, ca 1900, lg mrgs, lt fox/sl, 16x12", SBY 2/23/89 **1,760**
Woman on a Canape, drypt/wove paper, ca 1900, p/s, lt fox/stn, 13x16", lot 279, SBY 2/23/89 OE **2,420**
Woman with Hat, Arms Folded; drypt, ca 1900, p/s, 12x8", lot 84, SWN 12/1/88 OE **825**
Woman with Hat & Stole, drypt, ca 1910, p/s, lt rpl img, lt sl/cr mrgs, 15x11", lot 218, SBY 2/25/88 OE **1,540**
Young Girl, a/p, dk brn drypt, ca 1910, p/s, lt stn, laid down, 14x9", lot 281, SBY 2/23/89 **1,320**
Young Woman with Harp, Facing Left; drypt/laid paper, ca 1898, sgn in blk crayon, lt fox/sl, 16x11", SBY 2/23/89 OE **3,850**
Young Woman with Harp, Facing Right; drypt/JW Turkey Mill, ca 1901, full mrgs, lt stn/sl/cr, 22x13", SBY 2/23/89 OE **4,125**

HENDEN (Norwegian, 20th C)
Trondheim, Norge, Vinterleker; clr litho/poster paper, 1939, 39x24", Norsk Lith Offkin, lot 255, FAP 2/24/89 UE **75**

HENDERSON, P.; after
China Limodoran, by Landseer, aqua/stpl engr/JW, trm mrgs, stn/nicked img, fox/sl mrgs/verso, P-21x16", C-NY 1/22/88 UE **110**
Nodding Renealmia, by Caldwell, 2nd/final state, clr aqua/stpl engr, scr img, sl/fox mrgs, L-13x14", C-NY 1/22/88 OE **1,980**
Pair: Blue Passion Flower, by Caldwall; Winged Passion Flower, by Warner; aqua/stpl engr, 1800/1802, C-NY 1/22/88 OE **2,200**
Pair: Indian Reed, by Caldwall; American Cowslip, by Warner; aqua/engr, trm mrgs, lt fox/stn, laid down, C-NY 1/22/88 OE **1,210**

HENRY, Edward Lamson; after (American, 1841-1919)
First Railway Train, hc collo/wove applique, 1894, lt stn/tr/cr, S-22x42", Klackner, lot 561, SBY 1/28/88 **660**

HERRING, John Frederick; after (British, 19th C)
Grand Stand Ascot, Caravan; by C Hunt, aqua/wove paper, 1852, trm/stn/fox, 20x30", Barnett Moss, lot 81A, C-NY 1/19/89 **1,870**

HERSCHFELD, Al (American, 20th C)
Jackie Gleason, 99/150, clr engr, p/s, 12" dia, lot 383, WG 10/19/88 **375**

HIGGINS, Eugene (American, 1874-1958)

Rock Quarry, clr monotype/thick wove paper, early 20th C, p/s, lt cr, tp in mrg, L-16x12", lot 182, C-NY 1/19/89 ... 330

HILL, John William (American, 1812-1879)

Configuration of the Masonic Hall, Chestnut Street, Philadelphia; engr, 1819, lt stn, 21x17", Kennedy/Smith, FAP 2/24/89 ... 375
New York, by Mottram, a/p, 3rd state, hc engr/aqua, ca 1855, lt cr img, lt stn, L-29x50", lot 83, C-NY 1/19/89 ... 1,320
Paterson, New Jersey; clr litho w/hc, 1834, trm/lstn/fox mrgs, rpr tr img/mrgs, laid down, L-8x13", C-NY 1/22/88 ... 242
Shoal of Sperm Whale, Off the Island of Hawaii...; hc aqua, 1838, rpr tr, laid down, S-20x25", lot 82, C-NY 1/19/89 OE ... 3,850

HILL, John William; after (American, 1812-1879)

Capturing a Sperm Whale, litho, lt tr/fox, unfr, 20x27", RAB 3/14/89 ... 175
New York, a/p, etch/aqua/thin wove applique, 1855, scr/sl/fox, laid down, L-29x51", Charden, lot 517, SBY 1/28/88 ... 1,320
New York, a/p, final state, etch/aqua/thin wove applique, 1855, lt scr img, sl/fox, laid down, L-29x51", SBY 1/28/88 ... 1,320
New York, 1865; by C Mottram, full mrgs, lt tstn, L-29x49", GW Smith of NY, RWS 8/20/88 OE ... 1,200
New York From Heights Near Brooklyn, by Margolies, clr aqua, 1949, p/s, lt fox/stn, laid down, P-15x21", C-NY 1/22/88 ... 440
New York From Steeple of St Paul's Church...; 3rd state, etch/aqua/India applique, 1855, stn, P-26x41", C-NY 1/22/88 OE ... 6,600

HINGRE, Louis Theophile (French, 19th/20th C)

Parfumerie, litho/poster paper, 26x21", lot 283, FAP 2/24/89 UE ... 300

HIRSCH, Joseph (American, 1910-)

Man & Beast, litho, p/s, 14x7", lt stn, L-14x7", lot 16, PHL 6/16/88 UE ... 100
Music, litho, p/s, stn, 10x8", Assn Am Artist, lot 146, WG 10/19/88 ... 60
Survivor, litho, p/s, lt stn, L-8x14", lot 18, PHL 6/16/88 ... 700

HOBBS, Morris Henry (American, 1892-)

Little Shop, Ursuline St, New Orleans; ed of 100, etch, p/s, titled, 7x8", lot 320, NA 2/6/88 UE ... 100
Rooftops of Old New Orleans, ed of 50, engr, p/s, no size given, lot 31, FAP 2/24/89 ... 40
St Louis Cathedral, a/p, p/s, P-8x13", lot 12, MG 5/28/88 ... 350

HOCKNEY, David (British, 1937-)

Amaryllis, 47/80, clr litho/wht HMP handmade, 1985, p/s, TGL bstp, full mrgs, 46x32", lot 1032, SBY 5/13/89 OE ... 68,750
Amaryllis in Vase, 74/80, clr litho/HMP handmade, 1985, p/s, TGL bstp, full mrgs, 46x33", lot 809, SBY 11/5/88 OE ... 37,400
Ann Putting on Lipstick, 24/75, litho/Okawara, 1979, sgn in orange crayon, Gemini bstp, 47x19", lot 802, SBY 11/5/88 ... 5,500
Beginning, Pl 9, 60/75, total ed of 670, etch/Crisbrook handmade, 1966, p/s, full mrgs, lt stn/cr, P-14x9", C-NY 11/1/88 ... 462
Big Celiaprint #1, a/p, VII/XV, litho/Arches, 1982, p/s, dtd 81, Gemini bstp, S-48x57", lot 655, C-NY 11/1/88 OE ... 9,900
Big Celiaprint #1, 74/100, litho/Arches Cover, 1982, p/s, Gemini bstp, S-47x57", lot 1030, SBY 5/13/89 OE ... 16,500
Black Tulips, APXII, litho/cream Rives BFK, 1980, p/s, TGL bstp, lt cr, S-44x30", SBY 5/14/88 OE ... 15,400
Black Tulips, 84/100, litho/BFK Rives, 1980, p/s, TGL bstp, full sheets, S-44x30", lot 653A, C-NY 11/1/88 ... 14,300
Black Tulips, 91/100, litho/BFK Rives, 1980, p/s, TGL bstp, lt cr/rub/rpr tr, S-44x30", lot 670, SBY 2/23/89 OE ... 14,300
Black Tulips, 95/100, litho/BFK Rives, 1980, p/s, TGL bstp, lt rub/cr, S-44x30", lot 805, SBY 11/5/88 ... 12,650
Blue Guitar: A Picture of Ourselves; 81/200, etch, 1976-77, p/s, full mrgs, 14x17", Petersburg, lot 513, SBY 2/25/88 OE ... 1,320
Book: Illustrations for Six Fairy Tales From the Brothers Grimm; Ed B 33/100, 1970, Petersburg, lot 1016, SBY 5/13/89 OE ... 7,700
Book: Illustrations for 14 Poems for CP Cavafy, Ed B; 372/500, 12 etch w/text, 1966, Alecto, lot 659, SBY 2/23/89 OE ... 2,310
Bora Bora, 60/100, clr litho, 1979, p/s, TGL bstp, full mrgs, lt stn/cr/scr, S-35x48", lot 514, SBY 2/25/88 OE ... 6,600
Celia in a Wicker Chair, 5/60, sftgr etch/BFK Rives, 1974, p/s, full mrgs, 27x21", Petersburg, lot 1020, SBY 5/13/89 ... 26,400
Celia in a Wicker Chair, 52/60, sftgr etch/BFK Rives, 1974, p/s, full mrgs, P-27x22", Petersburg, lot 451, C-NY 5/11/88 ... 17,600
Celia in the Director's Chair, 22/100, litho, 1981, 41x37", lot 194A, LH 10/16/88 ... 5,000
Celia in the Director's Chair, 3/100, litho/Kurotani, 1981, p/s, dtd 80, Gemini bstp, S-42x38", lot 807, SBY 11/5/88 OE ... 6,050
Celia Musing, 96/100, litho/Toyoshi #80, 1979, sgn in bl crayon, Gemini bstp, lt cr, S-41x30", lot 1024, SBY 5/13/89 ... 6,600
Celia Observing, 39/60, clr etch/BFK Rives, 1976, p/s, full mrgs, P-27x22", Petersburg, lot 453, C-NY 5/11/88 ... 12,100
Celia Seated in a Wicker Chair, 9/20, sftgr etch, 1974, p/s, P-27x22", Petersburg, lot 653, C-NY 11/1/88 OE ... 15,400
Celia Seated in an Office Chair, a/p, II/IV, etch, 1974, p/s, P-27x22", Petersburg, lot 652, C-NY 11/1/88 OE ... 13,200
Celia Seated in an Office Chair, 22/60, etch/BFK Rives, 1974, full mrgs, P-27x22", Petersburg, lot 452, C-NY 5/11/88 OE ... 18,700
Celia with Green Hat, 82/98, clr litho/HMP handmade, 1985, p/s, TGL bstp, lt stn, S-30x22", lot 656, C-NY 11/1/88 OE ... 17,600
Celia with Green Hat, 85/98, clr litho/wht HMP handmade, 1985, TGL bstp, S-30x23", lot 1034, SBY 5/13/89 OE ... 30,800
Celia with Green Hat, 94/98, litho/HMP handmade, 1985, p/s, Tyler Graphics bstp, S-30x22", lot 462, C-NY 5/11/88 OE ... 10,450
Celia with Green Hat, 97/98, clr litho, 1985, p/s, TGL bstp, S-30x23", lot 810, SBY 11/5/88 OE ... 17,600
Celia-Amused; 19/100, litho/Toyoshi #80, 1979, p/s, Gemini bstp, lt cr/fox, S-40x29", lot 457, C-NY 5/11/88 ... 3,520
Celia-Elegant; 17/100, litho/Toyoshi #80, 1979, p/s, Gemini bstp, full sheet, lt cr, S-40x29", lot 459, C-NY 5/11/88 OE ... 4,400
Celia-Inquiring; 19/78, litho/Toyoshi #80, p/s, Gemini bstp, full sheet, S-40x29", lot 458, C-NY 5/11/88 OE ... 4,180
Celia-Musing; 19/100, litho/Toyoshi #80, 1979, p/s, Gemini bstp, full sheet, lt cr, S-40x29", lot 455, C-NY 5/11/88 ... 3,300
Celia-Weary; 19/100, litho/Toyoshi #80, 1979, p/s, Gemini bstp, full sheet, S-40x29", lot 456, C-NY 5/11/89 ... 1,870
Celia-Weary; 92/100, litho/Toyoshi #80, 1979, Gemini bstp, lt cr, S-40x30", lot 803, SBY 11/5/88 OE ... 7,150
Colored Flowers Made of Paper & Ink, aside from ed of 50, litho, 1971, p/s, S-39x38", Petersburg, SBY 5/14/80 OE ... 20,350
Commissioner, 37/50, litho/peach TGL handmade, 1980, p/s, Tyler Graphic bstp, lt cr, S-16x20", lot 461, C-NY 5/11/88 OE ... 660
Contrejour in the French Style, 43/75, clr etch/aqua, 1974, full mrgs, lt cr/sl/stn, 29x29", Petersburg, SBY 5/13/89 OE ... 44,000
Conversation in the Studio, 17/45, clr litho/TGL handmade, 1984, p/s, TGL bstp, full mrgs, 27x32", lot 808, SBY 11/5/88 ... 17,600
Cushions, 18/75, etch/aqua, 1968, p/s, full mrgs, lt cr/stn, 15x14", Alecto, lot 794, SBY 11/5/88 OE ... 4,400
Etch & Litho for Editions Alecto, 56/100, etch/litho/English mould made, 1973, S-36x25", Alecto, lot 450, C-NY 5/11/88 ... 605
Felicite Sleeping with Parrot: Illustration for Simple Heart of Gustave Flaubert; 66/100, 1978, 9x10", SBY 2/23/89 OE ... 2,420
Fires of Furious Desire, 43/75, etch/aqua, 1961, p/s, full mrgs, 6x11", Petersburg, lot 657, SBY 2/23/89 OE ... 1,210
Flowers, Apple, & Pear on a Table, July 1986; 16/59, clr handmade print/Arches, 1986, S-22x17", Hockney, SBY 5/13/89 OE ... 15,400
Gregory, 43/75, clr etch, 1974, p/s, full mrgs, lt scr/old hinge remains, 27x22", Petersburg, lot 1023, SBY 5/13/89 ... 8,800
Gregory, 67/75, clr etch, 1974, p/s, full mrgs, 27x22", Petersburg, lot 667, SBY 2/23/89 ... 8,800
Gregory Evans, 20/90, litho/buff Arches Cover, 1976, p/s, Gemini bstp, lt cr, S-42x30", lot 668, SBY 2/23/89 OE ... 3,410
Gregory Evans, 27/90, litho/buff Arches, 1976, p/s, Gemini bstp, lt stn/scr, 41x29", lot 511, SBY 2/25/88 ... 1,100

Gregory Thinking of Henry, 9/30, litho, 1977, sgn in orange crayon, Gemini bstp, S-36x23", lot 669, SBY 2/23/89 ... 1,430
Henry & Christopher, 3/15, gray litho/collage, 1967, p/s, Gemini bstp, full mrgs, S-22x30", lot 1014, SBY 5/13/89 OE ... 13,750
Hotel Acatlan: First Day; 50/70, clr litho/2 sheets wht HMP, 1985, p/s, TGL bstp, full mrgs, S-29x74", SBY 11/5/88 OE ... 26,400
Hotel Acatlan: Second Day, 76/98, clr litho/2 sheets TGL handmade, 1985, p/s, TGL bstp, S-29x78", lot 663, C-NY 11/1/88 ... 28,600
Hotel Acatlan: Second Day; clr litho/2 sheets wht TGL handmade, 1984-85, TGL bstp, S-29x76", lot 1040, SBY 5/13/89 OE ... 66,000
Hotel Acatlan: Second Day; 97/98, clr litho/2 sheets wht TGL, 1985, p/s, TGL bstp, S-29x76", lot 817, SBY 11/5/88 OE ... 33,000
Hotel Acatlan: Two Weeks Later; 12/98, clr litho/2 sheets HMP handmade, 1985, TGL bstp, 29x74" overall, SBY 5/13/89 OE ... 93,500
House Doodle, 32/60, etch, 1984, p/s, Gemini bstp, full mrgs, lt stn, 24x36", lot 671, SBY 2/23/89 OE ... 3,520
Illustration for the Six Fairy Tales From the Brothers Grimm, Ed C; 16/100, 1970, Petersburg, lot 796, SBY 11/5/88... 5,500
Image of Celia, State I; 8/10, clr litho/TGL handmade, 1986, Tyler Graphics bstp, S-50x39", lot 469, C-NY 5/11/88 ... 46,200
Image of Celia, 32/40, litho/scrpt/collage/TGL handmade, 1986, Tyler Graphics bstp, S-60x41", lot 468, C-NY 5/11/88 ... 71,500
Image of Celia, 6/40, litho/scrpt/collage/TGL handmade, 1986, p/s, TGL bstp, lt scr, S-60x41", lot 666, C-NY 11/1/88... 93,500
Image of Celia Study, 11/60, etch/aqua/litho/HMP handmade, 1986, Tyler Graphics bstp, S-23x18", lot 470, C-NY 5/11/88 OE ... 3,520
Image of Gregory, 17/75, clr litho/collage/TGL handmade, 1985, p/s, TGL bstp, 87x42" overall, lot 1041, SBY 5/13/89 OE ... 60,500
Image of Gregory, 51/75, litho/collage/2 sheets of TGL handmade, 1985, TGL bstp, S-98x42", lot 664, C-NY 11/1/88... 28,600
Image of Gregory, 61/75, clr litho/collage/2 sheets wht TGL, 1985, p/s, S-87x42", Tyler Graphics, lot 818, SBY 11/5/88 ... 30,800
Image of Ken, 14/20, litho/Moulin du Verger, 1987, p/s, dtd 85, TGL bstp, full mrgs, 28x21", lot 1046, SBY 5/13/89 ... 4,950
Image of Ken, 15/20, litho/Moulin du Verger, 1987, p/s, dtd 85, TGL bstp, full mrgs, 28x21", lot 823, C-NY 11/5/88 ... 3,300
Jungle Boy, 48/50, blk & red etch/aqua, 1964, full mrgs, lt stn/cr, 16x20", Assn Am Artists, lot 792, SBY 11/5/88 OE... 7,700
Lathe & Fire, 87/100, etch/aqua, 1970, p/s, full mrgs, P-6x7", lot 123, PHL 10/28/88... 400
Lightning, 47/98, clr litho/slksc, 1973, sgn/dtd in red crayon, Gemini bstp, full mrgs, 31x25", lot 800, SBY 11/5/88... 4,125
Litho of Water Made of Lines, a Green Wash, & a Blue Wash; 9/37, TGL bstp, full mrgs, 20x28", lot 1026, SBY 5/13/89 OE... 14,300
Lithograph of Water Made of Lines with Two Light Blue Washes, 15/35, 1978-80, TGL bstp, 20x28", lot 1027, SBY 5/13/89 OE ... 15,400

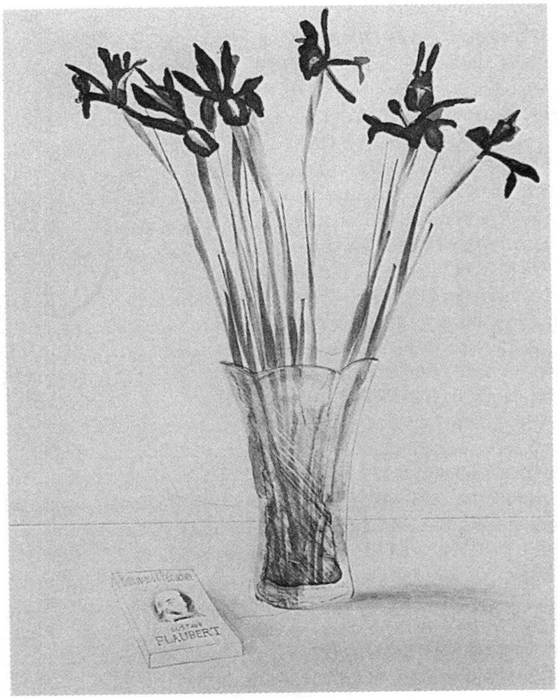

Still Life with Book, 72/88, clr litho/Arjomari, 1973, sgn in bl pencil, dtd/titled, 27x22", B/B 4/12/89; $24,750

Lithograph of Water Made of Lines with Two Light Blue Washes, APX, 1980, p/s, TGL bstp, 20x28", lot 804, SBY 11/5/88 OE ... 11,000
Lithograph of Water Made of Thick & Thin Lines,...; PPII, litho/TGL handmade, 1980, L-20x28", SBY 5/14/88 OE ... 9,625
Lithograph of Water Made of Thick & Thin Lines & a Light Blue & Dark Blue Wash, S-26x34", lot 460, C-NY 5/11/88 OE ... 7,150
Livingroom & Terrace, July 1986; 32/60, clr handmade print/Arches, 1986, S-17x22", Hockney, lot 1045, SBY 5/13/89 OE... 12,100
Livingroom & Terrace, July 1986; 43/60, hc print/2 sheets Arches, 1986, p/s, S-17x22", Hockney, lot 822, SBY 11/5/88 OE ... 8,800
Marguerites, 1/100, clr etch/aqua, 1973, p/s, full mrgs, 10x7", Petersburg, lot 1019, SBY 5/13/89 ... 9,900
My Bonnie Lies Over the Ocean, a/p, clr etch/aqua/collage, 1962, full mrgs, cr/stn/sl, 18x18", lot 790, SBY 11/5/88 OE... 12,100
My Pool & Terrace, 85/250, clr etch, 1984, p/s, full mrgs, lt cr, 24x26", lot 672, SBY 2/23/89 OE ... 4,400
Nicholas Wilder, 87/95, litho, 1976, p/s, Gemini bstp, lt cr, 33x25", lot 512, SBY 2/25/88 OE ... 1,430
Old Rink-Rank Threatens the Princess, 87/100, etch/aqua, 1970, p/s, full mrgs, P-9x11", lot 122, PHL 10/28/88 ... 800
Olympische Spiele Munchen 1972, 40/200, clr litho/Rives, 1970, p/s, full mrgs, L-35x26", lot 647, C-NY 11/1/88 OE ... 2,200
Pair: Ossie & Mo; Wooded Landscape; 47/75 & 99/100, etch, 1968/1969, 13x14"/16x11", Petersburg, SBY 5/14/88 OE ... 1,980
Panama Hat, 71/125, etch/aqua/Crisbrook handmade, 1972, p/s, 16x13", Petersburg/Brooke Alexander, lot 649, C-NY 11/1/88 ... 13,200
Panama Hat, 98/125, aqua, 1972, p/s, lt cr, S-17x13", Petersburg/Brooke Alexander, lot 799, SBY 11/5/88 ... 12,100
Pembroke Studio Interior, 44/70, clr litho/TGL handmade, 1985, p/s, TGL handmade, S-46x55", lot 1037, SBY 5/13/89 OE... 49,500
Pembroke Studio Interior, 55/70, clr litho/TGL handmade, 1985, p/s, Tyler Graphics bstp, S-46x55", SBY 5/14/88 OE ... 28,600
Pembroke Studio with Blue Chair & Lamp, 55/98, clr litho/wht HMP, 1985, p/s, TGL bstp, 17x20", lot 807A, SBY 11/5/88 OE ... 5,500
Pembroke Studio with Blue Chairs & Lamp, 6/98, clr litho/HMP handmade, 1985, TGL bstp, S-19x22", lot 657, C-NY 11/1/88... 4,950

Pembroke Studio with Blue Chairs & Lamp, 67/98, clr litho/HMP handmade, 1985, S-19x22", lot 463, C-NY 5/11/88 OE	5,280
Pembroke Studio with Blue Chairs & Lamp, 79/98, clr litho/wht HMP handmade, 1985, Tyler Graphics bstp, SBY 5/14/88 OE	5,775
Perspective Lesson, 25/50, clr litho/gray HMP handmade, 1985, p/s, dtd 1984, TGL bstp, 30x22", lot 1036, SBY 5/13/89 OE	9,900
Peter, 45/75, etch, 1969, p/s, full mrgs, lt rub/cr/sl, 27x21", Petersburg, lot 661, SBY 2/23/89 OE	1,320
Picture of Two Chairs, 23/60, clr etch/offset litho/HMP, 1986, p/s, TGL bstp, S-19x22", lot 820, SBY 11/5/88	4,125
Picture of Two Chairs, 6/60, clr etch/litho/HMP handmade, 1986, Tyler Graphics bstp, S-19x22", lot 467, C-NY 5/11/88 OE	2,200
Picture of Two Chairs, 6/60, etch/offset litho/wht HMP handmade, 1985-86, TGL bstp, 19x22", lot 1043, SBY 5/13/89 OE	9,350
Portfolio: Illustrations for Six Fairy Tales From the Brothers Grimm; 51/100, 1970, Petersburg, lot 795, SBY 11/5/88 OE	60,500
Portfolio: Rake's Progress; 37/50, 16 etch/aqua/Barcham Green, 1961-63, S-20x25", Alecto, lot 791, SBY 11/5/88 OE	7,700
Portrait of Felix Mann, 33/65, gray litho, 1969, p/s, lt stn, S-26x20", lot 663, SBY 2/23/89	1,980
Portrait of My Mother III, 9/25, clr litho, 1987, p/s, TGL bstp, full mrgs, 20x17", lot 673, SBY 2/23/89 OE	2,090
Potted Daffodils, APXIV, litho/cream BFK Rives, 1980, p/s, TGL bstp, lt cr, S-44x30", lot 806, SBY 11/5/88	14,850
Potted Daffodils, APXV, litho/BFK Rives, 1980, p/s, TGL bstp, S-44x30", lot 1028, SBY 5/13/89 OE	20,900
Potted Daffodils, 19/98, litho/BFK Rives, 1980, p/s, TGL bstp, full sheet, S-44x30", lot 654, C-NY 11/1/88	15,400
Pretty Tulips, 107/200, clr litho, 1969, p/s, S-29x20", Petersburg, lot 1015, SBY 5/13/89 OE	34,100
Pretty Tulips, 116/200, clr litho, 1969/1970, p/s, titled, lt cr, S-29x20", Petersburg, lot 797, SBY 11/5/88 OE	19,800
Rain, Pl 2, 91/98, clr litho/Arjomari, 1973, sgn in gr pencil, Gemini bstp, full mrgs, 39x32", lot 650, C-NY 11/1/88 UE	5,500
Red Celia, 40/82, red toned litho/HMP handmade, 1985, p/s, Tyler Graphics bstp, S-30x22", SBY 5/14/88 OE	23,100
Red Celia, 74/82, red litho/wht HMP handmade, 1985, p/s, TGL bstp, S-30x22", lot 1033, SBY 5/13/89 OE	45,100
Red Flowers & Green Leaves, Separate, May 1988; 24/70, clr print/2 sheets Arches, 1988, 14x17", lot 674, SBY 2/23/89 OE	9,900
Red Flowers & Green Leaves, Separate, May 1988; 63/70, a/bstp, 14x17", Metropolitan Mus, lot 1047, SBY 5/13/89 OE	14,300
Rue de Seine, a/p, etch, 1971, p/s, full mrgs, 21x17", Petersburg, lot 798, SBY 11/5/88 OE	24,200
Rue de Seine, 38/150, etch, 1971, p/s, dtd 1972, full mrgs, lt cr, P-21x17", Petersburg, SBY 5/14/88 OE	20,350
Rue de Seine, 57/100, etch/J Green mould made, p/s, dtd 72, P-21x17", Petersburg, lot 648, C-NY 11/1/88 OE	13,200
Small Study of Lightning, 28/75, clr litho, 1973, p/s, Gemini bstp, full mrgs, lt cr, 13x10", lot 664, SBY 2/23/89 OE	2,860
Still Life, 45/75, etch, 1969, p/s, 1969, full mrgs, 21x27", Petersburg, lot 662, SBY 2/23/89 OE	5,225
Study for Rumpelstiltskin; 2/15, 4 etch/aqua on 1 sheet, 1961, p/s, full mrgs, lt rub, 5x14" overall, SBY 2/23/89 OE	2,750
Suite: Rake's Progress; 23/50, 16 etch/aqua/Barcham Green handmade, 1961-63, 20x24", Ed Alecto, lot 113, SBY 5/13/89	66,000
Three Kings & a Queen, ed of about 50, etch/aqua/English handmade, p/s, lt stn/cr/sl, P-9x25", lot 448, C-NY 5/11/88	1,980
Tulips, a/p, ed of 16, etch, 1973, p/s, full mrgs, lt cr, 27x21", Petersburg, lot 801, SBY 11/5/88	8,800
Tulips, 13/75, etch/German mould made Museum Board, 1973, p/s, full mrgs, P-27x21", Petersburg, lot 651, C-NY 11/1/88	7,700
Two Pembroke Studio Chairs, 13/98, clr litho/wht HMP, 1985, p/s, dtd 84, TGL bstp, full mrgs, 16x19", SBY 11/5/88	4,400
Two Pembroke Studio Chairs, 68/98, clr litho/HMP handmade, p/s, Tyler Graphic bstp, S-19x22", lot 464, C-NY 5/11/88 OE	4,400
Two Pembroke Studio Chairs, 83/98, clr litho/wht HMP handmade, 1985, Tyler Graphics bstp, L-16x19", SBY 5/14/88 OE	4,675
Two Pembroke Studio Chairs, 84/98, clr litho/HMP handmade, 1985, p/s, TGL bstp, S-19x22", lot 658, C-NY 11/1/88	4,620
Two Pembroke Studio Chairs, 89/98, clr litho, 1985, p/s, TGL bstp, full mrgs, 16x19", lot 1035, SBY 5/13/89 OE	8,800
Two Vases in the Louvre, 43/75, etch/aqua, 1974, p/s, full mrgs, lt cr/stn, 29x29", Petersburg, lot 1022, SBY 5/13/89 OE	42,900
Two Vases of Cut Flowers & a Liriope Plant, PPII, litho/Toyoshi 80, 1979, Gemini bstp, 42x59", lot 3021, B/B 4/19/88	8,800
Two Vases of Cut Flowers & a Liriope Plant, 79/98, litho/Toyoshi 80, 1981, Gemini bstp, S-42x59", lot 1029, SBY 5/13/89	27,500
Tyler Dining Room, 4/98, clr litho/TGL handmade, 1985, p/s, Tyler Graphics bstp, S-33x40", lot 465, C-NY 5/11/88 OE	17,600
Tyler Dining Room, 45/98, clr litho/wht TGL handmade, 1985, p/s, full mrgs, cr, L-29x37", Tyler Graphics, SBY 5/14/88 OE	15,125
Tyler Dining Room, 68/98, clr litho/TGL handmade, p/s, TGL bstp, S-32x40", lot 659, C-NY 11/1/88	17,600
Tyler Dining Room, 75/98, clr litho/wht TGL handmade, 1985, p/s, TGL bstp, full mrgs, 29x37", lot 812, SBY 11/5/88 OE	16,500
Vase & Flowers, 7/75, etch/Crisbrook handmade, 1969, p/s, full mrgs, lt fox, S-36x28", Petersburg, lot 449, C-NY 5/11/88	9,900
Views of Hotel III, 62/80, clr litho/TGL handmade, 1985, p/s, TGL bstp, S-49x39", lot 662, C-NY 11/1/88	24,200
Views of Hotel Well I, APXIV/XIV, clr litho/TGL handmade, 1985, p/s, TGL bstp, full mrgs, S-27x47", lot 814, SBY 11/5/88	19,800
Views of Hotel Well I, 3/75, clr litho/TGL handmade, 1985, Tyler Graphics bstp, S-31x42", lot 466, C-NY 5/11/88 OE	17,600
Views of Hotel Well I, 47/75, clr litho/TGL handmade, 1985, p/s, TGL bstp, S-31x42", lot 660, C-NY 11/1/88	19,800
Views of Hotel Well II, 18/80, clr litho/TGL handmade, 1985, p/s, TGL bstp, full mrgs, 46x35", lot 816, SBY 11/5/88 OE	37,400
Views of Hotel Well II, 30/75, clr litho/TGL handmade, 1985, p/s, TGL bstp, S-25x32", lot 661, C-NY 11/1/88	22,000
Views of Hotel Well II, 60/75, clr litho/wht HMP, 1985, p/s, TGL bstp, full mrgs, S-30x37", lot 815, SBY 11/5/88	19,800
Views of Hotel Well III, 57/80, clr litho/wht TGL handmade, 1985, p/s, Tyler Graphics bstp, L-46x35", SBY 5/14/88 OE	23,100
Views of Hotel Well III, 6/80, clr litho/TGL handmade, 1985, p/s, TGL bstp, full mrgs, 46x35", lot 1039, SBY 5/13/89 OE	99,000
Walking Past Two Chairs, PPII, clr litho/wht TGL, 1984-86, p/s, 38x46", Tyler Graphics, lot 819, SBY 11/5/88 OE	51,700
Walking Past Two Chairs, 25/38, clr litho/wht TGL handmade, 1984-86, p/s, TGL bstp, 28x46", lot 1031, SBY 5/13/89 OE	82,500
Walking Past Two Chairs, 6/38, litho/scrpt/TGL handmade/plexiglas, 1984-86, 22x40", Tyler Graphics, lot 665, C-NY 11/1/88	46,200
Weather Series: Mist; a/p, ed of 3, clr litho/Arjomari, 1972, Gemini bstp, full mrgs, lt sl/cr, 29x25", SBY 5/13/89 OE	17,600
Weather Series: Wind; 49/98, clr litho, 1973, sgn/titled, Gemini bstp, full mrgs, cr, 31x24", lot 1018, SBY 5/13/89 OE	11,000
White Porcelain, a/p, XV/XVI, etch/offset litho/HMP handmade, TGL bstp, S-19x22", lot 667, C-NY 11/1/88 OE	11,000
White Porcelain, 17/80, clr etch/offset litho, 1986, p/s, TGL bstp, S-19x22", lot 821, SBY 11/5/88 OE	11,000

HODGKIN, Howard (British, 1932-)

After Lunch, 68/100, sftgr etch/aqua/Velin Arches mould made, 1980, intl, S-22x30", Petersburg, lot 668, C-NY 11/1/88	770
Alexander Stree, 85/90, clr litho, p/s, 14x24", SLK 4/7/89	320
Birthday Party, 21/50, clr litho, p/s, 1977, 16x24", SLK 4/7/89	225
David's Pool, 19/100, sftgr etch/aqua/Hahnemuhl, 1979/1985, p/s, S-25x31", Petersburg, lot 825, SBY 11/5/88 OE	5,500
David's Pool, 38/100, sftgr etch/aqua/Hahnemuhl, 1979/1985, intl, S-25x31", Petersburg, lot 1048, SBY 5/13/89 OE	9,350
David's Pool, 49/100, sftgr etch/aqua/cream Hahnemuhl, 1979, intl, S-25x31", Petersburg, lot 675, SBY 2/23/89	5,050
David's Pool at Night, 37/100, sftgr etch/aqua/wht Hahnemuhl, 1985, intl, S-25x31", Petersburg, SBY 5/14/88	1,430
For John Constable, 7/100, clr litho, p/s, 1976, 18x22", SLK 4/7/89	190
Furnished Room, 64/100, clr sftgr etch/aqua, 1977, p/s, lt cr, S-21x27", Petersburg, lot 683, SBY 5/14/88	1,100
Moonlight, 17/100, clr litho/2 sheets buff BFK Rives, 1980, intl, 44x56", Bernard Jacobson, SBY 5/14/88 OE	7,425

Nick, 64/100, clr sftgr etch/aqua, 1977, p/s, full mrgs, lt cr mrg, 18x22", Petersburg Press, SBY 5/14/88 OE ... **3,410**
Pair: Jarid's Porch; Nick's Room; 64/100, clr litho, 1977, p/s, S-21x24", Petersburg, lot 684, SBY 5/14/88 ... **1,540**
Red Palm, 23/85, hc litho, 1986, intl/dtd, lt cr, S-42x49", Waddington, lot 1050, SBY 5/13/89 OE ... **6,050**
Sand, 22/50, clr litho w/hc watercolor, 1983, intl, S-31x40", Petersburg, SBY 5/14/88 ... **2,475**
Set: Indian View A-L; ed of 75, 12 clr scpt, p/s, Kelpra Studio stp, 1971, 23x31", SLK 4/7/89 ... **525**
Storm, a/p, clr litho, 1977, p/s, S-21x24", Petersburg, lot 824, SBY 11/5/88 OE ... **3,575**
Storm, 64/100, clr litho, 1977, p/s, S-21x24", Petersburg, SBY 5/14/88 OE ... **3,190**
Two To Go, 84/100, grays & blk litho/Velin Arches, 1982, intl, 36x48", Bernard Jacobson, lot 669, C-NY 11/1/88 ... **1,210**

HOEFNAGLE, Joris (George); after (Flemish, 1545-1601)
Blanmont au Pays de Vavge en Loreyne, clr engr, lt cr, 11x18", lot 80, FAP 2/24/89 UE ... **80**

HOERNES, T.K.
New York City From Central Park, 48/250, clr etch, p/s, 21x25", lot 29, GAI 3/3/89 ... **90**

HOERTZ, Frederick J. (American, 1959-)
Your Work Means Vistory, Build Another One; clr litho/poster paper, ca 1918, laid down, 37x28", lot 172, FAP 2/24/89 OE ... **173**

HOFER, Karl (German, 1878-1955)
Pair: Embracing Couple; Three Women; ed of 60, litho, 1923, p/s, full mrgs, 19x13", lot 116, SWN 6/15/89 ... **605**

HOFFMAN, Irwin (20th C)
Pair: Mexican Folk Band; Barber Shop; ed of 250, cream laid paper, 1936 & 1938, 8x11", Assn Am Artists, B/B 2/16/88 ... **275**

HOGARTH, William; after (British, 1697-1764)
Set of 6: Marriage a la Mode; engr & restrikes, 14x18", lot 19, FAP 2/24/89 ... **200**

HOLBEIN, Hans; after (18th C)
In His Majesty's Collection, stpl engr/laid paper, 1793, lt cr/stn, 14x10", Chamberlaine, lot 2807, B/B 4/19/88 ... **605**

HOLLAR, Wenceslaus (Bohemian, 1607-1677)
American Indian, 2nd state, etch, 1645, pl/s, 4x3", lot 85, SWN 12/1/88 UE ... **195**

HOMER, Winslow (American, 1836-1910)
Eight Bells, #11, ed of about 100, etch/stiff Japan, 1887, p/s, lt cr/tr, unfr, S-25x32", Klackner, SBY 5/12/88 OE ... **20,900**
Eight Bells, brn-blk etch/cream Japan, 1887, lg mrgs, lt stn/tr, S-24x29", lot 31, SBY 2/23/89 OE ... **13,750**
Eight Bells, ed of about 100, etch/vellum, 1887, anchor between 2 dials remarque, 19x24", Klackner, lot 234, SBY 5/11/89 ... **30,800**
Perils of the Sea, brn-blk etch/vellum, 1888, p/s, remarques, lt fox/stn/rpr tr, P-13x20", lot 27, C-NY 5/11/88 ... **19,800**
Saved, etch/simile Japan, 1889, inscr GWH Ritchie imp, lt sl/cr, S-26x35", lot 28, SBY 11/3/88 ... **9,350**
Yachting Girl, body clr litho/thick wove paper, 1880, sgn/bstp, lt fox/stn mrg, laid down, S-16x21", C-NY 1/22/88 OE ... **52,800**

HOMER, Winslow; after (American, 1836-1910)
Pair: Snap-the-Whip; Army of the Potomac-Sharpshooter on Picket Duty; wood engr/nspt, 1873/1862, C-NY 1/22/88 OE ... **660**

HOPFER, Daniel (14th C)
Last Judgement, 2nd state, etch, ca 1525, lt fox/stn, 12x17", lot 72, SBY 5/11/89 ... **1,430**

HOPPER, Edward (American, 1882-1967)
American Landscape, etch/wht wove paper, 1920, p/s, titled, full mrgs, lt stn/sl, 7x12", lot 31, SBY 2/25/88 OE ... **19,800**
Cat Boat, etch/wove paper, 1922, p/s, full mrgs, gstn mrgs/verso, lt lstn, P-8x10", C-NY 1/22/88 OE ... **27,500**
East Side Interior, ed of up to 100, etch, 1922, p/s, full mrgs, lt stn/fox mrg & verso, 8x10", lot 235, SBY 5/11/89 OE ... **39,600**
East Side Interior, ed of up to 100, etch, 1922, p/s, lg mrgs, lt stn/fox, 8x10", lot 29, SBY 11/3/88 OE ... **23,100**
Monhegan Boat, etch, 1919, p/s, inscr, full mrgs, lt tp stn/glue to mrg corners, P-7x9", SBY 5713 ... **28,600**
Night in the Park, ed of about 100, etch, 1921, p/s, full mrgs, lt stn, 7x8", lot 236, SBY 5/11/89 OE ... **34,100**
Night Shadows, ed of about 500, etch/wove paper, 1921, p/s, full mrgs, lt stn, P-7x8", lot 185, C-NY 1/19/89 OE ... **7,150**
Night Shadows, ed of at least 500, etch/wove paper, 1921/1924, p/s, unfr, P-7x8", New Republic, C-NY 1/22/88 OE ... **7,150**
Night Shadows, ed of between 500-600, etch/cream wove paper, 1921, p/s, lt cr, S-10x11", lot 31A, SBY 2/23/89 OE ... **12,100**
Night Shadows, ed of between 500-600, etch/cream wove paper, 1921, p/s, rpr tr, S-9x10", lot 30, SBY 11/3/88 OE ... **14,300**
Night Shadows, ed of 500-600, etch/cream wove paper, 1921, p/s, lt stn, 7x8", lot 237, SBY 5/11/89 OE ... **12,100**
Night Shadows, etch, 1921, p/s, full mrgs, 7x8", lot 118, WG 10/19/89 ... **11,000**

HORNYANSKY, Nicholas (1896-1965)
Lips Are Silent (France), 20/250, clr aqua, p/s, titled, 12x16", lot 880, WAD 6/12/89 ... **425**
Mill Stream in Winter, clr aqua, p/s, titled, 4x4", lot 1208, WAD 11/28/88 ... **310**

HUET, Jean Baptiste; after (French, 1745-1811)
Pygmalion & Galatea, by Jubier, aqua, P-10x7", C-E 11/15/88 ... **66**

HUGGINS, William John (British, 1781-1845)
Ships of the General Steam Navigation Company, hc litho, 19x28", lot 12, GAI 5/26/89 ... **475**
South Sea Whale Fishery, by Sutherland, etch/aqua/wove paper, 1825, lt fox/rub/sl/stn, P-17x22", lot 84, C-NY 1/19/89 UE ... **220**
South Sea Whale Fishery, engr, dtd 1825, no size given, RAB 8/1/88 UE ... **200**

HUGGINS, William John; after (British, 1781-1845)
South Sea Fishery, aqua/engr, full mrgs, lt fox, 1825, orig fr, no size given, RAB 11/10/88 OE ... **800**
South Sea Whale Fishery, litho, fox, laid down on cardboard, no size given, RAB 11/10/88 ... **350**

HUNDERTWASSER, Friedensreich (Austrian, 1929-)
Journey I, HC1/14, clr etch, 1967, sgn in ink, full mrgs, 13x9", Lazar-Vernet, lot 282, SBY 2/23/89 OE ... **2,310**
Journey II & Travel by Rail, 117/267, clr litho, 1967, sgn in ink, S-26x20", Krugier & Moos, lot 220, SBY 2/25/88 ... **1,430**
Occidental, 57/220, clr etch/aqua, 1977, sgn in pen, full mrgs, lt fox, 20x13", Gruener Janura AG, lot 522, SBY 5/11/89 ... **1,540**
One of the Five Seaman il Marinaio, 149/250, clr slksc/Red Indian brn paper, 1975, S-34x24", lot 521, SBY 5/11/89 ... **1,540**
Shadow of the Stars, 134/150, clr litho, 1967, sgn in ink, full mrgs, 17x21", Krugier & Moos/Kunstverein, SBY 2/25/88 OE ... **1,320**
Untitled (Venzia), 111/250, clr & metallic wc/wove paper, 1968, sgn in ink, tp to mat, 22x18", lot 2857, B/B 2/16/88 ... **1,870**

HUNT, Bryan (American, 1947-)
Fall with Bend, AP VI, etch/aqua, 1979, Crown Point bstp, full mrgs, P-84x15", lot 471, C-NY 5/11/88 ... **5,500**

HUNT, William Morris; after (American, 1824-1879)
Bugler, by DC Fabronius, litho/laid India, 1863, rpr tr mrgs, lt fox/stn, 17x14", lot 545A, SBY 1/28/88 ... **330**

HURD, Peter (American, 1904-)

Dona Nestorita, ed of about 50, litho, 1942, p/s, titled, 13x11", Assn Am Artists, lot 87, SWN 12/1/88 360
Late Call, ed of unknown size, litho/wove paper, 1949, p/s, full mrgs, lt stn/fox, L-14x18", lot 186, C-NY 1/19/89 OE 1,210
Sermon From Revelations, litho, p/s, titled, 14x19", lot 212, WG 10/19/88 400

HUTCHINSON, H.S.; & CO.

Sperm Whaling with Its Varieties, litho, copyright mk, 1901, orig fr, lg folio, RAB 11/10/88 400

HYDE, Helen (American, 1868-1919)

Pair: Dwarf Trees; New Brooms; #18 & #181, clr wc/Japan, 1910, p/s, lt stn/sl, laid down, lot 187, C-NY 1/19/89 308
Sacred Calf, In the Bazaar at Agra; clr woodblock on tissue, sgn/dtd/titled, unfr, L-9x10", RWS 4/22/89 225

ICART, Louis (French, 1888-1950)

Angry Steed (Le Coursier en Colere), a/p, etch/drypt, ca 1917, p/s, trm mrgs, 16x10", lot 293, SBY 12/12/88 1,100
Apache Dance, clr etch/drypt, 1929, p/s, a/bstp, 21x14", lot 300, SBY 12/12/88 1,430
At Water's Edge, photogr, ca 1947, copyright, 18x14", Draegar Imp, C-E 9/16/88 286
Attic Room, photogr, ca 1946, artist copyright, 13x16", Draeger Imp, C-E 9/16/88 198
Autumn Leaves, #350, clr etch/drypt, ca 1926, sgn/bstp, 20x16", C-E 6/16/88 OE 1,320
Ballerina (Repos), clr etch/drypt, 1935, p/s, a/bstp, 15x19", lot 326, SBY 12/12/88 OE 2,530
Bathing Beauties (Baigneuses), 4/170, clr etch/aqua, 1931, p/s, a/bstp, laid down, P-26x18", lot 38, PHL 6/16/88 OE 2,100
Behind the Fan, a/p, clr etch/drypt, 1922, p/s, 15x20", L'Estampe Moderne/Bresler, lot 302, SBY 12/12/88 660
Belle Rose, clr etch/drypt, ca 1933, p/s, a/bstp, 17x21", lot 453, C-E 9/20/89 2,860
Belle Rose, clr etch/drypt, ca 1933, sgn, a/bstp, 17x21", C-E 9/16/88 OE 1,870
Belle Rose, clr etch/drypt, 1933, p/s, bstp, stn, 17x21", Icart Soc, SBY 6/10/88 880

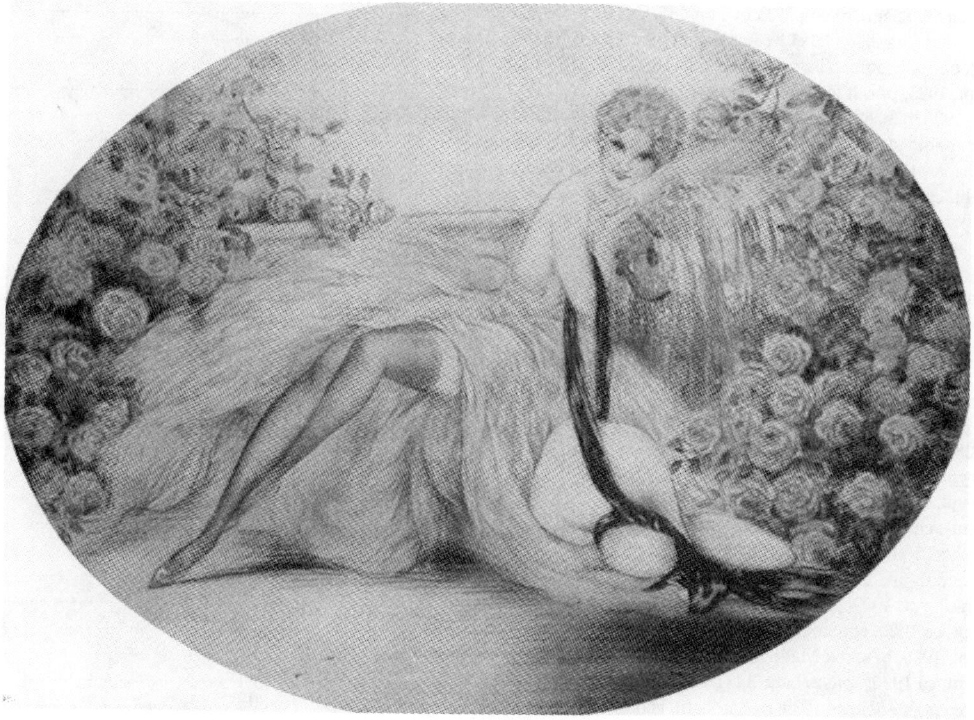

Belle Rose, clr etch/drypt, ca 1933, p/s, a/bstp, 17x21", lot 453, C-E 9/20/89: $2,860

Bird of Prey, 66/100, clr etch/drypt, ca 1918, p/s, cr, 19x13", SBY 6/10/88 770
Bird Seller, 270/500, clr etch/drypt, ca 1929, sgn/bstp, 19x14", C-E 6/16/88 OE 1,210
Black Lace, #118, clr etch/drypt, ca 1924, 12x9", C-E 3/24/88 OE 880
Black Mask, clr etch/drypt, ca 1933, sgn/bstp, 13x9", C-E 6/16/88 OE 1,540
Black Shawl, #240, clr etch/drypt, ca 1925, p/s, 17x13", lot 454, C-E 9/20/89 1,540
Black Shawl, clr etch/drypt, ca 1925, sgn, 17x13", C-E 9/16/88 352
Blue Alcove, clr etch/drypt, ca 1929, p/s, a/bstp, 11x13", lot 455, C-E 9/20/89 1,870
Blue Bandana, #173, clr etch/drypt, ca 1925, sgn, a/bstp, 14x18", lot 456, C-E 9/20/89 OE 2,420
Blue Bonnet, ca 1930, titled, 16x20", lot 451, C-E 9/20/89 240
Blue Buddah, #311, clr etch/drypt, ca 1924, 16x21", C-E 3/24/88 990
Blue Buddha, drypt/etch, ca 1934, p/s, L-26x21", lot 1006, DM 2/19/88 1,000
Bluebirds, #17, clr etch/drypt, 1925, p/s, 19x15", Graveurs Modernes, SBY 6/10/88 990
Broken Jug, #165, clr etch/drypt, ca 1922, p/s, 18x13", lot 457, C-E 9/20/89 1,650
Carmen, #162, clr etch/drypt, ca 1927, sgn, a/bstp, 20x14", lot 458, C-E 9/20/89 OE 1,650
Carmen, #420, clr etch/drypt, 1927, p/s, bstp, 21x14", Graveurs Modernes, SBY 6/10/88 1,100
Carmen, #48, clr etch/drypt, ca 1929, sgn, a/bstp, lt fox mrgs, 20x13", C-E 9/16/88 1,210

Carmen, clr etch/drypt, ca 1927, sgn, a/bstp, 20x14", C-E 3/24/88	**935**
Casanova, #487, clr etch/drypt, ca 1928, sgn, a/bstp, 21x14", C-E 9/16/88	**1,540**
Casanova, clr etch/drypt, ca 1928, sgn, 21x14", lot 459, C-E 9/20/89	**1,650**
Casanova, clr etch/drypt, 1928, p/s, bstp, 21x14", Art Devambez, SBY 6/10/88	**990**
Casanova, 406/500, clr etch/drypt, 1928, p/s, a/bstp, lt stn, 21x14", Ed d'Art Devambez, lot 289, SBY 12/12/88	**1,210**
Chanel, clr litho, 10x13", lot 973, LH 3/20/88 OE	**300**
Chestnut Vendor, #A2, clr etch/drypt, ca 1928, sgn, a/bstp, 19x14", C-E 9/16/88 OE	**1,045**
Choice Morsel, clr etch/drypt, ca 1927, sgn, a/bstp, 18x14", C-E 9/16/88	**1,045**
Coach, #395, clr etch/drypt, p/s, a/bstp, lt stn, 22x18", lot 290, SBY 12/12/88 OE	**1,650**
Conchita, clr etch/drypt, 1929, p/s, a/bstp, 21x14", lot 291, SBY 12/12/88	**1,100**
Conchita, clr etch/drypt, 1929, p/s, bstp, 20x14", SBY 6/10/88	**880**
Coursing II, clr etch/drypt, ca 1929, sgn, a/bstp, 16x26", C-E 3/24/88	**2,970**
Coursing II, E361/500, clr etch/drypt, ca 1929, sgn, a/bstp, 16x26", lot 460, C-E 9/20/89	**5,500**
Coursing II, 2/182, clr etch/drypt, 1929, p/s, a/bstp, 16x26", lot 295, SBY 12/12/88 OE	**4,675**
Coursing II, 327/500, clr etch/drypt, 1929, p/s, bstp, fox, glued to mat, 16x26", SBY 6/10/88	**2,860**
Coursing II, 491/500, etch/drypt, 1929, p/s, a/bstp, 16x26", lot 294, SBY 12/12/89 OE	**5,775**
Coursing III, clr etch/drypt, ca 1930, sgn, a/bstp, NY Graphic Soc bstp, 16x25", C-E 9/16/88	**4,950**
Crossing, #162, clr etch/drypt, ca 1926, sgn, a/bstp, 19x14", lot 461, C-E 9/20/89 OE	**1,760**
Dalila, a/p, clr etch/drypt, ca 1929, sgn, a/bstp, 21x14", lot 462, C-E 9/20/89	**1,650**
Dear Friends, clr etch/drypt, ca 1929, sgn, a/bstp, 14x11", C-E 3/24/88	**1,210**
Don Juan, #211, clr etch/drypt, 1928, sgn, a/bstp, lt stn, 21x14", Devambez, lot 303, SBY 12/12/88	**1,210**
Don Juan, A112/500, clr etch/drypt, ca 1928, sgn, a/bstp, 21x14", C-E 9/16/88	**770**
Don Juan, clr etch/drypt, ca 1928, sgn, a/bstp, 21x14", lot 465, C-E 9/20/89	**1,430**
Don Juan, clr etch/drypt, 1928, p/s, bstp, 21x14", Art Devambez, SBY 6/10/88	**880**
Dreaming, clr etch/drypt, ca 1935, sgn, a/bstp, 28x18", lot 466, C-E 9/20/89	**4,620**
Elephants, 142, etch/drypt, 1925, p/s, lt fox/stn, laid down, matted, unfr, L-17x12", Les Graveurs, RWS 3/16/89	**1,200**
Eve, #110, clr etch/drypt, 1928, p/s, a/bstp, trm mrgs, stn, laid down, 14x20", Jaubert, lot 305, SBY 12/12/88	**1,100**
Eve, A164/500, Eve, clr etch/drypt, ca 1928, sgn, a/bstp, 14x20", C-E 9/16/88	**1,430**
Eve, clr etch/drypt/rice paper, 1928, p/s, 13x20", Jaubert et Cie, SBY 6/10/88	**1,100**
Fair Dancer, clr etch/drypt, ca 1939, sgn, a/bstp, 19x22", lot 467, C-E 9/20/89	**2,090**
Fair Dancer, clr etch/drypt, 1939, p/s, bstp, laid down, 20x23", SBY 6/10/88	**1,760**
Fair Dancer, 144/500, clr etch/drypt, 20x14", lot 40, FAP 2/24/89	**875**
Fair Dancer (Music Hall), #289, clr etch/drypt, p/s, 20x23", lot 320, SBY 12/12/88 OE	**2,475**
Fall, Fall; #206, clr etch/drypt, ca 1920, sgn/Estampe Moderne bstp, 16x11", C-E 9/16/88 OE	**1,100**
Fanny & Pussycat, #203, clr etch/drypt, ca 1927, sgn, a/bstp, 18x17", lot 468, C-E 9/20/89	**4,620**
Farewell, a/p, etch/drypt, ca 1927, p/s, a/bstp, 15x20", lot 283, SBY 12/12/88 OE	**1,320**
Faust, #278, clr etch/drypt, ca 1928, sgn, a/bstp, 21x13", C-E 9/16/88	**1,210**
Faust, #301, clr etch/drypt, 1928, p/s, a/bstp, 21x24", lot 306, SBY 12/12/88	**1,100**
Faust, #434, clr etch/drypt, sgn/titled, a/bstp, 21x13", C-E 3/24/88	**1,320**
Faust, clr etch/drypt, 1928, p/s, bstp, 21x14", Graveurs Modernes, SBY 6/10/88	**1,485**
Faust, E/124, clr etch/drypt, ca 1928, sgn/bstp, 23x13", C-E 6/16/88 OE	**1,320**
Faust, E/393, clr etch/drypt, 1928, 13x21", lot 130, WG 10/19/88	**1,000**
Favorite (Brebis et Agneau), clr etch/drypt, ca 1926, p/s, a/bstp, fox, 16x16", lot 286, SBY 12/12/88	**1,320**
Fidelity, drypt/etch, p/s, 20x15", lot 13, DM 10/14/88	**1,000**
Findande, mortally wounded figure against Findland's flag; aqua/drypt/rlt, 1940, a/bstp, 14x21", lot 18, RWS 9/29/88	**1,000**
Four Dears, #108, clr etch/drypt, 1929, p/s, full mrgs, 22x16", Estampe Moderne, SBY 6/10/88	**1,320**
Four Dears, clr etch/drypt, ca 1929, sgn, a/bstp, 21x15", C-E 3/24/88	**1,320**
Four Dears, clr etch/drypt, 1929, p/s, mk Made in France, full mrg, lt tr, 22x16", Estampe Moderne, SBY 6/10/88	**1,320**
French Doll, clr etch/drypt, ca 1926, sgn, a/bstp, 14x18", C-E 9/16/88	**825**
Gay Senorita, 241, aqua/drypt/stencil, ca 1939, p/s, a/bstp, laid down, L-18x22", Icart Studios, RWS 3/16/89	**1,200**
Gay Trio, clr etch/drypt, ca 1936, sgn, a/bstp, 20x12", C-E 9/16/88 OE	**5,280**
Girl in Crinoline, clr etch/drypt, ca 1937, sgn, 23x19", lot 469, C-E 9/20/89 OE	**2,200**
Girl in Crinoline, clr etch/drypt, ca 1937, sgn/bstp, 23x19", C-E 6/16/88	**1,540**
Girl in Crinoline, clr etch/drypt, 1937, p/s, a/bstp, 23x20", Icart Soc, lot 317, SBY 12/12/88 OE	**2,475**
Golden Veil, clr etch/drypt, ca 1930, sgn, a/bstp, 15x20", NY Graphic Soc, C-E 9/16/88 OE	**2,200**
Golden Veil, clr etch/drypt, ca 1930, sgn/bstp, 15x20", C-E 6/16/88 OE	**2,200**
Gossip, 16/350, clr etch/drypt, ca 1926, sgn, a/bstp, 17x13", lot 470, C-E 9/20/89 OE	**1,650**
Grand Eve, clr etch/drypt, ca 1934, sgn, a/bstp, 31x20", C-E 9/16/88 OE	**22,000**
Group of 4: Bookplates, La Nuit et Le Moment; clr etch, ca 1946, p/s, 8x5", lot 454, C-E 9/16/88	**1,045**
Guardians (Berger et Bergeres), clr etch/drypt, 1936, p/s, a/bstp, 16x16", Icart Soc, lot 285, SBY 12/12/88	**1,760**
Gust of Wind, clr etch/drypt, ca 1925, sgn/bstp, 21x18", C-E 6/16/88 OE	**1,650**
Gust of Wind, clr etch/drypt, 1925, p/s, scr, 22x18", Graveurs Modernes, SBY 6/10/88	**1,100**
Hiver, clr etch, sgn/titled, 9x7", lot 380, FB 5/28/89	**1,200**
Homage to Guynemere, 12/100, clr etch/drypt, ca 1918, sgn, 19x15", C-E 9/16/88	**2,090**
Homage to Guynemere, 12/100, clr etch/drypt, 1918, p/s, fox, 20x16", SBY 6/10/88	**1,540**
Hop La, #244, clr etch/drypt, 1935, p/s, bstp/titled, 9x12", Icart Soc, SBY 6/10/88	**2,200**
Hydrangeas, clr etch/drypt, ca 1929, sgn, a/bstp, 17x21", lot 471, C-E 9/20/89 OE	**2,090**
Hydrangeas, clr etch/drypt, ca 1929, sgn/bstp, 21x17", C-E 6/16/88 OE	**1,210**
Hydrangeas, clr etch/drypt/aqua, 1929, a/bstp, full mrgs, lt stn, laid down, L-16x20", Icart, lot 15, RWS 9/8/89 OE	**2,200**
Hydrangeas, drypt/etch, 1929, p/s, 21x17" oval, lot 137, WG 1/19/89	**1,100**
Hydrangeas, etch/drypt, p/s, bstp/dtd Paris 1929, laid down on board, oval, 17x21", SLK 2/11/89	**3,500**

In Homage to Beethoven, photogr, ca 1946, artist copyright, 13x16", Draeger Imp, C-E 9/16/88	**209**
Intimacy, #108, clr etch/drypt, sgn/bstp, 16x18", C-E 6/16/88 OE	**1,650**
Japanese Garden, #260, clr etch/drypt, ca 1931, sgn, 21x18", lot 472, C-E 9/20/89	**1,430**
Jitterbug, La Ronde des Danses; 38/50, clr etch/drypt, ca 1938, p/s, 7x6", lot 308, SBY 12/12/88	**825**
Joy of Life, drypt/etch, ca 1929, p/s, L-25x16", lot 1007, DM 2/19/88 OE	**3,000**
L'Automne, clr etch, sgn/titled, 9x7", lot 379, FB 5/28/89	**1,100**
La Vie Seins, drypt/etch, sgn, 8x10", lot 407, FB 5/28/89	**450**
Lady of the Camelias, a/p, clr etch/drypt, ca 1927, sgn, a/bstp, 17x21", lot 396,, C-E 3/24/88	**1,100**
Lady of the Camelias, clr etch/drypt, ca 1927, sgn, 17x21", lot 462, C-E 9/20/89	**2,090**
Lady of the Camelias, clr etch/drypt, ca 1927, sgn/bstp, 17x20", C-E 6/16/88 OE	**1,320**
Lady of the Camelias, E149, clr etch/drypt, ca 1927, sgn, a/bstp, lt stn, 17x21", lot 464, C-E 9/20/89	**1,430**
Lady of the Camelias, H273/500, clr etch/drypt, 1927, p/s, bstp, 21x17", Graveurs Modernes, SBY 6/10/88 OE	**1,265**
Lady of the Camelias (La Dame aux Camelias), etch/drypt, p/s, bstp/dtd 1927, ls to corner, 17x21", SLK 4/7/89	**525**
Laughing, A/151, clr etch, ca 1939, sgn, a/bstp, 12x17", C-E 3/24/88	**1,430**
Laughing, photogr, ca 1946, artist's copyright, 13x16", Draegar Imp, C-E 9/16/88	**264**
Laughing (Rieuse), #A/217, clr etch/drypt, 1930, p/s, a/bstp, 12x17", Icart, lot 327, SBY 12/12/88 OE	**2,475**
Laziness, #171, clr etch/drypt, 1925, p/s, 16x20", Graveurs Modernes, SBY 6/10/88 OE	**2,200**
Laziness, a/p, clr etch/drypt, ca 1925, sgn, 15x19", lot 405, C-E 3/24/88	**1,650**
Leda & the Swan, #119, clr etch/drypt (lacquered), ca 1934, sgn/bstp, S-21x31", C-E 6/16/88 OE	**7,700**
Leda & the Swan, #188, clr etch/drypt, 1934, p/s, a/bstp, 21x31", Icart Soc, lot 309, SBY 12/12/88	**11,550**
Leda & the Swan, clr etch/drypt (lacquered), ca 1934, sgn, 21x31", C-E 3/24/88	**7,260**
Lesson of Love (Lecon d'Amour), #11, clr drypt, 1927, p/s, a/bstp, P-10x11", lot 39, PHL 6/16/88 OE	**1,200**
Lilies, clr drypt/etch, 1934, p/s, a/bstp, 29x19", lot 310, 29x19", lot 310, SBY 12/12/88 OE	**4,675**
Lilies, clr etch/drypt, ca 1934, sgn, a/bstp, 28x20", C-E 3/24/88	**2,420**
Lilies, clr etch/drypt, ca 1934, sgn/bstp, 28x20", lot 220, C-E 6/16/88	**3,300**
Lilies, clr etch/drypt, ca 1934, trm mrgs, 28x19", lot 219, C-E 6/16/88	**2,200**
Lilies, clr etch/drypt, 1934, p/s, a/bstp, varnished, 28x20", Icart, lot 311, SBY 12/12/88 OE	**5,775**
Lilies, clr etch/drypt, 1934, p/s, bstp, laid down, lt varnished, 29x20", lot 32, SBY 6/10/88	**3,740**
Lilies, clr etch/drypt, 1934, p/s, bstp, varnished, 28x20", lot 31, SBY 6/10/88 OE	**3,960**
Lilies, E166, clr etch/drypt, ca 1934, sgn, a/bstp, 28x20", lot 474, C-E 9/20/89	**5,500**
Lilies, Les Lis; etch, sgn, full mrgs, 1934, L-28x19", RAB 3/27/89 OE	**3,700**
Little Butterflies (Petits Papillons), #299, clr etch/drypt, 1926, p/s, 15x20", lot 325, SBY 12/12/88	**2,200**
Look, clr etch/drypt, ca 1928, sgn, a/bstp, 21x14", lot 475, C-E 9/20/89	**1,870**
Louise, #130, clr etch/drypt, 1927, p/s, a/bstp, 21x14", lot 312, SBY 12/12/88 OE	**1,760**
Louise, a/p, clr drypt/aqua, 1927, p/s, a/bstp, lt stn, P-21x14", lot 40, PHL 6/16/88 OE	**1,200**
Love's Awakening, clr etch/drypt, ca 1933, sgn, a/bstp, 15x16", lot 478, C-E 9/20/89	**1,650**
Lovers, clr etch/drypt, ca 1930, sgn, a/bstp, 21x14", lot 477, C-E 9/20/89	**1,760**
Lovers, E161/500, clr etch/drypt, ca 1930, sgn, a/bstp, 21x14", C-E 9/16/88 OE	**1,430**
Madame Bovary, clr etch/drypt, 1929, p/s, a/bstp, 17x21", lot 314, SBY 12/12/88 OE	**2,090**
Madame Butterfly, #22(?), clr etch/drypt, 1927, p/s, bstp, wstn, 21x14", Graveurs Modernes, SBY 6/10/88	**990**
Madame Butterfly, #242, clr aqua/drypt/wove paper, 1927, p/s, a/bstp, L-20x13", Modernes Rue de Rivoli, RWS 9/8/89	**1,300**
Manon, #B72, clr etch/drypt, 1927, p/s, a/bstp, lt stn, 21x14", lot 315, SBY 12/12/88 OE	**1,430**
Manon, a/p, clr etch/drypt, ca 1927, sgn, a/bstp, 20x13", C-E 9/20/89	**1,485**
Marchande de Fleurs, a/p, total ed of 500, etch/drypt, 1928, laid down, L-19x14", Graveurs Modernes, RWS 3/16/89	**1,200**
Mardi Gras, clr etch/drypt, 1936, p/s, bstp, laid down, stn/scr, 20x19", Icart Soc, SBY 6/10/88	**3,025**
Martini, clr etch/bstp, ca 1932, sgn, a/bstp, 13x17", C-E 3/24/88	**4,070**
Meditation, a/p, clr etch/drypt, ca 1928, sgn/bstp, 12x17", C-E 6/16/88 OE	**1,265**
Melody Hour, clr etch/drypt, ca 1934, sgn, a/bstp, 19x23", C-E 9/16/88 OE	**7,700**
Mimi, #392, clr etch/drypt, 1927, p/s, bstp, 21x14", Graveurs Modernes, SBY 6/10/88	**1,210**
Mimi, 1st state, etch/drypt, ca 1927, p/s, rpr tr, 21x14", SBY 6/10/88	**880**
Minuet, #40, clr etch/drypt, ca 1929, sgn, a/bstp, 21x13", C-E 3/24/88	**990**
Minuet, clr etch/drypt, 1929, p/s, bstp/mk Gravure Garantie Originale, full mrgs, 21x14", SBY 6/10/88	**1,100**
Miroir de Venice, etch, sgn, full mrgs, 1937, L-22x19", Louis Icart Studio, RAB 3/27/89 OE	**1,800**
Mockery, #E55, clr etch/drypt, ca 1928, sgn/bstp, 16x18", C-E 6/16/88 OE	**1,540**
Model I (My Model), ca 1932, sgn, a/bstp, 21x17", lot 481, C-E 9/20/89 OE	**3,300**
Monmartre I, clr etch/drypt, 1928, p/s, bstp/mk Gravure Garantie Originale, full mrgs, 21x15", SBY 6/10/88	**1,320**
Monte Carlo, clr litho, sgn, 28x43", Monegasque, SBY 6/10/88	**2,530**
Muff, #172, clr etch/drypt, ca 1914, sgn/bstp, 21x12", C-E 6/16/88 OE	**1,210**
My Model, #148, clr etch/drypt, 1933, p/s, a/bstp, 22x17", Icart Soc, lot 319, SBY 12/12/88 OE	**3,575**
On the Quais, clr etch/drypt, 1929, p/s, bstp, 13x7", SBY 6/10/88	**990**
Open Cage, #267, clr etch, 1926, p/s, 13x18" oval, Les Graveurs Moderns, lot 418, MG 7/30/88	**1,200**
Orange Seller, #65, a/p, clr etch/drypt, 1929, p/s, a/bstp, 19x15", Icart Soc, lot 316, SBY 12/12/89	**1,100**
Orange Seller, 308/500, clr etch/drypt, ca 1929, sgn/bstp, lt ls, 19x14", C-E 6/16/88	**935**
Orchids, clr etch/drypt, ca 1937, sgn, 28x20", C-E 3/24/88	**2,970**
Orchids, clr etch/drypt, ca 1937, sgn/bstp, 28x20", C-E 6/16/88	**2,860**
Orchids, clr etch/drypt, 1937, p/s, a/bstp, lt varnished, 28x20", lot 324, SBY 12/12/88 OE	**6,325**
Orchids, clr etch/drypt, 1937, p/s, a/bstp, 28x20", lot 323, SBY 12/12/88 OE	**5,225**
Orchids, clr etch/drypt, 1937, p/s, bstp, varnished, 28x20", Icart Soc, SBY 6/10/88 OE	**4,180**
Pair: Guardians, Berger et Bergere; Favorite Berbis et Agneau; etch/drypt, 86 & 96, 1927, p/s, bstp, 10x10", SLK 5/6/88	**1,250**
Pair: Staircase Romance; Boudoir Mirror; brn aqua, ca 1946, p/s, titled on verso, 8x6"/8x5", RWS 6/17/89 OE	**1,700**
Pair: The Kiss; Garden of Love; brn aqua, 1946, p/s, P-8x5", RWS 6/17/89	**1,000**

Paris Flowers, 156/500, clr etch/drypt, ca 1930, sgn/bstp, 15x19", C-E 6/16/88 OE 1,430
Perfect Harmony, clr etch/drypt, ca 1932, sgn, 13x17", C-E 6/16/88 OE 3,520
Perfect Harmony, etch/drypt, 1932, p/s, a/bstp, titled, lt stn, 13x17", lot 281, SBY 12/12/88 OE 5,500
Puff of Smoke, clr etch/drypt, 1922, p/s, Estampe Moderne bstp, 19x14", SBY 6/10/88 1,430
Puppies, #336, clr drypt/etch, ca 1925, sgn, 16x21", C-E 9/16/88 990
Rainbow, clr etch/drypt, ca 1930, p/s, 25x17", C-E 9/16/88 2,200
Rainbow, clr etch/drypt, ca 1930, sgn/inscr Epreuve d'artist, a/bstp, 25x17", C-E 3/24/88 1,540
Red Cage, #244, clr etch/drypt, p/s, bstp, tstn, 12x10", SBY 6/10/88 770
Repose (Sommeil), #112, clr etch/drypt, 1937, p/s, a/bstp, 20x47", Icart Soc, lot 330, SBY 12/12/88 14,300
Sapho, clr etch/drypt, 1929, p/s, full mrgs, 17x21", lot 329, SBY 12/12/88 1,870
Seduction, #266, clr etch/drypt, ca 1921, sgn, L'Estampe Moderne bstp, 15x19", lot 482, C-E 9/20/89 1,650
Seville, #281, clr etch/drypt, ca 1928, sgn/bstp, 20x13", C-E 6/16/88 1,045
Seville, #52, clr etch/drypt, ca 1928, sgn, a/bstp, 20x13", C-E 3/24/88 990
Seville, drypt/etch, ca 1928, p/s, L-21x14", lot 1008, DM 2/19/88 900

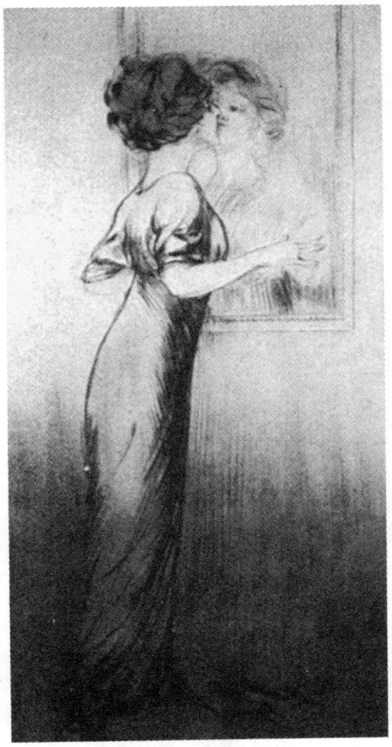

Woman Kissing Herself in Mirror, clr etch/drypt, sgn, a/bstp, 18x10", C-E 9/20/89 OE; $2,750

Silk Robe (La Robe de Chine), #24, clr etch/drypt, 1926, p/s, a/bstp, 16x19", Les Graveurs Modernes, SBY 12/12/88 2,200
Singing Lesson, 120/350, clr etch/drypt, ca 1926, p/s, bstp, rpr tr mrgs, 15x19", SBY 6/10/88 1,155
Sleeping Beauty, clr etch/drypt, 1927, p/s, a/bstp, lt fox, 15x19", Artistes Modernes, SBY 6/10/88 880
Smoke, #B107, clr etch/drypt, ca 1926, sgn, a/bstp, 15x21", C-E 3/24/88 2,200
Smoke, clr etch/drypt, ca 1926, sgn, 15x21", C-E 6/16/88 OE 3,080
Smoke, E/408, clr etch/drypt, ca 1926, sgn, a/bstp, 15x20", C-E 9/16/88 1,320
Smoke, 8/41A, clr etch/drypt, ca 1925, sgn, a/bstp, 15x21", lot 483, C-E 9/20/89 2,420
Sofa, clr etch/drypt, ca 1937, sgn, a/bstp, 17x25", lot 484, C-E 9/20/89 6,600
Spanish Dance, #110, clr etch/drypt, 1929, p/s, bstp, 21x14", David Ashley Inc, SBY 6/10/88 OE 1,540
Spanish Dancer, #346, clr etch/drypt, ca 1929, sgn/titled, a/bstp, 21x13", lot 416, C-E 3/24/88 1,045
Spanish Nights (Nuit Espangnole), #140, clr etch/drypt, sgn/titled, 21x13", C-E 3/24/88 990
Speed, #480, clr etch/drypt, ca 1927, sgn, a/bstp, 16x25", C-E 9/16/88 OE 4,180
Speed, #91, clr etch/drypt, 1927, p/s, bstp/inscr Les Levriers, lt fox, laid down, 15x26", SBY 6/10/88 OE 3,300
Speed, clr etch/drypt, ca 1933, trm mrgs, 15x25", C-E 3/24/88 935
Speed II, clr etch/drypt, ca 1933, sgn, a/bstp, 16x25", lot 485, C-E 9/20/89 5,500
Speed II, clr etch/drypt, 1933, p/s, bstp, fox, 16x26", Icart Soc, SBY 6/10/88 3,410
Speed II (Vitesse II), clr etch/drypt, 1933, p/s, a/bstp, 16x26", Icart Soc, lot 333, SBY 12/12/88 OE 6,050
Spilled Apples (Le Panier Renversee), a/p, clr drypt/aqua, 1928, p/s, a/bstp, P-21x13", lot 41, PHL 6/16/88 OE 1,200
Spilled Milk, a/p, clr etch/drypt, 1925, p/s, lt stn, 17x21", Les Graveurs Modernes, lot 331, SBY 12/12/88 1,650
Spilled Milk, E490/500, clr etch/aqua, 1928, p/s, trm mrgs, P-16x21", lot 42, PHL 6/16/88 1,300
Spring, #84, clr etch/drypt, ca 1920, sgn/Estampe Moderne bstp, 16x11", C-E 9/16/88 OE 1,320
Spring Again, 60/100, clr etch/drypt, ca 1925, sgn, 11x8", lot 486, C-E 9/20/89 1,540
Storyteller, 275/350, clr etch/drypt, sgn, a/bstp, 14x17", C-E 3/24/88 1,100
Success, #176, clr etch/drypt, ca 1927, sgn, a/bstp, 15x18", lot 487, C-E 9/20/89 2,420
Suite: 4 Seasons; 145/150, clr etch/drypt, sgn, 11x8", lot 403, C-E 3/24/88 4,510
Sweet Mystery, clr etch/drypt, ca 1935, sgn, a/bstp, 21x16", C-E 3/24/88 3,080
Sweet Mystery, clr etch/drypt, sgn, a/bstp, 21x16", C-E 9/16/88 3,080

Sweet Mystery, clr etch/drypt (lacquered), ca 1925, sgn/bstp, 21x16", C-E 6/16/88 OE 3,080
Swing, #268, clr etch/drypt, sgn, a/bstp, 20x14", C-E 3/24/88 OE 2,640
Symphony in Blue, clr etch/drypt, ca 1936, sgn/bstp, 23x20", C-E 6/16/88 1,760
Symphony in Blue, clr etch/drypt, 1926, p/s, a/bstp, 23x19", Icart Soc, lot 332, SBY 12/12/88 OE 3,300
Symphony in White, a/p, clr etch/drypt, ca 1932, sgn/bstp, 20x16", C-E 6/16/88 OE 2,860
Tete a Tete, photogr, ca 1946, artist copyright/Dragar Imp, 13x16", lot 457, C-E 9/16/88 220
Thais, A127, clr etch/drypt, ca 1927, sgn, a/bstp, 16x20", C-E 9/20/89 4,620
The Red Cage (La Cage Rouge), clr etch/drypt, 1928, p/s, a/bstp, 12x9", Icart, lot 288, SBY 12/12/88 1,100
Tosca, #111, clr etch/drypt, ca 1928, sgn/bstp, 21x13", C-E 6/16/88 OE 1,320
Tosca, A259/500, clr etch/drypt, 1928, p/s, bstp, tr mrgs, 21x13", Graveurs Modernes, SBY 6/10/88 OE 1,650
Tosca, clr etch/drypt, ca 1928, sgn, a/bstp, 21x13", C-E 3/24/88 1,100
Two Beauties, clr etch/drypt, ca 1931, sgn, a/bstp, 17x24", lot 490, C-E 9/20/89 11,000
Unititled (lady in masquerade dress/tri-corner hat holds fan), Dessins des Femmes; litho, sgn, 18x14", C-E 9/16/88 OE 605
Unmasked, clr etch/drypt, ca 1933, sgn, a/bstp, 21x13", C-E 3/24/88 990
Venetian Night (Nuit Venitienne), #120, clr etch/drypt, 1926, laid down, 21x14", Les Graveurs Modernes, SBY 12/12/88 1,430
Volupte, clr etch/drypt, 1935, p/s, 1935, 18x16", SBY 5/6/88 1,950
Waltz Dream, clr etch/drypt, 1931, p/s, bstp, fox, laid down, 15x17", Icart Soc, SBY 6/10/88 7,425
Waterfall, cir etch/drypt, 1936, p/s, bstp/inscr Le jet d'eau, full mrgs, 21x9", Icart Soc, SBY 6/10/88 3,850
Werther, #86, clr etch/drypt, ca 1928, sgn, a/bstp, 20x13", lot 491, C-E 9/20/89 OE 1,870
White Underwear, a/p, clr etch/drypt, ca 1925, sgn, 15x19", lot 482, C-E 9/16/88 1,870
Winsome, clr etch/drypt, 1935, p/s, bstp, 17x15", Icart Soc, SBY 6/10/88 1,980
Wishing Well, #326, clr etch/drypt, ca 1925, sgn, 18x12", lot 492, C-E 9/20/89 1,430
Woman Dancing with Elephants, clr etch/drypt, p/s, fox img/mrgs, 17x12", lot 41, FAP 2/24/89 OE 925
Woman in Boudoir, #82, clr etch/drypt, p/s, inscr Le Reve, 8x12", lot 334, SBY 12/12/88 OE 1,540
Woman in Doorway, clr etch/drypt, 1929, p/s, a/bstp, lt stn, 15x19", lot 335, SBY 12/12/88 OE 1,320
Woman in Wings, clr etch/drypt, 1936, p/s, bstp, varnished, 7x10", Icart Soc, SBY 6/10/88 3,850
Woman Kissing Herself in Mirror, sgn, a/bstp, 18x10", lot 493, C-E 9/20/89 OE 2,750
Woman Watching a Coach Pass By, clr etch/drypt, 1929, p/s, bstp, 15x19", SBY 6/10/88 825
Woman Wearing Blue Bandana Holding Three Kittens, a/p, clr drypt/aqua, 1925, p/s, P-18x15", lot 43, PHL 6/16/88 OE 1,600
Woman with Doves, #228, clr etch/drypt, 1926, p/s, 19x11", SBY 6/10/88 1,320
Woman with Parakeets & a Kitten, #23, clr etch/drypt, 1927, p/s, bstp, 10x10", Graveurs Modernes, SBY 6/10/88 770
Wounded Dove, #13, clr etch/drypt, ca 1923, sgn, a/bstp, 21x16", lot 494, C-E 9/20/89 OE 1,870
Young Woman with a Dog, #179, clr etch/drypt, ca 1924, sgn/bstp, 12x10", C-E 6/16/88 OE 880
Zest, #211, clr etch/drypt, ca 1928, sgn, a/bstp, 19x14", lot 495, C-E 9/20/89 4,400
1830, #6.26, clr etch/drypt, ca 1929, sgn, a/bstp, 15x18", C-E 3/24/88 990

ART, Louis; style of (French, 1888-1950)

Country Scene of a Girl with a Dog, 129/310, clr etch/drypt, sgn WL Laurbrecht(?), 20x15", C-E 6/16/88 UE 66

STED, Peter (Danish, 1861-1933)

Sunshine, clr mezzo/Chine colle, 1902, p/s, lt stn/cr img & mrgs, lt fox mrgs & verso, 13x11", lot 631, C-NY 5/10/89 OE 4,180
Woman Reading, 125/43, mezzo/Japan, 1925, p/s, lt cr/stn mrgs, ls in mrg corners, P-14x12", lot 633, C-NY 5/10/89 OE 715
2 Little Girls Playing, 103/150, mezzo/wove paper, 1911, p/s, lt scr/fox img, stn mrg, 19x18", lot 632, C-NY 5/10/89 OE 3,080

IMENDORF, Jorg (German, 20th C)

Krieg's Blatt, clr litho, 1982, sgn/dtd 83, S-25x35", lot 827, SBY 11/5/88 2,200
Neue Mehrheit, 5(?)/10, clr linocut over watercolor, 1983, p/s, full mrgs, lt tack holes, 62x82", SBY 5/14/88 OE 4,950
Quadriga, blk/red/yel linocut on glazed wove paper, 1983, sgn, full sheet, lt tr/rpl, S-34x24", lot 472, C-NY 5/11/88 1,980

DIANA, Robert (American, 1928-)

American Dream, 20/25, clr scpt/wove paper, 1971, sgn/dtd, full mrgs, S-39x32", orig folder, C-E 5/13/88 242
Figure Five, 122/201, clr slksc, 1971, p/s, lt cr, L-26x30", lot 124, PHL 10/28/88 350
Set of 4: American Dream No 2; 51/100, clr scrpt/Fabriano, 1982, Domberger bstp, S-27x27", lot 671, C-NY 11/1/88 825
Set of 5: Golden Five; 32/100, clr scrpt, 1980, Domberger bstp, full sheet, S-27x27", orig box, lot 473, C-NY 5/11/88 OE 1,210
Set of 5: Golden Five; 91/100, clr scrpt/Fabrino, 1980, Domberger bstp, S-27x27", Prestige Art, lot 670, C-NY 11/1/88 OE 1,650
Suite: Garden of Love; 87/100, 6 clr slksc, 1982, p/s, titled, full mrgs, lt cr, S-27x27", Prestige Art, SBY 2/23/89 1,430

TOURIST

Batumi, clr litho/poster paper, 40x25", s/wrp, lot 157, FAP 2/24/89 UE 90
Pair: Baku; Castle Above the Sea; clr litho/poster paper, 40x25", s/wrp, lot 158, FAP 2/24/89 150

COBY, J.H. (19th C)

New York & Manhattan Beach Railway Co Parlor Cars to Manhattan Beach, chromolitho, ca 1865, S-11x16", SBY 1/28/88 990

COULET, Paul (French, 1902-1960)

Bergers des Hautes Montagnes Coree, ed of 350, clr wc, 1941, p/s, trm mrgs, lt cr, unfr, 16x12", lot 25, RWS 9/29/88 350
La Chenille Verte, clr woodblock, ca 1940, p/s, 16x12", lot 338, LH 5/15/88 275
Le Bocal de Poissons Rouge, ed of 150, clr wc, 1942, p/s, unfr, full mrgs, lt stn, L-16x12", lot 23, RWS 9/29/89 UE 550

CQUE, Charles (French, 1813-1894)

Interior of Smithy, #3B, etch, pl/s, dtd 1843/titled, L-2x2", lot 1010, S/A 2/18/89 160
Le Retour des Champs, 1st state, etch/drypt, 1865, 7x10", lot 91, SWN 12/1/88 120
Shepherd, a/p before title, etch, ca 1865, 11x8", lot 90, SWN 12/1/88 300

CQUET, Alain (20th C)

Thomas Eakins' Swimming Hole, photo-slksc on cotton, sgn/dtd 1966-67, 32x21", C-E 5/9/89 OE 6,050

CQUETTE, Yvonne (American, 1934-)

Glimpse of Lower Manhattan, Night; 34/60, litho, 1986, p/s, plexiglas box, 21x15x4", Shark's Inc, lot 1051, SBY 5/13/89 2,475
Two Ferries Passing, 39/50, clr aqua, 1982, p/s, full mrgs, 16x16", Brooke Alexander, lot 678, SBY 2/23/89 1,210

JAMES, Clifford R.
New York & London Packet Ship Victoria 1000 Tons, litho, lt fox, lg folio, lot 320, RAB 11/25/88 .... **225**
JANSEM, Jean (Armenian, 1920-)
Female Nude Model, 97/120, litho, p/s, 23x20", lot 402, FAP 4/15/88 UE **33**
Japanese School (19th C)
Triptych: Village View; woodblock/paper, 14x10", lot 15, FAP 2/24/89 .... **80**
Japanese School (20th C)
School of Fish, 30/55, clr etch, p/s, dtd 53, 17x22", lot 837, PHL 3/20/88 .... **100**
Yoshitoshi Courtesan, clr woodblock, oban size, lot 11, LH 3/20/88 .... **50**
JAWLENSKY, Alexei (Russian, 1864-1941)
Kauernde, total ed of 75, clr litho/thick laid paper, 1921, p/s, lt sl/stn/cr, 10x16", lot 522A, SBY 5/11/89 OE **5,775**
JENKINS, Paul (American, 1927-)
Four Winds (I), litho, 1980, p/s, S-48x33", Tyler Graphics, lot 516, SBY 2/25/88 .... **1,320**
JOFFEY, Edith (American, 20th C)
Pair: Reviewing Stand; Heroes on Parade; litho, 1949, p/s, titled, 10x11"/13x17", FAP 6/16/89 UE **15**
JOHN, Augustus (British, 1878-1961)
Pair: Quarry Folk; Fruit Sellers; ed of 25 & 50, etch, ca 1906, p/s, 4x5"/8x5", lot 122, SWN 6/15/89 .... **248**
JOHNS, Jasper (American, 1930-)
#4 (After Untitled 1975), AP13/13, clr litho/Rives nspt clr paper, 1976, p/s, Gemini bstp, lt cr, 29x29", SBY 2/23/89 OE **17,050**
Ale Cans, 14/31, litho/wm Japan wove Japan, 1964, p/s, ULAE bstp, full mrgs, lt cr/stn, S-23x18", lot 674, C-NY 11/1/88 .... **132,000**
Black & White Numerals: Figure 4; 4/70, blk/gray litho, 1968, p/s, Gemini bstp, full mrgs, 28x21", lot 1066, SBY 5/13/89 .... **20,900**
Black & White Numerals: Figure 6; 6/70, blk/gray litho, 1968, p/s, Gemini bstp, full mrgs, 28x21", SBY 5/13/89 .... **19,800**
Black & White Numerals: Figure 7; APIV/X, blk/gray litho, 1968, Gemini bstp, full mrgs, 28x22", lot 835, SBY 11/5/88 OE **55,000**
Black & White Numerals: Figure 7; 57/70, blk/gray litho, 1968, p/s, Gemini bstp, full mrgs, 28x22", SBY 5/13/89 .... **77,000**
Black & White Numerals: Figure 8; 57/70, blk/gray litho, 1968, p/s, Gemini bstp, full mrgs, 28x22", SBY 5/13/89 OE **28,600**
Book: Fizzles (Foirades); by Samuel Beckett, HC7/20, 1975-76, sgns, Petersburg/Crommelynck, lot 845, SBY 11/5/88 OE **22,000**
Book: Fizzles (Foirades); by Samuel Beckett, XVIII/XXX, 1975-76, Petersburg/Crommelynck, lot 683, SBY 2/23/89 OE **56,100**
Book: Fizzles; by Samuel Beckett, 79/250, 31 etch w/text on Richard de Bas, 1975-76, Petersburg, lot 1100, SBY 5/13/89 .... **66,000**
Book: Poems; by Wallace Stevens, 142, ed of 320, 1985, p/s, orig wrappers, Arion, lot 1119, SBY 5/13/89 OE **7,150**
Book: Poems; by Wallace Stevens, 111/320, 1 etch/aqua, 1985, p/s, orig binding, Arion, SBY 5/14/88 OE **3,575**
Book: Poems; by Wallace Stevens, 259/300, aqua w/text, 1985, sgn, orig wrappers, Arion, lot 688, C-NY 11/1/88 OE **4,620**
Bread, 41/60, lead relief/laminated embossed paper, 1969, orig aluminum fr, 23x17", Gemini, lot 838, SBY 11/5/88 OE **15,950**
Casts From Untitled: Knee; 38/47, blk/wht litho, 1974, p/s, Gemini bstp, full mrgs, 15x15", lot 681, SBY 2/23/89 OE **8,525**
Casts From Untitled: Sketch From Untitled, I; 24/50, clr litho/Angoumois, 1974, p/s, S-43x29", lot 1092, SBY 5/13/89 OE **4,400**
Casts From Untitled: Sketch From Untitled, II; 24/50, litho/Washi No Mise, 1974, Gemini bstp, 28x19", SBY 5/13/89 OE **6,050**
Casts from Untitled: Sketch From Untitled I; PPII, clr litho, 1973-74, p/s, Gemini bstp, S-43x28", SBY 5/14/88 OE **2,200**
Casts From Untitled: Sketch From Untitled I; 14/50, clr litho, 1973-74, p/s, Gemini bstp, 43x28", lot 518, SBY 2/25/88 .... **1,540**
Cicada, 26/58, clr litho/Arches, 1981, p/s, Gemini bstp, full mrgs, S-35x26", lot 687, C-NY 11/1/88 OE **19,800**
Color Numerals: Figure 6; 40/40, clr litho/Japan Arjomari, 1968-69, Gemini bstp, 21x28", lot 1071, SBY 5/13/89 OE **41,800**
Color Numerals: Figure 7; 20/40, clr litho/Japan Arjomari, 1968-69, Gemini bstp, S-38x21", lot 1073, SBY 5/13/89 .... **231,000**
Color Numerals: Figure 8; 20/40, clr litho/Japan Arjomari, 1968-69, Gemini bstp, full mrgs, 27x22", SBY 5/13/89 OE **55,000**
Corpse & Mirror (Screenprint), 43/65, clr slksc/ivory Nishinouchi Kizuki Kozo, 1976, Simca bstp, 43x53", SBY 5/13/89 OE **176,000**
Corpse & Mirror (Screenprint), 51/65, clr slksc/ivory Nishinouchi Kizuki Kozo, 1976, Simca bstp, 43x53", SBY 11/5/88 OE **154,000**
Cup Four Picasso, 15/39, litho/Japan, 1972, p/s, ULAE bstp, S-14x32", lot 3032, B/B 4/19/88 .... **6,050**
Cups Two Picasso, clr litho, sgn in stone, 12x7", lot 974, FAP 12/8/88 .... **300**
Decoy, 25/55, clr litho/BFK Rives, 1971, p/s, ULAE bstp, S-42x30", lot 839, SBY 11/5/88 .... **154,000**
Decoy, 27/55, clr litho/BFK Rives, 1971, p/s, ULAE bstp, full sheet, S-42x30", lot 676, C-NY 11/1/88 .... **132,000**
Decoy, 47/55, clr litho/BFK Rives, 1971, p/s, ULAE bstp, S-42x30", lot 1079, SBY 5/13/89 OE **220,000**
Decoy, 54/55, clr litho/BFK Rives, 1971, p/s, dtd, ULAE bstp, S-42x30", SBY 5/14/88 OE **143,000**
Device, HC6/8, brn litho/English Crisbrook handmade, 1962, p/s, ULAE bstp, lt stn, S-32x23", lot 637, C-NY 11/1/88 .... **26,400**
Device, 2/6, brn-blk litho/English Crisbrook, 1962, p/s, ULAE bstp, full mrgs, 30x20", lot 829, SBY 11/5/88 .... **44,000**
Dutch Wives, 28x53, clr slksc/Japan, 1978, p/s, Simca bstp, full mrgs, lt cr mrg, S-43x56", SBY 5/14/88 .... **14,300**
Dutch Wives, 29/70, clr slksc/Japan, 1977, p/s, Simca bstp, full mrgs, S-43x56", SBY 5/14/88 OE **24,200**
Dutch Wives, 9/53, clr slksc/handmade Japan, 1978, p/s, Simca bstp, full mrgs, lt cr, 43x56", lot 1105, SBY 5/13/89 .... **37,400**
Embossed Alphabet, PPII, uninked embossing, 1968-69, Gemini bstp, full mrgs, L-28x34", lot 1074, SBY 5/13/89 OE **11,000**
Evion, 59/74, clr litho/Angoumois, 1971-72, p/s, Gemini bstp, lt scr/old tp, S-44x30", lot 1088, SBY 5/13/89 .... **13,200**
False Start I, 21/38I, clr litho, 1962, red crayon sgn, ULAE bstp, full mrgs, lt disclr/cr, L-18x14", SBY 5/14/88 OE **88,000**
False Start I, 3/38, clr litho/BFK Rives, 1962, p/s, ULAE bstp, full mrgs, S-30x22", lot 475, C-NY 5/11/88 OE **82,500**
False Start I, 5/38, clr litho, 1962, sgn in red crayon, ULAE bstp, full mrgs, cr/stn, 30x22", lot 1053, SBY 5/13/89 OE **231,000**
Flag I, AP6/7, clr slksc/JB Green, 1973, p/s, Simca bstp, S-27x35", lot 1092, SBY 5/13/89 .... **308,000**
Flag I, 36/65, clr slksc/JB Green, 1973, p/s, inscr I, Simca bstp, S-28x35", lot 842, SBY 11/5/88 OE **275,000**
Flags, 39/43, clr litho/handmade India, 1967-68, p/s, ULAE bstp, S-35x26", lot 1064, SBY 5/13/89 .... **99,000**
Flashlight, 1st Etchings, 2nd State; 34/40, etch/aqua/Richard de Bas, 1967, P-9x13", ULAE, lot 477, C-NY 5/11/88 OE **2,692**
Fool's House, 22/67, clr litho/Angoumois, 1971-72, p/s, Gemini bstp, full mrgs, lt cr, 41x20", lot 840, SBY 11/5/88 OE **28,600**
Fool's House, 27/67, clr litho/Angoumois, Gemini bstp, full mrgs, 41x20", lot 1084, SBY 5/13/89 OE **33,000**
Fool's House: Black State; 5/18, clr litho/wht Arjomari, 1972, p/s, Gemini bstp, lt sl, 41x20", lot 1085, SBY 5/13/89 .... **24,200**
Fragments, According to What: Bent Blue (Second State); 28/66, clr litho, 1971, Gemini bstp, S-25x29", SBY 5/13/89 .... **25,300**
Fragments, According to What: Bent Stencil; 14/79, clr litho, 1971, p/s, Gemini bstp, S-28x20", SBY 5/14/88 OE **1,925**
Fragments, According to What: Bent U; 38/69, clr litho, 1971, Gemini bstp, lt cr/sl, S-25x20", lot 1082, SBY 5/13/89 OE **8,800**
Fragments, According to What: Hinged Canvas; APXI/XII, clr litho, 1971, Gemini bstp, cr, 36x30", lot 680, SBY 2/23/89 OE **7,700**
Fragments, According to What: Hinged Canvas; PP2, clr litho, Gemini bstp, lt cr, S-36x30", lot 1081, SBY 5/13/89 OE **8,800**

Fragments, According to What: Leg & Chair; 48/68, clr litho, 1971, bl crayon sgn, Gemini bstp, S-35x30", SBY 5/14/88 OE	2,200
Good Time Charley, 27/69, clr litho/Angoumois, 1971-72, Gemini bstp, full mrgs, 38x25", lot 1083, SBY 5/13/89 OE	16,500
Good Time Charley; 48/69, clr litho/Angoumois, 1972, p/s, Gemini bstp, full mrgs, 38x25", lot 841, SBY 11/3/88 OE	11,550
Gray Alphabets, 8/59, litho, 1968, p/s, Gemini bstp, full mrgs, 51x34", lot 836, SBY 11/5/88 OE	170,500
High School Days, 45/60, lead relief w/mirror, 1969, sgn, orig frame/plexiglas box, 23x17", Gemini, SBY 5/14/88	14,300
Land's End, 35/70, litho/Kurotani, 1979, p/s, Gemini bstp, S-52x36", lot 850, SBY 11/5/88 OE	23,100
Land's End, 48/70, litho/Kurotani, 1979, p/s, Gemini bstp, S-52x36", SBY 5/14/88 OE	18,150
Land's End, 60/70, litho/Kurotani, 1979, p/s, Gemini bstp, S-52x36", lot 1106, SBY 5/13/89	29,700
Land's End, 65/70, litho/Kurotani, 1979, p/s, Gemini bstp, full mrgs, S-52x36", lot 683, C-NY 11/1/88 OE	24,200
Land's End II, 39/60, etch/aqua/Arches, 1979, p/s, full mrgs, P-34x25", Petersburg, lot 684, C-NY 11/1/88 OE	7,700
Light Blub, 20/48, gray & blk litho/JW 1956, 1976, p/s, ULAE bstp, full mrgs, S-17x14", lot 1098, SBY 5/13/89 OE	20,900
Light Bulb, 4/45, gray/blk litho/JW 1952, 1966, p/s, ULAE bstp, full mrgs, 9x15", lot 1057, SBY 5/13/89 OE	15,400
M: Black State; 4/16, clr litho/wht Arjomari, 1972, p/s, Gemini bstp, lt cr, 28x19", lot 1087, SBY 5/13/89 OE	15,400
No (contemporary), 26/80, gray/slvr litho/metal collage/embossing, 1968-69, Gemini bstp, 46x28", lot 1075, SBY 5/13/89	19,800
No (contemporary), 70/80, gray/slvr litho with collage, 1968-69, p/s, Gemini bstp, full mrgs, 46x28", SBY 11/5/88	18,700
Number 0, 0-9; 48/100, etch/aqua/sftgr/open-bite/Barcham Green, 1973, p/s, full mrgs, 2x2", Petersburg, SBY 2/23/89 OE	6,050
Numbers, 25/35, gray & blk litho/Angoumois, 1967, p/s, ULAE bstp, full mrgs, lt fox/stn, 23x20", lot 1061, SBY 5/13/89	35,750
Numbers, 30/35, gray & blk litho/Angoumois a la Main, 1967, ULAE bstp, full mrgs, 23x20", lot 832, SBY 11/5/88 OE	41,250
Numbers, 7/35, litho/Angoumois handmade, 1967, ULAE bstp, full mrgs, S-28x24", lot 675, C-NY 11/1/88 OE	44,000
Painting with a Ball, 15/42, litho/JW 1962, 1972-73, p/s, ULAE bstp, full mrgs, lt cr, 31x23", lot 1091, SBY 5/13/89 OE	8,800
Painting with Two Balls, 23/59, clr slksc, 1971, p/s, full mrgs, lt cr, 30x25", Johns/Heinrici, lot 1078, SBY 5/13/89 OE	41,800
Painting with Two Balls, 23/59, clr slksc, 1971, p/s, full mrgs, lt cr, 22x25", Jasper Johns, SBY 5/14/88 OE	12,650
Painting with Two Balls (Grays), 7/66, slksc, 1971, p/s, full mrgs, lt fox, 30x25", Jasper Johns, SBY 5/14/88 OE	8,250
Painting with Two Balls I, 14/39, clr litho/Kochi Japan, 1962, ULAE bstp, lt fox/stn, S-26x20", lot 672, C-NY 11/1/88 OE	33,000
Pair: Flashlight I; Lightbulb I; 8/40, etch/engr, 1967-69, p/s, ULAE bstp, full mrgs, S-26x20", lot 833, SBY 11/5/88 OE	15,400
Passage I, PPI2/2, clr litho/handmade Italia, 1966, p/s, ULAE bstp, full mrgs, lt cr, S-28x36", lot 1058, SBY 5/13/89 OE	60,500
Periscope, AP10/12, clr etch/aqua/buff Rives, 1981, p/s, full mrgs, lt cr, 34x24", Petersburg, lot 1116, SBY 5/13/89 OE	33,000
Periscope, 33/65, clr litho/Kurotani, 1979, p/s, Gemini bstp, S-51x36", lot 1107, SBY 5/13/89	46,750
Periscope, 84/88, clr etch/aqua, 1981, p/s, full mrgs, lt cr/tr, 34x24", Petersburg, lot 858, SBY 11/5/88 OE	15,950
Periscope I, 40/65, clr litho/Kurotani, 1979, p/s, Gemini bstp, S-51x36", lot 851, SBY 11/5/88 OE	58,300
Periscope II, 18/28, litho, 1979, p/s, Gemini bstp, full mrgs, lt cr, 52x39", SBY 5/14/88	8,250
Portfolio: 1st Etchings; 26/26, 6 etch & engr/unbleached Angoumois, 1967-68, orig wrappers, lot 1065, SBY 5/13/89 OE	66,000
Recent Still Life, 100/100, gray/blk litho, 1965-66, p/s, ULAE bstp, full mrgs, lt cr, S-35x20", lot 1056, SBY 5/13/89	12,100
Recent Still Life, 26/100, gray/blk litho, 1965-66, p/s, ULAE bstp, full mrgs, lt stn, S-35x20", lot 679, SBY 2/23/89 OE	14,300
Savarin, APIII/X, clr litho/handmade Twinrocker, 1977, p/s, ULAE bstp, S-45x34", lot 1101, SBY 5/13/89 OE	297,000
Savarin, 4/50, clr litho/Twinrocker, 1977, p/s, ULAE bstp, full mrgs, lt sl, S-45x34", lot 847, SBY 11/5/88 OE	198,000
Savarin, 47/60, clr litho, 1977-81, p/s, ULAE bstp, full mrgs, lt rub, 40x30", lot 1102, SBY 5/13/89 OE	121,000
Savarin 5 (Corpse & Mirror), APIV/V, clr litho/Auvergne Richard de Bas, 1978, p/s, full mrgs, S-26x20", SBY 5/13/89 OE	44,000
Scent, 23/42, clr litho/linocut/wc/Twinrocker, 1975-76, p/s, ULAE bstp, full mrgs, S-32x47", lot 843, SBY 11/5/88 OE	159,500
Scent, 26/42, clr litho/linocut/wc/Twinrocker, 1975-76, p/s, ULAE bstp, full mrgs, S-32x48", lot 1096A, SBY 5/13/89	143,000
Scott Fagan Record, 17/20, clr litho/Angoumois a la main, 1970, sgn, ULAE bstp, full mrgs, S-16x16", SBY 5/14/88	3,850
Souvenir, 50/50, clr litho/off-wht handmade English, 1970, p/s, ULAE bstp, full mrgs, 23x18", lot 1077, SBY 5/13/89	27,500
Souvenir I, PP2, ed of 62, clr litho/Angoumois, 1971-72, p/s, Gemini bstp, full sheet, S-39x29", lot 478, C-NY 5/11/88	4,620
Souvenir I, 56/63, clr litho/Angoumois, 1971-72, p/s, Gemini bstp, full mrgs, 27x21", lot 1086, SBY 5/13/89	14,300
Suite: Color Numerals: Figures From 0 to 9; 12/40, 10 clr litho/Japan Arjomari, 1968-69, S-38x31", SBY 5/13/89	770,000
Suite: Seasons: Spring; Summer; Fall; Winter; 33/73, etch/aqua, 1987, p/s, ULAE bstp, full mrgs, S-26x19", SBY 5/13/89	231,000
Suite: Six Lithographs (After Untitled 1975); 29/60, litho/gray Rives nspt, 1976, S-30x30", Gemini, SBY 5/13/89 OE	88,000
Target, 51/70, clr scrpt/JB Green, 1974, p/s, Simca bstp, full mrgs, S-35x28", lot 479, C-NY 5/11/88 OE	77,000
Target, 52/70, clr scrpt/JB Green, 1974, p/s, Simca bstp, full mrgs, S-35x27", lot 680, C-NY 11/1/88 OE	220,000
Target, 58/70, clr slksc/JB Green, 1974, p/s, Simca bstp, S-35x27", lot 1094, SBY 5/13/89 OE	164,000
Target with Four Faces, aside from #d ed of 88, clr etch/aqua, 1979, p/s, full mrgs, 24x18", lot 1109, SBY 5/13/89 OE	52,250
Target with Plaster Casts, AP10/13, clr etch/aqua, 1978-80, p/s, full mrgs, 23x18", Petersburg, lot 519, SBY 2/25/88	9,350
Target with Plaster Casts, 26/88, clr etch/aqua, 1978-80, p/s, full mrgs, 24x18", Petersburg, lot 1110, SBY 5/13/89 OE	55,000
Target with Plaster Casts, 51/88, clr aqua/etch, 1978-80, p/s, full mrgs, 23x18", Petersburg, SBY 5/14/88 OE	17,600
Targets, 25/42, clr litho/handmade India, 1967-68, p/s, ULAE bstp, lt stn, S-34x26", lot 1063, SBY 5/13/89	82,500
Triptych: Untitled (Red); Untitled (Yellow); Untitled (Blue); AP11/14, etch, 1982, ea 42x30", SBY 5/14/88 OE	16,500
Triptych: Untitled (Red); Untitled (Yellow); Untitled (Blue); 73/77, etch, 1982, ea 42x30", lot 859, SBY 11/5/88	19,800
Triptych: Voice 2; 28/54, clr litho/Japan Hanga, 1982, p/s, ULAE bstp, full mrgs, S-36x24", lot 1118, SBY 5/13/89 OE	176,000
Two Flags, 26/56, litho/ivory Nishinouchi Kizuki, 1980, p/s, Gemini bstp, S-47x36", lot 854, SBY 11/5/88 OE	19,800
Two Flags, 30/55, litho/ivory Nishinouchi Kizuki, 1980, p/s, Gemini bstp, S-48x36", lot 1112, SBY 5/13/89	18,700
Two Flags (Black), 12/40, litho/India, 1970-72, p/s, ULAE bstp, full mrgs, S-32x24", lot 1089, SBY 5/13/89 OE	37,400
Two Flags (Gray), 21/36, litho/Japan, 1970-72, sgn in blk crayon, ULAE bstp, full mrgs, S-27x33", lot 1090, SBY 5/13/89	42,900
Two Flags (Gray), 8/36, litho/Japan, p/s, 1970-72, p/s, ULAE bstp, full sheet, S-27x32", lot 678, C-NY 11/1/88 OE	25,300
Two Flags (Whitney Anniversary), 12/51, clr litho, 1980, p/s, Gemini bstp, full mrgs, lt cr, S-50x34", SBY 5/14/88	14,300
Two Maps II, 5/30, blk litho/wht laid Japan/blk laid Fabriano, 1966, ULAE bstp, S-34x26", lot 830, SBY 11/5/88 OE	121,000
Untitled (abstract lineation), 6/130, slksc/Rives Moulin du Gue, 1977, p/s, artist/Simca bstps, 10x10", SBY 5/14/88 OE	9,900
Untitled (contemporary Savannah coffee), 40/53, litho/JB Green, 1977, p/s, ULAE bstp, S-28x40", lot 681, C-NY 11/1/88 OE	82,500
Untitled (contemporary), clr litho/Kurotani, 1977-80, sgn in wht crayon, Gemini bstp, S-34x30", lot 853, SBY 11/5/88 OE	8,250
Untitled (Ruler & Fork) II, 2/9, gray aqua/etch/Barcham Green, 1969, p/s, ULAE bstp, lt cr/fox/sl, 29x20", SBY 5/14/88	3,300
Untitled (Savarin coffee can/contemporary), 4/53, litho/JB Green, 1977, p/s, ULAE bstp, 27x40", lot 846, SBY 11/5/88	71,500
Untitled I (Hatching), 34/55, clr etch/aqua, 1976, p/s, full mrgs, lt fox, 13x19", Petersburg, lot 1099, SBY 5/13/89 OE	25,300

Usuyuki, AP2/15, clr slksc/handmade Japan, 1979-81, p/s, Simca bstp, full mrgs, 28x45", lot 1111, SBY 5/13/89 OE **165,000**
Usuyuki, 23/57, clr litho/BFK Rives, 1980, p/s, ULAE bstp, S-52x20", lot 686, C-NY 11/1/88 OE **77,000**
Usuyuki, 28/49, clr litho, 1979, p/s, ULAE bstp, full mrgs, 35x50", lot 852, SBY 11/5/88 .... **49,500**
Usuyuki, 3/52, clr slksc/handmade Kurotani, 1982, p/s, Simca bstp, full mrgs, S-28x46", lot 1117, SBY 5/13/89 OE **154,000**
Usuyuki, 36/57, clr litho, 1980, p/s, ULAE bstp, 46x15", lot 855, SBY 11/5/88 OE **79,750**
Usuyuki, 41/57, clr litho/BFK Rives, 1980, p/s, ULAE bstp, full mrgs, S-53x20", lot 480, C-NY 5/11/88 OE **38,500**
Usuyuki, 42/49, clr litho, 1979, p/s, ULAE bstp, full mrgs, S-34x50", SBY 5/14/88 OE **39,600**
Usuyuki, 52/90, clr slksc/handmade Japan, dyed w/bamboo, 1980, p/s, Simca bstp, full mrgs, S-52x20", SBY 5/14/88 OE **44,000**
Usuyuki, 68/90, clr slksc/Japan, 1980, p/s, Simca bstp, full mrgs, S-52x20", lot 1113, SBY 5/13/89 .... **82,500**
Usuyuki, 80/90, clr scrpt/Japanese handmade dyed with bamboo, 1980, p/s, S-52x20", Simca, lot 684, C-NY 11/1/88 OE **71,500**

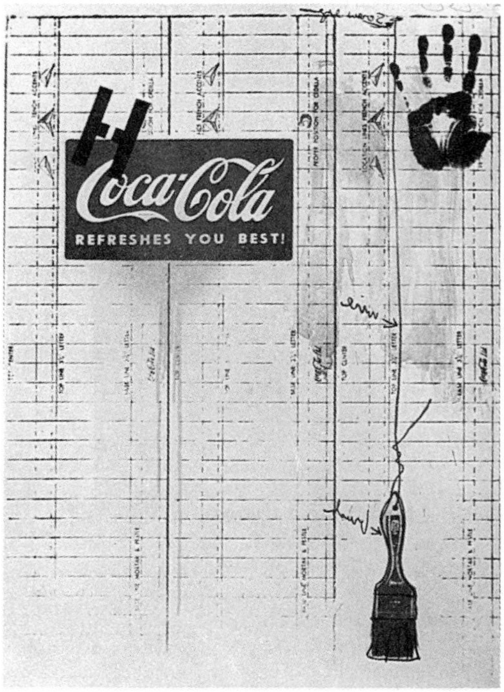

Untitled, APXI/XII, aside from #d ed of 66, clr litho/Arches, p/s, Gemini bstp, 34x26", lot 3545, B/B 4/12/89 OE; $18,700

Voice, 28/30, blk/slvr/handmade JW 1957, 1966-67, ULAE bstp, full mrgs, lt cr, S-48x32", lot 1059, SBY 5/13/89 .... **31,900**
Watchman, 36/40, clr litho/handmade Angoumois a la Main, 1967, ULAE bstp, S-36x24", lot 831, SBY 11/5/88 OE **68,750**
Watchman, 6/40, clr litho/unbleached Angoumois, 1967, p/s, ULAE bstp, S-36x24", lot 1060, SBY 5/13/89 OE **8,800**
0 Through 9, AP IX/XV, tones of bl litho/La Paloma, 1978, p/s, Gemini bstp, full mrgs, 6x5", lot 849, SBY 11/5/88 OE **18,700**
0 Through 9, AP9/10, yel/red/bl/wht litho on Japan & English Chatham, 1967, ULAE bstp, 12x10", lot 1062, SBY 5/13/89 OE **93,500**
0 Through 9, 13/35, litho/Arches, 1960, p/s, ULAE bstp, lt rub/sl/tr/scr, S-29x21", lot 1052, SBY 5/13/89 .... **165,000**
0 Through 9, 26/35, litho/Arches, 1960, p/s, ULAE bstp, full mrgs, lt cr, S-30x22", lot 474, C-NY 5/11/88 .... **121,000**
0 Through 9, 43/60, tones of burnt orange litho/La Paloma handmade, 1978, Gemini bstp, 6x5", lot 848, SBY 11/5/88 OE **10,450**
0 Through 9, 45/60, bl litho/La Paloma, 1978, p/s, Gemini bstp, full mrgs, 6x5", lot 1103, SBY 5/13/89 OE **52,800**
0 Through 9, 8/35, litho/Arches, 1960, p/s, ULAE bstp, full mrgs, 25x19", lot 828, SBY 11/5/88 OE **187,000**
1st Etchings, 2nd State: Flashlight I; 28/40, etch over photoengr, 1967-69, ULAE bstp, lt fox, S-26x20", SBY 5/14/88 OE **2,860**
6 Lithographs (after Untitled 1975): #1; 52/60, litho/gray Rives Newsprint, 1976, Gemini bstp, S-30x30", SBY 5/14/88 OE **4,400**
6 Lithographs (after Untitled 1975): #3; 48/60, litho/gray Rives Newsprint, 1976, Gemini bstp, cr, S-20x20", SBY 5/14/88 .... **3,025**
6 Lithographs (after Untitled 1975): #4; 40/60, litho/gray Rives Newsprint, 1976, Gemini bstp, S-30x30", SBY 5/14/88 .... **3,025**
6 Lithographs (after Untitled): #4; 48/60, clr litho/gray Rives Newsprint, 1976, Gemini bstp, S-30x30", SBY 5/14/88 .... **3,025**

JONES, Joe (American, 1909-1963)
Missouri Wheat Farmers, litho, p/s, 17x12", Assn Am Aritsts, lot 185, WG 10/19/88 .... **450**

JONGKIND, Johan Barthold (Dutch, 1819-1891)
Album: Cahier de Six Eaux-Fortes; 6 etch/Hallines or Hudelist, 1862, S-15x21", orig wrappers, lot 62, C-NY 11/1/88 .... **11,000**
Moulins en Holland, Rotterdam; 1st ed, etch, 1967, 6x8", lot 92, SWN 12/1/88 .... **330**
Vue de Port au Chemin de Fer, Honfleur; 2nd state, etch/laid paper, 1866, 10x13", Cadart/Delatre, lot 93, SWN 12/1/88 .... **358**

JOPLING, Frederic Waistell (1860-1945)
Portrait of H Rutley, engr, 1928, p/s, titled, 9x5", lot 1200, WAD 11/28/88 .... **100**

JOUVE, Paul
Gorilla Approaching Statue of a Woman, etch/drypt, ca 1925, sgn, 16x21", SBY 6/10/88 .... **660**

JUDD, Donald (American, 1928-)
Paragon 6, 13/175, aqua/cream wove paper, p/s, Styria bstp, lt cr, 35x25", lot 3033, B/B 4/19/88 .... **358**
Untitled (No 2), 22/25, cadmium orange wc/Cartridge, 1961-78, p/s, full mrgs, 10x17", Heiner Friedrich, SBY 2/23/89 OE **2,310**

JULES, Mervin (American, 1912-)
Trio (expressionistic interior scene w/musicians), ed of 75 , clr wc, sgn/titled, L-13x18", lot 57, RWS 9/29/88 UE **100**

KAGY, Sheffield (American, 1907-)
Judgement, relief cut/handmade paper, 1933, p/s, dtd March 1933, 10x10", Cleveland Print Club, lot 179, WG 10/19/88 .... **40**

KAHLO, Frida (Mexican, 1910-1954)
Frida & the Abortion (surrealistic), 12th imp, litho/thin Japan, p/s, dtd 1936, 1932, 8x6", SBY 11/21/88 OE **20,900**
KAHN, Max
Swift in the Moonlight, 2/122, wc, sgn, 22x31", lot 956, LH 5/15/88 UE **40**
KAINEN, Jacob (American, 1909-)
Dead End, litho, p/s, 8x11", Federal Arts Project, lot 175, WG 10/19/88 OE **230**
KAISER, Amanda (American, 20th C)
Bitch in Heat, 4/12, etch, p/s, titled, 18x13", lot 443, WG 10/19/88 .... **50**
KANDINSKY, Wassily (American, 1866-1944)
Holzschnitt fur die Ganymed-Mappe, ed of 100, wc/Advertisers Text, 1924, p/s, lt stn, L-6x8", lot 327, C-NY 11/1/88 .... **2,200**
Im Sommer, clr wc/support sheet, 1904, lt stn/cr, S-20x12", lot 523, SBY 5/11/89 .... **93,500**
Kleine Welten I, ed of 200, clr litho, 1922, p/s, full mrgs, lt stn/fox, 10x9", lot 283, SBY 2/23/89 .... **7,975**
Kleine Welten I, ed of 200, clr litho/wove paper, 1922, lt stn/scr, S-14x11", lot 634, C-NY 5/10/89 OE **28,600**
Kleine Welten II, ed of 200, clr litho/wove paper, 1922, p/s, full mrgs, lt stn, 10x8", lot 284, SBY 2/23/89 .... **15,400**
Kleine Welten II, ed of 200, clr litho/wove paper, 1922, p/s, lg mrgs, lt fox/cr, 10x8", lot 525, SBY 5/11/89 .... **13,200**
Kleine Welten II, ed of 200, clr litho/wove paper, 1922, p/s, full mrgs, lt fox/stn/scr, 10x8", lot 229, SBY 11/3/88 OE **26,400**
Kleine Welten IV, ed of 200, clr litho/wove paper, 1922, p/s, lt fox/stn, 10x10", lot 224, SBY 2/25/88 OE **6,875**
Kleine Welten IV, ed of 200, clr litho/wove paper, 1922, p/s, full mrgs, lt stn/tr, 11x10", lot 526, SBY 5/11/89 OE **25,300**
Kleine Welten IX, ed of 200, drypt, 1922, p/s, full mrgs, lt tr/cr in mrgs, P-9x8", lot 180, C-NY 5/11/88 OE **4,180**
Kleine Welten V, ed of 200, clr wc/wove paper, 1922, p/s, full mrgs, lt stn/sl/stn, S-14x11", lot 635, C-NY 5/10/89 OE **14,300**
Kleine Welten VI, ed of 200, wc/wove paper, 1922, p/s, full mrgs, lt stn/cr, 11x9", lot 285, SBY 2/23/89 OE **7,150**
Kleine Welten VII, ed of 200, clr wc/wove paper, 1922, p/s, lt stn/skinned, 11x9", lot 527, SBY 5/11/89 OE **29,700**
Kleine Welten X, ed of 200, drypt/wove paper, 1922, p/s, large mrgs, lt stn/fox, 9x8", lot 230, SBY 11/3/88 .... **2,475**
Kleine Welten XII, ed of 200, drypt/wove paper, 1922, p/s, full mrgs, lt stn/fox, 9x8", lot 231, SBY 11/3/88 OE **6,500**
Landscape, From Klange; clr wc/cream wove paper, 1938, lt cr, 5x8", lot 2858, B/B 2/16/88 .... **358**
Pair: Lithographie Blau; Holzschnitt fur Xxieme Siecle; clr litho & wc, 1922 & 1939, 8x6"/9x11", lot 528, SBY 5/11/89 OE **3,300**
Portfolio: Kleine Welten; 51/200, 1922, p/s, full sheets, lt stn, S-19x14", orig wrappers, Verlag, lot 65, C-NY 11/1/88 .... **143,000**
Postkarte fur die Bauhaus Ausstellung, clr litho/wove paper, 1923, S-6x4", lot 232, SBY 11/3/88 .... **2,200**
Radierung fur die Deutsche Kunstgemeinschaft, drypt, 1926, p/s, full mrgs, lt cr, P-6x5", lot 328, C-NY 11/1/88 OE **6,380**
Sangerin, 2nd state, hc wc/Japan, 1903, p/s, lt cr/fox, S-8x6", lot 64, C-NY 11/1/88 OE **71,500**
Suite: Kleine Welten; #160, total ed of 230, 12 prints, 1922, full mrgs, orig portfolio, Verlag, lot 524, SBY 5/11/89 OE **330,000**
Zwei Madchen, hc linocut/soft fibrous Japan, 1907, lt fox, S-10x5", lot 63, C-NY 11/1/88 OE **110,000**
KAPLAN, Jerome (American, 1920-)
Waterworks, clr engr, p/s, 12x15", lot 64, FAP 2/24/89 .... **70**
KAPPEL, Philip (American, 1901-)
At Jacmel, Haiti; drypt/van Gelder, 1933, p/s, 8x4", Cleveland Print Club, lot 192, WG 10/19/88 .... **55**
Away Forward, a/p, etch/laid paper, p/s, titled, 8x10", lot 2953, B/B 2/16/88 .... **137**
Group of 3: In Tow; To the Marshlands, 1954; Nude; etch/drypt, p/s, unfr, 7x6"/8x6"/7x5", RWS 3/16/89 .... **225**
Pair: Ghosting Along; Chatham Bar, Cape Cod (marine scenes); sftgr etch/drypt & aqua, 1978, lot 41, RWS 9/8/89 .... **225**
KASAMATSU, Shiro (Japanese, 1898-)
House in Evening, 104/200, clr wc, 1967, sgn, 15x10", lot 427, WG 10/19/88 .... **70**
KASIMIR, Luigi (Austrian, 1881-1962)
Arch of Septimius Severus in Rome, clr etch/aqua, p/s, 27x19", lot 1455, LH 12/4/88 OE **525**
Beethovenhaus in Wien, clr etch, p/s, dtd September 1817, P-10x9", lot 1004, S/A 2/18/89 .... **150**
Brooklyn Bridge, 8/150, clr etch/aqua, 1927, p/s, lt sl, laid down/sealed in mat, P-12x17", lot 188, C-NY 1/19/89 .... **330**
Freiburg, Germany; clr etch/wove paper, p/s, lt stn/scr, old tp on verso, 19x13", lot 2859, B/B 2/16/88 .... **440**
Group of 3: Public Library; Broad Street; Brooklyn Bridge; clr etch/aqua, 1927, p/s, lt fox/stn, lot 189, C-NY 1/19/89 .... **1,045**
Schubert House Vienna, clr etch, p/s, titled, P-8x11", lot 1002, S/A 2/18/89 .... **150**
Stanford University, etch/wove paper, p/s, full mrgs, 11x15", lot 2860, B/B 2/16/88 .... **285**
Thames River, London; etch, sgn/dtd 1912-1922, full mrgs, 13x20", SBY 8/8/89 UE **200**
View of New York, clr etch/aqua, p/s, 12x15", lot 250, LH 12/4/88 OE **250**
Wien Schuberthaus, clr etch, p/s, P-10x8", lot 1003, S/A 2/18/89 .... **125**
KATZ, Alex (American, 1927-)
Ada Four Times, 74/120, litho/slksc/4 separate sheets, 1979, p/s, ea 30x23", GHJ Graphics, lot 523, SBY 2/25/89 OE **4,400**
Ada with Flowers, 1/65, clr slksc, 1980, p/s, a/bstp, Simca bstp, 48x36", lot 861, SBY 11/5/88 OE **4,400**
Ada with Flowers, 2/65, clr slksc, 1980, p/s, Simca bstp, S-48x36", lot 1121, SBY 5/13/89 OE **7,700**
Bicycle Rider, 108/250, clr litho/Arches, 1982, p/s, full sheet, S-20x33", NY Graphic Soc, lot 693, C-NY 11/1/88 .... **825**
Blue Rider, 3/250, clr litho/wove paper, 1982, p/s, full sheet, S-22x30", NY Graphic Soc, lot 484, C-NY 5/11/88 OE **1,100**
Blue Umbrella, 2/120, clr litho/Arches, 1979-80, p/s, full sheet, S-20x30", GHJ Graphics, lot 483, C-NY 5/11/88 .... **6,050**
Blue Umbrella, 3/120, clr litho, 1979-80, p/s, 20x30", GHJ Graphics, lot 692, SBY 2/23/89 .... **5,500**
Blue Umbrella, 89/120, clr litho/Arches, 1979-80, p/s, full sheet, S-20x30", GHJ Graphics, lot 692, C-NY 11/1/88 OE **7,150**
Five Women, 18/100, clr scrpt/Japan, 1977, p/s, full sheet, S-18x47", Abrams, lot 690, C-NY 11/1/88 .... **4,400**
Five Women, 62/100, clr slksc/Japan, 1977, p/s, S-18x47", Abrams, lot 860, SBY 11/5/88 .... **3,300**
Group of 4: Night, William Dunas Dance, No 1, 2, 3, 4; ed of 125, clr srgph, 25x31", lot 124, SWN 6/15/89 OE **3,900**
Homage to Frank O'Hara: William Dunas; 42/90, clr litho, 1972, p/s, lt cr/sl, 33x25", lot 522, SBY 2/25/88 .... **770**
Joan, a/p, #7, clr aqua/Somerset, 1986, p/s, full sheet, S-31x39", Crown Point, lot 694, C-NY 11/1/88 OE **7,150**
Joan, AP8, ed of 12 a/p, clr aqua, 1986, p/s, S-31x39", Crown Point, lot 1123, SBY 5/13/89 OE **10,450**
Orange Band, 43/80, clr scrpt/Arches, 1979, p/s, full sheet, S-40x28", Simca, lot 691, C-NY 11/1/88 .... **3,520**
Portfolio: Tremor in the Morning; by Vincent Katz, 16/45, 1986, sgns, Blum, lot 862, SBY 11/5/88 .... **3,575**
Red Coat, 32/73, clr slksc/Stonehenge, 1983, p/s, Simca bstp, S-58x29", Katz/Simca, lot 1122, SBY 5/13/89 OE **26,400**
Samantha, 35/80, clr slksc, 1987, p/s, S-66x29", Katz/Simca, lot 1125, SBY 5/13/89 .... **6,600**

Samantha, 38/80, clr slksc, 1987, p/s, S-66x29", Katz/Simca, lot 863, SBY 11/5/88 OE **7,700**
Superb Lilies, 28/90, clr litho/wove paper, 1972, p/s, full sheet, S-19x20", Marlborough, lot 482, C-NY 5/11/88 OE **880**
Susan, XXXVI/L, ed of 50, clr slksc/Tronko Japan, 1976, p/s, S-26x20", Transworld, lot 689, SBY 2/23/89 .... **1,320**
Susan, 40/175, scrpt/Arches, 1976, p/s, Transworld bstp, full sheet, S-26x20", lot 689, C-NY 11/1/88 .... **605**
Swamp Maple I, 54/84, clr litho/Arches, 1970, p/s, S-41x28", Brooke Alexander/Fishbach Gallery, lot 481, C-NY 5/11/88 .... **1,100**
Swamp Maple I, 59/84, clr litho, 1970, p/s, lt scr/cr, S-41x28", Brooke Alexander/Mourlot, lot 520, SBY 2/25/88 .... **1,320**
Swamp Maple I, 81/84, clr litho, 1970, p/s, S-41x27", Brooke Alexander/Fishbach Gallery, lot 688, SBY 2/23/89 .... **1,430**
Swamp Maple II, 26/90, clr litho, 1970, p/s, lt cr/scr, 40x27", Brooke Alexander/Fishbach Gallery, lot 521, SBY 2/25/88 .... **880**
Swimmer, 18/80, aqua, 1974, p/s, lt scuff/cr, S-28x36", Brooke Alexander/Marlborough Graphics, SBY 5/14/88 OE **2,750**

KAUFFMAN, Edwin (American, 20th C)
Brooklyn Bridge, 13/50, etch, p/s, titled, stn, 6x4", lot 150, WG 10/19/88 .... **40**

KEITH, Elizabeth (British, 1887-1956)
Pair: Kamakura Daibutsu; River Scene; clr woodblock & brn etch, ca 1920/ca 1926, unfr, 18x13"/10x13", RWS 3/16/89 .... **325**
Pair: Kamakura Summer Reflections; Street Scene with Bridge Over Narrow River; wc, 1922, 10x15", lot 26, RWS 9/29/88 .... **650**
Pair: Korean Mother & Child; Chinese Scholar; aqua/etch & aqua/woodblock, ca 1929 & 1931, 13x10"/14x8", RWS 3/16/89 UE **200**
Pair: Tokyo; New Year's Lanterns Evening, Malacca; ed of 100, clr wc, 1932, 15x10"/17x11", lot 24, RWS 9/29/88 .... **425**

KELLER, Henry G. (American, 1869-1949)
Cart Horses Resting, litho, 1935, p/s, no size given, Cleveland Print Club, lot 221, WG 10/19/88 UE **60**
Fighting Horses, #13, litho, 1933, p/s, 15x20", Cleveland Print Club, lot 190, WG 10/19/88 .... **125**

KELLOGG
James Madison, hc litho, 13x17", lot 36, GAI 3/17/89 .... **85**
John Tyler, full-length & standing before window in his study; litho, 1841, titled, 11x14", C-E 4/26/88 UE **220**
Lieutenant-General Ulysses S Grant, hc litho, 16x12", lot 68, GAI 9/22/89 .... **45**
Lincoln at Home, hc litho, 10x14", lot 45, GAI 3/17/89 .... **275**
Nellie, hc litho, lt stn, 13x17", lot 156, GAI 9/23/88 .... **45**
Stephen A Douglas, hc litho, lt stn, 10x14", lot 547, GAI 3/17/89 .... **85**
Storming of Fort Donelson, February 16, 1862; hc litho, trm mrgs, stn, 10x13", lot 409, GAI 3/17/89 .... **125**
Three Friends, litho, 14x10", lot 195, DM 10/14/88 .... **65**

KELLOGG & COMSTOCK
Cass & Butler, hc litho, stn, 13x17", lot 143, GAI 3/17/89 .... **225**
Millard Fillmore, hc litho, 1848, lt stn, 10x14", lot 204, GAI 3/17/89 .... **125**
Pierce & King, hc litho, lt stn/tr mrg, 13x17", lot 147, GAI 3/17/89 .... **300**

KELLOGG & THAYER
Look at Mamma, hc litho, trm mrgs, lt stn, 12x17", lot 130, GAI 2/10/89 .... **30**
Washington (full-figure portrait), hc litho, lt trm/stn, 10x14", lot 286, GAI 3/17/89 .... **115**

KELLY, Ellsworth (American, 1923-)
Camellia III, 51/75, litho/BFK Rives, 1964-65, p/s, full sheet, lt cr/sl/stn, S-35x24", Maeght, lot 485, C-NY 5/11/88 OE **935**
Colored Paper Image XI, 17/18, brn/gray pulp laminated to handmade, 1976, p/s, TGL bstp, 46x32", lot 695, SBY 2/23/89 .... **3,300**
Colored Paper Image XIV, 23/24, total ed of 32, 1976, p/s, a/bstp, TGL bstp, full sheet, S-32x31", lot 696, C-NY 11/1/88 .... **3,300**
Colored Paper Image XV, 13/23, total ed of 31, p/s, a/bstp, TGL bstp, full sheet, S-32x31", lot 697, C-NY 11/1/88 .... **3,520**
Colored Paper Image XV, 23/23, dk gray/bl pressed paper pulp, 1976, p/s, TGL bstp, S-32x32", lot 865, SBY 11/5/88 .... **2,750**
Colored Paper Image XVII, 17/22, laminated gr/gray/blk pulp on handmade, 1976, S-32x31", Tyler Graphics, SBY 5/14/88 .... **3,850**
Concorde IV (State), 11/18, aqua/Arches, 1982, p/s, inscr State, Gemini bstp, S-34x26", lot 698, C-NY 11/1/88 OE **1,320**
Dracena I, 8/30, litho/BFK Rives, 1983-85, p/s, Gemini bstp, full sheet, S-43x32", lot 487, C-NY 5/11/88 OE **1,210**
Dracena II, 8/30, litho/BFK Rives, 1983-85, p/s, Gemini bstp, full sheet, S-43x32", lot 488, C-NY 5/11/88 OE **990**
Eight by Eight To Celebrate the Temporary Contemporary: Untitled; 85/250, bl litho, 1983, p/s, 29x41", SBY 2/23/89 OE **2,310**
Nine Squares, 12/44, clr slksc/litho/wht BFK Rives, 1977, p/s, TGL bstp, full mrgs, S-40x40", lot 1127, SBY 5/13/89 OE **7,700**
Spectrum, 21/34, clr scrpt/Arches, 1973, p/s, Gemini bstp, lt stn/cr/fox, S-34x84", lot 695, C-NY 11/1/88 .... **6,600**
Spectrum, TPV, ed of 6 trial proofs, clr slksc, 1973, p/s, Gemini bstp, full mrgs, 17x67", lot 1126, SBY 5/13/89 OE **18,700**
Two Whites & Black, 17/75, slksc/Arjomari, 1973, p/s, Gemini bstp, 23x47", lot 3034, B/B 4/19/88 .... **600**
Wall, AP16/16, etch/aqua, 1976-79, p/s, TGL bstp, full mrgs, 16x14", lot 866, SBY 11/5/88 OE **3,575**
Wall, 24/50, etch/aqua/Arches Cover, 1976-79, p/s, Tyler Graphics bstp, S-32x28", lot 486, C-NY 5/11/88 OE **6,050**

KELLY, Thomas (American, 19th C)
American Hunting Scene, Wild Duck Shooting; hc litho, ca 1869, rpr trs, stn mrgs, tp verso, P-18x25", C-NY 1/22/88 UE **176**
American Prize Fruit with Basket, hc litho, 1869, lt lstn, cr img, rpr tr/sl mrgs, laid down, L-18x25", C-NY 1/22/88 .... **528**

KEMP, Robert (American, 20th C)
Uncle Tom's Cabin, clr litho/3 sheets poster paper, 88x40", Moody Brothers, lot 245, FAP 2/24/88 .... **225**

KENT, Rockwell (American, 1882-1971)
Beowulf, ed of 150, litho, 1931, p/s, 14x11", lot 161, WG 10/19/88 .... **550**
Beowulf, ed of 150, litho/cream wove paper, 1931, p/s, titled, full mrgs, 14x11", lot 2954, B/B 4/19/88 .... **468**
Beowulf: Beowulf & Grendel's Mother; ed of 150, litho/cream wove paper, p/s, lg mrgs, 14x10", lot 2955, B/B 2/16/88 .... **605**
Climbing the Bars, litho, 1928, p/s, 11x7", lot 163, WG 10/19/88 .... **425**
Convalescent, wood engr/cream wove paper, p/s, titled, sm mrgs, 16x12", lot 58, FAP 2/24/89 .... **170**
Diver, ed of 150, wood engr/cream wove paper, 1931, p/s, lg mrgs, lt stn, 8x5", lot 2956, B/B 2/16/88 OE **660**
Europe, litho/wove paper, 1946, p/s, titled, lt stn, tp to overmat, L-14x10", lot 191, C-NY 1/19/89 OE **825**
Fire, ed of 100, litho/BFK Rives, 1948, p/s, titled, full mrgs, lt stn, 14x10", lot 2958, B/B 2/16/88 .... **412**
Girl on Cliff, ed of 1750, wood engr/wove paper, 1920, p/s, full mrgs, cr/stn/sl mrgs, fox verso, L-7x5", C-NY 1/22/88 .... **418**
Girl on Cliff, ed of 1750, wood engr/wove paper, 1930, p/s, lt fox/stn mrgs, unfr, L-7x5", C-NY 1/22/88 .... **418**
Godspeed, ed of 150, wood engr/wove paper, 1931, p/s, lt stn/fox, old tp on verso, L-5x7", lot 190, C-NY 1/19/89 OE **935**
Greenland Kayaker, ed of 150, litho/BFK Rives, 1933, p/s, titled, full mrgs, 9x7", lot 2957, B/B 2/16/88 .... **468**
Greenland Mother Nursing, ed of 250, litho/BFK Rives, 1934, p/s, 8x6", Cleveland Print Club, lot 204, WG 10/19/88 .... **350**

Lovers, wood engr, 1928, p/s, full mrgs, lt scr img, lt stn, 7x10", lot 38, SBY 2/25/88 OE 2,420
Mountain Climber, ed of 235, state 3, wood engr/Shogun, 1933, p/s, 8x6", Cleveland Print Club, lot 183, WG 10/19/88 700
Northern Night (N by E), ed of 120, wood engr/linocut, 1930, p/s, lt stn mrgs, 6x8", lot 125, SWN 6/15/89 825
Oarsman, ed of 150, engr/wm Japan, 1931, lt mstn, lt cr mrg edge, L-5x7", lot 30, C-NY 5/11/88 660
Pair: Prometheus; Beouwulf: Beowulf; ed of 170/150, wood engr & litho, 1931, p/s, C-NY 1/22/88 440
Self-Portrait, ed of 150, litho/wove paper, 1934, p/s, inscr It's Me O Lord!, lt stn/sl, unfr, L-14x10", C-NY 1/22/88 1,430
Starlight, ed of 120, engr/wove paper, 1930, p/s, lt stn, L-6x7", lot 48, RWS 9/8/89 OE 1,100
Starry Night, ed of 1750, wood engr, 1933, p/s, full mrgs, lt stn, L-7x5", lot 19, PHL 6/16/88 250
Starry Night, wood engr, 1933, p/s, 7x5", lot 162, WG 10/19/88 400
Starry Night, wood engr/thin Japan, 1933, p/s, hinged to mat, 7x5", lot 2954, B/B 2/16/88 OE 715
Starry Night, wood engr/thin Japan, 1933, p/s, lt trm mrgs, lt fox, old tp on verso, 7x5", lot 2955, B/B 4/19/88 UE 300
Starry Night, wood engr/thin Japan, 1933, p/s, 3 lt trm mrgs, lt mstn, 7x5", lot 2956, B/B 4/19/88 248
Workers of the World Unite, ed of 150, engr, 1937, p/s, lt scr img, lt fox/tstn mrgs, L-8x6", lot 31, C-NY 5/11/88 OE 880

KIRCHNER, Ernst Ludwig (German, 1880-1938)

Alte und Junge Frau, ed of 100, wc, 1921, stp/s, lt sl, L-13x9", lot 329, C-NY 11/1/88 1,320
Badende, clr wc/cream wove paper, 1923, 2x4", lot 2854, B/B 4/19/88 248
Badende Frauen Zwischen Weissen Steinen, #KFH39, clr wc/Japan, 1912, p/s, lt cr, S-19x14", lot 72, C-NY 11/1/88 110,000
Bildnis van Vloten, #KH83, wc/firm Japan, 1918, sgn/inscr Eigendruck by Erna Kirchner, S-26x17", lot 76, C-NY 11/1/88 49,500
Die Frau und die Manner, #KH59, wc/thin Japan, 1937, p/s, Swiss Customs stp, lt stn, S-25x18", lot 80, C-NY 11/1/88 7,700
Dodokopf, #KR20, drypt/thick fibrous lt bl wove paper, 1909, p/s, inscr Eigendruck, S-15x15", lot 71, C-NY 11/1/88 OE 17,600
Kinderportrat, 2nd state, wc/wove paper, 1908, p/s, lt rub/old hinges, L-20x15", lot 636, C-NY 5/10/89 19,800
Liegender Madchenkopf, bl etch/stiff wove paper, 1917, inscr Eigendruck, Kirchner estate stp, P-10x10", SBY 5/12/88 OE 4,400
Moritzburger Badende und Mandoline Spielender Mann, drypt/burnishing/buff laid paper, 1909, 8x9", lot 529, SBY 5/11/89 9,900
Muggelsee, 1st state, blk/gr/purple wc, 1912, p/s, inscr Eigendruck, rpr tr, lt cr/fox, S-20x16", lot 637, C-NY 5/10/89 82,500
Neben der Heerstrasse, wc, titled, 3x3", lot 1018, S/A 2/18/89 320
Plakat der Neue Kunstsalon 1912, wc/bl wove paper, 1912, lt stn/cr/tr, canvas backed, S-37x28", lot 199, C-NY 11/1/88 11,000
Ruhender Madchenakt, wc/thin Japan, 1905, p/s, inscr Akt Reihe das Modell, lt fox/cr, S-6x7", lot 66, C-NY 11/1/88 8,250
Steinbruch, brn drypt/smooth wove paper, 1924, p/s, lt sl/scuff, 10x7", lot 286, SBY 2/23/89 880
Strassenkreuzung, #16, wc/firm wove paper, 1908, p/s, inscr Handdruck, lt cr, S-17x22", lot 70, C-NY 11/1/88 38,500
Topfmarkt, wc/firm gray laid paper, 1905, p/s, inscr Handdruck, lt stn, S-6x7", lot 67, C-NY 11/1/88 4,400
Unterhaltung von Drei Frauen, 1st state, clr wc/fibrous cream laid paper, 1907, p/s, S-19x17", lot 69, C-NY 11/1/88 93,500
Weisses Haus in Wiesen, #K11, wc/soft tan wove paper, 1920, p/s, inscr Eigendruck, S-17x23", lot 78, C-NY 11/1/88 44,000

KLEE, Paul (Swiss, 1879-1940)

Abstrakton II, etch/cream simili Japan, 1913, p/s, dtd 1932, lt cr, S-7x9", lot 82, C-NY 11/1/88 17,600
Baumwollpfluckerin-Poster for Kunstschau Wien-Mai-Oktober 1908; clr litho, 1908, S-35x22", Berger, lot 233A, SBY 11/3/88 3,850
Jungfrau im Baum (Jungfrau Tramend), a/p, aside from ed of 30, etch, 1903, p/s, cr/scr, 13x17", lot 81, C-NY 11/1/88 OE 49,500
Night Ended, #K10, etch/Japan, 1930, full mrgs, lt cr, 7x5", Cahiers d'Art, lot 225, SBY 2/25/88 OE 3,575
Seiltanzer, #138, blk & rose litho/BSB laid paper, 1923, p/s, Piper bstp, lt stn/tr, S-21x15", lot 233, SBY 11/3/88 OE 25,300

KLEIBER, Hans (American, 1887-1967)

Grand Teton, etch, p/s, titled, 12x9", Assn Am Artists, lot 287, WG 10/19/88 75
Pair: Deep in the Rockies; Fall in the Rockies; etch/drypt & etch, p/s, full mrgs, P-8x11"/P-11x10", PHL 6/16/88 UE 190
Pair: Disturbed Pintails; Evening; etch, p/s, titled, no size given, Assn Am Artists, lot 274, WG 10/19/88 OE 160
Pintails Feeding, etch, p/s, titled, 9x7", Assn Am Artists, lot 143, WG 10/19/88 80

KLEINHOF, H. (20th C)

Head of a Body, clr slksc, 1985, sgn/dtd, 18x24", lot 137, MG 5/28/88 45

KLINGER, Max (German, 1857-1920)

Atelierszene, #3, etch/engr/drypt/laid paper, ca 1893, p/s, tstn, P-5x7", lot 344, C-NY 1/19/89 462
House on a River, etch/aqua/heavy wove paper, lt skinned, tr, 15x22", lot 2862, B/B 2/16/88 165
Stillbirth, #10, etch/aqua/cream wove paper, 1903, lt cr, 13x18", lot 2861, B/B 2/16/88 220

KLOSS, Gene (American, 1903-)

Interpreter, etch, intl/titled, 8x7", lot 933, LH 10/16/88 OE 275
Pair: Christmas Eve; Taos Pueblo; etch, p/s, 11x14", lot 235, MG 11/19/88 150
Pair: Roadside Pottery; Trip to Town; 13/35 & 11/25, etch/Somerset & etch/wove paper, 1979, p/s, trm mrgs, C-NY 1/22/88 209
Riders at Sundown, ed of 75, drypt/aqua/cream wove paper, 1953, p/s, titled, lt trm mrgs, 8x12", lot 2957, B/B 4/19/88 275

KNIGHT, Daniel Ridgeway (American, 1840-1924)

Afternoon Nap, litho, sgn/inscr Nellie Rose Potel, full mrgs, L-11x12", RAB 3/27/89 75

KNOBEL, E. (American, 19th C)

Southern Hotel, clr litho, lt ls/stn in corner, 18x24", SLK 5/6/88 250

KOCH, Walther (German, 1875-1915)

Wintersport in Graubunden, 55/500, clr litho, 23x28", Wolfenberger, lot 154, FAP 2/24/89 UE 155

KOEHLER, Joseph

Pair: New York & Brooklyn Bridge; New York & Williamsburg Bridge; chromolitho, 1916, stn, 16x23", lot 535, SBY 1/28/88 880

KOHN, Misch (American, 1916-)

The General, clr aqua, ca 1961, p/s, dtd 1961, 17x9", lot 998, LH 5/15/88 250

KOKOSCHKA, Oskar (Austrian, 1886-1980)

Baumwollpfluckerin Poster for Kunstschau Wein Mai-Oktober 1908, litho, 1908, unfr, S-35x22", Kunstschau, SBY 5/12/88 UE 3,300
Book: Die Traumenden Knaben; orig ed of 225, 1908, Wiener Werkstatte/Verlag, lot 530, SBY 5/11/89 OE 14,300
Book: Die Traumenden Knaben; 270/275, 18 litho w/text on wove paper, 1917, orig boards, Verlag, lot 639, C-NY 5/10/89 OE 15,400

KOLLER, Rudolf (Swiss, 1828-1905)

Jubilaums, Asstellung, Zurich; clr litho, 1898, Maitres de l'Affiche bstp, 12x9", lot 329, LH 9/10/89 170

KOLLWITZ, Kathe (German, 1867-1945)

Arbeiterfrau Im Profil Nach Links, 2nd state of 3, dk brn litho/buff laid paper, 1903, p/s, L-17x12", SBY 5/12/88 OE **3,850**
Aufruhr, final state, dk brn etch/stiff Japan, 1899, large mrgs, lt rub/fox/sl, 12x13", lot 234, SBY 11/3/88 ..... **1,100**
Aus Vielen Wunden Blutest Du, Oh Volk; etch/aqua, 1986, p/s, full mrgs, lt stn, 5x13", lot 532, SBY 5/11/89 OE **1,540**
Beim Dengeln, etch, 1905/1921, p/s, 11x11", lot 95, WG 10/19/88 ..... **1,900**
Beim Dengeln, 9th state of 12, etch/sftgr/simili Japan, 1905, p/s, trm mrgs, lt cr/stn, S-14x13", C-NY 1/22/88 OE **1,650**
Beratung, etch, 1895/1945, Berlin-Halensee bstp, lt stn, P-11x7", RWS 3/16/89 ..... **250**
Besuch im Krankenhous, 5th state, wc/Japan, 1929, p/s, full mrgs, lt mstn/fox, 11x14", lot 536, SBY 5/11/89 OE **6,050**
Birth, restrike, sgn in pl, 18x18", FAP 6/16/89 ..... **225**
Die Carmagnole, dk brn aqua/etch, 1901, p/s, full mrgs, lt sl/ls to img, fox/stn, unfr, P-16x14", SBY 5/12/88 OE **3,025**

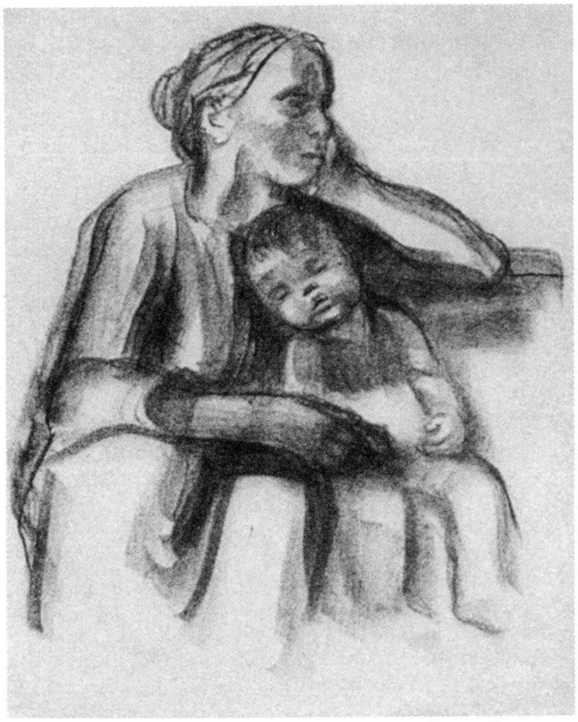

Arbeiterfrau mit Schlafendem Jungen, #82, total ed of 100, litho/thick wove paper, 1927, lt fox/stn/sl, L-15x13", lot 641, C-NY 5/10/89; $8,250

Die Eltern der Kunstlerin, ed of 275, litho/JW Zanders, 1919, p/s, full mrgs, lt cr, L-12x19", SBY 5/12/88 ..... **1,980**
Die Pfluger, 7th state, dk brn etch/aqua/cream laid paper, 1921, full mrgs, stn/sl/fox, 12x18", lot 533, SBY 5/11/89 OE **4,400**
Die Pfluger, 7th state, etch/aqua/heavy wove paper, 1906, full mrgs, lt sl/cr, 12x18", lot 237, SBY 11/3/88 OE **2,750**
Frau mit Totem Kind, 9th state, etch/wove paper, 1903, p/s, lt stn, 17x19", Richter/Felsing, lot 236, SBY 11/3/88 OE **5,500**
Gefallen, a/p, 1st state, litho/Butten, 1921, p/s, inscr Stein II, full mrgs, lt stn, 16x15", lot 238, SBY 11/3/88 OE **3,300**
Girl Praying, posthumous ed, etch/aqua, 1892, 8x6", lot 128, SWN 6/15/89 ..... **330**
Helft Russland, 3rd state, litho, 1921, p/s, full mrgs, lt cr img/mrgs, tp on verso, L-16x19", lot 332, C-NY 11/1/88 OE **1,650**
Junges Paar, 4th state, etch/wove paper, 1904, stp/s, full mrgs, lt stn/sl, 11x12", lot 287, SBY 2/23/89 ..... **4,400**
Kleiner Selbstbildnis Nach Links, ed of 200, litho/wove paper, 1922, p/s, full mrgs, lt stn/fox, S-14x10", RWS 3/16/89 ..... **2,000**
Kleines Selbstbildnis, 1st state, litho/Japan nacre, 1920, p/s, full mrgs, stn/fox, 13x8", lot 534, SBY 5/11/89 ..... **3,575**
Mutter mit Jungen, state IIa, litho, 1931, p/s, full mrgs, lt cr img, lt stn/sl mrgs, L-14x9", lot 334, C-NY 11/1/88 ..... **6,380**
Mutter mit Kind auf dem Arm, state IIIb, brn-blk etch/cream wove paper, 1910, P-8x5", Felsing, lot 182, C-NY 5/11/88 OE **3,520**
Not, Pl 1, 2nd state, litho/thick Japan, 1867, lt stn, tp to overmat on verso, L-6x6", lot 640, C-NY 5/10/89 ..... **1,980**
Pair: Girl Praying; Woman with Folded Arms; drypt/etch/aqua, 8x6"/11x9", lot 101, SWN 12/1/88 ..... **550**
Pair: Mutter Gebt von Euerm Eberfluss; Selbstbildnis im Profil Nach Rechts; litho, 1926 & 1938, lot 535, SBY 5/11/89 OE **5,500**
Portrait of a Woman, etch/aqua/heavy wove paper, lg mrgs, lt stn, 14x9", lot 2866, B/B 2/16/88 ..... **385**
Selbstbildnis, ed of 80, litho/wove paper, 1934, p/s, full mrgs, rpr tr/mstn, 8x7", lot 537, SBY 5/11/89 OE **4,400**
Selbstbildnis am Tisch II, state IIIb, etch/aqua, ca 1893, p/s, lt stn/cr, P-7x5", lot 330, C-NY 11/1/88 OE **2,750**
Selbstbildnis von Vorn, ed of 275, final state, wc/cream wove paper, 1923, p/s, 6x6", Richter, lot 239, SBY 11/3/88 OE **2,750**
Selbstbildnis, aside from #d ed of 80, litho/wove paper, 1934, p/s, full mrgs, lt stn, L-8x7", lot 69, PHL 10/28/88 ..... **2,800**
Set of 8: Tod; ed of 100, litho/cream wove paper, 1934-35, p/s, lt cr/sl, S-26x21", lot 83, C-NY 11/1/88 OE **46,200**
Stehender Weiblicher Akt, state IIa, etch/wove paper, 1900, p/s, lt cr/tp, P-7x5", Felsing, lot 181, C-NY 5/11/88 ..... **1,650**
Sturm, state IIa, etch, 1987, p/s, inscr Felsing, lt lstn/fox, P-9x12", lot 331, C-NY 11/1/88 ..... **1,650**
Swei Schwartzende Frauen mit Zwei Kindern, ed of 150, litho/stiff paper, 1930, p/s, lt stn, L-12x11", PHL 10/28/88 OE **3,250**
Tod im Wasser, Pl 7, 13/100, litho, ca 1934, p/s, full mrgs, 20x16", lot 100, SWN 12/1/88 ..... **1,210**
Widow-1, posthumous ed, wc, 1922-23, 2 tr to upper mrg, 15x9", lot 127, SWN 6/15/89 ..... **165**
Zertretene, 4th state, etch/thick wove paper, 1900, p/s, full mrgs, lt fox/sl, 9x8", lot 235, SBY 11/3/88 ..... **2,200**
Zwei Schwatzende Frauen mit Zwei Kindern, ed of 150, litho, 1930, p/s, lt cr/stn/sl, L-12x10", lot 333, C-NY 11/1/88 ..... **3,300**

KRASNER, Lee (American, 1911-)

Primary Series: Rose Stone; Blue Stone; Gold Stone; 3 clr litho, 1969, full sheet, Marlborough, lot 489, C-NY 5/11/88 ..... **660**

KRUGER, Barbara (Austrian, 1945-)
We Are Ordered To Enter the Sphere of Fixation, photo slksc on paper, 1985, 73x49", SBY 10/8/88 OE ... 17,600
KUBINYI, Kalman (American, 1906-1973)
Lake Port, engr, p/s, titled, 8x9", lot 132, WG 10/19/88 ... 200
Saraband, mezzo/handmade paper, 1932, p/s, titled, 11x9", Cleveland Print Club, lot 173, WG 10/19/88 ... 175
KUHN, Walt (American, 1877-1949)
Americans, 32/50, litho, ca 1925, sgn/titled, 9x10", lot 102, SWN 12/1/88 ... 275
Angel, #31-P, litho/Basinwerk, 1929, p/s, titled, 12x8", lot 132, SWN 6/15/89 ... 605
Angel in a Sensual Pose, ed of no more than 50, etch/laid paper, 1925, p/s, pl/s, 8x9", lot 103, SWN 12/1/88 OE ... 523
Hulda, ed of 50, ltiho, 1929, p/s, S-20x12", lot 104, SWN 12/1/88 ... 358
Large Head, ed of 35, litho, 1923, p/s, 22x18", lot 131, SWN 6/15/89 OE ... 1,320
Reclining Nude, etch/wove paper, 1925, p/s, full mrgs, P-8x6", RWS 3/16/89 OE ... 350
Rhoda, ed of less than 50, litho, 1929, p/s, 13x10", lot 130, SWN 6/15/89 ... 495
Vessel, ed of 50, litho, 1923, p/s, 19x16", lot 105, SWN 12/1/88 ... 770
KUNICHIKA (Japanese, Meiji period)
Man with Sword, woodblock, sgn/dtd 1876, 10x14", lot 16A, MG 5/28/88 UE ... 110
Pair: Courtesans; clr woodblock, ca 1870, oban size, lot 737, LH 5/15/88 ... 100
Woman in Kimono, woodblock, sgn/dtd 1876, 10x14", lot 16B, MG 5/28/88 UE ... 90
KUNIYOSHI, Yasuo (American, 1893-1953)
Aerialist, litho/China, p/s, inscr 30 Proofs, mrg corners trm, lt stn, 9x10", lot 241, SBY 5/11/89 OE ... 15,400
Artificial Flowers, ed of 30, litho/Chine applique, 1934, p/s, inscr 30P, full mrgs, stn, L-16x10", SBY 5/12/88 OE ... 6,050
Cafe, presumed ed of 30, litho/wove paper, 1934, intl, trm to img, laid down, L-10x8", lot 194, C-NY 1/19/89 OE ... 1,210
Cafe No 2, Ed 100, litho/BFK Rives, 1936, p/s, Hamilton Easter Field bstp, full mrgs, cr/sl, L-13x10", C-NY 1/22/88 OE ... 14,300
Cafe No 2, litho/cream BFK Rives, 1935, p/s, inscr 100 Ed, lt stn/fox, 13x10", George Miller, lot 37, SBY 2/25/88 ... 17,600
Cafe No 2, litho/wove paper, 1935, p/s, dtd 36, lt trm mrg, lt ls/stn, L-13x10", lot 195, C-NY 1/19/89 ... 14,300
Carnival, litho/wove paper, ca 1965, p/s, lt trm mrgs, lt stn, 16x10", lot 2958, B/B 4/19/88 OE ... 1,650
Circus Girl with Plumed Hat, #25P, litho/wht wove paper, 1933, p/s, lt rpr tr, lt sl/ls, 13x10", lot 35, SBY 11/3/88 ... 2,200
Cyclist, ed of 250, litho/Rives, 1939, p/s, full mrgs, lt stn/old tp, L-13x9", lot 445, C-NY 5/10/89 ... 9,900
Cyclist, ed of 250, litho/wove paper, 1939, p/s, full mrgs, lt fox/stn mrgs, tp verso, mstn, L-13x9", C-NY 1/22/88 OE ... 7,700
Flowers in a Friend's Window, 26/26, litho/tan Chine applique, 1928, lt stn, 13x9", Desjobert, lot 36, C-NY 2/25/88 OE ... 6,325
Fruit in White Bowl, 5/50, litho/BFK Rives, 1927, p/s, full mrgs, lt stn/fox, L-14x16", SBY 5/12/88 OE ... 6,875
Girl at Table, 27/30, litho/Chine applique, 1928, p/s, full mrgs, lt rpr tr, 9x6", Desjobert, lot 238, SBY 5/11/89 OE ... 13,200
Girl in a Wicker Chair, ed of 50, litho/wove paper, 1927, p/s, inscr, trm mrg, lt lstn/cr/sl, L-18x12", C-NY 1/22/88 OE ... 8,250
Girl in Feathered Hat, 11/26, litho/India applique, p/s, dtd, trm mrg, lt stn/sl, tr mrg, unfr, L-8x6", C-NY 1/22/88 OE ... 4,950
Girl on Trapeze, ed of 100, litho/wove paper, 1936, p/s, WPA bstp, trm/ls to mrgs, laid down, L-13x10", C-NY 1/22/88 OE ... 5,500
Girl Putting on a Chemise, 21/32, litho/Chine applique, 1928, p/s, lg mrgs, 9x5", Desjobert, lot 31, SBY 11/3/88 OE ... 13,200
Grapes & Sculpture, #30P, ed of 30, litho, 1932, p/s, dtd 33, lt sl/cr/ls/fox, 10x11", lot 34, SBY 2/23/89 ... 4,125

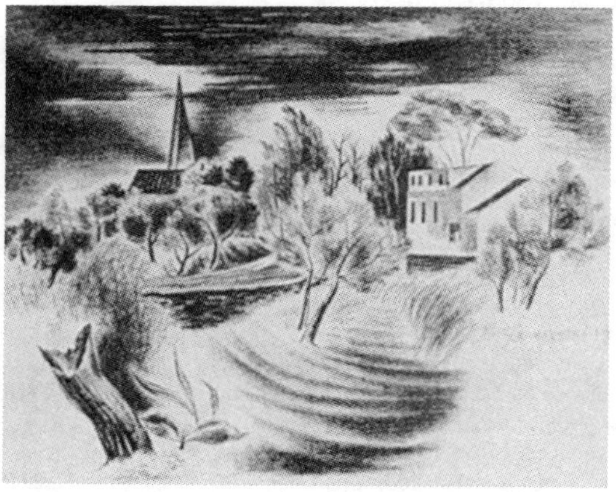

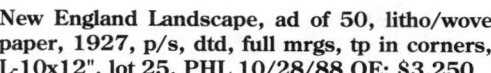

New England Landscape, ad of 50, litho/wove paper, 1927, p/s, dtd, full mrgs, tp in corners, L-10x12", lot 25, PHL 10/28/88 OE; $3,250

Nude at Door, 20/36, litho/Chine applique, 1928, p/s, lt stn/cr mrgs, mstn verso, L-13x7", lot 444, C-NY 5/10/89 ... 8,800
Nude at Door, 21/36, litho/Chine applique, 1928, lg mrgs, lt sl/cr/tr, 13x8", Desjobert, lot 239, SBY 5/11/89 OE ... 13,200
Pair: Bullfight; Winter; litho, 1928 & 1934, 9x10"/9x12", lot 32, SBY 11/3/88 OE ... 5,500
Pears & Grapes, 17/44, litho/Chine applique, 1928, p/s, full mrgs, lt stn/rpr, 8x11", Desjobert, lot 240, SBY 5/11/89 OE ... 9,250
Pears & Grapes, 25/44, litho/Chine applique, 1928, p/s, full mrgs, lt fox/cr/stn, 8x11", lot 33, SBY 11/3/88 OE ... 7,150
Pears & Grapes, 6/44, litho/Chine applique, 1928, p/s, full mrgs, fox/sl/stn, 8x11", Desjobert, lot 34, SBY 11/3/88 OE ... 5,500
Shower, #30, litho/cream wove paper, 1932, p/s, lt scr img, lt stn/old tp, L-10x14", lot 193, C-NY 1/19/89 ... 1,760
South Berwick, Maine; ed of 250, litho/wove paper, 1934, p/s, full mrgs, 9x13", lot 36, SBY 11/3/88 OE ... 4,125
Still Life at Window, 25/25, litho/tan Chine applique, 1928, p/s, lt stn, 12x9", Desjobert, lot 35, SBY 2/25/88 OE ... 5,775
Striped Vase, 7/50, litho/wove paper, 1927, p/s, lt trm mrgs, lt lstn/mstn/sl, unfr, L-15x8", SBY 5/12/88 OE ... 4,950
Two Acrobats, 2/26, litho/tan Chine applique, 1928, p/s, full mrgs, lt stn/rpr tr/ls, 13x9", Desjobert, SBY 2/25/88 ... 9,350
Western Landscape, ed of 30, litho/wove paper, 1935, p/s, inscr 35P, lt trm, lt stn, L-11x15", SBY 5/12/88 OE ... 6,875
Wire Performer, ed of 100, litho/wove paper, 1938, p/s, full mrgs, rpr tr/cr, scr verso, unfr, L-16x12", C-NY 1/22/88 OE ... 5,280
Wire Walker, 2/20, litho/tan Chine applique, 1928, p/s, lt stn/rub, 8x9", Desjobert, lot 34, SBY 2/25/88 ... 7,700

KURTZ & ALLISON
George Washington at Mount Vernon, hc litho, 1889, trm mrgs , lt stn/ls, 20x24", lot 61, GAI 11/25/88 .... **70**
KURZWEIL, Maximilian (Austrian, 1867-1916)
Der Polster, clr wc, 1903, 12x10", lot 299, LH 3/20/88 .... **1,000**
Der Polster, clr wc/fibrous laid Japan, 1903, full mrgs, lt mstn, L-11x10", Verlag, lot 335, C-NY 11/1/88 UE **700**
Der Polster, clr wc/fibrous laid Japan, 1903, full mrgs, lt mstn, L-11x10", Verlag, lot 183, C-NY 5/11/88 .... **990**
KUSHNER, Robert (American, 1949-)
Cupids Making Borscht, 3/30, clr litho/2 sheets of Arches, 1981, p/s, S-22x60", Holly Solomon, lot 701, C-NY 11/1/88 .... **880**
KUZNETSOV, Pavel (Russian, 20th C)
Set of 15: Turkestan, Autolithografienp; ed of unknown size, litho/wove paper, 1923, orig folder, lot 336, C-NY 11/1/88 .... **935**
LABOUREUR, Jean Emile (French, 1877-1943)
La Fille aux Oies, 27/40, drypt/laid MBM, 1916, p/s, full mrgs, lt mstn, P-7x6", lot 345, C-NY 1/19/89 OE **715**
La Promenade sur Le Porl, total ed of 250, 2nd state, etch/engr, 1933, Cleveland Print Club, lot 222, WG 10/19/88 .... **375**
LAM, Wilfredo (Cuban, 1902-1982)
Suite: Le Regard Vertical; HC XXVI/XXXI, 6 clr litho, 1973, S-26x20", Ed Aguri/LaMata, lot 37, SBY 11/3/88 .... **2,750**
LANDACRE, Paul (American, 1893-1963)
Group of 3: Sultry Day; Rima; Forest Girl; engr/wove Vidalon, 1937, full mrgs, Am Artist Group, lot 2959, B/B 4/19/88 .... **825**
Nimbus, 15/60, wood engr/Japan, 1934, p/s, titled, corners tp to mat, lt stn, 5x8", lot 2960, B/B 4/19/88 OE **825**
Pair: Rima; Forest Girl; wood engr/cream wove paper, 1937, pl/s, full mrgs, Assn Am Artists, lot 2962, B/B 2/16/88 .... **330**
Pair: Rima; Sultry Day; wood engr, 1936-37, 9x6", Am Artist Group, lot 228, WG 10/19/88 .... **250**
Sultry Day, wood engr/cream wove paper, 1937, sgn/dtd in block, lg mrgs, lt fox verso, 8x6", lot 2961, B/B 2/16/88 OE **1,210**
LANDEAU, R. (French, 19th/20th C)
Exposition de Horticulture, clr litho/poster paper, 1929, linen backed, unfr, 47x31", Bedos & Cie, lot 22, FAP 2/24/89 .... **225**
LANDECK, Armin (American, 1905-)
Black House, Bleecker Street; ed of 100, etch, 1972, p/s, 24x18", lot 436, WG 10/19/88 .... **550**
Fish, ed of 100, final state, engr, 1963, p/s, 18x24", lot 107, SWN 12/1/88 UE **300**
Housetops, 14th Street; ed of 100, drypt/etch/wove paper, 1937, p/s, lt rpr/sl, P-8x11", lot 199, C-NY 1/19/89 OE **935**
Manhattan Canyon, Ed 100, drypt, 1934, full mrgs, lt stn, 14x7", lot 38, SBY 11/3/88 .... **2,750**
Manhattan Vista, Ed 100, drypt, 1934, p/s, full mrgs, lt rub/sl mrgs, stn verso, 10x9", lot 39, SBY 11/3/88 .... **1,760**
Pair: Manhattan Vista; Paris Metro; ed of 100, drypt/BFK Rives & engr/wove paper, p/s, lt stn/ink, C-NY 1/22/88 .... **1,650**
Pair: On West 13th Street; Window on 14th Street; drypt & engr/drypt, 1980 & 1949, unfr, no size given, C-NY 1/22/88 .... **330**
Pair: Rooftop with Ventilators; Stairhall; engr & drypt/engr, 1942 & 1950, p/s, lt stn, lot 200, C-NY 1/19/89 OE **1,210**
Pair: Ski Jump No 1; Engraver's Tools; litho & engr, 1935/1974, w/mrgs, lt stn/sl, L-10x14"/P-16x18", SBY 5/12/88 UE **770**
Pop's Tavern, ed of 100, aqua/drypt, 1934, p/s, tp in mrg, lt sl on verso, P-6x10", lot 32, C-NY 5/11/88 .... **2,420**
Pop's Tavern, ed of 100, aqua/drypt/wove paper, 1934, p/s, trm mrgs, lt ink/rub mrgs, P-6x10", C-NY 1/22/88 .... **3,520**
Restaurant, Ed 100, engr/wove paper, 1951, p/s, full mrgs, lt cr mrgs, unfr, P-12x16", C-NY 1/22/88 .... **385**
Rooftops, ed of 100, engr, 1941, sgn w/thumbprint, 5x9", lot 133, SWN 6/15/89 .... **660**
Studio Interior No 1, a/p, drypt/wove paper, 1935, p/s, full mrgs, P-8x11", lot 196, C-NY 1/19/89 OE **1,045**
LANE, Fitz Hugh (American, 1804-1865)
View of Newburyport, From Salisbury; hc litho, 1846-48, tr img, lt cr/sl mrgs, S-19x27", lot 513, SBY 1/28/88 .... **3,025**
LANE, Lois (American, 1948-)
Untitled, 6 Aquatints; 39/45, blk & pk aqua/Moulin du Gue, 1979, full mrgs, 30x23", Parasol, lot 702, C-NY 11/1/88 OE **220**
LANE, William (American, 18th C)
Encampment of the Convention Army, engr/laid paper, 1789, trm mrgs, lt stn/fld/fox, P-10x17", lot 85, C-NY 1/19/89 UE **550**
LANKES, Julius J. (American, 1884-1960)
Group of 3: Church at Jamestown; New Moon; Haying; wood engr, ca 1930s, p/s, various sizes, lot 158, WG 10/19/88 .... **185**
Winter Twilight, wc, 1929, p/s, 12x16", lot 244, WG 10/19/88 UE **150**
LAPORTE, George; after (German, 1789-1873)
Pair Going In; Going Away (hunt scenes); engr, 12x23", WT Davey, lot 968, FAP 12/8/88 .... **575**
LARIONOV, Mikhail (Russian, 1881-1964)
Costume Design: A Male Character; ed of 500, gouache/pochoir, sgn, 1919, 18x12", La Cible, C-L 10/8/88 OE **2,975**
Cover of La Cible Portfolio, ed of 500, wc, sgn on separate sheet, 19x13", C-L 10/8/88 .... **930**
LASANSKY, Mauricio L. (American, 1914-)
Boy with Cat, 37/50, mixed media etch, 1964, p/s, titled, full mrgs, lt cr, 53x24", lot 36, SBY 2/23/89 OE **7,425**
Old Lady with Bonnet, 37/70, etch/drypt, 1969, p/s, titled, full mrgs, lt rub/sl, 22x18", lot 37, SBY 2/23/89 .... **550**
LAURENCIN, Marie (French, 1885-1956)
Anne et les Pingouins, Pl 6, 38/115, bl/blk litho, 1930, full mrgs, lt stn/tr, L-13x10", lot 644, C-NY 5/10/89 .... **2,090**
Augusta, 14/100, clr litho/Japan, 1930, p/s, Jacquart bstp, full mtgs, lt fox/sl/stn, 16x11", lot 234, SBY 2/25/88 .... **5,500**
Augusta, 7/100, clr litho/Japan, 1930, p/s, Jacquart bstp, lt stn/scr, L-16x11", lot 344, C-NY 11/1/88 OE **8,250**
Auto-Portrait, total ed of 80, sanguine litho, 1920, sgn in bl crayon, lt stn, 9x6", lot 240, SBY 11/3/88 .... **1,650**
Boubou, ed of 25, 2nd state, clr litho/Japan, 1931, p/s, Jacquart bstp, lt rub/cr, 15x11", lot 253, SBY 11/3/88 .... **7,150**
Boubou, 18/125, bl & blk litho/Japan, 1931, p/s, lt scr/rub/stn/fox, 15x11", lot 253A, SBY 11/3/88 .... **7,150**
Boubou, 78/125, bl & blk litho/Arches, 1931, p/s, full mrgs, lt cr/fox, 15x11", lot 235, SBY 2/25/88 .... **7,150**
Boubou, 78/125, bl & blk litho/Arches, 1932, p/s, full mrgs, lt cr/fox/tr, L-15x11", SBY 5/12/88 OE **11,000**
Boubou, 92/125, clr litho, 1931, p/s, lg mrgs, lt stn, laid down, 15x12", lot 548, SBY 5/11/89 .... **9,350**
Chanson, Ou le Rideau Noir; 8/55, etch, 1921, lg mrgs, lt stn, 7x5", lot 288, SBY 2/23/89 .... **2,310**
Chanson, Ou le Rideau Noir; 14/55, final state, etch, 1921, p/s, full mrgs, lt stn/sl/cr, 7x6", lot 242, SBY 11/3/88 .... **2,640**
Christine, Ou l'Amazone; Pl 5, 41/115, clr litho/wove paper, 1930, p/s, lt stn, L-12x16", lot 643, C-NY 5/10/89 OE **9,350**
Christine, Ou l'Amazone; 102/115, clr litho, 1930, p/s, full mrgs, lt stn, 12x15", Quatre-Chemins, lot 297, SBY 2/23/89 .... **6,050**
Colombine, litho/stiff Japan, 1928, p/s, lg mrgs, lt stn/cr, 15x11", Weyhe Gallery, lot 248, SBY 11/3/88 OE **11,000**
Dinah, 108/125, final state, clr litho/stiff Japan, 1931, p/s, lg mrgs, 15x11", Jacquart, lot 252, SBY 11/3/88 OE **12,100**

Dinah, 35/125, clr litho/smooth cream wove paper, 1931, p/s, lt cr/skinned, 15x11", Jacquart, lot 298, SBY 2/23/89 9,900
Dinah, 50/125, clr litho/Japan, 1931, p/s, Jacquart bstp, full mrgs, lt stn, 16x11", lot 547, SBY 5/11/89 12,100
Dix Filles dan un Pre: Tois Jeune Filles Jouant a'l'Arc; total ed of about 995, etch, 1926, p/s, 5x3", SBY 2/23/89 1,320
Elvire, 2/125, clr litho/Japan, 1930, p/s, lt scr/stn/cr/sl, 15x11", Jacquart, lot 546, SBY 5/11/89 OE 13,200
Elvire, 47/125, clr litho/Japan, 1930, p/s, lt stn, 15x11", Jacquart, lot 296, SBY 2/23/89 OE 9,350
Elvire, 68/125, clr litho/stiff Japan, 1930, p/s, lt stn/cr, 15x11", Jacquart, lot 251, SBY 11/3/88 OE 11,550
Emilie, for Rene Crevel; 70/115, litho/van Gelder, 1930, full mrgs, L-10x8", Quatre-Chemins, lot 186, C-NY 5/11/88 OE 3,080
Emilie, Pl 2, 37/115, clr litho, 1943, p/s, lt stn, 10x8", Quatre-Chemins, lot 250, SBY 11/3/88 2,200
Europe, 135/150, clr litho/Japan, 1932, p/s, Jacquart bstp, lt stn/scr mrg, S-22x15", lot 187, C-NY 5/11/88 OE 5,500
Europe, 2nd state, clr litho/simili Japan, 1932, lt stn/scr, L-17x12", lot 645, C-NY 5/10/89 2,750
Europe, 82/150, final state, clr litho/stiff Japan, 1932, p/s, Jacquart bstp, lt stn, 17x12", lot 254, SBY 11/3/88 9,350

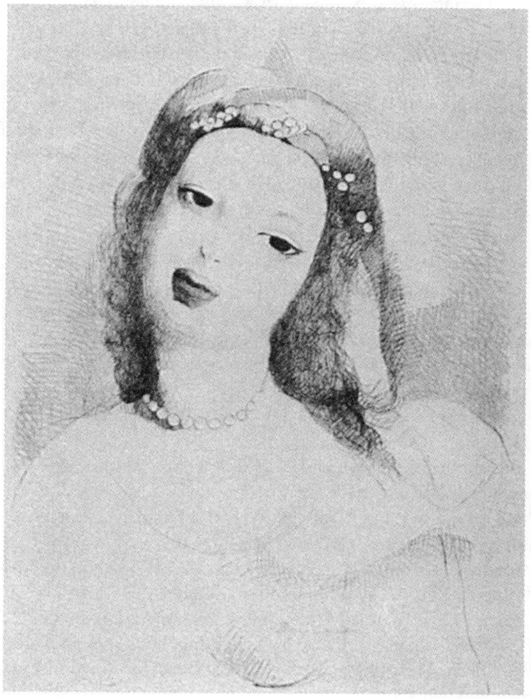

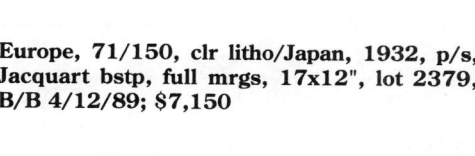

Europe, 71/150, clr litho/Japan, 1932, p/s, Jacquart bstp, full mrgs, 17x12", lot 2379, B/B 4/12/89; $7,150

Girl with Mandolin, restrike, clr etch/cream wove paper, pl/s, 8x7", lot 2867, B/B 2/16/88 137
Green Hat, 76/200, clr aqua, p/s, no size given, lot 538, LH 5/15/88 OE 2,800
Group of 3: Portrait of Alice; Alice, Outside the White Rabbit's House; Can You Play Croquet...; lot 136, SWN 6/15/89 OE 1,760
Jeune Fille a Balcon, Pl 5, 3rd state, ed of 33, clr etch, 1925, p/s, P-8x6", Ed l'Etoile, lot 342, C-NY 11/1/88 OE 7,700
Jeune Fille a la Fleur, Pl 1, 2/33, etch/smili Japan, 1925, p/s, lt stn, P-8x6", Ed l'Etoile, lot 339, C-NY 11/1/88 880
Jeune Fille au Chapeau Bleu, 80/80, etch, 1926, p/s, lt mstn, 4x3", lot 292, SBY 2/23/89 1,210
Jeune Fille aux Trois Ornaments de Perls, 29/100, clr litho, 1955, p/s, lt cr/fox, 16x12", lot 346, C-NY 11/1/88 OE 11,000
Jeune Fille avec Guitare, Alternace; 2nd state, etch/drypt/watercolor, 1946/wove paper, P-8x7", C-E 5/13/88 OE 770
Joueuse de Mandoline, 13/100, 3rd/final state, clr etch/wove paper, 1928, lt stn, laid down, P-7x10", C-NY 1/22/88 OE 3,300
Joueuse de Mandoline, 50/100, clr etch/Japan, 1928, p/s, Jacquart bstp, lt stn, 7x10", lot 246, SBY 11/3/88 3,850
Joueuse de Mandoline, 72/100, clr etch/wove paper, 1928, p/s, lt stn/sl, 7x10", Jacquart, lot 544, SBY 5/11/89 OE 6,600
Juene Fille a la Guitare, for Thierry Maulnier; hc etch/wove paper, 1946, pl/s, lt stn/fox, L-8x7", C-NY 1/22/88 OE 330
L'Amazone, total ed of 80, litho/stiff Japan, 1920, p/s, lt stn/cr, 8x8", lot 241, SBY 11/3/88 2,850
L'Arlequine, 77/100, clr etch/Japan, 1927, p/s, full mrgs, lt sl/cr, unfr, P-10x7", Nouvel Essor, SBY 5/12/88 OE 8,800
L'Arlequine, 96/100, etch/rlt, 1927, p/s, lt stn, 10x7", Jacquart, lot 233, SBY 2/25/88 7,150
L'Ecuyere, 6/80, etch/laid paper, 1926, p/s, Jacquart bstp, full mrgs, lt stn/cr, P-7x5", SBY 5/12/88 OE 5,775
L'Eventail Rose, 83/100, etch/drypt/rlt, 1927, p/s, laid down, 12x10", Calerie Marcel Guiot, lot 295, SBY 2/23/89 OE 8,800
La Creole, 56/100, litho, 1924, p/s, full mrgs, lt fox, mst mrgs/verso, 16x12", lot 290, SBY 2/23/89 3,575
La Dame Jaune, 53/110, yel & blk litho/Chine volant, 1926, p/s, lg mrgs, lt stn/fox, 9x11", lot 541, SBY 5/11/89 OE 5,500
La Fete de la Danse, 2/100, clr litho, 1937, full mrgs, lt stn/fox/cr, 14x17", lot 299, SBY 2/23/89 OE 11,550
La Mort d'Aimee, Pl 3, ed of 90, 2nd state, litho/wove paper, 1930, lt scr/stn, laid down, 11x12", lot 642, C-NY 5/10/89 3,080
La Premiere Voiture Renault, 3rd state, litho/wove paper, 1936, sgn by artist/sitter, L-14x11", lot 188, C-NY 5/11/88 OE 3,300
La Promenade a Cheval, 44/100, final state, clr etch/rlt/wove paper, 1928, Jacquart bstp, 10x7", lot 247, SBY 11/3/88 6,600
La Ronde, 27/110, gold & blk litho/Chine volant, 1926, p/s, lt cr img, unfr, L-7x9", SBY 5/12/88 OE 4,675
La Semeuse, Pl 2, 1st state, 1/3, etch/simili Japan, 1925, lt stn/fox, P-8x6", Ed L'Etoile, lot 340, C-NY 11/1/88 UE 880
La Vie de Chateau: La Cavaliere; total ed of 120, clr litho/Japan, 1925, p/s, lt stn, laid down, 10x8", SBY 2/23/89 OE 5,225
Le Bal, ed of 80, final state, etch/BFK Rives, 1927, full mrgs, lt stn/fox, 10x11", lot 244, SBY 11/3/88 2,750
Le Chat, 75/150, 3rd state, clr litho, 1945, p/s, lt trm/stn, 13x18", Nouvel Essor/Jacquart, lot 256, SBY 11/3/88 OE 17,600
Le Cirque des Enfants, 8/110, etch/cream Japan, 1927, p/s, full mrgs, lt cr/stn, 10x11", lot 542, SBY 5/11/89 2,750
Le Cirque des Enfants, 81/110, 2nd state, etch/thin laid paper, 1927, 10x11", Bernheim-Jeune, lot 245, SBY 11/3/88 OE 2,200

Le Concert, deluxe ed of 10, clr litho/Japan Imperial, 1926, p/s, laid down, 9x7", lot 230, SBY 2/25/88 4,125
Le Concert, ed of 110, clr litho/Chine volant, 1926, p/s, lt cr/stn, 10x8", Quatres-Chemins, lot 231, SBY 2/25/88 1,540
Le Concert, 25/110, clr litho, 1926, p/s, lt faded/mstn/fox, gstn verso, unfr, L-9x8", SBY 5/12/88 OE 4,400
Le Cygne, 25/110, clr litho/laid China paper, 1926, p/s, full mrgs, lt stn, 10x7", lot 540, SBY 5/11/89 OE 5,500
Le Poney, 69/100, litho/Vidalon, 1924, p/s, mstn/scr/lt ls, L-11x9", lot 338, C-NY 11/1/88.......... 2,860
Le Promenoir, 29/80, etch/wove paper, 1926, p/s, full mrgs, lt stn/cr, 7x4", Jacquart, lot 232, SBY 2/25/89 2,090
Le Promenoir, 67/80, final state, etch, 1926, p/s, Jacquart bstp, full mrgs, lt stn, 7x4", lot 243, SBY 11/3/88 OE 2,420
Les Biches, 22/70, etch, 1924, p/s, full mrgs, lt stn, 8x10", lot 289, SBY 2/23/89 4,675
Les Deux Espagnoles, 23/75, 2nd state, etch/laid paper, 1924, p/s, lt stn/rpr tr, P-11x8", lot 185, C-NY 5/11/88 OE 2,860
Les Enfants du Chateau, 94/100, final state, etch, 1943, p/s, lt stn, 10x14", Sagot, lot 255, SBY 11/3/88 OE.......... 4,125
Les Trois Soeurs, 10/30, 1st state before letters, litho, 1930, p/s, lt stn/rub, 6x7", lot 545, SBY 5/11/89 2,200
Pair: Jeune Fille a la Guitar; Portrait de Jeune Fille; hc etch/heavy wove paper, no size given, lot 2858, B/B 4/19/88.......... 385
Pair: Young Woman with a Hat; Young Woman with a Guitar; hc etch/wove paper, 3x3"/8x7", lot 135, SWN 6/15/89 OE 935
Portrait de l'Artiste, 92/100, litho/stiff Japan, 1927, p/s, full mrgs, lt sl, 15x11", lot 543, SBY 5/11/89 7,150
Portrait de la Baronne Gourgaud, 2nd state, hc red & bl litho/glazed wove paper, 1923, L-12x7", lot 184, C-NY 5/11/88 OE.......... 4,180
Portrait of Two Women, 34/50, clr etch/cream wove paper, p/s, lt stn, 7x9", lot 2859, B/B 4/19/88 OE.......... 935
Set of 4: Mariana; ed of 30, litho w/text on Chine, 1932, untrm, orig wrappers, Bernouard, lot 345, C-NY 11/1/88 OE 9,350
Tete d'Arlequine, 92/100, blk/bl etch, 1928, p/s, Jacquart Ed bstp, lt cr/fox/stn, P-10x7", lot 343, C-NY 11/1/88 3,520
Tete de Femme au Noeud Noir, unsgn ed of 100, final state, etch/cream wove paper, 1928, 8x6", lot 249, SBY 11/3/88 OE 2,640
Trois Courtisanes, La Princesse de Cleves; 5/15, 3rd state, clr etch, 1947, p/s, lt stn, P-7x5", C-E 5/13/88 OE 880
Trois Jeunes Filles, posthumous ed, etch/Arches, full mrgs, P-10x8", lot 71, PHL 10/28/88 90
Two Girls & a Dog, 26/30, clr litho/Japan nacre, ca 1955, p/s, full mrgs, lt stn/cr, 14x10", lot 549, SBY 5/11/89 OE.......... 9,350
Vendredi, 1st state, wc/Japan, 1912, lt fox/ls, L-6x5", lot 337, C-NY 11/1/88 2,750
Young Woman, 133/200, clr aqua, ca 1938, p/s, Jacquart bstp, lt trm/stn/fox, 18x15", lot 258, SBY 11/3/88 6,050

LAURENCIN, Marie; after (French, 1885-1956)

Dialogue sur la Danse, a/p, total ed of 170, clr aqua, sgn, 15x11", lot 137, SWN 6/15/89 OE 3,740
Three Ladies at a Table, clr etch/aqua/rlt, 1937, p/s, pl/s, trm mrgs, lt stn/ls, 19x13", lot 138, SWN 6/15/89 OE 3,080

LAURENS, Henri (French, 1885-1954)

Book: Lucien, Dialogues; 155/275, 33 wc, 1951, lt fox/sl, orig wrappers/folder/case, Teriade, lot 238, SBY 2/25/89 UE 770

LAWLER, Thomas (19th C)

Mount Vernon, by Knirsch, hc litho/wove paper, 1867, lt tr/fox/stn, L-18x25", lot 86, C-NY 1/19/89 UE 55

LAZZARI, Pietro (American/Italian, 20th C)

Self-Portrait, etch, 1945, p/s, titled, 12x9", lot 302, WG 10/19/88 UE.......... 20

LAZZELL, Nettie Blanche (American, 1878-1956)

Exhibition Announcement, blk/orange linocut on laid Japan, ca 1930, intl, full mrgs, S-11x6", lot 201, C-NY 1/19/89 OE.......... 1,760
Little Church, clr wc/Japan, 1951-52, sgn/titled/dtd in ink, lt stn, L-12x14", lot 202, C-NY 1/19/89.......... 10,450
Planes, clr wc/laid Japan, 1952, sgn/titled/dtd in ink, lt fox/stn/old tp, L-14x12", lot 203, C-NY 1/19/89.......... 15,400
Provincetown Wharf, wc/laid paper, ca 1927, p/s, lt ls to img, lt stn, L-6x5", lot 54, RWS 9/8/89 UE 350
Yellow Petunia, clr wc/fibrous wove paper, 1928, p/s, inscr Provincetown MA Dec 28, cr, unfr, L-14x12", C-NY 1/22/88 OE 4,180

LE CLERC, after (French, 19th C)

Pair: 19th C French Fashion Plates; by Patas, hc engr, P-10x7", C-E 11/15/88 OE 132

LE CORBUSIER (Charles Edouard Janneret)(French, 1887-1965)

Portfolio: Poeme de l'Angle Droit; 31/60, 19 clr litho, 1955, orig wrappers, 19x15", Teriade, lot 175, SBY 2/25/88 OE 13,200

LE PACON, after

General Washington, by Le Mire, engr, 16x13", C-E 3/22/88 132

LEGER, Fernand (French, 1881-1955)

Acrobats, ed of 300, clr litho/collotype/Arches, 1953, p/s, full mrgs, lt stn/fox, L-19x26", lot 62, RWS 9/8/89 750
Album: Andre Malraux, Lunes en Papier; 40/90, wc/van Gelder, 1921, S-13x9", Galerie Simon, lot 85, C-NY 11/1/88 OE.......... 7,700
Album: Cirque; #271, blk & clr lithos w/text on Arches, 1950, S-17x14", orig wrappers, Verve, lot 86, C-NY 11/1/88.......... 18,700
Book: Cirque; 6/300, 63 litho, 22 illuminations, manuscript text, sgn in bl ballpoint pen, S-17x13", Verve, SBY 5/12/88.......... 15,950
Composition sur Fond Jaune, 63/75, clr litho/Arches, 1954, full mrgs, L-17x21", Galerie Louise Leiris, SBY 5/12/88 OE 2,200
Femme Tenant un Vase From Teriade, ed of 52, litho/thick wove paper, 1928, p/s, full mrgs, 10x7", lot 347, C-NY 11/1/88 7,700
Groupe, ed of 1000, slksc poster, 1954-45, inscr FL 50.51, lt stn/scr, L-18x13", LA Guilde, RWS 3/16/89 OE.......... 700
L'Ouvrier, ed of 800, clr litho, 1951, full mrgs, lt stn/cr, S-30x21", Maison Pensee/Mourlot, lot 260, SBY 11/3/88 OE 1,650
La Femme et la Fleur, 44/75, clr litho, 1954, sgn in pen, trm mrgs, lt stn/fox, 23x21", lot 261, SBY 11/3/88 OE 7,975
La Lecture, HC, ed of 350, clr litho/Arches, ca 1950, sgn in ink, full mrgs, lt cr, L-17x22", lot 351, C-NY 11/1/88 OE.......... 2,310
La Ville, le Remoroueur; 3/180, clr litho, p/s, 15x12", lot 131, WG 10/19/88.......... 1,000
Le Vase, 2/100(?), clr litho/Arches, 1927, p/s, lt sl/cr, glue on verso, 29x22", Galerie Simon, lot 84, C-NY 11/1/88 OE 28,600
Les Constructeurs, 59/75, bl/blk litho, 1951, ink sgn, full mrgs, lt stn, L-17x14", Mourlot, SBY 5/12/88 OE 4,950
Les Femmes au Perroquet, 33/75, clr litho/Arches, 1952, sgn in ink, full mrgs, 17x24", Mourlot, lot 349, C-NY 11/1/88 OE 14,300
Les Femmes au Perroquet, 64/75, total ed of 110, litho/Arches, 1952, sgn, full mrgs, cr, unfr, L-16x24", SBY 5/12/88.......... 4,400
Nature Morte aux Fruits, 45/75, clr litho, 1948, p/s, lg mrgs, lt fox, 14x18", lot 300, SBY 2/23/89 880
Nature Morte aux Fruits, 59/75, clr litho, 1948, p/s, trm mrgs, lt stn, 14x18", lot 259, SBY 11/3/88 OE 2,200
Tete de Femme, aside from ed of 300, clr litho, 1949, lg mrgs, lt stn, 23x14", Desjobert, lot 301, SBY 2/23/89 OE 2,420
Untitled Abstract Composition, 64/300, litho, Musee Biot stp, 22x9", FAP 6/16/89.......... 550

LEGER, Fernand; after (French, 1881-1955)

Composition Mecanique, 243/300, clr srgph/cream wove paper, ca 1919, lt stn, 17x12", lot 2860, B/B 4/19/88 220
Contraste de Formes, 36/100, clr repro/Arches, stp sgn, lt lstn/mstn, L-16x12", C-NY 1/22/88 OE 132
Femme a la Cruche, by Jacques Villon, 8/200, clr aqua, 1928, full mrgs, 19x12", Bernheim-Jeune, lot 590, SBY 11/3/88 OE 3,025
La Lecture, HC, ed of 350, clr litho/Arches, ca 1950, sgn in ink, full mrgs, lt stn/cr, 17x22", lot 647, C-NY 5/10/89 OE.......... 4,400
La Parade, a/p, apart from ed of 285, clr litho, ca 1953, sgn in ink, lt cr/stn, L-14x18", lot 648, C-NY 5/10/89 OE 1,430

Portfolio: La Ville; 5/180, 29 clr litho, 1959, p/s, S-26x20", orig wrappers, Teriade, SBY 5/12/88 OE ... 9,900

LEGRAND, Louis (French, 1863-1951)

Fleur-de-Lis, ed of about 100, aqua/drypt, 1896, p/s, titled in pl, 10x7", lot 141, SWN 6/15/89 UE ... 220
La Fille et sa Tante, ed of 100, etch/aqua/Japan, 1893, p/s, pl/s, titled, 14x9", lot 140, SWN 6/15/89 ... 468
Realisme, 39/50, drypt, ca 1902, p/s, Pellet bstp, full mrgs, lt stn, 11x7", lot 142, SWN 6/15/89 ... 715

LEGROS, Alphonse (French, 1837-1911)

Chateaux des Revenants, 3rd state, etch, ca 1890, p/s, 7x9", lot 143, SWN 6/15/89 ... 143
Le Village Abondonne, ed of 100, etch/drypt, ca 1880, p/s, 4x8", lot 334, LH 9/10/89 UE ... 50

LEHMAN & DUVAL

View of the Great Treaty Held at Prairie du Chien, hc litho, stn/tr, 12x15", lot 101, GAI 5/26/89 ... 150
Waa-Pa-Shaw, Sioux Chief (Indian portrait); hc litho, 1836, lt fox/stn, 15x21", Key & Biddle, lot 511, GAI 3/17/89 ... 130

LEIGHTON, Claire (British, 1900-)

Net Menders, wood engr, p/s, 6x8", lot 176, WG 10/19/88 ... 200

LEIGHTON, Scott; after (American, 1849-1898)

Brush for the Lead, litho, full mrgs, lt tr/fox, White & Piplar, RAB 11/25/88 UE ... 375
End of the Brush, litho, full mrgs, lt fox, orig fr, White & Piplar, RAB 11/25/88 UE ... 400
Fearnaught Stallions, litho, lt rpr/fox, 3" tr in mrg, Haskell & Allen, RAB 11/25/88 UE ... 150
Smuggler (trotting horse/rig), litho, tr, lt fox, 1874, Haskell & Leighton, RAB 11/25/88 ... 300

LEIZELT, Frederic (18th C)

Salem (18th-C view), aqua/engr, lt fox, 12x17", RAB 3/14/89 ... 600

LENOIR, Marcel (French, 1872-1931)

L'Education, clr litho/poster paper, 44x30", lot 237, FAP 2/24/89 ... 250
Le Aptaude, clr litho, trm mrgs, laid down, 16x29", lot 252, FAP 2/24/89 ... 350
Le Monstre, 118/175, p/s, lt fox mrgs, 28x19", lot 287, FAP 2/24/89 ... 450

LEPERE, Auguste

Pair: Le Czar en Costume Sacre; L'Empereur d'Autriche; wc/cream wove paper, p/s, Sagot bstp, 8x6", lot 2861, B/B 4/19/88 ... 165

LESLIE, Kenneth (American, 20th C)

House in a Landscape, clr litho, p/s, 16x22", lot 106, FAP 2/24/89 UE ... 50

LEUTZE, Emanuel Gottlieb; after (German, 1816-1868)

Washington Crossing the Delaware, by Paul Girardet, engr/rlt, ca 1855, lt stn/fox, 14x24", Goupil, lot 87, C-NY 1/19/89 ... 660

LEVINE, Jack (American, 1915-)

Art Lover, 81/100, clr litho, 1967, p/s, 22x18", lot 849, LH 10/16/88 ... 300
Ashkenazi I, 58/100, etch, 1963, p/s, 10x8", lot 1203, LH 10/16/88 ... 150
Bechtiana, 6/100, litho, 1966, p/s, 15x17", lot 852, LH 10/16/88 ... 150
Blue Angel, 15/120, total ed of about 140, clr litho/Rives, 1967, p/s, L-20x26", lot 73, RWS 9/8/89 OE ... 700
Boudoin, 25/50, etch/drypt, 1968, p/s, 8x10", lot 1200, LH 10/16/88 ... 100
Careless Love, 80/100, total ed of about 120, etch/aqua/Rives, 1965, p/s, lt sl, unfr, 18x22", lot 75, RWS 9/8/89 OE ... 1,000
End of the Weimar Republic, 86/100, etch/mezzo, 1967, p/s, 18x15", lot 851, LH 10/16/88 UE ... 120
Gangster's Funeral, 101/120, etch, p/s, 20x26", lot 462, FAP 4/15/88 ... 250
Je Me Souviens de M Watteau, 1/100, clr litho, 1965, p/s, 17x23", lot 853, LH 10/16/88 ... 200
Marianne & the Goddess of Liberty, 83/125, litho, 1967, p/s, 27x21", lot 848, LH 10/16/88 UE ... 70
On the Convention Floor, a/p, litho, 1968, p/s, 19x25", lot 1202, LH 10/16/88 ... 150
Pair: Venetian Lady; Great Society; a/p & 35/100, etch, 1964 & 1968, 8x10", lot 1198, LH 10/16/88 ... 110
Prussian General, 108/120, 2nd state, etch/aqua, 1966, p/s, 10x8", lot 1201, LH 10/16/88 UE ... 70
Texas Delegate, 112/120, litho, 1970, p/s, 16x20", lot 1204, LH 10/16/88 UE ... 100
Vernissage, 94/125, litho, 1967, p/s, 17x22", lot 850, LH 10/16/88 UE ... 130
Warsaw Ghetto, 14/120, litho, 1969, p/s, 19x25", lot 847, LH 10/16/88 UE ... 100
Weimer Republic, 55/100, etch, 1967, p/s, full mrgs, 18x15", lot 147, SWN 6/15/89 ... 275

LEWANDOWSKI, Edmund D. (American, 1914-)

Three Architectural Abstractions, clr slksc, ca 1940, p/s, lt stn, laid down, S-9x12", lot 39, C-NY 2/25/88 OE ... 2,200

LEWIS, Martin (American, 1883-1962)

Bands of Lines One-Inch Wide in Four Directions & Four Colors, 10/20, slksc, 1985, p/s, 29x95", lot 1129, SBY 5/13/89 OE ... 4,950
Bands of Lines One-Inch Wide in Four Directions in Black & Gray, 12/20, slksc, 1985, p/s, S-29x96", SBY 5/13/89 OE ... 4,675
Boss of the Block, ed of about 200, etch/aqua/drypt, 1928/1944, L-11x8", lot 54, RWS 9/29/88 ... 375
Building a Babylon, ed of 100, drypt, 1929, p/s, full mrgs, lt scr/stn/fox, 13x8", lot 43, SBY 2/23/89 OE ... 3,300
Building a Babylon, ed of 100, drypt, 1929, p/s, full mrgs, 13x8", lot 40, SBY 11/3/88 ... 2,475
Chance Meeting, ed of 100, drypt/cream laid paper, 1941, p/s, lt stn, P-10x7", Soc Am Etchers, lot 211, C-NY 1/19/89 OE ... 3,520
Chance Meeting, ed of 100, drypt/laid paper, p/s, full mrgs, loose hinges, unfr, P-11x8", RWS 3/16/89 OE ... 3,800
Circus Night, ed of ca 100, drypt w/sandpaper ground, 1933, p/s, lt stn/sl/cr mrgs, unfr, 11x15", SBY 5/12/88 OE ... 11,000
Clearing Rain-Evening, Japan; ed of 100, drypt/sandpaper ground/wove paper, 1927, p/s, P-15x9", lot 205, C-NY 1/19/89 OE ... 715
Corner Shadows, drypt/cream wove paper, 1929, p/s, lt stn, 8x9", lot 2961, B/B 4/19/88 ... 3,025
Corner Shadows, ed of 250, drypt/laid paper, 1929, tp stn mrgs, unfr, P-9x9", Cleveland Print Club, C-NY 1/22/88 OE ... 2,860
Cronies, ed of about 100, aqua, 1932, p/s, lt mstn, P-10x11", lot 34, C-NY 5/11/88 OE ... 880
Day's End, ed of 100, drypt, 1937, p/s, full mrgs, lt stn/fox/cr, 10x13", lot 45, SBY 2/23/89 OE ... 5,775
Derricks, ed of 100, brn-blk drypt, 1927, p/s, full mrgs, lt stn, 8x12", lot 40, C-NY 2/25/88 ... 1,760
East Side Night-Williamsburg Bridge, ed of 85, etch/wm Armorial, 1928, p/s, inscr Imp, stn, unfr, P-10x12", C-NY 1/22/88 ... 1,540
Glow of the City, ed of 100, drypt/gr fibrous wove paper, 1929, p/s, full mrgs, lt stn, 12x14", lot 44, SBY 2/23/89 OE ... 16,500
Great Shadow, ed of 100, drypt/wove paper, 1925, p/s, P-10x7", lot 204, C-NY 1/19/89 OE ... 3,080
H'anted, ed of about 100, drypt/sandpaper ground, 1932, p/s, old tp hinge, lt stn, 13x9", lot 41, SBY 2/25/88 ... 1,540
Little Penthouse, ed of 75, drypt/laid paper, 1931, p/s, full mrgs, P-10x7", lot 210, C-NY 1/19/89 OE ... 8,250
Night in New York, ed of about 135, etch/cream laid paper, 1926, Chicago Soc Etchers bstp, P-8x9", C-NY 5/10/89 OE ... 3,850

Night in New York, ed of 135, etch, 1932, p/s, Chicago Soc Etchers bstp, lt stn, 9x9", lot 38, SBY 2/23/89 OE 2,640
Night in New York, ed of 25 to 50, etch/cream laid paper, 1926, p/s, Chicago Soc Etchers bstp, rpr, P-9x9", C-NY 5/11/88..... 2,860
Quarter of Nine, Saturday's Children; ed of 100, drypt, 1929, p/s, stn/fox mrgs & verso, 10x13", lot 242, SBY 5/11/89 OE 9,350
Rain on Murry Hill, ed of 100, drypt/wove paper, 1928, p/s, wide mrgs, lt lstn, unfr, P-8x12", C-NY 1/22/88 OE..... 3,520
Relics, ed of 100, drypt/Etruria Italy, 1928, p/s, full mrgs, lt sl mrgs, P-12x10", lot 207, C-NY 1/19/89 OE 11,000
Spring Night, Greenwich Village; ed of 100, drypt/laid paper, 1930, p/s, lt scr/stn, P-10x12", lot 209, C-NY 1/19/89 OE 3,300
Spring Night, Greenwich Village; ed of 100, drypt/laid paper, 1930, p/s, lt stn, P-10x12", lot 449, C-NY 5/10/89 OE 5,280
Street Booth, Tokyo-New Year's Eve; ed of 100, drypt/wove paper, 1927, p/s, lt sl/fox, 14x10", lot 206, C-NY 1/19/89 OE 990
Tree, Manhattan; drypt/sandpaper ground/cream laid paper, 1930, p/s, stn/sl, P-13x10", lot 208, C-NY 1/19/89 OE 5,280
Under the Street Lamp, ed of 100, etch, 1928, p/s, inscr Imp, full mrgs, lt stn, 15x10", lot 40, SBY 2/23/89 OE 2,750
Wet Saturday, ed of 75, drypt/laid paper, 1929, p/s, inscr Imp, w/mrgs, 10x11", SBY 5/12/88 OE..... 2,640
Winter on White Street, ed of 25 to 50, drypt/sandpaper ground/wove paper, 1934, lt stn/fox, P-11x7", C-NY 5/11/88 OE 3,300

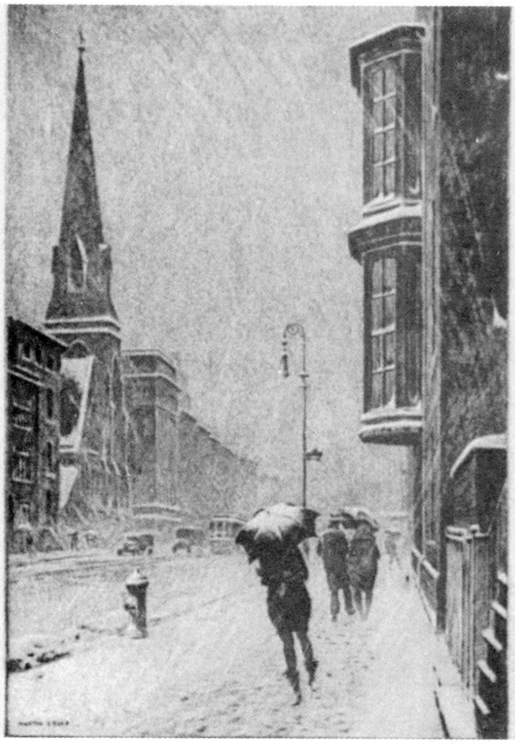

Bay Windows, drypt/sandpaper ground, 1930, p/s, inscr Imp, 12x8", lot 87, WD 12/8/88 OE; $8,500

LEWITT, Sol (American, 1928-)
Book: Grids, Using Straight Lines, No-Straight Lines...; 9/25, 28 etch, 1973, slipcase, Parasol, lot 490, C-NY 5/11/88..... 1,540
Book: Location of Lines; 2/25, 5 etch, 1975, full sheets, orig portfolio, Parasol, lot 491, C-NY 5/11/88..... 825
Set of 16: Bands of Color in Four Directions & All Combinations; etch/BFK Rives, 1971, 21x21", lot 702A, C-NY 11/1/ 88..... 3,300
Suite: Squares with a Different Line Direction in Each Half Square; 9/25, 10 etch, 1971, 15x15", lot 699, SBY 2/23/89 OE..... 2,200
LICHTENSTEIN, Roy (American, 1923-)
Against Apartheid, AP29/30, clr slksc, 1983, p/s, S-34x24", Maeght, lot 536, SBY 2/25/89 OE 3,850
American Indian Theme I, AP18, wc/wht Suzuki handmade Japan, 1980, TGL bstp, 25x24", lot 745, SBY 5/14/88 OE..... 5,060
American Indian Theme I, 2/50, clr wc/Suzuki handmade, 1980, p/s, TGL bstp, S-33x32", lot 717, C-NY 11/1/88 OE..... 6,600
American Indian Theme I, 3/50, clr wc/wht Suzuki, 1980, p/s, TGL bstp, full mrgs, 24x24", lot 888, SBY 11/5/88..... 5,500
American Indian Theme I, 43/50, clr wc/wht Suzuki, 1980, p/s, TGL bstp, full mrgs, 24x24", lot 1143, SBY 5/13/89..... 6,600
American Indian Theme VI, 40/50, clr wc/wht Suzuki, 1980, p/s, TGL bstp, full mrgs, 30x42", lot 1144, SBY 5/13/89 7,150
Apple & Lemon, AP14/14, ed of 60, clr wc/Japan, 1982, p/s, full mrgs, lt cr, S-31x40", Petersburg, lot 718, C-NY 11/1/88..... 2,200
Apple on Gray Ground, 48/60, clr wc/Japan, 1982, p/s, dtd 83, full mrgs, S-30x33", Petersburg, lot 509, C-NY 5/11/88 OE 2,750
As I Opened Fire, I Knew Why Tex Hadn't Buzzed Me...; offset litho/3 sheets, ca 1968, 26x21", lot 149, SWN 6/15/89 OE 2,420
As I Opened Fire...; slksc/paper, 1964, intl, unfr, S-25x21", lot 99, RWS 9/8/89 OE 1,600
Brushstroke, 57/280, yel/bl/blk slksc, 1965, p/s, full mrgs, lt darkening/scuff, 22x29", Castelli, SBY 5/14/88 OE 6,875
Brushstrokes, ed of 300, clr scrpt, 1967, p/s, full mrgs, lt scr/sl, L-22x30", Pasadena Art Museum, lot 707, C-NY 11/1/88..... 3,520
Brushstrokes, 194/300, clr slksc, 1967, p/s, full mrgs, lt cr/scr/sl, 22x30", Pasadena Art Museum, lot 1137, SBY 5/13/89 OE..... 9,900
Brushstrokes, 217/300, clr scrpt, 1967, p/s, lt scr/sl/fox/stn, L-22x30", Pasadena Art Museum, lot 497, C-NY 5/11/88 OE 3,080
Crak!, apart from #d ed of 300, offset litho, 1964, full mrgs, cr/sl, S-20x29", Leo Castelli, lot 494, C-NY 5/11/88 OE..... 6,600
Crak!, apart from #d ed of 300, offset litho, 1964, p/s, lt cr/stn/fox, S-20x28", Castelli, lot 704, C-NY 11/1/88 4,400
Crak!, aside from #d ed of 300, offset litho, 1964, p/s, full mrgs, lt stn, 19x27", lot 530, SBY 2/25/89 OE 8,800
Crak!, aside from #d ed of 300, offset litho, 1964, p/s, laid down, 19x27", Leo Castelli, lot 531, SBY 2/25/88 OE 2,310
Crak!, ed of 300, offset litho, 1964, p/s, lt stn/rub, 19x27", Castelli, lot 702, SBY 2/23/89 5,225
Crak!, 231/300, clr litho, 1964, p/s, full mrgs, lt rpr tr mrgs, lt ls, 19x27", Castelli, lot 1133, SBY 5/13/89 OE..... 7,150
Crak!, 69/300, clr offset litho, 1964, p/s, full mrgs, lt stn/cr, 19x27", Castelli, lot 870, SBY 11/5/88..... 7,700
Crying Girl, clr offset litho, 1963, p/s, full mrgs, laid down, 17x23", Castelli, lot 701, SBY 2/23/89 OE 3,520

Crying Girl, clr offset litho, 1963, p/s, full mrgs, lt stn/cr, 17x23", Castelli, lot 700, SBY 2/23/89	**8,250**
Crying Girl, ed of unknown size, clr offset litho, 1963, p/s, lt scr/cr/ls, 18x24", Castelli, lot 703, C-NY 11/1/88	**2,420**
Crying Girl, ed of unknown size, offset litho, 1963, full mrgs, rpr tr, 18x24", Castelli, lot 493, C-NY 5/11/88 OE	**13,200**
Crying Girl, unnumbered ed, clr offset litho, 1963, p/s, full mrgs, lt cr, 17x23", Castelli, lot 1131, SBY 5/13/89 OE	**28,600**
Crying Girl, unnumbered ed, clr offset litho, 1963, p/s, full mrgs, lt rpr/tr/disclr, L-17x23", Castelli, SBY 5/14/88	**5,500**
Crying Girl, unnumbered ed, clr offset litho, 1963, p/s, full mrgs, 17x23", Castelli, lot 869, SBY 11/5/88 OE	**13,200**
Crying Girl, unnumbered ed, clr offset litho, 1983, p/s, full mrgs, lt cr/stn, 17x23", Castelli, lot 1132, SBY 5/13/89	**9,900**

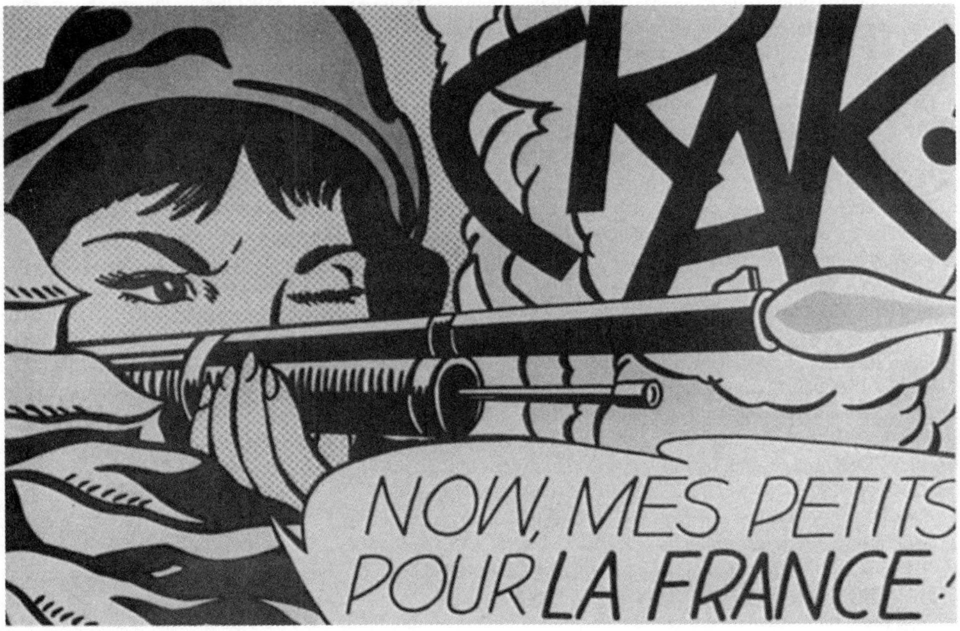

Crak!; 5/300, clr offset litho, 1964, p/s, dtd, 19x27", Castelli, lot 3556, B/B 4/12/89; $5,225

Dancing Figures, 7/32, clr etch/aqua/engr, 1980, p/s, full mrgs, 11x10", Tyler Graphics, SBY 5/14/88 OE	**4,125**
Dr Waldmann, 4/50, clr wc/Arches, 1980, p/s, Gemini bstp, full mrgs, S-42x34", lot 507, C-NY 5/11/88 OE	**6,050**
Dr Waldmann, 48/50, clr wc/Arches, 1980, p/s, Gemini bstp, full mrgs, S-42x34", lot 715, C-NY 11/1/88	**6,050**
Explosion, ed of 100, clr litho, 1967, p/s, S-22x17", Hollander, lot 876, SBY 11/5/88 OE	**3,300**
Figure with Teepee, 20/32, etch/engr/wht Lanan mold made, 1980, TGL bstp, full mrgs, 11x9", lot 1145, SBY 5/13/89 OE	**3,300**
Foot & Hand, 48/300, clr offset litho, 1962, p/s, full mrgs, lt cr, L-17x21", Castelli, SBY 5/14/88 OE	**3,300**
Foot & Hand, 50/300, clr offset litho, 1962, p/s, full mrgs, lt cr, 17x21", Castelli, lot 868, SBY 11/5/88	**3,300**
Foot & Hand, 58/200, offset litho, 1962, p/s, full mrgs, S-17x22", Leo Castelli, lot 492, C-NY 5/11/88 OE	**3,850**
Foot & Hand, 88/300, offset litho, 1962, p/s, full mrgs, lt ls to mrg, 21x21", Castelli, lot 529, SBY 2/25/88 OE	**3,575**
Forms in Space (American Flag), PP3/5, clr scrpt/BFK Rives, S-36x52", Inst Contemporary Art, lot 514, C-NY 5/11/88 OE	**4,180**
Green Lamp, 51/60, wc/litho/slksc, 1984, p/s, Gemini bstp, full mrgs, lt cr/rub, 36x50", lot 895, SBY 11/5/88 OE	**13,750**
Haystack, 29/50, clr slksc, 1969, p/s, Mazzotta bstp, full mrgs, 15x17", lot 879, SBY 11/5/88	**2,750**
Haystacks #4, 16/100, clr litho/scrpt/BFK Rives, p/s, full mrgs, lt scr, S-21x31", Gemini, lot 500, C-NY 5/11/88 OE	**1,045**
Head with Braids, 29/32, clr etch/aqua/engr, 1980, p/s, Tyler Graphics bstp, full mrgs, 10x8", SBY 5/14/88	**1,430**
Huh?, 46/100, clr slksc, 1976, p/s, full mrgs, lt scuff/cr, S-42x30", Castelli/Multiples, lot 887, SBY 11/5/88 OE	**8,250**
Ice Cream Deserts, a/p, clr etch/aqua, 1975-76, p/s, full mrgs, 14x21", Petersburg, lot 740, SBY 2/23/89 OE	**2,750**
Industry & Melody, 23/250, litho/CM Fabriano Cotone, 1969, p/s, Gabriel Mazzotta bstp, 26x19", lot 710, C-NY 11/1/88	**3,850**
Industry & Melody, 29/250, clr litho/CM Fabriano Cotone, 1969, Gabriel Mazzotta bstp, L-17x14", lot 503, C-NY 5/11/88 OE	**4,180**
Knock, Knock; ed of unknown size (only 100 were sgn), litho, 1975, p/s, full sheet, S-26x19", lot 713, C-NY 11/1/88 OE	**2,200**
Lamp, PPI, clr wc/Okawara, 1981, p/s, TGL bstp, full mrgs, 20x8", lot 892, SBY 11/5/88 OE	**5,775**
Landscape 1, 8/100, red/yel/bl/blk scrpt, 1967, p/s, full sheet, S-11x18", Orig Ed, lot 498, C-NY 5/11/88 OE	**2,200**
Lincoln Center Poster, 7/100, clr slksc/slvr paper, 1966, sgn in felt pen, lt cr/scr, S-46x30", lot 535, SBY 2/25/88 OE	**2,640**
Melody Haunts My Reverie, #d ed of 200, slksc, 1965, p/s, full mrgs, scr/cr, 27x23", Orig Ed, lot 1135, SBY 5/13/89 OE	**39,600**
Melody Haunts My Reverie, 145/200, clr slksc, 1965, p/s, full mrgs, lt scuff/cr/sl, 27x23", Orig Ed, SBY 5/14/88	**23,100**
Melody Haunts My Reverie, 145/200, clr slksc, 1965, p/s, full mrgs, lt scuff, 27x23", Orig Ed, lot 872, SBY 11/5/88 OE	**30,800**
Merton of the Movies, 291/450, slvr/red/yel/blk scrpt, 1968, p/s, S-30x20", HKL Ltd, lot 499, C-NY 5/11/88 OE	**1,430**
Mirror #1, 29/80, linecut/slksc/embossing, 1972, p/s, Gemini bstp, full mrgs, S-28x28", lot 715, SBY 2/23/89 OE	**4,950**
Modern Art Poster, 115/300, clr slksc, 1967, p/s, full mrgs, lt scuff/stn, 8x11", Castelli, lot 701, SBY 2/23/89 OE	**3,575**
Modern Art Poster, 99/300, clr slksc, 1967, p/s, full mrgs, 8x11", Castelli, lot 1138, SBY 5/13/89 OE	**4,950**
Modern Head #3, 6/100, embossed linecut, 1970, p/s, Gemini bstp, lt scuff, S-24x18", SBY 5/14/88 OE	**3,300**
Modern Head #3, 61/100, embossed linecut, 1970, p/s, Gemini bstp, lt cr/scuff/rub, S-24x18", lot 883, SBY 11/5/88 OE	**4,400**
Modern Head #5, 99/100, embossed graphite w/die-cut paper overlay, 1970, p/s, orig fr, 28x20", Gemini, SBY 5/14/88	**2,640**
Modern Print, 191/200, clr litho/slksc, 1971, p/s, Gemini bstp, full mrgs, lt cr, 24x24", SBY 5/14/88 OE	**2,640**

Moonscape, 11 Pop Artist I; a/p, ed of 200, clr scrpt/Rowlux, 1965, p/s, S-20x24", Orig Ed, lot 706, C-NY 11/1/88 OE	3,520
Moonscape, 2/60, clr litho/wc/slksc, 1985, p/s, Gemini bstp, full mrgs, L-34x56", SBY 5/14/88 OE	14,850
Morton a Mort, ed of 8, clr wc/Arches cover, 1980, p/s, full mrgs, 23x33", Gemini, lot 3038, B/B 4/19/88	3,850
Night Scene, 16/32, clr etch/aqua/engr, 1980, p/s, Tyler Graphics bstp, full mrgs, 7x10", SBY 5/14/88 OE	4,675
No Thank You, offset litho/poster paper, 1984, p/s, S-36x25", Goodman Gallery, lot 150, SWN 6/15/89 UE	550
Nude in the Woods, 48/50, clr wc/Arches, 1980, p/s, Gemini bstps, full mrgs, S-40x36", lot 716, C-NY 11/1/88 OE	8,250
Painting on Blue & Yellow Wall, 3/60, clr wc/litho/Arches, 1984, p/s, Gemini bstp, S-47x31", lot 513, C-NY 5/11/88	3,300
Painting on Blue & Yellow Wall, 34/60, clr litho/wc/Arches 88, 1984, p/s, Gemini bstp, full mrgs, 44x29", SBY 5/13/89 OE	9,900
Painting on Canvas, 27/60, wc/litho/slksc/collage, 1984, p/s, Gemini bstp, lt cr, 31x26", lot 717, SBY 2/23/89 OE	8,250
Painting on Canvas, 28/60, clr wc/litho/scrpt/collage/Arches, 1984, p/s, Gemini bstp, S-34x29", lot 721, C-NY 11/1/88 OE	4,950
Painting on Canvas, 3/60, wc/litho/scrpt/collage/Arches, 1984, Gemini bstp, full mrgs, S-34x29", lot 512, C-NY 5/11/88	3,300
Pair: Aspen Winter Jazz; Merton of the Movies; clr scrpt, 1967 & 1968, lot 708, C-NY 11/1/88 OE	3,850
Pair: Haystack; Litho/Litho; A/P VII & 5/54, litho with slksc & clr litho, 1969/1970, 13x23"/28x40", SBY 5/14/88 OE	2,200
Pair: Mirror #5; Mirror #7; 3/80 & A/P VIII, clr litho/slksc, 1972, p/s, full mrgs, S-44x33"/S-39x25", SBY 5/14/88 OE	2,420
Paris Review Poster, 5/150, clr slksc, 1966, p/s, Chiron bstp, S-40x25", Paris Review, lot 709, SBY 2/23/89 OE	6,050
Peace Through Chemistry IV, 53/56, yel/bl/blk litho, 1970, p/s, Gemini bstp, full mrgs, 25x45", lot 881, SBY 11/5/88 OE	13,200
Picture & Picture, 10/30, clr wc/natural Okawara, 1981, p/s, TGL bstp, full mrgs, S-25x19", lot 893, SBY 11/3/89 OE	5,775
Pyramid, 51/100, blk/yel slksc on composition board in plexiglas box, 1968, p/s, 20x20x20", lot 1139, SBY 5/13/89 OE	3,850
Reclining Nude, ed of 50, wc/Arches cover, 1980, p/s, 28x34", Gemini, lot 3037, B/B 4/19/88	6,050
Red & Yellow Apple, 48/60, clr wc/Japan, 1982, p/s, full mrgs, S-29x38", Petersburg, lot 511, C-NY 5/11/88 OE	2,200
Red Apple, 48/60, clr wc/Japan, 1982, p/s, dtd 83, full mrgs, S-30x37", Petersburg, lot 510, C-NY 5/11/88 OE	2,090
Red Apple & Yellow Apple, 52/60, clr wc/Japan, 1982, full mrgs, lt cr, S-28x38", Petersburg, lot 719, C-NY 11/1/88 OE	3,850
Red Barn, 16/250, clr slksc, 1969, p/s, Editore Gabriele Mazzotta bstp, full mrgs, lt cr, 15x17", SBY 5/14/88 OE	4,950
Red Barn, 193/250, clr slksc, 1969, p/s, Mazzotta bstp, full mrgs, lt cr, 15x17", lot 880, SBY 11/5/88	4,950
Red Barn, 67/250, clr litho/CM Fabriano Cotone, 1969, Gabriele Mazzotta bstp, L-14x17", lot 504, C-NY 5/11/88 OE	4,620
Red Barn, 77/250, clr litho/CM Fabriano Cotone, 1969, Gabriele Mazzotta bstp, full mrgs, S-19x26", lot 711, C-NY 11/1/88	4,620
River, 29/60, litho/wc/slksc, 1985, p/s, Gemini bstp, full mrgs, 37x52", lot 1149, SBY 5/13/89 OE	37,400
Road Before the Forest, total ed of 71, litho/wc/scrpt, 1985, inscr RTP, Gemini bstp, S-37x52", lot 515, C-NY 5/11/88 OE	12,100
Road Before the Forest, 29/60, litho/wc/slksc, 1985, p/s, Gemini bstp, full mrgs, 37x53", lot 1148, SBY 5/13/89 OE	27,500
Rouen Cathedral, 16/75, clr litho, 1969, p/s, Gemini bstp, L-42x27", lot 502, C-NY 5/11/88	1,980
Rouen Cathedral, 55/75, bl/blk litho, 1969, p/s, Gemini bstp, full mrgs, lt scuff/sl, L-42x27", SBY 5/14/88 OE	2,750
Rouen Cathedral, 59/75, clr litho, 1969, p/s, Gemini bstp, full mrgs, S-49x33", lot 709, C-NY 11/1/88	3,080
Rouen Cathedral, 66/75, bl litho, 1969, p/s, Gemini bstp, full mrgs, lt cr/toned, L-42x27", SBY 5/14/88 OE	2,640
Rouen Cathedral #1, 54/75, yel litho/slksc, 1969, p/s, full mrgs, 42x27", Gemini, lot 877, SBY 11/5/88	3,025
Rouen Cathedral #1, 69/75, yel/wht litho, 1969, p/s, Gemini bstp, full mrgs, 42x27", lot 1140, SBY 5/13/89	3,300
Rouen Cathedral #2, 70/75, red/bl litho, 1969, p/s, Gemini bstp, full mrgs, lt cr/sl, 42x27", lot 1141, SBY 5/13/89	3,575
Rouen Cathedral #4, 74/75, bl & red litho/slksc, 1969, p/s, Gemini bstp, full mrgs, lt cr, 42x27", lot 1142, SBY 5/13/89	3,575
Rouen Cathedral #5, 66/75, blk & yel litho/slksc, 1969, p/s, Gemini bstp, full mrgs, 42x27", lot 878, SBY 11/5/88	3,850
Seascape, 9/60, litho/wc/slksc, 1985, p/s, Gemini bstp, full mrgs, 37x53", lot 1147, SBY 5/13/89 OE	27,500
Set of 3: As I Opened Fire...; ed of 3000, clr litho/sturdy wove paper, 1964, Stedelijk Mus, lot 1134, SBY 5/13/89 OE	13,200
Set of 3: As I Opened Fire...; ed of 3000, clr offset litho, 1964, full mrgs, 25x21", Stedelijk, lot 703, SBY 2/23/89 OE	12,100
Set of 3: Bull Head Series; ed of 100, litho/scrpt/linocut, 1973, Gemini bstp, S-25x33", lot 506, C-NY 5/11/88 OE	7,700
Set of 7: Haystack Series; 84/100, clr litho/BFK Rives, 1969, sgn/dtd, Gemini bstp, S-21x31", lot 501, C-NY 5/11/88 OE	8,250
Set of 7: Reclining Nude; Dr. Waldman; Nude in the Woods; The Couple; The Student; Morton A Mort; lot 890, SBY 11/5/88	71,500
Set: Bull Profile Series I-VI; clr linecut/litho/slksc, 1973, p/s, Gemini bstp, ea S-27x35", SBY 5/14/88 OE	66,000
Shipboard Girl, clr offset litho, 1965, p/s, full mrgs, lt cr/tr/nick, old hinges on verso, 26x19", lot 706, SBY 2/23/89	11,000
Shipboard Girl, offset litho, 1965, full mrgs, 26x19", Leo Castelli, lot 532, SBY 2/25/88 OE	4,400
Shipboard Girl, offset litho, 1965, p/s, full mrgs, lt cr, 26x19", Castelli, lot 708, SBY 2/23/89 OE	4,950
Shipboard Girl, offset litho, 1965, p/s, full mrgs, lt stn/cr, 26x19", Castelli, lot 707, SBY 2/23/89 OE	6,050
Shipboard Girl, unnumbered ed, clr litho, 1965, p/s, full mrgs, lt cr, 26x19", Castelli, lot 1136, SBY 5/13/89 OE	17,600
Shipboard Girl, unnumbered ed, clr offset litho, 1963, full mrgs, 26x19", Castelli, lot 874, SBY 11/5/88 OE	6,875
Shipboard Girl, unnumbered ed, clr offset litho, 1965, full mrgs, lt cr/sl, 26x19", Castelli, SBY 5/14/88 OE	15,400
Solomon R Guggenheim, 177/250, clr litho, 1969, p/s, full mrgs, lt stn/cr, 29x29", Castelli/Poster Orig, SBY 2/23/89 OE	5,500
Sower, 26/60, clr litho/wc/slksc, 1985, p/s, full mrgs, L-38x52", Gemini, SBY 5/14/88 OE	1,980
Still Life, a/p, clr slksc on aluminum, 1968, p/s, lt scuff/scr/sl, mounted for hanging, 34x34", lot 711, SBY 2/23/89 OE	5,775
Still Life with Crystal Bowl, AP8/10, scrpt/litho, 1976, p/s, Multiples/Styria bstps, L-32x44", lot 714, C-NY 11/1/88 OE	6,600
Still Life with Pitcher & Flowers, 94/100, litho/slksc, 1974, Styria bstp, 30x45", Multiples/Castelli, SBY 2/23/89 OE	5,775
Still Life with Pitcher & Flowers, 96/100, litho/slksc, 1974, Styria bstp, 30x45", Multiples, SBY 5/14/88 OE	7,150
Student, 37/50, clr embossed wc, 1980, p/s, Gemini bstp, full mrgs, L-32x27", SBY 5/14/88 OE	6,600
Suite: American Indian Theme I-VI; 44/55, clr wc/Suzuki handmade, 1980, p/s, TGL bstps, lot 891, SBY 11/5/88	30,250
Sunrise, offset litho, 1965, p/s, full mrgs, lt cr, 17x24", Castelli, lot 534, SBY 2/25/88 OE	1,760
Sunrise, unnumbered ed, clr offset litho, 1965, p/s, full mrgs, lt cr, 17x24", Castelli, lot 875, SBY 11/5/88 OE	22,000
Sweet Dreams Baby!, XXIX, clr slksc, 1965, p/s, full mrgs, lt scuff img, 36x26", Orig Ed, lot 871, SBY 11/5/88 OE	29,700
Sweet Dreams Baby!, 41/200, clr slksc, 1965, p/s, lt fox/skinned/old tp, 36x26", Orig Ed, lot 705, SBY 2/23/89 OE	7,975
Sweet Dreams Baby!, 56/200, clr scrpt, 1965, p/s, lt cr/sl/stn, sl/scr verso, S-37x28", Orig Ed, lot 496, C-NY 5/11/88	11,000
Sweet Dreams Baby!, 63/200, clr slksc, 1965, p/s, full mrgs, lt stn/scuff/sl, 36x26", Orig Ed, SBY 5/14/88	14,300
Temple, 138/300, offset litho/wove paper, 1964, p/s, full mrgs, lt stn/cr, S-24x18", Castelli, lot 167, C-NY 2/14/89	1,980
Temple, 144/300, bl/blk offset litho, 1964, p/s, full mrgs, lt stn, S-24x18", Castelli, lot 494, C-NY 5/11/88	1,760
This Must Be the Place, offset litho, 1965, p/s, full mrgs, 21x16", Am Cartoonist Soc, 21x16", lot 533, SBY 2/25/88 OE	3,300
Turkey Shopping Bag, ed of 200, clr slksc, 1964, p/s, lt cr, S-24x17", Bianchini, lot 704, SBY 2/23/89 OE	2,860
Turkey Shopping Bag, ed of 200, scrpt/wove paper shopping bag, 1964, p/s, 19x17", Bianchini, lot 705, C-NY 11/1/88 OE	2,420

Twin Mirrors, 233/250, clr slksc, 1970, p/s, lt cr/scuff, 34x21", Guggenheim Mus, lot 714, SBY 2/23/89 OE ... 5,775
Two Figures with Teepee, 12/32, etch/aqua/engr/wht Lana mould made, 1980, p/s, TGL bstp, 10x9", lot 889, SBY 11/5/88... 5,500
Two Figures with Teepee, 31/32, etch/aqua/engr/Lana mould made, 1980, TGL bstp, full mrgs, 24x21", lot 508, C-NY 5/11/88... 3,300
Vertical Apple, 44/60, clr wc/Japan, 1982, sgn/dtd 83, lt scr, L-29x27", Petersburg, lot 720, C-NY 11/1/88 OE ... 2,640
View From the Window, 56/60, clr litho/wc/slksc, 1985, p/s, Gemini bstp, full mrgs, 76x31", lot 1150, SBY 5/13/89 OE... 49,500
Yellow Haystack, 52/250, litho/CM Fabriano Cotone, p/s, Gabriele Mazzotta bstp, full mrgs, 19x26", lot 712, C-NY 11/1/88... 2,420
Yellow Haystack, 56/250, clr litho/CM Fabriano Cotone, 1969, Gabriele Mazzotta bstp, L-14x17", lot 505, C-NY 5/11/88... 2,420

LIEBERMANN, Max (German, 1847-1935)
Women in the Field, etch/wove paper, ca 1890, p/s, lt cr/stn mrgs, lt sl, P-9x12", lot 354, C-NY 11/1/88... 495

LILIEN, Ephraim M. (German, 1874-1925)
Water Carrier, etch, p/s, stn, 6x5", lot 57, WG 10/19/89 UE ... 75

LILLIE, Ella Fillmore (American, 1887-)
Pair: Marblehead; Old Town Square, Marblehead; Ed/25, litho/Rives, ca 1939, p/s, 8x13"/9x12", lot 36, RWS 9/8/89 UE ... 100

LIMBACH, Russell (American, 1904-1975)
Downtown, litho, p/s, titled, 6x6", lot 343, WG 10/19/88 OE ... 100
Strictly Kosher, ed of 250, litho/BFK Rives, 1934, p/s, 10x12", Cleveland Print Club, lot 205, WG 10/19/88... 75

LINDENMUTH, Tod (American, 1885-)
Gill Net, clr litho/Japan, ca 1915, p/s, titled, full mrgs, lt stn/fox, L-12x16", lot 212, C-NY 1/19/89 OE... 2,750
On the Mooring, clr linocut/Japan, ca 1915, p/s, titled, full mrgs, lt stn, L-13x15", lot 213, C-NY 1/19/89 OE... 2,750

LINDNER, Richard (American, 1901-1978)
Banner #4, 10/18, collage, 1971, 75x53", Multiples, lot 896, SBY 11/5/88 OE ... 5,775
Man & Woman, 75/100, clr litho, 1967, sgn in ink, lt stn, L-27x20", lot 109, PHL 6/16/88 UE ... 250
Portfolio: Untitled 1975; 108/125, 10 clr litho w/text, 1976, full mrgs, orig wrappers, Mazo, lot 1150A, SBY 5/13/89... 6,600
Portfolio: Untitled 1975; 111/125, 10 clr litho w/text, p/s, 28x21", Mourlot/AC Maxo, lot 752, SBY 5/14/88 ... 6,600
Red Head, 20/120, clr litho, p/s, S-29x22", lot 110, PHL 6/16/88 UE ... 200
Set of 14: Fun City; 41/265, litho/wove paper, 1971, orig plexiglas box, Shorewood Atelier, lot 516, C-NY 5/11/88 OE... 7,150
Shoot, clr litho, 1971, p/s, 39x27", lot 434, WG 10/19/88 ... 800
Spoleto 1957-1967, 68/100, clr slksc, p/s, S-40x27", lot 111, PHL 6/16/88 UE... 160

LINDSAY, Lionel (American, 20th C)
Peacock, ed of 200, wc, p/s, 9x5", lot 208, WG 10/19/88 ... 175

LINSEY, Martin (American, 20th C)
Columbus Road Ramp, litho, p/s, titled, 12x16", lot 122, WG 10/19/88... 80

LIPCHITZ, Jacques (American, 1891-1973)
Figure & Dog, 40/75, clr litho, p/s, lt cr/ls in corners, S-26x22", lot 73, PHL 10/28/88... 300
Le Chemin de l'Exile, a/p, etch/engr/aqua/wove paper, 1944, sgn, lt tr/sl, P-14x10", lot 451, C-NY 5/10/89 OE ... 1,980
Theseus, a/p, etch/engr/aqua/Vidalon les Annonay, 1943, sgn, stn/sl/fox, P-14x11", Atelier 17, lot 450, C-NY 5/10/89 OE ... 3,850

LISSITZKY, Lazar (El)(Russian, 1890-1941)
Book: Tale of a Goat; 11 litho/thick cream wove paper, 1919, w/rare litho dust jacket, lot 355, C-NY 11/1/88 OE ... 110,000
Book: V Maiakovskii, El Lissitzky, Dlia Golosa (For the Voice); 1923, 8x5", Lutze/Vogt, lot 551, SBY 5/11/89 OE ... 4,675
Portfolio: Die Plastische Gestaltung der Elektro-Mechanischen Schau Sieg uber die Sonne; 1923, lot 87, C-NY 11/1/88 OE... 154,000
Suite: Chad Gadya (The Tale of the Goat); only known copy of blk stones only, 1919, S-12x11", lot 550, SBY 5/11/89 OE ... 66,000

LLOYD, H.H. (19th C)
Major-General George B McClellan, hc engr, trm mrgs, lt stn, 12x16", lot 129, GAI 2/10/89 ... 40

LOCKE, Walter R. (American, 1883-)
Along the Gulf of Mexico, etch, 1934, p/s, titled, 11x8", Assn Am Artists, lot 209, WG 10/19/88 UE ... 35

LONGACRE, Margaret Green (American, 1910-1976)
Point Lobos, California; 4/19, wc, p/s, lt stn, 11x8", lot 397, WG 10/19/88 UE... 20

LONGO, Robert (American, 1953-)
Group of 3: Jules; Gretchen; Mark; PP1/4, clr litho/3 separate sheets, 1982-83, S-37x21", Brooke Alexander, SBY 5/13/89 ... 8,250
Jules, Gretchen, Mark, State II; 27/30, litho, 1982-83, p/s, full mrgs, S-37x68", Brooke Alexander, SBY 5/14/88 OE... 8,800
Pair: Eric; Cindy; 1/38, clr litho, p/s, full mrgs, S-68x39", Brooke Alexander, lot 1152, SBY 5/13/89 ... 29,700
Pair: Men in the Cities: Eric; Gretchen; 29/48, clr litho, 1985, p/s, S-72x36", Schellmann, lot 1153, SBY 5/13/89 OE ... 15,400
Pair: Men in the Cities: Larry; Joanna; 28/48, clr litho, 1983, p/s, S-72x36", Schellmann, lot 1151, SBY 5/13/89... 14,300

LORAIN, G. (French, 19th/20th C)
Art & Decoration, clr litho/poster, 1898, lt tr img/cr, 26x18", Lemercier, lot 271, FAP 2/24/89 UE... 170

LORD, Elyse Ashe (British, -1971)
Asian Interior/Blowing Bubbles, 71/100, etch/clr woodblock, p/s, mount stn, laid down, 13x18", RWS 3/16/89... 350
Pair: Immortals; hc etch/aqua, sgn, 17x21", Ackermann, lot 16, MG 5/28/88 OE... 550

LORRAIN, Claude; see Gellee, Claude

LOUPOT, Charles (French, 20th C)
Exposition Internationale Arts Decoratifs, Paris 1925; litho/poster paper, linen backed, unfr, 38x24", FAP 2/24/89 OE ... 725

LOVING, Eugene E. (American, 20th C)
Private Alley, New Orleans; ed of 200, etch, p/s, titled, 10x7", lot 325, WG 10/19/88 ... 110

LOZOWICK, Louis (American, 1892-1973)
Bridge in Shadow, a/p, litho/wht wove paper, 1930, p/s, wide mrgs, 12x8", lot 152, SWN 6/15/89 OE ... 1,320
Conversation in Haiti, ed of 20, litho, 1955, p/s, titled, 14x8", lot 361, WG 10/19/88... 275
Guts of Manhattan, 2/20, litho/GCM wove paper, 1939, p/s, full mrgs, lt stn/sl/rub, L-13x9", lot 218, C-NY 1/19/89 OE ... 1,650
Hells Gate Bridge, litho, 1928, p/s, dtd, full mrgs, lt sl mrgs, 13x10", lot 126, FAP 2/24/89 ... 1,050
Hudson Bridge (George Washington Bridge), litho, 1931, p/s, lt stn/cr, L-14x9", RWS 3/16/89 ... 1,200
Mural Study: Lower Manhattan; recorded ed of 10 or less, litho, 1936, p/s, trm mrgs, L-13x7", lot 453, C-NY 5/10/89 OE... 2,750
Mural Study: Triborough Bridge; recorded ed of 10 or less, litho/BFK Rives, 1936, L-14x7", lot 454, C-NY 5/10/89... 1,980

Pair: Breakfast (Still Life, Breakfast); Still Life #1 (Still Life with Guitar); litho, 1929, lot 243, SBY 5/11/89 1,980
Queensboro Bridge, ed of 50, litho, 1930, p/s, full mrgs, lt stn, L-14x8", lot 22, PHL 6/16/88 OE 1,700
Queensboro Bridge, ed of 50, litho, 1930, p/s, full mrgs, lt sl/rpl mrgs, 14x8", lot 246, SBY 5/11/89 1,430
Quiet Harbor (Swimming Hole), total ed of 260, litho/wove paper, 1932, p/s, L-9x13", lot 37, C-NY 5/11/88 UE 286
Red Teapot (Tea for One), 3/50, litho, 1973, sgn by Adele Lozowick, full mrgs, L-9x15", lot 26, PHL 10/28/88 225
Self-Portrait in Spring, 6/20, litho, 1943, p/s, lt ls/tp stn mrg/recto, lt mstn, L-11x8", SBY 5/12/88 880
Summer Home, ed of 15, litho/wove paper, 1930, sgn/dtd 45, lt stn, L-13x9", lot 216, C-NY 1/19/89 OE 770
Tanks #2, ed of 50, litho/wove paper, 1929/1930, p/s, lt cr/sl, L-14x9", George Miller, lot 214, C-NY 1/19/89 3,300
Thanksgiving Dinner, V/X, litho/wove paper, 1938, p/s, full mrgs, L-13x8", Miller & Miller, lot 38, C-NY 5/11/88 OE 735
Through Brooklyn Bridge Cables, ed of 250, litho, 1938, p/s, L-10x13", lot 55A, RWS 9/29/89 OE 3,750
Untitled (Hudson Bridge?), litho/MBM France, 1936, p/s, trm mrgs, lt stn/old glue, L-13x9", lot 455, C-NY 5/10/89 1,980
White Tanks, I/X, litho/wove paper, 1930, p/s, full mrgs, L-11x8", Burr Miller, lot 217, C-NY 1/19/89 660
Winter Fun, ed of 270, litho/wove paper, 1940, p/s, cut mrgs, ls/cr/stn, stn verso, unfr, L-10x13", C-NY 1/22/88 209
3rd Avenue (3rd Avenue El), ed of 15, litho, 1929, p/s, dtd 31, full mrgs, lt tr/cr, 12x8", lot 245, SBY 5/11/89 OE 5,775
57th Street (Rubber Center), ed of 40, litho, 1929, p/s, full mrgs, lt rpr tr/sl, 15x8", lot 244, SBY 5/11/89 3,300

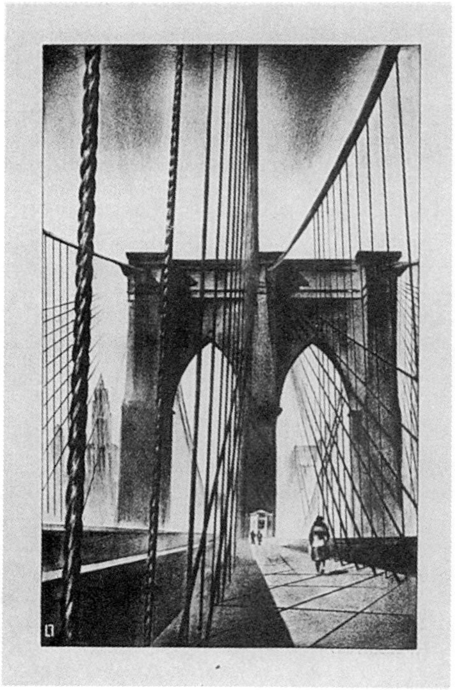

Brooklyn Bridge, ed of 100, litho/BFK Rives, 1930, p/s, full mrgs, lt stn, L-13x8", lot 215, C-NY 1/19/88 OE; $11,000

LUCAS, David (19th C)
Group of 4: Stonehenge; A Mill; Lock on the Stour, Suffolk; Summer Afternoon, After a Shower; mezzo, 1855, SWN 6/15/89 495
LUCE, Maximilien; after (French, 1858-1941)
Londres, by Jacques Villon, 1/200, clr aqua/Japan, 1929, sgn by Luce/Villon, full mrgs, 14x20", lot 592, SBY 11/3/88 OE 3,850
LUCIONI, Luigi (American, 1900-)
Barn in Vermont, engr, p/s, 6x9", lot 218, WG 10/19/89 90
Group of 3: Birch Grove; On a Vermont Highway; Elms on the Lake; ed of 250, various sizes, Assn Am Artists, SWN 6/15/89 330
Group of 3: Shadow & Substance; Rhythm in White; Peaceful Pastures; p/s, various sizes, Assn Am Artists, SWN 6/15/89 300
Steeple in the Mountains (church/landscape), etch, p/s, 12x9", Assn Am Artists, lot 282, WG 10/19/88 85
LUM, Bertha Boynton (American, 1879-1954)
Cherry Blossoms, hc woodblock, 1913, p/s, orig label, unfr, 17x12", RWS 4/22/89 950
Junks in a Lake, clr woodblock on laid paper, lt stn/cr, unfr, 12x9", RWS 4/22/89 OE 850
LUNS, Huib (Dutch, 1915-)
Green Grass/Kills Flies/Be Tidy/& You Save Human Lives...; blk/gr linocut poster, 1915, cr/sl, S-33x20", RWS 3/16/89 2,000
LYENDECKER, Joseph Christian (American, 19th/20th C)
USA Bonds, Weapons for Liberty; clr litho/poster paper, laid down, 30x20", lot 182, FAP 2/24/89 120
MAAS, George Jo (American, 1910-)
Main Street, 24/100, aqua, p/s, 10x14", lot 121, WG 10/19/88 110
MAC COY, Guy (American, 1904-)
Belleville Harbor, clr etch, p/s, titled, 6x8", lot 752, WAD 6/12/89 OE 420
Blue Birds, clr scpt/thick wove paper, 1949, p/s, full mrgs, sl/stn mrgs/verso, cr mrg, unfr, L-11x14", C-NY 1/22/88 UE 8,250
MAC LEAN, William (American, 1860-1940)
Evening Visit, etch, p/s, titled, lt stn, 10x12", Assn Am Artists, lot 241, WG 10/19/88 90
Snow Valley, etch, p/s, titled, 10x12", Assn Am Artists, lot 298, WG 10/19/88 UE 45
MAGNUS, Charles (19th C)
Bird's-Eye View of City of Annapolis, Maryland; litho, 1864, inscr, trm mrgs, rpr img, lstn, L-10x17", C-NY 1/22/88 OE 528

MAGRITTE, Rene (Belgian, 1898-1967)
Ceci n'est pas une Pipe (L'Air et le Chanson), 37/60, etch, 1962, p/s, full mrgs, 5x6", Schwarz, lot 263, SBY 11/3/88 UE **2,200**
Les Travaux d'Alexandre, a/p, etch, 1962, p/s, full mrgs, tp hinge, 5x6", Schwartz, lot 303, SBY 2/23/89 OE **2,750**
Les Travaux d'Alexandre, XVI/XXV, etch, 1962, p/s, full mrgs, tp hinges, 5x6", lot 262, SBY 11/3/88 **2,200**
Paysage de Baucis, HC, blk/gr-wht etch, 1966, p/s, full mrgs, lt stn/sl/cr, 9x7", Visat, lot 570, SBY 5/11/89 OE **8,250**
Paysage de Baucis, HC, blk/pale gr etch, 1966, p/s, full mrgs, lt cr, 9x7", Visat, lot 304, SBY 2/23/89 **3,575**
Paysage de Baucis, HC, blk/wht etch, 1966, p/s, full mrgs, lt cr, 9x7", Visat, lot 265, SBY 11/3/88 OE **6,050**
Salon de Mai 1965, 74/107, clr litho, 1965, sgn in pen, full mrgs, lt stn, 19x16", Musse d'Art, lot 569, SBY 5/11/89 OE **6,600**
Salon de Mai 1965, 74/107, clr litho, 1965, sgn in pen, full mrgs, lt stn, 19x16", Musee, lot 264, SBY 11/3/88 **4,950**

MAGRITTE, Rene; after (Belgian, 1898-1967)
Bird's Nest, 157/200, clr litho, p/s by Georgette Magritte, L-22x17", lot 74, PHL 10/28/88 **350**

MAILLOL, Aristide (French, 1861-1944)
Epanouissement, 25/50, 1st state, litho, p/s, 10x15", lot 117, SWN 12/1/88 **358**
Femme de Dos, Drapee; 1st state, litho/Montval, ca 1924, Galerie Peintres-Graveurs bstp, P-11x5", C-NY 1/22/88 UE **242**
Femme en Berceau...; 23/25, litho/simili Japan, ca 1920s, Galerie Peintres-Graveurs bstp, unfr, L-6x7", C-NY 1/22/88 UE **275**
Femme Nue de dos Tenant une Echarpe, 13/35, 1st state, litho Galerie Peintres-Graveurs bstp, L-11x4", C-NY 1/22/88 **660**
Group of 3: Galatea in the Waves; Galatea, Daughter of Nereus; Gallus Hunging the Fierce Wild Boar; wc, SWN 6/15/89 **132**
Junon, #21, litho, ca 1925, intl, Peintres Graveurs bstp, full mrgs, lt sl/cr, 8x10", lot 306, SBY 2/23/89 **1,100**
La Vague, 32/60, 2nd state, wc/Chine, 1895-98, intl/Petiet bstp, cr/fox img, stn mrg, L-7x8", lot 190, C-NY 5/11/88 OE **10,450**
Nudebout, 182/275, litho, sgn in stone, 14x7", lot 1163, LH 10/16/88 UE **60**

MAJOR & KNAPP
New Berne, litho, 1864, lt scuff/scr/stn, backed w/Japan, 19x30", Voltaire Combe, lot 525, SBY 1/28/88 OE **2,090**

MAKI, Naku (Japanese, 1924-)
Work 74-22, 68/100, clr intg, p/s, titled, 5x8", Cleveland Print Club, lot 419, WG 10/19/88 **130**

MALEVITCH, Kasimir (Russian, 1878-1935)
Book: A Kruchenykh, V Klebnikov, EG Guro, Troe (The Three); 1913, 8x7", Crane, lot 552, SBY 5/11/89 OE **5,225**

MAN-RAY (Emmanuel Radinski)(American, 1890-1976)
Abstract Composition, 53/100, clr litho/cream wove paper, p/s, full mrgs, 13x19", lot 2893, B/B 4/19/88 **330**
Landscape with a Cow, 36/75, leather/blk plexiglas collage/bl wove paper, 1974, Galleria il Fauno, lot 812, C-NY 5/10/89 **1,430**
Portfolio: Revolving Doors; #86, ed of 105, 10 pochoirs/wove paper, 1916-17, lt fox/sl, 22x15", lot 536, SBY 11/3/88 OE **10,450**
Still Life, 99/175, clr litho, ca 1973, p/s, 25x19", lot 119, SWN 12/1/88 **468**
Suite: Les Anatomes; 30/100, 11 clr etch, 1970, p/s, full mrgs, cr/lt sl mrg & verso, S-26x20", SBY 5/14/88 **1,100**

MANET, Edouard (French, 1832-1883)
Au Paradis, 2, brush litho/thin China, 1877, trm, lt fox/cr, S-10x14", SBY 5/12/88 **6,600**
Beaudelaire en Face, etch, 1865, pl/s, 4x3", lot 303, FB 5/28/89 **170**
Charles Baudelaire, 4th/final state, etch/laid paper, 1865, P-4x3", C-NY 1/22/88 OE **242**
Guerre Civile, 2nd state, litho/pk-bl Chine applique, 1871, lt tr/ls/cr/sl/stn, S-20x26", lot 89, C-NY 11/1/88 OE **20,900**
Le Chanteur Espagnol ou le Guitarero, etch/rlt/laid paper, 1861-62, lt cr, 12x10", lot 242, SBY 2/25/88 OE **3,850**
Le Chanteur Espagnol ou le Guitarero, etch/rlt/laid paper, 1861-62, 12x10", L'Artiste, lot 266, SBY 11/3/88 OE **8,525**
Le Chat et les Fleurs, etch/aqua/BFK Rives, 1869, pl/s, 8x7", lot 2867, B/B 2/16/88 **220**
Le Gamin, 2nd state, litho/pk-bl Chine applique, 1962-74, lt fox/sl, S-23x17", Lemercier, lot 88, C-NY 11/1/88 **18,700**
Lola de Valence, Guerin's 3rd state, etch/aqua/laid paper, 1862-3, Societe des Aquafortistes bstp, 10x7", C-NY 5/11/88 **1,100**
Pair: Baudelaire de Profile en Chapeau, 1862; Baudelaire de Face, 1865; etch, Salmon/Asselineaux, lot 158, SWN 6/15/89 **550**
Polichinelle, gouache/watercolor/blk litho, 1974, w/verse by Theodore de Banville, lt stn/sl, S-19x23", SBY 5/12/88 OE **187,000**
Polichinelle, 2nd ed, final state, clr litho, sepia ink sgn/inscr, trm, backed w/Japan, S-19x12", SBY 5/12/88 OE **7,150**
Polichinelle, 2nd ed, final state, clr litho/wht wove paper, 1874, lt fox/sl, 20x13", lot 267, SBY 11/3/88 **5,500**
Polichinelle, 2nd ed, 3rd state, clr litho/wove paper, 1876, lt rpr/ls to img/lt stn, L-19x13", lot 654, C-NY 5/10/89 OE **1,870**
Untitled, Portrait of a Woman; etch/laid paper, 9x6", lot 2865, B/B 4/19/88 **825**

MANET, Edouard; after (French, 1832-1883)
Dejeuner sur l'Herbe, by Jacques Villon, 99/200, aqua, 1929, p/s, full mrgs, lt stn/cr, P-10x25", lot 84, PHL 6/16/88 OE **3,400**

MANSFIELD, Louise Buckingham (American, 1876-)
Good Children Street, clr woodblock, sgn, matted, unfr, 7x7", RWS 4/22/89 **200**

MANSOUROFF, Paul (European, 1896-)
Set of 6: Untitled; 27/100, clr litho/Arches, 1970, full mrgs, orig portfolio, Gervis/Parasol, lot 517, C-NY 5/11/88 UE **143**

MARA, Kim (British, 20th C)
Stage & Television Today, 20/40, litho, p/s, dtd 1975, 35x46", SLK 4/7/89 **40**

MARC, Franz (German, 1880-1916)
Reitschule Nach Ridinger, wc/gray Japan, 1913, lt lstn, glue at mrg edges, L-11x12", lot 360, C-NY 11/1/88 **3,300**
Schafende Hirtin, wc/Japan, 1912, sgn by Maria Marc on verso, lt stn/cr, L-8x10", lot 359, C-NY 11/1/88 **1,210**
Tierlegende, wc/wove paper, 1912-13/1919, titled on verso, trm mrgs, lt stn, 8x10", lot 2867, B/B 4/19/88 **412**
Zwei Katzen, clr litho, 1909-10, lt fld/fox/stn, linen backed, S-36x25", Eigner, lot 90, C-NY 11/1/88 OE **30,800**

MARCKS, Gerhard Alexander (German, 1864-1905)
Bat (Die Fledermaus), ed of unknown size, wc/wove paper, 20th C, p/s, mstn/old glue, S-15x11", lot 655, C-NY 5/10/89 OE **440**
Picador II, 12/50, wc/heavy wove paper, 1950, p/s, 10x10", lot 2869, B/B 2/16/88 **250**

MARCOUSSIS, Louis (Polish, 1878-1941)
La Table, 12/20, clr etch/Japan, 1930, p/s, rpl/sl in mrg & verso, P-10x7", lot 194, C-NY 5/11/88 **4,180**
La Table, 41/120, clr etch/wove paper, 1930, p/s, lt stn img, lt stn mrg, P-10x7", lot 361, C-NY 11/1/88 **4,180**
Le Comptoir, ed of 100, drypt/cream wove paper, 1921, S-16x12", Die Schaffenden, lot 93, C-NY 11/1/88 OE **3,300**
Le Comptoir, ed of 125, aqua/etch/drypt/Japan, brn ink w/pl tone, 1921, p/s, full mrgs, lt cr/fox, 7x10", SBY 5/12/88 OE **7,150**
Nature Morte, 46/50, drypt/MBM wove paper, ca 1920, p/s, lt cr/sl/tp, S-19x13", lot 92, C-NY 11/1/88 OE **6,050**
Suite: Eaux-Fortes Theatrales pour MG...; 11/30, 11 etch/Arches, lt fox/ls, 16x13", Montagne, lot 204A, SBY 5/12/88 OE **2,200**

MARDEN, Brice (American, 1938-)	
Pair: Untitled (Grids-Black); Untitled (Grids-White); 22/50, scrpt, 1974, full mrgs, S-30x22", lot 519, C-NY 5/11/88 OE	**1,320**
Pair: Untitled; Five Plates; 40/50, etch/aqua/wove paper, 1973, p/s, S-40x30", Parasol, lot 518, C-NY 5/11/88 OE	**825**
Portfolio: Adriatics; Adriatics, Grids; 35/40, 3 aqua & 4 etch, 1973, S-33x37", Parasol, lot 1157, SBY 5/13/89	**7,700**
Portfolio: Five Threes; 14/25, 5 clr aqua, 1977, p/s, full mrgs, orig wrappers, Parasol, lot 1158, SBY 5/13/89	**8,800**
Portfolio: 6/30, 8 etch, 1972, p/s, orig wrappers, S-22x30", Parasol, lot 1159, SBY 5/13/89 OE	**13,200**
Skowhegan School, 33/40, etch/wove paper, 1979, p/s, Aeropress bstp, full mrgs, P-6x5", lot 521, C-NY 5/11/88 OE	**880**
Untitled (Grids-Black), 22/50, scrpt/wove paper, 1974, p/s, full mrgs, lt sl/scr mrgs, S-30x22", lot 520, C-NY 5/11/88	**462**
MARGOLIES, Samuel L. (American, 1897-)	
Beware of the Dog, etch, p/s, titled, 7x10", Federal Art Project, lot 129, WG 10/19/88	**175**
Man's Canyons, aqua/etch/cream laid paper, 1936, p/s, titled, lt stn/old tp, P-12x9", lot 219, C-NY 1/19/89 OE	**7,700**
Men of Steel, ed of 250, drypt/BFK Rives, ca 1940, p/s, titled, lt scuff/scr, P-15x12", lot 220, C-NY 1/19/89 OE	**3,520**
Winter Wonderland, aqua/wove paper, p/s, lt fox/stn, orig mount, L-9x12", Assn Am Artists, RWS 3/16/89 UE	**110**
MARGULIES, Joseph (American, 1896-)	
Fishing Boats & Dinghies, etch, p/s, 8x12", lot 288, WG 10/19/88	**90**
Group of 4: Peaceful Harbor; Light & Shadow; Chess; Man With Drink; litho, p/s, Assn Am Artists, WG 10/19/88	**200**
MARIN, John (American, 1870-1953)	
Downtown the El, etch, 1921, p/s, full mrgs, lt stn/cr, 7x9", New Republic, lot 48, SBY 2/25/88	**1,210**
From Ponte S Pantaleo, Venice; ed of about 30, etch/Japan, 1907, p/s, lt mstn/cr, P-8x6", lot 456, C-NY 5/10/89	**715**
Lobster Fisherman, ed of 125, etch/wove paper, 1948, p/s, full mrgs, lt sl, P-9x7", lot 222, C-NY 1/19/89 OE	**352**
Lobster Fisherman, 31/125, etch/wove paper, 1949, p/s, full mrgs, lt cr mrg, lt lstn/mstn, P-9x7", C-NY 1/22/88	**220**
Old Houses, Rue des Arpents, Rouen, I; 2nd state, etch/wove paper, 1909, p/s, full mrgs, lt stn, P-7x9", SBY 1/19/89	**440**
Pair: Near Quai D'Ivry; Campiello S Rocco, Venice; ed of about 30, etch, 1906 & 1907, 6x8"/6x5", lot 46, SBY 2/25/88	**880**
Woolworth Building (The Dance), ed of about 30, etch/drypt/wove paper, 1913, p/s, P-13x11", lot 41, SBY 11/3/88 OE	**57,200**
MARINI, Marino (Italian, 1901-1980)	
Ceramica II, a/p, ed of 80, clr litho/Arches, 1955, p/s, lt sl/cr, tp verso, S-26x20", RWS 3/16/89 OE	**1,200**
Cheval Rouge sur Fond Vert, 10/25, total ed of 175, clr litho, 1955, p/s, lt stn, L-20x14", lot 657, C-NY 5/10/89 OE	**1,540**
Chevaux et Cavaliers, 29/50, clr litho/Arches, 1972, p/s, L-15x20", lot 196, C-NY 5/11/88 OE	**1,320**
Composition, 29/50, clr litho/Arches, ca 1972, p/s, L-15x20", C-NY 5/11/88 OE	**1,760**
Composition (Juggler), clr etch, after 1970, p/s, lt cr mrgs, 12x10", Guastalla & Toninelli, lot 161, SWN 6/15/89 OE	**770**
Devastation & Reconstruction, 18/50, total ed of 128, etch/Arches, 1963, p/s, lt stn, P-16x12", lot 362, C-NY 11/1/88 OE	**1,540**
Dream of the Rider, HC V/XV, ed of 33, etch/Rives, 1960, p/s, P-14x12", lot 658, C-NY 5/10/89 OE	**880**
Miracolo, 11/125, litho/Rives, ca 1965, p/s, full mrgs, lt mstn, L-29x21", lot 364, C-NY 11/1/88	**605**
Miracolo, Pl 4, HC, clr etch/aqua, 1971, p/s, full mrgs, lt stn, 16x11", XXe Siecle/Amiel, lot 307, SBY 2/23/89	**660**
Pair: Miracolo; Horse & Rider; ed of 75, etch/aqua & aqua, 1978, full mrgs, 22x17"/20x18", lot 269A, SBY 11/3/88	**1,925**
Rider Survivor, 18/50, clr etch/Arches, 1963, p/s, full mrgs, lt tstn, P-16x12", lot 363, C-NY 11/1/88	**715**
Spartaco, 11/175, etch/aqua, 1975, p/s, full mrgs, P-15x20", Transworld/Crommelynck, lot 114, PHL 6/16/88	**425**
Suite: Marino From Goethe I-IV; XVI/L, 4 etch/aqua, 1979, p/s, full mrgs, 25x20", lot 269, SBY 11/3/88	**8,250**
Suite: Marino From Shakespeare II; VII/L, 8 aqua/etch/drypt/Arches, p/s, full mrgs, lt stn/sl, ea 19x15", SBY 5/12/88 OE	**23,100**
Suite: Marino From Shakespeare II; XLII/L, 8 etch/drypt/aqua/Arches, 1978, full mrgs, S-19x15", lot 268, SBY 11/3/88	**18,700**
Trois Chevaux, 32/50, clr litho/Arches, 1971, p/s, full mrgs, L-12x10", lot 365, C-NY 11/1/88	**1,045**
Warrior, 30/50, clr etch/aqua, 1963, lt cr mrgs, 16x12", Gustalla & Toninelli/Commelynck, lot 160, SWN 6/15/89 OE	**880**
MARKHAM, Kyra (American, 1891-1967)	
Bleeker St Fire Hydrant, litho/wove paper, 1942, p/s, dtd, tp, unfr, L-9x11", RWS 3/16/89 OE	**900**
Pair: Fit Yourself Shop; And He Said; 39/50 & 50/50, litho/wove paper, 1935/1943, p/s, dtd, full mrg, unfr, C-NY 1/22/88	**528**
MARSH, Reginald (American, 1898-1954)	
Along the Seine, a/p, litho/Chine applique, 1928, p/s, lg mrgs, lt stn corner, 9x11", lot 2962, B/B 4/19/88	**600**
Along the Seine, litho/Chine applique, 1928, p/s, inscr 40 Proofs, lt sl/tstn/tp, unfr, L-9x11", C-NY 1/22/88 UE	**275**
Bowery-Upright, 9/21, litho/India applique, 1932, p/s, full mrgs, scr/cr/sl mrgs, lt fox, unfr, L-9x7", C-NY 1/22/88 OE	**1,320**
Cafe Dome, ed of 21, litho, p/s, 8x7", lot 56, LH 3/20/88	**1,500**
Cafe Dome, 14/21, litho/India applique, 1932, p/s, lt sl, fld mrgs, L-8x6", lot 226, C-NY 1/19/89	**990**
Cafe Dome, 6/21, litho/India applique, 1932, p/s, full mrgs, lt cr/sl/tr/fox mrgs, lt tstn, unfr, L-9x7", C-NY 1/22/88	**990**
Diana Dancing Academy, ed of 12, 5th state, engr/laid paper, 1939, p/s, lt stn/sl, P-8x10", lot 234, C-NY 1/19/89	**1,870**
Drum Majorette, ed of 300, final state, engr, 1940, p/s, P-12x6", Atelier 17, lot 53, RWS 9/29/88	**400**
Drum Majorette, presumed ed of 300, 4th state, engr/wove paper, 1940, p/s, lt sl mrgs, P-12x6", lot 235, C-NY 1/19/89	**440**
Eltinge Follies, ed of 15, final state, engr/laid England, 1940, p/s, lt tr/ls/stn, 12x10", lot 48, SBY 2/23/89	**3,850**
Erie RR & Factories, #45, 6th state, etch/engr/wove paper, 1930, p/s, lt stn/sl, P-8x12", lot 229, C-NY 1/19/89	**1,870**
Erie RR Yards, litho/India applique, 1928, p/s, inscr 35 Proofs, full mrgs, mstn/cr/sl, unfr, L-9x13", C-NY 1/22/88	**825**
Erie RR Yards, litho/India applique, 1928, p/s, inscr 35 Proofs, Downtown Gallery stp, sl, unfr, L-9x13", C-NY 1/22/88	**715**
Gaiety Burlesque, 36/40, etch, 1930, p/s, lt sl/stn, 12x10", lot 248, SBY 5/11/89 OE	**6,325**
Girl Walking, litho, p/s, 11x8", Assn Am Artists, lot 184, WG 10/19/88 OE	**850**
Girl Walking (Elevated), ed of 150, litho, 1945, p/s, full mrgs, lt stn, L-11x8", Assn Am Arists, lot 25, PHL 6/16/88 OE	**1,100**
Girl Walking-Pillar-Soldier; engr/wove paper, 1942, p/s, intl/dtd, lt stn, P-6x4", lot 29, RWS 9/8/89 OE	**425**
Huber's Museum, litho/India applique, 1928, p/s, inscr 35 Proofs, full mrgs, lt fox/cr/sl, unfr, L-9x14", C-NY 1/22/88	**1,320**
Iron Steamboat Co, #15, etch, 1932, p/s, full mrgs, lt mstn/sl, 7x9", lot 249, SBY 5/11/89	**1,980**
Irving Place Burlesque, ed of 25, litho/Chine applique, 1928, p/s, trm mrgs, lt rub, laid down, L-10x11", C-NY 1/19/89	**1,100**
Irving Place Burlesque, ed of 25, litho/mounted thin paper, 1928, p/s, inscr 25 Proofs, unfr, L-10x12", RWS 3/16/89	**2,000**
Irving Place Burlesque, 10/50, 3rd state, etch/laid paper, 1929, p/s, lt stn, P-8x10", lot 228, C-NY 1/19/89 OE	**3,300**
Loco-Erie Watering, 4th/final state, etch, 1929, p/s, full mrgs, cr/stn/fox, unfr, P-7x10", Friends Am Art, C-NY 1/22/88	**1,210**
Merry-Go-Round, 53/59, etch, 1930, p/s, lt sl/stn mrgs & verso, 7x10", lot 247, SBY 5/11/89	**3,850**
Old Paris, litho/India applique, 1928, p/s, lt stn/sl mrgs, L-13x9", lot 223, C-NY 1/19/89	**1,430**

Pair: Ormond House; Kenneth Hayes Miller; 12/18 & 19/24, etch/JW & etch/Rives, 1931, p/s, inscr, C-NY 1/22/88 UE 220
Skyline From Pier 10 Brooklyn, 4th state, etch/wove paper, 1931, full mrgs, lt sl/fox, P-6x12", lot 457, C-NY 5/10/89 1,430
St Jean de Luz, ed of 40 a/p, litho/Chine colle, ca 1928, p/s, pl/s, lt stn mrgs, 8x13", lot 162, SWN 6/15/89 1,100
Steeplechase Swings, 7/75, etch, 1935, p/s, lt stn/sl/old tp hinges, 9x13", lot 250, SBY 5/11/89 3,850
Switch Engines, Erie Yards, Jersey City, Store No 3; ed of 250, litho, 1948, p/s, 9x14", George Miller, SBY 2/25/88 990
Switch Engines, Erie Yards, Jersey City, Store No 3; total ed of 263, litho, 1948, Cleveland Print Club, C-NY 1/19/89 1,100
Tattoo-Shave-Haircut; 10th state, etch/engr, 1932, p/s, full mrgs, lt stn/sl/tp, P-10x10", Jones, lot 39, C-NY 5/11/88 4,180
Tenth Avenue at 27th Street, ed of 17, 3rd/final state, etch/JW, 1931, lt lstn/tstn, P-8x11", C-NY 1/22/88 3,300
Tenth Avenue, 81/100, etch, no size given, Whitney Mus, lot 354, WG 10/19/88 275
Third Avenue El, posthumous ed of 13, etch/BFK Rives, full mrgs, lt sl mrgs/verso, P-6x9", lot 230, C-NY 1/19/89 715
Tugboat New York, clr scrpt/wove paper, ca 1930s, sgn in img, Living Am Art stp, 16x20", lot 225, C-NY 1/19/89 UE 165
US Marine, #8, 3rd state, etch/wove paper, 1934, p/s, lt stn, P-8x6", lot 233, C-NY 1/19/89 OE 1,045

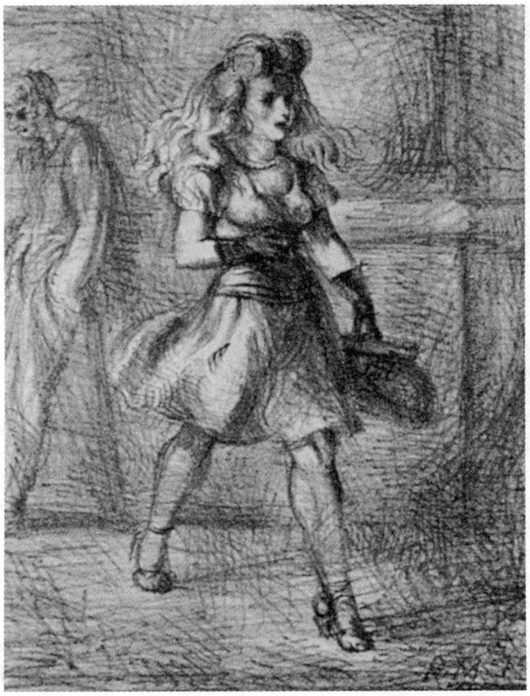

Girl Walking (Elevated), ed of 150, litho, 1945, p/s, full mrgs, lt stn, L-11x18", Assn Am Artists, lot 25, PHL 6/16/88 OE; $1,100

MARSHALL, Benjamin; after (British, 1767-1835)
Thomas Oldaker, Twenty-Six Years Huntsman to the Berkeley Hounds; lt stn, 16x19", lot 112, FAP 2/24/89 UE 120

MARTENS, Conrad (1801-1878)
View of Part of Port Jackson, with Garden Island From Darling Point; hc litho, L-6x9", lot 170, C-SK 5/25/89 2,390

MARTIN, Fletcher (American, 1904-1979)
Arab Children, litho, p/s, 17x13", Assn Am Artists, lot 289, WG 10/19/88 60

MARTIN, John (British, 1789-1854)
Fall of Man, a/p, engr, 1826, sm tr in mrg, lt sl, 6x8", lot 2868, B/B 4/19/88 110
Set of 6: Paradise Lost; a/p, mezzo/etch/rlt, 1827, full mrgs, lt fox, S-7x10", lot 245, SBY 2/25/88 1,210

MARTIN, Sam (American, 1928-)
Eby Print, 52/125, clr srgph, p/s, 26x20", lot 435, FAP 4/15/88 OE 55

MARVAL, Jacqueline (French, 1866-1932)
Une Nuit a Chang-Hai, clr litho/poster paper, sgn, S-45x30", lot 46, RWS 9/29/88 300

MASSARD, Jules (French, 19th C)
Mother & Child, engr, p/s, lt fox, no size given, lot 13, FAP 2/24/89 100

MASSON, Andre (French, 1896-)
Book: Anatomy of My Universe; 5/30, 1943, lt sl/rpr tr, Valentin, lot 574, SBY 5/11/89 9,350
Book: Anatomy of My Universe; 5/30, 1943, orig wrappers, Curt Valentin, lot 271, SBY 11/3/88 OE 8,800
Book: Une Etoile de Craie; by Patrick Waldberg, 75/101, 1973, orig wrappers, Au Pont des Arts, lot 575, SBY 5/11/89 4,070
Le Genie de L'Espece, 14/30, engr/drypt/sanguine/tone, 1942, p/s, lt cr/ink, 14x11", Buchholz Gallery, SBY 5/12/88 OE 7,150
Les Fruits de l'Abime, proposed ed of 50, sftgr etch, 1942, p/s, full mrgs, lt sl/stn, 12x8", lot 573, SBY 5/11/89 2,200
Les Fruits de l'Abime, proposed ed of 50, sftgr etch, 1942, p/s, full mrgs, lt stn, 12x8", lot 270, SBY 11/3/88 2,750
Les Fruits de l'Abime, proposed ed of 50, sftgr etch/wove paper, 1942, p/s, full mrgs, lt cr/tr, P-12x8", SBY 5/12/88 OE 3,875

MATHAM, Jacob (Dutch, 17th C)
Set of 8: Divinities of Fable; engr/wm double-headed eagle paper, lt nick/rpr, lot 74, SBY 5/11/89 1,210
Three Fates, Weigel's 1st state of 2, engr, 1587, trm/cr/fox/stn, 13" dia, lot 641, SBY 2/25/88 OE 1,870

MATISSE, Henri (French, 1869-1954)
Arabesque, Pl 58, 7/50, litho, 1924, p/s, full mrgs, lt tr/rpr/sl mrgs, 19x12", lot 280, SBY 11/3/88 OE 14,850
Bedouine au Grand Voile, Pl 331, a/p, aqua/wove paper, 1947, full mrgs, lt cr, 13x10", lot 323, SBY 2/23/89 8,250
Book: Jazz; 87/200, ed of 250, 1947, orig wrappers/slipcase, Teriade, lot 299, SBY 11/3/88 OE 187,000
Book: Poemes de Charles d'Orleans; 54 clr litho w/text on Arches, 1950, orig wrappers, slipcase, lot 670, C-NY 5/10/89 2,420

Book: Portraits; #2474, 1954, orig wrappers, Sauret/Mourlot, lot 254, SBY 2/25/88	**385**
Book: Repli; by Andre Rouveyre, 229/270, 1947, orig wrappers, Eds Du Belier/Mourlot, lot 251, SBY 2/25/88	**1,650**
Book: Ulysses; by James Joyce, #1028, ed of 1500, 1935, Ltd Ed Club, lot 295, SBY 11/3/88 OE	**3,960**
Book: Ulysses; by James Joyce, ed of 1500, 1935, Ltd Ed Club, lot 316, SBY 2/23/89 OE	**4,125**
Danseuse Assise (En Hauteur), Pl 93 or 91, 22/130, litho/Arches, 1927, p/s, full mrgs, 17x11", lot 313, SBY 2/23/89 OE	**14,300**
Danseuse au Fauteuil en Bois, Pl 4, 6/15, litho/Japan, 1925-26, p/s, lt sl, S-20x13", lot 95, C-NY 11/1/88	**10,450**
Danseuse au Fauteuil en Bois, Pl 95 or 97, litho/Arches, 1927, p/s, 18x11", Galerie d'Art Contemporain, SBY 11/3/88	**9,075**
Danseuse au Tabouret, Pl 90 or 95, 112/130, litho/Arches, 1927, p/s, 18x11", Galerie d'Art Contemporain, SBY 11/3/88 OE	**20,900**
Danseuse Couchee, Pl 96, 1/130, litho/Arches, 1927, p/s, full mrgs, lt sl/stn, 11x18", Galerie Contemporain, SBY 2/25/88	**11,000**
Danseuse Debout, Accoudee; Pl 99 or 91, 16/130, litho/Arches, 1927, p/s, 18x11", Galerie d'Art, lot 585, SBY 5/11/89	**13,200**
Danseuse Endormie au Divan, 8/15, litho/Japan, 1927, p/s, lt cr/rub mrgs, L-11x18", lot 370, C-NY 11/1/88 OE	**18,700**
Danseuse Endormie au Divan, 91 or 99, 36/130, litho, p/s, 1927, full mrgs, lt scr/fox, unfr, L-13x20", SBY 5/12/88 OE	**15,400**
Danseuse Etendue au Divan (Mains a la Nuque), 92, 44/130, litho/Arches, 1927, p/s, full mrgs, L-11x18", SBY 5/12/88 OE	**12,100**
Danseuse Reflectee dans la Glace, Pl 87, 7/50, litho/Chine volant, 1927, p/s, full mrgs, 16x11", lot 586, SBY 5/11/89 OE	**51,700**
Deux Femmes en Costume de Ville, 25/30, drypt/wove paper, 1900-03, sgn in ink, lt stn/sl, P-6x4", lot 366, C-NY 11/1/88	**3,300**
Duex Nus, Deux Tetes d'Enfants; Pl 55B, 30/30, drypt/van Gelder, 1900-03, full mrgs, lt sl, 6x4", lot 272, SBY 11/3/88	**4,675**
Femme Assise au Costume, 19/25, litho/Chine applique, 1942-43, p/s, full mrgs, lt cr, L-14x8", lot 374, C-NY 11/1/88	**9,900**
Figure Devant Tapa African, Pl 126, 30/50, litho/cream Japan, 1929, p/s, full mrgs, lt stn, 21x17", lot 288, SBY 11/3/88	**12,650**
Figure Mains Jointes et Nappe a Decor Persan, Pl 154, 3/25, etch/Chine applique, 1929, 5x4", lot 290, SBY 11/3/88 OE	**12,100**
Formes, total fld book ed of 270, clr pochoir/Arches, 1947, lt stn, S-17x26", lot 666, C-NY 5/10/89	**2,200**
Garcon aux Cheveux Boucles, Pl 328, aqua/Chine applique, 1946, p/s, trm/fox/stn, 12x9", lot 297, SBY 11/3/88	**9,900**
Grand Nu Assis, Bras Releves; 17/250, etch/Chine applique, 1932, full mrgs, P-15x11", Cleveland Print, C-NY 5/10/89 OE	**3,300**
Grand Nu Assis, Bras Releves; 89/250, etch/Chine applique, 1932, p/s, P-14x11", Cleveland Print Club, C-NY 5/11/88 OE	**5,280**
Grande Odalisque a la Culotte Bayadere, ed of 50, litho/Chine, 1925, lt cr, L-21x17", lot 201, C-NY 5/11/88 OE	**187,000**
Haitienne, Pl 273, 167/200, litho, 1945, p/s, lt stn, 16x12", lot 318, SBY 2/23/89 OE	**6,600**
Haitienne, 134/200, litho/BFK Rives, 1945, p/s, tp on verso, S-15x12", lot 96, C-NY 11/1/88 OE	**6,600**
Jeune Femme, La Cordeliere de Son Peignoir en Collier; 148, 9/25, etch/Chine, 1929, unfr, P-5x7", SBY 5/12/88 OE	**11,000**
Jeune Fille Assise au Bouquet de Fleurs, Pl 51, 55/60, litho/Japan, 1923, full mrgs, 11x7", lot 583, SBY 5/11/89 OE	**37,400**
Jeune Fille au Col d'Organdi, Pl 45, 47/50, litho/Chine volant, 1923, p/s, lg mrgs, 8x6", lot 581, SBY 5/11/89 OE	**2,530**
Jeune Fille aux Boucles Brune, 53/100, litho/Arches, 1924, p/s, full mrgs, lt fox/stn, L-7x5", lot 200, C-NY 5/11/88 OE	**8,800**
Jeune Fille aux Boucles Brune, 75/100, litho, 1924, p/s, full mrgs, lt stn/cr mrgs, L-7x5", lot 369, C-NY 11/1/88 OE	**16,500**
Jeune Fille de Face, Flot de Ruban sur l'Epaule Gauche; Pl 157, 20/25, etch/Chine applique, 1929, 7x5", SBY 11/3/88	**3,300**
Jeune Hindoue, litho/Arches, 1929, p/s, inscr Essai, full mrgs, lt stn/old glue, L-11x14", lot 671, C-NY 5/10/89	**38,500**
Josette Gris, Pl 28, 12/15, etch/Chine applique, 1914-15, sgn in ink, full mrgs, ls/stn/fox, 4x2", lot 577, SBY 5/11/89	**3,850**
Josette Gris, Visage de Trois-Quarts; 11/15, etch/Chine applique, 1915, full mrgs, lt sl, P-6x4", lot 198, C-NY 5/11/88	**3,300**
L-Homme Endormi, VII/XXIV, aqua/Montval, 1936, p/s, full mrgs, lt stn/scr, P-10x7", lot 673, C-NY 5/10/89	**14,300**
La Nageuse dans l'Aquarium; total fld book ed of 270, pochoir/Arches, 1947, lt stn, S-17x26", lot 667, C-NY 5/10/89	**3,080**
La Persane, Pl 100, 27/50, litho, 1929, p/s, lt stn, S-22x14", lot 286, SBY 11/3/88	**8,800**
La Persane, Pl 100, 50/50, litho, 1929, p/s, Petiet bstp, full mrgs, lt stn, 18x11", lot 588, SBY 5/11/89 OE	**154,000**
La Persane, 100, 33/50, litho, 1929, p/s, lt skinned corners, S-25x14", SBY 5/12/88 OE	**99,000**
La Robe d'Organdi, Pl 38, 49/50, litho/Chine volant, 1922, sgn in ink, full mrgs, stn, 17x11", lot 579, SBY 5/11/89 OE	**31,900**
La Robe Jaune au Ruban Noir, Pl 34, 31/50, litho/Chine volant, 1922, full mrgs, lt tr, 16x11", lot 580, SBY 5/11/89 OE	**15,950**
Lassitude, Pl 62, 38/50, litho/cream Japan, 1925, p/s, full mrgs, lt cr, 8x5", lot 281, SBY 11/3/88	**5,500**
Le Bonnet Fleuri, 110, drypt/Chine applique, p/s, inscr, lt cr/stn, skinned/gstn verso, unfr, 5x6", SBY 5/12/88 OE	**7,150**
Le Cheval, l'Ecuyere et le Clown; unfld portfolio ed of 100, stencil, 1974, 17x26", Teriade, lot 595, SBY 5/11/89 OE	**16,500**
Le Cirque, portfolio ed of 100, stencil/Arches, 1947, full mrgs, lt scr/sl, 14x22", Teriade, lot 301, SBY 11/3/88	**8,800**
Le Cite-Notre-Dame, ed of 500, etch/laid paper, 1937, pl/s, laid down/sealed in mat, P-13x10", lot 663, C-NY 5/10/89 OE	**715**
Le Coeur, total unfld portfolio ed of 100, clr pochoir/Arches, 1947, lt cr/stn, S-17x26", lot 664, C-NY 5/10/89 OE	**8,800**
Le Cow-Boy, unfld portfolio ed of 100, stencil/Arches, 1947, S-17x26", Teriade, lot 598, SBY 5/11/89	**5,500**
Le Jour, Pl 33, litho/stiff cream Japan, 1922, sgn in ink, full mrgs, lt fox/tp, 10x11", lot 311, SBY 2/23/89 OE	**12,100**
Le Lagon, portfolio ed of 100, stencil, 1947, lt cr/fox, S-17x26", Teriade, lot 302, SBY 11/3/88 OE	**8,800**
Le Lagon, total fld book ed of 270, clr pochoir/Arches, 1947, full sheet, lt scr/stn, S-17x26", lot 669, C-NY 5/10/89	**2,200**
Le Loup, portfolio ed of 100, stencil/Arches, 1947, full sheet, lt fox, S-17x26", Teriade, lot 300, SBY 11/3/88 OE	**7,700**
Le Renard Blanc, Pl 123, 45/75, litho, 1929, p/s, S-23x17", lot 287, SBY 11/3/88	**66,000**
Le Repos du Modele, Pl 29, ed of 100, 1st state, litho/Chine volant, 1922, lt fox, 9x12", Frapier, lot 578A, SBY 5/11/89	**8,800**
Le Repos du Modele, Pl 29, litho/stiff Japan, 1922, Frapier bstp, full mrgs, lt cr/rub/stn, 9x12", lot 276, SBY 11/3/88	**9,900**
Le Repos du Modele, Pl 29, 1st state, litho/Chine volant, 1922, Frapier bstp, full mrgs, lt fox, 9x12", SBY 2/23/89	**7,700**
Le Repos du Modele, 37/50, litho/Chine, 1922, p/s, Frapier stp, full mrgs, lt cr, L-9x12", lot 368, C-NY 11/1/88	**7,150**
Le Repos sur le Lit, Pl 85, a/p, etch/Chine applique, 1929, p/s, full mrgs, lt rub, SBY 11/3/88	**19,800**
Les Trois Coloquintes, monotype/wove paper, 1916, sgn, full mrgs, lt stn/sl, 5x7", lot 578, SBY 5/11/89 OE	**51,700**
Loulou Masque-Chapeau Fleuri, 10/15, etch/Chine applique, 1914-15, p/s, full mrgs, lt stn/cr, P-16x2", SBY 5/12/88 OE	**7,700**
Loulou Masque-Chapeau Fleuri; Pl 58, 8/15, etch/Chine applique, 1914-15, p/s, full mrgs, 6x3", lot 274, SBY 11/3/88	**7,150**
Martiniquaise, Pl 304, 11/25, etch/Annam applique, 1946, p/s, full mrgs, lt stn, 10x8", lot 321, SBY 2/23/89	**6,050**
Martiniquaise, Pl 305, 9/25, etch/Chine applique, 1946, p/s, full mrgs, lt sl/cr, 10x8", lot 296, SBY 11/3/88	**7,150**
Masque Aigu (Ida Chagall), 4/25, aqua/BFK Rives, 1948, p/s, full mrgs, P-14x10", lot 378, C-NY 11/1/88	**8,800**
Mme Vignier, Pl 1, 14/15, etch/Chine applique, 1914, sgn in ink, full mrgs, lt stn, 4x3", lot 576, SBY 5/11/89 OE	**4,675**
Nadia au Visage Rond, Pl 357, 17/25, aqua, 1948, p/s, trm mrgs, lt stn/fox/tp, 17x14", lot 303, SBY 11/3/88 OE	**24,200**
Notre Dame, etch/cream laid paper, pl/s, 13x10", lot 2874, B/B 2/16/88	**300**
Notre Dame, late imp, etch/MBM Ingres Arches, pl/s, 13x10", lot 2869, B/B 4/19/88 OE	**522**
Nu, Mains au Visage (standing nude); total ed of 41, drypt, ca 1903, lt stn, P-6x4", lot 5, RWS 9/8/89 OE	**4,400**
Nu Accroupi I, Pl 363, a/p, aqua, 1947, intl, full mrgs, lt stn/fox, fox on verso, 11x9", lot 324, SBY 2/23/89 UE	**7,700**

Nu Allonge, aux Babouches de Paille Tressee; 169, 8x25, etch/Chine applique, 1931, lt cr, unfr, 5x10", SBY 5/12/88 OE **11,550**
Nu Allonge sur Fond a Motifs Circulaires, Pl 172, 7/25, etch/Chine applique, 1929, p/s, 6x8", lot 292, SBY 11/3/88 OE **14,850**
Nu Assis, Vu de Dos; 42/50, litho/Japan, 1913, intl in stone, lt stn/cr, L-17x10", lot 367, C-NY 11/1/88 OE **14,300**
Nu Assis a la Chemise de Tulle, Pl 69, 18/50, litho, 1925, p/s, lt rpr, S-22x15", lot 282, SBY 11/3/88 OE **37,400**
Nu Assis dans un Fauteuil au Decor Fleuri, Pl 54, 240/280, litho/Chine volant, 1924, S-23x15", lot 279, SBY 11/3/88 OE **23,100**
Nu Assis dans un Fauteuil au Decor Fleuri, Pl 54, 48/250, litho/Chine volant, 1924, p/s, lt rpr, 19x13", SBY 2/23/89 ..... **20,900**
Nu Assis sur la Jambe Droite, Bras Leves; Pl 163, 10/25, etch, 1931, p/s, lg mrgs, lt stn, 5x3", lot 590, SBY 5/11/89 ..... **6,875**
Nu au Collier et aux Cheveux Longs, Pl 61, 15/25, etch/Chine applique, ca 1920, p/s, lt stn/fox, S-8x10", SBY 11/3/88 ..... **12,100**
Nu au Coussin Bleu, AP 8/10, litho/Arches, 1924, p/s, full mrgs, lt stn/cr, L-24x19", lot 661, C-NY 5/10/89 ..... **88,000**
Nu au Coussin Bleu, Pl 55, 37/50, litho/MBM Arches J Perricot, 1924, p/s, full mrgs, 24x19", lot 584, SBY 5/11/89 OE **60,500**
Nu aux Boucles d'Oreilles, #64, aside from ed of 25, etch/BFK Rives, 1929, full mrgs, unfr, P-5x7", SBY 5/12/88 ..... **2,200**
Nu de Profil sur une Chaise Longue, 10/50, wc/van Gelder laid paper, 1906, full mrgs, S-23x18", lot 94, C-NY 11/1/88 OE **46,200**
Nu pour Cleveland, Pl 194 or 200, 149/250, etch/Chine applique, 1932, p/s, 15x11", Cleveland Print Club, SBY 11/3/88 OE **13,750**
Nu pour Cleveland, 194 or 200, 174/250, etch/Chine applique, 1932, unfr, P-14x11", Cleveland Print Club, SBY 5/12/88 OE **9,350**
Odalisque, Brasero et Coupe de Fruits; 122, 17/100, litho/Arches, 1929, p/s, full mrg, fox, unfr, 11x15", SBY 5/12/88 OE **28,600**
Odalisque, Brasero et Coupe de Fruits; 80/100, litho/Arches, 1929, p/s, full mrgs, L-11x15", lot 371, C-NY 11/1/88 ..... **28,600**
Odalisque, Brasero et Couple de Fruits; Pl 122, 45/100, litho/Arches, 1929, p/s, full mrgs, 11x15", lot 587, SBY 5/11/89 ..... **26,400**
Odalisque, 5/250, etch/Chine colle, 1934, p/s, lt stn, 14x11", Cleveland Print Club, lot 2870, B/B 4/19/88 ..... **4,400**
Odalisque a la Coupe de Fruits, Pl 72, 17/50, litho/laid Chine volant, 1925, p/s, full mrgs, lt stn, 13x10", SBY 11/3/88 ..... **41,250**
Odalisque a la Culotte de Satin Rouge, 66, 8/10, litho, 1925, p/s, inscr Epr d'Artiste, unfr, L-8x11", SBY 5/12/88 OE **77,000**
Odalisque Assise a la Jupe de Tulle, Pl 52, 17/50, litho/Chine volant, 1924, p/s, lt stn, S-20x14", lot 278, SBY 11/3/88 ..... **60,500**
Odalisque au Magnolia, Pl 42, 18/50, litho/cream simili Japan, 1923, p/s, lt stn, S-15x20", lot 582, SBY 5/11/89 ..... **57,750**
Odalisque au Magnolia, Pl 42, 25/50, litho/simili Japan, 1923, p/s, lt fox/stn, S-16x21", lot 277, SBY 11/3/88 ..... **49,500**
Orientale, Tatouage en Croix sur la Poitrine; 120, 23/25, drypt/Chine applique, 1929, p/s, lt sl, 6x4", SBY 5/12/88 OE **11,550**
Orientale sur Lit de Repose, sol de Carreaux Rouges; Pl 112, 34/50, litho/stiff wove paper, 1929, 10x19", SBY 5/11/89 OE **28,600**
Patitcha, Pl 364, a/p, aqua/wove paper, 1947, full mrgs, lt scuff/fox, 12x9", lot 325, SBY 2/23/89 ..... **18,150**
Patitcha Masque, Pl 367, aqua, 1947, intl/inscr Essai, full mrgs, 14x11", lot 298, SBY 11/3/88 ..... **13,700**
Petite Irene Vignier, 7/15, etch/Chine applique, 1914, p/s, lt stn, 4x2", lot 273, SBY 11/3/88 ..... **2,475**
Pierres Levees: Frontispiece, Tete de Femme (Le Yeux Clos); 122/300, litho, 1948, p/s, 6x6", lot 252, SBY 2/25/88 ..... **1,980**
Poems de Charles d'Orleans, Pl 329, 17/25, litho/Chine applique, 1942-43, p/s, full mrgs, 14x8", lot 593, SBY 5/11/89 ..... **7,700**
Poems de Charles d'Orleans, Pl 330, litho/Chine applique, 1950, p/s, full mrgs, 15x9", Teriade, lot 317, SBy 2/23/89 OE **10,450**
Polypheme, 3, 45/150, etch/wove paper, p/s, lt cr mrg, glue/sl/tp verso, unfr, P-11x9", C-NY 1/22/88 OE **1,760**
Suite: Ulysses; 40/150, 6 sftgr etch/Arches, 1935, full mrgs, orig wrappers/portfolio, lot 373, C-NY 11/1/88 ..... **16,500**
Suite: Ulysses; text by James Joyce, 112/150, 1935, Ltd Ed Club of NY, lot 592, SBY 5/11/89 ..... **18,700**
Suite: Ulysses; 110/150, 1935, p/s, orig wrappers, S-6x13", Ltd Ed Club, lot 294, SBY 11/3/88 OE **22,000**
Suite: Ulysses; 129/150, aside from book ed of 1500, 6 sftgr etch, 1935, p/s, S-6x13", Ltd Ed Club, SBY 5/12/88 OE **22,000**
Tenny, ed of 500, linocut/wove paper, 1938, intl, lt stn/sl, tstn verso, L-12x9", C-NY 1/22/88 ..... **385**
Tete d'Homme, total ed of 125, linocut/wove paper, 1944, a/bstp, 10x6", lot 2872, B/B 2/16/88 ..... **440**
Tete d'Homme de Profil, 50/100, linocut/wove paper, 1944, a/bstp, old hinge stn, 11x9", lot 2873, B/B 2/16/88 ..... **357**
Tete de Marguerite II, ed of 1000, etch/Chine applique, 1920, sgn, lt stn, lt fox mrgs, P-6x4", lot 199, C-NY 5/11/88 ..... **2,200**
Vierge a l'Enfant Debout, Pl 345, 111/200, litho/Chine applique, 1950-51, full mrgs, cr, 11x5", lot 253, SBY 2/25/88 OE **4,125**
Vierge et Enfant sur Fond de Fleurs et d'Etoiles, 94/200, litho/Chine applique, ca 1950, tstn, L-12x9", C-NY 5/10/89 OE **10,450**
Vierge et Enfant sur Fond Etoile, Pl 346, 81/100, litho/Chine applique, 1950, full mrgs, 12x9", lot 594, SBY 5/11/89 OE **16,500**
Vierge et Enfant sur Fond Etoile, 87/100, litho/Chine applique, ca 1950, full mrgs, L-13x10", lot 377, C-NY 11/1/88 OE **10,450**
Visage de Femme, Pl 326, 3/25, etch/Annam applique, p/s, full mrgs, lt stn/fox, 9x6", lot 322, SBY 2/23/89 OE **8,250**
Visage de Jeune Femme, Pl 371, 17x25, aqua/BFK Rives, 1948, p/s, full mrgs, lt cr, 14x10", lot 326, SBY 2/23/89 ..... **7,700**
Visage: Etude pour la Vierge; ed of 100, litho/Japan applique, 1950-51, p/s, lt stn/cr/fox, S-14x10", C-NY 1/19/89 OE **5,720**

IATISSE, Henri; after (French, 1869-1954)
L'Espagnole, by Jacques Villon, aqua/etch, 1925-26, P-18x12", Bernheim Jeune/Chalographie du Louvre, lot 85, PHL 6/16/88 ..... **300**

IATTA, Roberto (Chilian, 1912-)
Fou Riez, 96/100, clr aqua/etch, 1972, p/s, full mrgs, lt lstn, lt disclr verso, P-15x19", SBY 5/12/88 OE **770**
Les Damnations, ed of 75, clr aqua/Arches, 1966, p/s, 14x10", Visat, lot 164, SWN 6/15/89 ..... **358**
Pair: Une Saison en Enfer: Je Suis Intact; Des Secrets Intacts; 97/100, clr etch/aqua, 1977, P-19x14", SBY 5/12/88 OE **1,430**
Suite: Le Transeport; 25/100, 6 aqua/etch/Arches, 1976, p/s, full mrgs, lt sl mrgs, SBY 5/12/88 OE **2,970**

IATULKA, Jan (American, 1890-1969)
Three-Quarter View of Nude Bather Seated Near Lamp, litho/buff Japan, 1925, p/s, S-15x11", lot 42, SBY 11/3/88 OE **1,870**

IAUFRA, Maxime Emilio Louise (French, 1861-1918)
Tonquedec, 45/100, 3rd state, etch/aqua/rlt/cream wove paper, ca 1894, full mrgs, lt stn, P-12x14", C-NY 5/10/89 OE **2,420**

IAURER, Louis; after (American/German, 1832-1932)
Last Shot, hc litho/gum arabic, 1858, lt stn, L-17x25", Currier & Ives, lot 54, RWS 10/27/89 ..... **1,300**

IAX, Peter (American, 1937-)
Pair: Moonscape 2; Flower Abstract; srgph & litho, 1977 & 1981, p/s, 19x25"/18x24", lot 169, SWN 6/15/89 UE **300**
Woman Seated at Table, 11/150, litho, p/s, no size given, lot 962, FAP 12/8/88 ..... **350**
Zero & Flowers, 83/300, transfer clr litho/wove paper, p/s, lt cr, L-16x21", lot 78, RWS 9/8/89 ..... **400**

IAYER
Cunard Royal Mail Steamship, litho, modern fr, lg folio, RAB 8/1/88 ..... **400**

IAYHEW, Nell Brooker
San Gabriel Mission, clr etch/cream wove paper, trm mrgs, 15x11", lot 2963, B/B 4/19/88 ..... **138**

IAZUR, Michael (American, 1935-)
View From Studio into Porch, 10/20, engr/stpl engr/magnesium/wove paper, 1974, p/s, L-18x23", RWS 3/16/89 UE **450**

MC BEY, James (British, 1889-1959)
Tartane Leaving Venice, XII, total ed of 80, etch, 1925, sgn, 7x13", lot 156, SWN 6/15/89 OE ... **770**
MC KNIGHT, Thomas Frederick (American, 1941-)
Venetian Scene, 19/20, litho, p/s, 16x18", lot 918, LH 5/15/88 UE ... **70**
MC MILLEN, Mildred
Lodging, wc/wove paper, 1915, p/s, dtd, lt cr, lt fox/pencil lines mrgs, unfr, L-15x12", C-NY 1/22/88 OE ... **770**
MC NALTY, William Charles (American, 1889-)
Whirlpool, drypt/wove paper, 1930s, p/s, titled, lt stn/old tp, P-14x7", lot 458, C-NY 5/10/89 ... **495**
MCARDELL, James; after (British, 18th C)
Rembrandt's Mother, etch, 1923, 14x10", Sayer, lot 226, MG 8/27/88 UE ... **30**
MCLEAN, James (American, 1928-)
Space Totem, 9/10, intg, 1968, sgn, 14x30", lot 146, MG 5/28/88 ... **100**
MEISSONIER, Jean Charles; after (French, 1848-1917)
Cavaliers Outside a Tavern, engr, sl mrgs, 14x11", lot 3, FAP 2/24/89 UE ... **25**
MELINCOFF (American, 20th C)
Bathers, woodblock, 15x20", FAP 6/16/89 UE ... **30**
MELROSE, Andrew W.; after (American, 1836-1901)
Harbor of New York & the Battery, chromolitho/gum arabic, 1887, trm mrgs, lt stn/fox, S-22x36", lot 532, SBY 1/28/88 ... **1,320**
MELVILLE, Harden Sidney (fl 1837-1876)
Group of 4: Tasmania; Java, Sourebaya, West Coast; Timor; Java; hc litho, largest: L-5x7", C-SK 6/9/88 ... **205**
MENIHAN, John C. (American, 1908-)
Winter Home, ed of 100, litho/Japan pelure, p/s, 6x9", lot 384, WG 10/19/88 ... **25**
MENPES, Mortimer L. (British, 1860-1938)
JA McNeill Whistler, with Monocle; drypt/antique laid paper, ca 1890, p/s, inscr Imp Only Proof, P-7x6", C-NY 1/22/88 ... **605**
MERIDA, Carlos (Mexican, 1891-1984)
Four Standing Figures, 64/115, clr slksc, 1975, p/s, full mrgs, lt cr/stn, 27x19", lot 43, SBY 11/3/88 ... **880**
Suite: Dances of Mexico; ed of 100, 10 litho, p/s, lt wstn/tstn edges, full sheets, orig wrappers, SBY 5/12/88 OE ... **1,430**
MERYON, Charles (French, 1821-1868)
Galerie Notre Dame, Paris; 3rd state, brn etch/Hudelist laid paper, 1853, lt stn/sl, P-11x7", lot 675, C-NY 5/10/89 ... **1,760**
L'Abside de Notre Dame de Paris, 4th state of 8, dk brn etch/laid Hudelist, 1854, lt stn, 7x12", lot 602, SBY 5/11/89 OE ... **9,350**
La Galerie Notre Dame, 3rd state, etch/JW, 1853, lg mrgs, lt mstn, rpr tr, 11x7", lot 304A, SBY 11/3/88 ... **3,575**

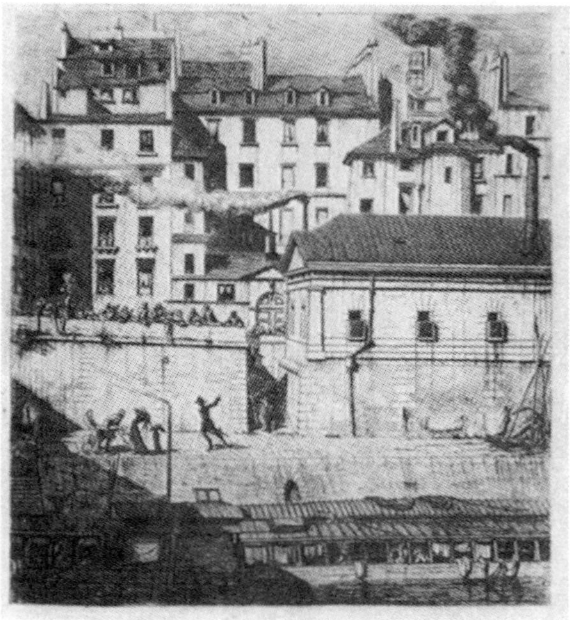

La Morgue, Paris; 2nd state, etch, 1854, lt stn/sl/cr, 9x8", lot 94, WD 12/8/88 OE; $13,000

La Morgue, Paris; 4th state, etch/drypt/India applique, 1854, lt fox/stn, P-9x8", lot 676, C-NY 5/10/89 ... **1,980**
La Morgue, Paris; 4th state of 7, etch/laid Hudelist, 1854, lt mstn/fox/sl, 9x8", lot 601, SBY 5/11/89 OE ... **6,050**
La Pavillon de Mademoiselle et une Partie du Louvre, 3rd state, etch, 1849, tstn, P-5x10", lot 380, C-NY 11/1/88 ... **550**
La Pompe Notre Dame, Paris; 6th state, etch/gr laid paper, 1852, lt fox/cr, 7x10", lot 599, SBY 5/11/89 OE ... **13,750**
La Pompe Notre Dame, 9th state, ed of 30, etch/laid paper, 1861, lt stn, cr mrgs, P-7x10", lot 207, C-NY 5/11/88 ... **385**
La Rue des Toiles a Bourges, 3rd state, etch/gr laid paper, 1853, lt fox/stn, S-10x6", lot 306, SBY 11/3/88 OE ... **4,950**
La Rue Pirouette aux Halles, Paris; 3rd state, ed of 20, etch/Hudelist, 1860, full mrgs, 6x5", lot 382, C-NY 11/1/88 ... **1,980**
La Tour de l'Horloge, Paris; 3rd state, etch/bl laid paper, 1852, lt stn, P-10x7", lot 206, C-NY 5/11/88 ... **3,080**
Le Petit Pont, Paris; etch/drypt/Chine applique/wht wove paper, 1850, lt stn/ls, 10x7", lot 170, SWN 6/15/89 ... **660**
Le Pont-au-Change, Paris; 5th state of 12, brn-blk etch/old laid paper, 1854, lt stn, 6x13", lot 600, SBY 5/11/89 OE ... **11,550**
Le Stryge, 5th state, etch/laid paper, 1852, lg mrgs, lt stn/sl/ls, 7x6", lot 304, SBY 11/3/88 ... **1,980**
Oceanie, Ilots a Uvea (Wallis), Peche aux Palmes, 1845; a/p, etch/Chine, 1863, lt fox, P-6x14", lot 383, C-NY 11/1/88 OE ... **9,900**
Oceanie, Ilots a Uvea (Wallis), Peche aux Palmes, 1845; 3rd state, etch/Hudelist, 1963, fox, 6x6", lot 257, SBY 2/25/88 ... **550**

Rue de la Bucherien, etch, 1853, sgn/titled, 7x6", lot 356, LH 3/20/88 OE 600
St Etienne du Mont, Paris; 4th state, etch/thin buff fibrous paper, 1852, lt sl, 10x5", lot 305, SBY 11/3/88 1,540
St Etienne du Mont, etch, 1852, sgn/titled, 7x10", lot 357, LH 3/20/88 OE 850

MEUNIER, Georges (French, 1869-1934)

Lox, clr litho, 1895, lt ls, S-47x32", Imprimerie Chaix, lot 274, SBY 12/12/88 330
Otart-Dupuy & Co, Cognac; clr litho, pl/s, 48x33", Chaix, C-E 3/24/88 OE 770

MEUNIER, Henri (French, 1869-1942)

Amueblements, clr litho/poster paper, 1897, lt fox/cr, linen backed, 20x14", Renette, lot 216, FAP 2/24/89 UE 80

MICHEL, Robert (European, 1897-)

Mez (Mitteleuropaische Zeit), #4, linocut/soft Japan, 1919-20, sgn in red ink, full mrgs, 18x15", lot 259, SBY 2/25/88 2,420
Mez (Mitteleuropaische Zeit), wht wc/blk paper, 1919-20, sgn in red ink, inscr MEX 1919/20 Weimar, 18x15", SBY 5/11/89 2,200

MIGNON, Jean (16th C)

Judgement of Paris, etch, ca 1545, trm/lt tr/cr/fox, lt fox verso, 12x17", lot 75, SBY 5/11/89 6,600

MILLAIS, John Everett; after (British, 1829-1896)

Hugeunot, by TO Barlow, hc engr/thin wove paper, 1857, lt stn, L-25x17", David Thomas White, lot 348, C-NY 1/19/89 OE 990

MILLER, Kenneth Hayes (American, 1876-1952)

Nurse & Child, ed of 20, etch/cream wove paper, 1928, p/s, lt sl, 7x5", lot 2965, B/B 4/19/88 275
Pair: Shoppers by an Awning; Nurse & Child; etch, p/s, full mrgs, P-6x5"/P-7x5", lot 27, PHL 10/28/88 OE 425
Three Shoppers, etch, 1936-37, 5x7", Am Artists Group, lot 229, WG 10/19/88 110

MILLET, Jean Francois (French, 1814-1875)

La Baratteuse, final state, etch/laid paper, 1855, full mrgs, lt mstn/cr mrgs, P-7x5", SBY 5/12/88 2,310
La Bouillie, final state, etch/cream wove paper, 1861/ca 1903-06, lt fox/cr, 7x6", lot 309, SBY 11/3/88 OE 4,125
La Bouillie, 5th state, brn etch/laid paper, 1861/ca 1903-06, lt sl/tp, P-7x6", lot 385, C-NY 11/1/88 OE 2,640
La Cardeuse, brn etch/laid tissue-thin Japan, ca 1850, old label on verso, P-4x3", lot 384, C-NY 11/1/88 OE 1,540
La Cardeuse, brn etch/thin Japan, ca 1858, full mrgs, lt disclr/fox/sl/cr, P-10x7", SBY 5/12/88 OE 3,025
La Cardeuse, etch/thin Japan, ca 1858, lt rpl, 10x7", lot 172, SWN 6/15/89 OE 2,280
La Couseuse, final state, etch/thin laid paper, 1855, lg mrgs, lt mstn/glue, 4x3", lot 329, SBY 2/23/89 1,870
La Fileuse Auvergnate, etch, 1869, pl/s, stn mrgs, rpr img, 8x5", lot 45, WG 10/19/88 UE 200
La Grande Vergere, etch/Japan, 1862, pl/s, lt trm mrgs, lt ls/cr edges, 13x9", lot 2872, B/B 4/19/88 5,500
Le Depart pour le Travail, final state, dk brn etch/pl tone/thin laid paper, lt stn/cr, unfr, P-15x12", SBY 5/12/88 8,250
Le Depart pour le Travail, final state, dk brn etch/thin Japan, lt stn/fox, 16x12", lot 604, SBY 5/11/89 OE 14,300
Le Depart pour le Travail, 3rd state, dk sepia etch/cream laid paper, 1861, lt fox/scr, S-24x16", lot 311, SBY 11/3/88 9,900
Le Depart pour le Travail, 4th state, brn etch/laid Japan, 1863, lt mstn, P-15x12", lot 209, C-NY 5/11/88 OE 12,100
Le Depart pour le Travail, 6th state, dk brn etch/thin laid Japan, 1863, lt stn/fox, 15x13", lot 312, SBY 11/3/88 12,100
Le Paysan Rentrant du Fumier, 4th state, brn etch/thin laid paper, full mrgs, fox/stn, P-6x5", lot 678, C-NY 5/10/89 OE 3,300
Le Semeur, final state, dk brn litho/Japan pelure, 1851, full mrgs, lt stn/fox/cr, 8x6", lot 605, SBY 5/11/89 OE 12,100
Le Semeur, litho/Japan pelure, 1851, trm mrgs, lt fox/stn, 7x6", lot 262, SBY 2/25/88 OE 7,150
Les Becheurs, final state, dk brn etch/laid paper, 1855, lt mstn/sl, 9x13", lot 308, SBY 11/3/88 OE 8,800
Les Glaneuses, final state, etch/laid paper, 1855-56, full mrgs, lt stn, 8x10", lot 307, SBY 11/3/88 OE 12,100
Les Glaneuses, 1st state, brn etch/India applique, ca 1855, rpr tr, lt scr/stn, P-7x10", lot 208, C-NY 5/11/88 OE 8,800
Paysan Rentrant au Fumier, 4th state, etch, full mrgs, P-7x5", lot 58, PHL 6/16/88 OE 2,600

MILLIERE, Maurice

Madame A Marson, #23, clr drypt/thick wove paper, 1908, p/s, wide mrgs, lt tr/ls, P-20x13", lot 75, PHL 10/28/88........ 275

MILTON, Peter (American, 1930-)

Collecting with Rudi, 7/25, final state, etch/stpl, 1974, p/s, full mrgs, 20x30", lot 175, SWN 6/15/89 UE 825
Country Pieces No 1, The Couple; a/p, etch/stpl, 1979, p/s, titled, full mrgs, 18x24", lot 176, SWN 6/15/89 660
Country Pieces No 2, In the Park; a/p, etch/stpl, 1979, p/s, titled, full mrgs, 18x24", lot 177, SWN 6/15/89 UE 660
Day Lilies, 129/160, total ed of 245, etch/engr, 1975, full mrgs, 20x32", Townsend, lot 44, SBY 11/3/88 3,850
Jolly Corner Suite 1:4; 34/90, etch/cream wove paper, 1971, p/s, full mrgs, 15x19", lot 3040, B/B 4/19/88 248

MIRO, Joan (Spanish, 1893-1983)

A L'Encre, HC, litho, 1972, p/s, lt cr, L-14x10", lot 63, PHL 6/16/88 OE 1,200
Abstract Composition, 12/30, p/s, lt stn, no size given, lot 100, FAP 2/24/89 2,000
Affiche, clr litho, p/s, 28x20", lot 219, LH 3/20/88 UE 450
Aieule des 10,000 Ages; 5/50, clr litho/wove paper, 1981, p/s, lt cr, S-23x34", lot 372, SBY 2/23/89 OE 3,300
Album 13: Pl 4; 15/75, litho, 1948, p/s, full mrgs, lt fox, 11x14", lot 317A, SBY 11/3/88 OE........ 2,750
Album 21, clr litho, sgn, 20x26", lot 304, MG 3/26/88 900
Album 21, 23/75, clr litho, 1978, p/s, full mrgs, 19x24", lot 363, SBY 2/23/89 OE 4,675
Album 21, 46/75, clr litho, 1978, p/s, full mrgs, lt cr, 25x18", lot 291, SBY 2/25/88 1,210
Altamira, 71/75, clr litho, 1958, p/s, full mrgs, lt stn/cr, 18x24", Maeght, lot 334, SBY 2/23/89 OE 4,125
Appelant Ecartele, 32/50, etch/aqua/cbrn, 1974, S-26x20", lot 231, C-NY 5/11/88 5,500
Archipel Sauvage II, HC, etch/aqua, 1970, p/s, full mrgs, lt sl/stn, 23x36", Maeght, lot 641, SBY 5/11/89 OE 6,600
Astre et Fumee, 39/75, clr aqua/etch/cbrn, p/s, full mrgs, lt cr/fox, 30x22", SBY 5/12/88 OE........ 6,050
Barcelona Series: Pl 1; 17/50, aqua/cbrn, 1973, p/s, lt cr/sl, 28x41", Gaspar/Torralba, lot 354A, SBY 2/23/89 OE........ 17,600
Barcelona Series: Pl 6; 49/50, aqua/cbrn, 1973, sgn in crayon, 1973, 28x41", Gaspar/Torralba, lot 644, SBY 5/11/89 OE 7,700
Barcelona Suite: Pl XIX; 1/5, litho, 1944, p/s, full mrgs, lt sl/cr, 25x18", Joan Prats, lot 313, SBY 11/3/88 6,710
Barcelona Suite: Pl XXI; 5/5, litho, 1944, p/s, full mrgs, lt cr/stn, 26x18", lot 314, SBY 11/3/88 OE 7,700
Barcelona Suite: Pl XXXIX; 4/5, litho, 1944, p/s, full mrgs, lt stn/fox, 25x18", Joan Prats, lot 265, SBY 2/25/88 OE........ 7,700
Barcelona Suite: Pl XXXVIII; 5/5, litho, 1944, p/s, full mrgs, lt stn/cr/scr, 24x19", lot 315, SBY 11/3/88 8,250
Bather, HC, ed of 75, litho/red & wht checked cloth/stiff wove paper, 1969, stn/sl, S-36x25", SBY 5/12/88 OE........ 4,400
Bather, 35/75, clr litho/checked cloth/stiff wove paper, 1969, p/s, S-34x24", Maeght, lot 342, SBY 11/3/88........ 2,420
Bethsabee, hc aqua, p/s, 27x21", lot 163, MG 5/28/88........ 3,000

Bird-Catchers, 26/75, clr litho/Rives, 1951, p/s, lt stn img, lt fox/stn verso, S-22x14", lot 389, C-NY 11/1/88	2,420
Birth of Dawn, 57/300, clr litho/Arches, p/s, lt stn, 23x16", lot 45, RWS 9/29/88	2,200
Bon Cop de Lluna, 50/75, clr litho, ca 1980, p/s, lt fox, 34x24", lot 370, SBY 2/23/89 OE	6,325
Book: Hai-Ku; by Philippe Jaccottet, 10/100, Deluxe ed, sgn on justification, Maeght, lot 325, SBY 11/3/88	9,900
Book: Miro Lithographs Volume II; 116/150, deluxe ed, 12 clr litho, 1975, orig wrappers, Amiel, SBY 5/12/88	2,750
Book: Parler Seul; by Parler Seul, 95/253, 70 litho w/text, 1948-50, sgn, slipcase, Maeght, lot 212, C-NY 5/11/88 OE	30,800
Cantic del Sol, 12/12, yel/bl aqua, 1874, p/s, full mrgs, lt cr, 16x21", Gustavo Gili, lot 651, SBY 5/11/89 OE	5,225
Chemin de Ronde III, 16/50, clr aqua/etch, 1966, p/s, full mrgs, P-14x10", Maeght, SBY 5/12/88 OE	5,225
Cloudy Figure, 27/50, clr litho/Arches, 1955, p/s, full mrgs, lt cr/tstn, L-30x22", lot 390, C-NY 11/1/88	2,860
Colombine a la Fenetre, 9/50, clr litho/Arches, 1981, p/s, full mrgs, lt cr/stn mrgs, L-30x21", Maeght, SBY 5/12/88 OE	4,950
Colombine Entre Chien et Loup, 6/50, clr etch/aqua, 1976, lt cr, 15x9", lot 2876, B/B 2/16/88	1,980
Comet Bird, 43/75, clr litho, 1951, p/s, dtd, full mrgs, lt scuff img, lt stn/cr, L-22x15", SBY 5/12/88 OE	3,410
Composition, Miro Lithographs I; 5/80, clr litho, 1972, p/s, full mrgs, lt cr, S-18x15", lot 228, C-NY 5/11/88 OE	2,860
Composition, 54/100, clr litho/Arches, ca 1980, p/s, full mrgs, lt stn, 30x24", lot 371, SBY 11/3/88 OE	3,850
Congres Juridic Catala, clr litho, 1971, p/s, dtd 13/X/71, inscr Moncha Josep Lluis, S-30x23", lot 226, C-NY 5/11/88	2,200
Constellations, a/p, clr litho, 1959, full mrgs, lt stn/scuff, 22x19", Berggruen/Mourlot, lot 613, SBY 5/11/89 OE	4,400
Constellations, 99/150, clr litho poster/Arches, 1959, p/s, full mrgs, lt cr, L-22x19", lot 391, C-NY 11/1/88	2,860
Couple d'Oiseaux I, 48/50, clr etch, 1966, p/s, full mrgs, lt scuff img, cr/tr, unfr, P-23x36", Maeght, SBY 5/12/88 OE	3,850
Couple d'Oiseaux II, 42/50, clr aqua/etch, 1966, p/s, full mrgs, lt stn/sl/fox, P-23x37", Maeght, SBY 5/12/88	3,300
Cover, Nous Avons; 4/40, etch/aqua/Japan ancien, 1959, p/s, full mrgs, lt lstn, S-5x16", lot 684, C-NY 5/10/89 OE	4,400
Cracheur de Flammes, 28/75, etch/aqua/carbor, 1969, p/s, lt fox, S-45x28", lot 340A, SBY 11/3/88	12,100
Diana of Ephesus, HC, litho, 1958, p/s, full mrgs, lt stn/fox, 22x16", lot 333, SBY 2/23/89 OE	3,850
Diana of Ephesus, 56/100, litho, 1958, p/s, full mrgs, lt stn recto/verso, unfr, L-22x16", SBY 5/12/88 OE	1,540
Dog Barking at the Moon, 10/80, clr litho, 1952, sgn in wht crayon, lt stn/fox, S-14x22", Verve, lot 610, SBY 5/11/89 OE	40,700
Dog Barking at the Moon, 11/80, clr litho, 1952, sgn in wht crayon, lt sl/fox, S-14x22", lot 318, SBY 11/3/88	20,900
Dog Barking at the Moon, 40/80, clr litho, 1952, sgn/dtd in wht crayon, fox on verso, S-14x22", lot 331, SBY 2/23/89 OE	23,100
Dormir sous la Lune, 42/75, etch/aqua/cbrn/drypt, 1969, p/s, S-29x41", lot 332, SBY 11/3/88 OE	12,650
El Gossos, HCXI/XV, clr aqua, 1979, p/s, lt stn/fox, S-29x46", Maeght/Joan Barbara, lot 370, SBY 11/3/88	11,000
El Gossos, 21/30, clr aqua, 1979, p/s, S-29x46", Maeght/Joan Barbara, lot 293, SBY 2/25/88	5,500
El Merma, 15/75, clr litho, 1978, p/s, full mrgs, lt fox, 37x26", Maeght/Litografies Artistques, lot 657, SBY 5/11/89 OE	12,650
El pi de Formentor, 14/50, from portfolio of 5, clr aqua/etch/relief, 1976, full mrgs, P-35x29", Gaspar, SBY 5/12/88	3,300
El pi de Formentor, 24/50, from portfolio of 5, clr aqua, 1976, p/s, full mrgs, S-41x35", Gaspar, lot 270, SBY 5/12/88	4,400
El pi de Formentor, 24/50, from portfolio of 5, clr aqua/etch/relief, 1976, p/s, 42x36", Gaspar, lot 268, SBY 5/12/88 OE	5,775
El pi de Formentor, 24/50, from portfolio of 5, clr etch/aqua/relief, 1976, p/s, P-37x31", Gaspar, lot 269, SBY 5/12/88	4,125
El pi de Formentor, 38/50, from portfolio of 5, aqua/etch, 1976, p/s, full mrgs, 35x29", Gaspar, lot 267, SBY 5/12/88	3,300
Els Gossos, 2, 13/30, from series of 9, clr aqua, 1979, p/s, lt skinned mrg, S-46x29", Barbara/Maeght, SBY 5/12/88 OE	7,975
Els Gossos, 23/30, clr aqua, 1979, p/s, S-46x29", Maeght/Joan Barbara, lot 369, SBY 11/3/88 OE	7,700
Emehpylop, HC, clr drypt/cbrn, 1968, p/s, lt cr/stn, S-41x29", Maeght, lot 624, SBY 5/11/89	7,150
Emehpylop, 46/75, aqua/drypt/intg, 1968, p/s, lt cr/tr, 41x29", SBY 5/12/88	3,850
Emephylop, 56/75, clr etch/aqua/cbrn, 1968, lt sl, S-41x30", Maeght, lot 626, SBY 5/11/89	7,700
Empress, 19/75, clr litho, 1964, p/s, full sheet, S-24x36", Maeght, lot 274, SBY 2/25/88 OE	1,760
Empress, 8/75, clr litho, 1964, p/s, lt stn/sl/cr, S-35x24", lot 339, SBY 2/23/89 OE	3,300
Entre Chien et Loup, 21/75, clr litho/Arches, ca 1980, p/s, lt cr, S-24x36", lot 371, SBY 2/23/89 OE	7,150
Equinoxe, 2/75, clr etch/aqua/cbrn, 1967, p/s, lt stn, S-41x29", Maeght, lot 622, SBY 5/11/89 OE	115,500
Equinoxe, 23/75, etch/aqua/cbrn, 1967, p/s, lt fox, S-41x28", Maeght, lot 326, SBY 11/3/88 OE	45,100
Equinoxe, 38/75, clr aqua/etch/cbrn, 1967, p/s, lt scuff/stn/fox, S-41x29", Maeght, SBY 5/12/88 OE	40,700
Escalade, 62/75, clr etch/aqua/cbrn/Arches, 1969, p/s, full mrgs, lt fox/stn/scr, L-26x19", lot 404, C-NY 11/1/88	4,620
Escalade vers la Lune, 28/75, etch/aqua/cbrn, 1969, p/s, lt stn/cr, S-41x30", lot 333, SBY 11/3/88 OE	8,800
Espriu-Miro, HC, clr etch/aqua/relief, 1974, p/s, lt cr/sl, S-35x28", Gaspar/Torralba, lot 358, SBY 2/23/89 OE	7,150
Espriu-Miro, Pl IV, 35/50, clr etch/aqua/relief, 1974, p/s, lt fox/cr, S-34x28", Gaspar/Torralba, lot 358A, SBY 11/3/88	5,500
Espriu-Miro, 33/50, 1 of set of 8, clr aqua/etch/relief, 1974, p/s, S-42x35", Gaspar/Torralba, SBY 5/12/88 OE	6,600
Espriu-Miro, 33/50, 1 of set of 8, clr aqua/etch/relief, 1974, p/s, lt stn, S-34x28", Gaspar/Torralba, SBY 5/12/88 OE	5,500
Essence de la Terre, ed of 60, litho/Japan nacre, 1970, p/s, hinged to mat on verso, 12x11", lot 2880, B/B 2/16/88	990
Exhibition at the Pasadena Art Museum, HC, clr litho before text, 1969, p/s, full mrgs, 26x19", lot 344, SBY 11/3/88	2,200
Fashion Frenzy-Aybergine Purple, HC, clr litho, 1969, p/s, full mrgs, lt stn/sl, 40x32", Maeght, lot 346, SBY 11/3/88	3,300
Fashion Frenzy-Yellow; 7/30, clr litho/Arches, 1969, p/s, full mrgs, lt cr, S-50x34", lot 224, C-NY 5/11/88	3,520
Femme au Miroir, a/p, aside from ed of 150, clr litho/Rives, sgn in wht crayon, L-15x22", Maeght, SBY 5/12/88 OE	44,000
Femme au Miroir, 9/150, clr litho/wove paper, 1956, p/s, lt scuff/stn, S-15x22", Maeght/Mourlot, lot 612, SBY 5/11/89 OE	85,250
Femme au Miroir, 93/150, clr litho/Rives, 1956, p/s, full mrgs, lt scr/stn/cr, S-15x22", lot 217, C-NY 5/11/88 OE	44,000
Femme et Oiseau Devant la Lune, 174/300, etch, 1947, p/s, full mrgs, lt sl/stn/cr, P-4x6", lot 387, C-NY 11/1/88	2,860
Femme et Oiseau Devant la Lune, 189/300, etch, 1947, p/s, full mrgs, lt stn/scr, P-4x6", lot 211, C-NY 5/11/88	2,200
Femme Toupie, 25/50, clr etch/aqua/cbrn/Arches, 1974, full mrgs, lt stn/fox, 46x29", Maeght, lot 648, SBY 5/11/89 OE	68,200
Figure, Fraternity; a/p, aside from ed of 113, etch/Montval, 1939, lt stn, S-9x7", Fraternity, lot 108, C-NY 11/1/88 OE	4,400
Figure, 26/50, clr litho, 1955, p/s, dtd, full sheet, L-21x29", Maeght, SBY 5/12/88 OE	6,600
Figure with a Red Sun, I; 18/40, clr litho/Arches, 1950, p/s, lstn, tp in mrg, L-23x17", lot 388, C-NY 11/1/88	2,090
Figure with Stars, a/p, clr litho/Vidalon, 1950, p/s, lt stn/sl img & mrg, lt cr mrg, L-25x18", lot 213, C-NY 5/11/88 OE	3,080
Fire Dance, 33/90, clr litho, 1963, p/s, lt stn/skinned, S-19x26", lot 338, SBY 2/23/89	2,750
Fissures, 44/75, clr etch/aqua, 1969, full mrgs, lt stn, 16x19", Maeght, lot 282, SBY 2/25/88	2,640
Fond Marin II, 8/50, clr aqua, 1963, p/s, full mrgs, lt stn/sl, unfr, 14x21", Maeght, SBY 5/12/88	2,090
Foreign Woman, 45/75, clr litho, 1958, p/s, full mrgs, lt stn, L-24x17", lot 65, PHL 6/16/88	1,900
Frappeuse de Silex, HC, etch/aqua/cbrn/Arches, 1973, p/s, S-29x41", Maeght, lot 642, SBY 5/11/89 OE	13,750

Frappeuse de Silex, 46/50, etch/aqua/cbrn, 1973, p/s, lt scr, S-29x41", Maeght/Morsang, lot 358A, SBY 11/3/88 **4,950**
Fusee, II/XV, bl & blk etch/aqua, 1959, p/s, full mrgs, lt stn/fox, 6x16", Broder/Crommelynck, lot 614, SBY 5/11/89 OE **3,300**
Fusees, 40/50, etch/aqua/stencil/gouache/BFK Rives, 1959, p/s, full mrgs, lt stn, P-5x7", lot 219, C-NY 5/11/88 OE **2,090**
Galatee, 8/50, clr etch/aqua/cbrn, ca 1976, full mrgs, lt stn/fox, 45x29", lot 665, SBY 5/11/89 OE **25,300**
Gaudi Suite: Pl 42; 47/50, clr aqua/etch, 1979, p/s, S-36x25", Maeght, lot 66, PHL 6/16/88 **6,000**
Giboulees, 41/90, clr aqua/sftgr etch, 1960, p/s, full mrgs, lts stn/fox, P-14x19", Maeght, SBY 5/12/88 **1,320**
Grand Duc I, HC, clr etch/aqua, 1965, p/s, lt cr, S-36x25", lot 619, SBY 5/11/89 OE **9,350**
Grand Duc I, 28/75, clr etch/aqua/Arches, 1965, p/s, full mrgs, lt stn/sl/scr, P-27x21", lot 395, C-NY 11/1/88 **5,720**
Grand Duc I, 52/75, clr etch/aqua, 1965, p/s, full sheet, lt cr/fox, S-38x25", Maeght, lot 275, SBY 2/25/88 **5,225**
Grand Duc II, 19/75, clr etch, 1965, p/s, full mrgs, lt cr/sl, 27x21", Maeght, lot 276, SBY 2/25/88 3,850

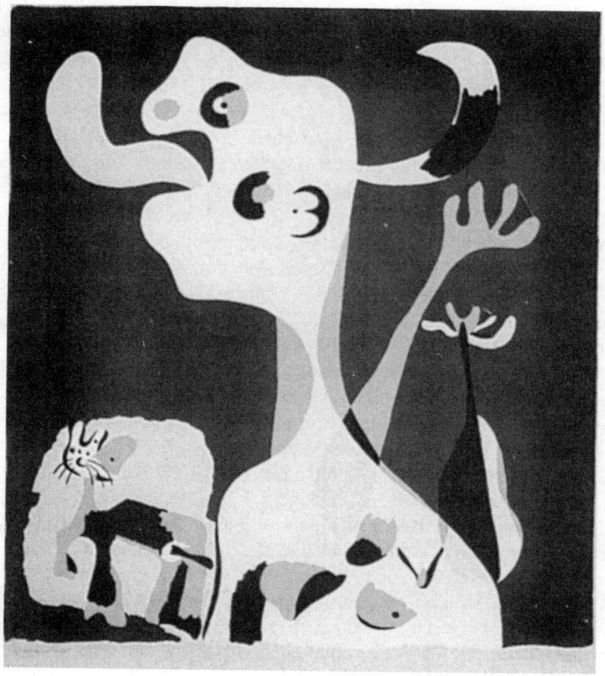

Femme et Chien Devant la Lune, ed of 60, clr scrpt, 1936, p/s, lt scr, S-22x18", Adlan, lot 210, C-NY 5/11/88 OE; $12,100

Grand Duc II, 61/75, clr etch, 1965, p/s, full mrgs, lt cr, 27x21", Maeght, lot 620, SBY 5/11/89 OE **8,800**
Grand Duc II, 73/75, clr etch, 1965, p/s, full mrgs, lt fox/stn, unfr, P-27x21", Maeght, SBY 5/12/88 **3,575**
Grans Rupestres, 21/30, clr aqua, 1979, p/s, S-35x27", Maeght, lot 365, SBY 11/3/88 **3,300**
Grans Rupestres, 22/30, clr aqua, 1979, p/s, lt cr edges, S-36x27", Maeght, lot 366, SBY 11/3/88 **3,575**
Grans Rupestres, 3/30, clr aqua, 1979, p/s, lt stn/scr, S-35x27", Maeght, lot 365, SBY 2/23/89 OE **6,050**
Homage a Miro, a/p, clr litho/Arches, 1972, p/s, full mrgs, 13x20", lot 287, SBY 2/25/88 OE **2,090**
Homenatage a Joan Prats, Pl XIV, 28/75, clr litho, 1971, p/s, full mrgs, 21x30", Poligrafa, lot 353, SBY 11/3/88 OE **3,575**
Inceste au Sahara, 20/50, clr etch/aqua, 1976, p/s, lt cr/sl, S-63x48", lot 666, SBY 5/11/89 OE **19,800**
Inceste au Sahara, 39/50, clr etch/aqua/wm Maeght, 1976, p/s, full sheet, lt cr/sl, S-64x58", lot 236, C-NY 5/11/88 OE **7,150**
Joan Miro Graphics, 135/150, clr litho/Arches, 1966, p/s, full mrgs, L-28x21", Assn Friends of Phil Mus, C-NY 11/1/88 **2,420**
Joan Miro Graphics, 42/150, clr litho/Arches, 1966, p/s, full mrgs, lt cr/stn/ls, S-26x21", lot 349, C-NY 1/19/89 **935**
Jongleur de Colombes, 21/75, clr litho, 1973, p/s, lt stn, S-32x23", Maeght, lot 288, SBY 2/25/88 OE **3,410**
L'Aieule Devant la Mer, 71/75, clr etch/aqua/cbrn/Arches, 1969, p/s, 42x28", Maeght/Morsang, lot 627, SBY 5/11/89 OE **26,400**
L'Aigle et la Femme la Nuit, 5/30, etch/drypt/Arches, 1938, full mrgs, lt stn/tr, 9x12", Loeb, lot 264, SBY 2/25/88 OE **9,900**
L'Aigrette Rouge, 32/50, clr aqua, 1976, p/s, full mrgs, lt sl/cr, 45x29", lot 664, SBY 5/11/89 OE **18,700**
L'Astre du Marecage, HC, etch/aqua/cbrn, 1967, p/s, lt stn, S-40x29", Maeght, lot 621, SBY 5/11/89 OE **12,100**
L'Astre Patagon, 104/150, clr litho, 1960, p/s, full mrgs, lt stn/sl, 15x21", lot 336, SBY 2/23/89 **1,430**
L'Ecoliere au Buisson, 41/50, clr etch/aqua, 1975, p/s, full mrgs, S-36x25", lot 234, C-NY 5/11/88 OE **8,800**
L'Enfance d'Ubu: Pl 10; 22/120, clr litho, 1975, p/s, lt stn, S-13x20", lot 233, C-NY 5/11/88 OE **2,420**
L'Enfance d'Ubu: Pl 14; 69/120, clr litho, 1952/1975, p/s, full mrgs, 12x18", Teriade, lot 267, SBY 2/25/89 OE **1,540**
L'Enrage, 32/75, clr aqua/etch/cbrn, 1967, p/s, S-35x24", Maeght, SBY 5/12/88 OE **12,100**
L'Etrangel, 45/50, etch/aqua/cbrn, 1974, p/s, rpl mrgs, P-45x29", lot 230, C-NY 5/11/88 OE **11,000**
L'Exile Noir, 19/75, etch/aqua/cbrn, 1969, p/s, lt cr, S-42x27", Maeght/Morsang, lot 281, SBY 2/25/88 **4,400**
L'Exile Vert, HC, clr aqua/etch/cbrn, 1969, p/s, lt stn/fox img, lt cr, 41x27", Maeght, SBY 5/12/88 OE **7,150**
L'Exile Vert, 52/75, etch/aqua/cbrn, 1969, p/s, S-41x28", Maeght, lot 334, SBY 11/3/88 OE **13,750**
L'Exile Vert, 54/75, clr etch/aqua/cbrn, 1969, p/s, S-41x28", Maeght, lot 343, SBY 2/23/89 OE **16,500**
L'Homme au Balancier, 20/75, etch/aqua/cbrn/Japan nacre, 1969, lt stn/fox, S-27x20", Maeght, lot 631, SBY 5/11/89 OE **13,200**
L'Invention du Regard, 19/75, etch/aqua/cbrn, 1970, p/s, lt stn/sl, S-20x26", Maeght, lot 349, SBY 11/3/88 OE **6,050**
L'Invitee du Dimanche, Fond Nor II; 43/75, clr etch/Arches, 1969, p/s, full mrgs, lt cr img, S-48x32", C-NY 5/11/88 **3,850**
L'Oiseau du Forgeron, 24/75, clr aqua/drypt/relief, 1963, p/s, lt fox/stn, S-26x19", Maeght, lot 617, SBY 5/11/89 **3,850**
L'Oiseu Destructeur, 5/75, etch/aqua/cbrn, 1969, p/s, lt cr, S-28x37", Maeght/Morsang, lot 337, SBY 11/3/88 OE **12,100**
La Bague d'Aurore: Pl 2; 56/60, clr etch/aqua, 1957, p/s, full mrgs, lt stn, 6x5", lot 319A, SBY 11/3/88 OE **3,630**

La Chevelure de Berenice I, 8/75, clr aqua/etch, 1963, p/s, full mrgs, lt sl/mstn/cr, unfr, 18x27", Maeght, SBY 5/12/88	1,320
La Commedia Dell'Arte, 13/30, clr etch/aqua, 1979, p/s, lt stn corners, S-22x30", Maeght/Joan Barbara, SBY 2/23/89 OE	2,750
La Corciere, 50/75, etch/aqua/cbrn, 1969, p/s, S-42x28", Maeght/Morsang, lot 634, SBY 5/11/89 OE	30,800
La Dandy, HC, aqua/drypt/cbrn, 1969, p/s, full mrgs, lt stn/rub, 16x17", Maeght, lot 629, SBY 5/11/89 OE	29,700
La Demoiselle a Bascule, 10/75, litho/cream wove paper, 1970, old tp stn on verso, S-23x19", lot 2875, B/B 2/16/88	2,750
La Femme aux Bijoux, 17/75, aqua/cbrn/Chiffon de Mandeure, 1968, p/s, full mrgs, stn, 18x13", lot 692, C-NY 5/10/89 OE	35,200
La Femme des Sables, 17/75, clr etch/aqua/cbrn, 1969, p/s, lt sl/cr/stn/skinned, S-41x26", lot 344, SBY 2/23/89 OE	14,300
La Femme des Sables, 18/75, aqua/etch/cbrn, 1969, p/s, lt fox, skinned mrg, unfr, S-41x26", SBY 5/12/88 OE	12,100
La Fronde, 27/75, clr aqua/etch/cbrn, 1969, wht crayon sgn, S-42x28", Maeght, SBY 5/12/88 OE	14,300
La Grande Ecalliere, 8/30, clr litho, 1975, p/s, full mrgs, S-87x43", Maeght, lot 359A, SBY 11/3/88	8,800
La Grande Ordinateur, 36/75, etch/aqua/cbrn, 1969, p/s, S-42x27", lot 335, SBY 11/3/88 OE	14,300
La Greve Noire, 12/50, etch/aqua/cbrn/wove paper, 1973, p/s, full sheet, lt cr/scuff, S-24x55", lot 699, C-NY 5/10/89	9,900
La Lune Bleu, 38/75, clr litho/wove paper, ca 1976, p/s, full mrgs, lt rub, L-25x17", lot 350, C-NY 1/19/89	1,870
La Metamorphose, 28/50, clr etch/aqua, 1978, p/s, full mrgs, 42x30", lot 364, SBY 2/23/89 OE	23,100
La Ruisselante Lunaire, 23/30, clr litho, 1976, p/s, S-62x46", lot 362, SBY 11/3/88	9,900
La Ruisselante Solaire, 24/30, clr litho, 1976, p/s, S-62x46", lot 363, SBY 11/3/88	9,900
La Sarrazin a l'Etoile Bleue, 27/50, clr etch/aqua/cbrn, 1973, p/s, S-54x24", lot 409, C-NY 11/1/88 OE	11,000
La Traca, 2/30, clr aqua, 1979, p/s, full sheet, lt cr, S-30x22", Joan Barbara, lot 292, SBY 2/25/88	1,650
La Traca, 30/30, clr aqua, 1979, p/s, lt cr edges, S-30x22", Barbara, SBY 5/12/88	1,870
La Traca, 8/30, clr aqua, 1979, p/s, lt sl on verso, S-30x23", Maeght/Joan Barbara, lot 367, SBY 2/23/89 OE	2,750
Le Barbare dans la Nuit, 44/50, clr etch/aqua, 1976, sgn in wht, full mrgs, S-42x30", lot 235, C-NY 5/11/88 OE	8,800
Le Bouvier, 6/30, clr etch/aqua, 1978, p/s, S-20x26", Maeght/Morsang, lot 656, SBY 5/11/89	3,300
Le Caissier, 56/75, clr aqua/etch/cbrn, 1969, p/s, lt fox, S-36x27", Maeght, lot 330, SBY 11/3/88 OE	13,750
Le Chat Enchantee, 58/75, clr litho, p/s, L-12x15", lot 64, PHL 6/16/88	1,200
Le Ciel du Fargeron, 7/75, clr etch, p/s, 23x19", lot 467, LH 5/15/88 Oe	1,300
Le Cosmonaute, aside from #d ed of 75, etch/aqua/cbrn/relief, 1969, full mrgs, S-21x26", lot 628, SBY 5/11/89 OE	7,150
Le Cosmonaute, 20/75, etch/aqua/cbrn, 1969, p/s, lt fox, S-20x26", lot 222, C-NY 5/11/88	4,180
Le Cosmonaute, 62/75, clr etch/aqua/cbrn/Chiffon de Mandeure, 1969, lt fox/cr, S-21x26", lot 403, C-NY 11/1/88 OE	6,600
Le Courtisan Grotesque: Pl XI; 10/12, clr etch/aqua, 1974, p/s, S-16x23", Iliazd/Lacouriere, lot 652, SBY 5/11/89 OE	7,150
Le Dandy, HC, aqua/drypt/cbrn, 1969, p/s, full mrgs, lt cr/sl, 16x17", Maeght, lot 342, SBY 2/23/89 OE	13,200
Le Dandy, HC, aqua/drypt/cbrn, 1969, p/s, full mrgs, lt fox, 16x17", Maeght, SBY 5/12/88	7,700
Le Dandy, HC, aqua/drypt/cbrn, 1969, p/s, full mrgs, lt fox/stn, 16x17", lot 331, SBY 11/3/88	11,000
Le Grand Ordinateur, hc aqua, p/s, 40x24", lot 164, MG 5/28/88	2,500
Le Grand Sorcier, HC, aqua/etch/cbrn, p/s, lt cr, S-35x27", Maeght, SBY 5/12/88	2,000
Le Guerrier Mongol, 3/50, clr litho/Arches, 1976, p/s, full mrgs, L-27x21", lot 704, C-NY 5/10/89	3,850
Le Hibou Blasphemateur, 19/50, clr etch/aqua/Arches, 1976, p/s, lt cr, S-48x60", lot 655, SBY 5/11/89 OE	60,500
Le Lezard aux Plumes d'Or, Pl 1, 3/50, clr litho/Japan, 1971, p/s, full mrgs, L-14x19", lot 227, C-NY 5/11/88 OE	2,420
Le Lezard aux Plumes d'Or, Pl 1, 9/50, clr litho/Rives, 1971, p/s, full mrgs, 13x19", Broder, lot 355, SBY 11/3/88	3,025
Le Lezard aux Plumes d'Or, Pl 5, 46/50, clr litho/Rives, 1971, p/s, 13x19", Broder/Mourlot, lot 356, SBY 11/3/88	3,025
Le Lezard aux Plumes d'Or, Pl 8, a/p, VIII/X, clr litho, 1971, sgn in wht crayon, 13x19", Broder/Mourlot, SBY 2/25/88 OE	2,640
Le Lezard aux Plumes d'Or, 14/20, clr litho/parchment, 1967, p/s, S-14x20", lot 323, SBY 11/3/88	3,575
Le Marteau sans Maitre, a/p, clr etch/aqua/Japan nacre, 1976, p/s, S-18x26", Au Vent d'Arles, lot 362, SBY 2/23/89 OE	3,575
Le Penseur Puissant, 2/75, aqua/etch/drypt/cbrn, 1969, p/s, S-42x27", Maeght/Morsang, lot 633, SBY 5/11/89 OE	23,100
Le Penseur Puissant, 66/75, etch/aqua/drypt/cbrn, 1969, p/s, lt cr/sl/stn, S-42x27", lot 405, C-NY 11/1/88	9,350
Le Permissionnaire, 31/50, clr etch/aqua/cbrn/Arches, 1974, p/s, full mrgs, stn/fox, 45x29", lot 649, SBY 5/11/89 OE	40,700
Le Porteur d'Eau III, 58/75, clr aqua, 1962, p/s, full mrgs, lt fox/cr, 22x31", lot 337, SBY 2/23/89	3,300
Le Porteur d'Eau III, 62/75, clr aqua, 1962, p/s, lt cr/stn/fox, 22x31", Maeght, lot 271, SBY 2/25/88 OE	1,320
Le Prophete la Nuit, 19/75, clr etch/Arches, 1965, p/s, full mrgs, lt stn, P-27x21", lot 396, C-NY 11/1/88 OE	4,620
Le Prophete la Nuit, 37/75, clr etch, 1965, p/s, full sheet, lt tr mrg, S-36x25", Maeght, lot 277, SBY 2/25/88 OE	3,410
Le Querrier Mongol, 4/50, clr litho/wht wove paper, 1976, p/s, full mrgs, lt cr, 27x20", lot 361, SBY 11/3/88 OE	4,125
Le Revenant, 39/75, clr litho, 1969, p/s, S-36x25", Maeght/Arte Adrien Maeght, lot 639, SBY 5/11/89	3,520
Le Vieil Irlandais, HCXXIII/XXIV, clr etch/aqua/cbrn, 1969, p/s, S-41x28", Maeght/Morsang, lot 635, SBY 5/11/89 OE	30,800
Le Vieil Irlandais, 20/75, etch/aqua/cbrn, 1969, sgn in wht crayon, S-42x28", Maeght/Morsang, lot 340, SBY 11/3/88 OE	14,300
Lea Magdaleniens, 22/75, clr etch/aqua, 1958, p/s, full mrgs, fox/stn, 5x6", Crommelynck/Maeght, lot 335, SBY 2/23/89 OE	2,640
Les Armes du Sommeil, 32/75, etch/aqua/cbrn, 1970, p/s, full mrgs, lt stn, 20x25", lot 347, SBY 11/3/88	11,000
Les Armes du Sommeil, 56/75, etch/aqua/cbrn, 1970, p/s, full mrgs, 21x25", Maeght, lot 348, SBY 11/3/88 OE	12,100
Les Deux Amis, 21/75, aqua/etch/cabor/drypt, 1969, full mrgs, lt stn, 28x42", lot 280, SBY 2/25/88 OE	6,600
Les Deux Amis, 61/75, clr etch/aqua/cbrn/Chiffon de Mandeure, 1969, Maeght/Atelier Maeght, lot 630, SBY 5/11/89 OE	42,900
Les Essencies de la Terra, 75A/100, litho/Japan nacre, 1968, full mrgs, lt cr, 16x13", Poligrafa, lot 279, SBY 2/25/88	1,100
Les Grandes Manoeuvers, 44/50, clr etch/aqua/cbrn, 1973, p/s, lt sl, S-55x24", Maeght, lot 643, SBY 5/11/89 OE	27,500
Les Orfeures, hc etch/wove paper, 1971-73, p/s, S-36x25", lot 406, C-NY 11/1/88 OE	7,700
Lezard aux Plumes d'Or, Pl XII, 24/50, clr litho, 1971, p/s, full mrgs, lt stn, 14x20", Broder, lot 357, SBY 11/3/88 OE	3,575
Literate Man-Green, 31/75, clr litho/cloth backed on wove paper, 1969, p/s, S-33x24", lot 343, SBY 11/3/88	2,475
Lithographie Originale (frontispiece for Mourlot catalog Vol IV 1969-72), litho/Arches, 12x11", lot 66, RWS 9/8/89 OE	1,800
Lithographie Originale V, HC, clr litho/Arches, 1972, p/s, lt stn, S-18x14", lot 64, RWS 9/8/89 OE	2,500
Little Girl in the Woods, 56/100, litho/Arches, 1958, p/s, full mrgs, 19x22", Maeght/Mourlot, lot 320, SBY 11/3/88	2,750
Ma de Proverbis, XI/XXV, clr litho/Japan nacre, 1970, p/s, full mrgs, S-22x30", lot 696, C-NY 5/10/89 OE	6,600
Ma de Proverbis, 34/75, clr litho/Arches, 1970, p/s, lt stn, S-22x30", lot 350, SBY 11/3/88 OE	2,090
Maja Negra, 22/50, clr etch/aqua/cbrn/wove paper, 1973, lt scr, S-24x54", lot 407, C-NY 11/1/88 OE	12,100
Maja Negra, 45/50, etch/aqua/cbrn, 1973, p/s, rpr tr, S-24x54", lot 229, C-NY 5/11/88	6,380
Man Picking Grapes, 22/75, clr litho, p/s, lt stn, 36x24", lot 340, SBY 2/23/89	5,225

Mannequin Parade in Bahia, 30/75, clr litho, 1969, p/s, full mrgs, lt cr/sl, 48x32", Maeght, lot 638, SBY 5/11/89 OE 15,950
Mannequin Parade in Lapland, 15/75, clr litho, 1969, p/s, full mrgs, lt sl mrgs/verso, 47x32", lot 345, SBY 11/3/88 5,500
Manoletina, 64/75, aqua/cbrn, 1969, p/s, S-28x41", Maeght, lot 336, SBY 11/3/88 13,200
Marteau Sans Maitre, 2/25, hc srgph, p/s, 9x11", lot 160, MG 5/28/88 900
Marti Pol, Pl IV, 30/50, clr etch/aqua, 1980, p/s, Gaspar bstp, full mrgs, 28x22", lot 370A, SBY 11/3/88 7,700
Marti Pol, 3, 38/50, clr aqua/etch, 1980, p/s, full mrgs, P-29x22", Gaspar, SBY 5/12/88 6,050
Marti Pol, 4, 28/50, clr aqua/etch, p/s, full mrgs, P-28x22", Gaspar, SBY 5/12/88 6,600
Marti Pol, 6, 28/50, clr aqua/etch, 1980, p/s, full mrgs, lt cr mrg/verso, P-29x22", Gaspar, SBY 5/12/88 OE 8,250
Montroig I, a/p, total ed of 40, clr litho/Arches, 1973, p/s, 30x23", Poligrafa, lot 2877, B/B 2/16/88 2,475
Montroig I, 8/30, clr litho, 1973, p/s, S-30x23", Maeght, lot 646, SBY 5/11/89 OE 13,200
Nestob, 5/50, clr litho, ca 1975, p/s, S-36x25", lot 359, SBY 11/3/88 OE 7,150
Nymphomaniac President, 46/50, clr litho, p/s, 47x31", lot 196, LH 5/15/88 OE 5,200
Oda a Joan Miro, a/p, aside from ed of 100, litho, 1973, p/s, full mrgs, L-35x24", Poligrafa, SBY 5/12/88 OE 6,600
Oda a Joan Miro, HC4/10, clr litho, 1973, p/s, lt stn/cr, S-30x23", Poligrafa, lot 647, SBY 5/11/89 OE 12,100
Oiseau Mongol, HC, etch/aqua/cbrn, 1969, sgn in wht crayon, lt cr/sl, S-41x28", Maeght, lot 632, SBY 5/11/89 OE 19,800
Oiseau Mongol, 65/75, etch/aqua/cbrn, 1969, sgn in wht crayon, S-41x28", Maeght/Morsang, lot 338, SBY 11/3/88 12,100
Original Lithograph, XIX/LXXX, clr litho, p/s, full mrgs, lt cr mrgs, L-13x10", lot 68, PHL 6/16/88 800
Original Lithograph I, XIX/LXXX, clr litho, 1975, p/s, full mrgs, lt cr, L-13x10", lot 67, PHL 6/16/88 750
Pair: Essencies de la Terra; 67/100 & 67A/100, litho/Japan nacre, 1968, S-20x14", Mourlot, lot 278A, SBY 2/25/88 1,980
Pair: Je Travaille Comme un Jardinier; Japanese Woman; ed of 125/150, litho, 1959/1971, S-16x13"/14x20", SBY 5/12/88 OE 3,410
Pair: Joan Miro; relief etch, 1947, inscr Personal proof, full mrgs, lt stn, 7x6", lot 266, SBY 2/25/88 OE 1,760
Pair: L'Enfance d'Ubu; ed of 120, clr litho, 1952, p/s, full mrgs, 12x19"/11x17", lot 332, SBY 2/23/89 OE 5,225
Pair: Le Lezard aux Plumes d'Or; 25/50 & 12/50, litho/Japan nacre, 1967, p/s, S-16x22"/15x19", lot 278, SBY 2/25/88 OE 3,630
Pair: Le Lezard aux Plumes d'Or: Pl XI; Bouquet de Reves pour Nelia; litho, 1967, p/s, S-16x22"/S-13x20", SBY 11/3/88 OE 4,400
Pair: Maravillas con Variacones Acrosticas en el Jardin de Miro; XI/XV, litho, 1975, 30x21", Poligrafa, SBY 2/23/89 OE 4,400
Pair: Maravillas con Variacones Acrostica en el Jardin de Miro; 63/75, litho, 1975, 18x13", Poligrafa, SBY 2/25/88 2,420
Pair: Maravillas con Variacones Acrosticas en el Jardin de Miro; HC, 1975, 18x12", Poligrafa, lot 361, SBY 2/23/89 OE 3,850
Pair: Miro, Grand Palais Exhibition, 1974; Lucifer; 43/100 & 24/75, litho, 1973-74, p/s, 24x17"/31x22", SBY 2/23/89 OE 5,500
Pair: Miro Lithographs, Vol III; IIIII/LXXX, clr litho, 1969, p/s, S-18x15", lot 640, SBY 5/11/89 OE 6,600
Pair: Per un Teatre a Catalunya; Quiriquibu; 14/50 & 40/99, litho, 1973 & 1976, 21x19"/30x22", lot 356, SBY 2/23/89 OE 5,500
Pair: Pierrot le Fou; The Drunken Horse; ed of 75, clr litho, 1964, p/s, S-24x36", Maeght, lot 272, SBY 2/25/88 OE 4,400
Pair: Series I: Blue & Red Graphism; Blue on Red Wash; ed of 30, clr litho/Rives, 1961, S-26x40", lot 615, SBY 5/11/89 3,575
Partie de Campagne I, 44/75, clr etch/aqua, 1967, p/s, full mrgs, lt mstn/cr/tr, P-23x36", Maeght, SBY 5/12/88 OE 12,100

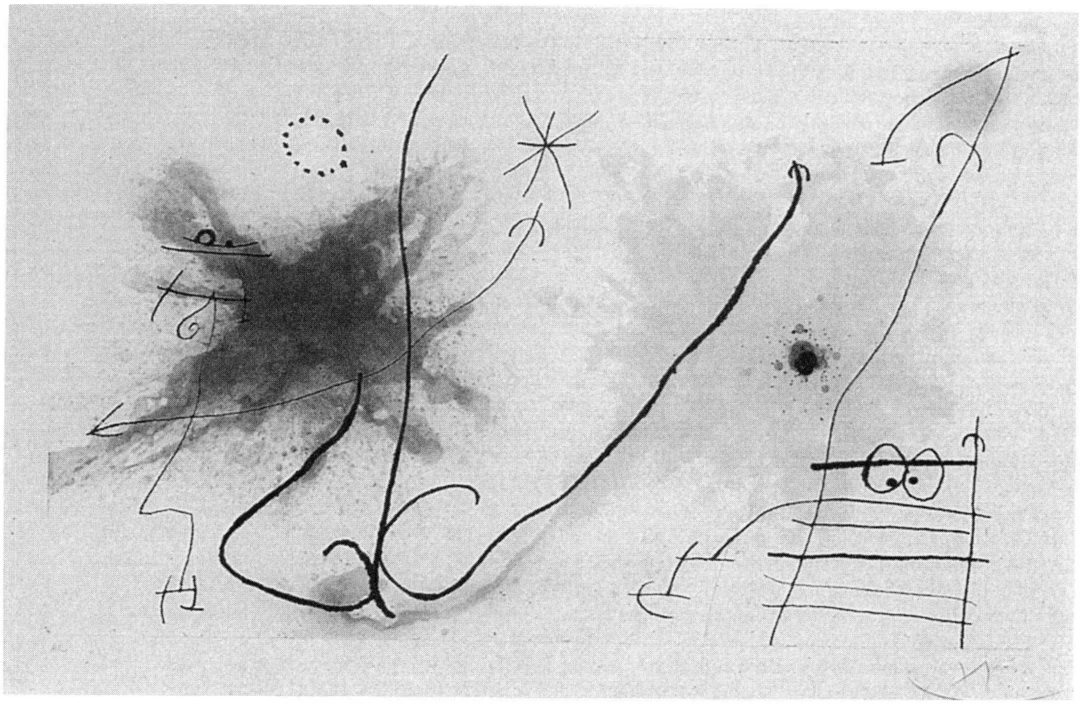

Partie de Campagne V, HC, etch/aqua/wove paper, 1967, p/s, full mrgs, lt cr/rub, P-23x37", C-NY 5/10/89 OE; $17,600

Peintures sur Papier, Dessins (poster); 27/150, clr litho/Arches, 1971, full sheet, lt scr, S-34x23", C-NY 5/10/89 OE 1,870
Penseur Puissant, 6/75, aqua/etch/drypt/cbrn, 1969, p/s, S-41x27", Maeght, lot 339, SBY 11/3/88 OE 12,100
People on a Black Background, 50/75, clr litho, 1949, p/s, full mrgs, lt stn, 12x18", Maeght, lot 608, SBY 5/11/89 OE 28,600
Person in a Garden, II; 26/75, clr litho, 1951, p/s, full mrgs, lt rpr tr/cr, 14x23", lot 330, SBY 2/23/89 OE 4,675

Personatge I Estels, 17/50, aqua/wc/collage, 1979, p/s, S-36x25", Maeght/Joan Barbara, lot 368, SBY 11/3/88 OE **5,225**
Personatge I Estels, 13/50, clr etch, 1979, p/s, S-35x25", Maeght/Joan Barbara, lot 659, SBY 5/11/89 OE **8,800**
Personatge I Estels, 20/50, clr aqua/wc/collage, 1979, p/s, lt stn, 36x25", Maeght/Joan Barbara, lot 367, SBY 11/3/88 OE **6,050**
Personatge I Estels, 6/50, clr aqua/wc/collage, 1979, p/s, S-36x25", Maeght, lot 368, SBY 2/23/89 OE **6,050**
Personatge I Estels #55, 37/50, aqua/wc/collage/wove paper, p/s, full sheet, S-36x25", lot 705, C-NY 5/10/89 OE **6,050**
Personatge I Estels #56, 14/50, aqua/wc/collage/wove paper, 1979, p/s, full sheet, S-36x25", lot 706, C-NY 5/10/89 OE **4,620**
Personnage Romantique, 8/50, clr etch/aqua/wht wove paper, 1975, p/s, full mrgs, lt cr, 17x16", lot 359, SBY 2/23/89 OE **3,300**
Petite Barriere, 22/75, clr aqua/drypt, 1967, p/s, full mrgs, lt stn/sl mrgs/verso, 11x4", Maeght, SBY 5/12/88 OE **6,325**
Petite Fete de Nuit, 15/50, clr litho/wove paper, 1974, p/s, full mrgs, lt cr, L-15x13", lot 701, C-NYU 5/10/89 OE **3,740**
Petite Fille au Bois, 74/100, litho/Arches, 1958, full mrgs, lt fox, S-20x26", lot 218, C-NY 5/11/88 OE **1,980**
Petite Fille au Bois, 74/100, litho/Arches, 1958, p/s, full mrgs, lt fox, S-20x26", lot 218, C-NY 5/11/88 .... **1,980**
Petite Fille Devant la Mer, 42/75, clr etch/aqua, 1967, p/s, full mrgs, P-23x36", Maeght, SBY 5/12/88 OE **11,550**
Pitre Rose, 19/50, clr etch/aqua/cbrn, 1974, p/s, lt cr/tr, P-46x29", Maeght, lot 410, C-NY 11/1/88 .... **16,500**
Portfolio No 1, a/p, etch, 1947, p/s, full mrgs, lt cr/stn/rpr tr, 12x9", lot 316, SBY 11/3/88 OE **13,200**
Portfolio No 1, 32/70, etch/wove paper, 1947, p/s, full mrgs, 12x9", Brunidor/Atelier 17, lot 607, SBY 5/11/89 OE **14,300**
Portfolio: Album 13; 16/75, 13 litho, 1948, p/s, full mrgs, orig wrappers/portfolio, S-22x18", lot 317, SBY 11/3/88 .... **20,900**
Portfolio: Fusees; V/XV, 15 etch/aqua/Japan ancien, 1959, p/s, full mrgs, Crommelynck/Broder, lot 322, SBY 11/3/88 OE **55,000**
Portfolio: L'Enfance d'Ubu; #31, total ed of 120, 1975, orig wrappers, Teriade/Mourlot, lot 653, SBY 5/11/89 OE **39,600**
Portfolio: L'Enfance d'Ubu; #6, total ed of 120, 1975, orig wrappers, Teriade/Mourlot, lot 360, SBY 11/3/88 .... **23,100**
Portfolio: Quelque Fleurs pour des Amis; total ed of 225, orig wrappers/portfolio, XXe Siecle, lot 322A, SBY 11/3/88 OE **10,450**
Poster for Cartons, 28/100, clr litho/Rives, 1965, p/s, full mrgs, lt stn/scr/cr, L-25x19", lot 686, C-NY 5/10/89 UE **1,100**
Poster for Miro Exhibition, 130/150, clr litho/BFK Rives, 1962, p/s, full mrgs, lt stn, L-23x18", lot 685, C-NY 5/10/89 .... **2,420**
Poster for the Exhibition Agora I, 23/125, clr litho before text, 1971, p/s, S-35x31", lot 352, SBY 11/3/88 OE **3,575**
Poster for the Exhibition Sculptures, 8/150, clr litho/wove paper, 1970, p/s, full mrgs, S-31x23", lot 695, C-NY 5/10/89 .... **1,430**
Poster for the Opening of the Mourlot Atelier in New York, 1/60, clr litho, 1967, p/s, S-29x22", SBY 5/12/88 OE **2,475**
Poster for the Publication of the Book, Le Lezard Aux Plumes D'Or; ed of 300, litho/Arches, unfr, 25x19", SBY 5/12/88 OE **2,200**
Pour Paul Eluard, HC, clr etch/aqua, 1973, p/s, lt cr/sl, S-26x20", Ed Cercle d'Art, lot 354C, SBY 2/23/89 OE **1,750**
Pour Paul Eluard, 63/100, clr etch/aqua, 1973, p/s, S-26x20", Cercle d'Art/Morsang, lot 645, SBY 5/11/89 OE **7,700**
Pygmies Sous la Lune, HC, clr etch/aqua, 1974, p/s, full mrgs, lt cr, 21x27", lot 289, SBY 2/25/88 OE **5,225**
Pygmies Sous la Lune, hc aqua, p/s, 27x21", lot 162, MG 5/28/88 .... **3,000**
Quiriquibu, 20/99, clr litho/Guarro, 1976, p/s, S-30x22", lot 654, SBY 5/11/89 .... **3,850**
Red & Blue, 35/100, clr litho/Arches, 1960, p/s, full mrgs, lt lstn, laid down, L-23x16", lot 392, C-NY 11/1/88 .... **1,210**
Red Bird I, 31/75, clr litho, 1951, p/s, full mrgs, lt stn/cr, 10x17", lot 609, SBY 5/11/89 .... **2,750**
Red Bird I, 61/75, clr litho/Rives, 1951, p/s, dtd 1950, lt stn, S-15x22", lot 214, C-NY 5/11/88 .... **2,860**
Rustics, aside from ed of 75, litho/red & wht checked cloth/stiff wove paper, 1969, p/s, lt cr, L-35x27", SBY 5/12/88 OE **3,300**
Rustics, 27/75, litho/checked cloth, 1969, full mrgs, 36x27", Maeght, lot 341, SBY 11/3/88 .... **2,750**
San Lazzaro et Ses Amis, 26/60, clr litho, ca 1979, p/s, full mrgs, 20x15", lot 661, SBY 5/11/89 .... **5,500**
Sculptures en Montagne Exhibition, 115/150, clr litho before letters, 1973, p/s, 31x22", Maeght, lot 358, SBY 11/3/88 OE **2,750**
Seers, ed of 75, clr litho, 1970, p/s, inscr 28/VII/69, lt cr mrg, unfr, S-26x20", Mourlot/Broder, SBY 5/12/88 OE **2,475**
Serie Barcelona, #6, 49/50, aqua/etch, 1972-73, sgn in wht crayon, lt cr, unfr, S-42x28", Gaspar, SBY 5/12/88 .... **4,125**
Serie Gaudi, 24/50, aqua/etch/collage, 1979, sgn in wht crayon, S-45x28", Maeght/Joan Barbara, lot 366A, SBY 11/3/88 OE **14,300**
Serie Gaudi, 29/50, clr etch/aqua, 1979, sgn in wht crayon, lt skinned, S-36x25", Maeght, lot 366, SBY 2/23/89 OE **20,900**
Serie Gaudi 30, 16/50, clr etch/aqua/wove applique, 1980, p/s, full mrgs, 15x16", lot 662, SBY 5/11/89 .... **8,800**
Serie Gaudi 33, 37/50, etch/aqua, 1980, p/s, full mrgs, lt stn, 14x10", Maeght, lot 663, SBY 5/11/89 OE **7,150**
Serie I: Plate I; 11/13, blk & gray etch/Arches, 1947, p/s, S-20x26", Maeght/Lacouriere, lot 99, C-NY 11/1/88 OE **11,000**
Serie I: Plate II; 11/13, etch/Rives, 1947, sgn/dtd 1953, lt scr, S-20x26", Maeght/Lacouriere, lot 100, C-NY 11/1/88 OE **12,100**
Serie I: Plate III; 11/13, clr etch/Arches, 1947, sgn/dtd 1952, S-20x26", Maeght/Lacouriere, lot 101, C-NY 11/1/88 OE **26,400**
Serie I: Plate IV; 11/13, clr etch/Rives, 1947, sgn/dtd 1953, S-20x26", Maeght/Lacouriere, lot 102, C-NY 11/1/88 OE **22,000**
Serie I: Plate V; 11/13, clr etch/Arches, 1947, sgn/dtd 1952, S-20x26", Maeght/Lacouriere, lot 103, C-NY 11/1/88 OE **33,000**
Serie I: Plate VI; 11/13, clr etch/Arches, 1947, sgn/dtd 1952, S-20x26", Maeght/Lacouriere, lot 104, C-NY 11/1/88 OE **30,800**
Serie I: Plate VII; 11/13, clr etch/drypt, 1947, sgn/dtd 1952, S-20x26", Maeght/Lacouriere, lot 105, C-NY 11/1/88 OE **28,600**
Serie I: Plate VII; 11/13, clr etch/Rives, 1947, sgn/dtd 1953, S-20x26", Maeght/Lacouriere, lot 106, C-NY 11/1/88 OE **28,600**
Serie I: Proof Plate; a/p, clr etch/soft wove paper, 1947, inscr New York 17/6/47, S-20x26", lot 98, C-NY 11/1/88 OE **38,500**
Serie II, 2/13, etch/Rives, 1952-3, sgn/dtd 1953, lt mstn, P-15x18", lot 216, C-NY 5/11/88 .... **5,500**
Serie III, III/XIII, hc etch, 1952-53, full but irregularly shaped sheet, lt sl, S-20x28", lot 611, SBY 5/11/89 .... **60,500**
Serie III, VI/XIII, hc etch/aqua/parchment, 1952-53, full sheet, lt rpl mrgs, S-17x30", lot 680, C-NY 5/10/89 .... **22,000**
Serie Noire et Rouge, 2/30, brick-red & blk drypt/Arches, 1938, full mrgs, lt stn/scr, 10x7", lot 263, SBY 2/25/88 .... **13,200**
Set of 20: L'Enfance d'Ubu; 16/120, clr litho w/text on Arches, full mrgs, Teriade, lot 703, C-NY 5/10/89 OE **35,200**
Sobreteixims, 37/40, clr litho, 1978, p/s, S-64x47", lot 364, SBY 11/3/88 .... **4,400**
Somnambule, 25/50, clr etch/aqua/cbrn/Arches, 1974, p/s, full mrgs, lt stn/fox, 45x29", Maeght, lot 650, SBY 5/11/89 .... **71,500**
Sous la Grele, 40/75, clr aqua/wove paper, 1969, p/s, full mrgs, lt stn/scr img, P-17x27", lot 694, C-NY 5/10/89 .... **7,150**
Stevedore, 39/50, clr litho, 1971, p/s, full mrgs, lt cr/stn, S-42x33", Maeght, lot 351, SBY 11/3/88 OE **4,950**
Surrealist Composition, for Cahiers d'Art; 30/48, orange/blk pochoir, 1934, lt scr/fox, 13x10", lot 386, C-NY 11/1/88 .... **10,450**
Terre Atteinte et Soleil Intact, 37/50, clr etch/aqua/wove paper, 1974, p/s, lt stn, P-27x21", lot 700, C-NY 5/10/89 .... **3,520**
Terres de Grand Feu, 35/200, before letters, clr litho, 1956, p/s, full mrgs, stn/fox/sl, L-27x20", Maeght, SBY 5/12/88 .... **2,860**
Trace sur la Paroi II, 49/75, etch/aqua/cbrn, 1967, p/s, full mrgs, rpl/stn, 23x37", Maeght, lot 624, SBY 5/11/89 OE **31,900**
Trace sur la Paroi V, 51/75, etch/aqua/cbrn, 1967, p/s, full mrgs, lt mstn, P-23x37", Maeght, SBY 5/12/88 OE **20,900**
Trace sur la Paroi VI, 32/75, etch/aqua/cbrn, 1967, p/s, full mrgs, lt stn/sl/cr, 23x37", lot 327, SBY 11/3/88 .... **18,700**
Tres Joan, XIV/XV, clr etch/aqua, 1979, p/s, full mrgs, lt stn, 21x42", lot 660, SBY 5/11/89 OE **18,150**
Twilight's Ring, 66/75, clr litho, 1964, p/s, lt stn, S-36x24", Maeght, lot 618, SBY 5/11/89 OE **6,600**
Ubu, Pl II; 21/75, clr litho/Arches, 1966, p/s, full mrgs, lt stn, L-16x25", lot 397, C-NY 11/1/88 OE **8,250**

Ubu, Pl VII; 31/75, clr litho/Arches, 1966, p/s, full mrgs, L-16x25", lot 398, C-NY 11/1/88 ... 3,520
Ubu Roi, Pl VII, 20/75, clr litho, full mrgs, lt stn, 17x25", lot 341, SBY 2/23/89 OE ... 9,350
Ubu Roi, Plate II; 16/75, clr litho, 1966, p/s, full mrgs, Teriade, SBY 5/12/88 OE ... 9,900
Ubu Roi, Plate XII, 35/75, clr litho, 1966, p/s, full mrgs, lt mstn/lstn, lt sl verso, L-16x25", Teriade, SBY 5/12/88 ... 2,740
Ubu Roi, 37/75, clr litho/Arches, 1966, p/s, full mrgs, lt stn/fox/tr, L-16x25", lot 220, C-NY 5/11/88 ... 6,050
Une Femme, ed of 300, clr litho, ca 1969, 18x15", p/s, pl/s, Maeght bstp, lt stn, 18x15", lot 179, SWN 6/15/89 OE ... 1,320
Une Telle et Son Petit Mari, 55/75, etch/aqua/cbrn, 1970, p/s, full mrgs, lt rpl, S-26x20", lot 225, C-NY 5/11/88 ... 4,950
Untitle, Ubu Roi; Pl 5, 63/75, clr litho/Arches, 1966, intl, full mrgs, L-16x25", lot 78, PHL 10/28/88 ... 800
Untitled, Album 13; 68/75, litho/Marais, p/s, full mrgs, lt stn/cr/scuff/sl, L-14x17", lot 679, C-NY 5/10/89 OE ... 3,520
Untitled, Album 19; Pl 10, 44/75, litho, 1961, intl, 26x20", lot 267, LH 5/15/88 ... 750
Untitled, Album 19; Pl 6, 45/75, clr litho/BFK Rives, 1961, full mrgs, lt scr, S-20x26", Maeght, lot 393, C-NY 11/1/88 ... 2,310
Untitled, Album 21; 46/75, clr litho/Arches, 1966, p/s, full mrgs, S-26x20", Maeght, lot 687, C-NY 5/10/89 ... 1,540
Untitled, Album 21; 46/76, clr litho/Arches, 1978, p/s, full mrgs, S-20x25", Maeght, lot 688, C-NY 5/10/89 ... 1,760
Untitled, El Pi de Formentor; 45/50, clr etch/aqua, 1976, p/s, Sala Gaspar bstp, P-35x29", lot 412, C-NY 11/1/88 ... 4,620
Untitled, Essencies de la Terra; IIh/xvh.c, litho/Japan nacre, 1970, p/s, lt stn, L-12x11", lot 86, PHL 10/28/88 ... 1,100
Untitled, Gaudi; Pl 33, HC9/15, clr etch/aqua, 1979, p/s, trm mrgs, S-14x20", Maeght, lot 413, C-NY 11/1/88 OE ... 4,180
Untitled, Grans Rupestres; 25/30, clr aqua/cbrn, 1979, p/s, full sheet, S-35x27", Maeght, lot 237, C-NY 5/11/88 OE ... 4,180
Untitled, Le Courtisan Grotesque; Pl 7, 10/12, etch/aqua/Japan, 1974, p/s, S-26x23", Iliazd, lot 702, C-NY 5/10/89 OE ... 3,520
Untitled, Le Lezard aux Plumes d'Or; Pl 2, a/p, litho/wm Miro wove paper, 1967, p/s, S-16x22", lot 402, C-NY 11/1/88 OE ... 2,200
Untitled, Le Lezard aux Plumes d'Or; Pl 3, IX/X, litho/Japan nacre, 1967, full mrgs, S-16x22", lot 689, C-NY 5/10/89 OE ... 3,520
Untitled, Le Lezard aux Plumes d'Or; Pl 8, 1/100, litho/wove paper, 1967, p/s, S-14x39", lot 401, C-NY 11/1/88 OE ... 5,280
Untitled, Le Vent Parmi les Roseaux; 37/140, clr etch/aqua/wove paper, 1971, full mrgs, lt stn, 13x10", C-NY 5/10/89 OE ... 3,740
Untitled, Les Essencies de la Terra; 76/100, clr litho/Japan nacre, 1968, inscr A-T, L-10x10", lot 691, C-NY 5/10/89 ... 1,320
Untitled, Marti Pol; Pl 6, 27/50, etch/aqua/Sala Gaspar wove paper, p/s, P-29x22", Sala Gaspar, lot 707, C-NY 5/10/89 OE ... 12,100
Untitled, Miro Lithographs II; Pl 7, 29/80, clr litho/Arches, 1975, p/s, full mrgs, 12x9", Maeght, lot 411, C-NY 11/1/88 ... 2,420
Untitled, Pl 6, Fernand Mourlot, Miro Lithographs II; 31/80, litho, 1975, full mrgs, S-18x14", lot 232, C-NY 5/11/88 OE ... 3,520
Untitled, Ubu Roi; Pl II, 63/75, clr litho/Arches, 1966, intl/titled, full mrgs, 16x25", lot 76, PHL 10/28/88 OE ... 900
Untitled, Ubu Roi; Pl 12, 63/75, clr litho/Arches, 1966, intl, full mrgs, L-16x25", lot 81, PHL 10/28/88 OE ... 850
Untitled, Ubu Roi; Pl 6, 63/75, clr litho/Arches, 1966, intl, full mrgs, L-16x25", lot 77, PHL 10/28/88 OE ... 900
Untitled, Ubu Roi; Pl 6, 63/75, clr litho/Arches, 1966, intl, full mrgs, L-16x25", lot 79, PHL 10/28/88 ... 650
Untitled, Ubu Roi; Pl 9, 63/75, clr litho/Arches, 1966, intl, full mrgs, L-16x25", lot 80, PHL 10/28/88 OE ... 900
Untitled (Red Sun), HC, clr litho, p/s, lt sl, 18x15", lot 180, SWN 6/15/89 ... 935
Vers la Gauche, HC, aqua/etch/cbrn, 1968, p/s, cr img, lt sl/stn mrgs, S-29x41", SBY 5/12/88 OE ... 19,800
Vers la Gauche, 15/75, clr etch/aqua/cbrn, 1968, p/s, S-29x41", lot 329, SBY 11/3/88 ... 18,700
Vers la Gauche, 29/75, clr aqua/etch/cbrn, 1968, p/s, lt cr mrg corner, lt fox, S-29x41", SBY 5/12/88 OE ... 17,600
Village d'Oiseaux, 60/75, clr etch/aqua/cbrn, 1969, p/s, full mrgs, lt cr/sl, 36x25", Maeght, lot 637, SBY 5/11/89 OE ... 13,200
Woman & Bird in Torment, 10/75, clr litho, 1967, p/s, full mrgs, mstn/cr, disclr verso, unfr, L-15x22", SBY 5/12/88 OE ... 1,870
Woman Picking Grapes, 71/75, clr litho/Arches, 1964, p/s, full mrgs, lt sl/stn, S-36x24", lot 394, C-NY 11/1/88 ... 3,520
Young Artists 1973 Exhibit (Harlequin Kicking the Bee), 24/75, clr litho, 1973, p/s, cr, S-35x24", Maeght, SBY 5/12/88 ... 3,850
Young Girl in the Moonlight, HC, ed of 75, clr litho/pur fil du Marais, 1951, S-22x30", lot 215, C-NY 5/11/88 OE ... 1,870

MITRA, Dan (American, 20th C)

Blue Heron, 200/750, clr litho, sgn, 23x32", lot 156, MG 5/28/88 UE ... 275
Louisiana Heron, 193/750, clr litho, sgn, 23x32", lot 157, MG 5/28/88 UE ... 250
Louisiana Heron, 193/750, clr litho, sgn, 23x32", lot 211, MG 12/10/88 ... 300

MOALE, John; after

Baltimore in 1752, by Wm Strickland, aqua w/varnish, 1817, lt tr/stn image, ls mrgs, stn verso, L-17x29", C-NY 1/22/88 ... 495
Baltimore Town in 1752, clr litho/wove paper, ca 1850, lstn/4 cr, rpr/ls mrg, tp undermat mrgs, L-7x18", C-NY 1/22/88 ... 242

MODIGLIANI, Amedeo; after (Italian, 1884-1920)

L'Italienne, by Jacques Villon, 161/200, clr aqua, 1926-27, Berheim Jeune bstp, lt cr/fox, 20x12", lot 589, SBY 11/3/88 ... 7,700

MOHOLY-NAGY, Laszlo (American/Hungarian, 1895-1946)

Konstruktion, Pl 4, ed of 50, red & blk litho/cream wove paper, 1923, S-24x18", Verlag, lot 110, C-NY 11/1/88 OE ... 5,500
Untitled-Construction; wc, ca 1920, p/s, full mrgs, lt fox/cr, 5x6", lot 372, SBY 11/3/88 ... 4,950
Untitled-Construction; wc, ca 1920, p/s, inscr Probedruck, lg mrgs, lt sl/cr, S-13x12", lot 373, SBY 11/3/88 OE ... 8,250
Untitled-Construction; wc, ca 1920, p/s, lg mrgs, lt scr/stn/tr, S-13x12", lot 374, SBY 11/3/88 ... 5,225

MOHUR, Johann Georg Paul (Danish, 1808-1843)

Refrain, still life of stylized string instrument; 2/99, clr etch, p/s, titled, 12x16", lot 356, GAI 8/12/88 ... 100

MOORE, Henry (British, 1898-1986)

Album: Elephant Skull; XII/XV, 1970, full mrgs, S-20x15", Cramer, lot 672, SBY 5/11/89 OE ... 17,050
Black on Red Image, 39/65, clr litho/Arches, 1963, full mrgs, lt stn, S-26x20", lot 709, C-NY 5/10/89 ... 550
Book: Shelter Sketchbook; 7 clr litho w/text on Japan nacre, 1967, orig wrappers, Marlborough, lot 416, C-NY 11/1/88 OE ... 16,500
Eight Reclining Figures, 21/125, clr litho/Japan nacre, 1967, p/s, lt stn/cr/tp, S-15x13", lot 241, C-NY 5/11/88 OE ... 1,870
Eight Reclining Figures, 91/125, clr litho/Japan nacre, 1967, p/s, full mrgs, S-30x22", lot 417, C-NY 11/1/88 OE ... 2,640
Eight Reclining Figures with Architectural Background, 54/64, clr litho, 1963, 17x13", lot 377, SBY 11/3/88 ... 2,090
Four Ideas for Sculpture, 31/50, clr litho/Rives, 1982, p/s, L-9x12", lot 717, C-NY 5/10/89 UE ... 550
Girl Reading at Window, IV/XV, gr/blk litho, 1977-78, p/s, full mrgs, 7x13", lot 379, SBY 2/23/89 ... 1,100
Large Reclining Figure & Small Motifs, Pl 5, 47/50, litho, 1967, full mrgs, S-23x31", lot 414, C-NY 11/1/88 ... 770
Mother & Child, 56/180, clr litho/Barcham Green, 1967, p/s, S-15x12", lot 240, C-NY 5/11/88 OE ... 1,210
Mother & Child Shell, 7/15, blk/brn/gray litho, 1976, p/s, full mrgs, tp hinge mrg, L-13x10", SBY 5/12/88 OE ... 1,540
Mother & Child with a Wave Background III, ed of 40, clr litho, 1976, p/s, full mrgs, 7x11", lot 181, SWN 6/15/89 ... 1,320
Pair: Reclining Nude I; Reclining Nude II; 28/50 & IX/X, etch/drypt, 1978, p/s, 6x8", Spencer, lot 301, SBY 2/25/88 OE ... 1,870
Pair: Two Reclining Figures; Two Reclining Figures; 29/100, etch & aqua/etch, 1977-78, 12x9", Visat, SBY 5/12/88 OE ... 5,500

Pair: Woman with Arms Crossed; Black on Red Image; 35/50 & 34/65, litho, 1979, 6x7"/21x19", lot 379, SBY 2/23/89 1,760
Pallas Heads, II/V, clr litho, 1973, p/s, full mrgs, lt fox/cr, 14x11", Pallas Gallery/Curwen, lot 299, SBY 2/25/89 1,320
Portfolio: Animals in the Zoo; 33/65, total ed of 80, orig wrappers, Spencer Ltd, lot 380, SBY 11/3/88 6,600
Portfolio: Elephant Skull Album; by Henry Seldis, XII/XV, orig wrappers, Cramer, lot 379, SBY 11/3/88 OE 15,400
Promethee: Death of Mira; deluxe ed of 18, clr litho, 1950/1951, p/s, lt stn/cr, 13x10", lot 376, SBY 11/3/88 OE 1,650
Promethee: Death of Mira; total ed of 183, clr litho, 1950/1951, p/s, full mrgs, lt cr/stn, 12x10", lot 668, SBY 5/11/89 2,200
Reclining Figure, 59/75, gray/brn/blk litho, 1974/1977, p/s, full mrgs, L-6x9", Poligrafa, lot 713, C-NY 5/10/89 OE 2,420
Reclining Figure & Torsos, 10/50, litho, 1968, p/s, full mrgs, 13x12", Marlborough/Wolfensberg, lot 376, SBY 2/23/89 1,430
Reclining Figure Arch Leg, 20/50, litho/TH Saunders, 1979, p/s, full mrgs, L-11x16", lot 243, C-NY 5/11/88 OE 2,200
Reclining Figure Idea for Metal Sculpture, 44/55, clr litho/Rives, 1982, p/s, glue on overmat, L-9x12", C-NY 5/10/89 880
Reclining Figure Piranesi Background II, 46/50, etch/BFK Rives, 1979, p/s, full mrgs, P-9x11", lot 715, C-NY 5/10/89 1,980
Reclining Figure 4, Pl 4, HC, aside from total ed of 65, etch, 1978, full mrgs, 9x12", Ganymed, lot 380, SBY 2/23/89 OE 1,650
Reclining Figures & Reclining Mother & Child, VIII/X, clr litho, p/s, full mrgs, L-12x10", lot 72, PHL 6/16/88 700
Reclining Woman I, 28x50, clr litho/Rives, 1980-81, p/s, L-21x23", lot 420, C-NY 11/1/88 OE 3,850
Reclining Woman on Sea Shore, 28/50, clr litho/Rives, 1980-81, p/s, L-17x24", lot 421, C-NY 11/1/88 OE 4,400
Red & Blue Standing Figures, 10/30, red/gray litho on Rives, 1951, p/s, lt rpl, L-12x9", lot 238, C-NY 5/11/88 OE 3,080
Seated Figures, 161/200, clr litho, 1957, p/s, lt stn, 21x14", Berggruen & Cie, lot 669, SBY 5/11/89 OE 12,100
Seated Mother & Child, Pl 13, 21/50, etch/drypt/Richard de Bas, 1951-66, full mrgs, P-9x11", lot 239, C-NY 5/11/88 1,320
Seated Mother & Child, 22/50, etch/Auvergne, 1951/1968, p/s, lt stn/fld mrgs, 9x11", Marlborough, lot 415, C-NY 11/1/88 1,430
Six Reclining Figures, X/XXV, dk brn/gray litho, 1973, p/s, lt cr, 13x15", LA Co Mus/Curwen, lot 300, SBY 2/25/88 OE 2,090
Six Reclining Figures, 10/100, clr litho/wove paper, 1973, p/s, lt glue/cr mrgs, unfr, L-13x15", C-NY 1/22/88 1,320
Six Reclining Figures, 10/25, gray & brn litho/TH Saunders, 1973, lt cr, L-13x15", LA Co Art Mus, lot 418, C-NY 11/1/88 1,980
Six Reclining Figures Black, 36/50, litho, 1963, p/s, full mrgs, lt cr, L-16x20", Curwen Prints/Much Hadham, SBY 5/12/88 2,090

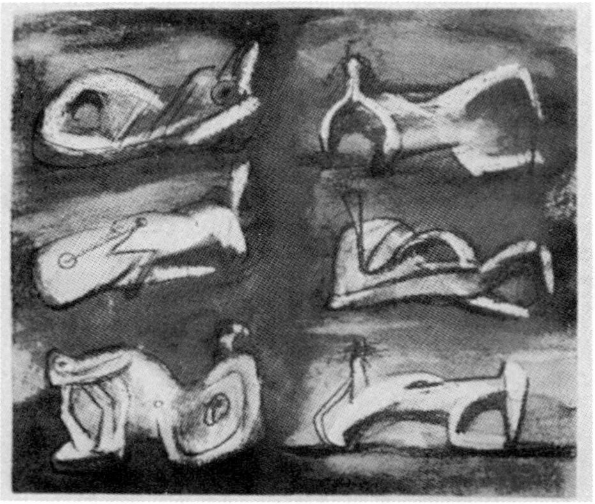

Six Reclining Figures with Red Background, 18/50, clr litho/TH Saunders, 1981, p/s, L-9x10", lot 716, C-NY 5/10/89 OE; $1,870

Square Forms, a/p, litho/Japan, 1963, p/s, full mrgs, lt cr, L-18x23", lot 87, PHL 10/28/88 OE 800
Standing Figures, 1949; 47/75, yel/bl-gray/blk colograph, 1949/1951, 15x19", Canymed, lot 1348, WL 2/26/88 3,700
Stone Reclining Figure II, 20/50, clr litho/BFK Rives, p/s, full mrgs, S-24x35", lot 419, C-NY 11/1/88 OE 3,520
Thirteen Standing Figures, litho/handmade English, 1958, lt sl/cr, 12x10", lot 2879, B/B 4/19/88 OE 495
Thirteen Standing Figures, 70/150, clr litho, 1958, p/s, lt stn/rub, 12x10", Rainbird Ltd, lot 671, SBY 5/11/89 1,925
Three Reclining Figures, 6/75, clr litho, 1971, p/s, full mrgs, 12x9", lot 298, SBY 2/25/88 1,540
Three Reclining Figures, 67/90, clr litho, 1971, p/s, full mrgs, lt cr, 12x9", Siecle/Curwen, lot 297, SBY 2/25/88 1,430
Three Reclining Figures, 70/90, clr litho/BFK Rives, p/s, full mrgs, lt cr, L-12x9", lot 711, C-NY 5/10/89 1,100
Two Black Forms, Metal Figures; 63/80, litho, 1973, p/s, full mrgs, L-13x11", Cramer, lot 89, PHL 10/28/88 300
Two Reclining Figures with River Background, 24/50, clr litho, 1963, p/s, lg mrgs, 12x25", lot 375, SBY 2/23/89 2,475
Two Reclining Figures with River Background, 24/50, litho, 1963, p/s, full mrgs, 12x25", Cramer, lot 378, SBY 11/3/88 1,760
Two Seated Figures with Children, 19/50, clr litho/wove paper, 1976, p/s, full mrgs, L-9x11", lot 714, C-NY 5/10/89 OE 1,430
Two Standing Figures No XII, 4/50, etch/aqua/drypt, 1970, full mrgs, 12x8", lot 296, SBY 2/25/88 1,320
Two Women Bathing Child II, HCIV/XXV, clr litho, 1973, p/s, full mrgs, 15x17", Transworld, lot 377, SBY 2/23/89 OE 2,200
Two Women Bathing Child II, 45/50, gray/buff/blk litho on Arches, 1973, p/s, L-15x17", lot 242, C-NY 5/11/88 2,640
Woman Holding Cat, 6/75, clr colograph, 1949/1951, p/s, full mrgs, lt fox, 12x19", Ganymed, lot 375, SBY 11/3/88 13,200
Woman Holding Cat, before ed of 75, clr colograph, 1949, p/s, full mrgs, lt cr, 12x19", Ganymed, lot 373, SBY 2/23/89 9,900
Woman Holding Cat, 60/75, clr colograph/wove paper, 1949, p/s, lt stn, 12x19", Orig Ed, lot 667, SBY 5/11/89 12,100
Woman with Dove, 35/50, clr litho, 1976, p/s, full mrgs, lt cr/scr, L-12x9", Levinson, lot 90, PHL 10/28/88 400

MORAN, Edward; after (American, 1862-1935)

Homeward Bound (ship) lt fox, tr mrg, 22x36", RAB 3/14/89 U E 70

MORAN, Mary Nimmo (American, 1842-1899)

Pair: Haunted House, East Hampton; Solitude; etch, 1885 & 1880, p/s & pl/s, no size given, lot 2965, B/B 2/16/88 412

MORAN, Peter (American, 1841-1914)

Cows in a Stream, etch, p/s, 8x12", lot 72, WG 10/19/88 75
Harbor Scene, etch, 1885, p/s, lt stn, 12x27", lot 71, WG 10/19/88 OE 1,300

Harvest at San Juan, New Mexico; etch/heavy wove paper, ca 1880/1883, pl/s, 6x12", Koehler, lot 182, SWN 6/15/89 UE ... 195

MORAN, Thomas (American, 1837-1926)

Castle of San Juan D'Ulloa, Vera Cruz, Mexico; brn etch/thin laid paper, 1884, p/s, lt cr/fox, P-11x10", C-NY 5/11/88 ... 418
Gate of Venice, etch/laid paper, p/s, lt buckling, 18x31", lot 2967, B/B 4/19/88 OE ... 2,090
Ruins, etch/heavy paper, 1883, p/s, 17x13", lot 243, FAP 2/24/89 ... 15
Tower of Cortez, Mexico; etch/rlt/Japan, 1883, p/s, printercr img, lt rub mrgs, laid down, P-12x10", C-NY 1/22/88 UE ... 352
Twilight in Arizona, etch/mezzo, ca 1884, pl/s, 6x9", lot 183, SWN 6/15/89 ... 440

MORAN, Thomas; after (American, 1837-1926)

Grand Canyon of Arizona From Hermit Rim Road, chromolitho/gum arabic, 1912-13, trm mrgs, lt ls, L-27x35", SBY 1/28/88 ... 2,420

MORANDI, Giorgio (Italian, 1890-1964)

Natura Morta con Compostiera, Bottiglia Lunga e Bottiglia Scannellata; 7/50, etch, 1928, L-10x7", lot 423, C-NY 11/1/88 ... 15,400
Paesaggio, 12/50, etch/wove paper, ca 1930, p/s, lt mstn/cr, tp on verso, P-7x8", lot 424, C-NY 11/1/88 OE ... 4,950
Vaso a Strisce con Fiori, 12/60, etch/India colle, 1924, p/s, 3 full mrgs, lt stn/sl, L-9x8", lot 422, C-NY 11/1/88 ... 8,520

MORISOT, Berthe Marie Pauline (French, 1841-1895)

Pair: Le lac du Bois; Canard et Roseaux; 3rd state, drypt/cream wove paper, lt stn, no size given, lot 3880, B/B 4/19/88 ... 522

MORLEY, Malcolm (British, 1931-)

Beach Scene, 37/58, clr litho, 1982, p/s, TGL bstp, S-38x51", lot 1160, SBY 5/13/89 ... 6,050
Family at the Beach, 25/60, slksc/Rives, ca 1975, p/s, full mrgs, lt stn, L-19x14", lot 101, RWS 9/8/89 UE ... 375
Parrots, 26/55, clr litho, 1982, p/s, Tyler Graphics bstp, full mrgs, lt cr/sl mrgs & verso, L-40x37", SBY 5/14/88 ... 1,650
Set of 5: Arles/Miami, Portfolio of 5 Lithographs; 31/150, 1973, Shorewood Atelier bstp, S-25x34", lot 729, C-NY 11/1/88 ... 605
Suite: Miami-Arles; 19/30, clr litho/Rives, 1975, S-24x34", Prestige Art Ltd, C-E 5/13/88 OE ... 825
Train Wreck, PP4/5, etch/aqua, 1975, p/s, Styria bstp, full mrgs, lt sl mrgs/verso, 33x44", lot 719, SBY 2/23/89 ... 1,100

MORPER, Daniel (American, 1937-)

Force Field, 27/100, slksc/paper, 1980, p/s, full mrgs, lt stn/cr, L-30x25", lot 100, RWS 9/8/89 ... 375

MOSKOWITZ, Ira (American, 1912-)

Newburgh Ferry, litho, p/s, full mrgs, unfr, 8x12", RAB 8/9/88 UE ... 100

MOTHERWELL, Robert (American, 1915-)

A la Pintura: End Page; a/p, aqua/sftgr etch/letterpress, 1971, intl, ULAE bstp, full mrgs, 14x27", SBY 2/23/89 OE ... 1,320
African Suite, No 1; 91/150, blk & cream slksc/JB Green, 1970, p/s, lt sl, L-32x24", Marlborough, lot 92, RWS 9/8/89 ... 2,700
African Suite, No 2; 141/150, blk & cream slksc/JB Green, 1970, intl, lt sl/stn, L-32x24", Marlborough, RWS 9/8/89 OE ... 3,100
African Suite, No 7; 48/150, blk & cream slksc/JB Green, 1970, p/s, lt stn, L-32x24", Marlborough, lot 91, RWS 9/8/89 ... 1,700
Alberti Elegy, 48/100, litho/Chine applique, 1981, sgn in ink, TGL bstp, full mrgs, S-14x15", lot 745, C-NY 11/1/88 OE ... 2,420
Alphabet Series, APIII/V, blk/red/brn etch, 1986-87, p/s, full mrgs, 30x22", lot 728, SBY 2/23/89 ... 16,500
Alphabet Series, ed of 26, blk/red/brn etch & aqua, 1986-87, p/s, full mrgs, 29x22", Motherwell, lot 1172, SBY 5/13/89 ... 25,300
American, La France Variation IV; 28/68, clr litho/collage/TGL handmade, 1984, 47x32", lot 1167, SBY 5/13/89 OE ... 6,600
Art 1981 Chicago Print, 142/150, clr litho/Arches, 1981, p/s, TGL bstp, full mrgs, S-34x25", lot 744, C-NY 11/1/88 OE ... 1,210
Automatism A, 36/100, litho/BFK Rives, 1965-6, brn crayon sgn, L-28x21", Hollander Workshop, RWS 3/16/89 OE ... 8,000
Automatism B, 12/100, litho/BFK Rives, 1965-6, p/s, lt sl, S-30x21", Hollander Workshop, RWS 3/16/89 OE ... 9,000
Automatism B, 47/100, litho/BFK Rives, 1965-66, p/s, Hollander bstp, full sheet, lt cr, S-30x21", lot 522, C-NY 5/11/88 ... 1,100
Basque Suite, 69/150, blk/gr/orange scrpt, 22x17", lot 101, FAP 2/24/89 UE ... 725
Bastos, APVII/XII, clr litho/Arjomari, 1974-75, p/s, TGL bstp, lt cr, S-62x40", lot 1165, SBY 5/13/89 ... 30,800
Black Douglas Stone, HC3/8, bl/blk litho, 1970-71, p/s, ULAE bstp, full mrgs, lt stn, S-48x32", lot 734, C-NY 11/1/88 ... 3,850
Black Sounds, PPI, tan/blk litho/letterpress, 1983-84, TGL bstp, S-39x25", lot 1168, SBY 5/13/89 ... 5,500
Black Sounds, 31/60, tan/blk litho/letterpress/collage, 1983-4, p/s, Tyler Graphics bstp, S-39x25", SBY 5/14/88 ... 3,850
Black with No Way Out, El Negro; 14/98, red/blk litho, 1983, TGL bstp, full sheet, S-15x38", lot 530, C-NY 5/11/88 OE ... 4,620
Black 4, total ed of 48, etch/aqua/letterpress/JB Green, 1969, ULAE bstp, full sheet, S-26x38", lot 524, C-NY 5/11/88 UE ... 275
Blue, London Series I; 57/150, scrpt/JB Green, 1970-71, p/s, a/bstp, P-36x24", Marlborough, lot 523, C-NY 5/11/88 ... 1,650
Blue Elegy, 28/30, clr relief/litho/6-clr handmade TGL, 1987, p/s, Tyler Graphics bstp, S-40x58", SBY 5/14/88 ... 23,100
Blue 6-11, a/p, total ed of 48, etch/aqua/letterpress/JB Green, 1971, ULAE bstp, S-26x38", lot 525, C-NY 5/11/88 ... 605
Book: El Negro; 8/51, 19 clr litho/handmade TGL, 1981-83, sgn, text Rafael Alberti, boxed, 16x16", SBY 5/14/88 ... 12,650
Burning Sun, 7/25, clr litho/wht Arches Cover, 1985, p/s, TGL bstp, S-43x29", lot 1169, SBY 5/13/89 ... 6,050
Dutch Linen Suite V, 18/24, etch/aqua/gray Dutch Linen handmade, 1974, a/bstp, 29x25", Brooke Alexander, C-NY 11/1/88 ... 660
Elegy Black-Black, 21/98, clr litho/wht handmade TGL, 1982-83, p/s, Tyler Graphics bstp, S-15x38", SBY 5/14/88 OE ... 12,100
Gauloises Bleues (Raw Umber Edge), 18/38, aqua/Auvergne, 1971, p/s, ULAE bstp, S-23x16", lot 733, C-NY 11/1/88 ... 1,210
Gauloises Bleues (White), 21/40, bl aqua/Auvergne a la main, 1970, p/s, ULAE bstp, S-23x16", lot 731, C-NY 11/1/88 OE ... 1,760
Gauloises Bleues (Yellow with Black Square), 27/35, aqua/linecut/Auvergne, 1971, 12x7", lot 904, SBY 11/5/88 OE ... 1,870
Glass Garden, 18/59, blk etch/aqua/collage/handmade Hawthorne Larroque, 1979-84, 10x23", lot 1170, SBY 5/13/89 ... 3,025
Glass Garden, 26/59, blk etch/aqua/collage/Hawthorne, 1979-84, p/s, a/bstp, 10x23", Tyler Graphics, lot 912, SBY 11/5/88 ... 3,300
Glass Garden, 48/59, etch/aqua/Hawthorne of Larroque/Moriki, 1979-84, S-18x30", Tyler Graphics, lot 747, C-NY 11/1/88 ... 2,080
Glass Garden, 9/59, etch/aqua/collage/Hawthorne/Moriki colle, 1979-84, S-18x30", Tyler Graphics, lot 533, C-NY 5/11/88 ... 2,420
Harvest, with Orange Stripe; 27/55, clr litho/collage/Hawthorne, 1973, Gemini bstp, full mrgs, 30x12", SBY 2/23/89 OE ... 5,225
Harvest with Two White Stripes, 18/75, clr litho/Hawthorne, 1973, Gemini bstp, full mrgs, 30x12", lot 905, SBY 11/5/88 ... 2,200
Hermitage, 158/200, clr litho/slksc, 1975, p/s, Tyler Graphics bstp, full mrgs, lt cr, L-40x29", SBY 5/14/88 OE ... 2,750
Hermitage, 186/200, clr litho/slksc, 1975, p/s, TGL bspt, full mrgs, lt cr/ls, 40x29", lot 908, SBY 11/5/88 OE ... 3,300
Mexican Night, 66/70, blk & red etch/aqua, 1984, p/s, a/bstp, full mrgs, 18x18", lot 1171, SBY 5/13/89 OE ... 22,000
Mexican Night II, 49/70, blk/red etch/aqua, 1984, p/s, artist bstp, full mrgs, 18x18", SBY 5/14/88 OE ... 4,675
On the Wing, 12/70, clr litho/collage/Arches, 1983-84, p/s, TGL bstp, full sheet, S-47x30", lot 532, C-NY 5/11/88 ... 5,500
Pair: A La Pintura: Blue 6-11; White 14-15; etch/aqua/letterpress, 1971, inscr Trial, 26x38", ULAE, SBY 5/14/88 ... 1,320
Pair: Beige Open; Gray Open with White Paint; 72/80 & 64/79, etch/pochoir/Auvergne, 20x27", Petersburg, C-NY 11/1/88 ... 770
Pair: Blue 2; Blue 2; lt gr etch & dk gr etch, 1969, inscr Trial #151 & Trial #153, full mrgs, P-11x4", SBY 5/14/88 ... 1,210
Pair: Primal Sign V (Cooper); Primal Sign VI (Moss), 20/28 & 28/32, aqua/Arches, 1981, 33x26", Petersburg, C-NY 11/1/88 ... 1,320

Perpetual Summer, HC, ed of 26, clr etch/aqua/collage/JW, 1986, p/s, S-32x25", Tyler Graphics, lot 534, C-NY 5/11/88 ... **4,620**
Persian II, 6/70, clr etch/aqua, 1984, p/s, a/bstp, full mrgs, 20x16", Tyler Graphics, lot 913, SBY 11/5/88 ... **1,925**
Put Out All Flags, 20/50, blk/red aqua, 1979-80, p/s, full mrgs, 12x20", Am Federation of Arts, lot 542, SBY 2/25/88 OE ... **4,125**
Put Out All Flags, 46/50, red/blk aqua, 1979-80, p/s, full mrgs, Am Federation Arts, lot 911, SBY 11/5/88 ... **4,950**
Red Sea II, 51/100, red/blk aqua, 1979, p/s, a/bstp, full mrgs, lt cr, 24x20", Abrams, SBY 5/14/88 ... **4,070**
Red Sea II, 54/100, red/blk aqua, 1979, p/s, a/bstp, full mrgs, lt cr, 24x20", Abrams, lot 910, SBY 11/5/88 ... **4,400**
Red 1-3, a/p, #170, red aqua/wht chalk, 1971, p/s, ULAE bstp, full mrgs, 5x10", lot 902, SBY 11/5/88 OE ... **4,950**
Redness of Red, 24/100, clr litho/slksc, 1985, intl, TGL bstp, S-24x16", lot 914, SBY 11/5/88 OE ... **7,700**
Redness of Red, 30/100, clr litho/slksc/collage, 1985, intl, Tyler Graphics bstp, S-24x16", SBY 5/14/88 ... **5,500**
Rite of Passage II, 41/51, blk/red/wht litho on TGL handmade, 1980, p/s, TGL Graphics, 23x29", lot 1166, SBY 5/13/89 OE ... **5,500**
Running Elegy, Yellow State; 7/10, etch/aqua/Hawthorne, 1983, a/p, full mrgs, S-18x36", lot 531, C-NY 5/11/88 OE ... **4,950**
Samurai II, 27/49, blk litho/Sekishu Natural/2 joined sheets Napal, 1979-80, intl, 57x25", Tyler Graphics, SBY 5/14/88 ... **3,575**
Set of 21: A la Pintura; 38/40, clr aqua w/text on JB Green, 1968-72, a/stp, S-26x38", lot 735, C-NY 11/1/88 OE ... **41,800**
Set of 5: London Series II; ed of 150, clr scrpt/JB Green, 1970-71, a/bstp, S-28x41", Marlborough, lot 732, C-NY 11/1/88 ... **2,640**
St Michael III, 6/99, clr litho/HMP handmade, 1975-79, intl, TGL bstp, S-41x33", lot 909, SBY 11/5/88 ... **5,500**
St Michael III, 7/99, clr litho/mottled gray HMP handmade, 1975-79, intl, full sheet, S-41x32", lot 741, C-NY 11/1/88 ... **4,620**
St Michael III, 85/99, clr litho/gray handmade HMP, 1975-79, intl, TGL bstp, S-41x33", lot 1164, SBY 5/13/89 OE ... **7,150**
Stoneness of the Stone, 6/75, blk litho/Twinrocker, 1974, p/s, TGL bstp, S-42x30", Brooke Alexander, SBY 11/5/88 OE ... **7,700**
Suite: Madrid Suite; 26/100, 10 litho/Arches, 1965-66, sgn in brn crayon, Hollander bstp, S-22x30", SBY 5/13/89 ... **4,950**
Summer Light Series: Harvest, in Scotland; APXI, clr litho/collage/Arjomari, 1973, Gemini bstp, 36x18", SBY 5/13/89 OE ... **6,050**
Summer Light Series: Harvest with Blue Bottom; 37/55, litho/Hawthorne, 1973, Gemini bstp, 35x19", lot 528, C-NY 5/11/88 ... **1,870**
Summer Light Series: Harvest with Leaf; 54/54, litho/Hawthorne of Larroque, 1973, 36x18", Gemini, lot 739, C-NY 11/1/88 ... **1,540**
Summer Light Series: Harvest with Two White Stripes; litho/pochoir, 1973, Gemini bstp, S-35x18", lot 529, C-NY 5/11/88 ... **1,760**
Summer Light Series: Pauillac, #1; 46/92, clr litho/Arjomari, 1973, a/bstp, Gemini bstp, 36x24", lot 736, C-NY 11/1/88 ... **1,980**
Summer Light Series: Pauillac, #2; 3/55, litho/scrpt/pochoir/Hawthorne of Larroque, 1973, 36x19", lot 737, C-NY 11/1/88 ... **1,870**
Summer Light Series: Pauillac, #3; litho/Hawthrone of Larroque, 1973, p/s, Gemini bstp, 36x18", lot 738, C-NY 11/1/88 OE ... **1,540**
Summer Light Series: Pauillac; a/p, litho/scrpt/pochoir/collage/Hawthorne, 1973, p/s, S-36x19", lot 527, C-NY 5/11/88 ... **1,760**
Tobacco Roth-Handle, 13/45, clr litho/slksc/HMP handmade, 1974-75, TGL bstp, full mrgs, S-40x30", lot 907, SBY 11/5/88 ... **9,350**
Untitled (contemporary), APV/XV, clr aqua/sftgr etch/buff Arches, 1975, a/bstp, Brooke Alexander, lot 541, SBY 2/25/88 ... **2,750**
White 10-13, 1 of about 240 proofs, orange etch/heavy wove paper, 1972, ULAE bstp, P-4x10", lot 526, C-NY 5/11/88 UE ... **330**

MOUNT, William Sidney; after (American, 1807-1868)

Coming to the Point, by Soulange Teissier, hc litho, 1855, lt tr/stn/ls, L-19x23", Schaus, lot 91, C-NY 1/19/89 OE ... **2,860**
Farmers Nooning, by Alfred Jones, steel engr/wove paper, 1843, trm mrgs, fox/stn, L-13x16", C-NY 1/22/88 UE ... **220**
Power of Music!; by Leon Noel, clr litho/wove paper, ca 1854, trm mrgs, lt scr/ls, laid down, L-15x19", C-NY 1/19/89 ... **715**

MUCHA, Alphonse (Czechoslovakian, 1860-1939)

Book: Ilsee Princesse de Tripoli; by Robert de Flers, Czech ed of 200, 1901, Koci, 12x9" overall, lot 361, SBY 6/8/88 ... **1,320**
Book: Le Pater; 131/510, 30 litho & monochrome heliograph/Japan, 1899, ea pl: 16x12", Champenois/Piazza, C-E 6/16/88 ... **2,640**
Clio, Illustrations de Mucha; lt tr, 8x5", lot 248, FAP 2/24/89 UE ... **20**
Cycles Perfecta, clr litho/poster paper, linen backed, unfr, 59x42", Champenois, lot 309, FAP 2/24/89 ... **6,300**
Exposition Universelle & Internationale de St Louis, litho, 1903, linen backed, unfr, 41x30", lot 298, FAP 2/24/89 ... **3,200**
Figures Decoratives, No 24; litho, 15x8", lot 1158, LH 10/16/88 ... **225**

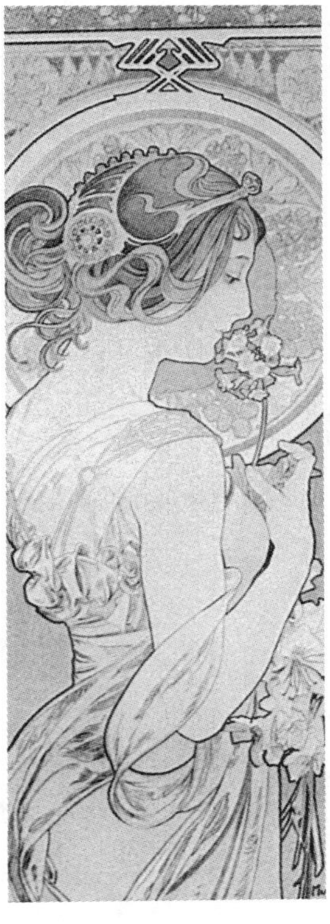

Girl with Primulas, clr litho/cream wove paper, 1899, sgn in stone, tp to mat on verso, 30x12", lot 2882, B/B 2/16/88 OE; $1,760

Gismonda, clr litho/2 joined sheets, 1894, lt stn/fox/tr/ls, S-86x29", Lemercier, lot 291, SBY 3/10/89 OE 5,775
Gismonda, litho, 1894, sgn in block, 85x29", C-NY 6/11/88 3,850
Hamlet, clr litho/2 joined sheets, 1899, lt tr/cr/sl, linen backed, S-82x30", Champenois, lot 292, SBY 3/10/89 OE 11,000
Iris, clr litho, 1897, sgn in stone, laid down/lt stn/scr, 40x17", RWS 6/17/89 1,000
Job, clr litho, lt cr, 20x15", Champenois, lot 310, FAP 2/24/89 OE 6,500
Job, clr litho, 1896, lt cr, 20x15", Champenois, lot 288, SBY 3/10/89 5,500
Job, clr litho, 1896, sgn in stone, 23x18", lot 151, C-NY 6/11/88 1,980
Job, clr litho, 1898, with mrgs, 55x36", Champenois, 55x36", lot 160, SBY 3/19/88 5,500
Job, clr litho, 1986, sgn in block, fr, 64x44", C-E 9/16/88 1,870
La Trappistine, clr litho/2 joined sheets, 1897, lt stn/sl/tr, S-81x31", Champenois, lot 290, SBY 3/10/89 6,600
Le Pater, ed of 510, litho, 1899, lt tr, 14x17", lot 84, WG 10/19/88 325
Lefevre Utile-Flirt; clr litho, 1900, pl/s, 24x10", Champenois, lot 192, C-E 6/16/88 1,980
Lefevre Utile-Flirt; clr litho, 1900, pl/s, 24x11", Champenois, lot 381, C-E 3/24/88 1,980
Lefevre Utile-Sarah Bernhardt, clr litho, 1904, p/s, 28x20", Champenois, C-E 3/24/88 3,850
Les Fruits, clr litho, pl/s, 22x14", C-E 3/24/88 OE 825
Leslie Carter, clr litho backed on linen, 1908, pl/s, 81x30", C-E 6/16/88 5,720
Leslie Carter, litho/2 joined sheets, 1908, lg mrgs, lt cr, linen backed, 83x31", Strobridge, lot 362, SBY 6/8/88 OE 6,050
Lorenzaccio, clr litho, 1896, pl/s, 41x15", lot 425, C-E 9/20/89 1,320
Lorenzaccio, clr litho backed on linen, 1896, pl/s, 41x15", C-E 6/16/88 1,760
Lorenzaccio, clr litho/2 joined sheets, 1896, lt trm/rpr, linen backed, S-79x28", Champenois, lot 289, SBY 3/10/89 OE 5,775
Moet et Chandon Champagne White Star, clr litho, 1899, 23x8", Champenois, lot 293, SBY 3/10/89 OE 3,300
Pair: La Primevere et la Plume; clr litho, 1899, trm/tr/rpr, linen backed, 19x9", Champenois, lot 294, SBY 3/10/89 OE 4,950
Repos de la Nuit, clr litho/cream wove paper, sgn in stone, lt scr, 40x15", lot 2882, B/B 4/19/88 OE 2,750
Reverie, clr litho, ca 1989, pl/s, cr, 28x22", C-E 6/19/88 1,045
Salome, litho/poster paper, lt cr, 16x13", lot 289, FAP 2/24/89 UE 350
Salome, litho/poster paper, unfr, 13x9", lot 281, FAP 2/24/89 UE 80
Sarah Bernhardt, American Tour; clr litho, 1895, pl/s, 78x30", lot 428, C-E 9/20/89 4,400
Sarah Bernhardt, American Tour; clr litho backed on linen, 1895, pl/s, 78x30", C-E 6/16/88 6,600
Vient de Paraitre, litho/poster paper, lt cr/tr, linen backed, 30x18", lot 306, FAP 2/24/89 600
Vin des Incas, litho/2 sheets poster paper, laid on paper, linen backed, 33x81", Champenois, lot 301, FAP 2/24/89 OE 7,500

MUELLER, Edward; after

USS Constitution Towing the HBM Ship Cyane Captured Feb 28th, 1815; litho, ca 1915, L-20x32", lot 92, C-NY 1/19/89 660

MUELLER, Hans A. (American, 1888-1962)

Don Quixote, total ed of 260, clr wc/Basingwerk, 1950, p/s, 13x10", Cleveland Print Club, WG 10/19/88 OE 125

MUELLER, Otto (German, 1874-1930)

Affindung des Moses, a/p, blk & gr-yel litho/buff-gray wove paper, ca 1920, p/s, lt stn, S-17x21", lot 119, C-NY 11/1/88 13,200
Am Ufer Sitzendes Madchen (Sitzendes Madchen in Landschaft), litho/Japan, 1922-26, S-23x18", lot 116, C-NY 11/1/88 60,500
Badendes und am Ufer Sitzendes Madchen (I), hc litho/firm tan wove paper, ca 1912, S-14x20", lot 113, C-NY 11/1/88 OE 16,500
Der Mord 3, #31, hc litho/crisp buff wove paper, 1919, p/s, lt cr/stn, S-20x15", lot 115, C-NY 11/1/88 7,150
Drei Madchen vor dem Spiegel, 28/50, litho/soft Japan, ca 1922, p/s, inscr Eig, cr/fox, S-19x14", lot 117, C-NY 11/1/88 6,050
Knabe Zwischen Blattpflanzen (Knabe im Schilf), 2nd state, wc, 1912, sgn/dtd 1920, S-15x19", lot 112, C-NY 11/1/88 OE 3,520
Selbstbildnis Nach Rechts, a/p, before #d ed of 30, litho, 1921-22, p/s, S-22x18", Neumann, lot 118, C-NY 11/1/88 7,700
Zigeuner Liebespaar 2, a/p, aside from #d ed of 30, litho/tissue thin Japan, 1921-22, S-20x15", lot 111, C-NY 11/1/88 OE 15,400
Zwei Madchen mit Gegabeltem Baum, litho/buff wove paper, 1914-18, p/s, lt cr/stn, S-15x21", lot 114, C-NY 11/1/88 OE 10,450

MULLER, Jan (German, 16th/17th C)

Mercury Leads a Young Man (G Spranger) to Minerva, 1st state, engr, trm, lt sl/fox, 10x7", lot 77, SBY 5/11/89 OE 9,350
Painting, Sculpture, & Architecture, Banned by the Turks, Withdrawn to Olympus; engr, 1597, 27x20", SBY 5/11/89 OE 3,190

MUNAKATA, Shiko (Japanese, 1903-1975)

Akasaka, shaded blk wc/cream Japan on sturdy Japan, ca 1958, p/s, red chop mk, sl/ink, unfr, L-17x12", SBY 5/12/88 4,675
Dragonfly, wc/Japan mounted as hanging scroll, 1957, p/s, artist's chop mk, 13x10", lot 673, SBY 5/11/89 9,900
Fish & Flower & Female Buddha, ed of 260, wc, 1957, p/s, artist's red seal, 13x9", Cleveland Print Club, SBY 2/25/88 3,410
Fish & Flower & Female Buddha, total ed of 260, wc/Japan, 1957, p/s, Cleveland Print Club bstp, L-13x9", C-NY 5/11/88 OE 4,620
Fish & Flower & Female Buddha, 1/260, wc/laid Kozo, 1959, sgn, full mrgs, 13x9", Cleveland Print Club, SBY 2/23/89 6,600
Fish & Flower & Female Buddha (Sakana, Hana to Butsujo), total ed of 260, wc/Japan, 1959, 13x9", lot 381, SBY 2/23/89 6,600
Fish & Flower & Female Buddha (Sakana, Hana to Butsujo), wc/Kozo, 1959, 12x9", Cleveland Print Club, SBY 5/11/89 OE 11,550
Fugen, ed of unknown size, hc wc/Japan, 1958, p/s, artist's seal, glue at edges, L-26x16", lot 247, C-NY 5/11/88 OE 26,400
Fukuroe, shaded blk wc/cream Japan mounted on sturdy Japan, 1958, p/s, red chop mk, lt sl/cr, L-12x17", SBY 5/12/88 3,300
Gautama & Bodhisattvas, ed of 10, wc/Kozo, 1958, p/s, artist's mk, unfr, L-9x13", Cleveland Print Club, SBU 5/12/88 OE 6,050
Gautama & Bodhisattvas, ed of 260, wc, 1958, p/s, artist's red mk, 9x13", Cleveland Print Club, lot 304, SBY 2/25/89 4,125
Gautama & Bodhisattvas, total ed of 260, wc/Japan, 1960, p/s, L-9x13", Clevland Print Club, lot 249, C-NY 5/11/88 OE 5,500
Gautama & Bodhisattvas (Gotama to Bosatsu), ed of 10, wc/Kozo, 1958, 9x13", Cleveland Print Club, lot 675, SBY 5/11/89 11,550
Gautama & Bodhisattvas (Gotama to Bosatsu), total ed of 260, wc/laid Japan, 1958, p/s, 9x13", lot 383, SBY 11/3/88 OE 6,875
Gautama & Bodhisattvas (Gotama to Bosatsu), total ed of 260, wc/laid Japan, 1958, sgn, lt stn/rpl, 9x13", SBY 2/23/89 6,655
Hamamatsu, wc/Japan, ca 1958, p/s, artist's mk, titled, cr/sl, mounted on sturdy Japan, 12x17", lot 386, SBY 2/23/89 OE 3,300
Hawk Woman, wc/Japan mounted as hanging scroll, 1957, p/s, artist's chop mk, lt fox, 16x12", lot 674, SBY 5/11/89 OE 11,000
Kooyo, shaded blk wc/cream Japan mounted on sturdy Japan, 1958, p/s, red mk, lt ink/cr, unfr, L-12x17", SBY 5/12/88 OE 5,225
Landscape with Fuji, ed of unknown size, hc wc/Japan, ca 1953, p/s, tp to overmat, S-17x14", lot 245, C-NY 5/11/88 OE 4,400
Maruko, wc/cream Japan, ca 1958, p/s, artist's red chop mk, titled, lt sl, 17x12", lot 387, SBY 2/23/89 UE 1,650
Mitsuke, wc/Japan, ca 1958, p/s, titled, lt sl/cr, mounted on sturdy Japan, 17x12", lot 385, SBY 2/23/89 1,650
Monju, hc wc/Japan, 1958, p/s, artist's red seal, glue at edges, L-26x16", lot 248, C-NY 5/11/88 OE 28,600
Pair: North Window; Nude Thinking of Springtime; wc/thin Japan, 1959, p/s, full mrgs, 6x8", lot 677, SBY 5/11/89 7,700

Pair: Two Kanjii Characters; wc/thin soft Japan, 1960, sgn in red crayon, 8x8", lot 679, SBY 5/11/89 ... 1,980
Shokeisho Series: Kaminari-No-Mon; wc/thin Japan, ca 1945, lt stn/ls/cr, S-15x20", lot 381, SBY 11/3/88 OE ... 23,100
Totsauka, shaded blk wc/cream Japan mounted on sturdy Japan, ca 1958, p/s, red chop mk, L-12x17", SBY 5/12/88 ... 4,675

MUNCH, Edvard (Norwegian, 1863-1944)
Bildnis Helge Rode, blk/beige litho on stiff cream cardboard, 1908-09, full mrgs, lt cr/tr, 13x8", lot 388, SBY 2/23/89 ... 1,650
Buchenwald Wiesbaden, ed of ca 30, transfer litho, ca 1920, Schutzmarke Schoellers-Hammer stp, L-19x15", RWS 3/16/89 ... 1,900
Das Kranke Madchen, #7, 2nd state of 3, litho/firm fibrous Japan, 1896, stp/s, lt stn, L-17x23", lot 250, C-NY 5/11/88 ... 99,000
Das Kranke Madchen, #97, clr litho litho/stiff Japan, 1896, p/s, lt trm/cr, 17x23", lot 680, SBY 5/11/89 OE ... 25,300
Der Kuss, blk/gray wc, 1897-1902, p/s, inscr Eget Tryk, lt scr/ls/cr/rpr tr, tp on verso, 23x22", lot 251, C-NY 5/11/88 ... 27,500
Der Tag Danach, aqua/drypt, 1895, p/s, lt scr, stn verso, P-8x12", C-NY 11/1/88 ... 15,400
Die Blume der Liebe, litho/laid Japan, 1896, p/s, lt stn mrgs, old glue, L-25x12", lot 719, C-NY 5/10/89 ... 8,800
Figures at the Shore, clr litho, 1898, titled/dtd, L-6x7", lot 1025, S/A 2/18/89 ... 650
Head of a Fisherman, etch/cream wove paper, lt cr, 5x3", lot 2881, B/B 4/19/88 OE ... 440
Oswald (Gespenster), litho/firm buff wove paper, 1920, p/s, lt cr/stn, S-20x26", lot 121, C-NY 11/1/88 OE ... 6,600
Portrat (Derr Dr A), 2nd/final state, drypt/wove paper, 1895, p/s, stn, tp overmat on verso, unfr, L-10x7", C-NY 1/22/88 ... 1,320
Portrat Strindberg, 1st state, litho/smooth cream wove paper, 1896, p/s, lt fox/scr, 25x17", Clot, lot 120, C-NY 11/1/88 ... 8,250
Portrat Strindberg, 1st state, litho/smooth cream wove paper, 1986, lt scr/fox, L-20x15", lot 720, C-NY 5/10/89 ... 6,050
Wascherinnen am Strand, brn-blk etch/aqua/ivory wove paper, 1903, p/s, lt cr, P-4x6", Felsing, lot 426, C-NY 11/1/88 ... 2,750

MUNDORFF, V. (German, 20th C)
Horch, litho/poster paper, lt tr corners, 28x40", Brandstetter, lot 229, FAP 2/24/89 OE ... 775

MURPHY, Katherine
Houses in Woodside, 64/75, litho/wove paper, p/s, titled, S-19x21", lot 237, C-NY 1/19/89 ... 330

MURRAY, Elizabeth (American, 1940-)
Mostly Mozart Festival, APXII/XIX, clr slksc/wove paper, 1979, 30x30", Lincoln Center/List Art Posters, SBY 2/23/89 OE ... 1,320
Mostly Mozart Festival, 111/144, scrpt, 1979, p/s, full mrgs, Lincoln Center/List Art Posters, lot 748, C-NY 11/1/88 ... 550
Untitled (Black Cup), 8/10, hc litho/Arches, 1984, p/s, full sheet, S-59x36", Cooper/Alexander, lot 535, C-NY 5/11/88 ... 2,860

MYERS, Jerome (American, 1867-1940)
On Ninth Avenue, a/p, etch/drypt/wove paper, ca 1930s, p/s, lt stn/ls, P-7x9", lot 26, C-NY 6/17/89 OE ... 440
Top Gallery, etch, p/s, titled, 6x7", lot 359, WG 10/19/88 ... 100

NAKAYAMA, T. (Japanese, 20th C)
Animal, wc, 27x23", lot 1098, LH 10/16/88 OE ... 350
Sun Child, wc, 22x15", lot 1097, LH 10/16/88 ... 180

NAKIAN, Reuben (American, 1897-)
Nymph & Goat, 12/62, drypt/Chine colle/Richard de Bas, ca 1979, P-14x17", lot 143, SWN 12/1/88 ... 495

NASH, Willard Ayer (American, 1898-1943)
Street Scene, ed of 6, litho/cream wove paper, 1932, p/s, lt sl/cr, 8x13", lot 2966, B/B 2/16/88 ... 220

NAUMAN, Bruce (American, 1941-)
M Ampere, 40/88, dk brn/tan litho, 1973, p/s, full mrgs, lt cr, L-30x44", lot 536, C-NY 5/11/88 OE ... 825

NEAL, Reginald (American, 1909-)
Gold Train, litho, p/s, 9x13", lot 295, WG 10/19/88 ... 55

NEEL, Alice (American, 1901-)
Victoria & Cat, 26/100, clr slksc/litho, 1981, p/s, Maurel Studio bstp, full mrgs, 40x26", lot 730, SBY 2/23/89 ... 1,210

NEIMAN, Leroy (American, 1926-)
Nantucket Sailing, 199/300, slksc, 1980, p/s, 19x24", Knoedler, lot 2101, DM 2/19/88 ... 1,300
Power Serve, 103/300, clr litho, 33x24", lot 308, MG 3/26/88 ... 700

NESBIT, Jackson Lee (American, 1913-)
Charging Hot Metal, Sheffield Steet Corporation; etch, p/s, titled, 12x9", lot 281, WG 10/19/88 ... 225
Soaking Pits, Sheffield Steel Conjugation; etch, p/s, titled, 10x14", lot 280, WG 10/19/88 ... 275

NESBITT, Lowell (American, 1933-)
Grapes, 5/175, clr litho/cream wove paper, 1977, p/s, dtd, 19x28", lot 3047, B/B 4/19/88 ... 258
Iris, 143/200, ed of 200, clr slksc/ wove paper, 1978, p/s, dtd, S-38x30", RWS 3/16/89 ... 400
National Air & Space Museum, a/p, litho/poster paper, 1976, p/s, 40x30", lot 102, FAP 2/24/89 UE ... 100

NEVELSON, Louise (American, 1900-)
Dancing Figure, 1/10, etch/drypt/laid paper, ca 1953-55, lt cr/tr/stn, P-21x14", lot 749, C-NY 11/1/88 ... 1,100
Dawnscape, 69/75, wht cast paper relief, 1975, p/s, full sheet, S-27x31", Pace, lot 754, C-NY 11/1/88 ... 4,180
East Landscape, 3/20, etch/BFK Rives, p/s, full mrgs, lt stn, P-14x21", lot 125, PHL 10/28/88 OE ... 1,200
Essences #5, 10/30, etch/Arches, 1977, p/s, full mrgs, S-42x29", Pace, lot 755, C-NY 11/1/88 UE ... 550
Figure, 1/20, etch/laid paper, 1952, p/s, inscr To Hjordis, lt stn, tp on verso, P-14x8", lot 537, C-NY 5/11/88 OE ... 880
Great Wall, 73/150, ingl collage, 1970, p/s, titled, full mrgs, orig aluminum fr, 24x18", Pace, lot 1176, SBY 5/13/89 OE ... 4,950
Moon Garden, 51/75, blk cast paper relief, 1976, p/s, S-33x22", Pace, lot 917, SBY 11/5/88 ... 3,850
Portfolio: Facade; 101/125, 12 slksc, 1966, orig wrappers, Abrams/Pace, lot 543, SBY 2/25/89 ... 3,300
Portfolio: Facade; 59/150, 12 clr slksc/collage, 1966, p/s, orig wrappers, Abrams/Pace, lot 1174, SBY 5/13/89 ... 3,850
Six-Pointed Star, 55/90, dk gr/wht cast paper relief, 1980, p/s, S-41x35", Pace, lot 918, SBY 11/5/88 ... 4,400
Six-Pointed Star, 72/90, dk gr/wht cast paper, 1980, p/s, S-40x34", lot 733, SBY 2/23/89 ... 3,575
Vertical Cloud II, 10/20, sftgr etch/collage/wove paper, 1977, p/s, S-30x22", lot 756, C-NY 11/1/88 UE ... 550

NEWMAN, Barnett (American, 1905-1970)
Etching No 1, a/p, etch/aqua/handmade British, 1969, p/s, dtd 1968, ULAE bstp, full mrgs, 15x24", SBY 5/14/88 OE ... 19,800
Moment, a/p, ed of 125, bl scrpt/masonite/plexiglas mounted on stretcher, 1966, 49x5", Multiples, lot 757, C-NY 11/1/88 ... 1,650
Moment, Four on Plexi; 12/125, bl scrpt/masonite/plexiglas/wooden stretcher, 1966, 49x5, lot 542, C-NY 5/11/88 OE ... 1,320
Portfolio: Eighteen Cantos; 4/18, 18 clr litho, 1963-64, p/s, full mrgs, boxed, ULAE, lot 1179, SBY 5/13/89 OE ... 407,000

NEWMAN, John (Canadian, 1933-)
Foldout, 30/60, etch/aqua/litho, 1985, p/s, full sheet, S-40x30", Vermilion, lot 758, C-NY 11/1/88 .... **990**
NICHOLS, Dale William (American, 1904-)
Pair: Grain Elevator; Partners; litho, p/s, L-10x12"/L-10x13", lot 26, PHL 6/16/88 .... **250**
NICHOLSON, Ben (British, 1894-1982)
Complicated Form, 36/50, etch/wove paper, 1967, p/s, full sheet, P-11x5", lot 544, C-NY 5/11/88 .... **1,320**
Large Jug, Small Mug; 7/100, etch, 1967, p/s, full mrgs, lt cr/stn, P-11x10", Marlborough, lot 543, C-NY 5/11/88 OE **1,045**
Single Turkish Form, 8/25, etch/wove paper, 1967, p/s, full sheet, P-12x14", lot 547, C-NY 5/11/88 .... **825**
Three Goblets, etch/wove paper, 1967, p/s, inscr Artist copy 2 on verso, full sheet, P-8x6", lot 545, C-NY 5/11/88 .... **1,430**
Turkish Form, 21/50, etch/wove paper, 1967, p/s, full sheet, lt cr, P-11x5", Waddington, lot 546, C-NY 5/11/88 .... **1,430**
NICOLL, James Craig (American, 1846-1918)
Harbor View, engr, 1885, p/s, P-11x16", lot 48, FAP 2/24/89 UE **40**
NOBLE, John A. (American, 1874-1935)
Floating Grain Elevators of New York, litho, p/s, lt fox, L-12x16", lot 28, PHL 10/28/88 .... **275**
NOLAND, Kenneth (American, 1924-)
Montes Coloreados, clr monotype/handmade paper, 1985, sgn on verso, S-38x59", lot 919, SBY 11/5/88 OE **8,250**
Montes Coloreados, hc monotype/thick fibrous handmade paper, 1985, p/s, a/bstp, S-38x60", lot 759, C-NY 11/1/88 .... **8,800**
NOLDE, Emil (German, 1867-1956)
Agypterin II, 2nd state, wc/firm wove paper, 1910, p/s, wide mrgs, lt cr, S-16x13", lot 128, C-NY 11/1/88 OE **9,900**
Burg, between Schiefler/Mosel's 4th & 5th states, wc/buff laid paper, 1906, S-15x10", lot 124, C-NY 11/1/88 OE **3,520**
Der Maler (Selbstbildnis), #6, 4th state, etch/wove paper, 1905-06, full mrgs, P-7x5", Felsing, lot 429, C-NY 11/1/88 OE **3,850**
Dusterer Mannerkopf, #10, bl-blk & crimson litho/crisp wove paper, 1907-15, p/s, S-24x17", lot 122, C-NY 11/1/88 .... **44,000**
EN (Selbstportrat), 2nd state, bl-gr etch/aqua/firm wove paper, 1908, p/s, S-22x17", lot 126, C-NY 11/1/88 OE **15,400**
Gefangene, 3rd state, wc/gray wove paper, 1906, p/s, full mrgs, 7x5", lot 385, SBY 11/3/88 .... **2,750**
Gerte, #II1, 2nd state, wc/wove paper, 1917, p/s, lt cr, S-15x12", lot 129, C-NY 11/1/88 .... **6,050**
Junge Madchen, ed of 100, deep bl litho/smooth wove paper, 1907, p/s, lt cr/fox, S-25x21", lot 125, C-NY 11/1/88 .... **6,600**
Junger Furst und Tanzerinnen, 1st state, etch/aqua/van Gelder laid paper, 1918, p/s, S-23x18", lot 130, C-NY 11/1/88 .... **7,150**
Junger Furst und Tanzerinnen, 2nd state, etch/aqua/wht wove paper, 1918, full mrgs, lt sl, 10x9", lot 386, SBY 11/3/88 .... **7,700**
Muhle am Wasser, rust/grays/blk litho on buff wove, inscr In dieser Fassung ein Druck, unfr, S-26x32", SBY 5/12/88 OE **121,000**
Russin, 3/20, dk bl/mustard/red litho on cream Japan, 1913, full mrgs, lt cr, S-28x23", lot 681, SBY 5/11/89 .... **46,200**
Salomo und Seine Frauen, 2nd state, etch/aqua/JW Zanders laid paper, 1911, p/s, S-25x19", lot 127, C-NY 11/1/88 OE **14,300**
Seltsame Wesen, 3rd state, etch/aqua/firm wove paper, 1922, p/s, wide mrgs, lt fld/sl, S-26x20", lot 131, C-NY 11/1/88 .... **6,050**
NORDELL, Carl J. (American, 1885-)
Pair: Passing Storm; Mt Chocorus; etch, p/s, titled, various sizes, lot 117, C-NY 1/19/88 UE **20**
NORFELDT, Bror Julius Olsson (American, 1987-1955)
Old Archway, Paris; etch/drypt, ca 1908, p/s, lt cr, 13x11", lot 145, SWN 12/1/88 .... **195**
NORMAN, Irving (American, 20th C)
From Work, a/p, litho/Arches, p/s, 19x25", Ed Press, lot 2967, B/B 2/16/88 .... **110**
NORTHOUSE, George (19th C)
To the Gentry, Farmers, Graziers, Dealers; Tradesmen...of Lincolnshire; litho, 19th C, L-17x24", lot 93, C-NY 1/19/89 .... **440**
OGE, Eugene (French, 19th C)
Velodrome de l'Est, clr litho, 1886, 32x47", lot 70, WG 10/19/88 .... **400**
OLDENBURG, Claes (Swedish, 1929-)
Alphabet in the Form of a Good Humor Bar, 150/250, clr offset litho, 1970, intl, lt stn, L-22x10", lot 115, PHL 6/16/88 .... **500**
Coffee Cup, 2/50, clr litho, 1973, p/s, 12x15", lot 855, LH 10/16/88 OE **400**
Dance Costume in the Form of a Fag End with a Fallen Dancer, 15/50, clr litho, 1971, 9x7", lot 738, SBY 2/23/89 .... **770**
Double-Nose/Purse/Punching Bag/Ashtray; 19/50, litho, 1970, intl, Gemini bstp, full mrgs, 14x13", lot 737, SBY 2/23/89 .... **440**
Oberlin Project, 45/60, clr etch, 1979, p/s, Aeropress bstp, full mrgs, 23x29", lot 547, SBY 2/25/88 OE **1,320**
Orpheum Sign, 37/60, aqua, 1962, p/s, full mrgs, lt scr, 6x4", Galleria Schwarz, lot 922, SBY 11/5/88 .... **1,430**
Orpheum Sign, 37/60, total ed of 100, aqua, 1962, p/s, full mrgs, L-6x4", Galleria Schwarz, SBY 5/14/88 OE **1,650**
Pair: Alphabet in the Form of a Good Humor Bar; Typewriter Eraser; offset litho, 1970, 21x10"/19x18", SBY 2/23/89 OE **4,675**
Pair: Hats, Bones, Q's, Etc; Hats, Bones, Q's, Etc.; brn or orange aqua, 1976, 18x15", Petersburg, lot 760, C-NY 11/1/88 .... **550**
Portfolio: Notes in Hand; 60/100, 1972, intl, S-10x8", Professional Prints/Petersburg, lot 923, SBY 11/5/88 OE **6,050**
Portfolio: Notes; 47/100, 12 clr litho w/text, 1968, full mrgs, orig wrappers, S-23x16", Gemini, lot 734, SBY 2/23/89 OE **9,900**
Profile Airflow, 32/75, molded polyurethane relief over 2-clr litho, 1969, p/s, orig fr, Gemini, lot 921, SBY 11/5/88 OE **37,400**
Proposed Colossal Monument for Battersea Park, 84/300, offset litho, 1966, p/s, S-24x35", lot 549, C-NY 5/11/88 OE **825**
Screw Arch Bridge, State II; APIII/XII, aqua/etch, 1980-1, p/s, Multiples bstp, full mrgs, 24x51", SBY 5/14/88 OE **29,700**
Screw Arch Bridge, State III; 12/35, etch/aqua/1980, p/s, Aeropress bstp, S-31x58", Multiples, lot 763, C-NY 11/1/88 .... **27,500**
Soft Drum Set, 41/68, litho/Angoumois a la Main, 1972, intl, Gemini bstps, full sheet, 29x40", lot 552, C-NY 5/11/88 .... **550**
Soft Screw in Waterfall, 15/35, litho, 1976, p/s, a/bstp, Gemini bstp, S-67x45", lot 761, C-NY 11/1/88 .... **1,650**
Store, 2/6, blk/hc litho, 1961, p/s, dtd Oct 1961, full mrgs, lt sl/cr, S-20x26", lot 920, SBY 11/5/88 OE **19,800**
Study for Tongue Cloud, 40/60, clr aqua/etch, 1976, p/s, full mrgs, 10x8", Petersburg, SBY 5/14/88 UE **550**
Tongue Cloud Over London, With Thames Ball; a/p, sftgr etch/aqua, 1976, full mrgs, 32x21", Petersburg, SBY 2/23/89 OE **2,530**
OLDENBURG, Claes; after (Swedish, 1929-)
Proposed Colossal Monument for Battersea Park, London, Drum Set, 1966; 243/300, S-24x35", lot 103, RWS 9/8/89 .... **425**
ORAZI, Manuel
Thais, clr litho, 1894, pl/s, 42x15", C-E 6/16/88 UE **55**
OROZCO, Jose Clemente (Mexican, 1883-1949)
Brothel, 112/130, litho/cream wove paper, p/s, 12x15", lot 2968, B/B 2/16/88 .... **467**
Brothel, 14/120, litho/thick wove paper, 1935, p/s, full mrgs, lt stn/sl, 12x16", lot 46, SBY 11/3/88 .... **990**
Las Turistas, litho/tissue-thin wove paper, ca 1928, p/s, inscr Trial Proof, lt cr/sl, L-12x17", C-NY 5/11/88 .... **385**

Mexican Peasants Working, 1928; 4/100, blk litho, sgn, 13x18", lot 1338, WL 2/26/88 OE 1,000
Mexican Soldiers, ed of 100, litho, 1928, p/s, full mrgs, lt rub/stn, 11x18", lot 256, SBY 5/11/89 3,300
Pair: Franciscan & the Indian; Hanged Men; ed of 100, litho, 1926 & 1933, p/s, 9x11"/13x9", lot 252, SBY 5/11/89 OE 3,410
Pair: Head of a Woman; Demented; ed of 100, litho & aqua, 1926 & 1944, fox/stn, 14x10"/11x7", lot 254, SBY 5/11/89 OE 3,520
Pair: Masses; Tourists; ed of 100, litho, 1935 & 1928, p/s, lt stn/fox, 13x17"/12x17", lot 259, SBY 5/11/89 OE 3,300
Pair: Mexican Peasants Working; Contortionists (II); litho & aqua, 1928 & 1944, p/s, 12x17"/12x18", lot 257, SBY 5/11/89 1,980
Pair: Soldier's Wife; Unemployed, Paris, 1932; ed of 100, litho, 1926 & 1932, p/s, 16x10"/14x11", lot 253, SBY 5/11/89 2,860
Rear Guard, ed of 100, litho, 1929, p/s, full mrgs, lt cr/stn, 14x19", lot 45, SBY 11/3/88 OE 7,425
Requiem, ed of 100, litho, 1928, p/s, full mrgs, lt stn/sl, 12x16", lot 255, SBY 5/11/89 5,500
Unemployed (Descocupado), 8/100, litho/cream wove paper, 1932, p/s, lt stn, L-14x10", Delphic, lot 238, C-NY 1/19/89 OE 660
Zapatistas, 4/120, litho/wove paper, 1936, p/s, full mrgs, lt stn/cr/skinned, 13x17", lot 50, SBY 2/23/89 OE 2,310

ORR, Alfred Everitt (American, 1886-)
For Home & Country, clr litho/poster paper, 1918, laid down, 40x30", lot 176, FA)P 2/24/89 OE 178

OVERALL, Charles (19th C)
View of St Louis From Lucas Place, litho, 1854, unfr, 19x29", SLK 5/6/88 200

PAILLOU, Peter; after (British, 1768-1805)
Common Pigeon, clr engr, 18x13", lot 130, FAP 2/24/89 UE 50

PALADINO, Mimmo (Italian, 1948-)
Muto, 27/35, etch/sugar-lift/aqua/collage, 1985, p/s, full mrgs, S-62x35", Schellmann, lot 925, SBY 11/5/88 OE 3,025
Set of 3: Camera de gli Sposi; Intermezzo; Chiaro di Luna; 30/40, 1985, p/s, full mrgs, P-10x13", lot 556, C-NY 5/11/88 1,870
Set of 4: Tra il Vento Fuoco; Guardar Misteri; Stelle Sulla Schena; Caverne Minacciose; lot 924, SBY 11/5/88 4,125
Set of 4: Tra Il Vento Fuoco; Guardar Misteri; Stelle Sulla Schena; Caverne Minacciose; 1982, Multiples, SBY 2/25/88 2,750
Set: Tra il Vento Fuoco; Guardar Misteri; Stelle Sulla Schena; Caverne Minacciose; 34/35, 1982, 31x23", SBY 5/14/88 OE 4,125
Tra Gli Ulivi, 22/35, etch/drypt/aqua/sugar-lift, 1984, p/s, full mrgs, S-52x38", lot 1181, SBY 5/13/89 OE 4,400
Tra Gli Ulivi, 34/35, etch/drypt/aqua/sugar-lift/Chine applique, 1984, Schellmann bstp, S-53x39", lot 555, C-NY 5/11/88 2,750

PALMER, Samuel (American, 19th C)
Early Ploughman; or, Morning Spread Upon the Mountains; state 8, etch/Hallines, 1861, 5x8", lot 192, RWS 6/15/89 UE 300

PARKER, Mary (American, 20th C)
School Days, litho, p/s, lt tr, 11x15", lot 290, WG 10/19/88 25

PARMIGIANINO, after (Italian, 16th/17th C)
Vision of St Jerome, by Giulio Bonasone, engr/wm crossbow in circle, lt cr/sl, 14x10", lot 586, SBY 2/25/88 1,540

PARRISH, Clara Weaver (American, -1925)
The (?) Makers (figures in street scene), etch, sgn twice/titled, fox/wstn, L-6x4", RAB 3/27/89 40

PARRISH, Maxfield (American, 1870-1966)
Century, August; clr litho, ca 1897, pl/s, linen backed, 20x14", lot 430, C-E 9/20/89 3,300
Evening, copyright mk, lt fld corner, Reinthal/Newman NY, RAB 4/25/89 90

PARRISH, Stephen (American, 1846-1938)
Fisherman's House, Cape Ann; etch, 1849, p/s, faded, 12x19", lot 47, WG 10/19/89 OE 250
Harbor Scene, etch, p/s, 18x12", lot 48, WG 10/19/88 375

PARSONS, Charles; after (American, 1821-1910)
Rail Road Suspension Bridge, 1856; hc litho, 1856, lt stn/fox, L-10x16", Currier & Ives, lot 53, RWS 10/27/89 475

PARTRIDGE, Roi (American, 1888-)
White Butterfly, etch, 1913, p/s, 18x10", lot 105, WG 10/19/89 OE 400

PASCIN, Jules (American, 1885-1930)
Pair: Prostitute; Two Prostitutes Relaxing; 10/25, litho/laid paper, ca 1925, pl/s, 12x9", lot 193, SWN 6/15/89 385

PATTERSON, Margaret Jordan (American, 1867-1950)
Belgium: House & Tall Trees; clr wc/wove paper, ca 1920, sgn on undermat, support sheet, unfr, S-9x6", C-NY 1/22/88 UE 385
Coast Cedars, Winter; clr woodblock, sgn, trm mrgs, laid down on board, 7x10", RWS 4/22/89 225
Heartsease, 13/100, clr woodblock w/embossing, 1921, p/s, lt stn, tp verso, 7x10", RWS 3/16/89 OE 950
In the High Hills, 3/100, woodblock, sgn/titled, lt stn, L-11x9", RWS 4/22/89 OE 1,200

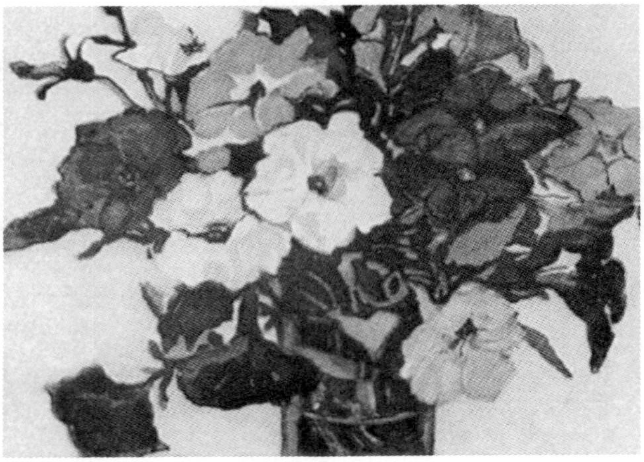

Petunias, 7/100, ed of 100, clr woodblock w/embossing, 1921, p/s, lt stn, tp verso, 7x10", RWS 3/16/89 OE; $1,000

Pair: Cathedral, Anacapri; Certosa, Capri; 30/50 & 17/50, wc/fibrous paper, ca 1923, unfr, S-11x13", C-NY 1/22/88 UE **110**
Pair: Chatham Beach; Beach at Chatham; clr wc/thick cream wove paper, lt rub, no size given, lot 239, C-NY 1/19/89 .... **770**
Pair: On the Canal; Cape Cod House; wc/stiff fibrous paper, ca 1920, p/s, unfr, C-NY 1/22/88 UE **550**
Pair: Tall Trees; On the Canal; wc/fibrous wove paper, ca 1920, trm to img, C-NY 1/22/88 UE **418**
Rugen, clr wc/fibrous wove paper, ca 1920, twice p/s, titled, ink mrgs, rub mrgs/verso, unfr, L-8x10", C-NY 1/22/88 UE **495**
Spring Flowers, clr woodblock w/embossing, 1921, p/s, 7x10", RWS 3/16/89 OE **850**
Tall Trees, ed of 50, clr woodblock, sgn/dtd 1901, L-7x10", RWS 4/22/89 OE **1,600**

AYOT, Henry (19th C)
View of San Francisco in 1860, litho, lt fox, orig fr, lg folio, RAB 11/10/88 OE **1,900**

EARLSTEIN, Philip (American, 1924-)
Nude in Rocker, 97/100, clr litho, p/s, S-23x34", Landfall, lot 126, PHL 10/28/88 .... **700**
Two Nudes, 9/20, litho/wht wove paper, p/s, lt ls/stn, S-27x39", lot 3051, B/B 4/19/88 .... **358**

ECHAUBES, Eugene (French, 1890-1967)
Group of 3: Plow Horses; Race Horses; Horses in the Field; hc litho, p/s, 19x24", lot 107, FAP 2/24/89 UE **225**

ECHSTEIN, Max Herman (German, 1881-1955)
Am Wasser, 1st state, wc/soft wove paper, 1907, p/s, titled, lt fox/cr, S-19x11", lot 133, C-NY 11/1/88 OE **5,280**
Badende I, blk/red/yel-ochre/bl/gr wc on smooth wove paper, 1911, p/s, lt tr/cr/sl, S-17x14", lot 140, C-NY 11/1/88 OE **82,500**
Frauenkopf, litho/cream stiff wove paper, 1917, p/s, inscr Probedruck, full mrgs, lt cr/fox, 12x14", SBY 2/23/89 UE **660**
Gesprach, #4, unrecorded 1st state before the signature, litho, 1908, lt ls/stn/sl, S-17x23", lot 137, C-NY 11/1/88 .... **4,620**
Italienische Bauern, III, gray-gr etch/aqua/firm wove paper, 1908, lt stn/sl, S-14x20", lot 135, C-NY 11/1/88 .... **3,300**
Italienische Landschaft, wc/tan wove paper, 1907, sgn/dtd Paris 07, lt stn, S-11x15", lot 134, C-NY 11/1/88 .... **3,520**
Mann und Dame, 13/50, wc/cream wove paper, p/s, lt trm mrgs, old tp in corners, 7x5", lot 2883, B/B 4/19/88 .... **770**
Nach dem Bad, etch/aqua, 1920, p/s, Die Schaffenden bstp, full mrgs, lt sl/rub, 10x8", lot 388, SBY 11/3/88 .... **2,090**
Pair: Araber; Malaie; wc/soft Japan, 1917, p/s, full mrgs, lt cr/fox mrgs, 10x8", lot 398, SBY 2/23/89 .... **990**
Portfolio: Reisebilder, #32, 50 litho/Japan, 1919, p/s, full mrgs, lt cr/sl, S-14x11", lot 387, SBY 11/3/88 OE **8,800**
Schlafende, #2, litho/wove paper, 1908, inscr Eigendruck, lt scr/tr/cr, S-23x17", lot 136, C-NY 11/1/88 .... **5,500**
Weiblicher Halbakt, blk & yel litho/thin smooth wove paper, 1910, p/s, wide mrgs, stn/tr/sl, S-22x16", C-NY 11/1/88 OE **13,200**
Weiblicher Profilkopf, litho/thin smooth wove paper, 1912, p/s, lt fox/tr, S-22x16", lot 141, C-NY 11/1/88 .... **5,500**

ENCK, A.R. (German, 1939-)
Set of 11: Ur End Standart; 46/90, scrpt/wove paper, 1972, full sheets, S-28x27", Jahn/Werner, lot 557, C-NY 5/11/88 .... **5,500**

ENCZ, Georg (16th C)
Virginius, engr, ca 1546-47, thread mrgs, lt fox, lt stn img, 5x3", lot 82, SBY 5/11/89 OE **1,870**

ENNELL, Joseph (American, 1860-1926)
Columbia Heights From Fulton Ferry, ed of 50, etch, 1924, p/s, lt stn, P-10x8", lot 55, RWS 9/29/88 .... **250**
Entrance to the Hall, Lincoln's Inn; ed of about 50, etch, 1905, p/s, lt ls/stn, 11x9", lot 55, SBY 2/25/88 .... **220**
Girard Trust Building, ed of 50, litho, 1912, p/s, laid down, L-22x17", lot 52, RWS 9/29/88 .... **125**
Golden Cornice, ed of about 90, etch/thin laid paper, 1904, p/s, lt stn/cr, unfr, P-11x7", C-NY 1/22/88 UE **143**
New York, From Brooklyn; ed of ca 80, etch/laid paper, 1915, p/s, inscr Imp, unfr, P-8x12", C-NY 1/22/88 .... **880**
On the Way to Bessemer, a/p, etch/laid paper, 1908-09, p/s, lt stn/fox, old tp in mrgs, P-11x7", lot 245, C-NY 1/19/89 .... **440**
Pair: Among the Skyscrapers; Standard Oil Building, etch/laid paper, 1908 & 1923, stn/old tp, lot 242, C-NY 1/19/89 OE **550**
Pair: Lair of the Locos, Philadelphia; Elevated; ed of about 50, etch, 1919 & 1921, laid down, lot 247, C-NY 1/19/89 OE **418**
Pair: Sunset From Williamsburg Bridge; Brasserie au Lion Rouge, etch, 1915 & 1893, laid down, lot 246, C-NY 1/19/89 .... **715**
Pair: Windmills; On the River; litho & etch, 1897, no size given, lot 2972, B/B 2/16/88 .... **300**
Tower Bridge, etch/laid paper, p/s, lt stn, 4x8", lot 2970, B/B 2/16/88 .... **220**
Wren's City, a/p, mezzo/wove paper, 1909, p/s, lt stn/tr, old tp in top mrg, P-10x12", lot 244, C-NY 1/19/89 .... **660**

EROT, Roger (French, 20th C)
Cycles Peugeot, litho/poster paper, 1931, linen backed, 31x47", Hachard, lot 297, FAP 2/24/89 UE **375**

ETERDI, Gabor (American, 1915-)
Pair: Bramble; Wisteria; etch/engr, 1951, p/s, lt stn, 13x18"/13x10", Cleveland Print Club, lot 195, SWN 6/15/89 .... **195**

ETHER, after (British, 18th/19th C)
Snowdrop, 1st state, hc mezzo/wove paper, 1804, glued to overmat, P-19x14", lot 102, C-NY 1/19/89 .... **825**

ETROVIC, Milan (American, 1893-)
Set of 6: Views of Venice; etch, p/s, titled, various sizes, lot 66, WG 10/19/88 OE **260**

HILLIPS, Peter (British, 1939-)
Gravy for the Navy, a/p, clr litho, p/s, 29x40", SLK 4/7/89 .... **70**
Pair: Race Cars; Stars/Dogs; 6/100 & 71/100, clr scrpt, ca 1960, p/s, lt scr/sl, lot 767, C-NY 11/1/88 UE **220**

HILLIPS, Thomas (British, 1770-1845)
Sir Joseph Banks, BT; engr, 1812, L-17x14", N Schiavonetti/London, C-SK 6/9/88 .... **706**

HILLIPS, Walter Joseph (Canadian, 1884-1963)
Diving Board, wc, p/s, intl on img, 9x6", lot 1209, WAD 11/28/88 .... **420**
Dock, 33/100, clr wc/laid paper, 1922, p/s, titled, old tp on verso, L-7x11", lot 249, C-NY 1/19/89 .... **330**
Folio: Northwest Coast Indian Scenes; 8 woodblock, p/s, 5x4"/5x6", lot 1206, WAD 11/28/88 .... **1,600**
Lake Shore, woodblock, p/s, titled in mrg, intl in img, 6x7", lot 1212, WAD 11/28/88 .... **450**
Mill Stream in Winter, clr aqua, p/s, titled, 4x4", lot 1208, WAD 11/28/88 .... **310**
Nasturtiums, 7/200, clr wc, p/s, intl/titled, 6x7", lot 888, WAD 6/12/89 .... **600**
Red River Road, 3/100, clr wc, p/s, a/bstp, 8x8", lot 803, WAD 6/12/89 .... **500**
Sunset Lake of the Woods, 26/50, clr woodblock, sgn/dtd 1919/titled, unfr, 8x11", RWS 4/22/89 .... **375**

HOENIX LITHOGRAPH CO. (Buffalo & Chicago)
Small Hopes & Lady Mac (fancy rig/horses), litho, lt fox, 1877, lg folio, RAB 11/25/88 .... **400**

IATTOLI, G.
Senza Cerece Bacco, hc engr, 12x8", C-E 11/15/88 .... **88**

PICASSO, Pablo (Spanish, 1881-1973)

A Pablo Picasso, total ed of 90, etch, 1945, p/s, full mrgs, lt stn, 7x7", lot 398, SBY 2/23/89 OE	4,675
Affiche Exposition de Ceramiques, brn/blk litho, 1958, sgn in bl pencil, L-24x16", lot 75, PHL 6/16/88	700
Affiche pour le Musee de Ceret, a/p, litho/Arches, 1957, sgn in red pencil, full mrgs, lt stn, L-25x19", C-NY 5/10/89	1,100
Alex Maguy, Galerie de L'Elysee; ed of unrecorded size, clr litho/Arches, 1962, sgn, stn, S-26x19", C-NY 1/22/88	660
Apres la Pique, 7/50, blk/tan/brn linocut, 1959, p/s, full mrgs, 21x25", SBY 5/12/88 OE	19,800
Au Cabaret, 36/50, etch w/burnishing on laid paper, 1934, stp/s, full mrgs, P-10x12", SBY 5/12/88	13,200
Au Cirque, ed of 250, drypt/van Gelder, 1905/1913, fld bottom mrg, tp/scr verso, 9x6", Vollard, lot 261, C-NY 5/11/88 OE	11,000
Au Cirque, ed of 250, drypt/van Gelder Zonen, 1905/1913, trm mrg, lt fox mrg/verso, 9x6", Vollard, SBY 5/12/88 OE	13,200
Avant la Pique, 7/50, brn/beige/blk linocut, 1959, p/s, full mrgs, 21x26", lot 461, SBY 11/3/88	15,400
Bacchanale au Hibou, 7/50, tan/blk linocut, 1959, p/s, full mrgs, 21x25", lot 735, SBY 5/11/89	20,900
Book: La Bout du Bonheur; by Jean Marcenac, #23, 1970, Abrams/Schunemman, lot 395, SBY 2/25/88	1,760
Book: Le Chef-d'Oeuvre Inconnu; by Honore de Balzac, 132/240, 1931, S-13x10", Vollard, lot 689, SBY 5/11/89 OE	27,500
Book: Lysistrata d'Aristophane; #1484, ed of 1500, 1934, orig boards, Ltd Ed Club, lot 709, SBY 5/11/89	2,750
Book: Lysistrata d'Aristophane; #448, 6 etch w/text, 1934, Ltd Ed Club, lot 317, SBY 2/25/88 OE	2,640
Book: Lysistrata d'Aristophane; 153, ed of 1500, 6 etch w/text, 1934, p/s, orig slipcase, Ltd Ed, SBY 5/12/88 OE	3,300
Book: Lysistrata; 229/1500, 1934, sgn on justification, orig wrappers, slipcase, Ltd Ed Club, lot 739, C-NY 5/10/89	2,420
Book: Picasso de 1916 a 1961; by Jean Cocteau, p/s by Picasso/Cocteau, 1962, Eds du Rocher, lot 333, SBY 2/25/88	1,320
Book: Picasso Lithographe (4 vol set); ed of 2500, 1956, Sauret/Mourlot, lot 394, SBY 2/25/88 OE	1,760
Buste de Femme, 38/50, aqua, 1966, p/s, full mrgs, 15x11", lot 380, SBY 2/25/88	3,410
Buste de Femme d'Apres Cranach, 28/50, clr linocut, 1958, sgn in crayon, lt stn, 26x21", lot 731, SBY 5/11/89 OE	264,000
Buste de'Homme, ed of 250, drypt/van Gelder, 1905/1913, full mrgs, lt cr/fox, P-5x4", Vollard, lot 255, C-NY 5/11/88 OE	12,100
Buste Modern Style, 2/6, litho/Arches, 1949, lt fox/stn, S-26x20", Mourlot, lot 718, SBY 5/11/89	41,800
Buste Modern Style, 34/50, litho/Arches, 1949, sgn, lt fox/sl, S-26x20", lot 149, C-NY 11/1/88 OE	44,000
Carmen des Carmen, 165/245, aqua, 14x10", lot 325, LH 5/15/88 UE	300
Carnaval, 127/160, clr linocut, 1965, p/s, full mrgs, lt scuff img, lt cr edge, 25x21", SBY 5/12/88	8,250
Carnaval, 159/160, brn/blk linocut, 1965, p/s, full mrgs, lt cr, 25x21", SBY 5/12/88	7,150
Carnaval, 68/160, brn/blk linocut, 1965, p/s, full mrgs, lt cr/fox/nicks, 25x21", lot 743, SBY 5/11/89	10,450
Carnaval, 82/160, brn & blk linocut/Arches, 1965, p/s, lt cr/stn/ls, L-25x21", lot 469, C-NY 11/1/88 OE	12,100
Citando al Toro con la Capa, La Tauromaquia; 5/12, aqua/Japan, 1957, full mrgs, P-8x11", lot 460, C-NY 11/1/88	7,150
Colombe Volant, 123/200, clr litho/Arches, 1952, p/s, full mrgs, lt sl/skinned, L-20x26", SBY 5/12/88 OE	7,975
Colombe Volant (A l'Arc-en-Ceil), 13/38, clr litho/Japon nacre, 1952, lt cr/scr/stn, L-20x26", lot 454, C-NY 11/1/88 OE	4,620
Colombe Volant (A l'Arc-en-Ciel), 198/200, clr litho/Arches, 1952, p/s, full mrgs, 20x26", lot 324, SBY 2/25/88 OE	3,300
Colombe Volant (A l'Arc-en-Ciel), 63/200, clr litho/Arches, sgn, full mrgs, lt stn, 20x26", lot 196, SWN 6/15/89 OE	4,180

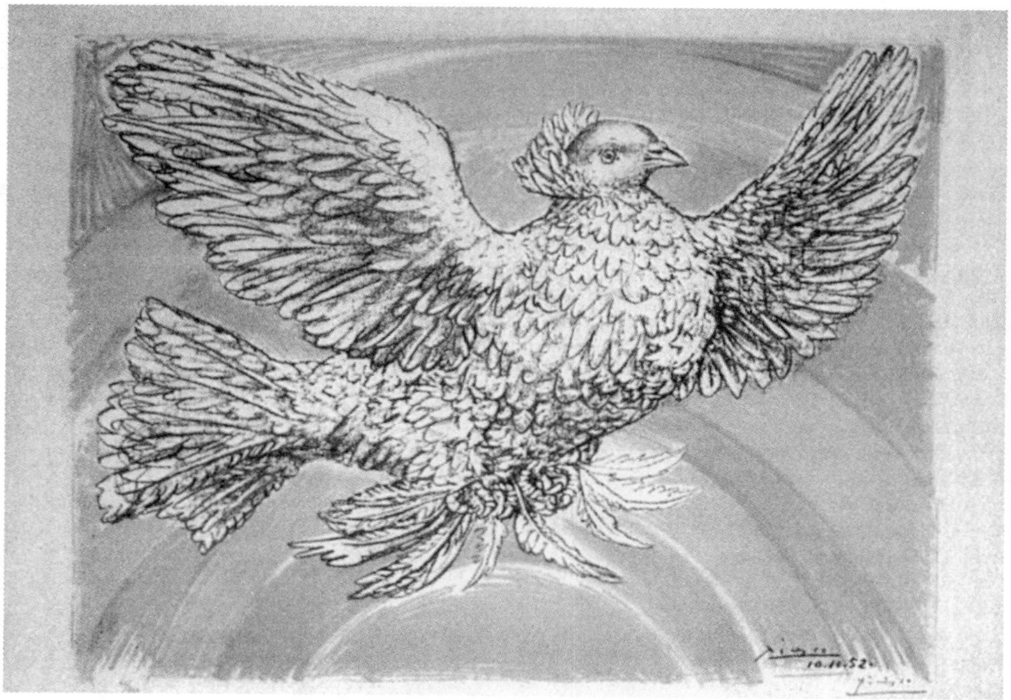

Colombe Volant (a 'Arc-en-Ciel), 61/200, clr litho/Arches, 1952, p/s, full mrgs, lt stn, L-20x25", lot 745, C-NY 5/10/89 OE; $7,150

Combat de Centaures, IV; 29/50, litho/Arches, 1959, p/s, full mrgs, lt lstn/cr, L-18x25", SBY 5/12/88 OE	4,400
Composition, 120/250, clr litho, 1957, sgn in red crayon, full mrgs, lt cr/stn, 24x13", lot 454, SBY 11/3/88	3,575
Composition (group of seated figures), 41/50, scr aqua/etch, 1966, stp/s, full mrgs, tp verso, P-9x13", SBY 5/12/88	2,090
Composition du 8 Aout 1947, 43/50, ochre/blk litho, 1947, p/s, tp verso edges, S-9x20", SBY 5/12/88 UE	1,100

Composition with a Couple Seated in Front of a Holy Man, 46/50, etch, 1966, stp/s, full mrgs, P-9x13", SBY 5/12/88	1,760
Composition with Models & Viewers, 34/50, etch/aqua/drypt, 1966, stp/s, full mrgs, 9x13", lot 745, SBY 5/11/89	3,850
Corrida, aside from #d ed of 50, litho/wove paper, 1961, p/s, lstn, L-19x13", lot 464, C-NY 11/1/88	1,980
Corrida, le Picador; 8/50, litho/Arches, 1949, p/s, lt cr/rpr tr, S-22x30", lot 151, C-NY 11/1/88	5,280
Couple et Chien Regardant une Tableau, 39/50, aqua/etch, 1966, stp/s, full mrgs, lt cr, tp verso, P-9x13", SBY 5/12/88	1,760
Danae, a/p, clr linocut/Arches, 1962, inscr Pour Albert Skira Picasso le 3.11.66, L-11x14", lot 467, C-NY 11/1/88 OE	39,600
Dans l'Atelier, 21/50, etch/aqua/BFK Rives, 1966, full mrgs, p/s, lt cr, P-16x22", lot 286, C-NY 5/11/88	3,520
Dans l'Atelier, 24/50, aqua/engr/drypt, 1963, p/s, full mrgs, lt lstn/fox, SBY 5/12/88	1,980
Dans l'Atelier, 33/50, aqua/drypt/wove paper, 1965, p/s, full mrgs, lt stn/fox, P-9x13", lot 470, C-NY 11/1/88	3,520
Dans l'Atelier, 38/50, aqua, 1965, p/s, full mrgs, 10x15", lot 365, SBY 2/25/88 OE	2,310
Dans l'Atelier, 38/50, aqua/burin/drypt, 1963, p/s, full mrgs, 8x10", lot 339, SBY 2/25/88 OE	2,640
Dans l'Atelier, 38/50, aqua/drypt, 1965, p/s, full mrgs, lt fox img, 9x13", lot 360, SBY 2/25/88 OE	2,420
Dans l'Atelier, 38/50, aqua/drypt, 1965, p/s, full mrgs, lt fox mrgs, 11x15", lot 361, SBY 2/25/88 OE	3,520
Dans l'Atelier, 38/50, aqua/drypt, 1965, p/s, full mrgs, lt stn mrgs, 10x15", lot 364, SBY 2/25/88 OE	3,575
Dans l'Atelier, 38/50, aqua/drypt, 1965, p/s, full mrgs, 10x15", lot 363, SBY 2/25/88 OE	3,080
Dans l'Atelier, 38/50, aqua/drypt, 1965, p/s, full mrgs, 13x18", lot 362, SBY 2/25/88 OE	5,500
Dans l'Atelier, 38/50, aqua/etch, 1965, p/s, full mrgs, lt stn mrgs, 16x22", lot 366, SBY 2/25/88	3,850
Dans L'Atelier, 38/50, drypt/aqua, 1963, p/s, full mrgs, 13x17", lot 346, SBY 2/25/88 OE	4,400
Dans l'Atelier, 38/50, etch/aqua, 1966, p/s, full mrgs, 13x19", lot 383, SBY 2/25/88 OE	3,960
Dans l'Atelier, 38/50, etch/aqua, 1966, p/s, full mrgs, 16x22", lot 377, SBY 2/25/88 OE	3,080
Dans l'Atelier, 9/50, aqua/drypt/Auvergne a la main, 1965, p/s, lt lstn, P-10x15", lot 471, C-NY 11/1/88	5,280
Danseurs et Musicien, 7/50, tan/blk linocut, 1959, p/s, full mrgs, 21x25", lot 736, SBY 5/11/89	23,100
David et Bethsabee, ed of 50, 1st state, litho, 1949, inscr Bon a tirer, full mrgs, 30x22", lot 717, SBY 5/11/89	28,600
David et Bethsabee, 35/50, litho/wove paper, 1947, sgn in red crayon, full mrgs, lt scr/stn/sl, 26x20", C-NY 5/10/89 OE	17,600
Deux Enfants Jouant et Femme Couchee, I; 29/50, etch, 1953/1980, full mrgs, lt cr, 9x14", lot 721, SBY 5/11/89	4,675
Deux Femmes a Leur Toilette, linocut/Arches, 1958, sgn in ink, old hinges, 28x22", lot 2883, B/B 2/16/88 OE	18,700
Deux Femmes Nues, a/p, ed of 125, etch, 1930, sgn in blk ink, full mrgs, lt rpr trs, P-12x9", lot 271, C-NY 5/11/88 OE	14,300
Deux Femmes Nues dans un Arbre, sgn ed of 100, etch, dtd 1931, 15x12", C-NY 10/6/88	4,950
Deux Femmes Nues dans un Arbre, 43/100, etch, 1931, sgn in ink, lt stn/cr, 15x12", lot 691, SBY 5/11/89	4,675
Deux Femmes sur la Plage, 25/50, litho/Arches, 1956, p/s, full mrgs, lt stn/fox, S-20x26", lot 746, C-NY 5/10/89	10,450
Deux Modeles Vetus, total ed of 300, etch, 1933, p/s, full mrgs, 11x12", Vollard, lot 392, SBY 2/23/89	9,350
Deux Modeles Vetus, total ed of 300, etch, 1933, p/s, full mrgs, lt mstn, P-11x8", Vollard, SBY 5/12/88 OE	8,250
Don Quichotte et Sancho Panca, II; 38/50, litho, 1951, p/s, full mrgs, 13x13", lot 323, SBY 2/25/88 OE	3,300
Dormeuse et Sculptures, 38/50, etch, 1933/1961, p/s, full mrgs, no size given, lot 707, SBY 5/11/89 OE	6,600
Echan Perros al Toros, La Touromaquia; 5/12, aqua/Japan, 1957, full mrgs, lt fox/stn, P-8x12", lot 461, C-NY 11/1/88	6,600
Etreinte, 38/50, etch, 1963, p/s, full mrgs, 17x23", lot 337, SBY 2/25/88 OE	3,300
Etreinte, 8/50, etch, 1963, p/s, lt stn/scr, 17x23", lot 465, SBY 11/3/88 OE	4,950
Exposition Ceramique, Vallauris 1959; 55/175, red-brn/blk linocut, p/s, full mrgs, 25x21", SBY 5/12/88 OE	3,025
Exposition Hispano-Americaine, litho/cream wove paper, ca 1951, sgn in stone, lt cr, 22x16", lot 2884, B/B 4/19/88	192
Exposition Vallauris 1957, 53/175, linocut, 1957, sgn in bl crayon, full mrgs, sl/fox, 25x21", lot 416, SBY 2/23/89 OE	2,750
Exposition Vallauris 1957, brn linocut, sgn in red pencil, full mrgs, lt cr/scr, L-25x21", lot 77, PHL 6/16/88 OE	1,400
Exposition Vallauris 1961, 36/175, clr linocut, p/s, full mrgs, 25x21", lot 371, SBY 2/25/88 OE	2,420
Exposition Vallauris 1961, 65/175, brn/beige linocut, 1961, p/s, full mrgs, lt fox, 25x21", SBY 5/12/88 OE	3,025
Exposition Vallauris 1961, 75/175, brn-gr/tan linocut, 1961, full mrgs, 25x21", lot 417, SBY 2/23/89 OE	3,850
Exposition Vallauris 1962, 134/175, yel/brn linocut, full mrgs, lt fox, 25x21", lot 419, SBY 2/23/89	1,320
Exposition Vallauris 1962, 137/175, yel/brn linocut, 1962, p/s, full mrgs, lt stn, 25x21", lot 418, SBY 2/23/89 OE	2,860
Exposition Vallauris 1962, 142/175, yel/brn linocut, 1962, p/s, full mrgs, 25x21", SBY 5/12/88 OE	1,650
Exposition Vallauris 1962, 144/175, yel/brn linocut, 1962, full mrgs, lt scr img, 25x21", lot 372, SBY 2/25/88 OE	2,420
Exposition Vallauris 1962, 153/175, brn & yel linocut/Arches, 1962, full mrgs, cr/stn, 25x21", lot 285, C-NY 5/11/88 OE	1,760
Exposition Vallauris 1964, 123/168, brn linocut, sgn in crayon, full mrgs, 25x21", SBY 5/12/88 OE	1,210
Exposition Vallauris 1964, 124/168, brn linocut, 1964, sgn in bl crayon, full mrgs, 25x21", lot 373, SBY 2/25/88	880
Famille de Saltimbanques, Pl 54, etch/Montval, 1933, p/s, full mrgs, lt stn, P-8x11", lot 730, C-NY 5/10/89	12,100
Famille de Saltimbanques, total ed of 300, etch, 1933, p/s, lt stn, 8x11", Vollard, lot 412, SBY 11/3/88 OE	10,450
Faune Devoilant une Femme, Pl 27, etch/aqua, 1936, p/s, full mrgs, lt fox, P-13x17", Vollard, lot 443A, C-NY 11/1/88	44,000
Faune Devoilant une Femme, total ed of 300, aqua, 1936, p/s, full mrgs, lt stn, 13x16", Vollard, lot 315, SBY 2/25/88	37,400
Faune Devoilant une Femme, total ed of 300, aqua, 1936, p/s, full mrgs, mstn/scr, unfr, 13x17", Vollard, SBY 5/12/88 OE	49,500
Faune Devoilant une Femme, total ed of 300, etch/aqua/Montval, 1936, lt stn, 12x16", Vollard, lot 706, SBY 5/11/89 OE	88,000
Faune Misicien No 4, 42/50, litho, 1948, p/s, lt fox/sl/tr, S-30x22", lot 400, SBY 2/23/89 OE	14,300
Faunes et Chevre, 3/50, clr linocut, 1959, p/s, full mrgs, lt tr/sl, 21x25", lot 460, SBY 11/3/88	40,700
Faunes et Chevre, 49/50, clr linocut, 1959, p/s, full mrgs, lt cr/stn/old hinges, 21x25", lot 407, SBY 2/23/89 OE	41,800
Femme Accoudee, 29/50, bl/blk linocut, 1922, p/s, full mrgs, lt cr/skinned mrg, unfr, 25x21", SBY 5/12/88	37,400
Femme Assise, 33/50, litho/cream wove paper, 1924, p/s, lstn/mstn, L-12x8", lot 266, C-NY 5/11/88 OE	9,900
Femme Assise dans un Fauteuil, 11/50, aqua/Rives, 1966, p/s, full mrgs, P-15x11", lot 756, C-NY 5/10/89	4,400
Femme Assise dans un Fauteuil, 25/50, aqua, 1966, p/s, full mrgs, 15x11", lot 422, SBY 2/23/89 OE	3,850
Femme au Balcon, 86/145, litho, p/s, 26x20", lot 293, LH 5/15/88	1,000
Femme au Chapeau, a/p, aside from ed of 50, linocut, 1962, inscr Pour Ynes, lt cr, 14x11", lot 462, SBY 11/3/88 OE	15,400
Femme au Chignon, 16/50, litho, 1957, red p/s, full mrgs, lt lstn/fox, lt gstn mrg, scr verso, L-22x17", SBY 5/12/88 OE	30,800
Femme au Collier, 15/50, blk/ochre/brn linocut, 1959, p/s, full mrgs, lt mstn/cr, 25x21", SBY 5/12/88	22,220
Femme au Collier, 29/50, brn/blk/beige linocut, 1959, p/s, full mrgs, lt stn, 25x21", lot 330, SBY 2/25/88	16,500
Femme au Corsage a Fleurs, 3/50, litho, 1958, p/s, lt cr, S-26x20", lot 730, SBY 5/11/89 OE	148,500
Femme au Corsage a Fleurs, 37/50, litho, 1958, p/s, lt stn, S-26x20", lot 328, SBY 2/25/88 OE	82,500

Femme au Fauteuil No 1, 44/50, litho, 1948, p/s, full mrgs, lt scr img, lt cr/stn, unfr, L-28x22", SBY 5/12/88 OE	68,750
Femme au Fauteuil No 4, 42/50, 5th state, litho, 1949, p/s, full mrgs, lt stn, 27x22", lot 321, SBY 2/25/89	27,500
Femme Couchee et Guitariste, 7/50, brn/beige/blk linocut, 1959, p/s, full mrgs, 21x25", lot 459, SBY 11/3/88	15,400
Femme dans un Fauteuil et Guitariste, 7/50, brn/tan/blk linocut, 1959, p/s, full mrgs, 21x25", lot 458, SBY 11/3/88	13,200
Femme et Enfant, 37/50, litho/beige wove paper, 1923, p/s, lt stn/cr, old tp on verso, L-8x12", lot 724, C-NY 5/10/89	6,050
Femme et Homme, 38/50, drypt, 1965, p/s, full mrgs, lt stn, 14x19", lot 356, SBY 2/25/88 OE	3,080
Femme Nue a la Jambe Pliee, Pl 8, aside from ed of 250, etch/Montval, 1931, fox/stn, P-12x9", lot 726, C-NY 5/10/89 OE	8,800
Femme Nue a la Jambe Pliee, total ed of 300, etch, 1931, p/s, full mrgs, stn/sl, P-13x7", Vollard, SBY 5/12/88 OE	6,600
Femme Nue Assise, la Tete Appuyee sur la Main; engr, 1934, p/s, full mrgs, lt stn, 11x8", Vollard, lot 425, SBY 11/3/88	8,250
Femme Nue Assise et Trois Tetes Barbues, ed of 300, etch/aqua, 1934, p/s, stn/fox, 5x7", Vollard, lot 702, SBY 5/11/89	5,775
Femme Nue Devant une Statue, Pl 6, ed of 250, etch/Montval wm Picasso, 1931, p/s, P-12x9", lot 272, C-NY 5/11/88 OE	7,700
Femme Nue et Homme a la Canne, 102/125, litho, 1969, p/s, full mrgs, lt lstn, 11x9", lot 746, SBY 5/11/89 OE	2,475
Femme Nue et Homme a la Canne, 74/125, litho/wove paper, 1969, lt stn, Ed Cercle d'Art, lot 473, C-NY 11/1/88 OE	1,760
Femme Vue de Dos, ed of 125, etch/wove MBM, 1956, p/s, full mrgs, lt sl/stn, P-15x11", lot 747, C-NY 5/10/89	1,320
Figure, 27/50, litho, 1949, sgn in bl crayon, lt fox/stn, S-26x20", lot 717A, SBY 5/11/89 OE	28,600
Figure au Corsage Raye, 19/50, clr litho/Arches, lt cr, S-26x20", lot 152, C-NY 11/1/88 OE	81,400
Figure Composee II, 45/50, litho, 1949, p/s, lt stn/fox/cr, S-26x20", lot 445, SBY 11/3/88 OE	15,400
Figure Noire, 36/50, litho, 1948, p/s, 2 pressure marks, lt lstn/mstn/fox, S-26x20", SBY 5/12/88 OE	14,850
Figure Noire, 44/50, litho/Arches, 1948, p/s, lt fox/scr, S-26x20", lot 150, C-NY 11/1/88	11,000
Figures, 38/50, etch, 1927/1960, full mrgs, 8x11", lot 688, SBY 5/11/89	6,600
Flutiste et Jeune Fille au Tambourin, Pl 20, etch/Montval, 1934, full mrgs, P-11x8", Vollard, lot 441, C-NY 11/1/88 OE	4,400
Flutiste et Trois Femmes Nues, total ed of 300, drypt, 1932, p/s, lt sl, 12x15", Vollard, lot 695, SBY 5/11/89 OE	4,400
Football, 22/200, clr litho, 1961, p/s, full mrgs, lt cr img, lt skinned/stn edges, L-19x25", SBY 5/12/88 OE	4,125
Francoise, 20/50, litho/Arches, 1946, p/s, lt scr/cr/stn, S-26x20", lot 742, C-NY 5/10/89	24,200
Francoise, 32/50, litho, 1946, p/s, full mrgs, lt stn/cr/sl, S-26x20", lot 716, SBY 5/11/89 OE	27,500
Francoise, 36/50, litho, 1946, p/s, lt rpr scr/fox, S-26x20", lot 438, SBY 11/3/88	22,000
Francoise, 7/50, litho, 1946, p/s, lt fox img, lt sl/fox edges, tp hinges, S-26x20", SBY 5/12/88 OE	27,500
Francoise sur Fond Gris, 18/50, litho/bl-gray Ingres laid paper on Arches, 1950, p/s, S-30x22", lot 153, C-NY 11/1/88 OE	66,000
Francoise sur Fond Gris, 49/50, litho/bl-gray Ingres mounted on Arches, 1950, p/s, 25x19", lot 720, SBY 5/11/89	77,000
Fueur, 42/50, clr sftgr etch, 1964, p/s, full mrgs, tp stn, lt fox, 17x12", SBY 5/12/88	11,000
Fumeur, clr aqua/Richard de Bas, 1964, p/s, full mrgs, lt fox/stn, 16x12", lot 741, SBY 5/11/89	8,250
Fumeur, 2/50, clr aqua/sftgr, 1964, p/s, full mrgs, lt fox/cr, 17x13", lot 412, SBY 2/23/89	11,000
Fumeur, 33/50, clr aqua, 1964, p/s, full mrgs, lt stn/fox, 17x9", lot 742, SBY 5/11/89 OE	15,400
Fumeur, 36/50, clr sftgr etch, 1964, p/s, 17x13", lot 368, LH 10/16/88	7,000
Fumeur, 4/50, sftgr etch, 1964, p/s, full mrgs, lt fox/cr, 16x13", lot 467, SBY 11/3/88	10,450
Girl at the Window, 274/5000, clr litho, 16x22", lot 151, MG 5/28/88	85
Grand Profil, 7/50, litho, 1947, p/s, full mrgs, lt stn/cr, 24x18", lot 441, SBY 11/3/88	13,200
Grande Nu de Femme, 31/50, clr linocut/Arches, 1962, p/s, lt cr/stn mrgs, L-25x21", lot 468, C-NY 11/1/88 OE	38,500
Grande Tete de Femme, 28/50, clr linocut/Arches, 1962, p/s, full mrgs, lt mstn/cr, L-25x21", lot 466, C-NY 11/1/88	30,800
Grande Tete de Femme au Chapeau Orne, 1/50, blk/beige linocut, 1962, p/s, full mrgs, 25x21", SBY 5/12/88 OE	71,500
Groupe de Trois Femmes, 90/100, drypt/etch/laid paper, 1922-23, p/s, full mrgs, stn/fox, 7x5", lot 400, SBY 11/3/88 OE	29,700
Head of a Young Woman in Profile, a/p (unpublished work), litho, 1963, full mrgs, lt stn, S-26x20", lot 408, SBY 2/23/89	3,575
Homme Barbu Couronne, 4/50, 3 tones brn & blk linocut/Arches, 1962, p/s, full mrgs, lt cr/stn, 14x11", SBY 5/12/88 OE	11,550
Homme Devoilant une Femme, total ed of 300, etch, 1931, lt stn/fox, 14x12", Vollard, lot 408, SBY 11/3/88	3,575
Homme et Femme, 38/50, aqua/drypt, 1965, p/s, full mrgs, lt stn, 9x13", lot 357, SBY 2/25/88 OE	3,520
Homme et Femme, 38/50, etch/aqua, 1966, p/s, full mrgs, lt stn mrgs, 10x15", lot 378, SBY 2/25/88 OE	3,080
Homme et Femme, 85/250, etch, 1927, sgn, lt scr/sl/cr mrgs, 8x11", lot 403, SBY 11/3/88 OE	4,950
Homme Nu Assis avec Femme Nue sur les Genoux, 34/50, etch, 1955/1961, stp/s, full mrgs, 10x12", lot 403A, SBY 2/23/89	2,475
Interieur, 18/50, etch/aqua/Rives, 1963, p/s, full mrgs, lt scr, P-12x16", lot 284, C-NY 5/11/88	1,760
Interieur, 38/50, aqua, 1963, p/s, full mrgs, 13x17", lot 342, SBY 2/25/88 OE	2,090
Jacqueline Lisant, 42/50, linocut, 1964, p/s, full mrgs, lt disclr mrgs, lt cr/skinned/stn, 25x21", SBY 5/12/88 OE	44,000
Jeune Femme, 23/75, litho/smooth wove paper mounted on sturdy wove Arches, 1949, lt stn, unfr, L-16x12", SBY 5/12/88 OE	8,250
Jeune Fille Inspiree par Cranch, 15/50, litho, 1949, p/s, full mrgs, lt scr/stn/fox, L-25x20", lot 279, C-NY 5/11/88 OE	30,800
Jeunesse, 38/50, litho, 1950, p/s, full mrgs, lt scuff/cr/stn, 20x26", lot 448, SBY 11/3/88 OE	44,000
L'Abreuvoir, ed of 250, etch/van Gelder, 1905/1913, full mrgs, lt fox/stn/ls, P-5x7", Vollard, lot 260, C-NY 5/11/88	4,400
L'Age de Soleil, etch, p/s, 9x7", lot 1267, LH 12/4/88 OE	600
L'Age de Soleil, etch, 1950, pl/s, 7x9", lot 332, LH 9/10/89	160
L'Age de Soleil, etch, 1950, 9x7", lot 1164, LH 10/16/88 UE	225
L'Atelier du Peintre, 38/50, aqua/drypt, 1963, p/s, full mrgs, 9x13", lot 345, SBY 2/25/88 OE	3,740
L'Ecuyere, litho/wove paper, 1960, sgn in stone, full mrgs, lt stn, L-20x25", lot 749, C-NY 5/10/89	440
L'Ecuyere, 19/200, litho/Arches, 1960, p/s, lt cr/stn in mrgs, S-21x27", lot 282, C-NY 5/11/88 OE	2,750
L'Ecuyere et les Clowns, 11/50, blk/gr/red litho, 1961, sgn in crayon, lt stn/cr, unfr, L-20x26", SBY 5/12/88	11,550
L'Espagnole, 5/50, brn/tan/blk linocut, 1962, p/s, full mrgs, lt stn/cr, 14x11", lot 464, SBY 11/3/88 OE	22,000
L'Homme a la Guitare, a/p, engr/Japan ancien, 1915/1929, 6x5", Leblanc/Trautmann, lot 685, SBY 5/11/89 OE	36,300
L'Homme au Chien, ed of 102, etch/wove paper, 1914, full mrgs, lt stn, 11x9", lot 684, SBY 5/11/89 OE	36,200
La Cogida, La Tauromaquia; 5/12, aqua/Japan, 1957, full mrgs, lt mstn, P-8x11", lot 462, C-NY 11/1/88	7,150
La Coiffure, 34/50, litho/van Gelder, 1923, p/s, full mrgs, lt stn/scr, L-10x7", lot 723, C-NY 5/10/89	9,900
La Danse, ed of 250, drypt/van Gelder Zonen, 1905, full mrgs, lt fox/stn, 7x9", Vollard, lot 1913, SBY 5/11/89 OE	5,225
La Danse, ed of 250, drypt/van Gelder Zonen, 1905/1913, full mrgs, lt fox/rub, 8x9", Vollard, lot 394, SBY 11/3/88	2,640
La Danse des Faunes, ed of 1000, beige/blk litho, 1957, stp/s, full mrgs, 16x21", lot 327, SBY 2/25/88 OE	2,970
La Danse des Faunes, ed of 1000, beige/blk litho/wove paper, 1957, stp/s, full mrgs, L-16x21", lot 748, C-NY 5/10/89	1,320

La Femme a la Fenetre, 31/50, aqua, 1952, p/s, full mrgs, lt stn, 33x19", lot 451, SBY 11/3/88	**93,500**
La Femme a la Resilie (Femme aux Chevaux Verts), a/p, before ed of 50, clr litho, 1949, S-26x20", lot 446, SBY 11/3/88	**143,000**
La Femme a la Resille (Femme Aux Cheveux Verts), 35/50, clr litho, 1949, sgn, stn/fox, S-26x20", lot 719, SBY 5/11/89	**99,000**
La Femme au Tambourin, 29/30, etch/scr aqua/Arches, 1939/1943, full mrgs, lt rpr/tr, 26x20", lot 435A, SBY 11/3/88	**165,000**
La Lecture, 75/100, litho, 1926, p/s, full mrgs, lt cr/sl, 13x10", lot 402, SBY 11/3/88 OE	**6,050**
La Petite Corrida, 4/50, clr litho, 1957, sgn, full mrgs, lt stn/skinned/old hinges, 11x10", lot 406, SBY 2/23/89 OE	**3,300**
La Petite Corrida-Cannes, ed of 2000, clr litho, 1957, sgn in stone, S-13x10", Mourlot, lot 198, SWN 6/15/89	**550**
La Pique, ed of 50, litho/cream wove paper, 1961, 10x12", lot 2886, B/B 2/16/88	**440**
La Plage, III; 27/50, total ed of 65, etch, 1932/1961, stp/s, full mrgs, lt mstn, P-6x5", lot 276, C-NY 5/11/88	**2,530**
La Plongeuse, etch/collage/cream wove paper, 1932, p/s, 16x5", lot 693, SBY 5/11/89 OE	**12,100**
La Pose Habilee, 40/50, litho, 1954, p/s, full mrgs, 22x15", lot 325, SBY 2/25/88 OE	**8,800**
La Pose Habille, 42/50, litho, 1945, p/s, full mrgs, lt stn/sl, 22x15", lot 403, SBY 2/23/89 OE	**1,210**
La Source, 49/100, engr/drypt/laid wm BP, 1921, 2 trm mrgs, lt tr/sl/stn mrgs, P-7x9", lot 264, C-NY 5/11/88 OE	**9,900**
La Toilette, 13/50, litho, 1923, p/s, full mrgs, lt stn, 11x8", lot 687, SBY 5/11/89	**9,900**
La Toilette, 16/50, litho, 1923, p/s, full mrgs, lt mstn/fox, L-11x8", SBY 5/12/88 OE	**9,900**
La Toilette de la Mere, ed of 250, drypt/van Gelder Zonen, 1905/1913, full mrgs, 9x7", Vollard, lot 392, SBY 11/3/88	**11,000**
La Toilette de la Mere, ed of 29, etch/Japan, 1905/1913, full mrgs, lt fox, P-9x7", Vollard, lot 263, C-NY 5/11/88 OE	**16,500**
La Vase de Fleurs (Epreuve Rincee), linocut w/encre de Chine on Arches, 1959, sgn, L-26x21", lot 457, C-NY 11/1/88	**16,500**
Le Chapeau a Fleurs, 21/50, clr linocut, 1963, p/s, full mrgs, 21x16", lot 347, SBY 2/25/88 OE	**40,700**
Le Combat, 30/50, etch, 1937, p/s, full mrgs, lt fox/stn, 16x19", lot 397, SBY 2/23/89	**14,300**
Le Danseur, 188/200, brn/blk linocut, 1965, p/s, full mrgs, lt cr/scr, 25x21", lot 469, SBY 11/3/88 OE	**7,425**
Le Dejeuner sur l'Herbe, 26/50, beige/brn/blk linocut, 1962, p/s, full mrgs, lt cr/sl, 21x25", lot 334, SBY 2/25/88 OE	**7,700**
Le Dejeuner sur l'Herbe, 32/50, clr linocut, 1962, p/s, full mrgs, lt cr img, lt stn, 21x25", lot 737, SBY 5/11/89 OE	**148,500**
Le Dejeuner sur l'Herbe, 35/150, litho/cream wove paper, 1962, p/s, full mrgs, lt cr, L-10x13", lot 76, PHL 6/16/88	**1,500**
Le Festin, Lysistrata; Pl 6, 150/145 (sic), etch, 1934, p/s, full mrgs, lt mstn, P-9x6", lot 277, C-NY 5/11/88 OE	**3,410**
Le Gout du Bonheur, ed of 105, etch, 1970, p/s, full mrgs, 4x6", lot 429, SBY 2/23/89 OE	**2,475**
Le Grand Hibou, 2/50, litho, 1948, p/s, full mrgs, lt sl/fox/stn, 27x22", SBY 11/3/88 OE	**6,050**
Le Modele, 28/50, aqua, 1965, p/s, full mrgs, 15x11", lot 354, SBY 2/25/88 OE	**4,400**
Le Modele Nu, 21/40, total ed of 150, etch/Japan, 1927, p/s, full mrgs, lt stn, 11x8", lot 404, SBY 11/3/88 OE	**6,050**
Le Peintre a la Palette, 28/150, linocut, 1963, p/s, lt stn/cr, 25x21", lot 739A, SBY 5/11/89 OE	**9,900**
Le Peintre et Son Modele, 38/50, aqua/drypt, 1963, p/s, full mrgs, lt mstn, 9x13", lot 344, SBY 2/25/88 OE	**4,125**
Le Peintre et Son Modele, 38/50, aqua/drypt, 1963, p/s, 15x19", lot 408, WG 10/19/88	**13,000**
Le Pitchet Noir et la Tete de Mort, 26/50, litho, 1946, p/s, full sheet, lt rpr tr, S-13x17", lot 451, C-NY 11/1/88	**4,950**
Le Repas Frugal, ed of 250, etch/van Gelder Zonen, 1904/1913, full mrgs, lt tr, 18x15", Vollard, lot 389, SBY 11/3/88 OE	**165,000**
Le Repas Frugal, ed of 250, etch/van Gelder Zonen, 1904/1913, lt mstn/fox, S-24x19", Vollard, SBY 5/12/88 OE	**115,500**
Le Repos du Sculpteur, III; total ed of 300, etch, 1933, p/s, full mrgs, lt stn, 8x11", Vollard, lot 415, SBY 11/3/88 OE	**7,150**
Le Repos du Sculpteur Devant des Chevaux et Taureau, total ed of 300, etch, 1933, 8x11", Vollard, lot 413, SBY 11/3/88	**5,500**
Le Repos du Sculpteur Devant le Petit Torse, total ed of 300, etch, 1933, p/s, full mrgs, stn/fox, 8x11", SBY 11/3/88 OE	**8,800**
Le Repos du Sculpteur Devant un Centaure et une Femme, total ed of 300, etch, 1933, 8x11", Vollard, lot 699, SBY 5/11/89	**11,000**
Le Repos du Sculpteur Devant un Nu a la Draperie, total ed of 300, etch, 1933, 11x8", Vollard, lot 698, SBY 5/11/89 OE	**9,900**
Le Repos du Sculpteur et le Modele au Masque, Pl 50, ed of 50, etch/Montval, 1933, full mrgs, P-11x8", C-NY 5/10/89	**8,250**
Le Repos du Sculpteur et le Modele au Masque, total ed of 300, etch, 1933, p/s, lt stn, 11x8", lot 410, SBY 11/3/88	**6,050**
Le Repos du Sculpteur I, total ed of 300, etch, 1933, p/s, lt mstn/fox, P-8x11", Vollard, SBY 5/12/88 OE	**9,900**
Le Saltimbanque au Repos, ed of 250, drypt/van Gelder, 1905/1913, full mrgs, P-5x3", Vollard, lot 262, C-NY 5/11/88 OE	**6,050**
Le Sauvetage, I; 28/50, etch, 1932/1961, stp/s, full mrgs, lt cr, 6x8", lot 316, SBY 2/25/89	**1,980**
Le Sauvetage II, 41/50, etch, 1932/1961, p/s, full mrgs, lt tr/cr, 6x8", lot 431, SBY 11/3/88	**3,850**
Le Sculpteur, 38/50, aqua, 1965, p/s, full mrgs, 15x11", lot 351, SBY 2/25/88 OE	**3,520**
Le Torero Blesse, 43/50, litho, 1956, p/s, full mrgs, lt stn/cr, 14x19", lot 724, SBY 5/11/89	**4,400**
Le Vieu Roi, ed of 200, litho/Arches, 1959, p/s, full mrgs, lt cr corners, L-26x20", lot 93, PHL 10/28/88 UE	**400**
Le Vieux Roi, ed of 1000, litho/Arches, 1959, S-26x20", lot 199, SWN 6/15/89	**715**
Le Vieux Roi, ed of 1000, litho/Arches, 1959, sgn in stone, lt stn/skinned/tp, unfr, L-26x20", C-NY 1/22/88 OE	**715**
Le Vieux Roi, 117/160, clr linocut, 1963, p/s, lt scuff/cr/stn, 26x21", lot 739, SBY 5/11/89 OE	**10,450**
Le Viol, IV; total ed of 300, etch/drypt, 1933, p/s, full mrgs, 8x11", Vollard, lot 700, SBY 5/11/89 OE	**4,950**
Le Viol, Pl 29, ed of 250, etch/aqua/drypt/Montval, 1933, p/s, lt fox/stn, P-8x11", lot 437, C-NY 11/1/88	**3,300**
Le Viol, VII; Pl 32, etch/Montval, 1934, p/s, full mrgs, lt stn, P-10x12", Vollard, lot 735, C-NY 5/10/89 OE	**8,250**
Le Viol Sous la Fenetre, total ed of 300, etch/aqua/drypt, 1933, p/s, full mrgs, 11x8", Vollard, lot 393, SBY 2/23/89 OE	**4,950**
Les Amies, 24/50, drypt, 1965, p/s, full mrgs, lt stn/sl, 9x13", lot 415, SBY 2/23/89 OE	**3,850**
Les Amies, 38/50, drypt, 1965, p/s, full mrgs, 9x13", lot 353, SBY 2/25/88	**2,200**
Les Banderilles, 7/50, blk/mauve/tan linocut, 1959, p/s, full mrgs, lt cr mrg corner, 21x26", SBY 5/12/88	**18,700**
Les Danseurs au Hibou, 8/50, brn/blk linocut, 1959, p/s, full mrgs, lt lstn/sl mrgs, unfr, 21x25", SBY 5/12/88	**7,700**
Les Deux Saltimbanques, ed of 250, drypt/van Gelder, 1905/1913, lt sl/stn, P-5x4", Vollard, lot 256, C-NY 5/11/88 OE	**14,300**
Les Jeux et la Lecture, a/p, before ed of 50, litho/Arches, 1953, full mrgs, lt stn, 19x25", lot 453, SBY 11/3/88 OE	**9,900**
Les Mains Liees II, 39/50, litho, 1952, p/s, lt fox/cr/sl, rub on verso, S-20x27", lot 402, SBY 2/23/89	**3,850**
Les Mains Liees IV, 38/50, litho, 1952, p/s, full mrgs, lt fox/scr, 19x23", lot 452, SBY 11/3/88	**3,850**
Les Menines et la Vie, total ed of 120, etch/Arches, 1958, p/s, full mrgs, lt cr, P-8x6", lot 456, C-NY 11/1/88 OE	**1,870**
Les Pauvres, ed of 250, etch/van Gelder Zonen, 1905/1913, full mrgs, lt stn/fox, 9x7", Vollard, lot 390, SBY 11/3/88	**14,300**
Les Pauvres, ed of 250, etch/van Gelder Zonen, 1913, lg mrgs, lt stn, 9x7", Vollard, lot 682, SBY 5/11/89 OE	**20,900**
Les Saltimbanques, ed of 250, drypt/van Gelder, 1905/1913, trm mrgs, lt fox/stn, 11x13", Vollard, lot 259, C-NY 5/11/88	**9,900**
Les Saltimbanques, ed of 250, drypt/van Gelder Zonen, 1905/1913, full mrgs, S-20x24", Vollard, lot 391, SBY 11/3/88 OE	**9,350**
Les Saltimbanques, ed of 250, drypt/van Gelder Zonen, 1913, lt fox/stn, 20x26", Vollard, lot 391, SBY 2/23/8 OE	**18,150**
Les Saltimbanques, 61/100, litho/Arches, 1958, sgn in red pencil, full mrgs, lt sl, L-9x6", lot 281, C-NY 5/11/88 OE	**1,760**

Les Tois Baigneuses, I; ed of 100, drypt/laid Japan, 1922-23, red crayon sgn, lt stn/fox, unfr, 7x5", SBY 5/12/88 OE	19,800
Les Trois Amies, 9/150, etch/Japan, 1927, sgn in red ink, lt fox/cr/mstn, P-17x12", lot 267, C-NY 5/11/88 OE	12,100
Les Trois Femmes, ed of 103, etch/wove paper, 1922/later, lt stn, 7x5", lot 399, SBY 11/3/88 OE	26,400
Les Trois Graces, total ed of 102, etch/wove paper, 1922-23, full mrgs, lt stn/fox, 7x5", lot 2884, B/B 2/16/88 OE	6,600
Les Trois Graces, 65/100, etch/wove paper, 1922-3, p/s, lt lstn/cr, tp/mstn on verso, P-13x8", lot 265, C-NY 5/11/88 OE	6,600
Les Trois Graces II, apart from #d ed of 100, etch/wove paper, 1922-23, lt stn/rpr tr, P-13x8", lot 722, C-NY 5/10/89	14,300
Les Trois Graces II, 15/100, etch/wove paper, 1922-23, p/s, Marcel Guiot bstp, full mrgs, P-13x8", lot 431, C-NY 11/1/88	5,720
Les Vendangeurs, 7/50, beige/blk/brn/mauve-tan linocut, 1959, p/s, full mrgs, 21x25", SBY 5/12/88 OE	14,300
Maison de la Pensee Francaise...Exposition de Ceramiques, ed of 500, litho, 1958, p/s, L-23x16", RWS 3/16/89 OE	800
March 25, 1971 I; 37/50, etch/aqua, 1971, stp/s, 8x6", lot 846, LH 12/4/88	750
Meleagre Tue le Sanglier de Calydon, sanguine etch/Japan, 1930, blk remarque, lt sl, 12x9", lot 407, SBY 11/3/88	1,650
Mere, Danseur et Musicien; 7/50, brn/tan/blk linocut, 1959, full mrgs, 25x21", lot 734, SBY 5/11/89 OE	23,100
Mere et Fils, 25/50, etch/laid paper, 1922/1961, stp/s, full mrgs, lt stn/cr, 5x5", lot 398, SBY 11/3/88	6,600
Minotaure, Buveur et Femmes; Pl 92, etch/Vollard laid paper, 1933, p/s, full mrgs, P-12x15", lot 734, C-NY 5/10/89	22,000
Minotaure, Buveur et Femmes; total ed of 300, etch, 1933, p/s, full mrgs, lt stn/fox, 12x14", lot 395, SBY 2/23/89 OE	24,200
Minotaure, Buveur et Femmes; total ed of 300, etch, 1933, p/s, full mrgs, lt stn/scr, P-12x14", Vollard, SBY 5/12/88 OE	17,600
Minotaure, un Coupe a la Main, et Jeune Fille; total ed of 300, etch, 1933, 8x11", Vollard, lot 419, SBY 11/3/88 OE	8,800
Minotaure Attaquant une Amazone, Pl 87, etch/Montval, 1933, p/s, full mrgs, stn, 7x11", Vollard, lot 439, C-NY 11/11/88	4,400
Minotaure Aveugle Guide par une Fillette, I; Pl 94, etch/Montval, 1934, p/s, full mrgs, stn/sl, 10x14", C-NY 5/10/89 OE	14,300
Minotaure Aveugle Guide par une Fillette dans la Nuit, Pl 97, etch/aqua/engr, 1934, P-10x14", Vollard, C-NY 5/11/88 OE	60,500
Minotaure Aveugle Guide par une Fillette dans la Nuit, Pl 97, etch/aqua/engr, 1934, p/s, P-10x14", lot 737, C-NY 5/10/89	71,500
Minotaure Aveugle Guide par une Fillette dans la Nuit, Pl 97, etch/aqua/engr/Montval, 1934, 10x14", C-NY 11/1/88	55,000
Minotaure Blesse, VI; Pl 88, etch/Montval, 1933, p/s, full mrgs, lt mstn, P-8x20", lot 733, C-NY 5/10/89 OE	5,280
Minotaure Caressant une Femme, ed of 300, etch, 1933, full mrgs, lt stn/fox, 12x15", Vollard, lot 701, SBY 5/11/89 OE	20,900
Minotaure Caressant une Femme, total ed of 300, etch/Montval, 1933, full mrgs, 12x14", Vollard, lot 394, SBY 2/23/89 OE	2,200
Minotaure Vaincu, total ed of 300, etch, 1933, p/s, full mrgs, lt stn, 8x11", Vollard, lot 421, SBY 11/3/88 OE	7,425
Modele Accoude sur un Tableau, Pl 43, ed of 250, etch/Montval, 1933, stn, P-11x8", lot 273, C-NY 5/11/88 OE	7,150
Modele Accoude sur un Tableau, Pl 43, ed of 250, etch/Montval, 1933, full mrgs, lt stn, P-11x8", lot 727, C-NY 5/10/89	9,900
Modele Accroupi, Sculpture de Dos et Tete Barbue; etch/aqua/Montval, 1933, p/s, full mrgs, P-11x8", C-NY 5/10/89	6,600
Modele au Fume-Cigarette, 24/50, etch/aqua/BFK Rives, 1966, p/s, full mrgs, P-11x15", lot 755, C-NY 5/10/89	3,300
Modele Contemplant un Groupe Sculpte, Pl 66, etch/wm Vollard laid paper, 1933, trm mrgs, 12x15", lot 436, C-NY 11/1/88	6,600
Modele Contemplant un Groupe Sculpte, total ed of 300, etch, 1933, p/s, full mrgs, 12x15", Vollard, lot 416, SBY 11/3/88	7,700
Modele Contemplant un Groupe Sculpte, total ed of 300, etch, 1933, p/s, full mrgs, P-12x15", Vollard, SBY 5/12/88 OE	8,250
Modele et Grande Sculpture de Dos, Pl 73, etch/scr/Montval wm Picasso, 1933, P-11x8", lot 274, C-NY 5/11/88 OE	7,700
Modele et Grande Tete Sculptee, Pl 61, etch/Montval, 1933, full mrgs, lt stn/fox, P-11x8", Vollard, C-NY 5/10/89 OE	7,700
Modele et Grande Tete Sculptee, Pl 61, etch/Montval, 1933, p/s, full mrgs, P-11x8", Vollard, lot 435, C-NY 11/1/88 OE	6,600
Monotaure Aveugle Guide par une Fillette, III; etch/engr, 1934, p/s, full mrgs, 9x12", Vollard, lot 427, SBY 11/3/88 OE	12,100
Nature Morte, Compotier; ed of 100, drypt, 1909, p/s, trm mrgs, lt stn, S-13x9", lot 395, SBY 11/3/88	7,150
Nature Morte, Compotier; ed of 100, drypt/laid paper, 1909, p/s, trm mrgs, lt stn/fox, unfr, S-16x15", SBY 5/12/88	11,000

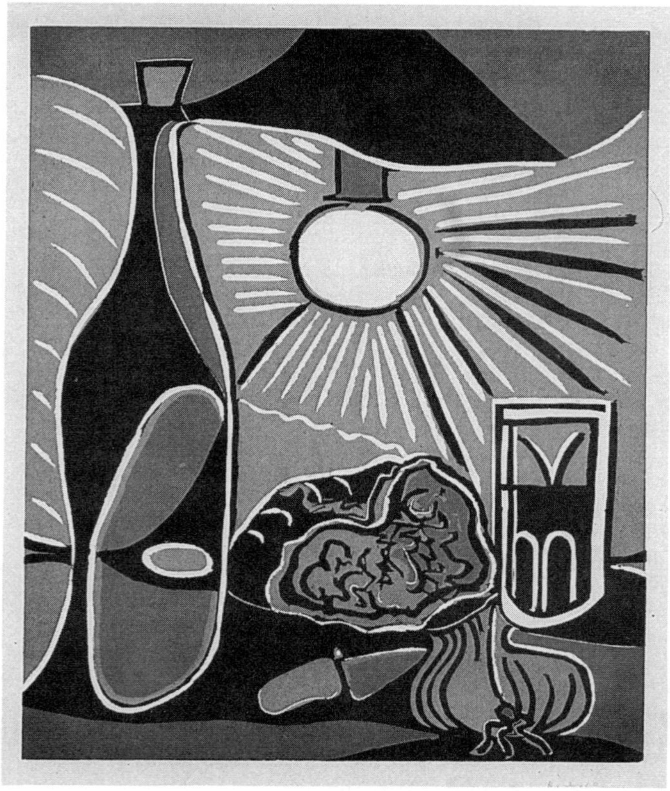

Nature Morte a la Bouteille, 14/50, blk/slate gray/burnt sienna linocut on Arches, 1962, lt stn, L-25x21", lot 751, C-NY 5/10/89; $38,500

Nature Morte a la Pasteque, aside from #d ed of 60, clr linocut, 1962, p/s, inscr, full mrgs, 24x28", SBY 5/12/88 OE **20,900**
Nature Morte Sous la Lampe, 14/50, clr linocut, 1962, p/s, full mrgs, lt stn, 25x21", lot 335, SBY 2/25/88 OE **93,500**
Neuf Tetes, 2/50, etch/drypt, 1934/1961, stp/s, full mrgs, lt sl mrgs, 12x9", lot 434, SBY 11/3/88 OE **5,500**
Neuf Tetes, 30/50, etch/drypt, 1934/1961, stp/s, full mrgs, lt cr/sl, 13x9", lot 318, SBY 2/25/88 OE **2,860**
Nu Assis Entoure d'Esquisses de Betes et d'Hommes, book ed of 340, etch, 1927, lt stn, P-8x11", lot 269, C-NY 5/11/88 OE **825**
One Hundred Fifty-Six Series: #79; 17/50, etch/wove paper, stp/s, 15x19", SLK 11/25/88 ..... **1,600**
Pablo Picasso (Paul Eluard), 4/25, etch, 1945, p/s, lt scr/stn, S-11x9", lot 437, SBY 11/3/88 OE **4,675**
Pair: La Biche; La Sauterelle; ed of 225, etch/aqua, 1941-42, tp on verso, S-17x13", lot 278, C-NY 5/11/88 OE **715**
Pair: Le Frere Mendiant; Portrait de Pepe Illo; 1/3 & 19/50, drypt, 1959/1963, unfr, 12x5"/8x7", SBY 5/12/88 ..... **1,760**
Pair: Sueno y Mentira de Franco; 230/850, etch/aqua, 1937, stp/s, 12x17", lot 365, LH 10/16/88 ..... **1,500**
Pair: Sueno y Mentira de Franco; 136/150, etch/aqua/smooth wove paper, 1937, full mrgs, 15x23", lot 710, SBY 5/11/89 ..... **17,600**
Pair: Sueno y Mentira de Franco; 33/150, etch/aqua/Chine applique, 1937, full mrgs, P-13x17", lot 450, C-NY 11/1/88 OE **16,500**
Pair: 156 Series: No 62 & No 68; 5/50, etch, 1971, stp/s, full mrgs, lt stn, 8x6", lot 428, SBY 2/23/89 OE **4,675**
Peintre au Travail, 33/50, etch/BFK Rives, 1963, p/s, full mrgs, lt mstn, P-13x17", lot 283, C-NY 5/11/88 ..... **2,420**
Peintre au Travail, 38/50, aqua, 1963, p/s, full mrgs, 13x17", lot 341, SBY 2/25/88 OE **3,740**
Peintre au Travail, 38/50, aqua, 1965, p/s, full mrgs, 15x11", lot 352, SBY 2/25/88 OE **3,080**
Peintre au Travail, 38/50, aqua/drypt, 1963, p/s, 8x10", lot 340, SBY 2/25/88 ..... **3,300**
Peintre au Travail, 38/50, aqua/etch/drypt, 1964, p/s, full mrgs, 13x19", lot 348, SBY 2/25/88 OE **4,400**
Peintre au Travail, 38/50, aqua/etch/drypt, 1964, p/s, full mrgs, 13x19", lot 349, SBY 2/25/88 OE **3,850**
Peintre Entre Deux Modeles, 24/99, etch, sgn, lt stn, 8x11", lot 405, SBY 11/3/88 OE **5,225**
Peintre et Modele, 15/50, aqua/drypt, 1965, p/s, full mrgs, lt mstn, 9x13", lot 744, SBY 5/11/89 OE **3,850**
Peintre et Modele, 24/50, drypt/BFK Rives, 1966, p/s, full mrgs, lt mstn, P-11x15", lot 754, C-NY 5/10/89 ..... **2,420**
Peintre et Modele, 38/50, aqua, 1963, p/s, full mrgs, 13x17", lot 343, SBY 2/25/88 OE **3,850**
Peintre et Modele, 38/50, aqua/drypt, 1965, p/s, full mrgs, 9x13", lot 359, SBY 2/25/88 OE **3,850**
Peintre et Modele, 38/50, aqua/drypt, 1965, p/s, full mrgs, 9x13", lot 358, SBY 2/25/88 OE **3,300**
Peintre et Modele, 38/50, etch/aqua, 1966, p/s, full mrgs, lt stn mrgs, 11x15", lot 375, SBY 2/25/88 OE **3,300**
Peintre et Modele, 38/50, etch/aqua, 1966, p/s, full mrgs, 16x22", lot 374, SBY 2/25/88 ..... **2,860**
Peintre et Modele, 38/50, etch/aqua, 1966, p/s, full mrgs, 13x19", lot 379, SBY 2/25/88 ..... **1,760**
Peintre et Modele Tricontant, Le Chef-d'Oeuvre Inconnu; 24/99, etch, 1927, P-8x11", lot 268, C-NY 5/11/88 OE **4,620**
Peintre Ramassant son Pinceau, Pl 7, 75/99, etch/van Gelder, full mrgs, lt stn, P-8x11", lot 432, C-NY 11/1/88 OE **6,600**
Personnages Masques et Femme Oiseau, ed of 300, aqua/etch, 1934, p/s, full mrgs, mstn, P-10x14", Vollard, SBY 5/12/88 OE **6,050**
Personnages Masques et Femme Oiseau, total ed of 300, etch/aqua, 1934, full mrgs, 10x14", lot 704, SBY 5/11/89 OE **8,250**
Personnages Masques et Femme Oiseau, total ed of 300, etch/aqua, 1934, p/s, full mrgs, 10x14", lot 428, SBY 11/3/88 ..... **5,500**
Picador, Femme et Cheval; 7/50, tan/blk linocut, 1959, p/s, full mrgs, 25x21", lot 457, SBY 11/3/88 ..... **12,650**
Picador et Cheval, 31/50, brn/blk linocut, 1959, p/s, full mrgs, lt stn, 25x21", lot 456, SBY 11/3/88 ..... **8,250**
Picasso, Dessins d'un Demi-Siecle; ed of 1000, clr litho/cream wove paper, sgn in stone, cr, 8x9", lot 2885, B/B 4/19/88 ..... **248**
Picasso Ceramiques et Pates Blanches, 41/125, clr linocut/Arches, 1958, full mrgs, unfr, 24x18", SBY 5/12/88 OE **3,300**
Pigeon au Fond Gris, 12/50, litho/Arches, sgn in red crayon, lt stn/scr, S-13x20", lot 146, C-NY 11/1/88 OE **12,100**
Pigeon au Fond Gris, 30/50, litho, 1947, sgn in red pencil, lt stn, 11x18", lot 399, SBY 2/23/89 OE **4,400**
Pigeonneau, 31/226, linocut/BFK Rives, 1939, sgn in blk crayon, full mrgs, lt stn, L-6x8", lot 741, C-NY 5/10/89 ..... **3,080**
Pique, 7/50, bl/blk linocut, 1959, p/s, full mrgs, lt print irregularity in corner, 21x25", SBY 5/12/88 OE **20,900**
Pique (Rouge et Jaune), 26/50, red/yel linocut, 1959, p/s, full mrgs, lt stn/sl, 21x25", lot 455, SBY 11/3/88 OE **23,100**
Planche pour B Geiser, 1/2, etch/Arches, 1933, full mrgs, 7x5", w/cancelled copper pl, lot 694, SBY 5/11/89 OE **28,600**
Plante aux Toritos (Epreuve Rincee), linocut w/encre de Chine/Arches, after 1960, sgn, L-27x23", lot 458, C-NY 11/1/88 ..... **16,500**
Portfolio: Papiers Colles 1910-1914; 68/100, p/s, orig wrappers, Au Pont des Artes, lot 367, SBY 2/25/88 OE **2,970**
Portrait de DH Kahnweiler, I; 42/50, litho, 1957, sgn in red crayon, S-26x20", lot 729, SBY 5/11/89 OE **3,850**
Portrait de Famille, Quatre Personnages Dont Trois Assis; 38/50, litho, 1962, full mrgs, 17x23", lot 332, SBY 2/25/88 OE **4,950**
Portrait de Jacqueline, aside from #d ed of 100, offset litho, 1956, lt stn/nick, 20x15", lot 404, SBY 2/23/89 OE **13,200**
Portrait de Mme Picasso, a/p, before ed of 65, drypt, 1919-20, p/s, full mrgs, S-12x8", lot 396, SBY 11/3/88 OE **46,750**
Portrait de Mme Picasso, I; 34/50, drypt/old bl laid paper, 1919-20/1961, stp/s, lt fox, 6x4", SBY 5/12/88 OE **9,900**
Portrait de Mme Rosengart, a/p, ed of 6, litho/Arches, 1964, p/s, lt cr/sl, 25x18", lot 740, SBY 5/11/89 OE **42,900**
Portrait de Vollard, II; Pl 98, aqua/Montval, ca 1937, full mrgs, lt stn/sl, P-14x10", Vollard, lot 444, C-NY 11/1/88 ..... **1,760**
Portrait de Vollard, II; Pl 98, aqua/wm Vollard Montval, ca 1937, sgn in red pencil, 14x10", lot 445, C-NY 11/1/88 ..... **2,860**
Portrait de Vollard, III; Pl 99, aqua/wm Vollard Montval, ca 1937, full mrgs, P-14x20", lot 446, C-NY 11/1/88 OE **2,860**
Portrait de Vollard, IV; Pl 100, aqua/wm Picasso Montval, ca 1937, full mrgs, fox/stn, 14x10", lot 447, C-NY 11/1/88 OE **3,520**
Profil, 8/50, etch/aqua, 1966, p/s, full mrgs, lt sl mrgs/verso, 11x15", lot 421, SBY 2/23/89 OE **3,300**
Profil au Fond Noir, a/p, before ed of 50, litho, 1947, full mrgs, lt fox/scr, 21x14", lot 440, SBY 11/3/88 OE **6,325**
Profil en Trois Couleurs, 3/50, clr litho/Arches, 1956, p/s, full mrgs, lt fox/stn, 20x13", lot 326, SBY 2/25/88 OE **10,450**
Profil et Femme, 25/50, aqua, 1965, p/s, full mrgs, 15x11", lot 468, SBY 11/3/88 ..... **3,300**
Profil et Femme, 38/50, aqua, 1965, p/s, full mrgs, 15x11", lot 350, SBY 2/25/88 OE **3,300**
Profile of Woman Looking to the Right, a/p (unpublished work), litho, 1963, full mrgs, lt fox/cr, SBY 2/23/89 OE **2,475**
Quatre Femmes Nues et Tete Sculptee, total ed of 300, etch, 1934, p/s, full mrgs, 9x12", Vollard, lot 426, SBY 11/3/88 ..... **20,900**
Rembrandt a la Palette, total ed of 300, etch, 1934, p/s, full mrgs, 11x8", Vollard, lot 422, SBY 11/3/88 OE **4,125**
Rembrandt et Femme au Voile, ed of 300, etch, 1934, p/s, full mrgs, lt stn, 11x8", Vollard, lot 423, SBY 11/3/88 ..... **5,775**
Sable Mouvant, VII/X, aqua/Auvergne, 1964, p/s, full mrgs, lt stn, 15x11", lot 414, SBY 2/23/89 ..... **3,300**
Sable Mouvant, 3/50, aqua/Auvergne, 1964, p/s, full mrgs, 15x12", lot 2887, B/B 4/19/88 OE **3,575**
Sable Mouvant, 3/50, aqua/Auvergne, 1965, p/s, full mrgs, 15x11", lot 2888, B/B 4/19/88 OE **3,300**
Salome, ed of 250, drypt/van Gelder Zonen, 1905/1913, full mrgs, lt fox/cr, 16x14", Vollard, lot 393, SBY 11/3/88 ..... **15,400**
Scene Antique, 45/50, litho, 1956, p/s, full mrgs, 18x14", lot 725, SBY 5/11/89 ..... **3,850**
Scene aux Quatre Personnages, 38/50, etch, 1959, p/s, full mrgs, lt cr/stn, 10x10", lot 329, SBY 2/25/88 ..... **2,420**
Scene aux Quatre Personnages, 41/50, etch/laid paper, 1959, p/s, lt cr mrgs, 9x10", lot 732, SBY 5/11/89 OE **3,850**

Scene Bachique au Minotaure, total ed of 300, etch, 1933, p/s, full mrgs, 12x14", Vollard, lot 420, SBY 11/3/88 ... 19,525
Scene Bachique au Minotaure, Pl 85, 6/15, etch/Montval, 1933, sgn in red ink, P-12x15", Vollard, lot 438, C-NY 11/1/88 ... 17,600
Scene d'Atelier, 15/50, etch/engr, 1963, p/s, S-15x19", lot 411, SBY 2/23/89 OE ... 2,750
Scene d'Interieur, 25/100, litho, 1926, p/s, full mrgs, lt tr/cr/sl, 9x11", lot 401, SBY 11/3/88 OE ... 3,300
Scene de Theatre, 21/50, aqua/BFK Rives, 1966, p/s, full mrgs, P-13x19", C-NY 5/11/88 ... 1,870
Scene de Theatre, 38/50, aqua, 1966, p/s, full mrgs, 13x19", lot 381, SBY 2/25/88 ... 1,980
Scene Familiale, 25/50, brn/blk linocut, 1963, p/s, full mrgs, lt stn, 16x21", lot 738, SBY 5/11/89 OE ... 15,400
Scene Mythologique, 38/50, drypt, 1966, p/s, full mrgs, 11x15", lot 382, SBY 2/25/88 OE ... 3,850
Sculpteur, Modele Accroupi et Tete Sculptee; Pl 39, etch/wm Picasso Montval, 1933, p/s, 10x8", lot 434, C-NY 11/1/88 OE ... 7,700
Sculpteur, Modele Accroupi et Tete Sculptee; total ed of 300, etch, 1933, 11x8", Vollard, lot 697, SBY 5/11/88 OE ... 13,200
Sculpteur, Modele Couche et Sculpture; total ed of 300, etch, 1937, p/s, 10x8", Vollard, lot 409, SBY 11/3/88 ... 7,150
Sculpteur, Modele et Sculpture Assise; total ed of 300, drypt, 1933, full mrgs, lt sl/stn, 13x7", Vollard, SBY 5/12/88 ... 4,950
Sculpteur avec Coupe et Modele Accroupi, Pl 44, ed of 250, etch/Montval, 1933, p/s, full mrgs, P-11x8", C-NY 5/10/89 OE ... 12,100
Sculpteur avec Coupe et Modele Accroupi, total ed of 300, etch, 1933, p/s, lt mstn, P-11x8", Vollard, SBY 5/12/88 OE ... 8,250
Sculpteur d'un Jeune Homme a la Coupe, total ed of 300, etch, 1933, full mrgs, 11x8", Vollard, lot 418, SBY 11/3/88 OE ... 6,050
Sculpteur et Modele Agenouille, ed of 300, etch, 1933, p/s, full mrgs, lt stn, 15x12", Vollard, lot 417, SBY 11/3/88 OE ... 26,400
Sculpteur et son Modele Devant une Fenetre, total ed of 300, etch, 1933, p/s, full mrgs, lt stn, 8x11", SBY 11/3/88 OE ... 13,200
Sculpteur et Trois Danseuses Sculptees, Pl 81, etch/Montval, 1934, p/s, full mrgs, 9x12", Vollard, lot 442, C-NY 11/1/88 ... 9,900
Sculpteur et Trois Danseuses Sculptees, total ed of 300, etch, 1934, full mrgs, 9x12", Vollard, lot 424, SBY 11/3/88 OE ... 11,000
Sculpteurs, Modeles et Sculpture; total ed of 300, etch, 1933, full mrgs, lt stn/fox, 8x11", lot 696, SBY 5/11/89 ... 9,900
Set of 6: Lysistrata d'Aristophane; 150/25, etch/Arches, 1934, p/s, 9x6", Ltd Ed Club, lot 708, SBY 5/11/89 OE ... 24,200
Six Contes Fantasques: Composition; 12/30, engr, 1944, sgn in crayon, full mrgs, stn, P-14x11", Flammarion, SBY 5/12/88 ... 1,540
Still Life with Vase of Flowers, a/p, 2nd state, litho, 1949, lt fox/scuff/cr/sl, S-20x22", lot 401, SBY 2/23/89 OE ... 13,200
Sur la Plage, I (2 Nus); 37/50, litho, 1921, p/s, full mrgs, lt stn, 4x9", lot 686, SBY 5/11/89 OE ... 4,125
Taureau Aile Contemple par Quatre Enfants, Pl 13, etch/Montval, 1934, p/s, full mrgs, lt stn, P-10x12", C-NY 5/10/89 ... 20,900
Taureau Aile Contemple par Quatre Enfants, total ed of 300, etch, 1934, p/s, fox/stn, 9x12", lot 705, SBY 5/11/89 ... 17,600
Taureau Aile Contemple par Quatre Enfants, total ed of 300, etch, 1934, p/s, full mrgs, 9x12", Vollard, SBY 11/3/88 OE ... 20,900
Taureau Attaquant un Cheval, ed of 101, etch/Japan, 1921, p/s, full mrgs, lt stn, 7x10", lot 397, SBY 11/3/88 ... 4,125
Taureau et Chevaux dans l'Arene, Pl 15, etch/Montval, 1933, p/s, full mrgs, 8x11", Vollard, lot 440, C-NY 11/1/88 ... 2,860
Taureu Aile Contemple par Quatre Enfants, Pl 13, ed of 300, etch, 1934, p/s, 9x12", lot 153, LH 12/4/88 ... 16,000
Tete, 40/50, clr aqua/Richard de Bas, 1964, p/s, full mrgs, lt lstn, P-16x13", lot 752, C-NY 5/10/89 ... 770
Tete de Femme, de Profil; ed of 250, drypt/van Gelder, 1905/1913, lt cr/stn, P-11x10", Vollard, lot 258, C-NY 5/11/88 ... 8,800
Tete de Femme, de Profil; ed of 250, drypt/van Gelder, 1905/1913, fox/stn, P-12x10", Vollard, lot 257, C-NY 5/11/88 OE ... 35,200
Tete de Femme, ed of 250, etch/van Gelder, 1905/1913, full mrgs, lt stn, P-5x3", Vollard, lot 254, C-NY 5/11/88 OE ... 18,700
Tete de Femme, 16/50, litho, 1945, p/s, lt stn/scr, 13x10", lot 715, SBY 5/11/89 ... 7,150
Tete de Femme, 40/50, beige/purple-brn/blk linocut, 1962, p/s, full mrgs, cr img, lt mstn, unfr, 25x21", SBY 5/12/88 OE ... 34,100
Tete de Femme (De Profil), brick/tan/blk linocut, 1959, p/s, full mrgs, lt stn, 25x21", lot 733, SBY 5/11/89 ... 38,500
Tete de Femme au Chignon, 30/50, litho/Arches, 1953, p/s, full mrgs, lt cr/scr/tstn, L-26x17", lot 455, C-NY 11/1/88 ... 5,280
Tete de Femme No 1, Portrait de Dora Maar; total ed of 80, aqua/drypt, 1939, full mrgs, 12x9", lot 436, SBY 11/3/88 ... 27,500
Tete de Femme No 6, Portrait de Dora Maar; aqua/grattoir, 1939, 12x9", Vollard/Lacouriere, lot 713, SBY 5/11/89 OE ... 23,100
Tete de Femme Tournee a Droite, 36/50, sftgr etch, 1933/1961, stp/s, full mrgs, lt cr/sl, 3x2", lot 432, SBY 11/3/88 OE ... 2,310
Tetes, 25/50, blk/brn/beige linocut on Arches, 1963, p/s, full mrgs, lt stn, 25x21", lot 336, SBY 2/25/88 OE ... 8,250
Tetes et Pierre, 4/50, litho/Arches, 1950, p/s, lt stn/fox/sl, L-18x24", lot 744, C-NY 5/10/89 ... 4,400
Tetes et Pierre, 42/50, litho/Arches, 1950, p/s, full mrgs, lt fox img, L-18x22", lot 280, C-NY 5/11/88 ... 4,180
Tetes et Pierre, 47/50, litho, 1950, p/s, full mrgs, lt fox/ls, 18x23", lot 450, SBY 11/3/88 OE ... 5,500
Toreo y Senorita, 12/245, clr litho/cream wove paper, 1960, p/s, lt trm mrgs, lt stn, 13x9", lot 2886, B/B 4/19/88 OE ... 2,200
Toros en Vallauris, clr linocut, 1955, sgn in red crayon, lt cr, 26x21", lot 368, SBY 2/25/88 OE ... 4,125
Toros en Vallauris, ed of 200, clr linocut, 1955, sgn in crayon, full mrgs, lt cr, 26x21", SBY 5/12/88 OE ... 4,950
Toros en Vallauris 1955, 130/200, litho, full mrgs, wstn/rpl, 31x23", RAB 3/27/89 UE ... 1,050
Toros en Vallauris 1957, 153/198, bl linocut, 1957, sgn in bl crayon, lt sl/fox/cr, 25x21", lot 728, SBY 5/11/89 ... 2,750
Trois Femmes, 32/50, etch/laid paper, 1938, p/s, full mrgs, lt stn, 12x8", lot 711, SBY 5/11/89 ... 13,200
Trois Femmes, 38/50, drypt, 1965, p/s, full mrgs, lt fox img/mrgs, 9x13", lot 355, SBY 2/25/88 OE ... 3,960
Two Dancers, etch/Deluxe Japan, 1943, pl/s, 11x8", lot 2885, B/B 2/16/88 OE ... 770
Un Couple d'Amateurs, 47/50, aqua, 1966, p/s, full mrgs, lt mstn/cr, skinned mrg/verso, 13x16", SBY 5/12/88 OE ... 4,950
Untitled, From Sueno y Mentira de Franco; Pl 1, 799/850, aqua/etch/Montval, 1937, stn, unfr, P-13x17", C-NY 1/22/88 OE ... 1,045
Untitled, Le Carmen des Carmen; XXIII/XXX, aqua/Japan nacre, sgn in gr pencil, full mrgs, 16x12", lot 750, C-NY 5/10/89 ... 7,150
Vallauris, Peintrue et Lumiere, Xe Anniversaire; 158/185, brn/yel/wht linocut, 1964, full mrgs, 25x21", SBY 2/23/89 OE ... 6,875
Vallauris 1956 Exposition, clr linocut/Arches, 1956, sgn in bl crayon, full mrgs, 26x21", lot 369, SBY 2/25/88 OE ... 6,325
Vallauris 1956 Toros, ed of 200, clr linocut/Arches, 1956, sgn in crayon, full mrgs, stn, unfr, 26x21", SBY 5/12/88 OE ... 6,050
Vallauris 1956 Toros, linocut/Arches, 1956, sgn in red crayon, full mrgs, 26x21", lot 727, SBY 5/11/89 OE ... 6,050
Vase de Fleurs, 7/50, clr litho, 1957/1961, stp/s, full mrgs, lt fox, L-20x17", SBY 5/12/88 OE ... 6,820
Venus et l'Amour, 2E Variation; a/p, before ed of 50, litho, 1949, S-26x20", lot 447, SBY 11/3/88 OE ... 6,600
Visage, 172/200, litho/Japan, 1928, p/s, full mrgs, lt stn/rub/fox, S-10x8", lot 406, SBY 11/3/88 ... 49,500
Visage, 2/25, litho/Chine volant, 1928, full mrgs, lt fox, S-11x8", lot 690, SBY 5/11/89 OE ... 66,000
Visage, 24/25, aside from ed of 200, litho, 1928, p/s, inscr HC, full mrgs, lt rub/cr/stn, S-11x8", SBY 5/12/88 OE ... 50,600
Visage, 33/50, blk/tan linocut, 1962, p/s, lg mrgs, lt stn, S-22x18", lot 463, SBY 11/3/88 ... 4,950
Young Woman, Full Face; a/p (unpublished work), litho, 1963, full mrgs, lt fox, 24x18", lot 410, SBY 2/23/89 ... 7,700
156 Series: No 107; 38/50, etch, 1971, stp/s, full mrgs, lt tr mrg, lt mstn, P-15x20", SBY 5/12/88 OE ... 3,850
156 Series: No 112; 45/50, etch, 1971, stp/s, full mrgs, 2 sm tr mrg, lt mstn, hinge stn, P-14x20", SBY 5/12/88 OE ... 4,400
156 Series: No 113; 17/50, etch, 1971, stp/s, full mrgs, 15x19", lot 481, SBY 11/3/88 ... 2,750
156 Series: No 13; IV/XV, etch/scraper, 1970, stp/s, full mrgs, 20x25", lot 749, SBY 5/11/89 ... 9,900

156 Series: No 15; IX/XV, etch/aqua/drypt/scraper, 1970, stp/s, full mrgs, 20x25", lot 750, SBY 5/11/89 ... 11,000
156 Series: No 35; 50/50, etch, 1970, stp/s, full mrgs, lt cr/disclr mrgs, gstn recto/verso, P-20x21", SBY 5/12/88 OE ... 4,675
156 Series: No 69; 38/50, etch, 1971, stp/s, full mrgs, 6x8", lot 393, SBY 2/25/88 ... 990
156 Series: No 73; 42/50, etch, 1971, stp/s, full mrgs, lt mstn, P-6x8", lot 294, C-NY 5/11/88 ... 1,320
156 Series: No 81; 34/50, etch, 1971, stp/s, full mrgs, lt mstn, P-15x19", SBY 5/12/88 OE ... 4,675
347 Series, No 324; 29/50, etch, 1968, p/s, full mrgs, lt sl/disclr mrgs, P-8x11", SBY 5/12/88 OE ... 4,675
347 Series: No 100; 22/50, etch/aqua, 1968, p/s, full mrgs, lt stn, P-12x14", lot 290, C-NY 5/11/88 OE ... 3,300
347 Series: No 11; 23/50, etch, 1968, p/s, full mrgs, 16x12", lot 471, SBY 11/3/88 OE ... 5,775
347 Series: No 114; 43/50, aqua, 1968, p/s, full mrgs, 9x13", SBY 5/12/88 ... 4,950
347 Series: No 13; 8/50, etch/wove paper, 1968, p/s, full mrgs, P-16x12", lot 757, C-NY 5/10/89 OE ... 5,280
347 Series: No 143; 20/50, aqua/wove paper, 1968, p/s, full mrgs, lt stn/sl, P-20x16", lot 758, C-NY 5/10/89 ... 4,180
347 Series: No 18; 20/50, aqua/etch, 1968, p/s, full mrgs, 15x11", lot 472, SBY 11/3/88 OE ... 8,525
347 Series: No 184; 35/50, etch, 1968, p/s, full mrgs, 9x4", lot 475, SBY 11/3/88 OE ... 4,125
347 Series: No 194; 31/50, etch, 1968, p/s, full mrgs, 8x6", lot 426, SBY 2/23/89 OE ... 3,300
347 Series: No 197; 4/50, etch, 1968, p/s, full mrgs, 11x15", SBY 5/12/88 OE ... 4,125
347 Series: No 20; 21/50, aqua, 1968, p/s, full mrgs, lt stn, 12x19", lot 473, SBY 11/3/88 OE ... 4,675
347 Series: No 20; 24/50, aqua, 1968, p/s, full mrgs, lt mstn, P-13x18", lot 289, C-NY 5/11/88 OE ... 2,420
347 Series: No 217; 27/50, etch, 1968, p/s, full mrgs, lt skinned mrg/verso, lt cr, P-12x12", SBY 5/12/88 OE ... 4,125
347 Series: No 220; 45/50, drypt w/sandpaper ground, 1968, p/s, full mrgs, lt mstn, 6x9", SBY 5/12/88 OE ... 2,475
347 Series: No 229; 25/50, etch, 1968, p/s, full mrgs, lt mstn mrgs, P-7x9", lot 291, C-NY 5/11/88 OE ... 1,980
347 Series: No 229; 45/50, etch, 1968, p/s, full mrgs, 7x9", lot 427, SBY 2/23/89 OE ... 4,125
347 Series: No 24; 32/50, etch, 1968, p/s, full mrgs, lt skinned/gstn mrg/verso, lt mstn, P-12x16", SBY 5/12/88 OE ... 8,525
347 Series: No 259; 21/50, etch, 1968, p/s, P-7x9", C-NY 5/11/88 OE ... 2,640
347 Series: No 28; 31/50, etch, 1968, p/s, full mrgs, 3x2", lot 423, SBY 2/23/89 OE ... 2,750
347 Series: No 299; 23/50, etch, 1968, p/s, full mrgs, 9x13", lot 748, SBY 5/11/89 OE ... 3,300
347 Series: No 300; 43/50, etch, 1968, p/s, full mrgs, lt stn, 16x20", lot 477, SBY 11/3/88 OE ... 4,675
347 Series: No 308; 24/50, etch, 1968, p/s, full mrgs, lt mstn, 6x8", lot 386, SBY 2/25/88 ... 1,320
347 Series: No 310; 24/50, etch, 1968, p/s, full mrgs, lt mstn, 6x8", lot 387, SBY 2/25/88 ... 1,650
347 Series: No 311; 24/50, etch, 1968, p/s, full mrgs, lt stn, 6x8", lot 388, SBY 2/25/88 ... 1,430
347 Series: No 312; 24/50, etch, 1968, p/s, full mrgs, lt stn, 6x8", lot 478, SBY 11/3/88 OE ... 3,025
347 Series: No 313; 24/50, etch, 1968, p/s, full mrgs, lt mstn, 6x8", lot 390, SBY 2/25/88 ... 1,320
347 Series: No 315; 25/50, etch, 1968, sgn, full mrgs, lt mstn, 6x8", lot 391, SBY 2/25/89 ... 1,320
347 Series: No 327; 18/50, aqua, 1968, p/s, full mrgs, lt mstn, 8x10", SBY 5/12/88 OE ... 4,125
347 Series: No 332; 25/50, etch/wove paper, 1968, p/s, full mrgs, lt mstn, P-8x11", lot 477, C-NY 11/1/88 ... 3,080
347 Series: No 334; 2/50, etch/wove paper, 1968, p/s, full mrgs, P-8x11", lot 478, C-NY 11/1/88 ... 2,860
347 Series: No 334; 4/50, etch, 1968, p/s, full mrgs, 8x11", lot 479, SBY 11/3/88 OE ... 5,500
347 Series: No 339; 25/50, etch, 1968, p/s, full mrgs, lt mstn/cr mrgs, P-8x11", lot 293, C-NY 5/11/88 OE ... 2,420
347 Series: No 343; 26/50, etch/drypt, 1968, p/s, full mrgs, 8x11", lot 392, SBY 2/25/88 OE ... 3,960
347 Series: No 347; 17/50, aqua, 1968, p/s, full mrgs, 9x13", lot 480, SBY 11/3/88 ... 9,350
347 Series: No 347; 8/50, aqua/wove paper, 1968, p/s, full mrgs, lt mstn mrgs, P-9x13", lot 480, C-NY 11/1/88 OE ... 7,700
347 Series: No 42; 18/50, aqua/drypt, 1968, p/s, full mrgs, 13x16", lot 747, SBY 5/11/89 OE ... 6,600
347 Series: No 45; 8/50, drypt/aqua, 1968, p/s, full mrgs, 12x16", lot 424, SBY 2/23/89 ... 4,400
347 Series: No 46; 21/50, etch, 1968, p/s, full mrgs, 11x15", lot 474, SBY 11/3/88 OE ... 6,600
347 Series: No 47; 4/50, etch, 1968, p/s, full mrgs, 11x15", lot 384, SBY 2/25/89 OE ... 4,125
347 Series: No 50; 18/50, aqua/wove paper, 1968, p/s, full mrgs, P-5x4", lot 474, C-NY 11/1/88 OE ... 2,420
347 Series: No 59; 8/50, etch, p/s, full mrgs, P-13x16", SBY 5/12/88 OE ... 3,850
347 Series: No 70; 4/50, etch, 1968, p/s, full mrgs, 12x16", lot 385, SBY 2/25/88 OE ... 5,225
347 Series: No 74; 8/50, etch, 1968, p/s, full mrgs, 12x16", lot 425, SBY 2/23/89 OE ... 4,400
347 Series: No 8; 5/50, etch, 1968, p/s, full mrgs, lt stn, 17x14", lot 470, SBY 11/3/88 OE ... 6,050
347 Series: No 92; 23/50, aqua/etch/Rives, 1968, p/s, full mrgs, P-7x8", lot 475, C-NY 11/1/88 ... 4,180
4 Mai 1945, aside from #d ed of 50, engr/wove paper, 1945, p/s, full mrgs, lt stn, 9x14", lot 319, SBY 2/25/89 OE ... 2,200

PICASSO, Pablo; after (Spanish, 1881-1973)
Bullfighting Arena, by Aldo Crommelynck, 187/200, aqua/Rives, 1960s, p/s, lt cr/sl, P-19x26", lot 761, C-NY 5/10/89 OE ... 5,500
Composition 2, AP4, ed of 500, etch, 1933, p/s, no size given, Marina Picasso, lot 200, SWN 6/15/89 UE ... 358
Femme dans L'Atelier, AP3, ed of 500, srgph, 1957, p/s, 16x20", Marina Picasso, lot 202, SWN 6/15/89 UE ... 358

PILOT, Robert Wakeham (Canadian, 1898-1967)
Cathedral & Trees No 3, engr, 1925, p/s, 9x11", lot 850A, WAD 6/12/89 ... 450

PINTO, Salvatore (American, 1905-)
On the Schuylkill, engr, 9x12", lot 66, FAP 2/24/89 ... 100

PIRANESI, Francesco (Italian, 1758-1810)
Altra Veduta del Tempio Della Sibilla in Tivoli, etch, lt fld/tr, unfr, no size given, lot 24, FAP 2/24/89 ... 110

PIRANESI, Giovanni Battista (Italian, 1720-1778)
Carceri: Drawbridge; Pl VII, Robison's 5th state, etch, ca 880s, lt scr/stn, 22x16", lot 88, SBY 5/11/89 ... 3,300
Carceri: Grand Piazza; Pl IV, Robison's 4th state, etch, ca 1749, lt stn, 22x16", lot 83, SBY 5/11/89 ... 2,310
Carceri: Lion Bas-Reliefs; Pl V, Robison's 2nd state, etch, 1761, lg mrgs, lt stn/tr, 22x16", lot 84, SBY 5/11/89 ... 3,300
Carceri: Man on the Rack (Pl II); Robison's 5th state, etch, ca 1761, lt scr img, 22x17", lot 646, SBY 2/25/88 OE ... 2,090
Carceri: Perspective of Arches with a Smoking Fire in the Center; Pl VI, etch, 1749, S-23x17", lot 86, SBY 5/11/89 ... 9,900
Carceri: Pier with the Lamp; Robison's 6th state, etch, ca 1749, full mrgs, lt fox, 16x22", lot 648, SBY 2/25/88 OE ... 2,530
Carceri: Prisoners on a Projecting Platform; Pl X, Robison's 1st state, etch, 1749, 16x21", lot 89, SBY 5/11/89 OE ... 10,450
Carceri: Smoking Fire; Pl VI, Robison's 5th state, etch, 1749, lg mrgs, lt stn, 21x16", lot 85, SBY 5/11/89 ... 3,025
Carceri: Vast Interior with Trophies at the Foot of a Broad Staircase...; Pl VIII, 1749, S-23x18", lot 87, SBY 5/11/89 ... 8,800

Marble Vessel Supported by Four Barbarians, etch, ca 1775, pl/s, 21x15", lot 1402, LH 12/4/88 OE 350
Pair: Carceri: Man on the Rack; Lion Bas-Reliefs; Robison's penultimate states, etch, ca 1761, lot 647, SBY 2/25/88 3,300
Pair: Veduta de Campo Vaccino; 1st Paris ed, etch, ca 1772, lt tstn, 16x22"/19x28", lot 5, RWS 9/29/88 UE 475
Pair: Vedute di Roma: Colonna Antonina; Obelisco Egizio; etch, 1758 & 1759, laid down, 22x16", lot 651, SBY 2/25/88 660
Palmi Romani Numero Sei, engr/laid paper, ca 18th C, lt stn/sl/cr, 25x16", lot 2810, B/B 4/19/88 220
Pier with Chains, Robison's 5th state, etch, ca 1749, full mrgs, 16x22", lot 649, SBY 2/25/88 2,640
Portico of Octavia: Entrance Porch Exterior; etch/heavy laid paper, 1748, S-16x24", lot 205, SWN 6/15/89 358
Prima Parte: Camera Sepolcrale; Robison's 2nd state, etch, 1743-44, sgn, lt ls/rpr/stn, 16x11", lot 645, SBY 2/25/88 2,310
Prospettiva della Scala della Conserva d'Acqua...; etch/heavy wove paper, Roman bstp, 16x12", lot 2811, B/B 2/16/88 137
Set of 13: Antichita Romane de Tempi della Repubblica; etch/laid paper, ca 1748, leather folio, lot 2813, B/B 2/16/88 990
Veduta Degli Avanzi del Foro di Nerva, etch, lt fld/tr, unfr, 15x24", lot 22, FAP 2/24/89 450
Veduta del Pantheon d'Agrippa, etch/heavy wove paper, lt fox/stn/tr, 19x28", lot 2812, B/B 2/16/88 66
Veduta del Tempio Della, Fortuna Vivile; engr, lt tr/sl/cr, 15x23", lot 20, FAP 2/24/89 300
Veduta Dell'Arco di Settimio Severo, posthumous ed, etch, 19x28", lot 994, LH 12/4/88 160
Veduta dell'Esterno della Gran Basilica di Pietro in Vaticano, engr/laid paper, lt cr/sl, 15x24", lot 2812, B/B 4/19/88 468
Vedute di Roma, engr/wove paper, ca 18th C, lt stn/cr, 16x21", lot 2811, B/B 4/19/88 495

PISSARRO, Camille (French, 1830-1903)

Convalescence (Lucien Pissarro), 11/11, litho/Chine applique, ca 1900, lt sl/stn, 13x19", lot 421, SBY 2/25/88 OE 18,150
Eglise et Ferme d'Eragny, gray/bl/red/yel etch on gray laid paper, 1894-95, lt cr, 11x13", lot 154, C-NY 11/1/88 OE 38,500
Enfant Tetant sa Mere, 4/20, after Delteil's 3rd state, etch/aqua/Arches, 1882, stp/s, 5x4", lot 419, SBY 2/25/88 OE 2,200
Groupe de Paysans, #4, ed of 14 or 15, litho/papier violace, 1899, p/s, full mrgs, sl/fox, 5x5", lot 795, SBY 5/11/89 OE 9,900
La Vache, #4, lifetime ed of 12, etch, 1885, intl, full mrgs, lt sl/cr/fox, 5x5", lot 420, SBY 2/25/88 OE 2,090
Le Charrue, clr litho/cream wove paper, full mrgs, lt stn, 9x6", Les Temps Nouveaux, lot 530, SBY 11/3/88 3,575
Le Charrue, clr litho/wove paper, 1901, full mrgs, lt sl/cr, 9x6", lot 796, SBY 5/11/89 OE 6,600
Paysanne Marchante, 3rd state, aqua/etch/wove paper, 1899, inscr LD 86, full mrgs, lt stn, P-5x4", RWS 3/16/89 1,100
Paysannes a l'Herbe, #209, clr etch, ca 1894, full mrgs, lt stn mrgs, P-5x6", lot 325, C-NY 5/11/88 OE 1,430
Paysans Portant du Foin, probably 7th state, etch/laid paper, 1900, laid down, P-5x3", lot 97, PHL 10/28/88 850
Quai des Menetriers, a Bruges; #2, a/p, final state, etch, 1894, lt stn/cr, P-5x6", SBY 5/12/88 OE 7,700
Vachere au Bord de l'Eau, etch/laid paper, 8x5", Gazette des Beaux Arts, lot 2891, B/B 4/19/88 275
Vachere au Bord de l'Eau, 8th state, etch/drypt/laid paper, 1890, lt cr/stn, P-8x5", lot 810, C-NY 5/10/89 495

PLATT, Charles Adams (American, 1861-1933)

Fish House Interior, etch, 1881, p/s, titled in mrg, full mrgs, 5x8", lot 17, RAB 8/9/88 300
Oxford Scene, England, 1883; etch, sgn/dtd 1883, full mrgs, 5x6", RAB 8/8/89 200

PLOWMAN, George Taylor (American, 1869-1932)

View of Boston & Boston Harbor, etch, p/s, full mrgs, 9x11", lot 12, RAB 8/9/88 275

POLIAKOFF, Serge (Russian, 1900-1969)

Composition, 94/100, clr etch/BFK Rives, 1960, full mrgs, lt cr/mstn, P-10x8", lot 326, C-NY 5/11/88 2,090
Composition Noire, Jaune et Brune; by Jean Signovert, 60/75, etch/aqua/burin/BFK Rives, 1962, 19x25", SBY 11/3/88 OE 3,850
Composition Noire, Jaune et Brune; 63/75, etch/aqua/engr/watercolor, 1962, stn, P-19x25", lot 327, C-NY 5/11/88 OE 2,090
Composition Rouge, Carmin et Jaune; 63/126, litho/BFK Rives, 1958, p/s, l'Oeuvre Gravee bstp, 25x19", C-NY 11/1/88 OE 3,520

POLLACK, Max (American, 1886-)

Guatamala Getting Water From the Lake, 21/100, clr etch, sgn, titled, 3x11", lot 356, WG 10/19/88 UE 300
Imperial Castle, Vienna; clr etch/aqua/cream wove paper, p/s, titled, lt buckling, 15x27", lot 2973, B/B 4/19/88 440
Mexico Market Day, 26/100, hc etch/cream wove paper, 10x12", lot 2888, B/B 2/16/88 192

POLLARD, James; after (British, 1797-1859)

West Country Mails at the Gloucester Coffee House, Piccadilly; clr print, no size given, lot 34, FAP 2/24/89 375

POLLOCK, Jackson (American, 1912-1956)

Silkscreen VI, slksc/heavy wht wove Strathmore, ink sgn, dtd 1952, full mrgs, 16x19", Pollock/McCoy, SBY 5/14/88 OE 12,650

PONTIUS, Paulus (17th C)

Peter Paul Rubens, Painter; final state, engr, 1630, lt cr/sl, 15x11", lot 654, SBY 2/25/88 OE 935

PORTER, Dorothy Rutka (American, -1985)

Pair: Occupation; Tropical Storm; etch, p/s, titled, 9x7"/7x6", lot 195, WG 10/19/88 45

PORTER, Fairfield (American, 1907-1975)

Apple Blossoms I, 36/50, clr litho, 1974, p/s, full mrgs, lt cr/stn, L-20x26", Brooke Alexander, lot 95, RWS 9/8/89 950
Christmas Tree, a/p, 1 of 10, litho/Arches, 1971, p/s, full mrgs, S-29x22", Brooke Alexander/Knoedler, C-NY 5/10/89 OE 1,210

PRANY & MAYER (19th C)

Bird's-Eye View of Harvard College, & of Old Cambridge; hc litho, ca 1858-60, rpr tr, stn, S-22x29", SBY 1/28/88 1,540

PRENDERGAST, Maurice Brazil (American, 1861-1924)

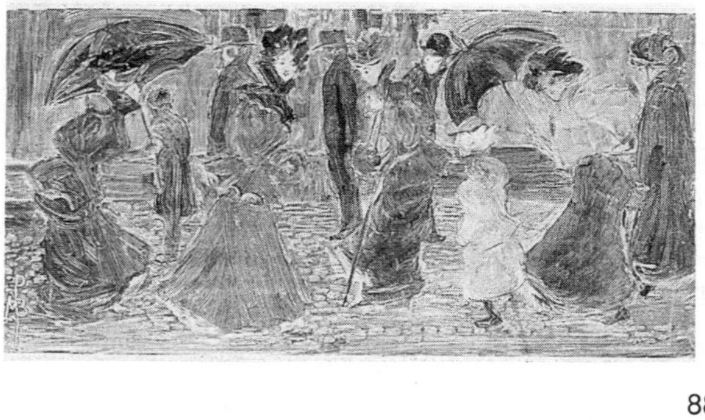

Rainy Day, Boston; clr monotype/laid paper, ca 1891-94, intl, full mrgs, lt scuff/stn/cr, L-5x10", lot 252, C-NY 1/19/89; $55,000

Children in the Park (Children at Play), clr monotype/thin Japan, ca 1895, lt stn, S-12x10", lot 48, SBY 11/3/88 .... **148,500**
Park Promenade, clr monotype/thin wht paper with mica, 1901, lt scr/sl, S-10x8", lot 47, SBY 11/3/88 OE **181,500**
Rainy Day, Boston; clr monotype/laid paper, ca 1891-94, intl, full mrgs, lt scuff/stn/cr, L-5x10", lot 252, C-NY 1/19/89 .... **55,000**

PRICE, Ken (American, 1925-)
Coffee Shop at the Chicago Art Institute, 31/75, clr slksc/Arjomari, 1971, p/s, Gemini bstp, 40x60", B/B 4/19/88 .... **1,430**
Coffee Shop at the Chicago Art Institute, 64/75, clr scrpt/Arjomari, 1971, p/s, S-40x60", Gemini, lot 773, C-NY 11/1/88 .... **715**
Figurine Cup III, 58/63, clr litho/slksc/Special Arjomari, 1970, p/s, titled, Gemini bstp, S-19x15", B/B 4/19/88 .... **248**

PRIVAT-LIVEMONT (20th C)
Absinthe-Robette; clr litho, 1986, pl/s, 43x33", Goffart, C-E 3/24/88 .... **1,650**

PUSHMAN, Hovsep (American, 1877-1966)
Still Life of Orientalia, chromolitho, p/s, 18x23", Frost & Reed, lot 124, WG 1/19/88 .... **250**

QUINTE, Lothar (American, 20th C)
Luna Yellow, 20/40, scrpt, 35x35", lot 91, FAP 2/24/89 UE **20**

RAFFAEL, Joseph (American, 1935-)
Celebration-Koi Fish; 28/44, clr litho/wht wove paper, 1980, Archer bstp, full mrgs, 28x22", lot 3056, B/B 4/19/88 .... **935**
Larkspur, monotype/BFK Rives, 1982, p/s, a/bstp on verso, full sheet, cr/scr, lt sl, S-40x30", lot 561, C-NY 5/11/88 UE **528**
Lily for Mathew, 16/20, litho/BFK Rives, 1980, p/s, titled, full mrgs, 28x40", lot 3057, B/B 4/19/88 .... **1,430**
Set of 11: Leta & the Swan; 2/100, clr scrpt/wove or metallic paper, full sheet, 30x24", lot 562, C-NY 5/11/88 UE **605**
Shadow Light, 12/89, clr litho/wove paper, 1984, p/s, S-40x26", lot 3058, B/B 4/19/88 .... **1,430**

RAFFAELLI, Jean Francois (French, 1850-1924)
Raffaelli, par Lui-Meme; 67/100, clr drypt/laid paper, 1983, p/s, L'Estampe Orig bstp, P-7x6", lot 523, C-NY 11/1/88 .... **385**

RAIMONDI, Marcantonio (Italian, 1480-1527)
Virgin with the Long Thigh, engr, trm/rpr mrgs, ls to img, stn, 16x11", lot 656, SBY 2/25/88 .... **990**

RAIMONDI, Marcantonio; after (Italian, 1480-1527)
Judgment of Paris, by Marco Dente da Ravenna, engr, trm/rpr/cr/stn, lt sl, 12x17", lot 90B, SBY 5/11/89 .... **3,300**

RALEIGH, Henry Patrick (American, 1880-1944)
Hun or Home?, clr litho/poster paper, laid down, 30x20", lot 190, FAP 2/24/89 OE **190**

RAMOS, Mel (American, 1935-)
Pair: Velasquez Vision; Leo; AP35/35 & 124/150, clr srgph, 1791, p/s, 14x18", lot 211, SWN 6/15/89 .... **195**
Pelicana, clr litho/cream wove paper, 1969, Collector Pr bstp, S-28x22", lot 3060, B/B 4/19/88 .... **138**
Tenerefe, clr litho/cream wove paper, 1981, p/s, dtd, Tamarind Inst bstp, 19x56", lot 3062, B/B 4/19/88 .... **990**
Untitled, Woman with Catsup; offset litho, 1972, p/s, dtd, 29x25", lot 3061, B/B 4/19/88 OE **330**

RANSON, Paul (French, 1864-1909)
Tristesse, clr litho/cream wove paper, 1896, trm mrgs, lt stn, 9x7", lot 2892, B/B 4/19/88 .... **330**

RAPHAEL, after (Italian, 1483-1520)
Vison of Ezekial, hc etch, P-12x15", Longhi, lot 225, MG 8/27/88 UE **45**

RASMUSSEN, Aage (Danish, 20th C)
Le Pont du Storstroem, clr litho, 1937, lt fox, 40x24", Andreasen/Lachmanin, lot 223, FAP 2/24/89 .... **175**

RASSENFUSSE, Andre Louis Armand (Belgian, 1862-1934)
L'Art Independent, red & blk litho/poster paper, ca 1896, 26x19", lot 436, C-E 9/20/89 UE **110**

RATTNER, Abraham (American, 1895-1978)
Portfolio: In the Beginning; ed of 22, 12 clr litho w/text, 1972, sgn, 20x26", LH 12/4/88 UE **300**
Portfolio: In the Beginning; 35/200, 12 litho w/text on Arches, 1972, sgn, orig wrappers/box, lot 253, C-NY 1/19/89 .... **770**

RAUSCHENBERG, Robert (American, 1925-)
Accident, 16/29, blk & gray litho/BFK Rives, 1963, p/s, ULAE bstp, full mrgs, stn/cr, S-41x30", lot 1192, SBY 5/13/89 OE **176,000**
American Pewter with Burroughs III, litho/Crisbrook, 1921, p/s, Gemini bstp, S-32x24", lot 3063, B/B 4/19/88 UE **660**
American Pewter with Burroughs V, PPII, litho/BFK Rives, 1981, p/s, Gemini bstp, S-32x23", lot 3064, B/B 4/19/88 .... **825**
Aquafix, 5/25, blk/orange/gr/purple etch & litho on Twinrocker, 1981, p/s, ULAE bstp, S-40x30", SBY 5/14/88 .... **2,420**
Arcanum VI, 39/85, clr scrpt/collage/thick wove paper, 1981, p/s, Styria bstp, S-23x16", lot 780, C-NY 11/1/88 .... **495**
Bait, 36/45, clr litho, 1970, p/s, Gemini bstp, lt cr/nick/sl, 35x26", lot 764, SBY 2/23/89 OE **1,870**
Cage, 112/125, clr slksc/collage, 1983, p/s, Styria bstp, lt cr/skinned, 41x30", lot 767, SBY 2/23/89 OE **2,970**
Drizzle, 21/29, clr litho/JW, 1967, p/s, ULAE bstp, lt fox, S-54x31", lot 935, SBY 11/5/88 OE **11,000**
Drizzle, 7/29, clr litho/JW 1955, 1967, p/s, ULAE bstp, full mrgs, lt stn/sl, 42x30", lot 1195, SBY 5/13/89 OE **16,500**
Earth Day, 45/50, blk & wht litho/collage/Rives, 1970, p/s, L-47x47, Gemini, lot 566, C-NY 5/11/88 .... **1,210**
Expo `67-Fire Pole 33` X 17`; 25/41, clr litho, 1967, p/s, ULAE bstp, S-34x19", lot 940, SBY 11/5/88 OE **11,550**
Front Roll, HC1/8, red & blk litho/BFK Rives, 1964, p/s, ULAE bstp, full sheet, S-41x30", lot 565, C-NY 5/11/88 OE **15,400**
Glacial Decoy Series: Etching V; ed of 22, purple etch/Swiss, 1979, ULAE bstp, S-25x17", lot 570, C-NY 5/11/88 .... **935**
Group of 3: Glacial Decoy Series: Etching I, III, & IV; clr etch, 1979, ULAE bstp, ea S-25x17", SBY 5/14/88 OE **2,640**
Hoarfrost Editions: Pull; 15/29, offset litho/collage, 1974, p/s, 85x48", Gemini bstp, lot 1197, SBY 5/13/89 .... **18,700**
Horsefeathers Thirteen VII, 15/84, engr/collage/slksc, p/s, 18x15", lot 233, LH 5/15/88 .... **900**
Howl, 7 Characters; 51/70, paper/collage/Xuan, 1982, p/s, S-41x27", Gemini, lot 781, C-NY 11/1/88 UE **3,520**
Killdevil Hill, 14/42, red & bl litho/2 sheets JW 1952, 1975, p/s, ULAE bstp, S-27x80", lot 1199, SBY 5/13/89 .... **38,500**
Kip-Up, a/p, ed of 33, litho/BFK Rives, 1964, p/s, ULAE bstp, full sheet, S-41x30", lot 563, C-NY 5/11/88 OE **12,100**
Kitty Hawk, 24/28, clr litho, 1974, sgn in blk crayon, ULAE bstp, 39x78", lot 1198, SBY 5/13/89 .... **85,250**
Lichen, 81/100, clr scrpt/wove paper, 1972, p/s, Styria bstp, full sheet, lt cr, S-42x30", lot 568, C-NY 5/11/88 .... **935**
Marilyn, 12/75, clr litho, 1974, p/s, full mrgs, lt stn/sl, 36x27", Petersburg, lot 941, SBY 11/5/88 OE **12,100**
More Distant Visible Part of the Sea, 93/100, clr scrpt/heavy wove paper, 1979, p/s, S-31x23", lot 778, C-NY 11/1/88 .... **660**
One More & We Will Be More Than Half Way There, 56/100, clr slksc, 1979, p/s, Styria bstp, 31x23", SBY 2/23/89 OE **1,650**
Pair: Arcanum VII; Arcanum IX; 58/85 & AP8/9, clr slksc/collage, p/s, Styria bstp, S-22x15", SBY 5/14/88 OE **2,530**
Paris Review Poster, 9/150, offset litho, 1965, sgn in ink, lt cr, lt sl verso, L-20x16", lot 775, C-NY 11/1/88 .... **880**
Razorback Bunch (Etching I), 8/40, clr etch/Twinrocker, 1980, p/s, ULAE bstp, S-30x22", lot 554, SBY 2/25/88 .... **880**

Razorback Bunch (Etching III), 8/26, clr etch/Twinrocker, 1981, p/s, ULAE bstp, S-44x31", lot 939, SBY 11/3/88 OE 3,300
Red Heart, 7 Characters; 40/70, paper/collage/fabric medallion/mirror/Xuan, 1982, 41x27", Gemini, lot 570A, C-NY 5/11/88..... 7,700
Set of 3: Romances: Elopement; Elysian; Castle; clr litho, 1977, p/s, Gemini bstp, full sheets, lot 569, C-NY 5/11/88 1,760
Set of 3: Stunt Man I-III; litho, 1962, p/s, ULAE bstp, full mrgs, S-23x18", lot 933, SBY 11/5/88 OE..... 28,600
Shoot From the Main Stem, 94/100, clr scrpt/heavy wove paper, 1979, p/s, Styria bstp, S-31x23", lot 779, C-NY 11/1/88 990
Spot, a/p, ed of 37, litho/BFK Rives, 1964, p/s, ULAE bstp, full sheet, S-41x30", lot 564, C-NY 5/11/88 OE 16,500
Suite: Chow Bags; 70/100, 6 mixed media prints, 1977, Styria/Untitled Press bstps, 48x36", lot 1200, SBY 5/13/89 OE 7,150
Test Stone 1, API, litho/wove paper, 1967, p/s, Gemini bstp, full mrgs, lt sl/scr, S-20x15", lot 776, C-NY 11/1/88 OE 3,520
Untitled (abstract), 36/75, clr slksc, 1982, p/s, S-29x22", Anthology Film Archives, SBY 5/14/88..... 1,210
Urban, 9/38, litho/BFK Rives, 1962, p/s, ULAE bstp, full mrgs, lt cr/tr, 30x23", lot 932, SBY 11/5/88 OE 13,750
Visitation II, a/p, litho/BFK Rives, 1965, p/s, ULAE bstp, lt cr/sl, 30x22", lot 1194, SBY 5/13/89 OE 15,400
Watch, 3/13, blind embossing/Angoumois a la main, 1968, p/s, ULAE bstp, S-24x8", lot 777, C-NY 11/1/88 OE 1,210
Waves, 26/27, litho, 1969, p/s, Gemini bstp, full mrgs, lt sl/cr/tr, S-89x42", lot 936, SBY 11/5/88 3,850
White Walk, 38/53, clr litho, 1970, p/s, Gemini bstp, lt fox, S-42x30", lot 765, SBY 2/23/89 OE 2,090

RAVENSCROFT, Ellen (American, 20th C)
Cranes, clr wc/brn wove paper, ca 1920-30s, p/s, lt sl/wstn mrgs, L-20x12", C-NY 1/22/88 1,320

REDON, Odilon (French, 1840-1916)
Bataille, ed of 25, 2nd state, etch/drypt/cream laid paper, lg mrgs, lt stn, 7x6", lot 537, SBY 11/3/88 5,775
Beatrice, a/p, clr litho/Chine applique, 1897, lt cr/rpr tr, lt stn/sl, L-13x12", Vollard, lot 331, C-NY 5/11/88..... 14,300
Christ, litho/Chine, 1887/later, lt stn, L-13x11", lot 330, C-NY 5/11/88..... 715
Femme de Profil vers la Gauche Coiffee d'un Hennin, Pl 1, litho/Chine, 1900, lt fox/tr, 12x9", lot 814, C-NY 5/10/89 OE 1,430
L'Aile, ed of 25, litho/Chine applique, 1893, p/s, lt fox/sl, S-23x16", Becquet, lot 155, C-NY 11/1/88..... 33,000
L'Art Celeste, ed of 50, litho/Chine applique, 1894, p/s, lg mrgs, lt sl verso, 12x10", lot 540, SBY 11/3/88 OE 31,900
La Peur, Harrison's 2nd state, etch/cream laid MBM, 1866, p/s, rpr tr, 6x9", lot 538, SBY 11/3/88 OE..... 13,200
Le Coursier, ed of 25, litho/Chine applique, 1894, p/s, lt sl/fox/stn, 9x8", Monrocq, lot 799, SBY 5/11/89 OE 19,800
Les Origines: Pl V, La Satyre au Cynique; ed of 25, litho/Chine applique, 1883, lt cr, 10x8", lot 425, SBY 2/25/88..... 2,420
Profil de Lumiere, reprint after ed of 50, litho/Chine volant, 1886, lt fox, L-13x10", SBY 5/12/88 OE 1,650
Quel est le but Tout Cela?, Pl 18, litho/laid Chine, 1896, full mrgs, lt cr, L-12x10", Vollard, lot 813, C-NY 5/10/89 OE..... 935
Sciapode, etch/drypt/laid MBM, 1982, full mrgs, lt scuff/fox, 8x6", lot 539, SBY 11/3/88..... 4,400
Vieux Chevalier, a/p, litho/Chine applique, 1896, intl, lt sl, S-22x17", Vollard, lot 156, C-NY 11/1/88 12,100

REED, Ethel (American, 1876-)
Boston Sunday Herald, clr litho backed on linen, pl/s, 19x12", C-E 6/16/88 OE 440

REEVE, R.G. (British, 19th C)
Group of 4: Hawking; The Departure; The Rendezvous; Fatal Stoop Disgorging; engr, 15x13", lot 805, LH 10/16/88 425

REINAGLE, Phillip; after (British, 1749-1833)
Aloe, by Medland, 2nd/final state, aqua/engr/gum arabic/1794 JW, trm mrgs, lt stn/fox, tp verso, S-21x17", C-NY 1/22/88 418
Cupid Inspiring Plants with Love, engr/aqua/heavy wove paper, 1805, lt sl/stn/ls, P-20x17", lot 101, C-NY 1/19/89 308
Narrow-Leaved Kalmia, by Caldwall, aqua/stpl engr/engr/gum arabic, 1804, lt mstn, stn/sl verso, L-18x14", C-NY 1/22/88..... 1,430
Queen Flower, clr engr/stpl engr/aqua/wove paper, 1812, full mrgs, lt sl/tstn mrgs/verso, P-21x16", C-NY 1/22/88 OE..... 1,320
Superb Lily, by Richard Earlom, 3rd/final state, aqua/stpl engr/engr, 1799, tstn edges, P-19x14", C-NY 1/22/88 OE 2,420
Superb Lily, by Ward, mezzo/gum arabic/1794 JW, trm mrgs, scr img, stn/fox/sl mrgs/verso, P-19x14", C-NY 1/22/88 1,760

REINHOLD, Bernhard (German, 1824-1892)
Pair: St Michael, Hamburg; Hamburg Canal; engr, p/s, 9x13"/10x13", lot 2, FAP 2/24/89 UE..... 20

REMBRANDT, Harmensz (Dutch, 1606-1669)
Abraham & Isaac, Hollander's only state, etch/burin, 1645, trm, 6x5", lot 660, SBY 2/25/88..... 5,225
Abraham Casting Out Hagar & Ismael, etch/drypt, 1637, narrow mrgs, lt stn/rub/scr, 5x4", lot 96, SBY 5/11/89 OE 34,100
Abraham Francen, Apothecary; Hollander's 9th state, etch/drypt, ca 1657, lt fox, 6x8", lot 684, SBY 2/25/88 OE..... 2,860
Adoration of the Shepherds, Night Piece; probably state 8, etch/drypt/wove paper, 1652, 6x8", lot 217, SWN 6/15/89 OE 880
Adoration of the Shepherds: With the Lamp; 1st state, etch, ca 1654, trm mrgs, 4x5", lot 99, SBY 5/11/89 OE 15,950
Angel Departing From the Family of Tobias, 3rd state of 4, etch/drypt, 1641, trm, 4x6", lot 2814, B/B 2/16/88 UE 1,650
Artist Drawing From a Live Model (unfinished pl), late imp, etch, ca 1648, P-9x7", RWS 9/29/88 OE 700
Artist Drawing From the Model, etch/drypt/burin, ca 1647, rpr corners, lt cr/fox, 9x7", lot 673, SBY 2/25/88 OE 6,050
Artist Drawing From the Model, Hollander's final state, etch/drypt/burin, ca 1647, 9x7", lot 119, SBY 5/11/89 OE..... 4,400
Beggar Man & Woman Conversing, Hollander's only state, etch/Strasburg, 1630, lt fox, 3x3", lot 116, SBY 5/11/89 4,125
Beggars Receiving Alms at the Door of a House, Hollander's 1st state, etch/drypt, 1648, 7x5", lot 118, SBY 5/11/89 OE 23,100
Bust of Old Man with Flowing Beard, etch, 1630, lt scr/thin spots, 4x3", lot 135, SBY 5/11/89 OE..... 7,700
Bust of Old Man with Flowing Beard, etch, 1630, trm mrgs, laid down, lt stn corner, 4x3", lot 690, SBY 2/25/88 OE 2,310
Christ & the Woman of Samaria, etch/drypt, 1658/later, pl/s, lt ls corner, 5x6", Bartsch, lot 215, SWN 6/15/89..... 1,045
Christ Carried to the Tomb, etch, ca 1645, trm, 5x4", lot 667, SBY 2/25/88 1,650
Christ Disputing with the Doctors, 2nd state of 3, etch/drypt, 1652/18th-C imp, 5x9", lot 662, SBY 2/25/88 OE 1,540
Christ Preaching (La Petite Tombe), blk sleeve imp, etch/drypt/burin, ca 1652, rpr tr, 6x8", lot 663, SBY 2/25/88 OE..... 115,500
Christ Preaching (La Petite Tombe), etch/drypt/burin/Arms-of-Amsterdam, ca 1652, 6x8", lot 664, SBY 2/25/88 OE 9,350
Circumcision: Small Plate; etch, ca 1630, sm mrgs, lt stn/fox, 4x3", lot 102, SBY 5/11/89 3,850
Clement de Jonghe, Printseller; Hollander's 5th state, etch, 1631, lt cr/tr/stn, 8x6", lot 129, SBY 5/11/89 3,575
Cottage Beside a Canal: View of Diemen; etch, ca 1645, trm mrgs, lt stn/fox/cr, 6x8", lot 122, SBy 5/11/89..... 22,000
Cottage with a White Paling, final state, etch/drypt, 1648, rpr ls in img/corner, 5x6", lot 123, SBY 5/11/89..... 28,600
Cottage with a White Paling, 3rd state, etch/drypt/Strasburg Lily, 1648, lt stn/rub, 5x6", lot 677, SBY 2/25/88 6,600
Death of the Virgin, Hollander's final state, etch/drypt, 1639, trm mrgs, lt cr/stn, 16x12", lot 111, SBY 5/11/89 OE 4,675
Death of the Virgin, Hollander's 2nd state, etch/drypt, 1639, lt cr/rpr, 16x12", lot 110, SBY 5/11/89 OE..... 11,000
Descent From the Cross, Pl 2, Hollander's 3rd state, etch/burin, 1633, lt rpr, 21x16", lot 107, SBY 5/11/89 5,500
Descent From the Cross by Torchlight, etch/drypt/wove paper, 1654, pl/s, thread mrgs, lt stn, L-8x6", lot 4, RWS 9/29/88 850

Descent From the Cross by Torchlight, Hollander's only state, etch/drypt, 1654, lt stn, 8x6", lot 666, SBY 2/25/88	57,750
Diana at the Bath, only state, etch/Fool's Cap, ca 1631, sm mrgs, lt rpr, 7x6", lot 120, SBY 5/11/89	12,100
Ephriam Bonus, Jewish Physician; Hollander's 2nd state, etch/drypt/burin, 1647, lt cr, 10x7", lot 686, SBY 2/25/88 OE	24,200
Faust, Hollander's final state from Basan ed, etch/drypt/burin, ca 1652, lt stn, 8x6", lot 683, SBY 2/25/88 OE	2,530
Faust, Hollander's 1st state, etch/drypt/burin, ca 1652, lt ls to corners, 8x6", lot 128, SBY 5/11/89	13,200
Faust in His Study Watching a Magic Disk, Hollander's 1st state, etch/drypt/burin, 1652, 8x6", lot 682, SBY 2/25/88 OE	13,750
Fourth Head, Hollander's 2nd state, etch, ca 1635, lt scr/stn/fox, 6x5", lot 692, SBY 2/25/88 OE	12,100
Great Jewish Bride, final state, etch/drypt/burin, 1635, lt rpr img/mrg, 9x7", lot 136, SBY 5/11/89	25,300
Hundred Guilder Print, etch/drypt, ca 1649, 11x16", lot 286, LH 10/16/88	17,000
Jacob's Ladder, 2nd state (from undivided pl), etch/drypt/Japan, 1655, lt cr/rpr ls, 4x3", lot 661, SBY 2/25/88 OE	10,725
Jan Asselyn, Painter; Hollander's final state, etch, 1647, rpr tr at edge, 9x7", lot 685, SBY 2/25/88 OE	1,760
Jan Cornelis Sylvius, Preacher; 2nd state, etch/drypt/burin, 1646, lt rpr/cr/fox, 11x8", lot 688, SBY 2/25/88 OE	16,500
Jan Lutma, Goldsmith; Hollander's 2nd state, etch/drypt/burin, 1656, lt cr, 8x6", lot 131, SBY 5/11/89 OE	7,920
Jan Lutma, Goldsmith; Hollander's 2nd state, etch/drypt/burin, 1656, lt stn, 8x6", lot 130, SBY 5/11/89	60,500
Jan Lutma, Goldsmith; 3rd state, etch/drypt/burin, 1656, trm mrgs, 8x6", lot 132, SBY 5/11/89	4,950
Jan Uytenbogaert, Preacher of the Remonstrants; etch/burin, 1635, trm mrgs, lt tr/cr, 9x7", lot 687, SBY 2/25/88	4,125
Joseph Telling His Dreams, etch, 1628, 4x3", lot 283, LH 10/16/88	1,800
Jupiter & Antiope: Smaller Plate; Hollander's 2nd state, etch, ca 1631, trm, lt sl, 3x4", lot 675, SBY 2/25/88	1,760
Jupiter & Antiope: Smaller Plate; 2nd state, etch, ca 1631, lt stn, rpr corner, 3x4", lot 121, SBY 5/11/89	13,200
La Petite Tombe, etch/laid paper, 19th C, lt stn, P-6x8", lot 4, PHL 10/28/88	750
Landscape with a Hay Barn & a Flock of Sheep, etch/drypt, 1652, lt fox/skinned, 3x7", lot 676, SBY 2/25/88 OE	17,050
Man at a Desk Wearing a Cross & Chain, Hollander's 2nd state, etch/drypt, 1641, 6x4", lot 124, SBY 5/11/89	6,600
Man Drawing From a Cast, etch, 1641, 4x3", lot 214, SWN 6/15/89 OE	1,100
Man in a Coat & Fur Cap Leaning Against a Bank, etch/laid paper, ca 1630, sm mrgs, 5x3", lot 1816, B/B 2/16/88	990

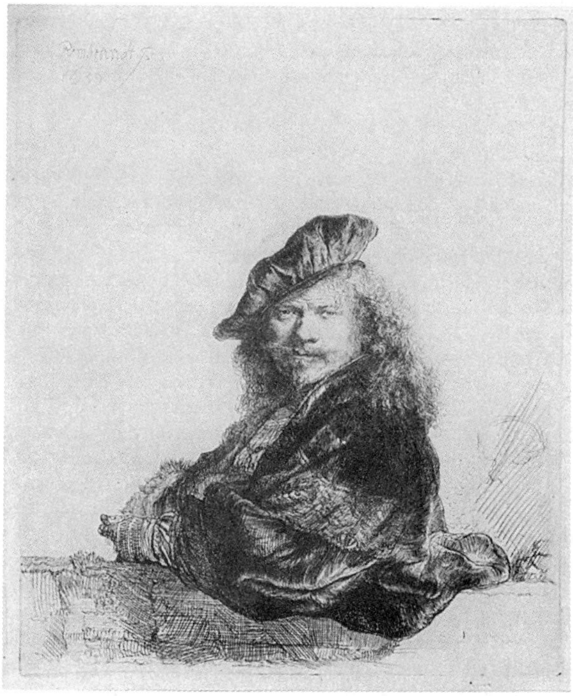

Self-Portrait Leaning on a Stone Sill, 2nd state, etch/wm paper, 1639, thin mrgs, lt sl, 8x6", lot 125, WD 12/8/88 OE; $28,000

Man in an Arbor, only state, etch, 1642, trm mrgs, lt cr/fox, 3x2", lot 678, SBY 2/25/88	2,970
Medea; or, The Marriage of Jason & Creusa; 4th state, etch/drypt, lt fox, 9x7", lot 113, SBY 5/11/89	3,300
Naked Woman Seated on a Mound, 2nd state, etch, ca 1631, lt tr, rpr corner, 7x6", lot 674, SBY 2/25/88	8,800
Old Bearded Man in a Fur Cap, etch, ca 1635, lt nick/tr/fox, 5x4", lot 134, SBY 5/11/89 OE	9,350
Old Man in Divided Fur Cap, 2nd state, etch/Arms-of-Amsterdam, 1640, lt tr/stn, 6x6", lot 125, SBY 5/11/89	3,300
Old Man Shading His Eyes with His Hand, etch/drypt, ca 1638, trm mrgs, lt fox/stn, 5x5", lot 679, SBY 2/25/88	3,410
Old Man with a Divided Fur Cap, 1st state of 2, etch, 1640, trm mrgs, lt ls/scr/fox, 6x5", lot 680, SBY 2/25/88 OE	6,325
Old Man with a Divided Fur Cap, 2nd state, etch/laid paper, 1640, lg mrgs, 6x6", lot 126, SBY 5/11/89	3,025
Old Man with a Flowing Beard: Bust; Hollander's 2nd state, etch, 1631, trm mrgs, 2x2", lot 689, SBY 2/25/88	1,870
Pair: Bathers; Virgin & Child with the Cat & Snake; etch, 1651 & 1654, 5x4"/4x6", lot 216, SWN 6/15/89 OE	1,210
Pair: Card Player; Jan Cornelis Sylvius; Hollander's final state, etch, 1641 & 1633, 4x3"/7x6", lot 671, SBY 2/25/88	3,080
Pair: Young Man in a Velvet Cap; Jews in a Synagogue; etch, 1637 & 1648, 4x3"/3x5", lot 681, SBY 2/25/88 OE	3,520
Pancake Woman, Basan or later ed, etch, 1635, pl/s, lt cr, no size given, lot 213, SWN 6/15/89	600
Pancake Woman, 2nd state, etch, 1635, trm mrgs, lt scr img, lt cr, 4x3", lot 115, SBY 5/11/89	1,430
Peasant in a High Cap, Standing Leaning on a Stick; Basan imp, etch, 1639, 3x2", lot 406, LH 9/10/89	550
Peter & John Healing the Cripple at the Gate of the Temple, Hollander's 4th, etch, 1659, 7x9", lot 109, SBY 5/11/89	1,980
Peter & John Healing the Cripple at the Gate of the Temple, 2nd state, etch/drypt/burin, 1659, 7x9", SBY 2/25/88	2,530

Presentation in the Temple with the Angel: Small Plate; etch, 1630, trm mrgs, 4x3", lot 104, SBY 5/11/89 OE **1,210**
Presentation in the Temple: Oblong; 2nd state, etch/drypt/Fool's Cap, ca 1639, 8x11", lot 103, SBY 5/11/89 .... **1,926**
Ragged Peasant with Hands Behind Him Holding a Stick, 5th state, etch/drypt, ca 1630, 4x3", lot 117, SBY 5/11/89 OE **11,000**
Raising of Lazarus: Small Plate; 1st state of 2, etch, 1642, lt cr/sl/tr, 6x4", lot 665, SBY 2/25/88 .... **1,650**
Rest on the Flight: Lightly Etched; etch/drypt, 1645, lt rpr/stn/cr, 5x5", lot 105, SBY 5/11/89 OE **5,775**
Return of the Prodigal Son, Basan ed, etch/India, 1636, sm mrgs, lt stn, 6x5", lot 108, SBY 5/11/89 OE **2,420**
Return of the Prodigal Son, only state, etch/laid paper, 1636, trm/fox/sl/stn, 6x5", lot 2815, B/B 2/16/88 .... **1,980**
Samuel Manasseh Ben Israel, Hollander's 3rd state, etch, 1636, lt cr/fox/stn, 6x4", lot 127, SBY 5/11/89 .... **5,775**
Self-Portrait in a Cap & Scarf with the Face Dark: Bust; Hollander's 2nd state, etch, 1633, 5x4", lot 92, SBY 5/11/89 OE **7,700**
Self-Portrait in a Cap & Scarf with the Face Dark: Bust; 2nd state, etch, 1633, fox/stn, 5x4", lot 658, SBY 2/25/88 OE **2,310**
Self-Portrait in a Heavy Fur Cap, etch/1631, trm, lt ls in corner, lt stn img, 3x2", lot 91, SBY 5/11/89 OE **9,900**
Self-Portrait in a Velvet Cap with Plume, Hollander's only state, etch, 1638, lt scr/fox/tp, 5x4", lot 93, SBY 5/11/89 .... **3,850**
Self-Portrait in Plumed Cap, 3rd state, etch, 1634, trm/rpr trs, 5x4", lot 659, SBY 2/25/88 .... **2,750**
Self-Portrait(?) with Plumed Cap & Lowered Sabre, early imp of Hollander's 3rd state, 1934, 5x4", lot 95, SBY 5/11/89 .... **12,650**
Self-Portrait(?) with Plumed Cap & Lowered Sabre, Hollander's 3rd state, etch, 1634, 5x4", lot 94, SBY 5/11/89 UE **8,800**
St Jerome Beside a Pollard Willow, 2nd state, etch/drypt, 1648, lt rpr edges, 7x5", lot 112, SBY 5/11/89 OE **137,500**
St Jerome Beside a Pollard Willow, 2nd state of 2, etch/drypt, 1648, lt tr/fox, 7x5", lot 670, SBY 2/25/88 OE **28,600**
St Jerome Reading, Hollander's only state, etch, 1634, trm/lt fox/rpr cut, 4x4", lot 669, SBY 2/25/88 .... **3,850**
Strolling Musicians, 1st state, etch, ca 1635, lt scr img, lt stn/rub, 6x5", lot 114, SBY 5/11/89 OE **9,350**
Three Heads of Woman, One Asleep; 1637, ca 1910, 6x4", lot 133, FAP 2/24/89 UE **2,100**
Three Heads of Woman: One Asleep; Hollander's only state, etch, 1637, lt fox/stn, 6x4", lot 694, SBY 2/25/88 .... **8,800**
Triumph of Mordecai, etch/drypt, ca 1641, sm mrgs, lt stn img, 7x8", lot 97, SBY 5/11/89 .... **5,500**
Turbaned Soldier on Horseback, Hollander's only state, etch, ca 1632, 3x2", lot 672, SBY 2/25/88 .... **4,675**
White Negress, etch, ca 1631, sm mrgs, lt cr img, lt fox verso, 4x3", lot 137, SBY 5/11/89 .... **1,760**
White Negress, 2nd state, etch/Wurtemburg, ca 1631, trm mrgs, clipped corner, 4x3", lot 138, SBY 5/11/89 .... **1,870**
Windmill, posthumous ed, etch, 1641, 6x8", lot 669, LH 12/4/88 .... **450**
Woman Reading, 2nd state, etch, 1634, trm mrgs, lt ls/rpr tr, 5x4", lot 691, SBY 2/25/88 OE **8,800**

REMINGTON, Frederick; after (American, 1861-1909)

Untitled (cowboy on rearing horse), copyright mk, 1894, 27x21", Harper Brothers, RAB 1/10/89 UE **100**

REMO, N. (Italian, 19th C)

Liquore del Reno, clr litho, ca 1909, pl/s, 22x14", lot 438, C-E 9/20/89 .... **270**

RENOIR, Pierre Auguste (French, 1841-1919)

Baigneuse Assise, ed of 525, bl sftgr etch/wove paper, 1897, full mrgs, lt sl/stn, P-9x5", lot 817, C-NY 5/10/89 OE **8,250**
Baigneuse Debout, en Pied; a/p, clr litho/laid paper, ca 1896, lt fox/cr/tstn, S-25x17", lot 334, C-NY 5/11/88 .... **23,100**
Baigneuse Debout, en Pied; 77, clr litho/laid paper, ca 1896, intl in stone, rpr tr, lt stn, S-23x18", SBY 5/12/88 .... **28,600**
Baigneuse Debout a Mi-Jambes, etch/cream laid paper, 1919, p/s, unfr, 7x4", Durets, S/A 3/12/88 .... **575**
Claude Renoir, fils de l'Artiste, de Profil; only state, etch, 1908/1920-28, stn mrg/verso, 6x4", lot 219, SWN 6/15/89 .... **300**
Claude Renoir, La Tete Baisee; total ed of 1000, litho/wove paper, 1904, full mrgs, lt stn/fox/cr, L-8x8", SBY 5/12/88 .... **1,540**
Claude Renoir, La Tete Baissee; ed of 1000, litho/wove paper, ca 1904, stp/s, 8x8", lot 431, C-NY 2/25/89 OE **2,530**
Claude Renoir, La Tete Baissee; ed of 1000, 2nd state, litho, ca 1904, stp/s, full mrgs, 8x8", lot 480, SBY 2/23/89 OE **2,310**
Claude Renoir, Tourne a Gauche; ed of 1000, litho/wove paper, ca 1904, lt cr/fox, tp hinge verso, L-5x5", SBY 5/12/88 OE **1,760**
Claude Renoir, Tourne a Gauche; 2nd state, litho/wove paper, ca 1904, full mrgs, lt fox, L-5x5", lot 822, C-NY 5/10/89 .... **1,430**
Claude Renoir, 2nd state, litho/wove paper, 1904, sgn in stone, full mrgs, lt stn, L-9x7", lot 821, C-NY 5/10/89 OE **2,750**
Enfants Jouant a la Balle, a/p, before ed of 200, clr litho, 1900, lt fox, S-28x23", lot 544, SBY 11/3/88 OE **104,500**
Enfants Jouant a la Balle, a/p, blk litho/wm MBM laid paper, ca 1900, trm mrgs, sgn, L-20x20", lot 528, C-NY 11/1/88 OE **14,300**
Enfants Jouant a la Balle, ed of 200, clr litho, ca 1900, rpr tr, lt mstn/sl/fox, S-30x22", lot 806, SBY 5/11/89 .... **77,000**
Etude de Femme Nue, Assise; 2nd state, litho/wove paper, ca 1904, full mrgs, S-13x10", Vollard, lot 530, C-NY 11/1/88 .... **1,980**
Etude pour une Baigneuse, ed of 1000, drypt/cream wove paper, ca 1906, stp/s, full mrgs, 9x7", lot 801, SBY 5/11/89 .... **2,475**
Etude pour une Baigneuse, total ed of 100, etch/drypt/cream Japan, ca 1906, stp/s, full mrgs, P-9x7", SBY 5/12/88 OE **4,125**
Etude pour une Baigneuse, total ed of 1000, 2nd state, etch/drypt, ca 1906, full mrgs, lt stn, 9x7", SBY 2/25/88 OE **2,750**
Etude pour une Baigneuse, 2nd state, drypt/wove paper, ca 1906, stp/s, lt stn, P-9x7", lot 818, C-NY 5/10/89 .... **3,520**
Femme Nue Assise, sftgr etch/cream laid paper, ca 1906, full mrgs, P-8x6", SBY 5/12/88 .... **2,475**
Femme nue Couchee (Tournee a Droit), only state, late imp, etch/laid paper, 6x8", lot 2895, B/B 4/19/88 .... **275**
Jeune Femme en Buste (Mlle Dieterle), ed of 100, gray/blk litho, ca 1899, lt rpr, S-21x16", lot 542, SBY 11/3/88 OE **60,500**
Jeune Fille en Buste et Etudes de Tetes, litho/Japan, ca 1903, lt cr/rub mrg, L-11x8", lot 825, C-NY 5/10/89 OE **1,100**
L'Enfant au Biscuit, ed of 100, blk/gr/yel-ochre/brick red litho on Arches, ca 1898, full mrgs, 13x10", SBY 11/3/88 OE **33,000**
L'Enfant au Biscuit, ed of 100, blk/gr/yel-ochre/flesh/rose litho, ca 1898, full mrgs, fox, 13x11", lot 478, SBY 2/23/89 .... **26,400**
L'Enfant au Biscuit, ed of 100, litho/Arches, ca 1898, lt stn, 13x10", lot 803, SBY 5/11/88 .... **20,900**
L'Enfant au Biscuit, ed of 100, 8-clr litho/wm MBM Ingres d'Arches, ca 1898-99, P-12x11", lot 335, C-NY 5/11/88 OE **49,500**
L'Enfant au Biscuit (Jean Renoir), ed of 100, clr litho/Arches, 1899, S-24x18", Vollard/Clot, lot 158, C-NY 11/1/88 OE **29,700**
L'Enfant au Biscuit (Jean Renoir), ed of 100, litho/wm MBM Ingres d'Arches, 1898-99, L-13x11", lot 526, C-NY 11/1/88 OE **35,200**
La Danse a la Campagne, 2e Planche; sftgr etch, ca 1890, stp/s, lt tstn/fox, P-8x5", lot 333, C-NY 5/11/88 .... **7,700**
La Danse a la Campagne, 2e Planche; sftgr etch, ca 1890, stp/s, lt cr/stn, P-9x5", lot 332, C-NY 5/11/88 .... **6,600**
La Danse a la Campagne, 2e Planche; sftgr etch, ca 1890, stp/s, lt stn/fox/sl, P-9x5", lot 524, C-NY 11/1/88 OE **11,000**
La Danse a la Campagne, 2e Planche; sftgr etch, 1890, stp/s full mrgs, lt stn/fox, 9x5", lot 427, SBY 2/25/88 .... **7,700**
La Danse a la Campagne, 2e Planche; sftgr etch, 1890, stp/s, full mrgs, lt pressure mk in mrg, P-95", SBY 5/12/88 OE **11,000**
La Pierre aux Trois Croquis, ed of 1000, litho, ca 1904, full mrgs, lt stn/tp hinge, 9x11", lot 481, SBY 2/23/89 .... **2,310**
La Pierre aux Trois Croquis, ed of 1000, litho/wove paper, ca 1904, full mrgs, lt fox/rpl, 9x11", lot 546, SBY 11/3/88 .... **3,025**
La Pierre aux Trois Croquis, ed of 1000, litho/wove paper, 1904, stp/s, full mrgs, lt fox, 9x11", lot 804, SBY 5/11/89 .... **3,850**
La Pierre aux Trois Croquis, 2nd state, litho/wove paper, ca 1904, sgn in stone, full mrgs, L-9x11", C-NY 5/10/89 .... **2,200**
Le Chapeau Epingle, posthumous ed, etch, P-5x3", lot 98A, PHL 10/28/88 OE **300**

Le Chapeau Epingle, 1Re Planche; a/p, gr litho/laid paper, ca 1897, full mrgs, lt rpr, L-24x19", lot 525, C-NY 11/1/88 ..... **24,200**
Le Chapeau Epingle, 1Re Planche; total ed of 200, sanguine litho/van Gelder Zonen, lt fox/rpl, L-23x20", SBY 5/12/88 OE **22,000**
Le Chapeau Epingle (La Fille de Berthe Morisot et sa Cousinte), etch/laid paper, ca 1894, 7x5", lot 2896, B/B 4/19/88 ..... **220**
Le Fleuve Scamandre, 1Re Planche; 2nd state, etch, ca 1900, stp/s, lt fox/stn, 9x7", lot 429, SBY 2/25/88 ..... **1,650**
Le Fleuve Scamandre, 2e Planche; ed of 1000, etch, ca 1909, stp/s, full mrgs, lt lstn/fox, P-10x7", SBY 5/12/88 ..... **990**
Le Petit Garcon au Porte-Plume (Claude Renoir Ecrivant), ed of about 50, litho, ca 1900, stn/fox, 12x16", SBY 2/23/89 OE **13,200**
Les Baigneuses, ed of about 30-50, transfer litho/Arches Ingres, ca 1900-12, lt tr/fox, 19x25", lot 432, SBY 2/25/88 OE **2,640**

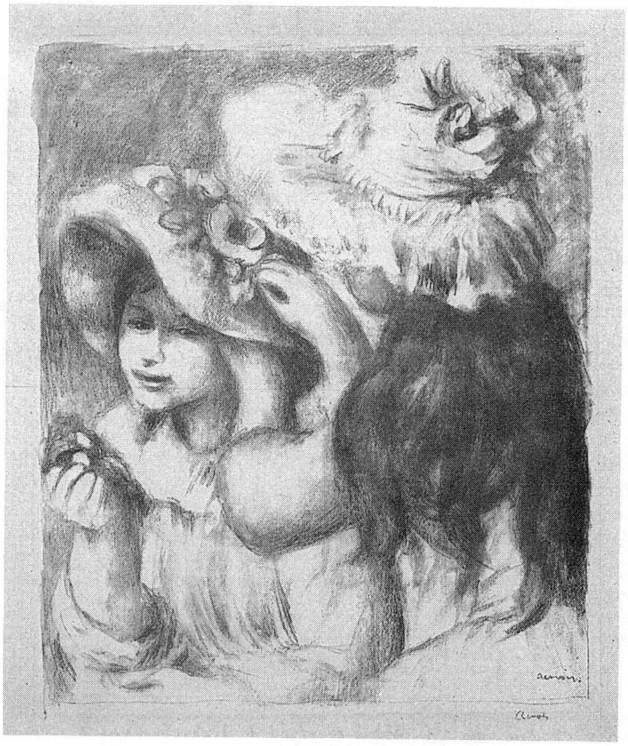

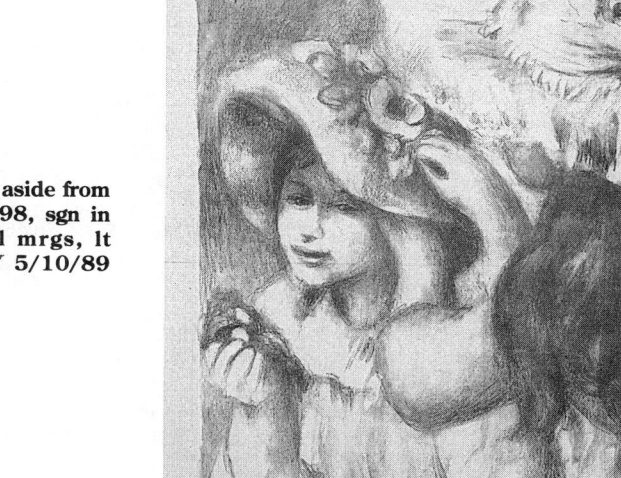

Le Chapeau Epingle, 2e Planche; a/p, aside from ed of 200, ash bl litho/Chine, ca 1898, sgn in stone, 2nd printed signature, full mrgs, lt fox/stn/cr, L-24x19", lot 819, C-NY 5/10/89 OE; $33,000

Louis Valtat, ed of 1000, litho, ca 1904, full mrgs, lt stn, laid down, L-12x10", Vollard, lot 98, PHL 10/28/88 ..... **1,600**
Louis Valtat, ed of 1000, litho/wove paper, ca 1904, lt fox/glue, 12x10", lot 430, SBY 2/25/88 OE **2,310**
Louis Valtat, part ed of 950, litho/wove paper, ca 1904, sgn in stone, full mrgs, S-13x10", lot 820, C-NY 5/10/89 OE **4,400**
Mere et Engant (Jean Renoir), a/p, clr etch/laid paper, ca 1896, 3 full mrgs, lt stn/cr, P-10x8", C-NY 5/10/89 OE **8,250**
Pair: Femme au Cep de Vigne; Femme au Cep de Vigne, 1Re Variante; ed of 1000, litho, ca 1904, 9x6"/8x5", SBY 5/12/88 OE **1,430**
Pair: Femme Nue Couchee; La Pierre aux Trois Croquis; drypt & litho, ca 1906/ca 1904, 5x8"/9x12", SBY 5/12/88 ..... **2,475**
Richard Wagner, ed of 100, litho, ca 1900, full mrgs, lt fox, lot 17x13", lot 479, SBY 2/23/89 OE **1,320**
Suite: Douze Lithographies Originales; 12 litho/wove paper, 1904-05/1919, full mrgs, Vollard, lot 545, SBY 11/3/88 OE **27,500**
Sur la Plage a Berneval, etch, pl/s, 5x4", lot 306, FB 5/28/89 OE **420**

RENOIR, Pierre Auguste; after (French, 1841-1919)

La Loge, by Jacques Villon, 106/200, clr aqua, full mrgs, lt stn/sl, 11x8", Bernheim-Jeune, lot 591, SBY 11/3/88 ..... **2,200**
Nu, by Jacques Villon, clr aqua, 1923, full mrgs, lt fox/stn, laid down on board, 23x17", lot 464, SBY 2/25/88 ..... **1,650**

REPPEN, Jack (1933-1964)

Kings Head, 1/1, monotype, titled twice, 14x14", lot 756, WAD 6/12/89 ..... **300**

REVERE, Paul (American, 1735-1818)

View of the Year, 1765; engr/laid paper, 1765-66, 10-12mm mrgs, lt tr/ls/cr mrg, lt sl/stn, S-7x9", C-NY 1/22/88 UE **11,000**

REYMOND, Carlos (French, 1884-)

Bal des Affiches, clr litho/poster paper, lt nick edges, linen backed, 22x15", lot 217, FAP 2/24/89 ..... **140**

RHEAD, Louis John (American, 1857-1926)

Femme au Paon, clr litho, 1897, Estampe Moderne bstp, 13x9", C-E 9/16/88 UE **165**
La Femme au Paon, clr litho, pl/s, 15x10", C-E 3/24/88 ..... **660**
Panneau Decoratif (Swans), clr litho, ca 1896, full mrgs, lt stn, 62x35", La Plume, lot 161, SBY 3/19/88 OE **2,420**

RIAB, L.; after

Pair: German Shorthair; English Setter; litho, p/s, 14x9", Wucher, lot 1073, DM 2/19/88 OE **500**

RICCI, Marco (Italian, 1676-1729)

Landscape with a Fruit Tree, etch, ca 1724/1730, lt cr/rub, 13x17", lot 697, SBY 2/25/88 OE **1,650**

RICHARDSON, Freeman (American, 19th C)

Horn Pond & Environs of Boston, Taken From Rag Rock in Woburn...; hc litho, 1863, S-22x30", lot 524, SBY 1/28/88 UE **660**

RICHARDT, Ferdinand; after

Great International Railway Suspension Bridge Over the Niagara River...; engr, 1859, trm/stn, S-26x35", SBY 1/28/88 ..... **1,100**

RIFKA, Judy (20th C)

Untitled, Modern Dance (contemporary female figure); AP2, litho, 1984, Solo bstp, S-29x22", lot 785, C-NY 11/1/88 ..... **440**

RIGGS, Robert (American, 1896-1970)
Baer-Carnera, #35, ed of unrecorded size, litho/BFK Rives, 1934, p/s, titled, lt stn, L-15x20", lot 254, C-NY 1/19/89 OE **6,600**
Clown Acrobatics, litho/Rives, ca 1937, p/s, titled, gstn mrgs, mstn verso, unfr, L-14x19", C-NY 1/22/88 OE **770**
Club Fighter, #42, ed of unknown size, litho/Rives, ca 1933-39, p/s, lt stn, L-14x18", lot 460, C-NY 5/10/89 OE **4,400**
Club Fighter, litho, p/s, titled, full mrgs, lt sl mrgs, 14x18", lot 117, FAP 2/24/89 ..... **2,600**
Elephant Act, litho/Rives, ca 1937, p/s, titled, full mrgs, mstn/tstn, unfr, L-14x20", C-NY 1/22/88 OE **1,320**
Pair: Clown Alley; On Stage Four; #45 & #42, litho, ca 1937-38, p/s, titled, 15x19"/14x19", lot 58, SBY 2/25/88 OE **2,640**
Pool (Germantown Boy's Club Pool), litho, ca 1938, p/s, lt sl mrgs/verso, lt cr mrg, unfr, L-15x20", SBY 5/12/88 ..... **1,980**
Psychopathic Ward, #22, litho/Rives, ca 1939, p/s, titled, full mrgs, lt scuff/rpr, unfr, L-14x19", C-NY 1/22/88 ..... **990**
Psychopathic Ward, #28, ed of about 50, litho/wove paper, ca 1940, p/s, titled, scr/cr, 14x19", lot 255, C-NY 1/19/89 OE **1,870**
Third Round, litho/wove wm Germany, 1932, p/s, titled, trm mrgs, lt cr, sl/stn mrgs/verso, unfr, L-14x20", C-NY 1/22/88 ..... **1,045**
Tightrope, litho, 15x21", lot 277, WG 10/19/88 ..... **1,000**

RIVERA, Diego (Mexican, 1886-1957)
Donna Fulana, linocut/Japan, 1955, p/s, titled, lt stn/scuff, L-15x11", lot 30, PHL 10/28/88 ..... **550**
El Nino del Taco, #12, ed of 100, litho, 1932, full mrgs, 17x12", lot 48A, SBY 11/3/88 ..... **3,410**
Emilio Zapata, 59/100, litho/wove paper, 1932, p/s, lstn/mstn, scr mrg edge, laid down, unfr, L-16x16", C-NY 1/22/88 OE **1,540**
Los Frutos de la Escuela, 77/100, litho, 1932, p/s, lt gstn/lstn/fox, unfr, 17x12", SBY 5/12/88 OE **5,500**
Mexican Flower Vendors, 67/100, litho/laid paper, 1930, p/s, lg mrgs, 11x16", lot 2975, B/B 2/16/88 ..... **935**
Nude Woman, 83/100, litho/wove paper, 1930, p/s, dtd, 18x11", lot 2973, B/B 2/16/88 ..... **1,980**
Nude Woman with Long Hair, 43/100, litho, 1930, p/s, full mrgs, lt disclr/sl/cr/stn, unfr, 17x9", SBY 5/12/88 ..... **1,540**
Open Air School (La Maestra Rural), 9/100, litho, 1932, p/s, full mrgs, lt stn/sl, 13x16", lot 60, SBY 2/25/88 ..... **3,630**
Seated Nude, 65/100, litho/laid paper, 1930, p/s, 17x11", lot 2974, B/B 2/16/88 ..... **1,870**
Seated Nude with Raised Arms, 43/100, litho, 1930, p/s, full mrgs, lt disclr/ls/stn, unfr, 17x11", SBY 5/12/88 OE **2,090**

RIVERS, Larry (American, 1923-)
Bronx Zoo, 3/250, clr litho/wove paper, 1983, p/s, Styria bstp, full sheet, S-26x34", lot 578, C-NY 5/11/88 ..... **715**
Bronx Zoo, 94/250, clr litho, 1983, p/s, Styria bstp, full sheet, S-26x34", lot 792, C-NY 11/1/88 OE **880**
Camel Quartet, ed of 125, clr scrpt/litho/wove paper, 1978, p/s, lt sl verso, S-23x21", lot 788, C-NY 11/1/88 OE **1,210**
Daniel Webster, 29/80, litho/BFK Rives, 1961, p/s, full sheet, S-22x29", lot 573, C-NY 5/11/88 ..... **605**
Dutch Masters, AP9/20, clr offset litho/scrpt/Fabriano, 1982, p/s, lt sl/stn, L-30x24", lot 791, C-NY 11/1/88 OE **1,760**
First New York Film Festival, 50/250, brn/blk/orange litho, 1963, cr/stn, S-45x30", lot 574, C-NY 5/11/88 ..... **242**
French Money, 14/32, clr litho, 1963, p/s, ULAE bstp, full mrgs, lt stn, hinged to mat, L-17x27", lot 786, C-NY 11/1/88 ..... **2,640**
French Money, 4 on Plexi; 12/125, scrpt/collaged plexiglas, 1966, p/s, 30x32", Multiples, lot 576, C-NY 5/11/88 OE **3,520**
Garbo Grossman, 10/38, clr litho/Twinrocker handmade, 1983, p/s, ULAE bstp, full mrgs, S-31x36", lot 793, C-NY 11/1/88 ..... **2,420**
Last Civil War Veteran, 20/20, litho, 1961, p/s, ULAE bstp, full mrgs, lt stn, 18x12", lot 556, SBY 2/25/88 UE **550**
Map with Fraser, ed of 14, clr scrpt/collage/wove paper, 1966, lt cr/sl/stn, S-25x20", lot 787, C-NY 11/1/88 ..... **770**
Peter's Cheetahs, ed of about 30, stencil/acrylic/airbrush, 1976, p/s, inscr For He Who Did It, 30x43", SBY 5/14/88 OE **2,090**
Portfolio: Boston Massacre; 34/150, 13 embossed/collaged clr slksc, 1970, p/s, 19x14", Kelpra/Marlborough, SBY 5/14/88 ..... **3,850**
Purim, a/p, ed of 45, clr litho/Richard de Bas, 1963, p/s, ULAE bstp, full sheet, stn, S-20x25", lot 575, C-NY 5/11/88 ..... **1,320**
Queen of Clubs, ed of 200, clr offset litho/scrpt/wove paper, 1979, p/s, lt rub/stn/scr, S-30x22", lot 789, C-NY 11/1/88 ..... **1,320**
Single Patriotic Stamp, ed of about 30, stencil/acrylic/airbrush/graphite, 1976, p/s, lt cr, S-30x23", SBY 5/14/88 ..... **1,210**
Swimmer, 71/100, clr scrpt/collage/plexiglas, 1970, sgn, lt scr, 10x10", Marlborough, lot 577, C-NY 5/11/88 ..... **352**
Webster, working proof(?), clr offset litho/scrpt, 1979, p/s, Styria bstp, full mrgs, S-26x30", lot 790, C-NY 11/1/88 ..... **825**

ROBBE, Manuel (French, 1872-1936)
Femme a l'Estampe, ed of about 100, aqua/drypt/rlt/Arches, ca 1906, pl/s, full mrgs, P-21x15", lot 826, C-NY 5/10/89 OE **1,650**
Girl by a Pond, 7/40, clr aqua/cream wove paper, p/s, 15x20", lot 2897, B/B 4/19/88 ..... **468**
Harbor (port scene), aqua, sgn, full mrgs, 19x12", RAB 8/8/89 ..... **475**
Le Choix de l'Epreuve, ed of 40, clr aqua, 1900, p/s, lg mrgs, lt stn, 17x12", Sagot, lot 486, SBY 2/23/89 OE **1,760**
Pair: La Bibliothecaire; La Jolie Menagerie; ed of about 100, drypt/aqua, 1906, 15x10"/19x15", lot 483, SBY 2/23/89 OE **3,850**
Parisian Market Place, Winter; 89, clr aqua/wove wm Idealys, p/s, Cercle Libraire stp, full mrgs, 20x16", RWS 3/16/89 OE **800**
Reflexion, a/p, before clr ed of 100, etch, ca 1902, p/s, 14x11", lot 162, SWN 12/1/88 ..... **600**
Reverie, ed of about 100, clr aqua/Arches, ca 1907, sgn in blk crayon, full mrgs, scuff/cr/fox, lot 485, SBY 2/23/89 OE **1,540**
Sardine Packing, #89, clr aqua, sgn, 18x23", lot 16, RWS 9/29/88 ..... **400**

ROBERTS, David (Scottish, 1796-1864)
Ashdod, hc litho, 1839, sgn in stone, 9x12", lot 1215, LH 12/4/88 ..... **100**
Bethany, hc litho, 1839, sgn in stone, 9x12", lot 1216, LH 12/4/88 ..... **100**
Bethlehem, hc litho, sgn in stone, 14x19", lot 1217, LH 12/4/88 ..... **150**
Christian & Mohamedan Chapels on the Summit of Sinai, hc litho, 9x14", FAP 6/16/89 ..... **250**
Convent of St Catherine, hc litho, 1839, sgn in stone, 19x14", lot 1218, LH 12/4/88 ..... **425**
Convent of the Tara Santa, hc litho, 1839, lt stn, 20x26", lot 216, GAI 6/17/89 ..... **135**

ROBY (20th C)
Kina Lillet, clr litho, 1937, sgn/dtd in pl, backed on linen, 79x52", C-E 7/12/88 ..... **242**

ROCKBURNE, Dorothea (American/Canadian, 20th C)
Locus Series #5, 16/42, etch/aqua/Strathmore, 1972-75, p/s, titled, S-40x30", Parasol, lot 771, SBY 2/23/89 OE **1,760**
Suite: Locus Series #1-6; 42/42, 6 etch/aqua/Strathmore, 1972-75, p/s, orig box, 40x30", Parasol, lot 1203, SBY 5/13/89 ..... **8,250**

ROCKMORE, Noel (American, 20th C, New Orleans)
Bon Voyage, a/p, srgph, 1980, sgn/dtd, 18x24", lot 95, MG 5/28/88 UE **100**
Jazz, 219/265, srgph, 1978, sgn/dtd, 18x24", lot 94, MG 5/28/88 ..... **100**
Moonlight Sonata, a/p, srgph, sgn, 17x24", lot 96, MG 5/28/88 UE **25**
Shroud of Turin, 73/86, srgph, 1979, sgn/dtd, 17x25", lot 97, MG 5/28/88 UE **45**
Susanna & the Elders, a/p, srgph, 1980, sgn/dtd, 10x14", lot 90, MG 5/28/88 ..... **196**
Venice, 190/258, clr srgph w/gold leaf, 1978, sgn/dtd, 18x24", lot 232, MG 11/19/88 UE **25**

ROCKWELL, Norman (American, 1894-1978)
Connoisseur, 68/200, clr collotype/Rives, 1980, L-24x20", Ettinger, lot 2200, DM 3/14/88 ... **1,700**
Top Hat & Tails, 63/200, clr litho, p/s, 34x28", lot 2199, DM 3/14/88 ... **1,700**
RODCHENKO, Alexander (Russian, 1891-1956)
Airplane Poster (Russian text), clr litho, sgn in stone, 14x19", SBY 7/7/88 OE ... **160,000**
ROGERS, Robert Bruce (American, 1907-)
Off in a Calm, linocut, p/s, titled, 8x11", lot 322, WG 10/19/88 ... **300**
Off in a Calm, litho, p/s, titled, full mrgs, 8x11", lot 13, RAB 8/9/88 UE ... **75**
ROHLFS, Christian (1849-1938)
Austreibung aus dem Paradies, dk brn wc/soft buff laid paper, ca 1917, p/s, lt cr/sl, S-21x28", lot 161, C-NY 11/1/88 ... **4,950**
Die Wierbung (Neger mit Tanzerin), wc/cream wove paper, 1913, sgn in img, lt fox/cr, S-15x11", lot 160, C-NY 11/1/88 OE ... **6,050**
Sintflut, a/p, 1st state, hc wc/thick bl-gray wove paper, ca 1918, intl, S-27x20", lot 159, C-NY 11/1/88 ... **12,100**
ROMAN, Giulio; after
Apollo & the Muses, by RU Massard, engr, P-21x30", C-E 7/26/88 UE ... **220**
ROSA, Salvatore (Italian, 1615-1673)
Apollo & the Cumaen Sibyl, 2nd state(?), etch, ca 1661, lt stn/rpr, 13x9", lot 165, SWN 12/1/88 ... **220**
ROSA, Salvatore; after (Italian, 1615-1673)
Saint John Seated Upon a Rock, etch, 17x13", lot 77, FAP 2/24/89 UE ... **60**
ROSENBERG, Louis (American, 1890-)
Ponte Fabricio, Rome; drypt, p/s, 9x7", lot 270A, WG 10/19/88 ... **125**
ROSENQUIST, James (American, 1933-)
Alphabet Avalanche, 16/16AP, clr litho/diecut, 1979, sgn in slvr crayon, Vermilion bstp, S-22x45", SBY 5/14/88 OE ... **1,870**
Cold Rolled, a/p, 11/12, clr litho/Arches, 1974-76, p/s, full sheet, lt sl, 34x74", JR Inc/USF, lot 579, C-NY 5/11/88 OE ... **3,080**
Dusting Off the Roses, 23/35, clr litho, 1965, p/s, titled, ULAE bstp, lt cr, 26x22", lot 772, SBY 2/23/89 OE ... **7,975**
Free For All, 14/50, clr litho/John Kohler, 1976, p/s, S-26x20", orig folder, Transworld, lot 794, C-NY 11/1/88 ... **660**
Gravity Seed, 25/78, clr etch/aqua/wove paper, 1978, p/s, dtd/titled, full mrgs, S-23x40", lot 795, C-NY 11/1/88 UE ... **605**
Hey, Let's Go for a Ride; a/p, clr litho/1972, p/s, full mrgs, lt cr, 22x23", Petersburg, lot 1204, SBY 5/13/89 OE ... **9,900**
Hey, Let's Go for a Ride; clr litho/Hodgkins handmade Woohe Hole, 1972, p/s, 23x22", Petersburg, lot 3065, B/B 4/19/88 ... **2,090**
Horse Blinders, 2/41, clr litho, 1968, p/s, titled, full mrgs, lt stn/cr, L-25x28", lot 129, PHL 10/28/88 OE ... **550**
L'Amour, 22/59, clr etch/aqua/Somerset Satin, 1982, p/s, titled/dtd 1981, P-23x16", Gemini, lot 580, C-NY 5/11/88 OE ... **2,420**
Light That Won't Fail, 24/75, clr litho/Arches Satine, 1972, sgn/dtd/titled, S-20x26", Petersburg, lot 8, C-E 7/26/88 UE ... **143**
Marilyn, 64/75, clr litho, 1974, p/s, full mrgs, lt stn, 35x27", lot 1207, SBY 5/13/89 OE ... **26,400**
More Points on a Bachelor's Tie, 38/78, clr etch/aqua, 1977, p/s, titled, full mrgs, lt cr, 18x36", SBY 2/23/89 OE ... **6,325**
More Points on a Bachelor's Tie, 74/78, clr etch/aqua, 1977, p/s, full mrgs, 18x36", lot 1209, SBY 5/13/89 ... **4,125**
One Million Tons per Square Inch, 28/78, clr litho, 1977, p/s, titled, 18x36", FAP 6/16/89 OE ... **1,300**
Pair: Spring Cheer; Star Proctor; ed of 78, etch/wove paper, 1978-80, p/s, P-18x36", Multiples, lot 796, C-NY 11/1/88 ... **935**
Paper Clip, 39/75, clr litho, 1974, p/s, S-36x69", Petersburg, lot 1205, SBY 5/13/89 OE ... **11,550**
Pulling Out, 33/39, clr litho, 1972, p/s, titled, lt cr/sl, S-26x30", Petersburg, lot 774, SBY 2/23/89 OE ... **3,410**
Pushbuttons, 26/75, litho/Hodgkins Handmade Oatmeal, 1972, sgn/dtd/titled, S-31x27", Petersburg, lot 7, C-E 7/26/88 UE ... **120**
Seesaw, 67/100, clr litho, 1968, p/s, titled, lt tr, S-24x35", lot 120A, PHL 6/16/88 OE ... **400**
Sight Seeing, 25/75, litho/scrpt/German wm PP paper, 1972, sgn/dtd/titled, S-23x29", C-E 7/26/88 UE ... **143**
Wall Street Journal, Dinner Triangle; 67/78, clr etch/aqua, 1977, p/s, titled, full mrgs, 18x36", lot 1208, SBY 5/13/894 ... **125**
Yellow Landing, 29/86, clr litho, 1974, p/s, S-33x74", Petersburg, lot 1206, SBY 5/13/89 ... **6,050**
ROSTIG (20th C)
Setters with Ducks, clr etch, 1938, 16x23", International Art, lot 1074, DM 2/19/88 OE ... **800**
ROTH, Ernest David (American, 1879-1964)
Old Houses, etch/drypt/Japan, 1906, p/s, full mrgs, lt fox, P-9x7", lot 100, PHL 10/28/88 UE ... **100**
Pair: Corner in Bayeux, 1914; Grand Canal, Venice, 1926; etch, p/s, lt stn mrgs, 10x7", lot 225, SWN 6/15/89 ... **195**
ROTHENBERG, Susan (American, 1945-)
Black Water, 9/16, blk & gray litho/Dieu Donne, 1984-85, p/s, ULAE bstp, full mrgs, 43x30", lot 1210, SBY 5/13/89 ... **12,100**
Plug, 20/29, blk/gray litho on Albrecht Durer British, 1983, p/s, ULAE bstp, S-30x22", lot 558, SBY 2/25/88 OE ... **1,870**
Tilting, 24/46, clr litho/wc/Supra 100, 1986, p/s, Gemini bstp, full mrgs, 46x50", lot 1211, SBY 5/13/89 OE ... **4,950**
Untitled (Hartford), 11/23, litho/Arches, 1980, p/s, full mrgs, S-35x30", Rothenberg/Hartford Art School, C-NY 11/1/88 ... **2,200**
Untitled (May #3), PPI, sugar-lift/spit-bite/sftgr/burin, 1979, p/s, full mrgs, 24x18", Parasol, SBY 11/5/88 OE ... **7,150**
ROUAULT, Georges (French, 1871-1958)
Abandonne, aqua/rlt/drypt/Arches, 1916-26/1948, full mrgs, lt sl, Ed l'Etoile, lot 535, C-NY 11/1/88 OE ... **2,640**
Aide-Bourreau Portant un des Bois de la Croix, aqua/cream paper, 1936, pl/s, 12x8", lot 2899, B/B 4/19/88 ... **300**
Amazone, ed of 270, clr aqua, 1930, full mrgs, lt stn, 12x9", lt 435, SBY 2/25/88 OE ... **15,400**
Amazone, total ed of 270, clr aqua, 1930, full mrgs, lt stn/cr, 12x9", lot 549, SBY 11/3/88 OE ... **20,900**
Amer Citron, total ed of 280, clr aqua, 1935, lt glue in mrgs/verso, 12x9", lot 438, SBY 2/25/88 OE ... **12,100**
Amer Citron, total ed of 280, clr aqua, 1935/1938, full mrgs, lt fox/stn, 12x9", Vollard, lot 498, SBY 2/23/89 OE ... **11,000**
Au Pressoir, le Raisin fut Foule; aqua/laid Arches, 1922, pl/s, full mrgs, stn, 16x19", Vollard, lot 2904, B/B 4/19/88 ... **660**
Au Vieux Faubourg des Longues Peines, Pl 10, aqua/drypt/Arches, 1923, L-22x17", Vollard, lot 9, RWS 9/8/89 Oe ... **2,200**
Augures, aqua/Arches, full mrgs, 20x17", Vollard, lot 2903, B/B 4/19/88 OE ... **935**
Augures, total ed of 450, drypt/aqua/burnished/rlt/heliogravure, 1923/1948, full mrgs, 20x17", lot 534, C-NY 11/1/88 OE ... **1,650**
Auto-Portrait III, 27/100, clr litho/Arches, 1926, p/s, full mrgs, lt cr/fox/ls, 14x10", lot 567, SBY 11/3/88 ... **6,600**
Automme, ed of 175, litho, 1927, sgn/dtd 1933/inscr 3e Tirage, full mrgs, lt stn, L-23x17", lot 340, C-NY 5/11/88 ... **6,050**
Automme, 92/175, clr aqua, 1938, sgn in ink, full mrgs, lt lstn, mstn verso, P-20x26", lot 541, C-NY 11/1/88 OE ... **52,800**
Automne, ed of 175, 11th state, litho/Montval, 1927-33, full mrgs, lt sl, S-22x29", Vollard/Clot, lot 163, C-NY 11/1/88 ... **6,600**
Automne, litho, 1927, sgn in ink, dtd 1933, full mrgs, lt stn/cr, 17x23", lot 568A, SBY 11/3/88 OE ... **9,350**
Automne, 11th state, litho, 1927, sgn/dtd 1933, inscr 3e Tirage, full mrgs, lt stn, L-17x23", lot 543, C-NY 11/1/88 OE ... **8,250**

Automne, 129/175, clr aqua, 1938, ink sgn, full mrgs, lt mstn/disclr/skinned, 20x26", SBY 5/12/88	34,100
Automne, 78/175, clr aqua, 1938, full mrgs, lt mstn, lt stn/sl mrgs, sl verso, 20x26", SBY 5/12/88	31,900
Autonme, ed of 60, litho/Montval, 1927-33, sgn in ink, full mrgs, lt cr/sl, 17x23", lot 568, SBY 11/3/88 OE	9,350
Ballerine, Cirque; total ed of 270, clr aqua, 1931, full mrgs, lt mstn, P-12x8", Vollard, lot 537, C-NY 11/1/88	4,950
Ballerine, total ed of 270, clr aqua, full mrgs, 12x8", lot 496, SBY 2/23/89 OE	8,800
Ballerine, total ed of 270, clr aqua, 1930, full mrgs, lt stn, 12x8", lot 497, SBY 2/23/89 OE	5,500
Book: Cirque de l'Etoile Filante; #28, deluxe ed of 35, 1938, Vollard, lot 437, SBY 2/25/88 OE	7,150
Celui qui Croit en Moi, Fut-il Mort, Vivva; etch/aqua/Arches, 1923, pl/s, full mrgs, 23x17", Vollard, B/B 2/16/88	300
Cheval Blanc, Saltimbanques; 4/10, 2nd state, litho, ca 1925, Peintres Graveurs bstp, L-12x9", lot 338, C-NY 5/11/88	462
Christ (de Profil), total ed of 270, clr aqua, 1935/1939, full mrgs, lt fox/stn, 12x9", Vollard, lot 813, SBY 5/11/89	12,100
Christ (de Profil), total ed of 270, clr aqua, 1935/1939, lt trm mrg, lt stn, 12x9", Vollard, lot 502, SBY 2/23/89	9,350
Christ aux Portes de la Ville, total ed of 270, clr aqua, 1935/1939, lt stn/fox, 12x9", Vollard, lot 811, SBY 5/11/89	3,850
Christ aux Portes de la Ville, total ed of 270, clr aqua, 1935/1939, full mrgs, lt stn, 12x9", Vollard, SBY 11/3/88 OE	7,700
Christ en Croix, a/p, 2nd state, litho/Japan, 1932, Frapier stp, lt rpl/sl mrgs, L-12x9", lot 342, C-NY 5/11/88 OE	1,870
Christ en Croix, aside from #d ed of 175, clr aqua, 1936, sgn in ink, lt stn/sl/cr, 26x20", lot 817, SBY 5/11/89 OE	57,750

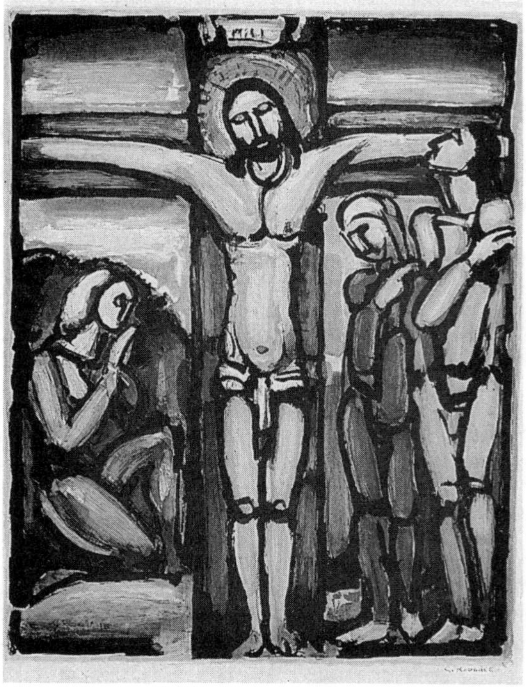

Christ en Croix, ed of 175, aqua/rlt/Montval, 1936, sgn in ink, lt stn mrgs/verso, P-26x20", lot 834, C-NY 5/10/89 OE; $55,000

Christ en Croix, 45/175, clr aqua, 1936, full mrgs, lt sl/fox/cr, 26x20", lot 565, SBY 11/3/88 OE	40,700
Christ et Disciples, total ed of 270, clr aqua, 1935/1939, full mrgs, lt stn, 12x9", Vollard, lot 560, SBY 11/3/88 OE	3,300
Christ et Disciples, total ed of 270, clr aqua, 1936, trm mrgs, laid down, 12x9", lot 441, SBY 2/25/88 OE	3,025
Clown au Chien, a/p, blk aqua/Montval, ca 1931, lt mstn, P-14x10", lot 341, C-NY 5/11/88 UE	1,100
Clown et Enfant, ed of 270, clr aqua, 1930, full mrgs, lt stn, 12x8", lot 493, SBY 2/23/89	6,600
Clownesse, 5/50, 3rd state, litho/heavy Arches, ca 1925-29, full mrgs, lt fox, 13x9", lot 227, SWN 6/15/89 OE	1,430
Courtisane aux Yeux Baisses, ed of 250, clr aqua, 1937, full mrgs, lt stn, 12x9", Lacouriere, lot 814, SBY 5/11/89 OE	8,250
Courtisane aux Yeux Baisses, ed of 250, clr aqua, 1937, full mrgs, lt stn/sl, 12x9", Lacouriere, lot 561, SBY 11/3/88	6,050
Courtisane Nue, etch/aqua/heavy wove paper, 1927, pl/s, 11x14", lot 2896, B/B 2/16/88	468
Dame a la Huppe, total ed of 270, clr aqua, 1935/1939, full mrgs, lt cr, 12x8", Vollard, SBY 5/12/88 OE	4,950
Dame a la Huppe, total ed of 270, clr aqua, 1935/1939, trm mrgs, lt gstn/skinned, fox, 12x8", Vollard, SBY 5/12/88 OE	4,125
Dame a la Huppe, total ed of 270, clr aqua, 1936/1939, lt stn, 12x9", Vollard, lot 504, SBY 2/23/89 OE	6,050
Dame du Haut-Quartier Croit Prendre pour le Ciel Place Reserve, aqua, 1922, full mrgs, 23x16", Vollard, B/B 4/19/88	935
Demain Sera Beau, Disait le Naufrage; Pl 11, aqua/drypt/collotype/Arches, 1922, 20x14", Vollard, lot 10, RWS 9/8/89 OE	1,800
Demain Sera Beau, Disait le Naufrage; 11, aqua/laid wm Ambrose Vollard Arches, 1922, lt stn, 20x14", RWS 3/16/89 OE	1,100
Des Ongles et du Bec, Pl 50, aqua/collotype/Arches, 1926, pl/s, lt stn, L-23x18", Vollard, lot 11, RWS 9/8/89 OE	2,200
Dors Mon Amour, total ed of 280, etch/aqua/rlt/Verge de Montval, 1935, sgn, P-12x9", Vollard, lot 540, C-NY 11/1/88 OE	8,800
Douce Amere, total ed of 280, clr aqua, 1934, full mrgs, lt stn/sl/fox, 12x8", Vollard, lot 810, SBY 5/11/89	9,900
Dura Lex sed Lex, Pl 52, aqua/stpl/collotype/Arches, 1926, pl/s, lt stn, L-23x17", Vollard, lot 12, RWS 9/8/89	900
Ecce Dolor, total ed of 270, clr aqua, 1935, lt stn, 12x9", lot 440, SBY 2/25/88 OE	9,350
Ecce Homo, total ed of 270, clr aqua, 1936/1939, full mrgs, lt mstn, 13x8", Suares/Vollard, lot 812, SBY 5/11/89	9,900
En les Temps Noirs de Jactance et d'Incroyance Notre Dame de la Fin des Terres Vigilante, lot 2895, B/B 2/16/88 OE	880
Enfant de la Balle, Pl 10, ed of 280, clr aqua/Montval, 1935, S-18x13", Vollard, lot 162, C-NY 11/1/88	6,600
Enfant de la Balle, total ed of 280, clr aqua, 1935/1938, full mrgs, lt stn, 12x8", Vollard, lot 501, SBY 2/23/89 OE	8,250
Et Veronique au Tendre Lin, Pass Encore sur le Chemin; Pl 33, aqua/collotype/Arches, 1922, 17x17", Vollard, RWS 9/8/89	900
Femme Affranchie, Quatorze Heures, Chante Midi; aqua/Arches, pl/s, full mrgs, 22x17", Vollard, lot 2901, B/B 4/19/88	990

Fiere Autant Qu'un Vivant, de Sa Noble Stature; ed of 250, clr aqua, 1937, full mrgs, lt cr/fox, 12x9", SBY 5/12/88	2,200
Fille au Cafe, clr monotype/thick wove paper, 1910, sepia ink sgn, skinned/disclr verso, S-13x8", SBY 5/12/88	35,200
Group of 3: Arrive Parfois...; Au Pays de la Soif...; Au Pressoir le Raisin Fut Foule; aqua, 1922/1948, SBY 5/12/88	3,025
Group of 3: Chantez Mantines le Jour Renait; Nous Sommes Fous...; La Mort L'A Pris Comme...; aqua, 1922, SBY 5/12/88	2,200
Hiver Lepre de la Terra, Pl 24, ed of 450, aqua, 20x14", lot 850, LH 12/4/88	600
Homme au Chapeau, 62/225, etch/aqua/heavy wove paper, 1928, sgn in ink, full mrgs, lt stn, 12x8", lot 2897, B/B 2/16/88	440
Jongleur, total ed of 280, clr aqua, 1934/1938, full mrgs, lt mstn, 12x8", Vollard, lot 500, SBY 2/23/89	9,250
Jongleur, total ed of 280, clr aqua, 1934/1938, lt stn/fox, 12x8", Vollard, lot 553, SBY 11/3/88	8,800
Juges, ed of 250, clr aqua, 1938, full mrgs, 12x9", Lacouriere, lot 457, SBY 5/12/88	2,530
Juges, ed of 250, clr aqua, 1938, lt mstn, 12x9", Lacouriere, lot 442, SBY 2/25/88	1,980
L'Administrateur, 75/225, etch/aqua/heavy wove paper, 1928, p/s, full mrgs, 11x7", lot 2897A, B/B 2/16/88	275
La Baie des Trepasses, 36/175, clr aqua, 1939, full mrgs, lt stn, 24x18", lot 566, SBY 11/3/88	5,500
La Lutteuse, litho/wove paper, p/s, 12x9", lot 2891, B/B 2/16/88	468
La Parade, Cirque; total ed of 270, clr aqua/Rives, 1930, full mrgs, lt stn, P-12x11", Vollard, lot 536, C-NY 11/1/88 OE	5,280
La Parade, total ed of 270, clr aqua, 1930, full mrgs, lt gstn mrgs, unfr, 12x11", SBY 5/12/88 OE	9,350
La Parade, total ed of 270, clr aqua/laid paper, 1930, pl/s, full mrgs, lt stn, tp on verso, P-12x11", C-NY 5/10/89 OE	1,750
La Petite Ecuyere, Cirque de l'Etoile Filante; etch/aqua/rlt/Verge de Montval, ca 1935, 12x8", lot 538, C-NY 11/1/88 OE	9,350
La Petite Ecuyere, total ed of 280, clr aqua, 1935/1938, full mrgs, lt stn, 12x9", Vollard, lot 554, SBY 11/3/88	9,900
Laquais, ed of 250, clr aqua, 1937, full mrgs, lt fox/sl, 12x9", Lacouriere, lot 562, SBY 11/3/88 OE	7,700
Laquais, ed of 250, clr aqua, 1937, full mrgs, lt stn, 12x8", Lacouriere, lot 815, SBY 5/11/89	6,600
Le Baie des Trepasses, 49/175, clr aqua, 1939, full mrgs, lt gstn/mstn/ls, 24x18", SBY 5/12/88 OE	6,600
Le Bilboquet, Grotesques; Pl 2, 40/50, 4th state, litho/Arches, ca 1925, Frapier stp, L-12x9", lot 339, C-NY 5/11/88	462
Le Boniment du Clown, ed of 50, litho, ca 1929, p/s, full mrgs, lt fox recto/verso, 12x9", lot 230, SWN 6/16/89	1,100
Le Christ et Mammon, ed of 270, clr aqua, 1936/1939, intl, full mrgs, lt stn/fox, 12x9", Vollard, lot 559, SBY 11/3/88	3,025
Le Christ et Mammon, total ed of 270, clr aqua, 1935/1939, full mrgs, lt cr, 12x9", Vollard, lot 505, SBY 2/23/89	5,500
Le Clown a la Grosse Caisse, total ed of 200, clr aqua, 1930, full mrgs, lt stn/tr, 12x8", Saures, lot 808, SBY 5/11/89	4,950
Le Clown a la Grosse Caisse, total ed of 200, clr aqua, 1930, full mrgs, lt stn/sl/cr, 12x8", lot 550, SBY 11/3/88	5,500
Le Clown a la Grosse Caisse, total ed of 270, clr aqua, 1930, full mrgs, lt stn, 12x8", lot 492, SBY 2/23/89	8,250
Le Clown a la Grosse Caisse, total ed of 270, clr aqua/Verge de Montval, 1930, full mrgs, lt stn, P-12x8", C-NY 5/10/89	5,280
Le Clown Jaune, total ed of 270, clr aqua, 1930, full mrgs, lt stn, 14x10", lot 551, SBY 11/3/88	6,050
Le Jongleur, ed of 270, clr aqua, 1930, full mrgs, lt stn, 12x9", lot 436, SBY 2/25/88 OE	3,520
Le Jongleur, total ed of 270, clr aqua, 1930, full mrgs, lt mstn, 13x9", lot 491, SBY 2/23/89	2,750
Le Petit Main, total ed of 280, clr aqua, 1935/1938, lt stn, 12x8", Vollard, lot 499, SBY 2/23/89	5,775
Le Pitre, ed of 25, 2nd state of 4, litho/Japan, 1924-32, p/s, pub stp, full mrgs, unfr, L-14x9", Frapier, SBY 5/12/88	770
Le Vieux Clown, total ed of 270, clr aqua, 1930, full mrgs, 13x9", lot 494, SBY 2/23/89 OE	8,800
Les Ballerines, Cirque de l'Etoile Filante; etch/aqua/rlt/Verge de Montval, 1934, P-12x8", lot 539, C-NY 11/1/88 OE	7,700
Les Ballerines, ed of 35, clr aqua/Chine applique, 1934/1938, lt rub/skinned, 12x8", Vollard, SBY 5/12/88 OE	8,800
Madame Carmencita, total ed of 280, clr aqua, 1935/1938, full mrgs, lt fox, 12x8", Vollard, lot 555, SBY 11/3/88	5,500
Madame Carmencita, total ed of 280, clr aqua/Japan Imperial, 1935, full mrgs, 12x8", lot 809, SBY 5/11/89	5,500
Madame Louison, etch/aqua/rlt/Verge de Montval, 1935, pl/s, full mrgs, lt fox/tp, P-12x8", lot 833, C-NY 5/10/89	6,050
Maitres et Petits Maitres d'Aujourd'Hou: Fille; 27/100, litho, 1926, p/s, lt stn/fox, L-13x9", Frapier, SBY 5/12/88 UE	440
Master Arthur, total ed of 280, clr aqua, 1934, full mrgs, lt stn/fox, 12x8", Vollard, lot 556, SBY 11/3/88 OE	10,450
Master Arthur, total ed of 280, clr aqua, 1935/1938, full mrgs, lt fox/disclr, 12x8", SBY 5/12/88 OE	9,350
Miserere: Bella Matribus Detestata; XLII, ed of 450, aqua/drypt, 1923, 23x21", L'Etoile Filante, lot 433, SBY 2/25/88 OE	4,125
Miserere: De Profondis...; Pl XLVII, ed of 450, aqua, 1948, full mrgs, lt stn, 17x24", L'Etoile Filante, SBY 2/25/88 OE	1,760
Miserere: Qui ne se Grime Pas?; Pl VIII, ed of 450, aqua/drypt, 1923, full mrgs, lt stn, 22x17", lot 488, SBY 2/23/89 OE	16,500
Ne Sommes-Nous pas Forcats?; #6, ed of 450, aqua, 1926, full mrgs, lt sl/2 tp stn in mrgs, unfr, 23x17", SBY 5/12/88	1,430
Ne Sommes-Nous Pas Forcats?; total ed of 450, etch/aqua/rlt/Arches, 1926, lt stn, 23x17", Vollard, lot 829, C-NY 5/10/89	1,870
Negresse en Profil, 62/225, etch/aqua/cream wove paper, 1928, sgn in ink, lg mrgs, lt stn, 12x8", lot 2899, B/B 2/16/88	825
Nous...C'est en sa Mort que Nous Avons ete Babtises; etch/aqua/cream wove paper, pl/s, 22x17", lot 2902, B/B 4/19/88	495
Nu Assis, Reincarnations du Pere Ubu; total ed of 575, etch/aqua/rlt/Arches, 1928, P-11x7", lot 827, C-NY 5/10/89	385
Obeissant Jusqu` a la Mort et a la Mort de la Croix, Pl 57, aqua/drypt/collotype/Arches, 23x17", Vollard, RWS 9/8/89 OE	2,400
Pair: Bon Candidat Boudoubadabou; Bon Electeur; before ed CR10d, etch/aqua/rlt, 1918, sgn/dtd, sl, lot 531, C-NY 11/1/88	462
Pair: Gustave Moreau; Confidences; ed of 35 & 10, litho, 1926, p/s, lt fox/stn, 9x7"/12x9", lot 229, SWN 6/15/89 OE	1,540
Pair: Le Condamne S'En Est Alle...; Hiver Lepre de la Terre; ed of 450, aqua, 1922/1948, 20x14"/20x15", SBY 5/12/88	1,650
Pair: Les Trois Croix; Tombeau; ed of 250, clr aqua, 1938 & 1936, 12x9"/12x8", Lacouriere, lot 564, SBY 11/3/88 OE	2,090
Pair: Miserere: En Ces Temps Noirs de Jactance...; Mon Doux Pays ou Etes-Vous?; aqua, 1927, 23x17"/16x24", SBY 2/23/89	7,700
Parade, ed of 270, clr aqua, 1930, full mrgs, 12x11", lot 495, SBY 2/23/89	7,150
Parade (Frontispiece), total ed of 280, clr aqua, 1934/1938, full mrgs, lt stn, 12x8", Vollard, lot 552, SBY 11/3/88	9,350
Passion, ed of 250, clr aqua, 1937, full mrgs, lt stn, 12x8", Lacouriere, lot 443, SBY 2/25/88 OE	9,350
Passion, ed of 250, clr aqua, 1938, full mrgs, lt stn, 13x9", Lacouriere, lot 506, SBY 2/23/89 OE	13,750
Paysage au Palmier, 74/225, etch/aqua/cream wove paper, 1918, 12x8", lot 2898, B/B 2/16/88	412
Pecheur, total ed of 270, clr aqua, 1936/1939, full mrgs, lt fox, 12x8", Vollard, lot 503, SBY 2/23/89 OE	4,400
Pierrot, total ed of 280, clr aqua, 1935/1938, lt stn, 12x9", Vollard, lot 557, SBY 11/3/88 OE	8,800
Plus le Coeur est Noble, Moins le Col est Roide; Pl 49, 3rd state, aqua/drypt/rlt, 1926, P-23x17", C-E 5/13/88 OE	605
Portfolio: Miserere; 35/425, 58 aqua/Arches, 1922-27, full mrgs, orig wrappers, Ed L'Etoile, lot 828, C-NY 5/10/89 OE	170,500
Portfolio: Miserere; 78/425, 58 aqua/Arches, 1922-27/1948, orig wrappers, Etoile Filante/Vollard, lot 807, SBY 5/11/89	176,000
Portrait of a Woman, etch, 11x7", lot 93, FAP 2/24/89 UE	200
Reincarnations du Pere Ubu, woodblock, 1932, 8x8", Vollard/Aubert, lot 548, SBY 11/3/88	2,200
Rue des Solitaires, etch/aqua/Arches, 1922, full mrgs, lt stn/sl, 14x20", Vollard, lot 2892, B/B 2/16/88	330
Son Avocat en Phrases Creuses...; total ed of 450, etch/aqua/heliogravure/Arches, 1922, 21x16", Vollard, C-NY 11/1/88	660

Squelette Laboureur, Pl 9, 249/425, aqua/Arches, 1966, 14x10", L'Etoile Filante, lot 2905, B/B 4/19/88 ..... **165**
Suite: Reincarnations du Pere Ubu (Edition Minature); total ed of 210, 23 etch/aqua, 1929, S-13x10", SBY 2/23/89 OE **3,080**
Sund Lacrimoe Rerum...; etch/aqua/laid paper, 1926, pl/s, trm mrgs, laid down, 17x23", lot 2893, B/B 2/16/88 ..... **275**
Sunt Lacrymae Rerum...; total ed of 450, aqua/wove paper, 1926, pl/s, lt stn, P-23x16", lot 830, C-NY 5/10/89 OE **1,870**
Trio, ed of 250, clr aqua, 1938, full mrgs, lt sl mrgs, 12x9", Lacouriere, lot 563, SBY 11/3/88 OE **5,775**
Tristes Os, total ed of 280, clr aqua, 1934, full mrgs, 12x8", Vollard, lot 439, SBY 2/25/88 OE **6,050**
Verloersie, litho, 1933, p/s, titled, 17x12", lot 181, WG 10/19/88 ..... **675**

ROUAULT, Georges; after (French, 1871-1958)
Fleurs Decoratives, 123/175, etch/aqua/rlt/Arches, 1960, pl/s, Lacouriere bstp, lt fox, P-22x15", lot 343, C-NY 5/11/88 ..... **7,700**
Fleurs Decoratives, 161/175, clr aqua, 1960, full mrgs, lt stn/old tp, 22x15", Lacouriere, lot 818, SBY 5/11/89 OE **9,900**
Fleurs Decoratives, 48/175, clr aqua, 1960, Lacouriere bstp, full mrgs, lt stn/sl/cr, 22x15", lot 444, SBY 2/25/88 OE **5,775**

ROUBILLE, Auguste Jean Baptiste
Les Meilleures Nourritures pour Chiens Gibiers Et Volailles, clr litho, ca 1910, pl/s, fr, 63x46", C-E 9/16/88 OE **4,400**

ROUSSEAU, Henri (Le Douanier)(French, 1844-1910)
La Guerre, pen litho/orange wove paper, 1894, S-10x16", Gourmont & Jarry, lot 164, C-NY 11/1/88 OE **4,180**

ROUSSEL, Ker Xavier (French, 1867-1944)
La Source, Pl 7, ed of 100, clr litho/Chine volant, ca 1900, full mrgs, lt stn/sl, 13x16", lot 819, SBY 5/11/89 ..... **1,100**
Set of 7: L'Album de Paysage; ed of 100, clr litho/Chine volant, ca 1900, L-13x16", lot 165, C-NY 11/1/88 OE **16,500**

ROVERSON, R. (British, 19th C)
American Express Trains, litho, wstn mrgs, 1874, lg folio, RAB 11/25/88 OE **750**

RUELLAN, Andree (American, 1905-)
Pair: Side Show; Dog Circus; litho, various sizes, Am Artists Group, lot 231, WG 10/19/88 ..... **100**

RUFFIE, Cathy (American, 20th C)
Hegged Town From Klee, 5/150, litho, p/s, 20x16", lot 1265, LH 12/4/88 ..... **950**

RUSCHA, Ed (American, 1937-)
Cheese Mold Standard with Olive, 28/150, scrpt/wove paper, 1969, p/s, lt cr, L-20x37", Ruscha, lot 800, C-NY 11/1/88 OE **2,640**

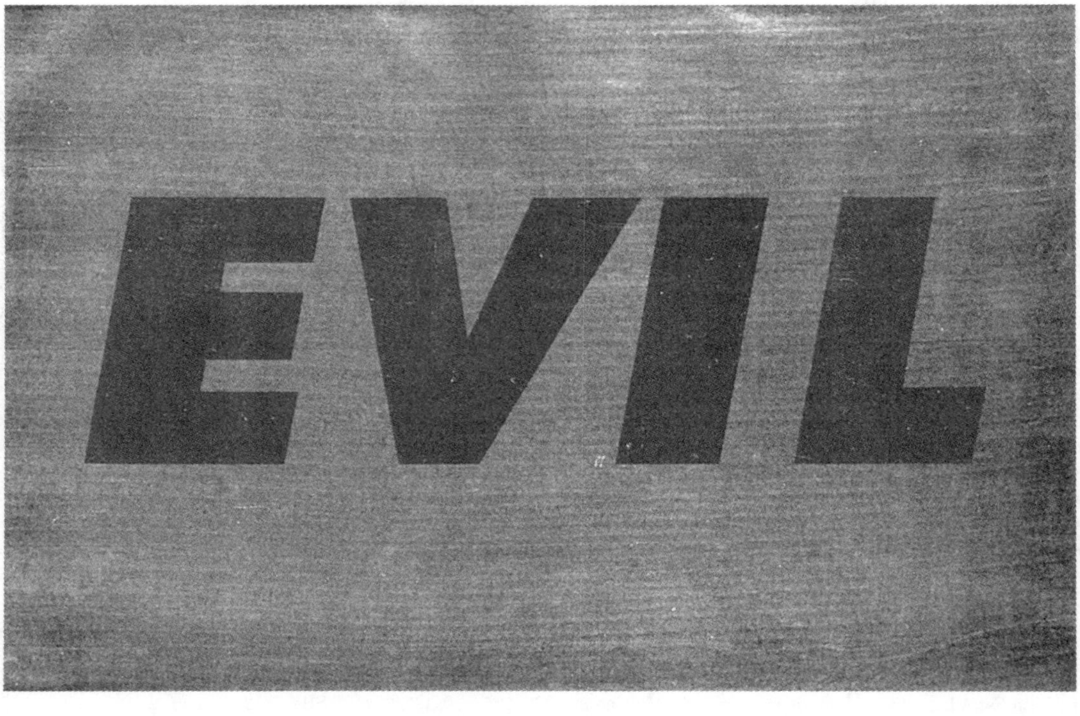

Evil, AP, blk/dk maroon scrpt on thin veneer-textured paper, 1973, sgn/dtd on verso, full sheet, S-20x30", Cirrus Ed, lot 21, C-NY 10/31/89 OE; $6,600

Fruit-Metrecal Hollywood; 38/89, clr slksc, 1971, p/s, full mrgs, 10x38", Jacobson/Ruscha, lot 946, SBY 11/5/88 OE **2,200**
Made in California, 70/100, wht/orange scrpt on Arches, 1971, p/s, S-20x28", Grunewald, lot 801, C-NY 11/1/88 OE **1,320**
Pair: Yes; Sea of Desire; 2/25, clr litho, 1984, p/s, full mrgs, 18x26", lot 559, SBY 2/25/88 OE **1,760**
Rabbit, 27/30, brn litho, 1985, p/s, Tamarind bstp, S-45x34", lot 1212, SBY 5/13/89 OE **7,700**
Some Los Angeles Apartments, Book Covers; #3, ed of 30, litho/Arches, 1970, USF bstp, S-16x20", lot 581, C-NY 5/11/88 ..... **605**

RUSSELL, Benjamin; after (American, 1804-1885)
Right Whaling in Behring Straights & Arctic Ocean, litho, trm mrgs, fox, unfr, lg folio, RAB 11/10/88 ..... **400**
Sperm Whaling with Its Varieties, litho, fox, orig fr, lg folio, JH Bufford of Boston, RAB 11/10/88 ..... **2,300**

RUTHVEN, John A. (American, 1924-)
Bald Eagle, 789/1000, litho, p/s, no size given, lot 1062, DM 2/19/88 ..... **350**
Spring Flowers, 244/600, p/s, 14x22", lot 616, GAI 12/9/88 ..... **65**

RYAN, Anne (American, 1889-1954)

Pair: Cancer; Window; 28/34 & 30/50, clr wc, 1946 & ca 1947, sgn, laid down, lot 257, C-NY 1/19/89 330
Pair: Untitled (figure); Untitled (abstract); etch & monotye, ca 1945-49 & 1945, p/s, inscr, lt fox/stn, C-NY 1/22/88 528
Untitled (female nude), etch/L'Aiglon, ca 1945-49, p/s, inscr verso, scr img, cr/sl mrgs/verso, P-8x4", C-NY 1/22/88 550

RYLAND, John (American, 20th C)

Dartmouth Winter Carnival, litho/poster paper, 34x22", lot 228, FAP 2/24/89 OE 175

RYLEY, Charles Reuben; after (British, 1752-1798)

Daniel Mendoza & Richard Humphreys, clr engr/glass, 11x13", lot 73, FAP 2/24/89 OE 650

RYMAN, Robert (American, 1930-)

Portfolio: Seven Aquatints; 26/50, aqua, 1972, p/s, orig wrapers, S-24x24"/20" dia, Parasol, lot 798,SBY 5/14/88 4,400
Portfolio: Six Aquatints; 1975; 31/50, clr aqua, 1975, p/s, orig wrappers, S-36x36", Parasol, lot 1212A, SBY 5/13/89 17,600
Portfolio: Six Aquatints; 37/50, buff aqua, 1975, full sheets, orig wrappers, Parasol, lot 582, C-NY 5/11/88 OE 7,150

SABATINI, Raphael (American, 1898-)

Three Men, 1/5, clr litho, no size given, lot 32, FAP 2/24/89 UE 10

SACHSE, E.; & Co. (19th C)

Bird's-Eye View of Baltimore City, clr litho, 1858, lt sl img, lt tstn/tr mrg, stn verso, L-24x40", C-NY 1/22/88 OE 8,800
Chesapeake Marine Railway...; clr litho/wove paper, 1868, stn/rpr tr img/mrgs, laid down, L-14x20", C-NY 1/22/88 OE 2,750
Fort Federal Hill, Baltimore, Maryland; 2nd state of 4, litho, 1862, lstn/fox, stn/ls mrg edges, L-14x20", C-NY 1/22/88 440

SAGE, Philip (American, 20th C, New Orleans)

Decatur Street, 158/200, litho, sgn, 4x6", lot 234, MG 11/19/88 UE 50

SAITO, Kiyoshi (Japanese, 20th C)

Geisha Girl, clr wc, p/s, no size given, lot 340, WG 10/19/88 200
Pair: Children in the Snow; woodblock, p/s, 14x10", lot 155, WG 10/19/88 300

SALLE, David (American, 1952-)

Drunken Chauffeur, 33/45, clr slksc, 1983, p/s, S-30x42", Parasol, SBY 5/14/88 OE 1,210
Paris Review, 63/100, clr slksc/BFK Rives, 1982, p/s, dtd, S-30x41", lot 3066, B/B 4/19/88 600
Set of 8: Until Photographs Could Be Taken From Earth Satellites; AP9/10, aqua/BFK Rives, 1981, lot 802, C-NY 11/1/88 22,000
Set of 8: Until Photographs Could Be Taken From Earth Satellites; AP6/10, aqua, 1981, Parasol, lot 583, C-NY 5/11/88 19,800
Set of 8: Until Photographs Could Be Taken From Earth Satellites; AP5/10, aqua, 1981, S-30x42", lot 1213, SBY 5/13/89 18,700
Until Photographs Could Be Taken From Earth's Satellites, 3/10, blk aqua, 1981, p/s, S-30x42", Parasol, SBY 2/23/89 1,540
Untitled, Grandiose Synonym for Church; 4/17, yel/olive-gr/blk aqua, 1985, S-61x48", Parasol, lot 584, C-NY 5/11/88 1,980
Untitled, Grandiose Synonym for Church; AP7/10, aqua, 1985, p/s, full mrgs, 48x38", Parasol, lot 1213A, SBY 5/13/89 3,850
Untitled, Grandiose Synonym for Church; 11/17, clr aqua, 1985, p/s, full mrgs, 48x38", Parasol, lot 947, SBY 11/5/88 1,925

SALOMUSMULLER, Matthaus Sigmund (German, 1696-1731)

Meridies Mittag le Midi, mezzo, 16x20", lot 18, FAP 2/24/89 UE 45

SALTONSTALL, Elizabeth (American, 1900-)

From the Sea, litho, sgn, L-13x10", RAB 8/8/89 150

SAMPLE, Paul (American, 1896-1974)

Two Children on a Horse, litho, p/s, 9x13", lot 279, WG 10/19/88 105

SANDZEN, Sven Birger (American, 1871-1954)

Smoky River, litho, p/s, titled, 10x14", lot 858, LH 5/15/88 120

SASSONE, Marco (Italian, 1942-)

Flood of Florence, 154/200, clr srgph/cream wove paper, p/s, 14x9", lot 3067, B/B 4/19/88 UE 88
Santo Cruz, 117/200, clr srgph, 1982, p/s, 24x28", lot 2211, DM 3/14/88 375
Studio Vista, 128/150, clr srgph/cream wove paper, p/s, 26x32", lot 3068, B/B 4/19/88 468

SCHAWBE, Carloz (French, 19th C)

Salon Rose Croix, clr litho/poster paper, cr, 78x32", lot 280, FAP 2/24/89 UE 90

SCHIELE, Egon (German, 1890-1918)

Bildnis Arthur Roessler, ed of 80, gr etch/firm cream wove paper, 1914, stp/sgn, S-14x20", lot 169, C-NY 11/1/88 OE 6,600
Kauernde, ed of 80, gr drypt/firm cream simili Japan, 1914, tp/s, lt cr, S-21x15", lot 168, C-NY 11/1/88 18,700
Mannliches Bildnis (Franz Hauer?), ed of 80, etch/firm cream simili Japan, 1914, stp/s, S-13x10", lot 166, C-NY 11/1/88 1,210
Selbstbildnis, ed of 80, etch/thick cream wove paper, 1914, stp/s, lt sl, S-8x7", lot 167, C-NY 11/1/88 OE 4,180

SCHLEMMER, Oskar (German, 1888-1943)

Figur von der Seite, a/p, litho/pk Japan, 1921, p/s, lt stn/tp, S-19x14", lot 171, C-NY 11/1/88 OE 5,280
Figurenplan, ed of 25, litho/wove paper, 1919-20, p/s, Euphorion Verlag bstp, cr/fox, S-16x12", lot 170, C-NY 11/1/88 OE 3,850
Konzentrische Gruppe (Figurenplan K1), a/p, litho/yel Japan, 1921, p/s, full mrgs, stn, 18x14", lot 172, C-NY 11/1/88 OE 9,900
Konzentrische Gruppe (Figurenplan K1), litho, 1921, p/s, Staatliches Bauhaus bstp, 19x14", lot 820, SBY 5/11/89 OE 12,100

SCHMIDT-ROTTLUFF, Karl (German, 1884-1976)

Album: 9 Holzschnitte; 71/75, wc/van Gelder laid paper, 1918, p/s, L-16x20", Verlag, lot 180, C-NY 11/1/88 OE 55,000
Christus und die Ehebrecherin, ed of 75, wc, 1918, p/s, lg mrgs, lt cr/sl, 16x35", lot 570, SBY 11/3/88 3,850
Drei am Tisch, a/p, wc/wm Crown laid paper, 1914/1919, p/s, full mrgs, cr/sl, S-24x20", Neumann, lot 178, C-NY 11/1/88 10,450
Dunen und Mole, ed of 100, blk & bl wc/wm Perfecta laid paper, 1917, p/s, S-17x20", Verlag, lot 179, C-NY 11/1/88 9,900
Frau Unter Baumen, wc/gray laid paper, 1914, p/s, lt cr/stn, S-25x20", lot 177, C-NY 11/1/88 OE 12,100
Gehoft im Moor (Motiv aus Dangastermoor), litho/cream wove paper, 1907, p/s, lt sl, S-13x18", lot 173, C-NY 11/1/88 OE 5,280
Hauser I, litho/wove paper, 1910, p/s, lt stn/sl, S-17x20", lot 174, C-NY 11/1/88 OE 13,200
Kopf Eines Mannes, ed of 100, wc, 1922/1923, p/s, lt sl, L-11x8", Deutsche Graphiker, lot 544, C-NY 11/1/88 1,045
Kopf Eines Mannes, ed of 100, wc/Imperial Japan, 1922, p/s, full mrgs, lt cr/stn, 11x8", lot 570A, SBY 11/3/88 2,475
Madchen vor dem Spiegel, a/p, wc/wm Rampant Lion, 1914/1919, p/s, full mrgs, S-24x20", Neumann, lot 176, C-NY 11/1/88 OE 16,500
Russische Madonna, drypt, 1921, p/s, inscr 21 15 St Gedr F Voight, lt cr/stn, 15x13", lot 569, SBY 11/3/88 UE 3,850
Segler auf der Elbe II, wc/wove paper, 1911, p/s, wide mrgs, lt cr/stn/tr/fld, S-26x32", lot 175, C-NY 11/1/88 19,800

SCHNABEL, Julian (American, 1951-)

Dream, 5/30, aqua, 1983, p/s, S-54x72", Parasol, lot 1216, SBY 5/13/89 3,575

For Anna Magnani, AP1, etch/2 sheets lithographic clr maps, 1981, p/s, S-74x54", Pace, lot 1214, SBY 5/13/89 OE **11,000**
Set of 9: Tod, Cage Without Bars; AP7/10, red-brn aqua/etch/Kozo Shoin, sgn, full sheets, lot 806, C-NY 11/1/88 .... **4,950**
Untitled, Tod, Cage Without Bars; a/p, red-brn aqua/Kozo Shoin, 1983, lt cr, S-29x24", Parasol, lot 805, C-NY 11/1/88 .... **715**
Untitled (contemporary), 26/75, brn/ochre aqua on 2 sheets, 1986-87, p/s, S-85x60", Parasol, lot 948, SBY 11/5/88 OE **4,125**

SCHOLDER, Fritz (American, 1937-)
New York Graphic Society Poster, litho, 1975, p/s, 23x17", lot 437, FAP 4/15/88 UE **77**

SCHONGAUER, Martin (German, 1445-1491)
Nativity, engr, ca 1480-90, lt cr/rub, rpr tr in img, lt fox, S-6x6", lot 700, SBY 2/25/88 .... **24,200**

SCHREIBER, Georges (American, 1904-1977)
Equilibrium, litho, p/s, 16x11", Assn Am Artists, lot 242, WG 10/19/88 .... **130**
In Tennessee, litho, p/s, 12x16", Assn Am Artists, lot 243, WG 10/19/88 .... **175**

SCHWITTERS, Kurt (German, 1887-1948)
Book: Die Kathedrale-Merz 8; 8 litho, 1920, orig covers/labels, Verlag, lot 821, SBY 5/11/89 OE **8,250**

SCULLY Sean (British, 1946-)
Block, 25/30, clr wc/Okawara handmade, 1986, p/s, full mrgs, S-37x43", s/wrp, Diane Villani, lot 807, C-NY 11/1/88 .... **1,430**
Pair: Block; Standing II; 11/30 & 14/35, clr wc, 1986, p/s, full mrgs, 30x35"/40x30", Villani, lot 951, SBY 11/5/88 .... **3,300**
Standing I, 26/35, clr wc/Korean Kozo, 1986, p/s, full mrgs, S-52x36", s/wrp, Diane Villani, lot 808, C-NY 11/1/88 OE **1,980**
This: Stand Within Feet; 8/18, wc/etch/linecut/collage/wht TGL & Oriental, 1985, p/s, 66x49", lot 952, SBY 11/5/88 .... **2,750**

SEARLE, Ronald (British, 1920-)
Le Nettoyage, 83/95, litho/wove paper, 1968, p/s, titled, lt sl/stn, L-14x23", lot 77, RWS 9/8/89 .... **275**
Pair: Great Vegetable City; Visit of the Magic Eyeball; 51/99, clr litho/wove paper, 1970, p/s, S-26x20", SWN 12/1/88 UE **220**

SEBRON, Hyppolite Victor Valentin; after (French, 1801-1879)
New York Winter Scene in Broadway, by P Girardet, etch/aqua, 1857, fox/wstn/scuff, P-28x39", C-NY 1/22/88 OE **2,200**

SEITZ, Emile (19th C)
Washington & His Generals, hc engr, 19th C, 30x40", lot 300, NA 2/6/88 .... **380**

SELBY, Prideaux John (European, 19th C)
Collard Pratincole (shore bird), Pl 63, hc engr, sgn, full mrgs, 21x26", lot 91, GAI 25/11/88 .... **45**

SERRA, Richard (American, 1939-)
Patience, 19/20, paint stick/slksc/coated paper, 1985, Gemini bstp, S-62x53", lot 1217, SBY 5/13/89 OE **9,900**
St Louis, paint stick/German Etching, 1982, p/s, full mrgs, stn, 43x31", lot 811, C-NY 11/1/88 OE **2,420**

SEVENSEEN, Hanna (19th C)
Life Oak, Carmel, California; linocut, 1933, p/s, 9x12", lot 926, LH 5/15/88 UE **60**

SEVERINI, Gino (Italian, 1883-1966)
Harlequins, 42/125, clr litho, p/s, 22x15", lot 437, WG 10/19/88 OE **950**
Le Concert, 136/200, clr litho/wove paper, 1955, p/s, L'Oeuvre Gravee bstp, lt stn, L-14x19", lot 837, C-NY 5/10/89 OE **1,870**
Les Arlequins, 111/220, clr litho/Pur Fil, 1954, Guilde de la Gravure bstp, lt stn, L-15x11", lot 836, C-NY 5/10/89 OE **2,420**
Suite: Carlo Ludovico Ragghianti & Giovanni Carandente; 53/85, 7 litho w/text, 1966, orig portfolio, C-NY 5/11/88 .... **4,620**
Suite: Fleurs et Masques; 34/125, 16 clr & gilt pochoir/cream wove, 1930, S-18x13", Etchells & MacDonald, SBY 5/12/88 OE **23,100**
Two Harlequin Musicians, ed of 220, clr litho, ca 1930s, p/s, lt stn, L-15x11", lot 344, C-NY 5/11/88 OE **770**
Two Harlequin Musicians, 90/220, clr litho/wove paper, ca 1930s, p/s, lt sl, L-15x11", lot 546, C-NY 11/1/88 OE **1,760**

SHAHN, Ben (American, 1898-1969)
All That Is Beautiful, ed of unknown size, clr scrpt/wove paper, 1965, lt stn/skinned, S-26x39", lot 261, C-NY 1/19/89 .... **3,080**
Flowering Brushes, ed of 200, clr litho, 1968, blk crayon/red chop mk, stn/cr, S-40x27", Kennedy Graphics, SBY 5/12/88 .... **3,575**
Large Owl, ed of 250, litho, 1968, p/s, 26x20", Mourlot, lot 233, SWN 6/15/89 OE **550**
Pair: Cat's Cradle; Skowhegan; blk/bl script & wood engr, 1959 & 1965, sgn/artist's chop mk, lt cr, unfr, C-NY 1/22/88 .... **990**
Passion of Sacco & Vanzetti, ed of unknown size, blk/brn slksc, 1958, full mrgs, lt sl/cr, 26x17", lot 49, SBY 11/3/88 .... **2,474**
Phoenix, ed of unknown size, hc slksc, ca 1968, sgn in blk crayon, lt cr, S-37x28", lot 50, SBY 11/3/88 OE **8,800**
Prenatal Cinic, ed of unrecorded size, scpt/thick wove paper, ink sgn, full mrgs, lt stn, unfr, L-14x22", C-NY 1/22/88 .... **1,870**
Rev Martin Luther King, 9 Drawings Portfolio; offset litho/Japan, 1965, sgn by King, S-22x17", lot 162, C-E 5/13/88 .... **660**
Self-Portrait, litho, 14x11", lot 976, FAP 12/8/88 .... **250**
Silent Music (Musical Chairs), ed of 97, srgph, 1950, sgn/dtd, lt fox/tstn, S-24x38", lot 60, RWS 9/29/88 OE **1,000**
Suite: Contemplative Man; Head of Man; Man & Woman; litho, pl/s, 22x18", FAP 6/16/89 UE **150**
Supermarket, ed of 80, blk/hc scpt, 1957, sgn w/brush, lt fox, S-26x40", SBY 5/12/88 OE **4,950**

SHALLUS, Francis (18th/19th C)
Plan of the City & Environs of Baltimore...; 2nd/final state, engr, 1801, stn/cr, laid down, L-19x29", C-NY 1/22/88 OE **1,430**

SHARP, William (American, fl 1840-1890)
Group of 4: Opening Bud; Opening Flower; Intermediate State of Bloom; Complete Bloom; chromo, 1854, C-NY 1/22/88 OE **13,200**

SHAW, Glenn M. (American, 1891-)
Pair: Houses in Taolmiha; Tapping the Blast Furnace; 5/25, wc, p/s, 9x12", lot 226, WG 10/19/88 .... **45**

SHAW, J.; after (19th C)
Jones Falls Near Baltimore, by John Hill, 1st state of 2, hc aqua, 1820, lstn/fox mrgs, L-10x13", C-NY 1/22/88 .... **308**

SHEELER, Charles (American, 1883-1965)
Delmonico Building, litho, 1926, p/s, dtd 1927, full mrgs, lt disclr/cr mrgs, unfr, L-10x7", SBY 5/12/88 .... **18,700**
Delmonico Building, litho, 1926, p/s, titled, lt stn, 10x7", lot 63, SBY 2/25/88 .... **17,600**
Industrial Series #1, litho, 1928, p/s, titled/dtd in mrgs, lt stn, 8x11", lot 64, SBY 2/25/88 .... **20,900**
Yachts, 11/35, litho/BFK Rives, 1924, p/s, lt rpr tr, stn, L-8x10", lot 263, C-NY 1/19/89 OE **28,600**

SHIELDS, Alan (American, 1944-)
Castle Window: Plastic Bucket; 5/10, linocut/etch/aqua/collage, 1981, p/s, Tyler Graphics bstp, S-35x28", SBY 5/14/88 .... **880**
Josh's Route, Raggedy Circumnavigation Series; 6/20, relief/slksc/collage, 1985, p/s, 47" dia, lot 783, SBY 2/23/89 OE **1,430**

SHUNNEY, A. (American, 20th C)
Industrial Waterway, 11/38, wc/wove paper, 1938, p/s, lt fox/cr, tp on verso, L-14x10", lot 53, RWS 9/8/89 UE **175**

SIGNAC, Paul (French, 1863-1935)
Au Temps d'Harmonie, a/p, clr litho/thick crisp simili Japan, 1895-96, lt cr/sl, S-17x23", lot 182, C-NY 11/1/88 OE **9,900**
Bridge of St Peres to Paris, etch, pl/s, unfr, 5x8", lot 1392, S/A 3/12/88..... **500**
La Seine en Crue, en 1910; ed of 100, 2nd state, litho/laid paper, 1923, p/s, full mrgs, L-6x9", lot 838, C-NY 5/10/89..... **1,210**
Le Pont des Arts avec Remorquers, etch/aqua/simili Japan, pl/s, 5x7", lot 2907, B/B 4/19/88 ..... **248**
Le Soir, a/p, litho/Chine volant, 1898, S-8x10", lot 445, SBY 2/25/88 ..... **770**
Les Bateaux a Flessingue, 9/20, 3rd state, clr litho/thin wove paper, 1895, S-16x21", Pellet, lot 181, C-NY 11/1/88 OE..... **16,500**
Saint-Tropez II, ed of 100, clr litho, 1894, p/s, Estampe Originale bstp, full mrgs, lt fox/stn, 11x15", SBY 11/3/88 OE **23,100**
Saint-Tropez: Le Port; 88/100, litho/fine wove paper, 1897-98, full mrgs, S-21x16", Vollard, lot 183, C-NY 11/1/88 OE **24,200**
SIMBARI, Nicholas (Italian, 1927-)
Beach Scene, 259/300, srgph, p/s, 27x33", lot 400, WG 10/19/88 UE **650**
SIMON, Tavik Frantisek (Czechoslovakian, 1877-1942)
Nocturne Tangiers, clr etch, sgn, 11x12", lot 90, WG 10/19/88 OE..... **150**
Pair: Au Marche; Devant Le Temple, Ceylon; etch, ca 1912 & ca 1913, p/s, 11x13", lot 169, SWN 12/1/88 UE..... **275**
SINDELAER, after
At the Spring, etch, bears signature/titled, 11x8", C-E 1/12/88 UE..... **66**
SIQUEIROS, David Alfaro (Mexican, 1896-1974)
Study for a Man, #EE, litho/cream wove paper, p/s, tp to mat, lt stn/cr, 12x9", lot 2977, B/B 2/16/88 UE **220**
SISLEY, Alfred (French, 1839-1899)
Bords de Riviere (Les Oies), ed of 100, litho/Chine applique, 1897, p/s, S-17x23", Vollard, lot 184, C-NY 11/1/88 OE..... **14,300**
SLOAN, John (American, 1871-1951)
Anshutz on Anatomy, etch, 1912, p/s, inscr Ernest Roth Imp, lg mrgs, lt sl, 8x9", lot 268, SBY 5/11/89..... **4,950**
Anshutz on Anatomy, etch, 1912, p/s, titled/inscr 100 Proofs, full mrgs, 8x9", Ernest Roth, lot 55, SBY 11/3/88 OE..... **5,610**
Anshutz on Anatomy, 8th/final state, etch, 1912, p/s, inscr 100 Proofs, lt sl/tstn mrgs, unfr, P-7x9", C-NY 1/22/88 OE..... **3,850**
Arch Conspirators, 3rd/final state, etch/wove paper, 1917, p/s, inscr 100 Proofs, full mrgs, unfr, P-4x6", C-NY 1/22/88 ..... **1,430**
Barber Shop, 3rd state, etch/aqua/cream wove paper, 1915, p/s, titled, lt stn, P-10x12", lot 268, C-NY 1/19/89 OE **12,100**
Bonfire, 2nd/final state, etch/laid paper, p/s, inscr 100 Proofs & JS Imp, full mrgs, lt stn, unfr, P-5x7", C-NY 1/22/88..... **1,650**
Book: Of Human Bondage; by Maugham, ed of 1500, 15 etch, 1938, Ltd Ed Club, lot 170, SWN 12/1/88..... **385**
Boys Sledding, a/p, etch/van Gelder, 1920, p/s, titled, full mrgs, lt stn/tr, P-5x7", lot 272, C-NY 1/19/89 ..... **990**
Boys Sledding, 3rd state, etch/van Gelder, 1920, p/s, lt stn/old tp, P-5x7", lot 465, C-NY 5/10/89 ..... **880**
Busses in Washington Square, 5th state, etch/van Gelder, 1925, p/s, dtd 1928, lt stn/cr, P-8x10", lot 466, C-NY 5/10/89 ..... **1,430**
Calf Love, ed of 100, etch/laid paper, p/s, titled, lg mrgs, 4x2", Ernest Roth, lot 2979, B/B 4/19/88 ..... **522**
Connoisseurs of Prints, ed of 105, etch/Arches, 1905, p/s, lt pl tone, lt mstn, unfr, P-5x7", SBY 5/12/88 OE..... **5,225**
Connoisseurs of Prints, etch, 1905, p/s, inscr Ernest Roth Imp, lt fox/stn, 5x7", lot 51, SBY 11/3/88 ..... **5,500**
Connoisseurs of Prints, etch/laid paper, 1905, p/s, titled/inscr 100 Proofs, lstn/mstn, mstn verso, P-5x7", C-NY 1/22/88..... **1,980**
Copyist at the Metropolitan Museum, etch, 1908, p/s, inscr 100 Proofs, full mrgs, 7x9", lot 267, SBY 5/11/89 OE **7,150**
Copyist at the Metropolitan Museum, etch, 1980, p/s, inscr 100 Proofs, full mrgs, 8x9", lot 53, SBY 11/3/88 OE..... **3,850**
Copyist at the Metropolitan Museum, 8th/final state, etch, 1908, inscr 100 Proofs, sl mrgs, unfr, P-8x9", C-NY 1/22/88 ..... **3,300**
Costume Ball Poster, brn linocut/wove paper, 1933, p/s, trm mrgs, lt cr/tr/sl/tstn, unfr, S-19x13", C-NY 1/22/88..... **880**
Easter Eve, Washington Square; etch/aqua, 1926, p/s, inscr 100 Proofs, lt stn/cr/sl, 10x8", lot 273, SBY 5/11/89 OE **4,675**
Expecting a Turkey From Uncle, etch, 1910, p/s, L-4x3", FAP 4/15/88 ..... **600**
Fashions of the Past, ed of 75, 6th state, aqua/etch/wove paper, 1926, p/s, full mrgs, unfr, P-8x10", C-NY 1/22/88 UE **825**
Fifth Avenue Critics, ed of 110, etch, 1905, p/s, full mrgs, lt stn/fox, laid down, 5x7", lot 55, SBY 2/23/89 OE..... **1,760**
Fourteenth Street, The Wigwam; a/p, 7th state, etch/van Gelder, 1928, p/s, full mrgs, P-10x7", lot 274, C-NY 1/19/89 OE **3,520**
Greetings, a/p, 2nd state, etch/laid paper, p/s, lt sl verso, P-4x2", lot 32, C-NY 6/17/89 OE **990**
Hell Hole, a/p, 2nd state, etch/aqua/wove paper, 1917, p/s, full mrgs, lt stn/cr/sl, P-8x10", lot 270, C-NY 1/19/89 OE **3,520**
Hell Hole, etch/aqua, 1917, p/s, inscr Peter Platt Imp, full mrgs, lt fox, 8x10", lot 5/11/89 OE..... **4,400**
Hell Hole, etch/aqua, 1917, p/s, inscr Peter Platt Imp 100 Proofs, full mrgs, lt fox, 8x10", lot 271, SBY 5/11/89 ..... **3,520**
Hell Hole, 2nd/final state, aqu/etch, 1917, p/s, inscr 100 Proofs & Peter Platt Imp, sl, unfr, P-8x10", C-NY 1/22/88 OE **3,080**
Knees & Aborigines, 2nd state, etch/heavy wove paper, 1927, intl, lt sl, P-7x6", lot 469, C-NY 5/10/89 OE **1,760**
Kraushaar's, etch, 1927, p/s, inscr 75 Ernest Roth Imp, lg mrgs, lt stn, 4x5", lot 57, SBY 2/23/89..... **880**
Kraushaar's, 8th state, etch/wove paper, 1926, p/s, titled/inscr 100 Proofs, full mrgs, unfr, P-4x5", C-NY 1/22/88..... **660**
Love on the Roof, a/p, 2nd state, etch/wove paper, 1914, intl, full mrgs, lt sl, P-6x4", lot 462, C-NY 5/10/89..... **1,650**
Love on the Roof, a/p, 2nd state, etch/wove paper, 1914, p/s, titled, lt sl/stn, P-6x4", lot 267, C-NY 1/19/89..... **2,640**
Love on the Roof, 1st state of 2, etch, 1914, p/s, inscr For John Quinn, full mrgs, unfr, P-6x4", C-NY 1/22/88 OE **2,420**
Man, Wife, & Child; a/p, 5th state, etch/Arms-of-Amsterdam, 1905, p/s, full mrgs, P-5x7", lot 265, C-NY 1/19/89 ..... **990**
McSorley's Back Room, a/p, 3rd state, etch/BFK Rives, 1916, p/s, full mrgs, lt sl, P-5x7", lot 269, C-NY 1/19/89 OE **2,640**
McSorley's Back Room, etch, 1916, p/s, inscr Ernest Roth Imp 100 Proofs, full mrgs, 5x7", lot 269, SBY 5/11/89 ..... **2,200**
Mosaic, aqua/etch, 1917, p/s, inscr 100 Proofs & Peter Platt Imp, full mrgs, lt sl/holes, unfr, P-8x10", C-NY 1/22/88 ..... **2,420**
Mother, p/p, ed of 100, etch, 1906, p/s, 9x7", Roth, lot 238, SWN 6/15/89 ..... **990**
Movey Troup, a/p, 4th state, etch/wove paper, 1920, p/s, full mrgs, lt sl verso, P-5x7", lot 464, C-NY 5/10/89 OE **2,640**
Night Windows, total ed of 110, etch, 1910, p/s, inscr Ernest Roth Imp, full mrgs, 5x7", lot 65, SBY 2/25/88 OE **5,500**
Nude Sketches, a/p, etch/wove paper, 1917, p/s, titled, full mrgs, lt stn/sl/cr, P-3x7", lot 271, C-NY 1/19/89 OE **660**
Pair: Boar Hunt; Return From Toil; etch, 1904 & 1915, full mrgs, P-5x6", lot 31, PHL 10/28/88 ..... **450**
Pair: Half Nude on Elbow; Nude by Bookcase; 6th/3rd state, etch/engr & etch, 1931, p/s, inscr 100 Proofs, C-NY 1/22/88 ..... **550**
Pair: Memory; Lafayette; etch, 1906 & 1928, p/s, 7x9"/5x7", lot 52, SBY 11/3/88 ..... **1,650**
Pair: Nude & Etching Press; Better Mouse Traps?; 2nd state, etch, 1931/1937, p/s, inscr 100 proofs, C-NY 1/22/88 UE **330**
Pair: Nude on Posing Stand; Nude & Arch; ed of 100, etch/engr/aqua, 1931 & 1933, p/s, lt cr/fox, lot 470, C-NY 5/10/89..... **1,210**
Pair: Nude on Posing Stand; Nude & Arch; ed of 100, 3rd state, etch, 1931 & 1933, matted together, lot 277, C-NY 1/19/89..... **1,210**
Pair: Nude Reading; Nude Resting on Elbow; 4th/2nd state, etch, 1928/1931, p/s, inscr 100 Proofs, unfr, C-NY 1/22/88..... **605**
Pair: Nude Reading; Nude with Furniture: 4th/3rd state, etch, 1928/1931, p/s, titled/inscr 100 Proofs, tp, C-NY 1/22/88 ..... **660**

Pair: Nude with Cigarette; Nude with Halo; 3rd state, etch/laid paper, 1931, p/s, inscr 100 Proofs, C-NY 1/22/88 ..... **660**
Pair: Portrait of CK Keller; Green Hour; etch, 1930, p/s, no size given, lot 43, C-NY 5/11/88 ..... **550**
Pair: Seeing New York; Green Hour; etch/laid paper, 1917/1930, p/s, inscr 100 Proofs, lt fox, C-NY 1/22/88 ..... **462**
Pair: Serenade: Dolly; 2nd/final state, etch on Japan/laid paper, 1912/1929, p/s, inscr 100 Proofs, C-NY 1/22/88 UE **275**
Picture Buyer, ed of 100, etch, 1911, p/s, full mrgs, lt stn, 5x7", lot 54, SBY 11/3/88 ..... **2,640**
Picture Buyer, 5th/final state, etch, 1911, p/s, titled/inscr 100 Proofs, lstn/mstn, mstn verso, P-5x7", C-NY 1/22/88 ..... **1,320**
Ping Pong Photographs, litho, 1908, p/s, inscr Proof For John Quinn, lt cr/sl/tr, sl verso, unfr, L-8x6", C-NY 1/22/88 ..... **990**
Reading in the Subway, ed of 85, 3rd state, etch/laid paper, 1926, p/s, inscr w/poem, unfr, P-5x4", C-NY 1/22/88 OE **825**
Robert Henri, Painter; 7th state of 8, etch/Rives, 1931, inscr 100 Proofs & 7th JS Imp, unfr, P-14x11", C-NY 1/22/88 ..... **4,180**
Romarye Marye in Christopher Street, 7th state, etch/laid paper, 1936, p/s, full mrgs, P-6x8", lot 278, C-NY 1/19/89 OE **1,870**
Roofs, Summer Night; ed of 110, 2nd state, etch/laid paper, 1906, p/s, lt stn, P-5x7", lot 266, C-NY 1/19/89 ..... **1,210**
Salesmanship, 6th (final state), etch/laid paper, 1930, p/s, inscr 100 Proofs, full mrgs, P-4x5", lot 44, C-NY 5/11/88 ..... **660**
Shine, Washington Square; a/p, 5th state, etch/laid paper, 1923, p/s, titled, full mrgs, 5x7", lot 273, C-NY 1/19/89 OE **1,650**
Shine, Washington Square; 5th state, etch, 1923, p/s, inscr Working Proof, lt cr/stn, unfr, P-5x7", C-NY 1/22/88 UE **1,320**
Shine, Washington Square; 5th state, etch, 1923, p/s, inscr 100 Proofs & Ernest Roth Imp, unfr, P-5x7", C-NY 1/22/88 UE **1,430**
Show Case, 2nd state, etch/wove paper, 1905, intl, full mrgs, lt sl mrgs/verso, P-5x7", lot 461, C-NY 5/10/89 ..... **770**
Show Case, 3rd state, etch/Japan, 1905, p/s, titled/inscr 100 Proofs, full mrgs, cr/stn/sl, unfr, P-5x7", C-NY 1/22/88 ..... **660**
Sixth Avenue, Greenwich Village; etch, 1923, p/s, inscr 100 Proofs Ernest Roth Imp, lt stn, unfr, P-5x7", SBY 5/12/88 OE **2,200**
Sixth Avenue, Greenwich Village; etch/Japan, 1923, p/s, titled/inscr 100 Proofs, full mrgs, 5x7", lot 56, SBY 11/3/88 ..... **1,650**
Snow Storm in the Village, 3rd state, etch, 1925, p/s, inscr JS Imp, full mrgs, lt cr/sl, unfr, P-7x5", C-NY 1/22/88 ..... **4,950**
Subway Stairs, a/p, 3rd state, etch/Japan, 1926, p/s, titled, lt stn/cr, P-7x5", lot 467, C-NY 5/10/89 ..... **2,640**
Their Appointed Rounds, ed of 50, mezzo/etch, 1938, p/s, titled/inscr 50 Proofs, 6x7", lot 825, LH 12/4/88 ..... **425**
Thirst for Art, total ed of 210, 4th state, etch, 1939, p/s, full mrgs, lt stn/cr mrg, P-4x6", lot 45, C-NY 5/11/88 ..... **935**
Turning Out the Light, ed of 100, etch, 1905, p/s, titled/inscr 100 Proofs, full mrgs, 5x7", lot 264, SBY 5/11/89 ..... **4,125**
Up the Line, Miss?; a/p, 5th state, etch/laid paper, 1930, p/s, titled, lt fox, P-6x7", lot 275, C-NY 1/19/89 OE **2,200**
Up the Line, Miss?; etch/fibrous laid paper, 1931, inscr Roth Imp 100 Proofs, lt cr/sl, 6x7", lot 275, SBY 5/11/89 ..... **1,760**
Wake on the Ferry, ed of 350, etch, 1919, p/s, Will Shuster bstp, full mrgs, lt stn/sl, 5x7", lot 276, SBY 5/11/89 ..... **770**
Wake on the Ferry, total ed of 350, 4th state, etch, 1949, p/s, inscr 200 Proofs, full mrgs, P-5x7", C-NY 5/11/88 ..... **770**
Woman's Page, 2nd/final state, etch, 1905, p/s, inscr 100 Proofs & Ernest Roth Imp, lt ls, unfr, P-5x7", C-NY 1/22/88 UE **1,540**
14th Street, Wigwam; etch, 1928, p/s, inscr Peter Platt Imp 100 Proofs, full mrgs, stn/sl, 10x7", lot 274, SBY 5/11/89 ..... **3,025**
25th Anniversary, 2nd state, etch, 1926, p/s, inscr 25th Anniversary Dolly & JS 1926, P-4x5", lot 468, C-NY 5/10/89 ..... **550**
5th Avenue 1909, 6th state, etch/laid paper, 1941, p/s, lt cr/tp, P-8x6", lot 471, C-NY 5/10/89 OE **1,760**

SLOWMAN, George T. (Continental, 19th/20th C)
Canal View, engr, 11x7", lot 30, FAP 2/24/89 UE **15**

SMITH, C.N.; after (19th C)
Cambridceshire Stakes, 1853: The Finish; clr engr, P-14x21", C-E 5/3/88 UE **176**
Cambridceshire Stakes, 1853: They Are Off; clr engr, P-14x21", C-E 5/3/88 UE **220**

SMITH, Jessie Wilcox (American, 1863-1935)
Have You a Red Cross Service Flag?; clr litho/poster paper, 1918, laid down, 28x22", lot 161, FAP 2/24/89 ..... **50**

SMITH, Lawrence Beal (American, 1909-)
At the Institute, litho, 1941, p/s, 1941, 13x13", lot 171, SWN 12/1/88 ..... **330**
Frolic, litho, lt stn, 9x13", Assn Am Artists, lot 235, WG 10/19/88 ..... **80**
Frolic, litho, p/s, lt stn, 9x12", Assn Am Artists, lot 196, WG 10/19/88 ..... **60**

SMITH, William (American, 18th/19th C)
Battle on Lake Erie Fought Sept 10th, 1813, Second View; hc engr, 19th C, full mrgs, P-20x29", lot 98, C-NY 1/19/89 ..... **550**

SNOW, Michael (1919-)
Foothills Road, 5/15, clr litho, p/s, titled, 15x20", lot 785, WAD 6/12/89 ..... **140**

SONEBERG, Jack (American, 20th C)
Literal Dimensions, 66/100, slksc/collage, p/s, unfr, no size given, lot 1507, LH 12/4/88 UE **50**

SORMAN, Steven (American, 1948-)
Group of 3: Games the French Play; 12/28, mixed media prints, 1980, p/s, no size given, Vermilion, lot 1218, SBY 5/13/89 ..... **3,025**

SOTTLOB, F. (French, 19th/20th C)
Second Exposition des Peintres Lithographes, 48x31", Lemercier, lot 275, FAP 2/24/89 OE **1,050**

SOYER, Isaac (American, 1907-)
Dancers, 192/250, brn litho, 18x19", lot 85, FAP 2/24/89 ..... **55**
Seated Woman in Blue, 29/150, clr litho/wove paper, p/s, full mrgs, tp mat, matted, unfr, L-19x13", RWS 3/16/89 ..... **200**

SOYER, Moses (American, 1899-1974)
Ballerina, litho, pl/s, 10x8", lot 387, WG 10/19/88 ..... **60**

SOYER, Raphael (American, 1899-1987)
Bronx Street, ed of 50, litho, 1928, p/s, lt tr/stn/sl, 7x9", lot 67, SBY 2/25/88 ..... **1,430**
Casting Office, litho, p/s, titled, full mrgs, lt stn, L-10x13", lot 31, PHL 6/16/88 OE **475**
Four Female Nudes, a/p, litho, p/s, 22x26", lot 442, FAP 4/15/88 ..... **165**
Friends, 160/250, etch, p/s, 12x15", lot 1500, LH 12/4/88 ..... **225**
Group of 3: Protected; Protected; Young Model; ed of 250, litho/GCM & Rives, full mrgs, lt stn, lot 47, C-NY 5/11/88 OE **1,100**
Interior with Figure, aside from ed of 85, etch/wove paper, 1963, full mrgs, lt stn, P-10x8", lot 28, C-NY 6/17/89 OE **528**
Model, ed of 250, litho, 1944, p/s, titled, lt stn, 12x8", Assn Am Artists, lot 240, SWN 6/15/89 OE **660**
Model (figure), litho, 1944, p/s, titled, 10x12", lot 292, WG 10/19/88 ..... **625**
Mother Nursing Her Child, clr litho, p/s, lg mrgs, 18x13", lot 172, SWN 12/1/88 ..... **385**
Pair: Girl with Puppies; Nude Model Standing; ed of 285, etch, 1979, p/s, 10x12"/14x10", Sorini, lot 242, SWN 6/15/89 ..... **600**
Pair: Protected; Model; litho/wove paper, 1938, p/s, titled, lt fox, no size given, lot 279, C-NY 1/19/89 OE **990**
Pensive Woman, 12/35, etch/wove paper, ca 1975, p/s, a/bstp, full mrgs, lt sl mrgs, P-9x7", lot 25, C-NY 6/17/89 ..... **418**

Portrait of a Girl, 63/75, litho/cream wove paper, p/s, lt stn/cr, 16x10", lot 2981, B/B 4/19/88 OE ... 550
Protected, litho, sgn/titled in ink, tp to mat, lt stn, L-14x6", lot 32, PHL 10/28/88 ... 325
Self-Portrait, 29/40, etch, p/s, 8x10", lot 438, FAP 4/15/88... 200
Self-Portrait, 84/85, etch/BFK Rives, 1963, full mrgs, 4x2", lot 2980, B/B 4/19/88 OE ... 660
Veterans, a/p, clr srgph, ca 1967-70, p/s, 15x18", lot 241, 15x18", lot 241, SWN 6/15/89... 550
Village Leader with Arms Folded, 136/150, clr litho, p/s, 23x17", lot 176, SWN 12/1/88... 600
Waiting (seated mother/child), ed of 250, drypt, 1942, p/s, titled, lt tstn, P-7x9", Assn Am Artists, RWS 9/29/88 OE... 500
Young Woman Drying Herself, 82/300, clr litho/wove paper, ca 1940, p/s, lt cr, S-19x12", lot 472, C-NY 5/10/89 OE ... 880

SOYLE, John (American, 1939-)

Suite: Cowboys; 4/75, 8 clr litho, 1974, p/s, titled, 48x36", lot 786, LH 10/16/88... 425
Suite: Cowboys; 57/75, 8 clr litho, 1974, p/s, titled, 48x36", w/3 text sheets, lot 787, LH 10/16/88... 425
Suite: Sharpshooters; 3/76, 11 clr litho, 1975, p/s, titled, 41x30", lot 788, LH 10/16/88 ... 550

SPRUANCE, Benton Murdoch (American, 1904-1967)

Adirondacks, The Sentinels; ed of 30, litho/wove paper, 1942, p/s, full mrgs, lt fox, unfr, L-10x14", RWS 9/8/89... 375

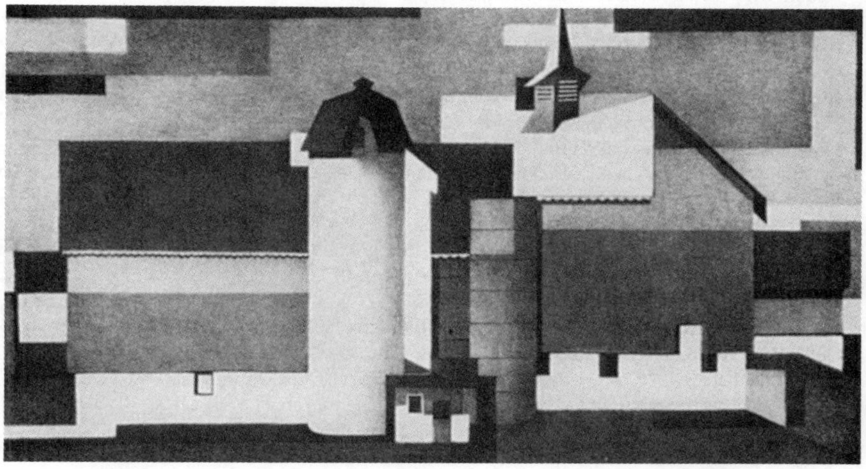

American Pattern, Barn; ed of 45, blk/tan litho, 1940, p/s, full mrgs, lt fox/tp, L-8x14", lot 55, RWS 9/8/89 OE; $7,500

Amusement Park, Vienna; 5/22, blk litho/cream Chine colle, 1928, p/s, full mrgs, L-10x10", lot 27, RWS 9/8/89 ... 600
Anabasis, ed of 30, clr litho, 1957, p/s, 18x24", lot 964, FAP 12/8/88... 180
Fencers, litho, 13x8", Am Artists Group, lot 230, WG 10/19/88 ... 110
Football Player, ed of 25, litho, 1933, p/s, titled, 15x8", lot 245, SWN 6/15/89 ... 1,100
Head, clr wc, 1951, p/s, titled, 14x12", lot 249, SWN 6/15/89 ... 440
Introduction to Love, ed of 35, litho/handmade Barcelona, 1935, p/s, 10x14", lot 247, SWN 6/15/89 OE... 1,650
Lamentation, ed of 35, litho, ca 1942, p/s, 12x18", lot 975, FAP 12/8/88... 400
Minotaur with Bronze Horns, ed of 30, clr litho, 1963, 23x15", lot 127, FAP 2/24/89 ... 210
Moby Dick 3: The Whiteness of the Whale-The Whale; a/p, ed of about 10, litho, 1966, p/s, 20x29", lot 33, RWS 9/8/89 OE ... 425
Set Pieces, ed of 30, litho, 1949, p/s, titled/dtd, full mrgs, 13x19", lot 248, SWN 6/15/89 ... 275
Solome & John, clr litho, p/s, 18x14", lot 959, FAP 12/8/88 ... 150
Street Scene in Germantown, 21/28, litho, p/s, titled, 12x11", lot 458, FAP 4/15/88 ... 330
Tarot No 1, ed of 30, litho, 1951, p/s, titled/dtd, lt cr, 15x20", lot 246, SWN 6/15/89 ... 275

STANCZAK, Julian (American/Polish, 1928-)

Abstract Design, Martha Jackson Gallery; litho, p/s, 30x25", lot 103, FAP 2/24/89 UE ... 35

STEINBERG, Saul (American, 1914-)

Main Street, 18/40, clr litho/Arches, 1972-73, p/s, ULAE bstp, full mrgs, S-23x30", lot 812, C-NY 11/1/88 OE... 2,640
Taxi, 77/150, clr litho/embossing/poster paper, 1977, p/s, full mrgs, 31x24", Maeght, lot 251, SWN 6/15/89... 935
Union Square, 45/75, clr litho, 1973, p/s, full mrgs, 26x19", lot 250, SWN 6/15/89... 1,100

STEINLEN, Theophile Alexandre (Swiss, 1859-1923)

Chat Noir, clr litho, lt fox/stn, linen backed, 24x16", Charles Verneau, lot 282, FAP 2/24/89 OE... 2,000
Deux Femmes, 1st state, aqua/etch, ca 1902, p/s, inscr Tire a 4ep, full mrgs, lt stn, P-16x11", lot 79, PHL 6/16/88 ... 1,300
Femme Couchee, sftgr aqua/cream paper, p/s, lg mrgs, lt cr/fox, old glue on verso, 12x12", lot 2910, B/B 4/19/88 OE ... 825
L'Ete-Chat sur une Balustrade, ed of 250, clr litho, 1909, lt scr, lt sl/tr mrgs, S-20x25", Sagot/Englemann, SBY 5/12/88... 4,950
L'Ete-Chat sur une Balustrade; ed of 250, clr litho, 1909, lt fox/cr, S-20x25", Sagot/Engelmann, lot 448, SBY 2/25/88 OE... 7,700
L'Ete-Chat sur une Balustrade; ed of 250, clr litho/thin wove paper, 1909, lt rpr tr, S-19x24", lot 840, C-NY 5/10/89 ... 3,300
L'Hiver-Chat sur un Coussin; ed of 250, clr litho, 1909, lt stn, linen backed, S-20x24", Sagot/Englemann, SBY 2/25/88 OE... 6,600
L'Hiver-Chat sur un Coussin; ed of 250, clr litho, 1909, p/s, lt cr, S-20x24", Sagot/Englemann, lot 572, SBY 11/3/88... 4,400
L'Hiver-Chat sur un Coussin; ed of 250, clr litho/wove paper, 1909, p/s, Sagot bstp, S-20x24", lot 841, C-NY 5/10/89... 4,180
Le Reve, clr litho, pl/s, 31x24", lot 441, C-E 9/20/89 UE ... 150
Le Reve, clr litho, pl/s, 31x24", s/wrp, lot 451, C-E 9/16/88 ... 462
Nu en Hauteur, 20/14, sftgr etch/BFK Rives, 1914, p/s, full mrgs, lt fox/cr, P-17x10", lot 102, PHL 10/28/88 ... 550
Ouvriers Sortant de l'Usine, litho/cream wove paper, p/s, Paris bstp, lt trm mrgs, lt cr, 9x12", lot 2909, B/B 4/19/88... 248
Pair: Aubade pour Elle; Standing Nude Model with Stockings; litho & etch/sftgr, 1901 & ca 1910, 10x8"/16x5", SWN 6/15/89... 220
Pair: Nurses & Children; Soldier, Mother & Child; litho/smooth wove paper, 1925, no size given, lot 547, C-NY 11/1/88 OE ... 462

STEIR, Pat (American, 1940-)

Set of 7: Burial Mound Series; 26/35, etch/drypt/aqua/rlt/HMP, 1976, P-10x10", Landfall, lot 587, C-NY 5/11/88 OE ... 2,750

STELLA, Frank (American, 1935-)

And the Holy One, Blessed Be He, Came & Smote the Angel of Death; Pl 10, ed of 60, 1982-84, 51x41", SBY 5/13/89 OE	**39,600**
Bermuda Petrel, 1/10, clr scrpt/Tycore panel, 1979, sgn, 63x82", Tyler Graphics, lot 1225, SBY 5/13/89	**28,600**
Black Stack, 29/56, litho, 1970, p/s, Gemini bstp, lt sl/stn, S-41x29", lot 787, SBY 2/23/89 OE	**2,475**
Bogoria VI, ed of 8, hc/dyed/collaged handmade paper multiple, 1975, p/s, TGL bstp, S-22x28", lot 958, SBY 11/5/88	**16,500**
Bonne Bay, 18/58, clr litho/scrpt/Special Arjomari, 1971, p/s, Gemini bstp, full mrgs, S-38x70", lot 820, C-NY 11/1/88	**19,800**
Butcher Came & Slew the Ox, Pl 8, 50/60, litho/linocut/slksc, 1982-84, p/s, S-57x53", Waddington, lot 1241, SBY 5/13/89	**25,300**
Butcher Came & Slew the Ox, Pl 8, 51/60, litho/linocut/slksc/collage, 1982-84, p/s, 57x53", Waddington, SBY 5/14/88 OE	**26,400**
Butcher Came & Slew the Ox, Pl 8, 57/60, litho/linocut/slksc, 1982-84, p/s, S-57x53", Waddington, lot 981, SBY 11/5/88	**20,900**
Casa Cornu, 11/75, gray litho/Special Arjomari, 1970, p/s, Gemini bstp, full mrgs, S-16x22", lot 815, C-NY 11/1/88 OE	**990**
Circuits: Estoril Five II; PPI, engr/relief-print etch/handmade dyed paper, 1982, p/s, 66x52", SBY 5/14/88 OE	**42,900**
Circuits: Imola Three IV; 19/30, relief-print etch/slksc/handmade TGL, 1984, S-66x52", Tyler Graphics, SBY 5/14/88 OE	**26,400**
Circuits: Imola Three IV; 2/30, etch/slksc/wht TGL handmade, 1984, p/s, TGL bstp, S-66x53", lot 1243, SBY 5/13/89 OE	**35,200**
Del Mar, 24/75, clr scrpt/Gemini rag board, 1972, Gemini bstp, full mrgs, lt stn/fox, 20x80", lot 821, C-NY 11/1/88 OE	**7,700**
Double Gray Scramble, APXXIV, clr scrpt, 1973, p/s, 23x43", lot 195, LH 10/16/88	**13,000**
Eskimo Curlew; 7/50, clr offset litho/slksc, 1977, p/s, Tyler Graphics bstp, L-27x34", SBY 5/14/88	**8,250**
Inaccessible Island Rail; 29/50, litho/slksc, 1977, p/s, TGL bstp, 32x43", lot 1224, SBY 5/13/89 OE	**20,900**
Group of 4: Eccentric Polygons: Conway; Wolfeboro; Ossipee; Effingham; litho, 1974, p/s, Gemini, lot 957, SBY 11/5/88 OE	**5,500**
Hungry Cat Ate Up the Goat, Pl 2, 24/60, litho/linocut/slksc/collage, 1982-84, 46x54", Waddington, lot 1238, SBY 5/13/89	**15,400**
Ifafa II, 67/100, litho/varnish/wove paper, 1965, p/s, Gemini bstp, lt cr/rpl/tp, L-11x20", lot 88, RWS 9/8/89 OE	**1,400**
Illustrations After El Lissitzky's Had Gadya: Back Cover: B; AP6, litho/linocut/slksc, 1982-84, p/s, 60x53", SBY 5/14/88	**16,500**
Illustrations After El Lissitzky's Had Gadya: Front Cover: A; APVI, litho/linocut/slksc, 1982-84, 42x34", SBY 11/5/88	**13,200**
Inaccessible Island Rail, APXII, clr litho/scrpt/Arches, 1977, p/s, TGL bstp, S-34x46", lot 593, C-NY 5/11/88	**12,100**
Inaccessible Island Rail, 39/50, offset litho/slksc, 1977, p/s, TGL bstp, full mrgs, lt stn, S-34x46", SBY 11/5/88	**13,200**
Jasper's Dilemma, 40/100, offset litho/J Green, 1973, p/s, full mrgs, S-16x22", Petersburg, lot 822, C-NY 11/1/88 OE	**1,650**
Multicolored Squares, 41/100, clr litho/wht wove paper, 1972, p/s, dtd, full mrgs, 16x21", lot 3071, B/B 4/19/88	**1,045**
Mysterious Bird of Ulieta, 30/50, offset litho/slksc, 1977, p/s, Tyler Graphics bstp, 32x42", SBY 5/14/88	**5,500**
Noguchi's Okinawa Woodpecker, 22/50, offset litho/slksc, 1977, p/s, TGL bstp, full mrgs, S-34x46", lot 960, SBY 11/5/88	**6,050**
Olyka III, ed of 26, paper multiple, 1975, p/s, TGL bstp, S-24x21", lot 1222, SBY 5/13/89 OE	**16,500**
Olyka III, ed of 26, 1975, p/s, Tyler Graphics bstp, tstn/lt sl, S-26x21", lot 825, C-NY 11/1/88	**7,150**
One Small Goat Papa Bought for Two Zuzim, Pl 1, APVI, litho/linocut/slksc, 1982-84, S-52x51", lot 1237, SBY 5/13/89	**18,700**
One Small Goat Papa Bought for Two Zuzim, Pl 1, 24/60, 52x51", SBY 11/5/88	**12,650**
One Small Goat Papa Bought for Two Zuzim; Pl 1, 16/60, litho/scrpt/linocut/collage, 1982, 52x51", C-NY 11/1/88	**16,500**
Pair: Eccentric Polygons: Wolfeboro; Ossippe; 47/100, clr litho/slksc, 1974, p/s, Gemini bstp, S-17x22", SBY 5/14/88 OE	**1,870**
Pair: Sabine Pass; Palmito Ranch; 36/100 & 54/100, litho/Arches, p/s, Gemini bstp, full sheet, lot 588, C-NY 5/11/88 OE	**1,650**
Pair: Star of Persia I; Star of Persia II; 26/92, clr litho/English Vellum, 1967, Gemini bstp, S-26x32", SBY 11/5/88 OE	**11,550**
Pair: Star of Persia I; Star of Persia II; 41/92, clr litho, 1967, p/s, Gemini bstp, 26x32", lot 786, SBY 2/23/89 OE	**12,650**
Pastel Stack, 42/100, clr slksc/English Vellum graph paper, 1970, p/s, Gemini bstp, S-41x28", lot 788, SBY 2/23/89 OE	**4,675**
Pergusa III, PPII, relief etch/wc/dyed TGL handmade, 1982, p/s, dtd 83, TGL bstp, S-67x52", lot 970, SBY 11/5/88	**77,000**
Polar Co-Ordinates for Ronnie Peterson II, 32/100, clr litho, slksc/letterpress, 1980, p/s, 39x38", SBY 2/23/89 OE	**16,500**
Polar Co-Ordinates for Ronnie Peterson III, AP9/20, offset litho/slksc/letterpress, 1980, p/s, S-38x39", SBY 5/14/88 OE	**11,550**
Polar Co-Ordinates for Ronnie Peterson IV, AP17/20, offset litho/slksc/letterpress, 1980, p/s, S-38x39", SBY 5/14/88	**6,600**
Polar Co-Ordinates for Ronnie Peterson IV, AP9/20, offset litho/slksc/letterpress, 1980, 38x39", Petersburg, SBY 11/5/88	**10,450**
Polar Co-Ordinates for Ronnie Peterson IV, 96/100, offset litho/slksc/letterpress, 1980, 38x39", SBY 5/13/89	**9,900**
Polar Co-Ordinates for Ronnie Peterson IV, 99/100, litho/slksc/letterpress, 1980, p/s, 38x39", lot 790, SBY 2/23/89	**11,550**
Polar Co-Ordinates for Ronnie Peterson V, AP9/20, offset litho/slksc/letterpress, 1980, p/s, S-38x39", SBY 5/14/88 OE	**11,000**
Polar Co-Ordinates for Ronnie Peterson VI, AP9/20, offset litho/slksc/letterpress, 1980, p/s, S-38x39", SBY 5/14/88	**9,900**
Polar Co-Ordinates for Ronnie Peterson VI, 81/100, litho/slksc/letterpress, 1980, 39x38", lot 1227, SBY 5/13/89 OE	**16,500**
Polar Co-Ordinates for Ronnie Peterson VIII, AP9/20, offset litho/slksc/1980, p/s, S-38x39", Petersburg, SBY 5/14/88 OE	**10,450**
Port aux Basques; AP VI, clr litho/slksc, 1971, p/s, Gemini bstp, lt cr, L-32x64", SBY 5/14/88 OE	**22,000**
Port aux Basques, 6/58, clr litho/scrpt/Special Arjomari, 1971, Gemini bstp, full mrgs, S-38x70", lot 819, C-NY 11/1/88	**19,800**
Puerto Rican Blue Pigeon, a/p, offset litho/scrpt/Arches, 1977, p/s, TGL bstp, full mrgs, 34x46", lot 826, C-NY 11/1/88	**17,600**
Puerto Rican Blue Pigeon, 48/50, clr offset litho/slksc, 1977, p/s, TGL bstp, full mrgs, S-34x46", lot 959, SBY 11/5/88	**13,200**
Puerto Rican Blue Pigeon; 8/50, litho/slksc, 1977, p/s, TGL bstp, S-34x46", SBY 5/13/89	**19,800**
Quathlamba I, 66/100, clr litho/Lowell, 1968, p/s, Gemini bstp, full sheet, lt stn/rpl, S-16x29", lot 814, C-NY 11/1/88	**715**
Quathlamba I, 66/100, clr litho/Lowell, 1968, p/s, Gemini bstp, lt stn/rpl, S-16x29", lot 814, C-NY 11/1/88	**715**
Race Track Series: Los Alamitos; APII, clr slksc, 1972, p/s, Gemini bstp, full mrgs, S-20x80", lot 1220, SBY 5/13/89 OE	**10,450**
River of Ponds I, APX, clr litho/Special Arjomari, 1971, p/s, Gemini bstp, full mrgs, lt scr/cr, S-38x38", C-NY 11/1/88	**7,150**
River of Ponds II, APVII, clr litho/Special Arjomari, 1971, p/s, Gemini bstp, full mrgs, S-38x38", lot 817, C-NY 11/1/88	**8,800**
River of Ponds III, 51/75, clr litho, 1971, p/s, Gemini bstp, full mrgs, lt cr/sl, 32x32", lot 955, SBY 11/5/88 OE	**8,800**
River of Ponds IV, APIII, clr litho/Special Arjomari, 1971, p/s, Gemini bstp, full mrgs, S-38x38", C-NY 11/1/88	**8,800**
Sanbornville, Eccentric Polygons; 93/100, litho/scrpt, 1974, p/s, Gemini bstp, S-17x22", lot 592, C-NY 5/11/88 OE	**1,430**
Set of 4: Jasper's Dilemma; 31/100, clr offset litho/J Green, full mrgs, S-16x22", Petersburg, lot 589, C-NY 5/11/88	**3,850**
Set of 4: Jasper's Dilemma; 33/100, offset litho/J Green, 1973, full mrgs, 16x22", Petersburg, lot 823, C-NY 11/1/88 OE	**6,050**
Set of 5: Les Indes Galantes; 31/100, clr offset litho/J Green, 1973, S-16x23", Petersburg, lot 589, C-NY 5/11/88 OE	**4,620**
Set of 5: Les Indes Galantes; 33/100, offset litho/J Green, 1973, sgn, S-16x22", Petersburg, lot 824, C-NY 11/1/88 OE	**8,800**
Set of 5: Shards I-V; APIX, clr offset litho/slksc, 1982, p/s, ea S-40x45", SBY 5/14/88 OE	**34,100**
Set of 5: Shards I-V; 11/100, offset litho/slksc, 1982, p/s, S-40x45", Petersburg, lot 1232, SBY 5/13/89 OE	**52,250**
Set of 5: Shards I-V; 84/100, offset litho/slksc, 1982, sgn/dtd, S-40x45", Petersburg, lot 971, SBY 11/5/88 OE	**38,500**
Shards I, 19/100, offset litho/scrpt/Arches, 1982, p/s, S-45x40", Petersburg, lot 829, C-NY 11/1/88 OE	**8,250**
Shards I, 83/100, offset litho/slksc, 1982, p/s, S-45x40", Petersburg, lot 791, SBY 2/23/89 OE	**8,800**

Shards II, 60/100, offset litho/slksc, 1982, p/s, S-40x45", lot 972, SBY 11/5/88 6,050
Shards IV, 60/100, clr offset litho/slksc, 1982, p/s, S-40x445", Petersburg, SBY 5/14/88 OE 8,800
Shards Variant IA, 27/38, offset litho/slksc, 1982, p/s, S-45x40", Petersburg, lot 973, SBY 11/5/88 OE 6,600
Shards Variant IIIA, 22/77, offset litho/slksc, 1982, p/s, S-45x40", Petersburg, lot 974, SBY 11/5/88 OE 9,350
Shards Variant IVA, 11/49, offset litho/slksc, 1982, p/s, S-40x46", Petersburg, lot 1233, SBY 5/13/89 12,100
Shards Variant IVA, 43/49, offset litho/slksc, 1982, p/s, S-40x45", Petersburg, lot 975, SBY 11/5/88 OE 10,450
Shards Variant VA, 20/30, offset litho/slksc, 1982, p/s, S-40x45", Petersburg, lot 976, SBY 11/5/88 OE 7,700
Sinjerli Variation Squared with Colored Ground I, 21/38, offset litho/slksc, 1981, S-32x32", Petersburg, SBY 5/14/88 OE 11,000
Sinjerli Variation Squared with Colored Ground IA, 41/61, offset litho/slksc, 1981, 32x32", Petersburg, SBY 5/13/89 14,300
Sinjerli Variation Squared with Colored Ground IA, 59/61, offset litho/slksc, 1981, p/s, 32x32", Petersburg, SBY 11/5/88 10,450
Sinjerli Variation Squared with Colored Ground II, PPIII, litho/slksc, 1981, 32x32", Petersburg, lot 967, SBY 11/5/88 9,350
Sinjerli Variation Squared with Colored Ground II, 23/50, offset litho/slksc, 1981, p/s, 32x32", lot 1229, SBY 5/13/89 13,200
Sinjerli Variation Squared with Colored Ground IIA, 23/29, offset litho/slksc, 1981, 32x32", lot 1230, SBY 5/13/89 OE 17,600
Sinjerli Variation Squared with Colored Ground III, CPT VIII, litho/scrpt, 1981, S-32x32", lot 595, C-NY 5/11/88 5,280
Sinjerli Variation Squared with Colored Ground III, 23/32, offset litho/slksc, 1981, 32x32", Petersburg, SBY 5/13/89 14,300
Star of Persia I, 91/92, clr litho/English Vellum Graph, 1967, p/s, Gemini bstp, full mrgs, S-26x32", C-NY 11/1/88 OE 3,850
Star of Persia II, 61/92, clr litho/English Vellum, 1967, p/s, Gemini bstp, full mrgs, 26x32", lot 1219, SBY 5/13/89 OE 14,300
Steller's Albatross; 31/50, clr offset litho/slksc, 1977, Tyler Graphics bstp, 32x43", SBY 5/14/88 11,000
Suite: Black Series II; 51/100, 8 litho, 1967, p/s, Gemini bstp, full mrgs, S-15x22", lot 954, SBY 11/5/88 OE 15,950
Suite: Illustrations After El Lissitsky's Had Gadya; 40/60, 12 prints, 1982-84, Waddington, lot 1236, SBY 5/13/89 OE 242,000
Swan Engraving, 7/30, etch/engr/TGL handmade, 1983, p/s, TGL bstp, full sheet, S-39x32", lot 596, C-NY 5/11/88 OE 3,300
Swan Engraving Blue, Green, Gray; APVI, relief etch/TGL handmade, 1985, p/s, S-66x52", lot 983, SBY 11/5/88 OE 14,300
Swan Engraving III, 4/30, intg/etch/wht TGL handmade, 1982, p/s, TGL bstp, S-66x52", lot 1234, SBY 5/13/89 OE 11,000
Swan Engraving IV, PP II, intg/relief-print etch/handmade TGL, 1982, p/s, bstp, S-65x51", Tyler Graphics, SBY 5/14/88 6,600
Swan Engraving Square IV, PPII, intg/etch/wht TGL handmade, 1982, p/s, TGL bstp, S-52x54", lot 1235, SBY 5/13/89 8,250
Then Came a Dog & Bit the Cat, Pl 3, 16/60, 1982-84, p/s, dtd 84, full sheet, 54x52", Waddington, lot 831, C-NY 11/1/88 26,400
Then Came a Fire & Burnt the Stick, Pl 5, 16/60, sgn/dtd 84, full sheet, S-52x53", Waddington, lot 832, C-NY 11/1/88 14,300

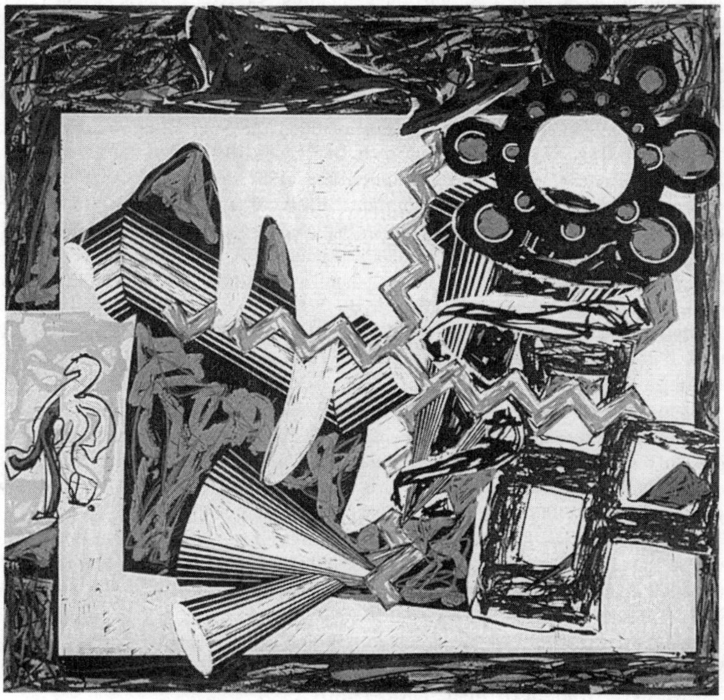

Then Came a Fire & Burnt the Stick, P1 5, 51/60, clr litho/script/linocut/collage, 1984, p/s, full sheet, S-52x53", lot 597, C-NY 5/11/88 OE; $19,800

Then Came an Ox & Drank the Water, Pl 7, 50/60, litho/linocut/slksc, 1982-84, S-54x52", lot 1240, SBY 5/13/89 19,800
Then Came an Ox & Drank the Water, Pl 7, 52/60, sgn/dtd 84, full sheet, lt ls img, S-54x52", Waddington, C-NY 11/1/88 14,300
Then Came Death & Took the Butcher, Pl 9, APVI, litho/linocut/slksc, 1982-84, p/s, 59x48", lot 982, SBY 11/5/88 15,400
Then Water Came & Quenched the Fire, Pl 6, 24/60, litho/linocut/slksc/collage, 1982-84, 54x52", Waddington, SBY 5/14/88 17,600
Then Water Came & Quenched the Fire, Pl 6, 57/60, litho/linocut/slksc, 1982-84, p/s, 54x52", Waddington, SBY 5/13/89 21,450
Then Water Came & Quenched the Fire; Pl 6, APVI, lot 980, SBY 11/5/88 19,800
Wake Island Rail, 1/10, clr scpt/Tycore panel, 1979, felt tip pen sgn, 62x82", Tyler Graphics, SBY 5/14/88 27,500
Yellow Journal, State I; 14/16, clr litho/Arches Cover, 1984, p/s, TGL bstp, S-53x38", lot 598, C-NY 5/11/88 4,950
Yellow Journal, 27/50, offset litho, 1982, p/s, TGL bstp, S-52x39", lot 793, SBY 2/23/89 OE 15,400
York Factory II, 47/100, clr slksc/blk Arches, 1974, p/s, Gemini bstp, full mrgs, 13x40", lot 1221, SBY 5/13/89 OE 34,100
York Factory II, 69/100, clr slksc/blk Arches, 1974, p/s, Gemini bstp, full mrgs, S-19x44", lot 956, SBY 11/5/88 OE 23,100
York Factory II, 77/100, clr scrpt/blk Arches, 1974, p/s, Gemini bstp, full sheet, S-19x45", lot 591, C-NY 5/11/88 OE 15,400

STEPHANOFF, J.; after

Pair: Kensington Palace; Hampton Court; etch, 8x12", lot 931, LH 10/16/89 UE 50

STERNBERG, Harry (American, 1904-)
Blast Furnace, etch/aqua/rlt, p/s, full mrgs, lt stn, P-12x9", lot 32, PHL 6/16/88 .... **400**
Pittsburgh Steel Mills, litho/wove paper, ca 1945, p/s, stone sgn, lt stn, tp, unfr, L-12x17", RWS 3/16/89 OE **375**
STERNMANN
Panorama of Rio de Janeiro, hc engr/2 sheets, L-6x40", lot 1, C-SK 5/25/89 .... **2,020**
STEVENS, Alice Barber (American, 1858-1932)
Concert at Rose Valley Guild Hall, litho poster, 23x25", FAP 6/16/89 UE **300**
STONER, J.J. (19th C)
Bird's-Eye View of the Town of Nantucket...; litho, 1881, lt stn/fox/ls, tr mrgs, S-21x30", Beck/Pauli, SBY 1/28/88 OE **3,410**
STORRS, John Bradley (American, 1887-1966)
Three Soldiers, ed of unknown but presumed sm size, wc/Japan, 1918, lt stn, L-4x4", lot 282, C-NY 1/19/89 OE **2,640**
STUBBS, George; after (British, 1724-1806)
Baronet, clr engr, 16x17", C-E 5/3/88 UE **264**
STURGES, Dwight Case (American, 1874-1940)
Guidance (Lincoln portrait), etch, sgn/titled, lt trm mrgs, 13x9", RAB 3/27/89 UE **25**
SUBLEYRAS, Pierre (French, 1699-1749)
La Madeleine aux Piedes de Jesus, 4th state, etch, 1738, trm, glued to 18th-C paper, 10x24", lot 140, SBY 5/11/89 OE **1,650**
SULTAN, Donald (American, 1951-)
Black Lemon, April 20, 1987; 4/14, aqua, 1987, intl/titled, full mrgs, S-49x63", Parasol, lot 839, C-NY 11/1/88 OE **13,200**
Black Lemon, May 18, 1987; a/p, 16/16, aqua, 1987, intl/titled, full mrgs, S-48x36", Parasol, lot 840, C-NY 11/1/88 OE **7,150**
Black Lemon, 10/14, aqua, 1987, intl/titled, full mrgs, 62x48", Parasol, lot 985, SBY 11/5/88 .... **12,100**
Black Lemon, 23/75, aqua, 1987, intl/dtd March 5 1987, full mrgs, 40x30", Parasol, lot 827, SBY 5/12/88 OE **4,125**
Black Lemon, 28/75, aqua, 1987, intl/titled, full mrgs, 40x30", Parasol, lot 987, SBY 11/5/88 OE **8,800**
Black Lemon, 43/75, aqua, 1987, intl/titled, full mrgs, 40x29", Parasol, lot 1246, SBY 5/13/89 .... **9,900**
Black Lemons, AP2/10, aqua, 1984-85, intl/titled, 62x48", Parasol, lot 984, SBY 11/5/88 OE **15,400**
Black Lemons, Dec 14, 1984; 1/10, aqua/open-bite/Somerset/Satin, 1984-85, p/s, S-63x49", Parasol, lot 836, C-NY 11/1/88 .... **4,400**
Black Lemons, 10/14, aqua, 1987, p/s, titled/dtd April 16 1987 full mrgs, 62x48", Parasol, SBY 5/14/88 OE **11,550**
Black Lemons, 4/14, aqua, 1987, intl/titled, full mrgs, S-49x63", Parasol, lot 838, C-NY 11/1/88 OE **14,300**
Black Lemons & Egg, April 14, 1987; 4/14, aqua, 1987, intl/titled, full mrgs, S-49x63", Parasol, lot 837, C-NY 11/1/88 .... **12,100**
Black Lemons & Egg, AP8/10, aqua, 1987, intl/titled, full mrgs, 62x48", Parasol, lot 986, SBY 11/5/88 .... **12,100**
Black Lemons & Egg, 10/14, aqua, 1987, intl/dtd April 14 1987, full mrgs, 62x48", Parasol, lot 828, SBY 5/14/88 OE **11,000**
Black Lemons & Egg, 2/14, aqua, 1987, intl/titled/dtd April 14 1987, full mrgs, 62x48", lot 1244, SBY 5/13/89 OE **29,700**
Black Tulips & Lemons, 43/54, aqua, 1986, intl/titled/dtd Nov 28 1986, full mrgs, 15x21", SBY 5/14/88 OE **1,540**
Canyon, February 28, 1980; AP2, aqua/etch/BFK Rives, 1980, intl, S-42x42", Parasol, lot 599, C-NY 5/11/88 .... **3,520**
Moon Beam, Dec 21, 1980; a/p, 3/10, litho/Arches, 1982, intl/titled, L-14x19", Parasol, lot 835, C-NY 11/1/88 OE **1,540**
Set of 8: Water Under the Bridge; 9/45, aqua/BFK Rives or Farnesworth, 1979, sgn, Parasol, lot 834, C-NY 11/1/88 .... **8,250**
Suite: Water Under the Bridge; a/p, 9 aqua, 1979, full mrgs, S-18x18", Parasol/Crown Point, lot 1243, SBY 5/13/89 OE **11,000**
Suite: Water Under the Bridge; AP7, ed of 20, 8 aqua, 1979, intl, S-18x18", Crown Point, lot 825, SBY 5/14/88 OE **6,600**
Three Black Lemons, 10/14, aqua, intl/titled, full mrgs, 62x48", Parasol, lot 1245, SBY 5/13/89 OE **20,900**
SUMMERS, Carol (American, 1925-)
Creation of Malwa, 35/75, wc, p/s, 37x37", lot 701, LH 5/15/88 .... **400**
Delta, 129/150, clr wc/laid Japan, p/s, S-20x16", lot 131, PHL 10/28/88 .... **200**
Esperanza, 9/100, clr wc/laid Japan, p/s, titled, S-30x30", lot 132, PHL 10/28/88 .... **225**
Fountain, 5/25, clr wc/fibrous laid Japan, 1964, p/s, full sheet, S-29x21", lot 600, C-NY 5/11/88 OE **1,045**
Group of 3: Esperanza; Burning Mountain; Family Portrait by the Sea; ed of 100, clr wc, ca 1980, lot 794, SBY 2/23/89 .... **1,980**
Group of 3: Himayaya; Pura Vida; The Likiang; 34/75, 48/125, & 101/150, clr wc, 1984/1985/1982, p/s, SBY 5/14/88 OE **1,980**
Group of 3: Pura Vida; Santa Maria del Oro; August 17th; 58/100, 51/100, & 74/100, wc, 1987/1985/1982, SBY 5/14/88 OE **1,870**
Lexington Fire, 24/100, clr wc/Japan, 1958, p/s, titled, lt buckling, S-37x37", lot 3073, B/B 4/19/88 UE **550**
Pair: Monsoon; Family Portrait by the Sea; ed of 100, clr wc/Japan, 1982 & 1981, S-37x37", lot 795, SBY 2/23/89 .... **1,320**
Sierra Madre, 32/75, clr wc/Japan, 1972, p/s, full sheet, lt stn, S-37x37", lot 842, C-NY 11/1/88 .... **1,320**
Sierra Madre, 6/75, clr wc/thin laid Japan, 1972, p/s, titled, S-37x37", L-37x37", SBY 5/14/88 .... **1,375**
SURVAGE, Leopold (French, 1879-1968)
Untitled (l'Oseau), 47/55, wc/wove paper, 1931, p/s, inscr Hollande Japan 1-5, full mrgs, L-8x12", lot 548, C-NY 11/1/88 .... **330**
Untitled (Two Nude Figures), 20/50, wc/wove paper, 1935, p/s, lt lstn, L-3x4", lot 549, C-NY 11/1/88 .... **286**
SUTHERLAND, Graham (British, 1903-1980)
Three Standing Forms in Black, 32/50, litho, 1953, p/s, 19x14", Curwen/Redfern, lot 253, SWN 6/15/89 UE **300**
Swedish School (20th C)
Faerdgels og Trafic, litho/poster paper, 34x25", Andersen/Lachman, lot 231, FAP 2/24/89 .... **125**
SZASZ, Frank (American, 1925-)
Many Faces of Man, 9/175, srgph, sgn, 29x21", lot 139, MG 5/28/88 .... **75**
TAMAYO, Rufino (Mexican, 1886-1957)
Affiche, II/XXV, pk/blk litho, 1969, p/s, lt tr/stn/cr, S-33x24", lot 277, SBY 5/11/89 OE **1,430**
Cabeza en Negro, 66/100, clr mixograph, 1978, Taller de Grafica Mexicana bstp, S-34x25", lot 281, SBY 5/11/89 .... **5,170**
Hombre Con Pipa, 64/100, mixograph, 1979, sgn in blk crayon, Taller de Grafica bstp, S-37x30", lot 283, SBY 5/11/89 .... **3,960**
Man Contemplating the Moon, 44/80, etch, 1947-48, p/s, lt cr, 8x6", lot 58, SBY 2/23/89 OE **1,430**
Mujer con los Brazos en Alto, 122/140, mixed media/embossing, S-30x23", Transworld/Taller, lot 121, PHL 6/16/88 .... **500**
Mujeres: Venus Negra; 109/150, clr litho, 1969, p/s, lt cr, 28x21", Touchstone/Desjobert, lot 68, SBY 2/25/88 .... **550**
Negress, clr litho, ca 1970, p/s, 21x27", lot 184, SWN 12/1/88 .... **600**
Pair: Guerrero de Nayarig; Sigura Femenina de Nayarig; ed of 100, litho, 1976, Kyron bstp, 21x17", lot 68A, SBY 2/25/88 .... **1,430**
Pair: Personaje con Sombrero; Fiugra Hombre en Azule con Fondo Gris; 5/99, etch, 1979, 30x22", Poligrafa, SBY 5/11/89 OE **2,640**
Pair: Torse de Jeune Fille; Untitled (standing figure); clr litho, 1969/ca 1969, p/s, sl, 28x21"/26x19", SBY 5/12/88 OE **1,760**

Pair: Wild Dog; Cat; 35/100 & 49/99, clr litho, ca 1975, sgn, 23x30"/19x26", lot 278, SBY 5/11/89 OE 2,420
Pair: Woman with Red Face; Boy with Airplane; 122/150 & 73/100, litho, ca 1975, 21x27"/26x20", lot 279, SBY 5/11/89 OE 2,420
Perfil en Oro, 54/100, clr mixograph, 1982, sgn in blk crayon, full mrgs, S-35x27", lot 284, SBY 5/11/89 2,750
Perro, 8/75, clr litho, 1973, sgn in wht crayon, S-22x30", Poligrafa, lot 60, SBY 11/3/88 1,430
Quetzalcoatl, 10/70, clr mixograph/handmade pulp, 1979, sgn, full mrgs, 24x48", Mixografia, lot 280, SBY 5/11/89 OE 3,025
Untitled (Standing Figure), 37/100, clr mixograph, ca 1975, sgn in crayon, tp hinge, S-30x22", SBY 5/12/88 OE 1,760
Watermelon Eater, 196/200, clr litho, ca 1950, p/s, full mrgs, lt stn/old hinges, 22x17", lot 59, SBY 11/3/88 OE 3,300

TANGUY, Yves (French, 1900-1955)
Ohne Titel, ed of 100, etch/monotype/laid paper, 1953, p/s, 4x3", Cercle des Arts/Atelier 17, lot 823, SBY 5/11/89 OE 4,125

TAPPAN & BRADFORD (19th C)
Dow & Hobart, Sail Makers, Province, Rhode Island; hc litho, ca 1850, lt rpr/ls, L-16x24", lot 100, C-NY 1/19/89 OE 1,045
Sporting, hc litho/gum arabic, ca 1845, trm mrgs, lt scuff img, lt stn/tr/scr/cr mrgs, S-17x22", lot 536, SBY 1/28/88 1,540

TAUBES, Frederic (American, 1900-1981)
Five Nudes, etch, p/s, 12x10", lot 960, FAP 12/8/88 OE 425

TAYLOR, James; after (19th C)
Sydney (scenic view), clr litho, ca 1821, S-11x34", lt stn/cr/rpr, Chabot/Pattison, C-SK 6/9/88 OE 1,860

TEICHMAN, Sabina (American, 1905-)
Cove, 3/60, litho/wove paper, p/s, titled, lt cr, lt stn verso, L-10x14", lot 74, RWS 9/8/89 UE 100

TENIERS, David; after (Flemish, 17th C)
Pair: Peasant at the Window; Peasants in a Tavern; mezzo/cream laid paper, 8x7", lot 2818, B/B 2/16/88 UE 110

THAL, Sam (American, 1903-)
Launching, etch, p/s, 9x12", Assn Am Artists, lot 285, WG 10/19/88 65
Wolfesboro, New York; etch, p/s, 9x12", Assn Am Artists, lot 286, WG 10/19/88 UE 60

THIEBAUD, Wayne (American, 1920-)
Barbecue Beef, 41/50, clr slksc, 1970, p/s, full mrgs, lt cr/sl/skinned, S-23x30", Parasol, lot 797, SBY 2/23/89 OE 2,420
Candy Apples, 61/200, clr wc/Tosa Kozo, 1987, p/s, Crown Point bstp, full mrgs, 15x17", lot 1250, SBY 5/13/89 OE 20,900
Candy Sticks, a/p, blk/hc etch, 1964, p/s, dtd 1965, full mrgs, 5x7", lot 989, SBY 11/5/88 OE 16,500
Clown, Recent Etchings I; 10/50, sftgr-etch/aqua/Somerset, 1979, p/s, Crown Point bstp, S-23x30", lot 845, C-NY 11/1/88 715
Coconut Cake, a/p, etch, 1964, p/s, titled, 5x5", lot 796, SBY 2/23/89 OE 2,640
Eight Lipsticks, 9/60, clr drypt/etch/Somerset, 1988, p/s, full mrgs, 7x6", Crown Point, lot 1249, SBY 5/13/89 OE 18,150
Group of 3: Candy Counter; Toy Counter; Chocolate Cake, 44/50, linocut, ca 1970, Parasol, lot 836, SBY 5/14/88 OE 4,125
Half Cakes, 26/50, scrpt/Arches, 1970, p/s, full mrgs, lt scr, S-30x23", Parasol, lot 601, C-NY 5/11/88 OE 990
Hill Street, 107/200, clr wc/Echizen Japan, 1987, p/s, printer sgn, Crown Point bstp, L-30x20", SB 5/14/88 5,775
Hill Street, 151/200, clr wc/Echizen Mashi Japan, 1987, p/s, Crown Point bstp, full mrgs, 30x20", lot 990, SBY 11/5/88 5,500
Portfolio: Delights; 93/100, 17 etch, 1965, titled/dtd 64, full mrgs, S-13x11", Crown Point, lot 1247A, SBY 5/13/89 OE 96,250
Portfolio: Recent Etchings I; 8 etch/aqua, 1979, p/s, Crown Point bstp, full mrgs, S-30x22", lot 988, SBY 11/5/88 31,900
Recent Etchings I: Down 18th; 28/50, bl etch, 1979, p/s, full mrgs, P-20x16", Crown Point/Parasol, SBY 5/14/88 990
Recent Etchings II: Boxed Balls; 32/50, clr aqua/drypt, 1979, p/s, Crown Point bstp, 25x20", lot 1248, SBY 5/13/89 OE 8,250
Six Desserts, 4/50, sftgr etch/Somerset, 1970, p/s, P-16x20", lot 602, C-NY 5/11/88 1,430
Slice of Pie, 8/60, etch/wove paper, 1964, p/s, full mrgs, lt sl, S-10x8", Arturo Schwarz, lot 844, C-NY 11/1/88 OE 1,540
Untitled (dessert table), 2/12, gr-blk litho, 1964, p/s, full mrgs, lt cr/stn mrgs, L-10x21", SBY 5/14/88 OE 5,775
Yo-Yo's, 41/60, etch/wove paper, 1962, p/s, S-10x8", Gallera Schwarz, lot 843, C-NY 11/1/88 1,100

THIEMANN, Carl (Czechoslovakian, 1881-)
Sailboat, clr wc/fibrous wove paper, ca 1915, p/s, sealed in mat, L-15x8", C-NY 1/22/88 275
View of a Tree-Lined Canal & Buildings, clr woodcut, unfr, L-23x15", RWS 4/22/89 UE 150

THOMPSON, Jacob (British, 1806-1879)
Crossing a Highland Lock, hc etch, 1858, pl/s, 23x34", lot 404, LH 9/10/89 275

THOMPSON, Jerome; after (American, 1814-1886)
Apple Catching, engr, lt sl/stn, 18x27", lot 46, FAP 2/24/89 225

THORNTON, Robert John; after (18th/19th C)
Roses, by Richard Earlom, 2nd/final state, etch/mezzo, 1805, full mrgs, lt stn mrgs/verso, P-19x15", C-NY 1/22/88 OE 3,850

TIEPOLO, Giovanni Battista (Italian, 1669-1770)
Scherzi: Satyr Family with an Obelisk; 1st state, etch, 1743, trm mrgs, lt stn, 9x7", lot 704, SBY 2/25/88 2,310
Scherzi di Fantasia: Frontispiece; etch, ca 1740, lg mrgs, lt scr/fox, 9x7", lot 141, SBY 5/11/89 OE 2,640
Scherzi di Fantasia: Mother with Two Children; #21, etch, ca 1740, lt fox/cr, 9x7", lot 145, SBY 5/11/89 OE 3,300
Scherzi di Fantasia: The Happy Satyr & His Family; #10, etch/laid paper, ca 1740, lt fox/cr, 9x7", lot 142, SBY 5/11/89 2,970
Scherzi di Fantasia: Two Astrologers & a Boy; #13, etch, ca 1740, lg mrgs, lt cr/fox, 9x7", lot 143, SBY 5/11/89 3,080
Scherzi di Fantasia: Two Magicians & Two Boys; #14, etch, ca 1740, lt fox/sl, 9x7", lot 144, SBY 5/11/89 3,080
Series of Heads: Old Man Seen From the Front; 1st state, etch, pre-1770, lt fox/cr, 5x4", lot 147, SBY 5/11/89 OE 6,325
Vari Capricci: Standing Philosopher & Two Other Figures; etch, ca 1740-43/1785, lt sl/stn, 5x7", lot 146, SBY 5/11/89 UE 880

TISSOT, James Jacques Joseph (French, 1836-1902)
Le Banc de Jardin, 3rd state, mezzo/Chine applique, 1883, full mrgs, lt fox, 16x22", lot 574, SBY 11/3/88 1,100
Le Foyer de la Comedie Francaise Pendant le Siege de Paris, ed of about 100, etch, 1877, 15x11", lot 573, SBY 11/3/88 1,100
Mavourneen, ed of about 100, etch/drypt/laid paper, 1877, pl s, lt stn/tp, laid down, P-15x8", lot 3, RWS 9/8/89 OE 5,750

TITIAN, after (Italian, 1477-1576)
Roger Liberating Angelica, by Cornelius Cort, 4th state, engr, 1563, lt cr, 12x18", lot 45, SWN 12/1/88 605

TITTLE, Walter Ernest (American, 1883-1960)
Grand Central, Night; drypt, ca 1930, p/s, lt stn, P-13x8", C-NY 5/11/88 OE 1,045
View of Central Park, brn drypt/wove paper, ca 1930, p/s, lt stn/tr, P-12x7", lot 286, C-NY 1/19/89 220

TOBEY, Mark (American, 1890-1976)
Companionship, 6/100, intg, p/s, 14x10", lot 342, LH 5/15/88 OE 700

Summer Reflection, 20/50, clr litho, p/s, full mrgs, L-11x9", Beaclair, lot 133, PHL 10/28/88 UE 160
Untitled (abstract), monotype on paper, sgn/dtd 64, 13x10", SBY 5/3/88 1,980

TOKITA, Ryotaro (20th C)
Pair: Y-SE020; Y-FE015; 14/15 & 20/40, slksc, p/s, 22x22", lot 86, FAP 2/24/89 100

TOLEDO, Francisco (Mexican, 1940-)
Group of 3: Woman & Beast; Woman Mounting Bull; Woman & Birthing Stag; litho, ca 1970, p/s, lot 69, SBY 2/25/88 770
Group of 4: Rabbit & Bucket; Horses; Deer; Cart; 3 litho & 1 etch, p/s, full mrgs, lot 70, SBY 2/25/88 1,100

TOOKER, George (American, 1920-)
Mirror, 115/125, blk & beige litho/Arches, 1978, p/s, Ed Press bstp, full mrgs, unfr, L-20x16", C-NY 1/22/88 OE 1,320
Mirror, 91/125, clr litho/Arches, p/s, full mrgs, L-20x16", lot 134, PHL 10/28/88 850
Sleep, 105/150, molded paper relief/wove paper, 1975, p/s, 1 trm mrg, lstn, P-7x10", C-NY 1/22/88 UE 165
Sleep, 38/150, moulded paper relief/heavy wove paper, 1975, p/s, full mrgs, 7x10", Ed Press, lot 2981, B/B 2/16/88 300
Voice, 89/125, litho/lt gray wove paper, 1977, p/s, full mrgs, L-11x10", lot 287, C-NY 1/19/89 935

TOOROP, Jan (Dutch, 1858-1928)
Voor de Arbeid Voor de Vrouw, a/p, litho/smooth wove paper, 35x26", Lankhout, lot 363, SBY 6/8/88 OE 1,925

TOT, Amerigo
Idyll, 63/100, lithȯ, p/s, 17x25", lot 1080, LH 5/15/88 UE 30

TOULOUSE-LAUTREC, Henri de (French, 1864-1901)
Achetez Me Belle Violettes, ed of 500, litho/Arches, 1895, 10x7", Mourlot, lot 2914, B/B 4/19/88 412
Adieu, ed of 500, litho/heavy Arches, 1895, 10x8", lot 2907, B/B 2/16/88 440
Ambassadeurs: Aristide Bruant; litho/2 sheets wove paper laid down on linen, 1892, L-52x36", lot 550, C-NY 11/1/88 24,200
Antoine et Gemier, dans Une Faillite; #20, blk litho, 1893, full mrgs, Kleinmann bstp, 12x15", lot 830, SBY 5/11/89 2,970
Au Pied de l'Echafaud, Adriani's 2nd state, clr litho, 1893, trm mrgs, lt ls/fox/rpr, S-33x24", lot 552, C-NY 11/1/88 OE 2,420
Babylone d'Allemagne, final state, clr litho, 1894, lt tr/sl/cr, linen backed, S-48x32", Chaix, lot 855, SBY 5/11/89 OE 33,000
Babylone d'Allemagne, 2nd/final state, clr litho, 1894, lt cr, S-47x32", Chaix/Wittrock, lot 483, SBY 5/12/88 9,900
Book: Au Pied du Sinai; by Georges Clemenceau, total ed of 380, 1898, Henri Floury, lot 839, SBY 5/11/89 11,550
Cafe Concert: Aristide Bruant; ed of 500, blk litho/wove paper, 1893, full mrgs, lt stn/fox, 11x8", lot 826, SBY 5/11/89 3,025
Cafe Concert: Chanteur American; ed of 500, blk litho/wove paper, 1893, full mrgs, 11x7", lot 827, SBY 5/11/89 2,200
Cafe Concert: Madame Abadala; ed of 500, litho, 1893, full mrgs, lt stn/cr, tp hinge, L-11x8", Estampe, SBY 5/12/88 770
Caudieux, clr litho/wove paper, 1893, lt stn/fld/ls, S-37x50", lot 844, C-NY 5/10/89 OE 9,900
Ce Que Dit la Pluie, ed of 500, litho/Arches, 1895, 7x7", Mourlot, lot 2912, B/B 4/19/88 385
Cecy Loftus, ed of 25, olive-gr litho/applied wove paper, 1894, lt sl, S-20x14", Kleinmann, lot 186, C-NY 11/1/88 OE 13,200
Couverture pour l'Exemple de Ninon de Lenclos Amoureuse, 1st state, litho, 1898, lt stn, 8x10", lot 580, SBY 11/3/88 OE 3,575
Cycle Michael, ed of 200, olive-gr litho, 1896, lt cr/tstn, S-35x50", lot 353, C-NY 5/11/88 4,400
Cycle Michael, olive-gr litho, 1896, lt cr/stn, laid down on masonite, S-35x49", lot 861, SBY 5/11/89 4,950
Cycle Michael, olive-gr litho, 1896, lt stn/tr/cr, S-36x50", lot 585, SBY 11/3/88 7,700
Debauche (Deuxieme Planche), Wittrock's 2nd ed, clr litho, 1896, full mrgs, 10x13", Arnould, lot 836, SBY 5/11/89 OE 11,000
Debauche (Deuxieme Planche), Wittrocks's 2nd state, clr litho, 1896, lt mstn/rpl, L-9x13", lot 555, C-NY 11/1/88 OE 4,180
Divan Japonais, clr litho, 1893, lt cr/tr, 32x25", lot 851, SBY 5/11/89 OE 74,250
Divan Japonais, clr litho, 1893, lt fld/tr/ls, linen backed, S-31x24", lot 516, SBY 2/23/89 OE 13,200
Divan Japonais, clr litho, 1893, lt scuff/cr/tr/ls, linen backed, 32x25", lot 515, SBY 2/23/89 OE 26,400
Divan Japonais, clr litho, 1893, rpr mrg, lt faded clr, cr/tr/sl, backed w/Japan, S-32x23", lot 481, SBY 5/12/88 7,700
Divan Japonais, clr litho/Japan, 1893, lt cr/tr/stn, S-32x24", lot 852, SBY 5/11/89 OE 29,700
Divan Japonais, clr litho/wove paper, 1893, lt scr img, lt ls/cr/stn mrgs, L-32x24", lot 551, C-NY 11/1/88 OE 14,300
Eldorado: Aristide Braunt; clr litho/2 sheets wove paper, 1892, rpr cr, lt sl, L-54x38", lot 843, C-NY 5/10/89 11,000
Elles: Affiche; litho/cream wove paper, 1896, lt fox/stn, S-25x19", lot 455, SBY 2/25/88 7,150
Elles: Frontispiece; #64, ed of 100, clr litho, 1896, lt cr, old tp hinges, S-21x16", lot 837, SBY 5/11/89 OE 33,000
Eros Vanne, litho/beige laid paper, ca 1910, intl, full mrgs, lt stn/fox/cr, 11x9", lot 2903, B/B 2/16/88 OE 2,200
Eros Vanne, litho/cream paper, lt stn, 10x7", lot 2913, B/B 4/19/88 660
Eros Vanne, 2nd state of 4, blk litho/tan laid paper, 1894/pre-1910, full mrgs, 11x9", Pellet, lot 831, SBY 5/11/89 3,025
Femme au Lit, Profil-Au Petit Lever; ed of 100, clr litho, 1896, Gustave Pellet bstp, 16x21", lot 579, SBY 11/3/88 OE 5,768
Femme au Tub, Le Tub; 74/100, clr litho/wove paper, 1896, S-16x21", Gustave Pellet, lot 578A, SBY 11/3/88 OE 93,500
Folies-Bergere: Les Pudeurs de Monsieur Prudhomme; 89/100, litho, 1893, full mrgs, L-15x11", lot 348, C-NY 5/11/88 4,950
Guy et Mealy, Paris qui Marche; ed of 100, dk violet litho/simili Japan, 1898, L-11x9", Goupil, lot 356, C-NY 5/11/88 5,500
Hommage a Moliere, Delteil's 2nd state, olive-gr litho w/bl text, 1897, full mrgs, lt cr, S-13x10", SBY 2/23/89 OE 1,540
Irish & American Bar, Rue Royale-The Chap Book; #30, litho, 1895, lt fox/scr/rpr tr, S-17x24", lot 555, C-NY 11/1/88 24,200
Irish & American Bar, Rue Royale-The Chap Book; ed of 100, clr litho, lt stn, S-17x24", lot 862, SBY 5/11/89 OE 60,500
Irish & American Bar, Rue Royale-The Chap Book; final state, clr litho, 1895, S-16x24", lot 863, SBY 5/11/89 OE 23,100
Irish & American Bar, Rue Royale-The Chap Book; 60/100, 1st state, litho, 1895, cr/sl, S-17x24", lot 351, C-NY 5/11/88 24,200
Jane Avril, clr litho/thin wove paper, 1899, lt tr/cr/fox, 22x15", lot 586, SBY 11/3/88 27,500
Jane Avril, clr litho/thin wove paper, 1899, rpr tr, lt cr/ls/fox, linen backed, S-22x15", lot 864, SBY 5/11/89 OE 60,500
Jane Avril, ed of sm but unknown size, clr litho/smooth wove paper, 1899, rpr tr, lt cr/stn, S-22x14", C-NY 11/1/88 28,600
Jane Avril (Jardin de Paris), final state w/letters, clr litho, 1893, lt cr/ls, linen backed, S-50x36", SBY 5/12/88 23,100
L'Argent 1893, litho, intl, full mrgs, 14x11", lot 18, RAB 8/9/88 650
L'Artisan Moderne, Adriani's 2nd state, clr litho, 1896, lt cr/rpr, laid down, S-36x26", lot 349, C-NY 5/11/88 16,500
La Chaine Simpson, litho, 1896, lt cr/tr/ls, linen backed, S-35x49", SBY 5/12/88 13,200
La Clownesse Assise (Mlle Cha-U-Ka-O), ed of 100, clr litho, 1986, S-21x16", Gustave Pellet, lot 578, SBY 11/3/88 OE 330,000
La Modiste, Renee Vert; 1st state, olive-gr/gray litho, 1893, lt cr/sl, 18x11", Ancourt, lot 575, SBY 11/3/88 3,025
La Passagere du 54-Promenade en Yacht; 3rd state, clr litho/wove paper, 1896, lt cr/sl/sl, S-24x16", C-NY 5/10/89 19,800
La Revue Blanche, final state, clr litho, 1895, laid down, S-49x35", Charpentier/Fasquelle, lot 458, SBY 2/25/88 5,775
La Revue Blanche, final state, clr litho, 1895, lt cr, S-50x36", Charpentier/Fasquelle, lot 457, SBY 2/25/88 16,500

La Revue Blanche, litho/2 sheets wove paper, 1895, trm mrgs, lt cr/stn, S-50x35", Charpentier/Fasquelle, C-NY 11/1/88	14,300
La Revue Blanche, 3rd state, clr litho, 1895, lt sl/cr/stn, S-51x37", lot 584, SBY 11/3/88 OE	13,200
La Revue Blanche, 3rd state, clr litho, 1895, lt stn/fox, linen backed, S-50x37", Charpentier, lot 857, SBY 5/11/89 OE	22,000
La Revue Blanche, 3rd state, litho, 1895, cr/stn/sl, linen backed, 50x36", Ancourt/Charpentier & Fasquelle, SBY 5/12/88	13,750
La Revue Blanche, 3rd state, litho, 1895, lt ls/cr, linen backed, S-50x37", Ancourt/Charpentier & Fasquelle, SBY 5/12/88	12,100
Le Coiffeur-Programme du Theatre Libre; ed of 100, 1st state, litho, 1893, 13x10", Kleinmann, lot 824, SBY 5/11/89 OE	7,150
Le Jockey, ed of 100, blk litho/China paper, 1899, lt scr/rpr tr/cr, 20x14", lot 846, SBY 5/11/89	27,500
Le Jockey, ed of 12, 2nd state, clr litho/Japan, 1899, S-20x14", Pierrefort/Stern, lot 357, C-NY 5/11/88	49,500
Le Logue au Mascaron Dore (Programme pour le Missionnaire), 2nd state, litho, 1893/1894, S-12x10", SBY 5/12/88 OE	8,800
Le Petit Trottin, olive-gr litho/wove paper, after 1901, lt fox/stn/cr, 11x8", lot 450, SBY 2/25/88 OE	2,200
Le Tocsin, gray-gr litho backed w/Japan, 1895, lt cr, S-22x17", Cassan Fis/Toulouse, lot 860, SBY 5/11/89	6,050
Lender de Dos, Dansant le Bolero dans Chilperic; ed of 50, olive-gr litho, 1895, 15x11", Kleinmann, lot 833, SBY 5/11/89	7,700
Les Vieux Papillons, ed of 500, litho/Arches, 1895, 9x7", lot 2905, B/B 2/16/88 UE	248
Les Vieux Papillons, ed of 500, litho/Arches, 1895, 9x8", lot 2906, B/B 2/16/88 UE	190
Louise Balthy (or Yvette Guilbert), ed of 40, litho/beige wove paper, 1898, lt stn, S-12x10", lot 454, SBY 2/25/88	1,430
Mademoiselle Marcelle Lender en Buste, clr litho, 1895, lt rpr/stn, S-15x11", lot 832, SBY 5/11/89 OE	25,300
Mademoiselle Marcelle Lender en Buste, clr litho, 1895, trm mrgs, lt stn mrgs/verso, S-14x11", lot 452, SBY 2/25/88	13,750
May Belfort, Whittrock's 2nd state, clr litho, 1895, trm mrgs, lt cr, S-31x24", lot 856, SBY 5/11/89	16,500
May Milton, Delteil's 2nd state, clr litho/Japan, 1895, rpr tr, S-32x24", lot 859, SBY 5/11/89	26,400
May Milton, 2nd state, clr litho, 1895, lt faded, tr/cr/ls, linen backed, S-31x24", lot 486, SBY 5/12/88 OE	4,400
Miss May Belfort Saluant, ed of 5, gr-blk litho/Japan, 1895, lt cr/sl, S-23x17", lot 187, C-NY 11/1/88 OE	17,600
Miss May Belfort Saluant, ed of 65, dk olive-gr litho, 1895, p/s, lt stn/cr, 15x11", Andre Marty, lot 835, SBY 5/11/89	30,800
Moulin Rouge, La Goulue; Wittrock's 2nd state, clr litho, 1891, lt cr/tr/sl, S-77x46", Affiches, lot 849, SBY 5/11/89 OE	58,300
Oscar Wilde et Romain Coolus, 4th state, litho/beige wove paper, 1896, 12x20", Theatre l'Oeuvre, lot 351A, C-NY 5/11/88	1,100
Partie de Campagne, #96, clr litho, 1897, a/bstp, lt cr/fox, S-16x20", Vollard, lot 581, SBY 11/3/88 OE	330,000
Portfolio: Le Cafe Concert; total ed of 550, 22 litho w/text, 1893, Estampe Originale, lot 576, SBY 11/3/88	22,000
Portfolio: Yvette Guilbert (Serie Anglaise); ed of 350, 1st ed, 1898, Bliss-Sands, lot 840, SBY 5/11/89	23,100
Pour Toi!...; 89/100, Adrian's 1st state, clr litho, 1893, Kleinmann bstp, lt stn/scr, L-11x8", lot 347, C-NY 5/11/88	2,970
Pourquoi Pas?...Une Fois N'est Pas Coutume; #38, litho, 1893, p/s, full mrgs, lt stn, L-13x10", lot 553, C-NY 11/1/88	6,600
Pourquoi Pas?...Une Fois N'est Pas Coutume; 8/100, litho, 1893, p/s, full mrgs, lt cr, 13x10", lot 577, SBY 11/3/88 OE	13,200
Prochainement au Theatre, Aristide Bruant; blk/red litho, 1893, lt stn/ls, S-32x23", lot 456, SBY 2/25/88 OE	3,850
Rejane et Galipaux, Dans Madame Sans-Gene; a/p, sanguine litho/cream laid Japan, 1893, S-18x11", lot 829, SBY 5/11/89 OE	12,100
Set of 9: Yvette Guilbert (Serie Anglaise); litho/simili Japan, 1898/1930, Brown/Phillips, lot 841, SBY 5/11/89	4,950
Ta Bouche, 77/100, Wittrock's 1st ed, gr litho w/stencil clr, 1893, p/s, trm/stn, L-10x7", Kleinmann, SBY 5/12/88 OE	3,300
Troupe de Mlle Eglantine, 3rd state w/letters, clr litho, 1896, tr, lt cr/tr/rpr, backed w/Japan, S-34x31", SBY 5/12/88	12,650
Un Monsieur et Une Dame, 2nd state, clr litho w/text, 1895, S-13x9", Theatre Libre/Verneau, lot 825, SBY 5/11/89	8,800
Yahne et Mayer, Dans l'Age Difficile; #23, olive-gr litho, 1895, full mrgs, 13x9", Kleinmann, lot 834, SBY 5/11/89	5,500

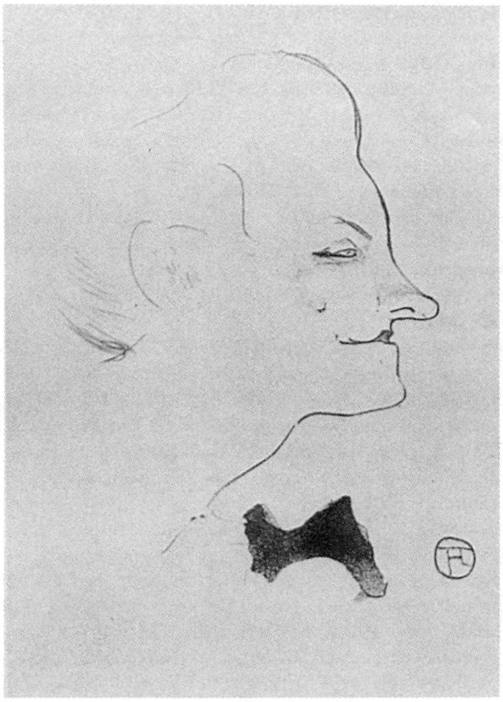

Yvette Guilbert, Pl 2, litho/wove paper, 1893, monogram stp, lt cr, 10x7", L'Estampe Originale, lot 2904, B/B 2/16/88 OE; $1,320

Yvette Guilbert, dans Colombine a Pierrot; litho/cream paper, lt sl, 15x11", lot 2911, B/B 4/19/88 OE	660
Yvette Guilbert, Linger, Longer, Loo; ed of 350, litho, 1898, lt trm/stn, 13x11", Bliss Sands, lot 843, SBY 5/11/89	3,025
Yvette Guilbert, Linger, Longer, Loo; ed of 350, litho, 1898, full mrgs, sl/stn, L-13x11", Bliss Sands, SBY 5/12/88 OE	3,520
Yvette Guilbert, Saluant le Public; ed of 350, litho, 1898, lt trm/sl/stn, 13x11", Bliss Sands, SBY 5/11/89	2,200

Yvette Guilbert, Sur la Scene; ed of 350, litho, 1898, lg mrgs, lt stn/sl, 13x11", Bliss Sands, lot 842, SBY 5/11/89 2,750
Yvette Guilbert-Pessima, ed of 350, litho w/beige tint stone, 1898, full mrgs, lt sl, L-13x11", Bliss Sands, SBY 5/12/88 1,870
Yvette Guilbert-Pessima, violet litho, 1898/1930, a/bstp, Leicester bstp, full mrgs, lt stn, 12x10", SBY 2/23/89 OE 3,300
Zamboula-Polka, Wittrock's 2nd ed, litho/cream wove paper, 1900/after 1901, lt sl/cr, 9x9", lot 848, SBY 5/11/89 1,925
Zamboula-Polka, 2nd ed of 50, olive-gr litho/simili Japan, 1900/after 1901, lt stn, L-9x8", lot 359, C-NY 5/11/88 1,100

TOYOKUNI, Utagwa (Japanese, 1769-1825)
Portrait of an Actor As Warrior, woodblock, no size given, lot 124, FAP 2/24/89 210

TOYOKUNI III (19th C)
Courtesan, clr woodblock, ca 1860, oban size, lot 682, LH 5/15/88 60

TRAVIS, Paul B. (American, 1891-1975)
Clearing in the Congo Forest, ed of 250, litho, 1933, p/s, titled, 9x11", lot 191, WG 10/19/88 90
Studio Window, litho, 1945, p/s, titled, 10x7", lot 301, WG 10/19/88 60

TROUVELOT, Etienne Leopold; after
Great Comet of 1881, #11, chromo/wove paper, lt stn/tstn, cr/ls mrgs, s/wrp, S-38x28", C-NY 1/22/88 1,210
November Meteors, #12, chromo/wove paper, 1868, lt stn, cr/lt ls mrgs, s/wrp, S-38x28", C-NY 1/22/88 OE 2,750
Pair: Mare Humorum; Great Nebula in Orion; chromo/wove paper, 1875/1876, tr/cr/sl, s/wrp, C-NY 1/22/88 UE 275
Pair: Solar Protruberance; Partial Eclipse of Moon; chromo/wove paper, 1873/1874, ls mrgs, 38x28", C-NY 1/22/88 242
Pair: Star Cluster in Hercules; Group of Sun Spots & Veiled Spots; chromo, tr/sl, s/wrp, C-NY 1/22/88 UE 220
Part of the Milky Way, #13, chromo, ca 1875, lt ls/stn, cr/tstn mrgs, s/wrp, S-38x28", C-NY 1/22/88 UE 198
Planet Mars, #8, chromo, 1877, 2 cr img, tr/cr/stn/glue mrg, tstn, s/wrp, S-28x38", C-NY 1/22/88 418
Planet Saturn, #10, chromo, 1874, cr img, tr/sl mrgs, tstn, s/wrp, S-28x38", C-NY 1/22/88 605
Total Eclipse of the Sun, #3, chromo, 1878, 1" tr to img, ltstn/tr mrg, s/wrp, S-28x38", C-NY 1/22/88 UE 352
Zodiacal Light, #5, chromolitho, 1876, cr/sl/tr/stn mrgs, s/wrp, S-38x28", C-NY 1/22/88 605

TROVA, Ernest (American, 1929-)
Four Figures in a Square, 38/50, srgph, 1965, p/s, 26x26", Chiron, lot 2279, DM 3/14/88 125

TRUCHET, Abel (French, 1857-1918)
La Danseuse, clr litho, ca 1895, pl/s, 26x33", lot 443, C-E 9/20/89 600
Quadrille, clr litho, ca 1895, pl/s, 26x33", lot 444, C-E 9/20/89 440
Quadrille, clr litho, pl/s, 26x34", Eugene Verneau, C-E 7/12/88 264

TURGISES (19th C)
Amerique: Vue Generale de New York, Vista General de New York; litho, ca 1855, trm mrgs, 16x23", lot 518, SBY 1/28/88 OE 2,090

TURNER, Francis Calcraft; after (British, 1782-1846)
Group of 4: Departure; Rendezvous; Fatal Stoop; Disgourging (hawking scenes); clr aqua, 1839, Reeve/Laird, FAP 2/24/89 925
Start for the Derby, by C Hunt, hc aqua/wove paper, 1852, trm mrgs, lt stn/scr/fox, L-20x20", lot 103A, C-NY 1/19/89 OE 1,760

TURNER, Joseph Mallord William (British, 1775-1851)
Junction of the Severn & Wye, sepia etch, full mrgs, fox, June 1811, L-7x10", JMW Turner, RAB 3/27/89 UE 150

TUSHINGHAM, Sidney (British, 20th C)
Market Place, Old Falmouth; etch, p/s, 5x12", lot 227, MG 8/27/88 UE 70

TWACHTMAN, John Henry (American, 1853-1902)
Fishing Boats, Gloucester Harbor; etch, ca 1901, intl by artist's son, 5x7", lot 257, SWN 6/15/89 275

TWOMBLY, Cy (American, 1929-)
Note I, 14/14, brn-blk etch/yel Auvergne, 1967, p/s, ULAE bstp, full mrgs, S-9x11", lot 1251, SBY 5/13/89 OE 30,800
Note II, 14/14, brn-blk etch/yel Auvergne, 1967, p/s, ULAE bstp, full mrgs, S-26x21", lot 1252, SBY 5/13/89 OE 29,700
Notes IV, 14/14, brn-blk etch/yel Avergne, 1967, p/s, ULAE bstp, full mrgs, S-26x21", lot 1253, SBY 5/13/89 OE 28,600
Suite: Roman Notes; 36/100, 6 offset litho, 1970, p/s, S-34x28", Neuendorf Verlag, lot 1254, SBY 5/13/89 OE 42,900

TYLER, James Gale; after (American, 1851-1931)
Victorious Volunteer, litho, modern fr, lg folio, Prang, RAB 11/10/88 1,000
Victorious Volunteer, litho, 1887, lg folio, Prang, RAB 8/1/88 900

ULEN, Jean Grigor (American, 1900-)
Corfe Dorset, aqua, p/s, titled, 9x11", lot 330, WG 10/19/88 55

UNGER, Hans (German, 1872-1936)
Nicode-Concert, clr litho, dtd 1897, 41x24", lot 291, FAP 2/24/89 300

UTRILLO, Maurice (French, 1883-1955)
Ferme Debray a Montmartre, 3/100, litho, p/s, no size given, FAP 6/16/89 1,000
La Ferme Debray, ed of about 25, litho/laid paper, 1924, p/s, full mrgs, lt fox, L-8x11", lot 104, PHL 10/28/88 2,000
Notre Dame de Paris, 53/100, total ed of 125, litho/Chine, 1925, p/s, full mrgs, lt stn, 7x9", lot 846, C-NY 5/10/89 OE 2,090
Pour le Bal de L'AAA (Aide Amicale aux Artistes), litho, 1925, linen backed, S-47x31", Affiches Gaillard, SBY 5/12/88 9,350

VAILLANT, Wallerant (Dutch, 1623-1677)
L'Atelier, etch/cream paper, 13x12", lot 2918, B/B 4/19/88 220

VALADON, Suzanne (French, 1865-1938)
Catherine Nue se Coiffant, a/p, sftgr etch/drypt/buff wove paper, 1895, S-12x10", lot 190, C-NY 11/1/88 OE 7,700
Pair: Femmes et Enfant au Bord de l'Eau; Catherine S'Epongeant; sftgr etch, 1904/1908, 8x9"/9x8", SBY 5/12/88 UE 990

VALLOTTON, Felix (Swiss, 1865-1925)
L'Anarchiste, 9/25, wc/Japan, 1892, a/bstp, full mrgs, L-7x10", lot 362, C-NY 5/11/88 330
L'Assassinat, ed of 75, wc/wove paper, 1983, p/s, lt cr/sl/stn, L-6x10", lot 847, C-NY 5/10/89 770
L'Emotion, 43/50, wc/Japan, 1898, intl, full mrgs, lt tstn, L-7x9", lot 376, C-NY 5/11/88 UE 242
L'Etranger, 1/25, wc/Japan, 1894, intl, a/bstp, full mrgs, lt cr mrgs, L-9x7", lot 368, C-NY 5/11/88 462
La Manifestation, 62/100, wc/cream wove paper, 1893, p/s, Estampe Originale bstp, S-9x14", lot 191, C-NY 11/1/88 1,210
La Modiste, ed of 60, wc/cream wove paper, 1894, p/s, lt stn, L-7x9", lot 369, C-NY 5/11/88 UE 2,090
La Paresse, #116, ed of about 180, wc/cream wove paper, 1896, full mrgs, tp on verso, L-7x9", lot 375, C-NY 5/11/88 17,600
La Paresse, 45/180, wc/cream wove paper, 1896, lt stn, S-10x13", lot 192, C-NY 11/1/88 OE 15,400

La Sortie, 10/25, wc/Japan, 1895, intl, a/bstp, full mrgs, old hinges on verso, L-7x9", lot 373, C-NY 5/11/88 OE **605**
Le Bain, 78/100, wc/cream wove paper, 1894, full mrgs, lt cr, L-7x9", Estampe Orig, lot 371, C-NY 5/11/88 ..... **8,800**
Le Bon Marche, ed of about 150, wc/wove paper, 1893, p/s, lt stn/tr, L-8x10", lot 364, C-NY 5/11/88 UE **1,430**
Le Confiant, 21/25, wc/Japan, 1895, intl, full mrgs, lt cr mrgs, tp on verso, L-7x9", lot 372, C-NY 5/11/88 UE **385**
Le Coup de Vent, ed of 60, wc/cream wove paper, sgn in bl crayon, full mrgs, lt stn, L-7x9", lot 370, C-NY 5/11/88 UE **1,540**
Le Couplet Patriotique, unsgn ed of 55, wc/wove paper, 1893, a/bstp, L-7x11", lot 365, C-NY 5/11/88 UE **352**
Les Raseurs, 24/100, litho/glazed wove paper, 1893, sgn, lt rpl/tstn, scr verso, S-15x11", lot 361, C-NY 5/11/88 ..... **1,100**
Monograph: Felix Vallotton; by Meir-Graefe, 15/25, 1898, sgn, Sagot/Stargardt, lot 848, C-NY 5/10/89 ..... **1,320**
Roger & Angelica, #30, ed of about 80, wc/cream wove paper, sgn, full mrgs, lt stn, L-7x9", lot 374, C-NY 5/11/88 UE **550**

VALOIS, E. (19th C)
Yale College, New Haven, Connecticut; hc litho, ca 1850, lt stn/fox, S-18x22", lot 514, SBY 1/28/88 ..... **1,100**

VALTAT, Louis (French, 1869-1952)
Modile de Face, 7/7, etch/laid paper, p/s, full mrgs, P-8x8", lot 105, PHL 10/28/88 ..... **800**

VAN CAULAUERT, Jean Dominique; after (French, 20th C)
Mistinguette, Feerie de Paris; clr litho/poster paper, ca 1937, pl/s, 24x17", lot 445, C-E 9/20/89 ..... **265**

VAN DYCK, Anthony; after (Flemish, 1599-1641)
Allegorical Figure, by JM Ardell, mezzo, mid-18th C, laid down, P-20x14", lot 5, PHL 10/28/88 UE **100**

VAN GOGH, Vincent (Dutch, 1853-1890)
L'Homme a la Pipe: Portrait du Docteur Gachet; etch, 1890, lt tr/stn/fox, S-13x20", Gachet Pere, lot 49, C-NY 11/1/88 ..... **99,000**

VAN GOGH, Vincent; after (Dutch, 1853-1890)
Les Roses, by Jacques Villon, 200/200, clr aqua, 1927, p/s, a/bstp, P-15x20", Bernheim Jeune, lot 86, PHL 6/16/88 ..... **1,900**

VAN HOESEN, Beth (American, 1926-)
Boris, 2/100, aqua/etch/drypt/wove paper, 1981, p/s, titled/dtd, 15x18", lot 3078, B/B 4/19/88 OE **1,430**

VAN LEYDEN, Lucas (Dutch, 1494-1538)
Pair: Abraham Repudiating Hagar; Rest on the Flight into Egypt; engr, 1516 & ca 1506, 6x5"/6x6", lot 634, SBY 2/25/88 ..... **3,575**
Pair: Man with the Torch; Woman Followed by a Fool; Four Soldiers in the Forest; engr, ca 1508, lot 637, SBY 2/25/88 ..... **2,750**
Virgin with Two Angels, blk engr, 1523, trm, lt stn, 6x4", lot 635, SBY 2/25/88 ..... **5,775**

VAN LOO, Carle; after (French, 1705-1765)
Queen Maria Polonia of France & Navarre, by L Cars, engr, 18x15", C-E 7/26/88 UE **380**

VAN OSTADE, Adriaen Janzoon (Dutch, 1610-1685)
Anglers, 2nd state, etch, ca 1684, thread mrgs, lt fox, 4x6", lot 78, SBY 5/11/89 UE **3,850**
Barn, etch, 1647, pl/s, 6x8", Hollstein, lot 189, SWN 6/15/89 ..... **248**
Breakfast, 8th state, etch/Fool's Cap, ca 1664, lt stn/fox/cr, 9x10", lot 80, SBY 5/11/89 OE **14,300**
Bust of a Laughing Peasant, etch/laid paper, lt cr, 3x3", lot 3808, B/B 4/19/88 ..... **220**
Cobbler, etch, 1671, pl/s, 7x5", lot 33, WG 10/19/88 ..... **300**
Couple Walking, etch/laid paper, ca 1638, lt cr, 3x3", lot 2810, B/B 2/16/88 ..... **300**
Laughing Peasant, 4th state of 9, etch, ca 1672, rpr tr in corner, 3x2", lot 643, SBY 2/25/88 ..... **1,430**
Pair: Backgammon Players; Man & Woman Conversing; etch, ca 1682 & 1675, p/s, lt fox, 4x4"/4x3", lot 191, SWN 6/15/89 OE **660**
Pair: Bust of a Laughing Peasant; Bust of a Peasant; etch/laid paper, ca 1636, 2x1"/1x1", lot 2809, B/B 2/16/88 OE **550**
Peasant Family Saying Grace Before Dinner, 2nd state, etch, 1653, pl/s, 6x5", lot 146, SWN 12/1/88 OE **468**
Peasants' Quarrel, 5th state, etch/Fool's Cap, 1653, trm mrgs, lt fox/stn/rub, 5x6", lot 79, SBY 5/11/89 ..... **1,980**
Smoker, etch/laid paper, ca 1640, sm mrgs, 3x2", lot 2809, B/B 4/19/88 ..... **220**
Smoker & the Drinker, 4th state of 6, etch, ca 1650(?), 3x3", lot 644, SBY 2/25/88 OE **2,530**

VAN ROSSEM, Ru (Dutch, 1924-)
Bullfight, clr litho, p/s, 14x19", lot 105, FAP 2/24/89 UE **50**
Horse Race, clr litho, p/s, dtd, 13x19", lot 105, FAP 2/24/89 UE **40**

VAN VLIET, Jan Joris (Dutch, 17th C)
Peasants' Feast, Dutuit's 1st state of 3, engr/wm Pot paper, ca 1655, trm mrgs, lt fox, 8x12", lot 709, SBY 2/25/88 OE **1,540**

VANDERHOOF, Charles A. (American, 1918-)
Set of 4: New York Waterfront; Yachting Scene, Newport; Levee, New Orleans; San Francisco; etch, 10x14", RAB 3/14/89 OE **550**

VARIN, Robert
Chicago in 1779, Called Eschikago, 1930; engr/aqua, p/s, 14x19", Ackerman, lot 90, LH 5/15/88 ..... **300**
Chicago Water Works, 1868; engr/aqua, 1929, p/s, 13x17", Ackerman, lot 86, LH 5/15/88 ..... **325**
Corner of State & Washington Streets, Chicago, 1965; engr/aqua, 1928, p/s, 17x22", Ackerman, lot 897, LH 5/15/88 ..... **400**
First House Built in Chicago, 1897; 96/125, clr aqua/engr, 1930, 22x27", lot 1221, LH 10/16/88 UE **375**
First House in Chicago, 1827; engr/aqua, 1930, p/s, 13x19", Ackerman, lot 88, LH 5/25/88 UE **225**
Michigan Avenue, Chicago, 1889; engr/aqua, 1931, p/s, no size given, Ackerman, lot 84, LH 3/20/88 ..... **300**
Michigan Avenue From Park Row, ed of 100, aqua, p/s, 17x22", lot 1218, LH 10/16/88 UE **40**
Old Fort Dearborn, 1929; engr/aqua, p/s, 14x17", Ackerman, lot 89, LH 5/15/88 ..... **275**
Pair: Corners of Lake & Lasalle Streets; Lasalle Street From Court House Square; aqua, p/s, 17x22", lot 915, LH 10/16/88 ..... **400**
Pair: Washington Between State & Dearborn; NW Corner of Dearborn & Monroe; aqua, p/s, 17x22", lot 914, LH 10/16/88 ..... **425**
Rush Street Bridge, Chicago, 1861; engr/aqua, 1930, p/s, 13x19", Ackerman, lot 85, LH 5/15/88 ..... **300**

VASARELY, Victor (Hungarian, 1908-)
Delocta, 275/275, clr srgph/cream wove paper, p/s, 24x24", lot 2921, B/B 4/19/88 ..... **330**
Harlequin, 54/150, srgph, p/s, 26x16", lot 144, MG 5/28/88 ..... **450**
Triangles, 222/425, clr srgph, p/s, 24x24", lot 924, LH 3/20/88 ..... **150**
Vi-Va, 9/250, clr srgph/cream wove paper, p/s, 31x31", lot 2922, B/B 4/19/88 ..... **330**

VEIT, Rudolf (German, 20th C)
Wartburg (Court View of Luther's Home), clr etch, p/s, titled, P-12x9", lot 1069, S/A 2/18/89 ..... **85**

VENEZIANO, Agostino (Italian, 16th C)
Procession of Silenus, engr, ca 1525, P-7x10", lot 187, SWN 12/1/88 ..... **358**

VENEZIANO, Agostino; att (Italian, 16th C)
Abduction of Helen of Troy, 2nd state, engr, ca 1525, trm mrgs, lt cr, 12x17", lot 188, SWN 12/1/88 ..... **195**
VERNET, Carle Antoine Charles; after (French, 1758-1836)
Pair: Cheval de Course au Moment du Dipart; Le Course au Premier Tournant; hc aqua, L-16x13", lot 1060, DM 2/19/88 ..... **450**
VERTES, Marcel (French, 1895-1961)
Dancers, a/p, litho, p/s, 25x17", lot 966, FAP 12/8/88 ..... **175**
Two Circus Performers, 206/250, clr litho, p/s, lt stn, laid down, 18x14", lot 260, SWN 6/15/89 UE **66**
Woman in a Landscape, clr litho, p/s, 5x7", lot 42, FAP 2/24/89 ..... **85**
Woman Reading a Letter, a/p, litho, p/s, 11x14", lot 965, FAP 12/8/88 ..... **200**
Woman Smelling Flowers, 2/2, a/p, hc litho, p/s, 11x9", lot 39, FAP 2/24/89 ..... **190**
VERTUE, G. (British, 18th C)
Seated Scribe, etch, 1755, pl/s, 14x9", lot 987, LH 12/4/88 OE **90**
Viennese School (20th C)
Ghanza, clr litho/poster paper, unfr, 38x49", lot 302, FAP 2/24/89 UE **130**
VIGNERES (French, 20th C)
Cycles Automobiles, Gladiator; litho/poster paper, tr corner, cr, linen backed, 63x44", lot 262, FAP 2/24/89 OE **500**
VILLON, Jacques Gaston Duchamp (French, 1875-1963)
Autre Temps, 1st state of 3, aqua/drypt/Arches, 1904, p/s, inscr Ep Avant l'Acierage, lt fox/sl, 17x14", SBY 5/12/88 OE **7,700**
Avenue du Bois, d'Apres Van Dongen; 191/200, aqua/Arches, sgn by Van Dongen, full mrgs, P-19x15", C-NY 5/10/89 ..... **1,760**
Bal du Moulin Rouge, IV/IV, etch, p/s, 9x4", lot 263, SWN 6/15/89 UE **248**
Bicycle Race, 6/15, clr litho, ca 1945, p/s, no size given, lot 264, SWN 6/15/89 UE **220**
Buste de Femme, d'Apres Derain; 189/200, clr aqua/wove paper, 1922, p/s, lt scr, P-24x19", lot 559, C-NY 11/1/88 UE **605**
Croquis de Plage, Mere et Engant; ed of 15, aqua/BFK Rives, 1907, p/s, full mrgs, lt sl/fox, 8x6", lot 520, SBY 2/23/89 ..... **1,210**
D'Oul'on Tourne l'Epaule a'la Vie, a/p, etch, sgn, 11x9", lot 287, LH 3/20/88 ..... **1,200**
Eventail pour le Bal Henri Monnier, clr litho (fld/mounted as fan), 1904, lt fox, 10x18", lot 587, SBY 11/3/88 ..... **2,750**
Femme a la Cruche, d'Apres Leger; 195/200, clr aqua/rlt, 1928, p/s, lstn, laid down, P-19x12", lot 382, C-NY 5/11/88 OE **1,540**
La Chasse au Tigre, d'Apres Le Douanier Rousseau; 163/200, aqua, 1924, pl/s, fox/stn, unfr, P-15x20", C-NY 1/22/88 OE **825**
La Faucheuse (Mouissons), a/p, drypt/fine laid paper, 1951, p/s, full mrgs, lt tr/cr, P-10x13", lot 108, PHL 10/28/88 ..... **650**
La Femme au Chien Colley, a/p, 2nd state, drypt/Arches, 1905, p/s, full mrgs, stn/fox, P-20x15", lot 379, C-NY 5/11/88 ..... **15,400**
La Femme au Mannequin (La Femme et la Pantin), 2nd state, etch/aqua, 1899, p/s, S-18x25", lot 193, C-NY 11/1/88 OE **4,620**
La Ferme de la Bendeliere, a/p, aside from ed of 50, clr etch/aqua, 1905, full mrgs, 18x23", lot 519, SBY 2/23/89 OE **4,675**
La Mere, 38/108, drypt, 1945-49, p/s, full mrgs, P-10x7", Graveurs Francois, lot 106, PHL 10/28/88 UE **170**
La Tasse de The, d'Apres Metzinger; 12/200, clr aqua/Arches, 1929, full mrgs, lt fox/stn, 19x18", lot 561, C-NY 11/1/88 ..... **935**
Le Cake Walk des Petites Filles, ed of 10, 2nd state, aqua/drypt, 1904, cr/stn, P-14x18", lot 378, C-NY 5/11/88 ..... **5,500**
Le Cake Walk des Petites Filles, 5/30, clr aqua/wove paper, 1904, p/s, lt sl, S-16x21", lot 194, C-NY 11/1/88 OE **17,600**
Le Peintre, 27/50, etch/drypt, sgn, 8x6", lot 273, LH 3/20/88 ..... **850**
Le Petit Equilibriste, drypt/Arches, 1914, p/s, inscr Tire a 50, full mrgs, P-9x7", Bruker, lot 849, C-NY 5/10/89 OE **13,200**
Le Pont de Beaugency, 25/45, etch/wove paper, 1939, p/s, lt mstn/tp, P-13x9", lot 850, C-NY 5/10/89 ..... **770**
Le Village d'Herouville, d'Apres Vlaminck; 93/200, clr aqua/Arches, 1923-24, p/s, lt stn, 19x23", lot 356, C-NY 1/19/89 ..... **1,430**
Les Deux Colombes, 3/25, drypt/wove paper, 1959, p/s, lt trm/stn/cr, P-4x6", lot 355, C-NY 1/19/89 ..... **132**

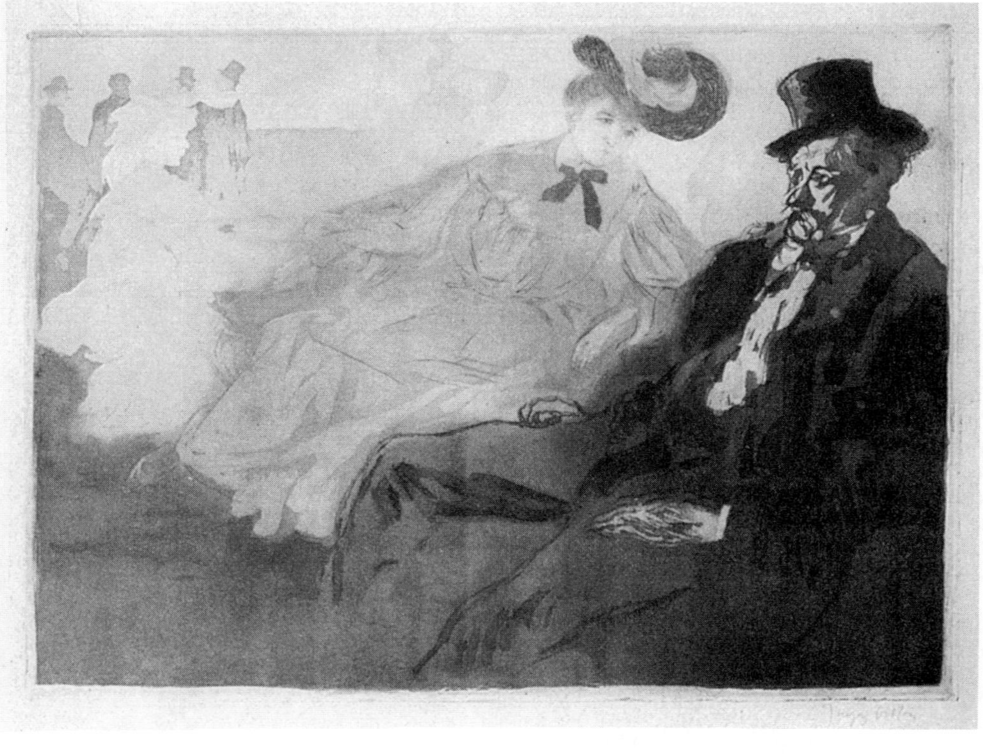

Nevers a Paris, ou Le Fetard; ed pf 50, 3rd state, clr drypt/aqua/wove paper, 1904, p/s, full mrgs, lt cr/stn/sl, P-14x18", lot 377, C-NY 5/11/88; $18,700

Nu, d'Apres Renoir; 166/200, aqua, ca 1923, pl/s, inscr Controlee par Pierre Renoir, trm, stn, P-24x17", C-NY 1/22/88 .... **1,430**
Pair: Miss Bea; Homme Debout; 14/50 & 9/30, etch/drypt & etch, 1955, p/s, 7x6"/10x6", lot 463, SBY 2/25/88 OE **1,100**
Petit Vase de Fleurs, 148/150, etch/laid paper, p/s, full mrgs, lt cr, P-8x5", lot 109, PHL 10/28/88.......... **180**
Portrait d'Acteur, ou l'Acteur; 12/32, drypt/laid BFK Rives, 1913, p/s, full mrgs, 16x12", lot 462, SBY 2/25/88 .... **26,400**
Sous la Tente, sur la Plage (Bondville); #6, ed of 50, aqua, 1905, Sagot bstp, lt stn/fox, 18x23", lot 588, SBY 11/3/88 .... **7,975**
Untitled, From Laus Veneris; ed of 150, etch/Arches, 1956, p/s, lt tstn, P-9x7", C-NY 1/22/88 OE.......... **264**
Yvonne D de Profil, 9/11, 2nd state, drypt, 1913, p/s, inscr Ler Etat, lt stn/fox, 22x16", lot 864A, SBY 5/11/89.......... **66,000**

VILLON, Jacques Gaston Duchamp; after (French, 1875-1963)
Moissons, 6/15, clr litho/laid Heart, 1959-60, lt fox, L-5x11", lot 357, C-NY 1/19/89 UE **110**

VOIRT, Joseph P. (American, 20th C)
Pair: Figures Working the Fields; Mules in a Field; litho, 1937, p/s, 9x6", lot 159, WG 10/19/88.......... **130**

VOLK, Douglas (American, 1856-1935)
They Shall Not Perish, clr litho/psoter paper, 1918, laid down, 40x28", lot 181, FAP 2/24/89.......... **100**

VOLKMAR, Charles (American, 1841-1914)
Duck by a Pond, engr, p/s, laid down, 16x9", lot 241, FAP 2/24/89 UE.......... **10**

VON NEUMANN, Robert (American, 1888-1976)
Beaching the Dory, litho, p/s, 9x14", Assn Am Artists, lot 803, PHL 3/20/88 UE **50**

VUILLARD, Edouard (French, 1868-1940)
Couverture de l'Album, ed of 100, clr litho/Chine, 1899, lt stn/rpr ls, L-20x15", lot 856, C-NY 5/10/89 OE.......... **2,750**
Couverture de l'Album, ed of 100, clr litho/Chine, 1899, lt scr, laid down, L-20x15", lot 564, C-NY 11/1/88 UE.......... **550**
Interieur au Canape (or Soir), 3rd state, etch/laid paper, ca 1930, pl/s, stn, P-4x6", Vuillard, lot 23, C-NY 6/17/89 OE.......... **990**
Interieur aux Tentures Roses I, Paysages et Interieurs; ed of 100, litho/Chine, 1899, L-14x11", lot 386, C-NY 5/11/88 .... **12,100**
Interieur aux Tentures Roses II, clr litho/China paper, 1899, full mrgs, 14x11", Vollard, lot 594, SBY 11/3/88 OE **20,350**
Interieur aux Tentures Roses III, clr litho/Chine volant, 1899, lt cr/fox, 14x11", Vollard/Clot, lot 866, SBY 5/11/89 OE.......... **26,400**
Jeux d'Enfants, Album des Pientres-Graveurs; ed of 100, litho/Chine, 1897, lt cr/tr, L-12x17", lot 385, C-NY 5/11/88.......... **15,400**
La Cuisiniere, Paysages et Interieurs; ed of 100, 2nd state, clr litho/Chine, 1899, S-15x12", lot 387, C-NY 5/11/88 OE **41,800**
La Naissance d'Annette, rare intermediary state, clr litho/Chine volant, ca 1899, lt sl, 17x23", lot 471, SBY 2/25/88 OE.......... **8,250**
Le Jardin des Tuileries, 6/100, litho/Chine volant, 1896, p/s, lt tr/stn, S-16x21", Vollard, lot 198, C-NY 11/1/88 OE **8,250**
Le Jardin Devant l'Atelier, aside from ed of 100, litho, 1901, p/s, lt cr/fox, 25x19", lot 472, SBY 2/25/88 OE.......... **1,540**
Les Deux Belles-Soeurs; 3rd state, clr litho/Chine, lt cr img, laid down, L-14x11", lot 857, C-NY 6850 .... **9,350**
Pair: Van Ryselberghe; Petites Etudes dans le Square: total ed of 170, etch & etch/aqua, ca 1898 & 1937, C-NY 6/17/89 .... **352**

WALKER, E.; after (British, 19th C)
Greenwich Hospital, clr engr, 12x16", Lloyd Brothers, lot 71, FAP 2/24/89 UE.......... **45**

WALKER, William Aiken (American, 1838-1921)
Red Cross Cotton From Start to Finish, clr litho, ca 1894, 21x30", Johnson & Johnson, lot 298A, N/A 5/13/89 .... **550**

WALKOWITZ, Abraham (Russian, 1878-1965)
New York #1, litho/wove paper, ca 1927, p/s, lt stn, L-16x10", lot 289, C-NY 1/10/89 OE **17,600**
Two Figures Seated Before a Window, brn monotype/laid Japan, ink sgn/dtd 3 times, lt cr/tp, P-9x12", C-NY 1/22/88 .... **385**

WALL, William Guy (American, 1792-1862)
Pair: View Near Jessup's Landing; Rapids Above Hadley Falls; litho, lt fox, modern fr, Megarey & Mill, RAB 9/8/88 UE.......... **750**

WALL, William Guy; after (American, 1792-1862)
Glenns Falls, Pl 6, 1st state, etch, 1822-23, lt cr/scuff/fox/stn/sl, S-18x24", Megarey, lot 507, SBY 1/28/88 OE.......... **1,760**

WALLACE, Harry Draper (Canadian, 1892-1977)
Set of 4: Grange; Dock at Toronto; Royal Museum; Cawthra House; etch, p/s, titled, 5x5", lot 1207, WAD 11/28/88 .... **175**

WARHOL, Andy (American, 1928-1987)
$ (dollar sgn), PP2/3, red/brn/gr/bl slksc on Lenox Museum board, 1983, 20x16", lot 4071, B/B 6/19/89 .... **4,125**
$ (dollar sgn), 20/60, orange/gr/bl slksc on Lenox Museum board, 1982, p/s, 20x15", lot 4070, B/B 6/19/89 .... **4,400**
$ (dollar sgn), 21/60, gr/purple slksc/Lenox Museum board, 1982, p/s, 20x16", lot 4068, B/B 6/19/89 .... **3,300**
$ (dollar sgn), 23/60, red/purple slksc/Lenox Museum board, 1982, p/s, 20x16", lot 4069, B/B 6/19/89.......... **3,300**
$9 (dollar sgn 9 times), clr slksc, 1982, p/s, 40x31", lot 4065, B/B 6/19/89 OE **9,350**
$9 (dollar sgn 9 times), 22/35, clr slksc, 1982, p/s, 40x31", lot 4066, B/B 6/19/89 .... **8,800**
$9 (dollar sgn 9 times), 22/35, clr slksc, 1982, 40x32", lot 4067, B/B 6/19/89.......... **8,250**
African Elephant, 54/150, clr slksc, 1983, p/s, S-38x38", Feldman Fine Arts, lot 1034, SBY 11/5/88 OE **4,400**
After the Party, 700/100, clr slksc/heavy wove paper, 1979, p/s, 21x30", Feldman Fine Arts, lot 4037, B/B 6/19/89 .... **3,575**
Albert Einstein, AP24/30, clr slksc, 1980, p/s, S-40x32", Feldman/Jonathan A Ed, lot 1028, SBY 11/5/88 OE **10,450**
Albert Einstein, AP29/30, slksc, 1980, p/s, 40x32", Feldman Fine Arts/Jonathan A Ed, lot 4049, B/B 6/19/89.......... **12,100**
Album: Wonderful World of Fleming-Joffe; 12 litho/collage, 1961, Fleming-Joffe, lot 995, SBY 11/5/88.......... **1,650**
Album: Wonderful World of Fleming-Joffe; 12 litho/collage, 1961, lt stn, S-20x14", Flemming-Joffe, lot 806, SBY 2/23/89 .... **1,320**
Anniversary Donald Duck, 24/30, clr slksc, 1985, p/s, S-31x25", Feldman Fine Arts, lot 1307, SBY 5/13/89 OE **23,100**
Apple, Ads; 169/200, slksc/Lenox Museum board, 1985, p/s, 38x38", Feldman Fine Arts, lot 4101, B/B 6/19/89 OE **9,350**
Bald Eagle, 107/150, clr slksc, 1983, p/s, lt nick, S-38x38", Feldman Fine Arts, lot 1301, SBY 5/13/89 OE **11,550**
Bald Eagle, 11/150, clr slksc/Lenox paper, 1983, p/s, 38x38", Feldman Fine Arts, lot 4073, B/B 6/19/89 OE **12,100**
Banana, #5, ed of about 300, pk/yel scrpt & plastic collage, S-30x40", Factory Additions, lot 610, C-NY 5/11/88 OE.......... **24,200**
Banana, ed of about 300, mixed media slksc, 1966, sgn/dtd 67 on verso, S-24x54", Factory Additions, lot 813, SBY 2/23/89.......... **14,300**
Beets, photolitho, p/s, lt cr/tr/ls/sl, L-9x7", lot 122, PHL 6/16/88 UE **200**
Bighorn Ram, 122/150, clr slksc, 1983, p/s, lt sl, S-38x38", Feldman Fine Arts, lot 852, SBY 2/23/89 OE **4,400**
Bighorn Ram, 54/150, clr slksc, 1983, p/s, S-38x38", Feldman Fine Arts, SBY 5/14/88 .... **3,575**
Birmingham Race Riot, ed of 500, scrpt, 1964, lt cr/scr, S-20x24", Wadsworth Atheneum, lot 851A, C-NY 11/1/88 OE.......... **3,300**
Black Rhinoceros, IX/X, clr scrpt/Lenox Museum board, 1983, S-38x38", Feldman Fine Arts, lot 893, C-NY 11/1/88.......... **3,520**
Blackglama (Judy Garland), 169/190, slksc/Lenox Museum board, 1985, 38x28", Feldman Fine Arts, lot 4096, B/B 6/19/89 OE **14,300**
Blackglama (Judy Garland), 53/190, clr slksc, 1985, p/s, S-38x38", Feldman Fine Arts, lot 1304, SBY 5/13/89 OE.......... **10,450**

Book: Andy Warhol's Index; offset lithos/pop-up illustrations/Velvet Underground record, 1967, lot 807, SBY 2/23/89 OE	1,760
Book: Andy Warhol's Index; trade ed of unlimited size, 1967, Random House, lot 859, C-NY 11/1/88 UE	605
Book: Gold Book; #12, ed of 100, 22 pages, 1957, sgn on justification, lt cr, S-14x11", lot 804, SBY 2/23/89 OE	4,950
Book: Gold Book; #40, ed of 100, 20 pages, 1957, sgn on justification, lt cr, S-14x11", lot 803, SBY 2/23/89	3,300
Book: Gold Book; aside from sgn/#d ed of 100, 1957, sgn, lot 1257, SBY 5/13/89	1,925
Book: Gold Book: 48/100, 1957, sgn in ink on justification, lot 993, SBY 11/5/88 OE	3,850
Book: Gold Book; 59/100, 19 letterpress, 1957, sgn on justification, lt tr/cr/scr, lot 606, C-NY 5/11/88 OE	1,980
Book: Holy Cats by Andy Warhol's Mother; 1954, lot 994, SBY 11/5/88	2,200
Book: Holy Cats by Andy Warhol's Mother; 20 pages, 1954, lt stn, S-9x6", lot 801, SBY 2/23/89	1,320
Book: In the Bottom of My Garden; ca 1956, gr suede slipcase, lot 992, SBY 11/5/88	2,640
Book: In the Bottom of My Garden; 12 hc prints, ca 1956, orig wrappers/boards, lot 1256, SBY 5/13/89	1,925
Book: In the Bottom of My Garden; 17 pages, ca 1956, lt stn, S-9x11", lot 802, SBY 2/23/89 OE	3,850
Book: Wild Raspberries; by Andy Warhol & Susie Frankfurt, 1959, lt stn, lot 1258, SBY 5/13/89	3,025
Book: Wild Raspberries; by Andy Warhol & Susie Frankfurt, 20 letterpress, 1959, lt tr/scr, lot 607, C-NY 5/11/88 OE	2,090
Book: Wild Raspberries; by Andy Warhol & Susie Frankfurt, 20pgs, lt stn/sl, S-17x11", lot 805, SBY 2/23/89	3,850
Book: 25 Cats Name(d) Sam & One Blue Pussy; by Charles Lisanby, #57, sgn, lt stn, lot 561, SBY 2/25/88 OE	4,950
Book: 25 Cats Name(d) Sam & One Blue Pussy; by Charles Lisanby, #32, ed of 190, ca 1954, lt stn/sl, lot 800, SBY 2/23/89	6,050
Book: 25 Cats Name(d) Sam & One Blue Pussy; by Charles Lisanby, ed of 190, ca 1954, sgn, lot 1255, SBY 5/13/89 OE	7,150
Book: 25 Cats Name(d) Sam & One Blue Pussy; by Charles Lisanby, 17 photolitho, ca 1954, 9x6", lot 840, SBY 5/14/88 OE	6,325
Book: 25 Cats Name(d) Sam & One Blue Pussy; by Charles Lisanby, 55/190, ca 1954, lot 991, SBY 11/5/88 OE	5,500
Brooklyn Bridge, litho/poster paper, 1983, sgn in pen, S-36x24", lot 266, SWN 6/15/89	880
Brooklyn Bridge, 85/200, clr slksc, 1983, p/s, 39x39", Feldman Fine Arts, lot 4077, B/B 6/19/89 OE	6,600
Campbell's Soup Shopping Bag, slksc/shopping bag, 1966, felt-tip pen sgn, 24x17", Inst Contemporary Art, SBY 5/14/88 OE	3,575
Campbell's Chicken with Rice Soup, clr slksc/2 plastic panels, 1966, sgn, lt ink ls, 4x9", lot 844, SBY 5/14/88 OE	3,300
Campbell's Soup Can II: Oyster Stew; 249/250, clr slksc, 1969, lt cr/sl, 32x19", Factory Additions, lot 566, SBY 2/25/88	1,980
Campbell's Soup Can on Shopping Bag for Institute of Contemporary Art...; scrpt, 1966, 19x17", lot 857, C-NY 11/1/88	3,080
Campbell's Soup Can on Shopping Bag for Institute of Contemporary Art...; scrpt, 1966, 19x17", lot 612, C-NY 5/11/88 OE	3,080
Campbell's Soup Can on Shopping Bag for Institute of Contemporary Art...; scrpt, 1966, 19x17", lot 611, C-NY 5/11/88 OE	3,520
Campbell's Soup Can Shopping Bag, ed of unknown size, slksc/shopping bag, 1966, p/s, 24x17", lot 998, SBY 11/5/88	3,300
Campbell's Soup I: Beef with Vegetables & Barley; 77/250, slksc, 1968, sgn on verso, S-35x23", lot 821, SBY 2/23/89 OE	3,300
Campbell's Soup I: Beef; 82/250, scrpt, 1968, full mrgs, lt cr/sl, S-35x23", Factory Additions, lot 863, C-NY 11/1/88 OE	4,400
Campbell's Soup I: Chicken Noodle; 21/250, scrpt, 1968, full mrgs, S-35x23", Factory Additions, lot 862, C-NY 11/1/88 OE	5,500

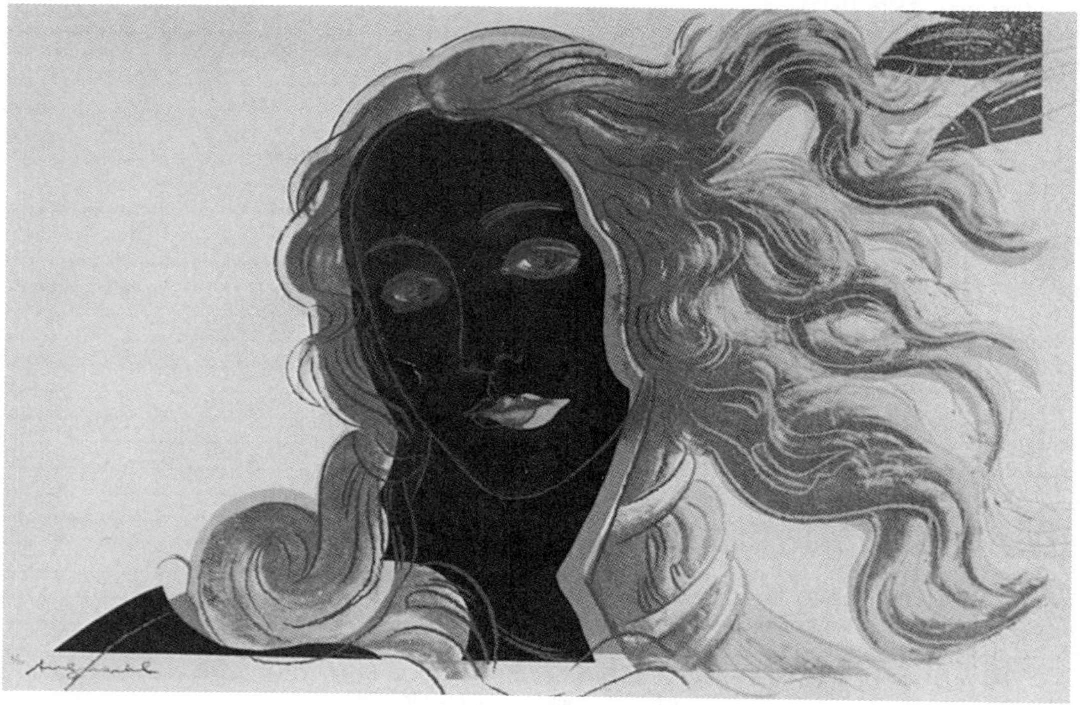

Detail of Renaissance Paintings (Botticelli, Birth of Venus), 1984; 18/70, clr slksc, 1984, p/s, full mrgs, 25x37", Schellmann & Kluser, lot 4090, B/B 6/19/89 OE; $12,100

Campbell's Soup I: Consomme (Beef); 21/250, scrpt, 1968, full mrgs, S-35x23", Factory Additions, lot 865, C-NY 11/1/88	4,180
Campbell's Soup I: Green Pea; 21/250, scrpt, 1968, full mrgs, lt stn, S-35x23", Factory Additions, lot 864, C-NY 11/1/88	4,180
Campbell's Soup II: Cheddar Cheese; 127/250, slksc, 1969, full mrgs, 35x23", Factory Additions, lot 567, SBY 2/25/88	2,200
Campbell's Soup II: Cheddar Cheese; 216/250, clr slksc, 1969, 35x23", Factory Additions, lot 1276, SBY 5/13/89 OE	3,850
Campbell's Soup II: Chicken 'N Dumplings; 147/250, scrpt, 1969, S-35x23", Factory Additions, lot 623, C-NY 5/11/88 OE	3,520
Campbell's Soup II: Chicken 'N Dumplings; 87/250, clr slksc, full mrgs, 25x23", Factory Additions, lot 4008, B/B 6/19/89	5,500

Campbell's Soup II: Golden Mushroom; 237/250, slksc/glazed wove paper, 35x23", Factory Additions, lot 4010, B/B 6/19/89	6,600
Campbell's Soup II: Hot Dog Bean; aside from ed of 250, clr slksc, 1969, S-35x23", Factory Additions, SBY 2/23/89 OE	3,575
Campbell's Soup II: Old Fashioned Vegetable; 127/250, scrpt, 1969, S-35x23", Factory Additions, lot 866, C-NY 11/1/88	3,740
Campbell's Soup II: Old Fashioned Vegetable; 215/250, slksc, 1969, 35x23, Factory Additions, lot 1275, SBY 5/13/89 OE	4,400
Campbell's Soup II: Oyster Stew; 249/250, clr slksc, 1969, full mrgs, lt scuff/cr, 32x19", lot 824, SBY 2/23/89	2,475
Campbell's Soup II: Tomato-Beef Noodle O's; 250/250, clr slksc, 1969, 36x23", Factory Additions, lot 4009, B/B 6/19/89	5,500
Campbell's Soup: Chicken Noodle; 19/250, clr slksc, 1968, sgn, lt cr, 35x23", Factory Additions, lot 820, SBY 2/23/89 OE	4,400
Chanel No 5, Ads; 169/190, slksc/Lenox Museum board, 1985, p/s, 38x38", Feldman Fine Arts, lot 4095, B/B 6/19/89 OE	17,600
Cologne Cathedral, AP9/15, clr scrpt/diamond dust/Lenox Museum board, 1985, 39x32", Wunsche, lot 650, C-NY 5/11/88	3,520
Committee 2000, 742/2000, clr slksc/Lenox Museum board, 1982, p/s, 30x20", Committee 2000/Warhol, lot 4062, B/B 6/19/89	3,025
Cow, pk & yel slksc/wallpaper, 1966, sgn in ink, lt tr/rpr ls, S-45x30", Factory Additions, lot 814, SBY 2/23/89	4,950
Cow, unlimited ed, blk/pk/purple scrpt, 1976, sgn in ink, S-46x30", Modern Art Pavilion, lot 639, C-NY 5/11/88 OE	2,420
Cow, unlimited ed, pk/yel slksc, 1966, p/s on verso, lt cr/tr, 46x30", Factory Additions, lot 4005, B/B 6/19/89	4,950
Cow, unlimited ed (about 100 were sgn), purple/dk salmon scrpt, 1971, sgn, S-46x30", Whitney Mus, lot 877, C-NY 11/1/88	1,980
Cow, 61/100, clr scrpt/wove paper, 1966, sgn in ink, S-45x30", Factory Additions, lot 613, C-NY 5/11/88 OE	5,500
Cow Wallpaper, ed of 100, bl/brn/blk slksc, 1979, sgn, lt scuff/skinned, S-45x30", Whitney Mus, lot 846, SBY 2/23/89	2,310
Cow Wallpaper, ed of 100, pk/blk/purple slksc, 1979, ink sgn, S-46x30", Modern Art Pavilion, SBY 5/14/88 OE	2,860
Cow Wallpaper, ed of 100, pk/blk/purple slksc, 1979, sgn, S-46x30", Modern Art Pavilion, lot 573, SBY 2/25/88 OE	1,980
Cow Wallpaper, ed of 100, pk/purple/blk slksc, 1979, sgn, lt scuff, 46x30", w/sgn certificate, lot 845, SBY 2/23/89 OE	3,300
Details of Renaissance Paintings (Botticelli, Birth of Venus), 18/70, slksc, 1984, sgn, 25x38", lot 4089, B/B 6/19/89 OE	8,800
Details of Renaissance Paintings (Botticelli, Birth of Venus), 18/70, slksc, 1984, sgn, 25x37", lot 4090, B/B 6/19/89 OE	12,100
Details of Renaissance Paintings (da Vinci, The Annunciation), 18/60, slksc, 1984, Schellmann, lot 4091, B/B 6/19/89	5,500
Details of Renaissance Paintings (da Vinci, The Annunciation), 18/60, slksc, 1984, Schellmann, lot 4092, B/B 6/19/89	4,400
Details of Renaissance Paintings (St George & Dragon), 18/50, slksc, 1984, 32x44", Schellmann, lot 4093, B/B 6/19/88	4,400
Diamond Dust Grapes, II/IV, clr slksc w/diamond dust, 1979, sgn, lt sl, 40x30", Warhol Ent, lot 4036, B/B 6/19/89	5,500
Double Mickey Mouse, 24/25, clr scrpt/diamond dust/Arches 88, 1981, 31x43", Feldman Fine Arts, lot 645, C-NY 5/11/88	19,800
Dracula, Myths; 84/200, slksc/Lenox Museum board, 1981, p/s, 38x38", Feldman Fine Arts, lot 4055, B/B 6/19/89	7,700
Dracula, 77/200, clr slksc, 1981, p/s, S-38x38", Feldman Fine Arts, lot 1031, SBY 11/5/88 OE	4,400
Electric Chair, a/p, XIX/L, scrpt, 1971, inscr Merry Christmas to Chris, 36x48", Bischofberger, lot 628, C-NY 5/11/88	1,980
Electric Chair, a/p, XLV/L, purple/orange scrpt, 1971, full sheet, S-36x48", Bischofberger, lot 629, C-NY 5/11/88	1,980
Electric Chair, a/p, XXII/L, shocking pk/yel, sgn, full sheet, lt cr, S-35x48", Bischofberger, lot 630, C-NY 5/11/88	1,870
Electric Chair, APXLV/L, pk/orange slksc, 1971, sgn/dtd on verso, 36x48", Bruno Bischofberger, lot 4013, B/B 6/19/89 OE	9,350
Electric Chair, APXLVII/L, clr slksc, 1971, sgn in pen on verso, lt stn, 36x48", Bischofberger, lot 832, SBY 2/23/89 OE	2,860
Electric Chair, 134/250, clr slksc, 1971, sgn in pen on verso, S-36x48", Bischofberger, lot 831, SBY 2/23/89 OE	3,025
Electric Chair, 134/250, gray/gr slksc, 1971, sgn, lt cr/sl, 36x48", Bruno Bischofberger, lot 4012, B/B 6/19/89 OE	5,225
Electric Chair, 148/250, clr slksc, 1971, sgn in pen, lt rub/sl/cr, S-36x48", Bischofberger, lot 830, SBY 2/23/89 OE	2,475
Eric Emerson, 6/75, scrpt/Somerset Satin, 1982, full mrgs, lt cr, 30x22", Anthology Film Archives, lot 647, C-NY 5/11/88	1,980
Eric Emerson, 73/75, slksc/Somerset Satin, p/s, full mrgs, 20x13", Anthology Film Archives, lot 4061, B/B 6/19/89	4,400
Eric Emerson (Chelsea Girls), 73/75, clr scrpt/Somerset Satin White, 1982, 30x22", Anthology Film Archives, C-NY 11/1/88	2,200
Fiesta Pig, AP6/10, clr slksc/cream wove paper, 1979, p/s, 22x31", Feldman Fine Arts, lot 4038, B/B 6/19/89 OE	6,050
Flowers, aside from #d ed of 250, clr slksc, 1970, sgn in pen, lt scuff/sl, S-36x36", Factory Additions, SBY 2/23/89 OE	7,150
Flowers, ed of about 300, offset clr litho, 1964, sgn/dtd, lt cr, 22x22", lot 4002, B/B 6/19/89	6,600
Flowers, ed of about 300, offset litho, 1964, p/s, full mrgs, lt stn, 22x22", Castelli, lot 808, SBY 2/23/89 OE	4,400
Flowers, ed of about 300, offset litho, 1964, trm to img, S-22x22", lot 135, PHL 10/28/88 OE	500
Flowers, ed of 250, clr slksc, 1970, sgn on verso, S-36x36", Factory Additions, lot 1279, SBY 5/13/89	5,500
Flowers, 1 of 26 a/p, clr scrpt/wove paper, sgn in ink, S-36x36", Factory Additions, lot 872, C-NY 11/1/88	5,500
Flowers, 1 of 26 a/p, X, clr scrpt/wove paper, 1970, sgn in ink, S-36x36", Factory Additions, lot 870, C-NY 11/1/88	6,050
Flowers, 118/250, clr slksc, 1970, sgn in pen, lt cr/sl verso, S-36x36", Factory Additions, SBY 5/14/88 OE	5,225
Flowers, 13/250, clr slksc, 1970, sgn on verso, lt sl/cr, 36x36", Factory Additions, lot 4011, B/B 6/19/89	9,900
Flowers, 139/250, clr slksc, 1970, sgn on verso, lt cr/tr, S-36x36", Factory Additions, lot 1281, SBY 5/13/89	6,600
Flowers, 147/250, scrpt/wove paper, 1970, sgn in ink, full sheet, S-36x36", Factory Additions, lot 626, C-NY 5/11/88 OE	5,500
Flowers, 147/250, scrpt/wove paper, 1970, sgn in ink, full sheet, 36x36", Factory Additions, lot 625, C-NY 5/11/88 OE	6,600
Flowers, 147/250, scrpt/wove paper, 1970, sgn in ink, full sheet, S-36x36", Factory Additions, lot 627, C-NY 5/11/88 OE	7,700
Flowers, 152/250, clr slksc, 1970, sgn, lt cr/scr/sl, S-36x36", Factory Additions, lot 1011, SBY 11/5/88 OE	7,700
Flowers, 153/250, clr slksc, 1970, sgn on verso, lt cr/rub, S-36x36", Factory Additions, lot 1014, SBY 11/5/88 OE	7,150
Flowers, 160/250, clr scrpt/wove paper, 1970, sgn in ink, S-36x36", Factory Additions, lot 875, C-NY 11/1/88	6,600
Flowers, 170/250, clr slksc, 1970, sgn in pen, lt cr/scuff/rub, S-36x36", Factory Additions, lot 829, SBY 2/23/89	5,500
Flowers, 171/250, clr slksc, 1970, sgn, lt cr, S-36x36", Factory Additions, SBY 5/14/88 OE	5,500
Flowers, 171/250, clr slksc, 1970, sgn on verso, lt cr/sl, S-36x36", Factory Additions, lot 1013, SBY 11/5/88	5,500
Flowers, 171/250, clr slksc, 1970, sgn on verso, lt cr/sl, S-36x36", Factory Additions, lot 1012, SBY 11/5/88	4,950
Flowers, 18/250, clr scrpt/wove paper, 1970, sgn/dtd in ink, S-36x36", Factory Additions, lot 876, C-NY 11/1/88 OE	8,800
Flowers, 192/250, clr scpt, 1970, pen sgn on verso, lt scuff/scr/cr/sl, S-36x36", Factory Additions, SBY 5/14/88	3,575
Flowers, 20/250, clr scrpt/wove paper, 1970, sgn in ink, S-36x36", Factory Additions, lot 869, C-NY 11/1/88 OE	7,700
Flowers, 248/250, clr scrpt/wove paper, 1970, sgn in ink, S-36x36", Factory Additions, lot 874, C-NY 11/1/88	6,050
Flowers, 28/250, clr slksc, 1970, sgn on verso, lt cr, S-36x36", Factory Additions, lot 1280, SBY 5/13/89 OE	7,700
Flowers (Hand Colored), AP4/50, hc blk/gray slksc, 1974, pl/intl, S-40x27", Brant/Castelli/Multiples, SBY 5/14/88 OE	2,475
Flowers (Hand Colored), PP/2, slksc, 1974, intl/sgn on verso, full mrgs, S-41x27", Brant/Castelli/Multiples, SBY 2/23/89	3,190
Flowers (Hand Colored), 247/250, hc slksc, 1974, intl/sgn on verso, S-41x27", Brant/Castelli/Multiples, SBY 2/23/89	2,200
Flowers (Hand Colored), 247/250, hc slksc, 1974, intl/sgn on verso, S-41x27", Brant/Castelli/Multiples, SBY 2/23/89 OE	3,025
General Custer, 38/50, clr slksc, 1986, p/s, 36x36", Gaultney-Klineman Art, lot 4108, B/B 6/19/89	6,600
George Gershwin, AP29/30, clr slksc/Lenox Museum board, 1980, 40x32", Feldman Fine Arts/Jonathan A Ed, B/B 6/19/89	7,700

Geronimo, 70/250, clr slksc/heavy wht paper, 1986, p/s, Gaultney-Klineman bstp, S-36x36", lot 3084, B/B 4/19/88	**3,025**
Golda Meir, AP10/30, scrpt/Lenox Museum board, 1980, S-40x32", Feldman Fine Arts/Jonathan A Ed, lot 643, C-NY 5/11/88	**3,850**
Golda Meir, AP29/30, slksc/Lenox Museum board, 1980, p/s, 40x32", Feldman Fine Arts/Jonathan A Ed, B/B 6/19/89	**7,150**
Grace Kelly, 130/225, clr slksc, 1984, p/s, lt cr, S-40x32", Inst Contemporary Arts, lot 1037, SBY 11/5/88 OE	**6,600**
Grace Kelly, 147/225, clr slksc, 1984, p/s, lt stn, S-40x32", Contemporary Arts, lot 853, SBY 5/23/89 OE	**16,500**
Grace Kelly, 186/225, clr slksc, 1984, p/s, lt scuff img, S-40x32", Inst Contemporary Art, lot 1302, SBY 5/13/89	**15,400**
Grace Kelly, 200/225, clr slksc, 1984, p/s, 40x32", Inst Contemporary Arts, lot 4078, B/B 6/19/89 OE	**19,800**
Grevy's Zebra, 122/150, clr slksc, 1983, p/s, lt scr/sl, S-38x38", Feldman Fine Arts, lot 851, SBY 2/23/89	**5,500**
Group of 2: Mick Jagger; 172/250, clr slksc/Arches, 1975, sgn Warhol/Jagger, 44x29", Seabird Ed, lot 4033, B/B 6/19/89	**15,400**
Group of 3: Hammer & Sickle; 22/50, clr slksc, 1977, p/s, S-30x39", Warhol Ent, lot 572, SBY 2/25/88	**3,025**
Group of 8: Campbell's Soup I; 231/250, clr slksc, 1969, sgn, S-35x23", Factory Additions, lot 855, SBY 5/14/88 OE	**20,900**
Group of 8: Campbell's Soup II; 143/250, clr slksc, 1969, sgn, S-35x23", Factory Additions, lot 856, SBY 5/14/88	**17,600**
Happy Bug Day, ed of unknown size, offset litho, ca 1955-60, sgn/titled, lt tr, S-13x9", lot 850, C-NY 11/1/88 UE	**1,100**
Happy Bug Day, hc offset litho, ca 1955-60, sgn/titled in ink, fld/tr/cr/stn, S-14x9", lot 608, C-NY 5/11/88 OE	**2,750**
Happy Butterfly Day, ed of unknown size, offset litho/wove paper, ca 1955, sgn, lt stn, L-13x10", lot 849, C-NY 11/1/88	**1,210**
Howdy Doody, Myths; 84/200, slksc/diamond dust/Lenox Museum board, 1981, 38x38", Feldman Fine Arts, B/B 6/19/89	**13,200**
Indian Head Nickel, 70/250, clr slksc/heavy wht paper, 1986, p/s, Gaultney-Klineman bstp, S-36x36", lot 380, B/B 4/19/88	**3,025**
Indian Mother & Child, 70/250, clr slksc/heavy wove paper, 1986, p/s, Gaultney-Klineman bstp, S-36x36", B/B 4/19/88	**2,750**
Ingrid Bergman As Nun, 244/250, clr slksc/Arches, 1983, p/s, 38x38", Galerie Borjeson, lot 4087, B/B 6/19/89	**8,250**
Ingrid Bergman Herself, 244/250, clr slksc/Arches, 1983, p/s, 38x38", Galerie Borjeson, lot 4086, B/B 6/19/89 OE	**13,200**
Ingrid Bergman with Hat, 244/250, clr slksc/Arches, 1983, p/s, 38x38", Galerie Borjeson, lot 4088, B/B 6/19/89 OE	**14,300**
Jackie, synthetic polymer slksc on canvas, sgn, ca 1964, 20x16", lot 211, SBY 10/8/88	**38,500**
Jackie, synthetic polymer slksc on canvas, sgn/dtd 1964 on verso, 20x16", lot 189, SBY 10/8/88	**38,500**
Jackie I, 11 Pop Artists I; 150/200, slvr scrpt/wove paper, stp/s, full mrgs, 24x20", Orig Ed, lot 614, C-NY 5/11/88 OE	**4,180**
Jackie I, 165/200, slvr slksc, 1966, stp sgn verso, full mrgs, lt cr/sl/stn, 21x17", Orig Ed, SBY 5/14/88 OE	**4,125**
Jackie II, a/p, ed of 200, blk/slvr-mauve scrpt, 1966, full sheet, lt scr/sl, S-24x30", Orig Ed, lot 855, C-NY 11/1/88	**3,520**
Jackie II, a/p, mauve/blk slksc, 1966, stp/s, lt scuff/cr, S-24x30", Orig Ed, lot 1260, SBY 5/13/89	**4,400**
Jackie II, aside from ed of 200, mauve/blk slksc, 1966, stp/s on verso, lt cr, S-24x30", Orig Ed, SBY 5/14/88 OE	**4,675**
Jackie II, 11 Pop Artists II; 91/200, blk/mauve scrpt, 1966, stp/s, lt scr, S-24x30", Orig Ed, lot 615, C-NY 5/11/88 OE	**4,620**
Jackie III, APXXXVIII, bl/blk slksc, 1966, stp/s on verso, lt cr, S-40x30", Orig Ed, lot 847, SBY 5/14/88 OE	**5,500**
Jackie III, XXIX, bl/blk slksc, 1966, stp/s, lt scr/cr, S-40x30", Orig Ed, lot 999, SBY 11/5/88	**5,500**
Jackie III, 11 Pop Artists III; 50/200, blk/slvr bl scrpt, 1966, lt ls, S-40x30", Orig Ed, lot 616, C-NY 5/11/88 OE	**8,250**
Jackie III, 198/200, clr scrpt, 1966, stp/s, full sheet, lt cr corners, S-40x30", Orig Ed, lot 856, C-NY 11/1/88	**6,600**
Jane Fonda, TP25/25, clr slksc/wove paper, 1982, p/s, 40x30", lot 4064, B/B 6/19/89	**7,150**
Jimmy Carter, AP12/25, clr slksc, 1976, p/s, ink sgn Carter, lt cr/sl, S-39x29", SBY 5/14/88 OE	**2,420**
Jimmy Carter I, a/p, II, scrpt/Strathmore, 1976, sgn Warhol/Carter, lt sl, S-39x30", Dem Nat Com, lot 640, C-NY 5/11/88	**1,760**
Jimmy Carter III, 8/100, litho/heavy wove paper, 1977, 28x21", lot 4034, B/B 6/19/89	**2,475**
Joseph Beuys (State III), TP39/45, clr slksc w/rayon flocking, p/s, 40x32", Schellman & Kluser, lot 4041, B/B 6/19/89 OE	**9,350**
Joseph Beuys (State III), 24/150, clr slksc w/rayon flock, 1980-83, p/s, S-40x32", Schellmann/Kluser, SBY 5/13/89 OE	**8,800**
Kachina Dolls, 70/250, clr slksc/heavy wht paper, 1986, p/s, Gaultney-Klineman bstp, S-36x36", lot 3081, B/B 4/19/88	**2,750**
Kiku, 181/300, clr slksc/heavy wove paper, 1983, p/s, pub bstp, 20x26", lot 4082, B/B 6/19/89	**3,575**
Kiku, 181/300, clr slksc/heavy wove paper, 1983, p/s, pub bstp, 20x26", lot 4081, B/B 6/19/89	**4,400**
Kiku, 181/300, slksc/heavy wove paper, 1983, p/s, pub bstp, 20x26", lot 4080, B/B 6/19/89 OE	**6,600**
Kimiko, ed of unknown size, clr scrpt w/text on wove paper, 1981, p/s, S-35x25", CO State U, lot 889, C-NY 11/1/88 UE	**660**
Kimiko, ed of unknown size, clr scrpt/wove paper, 1981, p/s, full mrgs, S-35x25", CO State U, lot 644, C-NY 5/11/88	**990**
Kiss, a/p, total ed of 100, scrpt/plexiglas, 1966, embossed signature, 13x6", Tanglewood, lot 854, C-NY 11/1/88 OE	**4,400**
Ladies & Gentleman, 61/125, clr scrpt/Arches, 1975, p/s, full mrgs, lt stn/sl, S-44x29", Mazzota, lot 884, C-NY 11/1/88	**1,430**
Ladies & Gentlemen, AP19/25, clr slksc, 1975, p/s on verso, S-44x29", Mazzotta, lot 1289, SBY 5/13/89 OE	**3,300**
Ladies & Gentlemen, AP6/25, clr slksc, 1975, p/s, full mrgs, 40x29", Gabriele Mazzotta, lot 4019, B/B 6/19/89 OE	**3,575**
Ladies & Gentlemen, AP6/25, clr slksc/Arches, 1975, p/s, full mrgs, 44x29", Gabriele Mazotta, lot 4022, B/B 6/19/89 OE	**2,750**
Ladies & Gentlemen, 35/125, clr slksc, 1975, p/s, lt sl, 40x29", Gabriele Mazzotta, lot 4020, B/B 6/19/89	**2,200**
Ladies & Gentlemen, 35/125, clr slksc/Arches, 1975, p/s, full mrgs, 44x29", Gabriele Mazotta, lot 4021, B/B 6/19/88 OE	**3,025**
Ladies & Gentlemen, 61/125, clr scrpt/Arches, 1975, p/s, full mrgs, lt stn/sl, 44x28", Mazzota, lot 883, C-NY 11/1/88 OE	**1,650**
Lemon (Volkswagen), Ads; 169/190, slksc/Lenox Museum board, 1985, p/s, 38x38", Feldman Fine Arts, lot 4100, B/B 6/19/89	**6,050**
Lenin, PP5/6, slksc/Arches, 1987, p/s, 40x30", Rupert Jasen Smith/Bernd Kluser, lot 4111, B/B 6/19/89	**6,600**
Life Savers, Ads; 169/190, slksc/Lenox Museum board, 1985, p/s, 38x38", Feldman Fine Arts, lot 4104, B/B 6/19/89	**8,250**
Lincoln Center Ticket, ed of about 200, scrpt/opaque acrylic, 1967, S-45x24", Leo Castelli, lot 618, C-NY 5/11/88 OE	**1,100**
Lincoln Center Ticket, 53/200, clr slksc/opaque acrylic, 1967, sgn, 45x24", Castelli, lot 818, SBY 2/23/89 OE	**2,750**
Liz, ca ed of 300, clr offset litho, 1964, sgn in pen/dtd 66, lt stn/cr mrgs, L-22x22", Castelli, SBY 5/14/88	**6,050**
Liz, ed of about 100, offset litho, 1964, sgn/dtd 66, full mrgs, lt stn/tr, 22x22", Castelli, lot 1258A, SBY 5/13/89	**10,450**
Liz, ed of about 300, clr offset litho, 1964, sgn, full mrgs, 22x22", Castelli, lot 996, SBY 11/5/88 OE	**8,800**
Liz, ed of about 300, clr offset litho, 1964, sgn/dtd in ink, full mrgs, 23x23", Castelli, lot 852, C-NY 11/1/88 OE	**6,050**
Liz, ed of about 300, clr offset litho/wove paper, 1964, full mrgs, S-23x23", Leo Castelli, lot 609, C-NY 5/11/88 OE	**7,150**
Liz, ed of about 300, offset clr litho, 1964, full mrgs, lt cr, 22x22", Leo Castelli, lot 4003, B/B 6/19/89	**13,200**
Liz, ed of about 300, offset litho, 1964, sgn in gr pen, dtd 66, 22x22", Leo Castelli, lot 562, SBY 2/25/88 OE	**3,300**
Liz, ed of about 300, offset litho, 1964, sgn in pen/dtd 65, full mrgs, lt cr, 22x22", Castelli, lot 810, SBY 2/23/89 OE	**13,200**
Liz, ed of ca 300, clr offset litho, 1964, sgn, full mrgs, lt cr/sl, L-22x22", Castelli, lot 842, SBY 5/14/88	**4,400**
Louis Brandeis, AP10/30, scrpt/Lenox Museum board, 1980, 40x32", Feldman Fine Arts/Jonathan A Ed, lot 642, C-NY 5/11/88	**3,520**
Louis Brandeis, 105/200, slksc/Lenox Museum board, 1980, 40x32", Feldman Fine Arts/Jonathan A Ed, lot 4042, B/B 6/19/89	**8,800**
Louis Brandeis, 193/200, scrpt/Lenox Museum board, 1980, S-40x32", Feldman Fine Arts/Jonathan A Ed, C-NY 11/1/88 OE	**2,640**
Louis Brandeis, 70/200, clr slksc, 1980, p/s, lt scr/cr, 40x32", Feldman Fine Arts/Jonathan A Ed, lot 574, SBY 2/25/88	**4,125**

Love, 51/100, clr slksc/heavy wove paper, 1983, p/s, pub bstp, 26x20", lot 4085, B/B 6/19/89	4,125
Love, 51/100, clr slksc/heavy wove paper, 1983, p/s, pub bstp, 26x20", lot 4084, B/B 6/19/89	3,850
Mammy, Myths; 84/200, slksc/diamond dust/Lenox Museum board, 1981, 38x38", Feldman Fine Arts, lot 4057, B/B 6/19/89 OE	9,350
Mao, unlimited ed, purple/blk scrpt on glazed wove paper, 1974, dtd 83, 40x30", Musee Galliera, lot 633, C-NY 5/11/88 OE	2,420
Mao Tse-Tung, AP13/50, clr slksc, 1972, p/s on verso, S-36x36", Brant, lot 834, SBY 2/23/89 OE	7,150
Mao Tse-Tung, ed of 250, clr slksc, sgn on verso, S-36x36", Brant, lot 1019, SBY 11/5/88	4,400
Mao Tse-Tung, 119/250, clr slksc, 1972, pen sgn on verso, lt cr, linen tp, S-36x36", Peter Brant, SBY 5/14/88 OE	4,125
Mao Tse-Tung, 119/250, clr slksc, 1972, sgn on verso, lt cr/ink ls, S-36x36", Peter Brant, SBY 5/14/88 OE	4,125
Mao Tse-Tung, 122/250, clr slksc, 1972, sgn on verso, lt stn, S-36x36", Brant, lot 1020, SBY 11/5/88	3,850
Mao Tse-Tung, 129/250, clr slksc, 1972, sgn on verso, lt ls, S-36x36", Brant, lot 1021, SBY 11/5/88	4,400
Mao Tse-Tung, 130/250, clr slksc, 1972, sgn on verso, 36x36", Peter Brant, lot 4014, B/B 6/19/89 OE	9,350
Mao Tse-Tung, 134/250, clr scrpt, 1972, sgn in ink, full sheet, lt cr, S-36x36", Peter Brant, lot 632, C-NY 5/11/88 OE	5,500
Mao Tse-Tung, 134/250, clr slksc, 1972, sgn on verso, lt cr/stn, S-36x36", Brant, lot 1287, SBY 5/13/89 OE	9,900
Mao Tse-Tung, 134/250, clr slksc, 1972, sgn on verso, lt cr/stn, S-36x36", Brant, lot 1285, SBY 5/13/89 OE	8,250
Mao Tse-Tung, 134/250, clr slksc, 1972, sgn on verso, lt stn, S-36x36", Brant, lot 1284, SBY 5/13/89 OE	12,100
Mao Tse-Tung, 135/250, clr slksc, 1972, sgn in pen on verso, lt ls/cr/tr, S-36x36", Brant, lot 835, SBY 2/23/89 OE	5,225
Mao Tse-Tung, 147/250, clr scrpt, 1972, sgn in ink, Styria bstp, S-36x36", Peter Brant, lot 881, C-NY 11/1/88	3,850
Mao Tse-Tung, 147/250, clr scrpt, 1972, sgn in ink, Styria bstp, S-36x36", Peter Brant, lot 880, C-NY 11/1/88	4,180
Mao Tse-Tung, 149/250, clr slksc, 1972, sgn in pen on verso, lt ls, S-36x36", Brant, lot 836, SBY 2/23/89 OE	6,325
Mao Tse-Tung, 149/250, slksc, 1972, sgn in pen on verso, lt cr/scr, S-36x36", Peter Brant, lot 568, SBY 2/25/88 OE	2,860
Mao Tse-Tung, 161/250, clr slksc, 1972, pen sgn on verso, S-36x36", Peter Brant, SBY 5/14/88 OE	4,675
Mao Tse-Tung, 236/250, clr scrpt, 1972, sgn in ink, Styria bstp, S-36x36", Peter Brant, lot 879, C-NY 11/1/88	4,620
Mao Wallpaper, ed of 100, purple/blk slksc, 1974, sgn, lt cr, S-40x30", lot 841, SBY 2/23/89	2,475
Marilyn, a/p, clr slksc, 1967, sgn twice on verso, lt cr, S-36x36", Factory Additions, lot 565, SBY 2/25/88 OE	5,225
Marilyn, a/p, pk/gr/yel slksc, 1967, inscr Trial Proof 1/1, full mrgs, lt scr/cr/sl, 39x37", lot 1004, SBY 11/5/88	13,200
Marilyn, AP, aside from ed of 250, blk/slvr scpt, 1967, p/s twice, lt cr, S-36x36, Factory Additions, SBY 5/14/88 OE	44,000
Marilyn, ed of about 5000, clr scrpt w/text, 1981, sgn/dtd 84, lt cr, S-12x12", Castelli, lot 646, C-NY 5/11/88 OE	3,300
Marilyn, ed of about 5000 (150 were sgn), clr scrpt w/text, 1981, sgn, S-12x12", Castelli, lot 890, C-NY 11/1/88 OE	3,850
Marilyn, ed of about 5000 (150 were sgn), clr slksc w/text, 1981, sgn, S-12x12", Castelli, lot 1033, SBY 11/5/88 OE	6,050
Marilyn, ed of about 5000 (150 were sgn), slksc, 1981, sgn, S-12x12", Castelli, lot 849, SBY 2/23/89 OE	8,800
Marilyn, 111/250, clr slksc, 1967, p/s, S-36x36", Factory Additions, lot 1268, SBY 5/13/89	27,500
Marilyn, 12/250, clr slksc, 1967, pl/intl & dtd verso, lt cr/ls/scuff, S-36x36", Factory Additions, SBY 5/14/88 OE	14,300
Marilyn, 15/250, clr slksc, 1967, intl, lt scuff/stn, S-36x36", Factory Additions, lot 1267, SBY 5/13/89	27,500
Marilyn, 15/250, clr slksc, 1967, intl on verso, S-36x36", Factory Additions, lot 564, SBY 2/25/88	9,900
Marilyn, 15/250, clr slksc, 1967, intl/dtd, lt cr img, S-36x36", Factory Additions, lot 1269, SBY 5/13/89	28,600
Marilyn, 154/250, clr scrpt/wove paper, 1967, p/s, full sheet, lt cr img, sl/stn verso, 36x36", lot 620, C-NY 5/11/88 OE	19,800
Marilyn, 156/250, clr slksc, 1967, p/s on verso, lt scr/cr, S-36x36", Factory Additions, lot 1006, SBY 11/5/88 OE	52,800
Marilyn, 157/250, blk/slvr slksc, 1967, p/s, lt cr/stn, S-36x36", Factory Additions, lot 1266, SBY 5/13/88 OE	66,000
Marilyn, 16/100, clr slksc, 1967, p/s, lt stn, S-6x6", lot 1263, SBY 5/13/89 OE	7,700
Marilyn, 16/250, clr slksc, 1967, intl on verso, lt cr/stn, S-36x36", Factory Additions, lot 1003, SBY 11/5/88 OE	20,900
Marilyn, 161/250, clr slksc, 1967, p/s, lt cr/scuff/sl, S-36x36", Factory Additions, lot 1264, SBY 5/13/89 OE	38,500
Marilyn, 191/250, clr slksc, 1967, p/s, lt cr/scuff/ink ls, lt disclr verso, S-36x36", Factory Additions, SBY 5/14/88 OE	22,000
Marilyn, 238/250, clr slksc, 1967, p/s on verso, lt scuff/ls/cr, S-36x36", Factory Additions, lot 1271, SBY 5/13/89 OE	88,000
Marilyn, 3/250, clr slksc, 1967, intl, lt cr/stn, S-36x36", Factory Additions, lot 1265, SBY 5/13/89	41,250
Marilyn, 3/250, clr slksc, 1967, p/s on verso, lt cr, S-36x36", Factory Additions, lot 1270, SBY 5/13/89	31,900
Marilyn, 38/250, clr slksc, 1967, lt cr/scr, 36x36", Factory Additions, lot 4006, B/B 6/19/89	27,500
Marilyn, 38/250, clr slksc, 1967, p/s on verso, 36x36", Factory Additions, lot 4007, B/B 6/19/89	29,700
Marilyn, 50/250, clr scrpt/wove paper, 1967, p/s, full sheet, S-36x36", Factory Additions, lot 619, C-NY 5/11/88 OE	14,300
Marilyn, 87/100, clr slksc, 1967, p/s on verso, S-6x6", lot 1001, SBY 11/5/88 OE	6,050
Marilyn, 9/250, clr slksc, 1967, p/s on verso, lt cr/stn, S-36x36", Factory Additions, lot 1002, SBY 11/5/88	41,800
Martha Graham: Lamentation; 95/100, slksc/Lenox Museum board, 1986, 36x36", Gaultney-Klineman Art, lot 4117, B/B 6/19/89	6,050
Martha Graham: Letter to the World; 95/100, slksc/Lenox Museum board, 1986, 36x36", Feldman Fine Art, B/B 6/19/89	6,600
Martha Graham: Satyric Festival Song; 95/100, slksc/Lenox Museum board, 1986, 36x36", Gaultney-Klineman Art, B/B 6/19/89	5,500
Martin Buber, 130/200, clr slksc, 1980, p/s, lt scuff/sl, S-40x32", Feldman Fine Arts/Jonathan A Ed, SBY 5/14/88 OE	4,950
Marx Brothers, AP29/30, clr slksc/Lenox Museum Board, 1980, 40x32", Feldman Fine Arts/Jonathan A Ed, B/B 6/19/89 OE	13,200
Merce Cunningham I, 41/100, scrpt/Japanese gift-wrapping paper, 1974, 30x20", Castelli/Multiples, lot 634, C-NY 5/11/88	2,090
Mick Jagger, AP 12/50, clr slksc, 1975, p/s Warhol, red felt-tip sgn Jagger, S-40x29", Seabird Ed, SBY 5/14/88	5,225
Mick Jagger, 10/250, clr slksc, 1975, p/s Warhol, blk felt-tip pen sgn Jagger, S-40x29", Seabird Ed, SBY 5/14/88	6,050
Mick Jagger, 127/250, blk/gray/yel-orange scrpt/Arches Watercolor, 1975, 44x29", Seabird Ed, lot 885, C-NY 11/1/88 OE	7,150
Mick Jagger, 135/250, clr slksc, 1975, blk felt-tip pen sgn Warhol/Jagger, S-40x29", Seabird Ed, SBY 5/14/88	5,500
Mick Jagger, 172/250, clr slksc/Arches, 1975, sgn Warhol/Jagger, 44x29", Seabird Ed, lot 4025, B/B 6/19/89 OE	13,200
Mick Jagger, 175/250, clr scrpt/Arches Watercolor, 1975, sgn Warhol/Jagger, 44x29", Seabird Ed, lot 637, C-NY 5/11/88	4,950
Mick Jagger, 178/250, clr slksc/Arches, 1975, sgn Warhol/Jagger, 44x29", Seabird Ed, lot 4031, B/B 6/19/89	7,700
Mick Jagger, 179/250, clr scrpt/Arches Watercolor, 1975, sgn Warhol/Jagger, 44x29", Seabird Ed, lot 636, C-NY 5/11/88	4,620
Mick Jagger, 179/250, clr slkcr/Arches, 1975, sgn Warhol/Jagger, 44x29", Seabird Ed, lot 4032, B/B 6/19/89	7,700
Mick Jagger, 179/250, clr slksc/Arches, sgn Warhol/Jagger, 44x29", Seabird Ed, lot 4028, B/B 6/19/89 OE	9,900
Mick Jagger, 179/250, clr slksc/Arches, 1975, sgn Warhol/Jagger, 44x29", Seabird Ed, lot 4030, B/B 6/19/89 OE	8,800
Mick Jagger, 179/250, clr slksc/Arches, 1975, sgn Warhol/Jagger, 44x29", Seabird Ed, lot 4029, B/B 6/19/89	7,150
Mick Jagger, 220/250, clr slksc, 1975, sgn Warhol/Jagger, lt scr, S-40x29", Seabird Ed, lot 1024A, SBY 11/5/88	5,500
Mick Jagger, 221/250, clr slksc, 1975, sgn Warhol/Jagger, full mrgs, S-40x29", Seabird Ed, lot 1025, SBY 11/5/88 OE	9,350
Mick Jagger, 224/250, clr slksc/Arches, 1975, sgn Warhol/Jagger, 44x29", Seabird Ed, lot 4026, B/B 6/19/89 OE	8,800

Mick Jagger, 233/250, clr slksc, 1975, p/s by Warhol, sgn in pen by Jagger, S-44x29", Seabird Ed, lot 1291, SBY 5/13/89 11,000
Mick Jagger, 249/250, clr slksc, 1975, sgn Warhol/Jagger, full mrgs, scr/sl, 40x29", Seabird Ed, lot 1026, SBY 11/5/88 4,950
Mick Jagger, 40/250, clr slksc, 1975, sgn Warhol/Jagger, lt sl/scuff, S-44x29", Seabird Ed, lot 1290, SBY 5/13/89 7,150
Mick Jagger, 8/250, clr slksc, 1975, sgn Warhol/Jagger, lt stn, S-44x29", Seabird Ed, lot 570, SBY 2/25/88 4,400

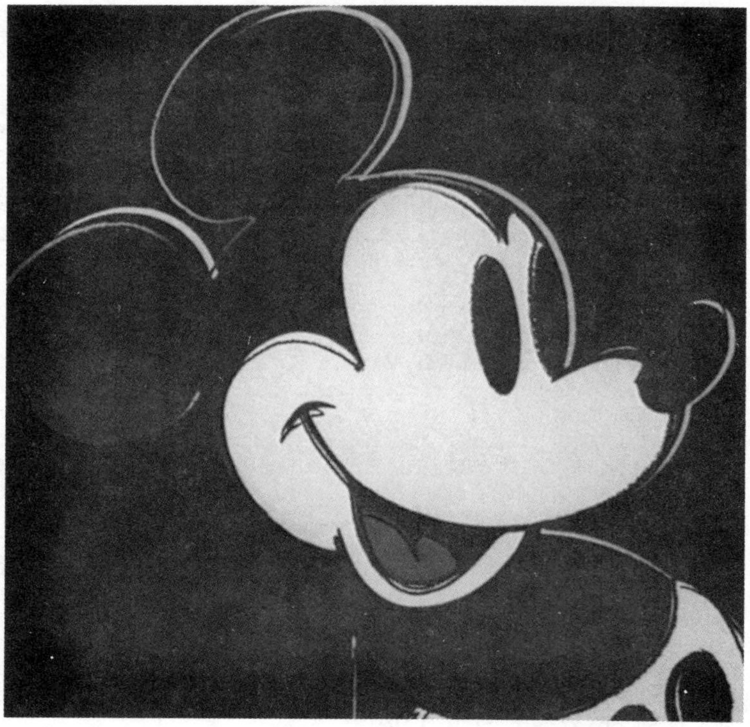

Mickey Mouse, Myths; 84/200, clr slksc/diamond dust/Lenox Museum board, 1981, Feldman Fine Arts bstp, S-38x38", lot 4050, B/B 6/19/89 OE; $38,500

Mobil, Ads; 169/190, clr slksc/Lenox Museum board, 1985, p/s, 38x38", Feldman Fine Arts, lot 4103, B/B 6/19/89 6,600
Moonwalk, 111/160, slksc/Lenox Museum board, 1986, p/s, 38x38", Feldman Fine Arts, lot 4112, B/B 6/19/89 11,000
Moonwalk, 111/160, slksc/Lenox Museum board, 1986, sgn, pub bstp, 38x38", Feldman Fine Arts, lot 4114, B/B 6/19/89 9,900
Moonwalk, 58/160, slksc/Lenox Museum board, 1986, p/s, 38x38", Feldman Fine Arts, lot 4113, B/B 6/19/89 9,900
Muhammed Ali, 45/150, clr slksc, 1978, sgn/inscr To Robert, lt cr/scr/tr, 39x30", lot 4035, B/B 6/19/89 3,300
Neuschwanstein, PP3/5, clr slksc, 1986, p/s, 34x24", Schellmann, lot 4110, B/B 6/19/89 3,025
New Spirit (Donald Duck), 169/190, slksc/Lenox Museum board, 1985, 38x38", Feldman Fine Arts, lot 4102, B/B 6/19/89 OE 16,500
Orangutan, 140/150, clr slksc, 1983, p/s, lt cr, S-38x38", Feldman Fine Arts, lot 850, SBY 2/23/89 4,125
Orangutan, 58/150, clr slksc, 1983, p/s, S-38x38", Feldman Fine Arts, lot 1035, SBY 11/5/88 OE 4,400
Pair: Flowers; Brillo; ed of unknown size, clr scrpt, 1964 & 1970, sgn, lt sl, lot 853, C-NY 11/1/88 3,080
Pair: Flowers; 174/250, hc slksc, 1974, pl/intl, sgn verso, lt sl, S-41x27", Brant/Castelli/Multiples, SBY 5/14/88 OE 4,950
Pair: Golda Meir; 445/550 & 452/550, clr litho/felt, ca 1973, sgn/label verso, Am Friends of Israel Mus, SBY 5/14/88 990
Pair: Space Fruit: Apples; Cantaloupes I; 83/150, clr slksc, 1979, sgn, S-30x40", Zivian, lot 1027, SBY 11/5/88 OE 3,850
Paloma Picasso, clr slksc/Arches, p/s, inscr HC, full mrgs, lt cr, 41x28", lot 4024, B/B 6/19/89 7,150
Paramount, Ads; 169/190, clr slksc/Lenox Museum board, 1985, 38x38", Feldman Fine Arts, B/B 6/19/89 9,350
Paris Review Poster, clr slksc w/diecut holes, 1967, p/s, lt cr, S-37x27", Paris Review, lot 817, SBY 2/23/89 OE 2,640
Paris Review Poster, 71/150, blk & red scrpt/cream wove paper, 1967, sgn, 37x27", Paris Review, lot 860, C-NY 11/1/88 OE 2,640
Pete Rose, 8/50, clr slksc, 1986, p/s, full mrgs, S-38x30", Cincinnati Art Mus, lot 1308, SBY 5/13/89 OE 9,350
Pine Barrens Tree Frog, 11/150, slksc/Lenox paper, 1983, p/s, 38x38", Feldman Fine Arts, lot 4072, B/B 6/19/89 6,050
Portfolio: Flash, November 22, 1963; #57, 11 slksc, 1968, sgn on verso, S-22x21", Racolin, lot 1007, SBY 11/5/88 OE 17,600
Portfolio: Flash, November 22, 1963; ed of 200, 11 slksc, 1968, sgn on verso, lt cr/scuff, orig box, SBY 5/13/89 22,000
Portfolio: Flash, November 22, 1963; G, 1 of 10 deluxe ed, clr slksc, 1968, ea S-22x21", Racolin Press, SBY 5/14/88 14,300
Queen Elizabeth II of the United Kingdom, AP10/10, scrpt/Lenox Museum board, 39x32", Mulder, lot 648, C-NY 5/11/88 OE 3,080
Rebel Without a Cause (James Dean), Ads; 169/190, slksc/Lenox Museum board, 1985, 38x38", lot 4098, B/B 6/19/89 OE 28,600
Rebel Without a Cause (James Dean), TP23/30, clr slksc, 1985, p/s, S-38x38", Feldman Fine Arts, lot 1305, SBY 5/13/89 OE 26,400
S&H Green Stamps, ed of about 300, offset clr litho, 1965, cr/stn, 23x22", Contemporary Art, lot 4004, B/B 6/19/89 OE 5,225
S&H Green Stamps, ed of about 300, offset clr litho, 1965, p/s, full mrgs, lt tr/cr, S-23x23", lot 997, SBY 11/5/88 OE 4,400
San Francisco Silverspot, IX/X, clr scrpt/Lenox Museum board, 1983, p/s, S-38x38", Feldman Fine Arts, C-NY 11/1/88 OE 4,180
San Francisco Silverspot, 58/150, clr slksc, 1983, p/s, S-38x38", Feldman Fine Arts, lot 1036, SBY 11/5/88 OE 4,950
Santa Claus, Myths; 84/200, slksc/diamond dust/Lenox Museum board, 1981, 38x38", Feldman Fine Arts, B/B 6/19/88 7,150
Santa Claus, 140/200, clr slksc, 1981, p/s, S-38x38", Feldman Fine Arts, lot 1032, SBY 11/5/88 OE 5,500
Sarah Bernhardt, AP29/30, slksc/Lenox Museum board, 1980, 40x32", Feldman Fine Arts/Jonathan A Ed, lot 4046, B/B 6/19/89 8,000
Self-Portrait, #165, blk/slvr scrpt, 1967, sgn in ink, full mrgs, cr/ls, 23x23", Leo Castelli, lot 617, C-NY 5/11/88 OE 6,600
Self-Portrait, ed of about 300, blk slksc/slvr-coated paper, 1967, lt cr, S-23x23", Castelli, lot 1261, SBY 5/13/89 6,600
Self-Portrait, HC, blk slksc/slvr paper, 1967, lt cr/rub, S-23x23", Castelli, lot 1000, SBY 11/5/88 OE 7,150
Self-Portrait, HC, blk slksc/slvr-coated paper, 1967, sgn, lt ls/cr, S-23x23", Castelli, SBY 5/14/88 4,400
Self-Portrait, 276/300, clr slksc, 1967, ink sgn, lt cr/scuff, S-23x23", Castelli, SBY 5/14/88 2,475
..... 3,575

Self-Portrait Wallpaper, blk/purple/pk scrpt, 1978, sgn in red ink, lt cr, S-42x30", lot 641, C-NY 5/11/88 OE	1,320
Set of 4: Queen Ntombi Twala of Swaziland; 33/44, clr slksc, 1985, p/s, S-40x32", Mulder, lot 1043, SBY 11/5/88	8,800
Shadow, Myths; AP12/30, clr slksc w/diamond dust, 1981, p/s, S-38x38", Feldman Fine Arts, lot 1299, SBY 5/13/89 OE	11,000
Shadow, Myths; AP6/30, clr slksc w/diamond dust, 1981, p/s, S-38x38", Feldman Fine Arts, lot 848, SBY 2/23/89 OE	8,250
Shadow, Myths; 84/200, slksc/diamond dust/Lenox Museum board, 38x38", Feldman Fine Arts, lot 4053, B/B 6/19/89 OE	13,200
Shoe, hc litho, sgn, unfr, 13x20", lot 353, SBY 10/7/89	2,970
Shoe, hc litho, sgn, unfr, 25x20", lot 359, SBY 10/7/89	2,310
Shoe & Leg, hc letterpress/wove paper, ca 1956, bears signature, lt cr img/mrg, mstn, S-25x14", lot 851, C-NY 11/1/88	880
Shoes, HC, aside from #d ed of 60, clr slksc w/diamond dust, 1980, p/s, S-40x60", Warhol, lot 1295, SBY 5/13/89 OE	13,200
Shoes I, 41/60, clr slksc/diamond dust/heavy Arches, 1980, p/s, 40x60", Warhol Ent, lot 4039, B/B 6/19/89 OE	12,100
Shoes II, 23/60, clr slksc/diamond dust/heavy Arches, 1980, p/s, 40x60", Warhol Ent, lot 4040, B/B 6/19/89 OE	13,200
Sidewalk, PP4/6, clr slksc/Dutch Etching paper, 1983, p/s, 29x42", Eight by Eight, lot 4076, B/B 6/19/89	5,500
Sigmund Freud, 91/200, slksc/Lenox Museum board, 1980, 40x32", Feldman Fine Arts/Jonathan A Ed, lot 4043, B/B 6/19/89	9,350
Speed Skater, CXXXI/CL, clr slksc/Arches, 1983, a/bstp on verso, 34x25", Visconti Art Spectrum, lot 4075, B/B 6/19/89	3,575
Speed Skater, LXX/CL, clr scrpt/Arches, 1983, p/s, S-34x25", Visconti Art Spectrum, lot 894, C-NY 11/1/88	1,540
Stamped Indelibly: Little Cow; lt purple imp, 1967, stp/s, intl in pen, full mrgs, 10x7", lot 819, SBY 2/23/89 OE	1,650
Star, Myths; 84/200, slksc/diamond dust/Lenox Museum board, 1981, 38x38", Feldman Fine Arts, lot 4051, B/B 6/19/89 OE	9,350
Suite: Ads; 119/190, clr slksc, 1985, p/s, S-38x38", Feldman, lot 1044, SBY 11/5/88 OE	66,000
Suite: Ads; 97/190, 10 clr slksc, 1985, p/s, lt scuff, orig box, S-38x38", Feldman Fine Arts, lot 1303, SBY 5/13/89 OE	85,250
Suite: Campbell's Soup I; 128/250, 10 clr slksc, 1968, sgn on verso, full mrgs, S-35x23", Factory Additions, SBY 5/13/89	60,500
Suite: Campbell's Soup I; 9/250, 10 slksc, 1969, sgn, full mrgs, S-35x23", Factory Additions, lot 1008, SBY 11/5/88 OE	55,000
Suite: Campbell's Soup II; 101/250, 10 slksc, 1969, full mrgs, S-35x23", Factory Additions, lot 1009, SBY 11/5/88 OE	36,300
Suite: Campbell's Soup II; 217/250, 10 slksc, 1969, sgn, full mrgs, S-35x23", Factory Additions, lot 822, SBY 2/23/89 OE	39,600
Suite: Campbell's Soup II; 38/250, 10 slksc, 1969, full mrgs, lt cr, orig box, S-35x23", lot 1274, SBY 5/13/89	49,500
Suite: Cowboys & Indians; TP21/36, 14 slksc, 1984, p/s, lt scuff/sl, 36x36", Gaultney-Klineman, lot 1309, SBY 5/13/89 OE	137,500
Suite: Electric Chair; APXXI/L, 10 clr slksc, 1971, sgn on verso, S-36x48", Bischofberger, lot 1282, SBY 5/13/89	31,900
Suite: Electric Chair; 60/125, 10 clr slksc, 1971, sgn on verso, S-36x48", Bischofberger, lot 1017, SBY 11/5/88 OE	29,700
Suite: Flowers (Hand Colored); AP40/50, 10 slksc/Arches, p/s, 41x28", Brant/Castelli/Multiples, lot 4018, B/B 6/19/89	28,600
Suite: Flowers (Hand Colored); 190/250, 10 clr slksc, 1974, S-41x27", Brant/Castelli/Multiples, lot 1023, SBY 11/5/88	26,400
Suite: Flowers (Hand Colored); 198/250, 10 hc slksc, 1974, p/s, boxed, S-41x27", Brant/Castelli/Multiples, SBY 5/13/89	27,500
Suite: Flowers; V, aside from ed of 250, 10 clr slksc, 1970, full mrgs, orig box, S-36x36", lot 1278, SBY 5/13/89 OE	99,000
Suite: Flowers; 91/250, 10 clr slksc, 1970, sgn in blk pen on verso, lt cr, S-36x36", Factory Additions, SBY 5/14/88	46 ,750
Suite: Grapes; 38/50, 6 clr slksc, 1979, sgn, orig box, S-40x30", Warhol Enterprises, lot 1292, SBY 5/13/89	28,600
Suite: Ladies & Gentlemen; 32/125, 10 clr slksc, 1975, p/s on verso, full mrgs, 40x29", Mazzotta, lot 1022, SBY 11/5/88	17,600
Suite: Love Is a Pink Cake; by Ralph Ward, ed of about 100, 1953, unbound, lt stn, lot 799, SBY 2/23/89 OE	2,640
Suite: Mao Tse-Tung; AP31/50, 10 clr slksc, 1972, sgn on verso, S-36x36", Brant, lot 1283, SBY 5/13/89 OE	71,500
Suite: Mao Tse-Tung; 17/250, 10 clr slksc, 1972, sgn on verso, lt tr/cr, S-36x36", Brant, lot 1018, SBY 11/5/88	55,000
Suite: Mao Tse-Tung; 228/250, 10 clr slksc, 1972, sgn in pen on verso, S-36x36", Brant, lot 833A, SBY 2/23/89	57,750
Suite: Marilyn; 8/250, 10 slksc, 1967, p/s on verso, lt cr, S-36x36", Factory Additons, lot 1262, SBY 5/13/89 OE	522,500
Suite: Mick Jagger; AP32/50, 10 slksc, 1975, sgn Warhol/Jagger, orig wrappers, Seabird Ed, lot 1024, SBY 11/5/88 OE	63,250
Suite: Mick Jagger; 237/250, 10 clr slksc, 1975, sgn Warhol/Jagger, boxed, S-44x29", Seabird Ed, SBY 5/14/88	49,500
Suite: Myths; AP27/30, 10 clr slksc, 1982, p/s, orig wrappers, S-38x38", Feldman, lot 1029, SBY 11/5/88 OE	77,000
Suite: Myths; AP28/30, 10 clr slksc, 1981, p/s, S-38x38", Feldman Fine Arts, lot 1296, SBY 5/13/89 OE	121,000
Suite: Myths; 133/200, 10 slksc/diamond dust (except Dracula), 1981, p/s, S-38x38", Feldman Fine Arts, SBY 5/14/88 OE	55,000
Suite: Ten Portraits of Jews of the Twentieth Century; 187/200, 1980, p/s, Feldman Fine Arts, lot 1293, SBY 5/13/89	74,250
Sunset & Evening Shoe, hc litho, titled, 9x13", lot 352, SBY 10/7/89	1,870
Superman, 84/200, slksc/diamond dust/Lenox Museum board, 1981, sgn, 38x38", Feldman Fine Arts, lot 4059, B/B 6/19/89 OE	30,800
Teddy Roosevelt, 60/250, clr slksc, 1986, p/s, 36x36", Gaultney-Klineman Art, lot 4109, B/B 6/19/89	5,500
Truck, 23/60, clr slksc/red background wove paper, 1986, p/s, 40x40", lot 4107, B/B 6/19/89	5,500
UN Stamp, 910/1000, clr offset litho/collage/Rives, 1979, S-9x11", UN Disaster Relief Org, lot 886, C-NY 11/1/88	990
Uncle Sam, Myths; 153/200, clr slksc w/diamond dust, 1981, p/s, S-38x38",	4,400
Uncle Sam, Myths; 84/200, slksc/diamond dust/Lenox Museum board, 1981, 38x38", Feldman Fine Arts, lot 4052, B/B 6/19/89	7,150
Uncle Sam, 140/200, clr slksc, 1981, p/s, S-38x38", Feldman Fine Arts, lot 1030, SBY 11/5/88	3,300
Untitled (Campbell's Tomato Soup), clr slksc, 1969, p/s, lt scuff/cr, 15x15", Multiples, lot 1277, SBY 5/13/89	3,850
Untitled (Campbell's Tomato Soup), ed of unknown size, clr slksc, 1969, S-15x15", Multiples, lot 1015, SBY 11/5/88	4,400
Untitled (Campbell's Tomato Soup), ed of unknown size, clr slksc, 1969, sgn, lt cr/scr, S-15x15", lot 825, SBY 2/23/89	3,850
Untitled (Campbell's Tomato Soup), ed of unknown size, clr slksc, 1969, p/s, scuff, S-15x15", Multiples, SBY 5/14/88 OE	4,950
Untitled (Scarf) (The Only Way Out...Is In!), scrpt, 1984, sgn/dtd in ink, S-35x25", lot 894B, C-NY 11/1/88	1,650
Untitled (Three Silver Fish), ed of unknown size, gray/blk/wht scrpt, ca 1983, S-43x30", lot 894A, C-NY 11/1/88	2,420
Untitled 12, 32/100, clr slksc/Arches, 1974, sgn, full mrgs, lt sl, 19x16", Meyer Shapiro, lot 4017, B/B 6/19/89 OE	4,125
Untitled 12, 49/100, blk/dk gr slksc, 1974, sgn, lt cr, S-19x16", Columbia U, lot 569, SBY 2/25/88 OE	1,430
Van Heusen (Ronald Reagan), 169/190, slksc/Lenox Museum board, 1985, 38x38", Feldman Fine Arts, lot 4099, B/B 6/19/89	9,350
Vote McGovern, 1/250, clr scrpt/Arches, 1972, sgn in ink, Gemini bstp, lt stn, S-42x42", lot 878, C-NY 11/1/88 OE	5,280
Vote McGovern, 1/250, clr scrpt/Arches, 1972, sgn in ink, Gemini bstp, lt stn/scr/stn, 42x42", lot 631, C-NY 5/11/88 OE	6,050
Vote McGovern, 20/250, clr slksc, 1972, sgn on verso, Gemini bstp, full mrgs, 42x42", lot 4016, B/B 6/19/89 OE	7,700
Vote McGovern, 214/250, clr slksc, 1972, sgn in pen on verso, Gemini bstp, full mrgs, 42x42", lot 833, SBY 2/23/89	5,225
Vote McGovern, 216/250, clr scrpt/Arches, 1972, sgn, Gemini bstp, lt cr/stn, S-42x42", lot 168, C-NY 2/14/89	3,300
Vote McGovern, 245/250, clr slksc, 1972, sgn, Gemini bstp, full mrgs, lt disclr, S-42x42", SBY 5/14/88 OE	4,950
Vote McGovern, 77/250, clr slksc, 1972, sgn on verso, Gemini bstp, full mrgs, stn/sl, S-42x42", lot 1016, SBY 11/5/88 OE	4,950
Watercolor Paint Kit with Brushes, 270/500, offset clr litho, 1982, sgn, 9x12", lot 4063, B/B 6/19/89 OE	3,850
Wayne Gretsky #99, 119/300, slksc/Lenox Museum board, 1984, sgn Warhol/Gretsky, 40x32", Wynans, lot 4079, B/B 6/19/89	3,850

Wayne Gretsky #99, 136/300, clr slksc, 1984, p/s, full mrgs, lt scr, S-40x32", Wynans, lot 1038, SBY 11/5/88 OE ... **3,850**
When I'm Calling Shoe, hc litho, titled, 9x13", lot 357, SBY 10/7/89 ... **935**
Witch, Myths; AP12/30, clr slksc w/diamond dust, 1981, p/s, lt cr, S-38x38", Feldman Fine Arts, lot 1298, SBY 5/13/89 OE ... **7,150**
Witch, Myths; 84/200, slksc/diamond dust/Lenox Museum board, 1981, 38x38", Feldman Fine Arts, lot 4056, B/B 6/19/89 OE ... **9,350**
10 Statues of Liberty, offset litho poster/wove paper, 1985, sgn in ink, S-39x27", s/wrp, lot 652, C-NY 5/11/88 OE ... **935**

WARRE, Henry James (American, 1819-1898)
Falls of the Kamanis Taquoh River, litho, 11x16", lot 783, LH 10/16/88 OE ... **275**

WATSON, Ernest W. (American, 1884-)
Foaming Lane, 30/100, linocut, 1926, p/s, titled, 10x9", lot 128, WG 10/19/88 ... **80**
Fummette, etch/drypt, pl/s, 7x4", lot 58, WG 10/19/89 ... **500**

WATTEAU, Jean Antoine; after (French, 1684-1721)
Pair: Abduction Scenes; aqua, 19th C, 6x8", lot 22, MG 5/28/88 UE ... **100**

WEAVER, Arthur (Scottish, 20th C)
16th Green, Cypress Point; clr chromolitho, 1962, p/s, 16x22", Frost & Reed, lot 401, WG 10/19/88 ... **110**

WEBER, Max (American, 1881-1961)
Balcony, ed of 30, litho/wove paper, ca 1928-29, p/s, lt stn/cr, L-7x9", lot 290, C-NY 1/19/89 ... **825**
Bathers & Sails, ed of 30, litho/Normandy Vellum France, ca 1929, p/s, full mrgs, cr/stn, L-8x10", lot 473, C-NY 5/10/88 ... **990**
Group of 3: Rose; Sabbath; Still Life with Apples; litho, 1928-32, p/s, lt stn, no size given, lot 59, SBY 2/23/89 ... **2,200**
Mirror, No 2; total ed of 103, litho/wove paper, 1928, p/s, lt stn/rpl/fox, L-8x13", lot 5A, RWS 9/8/89 ... **700**
Solo, litho/wove paper, ca 1928, p/s, lt stn mrgs, L-8x6", lot 291, C-NY 1/19/89 ... **880**

WEBER, Paul; after (American, 1823-1916)
Philadelphia, View From Peters Farm; engr/thin wove applique, ca 1850, lt scr/sl/tr, 18x27", Serz, lot 515, SBY 1/28/88 ... **1,430**

WEIDENAAR, Reynold H. (American, 1915-)
Reverie, no media given, sgn/titled, lt fox, 13x11", Assn Am Artists, lot 272, WG 10/19/88 OE ... **200**

WELLIVER, Neil (American, 1929-)
Pair: Brigg's Meadow; Greer's Bog; 131/144, scrpt, 1973, p/s, S-40x40", Vera List/Barbara Krakow, lot 895, C-NY 11/1/88 ... **825**
Portfolio: Landscapes; 96/144, 6 slksc, 1973, p/s, full mrgs, S-40x40", HKL Ltd, lot 854, SBY 2/23/89 OE ... **5,225**
Set of 4: Brook; Duck Trap; Maiden's Cliff; Si's Hill; 131/144, scrpt, S-40x40", Vera List/Barbara Krakow, C-NY 11/1/88 ... **1,650**

WENGENROTH, Stow (American, 1906-1978)
Blue Jay, ed of 58, litho, 15x8", FAP 6/16/89 UE ... **90**
Coming Home, ed of 75, litho, sgn, full mrgs, L-9x15", RAB 8/8/89 ... **275**
Deep Water, Winter Harbor, Maine, October; ed of 50, litho, 1941, p/s, titled, lt stn, L-12x17", lot 40, RWS 9/8/89 ... **450**
Delaware Church, ed of 60, litho/wht wove paper, p/s, titled, lt trm, 9x14", lot 2987, B/B 4/19/88 ... **330**

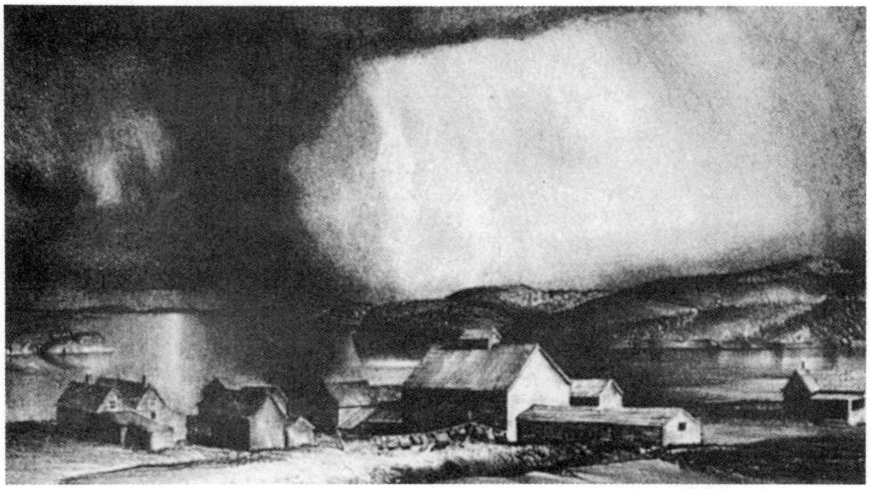

Descending Skies, ed of 75, litho, 1932, 7x13", lot 269, SWN 6/15/89 OE; $1,320

Fisherman's House, ed of 50, litho/wove paper, 1932, p/s, full mrgs, lt sl/stn mrgs, L-8x9", lot 49, C-NY 5/11/88 ... **385**
Group of 3: Cape Ann Marshes; Afternoon Light; Wild Coast; litho/wove paper, 2 1972/1973, p/s, lt sl, C-NY 1/22/88 UE ... **352**
Growth of the Rocks (Eastport, Maine), ed of 25, litho, 1931, p/s, lt stn, L-6x9", lot 34, RWS 9/8/89 ... **550**
Judge's House, ed of 40, litho/wove paper, 1961, p/s, full mrgs, lt cr/sl/rub, L-10x16", lot 292, C-NY 1/19/89 ... **462**
Little One, ed of 100, litho/heavy wove paper, p/s, titled, lt trm mrg, 9x14", lot 2988, B/B 4/19/88 ... **550**
Maine Lobstermen, ed of 212, litho, 1945, p/s, full mrgs, lstn, unfr, L-8x12", Print Club Cleveland, C-NY 1/22/88 OE ... **495**
New England Village, Coastline, Maine; ed of less than 100, litho, 1940, p/s, titled, 8x14", lot 268, SWN 6/15/89 ... **440**
Nuthatches on Bough, ed of 60, litho, 11x15", FAP 6/16/89 UE ... **120**
Old North Church, ED/76, litho, 1976, p/s, full mrgs, lt cr, L-16x12", lot 51, C-NY 5/11/88 UE ... **242**
Pair: Cape Ann Marshes; Sentinel Tree; Ed/75, litho/wove paper, 1972/1973, full mrgs, lt sl, C-NY 1/22/88 UE ... **220**
Pair: House, Eastport, Maine; The Quarry; ed of 54 & 40, litho, 1931 & 1935, various sizes, lot 267, SWN 6/15/89 ... **935**
Pair: Season's End; Sunlight Wicasset; ed of 40 & 75, litho, 1955, sgn, 9x16", lot 36, RWS 9/29/89 OE ... **1,600**
Pair: Summer Morning; Foundry Interior; litho/wove paper, 1933/1934, p/s, unfr, C-NY 1/22/88 OE ... **770**
Pair: Three Trees; Strange Visitors; ed of 50 & 60, litho, 1932 & 1944, sgn, 9x13"/11x9", lot 196, SWN 12/1/88 OE ... **1,100**
Quiet Day, Wellfleet, Massachusetts; March 1939; litho, full mrgs, 6x11", lot 7, RAB 8/9/88 ... **225**
Serenity, ed of 100, litho, 1951, p/s, unfr, 12x18", lot 37, RWS 9/29/88 OE ... **1,100**

Three Trees, ed of 50, litho/wm France, 1932, p/s, inscr To George Miller, full mrgs, lt stn, L-8x13", C-NY 5/11/88 440
Untamed, Monhegan, Maine, July; Ed/65, litho/wove paper, 1946, p/s, lt stn, L-12x18", lot 32, RWS 9/8/89 OE 1,700

WESSELMANN, Tom (American, 1931-)

Bedroom Face Print, 17/100, clr scrpt, 1987, p/s, L-47x53", International Img, lot 898, C-NY 11/1/88 OE 9,350
Claire Nude, 139/200, clr scrpt/litho/wove paper, 1980, p/s, full mrgs, S-31x30", Transworld Art, lot 655, C-NY 5/11/88 1,650
Metropolitan Opera Fine Art: Lulu; aside from ed of 250, litho, 1982/1984, full mrgs, 17x25", lot 857, SBY 2/23/89 OE 2,750
Nude Collage Edition, 30/40, acrylic/collage on board, 1970, sgn/titled, oval 6x9", lot 1045, SBY 11/5/88 OE 4,950
Pair: Helen Nude; Cynthia in the Bedroom; 127/150 & 86/100, clr slksc, 1981, p/s, 31x32"/31x27", Transworld, SBY 5/14/88 1,980
Smoker, American Portrait, 1776-1976; VIII/L, clr scrpt, p/s, Transworld Art bstp, S-26x20", lot 897, C-NY 11/1/88 OE 1,980
Smoker, American Portrait, 1776-1976; XXV/L, scrpt/wove board, 1976, 26x20", Transworld Art, lot 654, C-NY 5/11/88 OE 770
Smoker, XIII/L, clr slksc, 1976, p/s, full mrgs, 17x16", Transworld, lot 855, SBY 2/23/89 1,870
Smoker, 9/175, clr slksc, 1976, p/s, full mrgs, 17x16", Transworld, lot 856, SBY 2/23/89 1,760
TV Still Life, 11 Pop Artists III; 86/200, clr scrpt/wht wove paper, 1965, S-29x38", Orig Ed, lot 653, C-NY 5/11/88 OE 770
TV Still Life, 151/200, clr slksc, 1965, p/s, lt stn, S-29x38", lot 123, PHL 6/16/88 325
Woman with Green Blouse, 55/100, slksc, 1988, p/s, full mrgs, L-47x58", International Images, lot 1310, SBY 5/13/89 OE 9,075

WEST, Benjamin; after (American, 1738-1820)

William Penn's Treaty with the Indians...in 1681; engr, 1775, L-17x23", Boydell, lot 453, S/A 3/12/88 225
William Penn's Treaty with the Indians, by John Hall, etch/engr/laid paper, lt stn/rpl/tr, P-19x24", C-NY 1/19/89 UE 110

WEST, Levon (American, 1900-1968)

Casa Blanca, Venice; etch/laid paper, ca 1930, p/s, lt sl mrgs/verso, 12x9", lot 2989, B/B 4/19/88 165
Pair: Canadian Riders; Two Riders in a Storm; aqua/etch & etch/drypt, ca 1929, p/s, inscr Imp, lt stn, C-NY 1/22/88 275

WESTON, Frank (American, 1862-1951)

Alarm, 1917; a/p, etch, p/s, full mrgs, titled, 8x10", lot 15, RAB 8/9/88 900
Evening Flight, 1927; a/p, litho, p/s, full mrgs, 8x10", lot 16, RAB 8/9/88 700
In Dropping Flight, 1926; a/p, ed of 4, etch, p/s, titled on verso, full mrgs, 11x14", lot 14, RAB 8/9/88 1,300

WHISTLER, James Abbott McNeill (American, 1834-1903)

Adam & Eve, Old Chelsea; 2nd state, blk etch/Japan pelure, 1879, lt stn/ls, 7x12", lot 71, SBY 2/23/89 OE 3,410
Balcony, 9th state, etch/drypt/laid paper, 1879-80/1886, sgn w/butterfly, lt cr, 12x8", lot 300, SBY 5/11/89 OE 17,600
Becquet, 4th state, etch/drypt/tissue thin laid paper, 1859, glue at corners, P-10x8", lot 476, C-NY 5/10/89 1,650
Beggars, 9th state, etch/drypt/fine laid paper, 1879-80, lt rpr ls, stn, 12x8", lot 73, SBY 2/23/89 OE 2,200
Bibi Lalouette, 2nd state, etch/laid paper, 1859, lg mrgs, lt stn/sl/cr, 9x6", lot 291, SBY 5/11/89 2,475
Bibi Lalouette, 2nd state, etch/tissue thin laid paper, 1859, lt cr/fox/stn/sl, P-9x6", lot 475, C-NY 5/10/89 OE 4,400
Bibi Lalouette, 2nd state, etch/very fine laid paper, 1859, lt mstn/fox, 9x6", lot 69, SBY 2/23/89 OE 3,960
Billingsgate, etch, 1859, 6x9", lot 62, WG 10/19/88 OE 700
Billingsgate, 6th or 7th state, etch/laid paper, 1859, pl/s, lt trm mrgs, lt stn/sl/cr, 6x9", lot 2990, B/B 4/19/88 468
Billingsgate, 7th (of 8) state, etch/laid paper, 1859, lt scr/tr/sl/stn mrg, rpr tr, P-6x9", lot 59, C-NY 5/11/88 OE 1,760
Billingsgate, 7th state, dk brn etch/drypt/laid Japan, 1859, lt cr/fox/stn, 6x9", lot 68, SBY 2/23/89 OE 2,420
Billingsgate, 7th state, etch/JW, 1859, lt stn, P-6x9", lot 33, PHL 10/28/88 850
Billingsgate, 7th state, etch/laid paper, 1859, lt rpr, lt stn on verso, P-6x9", lot 297, C-NY 1/19/89 825
Billingsgate, 7th state of 8, etch/laid paper, 1859, tp/wht label on verso mrg, P-6x9", C-NY 1/22/88 660
Black Lion Wharf, 3rd state, etch/fine laid paper, 1859, p/s, butterfly stp, lt cr/sl, P-6x9", lot 57, C-NY 5/11/88 OE 6,050
Bridge, Amsterdam; 3rd state, etch, 1889, sgn w/butterfly, inscr Imp, lt ls/rpr/fox, 7x10", lot 302, SBY 5/11/89 OE 23,100
Bridge Over River, etch, fox, no size given, lot 61, WG 10/19/88 300
Cafe Corazzo, Palais Royal; dk brn etch/fibrous laid paper, 1892-93, lt nick, 5x9", lot 303, SBY 5/11/89 OE 2,750
Chinese Ginger Shop San Francisco, etch/J Head handmade paper, 1922, sgn in mrg, 7x11", lot 200, SWN 12/1/88 UE 195
Comte Robert de Montesquio, litho/Chine volant, 1895, full mrgs, lt stn/cr, 8x4", lot 307, SBY 5/11/89 OE 3,300
Courtyard, Brussels; brn-blk etch/thin laid Japan, 1887, lt rpr, 9x5", lot 70, SBY 11/3/88 3,575
Cutler Street, Houndsditch; 2nd state, brn etch/antique laid paper, ca 1880, inscr Imp, unfr, S-7x5", C-NY 1/22/88 OE 3,850
Dancing Girl, ed of 32, litho/wove mounted on sturdier wove paper, 1890, sgn w/butterfly, L-7x6", Way, SBY 5/12/88 OE 1,650
Doorway, 7th state, etch/Japan pelure, 1879-80/1881, sgn w/butterfly, inscr Imp, 12x8", lot 299, SBY 5/11/89 OE 20,900
Draped Figure, Seated; ed of 100, litho/Japan, 1893, sgn w/butterfly, 7x6", lot 252, LH 10/16/88 OE 5,000
Draped Figure, Seated; ed of 15, litho/tan simile Japan, 1893, butterfly sgn, lt stn, 7x6", lot 72, SBY 11/3/88 4,950
Draped Figure, Seated; litho/laid China paper, 1893, sgn w/ butterfly, lt stn/sl/scr, 7x6", lot 73, SBY 11/3/88 1,430
Drouet, final state, etch/drypt/thin wove paper, 1859, sgn w/butterfly, lt fox/stn, 9x6", lot 70, SBY 2/23/89 3,850
Drouet, 2nd state, etch/drypt/tissue thin laid paper, 1859, lt fox img, lt stn mrgs, P-9x6", lot 477, C-NY 5/10/89 1,540
Eagle Wharf, dk brn etch/thin laid paper, 1859, trm mrgs, lt fox, lt stn, P-5x8", lot 295, C-NY 1/19/89 OE 1,650
Eagle Wharf, etch/wm Shield & Beehive, 1859, lt scr verso, P-5x8", lot 56, C-NY 5/11/88 OE 2,750
Early Morning, Battersea; etch/drypt, ca 1861, lt sl mrgs, P-4x6", lot 62, C-NY 5/11/88 OE 550
Early Morning, lithotint/wove paper, 1878, sm mrgs, lt tp stn/cr, 7x10", lot 295, SBY 5/11/89 OE 3,025
Evening, Little Waterloo Bridge; ed of 26, litho, 1896, Birnie Philip stp on verso, 5x8", lot 84, SBY 2/25/88 880
Firelight: Joseph Pennell, No 1; litho/van Gelder, 1898, full mrgs, lt sl/glue, S-14x10", lot 70, C-NY 5/11/88 242
Fish Shop, Venice; 7th state, etch/thin Japan, 1879-80, butterfly sgn, lt stn/rpl, 5x9", lot 68, SBY 11/3/88 OE 3,575
Florence Leyland, 9th state, blk drypt, 1870-73, lt stn, 8x6", lot 80, SBY 2/25/88 1,320
Forge, etch/laid paper, 1866, pl/s, lt stn, mrgs tp to mat, 8x13", lot 3010, B/B 2/16/88 OE 660
Forge, 4th state, drypt/tissue-thin Japan, 1861, lt stn/cr mrg, P-8x13", lot 60, C-NY 5/11/88 880
Forge: Passage du Dragon; Way's 1st state, litho/laid paper, 1894, full mrgs, lt cr/fox, 9x6", lot 304, SBY 5/11/89 1,320
Free Trade Wharf, 5th state, etch/laid paper, 1877, full mrgs, lt stn/fox, 4x7", lot 294, SBY 5/11/89 1,320
Fullham, etch, 5x8", lot 60, WG 10/19/88 400
Gants de Suede, ed of 28, litho/laid wm Crowned GR, sgn w/butterfly, tp stn, lt fox/ls, L-9x4", Way, SBY 5/12/88 OE 3,520
Gants de Suede, litho/fine laid wm D&C Blauw, 1890/1903, full mrgs, lt mstn, S-14x9", C-NY 1/22/88 990
Girl with Bowl, blk litho/wove paper, 1895, sgn w/butterfly, full mrgs, lt cr, 5x3", lot 305, SBY 5/11/89 OE 2,750

Hurlingham, 3rd state, etch/laid paper, ca 1879, P-5x8", lot 301, C-NY 1/19/89 OE **825**
Kitchen, 2nd state, brn etch/laid paper, 1858, lg mrgs, lt fox/cr/stn, 9x6", lot 287, SBY 5/11/89 OE..... **3,575**
Kitchen, 2nd state of 3, etch/tan Chine applique, 1858, lt stn/sl, S-17x12", lot 63, SBY 11/3/88 OE **4,125**
La Mere Malade, litho/Japan, ca 1893-94, full mrgs, cr/mstn mrgs, tp verso mrg, L-8x6", C-NY 1/22/88 OE **935**
La Vieille aux Loques, 3rd/final state, etch/drypt/laid paper, 1858, trm mrgs, lt fox/stn, unfr, P-9x6", C-NY 1/22/88 ..... **495**
La Vieille aux Loques, 3rd/final state, etch/drypt/tissue thin laid Japan, 1858, trm/stn/cr, unfr, P-9x6", C-NY 1/22/88 ..... **660**
La Vielle aux Loques, 3rd state, etch/drypt/Japan applique, lt sl mrgs, P-8x6", lot 294, C-NY 1/19/89 ..... **770**
Landscape with the Horse, 2nd state, etch/drypt/Arches, 1859, lt nick/stn, 5x8", lot 65, SBY 2/23/89 OE **1,650**
Large Pool, 7th state, dk brn etch/drypt, 1879, sgn w/butterfly, rpr trs in img, P-7x11", SBY 5/12/88 OE..... **3,300**

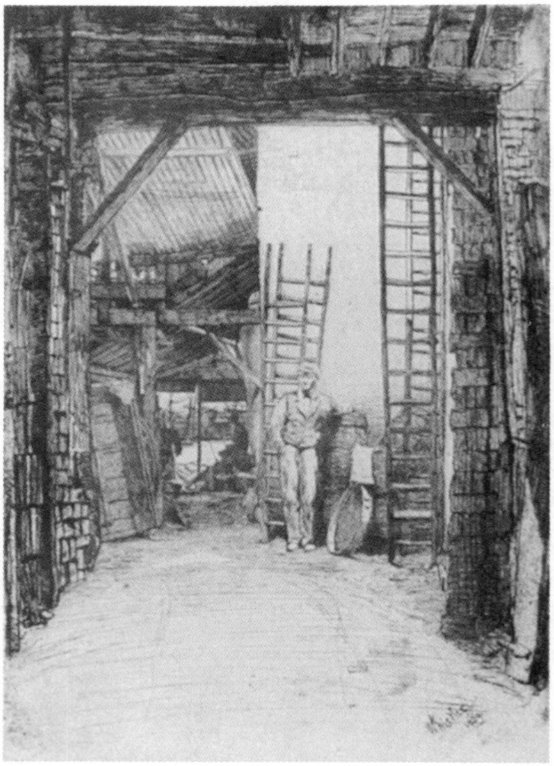

Lime-Burner, etch/drypt/laid w/illegible wm paper, 1859, p/s, full mrgs, tp/glue on verso, lt sl, P-10x7", lot 3, RWS 3/16/89 OE: $3,750

Lime-Burner, 2nd state, dk brn etch/drypt/laid paper, 1959, lt stn/fox, laid down, 10x7", lot 67, SBY 2/23/89 OE..... **4,675**
Lime-Burner, 2nd state, etch, 1859, lt stn, P-10x7", lot 33, PHL 6/16/88..... **2,600**
Lime-Burner, 2nd state, etch/drypt/Japan pelure, 1859/1871, lg mrgs, lt mstn/fox, 10x7", lot 290, SBY 5/11/89 ..... **4,125**
Lime-Burner, 2nd state, etch/Honig, 1859, lt cr img, lt ls to corner, lt stn/glue in mrg, P-10x7", lot 58, C-NY 5/11/88 ..... **3,300**
Limehouse, 3rd state, etch/fine laid paper, 1859, lt fox/stn/cr in mrgs & verso, P-5x8", lot 54, C-NY 5/11/88 OE..... **1,980**
Limehouse, 3rd state, etch/thin Japan, 1859, p/s, butterfly stp, lt cr/ls, P-5x8", lot 55, C-NY 5/11/88 OE..... **4,180**
Limehouse, 3rd state, etch/thin laid paper, 1859, lt mstn, lt fox img, 5x8", lot 288, SBY 5/11/89 ..... **2,200**
Little Butler Street, etch/laid paper, ca 1888, sgn/titled, S-7x3", lot 303, C-NY 1/19/89 OE..... **3,080**
Little Evelyn, litho/laid paper, 1896, full mrgs, hinged to mat on verso, lt stn, 8x6", lot 3008, B/B 2/16/88 ..... **468**
Little Lagoon, dk brn etch/old laid paper, 1879-80/1881, lt fox, 9x6", lot 66, SBY 11/3/88 OE **4,400**
Little Lagoon, 2nd state, drypt/laid paper, 1880, sgn, lt fox/scr, laid down, P-9x6", lot 302, C-NY 1/19/89 ..... **4,620**
Little Lagoon, 2nd state, etch/drypt/stiff Japan, ca 1880, lt sl/lstn, unfr, P-9x6", C-NY 1/22/88 ..... **1,650**
Little London, litho/antique laid wm Coat-of-Arms, 1896, lt fox/stn/tp, L-7x5", Goulding, lot 71, C-NY 5/11/88 UE **198**
Little Mast, 3rd state, brn etch/fine laid paper, 1880, p/s, butterfly stp, lt cr/ls, P-11x7", lot 66, C-NY 5/11/88 UE..... **495**
Little Mast, 4th state, etch/wm 1844 laid paper, 1879-80/1881, sgn w/butterfly, 10x7", lot 297, SBY 5/11/89 ..... **4,400**
Little Nude Model, Reading; posthumous imp, litho/laid paper, 1890, lt fox/stn, L-7x7", Goulding, SBY 5/12/88 OE **1,925**
Little Nude Model, Reading; transfer litho/D&C Blauw, 1890, lt stn/fox, 7x7", Goulding, lot 81, SBY 2/25/88 ..... **1,760**
Little Pool, etch, 4x5", lot 59, WG 10/19/89..... **450**
Little Pool, 8th state, etch/drypt, 1861, lt sl mrgs, lt scr verso, P-4x5", lot 61, C-NY 5/11/88 OE **1,100**
Little Pool, 8th state, etch/Rampant Lion in Crowned Circle, 1861, full mrgs, lt stn/tr, P-4x5", lot 299, C-NY 1/19/89..... **990**
Little Putney, No 1; 2nd state, etch/thin fibrous laid paper, 1879, lt fox, 5x8", lot 72, SBY 2/23/89 ..... **1,100**
Little Putney, 2nd state, etch/drypt/simili Japan, ca 1878, lt stn, glue in corners, P-5x8", lot 65, C-NY 5/11/88 ..... **462**
Little Venice, dk brn etch, 1879-80/1881, sgn w/butterfly, inscr Imp, lt fox,7x11", lot 296, SBY 5/11/89..... **14,300**
Longshoremen, etch/drypt/thin laid Japan, 1859, lt fox/cr/stn, 6x9", lot 78, SBY 2/25/88 OE **1,760**
Market Place, Vitre; litho/fine laid paper, 1893, lt fox, 8x6", lot 82, SBY 2/25/88 ..... **495**
Maunder's Fish Shop, Chelsea; litho, 1890, sgn w/butterfly, lt stn/cr, L-8x7", lot 34, PHL 10/28/88 ..... **650**
Maunder's Fish Shop, Chelsea; litho/Rampant Lion in Crowned Circle, 1890, full mrgs, L-8x7", lot 305, C-NY 1/19/89 OE **990**
Mother & Child, No 1; ed of 33, transfer litho/old wm fleur-de-lys Dutch, 1895, lt fox/stn, L-9x8", Way, SBY 5/12/88..... **3,025**
Nocturne, 3rd state of 5, etch/drypt/cream simili Japan, 1879-80, p/s, lt sl/rub/cr, S-13x18", lot 65, SBY 11/3/88..... **19,800**
Old Battersea Bridge, ed of 100, litho/cream laid paper, 1879, lt cr/tr, L-8x14", lot 35, PHL 10/28/88 OE **2,000**

Old Westminster Bridge, 2nd state, etch/drypt/fine laid paper, 1859, butterfly stp, rpr, P-3x8", lot 53, C-NY 5/11/88 OE 3,520
Pair: Early Morning Battersea; Street at Saverne; etch, 1861 & 1858, 4x6"/8x6", lot 79, SBY 2/25/88 880
Pair: La Robe Rouge; Gants de Suede; litho, 1894, trm mrgs, lt stn, no size given, lot 2991, B/B 4/19/88 600
Pair: Maunder's Fish Shop, Chelsea; Gaiety Stage Door; litho, 1890 & 1879, lt fox, L-8x7"/L-5x8", SBY 5/12/88 OE 2,750
Pair: Music Room; Billingsgate; 2nd/7th state, etch/drypt/laid paper, 1859, inscr, C-NY 1/22/88 OE 1,320
Pair: Thames Warehouse; Billingsgate; etch, 1858, lt stn, 3x8"/6x9", lot 76, SBY 2/25/88 OE 2,420
Pair: Winged Hat; St Giles-in-the-Field; litho/glazed wove paper/tissue thin Japan, 1890/1896, lt sl, C-NY 1/22/88 880
Palaces, 2nd state, etch/drypt/Arms-of-Amsterdam, 1879-80/1881, lt cr/stn, 10x14", lot 298, SBY 5/11/89 OE 20,900
Piazetta, 3rd state of 5, brn etch, 1879-80, sgn w/butterfly, inscr imp, trm, P-10x7", SBY 5/12/88 OE 4,400
Piazetta, 5th state, etch/laid paper, 1880, butterfly stp, inscr IP, rpr edge, P-10x7", lot 67, C-NY 5/11/88 4,400
Pool, 3rd state of 4, etch/laid fibrous Japan, 1859, lt mstn/fox, 6x8", lot 63A, SBY 11/3/88 OE 3,300
Portrait (Miss Howells), ed of 6, litho/thin laid China, 1895, tp stn, lt fox/disclr, L-9x8", Way, SBY 5/12/88 OE 5,060
Riva, No 1; 3rd state, brn-blk etch/drypt/Fellows, ca 1879-80, butterfly stp, lt stn, P-8x12", lot 68, C-NY 5/11/88 5,500
Riva, No 2; 1st state of 2, etch/drypt, 1879-80/1886, butterfly sgn, lt scr, 8x12", lot 67, SBY 11/3/88 6,050
Riva, No 2; 2nd state, brn etch/drypt/laid paper, 1880, p/s, inscr Imp, rpr edge, P-8x12", lot 69, C-NY 5/11/88 7,150
Rotherhithe, etch/drypt/laid paper, 1860, lt stn verso, P-11x8", SBY 5/12/88 OE 6,600
Rotherhithe, final state, etch/drypt/laid paper, 1860/1871, lt fox/cr, 11x8", lot 293, SBY 5/11/89 10,450
Rotherhithe, 1st state, etch/drypt/wht wove paper backed with Japan, 1860/1871, S-12x9", lot 292, SBY 5/11/89 OE 3,850
Sketch From Billingsgate, 6th State, drypt/wm BTH in cartouch, ca 1878-79, lt stn/sl, P-6x9", lot 64, C-NY 5/11/88 1,650
Smith's Yard, litho/old laid paper, 1895, butterfly sgn, Virnie Philip stp, lt fox/stn, S-13x8", lot 74, SBY 11/3/88 1,100
Smithy, 5th state, etch, 1883, p/s, lt tr/cr, 7x9", lot 69, SBY 11/3/88 OE 2,200
Soupe a Trois Sous, etch/drypt/India colle, ca 1859, stn mrgs/verso, P-6x9", lot 298, C-NY 1/19/89 990
Street at Saverne, 4th state, etch/bl Chine applique, 1858, lg mrgs, lt stn, 8x6", lot 61, SBY 2/23/89 1,980
Street in London, etch, ca 1901, sgn w/butterfly, 7x4", lot 199, SWN 12/1/88 195
TA Nash's Fruit Shop, 4th state, etch, ca 1886, sgn w/butterfly, 7x5", lot 301, SBY 5/11/89 OE 4,400
Thames, posthumous ed, lithotint/cream applique, 1896/1903-04, full mrgs, 11x8", Goulding, lot 308, SBY 5/11/89 OE 7,150
Thames Police, 3rd state, blk etch/drypt/fine laid paper, 1859/1871, lt stn, 6x9", lot 63B, SBY 11/3/88 OE 3,025
Thames Police, 3rd state, etch/drypt/laid paper, 1859, lt fox/stn, 6x9", lot 289, SBY 5/11/89 2,640
Troubled Thames, 3rd state, etch/drypt, ca 1870, lt cr/sl, rpr mrg edges, P-5x9", lot 63, C-NY 5/11/88 1,100
Tyresmith, 1 of 8 imp, litho/smooth gray-wht paper on wht wove paper, 1890, p/s, S-15x11", lot 71, SBY 11/3/88 OE 3,025
Unfinished Sketch of Lady Haden, litho/Chine, 1895, lt rub/cr, L-12x8", lot 480, C-NY 5/10/89 UE 550
Victoria Clug, litho/laid paper, 1879, sgn w/butterfly, full mrgs, lt tr, L-8x5", lot 34, PHL 6/16/88 OE 2,100
Wine Glass, 2nd state, etch/drypt/laid Japan, ca 1857, full mrg, lt sl/glue on mrgs/verso, P-3x2", lot 52, C-NY 5/11/88 495
Winged Hat, litho/laid wm Foolscap, 1890, lt fox, lt mstn/ls to mrg edges, unfr, L-7x7", C-NY 1/22/88 715
Winged Hat, litho/smooth wove paper, 1890, inscr Art Workers Guild 5-5-93, lt sl/cr, L-7x7", lot 478, C-NY 5/10/89 OE 1,760

WHITE, Stephen (American, 1944-)
Irises, 11/200, woodblock/mulberry paper, 1976, sgn/dtd, no size given, lot 27, FAP 2/24/89 UE 70

WHITEHEAD, Buell (20th C)
Tobacco Barns, litho, ca 1930, p/s, titled, stn/glue on overmat mrg edges, mstn verso, unfr, L-14x17", C-NY 1/22/88 UE 187

WHITEHEAD, Walter (American, 1874-1956)
Come On!; clr litho/poster paper, 1918, laid down, 29x19", lot 178, FAP 2/24/89 OE 180

WHITFIELD, E. (19th C)
View of Baltimore, Maryland; clr litho, 1847, rpl, rpr tr in img/mrg, stn/fox recto/verso, L-18x41", C-NY 1/22/88 OE 2,750

WICKE, William Hancock (American, 1879-1958)
Bay From Telegraph Hill, woodblock, p/s, 8x12", lot 65, FAP 2/24/89 UE 35

WILD, John Caspar (Casper)(American, 1806-1846)
Steam Alex, Scott, Captain JC Swon; clr litho, tr mrgs, lt cr/tstn, 24x32", SLK 5/6/88 3,600
University of Pennsylvania, litho, 5x7", lot 61, FAP 2/24/89 UE 25

WILEY, William T. (American, 1937-)
Eerie Grotto? Okini; 37/200, clr wc/Japan, 1982, p/s, full mrgs, 21x27", Crown Point, SBY 11/5/88 OE 2,970
I Keep Foolin' Around Hopin' I Won't Have to Start Here, 2/4, clr etch, 1981, p/s, Teaberry bstp, 18x18", B/B 4/19/88 880
Optag for PB, 2/4, etch/aqua/cream wove paper, 1981, p/s, Teaberry bstp, lt trm mrgs, 16x21", lot 3089, B/B 4/19/88 412
Pair: Scarecrow; Mr Unatural; 56/60 & 21/65, clr aqua & litho, 1975/1976, 10x8"/S-36x25", Landfall, SBY 5/14/88 1,320
Plank Pool, p/p, etch/cream wove paper, 1980, p/s, inscr TB Imp I, Teaberry bstp, full mrgs, 20x20", B/B 4/19/88 UE 358
Studio Light, 2/4, etch/cream wove paper, 1981, p/s, inscr TP Imp, Teaberry bstp, 12x9", lot 3088, B/B 4/19/88 192
Thank Yute Rubble, 16/80, litho, 1972, p/s, titled, 22x30", lot 1076, LH 10/16/88 170
Upside Down, 2/4, etch/cream wove paper, 1981, p/s, inscr TP Imp, Teaberry bstp, 3x3", lot 3087, B/B 4/19/88 UE 100

WILSON, C.Y.A. (American, 20th C)
Gloucestermen, etch, sgn/titled, full mrgs, lt stn, L-5x3", RAB 3/27/89 UE 50

WILSON, Edward A. (American, 1886-)
Hog Back Meeting House #6, litho, 1936, p/s, inscr To Bill & Mary 8/12/45, lt fox/stn, unfr, L-10x14", RWS 3/16/89 200

WILSON, J. Coggeshall (American, 19th C)
Set of 4: Untitled (pilot boats); etch, 5x6", RAB 3/14/89 OE 450

WILSON, John (American, 1922-)
Boulevard de Strasbourg, a/p, blk/ochre litho, 1950, p/s, titled, lt stn, ink in mrgs, L-12x17", lot 52, RWS 9/8/89 500
El Cargador, 4/30, litho/wove paper, 1952, p/s, lt sl/cr/tp, L-12x12", lot 49, RWS 9/8/89 UE 150
Trabagador, 16/30, litho/wove paper, 1951, p/s, lt stn mrg/verso, L-19x13", lot 51, RWS 9/8/89 400

WINKLER, John W. (American, 1890-)
Duck Seller, etch/BFK Rives, p/s, full mrgs, lt cr, 12x7", lot 3012, B/B 2/16/88 220
Festival Banners, etch/laid paper, p/s, lt cr, 10x5", lot 3013, B/B 2/16/88 220
Pair: Untitled; Warming Over a Fire; etch/laid or Japan paper, p/s, no size given, lot 3014, B/B 2/16/88 300

WINTERS, Terry (20th C)
Set of 3: Morula I, II, & III; clr litho/handmade Toyoshi, 1983-84, ULAE bstp, no size given, lot 1311, SBY 5/13/89 OE ... **61,600**
Untitled (contemporary), 14/75, clr litho, 1986, intl/dtd, S-30x22", ULAE/Parasol, lot 1312, SBY 5/13/89 OE ... **6,600**
WOEHRMAN, Ralph (American, 20th C)
Pair: Bramacidi; Itine's Last; intg, sgn/titled, various sizes, lot 403, WG 10/19/88 UE ... **225**
Pair: Still Life for FG; Toys & Taxidermy; intg, p/s, titled, various sizes, lot 402, WG 10/19/88 UE ... **200**
WOLSTENHOLME, Dean; after (British, 1757-1837)
Set of 4: Untitled (hunt scenes); prints/brn paper, 9x26", Burkitt & Hudson, lot 111, FAP 2/24/89 ... **500**
WOOD, Grant (American, 1892-1942)
Approaching Storm, ed of 250, litho, 1940, full mrgs, lt stn, 12x9", Assn Am Artists, lot 78, SBY 11/3/88 OE ... **4,125**
Approaching Storm, ed of 250, litho, 1941, p/s, lt stn, 12x9", Assn Am Artists, lot 92, SBY 2/25/88 OE ... **2,530**
Approaching Storm, ed of 250, litho/BFK Rives, 1941, p/s, full mrgs, stn, 12x9", Assn Am Artists, lot 2993, B/B 4/19/88 ... **3,300**
Approaching Storm, ed of 250, litho/wove paper, 1940, p/s, trm mrgs, lstn, tp verso mrg, L-12x9", C-NY 1/22/88 OE ... **1,760**
Approaching Storm, ed of 250, litho/wove paper, 1940, p/s, trm mrgs, lt mstn, tp verso mrg, L-12x9", C-NY 1/22/88 ... **1,870**
December Afternoon, ed of 250, litho, 1941, full mrgs, lt stn/fox/tp hinges, 9x12", Assn Am Artists, lot 94, SBY 2/25/88 ... **1,760**
December Afternoon, ed of 250, litho/BFK Rives, 1941, p/s, L-9x12", RWS 3/16/89 ... **1,900**
December Afternoon, ed of 250, litho/wove paper, 1940, p/s, trm mrgs, lt stn/sl, stn verso, unfr, L-9x12", C-NY 1/22/88 ... **1,100**
February, ed of 250, litho, 1941, p/s, full mrgs, Assn Am Artists, lot 81, SBY 2/23/89 OE ... **4,400**
February, ed of 250, litho, 1941, p/s, full mrgs, lt stn mrgs, 9x12", Assn Am Artists, lot 93, SBY 2/25/88 OE ... **3,190**
February, ed of 250, litho, 1941, p/s, full mrgs, 9x12", Assn Am Aritsts, lot 309, SBY 5/11/89 OE ... **5,720**
February, ed of 250, litho, 1941, p/s, lt lstn, 9x12", Assn Am Artists, lot 310, SBY 5/11/89 OE ... **6,050**
February, ed of 250, litho/GCM, 1940, p/s, full mrgs, lt mstn, L-9x12", lot 315, C-NY 1/19/89 OE ... **4,180**
Fertility, ed of 250, litho/cream wove GMC, 1945, p/s, full mrgs, lt cr/fox, 9x12", Assn Am Artists, B/B 2/16/88 ... **1,540**
Fertility, ed of 250, litho/wove paper, 1939, p/s, lt stn/fox, top on verso, L-9x12", lot 483, C-NY 5/10/89 ... **3,080**
Fertility, ed of 250, litho/wove paper, 1939, p/s, lt trm mrgs, lt stn/skinned, L-9x12", lot 314, C-NY 1/19/89 OE ... **3,740**
Fertility, ed of 250, litho/wove paper, 1939, p/s, trm mrgs, lstn/mstn, stn/tp verso, unfr, L-9x12", C-NY 1/22/88 OE ... **990**
Fertility, litho, 1939, p/s, titled/dtd, full mrgs, lt stn, 9x12", lot 77, SBY 11/3/88 OE ... **3,300**
Froup of 4: Fruits; Vegetables; Tame Flowers; Wildflowers; ed of 250, hc litho, lt stn/fox, L-7x10", C-NY 5/11/88 UE ... **2,420**
Fruits, ed of 250, hc litho, 1938, p/s, full mrgs, lt stn, 7x10", Assn Am Artists, lot 76, SBY 11/3/88 ... **990**
Fruits, ed of 250, hc litho, 1938, p/s, lt stn/fox, 7x10", Assn Am Artists, lot 85, SBY 2/25/88 UE ... **1,100**
Honorary Degree, ed of 250, litho, 1937, p/s, lt stn, no size given, Assn Am Artists, lot 238, WG 10/19/88 ... **1,100**
Honorary Degree, ed of 250, litho, 1937, p/s, lt stn/tr, 12x7", Assn Am Artists, lot 80, SBY 2/23/89 ... **1,430**
Honorary Degree, litho/Rives, 1938, ink sgn/inscr To Dr Carmon Ross Jan 9-1940, full mrgs, L-12x7", C-NY 1/22/88 ... **825**
In the Spring, ed of 250, litho, 1938, p/s, full mrgs, lt cr/stn, 9x12", Assn Am Artists, lot 90, SBY 2/25/88 ... **1,650**
In the Spring, ed of 250, litho/BFK Rives, 1939, p/s, lt stn verso, 9x12", Assn Am Artists, lot 2992, B/B 4/19/88 OE ... **2,750**
January, ed of 250, litho/wm GCM, 1939, p/s, full mrgs, tp in mrg corners, L-9x12", lot 72, C-NY 5/11/88 OE ... **3,300**
July Fifteenth, ed of 250, litho/wove paper, 1935, p/s, lt trm mrgs, lt stn, 9x12", lot 3016, B/B 2/16/88 ... **2,200**
July Fifteenth, ed of 250, litho/wove wm GCM, p/s, full mrgs, lt lstn, unfr, L-9x12", C-NY 1/22/88 ... **1,980**
March, ed of 250, litho/cream wove paper, 1939, p/s, trm mrgs, lt stn, 9x12", Assn Am Artists, lot 3017, B/B 2/16/88 ... **1,980**
March, ed of 250, litho/wove paper, 1939, p/s, full mrgs, L-9x12", lot 482, C-NY 5/10/89 OE ... **4,400**
Midnight Alarm, ed of 250, litho/BFK Rives, 1939, p/s, full mrgs, lt stn, L-12x7", lot 313, C-NY 1/19/89 OE ... **1,210**
Pair: Tame Flowers; Wildflowers; ed of 250, hc litho, 1938, p/s, lt stn, 7x10", Assn Am Artists, lot 89, SBY 2/25/88 ... **2,860**
Seed Time & Harvest, ed of 250, litho, 1937, p/s, full mrgs, lt fox/rpl, 8x12", lot 75, SBY 11/3/88 OE ... **3,300**
Seed Time & Harvest, ed of 250, litho/GMC, 1937, p/s, full mrgs, lt fox, lt stn, L-7x12", lot 307, C-NY 1/19/89 ... **2,200**
Seed Time & Harvest, ed of 250, litho/wove paper, 1937, p/s, lt stn/sl, L-8x12", lot 308, C-NY 1/19/89 ... **2,200**
Seed Time & Harvest, ed of 250, litho/wove wm GCM, 1937, p/s, dtd, full mrgs, unfr, L-8x12", C-NY 1/22/88 ... **1,980**
Set of 4: Fruits; Vegetables; Tame Flowers; Wildflowers; ed of 250, litho, 1939, L-7x10", lot 311, C-NY 1/19/89 OE ... **7,150**
Shrine Quartet, ed of 250, litho/BFK Rives, 1939, p/s, full mrgs, lt stn/fox, L-8x12", lot 312, C-NY 1/19/89 OE ... **2,200**
Shrine Quartet, ed of 250, litho/GCM wove paper, 1939, full mrgs, lt stn/tp, L-8x12", lot 481, C-NY 5/10/89 ... **1,430**
Shrine Quartet, ed of 250, litho, 1940, p/s, 8x12", lot 270, WG 10/19/88 ... **1,600**
Sultry Night, ed of 100, litho/BFK Rives, 1939, full mrgs, lt skinned/cr, L-9x12", lot 309, C-NY 1/19/89 ... **4,950**
Tame Flowers, ed of 250, litho/wove paper, 1939, lt stn/skinned, L-7x10", lot 310, C-NY 1/19/89 OE ... **1,430**
Vegetables, ed of 250, hc litho, 1938, p/s, glue stn mrgs/verso, 7x10", Assn Am Artists, lot 88, SBY 2/25/88 ... **1,650**
Vegetables, ed of 250, hc litho, 1938, p/s, lt stn/fox, 7x10", Assn Am Artists, lot 87, SBY 2/25/89 ... **1,570**
WOODBURY, Charles Herbert (American, 1864-1940)
Old Salt Box (house in landscape), etch, sgn, full mrgs, L-6x10", lot 2, RAB 8/9/88 ... **275**
Tide Rips, Portsmouth; etch, full mrgs, 9x11", lot 6", RAB 8/9/88 ... **250**
WOODVILLE, Richard Caton; after (British, 1856-1927)
Mexican News, by Alfred Jones, hc engr, 1851/1853, lt nick/stn, L-21x19", Am Art Union, lot 107A, C-NY 1/19/89 ... **605**
WOODWARD, Ellsworth (American, 1861-1939)
Coast Guard, etch/drypt, p/s, titled, 11x7", lot 244, NA 3/26/88 UE ... **75**
Pralines, etch/aqua, p/s, titled, P-9x8", lot 246, NA 3/26/88 OE ... **380**
Ursuline Convent, New Orleans; a/p, etch, p/s, 10x11", lot 258, NA 6/12/89 OE ... **550**
WOOLF, Samuel J. (American, 1880-1948)
Franklin Delano Roosevelt, ed of 250, litho, 1945, p/s, 13x9", lot 300, WG 10/19/88 UE ... **30**
WRINCH, Mary Evelyn (Canadian, 1878-1969)
Village by the St Lawrence, 19/100, clr wc, p/s, titled, 8x10", lot 770, WAD 6/12/89 OE ... **400**
WUNDERLICH, Paul (German, 1927-)
Pair: Twilight, Pl 4; Twilight, Pl 6; 79/125, clr litho/Rives, 1971, p/s, full mrgs, lt scr/cr, L-29x22", C-NY 5/10/89 ... **440**
WYETH, James (American, 1946-)
Portfolio: The Farm; Runaway Pig; Bee Shadows; Chicken Basket; 83/150, etch/drypt, full mrgs, lot 59, RWS 9/29/88 ... **1,700**

WYLLIE, Harold (British, 1880-)
US 44-Gun Frigate Constitution, litho, 1924, lt faded, orig fr, 16x21", FH Bresler, RAB 11/25/88 UE **100**
YERMEL (20th C)
Richard Cocktail, clr litho/poster paper, ca 1928, pl/s, 26x20", lot 446, C-E 9/20/89 OE **352**
YOSHIDA, Hiroshi (Japanese, 1876-1950)
Calm Wind, clr wc, 12x9", lot 910, LH 12/4/88 .... **250**
Fujiyama From Miko, clr wc, 10x15", lot 911, LH 12/4/88 .... **425**
Misty Day in Nikko, clr wc, 15x10", lot 909, LH 12/4/88 .... **300**
Three Little Islands, woodblock, 1880, sgn/dtd, no size given, lot 17, MG 5/28/88 .... **175**
Yoshibara, clr wc, 10x15", lot 912, LH 12/4/88.......... **275**
YOUKELES, Anne (American, 20th C)
Celebration II, 33/50, slksc, 22x22", lot 81, FAP 2/24/89 .... **45**
YOUNG, Charles Jac (American, 1880-1940)
Snow in the Air, etch, p/s, 7x10", Assn Am Artists, lot 283, WG 10/19/88.......... **85**
YOUNGERMAN, Jack (American, 1926-)
Suite: Untitled A-H; 20/50, 8 clr scpt/wove paper, 1980, sgn/dtd/#d, full mrgs, S-29x28", C-E 5/13/88 OE **495**
Untitled Suite, 14/100, 6 clr scrpt/wove paper, 1978, full sheets, S-45x52", lot 900, C-NY 11/1/88 OE **495**
ZABOLY, Bela (American, 1910-)
Trees, #18, ed of 250, drypt/BFK Rives, 1933, sgn in ink, pl/s, 7x4", Cleveland Print Club, lot 189, WG 10/19/88 .... **50**
ZADKINE, Ossip (French, 1890-1967)
Femme a la Gitare, ed of 90, clr drypt/etch, 1962, p/s, 21x16", L'Oeuvre Gravee, lot 202, SWN 12/1/88 .... **220**
Woman Playing a Guitar, 75/90, clr etch/drypt, 1962, p/s, 21x16", L'Oeuvre Gravee, SWN 6/15/89 .... **193**
ZAKANITCH, Robert (American, 1935-)
Untitled (contemporary), 6/31, slksc/gouache/paper, 1978, p/s, S-40x57", lot 93, RWS 9/8/89 UE **400**
ZOELLNER, Richard (American, 1908-)
Pair: Pine Trees; Forest; etch/aqua, p/s, titled, various sizes, lot 363, WG 10/19/88 .... **55**
ZORACH, Marguerite (American, 1887-1968)
Calvin's House, Paris; etch/sand ground/wove paper, ca 1908-1911, p/s, lt fox/sl, P-10x4", RWS 3/16/89 .... **250**
ZORACH, William (American, 1887-1966)
Mountain Stream, linocut/China paper, ca 1916, p/s, 11x14", lot 311, SBY 5/11/89 OE **2,530**
ZORN, Anders (Swedish, 1860-1920)

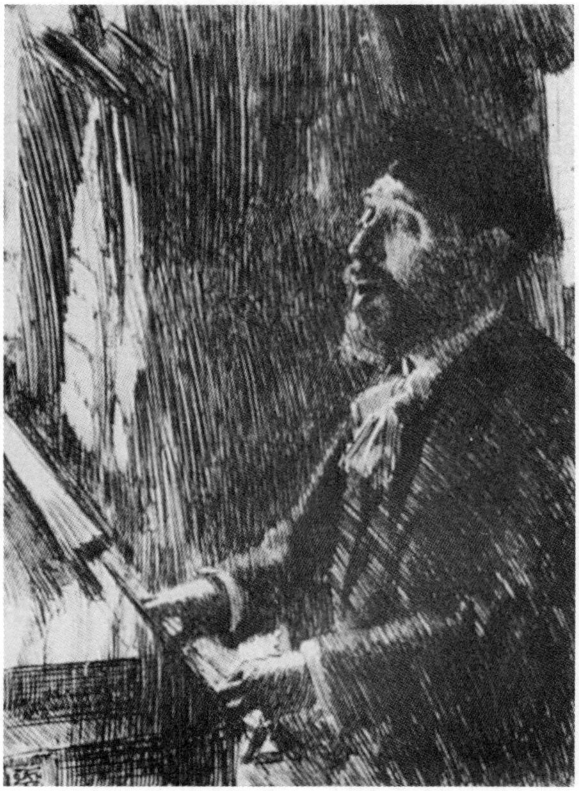

Singer, 1st state, etch/laid paper w/elaborate wm, 1891, p/s, lg mrgs, 9x6", lot 272, SWN 6/15/89 OE; $1,980

Cabin, etch/van Gelder, 1917, p/s, full mrgs, lt stn, laid down, P-12x8", lot 364, C-NY 1/19/89 OE **1,210**
Dance at Gopsmor, ed of 75, etch/laid paper, 1906, lt stn, 12x8", lot 2915, B/B 2/16/88 .... **522**
Dance at Gopsmor, 2nd state, etch/van Gelder, 1906, p/s, full mrgs, lt fox/lstn, stn verso, unfr, P-12x8", C-NY 1/22/88 .... **605**
Ernest Renan, presumed 5th state, etch/thick laid paper, 1892, p/s, thin spots, lt stn, unfr, P-9x13", C-NY 1/22/88 .... **935**
Galli I, 2nd state, drypt/wove paper, 1914, p/s, P-5x4", lot 21, RWS 9/29/88.......... **325**
Group of 4: ER Bacon; Self-Portrait with Model II; Col Lamont III; Self-Portrait 1916; lot 475, SBY 2/25/88 OE.......... **3,080**
Letter (bust-length portrait of lady), etch, sgn/dtd 1913, full mrgs, L-6x5", RAB 3/27/89 OE.......... **450**

Oles Maria, etch/laid paper, 1919, p/s, lt tr mrgs, 8x12", lot 2926, B/B 4/19/88 **495**
Omnibus, ed of 75, etch, 1892, p/s, full mrgs, lt lstn/fox, unfr, P-11x8", SBY 5/12/88 OE **4,950**
Omnibus, ed of 75, 3rd state, dk brn etch/laid paper, 1892, lt stn, P-11x8", lot 859, C-NY 5/10/89 **3,080**
Pair: An Irish Girl, or Annie; Wet; etch, 1894 & 1911, p/s, lt stn, 11x8"/6x5", lot 474, SBY 2/25/89 OE **1,980**
Pair: Edo; Pilot-Lots; etch & etch/van Gelder, 1907/1919, p/s, C-NY 1/22/88 **715**
Pilot, etch, 1919, p/s, lt stn, P-7x5", lot 20, RWS 9/29/88 **400**
Prince Paul Troubetzkoy II, etch/laid paper, 1909, p/s, lstn/tstn, stn verso, P-10x7", C-NY 1/22/88 UE **165**
Sappho, etch, 1917, sgn, stn recto/verso, 8x7", lot 203, SWN 12/1/88 **385**
Self-Portrait I, etch/drypt, 1904, p/s, lt fox mrg, P-7x5", lot 22, RWS 9/29/88 **325**
Shallow, etch, 1913, pl/s, p/s, full mrgs, lt lstn, 12x8", lot 17, RWS 9/29/88 **550**
Summer, sm ed of unknown size, etch, 1907, p/s, wide mrgs, lt stn, rpr tr mrg, 7x5", lot 273, SWN 6/15/89 OE **880**
Three Graces, 2nd state, etch/laid paper, 1910, pl/s, full mrgs, lt stn verso, 6x5", lot 19, RWS 9/29/88 **325**
Two, a/p, etch/laid wm Unicorn, 1916, p/s, pl/s & dtd, lt tr, P-8x6", RWS 3/16/89 **550**
Two (nude couple in landscape), etch, 1916, p/s, lt stn/sl, P-8x6", lot 4, RWS 9/8/89 OE **800**
Valkulla, only state, etch/van Gelder Zonen, 1912, p/s, pl/s, lt stn, 12x8", lot 274, SWN 6/15/89 OE **1,430**
Zorn with Bust of Troubetskey, etch, p/s, 10x7", lot 107, WG 10/19/89 OE **550**

ZUNIGA, Francisco (Costa Rican, 1913-)

Cuatro Figuras, 55/100, blk/golden litho, 1972, p/s, Ed Press bstp, S-17x23", lot 79, SBY 11/3/88 **880**
El Umbral, 26/47, blk & wht litho/scrpt/beige Amate, 1974, p/s, S-16x24", Kyron/Tasende, SBY 5/12/88 **1,100**
Group of 3: Muchacha en una Silla; Hombres con Barca, I; Hombres con Barca, II; litho, Brewster, lot 313, SBY 5/11/89 **2,860**
Grupo de Mujeres Sentadas, I; 11/92, clr litho, 1974, p/s, pub bstp, S-21x27", Kyron/Tasende, SBY 5/12/88 OE **1,980**
Grupo de Mujeres Sentadas, I; 24/92, clr litho, 1974, p/s, Kyron bstp, lt stn, S-21x27", Tasende, lot 80, SBY 11/3/88 **1,650**
La Escalera, 147/150, clr litho, 1986, p/s, printer bstp, unfr, S-30x21", Mourlot/Brewster, SBY 5/12/88 **1,430**
La Visita, 11/60, litho/Arches, 1974, Kyron bstp, S-22x29", lot 3021, B/B 2/16/88 **385**
Madre Juchiteca, 69/100, clr litho/Arches, 1973, p/s, Ed Press bstp, S-22x30", lot 3019, B/B 2/16/88 OE **1,760**
Mujer Sentada con Rebozo, 57/83, litho/Arches, 1974, p/s, Kyron bstp, S-28x19", lot 3020, B/B 2/16/88 **825**
Mujeres con Nino en la Puerta, total ed of 160, litho/German Etching, 1977, p/s, 32x24", lot 3023, B/B 2/16/88 **825**
Pair: El Rebozo Blanco; Yucatecas en el Parque; clr litho, 1986, p/s, S-30x21", Brewster/Mourlot, lot 314, SBY 5/11/89 **3,080**
Pair: El Rebozo; La Senal; 116/135 & 83/135, p/s, Mourlot bstp, S-22x30", Brewster/Mourlot, lot 312, SBY 5/11/89 OE **2,200**
Pair: El Robozo; Tres Mujeres de Pie, II; 100/135 & 83/135, litho, 1982, S-22x30"/S-23x16", Mourlot/Kyron, SBY 5/12/88 **2,200**
Pair: La Senal; Muchacha en una Silla; 106/135 & 55/135, litho, 1982, S-22x30"/S-23x17", Mourlot/Kyron, SBY 5/12/88 **1,980**
Rebolo Blanco, 96/135, clr litho, 1986, p/s, printer bstp, unfr, S-30x21", Mourlot/Brewster, SBY 5/12/88 **1,210**
Tres Mujeres de Pie, 1; 61/83, litho/Arches, 1974, p/s, Kyron bstp, S-27x22", lot 3022, B/B 2/16/88 OE **935**
Yucatecas en el Parque, 130/150, clr litho, 1986, p/s, printer bstp, unfr, S-21x30", Mourlot/Brewster, SBY 5/12/88 OE **2,090**

Glossary of Terms

Terms often used in auction catalogs (and in this price guide) may be confusing to the novice collector. Those most commonly used are listed below. While not every statement concerning authorship and authenticity made by the galleries whose catalogs were used are 100% guaranteed by them, we have been discerning in choosing only the most reputable companies to include in our report.

After: a copy of the known work by the artist

Attributed (att): a work of the period and in the style of the artist, which may actually be by the artist but for which a positive identification cannot be made

Bears date: is so dated and was probably executed at that time; possibly added by someone other than the artist

Bears signature: has a signature which (in the opinion of the gallery) may be that of the artist

Circle of: a work of the period by someone who was closely associated with the artist, who perhaps worked in the artist's studio, or whose style was closely related to the artist's

Dated: is so dated and upon examination appears to have been executed at that time

Follower of: see Style of

Manner of: a work done in the style of the artist, possibly produced during a later period

School of: a work done by a pupil or a follower of the artist, in his style

Signed: has the signature of the artist

Studio of: a work produced under the tutelage of the artist

Style of: done in the style of the artist, during the same approximate period

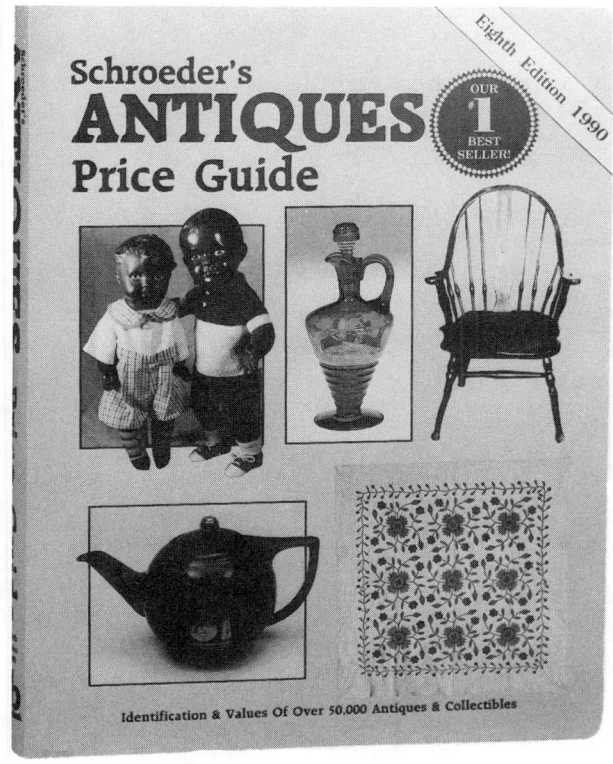